Ingenix Has You Covered!

April ICD-9-CM Updates

With semi-annual ICD-9-CM changes effective April 1 and October 1, it is more important than ever to have up-to-date ICD-9-CM coding information in order to stay in compliance with HIPAA regulations.

Ingenix is committed to providing you and your staff with the ICD-9-CM code update information you need to code accurately and efficiently. We are offering several ways to make sure you are always up-to-date.

- **Updateable *Expert* ICD-9-CM editions code books.** The February update will have the new April 1 codes.

- **Annual *Expert* and *Professional* ICD-9-CM editions.** Just visit IngenixOnline and look for the ICD-9-CM Special Updates link under the Quick Access Resources menu.

No extra charges for code changes. No additional cost for updated books. No hassle for you or your staff.

Revised Coding Guidelines

Revised official ICD-9-CM guidelines have been released and became effective April 1, 2005. Significant revisions were made to chapter-specific guidelines, the V code table and the use of terminology.

Only this set of guidelines, approved by the Cooperating Parties, is official. Adherence to these guidelines when assigning ICD-9-CM diagnosis and procedure codes is required under the Health Insurance Portability and Accountability Act (HIPAA).

Medicare Code Edits Notice

Not all Medicare edits for the new 2006 ICD-9-CM codes were released in time to be published in this edition. Once these edits are released we will post them on our Web site. Please visit www.ingenixonline.com and click on the ICD-9-CM Special Updates link under the Quick Access Resources menu to view these edits.

New! ICD-10 Corner on Ingenix Online

Ingenix is committed to keeping you informed of the very latest developments in ICD-10 and hopes that providing you with ICD-10 information will assist you in a successful transition to this new coding system. While no implementation date has been set at this time, it is not too early to begin preparing. Establishing your individual implementation plan is the path to success.

Visit IngenixOnline and look for the ICD-10 Corner link under Quick Access Resources for more information on ICD-10 history, structure and conventions, regulatory process, implementation tips, regulatory web sites and frequently asked questions. You can also find out about these Ingenix resources to help you prepare:

- *ICD-10-CM: A Preview of the Structure and Conventions of ICD-10-CM*

- *ICD-10-PCS: A Preview of the Structure and Conventions of ICD-10-PCS*

- *Ingenix Coding Lab: Implementing ICD-10*

SAVE MORE and qualify for REWARDS when you order at IngenixOnline.com.

Here are the top three reasons to place your order online:

1. Save an additional 5% when you order online*— use source **FOBW6**.

2. Get rewards for every $500 you spend at Ingenix Online with our eSmart program.**

3. Experience a quick, hassle-free purchase process with streamlined checkout options.

ingenix *e*smart

ingenix online frequent buyer program

Get rewards when you order online.

Ingenix eSmart is a program designed to reward our best Ingenix Online customers. If you are a registered online customer and qualify to participate**, all you have to do is use the returning customer checkout option for your web purchases every time you shop online. We keep track of your purchases. Once you reach $500, we send you a FREE product—it's that easy!

If you are not yet registered, go to IngenixOnline.com and register right away so we can get you started with the Ingenix eSmart program.

Are you part of our Medallion or Gold Medallion programs?

Ingenix Online has enhanced options for you, for a hassle-free, streamlined purchase and account management experience!

To view your enhanced online account options, simply register with us at IngenixOnline.com. You will then be able to easily place orders for items already reflecting your Price List discounts, get access to your purchase history, track shipments, change your profile, manage your address book and much more.

Could you benefit from an easy, quick way to consolidate orders for your company?

The Ingenix web-based consolidation tool is designed to streamline the purchasing process and enhance your productivity. For more information log into your account or visit www.ingenixonline.com/orderconsolidation.

(*) 5% offer valid online, cannot be combined with any other offer and is not applicable to Partner accounts. Bookstore products, packages, co-branded credentialing items and conferences not included.

(**) eSmart program valid for Ingenix customers who are NOT part of Medallion, Gold Medallion or Partner Accounts programs. You must be registered at Ingenix Online to have your online purchases tracked for rewards purposes. Shipping charges and taxes still apply and cannot be used for rewards. eSmart reward offers valid online only.

100% Money Back Guarantee:

If our merchandise* ever fails to meet your expectations, please contact our Customer Service Department toll-free at 1.800.INGENIX (464.3649), option 1, for an immediate response.

*Software/Data Files: Credit will be granted for unopened packages only.

SAVE 5% when you order at www.ingenixonline.com (reference source code FOBW6)

or call toll-free 1.800.INGENIX (464.3649), option 1.

Also available from your medical bookstore or distributor.

2006 Web Products

Fast Code Lookup and Access to Real-Time Updates All Year.

IngenixExpert.com

CPT® Expert.com
Item No.: 1400   **$74.95***

HCPCS Expert.com
Item No.: 1401   **$69.95***

ICD-9-CM Expert.com
for Physicians
Item No.: 1402   **$79.95***

ICD-9-CM Expert.com
for Hospitals
Item No.: 1403   **$89.95***

Available: Now   *Call for multi-user pricing.

*I*ngenixExpert.com allows you to look up every code found in your *Expert* code book by using our online search engine or index. Affordable and convenient, this online solution delivers every description, guideline and instruction found in the Ingenix *Expert* code books.

- **Look up CPT®, ICD-9-CM and HCPCS Level II codes faster than ever.** Locate the code you need with a term search or scroll through the index to access sections from the code book.

- **Get immediate guidance from Ingenix and Medicare with color code edits, guidelines and instructions.** Spend less time searching for information; avoid having to thumb through multiple pages or various books.

- **Up-to-date code descriptions and clinical information.** Code more confidently by accessing, up-to-date, extensive appendices, commonly miscoded procedures, Medicare requirements and glossaries with a click of the mouse.

- **Anatomical illustrations.** Large display of anatomical illustrations on your screen will help you to better understand of procedures and anatomy, so you can make the best possible coding selection.

100% Money Back Guarantee:

If our merchandise* ever fails to meet your expectations, please contact our Customer Service Department toll-free at 1.800.INGENIX (464.3649), option 1, for an immediate response.

*Software/Data Files: Credit will be granted for unopened packages only.

CPT is a registered trademark of the American Medical Association.

SAVE 5% when you order at www.ingenixonline.com (reference source code FOBW6)

or call toll-free 1.800.INGENIX (464.3649), option 1.

Also available from your medical bookstore or distributor.

FOBA6

All Three Code Books in One Powerful Package.

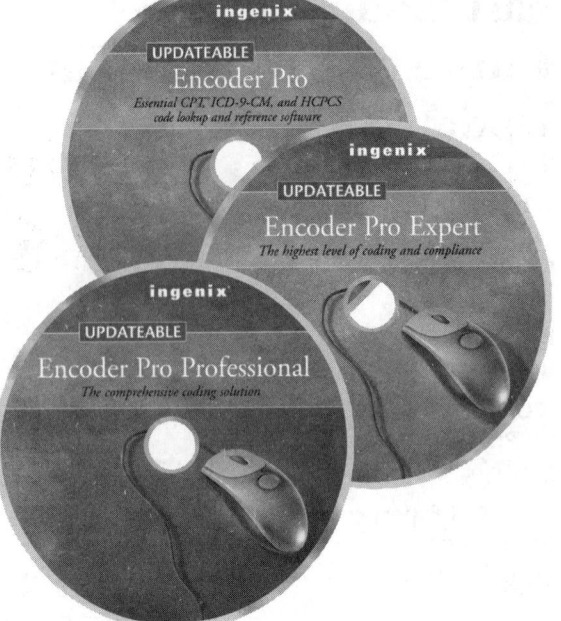

Encoder Pro

Item No.: 3310

$249.95*
*Call for multi-user pricing.

Encoder Pro Professional

Item No.: 2717

$499.95*
*Call for multi-user pricing.

Encoder Pro Expert

Item No.: 3460

$899.95*
*Call for multi-user pricing.

All available: Now

Encoder Pro is the coder's essential CPT®, ICD-9-CM and HCPCS Level II code lookup software. It gives users fast search capabilities across all three code sets. *Encoder Pro* can greatly reduce the time it takes to build or review a claim and help improve overall coding accuracy.

- **Powerful Ingenix CodeLogic™ search engine.** Improve productivity by eliminating time-consuming code lookup in outdated code books. Search all three code sets simultaneously using lay terms, acronyms, abbreviations and even misspelled words.

- **Color-coded edits.** Reduce research time, improve coding accuracy and become more efficient by delivering cleaner claims the first time.

- **Quarterly update service.** Rest assured you are always using accurate codes. You can code confidently throughout the year with free code updates.

- **Receive *Coders' Desk Reference* lay descriptions for thousands of CPT® codes.** Enhance your understanding of procedures with easy-to-understand descriptions.

Exclusive to Encoder Pro Professional

- **Access Local Medical Review Policies/Local Coverage Determinations and Medicare's Pub 100.** Check procedures for Medicare coverage instructions and medical necessity edits.

- **Modifier crosswalk.** Guides you to the correct modifiers when billing payers and helps you associate modifiers with selected procedures and services.

Exclusive to Encoder Pro Expert

- **Exclusive—Compliance editor.** Check for coding accuracy and review your code selections for CCI unbundle edits, ICD-9-CM specificity, age, medical necessity, gender and more.

- **Audit your E/M code selection with a detailed level-of-service review.**

SAVE 5% when you order at www.ingenixonline.com (reference source code FOBW6)

or call toll-free 1.800.INGENIX (464.3649), option 1.

Also available from your medical bookstore or distributor.

FOBA6

Let the Experts Guide You Through the Official 2006 CPT® Code Set.

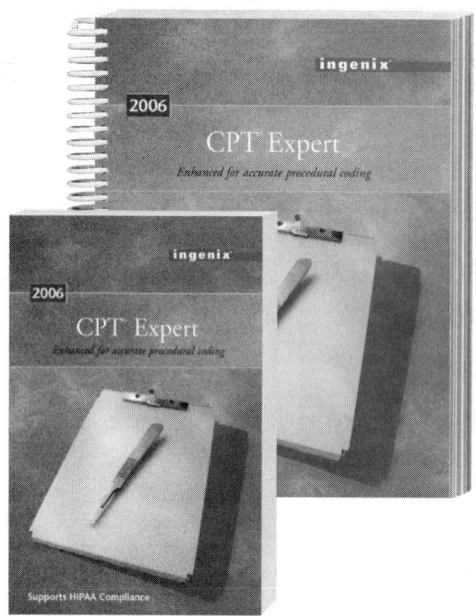

2006 CPT® Expert (Spiral)

Item No.: 4574   **$97.95**

Available: December 2005   ISBN: 1-56337-682-2

2006 CPT® Expert (Compact)

Item No.: 4621   **$82.95**

Available: December 2005   ISBN: 1-56337-683-0

A one-of-a-kind resource, the *CPT® Expert* provides physician office coders with all of the CPT® codes, plus detailed guidance on how to improve coding accuracy, increase coding efficiency and expedite claim submission by clarifying annual CPT® code changes and detailing the implications of the changes.

- **All 2006 CPT® codes with official, full descriptions.** Access a complete, comprehensive listing of CPT® codes—improving coding accuracy.

- **CPT® Assistant references.** Provides guidance and practical advice so you know exactly how to best apply a CPT® code.

- **Information from the AMA, CMS, Medicare Pub 100, National Coverage Decisions and Ingenix experts.** Better understand the rules and regulations and improve the precision of CPT® code selection.

- **Edit symbols distinguish codes meant for specific populations.** Prevent denials due to restrictions based on age or sex.

- **Illustrations.** Better understand procedures so that you can select the right codes the first time.

- **Color keys mark the CPT® codes that can affect your Medicare reimbursement.** Easily identify commonly miscoded codes, unlisted codes and codes not covered by Medicare.

- **APC and ASC edits help you determine payment.** Start off on the right foot by knowing what status or group your service falls under.

- **Alerts sent via email provide valuable code change information.** Keep current with corrections to CPT® codes and other late-breaking news.

- **Crosswalk from CPT® to equivalent HCPCS Level II codes.** Facilitates Medicare billing.

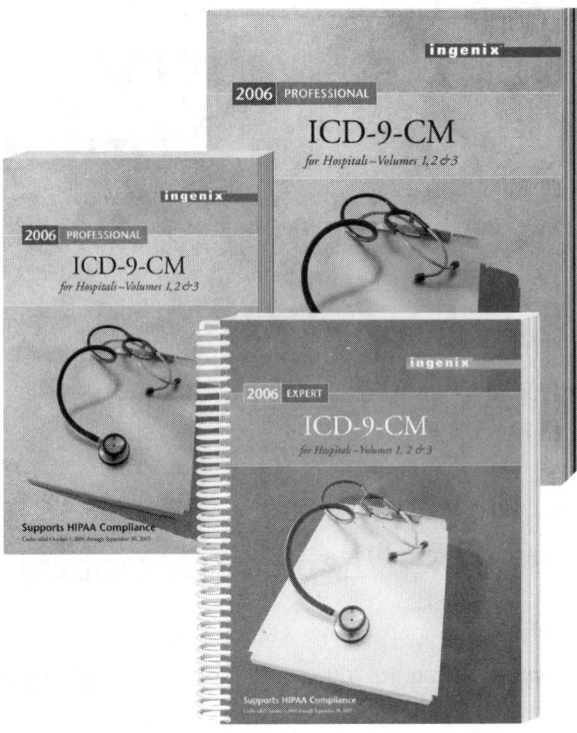

Critical ICD-9-CM Coding and Reimbursement Alerts on the Same Page as the Code You Want.

2006 ICD-9-CM for Hospitals, Vols. 1, 2 & 3

Softbound
Item No.: IHB06   **$87.95**
ISBN: 1-56337-701-2   Available: September 2005

Compact
Item No.: IHC06   **$82.95**
(ISBN: 1-56337-702-0)   Available: September 2005

Spiral
Item No.: IH506   **$97.95**
ISBN: 1-56337-703-9   Available: September 2005

Updateable Binder
Item No.: 3539   **$159.95**
                         Available: Now

Code with more precision and efficiency using the *ICD-9-CM for Hospitals, Volumes 1, 2 & 3* with critical coding and reimbursement edit alerts on the same page as the code you want. This product supports HIPAA compliance by providing the approved standard code set, the official coding guidelines, references for official coding advice, coding instructions and conventions required under HIPAA. Do it right… in less time.

- **Ingenix Edge—Exclusive color coding and symbols for all critical coding and reimbursement alerts.** Improve coding accuracy and efficiency with intuitive symbols and color coding that alert you to all crucial Medicare diagnosis and procedure coding and reimbursement edits.

- **Ingenix Edge—CC principal diagnosis exclusions listed right with the CC code.** Know at a glance if the CC code you are assigning will affect DRG assignment based upon the established principal diagnosis (PDx).

- **Ingenix Edge—AHA's *Coding Clinic for ICD-9-CM* references for official coding advice.** AHA's *Coding Clinic* provides the official coding advice that every coder in every health care setting must follow for ICD-9-CM.

- **Ingenix Edge—Additional digit symbol in both tabulars and indexes.** Color-coded symbols alert the coder as to whether the code is invalid without a fourth or fifth digit.

- **Ingenix Edge—DRG alert symbols.** Easily identiify Dx codes that are assigned to a targeted DRG, are major HIV-related conditions, or are major or complex cardiovascular conditions.

- **Current official code set with instructional notes and conventions, and complete official coding guidelines.** Be in compliance with HIPAA Transaction and Code Set requirements to avoid delayed or denied claims.

- **Illustrations and definitions.**

Exclusive to the Expert Editions:

- **Pharmalogical listings, complete list of all CC codes and Dx/MDC/DRG list for quick audits.**

- **Valid Three-digit Code List.** Know whether a three-digit code is valid for submitting a claim.

- **Email Alerts.** Know when crucial information is posted on our website concerning the latest ICD-9-CM news.

Exclusive to the Updateable Expert Edition:

- **Three updates per year allow you to stay current with changes throughout the year.**

SAVE 5% when you order at www.ingenixonline.com (reference source code FOBW6)

or call toll-free 1.800.INGENIX (464.3649), option 1.

Also available from your medical bookstore or distributor.

ingenix

HCPCS Level II Doesn't Have to be Difficult. The Expert is On Your Side.

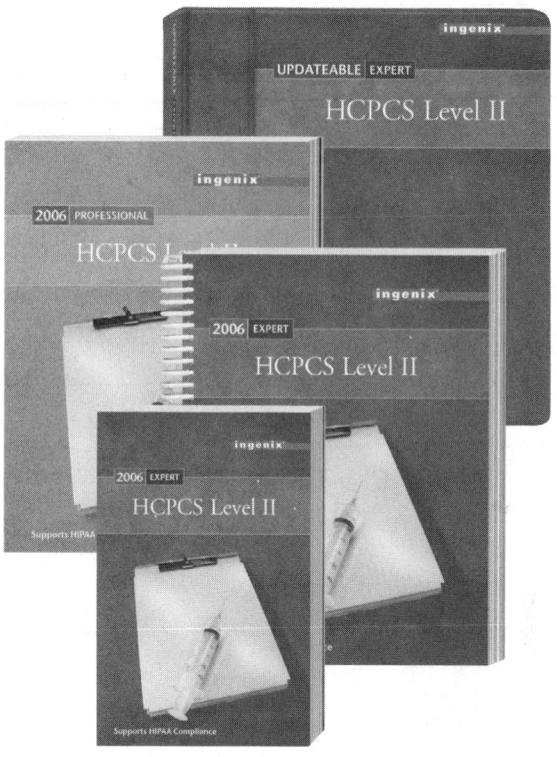

2006 HCPCS Level II Expert (Spiral)

Item No.: HS06   **$94.95**

Available: December 2005   ISBN: 1-56337-684-9

2006 HCPCS Level II Expert (Compact)

Item No.: HC06   **$79.95**

Available: December 2005   ISBN: 1-56337-685-7

2006 HCPCS Level II Expert (Updateable Binder)

Item No.: 4524   **$139.95**

Available: Now

2006 HCPCS Level II Professional (Softbound)

Item No.: HB06   **$69.95**

Available: December 2005   ISBN: 1-56337-687-3

Ingenix HCPCS Level II products enable customers to receive timely and appropriate reimbursement for supplies and services not found in their CPT® code book. HCPCS Level II codes are essential when billing for Medicare reimbursement or under APCs.

- **Includes all 2006 HCPCS Level II codes and modifiers.** Code with the most up-to-date information to submit accurate claims.

- **National Medicare and commercial fees for most HCPCS codes.** Helps identify reimbursement based on Medicare and private payer fee data for HCPCS Level II codes.

- **APC status indicators.** Determine which codes are payable under OPPS.

- **Email alerts inform you of the latest changes to HCPCS Level II from CMS.** Keep current with late-breaking news through special reports and code using the most up-to-date codes and regulations.

- **DMEPOS icon distinguishes codes paid under that fee schedule.** Improve efficiency when coding for supplies that should be submitted under the DMEPOS to your DME.

- **In-depth illustrations.** Makes coding various supplies and services easier and more accurate.

- **Color-coded bars and icons denote the government's coverage and rules for each code.** Pub. 100 references are included.

- **ASC group symbols.** Quickly determine which codes can be billed using ASC groupings and ensure appropriate billing for ASCs.

- **Enhanced Table of Drugs with generic and brand drug names and their corresponding codes.** This comprehensive table also includes the amount and route of administration.

100% Money Back Guarantee:

If our merchandise* ever fails to meet your expectations, please contact our Customer Service Department toll-free at 1.800.INGENIX (464.3649), option 1, for an immediate response.

*Software/Data Files: Credit will be granted for unopened packages only.

CPT is a registered trademark of the American Medical Association.

SAVE 5% when you order at www.ingenixonline.com (reference source code FOBW6)

or call toll-free 1.800.INGENIX (464.3649), option 1.

Also available from your medical bookstore or distributor.

FOBA6

Four simple ways to place an order.

Call
1.800.ingenix (464.3649), **option 1.** Mention source code FOBA6 when ordering.

Mail
PO Box 27116
Salt Lake City, UT 84127-0116
With payment and/or purchase order.

Fax
801.982.4033
With credit card information and/or purchase order.

Click
www.ingenixonline.com
Save 5% when you order online today—use source code FOBW6.

ingenix *e*smart
Ingenix online frequent buyer program

GET REWARDS FOR SHOPPING ONLINE!
To find out more, visit IngenixOnline.com

eSmart program available only to Ingenix customers who are not part of Medallion, Gold Medallion or Partner Accounts programs. You must be registered at Ingenix Online to have your online purchases tracked for rewards purposes. Shipping charges and taxes still apply and cannot be used for rewards. Offer valid online only.

100% Money Back Guarantee
If our merchandise* ever fails to meet your expectations, please contact our Customer Service Department toll-free at 1.800.ingenix (464.3649), option 1 for an immediate response.

*Software: Credit will be granted for unopened packages only.

Customer Service Hours
7:00 am - 5:00 pm Mountain Time
9:00 am - 7:00 pm Eastern Time

Shipping and Handling

no. of items	fee
1	$10.95
2-4	$12.95
5-7	$14.95
8-10	$19.95
11+	Call

---

ingenix FOBA6

Order Form

Information

Customer No. _____   Contact No. _____

Source Code _____

Contact Name _____

Title _____   Specialty _____

Company _____

Street Address _____

City _____ NO PO BOXES, PLEASE _____ State _____ Zip _____

Telephone (___) _____ Fax (___) _____

IN CASE WE HAVE QUESTIONS ABOUT YOUR ORDER

E-mail _____ @ _____
REQUIRED FOR ORDER CONFIRMATION AND SELECT PRODUCT DELIVERY.

Ingenix respects your right to privacy. We will not sell or rent your e-mail address or fax number to anyone outside Ingenix and its business partners. If you would like to remove your name from Ingenix promotion, please call 1.800.ingenix (464.3649), option 1.

Product

Item No.	Qty	Description	Price	Total

Subtotal _____

UT & VA residents, please add applicable Sales tax _____

(See chart on the left) Shipping & handling charges _____
All foreign orders, please call for shipping costs

Total _____

Payment

○ Please bill my credit card   ○ MasterCard   ○ VISA   ○ Amex   ○ Discover

Card No. | | | | | | | | | | | | | | | | | Expires | |
                                                        MONTH   YEAR

Signature _____

○ Check enclosed, made payable to: Ingenix, Inc.   ○ Please bill my office

Purchase Order No. _____
ATTACH COPY OF PURCHASE ORDER

FOBA6

2006

ingenix®

ICD-9-CM
Expert

for Home Health Services, Nursing Facilities, and Hospices
Volumes 1, 2 & 3

International Classification of Diseases
9th Revision
Clinical Modification

Sixth Edition

Edited by:
Anita C. Hart, RHIA, CCS, CCS-P
Catherine A. Hopkins
Beth Ford, RHIT, CCS

Ingenix is committed to providing you with the ICD-9-CM code update information you need to code accurately and to be in compliance with HIPAA regulations. In the case of adoption of additional ICD-9-CM code changes effective April 1, 2006, Ingenix will provide these code changes to you at no additional cost! Just check back at http://www.IngenixOnline.com and look for the ICD-9-CM Update icon to review the latest information concerning any new code changes.

Codes Valid October 1, 2005, through September 30, 2006

PUBLISHER'S NOTICE

All the codes, indexes and other material in the ICD-9-CM are compiled from official ICD-9-CM codes and instructions as well as the Medicare regulations and manuals issued or authorized by the Centers for Medicare and Medicaid Services. The code book is designed to provide accurate and authoritative information in regard to the subject covered, and every reasonable effort has been made to ensure the accuracy of the information within these pages. However, the ultimate responsibility for correct coding lies with the provider of services.

Ingenix, Inc., its employees, agents and staff make no representation, warranty or guarantee that this compilation of codes and narratives is error-free or that the use of this code book will prevent differences of opinion or disputes with Medicare or other third-party payers as to the codes that are accepted or the amounts that will be paid to providers of services, and will bear no responsibility or liability for the results or consequences of the use of this code book.

CONTINUING EDUCATION UNITS FOR AAPC CERTIFIED MEMBERS

This publication has prior approval by the American Academy of Professional Coders for continuing education units. Granting of prior approval in no way constitutes endorsement by AAPC of the publication content nor the publisher. Instructions to submit CEUs are available at www.aapc.com/education/ceus.htm.

OUR COMMITMENT TO ACCURACY

Ingenix is committed to producing accurate and reliable materials. To report corrections, please visit www.ingenixonline.com/accuracy or email accuracy@ingenix.com. You can also reach customer service by calling 1.800.INGENIX (464.3649), option 1.

SPECIAL REPORTS AND ANNOUNCEMENTS

Purchase of this publication entitles you to Special Reports and announcements via e-mail. Please call customer service at 800 INGENIX (464-3649) or contact your bookstore to take advantage of this exciting free service that will keep you abreast of important code changes and regulatory developments.

Review, download, and print the Special Reports in .pdf format. Log on to http://www.ingenixonline.com/content/2006I9Expert

Preface

As more and more services are being performed in nonhospital settings, the pressure is on to use, understand and code accurately with ICD-9-CM. Physicians now are required by law to submit ICD-9-CM codes for Medicare reimbursement. And since most third-party payers will no longer fill in an ICD-9-CM code when a claim is submitted without valid codes, nursing homes, home health agencies and hospices have had to become proficient in coding.

ICD-9-CM Expert for Home Health Services, Nursing Facilities, and Hospices, Volumes 1, 2 & 3 has been designed with the coder in mind. All three volumes of the most recent official government version of ICD-9-CM have been combined into one book. Additional features have been added that address issues specific to Home Health Services, Hospice Care and Skilled Nursing Facilities.

Our technical experts have drawn upon their extensive hands-on experience to enhance the government's book with valuable features essential to correct coding and reimburse-ment. Without these enhancements, health information management departments would spend hours locating the information required to code each record accurately. Because of the thoroughness, accuracy, timeliness and ease of use of *ICD-9-CM Expert for Home Health Services, Nursing Facilities, and Hospices, Volumes 1, 2 & 3* health information management departments nationwide have turned to them for their coding needs.

ICD-9-CM Expert for Home Health Services, Nursing Facilities, and Hospices, Volumes 1, 2 & 3 includes many of the enhancements described below in direct response to requests from our subscribers. As you review the content, you'll find the following:

- ICD-9-CM official guidelines for coding and reporting, published by the U.S. Department of Health and Human Services and approved by the cooperating parties (American Hospital Association (AHA), American Health Information Management Association (AHIMA), Centers for Medicare and Medicaid Services (formerly know as Health Care Financing Administration) and National Center for Health Statisics (NCHS))
- All the official ICD-9-CM codes, indices, notes, footnotes and symbols
- Additional symbols that alert coders to coding and reimbursement issues, such as codes requiring a fourth- or fifth-digit assignment to complete the code and V code sequencing guidelines.
- The American Hospital Association (AHA) *Coding Clinic for ICD-9-CM* references, integrated beneath the applicable codes to provide easy reference to official coding advice as designated by the four cooperating parties (AHA, AHIMA, CMS and NCHS)
- The official coding guidelines for long term care facilities
- A reference section that summarizes the proposed Home Health Agency Prospective Payment System
- An explanation of the basic ICD-9-CM coding conventions
- The 10 Steps to Correct Coding feature
- A summary of code changes
- Reference section addressing the qualifications for coverage of Medicare home health services
- Exclusive symbols to identify diagnosis codes that are considered primary or secondary diagnosis in the Clinical Dimension of the home health case mix classification system
- Explanation of the criteria for Medicare noncancer hospice care coverage
- Exclusive color coding system that alerts coders of noncancer diagnoses that may satisfy the medical necessity criteria for Medicare coverage of hospice care
- Background on the Resource Utilization Groups (RUG-III) classification system
- Exclusive color coding system that identifies disease and procedure codes that may be a contributory factor in assigning a RUG-III clinical category level as part of the skilled nursing facility (SNF) prospective payment system.

Please review "How to Use" *ICD-9-CM Expert for Home Health Services, Nursing Facilities, and Hospices, Volumes 1, 2 & 3* in this section to learn about the features that will help you assign and report correct codes, ensuring appropriate reimbursement.

USE OF OFFICIAL SOURCES

The *ICD-9-CM Expert for Home Health Services, Nursing Facilities, and Hospices, Volumes 1, 2 & 3* contains the official U.S. Department of Health and Human Services, Ninth Revision, Sixth Edition, ICD-9-CM codes, effective for the current year.

The color-coding, footnotes and symbols, which identify coding and reimbursement issues, are derived from official federal government sources, including the Medicare Code Edits (MCE) Version 23.0. Other sources of edits include: Prospective Payment System and Consolidated Billing for Skilled Nursing Facilities, Final Rule, *Federal Register* May 12, 1998, updates through July 30, 2004; Home Health Prospective Payment System, Final Rule, published in the *Federal Register* July 3, 2000 and updates through October 22, 2004. The hospice noncancer coverage information was obtained from the CMS Manual Publication 100-2, Medicare Benefits Policy Chapter 9.

The American Hospital Association's (AHA) *Coding Clinic for ICD-9-CM* references are used with permission of the AHA.

TECHNICAL EDITORS

Anita C. Hart, RHIA, CCS, CCS-P
Product Manager, Ingenix, Inc.
Ms. Hart's experience includes conducting and publishing research in clinical medicine and human genetics for Yale University, Massachusetts General Hospital, and Massachusetts Institute of Technology. In addition, Ms. Hart has supervised medical records management, health information management, coding and reimbursement, and worker's compensation issues as the office manager for a physical therapy rehabilitation clinic. Ms. Hart is an expert in physician and facility coding, reimbursement systems, and compliance issues. Ms. Hart developed the *ICD-9-CM Changes: An Insider's View* and served as technical consultant for numerous other publications for hospital and physician practices. Currrently, Ms. Hart is the Product Manager for the ICD-9-CM, ICD-10-CM/PCS and DRG product lines.

Catherine A. Hopkins
Clinical/Technical Editor, Ingenix, Inc.
Ms. Hopkins has 17 years of experience in the health care field. Her experience includes six years as office manager and senior coding specialist for a large multi-specialty practice. Ms. Hopkins has written several coding manuals and newsletters and has taught seminars on CPT, HCPCS, and ICD-9-CM coding. She also serves as technical support for various software products.

Beth Ford, RHIT, CCS
Clinical/Technical Editor, Ingenix, Inc.
Ms. Ford is a clinical/technical editor for Ingenix. She has extensive background in both the professional and technical components of CPT/HCPCS and ICD-9-CM coding. Ms. Ford has served as a coding supervisor and coding consultant, as well as a health information management director. She is an active member of the American Heath Information Management Association (AHIMA).

In addition to the editors, the following people have contributed to this book:

Stacy Perry, *Desktop Publishing Manager*
Kerrie Hornsby, *Desktop Publishing Specialist*
Tracy Betzler, *Desktop Publishing Specialist*
Irene Day, *Desktop Publishing Specialist*
Hope Dunn, *Desktop Publishing Specialist*
Sheri Bernard, *Senior Product Director*
Lynn Speirs, *Senior Director, Publishing Services*

WHAT TO DO IF YOU HAVE QUESTIONS

If you have any questions call our customer service department toll-free at 800-INGENIX (464-3649), option 1.

If you have comments on the content of this book, please e-mail them to customerservice@ingenix.com or fax to 801-982-4033.

ADDITIONAL COPIES

Contact the customer service order department toll-free at 800-INGENIX (464-3649), option 1.

Introduction

HISTORY AND FUTURE OF ICD-9

The *International Classification of Diseases, Ninth Revision, Clinical Modification* (ICD-9-CM) is based on the official version of the World Health Organization's Ninth Revision, International Classification of Diseases (ICD-9). ICD-9 classifies morbidity and mortality information for statistical purposes, and for the indexing of hospital records by disease and operations, for data storage and retrieval.

This modification of ICD-9 supplants the Eighth Revision International Classification of Diseases, Adapted for Use in the United States (ICDA-8) and the Hospital Adaptation of ICDA (H-ICDA).

The concept of extending the International Classification of Diseases for use in hospital indexing was originally developed in response to a need for a more efficient basis for storage and retrieval of diagnostic data. In 1950, the U.S. Public Health Service and the Veterans Administration began independent tests of the International Classification of Diseases for hospital indexing purposes. The following year, the Columbia Presbyterian Medical Center in New York City adopted the International Classification of Diseases, Sixth Revision, with some modifications for use in its medical record department. A few years later, the Commission on Professional and Hospital Activities (CPHA) in Ann Arbor, Mich., adopted the International Classification of Diseases with similar modifications for use in hospitals participating in the Professional Activity Study.

The problem of adapting ICD for indexing hospital records was taken up by the U.S. National Committee on Vital and Health Statistics through its subcommittee on hospital statistics. The subcommittee reviewed the modifications made by the various users of ICD and proposed that uniform changes be made. This was done by a small working party.

In view of the growing interest in the use of the International Classification of Diseases for hospital indexing, a study was undertaken in 1956 by the American Hospital Association and the American Medical Record Association (then the American Association of Medical Record Librarians) of the relative efficiencies of coding systems for diagnostic indexing. This study indicated the International Classification of Diseases provided a suitable and efficient framework for indexing hospital records. The major users of the International Classification of Diseases for hospital indexing purposes then consolidated their experiences, and an adaptation was first published in December 1959. A revision was issued in 1962 and the first "Classification of Operations and Treatments" was included.

In 1966, the international conference for revising the International Classification of Diseases noted the eighth revision of ICD had been constructed with hospital indexing in mind and considered the revised classification suitable, in itself, for hospital use in some countries. However, it was recognized that the basic classification might provide inadequate detail for diagnostic indexing in other countries. A group of consultants was asked to study the eighth revision of ICD (ICD-8) for applicability to various users in the United States. This group recommended that further detail be provided for coding of hospital and morbidity data. The American Hospital Association was requested to develop the needed adaptation proposals. This was done by an advisory committee (the Advisory Committee to the Central Office on ICDA). In 1968 the United States Public Health Service published the product, Eighth Revision International Classification of Diseases, Adapted for Use in the United States. This became commonly known as ICDA-8, and beginning in 1968 it served as the basis for coding diagnostic data for both official morbidity and mortality statistics in the United States.

In 1968, the CPHA published the Hospital Adaptation of ICDA (H-ICDA) based on both the original ICD-8 and ICDA-8. In 1973, CPHA published a revision of H-ICDA, referred to as H-ICDA-2. Hospitals throughout the United States were divided in their use of these classifications until January 1979, when ICD-9-CM was made the single classification intended primarily for use in the United States, replacing these earlier related, but somewhat dissimilar, classifications.

Physicians have been required by law to submit diagnosis codes for Medicare reimbursement since the passage of the Medicare Catastrophic Coverage Act of 1988. This act requires physician offices to include the appropriate diagnosis codes when billing for services provided to Medicare beneficiaries on or after April 1, 1989. The Health Care Financing Administration designated ICD-9-CM as the coding system physicians must use.

In 1993 the World Health Organization published the newest version of International Classification of Diseases, Tenth Revision, ICD-10. This version contains the greatest number of changes in the history of ICD. There are more codes (5,500 more than ICD-9) to allow more specific reporting of diseases and newly recognized conditions. ICD-10 consists of three volumes; Tabular List (volume I), instructions (volume 2) and the Alphabetic Index (volume 3). It contains 21 chapters including two supplementary ones. The codes are alphanumeric (A00–T98, V01–Y98 and Z00–Z99). Currently ICD-10 is being used in some European countries with implementation expected after the year 2008 in the United States.

ICD-9-CM BACKGROUND

In February 1977, a steering committee was convened by the National Center for Health Statistics to provide advice and counsel in developing a clinical modification of ICD-9. The organizations represented on the steering committee included the following:

- American Association of Health Data Systems
- American Hospital Association
- American Medical Record Association
- Association for Health Records
- Council on Clinical Classifications
- Centers for Medicare and Medicaid Services, Department of Health and Human Services
- WHO Center for Classification of Diseases for North America, sponsored by the National Center for Health Statistics, Department of Health and Human Services

The Council on Clinical Classifications was sponsored by the following:

- American Academy of Pediatrics
- American College of Obstetricians and Gynecologists
- American College of Physicians
- American College of Surgeons
- American Psychiatric Association
- Commission on Professional and Hospital Activities

The steering committee met periodically in 1977. Clinical guidance and technical input were provided by task forces on classification from the Council on Clinical Classification's sponsoring organizations.

ICD-9-CM is a clinical modification of the World Health Organization's ICD-9. The term "clinical" is used to emphasize the modification's intent: to serve as a useful tool to classify morbidity data for indexing medical records, medical care review, and ambulatory and other medical care programs, as well as for basic health statistics. To describe the clinical picture of the patient, the codes must be more precise than those needed only for statistical groupings and trend analysis.

CHARACTERISTICS OF ICD-9-CM

ICD-9-CM far exceeds its predecessors in the number of codes provided. The disease classification has been expanded to include health-related conditions and to provide greater specificity at the fifth-digit level of detail. These fifth digits are not optional; they are intended for use in recording the information substantiated in the clinical record.

Volume I (Tabular List) of ICD-9-CM contains four appendices:

Appendix A:	Morphology of Neoplasms
Appendix B:	Deleted effective October 1, 2004
Appendix C:	Classification of Drugs by American Hospital Formulary Service List Number and Their ICD-9-CM Equivalents
Appendix D:	Classification of Industrial Accidents According to Agency
Appendix E:	List of Three-Digit Categories

These appendices are included as a reference to provide further information about the patient's clinical picture, to further define a diagnostic statement, to aid in classifying new drugs or to reference three-digit categories.

Volume 2 (Alphabetic Index) of ICD-9-CM contains many diagnostic terms that do not appear in volume I since the index includes most diagnostic terms currently in use.

Volume 3 (procedure index and procedure tabular) of ICD-9-CM contains codes for operations and procedures. The format for the tabular is the same as Volume 1 Disease Tabular, except the codes consist of two digits with one or two digits following the decimal point. Conventions in the index follow volume 2 conventions except some subterms appear immediately below the main term rather than following alphabetizing rules

THE DISEASE CLASSIFICATION

ICD-9-CM is totally compatible with its parent system, ICD-9, thus meeting the need for comparability of morbidity and mortality statistics at the international level. A few fourth-digit codes were created in existing three-digit rubrics only when the necessary detail could not be accommodated by the use of a fifth-digit subclassification. To ensure that each rubric of ICD-9-CM collapses back to its ICD-9 counterpart the following specifications governed the ICD-9-CM disease classification:

Specifications for the Tabular List:

1. Three-digit rubrics and their contents are unchanged from ICD-9.

2. The sequence of three-digit rubrics is unchanged from ICD-9.

3. Three-digit rubrics are not added to the main body of the classification.

4. Unsubdivided three-digit rubrics are subdivided where necessary to
   - add clinical detail
   - isolate terms for clinical accuracy

5. The modification in ICD-9-CM is accomplished by adding a fifth digit to existing ICD-9 rubrics, except as noted under #7 below.

6. The optional dual classification in ICD-9 is modified.
   - Duplicate rubrics are deleted:
     - four-digit manifestation categories duplicating etiology entries
     - manifestation inclusion terms duplicating etiology entries
   - Manifestations of disease are identified, to the extent possible, by creating five-digit codes in the etiology rubrics.
   - When the manifestation of a disease cannot be included in the etiology rubrics, provision for its identification is made by retaining the ICD-9 rubrics used for classifying manifestations of disease.

7. The format of ICD-9-CM is revised from that used in ICD-9.
   - American spelling of medical terms is used.
   - Inclusion terms are indented beneath the titles of codes.
   - Codes not to be used for primary tabulation of disease are printed in italics with the notation, "code first underlying disease."

Specifications for the Alphabetic Index:

1. The format of the Alphabetic Index follows that of ICD-9.

2. When two codes are required to indicate etiology and manifestation, the optional manifestation code appears in brackets (e.g., diabetic cataract 250.5 [*366.41*]).

THE ICD-9-CM COORDINATION AND MAINTENANCE COMMITTEE

The four cooperating parties involved in maintaining the ICD-9-CM classification system include representatives of the American Hospital Association (AHA), the Centers for Medicare and Medicaid Services (CMS), the National Center for Health Statistics (NCHS), and the American Health Information Management Association (AHIMA).

Proposals for changes to the ICD-9-CM classification system are submitted and discussed in two open forum meetings held in April and October of each year at the Headquarters of the Centers for Medicare and Medicaid Services, Baltimore, Maryland. Comments received during and after the meetings are then discussed by the Committee. A notice of the new codes and code revisions approved by the Committee are published in the Federal Register as part of the proposed and final rule for the changes to the inpatient prospective payment system. The complete official document of changes to the classification system is released as the Addenda for the *International Classification of Diseases, Ninth Revision, Clinical Modification, Sixth Edition, Volumes 1, 2 and 3.*

How to Use the ICD-9-CM Expert for Home Health Services, Nursing Facilities and Hospices (Volumes 1, 2, & 3)

This *ICD-9-CM Expert for Home Health Services, Nursing Facilities, and Hospices, Volumes 1, 2 & 3* is based on the official version of the International Classification of Diseases, Ninth Revision, Clinical Modification, Sixth Edition, issued by the U.S. Department of Health and Human Services. Annual code changes are implemented by the government and are effective Oct. 1 and valid through Sept. 30 of the following year.

The code book is totally compatible with its parent system, ICD-9, thus meeting the need for comparability of morbidity and mortality statistics at the international level.

This book is consistent with the content of the government's version of ICD-9-CM. However, to accommodate the coder's approach to coding, the Alphabetic Index has been placed before the Tabular List in both the disease and procedure classifications. This allows the user to locate the correct codes in a logical, natural manner by locating the term in the index, then confirming the accuracy of the code in the Tabular List.

STEPS TO CORRECT CODING

1. Look up the main term in the Alphabetic Index and scan the subterm entries as appropriate. Follow any cross-references such as "*see*" and "*see also*." Do not code from the Alphabetic Index without verifying the accuracy of the code in the Tabular List.

2. Locate the code in the numerically arranged Tabular List.

3. Observe the punctuation, footnotes, cross-references, color-coded prompts and other conventions described in the 'Conventions' section.

4. To determine the appropriateness of the code selection, read all instructional material:
   - "includes" and "*excludes*" notes
   - "*see*," "*see also*" and "*see category*" cross-references
   - "use additional code" and "*code first underlying disease*" instructions
   - "code also" and "*omit code*" notes
   - fourth- and fifth-digit requirements

5. Consult definitions, relevant illustrations, CC exclusions, color coding and reimbursement prompts, the check fourth- and fifth-digit, age and sex symbols. Refer to the color/symbol legend at the bottom of each page for symbols. Refer to the list of footnotes that is included in the "Additional Conventions" section of this book for a full explanation of a footnote associated with a code.

6. Consult the official ICD-9-CM guidelines for coding and reporting, and refer to the AHA's *Coding Clinic for ICD-9-CM* for coding guidelines governing the use of specific codes.

7. Confirm and transcribe the correct code.

ORGANIZATION

Introduction
The introductory material in this book includes the history and future of ICD-9-CM as well as an overview of the classification system

Official ICD-9-CM Conventions
This section provides a full explanation of all the official footnotes, symbols, instructional notes, and conventions found in the official government version

Additional Conventions
Exclusive color-coding, symbols, and notations have been included in the *ICD-9-CM Expert for Home Health Services, Nursing Facilities, and Hospices, Volumes 1, 2 & 3* to alert coders to important coding and reimbursement issues. This section provides a full explanation of the additional conventions used throughout this book.

Summary of Code Changes
This section includes a complete listing of all new code changes for the current year.

Coding Guidelines
Included in this book are the official ICD-9-CM coding guidelines as approved by the four cooperating parties of the ICD-9-CM Coordination and Maintenance Committee. Failure to comply with the official coding guidelines may result in denied or delayed claims.

Disease Classification: Alphabetic Index to Diseases

The Alphabetic Index to Diseases contains diagnostic terms for illnesses, injuries and reasons for encounters with health care professionals. Both the Table of Drugs and Chemicals and the Alphabetic Index to External Causes of Injury and Poisoning are located in this section.

Disease Classification: Tabular List of Diseases
The Tabular List of Diseases arranges the ICD-9-CM codes and descriptors numerically.

The Tabular List includes two supplementary classifications:

- V Codes—Supplementary Classification of Factors Influencing Health Status and Contact with Health Services (V01–V85)
- E Codes—Supplementary Classification of External Causes of Injury and Poisoning (E800–E999)

ICD-9-CM includes four official appendixes.

- Appendix A   Morphology of Neoplasms
- Appendix B   Deleted effective October 1, 2004
- Appendix C   Classification of Drugs by AHFS List
- Appendix D   Classification of Industrial Accidents According to Agency
- Appendix E   List of Three-digit Categories

These appendices are included as a reference to provide further information about the patient's circumstances, help further define a diagnostic statement, maintain a tumor registry and aid in classifying new drugs.

Procedure Classification: Alphabetic Index to Procedures
The Alphabetic Index to Procedures lists common surgical and procedural terminology.

Procedure Classification: Tabular List of Procedures
The Tabular List of Procedures numerically arranges the procedure codes and their descriptors.

RESOURCES
Listed below are the exclusive resources in the *ICD-9-CM Expert for Home Health Services, Nursing Facilities, and Hospices, Volumes 1, 2 & 3* books.

Home Health: Qualifications for Medicare Coverage of Home Health Services
This section describes the criteria that must be met by the patient to qualify for Medicare coverage of home health services.

Home Health: Overview of the Proposed Home Health Agency Prospective Payment System

A prospective payment system for home health agencies (HHA) is required by the Balanced Budget Act of 1997. An overview of the framework of the proposed HHA prospective payment system is provided.

Hospice: Criteria for Medicare Coverage of Noncancer Hospice Care

Patients considered to be in the terminal stage of noncancer illness must meet certain criteria to be eligible for Medicare coverage of hospice care. A detailed explanation of the policies that have been developed concerning noncancer hospice care are provided.

Skilled Nursing Facility: Background on the Resource Utilization Groups (RUG-III) Classification System

The Balanced Budget Act of 1997 requires the implementation of a Medicare Skilled Nursing Facility (SNF) prospective payment system (PPS). Background on the Resource Utilization Groups (RUG-III) classification system that is part of the new PPS for skilled nursing facilities is provided.

Skilled Nursing Facility: Official Coding Guidelines for Long Term Care

The official guidelines for coding and sequencing diagnosis codes in the long term care setting are presented with examples to demonstrate the application of the guidelines to actual case scenarios.

10 Steps to Correct Coding

This is a valuable resource that takes the coder step by step through the coding process with detailed explanations accompanied by coding examples to demonstrate the practical application of the 10 steps.

Valid Three-digit Code Table

ICD-9-CM is composed of codes with either 3, 4, or 5 digits. A code is invalid if it has not been coded to the full number of digits required for that code. There are a certain number codes that are valid for reporting as three digit codes. A list of the valid three-digit code is included as a convenient reference when auditing claims.

ICD-9-CM Official Conventions

ICD-9-CM FOOTNOTES, SYMBOLS, INSTRUCTIONAL NOTES AND CONVENTIONS

This *ICD-9-CM Expert for Home Health Services, Nursing Facilities, and Hospices, Volumes 1, 2 & 3* preserves all the footnotes, symbols, instructional notes and conventions found in the government's official version. Accurate coding depends upon understanding the meaning of these elements.

The following appear in the disease Tabular List, unless otherwise noted.

OFFICIAL GOVERNMENT SYMBOLS

§   The section mark preceding a code denotes a footnote on the page. This symbol is used in the Tabular List of Diseases and in the Tabular List of Procedures.

ICD-9-CM CONVENTIONS USED IN THE TABULAR LIST

In addition to the symbols and footnotes above, the ICD-9-CM disease tabular has certain abbreviations, punctuation, symbols and other conventions. Our *ICD-9-CM Expert for Home Health Services, Nursing Facilities, and Hospices, Volumes 1, 2 & 3* preserves these conventions. Proper use of the conventions will lead to efficient and accurate coding.

Abbreviations

NEC   Not elsewhere classifiable

This abbreviation is used when the ICD-9-CM system does not provide a code specific for the patient's condition.

NOS   Not otherwise specified

This abbreviation is the equivalent of 'unspecified' and is used only when the coder lacks the information necessary to code to a more specific four-digit subcategory.

[ ]   Brackets enclose synonyms, alternative terminology or explanatory phrases:

    482.2   Pneumonia due to Hemophilus influenzae [H. influenzae]

Brackets that appear beneath a code indicate the fifth digits that are considered valid fifth digits for the code. This convention is applied for those instances in ICD-9-CM where not all common fifth digits are considered valid for each subcategory with in a category.

    715.0   Osteoarthrosis, generalized
    [0,4,9]

Generalized arthrosis can only be assigned in cases for which the degenerative joint disease involves multiple joints. Therefore, this code is considered for arthrosis in the sites described as unspecified, hand (which consists of multiple joints), or multiple sites. Therefore, only fifth digits 0, 4, and 9 are valid with subcategory 715.0.

[ ]   Slanted brackets that appear in the Alphabetic Indexes indicate mandatory multiple coding. Both codes must be assigned to fully describe the condition and are sequenced in the order listed.

    Tachycardia
       ventricular (paroxysmal)
          psychogenic 316 *[427.1]*

Psychogenic paroxysmal tachycardia is reported using both 316, Psychogenic factors associated with diseases classified elsewhere, and 427.1, Paroxysmal ventricular tachydcardia.

Diversion

    biliopancratic (BPD) 43.7 *[45.51] [45.91]*

Code assignment of biliopancratic diversion is reported using all three codes 43.7, Partial gastrectomy with anastomosis to jejunum, 45.51, Isolation of segment of small intestine, and 45.91, Small-to-small intestinal anastomosis.

( )   Parentheses enclose supplementary words, called nonessential modifiers, that may be present in the narrative description of a disease without affecting the code assignment:

    198.4   Other parts of nervous system
       Meninges (cerebral) (spinal)

:   Colons are used in the Tabular List after an incomplete term that needs one or more of the modifiers that follow in order to make it assignable to a given category:

    021.1   Enteric tularemia
       Tularemia:
          cryptogenic
          intestinal
          typhoidal

}   Braces enclose a series of terms, each of which is modified by the statement appearing to the right of the brace:

    560.2   Volvulus

       Knotting
       Strangulation   } of intestine, bowel, or colon
       Torsion
       Twist

OTHER CONVENTIONS

Boldface   Boldface type is used for all codes and titles in the Tabular List.

Italicized   Italicized type is used for all exclusion notes and to identify codes that should not be used for describing the primary diagnosis.

INSTRUCTIONAL NOTES

These notes appear only in the Tabular List of Diseases:

Includes   An includes note further defines or clarifies the content of the chapter, subchapter, category, subcategory or subclassification. The includes note in the example below applies only to category 461.

Excludes   Terms following the word "*Excludes*" are not classified to the chapter, subchapter, category, subcategory or specific subclassification code under which it is found. The note also may provide the location of the excluded diagnosis. Excludes notes are italicized.

    461   Acute sinusitis

      INCLUDES   abscess
                  empyema   acute, of sinus
                  infection   } (accessory)
                  inflammation   (nasal)
                  suppuration

      EXCLUDES   *chronic or unspecified sinusitis (473.0-473.9)*

Use additional code:

This instruction signals the coder that an additional code should be used if the information is available to provide a more complete picture of that diagnosis.

    362.13 Changes in vascular appearance
       Vascular sheathing of retina
       Use additional code for any associated atherosclerosis (440.8)

There are coding circumstances outside of the etiology/manifestation convention when multiple coding for a single condition is required. The 'Use additional code' note will be found under the associated condition code in the tabular. In the index, the multiple coding requirement is indicated by the use of the slanted bracket. The two codes are to be sequenced as listed in the index. For example, retinal arterisosclerosis must be coded using two codes sequenced as listed in the index.

Arteriosclerosis, arteriosclerotic

retinal (vascular) 440.8 *[362.13]*

Code first underlying disease:

The *Code first underlying disease* instructional note found under certain codes is a mandatory sequencing rule. Most often this sequencing rule applies to the etiology/manifestation convention and is found under at the manifestation code. The manifestation code may never be used alone or as a primary diagnosis (i.e., sequenced first). The instructional note, the code and its descriptor appear in italics in the Tabular List.

The code and its descriptor appear in italics in the Tabular List. The instruction "*Code first underlying disease*" is usually followed by the code or codes for the most common underlying disease (etiology). Record the code for the etiology or origin of the disease, and then record the italicized manifestation code in the next position.

590.81 *Pyelitis or pyelonephritis in diseases classified elsewhere*
   Code first underlying disease as:
      tuberculosis (016.0)

Not all codes with a 'Code first underlying disease' instructional note are part of the etiology/manifestation convention. The 'Code first' note will appear, but the title of the code and the instructional note are not in italics. These codes may be reported alone or as the secondary diagnosis. For example, disseminated chorioretinitis may be reported as a principal diagnosis. However, if the underlying condition that caused disseminated chorioretinitis is known, such as tuberculous disseminated chorioretinitis, two codes are required and sequenced as listed in the index.

363.13 Disseminated choroiditis and chorioretinitis, generalized
   Code first underlying disease as:
      tuberculosis (017.3)

Code, if applicable, any causal condition first:

A code with this note indicates that this code may be assigned as a principal diagnosis when the causal condition is unknown or not applicable. If a causal condition is known, then the code for that condition should be sequenced as the principal or first-listed diagnosis.

590.0 **Chronic pyelonephritis**
   Chronic pyelitis
   Chronic pyonephrosis
   Code, if applicable, any causal condition first

Modifiers

The physician's diagnostic statement usually contains several medical terms. To translate these terms into diagnosis codes, choose only one, the term for the condition, as the main term. The accompanying words, the modifiers, further describe the main term. Modifiers are found in the Alphabetic Index following the main term.

There are two types of modifiers: nonessential and essential.

- Nonessential modifiers are shown in parentheses after the term it modifies. These modifiers do not affect the code selection.
- Essential modifiers, those that do affect the code selection, are indented under the main term. Use these modifiers in the coding process only if they are specified in the physician's diagnosis.

For example, to locate a code for acute purulent lobar pneumonia in the Alphabetic Index, choose "Pneumonia" as the main term, with "acute," "purulent," and "lobar" as the modifiers.

Nonessential Modifiers	**Pneumonia** (acute) (Alpenstich) (benign) (bilateral) (brain) (cerebral) (circumscribed) (congestive) (creeping) (delayed resolution) (double) (epidemic) (fever) (flash) (fulminant) (fungoid) (granulomatous) (hemorrhagic) (incipient) (infantile) (infectious) (infiltration) (insular) (intermittent) (latent) (lobe) (migratory) (newborn) (organized) (overwhelming) (primary) (progressive) (pseudolobar) (purulent) (resolved) (secondary) (senile) (septic) (suppurative) (terminal) (true) (unresolved) (vesicular) 486
Essential	due to Eaton's agent 483.0

Essential	lobar (diplococcal) (disseminated) (double) (interstitial) (pneumococcal, any type) 481
	   with influenza 487.0
	   bacterial 482.9

Code 486 would be used for acute purulent pneumonia. The nonessential modifiers "acute" and "purulent" do not affect the code selection. However, lobar pneumonia and acute purulent lobar pneumonia would be coded 481. The essential modifier "lobar" changes the code selection.

Default Codes

The default code listing for any condition is to the unspecified form of the condition. Coders should go to the Tabular List to the category of the unspecified code listed to determine whether a more specific code should be assigned to the condition.

Example: **German measles** 056.9

Turning to the Tabular List to code 056, Rubella, the coder now has more information available for assigning a code. Is the condition truly rubella with no mention of complication? Or should a code be assigned indicating a specific complication such as 056.01, Encephalomyelitis due to the rubella?

Cross-references

ICD-9-CM provides assistance in locating codes through cross-references. They are found only in the Alphabetic Index. There are three types of cross-references: see, see also and see category.

The *see* cross-reference directs the coder elsewhere in the Alphabetic Index. This is a mandatory instruction.

The *see also* cross-reference provides the coder with the option to check another main term in the Alphabetic Index. This option should be chosen when the appropriate description is not found under the initial main term.

The see category cross-reference provides the coder with a category main term in the Tabular List to which the coder must refer in order to select an appropriate code.

Parencephalitis (*see also* Encephalitis)   323.9
   late effect — *see* category 326
Paresis (*see also* Paralysis)   344.9
   accommodation   367.51
   bladder (spastic) (sphincter) (*see also* Paralysis, bladder) 596.53
      tabetic   094.0
   bowel, colon, or intestine (*see also* Ileus)   560.1
   brain or cerebral — *see* Paralysis, brain
   extrinsic muscle, eye   378.55
   general   094.1
      arrested   094.1
      brain   094.1
      cerebral   094.1
      insane   094.1
      juvenile   090.40
         remission   090.49
      progressive   094.1
      remission (sustained)   094.1
      tabetic   094.1
   heart (*see also* Failure, heart)   428.9
   infantile (*see also* Poliomyelitis)   045.9 ☑
   insane   094.1
   juvenile   090.40
   late effect — *see* Paralysis, late effect

The *see also* condition directs the coder to search the Index under the main term describing the condition rather than an anatomical site or cause.

> **Abdomen, abdominal** — *see also* condition

The Index directs the coder to search by the main term describing the condition rather than the body site. The coder might need to locate a term such as ascites for accumulation of fluid in the abdominal cavity.

Omit code:

"*Omit code*" is used to instruct the coder that no code is to be assigned. When this instruction is found in the Alphabetic Index to Diseases the medical term should not be coded as a diagnosis.

> **Metaplasia**
>
> cervix — *omit code*

When used in Volume 3, 'omit code' is meant to indicate procedures that do not merit separate code assignments, such as minor procedures performed in conjunction with more extensive procedures or procedures that represent an operative approach.

> **Arthrotomy 80.10**
>
> as operative approach — *omit code*

See Condition:

The "see condition' note found in the Alphabetic Index to Disease instructs the coder to refer to a main term for the condition. This note will follow index terms that are nouns for anatomical sites or adjectival forms of disease term. In the example below, the index terms 'Cervix' and 'Diffuse' are followed by the — *see* condition. Coders should search the index using a condition term such as atrophy or prolapse.

> **Cervix** — *see* condition
>
> **Diffuse** — *see* condition

Morphology Codes

For each neoplastic disease listed in the index, a morphology code is provided that identifies histological type and behavior.

Example:

> **Myelolipoma** (M8870/0) — *see* Neoplasm, by site, benign

The histology is identified by the first four digits and the behavior is identified by the digit following the slash. Appendix A of Volume 1 contains a listing of morphology codes. This appendix is helpful when the pathology report identifies the neoplasm by using an M code. The coder may refer to Appendix A to determine the nomenclature of the neoplasm that will be the main term to search in the Index. The behavior classification is as follows:

0	Benign
1	Uncertain behavior
2	Carcinoma in situ
3	Malignant, primary site
6	Malignant, secondary site.

Mandatory Dual Coding

ICD-9-CM employs the slanted bracket to indicate mandatory coding of both etiology and manifestation. This is referred to as mandatory dual coding. The Alphabetic Index identifies mandatory dual coding by using the slanted bracket [ ] with the code in italics.

Example:

> **Arthritis, arthritic** (acute) (chronic) (subacute)
> due to or associated with
> acromegaly 253.0 *[713.0]*

In this example, the coding sequence must be 253.0, the etiology, listed first, followed by 713.0, the manifestation.

Instructional Notes

The Alphabetic Index contains notes that define terms, give instructions or list fifth-digit subclassifications. Each note is enclosed in a box, and the information within it is printed in italics. An example is shown below:

> **Diabetes, diabetic** (brittle) (congenital) (familial) (mellitus) (poorly controlled) (severe) (slight) (without complication)   250.0 ☑

> Note: Use the following fifth-digit subclassification with category 250:
>
> **0 type II or unspecified type, not stated as uncontrolled**
> Fifth-digit 0 is for use for type II patients, even if the patient requires insulin
> **1 type I [juvenile type], not stated as uncontrolled**
> **2 type II or unspecified type, uncontrolled**
> Fifth-digit 2 is for use for type II patients, even if the patient requires insulin
> **3 type I [juvenile type], uncontrolled**

This note under the main term "Diabetes" gives instructions concerning the need to use a fifth-digit when coding diabetes.

Additional Conventions

NEW AND REVISED TEXT SYMBOLS

● A bullet at a code or line of text indicates that that the entry is new.

▲ A triangle in the Tabular List indicates that the code title is revised. In the Alphabetic Index the triangle indicates that a code has changed.

►◄ These symbols appear at the beginning and at the end of a section of new or revised text.

When these symbols appear on a page there will be a date on the lower outside corner of the page indicating the date of the change, (e.g., October 2005).

ADDITIONAL DIGITS REQUIRED

✓3ʳᵈ This symbol indicates that the code requires a third digit.

✓4ᵗʰ This symbol indicates that the code requires a fourth digit.

✓5ᵗʰ This symbol indicates that a code requires a fifth digit.

☑ This symbol found only in the Alphabetic Index sections and the Table of Drugs and Chemicals indicates that an additional digit is required. Referring to the tabular section is essential to locate the appropriate additional digit.

Example:

Locate the following code:

☑4ᵗʰ 79.0 **Closed reduction of fracture without internal**
[0-9] **fixation**

The ☑4ᵗʰ symbol to the left of subcategory code 79.0 indicates that a fourth-digit subclassification must be assigned to complete the code. One other notation appears with this subcategory code: the numbers in brackets [0–9] below the code. The numbers 0–9 represent the valid fourth digits assigned to complete the code. To complete the code, the appropriate fourth digit should be assigned based on the procedure statement.

The following explains the footnotes used in the procedure Tabular List:

§ Requires fourth digit—reminds the coder that valid fourth digits are listed in brackets under the code.

DEFINITIONS

DEF: This symbol indicates a definition of disease or procedure term. The definition will appear in blue type in the Tabular Lists.

AHA's *CODING CLINIC FOR ICD-9-CM* REFERENCES

The four cooperating parties have designated the AHA's *Coding Clinic for ICD-9-CM* as the official publication for coding guidelines. The references are identified by the notation **AHA:** followed by the issue, year and page number.

In the example below, AHA's *Coding Clinic for ICD-9-CM*, third quarter 1991, page 15, contains a discussion on code assignment for vitreous hemorrhage:

379.23 Vitreous hemorrhage
AHA: 3Q, '91, 15

The table below explains the abbreviations in the *Coding Clinic* references:

J-F	January/February
M-A	March/April
M-J	May/June
J-A	July/August
S-O	September/October
N-D	November/December
1Q	First quarter
2Q	Second quarter
3Q	Third quarter
4Q	Fourth quarter

Age and Sex Edit Symbols

The age edits below address MCE edit 4 and are used to detect inconsistencies between the patient's age and diagnosis. They appear in the Tabular List of Diseases to the right of the code description.

Newborn Age: 0

These diagnoses are intended for newborns and neonates and the patient's age must be 0 years

Pediatric Age: 0-17

These diagnoses are intended for children and the patient's age must between 0 and 17 years

Maternity Age: 12-55

These diagnoses are intended for the patients between the age of 12 and 55 years

Adult Age: 15-124

These diagnoses are intended for the patients between the age of 15 and 124 years.

The sex symbols below address MCE edit 5 and are used to detect inconsistencies between the patient's sex and diagnosis and/or procedure. They appear in the Tabular Lists to the right of the code description:

♂ **Male diagnosis or procedure only**

This symbol appears to the right of the code description. This reference appears in the disease and procedure Tabular List.

♀ **Female diagnosis or procedure only**

This symbol appears to the right of the code description. This reference appears in the disease and procedure Tabular List.

PDx This symbol identifies a V code that can only be used as a primary diagnosis.

SDx This symbol identifies a V code that can only be used as a secondary diagnosis.

Note: A V code with out a symbol may be used as either a primary or secondary diagnosis.

Adj These adjunct codes are not to be reported alone. Adjunct codes are assigned only in addition to a primary procedure. Their purpose is to provide supplemental information about the primary procedure performed. Adjunct codes are not procedure codes, but serve to provide additional detail about the primary procedure.

Example:

PTCA balloon inflation of two vessels, with insertion of one intravascular coronary stent.

Code assignment:

00.66 **Percutaneous transluminal coronary angioplasty [PTCA] or athrectomy**

00.41 **Procedure on two vessels**

00.45 **Insertion of one vascular stent**

In the above example, codes 00.41 and 00.45 are adjunct codes that provide specific detail about the PTCA procedure performed.

CD PDx Primary diagnosis in the Clinical Dimension of the HHA case mix classification system.

CD SDx Secondary diagnosis in the Clinical Dimension of the HHA case mix classification system.

The prospective payment system for home health agencies is based upon a case mix classification system using selected data from the OASIS assessment instrument. The data elements are organized into three dimensions; clinical, functional, and service utilization. The clinical dimension is defined by certain primary and secondary diagnosis codes as reported on the OASIS assessment instrument under data elements M0230 and M0240. Refer to the "Overview of the Home Health Agency Prospective Payment System" resource in your code book for a more detailed discussion of the case mix classification system.

Reminder: All codes should be reported to the highest level of specificity. Codes indicated at the three and four digit levels include all related four and five digit codes. Diagnosis codes with four and five digits must be coded to that level on the OASIS assessment instrument.

Color Coding

For a quick reference to the color codes and their meaning, refer to the color/symbol legend located at the bottom of each page.

To alert the coder to important reimbursement issues affected by the code assignment, color bars have been added. The colors represent reimbursement issues as for the prospective payment systems cited.

Color coding appears in both Tabular Lists. Some codes carry more than one color. Please note that the same color may appear in the disease and procedure Tabular Lists, but with different meanings.

Disease Tabular List

Manifestation Code

These codes will appear in italic type as well as with a blue color bar over the code title. A manifestation code is not allowed to be reported as a primary diagnosis because each describes a manifestation of some other underlying disease, not the disease itself. This is referred to as mandatory multiple coding of etiology and manifestation. Code the underlying disease first. A *Code first underlying disease* instructional note will appear with underlying disease codes identified. In the Alphabetic Index these codes are listed as the secondary code in slanted bracket with the code for the underlying disease listed first.

RUG III Special Care Dx

A red color bar over the code description indicates a RUG-III Category Three, Special Care, diagnosis that may qualify a resident of a skilled nursing facility (SNF) for this clinical category. Before a resident is assigned to this category, other qualifications must be met. Please refer to the resource titled RUG-III Classification System in the Skilled Nursing Facility located at the back of this book.

RUG III Clinically Complex Dx

A yellow color bar over the code description indicates a RUG-III Category Four, Clinically Complex, diagnosis that may qualify a resident of a skilled nursing facility (SNF) for this clinical category. Before a resident is assigned to this category, other qualifications must be met. Please refer to the resource titled RUG-III Classification System in the Skilled Nursing Facility located at the back of this book.

Hospice Noncancer Dx

A gray color bar over a code description indicates a noncancer diagnosis that may satisfy the medical necessity criteria for Medicare coverage of hospice care. The diagnosis alone does not support medical necessity, but represents one of many factors that establish medical necessity. For a more detailed explanation of the noncancer diagnosis policies for hospice care please refer to the resource titled Criteria for Medicare Coverage of Noncancer Hospice Care located at the back of this book.

Procedure Tabular List

RUG III Rehabilitation Code

A blue color bar over the code description indicates a RUG-III Category One, Rehabilitation, procedure that may qualify a resident of a skilled nursing facility (SNF) for this clinical category. Before a resident is assigned to this category, other qualifications must be met. Please refer to the resource titled RUG-III Classification System in the Skilled Nursing Facility located at the back of this book.

RUG III Extensive Service Code

A gray color bar over the code description indicates a RUG-III Category Two, Extensive Service, procedure that may qualify a resident of a skilled nursing facility (SNF) for this clinical category. Before a resident is assigned to this category, other qualifications must be met. Please refer to the resource titled RUG-III Classification System in the Skilled Nursing Facility located at the back of this book.

RUG III Special Care Code

A red color bar over the code description indicates a RUG-III Category Three, Special Care, procedure that may qualify a resident of a skilled nursing facility (SNF) for this clinical category. Before a resident is assigned to this category, other qualifications must be met. Please refer to the resource titled RUG-III Classification System in the Skilled Nursing Facility located at the back of this book.

RUG III Clinically Complex Code

A yellow color bar over the code description indicates a RUG-III Category Four, Clinically Complex, procedure that may qualify a resident of a skilled nursing facility (SNF) for this clinical category. Before a resident is assigned to this category, other qualifications must be met. Please refer to the resource titled RUG-III Classification System in the Skilled Nursing Facility located at the back of this book.

Summary of Code Changes

DISEASE TABULAR LIST (VOLUME 1)

238.7   Includes term added
250.4   Use additional code note term added
250.5   Use additional code note term added
       Use additional code note terms revised
257.8   Includes terms deleted
       Excludes term added
● 259.5   Androgen insensitivity syndrome
       Includes terms added
276.5   Includes terms deleted
● 276.50   Volume depletion, unspecified
● 276.51   Dehydration
● 276.52   Hypovolemia
       Includes term added
▲ 278   ►Overweight,◄ obesity and other hyperalimentation
▲ 278.0   ►Overweight and◄ obesity
       Use additional code note added
● 278.02   Overweight
282.49   Includes term added
282.7   Includes term deleted
283.0   Excludes term revised
284.9   Includes term deleted
       Excludes note added
285.0   Includes term deleted
       Excludes note added
▲ 285.21   Anemia in ~~end stage renal disease~~ ►chronic kidney disease◄
       Includes term added
287.0   Excludes term revised
287.3   Includes terms deleted
● 287.30   Primary thrombocytopenia, unspecified
       Includes term added
● 287.31   Immune thrombocytopenic purpura
       Includes terms added
● 287.32   Evans' syndrome
● 287.33   Congenital and hereditary thrombocytopenic purpura
       Includes terms added
       Excludes note added
● 287.39   Other primary thrombocytopenia
Chapter 5. Mental Disorders (290-319)-Chapter introductory paragraphs deleted
● 291.82   Alcohol induced sleep disorders
       Includes terms added
291.89   Includes term deleted
● 292.85   Drug induced sleep disorders
       Includes terms added
292.89   Includes term deleted
307.4   Excludes terms added
307.41   Includes terms added
307.42   Includes terms added
307.44   Includes terms added
       Excludes term added
▲ 307.45   Circadian rhythm sleep disorder ►of nonorganic origin◄
       Includes terms deleted
307.59   Includes term revised
323.6   Includes term added
323.8   Includes term added
● 327   Organic sleep disorders
● 327.0   Organic disorders of initiating and maintaining sleep [Organic insomnia]
       Excludes terms added
● 327.00   Organic insomnia, unspecified
● 327.01   Insomnia due to medical condition classified elsewhere
       Code first note added
       Excludes note added
● 327.02   Insomnia due to mental disorder
       Code first note added
       Excludes note added
● 327.09   Other organic insomnia
● 327.1   Organic disorders of excessive somnolence [Organic hypersomnia]
       Excludes note added
● 327.10   Organic hypersomnia, unspecified
● 327.11   Idiopathic hypersomnia with long sleep time

● 327.12   Idiopathic hypersomnia without long sleep time
● 327.13   Recurrent hypersomnia
       Includes terms added
● 327.14   Hypersomnia due to medical condition classified elsewhere
       Code first note added
       Excludes note added
● 327.15   Hypersomnia due to mental disorder
       Code first note added
       Excludes note added
● 327.19   Other organic hypersomnia
● 327.2   Organic sleep apnea
       Includes term added
● 327.20   Organic sleep apnea, unspecified
● 327.21   Primary central sleep apnea
● 327.22   High altitude periodic breathing
● 327.23   Obstructive sleep apnea (adult) (pediatric)
● 327.24   Idiopathic sleep related nonobstructive alveolar hypoventilation
       Includes term added
● 327.25   Congenital central alveolar hypoventilation syndrome
● 327.26   Sleep related hypoventilation/hypoxemia in conditions classifiable elsewhere
       Code first note added
● 327.27   Central sleep apnea in conditions classified elsewhere
       Code first note added
● 327.29   Other organic sleep apnea
● 327.3   Circadian rhythm sleep disorder
       Includes terms added
       Excludes note added
● 327.30   Circadian rhythm sleep disorder, unspecified
● 327.31   Circadian rhythm sleep disorder, delayed sleep phase type
● 327.32   Circadian rhythm sleep disorder, advanced sleep phase type
● 327.33   Circadian rhythm sleep disorder, irregular sleep-wake type
● 327.34   Circadian rhythm sleep disorder, free-running type
● 327.35   Circadian rhythm sleep disorder, jet lag type
● 327.36   Circadian rhythm sleep disorder, shift work type
● 327.37   Circadian rhythm sleep disorder in conditions classified elsewhere
       Code first note added
● 327.39   Other circadian rhythm sleep disorder
● 327.4   Organic parasomnia
       Excludes note added
● 327.40   Organic parasomnia, unspecified
● 327.41   Confusional arousals
● 327.42   REM sleep behavior disorder
● 327.43   Recurrent isolated sleep paralysis
● 327.44   Parasomnia in conditions classified elsewhere
       Code first note added
● 327.49   Other organic parasomnia
● 327.5   Organic sleep related movement disorders
       Excludes note added
● 327.51   Periodic limb movement disorder
       Includes term added
● 327.52   Sleep related leg cramps
● 327.53   Sleep related bruxism
● 327.59   Other organic sleep related movement disorders
● 327.8   Other organic sleep disorders
332.1   Includes term added
333   Excludes term added
333.1   Includes term added
333.7   Includes term added
333.82   Includes term added
333.90   Includes term added
       Use additional code note added
333.99   Includes term added
       Use additional code note added
357.4   Code first note revised

362.01   Includes terms deleted
● 362.03   Nonproliferative diabetic retinopathy NOS
● 362.04   Mild nonproliferative diabetic retinopathy
● 362.05   Moderate nonproliferative diabetic retinopathy
● 362.06   Severe nonproliferative diabetic retinopathy
● 362.07   Diabetic macular edema
       Includes term added
       Instructional note added
402   Use additional code note revised
▲ 403   Hypertensive ~~renal~~ ►kidney◄ disease
       Use additional code note added
▲ 403.0   Hypertensive ~~renal~~ ►kidney◄ disease, Malignant
▲ 403.00   Hypertensive ~~renal~~ ►kidney◄ disease, malignant, without ~~mention of renal failure~~ ►chronic kidney disease◄
▲ 403.01   Hypertensive ~~renal~~ ►kidney◄ disease, malignant, with ~~renal failure~~ ►chronic kidney disease◄
▲ 403.1   Hypertensive ~~renal~~ ►kidney◄ disease, Benign
▲ 403.10   Hypertensive ~~renal~~ ►kidney◄ disease, benign, without ~~mention of renal failure~~ ►chronic kidney disease◄
▲ 403.11   Hypertensive ~~renal~~ ►kidney◄ disease, benign, with ~~renal failure~~ ►chronic kidney disease◄
▲ 403.9   Hypertensive ~~renal~~ ►kidney◄ disease, Unspecified
▲ 403.90   Hypertensive ~~renal~~ ►kidney◄ disease, unspecified, without ~~mention of renal failure~~ ►chronic kidney disease◄
▲ 403.91   Hypertensive ~~renal~~ ►kidney◄ disease, unspecified, with ~~renal failure~~ ►chronic kidney disease◄
▲ 404   Hypertensive heart and ~~renal~~ ►kidney◄ disease
       Use additional code note revised
       Use additional code note added
▲ 404.0   Hypertensive heart and ~~renal~~ ►kidney◄ disease, Malignant
▲ 404.00   Hypertensive heart and ~~renal~~ ►kidney◄ disease, malignant, without ~~mention of~~ heart failure or ~~renal failure~~ ► chronic kidney disease◄
▲ 404.02   Hypertensive heart and ~~renal~~ ►kidney◄ disease, malignant, with ~~renal failure~~ ►chronic kidney disease◄
▲ 404.03   Hypertensive heart and ~~renal~~ ►kidney◄ disease, malignant, with heart failure and ~~renal failure~~ ►chronic kidney disease◄
▲ 404.1   Hypertensive heart and ~~renal~~ ►kidney◄ disease, Benign
▲ 404.10   Hypertensive heart and ~~renal~~ ►kidney◄ disease, benign, without ~~mention of~~ heart failure or ~~renal failure~~ ► chronic kidney disease◄
▲ 404.12   Hypertensive heart and ~~renal~~ ►kidney◄ disease, benign, with ~~renal failure~~ ►chronic kidney disease◄
▲ 404.13   Hypertensive heart and ~~renal~~ ►kidney◄ disease, benign, with heart failure and ~~renal failure~~ ►chronic kidney disease◄
▲ 404.9   Hypertensive heart and ~~renal~~ ►kidney◄ disease, Unspecified
▲ 404.90   Hypertensive heart and ~~renal~~ ►kidney◄ disease, unspecified, without ~~mention of~~ heart failure or ~~renal failure~~ ► chronic kidney disease◄
▲ 404.92   Hypertensive heart and ~~renal~~ ►kidney◄ disease, unspecified, with ~~renal failure~~ ►chronic kidney disease◄
▲ 404.93   Hypertensive heart and ~~renal~~ ►kidney◄ disease, unspecified, with heart failure and ~~renal failure~~ ►chronic kidney disease◄
410   Includes term added
410.0   Includes term added
410.1   Includes term added

►◄ Revised Text   ● New Code   ▲ Revised Code Title

410.2	Includes term added
410.3	Includes term added
410.4	Includes term added
410.5	Includes term added
410.6	Includes term added
410.7	Includes term added
410.8	Includes term added
410.9	Includes term added
420.0	Code first note revised
● 426.82	Long QT syndrome
● 443.82	Erythromelalgia
443.89	Includes term deleted
Section	PNEUMONIA AND INFLUENZA (480-487)
	Excludes term revised
487	Excludes term deleted
487.0	Use additional code note added
507	Excludes term revised
524.51	Includes term deleted
525.1	Code first note added
525.10	Includes term deleted
● 525.4	Complete edentulism
	Use additional code note added
● 525.40	Complete edentulism, unspecified
	Includes term added
● 525.41	Complete edentulism, class I
● 525.42	Complete edentulism, class II
● 525.43	Complete edentulism, class III
● 525.44	Complete edentulism, class IV
● 525.5	Partial edentulism
	Use additional code note added
● 525.50	Partial edentulism, unspecified
● 525.51	Partial edentulism, class I
● 525.52	Partial edentulism, class II
● 525.53	Partial edentulism, class III
● 525.54	Partial edentulism, class IV
552.8	Excludes note added
▲ 567	Peritonitis ▶and retroperitoneal infections◀
567.2	Includes terms deleted
● 567.21	Peritonitis (acute) generalized
	Includes term added
● 567.22	Peritoneal abscess
	Includes terms added
● 567.23	Spontaneous bacterial peritonitis
● 567.29	Other suppurative peritonitis
	Includes term added
● 567.3	Retroperitoneal infections
● 567.31	Psoas muscle abscess
● 567.38	Other retroperitoneal abscess
● 567.39	Other retroperitoneal infections
567.8	Includes terms deleted
● 567.81	Choleperitonitis
	Includes term added
● 567.82	Sclerosing mesenteritis
	Includes terms added
● 567.89	Other specified peritonitis
	Includes terms added
▲ 585	Chronic renal failure ▶kidney disease (CKD)◀
	Use additional code note added
● 585.1	Chronic kidney disease, Stage I
● 585.2	Chronic kidney disease, Stage II (mild)
● 585.3	Chronic kidney disease, Stage III (moderate)
● 585.4	Chronic kidney disease, Stage IV (severe)
● 585.5	Chronic kidney disease, Stage V
● 585.6	End stage renal disease
● 585.9	Chronic kidney disease, unspecified
	Includes terms added
593.9	Includes term added
	Includes terms revised
	Excludes term added
	Excludes terms deleted
▲ 599.6	Urinary obstruction, unspecified
	Includes terms deleted
	Includes terms added
● 599.60	Urinary obstruction, unspecified
	Includes terms added
● 599.69	Urinary obstruction, not elsewhere classified
607.84	Excludes term revised
648.8	Instructional note revised
	Use additional code note added
● 651.7	Multiple gestation following (elective) fetal reduction
	Includes term added

● 651.70	Multiple gestation following (elective) fetal reduction, unspecified as to episode of care or not applicable
● 651.71	Multiple gestation following (elective) fetal reduction, delivered, with or without mention of antepartum condition
● 651.73	Multiple gestation following (elective) fetal reduction, antepartum condition or complication
660.8	Use additional code note added
▲ 728.87	Muscle weakness ▶(generalized)◀
742	Excludes note added
748	Excludes note added
752	Excludes term revised
752.11	Includes term deleted
752.41	Includes term added
752.7	Excludes term revised
Chapter 15.	CERTAIN CONDITIONS ORIGINATING IN THE PERINATAL PERIOD (760-779)
	Includes note revised
760.74	Includes term added
● 760.77	Noxious influences affecting fetus or newborn via placenta or breast milk, Anticonvulsants
	Includes terms added
● 760.78	Noxious influences affecting fetus or newborn via placenta or breast milk, Antimetabolic agents
	Includes terms added
● 763.84	Meconium passage during delivery
	Excludes note added
▲ 770.1	Meconium ▶Fetal and newborn◀ aspiration syndrome
	Includes term deleted
	Excludes terms added
● 770.10	Fetal and newborn aspiration, unspecified
● 770.11	Meconium aspiration without respiratory symptoms
	Includes term added
● 770.12	Meconium aspiration with respiratory symptoms
	Includes terms added
	Use additional code note added
● 770.13	Aspiration of clear amniotic fluid without respiratory symptoms
	Includes term added
● 770.14	Aspiration of clear amniotic fluid with respiratory symptoms
	Includes terms added
	Use additional code note added
● 770.15	Aspiration of blood without respiratory symptoms
	Includes term added
● 770.16	Aspiration of blood with respiratory symptoms
	Includes terms added
	Use additional code note added
● 770.17	Other fetal and newborn aspiration without respiratory symptoms
● 770.18	Other fetal and newborn aspiration with respiratory symptoms
	Includes terms added
	Use additional code note added
● 770.85	Aspiration of postnatal stomach contents without respiratory symptoms
	Includes term added
● 770.86	Aspiration of postnatal stomach contents with respiratory symptoms
	Includes terms added
	Use additional code note added
771	Includes note revised
● 779.84	Meconium staining
	Includes terms added
779.89	Use additional code note added
780.5	Excludes terms added
▲ 780.51	Insomnia with sleep apnea, ▶unspecified◀
▲ 780.52	Other Insomnia, ▶unspecified◀
	Includes term deleted
▲ 780.53	Hypersomnia with sleep apnea, ▶unspecified◀
▲ 780.54	Other Hypersomnia, ▶unspecified◀
	Includes term deleted
▲ 780.55	Disruption of 24 hour sleep wake cycle, ▶unspecified◀
	Includes terms deleted
▲ 780.57	Other and Unspecified sleep apnea

▲ 780.58	Sleep related movement disorder, ▶unspecified◀
	Includes term deleted
780.92	Excludes note added
● 780.95	Other excessive crying
	Excludes note added
783.2	Use additional code note added
783.9	Excludes term revised
788.2	Excludes term added
794.31	Excludes note added
795.09	Includes term added
▲ 799.0	Asphyxia ▶and hypoxemia◀
	Excludes term revised
	Excludes term added
● 799.01	Asphyxia
● 799.02	Hypoxemia
996	Excludes term added
996.4	Use additional code note added
● 996.40	Unspecified mechanical complication of internal orthopedic device, implant, and graft
● 996.41	Mechanical loosening of prosthetic joint
	Includes term added
● 996.42	Dislocation of prosthetic joint
	Includes terms added
● 996.43	Prosthetic joint implant failure
	Includes term added
● 996.44	Peri-prosthetic fracture around prosthetic joint
● 996.45	Peri-prosthetic osteolysis
● 996.46	Articular bearing surface wear of prosthetic joint
● 996.47	Other mechanical complication of prosthetic joint implant
	Includes term added
● 996.49	Other mechanical complication of other internal orthopedic device, implant, and graft
	Excludes term added
996.66	Use additional code note added
	SUPPLEMENTARY CLASSIFICATION OF FACTORS INFLUENCING HEALTH STATUS AND CONTACT WITH HEALTH SERVICES ▶(V01-V85)◀
V03	Excludes term revised
V07.39	Excludes term revised
V12.0	Excludes note added
● V12.42	Personal history of, Infections of the central nervous system
	Includes terms added
V12.6	Excludes term added
● V12.60	Personal history of, Unspecified disease of respiratory system
● V12.61	Personal history of, Pneumonia (recurrent)
● V12.69	Personal history of, Other diseases of respiratory system
● V13.02	Personal history of, Urinary (tract) infection
● V13.03	Personal history of, Nephrotic syndrome
● V15.88	Personal history of, History of fall
	Includes term added
● V17.81	Family history of, Osteoporosis
● V17.89	Family history of, Other musculoskeletal diseases
● V18.9	Family history of, Genetic disease carrier
V26.21	Excludes term revised
● V26.31	Testing for genetic disease carrier status
● V26.32	Other genetic testing
● V26.33	Genetic counseling
V45.1	Includes terms added
▲ 46.1	Other dependence on machines, Respirator ▶[Ventilator]◀
● V46.13	Encounter for weaning from respirator [ventilator]
● V46.14	Mechanical complication of respirator [ventilator]
	Includes term added
● V49.84	Bed confinement status
V54	Excludes term revised
V54.0	Excludes term revised
▲ V58.1	▶Encounter for antineoplastic◀ chemotherapy ▶and immunotherapy◀
	Excludes term added
● V58.11	Encounter for antineoplastic chemotherapy
● V58.12	Encounter for antineoplastic immunotherapy
● V59.7	Donors, Egg (oocyte) (ovum)

▶◀ Revised Text ● New Code ▲ Revised Code Title

● V59.70 Egg (oocyte) (ovum) donor, unspecified
● V59.71 Egg (oocyte) (ovum) donor, under age 35, anonymous recipient
Includes term added
● V59.72 Egg (oocyte) (ovum) donor, under age 35, designated recipient
● V59.73 Egg (oocyte) (ovum) donor, age 35 and over, anonymous recipient
Includes term added
● V59.74 Egg (oocyte) (ovum) donor, age 35 and over, designated recipient
V61.10 Includes terms added
V61.20 Includes term added
V61.8 Includes term added
V62.2 Includes term added
V62.3 Includes term added
V62.4 Includes term added
V62.81 Includes term added
● V62.84 Suicidal ideation
Excludes term added
V62.89 Includes terms added
▲V64.0 Vaccination not carried out ~~because of contraindication~~
● V64.00 Vaccination not carried out, unspecified reason
● V64.01 Vaccination not carried out because of acute illness
● V64.02 Vaccination not carried out because of chronic illness or condition
● V64.03 Vaccination not carried out because of immune compromised state
● V64.04 Vaccination not carried out because of allergy to vaccine or component
● V64.05 Vaccination not carried out because of caregiver refusal
● V64.06 Vaccination not carried out because of patient refusal
● V64.07 Vaccination not carried out for religious reasons
● V64.08 Vaccination not carried out because patient had disease being vaccinated against
● V64.09 Vaccination not carried out for other reason
V65.4 Excludes term revised
● V69.5 Behavioral insomnia of childhood
PERSONS WITHOUT REPORTED DIAGNOSIS ENCOUNTERED DURING EXAMINATION AND INVESTIGATION OF INDIVIDUALS AND POPULATIONS ▶(V70-V85)◀
V70.0 Excludes term added
V72.4 Excludes term deleted
● V72.42 Pregnancy examination or test, positive result
V72.81 Includes term added
V72.82 Includes term added
V72.83 Includes terms added
Excludes term added
V72.84 Includes term added
● V72.86 Encounter for blood typing
● V85 Body Mass Index
Includes term added
Instructional note added
● V85.0 Body Mass Index less than 19, adult
● V85.1 Body Mass Index between 19-24, adult
● V85.2 Body Mass Index between 25-29, adult
● V85.21 Body Mass Index 25.0-25.9, adult
● V85.22 Body Mass Index 26.0-26.9, adult
● V85.23 Body Mass Index 27.0-27.9, adult
● V85.24 Body Mass Index 28.0-28.9, adult
● V85.25 Body Mass Index 29.0-29.9, adult
● V85.3 Body Mass Index between 30-39, adult
● V85.30 Body Mass Index 30.0-30.9, adult
● V85.31 Body Mass Index 31.0-31.9, adult
● V85.32 Body Mass Index 32.0-32.9, adult
● V85.33 Body Mass Index 33.0-33.9, adult
● V85.34 Body Mass Index 34.0-34.9, adult
● V85.35 Body Mass Index 35.0-35.9, adult
● V85.36 Body Mass Index 36.0-36.9, adult
● V85.37 Body Mass Index 37.0-37.9, adult
● V85.38 Body Mass Index 38.0-38.9, adult
● V85.39 Body Mass Index 39.0-39.9, adult
● V85.4 Body Mass Index 40 and over, adult
E904.2 Excludes term revised

PROCEDURE TABULAR (VOLUME 3)

00.02 Excludes term revised
● 00.18 Infusion of immunosuppressive antibody therapy during induction phase of solid organ transplantation
Includes terms added
00.2 Includes term added
Instructional note added
Excludes terms added
● 00.4 Adjunct vascular system procedures
Instructional note added
Code also note added
● 00.40 Adjunct vascular system procedure, Procedure on single vessel
Includes term added
Excludes terms added
● 00.41 Adjunct vascular system procedure, Procedure on two vessels
Excludes terms added
● 00.42 Adjunct vascular system procedure, Procedure on three vessels
Excludes terms added
● 00.43 Adjunct vascular system procedure, Procedure on four or more vessels
Excludes terms added
● 00.45 Adjunct vascular system procedure, Insertion of one vascular stent
Includes term added
● 00.46 Adjunct vascular system procedure, Insertion of two vascular stents
● 00.47 Adjunct vascular system procedure, Insertion of three vascular stents
● 00.48 Adjunct vascular system procedure, Insertion of four or more vascular stents
00.50 Includes term added
00.51 Includes term added
00.55 Code also note revised
Code also terms added
00.6 Excludes terms deleted
00.61 Code also terms added
00.62 Code also terms added
00.63 Code also note revised
Code also terms added
Excludes terms added
00.64 Code also note added
Code also terms added
Excludes terms added
00.65 Code also note revised
Code also terms added
Excludes terms added
● 00.66 Percutaneous transluminal coronary angioplasty [PTCA] or coronary atherectomy
Includes terms added
Code also note added
● 00.7 Other hip procedures
● 00.70 Revision of hip replacement, both acetabular and femoral components
Includes term added
Code also note added
Excludes note added
● 00.71 Revision of hip replacement, acetabular component
Includes terms added
Code also note added
Excludes note added
● 00.72 Revision of hip replacement, femoral component
Includes terms added
Code also note added
Excludes note added
● 00.73 Revision of hip replacement, acetabular liner and/or femoral head only
Code also note added
● 00.74 Hip replacement bearing surface, metal on polyethylene
● 00.75 Hip replacement bearing surface, metal-on-metal
● 00.76 Hip replacement bearing surface, ceramic-on-ceramic
● 00.8 Other knee procedures
Instructional note added
● 00.80 Revision of knee replacement, total (all components)
Includes term added
Code also note added
Excludes note added

● 00.81 Revision of knee replacement, tibial component
Includes term added
Excludes note added
● 00.82 Revision of knee replacement, femoral component
Includes term added
Excludes note added
● 00.83 Revision of knee replacement, patellar component
Excludes note added
● 00.84 Revision of total knee replacement, tibial insert (liner)
Includes term added
Excludes note added
● 01.26 Insertion of catheter into cranial cavity
Code also note added
● 01.27 Removal of catheter from cranial cavity
03.53 Excludes terms revised
36 Code also note revised
Code also term added
36.01 Code deleted
36.02 Code deleted
36.03 Code also note revised
Code also terms added
36.04 Excludes term revised
36.05 Code deleted
36.06 Code also note revised
Code also terms added
36.07 Code also note revised
Code also terms added
36.09 Code also note added
Excludes term revised
36.1 Instructional note added
● 37.41 Implantation of prosthetic cardiac support device around the heart
Includes terms added
Code also note added
Excludes note added
● 37.49 Other repair of heart and pericardium
37.6 Excludes note added
▲37.7 Insertion, revision, replacement, and removal of pacemaker leads; insertion of temporary pacemaker system; or revision of ▶cardiac device◀ pocket
▲37.79 Revision or relocation of ~~pacemaker~~ ▶cardiac device◀ pocket
Includes term added
Excludes terms added
37.99 Includes term added
38.1 Code also note added
38.2 Excludes note added
39.50 Code also terms added
● 39.73 Endovascular implantation of graft in thoracic aorta
Includes terms added
Excludes note added
39.79 Excludes terms added
39.90 Code also terms added
77.8 Excludes term revised
▲78.1 Application of external ▶fixator◀ ~~fixation~~ device
Includes term revised
Code also note added
79 Code also note revised
Code also note added
80.0 Includes term deleted
Code also note added
81.0 Code also note deleted
81.06 Includes term added
81.08 Includes terms added
▲81.1 Arthrodesis ▶and arthroereisis◀ of foot and ankle
81.13 Excludes term added
● 81.18 Subtalar joint arthroereisis
81.3 Code also note deleted
81.36 Includes term added
81.38 Includes terms added
81.51 Code also note added
81.52 Code also note added
▲81.53 Revision of hip replacement, ▶not otherwise specified◀
Includes terms deleted
Includes term added
Code also note added
Excludes note added

▶◀ Revised Text   ● New Code   ▲ Revised Code Title

▲ 81.55 Revision of knee replacement, ▶not otherwise specified◀
Code also note added
Excludes term added

81.61 Code deleted

● 84.56 Insertion of (cement) spacer
Includes term added

● 84.57 Removal of (cement) spacer
Includes term added

● 84.58 Implantation of interspinous process decompression device
Excludes note added

● 84.7 Adjunct codes for external fixator devices
Code also note added

● 84.71 Adjunct codes for external fixator devices, monoplanar system
Excludes note added

● 84.72 Application of external fixator device, ring system
Includes terms added
Excludes note added

● 84.73 Application of hybrid external fixator device
Includes term added
Excludes terms added

86.09 Includes terms deleted
Excludes terms added

▲ 86.94 Insertion or replacement of single array neurostimulator pulse generator, ▶not specified as rechargeable◀
Excludes term added

▲ 86.95 Insertion or replacement of dual array neurostimulator pulse generator, ▶not specified as rechargeable◀
Excludes note added

86.96 Excludes terms revised

● 86.97 Insertion or replacement of single array rechargeable neurostimulator pulse generator
Includes term added
Code also note added

● 86.98 Insertion or replacement of dual array rechargeable neurostimulator pulse generator
Includes term added
Code also note added

88.77 Excludes term added

● 92.20 Infusion of liquid brachytherapy radioisotope
Includes terms added
Includes note added

92.27 Excludes term added

92.28 Excludes term added

93.5 Excludes term added

99.10 Excludes term deleted

▶◀ Revised Text   ● New Code   ▲ Revised Code Title

ICD-9-CM OFFICIAL GUIDELINES FOR CODING AND REPORTING

Effective April 1, 2005
Narrative changes appear in bold text
The guidelines have been updated to include the V Code Table.

The Centers for Medicare and Medicaid Services (CMS) and the National Center for Health Statistics (NCHS), two departments within the U.S. Federal Government's Department of Health and Human Services (DHHS) provide the following guidelines for coding and reporting using the International Classification of Diseases, 9th Revision, Clinical Modification (ICD-9-CM). These guidelines should be used as a companion document to the official version of the ICD-9-CM as published on CD-ROM by the U.S. Government Printing Office (GPO).

These guidelines have been approved by the four organizations that make up the Cooperating Parties for the ICD-9-CM: the American Hospital Association (AHA), the American Health Information Management Association (AHIMA), CMS, and NCHS. These guidelines are included in the official government version of the ICD-9-CM and also appear in *Coding Clinic for ICD-9-CM*, published by the AHA.

These guidelines are a set of rules that have been developed to accompany and complement the official conventions and instructions provided within the ICD-9-CM itself. These guidelines are based on the coding and sequencing instructions in Volumes 1, 2, and 3 of ICD-9-CM, but provide additional instruction. **Adherence to these guidelines when assigning ICD-9-CM diagnosis and procedure codes is required under the Health Insurance Portability and Accountability Act (HIPAA). The diagnosis codes (Volumes 1-2) have been adopted under HIPAA for all health care settings. Volume 3 procedure codes have been adopted for inpatient procedures reported by hospitals.** A joint effort between the health care provider and the coder is essential to achieve complete and accurate documentation, code assignment, and reporting of diagnoses and procedures. These guidelines have been developed to assist both the health care provider and the coder in identifying those diagnoses and procedures that are to be reported. The importance of consistent, complete documentation in the medical record cannot be overemphasized. Without such documentation accurate coding cannot be achieved. **The entire record should be reviewed to determine the specific reason for the encounter and the conditions treated.**

The term "encounter" is used for all settings, including hospital admissions. In the context of these guidelines, the term "provider" is used throughout the guidelines to mean physician or any qualified health care practitioner who is legally accountable for establishing the patient's diagnosis. Only this set of guidelines, approved by the cooperating parties, is official.

The guidelines are organized into sections. Section I includes the structure and conventions of the classification and general guidelines that apply to the entire classification, and chapter-specific guidelines that correspond to the chapters as they are arranged in the classification. Section II includes guidelines for selection of principal diagnosis for non-outpatient settings. Section III includes guidelines for reporting additional diagnoses in non-outpatient settings. Section IV is for outpatient coding and reporting.

Section I. Conventions, general coding guidelines and chapter-specific guidelines

A. Conventions for the ICD-9-CM
 1. Format
 2. Abbreviations
   a. **Index abbreviations**
   b. **Tabular abbreviations**
 3. Punctuation
 4. Includes and excludes notes and inclusion terms
 5. Other and Unspecified codes
   a. **"Other" codes**
   b. **"Unspecified" codes**
 6. Etiology/manifestation convention ("code first," "use additional code," and "in diseases classified elsewhere" notes)
 7. "And"
 8. "With"
 9. "See" and "see also"
B. General coding guidelines
 1. Use of both Alphabetic Index and Tabular List
 2. Locate each term in the Alphabetic Index
 3. Level of detail in coding
 4. Code or codes from 001.0 through V85.4
 5. Selection of codes 001.0 through 999.9
 6. Signs and symptoms
 7. Conditions that are an integral part of a disease process
 8. Conditions that are not an integral part of a disease process
 9. Multiple coding for a single condition
 10. Acute and chronic conditions
 11. Combination code
 12. Late effects
 13. Impending or threatened condition
C. Chapter-specific coding guidelines
 1. Chapter 1: Infectious and Parasitic Diseases (001–139)
   a. **Human immunodeficiency virus (HIV) infections**
   b. **Septicemia, systemic inflammatory response syndrome (SIRS), sepsis, severe sepsis, and septic shock**
 2. Chapter 2: Neoplasms (140–239)
   a. **Treatment directed at the malignancy**
   b. **Treatment of secondary site**
   c. **Coding and sequencing of complications**
   d. **Primary malignancy previously excised**
   e. **Admissions/encounters involving chemotherapy and radiation therapy**
   f. **Admission/encounter to determine extent of malignancy**
   g. **Symptoms, signs, and ill-defined conditions listed in chapter 16**
   h. **Encounter for prophylactic organ removal**
 3. Chapter 3: Endocrine, Nutritional, and Metabolic Diseases and Immunity Disorders (240–279)
   a. **Diabetes mellitus**
 4. Chapter 4: Diseases of Blood and Blood-Forming Organs (280–289)
   Reserved for future guideline expansion
 5. Chapter 5: Mental Disorders (290–319)
   Reserved for future guideline expansion
 6. Chapter 6: Diseases of Nervous System and Sense Organs (320–389)
   Reserved for future guideline expansion
 7. Chapter 7: Diseases of Circulatory System (390–459)
   a. **Hypertension**
   b. **Cerebral infarction/stroke/cerebrovascular accident (CVA)**
   c. **Postoperative cerebrovascular accident**
   d. **Late effects of cerebrovascular disease**
 8. Chapter 8: Diseases of Respiratory System (460–519)
   a. **Chronic obstructive pulmonary disease [COPD] and asthma**
   b. **Chronic obstructive pulmonary disease [COPD] and bronchitis**
 9. Chapter 9: Diseases of Digestive System (520–579)
   Reserved for future guideline expansion
 10. Chapter 10: Diseases of Genitourinary System (580–629)
   Reserved for future guideline expansion
 11. Chapter 11: Complications of Pregnancy, Childbirth, and the Puerperium (630–677)
   a. **General rules for obstetric cases**
   b. **Selection of OB principal or first-listed diagnosis**
   c. **Fetal conditions affecting the management of the mother**
   d. **HIV infection in pregnancy, childbirth and the puerperium**
   e. **Current conditions complicating pregnancy**
   f. **Diabetes mellitus in pregnancy**
   g. **Gestational diabetes**
   h. **Normal delivery, code 650**

Section I. Conventions, general coding guidelines and chapter-specific guidelines

The conventions, general guidelines, and chapter-specific guidelines are applicable to all health care settings unless otherwise indicated.

A. Conventions for the ICD-9-CM

The conventions for the ICD-9-CM are the general rules for use of the classification independent of the guidelines. These conventions are incorporated within the index and tabular of the ICD-9-CM as instructional notes. The conventions are as follows:

1. **Format:**
    The ICD-9-CM uses an indented format for ease in reference

2. **Abbreviations**

    a. Index abbreviations
    NEC "Not elsewhere classifiable"—This abbreviation in the index represents "other specified." When a specific code is not available for a condition, the index directs the coder to the "other specified" code in the tabular.

    b. Tabular abbreviations
    NEC "Not elsewhere classifiable"—This abbreviation in the tabular represents "other specified." When a specific code is not available for a condition, the tabular includes an NEC entry under a code to identify the code as the "other specified" code (See section I.A.5.a.,"Other" codes).

    NOS "Not otherwise specified"—This abbreviation is the equivalent of unspecified. (See section I.A.5.b., "Unspecified" codes)

3. **Punctuation**

    [ ] Brackets are used in the Tabular List to enclose synonyms, alternative wording, or explanatory phrases. Brackets are used in the index to identify manifestation codes. (See section I.A.6., Etiology/manifestations)

    ( ) Parentheses are used in both the index and tabular to enclose supplementary words that may be present or absent in the statement of a disease or procedure without affecting the code number to which it is assigned. The terms within the parentheses are referred to as nonessential modifiers.

    : Colons are used in the Tabular List after an incomplete term needs one or more of the modifiers following the colon to make it assignable to a given category.

4. **Includes and excludes notes and inclusion terms**

    Includes: This note appears immediately under a three-digit code title to further define, or give examples of, the content of the category.

    Excludes: An excludes note under a code indicates that the terms excluded from the code are to be coded elsewhere. In some cases the codes for the excluded terms should not be used in conjunction with the code from which they are excluded. An example of this is a congenital condition excluded from an acquired form of the same condition. The congenital and acquired codes should not be used together. In other cases, the excluded terms may be used together with an excluded code. An example of this is when fractures of different bones are coded to different codes. Both codes may be used together if both types of fractures are present.

    Inclusion terms: List of terms included under certain four- and five-digit codes. These terms are the conditions for which that code number is to be used. The terms may be synonyms of the code title,

Revised text in bold font

or, in the case of "other specified" codes, the terms are a list of the various conditions assigned to that code. The inclusion terms are not necessarily exhaustive. Additional terms found only in the index may also be assigned to a code.

5. **Other and unspecified codes**

   a. **"Other" codes**—Codes titled "other" or "other specified" (usually a code with a fourth digit of 8 or fifth digit of 9 for diagnosis codes) are for use when the information in the medical record provides detail for which a specific code does not exist. Index entries with NEC in the line designate "other" codes in the tabular. These index entries represent specific disease entities for which no specific code exists so the term is included within an "other" code.

   b. **"Unspecified" codes**—Codes (usually a code with a fourth digit of 9 or fifth of 0 for diagnosis codes) titled "unspecified" are for use when the information in the medical record is insufficient to assign a more specific code.

6. **Etiology/manifestation convention ("code first," "use additional code," and "in diseases classified elsewhere" notes)**—Certain conditions have both an underlying etiology and multiple body system manifestations due to the underlying etiology. For such conditions, the ICD-9-CM has a coding convention that requires the underlying condition to be sequenced first followed by the manifestation. Wherever such a combination exists, there is a "use additional code" note at the etiology code, and a "code first" note at the manifestation code. These instructional notes indicate the proper sequencing order of the codes, etiology followed by manifestation.

In most cases the manifestation codes will have in the code title, "in diseases classified elsewhere." Codes with this title are a component of the etiology/manifestation convention. The code title indicates that it is a manifestation code. "In diseases classified elsewhere," codes are never permitted to be used as first listed or principal diagnosis codes. They must be used in conjunction with an underlying condition code, and they must be listed following the underlying condition.

There are manifestation codes that do not have "in diseases classified elsewhere" in the title. For such codes a "use additional code" note will still be present and the rules for sequencing apply.

In addition to the notes in the tabular, these conditions also have a specific index entry structure. In the index both conditions are listed together with the etiology code first followed by the manifestation codes in brackets. The code in brackets is always to be sequenced second.

The most commonly used etiology/manifestation combinations are the codes for diabetes mellitus, category 250. For each code under category 250 there is a use additional code note for the manifestation that is specific for that particular diabetic manifestation. Should a patient have more than one manifestation of diabetes, more than one code from category 250 may be used with as many manifestation codes as are needed to fully describe the patient's complete diabetic condition. The category 250 diabetes codes should be sequenced first, followed by the manifestation codes.

"Code first" and "use additional code" notes are also used as sequencing rules in the classification for certain codes that are not part of an etiology/manifestation combination. See section I.B.9., "Multiple coding for a single condition."

7. **"And"**
The word "and" should be interpreted to mean either "and" or "or" when it appears in a title.

8. **"With"**
The word "with" in the Alphabetic Index is sequenced immediately following the main term, not in alphabetical order.

9. **"See" and "see also"**
The "see" instruction following a main term in the index indicates that another term should be referenced. It is necessary to go to the main term referenced with the "see" note to locate the correct code.

A "see also" instruction following a main term in the index instructs that there is another main term that may also be referenced that may provide additional index entries that may be useful. It is not necessary to follow the "see also" note when the original main term provides the necessary code.

B. General coding guidelines

1. **Use of both Alphabetic Index and Tabular List**—Use both the Alphabetic Index and the Tabular List when locating and assigning a code. Reliance on only the Alphabetic Index or the Tabular List leads to errors in code assignments and less specificity in code selection.

2. **Locate each term in the alphabetic index**—Locate each term in the Alphabetic Index and verify the code selected in the Tabular List. Read and be guided by instructional notations that appear in both the Alphabetic Index and the Tabular List.

3. **Level of detail in coding**—Diagnosis and procedure codes are to be used at their highest number of digits available.

ICD-9-CM diagnosis codes are composed of codes with either three, four, or five digits. Codes with three digits are included in ICD-9-CM as the heading of a category of codes that may be further subdivided by the use of four and/or fifth digits, which provide greater detail.

A three-digit code is to be used only if it is not further subdivided. Where fourth-digit subcategories and/or fifth-digit subclassifications are provided, they must be assigned. A code is invalid if it has not been coded to the full number of digits required for that code. For example, acute myocardial infarction, code 410, has fourth digits that describe the location of the infarction (e.g., 410.2 Of inferolateral wall), and fifth digits that identify the episode of care. It would be incorrect to report a code in category 410 without a fourth and fifth digit.

ICD-9-CM Volume 3 procedure codes are composed of codes with either three or four digits. Codes with two digits are included in ICD-9-CM as the heading of a category of codes that may be further subdivided by the use of third and/or fourth digits, which provide greater detail.

4. **Code or codes from 001.0 through V85.4**—The appropriate code or codes from 001.0 through V85.4 must be used to identify diagnoses, symptoms, conditions, problems, complaints, or other reason(s) for the encounter/visit.

5. **Selection of codes 001.0 through 999.9**—The selection of codes 001.0 through 999.9 will frequently be used to describe the reason for the admission/encounter. These codes are from the section of ICD-9-CM for the classification of diseases and injuries (e.g., infectious and parasitic diseases; neoplasms; symptoms, signs, and ill-defined conditions, etc.).

6. **Signs and symptoms**—Codes that describe symptoms and signs, as opposed to diagnoses, are acceptable for reporting purposes when a related definitive diagnosis has not been established (confirmed) by the provider. Chapter 16 of ICD-9-CM, "Symptoms, Signs, and Ill-defined Conditions" (codes 780.0-799.9) contain many, but not all, codes for symptoms.

7. **Conditions that are an integral part of a disease process**—Signs and symptoms that are integral to the disease process should not be assigned as additional codes.

8. **Conditions that are not an integral part of a disease process**—Additional signs and symptoms that may not be associated routinely with a disease process should be coded when present.

9. **Multiple coding for a single condition**—In addition to the etiology/manifestation convention that requires two codes to fully describe a single condition that affects multiple body systems, there are other single conditions that also require more than one code. "Use additional code" notes are found in the tabular at codes that are not part of an etiology/manifestation pair where a secondary code is useful to fully describe a condition. The sequencing rule is the same as the etiology/manifestation pair where a secondary code is useful to fully describe a condition. The sequencing rule is the same; "use additional code" indicates that a secondary code should be added.

For example, for infections that are not included in chapter 1, a secondary code from category 041 Bacterial infection in conditions classified elsewhere and of unspecified site, may be required to identify the bacterial organism causing the infection. A "use additional code" note will normally be found at the infectious disease code, indicating a need for the organism code to be added as a secondary code.

"Code first" notes are also under certain codes that are not specifically manifestation codes but may be due to an underlying cause. When a "code first" note is present and an underlying condition is present, the underlying condition should be sequenced first.

"Code, if applicable, any causal condition first" notes indicate that this code may be assigned as a principal diagnosis when the causal condition is unknown or not applicable. If a causal condition is known, then the code for that condition should be sequenced as the principal or first-listed diagnosis.

Multiple codes may be needed for late effects, complication codes, and obstetric codes to more fully describe a condition. See the specific guidelines for these conditions for further instruction.

10. **Acute and chronic conditions**—If the same condition is described as both acute (subacute) and chronic, and separate subentries exist in the Alphabetic Index at the same indentation level, code both and sequence the acute (subacute) code first.

11. **Combination code**—A combination code is a single code used to classify:
- Two diagnoses
- A diagnosis with an associated secondary process (manifestation)
- A diagnosis with an associated complication

Combination codes are identified by referring to subterm entries in the Alphabetic Index and by reading the inclusion and exclusion notes in the Tabular List.

Assign only the combination code when that code fully identifies the diagnostic conditions involved or when the Alphabetic Index so directs. Multiple coding should not be used when the classification provides a combination code that clearly identifies all of the elements documented in the diagnosis. When the combination code lacks necessary specificity in describing the manifestation or complication, an additional code should be used as a secondary code.

12. **Late effects**—A late effect is the residual effect (condition produced) after the acute phase of an illness or injury has terminated. There is no time limit on when a late effect code can be used. The residual may be apparent early, such as in cerebrovascular accident cases, or it may occur months or years later, such as that due to a previous injury. Coding of late effects generally requires two codes sequenced in the following order: The condition or nature of the late effect is sequenced first... The late effect code is sequenced second.

An exception to the above guidelines are those instances where the code for late effect is followed by a manifestation code identified in the Tabular List and title, or the late effect code has been expanded (at the fourth- and fifth-digit levels) to include the manifestation(s). The code for the acute phase of an illness or injury that led to the late effect is never used with a code for the late effect.

13. **Impending or threatened condition**—Code any condition described at the time of discharge as "impending" or "threatened" as follows:

If it did occur, code as confirmed diagnosis. If it did not occur, reference the Alphabetic Index to determine if the condition has a subentry term for "impending" or "threatened" and also reference main term entries for "Impending" and for "Threatened." If the subterms are listed, assign the given code. If the subterms are not listed, code the existing underlying condition(s) and not the condition described as impending or threatened.

C. Chapter-specific coding guidelines

In addition to general coding guidelines, there are guidelines for specific diagnoses and/or conditions in the classification. Unless otherwise indicated, these guidelines apply to all health care settings. Please refer to section II for guidelines on the selection of principal diagnosis.

1.   **Chapter 1: Infectious and Parasitic Diseases (001-139)**

  a. **Human immunodeficiency virus (HIV) infections**

   1) **Code only confirmed cases**—Code only confirmed cases of HIV infection/illness. This is an exception to the hospital inpatient guideline section II, H.

   In this context, "confirmation" does not require documentation of positive serology or culture for HIV; the provider's diagnostic statement that the patient is HIV positive or has an HIV-related illness is sufficient.

   2) **Selection and sequencing of HIV codes**
   (a) **Patient admitted for HIV-related condition**—If a patient is admitted for an HIV-related condition, the principal diagnosis should be 042, followed by additional diagnosis codes for all reported HIV-related conditions.

   (b) **Patient with HIV disease admitted for unrelated condition**—If a patient with HIV disease is admitted for an unrelated condition (such as a traumatic injury), the code for the unrelated condition (e.g., the nature of injury code) should be the principal diagnosis. Other diagnoses would be 042 followed by additional diagnosis codes for all reported HIV-related conditions.

   (c) **Whether the patient is newly diagnosed**—Whether the patient is newly diagnosed or has had previous admissions/encounters for HIV conditions is irrelevant to the sequencing decision.
   (d) **Asymptomatic human immunodeficiency virus**—V08
   Asymptomatic human immunodeficiency virus [HIV] infection, is to be applied when the patient without any documentation of symptoms is listed as being "HIV positive," "known HIV," "HIV test positive," or similar terminology. Do not use this code if the term "AIDS" is used or if the patient is treated for any HIV-related illness or is described as having any condition(s) resulting from his/her HIV positive status; use 042 in these cases.

   (e) **Patients with inconclusive HIV serology**—Patients with inconclusive HIV serology, but no definitive diagnosis or manifestations of the illness, may be assigned code 795.71 Inconclusive serologic test for human immunodeficiency virus [HIV].

   (f) **Previously diagnosed HIV-related illness**—Patients with any known prior diagnosis of an HIV-related illness should be coded to 042. Once a patient has developed an HIV-related illness, the patient should always be assigned code 042 on every subsequent admission/encounter. Patients previously diagnosed with any HIV illness (042) should never be assigned to 795.71 or V08.

   (g) **HIV infection in pregnancy, childbirth and the puerperium**—During pregnancy, childbirth, or the puerperium, a patient admitted (or presenting for a health care encounter) because of an HIV-related illness should receive a principal diagnosis code of 647.6x Other specified infectious and parasitic diseases in the mother classifiable elsewhere but complicating the pregnancy, childbirth or the puerperium, followed by 042 and the code(s) for the HIV-related illness(es). Codes from chapter 15 always take sequencing priority.

   Patients with asymptomatic HIV infection status admitted (or presenting for a health care encounter) during pregnancy, childbirth, or the puerperium should receive codes of 647.6x and V08.

   (h) **Encounters for testing for HIV**—If a patient is being seen to determine his/her HIV status, use code V73.89 Screening for other specified viral disease. Use code V69.8 Other problems related to lifestyle, as a secondary code if an asymptomatic patient is in a known high risk group for HIV. Should a patient with signs or symptoms or illness, or a confirmed HIV related diagnosis be tested for HIV, code the signs and symptoms or the diagnosis. An additional counseling code V65.44 may be used if counseling is provided during the encounter for the test.

   When a patient returns to be informed of his/her HIV test results, use code V65.44 HIV counseling, if the results of the test are negative.

   If the results are positive but the patient is asymptomatic, use code V08 Asymptomatic HIV infection. If the results are positive and the patient is symptomatic, use code 042 HIV infection, with codes for the HIV-related symptoms or diagnosis. The HIV counseling code may also be used if counseling is provided for patients with positive test results.

  b. **Septicemia, systemic inflammatory response syndrome (SIRS), sepsis, severe sepsis, and septic shock**

   1) **Sepsis as principal diagnosis or secondary diagnosis**
   (a) **Sepsis as principal diagnosis—If sepsis is present on admission and meets the definition of principal diagnosis, the underlying systemic infection code (e.g., 038.xx, 112.5, etc.) should be assigned as the principal diagnosis, followed by code 995.91 Systemic inflammatory response syndrome due to infectious process without organ dysfunction, as required by the sequencing rules in the Tabular List. Codes from subcategory 995.9 can never be assigned as a principal diagnosis.**
   (b) **Sepsis as secondary diagnoses—When sepsis develops during the encounter (it was not present on admission), the sepsis codes may be assigned as secondary diagnoses, following the sequencing rules provided in the Tabular List.**
   (c) **Documentation unclear as to whether sepsis present on admission—If the documentation is not clear whether the sepsis was present on admission, the provider should be queried. After provider query, if sepsis is determined at that point to have met the definition of principal diagnosis, the underlying systemic infection (038.xx, 112.5, etc.) may be used as the principal diagnosis along with code 995.91 Systemic inflammatory response syndrome due to infectious process without organ dysfunction.**

   2) **Septicemia/sepsis**—In most cases, it will be a code from category 038 Septicemia, that will be used in conjunction with a code from subcategory 995.9 such as the following:

(a) Streptococcal sepsis—If the documentation in the record states streptococcal sepsis, codes 038.0 and code 995.91 should be used, in that sequence.

(b) Streptococcal septicemia—If the documentation states streptococcal septicemia, only code 038.0 should be assigned; however, the provider should be queried whether the patient has sepsis, an infection with SIRS.

(c) Sepsis or SIRS must be documented—Either the term sepsis or SIRS must be documented to assign a code from subcategory 995.9.

3) **Terms "sepsis," " severe sepsis," or "SIRS"**—If the terms sepsis, severe sepsis, or SIRS are used with an underlying infection other than septicemia, such as pneumonia, cellulitis, or a nonspecified urinary tract infection, a code from category 038 should be assigned first, then code 995.91, followed by the code for the initial infection. The use of the terms sepsis or SIRS indicates that the patient's infection has advanced to the point of a systemic infection so the systemic infection should be sequenced before the localized infection. The instructional note under subcategory 995.9 instructs to assign the underlying systemic infection first.

Note: The term "urosepsis" is a nonspecific term. If that is the only term documented then only code 599.0 should be assigned based on the default for the term in the ICD-9-CM index, in addition to the code for the causal organism if known.

4) **Severe sepsis**—For patients with severe sepsis, the code for the systemic infection (e.g., 038.xx, 112.5, etc) or trauma should be sequenced first, followed by either code 995.92 Systemic inflammatory response syndrome due to infectious process with organ dysfunction, or code 995.94 Systemic inflammatory response syndrome due to noninfectious process with organ dysfunction. Codes for the specific organ dysfunctions should also be assigned.

5) **Septic shock**

(a) Sequencing of septic shock—Septic shock is a form of organ dysfunction associated with severe sepsis. A code for the initiating underlying systemic infection followed by a code for SIRS (code 995.92) must be assigned before the code for septic shock. As noted in the sequencing instructions in the Tabular List, the code for septic shock cannot be assigned as a principal diagnosis.

(b) Septic shock without documentation of severe sepsis—Septic shock cannot occur in the absence of severe sepsis. A code from subcategory 995.9 must be sequenced before the code for septic shock. The use additional code notes and the code first note provide sequencing instructions.

6) **Sepsis and septic shock associated with abortion**—Sepsis and septic shock associated with abortion, ectopic pregnancy, and molar pregnancy are classified to category codes in chapter 11 (630-639).

7) **Negative or inconclusive blood cultures**—Negative or inconclusive blood cultures do not preclude a diagnosis of septicemia or sepsis in patients with clinical evidence of the condition; however, the provider should be queried.

8) **Newborn sepsis**—See section I.C.15.j for information on the coding of newborn sepsis.

9) **Sepsis due to a postprocedural infection**—Sepsis resulting from a postprocedural infection is a complication of care. For such cases code 998.59 Other postoperative infections, should be coded first followed by the appropriate codes for the sepsis. The other guidelines for coding sepsis should then be followed for the assignment of additional codes.

10) **External cause of injury codes with SIRS**—An external cause code is not needed with codes 995.91 Systemic inflammatory response syndrome due to infectious process without organ dysfunction, or 995.92 Systemic inflammatory response syndrome due to infectious process with organ dysfunction.

Refer to section I.C.19.a.7 for instruction on the use of external cause of injury codes with codes for SIRS resulting from trauma.

2. Chapter 2: Neoplasms (140-239)
General guidelines

Chapter 2 of the ICD-9-CM contains the codes for most benign and all malignant neoplasms. Certain benign neoplasms, such as prostatic adenomas, may be found in the specific body system chapters. To properly code a neoplasm it is necessary to determine from the record if the neoplasm is benign, in situ, malignant, or of uncertain histologic behavior. If malignant, any secondary (metastatic) sites should also be determined.

The neoplasm table in the Alphabetic Index should be referenced first. However, if the histological term is documented, that term should be referenced first, rather than going immediately to the neoplasm table, in order to determine which column in the neoplasm table is appropriate. For example, if the documentation indicates "adenoma," refer to the term in the Alphabetic Index to review the entries under this term and the instructional note to "see also neoplasm, by site, benign." The table provides the proper code based on the type of neoplasm and the site. It is important to select the proper column in the table that corresponds to the type of neoplasm. The tabular should then be referenced to verify that the correct code has been selected from the table and that a more specific site code does not exist.

See section I. C. 18.d.4. for information regarding V codes for genetic susceptibility to cancer.

a. **Treatment directed at the malignancy**—If the treatment is directed at the malignancy, designate the malignancy as the principal diagnosis.

b. **Treatment of secondary site**—When a patient is admitted because of a primary neoplasm with metastasis and treatment is directed toward the secondary site only, the secondary neoplasm is designated as the principal diagnosis even though the primary malignancy is still present.

c. **Coding and sequencing of complications**—Coding and sequencing of complications associated with the malignancies or with the therapy thereof are subject to the following guidelines:

1) **Anemia associated with malignancy**—When admission/encounter is for management of an anemia associated with the malignancy, and the treatment is only for anemia, the anemia is designated at the principal diagnosis and is followed by the appropriate code(s) for the malignancy.

2) **Anemia associated with chemotherapy**—When the admission/encounter is for management of an anemia associated with chemotherapy or radiotherapy and the only treatment is for the anemia, the anemia is sequenced first followed by the appropriate code(s) for the malignancy.

3) **Management of dehydration due to the malignancy**—When the admission/encounter is for management of dehydration due to the malignancy or the therapy, or a combination of both, and only the dehydration is being treated (intravenous rehydration), the dehydration is sequenced first, followed by the code(s) for the malignancy.

4) **Treatment of a complication resulting from a surgical procedure**—When the admission/encounter is for treatment of a complication resulting from a surgical procedure, designate the complication as the principal or first-listed diagnosis if treatment is directed at resolving the complication.

d. **Primary malignancy previously excised**—When a primary malignancy has been previously excised or eradicated from its site and there is no further treatment directed to that site and there is no evidence of any existing primary malignancy, a code from category V10 Personal history of malignant neoplasm, should be used to indicate the former site of the malignancy. Any mention of extension, invasion, or metastasis to another site is coded as a secondary malignant neoplasm to that site. The secondary site may be the principal or first-listed with the V10 code used as a secondary code.

e. **Admissions/encounters involving chemotherapy and radiation therapy**

1) **Episode of care involves surgical removal of neoplasm**—When an episode of care involves the surgical removal of a neoplasm, primary or secondary site, followed by adjunct chemotherapy or radiation treatment, the neoplasm code should be assigned as principal or first-listed diagnosis, using codes in the 140-198 series or where appropriate in the 200-203 series.

2) **Patient admission/encounter solely for administration of chemotherapy**—If a patient admission/encounter is solely for the administration of chemotherapy or radiation therapy code V58.0 Encounter for radiation therapy, or V58.1 Encounter for chemotherapy, should be the first-listed or principal diagnosis. If a patient receives both chemotherapy and radiation therapy both codes should be listed, in either order of sequence.

3) **Patient admitted for radiotherapy/chemotherapy and develops complications**—When a patient is admitted for the purpose of radiotherapy or chemotherapy and develops complications such as uncontrolled nausea and vomiting or dehydration, the principal or first-listed diagnosis is V58.0 Encounter for radiotherapy, or V58.1

Encounter for chemotherapy, followed by any codes for the complications.

See section I.C.18.d.8. for additional information regarding aftercare V codes.

f. **Admission/encounter to determine extent of malignancy**—When the reason for admission/encounter is to determine the extent of the malignancy, or for a procedure such as paracentesis or thoracentesis, the primary malignancy or appropriate metastatic site is designated as the principal or first-listed diagnosis, even though chemotherapy or radiotherapy is administered.

g. **Symptoms, signs, and ill-defined conditions listed in chapter 16**—Symptoms, signs, and ill-defined conditions listed in chapter 16 characteristic of, or associated with, an existing primary or secondary site malignancy cannot be used to replace the malignancy as principal or first-listed diagnosis, regardless of the number of admissions or encounters for treatment and care of the neoplasm.

h. **Encounter for prophylactic organ removal**—For encounters specifically for prophylactic removal of breasts, ovaries, or another organ due to a genetic susceptibility to cancer or a family history of cancer, the principal or first-listed code should be a code from subcategory V50.4 Prophylactic organ removal, followed by the appropriate genetic susceptibility code and the appropriate family history code.

If the patient has a malignancy of one site and is having prophylactic removal of another site to prevent either a new primary malignancy or metastatic disease, a code for the malignancy should also be assigned in addition to a code from subcategory V50.4. A V50.4 code should not be assigned if the patient is having organ removal for treatment of a malignancy, such as the removal of the testes for the treatment of prostate cancer.

3. **Chapter 3: Endocrine, Nutritional, and Metabolic Diseases and Immunity Disorders (240-279)**

a. **Diabetes mellitus**—Codes under category 250 Diabetes mellitus, identify complications/manifestations associated with diabetes mellitus. A fifth-digit is required for all category 250 codes to identify the type of diabetes mellitus and whether the diabetes is controlled or uncontrolled.

1) **Fifth digits for category 250:** The following are the fifth digits for the codes under category 250:

0 type II or unspecified type, not stated as uncontrolled
1 type I, [juvenile type], not stated as uncontrolled
2 type II or unspecified type, uncontrolled
3 type I, [juvenile type], uncontrolled

The age of a patient is not the sole determining factor, though most type I diabetics develop the condition before reaching puberty. For this reason type I diabetes mellitus is also referred to as juvenile diabetes.

2) **Type of diabetes mellitus not documented**—If the type of diabetes mellitus is not documented in the medical record the default is type II.

3) **Diabetes mellitus and the use of insulin**—All type I diabetics must use insulin to replace what their bodies do not produce. However, the use of insulin does not mean that a patient is a type I diabetic. Some patients with type II diabetes mellitus are unable to control their blood sugar through diet and oral medication alone and do require insulin. If the documentation in a medical record does not indicate the type of diabetes but does indicate that the patient uses insulin, the appropriate fifth digit for type II must be used. For type II patients who routinely use insulin, code V58.67 Long-term (current) use of insulin, should also be assigned to indicate that the patient uses insulin. Code V58.67 should not be assigned if insulin is given temporarily to bring a type II patient's blood sugar under control during an encounter.

4) **Assigning and sequencing diabetes codes and associated conditions**—When assigning codes for diabetes and its associated conditions, the code(s) from category 250 must be sequenced before the codes for the associated conditions. The diabetes codes and the secondary codes that correspond to them are paired codes that follow the etiology/manifestation convention of the classification (See section I.A.6., Etiology/manifestation convention). Assign as many codes from

category 250 as needed to identify all of the associated conditions that the patient has. The corresponding secondary codes are listed under each of the diabetes codes.

5) **Diabetes mellitus in pregnancy and gestational diabetes**
(a) For diabetes mellitus complicating pregnancy, see aection I.C.11.f., Diabetes mellitus in pregnancy.
(b) For gestational diabetes, see section I.C.11, g., Gestational diabetes.

6) **Insulin pump malfunction**
(a) **Underdose of insulin due to insulin pump failure An underdose of insulin due to an insulin pump failure should be assigned 996.57 Mechanical complication due to insulin pump, as the principal or first listed code, followed by the appropriate diabetes mellitus code based on documentation.**
(b) **Overdose of insulin due to insulin pump failure The principal or first-listed code for an encounter due to an insulin pump malfunction resulting in an overdose of insulin should also be 996.57 Mechanical complication due to insulin pump, followed by code 962.3 Poisoning by insulins and antidiabetic agents, and the appropriate diabetes mellitus code based on documentation.**

4. **Chapter 4: Diseases of Blood and Blood Forming Organs (280-289)**
Reserved for future guideline expansion

5. **Chapter 5: Mental Disorders (290-319)**
Reserved for future guideline expansion

6. **Chapter 6: Diseases of Nervous System and Sense Organs (320-389)**
Reserved for future guideline expansion

7. **Chapter 7: Diseases of Circulatory System (390-459)**
a. **Hypertension**

Hypertension Table

The hypertension table, found under the main term, "Hypertension," in the Alphabetic Index, contains a complete listing of all conditions due to or associated with hypertension and classifies them according to malignant, benign, and unspecified.

1) **Hypertension, essential, or NOS**—Assign hypertension (arterial) (essential) (primary) (systemic) (NOS) to category code 401 with the appropriate fourth digit to indicate malignant (.0), benign (.1), or unspecified (.9). Do not use either .0 malignant or .1 benign unless medical record documentation supports such a designation.

2) **Hypertension with heart disease**—Heart conditions (425.8, 429.0–429.3, 429.8, 429.9) are assigned to a code from category 402 when a causal relationship is stated (due to hypertension) or implied (hypertensive). Use an additional code from category 428 to identify the type of heart failure in those patients with heart failure. More than one code from category 428 may be assigned if the patient has systolic or diastolic failure and congestive heart failure.

The same heart conditions (425.8, 429.0–429.3, 429.8, 429.9) with hypertension, but without a stated casual relationship, are coded separately. Sequence according to the circumstances of the admission/encounter.

3) **Hypertensive renal disease with chronic renal failure**—Assign codes from category 403, Hypertensive renal disease, when conditions classified to categories 585-587 are present. Unlike hypertension with heart disease, ICD-9-CM presumes a cause-and-effect relationship and classifies renal failure with hypertension as hypertensive renal disease.

4) **Hypertensive heart and renal disease**—Assign codes from combination category 404, Hypertensive heart and renal disease, when both hypertensive renal disease and hypertensive heart disease are stated in the diagnosis. Assume a relationship between the hypertension and the renal disease, whether or not the condition is so designated. Assign an additional code from category 428 to identify the type of heart failure. More than one code from category 428 may be assigned if the patient has systolic or diastolic failure and congestive heart failure.

5) **Hypertensive cerebrovascular disease**—First assign codes from 430-438 Cerebrovascular disease, then the appropriate hypertension code from categories 401–405.

6) **Hypertensive retinopathy**—Two codes are necessary to identify the condition. First assign the code from subcategory 362.11 Hypertensive retinopathy, then the appropriate code from categories 401–405 to indicate the type of hypertension.

7) **Hypertension, secondary**—Two codes are required: one to identify the underlying etiology and one from category 405 to identify the hypertension. Sequencing of codes is determined by the reason for admission/encounter.

8) **Hypertension, transient**—Assign code 796.2 Elevated blood pressure reading without diagnosis of hypertension, unless patient has an established diagnosis of hypertension. Assign code 642.3x for transient hypertension of pregnancy.

9) **Hypertension, controlled**—Assign appropriate code from categories 401–405. This diagnostic statement usually refers to an existing state of hypertension under control by therapy.

10) **Hypertension, uncontrolled**—Uncontrolled hypertension may refer to untreated hypertension or hypertension not responding to current therapeutic regimen. In either case, assign the appropriate code from categories 401-405 to designate the stage and type of hypertension. Code to the type of hypertension.

11) **Elevated blood pressure**—For a statement of elevated blood pressure without further specificity, assign code 796.2, Elevated blood pressure reading without diagnosis of hypertension, rather than a code from category 401.

b. **Cerebral infarction/stroke/cerebrovascular accident (CVA)—The terms stroke and CVA are often used interchangeably to refer to a cerebral infarction. The terms stroke, CVA, and cerebral infarction NOS are all indexed to the default code 434.91, Cerebral artery occlusion, unspecified, with infarction. Code 436, Acute, but ill-defined, cerebrovascular disease, should not be used when the documentation states stroke or CVA.**

c. **Postoperative cerebrovascular accident—A cerebrovascular hemorrhage or infarction that occurs as a result of medical intervention is coded to 997.02, Iatrogenic cerebrovascular infarction or hemorrhage. Medical record documentation should clearly specify the cause- and-effect relationship between the medical intervention and the cerebrovascular accident in order to assign this code. A secondary code from the code range 430-432 or from a code from subcategories 433 or 434 with a fifth digit of "1" should also be used to identify the type of hemorrhage or infarct.**

This guideline conforms to the use additional code note instruction at category 997. Code 436, Acute, but ill-defined, cerebrovascular disease, should not be used as a secondary code with code 997.02.

d. Late effects of cerebrovascular disease

1) **Category 438, late effects of cerebrovascular disease**—Category 438 is used to indicate conditions classifiable to categories 430–437 as the causes of late effects (neurologic deficits), themselves classified elsewhere. These "late effects" include neurologic deficits that persist after initial onset of conditions classifiable to 430–437. The neurologic deficits caused by cerebrovascular disease may be present from the onset or may arise at any time after the onset of the condition classifiable to 430-437.

2) **Codes from category 438 with codes from 430–437**—Codes from category 438 may be assigned on a health care record with codes from 430–437, if the patient has a current cerebrovascular accident (CVA) and deficits from an old CVA.

3) **Code V12.59**—Assign code V12.59 (and not a code from category 438) as an additional code for history of cerebrovascular disease when no neurologic deficits are present.

8. Chapter 8: Diseases of Respiratory System (460-519)

a. **Chronic obstructive pulmonary disease [COPD] and asthma**

1) **Conditions that comprise COPD and asthma—The conditions that comprise COPD are obstructive chronic bronchitis, subcategory 491.2, and emphysema, category 492. All asthma codes are under category 493 Asthma. Code 496 Chronic airway obstruction, not elsewhere classified, is a nonspecific code that should be used only when the documentation in a medical record does not specify the type of COPD being treated.**

2) **Acute exacerbation of chronic obstructive bronchitis and asthma—The codes for chronic obstructive bronchitis and asthma distinguish between uncomplicated cases and those in acute exacerbation. An acute exacerbation is a worsening or a decompensation of a chronic condition. An acute exacerbation is not equivalent to an infection superimposed on a chronic condition, though an exacerbation may be triggered by an infection.**

3) **Overlapping nature of the conditions that comprise COPD and asthma—Due to the overlapping nature of the conditions that make up COPD and asthma, there are many variations in the way these conditions are documented. Code selection must be based on the terms as documented. When selecting the correct code for the documented type of COPD and asthma, it is essential to first review the index and then verify the code in the Tabular List. There are many instructional notes under the different COPD subcategories and codes. It is important that all such notes be reviewed to ensure correct code assignment.**

4) **Acute exacerbation of asthma and status asthmaticus—An acute exacerbation of asthma is an increased severity of the asthma symptoms, such as wheezing and shortness of breath. Status asthmaticus refers to a patient's failure to respond to therapy administered during an asthmatic episode and is a life-threatening complication that requires emergency care. If status asthmaticus is documented by the provider with any type of COPD or with acute bronchitis, the status asthmaticus should be sequenced first. It supersedes any type of COPD, including that with acute exacerbation or acute bronchitis. It is inappropriate to assign an asthma code with fifth-digit 2, with acute exacerbation, together with an asthma code with fifth-digit 1, with status asthmaticus. Only the fifth-digit 1 should be assigned.**

b. **Chronic obstructive pulmonary disease [COPD] and bronchitis**

1) **Acute bronchitis with COPD—Acute bronchitis, code 466.0, is due to an infectious organism. When acute bronchitis is documented with COPD, code 491.22 Obstructive chronic bronchitis with acute bronchitis, should be assigned. It is not necessary to also assign code 466.0. If a medical record documents acute bronchitis with COPD with acute exacerbation, only code 491.22 should be assigned. The acute bronchitis included in code 491.22 supersedes the acute exacerbation. If a medical record documents COPD with acute exacerbation without mention of acute bronchitis, only code 491.21 should be assigned.**

9. Chapter 9: Diseases of Digestive System (520-579)
Reserved for future guideline expansion

10. Chapter 10: Diseases of Genitourinary System (580-629)
Reserved for future guideline expansion

11. Chapter 11: Complications of Pregnancy, Childbirth, and the Puerperium (630-677)

a. **General rules for obstetric cases**

1) **Codes from chapter 11 and sequencing priority**—Obstetric cases require codes from chapter 11, codes in the range 630-677 Complications of pregnancy, childbirth, and the puerperium. Chapter 11 codes have sequencing priority over codes from other chapters. Additional codes from other chapters may be used in conjunction with chapter 11 codes to further specify conditions. Should the provider document that the pregnancy is incidental to the encounter, then code V22.2 should be used in place of any chapter 11 codes. It is the provider's responsibility to state that the condition being treated is not affecting the pregnancy.

2) **Chapter 11 codes used only on the maternal record**—Chapter 11 codes are to be used only on the maternal record, never on the record of the newborn.

3) **Chapter 11 fifth digits**—Categories 640-648, 651-676 have required fifth-digits, which indicate whether the encounter is antepartum, postpartum and whether a delivery has also occurred.

4) **Fifth digits, appropriate for each code**—The fifth digits, which are appropriate for each code number, are listed in brackets under each code. The fifth digits on each code should all be consistent with each other. That is, should a delivery occur all of the fifth digits should indicate the delivery.

b. Selection of OB principal or first-listed diagnosis

1) **Routine outpatient prenatal visits**—For routine outpatient prenatal visits when no complications are present, codes V22.0 Supervision of normal first pregnancy, and V22.1 Supervision of other normal pregnancy, should be used as the first-listed diagnoses. These codes should not be used in conjunction with chapter 11 codes.

2) **Prenatal outpatient visits for high-risk patients**—For prenatal outpatient visits for patients with high-risk pregnancies, a code from category V23 Supervision of high-risk pregnancy, should be used as the principal or first-listed diagnosis. Secondary chapter 11 codes may be used in conjunction with these codes if appropriate.

3) **Episodes when no delivery occurs**—In episodes when no delivery occurs, the principal diagnosis should correspond to the principal complication of the pregnancy, which necessitated the encounter. Should more than one complication exist, all of which are treated or monitored, any of the complication codes may be sequenced first.

4) **When a delivery occurs**—When a delivery occurs, the principal diagnosis should correspond to the main circumstances or complication of the delivery. In cases of cesarean delivery, the selection of the principal diagnosis should correspond to the reason the cesarean delivery was performed unless the reason for admission/encounter was unrelated to the condition resulting in the cesarean delivery.

5) **Outcome of delivery**—An outcome of delivery code, V27.0-V27.9, should be included on every maternal record when a delivery has occurred. These codes are not to be used on subsequent records or on the newborn record.

c. Fetal conditions affecting the management of the mother

1) **Fetal condition responsible for modifying the management of the mother**—Codes from category 655 Known or suspected fetal abnormality affecting management of the mother, and category 656 Other fetal and placental problems affecting the management of the mother, are assigned only when the fetal condition is actually responsible for modifying the management of the mother, i.e., by requiring diagnostic studies, additional observation, special care, or termination of pregnancy. The fact that the fetal condition exists does not justify assigning a code from this series to the mother's record.

2) **In utero surgery**—In cases when surgery is performed on the fetus, a diagnosis code from category 655 Known or suspected fetal abnormalities affecting management of the mother, should be assigned identifying the fetal condition. Procedure code 75.36 Correction of fetal defect, should be assigned on the hospital inpatient record.

No code from chapter 15, the perinatal codes, should be used on the mother's record to identify fetal conditions. Surgery performed in utero on a fetus is still to be coded as an obstetric encounter.

d. HIV infection in pregnancy, childbirth and the puerperium
During pregnancy, childbirth, or the puerperium, a patient admitted because of an HIV-related illness should receive a principal diagnosis of 647.6X Other specified infectious and parasitic diseases in the mother classifiable elsewhere, but complicating the pregnancy, childbirth, or the puerperium, followed by 042 and the code(s) for the HIV-related illness(es).

Patients with asymptomatic HIV infection status admitted during pregnancy, childbirth, or the puerperium should receive codes of 647.6X and V08.

e. Current conditions complicating pregnancy—Assign a code from subcategory 648.x for patients that have current conditions when the condition affects the management of the pregnancy, childbirth, or the puerperium. Use additional secondary codes from other chapters to identify the conditions, as appropriate.

f. Diabetes mellitus in pregnancy—Diabetes mellitus is a significant complicating factor in pregnancy. Pregnant women who are diabetic should be assigned code 648.0x Diabetes mellitus complicating pregnancy, and a secondary code from category 250 Diabetes mellitus, to identify the type of diabetes.

Code V58.67 Long-term (current) use of insulin, should also be assigned if the diabetes mellitus is being treated with insulin.

g. Gestational diabetes—Gestational diabetes can occur during the second and third trimester of pregnancy in women who were not diabetic prior to pregnancy. Gestational diabetes can cause complications in the pregnancy similar to those of pre-existing diabetes mellitus. It also puts the woman at greater risk of developing diabetes after the pregnancy. Gestational diabetes is coded to 648.8x Abnormal glucose tolerance. Codes 648.0x and 648.8x should never be used together on the same record.

Code V58.67 Long-term (current) use of insulin, should also be assigned if the gestational diabetes is being treated with insulin.

h. Normal delivery, code 650

1) **Normal delivery**—Code 650 is for use in cases when a woman is admitted for a full-term normal delivery and delivers a single, healthy infant without any complications antepartum, during the delivery, or postpartum during the delivery episode. **Code 650 is always a principal diagnosis. It is not to be used if any other code from chapter 11 is needed to describe a current complication of the antenatal, delivery, or perinatal period. Additional codes from other chapters may be used with code 650 if they are not related to or are in any way complicating the pregnancy.**

2) **Normal delivery with resolved antepartum complication**—Code 650 may be used if the patient had a complication at some point during her pregnancy, but the complication is not present at the time of the admission for delivery.

3) **V27.0 Single liveborn, outcome of delivery**—V27.0 Single liveborn, is the only outcome of the delivery code appropriate for use with 650.

i. The postpartum and peripartum periods

1) **Postpartum and peripartum periods**—The postpartum period begins immediately after delivery and continues for six weeks following delivery. The peripartum period is defined as the last month of pregnancy to five months postpartum.

2) **Postpartum complication**—A postpartum complication is any complication occurring within the six-week period.

3) **Pregnancy-related complications after six-week period**—Chapter 11 codes may also be used to describe pregnancy-related complications after the six-week period should the provider document that a condition is pregnancy related.

4) **Postpartum complications occurring during the same admission as delivery**—Postpartum complications that occur during the same admission as the delivery are identified with a fifth digit of 2. Subsequent admissions/encounters for postpartum complications should be identified with a fifth digit of 4.

5) **Admission for routine postpartum care following delivery outside hospital**—When the mother delivers outside the hospital prior to admission and is admitted for routine postpartum care and no complications are noted, code V24.0 Postpartum care and examination immediately after delivery, should be assigned as the principal diagnosis.

6) **Admission following delivery outside hospital with postpartum conditions**—A delivery diagnosis code should not be used for a woman who has delivered prior to admission to the hospital. Any postpartum conditions and/or postpartum procedures should be coded.

j. Code 677 Late effect of complication of pregnancy

1) **Code 677**—Code 677 Late effect of complication of pregnancy, childbirth, and the puerperium is for use in those cases when an initial complication of a pregnancy develops a sequelae requiring care or treatment at a future date.

2) **After the initial postpartum period**—This code may be used at any time after the initial postpartum period.

3) **Sequencing of code 677**—This code, like all late effect codes, is to be sequenced following the code describing the sequelae of the complication.

k. Abortions

1) **Fifth digits required for abortion categories**—Fifth digits are required for abortion categories 634-637. Fifth-digit 1, incomplete, indicates that all of the products of conception have not been expelled from the uterus. Fifth-digit 2, complete, indicates that all

products of conception have been expelled from the uterus prior to the episode of care.

2) Code from categories 640-648 and 651-659—A code from categories 640-648 and 651-659 may be used as additional codes with an abortion code to indicate the complication leading to the abortion.

Fifth-digit 3 is assigned with codes from these categories when used with an abortion code because the other fifth digits will not apply. Codes from the 660-669 series are not to be used for complications of abortion.

3) Code 639 for complications—Code 639 is to be used for all complications following abortion. Code 639 cannot be assigned with codes from categories 634-638.

4) Abortion with liveborn fetus—When an attempted termination of pregnancy results in a liveborn fetus assign code 644.21 Early onset of delivery, with an appropriate code from category V27 Outcome of delivery. The procedure code for the attempted termination of pregnancy should also be assigned.

5) Retained products of conception following an abortion—Subsequent admissions for retained products of conception following a spontaneous or legally induced abortion are assigned the appropriate code from category 634 Spontaneous abortion, or 635 Legally induced abortion, with a fifth digit of 1 (incomplete). This advice is appropriate even when the patient was discharged previously with a discharge diagnosis of complete abortion.

12. Chapter 12: Diseases of Skin and Subcutaneous Tissue (680-709)

Reserved for future guideline expansion

13. Chapter 13: Diseases of Musculoskeletal and Connective Tissue (710-739)

Reserved for future guideline expansion

14. Chapter 14: Congenital Anomalies (740-759)

a. **Codes in categories 740-759 Congenital anomalies**—Assign an appropriate code(s) from categories 740-759, Congenital anomalies, when an anomaly is documented. A congenital anomaly may be the principal/first-listed diagnosis on a record or a secondary diagnosis. Use additional secondary codes from other chapters to specify conditions associated with the anomaly, if applicable. Codes from chapter 14 may be used throughout the life of the patient. If a congenital anomaly has been corrected, a personal history code should be used to identify the history of the anomaly.

For the birth admission, the appropriate code from category V30 Liveborn infants, according to type of birth should be sequenced as the principal diagnosis, followed by any congenital anomaly codes, 740-759.

15. Chapter 15: Newborn (Perinatal) Guidelines (760-779)
For coding and reporting purposes the perinatal period is defined as birth through the 28th day following birth. The following guidelines are provided for reporting purposes. Hospitals may record other diagnoses as needed for internal data use.

a. **General perinatal rules**

1) Chapter 15 codes—They are never for use on the maternal record. Codes from chapter 11, the obstetric chapter, are never permitted on the newborn record. Chapter 15 code may be used throughout the life of the patient if the condition is still present.

2) Sequencing of perinatal codes—Generally, codes from chapter 15 should be sequenced as the principal/first-listed diagnosis on the newborn record, with the exception of the appropriate V30 code for the birth episode, followed by codes from any other chapter that provide additional detail. The "use additional code" note at the beginning of the chapter supports this guideline. If the index does not provide a specific code for a perinatal condition, assign code 779.89 Other specified conditions originating in the perinatal period, followed by the code from another chapter that specifies the condition. Codes for signs and symptoms may be assigned when a definitive diagnosis has not been established.

3) Birth process or community acquired conditions—If a newborn has a condition that may be either due to the birth process or community acquired and the documentation does not indicate which it is, the default is due to the birth process and the code

from chapter 15 should be used. If the condition is community acquired, a code from chapter 15 should not be assigned.

4) Code all clinically significant conditions—All clinically significant conditions noted on routine newborn examination should be coded. A condition is clinically significant if it requires:

- Clinical evaluation; or
- Therapeutic treatment; or
- Diagnostic procedures; or
- Extended length of hospital stay; or
- Increased nursing care and/or monitoring; or
- Has implications for future health care needs

Note: The perinatal guidelines listed above are the same as the general coding guidelines for "additional diagnoses," except for the final point regarding implications for future health care needs. **Codes should be assigned for conditions that have been specified by the provider as having implications for future health care needs. Codes from the perinatal chapter should not be assigned unless the provider has established a definitive diagnosis.**

b. **Use of codes V30-V39**—When coding the birth of an infant, assign a code from categories V30-V39, according to the type of birth. A code from this series is assigned as a principal diagnosis and assigned only once to a newborn at the time of birth.

c. **Newborn transfers**—If the newborn is transferred to another institution, the V30 series is not used at the receiving hospital.

d. **Use of category V29**

1) Assigning a code from category V29—Assign a code from category V29 Observation and evaluation of newborns and infants for suspected conditions not found, to identify those instances when a healthy newborn is evaluated for a suspected condition that is determined after study not to be present. Do not use a code from category V29 when the patient has identified signs or symptoms of a suspected problem; in such cases, code the sign or symptom.

A code from category V29 may also be assigned as a principal diagnosis for readmissions or encounters when the V30 code no longer applies. Codes from category V29 are for use only for healthy newborns and infants for which no condition after study is found to be present.

2) V29 code on a birth record—A V29 code is to be used as a secondary code after the V30 Outcome of delivery, code.

e. **Use of other V codes on perinatal records**—V codes other than V30 and V29 may be assigned on a perinatal or newborn record code. The codes may be used as a principal or first-listed diagnosis for specific types of encounters or for readmissions or encounters when the V30 code no longer applies.

See section I.C.18 for information regarding the assignment of V codes.

f. **Maternal causes of perinatal morbidity**—Codes from categories 760-763 Maternal causes of perinatal morbidity and mortality, are assigned only when the maternal condition has actually affected the fetus or newborn. The fact that the mother has an associated medical condition or experiences some complication of pregnancy, labor, or delivery does not justify the routine assignment of codes from these categories to the newborn record.

g. **Congenital anomalies in newborns**—For the birth admission, the appropriate code from category V30 Liveborn infants according to type of birth, should be used, followed by any congenital anomaly codes, categories 740-759. **Use additional secondary codes from other chapters to specify conditions associated with the anomaly, if applicable.**

Also, see section I.C.14 for information on the coding of congenital anomalies.

h. **Coding additional perinatal diagnoses**

1) Assigning codes for conditions that require treatment—Assign codes for conditions that require treatment or further investigation, prolong the length of stay, or require resource utilization.

2) Codes for conditions specified as having implications for future health care needs—Assign codes for conditions that have been specified by the provider as having implications for future health care needs.

Note: This guideline should not be used for adult patients.

3) Codes for newborn conditions originating in the perinatal period—Assign a code for newborn conditions originating in the perinatal period (categories 760-779), as well as complications arising during the current episode of care classified in other chapters, only if the diagnoses have been documented by the responsible provider at the time of transfer or discharge as having affected the fetus or newborn.

i. Prematurity and fetal growth retardation—Providers utilize different criteria in determining prematurity. A code for prematurity should not be assigned unless it is documented. The fift-digit assignment for codes from category 764 and subcategories 765.0 and 765.1 should be based on the recorded birth weight and estimated gestational age.

A code from subcategory 765.2 Weeks of gestation, should be assigned as an additional code with category 764 and codes from 765.0 and 765.1 to specify weeks of gestation as documented by the provider in the record.

j. Newborn sepsis—Code 771.81 Septicemia [sepsis] of newborn, should be assigned with a secondary code from category 041 Bacterial infections in conditions classified elsewhere and of unspecified site, to identify the organism. It is not necessary to use a code from subcategory 995.9 Systemic inflammatory response syndrome (SIRS), on a newborn record. A code from category 038 Septicemia, should not be used on a newborn record. Code 771.81 describes the sepsis.

16. Chapter 16: Signs, Symptoms and Ill-Defined Conditions (780-799)

Reserved for future guideline expansion

17. Chapter 17: Injury and Poisoning (800-999)

a. Coding of injuries—When coding injuries, assign separate codes for each injury unless a combination code is provided, in which case the combination code is assigned. Multiple injury codes are provided in ICD-9-CM but should not be assigned unless information for a more specific code is not available. These codes are not to be used for normal, healing surgical wounds or to identify complications of surgical wounds.

The code for the most serious injury, as determined by the provider and the focus of treatment, is sequenced first.

1) Superficial injuries—Superficial injuries such as abrasions or contusions are not coded when associated with more severe injuries of the same site.

2) Primary injury with damage to nerves/blood vessels—When a primary injury results in minor damage to peripheral nerves or blood vessels, the primary injury is sequenced first with additional code(s) from categories 950-957 Injury to nerves and spinal cord, and/or 900-904 Injury to blood vessels. When the primary injury is to the blood vessels or nerves, that injury should be sequenced first.

b. Coding of fractures—The principles of multiple coding of injuries should be followed in coding fractures. Fractures of specified sites are coded individually by site in accordance with both the provisions within categories 800-829 and the level of detail furnished by medical record content. Combination categories for multiple fractures are provided for use when there is insufficient detail in the medical record (such as trauma cases transferred to another hospital), when the reporting form limits the number of codes that can be used in reporting pertinent clinical data, or when there is insufficient specificity at the fourth-digit or fifth-digit level. More specific guidelines are as follows:

1) Multiple fractures of same limb—Multiple fractures of same limb classifiable to the same three-digit or four-digit category are coded to that category.

2) Multiple unilateral or bilateral fractures of same bone—Multiple unilateral or bilateral fractures of same bone(s) but classified to different fourth-digit subdivisions (bone part) within the same three-digit category are coded individually by site.

3) Multiple fracture categories 819 and 828—Multiple fracture categories 819 and 828 classify bilateral fractures of both upper limbs (819) and both lower limbs (828), but without any detail at the fourth-digit level other than open and closed type of fractures.

4) Multiple fractures sequencing—Multiple fractures are sequenced in accordance with the severity of the fracture. The provider should be asked to list the fracture diagnoses in the order of severity.

c. Coding of burns—Current burns (940-948) are classified by depth, extent, and by agent (E code). Burns are classified by depth as first degree (erythema), second degree (blistering), and third degree (full-thickness involvement).

1) Sequencing of burn codes—Sequence first the code that reflects the highest degree of burn when more than one burn is present.

2) Burns of the same local site—Classify burns of the same local site (three-digit category level, 940-947) but of different degrees to the subcategory identifying the highest degree recorded in the diagnosis.

3) Non-healing burns—Non-healing burns are coded as acute burns. Necrosis of burned skin should be coded as a non-healed burn.

4) Code 958.3 Posttraumatic wound infection—Assign code 958.3 Posttraumatic wound infection, not elsewhere classified, as an additional code for any documented infected burn site.

5) Assign separate codes for each burn site—When coding burns, assign separate codes for each burn site. Category 946 Burns of multiple specified sites, should only be used if the locations of the burns are not documented. Category 949 Burn, unspecified, is extremely vague and should rarely be used.

6) Burns classified according to extent of body surface involved—Assign codes from category 948 Burns, when the site of the burn is not specified or when there is a need for additional data. It is advisable to use category 948 as additional coding when needed to provide data for evaluating burn mortality, such as that needed by burn units. It is also advisable to use category 948 as an additional code for reporting purposes when there is mention of a third-degree burn involving 20 percent or more of the body surface.

In assigning a code from category 948:

- Fourth-digit codes are used to identify the percentage of total body surface involved in a burn (all degree).

- Fifth digits are assigned to identify the percentage of body surface involved in third-degree burn.

- Fifth-digit zero (0) is assigned when less than 10 percent or when no body surface is involved in a third-degree burn.

- Category 948 is based on the classic "rule of nines" in estimating body surface involved: head and neck are assigned 9 percent, each arm 9 percent, each leg 18 percent, the anterior trunk 18 percent, posterior trunk 18 percent, and genitalia 1 percent. Providers may change these percentage assignments where necessary to accommodate infants and children who have proportionately larger heads than adults and patients who have large buttocks, thighs, or abdomen that involve burns.

7) Encounters for treatment of late effects of burns—Encounters for the treatment of the late effects of burns (i.e., scars or joint contractures) should be coded to the residual condition (sequelae) followed by the appropriate late effect code (906.5-906.9). A late effect E code may also be used, if desired.

8) Sequelae with a late effect code and current burn—When appropriate, both a sequelae with a late effect code, and a current burn code may be assigned on the same record **(when both a current burn and sequelae of an old burn exist).**

d. Coding of debridement of wound, infection, or burn—Excisional debridement involves an excisional debridement (surgical removal or cutting away), as opposed to a mechanical (brushing, scrubbing, washing) debridement.

For coding purposes, excisional debridement **is assigned to code 86.22.**

Nonexcisional debridement is assigned to **code 86.28.**

e. Adverse effects, poisoning and toxic effects—The properties of certain drugs, medicinal and biological substances, or combinations of such substances, may cause toxic reactions. The occurrence of drug toxicity is classified in ICD-9-CM as follows:

1) Adverse effect—When the drug was correctly prescribed and properly administered, code the reaction plus the appropriate code from the E930-E949 series. Codes from the E930-E949 series must be used to identify the causative substance for an adverse effect of drug, medicinal and biological substances, correctly prescribed and properly administered. The effect, such as tachycardia, delirium, gastrointestinal hemorrhaging, vomiting, hypokalemia, hepatitis, renal failure, or respiratory failure, is coded and followed by the appropriate code from the E930-E949 series.

Adverse effects of therapeutic substances correctly prescribed and properly administered (toxicity, synergistic reaction, side effect, and idiosyncratic reaction) may be due to (1) differences among patients, such as age, sex, disease, and genetic factors, and (2) drug-related factors, such as type of drug, route of administration, duration of therapy, dosage, and bioavailability.

2) Poisoning

(a) Error was made in drug prescription—Errors made in drug prescription or in the administration of the drug by provider, nurse, patient, or other person, use the appropriate poisoning code from the 960-979 series.

(b) Overdose of a drug intentionally taken—If an overdose of a drug was intentionally taken or administered and resulted in drug toxicity, it would be coded as a poisoning (960-979 series).

(c) Nonprescribed drug taken with correctly prescribed and properly administered drug—If a nonprescribed drug or medicinal agent was taken in combination with a correctly prescribed and properly administered drug, any drug toxicity or other reaction resulting from the interaction of the two drugs would be classified as a poisoning.

(d) Sequencing of poisoning—When coding a poisoning or reaction to the improper use of a medication (e.g., wrong dose, wrong substance, wrong route of administration) the poisoning code is sequenced first, followed by a code for the manifestation. If there is also a diagnosis of drug abuse or dependence to the substance, the abuse or dependence is coded as an additional code.

See section I.C.3.a.6.b. if poisoning is the result of insulin pump malfunctions and section I.C.19 for general use of E codes.

3) Toxic effects

(a) Toxic effect codes—When a harmful substance is ingested or comes in contact with a person, this is classified as a toxic effect. The toxic effect codes are in categories 980-989.

(b) Sequencing toxic effect codes—A toxic effect code should be sequenced first, followed by the codes that identify the result of the toxic effect.

(c) External cause codes for toxic effects—An external cause code from categories E860-E869 for accidental exposure, code E950.6 or E950.7 for intentional self-harm, category E962 for assault, or categories E980-E982 for undetermined, should also be assigned to indicate intent.

18. Classification of Factors Influencing Health Status and Contact with Health Service (Supplemental V01-V85)
Note: The chapter-specific guidelines provide additional information about the use of V codes for specified encounters.

a. Introduction—ICD-9-CM provides codes to deal with encounters for circumstances other than a disease or injury. The Supplementary Classification of Factors Influencing Health Status and Contact with Health Services (V01-V85) is provided to deal with occasions when circumstances other than a disease or injury (codes 001-999) are recorded as a diagnosis or problem.

There are four primary circumstances for the use of V codes:

1) A person who is not currently sick encounters the health services for some specific reason, such as to act as an organ donor, to receive prophylactic care, such as inoculations or health screenings, or to receive counseling on health related issues.

2) A person with a resolving disease or injury, or a chronic, long-term condition requiring continuous care, encounters the health care system for specific aftercare of that disease or injury (e.g., dialysis for renal disease; chemotherapy for malignancy; cast change). A diagnosis/symptom code should be used whenever a current, acute diagnosis is being treated or a sign or symptom is being studied.

3) Circumstances or problems influence a person's health status but are not in themselves a current illness or injury.

4) Newborns, to indicate birth status

b. V codes use in any health care setting—V codes are for use in any healthcare setting. V codes may be used as either a first-listed (principal diagnosis code in the inpatient setting) or secondary code, depending on the circumstances of the encounter. Certain V codes may only be used as first listed, others only as secondary codes. See section I.C.18.e, V code table.

c. V codes indicate a reason for an encounter—They are not procedure codes. A corresponding procedure code must accompany a V code to describe the procedure performed.

d. Categories of V codes

1) Contact/exposure—Category V01 indicates contact with or exposure to communicable diseases. These codes are for patients who do not show any sign or symptom of a disease but have been exposed to it by close personal contact with an infected individual or are in an area where a disease is epidemic. These codes may be used as a first-listed code to explain an encounter for testing, or, more commonly, as a secondary code to identify a potential risk.

2) Inoculations and vaccinations—Categories V03-V06 are for encounters for inoculations and vaccinations. They indicate that a patient is being seen to receive a prophylactic inoculation against a disease. The injection itself must be represented by the appropriate procedure code. A code from V03-V06 may be used as a secondary code if the inoculation is given as a routine part of preventive health care, such as a well-baby visit.

3) Status—Status codes indicate that a patient is either a carrier of a disease or has the sequelae or residual of a past disease or condition. This includes such things as the presence of prosthetic or mechanical devices resulting from past treatment.

A status code is informative, because the status may affect the course of treatment and its outcome. A status code is distinct from a history code. The history code indicates that the patient no longer has the condition.

A status code should not be used with a diagnosis code from one of the body system chapters, if the diagnosis code includes the information provided by the status code. For example, code V42.1 Heart transplant status, should not be used with code 996.83 Complications of transplanted heart. The status code does not provide additional information. The complication code indicates that the patient is a heart transplant patient.

The status V codes/categories are:

V02	Carrier or suspected carrier of infectious diseases—Carrier status indicates that a person harbors the specific organisms of a disease without manifest symptoms and is capable of transmitting the infection.
V08	Asymptomatic HIV infection status—This code indicates that a patient has tested positive for HIV but has manifested no signs or symptoms of the disease.
V09	Infection with drug-resistant microorganisms—This category indicates that a patient has an infection that is resistant to drug treatment. Sequence the infection code first.
V21	Constitutional states in development
V22.2	Pregnant state, incidental—This code is a secondary code only for use when the pregnancy is in no way complicating the reason for visit. Otherwise, a code from the obstetric chapter is required.
V26.5x	Sterilization status
V42	Organ or tissue replaced by transplant
V43	Organ or tissue replaced by other means
V44	Artificial opening status
V45	Other postsurgical states
V46	Other dependence on machines
V49.6	Upper limb amputation status
V49.7	Lower limb amputation status
V49.81	Postmenopausal status
V49.82	Dental sealant status
V49.83	**Awaiting organ transplant status**
V58.6	Long-term (current) drug use—This subcategory indicates a patient's continuous use of a prescribed drug (including such things as aspirin therapy) for the long-term treatment of a condition or for prophylactic use. It is not for use for patients who have addictions to drugs.
V83	Genetic carrier status—**Genetic carrier status indicates that a person carries a gene, associated with a particular disease, which may be passed to offspring who may develop that disease. The person does not have the disease and is not at risk of developing the disease.**
V84	**Genetic susceptibility status—Genetic susceptibility indicates that a person has a gene that increases the risk of that person developing the disease.**

Note: Categories V42-V46, and subcategories V49.6, V49.7 are for use only if there are no complications or malfunctions of the organ or tissue replaced, the amputation site, or the equipment on which the patient is dependent. These are always secondary codes.

4) History (of)—There are two types of history V codes, personal and family. Personal history codes explain a patient's past medical condition that no longer exists and is not receiving any treatment but that has the potential for recurrence, and therefore may require continued monitoring. The exceptions to this general rule are category V14 Personal history of allergy to medicinal agents, and subcategory V15.0 Allergy, other than to medicinal agents. A person who has had an allergic episode to a substance or food in the past should always be considered allergic to the substance.

Family history codes are for use when a patient has a family member(s) who has had a particular disease that causes the patient to be at higher risk of also contracting the disease.

Personal history codes may be used in conjunction with follow-up codes and family history codes may be used in conjunction with screening codes to explain the need for a test or procedure. History codes are also acceptable on any medical record regardless of the reason for visit. A history of an illness, even if no longer present, is important information that may alter the type of treatment ordered.

The history V code categories are:

V10	Personal history of malignant neoplasm
V12	Personal history of certain other diseases
V13	Personal history of other diseases

Except: V13.4 Personal history of arthritis, and V13.6 Personal history of congenital malformations. These conditions are life-long so are not true history codes.

V14	Personal history of allergy to medicinal agents
V15	Other personal history presenting hazards to health

Except: V15.7 Personal history of contraception

V16	Family history of malignant neoplasm
V17	Family history of certain chronic disabling diseases
V18	Family history of certain other specific diseases
V19	Family history of other conditions

5) Screening—Screening is the testing for disease or disease precursors in seemingly well individuals so that early detection and treatment can be provided for those who test positive for the disease. Screenings that are recommended for many subgroups in a population include routine mammograms for women over 40, a fecal occult blood test for everyone over 50, an amniocentesis to rule out a fetal anomaly for pregnant women over 35, because the incidence of breast cancer and colon cancer in these subgroups is higher than in the general population, as is the incidence of Down's syndrome in older mothers.

The testing of a person to rule out or confirm a suspected diagnosis because the patient has some sign or symptom is a diagnostic examination, not a screening. In these cases, the sign or symptom is used to explain the reason for the test.

A screening code may be a first-listed code if the reason for the visit is specifically the screening exam. It may also be used as an additional code if the screening is done during an office visit for other health problems. A screening code is not necessary if the screening is inherent to a routine examination, such as a Pap smear done during a routine pelvic examination.

Should a condition be discovered during the screening then the code for the condition may be assigned as an additional diagnosis.

The V code indicates that a screening exam is planned. A procedure code is required to confirm that the screening was performed.

The screening V code categories:

V28	Antenatal screening
V73-V82	Special screening examinations

6) Observation—There are two observation V code categories. They are for use in very limited circumstances when a person is being observed for a suspected condition that is ruled out. The observation codes are not for use if an injury or illness or any signs or symptoms related to the suspected condition are present. In such cases the diagnosis/symptom code is used with the corresponding E code to identify any external cause.

The observation codes are to be used as principal diagnosis only. The only exception to this is when the principal diagnosis is required to be a code from the V30 Live born infant, category. Then

the V29 observation code is sequenced after the V30 code. Additional codes may be used in addition to the observation code but only if they are unrelated to the suspected condition being observed.

The observation V code categories:

V29	Observation and evaluation of newborns for suspected condition not found

For the birth encounter, a code from category V30 should be sequenced before the V29 code.

V71	Observation and evaluation for suspected condition not found

7) Aftercare—Aftercare visit codes cover situations when the initial treatment of a disease or injury has been performed and the patient requires continued care during the healing or recovery phase, or for the long-term consequences of the disease. The aftercare code should not be used if treatment is directed at a current, acute disease or injury, the diagnosis code is to be used in these cases. Exceptions to this rule are codes V58.0 Radiotherapy, and V58.1 Chemotherapy. These codes are to be first listed, followed by the diagnosis code when a patient's encounter is solely to receive radiation therapy or chemotherapy for the treatment of a neoplasm. Should a patient receive both chemotherapy and radiation therapy during the same encounter, codes V58.0 and V58.1 may be used together on a record with either one being sequenced first.

The aftercare codes are generally first listed to explain the specific reason for the encounter. An aftercare code may be used as an additional code when some type of aftercare is provided in addition to the reason for admission and no diagnosis code is applicable. An example of this would be the closure of a colostomy during an encounter for treatment of another condition.

Certain aftercare V code categories need a secondary diagnosis code to describe the resolving condition or sequelae, for others, the condition is inherent in the code title.

Additional V code aftercare category terms include fitting and adjustment, and attention to artificial openings.

Status V codes may be used with aftercare V codes to indicate the nature of the aftercare. For example code V45.81 Aortocoronary bypass status, may be used with code V58.73 Aftercare following surgery of the circulatory system, NEC, to indicate the surgery for which the aftercare is being performed. Also, a transplant status code may be used following code V58.44 Aftercare following organ transplant, to identify the organ transplanted. A status code should not be used when the aftercare code indicates the type of status, such as using V55.0 Attention to tracheostomy with V44.0 Tracheostomy status.

The aftercare V category/codes:

V52	Fitting and adjustment of prosthetic device and implant
V53	Fitting and adjustment of other device
V54	Other orthopedic aftercare
V55	Attention to artificial openings
V56	Encounter for dialysis and dialysis catheter care
V57	Care involving the use of rehabilitation procedures
V58.0	Radiotherapy
V58.1	Chemotherapy
V58.3	Attention to surgical dressings and sutures
V58.41	Encounter for planned post-operative wound closure
V58.42	Aftercare, surgery, neoplasm
V58.43	Aftercare, surgery, trauma
V58.44	**Aftercare involving organ transplant**
V58.49	Other specified aftercare following surgery
V58.7x	Aftercare following surgery
V58.81	Fitting and adjustment of vascular catheter
V58.82	Fitting and adjustment of non-vascular catheter
V58.83	Monitoring therapeutic drug
V58.89	Other specified aftercare

8) Follow-up—The follow-up codes are used to explain continuing surveillance following completed treatment of a disease, condition, or injury. They imply that the condition has been fully treated and no longer exists. They should not be confused with aftercare codes that explain current treatment for a healing condition or its sequelae. Follow-up codes may be used in conjunction with history codes to provide the full picture of the healed condition and its treatment. The follow-up code is sequenced first, followed by the history code.

A follow-up code may be used to explain repeated visits. Should a condition be found to have recurred on the follow-up visit, then the diagnosis code should be used in place of the follow-up code.

The follow-up V code categories:

V24 Postpartum care and evaluation
V67 Follow-up examination

9) Donor—Category V59 is the donor codes. They are used for living individuals who are donating blood or other body tissue. These codes are only for individuals donating for others, not for self-donations. They are not for use to identify cadaveric donations.

10) Counseling—Counseling V codes are used when a patient or family member receives assistance in the aftermath of an illness or injury, or when support is required in coping with family or social problems. They are not necessary for use in conjunction with a diagnosis code when the counseling component of care is considered integral to standard treatment.

The counseling V categories/codes:

V25.0 General counseling and advice for contraceptive management
V26.3 Genetic counseling
V26.4 General counseling and advice for procreative management
V61 Other family circumstances
V65.1 Person consulted on behalf of another person
V65.3 Dietary surveillance and counseling
V65.4 Other counseling, not elsewhere classified

11) Obstetrics and related conditions—See section I.C.11., the obstetrics guidelines for further instruction on the use of these codes.

V codes for pregnancy are for use in those circumstances when none of the problems or complications included in the codes from the obstetrics chapter exist (a routine prenatal visit or postpartum care). Codes V22.0 Supervision of normal first pregnancy, and V22.1 Supervision of other normal pregnancy, are always first listed and are not to be used with any other code from the OB chapter.

The outcome of delivery, category V27, should be included on all maternal delivery records. It is always a secondary code.

V codes for family planning (contraceptive) or procreative management and counseling should be included on an obstetric record either during the pregnancy or the postpartum stage, if applicable.

Obstetrics and related conditions V code categories:

V22 Normal pregnancy
V23 Supervision of high-risk pregnancy
    Except: V23.2 Pregnancy with history of abortion. Code 646.3 Habitual aborter, from the OB chapter is required to indicate a history of abortion during a pregnancy.
V24 Postpartum care and evaluation
V25 Encounter for contraceptive management
    Except V25.0x (See section I.C.18.d.11, Counseling)
V26 Procreative management
    Except V26.5x Sterilization status, V26.3 and V26.4 (See section I.C.18.d.11., Counseling)
V27 Outcome of delivery
V28 Antenatal screening (See section I.C.18.d.6., Screening)

12) Newborn, infant and child—See section I.C.15, the newborn guidelines, for further instruction on the use of these codes.

Newborn V code categories:

V20 Health supervision of infant or child
V29 Observation and evaluation of newborns for suspected condition not found (See section I.C.18.d.7, Observation).
V30-V39 Liveborn infant according to type of birth

13) Routine and administrative examinations—The V codes allow for the description of encounters for routine examinations, such as a general check-up or, examinations for administrative purposes, such as a pre-employment physical. The codes are for use as first-listed codes only, and are not to be used if the examination is for diagnosis of a suspected condition or for treatment purposes. In such cases the diagnosis code is used. During a routine exam, should a diagnosis or condition be discovered, it should be coded as an additional code. Pre-existing and chronic conditions and history codes may also be included as additional codes as long as the examination is for administrative purposes and not focused on any particular condition.

Preoperative examination V codes are for use only in those situations when a patient is being cleared for surgery and no treatment is given.

The V code categories/code for routine and administrative examinations:

V20.2 Routine infant or child health check Any injections given should have a corresponding procedure code.
V70 General medical examination
V72 Special investigations and examinations
    Except V72.5 and V72.6

14) Miscellaneous V codes—The miscellaneous V codes capture a number of other health care encounters that do not fall into one of the other categories.

Certain of these codes identify the reason for the encounter, others are for use as additional codes that provide useful information on circumstances that may affect a patient's care and treatment.

Miscellaneous V code categories/codes:

V07 Need for isolation and other prophylactic measures
V50 Elective surgery for purposes other than remedying health states
V58.5 Orthodontics
V60 Housing, household, and economic circumstances
V62 Other psychosocial circumstances
V63 Unavailability of other medical facilities for care
V64 Persons encountering health services for specific procedures, not carried out
V66 Convalescence and palliative care
V68 Encounters for administrative purposes
V69 Problems related to lifestyle

15) Nonspecific V codes—Certain V codes are so nonspecific, or potentially redundant with other codes in the classification, that there can be little justification for their use in the inpatient setting. Their use in the outpatient setting should be limited to those instances when there is no further documentation to permit more precise coding. Otherwise, any sign or symptom or any other reason for a visit that is captured in another code should be used.

Nonspecific V code categories/codes:

V11 Personal history of mental disorder—A code from the mental disorders chapter, with an in remission fifth digit, should be used.
V13.4 Personal history of arthritis
V13.6 Personal history of congenital malformations
V15.7 Personal history of contraception
V23.2 Pregnancy with history of abortion
V40 Mental and behavioral problems
V41 Problems with special senses and other special functions
V47 Other problems with internal organs
V48 Problems with head, neck, and trunk
V49 Problems with limbs and other problems
    Exceptions:
    V49.6 Upper limb amputation status
    V49.7 Lower limb amputation status
    V49.81 Postmenopausal status
    V49.82 Dental sealant status
V49.83 Awaiting organ transplant status
V51 Aftercare involving the use of plastic surgery
V58.2 Blood transfusion, without reported diagnosis
V58.9 Unspecified aftercare
V72.5 Radiological examination, NEC
V72.6 Laboratory examination
    Codes V72.5 and V72.6 are not to be used if any sign or symptoms, or reason for a test is documented. See section IV.K. and section IV.L. of the outpatient guidelines.

V Code Table

Items in bold indicate a change from the October 2003 table. Items underlined have been moved within the table since October 2003.

FIRST LISTED: V codes/categories/subcategories which are only acceptable as principal/first listed.

Codes:

V22.0	Supervision of normal first pregnancy
V22.1	Supervision of other normal pregnancy
V46.12	Encounter for respirator dependence during power failure
V56.0	Extracorporeal dialysis
V58.0	Radiotherapy
V58.1	Chemotherapy

V58.0 and V58.1 may be used together on a record with either one being sequenced first, when a patient receives both chemotherapy and radiation therapy during the same encounter.

Categories/Subcategories:

V20	Health supervision of infant or child
V24	Postpartum care and examination
V29	Observation and evaluation of newborns for suspected condition not found

Exception: A code from the V30-V39 may be sequenced before the V29 if it is the newborn record.

V30-V39	Liveborn infants according to type of birth
V59	Donors
V66	Convalescence and palliative care

Exception: V66.7 Palliative care

V68	Encounters for administrative purposes
V70	General medical examination

Exception: V70.7 Examination of participant in clinical trial

V71	Observation and evaluation for suspected conditions not found
V72	Special investigations and examinations

Exceptions:
V72.5 Radiological examination, NEC
V72.6 Laboratory examination

FIRST OR ADDITIONAL: V code categories/subcategories which may be either principal/first-listed, or additional codes.

Codes:

V43.22	Fully implantable artificial heart status
V49.81	Asymptomatic postmenopausal status (age-related) (natural)
V70.7	Examination of participant in clinical trial

Categories/Subcategories:

V01	Contact with or exposure to communicable diseases
V02	Carrier or suspected carrier of infectious diseases
V03-V06	Need for prophylactic vaccination and inoculations
V07	Need for isolation and other prophylactic measures
V08	Asymptomatic HIV infection status
V10	Personal history of malignant neoplasm
V12	Personal history of certain other diseases
V13	Personal history of other diseases

Exception:

V13.4   Personal history of arthritis
V13.69 Personal history of other congenital malformations

V16-V19	Family history of disease
V23	Supervision of high-risk pregnancy
V25	Encounter for contraceptive management
V26	Procreative management

Exception: V26.5 Sterilization status

V28	Antenatal screening
V45.7	Acquired absence of organ
V50	Elective surgery for purposes other than remedying health states
V52	Fitting and adjustment of prosthetic device and implant
V53	Fitting and adjustment of other device
V54	Other orthopedic aftercare
V55	Attention to artificial openings
V56	Encounter for dialysis and dialysis catheter care

Exception: V56.0 Extracorporeal dialysis

V57	Care involving use of rehabilitation procedures
V58.3	Attention to surgical dressings and sutures
V58.4	Other aftercare following surgery
V58.6	Long-term (current) drug use

V58.7	Aftercare following surgery to specified body systems, not elsewhere classified
V58.8	Other specified procedures and aftercare
V61	Other family circumstances
V63	Unavailability of other medical facilities for care
V65	Other persons seeking consultation without complaint or sickness
V67	Follow-up examination
V69	Problems related to lifestyle
V73-V82	Special screening examinations
V83	Genetic carrier status

ADDITIONAL ONLY: V code categories/subcategories which may only be used as additional codes, not principal/first listed.

Codes:

V13.61	Personal history of hypospadias
V22.2	Pregnancy state, incidental
V49.82	Dental sealant status
V49.83	Awaiting organ transplant status
V66.7	Palliative care
V85	Body mass index

Categories/Subcategories:

V09	Infection with drug-resistant microorganisms
V14	Personal history of allergy to medicinal agents
V15	Other personal history presenting hazards to health

Exception: V15.7 Personal history of contraception

V21	Constitutional states in development
V26.5	Sterilization status
V27	Outcome of delivery
V42	Organ or tissue replaced by transplant
V43	Organ or tissue replaced by other means

Exception: V43.22 Fully implantable artificial heart status

V44	Artificial opening status
V45	Other postsurgical states

Exception: Subcategory V45.7 Acquired absence of organ

V46	Other dependence on machines

Exception: V46.12 Encounter for respirator dependence during power failure

V49.6x	Upper limb amputation status
V49.7x	Lower limb amputation status
V60	Housing, household, and economic circumstances
V62	Other psychosocial circumstances
V64	Persons encountering health services for specified procedure, not carried out
V84	**Genetic susceptibility to disease**

NONSPECIFIC CODES AND CATEGORIES:

V11	Personal history of mental disorder
V13.4	Personal history of arthritis
V13.69	Personal history of congenital malformations
V15.7	Personal history of contraception
V40	Mental and behavioral problems
V41	Problems with special senses and other special functions
V47	Other problems with internal organs
V48	Problems with head, neck, and trunk
V49	Problems with limbs and other problems

Exceptions:

V49.6	Upper limb amputation status
V49.7	Lower limb amputation status
V49.81	Postmenopausal status (age-related) (natural)
V49.82	Dental sealant status
V49.83	Awaiting organ transplant status

V51	Aftercare involving the use of plastic surgery
V58.2	Blood transfusion, without reported diagnosis
V58.5	Orthodontics
V58.9	Unspecified aftercare
V72.5	Radiological examination, NEC
V72.6	Laboratory examination

19. Supplemental Classification of External Causes of Injury and Poisoning (E-codes, E800-E999)

Introduction: These guidelines are provided for those who are currently collecting E codes in order that there will be standardization in the process. If your institution plans to begin collecting E codes, these guidelines are to be applied. The use of E codes is supplemental to the application of ICD-9-CM diagnosis codes. E codes are never to be recorded as principal diagnoses (first-listed in non-inpatient setting) and are not required for reporting to CMS.

External causes of injury and poisoning codes (E codes) are intended to provide data for injury research and evaluation of injury prevention strategies. E codes capture how the injury or poisoning happened (cause), the intent (unintentional or accidental; or intentional, such as suicide or assault), and the place where the event occurred.

Some major categories of E codes include:

- Transport accidents
- Poisoning and adverse effects of drugs, medicinal substances and biologicals
- Accidental falls
- Accidents caused by fire and flames
- Accidents due to natural and environmental factors
- Late effects of accidents, assaults or self injury
- Assaults or purposely inflicted injury
- Suicide or self inflicted injury

These guidelines apply to the coding and collection of E codes from records in hospitals, outpatient clinics, emergency departments, other ambulatory care settings and provider offices, and nonacute care settings, except when other specific guidelines apply.

a. **General E code coding guidelines**

1) **Used with any code in the range of 001-V85.4**—An E code may be used with any code in the range of 001-V85.4, which indicates an injury, poisoning, or adverse effect due to an external cause.

2) **Assign the appropriate E code for all initial treatments**—Assign the appropriate E code for the initial encounter of an injury, poisoning, or adverse effect of drugs, **not for subsequent treatment.**

3) **Use the full range of E codes**—Use the full range of E codes to completely describe the cause, the intent and the place of occurrence, if applicable, for all injuries, poisonings, and adverse effects of drugs.

4) **Assign as many E codes as necessary**
Assign as many E codes as necessary to fully explain each cause. If only one E code can be recorded, assign the E code most related to the principal diagnosis.

5) **The selection of the appropriate E code**—The selection of the appropriate E code is guided by the Index to External Causes, which is located after the Alphabetical Index to Diseases and by inclusion and exclusion notes in the Tabular List.

6) **E code can never be a principal diagnosis**—An E code can never be a principal (first-listed) diagnosis.

7) **External cause code(s) with systemic inflammatory response syndrome (SIRS)**—An external cause code(s) may be used with codes 995.93 Systemic inflammatory response syndrome due to noninfectious process without organ dysfunction, and 995.94 Systemic inflammatory response syndrome due to noninfectious process with organ dysfunction, if trauma was the initiating insult that precipitated the SIRS. The external cause(s) code should correspond to the most serious injury resulting from the trauma. The external cause(s) code should only be assigned if the trauma necessitated the admission in which the patient also developed SIRS. If a patient is admitted with SIRS but the trauma has been treated previously, the external cause codes should not be used.

b. **Place of occurrence guideline**—Use an additional code from category E849 to indicate the place of occurrence for injuries and poisonings. The place of occurrence describes the place where the event occurred and not the patient's activity at the time of the event.

Do not use E849.9 if the place of occurrence is not stated.

c. **Adverse effects of drugs, medicinal and biological substances guidelines**

1) **Do not code directly from the Table of Drugs**—Do not code directly from the Table of Drugs and Chemicals. Always refer back to the Tabular List.

2) **Use as many codes as necessary to describe**—Use as many codes as necessary to describe completely all drugs, medicinal or biological substances.

3) **If the same E code would describe the causative agent**—If the same E code would describe the causative agent for more than one adverse reaction, assign the code only once.

4) **If two or more drugs, medicinal or biological substances**—If two or more drugs, medicinal or biological substances are reported, code each individually unless the combination code is listed in the Table of Drugs and Chemicals. In that case, assign the E code for the combination.

5) **When a reaction results from the interaction of a drug(s)**—When a reaction results from the interaction of a drug(s) and alcohol, use poisoning codes and E codes for both.

6) **If the reporting format limits the number of E codes**—If the reporting format limits the number of E codes that can be used in reporting clinical data, code the one most related to the principal diagnosis. Include at least one from each category (cause, intent, place) if possible.

If there are different fourth-digit codes in the same three-digit category, use the code for "other specified" of that category. If there is no "other specified" code in that category, use the appropriate "unspecified" code in that category.

If the codes are in different three-digit categories, assign the appropriate E code for other multiple drugs and medicinal substances.

7) **Codes from the E930-E949 series**—Codes from the E930-E949 series must be used to identify the causative substance for an adverse effect of drug, medicinal and biological substances, correctly prescribed and properly administered. The effect, such as tachycardia, delirium, gastrointestinal hemorrhaging, vomiting, hypokalemia, hepatitis, renal failure, or respiratory failure, is coded and followed by the appropriate code from the E930-E949 series.

d. **Multiple cause E code coding guidelines**—If two or more events cause separate injuries, an E code should be assigned for each cause. The first listed E code will be selected in the following order:

E codes for child and adult abuse take priority over all other E codes. See section I.C.19.e., Child and adult abuse guidelines.

E codes for terrorism events take priority over all other E codes except child and adult abuse.

E codes for cataclysmic events take priority over all other E codes except child and adult abuse and terrorism.

E codes for transport accidents take priority over all other E codes except cataclysmic events and child and adult abuse and terrorism.

The first-listed E code should correspond to the cause of the most serious diagnosis due to an assault, accident, or self-harm, following the order of hierarchy listed above.

e. **Child and adult abuse guideline**

1) **Intentional injury**—When the cause of an injury or neglect is intentional child or adult abuse, the first-listed E code should be assigned from categories E960-E968 Homicide and injury purposely inflicted by other persons, (except category E967). An E code from category E967 Child and adult battering and other maltreatment, should be added as an additional code to identify the perpetrator, if known.

2) **Accidental intent**—In cases of neglect when the intent is determined to be accidental E code E904.0 Abandonment or neglect of infant and helpless person, should be the first-listed E code.

f. **Unknown or suspected intent guideline**

1) **If the intent (accident, self-harm, assault) of the cause of an injury or poisoning is unknown**—If the intent (accident, self-harm, assault) of the cause of an injury or poisoning is unknown or unspecified, code the intent as undetermined, E980-E989.

2) **If the intent (accident, self-harm, assault) of the cause of an injury or poisoning is questionable**—If the intent (accident, self-harm, assault) of the cause of an injury or poisoning is questionable, probable or suspected, code the intent as undetermined, E980-E989.

g. **Undetermined cause**—When the intent of an injury or poisoning is known, but the cause is unknown, use codes E928.9 Unspecified accident, E958.9 Suicide and self-inflicted injury by unspecified means, and E968.9 Assault by unspecified means.

These E codes should rarely be used, as the documentation in the medical record, in both the inpatient outpatient and other settings, should normally provide sufficient detail to determine the cause of the injury.

h. **Late effects of external cause guidelines**

1) **Late effect E codes**—Late effect E codes exist for injuries and poisonings but not for adverse effects of drugs, misadventures, and surgical complications.

2) **Late effect E codes (E929, E959, E969, E977, E989, or E999.1)**—A late effect E code (E929, E959, E969, E977, E989, or E999.1) should be used with any report of a late effect or sequela resulting from a previous injury or poisoning (905-909).

3) **Late effect E code with a related current injury**—A late effect E code should never be used with a related current nature of injury code.

4) **Use of late effect E codes for subsequent visits**—Use a late effect E code for subsequent visits when a late effect of the initial injury or poisoning is being treated. There is no late effect E code for adverse effects of drugs. Do not use a late effect E code for subsequent visits for follow-up care (e.g., to assess healing, to receive rehabilitative therapy) of the injury or poisoning when no late effect of the injury has been documented.

i. **Misadventures and complications of care guidelines**

1) **Code range E870-E876**—Assign a code in the range of E870-E876 if misadventures are stated by the provider.

2) **Code range E878-E879**—Assign a code in the range of E878-E879 if the provider attributes an abnormal reaction or later complication to a surgical or medical procedure, but does not mention misadventure at the time of the procedure as the cause of the reaction.

j. **Terrorism guidelines**

1) **Cause of injury identified by the federal government (FBI) as terrorism**—When the cause of an injury is identified by the federal government (FBI) as terrorism, the first-listed E code should be a code from category E979 Terrorism. The definition of terrorism employed by the FBI is found at the inclusion note at E979. The terrorism E code is the only E code that should be assigned. Additional E codes from the assault categories should not be assigned.

2) **Cause of an injury is suspected to be the result of terrorism**—When the cause of an injury is suspected to be the result of terrorism a code from category E979 should not be assigned. Assign a code in the range of E codes based on the documentation of intent and mechanism.

3) **Code E979.9 Terrorism, secondary effects**—Assign code E979.9 Terrorism, secondary effects, for conditions occurring subsequent to the terrorist event. This code should not be assigned for conditions that are due to the initial terrorist act.

4) **Statistical tabulation of terrorism codes**—For statistical purposes these codes will be tabulated within the category for assault, expanding the current category from E960-E969 to include E979 and E999.1.

Section II. Selection of Principal Diagnosis

The circumstances of inpatient admission always govern the selection of principal diagnosis. The principal diagnosis is defined in the Uniform Hospital Discharge Data Set (UHDDS) as "that condition established after study to be chiefly responsible for occasioning the admission of the patient to the hospital for care."

The UHDDS definitions are used by hospitals to report inpatient data elements in a standardized manner. These data elements and their definitions can be found in the July 31, 1985, *Federal Register* (vol. 50, no. 147), pp. 31038-40.

Since that time the application of the UHDDS definitions has been expanded to include all non-outpatient settings (acute care, short-term, long-term care and psychiatric hospitals; home health agencies; rehab facilities; nursing homes, etc.).

In determining principal diagnosis the coding conventions in the ICD-9-CM, Volumes 1 and 2 take precedence over these official coding guidelines. (See section I.A., Conventions, for the ICD-9-CM).

The importance of consistent, complete documentation in the medical record cannot be overemphasized. Without such documentation the application of all coding guidelines is a difficult, if not impossible, task.

A. Codes for symptoms, signs, and ill-defined conditions

Codes for symptoms, signs, and ill-defined conditions from chapter 16 are not to be used as principal diagnosis when a related definitive diagnosis has been established.

B. Two or more interrelated conditions, each potentially meeting the definition for principal diagnosis.

When there are two or more interrelated conditions (such as diseases in the same ICD-9-CM chapter or manifestations characteristically associated with a certain disease) potentially meeting the definition of principal diagnosis, either condition may be sequenced first, unless the circumstances of the admission, the therapy provided, the Tabular List, or the Alphabetic Index indicate otherwise.

C. Two or more diagnoses that equally meet the definition for principal diagnosis

In the unusual instance when two or more diagnoses equally meet the criteria for principal diagnosis as determined by the circumstances of admission, diagnostic workup and/or therapy provided, and the Alphabetic Index, Tabular List, or another coding guidelines do not provide sequencing direction, any one of the diagnoses may be sequenced first.

D. Two or more comparative or contrasting conditions.

In those rare instances when two or more contrasting or comparative diagnoses are documented as "either/or" (or similar terminology), they are coded as if the diagnoses were confirmed and the diagnoses are sequenced according to the circumstances of the admission. If no further determination can be made as to which diagnosis should be principal, either diagnosis may be sequenced first.

E. A symptom(s) followed by contrasting/comparative diagnoses

When a symptom(s) is followed by contrasting/comparative diagnoses, the symptom code is sequenced first. All the contrasting/comparative diagnoses should be coded as additional diagnoses.

F. Original treatment plan not carried out

Sequence as the principal diagnosis the condition, which after study occasioned the admission to the hospital, even though treatment may not have been carried out due to unforeseen circumstances.

G. Complications of surgery and other medical care

When the admission is for treatment of a complication resulting from surgery or other medical care, the complication code is sequenced as the principal diagnosis. If the complication is classified to the 996-999 series and the code lacks the necessary specificity in describing the complication, an additional code for the specific complication should be assigned.

H. Uncertain diagnosis

If the diagnosis documented at the time of discharge is qualified as "probable," "suspected," "likely," "questionable," "possible," or "still to be ruled out," code the condition as if it existed or was established. The bases for these guidelines are the diagnostic workup, arrangements for further workup or observation, and initial therapeutic approach that correspond most closely with the established diagnosis.

Note: This guideline is applicable only to short-term, acute, long-term care and psychiatric hospitals.

Section III. Reporting Additional Diagnoses

GENERAL RULES FOR OTHER (ADDITIONAL) DIAGNOSES

For reporting purposes the definition for "other diagnoses" is interpreted as additional conditions that affect patient care in terms of requiring:

- Clinical evaluation; or
- Therapeutic treatment; or
- Diagnostic procedures; or
- Extended length of hospital stay; or
- Increased nursing care and/or monitoring.

The UHDDS item #11-b defines other diagnoses as "all conditions that coexist at the time of admission, that develop subsequently, or that affect the treatment received and/or the length of stay. Diagnoses that relate to an earlier episode which have no bearing on the current hospital stay are to be excluded." UHDDS definitions apply to inpatients in acute care, short-term, long-term care and psychiatric hospital settings. The UHDDS definitions are used by acute care short-term hospitals to report inpatient data elements in a standardized manner. These data elements and their definitions can be found in the July 31, 1985, *Federal Register* (vol. 50, no. 147), pp. 31038-40.

Since that time the application of the UHDDS definitions has been expanded to include all non-outpatient settings (acute care, short-term,

long-term care and psychiatric hospitals; home health agencies; rehab facilities; nursing homes, etc.).

The following guidelines are to be applied in designating other diagnoses when neither the Alphabetic Index nor the Tabular List in ICD-9-CM provides direction. The listing of the diagnoses in the patient record is the responsibility of the attending provider.

A. Previous conditions
If the provider has included a diagnosis in the final diagnostic statement, such as the discharge summary or the face sheet, it should ordinarily be coded. Some providers include in the diagnostic statement resolved conditions or diagnoses and status-post procedures from previous admission that have no bearing on the current stay. Such conditions are not to be reported and are coded only if required by hospital policy.

However, history codes (V10-V19) may be used as secondary codes if the historical condition or family history has an impact on current care or influences treatment.

B. Abnormal findings
Abnormal findings (laboratory, x-ray, pathologic, and other diagnostic results) are not coded and reported unless the provider indicates their clinical significance. If the findings are outside the normal range and the **attending** provider has ordered other tests to evaluate the condition or prescribed treatment, it is appropriate to ask the provider whether the abnormal finding should be added.

Please note: This differs from the coding practices in the outpatient setting for coding encounters for diagnostic tests that have been interpreted by a provider.

C. Uncertain Diagnosis
If the diagnosis documented at the time of discharge is qualified as "probable," "suspected," "likely," "questionable," "possible," or "still to be ruled out," code the condition as if it existed or was established. The bases for these guidelines are the diagnostic workup, arrangements for further workup or observation, and initial therapeutic approach that correspond most closely with the established diagnosis.

Note: This guideline is applicable only to short-term, acute, long-term care and psychiatric hospitals.

Section IV. Diagnostic Coding and Reporting Guidelines for Outpatient Services
These coding guidelines for outpatient diagnoses have been approved for use by hospitals/providers in coding and reporting hospital-based outpatient services and provider-based office visits.

Information about the use of certain abbreviations, punctuation, symbols, and other conventions used in the ICD-9-CM Tabular List (code numbers and titles), can be found in section IA of these guidelines, under "Conventions for the ICD-9-CM." Information about the correct sequence to use in finding a code is also described in section I.

The terms "encounter" and "visit" are often used interchangeably in describing outpatient service contacts and, therefore, appear together in these guidelines without distinguishing one from the other.

Though the conventions and general guidelines apply to all settings, coding guidelines for outpatient and provider reporting of diagnoses will vary in a number of instances from those for inpatient diagnoses, recognizing that:

- The Uniform Hospital Discharge Data Set (UHDDS) definition of principal diagnosis applies only to inpatients in acute, short-term, long-term care **and psychiatric** hospitals.
- Coding guidelines for inconclusive diagnoses (probable, suspected, rule out, etc.) were developed for inpatient reporting and do not apply to outpatients.

A. Selection of first-listed condition
In the outpatient setting, the term "first-listed diagnosis" is used in lieu of principal diagnosis.

In determining the first-listed diagnosis the coding conventions of ICD-9-CM, as well as the general and disease-specific guidelines take precedence over the outpatient guidelines.

Diagnoses often are not established at the time of the initial encounter/visit. It may take two or more visits before the diagnosis is confirmed.

The most critical rule involves beginning the search for the correct code assignment through the Alphabetic Index. Never begin searching initially in the Tabular List as this will lead to coding errors.

B. Codes from 001.0 through V85.4
The appropriate code or codes from 001.0 through V84.8 must be used to identify diagnoses, symptoms, conditions, problems, complaints, or other reason(s) for the encounter/visit.

C. Accurate reporting of ICD-9-CM diagnosis codes
For accurate reporting of ICD-9-CM diagnosis codes, the documentation should describe the patient's condition, using terminology which includes specific diagnoses as well as symptoms, problems, or reasons for the encounter. There are ICD-9-CM codes to describe all of these.

D. Selection of codes 001.0 through 999.9
The selection of codes 001.0 through 999.9 will frequently be used to describe the reason for the encounter. These codes are from the section of ICD-9-CM for the classification of diseases and injuries (e.g. infectious and parasitic diseases; neoplasms; symptoms, signs, and ill-defined conditions, etc.).

E. Codes that describe symptoms and signs
Codes that describe symptoms and signs, as opposed to diagnoses, are acceptable for reporting purposes when a diagnosis has not been established (confirmed) by the provider. Chapter 16 of ICD-9-CM, Symptoms, Signs, and Ill-defined Conditions (codes 780.0-799.9) contain many, but not all, codes for symptoms.

F. Encounters for circumstances other than a disease or injury
ICD-9-CM provides codes to deal with encounters for circumstances other than a disease or injury. The Supplementary Classification of Factors Influencing Health Status and Contact with Health Services (V01.0-V84.8) is provided to deal with occasions when circumstances other than a disease or injury are recorded as diagnosis or problems.

G. Level of Detail in Coding
1. **ICD-9-CM codes with three, four, or five digits**—ICD-9-CM is composed of codes with either three, four, or five digits. Codes with three digits are included in ICD-9-CM as the heading of a category of codes that may be further subdivided by the use of fourth and/or fifth digits, which provide greater specificity.

2. **Use of full number of digits required for a code**—A three-digit code is to be used only if it is not further subdivided. Where fourth-digit subcategories and/or fifth-digit subclassifications are provided, they must be assigned. A code is invalid if it has not been coded to the full number of digits required for that code. See also discussion under section I.b.3., General coding guidelines, Level of detail in coding.

H. ICD-9-CM code for the diagnosis, condition, problem, or other reason for encounter/visit
List first the ICD-9-CM code for the diagnosis, condition, problem, or other reason for encounter/visit shown in the medical record to be chiefly responsible for the services provided. List additional codes that describe any coexisting conditions. **In some cases the first-listed diagnosis may be a symptom when a diagnosis has not been established (confirmed) by the physician.**

I. "Probable," "suspected," "questionable," "rule out," or "working diagnosis"
Do not code diagnoses documented as "probable," "suspected," "questionable," "rule out," or "working diagnosis." Rather, code the condition(s) to the highest degree of certainty for that encounter/visit, such as symptoms, signs, abnormal test results, or other reason for the visit. **Please note:** This differs from the coding practices used by **short-term, acute care, long-term care, and psychiatric** hospitals.

J. Chronic diseases
Chronic diseases treated on an ongoing basis may be coded and reported as many times as the patient receives treatment and care for the condition(s).

K. Code all documented conditions that coexist
Code all documented conditions that coexist at the time of the encounter/ visit, and require or affect patient care treatment or management. Do not code conditions that were previously treated and no longer exist. However, history codes (V10-V19) may be used as secondary codes if the historical condition or family history has an impact on current care or influences treatment.

L. Patients receiving diagnostic services only
For patients receiving diagnostic services only during an encounter/visit, sequence first the diagnosis, condition, problem, or other reason for encounter/visit shown in the medical record to be chiefly responsible for the outpatient services provided during the encounter/visit. Codes for other diagnoses (e.g., chronic conditions) may be sequenced as additional diagnoses.

For outpatient encounters for diagnostic tests that have been interpreted by a physician and the final report is available at the time of coding, code any confirmed or definitive diagnosis(es) documented in the interpretation. Do not code related signs and symptoms as additional diagnoses.

Please note: This differs from the coding practice in the hospital inpatient setting regarding abnormal findings on test results.

M. Patients receiving therapeutic services only

For patients receiving therapeutic services only during an encounter/visit, sequence first the diagnosis, condition, problem, or other reason for encounter/visit shown in the medical record to be chiefly responsible for the outpatient services provided during the encounter/visit. Codes for other diagnoses (e.g., chronic conditions) may be sequenced as additional diagnoses.

The only exception to this rule is that when the primary reason for the admission/encounter is chemotherapy, radiation therapy, or rehabilitation, the appropriate V code for the service is listed first, and the diagnosis or problem for which the service is being performed is listed second.

N. Patients receiving preoperative evaluations only

For patients receiving preoperative evaluations only, sequence **first** a code from category V72.8 Other specified examinations, to describe the pre-op consultations. Assign a code for the condition to describe the reason for the surgery as an additional diagnosis. Code also any findings related to the pre-op evaluation.

O. Ambulatory surgery

For ambulatory surgery, code the diagnosis for which the surgery was performed. If the postoperative diagnosis is known to be different from the preoperative diagnosis at the time the diagnosis is confirmed, select the postoperative diagnosis for coding, since it is the most definitive.

P. Routine outpatient prenatal visits

For routine outpatient prenatal visits when no complications are present, code V22.0 Supervision of normal first pregnancy, **or** V22.1 Supervision of other normal pregnancy, should be used as **the** principal diagnosis. These codes should not be used in conjunction with chapter 11 codes.

Revised text in bold font

A

AAT (alpha-1 antitrypsin) deficiency 273.4

AAV (disease) (illness) (infection) — *see* Human immunodeficiency virus (disease) (illness) (infection)

Abactio — *see* Abortion, induced

Abactus venter — *see* Abortion, induced

Abarognosis 781.99

Abasia (-astasia) 307.9
  atactica 781.3
  choreic 781.3
  hysterical 300.11
  paroxysmal trepidant 781.3
  spastic 781.3
  trembling 781.3
  trepidans 781.3

Abderhalden-Kaufmann-Lignac syndrome (cystinosis) 270.0

Abdomen, abdominal — *see also* condition
  accordion 306.4
  acute 789.0 ☑
  angina 557.1
  burst 868.00
  convulsive equivalent (*see also* Epilepsy) 345.5 ☑
  heart 746.87
  muscle deficiency syndrome 756.79
  obstipum 756.79

Abdominalgia 789.0 ☑
  periodic 277.3

Abduction contracture, hip or other joint — *see* Contraction, joint

Abercrombie's syndrome (amyloid degeneration) 277.3

Aberrant (congenital) — *see also* Malposition, congenital
  adrenal gland 759.1
  blood vessel NEC 747.60
    arteriovenous NEC 747.60
    cerebrovascular 747.81
    gastrointestinal 747.61
    lower limb 747.64
    renal 747.62
    spinal 747.82
    upper limb 747.63
  breast 757.6
  endocrine gland NEC 759.2
  gastrointestinal vessel (peripheral) 747.61
  hepatic duct 751.69
  lower limb vessel (peripheral) 747.64
  pancreas 751.7
  parathyroid gland 759.2
  peripheral vascular vessel NEC 747.60
  pituitary gland (pharyngeal) 759.2
  renal blood vessel 747.62
  sebaceous glands, mucous membrane, mouth 750.26
  spinal vessel 747.82
  spleen 759.0
  testis (descent) 752.51
  thymus gland 759.2
  thyroid gland 759.2
  upper limb vessel (peripheral) 747.63

Aberratio
  lactis 757.6
  testis 752.51

Aberration — *see also* Anomaly
  chromosome — *see* Anomaly, chromosome(s)
  distantial 368.9
  mental (*see also* Disorder, mental, nonpsychotic) 300.9

Abetalipoproteinemia 272.5

Abionarce 780.79

Abiotrophy 799.89

Ablatio
  placentae — *see* Placenta, ablatio
  retinae (*see also* Detachment, retina) 361.9

Ablation
  pituitary (gland) (with hypofunction) 253.7
  placenta — *see* Placenta, ablatio
  uterus 621.8

Ablepharia, ablepharon, ablephary 743.62

Ablepsia — *see* Blindness

Ablepsy — *see* Blindness

Ablutomania 300.3

Abnormal, abnormality, abnormalities — *see also* Anomaly
  acid-base balance 276.4
    fetus or newborn — *see* Distress, fetal
  adaptation curve, dark 368.63
  alveolar ridge 525.9
  amnion 658.9 ☑
    affecting fetus or newborn 762.9
  anatomical relationship NEC 759.9
  apertures, congenital, diaphragm 756.6
  auditory perception NEC 388.40
  autosomes NEC 758.5
    13 758.1
    18 758.2
    21 or 22 758.0
    D₁ 758.1
    E₃ 758.2
    G 758.0
  ballistocardiogram 794.39
  basal metabolic rate (BMR) 794.7
  biosynthesis, testicular androgen 257.2
  blood level (of)
    cobalt 790.6
    copper 790.6
    iron 790.6
    lithium 790.6
    magnesium 790.6
    mineral 790.6
    zinc 790.6
  blood pressure
    elevated (without diagnosis of hypertension) 796.2
    low (*see also* Hypotension) 458.9
      reading (incidental) (isolated) (nonspecific) 796.3
  bowel sounds 787.5
  breathing behavior — *see* Respiration
  caloric test 794.19
  cervix (acquired) NEC 622.9
    congenital 752.40
    in pregnancy or childbirth 654.6 ☑
      causing obstructed labor 660.2 ☑
        affecting fetus or newborn 763.1
  chemistry, blood NEC 790.6
  chest sounds 786.7
  chorion 658.9 ☑
    affecting fetus or newborn 762.9
  chromosomal NEC 758.89
    analysis, nonspecific result 795.2
    autosomes (*see also* Abnormal, autosomes NEC) 758.5
    fetal, (suspected) affecting management of pregnancy 655.1 ☑
    sex 758.81
  clinical findings NEC 796.4
  communication — *see* Fistula
  configuration of pupils 379.49
  coronary
    artery 746.85
    vein 746.9
  cortisol-binding globulin 255.8
  course, Eustachian tube 744.24
  dentofacial NEC 524.9
    functional 524.50
    specified type NEC 524.89
  development, developmental NEC 759.9
    bone 756.9
    central nervous system 742.9
  direction, teeth 524.30
  Dynia (*see also* Defect, coagulation) 286.9
  Ebstein 746.2
  echocardiogram 793.2
  echoencephalogram 794.01
  echogram NEC — *see* Findings, abnormal, structure
  electrocardiogram (ECG) (EKG) 794.31
  electroencephalogram (EEG) 794.02
  electromyogram (EMG) 794.17
    ocular 794.14
  electro-oculogram (EOG) 794.12
  electroretinogram (ERG) 794.11
  erythrocytes 289.9
    congenital, with perinatal jaundice 282.9 *[774.0]*

Abnormal, abnormality, abnormalities — *see also* Anomaly — *continued*
  Eustachian valve 746.9
  excitability under minor stress 301.9
  fat distribution 782.9
  feces 787.7
  fetal heart rate — *see* Distress, fetal
  fetus NEC
    affecting management of pregnancy — *see* Pregnancy, management affected by, fetal
    causing disproportion 653.7 ☑
      affecting fetus or newborn 763.1
      causing obstructed labor 660.1 ☑
        affecting fetus or newborn 763.1
    findings without manifest disease — *see* Findings, abnormal
  fluid
    amniotic 792.3
    cerebrospinal 792.0
    peritoneal 792.9
    pleural 792.9
    synovial 792.9
    vaginal 792.9
  forces of labor NEC 661.9 ☑
    affecting fetus or newborn 763.7
  form, teeth 520.2
  function studies
    auditory 794.15
    bladder 794.9
    brain 794.00
    cardiovascular 794.30
    endocrine NEC 794.6
    kidney 794.4
    liver 794.8
    nervous system
      central 794.00
      peripheral 794.19
    oculomotor 794.14
    pancreas 794.9
    placenta 794.9
    pulmonary 794.2
    retina 794.11
    special senses 794.19
    spleen 794.9
    thyroid 794.5
    vestibular 794.16
  gait 781.2
    hysterical 300.11
  gastrin secretion 251.5
  globulin
    cortisol-binding 255.8
    thyroid-binding 246.8
  glucagon secretion 251.4
  glucose 790.29
    in pregnancy, childbirth, or puerperium 648.8 ☑
      fetus or newborn 775.0
    non-fasting 790.29
  gravitational (G) forces or states 994.9
  hair NEC 704.2
  hard tissue formation in pulp 522.3
  head movement 781.0
  heart
    rate
      fetus, affecting liveborn infant
        before the onset of labor 763.81
        during labor 763.82
        unspecified as to time of onset 763.83
      intrauterine
        before the onset of labor 763.81
        during labor 763.82
        unspecified as to time of onset 763.83
      newborn
        before the onset of labor 763.81
        during labor 763.82
        unspecified as to time of onset 763.83
    shadow 793.2
    sounds NEC 785.3
  hemoglobin (*see also* Disease, hemoglobin) 282.7
    trait — *see* Trait, hemoglobin, abnormal
  hemorrhage, uterus — *see* Hemorrhage, uterus
  histology NEC 795.4

Abnormal, abnormality, abnormalities — *see also* Anomaly — *continued*

increase
  in
    appetite 783.6
    development 783.9
involuntary movement 781.0
jaw closure 524.51
karyotype 795.2
knee jerk 796.1
labor NEC 661.9 ☑
  affecting fetus or newborn 763.7
laboratory findings — *see* Findings, abnormal
length, organ or site, congenital — *see* Distortion
loss of height 781.91
loss of weight 783.21
lung shadow 793.1
mammogram 793.80
  microcalcification 793.81
Mantoux test 795.5
membranes (fetal)
  affecting fetus or newborn 762.9
  complicating pregnancy 658.8 ☑
menstruation — *see* Menstruation
metabolism (*see also* condition) 783.9
movement 781.0
  disorder NEC 333.90
    sleep related, ▶unspecified◀ 780.58
    specified NEC 333.99
  head 781.0
  involuntary 781.0
  specified type NEC 333.99
muscle contraction, localized 728.85
myoglobin (Aberdeen) (Annapolis) 289.9
narrowness, eyelid 743.62
optokinetic response 379.57
organs or tissues of pelvis NEC
  in pregnancy or childbirth 654.9 ☑
    affecting fetus or newborn 763.89
    causing obstructed labor 660.2 ☑
      affecting fetus or newborn 763.1
origin — *see* Malposition, congenital
palmar creases 757.2
Papanicolaou (smear)
  cervix 795.00
    with
      atypical squamous cells
        cannot exclude high grade
          squamous intraepithelial
          lesion (ASC-H) 795.02
        of undetermined significance
          (ASC-US) 795.01
      high grade squamous intraepithelial
        lesion (HGSIL) 795.04
      low grade squamous intraepithelial
        lesion (LGSIL) 795.03
      nonspecific finding NEC 795.09
    other site 795.1
parturition
  affecting fetus or newborn 763.9
  mother — *see* Delivery, complicated
pelvis (bony) — *see* Deformity, pelvis
percussion, chest 786.7
periods (grossly) (*see also* Menstruation) 626.9
phonocardiogram 794.39
placenta — *see* Placenta, abnormal
plantar reflex 796.1
plasma protein — *see* Deficiency, plasma, protein
pleural folds 748.8
position — *see also* Malposition
  gravid uterus 654.4 ☑
    causing obstructed labor 660.2 ☑
      affecting fetus or newborn 763.1
posture NEC 781.92
presentation (fetus) — *see* Presentation, fetus, abnormal
product of conception NEC 631
puberty — *see* Puberty
pulmonary
  artery 747.3
  function, newborn 770.89

Abnormal, abnormality, abnormalities — *see also* Anomaly — *continued*

pulmonary — *continued*
  test results 794.2
  ventilation, newborn 770.89
    hyperventilation 786.01
pulsations in neck 785.1
pupil reflexes 379.40
quality of milk 676.8 ☑
radiological examination 793.9
  abdomen NEC 793.6
  biliary tract 793.3
  breast 793.89
    mammogram NOS 793.80
      mammographic microcalcification 793.81
  gastrointestinal tract 793.4
  genitourinary organs 793.5
  head 793.0
  intrathoracic organ NEC 793.2
  lung (field) 793.1
  musculoskeletal system 793.7
  retroperitoneum 793.6
  skin and subcutaneous tissue 793.9
  skull 793.0
red blood cells 790.09
  morphology 790.09
  volume 790.09
reflex NEC 796.1
renal function test 794.4
respiration signs — *see* Respiration
response to nerve stimulation 794.10
retinal correspondence 368.34
rhythm, heart — *see also* Arrhythmia
  fetus — *see* Distress, fetal
saliva 792.4
scan
  brain 794.09
  kidney 794.4
  liver 794.8
  lung 794.2
  thyroid 794.5
secretion
  gastrin 251.5
  glucagon 251.4
semen 792.2
serum level (of)
  acid phosphatase 790.5
  alkaline phosphatase 790.5
  amylase 790.5
  enzymes NEC 790.5
  lipase 790.5
shape
  cornea 743.41
  gallbladder 751.69
  gravid uterus 654.4 ☑
    affecting fetus or newborn 763.89
    causing obstructed labor 660.2 ☑
      affecting fetus or newborn 763.1
  head (*see also* Anomaly, skull) 756.0
  organ or site, congenital NEC — *see* Distortion
sinus venosus 747.40
size
  fetus, complicating delivery 653.5 ☑
    causing obstructed labor 660.1 ☑
  gallbladder 751.69
  head (*see also* Anomaly, skull) 756.0
  organ or site, congenital NEC — *see* Distortion
  teeth 520.2
skin and appendages, congenital NEC 757.9
soft parts of pelvis — *see* Abnormal, organs or tissues of pelvis
spermatozoa 792.2
sputum (amount) (color) (excessive) (odor) (purulent) 786.4
stool NEC 787.7
  bloody 578.1
    occult 792.1
  bulky 787.7
  color (dark) (light) 792.1
  content (fat) (mucus) (pus) 792.1
  occult blood 792.1
synchondrosis 756.9
test results without manifest disease — *see* Findings, abnormal

Abnormal, abnormality, abnormalities — *see also* Anomaly — *continued*

thebesian valve 746.9
thermography — *see* Findings, abnormal, structure
threshold, cones or rods (eye) 368.63
thyroid-binding globulin 246.8
thyroid product 246.8
toxicology (findings) NEC 796.0
tracheal cartilage (congenital) 748.3
transport protein 273.8
ultrasound results — *see* Findings, abnormal, structure
umbilical cord
  affecting fetus or newborn 762.6
  complicating delivery 663.9 ☑
  specified NEC 663.8 ☑
union
  cricoid cartilage and thyroid cartilage 748.3
  larynx and trachea 748.3
  thyroid cartilage and hyoid bone 748.3
urination NEC 788.69
  psychogenic 306.53
  stream
    intermittent 788.61
    slowing 788.62
    splitting 788.61
    weak 788.62
  urgency 788.63
urine (constituents) NEC 791.9
uterine hemorrhage (*see also* Hemorrhage, uterus) 626.9
  climacteric 627.0
  postmenopausal 627.1
vagina (acquired) (congenital)
  in pregnancy or childbirth 654.7 ☑
    affecting fetus or newborn 763.89
    causing obstructed labor 660.2 ☑
      affecting fetus or newborn 763.1
vascular sounds 785.9
vectorcardiogram 794.39
visually evoked potential (VEP) 794.13
vulva (acquired) (congenital)
  in pregnancy or childbirth 654.8 ☑
    affecting fetus or newborn 763.89
    causing obstructed labor 660.2 ☑
      affecting fetus or newborn 763.1
weight
  gain 783.1
    of pregnancy 646.1 ☑
      with hypertension — *see* Toxemia, of pregnancy
  loss 783.21
x-ray examination — *see* Abnormal, radiological examination

Abnormally formed uterus — *see* Anomaly, uterus

Abnormity (any organ or part) — *see* Anomaly

ABO
  hemolytic disease 773.1
  incompatibility reaction 999.6

Abocclusion 524.20

Abolition, language 784.69

Aborter, habitual or recurrent NEC
  without current pregnancy 629.9
  current abortion (*see also* Abortion, spontaneous) 634.9 ☑
    affecting fetus or newborn 761.8
  observation in current pregnancy 646.3 ☑

Abortion (complete) (incomplete) (inevitable) (with retained products of conception) 637.9 ☑

Note — *Use the following fifth-digit subclassification with categories 634–637:*

0	*unspecified*
1	*incomplete*
2	*complete*

with
  complication(s) (any) following previous abortion — *see* category 639 ☑
  damage to pelvic organ (laceration) (rupture) (tear) 637.2 ☑

Abortion — *continued*
  with — *continued*
    embolism (air) (amniotic fluid) (blood clot)
        (pulmonary) (pyemic) (septic) (soap)
        637.6 ☑
    genital tract and pelvic infection 637.0 ☑
    hemorrhage, delayed or excessive 637.1 ☑
    metabolic disorder 637.4 ☑
    renal failure (acute) 637.3 ☑
    sepsis (genital tract) (pelvic organ) 637.0 ☑
        urinary tract 637.7 ☑
    shock (postoperative) (septic) 637.5 ☑
    specified complication NEC 637.7 ☑
    toxemia 637.3 ☑
    unspecified complication(s) 637.8 ☑
    urinary tract infection 637.7 ☑
  accidental — *see* Abortion, spontaneous
  artificial — *see* Abortion, induced
  attempted (failed) — *see* Abortion, failed
  criminal — *see* Abortion, illegal
  early — *see* Abortion, spontaneous
  elective — *see* Abortion, legal
  failed (legal) 638.9
    with
      damage to pelvic organ (laceration)
          (rupture) (tear) 638.2
      embolism (air) (amniotic fluid) (blood clot)
          (pulmonary) (pyemic) (septic) (soap)
          638.6
      genital tract and pelvic infection 638.0
      hemorrhage, delayed or excessive 638.1
      metabolic disorder 638.4
      renal failure (acute) 638.3
      sepsis (genital tract) (pelvic organ) 638.0
          urinary tract 638.7
      shock (postoperative) (septic) 638.5
      specified complication NEC 638.7
      toxemia 638.3
      unspecified complication(s) 638.8
      urinary tract infection 638.7
  fetal indication — *see* Abortion, legal
  fetus 779.6
  following threatened abortion — *see* Abortion,
      by type
  habitual or recurrent (care during pregnancy)
      646.3 ☑
    with current abortion (*see also* Abortion,
        spontaneous) 634.9 ☑
    affecting fetus or newborn 761.8
    without current pregnancy 629.9
  homicidal — *see* Abortion, illegal
  illegal 636.9 ☑
    with
      damage to pelvic organ (laceration)
          (rupture) (tear) 636.2 ☑
      embolism (air) (amniotic fluid) (blood clot)
          (pulmonary) (pyemic) (septic) (soap)
          636.6 ☑
      genital tract and pelvic infection 636.0 ☑
      hemorrhage, delayed or excessive
          636.1 ☑
      metabolic disorder 636.4 ☑
      renal failure 636.3 ☑
      sepsis (genital tract) (pelvic organ)
          636.0 ☑
          urinary tract 636.7 ☑
      shock (postoperative) (septic) 636.5 ☑
      specified complication NEC 636.7 ☑
      toxemia 636.3 ☑
      unspecified complication(s) 636.8 ☑
      urinary tract infection 636.7 ☑
  fetus 779.6
  induced 637.9 ☑
    illegal — *see* Abortion, illegal
    legal indications — *see* Abortion, legal
    medical indications — *see* Abortion, legal
    therapeutic — *see* Abortion, legal
  late — *see* Abortion, spontaneous
  legal (legal indication) (medical indication)
      (under medical supervision) 635.9 ☑
    with
      damage to pelvic organ (laceration)
          (rupture) (tear) 635.2 ☑
      embolism (air) (amniotic fluid) (blood clot)
          (pulmonary) (pyemic) (septic) (soap)
          635.6 ☑
      genital tract and pelvic infection 635.0 ☑

Abortion — *continued*
  legal — *continued*
    with — *continued*
      hemorrhage, delayed or excessive
          635.1 ☑
      metabolic disorder 635.4 ☑
      renal failure (acute) 635.3 ☑
      sepsis (genital tract) (pelvic organ)
          635.0 ☑
          urinary tract 635.7 ☑
      shock (postoperative) (septic) 635.5 ☑
      specified complication NEC 635.7 ☑
      toxemia 635.3 ☑
      unspecified complication(s) 635.8 ☑
      urinary tract infection 635.7 ☑
    fetus 779.6
  medical indication — *see* Abortion, legal
  mental hygiene problem — *see* Abortion, legal
  missed 632
  operative — *see* Abortion, legal
  psychiatric indication — *see* Abortion, legal
  recurrent — *see* Abortion, spontaneous
  self-induced — *see* Abortion, illegal
  septic — *see* Abortion, by type, with sepsis
  spontaneous 634.9 ☑
    with
      damage to pelvic organ (laceration)
          (rupture) (tear) 634.2 ☑
      embolism (air) (amniotic fluid) (blood clot)
          (pulmonary) (pyemic) (septic) (soap)
          634.6 ☑
      genital tract and pelvic infection 634.0 ☑
      hemorrhage, delayed or excessive
          634.1 ☑
      metabolic disorder 634.4 ☑
      renal failure 634.3 ☑
      sepsis (genital tract) (pelvic organ)
          634.0 ☑
          urinary tract 634.7 ☑
      shock (postoperative) (septic) 634.5 ☑
      specified complication NEC 634.7 ☑
      toxemia 634.3 ☑
      unspecified complication(s) 634.8 ☑
      urinary tract infection 634.7 ☑
    fetus 761.8
    threatened 640.0 ☑
      affecting fetus or newborn 762.1
  surgical — *see* Abortion, legal
  therapeutic — *see* Abortion, legal
  threatened 640.0 ☑
    affecting fetus or newborn 762.1
  tubal — *see* Pregnancy, tubal
  voluntary — *see* Abortion, legal

Abortus fever 023.9
Aboulomania 301.6
Abrachia 755.20
Abrachiatism 755.20
Abrachiocephalia 759.89
Abrachiocephalus 759.89
Abrami's disease (acquired hemolytic jaundice)
    283.9
Abramov-Fiedler myocarditis (acute isolated
    myocarditis) 422.91
Abrasion — *see also* Injury, superficial, by site
  cornea 918.1
  dental 521.20
    extending into
      dentine 521.22
      pulp 521.23
    generalized 521.25
    limited to enamel 521.21
    localized 521.24
  teeth, tooth (dentifrice) (habitual) (hard tissues)
      (occupational) (ritual) (traditional) (wedge
      defect) (*see also* Abrasion, dental) 521.20
Abrikossov's tumor (M9580/0) — *see also*
    Neoplasm, connective tissue, benign
  malignant (M9580/3) — *see* Neoplasm,
      connective tissue, malignant
Abrism 988.8
Abruption, placenta — *see* Placenta, abruptio
Abruptio placentae — *see* Placenta, abruptio

Abscess (acute) (chronic) (infectional)
      (lymphangitic) (metastatic) (multiple)
      (pyogenic) (septic) (with lymphangitis) (*see
      also* Cellulitis) 682.9
  abdomen, abdominal
    cavity 567.22   ▲
    wall 682.2
  abdominopelvic 567.22   ▲
  accessory sinus (chronic) (*see also* Sinusitis)
      473.9
  adrenal (capsule) (gland) 255.8
  alveolar 522.5
    with sinus 522.7
  amebic 006.3
    bladder 006.8
    brain (with liver or lung abscess) 006.5
    liver (without mention of brain or lung
        abscess) 006.3
      with
        brain abscess (and lung abscess)
            006.5
        lung abscess 006.4
    lung (with liver abscess) 006.4
      with brain abscess 006.5
    seminal vesicle 006.8
    specified site NEC 006.8
    spleen 006.8
  anaerobic 040.0
  ankle 682.6
  anorectal 566
  antecubital space 682.3
  antrum (chronic) (Highmore) (*see also* Sinusitis,
      maxillary) 473.0
  anus 566
  apical (tooth) 522.5
    with sinus (alveolar) 522.7
  appendix 540.1
  areola (acute) (chronic) (nonpuerperal) 611.0
    puerperal, postpartum 675.1 ☑
  arm (any part, above wrist) 682.3
  artery (wall) 447.2
  atheromatous 447.2
  auditory canal (external) 380.10
  auricle (ear) (staphylococcal) (streptococcal)
      380.10
  axilla, axillary (region) 682.3
    lymph gland or node 683
  back (any part) 682.2
  Bartholin's gland 616.3
    with
      abortion — *see* Abortion, by type, with
          sepsis
      ectopic pregnancy (*see also* categories
          633.0-633.9) 639.0
      molar pregnancy (*see also* categories 630-
          632) 639.0
    complicating pregnancy or puerperium
        646.6 ☑
    following
      abortion 639.0
      ectopic or molar pregnancy 639.0
  bartholinian 616.3
  Bezold's 383.01
  bile, biliary, duct or tract (*see also*
      Cholecystitis) 576.8
  bilharziasis 120.1
  bladder (wall) 595.89
    amebic 006.8
  bone (subperiosteal) (*see also* Osteomyelitis)
      730.0 ☑
    accessory sinus (chronic) (*see also* Sinusitis)
        473.9
    acute 730.0 ☑
    chronic or old 730.1 ☑
    jaw (lower) (upper) 526.4
    mastoid — *see* Mastoiditis, acute
    petrous (*see also* Petrositis) 383.20
    spinal (tuberculous) (*see also* Tuberculosis)
        015.0 ☑ *[730.88]*
      nontuberculous 730.08
  bowel 569.5
  brain (any part) 324.0
    amebic (with liver or lung abscess) 006.5
    cystic 324.0
    late effect — *see* category 326
    otogenic 324.0
    tuberculous (*see also* Tuberculosis) 013.3 ☑

Abscess (*see also* Cellulitis) — *continued*
  breast (acute) (chronic) (nonpuerperal) 611.0
    newborn 771.5
    puerperal, postpartum 675.1 ☑
    tuberculous (*see also* Tuberculosis) 017.9 ☑
  broad ligament (chronic) (*see also* Disease, pelvis, inflammatory) 614.4
    acute 614.3
  Brodie's (chronic) (localized) (*see also* Osteomyelitis) 730.1 ☑
  bronchus 519.1
  buccal cavity 528.3
  bulbourethral gland 597.0
  bursa 727.89
    pharyngeal 478.29
  buttock 682.5
  canaliculus, breast 611.0
  canthus 372.20
  cartilage 733.99
  cecum 569.5
    with appendicitis 540.1
  cerebellum, cerebellar 324.0
    late effect — *see* category 326
  cerebral (embolic) 324.0
    late effect — *see* category 326
  cervical (neck region) 682.1
    lymph gland or node 683
    stump (*see also* Cervicitis) 616.0
  cervix (stump) (uteri) (*see also* Cervicitis) 616.0
  cheek, external 682.0
    inner 528.3
  chest 510.9
    with fistula 510.0
    wall 682.2
  chin 682.0
  choroid 363.00
  ciliary body 364.3
  circumtonsillar 475
  cold (tuberculous) — *see also* Tuberculosis, abscess
    articular — *see* Tuberculosis, joint
  colon (wall) 569.5
  colostomy or enterostomy 569.61
  conjunctiva 372.00
  connective tissue NEC 682.9
  cornea 370.55
    with ulcer 370.00
  corpus
    cavernosum 607.2
    luteum (*see also* Salpingo-oophoritis) 614.2
  Cowper's gland 597.0
  cranium 324.0
  cul-de-sac (Douglas') (posterior) (*see also* Disease, pelvis, inflammatory) 614.4
    acute 614.3
  dental 522.5
    with sinus (alveolar) 522.7
  dentoalveolar 522.5
    with sinus (alveolar) 522.7
  diaphragm, diaphragmatic 567.22 ▲
  digit NEC 681.9
  Douglas' cul-de-sac or pouch (*see also* Disease, pelvis, inflammatory) 614.4
    acute 614.3
  Dubois' 090.5
  ductless gland 259.8
  ear
    acute 382.00
    external 380.10
    inner 386.30
    middle — *see* Otitis media
  elbow 682.3
  endamebic — *see* Abscess, amebic
  entamebic — *see* Abscess, amebic
  enterostomy 569.61
  epididymis 604.0
  epidural 324.9
    brain 324.0
    late effect — *see* category 326
    spinal cord 324.1
  epiglottis 478.79
  epiploon, epiploic 567.22 ▲
  erysipelatous (*see also* Erysipelas) 035
  esophagostomy 530.86
  esophagus 530.19
  ethmoid (bone) (chronic) (sinus) (*see also* Sinusitis, ethmoidal) 473.2

Abscess (*see also* Cellulitis) — *continued*
  external auditory canal 380.10
  extradural 324.9
    brain 324.0
    late effect — *see* category 326
    spinal cord 324.1
  extraperitoneal — *see* Abscess, peritoneum
  eye 360.00
  eyelid 373.13
  face (any part, except eye) 682.0
  fallopian tube (*see also* Salpingo-oophoritis) 614.2
  fascia 728.89
  fauces 478.29
  fecal 569.5
  femoral (region) 682.6
  filaria, filarial (*see also* Infestation, filarial) 125.9
  finger (any) (intrathecal) (periosteal) (subcutaneous) (subcuticular) 681.00
  fistulous NEC 682.9
  flank 682.2
  foot (except toe) 682.7
  forearm 682.3
  forehead 682.0
  frontal (sinus) (chronic) (*see also* Sinusitis, frontal) 473.1
  gallbladder (*see also* Cholecystitis, acute) 575.0
  gastric 535.0 ☑
  genital organ or tract NEC
    female 616.9
      with
        abortion — *see* Abortion, by type, with sepsis
        ectopic pregnancy (*see also* categories 633.0-633.9) 639.0
        molar pregnancy (*see also* categories 630-632) 639.0
      following
        abortion 639.0
        ectopic or molar pregnancy 639.0
      puerperal, postpartum, childbirth 670.0 ☑
    male 608.4
  genitourinary system, tuberculous (*see also* Tuberculosis) 016.9 ☑
  gingival 523.3
  gland, glandular (lymph) (acute) NEC 683
  glottis 478.79
  gluteal (region) 682.5
  gonorrheal NEC (*see also* Gonococcus) 098.0
  groin 682.2
  gum 523.3
  hand (except finger or thumb) 682.4
  head (except face) 682.8
  heart 429.89
  heel 682.7
  helminthic (*see also* Infestation, by specific parasite) 128.9
  hepatic 572.0
    amebic (*see also* Abscess, liver, amebic) 006.3
    duct 576.8
  hip 682.6
    tuberculous (active) (*see also* Tuberculosis) 015.1 ☑
  ileocecal 540.1
  ileostomy (bud) 569.61
  iliac (region) 682.2
    fossa 540.1
  iliopsoas 567.31 ▲
    tuberculous (*see also* Tuberculosis) 015.0 ☑ [730.88] ●
  infraclavicular (fossa) 682.3
  inguinal (region) 682.2
    lymph gland or node 683
  intersphincteric (anus) 566
  intestine, intestinal 569.5
    rectal 566
  intra-abdominal (*see also* Abscess, peritoneum) 567.22 ▲
    postoperative 998.59
  intracranial 324.0
    late effect — *see* category 326
  intramammary — *see* Abscess, breast
  intramastoid (*see also* Mastoiditis, acute) 383.00
  intraorbital 376.01
  intraperitoneal 567.22 ▲

Abscess (*see also* Cellulitis) — *continued*
  intraspinal 324.1
    late effect — *see* category 326
  intratonsillar 475
  iris 364.3
  ischiorectal 566
  jaw (bone) (lower) (upper) 526.4
    skin 682.0
  joint (*see also* Arthritis, pyogenic) 711.0 ☑
    vertebral (tuberculous) (*see also* Tuberculosis) 015.0 ☑ [730.88]
    nontuberculous 724.8
  kidney 590.2
    with
      abortion — *see* Abortion, by type, with urinary tract infection
      calculus 592.0
      ectopic pregnancy (*see also* categories 633.0-633.9) 639.8
      molar pregnancy (*see also* categories 630-632) 639.8
      complicating pregnancy or puerperium 646.6 ☑
        affecting fetus or newborn 760.1
      following
        abortion 639.8
        ectopic or molar pregnancy 639.8
  knee 682.6
    joint 711.06
    tuberculous (active) (*see also* Tuberculosis) 015.2 ☑
  labium (majus) (minus) 616.4
    complicating pregnancy, childbirth, or puerperium 646.6 ☑
  lacrimal (passages) (sac) (*see also* Dacryocystitis) 375.30
    caruncle 375.30
    gland (*see also* Dacryoadenitis) 375.00
  lacunar 597.0
  larynx 478.79
  lateral (alveolar) 522.5
    with sinus 522.7
  leg, except foot 682.6
  lens 360.00
  lid 373.13
  lingual 529.0
    tonsil 475
  lip 528.5
  Littre's gland 597.0
  liver 572.0
    amebic 006.3
      with
        brain abscess (and lung abscess) 006.5
        lung abscess 006.4
      due to Entamoeba histolytica 006.3
    dysenteric (*see also* Abscess, liver, amebic) 006.3
    pyogenic 572.0
    tropical (*see also* Abscess, liver, amebic) 006.3
  loin (region) 682.2
  lumbar (tuberculous) (*see also* Tuberculosis) 015.0 ☑ [730.88]
    nontuberculous 682.2
  lung (miliary) (putrid) 513.0
    amebic (with liver abscess) 006.4
      with brain abscess 006.5
  lymph, lymphatic, gland or node (acute) 683
    any site, except mesenteric 683
    mesentery 289.2
  lymphangitic, acute — *see* Cellulitis
  malar 526.4
  mammary gland — *see* Abscess, breast
  marginal (anus) 566
  mastoid (process) (*see also* Mastoiditis, acute) 383.00
    subperiosteal 383.01
  maxilla, maxillary 526.4
    molar (tooth) 522.5
      with sinus 522.7
    premolar 522.5
    sinus (chronic) (*see also* Sinusitis, maxillary) 473.0
  mediastinum 513.1
  meibomian gland 373.12
  meninges (*see also* Meningitis) 320.9

Abscess (*see also* Cellulitis) — *continued*
mesentery, mesenteric 567.22 ▲
mesosalpinx (*see also* Salpingo-oophoritis) 614.2
milk 675.1 ☑
Monro's (psoriasis) 696.1
mons pubis 682.2
mouth (floor) 528.3
multiple sites NEC 682.9
mural 682.2
muscle 728.89
 psoas 567.31 ●
myocardium 422.92
nabothian (follicle) (*see also* Cervicitis) 616.0
nail (chronic) (with lymphangitis) 681.9
 finger 681.02
 toe 681.11
nasal (fossa) (septum) 478.1
 sinus (chronic) (*see also* Sinusitis) 473.9
nasopharyngeal 478.29
nates 682.5
navel 682.2
 newborn NEC 771.4
neck (region) 682.1
 lymph gland or node 683
nephritic (*see also* Abscess, kidney) 590.2
nipple 611.0
 puerperal, postpartum 675.0 ☑
nose (septum) 478.1
 external 682.0
omentum 567.22 ▲
operative wound 998.59
orbit, orbital 376.01
ossifluent — *see* Abscess, bone
ovary, ovarian (corpus luteum) (*see also* Salpingo-oophoritis) 614.2
oviduct (*see also* Salpingo-oophoritis) 614.2
palate (soft) 528.3
 hard 526.4
palmar (space) 682.4
pancreas (duct) 577.0
paradontal 523.3
parafrenal 607.2
parametric, parametrium (chronic) (*see also* Disease, pelvis, inflammatory) 614.4
 acute 614.3
paranephric 590.2
parapancreatic 577.0
parapharyngeal 478.22
pararectal 566
parasinus (*see also* Sinusitis) 473.9
parauterine (*see also* Disease, pelvis, inflammatory) 614.4
 acute 614.3
paravaginal (*see also* Vaginitis) 616.10
parietal region 682.8
parodontal 523.3
parotid (duct) (gland) 527.3
 region 528.3
parumbilical 682.2
 newborn 771.4
pectoral (region) 682.2
pelvirectal 567.22 ▲
pelvis, pelvic
 female (chronic) (*see also* Disease, pelvis, inflammatory) 614.4
 acute 614.3
 male, peritoneal (cellular tissue) — *see* Abscess, peritoneum
 tuberculous (*see also* Tuberculosis) 016.9 ☑
penis 607.2
 gonococcal (acute) 098.0
 chronic or duration of 2 months or over 098.2
perianal 566
periapical 522.5
 with sinus (alveolar) 522.7
periappendiceal 540.1
pericardial 420.99
pericecal 540.1
pericemental 523.3
pericholecystic (*see also* Cholecystitis, acute) 575.0
pericoronal 523.3
peridental 523.3
perigastric 535.0 ☑

Abscess (*see also* Cellulitis) — *continued*
perimetric (*see also* Disease, pelvis, inflammatory) 614.4
 acute 614.3
perinephric, perinephritic (*see also* Abscess, kidney) 590.2
perineum, perineal (superficial) 682.2
 deep (with urethral involvement) 597.0
 urethra 597.0
periodontal (parietal) 523.3
 apical 522.5
periosteum, periosteal (*see also* Periostitis) 730.3 ☑
 with osteomyelitis (*see also* Osteomyelitis) 730.2 ☑
 acute or subacute 730.0 ☑
 chronic or old 730.1 ☑
peripleuritic 510.9
 with fistula 510.0
periproctic 566
periprostatic 601.2
perirectal (staphylococcal) 566
perirenal (tissue) (*see also* Abscess, kidney) 590.2
perisinuous (nose) (*see also* Sinusitis) 473.9
peritoneum, peritoneal (perforated) (ruptured) 567.22 ▲
 with
 abortion — *see* Abortion, by type, with sepsis
 appendicitis 540.1
 ectopic pregnancy (*see also* categories 633.0-633.9) 639.0
 molar pregnancy (*see also* categories 630-632) 639.0
 following
 abortion 639.0
 ectopic or molar pregnancy 639.0
 pelvic, female (*see also* Disease, pelvis, inflammatory) 614.4
 acute 614.3
 postoperative 998.59
 puerperal, postpartum, childbirth 670.0 ☑
 tuberculous (*see also* Tuberculosis) 014.0 ☑
peritonsillar 475
perityphlic 540.1
periureteral 593.89
periurethral 597.0
 gonococcal (acute) 098.0
 chronic or duration of 2 months or over 098.2
periuterine (*see also* Disease, pelvis, inflammatory) 614.4
 acute 614.3
perivesical 595.89
pernicious NEC 682.9
petrous bone — *see* Petrositis
phagedenic NEC 682.9
 chancroid 099.0
pharynx, pharyngeal (lateral) 478.29
phlegmonous NEC 682.9
pilonidal 685.0
pituitary (gland) 253.8
pleura 510.9
 with fistula 510.0
popliteal 682.6
postanal 566
postcecal 540.1
postlaryngeal 478.79
postnasal 478.1
postpharyngeal 478.24
posttonsillar 475
posttyphoid 002.0
Pott's (*see also* Tuberculosis) 015.0 ☑ *[730.88]*
pouch of Douglas (chronic) (*see also* Disease, pelvis, inflammatory) 614.4
premammary — *see* Abscess, breast
prepatellar 682.6
prostate (*see also* Prostatitis) 601.2
 gonococcal (acute) 098.12
 chronic or duration of 2 months or over 098.32
psoas 567.31 ▲
 tuberculous (*see also* Tuberculosis) ●
 015.0 ☑ *[730.88]* ●
pterygopalatine fossa 682.8
pubis 682.2

Abscess (*see also* Cellulitis) — *continued*
puerperal — *see* Puerperal, abscess, by site
pulmonary — *see* Abscess, lung
pulp, pulpal (dental) 522.0
 finger 681.01
 toe 681.10
pyemic — *see* Septicemia
pyloric valve 535.0 ☑
rectovaginal septum 569.5
rectovesical 595.89
rectum 566
regional NEC 682.9
renal (*see also* Abscess, kidney) 590.2
retina 363.00
retrobulbar 376.01
retrocecal 567.22 ▲
retrolaryngeal 478.79
retromammary — *see* Abscess, breast
retroperineal 682.2
retroperitoneal 567.38 ▲
retropharyngeal 478.24
 tuberculous (*see also* Tuberculosis) 012.8 ☑
retrorectal 566
retrouterine (*see also* Disease, pelvis, inflammatory) 614.4
 acute 614.3
retrovesical 595.89
root, tooth 522.5
 with sinus (alveolar) 522.7
round ligament (*see also* Disease, pelvis, inflammatory) 614.4
 acute 614.3
rupture (spontaneous) NEC 682.9
sacrum (tuberculous) (*see also* Tuberculosis) 015.0 ☑ *[730.88]*
 nontuberculous 730.08
salivary duct or gland 527.3
scalp (any part) 682.8
scapular 730.01
sclera 379.09
scrofulous (*see also* Tuberculosis) 017.2 ☑
scrotum 608.4
seminal vesicle 608.0
 amebic 006.8
septal, dental 522.5
 with sinus (alveolar) 522.7
septum (nasal) 478.1
serous (*see also* Periostitis) 730.3 ☑
shoulder 682.3
side 682.2
sigmoid 569.5
sinus (accessory) (chronic) (nasal) (*see also* Sinusitis) 473.9
 intracranial venous (any) 324.0
 late effect — *see* category 326
Skene's duct or gland 597.0
skin NEC 682.9
 tuberculous (primary) (*see also* Tuberculosis) 017.0 ☑
sloughing NEC 682.9
specified site NEC 682.8
 amebic 006.8
spermatic cord 608.4
sphenoidal (sinus) (*see also* Sinusitis, sphenoidal) 473.3
spinal
 cord (any part) (staphylococcal) 324.1
 tuberculous (*see also* Tuberculosis) 013.5 ☑
 epidural 324.1
spine (column) (tuberculous) (*see also* Tuberculosis) 015.0 ☑ *[730.88]*
 nontuberculous 730.08
spleen 289.59
 amebic 006.8
staphylococcal NEC 682.9
stitch 998.59
stomach (wall) 535.0 ☑
strumous (tuberculous) (*see also* Tuberculosis) 017.2 ☑
subarachnoid 324.9
 brain 324.0
 cerebral 324.0
 late effect — *see* category 326
 spinal cord 324.1
subareolar — *see also* Abscess, breast
 puerperal, postpartum 675.1 ☑

☑ Additional Digit Required — Refer to the Tabular List (Numeric Code Section) for Additional Digit Selection
▶◀ Revised Text ● New Line ▲ Revised Code

2006 ICD-9-CM
October 2005 • Volume 2 — 5

Abscess (*see also* Cellulitis) — *continued*
  subcecal 540.1
  subcutaneous NEC 682.9
  subdiaphragmatic 567.22 ▲
  subdorsal 682.2
  subdural 324.9
    brain 324.0
    late effect — *see* category 326
    spinal cord 324.1
  subgaleal 682.8
  subhepatic 567.22 ▲
  sublingual 528.3
    gland 527.3
  submammary — *see* Abscess, breast
  submandibular (region) (space) (triangle) 682.0
    gland 527.3
  submaxillary (region) 682.0
    gland 527.3
  submental (pyogenic) 682.0
    gland 527.3
  subpectoral 682.2
  subperiosteal — *see* Abscess, bone
  subperitoneal 567.22 ▲
  subphrenic — *see also* Abscess, peritoneum
      567.22 ▲
    postoperative 998.59
  subscapular 682.2
  subungual 681.9
  suburethral 597.0
  sudoriparous 705.89
  suppurative NEC 682.9
  supraclavicular (fossa) 682.3
  suprahepatic 567.22 ▲
  suprapelvic (*see also* Disease, pelvis,
      inflammatory) 614.4
    acute 614.3
  suprapubic 682.2
  suprarenal (capsule) (gland) 255.8
  sweat gland 705.89
  syphilitic 095.8
  teeth, tooth (root) 522.5
    with sinus (alveolar) 522.7
    supporting structures NEC 523.3
  temple 682.0
  temporal region 682.0
  temporosphenoidal 324.0
    late effect — *see* category 326
  tendon (sheath) 727.89
  testicle — *see* Orchitis
  thecal 728.89
  thigh (acquired) 682.6
  thorax 510.9
    with fistula 510.0
  throat 478.29
  thumb (intrathecal) (periosteal) (subcutaneous)
      (subcuticular) 681.00
  thymus (gland) 254.1
  thyroid (gland) 245.0
  toe (any) (intrathecal) (periosteal)
      (subcutaneous) (subcuticular) 681.10
  tongue (staphylococcal) 529.0
  tonsil(s) (lingual) 475
  tonsillopharyngeal 475
  tooth, teeth (root) 522.5
    with sinus (alveolar) 522.7
    supporting structure NEC 523.3
  trachea 478.9
  trunk 682.2
  tubal (*see also* Salpingo-oophoritis) 614.2
  tuberculous — *see* Tuberculosis, abscess
  tubo-ovarian (*see also* Salpingo-oophoritis)
      614.2
  tunica vaginalis 608.4
  umbilicus NEC 682.2
    newborn 771.4
  upper arm 682.3
  upper respiratory 478.9
  urachus 682.2
  urethra (gland) 597.0
  urinary 597.0
  uterus, uterine (wall) (*see also* Endometritis)
      615.9
    ligament (*see also* Disease, pelvis,
        inflammatory) 614.4
      acute 614.3
    neck (*see also* Cervicitis) 616.0
  uvula 528.3

Abscess (*see also* Cellulitis) — *continued*
  vagina (wall) (*see also* Vaginitis) 616.10
  vaginorectal (*see also* Vaginitis) 616.10
  vas deferens 608.4
  vermiform appendix 540.1
  vertebra (column) (tuberculous) (*see also*
      Tuberculosis) 015.0 ☑ *[730.88]*
    nontuberculous 730.0 ☑
  vesical 595.89
  vesicouterine pouch (*see also* Disease, pelvis,
      inflammatory) 614.4
  vitreous (humor) (pneumococcal) 360.04
  vocal cord 478.5
  von Bezold's 383.01
  vulva 616.4
    complicating pregnancy, childbirth, or
        puerperium 646.6 ☑
  vulvovaginal gland (*see also* Vaginitis) 616.3
  web-space 682.4
  wrist 682.4
Absence (organ or part) (complete or partial)
  acoustic nerve 742.8
  adrenal (gland) (congenital) 759.1
    acquired V45.79
  albumin (blood) 273.8
  alimentary tract (complete) (congenital) (partial)
      751.8
    lower 751.5
    upper 750.8
  alpha-fucosidase 271.8
  alveolar process (acquired) 525.8
    congenital 750.26
  anus, anal (canal) (congenital) 751.2
  aorta (congenital) 747.22
  aortic valve (congenital) 746.89
  appendix, congenital 751.2
  arm (acquired) V49.60
    above elbow V49.66
    below elbow V49.65
    congenital (*see also* Deformity, reduction,
        upper limb) 755.20
      lower — *see* Absence, forearm, congenital
      upper (complete) (partial) (with absence of
          distal elements, incomplete) 755.24
        with
          complete absence of distal elements
              755.21
          forearm (incomplete) 755.23
  artery (congenital) (peripheral) NEC (*see also*
      Anomaly, peripheral vascular system)
      747.60
    brain 747.81
    cerebral 747.81
    coronary 746.85
    pulmonary 747.3
    umbilical 747.5
  atrial septum 745.69
  auditory canal (congenital) (external) 744.01
  auricle (ear) (with stenosis or atresia of
      auditory canal), congenital 744.01
  bile, biliary duct (common) or passage
      (congenital) 751.61
  bladder (acquired) V45.74
    congenital 753.8
  bone (congenital) NEC 756.9
    marrow 284.9
      acquired (secondary) 284.8
      congenital 284.0
      hereditary 284.0
      idiopathic 284.9
    skull 756.0
  bowel sounds 787.5
  brain 740.0
    specified part 742.2
  breast(s) (acquired) V45.71
    congenital 757.6
  broad ligament (congenital) 752.19
  bronchus (congenital) 748.3
  calvarium, calvaria (skull) 756.0
  canaliculus lacrimalis, congenital 743.65
  carpal(s) (congenital) (complete) (partial) (with
      absence of distal elements, incomplete)
      (*see also* Deformity, reduction, upper
      limb) 755.28
    with complete absence of distal elements
        755.21
  cartilage 756.9

Absence — *continued*
  caudal spine 756.13
  cecum (acquired) (postoperative)
      (posttraumatic) V45.72
    congenital 751.2
  cementum 520.4
  cerebellum (congenital) (vermis) 742.2
  cervix (acquired) (uteri) V45.77
    congenital 752.49
  chin, congenital 744.89
  cilia (congenital) 743.63
    acquired 374.89
  circulatory system, part NEC 747.89
  clavicle 755.51
  clitoris (congenital) 752.49
  coccyx, congenital 756.13
  cold sense (*see also* Disturbance, sensation) 782.0
  colon (acquired) (postoperative) V45.72
    congenital 751.2
  congenital
    lumen — *see* Atresia
    organ or site NEC — *see* Agenesis
    septum — *see* Imperfect, closure
  corpus callosum (congenital) 742.2
  cricoid cartilage 748.3
  diaphragm (congenital) (with hernia) 756.6
    with obstruction 756.6
  digestive organ(s) or tract, congenital (complete)
      (partial) 751.8
    acquired V45.79
    lower 751.5
    upper 750.8
  ductus arteriosus 747.89
  duodenum (acquired) (postoperative) V45.72
    congenital 751.1
  ear, congenital 744.09
    acquired V45.79
    auricle 744.01
    external 744.01
    inner 744.05
    lobe, lobule 744.21
    middle, except ossicles 744.03
      ossicles 744.04
    ossicles 744.04
  ejaculatory duct (congenital) 752.89
  endocrine gland NEC (congenital) 759.2
  epididymis (congenital) 752.89
    acquired V45.77
  epiglottis, congenital 748.3
  epileptic (atonic) (typical) (*see also* Epilepsy)
      345.0 ☑
  erythrocyte 284.9
  erythropoiesis 284.9
    congenital 284.0
  esophagus (congenital) 750.3
  Eustachian tube (congenital) 744.24
  extremity (acquired)
    congenital (*see also* Deformity, reduction)
        755.4
    lower V49.70
    upper V49.60
  extrinsic muscle, eye 743.69
  eye (acquired) V45.78
    adnexa (congenital) 743.69
    congenital 743.00
    muscle (congenital) 743.69
  eyelid (fold), congenital 743.62
    acquired 374.89
  face
    bones NEC 756.0
    specified part NEC 744.89
  fallopian tube(s) (acquired) V45.77
    congenital 752.19
  femur, congenital (complete) (partial) (with
      absence of distal elements, incomplete)
      (*see also* Deformity, reduction, lower
      limb) 755.34
    with
      complete absence of distal elements 755.31
      tibia and fibula (incomplete) 755.33
  fibrin 790.92
  fibrinogen (congenital) 286.3
    acquired 286.6
  fibula, congenital (complete) (partial) (with
      absence of distal elements, incomplete)
      (*see also* Deformity, reduction, lower
      limb) 755.37

Absence — *continued*
  fibula, congenital (*see also* Deformity,
      reduction, lower limb) — *continued*
    with
      complete absence of distal elements
          755.31
        tibia 755.35
          with
            complete absence of distal elements
                755.31
              femur (incomplete) 755.33
                with complete absence of distal
                    elements 755.31
  finger (acquired) V49.62
    congenital (complete) (partial) (*see also*
        Deformity, reduction, upper limb)
        755.29
      meaning all fingers (complete) (partial)
          755.21
      transverse 755.21
  fissures of lungs (congenital) 748.5
  foot (acquired) V49.73
    congenital (complete) 755.31
  forearm (acquired) V49.65
    congenital (complete) (partial) (with absence
        of distal elements, incomplete) (*see
        also* Deformity, reduction, upper limb)
        755.25
      with
        complete absence of distal elements
            (hand and fingers) 755.21
          humerus (incomplete) 755.23
  fovea centralis 743.55
  fucosidase 271.8
  gallbladder (acquired) V45.79
    congenital 751.69
  gamma globulin (blood) 279.00
  genital organs
    acquired V45.77
    congenital
      female 752.89
        external 752.49
        internal NEC 752.89
      male 752.89
        penis 752.69
  genitourinary organs, congenital NEC 752.89
  glottis 748.3
  gonadal, congenital NEC 758.6
  hair (congenital) 757.4
    acquired — *see* Alopecia
  hand (acquired) V49.63
    congenital (complete) (*see also* Deformity,
        reduction, upper limb) 755.21
  heart (congenital) 759.89
    acquired — *see* Status, organ replacement
  heat sense (*see also* Disturbance, sensation)
      782.0
  humerus, congenital (complete) (partial) (with
      absence of distal elements, incomplete)
      (*see also* Deformity, reduction, upper
      limb) 755.24
    with
      complete absence of distal elements
          755.21
        radius and ulna (incomplete) 755.23
  hymen (congenital) 752.49
  ileum (acquired) (postoperative) (posttraumatic)
      V45.72
    congenital 751.1
  immunoglobulin, isolated NEC 279.03
    IgA 279.01
    IgG 279.03
    IgM 279.02
  incus (acquired) 385.24
    congenital 744.04
  internal ear (congenital) 744.05
  intestine (acquired) (small) V45.72
    congenital 751.1
      large 751.2
    large V45.72
      congenital 751.2
  iris (congenital) 743.45
  jaw — *see* Absence, mandible
  jejunum (acquired) V45.72
    congenital 751.1
  joint, congenital NEC 755.8
  kidney(s) (acquired) V45.73
    congenital 753.0

Absence — *continued*
  labium (congenital) (majus) (minus) 752.49
  labyrinth, membranous 744.05
  lacrimal apparatus (congenital) 743.65
  larynx (congenital) 748.3
  leg (acquired) V49.70
    above knee V49.76
    below knee V49.75
    congenital (partial) (unilateral) (*see also*
        Deformity, reduction, lower limb)
        755.31
      lower (complete) (partial) (with absence of
          distal elements, incomplete) 755.35
        with
          complete absence of distal elements
              (foot and toes) 755.31
            thigh (incomplete) 755.33
              with complete absence of distal
                  elements 755.31
      upper — *see* Absence, femur
  lens (congenital) 743.35
    acquired 379.31
  ligament, broad (congenital) 752.19
  limb (acquired)
    congenital (complete) (partial) (*see also*
        Deformity, reduction) 755.4
      lower 755.30
        complete 755.31
        incomplete 755.32
        longitudinal — *see* Deficiency, lower
            limb, longitudinal
        transverse 755.31
      upper 755.20
        complete 755.21
        incomplete 755.22
        longitudinal — *see* Deficiency, upper
            limb, longitudinal
        transverse 755.21
    lower NEC V49.70
    upper NEC V49.60
  lip 750.26
  liver (congenital) (lobe) 751.69
  lumbar (congenital) (vertebra) 756.13
    isthmus 756.11
    pars articularis 756.11
  lumen — *see* Atresia
  lung (bilateral) (congenital) (fissure) (lobe)
      (unilateral) 748.5
    acquired (any part) V45.76
  mandible (congenital) 524.09
  maxilla (congenital) 524.09
  menstruation 626.0
  metacarpal(s), congenital (complete) (partial)
      (with absence of distal elements,
      incomplete) (*see also* Deformity,
      reduction, upper limb) 755.28
    with all fingers, complete 755.21
  metatarsal(s), congenital (complete) (partial)
      (with absence of distal elements,
      incomplete) (*see also* Deformity,
      reduction, lower limb) 755.38
    with complete absence of distal elements
        755.31
  muscle (congenital) (pectoral) 756.81
    ocular 743.69
  musculoskeletal system (congenital) NEC 756.9
  nail(s) (congenital) 757.5
  neck, part 744.89
  nerve 742.8
  nervous system, part NEC 742.8
  neutrophil 288.0
  nipple (congenital) 757.6
  nose (congenital) 748.1
    acquired 738.0
  nuclear 742.8
  ocular muscle (congenital) 743.69
  organ
    of Corti (congenital) 744.05
    or site
      acquired V45.79
      congenital NEC 759.89
  osseous meatus (ear) 744.03
  ovary (acquired) V45.77
    congenital 752.0
  oviduct (acquired) V45.77
    congenital 752.19

Absence — *continued*
  pancreas (congenital) 751.7
    acquired (postoperative) (posttraumatic)
        V45.79
  parathyroid gland (congenital) 759.2
  parotid gland(s) (congenital) 750.21
  patella, congenital 755.64
  pelvic girdle (congenital) 755.69
  penis (congenital) 752.69
    acquired V45.77
  pericardium (congenital) 746.89
  perineal body (congenital) 756.81
  phalange(s), congenital 755.4
    lower limb (complete) (intercalary) (partial)
        (terminal) (*see also* Deformity,
        reduction, lower limb) 755.39
      meaning all toes (complete) (partial)
          755.31
      transverse 755.31
    upper limb (complete) (intercalary) (partial)
        (terminal) (*see also* Deformity,
        reduction, upper limb) 755.29
      meaning all digits (complete) (partial)
          755.21
      transverse 755.21
  pituitary gland (congenital) 759.2
  postoperative — *see* Absence, by site, acquired
  prostate (congenital) 752.89
    acquired V45.77
  pulmonary
    artery 747.3
    trunk 747.3
    valve (congenital) 746.01
    vein 747.49
  punctum lacrimale (congenital) 743.65
  radius, congenital (complete) (partial) (with
      absence of distal elements, incomplete)
      755.26
    with
      complete absence of distal elements
          755.21
        ulna 755.25
          with
            complete absence of distal elements
                755.21
              humerus (incomplete) 755.23
  ray, congenital 755.4
    lower limb (complete) (partial) (*see also*
        Deformity, reduction, lower limb)
        755.38
      meaning all rays 755.31
      transverse 755.31
    upper limb (complete) (partial) (*see also*
        Deformity, reduction, upper limb)
        755.28
      meaning all rays 755.21
      transverse 755.21
  rectum (congenital) 751.2
    acquired V45.79
  red cell 284.9
    acquired (secondary) 284.8
    congenital 284.0
    hereditary 284.0
    idiopathic 284.9
  respiratory organ (congenital) NEC 748.9
  rib (acquired) 738.3
    congenital 756.3
  roof of orbit (congenital) 742.0
  round ligament (congenital) 752.89
  sacrum, congenital 756.13
  salivary gland(s) (congenital) 750.21
  scapula 755.59
  scrotum, congenital 752.89
  seminal tract or duct (congenital) 752.89
    acquired V45.77
  septum (congenital) — *see also* Imperfect,
      closure, septum
    atrial 745.69
      and ventricular 745.7
    between aorta and pulmonary artery 745.0
    ventricular 745.3
      and atrial 745.7
  sex chromosomes 758.81
  shoulder girdle, congenital (complete) (partial)
      755.59
  skin (congenital) 757.39

Absence — *continued*
  skull bone 756.0
    with
      anencephalus 740.0
      encephalocele 742.0
      hydrocephalus 742.3
        with spina bifida (*see also* Spina
          bifida) 741.0 ☑
      microcephalus 742.1
  spermatic cord (congenital) 752.89
  spinal cord 742.59
  spine, congenital 756.13
  spleen (congenital) 759.0
    acquired V45.79
  sternum, congenital 756.3
  stomach (acquired) (partial) (postoperative)
    V45.75
    with postgastric surgery syndrome 564.2
    congenital 750.7
  submaxillary gland(s) (congenital) 750.21
  superior vena cava (congenital) 747.49
  tarsal(s), congenital (complete) (partial) (with
    absence of distal elements, incomplete)
    (*see also* Deformity, reduction, lower
    limb) 755.38
  teeth, tooth (congenital) 520.0
    with abnormal spacing 524.30
    acquired 525.10
      with malocclusion 524.30
      due to
        caries 525.13
        extraction 525.10
        periodontal disease 525.12
        trauma 525.11
  tendon (congenital) 756.81
  testis (congenital) 752.89
    acquired V45.77
  thigh (acquired) 736.89
  thumb (acquired) V49.61
    congenital 755.29
  thymus gland (congenital) 759.2
  thyroid (gland) (surgical) 246.8
    with hypothyroidism 244.0
    cartilage, congenital 748.3
    congenital 243
  tibia, congenital (complete) (partial) (with
    absence of distal elements, incomplete)
    (*see also* Deformity, reduction, lower
    limb) 755.36
    with
      complete absence of distal elements
        755.31
      fibula 755.35
        with
          complete absence of distal elements
            755.31
        femur (incomplete) 755.33
          with complete absence of distal
            elements 755.31
  toe (acquired) V49.72
    congenital (complete) (partial) 755.39
      meaning all toes 755.31
      transverse 755.31
    great V49.71
  tongue (congenital) 750.11
  tooth, teeth (congenital) 520.0
    with abnormal spacing 524.30
    acquired 525.10
      with malocclusion 524.30
      due to
        caries 525.13
        extraction 525.10
        periodontal disease 525.12
        trauma 525.11
  trachea (cartilage) (congenital) (rings) 748.3
  transverse aortic arch (congenital) 747.21
  tricuspid valve 746.1
  ulna, congenital (complete) (partial) (with
    absence of distal elements, incomplete)
    (*see also* Deformity, reduction, upper
    limb) 755.27
    with
      complete absence of distal elements
        755.21
      radius 755.25

Absence — *continued*
  ulna, congenital (*see also* Deformity, reduction,
    upper limb) — *continued*
    with — *continued*
      radius — *continued*
        with
          complete absence of distal elements
            755.21
          humerus (incomplete) 755.23
  umbilical artery (congenital) 747.5
  ureter (congenital) 753.4
    acquired V45.74
  urethra, congenital 753.8
    acquired V45.74
  urinary system, part NEC, congenital 753.8
    acquired V45.74
  uterus (acquired) V45.77
    congenital 752.3
  uvula (congenital) 750.26
  vagina, congenital 752.49
    acquired V45.77
  vas deferens (congenital) 752.89
    acquired V45.77
  vein (congenital) (peripheral) NEC (*see also*
    Anomaly, peripheral vascular system)
    747.60
    brain 747.81
    great 747.49
    portal 747.49
    pulmonary 747.49
  vena cava (congenital) (inferior) (superior)
    747.49
  ventral horn cell 742.59
  ventricular septum 745.3
  vermis of cerebellum 742.2
  vertebra, congenital 756.13
  vulva, congenital 752.49
Absentia epileptica (*see also* Epilepsy) 345.0 ☑
Absinthemia (*see also* Dependence) 304.6 ☑
Absinthism (*see also* Dependence) 304.6 ☑
Absorbent system disease 459.89
Absorption
  alcohol, through placenta or breast milk
    760.71
  antibiotics, through placenta or breast milk
    760.74
  anticonvulsants, through placenta or   ●
    breast milk 760.77   ●
  antifungals, through placenta or breast   ●
    milk 760.74   ●
  anti-infective, through placenta or breast milk
    760.74
  antimetabolics, through placenta or breast   ●
    milk 760.78   ●
  chemical NEC 989.9
    specified chemical or substance — *see* Table
      of Drugs and Chemicals
    through placenta or breast milk (fetus or
      newborn) 760.70
      alcohol 760.71
      anticonvulsants 760.77   ●
      antifungals 760.74   ●
      anti-infective agents 760.74
      antimetabolics 760.78   ●
      cocaine 760.75
      "crack" 760.75
      diethylstilbestrol [DES] 760.76
      hallucinogenic agents 760.73
      medicinal agents NEC 760.79
      narcotics 760.72
      obstetric anesthetic or analgesic drug
        763.5
      specified agent NEC 760.79
      suspected, affecting management of
        pregnancy 655.5 ☑
  cocaine, through placenta or breast milk
    760.75
  drug NEC (*see also* Reaction, drug)
    through placenta or breast milk (fetus or
      newborn) 760.70
      alcohol 760.71
      anticonvulsants 760.77   ●
      antifungals 760.74   ●
      anti-infective agents 760.74   ●
      antimetabolics 760.78   ●
      cocaine 760.75
      "crack" 760.75

Absorption — *continued*
  drug NEC (*see also* Reaction, drug) — *continued*
    through placenta or breast milk — *continued*
      diethylstilbestrol [DES] 760.76
      hallucinogenic agents 760.73
      medicinal agents NEC 760.79
      narcotics 760.72
      obstetric anesthetic or analgesic drug
        763.5
      specified agent NEC 760.79
      suspected, affecting management of
        pregnancy 655.5 ☑
  fat, disturbance 579.8
  hallucinogenic agents, through placenta or
    breast milk 760.73
  immune sera, through placenta or breast milk
    760.79
  lactose defect 271.3
  medicinal agents NEC, through placenta or
    breast milk 760.79
  narcotics, through placenta or breast milk
    760.72
  noxious substance — *see* Absorption, chemical
  protein, disturbance 579.8
  pus or septic, general — *see* Septicemia
  quinine, through placenta or breast milk
    760.74
  toxic substance — *see* Absorption, chemical
  uremic — *see* Uremia
Abstinence symptoms or syndrome
  alcohol 291.81
  drug 292.0
Abt-Letterer-Siwe syndrome (acute histiocytosis
  X) (M9722/3) 202.5 ☑
Abulia 799.89
Abulomania 301.6
Abuse
  adult 995.80
    emotional 995.82
    multiple forms 995.85
    neglect (nutritional) 995.84
    physical 995.81
    psychological 995.82
    sexual 995.83
  alcohol (*see also* Alcoholism) 305.0 ☑
    dependent 303.9 ☑
    nondependent 305.0 ☑
  child 995.50
    counseling
      perpetrator
        non-parent V62.83
        parent V61.22
      victim V61.21
    emotional 995.51
    multiple forms 995.59
    neglect (nutritional) 995.52
    psychological 995.51
    physical 995.54
      shaken infant syndrome 995.55
    sexual 995.53
  drugs, nondependent 305.9 ☑

> *Note* — Use the following fifth-digit
> subclassification with the following codes:
> 305.0, 305.2-305.9:
>
> | 0 | unspecified | 2 | episodic |
> |---|---|---|---|
> | 1 | continuous | 3 | in remission |

    amphetamine type 305.7 ☑
    antidepressants 305.8 ☑
    anxiolytic 305.4 ☑
    barbiturates 305.4 ☑
    caffeine 305.9 ☑
    cannabis 305.2 ☑
    cocaine type 305.6 ☑
    hallucinogens 305.3 ☑
    hashish 305.2 ☑
    hypnotic 305.4 ☑
    inhalant 305.9 ☑
    LSD 305.3 ☑
    marijuana 305.2 ☑
    mixed 305.9 ☑
    morphine type 305.5 ☑
    opioid type 305.5 ☑
    phencyclidine (PCP) 305.9 ☑

Abuse — *continued*
  drugs, nondependent — *continued*
    sedative 305.4 ☑
    specified NEC 305.9 ☑
    tranquilizers 305.4 ☑
  spouse 995.80
  tobacco 305.1
Acalcerosis 275.40
Acalcicosis 275.40
Acalculia 784.69
  developmental 315.1
Acanthocheilonemiasis 125.4
Acanthocytosis 272.5
Acanthokeratodermia 701.1
Acantholysis 701.8
  bullosa 757.39
Acanthoma (benign) (M8070/0) — *see also*
  Neoplasm, by site, benign
  malignant (M8070/3) — *see* Neoplasm, by site,
    malignant
Acanthosis (acquired) (nigricans) 701.2
  adult 701.2
  benign (congenital) 757.39
  congenital 757.39
  glycogenic
    esophagus 530.89
  juvenile 701.2
  tongue 529.8
Acanthrocytosis 272.5
Acapnia 276.3
Acarbia 276.2
Acardia 759.89
Acardiacus amorphus 759.89
Acardiotrophia 429.1
Acardius 759.89
Acariasis 133.9
  sarcoptic 133.0
Acaridiasis 133.9
Acarinosis 133.9
Acariosis 133.9
Acarodermatitis 133.9
  urticarioides 133.9
Acarophobia 300.29
Acatalasemia 277.89
Acatalasia 277.89
Acatamathesia 784.69
Acataphasia 784.5
Acathisia 781.0
  due to drugs 333.99
Acceleration, accelerated
  atrioventricular conduction 426.7
  idioventricular rhythm 427.89
Accessory (congenital)
  adrenal gland 759.1
  anus 751.5
  appendix 751.5
  atrioventricular conduction 426.7
  auditory ossicles 744.04
  auricle (ear) 744.1
  autosome(s) NEC 758.5
    21 or 22 758.0
  biliary duct or passage 751.69
  bladder 753.8
  blood vessels (peripheral) (congenital) NEC (*see
    also* Anomaly, peripheral vascular
    system) 747.60
    cerebral 747.81
    coronary 746.85
  bone NEC 756.9
    foot 755.67
  breast tissue, axilla 757.6
  carpal bones 755.56
  cecum 751.5
  cervix 752.49
  chromosome(s) NEC 758.5
    13-15 758.1
    16-18 758.2
    21 or 22 758.0
    autosome(s) NEC 758.5
    D_1 758.1
    E_3 758.2

Accessory — *continued*
  chromosome(s) — *continued*
    G 758.0
    sex 758.81
  coronary artery 746.85
  cusp(s), heart valve NEC 746.89
    pulmonary 746.09
  cystic duct 751.69
  digits 755.00
  ear (auricle) (lobe) 744.1
  endocrine gland NEC 759.2
  external os 752.49
  eyelid 743.62
  eye muscle 743.69
  face bone(s) 756.0
  fallopian tube (fimbria) (ostium) 752.19
  fingers 755.01
  foreskin 605
  frontonasal process 756.0
  gallbladder 751.69
  genital organ(s)
    female 752.89
      external 752.49
      internal NEC 752.89
    male NEC 752.89
    penis 752.69
  genitourinary organs NEC 752.89
  heart 746.89
    valve NEC 746.89
      pulmonary 746.09
  hepatic ducts 751.69
  hymen 752.49
  intestine (large) (small) 751.5
  kidney 753.3
  lacrimal canal 743.65
  leaflet, heart valve NEC 746.89
    pulmonary 746.09
  ligament, broad 752.19
  liver (duct) 751.69
  lobule (ear) 744.1
  lung (lobe) 748.69
  muscle 756.82
  navicular of carpus 755.56
  nervous system, part NEC 742.8
  nipple 757.6
  nose 748.1
  organ or site NEC — *see* Anomaly, specified
    type NEC
  ovary 752.0
  oviduct 752.19
  pancreas 751.7
  parathyroid gland 759.2
  parotid gland (and duct) 750.22
  pituitary gland 759.2
  placental lobe — *see* Placenta, abnormal
  preauricular appendage 744.1
  prepuce 605
  renal arteries (multiple) 747.62
  rib 756.3
    cervical 756.2
  roots (teeth) 520.2
  salivary gland 750.22
  sesamoids 755.8
  sinus — *see* condition
  skin tags 757.39
  spleen 759.0
  sternum 756.3
  submaxillary gland 750.22
  tarsal bones 755.67
  teeth, tooth 520.1
    causing crowding 524.31
  tendon 756.89
  thumb 755.01
  thymus gland 759.2
  thyroid gland 759.2
  toes 755.02
  tongue 750.13
  tragus 744.1
  ureter 753.4
  urethra 753.8
  urinary organ or tract NEC 753.8
  uterus 752.2
  vagina 752.49
  valve, heart NEC 746.89
    pulmonary 746.09
  vertebra 756.19
  vocal cords 748.3
  vulva 752.49

Accident, accidental — *see also* condition
  birth NEC 767.9
  cardiovascular (*see also* Disease,
    cardiovascular) 429.2
  cerebral (*see also* Disease, cerebrovascular,
    acute) 434.91
  cerebrovascular (current) (CVA) (*see also*
    Disease, cerebrovascular, acute) 434.91
    embolic 434.11
    healed or old V12.59
    hemorrhagic — *see* Hemorrhage, brain ●
    impending 435.9
    ischemic 434.91
    late effect — *see* Late effect(s) (of)
      cerebrovascular disease
    postoperative 997.02
    thrombotic 434.01
  coronary (*see also* Infarct, myocardium)
    410.9 ☑
  craniovascular (*see also* Disease,
    cerebrovascular, acute) 436
  during pregnancy, to mother, affecting fetus or
    newborn 760.5
  heart, cardiac (*see also* Infarct, myocardium)
    410.9 ☑
  intrauterine 779.89
  vascular — *see* Disease, cerebrovascular, acute
Accommodation
  disorder of 367.51
    drug-induced 367.89
      toxic 367.89
  insufficiency of 367.4
  paralysis of 367.51
    hysterical 300.11
  spasm of 367.53
Accouchement — *see* Delivery
Accreta placenta (without hemorrhage) 667.0 ☑
  with hemorrhage 666.0 ☑
Accretio cordis (nonrheumatic) 423.1
Accretions on teeth 523.6
Accumulation secretion, prostate 602.8
Acephalia, acephalism, acephaly 740.0
Acephalic 740.0
Acephalobrachia 759.89
Acephalocardia 759.89
Acephalocardius 759.89
Acephalochiria 759.89
Acephalochirus 759.89
Acephalogaster 759.89
Acephalostomus 759.89
Acephalothorax 759.89
Acephalus 740.0
Acetonemia 790.6
  diabetic 250.1 ☑
Acetonglycosuria 982.8
Acetonuria 791.6
Achalasia 530.0
  cardia 530.0
  digestive organs congenital NEC 751.8
  esophagus 530.0
  pelvirectal 751.3
  psychogenic 306.4
  pylorus 750.5
  sphincteral NEC 564.89
Achard-Thiers syndrome (adrenogenital) 255.2
Ache(s) — *see* Pain
Acheilia 750.26
Acheiria 755.21
Achillobursitis 726.71
Achillodynia 726.71
Achlorhydria, achlorhydric 536.0
  anemia 280.9
  diarrhea 536.0
  neurogenic 536.0
  postvagotomy 564.2
  psychogenic 306.4
  secondary to vagotomy 564.2
Achloroblepsia 368.52
Achloropsia 368.52
Acholia 575.8

Acholuric jaundice (familial) (splenomegalic) (*see also* Spherocytosis) 282.0
  acquired 283.9
Achondroplasia 756.4
Achrestic anemia 281.8
Achroacytosis, lacrimal gland 375.00
  tuberculous (*see also* Tuberculosis) 017.3 ☑
Achroma, cutis 709.00
Achromate (congenital) 368.54
Achromatopia 368.54
Achromatopsia (congenital) 368.54
Achromia
  congenital 270.2
  parasitica 111.0
  unguium 703.8
Achylia
  gastrica 536.8
    neurogenic 536.3
    psychogenic 306.4
  pancreatica 577.1
Achylosis 536.8
Acid
  burn — *see also* Burn, by site
    from swallowing acid — *see* Burn, internal
      organs
  deficiency
    amide nicotinic 265.2
    amino 270.9
    ascorbic 267
    folic 266.2
    nicotinic (amide) 265.2
    pantothenic 266.2
  intoxication 276.2
  peptic disease 536.8
  stomach 536.8
    psychogenic 306.4
Acidemia 276.2
  arginosuccinic 270.6
  fetal
    affecting management of pregnancy 656.3 ☑
    before onset of labor, in liveborn infant
      768.2
    during labor, in liveborn infant 768.3
    intrauterine 656.3 ☑
    unspecified as to time of onset, in liveborn
      infant 768.4
  pipecolic 270.7
Acidity, gastric (high) (low) 536.8
  psychogenic 306.4
Acidocytopenia 288.0
Acidocytosis 288.3
Acidopenia 288.0
Acidosis 276.2
  diabetic 250.1 ☑
  fetal, affecting management of pregnancy
    756.8 ☑
  fetal, affecting newborn 768.9
  kidney tubular 588.89
  lactic 276.2
  metabolic NEC 276.2
    with respiratory acidosis 276.4
    late, of newborn 775.7
  renal
    hyperchloremic 588.89
    tubular (distal) (proximal) 588.89
  respiratory 276.2
    complicated by
      metabolic acidosis 276.4
      metabolic alkalosis 276.4
Aciduria 791.9
  arginosuccinic 270.6
  beta-aminoisobutyric (BAIB) 277.2
  glutaric
    type I 270.7
    type II (type IIA, IIB, IIC) 277.85
    type III 277.86
  glycolic 271.8
  methylmalonic 270.3
    with glycinemia 270.7
  organic 270.9
  orotic (congenital) (hereditary) (pyrimidine
    deficiency) 281.4
Acladiosis 111.8
  skin 111.8

Aclasis
  diaphyseal 756.4
  tarsoepiphyseal 756.59
Acleistocardia 745.5
Aclusion 524.4
Acmesthesia 782.0
Acne (pustular) (vulgaris) 706.1
  agminata (*see also* Tuberculosis) 017.0 ☑
  artificialis 706.1
  atrophica 706.0
  cachecticorum (Hebra) 706.1
  conglobata 706.1
  conjunctiva 706.1
  cystic 706.1
  decalvans 704.09
  erythematosa 695.3
  eyelid 706.1
  frontalis 706.0
  indurata 706.1
  keloid 706.1
  lupoid 706.0
  necrotic, necrotica 706.0
    miliaris 704.8
  neonatal 706.1   ●
  nodular 706.1
  occupational 706.1
  papulosa 706.1
  rodens 706.0
  rosacea 695.3
  scorbutica 267
  scrofulosorum (Bazin) (*see also* Tuberculosis)
    017.0 ☑
  summer 692.72
  tropical 706.1
  varioliformis 706.0
Acneiform drug eruptions 692.3
Acnitis (primary) (*see also* Tuberculosis) 017.0 ☑
Acomia 704.00
Acontractile bladder 344.61
Aconuresis (*see also* Incontinence) 788.30
Acosta's disease 993.2
Acousma 780.1
Acoustic — *see* condition
Acousticophobia 300.29
Acquired — *see* condition
Acquired immune deficiency syndrome — *see*
  Human immunodeficiency virus (disease)
  (illness) (infection)
Acquired immunodeficiency syndrome — *see*
  Human immunodeficiency virus (disease)
  (illness) (infection)
Acragnosis 781.99
Acrania 740.0
Acroagnosis 781.99
Acroasphyxia, chronic 443.89
Acrobrachycephaly 756.0
Acrobystiolith 608.89
Acrobystitis 607.2
Acrocephalopolysyndactyly 755.55
Acrocephalosyndactyly 755.55
Acrocephaly 756.0
Acrochondrohyperplasia 759.82
Acrocyanosis 443.89
  newborn 770.83
    meaning transient blue hands and feet ●
    — *omit code*   ●
Acrodermatitis 686.8
  atrophicans (chronica) 701.8
  continua (Hallopeau) 696.1
  enteropathica 686.8
  Hallopeau's 696.1
  perstans 696.1
  pustulosa continua 696.1
  recalcitrant pustular 696.1
Acrodynia 985.0
Acrodysplasia 755.55
Acrohyperhidrosis (*see also* Hyperhidrosis) 780.8
Acrokeratosis verruciformis 757.39
Acromastitis 611.0
Acromegaly, acromegalia (skin) 253.0
Acromelalgia 443.82   ▲

Acromicria, acromikria 756.59
Acronyx 703.0
Acropachy, thyroid (*see also* Thyrotoxicosis)
  242.9 ☑
Acropachyderma 757.39
Acroparesthesia 443.89
  simple (Schultz's type) 443.89
  vasomotor (Nothnagel's type) 443.89
Acropathy thyroid (*see also* Thyrotoxicosis)
  242.9 ☑
Acrophobia 300.29
Acroposthitis 607.2
Acroscleriasis (*see also* Scleroderma) 710.1
Acroscleroderma (*see also* Scleroderma) 710.1
Acrosclerosis (*see also* Scleroderma) 710.1
Acrosphacelus 785.4
Acrosphenosyndactylia 755.55
Acrospiroma, eccrine (M8402/0) — *see*
  Neoplasm, skin, benign
Acrostealgia 732.9
Acrosyndactyly (*see also* Syndactylism) 755.10
Acrotrophodynia 991.4
Actinic — *see also* condition
  cheilitis (due to sun) 692.72
    chronic NEC 692.74
    due to radiation, except from sun 692.82
  conjunctivitis 370.24
  dermatitis (due to sun) (*see also* Dermatitis,
    actinic) 692.70
    due to
      roentgen rays or radioactive substance
        692.82
      ultraviolet radiation, except from sun
        692.82
      sun NEC 692.70
  elastosis solare 692.74
  granuloma 692.73
  keratitis 370.24
  ophthalmia 370.24
  reticuloid 692.73
Actinobacillosis, general 027.8
Actinobacillus
  lignieresii 027.8
  mallei 024
  muris 026.1
Actinocutitis NEC (*see also* Dermatitis, actinic)
  692.70
Actinodermatitis NEC (*see also* Dermatitis,
  actinic) 692.70
Actinomyces
  israelii (infection) — *see* Actinomycosis
  muris-ratti (infection) 026.1
Actinomycosis, actinomycotic 039.9
  with
    pneumonia 039.1
  abdominal 039.2
  cervicofacial 039.3
  cutaneous 039.0
  pulmonary 039.1
  specified site NEC 039.8
  thoracic 039.1
Actinoneuritis 357.89
Action, heart
  disorder 427.9
    postoperative 997.1
  irregular 427.9
    postoperative 997.1
    psychogenic 306.2
Active — *see* condition
Activity decrease, functional 780.99
Acute — *see also* condition
  abdomen NEC 789.0 ☑
  gallbladder (*see also* Cholecystitis, acute) 575.0
Acyanoblepsia 368.53
Acyanopsia 368.53
Acystia 753.8
Acystinervia — *see* Neurogenic, bladder
Acystineuria — *see* Neurogenic, bladder

Adactylia, adactyly (congenital) 755.4
   lower limb (complete) (intercalary) (partial)
      (terminal) (*see also* Deformity, reduction,
      lower limb) 755.39
      meaning all digits (complete) (partial) 755.31
      transverse (complete) (partial) 755.31
   upper limb (complete) (intercalary) (partial)
      (terminal) (*see also* Deformity, reduction,
      upper limb) 755.29
      meaning all digits (complete) (partial) 755.21
      transverse (complete) (partial) 755.21

Adair-Dighton syndrome (brittle bones and blue
   sclera, deafness) 756.51

Adamantinoblastoma (M9310/0) — *see*
   Ameloblastoma

Adamantinoma (M9310/0) — *see* Ameloblastoma

Adamantoblastoma (M9310/0) — *see*
   Ameloblastoma

Adams-Stokes (-Morgagni) disease or syndrome
   (syncope with heart block) 426.9

Adaptation reaction (*see also* Reaction,
   adjustment) 309.9

Addiction — *see also* Dependence
   absinthe 304.6 ☑
   alcoholic (ethyl) (methyl) (wood) 303.9 ☑
      complicating pregnancy, childbirth, or
         puerperium 648.4 ☑
         affecting fetus or newborn 760.71
      suspected damage to fetus affecting
         management of pregnancy 655.4 ☑
   drug (*see also* Dependence) 304.9 ☑
   ethyl alcohol 303.9 ☑
   heroin 304.0 ☑
   hospital 301.51
   methyl alcohol 303.9 ☑
   methylated spirit 303.9 ☑
   morphine (-like substances) 304.0 ☑
   nicotine 305.1
   opium 304.0 ☑
   tobacco 305.1
   wine 303.9 ☑

Addison's
   anemia (pernicious) 281.0
   disease (bronze) (primary adrenal insufficiency)
      255.4
      tuberculous (*see also* Tuberculosis) 017.6 ☑
   keloid (morphea) 701.0
   melanoderma (adrenal cortical hypofunction)
      255.4

Addison-Biermer anemia (pernicious) 281.0

Addison-Gull disease — *see* Xanthoma

Addisonian crisis or melanosis (acute
   adrenocortical insufficiency) 255.4

Additional — *see also* Accessory
   chromosome(s) 758.5
      13-15 758.1
      16-18 758.2
      21 758.0
      autosome(s) NEC 758.5
      sex 758.81

Adduction contracture, hip or other joint — *see*
   Contraction, joint

ADEM (acute disseminated encephalomyelitis) ●
   (postinfectious) 136.9 *[323.6]* ●
   infectious 323.6 ●
   noninfectious 323.8 ●

Adenasthenia gastrica 536.0

Aden fever 061

Adenitis (*see also* Lymphadenitis) 289.3
   acute, unspecified site 683
      epidemic infectious 075
   axillary 289.3
      acute 683
      chronic or subacute 289.1
   Bartholin's gland 616.8
   bulbourethral gland (*see also* Urethritis) 597.89
   cervical 289.3
      acute 683
      chronic or subacute 289.1
   chancroid (Ducrey's bacillus) 099.0
   chronic (any lymph node, except mesenteric)
      289.1
      mesenteric 289.2
   Cowper's gland (*see also* Urethritis) 597.89

Adenitis — *continued*
   epidemic, acute 075
   gangrenous 683
   gonorrheal NEC 098.89
   groin 289.3
      acute 683
      chronic or subacute 289.1
   infectious 075
   inguinal (region) 289.3
      acute 683
      chronic or subacute 289.1
   lymph gland or node, except mesenteric 289.3
      acute 683
      chronic or subacute 289.1
      mesenteric (acute) (chronic) (nonspecific)
         (subacute) 289.2
   mesenteric (acute) (chronic) (nonspecific)
      (subacute) 289.2
      due to Pasteurella multocida (P. septica)
         027.2
   parotid gland (suppurative) 527.2
   phlegmonous 683
   salivary duct or gland (any) (recurring)
      (suppurative) 527.2
   scrofulous (*see also* Tuberculosis) 017.2 ☑
   septic 289.3
   Skene's duct or gland (*see also* Urethritis)
      597.89
   strumous, tuberculous (*see also* Tuberculosis)
      017.2 ☑
   subacute, unspecified site 289.1
   sublingual gland (suppurative) 527.2
   submandibular gland (suppurative) 527.2
   submaxillary gland (suppurative) 527.2
   suppurative 683
   tuberculous — *see* Tuberculosis, lymph gland
   urethral gland (*see also* Urethritis) 597.89
   venereal NEC 099.8
   Wharton's duct (suppurative) 527.2

Adenoacanthoma (M8570/3) — *see* Neoplasm, by
   site, malignant

Adenoameloblastoma (M9300/0) 213.1
   upper jaw (bone) 213.0

Adenocarcinoma (M8140/3) — *see also*
   Neoplasm, by site, malignant

> *Note* — The list of adjectival modifiers below is
> not exhaustive. A description of adenocarcinoma
> that does not appear in this list should be coded
> in the same manner as carcinoma with that
> description. Thus, "mixed acidophil-basophil
> adenocarcinoma," should be coded in the same
> manner as "mixed acidophil-basophil
> carcinoma," which appears in the list under
> "Carcinoma."
>
> Except where otherwise indicated, the
> morphological varieties of adenocarcinoma in the
> list below should be coded by site as for
> "Neoplasm, malignant."

   with
      apocrine metaplasia (M8573/3)
      cartilaginous (and osseous) metaplasia
         (M8571/3)
      osseous (and cartilaginous) metaplasia
         (M8571/3)
      spindle cell metaplasia (M8572/3)
      squamous metaplasia (M8570/3)
   acidophil (M8280/3)
      specified site — *see* Neoplasm, by site,
         malignant
      unspecified site 194.3
   acinar (M8550/3)
   acinic cell (M8550/3)
   adrenal cortical (M8370/3) 194.0
   alveolar (M8251/3)
      and
         epidermoid carcinoma, mixed (M8560/3)
         squamous cell carcinoma, mixed
            (M8560/3)
   apocrine (M8401/3)
      breast — *see* Neoplasm, breast, malignant
      specified site NEC — *see* Neoplasm, skin,
         malignant
      unspecified site 173.9

Adenocarcinoma (M8140/3) — *continued*
   basophil (M8300/3)
      specified site — *see* Neoplasm, by site,
         malignant
      unspecified site 194.3
   bile duct type (M8160/3)
      liver 155.1
      specified site NEC — *see* Neoplasm, by site,
         malignant
      unspecified site 155.1
   bronchiolar (M8250/3) — *see* Neoplasm, lung,
      malignant
   ceruminous (M8420/3) 173.2
   chromophobe (M8270/3)
      specified site — *see* Neoplasm, by site,
         malignant
      unspecified site 194.3
   clear cell (mesonephroid type) (M8310/3)
   colloid (M8480/3)
   cylindroid type (M8200/3)
   diffuse type (M8145/3)
      specified site — *see* Neoplasm, by site,
         malignant
      unspecified site 151.9
   duct (infiltrating) (M8500/3)
      with Paget's disease (M8541/3) — *see*
         Neoplasm, breast, malignant
      specified site — *see* Neoplasm, by site,
         malignant
      unspecified site 174.9
   embryonal (M9070/3)
   endometrioid (M8380/3) — *see* Neoplasm, by
      site, malignant
   eosinophil (M8280/3)
      specified site — *see* Neoplasm, by site,
         malignant
      unspecified site 194.3
   follicular (M8330/3)
      and papillary (M8340/3) 193
      moderately differentiated type (M8332/3) 193
      pure follicle type (M8331/3) 193
      specified site — *see* Neoplasm, by site,
         malignant
      trabecular type (M8332/3) 193
      unspecified type 193
      well differentiated type (M8331/3) 193
   gelatinous (M8480/3)
   granular cell (M8320/3)
   Hürthle cell (M8290/3) 193
   in
      adenomatous
         polyp (M8210/3)
         polyposis coli (M8220/3) 153.9
      polypoid adenoma (M8210/3)
      tubular adenoma (M8210/3)
      villous adenoma (M8261/3)
   infiltrating duct (M8500/3)
      with Paget's disease (M8541/3) — *see*
         Neoplasm, breast, malignant
      specified site — *see* Neoplasm, by site,
         malignant
      unspecified site 174.9
   inflammatory (M8530/3)
      specified site — *see* Neoplasm, by site,
         malignant
      unspecified site 174.9
   in situ (M8140/2) — *see* Neoplasm, by site, in
      situ
   intestinal type (M8144/3)
      specified site — *see* Neoplasm, by site,
         malignant
      unspecified site 151.9
   intraductal (noninfiltrating) (M8500/2)
      papillary (M8503/2)
         specified site — *see* Neoplasm, by site, in
            situ
         unspecified site 233.0
      specified site — *see* Neoplasm, by site, in
         situ
      unspecified site 233.0
   islet cell (M8150/3)
      and exocrine, mixed (M8154/3)
         specified site — *see* Neoplasm, by site,
            malignant
      unspecified site 157.9
   pancreas 157.4

☑ Additional Digit Required — Refer to the Tabular List (Numeric Code Section) for Additional Digit Selection
▶◀ Revised Text   ● New Line   ▲ Revised Code

2006 ICD-9-CM   October 2005 • Volume 2 — 11

Adenocarcinoma (M8140/3) — *continued*
  islet cell — *continued*
    specified site NEC — *see* Neoplasm, by site,
      malignant
    unspecified site 157.4
  lobular (M8520/3)
    specified site — *see* Neoplasm, by site,
      malignant
    unspecified site 174.9
  medullary (M8510/3)
  mesonephric (M9110/3)
  mixed cell (M8323/3)
  mucinous (M8480/3)
  mucin-producing (M8481/3)
  mucoid (M8480/3) — *see also* Neoplasm, by
    site, malignant
    cell (M8300/3)
      specified site — *see* Neoplasm, by site,
        malignant
      unspecified site 194.3
  nonencapsulated sclerosing (M8350/3) 193
  oncocytic (M8290/3)
  oxyphilic (M8290/3)
  papillary (M8260/3)
    and follicular (M8340/3) 193
    intraductal (noninfiltrating) (M8503/2)
      specified site — *see* Neoplasm, by site, in
        situ
      unspecified site 233.0
    serous (M8460/3)
      specified site — *see* Neoplasm, by site,
        malignant
      unspecified site 183.0
  papillocystic (M8450/3)
    specified site — *see* Neoplasm, by site,
      malignant
    unspecified site 183.0
  pseudomucinous (M8470/3)
    specified site — *see* Neoplasm, by site,
      malignant
    unspecified site 183.0
  renal cell (M8312/3) 189.0
  sebaceous (M8410/3)
  serous (M8441/3) — *see also* Neoplasm, by
    site, malignant
    papillary
      specified site — *see* Neoplasm, by site,
        malignant
      unspecified site 183.0
  signet ring cell (M8490/3)
  superficial spreading (M8143/3)
  sweat gland (M8400/3) — *see* Neoplasm, skin,
    malignant
  trabecular (M8190/3)
  tubular (M8211/3)
  villous (M8262/3)
  water-clear cell (M8322/3) 194.1
Adenofibroma (M9013/0)
  clear cell (M8313/0) — *see* Neoplasm, by site,
    benign
  endometrioid (M8381/0) 220
    borderline malignancy (M8381/1) 236.2
    malignant (M8381/3) 183.0
  mucinous (M9015/0)
    specified site — *see* Neoplasm, by site,
      benign
    unspecified site 220
  prostate 600.20
    with urinary retention 600.21
  serous (M9014/0)
    specified site — *see* Neoplasm, by site,
      benign
    unspecified site 220
  specified site — *see* Neoplasm, by site, benign
  unspecified site 220
Adenofibrosis
  breast 610.2
  endometrioid 617.0
Adenoiditis 474.01
  acute 463
  chronic 474.01
    with chronic tonsillitis 474.02
Adenoids (congenital) (of nasal fossa) 474.9
  hypertrophy 474.12
  vegetations 474.2
Adenolipomatosis (symmetrical) 272.8

Adenolymphoma (M8561/0)
  specified site — *see* Neoplasm, by site, benign
  unspecified 210.2
Adenoma (sessile) (M8140/0) — *see also*
  Neoplasm, by site, benign

> *Note* — Except where otherwise indicated, the
> morphological varieties of adenoma in the list
> below should be coded by site as for "Neoplasm,
> benign."

  acidophil (M8280/0)
    specified site — *see* Neoplasm, by site,
      benign
    unspecified site 227.3
  acinar (cell) (M8550/0)
  acinic cell (M8550/0)
  adrenal (cortex) (cortical) (functioning)
    (M8370/0) 227.0
    clear cell type (M8373/0) 227.0
    compact cell type (M8371/0) 227.0
    glomerulosa cell type (M8374/0) 227.0
    heavily pigmented variant (M8372/0) 227.0
    mixed cell type (M8375/0) 227.0
  alpha cell (M8152/0)
    pancreas 211.7
    specified site NEC — *see* Neoplasm, by site,
      benign
    unspecified site 211.7
  alveolar (M8251/0)
  apocrine (M8401/0)
    breast 217
    specified site NEC — *see* Neoplasm, skin,
      benign
    unspecified site 216.9
  basal cell (M8147/0)
  basophil (M8300/0)
    specified site — *see* Neoplasm, by site,
      benign
    unspecified site 227.3
  beta cell (M8151/0)
    pancreas 211.7
    specified site NEC — *see* Neoplasm, by site,
      benign
    unspecified site 211.7
  bile duct (M8160/0) 211.5
  black (M8372/0) 227.0
  bronchial (M8140/1) 235.7
    carcinoid type (M8240/3) — *see* Neoplasm,
      lung, malignant
    cylindroid type (M8200/3) — *see* Neoplasm,
      lung, malignant
  ceruminous (M8420/0) 216.2
  chief cell (M8321/0) 227.1
  chromophobe (M8270/0)
    specified site — *see* Neoplasm, by site,
      benign
    unspecified site 227.3
  clear cell (M8310/0)
  colloid (M8334/0)
    specified site — *see* Neoplasm, by site,
      benign
    unspecified site 226
  cylindroid type, bronchus (M8200/3) — *see*
    Neoplasm, lung, malignant
  duct (M8503/0)
  embryonal (M8191/0)
  endocrine, multiple (M8360/1)
    single specified site — *see* Neoplasm, by site,
      uncertain behavior
    two or more specified sites 237.4
    unspecified site 237.4
  endometrioid (M8380/0) — *see also* Neoplasm,
    by site, benign
    borderline malignancy (M8380/1) — *see*
      Neoplasm, by site, uncertain behavior
  eosinophil (M8280/0)
    specified site — *see* Neoplasm, by site,
      benign
    unspecified site 227.3
  fetal (M8333/0)
    specified site — *see* Neoplasm, by site,
      benign
    unspecified site 226
  follicular (M8330/0)
    specified site — *see* Neoplasm, by site,
      benign
    unspecified site 226

Adenoma (M8140/0) — *see also* Neoplasm, by
  site, benign — *continued*
  hepatocellular (M8170/0) 211.5
  Hürthle cell (M8290/0) 226
  intracystic papillary (M8504/0)
  islet cell (functioning) (M8150/0)
    pancreas 211.7
    specified site NEC — *see* Neoplasm, by site,
      benign
    unspecified site 211.7
  liver cell (M8170/0) 211.5
  macrofollicular (M8334/0)
    specified site NEC — *see* Neoplasm, by site,
      benign
    unspecified site 226
  malignant, malignum (M8140/3) — *see*
    Neoplasm, by site, malignant
  mesonephric (M9110/0)
  microfollicular (M8333/0)
    specified site — *see* Neoplasm, by site,
      benign
    unspecified site 226
  mixed cell (M8323/0)
  monomorphic (M8146/0)
  mucinous (M8480/0)
  mucoid cell (M8300/0)
    specified site — *see* Neoplasm, by site,
      benign
    unspecified site 227.3
  multiple endocrine (M8360/1)
    single specified site — *see* Neoplasm, by site,
      uncertain behavior
    two or more specified sites 237.4
    unspecified site 237.4
  nipple (M8506/0) 217
  oncocytic (M8290/0)
  oxyphilic (M8290/0)
  papillary (M8260/0) — *see also* Neoplasm, by
    site, benign
    intracystic (M8504/0)
  papillotubular (M8263/0)
  Pick's tubular (M8640/0)
    specified site — *see* Neoplasm, by site,
      benign
    unspecified site
      female 220
      male 222.0
  pleomorphic (M8940/0)
  polypoid (M8210/0)
  prostate (benign) 600.20
    with urinary retention 600.21
  rete cell 222.0
  sebaceous, sebaceum (gland) (senile) (M8410/0)
    — *see also* Neoplasm, skin, benign
    disseminata 759.5
  Sertoli cell (M8640/0)
    specified site — *see* Neoplasm, by site,
      benign
    unspecified site
      female 220
      male 222.0
  skin appendage (M8390/0) — *see* Neoplasm,
    skin, benign
  sudoriferous gland (M8400/0) — *see* Neoplasm,
    skin, benign
  sweat gland or duct (M8400/0) — *see*
    Neoplasm, skin, benign
  testicular (M8640/0)
    specified site — *see* Neoplasm, by site, benign
    unspecified site
      female 220
      male 222.0
  thyroid 226
  trabecular (M8190/0)
  tubular (M8211/0) — *see also* Neoplasm, by
    site, benign
    papillary (M8460/3)
    Pick's (M8640/0)
      specified site — *see* Neoplasm, by site,
        benign
      unspecified site
        female 220
        male 222.0
  tubulovillous (M8263/0)
  villoglandular (M8263/0)
  villous (M8261/1) — *see* Neoplasm, by site,
    uncertain behavior

Adenoma (M8140/0) — *see also* Neoplasm, by
site, benign — *continued*
  water-clear cell (M8322/0) 227.1
  wolffian duct (M9110/0)
Adenomatosis (M8220/0)
  endocrine (multiple) (M8360/1)
    single specified site — *see* Neoplasm, by site,
     uncertain behavior
    two or more specified sites 237.4
    unspecified site 237.4
  erosive of nipple (M8506/0) 217
  pluriendocrine — *see* Adenomatosis, endocrine
  pulmonary (M8250/1) 235.7
    malignant (M8250/3) — *see* Neoplasm, lung,
     malignant
  specified site — *see* Neoplasm, by site, benign
  unspecified site 211.3
Adenomatous
  cyst, thyroid (gland) — *see* Goiter, nodular
  goiter (nontoxic) (*see also* Goiter, nodular)
    241.9
    toxic or with hyperthyroidism 242.3 ☑
Adenomyoma (M8932/0) — *see also* Neoplasm,
by site, benign
  prostate 600.20
    with urinary retention 600.21
Adenomyometritis 617.0
Adenomyosis (uterus) (internal) 617.0
Adenopathy (lymph gland) 785.6
  inguinal 785.6
  mediastinal 785.6
  mesentery 785.6
  syphilitic (secondary) 091.4
  tracheobronchial 785.6
    tuberculous (*see also* Tuberculosis) 012.1 ☑
     primary, progressive 010.8 ☑
  tuberculous (*see also* Tuberculosis, lymph
    gland) 017.2 ☑
    tracheobronchial 012.1 ☑
     primary, progressive 010.8 ☑
Adenopharyngitis 462
Adenophlegmon 683
Adenosalpingitis 614.1
Adenosarcoma (M8960/3) 189.0
Adenosclerosis 289.3
Adenosis
  breast (sclerosing) 610.2
  vagina, congenital 752.49
Adentia (complete) (partial) (*see also* Absence,
teeth) 520.0
Adherent
  labium (minus) 624.4
  pericardium (nonrheumatic) 423.1
    rheumatic 393
  placenta 667.0 ☑
    with hemorrhage 666.0 ☑
  prepuce 605
  scar (skin) NEC 709.2
  tendon in scar 709.2
Adhesion(s), adhesive (postinfectional)
(postoperative)
  abdominal (wall) (*see also* Adhesions,
    peritoneum) 568.0
  amnion to fetus 658.8 ☑
    affecting fetus or newborn 762.8
  appendix 543.9
  arachnoiditis — *see* Meningitis
  auditory tube (Eustachian) 381.89
  bands — *see also* Adhesions, peritoneum
    cervix 622.3
    uterus 621.5
  bile duct (any) 576.8
  bladder (sphincter) 596.8
  bowel (*see also* Adhesions, peritoneum) 568.0
  cardiac 423.1
    rheumatic 398.99
  cecum (*see also* Adhesions, peritoneum) 568.0
  cervicovaginal 622.3
    congenital 752.49
    postpartal 674.8 ☑
     old 622.3
  cervix 622.3
  clitoris 624.4
  colon (*see also* Adhesions, peritoneum) 568.0

Adhesion(s), adhesive — *continued*
  common duct 576.8
  congenital — *see also* Anomaly, specified type
    NEC
    fingers (*see also* Syndactylism, fingers)
     755.11
    labium (majus) (minus) 752.49
    omental, anomalous 751.4
    ovary 752.0
    peritoneal 751.4
    toes (*see also* Syndactylism, toes) 755.13
    tongue (to gum or roof of mouth) 750.12
  conjunctiva (acquired) (localized) 372.62
    congenital 743.63
    extensive 372.63
  cornea — *see* Opacity, cornea
  cystic duct 575.8
  diaphragm (*see also* Adhesions, peritoneum)
    568.0
  due to foreign body — *see* Foreign body
  duodenum (*see also* Adhesions, peritoneum)
    568.0
    with obstruction 537.3
  ear, middle — *see* Adhesions, middle ear
  epididymis 608.89
  epidural — *see* Adhesions, meninges
  epiglottis 478.79
  Eustachian tube 381.89
  eyelid 374.46
    postoperative 997.99
     surgically created V45.69
  gallbladder (*see also* Disease, gallbladder)
    575.8
  globe 360.89
  heart 423.1
    rheumatic 398.99
  ileocecal (coil) (*see also* Adhesions, peritoneum)
    568.0
  ileum (*see also* Adhesions, peritoneum) 568.0
  intestine (postoperative) (*see also* Adhesions,
    peritoneum) 568.0
    with obstruction 560.81
     with hernia — *see also* Hernia, by site,
      with obstruction
       gangrenous — *see* Hernia, by site,
        with gangrene
  intra-abdominal (*see also* Adhesions,
    peritoneum) 568.0
  iris 364.70
    to corneal graft 996.79
  joint (*see also* Ankylosis) 718.5 ☑
  kidney 593.89
  labium (majus) (minus), congenital 752.49
  liver 572.8
  lung 511.0
  mediastinum 519.3
  meninges 349.2
    cerebral (any) 349.2
     congenital 742.4
    congenital 742.8
    spinal (any) 349.2
     congenital 742.59
    tuberculous (cerebral) (spinal) (*see also*
     Tuberculosis, meninges) 013.0 ☑
  mesenteric (*see also* Adhesions, peritoneum)
    568.0
  middle ear (fibrous) 385.10
    drum head 385.19
     to
      incus 385.11
      promontorium 385.13
      stapes 385.12
    specified NEC 385.19
  nasal (septum) (to turbinates) 478.1
  nerve NEC 355.9
    spinal 355.9
     root 724.9
      cervical NEC 723.4
      lumbar NEC 724.4
      lumbosacral 724.4
      thoracic 724.4
  ocular muscle 378.60
  omentum (*see also* Adhesions, peritoneum)
    568.0
  organ or site, congenital NEC — *see* Anomaly,
    specified type NEC

Adhesion(s), adhesive — *continued*
  ovary 614.6
    congenital (to cecum, kidney, or omentum)
     752.0
  parauterine 614.6
  parovarian 614.6
  pelvic (peritoneal)
    female (postoperative) (postinfection) 614.6
    male (postoperative) (postinfection) (*see also*
     Adhesions, peritoneum) 568.0
    postpartal (old) 614.6
    tuberculous (*see also* Tuberculosis) 016.9 ☑
  penis to scrotum (congenital) 752.69
  periappendiceal (*see also* Adhesions,
    peritoneum) 568.0
  pericardium (nonrheumatic) 423.1
    rheumatic 393
    tuberculous (*see also* Tuberculosis) 017.9 ☑
     [420.0]
  pericholecystic 575.8
  perigastric (*see also* Adhesions, peritoneum)
    568.0
  periovarian 614.6
  periprostatic 602.8
  perirectal (*see also* Adhesions, peritoneum)
    568.0
  perirenal 593.89
  peritoneum, peritoneal (fibrous) (postoperative)
    568.0
    with obstruction (intestinal) 560.81
     with hernia — *see also* Hernia, by site,
      with obstruction
       gangrenous — *see* Hernia, by site,
        with gangrene
     duodenum 537.3
    congenital 751.4
    female (postoperative) (postinfective) 614.6
    pelvic, female 614.6
    pelvic, male 568.0
    postpartal, pelvic 614.6
    to uterus 614.6
  peritubal 614.6
  periureteral 593.89
  periuterine 621.5
  perivesical 596.8
  perivesicular (seminal vesicle) 608.89
  pleura, pleuritic 511.0
    tuberculous (*see also* Tuberculosis, pleura)
     012.0 ☑
  pleuropericardial 511.0
  postoperative (gastrointestinal tract) (*see also*
    Adhesions, peritoneum) 568.0
    eyelid 997.99
     surgically created V45.69
    pelvic female 614.9
    pelvic male 568.0
    urethra 598.2
  postpartal, old 624.4
  preputial, prepuce 605
  pulmonary 511.0
  pylorus (*see also* Adhesions, peritoneum) 568.0
  Rosenmüller's fossa 478.29
  sciatic nerve 355.0
  seminal vesicle 608.89
  shoulder (joint) 726.0
  sigmoid flexure (*see also* Adhesions,
    peritoneum) 568.0
  spermatic cord (acquired) 608.89
    congenital 752.89
  spinal canal 349.2
    nerve 355.9
     root 724.9
      cervical NEC 723.4
      lumbar NEC 724.4
      lumbosacral 724.4
      thoracic 724.4
  stomach (*see also* Adhesions, peritoneum)
    568.0
  subscapular 726.2
  tendonitis 726.90
    shoulder 726.0
  testicle 608.89
  tongue (congenital) (to gum or roof of mouth)
    750.12
    acquired 529.8
  trachea 519.1
  tubo-ovarian 614.6

☑ Additional Digit Required — Refer to the Tabular List (Numeric Code Section) for Additional Digit Selection
►◄ Revised Text   ● New Line   ▲ Revised Code

Index

Adhesion(s), adhesive — Admission

Admission — *continued*
  for — *continued*
    counseling (*see also* Counseling) — *continued*
      HIV V65.44
      human immunodeficiency virus V65.44
      injury prevention V65.43
      insulin pump training V65.46
      procreative management V26.4
      sexually transmitted disease NEC V65.45
        HIV V65.44
      specified reason NEC V65.49
      substance use and abuse V65.42
      syphilis V65.45
      victim of abuse
        child V61.21
        partner or spouse V61.11
    desensitization to allergens V07.1
    dialysis V56.0
      catheter
        fitting and adjustment
          extracorporeal V56.1
          peritoneal V56.2
        removal or replacement
          extracorporeal V56.1
          peritoneal V56.2
      extracorporeal (renal) V56.0
      peritoneal V56.8
      renal V56.0
    dietary surveillance and counseling V65.3
    drug monitoring, therapeutic V58.83
    ear piercing V50.3
    elective surgery V50.9
      breast
        augmentation or reduction V50.1
        removal, prophylactic V50.41
      circumcision, ritual or routine (in absence of medical indication) V50.2
      cosmetic NEC V50.1
        following healed injury or operation V51
      ear piercing V50.3
      face-lift V50.1
      hair transplant V50.0
      plastic
        cosmetic NEC V50.1
        following healed injury or operation V51
      prophylactic organ removal V50.49
        breast V50.41
        ovary V50.42
      repair of scarred tissue (following healed injury or operation) V51
      specified type NEC V50.8
    end-of-life care V66.7
    examination (*see also* Examination) V70.9
      administrative purpose NEC V70.3
      adoption V70.3
      allergy V72.7
      at health care facility V70.0
      athletic team V70.3
      camp V70.3
      cardiovascular, preoperative V72.81
      clinical research investigation (control) (participant) V70.7
      dental V72.2
      developmental testing (child) (infant) V20.2
      donor (potential) V70.8
      driver's license V70.3
      ear V72.1
      employment V70.5
      eye V72.0
      follow-up (routine) — *see* Examination, follow-up
      for admission to
        old age home V70.3
        school V70.3
      general V70.9
        specified reason NEC V70.8
      gynecological V72.31
      health supervision (child) (infant) V20.2
      hearing V72.1
      immigration V70.3
      insurance certification V70.3
      laboratory V72.6

Admission — *continued*
  for — *continued*
    examination (*see also* Examination) — *continued*
      marriage license V70.3
      medical (general) (*see also* Examination, medical) V70.9
      medicolegal reasons V70.4
      naturalization V70.3
      pelvic (annual) (periodic) V72.31
      postpartum checkup V24.2
      pregnancy (possible) (unconfirmed) V72.40
        negative result V72.41
        positive result V72.42 ●
      preoperative V72.84
        cardiovascular V72.81
        respiratory V72.82
        specified NEC V72.83
      preprocedural V72.84 ●
        cardiovascular V72.81 ●
        general physical V72.83 ●
        respiratory V72.82 ●
        specified NEC V72.83 ●
      prison V70.3
      psychiatric (general) V70.2
        requested by authority V70.1
      radiological NEC V72.5
      respiratory, preoperative V72.82
      school V70.3
      screening — *see* Screening
      skin hypersensitivity V72.7
      specified type NEC V72.85
      sport competition V70.3
      vision V72.0
      well baby and child care V20.2
    exercise therapy V57.1
    face-lift, cosmetic reason V50.1
    fitting (of)
      artificial
        arm (complete) (partial) V52.0
        eye V52.2
        leg (complete) (partial) V52.1
      biliary drainage tube V58.82
      brain neuropacemaker V53.02
      breast V52.4
        implant V52.4
        prosthesis V52.4
      cardiac pacemaker V53.31
      catheter
        non-vascular V58.82
        vascular V58.81
      cerebral ventricle (communicating) shunt V53.01
      chest tube V58.82
      colostomy belt V55.2
      contact lenses V53.1
      cystostomy device V53.6
      dental prosthesis V52.3
      device, unspecified type V53.90
        abdominal V53.5
        cerebral ventricle (communicating) shunt V53.01
        insulin pump V53.91
        intrauterine contraceptive V25.1
        nervous system V53.09
        orthodontic V53.4
        other device V53.99
        prosthetic V52.9
          breast V52.4
          dental V52.3
          eye V52.2
          special senses V53.09
        substitution
          auditory V53.09
          nervous system V53.09
          visual V53.09
      diaphragm (contraceptive) V25.02
      fistula (sinus tract) drainage tube V58.82
      growth rod V54.02
      hearing aid V53.2
      ileostomy device V55.2
      intestinal appliance or device NEC V53.5
      intrauterine contraceptive device V25.1
      neuropacemaker (brain) (peripheral nerve) (spinal cord) V53.02

Admission — *continued*
  for — *continued*
    fitting (of) — *continued*
      orthodontic device V53.4
      orthopedic (device) V53.7
        brace V53.7
        cast V53.7
        shoes V53.7
      pacemaker
        brain V53.02
        cardiac V53.31
        carotid sinus V53.39
        spinal cord V53.02
      pleural drainage tube V58.82
      prosthesis V52.9
        arm (complete) (partial) V52.0
        breast V52.4
        dental V52.3
        eye V52.2
        leg (complete) (partial) V52.1
        specified type NEC V52.8
      spectacles V53.1
      wheelchair V53.8
    follow-up examination (routine) (following) V67.9
      cancer chemotherapy V67.2
      chemotherapy V67.2
      high-risk medication NEC V67.51
      injury NEC V67.59
      psychiatric V67.3
      psychotherapy V67.3
      radiotherapy V67.1
      specified surgery NEC V67.09
      surgery V67.00
        vaginal pap smear V67.01
      treatment (for) V67.9
        combined V67.6
        fracture V67.4
        involving high-risk medication NEC V67.51
        mental disorder V67.3
        specified NEC V67.59
    hair transplant, for cosmetic reason V50.0
    health advice, education, or instruction V65.4 ☑
    hormone replacement therapy (postmenopausal) V07.4
    hospice care V66.7
    immunotherapy, antineoplastic V58.12 ●
    insertion (of)
      subdermal implantable contraceptive V25.5
    insulin pump titration V53.91
    insulin pump training V65.46
    intrauterine device
      insertion V25.1
      management V25.42
    investigation to determine further disposition V63.8
    isolation V07.0
    issue of
      medical certificate NEC V68.0
      repeat prescription NEC V68.1
        contraceptive device NEC V25.49
    kidney dialysis V56.0
    lengthening of growth rod V54.02
    mental health evaluation V70.2
      requested by authority V70.1
    nonmedical reason NEC V68.89
    nursing care evaluation V63.8
    observation (without need for further medical care) (*see also* Observation) V71.9
      accident V71.4
      alleged rape or seduction V71.5
      criminal assault V71.6
      following accident V71.4
        at work V71.3
      foreign body ingestion V71.89
      growth and development variations, childhood V21.0
      inflicted injury NEC V71.6
      ingestion of deleterious agent or foreign body V71.89
      injury V71.6
      malignant neoplasm V71.1
      mental disorder V71.09

Admission — *continued*
  for — *continued*
    observation (*see also* Observation) — *continued*
      newborn — *see* Observation, suspected, condition, newborn
      rape V71.5
      specified NEC V71.89
      suspected disorder V71.9
        abuse V71.81
        accident V71.4
          at work V71.3
        benign neoplasm V71.89
        cardiovascular V71.7
        exposure
          anthrax V71.82
          biological agent NEC V71.83
          SARS V71.83
        heart V71.7
        inflicted injury NEC V71.6
        malignant neoplasm V71.1
        mental NEC V71.09
        neglect V71.81
        specified condition NEC V71.89
        tuberculosis V71.2
      tuberculosis V71.2
    occupational therapy V57.21
    organ transplant, donor — *see* Donor
    ovary, ovarian removal, prophylactic V50.42
    palliative care V66.7
    Papanicolaou smear
      cervix V76.2
        for suspected malignant neoplasm V76.2
          no disease found V71.1
        routine, as part of gynecological examination V72.31
        to confirm findings of recent normal smear following initial abnormal smear V72.32
      vaginal V76.47
        following hysterectomy for malignant condition V67.01
    passage of sounds or bougie in artificial opening — *see* Attention to, artificial, opening
    paternity testing V70.4
    peritoneal dialysis V56.32
    physical therapy NEC V57.1
    plastic surgery
      cosmetic NEC V50.1
      following healed injury or operation V51
    postmenopausal hormone replacement therapy V07.4
    postpartum observation
      immediately after delivery V24.0
      routine follow-up V24.2
    poststerilization (for restoration) V26.0
    procreative management V26.9
      specified type NEC V26.8
    prophylactic
      administration of
        antibiotics V07.39
        antitoxin, any V07.2
        antivenin V07.2
        chemotherapeutic agent NEC V07.39
        chemotherapy NEC V07.39
        diphtheria antitoxin V07.2
        fluoride V07.31
        gamma globulin V07.2
        immune sera (gamma globulin) V07.2
        RhoGAM V07.2
        tetanus antitoxin V07.2
      breathing exercises V57.0
      chemotherapy NEC V07.39
        fluoride V07.31
      measure V07.9
        specified type NEC V07.8
      organ removal V50.49
        breast V50.41
        ovary V50.42
    psychiatric examination (general) V70.2
      requested by authority V70.1
    radiation management V58.0
    radiotherapy V58.0
    reforming of artificial opening — *see* Attention to, artificial, opening

Admission — *continued*
  for — *continued*
    rehabilitation V57.9
      multiple types V57.89
      occupational V57.21
      orthoptic V57.4
      orthotic V57.81
      physical NEC V57.1
      specified type NEC V57.89
      speech V57.3
      vocational V57.22
    removal of
      cardiac pacemaker V53.31
      cast (plaster) V54.89
      catheter from artificial opening — *see* Attention to, artificial, opening
      cerebral ventricle (communicating) shunt V53.01
      cystostomy catheter V55.5
      device
        cerebral ventricle (communicating) shunt V53.01
        fixation
          external V54.89
          internal V54.01
        intrauterine contraceptive V25.42
        traction, external V54.89
      dressing V58.3
      fixation device
        external V54.89
        internal V54.01
      intrauterine contraceptive device V25.42
      Kirschner wire V54.89
      neuropacemaker (brain) (peripheral nerve) (spinal cord) V53.02
      orthopedic fixation device
        external V54.89
        internal V54.01
      pacemaker device
        brain V53.02
        cardiac V53.31
        carotid sinus V53.39
        nervous system V53.02
      plaster cast V54.89
      plate (fracture) V54.01
      rod V54.01
      screw (fracture) V54.01
      splint, traction V54.89
      Steinmann pin V54.89
      subdermal implantable contraceptive V25.43
      surgical dressing V58.3
      sutures V58.3
      traction device, external V54.89
      ureteral stent V53.6
    repair of scarred tissue (following healed injury or operation) V51
    reprogramming of cardiac pacemaker V53.31
    respirator ►[ventilator]◄ dependence   ●
      during   ●
        mechanical failure V46.14   ●
        power failure V46.12   ●
      for weaning V46.13   ●
    restoration of organ continuity (poststerilization) (tuboplasty) (vasoplasty) V26.0
    sensitivity test — *see also* Test, skin
      allergy NEC V72.7
      bacterial disease NEC V74.9
      Dick V74.8
      Kveim V82.89
      Mantoux V74.1
      mycotic infection NEC V75.4
      parasitic disease NEC V75.8
      Schick V74.3
      Schultz-Charlton V74.8
    social service (agency) referral or evaluation V63.8
    speech therapy V57.3
    sterilization V25.2
    suspected disorder (ruled out) (without need for further care) — *see* Observation
    terminal care V66.7
    tests only — *see* Test
    therapeutic drug monitoring V58.83

Admission — *continued*
  for — *continued*
    therapy
      blood transfusion, without reported diagnosis V58.2
      breathing exercises V57.0
      chemotherapy, ►antineoplastic◄ V58.11   ▲
        prophylactic NEC V07.39
        fluoride V07.31
      dialysis (intermittent) (treatment)
        extracorporeal V56.0
        peritoneal V56.8
        renal V56.0
        specified type NEC V56.8
      exercise (remedial) NEC V57.1
        breathing V57.0
      immunotherapy, antineoplastic V58.12   ● ●
      long-term (current) drug use NEC V58.69
        antibiotics V58.62
        anticoagulants V58.61
        anti-inflammatories, non-steroidal (NSAID) V58.64
        antiplatelets V58.63
        antithrombotics V58.63
        aspirin V58.66
        insulin V58.67
        steroids V58.65
      occupational V57.21
      orthoptic V57.4
      physical NEC V57.1
      radiation V58.0
      speech V57.3
      vocational V57.22
    toilet or cleaning
      of artificial opening — *see* Attention to, artificial, opening
      of non-vascular catheter V58.82
      of vascular catheter V58.81
    tubal ligation V25.2
    tuboplasty for previous sterilization V26.0
    vaccination, prophylactic (against)
      arthropod-borne virus, viral NEC V05.1
        disease NEC V05.1
        encephalitis V05.0
      Bacille Calmette Guérin (BCG) V03.2
      BCG V03.2
      chickenpox V05.4
      cholera alone V03.0
        with typhoid-paratyphoid (cholera + TAB) V06.0
      common cold V04.7
      dengue V05.1
      diphtheria alone V03.5
      diphtheria-tetanus-pertussis (DTP) (DTaP) V06.1
        with
          poliomyelitis (DTP + polio) V06.3
          typhoid-paratyphoid (DTP + TAB) V06.2
      diphtheria-tetanus [Td] [DT] without pertussis V06.5
      disease (single) NEC V05.9
        bacterial NEC V03.9
          specified type NEC V03.89
        combinations NEC V06.9
          specified type NEC V06.8
        specified type NEC V05.8
        viral NEC V04.89
      encephalitis, viral, arthropod-borne V05.0
      Hemophilus influenzae, type B [Hib] V03.81
      hepatitis, viral V05.3
      immune sera (gamma globulin) V07.2
      influenza V04.81
        with
          Streptococcus pneumoniae [pneumococcus] V06.6
      Leishmaniasis V05.2
      measles alone V04.2
      measles-mumps-rubella (MMR) V06.4
      mumps alone V04.6
        with measles and rubella (MMR) V06.4
      not done because of contraindication V64.09   ▲
      pertussis alone V03.6

☑ Additional Digit Required — Refer to the Tabular List (Numeric Code Section) for Additional Digit Selection

Admission — *continued*
  for — *continued*
    vaccination, prophylactic — *continued*
      plague V03.3
      pneumonia V03.82
      poliomyelitis V04.0
        with diphtheria-tetanus-pertussis
          (DTP+ polio) V06.3
      rabies V04.5
      respiratory syncytial virus (RSV) V04.82
      rubella alone V04.3
        with measles and mumps (MMR)
          V06.4
      smallpox V04.1
      specified type NEC V05.8
      Streptococcus pneumoniae
        [pneumococcus] V03.82
        with
          influenza V06.6
      tetanus toxoid alone V03.7
        with diphtheria [Td] [DT] V06.5
          and pertussis (DTP) (DTaP) V06.1
      tuberculosis (BCG) V03.2
      tularemia V03.4
      typhoid alone V03.1
        with diphtheria-tetanus-pertussis (TAB
          + DTP) V06.2
      typhoid-paratyphoid alone (TAB) V03.1
      typhus V05.8
      varicella (chicken pox) V05.4
      viral encephalitis, arthropod-borne V05.0
      viral hepatitis V05.3
      yellow fever V04.4
    vasectomy V25.2
    vasoplasty for previous sterilization V26.0
    vision examination V72.0
    vocational therapy V57.22
    waiting period for admission to other facility
      V63.2
      undergoing social agency investigation
        V63.8
    well baby and child care V20.2
    x-ray of chest
      for suspected tuberculosis V71.2
      routine V72.5

Adnexitis (suppurative) (*see also* Salpingo-
  oophoritis) 614.2

Adolescence NEC V21.2

Adoption
  agency referral V68.89
  examination V70.3
  held for V68.89

Adrenal gland — *see* condition

Adrenalism 255.9
  tuberculous (*see also* Tuberculosis) 017.6 ☑

Adrenalitis, adrenitis 255.8
  meningococcal hemorrhagic 036.3

Adrenarche, precocious 259.1

Adrenocortical syndrome 255.2

Adrenogenital syndrome (acquired) (congenital)
  255.2
  iatrogenic, fetus or newborn 760.79

Adrenoleukodystrophy 277.86
  neonatal 277.86
  x-linked 277.86

Adrenomyeloneuropathy 277.86

Adventitious bursa — *see* Bursitis

Adynamia (episodica) (hereditary) (periodic) 359.3

Adynamic
  ileus or intestine (*see also* Ileus) 560.1
  ureter 753.22

Aeration lung, imperfect, newborn 770.5

Aerobullosis 993.3

Aerocele — *see* Embolism, air

Aerodermectasia
  subcutaneous (traumatic) 958.7
    surgical 998.81
  surgical 998.81

Aerodontalgia 993.2

Aeroembolism 993.3

Aerogenes capsulatus infection (*see also*
  Gangrene, gas) 040.0

Aero-otitis media 993.0

Aerophagy, aerophagia 306.4
  psychogenic 306.4

Aerosinusitis 993.1

Aerotitis 993.0

Affection, affections — *see also* Disease
  sacroiliac (joint), old 724.6
  shoulder region NEC 726.2

Afibrinogenemia 286.3
  acquired 286.6
  congenital 286.3
  postpartum 666.3 ☑

African
  sleeping sickness 086.5
  tick fever 087.1
  trypanosomiasis 086.5
    Gambian 086.3
    Rhodesian 086.4

Aftercare V58.9
  artificial openings — *see* Attention to, artificial,
    opening
  blood transfusion without reported diagnosis
    V58.2
  breathing exercise V57.0
  cardiac device V53.39
    defibrillator, automatic implantable V53.32
    pacemaker V53.31
      carotid sinus V53.39
  carotid sinus pacemaker V53.39
  cerebral ventricle (communicating) shunt
    V53.01
  chemotherapy session (adjunctive)
    (maintenance) V58.11 ▲
  defibrillator, automatic implantable cardiac
    V53.32
  exercise (remedial) (therapeutic) V57.1
    breathing V57.0
  extracorporeal dialysis (intermittent)
    (treatment) V56.0
  following surgery NEC V58.49
    for
      injury V58.43
      neoplasm V58.42
      organ transplant V58.44
      trauma V58.43
    joint replacement V54.81
    of
      circulatory system V58.73
      digestive system V58.75
      genital organs V58.76
      genitourinary system V58.76
      musculoskeletal system V58.78
      nervous system V58.72
      oral cavity V58.75
      respiratory system V58.74
      sense organs V58.71
      skin V58.77
      subcutaneous tissue V58.77
      teeth V58.75
      urinary system V58.76
    wound closure, planned V58.41
  fracture V54.9
    healing V54.89
      pathologic
        ankle V54.29
        arm V54.20
          lower V54.22
          upper V54.21
        finger V54.29
        foot V54.29
        hand V54.29
        hip V54.23
        leg V54.24
          lower V54.26
          upper V54.25
        pelvis V54.29
        specified site NEC V54.29
        toe(s) V54.29
        vertebrae V54.27
        wrist V54.29
      traumatic
        ankle V54.19
        arm V54.10
          lower V54.12
          upper V54.11
        finger V54.19
        foot V54.19

Aftercare — *continued*
  fracture — *continued*
    healing — *continued*
      traumatic — *continued*
        hand V54.19
        hip V54.13
        leg V54.14
          lower V54.16
          upper V54.15
        pelvis V54.19
        specified site NEC V54.19
        toe(s) V54.19
        vertebrae V54.17
        wrist V54.19
    removal of
      external fixation device V54.89
      internal fixation device V54.01
    specified care NEC V54.89
  gait training V57.1
    for use of artificial limb(s) V57.81
  internal fixation device V54.09
  involving
    dialysis (intermittent) (treatment)
      extracorporeal V56.0
      peritoneal V56.8
      renal V56.0
    gait training V57.1
      for use of artificial limb(s) V57.81
    growth rod
      adjustment V54.02
      lengthening V54.02
    internal fixation device V54.09
    orthoptic training V57.4
    orthotic training V57.81
    radiotherapy session V58.0
    removal of
      dressings V58.3
      fixation device
        external V54.89
        internal V54.01
      fracture plate V54.01
      pins V54.01
      plaster cast V54.89
      rods V54.01
      screws V54.01
      surgical dressings V58.3
      sutures V58.3
      traction device, external V54.89
  neuropacemaker (brain) (peripheral nerve)
    (spinal cord) V53.02
  occupational therapy V57.21
  orthodontic V58.5
  orthopedic V54.9
    change of external fixation or traction device
      V54.89
    following joint replacement V54.81
    internal fixation device V54.09
    removal of fixation device
      external V54.89
      internal V54.01
    specified care NEC V54.89
  orthoptic training V57.4
  orthotic training V57.81
  pacemaker
    brain V53.02
    cardiac V53.31
    carotid sinus V53.39
    peripheral nerve V53.02
    spinal cord V53.02
  peritoneal dialysis (intermittent) (treatment)
    V56.8
  physical therapy NEC V57.1
    breathing exercises V57.0
  radiotherapy session V58.0
  rehabilitation procedure V57.9
    breathing exercises V57.0
    multiple types V57.89
    occupational V57.21
    orthoptic V57.4
    orthotic V57.81
    physical therapy NEC V57.1
    remedial exercises V57.1
    specified type NEC V57.89
    speech V57.3
    therapeutic exercises V57.1
    vocational V57.22
  renal dialysis (intermittent) (treatment) V56.0

Aftercare — continued
  specified type NEC V58.89
    removal of non-vascular catheter V58.82
    removal of vascular catheter V58.81
  speech therapy V57.3
  vocational rehabilitation V57.22
After-cataract 366.50
  obscuring vision 366.53
  specified type, not obscuring vision 366.52
Agalactia 676.4 ☑
Agammaglobulinemia 279.00
  with lymphopenia 279.2
  acquired (primary) (secondary) 279.06
  Bruton's X-linked 279.04
  infantile sex-linked (Bruton's) (congenital) 279.04
  Swiss-type 279.2
Aganglionosis (bowel) (colon) 751.3
Age (old) (see also Senile) 797
Agenesis — see also Absence, by site, congenital
  acoustic nerve 742.8
  adrenal (gland) 759.1
  alimentary tract (complete) (partial) NEC 751.8
    lower 751.2
    upper 750.8
  anus, anal (canal) 751.2
  aorta 747.22
  appendix 751.2
  arm (complete) (partial) (see also Deformity, reduction, upper limb) 755.20
  artery (peripheral) NEC (see also Anomaly, peripheral vascular system) 747.60
    brain 747.81
    coronary 746.85
    pulmonary 747.3
    umbilical 747.5
  auditory (canal) (external) 744.01
  auricle (ear) 744.01
  bile, biliary duct or passage 751.61
  bone NEC 756.9
  brain 740.0
    specified part 742.2
  breast 757.6
  bronchus 748.3
  canaliculus lacrimalis 743.65
  carpus NEC (see also Deformity, reduction, upper limb) 755.28
  cartilage 756.9
  cecum 751.2
  cerebellum 742.2
  cervix 752.49
  chin 744.89
  cilia 743.63
  circulatory system, part NEC 747.89
  clavicle 755.51
  clitoris 752.49
  coccyx 756.13
  colon 751.2
  corpus callosum 742.2
  cricoid cartilage 748.3
  diaphragm (with hernia) 756.6
  digestive organ(s) or tract (complete) (partial) NEC 751.8
    lower 751.2
    upper 750.8
  ductus arteriosus 747.89
  duodenum 751.1
  ear NEC 744.09
    auricle 744.01
    lobe 744.21
  ejaculatory duct 752.89
  endocrine (gland) NEC 759.2
  epiglottis 748.3
  esophagus 750.3
  Eustachian tube 744.24
  extrinsic muscle, eye 743.69
  eye 743.00
    adnexa 743.69
  eyelid (fold) 743.62
  face
    bones NEC 756.0
    specified part NEC 744.89
  fallopian tube 752.19
  femur NEC (see also Absence, femur, congenital) 755.34

Agenesis — see also Absence, by site, congenital — continued
  fibula NEC (see also Absence, fibula, congenital) 755.37
  finger NEC (see also Absence, finger, congenital) 755.29
  foot (complete) (see also Deformity, reduction, lower limb) 755.31
  gallbladder 751.69
  gastric 750.8
  genitalia, genital (organ)
    female 752.89
      external 752.49
      internal NEC 752.89
    male 752.89
      penis 752.69
  glottis 748.3
  gonadal 758.6
  hair 757.4
  hand (complete) (see also Deformity, reduction, upper limb) 755.21
  heart 746.89
    valve NEC 746.89
      aortic 746.89
      mitral 746.89
      pulmonary 746.01
  hepatic 751.69
  humerus NEC (see also Absence, humerus, congenital) 755.24
  hymen 752.49
  ileum 751.1
  incus 744.04
  intestine (small) 751.1
    large 751.2
  iris (dilator fibers) 743.45
  jaw 524.09
  jejunum 751.1
  kidney(s) (partial) (unilateral) 753.0
  labium (majus) (minus) 752.49
  labyrinth, membranous 744.05
  lacrimal apparatus (congenital) 743.65
  larynx 748.3
  leg NEC (see also Deformity, reduction, lower limb) 755.30
  lens 743.35
  limb (complete) (partial) (see also Deformity, reduction) 755.4
    lower NEC 755.30
    upper 755.20
  lip 750.26
  liver 751.69
  lung (bilateral) (fissures) (lobe) (unilateral) 748.5
  mandible 524.09
  maxilla 524.09
  metacarpus NEC 755.28
  metatarsus NEC 755.38
  muscle (any) 756.81
  musculoskeletal system NEC 756.9
  nail(s) 757.5
  neck, part 744.89
  nerve 742.8
  nervous system, part NEC 742.8
  nipple 757.6
  nose 748.1
  nuclear 742.8
  organ
    of Corti 744.05
    or site not listed — see Anomaly, specified type NEC
  osseous meatus (ear) 744.03
  ovary 752.0
  oviduct 752.19
  pancreas 751.7
  parathyroid (gland) 759.2
  patella 755.64
  pelvic girdle (complete) (partial) 755.69
  penis 752.69
  pericardium 746.89
  perineal body 756.81
  pituitary (gland) 759.2
  prostate 752.89
  pulmonary
    artery 747.3
    trunk 747.3
    vein 747.49
  punctum lacrimale 743.65

Agenesis — see also Absence, by site, congenital — continued
  radioulnar NEC (see also Absence, forearm, congenital) 755.25
  radius NEC (see also Absence, radius, congenital) 755.26
  rectum 751.2
  renal 753.0
  respiratory organ NEC 748.9
  rib 756.3
  roof of orbit 742.0
  round ligament 752.89
  sacrum 756.13
  salivary gland 750.21
  scapula 755.59
  scrotum 752.89
  seminal duct or tract 752.89
  septum
    atrial 745.69
    between aorta and pulmonary artery 745.0
    ventricular 745.3
  shoulder girdle (complete) (partial) 755.59
  skull (bone) 756.0
    with
      anencephalus 740.0
      encephalocele 742.0
      hydrocephalus 742.3
        with spina bifida (see also Spina bifida) 741.0 ☑
      microcephalus 742.1
  spermatic cord 752.89
  spinal cord 742.59
  spine 756.13
    lumbar 756.13
      isthmus 756.11
      pars articularis 756.11
  spleen 759.0
  sternum 756.3
  stomach 750.7
  tarsus NEC 755.38
  tendon 756.81
  testicular 752.89
  testis 752.89
  thymus (gland) 759.2
  thyroid (gland) 243
    cartilage 748.3
  tibia NEC (see also Absence, tibia, congenital) 755.36
  tibiofibular NEC 755.35
  toe (complete) (partial) (see also Absence, toe, congenital) 755.39
  tongue 750.11
  trachea (cartilage) 748.3
  ulna NEC (see also Absence, ulna, congenital) 755.27
  ureter 753.4
  urethra 753.8
  urinary tract NEC 753.8
  uterus 752.3
  uvula 750.26
  vagina 752.49
  vas deferens 752.89
  vein(s) (peripheral) NEC (see also Anomaly, peripheral vascular system) 747.60
    brain 747.81
    great 747.49
    portal 747.49
    pulmonary 747.49
  vena cava (inferior) (superior) 747.49
  vermis of cerebellum 742.2
  vertebra 756.13
    lumbar 756.13
      isthmus 756.11
      pars articularis 756.11
  vulva 752.49
Ageusia (see also Disturbance, sensation) 781.1
Aggressiveness 301.3
Aggressive outburst (see also Disturbance, conduct) 312.0 ☑
  in children or adolescents 313.9
Aging skin 701.8
Agitated — see condition
Agitation 307.9
  catatonic (see also Schizophrenia) 295.2 ☑
Aglossia (congenital) 750.11

Aglycogenosis 271.0

Agnail (finger) (with lymphangitis) 681.02

Agnosia (body image) (tactile) 784.69
  verbal 784.69
    auditory 784.69
      secondary to organic lesion 784.69
    developmental 315.8
    secondary to organic lesion 784.69
    visual 784.69
      developmental 315.8
      secondary to organic lesion 784.69
  visual 368.16
    developmental 315.31

Agoraphobia 300.22
  with panic disorder 300.21

Agrammatism 784.69

Agranulocytopenia 288.0

Agranulocytosis (angina) (chronic) (cyclical)
    (genetic) (infantile) (periodic) (pernicious)
    288.0

Agraphia (absolute) 784.69
  with alexia 784.61
  developmental 315.39

Agrypnia (*see also* Insomnia) 780.52

Ague (*see also* Malaria) 084.6
  brass-founders' 985.8
  dumb 084.6
  tertian 084.1

Agyria 742.2

Ahumada-del Castillo syndrome (nonpuerperal
    galactorrhea and amenorrhea) 253.1

AIDS 042

AIDS-associated retrovirus (disease) (illness) 042
  infection — *see* Human immunodeficiency
      virus, infection

AIDS-associated virus (disease) (illness) 042
  infection — *see* Human immunodeficiency
      virus, infection

AIDS-like disease (illness) (syndrome) 042

AIDS-related complex 042

AIDS-related conditions 042

AIDS-related virus (disease) (illness) 042
  infection — *see* Human immunodeficiency
      virus, infection

AIDS virus (disease) (illness) 042
  infection — *see* Human immunodeficiency
      virus, infection

Ailment, heart — *see* Disease, heart

Ailurophobia 300.29

Ainhum (disease) 136.0

Air
  anterior mediastinum 518.1
  compressed, disease 993.3
  embolism (any site) (artery) (cerebral) 958.0
    with
      abortion — *see* Abortion, by type, with
          embolism
      ectopic pregnancy (*see also* categories
          633.0-633.9) 639.6
      molar pregnancy (*see also* categories 630-
          632) 639.6
    due to implanted device — *see*
        Complications, due to (presence of)
        any device, implant, or graft classified
        to 996.0-996.5 NEC
    following
      abortion 639.6
      ectopic or molar pregnancy 639.6
    infusion, perfusion, or transfusion 999.1
    in pregnancy, childbirth, or puerperium
        673.0 ☑
    traumatic 958.0
  hunger 786.09
    psychogenic 306.1
  leak (lung) (pulmonary) (thorax) 512.8
    iatrogenic 512.1
    postoperative 512.1
  rarefied, effects of — *see* Effect, adverse, high
      altitude
  sickness 994.6

Airplane sickness 994.6

Akathisia, acathisia 781.0
  due to drugs 333.99
  neuroleptic-induced acute 333.99 ●

Akinesia algeria 352.6

Akiyami 100.89

Akureyri disease (epidemic neuromyasthenia)
    049.8

Alacrima (congenital) 743.65

Alactasia (hereditary) 271.3

Alagille syndrome 759.89 ●

Alalia 784.3
  developmental 315.31
    receptive-expressive 315.32
  secondary to organic lesion 784.3

Alaninemia 270.8

Alastrim 050.1

Albarrán's disease (colibacilluria) 791.9

Albers-Schönberg's disease (marble bones)
    756.52

Albert's disease 726.71

Albinism, albino (choroid) (cutaneous) (eye)
    (generalized) (isolated) (ocular)
    (oculocutaneous) (partial) 270.2

Albinismus 270.2

Albright (-Martin) (-Bantam) disease
    (pseudohypoparathyroidism) 275.49

Albright (-McCune) (-Sternberg) syndrome
    (osteitis fibrosa disseminata) 756.59

Albuminous — *see* condition

Albuminuria, albuminuric (acute) (chronic)
    (subacute) 791.0
  Bence-Jones 791.0
  cardiac 785.9
  complicating pregnancy, childbirth, or
      puerperium 646.2 ☑
    with hypertension — *see* Toxemia, of
        pregnancy
    affecting fetus or newborn 760.1
  cyclic 593.6
  gestational 646.2 ☑
  gravidarum 646.2 ☑
    with hypertension — *see* Toxemia, of
        pregnancy
    affecting fetus or newborn 760.1
  heart 785.9
  idiopathic 593.6
  orthostatic 593.6
  postural 593.6
  pre-eclamptic (mild) 642.4 ☑
    affecting fetus or newborn 760.0
    severe 642.5 ☑
      affecting fetus or newborn 760.0
  recurrent physiologic 593.6
  scarlatinal 034.1

Albumosuria 791.0
  Bence-Jones 791.0
  myelopathic (M9730/3) 203.0 ☑

Alcaptonuria 270.2

Alcohol, alcoholic
  abstinence 291.81
  acute intoxication 305.0 ☑
    with dependence 303.0 ☑
  addiction (*see also* Alcoholism) 303.9 ☑
    maternal
      with suspected fetal damage affecting
          management of pregnancy 655.4 ☑
      affecting fetus or newborn 760.71
  amnestic disorder, persisting 291.1
  anxiety 291.89
  brain syndrome, chronic 291.2
  cardiopathy 425.5
  chronic (*see also* Alcoholism) 303.9 ☑
  cirrhosis (liver) 571.2
  delirium 291.0
    acute 291.0
    chronic 291.1
    tremens 291.0
    withdrawal 291.0
  dementia NEC 291.2
  deterioration 291.2
  drunkenness (simple) 305.0 ☑
  hallucinosis (acute) 291.3

Alcohol, alcoholic — *continued*
  induced
    circadian rhythm sleep disorder 291.82 ●
    hypersomnia 291.82 ●
    insomnia 291.82 ●
    mental disorder 291.9
      anxiety 291.89
      mood 291.89
      sexual 291.89
      sleep 291.82 ▲
      specified type 291.89
    parasomnia 291.82 ●
    persisting
      amnestic disorder 291.1
      dementia 291.2
    psychotic disorder
      with
        delusions 291.5
        hallucinations 291.3
    sleep disorder 291.82 ●
  insanity 291.9
  intoxication (acute) 305.0 ☑
    with dependence 303.0 ☑
    pathological 291.4
  jealousy 291.5
  Korsakoff's, Korsakov's, Korsakow's 291.1
  liver NEC 571.3
    acute 571.1
    chronic 571.2
  mania (acute) (chronic) 291.9
  mood 291.89
  paranoia 291.5
  paranoid (type) psychosis 291.5
  pellagra 265.2
  poisoning, accidental (acute) NEC 980.9
    specified type of alcohol — *see* Table of
        Drugs and Chemicals
  psychosis (*see also* Psychosis, alcoholic) 291.9
    Korsakoff's, Korsakov's, Korsakow's 291.1
    polyneuritic 291.1
      with
        delusions 291.5
        hallucinations 291.3
  related disorder 291.9
  withdrawal symptoms, syndrome NEC 291.81
    delirium 291.0
    hallucinosis 291.3

Alcoholism 303.9 ☑

---

*Note — Use the following fifth-digit
subclassification with category 303:*

  0   unspecified
  1   continuous
  2   episodic
  3   in remission

---

  with psychosis (*see also* Psychosis, alcoholic)
      291.9
  acute 303.0 ☑
  chronic 303.9 ☑
    with psychosis 291.9
  complicating pregnancy, childbirth, or
      puerperium 648.4 ☑
    affecting fetus or newborn 760.71
  history V11.3
  Korsakoff's, Korsakov's, Korsakow's 291.1
  suspected damage to fetus affecting
      management of pregnancy 655.4 ☑

Alder's anomaly or syndrome (leukocyte
    granulation anomaly) 288.2

Alder-Reilly anomaly (leukocyte granulation)
    288.2

Aldosteronism (primary) 255.10
  congenital 255.10
  familial type I 255.11
  glucocorticoid-remediable 255.11
  secondary 255.14

Aldosteronoma (M8370/1) 237.2

Aldrich (-Wiskott) syndrome (eczema-
    thrombocytopenia) 279.12

Aleppo boil 085.1

Aleukemic — *see* condition

Aleukia
  congenital 288.0

Aleukia — *continued*
  hemorrhagica 284.9
    acquired (secondary) 284.8
    congenital 284.0
    idiopathic 284.9
  splenica 289.4
Alexia (congenital) (developmental) 315.01
  secondary to organic lesion 784.61
Algoneurodystrophy 733.7
Algophobia 300.29
Alibert's disease (mycosis fungoides) (M9700/3) 202.1 ☑
Alibert-Bazin disease (M9700/3) 202.1 ☑
Alice in Wonderland syndrome 293.89
Alienation, mental (*see also* Psychosis) 298.9
Alkalemia 276.3
Alkalosis 276.3
  metabolic 276.3
    with respiratory acidosis 276.4
  respiratory 276.3
Alkaptonuria 270.2
Allen-Masters syndrome 620.6
Allergic bronchopulmonary aspergillosis 518.6
Allergy, allergic (reaction) 995.3
  air-borne substance (*see also* Fever, hay) 477.9
    specified allergen NEC 477.8
  alveolitis (extrinsic) 495.9
    due to
      Aspergillus clavatus 495.4
      cryptostroma corticale 495.6
      organisms (fungal, thermophilic actinomycete, other) growing in ventilation (air conditioning systems) 495.7
    specified type NEC 495.8
  anaphylactic shock 999.4
    due to food — *see* Anaphylactic shock, due to, food
  angioneurotic edema 995.1
  animal (cat) (dog) (epidermal) 477.8
    dander 477.2
    hair 477.2
  arthritis (*see also* Arthritis, allergic) 716.2 ☑
  asthma — *see* Asthma
  bee sting (anaphylactic shock) 989.5
  biological — *see* Allergy, drug
  bronchial asthma — *see* Asthma
  conjunctivitis (eczematous) 372.14
  dander, animal (cat) (dog) 477.2
  dandruff 477.8
  dermatitis (venenata) — *see* Dermatitis
  diathesis V15.09
  drug, medicinal substance, and biological (any) (correct medicinal substance properly administered) (external) (internal) 995.2
    wrong substance given or taken NEC 977.9
      specified drug or substance — *see* Table of Drugs and Chemicals
  dust (house) (stock) 477.8
  eczema — *see* Eczema
  endophthalmitis 360.19
  epidermal (animal) 477.8
  feathers 477.8
  food (any) (ingested) 693.1
    atopic 691.8
    in contact with skin 692.5
  gastritis 535.4 ☑
  gastroenteritis 558.3
  gastrointestinal 558.3
  grain 477.0
  grass (pollen) 477.0
    asthma (*see also* Asthma) 493.0 ☑
    hay fever 477.0
  hair, animal (cat) (dog) 477.2
  hay fever (grass) (pollen) (ragweed) (tree) (*see also* Fever, hay) 477.9
  history (of) V15.09
    to
      eggs V15.03
      food additives V15.05
      insect bite V15.06
      latex V15.07
      milk products V15.02

Allergy, allergic — *continued*
  history — *continued*
    to — *continued*
      nuts V15.05
        peanuts V15.01
      radiographic dye V15.08
      seafood V15.04
      specified food NEC V15.05
      spider bite V15.06
  horse serum — *see* Allergy, serum
  inhalant 477.9
    dust 477.8
    pollen 477.0
    specified allergen other than pollen 477.8
  kapok 477.8
  medicine — *see* Allergy, drug
  migraine 346.2 ☑
  milk protein 558.3
  pannus 370.62
  pneumonia 518.3
  pollen (any) (hay fever) 477.0
    asthma (*see also* Asthma) 493.0 ☑
  primrose 477.0
  primula 477.0
  purpura 287.0
  ragweed (pollen) (Senecio jacobae) 477.0
    asthma (*see also* Asthma) 493.0 ☑
    hay fever 477.0
  respiratory (*see also* Allergy, inhalant) 477.9
    due to
      drug — *see* Allergy, drug
      food — *see* Allergy, food
  rhinitis (*see also* Fever, hay) 477.9
    due to food 477.1
  rose 477.0
  Senecio jacobae 477.0
  serum (prophylactic) (therapeutic) 999.5
    anaphylactic shock 999.4
  shock (anaphylactic) (due to adverse effect of correct medicinal substance properly administered) 995.0
    food — *see* Anaphylactic shock, due to, food
    from serum or immunization 999.5
      anaphylactic 999.4
  sinusitis (*see also* Fever, hay) 477.9
  skin reaction 692.9
    specified substance — *see* Dermatitis, due to
  tree (any) (hay fever) (pollen) 477.0
    asthma (*see also* Asthma) 493.0 ☑
  upper respiratory (*see also* Fever, hay) 477.9
  urethritis 597.89
  urticaria 708.0
  vaccine — *see* Allergy, serum
Allescheriosis 117.6
Alligator skin disease (ichthyosis congenita) 757.1
  acquired 701.1
Allocheiria, allochiria (*see also* Disturbance, sensation) 782.0
Almeida's disease (Brazilian blastomycosis) 116.1
Alopecia (atrophicans) (pregnancy) (premature) (senile) 704.00
  adnata 757.4
  areata 704.01
  celsi 704.01
  cicatrisata 704.09
  circumscripta 704.01
  congenital, congenitalis 757.4
  disseminata 704.01
  effluvium (telogen) 704.02
  febrile 704.09
  generalisata 704.09
  hereditaria 704.09
  marginalis 704.01
  mucinosa 704.09
  postinfectional 704.09
  seborrheica 704.09
  specific 091.82
  syphilitic (secondary) 091.82
  telogen effluvium 704.02
  totalis 704.09
  toxica 704.09
  universalis 704.09
  x-ray 704.09
Alpers' disease 330.8

Alpha-lipoproteinemia 272.4
Alpha thalassemia 282.49
Alphos 696.1
Alpine sickness 993.2
Alport's syndrome (hereditary hematurianephropathy-deafness) 759.89
Alteration (of), altered
  awareness 780.09
    transient 780.02
  consciousness 780.09
    persistent vegetative state 780.03
    transient 780.02
  mental status 780.99
    amnesia (retrograde) 780.93
    memory loss 780.93
Alternaria (infection) 118
Alternating — *see* condition
Altitude, high (effects) — *see* Effect, adverse, high altitude
Aluminosis (of lung) 503
Alvarez syndrome (transient cerebral ischemia) 435.9
Alveolar capillary block syndrome 516.3
Alveolitis
  allergic (extrinsic) 495.9
    due to organisms (fungal, thermophilic actinomycete, other) growing in ventilation (air conditioning systems) 495.7
    specified type NEC 495.8
  due to
    Aspergillus clavatus 495.4
    Cryptostroma corticale 495.6
  fibrosing (chronic) (cryptogenic) (lung) 516.3
    idiopathic 516.3
    rheumatoid 714.81
  jaw 526.5
  sicca dolorosa 526.5
Alveolus, alveolar — *see* condition
Alymphocytosis (pure) 279.2
Alymphoplasia, thymic 279.2
Alzheimer's
  dementia (senile)
    with behavioral disturbance 331.0 [294.11]
    without behavioral disturbance 331.0 [294.10]
  disease or sclerosis 331.0
    with dementia — *see* Alzheimer's, dementia
Amastia (*see also* Absence, breast) 611.8
Amaurosis (acquired) (congenital) (*see also* Blindness) 369.00
  fugax 362.34
  hysterical 300.11
  Leber's (congenital) 362.76
  tobacco 377.34
  uremic — *see* Uremia
Amaurotic familial idiocy (infantile) (juvenile) (late) 330.1
Ambisexual 752.7
Amblyopia (acquired) (congenital) (partial) 368.00
  color 368.59
    acquired 368.55
  deprivation 368.02
  ex anopsia 368.00
  hysterical 300.11
  nocturnal 368.60
    vitamin A deficiency 264.5
  refractive 368.03
  strabismic 368.01
  suppression 368.01
  tobacco 377.34
  toxic NEC 377.34
  uremic — *see* Uremia
Ameba, amebic (histolytica) — *see also* Amebiasis
  abscess 006.3
    bladder 006.8
    brain (with liver and lung abscess) 006.5
    liver 006.3
      with
        brain abscess (and lung abscess) 006.5
        lung abscess 006.4

Ameba, amebic (histolytica) — *see also* Amebiasis
— *continued*
  abscess — *continued*
    lung (with liver abscess) 006.4
      with brain abscess 006.5
    seminal vesicle 006.8
    spleen 006.8
  carrier (suspected of) V02.2
  meningoencephalitis
    due to Naegleria (gruberi) 136.2
    primary 136.2
Amebiasis NEC 006.9
  with
    brain abscess (with liver or lung abscess)
      006.5
    liver abscess (without mention of brain or
      lung abscess) 006.3
    lung abscess (with liver abscess) 006.4
      with brain abscess 006.5
  acute 006.0
  bladder 006.8
  chronic 006.1
  cutaneous 006.6
  cutis 006.6
  due to organism other than Entamoeba
    histolytica 007.8
  hepatic (*see also* Abscess, liver, amebic) 006.3
  nondysenteric 006.2
  seminal vesicle 006.8
  specified
    organism NEC 007.8
    site NEC 006.8
Ameboma 006.8
Amelia 755.4
  lower limb 755.31
  upper limb 755.21
Ameloblastoma (M9310/0) 213.1
  jaw (bone) (lower) 213.1
    upper 213.0
  long bones (M9261/3) — *see* Neoplasm, bone,
    malignant
  malignant (M9310/3) 170.1
    jaw (bone) (lower) 170.1
      upper 170.0
  mandible 213.1
  tibial (M9261/3) 170.7
Amelogenesis imperfecta 520.5
  nonhereditaria (segmentalis) 520.4
Amenorrhea (primary) (secondary) 626.0
  due to ovarian dysfunction 256.8
  hyperhormonal 256.8
Amentia (*see also* Retardation, mental) 319
  Meynert's (nonalcoholic) 294.0
    alcoholic 291.1
  nevoid 759.6
American
  leishmaniasis 085.5
  mountain tick fever 066.1
  trypanosomiasis — *see* Trypanosomiasis,
    American
Ametropia (*see also* Disorder, accommodation)
  367.9
Amianthosis 501
Amimia 784.69
Amino acid
  deficiency 270.9
    anemia 281.4
  metabolic disorder (*see also* Disorder, amino
    acid) 270.9
Aminoaciduria 270.9
  imidazole 270.5
Amnesia (retrograde) 780.93
  auditory 784.69
    developmental 315.31
    secondary to organic lesion 784.69
  dissociative 300.12
  hysterical or dissociative type 300.12
  psychogenic 300.12
  transient global 437.7
Amnestic (confabulatory) **syndrome** 294.0
  alcohol-induced persisting 291.1
  drug-induced persisting 292.83
  posttraumatic 294.0

Amniocentesis screening (for) V28.2
  alphafetoprotein level, raised V28.1
  chromosomal anomalies V28.0
Amnion, amniotic — *see also* condition
  nodosum 658.8 ☑
Amnionitis (complicating pregnancy) 658.4 ☑
  affecting fetus or newborn 762.7
Amoral trends 301.7
Amotio retinae (*see also* Detachment, retina)
  361.9
Ampulla
  lower esophagus 530.89
  phrenic 530.89
Amputation
  any part of fetus, to facilitate delivery 763.89
  cervix (supravaginal) (uteri) 622.8
    in pregnancy or childbirth 654.6 ☑
      affecting fetus or newborn 763.89
  clitoris — *see* Wound, open, clitoris
  congenital
    lower limb 755.31
    upper limb 755.21
  neuroma (traumatic) — *see also* Injury, nerve,
    by site
    surgical complication (late) 997.61
  penis — *see* Amputation, traumatic, penis
  status (without complication) — *see* Absence,
    by site, acquired
  stump (surgical) (posttraumatic)
    abnormal, painful, or with complication
      (late) 997.60
    healed or old NEC — *see also* Absence, by
      site, acquired
      lower V49.70
      upper V49.60
  traumatic (complete) (partial)

> *Note* — "Complicated" includes traumatic
> amputation with delayed healing, delayed
> treatment, foreign body, or infection.

    arm 887.4
      at or above elbow 887.2
        complicated 887.3
      below elbow 887.0
        complicated 887.1
      both (bilateral) (any level(s)) 887.6
        complicated 887.7
      complicated 887.5
      finger(s) (one or both hands) 886.0
        with thumb(s) 885.0
          complicated 885.1
        complicated 886.1
      foot (except toe(s) only) 896.0
        and other leg 897.6
          complicated 897.7
        both (bilateral) 896.2
          complicated 896.3
        complicated 896.1
        toe(s) only (one or both feet) 895.0
          complicated 895.1
      genital organ(s) (external) NEC 878.8
        complicated 878.9
      hand (except finger(s) only) 887.0
        and other arm 887.6
          complicated 887.7
        both (bilateral) 887.6
          complicated 887.7
        complicated 887.1
      finger(s) (one or both hands) 886.0
        with thumb(s) 885.0
          complicated 885.1
        complicated 886.1
      thumb(s) (with fingers of either hand)
        885.0
        complicated 885.1
      head 874.9
      late effect — *see* Late, effects (of),
        amputation
      leg 897.4
        and other foot 897.6
          complicated 897.7
        at or above knee 897.2
          complicated 897.3
        below knee 897.0
          complicated 897.1

Amputation — *continued*
  traumatic — *continued*
    leg — *continued*
      both (bilateral) 897.6
        complicated 897.7
      complicated 897.5
    lower limb(s) except toe(s) — *see*
      Amputation, traumatic, leg
    nose — *see* Wound, open, nose
    penis 878.0
      complicated 878.1
    sites other than limbs — *see* Wound, open,
      by site
    thumb(s) (with finger(s) of either hand) 885.0
      complicated 885.1
    toe(s) (one or both feet) 895.0
      complicated 895.1
    upper limb(s) — *see* Amputation, traumatic,
      arm
Amputee (bilateral) (old) — *see also* Absence, by
  site, acquired V49.70
Amusia 784.69
  developmental 315.39
  secondary to organic lesion 784.69
Amyelencephalus 740.0
Amyelia 742.59
Amygdalitis — *see* Tonsillitis
Amygdalolith 474.8
Amyloid disease or degeneration 277.3
  heart 277.3 *[425.7]*
Amyloidosis (familial) (general) (generalized)
  (genetic) (primary) (secondary) 277.3
  with lung involvement 277.3 *[517.8]*
  heart 277.3 *[425.7]*
  nephropathic 277.3 *[583.81]*
  neuropathic (Portuguese) (Swiss) 277.3 *[357.4]*
  pulmonary 277.3 *[517.8]*
  systemic, inherited 277.3
Amylopectinosis (brancher enzyme deficiency)
  271.0
Amylophagia 307.52
Amyoplasia, congenita 756.89
Amyotonia 728.2
  congenita 358.8
Amyotrophia, amyotrophy, amyotrophic 728.2
  congenita 756.89
  diabetic 250.6 ☑ *[358.1]*
  lateral sclerosis (syndrome) 335.20
  neuralgic 353.5
  sclerosis (lateral) 335.20
  spinal progressive 335.21
Anacidity, gastric 536.0
  psychogenic 306.4
Anaerosis of newborn 768.9
Analbuminemia 273.8
Analgesia (*see also* Anesthesia) 782.0
Analphalipoproteinemia 272.5
Anaphylactic shock or reaction (correct
  substance properly administered) 995.0
  due to
    food 995.60
      additives 995.66
      crustaceans 995.62
      eggs 995.68
      fish 995.65
      fruits 995.63
      milk products 995.67
      nuts (tree) 995.64
      peanuts 995.61
      seeds 995.64
      specified NEC 995.69
      tree nuts 995.64
      vegetables 995.63
    immunization 999.4
    overdose or wrong substance given or taken
      977.9
    specified drug — *see* Table of Drugs and
      Chemicals
    serum 999.4
  following sting(s) 989.5
  purpura 287.0
  serum 999.4

☑ Additional Digit Required — Refer to the Tabular List (Numeric Code Section) for Additional Digit Selection
▶◀ Revised Text   ● New Line   ▲ Revised Code

2006 ICD-9-CM   **Volume 2 — 21**

Anaphylactoid shock or reaction — *see* Anaphylactic shock

Anaphylaxis — *see* Anaphylactic shock

Anaplasia, cervix 622.10

Anarthria 784.5

Anarthritic rheumatoid disease 446.5

Anasarca 782.3
cardiac (*see also* Failure, heart) 428.0
fetus or newborn 778.0
lung 514
nutritional 262
pulmonary 514
renal (*see also* Nephrosis) 581.9

Anaspadias 752.62

Anastomosis
aneurysmal — *see* Aneurysm
arteriovenous, congenital NEC (*see also* Anomaly, arteriovenous) 747.60
ruptured, of brain (*see also* Hemorrhage, subarachnoid) 430
intestinal 569.89
complicated NEC 997.4
involving urinary tract 997.5
retinal and choroidal vessels 743.58
acquired 362.17

Anatomical narrow angle (glaucoma) 365.02

Ancylostoma (infection) (infestation) 126.9
americanus 126.1
braziliense 126.2
caninum 126.8
ceylanicum 126.3
duodenale 126.0
Necator americanus 126.1

Ancylostomiasis (intestinal) 126.9
ancylostoma
americanus 126.1
caninum 126.8
ceylanicum 126.3
duodenale 126.0
braziliense 126.2
Necator americanus 126.1

Anders' disease or syndrome (adiposis tuberosa simplex) 272.8

Andersen's glycogen storage disease 271.0

Anderson's disease 272.7

Andes disease 993.2

Andrews' disease (bacterid) 686.8

Androblastoma (M8630/1)
benign (M8630/0)
specified site — *see* Neoplasm, by site, benign
unspecified site
female 220
male 222.0
malignant (M8630/3)
specified site — *see* Neoplasm, by site, malignant
unspecified site
female 183.0
male 186.9
specified site — *see* Neoplasm, by site, uncertain behavior
tubular (M8640/0)
with lipid storage (M8641/0)
specified site — *see* Neoplasm, by site, benign
unspecified site
female 220
male 222.0
specified site — *see* Neoplasm, by site, benign
unspecified site
female 220
male 222.0
unspecified site
female 236.2
male 236.4

Android pelvis 755.69
with disproportion (fetopelvic) 653.3 ☑
affecting fetus or newborn 763.1
causing obstructed labor 660.1 ☑
affecting fetus or newborn 763.1

Anectasis, pulmonary (newborn or fetus) 770.5

Anemia 285.9
with
disorder of
anaerobic glycolysis 282.3
pentose phosphate pathway 282.2
koilonychia 280.9
6-phosphogluconic dehydrogenase deficiency 282.2
achlorhydric 280.9
achrestic 281.8
Addison's (pernicious) 281.0
Addison-Biermer (pernicious) 281.0
agranulocytic 288.0
amino acid deficiency 281.4
aplastic 284.9
acquired (secondary) 284.8
congenital 284.0
constitutional 284.0
due to
chronic systemic disease 284.8
drugs 284.8
infection 284.8
radiation 284.8
idiopathic 284.9
myxedema 244.9
of or complicating pregnancy 648.2 ☑
red cell (acquired) (pure) (with thymoma) 284.8
congenital 284.0
specified type NEC 284.8
toxic (paralytic) 284.8
aregenerative 284.9
congenital 284.0
asiderotic 280.9
atypical (primary) 285.9
autohemolysis of Selwyn and Dacie (type I) 282.2
autoimmune hemolytic 283.0
Baghdad Spring 282.2
Balantidium coli 007.0
Biermer's (pernicious) 281.0
blood loss (chronic) 280.0
acute 285.1
bothriocephalus 123.4
brickmakers' (*see also* Ancylostomiasis) 126.9
cerebral 437.8
childhood 282.9
chlorotic 280.9
chronica congenita aregenerativa 284.0
chronic simple 281.9
combined system disease NEC 281.0 *[336.2]*
due to dietary deficiency 281.1 *[336.2]*
complicating pregnancy or childbirth 648.2 ☑
congenital (following fetal blood loss) 776.5
aplastic 284.0
due to isoimmunization NEC 773.2
Heinz-body 282.7
hereditary hemolytic NEC 282.9
nonspherocytic
type I 282.2
type II 282.3
pernicious 281.0
spherocytic (*see also* Spherocytosis) 282.0
Cooley's (erythroblastic) 282.49
crescent — *see* Disease, sickle-cell
cytogenic 281.0
Dacie's (nonspherocytic)
type I 282.2
type II 282.3
Davidson's (refractory) 284.9
deficiency 281.9
2, 3 diphosphoglycurate mutase 282.3
2, 3 PG 282.3
6-PGD 282.2
6-phosphogluronic dehydrogenase 282.2
amino acid 281.4
combined B₁₂ and folate 281.3
enzyme, drug-induced (hemolytic) 282.2
erythrocytic glutathione 282.2
folate 281.2
dietary 281.2
drug-induced 281.2
folic acid 281.2
dietary 281.2
drug-induced 281.2
G-6-PD 282.2
GGS-R 282.2

Anemia — *continued*
deficiency — *continued*
glucose-6-phosphate dehydrogenase (G-6-PD) 282.2
glucose-phosphate isomerase 282.3
glutathione peroxidase 282.2
glutathione reductase 282.2
glyceraldehyde phosphate dehydrogenase 282.3
GPI 282.3
G SH 282.2
hexokinase 282.3
iron (Fe) 280.9
specified NEC 280.8
nutritional 281.9
with
poor iron absorption 280.9
specified deficiency NEC 281.8
due to inadequate dietary iron intake 280.1
specified type NEC 281.8
of or complicating pregnancy 648.2 ☑
pentose phosphate pathway 282.2
PFK 282.3
phosphofructo-aldolase 282.3
phosphofructokinase 282.3
phosphoglycerate kinase 282.3
PK 282.3
protein 281.4
pyruvate kinase (PK) 282.3
TPI 282.3
triosephosphate isomerase 282.3
vitamin B₁₂ NEC 281.1
dietary 281.1
pernicious 281.0
Diamond-Blackfan (congenital hypoplastic) 284.0
dibothriocephalus 123.4
dimorphic 281.9
diphasic 281.8
diphtheritic 032.89
Diphyllobothrium 123.4
drepanocytic (*see also* Disease, sickle-cell) 282.60
due to
blood loss (chronic) 280.0
acute 285.1
defect of Embden-Meyerhof pathway glycolysis 282.3
disorder of glutathione metabolism 282.2
fetal blood loss 776.5
fish tapeworm (D. latum) infestation 123.4
glutathione metabolism disorder 282.2
hemorrhage (chronic) 280.0
acute 285.1
hexose monophosphate (HMP) shunt deficiency 282.2
impaired absorption 280.9
loss of blood (chronic) 280.0
acute 285.1
myxedema 244.9
Necator americanus 126.1
prematurity 776.6
selective vitamin B₁₂ malabsorption with proteinuria 281.1
Dyke-Young type (secondary) (symptomatic) 283.9
dyserythropoietic (congenital) (types I, II, III) 285.8
dyshemopoietic (congenital) 285.8
Egypt (*see also* Ancylostomiasis) 126.9
elliptocytosis (*see also* Elliptocytosis) 282.1
enzyme deficiency, drug-induced 282.2
epidemic (*see also* Ancylostomiasis) 126.9
EPO resistant 285.21
erythroblastic
familial 282.49
fetus or newborn (*see also* Disease, hemolytic) 773.2
late 773.5
erythrocytic glutathione deficiency 282.2
erythropoietin-resistant (EPO resistant anemia) 285.21
essential 285.9
Faber's (achlorhydric anemia) 280.9
factitious (self-induced blood letting) 280.0
familial erythroblastic (microcytic) 282.49

Anemia — *continued*
Fanconi's (congenital pancytopenia) 284.0
favism 282.2
fetal, following blood loss 776.5
fetus or newborn
  due to
    ABO
      antibodies 773.1
      incompatibility, maternal/fetal 773.1
      isoimmunization 773.1
    Rh
      antibodies 773.0
      incompatibility, maternal/fetal 773.0
      isoimmunization 773.0
  following fetal blood loss 776.5
fish tapeworm (D. latum) infestation 123.4
folate (folic acid) deficiency 281.2
  dietary 281.2
  drug-induced 281.2
folate malabsorption, congenital 281.2
folic acid deficiency 281.2
  dietary 281.2
  drug-induced 281.2
G-6-PD 282.2
general 285.9
glucose-6-phosphate dehydrogenase deficiency 282.2
glutathione-reductase deficiency 282.2
goat's milk 281.2
granulocytic 288.0
Heinz-body, congenital 282.7
hemoglobin deficiency 285.9
hemolytic 283.9
  acquired 283.9
    with hemoglobinuria NEC 283.2
    autoimmune (cold type) (idiopathic) (primary) (secondary) (symptomatic) (warm type) 283.0
    due to
      cold reactive antibodies 283.0
      drug exposure 283.0
      warm reactive antibodies 283.0
    fragmentation 283.19
    idiopathic (chronic) 283.9
    infectious 283.19
      autoimmune 283.0
    non-autoimmune 283.10
    toxic 283.19
    traumatic cardiac 283.19
  acute 283.9
    due to enzyme deficiency NEC 282.3
    fetus or newborn (*see also* Disease, hemolytic) 773.2
      late 773.5
    Lederer's (acquired infectious hemolytic anemia) 283.19
  autoimmune (acquired) 283.0
  chronic 282.9
    idiopathic 283.9
  cold type (secondary) (symptomatic) 283.0
  congenital (spherocytic) (*see also* Spherocytosis) 282.0
    nonspherocytic — *see* Anemia, hemolytic, nonspherocytic, congenital
  drug-induced 283.0
    enzyme deficiency 282.2
  due to
    cardiac conditions 283.19
    drugs 283.0
    enzyme deficiency NEC 282.3
      drug-induced 282.2
    presence of shunt or other internal prosthetic device 283.19
    thrombotic thrombocytopenic purpura 446.6
  elliptocytotic (*see also* Elliptocytosis) 282.1
  familial 282.9
  hereditary 282.9
    due to enzyme deficiency NEC 282.3
    specified NEC 282.8
  idiopathic (chronic) 283.9
  infectious (acquired) 283.19
  mechanical 283.19
  microangiopathic 283.19
  non-autoimmune NEC 283.10

Anemia — *continued*
hemolytic — *continued*
  nonspherocytic
    congenital or hereditary NEC 282.3
      glucose-6-phosphate dehydrogenase deficiency 282.2
      pyruvate kinase (PK) deficiency 282.3
      type I 282.2
      type II 282.3
    type I 282.2
    type II 282.3
    of or complicating pregnancy 648.2 ☑
    resulting from presence of shunt or other internal prosthetic device 283.19
  secondary 283.19
    autoimmune 283.0
  sickle-cell — *see* Disease, sickle-cell
  Stransky-Regala type (Hb-E) (*see also* Disease, hemoglobin) 282.7
  symptomatic 283.19
    autoimmune 283.0
  toxic (acquired) 283.19
  uremic (adult) (child) 283.11
  warm type (secondary) (symptomatic) 283.0
hemorrhagic (chronic) 280.0
  acute 285.1
HEMPAS 285.8
hereditary erythroblast multinuclearity-positive acidified serum test 285.8
Herrick's (hemoglobin S disease) 282.61
hexokinase deficiency 282.3
high A₂ 282.49
hookworm (*see also* Ancylostomiasis) 126.9
hypochromic (idiopathic) (microcytic) (normoblastic) 280.9
  with iron loading 285.0
  due to blood loss (chronic) 280.0
    acute 285.1
  familial sex linked 285.0
  pyridoxine-responsive 285.0
hypoplasia, red blood cells 284.8
  congenital or familial 284.0
hypoplastic (idiopathic) 284.9
  congenital 284.0
  familial 284.0
  of childhood 284.0
idiopathic 285.9
  hemolytic, chronic 283.9
in
  chronic illness NEC 285.29
  chronic kidney disease 285.21   ●
  end-stage renal disease 285.21
  neoplastic disease 285.22
infantile 285.9
infective, infectional 285.9
intertropical (*see also* Ancylostomiasis) 126.9
iron (Fe) deficiency 280.9
  due to blood loss (chronic) 280.0
    acute 285.1
  of or complicating pregnancy 648.2 ☑
  specified NEC 280.8
Jaksch's (pseudoleukemia infantum) 285.8
Joseph-Diamond-Blackfan (congenital hypoplastic) 284.0
labyrinth 386.50
Lederer's (acquired infectious hemolytic anemia) 283.19
leptocytosis (hereditary) 282.49
leukoerythroblastic 285.8
macrocytic 281.9
  nutritional 281.2
  of or complicating pregnancy 648.2 ☑
  tropical 281.2
malabsorption (familial), selective B₁₂ with proteinuria 281.1
malarial (*see also* Malaria) 084.6
malignant (progressive) 281.0
malnutrition 281.9
marsh (*see also* Malaria) 084.6
Mediterranean (with hemoglobinopathy) 282.49
megaloblastic 281.9
  combined B₁₂ and folate deficiency 281.3
  nutritional (of infancy) 281.2
  of infancy 281.2
  of or complicating pregnancy 648.2 ☑
  refractory 281.3
  specified NEC 281.3

Anemia — *continued*
megalocytic 281.9
microangiopathic hemolytic 283.19
microcytic (hypochromic) 280.9
  due to blood loss (chronic) 280.0
    acute 285.1
  familial 282.49
  hypochromic 280.9
microdrepanocytosis 282.49
miners' (*see also* Ancylostomiasis) 126.9
myelopathic 285.8
myelophthisic (normocytic) 285.8
newborn (*see also* Disease, hemolytic) 773.2
  due to isoimmunization (*see also* Disease, hemolytic) 773.2
  late, due to isoimmunization 773.5
  posthemorrhagic 776.5
nonregenerative 284.9
nonspherocytic hemolytic — *see* Anemia, hemolytic, nonspherocytic
normocytic (infectional) (not due to blood loss) 285.9
  due to blood loss (chronic) 280.0
    acute 285.1
  myelophthisic 284.8
nutritional (deficiency) 281.9
  with
    poor iron absorption 280.9
    specified deficiency NEC 281.8
  due to inadequate dietary iron intake 280.1
  megaloblastic (of infancy) 281.2
of childhood 282.9
of chronic illness NEC 285.29
of or complicating pregnancy 648.2 ☑
  affecting fetus or newborn 760.8
of prematurity 776.6
orotic aciduric (congenital) (hereditary) 281.4
osteosclerotic 289.89
ovalocytosis (hereditary) (*see also* Elliptocytosis) 282.1
paludal (*see also* Malaria) 084.6
pentose phosphate pathway deficiency 282.2
pernicious (combined system disease) (congenital) (dorsolateral spinal degeneration) (juvenile) (myelopathy) (neuropathy) (posterior sclerosis) (primary) (progressive) (spleen) 281.0
  of or complicating pregnancy 648.2 ☑
pleochromic 285.9
  of sprue 281.8
portal 285.8
posthemorrhagic (chronic) 280.0
  acute 285.1
  newborn 776.5
postoperative
  due to blood loss 285.1
  other 285.9
postpartum 648.2 ☑
pressure 285.9
primary 285.9
profound 285.9
progressive 285.9
  malignant 281.0
  pernicious 281.0
protein-deficiency 281.4
pseudoleukemica infantum 285.8
puerperal 648.2 ☑
pure red cell 284.8
  congenital 284.0
pyridoxine-responsive (hypochromic) 285.0
pyruvate kinase (PK) deficiency 282.3
refractoria sideroblastica 238.7   ▲
refractory (primary) 238.7   ▲
  with hemochromatosis 238.7   ▲
  megaloblastic 281.3
  sideroblastic 238.7   ▲
  sideropenic 280.9
Rietti-Greppi-Micheli (thalassemia minor) 282.49
scorbutic 281.8
secondary (to) 285.9
  blood loss (chronic) 280.0
    acute 285.1
  hemorrhage 280.0
    acute 285.1
  inadequate dietary iron intake 280.1
semiplastic 284.9

Anemia — *continued*
   septic 285.9
   sickle-cell (*see also* Disease, sickle-cell) 282.60
   sideroachrestic 285.0
   sideroblastic (acquired) (any type) (congenital)
      (drug-induced) (due to disease)
      (hereditary) (primary) (secondary) (sex-
      linked hypochromic) (vitamin B_6
      responsive) 285.0
      refractory 238.7   ●
   sideropenic (refractory) 280.9
      due to blood loss (chronic) 280.0
         acute 285.1
   simple chronic 281.9
   specified type NEC 285.8
   spherocytic (hereditary) (*see also* Spherocytosis)
      282.0
   splenic 285.8
      familial (Gaucher's) 272.7
   splenomegalic 285.8
   stomatocytosis 282.8
   syphilitic 095.8
   target cell (oval) 282.49
   thalassemia 282.49
   thrombocytopenic (*see also* Thrombocytopenia)
      287.5
   toxic 284.8
   triosephosphate isomerase deficiency 282.3
   tropical, macrocytic 281.2
   tuberculous (*see also* Tuberculosis) 017.9 ☑
   vegan's 281.1
   vitamin
      B_6-responsive 285.0
      B_{12} deficiency (dietary) 281.1
         pernicious 281.0
   von Jaksch's (pseudoleukemia infantum) 285.8
   Witts' (achlorhydric anemia) 280.9
   Zuelzer (-Ogden) (nutritional megaloblastic
      anemia) 281.2
Anencephalus, anencephaly 740.0
   fetal, affecting management of pregnancy
      655.0 ☑
Anergasia (*see also* Psychosis, organic) 294.9
   senile 290.0
Anesthesia, anesthetic 782.0
   complication or reaction NEC 995.2
      due to
         correct substance properly administered
            995.2
         overdose or wrong substance given 968.4
         specified anesthetic — *see* Table of
            Drugs and Chemicals
   cornea 371.81
   death from
      correct substance properly administered
         995.4
      during delivery 668.9 ☑
      overdose or wrong substance given 968.4
      specified anesthetic — *see* Table of Drugs
         and Chemicals
   eye 371.81
   functional 300.11
   hyperesthetic, thalamic 348.8
   hysterical 300.11
   local skin lesion 782.0
   olfactory 781.1
   sexual (psychogenic) 302.72
   shock
      due to
         correct substance properly administered
            995.4
         overdose or wrong substance given 968.4
         specified anesthetic — *see* Table of Drugs
            and Chemicals
   skin 782.0
   tactile 782.0
   testicular 608.9
   thermal 782.0
Anetoderma (maculosum) 701.3
Aneuploidy NEC 758.5
Aneurin deficiency 265.1
Aneurysm (anastomotic) (artery) (cirsoid) (diffuse)
   (false) (fusiform) (multiple) (ruptured)
   (saccular) (varicose) 442.9
   abdominal (aorta) 441.4
      ruptured 441.3

Aneurysm — *continued*
   abdominal — *continued*
      syphilitic 093.0
   aorta, aortic (nonsyphilitic) 441.9
      abdominal 441.4
         dissecting 441.02
         ruptured 441.3
         syphilitic 093.0
      arch 441.2
         ruptured 441.1
      arteriosclerotic NEC 441.9
         ruptured 441.5
      ascending 441.2
         ruptured 441.1
      congenital 747.29
      descending 441.9
         abdominal 441.4
            ruptured 441.3
         ruptured 441.5
         thoracic 441.2
            ruptured 441.1
      dissecting 441.00
         abdominal 441.02
         thoracic 441.01
         thoracoabdominal 441.03
      due to coarctation (aorta) 747.10
      ruptured 441.5
      sinus, right 747.29
      syphilitic 093.0
      thoracoabdominal 441.7
         ruptured 441.6
      thorax, thoracic (arch) (nonsyphilitic) 441.2
         dissecting 441.01
         ruptured 441.1
         syphilitic 093.0
      transverse 441.2
         ruptured 441.1
      valve (heart) (*see also* Endocarditis, aortic)
         424.1
   arteriosclerotic NEC 442.9
      cerebral 437.3
         ruptured (*see also* Hemorrhage,
            subarachnoid) 430
   arteriovenous (congenital) (peripheral) NEC (*see*
      also Anomaly, arteriovenous) 747.60
      acquired NEC 447.0
         brain 437.3
            ruptured (*see also* Hemorrhage,
               subarachnoid) 430
         coronary 414.11
         pulmonary 417.0
      brain (cerebral) 747.81
         ruptured (*see also* Hemorrhage,
            subarachnoid) 430
      coronary 746.85
      pulmonary 747.3
      retina 743.58
      specified site NEC 747.89
         acquired 447.0
      traumatic (*see also* Injury, blood vessel, by
         site) 904.9
   basal — *see* Aneurysm, brain
   berry (congenital) (ruptured) (*see also*
      Hemorrhage, subarachnoid) 430
   brain 437.3
      arteriosclerotic 437.3
         ruptured (*see also* Hemorrhage,
            subarachnoid) 430
      arteriovenous 747.81
         acquired 437.3
            ruptured (*see also* Hemorrhage,
               subarachnoid) 430
         ruptured (*see also* Hemorrhage,
            subarachnoid) 430
      berry (congenital) (ruptured) (*see also*
         Hemorrhage, subarachnoid) 430
      congenital 747.81
         ruptured (*see also* Hemorrhage,
            subarachnoid) 430
      meninges 437.3
         ruptured (*see also* Hemorrhage,
            subarachnoid) 430
      miliary (congenital) (ruptured) (*see also*
         Hemorrhage, subarachnoid) 430

Aneurysm — *continued*
   brain — *continued*
      mycotic 421.0
         ruptured (*see also* Hemorrhage,
            subarachnoid) 430
      nonruptured 437.3
      ruptured (*see also* Hemorrhage,
         subarachnoid) 430
         syphilitic 094.87
      syphilitic (hemorrhage) 094.87
      traumatic — *see* Injury, intracranial
   cardiac (false) (*see also* Aneurysm, heart)
      414.10
   carotid artery (common) (external) 442.81
      internal (intracranial portion) 437.3
         extracranial portion 442.81
         ruptured into brain (*see also*
            Hemorrhage, subarachnoid) 430
      syphilitic 093.89
         intracranial 094.87
   cavernous sinus (*see also* Aneurysm, brain)
      437.3
      arteriovenous 747.81
         ruptured (*see also* Hemorrhage,
            subarachnoid) 430
      congenital 747.81
         ruptured (*see also* Hemorrhage,
            subarachnoid) 430
   celiac 442.84
   central nervous system, syphilitic 094.89
   cerebral — *see* Aneurysm, brain
   chest — *see* Aneurysm, thorax
   circle of Willis (*see also* Aneurysm, brain) 437.3
      congenital 747.81
         ruptured (*see also* Hemorrhage,
            subarachnoid) 430
      ruptured (*see also* Hemorrhage,
         subarachnoid) 430
   common iliac artery 442.2
   congenital (peripheral) NEC 747.60
      brain 747.81
         ruptured (*see also* Hemorrhage,
            subarachnoid) 430
      cerebral — *see* Aneurysm, brain, congenital
      coronary 746.85
      gastrointestinal 747.61
      lower limb 747.64
      pulmonary 747.3
      renal 747.62
      retina 743.58
      specified site NEC 747.89
      spinal 747.82
      upper limb 747.63
   conjunctiva 372.74
   conus arteriosus (*see also* Aneurysm, heart)
      414.10
   coronary (arteriosclerotic) (artery) (vein) (*see*
      also Aneurysm, heart) 414.11
      arteriovenous 746.85
      congenital 746.85
      syphilitic 093.89
   cylindrical 441.9
      ruptured 441.5
      syphilitic 093.9
   dissecting 442.9
      aorta 441.00
         abdominal 441.02
         thoracic 441.01
         thoracoabdominal 441.03
      syphilitic 093.9
   ductus arteriosus 747.0
   embolic — *see* Embolism, artery
   endocardial, infective (any valve) 421.0
   femoral 442.3
   gastroduodenal 442.84
   gastroepiploic 442.84
   heart (chronic or with a stated duration of over
      8 weeks) (infectional) (wall) 414.10
      acute or with a stated duration of 8 weeks
         or less (*see also* Infarct, myocardium)
         410.9 ☑
      congenital 746.89
      valve — *see* Endocarditis
   hepatic 442.84
   iliac (common) 442.2
   infective (any valve) 421.0

Aneurysm — *continued*
  innominate (nonsyphilitic) 442.89
    syphilitic 093.89
  interauricular septum (*see also* Aneurysm,
    heart) 414.10
  interventricular septum (*see also* Aneurysm,
    heart) 414.10
  intracranial — *see* Aneurysm, brain
  intrathoracic (nonsyphilitic) 441.2
    ruptured 441.1
    syphilitic 093.0
  jugular vein 453.8
  lower extremity 442.3
  lung (pulmonary artery) 417.1
  malignant 093.9
  mediastinal (nonsyphilitic) 442.89
    syphilitic 093.89
  miliary (congenital) (ruptured) (*see also*
    Hemorrhage, subarachnoid) 430
  mitral (heart) (valve) 424.0
  mural (arteriovenous) (heart) (*see also*
    Aneurysm, heart) 414.10
  mycotic, any site 421.0
    ruptured, brain (*see also* Hemorrhage,
      subarachnoid) 430
  myocardium (*see also* Aneurysm, heart) 414.10
  neck 442.81
  pancreaticoduodenal 442.84
  patent ductus arteriosus 747.0
  peripheral NEC 442.89
    congenital NEC (*see also* Aneurysm,
      congenital) 747.60
  popliteal 442.3
  pulmonary 417.1
    arteriovenous 747.3
      acquired 417.0
    syphilitic 093.89
    valve (heart) (*see also* Endocarditis,
      pulmonary) 424.3
  racemose 442.9
    congenital (peripheral) NEC 747.60
  radial 442.0
  Rasmussen's (*see also* Tuberculosis) 011.2 ☑
  renal 442.1
  retinal (acquired) 362.17
    congenital 743.58
    diabetic 250.5 ☑ *[362.01]*
  sinus, aortic (of Valsalva) 747.29
  specified site NEC 442.89
  spinal (cord) 442.89
    congenital 747.82
    syphilitic (hemorrhage) 094.89
  spleen, splenic 442.83
  subclavian 442.82
    syphilitic 093.89
  superior mesenteric 442.84
  syphilitic 093.9
    aorta 093.0
    central nervous system 094.89
    congenital 090.5
    spine, spinal 094.89
  thoracoabdominal 441.7
    ruptured 441.6
  thorax, thoracic (arch) (nonsyphilitic) 441.2
    dissecting 441.01
    ruptured 441.1
    syphilitic 093.0
  traumatic (complication) (early) — *see* Injury,
    blood vessel, by site
  tricuspid (heart) (valve) — *see* Endocarditis,
    tricuspid
  ulnar 442.0
  upper extremity 442.0
  valve, valvular — *see* Endocarditis
  venous 456.8
    congenital NEC (*see also* Aneurysm,
      congenital) 747.60
  ventricle (arteriovenous) (*see also* Aneurysm,
    heart) 414.10
  visceral artery NEC 442.84
Angiectasis 459.89
Angiectopia 459.9
Angiitis 447.6
  allergic granulomatous 446.4
  hypersensitivity 446.20
    Goodpasture's syndrome 446.21

Angiitis — *continued*
  hypersensitivity — *continued*
    specified NEC 446.29
  necrotizing 446.0
  Wegener's (necrotizing respiratory
    granulomatosis) 446.4
Angina (attack) (cardiac) (chest) (effort) (heart)
  (pectoris) (syndrome) (vasomotor) 413.9
  abdominal 557.1
  accelerated 411.1
  agranulocytic 288.0
  aphthous 074.0
  catarrhal 462
  crescendo 411.1
  croupous 464.4
  cruris 443.9
    due to atherosclerosis NEC (*see also*
      Arteriosclerosis, extremities) 440.20
  decubitus 413.0
  diphtheritic (membranous) 032.0
  erysipelatous 034.0
  erythematous 462
  exudative, chronic 476.0
  faucium 478.29
  gangrenous 462
    diphtheritic 032.0
  infectious 462
  initial 411.1
  intestinal 557.1
  ludovici 528.3
  Ludwig's 528.3
  malignant 462
    diphtheritic 032.0
  membranous 464.4
    diphtheritic 032.0
  mesenteric 557.1
  monocytic 075
  nocturnal 413.0
  phlegmonous 475
    diphtheritic 032.0
  preinfarctional 411.1
  Prinzmetal's 413.1
  progressive 411.1
  pseudomembranous 101
  psychogenic 306.2
  pultaceous, diphtheritic 032.0
  scarlatinal 034.1
  septic 034.0
  simple 462
  stable NEC 413.9
  staphylococcal 462
  streptococcal 034.0
  stridulous, diphtheritic 032.3
  syphilitic 093.9
    congenital 090.5
  tonsil 475
  trachealis 464.4
  unstable 411.1
  variant 413.1
  Vincent's 101
Angioblastoma (M9161/1) — *see* Neoplasm,
  connective tissue, uncertain behavior
Angiocholecystitis (*see also* Cholecystitis, acute)
  575.0
Angiocholitis (*see also* Cholecystitis, acute) 576.1
Angiodysgensis spinalis 336.1
Angiodysplasia (intestinalis) (intestine) 569.84
  with hemorrhage 569.85
  duodenum 537.82
    with hemorrhage 537.83
  stomach 537.82
    with hemorrhage 537.83
Angioedema (allergic) (any site) (with urticaria)
  995.1
  hereditary 277.6
Angioendothelioma (M9130/1) — *see also*
  Neoplasm, by site, uncertain behavior
  benign (M9130/0) (*see also* Hemangioma, by
    site) 228.00
  bone (M9260/3) — *see* Neoplasm, bone,
    malignant
  Ewing's (M9260/3) — *see* Neoplasm, bone,
    malignant
  nervous system (M9130/0) 228.09

Angiofibroma (M9160/0) — *see also* Neoplasm,
  by site, benign
  juvenile (M9160/0) 210.7
    specified site — *see* Neoplasm, by site,
      benign
    unspecified site 210.7
Angiohemophilia (A) (B) 286.4
Angioid streaks (choroid) (retina) 363.43
Angiokeratoma (M9141/0) — *see also* Neoplasm,
  skin, benign
  corporis diffusum 272.7
Angiokeratosis
  diffuse 272.7
Angioleiomyoma (M8894/0) — *see* Neoplasm,
  connective tissue, benign
Angioleucitis 683
Angiolipoma (M8861/0) (*see also* Lipoma, by site)
  214.9
  infiltrating (M8861/1) — *see* Neoplasm,
    connective tissue, uncertain behavior
Angioma (M9120/0) (*see also* Hemangioma, by
  site) 228.00
  capillary 448.1
  hemorrhagicum hereditaria 448.0
  malignant (M9120/3) — *see* Neoplasm,
    connective tissue, malignant
  pigmentosum et atrophicum 757.33
  placenta — *see* Placenta, abnormal
  plexiform (M9131/0) — *see* Hemangioma, by
    site
  senile 448.1
  serpiginosum 709.1
  spider 448.1
  stellate 448.1
Angiomatosis 757.32
  bacillary 083.8
  corporis diffusum universale 272.7
  cutaneocerebral 759.6
  encephalocutaneous 759.6
  encephalofacial 759.6
  encephalotrigeminal 759.6
  hemorrhagic familial 448.0
  hereditary familial 448.0
  heredofamilial 448.0
  meningo-oculofacial 759.6
  multiple sites 228.09
  neuro-oculocutaneous 759.6
  retina (Hippel's disease) 759.6
  retinocerebellosa 759.6
  retinocerebral 759.6
  systemic 228.09
Angiomyolipoma (M8860/0)
  specified site — *see* Neoplasm, connective
    tissue, benign
  unspecified site 223.0
Angiomyoliposarcoma (M8860/3) — *see*
  Neoplasm, connective tissue, malignant
Angiomyoma (M8894/0) — *see* Neoplasm,
  connective tissue, benign
Angiomyosarcoma (M8894/3) — *see* Neoplasm,
  connective tissue, malignant
Angioneurosis 306.2
Angioneurotic edema (allergic) (any site) (with
  urticaria) 995.1
  hereditary 277.6
Angiopathia, angiopathy 459.9
  diabetic (peripheral) 250.7 ☑ *[443.81]*
  peripheral 443.9
    diabetic 250.7 ☑ *[443.81]*
    specified type NEC 443.89
  retinae syphilitica 093.89
  retinalis (juvenilis) 362.18
    background 362.10
    diabetic 250.5 ☑ *[362.01]*
    proliferative 362.29
    tuberculous (*see also* Tuberculosis) 017.3 ☑
      [362.18]
Angiosarcoma (M9120/3) — *see* Neoplasm,
  connective tissue, malignant
Angiosclerosis — *see* Arteriosclerosis
Angioscotoma, enlarged 368.42
Angiospasm 443.9
  brachial plexus 353.0

Angiospasm — *continued*
  cerebral 435.9
  cervical plexus 353.2
  nerve
    arm 354.9
      axillary 353.0
      median 354.1
      ulnar 354.2
    autonomic (*see also* Neuropathy, peripheral,
      autonomic) 337.9
    axillary 353.0
    leg 355.8
      plantar 355.6
    lower extremity — *see* Angiospasm, nerve,
      leg
    median 354.1
    peripheral NEC 355.9
    spinal NEC 355.9
    sympathetic (*see also* Neuropathy,
      peripheral, autonomic) 337.9
    ulnar 354.2
    upper extremity — *see* Angiospasm, nerve,
      arm
  peripheral NEC 443.9
  traumatic 443.9
    foot 443.9
    leg 443.9
  vessel 443.9
Angiospastic disease or edema 443.9
Angle's
  class I 524.21
  class II 524.22
  class III 524.23
Anguillulosis 127.2
Angulation
  cecum (*see also* Obstruction, intestine) 560.9
  coccyx (acquired) 738.6
    congenital 756.19
  femur (acquired) 736.39
    congenital 755.69
  intestine (large) (small) (*see also* Obstruction,
    intestine) 560.9
  sacrum (acquired) 738.5
    congenital 756.19
  sigmoid (flexure) (*see also* Obstruction,
    intestine) 560.9
  spine (*see also* Curvature, spine) 737.9
  tibia (acquired) 736.89
    congenital 755.69
  ureter 593.3
  wrist (acquired) 736.09
    congenital 755.59
Angulus infectiosus 686.8
Anhedonia 302.72
Anhidrosis (lid) (neurogenic) (thermogenic) 705.0
Anhydration 276.51   ▲
  with
    hypernatremia 276.0
    hyponatremia 276.1
Anhydremia 276.52   ▲
  with
    hypernatremia 276.0
    hyponatremia 276.1
Anidrosis 705.0
Aniridia (congenital) 743.45
Anisakiasis (infection) (infestation) 127.1
Anisakis larva infestation 127.1
Aniseikonia 367.32
Anisocoria (pupil) 379.41
  congenital 743.46
Anisocytosis 790.09
Anisometropia (congenital) 367.31
Ankle — *see* condition
Ankyloblepharon (acquired) (eyelid) 374.46
  filiforme (adnatum) (congenital) 743.62
  total 743.62
Ankylodactly (*see also* Syndactylism) 755.10
Ankyloglossia 750.0
Ankylosis (fibrous) (osseous) 718.50
  ankle 718.57
  any joint, produced by surgical fusion V45.4
  cricoarytenoid (cartilage) (joint) (larynx) 478.79
  dental 521.6

Ankylosis — *continued*
  ear ossicle NEC 385.22
    malleus 385.21
  elbow 718.52
  finger 718.54
  hip 718.55
  incostapedial joint (infectional) 385.22
  joint, produced by surgical fusion NEC V45.4
  knee 718.56
  lumbosacral (joint) 724.6
  malleus 385.21
  multiple sites 718.59
  postoperative (status) V45.4
  sacroiliac (joint) 724.6
  shoulder 718.51
  specified site NEC 718.58
  spine NEC 724.9
  surgical V45.4
  teeth, tooth (hard tissues) 521.6
  temporomandibular joint 524.61
  wrist 718.53
Ankylostoma — *see* Ancylostoma
Ankylostomiasis (intestinal) — *see*
  Ancylostomiasis
Ankylurethria (*see also* Stricture, urethra) 598.9
Annular — *see also* condition
  detachment, cervix 622.8
  organ or site, congenital NEC — *see* Distortion
  pancreas (congenital) 751.7
Anodontia (complete) (partial) (vera) 520.0
  with abnormal spacing 524.30
  acquired 525.10
    causing malocclusion 524.30
    due to
      caries 525.13
      extraction 525.10
      periodontal disease 525.12
      trauma 525.11
Anomaly, anomalous (congenital) (unspecified
    type) 759.9
  abdomen 759.9
  abdominal wall 756.70
  acoustic nerve 742.9
  adrenal (gland) 759.1
  Alder (-Reilly) (leukocyte granulation) 288.2
  alimentary tract 751.9
    lower 751.5
    specified type NEC 751.8
    upper (any part, except tongue) 750.9
      tongue 750.10
        specified type NEC 750.19
  alveolar 524.70
    ridge (process) 525.8
    specified NEC 524.79
  ankle (joint) 755.69
  anus, anal (canal) 751.5
  aorta, aortic 747.20
    arch 747.21
    coarctation (postductal) (preductal) 747.10
    cusp or valve NEC 746.9
    septum 745.0
    specified type NEC 747.29
  aorticopulmonary septum 745.0
  apertures, diaphragm 756.6
  appendix 751.5
  aqueduct of Sylvius 742.3
    with spina bifida (*see also* Spina bifida)
      741.0 ☑
  arm 755.50
    reduction (*see also* Deformity, reduction,
      upper limb) 755.20
  arteriovenous (congenital) (peripheral) NEC
      747.60
    brain 747.81
    cerebral 747.81
    coronary 746.85
    gastrointestinal 747.61
      acquired — *see* Angiodysplasia   ●
    lower limb 747.64
    renal 747.62
    specified site NEC 747.69
    spinal 747.82
    upper limb 747.63
  artery (*see also* Anomaly, peripheral vascular
      system) NEC 747.60
    brain 747.81

Anomaly, anomalous — *continued*
  artery (*see also* Anomaly, peripheral vascular
      system) — *continued*
    cerebral 747.81
    coronary 746.85
    eye 743.9
    pulmonary 747.3
    renal 747.62
    retina 743.9
    umbilical 747.5
  arytenoepiglottic folds 748.3
  atrial
    bands 746.9
    folds 746.9
    septa 745.5
  atrioventricular
    canal 745.69
    common 745.69
    conduction 426.7
    excitation 426.7
    septum 745.4
  atrium — *see* Anomaly, atrial
  auditory canal 744.3
    specified type NEC 744.29
      with hearing impairment 744.02
  auricle
    ear 744.3
      causing impairment of hearing 744.02
    heart 746.9
      septum 745.5
  autosomes, autosomal NEC 758.5
  Axenfeld's 743.44
  back 759.9
  band
    atrial 746.9
    heart 746.9
    ventricular 746.9
  Bartholin's duct 750.9
  biliary duct or passage 751.60
    atresia 751.61
  bladder (neck) (sphincter) (trigone) 753.9
    specified type NEC 753.8
  blood vessel 747.9
    artery — *see* Anomaly, artery
    peripheral vascular — *see* Anomaly,
      peripheral vascular system
    vein — *see* Anomaly, vein
  bone NEC 756.9
    ankle 755.69
    arm 755.50
    chest 756.3
    cranium 756.0
    face 756.0
    finger 755.50
    foot 755.67
    forearm 755.50
    frontal 756.0
    head 756.0
    hip 755.63
    leg 755.60
    lumbosacral 756.10
    nose 748.1
    pelvic girdle 755.60
    rachitic 756.4
    rib 756.3
    shoulder girdle 755.50
    skull 756.0
      with
        anencephalus 740.0
        encephalocele 742.0
        hydrocephalus 742.3
          with spina bifida (*see also* Spina
            bifida) 741.0 ☑
        microcephalus 742.1
    toe 755.66
  brain 742.9
    multiple 742.4
    reduction 742.2
    specified type NEC 742.4
    vessel 747.81
  branchial cleft NEC 744.49
    cyst 744.42
    fistula 744.41
    persistent 744.41
    sinus (external) (internal) 744.41
  breast 757.9

Anomaly, anomalous — *continued*
  broad ligament 752.10
    specified type NEC 752.19
  bronchus 748.3
  bulbar septum 745.0
  bulbus cordis 745.9
    persistent (in left ventricle) 745.8
  bursa 756.9
  canal of Nuck 752.9
  canthus 743.9
  capillary NEC (*see also* Anomaly, peripheral
      vascular system) 747.60
  cardiac 746.9
    septal closure 745.9
      acquired 429.71
    valve NEC 746.9
      pulmonary 746.00
        specified type NEC 746.89
  cardiovascular system 746.9
    complicating pregnancy, childbirth, or
        puerperium 648.5 ☑
  carpus 755.50
  cartilage, trachea 748.3
  cartilaginous 756.9
  caruncle, lacrimal, lachrymal 743.9
  cascade stomach 750.7
  cauda equina 742.59
  cecum 751.5
  cerebral — *see also* Anomaly, brain vessels
      747.81
  cerebrovascular system 747.81
  cervix (uterus) 752.40
    with doubling of vagina and uterus 752.2
    in pregnancy or childbirth 654.6 ☑
      affecting fetus or newborn 763.89
      causing obstructed labor 660.2 ☑
        affecting fetus or newborn 763.1
  Chédiak-Higashi (-Steinbrinck) (congenital
      gigantism of peroxidase granules) 288.2
  cheek 744.9
  chest (wall) 756.3
  chin 744.9
    specified type NEC 744.89
  chordae tendineae 746.9
  choroid 743.9
    plexus 742.9
  chromosomes, chromosomal 758.9
    13 (13-15) 758.1
    18 (16-18) 758.2
    21 or 22 758.0
    autosomes NEC (*see also* Abnormal,
        autosomes) 758.5
      deletion 758.39
    Christchurch 758.39
    D₁ 758.1
    E₃ 758.2
    G 758.0
    mitochondrial 758.9
    mosaics 758.89
    sex 758.81
      complement, XO 758.6
      complement, XXX 758.81
      complement, XXY 758.7
      complement, XYY 758.81
      gonadal dysgenesis 758.6
      Klinefelter's 758.7
      Turner's 758.6
    trisomy 21 758.0
  cilia 743.9
  circulatory system 747.9
    specified type NEC 747.89
  clavicle 755.51
  clitoris 752.40
  coccyx 756.10
  colon 751.5
  common duct 751.60
  communication
    coronary artery 746.85
    left ventricle with right atrium 745.4
  concha (ear) 744.3
  connection
    renal vessels with kidney 747.62
    total pulmonary venous 747.41
  connective tissue 756.9
    specified type NEC 756.89
  cornea 743.9
    shape 743.41

Anomaly, anomalous — *continued*
  cornea — *continued*
    size 743.41
    specified type NEC 743.49
  coronary
    artery 746.85
    vein 746.89
  cranium — *see* Anomaly, skull
  cricoid cartilage 748.3
  cushion, endocardial 745.60
    specified type NEC 745.69
  cystic duct 751.60
  dental arch relationship 524.20
    angle's class I 524.21
    angle's class II 524.22
    angle's class III 524.23
    articulation
      anterior 524.27
      posterior 524.27
      reverse 524.27
    disto-occlusion 524.22
      division I 524.22
      division II 524.22
    excessive horizontal overlap 524.26
    interarch distance (excessive) (inadequate)
        524.28
    mesio-occlusion 524.23
    neutro-occlusion 524.21
    open
      anterior occlusal relationship 524.24
      posterior occlusal relationship 524.25
    specified NEC 524.29
  dentition 520.6
  dentofacial NEC 524.9
    functional 524.50
    specified type NEC 524.89
  dermatoglyphic 757.2
  Descemet's membrane 743.9
    specified type NEC 743.49
  development
    cervix 752.40
    vagina 752.40
    vulva 752.40
  diaphragm, diaphragmatic (apertures) NEC
      756.6
  digestive organ(s) or system 751.9
    lower 751.5
    specified type NEC 751.8
    upper 750.9
  distribution, coronary artery 746.85
  ductus
    arteriosus 747.0
    Botalli 747.0
  duodenum 751.5
  dura 742.9
    brain 742.4
    spinal cord 742.59
  ear 744.3
    causing impairment of hearing 744.00
      specified type NEC 744.09
    external 744.3
      causing impairment of hearing 744.02
      specified type NEC 744.29
    inner (causing impairment of hearing)
        744.05
    middle, except ossicles (causing impairment
        of hearing) 744.03
      ossicles 744.04
    ossicles 744.04
    prominent auricle 744.29
    specified type NEC 744.29
      with hearing impairment 744.09
  Ebstein's (heart) 746.2
    tricuspid valve 746.2
  ectodermal 757.9
  Eisenmenger's (ventricular septal defect) 745.4
  ejaculatory duct 752.9
    specified type NEC 752.89
  elbow (joint) 755.50
  endocardial cushion 745.60
    specified type NEC 745.69
  endocrine gland NEC 759.2
  epididymis 752.9
  epiglottis 748.3
  esophagus 750.9
    specified type NEC 750.4

Anomaly, anomalous — *continued*
  Eustachian tube 744.3
    specified type NEC 744.24
  eye (any part) 743.9
    adnexa 743.9
      specified type NEC 743.69
    anophthalmos 743.00
    anterior
      chamber and related structures 743.9
        angle 743.9
          specified type NEC 743.44
        specified type NEC 743.44
      segment 743.9
        combined 743.48
        multiple 743.48
        specified type NEC 743.49
    cataract (*see also* Cataract) 743.30
    glaucoma (*see also* Buphthalmia) 743.20
    lid 743.9
      specified type NEC 743.63
    microphthalmos (*see also* Microphthalmos)
        743.10
    posterior segment 743.9
      specified type NEC 743.59
      vascular 743.58
      vitreous 743.9
        specified type NEC 743.51
    ptosis (eyelid) 743.61
    retina 743.9
      specified type NEC 743.59
    sclera 743.9
      specified type NEC 743.47
    specified type NEC 743.8
  eyebrow 744.89
  eyelid 743.9
    specified type NEC 743.63
  face (any part) 744.9
    bone(s) 756.0
    specified type NEC 744.89
  fallopian tube 752.10
    specified type NEC 752.19
  fascia 756.9
    specified type NEC 756.89
  femur 755.60
  fibula 755.60
  finger 755.50
    supernumerary 755.01
    webbed (*see also* Syndactylism, fingers)
        755.11
  fixation, intestine 751.4
  flexion (joint) 755.9
    hip or thigh (*see also* Dislocation, hip,
        congenital) 754.30
  folds, heart 746.9
  foot 755.67
  foramen
    Botalli 745.5
    ovale 745.5
  forearm 755.50
  forehead (*see also* Anomaly, skull) 756.0
  form, teeth 520.2
  fovea centralis 743.9
  frontal bone (*see also* Anomaly, skull) 756.0
  gallbladder 751.60
  Gartner's duct 752.41   ▲
  gastrointestinal tract 751.9
    specified type NEC 751.8
    vessel 747.61
  genitalia, genital organ(s) or system
    female 752.9
      external 752.40
        specified type NEC 752.49
      internal NEC 752.9
    male (external and internal) 752.9
      epispadias 752.62
      hidden penis 752.65
      hydrocele, congenital 778.6
      hypospadias 752.61
      micropenis 752.64
      testis, undescended 752.51
        retractile 752.52
    specified type NEC 752.89
  genitourinary NEC 752.9
  Gerbode 745.4
  globe (eye) 743.9
  glottis 748.3

☑ Additional Digit Required — Refer to the Tabular List (Numeric Code Section) for Additional Digit Selection

Anomaly, anomalous — *continued*
  paraurethral ducts 753.9
  parotid (gland) 750.9
  patella 755.64
  Pelger-Huët (hereditary hyposegmentation) 288.2
  pelvic girdle 755.60
    specified type NEC 755.69
  pelvis (bony) 755.60
    complicating delivery 653.0 ☑
      rachitic 268.1
        fetal 756.4
  penis (glans) 752.69
  pericardium 746.89
  peripheral vascular system NEC 747.60
    gastrointestinal 747.61
    lower limb 747.64
    renal 747.62
    specified site NEC 747.69
    spinal 747.82
    upper limb 747.63
  Peter's 743.44
  pharynx 750.9
    branchial cleft 744.41
    specified type NEC 750.29
  Pierre Robin 756.0
  pigmentation 709.00
    congenital 757.33
    specified NEC 709.09
  pituitary (gland) 759.2
  pleural folds 748.8
  portal vein 747.40
  position tooth, teeth 524.30
    crowding 524.31
    displacement 524.30
      horizontal 524.33
      vertical 524.34
    distance
      interocclusal
        excessive 524.37
        insufficient 524.36
    excessive spacing 524.32
    rotation 524.35
    specified NEC 524.39
  preauricular sinus 744.46
  prepuce 752.9
  prostate 752.9
  pulmonary 748.60
    artery 747.3
    circulation 747.3
    specified type NEC 748.69
    valve 746.00
      atresia 746.01
      insufficiency 746.09
      specified type NEC 746.09
      stenosis 746.02
        infundibular 746.83
        subvalvular 746.83
    vein 747.40
    venous
      connection 747.49
        partial 747.42
        total 747.41
      return 747.49
        partial 747.42
        total (TAPVR) (complete)
          (subdiaphragmatic)
          (supradiaphragmatic) 747.41
  pupil 743.9
  pylorus 750.9
    hypertrophy 750.5
    stenosis 750.5
  rachitic, fetal 756.4
  radius 755.50
  rectovaginal (septum) 752.40
  rectum 751.5
  refraction 367.9
  renal 753.9
    vessel 747.62
  respiratory system 748.9
    specified type NEC 748.8
  rib 756.3
    cervical 756.2
  Rieger's 743.44
  rings, trachea 748.3

Anomaly, anomalous — *continued*
  rotation — *see also* Malrotation
    hip or thigh (*see also* Subluxation,
      congenital, hip) 754.32
  round ligament 752.9
  sacroiliac (joint) 755.69
  sacrum 756.10
  saddle
    back 754.2
    nose 754.0
      syphilitic 090.5
  salivary gland or duct 750.9
    specified type NEC 750.26
  scapula 755.50
  sclera 743.9
    specified type NEC 743.47
  scrotum 752.9
  sebaceous gland 757.9
  seminal duct or tract 752.9
  sense organs 742.9
    specified type NEC 742.8
  septum
    heart — *see* Anomaly, heart, septum
    nasal 748.1
  sex chromosomes NEC (*see also* Anomaly,
      chromosomes) 758.81
  shoulder (girdle) (joint) 755.50
    specified type NEC 755.59
  sigmoid (flexure) 751.5
  sinus of Valsalva 747.29
  site NEC 759.9
  skeleton generalized NEC 756.50
  skin (appendage) 757.9
    specified type NEC 757.39
  skull (bone) 756.0
    with
      anencephalus 740.0
      encephalocele 742.0
      hydrocephalus 742.3
        with spina bifida (*see also* Spina
          bifida) 741.0 ☑
      microcephalus 742.1
  specified type NEC
    adrenal (gland) 759.1
    alimentary tract (complete) (partial) 751.8
      lower 751.5
      upper 750.8
    ankle 755.69
    anus, anal (canal) 751.5
    aorta, aortic 747.29
      arch 747.21
    appendix 751.5
    arm 755.59
    artery (peripheral) NEC (*see also* Anomaly,
        peripheral vascular system) 747.60
      brain 747.81
      coronary 746.85
      eye 743.58
      pulmonary 747.3
      retinal 743.58
      umbilical 747.5
    auditory canal 744.29
      causing impairment of hearing 744.02
    bile duct or passage 751.69
    bladder 753.8
      neck 753.8
    bone(s) 756.9
      arm 755.59
      face 756.0
      leg 755.69
      pelvic girdle 755.69
      shoulder girdle 755.59
      skull 756.0
        with
          anencephalus 740.0
          encephalocele 742.0
          hydrocephalus 742.3
            with spina bifida (*see also* Spina
              bifida) 741.0 ☑
          microcephalus 742.1
    brain 742.4
    breast 757.6
    broad ligament 752.19
    bronchus 748.3
    canal of Nuck 752.89
    cardiac septal closure 745.8
    carpus 755.59

Anomaly, anomalous — *continued*
  specified type — *continued*
    cartilaginous 756.9
    cecum 751.5
    cervix 752.49
    chest (wall) 756.3
    chin 744.89
    ciliary body 743.46
    circulatory system 747.89
    clavicle 755.51
    clitoris 752.49
    coccyx 756.19
    colon 751.5
    common duct 751.69
    connective tissue 756.89
    cricoid cartilage 748.3
    cystic duct 751.69
    diaphragm 756.6
    digestive organ(s) or tract 751.8
      lower 751.5
      upper 750.8
    duodenum 751.5
    ear 744.29
      auricle 744.29
        causing impairment of hearing 744.02
      causing impairment of hearing 744.09
      inner (causing impairment of hearing)
          744.05
      middle, except ossicles 744.03
        ossicles 744.04
    ejaculatory duct 752.89
    endocrine 759.2
    epiglottis 748.3
    esophagus 750.4
    Eustachian tube 744.24
    eye 743.8
      lid 743.63
      muscle 743.69
    face 744.89
      bone(s) 756.0
    fallopian tube 752.19
    fascia 756.89
    femur 755.69
    fibula 755.69
    finger 755.59
    foot 755.67
    fovea centralis 743.55
    gallbladder 751.69
    Gartner's duct 752.89
    gastrointestinal tract 751.8
    genitalia, genital organ(s)
      female 752.89
        external 752.49
        internal NEC 752.89
      male 752.89
        penis 752.69
        scrotal transposition 752.81
    genitourinary tract NEC 752.89
    glottis 748.3
    hair 757.4
    hand 755.59
    heart 746.89
      valve NEC 746.89
        pulmonary 746.09
    hepatic duct 751.69
    hydatid of Morgagni 752.89
    hymen 752.49
    integument 757.8
    intestine (large) (small) 751.5
      fixational type 751.4
    iris 743.46
    jejunum 751.5
    joint 755.8
    kidney 753.3
    knee 755.64
    labium (majus) (minus) 752.49
    labyrinth, membranous 744.05
    larynx 748.3
    leg 755.69
    lens 743.39
    limb, except reduction deformity 755.8
      lower 755.69
        reduction deformity (*see also*
            Deformity, reduction, lower limb)
            755.30

☑ Additional Digit Required — Refer to the Tabular List (Numeric Code Section) for Additional Digit Selection
▶◀ Revised Text   ● New Line   ▲ Revised Code

2006 ICD-9-CM

Volume 2 — 29

Anomaly, anomalous — *continued*
  specified type — *continued*
    limb, except reduction deformity —
      continued
        upper 755.59
          reduction deformity (*see also*
            Deformity, reduction, upper
            limb) 755.20
    lip 750.26
    liver 751.69
    lung (fissure) (lobe) 748.69
    meatus urinarius 753.8
    metacarpus 755.59
    mouth 750.26
    muscle 756.89
      eye 743.69
    musculoskeletal system, except limbs 756.9
    nail 757.5
    neck 744.89
    nerve 742.8
      acoustic 742.8
      optic 742.8
    nervous system 742.8
    nipple 757.6
    nose 748.1
    organ NEC 759.89
      of Corti 744.05
    osseous meatus (ear) 744.03
    ovary 752.0
    oviduct 752.19
    pancreas 751.7
    parathyroid 759.2
    patella 755.64
    pelvic girdle 755.69
    penis 752.69
    pericardium 746.89
    peripheral vascular system NEC (*see also*
      Anomaly, peripheral vascular system)
      747.60
    pharynx 750.29
    pituitary 759.2
    prostate 752.89
    radius 755.59
    rectum 751.5
    respiratory system 748.8
    rib 756.3
    round ligament 752.89
    sacrum 756.19
    salivary duct or gland 750.26
    scapula 755.59
    sclera 743.47
    scrotum 752.89
      transposition 752.81
    seminal duct or tract 752.89
    shoulder girdle 755.59
    site NEC 759.89
    skin 757.39
    skull (bone(s)) 756.0
      with
        anencephalus 740.0
        encephalocele 742.0
        hydrocephalus 742.3
          with spina bifida (*see also* Spina
            bifida) 741.0 ☑
        microcephalus 742.1
    specified organ or site NEC 759.89
    spermatic cord 752.89
    spinal cord 742.59
    spine 756.19
    spleen 759.0
    sternum 756.3
    stomach 750.7
    tarsus 755.67
    tendon 756.89
    testis 752.89
    thorax (wall) 756.3
    thymus 759.2
    thyroid (gland) 759.2
      cartilage 748.3
    tibia 755.69
    toe 755.66
    tongue 750.19
    trachea (cartilage) 748.3
    ulna 755.59
    urachus 753.7
    ureter 753.4
      obstructive 753.29

Anomaly, anomalous — *continued*
  specified type — *continued*
    urethra 753.8
      obstructive 753.6
    urinary tract 753.8
    uterus 752.3
    uvula 750.26
    vagina 752.49
    vascular NEC (*see also* Anomaly, peripheral
      vascular system) 747.60
      brain 747.81
    vas deferens 752.89
    vein(s) (peripheral) NEC (*see also* Anomaly,
      peripheral vascular system) 747.60
      brain 747.81
      great 747.49
      portal 747.49
      pulmonary 747.49
    vena cava (inferior) (superior) 747.49
    vertebra 756.19
    vulva 752.49
  spermatic cord 752.9
  spine, spinal 756.10
    column 756.10
    cord 742.9
      meningocele (*see also* Spina bifida)
        741.9 ☑
      specified type NEC 742.59
      spina bifida (*see also* Spina bifida)
        741.9 ☑
      vessel 747.82
    meninges 742.59
    nerve root 742.9
  spleen 759.0
  Sprengel's 755.52
  sternum 756.3
  stomach 750.9
    specified type NEC 750.7
  submaxillary gland 750.9
  superior vena cava 747.40
  talipes — *see* Talipes
  tarsus 755.67
    with complete absence of distal elements
      755.31
  teeth, tooth NEC 520.9
    position 524.30
      crowding 524.31
      displacement 524.30
        horizontal 524.33
        vertical 524.34
      distance
        interocclusal
          excessive 524.37
          insufficient 524.36
        excessive spacing 524.32
      rotation 524.35
      specified NEC 524.39
    spacing 524.30
  tendon 756.9
    specified type NEC 756.89
  termination
    coronary artery 746.85
  testis 752.9
  thebesian valve 746.9
  thigh 755.60
    flexion (*see also* Subluxation, congenital,
      hip) 754.32
  thorax (wall) 756.3
  throat 750.9
  thumb 755.50
    supernumerary 755.01
  thymus gland 759.2
  thyroid (gland) 759.2
    cartilage 748.3
  tibia 755.60
    saber 090.5
  toe 755.66
    supernumerary 755.02
    webbed (*see also* Syndactylism, toes) 755.13
  tongue 750.10
    specified type NEC 750.19
  trachea, tracheal 748.3
    cartilage 748.3
    rings 748.3
  tragus 744.3
  transverse aortic arch 747.21
  trichromata 368.59

Anomaly, anomalous — *continued*
  trichromatopsia 368.59
  tricuspid (leaflet) (valve) 746.9
    atresia 746.1
    Ebstein's 746.2
    specified type NEC 746.89
    stenosis 746.1
  trunk 759.9
  Uhl's (hypoplasia of myocardium, right
    ventricle) 746.84
  ulna 755.50
  umbilicus 759.9
    artery 747.5
  union, trachea with larynx 748.3
  unspecified site 759.9
  upper extremity 755.50
    vessel 747.63
  urachus 753.7
    specified type NEC 753.7
  ureter 753.9
    obstructive 753.20
    specified type NEC 753.4
      obstructive 753.29
  urethra (valve) 753.9
    obstructive 753.6
    specified type NEC 753.8
  urinary tract or system (any part, except
    urachus) 753.9
    specified type NEC 753.8
    urachus 753.7
  uterus 752.3
    with only one functioning horn 752.3
    in pregnancy or childbirth 654.0 ☑
      affecting fetus or newborn 763.89
      causing obstructed labor 660.2 ☑
        affecting fetus or newborn 763.1
  uvula 750.9
  vagina 752.40
  valleculae 748.3
  valve (heart) NEC 746.9
    formation, ureter 753.29
    pulmonary 746.00
    specified type NEC 746.89
  vascular NEC (*see also* Anomaly, peripheral
    vascular system) 747.60
    ring 747.21
  vas deferens 752.9
  vein(s) (peripheral) NEC (*see also* Anomaly,
    peripheral vascular system) 747.60
    brain 747.81
    cerebral 747.81
    coronary 746.89
    great 747.40
      specified type NEC 747.49
    portal 747.40
    pulmonary 747.40
    retina 743.9
  vena cava (inferior) (superior) 747.40
  venous return (pulmonary) 747.49
    partial 747.42
    total 747.41
  ventricle, ventricular (heart) 746.9
    bands 746.9
    folds 746.9
    septa 745.4
  vertebra 756.10
  vesicourethral orifice 753.9
  vessels NEC (*see also* Anomaly, peripheral
    vascular system) 747.60
    optic papilla 743.9
  vitelline duct 751.0
  vitreous humor 743.9
    specified type NEC 743.51
  vulva 752.40
  wrist (joint) 755.50
Anomia 784.69
Anonychia 757.5
  acquired 703.8
Anophthalmos, anophthalmus (clinical)
  (congenital) (globe) 743.00
  acquired V45.78
Anopsia (altitudinal) (quadrant) 368.46
Anorchia 752.89
Anorchism, anorchidism 752.89

Anorexia 783.0
  hysterical 300.11
  nervosa 307.1
Anosmia (*see also* Disturbance, sensation) 781.1
  hysterical 300.11
  postinfectional 478.9
  psychogenic 306.7
  traumatic 951.8
Anosognosia 780.99
Anosphrasia 781.1
Anosteoplasia 756.50
Anotia 744.09
Anovulatory cycle 628.0
Anoxemia 799.02 ▲
  newborn 768.9
Anoxia 799.02 ▲
  altitude 993.2
  cerebral 348.1
    with
      abortion — *see* Abortion, by type, with
        specified complication NEC
      ectopic pregnancy (*see also* categories
        633.0-633.9) 639.8
      molar pregnancy (*see also* categories 630-
        632) 639.8
    complicating
      delivery (cesarean) (instrumental)
        669.4 ☑
      ectopic or molar pregnancy 639.8
      obstetric anesthesia or sedation 668.2 ☑
    during or resulting from a procedure 997.01
    following
      abortion 639.8
      ectopic or molar pregnancy 639.8
    newborn (*see also* Distress, fetal, liveborn
      infant) 768.9
  due to drowning 994.1
  fetal, affecting newborn 768.9
  heart — *see* Insufficiency, coronary
  high altitude 993.2
  intrauterine
    fetal death (before onset of labor) 768.0
      during labor 768.1
    liveborn infant — *see* Distress, fetal,
      liveborn infant
  myocardial — *see* Insufficiency, coronary
  newborn 768.9
    mild or moderate 768.6
    severe 768.5
  pathological 799.02 ▲
Anteflexion — *see* Anteversion
Antenatal
  care, normal pregnancy V22.1
    first V22.0
  screening (for) V28.9
    based on amniocentesis NEC V28.2
      chromosomal anomalies V28.0
      raised alphafetoprotein levels V28.1
    chromosomal anomalies V28.0
    fetal growth retardation using ultrasonics
      V28.4
    isoimmunization V28.5
    malformations using ultrasonics V28.3
    raised alphafetoprotein levels in amniotic
      fluid V28.1
    specified condition NEC V28.8
    Streptococcus B V28.6
Antepartum — *see* condition
Anterior — *see also* condition
  spinal artery compression syndrome 721.1
Antero-occlusion 524.24
Anteversion
  cervix (*see also* Anteversion, uterus) 621.6
  femur (neck), congenital 755.63
  uterus, uterine (cervix) (postinfectional)
    (postpartal, old) 621.6
    congenital 752.3
    in pregnancy or childbirth 654.4 ☑
      affecting fetus or newborn 763.89
      causing obstructed labor 660.2 ☑
        affecting fetus or newborn 763.1
Anthracosilicosis (occupational) 500
Anthracosis (lung) (occupational) 500
  lingua 529.3

Anthrax 022.9
  with pneumonia 022.1 *[484.5]*
  colitis 022.2
  cutaneous 022.0
  gastrointestinal 022.2
  intestinal 022.2
  pulmonary 022.1
  respiratory 022.1
  septicemia 022.3
  specified manifestation NEC 022.8
Anthropoid pelvis 755.69
  with disproportion (fetopelvic) 653.2 ☑
    affecting fetus or newborn 763.1
    causing obstructed labor 660.1 ☑
      affecting fetus or newborn 763.1
Anthropophobia 300.29
Antibioma, breast 611.0
Antibodies
  maternal (blood group) (*see also*
    Incompatibility) 656.2 ☑
    anti-D, cord blood 656.1 ☑
      fetus or newborn 773.0
Antibody deficiency syndrome
  agammaglobulinemic 279.00
  congenital 279.04
  hypogammaglobulinemic 279.00
Anticoagulant, circulating (*see also* Circulating
  anticoagulants) 286.5
Antimongolism syndrome 758.39
Antimonial cholera 985.4
Antisocial personality 301.7
Antithrombinemia (*see also* Circulating
  anticoagulants) 286.5
Antithromboplastinemia (*see also* Circulating
  anticoagulants) 286.5
Antithromboplastinogenemia (*see also*
  Circulating anticoagulants) 286.5
Antitoxin complication or reaction — *see*
  Complications, vaccination
Anton (-Babinski) syndrome
  (hemiasomatognosia) 307.9
Antritis (chronic) 473.0
  maxilla 473.0 ●
    acute 461.0 ●
  stomach 535.4 ☑ ●
Antrum, antral — *see* condition
Anuria 788.5
  with
    abortion — *see* Abortion, by type, with renal
      failure
    ectopic pregnancy (*see also* categories
      633.0-633.9) 639.3
    molar pregnancy (*see also* categories 630-
      632) 639.3
  calculus (impacted) (recurrent) 592.9
    kidney 592.0
    ureter 592.1
  congenital 753.3
  due to a procedure 997.5
  following
    abortion 639.3
    ectopic or molar pregnancy 639.3
  newborn 753.3
  postrenal 593.4
  puerperal, postpartum, childbirth 669.3 ☑
  specified as due to a procedure 997.5
  sulfonamide
    correct substance properly administered
      788.5
    overdose or wrong substance given or taken
      961.0
  traumatic (following crushing) 958.5
Anus, anal — *see* condition
Anusitis 569.49
Anxiety (neurosis) (reaction) (state) 300.00
  alcohol-induced 291.89
  depression 300.4
  drug-induced 292.89
  due to or associated with physical condition
    293.84
  generalized 300.02
  hysteria 300.20

Anxiety — *continued*
  in
    acute stress reaction 308.0
    transient adjustment reaction 309.24
  panic type 300.01
  separation, abnormal 309.21
  syndrome (organic) (transient) 293.84
Aorta, aortic — *see* condition
Aortectasia 441.9
Aortitis (nonsyphilitic) 447.6
  arteriosclerotic 440.0
  calcific 447.6
  Döhle-Heller 093.1
  luetic 093.1
  rheumatic (*see also* Endocarditis, acute,
    rheumatic) 391.1
  rheumatoid — *see* Arthritis, rheumatoid
  specific 093.1
  syphilitic 093.1
    congenital 090.5
Apathetic thyroid storm (*see also* Thyrotoxicosis)
  242.9 ☑
Apepsia 536.8
  achlorhydric 536.0
  psychogenic 306.4
Aperistalsis, esophagus 530.0
Apert's syndrome (acrocephalosyndactyly) 755.55
Apert-Gallais syndrome (adrenogenital) 255.2
Apertognathia 524.20
Aphagia 787.2
  psychogenic 307.1
Aphakia (acquired) (bilateral) (postoperative)
  (unilateral) 379.31
  congenital 743.35
Aphalangia (congenital) 755.4
  lower limb (complete) (intercalary) (partial)
    (terminal) 755.39
    meaning all digits (complete) (partial) 755.31
    transverse 755.31
  upper limb (complete) (intercalary) (partial)
    (terminal) 755.29
    meaning all digits (complete) (partial) 755.21
    transverse 755.21
Aphasia (amnestic) (ataxic) (auditory) (Broca's)
  (choreatic) (classic) (expressive) (global)
  (ideational) (ideokinetic) (ideomotor) (jargon)
  (motor) (nominal) (receptive) (semantic)
  (sensory) (syntactic) (verbal) (visual)
  (Wernicke's) 784.3
  developmental 315.31
  syphilis, tertiary 094.89
  uremic — *see* Uremia
Aphemia 784.3
  uremic — *see* Uremia
Aphonia 784.41
  clericorum 784.49
  hysterical 300.11
  organic 784.41
  psychogenic 306.1
Aphthae, aphthous — *see also* condition
  Bednar's 528.2
  cachectic 529.0
  epizootic 078.4
  fever 078.4
  oral 528.2
  stomatitis 528.2
  thrush 112.0
  ulcer (oral) (recurrent) 528.2
    genital organ(s) NEC
      female 629.8
      male 608.89
    larynx 478.79
Apical — *see* condition
Apical ballooning syndrome 429.89 ●
Aplasia — *see also* Agenesis
  alveolar process (acquired) 525.8
    congenital 750.26
  aorta (congenital) 747.22
  aortic valve (congenital) 746.89
  axialis extracorticalis (congenital) 330.0
  bone marrow (myeloid) 284.9
    acquired (secondary) 284.8
    congenital 284.0

Aplasia — *see also* Agenesis — *continued*
bone marrow — *continued*
idiopathic 284.9
brain 740.0
specified part 742.2
breast 757.6
bronchus 748.3
cementum 520.4
cerebellar 742.2
congenital pure red cell 284.0
corpus callosum 742.2
erythrocyte 284.8
congenital 284.0
extracortical axial 330.0
eye (congenital) 743.00
fovea centralis (congenital) 743.55
germinal (cell) 606.0
iris 743.45
labyrinth, membranous 744.05
limb (congenital) 755.4
lower NEC 755.30
upper NEC 755.20
lung (bilateral) (congenital) (unilateral) 748.5
nervous system NEC 742.8
nuclear 742.8
ovary 752.0
Pelizaeus-Merzbacher 330.0
prostate (congenital) 752.89
red cell (pure) (with thymoma) 284.8
acquired (secondary) 284.8
congenital 284.0
hereditary 284.0
of infants 284.0
primary 284.0
round ligament (congenital) 752.89
salivary gland 750.21
skin (congenital) 757.39
spinal cord 742.59
spleen 759.0
testis (congenital) 752.89
thymic, with immunodeficiency 279.2
thyroid 243
uterus 752.3
ventral horn cell 742.59

Apleuria 756.3

Apnea, apneic (spells) 786.03
newborn, neonatorum 770.81
essential 770.81
obstructive 770.82
primary 770.81
sleep 770.81
specified NEC 770.82
psychogenic 306.1
sleep, ▶unspecified◀ 780.57
with
hypersomnia, ▶unspecified◀ 780.53
hyposomnia, ▶unspecified◀ 780.51
insomnia, ▶unspecified◀ 780.51
sleep disturbance 780.57
central, in conditions classified ●
elsewhere 327.27 ●
obstructive (adult) (pediatric) 327.23 ●
organic 327.20 ●
other 327.29 ●
primary central 327.21 ●

Apneumatosis newborn 770.4

Apodia 755.31

Apophysitis (bone) (*see also* Osteochondrosis) 732.9
calcaneus 732.5
juvenile 732.6

Apoplectiform convulsions (*see also* Disease, cerebrovascular, acute) 436

Apoplexia, apoplexy, apoplectic (*see also* Disease, cerebrovascular, acute) 436
abdominal 569.89
adrenal 036.3
attack 436
basilar (*see also* Disease, cerebrovascular, acute) 436
brain (*see also* Disease, cerebrovascular, acute) 436
bulbar (*see also* Disease, cerebrovascular, acute) 436

Apoplexia, apoplexy, apoplectic (*see also* Disease, cerebrovascular, acute) — *continued*
capillary (*see also* Disease, cerebrovascular, acute) 436
cardiac (*see also* Infarct, myocardium) 410.9 ☑
cerebral (*see also* Disease, cerebrovascular, acute) 436
chorea (*see also* Disease, cerebrovascular, acute) 436
congestive (*see also* Disease, cerebrovascular, acute) 436
newborn 767.4
embolic (*see also* Embolism, brain) 434.1 ☑
fetus 767.0
fit (*see also* Disease, cerebrovascular, acute) 436
healed or old V12.59
heart (auricle) (ventricle) (*see also* Infarct, myocardium) 410.9 ☑
heat 992.0
hemiplegia (*see also* Disease, cerebrovascular, acute) 436
hemorrhagic (stroke) (*see also* Hemorrhage, brain) 432.9
ingravescent (*see also* Disease, cerebrovascular, acute) 436
late effect — *see* Late effect(s) (of) cerebrovascular disease
lung — *see* Embolism, pulmonary
meninges, hemorrhagic (*see also* Hemorrhage, subarachnoid) 430
neonatorum 767.0
newborn 767.0
pancreatitis 577.0
placenta 641.2 ☑
progressive (*see also* Disease, cerebrovascular, acute) 436
pulmonary (artery) (vein) — *see* Embolism, pulmonary
sanguineous (*see also* Disease, cerebrovascular, acute) 436
seizure (*see also* Disease, cerebrovascular, acute) 436
serous (*see also* Disease, cerebrovascular, acute) 436
spleen 289.59
stroke (*see also* Disease, cerebrovascular, acute) 436
thrombotic (*see also* Thrombosis, brain) 434.0 ☑
uremic — *see* Uremia
uteroplacental 641.2 ☑

Appendage
fallopian tube (cyst of Morgagni) 752.11
intestine (epiploic) 751.5
preauricular 744.1
testicular (organ of Morgagni) 752.89

Appendicitis 541
with
perforation, peritonitis (generalized), or rupture 540.0
with peritoneal abscess 540.1
peritoneal abscess 540.1
acute (catarrhal) (fulminating) (gangrenous) (inflammatory) (obstructive) (retrocecal) (suppurative) 540.9
with
perforation, peritonitis, or rupture 540.0
with peritoneal abscess 540.1
peritoneal abscess 540.1
amebic 006.8
chronic (recurrent) 542
exacerbation — *see* Appendicitis, acute
fulminating — *see* Appendicitis, acute
gangrenous — *see* Appendicitis, acute
healed (obliterative) 542
interval 542
neurogenic 542
obstructive 542
pneumococcal 541
recurrent 542
relapsing 542
retrocecal 541
subacute (adhesive) 542
subsiding 542

Appendicitis — *continued*
suppurative — *see* Appendicitis, acute
tuberculous (*see also* Tuberculosis) 014.8 ☑

Appendiclausis 543.9

Appendicolithiasis 543.9

Appendicopathia oxyurica 127.4

Appendix, appendicular — *see also* condition
Morgagni (male) 752.89
fallopian tube 752.11

Appetite
depraved 307.52
excessive 783.6
psychogenic 307.51
lack or loss (*see also* Anorexia) 783.0
nonorganic origin 307.59
perverted 307.52
hysterical 300.11

Apprehension, apprehensiveness (abnormal) (state) 300.00
specified type NEC 300.09

Approximal wear 521.10

Apraxia (classic) (ideational) (ideokinetic) (ideomotor) (motor) 784.69
oculomotor, congenital 379.51
verbal 784.69

Aptyalism 527.7

Aqueous misdirection 365.83

Arabicum elephantiasis (*see also* Infestation, filarial) 125.9

Arachnidism 989.5

Arachnitis — *see* Meningitis

Arachnodactyly 759.82

Arachnoidism 989.5

Arachnoiditis (acute) (adhesive) (basic) (brain) (cerebrospinal) (chiasmal) (chronic) (spinal) (*see also* Meningitis) 322.9
meningococcal (chronic) 036.0
syphilitic 094.2
tuberculous (*see also* Tuberculosis, meninges) 013.0 ☑

Araneism 989.5

Arboencephalitis, Australian 062.4

Arborization block (heart) 426.6

Arbor virus, arbovirus (infection) NEC 066.9

ARC 042

Arches — *see* condition

Arcuatus uterus 752.3

Arcus (cornea)
juvenilis 743.43
interfering with vision 743.42
senilis 371.41

Arc-welders' lung 503

Arc-welders' syndrome (photokeratitis) 370.24

Areflexia 796.1

Areola — *see* condition

Argentaffinoma (M8241/1) — *see also* Neoplasm, by site, uncertain behavior
benign (M8241/0) — *see* Neoplasm, by site, benign
malignant (M8241/3) — *see* Neoplasm, by site, malignant
syndrome 259.2

Argentinian hemorrhagic fever 078.7

Arginosuccinicaciduria 270.6

Argonz-Del Castillo syndrome (nonpuerperal galactorrhea and amenorrhea) 253.1

Argyll-Robertson phenomenon, pupil, or syndrome (syphilitic) 094.89
atypical 379.45
nonluetic 379.45
nonsyphilitic 379.45
reversed 379.45

Argyria, argyriasis NEC 985.8
conjunctiva 372.55
cornea 371.16
from drug or medicinal agent
correct substance properly administered 709.09
overdose or wrong substance given or taken 961.2

Arhinencephaly 742.2
Arias-Stella phenomenon 621.30
Ariboflavinosis 266.0
Arizona enteritis 008.1
Arm — *see* condition
Armenian disease 277.3
Arnold-Chiari obstruction or syndrome (*see also*
    Spina bifida) 741.0 ☑
  type I 348.4
  type II (*see also* Spina bifida) 741.0 ☑
  type III 742.0
  type IV 742.2
Arousals   ●
  confusional 327.41   ●
Arrest, arrested
  active phase of labor 661.1 ☑
    affecting fetus or newborn 763.7
  any plane in pelvis
    complicating delivery 660.1 ☑
      affecting fetus or newborn 763.1
  bone marrow (*see also* Anemia, aplastic) 284.9
  cardiac 427.5
    with
      abortion — *see* Abortion, by type, with
        specified complication NEC
      ectopic pregnancy (*see also* categories
        633.0-633.9) 639.8
      molar pregnancy (*see also* categories 630-
        632) 639.8
    complicating
      anesthesia
        correct substance properly
          administered 427.5
        obstetric 668.1 ☑
        overdose or wrong substance given 968.4
          specified anesthetic — *see* Table of
            Drugs and Chemicals
      delivery (cesarean) (instrumental)
        669.4 ☑
      ectopic or molar pregnancy 639.8
      surgery (nontherapeutic) (therapeutic)
        997.1
    fetus or newborn 779.89
    following
      abortion 639.8
      ectopic or molar pregnancy 639.8
    postoperative (immediate) 997.1
      long-term effect of cardiac surgery 429.4
  cardiorespiratory (*see also* Arrest, cardiac)
    427.5
  deep transverse 660.3 ☑
    affecting fetus or newborn 763.1
  development or growth
    bone 733.91
    child 783.40
    fetus 764.9 ☑
      affecting management of pregnancy 656.5
        ☑
    tracheal rings 748.3
  epiphyseal 733.91
  granulopoiesis 288.0
  heart — *see* Arrest, cardiac
  respiratory 799.1
    newborn 770.89
  sinus 426.6
  transverse (deep) 660.3 ☑
    affecting fetus or newborn 763.1
Arrhenoblastoma (M8630/1)
  benign (M8630/0)
    specified site — *see* Neoplasm, by site,
      benign
    unspecified site
      female 220
      male 222.0
  malignant (M8630/3)
    specified site — *see* Neoplasm, by site,
      malignant
    unspecified site
      female 183.0
      male 186.9
  specified site — *see* Neoplasm, by site,
    uncertain behavior
  unspecified site
    female 236.2
    male 236.4

Arrhinencephaly 742.2
  due to
    trisomy 13 (13-15) 758.1
    trisomy 18 (16-18) 758.2
Arrhythmia (auricle) (cardiac) (cordis) (gallop
    rhythm) (juvenile) (nodal) (reflex) (sinus)
    (supraventricular) (transitory) (ventricle)
    427.9
  bigeminal rhythm 427.89
  block 426.9
  bradycardia 427.89
  contractions, premature 427.60
  coronary sinus 427.89
  ectopic 427.89
  extrasystolic 427.60
  postoperative 997.1
  psychogenic 306.2
  vagal 780.2
Arrillaga-Ayerza syndrome (pulmonary artery
    sclerosis with pulmonary hypertension)
    416.0
Arsenical
  dermatitis 692.4
  keratosis 692.4
  pigmentation 985.1
    from drug or medicinal agent
      correct substance properly administered
        709.09
      overdose or wrong substance given or
        taken 961.1
Arsenism 985.1
  from drug or medicinal agent
    correct substance properly administered
      692.4
    overdose or wrong substance given or taken
      961.1
Arterial — *see* condition
Arteriectasis 447.8
Arteriofibrosis — *see* Arteriosclerosis
Arteriolar sclerosis — *see* Arteriosclerosis
Arteriolith — *see* Arteriosclerosis
Arteriolitis 447.6
  necrotizing, kidney 447.5
  renal — *see* Hypertension, kidney
Arteriolosclerosis — *see* Arteriosclerosis
Arterionephrosclerosis (*see also* Hypertension,
    kidney) 403.90
Arteriopathy 447.9
Arteriosclerosis, arteriosclerotic (artery)
    (deformans) (diffuse) (disease) (endarteritis)
    (general) (obliterans) (obliterative) (occlusive)
    (senile) (with calcification) 440.9
  with
    gangrene 440.24
    psychosis (*see also* Psychosis,
      arteriosclerotic) 290.40
    ulceration 440.23
  aorta 440.0
  arteries of extremities — *see* Arteriosclerosis,
    extremities
  basilar (artery) (*see also* Occlusion, artery,
    basilar) 433.0 ☑
  brain 437.0
  bypass graft
    coronary artery 414.05
      autologous artery (gastroepiploic)
        (internal mammary) 414.04
      autologous vein 414.02
      nonautologous biological 414.03
      of transplanted heart 414.07
    extremity 440.30
      autologous vein 440.31
      nonautologous biological 440.32
  cardiac — *see* Arteriosclerosis, coronary
  cardiopathy — *see* Arteriosclerosis, coronary
  cardiorenal (*see also* Hypertension, cardiorenal)
    404.90
  cardiovascular (*see also* Disease,
    cardiovascular) 429.2
  carotid (artery) (common) (internal) (*see also*
    Occlusion, artery, carotid) 433.1 ☑
  central nervous system 437.0
  cerebral 437.0
    late effect — *see* Late effect(s) (of)
      cerebrovascular disease

Arteriosclerosis, arteriosclerotic — *continued*
  cerebrospinal 437.0
  cerebrovascular 437.0
  coronary (artery) 414.00
    graft — *see* Arteriosclerosis, bypass graft
    native artery 414.01
      of transplanted heart 414.06
  extremities (native artery) NEC 440.20
    bypass graft 440.30
      autologous vein 440.31
      nonautologous biological 440.32
    claudication (intermittent) 440.21
      and
        gangrene 440.24
        rest pain 440.22
          and
            gangrene 440.24
            ulceration 440.23
              and gangrene 440.24
        ulceration 440.23
          and gangrene 440.24
    gangrene 440.24
    rest pain 440.22
      and
        gangrene 440.24
        ulceration 440.23
          and gangrene 440.24
    specified site NEC 440.29
    ulceration 440.23
      and gangrene 440.24
  heart (disease) — *see also* Arteriosclerosis,
    coronary
    valve 424.99
      aortic 424.1
      mitral 424.0
      pulmonary 424.3
      tricuspid 424.2
  kidney (*see also* Hypertension, kidney) 403.90
  labyrinth, labyrinthine 388.00
  medial NEC (*see also* Arteriosclerosis,
    extremities) 440.20
  mesentery (artery) 557.1
  Mönckeberg's (*see also* Arteriosclerosis,
    extremities) 440.20
  myocarditis 429.0
  nephrosclerosis (*see also* Hypertension, kidney)
    403.90
  peripheral (of extremities) — *see*
    Arteriosclerosis, extremities
  precerebral 433.9 ☑
    specified artery NEC 433.8 ☑
  pulmonary (idiopathic) 416.0
  renal (*see also* Hypertension, kidney) 403.90
    arterioles (*see also* Hypertension, kidney)
      403.90
    artery 440.1
  retinal (vascular) 440.8 [362.13]
  specified artery NEC 440.8
    with gangrene 440.8 [785.4]
  spinal (cord) 437.0
  vertebral (artery) (*see also* Occlusion, artery,
    vertebral) 433.2 ☑
Arteriospasm 443.9
Arteriovenous — *see* condition
Arteritis 447.6
  allergic (*see also* Angiitis, hypersensitivity)
    446.20
  aorta (nonsyphilitic) 447.6
    syphilitic 093.1
  aortic arch 446.7
  brachiocephalica 446.7
  brain 437.4
    syphilitic 094.89
  branchial 446.7
  cerebral 437.4
    late effect — *see* Late effect(s) (of)
      cerebrovascular disease
    syphilitic 094.89
  coronary (artery) — *see also* Arteriosclerosis,
    coronary
    rheumatic 391.9
      chronic 398.99
    syphilitic 093.89
  cranial (left) (right) 446.5
  deformans — *see* Arteriosclerosis
  giant cell 446.5

Arteritis — *continued*
  necrosing or necrotizing 446.0
  nodosa 446.0
  obliterans — *see also* Arteriosclerosis
      subclaviocarotica 446.7
  pulmonary 417.8
  retina 362.18
  rheumatic — *see* Fever, rheumatic
  senile — *see* Arteriosclerosis
  suppurative 447.2
  syphilitic (general) 093.89
      brain 094.89
      coronary 093.89
      spinal 094.89
  temporal 446.5
  young female, syndrome 446.7
Artery, arterial — *see* condition
Arthralgia (*see also* Pain, joint) 719.4 ☑
  allergic (*see also* Pain, joint) 719.4 ☑
  in caisson disease 993.3
  psychogenic 307.89
  rubella 056.71
  Salmonella 003.23
  temporomandibular joint 524.62
Arthritis, arthritic (acute) (chronic) (subacute)
      716.9 ☑
  meaning Osteoarthritis — *see* Osteoarthrosis

---

*Note — Use the following fifth-digit
subclassification with categories 711-712, 715-
716:*

  0   site unspecified
  1   shoulder region
  2   upper arm
  3   forearm
  4   hand
  5   pelvic region and thigh
  6   lower leg
  7   ankle and foot
  8   other specified sites
  9   multiple sites

---

  allergic 716.2 ☑
  ankylosing (crippling) (spine) 720.0
      sites other than spine 716.9 ☑
  atrophic 714.0
      spine 720.9
  back (*see also* Arthritis, spine) 721.90
  Bechterew's (ankylosing spondylitis) 720.0
  blennorrhagic 098.50
  cervical, cervicodorsal (*see also* Spondylosis,
      cervical) 721.0
  Charcôt's 094.0 *[713.5]*
      diabetic 250.6 ☑ *[713.5]*
      syringomyelic 336.0 *[713.5]*
      tabetic 094.0 *[713.5]*
  chylous (*see also* Filariasis) 125.9 *[711.7]* ☑
  climacteric NEC 716.3 ☑
  coccyx 721.8
  cricoarytenoid 478.79
  crystal (-induced) — *see* Arthritis, due to
      crystals
  deformans (*see also* Osteoarthrosis) 715.9 ☑
      spine 721.90
          with myelopathy 721.91
  degenerative (*see also* Osteoarthrosis) 715.9 ☑
      idiopathic 715.09
      polyarticular 715.09
      spine 721.90
          with myelopathy 721.91
  dermatoarthritis, lipoid 272.8 *[713.0]*
  due to or associated with
      acromegaly 253.0 *[713.0]*
      actinomycosis 039.8 *[711.4]* ☑
      amyloidosis 277.3 *[713.7]*
      bacterial disease NEC 040.89 *[711.4]* ☑
      Behçet's syndrome 136.1 *[711.2]* ☑
      blastomycosis 116.0 *[711.6]* ☑
      brucellosis (*see also* Brucellosis)
          023.9 *[711.4]* ☑
      caisson disease 993.3
      coccidioidomycosis 114.3 *[711.6]* ☑
      coliform (Escherichia coli) 711.0 ☑

Arthritis, arthritic — *continued*
  due to or associated with — *continued*
      colitis, ulcerative (*see also* Colitis, ulcerative)
          556.9 *[713.1]*
      cowpox 051.0 *[711.5]* ☑
      crystals (*see also* Gout)
          dicalcium phosphate 275.49 *[712.1]* ☑
          pyrophosphate 275.49 *[712.2]* ☑
          specified NEC 275.49 *[712.8]* ☑
      dermatoarthritis, lipoid 272.8 *[713.0]*
      dermatological disorder NEC 709.9 *[713.3]*
      diabetes 250.6 ☑ *[713.5]*
      diphtheria 032.89 *[711.4]* ☑
      dracontiasis 125.7 *[711.7]* ☑
      dysentery 009.0 *[711.3]* ☑
      endocrine disorder NEC 259.9 *[713.0]*
      enteritis NEC 009.1 *[711.3]* ☑
          infectious (*see also* Enteritis, infectious)
              009.0 *[711.3]* ☑
              specified organism NEC 008.8
                  [711.3] ☑
          regional (*see also* Enteritis, regional)
              555.9 *[713.1]*
          specified organism NEC 008.8 *[711.3]* ☑
      epiphyseal slip, nontraumatic (old) 716.8 ☑
      erysipelas 035 *[711.4]* ☑
      erythema
          epidemic 026.1
          multiforme 695.1 *[713.3]*
          nodosum 695.2 *[713.3]*
      Escherichia coli 711.0 ☑
      filariasis NEC 125.9 *[711.7]* ☑
      gastrointestinal condition NEC 569.9 *[713.1]*
      glanders 024 *[711.4]* ☑
      Gonococcus 098.50
      gout 274.0
      H. influenzae 711.0 ☑
      helminthiasis NEC 128.9 *[711.7]* ☑
      hematological disorder NEC 289.9 *[713.2]*
      hemochromatosis 275.0 *[713.0]*
      hemoglobinopathy NEC (*see also* Disease,
          hemoglobin) 282.7 *[713.2]*
      hemophilia (*see also* Hemophilia) 286.0
          [713.2]
      Hemophilus influenzae (H. influenzae)
          711.0 ☑
      Henoch (-Schönlein) purpura 287.0 *[713.6]*
      histoplasmosis NEC (*see also*
          Histoplasmosis) 115.99 *[711.6]* ☑
      hyperparathyroidism 252.00 *[713.0]*
      hypersensitivity reaction NEC 995.3 *[713.6]*
      hypogammaglobulinemia (*see also*
          Hypogamma-globulinemia) 279.00
          [713.0]
      hypothyroidism NEC 244.9 *[713.0]*
      infection (*see also* Arthritis, infectious)
          711.9 ☑
      infectious disease NEC 136.9 *[711.8]* ☑
      leprosy (*see also* Leprosy) 030.9 *[711.4]* ☑
      leukemia NEC (M9800/3) 208.9 ☑ *[713.2]*
      lipoid dermatoarthritis 272.8 *[713.0]*
      Lyme disease 088.81 *[711.8]* ☑
      Mediterranean fever, familial 277.3 *[713.7]*
      meningococcal infection 036.82
      metabolic disorder NEC 277.9 *[713.0]*
      multiple myelomatosis (M9730/3) 203.0 ☑
          [713.2]
      mumps 072.79 *[711.5]* ☑
      mycobacteria 031.8 *[711.4]* ☑
      mycosis NEC 117.9 *[711.6]* ☑
      neurological disorder NEC 349.9 *[713.5]*
      ochronosis 270.2 *[713.0]*
      O'Nyong Nyong 066.3 *[711.5]* ☑
      parasitic disease NEC 136.9 *[711.8]* ☑
      paratyphoid fever (*see also* Fever,
          paratyphoid) 002.9 *[711.3]* ☑
      Pneumococcus 711.0 ☑
      poliomyelitis (*see also* Poliomyelitis) 045.9 ☑
          [711.5] ☑
      Pseudomonas 711.0 ☑
      psoriasis 696.0
      pyogenic organism (E. coli) (H. influenzae)
          (Pseudomonas) (Streptococcus)
          711.0 ☑
      rat-bite fever 026.1 *[711.4]* ☑
      regional enteritis (*see also* Enteritis,
          regional) 555.9 *[713.1]*

Arthritis, arthritic — *continued*
  due to or associated with — *continued*
      Reiter's disease 099.3 *[711.1]* ☑
      respiratory disorder NEC 519.9 *[713.4]*
      reticulosis, malignant (M9720/3) 202.3 ☑
          [713.2]
      rubella 056.71
      salmonellosis 003.23
      sarcoidosis 135 *[713.7]*
      serum sickness 999.5 *[713.6]*
      Staphylococcus 711.0 ☑
      Streptococcus 711.0 ☑
      syphilis (*see also* Syphilis) 094.0 *[711.4]* ☑
      syringomyelia 336.0 *[713.5]*
      thalassemia 282.49 *[713.2]*
      tuberculosis (*see also* Tuberculosis,
          arthritis) 015.9 ☑ *[711.4]* ☑
      typhoid fever 002.0 *[711.3]* ☑
      ulcerative colitis (*see also* Colitis, ulcerative)
          556.9 *[713.1]*
      urethritis
          nongonococcal (*see also* Urethritis,
              nongonococcal) 099.40 *[711.1]* ☑
          nonspecific (*see also* Urethritis,
              nongonococcal) 099.40 *[711.1]* ☑
          Reiter's 099.3 *[711.1]* ☑
      viral disease NEC 079.99 *[711.5]* ☑
  erythema epidemic 026.1
  gonococcal 098.50
  gouty (acute) 274.0
  hypertrophic (*see also* Osteoarthrosis) 715.9 ☑
      spine 721.90
          with myelopathy 721.91
  idiopathic, blennorrheal 099.3
  in caisson disease 993.3 *[713.8]*
  infectious or infective (acute) (chronic)
      (subacute) NEC 711.9 ☑
      nonpyogenic 711.9 ☑
      spine 720.9
  inflammatory NEC 714.9
  juvenile rheumatoid (chronic) (polyarticular)
      714.30
      acute 714.31
      monoarticular 714.33
      pauciarticular 714.32
  lumbar (*see also* Spondylosis, lumbar) 721.3
  meningococcal 036.82
  menopausal NEC 716.3 ☑
  migratory — *see* Fever, rheumatic
  neuropathic (Charcôt's) 094.0 *[713.5]*
      diabetic 250.6 ☑ *[713.5]*
      nonsyphilitic NEC 349.9 *[713.5]*
      syringomyelic 336.0 *[713.5]*
      tabetic 094.0 *[713.5]*
  nodosa (*see also* Osteoarthrosis) 715.9 ☑
      spine 721.90
          with myelopathy 721.91
  nonpyogenic NEC 716.9 ☑
      spine 721.90
          with myelopathy 721.91
  ochronotic 270.2 *[713.0]*
  palindromic (see also Rheumatism,
      palindromic) 719.3 ☑
  pneumococcal 711.0 ☑
  postdysenteric 009.0 *[711.3]* ☑
  postrheumatic, chronic (Jaccoud's) 714.4
  primary progressive 714.0
      spine 720.9
  proliferative 714.0
      spine 720.0
  psoriatic 696.0
  purulent 711.0 ☑
  pyogenic or pyemic 711.0 ☑
  rheumatic 714.0
      acute or subacute — *see* Fever, rheumatic
      chronic 714.0
      spine 720.9
  rheumatoid (nodular) 714.0
      with
          splenoadenomegaly and leukopenia 714.1
          visceral or systemic involvement 714.2
      aortitis 714.89
      carditis 714.2
      heart disease 714.2
      juvenile (chronic) (polyarticular) 714.30
          acute 714.31
          monoarticular 714.33

Arthritis, arthritic — *continued*
  rheumatoid — *continued*
    juvenile — *continued*
      pauciarticular 714.32
      spine 720.0
  rubella 056.71
  sacral, sacroiliac, sacrococcygeal (*see also*
    Spondylosis, sacral) 721.3
  scorbutic 267
  senile or senescent (*see also* Osteoarthrosis)
    715.9 ☑
    spine 721.90
      with myelopathy 721.91
  septic 711.0 ☑
  serum (nontherapeutic) (therapeutic) 999.5
    [713.6]
  specified form NEC 716.8 ☑
  spine 721.90
    with myelopathy 721.91
    atrophic 720.9
    degenerative 721.90
      with myelopathy 721.91
    hypertrophic (with deformity) 721.90
      with myelopathy 721.91
    infectious or infective NEC 720.9
    Marie-Strümpell 720.0
    nonpyogenic 721.90
      with myelopathy 721.91
    pyogenic 720.9
    rheumatoid 720.0
    traumatic (old) 721.7
    tuberculous (*see also* Tuberculosis) 015.0 ☑
      [720.81]
  staphylococcal 711.0 ☑
  streptococcal 711.0 ☑
  suppurative 711.0 ☑
  syphilitic 094.0 *[713.5]*
    congenital 090.49 *[713.5]*
  syphilitica deformans (Charcôt) 094.0 *[713.5]*
  temporomandibular joint 524.69
  thoracic (*see also* Spondylosis, thoracic) 721.2
  toxic of menopause 716.3 ☑
  transient 716.4 ☑
  traumatic (chronic) (old) (post) 716.1 ☑
    current injury — *see* nature of injury
  tuberculous (*see also* Tuberculosis, arthritis)
    015.9 ☑ *[711.4]* ☑
  urethritica 099.3 *[711.1]* ☑
  urica, uratic 274.0
  venereal 099.3 *[711.1]* ☑
  vertebral (*see also* Arthritis, spine) 721.90
  villous 716.8 ☑
  von Bechterew's 720.0
Arthrocele (*see also* Effusion, joint) 719.0 ☑
Arthrochondritis — *see* Arthritis
Arthrodesis status V45.4
Arthrodynia (*see also* Pain, joint) 719.4 ☑
  psychogenic 307.89
Arthrodysplasia 755.9
Arthrofibrosis, joint (*see also* Ankylosis) 718.5 ☑
Arthrogryposis 728.3
  multiplex, congenita 754.89
Arthrokatadysis 715.35
Arthrolithiasis 274.0
Arthro-onychodysplasia 756.89
Arthro-osteo-onychodysplasia 756.89
Arthropathy (*see also* Arthritis) 716.9 ☑

  Note — Use the following fifth-digit
  subclassification with categories 711-712, 716:

    0   *site unspecified*
    1   *shoulder region*
    2   *upper arm*
    3   *forearm*
    4   *hand*
    5   *pelvic region and thigh*
    6   *lower leg*
    7   *ankle and foot*
    8   *other specified sites*
    9   *multiple sites*

  Behçet's 136.1 *[711.2]* ☑

Arthropathy (*see also* Arthritis) — *continued*
  Charcôt's 094.0 *[713.5]*
    diabetic 250.6 ☑ *[713.5]*
    syringomyelic 336.0 *[713.5]*
    tabetic 094.0 *[713.5]*
  crystal (-induced) — *see* Arthritis, due to
    crystals
  gouty 274.0
  neurogenic, neuropathic (Charcôt's) (tabetic)
    094.0 *[713.5]*
    diabetic 250.6 ☑ *[713.5]*
    nonsyphilitic NEC 349.9 *[713.5]*
    syringomyelic 336.0 *[713.5]*
  postdysenteric NEC 009.0 *[711.3]* ☑
  postrheumatic, chronic (Jaccoud's) 714.4
  psoriatic 696.0
  pulmonary 731.2
  specified NEC 716.8 ☑
  syringomyelia 336.0 *[713.5]*
  tabes dorsalis 094.0 *[713.5]*
  tabetic 094.0 *[713.5]*
  transient 716.4 ☑
  traumatic 716.1 ☑
  uric acid 274.0
Arthrophyte (*see also* Loose, body, joint) 718.1 ☑
Arthrophytis 719.80
  ankle 719.87
  elbow 719.82
  foot 719.87
  hand 719.84
  hip 719.85
  knee 719.86
  multiple sites 719.89
  pelvic region 719.85
  shoulder (region) 719.81
  specified site NEC 719.88
  wrist 719.83
Arthropyosis (*see also* Arthritis, pyogenic)
  711.0 ☑
**Arthroscopic surgical procedure converted to
  open procedure** V64.43
Arthrosis (deformans) (degenerative) (*see also*
  Osteoarthrosis) 715.9 ☑
  Charcôt's 094.0 *[713.5]*
  polyarticular 715.09
  spine (*see also* Spondylosis) 721.90
Arthus' phenomenon 995.2
  due to
    correct substance properly administered
      995.2
    overdose or wrong substance given or taken
      977.9
      specified drug — *see* Table of Drugs and
        Chemicals
    serum 999.5
Articular — *see also* condition
  disc disorder (reducing or non-reducing)
    524.63
  spondylolisthesis 756.12
Articulation
  anterior 524.27
  posterior 524.27
  reverse 524.27
Artificial
  device (prosthetic) — *see* Fitting, device
  insemination V26.1
  menopause (states) (symptoms) (syndrome)
    627.4
  opening status (functioning) (without
    complication) V44.9
    anus (colostomy) V44.3
    colostomy V44.3
    cystostomy V44.50
      appendico-vesicostomy V44.52
      cutaneous-vesicostomy V44.51
      specified type NEC V44.59
    enterostomy V44.4
    gastrostomy V44.1
    ileostomy V44.2
    intestinal tract NEC V44.4
    jejunostomy V44.4
    nephrostomy V44.6
    specified site NEC V44.8
    tracheostomy V44.0
    ureterostomy V44.6

Artificial — *continued*
  opening status — *continued*
    urethrostomy V44.6
    urinary tract NEC V44.6
    vagina V44.7
    vagina status V44.7
ARV (disease) (illness) (infection) — *see* Human
  immunodeficiency virus (disease) (illness)
  (infection)
Arytenoid — *see* condition
Asbestosis (occupational) 501
Asboe-Hansen's disease (incontinentia pigmenti)
  757.33
Ascariasis (intestinal) (lung) 127.0
Ascaridiasis 127.0
Ascaridosis 127.0
Ascaris 127.0
  lumbricoides (infestation) 127.0
  pneumonia 127.0
Ascending — *see* condition
Aschoff's bodies (*see also* Myocarditis,
  rheumatic) 398.0
Ascites 789.5
  abdominal NEC 789.5
  cancerous (M8000/6) 197.6
  cardiac 428.0
  chylous (nonfilarial) 457.8
    filarial (*see also* Infestation, filarial) 125.9
  congenital 778.0
  due to S. japonicum 120.2
  fetal, causing fetopelvic disproportion 653.7 ☑
  heart 428.0
  joint (*see also* Effusion, joint) 719.0 ☑
  malignant (M8000/6) 197.6
  pseudochylous 789.5
  syphilitic 095.2
  tuberculous (*see also* Tuberculosis) 014.0 ☑
Ascorbic acid (vitamin C) **deficiency** (scurvy) 267
ASC-US (atypical squamous cells of undetermined
  significance) 795.01
ASC-H (atypical squamous cells cannot exclude
  high grade squamous intraepithelial lesion)
  795.02
ASCVD (arteriosclerotic cardiovascular disease)
  429.2
Aseptic — *see* condition
Asherman's syndrome 621.5
Asialia 527.7
Asiatic cholera (*see also* Cholera) 001.9
Asocial personality or trends 301.7
Asomatognosia 781.8
Aspergillosis 117.3
  with pneumonia 117.3 *[484.6]*
  allergic bronchopulmonary 518.6
  nonsyphilitic NEC 117.3
Aspergillus (flavus) (fumigatus) (infection)
  (terreus) 117.3
Aspermatogenesis 606.0
Aspermia (testis) 606.0
Asphyxia, asphyxiation (by) 799.01   ▲
  antenatal — *see* Distress, fetal
  bedclothes 994.7
  birth (*see also* Asphyxia, newborn) 768.9
  bunny bag 994.7
  carbon monoxide 986
  caul (*see also* Asphyxia, newborn) 768.9
  cave-in 994.7
    crushing — *see* Injury, internal,
      intrathoracic organs
  constriction 994.7
  crushing — *see* Injury, internal, intrathoracic
    organs
  drowning 994.1
  fetal, affecting newborn 768.9
  food or foreign body (in larynx) 933.1
    bronchioles 934.8
    bronchus (main) 934.1
    lung 934.8
    nasopharynx 933.0
    nose, nasal passages 932
    pharynx 933.0

Asphyxia, asphyxiation — *continued*
  food or foreign body — *continued*
    respiratory tract 934.9
      specified part NEC 934.8
    throat 933.0
    trachea 934.0
  gas, fumes, or vapor NEC 987.9
    specified — *see* Table of Drugs and
      Chemicals
  gravitational changes 994.7
  hanging 994.7
  inhalation — *see* Inhalation
  intrauterine
    fetal death (before onset of labor) 768.0
      during labor 768.1
    liveborn infant — *see* Distress, fetal,
      liveborn infant
  local 443.0
  mechanical 994.7
    during birth (*see also* Distress, fetal) 768.9
  mucus 933.1
    bronchus (main) 934.1
    larynx 933.1
    lung 934.8
    nasal passages 932
    newborn 770.18　▲
    pharynx 933.0
    respiratory tract 934.9
      specified part NEC 934.8
    throat 933.0
    trachea 934.0
    vaginal (fetus or newborn) 770.18　▲
  newborn 768.9
    with neurologic involvement 768.5
    blue 768.6
    livida 768.6
    mild or moderate 768.6
    pallida 768.5
    severe 768.5
    white 768.5
  pathological 799.01　▲
  plastic bag 994.7
  postnatal (*see also* Asphyxia, newborn) 768.9
    mechanical 994.7
  pressure 994.7
  reticularis 782.61
  strangulation 994.7
  submersion 994.1
  traumatic NEC — *see* Injury, internal,
    intrathoracic organs
  vomiting, vomitus — *see* Asphyxia, food or
    foreign body

Aspiration
  acid pulmonary (syndrome) 997.3
    obstetric 668.0 ☑
  amniotic fluid 770.13　▲
    with respiratory symptoms 770.14　●
  bronchitis 507.0
  clear amniotic fluid 770.13　●
    with　●
      pneumonia 770.14　●
      pneumonitis 770.14　●
      respiratory symptoms 770.14　●
  contents of birth canal 770.17　▲
    with respiratory symptoms 770.18　●
  fetal 770.10　●
    blood 770.15　●
      with　●
        pneumonia 770.16　●
        pneumonitis 770.16　●
    pneumonitis 770.18　●
  food, foreign body, or gasoline (with asphyxiation)
    — *see* Asphyxia, food or foreign body
  meconium 770.11　▲
    with　●
      pneumonia 770.12　●
      pneumonitis 770.12　●
      respiratory symptoms 770.12　●
    below vocal cords 770.11　●
      with respiratory symptoms 770.12　●
  mucus 933.1
    into
      bronchus (main) 934.1
      lung 934.8
      respiratory tract 934.9
        specified part NEC 934.8

Aspiration — *continued*
  mucus — *continued*
    into — *continued*
      trachea 934.0
    newborn 770.17　▲
    vaginal (fetus or newborn) 770.17　▲
  newborn 770.10　▲
    with respiratory symptoms 770.18　●
    blood 770.15　●
      with　●
        pneumonia 770.16　●
        pneumonitis 770.16　●
        respiratory symptoms 770.16　●
  pneumonia 507.0　●
    fetus or newborn 770.18　●
      meconium 770.12　●
  pneumonitis 507.0　●
    fetus or newborn 770.18　▲
      meconium 770.12　●
    obstetric 668.0 ☑
  postnatal stomach contents 770.85　●
    with　●
      pneumonia 770.86　●
      pneumonitis 770.86　●
      respiratory symptoms 770.86　●
  syndrome of newborn (massive) 770.18　▲
    meconium 770.12　●
  vernix caseosa 770.17　▲

Asplenia 759.0
  with mesocardia 746.87

Assam fever 085.0

Assimilation, pelvis
  with disproportion 653.2 ☑
    affecting fetus or newborn 763.1
    causing obstructed labor 660.1 ☑
      affecting fetus or newborn 763.1

Assmann's focus (*see also* Tuberculosis) 011.0 ☑

Astasia (-abasia) 307.9
  hysterical 300.11

Asteatosis 706.8
  cutis 706.8

Astereognosis 780.99

Asterixis 781.3
  in liver disease 572.8

Asteroid hyalitis 379.22

Asthenia, asthenic 780.79
  cardiac (*see also* Failure, heart) 428.9
    psychogenic 306.2
  cardiovascular (*see also* Failure, heart) 428.9
    psychogenic 306.2
  heart (*see also* Failure, heart) 428.9
    psychogenic 306.2
  hysterical 300.11
  myocardial (*see also* Failure, heart) 428.9
    psychogenic 306.2
  nervous 300.5
  neurocirculatory 306.2
  neurotic 300.5
  psychogenic 300.5
  psychoneurotic 300.5
  psychophysiologic 300.5
  reaction, psychoneurotic 300.5
  senile 797
  Stiller's 780.79
  tropical anhidrotic 705.1

Asthenopia 368.13
  accommodative 367.4
  hysterical (muscular) 300.11
  psychogenic 306.7

Asthenospermia 792.2

Asthma, asthmatic (bronchial) (catarrh)
  (spasmodic) 493.9 ☑

Note — *The following fifth-digit subclassification
is for use with codes 493.0-493.2, 493.9:*

> *0　unspecified*
>
> *1　with status asthmaticus*
>
> *2　with (acute) exacerbation*

  with
    chronic obstructive pulmonary disease
      (COPD) 493.2 ☑
    hay fever 493.0 ☑
    rhinitis, allergic 493.0 ☑

Asthma, asthmatic — *continued*
  allergic 493.9 ☑
    stated cause (external allergen) 493.0 ☑
  atopic 493.0 ☑
  cardiac (*see also* Failure, ventricular, left) 428.1
  cardiobronchial (*see also* Failure, ventricular,
    left) 428.1
  cardiorenal (*see also* Hypertension, cardiorenal)
    404.90
  childhood 493.0 ☑
  Colliers' 500
  cough variant 493.82
  croup 493.9 ☑
  detergent 507.8
  due to
    detergent 507.8
    inhalation of fumes 506.3
    internal immunological process 493.0 ☑
  endogenous (intrinsic) 493.1 ☑
  eosinophilic 518.3
  exercise induced bronchospasm 493.81
  exogenous (cosmetics) (dander or dust) (drugs)
    (dust) (feathers) (food) (hay) (platinum)
    (pollen) 493.0 ☑
  extrinsic 493.0 ☑
  grinders' 502
  hay 493.0 ☑
  heart (*see also* Failure, ventricular, left) 428.1
  IgE 493.0 ☑
  infective 493.1 ☑
  intrinsic 493.1 ☑
  Kopp's 254.8
  late-onset 493.1 ☑
  meat-wrappers' 506.9
  Millar's (laryngismus stridulus) 478.75
  millstone makers' 502
  miners' 500
  Monday morning 504
  New Orleans (epidemic) 493.0 ☑
  platinum 493.0 ☑
  pneumoconiotic (occupational) NEC 505
  potters' 502
  psychogenic 316 *[493.9]* ☑
  pulmonary eosinophilic 518.3
  red cedar 495.8
  Rostan's (*see also* Failure, ventricular, left)
    428.1
  sandblasters' 502
  sequoiosis 495.8
  stonemasons' 502
  thymic 254.8
  tuberculous (*see also* Tuberculosis, pulmonary)
    011.9 ☑
  Wichmann's (laryngismus stridulus) 478.75
  wood 495.8

Astigmatism (compound) (congenital) 367.20
  irregular 367.22
  regular 367.21

Astroblastoma (M9430/3)
  nose 748.1
  specified site — *see* Neoplasm, by site,
    malignant
  unspecified site 191.9

Astrocytoma (cystic) (M9400/3)
  anaplastic type (M9401/3)
    specified site — *see* Neoplasm, by site,
      malignant
    unspecified site 191.9
  fibrillary (M9420/3)
    specified site — *see* Neoplasm, by site,
      malignant
    unspecified site 191.9
  fibrous (M9420/3)
    specified site — *see* Neoplasm, by site,
      malignant
    unspecified site 191.9
  gemistocytic (M9411/3)
    specified site — *see* Neoplasm, by site,
      malignant
    unspecified site 191.9
  juvenile (M9421/3)
    specified site — *see* Neoplasm, by site,
      malignant
    unspecified site 191.9
  nose 748.1
  pilocytic (M9421/3)
    specified site — *see* Neoplasm, by site,
      malignant

Astrocytoma — *continued*
  pilocytic — *continued*
    unspecified site 191.9
  piloid (M9421/3)
    specified site — *see* Neoplasm, by site,
      malignant
    unspecified site 191.9
  protoplasmic (M9410/3)
    specified site — *see* Neoplasm, by site,
      malignant
    unspecified site 191.9
  specified site — *see* Neoplasm, by site,
      malignant
  subependymal (M9383/1) 237.5
    giant cell (M9384/1) 237.5
  unspecified site 191.9
Astroglioma (M9400/3)
  nose 748.1
  specified site — *see* Neoplasm, by site,
      malignant
  unspecified site 191.9
Asymbolia 784.60
Asymmetrical breathing 786.09
Asymmetry — *see also* Distortion
  chest 786.9
  face 754.0
  jaw NEC 524.12
    maxillary 524.11
  pelvis with disproportion 653.0 ☑
    affecting fetus or newborn 763.1
    causing obstructed labor 660.1 ☑
      affecting fetus or newborn 763.1
Asynergia 781.3
Asynergy 781.3
  ventricular 429.89
Asystole (heart) (*see also* Arrest, cardiac) 427.5
Ataxia, ataxy, ataxic 781.3
  acute 781.3
  brain 331.89
  cerebellar 334.3
    hereditary (Marie's) 334.2
    in
      alcoholism 303.9 ☑ *[334.4]*
      myxedema (*see also* Myxedema) 244.9
        [334.4]
      neoplastic disease NEC 239.9 *[334.4]*
  cerebral 331.89
  family, familial 334.2
    cerebral (Marie's) 334.2
    spinal (Friedreich's) 334.0
  Friedreich's (heredofamilial) (spinal) 334.0
  frontal lobe 781.3
  gait 781.2
    hysterical 300.11
  general 781.3
  hereditary NEC 334.2
    cerebellar 334.2
    spastic 334.1
    spinal 334.0
  heredofamilial (Marie's) 334.2
  hysterical 300.11
  locomotor (progressive) 094.0
    diabetic 250.6 ☑ *[337.1]*
  Marie's (cerebellar) (heredofamilial) 334.2
  nonorganic origin 307.9
  partial 094.0
  postchickenpox 052.7
  progressive locomotor 094.0
  psychogenic 307.9
  Sanger-Brown's 334.2
  spastic 094.0
    hereditary 334.1
    syphilitic 094.0
  spinal
    hereditary 334.0
    progressive locomotor 094.0
  telangiectasia 334.8
Ataxia-telangiectasia 334.8
Atelectasis (absorption collapse) (complete)
    (compression) (massive) (partial)
    (postinfective) (pressure collapse)
    (pulmonary) (relaxation) 518.0
  newborn (congenital) (partial) 770.5
    primary 770.4

Atelectasis — *continued*
  primary 770.4
  tuberculous (*see also* Tuberculosis, pulmonary)
    011.9 ☑
Ateleiosis, ateliosis 253.3
Atelia — *see* Distortion
Ateliosis 253.3
Atelocardia 746.9
Atelomyelia 742.59
Athelia 757.6
Atheroembolism
  extremity
    lower 445.02
    upper 445.01
  kidney 445.81
  specified site NEC 445.89
Atheroma, atheromatous (*see also*
    Arteriosclerosis) 440.9
  aorta, aortic 440.0
    valve (*see also* Endocarditis, aortic) 424.1
  artery — *see* Arteriosclerosis
  basilar (artery) (*see also* Occlusion, artery,
    basilar) 433.0 ☑
  carotid (artery) (common) (internal) (*see also*
    Occlusion, artery, carotid) 433.1 ☑
  cerebral (arteries) 437.0
  coronary (artery) — *see* Arteriosclerosis,
    coronary
  degeneration — *see* Arteriosclerosis
  heart, cardiac — *see* Arteriosclerosis, coronary
  mitral (valve) 424.0
  myocardium, myocardial — *see*
    Arteriosclerosis, coronary
  pulmonary valve (heart) (*see also* Endocarditis,
    pulmonary) 424.3
  skin 706.2
  tricuspid (heart) (valve) 424.2
  valve, valvular — *see* Endocarditis
  vertebral (artery) (*see also* Occlusion, artery,
    vertebral) 433.2 ☑
Atheromatosis — *see also* Arteriosclerosis
  arterial, congenital 272.8
Atherosclerosis — *see* Arteriosclerosis
Athetosis (acquired) 781.0
  bilateral 333.7
  congenital (bilateral) 333.7
  double 333.7
  unilateral 781.0
Athlete's
  foot 110.4
  heart 429.3
Athletic team examination V70.3
Athrepsia 261
Athyrea (acquired) (*see also* Hypothyroidism)
    244.9
  congenital 243
Athyreosis (congenital) 243
  acquired — *see* Hypothyroidism
Athyroidism (acquired) (*see also* Hypothyroidism)
    244.9
  congenital 243
Atmospheric pyrexia 992.0
Atonia, atony, atonic
  abdominal wall 728.2
  bladder (sphincter) 596.4
    neurogenic NEC 596.54
      with cauda equina syndrome 344.61
  capillary 448.9
  cecum 564.89
    psychogenic 306.4
  colon 564.89
    psychogenic 306.4
  congenital 779.89
  dyspepsia 536.3
    psychogenic 306.4
  intestine 564.89
    psychogenic 306.4
  stomach 536.3
    neurotic or psychogenic 306.4
    psychogenic 306.4
  uterus 666.1 ☑
    affecting fetus or newborn 763.7
  vesical 596.4

Atopy NEC V15.09
Atransferrinemia, congenital 273.8
Atresia, atretic (congenital) 759.89
  alimentary organ or tract NEC 751.8
    lower 751.2
    upper 750.8
  ani, anus, anal (canal) 751.2
  aorta 747.22
    with hypoplasia of ascending aorta and
      defective development of left ventricle
      (with mitral valve atresia) 746.7
    arch 747.11
    ring 747.21
  aortic (orifice) (valve) 746.89
    arch 747.11
  aqueduct of Sylvius 742.3
    with spina bifida (*see also* Spina bifida)
      741.0 ☑
  artery NEC (*see also* Atresia, blood vessel)
      747.60
    cerebral 747.81
    coronary 746.85
    eye 743.58
    pulmonary 747.3
    umbilical 747.5
  auditory canal (external) 744.02
  bile, biliary duct (common) or passage 751.61
    acquired (*see also* Obstruction, biliary)
      576.2
  bladder (neck) 753.6
  blood vessel (peripheral) NEC 747.60
    cerebral 747.81
    gastrointestinal 747.61
    lower limb 747.64
    pulmonary artery 747.3
    renal 747.62
    spinal 747.82
    upper limb 747.63
  bronchus 748.3
  canal, ear 744.02
  cardiac
    valve 746.89
      aortic 746.89
      mitral 746.89
      pulmonary 746.01
      tricuspid 746.1
  cecum 751.2
  cervix (acquired) 622.4
    congenital 752.49
    in pregnancy or childbirth 654.6 ☑
      affecting fetus or newborn 763.89
      causing obstructed labor 660.2 ☑
        affecting fetus or newborn 763.1
  choana 748.0
  colon 751.2
  cystic duct 751.61
    acquired 575.8
      with obstruction (*see also* Obstruction,
        gallbladder) 575.2
  digestive organs NEC 751.8
  duodenum 751.1
  ear canal 744.02
  ejaculatory duct 752.89
  epiglottis 748.3
  esophagus 750.3
  Eustachian tube 744.24
  fallopian tube (acquired) 628.2
    congenital 752.19
  follicular cyst 620.0
  foramen of
    Luschka 742.3
      with spina bifida (*see also* Spina bifida)
        741.0 ☑
    Magendie 742.3
      with spina bifida (*see also* Spina bifida)
        741.0 ☑
  gallbladder 751.69
  genital organ
    external
      female 752.49
      male NEC 752.89
        penis 752.69
    internal
      female 752.89
      male 752.89
  glottis 748.3

☑ Additional Digit Required — Refer to the Tabular List (Numeric Code Section) for Additional Digit Selection
▶◀ Revised Text   ● New Line   ▲ Revised Code

Atresia, atretic — *continued*
  gullet 750.3
  heart
    valve NEC 746.89
      aortic 746.89
      mitral 746.89
      pulmonary 746.01
      tricuspid 746.1
    hymen 752.42
      acquired 623.3
      postinfective 623.3
    ileum 751.1
    intestine (small) 751.1
      large 751.2
    iris, filtration angle (*see also* Buphthalmia)
      743.20
    jejunum 751.1
    kidney 753.3
    lacrimal, apparatus 743.65
      acquired — *see* Stenosis, lacrimal
    larynx 748.3
    ligament, broad 752.19
    lung 748.5
    meatus urinarius 753.6
    mitral valve 746.89
      with atresia or hypoplasia of aortic orifice or
        valve, with hypoplasia of ascending
        aorta and defective development of left
        ventricle 746.7
    nares (anterior) (posterior) 748.0
    nasolacrimal duct 743.65
    nasopharynx 748.8
    nose, nostril 748.0
      acquired 738.0
    organ or site NEC — *see* Anomaly, specified
      type NEC
    osseous meatus (ear) 744.03
    oviduct (acquired) 628.2
      congenital 752.19
    parotid duct 750.23
      acquired 527.8
    pulmonary (artery) 747.3
      valve 746.01
      vein 747.49
    pulmonic 746.01
    pupil 743.46
    rectum 751.2
    salivary duct or gland 750.23
      acquired 527.8
    sublingual duct 750.23
      acquired 527.8
    submaxillary duct or gland 750.23
      acquired 527.8
    trachea 748.3
    tricuspid valve 746.1
    ureter 753.29
    ureteropelvic junction 753.21
    ureterovesical orifice 753.22
    urethra (valvular) 753.6
    urinary tract NEC 753.29
    uterus 752.3
      acquired 621.8
    vagina (acquired) 623.2
      congenital 752.49
      postgonococcal (old) 098.2
      postinfectional 623.2
      senile 623.2
    vascular NEC (*see also* Atresia, blood vessel)
      747.60
      cerebral 747.81
    vas deferens 752.89
    vein NEC (*see also* Atresia, blood vessel) 747.60
      cardiac 746.89
      great 747.49
      portal 747.49
      pulmonary 747.49
    vena cava (inferior) (superior) 747.49
    vesicourethral orifice 753.6
    vulva 752.49
      acquired 624.8

Atrichia, atrichosis 704.00
  congenital (universal) 757.4

Atrioventricularis commune 745.69

At risk for falling V15.88 ●

Atrophia — *see also* Atrophy
  alba 709.09

Atrophia — *see also* Atrophy — *continued*
  cutis 701.8
    idiopathica progressiva 701.8
    senilis 701.8
  dermatological, diffuse (idiopathic) 701.8
  flava hepatis (acuta) (subacuta) (*see also*
    Necrosis, liver) 570
  gyrata of choroid and retina (central) 363.54
    generalized 363.57
  senilis 797
    dermatological 701.8
  unguium 703.8
    congenita 757.5

Atrophoderma, atrophodermia 701.9
  diffusum (idiopathic) 701.8
  maculatum 701.3
    et striatum 701.3
      due to syphilis 095.8
    syphilitic 091.3
  neuriticum 701.8
  pigmentosum 757.33
  reticulatum symmetricum faciei 701.8
  senile 701.8
  symmetrical 701.8
  vermiculata 701.8

Atrophy, atrophic
  adrenal (autoimmune) (capsule) (cortex) (gland)
    255.4
    with hypofunction 255.4
  alveolar process or ridge (edentulous) 525.20
    mandible 525.20
      minimal 525.21
      moderate 525.22
      severe 525.23
    maxilla 525.20
      minimal 525.24
      moderate 525.25
      severe 525.26
  appendix 543.9
  Aran-Duchenne muscular 335.21
  arm 728.2
  arteriosclerotic — *see* Arteriosclerosis
  arthritis 714.0
    spine 720.9
  bile duct (any) 576.8
  bladder 596.8
  blanche (of Milian) 701.3
  bone (senile) 733.99
    due to
      disuse 733.7
      infection 733.99
      tabes dorsalis (neurogenic) 094.0
    posttraumatic 733.99
  brain (cortex) (progressive) 331.9
    with dementia 290.10
    Alzheimer's 331.0
      with dementia — *see* Alzheimer's,
        dementia
    circumscribed (Pick's) 331.11
      with dementia
        with behavioral disturbance
          331.11 *[294.11]*
        without behavioral disturbance
          331.11 *[294.10]*
    congenital 742.4
    hereditary 331.9
    senile 331.2
  breast 611.4
    puerperal, postpartum 676.3 ☑
  buccal cavity 528.9
  cardiac (brown) (senile) (*see also* Degeneration,
    myocardial) 429.1
  cartilage (infectional) (joint) 733.99
  cast, plaster of Paris 728.2
  cerebellar — *see* Atrophy, brain
  cerebral — *see* Atrophy, brain
  cervix (endometrium) (mucosa) (myometrium)
    (senile) (uteri) 622.8
    menopausal 627.8
  Charcôt-Marie-Tooth 356.1
  choroid 363.40
    diffuse secondary 363.42
    hereditary (*see also* Dystrophy, choroid)
      363.50
    gyrate
      central 363.54

Atrophy, atrophic — *continued*
  choroid — *continued*
    hereditary (*see also* Dystrophy, choroid) —
      continued
      gyrate — *continued*
        diffuse 363.57
        generalized 363.57
    senile 363.41
  ciliary body 364.57
  colloid, degenerative 701.3
  conjunctiva (senile) 372.89
  corpus cavernosum 607.89
  cortical (*see also* Atrophy, brain) 331.9
  Cruveilhier's 335.21
  cystic duct 576.8
  dacryosialadenopathy 710.2
  degenerative
    colloid 701.3
    senile 701.3
  Déjérine-Thomas 333.0
  diffuse idiopathic, dermatological 701.8
  disuse
    bone 733.7
    muscle 728.2
    pelvic muscles and anal sphincter 618.83
  Duchenne-Aran 335.21
  ear 388.9
  edentulous alveolar ridge 525.20
    mandible 525.20
      minimal 525.21
      moderate 525.22
      severe 525.23
    maxilla 525.20
      minimal 525.24
      moderate 525.25
      severe 525.26
  emphysema, lung 492.8
  endometrium (senile) 621.8
    cervix 622.8
  enteric 569.89
  epididymis 608.3
  eyeball, cause unknown 360.41
  eyelid (senile) 374.50
  facial (skin) 701.9
  facioscapulohumeral (Landouzy-Déjérine) 359.1
  fallopian tube (senile), acquired 620.3
  fatty, thymus (gland) 254.8
  gallbladder 575.8
  gastric 537.89
  gastritis (chronic) 535.1 ☑
  gastrointestinal 569.89
  genital organ, male 608.89
  glandular 289.3
  globe (phthisis bulbi) 360.41
  gum (*see also* Recession, gingival) 523.20
  hair 704.2
  heart (brown) (senile) (*see also* Degeneration,
    myocardial) 429.1
  hemifacial 754.0
    Romberg 349.89
  hydronephrosis 591
  infantile 261
    paralysis, acute (*see also* Poliomyelitis, with
      paralysis) 045.1 ☑
  intestine 569.89
  iris (generalized) (postinfectional) (sector
    shaped) 364.59
    essential 364.51
    progressive 364.51
    sphincter 364.54
  kidney (senile) (*see also* Sclerosis, renal) 587
    with hypertension (*see also* Hypertension,
      kidney) 403.90
    congenital 753.0
    hydronephrotic 591
    infantile 753.0
  lacrimal apparatus (primary) 375.13
    secondary 375.14
  Landouzy-Déjérine 359.1
  laryngitis, infection 476.0
  larynx 478.79
  Leber's optic 377.16
  lip 528.5
  liver (acute) (subacute) (*see also* Necrosis, liver)
    570
    chronic (yellow) 571.8

Atrophy, atrophic — *continued*
liver — *continued*
  yellow (congenital) 570
    with
      abortion — *see* Abortion, by type, with
        specified complication NEC
      ectopic pregnancy (*see also* categories
        633.0-633.9) 639.8
      molar pregnancy (*see also* categories
        630-632) 639.8
    chronic 571.8
    complicating pregnancy 646.7 ☑
    following
      abortion 639.8
      ectopic or molar pregnancy 639.8
    from injection, inoculation or transfusion
      (onset within 8 months after
      administration) — *see* Hepatitis,
      viral
    healed 571.5
    obstetric 646.7 ☑
    postabortal 639.8
    postimmunization — *see* Hepatitis, viral
    posttransfusion — *see* Hepatitis, viral
    puerperal, postpartum 674.8 ☑
liver (senile) 518.89
  congenital 748.69
macular (dermatological) 701.3
  syphilitic, skin 091.3
    striated 095.8
muscle, muscular 728.2
  disuse 728.2
  Duchenne-Aran 335.21
  extremity (lower) (upper) 728.2
  familial spinal 335.11
  general 728.2
  idiopathic 728.2
  infantile spinal 335.0
  myelopathic (progressive) 335.10
  myotonic 359.2
  neuritic 356.1
  neuropathic (peroneal) (progressive) 356.1
  peroneal 356.1
  primary (idiopathic) 728.2
  progressive (familial) (hereditary) (pure)
    335.21
    adult (spinal) 335.19
    infantile (spinal) 335.0
    juvenile (spinal) 335.11
    spinal 335.10
      adult 335.19
      hereditary or familial 335.11
      infantile 335.0
  pseudohypertrophic 359.1
  spinal (progressive) 335.10
    adult 335.19
    Aran-Duchenne 335.21
    familial 335.11
    hereditary 335.11
    infantile 335.0
    juvenile 335.11
  syphilitic 095.6
myocardium (*see also* Degeneration,
  myocardial) 429.1
myometrium (senile) 621.8
  cervix 622.8
myotatic 728.2
myotonia 359.2
nail 703.8
  congenital 757.5
nasopharynx 472.2
nerve — *see also* Disorder, nerve
  abducens 378.54
  accessory 352.4
  acoustic or auditory 388.5
  cranial 352.9
    first (olfactory) 352.0
    second (optic) (*see also* Atrophy, optic
      nerve) 377.10
    third (oculomotor)(partial) 378.51
      total 378.52
    fourth (trochlear) 378.53
    fifth (trigeminal) 350.8
    sixth (abducens) 378.54
    seventh (facial) 351.8
    eighth (auditory) 388.5
    ninth (glossopharyngeal) 352.2

Atrophy, atrophic — *continued*
nerve — *see also* Disorder, nerve — *continued*
  cranial — *continued*
    tenth (pneumogastric) (vagus) 352.3
    eleventh (accessory) 352.4
    twelfth (hypoglossal) 352.5
  facial 351.8
  glossopharyngeal 352.2
  hypoglossal 352.5
  oculomotor (partial) 378.51
    total 378.52
  olfactory 352.0
  peripheral 355.9
  pneumogastric 352.3
  trigeminal 350.8
  trochlear 378.53
  vagus (pneumogastric) 352.3
nervous system, congenital 742.8
neuritic (*see also* Disorder, nerve) 355.9
neurogenic NEC 355.9
  bone
    tabetic 094.0
nutritional 261
old age 797
olivopontocerebellar 333.0
optic nerve (ascending) (descending)
  (infectional) (nonfamilial) (papillomacular
  bundle) (postretinal) (secondary NEC)
  (simple) 377.10
  associated with retinal dystrophy 377.13
  dominant hereditary 377.16
  glaucomatous 377.14
  hereditary (dominant) (Leber's) 377.16
  Leber's (hereditary) 377.16
  partial 377.15
  postinflammatory 377.12
  primary 377.11
  syphilitic 094.84
    congenital 090.49
    tabes dorsalis 094.0
orbit 376.45
ovary (senile), acquired 620.3
oviduct (senile), acquired 620.3
palsy, diffuse 335.20
pancreas (duct) (senile) 577.8
papillary muscle 429.81
paralysis 355.9
parotid gland 527.0
patches skin 701.3
  senile 701.8
penis 607.89
pharyngitis 472.1
pharynx 478.29
pluriglandular 258.8
polyarthritis 714.0
prostate 602.2
pseudohypertrophic 359.1
renal (*see also* Sclerosis, renal) 587
reticulata 701.8
retina (*see also* Degeneration, retina) 362.60
  hereditary (*see also* Dystrophy, retina)
    362.70
rhinitis 472.0
salivary duct or gland 527.0
scar NEC 709.2
sclerosis, lobar (of brain) 331.0
  with dementia
    with behavioral disturbance
      331.0 *[294.11]*
    without behavioral disturbance
      331.0 *[294.10]*
scrotum 608.89
seminal vesicle 608.89
senile 797
  degenerative, of skin 701.3
skin (patches) (senile) 701.8
spermatic cord 608.89
spinal (cord) 336.8
  acute 336.8
  muscular (chronic) 335.10
    adult 335.19
    familial 335.11
    juvenile 335.10
  paralysis 335.10
    acute (*see also* Poliomyelitis, with
      paralysis) 045.1 ☑
  spine (column) 733.99

Atrophy, atrophic — *continued*
spleen (senile) 289.59
spots (skin) 701.3
  senile 701.8
stomach 537.89
striate and macular 701.3
  syphilitic 095.8
subcutaneous 701.9
  due to injection 999.9
sublingual gland 527.0
submaxillary gland 527.0
Sudeck's 733.7
suprarenal (autoimmune) (capsule) (gland)
  255.4
  with hypofunction 255.4
tarso-orbital fascia, congenital 743.66
testis 608.3
thenar, partial 354.0
throat 478.29
thymus (fat) 254.8
thyroid (gland) 246.8
  with
    cretinism 243
    myxedema 244.9
  congenital 243
tongue (senile) 529.8
  papillae 529.4
  smooth 529.4
trachea 519.1
tunica vaginalis 608.89
turbinate 733.99
tympanic membrane (nonflaccid) 384.82
  flaccid 384.81
ulcer (*see also* Ulcer, skin) 707.9
upper respiratory tract 478.9
uterus, uterine (acquired) (senile) 621.8
  cervix 622.8
  due to radiation (intended effect) 621.8
vagina (senile) 627.3
vascular 459.89
vas deferens 608.89
vertebra (senile) 733.99
vulva (primary) (senile) 624.1
Werdnig-Hoffmann 335.0
yellow (acute) (congenital) (liver) (subacute) (*see
  also* Necrosis, liver) 570
  chronic 571.8
  resulting from administration of blood,
    plasma, serum, or other biological
    substance (within 8 months of
    administration) — *see* Hepatitis, viral

Attack
akinetic (*see also* Epilepsy) 345.0 ☑
angina — *see* Angina
apoplectic (*see also* Disease, cerebrovascular,
  acute) 436
benign shuddering 333.93
bilious — *see* Vomiting
cataleptic 300.11
cerebral (*see also* Disease, cerebrovascular,
  acute) 436
coronary (*see also* Infarct, myocardium)
  410.9 ☑
cyanotic, newborn 770.83
epileptic (*see also* Epilepsy) 345.9 ☑
epileptiform 780.39
heart (*see also* Infarct, myocardium) 410.9 ☑
hemiplegia (*see also* Disease, cerebrovascular,
  acute) 436
hysterical 300.11
jacksonian (*see also* Epilepsy) 345.5 ☑
myocardium, myocardial (*see also* Infarct,
  myocardium) 410.9 ☑
myoclonic (*see also* Epilepsy) 345.1 ☑
panic 300.01
paralysis (*see also* Disease, cerebrovascular,
  acute) 436
paroxysmal 780.39
psychomotor (*see also* Epilepsy) 345.4 ☑
salaam (*see also* Epilepsy) 345.6 ☑
schizophreniform (*see also* Schizophrenia)
  295.4 ☑
sensory and motor 780.39
syncope 780.2
toxic, cerebral 780.39
transient ischemic (TIA) 435.9

2006 ICD-9-CM

☑ Additional Digit Required — Refer to the Tabular List (Numeric Code Section) for Additional Digit Selection
▶◀ Revised Text   ● New Line   ▲ Revised Code

Volume 2 — 39

Attack — *continued*
  unconsciousness 780.2
    hysterical 300.11
  vasomotor 780.2
  vasovagal (idiopathic) (paroxysmal) 780.2
Attention to
  artificial opening (of) V55.9
    digestive tract NEC V55.4
    specified site NEC V55.8
    urinary tract NEC V55.6
    vagina V55.7
  colostomy V55.3
  cystostomy V55.5
  gastrostomy V55.1
  ileostomy V55.2
  jejunostomy V55.4
  nephrostomy V55.6
  surgical dressings V58.3
  sutures V58.3
  tracheostomy V55.0
  ureterostomy V55.6
  urethrostomy V55.6
Attrition
  gum (*see also* Recession, gingival) 523.20
  teeth (hard tissues) 521.10
    excessive 521.10
      extending into
        dentine 521.12
        pulp 521.13
      generalized 521.15
      limited to enamel 521.11
      localized 521.14
Atypical — *see also* condition
  cells
    endocervical 795.00
    endometrial 795.00
    glandular 795.00
  distribution, vessel (congenital) (peripheral)
    NEC 747.60
  endometrium 621.9
  kidney 593.89
Atypism, cervix 622.10
Audible tinnitus (*see also* Tinnitus) 388.30
Auditory — *see* condition
Audry's syndrome (acropachyderma) 757.39
Aujeszky's disease 078.89
Aura, jacksonian (*see also* Epilepsy) 345.5 ☑
Aurantiasis, cutis 278.3
Auricle, auricular — *see* condition
Auriculotemporal syndrome 350.8
Australian
  Q fever 083.0
  X disease 062.4
Autism, autistic (child) (infantile) 299.0 ☑
Autodigestion 799.89
Autoerythrocyte sensitization 287.2
Autographism 708.3
Autoimmune
  cold sensitivity 283.0
  disease NEC 279.4
  hemolytic anemia 283.0
  thyroiditis 245.2
Autoinfection, septic — *see* Septicemia
Autointoxication 799.89
Automatism 348.8
  epileptic (*see also* Epilepsy) 345.4 ☑
  paroxysmal, idiopathic (*see also* Epilepsy)
    345.4 ☑
Autonomic, autonomous
  bladder 596.54
    neurogenic 596.54
      with cauda equina 344.61
  dysreflexia 337.3
  faciocephalalgia (*see also* Neuropathy,
    peripheral, autonomic) 337.9
  hysterical seizure 300.11
  imbalance (*see also* Neuropathy, peripheral,
    autonomic) 337.9
Autophony 388.40
Autosensitivity, erythrocyte 287.2
Autotopagnosia 780.99
Autotoxemia 799.89

Autumn — *see* condition
Avellis' syndrome 344.89
Aviators
  disease or sickness (*see also* Effect, adverse,
    high altitude) 993.2
  ear 993.0
  effort syndrome 306.2
Avitaminosis (multiple NEC) (*see also* Deficiency,
    vitamin) 269.2
  A 264.9
  B 266.9
    with
      beriberi 265.0
      pellagra 265.2
  B_1 265.1
  B_2 266.0
  B_6 266.1
  B_{12} 266.2
  C (with scurvy) 267
  D 268.9
    with
      osteomalacia 268.2
      rickets 268.0
  E 269.1
  G 266.0
  H 269.1
  K 269.0
  multiple 269.2
  nicotinic acid 265.2
  P 269.1
Avulsion (traumatic) 879.8
  blood vessel — *see* Injury, blood vessel, by site
  cartilage — *see also* Dislocation, by site
    knee, current (*see also* Tear, meniscus)
      836.2
    symphyseal (inner), complicating delivery
      665.6 ☑
  complicated 879.9
  diaphragm — *see* Injury, internal, diaphragm
  ear — *see* Wound, open, ear
  epiphysis of bone — *see* Fracture, by site
  external site other than limb — *see* Wound,
    open, by site
  eye 871.3
  fingernail — *see* Wound, open, finger
  fracture — *see* Fracture, by site
  genital organs, external — *see* Wound, open,
    genital organs
  head (intracranial) NEC — *see also* Injury,
    intracranial, with open intracranial
    wound
    complete 874.9
    external site NEC 873.8
      complicated 873.9
  internal organ or site — *see* Injury, internal, by
    site
  joint — *see also* Dislocation, by site
    capsule — *see* Sprain, by site
  ligament — *see* Sprain, by site
  limb — *see also* Amputation, traumatic, by site
    skin and subcutaneous tissue — *see*
      Wound, open, by site
  muscle — *see* Sprain, by site
  nerve (root) — *see* Injury, nerve, by site
  scalp — *see* Wound, open, scalp
  skin and subcutaneous tissue — *see* Wound,
    open, by site
  symphyseal cartilage (inner), complicating
    delivery 665.6 ☑
  tendon — *see also* Sprain, by site
    with open wound — *see* Wound, open, by
      site
  toenail — *see* Wound, open, toe(s)
  tooth 873.63
    complicated 873.73
Awaiting organ transplant status V49.83
Awareness of heart beat 785.1
Axe grinders' disease 502
Axenfeld's anomaly or syndrome 743.44
Axilla, axillary — *see also* condition
  breast 757.6
Axonotmesis — *see* Injury, nerve, by site
Ayala's disease 756.89

Ayerza's disease or syndrome (pulmonary artery
    sclerosis with pulmonary hypertension)
    416.0
Azoospermia 606.0
Azotemia 790.6
  meaning uremia (*see also* Uremia) 586
Aztec ear 744.29
Azorean disease (of the nervous system) 334.8
Azygos lobe, lung (fissure) 748.69

B

Baader's syndrome (erythema multiforme
    exudativum) 695.1
Baastrup's syndrome 721.5
Babesiasis 088.82
Babesiosis 088.82
Babington's disease (familial hemorrhagic
    telangiectasia) 448.0
Babinski's syndrome (cardiovascular syphilis)
    093.89
Babinski-Fröhlich syndrome (adiposogenital
    dystrophy) 253.8
Babinski-Nageotte syndrome 344.89
Bacillary — *see* condition
Bacilluria 791.9
  asymptomatic, in pregnancy or puerperium
    646.5 ☑
  tuberculous (*see also* Tuberculosis) 016.9 ☑
Bacillus — *see also* Infection, bacillus
  abortus infection 023.1
  anthracis infection 022.9
  coli
    infection 041.4
      generalized 038.42
      intestinal 008.00
    pyemia 038.42
    septicemia 038.42
  Flexner's 004.1
  fusiformis infestation 101
  mallei infection 024
  Shiga's 004.0
  suipestifer infection (*see also* Infection,
    Salmonella) 003.9
Back — *see* condition
Backache (postural) 724.5
  psychogenic 307.89
  sacroiliac 724.6
Backflow (pyelovenous) (*see also* Disease, renal)
    593.9
Backknee (*see also* Genu, recurvatum) 736.5
Bacteremia 790.7
  newborn 771.83
Bacteria
  in blood (*see also* Bacteremia) 790.7
  in urine (*see also* Bacteriuria) 599.0
Bacterial — *see* condition
Bactericholia (*see also* Cholecystitis, acute) 575.0
Bacterid, bacteride (Andrews' pustular) 686.8
Bacteriuria, bacteruria 791.9
  with
    urinary tract infection 599.0
  asymptomatic 791.9
    in pregnancy or puerperium 646.5 ☑
      affecting fetus or newborn 760.1
Bad
  breath 784.9
  heart — *see* Disease, heart
  trip (*see also* Abuse, drugs, nondependent)
    305.3 ☑
Baehr-Schiffrin disease (thrombotic
    thrombocytopenic purpura) 446.6
Baelz's disease (cheilitis glandularis
    apostematosa) 528.5
Baerensprung's disease (eczema marginatum)
    110.3
Bagassosis (occupational) 495.1
Baghdad boil 085.1
Bagratuni's syndrome (temporal arteritis) 446.5

Behçet's syndrome 136.1
Behr's disease 362.50
Beigel's disease or morbus (white piedra) 111.2
Bejel 104.0
Bekhterev's disease (ankylosing spondylitis) 720.0
Bekhterev-Strümpell-Marie syndrome (ankylosing spondylitis) 720.0
Belching (see also Eructation) 787.3
Bell's
  disease (see also Psychosis, affective) 296.0 ☑
  mania (see also Psychosis, affective) 296.0 ☑
  palsy, paralysis 351.0
    infant 767.5
    newborn 767.5
    syphilitic 094.89
  spasm 351.0
Bence-Jones albuminuria, albuminosuria, or proteinuria 791.0
Bends 993.3
Benedikt's syndrome (paralysis) 344.89
Benign — see also condition
  cellular changes, cervix 795.09
  prostate
    hyperplasia 600.20
      with urinary retention 600.21
    neoplasm 222.2
Bennett's
  disease (leukemia) 208.9 ☑
  fracture (closed) 815.01
    open 815.11
Benson's disease 379.22
Bent
  back (hysterical) 300.11
  nose 738.0
    congenital 754.0
Bereavement V62.82
  as adjustment reaction 309.0
Berger's paresthesia (lower limb) 782.0
Bergeron's disease (hysteroepilepsy) 300.11
Beriberi (acute) (atrophic) (chronic) (dry) (subacute) (wet) 265.0
  with polyneuropathy 265.0 [357.4]
  heart (disease) 265.0 [425.7]
  leprosy 030.1
  neuritis 265.0 [357.4]
Berlin's disease or edema (traumatic) 921.3
Berloque dermatitis 692.72
Bernard-Horner syndrome (see also Neuropathy, peripheral, autonomic) 337.9
Bernard-Sergent syndrome (acute adrenocortical insufficiency) 255.4
Bernard-Soulier disease or thrombopathy 287.1
Bernhardt's disease or paresthesia 355.1
Bernhardt-Roth disease or syndrome (paresthesia) 355.1
Bernheim's syndrome (see also Failure, heart) 428.0
Bertielliasis 123.8
Bertolotti's syndrome (sacralization of fifth lumbar vertebra) 756.15
Berylliosis (acute) (chronic) (lung) (occupational) 503
Besnier's
  lupus pernio 135
  prurigo (atopic dermatitis) (infantile eczema) 691.8
Besnier-Boeck disease or sarcoid 135
Besnier-Boeck-Schaumann disease (sarcoidosis) 135
Best's disease 362.76
Bestiality 302.1
Beta-adrenergic hyperdynamic circulatory state 429.82
Beta-aminoisobutyric aciduria 277.2
Beta-mercaptolactate-cysteine disulfiduria 270.0
Beta thalassemia (major) (minor) (mixed) 282.49
Beurmann's disease (sporotrichosis) 117.1

Bezoar 938
  intestine 936
  stomach 935.2
Bezold's abscess (see also Mastoiditis) 383.01
Bianchi's syndrome (aphasia-apraxia-alexia) 784.69
Bicornuate or bicornis uterus 752.3
  in pregnancy or childbirth 654.0 ☑
    with obstructed labor 660.2 ☑
      affecting fetus or newborn 763.1
    affecting fetus or newborn 763.89
Bicuspid aortic valve 746.4
Biedl-Bardet syndrome 759.89
Bielschowsky's disease 330.1
Bielschowsky-Jansky
  amaurotic familial idiocy 330.1
  disease 330.1
Biemond's syndrome (obesity, polydactyly, and mental retardation) 759.89
Biermer's anemia or disease (pernicious anemia) 281.0
Biett's disease 695.4
Bifid (congenital) — see also Imperfect, closure
  apex, heart 746.89
  clitoris 752.49
  epiglottis 748.3
  kidney 753.3
  nose 748.1
  patella 755.64
  scrotum 752.89
  toe 755.66
  tongue 750.13
  ureter 753.4
  uterus 752.3
  uvula 749.02
    with cleft lip (see also Cleft, palate, with cleft lip) 749.20
Biforis uterus (suprasimplex) 752.3
Bifurcation (congenital) — see also Imperfect, closure
  gallbladder 751.69
  kidney pelvis 753.3
  renal pelvis 753.3
  rib 756.3
  tongue 750.13
  trachea 748.3
  ureter 753.4
  urethra 753.8
  uvula 749.02
    with cleft lip (see also Cleft, palate, with cleft lip) 749.20
  vertebra 756.19
Bigeminal pulse 427.89
Bigeminy 427.89
Big spleen syndrome 289.4
Bilateral — see condition
Bile duct — see condition
Bile pigments in urine 791.4
Bilharziasis (see also Schistosomiasis) 120.9
  chyluria 120.0
  cutaneous 120.3
  galacturia 120.0
  hematochyluria 120.0
  intestinal 120.1
  lipemia 120.9
  lipuria 120.0
  Oriental 120.2
  piarhemia 120.9
  pulmonary 120.2
  tropical hematuria 120.0
  vesical 120.0
Biliary — see condition
Bilious (attack) — see also Vomiting
  fever, hemoglobinuric 084.8
Bilirubinuria 791.4
Biliuria 791.4
Billroth's disease
  meningocele (see also Spina bifida) 741.9 ☑
Bilobate placenta — see Placenta, abnormal
Bilocular
  heart 745.7
  stomach 536.8

Bing-Horton syndrome (histamine cephalgia) 346.2 ☑
Binswanger's disease or dementia 290.12
Biörck (-Thorson) syndrome (malignant carcinoid) 259.2
Biparta, bipartite — see also Imperfect, closure
  carpal scaphoid 755.59
  patella 755.64
  placenta — see Placenta, abnormal
  vagina 752.49
Bird
  face 756.0
  fanciers' lung or disease 495.2
Bird's disease (oxaluria) 271.8
Birth
  abnormal fetus or newborn 763.9
  accident, fetus or newborn — see Birth, injury
  complications in mother — see Delivery, complicated
  compression during NEC 767.9
  defect — see Anomaly
  delayed, fetus 763.9
  difficult NEC, affecting fetus or newborn 763.9
  dry, affecting fetus or newborn 761.1
  forced, NEC, affecting fetus or newborn 763.89
  forceps, affecting fetus or newborn 763.2
  hematoma of sternomastoid 767.8
  immature 765.1 ☑
    extremely 765.0 ☑
  inattention, after or at 995.52
  induced, affecting fetus or newborn 763.89
  infant — see Newborn
  injury NEC 767.9
    adrenal gland 767.8
    basal ganglia 767.0
    brachial plexus (paralysis) 767.6
    brain (compression) (pressure) 767.0
    cerebellum 767.0
    cerebral hemorrhage 767.0
    conjunctiva 767.8
    eye 767.8
    fracture
      bone, any except clavicle or spine 767.3
      clavicle 767.2
      femur 767.3
      humerus 767.3
      long bone 767.3
      radius and ulna 767.3
      skeleton NEC 767.3
      skull 767.3
      spine 767.3
      tibia and fibula 767.3
    hematoma 767.8
      liver (subcapsular) 767.8
      mastoid 767.8
      skull 767.19
      sternomastoid 767.8
      testes 767.8
      vulva 767.8
    intracranial (edema) 767.0
    laceration
      brain 767.0
      by scalpel 767.8
      peripheral nerve 767.7
    liver 767.8
    meninges
      brain 767.0
      spinal cord 767.4
    nerves (cranial, peripheral) 767.7
      brachial plexus 767.6
      facial 767.5
    paralysis 767.7
      brachial plexus 767.6
      Erb (-Duchenne) 767.6
      facial nerve 767.5
      Klumpke (-Déjérine) 767.6
      radial nerve 767.6
      spinal (cord) (hemorrhage) (laceration) (rupture) 767.4
    rupture
      intracranial 767.0
      liver 767.8
      spinal cord 767.4
      spleen 767.8
      viscera 767.8

Birth — *continued*
  injury NEC — *continued*
    scalp 767.19
    scalpel wound 767.8
    skeleton NEC 767.3
    specified NEC 767.8
    spinal cord 767.4
    spleen 767.8
    subdural hemorrhage 767.0
    tentorial, tear 767.0
    testes 767.8
    vulva 767.8
  instrumental, NEC, affecting fetus or newborn 763.2
  lack of care, after or at 995.52
  multiple
    affected by maternal complications of pregnancy 761.5
    healthy liveborn — *see* Newborn, multiple
  neglect, after or at 995.52
  newborn — *see* Newborn
  palsy or paralysis NEC 767.7
  precipitate, fetus or newborn 763.6
  premature (infant) 765.1 ☑
  prolonged, affecting fetus or newborn 763.9
  retarded, fetus or newborn 763.9
  shock, newborn 779.89
  strangulation or suffocation
    due to aspiration of ►clear◄ amniotic fluid 770.13 ▲
      with respiratory symptoms 770.14 ●
    mechanical 767.8
  trauma NEC 767.9
  triplet
    affected by maternal complications of pregnancy 761.5
    healthy liveborn — *see* Newborn, multiple
  twin
    affected by maternal complications of pregnancy 761.5
    healthy liveborn — *see* Newborn, twin
  ventouse, affecting fetus or newborn 763.3
Birthmark 757.32
Bisalbuminemia 273.8
Biskra button 085.1
Bite(s)
  with intact skin surface — *see* Contusion
  animal — *see* Wound, open, by site
    intact skin surface — *see* Contusion
  centipede 989.5
  chigger 133.8
  fire ant 989.5
  flea — *see* Injury, superficial, by site
  human (open wound) — *see also* Wound, open, by site
    intact skin surface — *see* Contusion
  insect
    nonvenomous — *see* Injury, superficial, by site
    venomous 989.5
  mad dog (death from) 071
  poisonous 989.5
  red bug 133.8
  reptile 989.5
    nonvenomous — *see* Wound, open, by site
  snake 989.5
    nonvenomous — *see* Wound, open, by site
  spider (venomous) 989.5
    nonvenomous — *see* Injury, superficial, by site
  venomous 989.5
Biting
  cheek or lip 528.9
  nail 307.9
Black
  death 020.9
  eye NEC 921.0
  hairy tongue 529.3
  lung disease 500
Blackfan-Diamond anemia or syndrome (congenital hypoplastic anemia) 284.0
Blackhead 706.1
Blackout 780.2
Blackwater fever 084.8
Bladder — *see* condition

Blast
  blindness 921.3
  concussion — *see* Blast, injury
  injury 869.0
    with open wound into cavity 869.1
    abdomen or thorax — *see* Injury, internal, by site
    brain (*see also* Concussion, brain) 850.9
      with skull fracture — *see* Fracture, skull
    ear (acoustic nerve trauma) 951.5
      with perforation, tympanic membrane — *see* Wound, open, ear, drum
    lung (*see also* Injury, internal, lung) 861.20
    otitic (explosive) 388.11
Blastomycosis, blastomycotic (chronic) (cutaneous) (disseminated) (lung) (pulmonary) (systemic) 116.0
  Brazilian 116.1
  European 117.5
  keloidal 116.2
  North American 116.0
  primary pulmonary 116.0
  South American 116.1
Bleb(s) 709.8
  emphysematous (bullous) (diffuse) (lung) (ruptured) (solitary) 492.0
  filtering, eye (postglaucoma) (status) V45.69
    with complication 997.99
    postcataract extraction (complication) 997.99
  lung (ruptured) 492.0
    congenital 770.5
  subpleural (emphysematous) 492.0
Bleeder (familial) (hereditary) (*see also* Defect, coagulation) 286.9
  nonfamilial 286.9
Bleeding (*see also* Hemorrhage) 459.0
  anal 569.3
  anovulatory 628.0
  atonic, following delivery 666.1 ☑
  capillary 448.9
  due to subinvolution 621.1
    puerperal 666.2 ☑
  ear 388.69
  excessive, associated with menopausal onset 627.0
  familial (*see also* Defect, coagulation) 286.9
  following intercourse 626.7
  gastrointestinal 578.9
  gums 523.8
  hemorrhoids — *see* Hemorrhoids, bleeding
  intermenstrual
    irregular 626.6
    regular 626.5
  intraoperative 998.11
  irregular NEC 626.4
  menopausal 627.0
  mouth 528.9
  nipple 611.79
  nose 784.7
  ovulation 626.5
  postclimacteric 627.1
  postcoital 626.7
  postmenopausal 627.1
    following induced menopause 627.4
  postoperative 998.11
  preclimacteric 627.0
  puberty 626.3
    excessive, with onset of menstrual periods 626.3
  rectum, rectal 569.3
  tendencies (*see also* Defect, coagulation) 286.9
  throat 784.8
  umbilical stump 772.3
  umbilicus 789.9
  unrelated to menstrual cycle 626.6
  uterus, uterine 626.9
    climacteric 627.0
    dysfunctional 626.8
    functional 626.8
    unrelated to menstrual cycle 626.6
  vagina, vaginal 623.8
    functional 626.8
  vicarious 625.8
Blennorrhagia, blennorrhagic — *see* Blennorrhea

Blennorrhea (acute) 098.0
  adultorum 098.40
  alveolaris 523.4
  chronic or duration of 2 months or over 098.2
  gonococcal (neonatorum) 098.40
  inclusion (neonatal) (newborn) 771.6
  neonatorum 098.40
Blepharelosis (*see also* Entropion) 374.00
Blepharitis (eyelid) 373.00
  angularis 373.01
  ciliaris 373.00
    with ulcer 373.01
  marginal 373.00
    with ulcer 373.01
  scrofulous (*see also* Tuberculosis) 017.3 ☑ [373.00]
  squamous 373.02
  ulcerative 373.01
Blepharochalasis 374.34
  congenital 743.62
Blepharoclonus 333.81
Blepharoconjunctivitis (*see also* Conjunctivitis) 372.20
  angular 372.21
  contact 372.22
Blepharophimosis (eyelid) 374.46
  congenital 743.62
Blepharoplegia 374.89
Blepharoptosis 374.30
  congenital 743.61
Blepharopyorrhea 098.49
Blepharospasm 333.81
Blessig's cyst 362.62
Blighted ovum 631
Blind
  bronchus (congenital) 748.3
  eye — *see also* Blindness
    hypertensive 360.42
    hypotensive 360.41
  loop syndrome (postoperative) 579.2
  sac, fallopian tube (congenital) 752.19
  spot, enlarged 368.42
  tract or tube (congenital) NEC — *see* Atresia
Blindness (acquired) (congenital) (both eyes) 369.00
  blast 921.3
    with nerve injury — *see* Injury, nerve, optic
  Bright's — *see* Uremia
  color (congenital) 368.59
    acquired 368.55
    blue 368.53
    green 368.52
    red 368.51
    total 368.54
  concussion 950.9
  cortical 377.75
  day 368.10
    acquired 368.10
    congenital 368.10
    hereditary 368.10
    specified type NEC 368.10
  due to
    injury NEC 950.9
    refractive error — *see* Error, refractive
  eclipse (total) 363.31
  emotional 300.11
  hysterical 300.11
  legal (both eyes) (USA definition) 369.4
    with impairment of better (less impaired) eye near-total 369.02
      with
        lesser eye impairment 369.02
          near-total 369.04
          total 369.03
      profound 369.05
        with
          lesser eye impairment 369.05
          near-total 369.07
          profound 369.08
          total 369.06
    severe 369.21
      with
        lesser eye impairment 369.21
        blind 369.11

Blindness — *continued*
  legal — *continued*
    with impairment of better eye — *continued*
      severe — *continued*
        with — *continued*
          lesser eye impairment — *continued*
            near-total 369.13
            profound 369.14
            severe 369.22
            total 369.12
      total
        with lesser eye impairment
          total 369.01
  mind 784.69
  moderate
    both eyes 369.25
      with impairment of lesser eye (specified as)
        blind, not further specified 369.15
        low vision, not further specified 369.23
        near-total 369.17
        profound 369.18
        severe 369.24
        total 369.16
    one eye 369.74
      with vision of other eye (specified as)
        near-normal 369.75
        normal 369.76
  near-total
    both eyes 369.04
      with impairment of lesser eye (specified as)
        blind, not further specified 369.02
        total 369.03
    one eye 369.64
      with vision of other eye (specified as)
        near-normal 369.65
        normal 369.66
  night 368.60
    acquired 368.62
    congenital (Japanese) 368.61
    hereditary 368.61
    specified type NEC 368.69
    vitamin A deficiency 264.5
  nocturnal — *see* Blindness, night
  one eye 369.60
    with low vision of other eye 369.10
  profound
    both eyes 369.08
      with impairment of lesser eye (specified as)
        blind, not further specified 369.05
        near-total 369.07
        total 369.06
    one eye 369.67
      with vision of other eye (specified as)
        near-normal 369.68
        normal 369.69
  psychic 784.69
  severe
    both eyes 369.22
      with impairment of lesser eye (specified as)
        blind, not further specified 369.11
        low vision, not further specified 369.21
        near-total 369.13
        profound 369.14
        total 369.12
    one eye 369.71
      with vision of other eye (specified as)
        near-normal 369.72
        normal 369.73
  snow 370.24
  sun 363.31
  temporary 368.12
  total
    both eyes 369.01
    one eye 369.61
      with vision of other eye (specified as)
        near-normal 369.62
        normal 369.63
  transient 368.12
  traumatic NEC 950.9
  word (developmental) 315.01
    acquired 784.61
    secondary to organic lesion 784.61

Blister — *see also* Injury, superficial, by site
  beetle dermatitis 692.89
  due to burn — *see* Burn, by site, second degree
  fever 054.9
  multiple, skin, nontraumatic 709.8

Bloating 787.3

Bloch-Siemens syndrome (incontinentia pigmenti) 757.33

Bloch-Stauffer dyshormonal dermatosis 757.33

Bloch-Sulzberger disease or syndrome
  (incontinentia pigmenti) (melanoblastosis) 757.33

Block
  alveolar capillary 516.3
  arborization (heart) 426.6
  arrhythmic 426.9
  atrioventricular (AV) (incomplete) (partial) 426.10
    with
      2:1 atrioventricular response block 426.13
      atrioventricular dissociation 426.0
    first degree (incomplete) 426.11
    second degree (Mobitz type I) 426.13
      Mobitz (type) II 426.12
    third degree 426.0
    complete 426.0
      congenital 746.86
    congenital 746.86
    Mobitz (incomplete)
      type I (Wenckebach's) 426.13
      type II 426.12
    partial 426.13
  auriculoventricular (*see also* Block, atrioventricular) 426.10
    complete 426.0
      congenital 746.86
    congenital 746.86
  bifascicular (cardiac) 426.53
  bundle branch (complete) (false) (incomplete) 426.50
    bilateral 426.53
    left (complete) (main stem) 426.3
      with right bundle branch block 426.53
      anterior fascicular 426.2
        with
          posterior fascicular block 426.3
          right bundle branch block 426.52
      hemiblock 426.2
      incomplete 426.2
        with right bundle branch block 426.53
      posterior fascicular 426.2
        with
          anterior fascicular block 426.3
          right bundle branch block 426.51
    right 426.4
      with
        left bundle branch block (incomplete) (main stem) 426.53
        left fascicular block 426.53
          anterior 426.52
          posterior 426.51
    Wilson's type 426.4
  cardiac 426.9
  conduction 426.9
    complete 426.0
  Eustachian tube (*see also* Obstruction, Eustachian tube) 381.60
  fascicular (left anterior) (left posterior) 426.2
  foramen Magendie (acquired) 331.3
    congenital 742.3
      with spina bifida (*see also* Spina bifida) 741.0 ☑
  heart 426.9
    first degree (atrioventricular) 426.11
    second degree (atrioventricular) 426.13
    third degree (atrioventricular) 426.0
    bundle branch (complete) (false) (incomplete) 426.50
      bilateral 426.53
      left (*see also* Block, bundle branch, left) 426.3
      right (*see also* Block, bundle branch, right) 426.4
    complete (atrioventricular) 426.0

Block — *continued*
  heart — *continued*
    congenital 746.86
    incomplete 426.13
    intra-atrial 426.6
    intraventricular NEC 426.6
    sinoatrial 426.6
    specified type NEC 426.6
  hepatic vein 453.0
  intraventricular (diffuse) (myofibrillar) 426.6
    bundle branch (complete) (false) (incomplete) 426.50
      bilateral 426.53
      left (*see also* Block, bundle branch, left) 426.3
      right (*see also* Block, bundle branch, right) 426.4
  kidney (*see also* Disease, renal) 593.9
    postcystoscopic 997.5
  myocardial (*see also* Block, heart) 426.9
  nodal 426.10
  optic nerve 377.49
  organ or site (congenital) NEC — *see* Atresia
  parietal 426.6
  peri-infarction 426.6
  portal (vein) 452
  sinoatrial 426.6
  sinoauricular 426.6
  spinal cord 336.9
  trifascicular 426.54
  tubal 628.2
  vein NEC 453.9

Blocq's disease or syndrome (astasia-abasia) 307.9

Blood
  constituents, abnormal NEC 790.6
  disease 289.9
    specified NEC 289.89
  donor V59.01
    other blood components V59.09
    stem cells V59.02
    whole blood V59.01
  dyscrasia 289.9
    with
      abortion — *see* Abortion, by type, with hemorrhage, delayed or excessive
      ectopic pregnancy (*see also* categories 633.0-633.9) 639.1
      molar pregnancy (*see also* categories 630-632) 639.1
    fetus or newborn NEC 776.9
    following
      abortion 639.1
      ectopic or molar pregnancy 639.1
    puerperal, postpartum 666.3 ☑
  flukes NEC (*see also* Infestation, Schistosoma) 120.9
  in
    feces (*see also* Melena) 578.1
      occult 792.1
    urine (*see also* Hematuria) 599.7
  mole 631
  occult 792.1
  poisoning (*see also* Septicemia) 038.9
  pressure
    decreased, due to shock following injury 958.4
    fluctuating 796.4
    high (*see also* Hypertension) 401.9
      incidental reading (isolated) (nonspecific), without diagnosis of hypertension 796.2
    low (*see also* Hypotension) 458.9
      incidental reading (isolated) (nonspecific), without diagnosis of hypotension 796.3
  spitting (*see also* Hemoptysis) 786.3
  staining cornea 371.12
  transfusion
    without reported diagnosis V58.2
    donor V59.01
      stem cells V59.02
    reaction or complication — *see* Complications, transfusion
  tumor — *see* Hematoma
  vessel rupture — *see* Hemorrhage

Blood — *continued*
  vomiting (*see also* Hematemesis) 578.0
Blood-forming organ disease 289.9
Bloodgood's disease 610.1
Bloodshot eye 379.93
Bloom (-Machacek) (-Torre) syndrome 757.39
Blotch, palpebral 372.55
Blount's disease (tibia vara) 732.4
Blount-Barber syndrome (tibia vara) 732.4
Blue
  baby 746.9
  bloater 491.20
    with
      acute bronchitis 491.22
      exacerbation (acute) 491.21
  diaper syndrome 270.0
  disease 746.9
  dome cyst 610.0
  drum syndrome 381.02
  sclera 743.47
    with fragility of bone and deafness 756.51
  toe syndrome 445.02
Blueness (*see also* Cyanosis) 782.5
Blurring, visual 368.8
Blushing (abnormal) (excessive) 782.62
BMI (body mass index)
  adult   ●
    25.0–25.9 V85.21   ●
    26.0–26.9 V85.22   ●
    27.0–27.9 V85.23   ●
    28.0–28.9 V85.24   ●
    29.0–29.9 V85.25   ●
    30.0–30.9 V85.30   ●
    31.0–31.9 V85.31   ●
    32.0–32.9 V85.32   ●
    33.0–33.9 V85.33   ●
    34.0–34.9 V85.34   ●
    35.0–35.9 V85.35   ●
    36.0–36.9 V85.36   ●
    37.0–37.9 V85.37   ●
    38.0–38.9 V85.38   ●
    39.0–39.9 V85.39   ●
    40 and over V85.4   ●
    between 19–24 V85.1   ●
    less than 19 V85.0   ●
Boarder, hospital V65.0
  infant V65.0
Bockhart's impetigo (superficial folliculitis) 704.8
Bodechtel-Guttmann disease (subacute
  sclerosing panencephalitis) 046.2
Boder-Sedgwick syndrome (ataxia-telangiectasia)
  334.8
Body, bodies
  Aschoff (*see also* Myocarditis, rheumatic) 398.0
  asteroid, vitreous 379.22
  choroid, colloid (degenerative) 362.57
    hereditary 362.77
  cytoid (retina) 362.82
  drusen (retina) (*see also* Drusen) 362.57
    optic disc 377.21
  fibrin, pleura 511.0
  foreign — *see* Foreign body
  Hassall-Henle 371.41
  loose
    joint (*see also* Loose, body, joint) 718.1 ☑
      knee 717.6
    knee 717.6
    sheath, tendon 727.82
  Mallory's 034.1
  mass index (BMI)
    adult   ●
      25.0–25.9 V85.21   ●
      26.0–26.9 V85.22   ●
      27.0–27.9 V85.23   ●
      28.0–28.9 V85.24   ●
      29.0–29.9 V85.25   ●
      30.0–30.9 V85.30   ●
      31.0–31.9 V85.31   ●
      32.0–32.9 V85.32   ●
      33.0–33.9 V85.33   ●
      34.0–34.9 V85.34   ●
      35.0–35.9 V85.35   ●
      36.0–36.9 V85.36   ●
      37.0–37.9 V85.37   ●

Body, bodies — *continued*
  mass index — *continued*
    adult — *continued*
      38.0–38.9 V85.38   ●
      39.0–39.9 V85.39   ●
      40 and over V85.4   ●
      between 19–24 V85.1   ●
      less than 19 V85.0   ●
  Mooser 081.0
  Negri 071
  rice (joint) (*see also* Loose, body, joint) 718.1 ☑
    knee 717.6
  rocking 307.3
Boeck's
  disease (sarcoidosis) 135
  lupoid (miliary) 135
  sarcoid 135
Boerhaave's syndrome (spontaneous esophageal
  rupture) 530.4
Boggy
  cervix 622.8
  uterus 621.8
Boil (*see also* Carbuncle) 680.9
  abdominal wall 680.2
  Aleppo 085.1
  ankle 680.6
  anus 680.5
  arm (any part, above wrist) 680.3
  auditory canal, external 680.0
  axilla 680.3
  back (any part) 680.2
  Baghdad 085.1
  breast 680.2
  buttock 680.5
  chest wall 680.2
  corpus cavernosum 607.2
  Delhi 085.1
  ear (any part) 680.0
  eyelid 373.13
  face (any part, except eye) 680.0
  finger (any) 680.4
  flank 680.2
  foot (any part) 680.7
  forearm 680.3
  Gafsa 085.1
  genital organ, male 608.4
  gluteal (region) 680.5
  groin 680.2
  hand (any part) 680.4
  head (any part, except face) 680.8
  heel 680.7
  hip 680.6
  knee 680.6
  labia 616.4
  lacrimal (*see also* Dacryocystitis) 375.30
    gland (*see also* Dacryoadenitis) 375.00
    passages (duct) (sac) (*see also*
      Dacryocystitis) 375.30
  leg, any part, except foot 680.6
  multiple sites 680.9
  natal 085.1
  neck 680.1
  nose (external) (septum) 680.0
  orbit, orbital 376.01
  partes posteriores 680.5
  pectoral region 680.2
  penis 607.2
  perineum 680.2
  pinna 680.0
  scalp (any part) 680.8
  scrotum 608.4
  seminal vesicle 608.0
  shoulder 680.3
  skin NEC 680.9
  specified site NEC 680.8
  spermatic cord 608.4
  temple (region) 680.0
  testis 608.4
  thigh 680.6
  thumb 680.4
  toe (any) 680.7
  tropical 085.1
  trunk 680.2
  tunica vaginalis 608.4
  umbilicus 680.2
  upper arm 680.3

Boil (*see also* Carbuncle) — *continued*
  vas deferens 608.4
  vulva 616.4
  wrist 680.4
Bold hives (*see also* Urticaria) 708.9
Bolivian hemorrhagic fever 078.7
Bombé, iris 364.74
Bomford-Rhoads anemia (refractory) 238.7 ▲
Bone — *see* condition
Bonnevie-Ullrich syndrome 758.6
Bonnier's syndrome 386.19
Bonvale Dam fever 780.79
Bony block of joint 718.80
  ankle 718.87
  elbow 718.82
  foot 718.87
  hand 718.84
  hip 718.85
  knee 718.86
  multiple sites 718.89
  pelvic region 718.85
  shoulder (region) 718.81
  specified site NEC 718.88
  wrist 718.83
Borderline
  intellectual functioning V62.89
  pelvis 653.1 ☑
    with obstruction during labor 660.1 ☑
      affecting fetus or newborn 763.1
  psychosis (*see also* Schizophrenia) 295.5 ☑
    of childhood (*see also* Psychosis, childhood)
      299.8 ☑
  schizophrenia (*see also* Schizophrenia) 295.5 ☑
Borna disease 062.9
Bornholm disease (epidemic pleurodynia) 074.1
Borrelia vincentii (mouth) (pharynx) (tonsils) 101
Bostock's catarrh (*see also* Fever, hay) 477.9
Boston exanthem 048
Botalli, ductus (patent) (persistent) 747.0
Bothriocephalus latus infestation 123.4
Botulism 005.1
Bouba (*see also* Yaws) 102.9
Bouffée délirante 298.3
Bouillaud's disease or syndrome (rheumatic
  heart disease) 391.9
Bourneville's disease (tuberous sclerosis) 759.5
Boutonneuse fever 082.1
Boutonniere
  deformity (finger) 736.21
  hand (intrinsic) 736.21
Bouveret (-Hoffmann) disease or syndrome
  (paroxysmal tachycardia) 427.2
Bovine heart — *see* Hypertrophy, cardiac
Bowel — *see* condition
Bowen's
  dermatosis (precancerous) (M8081/2) — *see*
    Neoplasm, skin, in situ
  disease (M8081/2) — *see* Neoplasm, skin, in
    situ
  epithelioma (M8081/2) — *see* Neoplasm, skin,
    in situ
  type
    epidermoid carcinoma in situ (M8081/2) —
      see Neoplasm, skin, in situ
    intraepidermal squamous cell carcinoma
      (M8081/2) — *see* Neoplasm, skin, in
      situ
Bowing
  femur 736.89
    congenital 754.42
  fibula 736.89
    congenital 754.43
  forearm 736.09
    away from midline (cubitus valgus) 736.01
    toward midline (cubitus varus) 736.02
  leg(s), long bones, congenital 754.44
  radius 736.09
    away from midline (cubitus valgus) 736.01
    toward midline (cubitus varus) 736.02
  tibia 736.89
    congenital 754.43

☑ Additional Digit Required — Refer to the Tabular List (Numeric Code Section) for Additional Digit Selection

Bowleg(s) 736.42
- congenital 754.44
- rachitic 268.1

Boyd's dysentery 004.2

Brachial — *see* condition

Brachman-de Lange syndrome (Amsterdam dwarf, mental retardation, and brachycephaly) 759.89

Brachycardia 427.89

Brachycephaly 756.0

Brachymorphism and ectopia lentis 759.89

Bradley's disease (epidemic vomiting) 078.82

Bradycardia 427.89
- chronic (sinus) 427.81
- newborn 779.81
- nodal 427.89
- postoperative 997.1
- reflex 337.0
- sinoatrial 427.89
  - with paroxysmal tachyarrhythmia or tachycardia 427.81
    - chronic 427.81
- sinus 427.89
  - with paroxysmal tachyarrhythmia or tachycardia 427.81
    - chronic 427.81
    - persistent 427.81
    - severe 427.81
  - tachycardia syndrome 427.81
- vagal 427.89

Bradypnea 786.09

Brailsford's disease 732.3
- radial head 732.3
- tarsal scaphoid 732.5

Brailsford-Morquio disease or syndrome (mucopolysaccharidosis IV) 277.5

Brain — *see also* condition
- death 348.8
- syndrome (acute) (chronic) (nonpsychotic) (organic) (with neurotic reaction) (with behavioral reaction) (*see also* Syndrome, brain) 310.9
  - with
    - presenile brain disease 290.10
    - psychosis, psychotic reaction (*see also* Psychosis, organic) 294.9
  - congenital (*see also* Retardation, mental) 319

Branched-chain amino-acid disease 270.3

Branchial — *see* condition

Brandt's syndrome (acrodermatitis enteropathica) 686.8

Brash (water) 787.1

Brass-founders' ague 985.8

Bravais-Jacksonian epilepsy (*see also* Epilepsy) 345.5 ☑

Braxton Hicks contractions 644.1 ☑

Braziers' disease 985.8

Brazilian
- blastomycosis 116.1
- leishmaniasis 085.5

BRBPR (bright red blood per rectum) 569.3

Break
- cardiorenal — *see* Hypertension, cardiorenal
- retina (*see also* Defect, retina) 361.30

Breakbone fever 061

Breakdown
- device, implant, or graft — *see* Complications, mechanical
- nervous (*see also* Disorder, mental, nonpsychotic) 300.9
  - perineum 674.2 ☑

Breast — *see* condition

Breast feeding difficulties 676.8 ☑

Breath
- foul 784.9
- holder, child 312.81
- holding spells 786.9
- shortness 786.05

Breathing
- asymmetrical 786.09
- bronchial 786.09
- exercises V57.0
- labored 786.09
- mouth 784.9
  - causing malocclusion 524.59 ●
- periodic 786.09
  - high altitude 327.22 ●
- tic 307.20

Breathlessness 786.09

Breda's disease (*see also* Yaws) 102.9

Breech
- delivery, affecting fetus or newborn 763.0
- extraction, affecting fetus or newborn 763.0
- presentation (buttocks) (complete) (frank) 652.2 ☑
  - with successful version 652.1 ☑
  - before labor, affecting fetus or newborn 761.7
  - during labor, affecting fetus or newborn 763.0

Breisky's disease (kraurosis vulvae) 624.0

Brennemann's syndrome (acute mesenteric lymphadenitis) 289.2

Brenner's
- tumor (benign) (M9000/0) 220
  - borderline malignancy (M9000/1) 236.2
  - malignant (M9000/3) 183.0
  - proliferating (M9000/1) 236.2

Bretonneau's disease (diphtheritic malignant angina) 032.0

Breus' mole 631

Brevicollis 756.16

Bricklayers' itch 692.89

Brickmakers' anemia 126.9

Bridge
- myocardial 746.85

Bright red blood per rectum (BRBPR) 569.3

Bright's
- blindness — *see* Uremia
- disease (*see also* Nephritis) 583.9
  - arteriosclerotic (*see also* Hypertension, kidney) 403.90

Brill's disease (recrudescent typhus) 081.1
- flea-borne 081.0
- louse-borne 081.1

Brill-Symmers disease (follicular lymphoma) (M9690/3) 202.0 ☑

Brill-Zinsser disease (recrudescent typhus) 081.1

Brinton's disease (linitis plastica) (M8142/3) 151.9

Brion-Kayser disease (*see also* Fever, paratyphoid) 002.9

Briquet's disorder or syndrome 300.81

Brissaud's
- infantilism (infantile myxedema) 244.9
- motor-verbal tic 307.23

Brissaud-Meige syndrome (infantile myxedema) 244.9

Brittle
- bones (congenital) 756.51
- nails 703.8
  - congenital 757.5

Broad — *see also* condition
- beta disease 272.2
- ligament laceration syndrome 620.6

Brock's syndrome (atelectasis due to enlarged lymph nodes) 518.0

Brocq's disease 691.8
- atopic (diffuse) neurodermatitis 691.8
- lichen simplex chronicus 698.3
- parakeratosis psoriasiformis 696.2
- parapsoriasis 696.2

Brocq-Duhring disease (dermatitis herpetiformis) 694.0

Brodie's
- abscess (localized) (chronic) (*see also* Osteomyelitis) 730.1 ☑
- disease (joint) (*see also* Osteomyelitis) 730.1 ☑

Broken
- arches 734
  - congenital 755.67
- back — *see* Fracture, vertebra, by site
- bone — *see* Fracture, by site
- compensation — *see* Disease, heart
- implant or internal device — *see* listing under Complications, mechanical
- neck — *see* Fracture, vertebra, cervical
- nose 802.0
  - open 802.1
- tooth, teeth 873.63
  - complicated 873.73

Bromhidrosis 705.89

Bromidism, bromism
- acute 967.3
  - correct substance properly administered 349.82
  - overdose or wrong substance given or taken 967.3
- chronic (*see also* Dependence) 304.1 ☑

Bromidrosiphobia 300.23

Bromidrosis 705.89

Bronchi, bronchial — *see* condition

Bronchiectasis (cylindrical) (diffuse) (fusiform) (localized) (moniliform) (postinfectious) (recurrent) (saccular) 494.0
- with acute exacerbation 494.1
- congenital 748.61
- tuberculosis (*see also* Tuberculosis) 011.5 ☑

Bronchiolectasis — *see* Bronchiectasis

Bronchiolitis (acute) (infectious) (subacute) 466.19
- with
  - bronchospasm or obstruction 466.19
  - influenza, flu, or grippe 487.1
- catarrhal (acute) (subacute) 466.19
- chemical 506.0
  - chronic 506.4
- chronic (obliterative) 491.8
- due to external agent — *see* Bronchitis, acute, due to
- fibrosa obliterans 491.8
- influenzal 487.1
- obliterans 491.8
  - with organizing pneumonia (B.O.O.P.) 516.8
  - status post lung transplant 996.84
- obliterative (chronic) (diffuse) (subacute) 491.8
  - due to fumes or vapors 506.4
- respiratory syncytial virus 466.11
- vesicular — *see* Pneumonia, broncho-

Bronchitis (diffuse) (hypostatic) (infectious) (inflammatory) (simple) 490
- with
  - emphysema — *see* Emphysema
  - influenza, flu, or grippe 487.1
  - obstruction airway, chronic 491.20
    - with
      - acute bronchitis 491.22
      - exacerbation (acute) 491.21
  - tracheitis 490
    - acute or subacute 466.0
      - with bronchospasm or obstruction 466.0
    - chronic 491.8
- acute or subacute 466.0
  - with
    - bronchospasm 466.0
    - obstruction 466.0
    - tracheitis 466.0
  - chemical (due to fumes or vapors) 506.0
  - due to
    - fumes or vapors 506.0
    - radiation 508.8
- allergic (acute) (*see also* Asthma) 493.9 ☑
- arachidic 934.1
- aspiration 507.0
  - due to fumes or vapors 506.0
- asthmatic (acute) 493.90
  - with
    - acute exacerbation 493.92
    - status asthmaticus 493.91
  - chronic 493.2 ☑
- capillary 466.19
  - with bronchospasm or obstruction 466.19

Bronchitis — *continued*
  capillary — *continued*
    chronic 491.8
  caseous (*see also* Tuberculosis) 011.3 ☑
  Castellani's 104.8
  catarrhal 490
    acute — *see* Bronchitis, acute
    chronic 491.0
  chemical (acute) (subacute) 506.0
    chronic 506.4
    due to fumes or vapors (acute) (subacute)
      506.0
      chronic 506.4
  chronic 491.9
    with
      tracheitis (chronic) 491.8
    asthmatic 493.2 ☑
    catarrhal 491.0
    chemical (due to fumes and vapors) 506.4
    due to
      fumes or vapors (chemical) (inhalation)
        506.4
      radiation 508.8
      tobacco smoking 491.0
    mucopurulent 491.1
    obstructive 491.20
      with
        acute bronchitis 491.22
        exacerbation (acute) 491.21
    purulent 491.1
    simple 491.0
    specified type NEC 491.8
  croupous 466.0
    with bronchospasm or obstruction 466.0
    due to fumes or vapors 506.0
  emphysematous 491.20
    with
      acute bronchitis 491.22
      exacerbation (acute) 491.21
  exudative 466.0
  fetid (chronic) (recurrent) 491.1
  fibrinous, acute or subacute 466.0
    with bronchospasm or obstruction 466.0
  grippal 487.1
  influenzal 487.1
  membranous, acute or subacute 466.0
    with bronchospasm or obstruction 466.0
  moulders' 502
  mucopurulent (chronic) (recurrent) 491.1
    acute or subacute 466.0
  obliterans 491.8
  obstructive (chronic) 491.20
    with
      acute bronchitis 491.22
      exacerbation (acute) 491.21
  pituitous 491.1
  plastic (inflammatory) 466.0
  pneumococcal, acute or subacute 466.0
    with bronchospasm or obstruction 466.0
  pseudomembranous 466.0
  purulent (chronic) (recurrent) 491.1
    acute or subacute 466.0
      with bronchospasm or obstruction 466.0
  putrid 491.1
  scrofulous (*see also* Tuberculosis) 011.3 ☑
  senile 491.9
  septic, acute or subacute 466.0
    with bronchospasm or obstruction 466.0
  smokers' 491.0
  spirochetal 104.8
  suffocative, acute or subacute 466.0
  summer (*see also* Asthma) 493.9 ☑
  suppurative (chronic) 491.1
    acute or subacute 466.0
  tuberculous (*see also* Tuberculosis) 011.3 ☑
  ulcerative 491.8
    Vincent's 101
  Vincent's 101
  viral, acute or subacute 466.0
Bronchoalveolitis 485
Bronchoaspergillosis 117.3
Bronchocele
  meaning
    dilatation of bronchus 519.1
    goiter 240.9
Bronchogenic carcinoma 162.9

Bronchohemisporosis 117.9
Broncholithiasis 518.89
  tuberculous (*see also* Tuberculosis) 011.3 ☑
Bronchomalacia 748.3
Bronchomoniliasis 112.89
Bronchomycosis 112.89
Bronchonocardiosis 039.1
Bronchopleuropneumonia — *see* Pneumonia,
  broncho-
Bronchopneumonia — *see* Pneumonia, broncho-
Bronchopneumonitis — *see* Pneumonia,
  broncho-
Bronchopulmonary — *see* condition
Bronchopulmonitis — *see* Pneumonia, broncho-
Bronchorrhagia 786.3
  newborn 770.3
  tuberculous (*see also* Tuberculosis) 011.3 ☑
Bronchorrhea (chronic) (purulent) 491.0
  acute 466.0
Bronchospasm 519.1
  with
    asthma — *see* Asthma
    bronchiolitis, acute 466.19
      due to respiratory syncytial virus 466.11
    bronchitis — *see* Bronchitis
    chronic obstructive pulmonary disease
      (COPD) 496
    emphysema — *see* Emphysema
    due to external agent — *see* Condition,
      respiratory, acute, due to
    exercise induced 493.81
Bronchospirochetosis 104.8
Bronchostenosis 519.1
Bronchus — *see* condition
Bronze, bronzed
  diabetes 275.0
  disease (Addison's) (skin) 255.4
    tuberculous (*see also* Tuberculosis) 017.6 ☑
Brooke's disease or tumor (M8100/0) — *see*
  Neoplasm, skin, benign
Brown's tendon sheath syndrome 378.61
Brown enamel of teeth (hereditary) 520.5
Brown-Séquard's paralysis (syndrome) 344.89
Brow presentation complicating delivery
  652.4 ☑
Brucella, brucellosis (infection) 023.9
  abortus 023.1
  canis 023.3
  dermatitis, skin 023.9
  melitensis 023.0
  mixed 023.8
  suis 023.2
Bruck's disease 733.99
Bruck-de Lange disease or syndrome
  (Amsterdam dwarf, mental retardation, and
  brachycephaly) 759.89
Brugada syndrome 746.89
Brugsch's syndrome (acropachyderma) 757.39
Brug's filariasis 125.1
Bruhl's disease (splenic anemia with fever) 285.8
Bruise (skin surface intact) — *see also* Contusion
  with
    fracture — *see* Fracture, by site
    open wound — *see* Wound, open, by site
  internal organ (abdomen, chest, or pelvis) —
    see Injury, internal, by site
  umbilical cord 663.6 ☑
    affecting fetus or newborn 762.6
Bruit 785.9
  arterial (abdominal) (carotid) 785.9
  supraclavicular 785.9
Brushburn — *see* Injury, superficial, by site
Bruton's X-linked agammaglobulinemia 279.04
Bruxism 306.8
  sleep related 327.53   ●
Bubbly lung syndrome 770.7
Bubo 289.3
  blennorrhagic 098.89
  chancroidal 099.0
  climatic 099.1

Bubo — *continued*
  due to Hemophilus ducreyi 099.0
  gonococcal 098.89
  indolent NEC 099.8
  inguinal NEC 099.8
    chancroidal 099.0
    climatic 099.1
    due to H. ducreyi 099.0
  scrofulous (*see also* Tuberculosis) 017.2 ☑
  soft chancre 099.0
  suppurating 683
  syphilitic 091.0
    congenital 090.0
  tropical 099.1
  venereal NEC 099.8
  virulent 099.0
Bubonic plague 020.0
Bubonocele — *see* Hernia, inguinal
Buccal — *see* condition
Buchanan's disease (juvenile osteochondrosis of
  iliac crest) 732.1
Buchem's syndrome (hyperostosis corticalis)
  733.3
Buchman's disease (osteochondrosis, juvenile)
  732.1
Bucket handle fracture (semilunar cartilage) (*see*
  also Tear, meniscus) 836.2
Budd-Chiari syndrome (hepatic vein thrombosis)
  453.0
Budgerigar-fanciers' disease or lung 495.2
Büdinger-Ludloff-Läwen disease 717.89
Buerger's disease (thromboangiitis obliterans)
  443.1
Bulbar — *see* condition
Bulbus cordis 745.9
  persistent (in left ventricle) 745.8
Bulging fontanels (congenital) 756.0
Bulimia 783.6
  nervosa 307.51
  nonorganic origin 307.51
Bulky uterus 621.2
Bulla(e) 709.8
  lung (emphysematous) (solitary) 492.0
Bullet wound — *see also* Wound, open, by site
  fracture — *see* Fracture, by site, open
  internal organ (abdomen, chest, or pelvis) —
    see Injury, internal, by site, with open
    wound
  intracranial — *see* Laceration, brain, with open
    wound
Bullis fever 082.8
Bullying (*see also* Disturbance, conduct) 312.0 ☑
Bundle
  branch block (complete) (false) (incomplete)
    426.50
    bilateral 426.53
    left (*see also* Block, bundle branch, left)
      426.3
      hemiblock 426.2
    right (*see also* Block, bundle branch, right)
      426.4
  of His — *see* condition
  of Kent syndrome (anomalous atrioventricular
    excitation) 426.7
Bungpagga 040.81
Bunion 727.1
Bunionette 727.1
Bunyamwera fever 066.3
Buphthalmia, buphthalmos (congenital) 743.20
  associated with
    keratoglobus, congenital 743.22
    megalocornea 743.22
    ocular anomalies NEC 743.22
  isolated 743.21
  simple 743.21
Bürger-Grütz disease or syndrome (essential
  familial hyperlipemia) 272.3
Buried roots 525.3
Burke's syndrome 577.8
Burkitt's
  tumor (M9750/3) 200.2 ☑

Burkitt's — *continued*
　type malignant, lymphoma, lymphoblastic, or undifferentiated (M9750/3) 200.2 ☑

Burn (acid) (cathode ray) (caustic) (chemical) (electric heating appliance) (electricity) (fire) (flame) (hot liquid or object) (irradiation) (lime) (radiation) (steam) (thermal) (x-ray) 949.0

Note — Use the following fifth-digit subclassification with category 948 to indicate the percent of body surface with third degree burn:	
0	*Less than 10% or unspecified*
1	*10–19%*
2	*20–29%*
3	*30–39%*
4	*40–49%*
5	*50–59%*
6	*60–69%*
7	*70–79%*
8	*80–89%*
9	*90% or more of body surface*

　with
　　blisters — *see* Burn, by site, second degree
　　erythema — *see* Burn, by site, first degree
　　skin loss (epidermal) — *see also* Burn, by site, second degree
　　　full thickness — *see also* Burn, by site, third degree
　　　　with necrosis of underlying tissues — *see* Burn, by site, third degree, deep
　first degree — *see* Burn, by site, first degree
　second degree — *see* Burn, by site, second degree
　third degree — *see* Burn, by site, third degree
　　deep — *see* Burn, by site, third degree, deep
　abdomen, abdominal (muscle) (wall) 942.03
　　with
　　　trunk — *see* Burn, trunk, multiple sites
　　first degree 942.13
　　second degree 942.23
　　third degree 942.33
　　　deep 942.43
　　　　with loss of body part 942.53
　ankle 945.03
　　with
　　　lower limb(s) — *see* Burn, leg, multiple sites
　　first degree 945.13
　　second degree 945.23
　　third degree 945.33
　　　deep 945.43
　　　　with loss of body part 945.53
　anus — *see* Burn, trunk, specified site NEC
　arm(s) 943.00
　　first degree 943.10
　　second degree 943.20
　　third degree 943.30
　　　deep 943.40
　　　　with loss of body part 943.50
　　lower — *see* Burn, forearm(s)
　　multiple sites, except hand(s) or wrist(s) 943.09
　　　first degree 943.19
　　　second degree 943.29
　　　third degree 943.39
　　　　deep 943.49
　　　　　with loss of body part 943.59
　　upper 943.03
　　　first degree 943.13
　　　second degree 943.23
　　　third degree 943.33
　　　　deep 943.43
　　　　　with loss of body part 943.53
　auditory canal (external) — *see* Burn, ear
　auricle (ear) — *see* Burn, ear
　axilla 943.04
　　with
　　　upper limb(s), except hand(s) or wrist(s) — *see* Burn, arm(s), multiple sites
　　first degree 943.14

Burn — *continued*
　axilla — *continued*
　　second degree 943.24
　　third degree 943.34
　　　deep 943.44
　　　　with loss of body part 943.54
　back 942.04
　　with
　　　trunk — *see* Burn, trunk, multiple sites
　　first degree 942.14
　　second degree 942.24
　　third degree 942.34
　　　deep 942.44
　　　　with loss of body part 942.54
　biceps
　　brachii — *see* Burn, arm(s), upper
　　femoris — *see* Burn, thigh
　breast(s) 942.01
　　with
　　　trunk — *see* Burn, trunk, multiple sites
　　first degree 942.11
　　second degree 942.21
　　third degree 942.31
　　　deep 942.41
　　　　with loss of body part 942.51
　brow — *see* Burn, forehead
　buttock(s) — *see* Burn, back
　canthus (eye) 940.1
　　chemical 940.0
　cervix (uteri) 947.4
　cheek (cutaneous) 941.07
　　with
　　　face or head — *see* Burn, head, multiple sites
　　first degree 941.17
　　second degree 941.27
　　third degree 941.37
　　　deep 941.47
　　　　with loss of body part 941.57
　chest wall (anterior) 942.02
　　with
　　　trunk — *see* Burn, trunk, multiple sites
　　first degree 942.12
　　second degree 942.22
　　third degree 942.32
　　　deep 942.42
　　　　with loss of body part 942.52
　chin 941.04
　　with
　　　face or head — *see* Burn, head, multiple sites
　　first degree 941.14
　　second degree 941.24
　　third degree 941.34
　　　deep 941.44
　　　　with loss of body part 941.54
　clitoris — *see* Burn, genitourinary organs, external
　colon 947.3
　conjunctiva (and cornea) 940.4
　　chemical
　　　acid 940.3
　　　alkaline 940.2
　cornea (and conjunctiva) 940.4
　　chemical
　　　acid 940.3
　　　alkaline 940.2
　costal region — *see* Burn, chest wall
　due to ingested chemical agent — *see* Burn, internal organs
　ear (auricle) (canal) (drum) (external) 941.01
　　with
　　　face or head — *see* Burn, head, multiple sites
　　first degree 941.11
　　second degree 941.21
　　third degree 941.31
　　　deep 941.41
　　　　with loss of a body part 941.51
　elbow 943.02
　　with
　　　hand(s) and wrist(s) — *see* Burn, multiple specified sites
　　　upper limb(s), except hand(s) or wrist(s) — *see also* Burn, arm(s), multiple sites
　　first degree 943.12

Burn — *continued*
　elbow — *continued*
　　second degree 943.22
　　third degree 943.32
　　　deep 943.42
　　　　with loss of body part 943.52
　electricity, electric current — *see* Burn, by site
　entire body — *see* Burn, multiple, specified sites
　epididymis — *see* Burn, genitourinary organs, external
　epigastric region — *see* Burn, abdomen
　epiglottis 947.1
　esophagus 947.2
　extent (percent of body surface)
　　less than 10 percent 948.0 ☑
　　10-19 percent 948.1 ☑
　　20-29 percent 948.2 ☑
　　30-39 percent 948.3 ☑
　　40-49 percent 948.4 ☑
　　50-59 percent 948.5 ☑
　　60-69 percent 948.6 ☑
　　70-79 percent 948.7 ☑
　　80-89 percent 948.8 ☑
　　90 percent or more 948.9 ☑
　extremity
　　lower — *see* Burn, leg
　　upper — *see* Burn, arm(s)
　eye(s) (and adnexa) (only) 940.9
　　with
　　　face, head, or neck 941.02
　　　　first degree 941.12
　　　　second degree 941.22
　　　　third degree 941.32
　　　　　deep 941.42
　　　　　　with loss of body part 941.52
　　　other sites (classifiable to more than one category in 940-945) — *see* Burn, multiple, specified sites
　　　resulting rupture and destruction of eyeball 940.5
　　specified part — *see* Burn, by site
　eyeball — *see also* Burn, eye
　　with resulting rupture and destruction of eyeball 940.5
　eyelid(s) 940.1
　　chemical 940.0
　face — *see* Burn, head
　finger (nail) (subungual) 944.01
　　with
　　　hand(s) — *see* Burn, hand(s), multiple sites
　　　other sites — *see* Burn, multiple, specified sites
　　　thumb 944.04
　　　　first degree 944.14
　　　　second degree 944.24
　　　　third degree 944.34
　　　　　deep 944.44
　　　　　　with loss of body part 944.54
　　first degree 944.11
　　second degree 944.21
　　third degree 944.31
　　　deep 944.41
　　　　with loss of body part 944.51
　multiple (digits) 944.03
　　with thumb — *see* Burn, finger, with thumb
　　first degree 944.13
　　second degree 944.23
　　third degree 944.33
　　　deep 944.43
　　　　with loss of body part 944.53
　flank — *see* Burn, abdomen
　foot 945.02
　　with
　　　lower limb(s) — *see* Burn, leg, multiple sites
　　first degree 945.12
　　second degree 945.22
　　third degree 945.32
　　　deep 945.42
　　　　with loss of body part 945.52
　forearm(s) 943.01
　　with
　　　upper limb(s), except hand(s) or wrist(s) — *see* Burn, arm(s), multiple sites

Burn — *continued*
  forearm(s) — *continued*
    first degree 943.11
    second degree 943.21
    third degree 943.31
      deep 943.41
        with loss of body part 943.51
  forehead 941.07
    with
      face or head — *see* Burn, head, multiple
        sites
    first degree 941.17
    second degree 941.27
    third degree 941.37
      deep 941.47
        with loss of body part 941.57
    fourth degree — *see* Burn, by site, third degree,
      deep
  friction — *see* Injury, superficial, by site
  from swallowing caustic or corrosive substance
    NEC — *see* Burn, internal organs
  full thickness — *see* Burn, by site, third degree
  gastrointestinal tract 947.3
  genitourinary organs
    external 942.05
      with
        trunk — *see* Burn, trunk, multiple
          sites
      first degree 942.15
      second degree 942.25
      third degree 942.35
        deep 942.45
          with loss of body part 942.55
    internal 947.8
  globe (eye) — *see* Burn, eyeball
  groin — *see* Burn, abdomen
  gum 947.0
  hand(s) (phalanges) (and wrist) 944.00
    first degree 944.10
    second degree 944.20
    third degree 944.30
      deep 944.40
        with loss of body part 944.50
    back (dorsal surface) 944.06
      first degree 944.16
      second degree 944.26
      third degree 944.36
        deep 944.46
          with loss of body part 944.56
    multiple sites 944.08
      first degree 944.18
      second degree 944.28
      third degree 944.38
        deep 944.48
          with loss of body part 944.58
  head (and face) 941.00
    eye(s) only 940.9
      specified part — *see* Burn, by site
    first degree 941.10
    second degree 941.20
    third degree 941.30
      deep 941.40
        with loss of body part 941.50
    multiple sites 941.09
      with eyes — *see* Burn, eyes, with face,
        head, or neck
      first degree 941.19
      second degree 941.29
      third degree 941.39
        deep 941.49
          with loss of body part 941.59
  heel — *see* Burn, foot
  hip — *see* Burn, trunk, specified site NEC
  iliac region — *see* Burn, trunk, specified site
    NEC
  infected 958.3
  inhalation (*see also* Burn, internal organs)
    947.9
  internal organs 947.9
    from caustic or corrosive substance
      (swallowing) NEC 947.9
    specified NEC (*see also* Burn, by site) 947.8
  interscapular region — *see* Burn, back
  intestine (large) (small) 947.3
  iris — *see* Burn, eyeball

Burn — *continued*
  knee 945.05
    with
      lower limb(s) — *see* Burn, leg, multiple
        sites
    first degree 945.15
    second degree 945.25
    third degree 945.35
      deep 945.45
        with loss of body part 945.55
  labium (majus) (minus) — *see* Burn,
    genitourinary organs, external
  lacrimal apparatus, duct, gland, or sac 940.1
    chemical 940.0
  larynx 947.1
  late effect — *see* Late, effects (of), burn
  leg 945.00
    first degree 945.10
    second degree 945.20
    third degree 945.30
      deep 945.40
        with loss of body part 945.50
    lower 945.04
      with other part(s) of lower limb(s) — *see*
        Burn, leg, multiple sites
      first degree 945.14
      second degree 945.24
      third degree 945.34
        deep 945.44
          with loss of body part 945.54
    multiple sites 945.09
      first degree 945.19
      second degree 945.29
      third degree 945.39
        deep 945.49
          with loss of body part 945.59
    upper — *see* Burn, thigh
  lightning — *see* Burn, by site
  limb(s)
    lower (including foot or toe(s)) — *see* Burn,
      leg
    upper (except wrist and hand) — *see* Burn,
      arm(s)
  lip(s) 941.03
    with
      face or head — *see* Burn, head, multiple
        sites
    first degree 941.13
    second degree 941.23
    third degree 941.33
      deep 941.43
        with loss of body part 941.53
  lumbar region — *see* Burn, back
  lung 947.1
  malar region — *see* Burn, cheek
  mastoid region — *see* Burn, scalp
  membrane, tympanic — *see* Burn, ear
  midthoracic region — *see* Burn, chest wall
  mouth 947.0
  multiple (*see also* Burn, unspecified) 949.0
    specified sites classifiable to more than one
      category in 940-945 946.0
      first degree 946.1
      second degree 946.2
      third degree 946.3
        deep 946.4
          with loss of body part 946.5
  muscle, abdominal — *see* Burn, abdomen
  nasal (septum) — *see* Burn, nose
  neck 941.08
    with
      face or head — *see* Burn, head, multiple
        sites
    first degree 941.18
    second degree 941.28
    third degree 941.38
      deep 941.48
        with loss of body part 941.58
  nose (septum) 941.05
    with
      face or head — *see* Burn, head, multiple
        sites
    first degree 941.15
    second degree 941.25
    third degree 941.35
      deep 941.45
        with loss of body part 941.55

Burn — *continued*
  occipital region — *see* Burn, scalp
  orbit region 940.1
    chemical 940.0
  oronasopharynx 947.0
  palate 947.0
  palm(s) 944.05
    with
      hand(s) and wrist(s) — *see* Burn, hand(s),
        multiple sites
    first degree 944.15
    second degree 944.25
    third degree 944.35
      deep 944.45
        with loss of a body part 944.55
  parietal region — *see* Burn, scalp
  penis — *see* Burn, genitourinary organs,
    external
  perineum — *see* Burn, genitourinary organs,
    external
  periocular area 940.1
    chemical 940.0
  pharynx 947.0
  pleura 947.1
  popliteal space — *see* Burn, knee
  prepuce — *see* Burn, genitourinary organs,
    external
  pubic region — *see* Burn, genitourinary organs,
    external
  pudenda — *see* Burn, genitourinary organs,
    external
  rectum 947.3
  sac, lacrimal 940.1
    chemical 940.0
  sacral region — *see* Burn, back
  salivary (ducts) (glands) 947.0
  scalp 941.06
    with
      face or neck — *see* Burn, head, multiple
        sites
    first degree 941.16
    second degree 941.26
    third degree 941.36
      deep 941.46
        with loss of body part 941.56
  scapular region 943.06
    with
      upper limb(s), except hand(s) or wrist(s)
        — *see* Burn, arm(s), multiple sites
    first degree 943.16
    second degree 943.26
    third degree 943.36
      deep 943.46
        with loss of body part 943.56
  sclera — *see* Burn, eyeball
  scrotum — *see* Burn, genitourinary organs,
    external
  septum, nasal — *see* Burn, nose
  shoulder(s) 943.05
    with
      hand(s) and wrist(s) — *see* Burn,
        multiple, specified sites
      upper limb(s), except hand(s) or wrist(s)
        — *see* Burn, arm(s), multiple sites
    first degree 943.15
    second degree 943.25
    third degree 943.35
      deep 943.45
        with loss of body part 943.55
  skin NEC (*see also* Burn, unspecified) 949.0
  skull — *see* Burn, head
  small intestine 947.3
  sternal region — *see* Burn, chest wall
  stomach 947.3
  subconjunctival — *see* Burn, conjunctiva
  subcutaneous — *see* Burn, by site, third
    degree
  submaxillary region — *see* Burn, head
  submental region — *see* Burn, chin
  sun — *see* Sunburn
  supraclavicular fossa — *see* Burn, neck
  supraorbital — *see* Burn, forehead
  temple — *see* Burn, scalp
  temporal region — *see* Burn, scalp
  testicle — *see* Burn, genitourinary organs,
    external

Burn — *continued*

testis — *see* Burn, genitourinary organs, external

thigh 945.06

  with

    lower limb(s) — *see* Burn, leg, multiple sites

  first degree 945.16

  second degree 945.26

  third degree 945.36

    deep 945.46

      with loss of body part 945.56

thorax (external) — *see* Burn, chest wall

throat 947.0

thumb(s) (nail) (subungual) 944.02

  with

    finger(s) — *see* Burn, finger, with other sites, thumb

    hand(s) and wrist(s) — *see* Burn, hand(s), multiple sites

  first degree 944.12

  second degree 944.22

  third degree 944.32

    deep 944.42

      with loss of body part 944.52

toe (nail) (subungual) 945.01

  with

    lower limb(s) — *see* Burn, leg, multiple sites

  first degree 945.11

  second degree 945.21

  third degree 945.31

    deep 945.41

      with loss of body part 945.51

tongue 947.0

tonsil 947.0

trachea 947.1

trunk 942.00

  first degree 942.10

  second degree 942.20

  third degree 942.30

    deep 942.40

      with loss of body part 942.50

  multiple sites 942.09

    first degree 942.19

    second degree 942.29

    third degree 942.39

      deep 942.49

        with loss of body part 942.59

  specified site NEC 942.09

    first degree 942.19

    second degree 942.29

    third degree 942.39

      deep 942.49

        with loss of body part 942.59

tunica vaginalis — *see* Burn, genitourinary organs, external

tympanic membrane — *see* Burn, ear

tympanum — *see* Burn, ear

ultraviolet 692.82

unspecified site (multiple) 949.0

  with extent of body surface involved specified

    less than 10 percent 948.0 ☑

    10-19 percent 948.1 ☑

    20-29 percent 948.2 ☑

    30-39 percent 948.3 ☑

    40-49 percent 948.4 ☑

    50-59 percent 948.5 ☑

    60-69 percent 948.6 ☑

    70-79 percent 948.7 ☑

    80-89 percent 948.8 ☑

    90 percent or more 948.9 ☑

  first degree 949.1

  second degree 949.2

  third degree 949.3

    deep 949.4

      with loss of body part 949.5

uterus 947.4

uvula 947.0

vagina 947.4

vulva — *see* Burn, genitourinary organs, external

wrist(s) 944.07

  with

    hand(s) — *see* Burn, hand(s), multiple sites

Burn — *continued*

wrist(s) — *continued*

  first degree 944.17

  second degree 944.27

  third degree 944.37

    deep 944.47

      with loss of body part 944.57

Burnett's syndrome (milk-alkali) 275.42

Burnier's syndrome (hypophyseal dwarfism) 253.3

Burning

feet syndrome 266.2

sensation (*see also* Disturbance, sensation) 782.0

tongue 529.6

Burns' disease (osteochondrosis, lower ulna) 732.3

Bursa — *see also* condition

pharynx 478.29

Bursitis NEC 727.3

Achilles tendon 726.71

adhesive 726.90

  shoulder 726.0

ankle 726.79

buttock 726.5

calcaneal 726.79

collateral ligament

  fibular 726.63

  tibial 726.62

Duplay's 726.2

elbow 726.33

finger 726.8

foot 726.79

gonococcal 098.52

hand 726.4

hip 726.5

infrapatellar 726.69

ischiogluteal 726.5

knee 726.60

occupational NEC 727.2

olecranon 726.33

pes anserinus 726.61

pharyngeal 478.29

popliteal 727.51

prepatellar 726.65

radiohumeral 727.3

scapulohumeral 726.19

  adhesive 726.0

shoulder 726.10

  adhesive 726.0

subacromial 726.19

  adhesive 726.0

subcoracoid 726.19

subdeltoid 726.19

  adhesive 726.0

subpatellar 726.69

syphilitic 095.7

Thornwaldt's, Tornwaldt's (pharyngeal) 478.29

toe 726.79

trochanteric area 726.5

wrist 726.4

Burst stitches or sutures (complication of surgery) (external) 998.32

internal 998.31

Buruli ulcer 031.1

Bury's disease (erythema elevatum diutinum) 695.89

Buschke's disease or scleredema (adultorum) 710.1

Busquet's disease (osteoperiostitis) (*see also* Osteomyelitis) 730.1 ☑

Busse-Buschke disease (cryptococcosis) 117.5

Buttock — *see* condition

Button

Biskra 085.1

Delhi 085.1

oriental 085.1

Buttonhole hand (intrinsic) 736.21

Bwamba fever (encephalitis) 066.3

Byssinosis (occupational) 504

Bywaters' syndrome 958.5

C

Cacergasia 300.9

Cachexia 799.4

cancerous (M8000/3) 199.1

cardiac — *see* Disease, heart

dehydration 276.51   ▲

  with

    hypernatremia 276.0

    hyponatremia 276.1

due to malnutrition 261

exophthalmic 242.0 ☑

heart — *see* Disease, heart

hypophyseal 253.2

hypopituitary 253.2

lead 984.9

  specified type of lead — *see* Table of Drugs and Chemicals

malaria 084.9

malignant (M8000/3) 199.1

marsh 084.9

nervous 300.5

old age 797

pachydermic — *see* Hypothyroidism

paludal 084.9

pituitary (postpartum) 253.2

renal (*see also* Disease, renal) 593.9

saturnine 984.9

  specified type of lead — *see* Table of Drugs and Chemicals

senile 797

Simmonds' (pituitary cachexia) 253.2

splenica 289.59

strumipriva (*see also* Hypothyroidism) 244.9

tuberculous NEC (*see also* Tuberculosis) 011.9 ☑

Café au lait spots 709.09

Caffey's disease or syndrome (infantile cortical hyperostosis) 756.59

Caisson disease 993.3

Caked breast (puerperal, postpartum) 676.2 ☑

Cake kidney 753.3

Calabar swelling 125.2

Calcaneal spur 726.73

Calcaneoapophysitis 732.5

Calcaneonavicular bar 755.67

Calcareous — *see* condition

Calcicosis (occupational) 502

Calciferol (vitamin D) **deficiency** 268.9

with

  osteomalacia 268.2

  rickets (*see also* Rickets) 268.0

Calcification

adrenal (capsule) (gland) 255.4

  tuberculous (*see also* Tuberculosis) 017.6 ☑

aorta 440.0

artery (annular) — *see* Arteriosclerosis

auricle (ear) 380.89

bladder 596.8

  due to S. hematobium 120.0

brain (cortex) — *see* Calcification, cerebral

bronchus 519.1

bursa 727.82

cardiac (*see also* Degeneration, myocardial) 429.1

cartilage (postinfectional) 733.99

cerebral (cortex) 348.8

  artery 437.0

cervix (uteri) 622.8

choroid plexus 349.2

conjunctiva 372.54

corpora cavernosa (penis) 607.89

cortex (brain) — *see* Calcification, cerebral

dental pulp (nodular) 522.2

dentinal papilla 520.4

disc, intervertebral 722.90

  cervical, cervicothoracic 722.91

  lumbar, lumbosacral 722.93

  thoracic, thoracolumbar 722.92

fallopian tube 620.8

falx cerebri — *see* Calcification, cerebral

fascia 728.89

gallbladder 575.8

general 275.40

Calcification — *continued*
  heart (*see also* Degeneration, myocardial) 429.1
    valve — *see* Endocarditis
  intervertebral cartilage or disc (postinfectional)
    722.90
    cervical, cervicothoracic 722.91
    lumbar, lumbosacral 722.93
    thoracic, thoracolumbar 722.92
  intracranial — *see* Calcification, cerebral
  intraspinal ligament 728.89
  joint 719.80
    ankle 719.87
    elbow 719.82
    foot 719.87
    hand 719.84
    hip 719.85
    knee 719.86
    multiple sites 719.89
    pelvic region 719.85
    shoulder (region) 719.81
    specified site NEC 719.88
    wrist 719.83
  kidney 593.89
    tuberculous (*see also* Tuberculosis) 016.0 ☑
  larynx (senile) 478.79
  lens 366.8
  ligament 728.89
    intraspinal 728.89
    knee (medial collateral) 717.89
  lung 518.89
    active 518.89
    postinfectional 518.89
    tuberculous (*see also* Tuberculosis,
      pulmonary) 011.9 ☑
  lymph gland or node (postinfectional) 289.3
    tuberculous (*see also* Tuberculosis, lymph
      gland) 017.2 ☑
  massive (paraplegic) 728.10
  medial NEC (*see also* Arteriosclerosis,
    extremities) 440.20
  meninges (cerebral) 349.2
  metastatic 275.40
  Mönckeberg's — *see* Arteriosclerosis
  muscle 728.10
    heterotopic, postoperative 728.13
  myocardium, myocardial (*see also*
    Degeneration, myocardial) 429.1
  ovary 620.8
  pancreas 577.8
  penis 607.89
  periarticular 728.89
  pericardium (*see also* Pericarditis) 423.8
  pineal gland 259.8
  pleura 511.0
    postinfectional 518.89
    tuberculous (*see also* Tuberculosis, pleura)
      012.0 ☑
  pulp (dental) (nodular) 522.2
  renal 593.89
  Rider's bone 733.99
  sclera 379.16
  semilunar cartilage 717.89
  spleen 289.59
  subcutaneous 709.3
  suprarenal (capsule) (gland) 255.4
  tendon (sheath) 727.82
    with bursitis, synovitis or tenosynovitis
      727.82
  trachea 519.1
  ureter 593.89
  uterus 621.8
  vitreous 379.29
Calcified — *see also* Calcification
  hematoma NEC 959.9
Calcinosis (generalized) (interstitial) (tumoral)
  (universalis) 275.49
  circumscripta 709.3
  cutis 709.3
  intervertebralis 275.49 *[722.90]*
  Raynaud's
    phenomenonsclerodactylytelangiectasis
    (CRST) 710.1
Calcium
  blood
    high (*see also* Hypercalcemia) 275.42
    low (*see also* Hypocalcemia) 275.41

Calcium — *continued*
  deposits — *see also* Calcification, by site
    in bursa 727.82
    in tendon (sheath) 727.82
      with bursitis, synovitis or tenosynovitis
        727.82
  salts or soaps in vitreous 379.22
Calciuria 791.9
Calculi — *see* Calculus
Calculosis, intrahepatic — *see*
  Choledocholithiasis
Calculus, calculi, calculous 592.9
  ampulla of Vater — *see* Choledocholithiasis
  anuria (impacted) (recurrent) 592.0
  appendix 543.9
  bile duct (any) — *see* Choledocholithiasis
  biliary — *see* Cholelithiasis
  bilirubin, multiple — *see* Cholelithiasis
  bladder (encysted) (impacted) (urinary) 594.1
    diverticulum 594.0
  bronchus 518.89
  calyx (kidney) (renal) 592.0
    congenital 753.3
  cholesterol (pure) (solitary) — *see* Cholelithiasis
  common duct (bile) — *see* Choledocholithiasis
  conjunctiva 372.54
  cystic 594.1
    duct — *see* Cholelithiasis
  dental 523.6
    subgingival 523.6
    supragingival 523.6
  epididymis 608.89
  gallbladder — *see also* Cholelithiasis
    congenital 751.69
  hepatic (duct) — *see* Choledocholithiasis
  intestine (impaction) (obstruction) 560.39
  kidney (impacted) (multiple) (pelvis) (recurrent)
    (staghorn) 592.0
    congenital 753.3
  lacrimal (passages) 375.57
  liver (impacted) — *see* Choledocholithiasis
  lung 518.89
  nephritic (impacted) (recurrent) 592.0
  nose 478.1
  pancreas (duct) 577.8
  parotid gland 527.5
  pelvis, encysted 592.0
  prostate 602.0
  pulmonary 518.89
  renal (impacted) (recurrent) 592.0
    congenital 753.3
  salivary (duct) (gland) 527.5
  seminal vesicle 608.89
  staghorn 592.0
  Stensen's duct 527.5
  sublingual duct or gland 527.5
    congenital 750.26
  submaxillary duct, gland, or region 527.5
  suburethral 594.8
  tonsil 474.8
  tooth, teeth 523.6
  tunica vaginalis 608.89
  ureter (impacted) (recurrent) 592.1
  urethra (impacted) 594.2
  urinary (duct) (impacted) (passage) (tract) 592.9
    lower tract NEC 594.9
      specified site 594.8
  vagina 623.8
  vesical (impacted) 594.1
  Wharton's duct 527.5
Caliectasis 593.89
California
  disease 114.0
  encephalitis 062.5
Caligo cornea 371.03
Callositas, callosity (infected) 700
Callus (infected) 700
  bone 726.91
  excessive, following fracture — *see also* Late,
    effect (of), fracture
Calvé (-Perthes) disease (osteochondrosis,
  femoral capital) 732.1
Calvities (*see also* Alopecia) 704.00

Cameroon fever (*see also* Malaria) 084.6
Camptocormia 300.11
Camptodactyly (congenital) 755.59
Camurati-Engelmann disease (diaphyseal
  sclerosis) 756.59
Canal — *see* condition
Canaliculitis (lacrimal) (acute) 375.31
  Actinomyces 039.8
  chronic 375.41
Canavan's disease 330.0
Cancer (M8000/3) — *see also* Neoplasm, by site,
  malignant

> *Note* — The term "cancer" when modified by an
> adjective or adjectival phrase indicating a
> morphological type should be coded in the same
> manner as "carcinoma" with that adjective or
> phrase. Thus, "squamous-cell cancer" should be
> coded in the same manner as "squamous-cell
> carcinoma," which appears in the list under
> "Carcinoma."

  bile duct type (M8160/3), liver 155.1
  hepatocellular (M8170/3) 155.0
Cancerous (M8000/3) — *see* Neoplasm, by site,
  malignant
Cancerphobia 300.29
Cancrum oris 528.1
Candidiasis, candidal 112.9
  with pneumonia 112.4
  balanitis 112.2
  congenital 771.7
  disseminated 112.5
  endocarditis 112.81
  esophagus 112.84
  intertrigo 112.3
  intestine 112.85
  lung 112.4
  meningitis 112.83
  mouth 112.0
  nails 112.3
  neonatal 771.7
  onychia 112.3
  otitis externa 112.82
  otomycosis 112.82
  paronychia 112.3
  perionyxis 112.3
  pneumonia 112.4
  pneumonitis 112.4
  skin 112.3
  specified site NEC 112.89
  systemic 112.5
  urogenital site NEC 112.2
  vagina 112.1
  vulva 112.1
  vulvovaginitis 112.1
Candidiosis — *see* Candidiasis
Candiru infection or infestation 136.8
Canities (premature) 704.3
  congenital 757.4
Canker (mouth) (sore) 528.2
  rash 034.1
Cannabinosis 504
Canton fever 081.9
Cap
  cradle 690.11
Capillariasis 127.5
Capillary — *see* condition
Caplan's syndrome 714.81
Caplan-Colinet syndrome 714.81
Capsule — *see* condition
Capsulitis (joint) 726.90
  adhesive (shoulder) 726.0
  hip 726.5
  knee 726.60
  labyrinthine 387.8
  thyroid 245.9
  wrist 726.4
Caput
  crepitus 756.0
  medusae 456.8
  succedaneum 767.19

Carapata disease 087.1

Carate — *see* Pinta

Carbohydrate-deficient glycoprotein ●
    syndrome (CDGS) 271.8 ●

Carboxyhemoglobinemia 986

Carbuncle 680.9
  abdominal wall 680.2
  ankle 680.6
  anus 680.5
  arm (any part, above wrist) 680.3
  auditory canal, external 680.0
  axilla 680.3
  back (any part) 680.2
  breast 680.2
  buttock 680.5
  chest wall 680.2
  corpus cavernosum 607.2
  ear (any part) (external) 680.0
  eyelid 373.13
  face (any part, except eye) 680.0
  finger (any) 680.4
  flank 680.2
  foot (any part) 680.7
  forearm 680.3
  genital organ (male) 608.4
  gluteal (region) 680.5
  groin 680.2
  hand (any part) 680.4
  head (any part, except face) 680.8
  heel 680.7
  hip 680.6
  kidney (*see also* Abscess, kidney) 590.2
  knee 680.6
  labia 616.4
  lacrimal
    gland (*see also* Dacryoadenitis) 375.00
    passages (duct) (sac) (*see also*
      Dacryocystitis) 375.30
  leg, any part except foot 680.6
  lower extremity, any part except foot 680.6
  malignant 022.0
  multiple sites 680.9
  neck 680.1
  nose (external) (septum) 680.0
  orbit, orbital 376.01
  partes posteriores 680.5
  pectoral region 680.2
  penis 607.2
  perineum 680.2
  pinna 680.0
  scalp (any part) 680.8
  scrotum 608.4
  seminal vesicle 608.0
  shoulder 680.3
  skin NEC 680.9
  specified site NEC 680.8
  spermatic cord 608.4
  temple (region) 680.0
  testis 608.4
  thigh 680.6
  thumb 680.4
  toe (any) 680.7
  trunk 680.2
  tunica vaginalis 608.4
  umbilicus 680.2
  upper arm 680.3
  urethra 597.0
  vas deferens 608.4
  vulva 616.4
  wrist 680.4

Carbunculus (*see also* Carbuncle) 680.9

Carcinoid (tumor) (M8240/1) — *see also*
  Neoplasm, by site, uncertain behavior
  and struma ovarii (M9091/1) 236.2
  argentaffin (M8241/1) — *see* Neoplasm, by site,
    uncertain behavior
    malignant (M8241/3) — *see* Neoplasm, by
      site, malignant
  benign (M9091/0) 220
  composite (M8244/3) — *see* Neoplasm, by site,
    malignant
  goblet cell (M8243/3) — *see* Neoplasm, by site,
    malignant
  malignant (M8240/3) — *see* Neoplasm, by site,
    malignant

Carcinoid (tumor) (M8240/1) — *see also*
  Neoplasm, by site, uncertain behavior —
  continued
  nonargentaffin (M8242/1) — *see also*
    Neoplasm, by site, uncertain behavior
    malignant (M8242/3) — *see* Neoplasm, by
      site, malignant
  strumal (M9091/1) 236.2
  syndrome (intestinal) (metastatic) 259.2
  type bronchial adenoma (M8240/3) — *see*
    Neoplasm, lung, malignant

Carcinoidosis 259.2

Carcinoma (M8010/3) — *see also* Neoplasm, by
  site, malignant

> Note — *Except where otherwise indicated, the*
> *morphological varieties of carcinoma in the list*
> *below should be coded by site as for "Neoplasm,*
> *malignant."*

  with
    apocrine metaplasia (M8573/3)
    cartilaginous (and osseous) metaplasia
      (M8571/3)
    osseous (and cartilaginous) metaplasia
      (M8571/3)
    productive fibrosis (M8141/3)
    spindle cell metaplasia (M8572/3)
    squamous metaplasia (M8570/3)
  acidophil (M8280/3)
    specified site — *see* Neoplasm, by site,
      malignant
    unspecified site 194.3
  acidophil-basophil, mixed (M8281/3)
    specified site — *see* Neoplasm, by site,
      malignant
    unspecified site 194.3
  acinar (cell) (M8550/3)
  acinic cell (M8550/3)
  adenocystic (M8200/3)
  adenoid
    cystic (M8200/3)
    squamous cell (M8075/3)
  adenosquamous (M8560/3)
  adnexal (skin) (M8390/3) — *see* Neoplasm,
    skin, malignant
  adrenal cortical (M8370/3) 194.0
  alveolar (M8251/3)
    cell (M8250/3) — *see* Neoplasm, lung,
      malignant
  anaplastic type (M8021/3)
  apocrine (M8401/3)
    breast — *see* Neoplasm, breast, malignant
    specified site NEC — *see* Neoplasm, skin,
      malignant
    unspecified site 173.9
  basal cell (pigmented) (M8090/3) — *see also*
    Neoplasm, skin, malignant
    fibro-epithelial type (M8093/3) — *see*
      Neoplasm, skin, malignant
    morphea type (M8092/3) — *see* Neoplasm,
      skin, malignant
    multicentric (M8091/3) — *see* Neoplasm,
      skin, malignant
  basaloid (M8123/3)
  basal-squamous cell, mixed (M8094/3) — *see*
    Neoplasm, skin, malignant
  basophil (M8300/3)
    specified site — *see* Neoplasm, by site,
      malignant
    unspecified site 194.3
  basophil-acidophil, mixed (M8281/3)
    specified site — *see* Neoplasm, by site,
      malignant
    unspecified site 194.3
  basosquamous (M8094/3) — *see* Neoplasm,
    skin, malignant
  bile duct type (M8160/3)
    and hepatocellular, mixed (M8180/3) 155.0
    liver 155.1
    specified site NEC — *see* Neoplasm, by site,
      malignant
    unspecified site 155.1
  branchial or branchiogenic 146.8
  bronchial or bronchogenic — *see* Neoplasm,
    lung, malignant

Carcinoma — *see also* Neoplasm, by site,
  malignant — *continued*
  bronchiolar (terminal) (M8250/3) — *see*
    Neoplasm, lung, malignant
  bronchiolo-alveolar (M8250/3) — *see*
    Neoplasm, lung, malignant
  bronchogenic (epidermoid) 162.9
  C cell (M8510/3)
    specified site — *see* Neoplasm, by site,
      malignant
    unspecified site 193
  ceruminous (M8420/3) 173.2
  chorionic (M9100/3)
    specified site — *see* Neoplasm, by site,
      malignant
    unspecified site
      female 181
      male 186.9
  chromophobe (M8270/3)
    specified site — *see* Neoplasm, by site,
      malignant
    unspecified site 194.3
  clear cell (mesonephroid type) (M8310/3)
  cloacogenic (M8124/3)
    specified site — *see* Neoplasm, by site,
      malignant
    unspecified site 154.8
  colloid (M8480/3)
  cribriform (M8201/3)
  cylindroid type (M8200/3)
  diffuse type (M8145/3)
    specified site — *see* Neoplasm, by site,
      malignant
    unspecified site 151.9
  duct (cell) (M8500/3)
    with Paget's disease (M8541/3) — *see*
      Neoplasm, breast, malignant
    infiltrating (M8500/3)
      specified site — *see* Neoplasm, by site,
        malignant
      unspecified site 174.9
  ductal (M8500/3)
  ductular, infiltrating (M8521/3)
  embryonal (M9070/3)
    and teratoma, mixed (M9081/3)
    combined with choriocarcinoma (M9101/3)
      — *see* Neoplasm, by site, malignant
    infantile type (M9071/3)
    liver 155.0
    polyembryonal type (M9072/3)
  endometrioid (M8380/3)
  eosinophil (M8280/3)
    specified site — *see* Neoplasm, by site,
      malignant
    unspecified site 194.3
  epidermoid (M8070/3) — *see also* Carcinoma,
    squamous cell
    and adenocarcinoma, mixed (M8560/3)
    in situ, Bowen's type (M8081/2) — *see*
      Neoplasm, skin, in situ
    intradermal — *see* Neoplasm, skin, in situ
  fibroepithelial type basal cell (M8093/3) — *see*
    Neoplasm, skin, malignant
  follicular (M8330/3)
    and papillary (mixed) (M8340/3) 193
    moderately differentiated type (M8332/3)
      193
    pure follicle type (M8331/3) 193
    specified site — *see* Neoplasm, by site,
      malignant
    trabecular type (M8332/3) 193
    unspecified site 193
    well differentiated type (M8331/3) 193
  gelatinous (M8480/3)
  giant cell (M8031/3)
    and spindle cell (M8030/3)
  granular cell (M8320/3)
  granulosa cell (M8620/3) 183.0
  hepatic cell (M8170/3) 155.0
  hepatocellular (M8170/3) 155.0
    and bile duct, mixed (M8180/3) 155.0
  hepatocholangiolitic (M8180/3) 155.0
  Hürthle cell (thyroid) 193
  hypernephroid (M8311/3)
  in
    adenomatous
      polyp (M8210/3)
      polyposis coli (M8220/3) 153.9

Carcinoma — *see also* Neoplasm, by site,
  malignant — *continued*
  in — *continued*
    pleomorphic adenoma (M8940/3)
    polypoid adenoma (M8210/3)
    situ (M8010/3) — *see* Carcinoma, in situ
    tubular adenoma (M8210/3)
    villous adenoma (M8261/3)
  infiltrating duct (M8500/3)
    with Paget's disease (M8541/3) — *see*
        Neoplasm, breast, malignant
    specified site — *see* Neoplasm, by site,
        malignant
    unspecified site 174.9
  inflammatory (M8530/3)
    specified site — *see* Neoplasm, by site,
        malignant
    unspecified site 174.9
  in situ (M8010/2) — *see also* Neoplasm, by
      site, in situ
    epidermoid (M8070/2) — *see also* Neoplasm,
        by site, in situ
      with questionable stromal invasion
          (M8076/2)
        specified site — *see* Neoplasm, by site,
            in situ
        unspecified site 233.1
      Bowen's type (M8081/2) — *see*
          Neoplasm, skin, in situ
    intraductal (M8500/2)
      specified site — *see* Neoplasm, by site, in
          situ
      unspecified site 233.0
    lobular (M8520/2)
      specified site — *see* Neoplasm, by site, in
          situ
      unspecified site 233.0
    papillary (M8050/2) — *see* Neoplasm, by
        site, in situ
    squamous cell (M8070/2) — *see also*
        Neoplasm, by site, in situ
      with questionable stromal invasion
          (M8076/2)
        specified site — *see* Neoplasm, by site,
            in situ
        unspecified site 233.1
    transitional cell (M8120/2) — *see* Neoplasm,
        by site, in situ
  intestinal type (M8144/3)
    specified site — *see* Neoplasm, by site,
        malignant
    unspecified site 151.9
  intraductal (noninfiltrating) (M8500/2)
    papillary (M8503/2)
      specified site — *see* Neoplasm, by site, in
          situ
      unspecified site 233.0
    specified site — *see* Neoplasm, by site, in
        situ
    unspecified site 233.0
  intraepidermal (M8070/3) — *see also*
      Neoplasm, skin, in situ
    squamous cell, Bowen's type (M8081/2) —
        see Neoplasm, skin, in situ
  intraepithelial (M8010/2) — *see also* Neoplasm,
      by site, in situ
    squamous cell (M8072/2) — *see* Neoplasm,
        by site, in situ
  intraosseous (M9270/3) 170.1
    upper jaw (bone) 170.0
  islet cell (M8150/3)
    and exocrine, mixed (M8154/3)
      specified site — *see* Neoplasm, by site,
          malignant
      unspecified site 157.9
    pancreas 157.4
    specified site NEC — *see* Neoplasm, by site,
        malignant
    unspecified site 157.4
  juvenile, breast (M8502/3) — *see* Neoplasm,
      breast, malignant
  Kulchitsky's cell (carcinoid tumor of intestine)
      259.2
  large cell (M8012/3)
    squamous cell, non-keratinizing type
        (M8072/3)

Carcinoma — *see also* Neoplasm, by site,
  malignant — *continued*
  Leydig cell (testis) (M8650/3)
    specified site — *see* Neoplasm, by site,
        malignant
    unspecified site 186.9
      female 183.0
      male 186.9
  liver cell (M8170/3) 155.0
  lobular (infiltrating) (M8520/3)
    non-infiltrating (M8520/3)
      specified site — *see* Neoplasm, by site, in
          situ
      unspecified site 233.0
    specified site — *see* Neoplasm, by site,
        malignant
    unspecified site 174.9
  lymphoepithelial (M8082/3)
  medullary (M8510/3)
    with
      amyloid stroma (M8511/3)
        specified site — *see* Neoplasm, by site,
            malignant
        unspecified site 193
      lymphoid stroma (M8512/3)
        specified site — *see* Neoplasm, by site,
            malignant
        unspecified site 174.9
  mesometanephric (M9110/3)
  mesonephric (M9110/3)
  metastatic (M8010/6) — *see* Metastasis, cancer
  metatypical (M8095/3) — *see* Neoplasm, skin,
      malignant
  morphea type basal cell (M8092/3) — *see*
      Neoplasm, skin, malignant
  mucinous (M8480/3)
  mucin-producing (M8481/3)
  mucin-secreting (M8481/3)
  mucoepidermoid (M8430/3)
  mucoid (M8480/3)
    cell (M8300/3)
      specified site — *see* Neoplasm, by site,
          malignant
      unspecified site 194.3
  mucous (M8480/3)
  nonencapsulated sclerosing (M8350/3) 193
  noninfiltrating
    intracystic (M8504/2) — *see* Neoplasm, by
        site, in situ
    intraductal (M8500/2)
      papillary (M8503/2)
        specified site — *see* Neoplasm, by site,
            in situ
        unspecified site 233.0
      specified site — *see* Neoplasm, by site, in
          situ
      unspecified site 233.0
    lobular (M8520/2)
      specified site — *see* Neoplasm, by site, in
          situ
      unspecified site 233.0
  oat cell (M8042/3)
    specified site — *see* Neoplasm, by site,
        malignant
    unspecified site 162.9
  odontogenic (M9270/3) 170.1
    upper jaw (bone) 170.0
  onocytic (M8290/3)
  oxyphilic (M8290/3)
  papillary (M8050/3)
    and follicular (mixed) (M8340/3) 193
    epidermoid (M8052/3)
    intraductal (noninfiltrating) (M8503/2)
      specified site — *see* Neoplasm, by site, in
          situ
      unspecified site 233.0
    serous (M8460/3)
      specified site — *see* Neoplasm, by site,
          malignant
      surface (M8461/3)
        specified site — *see* Neoplasm, by site,
            malignant
        unspecified site 183.0
      unspecified site 183.0
    squamous cell (M8052/3)
    transitional cell (M8130/3)

Carcinoma — *see also* Neoplasm, by site,
  malignant — *continued*
  papillocystic (M8450/3)
    specified site — *see* Neoplasm, by site,
        malignant
    unspecified site 183.0
  parafollicular cell (M8510/3)
    specified site — *see* Neoplasm, by site,
        malignant
    unspecified site 193
  pleomorphic (M8022/3)
  polygonal cell (M8034/3)
  prickle cell (M8070/3)
  pseudoglandular, squamous cell (M8075/3)
  pseudomucinous (M8470/3)
    specified site — *see* Neoplasm, by site,
        malignant
    unspecified site 183.0
  pseudosarcomatous (M8033/3)
  regaud type (M8082/3) — *see* Neoplasm,
      nasopharynx, malignant
  renal cell (M8312/3) 189.0
  reserve cell (M8041/3)
  round cell (M8041/3)
  Schmincke (M8082/3) — *see* Neoplasm,
      nasopharynx, malignant
  Schneiderian (M8121/3)
    specified site — *see* Neoplasm, by site,
        malignant
    unspecified site 160.0
  scirrhous (M8141/3)
  sebaceous (M8410/3) — *see* Neoplasm, skin,
      malignant
  secondary (M8010/6) — *see* Neoplasm, by site,
      malignant, secondary
  secretory, breast (M8502/3) — *see* Neoplasm,
      breast, malignant
  serous (M8441/3)
    papillary (M8460/3)
      specified site — *see* Neoplasm, by site,
          malignant
      unspecified site 183.0
    surface, papillary (M8461/3)
      specified site — *see* Neoplasm, by site,
          malignant
      unspecified site 183.0
  Sertoli cell (M8640/3)
    specified site — *see* Neoplasm, by site,
        malignant
    unspecified site 186.9
  signet ring cell (M8490/3)
    metastatic (M8490/6) — *see* Neoplasm, by
        site, secondary
  simplex (M8231/3)
  skin appendage (M8390/3) — *see* Neoplasm,
      skin, malignant
  small cell (M8041/3)
    fusiform cell type (M8043/3)
    squamous cell, non-keratinizing type
        (M8073/3)
  solid (M8230/3)
    with amyloid stroma (M8511/3)
      specified site — *see* Neoplasm, by site,
          malignant
      unspecified site 193
  spheroidal cell (M8035/3)
  spindle cell (M8032/3)
    and giant cell (M8030/3)
  spinous cell (M8070/3)
  squamous (cell) (M8070/3)
    adenoid type (M8075/3)
    and adenocarcinoma, mixed (M8560/3)
    intraepidermal, Bowen's type — *see*
        Neoplasm, skin, in situ
    keratinizing type (large cell) (M8071/3)
    large cell, non-keratinizing type (M8072/3)
    microinvasive (M8076/3)
      specified site — *see* Neoplasm, by site,
          malignant
      unspecified site 180.9
    non-keratinizing type (M8072/3)
    papillary (M8052/3)
    pseudoglandular (M8075/3)
    small cell, non-keratinizing type (M8073/3)
    spindle cell type (M8074/3)
    verrucous (M8051/3)
  superficial spreading (M8143/3)

☑ Additional Digit Required — Refer to the Tabular List (Numeric Code Section) for Additional Digit Selection

Carcinoma — *see also* Neoplasm, by site,
     malignant — *continued*
  sweat gland (M8400/3) — *see* Neoplasm, skin,
       malignant
  theca cell (M8600/3) 183.0
  thymic (M8580/3) 164.0
  trabecular (M8190/3)
  transitional (cell) (M8120/3)
    papillary (M8130/3)
    spindle cell type (M8122/3)
  tubular (M8211/3)
  undifferentiated type (M8020/3)
  urothelial (M8120/3)
  ventriculi 151.9
  verrucous (epidermoid) (squamous cell)
       (M8051/3)
  villous (M8262/3)
  water-clear cell (M8322/3) 194.1
  wolffian duct (M9110/3)
Carcinomaphobia 300.29
Carcinomatosis
  peritonei (M8010/6) 197.6
  specified site NEC (M8010/3) — *see* Neoplasm,
       by site, malignant
  unspecified site (M8010/6) 199.0
Carcinosarcoma (M8980/3) — *see also* Neoplasm,
     by site, malignant
  embryonal type (M8981/3) — *see* Neoplasm, by
       site, malignant
Cardia, cardial — *see* condition
Cardiac — *see also* condition
  death — *see* Disease, heart
  device
    defibrillator, automatic implantable V45.02
    in situ NEC V45.00
    pacemaker
      cardiac
        fitting or adjustment V53.31
        in situ V45.01
      carotid sinus
        fitting or adjustment V53.39
        in situ V45.09
  pacemaker — *see* Cardiac, device, pacemaker
  tamponade 423.9
Cardialgia (*see also* Pain, precordial) 786.51
Cardiectasis — *see* Hypertrophy, cardiac
Cardiochalasia 530.81
Cardiomalacia (*see also* Degeneration,
     myocardial) 429.1
Cardiomegalia glycogenica diffusa 271.0
Cardiomegaly (*see also* Hypertrophy, cardiac)
     429.3
  congenital 746.89
  glycogen 271.0
  hypertensive (*see also* Hypertension, heart)
       402.90
  idiopathic 429.3
Cardiomyoliposis (*see also* Degeneration,
     myocardial) 429.1
Cardiomyopathy (congestive) (constrictive)
     (familial) (infiltrative) (obstructive)
     (restrictive) (sporadic) 425.4
  alcoholic 425.5
  amyloid 277.3 [*425.7*]
  beriberi 265.0 [*425.7*]
  cobalt-beer 425.5
  congenital 425.3
  due to
    amyloidosis 277.3 [*425.7*]
    beriberi 265.0 [*425.7*]
    cardiac glycogenosis 271.0 [*425.7*]
    Chagas' disease 086.0
    Friedreich's ataxia 334.0 [*425.8*]
    hypertension — *see* Hypertension, with,
         heart involvement
    mucopolysaccharidosis 277.5 [*425.7*]
    myotonia atrophica 359.2 [*425.8*]
    progressive muscular dystrophy 359.1
         [*425.8*]
    sarcoidosis 135 [*425.8*]
  glycogen storage 271.0 [*425.7*]
  hypertensive — *see* Hypertension, with, heart
       involvement

Cardiomyopathy — *continued*
  hypertrophic
    nonobstructive 425.4
    obstructive 425.1
      congenital 746.84
  idiopathic (concentric) 425.4
  in
    Chagas' disease 086.0
    sarcoidosis 135 [*425.8*]
  ischemic 414.8
  metabolic NEC 277.9 [*425.7*]
    amyloid 277.3 [*425.7*]
    thyrotoxic (*see also* Thyrotoxicosis) 242.9 ☑
         [*425.7*]
    thyrotoxicosis (*see also* Thyrotoxicosis)
         242.9 ☑ [*425.7*]
  newborn 425.4   ●
    congenital 425.3   ●
  nutritional 269.9 [*425.7*]
    beriberi 265.0 [*425.7*]
  obscure of Africa 425.2
  peripartum 674.5 ☑
  postpartum 674.5 ☑
  primary 425.4
  secondary 425.9
  takotsubo 429.89   ●
  thyrotoxic (*see also* Thyrotoxicosis) 242.9 ☑
       [*425.7*]
  toxic NEC 425.9
  tuberculous (*see also* Tuberculosis) 017.9 ☑
       [*425.8*]
Cardionephritis — *see* Hypertension, cardiorenal
Cardionephropathy — *see* Hypertension,
     cardiorenal
Cardionephrosis — *see* Hypertension, cardiorenal
Cardioneurosis 306.2
Cardiopathia nigra 416.0
Cardiopathy (*see also* Disease, heart) 429.9
  hypertensive (*see also* Hypertension, heart)
       402.90
  idiopathic 425.4
  mucopolysaccharidosis 277.5 [*425.7*]
Cardiopericarditis (*see also* Pericarditis) 423.9
Cardiophobia 300.29
Cardioptosis 746.87
Cardiorenal — *see* condition
Cardiorrhexis (*see also* Infarct, myocardium)
     410.9 ☑
Cardiosclerosis — *see* Arteriosclerosis, coronary
Cardiosis — *see* Disease, heart
Cardiospasm (esophagus) (reflex) (stomach) 530.0
  congenital 750.7
Cardiostenosis — *see* Disease, heart
Cardiosymphysis 423.1
Cardiothyrotoxicosis — *see* Hyperthyroidism
Cardiovascular — *see* condition
Carditis (acute) (bacterial) (chronic) (subacute)
     429.89
  Coxsackie 074.20
  hypertensive (*see also* Hypertension, heart)
       402.90
  meningococcal 036.40
  rheumatic — *see* Disease, heart, rheumatic
  rheumatoid 714.2
Care (of)
  child (routine) V20.1
  convalescent following V66.9
    chemotherapy V66.2
    medical NEC V66.5
    psychotherapy V66.3
    radiotherapy V66.1
    surgery V66.0
    surgical NEC V66.0
    treatment (for) V66.5
      combined V66.6
      fracture V66.4
      mental disorder NEC V66.3
      specified type NEC V66.5
  end-of-life V66.7
  family member (handicapped) (sick)
    creating problem for family V61.49
    provided away from home for holiday relief
         V60.5

Care (of) — *continued*
  family member — *continued*
    unavailable, due to
      absence (person rendering care) (sufferer)
           V60.4
      inability (any reason) of person rendering
           care V60.4
  holiday relief V60.5
  hospice V66.7
  lack of (at or after birth) (infant) (child) 995.52
    adult 995.84
  lactation of mother V24.1
  palliative V66.7
  postpartum
    immediately after delivery V24.0
    routine follow-up V24.2
  prenatal V22.1
    first pregnancy V22.0
    high-risk pregnancy V23.9
      specified problem NEC V23.89
  terminal V66.7
  unavailable, due to
    absence of person rendering care V60.4
    inability (any reason) of person rendering
         care V60.4
  well baby V20.1
Caries (bone) (*see also* Tuberculosis, bone)
     015.9 ☑ [*730.8*] ☑
  arrested 521.04
  cementum 521.03
  cerebrospinal (tuberculous) 015.0 ☑ [*730.88*]
  dental (acute) (chronic) (incipient) (infected)
       521.00
    with pulp exposure 521.03
    extending to
      dentine 521.02
      pulp 521.03
    other specified NEC 521.09
    pit and fissure 521.06
    root surface 521.08
    smooth surface 521.07
  dentin (acute) (chronic) 521.02
  enamel (acute) (chronic) (incipient) 521.01
  external meatus 380.89
  hip (*see also* Tuberculosis) 015.1 ☑ [*730.85*]
  initial 521.01
  knee 015.2 ☑ [*730.86*]
  labyrinth 386.8
  limb NEC 015.7 ☑ [*730.88*]
  mastoid (chronic) (process) 383.1
  middle ear 385.89
  nose 015.7 ☑ [*730.88*]
  orbit 015.7 ☑ [*730.88*]
  ossicle 385.24
  petrous bone 383.20
  sacrum (tuberculous) 015.0 ☑ [*730.88*]
  spine, spinal (column) (tuberculous) 015.0 ☑
       [*730.88*]
  syphilitic 095.5
    congenital 090.0 [*730.8*] ☑
  teeth (internal) 521.00
    initial 521.01
  vertebra (column) (tuberculous) 015.0 ☑
       [*730.88*]
Carini's syndrome (ichthyosis congenita) 757.1
Carious teeth 521.00
Carneous mole 631
Carnosinemia 270.5
Carotid body or sinus syndrome 337.0
Carotidynia 337.0
Carotinemia (dietary) 278.3
Carotinosis (cutis) (skin) 278.3
Carpal tunnel syndrome 354.0
Carpenter's syndrome 759.89
Carpopedal spasm (*see also* Tetany) 781.7
Carpoptosis 736.05
Carrier (suspected) **of**
  amebiasis V02.2
  bacterial disease (meningococcal,
       staphylococcal) NEC V02.59
  cholera V02.0
  cystic fibrosis gene V83.81
  defective gene V83.89
  diphtheria V02.4

Carrier (suspected) of — *continued*
dysentery (bacillary) V02.3
amebic V02.2
Endamoeba histolytica V02.2
gastrointestinal pathogens NEC V02.3
genetic defect V83.89
gonorrhea V02.7
group B streptococcus V02.51
HAA (hepatitis Australian-antigen) V02.61
hemophilia A (asymptomatic) V83.01
symptomatic V83.02
hepatitis V02.60
Australian-antigen (HAA) V02.61
B V02.61
C V02.62
serum V02.61
specified type NEC V02.69
viral V02.60
infective organism NEC V02.9
malaria V02.9
paratyphoid V02.3
Salmonella V02.3
typhosa V02.1
serum hepatitis V02.61
Shigella V02.3
Staphylococcus NEC V02.59
Streptococcus NEC V02.52
group B V02.51
typhoid V02.1
venereal disease NEC V02.8

Carrión's disease (Bartonellosis) 088.0

Car sickness 994.6

Carter's
relapsing fever (Asiatic) 087.0

Cartilage — *see* condition

Caruncle (inflamed)
abscess, lacrimal (*see also* Dacryocystitis)
375.30
conjunctiva 372.00
acute 372.00
eyelid 373.00
labium (majus) (minus) 616.8
lacrimal 375.30
urethra (benign) 599.3
vagina (wall) 616.8

Cascade stomach 537.6

Caseation lymphatic gland (*see also*
Tuberculosis) 017.2 ☑

Caseous
bronchitis — *see* Tuberculosis, pulmonary
meningitis 013.0 ☑
pneumonia — *see* Tuberculosis, pulmonary

Cassidy (-Scholte) syndrome (malignant
carcinoid) 259.2

Castellani's bronchitis 104.8

Castleman's tumor or lymphoma (mediastinal
lymph node hyperplasia) 785.6

Castration, traumatic 878.2
complicated 878.3

Casts in urine 791.7

Cat's ear 744.29

Catalepsy 300.11
catatonic (acute) (*see also* Schizophrenia)
295.2 ☑
hysterical 300.11
schizophrenic (*see also* Schizophrenia) 295.2 ☑

Cataphasia 307.0

Cataplexy (idiopathic) — *see* Narcolepsy

Cataract (anterior cortical) (anterior polar) (black)
(capsular) (central) (cortical) (hypermature)
(immature) (incipient) (mature) 366.9
anterior
and posterior axial embryonal 743.33
pyramidal 743.31
subcapsular polar
infantile, juvenile, or presenile 366.01
senile 366.13
associated with
calcinosis 275.40 *[366.42]*
craniofacial dysostosis 756.0 *[366.44]*
galactosemia 271.1 *[366.44]*
hypoparathyroidism 252.1 *[366.42]*
myotonic disorders 359.2 *[366.43]*

Cataract — *continued*
associated with — *continued*
neovascularization 366.33
blue dot 743.39
cerulean 743.39
complicated NEC 366.30
congenital 743.30
capsular or subcapsular 743.31
cortical 743.32
nuclear 743.33
specified type NEC 743.39
total or subtotal 743.34
zonular 743.32
coronary (congenital) 743.39
acquired 366.12
cupuliform 366.14
diabetic 250.5 ☑ *[366.41]*
drug-induced 366.45
due to
chalcosis 360.24 *[366.34]*
chronic choroiditis (*see also* Choroiditis)
363.20 *[366.32]*
degenerative myopia 360.21 *[366.34]*
glaucoma (*see also* Glaucoma) 365.9
[366.31]
infection, intraocular NEC 366.32
inflammatory ocular disorder NEC 366.32
iridocyclitis, chronic 364.10 *[366.33]*
pigmentary retinal dystrophy 362.74
[366.34]
radiation 366.46
electric 366.46
glassblowers' 366.46
heat ray 366.46
heterochromic 366.33
in eye disease NEC 366.30
infantile (*see also* Cataract, juvenile) 366.00
intumescent 366.12
irradiational 366.46
juvenile 366.00
anterior subcapsular polar 366.01
combined forms 366.09
cortical 366.03
lamellar 366.03
nuclear 366.04
posterior subcapsular polar 366.02
specified NEC 366.09
zonular 366.03
lamellar 743.32
infantile, juvenile, or presenile 366.03
morgagnian 366.18
myotonic 359.2 *[366.43]*
myxedema 244.9 *[366.44]*
nuclear 366.16
posterior, polar (capsular) 743.31
infantile, juvenile, or presenile 366.02
senile 366.14
presenile (*see also* Cataract, juvenile) 366.00
punctate
acquired 366.12
congenital 743.39
secondary (membrane) 366.50
obscuring vision 366.53
specified type, not obscuring vision 366.52
senile 366.10
anterior subcapsular polar 366.13
combined forms 366.19
cortical 366.15
hypermature 366.18
immature 366.12
incipient 366.12
mature 366.17
nuclear 366.16
posterior subcapsular polar 366.14
specified NEC 366.19
total or subtotal 366.17
snowflake 250.5 ☑ *[366.41]*
specified NEC 366.8
subtotal (senile) 366.17
congenital 743.34
sunflower 360.24 *[366.34]*
tetanic NEC 252.1 *[366.42]*
total (mature) (senile) 366.17
congenital 743.34
localized 366.21
traumatic 366.22
toxic 366.45

Cataract — *continued*
traumatic 366.20
partially resolved 366.23
total 366.22
zonular (perinuclear) 743.32
infantile, juvenile, or presenile 366.03

Cataracta 366.10
brunescens 366.16
cerulea 366.16
complicata 366.30
congenita 743.30
coralliformis 743.39
coronaria (congenital) 743.39
acquired 366.12
diabetic 250.5 ☑ *[366.41]*
floriformis 360.24 *[366.34]*
membranacea
accreta 366.50
congenita 743.39
nigra 366.16

Catarrh, catarrhal (inflammation) (*see also*
condition) 460
acute 460
asthma, asthmatic (*see also* Asthma) 493.9 ☑
Bostock's (*see also* Fever, hay) 477.9
bowel — *see* Enteritis
bronchial 490
acute 466.0
chronic 491.0
subacute 466.0
cervix, cervical (canal) (uteri) — *see* Cervicitis
chest (*see also* Bronchitis) 490
chronic 472.0
congestion 472.0
conjunctivitis 372.03
due to syphilis 095.9
congenital 090.0
enteric — *see* Enteritis
epidemic 487.1
Eustachian 381.50
eye (acute) (vernal) 372.03
fauces (*see also* Pharyngitis) 462
febrile 460
fibrinous acute 466.0
gastroenteric — *see* Enteritis
gastrointestinal — *see* Enteritis
gingivitis 523.0
hay (*see also* Fever, hay) 477.9
infectious 460
intestinal — *see* Enteritis
larynx (*see also* Laryngitis, chronic) 476.0
liver 070.1
with hepatic coma 070.0
lung (*see also* Bronchitis) 490
acute 466.0
chronic 491.0
middle ear (chronic) — *see* Otitis media,
chronic
mouth 528.0
nasal (chronic) (*see also* Rhinitis) 472.0
acute 460
nasobronchial 472.2
nasopharyngeal (chronic) 472.2
acute 460
nose — *see* Catarrh, nasal
ophthalmia 372.03
pneumococcal, acute 466.0
pulmonary (*see also* Bronchitis) 490
acute 466.0
chronic 491.0
spring (eye) 372.13
suffocating (*see also* Asthma) 493.9 ☑
summer (hay) (*see also* Fever, hay) 477.9
throat 472.1
tracheitis 464.10
with obstruction 464.11
tubotympanal 381.4
acute (*see also* Otitis media, acute,
nonsuppurative) 381.00
chronic 381.10
vasomotor (*see also* Fever, hay) 477.9
vesical (bladder) — *see* Cystitis

Catarrhus aestivus (*see also* Fever, hay) 477.9

Catastrophe, cerebral (*see also* Disease,
cerebrovascular, acute) 436

Catatonia, catatonic (acute) 781.99
  with
      affective psychosis — see Psychosis,
          affective
  agitation 295.2 ☑
  dementia (praecox) 295.2 ☑
  due to or associated with physical condition
      293.89
  excitation 295.2 ☑
  excited type 295.2 ☑
  in conditions classified elsewhere 293.89
  schizophrenia 295.2 ☑
  stupor 295.2 ☑
Cat-scratch — see also Injury, superficial
  disease or fever 078.3
Cauda equina — see also condition
  syndrome 344.60
Cauliflower ear 738.7
Caul over face 768.9
Causalgia 355.9
  lower limb 355.71
  upper limb 354.4
Cause
  external, general effects NEC 994.9
  not stated 799.9
  unknown 799.9
Caustic burn — see also Burn, by site
  from swallowing caustic or corrosive substance
      — see Burn, internal organs
Cavare's disease (familial periodic paralysis)
  359.3
Cave-in, injury
  crushing (severe) (see also Crush, by site)
      869.1
  suffocation 994.7
Cavernitis (penis) 607.2
  lymph vessel — see Lymphangioma
Cavernositis 607.2
Cavernous — see condition
Cavitation of lung (see also Tuberculosis)
  011.2 ☑
  nontuberculous 518.89
  primary, progressive 010.8 ☑
Cavity
  lung — see Cavitation of lung
  optic papilla 743.57
  pulmonary — see Cavitation of lung
  teeth 521.00
  vitreous (humor) 379.21
Cavovarus foot, congenital 754.59
Cavus foot (congenital) 754.71
  acquired 736.73
Cazenave's
  disease (pemphigus) NEC 694.4
  lupus (erythematosus) 695.4
CDGS (carbohydrate-deficient glycoprotein ●
  syndrome) 271.8   ●
Cecitis — see Appendicitis
Cecocele — see Hernia
Cecum — see condition
Celiac
  artery compression syndrome 447.4
  disease 579.0
  infantilism 579.0
Cell, cellular — see also condition
  anterior chamber (eye) (positive aqueous ray)
      364.04
Cellulitis (diffuse) (with lymphangitis) (see also
      Abscess) 682.9
  abdominal wall 682.2
  anaerobic (see also Gas gangrene) 040.0
  ankle 682.6
  anus 566
  areola 611.0
  arm (any part, above wrist) 682.3
  auditory canal (external) 380.10
  axilla 682.3
  back (any part) 682.2
  breast 611.0
      postpartum 675.1 ☑
  broad ligament (see also Disease, pelvis,
      inflammatory) 614.4
      acute 614.3

Cellulitis (see also Abscess) — continued
  buttock 682.5
  cervical (neck region) 682.1
  cervix (uteri) (see also Cervicitis) 616.0
  cheek, external 682.0
      internal 528.3
  chest wall 682.2
  chronic NEC 682.9
  colostomy 569.61
  corpus cavernosum 607.2
  digit 681.9
  Douglas' cul-de-sac or pouch (chronic) (see also
      Disease, pelvis, inflammatory) 614.4
      acute 614.3
  drainage site (following operation) 998.59
  ear, external 380.10
  enterostomy 569.61
  erysipelar (see also Erysipelas) 035
  esophagostomy 530.86
  eyelid 373.13
  face (any part, except eye) 682.0
  finger (intrathecal) (periosteal) (subcutaneous)
      (subcuticular) 681.00
  flank 682.2
  foot (except toe) 682.7
  forearm 682.3
  gangrenous (see also Gangrene) 785.4
  genital organ NEC
      female — see Abscess, genital organ, female
      male 608.4
  glottis 478.71
  gluteal (region) 682.5
  gonococcal NEC 098.0
  groin 682.2
  hand (except finger or thumb) 682.4
  head (except face) NEC 682.8
  heel 682.7
  hip 682.6
  jaw (region) 682.0
  knee 682.6
  labium (majus) (minus) (see also Vulvitis)
      616.10
  larynx 478.71
  leg, except foot 682.6
  lip 528.5
  mammary gland 611.0
  mouth (floor) 528.3
  multiple sites NEC 682.9
  nasopharynx 478.21
  navel 682.2
      newborn NEC 771.4
  neck (region) 682.1
  nipple 611.0
  nose 478.1
      external 682.0
  orbit, orbital 376.01
  palate (soft) 528.3
  pectoral (region) 682.2
  pelvis, pelvic
      with
          abortion — see Abortion, by type, with
              sepsis
          ectopic pregnancy (see also categories
              633.0— 633.9) 639.0
          molar pregnancy (see also categories
              630— 632) 639.0
      female (see also Disease, pelvis,
          inflammatory) 614.4
          acute 614.3
      following
          abortion 639.0
          ectopic or molar pregnancy 639.0
      male (see also Abscess, peritoneum)
          567.21   ▲
      puerperal, postpartum, childbirth 670.0 ☑
  penis 607.2
  perineal, perineum 682.2
  perirectal 566
  peritonsillar 475
  periurethral 597.0
  periuterine (see also Disease, pelvis,
      inflammatory) 614.4
      acute 614.3
  pharynx 478.21
  phlegmonous NEC 682.9
  rectum 566
  retromammary 611.0

Cellulitis (see also Abscess) — continued
  retroperitoneal (see also Peritonitis) 567.38 ▲
  round ligament (see also Disease, pelvis,
      inflammatory) 614.4
      acute 614.3
  scalp (any part) 682.8
      dissecting 704.8
  scrotum 608.4
  seminal vesicle 608.0
  septic NEC 682.9
  shoulder 682.3
  specified sites NEC 682.8
  spermatic cord 608.4
  submandibular (region) (space) (triangle) 682.0
      gland 527.3
  submaxillary 528.3
      gland 527.3
  submental (pyogenic) 682.0
      gland 527.3
  suppurative NEC 682.9
  testis 608.4
  thigh 682.6
  thumb (intrathecal) (periosteal) (subcutaneous)
      (subcuticular) 681.00
  toe (intrathecal) (periosteal) (subcutaneous)
      (subcuticular) 681.10
  tonsil 475
  trunk 682.2
  tuberculous (primary) (see also Tuberculosis)
      017.0 ☑
  tunica vaginalis 608.4
  umbilical 682.2
      newborn NEC 771.4
  vaccinal 999.3
  vagina — see Vaginitis
  vas deferens 608.4
  vocal cords 478.5
  vulva (see also Vulvitis) 616.10
  wrist 682.4
Cementoblastoma, benign (M9273/0) 213.1
  upper jaw (bone) 213.0
Cementoma (M9273/0) 213.1
  gigantiform (M9276/0) 213.1
      upper jaw (bone) 213.0
  upper jaw (bone) 213.0
Cementoperiostitis 523.4
Cephalgia, cephalalgia (see also Headache) 784.0
  histamine 346.2 ☑
  nonorganic origin 307.81
  psychogenic 307.81
  tension 307.81
Cephalhematocele, cephalematocele
  due to birth injury 767.19
  fetus or newborn 767.19
  traumatic (see also Contusion, head) 920
Cephalhematoma, cephalematoma (calcified)
  due to birth injury 767.19
  fetus or newborn 767.19
  traumatic (see also Contusion, head) 920
Cephalic — see condition
Cephalitis — see Encephalitis
Cephalocele 742.0
Cephaloma — see Neoplasm, by site, malignant
Cephalomenia 625.8
Cephalopelvic — see condition
Cercomoniasis 007.3
Cerebellitis — see Encephalitis
Cerebellum (cerebellar) — see condition
Cerebral — see condition
Cerebritis — see Encephalitis
Cerebrohepatorenal syndrome 759.89
Cerebromacular degeneration 330.1
Cerebromalacia (see also Softening, brain)
  434.9 ☑
Cerebrosidosis 272.7
Cerebrospasticity — see Palsy, cerebral
Cerebrospinal — see condition
Cerebrum — see condition
Ceroid storage disease 272.7
Cerumen (accumulation) (impacted) 380.4

Cervical — *see also* condition
    auricle 744.43
    high risk human papillomavirus (HPV) DNA
        test positive 795.05
    low risk human papillomavirus (HPV) DNA test
        positive 795.09
    rib 756.2
Cervicalgia 723.1
Cervicitis (acute) (chronic) (nonvenereal)
        (subacute) (with erosion or ectropion) 616.0
    with
        abortion — *see* Abortion, by type, with
            sepsis
        ectopic pregnancy (*see also* categories
            633.0-633.9) 639.0
        molar pregnancy (*see also* categories 630-
            632) 639.0
        ulceration 616.0
    chlamydial 099.53
    complicating pregnancy or puerperium
        646.6 ☑
        affecting fetus or newborn 760.8
    following
        abortion 639.0
        ectopic or molar pregnancy 639.0
    gonococcal (acute) 098.15
        chronic or duration of 2 months or more
            098.35
    senile (atrophic) 616.0
    syphilitic 095.8
    trichomonal 131.09
    tuberculous (*see also* Tuberculosis) 016.7 ☑
Cervicoaural fistula 744.49
Cervicocolpitis (emphysematosa) (*see also*
        Cervicitis) 616.0
Cervix — *see* condition
Cesarean delivery, operation or section NEC
        669.7 ☑
    affecting fetus or newborn 763.4
    post mortem, affecting fetus or newborn 761.6
    previous, affecting management of pregnancy
        654.2 ☑
Céstan's syndrome 344.89
Céstan-Chenais paralysis 344.89
Céstan-Raymond syndrome 433.8 ☑
Cestode infestation NEC 123.9
    specified type NEC 123.8
Cestodiasis 123.9
Chabert's disease 022.9
Chacaleh 266.2
Chafing 709.8
Chagas' disease (*see also* Trypanosomiasis,
        American) 086.2
    with heart involvement 086.0
Chagres fever 084.0
Chalasia (cardiac sphincter) 530.81
Chalazion 373.2
Chalazoderma 757.39
Chalcosis 360.24
    cornea 371.15
    crystalline lens 360.24 [366.34]
    retina 360.24
Chalicosis (occupational) (pulmonum) 502
Chancre (any genital site) (hard) (indurated)
        (infecting) (primary) (recurrent) 091.0
    congenital 090.0
    conjunctiva 091.2
    Ducrey's 099.0
    extragenital 091.2
    eyelid 091.2
    Hunterian 091.0
    lip (syphilis) 091.2
    mixed 099.8
    nipple 091.2
    Nisbet's 099.0
    of
        carate 103.0
        pinta 103.0
        yaws 102.0
    palate, soft 091.2
    phagedenic 099.0
    Ricord's 091.0

Chancre — *continued*
    Rollet's (syphilitic) 091.0
    seronegative 091.0
    seropositive 091.0
    simple 099.0
    soft 099.0
        bubo 099.0
        urethra 091.0
        yaws 102.0
Chancriform syndrome 114.1
Chancroid 099.0
    anus 099.0
    penis (Ducrey's bacillus) 099.0
    perineum 099.0
    rectum 099.0
    scrotum 099.0
    urethra 099.0
    vulva 099.0
Chandipura fever 066.8
Chandler's disease (osteochondritis dissecans,
        hip) 732.7
Change(s) (of) — *see also* Removal of
    arteriosclerotic — *see* Arteriosclerosis
    battery
        cardiac pacemaker V53.31
    bone 733.90
        diabetic 250.8 ☑ [731.8]
        in disease, unknown cause 733.90
    bowel habits 787.99
    cardiorenal (vascular) (*see also* Hypertension,
            cardiorenal) 404.90
    cardiovascular — *see* Disease, cardiovascular
    circulatory 459.9
    cognitive or personality change of other type,
            nonpsychotic 310.1
    color, teeth, tooth
        during formation 520.8
        extrinsic 523.6
        intrinsic posteruptive 521.7
    contraceptive device V25.42
    cornea, corneal
        degenerative NEC 371.40
        membrane NEC 371.30
        senile 371.41
    coronary (*see also* Ischemia, heart) 414.9
    degenerative
        chamber angle (anterior) (iris) 364.56
        ciliary body 364.57
        spine or vertebra (*see also* Spondylosis)
            721.90
    dental pulp, regressive 522.2
    dressing V58.3
    fixation device V54.89
        external V54.89
        internal V54.01
    heart — *see* Disease, heart
    hip joint 718.95
    hyperplastic larynx 478.79
    hypertrophic
        nasal sinus (*see also* Sinusitis) 473.9
        turbinate, nasal 478.0
        upper respiratory tract 478.9
    inflammatory — *see* Inflammation
    joint (*see also* Derangement, joint) 718.90
        sacroiliac 724.6
    Kirschner wire V54.89
    knee 717.9
    macular, congenital 743.55
    malignant (M— /3) — *see also* Neoplasm, by
            site, malignant

> *Note* — *for malignant change occurring in a
> neoplasm, use the appropriate M code with
> behavior digit /3 e.g., malignant change in
> uterine fibroid — M8890/3. For malignant
> change occurring in a nonneoplastic condition
> (e.g., gastric ulcer) use the M code M8000/3.*

    mental (status) NEC 780.99
        due to or associated with physical condition
            — *see* Syndrome, brain
    myocardium, myocardial — *see* Degeneration,
            myocardial
    of life (*see also* Menopause) 627.2
    pacemaker battery (cardiac) V53.31
    peripheral nerve 355.9

Change(s) (of) — *see also* Removal of — *continued*
    personality (nonpsychotic) NEC 310.1
    plaster cast V54.89
    refractive, transient 367.81
    regressive, dental pulp 522.2
    retina 362.9
        myopic (degenerative) (malignant) 360.21
        vascular appearance 362.13
    sacroiliac joint 724.6
    scleral 379.19
        degenerative 379.16
    senile (*see also* Senility) 797
    sensory (*see also* Disturbance, sensation) 782.0
    skin texture 782.8
    spinal cord 336.9
    splint, external V54.89
    subdermal implantable contraceptive V25.5
    suture V58.3
    traction device V54.89
    trophic 355.9
        arm NEC 354.9
        leg NEC 355.8
        lower extremity NEC 355.8
        upper extremity NEC 354.9
    vascular 459.9
    vasomotor 443.9
    voice 784.49
        psychogenic 306.1
Changing sleep-work schedule, affecting sleep
        327.36 ▲
Changuinola fever 066.0
Chapping skin 709.8
Character
    depressive 301.12
Charcôt's
    arthropathy 094.0 [713.5]
    cirrhosis — *see* Cirrhosis, biliary
    disease 094.0
        spinal cord 094.0
    fever (biliary) (hepatic) (intermittent) — *see*
            Choledocholithiasis
    joint (disease) 094.0 [713.5]
        diabetic 250.6 ☑ [713.5]
        syringomyelic 336.0 [713.5]
    syndrome (intermittent claudication) 443.9
        due to atherosclerosis 440.21
Charcôt-Marie-Tooth disease, paralysis, or
        syndrome 356.1
CHARGE association (syndrome) 759.89
Charleyhorse (quadriceps) 843.8
    muscle, except quadriceps — *see* Sprain, by
            site
Charlouis' disease (*see also* Yaws) 102.9
Chauffeur's fracture — *see* Fracture, ulna, lower
        end
Cheadle (-Möller) (-Barlow) disease or syndrome
        (infantile scurvy) 267
Checking (of)
    contraceptive device (intrauterine) V25.42
    device
        fixation V54.89
            external V54.89
            internal V54.09
        traction V54.89
    Kirschner wire V54.89
    plaster cast V54.89
    splint, external V54.89
Checkup
    following treatment — *see* Examination
    health V70.0
    infant (not sick) V20.2
    pregnancy (normal) V22.1
        first V22.0
        high-risk pregnancy V23.9
            specified problem NEC V23.89
Chédiak-Higashi (-Steinbrinck) anomaly,
        disease, or syndrome (congenital gigantism
        of peroxidase granules) 288.2
Cheek — *see also* condition
    biting 528.9
Cheese itch 133.8
Cheese washers' lung 495.8

Cheilitis 528.5
actinic (due to sun) 692.72
chronic NEC 692.74
due to radiation, except from sun 692.82
due to radiation, except from sun 692.82
acute 528.5
angular 528.5
catarrhal 528.5
chronic 528.5
exfoliative 528.5
gangrenous 528.5
glandularis apostematosa 528.5
granulomatosa 351.8
infectional 528.5
membranous 528.5
Miescher's 351.8
suppurative 528.5
ulcerative 528.5
vesicular 528.5
Cheilodynia 528.5
Cheilopalatoschisis (*see also* Cleft, palate, with cleft lip) 749.20
Cheilophagia 528.9
Cheiloschisis (*see also* Cleft, lip) 749.10
Cheilosis 528.5
with pellagra 265.2
angular 528.5
due to
dietary deficiency 266.0
vitamin deficiency 266.0
Cheiromegaly 729.89
Cheiropompholyx 705.81
Cheloid (*see also* Keloid) 701.4
Chemical burn — *see also* Burn, by site
from swallowing chemical — *see* Burn, internal organs
Chemodectoma (M8693/1) — *see* Paraganglioma, nonchromaffin
Chemoprophylaxis NEC V07.39
Chemosis, conjunctiva 372.73
Chemotherapy
convalescence V66.2
encounter (for) V58.11 ▲
maintenance V58.11 ▲
prophylactic NEC V07.39
fluoride V07.31
Cherubism 526.89
Chest — *see* condition
Cheyne-Stokes respiration (periodic) 786.04
Chiari's
disease or syndrome (hepatic vein thrombosis) 453.0
malformation
type I 348.4
type II (*see also* Spina bifida) 741.0 ☑
type III 742.0
type IV 742.2
network 746.89
Chiari-Frommel syndrome 676.6 ☑
Chicago disease (North American blastomycosis) 116.0
Chickenpox (*see also* Varicella) 052.9
exposure to V01.71
vaccination and inoculation (prophylactic) V05.4
Chiclero ulcer 085.4
Chiggers 133.8
Chignon 111.2
fetus or newborn (from vacuum extraction) 767.19
Chigoe disease 134.1
Chikungunya fever 066.3
Chilaiditi's syndrome (subphrenic displacement, colon) 751.4
Chilblains 991.5
lupus 991.5
Child
behavior causing concern V61.20
Childbed fever 670 ☑
Childbirth — *see also* Delivery
puerperal complications — *see* Puerperal

Childhood, period of rapid growth V21.0
Chill(s) 780.99
with fever 780.6
congestive 780.99
in malarial regions 084.6
septic — *see* Septicemia
urethral 599.84
Chilomastigiasis 007.8
Chin — *see* condition
Chinese dysentery 004.9
Chiropractic dislocation (*see also* Lesion, nonallopathic, by site) 739.9
Chitral fever 066.0
Chlamydia, chlamydial — *see* condition
Chloasma 709.09
cachecticorum 709.09
eyelid 374.52
congenital 757.33
hyperthyroid 242.0 ☑
gravidarum 646.8 ☑
idiopathic 709.09
skin 709.09
symptomatic 709.09
Chloroma (M9930/3) 205.3 ☑
Chlorosis 280.9
Egyptian (*see also* Ancylostomiasis) 126.9
miners' (*see also* Ancylostomiasis) 126.9
Chlorotic anemia 280.9
Chocolate cyst (ovary) 617.1
Choked
disk or disc — *see* Papilledema
on food, phlegm, or vomitus NEC (*see also* Asphyxia, food) 933.1
phlegm 933.1
while vomiting NEC (*see also* Asphyxia, food) 933.1
Chokes (resulting from bends) 993.3
Choking sensation 784.9
Cholangiectasis (*see also* Disease, gallbladder) 575.8
Cholangiocarcinoma (M8160/3)
and hepatocellular carcinoma, combined (M8180/3) 155.0
liver 155.1
specified site NEC — *see* Neoplasm, by site, malignant
unspecified site 155.1
Cholangiohepatitis 575.8
due to fluke infestation 121.1
Cholangiohepatoma (M8180/3) 155.0
Cholangiolitis (acute) (chronic) (extrahepatic) (gangrenous) 576.1
intrahepatic 575.8
paratyphoidal (*see also* Fever, paratyphoid) 002.9
typhoidal 002.0
Cholangioma (M8160/0) 211.5
malignant — *see* Cholangiocarcinoma
Cholangitis (acute) (ascending) (catarrhal) (chronic) (infective) (malignant) (primary) (recurrent) (sclerosing) (secondary) (stenosing) (suppurative) 576.1
chronic nonsuppurative destructive 571.6
nonsuppurative destructive (chronic) 571.6
Cholecystdocholithiasis — *see* Choledocholithiasis
Cholecystitis 575.10
with
calculus, stones in
bile duct (common) (hepatic) — *see* Choledocholithiasis
gallbladder — *see* Cholelithiasis
acute 575.0
acute and chronic 575.12
chronic 575.11
emphysematous (acute) (*see also* Cholecystitis, acute) 575.0
gangrenous (*see also* Cholecystitis, acute) 575.0
paratyphoidal, current (*see also* Fever, paratyphoid) 002.9

Cholecystitis — *continued*
suppurative (*see also* Cholecystitis, acute) 575.0
typhoidal 002.0
Choledochitis (suppurative) 576.1
Choledocholith — *see* Choledocholithiasis
Choledocholithiasis 574.5 ☑

> *Note* — *Use the following fifth-digit subclassification with category 574:*
>
> 0   *without mention of obstruction*
> 1   *with obstruction*

with
cholecystitis 574.4 ☑
acute 574.3 ☑
chronic 574.4 ☑
cholelithiasis 574.9 ☑
with
cholecystitis 574.7 ☑
acute 574.6 ☑
and chronic 574.8 ☑
chronic 574.7 ☑
Cholelithiasis (impacted) (multiple) 574.2 ☑

> *Note* — *Use the following fifth-digit subclassification with category 574:*
>
> 0   *without mention of obstruction*
> 1   *with obstruction*

with
cholecystitis 574.1 ☑
acute 574.0 ☑
chronic 574.1 ☑
choledocholithiasis 574.9 ☑
with
cholecystitis 574.7 ☑
acute 574.6 ☑
and chronic 574.8 ☑
chronic cholecystitis 574.7 ☑
Cholemia (*see also* Jaundice) 782.4
familial 277.4
Gilbert's (familial nonhemolytic) 277.4
Cholemic gallstone — *see* Cholelithiasis
Choleperitoneum, choleperitonitis (*see also* Disease, gallbladder) 567.81 ▲
Cholera (algid) (Asiatic) (asphyctic) (epidemic) (gravis) (Indian) (malignant) (morbus) (pestilential) (spasmodic) 001.9
antimonial 985.4
carrier (suspected) of V02.0
classical 001.0
contact V01.0
due to
Vibrio
cholerae (Inaba, Ogawa, Hikojima serotypes) 001.0
El Tor 001.1
El Tor 001.1
exposure to V01.0
vaccination, prophylactic (against) V03.0
Cholerine (*see also* Cholera) 001.9
Cholestasis 576.8
Cholesteatoma (ear) 385.30
attic (primary) 385.31
diffuse 385.35
external ear (canal) 380.21
marginal (middle ear) 385.32
with involvement of mastoid cavity 385.33
secondary (with middle ear involvement) 385.33
mastoid cavity 385.30
middle ear (secondary) 385.32
with involvement of mastoid cavity 385.33
postmastoidectomy cavity (recurrent) 383.32
primary 385.31
recurrent, postmastoidectomy cavity 383.32
secondary (middle ear) 385.32
with involvement of mastoid cavity 385.33
Cholesteatosis (middle ear) (*see also* Cholesteatoma) 385.30
diffuse 385.35
Cholesteremia 272.0

Cholesterin
  granuloma, middle ear 385.82
  in vitreous 379.22
Cholesterol
  deposit
    retina 362.82
    vitreous 379.22
  imbibition of gallbladder (see also Disease,
    gallbladder) 575.6
Cholesterolemia 272.0
  essential 272.0
  familial 272.0
  hereditary 272.0
Cholesterosis, cholesterolosis (gallbladder) 575.6
  with
    cholecystitis — see Cholecystitis
    cholelithiasis — see Cholelithiasis
    middle ear (see also Cholesteatoma) 385.30
Cholocolic fistula (see also Fistula, gallbladder)
  575.5
Choluria 791.4
Chondritis (purulent) 733.99
  auricle 380.03
  costal 733.6
    Tietze's 733.6
  patella, posttraumatic 717.7
  pinna 380.03
  posttraumatica patellae 717.7
  tuberculous (active) (see also Tuberculosis)
    015.9 ☑
      intervertebral 015.0 ☑ [730.88]
Chondroangiopathia calcarea seu punctate
  756.59
Chondroblastoma (M9230/0) — see also
  Neoplasm, bone, benign
  malignant (M9230/3) — see Neoplasm, bone,
    malignant
Chondrocalcinosis (articular) (crystal deposition)
  (dihydrate) (see also Arthritis, due to,
  crystals) 275.49 [712.3] ☑
  due to
    calcium pyrophosphate 275.49 [712.2] ☑
    dicalcium phosphate crystals
      275.49 [712.1] ☑
    pyrophosphate crystals 275.49 [712.2] ☑
Chondrodermatitis nodularis helicis 380.00
Chondrodysplasia 756.4
  angiomatose 756.4
  calcificans congenita 756.59
  epiphysialis punctata 756.59
  hereditary deforming 756.4
  rhizomelic punctata 277.86
Chondrodystrophia (fetalis) 756.4
  calcarea 756.4
  calcificans congenita 756.59
  fetalis hypoplastica 756.59
  hypoplastica calcinosa 756.59
  punctata 756.59
  tarda 277.5
Chondrodystrophy (familial) (hypoplastic) 756.4
Chondroectodermal dysplasia 756.55
Chondrolysis 733.99
Chondroma (M9220/0) — see also Neoplasm
  cartilage, benign
  juxtacortical (M9221/0) — see Neoplasm, bone,
    benign
  periosteal (M9221/0) — see Neoplasm, bone,
    benign
Chondromalacia 733.92
  epiglottis (congenital) 748.3
  generalized 733.92
  knee 717.7
  larynx (congenital) 748.3
  localized, except patella 733.92
  patella, patellae 717.7
  systemic 733.92
  tibial plateau 733.92
  trachea (congenital) 748.3
Chondromatosis (M9220/1) — see Neoplasm,
  cartilage, uncertain behavior
Chondromyxosarcoma (M9220/3) — see
  Neoplasm, cartilage, malignant

Chondro-osteodysplasia (Morquio-Brailsford type)
  277.5
Chondro-osteodystrophy 277.5
Chondro-osteoma (M9210/0) — see Neoplasm,
  bone, benign
Chondropathia tuberosa 733.6
Chondrosarcoma (M9220/3) — see also
  Neoplasm, cartilage, malignant
  juxtacortical (M9221/3) — see Neoplasm, bone,
    malignant
  mesenchymal (M9240/3) — see Neoplasm,
    connective tissue, malignant
Chordae tendineae rupture (chronic) 429.5
Chordee (nonvenereal) 607.89
  congenital 752.63
  gonococcal 098.2
Chorditis (fibrinous) (nodosa) (tuberosa) 478.5
Chordoma (M9370/3) — see Neoplasm, by site,
  malignant
Chorea (gravis) (minor) (spasmodic) 333.5
  with
    heart involvement — see Chorea with
      rheumatic heart disease
    rheumatic heart disease (chronic, inactive,
      or quiescent) (conditions classifiable to
      393-398) — see rheumatic heart
      condition involved
      active or acute (conditions classifiable to
        391) 392.0
  acute — see Chorea, Sydenham's
  apoplectic (see also Disease, cerebrovascular,
    acute) 436
  chronic 333.4
  electric 049.8
  gravidarum — see Eclampsia, pregnancy
  habit 307.22
  hereditary 333.4
  Huntington's 333.4
  posthemiplegic 344.89
  pregnancy — see Eclampsia, pregnancy
  progressive 333.4
    chronic 333.4
    hereditary 333.4
  rheumatic (chronic) 392.9
    with heart disease or involvement — see
      Chorea, with rheumatic heart disease
  senile 333.5
  Sydenham's 392.9
    with heart involvement — see Chorea, with
      rheumatic heart disease
    nonrheumatic 333.5
  variabilis 307.23
Choreoathetosis (paroxysmal) 333.5
Chorioadenoma (destruens) (M9100/1) 236.1
Chorioamnionitis 658.4 ☑
  affecting fetus or newborn 762.7
Chorioangioma (M9120/0) 219.8
Choriocarcinoma (M9100/3)
  combined with
    embryonal carcinoma (M9101/3) — see
      Neoplasm, by site, malignant
    teratoma (M9101/3) — see Neoplasm, by
      site, malignant
  specified site — see Neoplasm, by site,
    malignant
  unspecified site
    female 181
    male 186.9
Chorioencephalitis, lymphocytic (acute) (serous)
  049.0
Chorioepithelioma (M9100/3) — see
  Choriocarcinoma
Choriomeningitis (acute) (benign) (lymphocytic)
  (serous) 049.0
Chorionepithelioma (M9100/3) — see
  Choriocarcinoma
Chorionitis (see also Scleroderma) 710.1
Chorioretinitis 363.20
  disseminated 363.10
    generalized 363.13
    in
      neurosyphilis 094.83
      secondary syphilis 091.51

Chorioretinitis — continued
  disseminated — continued
    peripheral 363.12
    posterior pole 363.11
    tuberculous (see also Tuberculosis) 017.3 ☑
      [363.13]
  due to
    histoplasmosis (see also Histoplasmosis)
      115.92
    toxoplasmosis (acquired) 130.2
      congenital (active) 771.2
  focal 363.00
    juxtapapillary 363.01
    peripheral 363.04
    posterior pole NEC 363.03
  juxtapapillaris, juxtapapillary 363.01
  progressive myopia (degeneration) 360.21
  syphilitic (secondary) 091.51
    congenital (early) 090.0 [363.13]
      late 090.5 [363.13]
    late 095.8 [363.13]
  tuberculous (see also Tuberculosis) 017.3 ☑
    [363.13]
Choristoma — see Neoplasm, by site, benign
Choroid — see condition
Choroideremia, choroidermia (initial stage) (late
  stage) (partial or total atrophy) 363.55
Choroiditis (see also Chorioretinitis) 363.20
  leprous 030.9 [363.13]
  senile guttate 363.41
  sympathetic 360.11
  syphilitic (secondary) 091.51
    congenital (early) 090.0 [363.13]
      late 090.5 [363.13]
    late 095.8 [363.13]
  Tay's 363.41
  tuberculous (see also Tuberculosis) 017.3 ☑
    [363.13]
Choroidopathy NEC 363.9
  degenerative (see also Degeneration, choroid)
    363.40
  hereditary (see also Dystrophy, choroid) 363.50
  specified type NEC 363.8
Choroidoretinitis — see Chorioretinitis
Choroidosis, central serous 362.41
Choroidretinopathy, serous 362.41
Christian's syndrome (chronic histiocytosis X)
  277.89
Christian-Weber disease (nodular nonsuppurative
  panniculitis) 729.30
Christmas disease 286.1
Chromaffinoma (M8700/0) — see also Neoplasm,
  by site, benign
  malignant (M8700/3) — see Neoplasm, by site,
    malignant
Chromatopsia 368.59
Chromhidrosis, chromidrosis 705.89
Chromoblastomycosis 117.2
Chromomycosis 117.2
Chromophytosis 111.0
Chromotrichomycosis 111.8
Chronic — see condition
Churg-Strauss syndrome 446.4
Chyle cyst, mesentery 457.8
Chylocele (nonfilarial) 457.8
  filarial (see also Infestation, filarial) 125.9
  tunica vaginalis (nonfilarial) 608.84
    filarial (see also Infestation, filarial) 125.9
Chylomicronemia (fasting) (with
  hyperprebetalipoproteinemia) 272.3
Chylopericardium (acute) 420.90
Chylothorax (nonfilarial) 457.8
  filarial (see also Infestation, filarial) 125.9
Chylous
  ascites 457.8
  cyst of peritoneum 457.8
  hydrocele 603.9
  hydrothorax (nonfilarial) 457.8
    filarial (see also Infestation, filarial) 125.9
Chyluria 791.1
  bilharziasis 120.0

Chyluria — continued
  due to
    Brugia (malayi) 125.1
    Wuchereria (bancrofti) 125.0
      malayi 125.1
  filarial (see also Infestation, filarial) 125.9
  filariasis (see also Infestation, filarial) 125.9
  nonfilarial 791.1
Cicatricial (deformity) — see Cicatrix
Cicatrix (adherent) (contracted) (painful) (vicious)
    709.2
  adenoid 474.8
  alveolar process 525.8
  anus 569.49
  auricle 380.89
  bile duct (see also Disease, biliary) 576.8
  bladder 596.8
  bone 733.99
  brain 348.8
  cervix (postoperative) (postpartal) 622.3
    in pregnancy or childbirth 654.6 ☑
      causing obstructed labor 660.2 ☑
  chorioretinal 363.30
    disseminated 363.35
    macular 363.32
    peripheral 363.34
    posterior pole NEC 363.33
  choroid — see Cicatrix, chorioretinal
  common duct (see also Disease, biliary) 576.8
  congenital 757.39
  conjunctiva 372.64
  cornea 371.00
    tuberculous (see also Tuberculosis) 017.3 ☑
      [371.05]
  duodenum (bulb) 537.3
  esophagus 530.3
  eyelid 374.46
    with
      ectropion — see Ectropion
      entropion — see Entropion
  hypopharynx 478.29
  knee, semilunar cartilage 717.5
  lacrimal
    canaliculi 375.53
    duct
      acquired 375.56
      neonatal 375.55
    punctum 375.52
    sac 375.54
  larynx 478.79
  limbus (cystoid) 372.64
  lung 518.89
  macular 363.32
    disseminated 363.35
    peripheral 363.34
  middle ear 385.89
  mouth 528.9
  muscle 728.89
  nasolacrimal duct
    acquired 375.56
    neonatal 375.55
  nasopharynx 478.29
  palate (soft) 528.9
  penis 607.89
  prostate 602.8
  rectum 569.49
  retina 363.30
    disseminated 363.35
    macular 363.32
    peripheral 363.34
    posterior pole NEC 363.33
  semilunar cartilage — see Derangement,
      meniscus
  seminal vesicle 608.89
  skin 709.2
    infected 686.8
    postinfectional 709.2
    tuberculous (see also Tuberculosis) 017.0 ☑
  specified site NEC 709.2
  throat 478.29
  tongue 529.8
  tonsil (and adenoid) 474.8
  trachea 478.9
  tuberculous NEC (see also Tuberculosis)
      011.9 ☑
  ureter 593.89

Cicatrix — continued
  urethra 599.84
  uterus 621.8
  vagina 623.4
    in pregnancy or childbirth 654.7 ☑
      causing obstructed labor 660.2 ☑
  vocal cord 478.5
  wrist, constricting (annular) 709.2
CIN I [cervical intraepithelial neoplasia I] 622.11
CIN II [cervical intraepithelial neoplasia II] 622.12
CIN III [cervical intraepithelial neoplasia III] 233.1
Cinchonism
  correct substance properly administered 386.9
  overdose or wrong substance given or taken
      961.4
Circine herpes 110.5
Circle of Willis — see condition
Circular — see also condition
  hymen 752.49
Circulating anticoagulants 286.5
  following childbirth 666.3 ☑
  postpartum 666.3 ☑
Circulation
  collateral (venous), any site 459.89
  defective 459.9
    congenital 747.9
    lower extremity 459.89
  embryonic 747.9
  failure 799.89
    fetus or newborn 779.89
    peripheral 785.59
  fetal, persistent 747.83
  heart, incomplete 747.9
Circulatory system — see condition
Circulus senilis 371.41
Circumcision
  in absence of medical indication V50.2
  ritual V50.2
  routine V50.2
Circumscribed — see condition
Circumvallata placenta — see Placenta,
      abnormal
Cirrhosis, cirrhotic 571.5
  with alcoholism 571.2
  alcoholic (liver) 571.2
  atrophic (of liver) — see Cirrhosis, portal
  Baumgarten-Cruveilhier 571.5
  biliary (cholangiolitic) (cholangitic) (cholestatic)
      (extrahepatic) (hypertrophic)
      (intrahepatic) (nonobstructive)
      (obstructive) (pericholangiolitic)
      (posthepatic) (primary) (secondary)
      (xanthomatous) 571.6
    due to
      clonorchiasis 121.1
      flukes 121.3
  brain 331.9
  capsular — see Cirrhosis, portal
  cardiac 571.5
    alcoholic 571.2
  central (liver) — see Cirrhosis, liver
  Charcôt's 571.6
  cholangiolitic — see Cirrhosis, biliary
  cholangitic — see Cirrhosis, biliary
  cholestatic — see Cirrhosis, biliary
  clitoris (hypertrophic) 624.2
  coarsely nodular 571.5
  congestive (liver) — see Cirrhosis, cardiac
  Cruveilhier-Baumgarten 571.5
  cryptogenic (of liver) 571.5
    alcoholic 571.2
  dietary (see also Cirrhosis, portal) 571.5
  due to
    bronzed diabetes 275.0
    congestive hepatomegaly — see Cirrhosis,
        cardiac
    cystic fibrosis 277.00
    hemochromatosis 275.0
    hepatolenticular degeneration 275.1
    passive congestion (chronic) — see
        Cirrhosis, cardiac
    Wilson's disease 275.1

Cirrhosis, cirrhotic — continued
  due to — continued
    xanthomatosis 272.2
  extrahepatic (obstructive) — see Cirrhosis,
      biliary
  fatty 571.8
    alcoholic 571.0
  florid 571.2
  Glisson's — see Cirrhosis, portal
  Hanot's (hypertrophic) — see Cirrhosis, biliary
  hepatic — see Cirrhosis, liver
  hepatolienal — see Cirrhosis, liver
  hobnail — see Cirrhosis, portal
  hypertrophic — see also Cirrhosis, liver
    biliary — see Cirrhosis, biliary
    Hanot's — see Cirrhosis, biliary
  infectious NEC — see Cirrhosis, portal
  insular — see Cirrhosis, portal
  intrahepatic (obstructive) (primary) (secondary)
      — see Cirrhosis, biliary
  juvenile (see also Cirrhosis, portal) 571.5
  kidney (see also Sclerosis, renal) 587
  Laennec's (of liver) 571.2
    nonalcoholic 571.5
  liver (chronic) (hepatolienal) (hypertrophic)
      (nodular) (splenomegalic) (unilobar) 571.5
    with alcoholism 571.2
    alcoholic 571.2
    congenital (due to failure of obliteration of
        umbilical vein) 777.8
    cryptogenic 571.5
      alcoholic 571.2
    fatty 571.8
      alcoholic 571.0
    macronodular 571.5
      alcoholic 571.2
    micronodular 571.5
      alcoholic 571.2
    nodular, diffuse 571.5
      alcoholic 571.2
    pigmentary 275.0
    portal 571.5
      alcoholic 571.2
    postnecrotic 571.5
      alcoholic 571.2
    syphilitic 095.3
  lung (chronic) (see also Fibrosis, lung) 515
  macronodular (of liver) 571.5
    alcoholic 571.2
  malarial 084.9
  metabolic NEC 571.5
  micronodular (of liver) 571.5
    alcoholic 571.2
  monolobular — see Cirrhosis, portal
  multilobular — see Cirrhosis, portal
  nephritis (see also Sclerosis, renal) 587
  nodular — see Cirrhosis, liver
  nutritional (fatty) 571.5
  obstructive (biliary) (extrahepatic) (intrahepatic)
      — see Cirrhosis, biliary
  ovarian 620.8
  paludal 084.9
  pancreas (duct) 577.8
  pericholangiolitic — see Cirrhosis, biliary
  periportal — see Cirrhosis, portal
  pigment, pigmentary (of liver) 275.0
  portal (of liver) 571.5
    alcoholic 571.2
  posthepatitic (see also Cirrhosis, postnecrotic)
      571.5
  postnecrotic (of liver) 571.5
    alcoholic 571.2
  primary (intrahepatic) — see Cirrhosis, biliary
  pulmonary (see also Fibrosis, lung) 515
  renal (see also Sclerosis, renal) 587
  septal (see also Cirrhosis, postnecrotic) 571.5
  spleen 289.51
  splenomegalic (of liver) — see Cirrhosis, liver
  stasis (liver) — see Cirrhosis, liver
  stomach 535.4 ☑
  Todd's (see also Cirrhosis, biliary) 571.6
  toxic (nodular) — see Cirrhosis, postnecrotic
  trabecular — see Cirrhosis, postnecrotic
  unilobar — see Cirrhosis, liver
  vascular (of liver) — see Cirrhosis, liver

Cirrhosis, cirrhotic — *continued*
　　xanthomatous (biliary) (*see also* Cirrhosis, biliary) 571.6
　　　due to xanthomatosis (familial) (metabolic) (primary) 272.2
Cistern, subarachnoid 793.0
Citrullinemia 270.6
Citrullinuria 270.6
Ciuffini-Pancoast tumor (M8010/3) (carcinoma, pulmonary apex) 162.3
Civatte's disease or poikiloderma 709.09
Clam diggers' itch 120.3
Clap — *see* Gonorrhea
Clark's paralysis 343.9
Clarke-Hadfield syndrome (pancreatic infantilism) 577.8
Clastothrix 704.2
Claude's syndrome 352.6
Claude Bernard-Horner syndrome (*see also* Neuropathy, peripheral, autonomic) 337.9
Claudication, intermittent 443.9
　　cerebral (artery) (*see also* Ischemia, cerebral, transient) 435.9
　　due to atherosclerosis 440.21
　　spinal cord (arteriosclerotic) 435.1
　　　syphilitic 094.89
　　spinalis 435.1
　　venous (axillary) 453.8
Claudicatio venosa intermittens 453.8
Claustrophobia 300.29
Clavus (infected) 700
Clawfoot (congenital) 754.71
　　acquired 736.74
Clawhand (acquired) 736.06
　　congenital 755.59
Clawtoe (congenital) 754.71
　　acquired 735.5
Clay eating 307.52
Clay shovelers' fracture — *see* Fracture, vertebra, cervical
Cleansing of artificial opening (*see also* Attention to artificial opening) V55.9
Cleft (congenital) — *see also* Imperfect, closure
　　alveolar process 525.8
　　branchial (persistent) 744.41
　　　cyst 744.42
　　clitoris 752.49
　　cricoid cartilage, posterior 748.3
　　facial (*see also* Cleft, lip) 749.10
　　lip 749.10
　　　with cleft palate 749.20
　　　　bilateral (lip and palate) 749.24
　　　　　with unilateral lip or palate 749.25
　　　　　complete 749.23
　　　　　incomplete 749.24
　　　　unilateral (lip and palate) 749.22
　　　　　with bilateral lip or palate 749.25
　　　　　complete 749.21
　　　　　incomplete 749.22
　　　　bilateral 749.14
　　　　　with cleft palate, unilateral 749.25
　　　　　complete 749.13
　　　　　incomplete 749.14
　　　　unilateral 749.12
　　　　　with cleft palate, bilateral 749.25
　　　　　complete 749.11
　　　　　incomplete 749.12
　　nose 748.1
　　palate 749.00
　　　with cleft lip 749.20
　　　　bilateral (lip and palate) 749.24
　　　　　with unilateral lip or palate 749.25
　　　　　complete 749.23
　　　　　incomplete 749.24
　　　　unilateral (lip and palate) 749.22
　　　　　with bilateral lip or palate 749.25
　　　　　complete 749.21
　　　　　incomplete 749.22
　　　　bilateral 749.04
　　　　　with cleft lip, unilateral 749.25
　　　　　complete 749.03
　　　　　incomplete 749.04

Cleft — *see also* Imperfect, closure — *continued*
　palate — *continued*
　　　unilateral 749.02
　　　　with cleft lip, bilateral 749.25
　　　　complete 749.01
　　　　incomplete 749.02
　　penis 752.69
　　posterior, cricoid cartilage 748.3
　　scrotum 752.89
　　sternum (congenital) 756.3
　　thyroid cartilage (congenital) 748.3
　　tongue 750.13
　　uvula 749.02
　　　with cleft lip (*see also* Cleft, lip, with cleft palate) 749.20
　　water 366.12
Cleft hand (congenital) 755.58
Cleidocranial dysostosis 755.59
Cleidotomy, fetal 763.89
Cleptomania 312.32
Clérambault's syndrome 297.8
　　erotomania 302.89
Clergyman's sore throat 784.49
Click, clicking
　　systolic syndrome 785.2
Clifford's syndrome (postmaturity) 766.22
Climacteric (*see also* Menopause) 627.2
　　arthritis NEC (*see also* Arthritis, climacteric) 716.3 ☑
　　depression (*see also* Psychosis, affective) 296.2 ☑
　　disease 627.2
　　　recurrent episode 296.3 ☑
　　　single episode 296.2 ☑
　　female (symptoms) 627.2
　　male (symptoms) (syndrome) 608.89
　　melancholia (*see also* Psychosis, affective) 296.2 ☑
　　　recurrent episode 296.3 ☑
　　　single episode 296.2 ☑
　　paranoid state 297.2
　　paraphrenia 297.2
　　polyarthritis NEC 716.39
　　　male 608.89
　　symptoms (female) 627.2
Clinical research investigation (control) (participant) V70.7
Clinodactyly 755.59
Clitoris — *see* condition
Cloaca, persistent 751.5
Clonorchiasis 121.1
Clonorchiosis 121.1
Clonorchis infection, liver 121.1
Clonus 781.0
Closed bite 524.20
Closed surgical procedure converted to open procedure
　　arthroscopic V64.43
　　laparoscopic V64.41
　　thoracoscopic V64.42
Closure
　　artificial opening (*see also* Attention to artificial opening) V55.9
　　congenital, nose 748.0
　　cranial sutures, premature 756.0
　　defective or imperfect NEC — *see* Imperfect, closure
　　fistula, delayed — *see* Fistula
　　fontanelle, delayed 756.0
　　foramen ovale, imperfect 745.5
　　hymen 623.3
　　interauricular septum, defective 745.5
　　interventricular septum, defective 745.4
　　lacrimal duct 375.56
　　　congenital 743.65
　　　neonatal 375.55
　　nose (congenital) 748.0
　　　acquired 738.0
　　vagina 623.2
　　valve — *see* Endocarditis
　　vulva 624.8

Clot (blood)
　　artery (obstruction) (occlusion) (*see also* Embolism) 444.9
　　bladder 596.7
　　brain (extradural or intradural) (*see also* Thrombosis, brain) 434.0 ☑
　　　late effect — *see* Late effect(s) (of) cerebrovascular disease
　　circulation 444.9
　　heart (*see also* Infarct, myocardium) 410.9 ☑
　　vein (*see also* Thrombosis) 453.9
Clotting defect NEC (*see also* Defect, coagulation) 286.9
Clouded state 780.09
　　epileptic (*see also* Epilepsy) 345.9 ☑
　　paroxysmal (idiopathic) (*see also* Epilepsy) 345.9 ☑
Clouding
　　corneal graft 996.51
Cloudy
　　antrum, antra 473.0
　　dialysis effluent 792.5
Clouston's (hidrotic) ectodermal dysplasia 757.31
Clubbing of fingers 781.5
Clubfinger 736.29
　　acquired 736.29
　　congenital 754.89
Clubfoot (congenital) 754.70
　　acquired 736.71
　　equinovarus 754.51
　　paralytic 736.71
Club hand (congenital) 754.89
　　acquired 736.07
Clubnail (acquired) 703.8
　　congenital 757.5
Clump kidney 753.3
Clumsiness 781.3
　　syndrome 315.4
Cluttering 307.0
Clutton's joints 090.5
Coagulation, intravascular (diffuse) (disseminated) (*see also* Fibrinolysis) 286.6
　　newborn 776.2
Coagulopathy (*see also* Defect, coagulation) 286.9
　　consumption 286.6
　　intravascular (disseminated) NEC 286.6
　　　newborn 776.2
Coalition
　　calcaneoscaphoid 755.67
　　calcaneus 755.67
　　tarsal 755.67
Coal miners'
　　elbow 727.2
　　lung 500
Coal workers' lung or pneumoconiosis 500
Coarctation
　　aorta (postductal) (preductal) 747.10
　　pulmonary artery 747.3
Coated tongue 529.3
Coats' disease 362.12
Cocainism (*see also* Dependence) 304.2 ☑
Coccidioidal granuloma 114.3
Coccidioidomycosis 114.9
　　with pneumonia 114.0
　　cutaneous (primary) 114.1
　　disseminated 114.3
　　extrapulmonary (primary) 114.1
　　lung 114.5
　　　acute 114.0
　　　chronic 114.4
　　　primary 114.0
　　meninges 114.2
　　primary (pulmonary) 114.0
　　　acute 114.0
　　prostate 114.3
　　pulmonary 114.5
　　　acute 114.0
　　　chronic 114.4
　　　primary 114.0
　　specified site NEC 114.3

Cirrhosis, cirrhotic — Coccidioidomycosis

☑ Additional Digit Required — Refer to the Tabular List (Numeric Code Section) for Additional Digit Selection
►◄ Revised Text　　　　● New Line　　　　▲ Revised Code

2006 ICD-9-CM　　　　　　　　　　　　　　　　　　　　　　　　　　Volume 2 — 61

Coccidioidosis 114.9
  lung 114.5
    acute 114.0
    chronic 114.4
    primary 114.0
  meninges 114.2
Coccidiosis (colitis) (diarrhea) (dysentery) 007.2
Cocciuria 791.9
Coccus in urine 791.9
Coccydynia 724.79
Coccygodynia 724.79
Coccyx — *see* condition
Cochin-China
  diarrhea 579.1
    anguilluliasis 127.2
  ulcer 085.1
Cock's peculiar tumor 706.2
Cockayne's disease or syndrome (microcephaly and dwarfism) 759.89
Cockayne-Weber syndrome (epidermolysis bullosa) 757.39
Cocked-up toe 735.2
Codman's tumor (benign chondroblastoma) (M9230/0) — *see* Neoplasm, bone, benign
Coenurosis 123.8
Coffee workers' lung 495.8
Cogan's syndrome 370.52
  congenital oculomotor apraxia 379.51
  nonsyphilitic interstitial keratitis 370.52
Coiling, umbilical cord — *see* Complications, umbilical cord
Coitus, painful (female) 625.0
  male 608.89
  psychogenic 302.76
Cold 460
  with influenza, flu, or grippe 487.1
  abscess — *see also* Tuberculosis, abscess
    articular — *see* Tuberculosis, joint
  agglutinin
    disease (chronic) or syndrome 283.0
    hemoglobinuria 283.0
      paroxysmal (cold) (nocturnal) 283.2
  allergic (*see also* Fever, hay) 477.9
  bronchus or chest — *see* Bronchitis
    with grippe or influenza 487.1
  common (head) 460
    vaccination, prophylactic (against) V04.7
  deep 464.10
  effects of 991.9
    specified effect NEC 991.8
  excessive 991.9
    specified effect NEC 991.8
  exhaustion from 991.8
  exposure to 991.9
    specified effect NEC 991.8
  grippy 487.1
  head 460
  injury syndrome (newborn) 778.2
  intolerance 780.99
  on lung — *see* Bronchitis
  rose 477.0
  sensitivity, autoimmune 283.0
  virus 460
Coldsore (*see also* Herpes, simplex) 054.9
Colibacillosis 041.4
  generalized 038.42
Colibacilluria 791.9
Colic (recurrent) 789.0 ☑
  abdomen 789.0 ☑
    psychogenic 307.89
  appendicular 543.9
  appendix 543.9
  bile duct — *see* Choledocholithiasis
  biliary — *see* Cholelithiasis
  bilious — *see* Cholelithiasis
  common duct — *see* Choledocholithiasis
  Devonshire NEC 984.9
    specified type of lead — *see* Table of Drugs and Chemicals
  flatulent 787.3
  gallbladder or gallstone — *see* Cholelithiasis
  gastric 536.8
  hepatic (duct) — *see* Choledocholithiasis

Colic — *continued*
  hysterical 300.11
  infantile 789.0 ☑
  intestinal 789.0 ☑
  kidney 788.0
  lead NEC 984.9
    specified type of lead — *see* Table of Drugs and Chemicals
  liver (duct) — *see* Choledocholithiasis
  mucous 564.9
    psychogenic 316 [564.9]
  nephritic 788.0
  painter's NEC 984.9
  pancreas 577.8
  psychogenic 306.4
  renal 788.0
  saturnine NEC 984.9
    specified type of lead — *see* Table of Drugs and Chemicals
  spasmodic 789.0 ☑
  ureter 788.0
  urethral 599.84
    due to calculus 594.2
  uterus 625.8
    menstrual 625.3
  vermicular 543.9
  virus 460
  worm NEC 128.9
Colicystitis (*see also* Cystitis) 595.9
Colitis (acute) (catarrhal) (croupous) (cystica superficialis) (exudative) (hemorrhagic) (noninfectious) (phlegmonous) (presumed noninfectious) 558.9
  adaptive 564.9
  allergic 558.3
  amebic (*see also* Amebiasis) 006.9
    nondysenteric 006.2
  anthrax 022.2
  bacillary (*see also* Infection, Shigella) 004.9
  balantidial 007.0
  chronic 558.9
    ulcerative (*see also* Colitis, ulcerative) 556.9
  coccidial 007.2
  dietetic 558.9
  due to radiation 558.1
  functional 558.9
  gangrenous 009.0
  giardial 007.1
  granulomatous 555.1
  gravis (*see also* Colitis, ulcerative) 556.9
  infectious (*see also* Enteritis, due to, specific organism) 009.0
    presumed 009.1
  ischemic 557.9
    acute 557.0
    chronic 557.1
    due to mesenteric artery insufficiency 557.1
  membranous 564.9
    psychogenic 316 [564.9]
  mucous 564.9
    psychogenic 316 [564.9]
  necrotic 009.0
  polyposa (*see also* Colitis, ulcerative) 556.9
  protozoal NEC 007.9
  pseudomembranous 008.45
  pseudomucinous 564.9
  regional 555.1
  segmental 555.1
  septic (*see also* Enteritis, due to, specific organism) 009.0
  spastic 564.9
    psychogenic 316 [564.9]
  Staphylococcus 008.41
    food 005.0
  thromboulcerative 557.0
  toxic 558.2
  transmural 555.1
  trichomonal 007.3
  tuberculous (ulcerative) 014.8 ☑
  ulcerative (chronic) (idiopathic) (nonspecific) 556.9
    entero- 556.0
    fulminant 557.0
    ileo- 556.1
    left-sided 556.5
    procto- 556.2

Colitis — *continued*
  ulcerative — *continued*
    proctosigmoid 556.3
    psychogenic 316 [556] ☑
    specified NEC 556.8
    universal 556.6
Collagen disease NEC 710.9
  nonvascular 710.9
  vascular (allergic) (*see also* Angiitis, hypersensitivity) 446.20
Collagenosis (*see also* Collagen disease) 710.9
  cardiovascular 425.4
  mediastinal 519.3
Collapse 780.2
  adrenal 255.8
  cardiorenal (*see also* Hypertension, cardiorenal) 404.90
  cardiorespiratory 785.51
    fetus or newborn 779.89
  cardiovascular (*see also* Disease, heart) 785.51
    fetus or newborn 779.89
  circulatory (peripheral) 785.59
    with
      abortion — *see* Abortion, by type, with shock
      ectopic pregnancy (*see also* categories 633.0-633.9) 639.5
      molar pregnancy (*see also* categories 630-632) 639.5
    during or after labor and delivery 669.1 ☑
    fetus or newborn 779.89
    following
      abortion 639.5
      ectopic or molar pregnancy 639.5
  during or after labor and delivery 669.1 ☑
    fetus or newborn 779.89
  external ear canal 380.50
    secondary to
      inflammation 380.53
      surgery 380.52
      trauma 380.51
  general 780.2
  heart — *see* Disease, heart
  heat 992.1
  hysterical 300.11
  labyrinth, membranous (congenital) 744.05
  lung (massive) (*see also* Atelectasis) 518.0
    pressure, during labor 668.0 ☑
  myocardial — *see* Disease, heart
  nervous (*see also* Disorder, mental, nonpsychotic) 300.9
  neurocirculatory 306.2
  nose 738.0
  postoperative (cardiovascular) 998.0
  pulmonary (see also Atelectasis) 518.0
    fetus or newborn 770.5
      partial 770.5
      primary 770.4
  thorax 512.8
    iatrogenic 512.1
    postoperative 512.1
  trachea 519.1
  valvular — *see* Endocarditis
  vascular (peripheral) 785.59
    with
      abortion — *see* Abortion, by type, with shock
      ectopic pregnancy (*see also* categories 633.0-633.9) 639.5
      molar pregnancy (*see also* categories 630-632) 639.5
    cerebral (*see also* Disease, cerebrovascular, acute) 436
    during or after labor and delivery 669.1 ☑
    fetus or newborn 779.89
    following
      abortion 639.5
      ectopic or molar pregnancy 639.5
  vasomotor 785.59
  vertebra 733.13
Collateral — *see also* condition
  circulation (venous) 459.89
  dilation, veins 459.89
Colles' fracture (closed) (reversed) (separation) 813.41
  open 813.51

Collet's syndrome 352.6
Collet-Sicard syndrome 352.6
Colliculitis urethralis (*see also* Urethritis) 597.89
Colliers'
    asthma 500
    lung 500
    phthisis (*see also* Tuberculosis) 011.4 ☑
Collodion baby (ichthyosis congenita) 757.1
Colloid milium 709.3
Coloboma NEC 743.49
    choroid 743.59
    fundus 743.52
    iris 743.46
    lens 743.36
    lids 743.62
    optic disc (congenital) 743.57
        acquired 377.23
    retina 743.56
    sclera 743.47
Coloenteritis — *see* Enteritis
Colon — *see* condition
Coloptosis 569.89
Color
    amblyopia NEC 368.59
        acquired 368.55
    blindness NEC (congenital) 368.59
        acquired 368.55
Colostomy
    attention to V55.3
    fitting or adjustment V55.3
    malfunctioning 569.62
    status V44.3
Colpitis (*see also* Vaginitis) 616.10
Colpocele 618.6
Colpocystitis (*see also* Vaginitis) 616.10
Colporrhexis 665.4 ☑
Colpospasm 625.1
Column, spinal, vertebral — *see* condition
Coma 780.01
    apoplectic (*see also* Disease, cerebrovascular,
        acute) 436
    diabetic (with ketoacidosis) 250.3 ☑
        hyperosmolar 250.2 ☑
    eclamptic (*see also* Eclampsia) 780.39
    epileptic 345.3
    hepatic 572.2
    hyperglycemic 250.2 ☑
    hyperosmolar (diabetic) (nonketotic) 250.2 ☑
    hypoglycemic 251.0
        diabetic 250.3 ☑
    insulin 250.3 ☑
        hyperosmolar 250.2 ☑
        non-diabetic 251.0
        organic hyperinsulinism 251.0
    Kussmaul's (diabetic) 250.3 ☑
    liver 572.2
    newborn 779.2
    prediabetic 250.2 ☑
    uremic — *see* Uremia
Combat fatigue (*see also* Reaction, stress, acute)
    308.9
Combined — *see* condition
Comedo 706.1
Comedocarcinoma (M8501/3) — *see also*
    Neoplasm, breast, malignant
    noninfiltrating (M8501/2)
        specified site — *see* Neoplasm, by site, in
            situ
        unspecified site 233.0
Comedomastitis 610.4
Comedones 706.1
    lanugo 757.4
Comma bacillus, carrier (suspected) of V02.3
Comminuted fracture — *see* Fracture, by site
Common
    aortopulmonary trunk 745.0
    atrioventricular canal (defect) 745.69
    atrium 745.69
    cold (head) 460
        vaccination, prophylactic (against) V04.7
    truncus (arteriosus) 745.0
    ventricle 745.3

Commotio (current)
    cerebri (*see also* Concussion, brain) 850.9
        with skull fracture — *see* Fracture, skull, by
            site
    retinae 921.3
    spinalis — *see* Injury, spinal, by site
Commotion (current)
    brain (without skull fracture) (*see also*
        Concussion, brain) 850.9
        with skull fracture — *see* Fracture, skull, by
            site
    spinal cord — *see* Injury, spinal, by site
Communication
    abnormal — *see also* Fistula
        between
            base of aorta and pulmonary artery 745.0
            left ventricle and right atrium 745.4
            pericardial sac and pleural sac 748.8
            pulmonary artery and pulmonary vein
                747.3
        congenital, between uterus and anterior
            abdominal wall 752.3
            bladder 752.3
            intestine 752.3
            rectum 752.3
        left ventricular— right atrial 745.4
        pulmonary artery— pulmonary vein 747.3
Compensation
    broken — *see* Failure, heart
    failure — *see* Failure, heart
    neurosis, psychoneurosis 300.11
Complaint — *see also* Disease
    bowel, functional 564.9
        psychogenic 306.4
    intestine, functional 564.9
        psychogenic 306.4
    kidney (*see also* Disease, renal) 593.9
    liver 573.9
    miners' 500
Complete — *see* condition
Complex
    cardiorenal (*see also* Hypertension, cardiorenal)
        404.90
    castration 300.9
    Costen's 524.60
    ego-dystonic homosexuality 302.0
    Eisenmenger's (ventricular septal defect) 745.4
    homosexual, ego-dystonic 302.0
    hypersexual 302.89
    inferiority 301.9
    jumped process
        spine — *see* Dislocation, vertebra
    primary, tuberculosis (*see also* Tuberculosis)
        010.0 ☑
    Taussig-Bing (transposition, aorta and
        overriding pulmonary artery) 745.11
Complications
    abortion NEC — *see* categories 634-639
    accidental puncture or laceration during a
        procedure 998.2
    amputation stump (late) (surgical) 997.60
        traumatic — *see* Amputation, traumatic
    anastomosis (and bypass) — *see also*
        Complications, due to (presence of) any
        device, implant, or graft classified to
        996.0-996.5 NEC
        hemorrhage NEC 998.11
        intestinal (internal) NEC 997.4
            involving urinary tract 997.5
        mechanical — *see* Complications,
            mechanical, graft
        urinary tract (involving intestinal tract)
            997.5
    anesthesia, anesthetic NEC (*see also*
        Anesthesia, complication) 995.2
        in labor and delivery 668.9 ☑
            affecting fetus or newborn 763.5
            cardiac 668.1 ☑
            central nervous system 668.2 ☑
            pulmonary 668.0 ☑
            specified type NEC 668.8 ☑
    aortocoronary (bypass) graft 996.03
        atherosclerosis — *see* Arteriosclerosis,
            coronary
        embolism 996.72

Complications — *continued*
    aortocoronary graft — *continued*
        occlusion NEC 996.72
        thrombus 996.72
    arthroplasty ►(*see also* Complications,
        prosthetic joint)◄ 996.49   ▲
    artificial opening
        cecostomy 569.60
        colostomy 569.60
        cystostomy 997.5
        enterostomy 569.60
        esophagostomy 530.87   ▲
            infection 530.86
            mechanical 530.87
        gastrostomy 536.40
        ileostomy 569.60
        jejunostomy 569.60
        nephrostomy 997.5
        tracheostomy 519.00
        ureterostomy 997.5
        urethrostomy 997.5
    bariatric surgery 997.4
    bile duct implant (prosthetic) NEC 996.79
        infection or inflammation 996.69
        mechanical 996.59
    bleeding (intraoperative) (postoperative) 998.11
    blood vessel graft 996.1
        aortocoronary 996.03
            atherosclerosis — *see* Arteriosclerosis,
                coronary
            embolism 996.72
            occlusion NEC 996.72
            thrombus 996.72
        atherosclerosis — *see* Arteriosclerosis,
            extremities
        embolism 996.74
        occlusion NEC 996.74
        thrombus 996.74
    bone growth stimulator NEC 996.78
        infection or inflammation 996.67
    bone marrow transplant 996.85
    breast implant (prosthetic) NEC 996.79
        infection or inflammation 996.69
        mechanical 996.54
    bypass — *see also* Complications, anastomosis
        aortocoronary 996.03
            atherosclerosis — *see* Arteriosclerosis,
                coronary
            embolism 996.72
            occlusion NEC 996.72
            thrombus 996.72
        carotid artery 996.1
            atherosclerosis — *see* Arteriosclerosis,
                extremities
            embolism 996.74
            occlusion NEC 996.74
            thrombus 996.74
    cardiac (*see also* Disease, heart) 429.9
        device, implant, or graft NEC 996.72
            infection or inflammation 996.61
            long-term effect 429.4
            mechanical (*see also* Complications,
                mechanical, by type) 996.00
                valve prosthesis 996.71
                    infection or inflammation 996.61
        postoperative NEC 997.1
            long-term effect 429.4
    cardiorenal (*see also* Hypertension, cardiorenal)
        404.90
    carotid artery bypass graft 996.1
        atherosclerosis — *see* Arteriosclerosis,
            extremities
        embolism 996.74
        occlusion NEC 996.74
        thrombus 996.74
    cataract fragments in eye 998.82
    catheter device NEC — *see also* Complications,
        due to (presence of) any device, implant,
        or graft classified to 996.0-996.5 NEC
        mechanical — *see* Complications,
            mechanical, catheter
    cecostomy 569.60
    cesarean section wound 674.3 ☑
    chin implant (prosthetic) NEC 996.79
        infection or inflammation 996.69
        mechanical 996.59
    colostomy (enterostomy) 569.60
        specified type NEC 569.69

☑ Additional Digit Required — Refer to the Tabular List (Numeric Code Section) for Additional Digit Selection

Complications — *continued*

contraceptive device, intrauterine NEC 996.76
    infection 996.65
    inflammation 996.65
    mechanical 996.32
cord (umbilical) — *see* Complications, umbilical
    cord
cornea
    due to
        contact lens 371.82
coronary (artery) bypass (graft) NEC 996.03
    atherosclerosis — *see* Arteriosclerosis,
        coronary
    embolism 996.72
    infection or inflammation 996.61
    mechanical 996.03
    occlusion NEC 996.72
    specified type NEC 996.72
    thrombus 996.72
cystostomy 997.5
delivery 669.9 ☑
    procedure (instrumental) (manual) (surgical)
        669.4 ☑
    specified type NEC 669.8 ☑
dialysis (hemodialysis) (peritoneal) (renal) NEC
    999.9
    catheter NEC — *see also* Complications, due
        to (presence of) any device, implant, or
        graft classified to 996.0-996.5 NEC
        infection or inflammation 996.62
           peritoneal 996.68
        mechanical 996.1
           peritoneal 996.56
due to (presence of) any device, implant, or
    graft classified to 996.0-996.5 NEC
    996.70
    with infection or inflammation — *see*
        Complications, infection or
        inflammation, due to (presence of) any
        device, implant, or graft classified to
        996.0-996.5 NEC
    arterial NEC 996.74
        coronary NEC 996.03
           atherosclerosis — *see* Arteriosclerosis,
               coronary
           embolism 996.72
           occlusion NEC 996.72
           specified type NEC 996.72
           thrombus 996.72
        renal dialysis 996.73
    arteriovenous fistula or shunt NEC 996.74
    bone growth stimulator 996.78
    breast NEC 996.79
    cardiac NEC 996.72
        defibrillator 996.72
        pacemaker 996.72
        valve prosthesis 996.71
    catheter NEC 996.79
        spinal 996.75
        urinary, indwelling 996.76
        vascular NEC 996.74
           renal dialysis 996.73
        ventricular shunt 996.75
    coronary (artery) bypass (graft) NEC 996.03
        atherosclerosis — *see* Arteriosclerosis,
           coronary
        embolism 996.72
        occlusion NEC 996.72
        thrombus 996.72
    electrodes
        brain 996.75
        heart 996.72
    esophagostomy 530.87   ●
    gastrointestinal NEC 996.79
    genitourinary NEC 996.76
    heart valve prosthesis NEC 996.71
    infusion pump 996.74
    insulin pump 996.57
    internal
        joint prosthesis 996.77
        orthopedic NEC 996.78
        specified type NEC 996.79
    intrauterine contraceptive device NEC
        996.76
    joint prosthesis, internal NEC 996.77
    mechanical — *see* Complications,
        mechanical
    nervous system NEC 996.75

Complications — *continued*

due to (presence of) any device, implant, or
    graft classified to 996.0-996.5 —
    continued
    ocular lens NEC 996.79
    orbital NEC 996.79
    orthopedic NEC 996.78
        joint, internal 996.77
    renal dialysis 996.73
    specified type NEC 996.79
    urinary catheter, indwelling 996.76
    vascular NEC 996.74
    ventricular shunt 996.75
during dialysis NEC 999.9
ectopic or molar pregnancy NEC 639.9
electroshock therapy NEC 999.9
enterostomy 569.60
    specified type NEC 569.69
esophagostomy 530.87   ▲
    infection 530.86
    mechanical 530.87
external (fixation) device with internal
    component(s) NEC 996.78
    infection or inflammation 996.67
    mechanical 996.49   ▲
extracorporeal circulation NEC 999.9
eye implant (prosthetic) NEC 996.79
    infection or inflammation 996.69
    mechanical
        ocular lens 996.53
        orbital globe 996.59
gastrointestinal, postoperative NEC (*see also*
    Complications, surgical procedures)
    997.4
gastrostomy 536.40
    specified type NEC 536.49
genitourinary device, implant or graft NEC
    996.76
    infection or inflammation 996.65
        urinary catheter, indwelling 996.64
    mechanical (*see also* Complications,
        mechanical, by type) 996.30
        specified NEC 996.39
graft (bypass) (patch) — *see also* Complications,
    due to (presence of) any device, implant,
    or graft classified to 996.0-996.5 NEC
    bone marrow 996.85
    corneal NEC 996.79
        infection or inflammation 996.69
        rejection or reaction 996.51
    mechanical — *see* Complications,
        mechanical, graft
    organ (immune or nonimmune cause)
        (partial) (total) 996.80
        bone marrow 996.85
        heart 996.83
        intestines 996.87
        kidney 996.81
        liver 996.82
        lung 996.84
        pancreas 996.86
        specified NEC 996.89
    skin NEC 996.79
        infection or inflammation 996.69
        rejection 996.52
           artificial 996.55
           decellularized allodermis 996.55
heart — *see also* Disease, heart transplant
    (immune or nonimmune cause) 996.83
hematoma (intraoperative) (postoperative)
    998.12
hemorrhage (intraoperative) (postoperative)
    998.11
hyperalimentation therapy NEC 999.9
immunization (procedure) — *see*
    Complications, vaccination
implant — *see also* Complications, due to
    (presence of) any device, implant, or graft
    classified to 996.0-996.5 NEC
    mechanical — *see* Complications,
        mechanical, implant

Complications — *continued*

infection and inflammation
    due to (presence of) any device, implant or
        graft classified to 996.0-996.5 NEC
        996.60
        arterial NEC 996.62
           coronary 996.61
           renal dialysis 996.62
        arteriovenous fistula or shunt 996.62
        artificial heart 996.61
        bone growth stimulator 996.67
        breast 996.69
        cardiac 996.61
        catheter NEC 996.69
           peritoneal 996.68
           spinal 996.63
           urinary, indwelling 996.64
           vascular NEC 996.62
           ventricular shunt 996.63
        coronary artery bypass 996.61
        electrodes
           brain 996.63
           heart 996.61
        gastrointestinal NEC 996.69
        genitourinary NEC 996.65
           indwelling urinary catheter 996.64
        heart assist device 996.61
        heart valve 996.61
        infusion pump 996.62
        insulin pump 996.69
        intrauterine contraceptive device 996.65
        joint prosthesis, internal 996.66
        ocular lens 996.69
        orbital (implant) 996.69
        orthopedic NEC 996.67
           joint, internal 996.66
        specified type NEC 996.69
        urinary catheter, indwelling 996.64
        ventricular shunt 996.63
infusion (procedure) 999.9
    blood — *see* Complications, transfusion
    infection NEC 999.3
    sepsis NEC 999.3
inhalation therapy NEC 999.9
injection (procedure) 999.9
    drug reaction (*see also* Reaction, drug) 995.2
    infection NEC 999.3
    sepsis NEC 999.3
    serum (prophylactic) (therapeutic) — *see*
        Complications, vaccination
    vaccine (any) — *see* Complications,
        vaccination
inoculation (any) — *see* Complications,
    vaccination
insulin pump 996.57
internal device (catheter) (electronic) (fixation)
    (prosthetic) — *see also* Complications,
    due to (presence of) any device, implant,
    or graft classified to 996.0-996.5 NEC
    mechanical — *see* Complications,
        mechanical
intestinal transplant (immune or nonimmune
    cause) 996.87
intraoperative bleeding or hemorrhage 998.11
intrauterine contraceptive device (*see also*
    Complications, contraceptive device)
    996.76
    with fetal damage affecting management of
        pregnancy 655.8 ☑
    infection or inflammation 996.65
jejunostomy 569.60
kidney transplant (immune or nonimmune
    cause) 996.81
labor 669.9 ☑
    specified condition NEC 669.8 ☑
liver transplant (immune or nonimmune cause)
    996.82
lumbar puncture 349.0
mechanical
    anastomosis — *see* Complications,
        mechanical, graft
    artificial heart 996.09
    bypass — *see* Complications, mechanical,
        graft
    catheter NEC 996.59
        cardiac 996.09
        cystostomy 996.39

Complications — *continued*
  mechanical — *continued*
    catheter NEC — *continued*
      dialysis (hemodialysis) 996.1
        peritoneal 996.56
      during a procedure 998.2
      urethral, indwelling 996.31
    colostomy 569.62
    device NEC 996.59
      balloon (counterpulsation), intra-aortic 996.1
      cardiac 996.00
        automatic implantable defibrillator 996.04
        long-term effect 429.4
        specified NEC 996.09
      contraceptive, intrauterine 996.32
      counterpulsation, intra-aortic 996.1
      fixation, external, with internal components 996.49 ▲
      fixation, internal (nail, rod, plate) 996.40 ▲
      genitourinary 996.30
        specified NEC 996.39
      insulin pump 996.57
      nervous system 996.2
      orthopedic, internal 996.40 ▲
        prosthetic joint (*see also* Complications, mechanical, device, orthopedic, prosthetic, joint) 996.47 ●
      prosthetic NEC 996.59 ●
        joint (*see also* Complications, prosthetic joint) 996.47 ●
        articular bearing surface wear 996.46 ●
        aseptic loosening 996.41 ●
        breakage 996.43 ●
        dislocation 996.42 ●
        failure 996.43 ●
        fracture 996.43 ●
          around prosthetic 996.44 ●
          peri-prosthetic 996.44 ●
        instability 996.42 ●
        loosening 996.41 ●
        peri-prosthetic osteolysis 996.45 ●
        subluxation 996.42 ●
        wear 996.46 ●
      umbrella, vena cava 996.1
      vascular 996.1
    dorsal column stimulator 996.2
    electrode NEC 996.59
      brain 996.2
      cardiac 996.01
      spinal column 996.2
    enterostomy 569.62
    esophagostomy 530.87
    fistula, arteriovenous, surgically created 996.1
    gastrostomy 536.42
    graft NEC 996.52
      aortic (bifurcation) 996.1
      aortocoronary bypass 996.03
      blood vessel NEC 996.1
      bone 996.49 ▲
      cardiac 996.00
      carotid artery bypass 996.1
      cartilage 996.49 ▲
      corneal 996.51
      coronary bypass 996.03
      decellularized allodermis 996.55
      genitourinary 996.30
        specified NEC 996.39
      muscle 996.49 ▲
      nervous system 996.2
      organ (immune or nonimmune cause) 996.80
        heart 996.83
        intestines 996.87
        kidney 996.81
        liver 996.82
        lung 996.84
        pancreas 996.86
        specified NEC 996.89
      orthopedic, internal 996.49 ▲
      peripheral nerve 996.2
      prosthetic NEC 996.59

Complications — *continued*
  mechanical — *continued*
    graft NEC — *continued*
      skin 996.52
        artificial 996.55
      specified NEC 996.59
      tendon 996.49 ▲
      tissue NEC 996.52
      tooth 996.59
      ureter, without mention of resection 996.39
      vascular 996.1
    heart valve prosthesis 996.02
      long-term effect 429.4
    implant NEC 996.59
      cardiac 996.00
        automatic implantable defibrillator 996.04
        long-term effect 429.4
        specified NEC 996.09
      electrode NEC 996.59
        brain 996.2
        cardiac 996.01
        spinal column 996.2
      genitourinary 996.30
      nervous system 996.2
      orthopedic, internal 996.49 ▲
      prosthetic NEC 996.59
        in
          bile duct 996.59
          breast 996.54
          chin 996.59
          eye
            ocular lens 996.53
            orbital globe 996.59
      vascular 996.1
    insulin pump 996.57
    nonabsorbable surgical material 996.59
    pacemaker NEC 996.59
      brain 996.2
      cardiac 996.01
      nerve (phrenic) 996.2
    patch — *see* Complications, mechanical, graft
    prosthesis NEC 996.59
      bile duct 996.59
      breast 996.54
      chin 996.59
      ocular lens 996.53
      reconstruction, vas deferens 996.39
    reimplant NEC 996.59
      extremity (*see also* Complications, reattached, extremity) 996.90
      organ (*see also* Complications, transplant, organ, by site) 996.80
    repair — *see* Complications, mechanical, graft
    respirator [ventilator] V46.14 ●
    shunt NEC 996.59
      arteriovenous, surgically created 996.1
      ventricular (communicating) 996.2
    stent NEC 996.59
    tracheostomy 519.02
    vas deferens reconstruction 996.39
    ventilator [respirator] V46.14 ●
  medical care NEC 999.9
    cardiac NEC 997.1
    gastrointestinal NEC 997.4
    nervous system NEC 997.00
    peripheral vascular NEC 997.2
    respiratory NEC 997.3
    urinary NEC 997.5
    vascular
      mesenteric artery 997.71
      other vessels 997.79
      peripheral vessels 997.2
      renal artery 997.72
  nephrostomy 997.5
  nervous system
    device, implant, or graft NEC 349.1
      mechanical 996.2
    postoperative NEC 997.00
  obstetric 669.9 ☑
    procedure (instrumental) (manual) (surgical) 669.4 ☑
    specified NEC 669.8 ☑
    surgical wound 674.3 ☑

Complications — *continued*
  ocular lens implant NEC 996.79
    infection or inflammation 996.69
    mechanical 996.53
  organ transplant — *see* Complications, transplant, organ, by site
  orthopedic device, implant, or graft
    internal (fixation) (nail) (plate) (rod) NEC 996.78
      infection or inflammation 996.67
      joint prosthesis 996.77
        infection or inflammation 996.66
      mechanical 996.40 ▲
  pacemaker (cardiac) 996.72
    infection or inflammation 996.61
    mechanical 996.01
  pancreas transplant (immune or nonimmune cause) 996.86
  perfusion NEC 999.9
  perineal repair (obstetrical) 674.3 ☑
    disruption 674.2 ☑
  pessary (uterus) (vagina) — *see* Complications, contraceptive device
  phototherapy 990
  postcystoscopic 997.5
  postmastoidectomy NEC 383.30
  postoperative — *see* Complications, surgical procedures
  pregnancy NEC 646.9 ☑
    affecting fetus or newborn 761.9
  prosthetic device, internal — *see also* Complications, due to (presence of) any device, implant or graft classified to 996.0-996.5 NEC
    mechanical NEC (*see also* Complications, mechanical) 996.59
  puerperium NEC (*see also* Puerperal) 674.9 ☑
  puncture, spinal 349.0
  pyelogram 997.5
  radiation 990
  radiotherapy 990
  reattached
    body part, except extremity 996.99
    extremity (infection) (rejection) 996.90
      arm(s) 996.94
      digit(s) (hand) 996.93
        foot 996.95
      finger(s) 996.93
      foot 996.95
      forearm 996.91
      hand 996.92
      leg 996.96
      lower NEC 996.96
      toe(s) 996.95
      upper NEC 996.94
  reimplant NEC — *see also* Complications, due to (presence of) any device, implant, or graft classified to 996.0-996.5 NEC
    bone marrow 996.85
    extremity (*see also* Complications, reattached, extremity) 996.90
      due to infection 996.90
    mechanical — *see* Complications, mechanical, reimplant
    organ (immune or nonimmune cause) (partial) (total) (*see also* Complications, transplant, organ, by site) 996.80
  renal allograft 996.81
  renal dialysis — *see* Complications, dialysis
  respirator [ventilator], mechanical V46.14 ●
  respiratory 519.9
    device, implant or graft NEC 996.79
      infection or inflammation 996.69
      mechanical 996.59
    distress syndrome, adult, following trauma or surgery 518.5
    insufficiency, acute, postoperative 518.5
    postoperative NEC 997.3
    therapy NEC 999.9
  sedation during labor and delivery 668.9 ☑
    affecting fetus or newborn 763.5
    cardiac 668.1 ☑
    central nervous system 668.2 ☑
    pulmonary 668.0 ☑
    specified type NEC 668.8 ☑
  seroma (intraoperative) (postoperative) (noninfected) 998.13

☑ Additional Digit Required — Refer to the Tabular List (Numeric Code Section) for Additional Digit Selection
▶◀ Revised Text   ● New Line   ▲ Revised Code

2006 ICD-9-CM   October 2005 • Volume 2 — 65

Complications — *continued*
seroma — *continued*
infected 998.51
shunt — *see also* Complications, due to
(presence of) any device, implant, or graft
classified to 996.0-996.5 NEC
mechanical — *see* Complications,
mechanical, shunt
specified body system NEC
device, implant, or graft — *see*
Complications, due to (presence of)
any device, implant, or graft classified
to 996.0-996.5 NEC
postoperative NEC 997.99
spinal puncture or tap 349.0
stoma, external
gastrointestinal tract
colostomy 569.60
enterostomy 569.60
esophagostomy 530.87   ▲
infection 530.86
mechanical 530.87
gastrostomy 536.40
urinary tract 997.5
stomach banding 997.4
stomach stapling 997.4
surgical procedures 998.9
accidental puncture or laceration 998.2
amputation stump (late) 997.60
anastomosis — *see* Complications,
anastomosis
burst stitches or sutures (external) 998.32
internal 998.31
cardiac 997.1
long-term effect following cardiac surgery
429.4
cataract fragments in eye 998.82
catheter device — *see* Complications,
catheter device
cecostomy malfunction 569.62
colostomy malfunction 569.62
cystostomy malfunction 997.5
dehiscence (of incision) (external) 998.32
internal 998.31
dialysis NEC (*see also* Complications,
dialysis) 999.9
disruption
anastomosis (internal) — *see*
Complications, mechanical, graft
internal suture (line) 998.31
wound (external) 998.32
internal 998.31
dumping syndrome (postgastrectomy) 564.2
elephantiasis or lymphedema 997.99
postmastectomy 457.0
emphysema (surgical) 998.81
enterostomy malfunction 569.62
esophagostomy malfunction 530.87
evisceration 998.32
fistula (persistent postoperative) 998.6
foreign body inadvertently left in wound
(sponge) (suture) (swab) 998.4
from nonabsorbable surgical material
(Dacron) (mesh) (permanent suture)
(reinforcing) (Teflon) — *see*
Complications, due to (presence of)
any device, implant, or graft classified
to 996.0-996.5 NEC
gastrointestinal NEC 997.4
gastrostomy malfunction 536.42
hematoma 998.12
hemorrhage 998.11
ileostomy malfunction 569.62
internal prosthetic device NEC (*see also*
Complications, internal device) 996.70
hemolytic anemia 283.19
infection or inflammation 996.60
malfunction — *see* Complications,
mechanical
mechanical complication — *see*
Complications, mechanical
thrombus 996.70
jejunostomy malfunction 569.62
nervous system NEC 997.00
obstruction, internal anastomosis — *see*
Complications, mechanical, graft
other body system NEC 997.99

Complications — *continued*
surgical procedures — *continued*
peripheral vascular NEC 997.2
postcardiotomy syndrome 429.4
postcholecystectomy syndrome 576.0
postcommissurotomy syndrome 429.4
postgastrectomy dumping syndrome 564.2
postmastectomy lymphedema syndrome
457.0
postmastoidectomy 383.30
cholesteatoma, recurrent 383.32
cyst, mucosal 383.31
granulation 383.33
inflammation, chronic 383.33
postvagotomy syndrome 564.2
postvalvulotomy syndrome 429.4
reattached extremity (infection) (rejection)
(*see also* Complications, reattached,
extremity) 996.90
respiratory NEC 997.3
seroma 998.13
shock (endotoxic) (hypovolemic) (septic)
998.0
shunt, prosthetic (thrombus) — *see also*
Complications, due to (presence of)
any device, implant, or graft classified
to 996.0-996.5 NEC
hemolytic anemia 283.19
specified complication NEC 998.89
stitch abscess 998.59
transplant — *see* Complications, graft
ureterostomy malfunction 997.5
urethrostomy malfunction 997.5
urinary NEC 997.5
vascular
mesenteric artery 997.71
other vessels 997.79
peripheral vessels 997.2
renal artery 997.72
wound infection 998.59
therapeutic misadventure NEC 999.9
surgical treatment 998.9
tracheostomy 519.00
transfusion (blood) (lymphocytes) (plasma) NEC
999.8
atrophy, liver, yellow, subacute (within 8
months of administration) — *see*
Hepatitis, viral
bone marrow 996.85
embolism
air 999.1
thrombus 999.2
hemolysis NEC 999.8
bone marrow 996.85
hepatitis (serum) (type B) (within 8 months
after administration) — *see* Hepatitis,
viral
incompatibility reaction (ABO) (blood group)
999.6
Rh (factor) 999.7
infection 999.3
jaundice (serum) (within 8 months after
administration) — *see* Hepatitis, viral
sepsis 999.3
shock or reaction NEC 999.8
bone marrow 996.85
subacute yellow atrophy of liver (within 8
months after administration) — *see*
Hepatitis, viral
thromboembolism 999.2
transplant NEC — *see also* Complications, due
to (presence of) any device, implant, or
graft classified to 996.0-996.5 NEC
bone marrow 996.85
organ (immune or nonimmune cause)
(partial) (total) 996.80
bone marrow 996.85
heart 996.83
intestines 996.87
kidney 996.81
liver 996.82
lung 996.84
pancreas 996.86
specified NEC 996.89
trauma NEC (early) 958.8
ultrasound therapy NEC 999.9

Complications — *continued*
umbilical cord
affecting fetus or newborn 762.6
complicating delivery 663.9 ☑
affecting fetus or newborn 762.6
specified type NEC 663.8 ☑
urethral catheter NEC 996.76
infection or inflammation 996.64
mechanical 996.31
urinary, postoperative NEC 997.5
vaccination 999.9
anaphylaxis NEC 999.4
cellulitis 999.3
encephalitis or encephalomyelitis 323.5
hepatitis (serum) (type B) (within 8 months
after administration) — *see* Hepatitis,
viral
infection (general) (local) NEC 999.3
jaundice (serum) (within 8 months after
administration) — *see* Hepatitis, viral
meningitis 997.09 *[321.8]*
myelitis 323.5
protein sickness 999.5
reaction (allergic) 999.5
Herxheimer's 995.0
serum 999.5
sepsis 999.3
serum intoxication, sickness, rash, or other
serum reaction NEC 999.5
shock (allergic) (anaphylactic) 999.4
subacute yellow atrophy of liver (within 8
months after administration) — *see*
Hepatitis, viral
vaccinia (generalized) 999.0
localized 999.3
vascular
device, implant, or graft NEC 996.74
infection or inflammation 996.62
mechanical NEC 996.1
cardiac (*see also* Complications,
mechanical, by type) 996.00
following infusion, perfusion, or transfusion
996.2
postoperative NEC 997.2
mesenteric artery 997.71
other vessels 997.79
peripheral vessels 997.2
renal artery 997.72
ventilation therapy NEC 999.9
ventilator [respirator], mechanical V46.14   ●
Compound presentation, complicating delivery
652.8 ☑
causing obstructed labor 660.0 ☑
Compressed air disease 993.3
Compression
with injury — *see* specific injury
arm NEC 354.9
artery 447.1
celiac, syndrome 447.4
brachial plexus 353.0
brain (stem) 348.4
due to
contusion, brain — *see* Contusion, brain
injury NEC — *see also* Hemorrhage,
brain, traumatic
birth — *see* Birth, injury, brain
laceration, brain — *see* Laceration, brain
osteopathic 739.0
bronchus 519.1
by cicatrix — *see* Cicatrix
cardiac 423.9
cauda equina 344.60
with neurogenic bladder 344.61
celiac (artery) (axis) 447.4
cerebral — *see* Compression, brain
cervical plexus 353.2
cord (umbilical) — *see* Compression, umbilical
cord
cranial nerve 352.9
second 377.49
third (partial) 378.51
total 378.52
fourth 378.53
fifth 350.8
sixth 378.54
seventh 351.8

Compression — *continued*
  divers' squeeze 993.3
  duodenum (external) (*see also* Obstruction, duodenum) 537.3
  during birth 767.9
  esophagus 530.3
    congenital, external 750.3
  Eustachian tube 381.63
  facies (congenital) 754.0
  fracture — *see* Fracture, by site
  heart — *see* Disease, heart
  intestine (*see also* Obstruction, intestine) 560.9
    with hernia — *see* Hernia, by site, with obstruction
  laryngeal nerve, recurrent 478.79
  leg NEC 355.8
  lower extremity NEC 355.8
  lumbosacral plexus 353.1
  lung 518.89
  lymphatic vessel 457.1
  medulla — *see* Compression, brain
  nerve NEC — *see also* Disorder, nerve
    arm NEC 354.9
    autonomic nervous system (*see also* Neuropathy, peripheral, autonomic) 337.9
    axillary 353.0
    cranial NEC 352.9
    due to displacement of intervertebral disc 722.2
      with myelopathy 722.70
      cervical 722.0
        with myelopathy 722.71
        lumbar, lumbosacral 722.10
          with myelopathy 722.73
        thoracic, thoracolumbar 722.11
          with myelopathy 722.72
    iliohypogastric 355.79
    ilioinguinal 355.79
    leg NEC 355.8
    lower extremity NEC 355.8
    median (in carpal tunnel) 354.0
    obturator 355.79
    optic 377.49
    plantar 355.6
    posterior tibial (in tarsal tunnel) 355.5
    root (by scar tissue) NEC 724.9
      cervical NEC 723.4
      lumbar NEC 724.4
      lumbosacral 724.4
      thoracic 724.4
    saphenous 355.79
    sciatic (acute) 355.0
    sympathetic 337.9
    traumatic — *see* Injury, nerve
    ulnar 354.2
    upper extremity NEC 354.9
  peripheral — *see* Compression, nerve
  spinal (cord) (old or nontraumatic) 336.9
    by displacement of intervertebral disc — *see* Displacement, intervertebral disc
    nerve
      root NEC 724.9
        postoperative 722.80
          cervical region 722.81
          lumbar region 722.83
          thoracic region 722.82
        traumatic — *see* Injury, nerve, spinal
      traumatic — *see* Injury, nerve, spinal
    spondylogenic 721.91
      cervical 721.1
      lumbar, lumbosacral 721.42
      thoracic 721.41
    traumatic — *see also* Injury, spinal, by site
      with fracture, vertebra — *see* Fracture, vertebra, by site, with spinal cord injury
  spondylogenic — *see* Compression, spinal cord, spondylogenic
  subcostal nerve (syndrome) 354.8
  sympathetic nerve NEC 337.9
  syndrome 958.5
  thorax 512.8
    iatrogenic 512.1
    postoperative 512.1
  trachea 519.1
    congenital 748.3

Compression — *continued*
  ulnar nerve (by scar tissue) 354.2
  umbilical cord
    affecting fetus or newborn 762.5
      cord prolapsed 762.4
    complicating delivery 663.2 ☑
      cord around neck 663.1 ☑
      cord prolapsed 663.0 ☑
  upper extremity NEC 354.9
  ureter 593.3
  urethra — *see* Stricture, urethra
  vein 459.2
  vena cava (inferior) (superior) 459.2
  vertebral NEC — *see* Compression, spinal (cord)

Compulsion, compulsive
  eating 307.51
  neurosis (obsessive) 300.3
  personality 301.4
  states (mixed) 300.3
  swearing 300.3
    in Gilles de la Tourette's syndrome 307.23
  tics and spasms 307.22
  water drinking NEC (syndrome) 307.9

Concato's disease (pericardial polyserositis) 423.2
  peritoneal 568.82
  pleural — *see* Pleurisy

Concavity, chest wall 738.3

Concealed
  hemorrhage NEC 459.0
  penis 752.65

Concentric fading 368.12

Concern (normal) **about sick person in family** V61.49

Concrescence (teeth) 520.2

Concretio cordis 423.1
  rheumatic 393

Concretion — *see also* Calculus
  appendicular 543.9
  canaliculus 375.57
  clitoris 624.8
  conjunctiva 372.54
  eyelid 374.56
  intestine (impaction) (obstruction) 560.39
  lacrimal (passages) 375.57
  prepuce (male) 605
    female (clitoris) 624.8
  salivary gland (any) 527.5
  seminal vesicle 608.89
  stomach 537.89
  tonsil 474.8

Concussion (current) 850.9
  with
    loss of consciousness 850.5
      brief (less than one hour)
        30 minutes or less 850.11
        31-59 minutes 850.12
      moderate (1-24 hours) 850.2
      prolonged (more than 24 hours) (with complete recovery) (with return to pre-existing conscious level) 850.3
      without return to pre-existing conscious level 850.4
    mental confusion or disorientation (without loss of consciousness) 850.0
    with loss of consciousness — *see* Concussion, with, loss of consciousness
  without loss of consciousness 850.0
  blast (air) (hydraulic) (immersion) (underwater) 869.0
    with open wound into cavity 869.1
    abdomen or thorax — *see* Injury, internal, by site
    brain — *see* Concussion, brain
    ear (acoustic nerve trauma) 951.5
      with perforation, tympanic membrane — *see* Wound, open, ear drum
    thorax — *see* Injury, internal, intrathoracic organs NEC

Concussion — *continued*
  brain or cerebral (without skull fracture) 850.9
    with
      loss of consciousness 850.5
        brief (less than one hour)
          30 minutes or less 850.11
          31-59 minutes 850.12
        moderate (1-24 hours) 850.2
        prolonged (more than 24 hours) (with complete recovery) (with return to pre-existing conscious level) 850.3
        without return to pre-existing conscious level 850.4
      mental confusion or disorientation (without loss of consciousness) 850.0
      with loss of consciousness — *see* Concussion, brain, with, loss of consciousness
    skull fracture — *see* Fracture, skull, by site
    without loss of consciousness 850.0
  cauda equina 952.4
  cerebral — *see* Concussion, brain
  conus medullaris (spine) 952.4
  hydraulic — *see* Concussion, blast
  internal organs — *see* Injury, internal, by site
  labyrinth — *see* Injury, intracranial
  ocular 921.3
  osseous labyrinth — *see* Injury, intracranial
  spinal (cord) — *see also* Injury, spinal, by site
    due to
      broken
        back — *see* Fracture, vertebra, by site, with spinal cord injury
        neck — *see* Fracture, vertebra, cervical, with spinal cord injury
      fracture, fracture dislocation, or compression fracture of spine or vertebra — *see* Fracture, vertebra, by site, with spinal cord injury
  syndrome 310.2
  underwater blast — *see* Concussion, blast

Condition — *see also* Disease
  psychiatric 298.9
  respiratory NEC 519.9
    acute or subacute NEC 519.9
      due to
        external agent 508.9
          specified type NEC 508.8
        fumes or vapors (chemical) (inhalation) 506.3
        radiation 508.0
    chronic NEC 519.9
      due to
        external agent 508.9
          specified type NEC 508.8
        fumes or vapors (chemical) (inhalation) 506.4
        radiation 508.1
    due to
      external agent 508.9
        specified type NEC 508.8
      fumes or vapors (chemical) (inhalation) 506.9

Conduct disturbance (*see also* Disturbance, conduct) 312.9
  adjustment reaction 309.3
  hyperkinetic 314.2

Condyloma NEC 078.10
  acuminatum 078.11
  gonorrheal 098.0
  latum 091.3
  syphilitic 091.3
    congenital 090.0
  venereal, syphilitic 091.3

Confinement — *see* Delivery

Conflagration — *see also* Burn, by site
  asphyxia (by inhalation of smoke, gases, fumes, or vapors) 987.9
    specified agent — *see* Table of Drugs and Chemicals

Conflict
  family V61.9
    specified circumstance NEC V61.8

Conflict — *continued*
  interpersonal NEC V62.81
  marital V61.10
    involving divorce or estrangement V61.0
  parent-child V61.20
  partner V61.10
Confluent — *see* condition
Confusion, confused (mental) (state) (*see also* State, confusional) 298.9
  acute 293.0
  epileptic 293.0
  postoperative 293.9
  psychogenic 298.2
  reactive (from emotional stress, psychological trauma) 298.2
  subacute 293.1
Confusional arousals 327.41 ●
Congelation 991.9
Congenital — *see also* condition
  aortic septum 747.29
  intrinsic factor deficiency 281.0
  malformation — *see* Anomaly
Congestion, congestive (chronic) (passive)
  asphyxia, newborn 768.9
  bladder 596.8
  bowel 569.89
  brain (*see also* Disease, cerebrovascular NEC) 437.8
    malarial 084.9
  breast 611.79
  bronchi 519.1
  bronchial tube 519.1
  catarrhal 472.0
  cerebral — *see* Congestion, brain
  cerebrospinal — *see* Congestion, brain
  chest 514
  chill 780.99
    malarial (*see also* Malaria) 084.6
  circulatory NEC 459.9
  conjunctiva 372.71
  due to disturbance of circulation 459.9
  duodenum 537.3
  enteritis — *see* Enteritis
  eye 372.71
  fibrosis syndrome (pelvic) 625.5
  gastroenteritis — *see* Enteritis
  general 799.89
  glottis 476.0
  heart (*see also* Failure, heart) 428.0
  hepatic 573.0
  hypostatic (lung) 514
  intestine 569.89
  intracranial — *see* Congestion, brain
  kidney 593.89
  labyrinth 386.50
  larynx 476.0
  liver 573.0
  lung 514
    active or acute (*see also* Pneumonia) 486
      congenital 770.0
    chronic 514
    hypostatic 514
    idiopathic, acute 518.5
    passive 514
  malaria, malarial (brain) (fever) (*see also* Malaria) 084.6
  medulla — *see* Congestion, brain
  nasal 478.1
  orbit, orbital 376.33
    inflammatory (chronic) 376.10
      acute 376.00
  ovary 620.8
  pancreas 577.8
  pelvic, female 625.5
  pleural 511.0
  prostate (active) 602.1
  pulmonary — *see* Congestion, lung
  renal 593.89
  retina 362.89
  seminal vesicle 608.89
  spinal cord 336.1
  spleen 289.51
    chronic 289.51
  stomach 537.89
  trachea 464.11
  urethra 599.84

Congestion, congestive — *continued*
  uterus 625.5
    with subinvolution 621.1
  viscera 799.89
Congestive — *see* Congestion
Conical
  cervix 622.6
  cornea 371.60
  teeth 520.2
Conjoined twins 759.4
  causing disproportion (fetopelvic) 653.7 ✓
Conjugal maladjustment V61.10
  involving divorce or estrangement V61.0
Conjunctiva — *see* condition
Conjunctivitis (exposure) (infectious) (nondiphtheritic) (pneumococcal) (pustular) (staphylococcal) (streptococcal) NEC 372.30
  actinic 370.24
  acute 372.00
    atopic 372.05
    contagious 372.03
    follicular 372.02
    hemorrhagic (viral) 077.4
  adenoviral (acute) 077.3
  allergic (chronic) 372.14
    with hay fever 372.05
  anaphylactic 372.05
  angular 372.03
  Apollo (viral) 077.4
  atopic 372.05
  blennorrhagic (neonatorum) 098.40
  catarrhal 372.03
  chemical 372.01   ▲
    allergic 372.05   ●
    meaning corrosion — *see* Burn,   ●
      conjunctiva   ●
  chlamydial 077.98
    due to
      Chlamydia trachomatis — *see* Trachoma
      paratrachoma 077.0
  chronic 372.10
    allergic 372.14
    follicular 372.12
    simple 372.11
    specified type NEC 372.14
    vernal 372.13
  diphtheritic 032.81
  due to
    dust 372.05
    enterovirus type 70 077.4
    erythema multiforme 695.1 [372.33]
    filariasis (*see also* Filariasis) 125.9 [372.15]
    mucocutaneous
      disease NEC 372.33
      leishmaniasis 085.5 [372.15]
    Reiter's disease 099.3 [372.33]
    syphilis 095.8 [372.10]
    toxoplasmosis (acquired) 130.1
      congenital (active) 771.2
    trachoma — *see* Trachoma
  dust 372.05
  eczematous 370.31
  epidemic 077.1
    hemorrhagic 077.4
  follicular (acute) 372.02
    adenoviral (acute) 077.3
    chronic 372.12
  glare 370.24
  gonococcal (neonatorum) 098.40
  granular (trachomatous) 076.1
    late effect 139.1
  hemorrhagic (acute) (epidemic) 077.4
  herpetic (simplex) 054.43
    zoster 053.21
  inclusion 077.0
  infantile 771.6
  influenzal 372.03
  Koch-Weeks 372.03
  light 372.05
  medicamentosa 372.05
  membranous 372.04
  meningococcic 036.89
  Morax-Axenfeld 372.02
  mucopurulent NEC 372.03
  neonatal 771.6
    gonococcal 098.40

Conjunctivitis — *continued*
  Newcastle's 077.8
  nodosa 360.14
  of Beal 077.3
  parasitic 372.15
    filariasis (*see also* Filariasis) 125.9 [372.15]
    mucocutaneous leishmaniasis 085.5 [372.15]
  Parinaud's 372.02
  petrificans 372.39
  phlyctenular 370.31
  pseudomembranous 372.04
    diphtheritic 032.81
  purulent 372.03
  Reiter's 099.3 [372.33]
  rosacea 695.3 [372.31]
  serous 372.01
    viral 077.99
  simple chronic 372.11
  specified NEC 372.39
  sunlamp 372.04
  swimming pool 077.0
  trachomatous (follicular) 076.1
    acute 076.0
    late effect 139.1
  traumatic NEC 372.39
  tuberculous (*see also* Tuberculosis) 017.3 ✓ [370.31]
  tularemic 021.3
  tularensis 021.3
  vernal 372.13
    limbar 372.13 [370.32]
  viral 077.99
    acute hemorrhagic 077.4
    specified NEC 077.8
Conjunctivochalasis 372.81
Conjunctoblepharitis — *see* Conjunctivitis
Conn (-Louis) syndrome (primary aldosteronism) 255.12
Connective tissue — *see* condition
Conradi (-Hünermann) syndrome or disease (chondrodysplasia calcificans congenita) 756.59
Consanguinity V19.7
Consecutive — *see* condition
Consolidated lung (base) — *see* Pneumonia, lobar
Constipation 564.00
  atonic 564.09
  drug induced
    correct substance properly administered 564.09
    overdose or wrong substance given or taken 977.9
      specified drug — *see* Table of Drugs and Chemicals
  neurogenic 564.09
  other specified NEC 564.09
  outlet dysfunction 564.02
  psychogenic 306.4
  simple 564.00
  slow transit 564.01
  spastic 564.09
Constitutional — *see also* condition
  arterial hypotension (*see also* Hypotension) 458.9
  obesity 278.00
    morbid 278.01
  psychopathic state 301.9
  short stature in childhood 783.43
  state, developmental V21.9
    specified development NEC V21.8
  substandard 301.6
Constitutionally substandard 301.6
Constriction
  anomalous, meningeal bands or folds 742.8
  aortic arch (congenital) 747.10
  asphyxiation or suffocation by 994.7
  bronchus 519.1
  canal, ear (*see also* Stricture, ear canal, acquired) 380.50
  duodenum 537.3
  gallbladder (*see also* Obstruction, gallbladder) 575.2
    congenital 751.69

Constriction — *continued*
  intestine (*see also* Obstruction, intestine) 560.9
  larynx 478.74
    congenital 748.3
  meningeal bands or folds, anomalous 742.8
  organ or site, congenital NEC — *see* Atresia
  prepuce (congenital) 605
  pylorus 537.0
    adult hypertrophic 537.0
    congenital or infantile 750.5
    newborn 750.5
  ring (uterus) 661.4 ☑
    affecting fetus or newborn 763.7
  spastic — *see also* Spasm
    ureter 593.3
    urethra — *see* Stricture, urethra
  stomach 537.89
  ureter 593.3
  urethra — *see* Stricture, urethra
  visual field (functional) (peripheral) 368.45
Constrictive — *see* condition
Consultation
  medical — *see also* Counseling, medical
  specified reason NEC V65.8
  without complaint or sickness V65.9
    feared complaint unfounded V65.5
    specified reason NEC V65.8
Consumption — *see* Tuberculosis
Contact
  with
    AIDS virus V01.79
    anthrax V01.81
    cholera V01.0
    communicable disease V01.9
      specified type NEC V01.89
      viral NEC V01.79
    Escherichia coli (E. coli) V01.83
    German measles V01.4
    gonorrhea V01.6
    HIV V01.79
    human immunodeficiency virus V01.79
    meningococcus V01.84
    parasitic disease NEC V01.89
    poliomyelitis V01.2
    rabies V01.5
    rubella V01.4
    SARS-associated coronavirus V01.82
    smallpox V01.3
    syphilis V01.6
    tuberculosis V01.1
    varicella V01.71
    venereal disease V01.6
    viral disease NEC V01.79
  dermatitis — *see* Dermatitis
Contamination, food (*see also* Poisoning, food) 005.9
Contraception, contraceptive
  advice NEC V25.09
    family planning V25.09
    fitting of diaphragm V25.02
    prescribing or use of
      oral contraceptive agent V25.01
      specified agent NEC V25.02
  counseling NEC V25.09
    emergency V25.03
    family planning V25.09
    fitting of diaphragm V25.02
    prescribing or use of
      oral contraceptive agent V25.01
        emergency V25.03
        postcoital V25.03
      specified agent NEC V25.02
  device (in situ) V45.59
    causing menorrhagia 996.76
    checking V25.42
    complications 996.32
    insertion V25.1
    intrauterine V45.51
    reinsertion V25.42
    removal V25.42
    subdermal V45.52
  fitting of diaphragm V25.02
  insertion
    intrauterine contraceptive device V25.1
    subdermal implantable V25.5

Contraception, contraceptive — *continued*
  maintenance V25.40
    examination V25.40
      subdermal implantable V25.43
        intrauterine device V25.42
      oral contraceptive V25.41
      specified method NEC V25.49
    intrauterine device V25.42
    oral contraceptive V25.41
    specified method NEC V25.49
    subdermal implantable V25.43
  management NEC V25.49
  prescription
    oral contraceptive agent V25.01
      emergency V25.03
      postcoital V25.03
      repeat V25.41
    specified agent NEC V25.02
      repeat V25.49
  sterilization V25.2
  surveillance V25.40
    intrauterine device V25.42
    oral contraceptive agent V25.41
      subdermal implantable V25.43
    specified method NEC V25.49
Contraction, contracture, contracted
  Achilles tendon (*see also* Short, tendon, Achilles) 727.81
  anus 564.89
  axilla 729.9
  bile duct (*see also* Disease, biliary) 576.8
  bladder 596.8
    neck or sphincter 596.0
  bowel (*see also* Obstruction, intestine) 560.9
  Braxton Hicks 644.1 ☑
  bronchus 519.1
  burn (old) — *see* Cicatrix
  cecum (*see also* Obstruction, intestine) 560.9
  cervix (*see also* Stricture, cervix) 622.4
    congenital 752.49
  cicatricial — *see* Cicatrix
  colon (*see also* Obstruction, intestine) 560.9
  conjunctiva trachomatous, active 076.1
    late effect 139.1
  Dupuytren's 728.6
  eyelid 374.41
  eye socket (after enucleation) 372.64
  face 729.9
  fascia (lata) (postural) 728.89
    Dupuytren's 728.6
    palmar 728.6
    plantar 728.71
  finger NEC 736.29
    congenital 755.59
    joint (*see also* Contraction, joint) 718.44
  flaccid, paralytic
    joint (*see also* Contraction, joint) 718.4 ☑
    muscle 728.85
    ocular 378.50
  gallbladder (*see also* Obstruction, gallbladder) 575.2
  hamstring 728.89
    tendon 727.81
  heart valve — *see* Endocarditis
  Hicks' 644.1 ☑
  hip (*see also* Contraction, joint) 718.4 ☑
  hourglass
    bladder 596.8
      congenital 753.8
    gallbladder (*see also* Obstruction, gallbladder) 575.2
      congenital 751.69
    stomach 536.8
      congenital 750.7
      psychogenic 306.4
    uterus 661.4 ☑
      affecting fetus or newborn 763.7
  hysterical 300.11
  infantile (*see also* Epilepsy) 345.6 ☑
  internal os (*see also* Stricture, cervix) 622.4
  intestine (*see also* Obstruction, intestine) 560.9
  joint (abduction) (acquired) (adduction) (flexion) (rotation) 718.40
    ankle 718.47

Contraction, contracture, contracted — *continued*
  joint — *continued*
    congenital NEC 755.8
      generalized or multiple 754.89
        lower limb joints 754.89
      hip (*see also* Subluxation, congenital, hip) 754.32
      lower limb (including pelvic girdle) not involving hip 754.89
      upper limb (including shoulder girdle) 755.59
    elbow 718.42
    foot 718.47
    hand 718.44
    hip 718.45
    hysterical 300.11
    knee 718.46
    multiple sites 718.49
    pelvic region 718.45
    shoulder (region) 718.41
    specified site NEC 718.48
    wrist 718.43
  kidney (granular) (secondary) (*see also* Sclerosis, renal) 587
    congenital 753.3
    hydronephritic 591
    pyelonephritic (*see also* Pyelitis, chronic) 590.00
    tuberculous (*see also* Tuberculosis) 016.0 ☑
  ligament 728.89
    congenital 756.89
  liver — *see* Cirrhosis, liver
  muscle (postinfectional) (postural) NEC 728.85
    congenital 756.89
      sternocleidomastoid 754.1
    extraocular 378.60
    eye (extrinsic) (*see also* Strabismus) 378.9
      paralytic (*see also* Strabismus, paralytic) 378.50
    flaccid 728.85
    hysterical 300.11
    ischemic (Volkmann's) 958.6
    paralytic 728.85
    posttraumatic 958.6
    psychogenic 306.0
      specified as conversion reaction 300.11
  myotonic 728.85
  neck (*see also* Torticollis) 723.5
    congenital 754.1
    psychogenic 306.0
  ocular muscle (*see also* Strabismus) 378.9
    paralytic (*see also* Strabismus, paralytic) 378.50
  organ or site, congenital NEC — *see* Atresia
  outlet (pelvis) — *see* Contraction, pelvis
  palmar fascia 728.6
  paralytic
    joint (*see also* Contraction, joint) 718.4 ☑
    muscle 728.85
      ocular (*see also* Strabismus, paralytic) 378.50
  pelvis (acquired) (general) 738.6
    affecting fetus or newborn 763.1
    complicating delivery 653.1 ☑
      causing obstructed labor 660.1 ☑
      generally contracted 653.1 ☑
        causing obstructed labor 660.1 ☑
      inlet 653.2 ☑
        causing obstructed labor 660.1 ☑
      midpelvic 653.8 ☑
        causing obstructed labor 660.1 ☑
      midplane 653.8 ☑
        causing obstructed labor 660.1 ☑
      outlet 653.3 ☑
        causing obstructed labor 660.1 ☑
  plantar fascia 728.71
  premature
    atrial 427.61
    auricular 427.61
    auriculoventricular 427.61
    heart (junctional) (nodal) 427.60
    supraventricular 427.61
    ventricular 427.69
  prostate 602.8
  pylorus (*see also* Pylorospasm) 537.81

2006 ICD-9-CM

☑ Additional Digit Required — Refer to the Tabular List (Numeric Code Section) for Additional Digit Selection
▶◀ Revised Text   ● New Line   ▲ Revised Code

Volume 2 — 69

Contraction, contracture, contracted —
  continued
  rectosigmoid (*see also* Obstruction, intestine)
    560.9
  rectum, rectal (sphincter) 564.89
    psychogenic 306.4
  ring (Bandl's) 661.4 ☑
    affecting fetus or newborn 763.7
  scar — *see* Cicatrix
  sigmoid (*see also* Obstruction, intestine) 560.9
  socket, eye 372.64
  spine (*see also* Curvature, spine) 737.9
  stomach 536.8
    hourglass 536.8
      congenital 750.7
    psychogenic 306.4
  tendon (sheath) (*see also* Short, tendon) 727.81
  toe 735.8
  ureterovesical orifice (postinfectional) 593.3
  urethra 599.84
  uterus 621.8
    abnormal 661.9 ☑
      affecting fetus or newborn 763.7
    clonic, hourglass or tetanic 661.4 ☑
      affecting fetus or newborn 763.7
    dyscoordinate 661.4 ☑
      affecting fetus or newborn 763.7
    hourglass 661.4 ☑
      affecting fetus or newborn 763.7
    hypotonic NEC 661.2 ☑
      affecting fetus or newborn 763.7
    incoordinate 661.4 ☑
      affecting fetus or newborn 763.7
    inefficient or poor 661.2 ☑
      affecting fetus or newborn 763.7
    irregular 661.2 ☑
      affecting fetus or newborn 763.7
    tetanic 661.4 ☑
      affecting fetus or newborn 763.7
  vagina (outlet) 623.2
  vesical 596.8
    neck or urethral orifice 596.0
  visual field, generalized 368.45
  Volkmann's (ischemic) 958.6

Contusion (skin surface intact) 924.9
  with
    crush injury — *see* Crush
    dislocation — *see* Dislocation, by site
    fracture — *see* Fracture, by site
    internal injury — *see also* Injury, internal,
      by site
      heart — *see* Contusion, cardiac
      kidney — *see* Contusion, kidney
      liver — *see* Contusion, liver
      lung — *see* Contusion, lung
      spleen — *see* Contusion, spleen
    intracranial injury — *see* Injury, intracranial
    nerve injury — *see* Injury, nerve
    open wound — *see* Wound, open, by site
  abdomen, abdominal (muscle) (wall) 922.2
    organ(s) NEC 868.00
  adnexa, eye NEC 921.9
  ankle 924.21
    with other parts of foot 924.20
  arm 923.9
    lower (with elbow) 923.10
    upper 923.03
      with shoulder or axillary region 923.09
  auditory canal (external) (meatus) (and other
    part(s) of neck, scalp, or face, except eye)
    920
  auricle, ear (and other part(s) of neck, scalp, or
    face except eye) 920
  axilla 923.02
    with shoulder or upper arm 923.09
  back 922.31
  bone NEC 924.9
  brain (cerebral) (membrane) (with hemorrhage)
    851.8 ☑

Contusion — *continued*
  brain — *continued*

> *Note* — *Use the following fifth-digit
> subclassification with categories 851-854:*
>
> 0 *unspecified state of consciousness*
> 1 *with no loss of consciousness*
> 2 *with brief [less than one hour] loss of
>   consciousness*
> 3 *with moderate [1-24 hours] loss of
>   consciousness*
> 4 *with prolonged [more than 24 hours] loss
>   of consciousness and return to pre-
>   existing conscious level*
> 5 *with prolonged [more than 24 hours] loss
>   of consciousness, without return to pre-
>   existing conscious level*
>   *Use fifth-digit 5 to designate when a patient
>   is unconscious and dies before regaining
>   consciousness, regardless of the duration
>   of the loss of consciousness*
> 6 *with loss of consciousness of unspecified
>   duration*
> 9 *with concussion, unspecified*

    with
      open intracranial wound 851.9 ☑
      skull fracture — *see* Fracture, skull, by
        site
    cerebellum 851.4 ☑
      with open intracranial wound 851.5 ☑
    cortex 851.0 ☑
      with open intracranial wound 851.1 ☑
    occipital lobe 851.4 ☑
      with open intracranial wound 851.5 ☑
    stem 851.4 ☑
      with open intracranial wound 851.5 ☑
  breast 922.0
  brow (and other part(s) of neck, scalp, or face,
    except eye) 920
  buttock 922.32
  canthus 921.1
  cardiac 861.01
    with open wound into thorax 861.11
  cauda equina (spine) 952.4
  cerebellum — *see* Contusion, brain, cerebellum
  cerebral — *see* Contusion, brain
  cheek(s) (and other part(s) of neck, scalp, or
    face, except eye) 920
  chest (wall) 922.1
  chin (and other part(s) of neck, scalp, or face,
    except eye) 920
  clitoris 922.4
  conjunctiva 921.1
  conus medullaris (spine) 952.4
  cornea 921.3
  corpus cavernosum 922.4
  cortex (brain) (cerebral) — *see* Contusion,
    brain, cortex
  costal region 922.1
  ear (and other part(s) of neck, scalp, or face,
    except eye) 920
  elbow 923.11
    with forearm 923.10
  epididymis 922.4
  epigastric region 922.2
  eye NEC 921.9
  eyeball 921.3
  eyelid(s) (and periocular area) 921.1
  face (and neck, or scalp, any part, except eye)
    920
  femoral triangle 922.2
  fetus or newborn 772.6
  finger(s) (nail) (subungual) 923.3
  flank 922.2
  foot (with ankle) (excluding toe(s)) 924.20
  forearm (and elbow) 923.10
  forehead (and other part(s) of neck, scalp, or
    face, except eye) 920
  genital organs, external 922.4
  globe (eye) 921.3
  groin 922.2
  gum(s) (and other part(s) of neck, scalp, or face,
    except eye) 920
  hand(s) (except fingers alone) 923.20
  head (any part, except eye) (and face) (and
    neck) 920

Contusion — *continued*
  heart — *see* Contusion, cardiac
  heel 924.20
  hip 924.01
    with thigh 924.00
  iliac region 922.2
  inguinal region 922.2
  internal organs (abdomen, chest, or pelvis) NEC
    — *see* Injury, internal, by site
  interscapular region 922.33
  iris (eye) 921.3
  kidney 866.01
    with open wound into cavity 866.11
  knee 924.11
    with lower leg 924.10
  labium (majus) (minus) 922.4
  lacrimal apparatus, gland, or sac 921.1
  larynx (and other part(s) of neck, scalp, or face,
    except eye) 920
  late effect — *see* Late, effects (of), contusion
  leg 924.5
    lower (with knee) 924.10
  lens 921.3
  lingual (and other part(s) of neck, scalp, or
    face, except eye) 920
  lip(s) (and other part(s) of neck, scalp, or face,
    except eye) 920
  liver 864.01
    with
      laceration — *see* Laceration, liver
      open wound into cavity 864.11
  lower extremity 924.5
    multiple sites 924.4
  lumbar region 922.31
  lung 861.21
    with open wound into thorax 861.31
  malar region (and other part(s) of neck, scalp,
    or face, except eye) 920
  mandibular joint (and other part(s) of neck,
    scalp, or face, except eye) 920
  mastoid region (and other part(s) of neck,
    scalp, or face, except eye) 920
  membrane, brain — *see* Contusion, brain
  midthoracic region 922.1
  mouth (and other part(s) of neck, scalp, or face,
    except eye) 920
  multiple sites (not classifiable to same three-
    digit category) 924.8
    lower limb 924.4
    trunk 922.8
    upper limb 923.8
  muscle NEC 924.9
  myocardium — *see* Contusion, cardiac
  nasal (septum) (and other part(s) of neck, scalp,
    or face, except eye) 920
  neck (and scalp, or face, any part, except eye)
    920
  nerve — *see* Injury, nerve, by site
  nose (and other part(s) of neck, scalp, or face,
    except eye) 920
  occipital region (scalp) (and neck or face, except
    eye) 920
    lobe — *see* Contusion, brain, occipital lobe
  orbit (region) (tissues) 921.2
  palate (soft) (and other part(s) of neck, scalp, or
    face, except eye) 920
  parietal region (scalp) (and neck, or face, except
    eye) 920
    lobe — *see* Contusion, brain
  penis 922.4
  pericardium — *see* Contusion, cardiac
  perineum 922.4
  periocular area 921.1
  pharynx (and other part(s) of neck, scalp, or
    face, except eye) 920
  popliteal space (*see also* Contusion, knee)
    924.11
  prepuce 922.4
  pubic region 922.4
  pudenda 922.4
  pulmonary — *see* Contusion, lung
  quadriceps femoralis 924.00
  rib cage 922.1
  sacral region 922.32
  salivary ducts or glands (and other part(s) of
    neck, scalp, or face, except eye) 920

☑ Additional Digit Required — Refer to the Tabular List (Numeric Code Section) for Additional Digit Selection

Contusion — *continued*
scalp (and neck, or face any part, except eye) 920
scapular region 923.01
with shoulder or upper arm 923.09
sclera (eye) 921.3
scrotum 922.4
shoulder 923.00
with upper arm or axillar regions 923.09
skin NEC 924.9
skull 920
spermatic cord 922.4
spinal cord — *see also* Injury, spinal, by site
cauda equina 952.4
conus medullaris 952.4
spleen 865.01
with open wound into cavity 865.11
sternal region 922.1
stomach — *see* Injury, internal, stomach
subconjunctival 921.1
subcutaneous NEC 924.9
submaxillary region (and other part(s) of neck, scalp, or face, except eye) 920
submental region (and other part(s) of neck, scalp, or face, except eye) 920
subperiosteal NEC 924.9
supraclavicular fossa (and other part(s) of neck, scalp, or face, except eye) 920
supraorbital (and other part(s) of neck, scalp, or face, except eye) 920
temple (region) (and other part(s) of neck, scalp, or face, except eye) 920
testis 922.4
thigh (and hip) 924.00
thorax 922.1
organ — *see* Injury, internal, intrathoracic
throat (and other part(s) of neck, scalp, or face, except eye) 920
thumb(s) (nail) (subungual) 923.3
toe(s) (nail) (subungual) 924.3
tongue (and other part(s) of neck, scalp, or face, except eye) 920
trunk 922.9
multiple sites 922.8
specified site — *see* Contusion, by site
tunica vaginalis 922.4
tympanum (membrane) (and other part(s) of neck, scalp, or face, except eye) 920
upper extremity 923.9
multiple sites 923.8
uvula (and other part(s) of neck, scalp, or face, except eye) 920
vagina 922.4
vocal cord(s) (and other part(s) of neck, scalp, or face, except eye) 920
vulva 922.4
wrist 923.21
with hand(s), except finger(s) alone 923.20
Conus (any type) (congenital) 743.57
acquired 371.60
medullaris syndrome 336.8
Convalescence (following) V66.9
chemotherapy V66.2
medical NEC V66.5
psychotherapy V66.3
radiotherapy V66.1
surgery NEC V66.0
treatment (for) NEC V66.5
combined V66.6
fracture V66.4
mental disorder NEC V66.3
specified disorder NEC V66.5
Conversion
closed surgical procedure to open procedure
arthroscopic V64.43
laparoscopic V64.41
thoracoscopic V64.42
hysteria, hysterical, any type 300.11
neurosis, any 300.11
reaction, any 300.11
Converter, tuberculosis (test reaction) 795.5
Convulsions (idiopathic) 780.39
apoplectiform (*see also* Disease, cerebrovascular, acute) 436
brain 780.39
cerebral 780.39

Convulsions — *continued*
cerebrospinal 780.39
due to trauma NEC — *see* Injury, intracranial
eclamptic (*see also* Eclampsia) 780.39
epileptic (*see also* Epilepsy) 345.9 ☑
epileptiform (*see also* Seizure, epileptiform) 780.39
epileptoid (*see also* Seizure, epileptiform) 780.39
ether
anesthetic
correct substance properly administered 780.39
overdose or wrong substance given 968.2
other specified type — *see* Table of Drugs and Chemicals
febrile 780.31
generalized 780.39
hysterical 300.11
infantile 780.39
epilepsy — *see* Epilepsy
internal 780.39
jacksonian (*see also* Epilepsy) 345.5 ☑
myoclonic 333.2
newborn 779.0
paretic 094.1
pregnancy (nephritic) (uremic) — *see* Eclampsia, pregnancy
psychomotor (*see also* Epilepsy) 345.4 ☑
puerperal, postpartum — *see* Eclampsia, pregnancy
recurrent 780.39
epileptic — *see* Epilepsy
reflex 781.0
repetitive 780.39
epileptic — *see* Epilepsy
salaam (*see also* Epilepsy) 345.6 ☑
scarlatinal 034.1
spasmodic 780.39
tetanus, tetanic (*see also* Tetanus) 037
thymic 254.8
uncinate 780.39
uremic 586
Convulsive — *see also* Convulsions
disorder or state 780.39
epileptic — *see* Epilepsy
equivalent, abdominal (*see also* Epilepsy) 345.5 ☑
Cooke-Apert-Gallais syndrome (adrenogenital) 255.2
Cooley's anemia (erythroblastic) 282.49
Coolie itch 126.9
Cooper's
disease 610.1
hernia — *see* Hernia, Cooper's
Coordination disturbance 781.3
Copper wire arteries, retina 362.13
Copra itch 133.8
Coprolith 560.39
Coprophilia 302.89
Coproporphyria, hereditary 277.1
Coprostasis 560.39
with hernia — *see also* Hernia, by site, with obstruction
gangrenous — *see* Hernia, by site, with gangrene
Cor
biloculare 745.7
bovinum — *see* Hypertrophy, cardiac
bovis — *see also* Hypertrophy, cardiac
pulmonale (chronic) 416.9
acute 415.0
triatriatum, triatrium 746.82
triloculare 745.8
biatriatum 745.3
biventriculare 745.69
Corbus' disease 607.1
Cord — *see also* condition
around neck (tightly) (with compression)
affecting fetus or newborn 762.5
complicating delivery 663.1 ☑
without compression 663.3 ☑
affecting fetus or newborn 762.6

Cord — *see also* condition — *continued*
bladder NEC 344.61
tabetic 094.0
prolapse
affecting fetus or newborn 762.4
complicating delivery 663.0 ☑
Cord's angiopathy (*see also* Tuberculosis) 017.3 ☑ *[362.18]*
Cordis ectopia 746.87
Corditis (spermatic) 608.4
Corectopia 743.46
Cori type glycogen storage disease — *see* Disease, glycogen storage
Cork-handlers' disease or lung 495.3
Corkscrew esophagus 530.5
Corlett's pyosis (impetigo) 684
Corn (infected) 700
Cornea — *see also* condition
donor V59.5
guttata (dystrophy) 371.57
plana 743.41
Cornelia de Lange's syndrome (Amsterdam dwarf, mental retardation, and brachycephaly) 759.89
Cornual gestation or pregnancy — *see* Pregnancy, cornual
Cornu cutaneum 702.8
Coronary (artery) — *see also* condition
arising from aorta or pulmonary trunk 746.85
Corpora — *see also* condition
amylacea (prostate) 602.8
cavernosa — *see* condition
Corpulence — *see* Obesity
Corpus — *see* condition
Corrigan's disease — *see* Insufficiency, aortic
Corrosive burn — *see* Burn, by site
Corsican fever (*see also* Malaria) 084.6
Cortical — *see also* condition
blindness 377.75
necrosis, kidney (bilateral) 583.6
Corticoadrenal — *see* condition
Corticosexual syndrome 255.2
Coryza (acute) 460
with grippe or influenza 487.1
syphilitic 095.8
congenital (chronic) 090.0
Costen's syndrome or complex 524.60
Costiveness (*see also* Constipation) 564.00
Costochondritis 733.6
Cotard's syndrome (paranoia) 297.1
Cot death 798.0
Cotungo's disease 724.3
Cough 786.2
with hemorrhage (*see also* Hemoptysis) 786.3
affected 786.2
bronchial 786.2
with grippe or influenza 487.1
chronic 786.2
epidemic 786.2
functional 306.1
hemorrhagic 786.3
hysterical 300.11
laryngeal, spasmodic 786.2
nervous 786.2
psychogenic 306.1
smokers' 491.0
tea tasters' 112.89
Counseling NEC V65.40
without complaint or sickness V65.49
abuse victim NEC V62.89
child V61.21
partner V61.11
spouse V61.11
child abuse, maltreatment, or neglect V61.21
contraceptive NEC V25.09
device (intrauterine) V25.02
maintenance V25.40
intrauterine contraceptive device V25.42
oral contraceptive (pill) V25.41
specified type NEC V25.49
subdermal implantable V25.43

☑ Additional Digit Required — Refer to the Tabular List (Numeric Code Section) for Additional Digit Selection
▶◀ Revised Text   ● New Line   ▲ Revised Code

2006 ICD-9-CM   Volume 2 — 71

Counseling NEC — *continued*
  contraceptive NEC — *continued*
    management NEC V25.9
    oral contraceptive (pill) V25.01
      emergency V25.03
      postcoital V25.03
    prescription NEC V25.02
      oral contraceptive (pill) V25.01
        emergency V25.03
        postcoital V25.03
        repeat prescription V25.41
      repeat prescription V25.40
    subdermal implantable V25.43
    surveillance NEC V25.40
  dietary V65.3
  exercise V65.41
  expectant mother, pediatric pre-birth visit
    V65.11
  explanation of
    investigation finding NEC V65.49
    medication NEC V65.49
  family planning V25.09
  for nonattending third party V65.19
  genetic V26.33   ▲
  gonorrhea V65.45
  health (advice) (education) (instruction) NEC
    V65.49
  HIV V65.44
  human immunodeficiency virus V65.44
  injury prevention V65.43
  insulin pump training V65.46
  marital V61.10
  medical (for) V65.9
    boarding school resident V60.6
    condition not demonstrated V65.5
    feared complaint and no disease found
      V65.5
    institutional resident V60.6
    on behalf of another V65.19
    person living alone V60.3
  parent-child conflict V61.20
    specified problem NEC V61.29
  partner abuse
    perpetrator V61.12
    victim V61.11
  pediatric pre-birth visit for expectant mother
    V65.11
  perpetrator of
    child abuse V62.83
      parental V61.22
    partner abuse V61.12
    spouse abuse V61.12
  procreative V65.49
  sex NEC V65.49
    transmitted disease NEC V65.45
      HIV V65.44
  specified reason NEC V65.49
  spousal abuse
    perpetrator V61.12
    victim V61.11
  substance use and abuse V65.42
  syphilis V65.45
  victim (of)
    abuse NEC V62.89
    child abuse V61.21
    partner abuse V61.11
    spousal abuse V61.11

Coupled rhythm 427.89

Couvelaire uterus (complicating delivery) — *see*
  Placenta, separation

Cowper's gland — *see* condition

Cowperitis (*see also* Urethritis) 597.89
  gonorrheal (acute) 098.0
    chronic or duration of 2 months or over
      098.2

Cowpox (abortive) 051.0
  due to vaccination 999.0
  eyelid 051.0 *[373.5]*
    postvaccination 999.0 *[373.5]*

Coxa
  plana 732.1
  valga (acquired) 736.31
    congenital 755.61
    late effect of rickets 268.1
  vara (acquired) 736.32
    congenital 755.62
    late effect of rickets 268.1

Coxae malum senilis 715.25

Coxalgia (nontuberculous) 719.45
  tuberculous (*see also* Tuberculosis) 015.1 ☑
    [730.85]

Coxalgic pelvis 736.30

Coxitis 716.65

Coxsackie (infection) (virus) 079.2
  central nervous system NEC 048
  endocarditis 074.22
  enteritis 008.67
  meningitis (aseptic) 047.0
  myocarditis 074.23
  pericarditis 074.21
  pharyngitis 074.0
  pleurodynia 074.1
  specific disease NEC 074.8

Crabs, meaning pubic lice 132.2

Crack baby 760.75

Cracked nipple 611.2
  puerperal, postpartum 676.1 ☑

Cradle cap 690.11

Craft neurosis 300.89

Craigiasis 007.8

Cramp(s) 729.82
  abdominal 789.0 ☑
  bathing 994.1
  colic 789.0 ☑
    psychogenic 306.4
  due to immersion 994.1
  extremity (lower) (upper) NEC 729.82
  fireman 992.2
  heat 992.2
  hysterical 300.11
  immersion 994.1
  intestinal 789.0 ☑
    psychogenic 306.4
  linotypist's 300.89
    organic 333.84
  muscle (extremity) (general) 729.82
    due to immersion 994.1
    hysterical 300.11
  occupational (hand) 300.89
    organic 333.84
  psychogenic 307.89
  salt depletion 276.1
  sleep related, leg 327.52
  stoker 992.2
  stomach 789.0 ☑
  telegraphers' 300.89
    organic 333.84
  typists' 300.89
    organic 333.84
  uterus 625.8
    menstrual 625.3
  writers' 333.84
    organic 333.84
    psychogenic 300.89

Cranial — *see* condition

Cranioclasis, fetal 763.89

Craniocleidodysostosis 755.59

Craniofenestria (skull) 756.0

Craniolacunia (skull) 756.0

Craniopagus 759.4

Craniopathy, metabolic 733.3

Craniopharyngeal — *see* condition

Craniopharyngioma (M9350/1) 237.0

Craniorachischisis (totalis) 740.1

Cranioschisis 756.0

Craniostenosis 756.0

Craniosynostosis 756.0

Craniotabes (cause unknown) 733.3
  rachitic 268.1
  syphilitic 090.5

Craniotomy, fetal 763.89

Cranium — *see* condition

Craw-craw 125.3

Creaking joint 719.60
  ankle 719.67
  elbow 719.62
  foot 719.67
  hand 719.64

Creaking joint — *continued*
  hip 719.65
  knee 719.66
  multiple sites 719.69
  pelvic region 719.65
  shoulder (region) 719.61
  specified site NEC 719.68
  wrist 719.63

Creeping
  eruption 126.9
  palsy 335.21
  paralysis 335.21

Crenated tongue 529.8

Creotoxism 005.9

Crepitus
  caput 756.0
  joint 719.60
    ankle 719.67
    elbow 719.62
    foot 719.67
    hand 719.64
    hip 719.65
    knee 719.66
    multiple sites 719.69
    pelvic region 719.65
    shoulder (region) 719.61
    specified site NEC 719.68
    wrist 719.63

Crescent or conus choroid, congenital 743.57

Cretin, cretinism (athyrotic) (congenital)
  (endemic) (metabolic) (nongoitrous)
  (sporadic) 243
  goitrous (sporadic) 246.1
  pelvis (dwarf type) (male type) 243
    with disproportion (fetopelvic) 653.1 ☑
      affecting fetus or newborn 763.1
      causing obstructed labor 660.1 ☑
        affecting fetus or newborn 763.1
  pituitary 253.3

Cretinoid degeneration 243

Creutzfeldt-Jakob disease (syndrome) ▶(new
  variant)◀ 046.1
  with dementia
    with behavioral disturbance 046.1 *[294.11]*
    without behavioral disturbance 046.1
      [294.10]

Crib death 798.0

Cribriform hymen 752.49

Cri-du-chat syndrome 758.31

Crigler-Najjar disease or syndrome (congenital
  hyperbilirubinemia) 277.4

Crimean hemorrhagic fever 065.0

Criminalism 301.7

Crisis
  abdomen 789.0 ☑
  addisonian (acute adrenocortical insufficiency)
    255.4
  adrenal (cortical) 255.4
  asthmatic — *see* Asthma
  brain, cerebral (*see also* Disease,
    cerebrovascular, acute) 436
  celiac 579.0
  Dietl's 593.4
  emotional NEC 309.29
    acute reaction to stress 308.0
    adjustment reaction 309.9
    specific to childhood or adolescence 313.9
  gastric (tabetic) 094.0
  glaucomatocyclitic 364.22
  heart (*see also* Failure, heart) 428.9
  hypertensive — *see* Hypertension
  nitritoid
    correct substance properly administered
      458.29
    overdose or wrong substance given or taken
      961.1
  oculogyric 378.87
    psychogenic 306.7
  Pel's 094.0
  psychosexual identity 302.6
  rectum 094.0
  renal 593.81
  sickle cell 282.62
  stomach (tabetic) 094.0

Crisis — *continued*
  tabetic 094.0
  thyroid (*see also* Thyrotoxicosis) 242.9 ☑
  thyrotoxic (*see also* Thyrotoxicosis) 242.9 ☑
  vascular — *see* Disease, cerebrovascular, acute
Crocq's disease (acrocyanosis) 443.89
Crohn's disease (*see also* Enteritis, regional)
  555.9
Cronkhite-Canada syndrome 211.3
Crooked septum, nasal 470
Cross
  birth (of fetus) complicating delivery 652.3 ☑
    with successful version 652.1 ☑
      causing obstructed labor 660.0 ☑
  bite, anterior or posterior 524.20
  eye (*see also* Esotropia) 378.00
Crossed ectopia of kidney 753.3
Crossfoot 754.50
Croup, croupous (acute) (angina) (catarrhal)
  (infective) (inflammatory) (laryngeal)
  (membranous) (nondiphtheritic)
  (pseudomembranous) 464.4
  asthmatic (*see also* Asthma) 493.9 ☑
  bronchial 466.0
  diphtheritic (membranous) 032.3
  false 478.75
  spasmodic 478.75
    diphtheritic 032.3
  stridulous 478.75
    diphtheritic 032.3
Crouzon's disease (craniofacial dysostosis) 756.0
Crowding, teeth 524.31
CRST syndrome (cutaneous systemic sclerosis)
  710.1
Cruchet's disease (encephalitis lethargica) 049.8
Cruelty in children (*see also* Disturbance,
  conduct) 312.9
Crural ulcer (*see also* Ulcer, lower extremity)
  707.10
Crush, crushed, crushing (injury) 929.9
  with
    fracture — *see* Fracture, by site
  abdomen 926.19
    internal — *see* Injury, internal, abdomen
  ankle 928.21
    with other parts of foot 928.20
  arm 927.9
    lower (and elbow) 927.10
    upper 927.03
      with shoulder or axillary region 927.09
  axilla 927.02
    with shoulder or upper arm 927.09
  back 926.11
  breast 926.19
  buttock 926.12
  cheek 925.1
  chest — *see* Injury, internal, chest
  ear 925.1
  elbow 927.11
    with forearm 927.10
  face 925.1
  finger(s) 927.3
    with hand(s) 927.20
      and wrist(s) 927.21
  flank 926.19
  foot, excluding toe(s) alone (with ankle) 928.20
  forearm (and elbow) 927.10
  genitalia, external (female) (male) 926.0
    internal — *see* Injury, internal, genital organ
      NEC
  hand, except finger(s) alone (and wrist) 927.20
  head — *see* Fracture, skull, by site
  heel 928.20
  hip 928.01
    with thigh 928.00
  internal organ (abdomen, chest, or pelvis) —
    see Injury, internal, by site
  knee 928.11
    with leg, lower 928.10
  labium (majus) (minus) 926.0
  larynx 925.2
  late effect — *see* Late, effects (of), crushing

Crush, crushed, crushing — *continued*
  leg 928.9
    lower 928.10
      and knee 928.11
    upper 928.00
  limb
    lower 928.9
      multiple sites 928.8
    upper 927.9
      multiple sites 927.8
  multiple sites NEC 929.0
  neck 925.2
  nerve — *see* Injury, nerve, by site
  nose 802.0
    open 802.1
  penis 926.0
  pharynx 925.2
  scalp 925.1
  scapular region 927.01
    with shoulder or upper arm 927.09
  scrotum 926.0
  shoulder 927.00
    with upper arm or axillary region 927.09
  skull or cranium — *see* Fracture, skull, by site
  spinal cord — *see* Injury, spinal, by site
  syndrome (complication of trauma) 958.5
  testis 926.0
  thigh (with hip) 928.00
  throat 925.2
  thumb(s) (and fingers) 927.3
  toe(s) 928.3
    with foot 928.20
      and ankle 928.21
  tonsil 925.2
  trunk 926.9
    chest — *see* Injury, internal, intrathoracic
      organs NEC
    internal organ — *see* Injury, internal, by site
    multiple sites 926.8
    specified site NEC 926.19
  vulva 926.0
  wrist 927.21
    with hand(s), except fingers alone 927.20
Crusta lactea 690.11
Crusts 782.8
Crutch paralysis 953.4
Cruveilhier's disease 335.21
**Cruveilhier-Baumgarten cirrhosis, disease, or
  syndrome** 571.5
Cruz-Chagas disease (*see also* Trypanosomiasis)
  086.2
Cryoglobulinemia (mixed) 273.2
Crypt (anal) (rectal) 569.49
Cryptitis (anal) (rectal) 569.49
Cryptococcosis (European) (pulmonary)
  (systemic) 117.5
Cryptococcus 117.5
  epidermicus 117.5
  neoformans, infection by 117.5
Cryptopapillitis (anus) 569.49
Cryptophthalmos (eyelid) 743.06
Cryptorchid, cryptorchism, cryptorchidism
  752.51
Cryptosporidiosis 007.4
Cryptotia 744.29
Crystallopathy
  calcium pyrophosphate (*see also* Arthritis)
    275.49 *[712.2]* ☑
  dicalcium phosphate (*see also* Arthritis)
    275.49 *[712.1]* ☑
  gouty 274.0
  pyrophosphate NEC (*see also* Arthritis)
    275.49 *[712.2]* ☑
  uric acid 274.0
Crystalluria 791.9
Csillag's disease (lichen sclerosus et atrophicus)
  701.0
Cuban itch 050.1
Cubitus
  valgus (acquired) 736.01
    congenital 755.59
    late effect of rickets 268.1

Cubitus — *continued*
  varus (acquired) 736.02
    congenital 755.59
    late effect of rickets 268.1
Cultural deprivation V62.4
Cupping of optic disc 377.14
Curling's ulcer — *see* Ulcer, duodenum
Curling esophagus 530.5
**Curschmann (-Batten) (-Steinert) disease or
  syndrome** 359.2
Curvature
  organ or site, congenital NEC — *see* Distortion
  penis (lateral) 752.69
  Pott's (spinal) (*see also* Tuberculosis) 015.0 ☑
    [737.43]
  radius, idiopathic, progressive (congenital)
    755.54
  spine (acquired) (angular) (idiopathic)
    (incorrect) (postural) 737.9
    congenital 754.2
    due to or associated with
      Charcôt-Marie-Tooth disease 356.1
        [737.40]
      mucopolysaccharidosis 277.5 *[737.40]*
      neurofibromatosis 237.71 *[737.40]*
      osteitis
        deformans 731.0 *[737.40]*
        fibrosa cystica 252.01 *[737.40]*
      osteoporosis (*see also* Osteoporosis)
        733.00 *[737.40]*
      poliomyelitis (*see also* Poliomyelitis) 138
        [737.40]
      tuberculosis (Pott's curvature) (*see also*
        Tuberculosis) 015.0 ☑ *[737.43]*
    kyphoscoliotic (*see also* Kyphoscoliosis)
      737.30
    kyphotic (*see also* Kyphosis) 737.10
    late effect of rickets 268.1 *[737.40]*
    Pott's 015.0 ☑ *[737.40]*
    scoliotic (*see also* Scoliosis) 737.30
    specified NEC 737.8
    tuberculous 015.0 ☑ *[737.40]*
Cushing's
  basophilism, disease, or syndrome (iatrogenic)
    (idiopathic) (pituitary basophilism)
    (pituitary dependent) 255.0
  ulcer — *see* Ulcer, peptic
Cushingoid due to steroid therapy
  correct substance properly administered 255.0
  overdose or wrong substance given or taken
    962.0
Cut (external) — *see* Wound, open, by site
Cutaneous — *see also* condition
  hemorrhage 782.7
  horn (cheek) (eyelid) (mouth) 702.8
  larva migrans 126.9
Cutis — *see also* condition
  hyperelastic 756.83
    acquired 701.8
  laxa 756.83
    senilis 701.8
  marmorata 782.61
  osteosis 709.3
  pendula 756.83
    acquired 701.8
  rhomboidalis nuchae 701.8
  verticis gyrata 757.39
    acquired 701.8
Cyanopathy, newborn 770.83
Cyanosis 782.5
  autotoxic 289.7
  common atrioventricular canal 745.69
  congenital 770.83
  conjunctiva 372.71
  due to
    endocardial cushion defect 745.60
    nonclosure, foramen botalli 745.5
    patent foramen botalli 745.5
    persistent foramen ovale 745.5
  enterogenous 289.7
  fetus or newborn 770.83
  ostium primum defect 745.61
  paroxysmal digital 443.0
  retina, retinal 362.10

Cycle
 anovulatory 628.0
 menstrual, irregular 626.4
Cyclencephaly 759.89
Cyclical vomiting 536.2
 psychogenic 306.4
Cyclitic membrane 364.74
Cyclitis (see also Iridocyclitis) 364.3
 acute 364.00
  primary 364.01
  recurrent 364.02
 chronic 364.10
  in
   sarcoidosis 135 [364.11]
   tuberculosis (see also Tuberculosis)
    017.3 ☑ [364.11]
 Fuchs' heterochromic 364.21
 granulomatous 364.10
 lens induced 364.23
 nongranulomatous 364.00
 posterior 363.21
 primary 364.01
 recurrent 364.02
 secondary (noninfectious) 364.04
  infectious 364.03
 subacute 364.00
  primary 364.01
  recurrent 364.02
Cyclokeratitis — see Keratitis
Cyclophoria 378.44
Cyclopia, cyclops 759.89
Cycloplegia 367.51
Cyclospasm 367.53
Cyclosporiasis 007.5
Cyclothymia 301.13
Cyclothymic personality 301.13
Cyclotropia 378.33
Cyesis — see Pregnancy
Cylindroma (M8200/3) — see also Neoplasm, by
  site, malignant
 eccrine dermal (M8200/0) — see Neoplasm,
   skin, benign
 skin (M8200/0) — see Neoplasm, skin, benign
Cylindruria 791.7
Cyllosoma 759.89
Cynanche
 diphtheritic 032.3
 tonsillaris 475
Cynorexia 783.6
Cyphosis — see Kyphosis
Cyprus fever (see also Brucellosis) 023.9
Cyriax's syndrome (slipping rib) 733.99
Cyst (mucus) (retention) (serous) (simple)

> Note — In general, cysts are not neoplastic and
> are classified to the appropriate category for
> disease of the specified anatomical site. This
> generalization does not apply to certain types of
> cysts which are neoplastic in nature, for
> example, dermoid, nor does it apply to cysts of
> certain structures, for example, branchial cleft,
> which are classified as developmental
> anomalies.
>
> The following listing includes some of the most
> frequently reported sites of cysts as well as
> qualifiers which indicate the type of cyst. The
> latter qualifiers usually are not repeated under
> the anatomical sites. Since the code assignment
> for a given site may vary depending upon the
> type of cyst, the coder should refer to the
> listings under the specified type of cyst before
> consideration is given to the site.

 accessory, fallopian tube 752.11
 adenoid (infected) 474.8
 adrenal gland 255.8
  congenital 759.1
 air, lung 518.89
 allantoic 753.7
 alveolar process (jaw bone) 526.2
 amnion, amniotic 658.8 ☑

Cyst — continued
 anterior chamber (eye) 364.60
  exudative 364.62
  implantation (surgical) (traumatic) 364.61
  parasitic 360.13
 anterior nasopalatine 526.1
 antrum 478.1
 anus 569.49
 apical (periodontal) (tooth) 522.8
 appendix 543.9
 arachnoid, brain 348.0
 arytenoid 478.79
 auricle 706.2
 Baker's (knee) 727.51
  tuberculous (see also Tuberculosis) 015.2 ☑
 Bartholin's gland or duct 616.2
 bile duct (see also Disease, biliary) 576.8
 bladder (multiple) (trigone) 596.8
 Blessig's 362.62
 blood, endocardial (see also Endocarditis)
   424.90
 blue dome 610.0
 bone (local) 733.20
  aneurysmal 733.22
  jaw 526.2
   developmental (odontogenic) 526.0
   fissural 526.1
   latent 526.89
  solitary 733.21
  unicameral 733.21
 brain 348.0
  congenital 742.4
  hydatid (see also Echinococcus) 122.9
  third ventricle (colloid) 742.4
 branchial (cleft) 744.42
 branchiogenic 744.42
 breast (benign) (blue dome) (pedunculated)
   (solitary) (traumatic) 610.0
  involution 610.4
  sebaceous 610.8
 broad ligament (benign) 620.8
  embryonic 752.11
 bronchogenic (mediastinal) (sequestration)
   518.89
  congenital 748.4
 buccal 528.4
 bulbourethral gland (Cowper's) 599.89
 bursa, bursal 727.49
  pharyngeal 478.26
 calcifying odontogenic (M9301/0) 213.1
  upper jaw (bone) 213.0
 canal of Nuck (acquired) (serous) 629.1
  congenital 752.41
 canthus 372.75
 carcinomatous (M8010/3) — see Neoplasm, by
   site, malignant
 cartilage (joint) — see Derangement, joint
 cauda equina 336.8
 cavum septi pellucidi NEC 348.0
 celomic (pericardium) 746.89
 cerebellopontine (angle) — see Cyst, brain
 cerebellum — see Cyst, brain
 cerebral — see Cyst, brain
 cervical lateral 744.42
 cervix 622.8
  embryonal 752.41
  nabothian (gland) 616.0
 chamber, anterior (eye) 364.60
  exudative 364.62
  implantation (surgical) (traumatic) 364.61
  parasitic 360.13
 chiasmal, optic NEC (see also Lesion, chiasmal)
   377.54
 chocolate (ovary) 617.1
 choledochal (congenital) 751.69
  acquired 576.8
 choledochus 751.69
 chorion 658.8 ☑
 choroid plexus 348.0
 chyle, mesentery 457.8
 ciliary body 364.60
  exudative 364.64
  implantation 364.61
  primary 364.63
 clitoris 624.8
 coccyx (see also Cyst, bone) 733.20

Cyst — continued
 colloid
  third ventricle (brain) 742.4
  thyroid gland — see Goiter
 colon 569.89
 common (bile) duct (see also Disease, biliary)
   576.8
 congenital NEC 759.89
  adrenal glands 759.1
  epiglottis 748.3
  esophagus 750.4
  fallopian tube 752.11
  kidney 753.10
   multiple 753.19
   single 753.11
  larynx 748.3
  liver 751.62
  lung 748.4
  mediastinum 748.8
  ovary 752.0
  oviduct 752.11
  pancreas 751.7
  periurethral (tissue) 753.8
  prepuce NEC 752.69
   penis 752.69
  sublingual 750.26
  submaxillary gland 750.26
  thymus (gland) 759.2
  tongue 750.19
  ureterovesical orifice 753.4
  vulva 752.41
 conjunctiva 372.75
 cornea 371.23
 corpora quadrigemina 348.0
 corpus
  albicans (ovary) 620.2
  luteum (ruptured) 620.1
 Cowper's gland (benign) (infected) 599.89
 cranial meninges 348.0
 craniobuccal pouch 253.8
 craniopharyngeal pouch 253.8
 cystic duct (see also Disease, gallbladder) 575.8
 Cysticercus (any site) 123.1
 Dandy-Walker 742.3
  with spina bifida (see also Spina bifida)
   741.0 ☑
 dental 522.8
  developmental 526.0
  eruption 526.0
  lateral periodontal 526.0
  primordial (keratocyst) 526.0
  root 522.8
 dentigerous 526.0
  mandible 526.0
  maxilla 526.0
 dermoid (M9084/0) — see also Neoplasm, by
   site, benign
  with malignant transformation (M9084/3)
   183.0
  implantation
   external area or site (skin) NEC 709.8
   iris 364.61
   skin 709.8
   vagina 623.8
   vulva 624.8
  mouth 528.4
  oral soft tissue 528.4
  sacrococcygeal 685.1
   with abscess 685.0
 developmental of ovary, ovarian 752.0
 dura (cerebral) 348.0
  spinal 349.2
 ear (external) 706.2
 echinococcal (see also Echinococcus) 122.9
 embryonal
  cervix uteri 752.41
  genitalia, female external 752.41
  uterus 752.3
  vagina 752.41
 endometrial 621.8
  ectopic 617.9
 endometrium (uterus) 621.8
  ectopic — see Endometriosis
 enteric 751.5
 enterogenous 751.5
 epidermal (inclusion) (see also Cyst, skin)
   706.2

☑ Additional Digit Required — Refer to the Tabular List (Numeric Code Section) for Additional Digit Selection

▶◀ Revised Text   ● New Line   ▲ Revised Code

Cyst — *continued*
  epidermoid (inclusion) (*see also* Cyst, skin)
    706.2
    mouth 528.4
    not of skin — *see* Cyst, by site
    oral soft tissue 528.4
  epididymis 608.89
  epiglottis 478.79
  epiphysis cerebri 259.8
  epithelial (inclusion) (*see also* Cyst, skin) 706.2
  epoophoron 752.11
  eruption 526.0
  esophagus 530.89
  ethmoid sinus 478.1
  eye (retention) 379.8
    congenital 743.03
    posterior segment, congenital 743.54
  eyebrow 706.2
  eyelid (sebaceous) 374.84
    infected 373.13
    sweat glands or ducts 374.84
  falciform ligament (inflammatory) 573.8
  fallopian tube 620.8
  female genital organs NEC 629.8
  fimbrial (congenital) 752.11
  fissural (oral region) 526.1
  follicle (atretic) (graafian) (ovarian) 620.0
    nabothian (gland) 616.0
  follicular (atretic) (ovarian) 620.0
    dentigerous 526.0
  frontal sinus 478.1
  gallbladder or duct 575.8
  ganglion 727.43
  Gartner's duct 752.41   ▲
  gas, of mesentery 568.89
  gingiva 523.8
  gland of moll 374.84
  globulomaxillary 526.1
  graafian follicle 620.0
  granulosal lutein 620.2
  hemangiomatous (M9121/0) (*see also*
    Hemangioma) 228.00
  hydatid (*see also* Echinococcus) 122.9
    fallopian tube (Morgagni) 752.11
    liver NEC 122.8
    lung NEC 122.9
    Morgagni 752.89
      fallopian tube 752.11
    specified site NEC 122.9
  hymen 623.8
    embryonal 752.41
  hypopharynx 478.26
  hypophysis, hypophyseal (duct) (recurrent) 253.8
    cerebri 253.8
  implantation (dermoid)
    anterior chamber (eye) 364.61
    external area or site (skin) NEC 709.8
    iris 364.61
    vagina 623.8
    vulva 624.8
  incisor, incisive canal 526.1
  inclusion (epidermal) (epithelial) (epidermoid)
    (mucous) (squamous) (*see also* Cyst, skin)
    706.2
    not of skin — *see* Neoplasm, by site, benign
  intestine (large) (small) 569.89
  intracranial — *see* Cyst, brain
  intraligamentous 728.89
    knee 717.89
  intrasellar 253.8
  iris (idiopathic) 364.60
    exudative 364.62
    implantation (surgical) (traumatic) 364.61
    miotic pupillary 364.55
    parasitic 360.13
  Iwanoff's 362.62
  jaw (bone) (aneurysmal) (extravasation)
    (hemorrhagic) (traumatic) 526.2
    developmental (odontogenic) 526.0
    fissural 526.1
  keratin 706.2
  kidney (congenital) 753.10
    acquired 593.2
    calyceal (*see also* Hydronephrosis) 591
    multiple 753.19
    pyelogenic (*see also* Hydronephrosis) 591

Cyst — *continued*
  kidney — *continued*
    simple 593.2
    single 753.11
    solitary (not congenital) 593.2
  labium (majus) (minus) 624.8
    sebaceous 624.8
  lacrimal
    apparatus 375.43
    gland or sac 375.12
  larynx 478.79
  lens 379.39
    congenital 743.39
  lip (gland) 528.5
  liver 573.8
    congenital 751.62
    hydatid (*see also* Echinococcus) 122.8
      granulosis 122.0
      multilocularis 122.5
  lung 518.89
    congenital 748.4
    giant bullous 492.0
  lutein 620.1
  lymphangiomatous (M9173/0) 228.1
  lymphoepithelial
    mouth 528.4
    oral soft tissue 528.4
  macula 362.54
  malignant (M8000/3) — *see* Neoplasm, by site,
    malignant
  mammary gland (sweat gland) (*see also* Cyst,
    breast) 610.0
  mandible 526.2
    dentigerous 526.0
    radicular 522.8
  maxilla 526.2
    dentigerous 526.0
    radicular 522.8
  median
    anterior maxillary 526.1
    palatal 526.1
  mediastinum (congenital) 748.8
  meibomian (gland) (retention) 373.2
    infected 373.12
  membrane, brain 348.0
  meninges (cerebral) 348.0
    spinal 349.2
  meniscus knee 717.5
  mesentery, mesenteric (gas) 568.89
    chyle 457.8
    gas 568.89
  mesonephric duct 752.89
  mesothelial
    peritoneum 568.89
    pleura (peritoneal) 568.89
  milk 611.5
  miotic pupillary (iris) 364.55
  Morgagni (hydatid) 752.89
    fallopian tube 752.11
  mouth 528.4
  mullerian duct 752.89
  multilocular (ovary) (M8000/1) 239.5
  myometrium 621.8
  nabothian (follicle) (ruptured) 616.0
  nasal sinus 478.1
  nasoalveolar 528.4
  nasolabial 528.4
  nasopalatine (duct) 526.1
    anterior 526.1
  nasopharynx 478.26
  neoplastic (M8000/1) — *see also* Neoplasm, by
    site, unspecified nature
    benign (M8000/0) — *see* Neoplasm, by site,
      benign
    uterus 621.8
  nervous system — *see* Cyst, brain
  neuroenteric 742.59
  neuroepithelial ventricle 348.0
  nipple 610.0
  nose 478.1
    skin of 706.2
  odontogenic, developmental 526.0
  omentum (lesser) 568.89
    congenital 751.8
  oral soft tissue (dermoid) (epidermoid)
    (lymphoepithelial) 528.4
  ora serrata 361.19

Cyst — *continued*
  orbit 376.81
  ovary, ovarian (twisted) 620.2
    adherent 620.2
    chocolate 617.1
    corpus
      albicans 620.2
      luteum 620.1
    dermoid (M9084/0) 220
    developmental 752.0
    due to failure of involution NEC 620.2
    endometrial 617.1
    follicular (atretic) (graafian) (hemorrhagic)
      620.0
    hemorrhagic 620.2
    in pregnancy or childbirth 654.4 ☑
      affecting fetus or newborn 763.89
      causing obstructed labor 660.2 ☑
        affecting fetus or newborn 763.1
    multilocular (M8000/1) 239.5
    pseudomucinous (M8470/0) 220
    retention 620.2
    serous 620.2
    theca lutein 620.2
    tuberculous (*see also* Tuberculosis) 016.6 ☑
    unspecified 620.2
  oviduct 620.8
  palatal papilla (jaw) 526.1
  palate 526.1
    fissural 526.1
    median (fissural) 526.1
  palatine, of papilla 526.1
  pancreas, pancreatic 577.2
    congenital 751.7
    false 577.2
    hemorrhagic 577.2
    true 577.2
  paranephric 593.2
  para ovarian 752.11
  paraphysis, cerebri 742.4
  parasitic NEC 136.9
  parathyroid (gland) 252.8
  paratubal (fallopian) 620.8
  paraurethral duct 599.89
  paroophoron 752.11
  parotid gland 527.6
    mucous extravasation or retention 527.6
  parovarian 752.11
  pars planus 364.60
    exudative 364.64
    primary 364.63
  pelvis, female
    in pregnancy or childbirth 654.4 ☑
      affecting fetus or newborn 763.89
      causing obstructed labor 660.2 ☑
        affecting fetus or newborn 763.1
  penis (sebaceous) 607.89
  periapical 522.8
  pericardial (congenital) 746.89
    acquired (secondary) 423.8
  pericoronal 526.0
  perineural (Tarlov's) 355.9
  periodontal 522.8
    lateral 526.0
  peripancreatic 577.2
  peripelvic (lymphatic) 593.2
  peritoneum 568.89
    chylous 457.8
  pharynx (wall) 478.26
  pilonidal (infected) (rectum) 685.1
    with abscess 685.0
    malignant (M9084/3) 173.5
  pituitary (duct) (gland) 253.8
  placenta (amniotic) — *see* Placenta, abnormal
  pleura 519.8
  popliteal 727.51
  porencephalic 742.4
    acquired 348.0
  postanal (infected) 685.1
    with abscess 685.0
  posterior segment of eye, congenital 743.54
  postmastoidectomy cavity 383.31
  preauricular 744.47
  prepuce 607.89
    congenital 752.69
  primordial (jaw) 526.0
  prostate 600.3

☑ Additional Digit Required — Refer to the Tabular List (Numeric Code Section) for Additional Digit Selection

►◄ Revised Text   ● New Line   ▲ Revised Code

Cyst — *continued*
  pseudomucinous (ovary) (M8470/0) 220
  pudenda (sweat glands) 624.8
  pupillary, miotic 364.55
    sebaceous 624.8
  radicular (residual) 522.8
  radiculodental 522.8
  ranular 527.6
  Rathke's pouch 253.8
  rectum (epithelium) (mucous) 569.49
  renal — *see* Cyst, kidney
  residual (radicular) 522.8
  retention (ovary) 620.2
  retina 361.19
    macular 362.54
    parasitic 360.13
    primary 361.13
    secondary 361.14
  retroperitoneal 568.89
  sacrococcygeal (dermoid) 685.1
    with abscess 685.0
  salivary gland or duct 527.6
    mucous extravasation or retention 527.6
  Sampson's 617.1
  sclera 379.19
  scrotum (sebaceous) 706.2
    sweat glands 706.2
  sebaceous (duct) (gland) 706.2
    breast 610.8
    eyelid 374.84
    genital organ NEC
      female 629.8
      male 608.89
    scrotum 706.2
  semilunar cartilage (knee) (multiple) 717.5
  seminal vesicle 608.89
  serous (ovary) 620.2
  sinus (antral) (ethmoidal) (frontal) (maxillary) (nasal) (sphenoidal) 478.1
  Skene's gland 599.89
  skin (epidermal) (epidermoid, inclusion) (epithelial) (inclusion) (retention) (sebaceous) 706.2
    breast 610.8
    eyelid 374.84
    genital organ NEC
      female 629.8
      male 608.89
    neoplastic 216.3
    scrotum 706.2
    sweat gland or duct 705.89
  solitary
    bone 733.21
    kidney 593.2
  spermatic cord 608.89
  sphenoid sinus 478.1
  spinal meninges 349.2
  spine (*see also* Cyst, bone) 733.20
  spleen NEC 289.59
    congenital 759.0
    hydatid (*see also* Echinococcus) 122.9
  spring water (pericardium) 746.89
  subarachnoid 348.0
    intrasellar 793.0
  subdural (cerebral) 348.0
    spinal cord 349.2
  sublingual gland 527.6
    mucous extravasation or retention 527.6
  submaxillary gland 527.6
    mucous extravasation or retention 527.6
  suburethral 599.89
  suprarenal gland 255.8
  suprasellar — *see* Cyst, brain
  sweat gland or duct 705.89
  sympathetic nervous system 337.9
  synovial 727.40
    popliteal space 727.51
  Tarlov's 355.9
  tarsal 373.2
  tendon (sheath) 727.42
  testis 608.89
  theca-lutein (ovary) 620.2
  Thornwaldt's, Tornwaldt's 478.26
  thymus (gland) 254.8
  thyroglossal (duct) (infected) (persistent) 759.2
  thyroid (gland) 246.2
    adenomatous — *see* Goiter, nodular

Cyst — *continued*
  thyroid — *continued*
    colloid (*see also* Goiter) 240.9
  thyrolingual duct (infected) (persistent) 759.2
  tongue (mucous) 529.8
  tonsil 474.8
  tooth (dental root) 522.8
  tubo-ovarian 620.8
    inflammatory 614.1
  tunica vaginalis 608.89
  turbinate (nose) (*see also* Cyst, bone) 733.20
  Tyson's gland (benign) (infected) 607.89
  umbilicus 759.89
  urachus 753.7
  ureter 593.89
  ureterovesical orifice 593.89
    congenital 753.4
  urethra 599.84
  urethral gland (Cowper's) 599.89
  uterine
    ligament 620.8
      embryonic 752.11
    tube 620.8
  uterus (body) (corpus) (recurrent) 621.8
    embryonal 752.3
  utricle (ear) 386.8
    prostatic 599.89
  utriculus masculinus 599.89
  vagina, vaginal (squamous cell) (wall) 623.8
    embryonal 752.41
    implantation 623.8
    inclusion 623.8
  vallecula, vallecular 478.79
  ventricle, neuroepithelial 348.0
  verumontanum 599.89
  vesical (orifice) 596.8
  vitreous humor 379.29
  vulva (sweat glands) 624.8
    congenital 752.41
    implantation 624.8
    inclusion 624.8
    sebaceous gland 624.8
  vulvovaginal gland 624.8
  wolffian 752.89

Cystadenocarcinoma (M8440/3) — *see also* Neoplasm, by site, malignant
  bile duct type (M8161/3) 155.1
  endometrioid (M8380/3) — *see* Neoplasm, by site, malignant
  mucinous (M8470/3)
    papillary (M8471/3)
      specified site — *see* Neoplasm, by site, malignant
      unspecified site 183.0
    specified site — *see* Neoplasm, by site, malignant
    unspecified site 183.0
  papillary (M8450/3)
    mucinous (M8471/3)
      specified site — *see* Neoplasm, by site, malignant
      unspecified site 183.0
    pseudomucinous (M8471/3)
      specified site — *see* Neoplasm, by site, malignant
      unspecified site 183.0
    serous (M8460/3)
      specified site — *see* Neoplasm, by site, malignant
      unspecified site 183.0
    specified site — *see* Neoplasm, by site, malignant
    unspecified 183.0
  pseudomucinous (M8470/3)
    papillary (M8471/3)
      specified site — *see* Neoplasm, by site, malignant
      unspecified site 183.0
    specified site — *see* Neoplasm, by site, malignant
    unspecified site 183.0
  serous (M8441/3)
    papillary (M8460/3)
      specified site — *see* Neoplasm, by site, malignant
      unspecified site 183.0

Cystadenocarcinoma (M8440/3) — *see also* Neoplasm, by site, malignant — *continued*
  serous — *continued*
    specified site — *see* Neoplasm, by site, malignant
    unspecified site 183.0

Cystadenofibroma (M9013/0)
  clear cell (M8313/0) — *see* Neoplasm, by site, benign
  endometrioid (M8381/0) 220
    borderline malignancy (M8381/1) 236.2
    malignant (M8381/3) 183.0
  mucinous (M9015/0)
    specified site — *see* Neoplasm, by site, benign
    unspecified site 220
  serous (M9014/0)
    specified site — *see* Neoplasm, by site, benign
    unspecified site 220
  specified site — *see* Neoplasm, by site, benign
  unspecified site 220

Cystadenoma (M8440/0) — *see also* Neoplasm, by site, benign
  bile duct (M8161/0) 211.5
  endometrioid (M8380/0) — *see also* Neoplasm, by site, benign
    borderline malignancy (M8380/1) — *see* Neoplasm, by site, uncertain behavior
    malignant (M8440/3) — *see* Neoplasm, by site, malignant
  mucinous (M8470/0)
    borderline malignancy (M8470/1)
      specified site — *see* Neoplasm, uncertain behavior
      unspecified site 236.2
    papillary (M8471/0)
      borderline malignancy (M8471/1)
        specified site — *see* Neoplasm, by site, uncertain behavior
        unspecified site 236.2
      specified site — *see* Neoplasm, by site, benign
      unspecified site 220
    specified site — *see* Neoplasm, by site, benign
    unspecified site 220
  papillary (M8450/0)
    borderline malignancy (M8450/1)
      specified site — *see* Neoplasm, by site, uncertain behavior
      unspecified site 236.2
    lymphomatosum (M8561/0) 210.2
    mucinous (M8471/0)
      borderline malignancy (M8471/1)
        specified site — *see* Neoplasm, by site, uncertain behavior
        unspecified site 236.2
      specified site — *see* Neoplasm, by site, benign
      unspecified site 220
    pseudomucinous (M8471/0)
      borderline malignancy (M8471/1)
        specified site — *see* Neoplasm, by site, uncertain behavior
        unspecified site 236.2
      specified site — *see* Neoplasm, by site, benign
      unspecified site 220
    serous (M8460/0)
      borderline malignancy (M8460/1)
        specified site — *see* Neoplasm, by site, uncertain behavior
        unspecified site 236.2
      specified site — *see* Neoplasm, by site, benign
      unspecified site 220
    specified site — *see* Neoplasm, by site, benign
    unspecified site 220
  pseudomucinous (M8470/0)
    borderline malignancy (M8470/1)
      specified site — *see* Neoplasm, by site, uncertain behavior
      unspecified site 236.2

Cystadenoma (M8440/0) — *see also* Neoplasm, by site, benign — *continued*
pseudomucinous — *continued*
   papillary (M8471/0)
      borderline malignancy (M8471/1)
         specified site — *see* Neoplasm, by site, uncertain behavior
         unspecified site 236.2
      specified site — *see* Neoplasm, by site, benign
      unspecified site 220
   specified site — *see* Neoplasm, by site, benign
   unspecified site 220
serous (M8441/0)
   borderline malignancy (M8441/1)
      specified site — *see* Neoplasm, by site, uncertain behavior
      unspecified site 236.2
   papillary (M8460/0)
      borderline malignancy (M8460/1)
         specified site — *see* Neoplasm, by site, uncertain behavior
         unspecified site 236.2
      specified site — *see* Neoplasm, by site, benign
      unspecified site 220
   specified site — *see* Neoplasm, by site, benign
   unspecified site 220
thyroid 226
Cystathioninemia 270.4
Cystathioninuria 270.4
Cystic — *see also* condition
breast, chronic 610.1
corpora lutea 620.1
degeneration, congenital
   brain 742.4
   kidney (*see also* Cystic, disease, degeneration, kidney) 753.10
disease
   breast, chronic 610.1
   kidney, congenital 753.10
      medullary 753.16
      multiple 753.19
      polycystic — *see* Polycystic, kidney
      single 753.11
      specified NEC 753.19
   liver, congenital 751.62
   lung 518.89
      congenital 748.4
   pancreas, congenital 751.7
   semilunar cartilage 717.5
duct — *see* condition
eyeball, congenital 743.03
fibrosis (pancreas) 277.00
   with
      manifestations
         gastrointestinal 277.03
         pulmonary 277.02
         specified NEC 277.09
      meconium ileus 277.01
      pulmonary exacerbation 277.02
hygroma (M9173/0) 228.1
kidney, congenital 753.10
   medullary 753.16
   multiple 753.19
   polycystic — *see* Polycystic, kidney
   single 753.11
   specified NEC 753.19
liver, congenital 751.62
lung 518.89
   congenital 748.4
mass — *see* Cyst
mastitis, chronic 610.1
ovary 620.2
pancreas, congenital 751.7
Cysticerciasis 123.1
Cysticercosis (mammary) (subretinal) 123.1
Cysticercus 123.1
cellulosae infestation 123.1
Cystinosis (malignant) 270.0
Cystinuria 270.0

Cystitis (bacillary) (colli) (diffuse) (exudative) (hemorrhagic) (purulent) (recurrent) (septic) (suppurative) (ulcerative) 595.9
with
   abortion — *see* Abortion, by type, with urinary tract infection
   ectopic pregnancy (*see also* categories 633.0-633.9) 639.8
   fibrosis 595.1
   leukoplakia 595.1
   malakoplakia 595.1
   metaplasia 595.1
   molar pregnancy (*see also* categories 630-632) 639.8
actinomycotic 039.8 [595.4]
acute 595.0
   of trigone 595.3
allergic 595.89
amebic 006.8 [595.4]
bilharzial 120.9 [595.4]
blennorrhagic (acute) 098.11
   chronic or duration of 2 months or more 098.31
bullous 595.89
calculus 594.1
   chlamydial 099.53
chronic 595.2
   interstitial 595.1
   of trigone 595.3
complicating pregnancy, childbirth, or puerperium 646.6 ☑
   affecting fetus or newborn 760.1
cystic(a) 595.81
diphtheritic 032.84
echinococcal
   granulosus 122.3 [595.4]
   multilocularis 122.6 [595.4]
emphysematous 595.89
encysted 595.81
follicular 595.3
following
   abortion 639.8
   ectopic or molar pregnancy 639.8
gangrenous 595.89
glandularis 595.89
gonococcal (acute) 098.11
   chronic or duration of 2 months or more 098.31
incrusted 595.89
interstitial 595.1
irradiation 595.82
irritation 595.89
malignant 595.89
monilial 112.2
of trigone 595.3
panmural 595.1
polyposa 595.89
prostatic 601.3
radiation 595.82
Reiter's (abacterial) 099.3
specified NEC 595.89
subacute 595.2
submucous 595.1
syphilitic 095.8
trichomoniasis 131.09
tuberculous (*see also* Tuberculosis) 016.1 ☑
ulcerative 595.1
Cystocele (-rectocele)
female (without uterine prolapse) 618.01
   with uterine prolapse 618.4
      complete 618.3
      incomplete 618.2
   lateral 618.02
   midline 618.01
   paravaginal 618.02
in pregnancy or childbirth 654.4 ☑
   affecting fetus or newborn 763.89
   causing obstructed labor 660.2 ☑
      affecting fetus or newborn 763.1
male 596.8
Cystoid
cicatrix limbus 372.64
degeneration macula 362.53
Cystolithiasis 594.1

Cystoma (M8440/0) — *see also* Neoplasm, by site, benign
endometrial, ovary 617.1
mucinous (M8470/0)
   specified site — *see* Neoplasm, by site, benign
   unspecified site 220
serous (M8441/0)
   specified site — *see* Neoplasm, by site, benign
   unspecified site 220
simple (ovary) 620.2
Cystoplegia 596.53
Cystoptosis 596.8
Cystopyelitis (*see also* Pyelitis) 590.80
Cystorrhagia 596.8
Cystosarcoma phyllodes (M9020/1) 238.3
benign (M9020/0) 217
malignant (M9020/3) — *see* Neoplasm, breast, malignant
Cystostomy status V44.50
appendico-vesicostomy V44.52
cutaneous-vesicostomy V44.51
specified type NEC V44.59
with complication 997.5
Cystourethritis (*see also* Urethritis) 597.89
Cystourethrocele (*see also* Cystocele)
female (without uterine prolapse) 618.09
   with uterine prolapse 618.4
      complete 618.3
      incomplete 618.2
male 596.8
Cytomegalic inclusion disease 078.5
congenital 771.1
Cytomycosis, reticuloendothelial (*see also* Histoplasmosis, American) 115.00
Cytopenia 289.9

D

Daae (-Finsen) disease (epidemic pleurodynia) 074.1

Dabney's grip 074.1

Da Costa's syndrome (neurocirculatory asthenia) 306.2

Dacryoadenitis, dacryadenitis 375.00
acute 375.01
chronic 375.02

Dacryocystitis 375.30
acute 375.32
chronic 375.42
neonatal 771.6
phlegmonous 375.33
syphilitic 095.8
congenital 090.0
trachomatous, active 076.1
late effect 139.1
tuberculous (*see also* Tuberculosis) 017.3 ☑

Dacryocystoblenorrhea 375.42

Dacryocystocele 375.43

Dacryolith, dacryolithiasis 375.57

Dacryoma 375.43

Dacryopericystitis (acute) (subacute) 375.32
chronic 375.42

Dacryops 375.11

Dacryosialadenopathy, atrophic 710.2

Dacryostenosis 375.56
congenital 743.65

Dactylitis 686.9
bone (*see also* Osteomyelitis) 730.2 ☑
sickle-cell 282.61
syphilitic 095.5
tuberculous (*see also* Tuberculosis) 015.5 ☑

Dactylolysis spontanea 136.0

Dactylosymphysis (*see also* Syndactylism) 755.10

Damage
arteriosclerotic — *see* Arteriosclerosis
brain 348.9
anoxic, hypoxic 348.1
during or resulting from a procedure 997.01
child NEC 343.9
due to birth injury 767.0
minimal (child) (*see also* Hyperkinesia) 314.9
newborn 767.0
cardiac — *see also* Disease, heart
cardiorenal (vascular) (*see also* Hypertension, cardiorenal) 404.90
central nervous system — *see* Damage, brain
cerebral NEC — *see* Damage, brain
coccyx, complicating delivery 665.6 ☑
coronary (*see also* Ischemia, heart) 414.9
eye, birth injury 767.8
heart — *see also* Disease, heart
valve — *see* Endocarditis
hypothalamus NEC 348.9
liver 571.9
alcoholic 571.3
myocardium (*see also* Degeneration, myocardial) 429.1
pelvic
joint or ligament, during delivery 665.6 ☑
organ NEC
with
abortion — *see* Abortion, by type, with damage to pelvic organs
ectopic pregnancy (*see also* categories 633.0-633.9) 639.2
molar pregnancy (*see also* categories 630-632) 639.2
during delivery 665.5 ☑
following
abortion 639.2
ectopic or molar pregnancy 639.2
renal (*see also* Disease, renal) 593.9
skin, solar 692.79
acute 692.72
chronic 692.74
subendocardium, subendocardial (*see also* Degeneration, myocardial) 429.1
vascular 459.9

Dameshek's syndrome (erythroblastic anemia) 282.49

Dana-Putnam syndrome (subacute combined sclerosis with pernicious anemia) 281.0 *[336.2]*

Danbolt (-Closs) syndrome (acrodermatitis enteropathica) 686.8

Dandruff 690.18

Dandy fever 061

Dandy-Walker deformity or syndrome (atresia, foramen of Magendie) 742.3
with spina bifida (*see also* Spina bifida) 741.0 ☑

Dangle foot 736.79

Danielssen's disease (anesthetic leprosy) 030.1

Danlos' syndrome 756.83

Darier's disease (congenital) (keratosis follicularis) 757.39
due to vitamin A deficiency 264.8
meaning erythema annulare centrifugum 695.0

Darier-Roussy sarcoid 135

Darling's
disease (*see also* Histoplasmosis, American) 115.00
histoplasmosis (*see also* Histoplasmosis, American) 115.00

Dartre 054.9

Darwin's tubercle 744.29

Davidson's anemia (refractory) 284.9

Davies' disease 425.0

Davies-Colley syndrome (slipping rib) 733.99

Dawson's encephalitis 046.2

Day blindness (*see also* Blindness, day) 368.60

Dead
fetus
retained (in utero) 656.4 ☑
early pregnancy (death before 22 completed weeks gestation) 632
late (death after 22 completed weeks gestation) 656.4 ☑
syndrome 641.3 ☑
labyrinth 386.50
ovum, retained 631

Deaf and dumb NEC 389.7

Deaf mutism (acquired) (congenital) NEC 389.7
endemic 243
hysterical 300.11
syphilitic, congenital 090.0

Deafness (acquired) (bilateral) (both ears) (complete) (congenital) (hereditary) (middle ear) (partial) (unilateral) 389.9
with blue sclera and fragility of bone 756.51
auditory fatigue 389.9
aviation 993.0
nerve injury 951.5
boilermakers' 951.5
central 389.14
with conductive hearing loss 389.2
conductive (air) 389.00
with sensorineural hearing loss 389.2
combined types 389.08
external ear 389.01
inner ear 389.04
middle ear 389.03
multiple types 389.08
tympanic membrane 389.02
emotional (complete) 300.11
functional (complete) 300.11
high frequency 389.8
hysterical (complete) 300.11
injury 951.5
low frequency 389.8
mental 784.69
mixed conductive and sensorineural 389.2
nerve 389.12
with conductive hearing loss 389.2
neural 389.12
with conductive hearing loss 389.2
noise-induced 388.12
nerve injury 951.5
nonspeaking 389.7

Deafness — *continued*
perceptive 389.10
with conductive hearing loss 389.2
central 389.14
combined types 389.18
multiple types 389.18
neural 389.12
sensory 389.11
psychogenic (complete) 306.7
sensorineural (*see also* Deafness, perceptive) 389.10
sensory 389.11
with conductive hearing loss 389.2
specified type NEC 389.8
sudden NEC 388.2
syphilitic 094.89
transient ischemic 388.02
transmission — *see* Deafness, conductive
traumatic 951.5
word (secondary to organic lesion) 784.69
developmental 315.31

Death
after delivery (cause not stated) (sudden) 674.9 ☑
anesthetic
due to
correct substance properly administered 995.4
overdose or wrong substance given 968.4
specified anesthetic — *see* Table of Drugs and Chemicals
during delivery 668.9 ☑
brain 348.8
cardiac — *see* Disease, heart
cause unknown 798.2
cot (infant) 798.0
crib (infant) 798.0
fetus, fetal (cause not stated) (intrauterine) 779.9
early, with retention (before 22 completed weeks gestation) 632
from asphyxia or anoxia (before labor) 768.0
during labor 768.1
late, affecting management of pregnancy (after 22 completed weeks gestation) 656.4 ☑
from pregnancy NEC 646.9 ☑
instantaneous 798.1
intrauterine (*see also* Death, fetus) 779.9
complicating pregnancy 656.4 ☑
maternal, affecting fetus or newborn 761.6
neonatal NEC 779.9
sudden (cause unknown) 798.1
during delivery 669.9 ☑
under anesthesia NEC 668.9 ☑
infant, syndrome (SIDS) 798.0
puerperal, during puerperium 674.9 ☑
unattended (cause unknown) 798.9
under anesthesia NEC
due to
correct substance properly administered 995.4
overdose or wrong substance given 968.4
specified anesthetic — *see* Table of Drugs and Chemicals
during delivery 668.9 ☑
violent 798.1

de Beurmann-Gougerot disease (sporotrichosis) 117.1

Debility (general) (infantile) (postinfectional) 799.3
with nutritional difficulty 269.9
congenital or neonatal NEC 779.9
nervous 300.5
old age 797
senile 797

Débove's disease (splenomegaly) 789.2

Decalcification
bone (*see also* Osteoporosis) 733.00
teeth 521.8

Decapitation 874.9
fetal (to facilitate delivery) 763.89

Decapsulation, kidney 593.89

Decay
dental 521.00
senile 797
tooth, teeth 521.00

☑ Additional Digit Required — Refer to the Tabular List (Numeric Code Section) for Additional Digit Selection

Decensus, uterus — see Prolapse, uterus
Deciduitis (acute)
  with
    abortion — see Abortion, by type, with sepsis
    ectopic pregnancy (see also categories
      633.0-633.9) 639.0
    molar pregnancy (see also categories 630-
      632) 639.0
  affecting fetus or newborn 760.8
  following
    abortion 639.0
    ectopic or molar pregnancy 639.0
  in pregnancy 646.6 ☑
  puerperal, postpartum 670.0 ☑
Deciduoma malignum (M9100/3) 181
Deciduous tooth (retained) 520.6
Decline (general) (see also Debility) 799.3
Decompensation
  cardiac (acute) (chronic) (see also Disease,
    heart) 429.9
    failure — see Failure, heart
  cardiorenal (see also Hypertension, cardiorenal)
    404.90
  cardiovascular (see also Disease,
    cardiovascular) 429.2
  heart (see also Disease, heart) 429.9
    failure — see Failure, heart
  hepatic 572.2
  myocardial (acute) (chronic) (see also Disease,
    heart) 429.9
    failure — see Failure, heart
  respiratory 519.9
Decompression sickness 993.3
Decrease, decreased
  blood
    platelets (see also Thrombocytopenia) 287.5
    pressure 796.3
      due to shock following
        injury 958.4
        operation 998.0
  cardiac reserve — see Disease, heart
  estrogen 256.39
    postablative 256.2
  fetal movements 655.7 ☑
  fragility of erythrocytes 289.89
  function
    adrenal (cortex) 255.4
      medulla 255.5
    ovary in hypopituitarism 253.4
    parenchyma of pancreas 577.8
    pituitary (gland) (lobe) (anterior) 253.2
      posterior (lobe) 253.8
  functional activity 780.99
  glucose 790.29
  haptoglobin (serum) NEC 273.8
  libido 799.81
  platelets (see also Thrombocytopenia) 287.5
  pulse pressure 785.9
  respiration due to shock following injury 958.4
  sexual desire 799.81
  tear secretion NEC 375.15
  tolerance
    fat 579.8
    salt and water 276.9
  vision NEC 369.9
Decubital gangrene 707.00 [785.4]
Decubiti (see also Decubitus) 707.00
Decubitus (ulcer) 707.00
  with gangrene 707.00 [785.4]
  ankle 707.06
  back
    lower 707.03
    upper 707.02
  buttock 707.05
  elbow 707.01
  head 707.09
  heel 707.07
  hip 707.04
  other site 707.09
  sacrum 707.03
  shoulder blades 707.02
Deepening acetabulum 718.85
Defect, defective 759.9
  3-beta-hydroxysteroid dehydrogenase 255.2
  11-hydroxylase 255.2

Defect, defective — continued
  21-hydroxylase 255.2
  abdominal wall, congenital 756.70
  aorticopulmonary septum 745.0
  aortic septal 745.0
  atrial septal (ostium secundum type) 745.5
    acquired 429.71
    ostium primum type 745.61
    sinus venosus 745.8
  atrioventricular
    canal 745.69
    septum 745.4
      acquired 429.71
  atrium secundum 745.5
    acquired 429.71
  auricular septal 745.5
    acquired 429.71
  bilirubin excretion 277.4
  biosynthesis, testicular androgen 257.2
  bulbar septum 745.0
  butanol-insoluble iodide 246.1
  chromosome — see Anomaly, chromosome
  circulation (acquired) 459.9
    congenital 747.9
    newborn 747.9
  clotting NEC (see also Defect, coagulation)
    286.9
  coagulation (factor) (see also Deficiency,
    coagulation factor) 286.9
    with
      abortion — see Abortion, by type, with
        hemorrhage
      ectopic pregnancy (see also categories
        634-638) 639.1
      molar pregnancy (see also categories
        630-632) 639.1
    acquired (any) 286.7
    antepartum or intrapartum 641.3 ☑
      affecting fetus or newborn 762.1
    causing hemorrhage of pregnancy or delivery
      641.3 ☑
    due to
      liver disease 286.7
      vitamin K deficiency 286.7
    newborn, transient 776.3
    postpartum 666.3 ☑
    specified type NEC 286.3
  conduction (heart) 426.9
    bone (see also Deafness, conductive) 389.00
  congenital, organ or site NEC — see also
    Anomaly
    circulation 747.9
    Descemet's membrane 743.9
      specified type NEC 743.49
    diaphragm 756.6
    ectodermal 757.9
    esophagus 750.9
    pulmonic cusps — see Anomaly, heart valve
    respiratory system 748.9
      specified type NEC 748.8
  cushion endocardial 745.60
  dentin (hereditary) 520.5
  Descemet's membrane (congenital) 743.9
    acquired 371.30
    specific type NEC 743.49
  deutan 368.52
  developmental — see also Anomaly, by site
    cauda equina 742.59
    left ventricle 746.9
      with atresia or hypoplasia of aortic orifice
        or valve, with hypoplasia of
        ascending aorta 746.7
      in hypoplastic left heart syndrome 746.7
    testis 752.9
    vessel 747.9
  diaphragm
    with elevation, eventration, or hernia — see
      Hernia, diaphragm
    congenital 756.6
      with elevation, eventration, or hernia
        756.6
      gross (with elevation, eventration, or
        hernia) 756.6
  ectodermal, congenital 757.9
  Eisenmenger's (ventricular septal defect) 745.4
  endocardial cushion 745.60
    specified type NEC 745.69

Defect, defective — continued
  esophagus, congenital 750.9
  extensor retinaculum 728.9
  fibrin polymerization (see also Defect,
    coagulation) 286.3
  filling
    biliary tract 793.3
    bladder 793.5
    gallbladder 793.3
    kidney 793.5
    stomach 793.4
    ureter 793.5
  fossa ovalis 745.5
  gene, carrier (suspected) of V83.89
  Gerbode 745.4
  glaucomatous, without elevated tension 365.89
  Hageman (factor) (see also Defect, coagulation)
    286.3
  hearing (see also Deafness) 389.9
  high grade 317
  homogentisic acid 270.2
  interatrial septal 745.5
    acquired 429.71
  interauricular septal 745.5
    acquired 429.71
  interventricular septal 745.4
    with pulmonary stenosis or atresia,
      dextraposition of aorta, and
      hypertrophy of right ventricle 745.2
    acquired 429.71
    in tetralogy of Fallot 745.2
  iodide trapping 246.1
  iodotyrosine dehalogenase 246.1
  kynureninase 270.2
  learning, specific 315.2
  mental (see also Retardation, mental) 319
  osteochondral NEC 738.8
  ostium
    primum 745.61
    secundum 745.5
  pericardium 746.89
  peroxidase-binding 246.1
  placental blood supply — see Placenta,
    insufficiency
  platelet (qualitative) 287.1
    constitutional 286.4
  postural, spine 737.9
  protan 368.51
  pulmonic cusps, congenital 746.00
  renal pelvis 753.9
    obstructive 753.29
    specified type NEC 753.3
  respiratory system, congenital 748.9
    specified type NEC 748.8
  retina, retinal 361.30
    with detachment (see also Detachment,
      retina, with retinal defect) 361.00
    multiple 361.33
      with detachment 361.02
    nerve fiber bundle 362.85
    single 361.30
      with detachment 361.01
  septal (closure) (heart) NEC 745.9
    acquired 429.71
    atrial 745.5
    specified type NEC 745.8
  speech NEC 784.5
    developmental 315.39
    secondary to organic lesion 784.5
  Taussig-Bing (transposition, aorta and
    overriding pulmonary artery) 745.11
  teeth, wedge 521.20
  thyroid hormone synthesis 246.1
  tritan 368.53
  ureter 753.9
    obstructive 753.29
  vascular (acquired) (local) 459.9
    congenital (peripheral) NEC 747.60
      gastrointestinal 747.61
      lower limb 747.64
      renal 747.62
      specified NEC 747.69
      spinal 747.82
      upper limb 747.63

Defect, defective — continued
- ventricular septal 745.4
  - with pulmonary stenosis or atresia, dextraposition of aorta, and hypertrophy of right ventricle 745.2
  - acquired 429.71
  - atrioventricular canal type 745.69
  - between infundibulum and anterior portion 745.4
  - in tetralogy of Fallot 745.2
  - isolated anterior 745.4
- vision NEC 369.9
- visual field 368.40
  - arcuate 368.43
  - heteronymous, bilateral 368.47
  - homonymous, bilateral 368.46
  - localized NEC 368.44
  - nasal step 368.44
  - peripheral 368.44
  - sector 368.43
- voice 784.40
- wedge, teeth (abrasion) 521.20

Defeminization syndrome 255.2

Deferentitis 608.4
- gonorrheal (acute) 098.14
  - chronic or duration of 2 months or over 098.34

Defibrination syndrome (see also Fibrinolysis) 286.6

Deficiency, deficient
- 3-beta-hydroxysteroid dehydrogenase 255.2
- 6-phosphogluconic dehydrogenase (anemia) 282.2
- 11-beta-hydroxylase 255.2
- 17-alpha-hydroxylase 255.2
- 18-hydroxysteroid dehydrogenase 255.2
- 20-alpha-hydroxylase 255.2
- 21-hydroxylase 255.2
- AAT (alpha-1 antitrypsin) 273.4
- abdominal muscle syndrome 756.79
- accelerator globulin (Ac G) (blood) (see also Defect, coagulation) 286.3
- AC globulin (congenital) (see also Defect, coagulation) 286.3
  - acquired 286.7
- activating factor (blood) (see also Defect, coagulation) 286.3
- adenohypophyseal 253.2
- adenosine deaminase 277.2
- aldolase (hereditary) 271.2
- alpha-1-antitrypsin 273.4
- alpha-1-trypsin inhibitor 273.4
- alpha-fucosidase 271.8
- alpha-lipoprotein 272.5
- alpha-mannosidase 271.8
- amino acid 270.9
- anemia — see Anemia, deficiency
- aneurin 265.1
  - with beriberi 265.0
- antibody NEC 279.00
- antidiuretic hormone 253.5
- antihemophilic
  - factor (A) 286.0
    - B 286.1
    - C 286.2
  - globulin (AHG) NEC 286.0
- antithrombin III 289.81
- antitrypsin 273.4
- argininosuccinate synthetase or lyase 270.6
- ascorbic acid (with scurvy) 267
- autoprothrombin
  - I (see also Defect, coagulation) 286.3
  - II 286.1
  - C (see also Defect, coagulation) 286.3
- bile salt 579.8
- biotin 266.2
- biotinidase 277.6
- bradykinase-1 277.6
- brancher enzyme (amylopectinosis) 271.0
- calciferol 268.9
  - with
    - osteomalacia 268.2
    - rickets (see also Rickets) 268.0
- calcium 275.40
  - dietary 269.3

Deficiency, deficient — continued
- calorie, severe 261
- carbamyl phosphate synthetase 270.6
- cardiac (see also Insufficiency, myocardial) 428.0
- carnitine 277.81
  - due to
    - hemodialysis 277.83
    - inborn errors of metabolism 277.82
    - valproic acid therapy 277.83
  - iatrogenic 277.83
  - palmitoyltransferase (CPT1, CPT2) 277.85
  - palmityl transferase (CPT1, CPT2) 277.85
  - primary 277.81
  - secondary 277.84
- carotene 264.9
- Carr factor (see also Defect, coagulation) 286.9
- central nervous system 349.9
- ceruloplasmin 275.1
- cevitamic acid (with scurvy) 267
- choline 266.2
- Christmas factor 286.1
- chromium 269.3
- citrin 269.1
- clotting (blood) (see also Defect, coagulation) 286.9
- coagulation factor NEC 286.9
  - with
    - abortion — see Abortion, by type, with hemorrhage
    - ectopic pregnancy (see also categories 634-638) 639.1
    - molar pregnancy (see also categories 630-632) 639.1
  - acquired (any) 286.7
  - antepartum or intrapartum 641.3 ☑
    - affecting fetus or newborn 762.1
  - due to
    - liver disease 286.7
    - vitamin K deficiency 286.7
  - newborn, transient 776.3
  - postpartum 666.3 ☑
  - specified type NEC 286.3
- color vision (congenital) 368.59
  - acquired 368.55
- combined, two or more coagulation factors (see also Defect, coagulation) 286.9
- complement factor NEC 279.8
- contact factor (see also Defect, coagulation) 286.3
- copper NEC 275.1
- corticoadrenal 255.4
- craniofacial axis 756.0
- cyanocobalamin (vitamin B_{12}) 266.2
- debrancher enzyme (limit dextrinosis) 271.0
- desmolase 255.2
- diet 269.9
- dihydrofolate reductase 281.2
- dihydropteridine reductase 270.1
- disaccharidase (intestinal) 271.3
- disease NEC 269.9
- ear(s) V48.8
- edema 262
- endocrine 259.9
- enzymes, circulating NEC (see also Deficiency, by specific enzyme) 277.6
- ergosterol 268.9
  - with
    - osteomalacia 268.2
    - rickets (see also Rickets) 268.0
- erythrocytic glutathione (anemia) 282.2
- eyelid(s) V48.8
- factor (see also Defect, coagulation) 286.9
  - I (congenital) (fibrinogen) 286.3
    - antepartum or intrapartum 641.3 ☑
      - affecting fetus or newborn 762.1
    - newborn, transient 776.3
    - postpartum 666.3 ☑
  - II (congenital) (prothrombin) 286.3
  - V (congenital) (labile) 286.3
  - VII (congenital) (stable) 286.3
  - VIII (congenital) (functional) 286.0
    - with
      - functional defect 286.0
      - vascular defect 286.4
  - IX (Christmas) (congenital) (functional) 286.1

Deficiency, deficient — continued
- factor (see also Defect, coagulation) — continued
  - X (congenital) (Stuart-Prower) 286.3
  - XI (congenital) (plasma thromboplastin antecedent) 286.2
  - XII (congenital) (Hageman) 286.3
  - XIII (congenital) (fibrin stabilizing) 286.3
  - Hageman 286.3
  - multiple (congenital) 286.9
    - acquired 286.7
- fibrinase (see also Defect, coagulation) 286.3
- fibrinogen (congenital) (see also Defect, coagulation) 286.3
  - acquired 286.6
- fibrin-stabilizing factor (congenital) (see also Defect, coagulation) 286.3
- finger — see Absence, finger
- fletcher factor (see also Defect, coagulation) 286.9
- fluorine 269.3
- folate, anemia 281.2
- folic acid (vitamin B_c) 266.2
  - anemia 281.2
- follicle-stimulating hormone (FSH) 253.4
- fructokinase 271.2
- fructose-1, 6-diphosphate 271.2
- fructose-1-phosphate aldolase 271.2
- FSH (follicle-stimulating hormone) 253.4
- fucosidase 271.8
- galactokinase 271.1
- galactose-1-phosphate uridyl transferase 271.1
- gamma globulin in blood 279.00
- glass factor (see also Defect, coagulation) 286.3
- glucocorticoid 255.4
- glucose-6-phosphatase 271.0
- glucose-6-phosphate dehydrogenase anemia 282.2
- glucuronyl transferase 277.4
- glutathione-reductase (anemia) 282.2
- glycogen synthetase 271.0
- growth hormone 253.3
- Hageman factor (congenital) (see also Defect, coagulation) 286.3
- head V48.0
- hemoglobin (see also Anemia) 285.9
- hepatophosphorylase 271.0
- hexose monophosphate (HMP) shunt 282.2
- HGH (human growth hormone) 253.3
- HG-PRT 277.2
- homogentisic acid oxidase 270.2
- hormone — see also Deficiency, by specific hormone
  - anterior pituitary (isolated) (partial) NEC 253.4
    - growth (human) 253.3
  - follicle-stimulating 253.4
  - growth (human) (isolated) 253.3
  - human growth 253.3
  - interstitial cell-stimulating 253.4
  - luteinizing 253.4
  - melanocyte-stimulating 253.4
  - testicular 257.2
- human growth hormone 253.3
- humoral 279.00
  - with
    - hyper-IgM 279.05
      - autosomal recessive 279.05
      - X-linked 279.05
    - increased IgM 279.05
  - congenital hypogammaglobulinemia 279.04
  - non-sex-linked 279.06
  - selective immunoglobulin NEC 279.03
    - IgA 279.01
    - IgG 279.03
    - IgM 279.02
      - increased 279.05
  - specified NEC 279.09
- hydroxylase 255.2
- hypoxanthine-guanine phosphoribosyltransferase (HG-PRT) 277.2
- ICSH (interstitial cell-stimulating hormone) 253.4

Deficiency, deficient — *continued*
immunity NEC 279.3
    cell-mediated 279.10
        with
            hyperimmunoglobulinemia 279.2
            thrombocytopenia and eczema 279.12
        specified NEC 279.19
    combined (severe) 279.2
        syndrome 279.2
    common variable 279.06
    humoral NEC 279.00
    IgA (secretory) 279.01
    IgG 279.03
    IgM 279.02
    immunoglobulin, selective NEC 279.03
        IgA 279.01
        IgG 279.03
        IgM 279.02
    inositol (B complex) 266.2
    interferon 279.4
    internal organ V47.0
    interstitial cell-stimulating hormone (ICSH)
        253.4
    intrinsic factor (Castle's) (congenital) 281.0
    intrinsic (urethral) sphincter (ISD) 599.82
    invertase 271.3
    iodine 269.3
    iron, anemia 280.9
    labile factor (congenital) (*see also* Defect,
        coagulation) 286.3
        acquired 286.7
    lacrimal fluid (acquired) 375.15
        congenital 743.64
    lactase 271.3
    Laki-Lorand factor (*see also* Defect,
        coagulation) 286.3
    lecithin-cholesterol acyltranferase 272.5
    LH (luteinizing hormone) 253.4
    limb V49.0
        lower V49.0
            congenital (*see also* Deficiency, lower
                limb, congenital) 755.30
        upper V49.0
            congenital (*see also* Deficiency, upper
                limb, congenital) 755.20
    lipocaic 577.8
    lipoid (high-density) 272.5
    lipoprotein (familial) (high density) 272.5
    liver phosphorylase 271.0
    long chain 3-hydroxyacyl CoA dehydrogenase
        (LCHAD) 277.85
    long chain/very long chain acyl CoA
        dehydrogenase (LCAD, VLCAD) 277.85
    lower limb V49.0
        congenital 755.30
            with complete absence of distal elements
                755.31
            longitudinal (complete) (partial) (with
                distal deficiencies, incomplete)
                755.32
                with complete absence of distal
                    elements 755.31
                combined femoral, tibial, fibular
                    (incomplete) 755.33
                femoral 755.34
                fibular 755.37
                metatarsal(s) 755.38
                phalange(s) 755.39
                    meaning all digits 755.31
                tarsal(s) 755.38
                tibia 755.36
                tibiofibular 755.35
            transverse 755.31
    luteinizing hormone (LH) 253.4
    lysosomal alpha-1, 4 glucosidase 271.0
    magnesium 275.2
    mannosidase 271.8
    medium chain acyl CoA dehydrogenase (MCAD)
        277.85
    melanocyte-stimulating hormone (MSH) 253.4
    menadione (vitamin K) 269.0
        newborn 776.0
    mental (familial) (hereditary) (*see also*
        Retardation, mental) 319
    mineral NEC 269.3
    molybdenum 269.3
    moral 301.7

Deficiency, deficient — *continued*
multiple, syndrome 260
myocardial (*see also* Insufficiency, myocardial)
    428.0
myophosphorylase 271.0
NADH (DPNH)-methemoglobin-reductase
    (congenital) 289.7
NADH-diaphorase or reductase (congenital)
    289.7
neck V48.1
niacin (amide) (-tryptophan) 265.2
nicotinamide 265.2
nicotinic acid (amide) 265.2
nose V48.8
number of teeth (*see also* Anodontia) 520.0
nutrition, nutritional 269.9
    specified NEC 269.8
ornithine transcarbamylase 270.6
ovarian 256.39
oxygen (*see also* Anoxia) 799.02   ▲
pantothenic acid 266.2
parathyroid (gland) 252.1
phenylalanine hydroxylase 270.1
phosphoenolpyruvate carboxykinase 271.8
phosphofructokinase 271.2
phosphoglucomutase 271.0
phosphohexosisomerase 271.0
phosphomannomutase 271.8   ●
phosphomannose isomerase 271.8   ●
phosphomannosyl mutase 271.8   ●
phosphorylase kinase, liver 271.0
pituitary (anterior) 253.2
    posterior 253.5
placenta — *see* Placenta, insufficiency
plasma
    cell 279.00
    protein (paraproteinemia) (pyroglobulinemia)
        273.8
        gamma globulin 279.00
    thromboplastin
        antecedent (PTA) 286.2
        component (PTC) 286.1
platelet NEC 287.1
    constitutional 286.4
polyglandular 258.9
potassium (K) 276.8
proaccelerin (congenital) (*see also* Defect,
    congenital) 286.3
    acquired 286.7
proconvertin factor (congenital) (*see also*
    Defect, coagulation) 286.3
    acquired 286.7
prolactin 253.4
protein 260
    anemia 281.4
    C 289.81
    plasma — *see* Deficiency, plasma, protein
    S 289.81
prothrombin (congenital) (*see also* Defect,
    coagulation) 286.3
    acquired 286.7
Prower factor (*see also* Defect, coagulation)
    286.3
PRT 277.2
pseudocholinesterase 289.89
psychobiological 301.6
PTA 286.2
PTC 286.1
purine nucleoside phosphorylase 277.2
pyracin (alpha) (beta) 266.1
pyridoxal 266.1
pyridoxamine 266.1
pyridoxine (derivatives) 266.1
pyruvate carboxylase 271.8
pyruvate dehydrogenase 271.8
pyruvate kinase (PK) 282.3
riboflavin (vitamin B_2) 266.0
saccadic eye movements 379.57
salivation 527.7
salt 276.1
secretion
    ovary 256.39
    salivary gland (any) 527.7
    urine 788.5
selenium 269.3
serum
    antitrypsin, familial 273.4

Deficiency, deficient — *continued*
serum — *continued*
    protein (congenital) 273.8
short chain acyl CoA dehydrogenase (SCAD)
    277.85
smooth pursuit movements (eye) 379.58
sodium (Na) 276.1
SPCA (*see also* Defect, coagulation) 286.3
specified NEC 269.8
stable factor (congenital) (*see also* Defect,
    coagulation) 286.3
    acquired 286.7
Stuart (-Prower) factor (*see also* Defect,
    coagulation) 286.3
sucrase 271.3
sucrase-isomaltase 271.3
sulfite oxidase 270.0
syndrome, multiple 260
thiamine, thiaminic (chloride) 265.1
thrombokinase (*see also* Defect, coagulation)
    286.3
    newborn 776.0
thrombopoieten 287.39   ▲
thymolymphatic 279.2
thyroid (gland) 244.9
tocopherol 269.1
toe — *see* Absence, toe
tooth bud (*see also* Anodontia) 520.0
trunk V48.1
UDPG-glycogen transferase 271.0
upper limb V49.0
    congenital 755.20
        with complete absence of distal elements
            755.21
        longitudinal (complete) (partial) (with
            distal deficiencies, incomplete)
            755.22
            carpal(s) 755.28
            combined humeral, radial, ulnar
                (incomplete) 755.23
            humeral 755.24
            metacarpal(s) 755.28
            phalange(s) 755.29
                meaning all digits 755.21
            radial 755.26
            radioulnar 755.25
            ulnar 755.27
        transverse (complete) (partial) 755.21
vascular 459.9
vasopressin 253.5
viosterol (*see also* Deficiency, calciferol) 268.9
vitamin (multiple) NEC 269.2
    A 264.9
        with
            Bitôt's spot 264.1
                corneal 264.2
                    with corneal ulceration 264.3
            keratomalacia 264.4
            keratosis, follicular 264.8
            night blindness 264.5
            scar of cornea, xerophthalmic 264.6
            specified manifestation NEC 264.8
                ocular 264.7
            xeroderma 264.8
            xerophthalmia 264.7
            xerosis
                conjunctival 264.0
                    with Bitôt's spot 264.1
                corneal 264.2
                    with corneal ulceration 264.3
    B (complex) NEC 266.9
        with
            beriberi 265.0
            pellagra 265.2
        specified type NEC 266.2
    B_1 NEC 265.1
        beriberi 265.0
    B_2 266.0
    B_6 266.1
    B_{12} 266.2
    B_c (folic acid) 266.2
    C (ascorbic acid) (with scurvy) 267
    D (calciferol) (ergosterol) 268.9
        with
            osteomalacia 268.2
            rickets (*see also* Rickets) 268.0
    E 269.1

Deficiency, deficient — *continued*
 vitamin (multiple) NEC — *continued*
  folic acid 266.2
  G 266.0
  H 266.2
  K 269.0
   of newborn 776.0
  nicotinic acid 265.2
  P 269.1
  PP 265.2
  specified NEC 269.1
 zinc 269.3

Deficient — *see also* Deficiency
 blink reflex 374.45
 craniofacial axis 756.0
 number of teeth (*see also* Anodontia) 520.0
 secretion of urine 788.5

Deficit
 neurologic NEC 781.99
  due to
   cerebrovascular lesion (*see also* Disease,
    cerebrovascular, acute) 436
   late effect — *see* Late effect(s) (of)
    cerebrovascular disease
   transient ischemic attack 435.9
 oxygen 799.02   ▲

Deflection
 radius 736.09
 septum (acquired) (nasal) (nose) 470
 spine — *see* Curvature, spine
 turbinate (nose) 470

Defluvium
 capillorum (*see also* Alopecia) 704.00
 ciliorum 374.55
 unguium 703.8

Deformity 738.9
 abdomen, congenital 759.9
 abdominal wall
  acquired 738.8
  congenital 756.70
  muscle deficiency syndrome 756.79
 acquired (unspecified site) 738.9
  specified site NEC 738.8
 adrenal gland (congenital) 759.1
 alimentary tract, congenital 751.9
  lower 751.5
  specified type NEC 751.8
  upper (any part, except tongue) 750.9
   specified type NEC 750.8
   tongue 750.10
    specified type NEC 750.19
 ankle (joint) (acquired) 736.70
  abduction 718.47
  congenital 755.69
  contraction 718.47
  specified NEC 736.79
 anus (congenital) 751.5
  acquired 569.49
 aorta (congenital) 747.20
  acquired 447.8
  arch 747.21
   acquired 447.8
  coarctation 747.10
 aortic
  arch 747.21
   acquired 447.8
  cusp or valve (congenital) 746.9
   acquired (*see also* Endocarditis, aortic)
    424.1
  ring 747.21
 appendix 751.5
 arm (acquired) 736.89
  congenital 755.50
 arteriovenous (congenital) (peripheral) NEC
  747.60
  gastrointestinal 747.61
  lower limb 747.64
  renal 747.62
  specified NEC 747.69
  spinal 747.82
  upper limb 747.63
 artery (congenital) (peripheral) NEC (*see also*
  Deformity, vascular) 747.60
  acquired 447.8
  cerebral 747.81

Deformity — *continued*
 artery NEC (*see also* Deformity, vascular) —
  continued
  coronary (congenital) 746.85
   acquired (*see also* Ischemia, heart) 414.9
  retinal 743.9
  umbilical 747.5
 atrial septal (congenital) (heart) 745.5
 auditory canal (congenital) (external) (*see also*
  Deformity, ear) 744.3
  acquired 380.50
 auricle
  ear (congenital) (*see also* Deformity, ear)
   744.3
   acquired 380.32
  heart (congenital) 746.9
 back (acquired) — *see* Deformity, spine
 Bartholin's duct (congenital) 750.9
 bile duct (congenital) 751.60
  acquired 576.8
   with calculus, choledocholithiasis, or
    stones — *see* Choledocholithiasis
 biliary duct or passage (congenital) 751.60
  acquired 576.8
   with calculus, choledocholithiasis, or
    stones — *see* Choledocholithiasis
 bladder (neck) (sphincter) (trigone) (acquired)
  596.8
  congenital 753.9
 bone (acquired) NEC 738.9
  congenital 756.9
  turbinate 738.0
 boutonniere (finger) 736.21
 brain (congenital) 742.9
  acquired 348.8
  multiple 742.4
  reduction 742.2
  vessel (congenital) 747.81
 breast (acquired) 611.8
  congenital 757.9
 bronchus (congenital) 748.3
  acquired 519.1
 bursa, congenital 756.9
 canal of Nuck 752.9
 canthus (congenital) 743.9
  acquired 374.89
 capillary (acquired) 448.9
  congenital NEC (*see also* Deformity,
   vascular) 747.60
 cardiac — *see* Deformity, heart
 cardiovascular system (congenital) 746.9
 caruncle, lacrimal (congenital) 743.9
  acquired 375.69
 cascade, stomach 537.6
 cecum (congenital) 751.5
  acquired 569.89
 cerebral (congenital) 742.9
  acquired 348.8
 cervix (acquired) (uterus) 622.8
  congenital 752.40
 cheek (acquired) 738.19
  congenital 744.9
 chest (wall) (acquired) 738.3
  congenital 754.89
  late effect of rickets 268.1
 chin (acquired) 738.19
  congenital 744.9
 choroid (congenital) 743.9
  acquired 363.8
  plexus (congenital) 742.9
   acquired 349.2
 cicatricial — *see* Cicatrix
 cilia (congenital) 743.9
  acquired 374.89
 circulatory system (congenital) 747.9
 clavicle (acquired) 738.8
  congenital 755.51
 clitoris (congenital) 752.40
  acquired 624.8
 clubfoot — *see* Clubfoot
 coccyx (acquired) 738.6
  congenital 756.10
 colon (congenital) 751.5
  acquired 569.89
 concha (ear) (congenital) (*see also* Deformity,
  ear) 744.3
  acquired 380.32

Deformity — *continued*
 congenital, organ or site not listed (*see also*
  Anomaly) 759.9
 cornea (congenital) 743.9
  acquired 371.70
 coronary artery (congenital) 746.85
  acquired (*see also* Ischemia, heart) 414.9
 cranium (acquired) 738.19
  congenital (*see also* Deformity, skull,
   congenital) 756.0
 cricoid cartilage (congenital) 748.3
  acquired 478.79
 cystic duct (congenital) 751.60
  acquired 575.8
 Dandy-Walker 742.3
  with spina bifida (*see also* Spina bifida)
   741.0 ☑
 diaphragm (congenital) 756.6
  acquired 738.8
 digestive organ(s) or system (congenital) NEC
  751.9
  specified type NEC 751.8
 ductus arteriosus 747.0
 duodenal bulb 537.89
 duodenum (congenital) 751.5
  acquired 537.89
 dura (congenital) 742.9
  brain 742.4
   acquired 349.2
  spinal 742.59
   acquired 349.2
 ear (congenital) 744.3
  acquired 380.32
  auricle 744.3
   causing impairment of hearing 744.02
  causing impairment of hearing 744.00
  external 744.3
   causing impairment of hearing 744.02
  internal 744.05
  lobule 744.3
  middle 744.03
   ossicles 744.04
  ossicles 744.04
 ectodermal (congenital) NEC 757.9
  specified type NEC 757.8
 ejaculatory duct (congenital) 752.9
  acquired 608.89
 elbow (joint) (acquired) 736.00
  congenital 755.50
  contraction 718.42
 endocrine gland NEC 759.2
 epididymis (congenital) 752.9
  acquired 608.89
  torsion 608.2
 epiglottis (congenital) 748.3
  acquired 478.79
 esophagus (congenital) 750.9
  acquired 530.89
 Eustachian tube (congenital) NEC 744.3
  specified type NEC 744.24
 extremity (acquired) 736.9
  congenital, except reduction deformity 755.9
   lower 755.60
   upper 755.50
  reduction — *see* Deformity, reduction
 eye (congenital) 743.9
  acquired 379.8
  muscle 743.9
 eyebrow (congenital) 744.89
 eyelid (congenital) 743.9
  acquired 374.89
  specified type NEC 743.62
 face (acquired) 738.19
  congenital (any part) 744.9
   due to intrauterine malposition and
    pressure 754.0
 fallopian tube (congenital) 752.10
  acquired 620.8
 femur (acquired) 736.89
  congenital 755.60
 fetal
  with fetopelvic disproportion 653.7 ☑
   affecting fetus or newborn 763.1
  causing obstructed labor 660.1 ☑
   affecting fetus or newborn 763.1
  known or suspected, affecting management
   of pregnancy 655.9 ☑

☑ Additional Digit Required — Refer to the Tabular List (Numeric Code Section) for Additional Digit Selection

2006 ICD-9-CM ▶◀ Revised Text ● New Line ▲ Revised Code **October 2005** • Volume 2 — **83**

Deformity — *continued*
finger (acquired) 736.20
boutonniere type 736.21
congenital 755.50
flexion contracture 718.44
swan neck 736.22
flexion (joint) (acquired) 736.9
congenital NEC 755.9
hip or thigh (acquired) 736.39
congenital (*see also* Subluxation, congenital, hip) 754.32
foot (acquired) 736.70
cavovarus 736.75
congenital 754.59
congenital NEC 754.70
specified type NEC 754.79
valgus (acquired) 736.79
congenital 754.60
specified type NEC 754.69
varus (acquired) 736.79
congenital 754.50
specified type NEC 754.59
forearm (acquired) 736.00
congenital 755.50
forehead (acquired) 738.19
congenital (*see also* Deformity, skull, congenital) 756.0
frontal bone (acquired) 738.19
congenital (*see also* Deformity, skull, congenital) 756.0
gallbladder (congenital) 751.60
acquired 575.8
gastrointestinal tract (congenital) NEC 751.9
acquired 569.89
specified type NEC 751.8
genitalia, genital organ(s) or system NEC
congenital 752.9
female (congenital) 752.9
acquired 629.8
external 752.40
internal 752.9
male (congenital) 752.9
acquired 608.89
globe (eye) (congenital) 743.9
acquired 360.89
gum (congenital) 750.9
acquired 523.9
gunstock 736.02
hand (acquired) 736.00
claw 736.06
congenital 755.50
minus (and plus) (intrinsic) 736.09
pill roller (intrinsic) 736.09
plus (and minus) (intrinsic) 736.09
swan neck (intrinsic) 736.09
head (acquired) 738.10
congenital (*see also* Deformity, skull, congenital) 756.0
specified NEC 738.19
heart (congenital) 746.9
auricle (congenital) 746.9
septum 745.9
auricular 745.5
specified type NEC 745.8
ventricular 745.4
valve (congenital) NEC 746.9
acquired — *see* Endocarditis
pulmonary (congenital) 746.00
specified type NEC 746.89
ventricle (congenital) 746.9
heel (acquired) 736.76
congenital 755.67
hepatic duct (congenital) 751.60
acquired 576.8
with calculus, choledocholithiasis, or stones — *see* Choledocholithiasis
hip (joint) (acquired) 736.30
congenital NEC 755.63
flexion 718.45
congenital (*see also* Subluxation, congenital, hip) 754.32
hourglass — *see* Contraction, hourglass
humerus (acquired) 736.89
congenital 755.50
hymen (congenital) 752.40
hypophyseal (congenital) 759.2

Deformity — *continued*
ileocecal (coil) (valve) (congenital) 751.5
acquired 569.89
ileum (intestine) (congenital) 751.5
acquired 569.89
ilium (acquired) 738.6
congenital 755.60
integument (congenital) 757.9
intervertebral cartilage or disc (acquired) — *see also* Displacement, intervertebral disc
congenital 756.10
intestine (large) (small) (congenital) 751.5
acquired 569.89
iris (acquired) 364.75
congenital 743.9
prolapse 364.8
ischium (acquired) 738.6
congenital 755.60
jaw (acquired) (congenital) NEC 524.9
due to intrauterine malposition and pressure 754.0
joint (acquired) NEC 738.8
congenital 755.9
contraction (abduction) (adduction) (extension) (flexion) — *see* Contraction, joint
kidney(s) (calyx) (pelvis) (congenital) 753.9
acquired 593.89
vessel 747.62
acquired 459.9
Klippel-Feil (brevicollis) 756.16
knee (acquired) NEC 736.6
congenital 755.64
labium (majus) (minus) (congenital) 752.40
acquired 624.8
lacrimal apparatus or duct (congenital) 743.9
acquired 375.69
larynx (muscle) (congenital) 748.3
acquired 478.79
web (glottic) (subglottic) 748.2
leg (lower) (upper) (acquired) NEC 736.89
congenital 755.60
reduction — *see* Deformity, reduction, lower limb
lens (congenital) 743.9
acquired 379.39
lid (fold) (congenital) 743.9
acquired 374.89
ligament (acquired) 728.9
congenital 756.9
limb (acquired) 736.9
congenital, except reduction deformity 755.9
lower 755.60
reduction (*see also* Deformity, reduction, lower limb) 755.30
upper 755.50
reduction (*see also* Deformity, reduction, upper limb) 755.20
specified NEC 736.89
lip (congenital) NEC 750.9
acquired 528.5
specified type NEC 750.26
liver (congenital) 751.60
acquired 573.8
duct (congenital) 751.60
acquired 576.8
with calculus, choledocholithiasis, or stones — *see* Choledocholithiasis
lower extremity — *see* Deformity, leg
lumbosacral (joint) (region) (congenital) 756.10
acquired 738.5
lung (congenital) 748.60
acquired 518.89
specified type NEC 748.69
lymphatic system, congenital 759.9
Madelung's (radius) 755.54
maxilla (acquired) (congenital) 524.9
meninges or membrane (congenital) 742.9
brain 742.4
acquired 349.2
spinal (cord) 742.59
acquired 349.2
mesentery (congenital) 751.9
acquired 568.89
metacarpus (acquired) 736.00
congenital 755.50

Deformity — *continued*
metatarsus (acquired) 736.70
congenital 754.70
middle ear, except ossicles (congenital) 744.03
ossicles 744.04
mitral (leaflets) (valve) (congenital) 746.9
acquired — *see* Endocarditis, mitral
Ebstein's 746.89
parachute 746.5
specified type NEC 746.89
stenosis, congenital 746.5
mouth (acquired) 528.9
congenital NEC 750.9
specified type NEC 750.26
multiple, congenital NEC 759.7
specified type NEC 759.89
muscle (acquired) 728.9
congenital 756.9
specified type NEC 756.89
sternocleidomastoid (due to intrauterine malposition and pressure) 754.1
musculoskeletal system, congenital NEC 756.9
specified type NEC 756.9
nail (acquired) 703.9
congenital 757.9
nasal — *see* Deformity, nose
neck (acquired) NEC 738.2
congenital (any part) 744.9
sternocleidomastoid 754.1
nervous system (congenital) 742.9
nipple (congenital) 757.9
acquired 611.8
nose, nasal (cartilage) (acquired) 738.0
bone (turbinate) 738.0
congenital 748.1
bent 754.0
squashed 754.0
saddle 738.0
syphilitic 090.5
septum 470
congenital 748.1
sinus (wall) (congenital) 748.1
acquired 738.0
syphilitic (congenital) 090.5
late 095.8
ocular muscle (congenital) 743.9
acquired 378.60
opticociliary vessels (congenital) 743.9
orbit (congenital) (eye) 743.9
acquired NEC 376.40
associated with craniofacial deformities 376.44
due to
bone disease 376.43
surgery 376.47
trauma 376.47
organ of Corti (congenital) 744.05
ovary (congenital) 752.0
acquired 620.8
oviduct (congenital) 752.10
acquired 620.8
palate (congenital) 750.9
acquired 526.89
cleft (congenital) (*see also* Cleft, palate) 749.00
hard, acquired 526.89
soft, acquired 528.9
pancreas (congenital) 751.7
acquired 577.8
parachute, mitral valve 746.5
parathyroid (gland) 759.2
parotid (gland) (congenital) 750.9
acquired 527.8
patella (acquired) 736.6
congenital 755.64
pelvis, pelvic (acquired) (bony) 738.6
with disproportion (fetopelvic) 653.0 ☑
affecting fetus or newborn 763.1
causing obstructed labor 660.1 ☑
affecting fetus or newborn 763.1
congenital 755.60
rachitic (late effect) 268.1
penis (glans) (congenital) 752.9
acquired 607.89
pericardium (congenital) 746.9
acquired — *see* Pericarditis

Deformity — *continued*
  pharynx (congenital) 750.9
    acquired 478.29
  Pierre Robin (congenital) 756.0
  pinna (acquired) 380.32
    congenital 744.3
  pituitary (congenital) 759.2
  pleural folds (congenital) 748.8
  portal vein (congenital) 747.40
  posture — *see* Curvature, spine
  prepuce (congenital) 752.9
    acquired 607.89
  prostate (congenital) 752.9
    acquired 602.8
  pulmonary valve — *see* Endocarditis,
    pulmonary
  pupil (congenital) 743.9
    acquired 364.75
  pylorus (congenital) 750.9
    acquired 537.89
  rachitic (acquired), healed or old 268.1
  radius (acquired) 736.00
    congenital 755.50
      reduction — *see* Deformity, reduction,
        upper limb
  rectovaginal septum (congenital) 752.40
    acquired 623.8
  rectum (congenital) 751.5
    acquired 569.49
  reduction (extremity) (limb) 755.4
    brain 742.2
    lower limb 755.30
      with complete absence of distal elements
        755.31
      longitudinal (complete) (partial) (with
        distal deficiencies, incomplete)
        755.32
        with complete absence of distal
          elements 755.31
        combined femoral, tibial, fibular
          (incomplete) 755.33
        femoral 755.34
        fibular 755.37
        metatarsal(s) 755.38
        phalange(s) 755.39
          meaning all digits 755.31
        tarsal(s) 755.38
        tibia 755.36
        tibiofibular 755.35
        transverse 755.31
    upper limb 755.20
      with complete absence of distal elements
        755.21
      longitudinal (complete) (partial) (with
        distal deficiencies, incomplete)
        755.22
        with complete absence of distal
          elements 755.21
        carpal(s) 755.28
        combined humeral, radial, ulnar
          (incomplete) 755.23
        humeral 755.24
        metacarpal(s) 755.28
        phalange(s) 755.29
          meaning all digits 755.21
        radial 755.26
        radioulnar 755.25
        ulnar 755.27
      transverse (complete) (partial) 755.21
  renal — *see* Deformity, kidney
  respiratory system (congenital) 748.9
    specified type NEC 748.8
  rib (acquired) 738.3
    congenital 756.3
    cervical 756.2
  rotation (joint) (acquired) 736.9
    congenital 755.9
    hip or thigh 736.39
      congenital (*see also* Subluxation,
        congenital, hip) 754.32
  sacroiliac joint (congenital) 755.69
    acquired 738.5
  sacrum (acquired) 738.5
    congenital 756.10
  saddle
    back 737.8
    nose 738.0
      syphilitic 090.5

Deformity — *continued*
  salivary gland or duct (congenital) 750.9
    acquired 527.8
  scapula (acquired) 736.89
    congenital 755.50
  scrotum (congenital) 752.9
    acquired 608.89
  sebaceous gland, acquired 706.8
  seminal tract or duct (congenital) 752.9
    acquired 608.89
  septum (nasal) (acquired) 470
    congenital 748.1
  shoulder (joint) (acquired) 736.89
    congenital 755.50
      specified type NEC 755.59
    contraction 718.41
  sigmoid (flexure) (congenital) 751.5
    acquired 569.89
  sinus of Valsalva 747.29
  skin (congenital) 757.9
    acquired NEC 709.8
  skull (acquired) 738.19
    congenital 756.0
      with
        anencephalus 740.0
        encephalocele 742.0
        hydrocephalus 742.3
          with spina bifida (*see also* Spina
            bifida) 741.0 ☑
        microcephalus 742.1
      due to intrauterine malposition and
        pressure 754.0
  soft parts, organs or tissues (of pelvis)
    in pregnancy or childbirth NEC 654.9 ☑
      affecting fetus or newborn 763.89
      causing obstructed labor 660.2 ☑
        affecting fetus or newborn 763.1
  spermatic cord (congenital) 752.9
    acquired 608.89
      torsion 608.2
  spinal
    column — *see* Deformity, spine
    cord (congenital) 742.9
      acquired 336.8
      vessel (congenital) 747.82
    nerve root (congenital) 742.9
      acquired 724.9
  spine (acquired) NEC 738.5
    congenital 756.10
      due to intrauterine malposition and
        pressure 754.2
    kyphoscoliotic (*see also* Kyphoscoliosis)
      737.30
    kyphotic (*see also* Kyphosis) 737.10
    lordotic (*see also* Lordosis) 737.20
    rachitic 268.1
    scoliotic (*see also* Scoliosis) 737.30
  spleen
    acquired 289.59
    congenital 759.0
  Sprengel's (congenital) 755.52
  sternum (acquired) 738.3
    congenital 756.3
  stomach (congenital) 750.9
    acquired 537.89
  submaxillary gland (congenital) 750.9
    acquired 527.8
  swan neck (acquired)
    finger 736.22
    hand 736.09
  talipes — *see* Talipes
  teeth, tooth NEC 520.9
  testis (congenital) 752.9
    acquired 608.89
      torsion 608.2
  thigh (acquired) 736.89
    congenital 755.60
  thorax (acquired) (wall) 738.3
    congenital 754.89
    late effect of rickets 268.1
  thumb (acquired) 736.20
    congenital 755.50
  thymus (tissue) (congenital) 759.2
  thyroid (gland) (congenital) 759.2
    cartilage 748.3
      acquired 478.79

Deformity — *continued*
  tibia (acquired) 736.89
    congenital 755.60
    saber 090.5
  toe (acquired) 735.9
    congenital 755.66
    specified NEC 735.8
  tongue (congenital) 750.10
    acquired 529.8
  tooth, teeth NEC 520.9
  trachea (rings) (congenital) 748.3
    acquired 519.1
  transverse aortic arch (congenital) 747.21
  tricuspid (leaflets) (valve) (congenital) 746.9
    acquired — *see* Endocarditis, tricuspid
    atresia or stenosis 746.1
    specified type NEC 746.89
  trunk (acquired) 738.3
    congenital 759.9
  ulna (acquired) 736.00
    congenital 755.50
  upper extremity — *see* Deformity, arm
  urachus (congenital) 753.7
  ureter (opening) (congenital) 753.9
    acquired 593.89
  urethra (valve) (congenital) 753.9
    acquired 599.84
  urinary tract or system (congenital) 753.9
    urachus 753.7
  uterus (congenital) 752.3
    acquired 621.8
  uvula (congenital) 750.9
    acquired 528.9
  vagina (congenital) 752.40
    acquired 623.8
  valve, valvular (heart) (congenital) 746.9
    acquired — *see* Endocarditis
    pulmonary 746.00
    specified type NEC 746.89
  vascular (congenital) (peripheral) NEC 747.60
    acquired 459.9
    gastrointestinal 747.61
    lower limb 747.64
    renal 747.62
    specified site NEC 747.69
    spinal 747.82
    upper limb 747.63
  vas deferens (congenital) 752.9
    acquired 608.89
  vein (congenital) NEC (*see also* Deformity,
    vascular) 747.60
    brain 747.81
    coronary 746.9
    great 747.40
  vena cava (inferior) (superior) (congenital)
    747.40
  vertebra — *see* Deformity, spine
  vesicourethral orifice (acquired) 596.8
    congenital NEC 753.9
    specified type NEC 753.8
  vessels of optic papilla (congenital) 743.9
  visual field (contraction) 368.45
  vitreous humor (congenital) 743.9
    acquired 379.29
  vulva (congenital) 752.40
    acquired 624.8
  wrist (joint) (acquired) 736.00
    congenital 755.50
    contraction 718.43
    valgus 736.03
      congenital 755.59
    varus 736.04
      congenital 755.59

Degeneration, degenerative
  adrenal (capsule) (gland) 255.8
    with hypofunction 255.4
    fatty 255.8
    hyaline 255.8
    infectional 255.8
    lardaceous 277.3
  amyloid (any site) (general) 277.3
  anterior cornua, spinal cord 336.8
  aorta, aortic 440.0
    fatty 447.8
    valve (heart) (*see also* Endocarditis, aortic)
      424.1

Degeneration, degenerative — *continued*
arteriovascular — *see* Arteriosclerosis
artery, arterial (atheromatous) (calcareous) —
   see also Arteriosclerosis
  amyloid 277.3
  lardaceous 277.3
  medial NEC (*see also* Arteriosclerosis,
    extremities) 440.20
articular cartilage NEC (*see also* Disorder,
    cartilage, articular) 718.0 ☑
  elbow 718.02
  knee 717.5
  patella 717.7
  shoulder 718.01
  spine (*see also* Spondylosis) 721.90
atheromatous — *see* Arteriosclerosis
bacony (any site) 277.3
basal nuclei or ganglia NEC 333.0
bone 733.90
brachial plexus 353.0
brain (cortical) (progressive) 331.9
  arteriosclerotic 437.0
  childhood 330.9
    specified type NEC 330.8
  congenital 742.4
  cystic 348.0
    congenital 742.4
  familial NEC 331.89
  grey matter 330.8
  heredofamilial NEC 331.89
  in
    alcoholism 303.9 ☑ *[331.7]*
    beriberi 265.0 *[331.7]*
    cerebrovascular disease 437.9 *[331.7]*
    congenital hydrocephalus 742.3 *[331.7]*
      with spina bifida (*see also* Spina
        bifida) 741.0 ☑ *[331.7]*
    Fabry's disease 272.7 *[330.2]*
    Gaucher's disease 272.7 *[330.2]*
    Hunter's disease or syndrome
      277.5 *[330.3]*
    lipidosis
      cerebral 330.1
      generalized 272.7 *[330.2]*
    mucopolysaccharidosis 277.5 *[330.3]*
    myxedema (*see also* Myxedema)
      244.9 *[331.7]*
    neoplastic disease NEC (M8000/1)
      239.9 *[331.7]*
    Niemann-Pick disease 272.7 *[330.2]*
    sphingolipidosis 272.7 *[330.2]*
    vitamin B$_{12}$ deficiency 266.2 *[331.7]*
  motor centers 331.89
  senile 331.2
  specified type NEC 331.89
breast — *see* Disease, breast
Bruch's membrane 363.40
bundle of His 426.50
  left 426.3
  right 426.4
calcareous NEC 275.49
capillaries 448.9
  amyloid 277.3
  fatty 448.9
  lardaceous 277.3
cardiac (brown) (calcareous) (fatty) (fibrous)
    (hyaline) (mural) (muscular) (pigmentary)
    (senile) (with arteriosclerosis) (*see also*
    Degeneration, myocardial) 429.1
  valve, valvular — *see* Endocarditis
cardiorenal (*see also* Hypertension, cardiorenal)
    404.90
cardiovascular (*see also* Disease,
    cardiovascular) 429.2
  renal (*see also* Hypertension, cardiorenal)
    404.90
cartilage (joint) — *see* Derangement, joint
cerebellar NEC 334.9
  primary (hereditary) (sporadic) 334.2
cerebral — *see* Degeneration, brain
cerebromacular 330.1
cerebrovascular 437.1
  due to hypertension 437.2
  late effect — *see* Late effect(s) (of)
    cerebrovascular disease
cervical plexus 353.2

Degeneration, degenerative — *continued*
cervix 622.8
  due to radiation (intended effect) 622.8
    adverse effect or misadventure 622.8
changes, spine or vertebra (*see also*
    Spondylosis) 721.90
chitinous 277.3
chorioretinal 363.40
  congenital 743.53
  hereditary 363.50
choroid (colloid) (drusen) 363.40
  hereditary 363.50
  senile 363.41
    diffuse secondary 363.42
cochlear 386.8
collateral ligament (knee) (medial) 717.82
  lateral 717.81
combined (spinal cord) (subacute) 266.2 *[336.2]*
  with anemia (pernicious) 281.0 *[336.2]*
    due to dietary deficiency 281.1 *[336.2]*
    due to vitamin B$_{12}$ deficiency anemia
      (dietary) 281.1 *[336.2]*
conjunctiva 372.50
  amyloid 277.3 *[372.50]*
cornea 371.40
  calcerous 371.44
  familial (hereditary) (*see also* Dystrophy,
    cornea) 371.50
    macular 371.55
    reticular 371.54
  hyaline (of old scars) 371.41
  marginal (Terrien's) 371.48
  mosaic (shagreen) 371.41
  nodular 371.46
  peripheral 371.48
  senile 371.41
cortical (cerebellar) (parenchymatous) 334.2
  alcoholic 303.9 ☑ *[334.4]*
  diffuse, due to arteriopathy 437.0
corticostriatal-spinal 334.8
cretinoid 243
cruciate ligament (knee) (posterior) 717.84
  anterior 717.83
cutis 709.3
  amyloid 277.3
dental pulp 522.2
disc disease — *see* Degeneration, intervertebral
    disc
dorsolateral (spinal cord) — *see* Degeneration,
    combined
endocardial 424.90
extrapyramidal NEC 333.90
eye NEC 360.40
  macular (*see also* Degeneration, macula)
    362.50
    congenital 362.75
    hereditary 362.76
fatty (diffuse) (general) 272.8
  liver 571.8
    alcoholic 571.0
  localized site — *see* Degeneration, by site,
    fatty
  placenta — *see* Placenta, abnormal
globe (eye) NEC 360.40
  macular — *see* Degeneration, macula
grey matter 330.8
heart (brown) (calcareous) (fatty) (fibrous)
    (hyaline) (mural) (muscular) (pigmentary)
    (senile) (with arteriosclerosis) (*see also*
    Degeneration, myocardial) 429.1
  amyloid 277.3 *[425.7]*
  atheromatous — *see* Arteriosclerosis,
    coronary
  gouty 274.82
  hypertensive (*see also* Hypertension, heart)
    402.90
  ischemic 414.9
  valve, valvular — *see* Endocarditis
hepatolenticular (Wilson's) 275.1
hepatorenal 572.4
heredofamilial
  brain NEC 331.89
  spinal cord NEC 336.8
hyaline (diffuse) (generalized) 728.9
  localized — *see also* Degeneration, by site
    cornea 371.41
    keratitis 371.41

Degeneration, degenerative — *continued*
hypertensive vascular — *see* Hypertension
infrapatellar fat pad 729.31
internal semilunar cartilage 717.3
intervertebral disc 722.6
  with myelopathy 722.70
  cervical, cervicothoracic 722.4
    with myelopathy 722.71
  lumbar, lumbosacral 722.52
    with myelopathy 722.73
  thoracic, thoracolumbar 722.51
    with myelopathy 722.72
intestine 569.89
  amyloid 277.3
  lardaceous 277.3
iris (generalized) (*see also* Atrophy, iris) 364.59
  pigmentary 364.53
  pupillary margin 364.54
ischemic — *see* Ischemia
joint disease (*see also* Osteoarthrosis) 715.9 ☑
  multiple sites 715.09
  spine (*see also* Spondylosis) 721.90
kidney (*see also* Sclerosis, renal) 587
  amyloid 277.3 *[583.81]*
  cyst, cystic (multiple) (solitary) 593.2
    congenital (*see also* Cystic, disease,
      kidney) 753.10
  fatty 593.89
  fibrocystic (congenital) 753.19
  lardaceous 277.3 *[583.81]*
  polycystic (congenital) 753.12
    adult type (APKD) 753.13
    autosomal dominant 753.13
    autosomal recessive 753.14
    childhood type (CPKD) 753.14
    infantile type 753.14
  waxy 277.3 *[583.81]*
Kuhnt-Junius (retina) 362.52
labyrinth, osseous 386.8
lacrimal passages, cystic 375.12
lardaceous (any site) 277.3
lateral column (posterior), spinal cord (*see also*
    Degeneration, combined) 266.2 *[336.2]*
lattice 362.63
lens 366.9
  infantile, juvenile, or presenile 366.00
  senile 366.10
lenticular (familial) (progressive) (Wilson's) (with
    cirrhosis of liver) 275.1
  striate artery 437.0
lethal ball, prosthetic heart valve 996.02
ligament
  collateral (knee) (medial) 717.82
    lateral 717.81
  cruciate (knee) (posterior) 717.84
    anterior 717.83
liver (diffuse) 572.8
  amyloid 277.3
  congenital (cystic) 751.62
  cystic 572.8
    congenital 751.62
  fatty 571.8
    alcoholic 571.0
  hypertrophic 572.8
  lardaceous 277.3
  parenchymatous, acute or subacute (*see*
    also Necrosis, liver) 570
  pigmentary 572.8
  toxic (acute) 573.8
  waxy 277.3
lung 518.89
lymph gland 289.3
  hyaline 289.3
  lardaceous 277.3
macula (acquired) (senile) 362.50
  atrophic 362.51
  Best's 362.76
  congenital 362.75
  cystic 362.54
  cystoid 362.53
  disciform 362.52
  dry 362.51
  exudative 362.52
  familial pseudoinflammatory 362.77
  hereditary 362.76
  hole 362.54
  juvenile (Stargardt's) 362.75

Degeneration, degenerative — *continued*
macula — *continued*
  nonexudative 362.51
  pseudohole 362.54
  wet 362.52
medullary — *see* Degeneration, brain
membranous labyrinth, congenital (causing impairment of hearing) 744.05
meniscus — *see* Derangement, joint
microcystoid 362.62
mitral — *see* Insufficiency, mitral
Mönckeberg's (*see also* Arteriosclerosis, extremities) 440.20
moral 301.7
motor centers, senile 331.2
mural (*see also* Degeneration, myocardial) 429.1
  heart, cardiac (*see also* Degeneration, myocardial) 429.1
  myocardium, myocardial (*see also* Degeneration, myocardial) 429.1
muscle 728.9
  fatty 728.9
  fibrous 728.9
  heart (*see also* Degeneration, myocardial) 429.1
  hyaline 728.9
muscular progressive 728.2
myelin, central nervous system NEC 341.9
myocardium, myocardial (brown) (calcareous) (fatty) (fibrous) (hyaline) (mural) (muscular) (pigmentary) (senile) (with arteriosclerosis) 429.1
  with rheumatic fever (conditions classifiable to 390) 398.0
    active, acute, or subacute 391.2
      with chorea 392.0
    inactive or quiescent (with chorea) 398.0
  amyloid 277.3 *[425.7]*
  congenital 746.89
  fetus or newborn 779.89
  gouty 274.82
  hypertensive (*see also* Hypertension, heart) 402.90
  ischemic 414.8
  rheumatic (*see also* Degeneration, myocardium, with rheumatic fever) 398.0
  syphilitic 093.82
nasal sinus (mucosa) (*see also* Sinusitis) 473.9
  frontal 473.1
  maxillary 473.0
nerve — *see* Disorder, nerve
nervous system 349.89
  amyloid 277.3 *[357.4]*
  autonomic (*see also* Neuropathy, peripheral, autonomic) 337.9
  fatty 349.89
  peripheral autonomic NEC (*see also* Neuropathy, peripheral, autonomic) 337.9
nipple 611.9
nose 478.1
oculoacousticocerebral, congenital (progressive) 743.8
olivopontocerebellar (familial) (hereditary) 333.0
osseous labyrinth 386.8
ovary 620.8
  cystic 620.2
  microcystic 620.2
pallidal, pigmentary (progressive) 333.0
pancreas 577.8
  tuberculous (*see also* Tuberculosis) 017.9 ☑
papillary muscle 429.81
paving stone 362.61
penis 607.89
peritoneum 568.89
pigmentary (diffuse) (general)
  localized — *see* Degeneration, by site
  pallidal (progressive) 333.0
  secondary 362.65
pineal gland 259.8
pituitary (gland) 253.8
placenta (fatty) (fibrinoid) (fibroid) — *see* Placenta, abnormal
popliteal fat pad 729.31

Degeneration, degenerative — *continued*
posterolateral (spinal cord) (*see also* Degeneration, combined) 266.2 *[336.2]*
pulmonary valve (heart) (*see also* Endocarditis, pulmonary) 424.3
pulp (tooth) 522.2
pupillary margin 364.54
renal (*see also* Sclerosis, renal) 587
  fibrocystic 753.19
  polycystic 753.12
    adult type (APKD) 753.13
    autosomal dominant 753.13
    autosomal recessive 753.14
    childhood type (CPKD) 753.14
    infantile type 753.14
reticuloendothelial system 289.89
retina (peripheral) 362.60
  with retinal defect (*see also* Detachment, retina, with retinal defect) 361.00
  cystic (senile) 362.50
  cystoid 362.53
  hereditary (*see also* Dystrophy, retina) 362.70
    cerebroretinal 362.71
    congenital 362.75
    juvenile (Stargardt's) 362.75
    macula 362.76
  Kuhnt-Junius 362.52
  lattice 362.63
  macular (*see also* Degeneration, macula) 362.50
  microcystoid 362.62
  palisade 362.63
  paving stone 362.61
  pigmentary (primary) 362.74
    secondary 362.65
  posterior pole (*see also* Degeneration, macula) 362.50
  secondary 362.66
  senile 362.60
    cystic 362.53
    reticular 362.64
saccule, congenital (causing impairment of hearing) 744.05
sacculocochlear 386.8
senile 797
  brain 331.2
  cardiac, heart, or myocardium (*see also* Degeneration, myocardial) 429.1
  motor centers 331.2
  reticule 362.64
  retina, cystic 362.50
  vascular — *see* Arteriosclerosis
silicone rubber poppet (prosthetic valve) 996.02
sinus (cystic) (*see also* Sinusitis) 473.9
  polypoid 471.1
skin 709.3
  amyloid 277.3
  colloid 709.3
spinal (cord) 336.8
  amyloid 277.3
  column 733.90
  combined (subacute) (*see also* Degeneration, combined) 266.2 *[336.2]*
    with anemia (pernicious) 281.0 *[336.2]*
  dorsolateral (*see also* Degeneration, combined) 266.2 *[336.2]*
  familial NEC 336.8
  fatty 336.8
  funicular (*see also* Degeneration, combined) 266.2 *[336.2]*
  heredofamilial NEC 336.8
  posterolateral (*see also* Degeneration, combined) 266.2 *[336.2]*
  subacute combined — *see* Degeneration, combined
  tuberculous (*see also* Tuberculosis) 013.8 ☑
spine 733.90
spleen 289.59
  amyloid 277.3
  lardaceous 277.3
stomach 537.89
  lardaceous 277.3
strionigral 333.0
sudoriparous (cystic) 705.89
suprarenal (capsule) (gland) 255.8
  with hypofunction 255.4

Degeneration, degenerative — *continued*
sweat gland 705.89
synovial membrane (pulpy) 727.9
tapetoretinal 362.74
  adult or presenile form 362.50
testis (postinfectional) 608.89
thymus (gland) 254.8
  fatty 254.8
  lardaceous 277.3
thyroid (gland) 246.8
tricuspid (heart) (valve) *see* Endocarditis, tricuspid
tuberculous NEC (*see also* Tuberculosis) 011.9 ☑
turbinate 733.90
uterus 621.8
  cystic 621.8
vascular (senile) — *see also* Arteriosclerosis
  hypertensive — *see* Hypertension
vitreoretinal (primary) 362.73
  secondary 362.66
vitreous humor (with infiltration) 379.21
wallerian NEC — *see* Disorder, nerve
waxy (any site) 277.3
Wilson's hepatolenticular 275.1

Deglutition
paralysis 784.9
  hysterical 300.11
pneumonia 507.0

Degos' disease or syndrome 447.8

Degradation disorder, branched-chain amino acid 270.3

Dehiscence
anastomosis — *see* Complications, anastomosis
cesarean wound 674.1 ☑
episiotomy 674.2 ☑
operation wound 998.32
  internal 998.31
perineal wound (postpartum) 674.2 ☑
postoperative 998.32
  abdomen 998.32
    internal 998.31
  internal 998.31
uterine wound 674.1 ☑

Dehydration (cachexia) 276.51   ▲
with
  hypernatremia 276.0
  hyponatremia 276.1
newborn 775.5

Deiters' nucleus syndrome 386.19

Déjérine's disease 356.0

Déjérine-Klumpke paralysis 767.6

Déjérine-Roussy syndrome 348.8

Déjérine-Sottas disease or neuropathy (hypertrophic) 356.0

Déjérine-Thomas atrophy or syndrome 333.0

de Lange's syndrome (Amsterdam dwarf, mental retardation, and brachycephaly) 759.89

Delay, delayed
adaptation, cones or rods 368.63
any plane in pelvis
  affecting fetus or newborn 763.1
  complicating delivery 660.1 ☑
birth or delivery NEC 662.1 ☑
  affecting fetus or newborn 763.89
  second twin, triplet, or multiple mate 662.3 ☑
closure — *see also* Fistula
  cranial suture 756.0
  fontanel 756.0
coagulation NEC 790.92
conduction (cardiac) (ventricular) 426.9
delivery NEC 662.1 ☑
  second twin, triplet, etc. 662.3 ☑
    affecting fetus or newborn 763.89
development
  in childhood 783.40
    physiological 783.40
  intellectual NEC 315.9
  learning NEC 315.2
  reading 315.00
  sexual 259.0
  speech 315.39
    associated with hyperkinesis 314.1

☑ Additional Digit Required — Refer to the Tabular List (Numeric Code Section) for Additional Digit Selection

Delay, delayed — *continued*
  development — *continued*
    spelling 315.09
  gastric emptying 536.8
  menarche 256.39
    due to pituitary hypofunction 253.4
  menstruation (cause unknown) 626.8
  milestone in childhood 783.42
  motility — *see* Hypomotility
  passage of meconium (newborn) 777.1
  primary respiration 768.9
  puberty 259.0
  separation of umbilical cord 779.83
  sexual maturation, female 259.0
Del Castillo's syndrome (germinal aplasia) 606.0
Déleage's disease 359.89
Deletion syndrome
  5p 758.31
  22q11.2 758.32
  autosomal NEC 758.39
Delhi (boil) (button) (sore) 085.1
Delinquency (juvenile) 312.9
  group (*see also* Disturbance, conduct) 312.2 ☑
  neurotic 312.4
Delirium, delirious 780.09
  acute (psychotic) 293.0
  alcoholic 291.0
    acute 291.0
    chronic 291.1
  alcoholicum 291.0
  chronic (*see also* Psychosis) 293.89
    due to or associated with physical condition
      — *see* Psychosis, organic
  drug-induced 292.81
  due to conditions classified elsewhere 293.0
  eclamptic (*see also* Eclampsia) 780.39
  exhaustion (*see also* Reaction, stress, acute)
    308.9
  hysterical 300.11
  in
    presenile dementia 290.11
    senile dementia 290.3
  induced by drug 292.81
  manic, maniacal (acute) (*see also* Psychosis,
    affective) 296.0 ☑
    recurrent episode 296.1 ☑
    single episode 296.0 ☑
  puerperal 293.9
  senile 290.3
  subacute (psychotic) 293.1
  thyroid (*see also* Thyrotoxicosis) 242.9 ☑
  traumatic — *see also* Injury, intracranial
    with
      lesion, spinal cord — *see* Injury, spinal,
        by site
      shock, spinal — *see* Injury, spinal, by site
  tremens (impending) 291.0
  uremic — *see* Uremia
  withdrawal
    alcoholic (acute) 291.0
      chronic 291.1
    drug 292.0
Delivery

> *Note* — *Use the following fifth-digit subclassification with categories 640-648, 651-676:*
>
>   *0*   *unspecified as to episode of care*
>   *1*   *delivered, with or without mention of antepartum condition*
>   *2*   *delivered, with mention of postpartum complication*
>   *3*   *antepartum condition or complication*
>   *4*   *postpartum condition or complication*

  breech (assisted) (buttocks) (complete) (frank)
    (spontaneous) 652.2 ☑
    affecting fetus or newborn 763.0
    extraction NEC 669.6 ☑
  cesarean (for) 669.7 ☑
    abnormal
      cervix 654.6 ☑
      pelvic organs or tissues 654.9 ☑
      pelvis (bony) (major) NEC 653.0 ☑

Delivery — *continued*
  cesarean — *continued*
    abnormal — *continued*
      presentation or position 652.9 ☑
        in multiple gestation 652.6 ☑
      size, fetus 653.5 ☑
      soft parts (of pelvis) 654.9 ☑
      uterus, congenital 654.0 ☑
      vagina 654.7 ☑
      vulva 654.8 ☑
    abruptio placentae 641.2 ☑
    acromion presentation 652.8 ☑
    affecting fetus or newborn 763.4
    anteversion, cervix or uterus 654.4 ☑
    atony, uterus 666.1 ☑
    bicornis or bicornuate uterus 654.0 ☑
    breech presentation (buttocks) (complete)
      (frank) 652.2 ☑
    brow presentation 652.4 ☑
    cephalopelvic disproportion (normally
      formed fetus) 653.4 ☑
    chin presentation 652.4 ☑
    cicatrix of cervix 654.6 ☑
    contracted pelvis (general) 653.1 ☑
      inlet 653.2 ☑
      outlet 653.3 ☑
    cord presentation or prolapse 663.0 ☑
    cystocele 654.4 ☑
    deformity (acquired) (congenital)
      pelvic organs or tissues NEC 654.9 ☑
      pelvis (bony) NEC 653.0 ☑
    displacement, uterus NEC 654.4 ☑
    disproportion NEC 653.9 ☑
    distress
      fetal 656.8 ☑
      maternal 669.0 ☑
    eclampsia 642.6 ☑
    face presentation 652.4 ☑
    failed
      forceps 660.7 ☑
      trial of labor NEC 660.6 ☑
      vacuum extraction 660.7 ☑
      ventouse 660.7 ☑
    fetal deformity 653.7 ☑
    fetal-maternal hemorrhage 656.0 ☑
    fetus, fetal
      distress 656.8 ☑
      prematurity 656.8 ☑
    fibroid (tumor) (uterus) 654.1 ☑
    footling 652.8 ☑
      with successful version 652.1 ☑
    hemorrhage (antepartum) (intrapartum) NEC
      641.9 ☑
    hydrocephalic fetus 653.6 ☑
    incarceration of uterus 654.3 ☑
    incoordinate uterine action 661.4 ☑
    inertia, uterus 661.2 ☑
      primary 661.0 ☑
      secondary 661.1 ☑
    lateroversion, uterus or cervix 654.4 ☑
    mal lie 652.9 ☑
    malposition
      fetus 652.9 ☑
        in multiple gestation 652.6 ☑
      pelvic organs or tissues NEC 654.9 ☑
      uterus NEC or cervix 654.4 ☑
    malpresentation NEC 652.9 ☑
      in multiple gestation 652.6 ☑
    maternal
      diabetes mellitus 648.0 ☑
      heart disease NEC 648.6 ☑
    meconium in liquor 656.8 ☑
      staining only 792.3
    oblique presentation 652.3 ☑
    oversize fetus 653.5 ☑
    pelvic tumor NEC 654.9 ☑
    placental insufficiency 656.5 ☑
    placenta previa 641.0 ☑
      with hemorrhage 641.1 ☑
    poor dilation, cervix 661.0 ☑
    pre-eclampsia 642.4 ☑
      severe 642.5 ☑
    previous
      cesarean delivery, section 654.2 ☑
      surgery (to)
        cervix 654.6 ☑
        gynecological NEC 654.9 ☑

Delivery — *continued*
  cesarean — *continued*
    previous — *continued*
      surgery — *continued*
        rectum 654.8 ☑
        uterus NEC 654.9 ☑
          previous cesarean delivery, section
          654.2 ☑
        vagina 654.7 ☑
    prolapse
      arm or hand 652.7 ☑
      uterus 654.4 ☑
    prolonged labor 662.1 ☑
    rectocele 654.4 ☑
    retroversion, uterus or cervix 654.3 ☑
    rigid
      cervix 654.6 ☑
      pelvic floor 654.4 ☑
      perineum 654.8 ☑
      vagina 654.7 ☑
      vulva 654.8 ☑
    sacculation, pregnant uterus 654.4 ☑
    scar(s)
      cervix 654.6 ☑
      cesarean delivery, section 654.2 ☑
      uterus NEC 654.9 ☑
        due to previous cesarean delivery,
          section 654.2 ☑
    Shirodkar suture in situ 654.5 ☑
    shoulder presentation 652.8 ☑
    stenosis or stricture, cervix 654.6 ☑
    transverse presentation or lie 652.3 ☑
    tumor, pelvic organs or tissues NEC
      654.4 ☑
    umbilical cord presentation or prolapse
      663.0 ☑
  completely normal case — *see* category 650
  complicated (by) NEC 669.9 ☑
    abdominal tumor, fetal 653.7 ☑
      causing obstructed labor 660.1 ☑
    abnormal, abnormality of
      cervix 654.6 ☑
        causing obstructed labor 660.2 ☑
      forces of labor 661.9 ☑
      formation of uterus 654.0 ☑
      pelvic organs or tissues 654.9 ☑
        causing obstructed labor 660.2 ☑
      pelvis (bony) (major) NEC 653.0 ☑
        causing obstructed labor 660.1 ☑
      presentation or position NEC 652.9 ☑
        causing obstructed labor 660.0 ☑
      size, fetus 653.5 ☑
        causing obstructed labor 660.1 ☑
      soft parts (of pelvis) 654.9 ☑
        causing obstructed labor 660.2 ☑
      uterine contractions NEC 661.9 ☑
      uterus (formation) 654.0 ☑
        causing obstructed labor 660.2 ☑
      vagina 654.7 ☑
        causing obstructed labor 660.2 ☑
    abnormally formed uterus (any type)
      (congenital) 654.0 ☑
      causing obstructed labor 660.2 ☑
    acromion presentation 652.8 ☑
      causing obstructed labor 660.0 ☑
    adherent placenta 667.0 ☑
      with hemorrhage 666.0 ☑
    adhesions, uterus (to abdominal wall)
      654.4 ☑
    advanced maternal age NEC 659.6 ☑
      multigravida 659.6 ☑
      primigravida 659.5 ☑
    air embolism 673.0 ☑
    amnionitis 658.4 ☑
    amniotic fluid embolism 673.1 ☑
    anesthetic death 668.9 ☑
    annular detachment, cervix 665.3 ☑
    antepartum hemorrhage — *see* Delivery,
      complicated, hemorrhage
    anteversion, cervix or uterus 654.4 ☑
      causing obstructed labor 660.2 ☑
    apoplexy 674.0 ☑
      placenta 641.2 ☑
    arrested active phase 661.1 ☑
    asymmetrical pelvis bone 653.0 ☑
      causing obstructed labor 660.1 ☑

☑ Additional Digit Required — Refer to the Tabular List (Numeric Code Section) for Additional Digit Selection

▶◀ Revised Text   ● New Line   ▲ Revised Code

Delivery — *continued*
  complicated (by) — *continued*
    atony, uterus (hypotonic) (inertia) 666.1 ☑
      hypertonic 661.4 ☑
    Bandl's ring 661.4 ☑
    battledore placenta — *see* Placenta, abnormal
    bicornis or bicornuate uterus 654.0 ☑
      causing obstructed labor 660.2 ☑
    birth injury to mother NEC 665.9 ☑
    bleeding (*see also* Delivery, complicated, hemorrhage) 641.9 ☑
    breech presentation (assisted) (buttocks) (complete) (frank) (spontaneous) 652.2 ☑
      with successful version 652.1 ☑
    brow presentation 652.4 ☑
    cephalopelvic disproportion (normally formed fetus) 653.4 ☑
      causing obstructed labor 660.1 ☑
    cerebral hemorrhage 674.0 ☑
    cervical dystocia 661.0 ☑
    chin presentation 652.4 ☑
      causing obstructed labor 660.0 ☑
    cicatrix
      cervix 654.6 ☑
        causing obstructed labor 660.2 ☑
      vagina 654.7 ☑
        causing obstructed labor 660.2 ☑
    colporrhexis 665.4 ☑
      with perineal laceration 664.0 ☑
    compound presentation 652.8 ☑
      causing obstructed labor 660.0 ☑
    compression of cord (umbilical) 663.2 ☑
      around neck 663.1 ☑
      cord prolapsed 663.0 ☑
    contraction, contracted pelvis 653.1 ☑
      causing obstructed labor 660.1 ☑
      general 653.1 ☑
        causing obstructed labor 660.1 ☑
      inlet 653.2 ☑
        causing obstructed labor 660.1 ☑
      midpelvic 653.8 ☑
        causing obstructed labor 660.1 ☑
      midplane 653.8 ☑
        causing obstructed labor 660.1 ☑
      outlet 653.3 ☑
        causing obstructed labor 660.1 ☑
    contraction ring 661.4 ☑
    cord (umbilical) 663.9 ☑
      around neck, tightly or with compression 663.1 ☑
        without compression 663.3 ☑
      bruising 663.6 ☑
      complication NEC 663.9 ☑
        specified type NEC 663.8 ☑
      compression NEC 663.2 ☑
      entanglement NEC 663.3 ☑
        with compression 663.2 ☑
      forelying 663.0 ☑
      hematoma 663.6 ☑
      marginal attachment 663.8 ☑
      presentation 663.0 ☑
      prolapse (complete) (occult) (partial) 663.0 ☑
      short 663.4 ☑
      specified complication NEC 663.8 ☑
      thrombosis (vessels) 663.6 ☑
      vascular lesion 663.6 ☑
      velamentous insertion 663.8 ☑
    Couvelaire uterus 641.2 ☑
    cretin pelvis (dwarf type) (male type) 653.1 ☑
      causing obstructed labor 660.1 ☑
    crossbirth 652.3 ☑
      with successful version 652.1 ☑
      causing obstructed labor 660.0 ☑
    cyst (Gartner's duct) 654.7 ☑
    cystocele 654.4 ☑
      causing obstructed labor 660.2 ☑
    death of fetus (near term) 656.4 ☑
      early (before 22 completed weeks gestation) 632
    deformity (acquired) (congenital)
      fetus 653.7 ☑
        causing obstructed labor 660.1 ☑

Delivery — *continued*
  complicated (by) — *continued*
    deformity — *continued*
      pelvic organs or tissues NEC 654.9 ☑
        causing obstructed labor 660.2 ☑
      pelvis (bony) NEC 653.0 ☑
        causing obstructed labor 660.1 ☑
    delay, delayed
      delivery in multiple pregnancy 662.3 ☑
      due to locked mates 660.5 ☑
      following rupture of membranes (spontaneous) 658.2 ☑
        artificial 658.3 ☑
    depressed fetal heart tones 659.7 ☑
    diastasis recti 665.8 ☑
    dilatation
      bladder 654.4 ☑
        causing obstructed labor 660.2 ☑
      cervix, incomplete, poor or slow 661.0 ☑
    diseased placenta 656.7 ☑
    displacement uterus NEC 654.4 ☑
      causing obstructed labor 660.2 ☑
    disproportion NEC 653.9 ☑
      causing obstructed labor 660.1 ☑
    disruptio uteri — *see* Delivery, complicated, rupture, uterus
    distress
      fetal 656.8 ☑
      maternal 669.0 ☑
    double uterus (congenital) 654.0 ☑
      causing obstructed labor 660.2 ☑
    dropsy amnion 657.0 ☑
    dysfunction, uterus 661.9 ☑
      hypertonic 661.4 ☑
      hypotonic 661.2 ☑
        primary 661.0 ☑
        secondary 661.1 ☑
      incoordinate 661.4 ☑
    dystocia
      cervical 661.0 ☑
      fetal — *see* Delivery, complicated, abnormal, presentation
      maternal — *see* Delivery, complicated, prolonged labor
      pelvic — *see* Delivery, complicated, contraction pelvis
      positional 652.8 ☑
      shoulder girdle 660.4 ☑
    eclampsia 642.6 ☑
    ectopic kidney 654.4 ☑
      causing obstructed labor 660.2 ☑
    edema, cervix 654.6 ☑
      causing obstructed labor 660.2 ☑
    effusion, amniotic fluid 658.1 ☑
    elderly multigravida 659.6 ☑
    elderly primigravida 659.5 ☑
    embolism (pulmonary) 673.2 ☑
      air 673.0 ☑
      amniotic fluid 673.1 ☑
      blood clot 673.2 ☑
      cerebral 674.0 ☑
      fat 673.8 ☑
      pyemic 673.3 ☑
      septic 673.3 ☑
    entanglement, umbilical cord 663.3 ☑
      with compression 663.2 ☑
      around neck (with compression) 663.1 ☑
    eversion, cervix or uterus 665.2 ☑
    excessive
      fetal growth 653.5 ☑
        causing obstructed labor 660.1 ☑
      size of fetus 653.5 ☑
        causing obstructed labor 660.1 ☑
    face presentation 652.4 ☑
      causing obstructed labor 660.0 ☑
      to pubes 660.3 ☑
    failure, fetal head to enter pelvic brim 652.5 ☑
      causing obstructed labor 660.0 ☑
    female genital mutilation 660.8 ☑   ●
    fetal
      acid-base balance 656.8 ☑
      death (near term) NEC 656.4 ☑
        early (before 22 completed weeks gestation) 632
      deformity 653.7 ☑
        causing obstructed labor 660.1 ☑

Delivery — *continued*
  complicated (by) — *continued*
    fetal — *continued*
      distress 656.8 ☑
      heart rate or rhythm 659.7 ☑
      reduction of multiple fetuses reduced   ●
        to single fetus 651.7 ☑   ●
    fetopelvic disproportion 653.4 ☑
      causing obstructed labor 660.1 ☑
    fever during labor 659.2 ☑
    fibroid (tumor) (uterus) 654.1 ☑
      causing obstructed labor 660.2 ☑
    fibromyomata 654.1 ☑
      causing obstructed labor 660.2 ☑
    forelying umbilical cord 663.0 ☑
    fracture of coccyx 665.6 ☑
    hematoma 664.5 ☑
      broad ligament 665.7 ☑
      ischial spine 665.7 ☑
      pelvic 665.7 ☑
      perineum 664.5 ☑
      soft tissues 665.7 ☑
      subdural 674.0 ☑
      umbilical cord 663.6 ☑
      vagina 665.7 ☑
      vulva or perineum 664.5 ☑
    hemorrhage (uterine) (antepartum) (intrapartum) (pregnancy) 641.9 ☑
      accidental 641.2 ☑
      associated with
        afibrinogenemia 641.3 ☑
        coagulation defect 641.3 ☑
          hyperfibrinolysis 641.3 ☑
          hypofibrinogenemia 641.3 ☑
      cerebral 674.0 ☑
      due to
        low-lying placenta 641.1 ☑
        placenta previa 641.1 ☑
        premature separation of placenta (normally implanted) 641.2 ☑
        retained placenta 666.0 ☑
        trauma 641.8 ☑
        uterine leiomyoma 641.8 ☑
      marginal sinus rupture 641.2 ☑
      placenta NEC 641.9 ☑
      postpartum (atonic) (immediate) (within 24 hours) 666.1 ☑
        with retained or trapped placenta 666.0 ☑
        delayed 666.2 ☑
        secondary 666.2 ☑
        third stage 666.0 ☑
    hourglass contraction, uterus 661.4 ☑
    hydramnios 657.0 ☑
    hydrocephalic fetus 653.6 ☑
      causing obstructed labor 660.1 ☑
    hydrops fetalis 653.7 ☑
      causing obstructed labor 660.1 ☑
    hypertension — *see* Hypertension, complicating pregnancy
    hypertonic uterine dysfunction 661.4 ☑
    hypotonic uterine dysfunction 661.2 ☑
    impacted shoulders 660.4 ☑
    incarceration, uterus 654.3 ☑
      causing obstructed labor 660.2 ☑
    incomplete dilation (cervix) 661.0 ☑
    incoordinate uterus 661.4 ☑
    indication NEC 659.9 ☑
      specified type NEC 659.8 ☑
    inertia, uterus 661.2 ☑
      hypertonic 661.4 ☑
      hypotonic 661.2 ☑
      primary 661.0 ☑
      secondary 661.1 ☑
    infantile
      genitalia 654.4 ☑
        causing obstructed labor 660.2 ☑
      uterus (os) 654.4 ☑
        causing obstructed labor 660.2 ☑
    injury (to mother) NEC 665.9 ☑
    intrauterine fetal death (near term) NEC 656.4 ☑
      early (before 22 completed weeks gestation) 632
    inversion, uterus 665.2 ☑
    kidney, ectopic 654.4 ☑
      causing obstructed labor 660.2 ☑

☑ Additional Digit Required — Refer to the Tabular List (Numeric Code Section) for Additional Digit Selection

▶◀ Revised Text   ● New Line   ▲ Revised Code

Delivery — *continued*
  complicated (by) — *continued*
    knot (true), umbilical cord 663.2 ☑
    labor, premature (before 37 completed weeks gestation) 644.2 ☑
    laceration 664.9 ☑
      anus (sphincter) 664.2 ☑
        with mucosa 664.3 ☑
      bladder (urinary) 665.5 ☑
      bowel 665.5 ☑
      central 664.4 ☑
      cervix (uteri) 665.3 ☑
      fourchette 664.0 ☑
      hymen 664.0 ☑
      labia (majora) (minora) 664.0 ☑
      pelvic
        floor 664.1 ☑
        organ NEC 665.5 ☑
      perineum, perineal 664.4 ☑
        first degree 664.0 ☑
        second degree 664.1 ☑
        third degree 664.2 ☑
        fourth degree 664.3 ☑
        central 664.4 ☑
        extensive NEC 664.4 ☑
        muscles 664.1 ☑
        skin 664.0 ☑
        slight 664.0 ☑
      peritoneum 665.5 ☑
      periurethral tissue 665.5 ☑
      rectovaginal (septum) (without perineal laceration) 665.4 ☑
        with perineum 664.2 ☑
          with anal or rectal mucosa 664.3 ☑
      skin (perineum) 664.0 ☑
      specified site or type NEC 664.8 ☑
      sphincter ani 664.2 ☑
        with mucosa 664.3 ☑
      urethra 665.5 ☑
      uterus 665.1 ☑
        before labor 665.0 ☑
      vagina, vaginal (deep) (high) (sulcus) (wall) (without perineal laceration) 665.4 ☑
        with perineum 664.0 ☑
        muscles, with perineum 664.1 ☑
      vulva 664.0 ☑
    lateroversion, uterus or cervix 654.4 ☑
      causing obstructed labor 660.2 ☑
    locked mates 660.5 ☑
    low implantation of placenta — *see* Delivery, complicated, placenta, previa
    mal lie 652.9 ☑
    malposition
      fetus NEC 652.9 ☑
        causing obstructed labor 660.0 ☑
      pelvic organs or tissues NEC 654.9 ☑
        causing obstructed labor 660.2 ☑
      placenta 641.1 ☑
        without hemorrhage 641.0 ☑
      uterus NEC or cervix 654.4 ☑
        causing obstructed labor 660.2 ☑
    malpresentation 652.9 ☑
      causing obstructed labor 660.0 ☑
    marginal sinus (bleeding) (rupture) 641.2 ☑
    maternal hypotension syndrome 669.2 ☑
    meconium in liquor 656.8 ☑
    membranes, retained — *see* Delivery, complicated, placenta, retained
    mentum presentation 652.4 ☑
      causing obstructed labor 660.0 ☑
    metrorrhagia (myopathia) — *see* Delivery, complicated, hemorrhage
    metrorrhexis — *see* Delivery, complicated, rupture, uterus
    multiparity (grand) 659.4 ☑
    myelomeningocele, fetus 653.7 ☑
      causing obstructed labor 660.1 ☑
    Nägele's pelvis 653.0 ☑
      causing obstructed labor 660.1 ☑
    nonengagement, fetal head 652.5 ☑
      causing obstructed labor 660.0 ☑
    oblique presentation 652.3 ☑
      causing obstructed labor 660.0 ☑
    obstetric
      shock 669.1 ☑
      trauma NEC 665.9 ☑

Delivery — *continued*
  complicated (by) — *continued*
    obstructed labor 660.9 ☑
      due to
        abnormality of pelvic organs or tissues (conditions classifiable to 654.0-654.9) 660.2 ☑
        deep transverse arrest 660.3 ☑
        impacted shoulders 660.4 ☑
        locked twins 660.5 ☑
        malposition and malpresentation of fetus (conditions classifiable to 652.0-652.9) 660.0 ☑
        persistent occipitoposterior 660.3 ☑
        shoulder dystocia 660.4 ☑
    occult prolapse of umbilical cord 663.0 ☑
    oversize fetus 653.5 ☑
      causing obstructed labor 660.1 ☑
    pathological retraction ring, uterus 661.4 ☑
    pelvic
      arrest (deep) (high) (of fetal head) (transverse) 660.3 ☑
      deformity (bone) — *see also* Deformity, pelvis, with disproportion
        soft tissue 654.9 ☑
          causing obstructed labor 660.2 ☑
        tumor NEC 654.9 ☑
          causing obstructed labor 660.2 ☑
    penetration, pregnant uterus by instrument 665.1 ☑
    perforation — *see* Delivery, complicated, laceration
    persistent
      hymen 654.8 ☑
        causing obstructed labor 660.2 ☑
      occipitoposterior 660.3 ☑
    placenta, placental
      ablatio 641.2 ☑
      abnormality 656.7 ☑
        with hemorrhage 641.2 ☑
      abruptio 641.2 ☑
      accreta 667.0 ☑
        with hemorrhage 666.0 ☑
      adherent (without hemorrhage) 667.0 ☑
        with hemorrhage 666.0 ☑
      apoplexy 641.2 ☑
      battledore placenta — *see* Placenta, abnormal
      detachment (premature) 641.2 ☑
      disease 656.7 ☑
      hemorrhage NEC 641.9 ☑
      increta (without hemorrhage) 667.0 ☑
        with hemorrhage 666.0 ☑
      low (implantation) 641.0 ☑
        without hemorrhage 641.0 ☑
      malformation 656.7 ☑
        with hemorrhage 641.2 ☑
      malposition 641.1 ☑
        without hemorrhage 641.0 ☑
      marginal sinus rupture 641.2 ☑
      percreta 667.0 ☑
        with hemorrhage 666.0 ☑
      premature separation 641.2 ☑
      previa (central) (lateral) (marginal) (partial) 641.1 ☑
        without hemorrhage 641.0 ☑
      retained (with hemorrhage) 666.0 ☑
        without hemorrhage 667.0 ☑
      rupture of marginal sinus 641.2 ☑
      separation (premature) 641.2 ☑
      trapped 666.0 ☑
        without hemorrhage 667.0 ☑
      vicious insertion 641.1 ☑
    polyhydramnios 657.0 ☑
    polyp, cervix 654.6 ☑
      causing obstructed labor 660.2 ☑
    precipitate labor 661.3 ☑
    premature
      labor (before 37 completed weeks gestation) 644.2 ☑
      rupture, membranes 658.1 ☑
        delayed delivery following 658.2 ☑
    presenting umbilical cord 663.0 ☑
    previous
      cesarean delivery, section 654.2 ☑
      surgery
        cervix 654.6 ☑
          causing obstructed labor 660.2 ☑

Delivery — *continued*
  complicated (by) — *continued*
    previous — *continued*
      surgery — *continued*
        gynecological NEC 654.9 ☑
          causing obstructed labor 660.2 ☑
        perineum 654.8 ☑
        rectum 654.8 ☑
        uterus NEC 654.9 ☑
          due to previous cesarean delivery, section 654.2 ☑
        vagina 654.7 ☑
          causing obstructed labor 660.2 ☑
        vulva 654.8 ☑
    primary uterine inertia 661.0 ☑
    primipara, elderly or old 659.5 ☑
    prolapse
      arm or hand 652.7 ☑
        causing obstructed labor 660.0 ☑
      cord (umbilical) 663.0 ☑
      fetal extremity 652.8 ☑
      foot or leg 652.8 ☑
        causing obstructed labor 660.0 ☑
      umbilical cord (complete) (occult) (partial) 663.0 ☑
      uterus 654.4 ☑
        causing obstructed labor 660.2 ☑
    prolonged labor 662.1 ☑
      first stage 662.0 ☑
      second stage 662.2 ☑
      active phase 661.2 ☑
      due to
        cervical dystocia 661.0 ☑
        contraction ring 661.4 ☑
        tetanic uterus 661.4 ☑
        uterine inertia 661.2 ☑
          primary 661.0 ☑
          secondary 661.1 ☑
      latent phase 661.0 ☑
    pyrexia during labor 659.2 ☑
    rachitic pelvis 653.2 ☑
      causing obstructed labor 660.1 ☑
    rectocele 654.4 ☑
      causing obstructed labor 660.2 ☑
    retained membranes or portions of placenta 666.2 ☑
      without hemorrhage 667.1 ☑
    retarded (prolonged) birth 662.1 ☑
    retention secundines (with hemorrhage) 666.2 ☑
      without hemorrhage 667.1 ☑
    retroversion, uterus or cervix 654.3 ☑
      causing obstructed labor 660.2 ☑
    rigid
      cervix 654.6 ☑
        causing obstructed labor 660.2 ☑
      pelvic floor 654.4 ☑
        causing obstructed labor 660.2 ☑
      perineum or vulva 654.8 ☑
        causing obstructed labor 660.2 ☑
      vagina 654.7 ☑
        causing obstructed labor 660.2 ☑
    Robert's pelvis 653.0 ☑
      causing obstructed labor 660.1 ☑
    rupture — *see also* Delivery, complicated, laceration
      bladder (urinary) 665.5 ☑
      cervix 665.3 ☑
      marginal sinus 641.2 ☑
      membranes, premature 658.1 ☑
      pelvic organ NEC 665.5 ☑
      perineum (without mention of other laceration) — *see* Delivery, complicated, laceration, perineum
      peritoneum 665.5 ☑
      urethra 665.5 ☑
      uterus (during labor) 665.1 ☑
        before labor 665.0 ☑
    sacculation, pregnant uterus 654.4 ☑
    sacral teratomas, fetal 653.7 ☑
      causing obstructed labor 660.1 ☑
    scar(s)
      cervix 654.6 ☑
        causing obstructed labor 660.2 ☑
      cesarean delivery, section 654.2 ☑
        causing obstructed labor 660.2 ☑

Delivery — *continued*
complicated (by) — *continued*
scar(s) — *continued*
perineum 654.8 ☑
causing obstructed labor 660.2 ☑
uterus NEC 654.9 ☑
causing obstructed labor 660.2 ☑
due to previous cesarean delivery,
section 654.2 ☑
vagina 654.7 ☑
causing obstructed labor 660.2 ☑
vulva 654.8 ☑
causing obstructed labor 660.2 ☑
scoliotic pelvis 653.0 ☑
causing obstructed labor 660.1 ☑
secondary uterine inertia 661.1 ☑
secundines, retained — *see* Delivery,
complicated, placenta, retained
separation
placenta (premature) 641.2 ☑
pubic bone 665.6 ☑
symphysis pubis 665.6 ☑
septate vagina 654.7 ☑
causing obstructed labor 660.2 ☑
shock (birth) (obstetric) (puerperal) 669.1 ☑
short cord syndrome 663.4 ☑
shoulder
girdle dystocia 660.4 ☑
presentation 652.8 ☑
causing obstructed labor 660.0 ☑
Siamese twins 653.7 ☑
causing obstructed labor 660.1 ☑
slow slope active phase 661.2 ☑
spasm
cervix 661.4 ☑
uterus 661.4 ☑
spondylolisthesis, pelvis 653.3 ☑
causing obstructed labor 660.1 ☑
spondylolysis (lumbosacral) 653.3 ☑
causing obstructed labor 660.1 ☑
spondylosis 653.0 ☑
causing obstructed labor 660.1 ☑
stenosis or stricture
cervix 654.6 ☑
causing obstructed labor 660.2 ☑
vagina 654.7 ☑
causing obstructed labor 660.2 ☑
sudden death, unknown cause 669.9 ☑
tear (pelvic organ) (*see also* Delivery,
complicated, laceration) 664.9 ☑
teratomas, sacral, fetal 653.7 ☑
causing obstructed labor 660.1 ☑
tetanic uterus 661.4 ☑
tipping pelvis 653.0 ☑
causing obstructed labor 660.1 ☑
transverse
arrest (deep) 660.3 ☑
presentation or lie 652.3 ☑
with successful version 652.1 ☑
causing obstructed labor 660.0 ☑
trauma (obstetrical) NEC 665.9 ☑
tumor
abdominal, fetal 653.7 ☑
causing obstructed labor 660.1 ☑
pelvic organs or tissues NEC 654.9 ☑
causing obstructed labor 660.2 ☑
umbilical cord (*see also* Delivery,
complicated, cord) 663.9 ☑
around neck tightly, or with compression
663.1 ☑
entanglement NEC 663.3 ☑
with compression 663.2 ☑
prolapse (complete) (occult) (partial)
663.0 ☑
unstable lie 652.0 ☑
causing obstructed labor 660.0 ☑
uterine
inertia (*see also* Delivery, complicated,
inertia, uterus) 661.2 ☑
spasm 661.4 ☑
vasa previa 663.5 ☑
velamentous insertion of cord 663.8 ☑
young maternal age 659.8 ☑
delayed NEC 662.1 ☑
following rupture of membranes
(spontaneous) 658.2 ☑
artificial 658.3 ☑

Delivery — *continued*
delayed NEC — *continued*
second twin, triplet, etc. 662.3 ☑
difficult NEC 669.9 ☑
previous, affecting management of
pregnancy or childbirth V23.49
specified type NEC 669.8 ☑
early onset (spontaneous) 644.2 ☑
footling 652.8 ☑
with successful version 652.1 ☑
forceps NEC 669.5 ☑
affecting fetus or newborn 763.2
missed (at or near term) 656.4 ☑
multiple gestation NEC 651.9 ☑
with fetal loss and retention of one or more
fetus(es) 651.6 ☑
following (elective) fetal reduction ●
651.7 ☑ ●
specified type NEC 651.8 ☑
with fetal loss and retention of one or
more fetus(es) 651.6 ☑
following (elective) fetal reduction ●
651.7 ☑ ●
nonviable infant 656.4 ☑
normal — *see* category 650
precipitate 661.3 ☑
affecting fetus or newborn 763.6
premature NEC (before 37 completed weeks
gestation) 644.2 ☑
previous, affecting management of
pregnancy V23.41
quadruplet NEC 651.2 ☑
with fetal loss and retention of one or more
fetus(es) 651.5 ☑
following (elective) fetal reduction ●
651.7 ☑ ●
quintuplet NEC 651.8 ☑
with fetal loss and retention of one or more
fetus(es) 651.6 ☑
following (elective) fetal reduction ●
651.7 ☑ ●
sextuplet NEC 651.8 ☑
with fetal loss and retention of one or more
fetus(es) 651.6 ☑
following (elective) fetal reduction ●
651.7 ☑ ●
specified complication NEC 669.8 ☑
stillbirth (near term) NEC 656.4 ☑
early (before 22 completed weeks gestation)
632
term pregnancy (live birth) NEC — *see* category
650
stillbirth NEC 656.4 ☑
threatened premature 644.2 ☑
triplets NEC 651.1 ☑
with fetal loss and retention of one or more
fetus(es) 651.4 ☑
delayed delivery (one or more mates)
662.3 ☑
following (elective) fetal reduction ●
651.7 ☑ ●
locked mates 660.5 ☑
twins NEC 651.0 ☑
with fetal loss and retention of one fetus
651.3 ☑
delayed delivery (one or more mates)
662.3 ☑
following (elective) fetal reduction ●
651.7 ☑ ●
locked mates 660.5 ☑
uncomplicated — *see* category 650
vacuum extractor NEC 669.5 ☑
affecting fetus or newborn 763.3
ventouse NEC 669.5 ☑
affecting fetus or newborn 763.3

Dellen, cornea 371.41

Delusions (paranoid) 297.9
grandiose 297.1
parasitosis 300.29
systematized 297.1

Dementia 294.8
alcohol-induced persisting (*see also* Psychosis,
alcoholic) 291.2
Alzheimer's — *see* Alzheimer's, dementia
arteriosclerotic (simple type) (uncomplicated)
290.40
with
acute confusional state 290.41

Dementia — *continued*
arteriosclerotic — *continued*
with — *continued*
delirium 290.41
delusions 290.42
depressed mood 290.43
depressed type 290.43
paranoid type 290.42
Binswanger's 290.12
catatonic (acute) (*see also* Schizophrenia)
295.2 ☑
congenital (*see also* Retardation, mental) 319
degenerative 290.9
presenile-onset — *see* Dementia, presenile
senile-onset — *see* Dementia, senile
developmental (*see also* Schizophrenia)
295.9 ☑
dialysis 294.8
transient 293.9
drug-induced persisting (*see also* Psychosis,
drug) 292.82
due to or associated with condition(s) classified
elsewhere
Alzheimer's
with behavioral disturbance
331.0 [294.11]
without behavioral disturbance
331.0 [294.10]
cerebral lipidoses
with behavioral disturbance
330.1 [294.11]
without behavioral disturbance
330.1 [294.10]
epilepsy
with behavioral disturbance
345.9 ☑ [294.11]
without behavioral disturbance
345.9 ☑ [294.10]
hepatolenticular degeneration
with behavioral disturbance
275.1 [294.11]
without behavioral disturbance
275.1 [294.10]
HIV
with behavioral disturbance 042 [294.11]
without behavioral disturbance
042 [294.10]
Huntington's chorea
with behavioral disturbance
333.4 [294.11]
without behavioral disturbance
333.4 [294.10]
Jakob-Creutzfeldt disease ▶(new variant)◀
with behavioral disturbance
046.1 [294.11]
without behavioral disturbance
046.1 [294.10]
Lewy bodies
with behavioral disturbance
331.82 [294.11]
without behavioral disturbance
331.82 [294.10]
multiple sclerosis
with behavioral disturbance 340 [294.11]
without behavioral disturbance
340 [294.10]
neurosyphilis
with behavioral disturbance
094.9 [294.11]
without behavioral disturbance
094.9 [294.10]
Parkinsonism
with behavioral disturbance
331.82 [294.11]
without behavioral disturbance
331.82 [294.10]
Pelizaeus-Merzbacher disease
with behavioral disturbance
333.0 [294.11]
without behavioral disturbance
333.0 [294.10]
Pick's disease
with behavioral disturbance
331.11 [294.11]
without behavioral disturbance
331.11 [294.10]
polyarteritis nodosa
with behavioral disturbance
446.0 [294.11]

☑ Additional Digit Required — Refer to the Tabular List (Numeric Code Section) for Additional Digit Selection

Dementia — *continued*
  due to or associated with condition(s) classified elsewhere — *continued*
    polyarteritis nodosa — *continued*
      without behavioral disturbance 446.0 *[294.10]*
    syphilis
      with behavioral disturbance 094.1 *[294.11]*
      without behavioral disturbance 094.1 *[294.10]*
    Wilson's disease
      with behavioral disturbance 275.1 *[294.11]*
      without behavioral disturbance 275.1 *[294.10]*
  frontal 331.19
    with behavioral disturbance 331.19 *[294.11]*
    without behavioral disturbance 331.19 *[294.10]*
  frontotemporal 331.19
    with behavioral disturbance 331.19 *[294.11]*
    without behavioral disturbance 331.19 *[294.10]*
  hebephrenic (acute) 295.1 ☑
  Heller's (infantile psychosis) (*see also* Psychosis, childhood) 299.1 ☑
  idiopathic 290.9
    presenile-onset — *see* Dementia, presenile
    senile-onset — *see* Dementia, senile
  in
    arteriosclerotic brain disease 290.40
    senility 290.0
  induced by drug 292.82
  infantile, infantilia (*see also* Psychosis, childhood) 299.0 ☑
  Lewy body 331.82
    with behavioral disturbance 331.82 *[294.11]*
    without behavioral disturbance 331.82 *[294.10]*
  multi-infarct (cerebrovascular) (*see also* Dementia, arteriosclerotic) 290.40
  old age 290.0
  paralytica, paralytic 094.1
    juvenilis 090.40
    syphilitic 094.1
      congenital 090.40
    tabetic form 094.1
  paranoid (*see also* Schizophrenia) 295.3 ☑
  paraphrenic (*see also* Schizophrenia) 295.3 ☑
  paretic 094.1
  praecox (*see also* Schizophrenia) 295.9 ☑
  presenile 290.10
    with
      acute confusional state 290.11
      delirium 290.11
      delusional features 290.12
      depressive features 290.13
    depressed type 290.13
    paranoid type 290.12
    simple type 290.10
    uncomplicated 290.10
  primary (acute) (*see also* Schizophrenia) 295.0 ☑
  progressive, syphilitic 094.1
  puerperal — *see* Psychosis, puerperal
  schizophrenic (*see also* Schizophrenia) 295.9 ☑
  senile 290.0
    with
      acute confusional state 290.3
      delirium 290.3
      delusional features 290.20
      depressive features 290.21
    depressed type 290.21
    exhaustion 290.0
    paranoid type 290.20
  simple type (acute) (*see also* Schizophrenia) 295.0 ☑
  simplex (acute) (*see also* Schizophrenia) 295.0 ☑
  syphilitic 094.1
  uremic — *see* Uremia
  vascular 290.40
    with
      delirium 290.41
      delusions 290.42
      depressed mood 290.43
Demerol dependence (*see also* Dependence) 304.0 ☑

Demineralization, ankle (*see also* Osteoporosis) 733.00
Demodex folliculorum (infestation) 133.8
de Morgan's spots (senile angiomas) 448.1
Demyelinating
  polyneuritis, chronic inflammatory 357.81
Demyelination, demyelinization
  central nervous system 341.9
    specified NEC 341.8
  corpus callosum (central) 341.8
  global 340
Dengue (fever) 061
  sandfly 061
  vaccination, prophylactic (against) V05.1
  virus hemorrhagic fever 065.4
Dens
  evaginatus 520.2
  in dente 520.2
  invaginatus 520.2
Density
  increased, bone (disseminated) (generalized) (spotted) 733.99
  lung (nodular) 518.89
Dental — *see also* condition
  examination only V72.2
Dentia praecox 520.6
Denticles (in pulp) 522.2
Dentigerous cyst 526.0
Dentin
  irregular (in pulp) 522.3
  opalescent 520.5
  secondary (in pulp) 522.3
  sensitive 521.8
Dentinogenesis imperfecta 520.5
Dentinoma (M9271/0) 213.1
  upper jaw (bone) 213.0
Dentition 520.7
  abnormal 520.6
  anomaly 520.6
  delayed 520.6
  difficult 520.7
  disorder of 520.6
  precocious 520.6
  retarded 520.6
Denture sore (mouth) 528.9
Dependence

> *Note* — *Use the following fifth-digit subclassification with category 304:*
>
> | 0 | *unspecified* |
> | 1 | *continuous* |
> | 2 | *episodic* |
> | 3 | *in remission* |

  with
    withdrawal symptoms
      alcohol 291.81
      drug 292.0
  14-hydroxy-dihydromorphinone 304.0 ☑
  absinthe 304.6 ☑
  acemorphan 304.0 ☑
  acetanilid(e) 304.6 ☑
  acetophenetidin 304.6 ☑
  acetorphine 304.0 ☑
  acetyldihydrocodeine 304.0 ☑
  acetyldihydrocodeinone 304.0 ☑
  Adalin 304.1 ☑
  Afghanistan black 304.3 ☑
  agrypnal 304.1 ☑
  alcohol, alcoholic (ethyl) (methyl) (wood) 303.9 ☑
    maternal, with suspected fetal damage affecting management of pregnancy 655.4 ☑
  allobarbitone 304.1 ☑
  allonal 304.1 ☑
  allylisopropylacetylurea 304.1 ☑
  alphaprodine (hydrochloride) 304.0 ☑
  Alurate 304.1 ☑
  Alvodine 304.0 ☑
  amethocaine 304.6 ☑
  amidone 304.0 ☑
  amidopyrine 304.6 ☑

Dependence — *continued*
  aminopyrine 304.6 ☑
  amobarbital 304.1 ☑
  amphetamine(s) (type) (drugs classifiable to 969.7) 304.4 ☑
  amylene hydrate 304.6 ☑
  amylobarbitone 304.1 ☑
  amylocaine 304.6 ☑
  Amytal (sodium) 304.1 ☑
  analgesic (drug) NEC 304.6 ☑
    synthetic with morphine-like effect 304.0 ☑
  anesthetic (agent) (drug) (gas) (general) (local) NEC 304.6 ☑
  Angel dust 304.6 ☑
  anileridine 304.0 ☑
  antipyrine 304.6 ☑
  anxiolytic 304.1 ☑
  aprobarbital 304.1 ☑
  aprobarbitone 304.1 ☑
  atropine 304.6 ☑
  Avertin (bromide) 304.6 ☑
  barbenyl 304.1 ☑
  barbital(s) 304.1 ☑
  barbitone 304.1 ☑
  barbiturate(s) (compounds) (drugs classifiable to 967.0) 304.1 ☑
  barbituric acid (and compounds) 304.1 ☑
  benzedrine 304.4 ☑
  benzylmorphine 304.0 ☑
  Beta-chlor 304.1 ☑
  bhang 304.3 ☑
  blue velvet 304.0 ☑
  Brevital 304.1 ☑
  bromal (hydrate) 304.1 ☑
  bromide(s) NEC 304.1 ☑
  bromine compounds NEC 304.1 ☑
  bromisovalum 304.1 ☑
  bromoform 304.1 ☑
  Bromo-seltzer 304.1 ☑
  bromural 304.1 ☑
  butabarbital (sodium) 304.1 ☑
  butabarpal 304.1 ☑
  butallylonal 304.1 ☑
  butethal 304.1 ☑
  buthalitone (sodium) 304.1 ☑
  Butisol 304.1 ☑
  butobarbitone 304.1 ☑
  butyl chloral (hydrate) 304.1 ☑
  caffeine 304.4 ☑
  cannabis (indica) (sativa) (resin) (derivatives) (type) 304.3 ☑
  carbamazepine 304.6 ☑
  Carbrital 304.1 ☑
  carbromal 304.1 ☑
  carisoprodol 304.6 ☑
  Catha (edulis) 304.4 ☑
  chloral (betaine) (hydrate) 304.1 ☑
  chloralamide 304.1 ☑
  chloralformamide 304.1 ☑
  chloralose 304.1 ☑
  chlordiazepoxide 304.1 ☑
  Chloretone 304.1 ☑
  chlorobutanol 304.1 ☑
  chlorodyne 304.1 ☑
  chloroform 304.6 ☑
  Cliradon 304.0 ☑
  coca (leaf) and derivatives 304.2 ☑
  cocaine 304.2 ☑
    hydrochloride 304.2 ☑
    salt (any) 304.2 ☑
  codeine 304.0 ☑
  combination of drugs (excluding morphine or opioid type drug) NEC 304.8 ☑
    morphine or opioid type drug with any other drug 304.7 ☑
  croton-chloral 304.1 ☑
  cyclobarbital 304.1 ☑
  cyclobarbitone 304.1 ☑
  dagga 304.3 ☑
  Delvinal 304.1 ☑
  Demerol 304.0 ☑
  desocodeine 304.0 ☑
  desomorphine 304.0 ☑
  desoxyephedrine 304.4 ☑
  DET 304.5 ☑
  dexamphetamine 304.4 ☑
  dexedrine 304.4 ☑

Dependence — *continued*
  dextromethorphan 304.0 ☑
  dextromoramide 304.0 ☑
  dextronorpseudoephedrine 304.4 ☑
  dextrorphan 304.0 ☑
  diacetylmorphine 304.0 ☑
  Dial 304.1 ☑
  diallylbarbituric acid 304.1 ☑
  diamorphine 304.0 ☑
  diazepam 304.1 ☑
  dibucaine 304.6 ☑
  dichloroethane 304.6 ☑
  diethyl barbituric acid 304.1 ☑
  diethylsulfone-diethylmethane 304.1 ☑
  difencloxazine 304.0 ☑
  dihydrocodeine 304.0 ☑
  dihydrocodeinone 304.0 ☑
  dihydrohydroxycodeinone 304.0 ☑
  dihydroisocodeine 304.0 ☑
  dihydromorphine 304.0 ☑
  dihydromorphinone 304.0 ☑
  dihydroxcodeinone 304.0 ☑
  Dilaudid 304.0 ☑
  dimenhydrinate 304.6 ☑
  dimethylmeperidine 304.0 ☑
  dimethyltriptamine 304.5 ☑
  Dionin 304.0 ☑
  diphenoxylate 304.6 ☑
  dipipanone 304.0 ☑
  d-lysergic acid diethylamide 304.5 ☑
  DMT 304.5 ☑
  Dolophine 304.0 ☑
  DOM 304.2 ☑
  Doriden 304.1 ☑
  dormiral 304.1 ☑
  Dormison 304.1 ☑
  Dromoran 304.0 ☑
  drug NEC 304.9 ☑
    analgesic NEC 304.6 ☑
    combination (excluding morphine or opioid
        type drug) NEC 304.8 ☑
      morphine or opioid type drug with any
          other drug 304.7 ☑
    complicating pregnancy, childbirth, or
        puerperium 648.3 ☑
      affecting fetus or newborn 779.5
    hallucinogenic 304.5 ☑
    hypnotic NEC 304.1 ☑
    narcotic NEC 304.9 ☑
    psychostimulant NEC 304.4 ☑
    sedative 304.1 ☑
    soporific NEC 304.1 ☑
    specified type NEC 304.6 ☑
    suspected damage to fetus affecting
        management of pregnancy 655.5 ☑
    synthetic, with morphine-like effect 304.0 ☑
    tranquilizing 304.1 ☑
  duboisine 304.6 ☑
  ectylurea 304.1 ☑
  Endocaine 304.6 ☑
  Equanil 304.1 ☑
  Eskabarb 304.1 ☑
  ethchlorvynol 304.1 ☑
  ether (ethyl) (liquid) (vapor) (vinyl) 304.6 ☑
  ethidene 304.6 ☑
  ethinamate 304.1 ☑
  ethoheptazine 304.6 ☑
  ethyl
    alcohol 303.9 ☑
    bromide 304.6 ☑
    carbamate 304.6 ☑
    chloride 304.6 ☑
    morphine 304.0 ☑
  ethylene (gas) 304.6 ☑
    dichloride 304.6 ☑
  ethylidene chloride 304.6 ☑
  etilfen 304.1 ☑
  etorphine 304.0 ☑
  etoval 304.1 ☑
  eucodal 304.0 ☑
  euneryl 304.1 ☑
  Evipal 304.1 ☑
  Evipan 304.1 ☑
  fentanyl 304.0 ☑
  ganja 304.3 ☑
  gardenal 304.1 ☑
  gardenpanyl 304.1 ☑

Dependence — *continued*
  gelsemine 304.6 ☑
  Gelsemium 304.6 ☑
  Gemonil 304.1 ☑
  glucochloral 304.1 ☑
  glue (airplane) (sniffing) 304.6 ☑
  glutethimide 304.1 ☑
  hallucinogenics 304.5 ☑
  hashish 304.3 ☑
  headache powder NEC 304.6 ☑
  Heavenly Blue 304.5 ☑
  hedonal 304.1 ☑
  hemp 304.3 ☑
  heptabarbital 304.1 ☑
  Heptalgin 304.0 ☑
  heptobarbitone 304.1 ☑
  heroin 304.0 ☑
    salt (any) 304.0 ☑
  hexethal (sodium) 304.1 ☑
  hexobarbital 304.1 ☑
  Hycodan 304.0 ☑
  hydrocodone 304.0 ☑
  hydromorphinol 304.0 ☑
  hydromorphinone 304.0 ☑
  hydromorphone 304.0 ☑
  hydroxycodeine 304.0 ☑
  hypnotic NEC 304.1 ☑
  Indian hemp 304.3 ☑
  inhalant 304.6 ☑
  intranarcon 304.1 ☑
  Kemithal 304.1 ☑
  ketobemidone 304.0 ☑
  khat 304.4 ☑
  kif 304.3 ☑
  Lactuca (virosa) extract 304.1 ☑
  lactucarium 304.1 ☑
  laudanum 304.0 ☑
  Lebanese red 304.3 ☑
  Leritine 304.0 ☑
  lettuce opium 304.1 ☑
  Levanil 304.1 ☑
  Levo-Dromoran 304.0 ☑
  levo-iso-methadone 304.0 ☑
  levorphanol 304.0 ☑
  Librium 304.1 ☑
  Lomotil 304.6 ☑
  Lotusate 304.1 ☑
  LSD (-25) (and derivatives) 304.5 ☑
  Luminal 304.1 ☑
  lysergic acid 304.5 ☑
    amide 304.5 ☑
  maconha 304.3 ☑
  magic mushroom 304.5 ☑
  marihuana 304.3 ☑
  MDA (methylene dioxyamphetamine) 304.4 ☑
  Mebaral 304.1 ☑
  Medinal 304.1 ☑
  Medomin 304.1 ☑
  megahallucinogenics 304.5 ☑
  meperidine 304.0 ☑
  mephobarbital 304.1 ☑
  meprobamate 304.1 ☑
  mescaline 304.5 ☑
  methadone 304.0 ☑
  methamphetamine(s) 304.4 ☑
  methaqualone 304.1 ☑
  metharbital 304.1 ☑
  methitural 304.1 ☑
  methobarbitone 304.1 ☑
  methohexital 304.1 ☑
  methopholine 304.6 ☑
  methyl
    alcohol 303.9 ☑
    bromide 304.6 ☑
    morphine 304.0 ☑
    sulfonal 304.1 ☑
  methylated spirit 303.9 ☑
  methylbutinol 304.6 ☑
  methyldihydromorphinone 304.0 ☑
  methylene
    chloride 304.6 ☑
    dichloride 304.6 ☑
    dioxyamphetamine (MDA) 304.4 ☑
  methylparafynol 304.1 ☑
  methylphenidate 304.4 ☑
  methyprylone 304.1 ☑
  metopon 304.0 ☑

Dependence — *continued*
  Miltown 304.1 ☑
  morning glory *seeds* 304.5 ☑
  morphinan(s) 304.0 ☑
  morphine (sulfate) (sulfite) (type) (drugs
      classifiable to 965.00-965.09) 304.0 ☑
  morphine or opioid type drug (drugs classifiable
      to 965.00-965.09) with any other drug
      304.7 ☑
  morphinol(s) 304.0 ☑
  morphinon 304.0 ☑
  morpholinylethylmorphine 304.0 ☑
  mylomide 304.1 ☑
  myristicin 304.5 ☑
  narcotic (drug) NEC 304.9 ☑
  nealbarbital 304.1 ☑
  nealbarbitone 304.1 ☑
  Nembutal 304.1 ☑
  Neonal 304.1 ☑
  Neraval 304.1 ☑
  Neravan 304.1 ☑
  neurobarb 304.1 ☑
  nicotine 305.1
  Nisentil 304.0 ☑
  nitrous oxide 304.6 ☑
  Noctec 304.1 ☑
  Noludar 304.1 ☑
  nonbarbiturate sedatives and tranquilizers with
      similar effect 304.1 ☑
  noptil 304.1 ☑
  normorphine 304.0 ☑
  noscapine 304.0 ☑
  Novocaine 304.6 ☑
  Numorphan 304.0 ☑
  nunol 304.1 ☑
  Nupercaine 304.6 ☑
  Oblivon 304.1 ☑
  on
    aspirator V46.0
    hemodialysis V45.1   ●
    hyperbaric chamber V46.8
    iron lung V46.11
    machine (enabling) V46.9
      specified type NEC V46.8
    peritoneal dialysis V45.1   ●
    Possum (Patient-Operated-Selector-
        Mechanism) V46.8
    renal dialysis machine V45.1
    respirator ►[ventilator]◄ V46.11
      encounter
        during   ●
          mechanical failure V46.14   ●
          power failure V46.12   ●
        for weaning V46.13   ●
    supplemental oxygen V46.2
  opiate 304.0 ☑
  opioids 304.0 ☑
  opioid type 304.0 ☑
    with any other drug 304.7 ☑
  opium (alkaloids) (derivatives) (tincture)
      304.0 ☑
  ortal 304.1 ☑
  Oxazepam 304.1 ☑
  oxycodone 304.0 ☑
  oxymorphone 304.0 ☑
  Palfium 304.0 ☑
  Panadol 304.6 ☑
  pantopium 304.0 ☑
  pantopon 304.0 ☑
  papaverine 304.0 ☑
  paracetamol 304.6 ☑
  paracodin 304.0 ☑
  paraldehyde 304.1 ☑
  paregoric 304.0 ☑
  Parzone 304.0 ☑
  PCP (phencyclidine) 304.6 ☑
  Pearly Gates 304.5 ☑
  pentazocine 304.0 ☑
  pentobarbital 304.1 ☑
  pentobarbitone (sodium) 304.1 ☑
  Pentothal 304.1 ☑
  Percaine 304.6 ☑
  Percodan 304.0 ☑
  Perichlor 304.1 ☑
  Pernocton 304.1 ☑
  Pernoston 304.1 ☑
  peronine 304.0 ☑

☑ Additional Digit Required — Refer to the Tabular List (Numeric Code Section) for Additional Digit Selection

Dependence — continued
pethidine (hydrochloride) 304.0 ☑
petrichloral 304.1 ☑
peyote 304.5 ☑
Phanodorn 304.1 ☑
phenacetin 304.6 ☑
phenadoxone 304.0 ☑
phenaglycodol 304.1 ☑
phenazocine 304.0 ☑
phencyclidine 304.6 ☑
phenmetrazine 304.4 ☑
phenobal 304.1 ☑
phenobarbital 304.1 ☑
phenobarbitone 304.1 ☑
phenomorphan 304.0 ☑
phenonyl 304.1 ☑
phenoperidine 304.0 ☑
pholcodine 304.0 ☑
piminodine 304.0 ☑
Pipadone 304.0 ☑
Pitkin's solution 304.6 ☑
Placidyl 304.1 ☑
polysubstance 304.8 ☑
Pontocaine 304.6 ☑
pot 304.3 ☑
potassium bromide 304.1 ☑
Preludin 304.4 ☑
Prinadol 304.0 ☑
probarbital 304.1 ☑
procaine 304.6 ☑
propanal 304.1 ☑
propoxyphene 304.6 ☑
psilocibin 304.5 ☑
psilocin 304.5 ☑
psilocybin 304.5 ☑
psilocyline 304.5 ☑
psilocyn 304.5 ☑
psychedelic agents 304.5 ☑
psychostimulant NEC 304.4 ☑
psychotomimetic agents 304.5 ☑
pyrahexyl 304.3 ☑
Pyramidon 304.6 ☑
quinalbarbitone 304.1 ☑
racemoramide 304.0 ☑
racemorphan 304.0 ☑
Rela 304.6 ☑
scopolamine 304.6 ☑
secobarbital 304.1 ☑
Seconal 304.1 ☑
sedative NEC 304.1 ☑
    nonbarbiturate with barbiturate effect 304.1 ☑
Sedormid 304.1 ☑
sernyl 304.1 ☑
sodium bromide 304.1 ☑
Soma 304.6 ☑
Somnal 304.1 ☑
Somnos 304.1 ☑
Soneryl 304.1 ☑
soporific (drug) NEC 304.1 ☑
specified drug NEC 304.6 ☑
speed 304.4 ☑
spinocaine 304.6 ☑
Stovaine 304.6 ☑
STP 304.5 ☑
stramonium 304.6 ☑
Sulfonal 304.1 ☑
sulfonethylmethane 304.1 ☑
sulfonmethane 304.1 ☑
Surital 304.1 ☑
synthetic drug with morphine-like effect
    304.0 ☑
talbutal 304.1 ☑
tetracaine 304.6 ☑
tetrahydrocannabinol 304.3 ☑
tetronal 304.1 ☑
THC 304.3 ☑
thebacon 304.0 ☑
thebaine 304.0 ☑
thiamil 304.1 ☑
thiamylal 304.1 ☑
thiopental 304.1 ☑
tobacco 305.1
toluene, toluol 304.6 ☑
tranquilizer NEC 304.1 ☑
    nonbarbiturate with barbiturate effect
        304.1 ☑
tribromacetaldehyde 304.6 ☑

Dependence — continued
tribromethanol 304.6 ☑
tribromomethane 304.6 ☑
trichloroethanol 304.6 ☑
trichoroethyl phosphate 304.1 ☑
triclofos 304.1 ☑
Trional 304.1 ☑
Tuinal 304.1 ☑
Turkish Green 304.3 ☑
urethan(e) 304.6 ☑
Valium 304.1 ☑
Valmid 304.1 ☑
veganin 304.0 ☑
veramon 304.1 ☑
Veronal 304.1 ☑
versidyne 304.6 ☑
vinbarbital 304.1 ☑
vinbarbitone 304.1 ☑
vinyl bitone 304.1 ☑
vitamin B$_6$ 266.1
wine 303.9 ☑
Zactane 304.6 ☑

Dependency
passive 301.6
reactions 301.6

Depersonalization (episode, in neurotic state)
    (neurotic) (syndrome) 300.6

Depletion
carbohydrates 271.9
complement factor 279.8
extracellular fluid 276.52   ▲
plasma 276.52   ▲
potassium 276.8
    nephropathy 588.89
salt or sodium 276.1
    causing heat exhaustion or prostration
        992.4
    nephropathy 593.9
volume 276.50   ▲
    extracellular fluid 276.52   ▲
    plasma 276.52   ▲

Deposit
argentous, cornea 371.16
bone, in Boeck's sarcoid 135
calcareous, calcium — see Calcification
cholesterol
    retina 362.82
    skin 709.3
    vitreous (humor) 379.22
conjunctival 372.56
cornea, corneal NEC 371.10
    argentous 371.16
    in
        cystinosis 270.0 [371.15]
        mucopolysaccharidosis 277.5 [371.15]
crystalline, vitreous (humor) 379.22
hemosiderin, in old scars of cornea 371.11
metallic, in lens 366.45
skin 709.3
teeth, tooth (betel) (black) (green) (materia alba)
    (orange) (soft) (tobacco) 523.6
urate, in kidney (see also Disease, renal) 593.9

Depraved appetite 307.52

Depression 311
acute (see also Psychosis, affective) 296.2 ☑
    recurrent episode 296.3 ☑
    single episode 296.2 ☑
agitated (see also Psychosis, affective) 296.2 ☑
    recurrent episode 296.3 ☑
    single episode 296.2 ☑
anaclitic 309.21
anxiety 300.4
arches 734
    congenital 754.61
autogenous (see also Psychosis, affective)
    296.2 ☑
    recurrent episode 296.3 ☑
    single episode 296.2 ☑
basal metabolic rate (BMR) 794.7
bone marrow 289.9
central nervous system 799.1
    newborn 779.2
cerebral 331.9
    newborn 779.2
cerebrovascular 437.8
    newborn 779.2

Depression — continued
chest wall 738.3
endogenous (see also Psychosis, affective)
    296.2 ☑
    recurrent episode 296.3 ☑
    single episode 296.2 ☑
functional activity 780.99
hysterical 300.11
involutional, climacteric, or menopausal (see
    also Psychosis, affective) 296.2 ☑
    recurrent episode 296.3 ☑
    single episode 296.2 ☑
manic (see also Psychosis, affective) 296.80
medullary 348.8
    newborn 779.2
mental 300.4
metatarsal heads — see Depression, arches
metatarsus — see Depression, arches
monopolar (see also Psychosis, affective)
    296.2 ☑
    recurrent episode 296.3 ☑
    single episode 296.2 ☑
nervous 300.4
neurotic 300.4
nose 738.0
postpartum 648.4 ☑
psychogenic 300.4
    reactive 298.0
psychoneurotic 300.4
psychotic (see also Psychosis, affective)
    296.2 ☑
    reactive 298.0
    recurrent episode 296.3 ☑
    single episode 296.2 ☑
reactive 300.4
    neurotic 300.4
    psychogenic 298.0
    psychoneurotic 300.4
    psychotic 298.0
recurrent 296.3 ☑
respiratory center 348.8
    newborn 770.89
scapula 736.89
senile 290.21
situational (acute) (brief) 309.0
    prolonged 309.1
skull 754.0
sternum 738.3
visual field 368.40

Depressive reaction — see also Reaction,
    depressive
acute (transient) 309.0
    with anxiety 309.28
prolonged 309.1
situational (acute) 309.0
    prolonged 309.1

Deprivation
cultural V62.4
emotional V62.89
    affecting
        adult 995.82
        infant or child 995.51
food 994.2
    specific substance NEC 269.8
protein (familial) (kwashiorkor) 260
sleep V69.4
social V62.4
    affecting
        adult 995.82
        infant or child 995.51
symptoms, syndrome
    alcohol 291.81
    drug 292.0
vitamins (see also Deficiency, vitamin) 269.2
water 994.3

de Quervain's
disease (tendon sheath) 727.04
thyroiditis (subacute granulomatous thyroiditis)
    245.1

Derangement
ankle (internal) 718.97
    current injury (see also Dislocation, ankle)
        837.0
    recurrent 718.37

Derangement — *continued*
  cartilage (articular) NEC (*see also* Disorder,
    cartilage, articular) 718.0 ☑
    knee 717.9
      recurrent 718.36
    recurrent 718.3 ☑
  collateral ligament (knee) (medial) (tibial)
    717.82
    current injury 844.1
      lateral (fibular) 844.0
    lateral (fibular) 717.81
      current injury 844.0
  cruciate ligament (knee) (posterior) 717.84
    anterior 717.83
      current injury 844.2
    current injury 844.2
  elbow (internal) 718.92
    current injury (*see also* Dislocation, elbow)
      832.00
    recurrent 718.32
  gastrointestinal 536.9
  heart — *see* Disease, heart
  hip (joint) (internal) (old) 718.95
    current injury (*see also* Dislocation, hip)
      835.00
    recurrent 718.35
  intervertebral disc — *see* Displacement,
    intervertebral disc
  joint (internal) 718.90
    ankle 718.97
    current injury — *see also* Dislocation, by
      site
      knee, meniscus or cartilage (*see also*
        Tear, meniscus) 836.2
    elbow 718.92
    foot 718.97
    hand 718.94
    hip 718.95
    knee 717.9
    multiple sites 718.99
    pelvic region 718.95
    recurrent 718.30
      ankle 718.37
      elbow 718.32
      foot 718.37
      hand 718.34
      hip 718.35
      knee 718.36
      multiple sites 718.39
      pelvic region 718.35
      shoulder (region) 718.31
      specified site NEC 718.38
      temporomandibular (old) 524.69
      wrist 718.33
    shoulder (region) 718.91
    specified site NEC 718.98
    spine NEC 724.9
    temporomandibular 524.69
    wrist 718.93
  knee (cartilage) (internal) 717.9
    current injury (*see also* Tear, meniscus)
      836.2
    ligament 717.89
      capsular 717.85
      collateral — *see* Derangement, collateral
        ligament
      cruciate — *see* Derangement, cruciate
        ligament
      specified NEC 717.85
    recurrent 718.36
  low back NEC 724.9
  meniscus NEC (knee) 717.5
    current injury (*see also* Tear, meniscus)
      836.2
    lateral 717.40
      anterior horn 717.42
      posterior horn 717.43
      specified NEC 717.49
    medial 717.3
      anterior horn 717.1
      posterior horn 717.2
    recurrent 718.3 ☑
    site other than knee — *see* Disorder,
      cartilage, articular
  mental (*see also* Psychosis) 298.9
  rotator cuff (recurrent) (tear) 726.10
    current 840.4

Derangement — *continued*
  sacroiliac (old) 724.6
    current — *see* Dislocation, sacroiliac
  semilunar cartilage (knee) 717.5
    current injury 836.2
      lateral 836.1
      medial 836.0
    recurrent 718.3 ☑
  shoulder (internal) 718.91
    current injury (*see also* Dislocation,
      shoulder) 831.00
    recurrent 718.31
  spine (recurrent) NEC 724.9
    current — *see* Dislocation, spine
  temporomandibular (internal) (joint) (old)
    524.69
    current — *see* Dislocation, jaw

Dercum's disease or syndrome (adiposis
  dolorosa) 272.8

Derealization (neurotic) 300.6

Dermal — *see* condition

Dermaphytid — *see* Dermatophytosis

Dermatergosis — *see* Dermatitis

Dermatitis (allergic) (contact) (occupational)
  (venenata) 692.9
  ab igne 692.82
  acneiform 692.9
  actinic (due to sun) 692.70
    acute 692.72
    chronic NEC 692.74
    other than from sun NEC 692.82
  ambustionis
    due to
      burn or scald — *see* Burn, by site
      sunburn (*see also* Sunburn) 692.71
  amebic 006.6
  ammonia 691.0
  anaphylactoid NEC 692.9
  arsenical 692.4
  artefacta 698.4
    psychogenic 316 *[698.4]*
  asthmatic 691.8
  atopic (allergic) (intrinsic) 691.8
    psychogenic 316 *[691.8]*
  atrophicans 701.8
    diffusa 701.8
    maculosa 701.3
  berlock, berloque 692.72
  blastomycetic 116.0
  blister beetle 692.89
  Brucella NEC 023.9
  bullosa 694.9
    striata pratensis 692.6
  bullous 694.9
    mucosynechial, atrophic 694.60
      with ocular involvement 694.61
    seasonal 694.8
  calorica
    due to
      burn or scald — *see* Burn, by site
      cold 692.89
      sunburn (*see also* Sunburn) 692.71
  caterpillar 692.89
  cercarial 120.3
  combustionis
    due to
      burn or scald — *see* Burn, by site
      sunburn (*see also* Sunburn) 692.71
  congelationis 991.5
  contusiformis 695.2
  diabetic 250.8 ☑
  diaper 691.0
  diphtheritica 032.85
  due to
    acetone 692.2
    acids 692.4
    adhesive plaster 692.4
    alcohol (skin contact) (substances
      classifiable to 980.0-980.9) 692.4
      taken internally 693.8
    alkalis 692.4
    allergy NEC 692.9
    ammonia (household) (liquid) 692.4
    animal
      dander (cat) (dog) 692.84
      hair (cat) (dog) 692.84

Dermatitis — *continued*
  due to — *continued*
    arnica 692.3
    arsenic 692.4
      taken internally 693.8
    blister beetle 692.89
    cantharides 692.3
    carbon disulphide 692.2
    caterpillar 692.89
    caustics 692.4
    cereal (ingested) 693.1
      contact with skin 692.5
    chemical(s) NEC 692.4
      internal 693.8
      irritant NEC 692.4
      taken internally 693.8
    chlorocompounds 692.2
    coffee (ingested) 693.1
      contact with skin 692.5
    cold weather 692.89
    cosmetics 692.81
    cyclohexanes 692.2
    dander, animal (cat) (dog) 692.84
    deodorant 692.81
    detergents 692.0
    dichromate 692.4
    drugs and medicinals (correct substance
      properly administered) (internal use)
      693.0
      external (in contact with skin) 692.3
        wrong substance given or taken 976.9
          specified substance — *see* Table of
            Drugs and Chemicals
      wrong substance given or taken 977.9
        specified substance — *see* Table of
          Drugs and Chemicals
    dyes 692.89
      hair 692.89
    epidermophytosis — *see* Dermatophytosis
    esters 692.2
    external irritant NEC 692.9
      specified agent NEC 692.89
    eye shadow 692.81
    fish (ingested) 693.1
      contact with skin 692.5
    flour (ingested) 693.1
      contact with skin 692.5
    food (ingested) 693.1
      in contact with skin 692.5
    fruit (ingested) 693.1
      contact with skin 692.5
    fungicides 692.3
    furs 692.84
    glycols 692.2
    greases NEC 692.1
    hair dyes 692.89
    hair, animal (cat) (dog) 692.84
    hot
      objects and materials — *see* Burn, by
        site
      weather or places 692.89
    hydrocarbons 692.2
    infrared rays, except from sun 692.82
      solar NEC (*see also* Dermatitis, due to,
        sun) 692.70
    ingested substance 693.9
      drugs and medicinals (*see also*
        Dermatitis, due to, drugs and
        medicinals) 693.0
      food 693.1
      specified substance NEC 693.8
    ingestion or injection of chemical 693.8
      drug (correct substance properly
        administered) 693.0
      wrong substance given or taken 977.9
        specified substance — *see* Table of
          Drugs and Chemicals
    insecticides 692.4
    internal agent 693.9
      drugs and medicinals (*see also*
        Dermatitis, due to, drugs and
        medicinals) 693.0
      food (ingested) 693.1
        in contact with skin 692.5
      specified agent NEC 693.8
    iodine 692.3
    iodoform 692.3
    irradiation 692.82

Dermatitis — *continued*
  due to — *continued*
    jewelry 692.83
    keratolytics 692.3
    ketones 692.2
    lacquer tree (Rhus verniciflua) 692.6
    light (sun) NEC (*see also* Dermatitis, due to,
      sun) 692.70
      other 692.82
    low temperature 692.89
    mascara 692.81
    meat (ingested) 693.1
      contact with skin 692.5
    mercury, mercurials 692.3
    metals 692.83
    milk (ingested) 693.1
      contact with skin 692.5
    Neomycin 692.3
    nylon 692.4
    oils NEC 692.1
    paint solvent 692.2
    pediculocides 692.3
    petroleum products (substances classifiable
      to 981) 692.4
    phenol 692.3
    photosensitiveness, photosensitivity (sun)
      692.72
      other light 692.82
    plants NEC 692.6
    plasters, medicated (any) 692.3
    plastic 692.4
    poison
      ivy (Rhus toxicodendron) 692.6
      oak (Rhus diversiloba) 692.6
      plant or vine 692.6
      sumac (Rhus venenata) 692.6
      vine (Rhus radicans) 692.6
    preservatives 692.89
    primrose (primula) 692.6
    primula 692.6
    radiation 692.82
      sun NEC (*see also* Dermatitis, due to,
        sun) 692.70
      tanning bed 692.82
    radioactive substance 692.82
    radium 692.82
    ragweed (Senecio jacobae) 692.6
    Rhus (diversiloba) (radicans) (toxicodendron)
      (venenata) (verniciflua) 692.6
    rubber 692.4
    scabicides 692.3
    Senecio jacobae 692.6
    solar radiation — *see* Dermatitis, due to,
      sun
    solvents (any) (substances classifiable to
      982.0-982.8) 692.2
      chlorocompound group 692.2
      cyclohexane group 692.2
      ester group 692.2
      glycol group 692.2
      hydrocarbon group 692.2
      ketone group 692.2
      paint 692.2
    specified agent NEC 692.89
    sun 692.70
      acute 692.72
      chronic NEC 692.74
      specified NEC 692.79
    sunburn (*see also* Sunburn) 692.71
    sunshine NEC (*see also* Dermatitis, due to,
      sun) 692.70
    tanning bed 692.82
    tetrachlorethylene 692.2
    toluene 692.2
    topical medications 692.3
    turpentine 692.2
    ultraviolet rays, except from sun 692.82
      sun NEC (*see also* Dermatitis, due to,
        sun) 692.70
    vaccine or vaccination (correct substance
      properly administered) 693.0
      wrong substance given or taken
        bacterial vaccine 978.8
          specified — *see* Table of Drugs and
            Chemicals
        other vaccines NEC 979.9
          specified — *see* Table of Drugs and
            Chemicals

Dermatitis — *continued*
  due to — *continued*
    varicose veins (*see also* Varicose, vein,
      inflamed or infected) 454.1
    x-rays 692.82
  dyshydrotic 705.81
  dysmenorrheica 625.8
  eczematoid NEC 692.9
    infectious 690.8
  eczematous NEC 692.9
  epidemica 695.89
  erysipelatosa 695.81
  escharotica — *see* Burn, by site
  exfoliativa, exfoliative 695.89
    generalized 695.89
    infantum 695.81
    neonatorum 695.81
  eyelid 373.31
    allergic 373.32
    contact 373.32
    eczematous 373.31
    herpes (zoster) 053.20
      simplex 054.41
    infective 373.5
      due to
        actinomycosis 039.3 *[373.5]*
        herpes
          simplex 054.41
          zoster 053.20
        impetigo 684 *[373.5]*
        leprosy (*see also* Leprosy)
          030.0 *[373.4]*
        lupus vulgaris (tuberculous) (*see also*
          Tuberculosis) 017.0 ☑ *[373.4]*
        mycotic dermatitis (*see also*
          Dermatomycosis) 111.9 *[373.5]*
        vaccinia 051.0 *[373.5]*
          postvaccination 999.0 *[373.5]*
        yaws (*see also* Yaws) 102.9 *[373.4]*
  facta, factitia 698.4
    psychogenic 316 *[698.4]*
  ficta 698.4
    psychogenic 316 *[698.4]*
  flexural 691.8
  follicularis 704.8
  friction 709.8
  fungus 111.9
    specified type NEC 111.8
  gangrenosa, gangrenous (infantum) (*see also*
    Gangrene) 785.4
  gestationis 646.8 ☑
  gonococcal 098.89
  gouty 274.89
  harvest mite 133.8
  heat 692.89
  herpetiformis (bullous) (erythematous)
    (pustular) (vesicular) 694.0
    juvenile 694.2
    senile 694.5
  hiemalis 692.89
  hypostatic, hypostatica 454.1
    with ulcer 454.2
  impetiginous 684
  infantile (acute) (chronic) (intertriginous)
    (intrinsic) (seborrheic) 690.12
  infectiosa eczematoides 690.8
  infectious (staphylococcal) (streptococcal) 686.9
    eczematoid 690.8
  infective eczematoid 690.8
  Jacquet's (diaper dermatitis) 691.0
  leptus 133.8
  lichenified NEC 692.9
  lichenoid, chronic 701.0
  lichenoides purpurica pigmentosa 709.1
  meadow 692.6
  medicamentosa (correct substance properly
    administered) (internal use) (*see also*
    Dermatitis, due to, drugs or medicinals)
    693.0
    due to contact with skin 692.3
  mite 133.8
  multiformis 694.0
    juvenile 694.2
    senile 694.5
  napkin 691.0
  neuro 698.3
  neurotica 694.0

Dermatitis — *continued*
  nummular NEC 692.9
  osteatosis, osteatotic 706.8
  papillaris capillitii 706.1
  pellagrous 265.2
  perioral 695.3
  perstans 696.1
  photosensitivity (sun) 692.72
    other light 692.82
  pigmented purpuric lichenoid 709.1
  polymorpha dolorosa 694.0
  primary irritant 692.9
  pruriginosa 694.0
  pruritic NEC 692.9
  psoriasiform nodularis 696.2
  psychogenic 316
  purulent 686.00
  pustular contagious 051.2
  pyococcal 686.00
  pyocyaneus 686.09
  pyogenica 686.00
  radiation 692.82
  repens 696.1
  Ritter's (exfoliativa) 695.81
  Schamberg's (progressive pigmentary
    dermatosis) 709.09
  schistosome 120.3
  seasonal bullous 694.8
  seborrheic 690.10
    infantile 690.12
  sensitization NEC 692.9
  septic (*see also* Septicemia) 686.00
    gonococcal 098.89
  solar, solare NEC (*see also* Dermatitis, due to,
    sun) 692.70
  stasis 459.81
    due to
      postphlebitic syndrome 459.12
        with ulcer 459.13
      varicose veins — *see* Varicose
    ulcerated or with ulcer (varicose) 454.2
  sunburn (*see also* Sunburn) 692.71
  suppurative 686.00
  traumatic NEC 709.8
  trophoneurotica 694.0
  ultraviolet, except from sun 692.82
    due to sun NEC (*see also* Dermatitis, due to,
      sun) 692.70
  varicose 454.1
    with ulcer 454.2
  vegetans 686.8
  verrucosa 117.2
  xerotic 706.8

Dermatoarthritis, lipoid 272.8 *[713.0]*

Dermatochalasia, dermatochalasis 374.87

Dermatofibroma (lenticulare) (M8832/0) — *see*
  also Neoplasm, skin, benign
  protuberans (M8832/1) — *see* Neoplasm, skin,
    uncertain behavior

Dermatofibrosarcoma (protuberans) (M8832/3)
  — *see* Neoplasm, skin, malignant

Dermatographia 708.3

Dermatolysis (congenital) (exfoliativa) 757.39
  acquired 701.8
  eyelids 374.34
  palpebrarum 374.34
  senile 701.8

Dermatomegaly NEC 701.8

Dermatomucomyositis 710.3

Dermatomycosis 111.9
  furfuracea 111.0
  specified type NEC 111.8

Dermatomyositis (acute) (chronic) 710.3

Dermatoneuritis of children 985.0

Dermatophiliasis 134.1

Dermatophytide — *see* Dermatophytosis

Dermatophytosis (Epidermophyton) (infection)
  (microsporum) (tinea) (Trichophyton) 110.9
  beard 110.0
  body 110.5
  deep seated 110.6
  fingernails 110.1
  foot 110.4
  groin 110.3

☑ Additional Digit Required — Refer to the Tabular List (Numeric Code Section) for Additional Digit Selection

Dermatophytosis — *continued*
　hand 110.2
　nail 110.1
　perianal (area) 110.3
　scalp 110.0
　scrotal 110.8
　specified site NEC 110.8
　toenails 110.1
　vulva 110.8
Dermatopolyneuritis 985.0
Dermatorrhexis 756.83
　acquired 701.8
Dermatosclerosis (*see also* Scleroderma) 710.1
　localized 701.0
Dermatosis 709.9
　Andrews' 686.8
　atopic 691.8
　Bowen's (M8081/2) — *see* Neoplasm, skin, in situ
　bullous 694.9
　　specified type NEC 694.8
　erythematosquamous 690.8
　exfoliativa 695.89
　factitial 698.4
　gonococcal 098.89
　herpetiformis 694.0
　　juvenile 694.2
　　senile 694.5
　hysterical 300.11
　Linear IgA 694.8
　menstrual NEC 709.8
　neutrophilic, acute febrile 695.89
　occupational (*see also* Dermatitis) 692.9
　papulosa nigra 709.8
　pigmentary NEC 709.00
　　progressive 709.09
　　Schamberg's 709.09
　　Siemens-Bloch 757.33
　progressive pigmentary 709.09
　psychogenic 316
　pustular subcorneal 694.1
　Schamberg's (progressive pigmentary) 709.09
　senile NEC 709.3
　specified NEC 702.8
　Unna's (seborrheic dermatitis) 690.10
Dermographia 708.3
Dermographism 708.3
Dermoid (cyst) (M9084/0) — *see also* Neoplasm, by site, benign
　with malignant transformation (M9084/3) 183.0
Dermopathy
　infiltrative, with thyrotoxicosis 242.0 ☑
　senile NEC 709.3
Dermophytosis — *see* Dermatophytosis
Descemet's membrane — *see* condition
Descemetocele 371.72
Descending — *see* condition
Descensus uteri (complete) (incomplete) (partial) (without vaginal wall prolapse) 618.1
　with mention of vaginal wall prolapse — *see* Prolapse, uterovaginal
Desensitization to allergens V07.1
Desert
　rheumatism 114.0
　sore (*see also* Ulcer, skin) 707.9
Desertion (child) (newborn) 995.52
　adult 995.84
Desmoid (extra-abdominal) (tumor) (M8821/1) — *see also* Neoplasm, connective tissue, uncertain behavior
　abdominal (M8822/1) — *see* Neoplasm, connective tissue, uncertain behavior
Despondency 300.4
Desquamative dermatitis NEC 695.89
Destruction
　articular facet (*see also* Derangement, joint) 718.9 ☑
　　vertebra 724.9
　bone 733.90
　　syphilitic 095.5
　joint (*see also* Derangement, joint) 718.9 ☑
　　sacroiliac 724.6

Destruction — *continued*
　kidney 593.89
　live fetus to facilitate birth NEC 763.89
　ossicles (ear) 385.24
　rectal sphincter 569.49
　septum (nasal) 478.1
　tuberculous NEC (*see also* Tuberculosis) 011.9 ☑
　tympanic membrane 384.82
　tympanum 385.89
　vertebral disc — *see* Degeneration, intervertebral disc
Destructiveness (*see also* Disturbance, conduct) 312.9
　adjustment reaction 309.3
Detachment
　cartilage — *see also* Sprain, by site
　　knee — *see* Tear, meniscus
　cervix, annular 622.8
　　complicating delivery 665.3 ☑
　choroid (old) (postinfectional) (simple) (spontaneous) 363.70
　　hemorrhagic 363.72
　　serous 363.71
　knee, medial meniscus (old) 717.3
　　current injury 836.0
　ligament — *see* Sprain, by site
　placenta (premature) — *see* Placenta, separation
　retina (recent) 361.9
　　with retinal defect (rhegmatogenous) 361.00
　　　giant tear 361.03
　　　multiple 361.02
　　　partial
　　　　with
　　　　　giant tear 361.03
　　　　　multiple defects 361.02
　　　　　retinal dialysis (juvenile) 361.04
　　　　　single defect 361.01
　　　　retinal dialysis (juvenile) 361.04
　　　　single 361.01
　　　　subtotal 361.05
　　　　total 361.05
　　delimited (old) (partial) 361.06
　　old
　　　delimited 361.06
　　　partial 361.06
　　　total or subtotal 361.07
　　pigment epithelium (RPE) (serous) 362.42
　　　exudative 362.42
　　　hemorrhagic 362.43
　　rhegmatogenous (*see also* Detachment, retina, with retinal defect) 361.00
　　serous (without retinal defect) 361.2
　　specified type NEC 361.89
　　traction (with vitreoretinal organization) 361.81
　vitreous humor 379.21
Detergent asthma 507.8
Deterioration
　epileptic
　　with behavioral disturbance 345.9 ☑ *[294.11]*
　　without behavioral disturbance 345.9 ☑ *[294.10]*
　heart, cardiac (*see also* Degeneration, myocardial) 429.1
　mental (*see also* Psychosis) 298.9
　myocardium, myocardial (*see also* Degeneration, myocardial) 429.1
　senile (simple) 797
　transplanted organ — *see* Complications, transplant, organ, by site
de Toni-Fanconi syndrome (cystinosis) 270.0
Deuteranomaly 368.52
Deuteranopia (anomalous trichromat) (complete) (incomplete) 368.52
Deutschländer's disease — *see* Fracture, foot
Development
　abnormal, bone 756.9
　arrested 783.40
　　bone 733.91
　　child 783.40
　　due to malnutrition (protein-calorie) 263.2
　　fetus or newborn 764.9 ☑
　　tracheal rings (congenital) 748.3

Development — *continued*
　defective, congenital — *see also* Anomaly
　　cauda equina 742.59
　　left ventricle 746.9
　　　with atresia or hypoplasia of aortic orifice or valve with hypoplasia of ascending aorta 746.7
　　　in hypoplastic left heart syndrome 746.7
　delayed (*see also* Delay, development) 783.40
　　arithmetical skills 315.1
　　language (skills) 315.31
　　　expressive 315.31
　　　mixed receptive-expressive 315.32
　　learning skill, specified NEC 315.2
　　mixed skills 315.5
　　motor coordination 315.4
　　reading 315.00
　　specified
　　　learning skill NEC 315.2
　　　type NEC, except learning 315.8
　　speech 315.39
　　　associated with hyperkinesia 314.1
　　　phonological 315.39
　　spelling 315.09
　　written expression 315.2
　imperfect, congenital — *see also* Anomaly
　　heart 746.9
　　lungs 748.60
　improper (fetus or newborn) 764.9 ☑
　incomplete (fetus or newborn) 764.9 ☑
　　affecting management of pregnancy 656.5 ☑
　　bronchial tree 748.3
　　organ or site not listed — *see* Hypoplasia
　　respiratory system 748.9
　sexual, precocious NEC 259.1
　tardy, mental (*see also* Retardation, mental) 319
Developmental — *see* condition
Devergie's disease (pityriasis rubra pilaris) 696.4
Deviation
　conjugate (eye) 378.87
　　palsy 378.81
　　spasm, spastic 378.82
　esophagus 530.89
　eye, skew 378.87
　mandible, opening and closing 524.53
　midline (jaw) (teeth) 524.29
　　specified site NEC — *see* Malposition
　occlusal plane 524.76
　organ or site, congenital NEC — *see* Malposition, congenital
　septum (acquired) (nasal) 470
　　congenital 754.0
　sexual 302.9
　　bestiality 302.1
　　coprophilia 302.89
　　ego-dystonic
　　　homosexuality 302.0
　　　lesbianism 302.0
　　erotomania 302.89
　　　Clérambault's 297.8
　　exhibitionism (sexual) 302.4
　　fetishism 302.81
　　　transvestic 302.3
　　frotteurism 302.89
　　homosexuality, ego-dystonic 302.0
　　　pedophilic 302.2
　　lesbianism, ego-dystonic 302.0
　　masochism 302.83
　　narcissism 302.89
　　necrophilia 302.89
　　nymphomania 302.89
　　pederosis 302.2
　　pedophilia 302.2
　　sadism 302.84
　　sadomasochism 302.84
　　satyriasis 302.89
　　specified type NEC 302.89
　　transvestic fetishism 302.3
　　transvestism 302.3
　　voyeurism 302.82
　　zoophilia (erotica) 302.1
　teeth, midline 524.29
　trachea 519.1
　ureter (congenital) 753.4
Devic's disease 341.0

Device
   cerebral ventricle (communicating) in situ
      V45.2
   contraceptive — *see* Contraceptive, device
   drainage, cerebrospinal fluid V45.2
Devil's
   grip 074.1
   pinches (purpura simplex) 287.2
Devitalized tooth 522.9
Devonshire colic 984.9
   specified type of lead — *see* Table of Drugs and
      Chemicals
Dextraposition, aorta 747.21
   with ventricular septal defect, pulmonary
      stenosis or atresia, and hypertrophy of
      right ventricle 745.2
   in tetralogy of Fallot 745.2
Dextratransposition, aorta 745.11
Dextrinosis, limit (debrancher enzyme deficiency)
   271.0
Dextrocardia (corrected) (false) (isolated)
   (secondary) (true) 746.87
   with
      complete transposition of viscera 759.3
      situs inversus 759.3
Dextroversion, kidney (left) 753.3
Dhobie itch 110.3
Diabetes, diabetic (brittle) (congenital) (familial)
   (mellitus) (poorly controlled) (severe) (slight)
   (without complication) 250.0 ☑

Note — *Use the following fifth-digit*
subclassification with category 250:

   0   *type II or unspecified type, not stated*
         as uncontrolled

   Fifth-digit 0 is for use for type II patients,
   even if the patient requires insulin

   1   *type I [juvenile type], not stated as*
         uncontrolled

   2   *type II or unspecified type,*
         uncontrolled

   Fifth-digit 2 is for use for type II patients,
   even if the patient requires insulin

   3   *type I [juvenile type], uncontrolled*

---

   with
      coma (with ketoacidosis) 250.3 ☑
         hyperosmolar (nonketotic) 250.2 ☑
      complication NEC 250.9 ☑
         specified NEC 250.8 ☑
      gangrene 250.7 ☑ *[785.4]*
      hyperosmolarity 250.2 ☑
      ketosis, ketoacidosis 250.1 ☑
      osteomyelitis 250.8 ☑ *[731.8]*
      specified manifestations NEC 250.8 ☑
   acetonemia 250.1 ☑
   acidosis 250.1 ☑
   amyotrophy 250.6 ☑ *[358.1]*
   angiopathy, peripheral 250.7 ☑ *[443.81]*
   asymptomatic 790.29
   autonomic neuropathy (peripheral)
      250.6 ☑ *[337.1]*
   bone change 250.8 ☑ *[731.8]*
   bronze, bronzed 275.0
   cataract 250.5 ☑ *[366.41]*
   chemical 790.29
      complicating pregnancy, childbirth, or
         puerperium 648.8 ☑
   coma (with ketoacidosis) 250.3 ☑
      hyperglycemic 250.3 ☑
      hyperosmolar (nonketotic) 250.2 ☑
      hypoglycemic 250.3 ☑
      insulin 250.3 ☑
   complicating pregnancy, childbirth, or
      puerperium (maternal) 648.0 ☑
      affecting fetus or newborn 775.0
   complication NEC 250.9 ☑
      specified NEC 250.8 ☑
   dorsal sclerosis 250.6 ☑ *[340]*
   dwarfism-obesity syndrome 258.1
   gangrene 250.7 ☑ *[785.4]*
   gastroparesis 250.6 ☑ *[536.3]*

Diabetes, diabetic — *continued*
   gestational 648.8 ☑
      complicating pregnancy, childbirth, or
         puerperium 648.8 ☑
   glaucoma 250.5 ☑ *[365.44]*
   glomerulosclerosis (intercapillary)
      250.4 ☑ *[581.81]*
   glycogenosis, secondary 250.8 ☑ *[259.8]*
   hemochromatosis 275.0
   hyperosmolar coma 250.2 ☑
   hyperosmolarity 250.2 ☑
   hypertension-nephrosis syndrome
      250.4 ☑ *[581.81]*
   hypoglycemia 250.8 ☑
   hypoglycemic shock 250.8 ☑
   insipidus 253.5
      nephrogenic 588.1
      pituitary 253.5
      vasopressin-resistant 588.1
   intercapillary glomerulosclerosis
      250.4 ☑ *[581.81]*
   iritis 250.5 ☑ *[364.42]*
   ketosis, ketoacidosis 250.1 ☑
   Kimmelstiel (-Wilson) disease or syndrome
      (intercapillary glomerulosclerosis)
      250.4 ☑ *[581.81]*
   Lancereaux's (diabetes mellitus with marked
      emaciation) 250.8 ☑ *[261]*
   latent (chemical) 790.29
      complicating pregnancy, childbirth, or
         puerperium 648.8 ☑
   lipoidosis 250.8 ☑ *[272.7]*
   macular edema 250.5 ☑ *[362.07]*   ▲
   maternal
      with manifest disease in the infant 775.1
      affecting fetus or newborn 775.0
   microaneurysms, retinal 250.5 ☑ *[362.01]*
   mononeuropathy 250.6 ☑ *[355.9]*
   neonatal, transient 775.1
   nephropathy 250.4 ☑ *[583.81]*
   nephrosis (syndrome) 250.4 ☑ *[581.81]*
   neuralgia 250.6 ☑ *[357.2]*
   neuritis 250.6 ☑ *[357.2]*
   neurogenic arthropathy 250.6 ☑ *[713.5]*
   neuropathy 250.6 ☑ *[357.2]*
   nonclinical 790.29
   osteomyelitis 250.8 ☑ *[731.8]*
   peripheral autonomic neuropathy
      250.6 ☑ *[337.1]*
   phosphate 275.3
   polyneuropathy 250.6 ☑ *[357.2]*
   renal (true) 271.4
   retinal
      edema 250.5 ☑ *[362.07]*   ▲
      hemorrhage 250.5 ☑ *[362.01]*
      microaneurysms 250.5 ☑ *[362.01]*
   retinitis 250.5 ☑ *[362.01]*
   retinopathy 250.5 ☑ *[362.01]*
      background 250.5 ☑ *[362.01]*
      nonproliferative 250.5 *[362.03]*   ●
         mild 250.5 ☑ *[362.04]*   ●
         moderate 250.5 ☑ *[362.05]*   ●
         severe 250.5 ☑ *[362.06]*   ●
      proliferative 250.5 ☑ *[362.02]*
   steroid induced
      correct substance properly administered
         251.8
      overdose or wrong substance given or taken
         962.0
   stress 790.29
   subclinical 790.29
   subliminal 790.29
   sugar 250.0 ☑
   ulcer (skin) 250.8 ☑ *[707.9]*
      lower extremity 250.8 ☑ *[707.10]*
         ankle 250.8 ☑ *[707.13]*
         calf 250.8 ☑ *[707.12]*
         foot 250.8 ☑ *[707.15]*
         heel 250.8 ☑ *[707.14]*
         knee 250.8 ☑ *[707.19]*
         specified site NEC 250.8 ☑ *[707.19]*
         thigh 250.8 ☑ *[707.11]*
         toes 250.8 ☑ *[707.15]*
      specified site NEC 250.8 ☑ *[707.8]*
   xanthoma 250.8 ☑ *[272.2]*
Diacyclothrombopathia 287.1

Diagnosis deferred 799.9
Dialysis (intermittent) (treatment)
   anterior retinal (juvenile) (with detachment)
      361.04
   extracorporeal V56.0
   hemodialysis V56.0   ●
      status only V45.1   ●
   peritoneal V56.8   ●
      status only V45.1   ●
   renal V56.0
      status only V45.1
   specified type NEC V56.8
Diamond-Blackfan anemia or syndrome
   (congenital hypoplastic anemia) 284.0
Diamond-Gardener syndrome (autoerythrocyte
   sensitization) 287.2
Diaper rash 691.0
Diaphoresis (excessive) NEC (*see also*
   Hyperhidrosis) 780.8
Diaphragm — *see* condition
Diaphragmalgia 786.52
Diaphragmitis 519.4
Diaphyseal aclasis 756.4
Diaphysitis 733.99
Diarrhea, diarrheal (acute) (autumn) (bilious)
   (bloody) (catarrhal) (choleraic) (chronic)
   (gravis) (green) (infantile) (lienteric)
   (noninfectious) (presumed noninfectious)
   (putrefactive) (secondary) (sporadic)
   (summer) (symptomatic) (thermic) 787.91
   achlorhydric 536.0
   allergic 558.3
   amebic (*see also* Amebiasis) 006.9
      with abscess — *see* Abscess, amebic
      acute 006.0
      chronic 006.1
      nondysenteric 006.2
   bacillary — *see* Dysentery, bacillary
   bacterial NEC 008.5
   balantidial 007.0
   bile salt-induced 579.8
   cachectic NEC 787.91
   chilomastix 007.8
   choleriformis 001.1
   coccidial 007.2
   Cochin-China 579.1
      anguilluliasis 127.2
      psilosis 579.1
   Dientamoeba 007.8
   dietetic 787.91
   due to
      achylia gastrica 536.8
      Aerobacter aerogenes 008.2
      Bacillus coli — *see* Enteritis, E. coli
      bacteria NEC 008.5
      bile salts 579.8
      Capillaria
         hepatica 128.8
         philippinensis 127.5
      Clostridium perfringens (C) (F) 008.46
      Enterobacter aerogenes 008.2
      enterococci 008.49
      Escherichia coli — *see* Enteritis, E. coli
      Giardia lamblia 007.1
      Heterophyes heterophyes 121.6
      irritating foods 787.91
      Metagonimus yokogawai 121.5
      Necator americanus 126.1
      Paracolobactrum arizonae 008.1
      Paracolon bacillus NEC 008.47
         Arizona 008.1
      Proteus (bacillus) (mirabilis) (Morganii) 008.3
      Pseudomonas aeruginosa 008.42
      S. japonicum 120.2
      specified organism NEC 008.8
         bacterial 008.49
         viral NEC 008.69
      Staphylococcus 008.41
      Streptococcus 008.49
         anaerobic 008.46
      Strongyloides stercoralis 127.2
      Trichuris trichiuria 127.3
      virus NEC (*see also* Enteritis, viral) 008.69
   dysenteric 009.2
      due to specified organism NEC 008.8

☑ Additional Digit Required — Refer to the Tabular List (Numeric Code Section) for Additional Digit Selection

Diarrhea, diarrheal — *continued*
dyspeptic 787.91
endemic 009.3
due to specified organism NEC 008.8
epidemic 009.2
due to specified organism NEC 008.8
fermentative 787.91
flagellate 007.9
Flexner's (ulcerative) 004.1
functional 564.5
following gastrointestinal surgery 564.4
psychogenic 306.4
giardial 007.1
Giardia lamblia 007.1
hill 579.1
hyperperistalsis (nervous) 306.4
infectious 009.2
due to specified organism NEC 008.8
presumed 009.3
inflammatory 787.91
due to specified organism NEC 008.8
malarial (*see also* Malaria) 084.6
mite 133.8
mycotic 117.9
nervous 306.4
neurogenic 564.5
parenteral NEC 009.2
postgastrectomy 564.4
postvagotomy 564.4
prostaglandin induced 579.8
protozoal NEC 007.9
psychogenic 306.4
septic 009.2
due to specified organism NEC 008.8
specified organism NEC 008.8
bacterial 008.49
viral NEC 008.69
Staphylococcus 008.41
Streptococcus 008.49
anaerobic 008.46
toxic 558.2
travelers' 009.2
due to specified organism NEC 008.8
trichomonal 007.3
tropical 579.1
tuberculous 014.8 ☑
ulcerative (chronic) (*see also* Colitis, ulcerative)
556.9
viral (*see also* Enteritis, viral) 008.8
zymotic NEC 009.2
Diastasis
cranial bones 733.99
congenital 756.0
joint (traumatic) — *see* Dislocation, by site
muscle 728.84
congenital 756.89
recti (abdomen) 728.84
complicating delivery 665.8 ☑
congenital 756.79
Diastema, teeth, tooth 524.30
Diastematomyelia 742.51
Diataxia, cerebral, infantile 343.0
Diathesis
allergic V15.09
bleeding (familial) 287.9
cystine (familial) 270.0
gouty 274.9
hemorrhagic (familial) 287.9
newborn NEC 776.0
oxalic 271.8
scrofulous (*see also* Tuberculosis) 017.2 ☑
spasmophilic (*see also* Tetany) 781.7
ulcer 536.9
uric acid 274.9
Diaz's disease or osteochondrosis 732.5
Dibothriocephaliasis 123.4
larval 123.5
Dibothriocephalus (infection) (infestation) (latus)
123.4
larval 123.5
Dicephalus 759.4
Dichotomy, teeth 520.2
Dichromat, dichromata (congenital) 368.59
Dichromatopsia (congenital) 368.59

Dichuchwa 104.0
Dicroceliasis 121.8
Didelphys, didelphic (*see also* Double uterus)
752.2
Didymitis (*see also* Epididymitis) 604.90
Died — *see also* Death
without
medical attention (cause unknown) 798.9
sign of disease 798.2
Dientamoeba diarrhea 007.8
Dietary
inadequacy or deficiency 269.9
surveillance and counseling V65.3
Dietl's crisis 593.4
Dieulafoy lesion (hemorrhagic)
of
duodenum 537.84
intestine 569.86
stomach 537.84
Difficult
birth, affecting fetus or newborn 763.9
delivery NEC 669.9 ☑
Difficulty
feeding 783.3
adult 783.3 ●
breast 676.8 ☑ ●
child 783.3 ●
elderly 783.3 ●
infant 783.3 ●
newborn 779.3
nonorganic (infant) NEC 307.59
mechanical, gastroduodenal stoma 537.89
reading 315.00
specific, spelling 315.09
swallowing (*see also* Dysphagia) 787.2
walking 719.7
Diffuse — *see* condition
Diffused ganglion 727.42
Digestive — *see* condition
Di George's syndrome (thymic hypoplasia)
279.11
Di Guglielmo's disease or syndrome (M9841/3)
207.0 ☑
Diktyoma (M9051/3) — *see* Neoplasm, by site,
malignant
Dilaceration, tooth 520.4
Dilatation
anus 564.89
venule — *see* Hemorrhoids
aorta (focal) (general) (*see also* Aneurysm,
aorta) 441.9
congenital 747.29
infectional 093.0
ruptured 441.5
syphilitic 093.0
appendix (cystic) 543.9
artery 447.8
bile duct (common) (cystic) (congenital) 751.69
acquired 576.8
bladder (sphincter) 596.8
congenital 753.8
in pregnancy or childbirth 654.4 ☑
causing obstructed labor 660.2 ☑
affecting fetus or newborn 763.1
blood vessel 459.89
bronchus, bronchi 494.0
with acute exacerbation 494.1
calyx (due to obstruction) 593.89
capillaries 448.9
cardiac (acute) (chronic) (*see also* Hypertrophy,
cardiac) 429.3
congenital 746.89
valve NEC 746.89
pulmonary 746.09
hypertensive (*see also* Hypertension, heart)
402.90
cavum septi pellucidi 742.4
cecum 564.89
psychogenic 306.4
cervix (uteri) — *see also* Incompetency, cervix
incomplete, poor, slow
affecting fetus or newborn 763.7
complicating delivery 661.0 ☑
affecting fetus or newborn 763.7

Dilatation — *continued*
colon 564.7
congenital 751.3
due to mechanical obstruction 560.89
psychogenic 306.4
common bile duct (congenital) 751.69
acquired 576.8
with calculus, choledocholithiasis, or
stones — *see* Choledocholithiasis
cystic duct 751.69
acquired (any bile duct) 575.8
duct, mammary 610.4
duodenum 564.89
esophagus 530.89
congenital 750.4
due to
achalasia 530.0
cardiospasm 530.0
Eustachian tube, congenital 744.24
fontanel 756.0
gallbladder 575.8
congenital 751.69
gastric 536.8
acute 536.1
psychogenic 306.4
heart (acute) (chronic) (*see also* Hypertrophy,
cardiac) 429.3
congenital 746.89
hypertensive (*see also* Hypertension, heart)
402.90
valve — *see also* Endocarditis
congenital 746.89
ileum 564.89
psychogenic 306.4
inguinal rings — *see* Hernia, inguinal
jejunum 564.89
psychogenic 306.4
kidney (calyx) (collecting structures) (cystic)
(parenchyma) (pelvis) 593.89
lacrimal passages 375.69
lymphatic vessel 457.1
mammary duct 610.4
Meckel's diverticulum (congenital) 751.0
meningeal vessels, congenital 742.8
myocardium (acute) (chronic) (*see also*
Hypertrophy, cardiac) 429.3
organ or site, congenital NEC — *see* Distortion
pancreatic duct 577.8
pelvis, kidney 593.89
pericardium — *see* Pericarditis
pharynx 478.29
prostate 602.8
pulmonary
artery (idiopathic) 417.8
congenital 747.3
valve, congenital 746.09
pupil 379.43
rectum 564.89
renal 593.89
saccule vestibularis, congenital 744.05
salivary gland (duct) 527.8
sphincter ani 564.89
stomach 536.8
acute 536.1
psychogenic 306.4
submaxillary duct 527.8
trachea, congenital 748.3
ureter (idiopathic) 593.89
congenital 753.20
due to obstruction 593.5
urethra (acquired) 599.84
vasomotor 443.9
vein 459.89
ventricular, ventricle (acute) (chronic) (*see also*
Hypertrophy, cardiac) 429.3
cerebral, congenital 742.4
hypertensive (*see also* Hypertension, heart)
402.90
venule 459.89
anus — *see* Hemorrhoids
vesical orifice 596.8
Dilated, dilation — *see* Dilatation
Diminished
hearing (acuity) (*see also* Deafness) 389.9
pulse pressure 785.9
vision NEC 369.9
vital capacity 794.2

Diminuta taenia 123.6
Diminution, sense or sensation (cold) (heat)
(tactile) (vibratory) (see also Disturbance,
sensation) 782.0
Dimitri-Sturge-Weber disease
(encephalocutaneous angiomatosis) 759.6
Dimple
parasacral 685.1
with abscess 685.0
pilonidal 685.1
with abscess 685.0
postanal 685.1
with abscess 685.0
Dioctophyma renale (infection) (infestation) 128.8
Dipetalonemiasis 125.4
Diphallus 752.69
Diphtheria, diphtheritic (gangrenous)
(hemorrhagic) 032.9
carrier (suspected) of V02.4
cutaneous 032.85
cystitis 032.84
faucial 032.0
infection of wound 032.85
inoculation (anti) (not sick) V03.5
laryngeal 032.3
myocarditis 032.82
nasal anterior 032.2
nasopharyngeal 032.1
neurological complication 032.89
peritonitis 032.83
specified site NEC 032.89
Diphyllobothriasis (intestine) 123.4
larval 123.5
Diplacusis 388.41
Diplegia (upper limbs) 344.2
brain or cerebral 437.8
congenital 343.0
facial 351.0
congenital 352.6
infantile or congenital (cerebral) (spastic)
(spinal) 343.0
lower limbs 344.1
syphilitic, congenital 090.49
Diplococcus, diplococcal — see condition
Diplomyelia 742.59
Diplopia 368.2
refractive 368.15
Dipsomania (see also Alcoholism) 303.9 ☑
with psychosis (see also Psychosis, alcoholic)
291.9
Dipylidiasis 123.8
intestine 123.8
Direction, teeth, abnormal 524.30
Dirt-eating child 307.52
Disability
heart — see Disease, heart
learning NEC 315.2
special spelling 315.09
Disarticulation (see also Derangement, joint)
718.9 ☑
meaning
amputation
status — see Absence, by site
traumatic — see Amputation, traumatic
dislocation, traumatic or congenital — see
Dislocation
Disaster, cerebrovascular (see also Disease,
cerebrovascular, acute) 436
Discharge
anal NEC 787.99
breast (female) (male) 611.79
conjunctiva 372.89
continued locomotor idiopathic (see also
Epilepsy) 345.5 ☑
diencephalic autonomic idiopathic (see also
Epilepsy) 345.5 ☑
ear 388.60
blood 388.69
cerebrospinal fluid 388.61
excessive urine 788.42
eye 379.93
nasal 478.1
nipple 611.79

Discharge — continued
patterned motor idiopathic (see also Epilepsy)
345.5 ☑
penile 788.7
postnasal — see Sinusitis
sinus, from mediastinum 510.0
umbilicus 789.9
urethral 788.7
bloody 599.84
vaginal 623.5
Discitis 722.90
cervical, cervicothoracic 722.91
lumbar, lumbosacral 722.93
thoracic, thoracolumbar 722.92
Discogenic syndrome — see Displacement,
intervertebral disc
Discoid
kidney 753.3
meniscus, congenital 717.5
semilunar cartilage 717.5
Discoloration
mouth 528.9
nails 703.8
teeth 521.7
due to
drugs 521.7
metals (copper) (silver) 521.7
pulpal bleeding 521.7
during formation 520.8
extrinsic 523.6
intrinsic posteruptive 521.7
Discomfort
chest 786.59
visual 368.13
Discomycosis — see Actinomycosis
Discontinuity, ossicles, ossicular chain 385.23
Discrepancy
centric occlusion maximum intercuspation
524.55
leg length (acquired) 736.81
congenital 755.30
uterine size-date 646.8 ☑
Discrimination
political V62.4
racial V62.4
religious V62.4
sex V62.4
Disease, diseased — see also Syndrome
Abrami's (acquired hemolytic jaundice) 283.9
absorbent system 459.89
accumulation — see Thesaurismosis
acid-peptic 536.8
Acosta's 993.2
Adams-Stokes (-Morgagni) (syncope with heart
block) 426.9
Addison's (bronze) (primary adrenal
insufficiency) 255.4
anemia (pernicious) 281.0
tuberculous (see also Tuberculosis) 017.6 ☑
Addison-Gull — see Xanthoma
adenoids (and tonsils) (chronic) 474.9
adrenal (gland) (capsule) (cortex) 255.9
hyperfunction 255.3
hypofunction 255.4
specified type NEC 255.8
ainhum (dactylolysis spontanea) 136.0
akamushi (scrub typhus) 081.2
Akureyri (epidemic neuromyasthenia) 049.8
Albarrán's (colibacilluria) 791.9
Albers-Schönberg's (marble bones) 756.52
Albert's 726.71
Albright (-Martin) (-Bantam) 275.49
Alibert's (mycosis fungoides) (M9700/3)
202.1 ☑
Alibert-Bazin (M9700/3) 202.1 ☑
alimentary canal 569.9
alligator skin (ichthyosis congenita) 757.1
acquired 701.1
Almeida's (Brazilian blastomycosis) 116.1
Alpers' 330.8
alpine 993.2
altitude 993.2
alveoli, teeth 525.9
Alzheimer's — see Alzheimer's
amyloid (any site) 277.3

Disease, diseased — see also Syndrome —
continued
anarthritic rheumatoid 446.5
Anders' (adiposis tuberosa simplex) 272.8
Andersen's (glycogenosis IV) 271.0
Anderson's (angiokeratoma corporis diffusum)
272.7
Andes 993.2
Andrews' (bacterid) 686.8
angiospastic, angiospasmodic 443.9
cerebral 435.9
with transient neurologic deficit 435.9
vein 459.89
anterior
chamber 364.9
horn cell 335.9
specified type NEC 335.8
antral (chronic) 473.0
acute 461.0
anus NEC 569.49
aorta (nonsyphilitic) 447.9
syphilitic NEC 093.89
aortic (heart) (valve) (see also Endocarditis,
aortic) 424.1
apollo 077.4
aponeurosis 726.90
appendix 543.9
aqueous (chamber) 364.9
arc-welders' lung 503
Armenian 277.3
Arnold-Chiari (see also Spina bifida) 741.0 ☑
arterial 447.9
occlusive (see also Occlusion, by site)
444.22
with embolus or thrombus — see
Occlusion, by site
due to stricture or stenosis 447.1
specified type NEC 447.8
arteriocardiorenal (see also Hypertension,
cardiorenal) 404.90
arteriolar (generalized) (obliterative) 447.9
specified type NEC 447.8
arteriorenal — see Hypertension, kidney
arteriosclerotic — see also Arteriosclerosis
cardiovascular 429.2
coronary — see Arteriosclerosis, coronary
heart — see Arteriosclerosis, coronary
vascular — see Arteriosclerosis
artery 447.9
cerebral 437.9
coronary — see Arteriosclerosis, coronary
specified type NEC 447.8
arthropod-borne NEC 088.9
specified type NEC 088.89
Asboe-Hansen's (incontinentia pigmenti) 757.33
atticoantral, chronic (with posterior or superior
marginal perforation of ear drum) 382.2
auditory canal, ear 380.9
Aujeszky's 078.89
auricle, ear NEC 380.30
Australian X 062.4
autoimmune NEC 279.4
hemolytic (cold type) (warm type) 283.0
parathyroid 252.1
thyroid 245.2
aviators' (see also Effect, adverse, high altitude)
993.2
ax(e)-grinders' 502
Ayala's 756.89
Ayerza's (pulmonary artery sclerosis with
pulmonary hypertension) 416.0
Azorean (of the nervous system) 334.8
Babington's (familial hemorrhagic
telangiectasia) 448.0
back bone NEC 733.90
bacterial NEC 040.89
zoonotic NEC 027.9
specified type NEC 027.8
Baehr-Schiffrin (thrombotic thrombocytopenic
purpura) 446.6
Baelz's (cheilitis glandularis apostematosa)
528.5
Baerensprung's (eczema marginatum) 110.3
Balfour's (chloroma) 205.3 ☑
balloon (see also Effect, adverse, high altitude
993.2
Baló's 341.1

☑ Additional Digit Required — Refer to the Tabular List (Numeric Code Section) for Additional Digit Selection

100 — Volume 2
►◄ Revised Text
● New Line
▲ Revised Code
2006 ICD-9-CM

Disease, diseased — *see also* Syndrome — *continued*
Bamberger (-Marie) (hypertrophic pulmonary osteoarthropathy) 731.2
Bang's (Brucella abortus) 023.1
Bannister's 995.1
Banti's (with cirrhosis) (with portal hypertension) — *see* Cirrhosis, liver
Barcoo (*see also* Ulcer, skin) 707.9
barium lung 503
Barlow (-Möller) (infantile scurvy) 267
barometer makers' 985.0
Barraquer (-Simons) (progressive lipodystrophy) 272.6
basal ganglia 333.90
    degenerative NEC 333.0
    specified NEC 333.89
Basedow's (exophthalmic goiter) 242.0 ☑
basement membrane NEC 583.89
    with
        pulmonary hemorrhage (Goodpasture's syndrome) 446.21 *[583.81]*
Bateman's 078.0
    purpura (senile) 287.2
Batten's 330.1 *[362.71]*
Batten-Mayou (retina) 330.1 *[362.71]*
Batten-Steinert 359.2
Battey 031.0
Baumgarten-Cruveilhier (cirrhosis of liver) 571.5
bauxite-workers' 503
Bayle's (dementia paralytica) 094.1
Bazin's (primary) (*see also* Tuberculosis) 017.1 ☑
Beard's (neurasthenia) 300.5
Beau's (*see also* Degeneration, myocardial) 429.1
Bechterew's (ankylosing spondylitis) 720.0
Becker's (idiopathic mural endomyocardial disease) 425.2
Begbie's (exophthalmic goiter) 242.0 ☑
Behr's 362.50
Beigel's (white piedra) 111.2
Bekhterev's (ankylosing spondylitis) 720.0
Bell's (*see also* Psychosis, affective) 296.0 ☑
Bennett's (leukemia) 208.9 ☑
Benson's 379.22
Bergeron's (hysteroepilepsy) 300.11
Berlin's 921.3
Bernard-Soulier (thrombopathy) 287.1
Bernhardt (-Roth) 355.1
beryllium 503
Besnier-Boeck (-Schaumann) (sarcoidosis) 135
Best's 362.76
Beurmann's (sporotrichosis) 117.1
Bielschowsky (-Jansky) 330.1
Biermer's (pernicious anemia) 281.0
Biett's (discoid lupus erythematosus) 695.4
bile duct (*see also* Disease, biliary) 576.9
biliary (duct) (tract) 576.9
    with calculus, choledocholithiasis, or stones — *see* Choledocholithiasis
Billroth's (meningocele) (*see also* Spina bifida) 741.9 ☑
Binswanger's 290.12
Bird's (oxaluria) 271.8
bird fanciers' 495.2
black lung 500
bladder 596.9
    specified NEC 596.8
bleeder's 286.0
Bloch-Sulzberger (incontinentia pigmenti) 757.33
Blocq's (astasia-abasia) 307.9
blood (-forming organs) 289.9
    specified NEC 289.89
    vessel 459.9
Bloodgood's 610.1
Blount's (tibia vara) 732.4
blue 746.9
Bodechtel-Guttmann (subacute sclerosing panencephalitis) 046.2
Boeck's (sarcoidosis) 135
bone 733.90
    fibrocystic NEC 733.29
        jaw 526.2
    marrow 289.9

Disease, diseased — *see also* Syndrome — *continued*
bone — *continued*
    Paget's (osteitis deformans) 731.0
    specified type NEC 733.99
    von Recklinghausen's (osteitis fibrosa cystica) 252.01
Bonfils' — *see* Disease, Hodgkin's
Borna 062.9
Bornholm (epidemic pleurodynia) 074.1
Bostock's (*see also* Fever, hay) 477.9
Bouchard's (myopathic dilatation of the stomach) 536.1
Bouillaud's (rheumatic heart disease) 391.9
Bourneville (-Brissaud) (tuberous sclerosis) 759.5
Bouveret (-Hoffmann) (paroxysmal tachycardia) 427.2
bowel 569.9
    functional 564.9
        psychogenic 306.4
Bowen's (M8081/2) — *see* Neoplasm, skin, in situ
Bozzolo's (multiple myeloma) (M9730/3) 203.0 ☑
Bradley's (epidemic vomiting) 078.82
Brailsford's 732.3
    radius, head 732.3
    tarsal, scaphoid 732.5
Brailsford-Morquio (mucopolysaccharidosis IV) 277.5
brain 348.9
    Alzheimer's 331.0
        with dementia — *see* Alzheimer's, dementia
    arterial, artery 437.9
    arteriosclerotic 437.0
    congenital 742.9
    degenerative — *see* Degeneration, brain
    inflammatory — *see also* Encephalitis
        late effect — *see* category 326
    organic 348.9
        arteriosclerotic 437.0
    parasitic NEC 123.9
    Pick's 331.11
        with dementia
            with behavioral disturbance 331.11 *[294.11]*
            without behavioral disturbance 331.11 *[294.10]*
    senile 331.2
braziers' 985.8
breast 611.9
    cystic (chronic) 610.1
    fibrocystic 610.1
    inflammatory 611.0
    Paget's (M8540/3) 174.0
    puerperal, postpartum NEC 676.3 ☑
    specified NEC 611.8
Breda's (*see also* Yaws) 102.9
Breisky's (kraurosis vulvae) 624.0
Bretonneau's (diphtheritic malignant angina) 032.0
Bright's (*see also* Nephritis) 583.9
    arteriosclerotic (*see also* Hypertension, kidney) 403.90
Brill's (recrudescent typhus) 081.1
    flea-borne 081.0
    louse-borne 081.1
Brill-Symmers (follicular lymphoma) (M9690/3) 202.0 ☑
Brill-Zinsser (recrudescent typhus) 081.1
Brinton's (leather bottle stomach) (M8142/3) 151.9
Brion-Kayser (*see also* Fever, paratyphoid) 002.9
broad
    beta 272.2
    ligament, noninflammatory 620.9
        specified NEC 620.8
Brocq's 691.8
    meaning
        atopic (diffuse) neurodermatitis 691.8
        dermatitis herpetiformis 694.0
        lichen simplex chronicus 698.3
        parapsoriasis 696.2
        prurigo 698.2
Brocq-Duhring (dermatitis herpetiformis) 694.0

Disease, diseased — *see also* Syndrome — *continued*
Brodie's (joint) (*see also* Osteomyelitis) 730.1 ☑
bronchi 519.1
bronchopulmonary 519.1
bronze (Addison's) 255.4
    tuberculous (*see also* Tuberculosis) 017.6 ☑
Brown-Séquard 344.89
Bruck's 733.99
Bruck-de Lange (Amsterdam dwarf, mental retardation and brachycephaly) 759.89
Bruhl's (splenic anemia with fever) 285.8
Bruton's (X-linked agammaglobulinemia) 279.04
buccal cavity 528.9
Buchanan's (juvenile osteochondrosis, iliac crest) 732.1
Buchman's (osteochondrosis juvenile) 732.1
Budgerigar-fanciers' 495.2
Büdinger-Ludloff-Läwen 717.89
Buerger's (thromboangiitis obliterans) 443.1
Bürger-Grütz (essential familial hyperlipemia) 272.3
Burns' (lower ulna) 732.3
bursa 727.9
Bury's (erythema elevatum diutinum) 695.89
Buschke's 710.1
Busquet's (*see also* Osteomyelitis) 730.1 ☑
Busse-Buschke (cryptococcosis) 117.5
C₂ (*see also* Alcoholism) 303.9 ☑
Caffey's (infantile cortical hyperostosis) 756.59
caisson 993.3
calculous 592.9
California 114.0
Calvé (-Perthes) (osteochondrosis, femoral capital) 732.1
Camurati-Engelmann (diaphyseal sclerosis) 756.59
Canavan's 330.0
capillaries 448.9
Carapata 087.1
cardiac — *see* Disease, heart
cardiopulmonary, chronic 416.9
cardiorenal (arteriosclerotic) (hepatic) (hypertensive) (vascular) (*see also* Hypertension, cardiorenal) 404.90
cardiovascular (arteriosclerotic) 429.2
    congenital 746.9
    hypertensive (*see also* Hypertension, heart) 402.90
        benign 402.10
        malignant 402.00
    renal (*see also* Hypertension, cardiorenal) 404.90
    syphilitic (asymptomatic) 093.9
carotid gland 259.8
Carrión's (Bartonellosis) 088.0
cartilage NEC 733.90
    specified NEC 733.99
Castellani's 104.8
cat-scratch 078.3
Cavare's (familial periodic paralysis) 359.3
Cazenave's (pemphigus) 694.4
cecum 569.9
celiac (adult) 579.0
    infantile 579.0
cellular tissue NEC 709.9
central core 359.0
cerebellar, cerebellum — *see* Disease, brain
cerebral (*see also* Disease, brain) 348.9
    arterial, artery 437.9
    degenerative — *see* Degeneration, brain
cerebrospinal 349.9
cerebrovascular NEC 437.9
    acute 436
        embolic — *see* Embolism, brain
        late effect — *see* Late effect(s) (of) cerebrovascular disease
        puerperal, postpartum, childbirth 674.0 ☑
        thrombotic — *see* Thrombosis, brain
    arteriosclerotic 437.0
    embolic — *see* Embolism, brain
    ischemic, generalized NEC 437.1
    late effect — *see* Late effect(s) (of) cerebrovascular disease
    occlusive 437.1

2006 ICD-9-CM

☑ Additional Digit Required — Refer to the Tabular List (Numeric Code Section) for Additional Digit Selection
▶◀ Revised Text   ● New Line   ▲ Revised Code

Volume 2 — 101

Disease, diseased — *see also* Syndrome — *continued*
  cerebrovascular NEC — *continued*
    puerperal, postpartum, childbirth 674.0 ☑
    specified type NEC 437.8
    thrombotic — *see* Thrombosis, brain
  ceroid storage 272.7
  cervix (uteri)
    inflammatory 616.9
      specified NEC 616.8
    noninflammatory 622.9
      specified NEC 622.8
  Chabert's 022.9
  Chagas' (*see also* Trypanosomiasis, American) 086.2
  Chandler's (osteochondritis dissecans, hip) 732.7
  Charcôt's (joint) 094.0 [713.5]
    spinal cord 094.0
  Charcôt-Marie-Tooth 356.1
  Charlouis' (*see also* Yaws) 102.9
  Cheadle (-Möller) (-Barlow) (infantile scurvy) 267
  Chédiak-Steinbrinck (-Higashi) (congenital gigantism of peroxidase granules) 288.2
  cheek, inner 528.9
  chest 519.9
  Chiari's (hepatic vein thrombosis) 453.0
  Chicago (North American blastomycosis) 116.0
  chignon (white piedra) 111.2
  chigoe, chigo (jigger) 134.1
  childhood granulomatous 288.1
  Chinese liver fluke 121.1
  chlamydial NEC 078.88
  cholecystic (*see also* Disease, gallbladder) 575.9
  choroid 363.9
    degenerative (*see also* Degeneration, choroid) 363.40
    hereditary (*see also* Dystrophy, choroid) 363.50
    specified type NEC 363.8
  Christian's (chronic histiocytosis X) 277.89
  Christian-Weber (nodular nonsuppurative panniculitis) 729.30
  Christmas 286.1
  ciliary body 364.9
  circulatory (system) NEC 459.9
    chronic, maternal, affecting fetus or newborn 760.3
    specified NEC 459.89
    syphilitic 093.9
      congenital 090.5
  Civatte's (poikiloderma) 709.09
  climacteric 627.2
    male 608.89
  coagulation factor deficiency (congenital) (*see also* Defect, coagulation) 286.9
  Coats' 362.12
  coccidioidal pulmonary 114.5
    acute 114.0
    chronic 114.4
    primary 114.0
    residual 114.4
  Cockayne's (microcephaly and dwarfism) 759.89
  Cogan's 370.52
  cold
    agglutinin 283.0
      or hemoglobinuria 283.0
        paroxysmal (cold) (nocturnal) 283.2
    hemagglutinin (chronic) 283.0
  collagen NEC 710.9
    nonvascular 710.9
    specified NEC 710.8
    vascular (allergic) (*see also* Angiitis, hypersensitivity) 446.20
  colon 569.9
    functional 564.9
      congenital 751.3
    ischemic 557.1
  combined system (of spinal cord) 266.2 [336.2]
    with anemia (pernicious) 281.0 [336.2]
  compressed air 993.3
  Concato's (pericardial polyserositis) 423.2
    peritoneal 568.82
    pleural — *see* Pleurisy
  congenital NEC 799.89

Disease, diseased — *see also* Syndrome — *continued*
  conjunctiva 372.9
    chlamydial 077.98
      specified NEC 077.8
    specified type NEC 372.89
    viral 077.99
      specified NEC 077.8
  connective tissue, diffuse (*see also* Disease, collagen) 710.9
  Conor and Bruch's (boutonneuse fever) 082.1
  Conradi (-Hünermann) 756.59
  Cooley's (erythroblastic anemia) 282.49
  Cooper's 610.1
  Corbus' 607.1
  cork-handlers' 495.3
  cornea (*see also* Keratopathy) 371.9
  coronary (*see also* Ischemia, heart) 414.9
    congenital 746.85
    ostial, syphilitic 093.20
      aortic 093.22
      mitral 093.21
      pulmonary 093.24
      tricuspid 093.23
  Corrigan's — *see* Insufficiency, aortic
  Cotugno's 724.3
  Coxsackie (virus) NEC 074.8
  cranial nerve NEC 352.9
  Creutzfeldt-Jakob ►(new variant)◄ 046.1
    with dementia
      with behavioral disturbance 046.1 [294.11]
      without behavioral disturbance 046.1 [294.10]
  Crigler-Najjar (congenital hyperbilirubinemia) 277.4
  Crocq's (acrocyanosis) 443.89
  Crohn's (intestine) (*see also* Enteritis, regional) 555.9
  Crouzon's (craniofacial dysostosis) 756.0
  Cruchet's (encephalitis lethargica) 049.8
  Cruveilhier's 335.21
  Cruz-Chagas (*see also* Trypanosomiasis, American) 086.2
  crystal deposition (*see also* Arthritis, due to, crystals) 712.9 ☑
  Csillag's (lichen sclerosus et atrophicus) 701.0
  Curschmann's 359.2
  Cushing's (pituitary basophilism) 255.0
  cystic
    breast (chronic) 610.1
    kidney, congenital (*see also* Cystic, disease, kidney) 753.10
    liver, congenital 751.62
    lung 518.89
      congenital 748.4
    pancreas 577.2
      congenital 751.7
    renal, congenital (*see also* Cystic, disease, kidney) 753.10
    semilunar cartilage 717.5
  cysticercus 123.1
  cystine storage (with renal sclerosis) 270.0
  cytomegalic inclusion (generalized) 078.5
    with
      pneumonia 078.5 [484.1]
    congenital 771.1
  Daae (-Finsen) (epidemic pleurodynia) 074.1
  dancing 297.8
  Danielssen's (anesthetic leprosy) 030.1
  Darier's (congenital) (keratosis follicularis) 757.39
    erythema annulare centrifugum 695.0
    vitamin A deficiency 264.8
  Darling's (histoplasmosis) (*see also* Histoplasmosis, American) 115.00
  Davies' 425.0
  de Beurmann-Gougerot (sporotrichosis) 117.1
  Débove's (splenomegaly) 789.2
  deer fly (*see also* Tularemia) 021.9
  deficiency 269.9
  degenerative — *see also* Degeneration
    disc — *see* Degeneration, intervertebral disc
  Degos' 447.8
  Déjérine (-Sottas) 356.0
  Déleage's 359.89

Disease, diseased — *see also* Syndrome — *continued*
  demyelinating, demyelinizating (brain stem) (central nervous system) 341.9
    multiple sclerosis 340
    specified NEC 341.8
  de Quervain's (tendon sheath) 727.04
    thyroid (subacute granulomatous thyroiditis) 245.1
  Dercum's (adiposis dolorosa) 272.8
  Deutschländer's — *see* Fracture, foot
  Devergie's (pityriasis rubra pilaris) 696.4
  Devic's 341.0
  diaphorase deficiency 289.7
  diaphragm 519.4
  diarrheal, infectious 009.2
  diatomaceous earth 502
  Diaz's (osteochondrosis astragalus) 732.5
  digestive system 569.9
  Di Guglielmo's (erythemic myelosis) (M9841/3) 207.0 ☑
  Dimitri-Sturge-Weber (encephalocutaneous angiomatosis) 759.6
  disc, degenerative — *see* Degeneration, intervertebral disc
  discogenic (*see also* Disease, intervertebral disc) 722.90
  diverticular — *see* Diverticula
  Down's (mongolism) 758.0
  Dubini's (electric chorea) 049.8
  Dubois' (thymus gland) 090.5
  Duchenne's 094.0
    locomotor ataxia 094.0
    muscular dystrophy 359.1
    paralysis 335.22
    pseudohypertrophy, muscles 359.1
  Duchenne-Griesinger 359.1
  ductless glands 259.9
  Duhring's (dermatitis herpetiformis) 694.0
  Dukes (-Filatov) 057.8
  duodenum NEC 537.9
    specified NEC 537.89
  Duplay's 726.2
  Dupré's (meningism) 781.6
  Dupuytren's (muscle contracture) 728.6
  Durand-Nicolas-Favre (climatic bubo) 099.1
  Duroziez's (congenital mitral stenosis) 746.5
  Dutton's (trypanosomiasis) 086.9
  Eales' 362.18
  ear (chronic) (inner) NEC 388.9
    middle 385.9
      adhesive (*see also* Adhesions, middle ear) 385.10
      specified NEC 385.89
  Eberth's (typhoid fever) 002.0
  Ebstein's
    heart 746.2
    meaning diabetes 250.4 ☑ [581.81]
  Echinococcus (*see also* Echinococcus) 122.9
  ECHO virus NEC 078.89
  Economo's (encephalitis lethargica) 049.8
  Eddowes' (brittle bones and blue sclera) 756.51
  Edsall's 992.2
  Eichstedt's (pityriasis versicolor) 111.0
  Ellis-van Creveld (chondroectodermal dysplasia) 756.55
  endocardium — *see* Endocarditis
  endocrine glands or system NEC 259.9
    specified NEC 259.8
  endomyocardial, idiopathic mural 425.2
  Engel-von Recklinghausen (osteitis fibrosa cystica) 252.01
  Engelmann's (diaphyseal sclerosis) 756.59
  English (rickets) 268.0
  Engman's (infectious eczematoid dermatitis) 690.8
  enteroviral, enterovirus NEC 078.89
    central nervous system NEC 048
  epidemic NEC 136.9
  epididymis 608.9
  epigastric, functional 536.9
    psychogenic 306.4
  Erb (-Landouzy) 359.1
  Erb-Goldflam 358.00
  Erichsen's (railway spine) 300.16
  esophagus 530.9
    functional 530.5
    psychogenic 306.4

Disease, diseased — *see also* Syndrome — *continued*
Eulenburg's (congenital paramyotonia) 359.2
Eustachian tube 381.9
Evans' (thrombocytopenic purpura) 287.32 ▲
external auditory canal 380.9
extrapyramidal NEC 333.90
eye 379.90
  anterior chamber 364.9
  inflammatory NEC 364.3
  muscle 378.9
eyeball 360.9
eyelid 374.9
eyeworm of Africa 125.2
Fabry's (angiokeratoma corporis diffusum) 272.7
facial nerve (seventh) 351.9
  newborn 767.5
Fahr-Volhard (malignant nephrosclerosis) 403.00
fallopian tube, noninflammatory 620.9
  specified NEC 620.8
familial periodic 277.3
  paralysis 359.3
Fanconi's (congenital pancytopenia) 284.0
Farber's (disseminated lipogranulomatosis) 272.8
fascia 728.9
  inflammatory 728.9
Fauchard's (periodontitis) 523.4
Favre-Durand-Nicolas (climatic bubo) 099.1
Favre-Racouchot (elastoidosis cutanea nodularis) 701.8
Fede's 529.0
Feer's 985.0
Felix's (juvenile osteochondrosis, hip) 732.1
Fenwick's (gastric atrophy) 537.89
Fernels' (aortic aneurysm) 441.9
fibrocaseous, of lung (*see also* Tuberculosis, pulmonary) 011.9 ☑
fibrocystic — *see also* Fibrocystic, disease
  newborn 277.01
Fiedler's (leptospiral jaundice) 100.0
fifth 057.0
Filatoff's (infectious mononucleosis) 075
Filatov's (infectious mononucleosis) 075
file-cutters' 984.9
  specified type of lead — *see* Table of Drugs and Chemicals
filterable virus NEC 078.89
fish skin 757.1
  acquired 701.1
Flajani (-Basedow) (exophthalmic goiter) 242.0 ☑
Flatau-Schilder 341.1
flax-dressers' 504
Fleischner's 732.3
flint 502
fluke — *see* Infestation, fluke
Følling's (phenylketonuria) 270.1
foot and mouth 078.4
foot process 581.3
Forbes' (glycogenosis III) 271.0
Fordyce's (ectopic sebaceous glands) (mouth) 750.26
Fordyce-Fox (apocrine miliaria) 705.82
Fothergill's
  meaning scarlatina anginosa 034.1
  neuralgia (*see also* Neuralgia, trigeminal) 350.1
Fournier's 608.83
fourth 057.8
Fox (-Fordyce) (apocrine miliaria) 705.82
Francis' (*see also* Tularemia) 021.9
Franklin's (heavy chain) 273.2
Frei's (climatic bubo) 099.1
Freiberg's (flattening metatarsal) 732.5
Friedländer's (endarteritis obliterans) — *see* Arteriosclerosis
Friedreich's
  combined systemic or ataxia 334.0
  facial hemihypertrophy 756.0
  myoclonia 333.2
Fröhlich's (adiposogenital dystrophy) 253.8
Frommel's 676.6 ☑
frontal sinus (chronic) 473.1
  acute 461.1
Fuller's earth 502

Disease, diseased — *see also* Syndrome — *continued*
fungus, fungous NEC 117.9
Gaisböck's (polycythemia hypertonica) 289.0
gallbladder 575.9
  congenital 751.60
Gamna's (sideriotic splenomegaly) 289.51
Gamstorp's (adynamia episodica hereditaria) 359.3
Gandy-Nanta (sideriotic splenomegaly) 289.51
gannister (occupational) 502
Garré's (*see also* Osteomyelitis) 730.1 ☑
gastric (*see also* Disease, stomach) 537.9
gastrointestinal (tract) 569.9
  amyloid 277.3
  functional 536.9
    psychogenic 306.4
Gaucher's (adult) (cerebroside lipidosis) (infantile) 272.7
Gayet's (superior hemorrhagic polioencephalitis) 265.1
Gee (-Herter) (-Heubner) (-Thaysen) (nontropical sprue) 579.0
generalized neoplastic (M8000/6) 199.0
genital organs NEC
  female 629.9
    specified NEC 629.8
  male 608.9
Gerhardt's (erythromelalgia) 443.82   ▲
Gerlier's (epidemic vertigo) 078.81
Gibert's (pityriasis rosea) 696.3
Gibney's (perispondylitis) 720.9
Gierke's (glycogenosis I) 271.0
Gilbert's (familial nonhemolytic jaundice) 277.4
Gilchrist's (North American blastomycosis) 116.0
Gilford (-Hutchinson) (progeria) 259.8
Gilles de la Tourette's (motor-verbal tic) 307.23
Giovannini's 117.9
gland (lymph) 289.9
Glanzmann's (hereditary hemorrhagic thrombasthenia) 287.1
glassblowers' 527.1
Glénard's (enteroptosis) 569.89
Glisson's (*see also* Rickets) 268.0
glomerular
  membranous, idiopathic 581.1
  minimal change 581.3
glycogen storage (Andersen's) (Cori types 1-7) (Forbes') (McArdle-Schmid-Pearson) (Pompe's) (types I-VII) 271.0
  cardiac 271.0 [425.7]
  generalized 271.0
  glucose-6-phosphatase deficiency 271.0
  heart 271.0 [425.7]
  hepatorenal 271.0
  liver and kidneys 271.0
  myocardium 271.0 [425.7]
  von Gierke's (glycogenosis I) 271.0
Goldflam-Erb 358.00
Goldscheider's (epidermolysis bullosa) 757.39
Goldstein's (familial hemorrhagic telangiectasia) 448.0
gonococcal NEC 098.0
Goodall's (epidemic vomiting) 078.82
Gordon's (exudative enteropathy) 579.8
Gougerot's (trisymptomatic) 709.1
Gougerot-Carteaud (confluent reticulate papillomatosis) 701.8
Gougerot-Hailey-Hailey (benign familial chronic pemphigus) 757.39
graft-versus-host (bone marrow) 996.85
  due to organ transplant NEC — *see* Complications, transplant, organ
grain-handlers' 495.8
Grancher's (splenopneumonia) — *see* Pneumonia
granulomatous (childhood) (chronic) 288.1
graphite lung 503
Graves' (exophthalmic goiter) 242.0 ☑
green monkey 078.89
Griesinger's (*see also* Ancylostomiasis) 126.9
grinders' 502
Grisel's 723.5
Gruby's (tinea tonsurans) 110.0
Guertin's (electric chorea) 049.8

Disease, diseased — *see also* Syndrome — *continued*
Guillain-Barré 357.0
Guinon's (motor-verbal tic) 307.23
Gull's (thyroid atrophy with myxedema) 244.8
Gull and Sutton's — *see* Hypertension, kidney
gum NEC 523.9
Günther's (congenital erythropoietic porphyria) 277.1
gynecological 629.9
  specified NEC 629.8
H 270.0
Haas' 732.3
Habermann's (acute parapsoriasis varioliformis) 696.2
Haff 985.1
Hageman (congenital factor XII deficiency) (*see also* Defect, congenital) 286.3
Haglund's (osteochondrosis os tibiale externum) 732.5
Hagner's (hypertrophic pulmonary osteoarthropathy) 731.2
Hailey-Hailey (benign familial chronic pemphigus) 757.39
hair (follicles) NEC 704.9
  specified type NEC 704.8
Hallervorden-Spatz 333.0
Hallopeau's (lichen sclerosus et atrophicus) 701.0
Hamman's (spontaneous mediastinal emphysema) 518.1
hand, foot, and mouth 074.3
Hand-Schüller-Christian (chronic histiocytosis X) 277.89
Hanot's — *see* Cirrhosis, biliary
Hansen's (leprosy) 030.9
  benign form 030.1
  malignant form 030.0
Harada's 363.22
Harley's (intermittent hemoglobinuria) 283.2
Hart's (pellagra-cerebellar ataxia-renal aminoaciduria) 270.0
Hartnup (pellagra-cerebellar ataxia-renal aminoaciduria) 270.0
Hashimoto's (struma lymphomatosa) 245.2
Hb — *see* Disease, hemoglobin
heart (organic) 429.9
  with
    acute pulmonary edema (*see also* Failure, ventricular, left) 428.1
    hypertensive 402.91
      with renal failure 404.93
      benign 402.11
        with renal failure 404.13
      malignant 402.01
        with renal failure 404.03
    kidney disease — *see* Hypertension, cardiorenal
    rheumatic fever (conditions classifiable to 390)
      active 391.9
        with chorea 392.0
      inactive or quiescent (with chorea) 398.90
  amyloid 277.3 [425.7]
  aortic (valve) (*see also* Endocarditis, aortic) 424.1
  arteriosclerotic or sclerotic (minimal) (senile) — *see* Arteriosclerosis, coronary
  artery, arterial — *see* Arteriosclerosis, coronary
  atherosclerotic — *see* Arteriosclerosis, coronary
  beer drinkers' 425.5
  beriberi 265.0 [425.7]
  black 416.0
  congenital NEC 746.9
    cyanotic 746.9
    maternal, affecting fetus or newborn 760.3
    specified type NEC 746.89
  congestive (*see also* Failure, heart) 428.0
  coronary 414.9
  cryptogenic 429.9
  due to
    amyloidosis 277.3 [425.7]
    beriberi 265.0 [425.7]

Disease, diseased — *see also* Syndrome — *continued*
  heart — *continued*
    due to — *continued*
      cardiac glycogenosis 271.0 *[425.7]*
      Friedreich's ataxia 334.0 *[425.8]*
      gout 274.82
      mucopolysaccharidosis 277.5 *[425.7]*
      myotonia atrophica 359.2 *[425.8]*
      progressive muscular dystrophy 359.1 *[425.8]*
      sarcoidosis 135 *[425.8]*
    fetal 746.9
      inflammatory 746.89
    fibroid (*see also* Myocarditis) 429.0
    functional 427.9
      postoperative 997.1
      psychogenic 306.2
    glycogen storage 271.0 *[425.7]*
    gonococcal NEC 098.85
    gouty 274.82
    hypertensive (*see also* Hypertension, heart) 402.90
      benign 402.10
      malignant 402.00
    hyperthyroid (*see also* Hyperthyroidism) 242.9 ☑ *[425.7]*
    incompletely diagnosed — *see* Disease, heart
    ischemic (chronic) (*see also* Ischemia, heart) 414.9
      acute (*see also* Infarct, myocardium) 410.9 ☑
        without myocardial infarction 411.89
          with coronary (artery) occlusion 411.81
      asymptomatic 412
      diagnosed on ECG or other special investigation but currently presenting no symptoms 412
    kyphoscoliotic 416.1
    mitral (*see also* Endocarditis, mitral) 394.9
    muscular (*see also* Degeneration, myocardial) 429.1
    postpartum 674.8 ☑
    psychogenic (functional) 306.2
    pulmonary (chronic) 416.9
      acute 415.0
      specified NEC 416.8
    rheumatic (chronic) (inactive) (old) (quiescent) (with chorea) 398.90
      active or acute 391.9
        with chorea (active) (rheumatic) (Sydenham's) 392.0
        specified type NEC 391.8
      maternal, affecting fetus or newborn 760.3
    rheumatoid — *see* Arthritis, rheumatoid
    sclerotic — *see* Arteriosclerosis, coronary
    senile (*see also* Myocarditis) 429.0
    specified type NEC 429.89
    syphilitic 093.89
      aortic 093.1
        aneurysm 093.0
      asymptomatic 093.89
      congenital 090.5
    thyroid (gland) (*see also* Hyperthyroidism) 242.9 ☑ *[425.7]*
    thyrotoxic (*see also* Thyrotoxicosis) 242.9 ☑ *[425.7]*
    tuberculous (*see also* Tuberculosis) 017.9 ☑ *[425.8]*
    valve, valvular (obstructive) (regurgitant) — *see also* Endocarditis
      congenital NEC (*see also* Anomaly, heart, valve) 746.9
        pulmonary 746.00
        specified type NEC 746.89
    vascular — *see* Disease, cardiovascular
  heavy-chain (gamma G) 273.2
  Heberden's 715.04
  Hebra's
    dermatitis exfoliativa 695.89
    erythema multiforme exudativum 695.1
    pityriasis
      maculata et circinata 696.3
      rubra 695.89
        pilaris 696.4
    prurigo 698.2

Disease, diseased — *see also* Syndrome — *continued*
  Heerfordt's (uveoparotitis) 135
  Heidenhain's 290.10
    with dementia 290.10
  Heilmeyer-Schöner (M9842/3) 207.1 ☑
  Heine-Medin (*see also* Poliomyelitis) 045.9 ☑
  Heller's (*see also* Psychosis, childhood) 299.1 ☑
  Heller-Döhle (syphilitic aortitis) 093.1
  hematopoietic organs 289.9
  hemoglobin (Hb) 282.7
    with thalassemia 282.49
    abnormal (mixed) NEC 282.7
      with thalassemia 282.49
    AS genotype 282.5
    Bart's 282.49   ▲
    C (Hb-C) 282.7
      with other abnormal hemoglobin NEC 282.7
      elliptocytosis 282.7
      Hb-S (without crisis) 282.63
        with
          crisis 282.64
          vaso-occlusive pain 282.64
      sickle-cell (without crisis) 282.63
        with
          crisis 282.64
          vaso-occlusive pain 282.64
      thalassemia 282.49
    constant spring 282.7
    D (Hb-D) 282.7
      with other abnormal hemoglobin NEC 282.7
      Hb-S (without crisis) 282.68
        with crisis 282.69
      sickle-cell (without crisis) 282.68
        with crisis 282.69
      thalassemia 282.49
    E (Hb-E) 282.7
      with other abnormal hemoglobin NEC 282.7
      Hb-S (without crisis) 282.68
        with crisis 282.69
      sickle-cell (without crisis) 282.68
        with crisis 282.69
      thalassemia 282.49
    elliptocytosis 282.7
    F (Hb-F) 282.7
    G (Hb-G) 282.7
    H (Hb-H) 282.49
    hereditary persistence, fetal (HPFH) ("Swiss variety") 282.7
    high fetal gene 282.7
    I thalassemia 282.49
    M 289.7
    S — *see also* Disease, sickle-cell, Hb-S
      thalassemia (without crisis) 282.41
        with
          crisis 282.42
          vaso-occlusive pain 282.42
    spherocytosis 282.7
    unstable, hemolytic 282.7
    Zurich (Hb-Zurich) 282.7
  hemolytic (fetus) (newborn) 773.2
    autoimmune (cold type) (warm type) 283.0
    due to or with
      incompatibility
        ABO (blood group) 773.1
        blood (group) (Duffy) (Kell) (Kidd) (Lewis) (M) (S) NEC 773.2
        Rh (blood group) (factor) 773.0
          Rh negative mother 773.0
      unstable hemoglobin 282.7
  hemorrhagic 287.9
    newborn 776.0
  Henoch (-Schönlein) (purpura nervosa) 287.0
  hepatic — *see* Disease, liver
  hepatolenticular 275.1
  heredodegenerative NEC
    brain 331.89
    spinal cord 336.8
  Hers' (glycogenosis VI) 271.0
  Herter (-Gee) (-Heubner) (nontropical sprue) 579.0
  Herxheimer's (diffuse idiopathic cutaneous atrophy) 701.8
  Heubner's 094.89

Disease, diseased — *see also* Syndrome — *continued*
  Heubner-Herter (nontropical sprue) 579.0
  high fetal gene or hemoglobin thalassemia 282.49
  Hildenbrand's (typhus) 081.9
  hip (joint) NEC 719.95
    congenital 755.63
    suppurative 711.05
    tuberculous (*see also* Tuberculosis) 015.1 ☑ *[730.85]*
  Hippel's (retinocerebral angiomatosis) 759.6
  Hirschfeld's (acute diabetes mellitus) (*see also* Diabetes) 250.0 ☑
  Hirschsprung's (congenital megacolon) 751.3
  His (-Werner) (trench fever) 083.1
  HIV 042
  Hodgkin's (M9650/3) 201.9 ☑

Note — Use the following fifth-digit subclassification with category 201:

  0   unspecified site
  1   lymph nodes of head, face, and neck
  2   intrathoracic lymph nodes
  3   intra-abdominal lymph nodes
  4   lymph nodes of axilla and upper limb
  5   lymph nodes of inguinal region and lower limb
  6   intrapelvic lymph nodes
  7   spleen
  8   lymph nodes of multiple sites

    lymphocytic
      depletion (M9653/3) 201.7 ☑
        diffuse fibrosis (M9654/3) 201.7 ☑
        reticular type (M9655/3) 201.7 ☑
      predominance (M9651/3) 201.4 ☑
    lymphocytic-histiocytic predominance (M9651/3) 201.4 ☑
    mixed cellularity (M9652/3) 201.6 ☑
    nodular sclerosis (M9656/3) 201.5 ☑
      cellular phase (M9657/3) 201.5 ☑
  Hodgson's 441.9
    ruptured 441.5
  Hoffa (-Kastert) (liposynovitis prepatellaris) 272.8
  Holla (*see also* Spherocytosis) 282.0
  homozygous-Hb-S 282.61
  hoof and mouth 078.4
  hookworm (*see also* Ancylostomiasis) 126.9
  Horton's (temporal arteritis) 446.5
  host-versus-graft (immune or nonimmune cause) 996.80
    bone marrow 996.85
    heart 996.83
    intestines 996.87
    kidney 996.81
    liver 996.82
    lung 996.84
    pancreas 996.86
    specified NEC 996.89
  HPFH (hereditary persistence of fetal hemoglobin) ("Swiss variety") 282.7
  Huchard's (continued arterial hypertension) 401.9
  Huguier's (uterine fibroma) 218.9
  human immunodeficiency (virus) 042
  hunger 251.1
  Hunt's
    dyssynergia cerebellaris myoclonica 334.2
    herpetic geniculate ganglionitis 053.11
  Huntington's 333.4
  Huppert's (multiple myeloma) (M9730/3) 203.0 ☑
  Hurler's (mucopolysaccharidosis I) 277.5
  Hutchinson's, meaning
    angioma serpiginosum 709.1
    cheiropompholyx 705.81
    prurigo estivalis 692.72
  Hutchinson-Boeck (sarcoidosis) 135
  Hutchinson-Gilford (progeria) 259.8
  hyaline (diffuse) (generalized) 728.9
    membrane (lung) (newborn) 769
  hydatid (*see also* Echinococcus) 122.9
  Hyde's (prurigo nodularis) 698.3

Disease, diseased — *see also* Syndrome —
continued
hyperkinetic (*see also* Hyperkinesia) 314.9
   heart 429.82
hypertensive (*see also* Hypertension) 401.9
hypophysis 253.9
   hyperfunction 253.1
   hypofunction 253.2
Iceland (epidemic neuromyasthenia) 049.8
I cell 272.7
ill-defined 799.89
immunologic NEC 279.9
immunoproliferative 203.8 ☑
inclusion 078.5
   salivary gland 078.5
infancy, early NEC 779.9
infective NEC 136.9
inguinal gland 289.9
internal semilunar cartilage, cystic 717.5
intervertebral disc 722.90
   with myelopathy 722.70
   cervical, cervicothoracic 722.91
     with myelopathy 722.71
   lumbar, lumbosacral 722.93
     with myelopathy 722.73
   thoracic, thoracolumbar 722.92
     with myelopathy 722.72
intestine 569.9
   functional 564.9
     congenital 751.3
     psychogenic 306.4
   lardaceous 277.3
   organic 569.9
   protozoal NEC 007.9
iris 364.9
iron
   metabolism 275.0
   storage 275.0
Isambert's (*see also* Tuberculosis, larynx)
   012.3 ☑
Iselin's (osteochondrosis, fifth metatarsal) 732.5
island (scrub typhus) 081.2
itai-itai 985.5
Jadassohn's (maculopapular erythroderma)
   696.2
Jadassohn-Pellizari's (anetoderma) 701.3
Jakob-Creutzfeldt ►(new variant)◄ 046.1
   with dementia
     with behavioral disturbance
       046.1 *[294.11]*
     without behavioral disturbance
       046.1 *[294.10]*
Jaksch (-Luzet) (pseudoleukemia infantum)
   285.8
Janet's 300.89
Jansky-Bielschowsky 330.1
jaw NEC 526.9
   fibrocystic 526.2
Jensen's 363.05
Jeune's (asphyxiating thoracic dystrophy) 756.4
jigger 134.1
Johnson-Stevens (erythema multiforme
   exudativum) 695.1
joint NEC 719.9 ☑
   ankle 719.97
   Charcôt 094.0 *[713.5]*
   degenerative (*see also* Osteoarthrosis)
     715.9 ☑
     multiple 715.09
     spine (*see also* Spondylosis) 721.90
   elbow 719.92
   foot 719.97
   hand 719.94
   hip 719.95
   hypertrophic (chronic) (degenerative) (*see
     also* Osteoarthrosis) 715.9 ☑
     spine (*see also* Spondylosis) 721.90
   knee 719.96
   Luschka 721.90
   multiple sites 719.99
   pelvic region 719.95
   sacroiliac 724.6
   shoulder (region) 719.91
   specified site NEC 719.98
   spine NEC 724.9
     pseudarthrosis following fusion 733.82
     sacroiliac 724.6
   wrist 719.93

Disease, diseased — *see also* Syndrome —
continued
Jourdain's (acute gingivitis) 523.0
Jüngling's (sarcoidosis) 135
Kahler (-Bozzolo) (multiple myeloma) (M9730/3)
   203.0 ☑
Kalischer's 759.6
Kaposi's 757.33
   lichen ruber 697.8
     acuminatus 696.4
     moniliformis 697.8
   xeroderma pigmentosum 757.33
Kaschin-Beck (endemic polyarthritis) 716.00
   ankle 716.07
   arm 716.02
     lower (and wrist) 716.03
     upper (and elbow) 716.02
   foot (and ankle) 716.07
   forearm (and wrist) 716.03
   hand 716.04
   leg 716.06
     lower 716.06
     upper 716.05
   multiple sites 716.09
   pelvic region (hip) (thigh) 716.05
   shoulder region 716.01
   specified site NEC 716.08
Katayama 120.2
Kawasaki 446.1
Kedani (scrub typhus) 081.2
kidney (functional) (pelvis) (*see also* Disease,
   renal) 593.9
   chronic 585.9   ●
     stage   ●
       I 585.1   ●
       II (mild) 585.2   ●
       III (moderate) 585.3 ●
       IV (severe) 585.4   ●
       V 585.5   ●
   cystic (congenital) 753.10
     multiple 753.19
     single 753.11
     specified NEC 753.19
   fibrocystic (congenital) 753.19
   in gout 274.10
   polycystic (congenital) 753.12
     adult type (APKD) 753.13
     autosomal dominant 753.13
     autosomal recessive 753.14
     childhood type (CPKD) 753.14
     infantile type 753.14
Kienböck's (carpal lunate) (wrist) 732.3
Kimmelstiel (-Wilson) (intercapillary
   glomerulosclerosis) 250.4 ☑ *[581.81]*
Kinnier Wilson's (hepatolenticular degeneration)
   275.1
kissing 075
Kleb's (*see also* Nephritis) 583.9
Klinger's 446.4
Klippel's 723.8
Klippel-Feil (brevicollis) 756.16
knight's 911.1
Köbner's (epidermolysis bullosa) 757.39
Koenig-Wichmann (pemphigus) 694.4
Köhler's
   first (osteoarthrosis juvenilis) 732.5
   second (Freiberg's infraction, metatarsal
     head) 732.5
   patellar 732.4
   tarsal navicular (bone) (osteoarthrosis
     juvenilis) 732.5
Köhler-Freiberg (infraction, metatarsal head)
   732.5
Köhler-Mouchet (osteoarthrosis juvenilis) 732.5
Köhler-Pellegrini-Stieda (calcification, knee
   joint) 726.62
Kok 759.89
König's (osteochondritis dissecans) 732.7
Korsakoff's (nonalcoholic) 294.0
   alcoholic 291.1
Kostmann's (infantile genetic agranulocytosis)
   288.0
Krabbe's 330.0
Kraepelin-Morel (*see also* Schizophrenia)
   295.9 ☑
Kraft-Weber-Dimitri 759.6
Kufs' 330.1

Disease, diseased — *see also* Syndrome —
continued
Kugelberg-Welander 335.11
Kuhnt-Junius 362.52
Kûmmell's (-Verneuil) (spondylitis) 721.7
Kundrat's (lymphosarcoma) 200.1 ☑
kuru 046.0
Kussmaul (-Meier) (polyarteritis nodosa) 446.0
Kyasanur Forest 065.2
Kyrle's (hyperkeratosis follicularis in cutem
   penetrans) 701.1
labia
   inflammatory 616.9
     specified NEC 616.8
   noninflammatory 624.9
     specified NEC 624.8
labyrinth, ear 386.8
lacrimal system (apparatus) (passages) 375.9
   gland 375.00
     specified NEC 375.89
Lafora's 333.2
Lagleyze-von Hippel (retinocerebral
   angiomatosis) 759.6
Lancereaux-Mathieu (leptospiral jaundice)
   100.0
Landry's 357.0
Lane's 569.89
lardaceous (any site) 277.3
Larrey-Weil (leptospiral jaundice) 100.0
Larsen (-Johansson) (juvenile osteopathia
   patellae) 732.4
larynx 478.70
Lasègue's (persecution mania) 297.9
Leber's 377.16
Lederer's (acquired infectious hemolytic
   anemia) 283.19
Legg's (capital femoral osteochondrosis) 732.1
Legg-Calvé-Perthes (capital femoral
   osteochondrosis) 732.1
Legg-Calvé-Waldenström (femoral capital
   osteochondrosis) 732.1
Legg-Perthes (femoral capital osteochrondosis)
   732.1
Legionnaires' 482.84
Leigh's 330.8
Leiner's (exfoliative dermatitis) 695.89
Leloir's (lupus erythematosus) 695.4
Lenegre's 426.0
lens (eye) 379.39
Leriche's (osteoporosis, posttraumatic) 733.7
Letterer-Siwe (acute histiocytosis X) (M9722/3)
   202.5 ☑
Lev's (acquired complete heart block) 426.0
Lewandowski's (*see also* Tuberculosis) 017.0 ☑
Lewandowski-Lutz (epidermodysplasia
   verruciformis) 078.19
Lewy body 331.82
   with dementia
     with behavioral disturbance
       331.82 *[294.11]*
     without behavioral disturbance
       331.82 *[294.10]*
Leyden's (periodic vomiting) 536.2
Libman-Sacks (verrucous endocarditis)
   710.0 *[424.91]*
Lichtheim's (subacute combined sclerosis with
   pernicious anemia) 281.0 *[336.2]*
ligament 728.9
light chain 203.0 ☑
Lightwood's (renal tubular acidosis) 588.89
Lignac's (cystinosis) 270.0
Lindau's (retinocerebral angiomatosis) 759.6
Lindau-von Hippel (angiomatosis
   retinocerebellosa) 759.6
lip NEC 528.5
lipidosis 272.7
lipoid storage NEC 272.7
Lipschütz's 616.50
Little's — *see* Palsy, cerebral
liver 573.9
   alcoholic 571.3
     acute 571.1
     chronic 571.3
   chronic 571.9
     alcoholic 571.3
   cystic, congenital 751.62
   drug-induced 573.3

Disease, diseased — *see also* Syndrome — *continued*

liver — *continued*
due to
chemicals 573.3
fluorinated agents 573.3
hypersensitivity drugs 573.3
isoniazids 573.3
fibrocystic (congenital) 751.62
glycogen storage 271.0
organic 573.9
polycystic (congenital) 751.62
Lobo's (keloid blastomycosis) 116.2
Lobstein's (brittle bones and blue sclera) 756.51
locomotor system 334.9
Lorain's (pituitary dwarfism) 253.3
Lou Gehrig's 335.20
Lucas-Championnière (fibrinous bronchitis) 466.0
Ludwig's (submaxillary cellulitis) 528.3
luetic — *see* Syphilis
lumbosacral region 724.6
lung NEC 518.89
black 500
congenital 748.60
cystic 518.89
congenital 748.4
fibroid (chronic) (*see also* Fibrosis, lung) 515
fluke 121.2
oriental 121.2
in
amyloidosis 277.3 [517.8]
polymyositis 710.4 [517.8]
sarcoidosis 135 [517.8]
Sjögren's syndrome 710.2 [517.8]
syphilis 095.1
systemic lupus erythematosus 710.0 [517.8]
systemic sclerosis 710.1 [517.2]
interstitial (chronic) 515
acute 136.3
nonspecific, chronic 496
obstructive (chronic) (COPD) 496
with
acute
bronchitis 491.22
exacerbation NEC 491.21
alveolitis, allergic (*see also* Alveolitis, allergic) 495.9
asthma (chronic) (obstructive) 493.2 ☑
bronchiectasis 494.0
with acute exacerbation 494.1
bronchitis (chronic) 491.20
with
acute bronchitis 491.22
exacerbation (acute) 491.21
emphysema NEC 492.8
diffuse (with fibrosis) 496
polycystic 518.89
asthma (chronic) (obstructive) 493.2 ☑
congenital 748.4
purulent (cavitary) 513.0
restrictive 518.89
rheumatoid 714.81
diffuse interstitial 714.81
specified NEC 518.89
Lutembacher's (atrial septal defect with mitral stenosis) 745.5
Lutz-Miescher (elastosis perforans serpiginosa) 701.1
Lutz-Splendore-de Almeida (Brazilian blastomycosis) 116.1
Lyell's (toxic epidermal necrolysis) 695.1
due to drug
correct substance properly administered 695.1
overdose or wrong substance given or taken 977.9
specific drug — *see* Table of Drugs and Chemicals
Lyme 088.81
lymphatic (gland) (system) 289.9
channel (noninfective) 457.9
vessel (noninfective) 457.9
specified NEC 457.8
lymphoproliferative (chronic) (M9970/1) 238.7

Disease, diseased — *see also* Syndrome — *continued*

Machado-Joseph 334.8
Madelung's (lipomatosis) 272.8
Madura (actinomycotic) 039.9
mycotic 117.4
Magitot's 526.4
Majocchi's (purpura annularis telangiectodes) 709.1
malarial (*see also* Malaria) 084.6
Malassez's (cystic) 608.89
Malibu 919.8
infected 919.9
malignant (M8000/3) — *see also* Neoplasm, by site, malignant
previous, affecting management of pregnancy V23.89
Manson's 120.1
maple bark 495.6
maple syrup (urine) 270.3
Marburg (virus) 078.89
Marchiafava (-Bignami) 341.8
Marfan's 090.49
congenital syphilis 090.49
meaning Marfan's syndrome 759.82
Marie-Bamberger (hypertrophic pulmonary osteoarthropathy) (secondary) 731.2
primary or idiopathic (acropachyderma) 757.39
pulmonary (hypertrophic osteoarthropathy) 731.2
Marie-Strümpell (ankylosing spondylitis) 720.0
Marion's (bladder neck obstruction) 596.0
Marsh's (exophthalmic goiter) 242.0 ☑
Martin's 715.27
mast cell 757.33
systemic (M9741/3) 202.6 ☑
mastoid (*see also* Mastoiditis) 383.9
process 385.9
maternal, unrelated to pregnancy NEC, affecting fetus or newborn 760.9
Mathieu's (leptospiral jaundice) 100.0
Mauclaire's 732.3
Mauriac's (erythema nodosum syphiliticum) 091.3
Maxcy's 081.0
McArdle (-Schmid-Pearson) (glycogenosis V) 271.0
mediastinum NEC 519.3
Medin's (*see also* Poliomyelitis) 045.9 ☑
Mediterranean (with hemoglobinopathy) 282.49
medullary center (idiopathic) (respiratory) 348.8
Meige's (chronic hereditary edema) 757.0
Meleda 757.39
Ménétrier's (hypertrophic gastritis) 535.2 ☑
Ménière's (active) 386.00
cochlear 386.02
cochleovestibular 386.01
inactive 386.04
in remission 386.04
vestibular 386.03
meningeal — *see* Meningitis
mental (*see also* Psychosis) 298.9
Merzbacher-Pelizaeus 330.0
mesenchymal 710.9
mesenteric embolic 557.0
metabolic NEC 277.9
metal polishers' 502
metastatic — *see* Metastasis
Mibelli's 757.39
microdrepanocytic 282.49
microvascular 413.9
Miescher's 709.3
Mikulicz's (dryness of mouth, absent or decreased lacrimation) 527.1
Milkman (-Looser) (osteomalacia with pseudofractures) 268.2
Miller's (osteomalacia) 268.2
Mills' 335.29
Milroy's (chronic hereditary edema) 757.0
Minamata 985.0
Minor's 336.1
Minot's (hemorrhagic disease, newborn) 776.0
Minot-von Willebrand-Jürgens (angiohemophilia) 286.4
Mitchell's (erythromelalgia) 443.82 ▲
mitral — *see* Endocarditis, mitral

Disease, diseased — *see also* Syndrome — *continued*

Mljet (mal de Meleda) 757.39
Möbius', Moebius' 346.8 ☑
Moeller's 267
Möller (-Barlow) (infantile scurvy) 267
Mönckeberg's (*see also* Arteriosclerosis, extremities) 440.20
Mondor's (thrombophlebitis of breast) 451.89
Monge's 993.2
Morel-Kraepelin (*see also* Schizophrenia) 295.9 ☑
Morgagni's (syndrome) (hyperostosis frontalis interna) 733.3
Morgagni-Adams-Stokes (syncope with heart block) 426.9
Morquio (-Brailsford) (-Ullrich) (mucopolysaccharidosis IV) 277.5
Morton's (with metatarsalgia) 355.6
Morvan's 336.0
Mouchet's (juvenile osteochondrosis, foot) 732.5
mouth 528.9
Moyamoya 437.5
Mucha's (acute parapsoriasis varioliformis) 696.2
mu-chain 273.2
mucolipidosis (I) (II) (III) 272.7
Münchmeyer's (exostosis luxurians) 728.11
Murri's (intermittent hemoglobinuria) 283.2
muscle 359.9
inflammatory 728.9
ocular 378.9
musculoskeletal system 729.9
mushroom workers' 495.5
Myà's (congenital dilation, colon) 751.3
mycotic 117.9
myeloproliferative (chronic) (M9960/1) 238.7
myocardium, myocardial (*see also* Degeneration, myocardial) 429.1
hypertensive (*see also* Hypertension, heart) 402.90
primary (idiopathic) 425.4
myoneural 358.9
Naegeli's 287.1
nail 703.9
specified type NEC 703.8
Nairobi sheep 066.1
nasal 478.1
cavity NEC 478.1
sinus (chronic) — *see* Sinusitis
navel (newborn) NEC 779.89
delayed separation of umbilical cord 779.83
nemaline body 359.0
neoplastic, generalized (M8000/6) 199.0
nerve — *see* Disorder, nerve
nervous system (central) 349.9
autonomic, peripheral (*see also* Neuropathy, peripheral, autonomic) 337.9
congenital 742.9
inflammatory — *see* Encephalitis
parasympathetic (*see also* Neuropathy, peripheral, autonomic) 337.9
peripheral NEC 355.9
specified NEC 349.89
sympathetic (*see also* Neuropathy, peripheral, autonomic) 337.9
vegetative (*see also* Neuropathy, peripheral, autonomic) 337.9
Nettleship's (urticaria pigmentosa) 757.33
Neumann's (pemphigus vegetans) 694.4
neurologic (central) NEC (*see also* Disease, nervous system) 349.9
peripheral NEC 355.9
neuromuscular system NEC 358.9
Newcastle 077.8
Nicolas (-Durand) — Favre (climatic bubo) 099.1
Niemann-Pick (lipid histiocytosis) 272.7
nipple 611.9
Paget's (M8540/3) 174.0
Nishimoto (-Takeuchi) 437.5
nonarthropod-borne NEC 078.89
central nervous system NEC 049.9
enterovirus NEC 078.89

☑ Additional Digit Required — Refer to the Tabular List (Numeric Code Section) for Additional Digit Selection

Disease, diseased — *see also* Syndrome — *continued*
nonautoimmune hemolytic NEC 283.10
Nonne-Milroy-Meige (chronic hereditary edema) 757.0
Norrie's (congenital progressive oculoacousticocerebral degeneration) 743.8
nose 478.1
nucleus pulposus — *see* Disease, intervertebral disc
nutritional 269.9
maternal, affecting fetus or newborn 760.4
oasthouse, urine 270.2
obliterative vascular 447.1
Odelberg's (juvenile osteochondrosis) 732.1
Oguchi's (retina) 368.61
Ohara's (*see also* Tularemia) 021.9
Ollier's (chondrodysplasia) 756.4
Opitz's (congestive splenomegaly) 289.51
Oppenheim's 358.8
Oppenheim-Urbach (necrobiosis lipoidica diabeticorum) 250.8 ☑ *[709.3]*
optic nerve NEC 377.49
orbit 376.9
specified NEC 376.89
Oriental liver fluke 121.1
Oriental lung fluke 121.2
Ormond's 593.4
Osgood's tibia (tubercle) 732.4
Osgood-Schlatter 732.4
Osler (-Vaquez) (polycythemia vera) (M9950/1) 238.4
Osler-Rendu (familial hemorrhagic telangiectasia) 448.0
osteofibrocystic 252.01
Otto's 715.35
outer ear 380.9
ovary (noninflammatory) NEC 620.9
cystic 620.2
polycystic 256.4
specified NEC 620.8
Owren's (congenital) (*see also* Defect, coagulation) 286.3
Paas' 756.59
Paget's (osteitis deformans) 731.0
with infiltrating duct carcinoma of the breast (M8541/3) — *see* Neoplasm, breast, malignant
bone 731.0
osteosarcoma in (M9184/3) — *see* Neoplasm, bone, malignant
breast (M8540/3) 174.0
extramammary (M8542/3) — *see also* Neoplasm, skin, malignant
anus 154.3
skin 173.5
malignant (M8540/3)
breast 174.0
specified site NEC (M8542/3) — *see* Neoplasm, skin, malignant
unspecified site 174.0
mammary (M8540/3) 174.0
nipple (M8540/3) 174.0
palate (soft) 528.9
Paltauf-Sternberg 201.9 ☑
pancreas 577.9
cystic 577.2
congenital 751.7
fibrocystic 277.00
Panner's 732.3
capitellum humeri 732.3
head of humerus 732.3
tarsal navicular (bone) (osteochondrosis) 732.5
panvalvular — *see* Endocarditis, mitral
parametrium 629.9
parasitic NEC 136.9
cerebral NEC 123.9
intestinal NEC 129
mouth 112.0
skin NEC 134.9
specified type — *see* Infestation
tongue 112.0
parathyroid (gland) 252.9
specified NEC 252.8
Parkinson's 332.0

Disease, diseased — *see also* Syndrome — *continued*
parodontal 523.9
Parrot's (syphilitic osteochondritis) 090.0
Parry's (exophthalmic goiter) 242.0 ☑
Parson's (exophthalmic goiter) 242.0 ☑
Pavy's 593.6
Paxton's (white piedra) 111.2
Payr's (splenic flexure syndrome) 569.89
pearl-workers' (chronic osteomyelitis) (*see also* Osteomyelitis) 730.1 ☑
Pel-Ebstein — *see* Disease, Hodgkin's
Pelizaeus-Merzbacher 330.0
with dementia
with behavioral disturbance 330.0 *[294.11]*
without behavioral disturbance 330.0 *[294.10]*
Pellegrini-Stieda (calcification, knee joint) 726.62
pelvis, pelvic
female NEC 629.9
specified NEC 629.8
gonococcal (acute) 098.19
chronic or duration of 2 months or over 098.39
infection (*see also* Disease, pelvis, inflammatory) 614.9
inflammatory (female) (PID) 614.9
with
abortion — *see* Abortion, by type, with sepsis
ectopic pregnancy (*see also* categories 633.0-633.9) 639.0
molar pregnancy (*see also* categories 630-632) 639.0
acute 614.3
chronic 614.4
complicating pregnancy 646.6 ☑
affecting fetus or newborn 760.8
following
abortion 639.0
ectopic or molar pregnancy 639.0
peritonitis (acute) 614.5
chronic NEC 614.7
puerperal, postpartum, childbirth 670.0 ☑
specified NEC 614.8
organ, female NEC 629.9
specified NEC 629.8
peritoneum, female NEC 629.9
specified NEC 629.8
penis 607.9
inflammatory 607.2
peptic NEC 536.9
acid 536.8
periapical tissues NEC 522.9
pericardium 423.9
specified type NEC 423.8
perineum
female
inflammatory 616.9
specified NEC 616.8
noninflammatory 624.9
specified NEC 624.8
male (inflammatory) 682.2
periodic (familial) (Reimann's) NEC 277.3
paralysis 359.3
periodontal NEC 523.9
specified NEC 523.8
periosteum 733.90
peripheral
arterial 443.9
autonomic nervous system (*see also* Neuropathy, autonomic) 337.9
nerve NEC (*see also* Neuropathy) 356.9
multiple — *see* Polyneuropathy
vascular 443.9
specified type NEC 443.89
peritoneum 568.9
pelvic, female 629.9
specified NEC 629.8
Perrin-Ferraton (snapping hip) 719.65
persistent mucosal (middle ear) (with posterior or superior marginal perforation of ear drum) 382.2
Perthes' (capital femoral osteochondrosis) 732.1

Disease, diseased — *see also* Syndrome — *continued*
Petit's (*see also* Hernia, lumbar) 553.8
Peutz-Jeghers 759.6
Peyronie's 607.85
Pfeiffer's (infectious mononucleosis) 075
pharynx 478.20
Phocas' 610.1
photochromogenic (acid-fast bacilli) (pulmonary) 031.0
nonpulmonary 031.9
Pick's
brain 331.11
with dementia
with behavioral disturbance 331.11 *[294.11]*
without behavioral disturbance 331.11 *[294.10]*
cerebral atrophy 331.11
with dementia
with behavioral disturbance 331.11 *[294.11]*
without behavioral disturbance 331.11 *[294.10]*
lipid histiocytosis 272.7
liver (pericardial pseudocirrhosis of liver) 423.2
pericardium (pericardial pseudocirrhosis of liver) 423.2
polyserositis (pericardial pseudocirrhosis of liver) 423.2
Pierson's (osteochondrosis) 732.1
pigeon fanciers' or breeders' 495.2
pineal gland 259.8
pink 985.0
Pinkus' (lichen nitidus) 697.1
pinworm 127.4
pituitary (gland) 253.9
hyperfunction 253.1
hypofunction 253.2
pituitary snuff-takers' 495.8
placenta
affecting fetus or newborn 762.2
complicating pregnancy or childbirth 656.7 ☑
pleura (cavity) (*see also* Pleurisy) 511.0
Plummer's (toxic nodular goiter) 242.3 ☑
pneumatic
drill 994.9
hammer 994.9
policeman's 729.2
Pollitzer's (hidradenitis suppurativa) 705.83
polycystic (congenital) 759.89
kidney or renal 753.12
adult type (APKD) 753.13
autosomal dominant 753.13
autosomal recessive 753.14
childhood type (CPKD) 753.14
infantile type 753.14
liver or hepatic 751.62
lung or pulmonary 518.89
congenital 748.4
ovary, ovaries 256.4
spleen 759.0
Pompe's (glycogenosis II) 271.0
Poncet's (tuberculous rheumatism) (*see also* Tuberculosis) 015.9 ☑
Posada-Wernicke 114.9
Potain's (pulmonary edema) 514
Pott's (*see also* Tuberculosis) 015.0 ☑ *[730.88]*
osteomyelitis 015.0 ☑ *[730.88]*
paraplegia 015.0 ☑ *[730.88]*
spinal curvature 015.0 ☑ *[737.43]*
spondylitis 015.0 ☑ *[720.81]*
Potter's 753.0
Poulet's 714.2
pregnancy NEC (*see also* Pregnancy) 646.9 ☑
Preiser's (osteoporosis) 733.09
Pringle's (tuberous sclerosis) 759.5
Profichet's 729.9
prostate 602.9
specified type NEC 602.8
protozoal NEC 136.8
intestine, intestinal NEC 007.9
pseudo-Hurler's (mucolipidosis III) 272.7
psychiatric (*see also* Psychosis) 298.9
psychotic (*see also* Psychosis) 298.9

Disease, diseased — *see also* Syndrome — *continued*
sinus — *see also* Sinusitis — *continued*
  specified NEC 478.1
Sirkari's 085.0
sixth 057.8
Sjögren (-Gougerot) 710.2
  with lung involvement 710.2 *[517.8]*
Skevas-Zerfus 989.5
skin NEC 709.9
  due to metabolic disorder 277.9
  specified type NEC 709.8
sleeping (*see also* Narcolepsy) 347.00
  meaning sleeping sickness (*see also* Trypanosomiasis) 086.5
small vessel 443.9
Smith-Strang (oasthouse urine) 270.2
Sneddon-Wilkinson (subcorneal pustular dermatosis) 694.1
South African creeping 133.8
Spencer's (epidemic vomiting) 078.82
Spielmeyer-Stock 330.1
Spielmeyer-Vogt 330.1
spine, spinal 733.90
  combined system (*see also* Degeneration, combined) 266.2 *[336.2]*
    with pernicious anemia 281.0 *[336.2]*
  cord NEC 336.9
    congenital 742.9
  demyelinating NEC 341.8
  joint (*see also* Disease, joint, spine) 724.9
  tuberculous 015.0 ☑ *[730.8]* ☑
spinocerebellar 334.9
  specified NEC 334.8
spleen (organic) (postinfectional) 289.50
  amyloid 277.3
  lardaceous 277.3
  polycystic 759.0
  specified NEC 289.59
sponge divers' 989.5
Stanton's (melioidosis) 025
Stargardt's 362.75
Startle 759.89
Steinert's 359.2
Sternberg's — *see* Disease, Hodgkin's
Stevens-Johnson (erythema multiforme exudativum) 695.1
Sticker's (erythema infectiosum) 057.0
Stieda's (calcification, knee joint) 726.62
Still's (juvenile rheumatoid arthritis) 714.30
Stiller's (asthenia) 780.79
Stokes' (exophthalmic goiter) 242.0 ☑
Stokes-Adams (syncope with heart block) 426.9
Stokvis (-Talma) (enterogenous cyanosis) 289.7
stomach NEC (organic) 537.9
  functional 536.9
    psychogenic 306.4
  lardaceous 277.3
stonemasons' 502
storage
  glycogen (*see also* Disease, glycogen storage) 271.0
  lipid 272.7
  mucopolysaccharide 277.5
striatopallidal system 333.90
  specified NEC 333.89
Strümpell-Marie (ankylosing spondylitis) 720.0
Stuart's (congenital factor X deficiency) (*see also* Defect, coagulation) 286.3
Stuart-Prower (congenital factor X deficiency) (*see also* Defect, coagulation) 286.3
Sturge (-Weber) (-Dimitri) (encephalocutaneous angiomatosis) 759.6
Stuttgart 100.89
Sudeck's 733.7
supporting structures of teeth NEC 525.9
suprarenal (gland) (capsule) 255.9
  hyperfunction 255.3
  hypofunction 255.4
Sutton's 709.09
Sutton and Gull's — *see* Hypertension, kidney
sweat glands NEC 705.9
  specified type NEC 705.89
sweating 078.2
Sweeley-Klionsky 272.4
Swift (-Feer) 985.0
swimming pool (bacillus) 031.1

Disease, diseased — *see also* Syndrome — *continued*
swineherd's 100.89
Sylvest's (epidemic pleurodynia) 074.1
Symmers (follicular lymphoma) (M9690/3) 202.0 ☑
sympathetic nervous system (*see also* Neuropathy, peripheral, autonomic) 337.9
synovium 727.9
syphilitic — *see* Syphilis
systemic tissue mast cell (M9741/3) 202.6 ☑
Taenzer's 757.4
Takayasu's (pulseless) 446.7
Talma's 728.85
Tangier (familial high-density lipoprotein deficiency) 272.5
Tarral-Besnier (pityriasis rubra pilaris) 696.4
Tay-Sachs 330.1
Taylor's 701.8
tear duct 375.69
teeth, tooth 525.9
  hard tissues NEC 521.9
  pulp NEC 522.9
tendon 727.9
  inflammatory NEC 727.9
terminal vessel 443.9
testis 608.9
Thaysen-Gee (nontropical sprue) 579.0
Thomsen's 359.2
Thomson's (congenital poikiloderma) 757.33
Thornwaldt's, Tornwaldt's (pharyngeal bursitis) 478.29
throat 478.20
  septic 034.0
thromboembolic (*see also* Embolism) 444.9
thymus (gland) 254.9
  specified NEC 254.8
thyroid (gland) NEC 246.9
  heart (*see also* Hyperthyroidism) 242.9 ☑ *[425.7]*
  lardaceous 277.3
  specified NEC 246.8
Tietze's 733.6
Tommaselli's
  correct substance properly administered 599.7
  overdose or wrong substance given or taken 961.4
tongue 529.9
tonsils, tonsillar (and adenoids) (chronic) 474.9
  specified NEC 474.8
tooth, teeth 525.9
  hard tissues NEC 521.9
  pulp NEC 522.9
Tornwaldt's (pharyngeal bursitis) 478.29
Tourette's 307.23
trachea 519.1
tricuspid — *see* Endocarditis, tricuspid
triglyceride-storage, type I, II, III 272.7
triple vessel (coronary arteries) — *see* Arteriosclerosis, coronary
trisymptomatic, Gougerot's 709.1
trophoblastic (*see also* Hydatidiform mole) 630
  previous, affecting management of pregnancy V23.1
tsutsugamushi (scrub typhus) 081.2
tube (fallopian), noninflammatory 620.9
  specified NEC 620.8
tuberculous NEC (*see also* Tuberculosis) 011.9 ☑
tubo-ovarian
  inflammatory (*see also* Salpingo-oophoritis) 614.2
  noninflammatory 620.9
  specified NEC 620.8
tubotympanic, chronic (with anterior perforation of ear drum) 382.1
tympanum 385.9
Uhl's 746.84
umbilicus (newborn) NEC 779.89
  delayed separation 779.83
Underwood's (sclerema neonatorum) 778.1
undiagnosed 799.9
Unna's (seborrheic dermatitis) 690.18
unstable hemoglobin hemolytic 282.7
Unverricht (-Lundborg) 333.2

Disease, diseased — *see also* Syndrome — *continued*
Urbach-Oppenheim (necrobiosis lipoidica diabeticorum) 250.8 ☑ *[709.3]*
Urbach-Wiethe (lipoid proteinosis) 272.8
ureter 593.9
urethra 599.9
  specified type NEC 599.84
urinary (tract) 599.9
  bladder 596.9
    specified NEC 596.8
  maternal, affecting fetus or newborn 760.1
Usher-Senear (pemphigus erythematosus) 694.4
uterus (organic) 621.9
  infective (*see also* Endometritis) 615.9
  inflammatory (*see also* Endometritis) 615.9
  noninflammatory 621.9
  specified type NEC 621.8
uveal tract
  anterior 364.9
  posterior 363.9
vagabonds' 132.1
vagina, vaginal
  inflammatory 616.9
    specified NEC 616.8
  noninflammatory 623.9
    specified NEC 623.8
Valsuani's (progressive pernicious anemia, puerperal) 648.2 ☑
  complicating pregnancy or puerperium 648.2 ☑
valve, valvular — *see* Endocarditis
van Bogaert-Nijssen (-Peiffer) 330.0
van Creveld-von Gierke (glycogenosis I) 271.0
van den Bergh's (enterogenous cyanosis) 289.7
van Neck's (juvenile osteochondrosis) 732.1
Vaquez (-Osler) (polycythemia vera) (M9950/1) 238.4
vascular 459.9
  arteriosclerotic — *see* Arteriosclerosis
  hypertensive — *see* Hypertension
  obliterative 447.1
    peripheral 443.9
  occlusive 459.9
  peripheral (occlusive) 443.9
    in diabetes mellitus 250.7 ☑ *[443.81]*
    specified type NEC 443.89
vas deferens 608.9
vasomotor 443.9
vasospastic 443.9
vein 459.9
venereal 099.9
  chlamydial NEC 099.50
    anus 099.52
    bladder 099.53
    cervix 099.53
    epididymis 099.54
    genitourinary NEC 099.55
      lower 099.53
      specified NEC 099.54
    pelvic inflammatory disease 099.54
    perihepatic 099.56
    peritoneum 099.56
    pharynx 099.51
    rectum 099.52
    specified site NEC 099.59
    testis 099.54
    vagina 099.53
    vulva 099.53
  complicating pregnancy, childbirth, or puerperium 647.2 ☑
  fifth 099.1
  sixth 099.1
  specified nature or type NEC 099.8
    chlamydial — *see* Disease, venereal, chlamydial
Verneuil's (syphilitic bursitis) 095.7
Verse's (calcinosis intervertebralis) 275.49 *[722.90]*
vertebra, vertebral NEC 733.90
  disc — *see* Disease, Intervertebral disc
vibration NEC 994.9
Vidal's (lichen simplex chronicus) 698.3
Vincent's (trench mouth) 101
Virchow's 733.99

☑ Additional Digit Required — Refer to the Tabular List (Numeric Code Section) for Additional Digit Selection
▶◀ Revised Text   ● New Line   ▲ Revised Code

2006 ICD-9-CM

Volume 2 — 109

Disease, diseased — *see also* Syndrome — *continued*
virus (filterable) NEC 078.89
  arbovirus NEC 066.9
  arthropod-borne NEC 066.9
  central nervous system NEC 049.9
    specified type NEC 049.8
  complicating pregnancy, childbirth, or puerperium 647.6 ☑
  contact (with) V01.79
    varicella V01.71
  exposure to V01.79
    varicella V01.71
  Marburg 078.89
  maternal
    with fetal damage affecting management of pregnancy 655.3 ☑
  nonarthropod-borne NEC 078.89
    central nervous system NEC 049.9
      specified NEC 049.8
  vaccination, prophylactic (against) V04.89
vitreous 379.29
vocal cords NEC 478.5
Vogt's (Cecile) 333.7
Vogt-Spielmeyer 330.1
Volhard-Fahr (malignant nephrosclerosis) 403.00
Volkmann's
  acquired 958.6
von Bechterew's (ankylosing spondylitis) 720.0
von Economo's (encephalitis lethargica) 049.8
von Eulenburg's (congenital paramyotonia) 359.2
von Gierke's (glycogenosis I) 271.0
von Graefe's 378.72
von Hippel's (retinocerebral angiomatosis) 759.6
von Hippel-Lindau (angiomatosis retinocerebellosa) 759.6
von Jaksch's (pseudoleukemia infantum) 285.8
von Recklinghausen's (M9540/1) 237.71
  bone (osteitis fibrosa cystica) 252.01
von Recklinghausen-Applebaum (hemochromatosis) 275.0
von Willebrand (-Jürgens) (angiohemophilia) 286.4
von Zambusch's (lichen sclerosus et atrophicus) 701.0
Voorhoeve's (dyschondroplasia) 756.4
Vrolik's (osteogenesis imperfecta) 756.51
vulva
  noninflammatory 624.9
    specified NEC 624.8
Wagner's (colloid milium) 709.3
Waldenström's (osteochondrosis capital femoral) 732.1
Wallgren's (obstruction of splenic vein with collateral circulation) 459.89
Wardrop's (with lymphangitis) 681.9
  finger 681.02
  toe 681.11
Wassilieff's (leptospiral jaundice) 100.0
wasting NEC 799.4
  due to malnutrition 261
  paralysis 335.21
Waterhouse-Friderichsen 036.3
waxy (any site) 277.3
Weber-Christian (nodular nonsuppurative panniculitis) 729.30
Wegner's (syphilitic osteochondritis) 090.0
Weil's (leptospiral jaundice) 100.0
  of lung 100.0
Weir Mitchell's (erythromelalgia) 443.82 ▲
Werdnig-Hoffmann 335.0
Werlhof's (*see also* Purpura, thrombocytopenic) 287.39 ▲
Wermer's 258.0
Werner's (progeria adultorum) 259.8
Werner-His (trench fever) 083.1
Werner-Schultz (agranulocytosis) 288.0
Wernicke's (superior hemorrhagic polioencephalitis) 265.1
Wernicke-Posadas 114.9
Whipple's (intestinal lipodystrophy) 040.2
whipworm 127.3
white
  blood cell 288.9
    specified NEC 288.8

Disease, diseased — *see also* Syndrome — *continued*
white — *continued*
  spot 701.0
White's (congenital) (keratosis follicularis) 757.39
Whitmore's (melioidosis) 025
Widal-Abrami (acquired hemolytic jaundice) 283.9
Wilkie's 557.1
Wilkinson-Sneddon (subcorneal pustular dermatosis) 694.1
Willis' (diabetes mellitus) (*see also* Diabetes) 250.0 ☑
Wilson's (hepatolenticular degeneration) 275.1
Wilson-Brocq (dermatitis exfoliativa) 695.89
winter vomiting 078.82
Wise's 696.2
Wohlfart-Kugelberg-Welander 335.11
Woillez's (acute idiopathic pulmonary congestion) 518.5
Wolman's (primary familial xanthomatosis) 272.7
wool-sorters' 022.1
Zagari's (xerostomia) 527.7
Zahorsky's (exanthem subitum) 057.8
Ziehen-Oppenheim 333.6
zoonotic, bacterial NEC 027.9
  specified type NEC 027.8

Disfigurement (due to scar) 709.2
  head V48.6
  limb V49.4
  neck V48.7
  trunk V48.7

Disgerminoma — *see* Dysgerminoma

Disinsertion, retina 361.04

Disintegration, complete, of the body 799.89
  traumatic 869.1

Disk kidney 753.3

Dislocatable hip, congenital (*see also* Dislocation, hip, congenital) 754.30

Dislocation (articulation) (closed) (displacement) (simple) (subluxation) 839.8

Note — "Closed" includes simple, complete, partial, uncomplicated, and unspecified dislocation.

"Open" includes dislocation specified as infected or compound and dislocation with foreign body.

"Chronic," "habitual," "old," or "recurrent" dislocations should be coded as indicated under the entry "Dislocation, recurrent," and "pathological" as indicated under the entry "Dislocation, pathological."

For late effect of dislocation see Late, effect, dislocation.

---

  with fracture — *see* Fracture, by site
  acromioclavicular (joint) (closed) 831.04
    open 831.14
  anatomical site (closed)
    specified NEC 839.69
      open 839.79
    unspecified or ill-defined 839.8
      open 839.9
  ankle (scaphoid bone) (closed) 837.0
    open 837.1
  arm (closed) 839.8
    open 839.9
  astragalus (closed) 837.0
    open 837.1
  atlanto-axial (closed) 839.01
    open 839.11
  atlas (closed) 839.01
    open 839.11
  axis (closed) 839.02
    open 839.12
  back (closed) 839.8
    open 839.9
  Bell-Daly 723.8
  breast bone (closed) 839.61
    open 839.71
  capsule, joint — *see* Dislocation, by site
  carpal (bone) — *see* Dislocation, wrist

Dislocation — *continued*
  carpometacarpal (joint) (closed) 833.04
    open 833.14
  cartilage (joint) — *see also* Dislocation, by site
    knee — *see* Tear, meniscus
  cervical, cervicodorsal, or cervicothoracic (spine) (vertebra) — *see* Dislocation, vertebra, cervical
  chiropractic (*see also* Lesion, nonallopathic) 739.9
  chondrocostal — *see* Dislocation, costochondral
  chronic — *see* Dislocation, recurrent
  clavicle (closed) 831.04
    open 831.14
  coccyx (closed) 839.41
    open 839.51
  collar bone (closed) 831.04
    open 831.14
  compound (open) NEC 839.9
  congenital NEC 755.8
    hip (*see also* Dislocation, hip, congenital) 754.30
    lens 743.37
    rib 756.3
    sacroiliac 755.69
    spine NEC 756.19
    vertebra 756.19
  coracoid (closed) 831.09
    open 831.19
  costal cartilage (closed) 839.69
    open 839.79
  costochondral (closed) 839.69
    open 839.79
  cricoarytenoid articulation (closed) 839.69
    open 839.79
  cricothyroid (cartilage) articulation (closed) 839.69
    open 839.79
  dorsal vertebrae (closed) 839.21
    open 839.31
  ear ossicle 385.23
  elbow (closed) 832.00
    anterior (closed) 832.01
      open 832.11
    congenital 754.89
    divergent (closed) 832.09
      open 832.19
    lateral (closed) 832.04
      open 832.14
    medial (closed) 832.03
      open 832.13
    open 832.10
    posterior (closed) 832.02
      open 832.12
    recurrent 718.32
    specified type NEC 832.09
      open 832.19
  eye 360.81
    lateral 376.36
  eyeball 360.81
    lateral 376.36
  femur
    distal end (closed) 836.50
      anterior 836.52
        open 836.62
      lateral 836.53
        open 836.63
      medial 836.54
        open 836.64
      open 836.60
      posterior 836.51
        open 836.61
    proximal end (closed) 835.00
      anterior (pubic) 835.03
        open 835.13
      obturator 835.02
        open 835.12
      open 835.10
      posterior 835.01
        open 835.11
  fibula
    distal end (closed) 837.0
      open 837.1
    proximal end (closed) 836.59
      open 836.69

Dislocation — *continued*
  finger(s) (phalanx) (thumb) (closed) 834.00
    interphalangeal (joint) 834.02
      open 834.12
    metacarpal (bone), distal end 834.01
      open 834.11
    metacarpophalangeal (joint) 834.01
      open 834.11
    open 834.10
    recurrent 718.34
  foot (closed) 838.00
    open 838.10
    recurrent 718.37
  forearm (closed) 839.8
    open 839.9
  fracture — *see* Fracture, by site
  glenoid (closed) 831.09
    open 831.19
  habitual — *see* Dislocation, recurrent
  hand (closed) 839.8
    open 839.9
  hip (closed) 835.00
    anterior 835.03
      obturator 835.02
        open 835.12
      open 835.13
    congenital (unilateral) 754.30
      with subluxation of other hip 754.35
      bilateral 754.31
    developmental 718.75
    open 835.10
    posterior 835.01
      open 835.11
    recurrent 718.35
  humerus (closed) 831.00
    distal end (*see also* Dislocation, elbow)
      832.00
    open 831.10
    proximal end (closed) 831.00
      anterior (subclavicular) (subcoracoid)
        (subglenoid) (closed) 831.01
        open 831.11
      inferior (closed) 831.03
        open 831.13
      open 831.10
      posterior (closed) 831.02
        open 831.12
  implant — *see* Complications, mechanical
  incus 385.23
  infracoracoid (closed) 831.01
    open 831.11
  innominate (pubic junction) (sacral junction)
    (closed) 839.69
    acetabulum (*see also* Dislocation, hip)
      835.00
    open 839.79
  interphalangeal (joint)
    finger or hand (closed) 834.02
      open 834.12
    foot or toe (closed) 838.06
      open 838.16
  jaw (cartilage) (meniscus) (closed) 830.0
    open 830.1
    recurrent 524.69
  joint NEC (closed) 839.8
    developmental 718.7 ☑
    open 839.9
    pathological — *see* Dislocation, pathological
    recurrent — *see* Dislocation, recurrent
  knee (closed) 836.50
    anterior 836.51
      open 836.61
    congenital (with genu recurvatum) 754.41
    habitual 718.36
    lateral 836.54
      open 836.64
    medial 836.53
      open 836.63
    old 718.36
    open 836.60
    posterior 836.52
      open 836.62
    recurrent 718.36
    rotatory 836.59
      open 836.69
  lacrimal gland 375.16

Dislocation — *continued*
  leg (closed) 839.8
    open 839.9
  lens (crystalline) (complete) (partial) 379.32
    anterior 379.33
    congenital 743.37
    ocular implant 996.53
    posterior 379.34
    traumatic 921.3
  ligament — *see* Dislocation, by site
  lumbar (vertebrae) (closed) 839.20
    open 839.30
  lumbosacral (vertebrae) (closed) 839.20
    congenital 756.19
    open 839.30
  mandible (closed) 830.0
    open 830.1
  maxilla (inferior) (closed) 830.0
    open 830.1
  meniscus (knee) — *see also* Tear, meniscus
    other sites — *see* Dislocation, by site
  metacarpal (bone)
    distal end (closed) 834.01
      open 834.11
    proximal end (closed) 833.05
      open 833.15
  metacarpophalangeal (joint) (closed) 834.01
    open 834.11
  metatarsal (bone) (closed) 838.04
    open 838.14
  metatarsophalangeal (joint) (closed) 838.05
    open 838.15
  midcarpal (joint) (closed) 833.03
    open 833.13
  midtarsal (joint) (closed) 838.02
    open 838.12
  Monteggia's — *see* Dislocation, hip
  multiple locations (except fingers only or toes
    only) (closed) 839.8
    open 839.9
  navicular (bone) foot (closed) 837.0
    open 837.1
  neck (*see also* Dislocation, vertebra, cervical)
    839.00
  Nélaton's — *see* Dislocation, ankle
  nontraumatic (joint) — *see* Dislocation,
    pathological
  nose (closed) 839.69
    open 839.79
  not recurrent, not current injury — *see*
    Dislocation, pathological
  occiput from atlas (closed) 839.01
    open 839.11
  old — *see* Dislocation, recurrent
  open (compound) NEC 839.9
  ossicle, ear 385.23
  paralytic (flaccid) (spastic) — *see* Dislocation,
    pathological
  patella (closed) 836.3
    congenital 755.64
    open 836.4
  pathological NEC 718.20
    ankle 718.27
    elbow 718.22
    foot 718.27
    hand 718.24
    hip 718.25
    knee 718.26
    lumbosacral joint 724.6
    multiple sites 718.29
    pelvic region 718.25
    sacroiliac 724.6
    shoulder (region) 718.21
    specified site NEC 718.28
    spine 724.8
      sacroiliac 724.6
    wrist 718.23
  pelvis (closed) 839.69
    acetabulum (*see also* Dislocation, hip)
      835.00
    open 839.79
  phalanx
    foot or toe (closed) 838.09
      open 838.19
    hand or finger (*see also* Dislocation, finger)
      834.00

Dislocation — *continued*
  postpoliomyelitic — *see* Dislocation,
    pathological
  prosthesis, internal — *see* Complications,
    mechanical
  radiocarpal (joint) (closed) 833.02
    open 833.12
  radioulnar (joint)
    distal end (closed) 833.01
      open 833.11
    proximal end (*see also* Dislocation, elbow)
      832.00
  radius
    distal end (closed) 833.00
      open 833.10
    proximal end (closed) 832.01
      open 832.11
  recurrent (*see also* Derangement, joint,
    recurrent) 718.3 ☑
    elbow 718.32
    hip 718.35
    joint NEC 718.38
    knee 718.36
    lumbosacral (joint) 724.6
    patella 718.36
    sacroiliac 724.6
    shoulder 718.31
    temporomandibular 524.69
  rib (cartilage) (closed) 839.69
    congenital 756.3
    open 839.79
  sacrococcygeal (closed) 839.42
    open 839.52
  sacroiliac (joint) (ligament) (closed) 839.42
    congenital 755.69
    open 839.52
    recurrent 724.6
  sacrum (closed) 839.42
    open 839.52
  scaphoid (bone)
    ankle or foot (closed) 837.0
      open 837.1
    wrist (closed) (*see also* Dislocation, wrist)
      833.00
      open 833.10
  scapula (closed) 831.09
    open 831.19
  semilunar cartilage, knee — *see* Tear, meniscus
  septal cartilage (nose) (closed) 839.69
    open 839.79
  septum (nasal) (old) 470
  sesamoid bone — *see* Dislocation, by site
  shoulder (blade) (ligament) (closed) 831.00
    anterior (subclavicular) (subcoracoid)
      (subglenoid) (closed) 831.01
      open 831.11
    chronic 718.31
    inferior 831.03
      open 831.13
    open 831.10
    posterior (closed) 831.02
      open 831.12
    recurrent 718.31
  skull — *see* Injury, intracranial
  Smith's — *see* Dislocation, foot
  spine (articular process) (*see also* Dislocation,
    vertebra) (closed) 839.40
    atlanto-axial (closed) 839.01
      open 839.11
      recurrent 723.8
    cervical, cervicodorsal, cervicothoracic
      (closed) (*see also* Dislocation,
      vertebrae, cervical) 839.00
      open 839.10
      recurrent 723.8
    coccyx 839.41
      open 839.51
    congenital 756.19
    due to birth trauma 767.4
    open 839.50
    recurrent 724.9
    sacroiliac 839.42
      recurrent 724.6
    sacrum (sacrococcygeal) (sacroiliac) 839.42
      open 839.52
  spontaneous — *see* Dislocation, pathological

2006 ICD-9-CM

☑ Additional Digit Required — Refer to the Tabular List (Numeric Code Section) for Additional Digit Selection
▶◀ Revised Text   ● New Line   ▲ Revised Code

Volume 2 — 111

Dislocation — *continued*
sternoclavicular (joint) (closed) 839.61
  open 839.71
sternum (closed) 839.61
  open 839.71
subastragalar — *see* Dislocation, foot
subglenoid (closed) 831.01
  open 831.11
symphysis
  jaw (closed) 830.0
    open 830.1
  mandibular (closed) 830.0
    open 830.1
  pubis (closed) 839.69
    open 839.79
tarsal (bone) (joint) 838.01
  open 838.11
tarsometatarsal (joint) 838.03
  open 838.13
temporomandibular (joint) (closed) 830.0
  open 830.1
  recurrent 524.69
thigh
  distal end (*see also* Dislocation, femur, distal
    end) 836.50
  proximal end (*see also* Dislocation, hip)
    835.00
thoracic (vertebrae) (closed) 839.21
  open 839.31
thumb(s) (*see also* Dislocation, finger) 834.00
thyroid cartilage (closed) 839.69
  open 839.79
tibia
  distal end (closed) 837.0
    open 837.1
  proximal end (closed) 836.50
    anterior 836.51
      open 836.61
    lateral 836.54
      open 836.64
    medial 836.53
      open 836.63
    open 836.60
    posterior 836.52
      open 836.62
    rotatory 836.59
      open 836.69
tibiofibular
  distal (closed) 837.0
    open 837.1
  superior (closed) 836.59
    open 836.69
toe(s) (closed) 838.09
  open 838.19
trachea (closed) 839.69
  open 839.79
ulna
  distal end (closed) 833.09
    open 833.19
  proximal end — *see* Dislocation, elbow
vertebra (articular process) (body) (closed)
    839.40
  cervical, cervicodorsal or cervicothoracic
    (closed) 839.00
    first (atlas) 839.01
      open 839.11
    second (axis) 839.02
      open 839.12
    third 839.03
      open 839.13
    fourth 839.04
      open 839.14
    fifth 839.05
      open 839.15
    sixth 839.06
      open 839.16
    seventh 839.07
      open 839.17
    congenital 756.19
    multiple sites 839.08
      open 839.18
    open 839.10
  congenital 756.19
  dorsal 839.21
    open 839.31
    recurrent 724.9

Dislocation — *continued*
vertebra — *continued*
  lumbar, lumbosacral 839.20
    open 839.30
  open NEC 839.50
  recurrent 724.9
  specified region NEC 839.49
    open 839.59
  thoracic 839.21
    open 839.31
wrist (carpal bone) (scaphoid) (semilunar)
    (closed) 833.00
  carpometacarpal (joint) 833.04
    open 833.14
  metacarpal bone, proximal end 833.05
    open 833.15
  midcarpal (joint) 833.03
    open 833.13
  open 833.10
  radiocarpal (joint) 833.02
    open 833.12
  radioulnar (joint) 833.01
    open 833.11
  recurrent 718.33
  specified site NEC 833.09
    open 833.19
xiphoid cartilage (closed) 839.61
  open 839.71
Dislodgement
  artificial skin graft 996.55
  decellularized allodermis graft 996.55
Disobedience, hostile (covert) (overt) (*see also*
    Disturbance, conduct) 312.0 ☑
Disorder — *see also* Disease
  academic underachievement, childhood and
    adolescence 313.83
  accommodation 367.51
    drug-induced 367.89
    toxic 367.89
  adjustment (*see also* Reaction, adjustment)
    309.9
    with
      anxiety 309.24
      anxiety and depressed mood 309.28
      depressed mood 309.0
      disturbance of conduct 309.3
      disturbance of emotions and conduct
        309.4
  adrenal (capsule) (cortex) (gland) 255.9
    specified type NEC 255.8
  adrenogenital 255.2
  affective (*see also* Psychosis, affective) 296.90
    atypical 296.81
  aggressive, unsocialized (*see also* Disturbance,
    conduct) 312.0 ☑
  alcohol, alcoholic (*see also* Alcohol) 291.9
  allergic — *see* Allergy
  amnestic (*see also* Amnestic syndrome) 294.8
    alcohol-induced persisting 291.1
    drug-induced persisting 292.83
    in conditions classified elsewhere 294.0
  amino acid (metabolic) (*see also* Disturbance,
    metabolism, amino acid) 270.9
    albinism 270.2
    alkaptonuria 270.2
    argininosuccinicaciduria 270.6
    beta-amino-isobutyricaciduria 277.2
    cystathioninuria 270.4
    cystinosis 270.0
    cystinuria 270.0
    glycinuria 270.0
    homocystinuria 270.4
    imidazole 270.5
    maple syrup (urine) disease 270.3
    neonatal, transitory 775.8
    oasthouse urine disease 270.2
    ochronosis 270.2
    phenylketonuria 270.1
    phenylpyruvic oligophrenia 270.1
    purine NEC 277.2
    pyrimidine NEC 277.2
    renal transport NEC 270.0
    specified type NEC 270.8
    transport NEC 270.0
      renal 270.0
    xanthinuria 277.2

Disorder — *see also* Disease — *continued*
  anaerobic glycolysis with anemia 282.3
  anxiety (*see also* Anxiety) 300.00
    due to or associated with physical condition
      293.84
  arteriole 447.9
    specified type NEC 447.8
  artery 447.9
    specified type NEC 447.8
  articulation — *see* Disorder, joint
  Asperger's 299.8 ☑
  attachment of infancy or early childhood
    313.89
  attention deficit 314.00
    with hyperactivity 314.01
    predominantly
      combined hyperactive/inattentive 314.01
      hyperactive/impulsive 314.01
      inattentive 314.00
    residual type 314.8
  autoimmune NEC 279.4
    hemolytic (cold type) (warm type) 283.0
    parathyroid 252.1
    thyroid 245.2
  autistic 299.0 ☑
  avoidant, childhood or adolescence 313.21
  balance
    acid-base 276.9
      mixed (with hypercapnia) 276.4
    electrolyte 276.9
    fluid 276.9
  behavior NEC (*see also* Disturbance, conduct)
    312.9
    disruptive 312.9
  bilirubin excretion 277.4
  bipolar (affective) (alternating) 296.80

> *Note* — *Use the following fifth-digit*
> *subclassification with categories 296.0-296.6:*
>
> 0 *unspecifed*
> 1 *mild*
> 2 *moderate*
> 3 *severe, without mention of psychotic*
>   *behavior*
> 4 *severe, specified as with psychotic*
>   *behavior*
> 5 *in partial or unspecified remission*
> 6 *in full remission*

    atypical 296.7
    currently
      depressed 296.5 ☑
      hypomanic 296.4 ☑
      manic 296.4 ☑
      mixed 296.6 ☑
    specified type NEC 296.89
    type I 296.7
      most recent episode (or current)
        depressed 296.5 ☑
        hypomanic 296.4 ☑
        manic 296.4 ☑
        mixed 296.6 ☑
        unspecified 296.7
      single manic episode 296.0
    type II (recurrent major depressive episodes
      with hypomania) 296.89
  bladder 596.9
    functional NEC 596.59
    specified NEC 596.8
  bone NEC 733.90
    specified NEC 733.99
  brachial plexus 353.0
  branched-chain amino-acid degradation 270.3
  breast 611.9
    puerperal, postpartum 676.3 ☑
    specified NEC 611.8
  Briquet's 300.81
  bursa 727.9
    shoulder region 726.10
  carbohydrate metabolism, congenital 271.9
  cardiac, functional 427.9
    postoperative 997.1
    psychogenic 306.2
  cardiovascular, psychogenic 306.2

Disorder — see also Disease — continued
  cartilage NEC 733.90
    articular 718.00
      ankle 718.07
      elbow 718.02
      foot 718.07
      hand 718.04
      hip 718.05
      knee 717.9
      multiple sites 718.09
      pelvic region 718.05
      shoulder region 718.01
      specified
        site NEC 718.08
        type NEC 733.99
      wrist 718.03
  catatonic — see Catatonia
  central auditory processing 315.32 ●
  cervical region NEC 723.9
  cervical root (nerve) NEC 353.2
  character NEC (see also Disorder, personality) 301.9
  coagulation (factor) (see also Defect, coagulation) 286.9
    factor VIII (congenital) (functional) 286.0
    factor IX (congenital) (functional) 286.1
    neonatal, transitory 776.3
  coccyx 724.70
    specified NEC 724.79
  colon 569.9
    functional 564.9
      congenital 751.3
  cognitive 294.9
  communication 307.9
  conduct (see also Disturbance, conduct) 312.9
    adjustment reaction 309.3
    adolescent onset type 312.82
    childhood onset type 312.81
    compulsive 312.30
      specified type NEC 312.39
    hyperkinetic 314.2
    onset unspecified 312.89
    socialized (type) 312.20
      aggressive 312.23
      unaggressive 312.21
    specified NEC 312.89
  conduction, heart 426.9
    specified NEC 426.89
  conflict
    sexual orientation 302.0
  congenital ●
    glycosylation (CDG) 271.8 ●
  convulsive (secondary) (see also Convulsions) 780.39
    due to injury at birth 767.0
    idiopathic 780.39
  coordination 781.3
  cornea NEC 371.89
    due to contact lens 371.82
  corticosteroid metabolism NEC 255.2
  cranial nerve — see Disorder, nerve, cranial
  cyclothymic 301.13
  degradation, branched-chain amino acid 270.3
  delusional 297.1
  dentition 520.6
  depersonalization 300.6
  depressive NEC 311
    atypical 296.82
    major (see also Psychosis, affective) 296.2 ☑
      recurrent episode 296.3 ☑
      single episode 296.2 ☑
  development, specific 315.9
    associated with hyperkinesia 314.1
    coordination 315.4
    language 315.31
    learning 315.2
      arithmetical 315.1
      reading 315.00
    mixed 315.5
    motor coordination 315.4
    specified type NEC 315.8
    speech 315.39
  diaphragm 519.4
  digestive 536.9
    fetus or newborn 777.9
      specified NEC 777.8
    psychogenic 306.4

Disorder — see also Disease — continued
  disintegrative, childhood 299.1 ☑
  dissociative 300.15
    identity 300.14
    nocturnal 307.47
  drug-related 292.9
  dysmorphic body 300.7
  dysthymic 300.4
  ear 388.9
    degenerative NEC 388.00
    external 380.9
      specified 380.89
    pinna 380.30
    specified type NEC 388.8
    vascular NEC 388.00
  eating NEC 307.50
  electrolyte NEC 276.9
    with
      abortion — see Abortion, by type, with metabolic disorder
      ectopic pregnancy (see also categories 633.0-633.9) 639.4
      molar pregnancy (see also categories 630-632) 639.4
    acidosis 276.2
      metabolic 276.2
      respiratory 276.2
    alkalosis 276.3
      metabolic 276.3
      respiratory 276.3
    following
      abortion 639.4
      ectopic or molar pregnancy 639.4
    neonatal, transitory NEC 775.5
  emancipation as adjustment reaction 309.22
  emotional (see also Disorder, mental, nonpsychotic) V40.9
  endocrine 259.9
    specified type NEC 259.8
  esophagus 530.9
    functional 530.5
    psychogenic 306.4
  explosive
    intermittent 312.34
    isolated 312.35
  expressive language 315.31
  eye 379.90
    globe — see Disorder, globe
    ill-defined NEC 379.99
    limited duction NEC 378.63
    specified NEC 379.8
  eyelid 374.9
    degenerative 374.50
    sensory 374.44
    specified type NEC 374.89
    vascular 374.85
  factitious (with combined psychological and physical signs and symptoms) (with predominantly physical signs and symptoms) 300.19
    with predominantly psychological signs and symptoms 300.16
  factor, coagulation (see also Defect, coagulation) 286.9
    VIII (congenital) (functional) 286.0
    IX (congenital) (funcitonal) 286.1
  fascia 728.9
  fatty acid oxidation 277.85
  feeding — see Feeding
  female sexual arousal 302.72
  fluid NEC 276.9
  gastric (functional) 536.9
    motility 536.8
    psychogenic 306.4
    secretion 536.8
  gastrointestinal (functional) NEC 536.9
    newborn (neonatal) 777.9
      specified NEC 777.8
    psychogenic 306.4
  gender (child) 302.6
    adult 302.85
  gender identity (childhood) 302.6
    adolescents 302.85
    adults (-life) 302.85
  genitourinary system, psychogenic 306.50
  globe 360.9
    degenerative 360.20
      specified NEC 360.29

Disorder — see also Disease — continued
  globe — continued
    specified type NEC 360.89
  hearing — see also Deafness
    conductive type (air) (see also Deafness, conductive) 389.00
    mixed conductive and sensorineural 389.2
    nerve 389.12
    perceptive (see also Deafness, perceptive) 389.10
    sensorineural type NEC (see also Deafness, perceptive) 389.10
  heart action 427.9
    postoperative 997.1
  hematological, transient neonatal 776.9
    specified type NEC 776.8
  hematopoietic organs 289.9
  hemorrhagic NEC 287.9
    due to intrinsic circulating anticoagulants 286.5
    specified type NEC 287.8
  hemostasis (see also Defect, coagulation) 286.9
  homosexual conflict 302.0
  hypomanic (chronic) 301.11
  identity
    childhood and adolescence 313.82
      gender 302.6
  immune mechanism (immunity) 279.9
    single complement (C1-C9) 279.8
    specified type NEC 279.8
  impulse control (see also Disturbance, conduct, compulsive) 312.30
  infant sialic acid storage 271.8
  integument, fetus or newborn 778.9
    specified type NEC 778.8
  interactional psychotic (childhood) (see also Psychosis, childhood) 299.1 ☑
  intermittent explosive 312.34
  intervertebral disc 722.90
    cervical, cervicothoracic 722.91
    lumbar, lumbosacral 722.93
    thoracic, thoracolumbar 722.92
  intestinal 569.9
    functional NEC 564.9
      congenital 751.3
      postoperative 564.4
    psychogenic 306.4
  introverted, of childhood and adolescence 313.22
  iron, metabolism 275.0
  isolated explosive 312.35
  joint NEC 719.90
    ankle 719.97
    elbow 719.92
    foot 719.97
    hand 719.94
    hip 719.95
    knee 719.96
    multiple sites 719.99
    pelvic region 719.95
    psychogenic 306.0
    shoulder (region) 719.91
    specified site NEC 719.98
    temporomandibular 524.60
      sounds on opening or closing 524.64
      specified NEC 524.69
    wrist 719.93
  kidney 593.9
    functional 588.9
      specified NEC 588.89
  labyrinth, labyrinthine 386.9
    specified type NEC 386.8
  lactation 676.9 ☑
  language (developmental) (expressive) 315.31
    mixed receptive-expressive 315.32
  learning 315.9
  ligament 728.9
  ligamentous attachments, peripheral — see also Enthesopathy
    spine 720.1
  limb NEC 729.9
    psychogenic 306.0
  lipid
    metabolism, congenital 272.9
    storage 272.7
  lipoprotein deficiency (familial) 272.5

Disorder — *see also* Disease — *continued*
low back NEC 724.9
  psychogenic 306.0
lumbosacral
  plexus 353.1
  root (nerve) NEC 353.4
lymphoproliferative (chronic) NEC (M9970/1)
  238.7
major depressive (*see also* Psychosis, affective)
  296.2 ☑
  recurrent episode 296.3 ☑
  single episode 296.2 ☑
male erectile 607.84 ▲
  ►nonorganic◄ origin 302.72 ▲
manic (*see also* Psychosis, affective) 296.0 ☑
  atypical 296.81
mathematics 315.1
meniscus NEC (*see also* Disorder, cartilage,
  articular) 718.0 ☑
menopausal 627.9
  specified NEC 627.8
menstrual 626.9
  psychogenic 306.52
  specified NEC 626.8
mental (nonpsychotic) 300.9
  affecting management of pregnancy,
    childbirth, or puerperium 648.4 ☑
  drug-induced 292.9
    hallucinogen persisting perception 292.89
    specified type NEC 292.89
  due to or associated with
    alcoholism 291.9
    drug consumption NEC 292.9
      specified type NEC 292.89
    physical condition NEC 293.9
  induced by drug 292.9
    specified type NEC 292.89
  neurotic (*see also* Neurosis) 300.9
  of infancy, childhood or adolescence 313.9
  persistent
    other
      due to conditions classified elsewhere
        294.8
    unspecified
      due to conditions classified elsewhere
        294.9
  presenile 310.1
    psychotic NEC 290.10
  previous, affecting management of
    pregnancy V23.89
  psychoneurotic (*see also* Neurosis) 300.9
  psychotic (*see also* Psychosis) 298.9
    brief 298.8
    senile 290.20
  specific, following organic brain damage
    310.9
    cognitive or personality change of other
      type 310.1
    frontal lobe syndrome 310.0
    postconcussional syndrome 310.2
    specified type NEC 310.8
  transient
    in conditions classified elsewhere 293.9
metabolism NEC 277.9
  with
    abortion — *see* Abortion, by type, with
      metabolic disorder
    ectopic pregnancy (*see also* categories
      633.0-633.9) 639.4
    molar pregnancy (*see also* categories 630-
      632) 639.4
  alkaptonuria 270.2
  amino acid (*see also* Disorder, amino acid)
    270.9
    specified type NEC 270.8
  ammonia 270.6
  arginine 270.6
  argininosuccinic acid 270.6
  basal 794.7
  bilirubin 277.4
  calcium 275.40
  carbohydrate 271.9
    specified type NEC 271.8
  cholesterol 272.9
  citrulline 270.6
  copper 275.1
  corticosteroid 255.2

Disorder — *see also* Disease — *continued*
metabolism NEC — *continued*
  cystine storage 270.0
  cystinuria 270.0
  fat 272.9
  fatty acid oxidation 277.85
  following
    abortion 639.4
    ectopic or molar pregnancy 639.4
  fructosemia 271.2
  fructosuria 271.2
  fucosidosis 271.8
  galactose-1-phosphate uridyl transferase
    271.1
  glutamine 270.7
  glycine 270.7
  glycogen storage NEC 271.0
    hepatorenal 271.0
  hemochromatosis 275.0
  in labor and delivery 669.0 ☑
  iron 275.0
  lactose 271.3
  lipid 272.9
    specified type NEC 272.8
    storage 272.7
  lipoprotein — *see also* Hyperlipemia
    deficiency (familial) 272.5
  lysine 270.7
  magnesium 275.2
  mannosidosis 271.8
  mineral 275.9
    specified type NEC 275.8
  mitochondrial 277.87
  mucopolysaccharide 277.5
  nitrogen 270.9
  ornithine 270.6
  oxalosis 271.8
  pentosuria 271.8
  phenylketonuria 270.1
  phosphate 275.3
  phosphorus 275.3
  plasma protein 273.9
    specified type NEC 273.8
  porphyrin 277.1
  purine 277.2
  pyrimidine 277.2
  serine 270.7
  sodium 276.9
  specified type NEC 277.89
  steroid 255.2
  threonine 270.7
  urea cycle 270.6
  xylose 271.8
micturition NEC 788.69
  psychogenic 306.53
misery and unhappiness, of childhood and
  adolescence 313.1
mitochondrial metabolism 277.87
mitral valve 424.0
mood (*see also* Disorder, bipolar) 296.90
  episodic 296.90
    specified NEC 296.99
  in conditions classified elsewhere 293.83
motor tic 307.20
  chronic 307.22
  transient (childhood) 307.21
movement NEC 333.90
  hysterical 300.11
  medication-induced 333.90 ●
  periodic limb 327.51 ▲
  sleep related, ►unspecified◄ 780.58
    other organic 327.59 ●
  specified type NEC 333.99
  stereotypic 307.3
mucopolysaccharide 277.5
muscle 728.9
  psychogenic 306.0
  specified type NEC 728.3
muscular attachments, peripheral — *see also*
  Enthesopathy
  spine 720.1
musculoskeletal system NEC 729.9
  psychogenic 306.0
myeloproliferative (chronic) NEC (M9960/1)
  238.7
myoneural 358.9
  due to lead 358.2

Disorder — *see also* Disease — *continued*
myoneural — *continued*
  specified type NEC 358.8
  toxic 358.2
myotonic 359.2
neck region NEC 723.9
nerve 349.9
  abducens NEC 378.54
  accessory 352.4
  acoustic 388.5
  auditory 388.5
  auriculotemporal 350.8
  axillary 353.0
  cerebral — *see* Disorder, nerve, cranial
  cranial 352.9
    first 352.0
    second 377.49
    third
      partial 378.51
      total 378.52
    fourth 378.53
    fifth 350.9
    sixth 378.54
    seventh NEC 351.9
    eighth 388.5
    ninth 352.2
    tenth 352.3
    eleventh 352.4
    twelfth 352.5
    multiple 352.6
  entrapment — *see* Neuropathy, entrapment
  facial 351.9
    specified NEC 351.8
  femoral 355.2
  glossopharyngeal NEC 352.2
  hypoglossal 352.5
  iliohypogastric 355.79
  ilioinguinal 355.79
  intercostal 353.8
  lateral
    cutaneous of thigh 355.1
    popliteal 355.3
  lower limb NEC 355.8
  medial, popliteal 355.4
  median NEC 354.1
  obturator 355.79
  oculomotor
    partial 378.51
    total 378.52
  olfactory 352.0
  optic 377.49
    ischemic 377.41
    nutritional 377.33
    toxic 377.34
  peroneal 355.3
  phrenic 354.8
  plantar 355.6
  pneumogastric 352.3
  posterior tibial 355.5
  radial 354.3
  recurrent laryngeal 352.3
  root 353.9
    specified NEC 353.8
  saphenous 355.79
  sciatic NEC 355.0
  specified NEC 355.9
    lower limb 355.79
    upper limb 354.8
  spinal 355.9
  sympathetic NEC 337.9
  trigeminal 350.9
    specified NEC 350.8
  trochlear 378.53
  ulnar 354.2
  upper limb NEC 354.9
  vagus 352.3
nervous system NEC 349.9
  autonomic (peripheral) (*see also* Neuropathy,
    peripheral, autonomic) 337.9
  cranial 352.9
  parasympathetic (*see also* Neuropathy,
    peripheral, autonomic) 337.9
  specified type NEC 349.89
  sympathetic (*see also* Neuropathy,
    peripheral, autonomic) 337.9
  vegetative (*see also* Neuropathy, peripheral,
    autonomic) 337.9

Disorder — *see also* Disease — *continued*
  neurohypophysis NEC 253.6
  neurological NEC 781.99
    peripheral NEC 355.9
  neuromuscular NEC 358.9
    hereditary NEC 359.1
    specified NEC 358.8
    toxic 358.2
  neurotic 300.9
    specified type NEC 300.89
  neutrophil, polymorphonuclear (functional) 288.1
  nightmare 307.47
  night terror 307.46
  obsessive-compulsive 300.3
  oppositional defiant, childhood and adolescence 313.81
  optic
    chiasm 377.54
      associated with
        inflammatory disorders 377.54
        neoplasm NEC 377.52
          pituitary 377.51
        pituitary disorders 377.51
        vascular disorders 377.53
    nerve 377.49
    radiations 377.63
    tracts 377.63
  orbit 376.9
    specified NEC 376.89
  orgasmic
    female 302.73
    male 302.74
  overanxious, of childhood and adolescence 313.0
  oxidation, fatty acid 277.85
  pancreas, internal secretion (other than diabetes mellitus) 251.9
    specified type NEC 251.8
  panic 300.01
    with agoraphobia 300.21
  papillary muscle NEC 429.81
  paranoid 297.9
    induced 297.3
    shared 297.3
  parathyroid 252.9
    specified type NEC 252.8
  paroxysmal, mixed 780.39
  pentose phosphate pathway with anemia 282.2
  periodic limb movement 327.51 ▲
  peroxisomal 277.86
  personality 301.9
    affective 301.10
    aggressive 301.3
    amoral 301.7
    anancastic, anankastic 301.4
    antisocial 301.7
    asocial 301.7
    asthenic 301.6
    avoidant 301.82
    borderline 301.83
    compulsive 301.4
    cyclothymic 301.13
    dependent-passive 301.6
    dyssocial 301.7
    emotional instability 301.59
    epileptoid 301.3
    explosive 301.3
    following organic brain damage 310.1
    histrionic 301.50
    hyperthymic 301.11
    hypomanic (chronic) 301.11
    hypothymic 301.12
    hysterical 301.50
    immature 301.89
    inadequate 301.6
    introverted 301.21
    labile 301.59
    moral deficiency 301.7
    narcissistic 301.81
    obsessional 301.4
    obsessive-compulsive 301.4
    overconscientious 301.4
    paranoid 301.0
    passive (-dependent) 301.6
    passive-aggressive 301.84
    pathological NEC 301.9

Disorder — *see also* Disease — *continued*
  personality — *continued*
    pseudosocial 301.7
    psychopathic 301.9
    schizoid 301.20
      introverted 301.21
      schizotypal 301.22
    schizotypal 301.22
    seductive 301.59
    type A 301.4
    unstable 301.59
  pervasive developmental 299.9
    childhood-onset 299.8 ☑
    specified NEC 299.8 ☑
  phonological 315.39
  pigmentation, choroid (congenital) 743.53
  pinna 380.30
    specified type NEC 380.39
  pituitary, thalamic 253.9
    anterior NEC 253.4
    iatrogenic 253.7
    postablative 253.7
    specified NEC 253.8
  pityriasis-like NEC 696.8
  platelets (blood) 287.1
  polymorphonuclear neutrophils (functional) 288.1
  porphyrin metabolism 277.1
  postmenopausal 627.9
    specified type NEC 627.8
  posttraumatic stress 309.81
    acute 309.81
    brief 309.81
    chronic 309.81
  premenstrual dysphoric (PMDD) 625.4
  psoriatic-like NEC 696.8
  psychic, with diseases classified elsewhere 316
  psychogenic NEC (*see also* condition) 300.9
    allergic NEC
      respiratory 306.1
    anxiety 300.00
      atypical 300.00
      generalized 300.02
    appetite 307.59   ▲
    articulation, joint 306.0
    asthenic 300.5
    blood 306.8
    cardiovascular (system) 306.2
    compulsive 300.3
    cutaneous 306.3
    depressive 300.4
    digestive (system) 306.4
    dysmenorrheic 306.52
    dyspneic 306.1
    eczematous 306.3
    endocrine (system) 306.6
    eye 306.7
    feeding 307.59
    functional NEC 306.9
    gastric 306.4
    gastrointestinal (system) 306.4
    genitourinary (system) 306.50
    heart (function) (rhythm) 306.2
    hemic 306.8
    hyperventilatory 306.1
    hypochondriacal 300.7
    hysterical 300.10
    intestinal 306.4
    joint 306.0
    learning 315.2
    limb 306.0
    lymphatic (system) 306.8
    menstrual 306.52
    micturition 306.53
    monoplegic NEC 306.0
    motor 307.9
    muscle 306.0
    musculoskeletal 306.0
    neurocirculatory 306.2
    obsessive 300.3
    occupational 300.89
    organ or part of body NEC 306.9
    organs of special sense 306.7
    paralytic NEC 306.0
    phobic 300.20
    physical NEC 306.9
    pruritic 306.3

Disorder — *see also* Disease — *continued*
  psychogenic NEC (*see also* condition) — *continued*
    rectal 306.4
    respiratory (system) 306.1
    rheumatic 306.0
    sexual (function) 302.70
      specified type NEC 302.79
    sexual orientation conflict 302.0
    skin (allergic) (eczematous) (pruritic) 306.3
    sleep 307.40
      initiation or maintenance 307.41
        persistent 307.42
        transient 307.41
      movement 780.58
      sleep terror 307.46
      specified type NEC 307.49
    specified part of body NEC 306.8
    stomach 306.4
  psychomotor NEC 307.9
    hysterical 300.11
  psychoneurotic (*see also* Neurosis) 300.9
    mixed NEC 300.89
  psychophysiologic (*see also* Disorder, psychosomatic) 306.9
  psychosexual identity (childhood) 302.6
    adult-life 302.85
  psychosomatic NEC 306.9
    allergic NEC
      respiratory 306.1
    articulation, joint 306.0
    cardiovascular (system) 306.2
    cutaneous 306.3
    digestive (system) 306.4
    dysmenorrheic 306.52
    dyspneic 306.1
    endocrine (system) 306.6
    eye 306.7
    gastric 306.4
    gastrointestinal (system) 306.4
    genitourinary (system) 306.50
    heart (functional) (rhythm) 306.2
    hyperventilatory 306.1
    intestinal 306.4
    joint 306.0
    limb 306.0
    lymphatic (system) 306.8
    menstrual 306.52
    micturition 306.53
    monoplegic NEC 306.0
    muscle 306.0
    musculoskeletal 306.0
    neurocirculatory 306.2
    organs of special sense 306.7
    paralytic NEC 306.0
    pruritic 306.3
    rectal 306.4
    respiratory (system) 306.1
    rheumatic 306.0
    sexual (function) 302.70
    specified type NEC 302.79
    skin 306.3
    specified part of body NEC 306.8
    stomach 306.4
  psychotic (*see also* Psychosis) 298.9
    brief 298.8
  purine metabolism NEC 277.2
  pyrimidine metabolism NEC 277.2
  reactive attachment of infancy or early childhood 313.89
  reading, developmental 315.00
  reflex 796.1
  REM sleep behavior 327.42   ●
  renal function, impaired 588.9
    specified type NEC 588.89
  renal transport NEC 588.89
  respiration, respiratory NEC 519.9
    due to
      aspiration of liquids or solids 508.9
      inhalation of fumes or vapors 506.9
    psychogenic 306.1
  retina 362.9
    specified type NEC 362.89
  rumination 307.53
  sacroiliac joint NEC 724.6
  sacrum 724.6

Disorder — *see also* Disease — *continued*
schizo-affective (*see also* Schizophrenia) 295.7 ☑
schizoid, childhood or adolescence 313.22
schizophreniform 295.4 ☑
schizotypal personality 301.22
secretion, thyrocalcitonin 246.0
seizure 780.39
  recurrent 780.39
    epileptic — *see* Epilepsy
sense of smell 781.1
  psychogenic 306.7
separation anxiety 309.21
sexual (*see also* Deviation, sexual) 302.9
  aversion 302.79
  desire, hypoactive 302.71
  function, psychogenic 302.70
shyness, of childhood and adolescence 313.21
single complement (C1-C9) 279.8
skin NEC 709.9
  fetus or newborn 778.9
    specified type 778.8
  psychogenic (allergic) (eczematous) (pruritic) 306.3
  specified type NEC 709.8
  vascular 709.1
sleep 780.50
  with apnea — *see* Apnea, sleep
  alcohol induced 291.82 ●
  arousal 307.46 ●
    confusional 327.41 ●
  circadian rhythm 327.30 ▲
    advanced sleep phase type 327.32 ●
    alcohol induced 291.82 ●
    delayed sleep phase type 327.31 ●
    drug induced 292.85 ●
    free running type 327.34 ●
    in conditions classified elsewhere 327.37 ●
    irregular sleep-wake type 327.33 ●
    jet lag type 327.35 ●
    other 327.39 ●
    shift work type 327.36 ●
  drug induced 292.85
  initiation or maintenance (*see also* Insomnia) 780.52
    nonorganic origin (transient) 307.41
      persistent 307.42
  nonorganic origin 307.40
    specified type NEC 307.49
  organic specified type NEC 327.8 ●
  periodic limb movement 327.51 ●
  specified NEC 780.59 ●
  wake ●
    cycle — *see* Disorder, sleep, circadian rhythm ●
    schedule — *see* Disorder, sleep, circadian rhythm ●
social, of childhood and adolescence 313.22
  specified NEC 780.59
soft tissue 729.9
somatization 300.81
somatoform (atypical) (undifferentiated) 300.82
  severe 300.81
  specified type NEC 300.89
speech NEC 784.5
  nonorganic origin 307.9
spine NEC 724.9
  ligamentous or muscular attachments, peripheral 720.1
steroid metabolism NEC 255.2
stomach (functional) (*see also* Disorder, gastric) 536.9
  psychogenic 306.4
storage, iron 275.0
stress (*see also* Reaction, stress, acute) 308.3
  posttraumatic
    acute 309.81
    brief 309.81
    chronic 309.81
substitution 300.11
suspected — *see* Observation
synovium 727.9
temperature regulation, fetus or newborn 778.4
temporomandibular joint NEC 524.60
  sounds on opening or closing 524.64
  specified NEC 524.69

Disorder — *see also* Disease — *continued*
tendon 727.9
  shoulder region 726.10
thoracic root (nerve) NEC 353.3
thyrocalcitonin secretion 246.0
thyroid (gland) NEC 246.9
  specified type NEC 246.8
tic 307.20
  chronic (motor or vocal) 307.22
  motor-verbal 307.23
  organic origin 333.1
  transient (of childhood) 307.21
tooth NEC 525.9
  development NEC 520.9
    specified type NEC 520.8
  eruption 520.6
  specified type NEC 525.8
Tourette's 307.23
transport, carbohydrate 271.9
  specified type NEC 271.8
tubular, phosphate-losing 588.0
tympanic membrane 384.9
unaggressive, unsocialized (*see also* Disturbance, conduct) 312.1 ☑
undersocialized, unsocialized (*see also* Disturbance, conduct)
  aggressive (type) 312.0 ☑
  unaggressive (type) 312.1 ☑
vision, visual NEC 368.9
  binocular NEC 368.30
  cortex 377.73
    associated with
      inflammatory disorders 377.73
      neoplasms 377.71
      vascular disorders 377.72
  pathway NEC 377.63
    associated with
      inflammatory disorders 377.63
      neoplasms 377.61
      vascular disorders 377.62
vocal tic
  chronic 307.22
wakefulness (*see also* Hypersomnia) 780.54
  nonorganic origin (transient) 307.43
    persistent 307.44
written expression 315.2
Disorganized globe 360.29
Displacement, displaced

> Note — For acquired displacement of bones, cartilage, joints, tendons, due to injury, see also Dislocation.
>
> Displacements at ages under one year should be considered congenital, provided there is no indication the condition was acquired after birth.

acquired traumatic of bone, cartilage, joint, tendon NEC (without fracture) (*see also* Dislocation) 839.8
  with fracture — *see* Fracture, by site
adrenal gland (congenital) 759.1
alveolus and teeth, vertical 524.75
appendix, retrocecal (congenital) 751.5
auricle (congenital) 744.29
bladder (acquired) 596.8
  congenital 753.8
brachial plexus (congenital) 742.8
brain stem, caudal 742.4
canaliculus lacrimalis 743.65
cardia, through esophageal hiatus 750.6
cerebellum, caudal 742.4
cervix (*see also* Malposition, uterus) 621.6
colon (congenital) 751.4
device, implant, or graft — *see* Complications, mechanical
epithelium
  columnar of cervix 622.10
  cuboidal, beyond limits of external os (uterus) 752.49
esophageal mucosa into cardia of stomach, congenital 750.4
esophagus (acquired) 530.89
  congenital 750.4
eyeball (acquired) (old) 376.36
  congenital 743.8
  current injury 871.3
  lateral 376.36

Displacement, displaced — *continued*
fallopian tube (acquired) 620.4
  congenital 752.19
  opening (congenital) 752.19
gallbladder (congenital) 751.69
gastric mucosa 750.7
  into
    duodenum 750.7
    esophagus 750.7
    Meckel's diverticulum, congenital 750.7
globe (acquired) (lateral) (old) 376.36
  current injury 871.3
graft
  artificial skin graft 996.55
  decellularized allodermis graft 996.55
heart (congenital) 746.87
  acquired 429.89
hymen (congenital) (upward) 752.49
internal prosthesis NEC — *see* Complications, mechanical
intervertebral disc (with neuritis, radiculitis, sciatica, or other pain) 722.2
  with myelopathy 722.70
  cervical, cervicodorsal, cervicothoracic 722.0
    with myelopathy 722.71
    due to major trauma — *see* Dislocation, vertebra, cervical
  due to major trauma — *see* Dislocation, vertebra
  lumbar, lumbosacral 722.10
    with myelopathy 722.73
    due to major trauma — *see* Dislocation, vertebra, lumbar
  thoracic, thoracolumbar 722.11
    with myelopathy 722.72
    due to major trauma — *see* Dislocation, vertebra, thoracic
intrauterine device 996.32
kidney (acquired) 593.0
  congenital 753.3
lacrimal apparatus or duct (congenital) 743.65
macula (congenital) 743.55
Meckel's diverticulum (congenital) 751.0
nail (congenital) 757.5
  acquired 703.8
opening of Wharton's duct in mouth 750.26
organ or site, congenital NEC — *see* Malposition, congenital
ovary (acquired) 620.4
  congenital 752.0
  free in peritoneal cavity (congenital) 752.0
  into hernial sac 620.4
oviduct (acquired) 620.4
  congenital 752.19
parathyroid (gland) 252.8
parotid gland (congenital) 750.26
punctum lacrimale (congenital) 743.65
sacroiliac (congenital) (joint) 755.69
  current injury — *see* Dislocation, sacroiliac
  old 724.6
spine (congenital) 756.19
spleen, congenital 759.0
stomach (congenital) 750.7
  acquired 537.89
subglenoid (closed) 831.01
sublingual duct (congenital) 750.26
teeth, tooth 524.30
  horizontal 524.33
  vertical 524.34
tongue (congenital) (downward) 750.19
trachea (congenital) 748.3
ureter or ureteric opening or orifice (congenital) 753.4
uterine opening of oviducts or fallopian tubes 752.19
uterus, uterine (*see also* Malposition, uterus) 621.6
  congenital 752.3
ventricular septum 746.89
  with rudimentary ventricle 746.89
xyphoid bone (process) 738.3
Disproportion 653.9 ☑
affecting fetus or newborn 763.1
caused by
  conjoined twins 653.7 ☑
  contraction, pelvis (general) 653.1 ☑
    inlet 653.2 ☑

Disproportion — *continued*
  caused by — *continued*
    contraction, pelvis — *continued*
      midpelvic 653.8 ☑
      midplane 653.8 ☑
      outlet 653.3 ☑
    fetal
      ascites 653.7 ☑
      hydrocephalus 653.6 ☑
      hydrops 653.7 ☑
      meningomyelocele 653.7 ☑
      sacral teratoma 653.7 ☑
      tumor 653.7 ☑
    hydrocephalic fetus 653.6 ☑
    pelvis, pelvic, abnormality (bony) NEC 653.0 ☑
    unusually large fetus 653.5 ☑
  causing obstructed labor 660.1 ☑
  cephalopelvic, normally formed fetus 653.4 ☑
    causing obstructed labor 660.1 ☑
  fetal NEC 653.5 ☑
    causing obstructed labor 660.1 ☑
  fetopelvic, normally formed fetus 653.4 ☑
    causing obstructed labor 660.1 ☑
  mixed maternal and fetal origin, normally formed fetus 653.4 ☑
  pelvis, pelvic (bony) NEC 653.1 ☑
    causing obstructed labor 660.1 ☑
  specified type NEC 653.8 ☑

Disruption
  cesarean wound 674.1 ☑
  family V61.0
  gastrointestinal anastomosis 997.4
  ligament(s) — *see also* Sprain
    knee
      current injury — *see* Dislocation, knee
      old 717.89
        capsular 717.85
        collateral (medial) 717.82
          lateral 717.81
        cruciate (posterior) 717.84
          anterior 717.83
        specified site NEC 717.85
  marital V61.10
    involving divorce or estrangement V61.0
  operation wound (external) 998.32
    internal 998.31
  organ transplant, anastomosis site — *see* Complications, transplant, organ, by site
  ossicles, ossicular chain 385.23
    traumatic — *see* Fracture, skull, base
  parenchyma
    liver (hepatic) — *see* Laceration, liver, major
    spleen — *see* Laceration, spleen, parenchyma, massive
  phase-shift, of 24 hour sleep wake cycle, ▶unspecified◀ 780.55
    nonorganic origin 307.45
  sleep wake cycle (24 hour), ▶unspecified◀ 780.55
    circadian rhythm 327.33 ▲
    nonorganic origin 307.45
  suture line (external) 998.32
    internal 998.31
  wound
    cesarean operation 674.1 ☑
    episiotomy 674.2 ☑
    operation 998.32
      cesarean 674.1 ☑
      internal 998.31
    perineal (obstetric) 674.2 ☑
    uterine 674.1 ☑

Disruptio uteri — *see also* Rupture, uterus
  complicating delivery — *see* Delivery, complicated, rupture, uterus

Dissatisfaction with
  employment V62.2
  school environment V62.3

Dissecting — *see* condition

Dissection
  aorta 441.00
    abdominal 441.02
    thoracic 441.01
    thoracoabdominal 441.03

Dissection — *continued*
  artery, arterial
    carotid 443.21
    coronary 414.12
    iliac 443.22
    renal 443.23
    specified NEC 443.29
    vertebral 443.24
  vascular 459.9
  wound — *see* Wound, open, by site

Disseminated — *see* condition

Dissociated personality NEC 300.15

Dissociation
  auriculoventricular or atrioventricular (any degree) (AV) 426.89
    with heart block 426.0
  interference 426.89
  isorhythmic 426.89
  rhythm
    atrioventricular (AV) 426.89
    interference 426.89

Dissociative
  identity disorder 300.14
  reaction NEC 300.15

Dissolution, vertebra (*see also* Osteoporosis) 733.00

Distention
  abdomen (gaseous) 787.3
  bladder 596.8
  cecum 569.89
  colon 569.89
  gallbladder 575.8
  gaseous (abdomen) 787.3
  intestine 569.89
  kidney 593.89
  liver 573.9
  seminal vesicle 608.89
  stomach 536.8
    acute 536.1
    psychogenic 306.4
  ureter 593.5
  uterus 621.8

Distichia, distichiasis (eyelid) 743.63

Distoma hepaticum infestation 121.3

Distomiasis 121.9
  bile passages 121.3
    due to Clonorchis sinensis 121.1
  hemic 120.9
  hepatic (liver) 121.3
    due to Clonorchis sinensis (clonorchiasis) 121.1
  intestinal 121.4
  liver 121.3
    due to Clonorchis sinensis 121.1
  lung 121.2
  pulmonary 121.2

Distomolar (fourth molar) 520.1
  causing crowding 524.31

Disto-occlusion (division I) (division II) 524.22

Distortion (congenital)
  adrenal (gland) 759.1
  ankle (joint) 755.69
  anus 751.5
  aorta 747.29
  appendix 751.5
  arm 755.59
  artery (peripheral) NEC (*see also* Distortion, peripheral vascular system) 747.60
    cerebral 747.81
    coronary 746.85
    pulmonary 747.3
    retinal 743.58
    umbilical 747.5
  auditory canal 744.29
    causing impairment of hearing 744.02
  bile duct or passage 751.69
  bladder 753.8
  brain 742.4
  bronchus 748.3
  cecum 751.5
  cervix (uteri) 752.49
  chest (wall) 756.3
  clavicle 755.51
  clitoris 752.49

Distortion — *continued*
  coccyx 756.19
  colon 751.5
  common duct 751.69
  cornea 743.41
  cricoid cartilage 748.3
  cystic duct 751.69
  duodenum 751.5
  ear 744.29
    auricle 744.29
      causing impairment of hearing 744.02
      causing impairment of hearing 744.09
    external 744.29
      causing impairment of hearing 744.02
    inner 744.05
    middle, except ossicles 744.03
      ossicles 744.04
    ossicles 744.04
  endocrine (gland) NEC 759.2
  epiglottis 748.3
  Eustachian tube 744.24
  eye 743.8
    adnexa 743.69
  face bone(s) 756.0
  fallopian tube 752.19
  femur 755.69
  fibula 755.69
  finger(s) 755.59
  foot 755.67
  gallbladder 751.69
  genitalia, genital organ(s)
    female 752.89
      external 752.49
      internal NEC 752.89
    male 752.89
      penis 752.69
  glottis 748.3
  gyri 742.4
  hand bone(s) 755.59
  heart (auricle) (ventricle) 746.89
    valve (cusp) 746.89
  hepatic duct 751.69
  humerus 755.59
  hymen 752.49
  ileum 751.5
  intestine (large) (small) 751.5
    with anomalous adhesions, fixation or malrotation 751.4
  jaw NEC 524.89
  jejunum 751.5
  kidney 753.3
  knee (joint) 755.64
  labium (majus) (minus) 752.49
  larynx 748.3
  leg 755.69
  lens 743.36
  liver 751.69
  lumbar spine 756.19
    with disproportion (fetopelvic) 653.0 ☑
      affecting fetus or newborn 763.1
      causing obstructed labor 660.1 ☑
  lumbosacral (joint) (region) 756.19
  lung (fissures) (lobe) 748.69
  nerve 742.8
  nose 748.1
  organ
    of Corti 744.05
    of site not listed — *see* Anomaly, specified type NEC
  ossicles, ear 744.04
  ovary 752.0
  oviduct 752.19
  pancreas 751.7
  parathyroid (gland) 759.2
  patella 755.64
  peripheral vascular system NEC 747.60
    gastrointestinal 747.61
    lower limb 747.64
    renal 747.62
    spinal 747.82
    upper limb 747.63
  pituitary (gland) 759.2
  radius 755.59
  rectum 751.5
  rib 756.3
  sacroiliac joint 755.69
  sacrum 756.19

2006 ICD-9-CM

☑ Additional Digit Required — Refer to the Tabular List (Numeric Code Section) for Additional Digit Selection
▶◀ Revised Text   ● New Line   ▲ Revised Code

October 2005 • Volume 2 — 117

Distortion — continued
- scapula 755.59
- shoulder girdle 755.59
- site not listed — see Anomaly, specified type NEC
- skull bone(s) 756.0
  - with
    - anencephalus 740.0
    - encephalocele 742.0
    - hydrocephalus 742.3
      - with spina bifida (see also Spina bifida) 741.0 ☑
    - microcephalus 742.1
- spinal cord 742.59
- spine 756.19
- spleen 759.0
- sternum 756.3
- thorax (wall) 756.3
- thymus (gland) 759.2
- thyroid (gland) 759.2
  - cartilage 748.3
- tibia 755.69
- toe(s) 755.66
- tongue 750.19
- trachea (cartilage) 748.3
- ulna 755.59
- ureter 753.4
  - causing obstruction 753.20
- urethra 753.8
  - causing obstruction 753.6
- uterus 752.3
- vagina 752.49
- vein (peripheral) NEC (see also Distortion, peripheral vascular system) 747.60
  - great 747.49
  - portal 747.49
  - pulmonary 747.49
- vena cava (inferior) (superior) 747.49
- vertebra 756.19
- visual NEC 368.15
  - shape or size 368.14
- vulva 752.49
- wrist (bones) (joint) 755.59

Distress
- abdomen 789.0 ☑
- colon 564.9
- emotional V40.9
- epigastric 789.0 ☑
- fetal (syndrome) 768.4
  - affecting management of pregnancy or childbirth 656.8 ☑
  - liveborn infant 768.4
    - first noted
      - before onset of labor 768.2
      - during labor or delivery 768.3
    - stillborn infant (death before onset of labor) 768.0
    - death during labor 768.1
- gastrointestinal (functional) 536.9
  - psychogenic 306.4
- intestinal (functional) NEC 564.9
  - psychogenic 306.4
- intrauterine — see Distress, fetal
- leg 729.5
- maternal 669.0 ☑
- mental V40.9
- respiratory 786.09
  - acute (adult) 518.82
  - adult syndrome (following shock, surgery, or trauma) 518.5
    - specified NEC 518.82
  - fetus or newborn 770.89
  - syndrome (idiopathic) (newborn) 769
- stomach 536.9
  - psychogenic 306.4

Distribution vessel, atypical NEC 747.60
- coronary artery 746.85
- spinal 747.82

Districhiasis 704.2

Disturbance — see also Disease
- absorption NEC 579.9
  - calcium 269.3
  - carbohydrate 579.8
  - fat 579.8
  - protein 579.8
  - specified type NEC 579.8
  - vitamin (see also Deficiency, vitamin) 269.2

Disturbance — see also Disease — continued
- acid-base equilibrium 276.9
- activity and attention, simple, with hyperkinesis 314.01
- amino acid (metabolic) (see also Disorder, amino acid) 270.9
  - imidazole 270.5
  - maple syrup (urine) disease 270.3
  - transport 270.0
- assimilation, food 579.9
- attention, simple 314.00
  - with hyperactivity 314.01
- auditory, nerve, except deafness 388.5
- behavior (see also Disturbance, conduct) 312.9
- blood clotting (hypoproteinemia) (mechanism) (see also Defect, coagulation) 286.9
- central nervous system NEC 349.9
- cerebral nerve NEC 352.9
- circulatory 459.9
- conduct 312.9

Note — Use the following fifth-digit subclassification with categories 312.0–312.2:

0	unspecified
1	mild
2	moderate
3	severe

- adjustment reaction 309.3
- adolescent onset type 312.82
- childhood onset type 312.81
- compulsive 312.30
  - intermittent explosive disorder 312.34
  - isolated explosive disorder 312.35
  - kleptomania 312.32
  - pathological gambling 312.31
  - pyromania 312.33
- hyperkinetic 314.2
- intermittent explosive 312.34
- isolated explosive 312.35
- mixed with emotions 312.4
- socialized (type) 312.20
  - aggressive 312.23
  - unaggressive 312.21
- specified type NEC 312.89
- undersocialized, unsocialized
  - aggressive (type) 312.0 ☑
  - unaggressive (type) 312.1 ☑
- coordination 781.3
- cranial nerve NEC 352.9
- deep sensibility — see Disturbance, sensation
- digestive 536.9
  - psychogenic 306.4
- electrolyte — see Imbalance, electrolyte
- emotions specific to childhood or adolescence 313.9
  - with
    - academic underachievement 313.83
    - anxiety and fearfulness 313.0
    - elective mutism 313.23
    - identity disorder 313.82
    - jealousy 313.3
    - misery and unhappiness 313.1
    - oppositional defiant disorder 313.81
    - overanxiousness 313.0
    - sensitivity 313.21
    - shyness 313.21
    - social withdrawal 313.22
    - withdrawal reaction 313.22
  - involving relationship problems 313.3
  - mixed 313.89
  - specified type NEC 313.89
- endocrine (gland) 259.9
  - neonatal, transitory 775.9
    - specified NEC 775.8
- equilibrium 780.4
- feeding (elderly) (infant) 783.3
  - newborn 779.3
    - nonorganic origin NEC 307.59
    - psychogenic NEC 307.59
- fructose metabolism 271.2
- gait 781.2
  - hysterical 300.11
- gastric (functional) 536.9
  - motility 536.8
  - psychogenic 306.4
  - secretion 536.8

Disturbance — see also Disease — continued
- gastrointestinal (functional) 536.9
  - psychogenic 306.4
- habit, child 307.9
- hearing, except deafness 388.40
- heart, functional (conditions classifiable to 426, 427, 428)
  - due to presence of (cardiac) prosthesis 429.4
  - postoperative (immediate) 997.1
    - long-term effect of cardiac surgery 429.4
  - psychogenic 306.2
- hormone 259.9
- innervation uterus, sympathetic, parasympathetic 621.8
- keratinization NEC
  - gingiva 523.1
  - lip 528.5
  - oral (mucosa) (soft tissue) 528.79
    - residual ridge mucosa
      - excessive 528.72
      - minimal 528.71
  - tongue 528.79
- labyrinth, labyrinthine (vestibule) 386.9
- learning, specific NEC 315.2
- memory (see also Amnesia) 780.93
  - mild, following organic brain damage 310.8
- mental (see also Disorder, mental) 300.9
  - associated with diseases classified elsewhere 316
- metabolism (acquired) (congenital) (see also Disorder, metabolism) 277.9
  - with
    - abortion — see Abortion, by type, with metabolic disorder
    - ectopic pregnancy (see also categories 633.0-633.9) 639.4
    - molar pregnancy (see also categories 630-632) 639.4
  - amino acid (see also Disorder, amino acid) 270.9
    - aromatic NEC 270.2
    - branched-chain 270.3
    - specified type NEC 270.8
    - straight-chain NEC 270.7
    - sulfur-bearing 270.4
    - transport 270.0
  - ammonia 270.6
  - arginine 270.6
  - argininosuccinic acid 270.6
  - carbohydrate NEC 271.9
  - cholesterol 272.9
  - citrulline 270.6
  - cystathionine 270.4
  - fat 272.9
  - following
    - abortion 639.4
    - ectopic or molar pregnancy 639.4
  - general 277.9
    - carbohydrate 271.9
    - iron 275.0
    - phosphate 275.3
    - sodium 276.9
  - glutamine 270.7
  - glycine 270.7
  - histidine 270.5
  - homocystine 270.4
  - in labor or delivery 669.0 ☑
  - iron 275.0
  - isoleucine 270.3
  - leucine 270.3
  - lipoid 272.9
    - specified type NEC 272.8
  - lysine 270.7
  - methionine 270.4
  - neonatal, transitory 775.9
    - specified type NEC 775.8
  - nitrogen 788.9
  - ornithine 270.6
  - phosphate 275.3
  - phosphatides 272.7
  - serine 270.7
  - sodium NEC 276.9
  - threonine 270.7
  - tryptophan 270.2
  - tyrosine 270.2
  - urea cycle 270.6
  - valine 270.3

Disturbance — *see also* Disease — *continued*
motor 796.1
nervous functional 799.2
neuromuscular mechanism (eye) due to
syphilis 094.84
nutritional 269.9
nail 703.8
ocular motion 378.87
psychogenic 306.7
oculogyric 378.87
psychogenic 306.7
oculomotor NEC 378.87
psychogenic 306.7
olfactory nerve 781.1
optic nerve NEC 377.49
oral epithelium, including tongue 528.79
residual ridge mucosa
excessive 528.72
minimal 528.71
personality (pattern) (trait) (*see also* Disorder,
personality) 301.9
following organic brain damage 310.1
polyglandular 258.9
psychomotor 307.9
pupillary 379.49
reflex 796.1
rhythm, heart 427.9
postoperative (immediate) 997.1
long-term effect of cardiac surgery 429.4
psychogenic 306.2
salivary secretion 527.7
sensation (cold) (heat) (localization) (tactile
discrimination localization) (texture)
(vibratory) NEC 782.0
hysterical 300.11
skin 782.0
smell 781.1
taste 781.1
sensory (*see also* Disturbance, sensation) 782.0
innervation 782.0
situational (transient) (*see also* Reaction,
adjustment) 309.9
acute 308.3
sleep 780.50
with apnea — *see* Apnea, sleep
initiation or maintenance (*see also*
Insomnia) 780.52
nonorganic origin 307.41
nonorganic origin 307.40
specified type NEC 307.49
specified NEC 780.59
nonorganic origin 307.49
wakefulness (*see also* Hypersomnia) 780.54
nonorganic origin 307.43
sociopathic 301.7
speech NEC 784.5
developmental 315.39
associated with hyperkinesis 314.1
secondary to organic lesion 784.5
stomach (functional) (*see also* Disturbance,
gastric) 536.9
sympathetic (nerve) (*see also* Neuropathy,
peripheral, autonomic) 337.9
temperature sense 782.0
hysterical 300.11
tooth
eruption 520.6
formation 520.4
structure, hereditary NEC 520.5
touch (*see also* Disturbance, sensation) 782.0
vascular 459.9
arteriosclerotic — *see* Arteriosclerosis
vasomotor 443.9
vasospastic 443.9
vestibular labyrinth 386.9
vision, visual NEC 368.9
psychophysical 368.16
specified NEC 368.8
subjective 368.10
voice 784.40
wakefulness (initiation or maintenance) (*see
also* Hypersomnia) 780.54
nonorganic origin 307.43

Disulfiduria, beta-mercaptolactate-cysteine
270.0

Disuse atrophy, bone 733.7

Ditthomska syndrome 307.81
Diuresis 788.42
Divers'
palsy or paralysis 993.3
squeeze 993.3
Diverticula, diverticulosis, diverticulum (acute)
(multiple) (perforated) (ruptured) 562.10
with diverticulitis 562.11
aorta (Kommerell's) 747.21
appendix (noninflammatory) 543.9
bladder (acquired) (sphincter) 596.3
congenital 753.8
broad ligament 620.8
bronchus (congenital) 748.3
acquired 494.0
with acute exacerbation 494.1
calyx, calyceal (kidney) 593.89
cardia (stomach) 537.1
cecum 562.10
with
diverticulitis 562.11
with hemorrhage 562.13
hemorrhage 562.12
congenital 751.5
colon (acquired) 562.10
with
diverticulitis 562.11
with hemorrhage 562.13
hemorrhage 562.12
congenital 751.5
duodenum 562.00
with
diverticulitis 562.01
with hemorrhage 562.03
hemorrhage 562.02
congenital 751.5
epiphrenic (esophagus) 530.6
esophagus (congenital) 750.4
acquired 530.6
epiphrenic 530.6
pulsion 530.6
traction 530.6
Zenker's 530.6
Eustachian tube 381.89
fallopian tube 620.8
gallbladder (congenital) 751.69
gastric 537.1
heart (congenital) 746.89
ileum 562.00
with
diverticulitis 562.01
with hemorrhage 562.03
hemorrhage 562.02
intestine (large) 562.10
with
diverticulitis 562.11
with hemorrhage 562.13
hemorrhage 562.12
congenital 751.5
small 562.00
with
diverticulitis 562.01
with hemorrhage 562.03
hemorrhage 562.02
congenital 751.5
jejunum 562.00
with
diverticulitis 562.01
with hemorrhage 562.03
hemorrhage 562.02
kidney (calyx) (pelvis) 593.89
with calculus 592.0
Kommerell's 747.21
laryngeal ventricle (congenital) 748.3
Meckel's (displaced) (hypertrophic) 751.0
midthoracic 530.6
organ or site, congenital NEC — *see* Distortion
pericardium (congenital) (cyst) 746.89
acquired (true) 423.8
pharyngoesophageal (pulsion) 530.6
pharynx (congenital) 750.27
pulsion (esophagus) 530.6
rectosigmoid 562.10
with
diverticulitis 562.11
with hemorrhage 562.13

Diverticula, diverticulosis, diverticulum —
continued
rectosigmoid — *continued*
with — *continued*
hemorrhage 562.12
congenital 751.5
rectum 562.10
with
diverticulitis 562.11
with hemorrhage 562.13
hemorrhage 562.12
renal (calyces) (pelvis) 593.89
with calculus 592.0
Rokitansky's 530.6
seminal vesicle 608.0
sigmoid 562.10
with
diverticulitis 562.11
with hemorrhage 562.13
hemorrhage 562.12
congenital 751.5
small intestine 562.00
with
diverticulitis 562.01
with hemorrhage 562.03
hemorrhage 562.02
stomach (cardia) (juxtacardia) (juxtapyloric)
(acquired) 537.1
congenital 750.7
subdiaphragmatic 530.6
trachea (congenital) 748.3
acquired 519.1
traction (esophagus) 530.6
ureter (acquired) 593.89
congenital 753.4
ureterovesical orifice 593.89
urethra (acquired) 599.2
congenital 753.8
ventricle, left (congenital) 746.89
vesical (urinary) 596.3
congenital 753.8
Zenker's (esophagus) 530.6
Diverticulitis (acute) (*see also* Diverticula) 562.11
with hemorrhage 562.13
bladder (urinary) 596.3
cecum (perforated) 562.11
with hemorrhage 562.13
colon (perforated) 562.11
with hemorrhage 562.13
duodenum 562.01
with hemorrhage 562.03
esophagus 530.6
ileum (perforated) 562.01
with hemorrhage 562.03
intestine (large) (perforated) 562.11
with hemorrhage 562.13
small 562.01
with hemorrhage 562.03
jejunum (perforated) 562.01
with hemorrhage 562.03
Meckel's (perforated) 751.0
pharyngoesophageal 530.6
rectosigmoid (perforated) 562.11
with hemorrhage 562.13
rectum 562.11
with hemorrhage 562.13
sigmoid (old) (perforated) 562.11
with hemorrhage 562.13
small intestine (perforated) 562.01
with hemorrhage 562.03
vesical (urinary) 596.3
Diverticulosis — *see* Diverticula
Division
cervix uteri 622.8
external os into two openings by frenum
752.49
external (cervical) into two openings by frenum
752.49
glans penis 752.69
hymen 752.49
labia minora (congenital) 752.49
ligament (partial or complete) (current) — *see
also* Sprain, by site
with open wound — *see* Wound, open, by
site

2006 ICD-9-CM

☑ Additional Digit Required — Refer to the Tabular List (Numeric Code Section) for Additional Digit Selection
►◄ Revised Text   ● New Line   ▲ Revised Code

Volume 2 — 119

Division — continued
  muscle (partial or complete) (current) — see also Sprain, by site
    with open wound — see Wound, open, by site
  nerve — see Injury, nerve, by site
  penis glans 752.69
  spinal cord — see Injury, spinal, by site
  vein 459.9
    traumatic — see Injury, vascular, by site
Divorce V61.0
Dix-Hallpike neurolabyrinthitis 386.12
Dizziness 780.4
  hysterical 300.11
  psychogenic 306.9
Doan-Wiseman syndrome (primary splenic neutropenia) 288.0
Dog bite — see Wound, open, by site
Döhle-Heller aortitis 093.1
Döhle body-panmyelopathic syndrome 288.2
Dolichocephaly, dolichocephalus 754.0
Dolichocolon 751.5
Dolichostenomelia 759.82
Donohue's syndrome (leprechaunism) 259.8
Donor
  blood V59.01
    other blood components V59.09
    stem cells V59.02
    whole blood V59.01
  bone V59.2
    marrow V59.3
  cornea V59.5
  egg (oocyte) (ovum) V59.70
    over age 35 V59.73
      anonymous recipient V59.73
      designated recipient V59.74
    under age 35 V59.71
      anonymous recipient V59.71
      designated recipient V59.72
  heart V59.8
  kidney V59.4
  liver V59.6
  lung V59.8
  lymphocyte V59.8
  organ V59.9
    specified NEC V59.8
  potential, examination of V70.8
  skin V59.1
  specified organ or tissue NEC V59.8
  sperm V59.8
  stem cells V59.02
  tissue V59.9
    specified type NEC V59.8
Donovanosis (granuloma venereum) 099.2
DOPS (diffuse obstructive pulmonary syndrome) 496
Double
  albumin 273.8
  aortic arch 747.21
  auditory canal 744.29
  auricle (heart) 746.82
  bladder 753.8
  external (cervical) os 752.49
  kidney with double pelvis (renal) 753.3
  larynx 748.3
  meatus urinarius 753.8
  organ or site NEC — see Accessory
  orifice
    heart valve NEC 746.89
      pulmonary 746.09
  outlet, right ventricle 745.11
  pelvis (renal) with double ureter 753.4
  penis 752.69
  tongue 750.13
  ureter (one or both sides) 753.4
    with double pelvis (renal) 753.4
  urethra 753.8
  urinary meatus 753.8
  uterus (any degree) 752.2
    with doubling of cervix and vagina 752.2
    in pregnancy or childbirth 654.0 ☑
      affecting fetus or newborn 763.89
  vagina 752.49
    with doubling of cervix and uterus 752.2

Double — continued
  vision 368.2
  vocal cords 748.3
  vulva 752.49
  whammy (syndrome) 360.81
Douglas' pouch, cul-de-sac — see condition
Down's disease or syndrome (mongolism) 758.0
Down-growth, epithelial (anterior chamber) 364.61
Dracontiasis 125.7
Dracunculiasis 125.7
Dracunculosis 125.7
Drainage
  abscess (spontaneous) — see Abscess
  anomalous pulmonary veins to hepatic veins or right atrium 747.41
  stump (amputation) (surgical) 997.62
  suprapubic, bladder 596.8
Dream state, hysterical 300.13
Drepanocytic anemia (see also Disease, sickle cell) 282.60
Dresbach's syndrome (elliptocytosis) 282.1
Dreschlera (infection) 118
  hawaiiensis 117.8
Dressler's syndrome (postmyocardial infarction) 411.0
Dribbling (post-void) 788.35
Drift, ulnar 736.09
Drinking (alcohol) — see also Alcoholism
  excessive, to excess NEC (see also Abuse, drugs, nondependent) 305.0 ☑
    bouts, periodic 305.0 ☑
    continual 303.9 ☑
    episodic 305.0 ☑
    habitual 303.9 ☑
    periodic 305.0 ☑
Drip, postnasal (chronic) — see Sinusitis
Drivers' license examination V70.3
Droop
  Cooper's 611.8
  facial 781.94
Drop
  finger 736.29
  foot 736.79
  hematocrit (precipitous) 790.01
  toe 735.8
  wrist 736.05
Dropped
  dead 798.1
  heart beats 426.6
Dropsy, dropsical (see also Edema) 782.3
  abdomen 789.5
  amnion (see also Hydramnios) 657.0 ☑
  brain — see Hydrocephalus
  cardiac (see also Failure, heart) 428.0
  cardiorenal (see also Hypertension, cardiorenal) 404.90
  chest 511.9
  fetus or newborn 778.0
    due to isoimmunization 773.3
  gangrenous (see also Gangrene) 785.4
  heart (see also Failure, heart) 428.0
  hepatic — see Cirrhosis, liver
  infantile — see Hydrops, fetalis
  kidney (see also Nephrosis) 581.9
  liver — see Cirrhosis, liver
  lung 514
  malarial (see also Malaria) 084.9
  neonatorum — see Hydrops, fetalis
  nephritic 581.9
  newborn — see Hydrops, fetalis
  nutritional 269.9
  ovary 620.8
  pericardium (see also Pericarditis) 423.9
  renal (see also Nephrosis) 581.9
  uremic — see Uremia
Drowned, drowning 994.1
  lung 518.5
Drowsiness 780.09
Drug — see also condition
  addiction (see also listing under Dependence) 304.9 ☑

Drug — see also condition — continued
  adverse effect NEC, correct substance properly administered 995.2
  dependence (see also listing under Dependence) 304.9 ☑
  habit (see also listing under Dependence) 304.9 ☑
  induced
    circadian rhythm sleep disorder 292.85 ●
    hypersomnia 292.85 ●
    insomnia 292.85 ●
    mental disorder 292.9
      anxiety 292.89
      mood 292.84
      sexual 292.89
      sleep 292.85 ▲
      specified type 292.89
    parasomnia 292.85 ●
    persisting
      amnestic disorder 292.83
      dementia 292.82
    psychotic disorder
      with
        delusions 292.11
        hallucinations 292.12
    sleep disorder 292.85 ●
  intoxication 292.89
  overdose — see Table of Drugs and Chemicals
  poisoning — see Table of Drugs and Chemicals
  therapy (maintenance) status NEC
    chemotherapy, antineoplastic V58.11 ●
    immunotherapy, antineoplastic V58.12 ●
    long-term (current) use V58.69
      antibiotics V58.62
      anticoagulants V58.61
      anti-inflammatories, non-steroidal (NSAID) V58.64
      antiplatelets V58.63
      antithrombotics V58.63
      aspirin V58.66
      insulin V58.67
      steroids V58.65
  wrong substance given or taken in error — see Table of Drugs and Chemicals
Drunkenness (see also Abuse, drugs, nondependent) 305.0 ☑
  acute in alcoholism (see also Alcoholism) 303.0 ☑
  chronic (see also Alcoholism) 303.9 ☑
  pathologic 291.4
  simple (acute) 305.0 ☑
    in alcoholism 303.0 ☑
  sleep 307.47
Drusen
  optic disc or papilla 377.21
  retina (colloid) (hyaloid degeneration) 362.57
    hereditary 362.77
Drusenfieber 075
Dry, dryness — see also condition
  eye 375.15
    syndrome 375.15
  larynx 478.79
  mouth 527.7
  nose 478.1
  skin syndrome 701.1
  socket (teeth) 526.5
  throat 478.29
DSAP (disseminated superficial actinic porokeratosis) 692.75
Duane's retraction syndrome 378.71
Duane-Stilling-Türk syndrome (ocular retraction syndrome) 378.71
Dubin-Johnson disease or syndrome 277.4
Dubini's disease (electric chorea) 049.8
Dubois' abscess or disease 090.5
Duchenne's
  disease 094.0
    locomotor ataxia 094.0
    muscular dystrophy 359.1
    pseudohypertrophy, muscles 359.1
  paralysis 335.22
  syndrome 335.22

Duchenne-Aran myelopathic, muscular atrophy
(nonprogressive) (progressive) 335.21
Duchenne-Griesinger disease 359.1
Ducrey's
bacillus 099.0
chancre 099.0
disease (chancroid) 099.0
Duct, ductus — *see* condition
Duengero 061
Duhring's disease (dermatitis herpetiformis) 694.0
Dukes (-Filatov) disease 057.8
Dullness
cardiac (decreased) (increased) 785.3
Dumb ague (*see also* Malaria) 084.6
Dumbness (*see also* Aphasia) 784.3
Dumdum fever 085.0
Dumping syndrome (postgastrectomy) 564.2
nonsurgical 536.8
Duodenitis (nonspecific) (peptic) 535.60
with hemorrhage 535.61
due to
Strongyloides stercoralis 127.2
Duodenocholangitis 575.8
Duodenum, duodenal — *see* condition
Duplay's disease, periarthritis, or syndrome
726.2
Duplex — *see also* Accessory
kidney 753.3
placenta — *see* Placenta, abnormal
uterus 752.2
Duplication — *see also* Accessory
anus 751.5
aortic arch 747.21
appendix 751.5
biliary duct (any) 751.69
bladder 753.8
cecum 751.5
and appendix 751.5
clitoris 752.49
cystic duct 751.69
digestive organs 751.8
duodenum 751.5
esophagus 750.4
fallopian tube 752.19
frontonasal process 756.0
gallbladder 751.69
ileum 751.5
intestine (large) (small) 751.5
jejunum 751.5
kidney 753.3
liver 751.69
nose 748.1
pancreas 751.7
penis 752.69
respiratory organs NEC 748.9
salivary duct 750.22
spinal cord (incomplete) 742.51
stomach 750.7
ureter 753.4
vagina 752.49
vas deferens 752.89
vocal cords 748.3
Dupré's disease or syndrome (meningism) 781.6
Dupuytren's
contraction 728.6
disease (muscle contracture) 728.6
fracture (closed) 824.4
ankle (closed) 824.4
open 824.5
fibula (closed) 824.4
open 824.5
radius (closed) 813.42
open 813.52
muscle contracture 728.6
Durand-Nicolas-Favre disease (climatic bubo)
099.1
Duroziez's disease (congenital mitral stenosis)
746.5
Dust
conjunctivitis 372.05
reticulation (occupational) 504

Dutton's
disease (trypanosomiasis) 086.9
relapsing fever (West African) 087.1
Dwarf, dwarfism 259.4
with infantilism (hypophyseal) 253.3
achondroplastic 756.4
Amsterdam 759.89
bird-headed 759.89
congenital 259.4
constitutional 259.4
hypophyseal 253.3
infantile 259.4
Levi type 253.3
Lorain-Levi (pituitary) 253.3
Lorain type (pituitary) 253.3
metatropic 756.4
nephrotic-glycosuric, with hypophosphatemic
rickets 270.0
nutritional 263.2
ovarian 758.6
pancreatic 577.8
pituitary 253.3
polydystrophic 277.5
primordial 253.3
psychosocial 259.4
renal 588.0
with hypertension — *see* Hypertension,
kidney
Russell's (uterine dwarfism and craniofacial
dysostosis) 759.89
Dyke-Young anemia or syndrome (acquired
macrocytic hemolytic anemia) (secondary)
(symptomatic) 283.9
Dynia abnormality (*see also* Defect, coagulation)
286.9
Dysacousis 388.40
Dysadrenocortism 255.9
hyperfunction 255.3
hypofunction 255.4
Dysarthria 784.5
Dysautonomia (*see also* Neuropathy, peripheral,
autonomic) 337.9
familial 742.8
Dysbarism 993.3
Dysbasia 719.7
angiosclerotica intermittens 443.9
due to atherosclerosis 440.21
hysterical 300.11
lordotica (progressiva) 333.6
nonorganic origin 307.9
psychogenic 307.9
Dysbetalipoproteinemia (familial) 272.2
Dyscalculia 315.1
Dyschezia (*see also* Constipation) 564.00
Dyschondroplasia (with hemangiomata) 756.4
Voorhoeve's 756.4
Dyschondrosteosis 756.59
Dyschromia 709.00
Dyscollagenosis 710.9
Dyscoria 743.41
Dyscraniopyophalangy 759.89
Dyscrasia
blood 289.9
with antepartum hemorrhage 641.3 ☑
fetus or newborn NEC 776.9
hemorrhage, subungual 287.8
puerperal, postpartum 666.3 ☑
ovary 256.8
plasma cell 273.9
pluriglandular 258.9
polyglandular 258.9
Dysdiadochokinesia 781.3
Dysectasia, vesical neck 596.8
Dysendocrinism 259.9
Dysentery, dysenteric (bilious) (catarrhal)
(diarrhea) (epidemic) (gangrenous)
(hemorrhagic) (infectious) (sporadic)
(tropical) (ulcerative) 009.0
abscess, liver (*see also* Abscess, amebic) 006.3
amebic (*see also* Amebiasis) 006.9
with abscess — *see* Abscess, amebic
acute 006.0

Dysentery, dysenteric — *continued*
amebic (*see also* Amebiasis) — *continued*
carrier (suspected) of V02.2
chronic 006.1
arthritis (*see also* Arthritis, due to, dysentery)
009.0 *[711.3]* ☑
bacillary 004.9 *[711.3]* ☑
asylum 004.9
bacillary 004.9
arthritis 004.9 *[711.3]* ☑
Boyd 004.2
Flexner 004.1
Schmitz (-Stutzer) 004.0
Shiga 004.0
Shigella 004.9
group A 004.0
group B 004.1
group C 004.2
group D 004.3
specified type NEC 004.8
Sonne 004.3
specified type NEC 004.8
bacterium 004.9
balantidial 007.0
Balantidium coli 007.0
Boyd's 004.2
Chilomastix 007.8
Chinese 004.9
choleriform 001.1
coccidial 007.2
Dientamoeba fragilis 007.8
due to specified organism NEC — *see* Enteritis,
due to, by organism
Embadomonas 007.8
Endolimax nana — *see* Dysentery, amebic
Entamoba, entamebic — *see* Dysentery, amebic
Flexner's 004.1
Flexner-Boyd 004.2
giardial 007.1
Giardia lamblia 007.1
Hiss-Russell 004.1
lamblia 007.1
leishmanial 085.0
malarial (*see also* Malaria) 084.6
metazoal 127.9
Monilia 112.89
protozoal NEC 007.9
Russell's 004.8
salmonella 003.0
schistosomal 120.1
Schmitz (-Stutzer) 004.0
Shiga 004.0
Shigella NEC (*see also* Dysentery, bacillary)
004.9
boydii 004.2
dysenteriae 004.0
Schmitz 004.0
Shiga 004.0
flexneri 004.1
group A 004.0
group B 004.1
group C 004.2
group D 004.3
Schmitz 004.0
Shiga 004.0
Sonnei 004.3
Sonne 004.3
strongyloidiasis 127.2
trichomonal 007.3
tuberculous (*see also* Tuberculosis) 014.8 ☑
viral (*see also* Enteritis, viral) 008.8
Dysequilibrium 780.4
Dysesthesia 782.0
hysterical 300.11
Dysfibrinogenemia (congenital) (*see also* Defect,
coagulation) 286.3
Dysfunction
adrenal (cortical) 255.9
hyperfunction 255.3
hypofunction 255.4
associated with sleep stages or arousal from
sleep 780.56
nonorganic origin 307.47
bladder NEC 596.59
bleeding, uterus 626.8
brain, minimal (*see also* Hyperkinesia) 314.9

☑ Additional Digit Required — Refer to the Tabular List (Numeric Code Section) for Additional Digit Selection
▶◀ Revised Text   ● New Line   ▲ Revised Code

2006 ICD-9-CM

Volume 2 — 121

Dysfunction — *continued*
  cerebral 348.30
  colon 564.9
    psychogenic 306.4
  colostomy or enterostomy 569.62
  cystic duct 575.8
  diastolic 429.9
    with heart failure — *see* Failure, heart
    due to
      cardiomyopathy — *see* Cardiomyopathy
      hypertension — *see* Hypertension, heart
  endocrine NEC 259.9
  endometrium 621.8
  enteric stoma 569.62
  enterostomy 569.62
  erectile 607.84   ●
    nonorganic condition 302.72   ●
  esophagostomy 530.87
  Eustachian tube 381.81
  gallbladder 575.8
  gastrointestinal 536.9
  gland, glandular NEC 259.9
  heart 427.9
    postoperative (immediate) 997.1
      long-term effect of cardiac surgery 429.4
  hemoglobin 288.8
  hepatic 573.9
  hepatocellular NEC 573.9
  hypophysis 253.9
    hyperfunction 253.1
    hypofunction 253.2
    posterior lobe 253.6
      hypofunction 253.5
  kidney (*see also* Disease, renal) 593.9
  labyrinthine 386.50
    specified NEC 386.58
  liver 573.9
    constitutional 277.4
  minimal brain (child) (*see also* Hyperkinesia)
      314.9
  ovary, ovarian 256.9
    hyperfunction 256.1
      estrogen 256.0
    hypofunction 256.39
      postablative 256.2
    postablative 256.2
    specified NEC 256.8
  papillary muscle 429.81
    with myocardial infarction 410.8 ☑
  parathyroid 252.8
    hyperfunction 252.00
    hypofunction 252.1
  pineal gland 259.8
  pituitary (gland) 253.9
    hyperfunction 253.1
    hypofunction 253.2
    posterior 253.6
      hypofunction 253.5
  placental — *see* Placenta, insufficiency
  platelets (blood) 287.1
  polyglandular 258.9
    specified NEC 258.8
  psychosexual 302.70
    with
      dyspareunia (functional) (psychogenic)
        302.76
      frigidity 302.72
      impotence 302.72
      inhibition
        orgasm
          female 302.73
          male 302.74
        sexual
          desire 302.71
          excitement 302.72
      premature ejaculation 302.75
      sexual aversion 302.79
      specified disorder NEC 302.79
      vaginismus 306.51
  pylorus 537.9
  rectum 564.9
    psychogenic 306.4
  segmental (*see also* Dysfunction, somatic)
      739.9
  senile 797
  sexual 302.70
  sinoatrial node 427.81

Dysfunction — *continued*
  somatic 739.9
    abdomen 739.9
    acromioclavicular 739.7
    cervical 739.1
    cervicothoracic 739.1
    costochondral 739.8
    costovertebral 739.8
    extremities
      lower 739.6
      upper 739.7
    head 739.0
    hip 739.5
    lumbar, lumbosacral 739.3
    occipitocervical 739.0
    pelvic 739.5
    pubic 739.5
    rib cage 739.8
    sacral 739.4
    sacrococcygeal 739.4
    sacroiliac 739.4
    specified site NEC 739.9
    sternochondral 739.8
    sternoclavicular 739.7
    temporomandibular 739.0
    thoracic, thoracolumbar 739.2
  stomach 536.9
    psychogenic 306.4
  suprarenal 255.9
    hyperfunction 255.3
    hypofunction 255.4
  symbolic NEC 784.60
    specified type NEC 784.69
  systolic 429.9   ●
    with heart failure — *see* Failure, heart   ●
  temporomandibular (joint) (joint-pain-
      syndrome) NEC 524.60
    sounds on opening or closing 524.64
    specified NEC 524.69
  testicular 257.9
    hyperfunction 257.0
    hypofunction 257.2
    specified type NEC 257.8
  thymus 254.9
  thyroid 246.9
    complicating pregnancy, childbirth, or
      puerperium 648.1 ☑
    hyperfunction — *see* Hyperthyroidism
    hypofunction — *see* Hypothyroidism
  uterus, complicating delivery 661.9 ☑
    affecting fetus or newborn 763.7
    hypertonic 661.4 ☑
    hypotonic 661.2 ☑
      primary 661.0 ☑
      secondary 661.1 ☑
  velopharyngeal (acquired) 528.9
    congenital 750.29
  ventricular 429.9
    with congestive heart failure (*see also*
      Failure, heart) 428.0
    due to
      cardiomyopathy — *see* Cardiomyopathy
      hypertension — *see* Hypertension, heart
  vesicourethral NEC 596.59
  vestibular 386.50
    specified type NEC 386.58

Dysgammaglobulinemia 279.06
Dysgenesis
  gonadal (due to chromosomal anomaly) 758.6
    pure 752.7
  kidney(s) 753.0
  ovarian 758.6
  renal 753.0
  reticular 279.2
  seminiferous tubules 758.6
  tidal platelet 287.31   ▲
Dysgerminoma (M9060/3)
  specified site — *see* Neoplasm, by site,
    malignant
  unspecified site
    female 183.0
    male 186.9
Dysgeusia 781.1
Dysgraphia 781.3
Dyshidrosis 705.81

Dysidrosis 705.81
Dysinsulinism 251.8
Dyskaryotic cervical smear 795.09
Dyskeratosis (*see also* Keratosis) 701.1
  bullosa hereditaria 757.39
  cervix 622.10
  congenital 757.39
  follicularis 757.39
    vitamin A deficiency 264.8
  gingiva 523.8
  oral soft tissue NEC 528.79
  tongue 528.79
  uterus NEC 621.8
Dyskinesia 781.3
  biliary 575.8
  esophagus 530.5
  hysterical 300.11
  intestinal 564.89
  neuroleptic-induced tardive 333.82   ●
  nonorganic origin 307.9
  orofacial 333.82
  psychogenic 307.9
  tardive (oral) 333.82
Dyslalia 784.5
  developmental 315.39
Dyslexia 784.61
  developmental 315.02
  secondary to organic lesion 784.61
Dyslipidemia 272.4
Dysmaturity (*see also* Immaturity) 765.1 ☑
  lung 770.4
  pulmonary 770.4
Dysmenorrhea (essential) (exfoliative) (functional)
    (intrinsic) (membranous) (primary)
    (secondary) 625.3
  psychogenic 306.52
Dysmetabolic syndrome X 277.7
Dysmetria 781.3
Dysmorodystrophia mesodermalis congenita
    759.82
Dysnomia 784.3
Dysorexia 783.0
  hysterical 300.11
Dysostosis
  cleidocranial, cleidocranialis 755.59
  craniofacial 756.0
  Fairbank's (idiopathic familial generalized
    osteophytosis) 756.50
  mandibularis 756.0
  mandibulofacial, incomplete 756.0
  multiplex 277.5
  orodigitofacial 759.89
Dyspareunia (female) 625.0
  male 608.89
  psychogenic 302.76
Dyspepsia (allergic) (congenital) (fermentative)
    (flatulent) (functional) (gastric)
    (gastrointestinal) (neurogenic) (occupational)
    (reflex) 536.8
  acid 536.8
  atonic 536.3
    psychogenic 306.4
  diarrhea 787.91
    psychogenic 306.4
  intestinal 564.89
    psychogenic 306.4
  nervous 306.4
  neurotic 306.4
  psychogenic 306.4
Dysphagia 787.2
  functional 300.11
  hysterical 300.11
  nervous 300.11
  psychogenic 306.4
  sideropenic 280.8
  spastica 530.5
Dysphagocytosis, congenital 288.1
Dysphasia 784.5
Dysphonia 784.49
  clericorum 784.49
  functional 300.11
  hysterical 300.11
  psychogenic 306.1
  spastica 478.79

Dyspigmentation — *see also* Pigmentation
　eyelid (acquired) 374.52
Dyspituitarism 253.9
　hyperfunction 253.1
　hypofunction 253.2
　posterior lobe 253.6
Dysplasia — *see also* Anomaly
　artery
　　fibromuscular NEC 447.8
　　　carotid 447.8
　　　renal 447.3
　bladder 596.8
　bone (fibrous) NEC 733.29
　　diaphyseal, progressive 756.59
　　jaw 526.89
　　monostotic 733.29
　　polyostotic 756.54
　　solitary 733.29
　brain 742.9
　bronchopulmonary, fetus or newborn 770.7
　cervix (uteri) 622.10
　　cervical intraepithelial neoplasia I [CIN I]
　　　622.11
　　cervical intraepithelial neoplasia II [CIN II]
　　　622.12
　　cervical intraepithelial neoplasia III [CIN III]
　　　233.1
　　CIN I 622.11
　　CIN II 622.12
　　CIN III 233.1
　　mild 622.11
　　moderate 622.12
　　severe 233.1
　chondroectodermal 756.55
　chondromatose 756.4
　colon 211.3　　　　　　　　　　　　　　　●
　craniocarpotarsal 759.89
　craniometaphyseal 756.89
　dentinal 520.5
　diaphyseal, progressive 756.59
　ectodermal (anhidrotic) (Bason) (Clouston's)
　　(congenital) (Feinmesser) (hereditary)
　　(hidrotic) (Marshall) (Robinson's) 757.31
　epiphysealis 756.9
　　multiplex 756.56
　　punctata 756.59
　epiphysis 756.9
　　multiple 756.56
　epithelial
　　epiglottis 478.79
　　uterine cervix 622.10
　erythroid NEC 289.89
　eye (*see also* Microphthalmos) 743.10
　familial metaphyseal 756.89
　fibromuscular, artery NEC 447.8
　　carotid 447.8
　　renal 447.3
　fibrous
　　bone NEC 733.29
　　diaphyseal, progressive 756.59
　　jaw 526.89
　　monostotic 733.29
　　polyostotic 756.54
　　solitary 733.29
　hip (congenital) 755.63
　　with dislocation (*see also* Dislocation, hip,
　　　congenital) 754.30
　high grade, focal — *see* Neoplasm, by site,　●
　　benign　　　　　　　　　　　　　　　　　●
　hypohidrotic ectodermal 757.31
　joint 755.8
　kidney 753.15
　leg 755.69
　linguofacialis 759.89
　lung 748.5
　macular 743.55
　mammary (benign) (gland) 610.9
　　cystic 610.1
　　specified type NEC 610.8
　metaphyseal 756.9
　　familial 756.89
　monostotic fibrous 733.29
　muscle 756.89
　myeloid NEC 289.89
　nervous system (general) 742.9
　neuroectodermal 759.6

Dysplasia — *see also* Anomaly — *continued*
　oculoauriculovertebral 756.0
　oculodentodigital 759.89
　olfactogenital 253.4
　osteo-onycho-arthro (hereditary) 756.89
　periosteum 733.99
　polyostotic fibrous 756.54
　progressive diaphyseal 756.59
　prostate 602.3
　　intraepithelial neoplasia I [PIN I] 602.3
　　intraepithelial neoplasia II [PIN II] 602.3
　　intraepithelial neoplasia III [PIN III] 233.4
　renal 753.15
　renofacialis 753.0
　retinal NEC 743.56
　retrolental 362.21
　spinal cord 742.9
　thymic, with immunodeficiency 279.2
　vagina 623.0
　vocal cord 478.5
　vulva 624.8
　　intraepithelial neoplasia I [VIN I] 624.8
　　intraepithelial neoplasia II [VIN II] 624.8
　　intraepithelial neoplasia III [VIN III] 233.3
　　VIN I 624.8
　　VIN II 624.8
　　VIN III 233.3
Dyspnea (nocturnal) (paroxysmal) 786.09
　asthmatic (bronchial) (*see also* Asthma)
　　493.9 ☑
　　with bronchitis (*see also* Asthma) 493.9 ☑
　　　chronic 493.2 ☑
　　cardiac (*see also* Failure, ventricular, left)
　　　428.1
　cardiac (*see also* Failure, ventricular, left) 428.1
　functional 300.11
　hyperventilation 786.01
　hysterical 300.11
　Monday morning 504
　newborn 770.89
　psychogenic 306.1
　uremic — *see* Uremia
Dyspraxia 781.3
　syndrome 315.4
Dysproteinemia 273.8
　transient with copper deficiency 281.4
Dysprothrombinemia (constitutional) (*see also*
　Defect, coagulation) 286.3
Dysreflexia, autonomic 337.3
Dysrhythmia
　cardiac 427.9
　　postoperative (immediate) 997.1
　　　long-term effect of cardiac surgery 429.4
　　specified type NEC 427.89
　cerebral or cortical 348.30
Dyssecretosis, mucoserous 710.2
Dyssocial reaction, without manifest
　psychiatric disorder
　adolescent V71.02
　adult V71.01
　child V71.02
Dyssomnia NEC 780.56
　nonorganic origin 307.47
Dyssplenism 289.4
Dyssynergia
　biliary (*see also* Disease, biliary) 576.8
　cerebellaris myoclonica 334.2
　detrusor sphincter (bladder) 596.55
　ventricular 429.89
Dystasia, hereditary areflexic 334.3
Dysthymia 300.4
Dysthymic disorder 300.4
Dysthyroidism 246.9
Dystocia 660.9 ☑
　affecting fetus or newborn 763.1
　cervical 661.0 ☑
　　affecting fetus or newborn 763.7
　contraction ring 661.4 ☑
　　affecting fetus or newborn 763.7
　fetal 660.9 ☑
　　abnormal size 653.5 ☑
　　affecting fetus or newborn 763.1
　　deformity 653.7 ☑

Dystocia — *continued*
　maternal 660.9 ☑
　　affecting fetus or newborn 763.1
　positional 660.0 ☑
　　affecting fetus or newborn 763.1
　shoulder (girdle) 660.4 ☑
　　affecting fetus or newborn 763.1
　uterine NEC 661.4 ☑
　　affecting fetus or newborn 763.7
Dystonia
　deformans progressiva 333.6
　due to drugs 333.7
　lenticularis 333.6
　musculorum deformans 333.6
　neuroleptic-induced acute 333.7　　　　●
　torsion (idiopathic) 333.6
　　fragments (of) 333.89
　　symptomatic 333.7
Dystonic
　movements 781.0
Dystopia kidney 753.3
Dystrophy, dystrophia 783.9
　adiposogenital 253.8
　asphyxiating thoracic 756.4
　Becker's type 359.1
　brevicollis 756.16
　Bruch's membrane 362.77
　cervical (sympathetic) NEC 337.0
　chondro-osseus with punctate epiphyseal
　　dysplasia 756.59
　choroid (hereditary) 363.50
　　central (areolar) (partial) 363.53
　　　total (gyrate) 363.54
　　circinate 363.53
　　circumpapillary (partial) 363.51
　　　total 363.52
　　diffuse
　　　partial 363.56
　　　total 363.57
　　generalized
　　　partial 363.56
　　　total 363.57
　　gyrate
　　　central 363.54
　　　generalized 363.57
　　helicoid 363.52
　　peripapillary — *see* Dystrophy, choroid,
　　　circumpapillary
　　serpiginous 363.54
　cornea (hereditary) 371.50
　　anterior NEC 371.52
　　Cogan's 371.52
　　combined 371.57
　　crystalline 371.56
　　endothelial (Fuchs') 371.57
　　epithelial 371.50
　　　juvenile 371.51
　　　microscopic cystic 371.52
　　granular 371.53
　　lattice 371.54
　　macular 371.55
　　marginal (Terrien's) 371.48
　　Meesman's 371.51
　　microscopic cystic (epithelial) 371.52
　　nodular, Salzmann's 371.46
　　polymorphous 371.58
　　posterior NEC 371.58
　　ring-like 371.52
　　Salzmann's nodular 371.46
　　stromal NEC 371.56
　dermatochondrocorneal 371.50
　Duchenne's 359.1
　due to malnutrition 263.9
　Erb's 359.1
　familial
　　hyperplastic periosteal 756.59
　　osseous 277.5
　foveal 362.77
　Fuchs', cornea 371.57
　Gowers' muscular 359.1
　hair 704.2
　hereditary, progressive muscular 359.1
　hypogenital, with diabetic tendency 759.81
　Landouzy-Déjérine 359.1
　Leyden-Möbius 359.1
　mesodermalis congenita 759.82

☑ Additional Digit Required — Refer to the Tabular List (Numeric Code Section) for Additional Digit Selection
▶◀ Revised Text　　　　● New Line　　　　▲ Revised Code

Dystrophy, dystrophia — continued
muscular 359.1
  congenital (hereditary) 359.0
    myotonic 359.2
  distal 359.1
  Duchenne's 359.1
  Erb's 359.1
  fascioscapulohumeral 359.1
  Gowers' 359.1
  hereditary (progressive) 359.1
  Landouzy-Déjérine 359.1
  limb-girdle 359.1
  myotonic 359.2
  progressive (hereditary) 359.1
    Charcôt-Marie-Tooth 356.1
  pseudohypertrophic (infantile) 359.1
myocardium, myocardial (see also
  Degeneration, myocardial) 429.1
myotonic 359.2
myotonica 359.2
nail 703.8
  congenital 757.5
neurovascular (traumatic) (see also
  Neuropathy, peripheral, autonomic) 337.9
nutritional 263.9
ocular 359.1
oculocerebrorenal 270.8
oculopharyngeal 359.1
ovarian 620.8
papillary (and pigmentary) 701.1
pelvicrural atrophic 359.1
pigmentary (see also Acanthosis) 701.2
pituitary (gland) 253.8
polyglandular 258.8
posttraumatic sympathetic — see Dystrophy,
  sympathetic
progressive ophthalmoplegic 359.1
retina, retinal (hereditary) 362.70
  albipunctate 362.74
  Bruch's membrane 362.77
  cone, progressive 362.75
  hyaline 362.77
  in
    Bassen-Kornzweig syndrome
      272.5 [362.72]
    cerebroretinal lipidosis 330.1 [362.71]
    Refsum's disease 356.3 [362.72]
    systemic lipidosis 272.7 [362.71]
  juvenile (Stargardt's) 362.75
  pigmentary 362.74
  pigment epithelium 362.76
  progressive cone (-rod) 362.75
  pseudoinflammatory foveal 362.77
  rod, progressive 362.75
  sensory 362.75
  vitelliform 362.76
Salzmann's nodular 371.46
scapuloperoneal 359.1
skin NEC 709.9
sympathetic (posttraumatic) (reflex) 337.20
  lower limb 337.22
  specified site NEC 337.29
  upper limb 337.21
tapetoretinal NEC 362.74
thoracic asphyxiating 756.4
unguium 703.8
  congenital 757.5
vitreoretinal (primary) 362.73
  secondary 362.66
vulva 624.0
Dysuria 788.1
psychogenic 306.53

E

Eagle-Barrett syndrome 756.71
Eales' disease (syndrome) 362.18
Ear — see also condition
ache 388.70
  otogenic 388.71
  referred 388.72
lop 744.29
piercing V50.3
swimmers' acute 380.12
tank 380.12
tropical 111.8 [380.15]
wax 380.4

Earache 388.70
otogenic 388.71
referred 388.72
Early satiety 780.94
Eaton-Lambert syndrome (see also Neoplasm, by
  site, malignant) 199.1 [358.1]
Eberth's disease (typhoid fever) 002.0
Ebstein's
anomaly or syndrome (downward displacement,
  tricuspid valve into right ventricle) 746.2
disease (diabetes) 250.4 ☑ [581.81]
Eccentro-osteochondrodysplasia 277.5
Ecchondroma (M9210/0) — see Neoplasm, bone,
  benign
Ecchondrosis (M9210/1) 238.0
Ecchordosis physaliphora 756.0
Ecchymosis (multiple) 459.89
conjunctiva 372.72
eye (traumatic) 921.0
eyelids (traumatic) 921.1
newborn 772.6
spontaneous 782.7
traumatic — see Contusion
Echinococciasis — see Echinococcus
Echinococcosis — see Echinococcus
Echinococcus (infection) 122.9
granulosus 122.4
  liver 122.0
  lung 122.1
  orbit 122.3 [376.13]
  specified site NEC 122.3
  thyroid 122.2
liver NEC 122.8
  granulosus 122.0
  multilocularis 122.5
lung NEC 122.9
  granulosus 122.1
  multilocularis 122.6
multilocularis 122.7
  liver 122.5
  specified site NEC 122.6
orbit 122.9 [376.13]
  granulosus 122.3 [376.13]
  multilocularis 122.6 [376.13]
specified site NEC 122.9
  granulosus 122.3
  multilocularis 122.6 [376.13]
thyroid NEC 122.9
  granulosus 122.2
  multilocularis 122.6
Echinorhynchiasis 127.7
Echinostomiasis 121.8
Echolalia 784.69
ECHO virus infection NEC 079.1
Eclampsia, eclamptic (coma) (convulsions)
  (delirium) 780.39
female, child-bearing age NEC — see
  Eclampsia, pregnancy
gravidarum — see Eclampsia, pregnancy
male 780.39
not associated with pregnancy or childbirth
  780.39
pregnancy, childbirth, or puerperium 642.6 ☑
  with pre-existing hypertension 642.7 ☑
  affecting fetus or newborn 760.0
uremic 586
Eclipse blindness (total) 363.31
Economic circumstance affecting care V60.9
specified type NEC V60.8
Economo's disease (encephalitis lethargica) 049.8
Ectasia, ectasis
aorta (see also Aneurysm, aorta) 441.9
  ruptured 441.5
breast 610.4
capillary 448.9
cornea (marginal) (postinfectional) 371.71
duct (mammary) 610.4
kidney 593.89
mammary duct (gland) 610.4
papillary 448.9
renal 593.89
salivary gland (duct) 527.8
scar, cornea 371.71
sclera 379.11

Ecthyma 686.8
contagiosum 051.2
gangrenosum 686.09
infectiosum 051.2
Ectocardia 746.87
Ectodermal dysplasia, congenital 757.31
Ectodermosis erosiva pluriorificialis 695.1
Ectopic, ectopia (congenital) 759.89
abdominal viscera 751.8
  due to defect in anterior abdominal wall
    756.79
ACTH syndrome 255.0
adrenal gland 759.1
anus 751.5
auricular beats 427.61
beats 427.60
bladder 753.5
bone and cartilage in lung 748.69
brain 742.4
breast tissue 757.6
cardiac 746.87
cerebral 742.4
cordis 746.87
endometrium 617.9
gallbladder 751.69
gastric mucosa 750.7
gestation — see Pregnancy, ectopic
heart 746.87
hormone secretion NEC 259.3
hyperparathyroidism 259.3
kidney (crossed) (intrathoracic) (pelvis) 753.3
  in pregnancy or childbirth 654.4 ☑
    causing obstructed labor 660.2 ☑
lens 743.37
lentis 743.37
mole — see Pregnancy, ectopic
organ or site NEC — see Malposition,
  congenital
ovary 752.0
pancreas, pancreatic tissue 751.7
pregnancy — see Pregnancy, ectopic
pupil 364.75
renal 753.3
sebaceous glands of mouth 750.26
secretion
  ACTH 255.0
  adrenal hormone 259.3
  adrenalin 259.3
  adrenocorticotropin 255.0
  antidiuretic hormone (ADH) 259.3
  epinephrine 259.3
  hormone NEC 259.3
  norepinephrine 259.3
  pituitary (posterior) 259.3
spleen 759.0
testis 752.51
thyroid 759.2
ureter 753.4
ventricular beats 427.69
vesicae 753.5
Ectrodactyly 755.4
finger (see also Absence, finger, congenital)
  755.29
toe (see also Absence, toe, congenital) 755.39
Ectromelia 755.4
lower limb 755.30
upper limb 755.20
Ectropion 374.10
anus 569.49
cervix 622.0
  with mention of cervicitis 616.0
cicatricial 374.14
congenital 743.62
eyelid 374.10
  cicatricial 374.14
  congenital 743.62
  mechanical 374.12
  paralytic 374.12
  senile 374.11
  spastic 374.13
iris (pigment epithelium) 364.54
lip (congenital) 750.26
  acquired 528.5
mechanical 374.12
paralytic 374.12

Ectropion — *continued*
  rectum 569.49
  senile 374.11
  spastic 374.13
  urethra 599.84
  uvea 364.54
Eczema (acute) (allergic) (chronic) (erythematous)
    (fissum) (occupational) (rubrum) (squamous)
    692.9
  asteatotic 706.8
  atopic 691.8
  contact NEC 692.9
  dermatitis NEC 692.9
  due to specified cause — *see* Dermatitis, due to
  dyshidrotic 705.81
  external ear 380.22
  flexural 691.8
  gouty 274.89
  herpeticum 054.0
  hypertrophicum 701.8
  hypostatic — *see* Varicose, vein
  impetiginous 684
  infantile (acute) (chronic) (due to any
      substance) (intertriginous) (seborrheic)
      690.12
  intertriginous NEC 692.9
    infantile 690.12
  intrinsic 691.8
  lichenified NEC 692.9
  marginatum 110.3
  nummular 692.9
  pustular 686.8
  seborrheic 690.18
    infantile 690.12
  solare 692.72
  stasis (lower extremity) 454.1
    ulcerated 454.2
  vaccination, vaccinatum 999.0
  varicose (lower extremity) — *see* Varicose, vein
  verrucosum callosum 698.3
Eczematoid, exudative 691.8
Eddowes' syndrome (brittle bones and blue
    sclera) 756.51
Edema, edematous 782.3
  with nephritis (*see also* Nephrosis) 581.9
  allergic 995.1
  angioneurotic (allergic) (any site) (with urticaria)
      995.1
    hereditary 277.6
  angiospastic 443.9
  Berlin's (traumatic) 921.3
  brain 348.5
    due to birth injury 767.8
    fetus or newborn 767.8
  cardiac (*see also* Failure, heart) 428.0
  cardiovascular (*see also* Failure, heart) 428.0
  cerebral — *see* Edema, brain
  cerebrospinal vessel — *see* Edema, brain
  cervix (acute) (uteri) 622.8
    puerperal, postpartum 674.8 ☑
  chronic hereditary 757.0
  circumscribed, acute 995.1
    hereditary 277.6
  complicating pregnancy (gestational) 646.1 ☑
    with hypertension — *see* Toxemia, of
      pregnancy
  conjunctiva 372.73
  connective tissue 782.3
  cornea 371.20
    due to contact lenses 371.24
    idiopathic 371.21
    secondary 371.22
  cystoid macular 362.53
  due to
    lymphatic obstruction — *see* Edema,
      lymphatic
    salt retention 276.0
  epiglottis — *see* Edema, glottis
  essential, acute 995.1
    hereditary 277.6
  extremities, lower — *see* Edema, legs
  eyelid NEC 374.82
  familial, hereditary (legs) 757.0
  famine 262
  fetus or newborn 778.5

Edema, edematous — *continued*
  genital organs
    female 629.8
    male 608.86
  gestational 646.1 ☑
    with hypertension — *see* Toxemia, of
      pregnancy
  glottis, glottic, glottides (obstructive) (passive)
      478.6
    allergic 995.1
      hereditary 277.6
    due to external agent — *see* Condition,
      respiratory, acute, due to specified
      agent
  heart (*see also* Failure, heart) 428.0
    newborn 779.89
  heat 992.7
  hereditary (legs) 757.0
  inanition 262
  infectious 782.3
  intracranial 348.5
    due to injury at birth 767.8
  iris 364.8
  joint (*see also* Effusion, joint) 719.0 ☑
  larynx (*see also* Edema, glottis) 478.6
  legs 782.3
    due to venous obstruction 459.2
    hereditary 757.0
  localized 782.3
    due to venous obstruction 459.2
      lower extremity 459.2
  lower extremities — *see* Edema, legs
  lung 514
    acute 518.4
      with heart disease or failure (*see also*
        Failure, ventricular, left) 428.1
        congestive 428.0
      chemical (due to fumes or vapors) 506.1
      due to
        external agent(s) NEC 508.9
          specified NEC 508.8
        fumes and vapors (chemical)
          (inhalation) 506.1
        radiation 508.0
    chemical (acute) 506.1
      chronic 506.4
    chronic 514
      chemical (due to fumes or vapors) 506.4
      due to
        external agent(s) NEC 508.9
          specified NEC 508.8
        fumes or vapors (chemical) (inhalation)
          506.4
        radiation 508.1
    due to
      external agent 508.9
        specified NEC 508.8
      high altitude 993.2
      near drowning 994.1
    postoperative 518.4
    terminal 514
  lymphatic 457.1
    due to mastectomy operation 457.0
  macula 362.83
    cystoid 362.53
    diabetic 250.5 ☑ *[362.07]*   ▲
  malignant (*see also* Gangrene, gas) 040.0
  Milroy's 757.0
  nasopharynx 478.25
  neonatorum 778.5
  nutritional (newborn) 262
    with dyspigmentation, skin and hair 260
  optic disc or nerve — *see* Papilledema
  orbit 376.33
    circulatory 459.89
  palate (soft) (hard) 528.9
  pancreas 577.8
  penis 607.83
  periodic 995.1
    hereditary 277.6
  pharynx 478.25
  pitting 782.3
  pulmonary — *see* Edema, lung
  Quincke's 995.1
    hereditary 277.6
  renal (*see also* Nephrosis) 581.9

Edema, edematous — *continued*
  retina (localized) (macular) (peripheral) 362.83
    cystoid 362.53
    diabetic 250.5 ☑ *[362.07]*   ▲
  salt 276.0
  scrotum 608.86
  seminal vesicle 608.86
  spermatic cord 608.86
  spinal cord 336.1
  starvation 262
  stasis (*see also* Hypertension, venous) 459.30
  subconjunctival 372.73
  subglottic (*see also* Edema, glottis) 478.6
  supraglottic (*see also* Edema, glottis) 478.6
  testis 608.86
  toxic NEC 782.3
  traumatic NEC 782.3
  tunica vaginalis 608.86
  vas deferens 608.86
  vocal cord — *see* Edema, glottis
  vulva (acute) 624.8
Edentia (complete) (partial) (*see also* Absence,
    tooth) 520.0
  acquired ▶(*see also* Edentulism)◀ 525.40   ▲
    due to
      caries 525.13
      extraction 525.10
      periodontal disease 525.12
      specified NEC 525.19
      trauma 525.11
  causing malocclusion 524.30
  congenital (deficiency of tooth buds) 520.0
Edentulism 525.40   ▲
  complete 525.40   ●
    class I 525.41   ●
    class II 525.42   ●
    class III 525.43   ●
    class IV 525.44   ●
  partial 525.50   ●
    class I 525.51   ●
    class II 525.52   ●
    class III 525.53   ●
    class IV 525.54   ●
Edsall's disease 992.2
Educational handicap V62.3
Edwards' syndrome 758.2
Effect, adverse NEC
  abnormal gravitational (G) forces or states
      994.9
  air pressure — *see* Effect, adverse, atmospheric
      pressure
  altitude (high) — *see* Effect, adverse, high
      altitude
  anesthetic
    in labor and delivery NEC 668.9 ☑
      affecting fetus or newborn 763.5
  antitoxin — *see* Complications, vaccination
  atmospheric pressure 993.9
    due to explosion 993.4
    high 993.3
    low — *see* Effect, adverse, high altitude
    specified effect NEC 993.8
  biological, correct substance properly
      administered (*see also* Effect, adverse,
      drug) 995.2
  blood (derivatives) (serum) (transfusion) — *see*
      Complications, transfusion
  chemical substance NEC 989.9
    specified — *see* Table of Drugs and
      Chemicals
  cobalt, radioactive (*see also* Effect, adverse,
      radioactive substance) 990
  cold (temperature) (weather) 991.9
    chilblains 991.5
    frostbite — *see* Frostbite
    specified effect NEC 991.8
  drugs and medicinals NEC 995.2
    correct substance properly administered
      995.2
    overdose or wrong substance given or taken
      977.9
    specified drug — *see* Table of Drugs and
      Chemicals
  electric current (shock) 994.8
    burn — *see* Burn, by site

☑ Additional Digit Required — Refer to the Tabular List (Numeric Code Section) for Additional Digit Selection

Effect, adverse — *continued*
electricity (electrocution) (shock) 994.8
  burn — *see* Burn, by site
exertion (excessive) 994.5
exposure 994.9
  exhaustion 994.4
external cause NEC 994.9
fallout (radioactive) NEC 990
fluoroscopy NEC 990
foodstuffs
  allergic reaction (*see also* Allergy, food)
    693.1
    anaphylactic shock due to food NEC
      995.60
  noxious 988.9
    specified type NEC (*see also* Poisoning, by
      name of noxious foodstuff) 988.8
gases, fumes, or vapors — *see* Table of Drugs
  and Chemicals
glue (airplane) sniffing 304.6 ☑
heat — *see* Heat
high altitude NEC 993.2
  anoxia 993.2
  on
    ears 993.0
    sinuses 993.1
  polycythemia 289.0
hot weather — *see* Heat
hunger 994.2
immersion, foot 991.4
immunization — *see* Complications,
  vaccination
immunological agents — *see* Complications,
  vaccination
implantation (removable) of isotope or radium
  NEC 990
infrared (radiation) (rays) NEC 990
  burn — *see* Burn, by site
  dermatitis or eczema 692.82
infusion — *see* Complications, infusion
ingestion or injection of isotope (therapeutic)
  NEC 990
irradiation NEC (*see also* Effect, adverse,
  radiation) 990
isotope (radioactive) NEC 990
lack of care (child) (infant) (newborn) 995.52
  adult 995.84
lightning 994.0
  burn — *see* Burn, by site
Lirugin — *see* Complications, vaccination
medicinal substance, correct, properly
  administered (*see also* Effect, adverse,
  drugs) 995.2
mesothorium NEC 990
motion 994.6
noise, inner ear 388.10
overheated places — *see* Heat
polonium NEC 990
psychosocial, of work environment V62.1
radiation (diagnostic) (fallout) (infrared) (natural
  source) (therapeutic) (tracer) (ultraviolet)
  (x-ray) NEC 990
  with pulmonary manifestations
    acute 508.0
    chronic 508.1
  dermatitis or eczema 692.82
    due to sun NEC (*see also* Dermatitis, due
      to, sun) 692.70
  fibrosis of lungs 508.1
  maternal with suspected damage to fetus
    affecting management of pregnancy
    655.6 ☑
  pneumonitis 508.0
radioactive substance NEC 990
  dermatitis or eczema 692.82
radioactivity NEC 990
radiotherapy NEC 990
  dermatitis or eczema 692.82
radium NEC 990
reduced temperature 991.9
  frostbite — *see* Frostbite
  immersion, foot (hand) 991.4
  specified effect NEC 991.8
roentgenography NEC 990
roentgenoscopy NEC 990
roentgen rays NEC 990
serum (prophylactic) (therapeutic) NEC 999.5

Effect, adverse — *continued*
specified NEC 995.89
  external cause NEC 994.9
strangulation 994.7
submersion 994.1
teletherapy NEC 990
thirst 994.3
transfusion — *see* Complications, transfusion
ultraviolet (radiation) (rays) NEC 990
  burn — *see* Burn, by site
    from sun (*see also* Sunburn) 692.71
  dermatitis or eczema 692.82
    due to sun NEC (*see also* Dermatitis, due
      to, sun) 692.70
uranium NEC 990
vaccine (any) — *see* Complications, vaccination
weightlessness 994.9
whole blood — *see also* Complications,
  transfusion
  overdose or wrong substance given (*see also*
    Table of Drugs and Chemicals) 964.7
working environment V62.1
x-rays NEC 990
  dermatitis or eczema 692.82
Effects, late — *see* Late, effect (of)
Effect, remote
of cancer — *see* condition
Effluvium, telogen 704.02
Effort
intolerance 306.2
syndrome (aviators) (psychogenic) 306.2
Effusion
amniotic fluid (*see also* Rupture, membranes,
  premature) 658.1 ☑
brain (serous) 348.5
bronchial (*see also* Bronchitis) 490
cerebral 348.5
cerebrospinal (*see also* Meningitis) 322.9
  vessel 348.5
chest — *see* Effusion, pleura
intracranial 348.5
joint 719.00
  ankle 719.07
  elbow 719.02
  foot 719.07
  hand 719.04
  hip 719.05
  knee 719.06
  multiple sites 719.09
  pelvic region 719.05
  shoulder (region) 719.01
  specified site NEC 719.08
  wrist 719.03
meninges (*see also* Meningitis) 322.9
pericardium, pericardial (*see also* Pericarditis)
  423.9
  acute 420.90
peritoneal (chronic) 568.82
pleura, pleurisy, pleuritic, pleuropericardial
  511.9
  bacterial, nontuberculous 511.1
  fetus or newborn 511.9
  malignant 197.2
  nontuberculous 511.9
    bacterial 511.1
  pneumococcal 511.1
  staphylococcal 511.1
  streptococcal 511.1
  traumatic 862.29
    with open wound 862.39
  tuberculous (*see also* Tuberculosis, pleura)
    012.0 ☑
    primary progressive 010.1 ☑
pulmonary — *see* Effusion, pleura
spinal (*see also* Meningitis) 322.9
thorax, thoracic — *see* Effusion, pleura
Egg (oocyte) (ovum)
donor V59.70 ●
  over age 35 V59.73 ●
    anonymous recipient V59.73 ●
    designated recipient V59.74 ●
  under age 35 V59.71 ●
    anonymous recipient V59.71 ●
    designated recipient V59.72 ●

Eggshell nails 703.8
  congenital 757.5
Ego-dystonic
homosexuality 302.0
lesbianism 302.0
sexual orientation 302.0
Egyptian splenomegaly 120.1
Ehlers-Danlos syndrome 756.83
Ehrlichiosis 082.40
chaffeensis 082.41
specified type NEC 082.49
Eichstedt's disease (pityriasis versicolor) 111.0
Eisenmenger's complex or syndrome
  (ventricular septal defect) 745.4
Ejaculation, semen
painful 608.89
  psychogenic 306.59
premature 302.75
retrograde 608.87
Ekbom syndrome (restless legs) 333.99
Ekman's syndrome (brittle bones and blue sclera)
  756.51
Elastic skin 756.83
acquired 701.8
Elastofibroma (M8820/0) — *see* Neoplasm,
  connective tissue, benign
Elastoidosis
cutanea nodularis 701.8
cutis cystica et comedonica 701.8
Elastoma 757.39
juvenile 757.39
Miescher's (elastosis perforans serpiginosa)
  701.1
Elastomyofibrosis 425.3
Elastosis 701.8
atrophicans 701.8
perforans serpiginosa 701.1
reactive perforating 701.1
senilis 701.8
solar (actinic) 692.74
Elbow — *see* condition
Electric
current, electricity, effects (concussion) (fatal)
  (nonfatal) (shock) 994.8
  burn — *see* Burn, by site
feet (foot) syndrome 266.2
Electrocution 994.8
Electrolyte imbalance 276.9
with
  abortion — *see* Abortion, by type, with
    metabolic disorder
  ectopic pregnancy (*see also* categories
    633.0-633.9) 639.4
  hyperemesis gravidarum (before 22
    completed weeks gestation) 643.1 ☑
  molar pregnancy (*see also* categories 630-
    632) 639.4
following
  abortion 639.4
  ectopic or molar pregnancy 639.4
Elephant man syndrome 237.71
Elephantiasis (nonfilarial) 457.1
arabicum (*see also* Infestation, filarial) 125.9
congenita hereditaria 757.0
congenital (any site) 757.0
due to
  Brugia (malayi) 125.1
  mastectomy operation 457.0
  Wuchereria (bancrofti) 125.0
    malayi 125.1
eyelid 374.83
filarial (*see also* Infestation, filarial) 125.9
filariensis (*see also* Infestation, filarial) 125.9
gingival 523.8
glandular 457.1
graecorum 030.9
lymphangiectatic 457.1
lymphatic vessel 457.1
  due to mastectomy operation 457.0
neuromatosa 237.71
postmastectomy 457.0
scrotum 457.1
streptococcal 457.1

Elephantiasis — *continued*
  surgical 997.99
    postmastectomy 457.0
  telangiectodes 457.1
  vulva (nonfilarial) 624.8
Elevated — *see* Elevation
Elevation
  17-ketosteroids 791.9
  acid phosphatase 790.5
  alkaline phosphatase 790.5
  amylase 790.5
  antibody titers 795.79
  basal metabolic rate (BMR) 794.7
  blood pressure (*see also* Hypertension) 401.9
    reading (incidental) (isolated) (nonspecific),
      no diagnosis of hypertension 796.2
  body temperature (of unknown origin) (*see also*
    Pyrexia) 780.6
  conjugate, eye 378.81
  C-reactive protein (CRP) 790.95
  CRP (C-reactive protein) 790.95
  diaphragm, congenital 756.6
  glucose
    fasting 790.21
    tolerance test 790.22
  immunoglobulin level 795.79
  indolacetic acid 791.9
  lactic acid dehydrogenase (LDH) level 790.4
  lipase 790.5
  lipoprotein a level 272.8 ●
  liver function test (LFT) 790.6 ●
  prostate specific antigen (PSA) 790.93
  renin 790.99
    in hypertension (*see also* Hypertension,
      renovascular) 405.91
  Rh titer 999.7
  scapula, congenital 755.52
  sedimentation rate 790.1
  SGOT 790.4
  SGPT 790.4
  transaminase 790.4
  vanillylmandelic acid 791.9
  venous pressure 459.89
  VMA 791.9
Elliptocytosis (congenital) (hereditary) 282.1
  Hb-C (disease) 282.7
  hemoglobin disease 282.7
  sickle-cell (disease) 282.60
    trait 282.5
Ellis-van Creveld disease or syndrome
  (chondroectodermal dysplasia) 756.55
Ellison-Zollinger syndrome (gastric
  hypersecretion with pancreatic islet cell
  tumor) 251.5
Elongation, elongated (congenital) — *see also*
  Distortion
  bone 756.9
  cervix (uteri) 752.49
    acquired 622.6
    hypertrophic 622.6
  colon 751.5
  common bile duct 751.69
  cystic duct 751.69
  frenulum, penis 752.69
  labia minora, acquired 624.8
  ligamentum patellae 756.89
  petiolus (epiglottidis) 748.3
  styloid bone (process) 733.99
  tooth, teeth 520.2
  uvula 750.26
    acquired 528.9
Elschnig bodies or pearls 366.51
El Tor cholera 001.1
Emaciation (due to malnutrition) 261
Emancipation disorder 309.22
Embadomoniasis 007.8
Embarrassment heart, cardiac — *see* Disease,
  heart
Embedded tooth, teeth 520.6
  root only 525.3
Embolic — *see* condition

Embolism 444.9
  with
    abortion — *see* Abortion, by type, with
      embolism
    ectopic pregnancy (*see also* categories
      633.0-633.9) 639.6
    molar pregnancy (*see also* categories 630-
      632) 639.6
  air (any site) 958.0
    with
      abortion — *see* Abortion, by type, with
        embolism
      ectopic pregnancy (*see also* categories
        633.0-633.9) 639.6
      molar pregnancy (*see also* categories 630-
        632) 639.6
    due to implanted device — *see*
      Complications, due to (presence of)
      any device, implant, or graft classified
      to 996.0-996.5 NEC
    following
      abortion 639.6
      ectopic or molar pregnancy 639.6
      infusion, perfusion, or transfusion 999.1
    in pregnancy, childbirth, or puerperium
      673.0 ☑
    traumatic 958.0
  amniotic fluid (pulmonary) 673.1 ☑
    with
      abortion — *see* Abortion, by type, with
        embolism
      ectopic pregnancy (*see also* categories
        633.0-633.9) 639.6
      molar pregnancy (*see also* categories 630-
        632) 639.6
    following
      abortion 639.6
      ectopic or molar pregnancy 639.6
  aorta, aortic 444.1
    abdominal 444.0
    bifurcation 444.0
    saddle 444.0
    thoracic 444.1
  artery 444.9
    auditory, internal 433.8 ☑
    basilar (*see also* Occlusion, artery, basilar)
      433.0 ☑
    bladder 444.89
    carotid (common) (internal) (*see also*
      Occlusion, artery, carotid) 433.1 ☑
    cerebellar (anterior inferior) (posterior
      inferior) (superior) 433.8 ☑
    cerebral (*see also* Embolism, brain) 434.1 ☑
    choroidal (anterior) 433.8 ☑
    communicating posterior 433.8 ☑
    coronary (*see also* Infarct, myocardium)
      410.9 ☑
      without myocardial infarction 411.81
    extremity 444.22
      lower 444.22
      upper 444.21
    hypophyseal 433.8 ☑
    mesenteric (with gangrene) 557.0
    ophthalmic (*see also* Occlusion, retina)
      362.30
    peripheral 444.22
    pontine 433.8 ☑
    precerebral NEC — *see* Occlusion, artery,
      precerebral
    pulmonary — *see* Embolism, pulmonary
    renal 593.81
    retinal (*see also* Occlusion, retina) 362.30
    specified site NEC 444.89
    vertebral (*see also* Occlusion, artery,
      vertebral) 433.2 ☑
  auditory, internal 433.8 ☑
  basilar (artery) (*see also* Occlusion, artery,
    basilar) 433.0 ☑
  birth, mother — *see* Embolism, obstetrical
  blood-clot
    with
      abortion — *see* Abortion, by type, with
        embolism
      ectopic pregnancy (*see also* categories
        633.0-633.9) 639.6
      molar pregnancy (*see also* categories 630-
        632) 639.6

Embolism — *continued*
  blood-clot — *continued*
    following
      abortion 639.6
      ectopic or molar pregnancy 639.6
    in pregnancy, childbirth, or puerperium
      673.2 ☑
  brain 434.1 ☑
    with
      abortion — *see* Abortion, by type, with
        embolism
      ectopic pregnancy (*see also* categories
        633.0-633.9) 639.6
      molar pregnancy (*see also* categories 630-
        632) 639.6
    following
      abortion 639.6
      ectopic or molar pregnancy 639.6
    late effect — *see* Late effect(s) (of)
      cerebrovascular disease
    puerperal, postpartum, childbirth 674.0 ☑
  capillary 448.9
  cardiac (*see also* Infarct, myocardium) 410.9 ☑
  carotid (artery) (common) (internal) (*see also*
    Occlusion, artery, carotid) 433.1 ☑
  cavernous sinus (venous) — *see* Embolism,
    intracranial venous sinus
  cerebral (*see also* Embolism, brain) 434.1 ☑
  cholesterol — *see* Atheroembolism
  choroidal (anterior) (artery) 433.8 ☑
  coronary (artery or vein) (systemic) (*see also*
    Infarct, myocardium) 410.9 ☑
    without myocardial infarction 411.81
  due to (presence of) any device, implant, or
    graft classifiable to 996.0-996.5 — *see*
    Complications, due to (presence of) any
    device, implant, or graft classified to
    996.0-996.5 NEC
  encephalomalacia (*see also* Embolism, brain)
    434.1 ☑
  extremities 444.22
    lower 444.22
    upper 444.21
  eye 362.30
  fat (cerebral) (pulmonary) (systemic) 958.1
    with
      abortion — *see* Abortion, by type, with
        embolism
      ectopic pregnancy (*see also* categories
        633.0-633.9) 639.6
      molar pregnancy (*see also* categories 630-
        632) 639.6
    complicating delivery or puerperium
      673.8 ☑
    following
      abortion 639.6
      ectopic or molar pregnancy 639.6
    in pregnancy, childbirth, or the puerperium
      673.8 ☑
  femoral (artery) 444.22
    vein 453.8
      deep 453.41
  following
    abortion 639.6
    ectopic or molar pregnancy 639.6
    infusion, perfusion, or transfusion
      air 999.1
      thrombus 999.2
  heart (fatty) (*see also* Infarct, myocardium)
    410.9 ☑
  hepatic (vein) 453.0
  iliac (artery) 444.81
  iliofemoral 444.81
  in pregnancy, childbirth, or puerperium
    (pulmonary) — *see* Embolism, obstetrical
  intestine (artery) (vein) (with gangrene) 557.0
  intracranial (*see also* Embolism, brain)
    434.1 ☑
    venous sinus (any) 325
      late effect — *see* category 326
      nonpyogenic 437.6
        in pregnancy or puerperium 671.5 ☑
  kidney (artery) 593.81
  lateral sinus (venous) — *see* Embolism,
    intracranial venous sinus
  longitudinal sinus (venous) — *see* Embolism,
    intracranial venous sinus

☑ Additional Digit Required — Refer to the Tabular List (Numeric Code Section) for Additional Digit Selection
▶◀ Revised Text   ● New Line   ▲ Revised Code

2006 ICD-9-CM   October 2005 • Volume 2 — 127

Embolism — *continued*
  lower extremity 444.22
  lung (massive) — *see* Embolism, pulmonary
  meninges (*see also* Embolism, brain) 434.1 ☑
  mesenteric (artery) (with gangrene) 557.0
  multiple NEC 444.9
  obstetrical (pulmonary) 673.2 ☑
    air 673.0 ☑
    amniotic fluid (pulmonary) 673.1 ☑
    blood-clot 673.2 ☑
    cardiac 674.8 ☑
    fat 673.8 ☑
    heart 674.8 ☑
    pyemic 673.3 ☑
    septic 673.3 ☑
    specified NEC 674.8 ☑
  ophthalmic (*see also* Occlusion, retina) 362.30
  paradoxical NEC 444.9
  penis 607.82
  peripheral arteries NEC 444.22
    lower 444.22
    upper 444.21
  pituitary 253.8
  popliteal (artery) 444.22
  portal (vein) 452
  postoperative NEC 997.2
    cerebral 997.02
    mesenteric artery 997.71
    other vessels 997.79
    peripheral vascular 997.2
    pulmonary 415.11
    renal artery 997.72
  precerebral artery (*see also* Occlusion, artery, precerebral) 433.9 ☑
  puerperal — *see* Embolism, obstetrical
  pulmonary (artery) (vein) 415.19
    with
      abortion — *see* Abortion, by type, with embolism
      ectopic pregnancy (*see also* categories 633.0-633.9) 639.6
      molar pregnancy (*see also* categories 630-632) 639.6
    following
      abortion 639.6
      ectopic or molar pregnancy 639.6
    iatrogenic 415.11
    in pregnancy, childbirth, or puerperium — *see* Embolism, obstetrical
    postoperative 415.11
  pyemic (multiple) 038.9
    with
      abortion — *see* Abortion, by type, with embolism
      ectopic pregnancy (*see also* categories 633.0-633.9) 639.6
      molar pregnancy (*see also* categories 630-632) 639.6
    Aerobacter aerogenes 038.49
    enteric gram-negative bacilli 038.40
    Enterobacter aerogenes 038.49
    Escherichia coli 038.42
    following
      abortion 639.6
      ectopic or molar pregnancy 639.6
    Hemophilus influenzae 038.41
    pneumococcal 038.2
    Proteus vulgaris 038.49
    Pseudomonas (aeruginosa) 038.43
    puerperal, postpartum, childbirth (any organism) 673.3 ☑
    Serratia 038.44
    specified organism NEC 038.8
    staphylococcal 038.10
      aureus 038.11
      specified organism NEC 038.19
    streptococcal 038.0
  renal (artery) 593.81
    vein 453.3
  retina, retinal (*see also* Occlusion, retina) 362.30
  saddle (aorta) 444.0
  septicemic — *see* Embolism, pyemic
  sinus — *see* Embolism, intracranial venous sinus

Embolism — *continued*
  soap
    with
      abortion — *see* Abortion, by type, with embolism
      ectopic pregnancy (*see also* categories 633.0-633.9) 639.6
      molar pregnancy (*see also* categories 630-632) 639.6
    following
      abortion 639.6
      ectopic or molar pregnancy 639.6
  spinal cord (nonpyogenic) 336.1
    in pregnancy or puerperium 671.5 ☑
    pyogenic origin 324.1
      late effect — *see* category 326
  spleen, splenic (artery) 444.89
  thrombus (thromboembolism) following infusion, perfusion, or transfusion 999.2
  upper extremity 444.21
  vein 453.9
    with inflammation or phlebitis — *see* Thrombophlebitis
    cerebral (*see also* Embolism, brain) 434.1 ☑
    coronary (*see also* Infarct, myocardium) 410.9 ☑
      without myocardial infarction 411.81
    hepatic 453.0
    lower extremity 453.8
      deep 453.40
        calf 453.42
        distal (lower leg) 453.42
        femoral 453.41
        iliac 453.41
        lower leg 453.42
        peroneal 453.42
        popliteal 453.41
        proximal (upper leg) 453.41
        thigh 453.41
        tibial 453.42
    mesenteric (with gangrene) 557.0
    portal 452
    pulmonary — *see* Embolism, pulmonary
    renal 453.3
    specified NEC 453.8
      with inflammation or phlebitis — *see* Thrombophlebitis
    vena cava (inferior) (superior) 453.2
  vessels of brain (*see also* Embolism, brain) 434.1 ☑

Embolization — *see* Embolism

Embolus — *see* Embolism

Embryoma (M9080/1) — *see also* Neoplasm, by site, uncertain behavior
  benign (M9080/0) — *see* Neoplasm, by site, benign
  kidney (M8960/3) 189.0
  liver (M8970/3) 155.0
  malignant (M9080/3) — *see also* Neoplasm, by site, malignant
    kidney (M8960/3) 189.0
    liver (M8970/3) 155.0
    testis (M9070/3) 186.9
      undescended 186.0
  testis (M9070/3) 186.9
    undescended 186.0

Embryonic
  circulation 747.9
  heart 747.9
  vas deferens 752.89

Embryopathia NEC 759.9

Embryotomy, fetal 763.89

Embryotoxon 743.43
  interfering with vision 743.42

Emesis — *see also* Vomiting
  gravidarum — *see* Hyperemesis, gravidarum

Emissions, nocturnal (semen) 608.89

Emotional
  crisis — *see* Crisis, emotional
  disorder (*see also* Disorder, mental) 300.9
  instability (excessive) 301.3
  overlay — *see* Reaction, adjustment
  upset 300.9

Emotionality, pathological 301.3

Emotogenic disease (*see also* Disorder, psychogenic) 306.9

Emphysema (atrophic) (centriacinar) (centrilobular) (chronic) (diffuse) (essential) (hypertrophic) (interlobular) (lung) (obstructive) (panlobular) (paracicatricial) (paracinar) (postural) (pulmonary) (senile) (subpleural) (traction) (unilateral) (unilobular) (vesicular) 492.8
  with bronchitis
    chronic 491.20
      with
        acute bronchitis 491.22
        exacerbation (acute) 491.21
  bullous (giant) 492.0
  cellular tissue 958.7
    surgical 998.81
  compensatory 518.2
  congenital 770.2
  conjunctiva 372.89
  connective tissue 958.7
    surgical 998.81
  due to fumes or vapors 506.4
  eye 376.89
  eyelid 374.85
    surgical 998.81
    traumatic 958.7
  fetus or newborn (interstitial) (mediastinal) (unilobular) 770.2
  heart 416.9
  interstitial 518.1
    congenital 770.2
    fetus or newborn 770.2
  laminated tissue 958.7
    surgical 998.81
  mediastinal 518.1
    fetus or newborn 770.2
  newborn (interstitial) (mediastinal) (unilobular) 770.2
  obstructive diffuse with fibrosis 492.8
  orbit 376.89
  subcutaneous 958.7
    due to trauma 958.7
    nontraumatic 518.1
    surgical 998.81
  surgical 998.81
  thymus (gland) (congenital) 254.8
  traumatic 958.7
  tuberculous (*see also* Tuberculosis, pulmonary) 011.9 ☑

Employment examination (certification) V70.5

Empty sella (turcica) syndrome 253.8

Empyema (chest) (diaphragmatic) (double) (encapsulated) (general) (interlobar) (lung) (medial) (necessitatis) (perforating chest wall) (pleura) (pneumococcal) (residual) (sacculated) (streptococcal) (supradiaphragmatic) 510.9
  with fistula 510.0
  accessory sinus (chronic) (*see also* Sinusitis) 473.9
  acute 510.9
    with fistula 510.0
  antrum (chronic) (*see also* Sinusitis, maxillary) 473.0
  brain (any part) (*see also* Abscess, brain) 324.0
  ethmoidal (sinus) (chronic) (*see also* Sinusitis, ethmoidal) 473.2
  extradural (*see also* Abscess, extradural) 324.9
  frontal (sinus) (chronic) (*see also* Sinusitis, frontal) 473.1
  gallbladder (*see also* Cholecystitis, acute) 575.0
  mastoid (process) (acute) (*see also* Mastoiditis, acute) 383.00
  maxilla, maxillary 526.4
    sinus (chronic) (*see also* Sinusitis, maxillary) 473.0
  nasal sinus (chronic) (*see also* Sinusitis) 473.9
  sinus (accessory) (nasal) (*see also* Sinusitis) 473.9
  sphenoidal (chronic) (sinus) (*see also* Sinusitis, sphenoidal) 473.3
  subarachnoid (*see also* Abscess, extradural) 324.9
  subdural (*see also* Abscess, extradural) 324.9

Empyema — *continued*
　tuberculous (*see also* Tuberculosis, pleura) 012.0 ☑
　ureter (*see also* Ureteritis) 593.89
　ventricular (*see also* Abscess, brain) 324.0
Enameloma 520.2
Encephalitis (bacterial) (chronic) (hemorrhagic) (idiopathic) (nonepidemic) (spurious) (subacute) 323.9
　acute — *see also* Encephalitis, viral
　　disseminated (postinfectious) NEC 136.9 *[323.6]*
　　　postimmunization or postvaccination 323.5
　　inclusional 049.8
　　inclusion body 049.8
　　necrotizing 049.8
　arboviral, arbovirus NEC 064
　arthropod-borne (*see also* Encephalitis, viral, arthropod-borne) 064
　Australian X 062.4
　Bwamba fever 066.3
　California (virus) 062.5
　Central European 063.2
　Czechoslovakian 063.2
　Dawson's (inclusion body) 046.2
　diffuse sclerosing 046.2
　due to
　　actinomycosis 039.8 *[323.4]*
　　cat-scratch disease 078.3 *[323.0]*
　　infectious mononucleosis 075 *[323.0]*
　　malaria (*see also* Malaria) 084.6 *[323.2]*
　　Negishi virus 064
　　ornithosis 073.7 *[323.0]*
　　prophylactic inoculation against smallpox 323.5
　　rickettsiosis (*see also* Rickettsiosis) 083.9 *[323.1]*
　　rubella 056.01
　　toxoplasmosis (acquired) 130.0
　　　congenital (active) 771.2 *[323.4]*
　　typhus (fever) (*see also* Typhus) 081.9 *[323.1]*
　　vaccination (smallpox) 323.5
　Eastern equine 062.2
　endemic 049.8
　epidemic 049.8
　equine (acute) (infectious) (viral) 062.9
　　Eastern 062.2
　　Venezuelan 066.2
　　Western 062.1
　Far Eastern 063.0
　following vaccination or other immunization procedure 323.5
　herpes 054.3
　Ilheus (virus) 062.8
　inclusion body 046.2
　infectious (acute) (virus) NEC 049.8
　influenzal 487.8 *[323.4]*
　　lethargic 049.8
　Japanese (B type) 062.0
　La Crosse 062.5
　Langat 063.8
　late effect — *see* Late, effect, encephalitis
　lead 984.9 *[323.7]*
　lethargic (acute) (infectious) (influenzal) 049.8
　lethargica 049.8
　louping ill 063.1
　lupus 710.0 *[323.8]*
　lymphatica 049.0
　Mengo 049.8
　meningococcal 036.1
　mumps 072.2
　Murray Valley 062.4
　myoclonic 049.8
　Negishi virus 064
　otitic NEC 382.4 *[323.4]*
　parasitic NEC 123.9 *[323.4]*
　periaxialis (concentrica) (diffusa) 341.1
　postchickenpox 052.0
　postexanthematous NEC 057.9 *[323.6]*
　postimmunization 323.5
　postinfectious NEC 136.9 *[323.6]*
　postmeasles 055.0
　posttraumatic 323.8
　postvaccinal (smallpox) 323.5

Encephalitis — *continued*
　postvaricella 052.0
　postviral NEC 079.99 *[323.6]*
　　postexanthematous 057.9 *[323.6]*
　　　specified NEC 057.8 *[323.6]*
　Powassan 063.8
　progressive subcortical (Binswanger's) 290.12
　Rio Bravo 049.8
　rubella 056.01
　Russian
　　autumnal 062.0
　　spring-summer type (taiga) 063.0
　saturnine 984.9 *[323.7]*
　Semliki Forest 062.8
　serous 048
　slow-acting virus NEC 046.8
　specified cause NEC 323.8
　St. Louis type 062.3
　subacute sclerosing 046.2
　subcorticalis chronica 290.12
　summer 062.0
　suppurative 324.0
　syphilitic 094.81
　　congenital 090.41
　tick-borne 063.9
　torula, torular 117.5 *[323.4]*
　toxic NEC 989.9 *[323.7]*
　toxoplasmic (acquired) 130.0
　　congenital (active) 771.2 *[323.4]*
　trichinosis 124 *[323.4]*
　Trypanosomiasis (*see also* Trypanosomiasis) 086.9 *[323.2]*
　tuberculous (*see also* Tuberculosis) 013.6 ☑
　type B (Japanese) 062.0
　type C 062.3
　van Bogaert's 046.2
　Venezuelan 066.2
　Vienna type 049.8
　viral, virus 049.9
　　arthropod-borne NEC 064
　　　mosquito-borne 062.9
　　　　Australian X disease 062.4
　　　　California virus 062.5
　　　　Eastern equine 062.2
　　　　Ilheus virus 062.8
　　　　Japanese (B type) 062.0
　　　　Murray Valley 062.4
　　　　specified type NEC 062.8
　　　　St. Louis 062.3
　　　　type B 062.0
　　　　type C 062.3
　　　　Western equine 062.1
　　　tick-borne 063.9
　　　　biundulant 063.2
　　　　Central European 063.2
　　　　Czechoslovakian 063.2
　　　　diphasic meningoencephalitis 063.2
　　　　Far Eastern 063.0
　　　　Langat 063.8
　　　　louping ill 063.1
　　　　Powassan 063.8
　　　　Russian spring-summer (taiga) 063.0
　　　　specified type NEC 063.8
　　　vector unknown 064
　　slow acting NEC 046.8
　　specified type NEC 049.8
　　vaccination, prophylactic (against) V05.0
　von Economo's 049.8
　Western equine 062.1
　West Nile type 066.41
Encephalocele 742.0
　orbit 376.81
Encephalocystocele 742.0
Encephalomalacia (brain) (cerebellar) (cerebral) (cerebrospinal) (*see also* Softening, brain) 434.9 ☑
　due to
　　hemorrhage (*see also* Hemorrhage, brain) 431
　　recurrent spasm of artery 435.9
　embolic (cerebral) (*see also* Embolism, brain) 434.1 ☑
　subcorticalis chronicus arteriosclerotica 290.12
　thrombotic (*see also* Thrombosis, brain) 434.0 ☑
Encephalomeningitis — *see* Meningoencephalitis

Encephalomeningocele 742.0
Encephalomeningomyelitis — *see* Meningoencephalitis
Encephalomeningopathy (*see also* Meningoencephalitis) 349.9
Encephalomyelitis (chronic) (granulomatous) (hemorrhagic necrotizing, acute) (myalgic, benign) (*see also* Encephalitis) 323.9
　abortive disseminated 049.8
　acute disseminated ▶(ADEM)◄ (postinfectious) 136.9 *[323.6]*
　　infectious 323.6　　　　　　　●
　　noninfectious 323.8　　　　　●
　　postimmunization 323.5
　due to or resulting from vaccination (any) 323.5
　equine (acute) (infectious) 062.9
　　Eastern 062.2
　　Venezuelan 066.2
　　Western 062.1
　funicularis infectiosa 049.8
　late effect — *see* Late, effect, encephalitis
　Munch-Peterson's 049.8
　postchickenpox 052.0
　postimmunization 323.5
　postmeasles 055.0
　postvaccinal (smallpox) 323.5
　rubella 056.01
　specified cause NEC 323.8
　syphilitic 094.81
　West Nile 066.41
Encephalomyelocele 742.0
Encephalomyelomeningitis — *see* Meningoencephalitis
Encephalomyeloneuropathy 349.9
Encephalomyelopathy 349.9
　subacute necrotizing (infantile) 330.8
Encephalomyeloradiculitis (acute) 357.0
Encephalomyeloradiculoneuritis (acute) 357.0
Encephalomyeloradiculopathy 349.9
Encephalomyocarditis 074.23
Encephalopathia hyperbilirubinemica, newborn 774.7
　due to isoimmunization (conditions classifiable to 773.0-773.2) 773.4
Encephalopathy (acute) 348.30
　alcoholic 291.2
　anoxic — *see* Damage, brain, anoxic
　arteriosclerotic 437.0
　　late effect — *see* Late effect(s) (of) cerebrovascular disease
　bilirubin, newborn 774.7
　　due to isoimmunization 773.4
　congenital 742.9
　demyelinating (callosal) 341.8
　due to
　　birth injury (intracranial) 767.8
　　dialysis 294.8
　　　transient 293.9
　　hyperinsulinism — *see* Hyperinsulinism
　　influenza (virus) 487.8
　　lack of vitamin (*see also* Deficiency, vitamin) 269.2
　　nicotinic acid deficiency 291.2
　　serum (nontherapeutic) (therapeutic) 999.5
　　syphilis 094.81
　　trauma (postconcussional) 310.2
　　　current (*see also* Concussion, brain) 850.9
　　　　with skull fracture — *see* Fracture, skull, by site, with intracranial injury
　　vaccination 323.5
　hepatic 572.2
　hyperbilirubinemic, newborn 774.7
　　due to isoimmunization (conditions classifiable to 773.0-773.2) 773.4
　hypertensive 437.2
　hypoglycemic 251.2
　hypoxic — *see* Damage, brain, anoxic
　infantile cystic necrotizing (congenital) 341.8
　lead 984.9 *[323.7]*
　leukopolio 330.0
　metabolic (*see also* Delirium) 348.31
　　toxic 349.82

☑ Additional Digit Required — Refer to the Tabular List (Numeric Code Section) for Additional Digit Selection
▶◀ Revised Text　　● New Line　　▲ Revised Code

Encephalopathy — continued
  necrotizing, subacute 330.8
  other specified type NEC 348.39
  pellagrous 265.2
  portal-systemic 572.2
  postcontusional 310.2
  posttraumatic 310.2
  saturnine 984.9 *[323.7]*
  septic 348.31
  spongioform, subacute (viral) 046.1
  subacute
    necrotizing 330.8
    spongioform 046.1
    viral, spongioform 046.1
  subcortical progressive (Schilder) 341.1
    chronic (Binswanger's) 290.12
  toxic 349.82
    metabolic 348.31
  traumatic (postconcussional) 310.2
    current (*see also* Concussion, brain) 850.9
      with skull fracture — *see* Fracture, skull,
        by site, with intracranial injury
  vitamin B deficiency NEC 266.9
  Wernicke's (superior hemorrhagic
    polioencephalitis) 265.1
Encephalorrhagia (*see also* Hemorrhage, brain)
  432.9
  healed or old V12.59
  late effect — *see* Late effect(s) (of)
    cerebrovascular disease
Encephalosis, posttraumatic 310.2
Enchondroma (M9220/0) — *see also* Neoplasm,
  bone, benign
  multiple, congenital 756.4
Enchondromatosis (cartilaginous) (congenital)
  (multiple) 756.4
Enchondroses, multiple (cartilaginous)
  (congenital) 756.4
Encopresis (*see also* Incontinence, feces) 787.6
  nonorganic origin 307.7
Encounter for — *see also* Admission for
  administrative purpose only V68.9
    referral of patient without examination or
      treatment V68.81
    specified purpose NEC V68.89
  chemotherapy, ▶antineoplastic◀ V58.11 ▲
  dialysis
    extracorporeal (renal) V56.0
    peritoneal V56.8
  end-of-life care V66.7
  hospice care V66.7
  immunotherapy, antineoplastic V58.12 ●
  palliative care V66.7
  paternity testing V70.4
  radiotherapy V58.0
  respirator ▶[ventilator]◀ dependence
    during
      mechanical failure V46.14 ●
      power failure V46.12 ●
    for weaning V46.13 ●
  screening mammogram NEC V76.12
    for high-risk patient V76.11
  terminal care V66.7
  weaning from respirator [ventilator] V46.13 ●
Encystment — *see* Cyst
End-of-life care V66.7
Endamebiasis — *see* Amebiasis
Endamoeba — *see* Amebiasis
Endarteritis (bacterial, subacute) (infective)
  (septic) 447.6
  brain, cerebral or cerebrospinal 437.4
    late effect — *see* Late effect(s) (of)
      cerebrovascular disease
  coronary (artery) — *see* Arteriosclerosis,
    coronary
  deformans — *see* Arteriosclerosis
  embolic (*see also* Embolism) 444.9
  obliterans — *see also* Arteriosclerosis
    pulmonary 417.8
  pulmonary 417.8
  retina 362.18
  senile — *see* Arteriosclerosis

Endarteritis — continued
  syphilitic 093.89
    brain or cerebral 094.89
    congenital 090.5
    spinal 094.89
  tuberculous (*see also* Tuberculosis) 017.9 ☑
Endemic — *see* condition
Endocarditis (chronic) (indeterminate) (interstitial)
  (marantis) (nonbacterial thrombotic)
  (residual) (sclerotic) (sclerous) (senile)
  (valvular) 424.90
  with
    rheumatic fever (conditions classifiable to
      390)
      active — *see* Endocarditis, acute,
        rheumatic
      inactive or quiescent (with chorea) 397.9
  acute or subacute 421.9
    rheumatic (aortic) (mitral) (pulmonary)
      (tricuspid) 391.1
      with chorea (acute) (rheumatic)
        (Sydenham's) 392.0
  aortic (heart) (nonrheumatic) (valve) 424.1
    with
      mitral (valve) disease 396.9
        active or acute 391.1
          with chorea (acute) (rheumatic)
            (Sydenham's) 392.0
          bacterial 421.0
      rheumatic fever (conditions classifiable to
        390)
        active — *see* Endocarditis, acute,
          rheumatic
        inactive or quiescent (with chorea)
          395.9
          with mitral disease 396.9
    acute or subacute 421.9
    arteriosclerotic 424.1
    congenital 746.89
    hypertensive 424.1
    rheumatic (chronic) (inactive) 395.9
      with mitral (valve) disease 396.9
        active or acute 391.1
          with chorea (acute) (rheumatic)
            (Sydenham's) 392.0
        active or acute 391.1
          with chorea (acute) (rheumatic)
            (Sydenham's) 392.0
    specified cause, except rheumatic 424.1
    syphilitic 093.22
  arteriosclerotic or due to arteriosclerosis
    424.99
  atypical verrucous (Libman-Sacks)
    710.0 *[424.91]*
  bacterial (acute) (any valve) (chronic) (subacute)
    421.0
  blastomycotic 116.0 *[421.1]*
  candidal 112.81
  congenital 425.3
  constrictive 421.0
  Coxsackie 074.22
  due to
    blastomycosis 116.0 *[421.1]*
    candidiasis 112.81
    Coxsackie (virus) 074.22
    disseminated lupus erythematosus
      710.0 *[424.91]*
    histoplasmosis (*see also* Histoplasmosis)
      115.94
    hypertension (benign) 424.99
    moniliasis 112.81
    prosthetic cardiac valve 996.61
    Q fever 083.0 *[421.1]*
    serratia marcescens 421.0
    typhoid (fever) 002.0 *[421.1]*
  fetal 425.3
  gonococcal 098.84
  hypertensive 424.99
  infectious or infective (acute) (any valve)
    (chronic) (subacute) 421.0
  lenta (acute) (any valve) (chronic) (subacute)
    421.0
  Libman-Sacks 710.0 *[424.91]*
  Loeffler's (parietal fibroplastic) 421.0
  malignant (acute) (any valve) (chronic)
    (subacute) 421.0

Endocarditis — continued
  meningococcal 036.42
  mitral (chronic) (double) (fibroid) (heart)
    (inactive) (valve) (with chorea) 394.9
  with
    aortic (valve) disease 396.9
      active or acute 391.1
        with chorea (acute) (rheumatic)
          (Sydenham's) 392.0
      rheumatic fever (conditions classifiable to
        390)
        active — *see* Endocarditis, acute,
          rheumatic
        inactive or quiescent (with chorea)
          394.9
          with aortic valve disease 396.9
    active or acute 391.1
      with chorea (acute) (rheumatic)
        (Sydenham's) 392.0
      bacterial 421.0
    arteriosclerotic 424.0
    congenital 746.89
    hypertensive 424.0
    nonrheumatic 424.0
      acute or subacute 421.9
    syphilitic 093.21
  monilial 112.81
  mycotic (acute) (any valve) (chronic) (subacute)
    421.0
  pneumococcic (acute) (any valve) (chronic)
    (subacute) 421.0
  pulmonary (chronic) (heart) (valve) 424.3
  with
    rheumatic fever (conditions classifiable to
      390)
      active — *see* Endocarditis, acute,
        rheumatic
      inactive or quiescent (with chorea)
        397.1
    acute or subacute 421.9
      rheumatic 391.1
        with chorea (acute) (rheumatic)
          (Sydenham's) 392.0
    arteriosclerotic or due to arteriosclerosis
      424.3
    congenital 746.09
    hypertensive or due to hypertension (benign)
      424.3
    rheumatic (chronic) (inactive) (with chorea)
      397.1
      active or acute 391.1
        with chorea (acute) (rheumatic)
          (Sydenham's) 392.0
    syphilitic 093.24
  purulent (acute) (any valve) (chronic) (subacute)
    421.0
  rheumatic (chronic) (inactive) (with chorea)
    397.9
    active or acute (aortic) (mitral) (pulmonary)
      (tricuspid) 391.1
      with chorea (acute) (rheumatic)
        (Sydenham's) 392.0
  septic (acute) (any valve) (chronic) (subacute)
    421.0
  specified cause, except rheumatic 424.99
  streptococcal (acute) (any valve) (chronic)
    (subacute) 421.0
  subacute — *see* Endocarditis, acute
  suppurative (any valve) (acute) (chronic)
    (subacute) 421.0
  syphilitic NEC 093.20
  toxic (*see also* Endocarditis, acute) 421.9
  tricuspid (chronic) (heart) (inactive) (rheumatic)
    (valve) (with chorea) 397.0
  with
    rheumatic fever (conditions classifiable to
      390)
      active — *see* Endocarditis, acute,
        rheumatic
      inactive or quiescent (with chorea)
        397.0
    active or acute 391.1
      with chorea (acute) (rheumatic)
        (Sydenham's) 392.0
    arteriosclerotic 424.2
    congenital 746.89
    hypertensive 424.2

Endocarditis — continued
 tricuspid — continued
  nonrheumatic 424.2
   acute or subacute 421.9
   specified cause, except rheumatic 424.2
  syphilitic 093.23
  tuberculous (see also Tuberculosis)
   017.9 ☑ [424.91]
  typhoid 002.0 [421.1]
 ulcerative (acute) (any valve) (chronic)
  (subacute) 421.0
 vegetative (acute) (any valve) (chronic)
  (subacute) 421.0
 verrucous (acute) (any valve) (chronic)
  (subacute) NEC 710.0 [424.91]
  nonbacterial 710.0 [424.91]
  nonrheumatic 710.0 [424.91]
Endocardium, endocardial — see also condition
 cushion defect 745.60
  specified type NEC 745.69
Endocervicitis (see also Cervicitis) 616.0
 due to
  intrauterine (contraceptive) device 996.65
 gonorrheal (acute) 098.15
  chronic or duration of 2 months or over
   098.35
 hyperplastic 616.0
 syphilitic 095.8
 trichomonal 131.09
 tuberculous (see also Tuberculosis) 016.7 ☑
Endocrine — see condition
Endocrinopathy, pluriglandular 258.9
Endodontitis 522.0
Endomastoiditis (see also Mastoiditis) 383.9
Endometrioma 617.9
Endometriosis 617.9
 appendix 617.5
 bladder 617.8
 bowel 617.5
 broad ligament 617.3
 cervix 617.0
 colon 617.5
 cul-de-sac (Douglas') 617.3
 exocervix 617.0
 fallopian tube 617.2
 female genital organ NEC 617.8
 gallbladder 617.8
 in scar of skin 617.6
 internal 617.0
 intestine 617.5
 lung 617.8
 myometrium 617.0
 ovary 617.1
 parametrium 617.3
 pelvic peritoneum 617.3
 peritoneal (pelvic) 617.3
 rectovaginal septum 617.4
 rectum 617.5
 round ligament 617.3
 skin 617.6
 specified site NEC 617.8
 stromal (M8931/1) 236.0
 umbilicus 617.8
 uterus 617.0
  internal 617.0
 vagina 617.4
 vulva 617.8
Endometritis (nonspecific) (purulent) (septic)
 (suppurative) 615.9
 with
  abortion — see Abortion, by type, with
   sepsis
  ectopic pregnancy (see also categories
   633.0-633.9) 639.0
  molar pregnancy (see also categories 630-
   632) 639.0
 acute 615.0
 blennorrhagic 098.16
  acute 098.16
  chronic or duration of 2 months or over
   098.36
 cervix, cervical (see also Cervicitis) 616.0
  hyperplastic 616.0
 chronic 615.1

Endometritis — continued
 complicating pregnancy 646.6 ☑
  affecting fetus or newborn 760.8
 decidual 615.9
 following
  abortion 639.0
  ectopic or molar pregnancy 639.0
 gonorrheal (acute) 098.16
  chronic or duration of 2 months or over
   098.36
 hyperplastic (see also Hyperplasia,
  endometrium) 621.30
  cervix 616.0
 polypoid — see Endometritis, hyperplastic
 puerperal, postpartum, childbirth 670.0 ☑
 senile (atrophic) 615.9
 subacute 615.0
 tuberculous (see also Tuberculosis) 016.7 ☑
Endometrium — see condition
Endomyocardiopathy, South African 425.2
Endomyocarditis — see Endocarditis
Endomyofibrosis 425.0
Endomyometritis (see also Endometritis) 615.9
Endopericarditis — see Endocarditis
Endoperineuritis — see Disorder, nerve
Endophlebitis (see also Phlebitis) 451.9
 leg 451.2
  deep (vessels) 451.19
  superficial (vessels) 451.0
 portal (vein) 572.1
 retina 362.18
 specified site NEC 451.89
 syphilitic 093.89
Endophthalmia (see also Endophthalmitis)
 360.00
 gonorrheal 098.42
Endophthalmitis (globe) (infective) (metastatic)
 (purulent) (subacute) 360.00
 acute 360.01
 chronic 360.03
 parasitic 360.13
 phacoanaphylactic 360.19
 specified type NEC 360.19
 sympathetic 360.11
Endosalpingioma (M9111/1) 236.2
Endosteitis — see Osteomyelitis
Endothelioma, bone (M9260/3) — see Neoplasm,
 bone, malignant
Endotheliosis 287.8
 hemorrhagic infectional 287.8
Endotoxic shock 785.52
Endotrachelitis (see also Cervicitis) 616.0
Enema rash 692.89
Engel-von Recklinghausen disease or syndrome
 (osteitis fibrosa cystica) 252.01
Engelmann's disease (diaphyseal sclerosis) 756.9
English disease (see also Rickets) 268.0
Engman's disease (infectious eczematoid
 dermatitis) 690.8
Engorgement
 breast 611.79
  newborn 778.7
  puerperal, postpartum 676.2 ☑
 liver 573.9
 lung 514
 pulmonary 514
 retina, venous 362.37
 stomach 536.8
 venous, retina 362.37
Enlargement, enlarged — see also Hypertrophy
 abdomen 789.3 ☑
 adenoids 474.12
  and tonsils 474.10
 alveolar process or ridge 525.8
 apertures of diaphragm (congenital) 756.6
 blind spot, visual field 368.42
 gingival 523.8
 heart, cardiac (see also Hypertrophy, cardiac)
  429.3
 lacrimal gland, chronic 375.03
 liver (see also Hypertrophy, liver) 789.1
 lymph gland or node 785.6

Enlargement, enlarged — see also Hypertrophy
 — continued
 orbit 376.46
 organ or site, congenital NEC — see Anomaly,
  specified type NEC
 parathyroid (gland) 252.01
 pituitary fossa 793.0
 prostate (simple) (soft) 600.00
  with urinary retention 600.01
 sella turcica 793.0
 spleen (see also Splenomegaly) 789.2
  congenital 759.0
 thymus (congenital) (gland) 254.0
 thyroid (gland) (see also Goiter) 240.9
 tongue 529.8
 tonsils 474.11
  and adenoids 474.10
 uterus 621.2
Enophthalmos 376.50
 due to
  atrophy of orbital tissue 376.51
  surgery 376.52
  trauma 376.52
Enostosis 526.89
Entamebiasis — see Amebiasis
Entamebic — see Amebiasis
Entanglement, umbilical cord(s) 663.3 ☑
 with compression 663.2 ☑
 affecting fetus or newborn 762.5
 around neck with compression 663.1 ☑
 twins in monoamniotic sac 663.2 ☑
Enteralgia 789.0 ☑
Enteric — see condition
Enteritis (acute) (catarrhal) (choleraic) (chronic)
 (congestive) (diarrheal) (exudative) (follicular)
 (hemorrhagic) (infantile) (lienteric)
 (noninfectious) (perforative) (phlegmonous)
 (presumed noninfectious)
 (pseudomembranous) 558.9
 adaptive 564.9
 aertrycke infection 003.0
 allergic 558.3
 amebic (see also Amebiasis) 006.9
  with abscess — see Abscess, amebic
  acute 006.0
   with abscess — see Abscess, amebic
   nondysenteric 006.2
  chronic 006.1
   with abscess — see Abscess, amebic
   nondysenteric 006.2
  nondysenteric 006.2
 anaerobic (cocci) (gram-negative) (gram-positive)
  (mixed) NEC 008.46
 bacillary NEC 004.9
 bacterial NEC 008.5
  specified NEC 008.49
 Bacteroides (fragilis) (melaninogeniscus) (oralis)
  008.46
 Butyrivibrio (fibriosolvens) 008.46
 Campylobacter 008.43
 Candida 112.85
 Chilomastix 007.8
 choleriformis 001.1
 chronic 558.9
  ulcerative (see also Colitis, ulcerative) 556.9
 cicatrizing (chronic) 555.0
 Clostridium
  botulinum 005.1
  difficile 008.45
  haemolyticum 008.46
  novyi 008.46
  perfringens (C) (F) 008.46
  specified type NEC 008.46
 coccidial 007.2
 dietetic 558.9
 due to
  achylia gastrica 536.8
  adenovirus 008.62
  Aerobacter aerogenes 008.2
  anaerobes (see also Enteritis, anaerobic)
   008.46
  Arizona (bacillus) 008.1
  astrovirus 008.66
  Bacillus coli — see Enteritis, E. coli

Enteritis — *continued*
due to — *continued*
bacteria NEC 008.5
specified NEC 008.49
Bacteroides (*see also* Enteritis, Bacteroides) 008.46
Butyrivibrio (fibriosolvens) 008.46
Calcivirus 008.65
Camplyobacter 008.43
Clostridium — *see* Enteritis, Clostridium
Cockle agent 008.64
Coxsackie (virus) 008.67
Ditchling agent 008.64
ECHO virus 008.67
Enterobacter aerogenes 008.2
enterococci 008.49
enterovirus NEC 008.67
Escherichia coli — *see* Enteritis, E. coli
Eubacterium 008.46
Fusobacterium (nucleatum) 008.46
gram-negative bacteria NEC 008.47
anaerobic NEC 008.46
Hawaii agent 008.63
irritating foods 558.9
Klebsiella aerogenes 008.47
Marin County agent 008.66
Montgomery County agent 008.63
Norwalk-like agent 008.63
Norwalk virus 008.63
Otofuke agent 008.63
Paracolobactrum arizonae 008.1
paracolon bacillus NEC 008.47
Arizona 008.1
Paramatta agent 008.64
Peptococcus 008.46
Peptostreptococcus 008.46
Proprionibacterium 008.46
Proteus (bacillus) (mirabilis) (morganii) 008.3
Pseudomonas aeruginosa 008.42
Rotavirus 008.61
Sapporo agent 008.63
small round virus (SRV) NEC 008.64
featureless NEC 008.63
structured NEC 008.63
Snow Mountain (SM) agent 008.63
specified
bacteria NEC 008.49
organism, nonbacterial NEC 008.8
virus NEC 008.69
Staphylococcus 008.41
Streptococcus 008.49
anaerobic 008.46
Taunton agent 008.63
Torovirus 008.69
Treponema 008.46
Veillonella 008.46
virus 008.8
specified type NEC 008.69
Wollan (W) agent 008.64
Yersinia enterocolitica 008.44
dysentery — *see* Dysentery
E. coli 008.00
enterohemorrhagic 008.04
enteroinvasive 008.03
enteropathogenic 008.01
enterotoxigenic 008.02
specified type NEC 008.09
el tor 001.1
embadomonial 007.8
epidemic 009.0
Eubacterium 008.46
fermentative 558.9
fulminant 557.0
Fusobacterium (nucleatum) 008.46
gangrenous (*see also* Enteritis, due to, by organism) 009.0
giardial 007.1
gram-negative bacteria NEC 008.47
anaerobic NEC 008.46
infectious NEC (*see also* Enteritis, due to, by organism) 009.0
presumed 009.1
influenzal 487.8
ischemic 557.9
acute 557.0
chronic 557.1
due to mesenteric artery insufficiency 557.1

Enteritis — *continued*
membranous 564.9
mucous 564.9
myxomembranous 564.9
necrotic (*see also* Enteritis, due to, by organism) 009.0
necroticans 005.2
necrotizing of fetus or newborn 777.5
neurogenic 564.9
newborn 777.8
necrotizing 777.5
parasitic NEC 129
paratyphoid (fever) (*see also* Fever, paratyphoid) 002.9
Peptococcus 008.46
Peptostreptococcus 008.46
Proprionibacterium 008.46
protozoal NEC 007.9
radiation 558.1
regional (of) 555.9
intestine
large (bowel, colon, or rectum) 555.1
with small intestine 555.2
small (duodenum, ileum, or jejunum) 555.0
with large intestine 555.2
Salmonella infection 003.0
salmonellosis 003.0
segmental (*see also* Enteritis, regional) 555.9
septic (*see also* Enteritis, due to, by organism) 009.0
Shigella 004.9
simple 558.9
spasmodic 564.9
spastic 564.9
staphylococcal 008.41
due to food 005.0
streptococcal 008.49
anaerobic 008.46
toxic 558.2
Treponema (denticola) (macrodentium) 008.46
trichomonal 007.3
tuberculous (*see also* Tuberculosis) 014.8 ☑
typhosa 002.0
ulcerative (chronic) (*see also* Colitis, ulcerative) 556.9
Veillonella 008.46
viral 008.8
adenovirus 008.62
enterovirus 008.67
specified virus NEC 008.69
Yersinia enterocolitica 008.44
zymotic 009.0
Enteroarticular syndrome 099.3
Enterobiasis 127.4
Enterobius vermicularis 127.4
Enterocele (*see also* Hernia) 553.9
pelvis, pelvic (acquired) (congenital) 618.6
vagina, vaginal (acquired) (congenital) 618.6
Enterocolitis — *see also* Enteritis
fetus or newborn 777.8
necrotizing 777.5
fulminant 557.0
granulomatous 555.2
hemorrhagic (acute) 557.0
chronic 557.1
necrotizing (acute) (membranous) 557.0
primary necrotizing 777.5
pseudomembranous 008.45
radiation 558.1
newborn 777.5
ulcerative 556.0
Enterocystoma 751.5
Enterogastritis — *see* Enteritis
Enterogenous cyanosis 289.7
Enterolith, enterolithiasis (impaction) 560.39
with hernia — *see also* Hernia, by site, with obstruction
gangrenous — *see* Hernia, by site, with gangrene
Enteropathy 569.9
exudative (of Gordon) 579.8
gluten 579.0
hemorrhagic, terminal 557.0
protein-losing 579.8

Enteroperitonitis (*see also* Peritonitis) 567.9
Enteroptosis 569.89
Enterorrhagia 578.9
Enterospasm 564.9
psychogenic 306.4
Enterostenosis (*see also* Obstruction, intestine) 560.9
Enterostomy status V44.4
with complication 569.60
Enthesopathy 726.90
ankle and tarsus 726.70
elbow region 726.30
specified NEC 726.39
hip 726.5
knee 726.60
peripheral NEC 726.8
shoulder region 726.10
adhesive 726.0
spinal 720.1
wrist and carpus 726.4
Entrance, air into vein — *see* Embolism, air
Entrapment, nerve — *see* Neuropathy, entrapment
Entropion (eyelid) 374.00
cicatricial 374.04
congenital 743.62
late effect of trachoma (healed) 139.1
mechanical 374.02
paralytic 374.02
senile 374.01
spastic 374.03
Enucleation of eye (current) (traumatic) 871.3
Enuresis 788.30
habit disturbance 307.6
nocturnal 788.36
psychogenic 307.6
nonorganic origin 307.6
psychogenic 307.6
Enzymopathy 277.9
Eosinopenia 288.0
Eosinophilia 288.3
allergic 288.3
hereditary 288.3
idiopathic 288.3
infiltrative 518.3
Loeffler's 518.3
myalgia syndrome 710.5
pulmonary (tropical) 518.3
secondary 288.3
tropical 518.3
Eosinophilic — *see also* condition
fasciitis 728.89
granuloma (bone) 277.89
infiltration lung 518.3
Ependymitis (acute) (cerebral) (chronic) (granular) (*see also* Meningitis) 322.9
Ependymoblastoma (M9392/3)
specified site — *see* Neoplasm, by site, malignant
unspecified site 191.9
Ependymoma (epithelial) (malignant) (M9391/3)
anaplastic type (M9392/3)
specified site — *see* Neoplasm, by site, malignant
unspecified site 191.9
benign (M9391/0)
specified site — *see* Neoplasm, by site, benign
unspecified site 225.0
myxopapillary (M9394/1) 237.5
papillary (M9393/1) 237.5
specified site — *see* Neoplasm, by site, malignant
unspecified site 191.9
Ependymopathy 349.2
spinal cord 349.2
Ephelides, ephelis 709.09
Ephemeral fever (*see also* Pyrexia) 780.6
Epiblepharon (congenital) 743.62
Epicanthus, epicanthic fold (congenital) (eyelid) 743.63

Epicondylitis (elbow) (lateral) 726.32
  medial 726.31
Epicystitis (*see also* Cystitis) 595.9
Epidemic — *see* condition
Epidermidalization, cervix — *see* condition
Epidermidization, cervix — *see* condition
Epidermis, epidermal — *see* condition
Epidermization, cervix — *see* condition
Epidermodysplasia verruciformis 078.19
Epidermoid
  cholesteatoma — *see* Cholesteatoma
  inclusion (*see also* Cyst, skin) 706.2
Epidermolysis
  acuta (combustiformis) (toxica) 695.1
  bullosa 757.39
  necroticans combustiformis 695.1
    due to drug
      correct substance properly administered 695.1
      overdose or wrong substance given or taken 977.9
        specified drug — *see* Table of Drugs and Chemicals
Epidermophytid — *see* Dermatophytosis
Epidermophytosis (infected) — *see* Dermatophytosis
Epidermosis, ear (middle) (*see also* Cholesteatoma) 385.30
Epididymis — *see* condition
Epididymitis (nonvenereal) 604.90
  with abscess 604.0
  acute 604.99
  blennorrhagic (acute) 098.0
    chronic or duration of 2 months or over 098.2
  caseous (*see also* Tuberculosis) 016.4 ☑
  chlamydial 099.54
  diphtheritic 032.89 *[604.91]*
  filarial 125.9 *[604.91]*
  gonococcal (acute) 098.0
    chronic or duration of 2 months or over 098.2
  recurrent 604.99
  residual 604.99
  syphilitic 095.8 *[604.91]*
  tuberculous (*see also* Tuberculosis) 016.4 ☑
Epididymo-orchitis (*see also* Epididymitis) 604.90
  with abscess 604.0
  chlamydial 099.54
  gonococcal (acute) 098.13
    chronic or duration of 2 months or over 098.33
Epidural — *see* condition
Epigastritis (*see also* Gastritis) 535.5 ☑
Epigastrium, epigastric — *see* condition
Epigastrocele (*see also* Hernia, epigastric) 553.29
Epiglottiditis (acute) 464.30
  with obstruction 464.31
  chronic 476.1
  viral 464.30
    with obstruction 464.31
Epiglottis — *see* condition
Epiglottitis (acute) 464.30
  with obstruction 464.31
  chronic 476.1
  viral 464.30
    with obstruction 464.31
Epignathus 759.4
Epilepsia
  partialis continua (*see also* Epilepsy) 345.7 ☑
  procursiva (*see also* Epilepsy) 345.8 ☑
Epilepsy, epileptic (idiopathic) 345.9 ☑

Note — use the following fifth-digit subclassification with categories 345.0, 345.1, 345.4–345.9:

  0   without mention of intractable epilepsy
  1   with intractable epilepsy

  abdominal 345.5 ☑
  absence (attack) 345.0 ☑

Epilepsy, epileptic — *continued*
  akinetic 345.0 ☑
    psychomotor 345.4 ☑
  automatism 345.4 ☑
  autonomic diencephalic 345.5 ☑
  brain 345.9 ☑
  Bravais-Jacksonian 345.5 ☑
  cerebral 345.9 ☑
  climacteric 345.9 ☑
  clonic 345.1 ☑
  clouded state 345.9 ☑
  coma 345.3
  communicating 345.4 ☑
  congenital 345.9 ☑
  convulsions 345.9 ☑
  cortical (focal) (motor) 345.5 ☑
  cursive (running) 345.8 ☑
  cysticercosis 123.1
  deterioration
    with behavioral disturbance 345.9 ☑ *[294.11]*
    without behavioral disturbance 345.9 ☑ *[294.10]*
  due to syphilis 094.89
  equivalent 345.5 ☑
  fit 345.9 ☑
  focal (motor) 345.5 ☑
  gelastic 345.8 ☑
  generalized 345.9 ☑
    convulsive 345.1 ☑
    flexion 345.1 ☑
    nonconvulsive 345.0 ☑
  grand mal (idiopathic) 345.1 ☑
  Jacksonian (motor) (sensory) 345.5 ☑
  Kojevnikoff's, Kojevnikov's, Kojewnikof's 345.7 ☑
  laryngeal 786.2
  limbic system 345.4 ☑
  major (motor) 345.1 ☑
  minor 345.0 ☑
  mixed (type) 345.9 ☑
  motor partial 345.5 ☑
  musicogenic 345.1 ☑
  myoclonus, myoclonic 345.1 ☑
    progressive (familial) 333.2
  nonconvulsive, generalized 345.0 ☑
  parasitic NEC 123.9
  partial (focalized) 345.5 ☑
    with
      impairment of consciousness 345.4 ☑
      memory and ideational disturbances 345.4 ☑
    abdominal type 345.5 ☑
    motor type 345.5 ☑
    psychomotor type 345.4 ☑
    psychosensory type 345.4 ☑
    secondarily generalized 345.4 ☑
    sensory type 345.5 ☑
    somatomotor type 345.5 ☑
    somatosensory type 345.5 ☑
    temporal lobe type 345.4 ☑
    visceral type 345.5 ☑
    visual type 345.5 ☑
  peripheral 345.9 ☑
  petit mal 345.0 ☑
  photokinetic 345.8 ☑
  progressive myoclonic (familial) 333.2
  psychic equivalent 345.5 ☑
  psychomotor 345.4 ☑
  psychosensory 345.4 ☑
  reflex 345.1 ☑
  seizure 345.9 ☑
  senile 345.9 ☑
  sensory-induced 345.5 ☑
  sleep (*see also* Narcolepsy) 347.00
  somatomotor type 345.5 ☑
  somatosensory 345.5 ☑
  specified type NEC 345.8 ☑
  status (grand mal) 345.3
    focal motor 345.7 ☑
    petit mal 345.2
    psychomotor 345.7 ☑
    temporal lobe 345.7 ☑
  symptomatic 345.9 ☑
  temporal lobe 345.4 ☑
  tonic (-clonic) 345.1 ☑

Epilepsy, epileptic — *continued*
  traumatic (injury unspecified) 907.0
    injury specified — *see* Late, effect (of) specified injury
  twilight 293.0
  uncinate (gyrus) 345.4 ☑
  Unverricht (-Lundborg) (familial myoclonic) 333.2
  visceral 345.5 ☑
  visual 345.5 ☑
Epileptiform
  convulsions 780.39
  seizure 780.39
Epiloia 759.5
Epimenorrhea 626.2
Epipharyngitis (*see also* Nasopharyngitis) 460
Epiphora 375.20
  due to
    excess lacrimation 375.21
    insufficient drainage 375.22
Epiphyseal arrest 733.91
  femoral head 732.2
Epiphyseolysis, epiphysiolysis (*see also* Osteochondrosis) 732.9
Epiphysitis (*see also* Osteochondrosis) 732.9
  juvenile 732.6
  marginal (Scheuermann's) 732.0
  os calcis 732.5
  syphilitic (congenital) 090.0
  vertebral (Scheuermann's) 732.0
Epiplocele (*see also* Hernia) 553.9
Epiploitis (*see also* Peritonitis) 567.9
Epiplosarcomphalocele (*see also* Hernia, umbilicus) 553.1
Episcleritis 379.00
  gouty 274.89 *[379.09]*
  nodular 379.02
  periodica fugax 379.01
    angioneurotic — *see* Edema, angioneurotic
  specified NEC 379.09
  staphylococcal 379.00
  suppurative 379.00
  syphilitic 095.0
  tuberculous (*see also* Tuberculosis) 017.3 ☑ *[379.09]*
Episode
  brain (*see also* Disease, cerebrovascular, acute) 436
  cerebral (*see also* Disease, cerebrovascular, acute) 436
  depersonalization (in neurotic state) 300.6
  hyporesponsive 780.09
  psychotic (*see also* Psychosis) 298.9
    organic, transient 293.9
  schizophrenic (acute) NEC (*see also* Schizophrenia) 295.4 ☑
Epispadias
  female 753.8
  male 752.62
Episplenitis 289.59
Epistaxis (multiple) 784.7
  hereditary 448.0
  vicarious menstruation 625.8
Epithelioma (malignant) (M8011/3) — *see also* Neoplasm, by site, malignant
  adenoides cysticum (M8100/0) — *see* Neoplasm, skin, benign
  basal cell (M8090/3) — *see* Neoplasm, skin, malignant
  benign (M8011/0) — *see* Neoplasm, by site, benign
  Bowen's (M8081/2) — *see* Neoplasm, skin, in situ
  calcifying (benign) (Malherbe's) (M8110/0) — *see* Neoplasm, skin, benign
  external site — *see* Neoplasm, skin, malignant
  intraepidermal, Jadassohn (M8096/0) — *see* Neoplasm, skin, benign
  squamous cell (M8070/3) — *see* Neoplasm, by site, malignant
Epitheliopathy
  pigment, retina 363.15
  posterior multifocal placoid (acute) 363.15

☑ Additional Digit Required — Refer to the Tabular List (Numeric Code Section) for Additional Digit Selection

Epithelium, epithelial — *see* condition
Epituberculosis (allergic) (with atelectasis) (*see also* Tuberculosis) 010.8 ☑
Eponychia 757.5
Epstein's
    nephrosis or syndrome (*see also* Nephrosis) 581.9
    pearl (mouth) 528.4
Epstein-Barr infection (viral) 075
    chronic 780.79 *[139.8]*
Epulis (giant cell) (gingiva) 523.8
Equinia 024
Equinovarus (congenital) 754.51
    acquired 736.71
Equivalent
    convulsive (abdominal) (*see also* Epilepsy) 345.5 ☑
    epileptic (psychic) (*see also* Epilepsy) 345.5 ☑
Erb's
    disease 359.1
    palsy, paralysis (birth) (brachial) (newborn) 767.6
        spinal (spastic) syphilitic 094.89
    pseudohypertrophic muscular dystrophy 359.1
Erb (-Duchenne) paralysis (birth injury) (newborn) 767.6
Erb-Goldflam disease or syndrome 358.00
Erdheim's syndrome (acromegalic macrospondylitis) 253.0
Erection, painful (persistent) 607.3
Ergosterol deficiency (vitamin D) 268.9
    with
        osteomalacia 268.2
        rickets (*see also* Rickets) 268.0
Ergotism (ergotized grain) 988.2
    from ergot used as drug (migraine therapy)
        correct substance properly administered 349.82
        overdose or wrong substance given or taken 975.0
Erichsen's disease (railway spine) 300.16
Erlacher-Blount syndrome (tibia vara) 732.4
Erosio interdigitalis blastomycetica 112.3
Erosion
    artery NEC 447.2
        without rupture 447.8
    arteriosclerotic plaque — *see* Arteriosclerosis, by site
    bone 733.99
    bronchus 519.1
    cartilage (joint) 733.99
    cervix (uteri) (acquired) (chronic) (congenital) 622.0
        with mention of cervicitis 616.0
    cornea (recurrent) (*see also* Keratitis) 371.42
        traumatic 918.1
    dental (idiopathic) (occupational) 521.30
        extending into
            dentine 521.32
            pulp 521.33
        generalized 521.35
        limited to enamel 521.31
        localized 521.34
    duodenum, postpyloric — *see* Ulcer, duodenum
    esophagus 530.89
    gastric 535.4 ☑
    intestine 569.89
    lymphatic vessel 457.8
    pylorus, pyloric (ulcer) 535.4 ☑
    sclera 379.16
    spine, aneurysmal 094.89
    spleen 289.59
    stomach 535.4 ☑
    teeth (idiopathic) (occupational) (*see also* Erosion, dental) 521.30
        due to
            medicine 521.30
            persistent vomiting 521.30
    urethra 599.84
    uterus 621.8
    vertebra 733.99
Erotomania 302.89
    Clérambault's 297.8

Error
    in diet 269.9
    refractive 367.9
        astigmatism (*see also* Astigmatism) 367.20
        drug-induced 367.89
        hypermetropia 367.0
        hyperopia 367.0
        myopia 367.1
        presbyopia 367.4
        toxic 367.89
Eructation 787.3
    nervous 306.4
    psychogenic 306.4
Eruption
    creeping 126.9
    drug — *see* Dermatitis, due to, drug
    Hutchinson, summer 692.72
    Kaposi's varicelliform 054.0
    napkin (psoriasiform) 691.0
    polymorphous
        light (sun) 692.72
        other source 692.82
    psoriasiform, napkin 691.0
    recalcitrant pustular 694.8
    ringed 695.89
    skin (*see also* Dermatitis) 782.1
        creeping (meaning hookworm) 126.9
        due to
            chemical(s) NEC 692.4
                internal use 693.8
            drug — *see* Dermatitis, due to, drug
            prophylactic inoculation or vaccination against disease — *see* Dermatitis, due to, vaccine
            smallpox vaccination NEC — *see* Dermatitis, due to, vaccine
        erysipeloid 027.1
        feigned 698.4
        Hutchinson, summer 692.72
        Kaposi's, varicelliform 054.0
            vaccinia 999.0
        lichenoid, axilla 698.3
        polymorphous, due to light 692.72
        toxic NEC 695.0
        vesicular 709.8
    teeth, tooth
        accelerated 520.6
        delayed 520.6
        difficult 520.6
        disturbance of 520.6
        in abnormal sequence 520.6
        incomplete 520.6
        late 520.6
        natal 520.6
        neonatal 520.6
        obstructed 520.6
        partial 520.6
        persistent primary 520.6
        premature 520.6
    vesicular 709.8
Erysipelas (gangrenous) (infantile) (newborn) (phlegmonous) (suppurative) 035
    external ear 035 *[380.13]*
    puerperal, postpartum, childbirth 670.0 ☑
Erysipelatoid (Rosenbach's) 027.1
Erysipeloid (Rosenbach's) 027.1
Erythema, erythematous (generalized) 695.9
    ab igne — *see* Burn, by site, first degree
    annulare (centrifugum) (rheumaticum) 695.0
    arthriticum epidemicum 026.1
    brucellum (*see also* Brucellosis) 023.9
    bullosum 695.1
    caloricum — *see* Burn, by site, first degree
    chronicum migrans 088.81
    circinatum 695.1
    diaper 691.0
    due to
        chemical (contact) NEC 692.4
            internal 693.8
        drug (internal use) 693.0
            contact 692.3
    elevatum diutinum 695.89
    endemic 265.2
    epidemic, arthritic 026.1
    figuratum perstans 695.0
    gluteal 691.0

Erythema, erythematous — *continued*
    gyratum (perstans) (repens) 695.1
    heat — *see* Burn, by site, first degree
    ichthyosiforme congenitum 757.1
    induratum (primary) (scrofulosorum) (*see also* Tuberculosis) 017.1 ☑
        nontuberculous 695.2
    infantum febrile 057.8
    infectional NEC 695.9
    infectiosum 057.0
    inflammation NEC 695.9
    intertrigo 695.89
    iris 695.1
    lupus (discoid) (localized) (*see also* Lupus, erythematosus) 695.4
    marginatum 695.0
        rheumaticum — *see* Fever, rheumatic
    medicamentosum — *see* Dermatitis, due to, drug
    migrans 529.1
        chronicum 088.81
    multiforme 695.1
        bullosum 695.1
        conjunctiva 695.1
        exudativum (Hebra) 695.1
        pemphigoides 694.5
    napkin 691.0
    neonatorum 778.8
    nodosum 695.2
        tuberculous (*see also* Tuberculosis) 017.1 ☑
    nummular, nummulare 695.1
    palmar 695.0
    palmaris hereditarium 695.0
    pernio 991.5
    perstans solare 692.72
    rash, newborn 778.8
    scarlatiniform (exfoliative) (recurrent) 695.0
    simplex marginatum 057.8
    solare (*see also* Sunburn) 692.71
    streptogenes 696.5
    toxic, toxicum NEC 695.0
        newborn 778.8
    tuberculous (primary) (*see also* Tuberculosis) 017.0 ☑
    venenatum 695.0
Erythematosus — *see* condition
Erythematous — *see* condition
Erythermalgia (primary) 443.82   ▲
Erythralgia 443.82   ▲
Erythrasma 039.0
Erythredema 985.0
    polyneuritica 985.0
    polyneuropathy 985.0
Erythremia (acute) (M9841/3) 207.0 ☑
    chronic (M9842/3) 207.1 ☑
    secondary 289.0
Erythroblastopenia (acquired) 284.8
    congenital 284.0
Erythroblastophthisis 284.0
Erythroblastosis (fetalis) (newborn) 773.2
    due to
        ABO
            antibodies 773.1
            incompatibility, maternal/fetal 773.1
            isoimmunization 773.1
        Rh
            antibodies 773.0
            incompatibility, maternal/fetal 773.0
            isoimmunization 773.0
Erythrocyanosis (crurum) 443.89
Erythrocythemia — *see* Erythremia
Erythrocytopenia 285.9
Erythrocytosis (megalosplenic)
    familial 289.6
    oval, hereditary (*see also* Elliptocytosis) 282.1
    secondary 289.0
    stress 289.0
Erythroderma (*see also* Erythema) 695.9
    desquamativa (in infants) 695.89
    exfoliative 695.89
    ichthyosiform, congenital 757.1
    infantum 695.89
    maculopapular 696.2
    neonatorum 778.8
    psoriaticum 696.1
    secondary 695.9

☑ Additional Digit Required — Refer to the Tabular List (Numeric Code Section) for Additional Digit Selection

Erythrogenesis imperfecta 284.0
Erythroleukemia (M9840/3) 207.0 ☑
Erythromelalgia 443.82   ▲
Erythromelia 701.8
Erythropenia 285.9
Erythrophagocytosis 289.9
Erythrophobia 300.23
Erythroplakia
  oral mucosa 528.79
  tongue 528.79
Erythroplasia (Queyrat) (M8080/2)
  specified site — *see* Neoplasm, skin, in situ
  unspecified site 233.5
Erythropoiesis, idiopathic ineffective 285.0
Escaped beats, heart 427.60
  postoperative 997.1
Esoenteritis — *see* Enteritis
Esophagalgia 530.89
Esophagectasis 530.89
  due to cardiospasm 530.0
Esophagismus 530.5
Esophagitis (alkaline) (chemical) (chronic)
    (infectional) (necrotic) (peptic) (postoperative)
    (regurgitant) 530.10
  acute 530.12
  candidal 112.84
  reflux 530.11
  specified NEC 530.19
  tuberculous (*see also* Tuberculosis) 017.8 ☑
  ulcerative 530.19
Esophagocele 530.6
Esophagodynia 530.89
Esophagomalacia 530.89
Esophagoptosis 530.89
Esophagospasm 530.5
Esophagostenosis 530.3
Esophagostomiasis 127.7
Esophagostomy
  complication 530.87   ▲
    infection 530.86
    malfunctioning 530.87
    mechanical 530.87
Esophagotracheal — *see* condition
Esophagus — *see* condition
Esophoria 378.41
  convergence, excess 378.84
  divergence, insufficiency 378.85
Esotropia (nonaccommodative) 378.00
  accommodative 378.35
  alternating 378.05
    with
        A pattern 378.06
        specified noncomitancy NEC 378.08
        V pattern 378.07
        X pattern 378.08
        Y pattern 378.08
    intermittent 378.22
  intermittent 378.20
    alternating 378.22
    monocular 378.21
  monocular 378.01
    with
        A pattern 378.02
        specified noncomitancy NEC 378.04
        V pattern 378.03
        X pattern 378.04
        Y pattern 378.04
    intermittent 378.21
Espundia 085.5
Essential — *see* condition
Esterapenia 289.89
Esthesioneuroblastoma (M9522/3) 160.0
Esthesioneurocytoma (M9521/3) 160.0
Esthesioneuroepithelioma (M9523/3) 160.0
Esthiomene 099.1
Estivo-autumnal
  fever 084.0
  malaria 084.0
Estrangement V61.0
Estriasis 134.0

Ethanolaminuria 270.8
Ethanolism (*see also* Alcoholism) 303.9 ☑
Ether dependence, dependency (*see also*
    Dependence) 304.6 ☑
Etherism (*see also* Dependence) 304.6 ☑
Ethmoid, ethmoidal — *see* condition
Ethmoiditis (chronic) (nonpurulent) (purulent)
    (*see also* Sinusitis, ethmoidal) 473.2
  influenzal 487.1
  Woakes' 471.1
Ethylism (*see also* Alcoholism) 303.9 ☑
Eulenburg's disease (congenital paramyotonia)
    359.2
Eunuchism 257.2
Eunuchoidism 257.2
  hypogonadotropic 257.2
European blastomycosis 117.5
Eustachian — *see* condition
Euthyroid sick syndrome 790.94
Euthyroidism 244.9
Evaluation
  fetal lung maturity 659.8 ☑
  for suspected condition (*see also* Observation)
    V71.9
    abuse V71.81
    exposure
        anthrax V71.82
        biologic agent NEC V71.83
        SARS V71.83
    neglect V71.81
    newborn — *see* Observation, suspected,
        condition, newborn
    specified condition NEC V71.89
  mental health V70.2
    requested by authority V70.1
  nursing care V63.8
  social service V63.8
▶**Evans'**◀ **syndrome** (thrombocytopenic purpura)
    287.32   ▲
Eventration
  colon into chest — *see* Hernia, diaphragm
  diaphragm (congenital) 756.6
Eversion
  bladder 596.8
  cervix (uteri) 622.0
    with mention of cervicitis 616.0
  foot NEC 736.79
    congenital 755.67
  lacrimal punctum 375.51
  punctum lacrimale (postinfectional) (senile)
    375.51
  ureter (meatus) 593.89
  urethra (meatus) 599.84
  uterus 618.1
    complicating delivery 665.2 ☑
        affecting fetus or newborn 763.89
    puerperal, postpartum 674.8 ☑
Evidence
  of malignancy
    cytologic
        without histologic confirmation 795.04
Evisceration
  birth injury 767.8
  bowel (congenital) — *see* Hernia, ventral
  congenital (*see also* Hernia, ventral) 553.29
  operative wound 998.32
  traumatic NEC 869.1
    eye 871.3
Evulsion — *see* Avulsion
Ewing's
  angioendothelioma (M9260/3) — *see* Neoplasm,
    bone, malignant
  sarcoma (M9260/3) — *see* Neoplasm, bone,
    malignant
  tumor (M9260/3) — *see* Neoplasm, bone,
    malignant
Exaggerated lumbosacral angle (with impinging
    spine) 756.12
Examination (general) (routine) (of) (for) V70.9
  allergy V72.7
  annual V70.0
  cardiovascular preoperative V72.81

Examination — *continued*
  cervical Papanicolaou smear V76.2
    as a part of routine gynecological
        examination V72.31
    to confirm findings of recent normal smear
        following initial abnormal smear
        V72.32
  child care (routine) V20.2
  clinical research investigation (normal control
    patient) (participant) V70.7
  dental V72.2
  developmental testing (child) (infant) V20.2
  donor (potential) V70.8
  ear V72.1
  eye V72.0
  following
    accident (motor vehicle) V71.4
    alleged rape or seduction (victim or culprit)
        V71.5
    inflicted injury (victim or culprit) NEC V71.6
    rape or seduction, alleged (victim or culprit)
        V71.5
    treatment (for) V67.9
        combined V67.6
        fracture V67.4
        involving high-risk medication NEC
            V67.51
        mental disorder V67.3
        specified condition NEC V67.59
  follow-up (routine) (following) V67.9
    cancer chemotherapy V67.2
    chemotherapy V67.2
    disease NEC V67.59
    high-risk medication NEC V67.51
    injury NEC V67.59
    population survey V70.6
    postpartum V24.2
    psychiatric V67.3
    psychotherapy V67.3
    radiotherapy V67.1
    specified surgery NEC V67.09
    surgery V67.00
        vaginal pap smear V67.01
  gynecological V72.31
    for contraceptive maintenance V25.40
        intrauterine device V25.42
        pill V25.41
        specified method NEC V25.49
  health (of)
    armed forces personnel V70.5
    checkup V70.0
    child, routine V20.2
    defined subpopulation NEC V70.5
    inhabitants of institutions V70.5
    occupational V70.5
    pre-employment screening V70.5
    preschool children V70.5
        for admission to school V70.3
    prisoners V70.5
        for entrance into prison V70.3
    prostitutes V70.5
    refugees V70.5
    school children V70.5
    students V70.5
  hearing V72.1
  infant V20.2
  laboratory V72.6
  lactating mother V24.1
  medical (for) (of) V70.9
    administrative purpose NEC V70.3
    admission to
        old age home V70.3
        prison V70.3
        school V70.3
    adoption V70.3
    armed forces personnel V70.5
    at health care facility V70.0
    camp V70.3
    child, routine V20.2
    clinical research (control) (normal
        comparison) (participant) V70.7
    defined subpopulation NEC V70.5
    donor (potential) V70.8
    driving license V70.3
    general V70.9
        routine V70.0
        specified reason NEC V70.8

☑ Additional Digit Required — Refer to the Tabular List (Numeric Code Section) for Additional Digit Selection

Examination — *continued*
  medical — *continued*
    immigration V70.3
    inhabitants of institutions V70.5
    insurance certification V70.3
    marriage V70.3
    medicolegal reasons V70.4
    naturalization V70.3
    occupational V70.5
    population survey V70.6
    pre-employment V70.5
    preschool children V70.5
      for admission to school V70.3
    prison V70.3
    prisoners V70.5
      for entrance into prison V70.3
    prostitutes V70.5
    refugees V70.5
    school children V70.5
    specified reason NEC V70.8
    sport competition V70.3
    students V70.5
  medicolegal reason V70.4
  pelvic (annual) (periodic) V72.31
  periodic (annual) (routine) V70.0
  postpartum
    immediately after delivery V24.0
    routine follow-up V24.2
  pregnancy (unconfirmed) (possible) V72.40
    negative result V72.41
    positive result V72.42   ●
  prenatal V22.1
    first pregnancy V22.0
    high-risk pregnancy V23.9
      specified problem NEC V23.89
  preoperative V72.84
    cardiovascular V72.81
    respiratory V72.82
    specified NEC V72.83   ●
  preprocedural V72.84   ●
    cardiovascular V72.81   ●
    general physical V72.83   ●
    respiratory V72.82   ●
    specified NEC V72.83   ●
  psychiatric V70.2
    follow-up not needing further care V67.3
    requested by authority V70.1
  radiological NEC V72.5
  respiratory preoperative V72.82
  screening — *see* Screening
  sensitization V72.7
  skin V72.7
    hypersensitivity V72.7
  special V72.9
  specified type or reason NEC V72.85
    preoperative V72.83
      specified NEC V72.83
  teeth V72.2
  vaginal Papanicolaou smear V76.47
    following hysterectomy for malignant
      condition V67.01
  victim or culprit following
    alleged rape or seduction V71.5
    inflicted injury NEC V71.6
  vision V72.0
  well baby V20.2

Exanthem, exanthema (*see also* Rash) 782.1
  Boston 048
  epidemic, with meningitis 048
  lichenoid psoriasiform 696.2
  subitum 057.8
  viral, virus NEC 057.9
    specified type NEC 057.8

Excess, excessive, excessively
  alcohol level in blood 790.3
  carbohydrate tissue, localized 278.1
  carotene (dietary) 278.3
  cold 991.9
    specified effect NEC 991.8
  convergence 378.84
  crying 780.95   ▲
    of infant (baby) 780.92   ●
  development, breast 611.1
  diaphoresis (*see also* Hyperhidrosis) 780.8
  distance, interarch 524.28
  divergence 378.85

Excess, excessive, excessively — *continued*
  drinking (alcohol) NEC (*see also* Abuse, drugs,
    nondependent) 305.0 ☑
    continual (*see also* Alcoholism) 303.9 ☑
    habitual (*see also* Alcoholism) 303.9 ☑
  eating 783.6
  eyelid fold (congenital) 743.62
  fat 278.02   ▲
    in heart (*see also* Degeneration, myocardial)
      429.1
    tissue, localized 278.1
  foreskin 605
  gas 787.3
  gastrin 251.5
  glucagon 251.4
  heat (*see also* Heat) 992.9
  horizontal overlap 524.26
  interarch distance 524.28
  interocclusal distance of teeth 524.37
  large
    colon 564.7
      congenital 751.3
    fetus or infant 766.0
      with obstructed labor 660.1 ☑
        affecting management of pregnancy
          656.6 ☑
      causing disproportion 653.5 ☑
    newborn (weight of 4500 grams or more)
      766.0
    organ or site, congenital NEC — *see*
      Anomaly, specified type NEC
  lid fold (congenital) 743.62
  long
    colon 751.5
    organ or site, congenital NEC — *see*
      Anomaly, specified type NEC
    umbilical cord (entangled)
      affecting fetus or newborn 762.5
      in pregnancy or childbirth 663.3 ☑
        with compression 663.2 ☑
  menstruation 626.2
  number of teeth 520.1
    causing crowding 524.31
  nutrients (dietary) NEC 783.6
  potassium (K) 276.7
  salivation (*see also* Ptyalism) 527.7
  secretion — *see also* Hypersecretion
    milk 676.6 ☑
    sputum 786.4
    sweat (*see also* Hyperhidrosis) 780.8
  short
    organ or site, congenital NEC — *see*
      Anomaly, specified type NEC
    umbilical cord
      affecting fetus or newborn 762.6
      in pregnancy or childbirth 663.4 ☑
  skin NEC 701.9
    eyelid 743.62
      acquired 374.30
  sodium (Na) 276.0
  spacing of teeth 524.32
  sputum 786.4
  sweating (*see also* Hyperhidrosis) 780.8
  tearing (ducts) (eye) (*see also* Epiphora) 375.20
  thirst 783.5
    due to deprivation of water 994.3
  tuberosity 524.07
  vitamin
    A (dietary) 278.2
      administered as drug (chronic) (prolonged
        excessive intake) 278.2
      reaction to sudden overdose 963.5
    D (dietary) 278.4
      administered as drug (chronic) (prolonged
        excessive intake) 278.4
      reaction to sudden overdose 963.5
  weight 278.02   ▲
    gain 783.1
      of pregnancy 646.1 ☑
    loss 783.21

Excitability, abnormal, under minor stress
  309.29

Excitation
  catatonic (*see also* Schizophrenia) 295.2 ☑
  psychogenic 298.1
  reactive (from emotional stress, psychological
    trauma) 298.1

Excitement
  manic (*see also* Psychosis, affective) 296.0 ☑
    recurrent episode 296.1 ☑
    single episode 296.0 ☑
  mental, reactive (from emotional stress,
    psychological trauma) 298.1
  state, reactive (from emotional stress,
    psychological trauma) 298.1

Excluded pupils 364.76

Excoriation (traumatic) (*see also* Injury,
  superficial, by site) 919.8
  neurotic 698.4

Excyclophoria 378.44

Excyclotropia 378.33

Exencephalus, exencephaly 742.0

Exercise
  breathing V57.0
  remedial NEC V57.1
  therapeutic NEC V57.1

Exfoliation, teeth due to systemic causes 525.0

Exfoliative — *see also* condition
  dermatitis 695.89

Exhaustion, exhaustive (physical NEC) 780.79
  battle (*see also* Reaction, stress, acute) 308.9
  cardiac (*see also* Failure, heart) 428.9
  delirium (*see also* Reaction, stress, acute)
    308.9
  due to
    cold 991.8
    excessive exertion 994.5
    exposure 994.4
  fetus or newborn 779.89
  heart (*see also* Failure, heart) 428.9
  heat 992.5
    due to
      salt depletion 992.4
      water depletion 992.3
  manic (*see also* Psychosis, affective) 296.0 ☑
    recurrent episode 296.1 ☑
    single episode 296.0 ☑
  maternal, complicating delivery 669.8 ☑
    affecting fetus or newborn 763.89
  mental 300.5
  myocardium, myocardial (*see also* Failure,
    heart) 428.9
  nervous 300.5
  old age 797
  postinfectional NEC 780.79
  psychogenic 300.5
  psychosis (*see also* Reaction, stress, acute)
    308.9
  senile 797
    dementia 290.0

Exhibitionism (sexual) 302.4

Exomphalos 756.79

Exophoria 378.42
  convergence, insufficiency 378.83
  divergence, excess 378.85

Exophthalmic
  cachexia 242.0 ☑
  goiter 242.0 ☑
  ophthalmoplegia 242.0 ☑ *[376.22]*

Exophthalmos 376.30
  congenital 743.66
  constant 376.31
  endocrine NEC 259.9 *[376.22]*
  hyperthyroidism 242.0 ☑ *[376.21]*
  intermittent NEC 376.34
  malignant 242.0 ☑ *[376.21]*
  pulsating 376.35
    endocrine NEC 259.9 *[376.22]*
  thyrotoxic 242.0 ☑ *[376.21]*

Exostosis 726.91
  cartilaginous (M9210/0) — *see* Neoplasm,
    bone, benign
  congenital 756.4
  ear canal, external 380.81
  gonococcal 098.89
  hip 726.5
  intracranial 733.3
  jaw (bone) 526.81
  luxurians 728.11
  multiple (cancellous) (congenital) (hereditary)
    756.4

Exostosis — *continued*
  nasal bones 726.91
  orbit, orbital 376.42
  osteocartilaginous (M9210/0) — *see* Neoplasm,
      bone, benign
  spine 721.8
      with spondylosis — *see* Spondylosis
  syphilitic 095.5
  wrist 726.4
Exotropia 378.10
  alternating 378.15
      with
          A pattern 378.16
          specified noncomitancy NEC 378.18
          V pattern 378.17
          X pattern 378.18
          Y pattern 378.18
      intermittent 378.24
  intermittent 378.20
      alternating 378.24
      monocular 378.23
  monocular 378.11
      with
          A pattern 378.12
          specified noncomitancy NEC 378.14
          V pattern 378.13
          X pattern 378.14
          Y pattern 378.14
      intermittent 378.23
Explanation of
  investigation finding V65.4 ☑
  medication V65.4 ☑
Exposure 994.9
  cold 991.9
      specified effect NEC 991.8
  effects of 994.9
  exhaustion due to 994.4
  to
      AIDS virus V01.79
      anthrax V01.81
      asbestos V15.84
      body fluids (hazardous) V15.85
      cholera V01.0
      communicable disease V01.9
          specified type NEC V01.89
      Escherichia coli (E. coli) V01.83
      German measles V01.4
      gonorrhea V01.6
      hazardous body fluids V15.85
      HIV V01.79
      human immunodeficiency virus V01.79
      lead V15.86
      meningococcus V01.84
      parasitic disease V01.89
      poliomyelitis V01.2
      potentially hazardous body fluids V15.85
      rabies V01.5
      rubella V01.4
      SARS-associated coronavirus V01.82
      smallpox V01.3
      syphilis V01.6
      tuberculosis V01.1
      varicella V01.71
      venereal disease V01.6
      viral disease NEC V01.79
      varicella V01.71
Exsanguination, fetal 772.0
Exstrophy
  abdominal content 751.8
  bladder (urinary) 753.5
Extensive — *see* condition
Extra — *see also* Accessory
  rib 756.3
      cervical 756.2
Extraction
  with hook 763.89
  breech NEC 669.6 ☑
      affecting fetus or newborn 763.0
  cataract postsurgical V45.61
  manual NEC 669.8 ☑
      affecting fetus or newborn 763.89
Extrasystole 427.60
  atrial 427.61
  postoperative 997.1
  ventricular 427.69

Extrauterine gestation or pregnancy — *see*
      Pregnancy, ectopic
Extravasation
  blood 459.0
      lower extremity 459.0
  chyle into mesentery 457.8
  pelvicalyceal 593.4
  pyelosinus 593.4
  urine 788.8
      from ureter 788.8
Extremity — *see* condition
Extrophy — *see* Exstrophy
Extroversion
  bladder 753.5
  uterus 618.1
      complicating delivery 665.2 ☑
          affecting fetus or newborn 763.89
      postpartal (old) 618.1
Extrusion
  alveolus and teeth 524.75
  breast implant (prosthetic) 996.54
  device, implant, or graft — *see* Complications,
      mechanical
  eye implant (ball) (globe) 996.59
  intervertebral disc — *see* Displacement,
      intervertebral disc
  lacrimal gland 375.43
  mesh (reinforcing) 996.59
  ocular lens implant 996.53
  prosthetic device NEC — *see* Complications,
      mechanical
  vitreous 379.26
Exudate, pleura — *see* Effusion, pleura
Exudates, retina 362.82
Exudative — *see* condition
Eye, eyeball, eyelid — *see* condition
Eyestrain 368.13
Eyeworm disease of Africa 125.2

F

Faber's anemia or syndrome (achlorhydric
      anemia) 280.9
Fabry's disease (angiokeratoma corporis
      diffusum) 272.7
Face, facial — *see* condition
Facet of cornea 371.44
Faciocephalalgia, autonomic (*see also*
      Neuropathy, peripheral, autonomic) 337.9
Facioscapulohumeral myopathy 359.1
Factitious disorder, illness — *see* Illness, factitious
Factor
  deficiency — *see* Deficiency, factor
  psychic, associated with diseases classified
      elsewhere 316
  risk — *see* Problem
Fahr-Volhard disease (malignant nephrosclerosis)
      403.00
Failure, failed
  adenohypophyseal 253.2
  attempted abortion (legal) (*see also* Abortion,
      failed) 638.9
  bone marrow (anemia) 284.9
      acquired (secondary) 284.8
      congenital 284.0
      idiopathic 284.9
  cardiac (*see also* Failure, heart) 428.9
      newborn 779.89
  cardiorenal (chronic) 428.9
      hypertensive (*see also* Hypertension,
          cardiorenal) 404.93
  cardiorespiratory 799.1
      specified during or due to a procedure 997.1
      long-term effect of cardiac surgery 429.4
  cardiovascular (chronic) 428.9
  cerebrovascular 437.8
  cervical dilatation in labor 661.0 ☑
      affecting fetus or newborn 763.7
  circulation, circulatory 799.89
      fetus or newborn 779.89
      peripheral 785.50
  compensation — *see* Disease, heart
  congestive (*see also* Failure, heart) 428.0

Failure, failed — *continued*
  coronary (*see also* Insufficiency, coronary)
      411.89
  descent of head (at term) 652.5 ☑
      affecting fetus or newborn 763.1
      in labor 660.0 ☑
          affecting fetus or newborn 763.1
  device, implant, or graft — *see* Complications,
      mechanical
  engagement of head NEC 652.5 ☑
      in labor 660.0 ☑
  extrarenal 788.9
  fetal head to enter pelvic brim 652.5 ☑
      affecting fetus or newborn 763.1
      in labor 660.0 ☑
          affecting fetus or newborn 763.1
  forceps NEC 660.7 ☑
      affecting fetus or newborn 763.1
  fusion (joint) (spinal) 996.49   ▲
  growth in childhood 783.43
  heart (acute) (sudden) 428.9
      with
          abortion — *see* Abortion, by type, with
              specified complication NEC
          acute pulmonary edema (*see also* Failure,
              ventricular, left) 428.1
              with congestion (*see also* Failure,
                  heart) 428.0
          decompensation (*see also* Failure, heart)
              428.0
          dilation — *see* Disease, heart
          ectopic pregnancy (*see also* categories
              633.0-633.9) 639.8
          molar pregnancy (*see also* categories 630-
              632) 639.8
      arteriosclerotic 440.9
      combined left-right sided 428.0
      combined systolic and diastolic 428.40
          acute 428.41
          acute on chronic 428.43
          chronic 428.42
      compensated (*see also* Failure, heart) 428.0
      complicating
          abortion — *see* Abortion, by type, with
              specified complication NEC
          delivery (cesarean) (instrumental)
              669.4 ☑
          ectopic pregnancy (*see also* categories
              633.0-633.9) 639.8
          molar pregnancy (*see also* categories 630-
              632) 639.8
          obstetric anesthesia or sedation 668.1 ☑
          surgery 997.1
      congestive (compensated) (decompensated)
          (*see also* Failure, heart) 428.0
          with rheumatic fever (conditions
              classifiable to 390)
              active 391.8
              inactive or quiescent (with chorea)
                  398.91
          fetus or newborn 779.89
          hypertensive (*see also* Hypertension,
              heart) 402.91
              with renal disease (*see also*
                  Hypertension, cardiorenal)
                  404.91
                  with renal failure 404.93
              benign 402.11
              malignant 402.01
          rheumatic (chronic) (inactive) (with
              chorea) 398.91
              active or acute 391.8
                  with chorea (Sydenham's) 392.0
      decompensated (*see also* Failure, heart)
          428.0
      degenerative (*see also* Degeneration,
          myocardial) 429.1
      diastolic 428.30
          acute 428.31
          acute on chronic 428.33
          chronic 428.32
      due to presence of (cardiac) prosthesis 429.4
      fetus or newborn 779.89
      following
          abortion 639.8
          cardiac surgery 429.4
          ectopic or molar pregnancy 639.8

Failure, failed — *continued*
  heart — *continued*
    high output NEC 428.9
    hypertensive (*see also* Hypertension, heart)
      402.91
      with renal disease (*see also* Hypertension,
        cardiorenal) 404.91
        with renal failure 404.93
      benign 402.11
      malignant 402.01
    left (ventricular) (*see also* Failure,
      ventricular, left) 428.1
      with right-sided failure (see also Failure,
        heart) 428.0
    low output (syndrome) NEC 428.9
    organic — *see* Disease, heart
    postoperative (immediate) 997.1
      long term effect of cardiac surgery 429.4
    rheumatic (chronic) (congestive) (inactive)
      398.91
    right (secondary to left heart failure, conditions
      classifiable to 428.1) (ventricular) (*see
      also* Failure, heart) 428.0
    senile 797
    specified during or due to a procedure 997.1
      long-term effect of cardiac surgery 429.4
    systolic 428.20
      acute 428.21
      acute on chronic 428.23
      chronic 428.22
    thyrotoxic (*see also* Thyrotoxicosis)
      242.9 ☑ [425.7]
    valvular — *see* Endocarditis
  hepatic 572.8
    acute 570
    due to a procedure 997.4
  hepatorenal 572.4
  hypertensive heart (*see also* Hypertension,
    heart) 402.91
    benign 402.11
    malignant 402.01
  induction (of labor) 659.1 ☑
    abortion (legal) (*see also* Abortion, failed)
      638.9
    affecting fetus or newborn 763.89
    by oxytocic drugs 659.1 ☑
    instrumental 659.0 ☑
    mechanical 659.0 ☑
    medical 659.1 ☑
    surgical 659.0 ☑
  initial alveolar expansion, newborn 770.4
  involution, thymus (gland) 254.8
  kidney — *see* Failure, renal
  lactation 676.4 ☑
  Leydig's cell, adult 257.2
  liver 572.8
    acute 570
  medullary 799.89
  mitral — *see* Endocarditis, mitral
  myocardium, myocardial (*see also* Failure,
    heart) 428.9
    chronic (*see also* Failure, heart) 428.0
    congestive (*see also* Failure, heart) 428.0
  ovarian (primary) 256.39
    iatrogenic 256.2
    postablative 256.2
    postirradiation 256.2
    postsurgical 256.2
  ovulation 628.0
  prerenal 788.9
  renal 586
    with
      abortion — *see* Abortion, by type, with
        renal failure
      ectopic pregnancy (*see also* categories
        633.0-633.9) 639.3
      edema (*see also* Nephrosis) 581.9
      hypertension (*see also* Hypertension,
        kidney) 403.91
      hypertensive heart disease (conditions
        classifiable to 402) 404.92
        with heart failure 404.93
        benign 404.12
          with heart failure 404.13
        malignant 404.02
          with heart failure 404.03

Failure, failed — *continued*
  renal — *continued*
    with — *continued*
      molar pregnancy (*see also* categories 630-
        632) 639.3
      tubular necrosis (acute) 584.5
    acute 584.9
      with lesion of
        necrosis
          cortical (renal) 584.6
          medullary (renal) (papillary) 584.7
          tubular 584.5
        specified pathology NEC 584.8
    chronic 585.9   ▲
      hypertensive or with hypertension (*see
        also* Hypertension, kidney) 403.91
    due to a procedure 997.5
    following
      abortion 639.3
      crushing 958.5
      ectopic or molar pregnancy 639.3
      labor and delivery (acute) 669.3 ☑
    hypertensive (*see also* Hypertension, kidney)
      403.91
    puerperal, postpartum 669.3 ☑
  respiration, respiratory 518.81
    acute 518.81
    acute and chronic 518.84
    center 348.8
      newborn 770.84
    chronic 518.83
    due to trauma, surgery or shock 518.5
    newborn 770.84
  rotation
    cecum 751.4
    colon 751.4
    intestine 751.4
    kidney 753.3
  segmentation — *see also* Fusion
    fingers (*see also* Syndactylism, fingers)
      755.11
    toes (*see also* Syndactylism, toes) 755.13
  seminiferous tubule, adult 257.2
  senile (general) 797
    with psychosis 290.20
  testis, primary (seminal) 257.2
  to progress 661.2 ☑
  to thrive
    adult 783.7
    child 783.41
  transplant 996.80
    bone marrow 996.85
    organ (immune or nonimmune cause) 996.80
      bone marrow 996.85
      heart 996.83
      intestines 996.87
      kidney 996.81
      liver 996.82
      lung 996.84
      pancreas 996.86
      specified NEC 996.89
    skin 996.52
      artificial 996.55
      decellularized allodermis 996.55
      temporary allograft or pigskin graft —
        omit code
  trial of labor NEC 660.6 ☑
    affecting fetus or newborn 763.1
  tubal ligation 998.89
  urinary 586
  vacuum extraction
    abortion — *see* Abortion, failed
    delivery NEC 660.7 ☑
      affecting fetus or newborn 763.1
  vasectomy 998.89
  ventouse NEC 660.7 ☑
    affecting fetus or newborn 763.1
  ventricular (*see also* Failure, heart) 428.9
    left 428.1
      with rheumatic fever (conditions
        classifiable to 390)
        active 391.8
          with chorea 392.0
        inactive or quiescent (with chorea)
          398.91

Failure, failed — *continued*
  ventricular (*see also* Failure, heart) —
    continued
    left — *continued*
      hypertensive (*see also* Hypertension,
        heart) 402.91
        benign 402.11
        malignant 402.01
      rheumatic (chronic) (inactive) (with
        chorea) 398.91
        active or acute 391.8
          with chorea 392.0
      right (*see also* Failure, heart) 428.0
    vital centers, fetus or newborn 779.89
    weight gain in childhood 783.41
Fainting (fit) (spell) 780.2
Falciform hymen 752.49
Fall, maternal, affecting fetus or newborn
  760.5
Fallen arches 734
Falling, any organ or part — *see* Prolapse
Fallopian
  insufflation
    fertility testing V26.21
    following sterilization reversal V26.22
  tube — *see* condition
Fallot's
  pentalogy 745.2
  tetrad or tetralogy 745.2
  triad or trilogy 746.09
Fallout, radioactive (adverse effect) NEC 990
False — *see also* condition
  bundle branch block 426.50
  bursa 727.89
  croup 478.75
  joint 733.82
  labor (pains) 644.1 ☑
  opening, urinary, male 752.69
  passage, urethra (prostatic) 599.4
  positive
    serological test for syphilis 795.6
    Wassermann reaction 795.6
  pregnancy 300.11
Family, familial — *see also* condition
  disruption V61.0
  Li-Fraumeni (syndrome) V84.01
  planning advice V25.09
  problem V61.9
    specified circumstance NEC V61.8
  retinoblastoma (syndrome) 190.5
Famine 994.2
  edema 262
Fanconi's anemia (congenital pancytopenia)
  284.0
Fanconi (-de Toni) (-Debré) syndrome
  (cystinosis) 270.0
Farber (-Uzman) syndrome or disease
  (disseminated lipogranulomatosis) 272.8
Farcin 024
Farcy 024
Farmers'
  lung 495.0
  skin 692.74
Farsightedness 367.0
Fascia — *see* condition
Fasciculation 781.0
Fasciculitis optica 377.32
Fasciitis 729.4
  eosinophilic 728.89
  necrotizing 728.86
  nodular 728.79
  perirenal 593.4
  plantar 728.71
  pseudosarcomatous 728.79
  traumatic (old) NEC 728.79
    current — *see* Sprain, by site
Fasciola hepatica infestation 121.3
Fascioliasis 121.3
Fasciolopsiasis (small intestine) 121.4
Fasciolopsis (small intestine) 121.4
Fast pulse 785.0

Fat
- embolism (cerebral) (pulmonary) (systemic) 958.1
  - with
    - abortion — *see* Abortion, by type, with embolism
    - ectopic pregnancy (*see also* categories 633.0-633.9) 639.6
    - molar pregnancy (*see also* categories 630-632) 639.6
    - complicating delivery or puerperium 673.8 ☑
  - following
    - abortion 639.6
    - ectopic or molar pregnancy 639.6
  - in pregnancy, childbirth, or the puerperium 673.8 ☑
- excessive 278.02 ▲
  - in heart (*see also* Degeneration, myocardial) 429.1
- general 278.02 ▲
- hernia, herniation 729.30
  - eyelid 374.34
  - knee 729.31
  - orbit 374.34
  - retro-orbital 374.34
  - retropatellar 729.31
  - specified site NEC 729.39
- indigestion 579.8
- in stool 792.1
- localized (pad) 278.1
  - heart (*see also* Degeneration, myocardial) 429.1
  - knee 729.31
  - retropatellar 729.31
- necrosis — *see also* Fatty, degeneration
  - breast (aseptic) (segmental) 611.3
  - mesentery 567.82 ▲
  - omentum 567.82 ▲
  - peritoneum 567.82 ●
- pad 278.1

Fatal syncope 798.1

Fatigue 780.79
- auditory deafness (*see also* Deafness) 389.9
- chronic, syndrome 780.71
- combat (*see also* Reaction, stress, acute) 308.9
- during pregnancy 646.8 ☑
- general 780.79
  - psychogenic 300.5
- heat (transient) 992.6
- muscle 729.89
- myocardium (*see also* Failure, heart) 428.9
- nervous 300.5
- neurosis 300.5
- operational 300.89
- postural 729.89
- posture 729.89
- psychogenic (general) 300.5
- senile 797
- syndrome NEC 300.5
  - chronic 780.71
- undue 780.79
- voice 784.49

Fatness 278.02 ▲

Fatty — *see also* condition
- apron 278.1
- degeneration (diffuse) (general) NEC 272.8
  - localized — *see* Degeneration, by site, fatty
  - placenta — *see* Placenta, abnormal
- heart (enlarged) (*see also* Degeneration, myocardial) 429.1
- infiltration (diffuse) (general) (*see also* Degeneration, by site, fatty) 272.8
  - heart (enlarged) (*see also* Degeneration, myocardial) 429.1
- liver 571.8
  - alcoholic 571.0
- necrosis — *see* Degeneration, fatty
- phanerosis 272.8

Fauces — *see* condition

Fauchard's disease (periodontitis) 523.4

Faucitis 478.29

Faulty — *see also* condition
- position of teeth 524.30

Favism (anemia) 282.2

Favre-Racouchot disease (elastoidosis cutanea nodularis) 701.8

Favus 110.9
- beard 110.0
- capitis 110.0
- corporis 110.5
- eyelid 110.8
- foot 110.4
- hand 110.2
- scalp 110.0
- specified site NEC 110.8

Fear, fearfulness (complex) (reaction) 300.20
- child 313.0
- of
  - animals 300.29
  - closed spaces 300.29
  - crowds 300.29
  - eating in public 300.23
  - heights 300.29
  - open spaces 300.22
    - with panic attacks 300.21
  - public speaking 300.23
  - streets 300.22
    - with panic attacks 300.21
  - travel 300.22
    - with panic attacks 300.21
  - washing in public 300.23
- transient 308.0

Feared complaint unfounded V65.5

Febricula (continued) (simple) (*see also* Pyrexia) 780.6

Febrile (*see also* Pyrexia) 780.6
- convulsion 780.31
- seizure 780.31

Febris (*see also* Fever) 780.6
- aestiva (*see also* Fever, hay) 477.9
- flava (*see also* Fever, yellow) 060.9
- melitensis 023.0
- pestis (*see also* Plague) 020.9
- puerperalis 672.0 ☑
- recurrens (*see also* Fever, relapsing) 087.9
  - pediculo vestimenti 087.0
- rubra 034.1
- typhoidea 002.0
- typhosa 002.0

Fecal — *see* condition

Fecalith (impaction) 560.39
- with hernia — *see also* Hernia, by site, with obstruction
  - gangrenous — *see* Hernia, by site, with gangrene
- appendix 543.9
- congenital 777.1

Fede's disease 529.0

Feeble-minded 317

Feeble rapid pulse due to shock following injury 958.4

Feeding
- faulty (elderly) (infant) 783.3
  - newborn 779.3
- formula check V20.2
- improper (elderly) (infant) 783.3
  - newborn 779.3
- problem (elderly) ▶(infant)◀ 783.3
  - newborn 779.3
- nonorganic origin 307.59

Feer's disease 985.0

Feet — *see* condition

Feigned illness V65.2

Feil-Klippel syndrome (brevicollis) 756.16

Feinmesser's (hidrotic) **ectodermal dysplasia** 757.31

Felix's disease (juvenile osteochondrosis, hip) 732.1

Felon (any digit) (with lymphangitis) 681.01
- herpetic 054.6

Felty's syndrome (rheumatoid arthritis with splenomegaly and leukopenia) 714.1

Feminism in boys 302.6

Feminization, testicular 259.5 ▲
- with pseudohermaphroditism, male 259.5 ▲

Femoral hernia — *see* Hernia, femoral

Femora vara 736.32

Femur, femoral — *see* condition

Fenestrata placenta — *see* Placenta, abnormal

Fenestration, fenestrated — *see also* Imperfect, closure
- aorta-pulmonary 745.0
- aorticopulmonary 745.0
- aortopulmonary 745.0
- cusps, heart valve NEC 746.89
  - pulmonary 746.09
- hymen 752.49
- pulmonic cusps 746.09

Fenwick's disease 537.89

Fermentation (gastric) (gastrointestinal) (stomach) 536.8
- intestine 564.89
  - psychogenic 306.4
- psychogenic 306.4

Fernell's disease (aortic aneurysm) 441.9

Fertile eunuch syndrome 257.2

Fertility, meaning multiparity — *see* Multiparity

Fetal alcohol syndrome 760.71

Fetalis uterus 752.3

Fetid
- breath 784.9
- sweat 705.89

Fetishism 302.81
- transvestic 302.3

Fetomaternal hemorrhage
- affecting management of pregnancy 656.0 ☑
- fetus or newborn 772.0

Fetus, fetal — *see also* condition
- papyraceous 779.89
- type lung tissue 770.4

Fever 780.6
- with chills 780.6
  - in malarial regions (*see also* Malaria) 084.6
- abortus NEC 023.9
- Aden 061
- African tick-borne 087.1
- American
  - mountain tick 066.1
  - spotted 082.0
- and ague (*see also* Malaria) 084.6
- aphthous 078.4
- arbovirus hemorrhagic 065.9
- Assam 085.0
- Australian A or Q 083.0
- Bangkok hemorrhagic 065.4
- biliary, Charcôt's intermittent — *see* Choledocholithiasis
- bilious, hemoglobinuric 084.8
- blackwater 084.8
- blister 054.9
- Bonvale Dam 780.79
- boutonneuse 082.1
- brain 323.9
  - late effect — *see* category 326
- breakbone 061
- Bullis 082.8
- Bunyamwera 066.3
- Burdwan 085.0
- Bwamba (encephalitis) 066.3
- Cameroon (*see also* Malaria) 084.6
- Canton 081.9
- catarrhal (acute) 460
  - chronic 472.0
- cat-scratch 078.3
- cerebral 323.9
  - late effect — *see* category 326
- cerebrospinal (meningococcal) (*see also* Meningitis, cerebrospinal) 036.0
- Chagres 084.0
- Chandipura 066.8
- changuinola 066.0
- Charcôt's (biliary) (hepatic) (intermittent) *see* Choledocholithiasis
- Chikungunya (viral) 066.3
  - hemorrhagic 065.4
- childbed 670.0 ☑
- Chitral 066.0
- Colombo (*see also* Fever, paratyphoid) 002.9
- Colorado tick (virus) 066.1

☑ Additional Digit Required — Refer to the Tabular List (Numeric Code Section) for Additional Digit Selection

Fever — *continued*
  congestive
    malarial (*see also* Malaria) 084.6
    remittent (*see also* Malaria) 084.6
  Congo virus 065.0
  continued 780.6
    malarial 084.0
  Corsican (*see also* Malaria) 084.6
  Crimean hemorrhagic 065.0
  Cyprus (*see also* Brucellosis) 023.9
  dandy 061
  deer fly (*see also* Tularemia) 021.9
  dehydration, newborn 778.4
  dengue (virus) 061
    hemorrhagic 065.4
  desert 114.0
  due to heat 992.0
  Dumdum 085.0
  enteric 002.0
  ephemeral (of unknown origin) (*see also* Pyrexia) 780.6
  epidemic, hemorrhagic of the Far East 065.0
  erysipelatous (*see also* Erysipelas) 035
  estivo-autumnal (malarial) 084.0
  etiocholanolone 277.3
  famine — *see also* Fever, relapsing
    meaning typhus — *see* Typhus
  Far Eastern hemorrhagic 065.0
  five day 083.1
  Fort Bragg 100.89
  gastroenteric 002.0
  gastromalarial (*see also* Malaria) 084.6
  Gibraltar (*see also* Brucellosis) 023.9
  glandular 075
  Guama (viral) 066.3
  Haverhill 026.1
  hay (allergic) (with rhinitis) 477.9
    with
      asthma (bronchial) (*see also* Asthma) 493.0 ☑
    due to
      dander, animal (cat) (dog) 477.2
      dust 477.8
      fowl 477.8
      hair, animal (cat) (dog) 477.2
      pollen, any plant or tree 477.0
      specified allergen other than pollen 477.8
  heat (effects) 992.0
  hematuric, bilious 084.8
  hemoglobinuric (malarial) 084.8
    bilious 084.8
  hemorrhagic (arthropod-borne) NEC 065.9
    with renal syndrome 078.6
    arenaviral 078.7
    Argentine 078.7
    Bangkok 065.4
    Bolivian 078.7
    Central Asian 065.0
    chikungunya 065.4
    Crimean 065.0
    dengue (virus) 065.4
    Ebola 065.8
    epidemic 078.6
      of Far East 065.0
    Far Eastern 065.0
    Junin virus 078.7
    Korean 078.6
    Kyasanur forest 065.2
    Machupo virus 078.7
    mite-borne NEC 065.8
    mosquito-borne 065.4
    Omsk 065.1
    Philippine 065.4
    Russian (Yaroslav) 078.6
    Singapore 065.4
    Southeast Asia 065.4
    Thailand 065.4
    tick-borne NEC 065.3
  hepatic (*see also* Cholecystitis) 575.8
    intermittent (Charcôt's) — *see* Choledocholithiasis
  herpetic (*see also* Herpes) 054.9
  Hyalomma tick 065.0
  icterohemorrhagic 100.0
  inanition 780.6
    newborn 778.4
  infective NEC 136.9

Fever — *continued*
  intermittent (bilious) (*see also* Malaria) 084.6
    hepatic (Charcôt) — *see* Choledocholithiasis
    of unknown origin (*see also* Pyrexia) 780.6
    pernicious 084.0
  iodide
    correct substance properly administered 780.6
    overdose or wrong substance given or taken 975.5
  Japanese river 081.2
  jungle yellow 060.0
  Junin virus, hemorrhagic 078.7
  Katayama 120.2
  Kedani 081.2
  Kenya 082.1
  Korean hemorrhagic 078.6
  Lassa 078.89
  Lone Star 082.8
  lung — *see* Pneumonia
  Machupo virus, hemorrhagic 078.7
  malaria, malarial (*see also* Malaria) 084.6
  Malta (*see also* Brucellosis) 023.9
  Marseilles 082.1
  marsh (*see also* Malaria) 084.6
  Mayaro (viral) 066.3
  Mediterranean (*see also* Brucellosis) 023.9
    familial 277.3
    tick 082.1
  meningeal — *see* Meningitis
  metal fumes NEC 985.8
  Meuse 083.1
  Mexican — *see* Typhus, Mexican
  Mianeh 087.1
  miasmatic (*see also* Malaria) 084.6
  miliary 078.2
  milk, female 672.0 ☑
  mill 504
  mite-borne hemorrhagic 065.8
  Monday 504
  mosquito-borne NEC 066.3
    hemorrhagic NEC 065.4
  mountain 066.1
    meaning
      Rocky Mountain spotted 082.0
      undulant fever (*see also* Brucellosis) 023.9
    tick (American) 066.1
  Mucambo (viral) 066.3
  mud 100.89
  Neapolitan (*see also* Brucellosis) 023.9
  neutropenic 288.0
  nine-mile 083.0
  nonexanthematous tick 066.1
  North Asian tick-borne typhus 082.2
  Omsk hemorrhagic 065.1
  O'nyong-nyong (viral) 066.3
  Oropouche (viral) 066.3
  Oroya 088.0
  paludal (*see also* Malaria) 084.6
  Panama 084.0
  pappataci 066.0
  paratyphoid 002.9
    A 002.1
    B (Schottmüller's) 002.2
    C (Hirschfeld) 002.3
  parrot 073.9
  periodic 277.3
  pernicious, acute 084.0
  persistent (of unknown origin) (*see also* Pyrexia) 780.6
  petechial 036.0
  pharyngoconjunctival 077.2
    adenoviral type 3 077.2
  Philippine hemorrhagic 065.4
  phlebotomus 066.0
  Piry 066.8
  Pixuna (viral) 066.3
  Plasmodium ovale 084.3
  pleural (*see also* Pleurisy) 511.0
  pneumonic — *see* Pneumonia
  polymer fume 987.8
  postoperative 998.89
    due to infection 998.59
  pretibial 100.89
  puerperal, postpartum 672.0 ☑
  putrid — *see* Septicemia

Fever — *continued*
  pyemic — *see* Septicemia
  Q 083.0
    with pneumonia 083.0 *[484.8]*
  quadrilateral 083.0
  quartan (malaria) 084.2
  Queensland (coastal) 083.0
    seven-day 100.89
  Quintan (A) 083.1
  quotidian 084.0
  rabbit (*see also* Tularemia) 021.9
  rat-bite 026.9
    due to
      Spirillum minor or minus 026.0
      Spirochaeta morsus muris 026.0
      Streptobacillus moniliformis 026.1
  recurrent — *see* Fever, relapsing
  relapsing 087.9
    Carter's (Asiatic) 087.0
    Dutton's (West African) 087.1
    Koch's 087.9
    louse-borne (epidemic) 087.0
    Novy's (American) 087.1
    Obermeyer's (European) 087.0
    spirillum NEC 087.9
    tick-borne (endemic) 087.1
  remittent (bilious) (congestive) (gastric) (*see also* Malaria) 084.6
  rheumatic (active) (acute) (chronic) (subacute) 390
    with heart involvement 391.9
      carditis 391.9
      endocarditis (aortic) (mitral) (pulmonary) (tricuspid) 391.1
      multiple sites 391.8
      myocarditis 391.2
      pancarditis, acute 391.8
      pericarditis 391.0
      specified type NEC 391.8
      valvulitis 391.1
    inactive or quiescent
      with cardiac hypertrophy 398.99
      carditis 398.90
      endocarditis 397.9
        aortic (valve) 395.9
          with mitral (valve) disease 396.9
        mitral (valve) 394.9
          with aortic (valve) disease 396.9
        pulmonary (valve) 397.1
        tricuspid (valve) 397.0
      heart conditions (classifiable to 429.3, 429.6, 429.9) 398.99
      failure (congestive) (conditions classifiable to 428.0, 428.9) 398.91
      left ventricular failure (conditions classifiable to 428.1) 398.91
      myocardial degeneration (conditions classifiable to 429.1) 398.0
      myocarditis (conditions classifiable to 429.0) 398.0
      pancarditis 398.99
      pericarditis 393
  Rift Valley (viral) 066.3
  Rocky Mountain spotted 082.0
  rose 477.0
  Ross river (viral) 066.3
  Russian hemorrhagic 078.6
  sandfly 066.0
  San Joaquin (valley) 114.0
  São Paulo 082.0
  scarlet 034.1
  septic — *see* Septicemia
  seven-day 061
    Japan 100.89
    Queensland 100.89
  shin bone 083.1
  Singapore hemorrhagic 065.4
  solar 061
  sore 054.9
  South African tick-bite 087.1
  Southeast Asia hemorrhagic 065.4
  spinal — *see* Meningitis
  spirillary 026.0
  splenic (*see also* Anthrax) 022.9
  spotted (Rocky Mountain) 082.0
    American 082.0

☑ Additional Digit Required — Refer to the Tabular List (Numeric Code Section) for Additional Digit Selection

Fever — *continued*
  spotted — *continued*
    Brazilian 082.0
    Colombian 082.0
    meaning
      cerebrospinal meningitis 036.0
      typhus 082.9
  spring 309.23
  steroid
    correct substance properly administered 780.6
    overdose or wrong substance given or taken 962.0
  streptobacillary 026.1
  subtertian 084.0
  Sumatran mite 081.2
  sun 061
  swamp 100.89
  sweating 078.2
  swine 003.8
  sylvatic yellow 060.0
  Tahyna 062.5
  tertian — *see* Malaria, tertian
  Thailand hemorrhagic 065.4
  thermic 992.0
  three day 066.0
    with Coxsackie exanthem 074.8
  tick
    American mountain 066.1
    Colorado 066.1
    Kemerovo 066.1
    Mediterranean 082.1
    mountain 066.1
    nonexanthematous 066.1
    Quaranfil 066.1
  tick-bite NEC 066.1
  tick-borne NEC 066.1
    hemorrhagic NEC 065.3
  transitory of newborn 778.4
  trench 083.1
  tsutsugamushi 081.2
  typhogastric 002.0
  typhoid (abortive) (ambulant) (any site) (hemorrhagic) (infection) (intermittent) (malignant) (rheumatic) 002.0
  typhomalarial (*see also* Malaria) 084.6
  typhus — *see* Typhus
  undulant (*see also* Brucellosis) 023.9
  unknown origin (*see also* Pyrexia) 780.6
  uremic — *see* Uremia
  uveoparotid 135
  valley (Coccidioidomycosis) 114.0
  Venezuelan equine 066.2
  Volhynian 083.1
  Wesselsbron (viral) 066.3
  West
    African 084.8
    Nile (viral) 066.40
      with
        cranial nerve disorders 066.42
        encephalitis 066.41
        optic neuritis 066.42
        other complications 066.49
        other neurologic manifestations 066.42
        polyradiculitis 066.42
  Whitmore's 025
  Wolhynian 083.1
  worm 128.9
  Yaroslav hemorrhagic 078.6
  yellow 060.9
    jungle 060.0
    sylvatic 060.0
    urban 060.1
    vaccination, prophylactic (against) V04.4
  Zika (viral) 066.3

Fibrillation
  atrial (established) (paroxysmal) 427.31
  auricular (atrial) (established) 427.31
  cardiac (ventricular) 427.41
  coronary (*see also* Infarct, myocardium) 410.9 ☑
  heart (ventricular) 427.41
  muscular 728.9
  postoperative 997.1
  ventricular 427.41

Fibrin
  ball or bodies, pleural (sac) 511.0
  chamber, anterior (eye) (gelatinous exudate) 364.04

Fibrinogenolysis (hemorrhagic) — *see* Fibrinolysis

Fibrinogenopenia (congenital) (hereditary) (*see also* Defect, coagulation) 286.3
  acquired 286.6

Fibrinolysis (acquired) (hemorrhagic) (pathologic) 286.6
  with
    abortion — *see* Abortion, by type, with hemorrhage, delayed or excessive
    ectopic pregnancy (*see also* categories 633.0-633.9) 639.1
    molar pregnancy (*see also* categories 630-632) 639.1
  antepartum or intrapartum 641.3 ☑
    affecting fetus or newborn 762.1
  following
    abortion 639.1
    ectopic or molar pregnancy 639.1
  newborn, transient 776.2
  postpartum 666.3 ☑

Fibrinopenia (hereditary) (*see also* Defect, coagulation) 286.3
  acquired 286.6

Fibrinopurulent — *see* condition

Fibrinous — *see* condition

Fibroadenoma (M9010/0)
  cellular intracanalicular (M9020/0) 217
  giant (intracanalicular) (M9020/0) 217
  intracanalicular (M9011/0)
    cellular (M9020/0) 217
    giant (M9020/0) 217
    specified site — *see* Neoplasm, by site, benign
    unspecified site 217
  juvenile (M9030/0) 217
  pericanicular (M9012/0)
    specified site — *see* Neoplasm, by site, benign
    unspecified site 217
  phyllodes (M9020/0) 217
  prostate 600.20
    with urinary retention 600.21
  specified site — *see* Neoplasm, by site, benign
  unspecified site 217

Fibroadenosis, breast (chronic) (cystic) (diffuse) (periodic) (segmental) 610.2

Fibroangioma (M9160/0) — *see also* Neoplasm, by site, benign
  juvenile (M9160/0)
    specified site — *see* Neoplasm, by site, benign
    unspecified site 210.7

Fibrocellulitis progressiva ossificans 728.11

Fibrochondrosarcoma (M9220/3) — *see* Neoplasm, cartilage, malignant

Fibrocystic
  disease 277.00
    bone NEC 733.29
    breast 610.1
    jaw 526.2
    kidney (congenital) 753.19
    liver 751.62
    lung 518.89
      congenital 748.4
    pancreas 277.00
  kidney (congenital) 753.19

Fibrodysplasia ossificans multiplex (progressiva) 728.11

Fibroelastosis (cordis) (endocardial) (endomyocardial) 425.3

Fibroid (tumor) (M8890/0) — *see also* Neoplasm, connective tissue, benign
  disease, lung (chronic) (*see also* Fibrosis, lung) 515
  heart (disease) (*see also* Myocarditis) 429.0
  induration, lung (chronic) (*see also* Fibrosis, lung) 515
  in pregnancy or childbirth 654.1 ☑
    affecting fetus or newborn 763.89
    causing obstructed labor 660.2 ☑
      affecting fetus or newborn 763.1

Fibroid (tumor) (M8890/0) — *see also* Neoplasm, connective tissue, benign — *continued*
  liver — *see* Cirrhosis, liver
  lung (*see also* Fibrosis, lung) 515
  pneumonia (chronic) (*see also* Fibrosis, lung) 515
  uterus (M8890/0) (*see also* Leiomyoma, uterus) 218.9

Fibrolipoma (M8851/0) (*see also* Lipoma, by site) 214.9

Fibroliposarcoma (M8850/3) — *see* Neoplasm, connective tissue, malignant

Fibroma (M8810/0) — *see also* Neoplasm, connective tissue, benign
  ameloblastic (M9330/0) 213.1
    upper jaw (bone) 213.0
  bone (nonossifying) 733.99
    ossifying (M9262/0) — *see* Neoplasm, bone, benign
  cementifying (M9274/0) — *see* Neoplasm, bone, benign
  chondromyxoid (M9241/0) — *see* Neoplasm, bone, benign
  desmoplastic (M8823/1) — *see* Neoplasm, connective tissue, uncertain behavior
  facial (M8813/0) — *see* Neoplasm, connective tissue, benign
  invasive (M8821/1) — *see* Neoplasm, connective tissue, uncertain behavior
  molle (M8851/0) (*see also* Lipoma, by site) 214.9
  myxoid (M8811/0) — *see* Neoplasm, connective tissue, benign
  nasopharynx, nasopharyngeal (juvenile) (M9160/0) 210.7
  nonosteogenic (nonossifying) — *see* Dysplasia, fibrous
  odontogenic (M9321/0) 213.1
    upper jaw (bone) 213.0
  ossifying (M9262/0) — *see* Neoplasm, bone, benign
  periosteal (M8812/0) — *see* Neoplasm, bone, benign
  prostate 600.20
    with urinary retention 600.21
  soft (M8851/0) (*see also* Lipoma, by site) 214.9

Fibromatosis
  abdominal (M8822/1) — *see* Neoplasm, connective tissue, uncertain behavior
  aggressive (M8821/1) — *see* Neoplasm, connective tissue, uncertain behavior
  Dupuytren's 728.6
  gingival 523.8
  plantar fascia 728.71
  proliferative 728.79
  pseudosarcomatous (proliferative) (subcutaneous) 728.79
  subcutaneous pseudosarcomatous (proliferative) 728.79

Fibromyalgia 729.1

Fibromyoma (M8890/0) — *see also* Neoplasm, connective tissue, benign
  uterus (corpus) (*see also* Leiomyoma, uterus) 218.9
    in pregnancy or childbirth 654.1 ☑
      affecting fetus or newborn 763.89
      causing obstructed labor 660.2 ☑
        affecting fetus or newborn 763.1

Fibromyositis (*see also* Myositis) 729.1
  scapulohumeral 726.2

Fibromyxolipoma (M8852/0) (*see also* Lipoma, by site) 214.9

Fibromyxoma (M8811/0) — *see* Neoplasm, connective tissue, benign

Fibromyxosarcoma (M8811/3) — *see* Neoplasm, connective tissue, malignant

Fibro-odontoma, ameloblastic (M9290/0) 213.1
  upper jaw (bone) 213.0

Fibro-osteoma (M9262/0) — *see* Neoplasm, bone, benign

Fibroplasia, retrolental 362.21

Fibropurulent — *see* condition

Fibrosarcoma (M8810/3) — *see also* Neoplasm, connective tissue, malignant
  ameloblastic (M9330/3) 170.1
    upper jaw (bone) 170.0

Fibrosarcoma — *see also* Neoplasm, connective tissue, malignant — *continued*
  congenital (M8814/3) — *see* Neoplasm, connective tissue, malignant
  fascial (M8813/3) — *see* Neoplasm, connective tissue, malignant
  infantile (M8814/3) — *see* Neoplasm, connective tissue, malignant
  odontogenic (M9330/3) 170.1
    upper jaw (bone) 170.0
  periosteal (M8812/3) — *see* Neoplasm, bone, malignant

Fibrosclerosis
  breast 610.3
  corpora cavernosa (penis) 607.89
  familial multifocal NEC 710.8
  multifocal (idiopathic) NEC 710.8
  penis (corpora cavernosa) 607.89

Fibrosis, fibrotic
  adrenal (gland) 255.8
  alveolar (diffuse) 516.3
  amnion 658.8 ☑
  anal papillae 569.49
  anus 569.49
  appendix, appendiceal, noninflammatory 543.9
  arteriocapillary — *see* Arteriosclerosis
  bauxite (of lung) 503
  biliary 576.8
    due to Clonorchis sinensis 121.1
  bladder 596.8
    interstitial 595.1
    localized submucosal 595.1
    panmural 595.1
  bone, diffuse 756.59
  breast 610.3
  capillary — *see also* Arteriosclerosis
    lung (chronic) (*see also* Fibrosis, lung) 515
  cardiac (*see also* Myocarditis) 429.0
  cervix 622.8
  chorion 658.8 ☑
  corpus cavernosum 607.89
  cystic (of pancreas) 277.00
    with
      manifestations
        gastrointestinal 277.03
        pulmonary 277.02
        specified NEC 277.09
      meconium ileus 277.01
      pulmonary exacerbation 277.02
  due to (presence of) any device, implant, or graft — *see* Complications, due to (presence of) any device, implant, or graft classified to 996.0-996.5 NEC
  ejaculatory duct 608.89
  endocardium (*see also* Endocarditis) 424.90
  endomyocardial (African) 425.0
  epididymis 608.89
  eye muscle 378.62
  graphite (of lung) 503
  heart (*see also* Myocarditis) 429.0
  hepatic — *see also* Cirrhosis, liver
    due to Clonorchis sinensis 121.1
  hepatolienal — *see* Cirrhosis, liver
  hepatosplenic — *see* Cirrhosis, liver
  infrapatellar fat pad 729.31
  interstitial pulmonary, newborn 770.7
  intrascrotal 608.89
  kidney (*see also* Sclerosis, renal) 587
  liver — *see* Cirrhosis, liver
  lung (atrophic) (capillary) (chronic) (confluent) (massive) (perialveolar) (peribronchial) 515
    with
      anthracosilicosis (occupational) 500
      anthracosis (occupational) 500
      asbestosis (occupational) 501
      bagassosis (occupational) 495.1
      bauxite 503
      berylliosis (occupational) 503
      byssinosis (occupational) 504
      calcicosis (occupational) 502
      chalicosis (occupational) 502
      dust reticulation (occupational) 504
      farmers' lung 495.0
      gannister disease (occupational) 502
      graphite 503

Fibrosis, fibrotic — *continued*
  lung — *continued*
    with — *continued*
      pneumoconiosis (occupational) 505
      pneumosiderosis (occupational) 503
      siderosis (occupational) 503
      silicosis (occupational) 502
      tuberculosis (*see also* Tuberculosis) 011.4 ☑
    diffuse (idiopathic) (interstitial) 516.3
    due to
      bauxite 503
      fumes or vapors (chemical) (inhalation) 506.4
      graphite 503
    following radiation 508.1
    postinflammatory 515
    silicotic (massive) (occupational) 502
    tuberculous (*see also* Tuberculosis) 011.4 ☑
  lymphatic gland 289.3
  median bar 600.90
    with urinary retention 600.91
  mediastinum (idiopathic) 519.3
  meninges 349.2
  muscle NEC 728.2
    iatrogenic (from injection) 999.9
  myocardium, myocardial (*see also* Myocarditis) 429.0
  oral submucous 528.8
  ovary 620.8
  oviduct 620.8
  pancreas 577.8
    cystic 277.00
      with
        manifestations
          gastrointestinal 277.03
          pulmonary 277.02
          specified NEC 277.09
        meconium ileus 277.01
        pulmonary exacerbation 277.02
  penis 607.89
  periappendiceal 543.9
  periarticular (*see also* Ankylosis) 718.5 ☑
  pericardium 423.1
  perineum, in pregnancy or childbirth 654.8 ☑
    affecting fetus or newborn 763.89
    causing obstructed labor 660.2 ☑
      affecting fetus or newborn 763.1
  perineural NEC 355.9
    foot 355.6
  periureteral 593.89
  placenta — *see* Placenta, abnormal
  pleura 511.0
  popliteal fat pad 729.31
  preretinal 362.56
  prostate (chronic) 600.90
    with urinary retention 600.91
  pulmonary (chronic) (*see also* Fibrosis, lung) 515
    alveolar capillary block 516.3
    interstitial
      diffuse (idiopathic) 516.3
      newborn 770.7
  radiation — *see* Effect, adverse, radiation
  rectal sphincter 569.49
  retroperitoneal, idiopathic 593.4
  sclerosing mesenteric (idiopathic) 567.82 ●
  scrotum 608.89
  seminal vesicle 608.89
  senile 797
  skin NEC 709.2
  spermatic cord 608.89
  spleen 289.59
    bilharzial (*see also* Schistosomiasis) 120.9
  subepidermal nodular (M8832/0) — *see* Neoplasm, skin, benign
  submucous NEC 709.2
    oral 528.8
    tongue 528.8
  syncytium — *see* Placenta, abnormal
  testis 608.89
    chronic, due to syphilis 095.8
  thymus (gland) 254.8
  tunica vaginalis 608.89
  ureter 593.89
  urethra 599.84

Fibrosis, fibrotic — *continued*
  uterus (nonneoplastic) 621.8
    bilharzial (*see also* Schistosomiasis) 120.9
    neoplastic (*see also* Leiomyoma, uterus) 218.9
  vagina 623.8
  valve, heart (*see also* Endocarditis) 424.90
  vas deferens 608.89
  vein 459.89
    lower extremities 459.89
  vesical 595.1

Fibrositis (periarticular) (rheumatoid) 729.0
  humeroscapular region 726.2
  nodular, chronic
    Jaccoud's 714.4
    rheumatoid 714.4
  ossificans 728.11
  scapulohumeral 726.2

Fibrothorax 511.0

Fibrotic — *see* Fibrosis

Fibrous — *see* condition

Fibroxanthoma (M8831/0) — *see also* Neoplasm, connective tissue, benign
  atypical (M8831/1) — *see* Neoplasm, connective tissue, uncertain behavior
  malignant (M8831/3) — *see* Neoplasm, connective tissue, malignant

Fibroxanthosarcoma (M8831/3) — *see* Neoplasm, connective tissue, malignant

Fiedler's
  disease (leptospiral jaundice) 100.0
  myocarditis or syndrome (acute isolated myocarditis) 422.91

Fiessinger-Leroy (-Reiter) syndrome 099.3

Fiessinger-Rendu syndrome (erythema muliforme exudativum) 695.1

Fifth disease (eruptive) 057.0
  venereal 099.1

Filaria, filarial — *see* Infestation, filarial

Filariasis (*see also* Infestation, filarial) 125.9
  bancroftian 125.0
  Brug's 125.1
  due to
    bancrofti 125.0
    Brugia (Wuchereria) (malayi) 125.1
    Loa loa 125.2
    malayi 125.1
    organism NEC 125.6
    Wuchereria (bancrofti) 125.0
      malayi 125.1
  Malayan 125.1
  ozzardi 125.5
  specified type NEC 125.6

Filatoff's, Filatov's, Filatow's disease (infectious mononucleosis) 075

File-cutters' disease 984.9
  specified type of lead — *see* Table of Drugs and Chemicals

Filling defect
  biliary tract 793.3
  bladder 793.5
  duodenum 793.4
  gallbladder 793.3
  gastrointestinal tract 793.4
  intestine 793.4
  kidney 793.5
  stomach 793.4
  ureter 793.5

Filtering bleb, eye (postglaucoma) (status) V45.69
  with complication or rupture 997.99
  postcataract extraction (complication) 997.99

Fimbrial cyst (congenital) 752.11

Fimbriated hymen 752.49

Financial problem affecting care V60.2

Findings, abnormal, without diagnosis (examination) (laboratory test) 796.4
  17-ketosteroids, elevated 791.9
  acetonuria 791.6
  acid phosphatase 790.5
  albumin-globulin ratio 790.99
  albuminuria 791.0
  alcohol in blood 790.3
  alkaline phosphatase 790.5

Findings, abnormal, without diagnosis — *continued*
  amniotic fluid 792.3
  amylase 790.5
  anisocytosis 790.09
  antenatal screening 796.5
  anthrax, positive 795.31
  antibody titers, elevated 795.79
  anticardiolipin antibody 795.79
  antigen-antibody reaction 795.79
  antiphospholipid antibody 795.79
  bacteriuria 791.9
  ballistocardiogram 794.39
  bicarbonate 276.9
  bile in urine 791.4
  bilirubin 277.4
  bleeding time (prolonged) 790.92
  blood culture, positive 790.7
  blood gas level (arterial) 790.91
  blood sugar level 790.29
    high 790.29
      fasting glucose 790.21
      glucose tolerance test 790.22
    low 251.2
  C-reactive protein (CRP) 790.95
  calcium 275.40
  carbonate 276.9
  casts, urine 791.7
  catecholamines 791.9
  cells, urine 791.7
  cerebrospinal fluid (color) (content) (pressure) 792.0
  cervical
    high risk human papillomavirus (HPV) DNA test positive 795.05
    low risk human papillomavirus (HPV) DNA test positive 795.09
  chloride 276.9
  cholesterol 272.9
  chromosome analysis 795.2
  chyluria 791.1
  circulation time 794.39
  cloudy dialysis effluent 792.5
  cloudy urine 791.9
  coagulation study 790.92
  cobalt, blood 790.6
  color of urine (unusual) NEC 791.9
  copper, blood 790.6
  crystals, urine 791.9
  culture, positive NEC 795.39
    blood 790.7
    HIV V08
    human immunodeficiency virus V08
    nose 795.39
    skin lesion NEC 795.39
    spinal fluid 792.0
    sputum 795.39
    stool 792.1
    throat 795.39
    urine 791.9
    viral
      human immunodeficiency V08
    wound 795.39
  echocardiogram 793.2
  echoencephalogram 794.01
  echogram NEC — *see* Findings, abnormal, structure
  electrocardiogram (ECG) (EKG) 794.31
  electroencephalogram (EEG) 794.02
  electrolyte level, urinary 791.9
  electromyogram (EMG) 794.17
    ocular 794.14
  electro-oculogram (EOG) 794.12
  electroretinogram (ERG) 794.11
  enzymes, serum NEC 790.5
  fibrinogen titer coagulation study 790.92
  filling defect — *see* Filling defect
  function study NEC 794.9
    auditory 794.15
    bladder 794.9
    brain 794.00
    cardiac 794.30
    endocrine NEC 794.6
      thyroid 794.5
    kidney 794.4
    liver 794.8

Findings, abnormal, without diagnosis — *continued*
  function study NEC — *continued*
    nervous system
      central 794.00
      peripheral 794.19
    oculomotor 794.14
    pancreas 794.9
    placenta 794.9
    pulmonary 794.2
    retina 794.11
    special senses 794.19
    spleen 794.9
    vestibular 794.16
  gallbladder, nonvisualization 793.3
  glucose 790.29
    elevated
      fasting 790.21
      tolerance test 790.22
  glycosuria 791.5
  heart
    shadow 793.2
    sounds 785.3
  hematinuria 791.2
  hematocrit
    drop (precipitous) 790.01
    elevated 282.7
    low 285.9
  hematologic NEC 790.99
  hematuria 599.7
  hemoglobin
    elevated 282.7
    low 285.9
  hemoglobinuria 791.2
  histological NEC 795.4
  hormones 259.9
  immunoglobulins, elevated 795.79
  indolacetic acid, elevated 791.9
  iron 790.6
  karyotype 795.2
  ketonuria 791.6
  lactic acid dehydrogenase (LDH) 790.4
  lipase 790.5
  lipids NEC 272.9
  lithium, blood 790.6
  liver function test 790.6   ●
  lung field (coin lesion) (shadow) 793.1
  magnesium, blood 790.6
  mammogram 793.80
    microcalcification 793.81
  mediastinal shift 793.2
  melanin, urine 791.9
  microbiologic NEC 795.39
  mineral, blood NEC 790.6
  myoglobinuria 791.3
  nasal swab, anthrax 795.31
  neonatal screening 796.6
  nitrogen derivatives, blood 790.6
  nonvisualization of gallbladder 793.3
  nose culture, positive 795.39
  odor of urine (unusual) NEC 791.9
  oxygen saturation 790.91
  Papanicolaou (smear) 795.1
    cervix 795.00
      with
        atypical squamous cells
          cannot exclude high grade squamous intraepithelial lesion (ASC-H) 795.02
          of undetermined significance (ASC-US) 795.01
        high grade squamous intraepithelial lesion (HGSIL) 795.04
        low grade squamous intraepithelial lesion (LGSIL) 795.03
      dyskaryotic 795.09
      nonspecific finding NEC 795.09
    other site 795.1
  peritoneal fluid 792.9
  phonocardiogram 794.39
  phosphorus 275.3
  pleural fluid 792.9
  pneumoencephalogram 793.0
  PO_2-oxygen ratio 790.91
  poikilocytosis 790.09
  potassium
    deficiency 276.8
    excess 276.7

Findings, abnormal, without diagnosis — *continued*
  PPD 795.5
  prostate specific antigen (PSA) 790.93
  protein, serum NEC 790.99
  proteinuria 791.0
  prothrombin time (partial) (prolonged) (PT) (PTT) 790.92
  pyuria 791.9
  radiologic (x-ray) 793.9
    abdomen 793.6
    biliary tract 793.3
    breast 793.89
      abnormal mammogram NOS 793.80
      mammographic microcalcification 793.81
    gastrointestinal tract 793.4
    genitourinary organs 793.5
    head 793.0
    intrathoracic organs NEC 793.2
    lung 793.1
    musculoskeletal 793.7
    placenta 793.9
    retroperitoneum 793.6
    skin 793.9
    skull 793.0
    subcutaneous tissue 793.9
  red blood cell 790.09
    count 790.09
    morphology 790.09
    sickling 790.09
    volume 790.09
  saliva 792.4
  scan NEC 794.9
    bladder 794.9
    bone 794.9
    brain 794.09
    kidney 794.4
    liver 794.8
    lung 794.2
    pancreas 794.9
    placental 794.9
    spleen 794.9
    thyroid 794.5
  sedimentation rate, elevated 790.1
  semen 792.2
  serological (for)
    human immunodeficiency virus (HIV)
      inconclusive 795.71
      positive V08
    syphilis — *see* Findings, serology for syphilis
  serology for syphilis
    false positive 795.6
    positive 097.1
      false 795.6
      follow-up of latent syphilis — *see* Syphilis, latent
      only finding — *see* Syphilis, latent
  serum 790.99
    blood NEC 790.99
    enzymes NEC 790.5
    proteins 790.99
  SGOT 790.4
  SGPT 790.4
  sickling of red blood cells 790.09
  skin test, positive 795.79
    tuberculin (without active tuberculosis) 795.5
  sodium 790.6
    deficiency 276.1
    excess 276.0
  spermatozoa 792.2
  spinal fluid 792.0
    culture, positive 792.0
  sputum culture, positive 795.39
    for acid-fast bacilli 795.39
  stool NEC 792.1
    bloody 578.1
      occult 792.1
    color 792.1
    culture, positive 792.1
    occult blood 792.1
  stress test 794.39
  structure, body (echogram) (thermogram) (ultrasound) (x-ray) NEC 793.9
    abdomen 793.6
    breast 793.89
      abnormal mammogram 793.80
      mammographic microcalcification 793.81

Findings, abnormal, without diagnosis —
continued
structure, body NEC — *continued*
  gastrointestinal tract 793.4
  genitourinary organs 793.5
  head 793.0
    echogram (ultrasound) 794.01
  intrathoracic organs NEC 793.2
  lung 793.1
  musculoskeletal 793.7
  placenta 793.9
  retroperitoneum 793.6
  skin 793.9
  subcutaneous tissue NEC 793.9
synovial fluid 792.9
thermogram — *see* Findings, abnormal,
  structure
throat culture, positive 795.39
thyroid (function) 794.5
  metabolism (rate) 794.5
  scan 794.5
  uptake 794.5
total proteins 790.99
toxicology (drugs) (heavy metals) 796.0
transaminase (level) 790.4
triglycerides 272.9
tuberculin skin test (without active
  tuberculosis) 795.5
ultrasound — *see also* Findings, abnormal,
  structure
  cardiogram 793.2
uric acid, blood 790.6
urine, urinary constituents 791.9
  acetone 791.6
  albumin 791.0
  bacteria 791.9
  bile 791.4
  blood 599.7
  casts or cells 791.7
  chyle 791.1
  culture, positive 791.9
  glucose 791.5
  hemoglobin 791.2
  ketone 791.6
  protein 791.0
  pus 791.9
  sugar 791.5
vaginal fluid 792.9
vanillylmandelic acid, elevated 791.9
vectorcardiogram (VCG) 794.39
ventriculogram (cerebral) 793.0
VMA, elevated 791.9
Wassermann reaction
  false positive 795.6
  positive 097.1
    follow-up of latent syphilis — *see*
      Syphilis, latent
    only finding — *see* Syphilis, latent
white blood cell 288.9
  count 288.9
    elevated 288.8
    low 288.0
  differential 288.9
  morphology 288.9
wound culture 795.39
xerography 793.89
zinc, blood 790.6

Finger — *see* condition
Fire, St. Anthony's (*see also* Erysipelas) 035
Fish
hook stomach 537.89
meal workers' lung 495.8
Fisher's syndrome 357.0
Fissure, fissured
abdominal wall (congenital) 756.79
anus, anal 565.0
  congenital 751.5
buccal cavity 528.9
clitoris (congenital) 752.49
ear, lobule (congenital) 744.29
epiglottis (congenital) 748.3
larynx 478.79
  congenital 748.3
lip 528.5
  congenital (*see also* Cleft, lip) 749.10

Fissure, fissured — *continued*
nipple 611.2
  puerperal, postpartum 676.1 ☑
palate (congenital) (*see also* Cleft, palate)
  749.00
postanal 565.0
rectum 565.0
skin 709.8
  streptococcal 686.9
spine (congenital) (*see also* Spina bifida)
  741.9 ☑
sternum (congenital) 756.3
tongue (acquired) 529.5
  congenital 750.13
Fistula (sinus) 686.9
abdomen (wall) 569.81
  bladder 596.2
  intestine 569.81
  ureter 593.82
  uterus 619.2
abdominorectal 569.81
abdominosigmoidal 569.81
abdominothoracic 510.0
abdominouterine 619.2
  congenital 752.3
abdominovesical 596.2
accessory sinuses (*see also* Sinusitis) 473.9
actinomycotic — *see* Actinomycosis
alveolar
  antrum (*see also* Sinusitis, maxillary) 473.0
  process 522.7
anorectal 565.1
antrobuccal (*see also* Sinusitis, maxillary)
  473.0
antrum (*see also* Sinusitis, maxillary) 473.0
anus, anal (infectional) (recurrent) 565.1
  congenital 751.5
  tuberculous (*see also* Tuberculosis) 014.8 ☑
aortic sinus 747.29
aortoduodenal 447.2
appendix, appendicular 543.9
arteriovenous (acquired) 447.0
  brain 437.3
    congenital 747.81
      ruptured (*see also* Hemorrhage,
        subarachnoid) 430
    ruptured (*see also* Hemorrhage,
      subarachnoid) 430
  cerebral 437.3
    congenital 747.81
  congenital (peripheral) 747.60
    brain — *see* Fistula, arteriovenous, brain,
      congenital
    coronary 746.85
    gastrointestinal 747.61
    lower limb 747.64
    pulmonary 747.3
    renal 747.62
    specified site NEC 747.69
    upper limb 747.63
  coronary 414.19
    congenital 746.85
  heart 414.19
  pulmonary (vessels) 417.0
    congenital 747.3
  surgically created (for dialysis) V45.1
    complication NEC 996.73
      atherosclerosis — *see* Arteriosclerosis,
        extremities
      embolism 996.74
      infection or inflammation 996.62
      mechanical 996.1
      occlusion NEC 996.74
      thrombus 996.74
  traumatic — *see* Injury, blood vessel, by site
artery 447.2
aural 383.81
  congenital 744.49
auricle 383.81
  congenital 744.49
Bartholin's gland 619.8
bile duct (*see also* Fistula, biliary) 576.4
biliary (duct) (tract) 576.4
  congenital 751.69
bladder (neck) (sphincter) 596.2
  into seminal vesicle 596.2

Fistula — *continued*
bone 733.99
brain 348.8
  arteriovenous — *see* Fistula, arteriovenous,
    brain
branchial (cleft) 744.41
branchiogenous 744.41
breast 611.0
  puerperal, postpartum 675.1 ☑
bronchial 510.0
bronchocutaneous, bronchomediastinal,
  bronchopleural,
  bronchopleuromediastinal (infective)
  510.0
  tuberculous (*see also* Tuberculosis) 011.3 ☑
bronchoesophageal 530.89
  congenital 750.3
buccal cavity (infective) 528.3
canal, ear 380.89
carotid-cavernous
  congenital 747.81
    with hemorrhage 430
  traumatic 900.82
    with hemorrhage (*see also* Hemorrhage,
      brain, traumatic) 853.0 ☑
    late effect 908.3
cecosigmoidal 569.81
cecum 569.81
cerebrospinal (fluid) 349.81
cervical, lateral (congenital) 744.41
cervicoaural (congenital) 744.49
cervicosigmoidal 619.1
cervicovesical 619.0
cervix 619.8
chest (wall) 510.0
cholecystocolic (*see also* Fistula, gallbladder)
  575.5
cholecystocolonic (*see also* Fistula, gallbladder)
  575.5
cholecystoduodenal (*see also* Fistula,
  gallbladder) 575.5
cholecystoenteric (*see also* Fistula, gallbladder)
  575.5
cholecystogastric (*see also* Fistula, gallbladder)
  575.5
cholecystointestinal (*see also* Fistula,
  gallbladder) 575.5
choledochoduodenal 576.4
cholocolic (*see also* Fistula, gallbladder) 575.5
coccyx 685.1
  with abscess 685.0
colon 569.81
colostomy 569.69
colovaginal (acquired) 619.1
common duct (bile duct) 576.4
congenital, NEC — *see* Anomaly, specified type
  NEC
cornea, causing hypotony 360.32
coronary, arteriovenous 414.19
  congenital 746.85
costal region 510.0
cul-de-sac, Douglas' 619.8
cutaneous 686.9
cystic duct (*see also* Fistula, gallbladder) 575.5
  congenital 751.69
dental 522.7
diaphragm 510.0
  bronchovisceral 510.0
  pleuroperitoneal 510.0
  pulmonoperitoneal 510.0
duodenum 537.4
ear (canal) (external) 380.89
enterocolic 569.81
enterocutaneous 569.81
enteroenteric 569.81
entero-uterine 619.1
  congenital 752.3
enterovaginal 619.1
  congenital 752.49
enterovesical 596.1
epididymis 608.89
  tuberculous (*see also* Tuberculosis) 016.4 ☑
esophagobronchial 530.89
  congenital 750.3
esophagocutaneous 530.89
esophagopleurocutaneous 530.89

Fistula — *continued*
  esophagotracheal 530.84
    congenital 750.3
  esophagus 530.89
    congenital 750.4
  ethmoid (*see also* Sinusitis, ethmoidal) 473.2
  eyeball (cornea) (sclera) 360.32
  eyelid 373.11
  fallopian tube (external) 619.2
  fecal 569.81
    congenital 751.5
  from periapical lesion 522.7
  frontal sinus (*see also* Sinusitis, frontal) 473.1
  gallbladder 575.5
    with calculus, cholelithiasis, stones (*see also* Cholelithiasis) 574.2 ☑
    congenital 751.69
  gastric 537.4
  gastrocolic 537.4
    congenital 750.7
    tuberculous (*see also* Tuberculosis) 014.8 ☑
  gastroenterocolic 537.4
  gastroesophageal 537.4
  gastrojejunal 537.4
  gastrojejunocolic 537.4
  genital
    organs
      female 619.9
        specified site NEC 619.8
      male 608.89
    tract-skin (female) 619.2
  hepatopleural 510.0
  hepatopulmonary 510.0
  horseshoe 565.1
  ileorectal 569.81
  ileosigmoidal 569.81
  ileostomy 569.69
  ileovesical 596.1
  ileum 569.81
  in ano 565.1
    tuberculous (*see also* Tuberculosis) 014.8 ☑
  inner ear (*see also* Fistula, labyrinth) 386.40
  intestine 569.81
  intestinocolonic (abdominal) 569.81
  intestinoureteral 593.82
  intestinouterine 619.1
  intestinovaginal 619.1
    congenital 752.49
  intestinovesical 596.1
  involving female genital tract 619.9
    digestive-genital 619.1
    genital tract-skin 619.2
    specified site NEC 619.8
    urinary-genital 619.0
  ischiorectal (fossa) 566
  jejunostomy 569.69
  jejunum 569.81
  joint 719.80
    ankle 719.87
    elbow 719.82
    foot 719.87
    hand 719.84
    hip 719.85
    knee 719.86
    multiple sites 719.89
    pelvic region 719.85
    shoulder (region) 719.81
    specified site NEC 719.88
    tuberculous — *see* Tuberculosis, joint
    wrist 719.83
  kidney 593.89
  labium (majus) (minus) 619.8
  labyrinth, labyrinthine NEC 386.40
    combined sites 386.48
    multiple sites 386.48
    oval window 386.42
    round window 386.41
    semicircular canal 386.43
  lacrimal, lachrymal (duct) (gland) (sac) 375.61
  lacrimonasal duct 375.61
  laryngotracheal 748.3
  larynx 478.79
  lip 528.5
    congenital 750.25
  lumbar, tuberculous (*see also* Tuberculosis) 015.0 ☑ [730.8] ☑
  lung 510.0

Fistula — *continued*
  lymphatic (node) (vessel) 457.8
  mamillary 611.0
  mammary (gland) 611.0
    puerperal, postpartum 675.1 ☑
  mastoid (process) (region) 383.1
  maxillary (*see also* Sinusitis, maxillary) 473.0
  mediastinal 510.0
  mediastinobronchial 510.0
  mediastinocutaneous 510.0
  middle ear 385.89
  mouth 528.3
  nasal 478.1
    sinus (*see also* Sinusitis) 473.9
  nasopharynx 478.29
  nipple — *see* Fistula, breast
  nose 478.1
  oral (cutaneous) 528.3
    maxillary (*see also* Sinusitis, maxillary) 473.0
    nasal (with cleft palate) (*see also* Cleft, palate) 749.00
  orbit, orbital 376.10
  oro-antral (*see also* Sinusitis, maxillary) 473.0
  oval window (internal ear) 386.42
  oviduct (external) 619.2
  palate (hard) 526.89
    soft 528.9
  pancreatic 577.8
  pancreaticoduodenal 577.8
  parotid (gland) 527.4
    region 528.3
  pelvoabdominointestinal 569.81
  penis 607.89
  perianal 565.1
  pericardium (pleura) (sac) (*see also* Pericarditis) 423.8
  pericecal 569.81
  perineal — *see* Fistula, perineum
  perineorectal 569.81
  perineosigmoidal 569.81
  perineo-urethroscrotal 608.89
  perineum, perineal (with urethral involvement) NEC 599.1
    tuberculous (*see also* Tuberculosis) 017.9 ☑
    ureter 593.82
  perirectal 565.1
    tuberculous (*see also* Tuberculosis) 014.8 ☑
  peritoneum (*see also* Peritonitis) 567.22 ▲
  periurethral 599.1
  pharyngo-esophageal 478.29
  pharynx 478.29
    branchial cleft (congenital) 744.41
  pilonidal (infected) (rectum) 685.1
    with abscess 685.0
  pleura, pleural, pleurocutaneous, pleuroperitoneal 510.0
    stomach 510.0
    tuberculous (*see also* Tuberculosis) 012.0 ☑
  pleuropericardial 423.8
  postauricular 383.81
  postoperative, persistent 998.6
  preauricular (congenital) 744.46
  prostate 602.8
  pulmonary 510.0
    arteriovenous 417.0
      congenital 747.3
    tuberculous (*see also* Tuberculosis, pulmonary) 011.9 ☑
  pulmonoperitoneal 510.0
  rectolabial 619.1
  rectosigmoid (intercommunicating) 569.81
  rectoureteral 593.82
  rectourethral 599.1
    congenital 753.8
  rectouterine 619.1
    congenital 752.3
  rectovaginal 619.1
    congenital 752.49
    old, postpartal 619.1
    tuberculous (*see also* Tuberculosis) 014.8 ☑
  rectovesical 596.1
    congenital 753.8
  rectovesicovaginal 619.1
  rectovulvar 619.1
    congenital 752.49

Fistula — *continued*
  rectum (to skin) 565.1
    tuberculous (*see also* Tuberculosis) 014.8 ☑
  renal 593.89
  retroauricular 383.81
  round window (internal ear) 386.41
  salivary duct or gland 527.4
    congenital 750.24
  sclera 360.32
  scrotum (urinary) 608.89
    tuberculous (*see also* Tuberculosis) 016.5 ☑
  semicircular canals (internal ear) 386.43
  sigmoid 569.81
    vesicoabdominal 596.1
  sigmoidovaginal 619.1
    congenital 752.49
  skin 686.9
    ureter 593.82
    vagina 619.2
  sphenoidal sinus (*see also* Sinusitis, sphenoidal) 473.3
  splenocolic 289.59
  stercoral 569.81
  stomach 537.4
  sublingual gland 527.4
    congenital 750.24
  submaxillary
    gland 527.4
      congenital 750.24
    region 528.3
  thoracic 510.0
    duct 457.8
  thoracicoabdominal 510.0
  thoracicogastric 510.0
  thoracicointestinal 510.0
  thoracoabdominal 510.0
  thoracogastric 510.0
  thorax 510.0
  thyroglossal duct 759.2
  thyroid 246.8
  trachea (congenital) (external) (internal) 748.3
  tracheoesophageal 530.84
    congenital 750.3
    following tracheostomy 519.09
  traumatic
    arteriovenous (*see also* Injury, blood vessel, by site) 904.9
    brain — *see* Injury, intracranial
  tuberculous — *see* Tuberculosis, by site
  typhoid 002.0
  umbilical 759.89
  umbilico-urinary 753.8
  urachal, urachus 753.7
  ureter (persistent) 593.82
  ureteroabdominal 593.82
  ureterocervical 593.82
  ureterorectal 593.82
  ureterosigmoido-abdominal 593.82
  ureterovaginal 619.0
  ureterovesical 596.2
  urethra 599.1
    congenital 753.8
    tuberculous (*see also* Tuberculosis) 016.3 ☑
  urethroperineal 599.1
  urethroperineovesical 596.2
  urethrorectal 599.1
    congenital 753.8
  urethroscrotal 608.89
  urethrovaginal 619.0
  urethrovesical 596.2
  urethrovesicovaginal 619.0
  urinary (persistent) (recurrent) 599.1
  uteroabdominal (anterior wall) 619.2
    congenital 752.3
  uteroenteric 619.1
  uterofecal 619.1
  uterointestinal 619.1
    congenital 752.3
  uterorectal 619.1
    congenital 752.3
  uteroureteric 619.0
  uterovaginal 619.8
  uterovesical 619.0
    congenital 752.3
  uterus 619.8
  vagina (wall) 619.8
    postpartal, old 619.8

Fistula — *continued*
- vaginocutaneous (postpartal) 619.2
- vaginoileal (acquired) 619.1
- vaginoperineal 619.2
- vesical NEC 596.2
- vesicoabdominal 596.2
- vesicocervicovaginal 619.0
- vesicocolic 596.1
- vesicocutaneous 596.2
- vesicoenteric 596.1
- vesicointestinal 596.1
- vesicometrorectal 619.1
- vesicoperineal 596.2
- vesicorectal 596.1
  - congenital 753.8
- vesicosigmoidal 596.1
- vesicosigmoidovaginal 619.1
- vesicoureteral 596.2
- vesicoureterovaginal 619.0
- vesicourethral 596.2
- vesicourethrorectal 596.1
- vesicouterine 619.0
  - congenital 752.3
- vesicovaginal 619.0
- vulvorectal 619.1
  - congenital 752.49

Fit 780.39
- apoplectic (*see also* Disease, cerebrovascular, acute) 436
  - late effect — *see* Late effect(s) (of) cerebrovascular disease
- epileptic (*see also* Epilepsy) 345.9 ☑
- fainting 780.2
- hysterical 300.11
- newborn 779.0

Fitting (of)
- artificial
  - arm (complete) (partial) V52.0
  - breast V52.4
  - eye(s) V52.2
  - leg(s) (complete) (partial) V52.1
- brain neuropacemaker V53.02
- cardiac pacemaker V53.31
- carotid sinus pacemaker V53.39
- cerebral ventricle (communicating) shunt V53.01
- colostomy belt V53.5
- contact lenses V53.1
- cystostomy device V53.6
- defibrillator, automatic implantable cardiac V53.32
- dentures V52.3
- device, unspecified type V53.90
  - abdominal V53.5
  - cardiac
    - defibrillator, automatic implantable V53.32
    - pacemaker V53.31
    - specified NEC V53.39
  - cerebral ventricle (communicating) shunt V53.01
  - insulin pump V53.91
  - intrauterine contraceptive V25.1
  - nervous system V53.09
  - orthodontic V53.4
  - orthoptic V53.1
  - other device V53.99
  - prosthetic V52.9
    - breast V52.4
    - dental V52.3
    - eye V52.2
    - specified type NEC V52.8
  - special senses V53.09
  - substitution
    - auditory V53.09
    - nervous system V53.09
    - visual V53.09
  - urinary V53.6
- diaphragm (contraceptive) V25.02
- glasses (reading) V53.1
- growth rod V54.02
- hearing aid V53.2
- ileostomy device V53.5
- intestinal appliance or device NEC V53.5
- intrauterine contraceptive device V25.1

Fitting — *continued*
- neuropacemaker (brain) (peripheral nerve) (spinal cord) V53.02
- orthodontic device V53.4
- orthopedic (device) V53.7
  - brace V53.7
  - cast V53.7
  - corset V53.7
  - shoes V53.7
- pacemaker (cardiac) V53.31
  - brain V53.02
  - carotid sinus V53.39
  - peripheral nerve V53.02
  - spinal cord V53.02
- prosthesis V52.9
  - arm (complete) (partial) V52.0
  - breast V52.4
  - dental V52.3
  - eye V52.2
  - leg (complete) (partial) V52.1
  - specified type NEC V52.8
- spectacles V53.1
- wheelchair V53.8

Fitz's syndrome (acute hemorrhagic pancreatitis) 577.0

Fitz-Hugh and Curtis syndrome 098.86
- due to
  - Chlamydia trachomatis 099.56
  - Neisseria gonorrhoeae (gonococcal peritonitis) 098.86

Fixation
- joint — *see* Ankylosis
- larynx 478.79
- pupil 364.76
- stapes 385.22
  - deafness (*see also* Deafness, conductive) 389.04
- uterus (acquired) — *see* Malposition, uterus
- vocal cord 478.5

Flaccid — *see also* condition
- foot 736.79
- forearm 736.09
- palate, congenital 750.26

Flail
- chest 807.4
  - newborn 767.3
- joint (paralytic) 718.80
  - ankle 718.87
  - elbow 718.82
  - foot 718.87
  - hand 718.84
  - hip 718.85
  - knee 718.86
  - multiple sites 718.89
  - pelvic region 718.85
  - shoulder (region) 718.81
  - specified site NEC 718.88
  - wrist 718.83

Flajani (-Basedow) syndrome or disease (exophthalmic goiter) 242.0 ☑

Flap, liver 572.8

Flare, anterior chamber (aqueous) (eye) 364.04

Flashback phenomena (drug) (hallucinogenic) 292.89

Flat
- chamber (anterior) (eye) 360.34
- chest, congenital 754.89
- electroencephalogram (EEG) 348.8
- foot (acquired) (fixed type) (painful) (postural) (spastic) 734
  - congenital 754.61
    - rocker bottom 754.61
    - vertical talus 754.61
  - rachitic 268.1
- rocker bottom (congenital) 754.61
- vertical talus, congenital 754.61
- organ or site, congenital NEC — *see* Anomaly, specified type NEC
- pelvis 738.6
  - with disproportion (fetopelvic) 653.2 ☑
    - affecting fetus or newborn 763.1
  - causing obstructed labor 660.1 ☑
    - affecting fetus or newborn 763.1
  - congenital 755.69

Flatau-Schilder disease 341.1

Flattening
- head, femur 736.39
- hip 736.39
- lip (congenital) 744.89
- nose (congenital) 754.0
  - acquired 738.0

Flatulence 787.3

Flatus 787.3
- vaginalis 629.8

Flax dressers' disease 504

Flea bite — *see* Injury, superficial, by site

Fleischer (-Kayser) ring (corneal pigmentation) 275.1 [371.14]

Fleischner's disease 732.3

Fleshy mole 631

Flexibilitas cerea (*see also* Catalepsy) 300.11

Flexion
- cervix (*see also* Malposition, uterus) 621.6
- contracture, joint (*see also* Contraction, joint) 718.4 ☑
- deformity, joint (*see also* Contraction, joint) 718.4 ☑
  - hip, congenital (*see also* Subluxation, congenital, hip) 754.32
- uterus (*see also* Malposition, uterus) 621.6

Flexner's
- bacillus 004.1
- diarrhea (ulcerative) 004.1
- dysentery 004.1

Flexner-Boyd dysentery 004.2

Flexure — *see* condition

Floater, vitreous 379.24

Floating
- cartilage (joint) (*see also* Disorder, cartilage, articular) 718.0 ☑
  - knee 717.6
- gallbladder (congenital) 751.69
- kidney 593.0
  - congenital 753.3
- liver (congenital) 751.69
- rib 756.3
- spleen 289.59

Flooding 626.2

Floor — *see* condition

Floppy
- infant NEC 781.99
- valve syndrome (mitral) 424.0

Flu — *see also* Influenza
- gastric NEC 008.8

Fluctuating blood pressure 796.4

Fluid
- abdomen 789.5
- chest (*see also* Pleurisy, with effusion) 511.9
- heart (*see also* Failure, heart) 428.0
- joint (*see also* Effusion, joint) 719.0 ☑
- loss (acute) 276.50   ▲
  - with
    - hypernatremia 276.0
    - hyponatremia 276.1
- lung — *see also* Edema, lung
  - encysted 511.8
- peritoneal cavity 789.5
- pleural cavity (*see also* Pleurisy, with effusion) 511.9
- retention 276.6

Flukes NEC (*see also* Infestation, fluke) 121.9
- blood NEC (*see also* Infestation, Schistosoma) 120.9
- liver 121.3

Fluor (albus) (vaginalis) 623.5
- trichomonal (Trichomonas vaginalis) 131.00

Fluorosis (dental) (chronic) 520.3

Flushing 782.62
- menopausal 627.2

Flush syndrome 259.2

Flutter
- atrial or auricular 427.32
- heart (ventricular) 427.42
  - atrial 427.32
- impure 427.32
- postoperative 997.1
- ventricular 427.42

Flux (bloody) (serosanguineous) 009.0
Focal — *see* condition
Fochier's abscess — *see* Abscess, by site
Focus, Assmann's (*see also* Tuberculosis) 011.0 ☑
Fogo selvagem 694.4
Foix-Alajouanine syndrome 336.1
Folds, anomalous — *see also* Anomaly, specified type NEC
  Bowman's membrane 371.31
  Descemet's membrane 371.32
  epicanthic 743.63
  heart 746.89
  posterior segment of eye, congenital 743.54
Folie à deux 297.3
Follicle
  cervix (nabothian) (ruptured) 616.0
  graafian, ruptured, with hemorrhage 620.0
  nabothian 616.0
Folliclis (primary) (*see also* Tuberculosis) 017.0 ☑
Follicular — *see also* condition
  cyst (atretic) 620.0
Folliculitis 704.8
  abscedens et suffodiens 704.8
  decalvans 704.09
  gonorrheal (acute) 098.0
    chronic or duration of 2 months or more 098.2
  keloid, keloidalis 706.1
  pustular 704.8
  ulerythematosa reticulata 701.8
Folliculosis, conjunctival 372.02
Følling's disease (phenylketonuria) 270.1
Follow-up (examination) (routine) (following) V67.9
  cancer chemotherapy V67.2
  chemotherapy V67.2
  fracture V67.4
  high-risk medication V67.51
  injury NEC V67.59
  postpartum
    immediately after delivery V24.0
    routine V24.2
  psychiatric V67.3
  psychotherapy V67.3
  radiotherapy V67.1
  specified condition NEC V67.59
  specified surgery NEC V67.09
  surgery V67.00
    vaginal pap smear V67.01
  treatment V67.9
    combined NEC V67.6
    fracture V67.4
    involving high-risk medication NEC V67.51
    mental disorder V67.3
    specified NEC V67.59
Fong's syndrome (hereditary osteoonychodysplasia) 756.89
Food
  allergy 693.1
  anaphylactic shock — *see* Anaphylactic shock, due to, food
  asphyxia (from aspiration or inhalation) (*see also* Asphyxia, food) 933.1
  choked on (*see also* Asphyxia, food) 933.1
  deprivation 994.2
    specified kind of food NEC 269.8
  intoxication (*see also* Poisoning, food) 005.9
  lack of 994.2
  poisoning (*see also* Poisoning, food) 005.9
  refusal or rejection NEC 307.59
  strangulation or suffocation (*see also* Asphyxia, food) 933.1
  toxemia (*see also* Poisoning, food) 005.9
Foot — *see also* condition
  and mouth disease 078.4
  process disease 581.3
Foramen ovale (nonclosure) (patent) (persistent) 745.5
Forbes' (glycogen storage) **disease** 271.0
Forbes-Albright syndrome (nonpuerperal amenorrhea and lactation associated with pituitary tumor) 253.1

Forced birth or delivery NEC 669.8 ☑
  affecting fetus or newborn NEC 763.89
Forceps
  delivery NEC 669.5 ☑
    affecting fetus or newborn 763.2
Fordyce's disease (ectopic sebaceous glands) (mouth) 750.26
Fordyce-Fox disease (apocrine miliaria) 705.82
Forearm — *see* condition
Foreign body

> Note — For foreign body with open wound or other injury, see Wound, open, or the type of injury specified.

  accidentally left during a procedure 998.4
  anterior chamber (eye) 871.6
    magnetic 871.5
      retained or old 360.51
    retained or old 360.61
  ciliary body (eye) 871.6
    magnetic 871.5
      retained or old 360.52
    retained or old 360.62
  entering through orifice (current) (old)
    accessory sinus 932
    air passage (upper) 933.0
      lower 934.8
    alimentary canal 938
    alveolar process 935.0
    antrum (Highmore) 932
    anus 937
    appendix 936
    asphyxia due to (*see also* Asphyxia, food) 933.1
    auditory canal 931
    auricle 931
    bladder 939.0
    bronchioles 934.8
    bronchus (main) 934.1
    buccal cavity 935.0
    canthus (inner) 930.1
    cecum 936
    cervix (canal) uterine 939.1
    coil, ileocecal 936
    colon 936
    conjunctiva 930.1
    conjunctival sac 930.1
    cornea 930.0
    digestive organ or tract NEC 938
    duodenum 936
    ear (external) 931
    esophagus 935.1
    eye (external) 930.9
      combined sites 930.8
      intraocular — *see* Foreign body, by site
      specified site NEC 930.8
    eyeball 930.8
      intraocular — *see* Foreign body, intraocular
    eyelid 930.1
      retained or old 374.86
    frontal sinus 932
    gastrointestinal tract 938
    genitourinary tract 939.9
    globe 930.8
      penetrating 871.6
        magnetic 871.5
          retained or old 360.50
        retained or old 360.60
    gum 935.0
    Highmore's antrum 932
    hypopharynx 933.0
    ileocecal coil 936
    ileum 936
    inspiration (of) 933.1
    intestine (large) (small) 936
    lacrimal apparatus, duct, gland, or sac 930.2
    larynx 933.1
    lung 934.8
    maxillary sinus 932
    mouth 935.0
    nasal sinus 932
    nasopharynx 933.0
    nose (passage) 932

Foreign body — *continued*
  entering through orifice — *continued*
    nostril 932
    oral cavity 935.0
    palate 935.0
    penis 939.3
    pharynx 933.0
    pyriform sinus 933.0
    rectosigmoid 937
      junction 937
    rectum 937
    respiratory tract 934.9
      specified part NEC 934.8
    sclera 930.1
    sinus 932
      accessory 932
      frontal 932
      maxillary 932
      nasal 932
      pyriform 933.0
    small intestine 936
    stomach (hairball) 935.2
    suffocation by (*see also* Asphyxia, food) 933.1
    swallowed 938
    tear ducts or glands 930.2
    throat 933.0
    tongue 935.0
      swallowed 933.0
    tonsil, tonsillar 933.0
      fossa 933.0
    trachea 934.0
    ureter 939.0
    urethra 939.0
    uterus (any part) 939.1
    vagina 939.2
    vulva 939.2
    wind pipe 934.0
  granuloma (old) 728.82
    bone 733.99
    in operative wound (inadvertently left) 998.4
      due to surgical material intentionally left — *see* Complications, due to (presence of) any device, implant, or graft classified to 996.0-996.5 NEC
    muscle 728.82
    skin 709.4
    soft tissue 709.4
    subcutaneous tissue 709.4
  in
    bone (residual) 733.99
    open wound — *see* Wound, open, by site complicated
    soft tissue (residual) 729.6
  inadvertently left in operation wound (causing adhesions, obstruction, or perforation) 998.4
  ingestion, ingested NEC 938
  inhalation or inspiration (*see also* Asphyxia, food) 933.1
  internal organ, not entering through an orifice — *see* Injury, internal, by site, with open wound
  intraocular (nonmagnetic) 871.6
    combined sites 871.6
      magnetic 871.5
        retained or old 360.59
      retained or old 360.69
    magnetic 871.5
      retained or old 360.50
    retained or old 360.60
    specified site NEC 871.6
      magnetic 871.5
        retained or old 360.59
      retained or old 360.69
  iris (nonmagnetic) 871.6
    magnetic 871.5
      retained or old 360.52
    retained or old 360.62
  lens (nonmagnetic) 871.6
    magnetic 871.5
      retained or old 360.53
    retained or old 360.63
  lid, eye 930.1
  ocular muscle 870.4
    retained or old 376.6

Foreign body — continued
old or residual
  bone 733.99
  eyelid 374.86
  middle ear 385.83
  muscle 729.6
    ocular 376.6
  retrobulbar 376.6
  skin 729.6
    with granuloma 709.4
  soft tissue 729.6
    with granuloma 709.4
  subcutaneous tissue 729.6
    with granuloma 709.4
operation wound, left accidentally 998.4
orbit 870.4
  retained or old 376.6
posterior wall, eye 871.6
  magnetic 871.5
    retained or old 360.55
  retained or old 360.65
respiratory tree 934.9
  specified site NEC 934.8
retained (old) (nonmagnetic) (in)
  anterior chamber (eye) 360.61
    magnetic 360.51
  ciliary body 360.62
    magnetic 360.52
  eyelid 374.86
  globe 360.60
    magnetic 360.50
  intraocular 360.60
    magnetic 360.50
    specified site NEC 360.69
      magnetic 360.59
  iris 360.62
    magnetic 360.52
  lens 360.63
    magnetic 360.53
  muscle 729.6
  orbit 376.6
  posterior wall of globe 360.65
    magnetic 360.55
  retina 360.65
    magnetic 360.55
  retrobulbar 376.6
  skin 729.6
    with granuloma 709.4
  soft tissue 729.6
    with granuloma 709.4
  subcutaneous tissue 729.6
    with granuloma 709.4
  vitreous 360.64
    magnetic 360.54
retina 871.6
  magnetic 871.5
    retained or old 360.55
  retained or old 360.65
superficial, without major open wound (see
    also Injury, superficial, by site) 919.6
swallowed NEC 938
vitreous (humor) 871.6
  magnetic 871.5
    retained or old 360.54
  retained or old 360.64

Forking, aqueduct of Sylvius 742.3
with spina bifida (see also Spina bifida)
  741.0 ☑

Formation
bone in scar tissue (skin) 709.3
connective tissue in vitreous 379.25
Elschnig pearls (postcataract extraction) 366.51
hyaline in cornea 371.49
sequestrum in bone (due to infection) (see also
  Osteomyelitis) 730.1 ☑
valve
  colon, congenital 751.5
  ureter (congenital) 753.29

Formication 782.0

Fort Bragg fever 100.89

Fossa — see also condition
pyriform — see condition

Foster-Kennedy syndrome 377.04

Fothergill's
disease, meaning scarlatina anginosa 034.1
neuralgia (see also Neuralgia, trigeminal) 350.1

Foul breath 784.9

Found dead (cause unknown) 798.9

Foundling V20.0

Fournier's disease (idiopathic gangrene) 608.83

Fourth
cranial nerve — see condition
disease 057.8
molar 520.1

Foville's syndrome 344.89

Fox's
disease (apocrine miliaria) 705.82
impetigo (contagiosa) 684

Fox-Fordyce disease (apocrine miliaria) 705.82

Fracture (abduction) (adduction) (avulsion)
(compression) (crush) (dislocation) (oblique)
(separation) (closed) 829.0

> Note — For fracture of any of the following sites
> with fracture of other bones — see Fracture,
> multiple.
>
> "Closed" includes the following descriptions of
> fractures, with or without delayed healing,
> unless they are specified as open or compound:
>
> | comminuted | linear |
> |---|---|
> | depressed | simple |
> | elevated | slipped epiphysis |
> | fissured | spiral |
> | greenstick | unspecified |
> | impacted | |
>
> "Open" includes the following descriptions of
> fractures, with or without delayed healing:
>
> | compound | puncture |
> |---|---|
> | infected | with foreign body |
> | missile | |
>
> For late effect of fracture, see Late, effect,
> fracture, by site.

with
  internal injuries in same region (conditions
    classifiable to 860-869) — see also
    Injury, internal, by site pelvic region —
    see Fracture, pelvis
acetabulum (with visceral injury) (closed) 808.0
  open 808.1
acromion (process) (closed) 811.01
  open 811.11
alveolus (closed) 802.8
  open 802.9
ankle (malleolus) (closed) 824.8
  bimalleolar (Dupuytren's) (Pott's) 824.4
    open 824.5
  bone 825.21
    open 825.31
  lateral malleolus only (fibular) 824.2
    open 824.3
  medial malleolus only (tibial) 824.0
    open 824.1
  open 824.9
  pathologic 733.16
  talus 825.21
    open 825.31
  trimalleolar 824.6
    open 824.7
antrum — see Fracture, skull, base
arm (closed) 818.0
  and leg(s) (any bones) 828.0
    open 828.1
  both (any bones) (with rib(s)) (with sternum)
    819.0
    open 819.1
  lower 813.80
    open 813.90
  open 818.1
  upper — see Fracture, humerus
astragalus (closed) 825.21
  open 825.31
atlas — see Fracture, vertebra, cervical, first
axis — see Fracture, vertebra, cervical, second
back — see Fracture, vertebra, by site
Barton's — see Fracture, radius, lower end
basal (skull) — see Fracture, skull, base
Bennett's (closed) 815.01
  open 815.11
bimalleolar (closed) 824.4
  open 824.5

Fracture — continued
bone (closed) NEC 829.0
  birth injury NEC 767.3
  open 829.1
  pathological NEC (see also Fracture,
    pathologic) 733.10
  stress NEC (see also Fracture, stress)
    733.95
boot top — see Fracture, fibula
boxers' — see Fracture, metacarpal bone(s)
breast bone — see Fracture, sternum
bucket handle (semilunar cartilage) — see Tear,
  meniscus
bursting — see Fracture, phalanx, hand, distal
calcaneus (closed) 825.0
  open 825.1
capitate (bone) (closed) 814.07
  open 814.17
capitellum (humerus) (closed) 812.49
  open 812.59
carpal bone(s) (wrist NEC) (closed) 814.00
  open 814.10
  specified site NEC 814.09
    open 814.19
cartilage, knee (semilunar) — see Tear,
  meniscus
cervical — see Fracture, vertebra, cervical
chauffeur's — see Fracture, ulna, lower end
chisel — see Fracture, radius, upper end
clavicle (interligamentous part) (closed) 810.00
  acromial end 810.03
    open 810.13
  due to birth trauma 767.2
  open 810.10
  shaft (middle third) 810.02
    open 810.12
  sternal end 810.01
    open 810.11
clayshovelers' — see Fracture, vertebra,
  cervical
coccyx — see also Fracture, vertebra, coccyx
  complicating delivery 665.6 ☑
collar bone — see Fracture, clavicle
Colles' (reversed) (closed) 813.41
  open 813.51
comminuted — see Fracture, by site
compression — see also Fracture, by site
  nontraumatic — see Fracture, pathologic
congenital 756.9
coracoid process (closed) 811.02
  open 811.12
coronoid process (ulna) (closed) 813.02
  mandible (closed) 802.23
    open 802.33
  open 813.12
corpus cavernosum penis 959.13
costochondral junction — see Fracture, rib
costosternal junction — see Fracture, rib
cranium — see Fracture, skull, by site
cricoid cartilage (closed) 807.5
  open 807.6
cuboid (ankle) (closed) 825.23
  open 825.33
cuneiform
  foot (closed) 825.24
    open 825.34
  wrist (closed) 814.03
    open 814.13
due to
  birth injury — see Birth injury, fracture
  gunshot — see Fracture, by site, open
  neoplasm — see Fracture, pathologic
  osteoporosis — see Fracture, pathologic
Dupuytren's (ankle) (fibula) (closed) 824.4
  open 824.5
  radius 813.42
    open 813.52
Duverney's — see Fracture, ilium
elbow — see also Fracture, humerus, lower end
  olecranon (process) (closed) 813.01
    open 813.11
  supracondylar (closed) 812.41
    open 812.51
ethmoid (bone) (sinus) — see Fracture, skull,
  base

Fracture — *continued*
  face bone(s) (closed) NEC 802.8
    with
      other bone(s) — *see* Fracture, multiple,
        skull
      skull — *see also* Fracture, skull
        involving other bones — *see* Fracture,
          multiple, skull
    open 802.9
  fatigue — *see* Fracture, march
  femur, femoral (closed) 821.00
    cervicotrochanteric 820.03
      open 820.13
    condyles, epicondyles 821.21
      open 821.31
    distal end — *see* Fracture, femur, lower end
    epiphysis (separation)
      capital 820.01
        open 820.11
      head 820.01
        open 820.11
      lower 821.22
        open 821.32
      trochanteric 820.01
        open 820.11
      upper 820.01
        open 820.11
    head 820.09
      open 820.19
    lower end or extremity (distal end) (closed)
      821.20
      condyles, epicondyles 821.21
        open 821.31
      epiphysis (separation) 821.22
        open 821.32
      multiple sites 821.29
        open 821.39
      open 821.30
      specified site NEC 821.29
        open 821.39
      supracondylar 821.23
        open 821.33
      T-shaped 821.21
        open 821.31
    neck (closed) 820.8
      base (cervicotrochanteric) 820.03
        open 820.13
      extracapsular 820.20
        open 820.30
      intertrochanteric (section) 820.21
        open 820.31
      intracapsular 820.00
        open 820.10
      intratrochanteric 820.21
        open 820.31
      midcervical 820.02
        open 820.12
      open 820.9
      pathologic 733.14
        specified part NEC 733.15
      specified site NEC 820.09
        open 820.19
      transcervical 820.02
        open 820.12
      transtrochanteric 820.20
        open 820.30
    open 821.10
    pathologic 733.14
      specified part NEC 733.15
    peritrochanteric (section) 820.20
      open 820.30
    shaft (lower third) (middle third) (upper
      third) 821.01
      open 821.11
    subcapital 820.09
      open 820.19
    subtrochanteric (region) (section) 820.22
      open 820.32
    supracondylar 821.23
      open 821.33
    transepiphyseal 820.01
      open 820.11
    trochanter (greater) (lesser) (*see also*
      Fracture, femur, neck, by site) 820.20
      open 820.30
    T-shaped, into knee joint 821.21
      open 821.31

Fracture — *continued*
  femur, femoral — *continued*
    upper end 820.8
      open 820.9
  fibula (closed) 823.81
    with tibia 823.82
      open 823.92
    distal end 824.8
      open 824.9
    epiphysis
      lower 824.8
        open 824.9
      upper — *see* Fracture, fibula, upper end
    head — *see* Fracture, fibula, upper end
    involving ankle 824.2
      open 824.3
    lower end or extremity 824.8
      open 824.9
    malleolus (external) (lateral) 824.2
      open 824.3
    open NEC 823.91
    pathologic 733.16
    proximal end — *see* Fracture, fibula, upper
      end
    shaft 823.21
      with tibia 823.22
        open 823.32
      open 823.31
    stress 733.93
    torus 823.41
      with tibia 823.42
    upper end or extremity (epiphysis) (head)
      (proximal end) (styloid) 823.01
      with tibia 823.02
        open 823.12
      open 823.11
  finger(s), of one hand (closed) (*see also*
    Fracture, phalanx, hand) 816.00
    with
      metacarpal bone(s), of same hand 817.0
        open 817.1
      thumb of same hand 816.03
        open 816.13
    open 816.10
  foot, except toe(s) alone (closed) 825.20
    open 825.30
  forearm (closed) NEC 813.80
    lower end (distal end) (lower epiphysis)
      813.40
      open 813.50
    open 813.90
    shaft 813.20
      open 813.30
    upper end (proximal end) (upper epiphysis)
      813.00
      open 813.10
  fossa, anterior, middle, or posterior — *see*
    Fracture, skull, base
  frontal (bone) — *see also* Fracture, skull, vault
    sinus — *see* Fracture, skull, base
  Galeazzi's — *see* Fracture, radius, lower end
  glenoid (cavity) (fossa) (scapula) (closed) 811.03
    open 811.13
  Gosselin's — *see* Fracture, ankle
  greenstick — *see* Fracture, by site
  grenade-throwers' — *see* Fracture, humerus,
    shaft
  gutter — *see* Fracture, skull, vault
  hamate (closed) 814.08
    open 814.18
  hand, one (closed) 815.00
    carpals 814.00
      open 814.10
      specified site NEC 814.09
        open 814.19
    metacarpals 815.00
      open 815.10
    multiple, bones of one hand 817.0
      open 817.1
    open 815.10
    phalanges (*see also* Fracture, phalanx,
      hand) 816.00
      open 816.10
  healing
    aftercare (*see also* Aftercare, fracture)
      V54.89
    change of cast V54.89

Fracture — *continued*
  healing — *continued*
    complications — *see* condition
    convalescence V66.4
    removal of
      cast V54.89
      fixation device
        external V54.89
        internal V54.01
  heel bone (closed) 825.0
    open 825.1
  hip (closed) (*see also* Fracture, femur, neck)
    820.8
    open 820.9
    pathologic 733.14
  humerus (closed) 812.20
    anatomical neck 812.02
      open 812.12
    articular process (*see also* Fracture
      humerus, condyle(s)) 812.44
      open 812.54
    capitellum 812.49
      open 812.59
    condyle(s) 812.44
      lateral (external) 812.42
        open 812.52
      medial (internal epicondyle) 812.43
        open 812.53
      open 812.54
    distal end — *see* Fracture, humerus, lower
      end
    epiphysis
      lower (*see also* Fracture, humerus,
        condyle(s)) 812.44
        open 812.54
      upper 812.09
        open 812.19
    external condyle 812.42
      open 812.52
    great tuberosity 812.03
      open 812.13
    head 812.09
      open 812.19
    internal epicondyle 812.43
      open 812.53
    lesser tuberosity 812.09
      open 812.19
    lower end or extremity (distal end) (*see also*
      Fracture, humerus, by site) 812.40
      multiple sites NEC 812.49
        open 812.59
      open 812.50
      specified site NEC 812.49
        open 812.59
    neck 812.01
      open 812.11
    open 812.30
    pathologic 733.11
    proximal end — *see* Fracture, humerus,
      upper end
    shaft 812.21
      open 812.31
    supracondylar 812.41
      open 812.51
    surgical neck 812.01
      open 812.11
    trochlea 812.49
      open 812.59
    T-shaped 812.44
      open 812.54
    tuberosity — *see* Fracture, humerus, upper
      end
    upper end or extremity (proximal end) (*see*
      also Fracture, humerus, by site)
      812.00
      open 812.10
      specified site NEC 812.09
        open 812.19
  hyoid bone (closed) 807.5
    open 807.6
  hyperextension — *see* Fracture, radius, lower
    end
  ilium (with visceral injury) (closed) 808.41
    open 808.51
  impaction, impacted — *see* Fracture, by site
  incus — *see* Fracture, skull, base

2006 ICD-9-CM

☑ Additional Digit Required — Refer to the Tabular List (Numeric Code Section) for Additional Digit Selection
    ▶◀ Revised Text   ● New Line   ▲ Revised Code

Volume 2 — 149

Fracture — *continued*
  innominate bone (with visceral injury) (closed)
      808.49
    open 808.59
  instep, of one foot (closed) 825.20
    with toe(s) of same foot 827.0
      open 827.1
    open 825.30
  internal
    ear — *see* Fracture, skull, base
    semilunar cartilage, knee — *see* Tear,
        meniscus, medial
  intertrochanteric — *see* Fracture, femur, neck,
      intertrochanteric
  ischium (with visceral injury) (closed) 808.42
    open 808.52
  jaw (bone) (lower) (closed) (*see also* Fracture,
      mandible) 802.20
    angle 802.25
      open 802.35
    open 802.30
    upper — *see* Fracture, maxilla
  knee
    cap (closed) 822.0
      open 822.1
    cartilage (semilunar) — *see* Tear, meniscus
  labyrinth (osseous) — *see* Fracture, skull, base
  larynx (closed) 807.5
    open 807.6
  late effect — *see* Late, effects (of), fracture
  Le Fort's — *see* Fracture, maxilla
  leg (closed) 827.0
    with rib(s) or sternum 828.0
      open 828.1
    both (any bones) 828.0
      open 828.1
    lower — *see* Fracture, tibia
      open 827.1
    upper — *see* Fracture, femur
  limb
    lower (multiple) (closed) NEC 827.0
      open 827.1
    upper (multiple) (closed) NEC 818.0
      open 818.1
  long bones, due to birth trauma — *see* Birth
      injury, fracture
  lumbar — *see* Fracture, vertebra, lumbar
  lunate bone (closed) 814.02
    open 814.12
  malar bone (closed) 802.4
    open 802.5
  Malgaigne's (closed) 808.43
    open 808.53
  malleolus (closed) 824.8
    bimalleolar 824.4
      open 824.5
    lateral 824.2
      and medial — *see also* Fracture,
          malleolus, bimalleolar
        with lip of tibia — *see* Fracture,
            malleolus, trimalleolar
      open 824.3
    medial (closed) 824.0
      and lateral — *see also* Fracture,
          malleolus, bimalleolar
        with lip of tibia — *see* Fracture,
            malleolus, trimalleolar
      open 824.1
    open 824.9
    trimalleolar (closed) 824.6
      open 824.7
  malleus — *see* Fracture, skull, base
  malunion 733.81
  mandible (closed) 802.20
    angle 802.25
      open 802.35
    body 802.28
      alveolar border 802.27
        open 802.37
      open 802.38
      symphysis 802.26
        open 802.36
    condylar process 802.21
      open 802.31
    coronoid process 802.23
      open 802.33

Fracture — *continued*
  mandible — *continued*
    multiple sites 802.29
      open 802.39
    open 802.30
    ramus NEC 802.24
      open 802.34
    subcondylar 802.22
      open 802.32
  manubrium — *see* Fracture, sternum
  march 733.95
    fibula 733.93
    metatarsals 733.94
    tibia 733.93
  maxilla, maxillary (superior) (upper jaw)
      (closed) 802.4
    inferior — *see* Fracture, mandible
    open 802.5
  meniscus, knee — *see* Tear, meniscus
  metacarpus, metacarpal (bone(s)), of one hand
      (closed) 815.00
    with phalanx, phalanges, hand (finger(s))
        (thumb) of same hand 817.0
      open 817.1
    base 815.02
      first metacarpal 815.01
        open 815.11
        open 815.12
      thumb 815.01
        open 815.11
    multiple sites 815.09
      open 815.19
    neck 815.04
      open 815.14
    open 815.10
    shaft 815.03
      open 815.13
  metatarsus, metatarsal (bone(s)), of one foot
      (closed) 825.25
    with tarsal bone(s) 825.29
      open 825.39
    open 825.35
  Monteggia's (closed) 813.03
    open 813.13
  Moore's — *see* Fracture, radius, lower end
  multangular bone (closed)
    larger 814.05
      open 814.15
    smaller 814.06
      open 814.16
  multiple (closed) 829.0

Note — *Multiple fractures of sites classifiable to
the same three- or four-digit category are coded
to that category, except for sites classifiable to
810-818 or 820-827 in different limbs.*
*Multiple fractures of sites classifiable to different
fourth-digit subdivisions within the same three-
digit category should be dealt with according to
coding rules.*
*Multiple fractures of sites classifiable to different
three-digit categories (identifiable from the
listing under "Fracture"), and of sites
classifiable to 810-818 or 820-827 in different
limbs should be coded according to the following
list, which should be referred to in the following
priority order: skull or face bones, pelvis or
vertebral column, legs, arms.*

  arm (multiple bones in same arm except in
      hand alone) (sites classifiable to 810-
      817 with sites classifiable to a
      different three-digit category in 810-
      817 in same arm) (closed) 818.0
    open 818.1
  arms, both or arm(s) with rib(s) or sternum
      (sites classifiable to 810-818 with sites
      classifiable to same range of categories
      in other limb or to 807) (closed) 819.0
    open 819.1
  bones of trunk NEC (closed) 809.0
    open 809.1
  hand, metacarpal bone(s) with phalanx or
      phalanges of same hand (sites
      classifiable to 815 with sites
      classifiable to 816 in same hand)
      (closed) 817.0
    open 817.1

Fracture — *continued*
  multiple — *continued*
    leg (multiple bones in same leg) (sites
        classifiable to 820-826 with sites
        classifiable to a different three-digit
        category in that range in same leg)
        (closed) 827.0
      open 827.1
    legs, both or leg(s) with arm(s), rib(s), or
        sternum (sites classifiable to 820-827
        with sites classifiable to same range of
        categories in other leg or to 807 or
        810-819) (closed) 828.0
      open 828.1
      open 829.1
    pelvis with other bones except skull or face
        bones (sites classifiable to 808 with
        sites classifiable to 805-807 or 810-
        829) (closed) 809.0
      open 809.1
    skull, specified or unspecified bones, or face
        bone(s) with any other bone(s) (sites
        classifiable to 800-803 with sites
        classifiable to 805-829) (closed)
        804.0 ☑

Note — *Use the following fifth-digit
subclassification with categories 800, 801, 803,
and 804:*
  0   *unspecified state of consciousness*
  1   *with no loss of consciousness*
  2   *with brief [less than one hour] loss of
       consciousness*
  3   *with moderate [1-24 hours] loss of
       consciousness*
  4   *with prolonged [more than 24 hours]
       loss of consciousness and return to pre-
       existing conscious level*
  5   *with prolonged [more than 24 hours]
       loss of consciousness, without return to
       pre-existing conscious level*
       *Use fifth-digit 5 to designate when a patient
       is unconscious and dies before
       regaining consciousness, regardless of
       the duration of the loss of
       consciousness*
  6   *with loss of consciousness of
       unspecified duration*
  9   *with concussion, unspecified*

    with
      contusion, cerebral 804.1 ☑
      epidural hemorrhage 804.2 ☑
      extradural hemorrhage 804.2 ☑
      hemorrhage (intracranial) NEC 804.3 ☑
      intracranial injury NEC 804.4 ☑
      laceration, cerebral 804.1 ☑
      subarachnoid hemorrhage 804.2 ☑
      subdural hemorrhage 804.2 ☑
    open 804.5 ☑
      with
        contusion, cerebral 804.6 ☑
        epidural hemorrhage 804.7 ☑
        extradural hemorrhage 804.7 ☑
        hemorrhage (intracranial) NEC
            804.8 ☑
        intracranial injury NEC 804.9 ☑
        laceration, cerebral 804.6 ☑
        subarachnoid hemorrhage 804.7 ☑
        subdural hemorrhage 804.7 ☑
    vertebral column with other bones, except
        skull or face bones (sites classifiable to
        805 or 806 with sites classifiable to
        807-808 or 810-829) (closed) 809.0
      open 809.1
  nasal (bone(s)) (closed) 802.0
    open 802.1
    sinus — *see* Fracture, skull, base
  navicular
    carpal (wrist) (closed) 814.01
      open 814.11
    tarsal (ankle) (closed) 825.22
      open 825.32

Fracture — *continued*
  neck — *see* Fracture, vertebra, cervical
  neural arch — *see* Fracture, vertebra, by site
  nonunion 733.82
  nose, nasal, (bone) (septum) (closed) 802.0
    open 802.1
  occiput — *see* Fracture, skull, base
  odontoid process — *see* Fracture, vertebra, cervical
  olecranon (process) (ulna) (closed) 813.01
    open 813.11
  open 829.1
  orbit, orbital (bone) (region) (closed) 802.8
    floor (blow-out) 802.6
      open 802.7
    open 802.9
    roof — *see* Fracture, skull, base
    specified part NEC 802.8
      open 802.9
  os
    calcis (closed) 825.0
      open 825.1
    magnum (closed) 814.07
      open 814.17
    pubis (with visceral injury) (closed) 808.2
      open 808.3
    triquetrum (closed) 814.03
      open 814.13
  osseous
    auditory meatus — *see* Fracture, skull, base
    labyrinth — *see* Fracture, skull, base
  ossicles, auditory (incus) (malleus) (stapes) — *see* Fracture, skull, base
  osteoporotic — *see* Fracture, pathologic
  palate (closed) 802.8
    open 802.9
  paratrooper — *see* Fracture, tibia, lower end
  parietal bone — *see* Fracture, skull, vault
  parry — *see* Fracture, Monteggia's
  patella (closed) 822.0
    open 822.1
  pathologic (cause unknown) 733.10
    ankle 733.16
    femur (neck) 733.14
      specified NEC 733.15
    fibula 733.16
    hip 733.14
    humerus 733.11
    radius (distal) 733.12
    specified site NEC 733.19
    tibia 733.16
    ulna 733.12
    vertebrae (collapse) 733.13
    wrist 733.12
  pedicle (of vertebral arch) — *see* Fracture, vertebra, by site
  pelvis, pelvic (bone(s)) (with visceral injury) (closed) 808.8
    multiple (with disruption of pelvic circle) 808.43
      open 808.53
    open 808.9
    rim (closed) 808.49
      open 808.59
  peritrochanteric (closed) 820.20
    open 820.30
  phalanx, phalanges, of one
    foot (closed) 826.0
      with bone(s) of same lower limb 827.0
        open 827.1
      open 826.1
    hand (closed) 816.00
      with metacarpal bone(s) of same hand 817.0
        open 817.1
      distal 816.02
        open 816.12
      middle 816.01
        open 816.11
      multiple sites NEC 816.03
        open 816.13
      open 816.10
      proximal 816.01
        open 816.11
    pisiform (closed) 814.04
      open 814.14
  pond — *see* Fracture, skull, vault

Fracture — *continued*
  Pott's (closed) 824.4
    open 824.5
  prosthetic device, internal — *see* Complications, mechanical
  pubis (with visceral injury) (closed) 808.2
    open 808.3
  Quervain's (closed) 814.01
    open 814.11
  radius (alone) (closed) 813.81
    with ulna NEC 813.83
      open 813.93
    distal end — *see* Fracture, radius, lower end
    epiphysis
      lower — *see* Fracture, radius, lower end
      upper — *see* Fracture, radius, upper end
    head — *see* Fracture, radius, upper end
    lower end or extremity (distal end) (lower epiphysis) 813.42
      with ulna (lower end) 813.44
        open 813.54
      torus 813.45
      open 813.52
    neck — *see* Fracture, radius, upper end
    open NEC 813.91
    pathologic 733.12
    proximal end — *see* Fracture, radius, upper end
    shaft (closed) 813.21
      with ulna (shaft) 813.23
        open 813.33
      open 813.31
    upper end 813.07
      with ulna (upper end) 813.08
        open 813.18
      epiphysis 813.05
        open 813.15
      head 813.05
        open 813.15
      multiple sites 813.07
        open 813.17
      neck 813.06
        open 813.16
      open 813.17
      specified site NEC 813.07
        open 813.17
  ramus
    inferior or superior (with visceral injury) (closed) 808.2
      open 808.3
    ischium — *see* Fracture, ischium
    mandible 802.24
      open 802.34
  rib(s) (closed) 807.0 ☑

Note — *Use the following fifth-digit subclassification with categories 807.0-807.1:*

0	*rib(s), unspecified*
1	*one rib*
2	*two ribs*
3	*three ribs*
4	*four ribs*
5	*five ribs*
6	*six ribs*
7	*seven ribs*
8	*eight or more ribs*
9	*multiple ribs, unspecified*

    with flail chest (open) 807.4
    open 807.1 ☑
  root, tooth 873.63
    complicated 873.73
  sacrum — *see* Fracture, vertebra, sacrum
  scaphoid
    ankle (closed) 825.22
      open 825.32
    wrist (closed) 814.01
      open 814.11
  scapula (closed) 811.00
    acromial, acromion (process) 811.01
      open 811.11
    body 811.09
      open 811.19

Fracture — *continued*
  scapula — *continued*
    coracoid process 811.02
      open 811.12
    glenoid (cavity) (fossa) 811.03
      open 811.13
    neck 811.03
      open 811.13
    open 811.10
  semilunar
    bone, wrist (closed) 814.02
      open 814.12
    cartilage (interior) (knee) — *see* Tear, meniscus
  sesamoid bone — *see* Fracture, by site
  Shepherd's (closed) 825.21
    open 825.31
  shoulder — *see also* Fracture, humerus, upper end
    blade — *see* Fracture, scapula
  silverfork — *see* Fracture, radius, lower end
  sinus (ethmoid) (frontal) (maxillary) (nasal) (sphenoidal) — *see* Fracture, skull, base
  Skillern's — *see* Fracture, radius, shaft
  skull (multiple NEC) (with face bones) (closed) 803.0 ☑

Note — *Use the following fifth-digit subclassification with categories 800, 801, 803, and 804:*

0	*unspecified state of consciousness*
1	*with no loss of consciousness*
2	*with brief [less than one hour] loss of consciousness*
3	*with moderate [1-24 hours] loss of consciousness*
4	*with prolonged [more than 24 hours] loss of consciousness and return to pre-existing conscious level*
5	*with prolonged [more than 24 hours] loss of consciousness, without return to pre-existing conscious level*

Use fifth-digit 5 to designate when a patient is unconscious and dies before regaining consciousness, regardless of the duration of loss of consciousness

6	*with loss of consciousness of unspecified duration*
9	*with concussion, unspecified*

    with
      contusion, cerebral 803.1 ☑
      epidural hemorrhage 803.2 ☑
      extradural hemorrhage 803.2 ☑
      hemorrhage (intracranial) NEC 803.3 ☑
      intracranial injury NEC 803.4 ☑
      laceration, cerebral 803.1 ☑
      other bones — *see* Fracture, multiple, skull
      subarachnoid hemorrhage 803.2 ☑
      subdural hemorrhage 803.2 ☑
    base (antrum) (ethmoid bone) (fossa) (internal ear) (nasal sinus) (occiput) (sphenoid) (temporal bone) (closed) 801.0 ☑
      with
        contusion, cerebral 801.1 ☑
        epidural hemorrhage 801.2 ☑
        extradural hemorrhage 801.2 ☑
        hemorrhage (intracranial) NEC 801.3 ☑
        intracranial injury NEC 801.4 ☑
        laceration, cerebral 801.1 ☑
        subarachnoid hemorrhage 801.2 ☑
        subdural hemorrhage 801.2 ☑
      open 801.5 ☑
        with
          contusion, cerebral 801.6 ☑
          epidural hemorrhage 801.7 ☑
          extradural hemorrhage 801.7 ☑
          hemorrhage (intracranial) NEC 801.8 ☑
          intracranial injury NEC 801.9 ☑
          laceration, cerebral 801.6 ☑
          subarachnoid hemorrhage 801.7 ☑
          subdural hemorrhage 801.7 ☑

Fracture — *continued*
  skull — *continued*
    birth injury 767.3
    face bones — *see* Fracture, face bones
    open 803.5 ☑
      with
        contusion, cerebral 803.6 ☑
        epidural hemorrhage 803.7 ☑
        extradural hemorrhage 803.7 ☑
        hemorrhage (intracranial) NEC
          803.8 ☑
        intracranial injury NEC 803.9 ☑
        laceration, cerebral 803.6 ☑
        subarachnoid hemorrhage 803.7 ☑
        subdural hemorrhage 803.7 ☑
    vault (frontal bone) (parietal bone) (vertex)
      (closed) 800.0 ☑
      with
        contusion, cerebral 800.1 ☑
        epidural hemorrhage 800.2 ☑
        extradural hemorrhage 800.2 ☑
        hemorrhage (intracranial) NEC
          800.3 ☑
        intracranial injury NEC 800.4 ☑
        laceration, cerebral 800.1 ☑
        subarachnoid hemorrhage 800.2 ☑
        subdural hemorrhage 800.2 ☑
      open 800.5 ☑
        with
          contusion, cerebral 800.6 ☑
          epidural hemorrhage 800.7 ☑
          extradural hemorrhage 800.7 ☑
          hemorrhage (intracranial) NEC
            800.8 ☑
          intracranial injury NEC 800.9 ☑
          laceration, cerebral 800.6 ☑
          subarachnoid hemorrhage 800.7 ☑
          subdural hemorrhage 800.7 ☑
  Smith's 813.41
    open 813.51
  sphenoid (bone) (sinus) — *see* Fracture, skull,
    base
  spine — *see also* Fracture, vertebra, by site due
    to birth trauma 767.4
  spinous process — *see* Fracture, vertebra, by
    site
  spontaneous — *see* Fracture, pathologic
  sprinters' — *see* Fracture, ilium
  stapes — *see* Fracture, skull, base
  stave — *see also* Fracture, metacarpus,
    metacarpal bone(s)
    spine — *see* Fracture, tibia, upper end
  sternum (closed) 807.2
    with flail chest (open) 807.4
    open 807.3
  Stieda's — *see* Fracture, femur, lower end
  stress 733.95
    fibula 733.93
    metatarsals 733.94
    specified site NEC 733.95
    tibia 733.93
  styloid process
    metacarpal (closed) 815.02
      open 815.12
    radius — *see* Fracture, radius, lower end
    temporal bone — *see* Fracture, skull, base
    ulna — *see* Fracture, ulna, lower end
  supracondylar, elbow 812.41
    open 812.51
  symphysis pubis (with visceral injury) (closed)
    808.2
    open 808.3
  talus (ankle bone) (closed) 825.21
    open 825.31
  tarsus, tarsal bone(s) (with metatarsus) of one
    foot (closed) NEC 825.29
    open 825.39
  temporal bone (styloid) — *see* Fracture, skull,
    base
  tendon — *see* Sprain, by site
  thigh — *see* Fracture, femur, shaft
  thumb (and finger(s)) of one hand (closed) (*see
    also* Fracture, phalanx, hand) 816.00
    with metacarpal bone(s) of same hand 817.0
      open 817.1
    metacarpal(s) — *see* Fracture, metacarpus
    open 816.10

Fracture — *continued*
  thyroid cartilage (closed) 807.5
    open 807.6
  tibia (closed) 823.80
    with fibula 823.82
      open 823.92
    condyles — *see* Fracture, tibia, upper end
    distal end 824.8
      open 824.9
    epiphysis
      lower 824.8
        open 824.9
      upper — *see* Fracture, tibia, upper end
    head (involving knee joint) — *see* Fracture,
      tibia, upper end
    intercondyloid eminence — *see* Fracture,
      tibia, upper end
    involving ankle 824.0
      open 824.9
    lower end or extremity (anterior lip)
      (posterior lip) 824.8
      open 824.9
    malleolus (internal) (medial) 824.0
      open 824.1
    open NEC 823.90
    pathologic 733.16
    proximal end — *see* Fracture, tibia, upper
      end
    shaft 823.20
      with fibula 823.22
        open 823.32
      open 823.30
    spine — *see* Fracture, tibia, upper end
    stress 733.93
    torus 823.40
      with fibula 823.42
    tuberosity — *see* Fracture, tibia, upper end
    upper end or extremity (condyle) (epiphysis)
      (head) (spine) (proximal end)
      (tuberosity) 823.00
      with fibula 823.02
        open 823.12
      open 823.10
  toe(s), of one foot (closed) 826.0
    with bone(s) of same lower limb 827.0
      open 827.1
    open 826.1
  tooth (root) 873.63
    complicated 873.73
  torus
    fibula 823.41
      with tibia 823.42
    radius 813.45
    tibia 823.40
      with fibula 823.42
  trachea (closed) 807.5
    open 807.6
  transverse process — *see* Fracture, vertebra, by
    site
  trapezium (closed) 814.05
    open 814.15
  trapezoid bone (closed) 814.06
    open 814.16
  trimalleolar (closed) 824.6
    open 824.7
  triquetral (bone) (closed) 814.03
    open 814.13
  trochanter (greater) (lesser) (closed) (*see also*
    Fracture, femur, neck, by site) 820.20
    open 820.30
  trunk (bones) (closed) 809.0
    open 809.1
  tuberosity (external) — *see* Fracture, by site
  ulna (alone) (closed) 813.82
    with radius NEC 813.83
      open 813.93
    coronoid process (closed) 813.02
      open 813.12
    distal end — *see* Fracture, ulna, lower end
    epiphysis
      lower — *see* Fracture, ulna, lower end
      upper — *see* Fracture, ulna, upper end
    head — *see* Fracture, ulna, lower end
    lower end (distal end) (head) (lower
      epiphysis) (styloid process) 813.43
      with radius (lower end) 813.44
        open 813.54

Fracture — *continued*
  ulna — *continued*
    lower end — *continued*
      open 813.53
    olecranon process (closed) 813.01
      open 813.11
    open NEC 813.92
    pathologic 733.12
    proximal end — *see* Fracture, ulna, upper
      end
    shaft 813.22
      with radius (shaft) 813.23
        open 813.33
      open 813.32
    styloid process — *see* Fracture, ulna, lower
      end
    transverse — *see* Fracture, ulna, by site
    upper end (epiphysis) 813.04
      with radius (upper end) 813.08
        open 813.18
      multiple sites 813.04
        open 813.14
      open 813.14
      specified site NEC 813.04
        open 813.14
  unciform (closed) 814.08
    open 814.18
  vertebra, vertebral (back) (body) (column)
    (neural arch) (pedicle) (spine) (spinous
    process) (transverse process) (closed)
    805.8
    with
      hematomyelia — *see* Fracture, vertebra,
        by site, with spinal cord injury
      injury to
        cauda equina — *see* Fracture,
          vertebra, sacrum, with spinal
          cord injury
        nerve — *see* Fracture, vertebra, by
          site, with spinal cord injury
        paralysis — *see* Fracture, vertebra, by
          site, with spinal cord injury
        paraplegia — *see* Fracture, vertebra,
          by site, with spinal cord injury
        quadriplegia — *see* Fracture, vertebra, by
          site, with spinal cord injury
      spinal concussion — *see* Fracture,
        vertebra, by site, with spinal cord
        injury
      spinal cord injury (closed) NEC 806.8

*Note — Use the following fifth-digit
subclassification with categories 806.0-806.3:
C_1-C_4 or unspecified level and D_1-D_6 (T_1-T_6) or
unspecified level with:*

0	*unspecified spinal cord injury*
1	*complete lesion of cord*
2	*anterior cord syndrome*
3	*central cord syndrome*
4	*specified injury NEC*

C_5-C_7 level and D_7-D_{12} level with:

5	*unspecified spinal cord injury*
6	*complete lesion of cord*
7	*anterior cord syndrome*
8	*central cord syndrome*
9	*specified injury NEC*

      cervical 806.0 ☑
        open 806.1 ☑
      dorsal, dorsolumbar 806.2 ☑
        open 806.3 ☑
        open 806.9
      thoracic, thoracolumbar 806.2 ☑
        open 806.3 ☑
    atlanto-axial — *see* Fracture, vertebra,
      cervical
    cervical (hangman) (teardrop) (closed) 805.00
      with spinal cord injury — *see* Fracture,
        vertebra, with spinal cord injury,
        cervical
      first (atlas) 805.01
        open 805.11
      second (axis) 805.02
        open 805.12

Fracture — *continued*
  vertebra, vertebral — *continued*
    cervical — *continued*
      third 805.03
        open 805.13
      fourth 805.04
        open 805.14
      fifth 805.05
        open 805.15
      sixth 805.06
        open 805.16
      seventh 805.07
        open 805.17
      multiple sites 805.08
        open 805.18
      open 805.10
    coccyx (closed) 805.6
      with spinal cord injury (closed) 806.60
        cauda equina injury 806.62
          complete lesion 806.61
            open 806.71
          open 806.72
          open 806.70
          specified type NEC 806.69
            open 806.79
      open 805.7
    collapsed 733.13
    compression, not due to trauma 733.13
    dorsal (closed) 805.2
      with spinal cord injury — *see* Fracture, vertebra, with spinal cord injury, dorsal
      open 805.3
    dorsolumbar (closed) 805.2
      with spinal cord injury — *see* Fracture, vertebra, with spinal cord injury, dorsal
      open 805.3
    due to osteoporosis 733.13
    fetus or newborn 767.4
    lumbar (closed) 805.4
      with spinal cord injury (closed) 806.4
        open 806.5
      open 805.5
    nontraumatic 733.13
    open NEC 805.9
    pathologic (any site) 733.13
    sacrum (closed) 805.6
      with spinal cord injury 806.60
        cauda equina injury 806.62
          complete lesion 806.61
            open 806.71
          open 806.72
          open 806.70
          specified type NEC 806.69
            open 806.79
      open 805.7
    site unspecified (closed) 805.8
      with spinal cord injury (closed) 806.8
        open 806.9
      open 805.9
    stress (any site) 733.95
    thoracic (closed) 805.2
      with spinal cord injury — *see* Fracture, vertebra, with spinal cord injury, thoracic
      open 805.3
  vertex — *see* Fracture, skull, vault
  vomer (bone) 802.0
    open 802.1
  Wagstaffe's — *see* Fracture, ankle
  wrist (closed) 814.00
    open 814.10
    pathologic 733.12
  xiphoid (process) — *see* Fracture, sternum
  zygoma (zygomatic arch) (closed) 802.4
    open 802.5
Fragile X syndrome 759.83
Fragilitas
  crinium 704.2
  hair 704.2
  ossium 756.51
    with blue sclera 756.51
  unguium 703.8
    congenital 757.5

Fragility
  bone 756.51
    with deafness and blue sclera 756.51
  capillary (hereditary) 287.8
  hair 704.2
  nails 703.8
Fragmentation — *see* Fracture, by site
Frambesia, frambesial (tropica) (*see also* Yaws) 102.9
  initial lesion or ulcer 102.0
  primary 102.0
Frambeside
  gummatous 102.4
  of early yaws 102.2
Frambesioma 102.1
Franceschetti's syndrome (mandibulofacial dysostosis) 756.0
Francis' disease (*see also* Tularemia) 021.9
Frank's essential thrombocytopenia (*see also* Purpura, thrombocytopenic) 287.39 ▲
Franklin's disease (heavy chain) 273.2
Fraser's syndrome 759.89
Freckle 709.09
  malignant melanoma in (M8742/3) — *see* Melanoma
  melanotic (of Hutchinson) (M8742/2) — *see* Neoplasm, skin, in situ
Freeman-Sheldon syndrome 759.89
Freezing 991.9
  specified effect NEC 991.8
Frei's disease (climatic bubo) 099.1
Freiberg's
  disease (osteochondrosis, second metatarsal) 732.5
  infraction of metatarsal head 732.5
  osteochondrosis 732.5
Fremitus, friction, cardiac 785.3
Frenulum linguae 750.0
Frenum
  external os 752.49
  tongue 750.0
Frequency (urinary) NEC 788.41
  micturition 788.41
  nocturnal 788.43
  polyuria 788.42
  psychogenic 306.53
Frey's syndrome (auriculotemporal syndrome) 705.22
Friction
  burn (*see also* Injury, superficial, by site) 919.0
  fremitus, cardiac 785.3
  precordial 785.3
  sounds, chest 786.7
Friderichsen-Waterhouse syndrome or disease 036.3
Friedländer's
  B (bacillus) NEC (*see also* condition) 041.3
    sepsis or septicemia 038.49
  disease (endarteritis obliterans) — *see* Arteriosclerosis
Friedreich's
  ataxia 334.0
  combined systemic disease 334.0
  disease 333.2
    combined systemic 334.0
  myoclonia 333.2
  sclerosis (spinal cord) 334.0
Friedrich-Erb-Arnold syndrome (acropachyderma) 757.39
Frigidity 302.72
  psychic or psychogenic 302.72
Fröhlich's disease or syndrome (adiposogenital dystrophy) 253.8
Froin's syndrome 336.8
Frommel's disease 676.6 ☑
Frommel-Chiari syndrome 676.6 ☑
Frontal — *see also* condition
  lobe syndrome 310.0
Frostbite 991.3
  face 991.0
  foot 991.2

Frostbite — *continued*
  hand 991.1
  specified site NEC 991.3
Frotteurism 302.89
Frozen 991.9
  pelvis 620.8
  shoulder 726.0
Fructosemia 271.2
Fructosuria (benign) (essential) 271.2
Fuchs'
  black spot (myopic) 360.21
  corneal dystrophy (endothelial) 371.57
  heterochromic cyclitis 364.21
Fucosidosis 271.8
Fugue 780.99
  dissociative 300.13
  hysterical (dissociative) 300.13
  reaction to exceptional stress (transient) 308.1
Fukuhara syndrome 277.87
Fuller Albright's syndrome (osteitis fibrosa disseminata) 756.59
Fuller's earth disease 502
Fulminant, fulminating — *see* condition
Functional — *see* condition
Functioning ●
  borderline intellectual V62.89 ●
Fundus — *see also* condition
  flavimaculatus 362.76
Fungemia 117.9
Fungus, fungous
  cerebral 348.8
  disease NEC 117.9
  infection — *see* Infection, fungus
  testis (*see also* Tuberculosis) 016.5 ☑ *[608.81]*
Funiculitis (acute) 608.4
  chronic 608.4
  endemic 608.4
  gonococcal (acute) 098.14
    chronic or duration of 2 months or over 098.34
  tuberculous (*see also* Tuberculosis) 016.5 ☑
Funnel
  breast (acquired) 738.3
    congenital 754.81
    late effect of rickets 268.1
  chest (acquired) 738.3
    congenital 754.81
    late effect of rickets 268.1
  pelvis (acquired) 738.6
    with disproportion (fetopelvic) 653.3 ☑
      affecting fetus or newborn 763.1
      causing obstructed labor 660.1 ☑
        affecting fetus or newborn 763.1
    congenital 755.69
    tuberculous (*see also* Tuberculosis) 016.9 ☑
FUO (*see also* Pyrexia) 780.6
Furfur 690.18
  microsporon 111.0
Furor, paroxysmal (idiopathic) (*see also* Epilepsy) 345.8 ☑
Furriers' lung 495.8
Furrowed tongue 529.5
  congenital 750.13
Furrowing nail(s) (transverse) 703.8
  congenital 757.5
Furuncle 680.9
  abdominal wall 680.2
  ankle 680.6
  anus 680.5
  arm (any part, above wrist) 680.3
  auditory canal, external 680.0
  axilla 680.3
  back (any part) 680.2
  breast 680.2
  buttock 680.5
  chest wall 680.2
  corpus cavernosum 607.2
  ear (any part) 680.0
  eyelid 373.13
  face (any part, except eye) 680.0
  finger (any) 680.4
  flank 680.2

Furuncle — *continued*
  foot (any part) 680.7
  forearm 680.3
  gluteal (region) 680.5
  groin 680.2
  hand (any part) 680.4
  head (any part, except face) 680.8
  heel 680.7
  hip 680.6
  kidney (*see also* Abscess, kidney) 590.2
  knee 680.6
  labium (majus) (minus) 616.4
  lacrimal
    gland (*see also* Dacryoadenitis) 375.00
    passages (duct) (sac) (*see also*
      Dacryocystitis) 375.30
  leg, any part except foot 680.6
  malignant 022.0
  multiple sites 680.9
  neck 680.1
  nose (external) (septum) 680.0
  orbit 376.01
  partes posteriores 680.5
  pectoral region 680.2
  penis 607.2
  perineum 680.2
  pinna 680.0
  scalp (any part) 680.8
  scrotum 608.4
  seminal vesicle 608.0
  shoulder 680.3
  skin NEC 680.9
  specified site NEC 680.8
  spermatic cord 608.4
  temple (region) 680.0
  testis 604.90
  thigh 680.6
  thumb 680.4
  toe (any) 680.7
  trunk 680.2
  tunica vaginalis 608.4

Furuncle — *continued*
  umbilicus 680.2
  upper arm 680.3
  vas deferens 608.4
  vulva 616.4
  wrist 680.4
Furunculosis (*see also* Furuncle) 680.9
  external auditory meatus 680.0 *[380.13]*
Fusarium (infection) 118
Fusion, fused (congenital)
  anal (with urogenital canal) 751.5
  aorta and pulmonary artery 745.0
  astragaloscaphoid 755.67
  atria 745.5
  atrium and ventricle 745.69
  auditory canal 744.02
  auricles, heart 745.5
  binocular, with defective stereopsis 368.33
  bone 756.9
  cervical spine — *see* Fusion, spine
  choanal 748.0
  commissure, mitral valve 746.5
  cranial sutures, premature 756.0
  cusps, heart valve NEC 746.89
    mitral 746.5
    tricuspid 746.89
  ear ossicles 744.04
  fingers (*see also* Syndactylism, fingers) 755.11
  hymen 752.42
  hymeno-urethral 599.89
    causing obstructed labor 660.1 ☑
      affecting fetus or newborn 763.1
  joint (acquired) — *see also* Ankylosis
    congenital 755.8
  kidneys (incomplete) 753.3
  labium (majus) (minus) 752.49
  larynx and trachea 748.3
  limb 755.8
    lower 755.69
    upper 755.59

Fusion, fused — *continued*
  lobe, lung 748.5
  lumbosacral (acquired) 724.6
    congenital 756.15
    surgical V45.4
  nares (anterior) (posterior) 748.0
  nose, nasal 748.0
  nostril(s) 748.0
  organ or site NEC — *see* Anomaly, specified
    type NEC
  ossicles 756.9
    auditory 744.04
  pulmonary valve segment 746.02
  pulmonic cusps 746.02
  ribs 756.3
  sacroiliac (acquired) (joint) 724.6
    congenital 755.69
    surgical V45.4
  skull, imperfect 756.0
  spine (acquired) 724.9
    arthrodesis status V45.4
    congenital (vertebra) 756.15
    postoperative status V45.4
  sublingual duct with submaxillary duct at
    opening in mouth 750.26
  talonavicular (bar) 755.67
  teeth, tooth 520.2
  testes 752.89
  toes (*see also* Syndactylism, toes) 755.13
  trachea and esophagus 750.3
  twins 759.4
  urethral-hymenal 599.89
  vagina 752.49
  valve cusps — *see* Fusion, cusps, heart valve
  ventricles, heart 745.4
  vertebra (arch) — *see* Fusion, spine
  vulva 752.49
Fusospirillosis (mouth) (tongue) (tonsil) 101
Fussy infant (baby) 780.91

G

Gafsa boil 085.1
Gain, weight (abnormal) (excessive) (*see also* Weight, gain) 783.1
Gaisböck's disease or syndrome (polycythemia hypertonica) 289.0
Gait
  abnormality 781.2
    hysterical 300.11
  ataxic 781.2
    hysterical 300.11
  disturbance 781.2
    hysterical 300.11
  paralytic 781.2
  scissor 781.2
  spastic 781.2
  staggering 781.2
    hysterical 300.11
Galactocele (breast) (infected) 611.5
  puerperal, postpartum 676.8 ☑
Galactophoritis 611.0
  puerperal, postpartum 675.2 ☑
Galactorrhea 676.6 ☑
  not associated with childbirth 611.6
Galactosemia (classic) (congenital) 271.1
Galactosuria 271.1
Galacturia 791.1
  bilharziasis 120.0
Galen's vein — *see* condition
Gallbladder — *see also* condition
  acute (*see also* Disease, gallbladder) 575.0
Gall duct — *see* condition
Gallop rhythm 427.89
Gallstone (cholemic) (colic) (impacted) — *see also* Cholelithiasis
  causing intestinal obstruction 560.31
Gambling, pathological 312.31
Gammaloidosis 277.3
Gammopathy 273.9
  macroglobulinemia 273.3
  monoclonal (benign) (essential) (idiopathic) (with lymphoplasmacytic dyscrasia) 273.1
Gamna's disease (siderotic splenomegaly) 289.51
Gampsodactylia (congenital) 754.71
Gamstorp's disease (adynamia episodica hereditaria) 359.3
Gandy-Nanta disease (siderotic splenomegaly) 289.51
Gang activity, without manifest psychiatric disorder V71.09
  adolescent V71.02
  adult V71.01
  child V71.02
Gangliocytoma (M9490/0) — *see* Neoplasm, connective tissue, benign
Ganglioglioma (M9505/1) — *see* Neoplasm, by site, uncertain behavior
Ganglion 727.43
  joint 727.41
  of yaws (early) (late) 102.6
  periosteal (*see also* Periostitis) 730.3 ☑
  tendon sheath (compound) (diffuse) 727.42
  tuberculous (*see also* Tuberculosis) 015.9 ☑
Ganglioneuroblastoma (M9490/3) — *see* Neoplasm, connective tissue, malignant
Ganglioneuroma (M9490/0) — *see also* Neoplasm, connective tissue, benign
  malignant (M9490/3) — *see* Neoplasm, connective tissue, malignant
Ganglioneuromatosis (M9491/0) — *see* Neoplasm, connective tissue, benign
Ganglionitis
  fifth nerve (*see also* Neuralgia, trigeminal) 350.1
  gasserian 350.1
  geniculate 351.1
    herpetic 053.11
    newborn 767.5
  herpes zoster 053.11
  herpetic geniculate (Hunt's syndrome) 053.11

Gangliosidosis 330.1
Gangosa 102.5
Gangrene, gangrenous (anemia) (artery) (cellulitis) (dermatitis) (dry) (infective) (moist) (pemphigus) (septic) (skin) (stasis) (ulcer) 785.4
  with
    arteriosclerosis (native artery) 440.24
      bypass graft 440.30
        autologous vein 440.31
        nonautologous biological 440.32
    diabetes (mellitus) 250.7 ☑ *[785.4]*
  abdomen (wall) 785.4
  adenitis 683
  alveolar 526.5
  angina 462
    diphtheritic 032.0
  anus 569.49
  appendices epiploicae — *see* Gangrene, mesentery
  appendix — *see* Appendicitis, acute
  arteriosclerotic — *see* Arteriosclerosis, with, gangrene
  auricle 785.4
  Bacillus welchii (*see also* Gangrene, gas) 040.0
  bile duct (*see also* Cholangitis) 576.8
  bladder 595.89
  bowel — *see* Gangrene, intestine
  cecum — *see* Gangrene, intestine
  Clostridium perfringens or welchii (*see also* Gangrene, gas) 040.0
  colon — *see* Gangrene, intestine
  connective tissue 785.4
  cornea 371.40
  corpora cavernosa (infective) 607.2
    noninfective 607.89
  cutaneous, spreading 785.4
  decubital (*see also* Decubitus) 707.00 *[785.4]*
  diabetic (any site) 250.7 ☑ *[785.4]*
  dropsical 785.4
  emphysematous (*see also* Gangrene, gas) 040.0
  epidemic (ergotized grain) 988.2
  epididymis (infectional) (*see also* Epididymitis) 604.99
  erysipelas (*see also* Erysipelas) 035
  extremity (lower) (upper) 785.4
  gallbladder or duct (*see also* Cholecystitis, acute) 575.0
  gas (bacillus) 040.0
    with
      abortion — *see* Abortion, by type, with sepsis
      ectopic pregnancy (*see also* categories 633.0-633.9) 639.0
      molar pregnancy (*see also* categories 630-632) 639.0
    following
      abortion 639.0
      ectopic or molar pregnancy 639.0
    puerperal, postpartum, childbirth 670.0 ☑
  glossitis 529.0
  gum 523.8
  hernia — *see* Hernia, by site, with gangrene
  hospital noma 528.1
  intestine, intestinal (acute) (hemorrhagic) (massive) 557.0
    with
      hernia — *see* Hernia, by site, with gangrene
      mesenteric embolism or infarction 557.0
      obstruction (*see also* Obstruction, intestine) 560.9
  laryngitis 464.00
    with obstruction 464.01
  liver 573.8
  lung 513.0
    spirochetal 104.8
  lymphangitis 457.2
  Meleney's (cutaneous) 686.09
  mesentery 557.0
    with
      embolism or infarction 557.0
      intestinal obstruction (*see also* Obstruction, intestine) 560.9
  mouth 528.1
  noma 528.1

Gangrene, gangrenous — *continued*
  orchitis 604.90
  ovary (*see also* Salpingo-oophoritis) 614.2
  pancreas 577.0
  penis (infectional) 607.2
    noninfective 607.89
  perineum 785.4
  pharynx 462
    septic 034.0
  pneumonia 513.0
  Pott's 440.24
  presenile 443.1
  pulmonary 513.0
  pulp, tooth 522.1
  quinsy 475
  Raynaud's (symmetric gangrene) 443.0 *[785.4]*
  rectum 569.49
  retropharyngeal 478.24
  rupture — *see* Hernia, by site, with gangrene
  scrotum 608.4
    noninfective 608.83
  senile 440.24
  sore throat 462
  spermatic cord 608.4
    noninfective 608.89
  spine 785.4
  spirochetal NEC 104.8
  spreading cutaneous 785.4
  stomach 537.89
  stomatitis 528.1
  symmetrical 443.0 *[785.4]*
  testis (infectional) (*see also* Orchitis) 604.99
    noninfective 608.89
  throat 462
    diphtheritic 032.0
  thyroid (gland) 246.8
  tonsillitis (acute) 463
  tooth (pulp) 522.1
  tuberculous NEC (*see also* Tuberculosis) 011.9 ☑
  tunica vaginalis 608.4
    noninfective 608.89
  umbilicus 785.4
  uterus (*see also* Endometritis) 615.9
  uvulitis 528.3
  vas deferens 608.4
    noninfective 608.89
  vulva (*see also* Vulvitis) 616.10
Gannister disease (occupational) 502
  with tuberculosis — *see* Tuberculosis, pulmonary
Ganser's syndrome, hysterical 300.16
Gardner-Diamond syndrome (autoerythrocyte sensitization) 287.2
Gargoylism 277.5
Garré's
  disease (*see also* Osteomyelitis) 730.1 ☑
  osteitis (sclerosing) (*see also* Osteomyelitis) 730.1 ☑
  osteomyelitis (*see also* Osteomyelitis) 730.1 ☑
Garrod's pads, knuckle 728.79
Gartner's duct
  cyst 752.41 ▲
  persistent 752.41 ▲
Gas
  asphyxia, asphyxiation, inhalation, poisoning, suffocation NEC 987.9
    specified gas — *see* Table of Drugs and Chemicals
  bacillus gangrene or infection — *see* Gas, gangrene
  cyst, mesentery 568.89
  excessive 787.3
  gangrene 040.0
    with
      abortion — *see* Abortion, by type, with sepsis
      ectopic pregnancy (*see also* categories 633.0-633.9) 639.0
      molar pregnancy (*see also* categories 630-632) 639.0
    following
      abortion 639.0
      ectopic or molar pregnancy 639.0
    puerperal, postpartum, childbirth 670.0 ☑

Gas — *continued*
on stomach 787.3
pains 787.3
Gastradenitis 535.0 ☑
Gastralgia 536.8
psychogenic 307.89
Gastrectasis, gastrectasia 536.1
psychogenic 306.4
Gastric — *see* condition
Gastrinoma (M8153/1)
malignant (M8153/3)
pancreas 157.4
specified site NEC — *see* Neoplasm, by site, malignant
unspecified site 157.4
specified site — *see* Neoplasm, by site, uncertain behavior
unspecified site 235.5
Gastritis 535.5 ☑

> *Note* — *Use the following fifth-digit subclassification for category 535:*
>
> 0   *without mention of hemorrhage*
> 1   *with hemorrhage*

acute 535.0 ☑
alcoholic 535.3 ☑
allergic 535.4 ☑
antral 535.4 ☑
atrophic 535.1 ☑
atrophic-hyperplastic 535.1 ☑
bile-induced 535.4 ☑
catarrhal 535.0 ☑
chronic (atrophic) 535.1 ☑
cirrhotic 535.4 ☑
corrosive (acute) 535.4 ☑
dietetic 535.4 ☑
due to diet deficiency 269.9 [535.4] ☑
eosinophilic 535.4 ☑
erosive 535.4 ☑
follicular 535.4 ☑
chronic 535.1 ☑
giant hypertrophic 535.2 ☑
glandular 535.4 ☑
chronic 535.1 ☑
hypertrophic (mucosa) 535.2 ☑
chronic giant 211.1
irritant 535.4 ☑
nervous 306.4
phlegmonous 535.0 ☑
psychogenic 306.4
sclerotic 535.4 ☑
spastic 536.8
subacute 535.0 ☑
superficial 535.4 ☑
suppurative 535.0 ☑
toxic 535.4 ☑
tuberculous (*see also* Tuberculosis) 017.9 ☑
Gastrocarcinoma (M8010/3) 151.9
Gastrocolic — *see* condition
Gastrocolitis — *see* Enteritis
Gastrodisciasis 121.8
Gastroduodenitis (*see also* Gastritis) 535.5 ☑
catarrhal 535.0 ☑
infectional 535.0 ☑
virus, viral 008.8
specified type NEC 008.69
Gastrodynia 536.8
Gastroenteritis (acute) (catarrhal) (congestive) (hemorrhagic) (noninfectious) (*see also* Enteritis) 558.9
aertrycke infection 003.0
allergic 558.3
chronic 558.9
ulcerative (*see also* Colitis, ulcerative) 556.9
dietetic 558.9
due to
food poisoning (*see also* Poisoning, food) 005.9
radiation 558.1
epidemic 009.0
functional 558.9

Gastroenteritis (*see also* Enteritis) — *continued*
infectious (*see also* Enteritis, due to, by organism) 009.0
presumed 009.1
salmonella 003.0
septic (*see also* Enteritis, due to, by organism) 009.0
toxic 558.2
tuberculous (*see also* Tuberculosis) 014.8 ☑
ulcerative (*see also* Colitis, ulcerative) 556.9
viral NEC 008.8
specified type NEC 008.69
zymotic 009.0
Gastroenterocolitis — *see* Enteritis
Gastroenteropathy, protein-losing 579.8
Gastroenteroptosis 569.89
Gastroesophageal laceration-hemorrhage syndrome 530.7
Gastroesophagitis 530.19
Gastrohepatitis (*see also* Gastritis) 535.5 ☑
Gastrointestinal — *see* condition
Gastrojejunal — *see* condition
Gastrojejunitis (*see also* Gastritis) 535.5 ☑
Gastrojejunocolic — *see* condition
Gastroliths 537.89
Gastromalacia 537.89
Gastroparalysis 536.3
diabetic 250.6 ☑ [536.3]
Gastroparesis 536.3
diabetic 250.6 ☑ [536.3]
Gastropathy 537.9   ▲
exudative 579.8   ●
Gastroptosis 537.5
Gastrorrhagia 578.0
Gastrorrhea 536.8
psychogenic 306.4
Gastroschisis (congenital) 756.79
acquired 569.89
Gastrospasm (neurogenic) (reflex) 536.8
neurotic 306.4
psychogenic 306.4
Gastrostaxis 578.0
Gastrostenosis 537.89
Gastrostomy
attention to V55.1
complication 536.40
specified type 536.49
infection 536.41
malfunctioning 536.42
status V44.1
Gastrosuccorrhea (continuous) (intermittent) 536.8
neurotic 306.4
psychogenic 306.4
Gaucher's
disease (adult) (cerebroside lipidosis) (infantile) 272.7
hepatomegaly 272.7
splenomegaly (cerebroside lipidosis) 272.7
Gayet's disease (superior hemorrhagic polioencephalitis) 265.1
Gayet-Wernicke's syndrome (superior hemorrhagic polioencephalitis) 265.1
Gee (-Herter) (-Heubner) (-Thaysen) disease or syndrome (nontropical sprue) 579.0
Gélineau's syndrome (*see also* Narcolepsy) 347.00
Gemination, teeth 520.2
Gemistocytoma (M9411/3)
specified site — *see* Neoplasm, by site, malignant
unspecified site 191.9
General, generalized — *see* condtion
Genetic
susceptibility to
neoplasm
malignant, of
breast V84.01
endometrium V84.04
other V84.09
ovary V84.02
prostate V84.03

Genetic — *continued*
susceptibility — *continued*
other disease V84.8
Genital — *see* condition
warts 078.19
Genito-anorectal syndrome 099.1
Genitourinary system — *see* condition
Genu
congenital 755.64
extrorsum (acquired) 736.42
congenital 755.64
late effects of rickets 268.1
introrsum (acquired) 736.41
congenital 755.64
late effects of rickets 268.1
rachitic (old) 268.1
recurvatum (acquired) 736.5
congenital 754.40
with dislocation of knee 754.41
late effects of rickets 268.1
valgum (acquired) (knock-knee) 736.41
congenital 755.64
late effects of rickets 268.1
varum (acquired) (bowleg) 736.42
congenital 755.64
late effect of rickets 268.1
Geographic tongue 529.1
Geophagia 307.52
Geotrichosis 117.9
intestine 117.9
lung 117.9
mouth 117.9
Gephyrophobia 300.29
Gerbode defect 745.4
Gerhardt's
disease (erythromelalgia) 443.82   ▲
syndrome (vocal cord paralysis) 478.30
Gerlier's disease (epidemic vertigo) 078.81
German measles 056.9
exposure to V01.4
Germinoblastoma (diffuse) (M9614/3) 202.8 ☑
follicular (M9692/3) 202.0 ☑
Germinoma (M9064/3) — *see* Neoplasm, by site, malignant
Gerontoxon 371.41
Gerstmann's syndrome (finger agnosia) 784.69
Gestation (period) — *see also* Pregnancy
ectopic NEC (*see also* Pregnancy, ectopic) 633.90
with intrauterine pregnancy 633.91
Gestational proteinuria 646.2 ☑
with hypertension — *see* Toxemia, of pregnancy
Ghon tubercle primary infection (*see also* Tuberculosis) 010.0 ☑
Ghost
teeth 520.4
vessels, cornea 370.64
Ghoul hand 102.3
Gianotti Crosti syndrome 057.8   ●
due to known virus — *see* Infection, virus ●
due to unknown virus 057.8   ●
Giant
cell
epulis 523.8
peripheral (gingiva) 523.8
tumor, tendon sheath 727.02
colon (congenital) 751.3
esophagus (congenital) 750.4
kidney 753.3
urticaria 995.1
hereditary 277.6
Giardia lamblia infestation 007.1
Giardiasis 007.1
Gibert's disease (pityriasis rosea) 696.3
Gibraltar fever — *see* Brucellosis
Giddiness 780.4
hysterical 300.11
psychogenic 306.9
Gierke's disease (glycogenosis I) 271.0
Gigantism (cerebral) (hypophyseal) (pituitary) 253.0

Gilbert's disease or cholemia (familial nonhemolytic jaundice) 277.4

Gilchrist's disease (North American blastomycosis) 116.0

Gilford (-Hutchinson) disease or syndrome (progeria) 259.8

Gilles de la Tourette's disease (motor-verbal tic) 307.23

Gillespie's syndrome (dysplasia oculodentodigitalis) 759.89

Gingivitis 523.1
  acute 523.0
    necrotizing 101
  catarrhal 523.0
  chronic 523.1
  desquamative 523.1
  expulsiva 523.4
  hyperplastic 523.1
  marginal, simple 523.1
  necrotizing, acute 101
  pellagrous 265.2
  ulcerative 523.1
    acute necrotizing 101
  Vincent's 101

Gingivoglossitis 529.0

Gingivopericementitis 523.4

Gingivosis 523.1

Gingivostomatitis 523.1
  herpetic 054.2

Giovannini's disease 117.9

GISA (glycopeptide intermediate staphylococcus aureus) V09.8

Gland, glandular — *see* condition

Glanders 024

Glanzmann (-Naegeli) disease or thrombasthenia 287.1

Glassblowers' disease 527.1

Glaucoma (capsular) (inflammatory) (noninflammatory) (primary) 365.9
  with increased episcleral venous pressure 365.82
  absolute 360.42
  acute 365.22
    narrow angle 365.22
    secondary 365.60
  angle closure 365.20
    acute 365.22
    chronic 365.23
    intermittent 365.21
    interval 365.21
    residual stage 365.24
    subacute 365.21
  borderline 365.00
  chronic 365.11
    noncongestive 365.11
    open angle 365.11
    simple 365.11
  closed angle — *see* Glaucoma, angle closure
  congenital 743.20
    associated with other eye anomalies 743.22
    simple 743.21
  congestive — *see* Glaucoma, narrow angle
  corticosteroid-induced (glaucomatous stage) 365.31
    residual stage 365.32
  hemorrhagic 365.60
  hypersecretion 365.81
  in or with
    aniridia 743.45 *[365.42]*
    Axenfeld's anomaly 743.44 *[365.41]*
    concussion of globe 921.3 *[365.65]*
    congenital syndromes NEC 759.89 *[365.44]*
    dislocation of lens
      anterior 379.33 *[365.59]*
      posterior 379.34 *[365.59]*
    disorder of lens NEC 365.59
    epithelial down-growth 364.61 *[365.64]*
    glaucomatocyclitic crisis 364.22 *[365.62]*
    hypermature cataract 366.18 *[365.51]*
    hyphema 364.41 *[365.63]*
    inflammation, ocular 365.62
    iridocyclitis 364.3 *[365.62]*
    iris
      anomalies NEC 743.46 *[365.42]*

Glaucoma — *continued*
  in or with — *continued*
    iris — *continued*
      atrophy, essential 364.51 *[365.42]*
      bombé 364.74 *[365.61]*
      rubeosis 364.42 *[365.63]*
    microcornea 743.41 *[365.43]*
    neurofibromatosis 237.71 *[365.44]*
    ocular
      cysts NEC 365.64
      disorders NEC 365.60
      trauma 365.65
      tumors NEC 365.64
    postdislocation of lens
      anterior 379.33 *[365.59]*
      posterior 379.34 *[365.59]*
    pseudoexfoliation of capsule 366.11 *[365.52]*
    pupillary block or seclusion 364.74 *[365.61]*
    recession of chamber angle 364.77 *[365.65]*
    retinal vein occlusion 362.35 *[365.63]*
    Rieger's anomaly or syndrome 743.44 *[365.41]*
    rubeosis of iris 364.42 *[365.63]*
    seclusion of pupil 364.74 *[365.61]*
    spherophakia 743.36 *[365.59]*
    Sturge-Weber (-Dimitri) syndrome 759.6 *[365.44]*
    systemic syndrome NEC 365.44
    tumor of globe 365.64
    vascular disorders NEC 365.63
  infantile 365.14
    congenital 743.20
      associated with other eye anomalies 743.22
      simple 743.21
  juvenile 365.14
  low tension 365.12
  malignant 365.83
  narrow angle (primary) 365.20
    acute 365.22
    chronic 365.23
    intermittent 365.21
    interval 365.21
    residual stage 365.24
    subacute 365.21
  newborn 743.20
    associated with other eye anomalies 743.22
    simple 743.21
  noncongestive (chronic) 365.11
  nonobstructive (chronic) 365.11
  obstructive 365.60
    due to lens changes 365.59
  open angle 365.10
    with
      borderline intraocular pressure 365.01
      cupping of optic discs 365.01
    primary 365.11
    residual stage 365.15
  phacolytic 365.51
    with hypermature cataract 366.18 *[365.51]*
  pigmentary 365.13
  postinfectious 365.60
  pseudoexfoliation 365.52
    with pseudoexfoliation of capsule 366.11 *[365.52]*
  secondary NEC 365.60
  simple (chronic) 365.11
  simplex 365.11
  steroid responders 365.03
  suspect 365.00
  syphilitic 095.8
  traumatic NEC 365.65
    newborn 767.8
  tuberculous (*see also* Tuberculosis) 017.3 ☑ *[365.62]*
  wide angle (*see also* Glaucoma, open angle) 365.10

Glaucomatous flecks (subcapsular) 366.31

Glazed tongue 529.4

Gleet 098.2

Glénard's disease or syndrome (enteroptosis) 569.89

Glinski-Simmonds syndrome (pituitary cachexia) 253.2

Glioblastoma (multiforme) (M9440/3)
  with sarcomatous component (M9442/3)
    specified site — *see* Neoplasm, by site, malignant
    unspecified site 191.9
  giant cell (M9441/3)
    specified site — *see* Neoplasm, by site, malignant
    unspecified site 191.9
  specified site — *see* Neoplasm, by site, malignant
  unspecified site 191.9

Glioma (malignant) (M9380/3)
  astrocytic (M9400/3)
    specified site — *see* Neoplasm, by site, malignant
    unspecified site 191.9
  mixed (M9382/3)
    specified site — *see* Neoplasm, by site, malignant
    unspecified site 191.9
  nose 748.1
  specified site NEC — *see* Neoplasm, by site, malignant
  subependymal (M9383/1) 237.5
  unspecified site 191.9

Gliomatosis cerebri (M9381/3) 191.0

Glioneuroma (M9505/1) — *see* Neoplasm, by site, uncertain behavior

Gliosarcoma (M9380/3)
  specified site — *see* Neoplasm, by site, malignant
  unspecified site 191.9

Gliosis (cerebral) 349.89
  spinal 336.0

Glisson's
  cirrhosis — *see* Cirrhosis, portal
  disease (*see also* Rickets) 268.0

Glissonitis 573.3

Globinuria 791.2

Globus 306.4
  hystericus 300.11

Glomangioma (M8712/0) (*see also* Hemangioma) 228.00

Glomangiosarcoma (M8710/3) — *see* Neoplasm, connective tissue, malignant

Glomerular nephritis (*see also* Nephritis) 583.9

Glomerulitis (*see also* Nephritis) 583.9

Glomerulonephritis (*see also* Nephritis) 583.9
  with
    edema (*see also* Nephrosis) 581.9
    lesion of
      exudative nephritis 583.89
      interstitial nephritis (diffuse) (focal) 583.89
      necrotizing glomerulitis 583.4
        acute 580.4
        chronic 582.4
      renal necrosis 583.9
        cortical 583.6
        medullary 583.7
      specified pathology NEC 583.89
        acute 580.89
        chronic 582.89
    necrosis, renal 583.9
      cortical 583.6
      medullary (papillary) 583.7
    specified pathology or lesion NEC 583.89
  acute 580.9
    with
      exudative nephritis 580.89
      interstitial nephritis (diffuse) (focal) 580.89
      necrotizing glomerulitis 580.4
    extracapillary with epithelial crescents 580.4
    poststreptococcal 580.0
    proliferative (diffuse) 580.0
    rapidly progressive 580.4
    specified pathology NEC 580.89
  arteriolar (*see also* Hypertension, kidney) 403.90
  arteriosclerotic (*see also* Hypertension, kidney) 403.90
  ascending (*see also* Pyelitis) 590.80

Glomerulonephritis — Goiter

Glomerulonephritis (*see also* Nephritis) — *continued*
  basement membrane NEC 583.89
    with
      pulmonary hemorrhage (Goodpasture's syndrome) 446.21 *[583.81]*
  chronic 582.9
    with
      exudative nephritis 582.89
      interstitial nephritis (diffuse) (focal) 582.89
      necrotizing glomerulitis 582.4
      specified pathology or lesion NEC 582.89
    endothelial 582.2
    extracapillary with epithelial crescents 582.4
    hypocomplementemic persistent 582.2
    lobular 582.2
    membranoproliferative 582.2
    membranous 582.1
      and proliferative (mixed) 582.2
      sclerosing 582.1
    mesangiocapillary 582.2
    mixed membranous and proliferative 582.2
    proliferative (diffuse) 582.0
    rapidly progressive 582.4
    sclerosing 582.1
  cirrhotic — *see* Sclerosis, renal
  desquamative — *see* Nephrosis
  due to or associated with
    amyloidosis 277.3 *[583.81]*
      with nephrotic syndrome 277.3 *[581.81]*
      chronic 277.3 *[582.81]*
    diabetes mellitus 250.4 ☑ *[583.81]*
      with nephrotic syndrome 250.4 ☑ *[581.81]*
    diphtheria 032.89 *[580.81]*
    gonococcal infection (acute) 098.19 *[583.81]*
      chronic or duration of 2 months or over 098.39 *[583.81]*
    infectious hepatitis 070.9 *[580.81]*
    malaria (with nephrotic syndrome) 084.9 *[581.81]*
    mumps 072.79 *[580.81]*
    polyarteritis (nodosa) (with nephrotic syndrome) 446.0 *[581.81]*
    specified pathology NEC 583.89
      acute 580.89
      chronic 582.89
    streptotrichosis 039.8 *[583.81]*
    subacute bacterial endocarditis 421.0 *[580.81]*
    syphilis (late) 095.4
      congenital 090.5 *[583.81]*
      early 091.69 *[583.81]*
    systemic lupus erythematosus 710.0 *[583.81]*
      with nephrotic syndrome 710.0 *[581.81]*
      chronic 710.0 *[582.81]*
    tuberculosis (*see also* Tuberculosis) 016.0 ☑ *[583.81]*
    typhoid fever 002.0 *[580.81]*
  extracapillary with epithelial crescents 583.4
    acute 580.4
    chronic 582.4
  exudative 583.89
    acute 580.89
    chronic 582.89
  focal (*see also* Nephritis) 583.9
    embolic 580.4
  granular 582.89
  granulomatous 582.89
  hydremic (*see also* Nephrosis) 581.9
  hypocomplementemic persistent 583.2
    with nephrotic syndrome 581.2
    chronic 582.2
  immune complex NEC 583.89
  infective (*see also* Pyelitis) 590.80
  interstitial (diffuse) (focal) 583.89
    with nephrotic syndrome 581.89
    acute 580.89
    chronic 582.89
  latent or quiescent 582.9
  lobular 583.2
    with nephrotic syndrome 581.2
    chronic 582.2
  membranoproliferative 583.2
    with nephrotic syndrome 581.2
    chronic 582.2

Glomerulonephritis (*see also* Nephritis) — *continued*
  membranous 583.1
    with nephrotic syndrome 581.1
    and proliferative (mixed) 583.2
      with nephrotic syndrome 581.2
      chronic 582.2
    chronic 582.1
    sclerosing 582.1
      with nephrotic syndrome 581.1
  mesangiocapillary 583.2
    with nephrotic syndrome 581.2
    chronic 582.2
  minimal change 581.3
  mixed membranous and proliferative 583.2
    with nephrotic syndrome 581.2
    chronic 582.2
  necrotizing 583.4
    acute 580.4
    chronic 582.4
  nephrotic (*see also* Nephrosis) 581.9
  old — *see* Glomerulonephritis, chronic
  parenchymatous 581.89
  poststreptococcal 580.0
  proliferative (diffuse) 583.0
    with nephrotic syndrome 581.0
    acute 580.0
    chronic 582.0
  purulent (*see also* Pyelitis) 590.80
  quiescent — *see* Nephritis, chronic
  rapidly progressive 583.4
    acute 580.4
    chronic 582.4
  sclerosing membranous (chronic) 582.1
    with nephrotic syndrome 581.1
  septic (*see also* Pyelitis) 590.80
  specified pathology or lesion NEC 583.89
    with nephrotic syndrome 581.89
    acute 580.89
    chronic 582.89
  suppurative (acute) (disseminated) (*see also* Pyelitis) 590.80
  toxic — *see* Nephritis, acute
  tubal, tubular — *see* Nephrosis, tubular
  type II (Ellis) — *see* Nephrosis
  vascular — *see* Hypertension, kidney

Glomerulosclerosis (*see also* Sclerosis, renal) 587
  focal 582.1
    with nephrotic syndrome 581.1
  intercapillary (nodular) (with diabetes) 250.4 ☑ *[581.81]*

Glossagra 529.6

Glossalgia 529.6

Glossitis 529.0
  areata exfoliativa 529.1
  atrophic 529.4
  benign migratory 529.1
  gangrenous 529.0
  Hunter's 529.4
  median rhomboid 529.2
  Moeller's 529.4
  pellagrous 265.2

Glossocele 529.8

Glossodynia 529.6
  exfoliativa 529.4

Glossoncus 529.8

Glossophytia 529.3

Glossoplegia 529.8

Glossoptosis 529.8

Glossopyrosis 529.6

Glossotrichia 529.3

Glossy skin 701.9

Glottis — *see* condition

Glottitis — *see* Glossitis

Glucagonoma (M8152/0)
  malignant (M8152/3)
    pancreas 157.4
    specified site NEC — *see* Neoplasm, by site, malignant
    unspecified site 157.4
  pancreas 211.7
  specified site NEC — *see* Neoplasm, by site, benign
  unspecified site 211.7

Glucoglycinuria 270.7

Glue ear syndrome 381.20

Glue sniffing (airplane glue) (*see also* Dependence) 304.6 ☑

Glycinemia (with methylmalonic acidemia) 270.7

Glycinuria (renal) (with ketosis) 270.0

Glycogen
  infiltration (*see also* Disease, glycogen storage) 271.0
  storage disease (*see also* Disease, glycogen storage) 271.0

Glycogenosis (*see also* Disease, glycogen storage) 271.0
  cardiac 271.0 *[425.7]*
  Cori, types I-VII 271.0
  diabetic, secondary 250.8 ☑ *[259.8]*
  diffuse (with hepatic cirrhosis) 271.0
  generalized 271.0
  glucose-6-phosphatase deficiency 271.0
  hepatophosphorylase deficiency 271.0
  hepatorenal 271.0
  myophosphorylase deficiency 271.0

Glycopenia 251.2

Glycopeptide
  intermediate staphylococcus aureus (GISA) V09.8
  resistant
    enterococcus V09.8
    staphylococcus aureus (GRSA) V09.8

Glycoprolinuria 270.8

Glycosuria 791.5
  renal 271.4

Gnathostoma (spinigerum) (infection) (infestation) 128.1
  wandering swellings from 128.1

Gnathostomiasis 128.1

Goiter (adolescent) (colloid) (diffuse) (dipping) (due to iodine deficiency) (endemic) (euthyroid) (heart) (hyperplastic) (internal) (intrathoracic) (juvenile) (mixed type) (nonendemic) (parenchymatous) (plunging) (sporadic) (subclavicular) (substernal) 240.9
  with
    hyperthyroidism (recurrent) (*see also* Goiter, toxic) 242.0 ☑
    thyrotoxicosis (*see also* Goiter, toxic) 242.0 ☑
  adenomatous (*see also* Goiter, nodular) 241.9
  cancerous (M8000/3) 193
  complicating pregnancy, childbirth, or puerperium 648.1 ☑
  congenital 246.1
  cystic (*see also* Goiter, nodular) 241.9
  due to enzyme defect in synthesis of thyroid hormone (butane-insoluble iodine) (coupling) (deiodinase) (iodide trapping or organification) (iodotyrosine dehalogenase) (peroxidase) 246.1
  dyshormonogenic 246.1
  exophthalmic (*see also* Goiter, toxic) 242.0 ☑
  familial (with deaf-mutism) 243
  fibrous 245.3
  lingual 759.2
  lymphadenoid 245.2
  malignant (M8000/3) 193
  multinodular (nontoxic) 241.1
    toxic or with hyperthyroidism (*see also* Goiter, toxic) 242.2 ☑
  nodular (nontoxic) 241.9
    with
      hyperthyroidism (*see also* Goiter, toxic) 242.3 ☑
      thyrotoxicosis (*see also* Goiter, toxic) 242.3 ☑
    endemic 241.9
    exophthalmic (diffuse) (*see also* Goiter, toxic) 242.0 ☑
    multinodular (nontoxic) 241.1
    sporadic 241.9
    toxic (*see also* Goiter, toxic) 242.3 ☑
    uninodular (nontoxic) 241.0
  nontoxic (nodular) 241.9
    multinodular 241.1
    uninodular 241.0
  pulsating (*see also* Goiter, toxic) 242.0 ☑

Goiter — continued
  simple 240.0
  toxic 242.0 ☑

Note — Use the following fifth-digit
subclassification with category 242:

  0   without mention of thyrotoxic crisis or
       storm
  1   with mention of thyrotoxic crisis or storm

    adenomatous 242.3 ☑
      multinodular 242.2 ☑
      uninodular 242.1 ☑
    multinodular 242.2 ☑
    nodular 242.3 ☑
      multinodular 242.2 ☑
      uninodular 242.1 ☑
    uninodular 242.1 ☑
  uninodular (nontoxic) 241.0
    toxic or with hyperthyroidism (see also
      Goiter, toxic) 242.1 ☑
Goldberg (-Maxwell) (-Morris) syndrome
    (testicular feminization) 259.5 ▲
Goldblatt's
  hypertension 440.1
  kidney 440.1
Goldenhar's syndrome (oculoauriculovertebral
    dysplasia) 756.0
Goldflam-Erb disease or syndrome 358.00
Goldscheider's disease (epidermolysis bullosa)
    757.39
Goldstein's disease (familial hemorrhagic
    telangiectasia) 448.0
Golfer's elbow 726.32
Goltz-Gorlin syndrome (dermal hypoplasia)
    757.39
Gonadoblastoma (M9073/1)
  specified site — see Neoplasm, by site,
      uncertain behavior
  unspecified site
    female 236.2
    male 236.4
Gonecystitis (see also Vesiculitis) 608.0
Gongylonemiasis 125.6
  mouth 125.6
Goniosynechiae 364.73
Gonococcemia 098.89
Gonococcus, gonococcal (disease) (infection) (see
    also condition) 098.0
  anus 098.7
  bursa 098.52
  chronic NEC 098.2
  complicating pregnancy, childbirth, or
      puerperium 647.1 ☑
    affecting fetus or newborn 760.2
  conjunctiva, conjunctivitis (neonatorum)
      098.40
  dermatosis 098.89
  endocardium 098.84
  epididymo-orchitis 098.13
    chronic or duration of 2 months or over
        098.33
  eye (newborn) 098.40
  fallopian tube (chronic) 098.37
    acute 098.17
  genitourinary (acute) (organ) (system) (tract)
      (see also Gonorrhea) 098.0
    lower 098.0
      chronic 098.2
    upper 098.10
      chronic 098.30
  heart NEC 098.85
  joint 098.50
  keratoderma 098.81
  keratosis (blennorrhagica) 098.81
  lymphatic (gland) (node) 098.89
  meninges 098.82
  orchitis (acute) 098.13
    chronic or duration of 2 months or over
        098.33
  pelvis (acute) 098.19
    chronic or duration of 2 months or over
        098.39

Gonococcus, gonococcal (see also condition) —
    continued
  pericarditis 098.83
  peritonitis 098.86
  pharyngitis 098.6
  pharynx 098.6
  proctitis 098.7
  pyosalpinx (chronic) 098.37
    acute 098.17
  rectum 098.7
  septicemia 098.89
  skin 098.89
  specified site NEC 098.89
  synovitis 098.51
  tendon sheath 098.51
  throat 098.6
  urethra (acute) 098.0
    chronic or duration of 2 months or over
        098.2
  vulva (acute) 098.0
    chronic or duration of 2 months or over
        098.2
Gonocytoma (M9073/1)
  specified site — see Neoplasm, by site,
      uncertain behavior
  unspecified site
    female 236.2
    male 236.4
Gonorrhea 098.0
  acute 098.0
  Bartholin's gland (acute) 098.0
    chronic or duration of 2 months or over
        098.2
  bladder (acute) 098.11
    chronic or duration of 2 months or over
        098.31
  carrier (suspected of) V02.7
  cervix (acute) 098.15
    chronic or duration of 2 months or over
        098.35
  chronic 098.2
  complicating pregnancy, childbirth, or
      puerperium 647.1 ☑
    affecting fetus or newborn 760.2
  conjunctiva, conjunctivitis (neonatorum)
      098.40
  contact V01.6
  Cowper's gland (acute) 098.0
    chronic or duration of 2 months or over
        098.2
  duration of two months or over 098.2
  exposure to V01.6
  fallopian tube (chronic) 098.37
    acute 098.17
  genitourinary (acute) (organ) (system) (tract)
      098.0
    chronic 098.2
    duration of two months or over 098.2
  kidney (acute) 098.19
    chronic or duration of 2 months or over
        098.39
  ovary (acute) 098.19
    chronic or duration of 2 months or over
        098.39
  pelvis (acute) 098.19
    chronic or duration of 2 months or over
        098.39
  penis (acute) 098.0
    chronic or duration of 2 months or over
        098.2
  prostate (acute) 098.12
    chronic or duration of 2 months or over
        098.32
  seminal vesicle (acute) 098.14
    chronic or duration of 2 months or over
        098.34
  specified site NEC — see Gonococcus
  spermatic cord (acute) 098.14
    chronic or duration of 2 months or over
        098.34
  urethra (acute) 098.0
    chronic or duration of 2 months or over
        098.2
  vagina (acute) 098.0
    chronic or duration of 2 months or over
        098.2

Gonorrhea — continued
  vas deferens (acute) 098.14
    chronic or duration of 2 months or over
        098.34
  vulva (acute) 098.0
    chronic or duration of 2 months or over
        098.2
Goodpasture's syndrome (pneumorenal) 446.21
Good's syndrome 279.06
Gopalan's syndrome (burning feet) 266.2
Gordon's disease (exudative enteropathy) 579.8
Gorlin-Chaudhry-Moss syndrome 759.89
Gougerot's syndrome (trisymptomatic) 709.1
Gougerot-Blum syndrome (pigmented purpuric
    lichenoid dermatitis) 709.1
Gougerot-Carteaud disease or syndrome
    (confluent reticulate papillomatosis) 701.8
Gougerot-Hailey-Hailey disease (benign familial
    chronic pemphigus) 757.39
Gougerot (-Houwer) - Sjögren syndrome
    (keratoconjunctivitis sicca) 710.2
Gouley's syndrome (constrictive pericarditis)
    423.2
Goundou 102.6
Gout, gouty 274.9
  with specified manifestations NEC 274.89
  arthritis (acute) 274.0
  arthropathy 274.0
  degeneration, heart 274.82
  diathesis 274.9
  eczema 274.89
  episcleritis 274.89 [379.09]
  external ear (tophus) 274.81
  glomerulonephritis 274.10
  iritis 274.89 [364.11]
  joint 274.0
  kidney 274.10
  lead 984.9
    specified type of lead — see Table of Drugs
        and Chemicals
  nephritis 274.10
  neuritis 274.89 [357.4]
  phlebitis 274.89 [451.9]
  rheumatic 714.0
  saturnine 984.9
    specified type of lead — see Table of Drugs
        and Chemicals
  spondylitis 274.0
  synovitis 274.0
  syphilitic 095.8
  tophi 274.0
    ear 274.81
    heart 274.82
    specified site NEC 274.82
Gowers'
  muscular dystrophy 359.1
  syndrome (vasovagal attack) 780.2
Gowers-Paton-Kennedy syndrome 377.04
Gradenigo's syndrome 383.02
Graft-versus-host disease (bone marrow) 996.85
  due to organ transplant NEC — see
      Complications, transplant, organ
Graham Steell's murmur (pulmonic
    regurgitation) (see also Endocarditis,
    pulmonary) 424.3
Grain-handlers' disease or lung 495.8
Grain mite (itch) 133.8
Grand
  mal (idiopathic) (see also Epilepsy) 345.1 ☑
    hysteria of Charcôt 300.11
    nonrecurrent or isolated 780.39
  multipara
    affecting management of labor and delivery
        659.4 ☑
    status only (not pregnant) V61.5
Granite workers' lung 502
Granular — see also condition
  inflammation, pharynx 472.1
  kidney (contracting) (see also Sclerosis, renal)
      587
  liver — see Cirrhosis, liver
  nephritis — see Nephritis

☑ Additional Digit Required — Refer to the Tabular List (Numeric Code Section) for Additional Digit Selection
▶◀ Revised Text   ● New Line   ▲ Revised Code

2006 ICD-9-CM   **October 2005 • Volume 2 — 159**

Granulation tissue, abnormal — *see also*
Granuloma
abnormal or excessive 701.5
postmastoidectomy cavity 383.33
postoperative 701.5
skin 701.5
Granulocytopenia, granulocytopenic (primary)
288.0
malignant 288.0
Granuloma NEC 686.1
abdomen (wall) 568.89
skin (pyogenicum) 686.1
from residual foreign body 709.4
annulare 695.89
anus 569.49
apical 522.6
appendix 543.9
aural 380.23
beryllium (skin) 709.4
lung 503
bone (*see also* Osteomyelitis) 730.1 ☑
eosinophilic 277.89
from residual foreign body 733.99
canaliculus lacrimalis 375.81
cerebral 348.8
cholesterin, middle ear 385.82
coccidioidal (progressive) 114.3
lung 114.4
meninges 114.2
primary (lung) 114.0
colon 569.89
conjunctiva 372.61
dental 522.6
ear, middle (cholesterin) 385.82
with otitis media — *see* Otitis media
eosinophilic 277.89
bone 277.89
lung 277.89
oral mucosa 528.9
exuberant 701.5
eyelid 374.89
facial
lethal midline 446.3
malignant 446.3
faciale 701.8
fissuratum (gum) 523.8
foot NEC 686.1
foreign body (in soft tissue) NEC 728.82
bone 733.99
in operative wound 998.4
muscle 728.82
skin 709.4
subcutaneous tissue 709.4
fungoides 202.1 ☑
gangraenescens 446.3
giant cell (central) (jaw) (reparative) 526.3
gingiva 523.8
peripheral (gingiva) 523.8
gland (lymph) 289.3
Hodgkin's (M9661/3) 201.1 ☑
ileum 569.89
infectious NEC 136.9
inguinale (Donovan) 099.2
venereal 099.2
intestine 569.89
iridocyclitis 364.10
jaw (bone) 526.3
reparative giant cell 526.3
kidney (*see also* Infection, kidney) 590.9
lacrimal sac 375.81
larynx 478.79
lethal midline 446.3
lipid 277.89
lipoid 277.89
liver 572.8
lung (infectious) (*see also* Fibrosis, lung) 515
coccidioidal 114.4
eosinophilic 277.89
lymph gland 289.3
Majocchi's 110.6
malignant, face 446.3
mandible 526.3
mediastinum 519.3
midline 446.3
monilial 112.3
muscle 728.82
from residual foreign body 728.82

Granuloma — *continued*
nasal sinus (*see also* Sinusitis) 473.9
operation wound 998.59
foreign body 998.4
stitch (external) 998.89
internal organ 996.7 ☑
internal wound 998.89
talc 998.7
oral mucosa, eosinophilic or pyogenic 528.9
orbit, orbital 376.11
paracoccidioidal 116.1
penis, venereal 099.2
periapical 522.6
peritoneum 568.89
due to ova of helminths NEC (*see also*
Helminthiasis) 128.9
postmastoidectomy cavity 383.33
postoperative — *see* Granuloma, operation
wound
prostate 601.8
pudendi (ulcerating) 099.2
pudendorum (ulcerative) 099.2
pulp, internal (tooth) 521.49
pyogenic, pyogenicum (skin) 686.1
maxillary alveolar ridge 522.6
oral mucosa 528.9
rectum 569.49
reticulohistiocytic 277.89
rubrum nasi 705.89
sarcoid 135
Schistosoma 120.9
septic (skin) 686.1
silica (skin) 709.4
sinus (accessory) (infectional) (nasal) (*see also*
Sinusitis) 473.9
skin (pyogenicum) 686.1
from foreign body or material 709.4
sperm 608.89
spine
syphilitic (epidural) 094.89
tuberculous (*see also* Tuberculosis)
015.0 ☑ *[730.88]*
stitch (postoperative) 998.89
internal wound 998.89
suppurative (skin) 686.1
suture (postoperative) 998.89
internal wound 998.89
swimming pool 031.1
talc 728.82
in operation wound 998.7
telangiectaticum (skin) 686.1
trichophyticum 110.6
tropicum 102.4
umbilicus 686.1
newborn 771.4
urethra 599.84
uveitis 364.10
vagina 099.2
venereum 099.2
vocal cords 478.5
Wegener's (necrotizing respiratory
granulomatosis) 446.4
Granulomatosis NEC 686.1
disciformis chronica et progressiva 709.3
infantiseptica 771.2
lipoid 277.89
lipophagic, intestinal 040.2
miliary 027.0
necrotizing, respiratory 446.4
progressive, septic 288.1
Wegener's (necrotizing respiratory) 446.4
Granulomatous tissue — *see* Granuloma
Granulosis rubra nasi 705.89
Graphite fibrosis (of lung) 503
Graphospasm 300.89
organic 333.84
Grating scapula 733.99
Gravel (urinary) (*see also* Calculus) 592.9
Graves' disease (exophthalmic goiter) (*see also*
Goiter, toxic) 242.0 ☑
Gravis — *see* condition
Grawitz's tumor (hypernephroma) (M8312/3)
189.0
Grayness, hair (premature) 704.3
congenital 757.4

Gray or grey syndrome (chloramphenicol)
(newborn) 779.4
Greenfield's disease 330.0
Green sickness 280.9
Greenstick fracture — *see* Fracture, by site
Greig's syndrome (hypertelorism) 756.0
Griesinger's disease (*see also* Ancylostomiasis)
126.9
Grinders'
asthma 502
lung 502
phthisis (*see also* Tuberculosis) 011.4 ☑
Grinding, teeth 306.8
Grip
Dabney's 074.1
devil's 074.1
Grippe, grippal — *see also* Influenza
Balkan 083.0
intestinal 487.8
summer 074.8
Grippy cold 487.1
Grisel's disease 723.5
Groin — *see* condition
Grooved
nails (transverse) 703.8
tongue 529.5
congenital 750.13
Ground itch 126.9
Growing pains, children 781.99
Growth (fungoid) (neoplastic) (new) (M8000/1) —
see also Neoplasm, by site, unspecified
nature
adenoid (vegetative) 474.12
benign (M8000/0) — *see* Neoplasm, by site,
benign
fetal, poor 764.9 ☑
affecting management of pregnancy 656.5 ☑
malignant (M8000/3) — *see* Neoplasm, by site,
malignant
rapid, childhood V21.0
secondary (M8000/6) — *see* Neoplasm, by site,
malignant, secondary
GRSA (glycopeptide resistant staphylococcus
aureus) V09.8
Gruber's hernia — *see* Hernia, Gruber's
Gruby's disease (tinea tonsurans) 110.0
G-trisomy 758.0
Guama fever 066.3
Gubler (-Millard) paralysis or syndrome 344.89
Guérin-Stern syndrome (arthrogryposis multiplex
congenita) 754.89
Guertin's disease (electric chorea) 049.8
Guillain-Barré disease or syndrome 357.0
Guinea worms (infection) (infestation) 125.7
Guinon's disease (motor-verbal tic) 307.23
Gull's disease (thyroid atrophy with myxedema)
244.8
Gull and Sutton's disease — *see* Hypertension,
kidney
Gum — *see* condition
Gumboil 522.7
Gumma (syphilitic) 095.9
artery 093.89
cerebral or spinal 094.89
bone 095.5
of yaws (late) 102.6
brain 094.89
cauda equina 094.89
central nervous system NEC 094.9
ciliary body 095.8 *[364.11]*
congenital 090.5
testis 090.5
eyelid 095.8 *[373.5]*
heart 093.89
intracranial 094.89
iris 095.8 *[364.11]*
kidney 095.4
larynx 095.8
leptomeninges 094.2
liver 095.3
meninges 094.2

Gumma — *continued*
myocardium 093.82
nasopharynx 095.8
neurosyphilitic 094.9
nose 095.8
orbit 095.8
palate (soft) 095.8
penis 095.8
pericardium 093.81
pharynx 095.8
pituitary 095.8
scrofulous (*see also* Tuberculosis) 017.0 ☑
skin 095.8
specified site NEC 095.8
spinal cord 094.89
tongue 095.8
tonsil 095.8
trachea 095.8
tuberculous (*see also* Tuberculosis) 017.0 ☑
ulcerative due to yaws 102.4
ureter 095.8
yaws 102.4
bone 102.6
Gunn's syndrome (jaw-winking syndrome) 742.8
Gunshot wound — *see also* Wound, open, by site
fracture — *see* Fracture, by site, open
internal organs (abdomen, chest, or pelvis) —
see Injury, internal, by site, with open
wound
intracranial — *see* Laceration, brain, with open
intracranial wound
Günther's disease or syndrome (congenital
erythropoietic porphyria) 277.1
Gustatory hallucination 780.1
Gynandrism 752.7
Gynandroblastoma (M8632/1)
specified site — *see* Neoplasm, by site,
uncertain behavior
unspecified site
female 236.2
male 236.4
Gynandromorphism 752.7
Gynatresia (congenital) 752.49
Gynecoid pelvis, male 738.6
Gynecological examination V72.31
for contraceptive maintenance V25.40
Gynecomastia 611.1
Gynephobia 300.29
Gyrate scalp 757.39

H

Haas' disease (osteochondrosis head of humerus)
732.3
Habermann's disease (acute parapsoriasis
varioliformis) 696.2
Habit, habituation
chorea 307.22
disturbance, child 307.9
drug (*see also* Dependence) 304.9 ☑
laxative (*see also* Abuse, drugs, nondependent)
305.9 ☑
spasm 307.20
chronic 307.22
transient (of childhood) 307.21
tic 307.20
chronic 307.22
transient (of childhood) 307.21
use of
nonprescribed drugs (*see also* Abuse, drugs,
nondependent) 305.9 ☑
patent medicines (*see also* Abuse, drugs,
nondependent) 305.9 ☑
vomiting 536.2
Hadfield-Clarke syndrome (pancreatic
infantilism) 577.8
Haff disease 985.1
Hageman factor defect, deficiency, or disease
(*see also* Defect, coagulation) 286.3
Haglund's disease (osteochondrosis os tibiale
externum) 732.5
Haglund-Läwen-Fründ syndrome 717.89

Hagner's disease (hypertrophic pulmonary
osteoarthropathy) 731.2
Hag teeth, tooth 524.39
Hailey-Hailey disease (benign familial chronic
pemphigus) 757.39
Hair — *see also* condition
plucking 307.9
Hairball in stomach 935.2
Hairy black tongue 529.3
Half vertebra 756.14
Halitosis 784.9
Hallermann-Streiff syndrome 756.0
Hallervorden-Spatz disease or syndrome 333.0
Hallopeau's
acrodermatitis (continua) 696.1
disease (lichen sclerosis et atrophicus) 701.0
Hallucination (auditory) (gustatory) (olfactory)
(tactile) 780.1
alcohol-induced 291.3
drug-induced 292.12
visual 368.16
Hallucinosis 298.9
alcohol-induced (acute) 291.3
drug-induced 292.12
Hallus — *see* Hallux
Hallux 735.9
malleus (acquired) 735.3
rigidus (acquired) 735.2
congenital 755.66
late effects of rickets 268.1
valgus (acquired) 735.0
congenital 755.66
varus (acquired) 735.1
congenital 755.66
Halo, visual 368.15
Hamartoblastoma 759.6
Hamartoma 759.6
epithelial (gingival), odontogenic, central, or
peripheral (M9321/0) 213.1
upper jaw (bone) 213.0
vascular 757.32
Hamartosis, hamartoses NEC 759.6
Hamman's disease or syndrome (spontaneous
mediastinal emphysema) 518.1
Hamman-Rich syndrome (diffuse interstitial
pulmonary fibrosis) 516.3
Hammer toe (acquired) 735.4
congenital 755.66
late effects of rickets 268.1
Hand — *see* condition
Hand-Schüller-Christian disease or syndrome
(chronic histiocytosis x) 277.89
Hand-foot syndrome 282.61
Hanging (asphyxia) (strangulation) (suffocation)
994.7
Hangnail (finger) (with lymphangitis) 681.02
Hangover (alcohol) (*see also* Abuse, drugs,
nondependent) 305.0 ☑
Hanot's cirrhosis or disease — *see* Cirrhosis,
biliary
Hanot-Chauffard (-Troisier) syndrome (bronze
diabetes) 275.0
Hansen's disease (leprosy) 030.9
benign form 030.1
malignant form 030.0
Harada's disease or syndrome 363.22
Hard chancre 091.0
Hard firm prostate 600.10
with urinary retention 600.11
Hardening
artery — *see* Arteriosclerosis
brain 348.8
liver 571.8
Hare's syndrome (M8010/3) (carcinoma,
pulmonary apex) 162.3
Harelip (*see also* Cleft, lip) 749.10
Harkavy's syndrome 446.0
Harlequin (fetus) 757.1
color change syndrome 779.89

Harley's disease (intermittent hemoglobinuria)
283.2
Harris'
lines 733.91
syndrome (organic hyperinsulinism) 251.1
Hart's disease or syndrome (pellagra-cerebellar
ataxia-renal aminoaciduria) 270.0
Hartmann's pouch (abnormal sacculation of
gallbladder neck) 575.8
of intestine V44.3
attention to V55.3
Hartnup disease (pellagra-cerebellar ataxia-renal
aminoaciduria) 270.0
Harvester lung 495.0
Hashimoto's disease or struma (struma
lymphomatosa) 245.2
Hassall-Henle bodies (corneal warts) 371.41
Haut mal (*see also* Epilepsy) 345.1 ☑
Haverhill fever 026.1
Hawaiian wood rose dependence 304.5 ☑
Hawkins' keloid 701.4
Hay
asthma (*see also* Asthma) 493.0 ☑
fever (allergic) (with rhinitis) 477.9
with asthma (bronchial) (*see also* Asthma)
493.0 ☑
allergic, due to grass, pollen, ragweed, or
tree 477.0
conjunctivitis 372.05
due to
dander, animal (cat) (dog) 477.2
dust 477.8
fowl 477.8
hair, animal (cat) (dog) 477.2
pollen 477.0
specified allergen other than pollen 477.8
Hayem-Faber syndrome (achlorhydric anemia)
280.9
Hayem-Widal syndrome (acquired hemolytic
jaundice) 283.9
Haygarth's nodosities 715.04
Hazard-Crile tumor (M8350/3) 193
Hb (abnormal)
disease — *see* Disease, hemoglobin
trait — *see* Trait
H disease 270.0
Head — *see also* condition
banging 307.3
Headache 784.0
allergic 346.2 ☑
cluster 346.2 ☑
due to
loss, spinal fluid 349.0
lumbar puncture 349.0
saddle block 349.0
emotional 307.81
histamine 346.2 ☑
lumbar puncture 349.0
menopausal 627.2
migraine 346.9 ☑
nonorganic origin 307.81
postspinal 349.0
psychogenic 307.81
psychophysiologic 307.81
sick 346.1 ☑
spinal 349.0
complicating labor and delivery 668.8 ☑
postpartum 668.8 ☑
spinal fluid loss 349.0
tension 307.81
vascular 784.0
migraine type 346.9 ☑
vasomotor 346.9 ☑
Health
advice V65.4 ☑
audit V70.0
checkup V70.0
education V65.4 ☑
hazard (*see also* History of) V15.9
falling V15.88
specified cause NEC V15.89
instruction V65.4 ☑

☑ Additional Digit Required — Refer to the Tabular List (Numeric Code Section) for Additional Digit Selection

Health — *continued*
services provided because (of)
boarding school residence V60.6
holiday relief for person providing home care
V60.5
inadequate
housing V60.1
resources V60.2
lack of housing V60.0
no care available in home V60.4
person living alone V60.3
poverty V60.3
residence in institution V60.6
specified cause NEC V60.8
vacation relief for person providing home
care V60.5

Healthy
donor (*see also* Donor) V59.9
infant or child
accompanying sick mother V65.0
receiving care V20.1
person
accompanying sick relative V65.0
admitted for sterilization V25.2
receiving prophylactic inoculation or
vaccination (*see also* Vaccination,
prophylactic) V05.9

Hearing examination V72.1

Heart — *see* condition

Heartburn 787.1
psychogenic 306.4

Heat (effects) 992.9
apoplexy 992.0
burn — *see also* Burn, by site
from sun (*see also* Sunburn) 692.71
collapse 992.1
cramps 992.2
dermatitis or eczema 692.89
edema 992.7
erythema — *see* Burn, by site
excessive 992.9
specified effect NEC 992.8
exhaustion 992.5
anhydrotic 992.3
due to
salt (and water) depletion 992.4
water depletion 992.3
fatigue (transient) 992.6
fever 992.0
hyperpyrexia 992.0
prickly 705.1
prostration — *see* Heat, exhaustion
pyrexia 992.0
rash 705.1
specified effect NEC 992.8
stroke 992.0
sunburn (*see also* Sunburn) 692.71
syncope 992.1

Heavy-chain disease 273.2

Heavy-for-dates (fetus or infant) 766.1
4500 grams or more 766.0
exceptionally 766.0

Hebephrenia, hebephrenic (acute) (*see also*
Schizophrenia) 295.1 ☑
dementia (praecox) (*see also* Schizophrenia)
295.1 ☑
schizophrenia (*see also* Schizophrenia) 295.1 ☑

Heberden's
disease or nodes 715.04
syndrome (angina pectoris) 413.9

Hebra's disease
dermatitis exfoliativa 695.89
erythema multiforme exudativum 695.1
pityriasis 695.89
maculata et circinata 696.3
rubra 695.89
pilaris 696.4
prurigo 698.2

Hebra, nose 040.1

Hedinger's syndrome (malignant carcinoid) 259.2

Heel — *see* condition

Heerfordt's disease or syndrome (uveoparotitis)
135

Hegglin's anomaly or syndrome 288.2

Heidenhain's disease 290.10
with dementia 290.10

Heilmeyer-Schöner disease (M9842/3) 207.1 ☑

Heine-Medin disease (*see also* Poliomyelitis)
045.9 ☑

Heinz-body anemia, congenital 282.7

Heller's disease or syndrome (infantile
psychosis) (*see also* Psychosis, childhood)
299.1 ☑

H.E.L.L.P 642.5 ☑

Helminthiasis (*see also* Infestation, by specific
parasite) 128.9
Ancylostoma (*see also* Ancylostoma) 126.9
intestinal 127.9
mixed types (types classifiable to more than
one of the categories 120.0-127.7)
127.8
specified type 127.7
mixed types (intestinal) (types classifiable to
more than one of the categories 120.0-
127.7) 127.8
Necator americanus 126.1
specified type NEC 128.8
Trichinella 124

Heloma 700

Hemangioblastoma (M9161/1) — *see also*
Neoplasm, connective tissue, uncertain
behavior
malignant (M9161/3) — *see* Neoplasm,
connective tissue, malignant

Hemangioblastomatosis, cerebelloretinal 759.6

Hemangioendothelioma (M9130/1) — *see also*
Neoplasm, by site, uncertain behavior
benign (M9130/0) 228.00
bone (diffuse) (M9130/3) — *see* Neoplasm,
bone, malignant
malignant (M9130/3) — *see* Neoplasm,
connective tissue, malignant
nervous system (M9130/0) 228.09

Hemangioendotheliosarcoma (M9130/3) — *see*
Neoplasm, connective tissue, malignant

Hemangiofibroma (M9160/0) — *see* Neoplasm,
by site, benign

Hemangiolipoma (M8861/0) — *see* Lipoma

Hemangioma (M9120/0) 228.00
arteriovenous (M9123/0) — *see* Hemangioma,
by site
brain 228.02
capillary (M9131/0) — *see* Hemangioma, by
site
cavernous (M9121/0) — *see* Hemangioma, by
site
central nervous system NEC 228.09
choroid 228.09
heart 228.09
infantile (M9131/0) — *see* Hemangioma, by site
intra-abdominal structures 228.04
intracranial structures 228.02
intramuscular (M9132/0) — *see* Hemangioma,
by site
iris 228.09
juvenile (M9131/0) — *see* Hemangioma, by site
malignant (M9120/3) — *see* Neoplasm,
connective tissue, malignant
meninges 228.09
brain 228.02
spinal cord 228.09
peritoneum 228.04
placenta — *see* Placenta, abnormal
plexiform (M9131/0) — *see* Hemangioma, by
site
racemose (M9123/0) — *see* Hemangioma, by
site
retina 228.03
retroperitoneal tissue 228.04
sclerosing (M8832/0) — *see* Neoplasm, skin,
benign
simplex (M9131/0) — *see* Hemangioma, by site
skin and subcutaneous tissue 228.01
specified site NEC 228.09
spinal cord 228.09
venous (M9122/0) — *see* Hemangioma, by site
verrucous keratotic (M9142/0) — *see*
Hemangioma, by site

Hemangiomatosis (systemic) 757.32
involving single site — *see* Hemangioma

Hemangiopericytoma (M9150/1) — *see also*
Neoplasm, connective tissue, uncertain
behavior
benign (M9150/0) — *see* Neoplasm, connective
tissue, benign
malignant (M9150/3) — *see* Neoplasm,
connective tissue, malignant

Hemangiosarcoma (M9120/3) — *see* Neoplasm,
connective tissue, malignant

Hemarthrosis (nontraumatic) 719.10
ankle 719.17
elbow 719.12
foot 719.17
hand 719.14
hip 719.15
knee 719.16
multiple sites 719.19
pelvic region 719.15
shoulder (region) 719.11
specified site NEC 719.18
traumatic — *see* Sprain, by site
wrist 719.13

Hematemesis 578.0
with ulcer — *see* Ulcer, by site, with
hemorrhage
due to S. japonicum 120.2
Goldstein's (familial hemorrhagic telangiectasia)
448.0
newborn 772.4
due to swallowed maternal blood 777.3

Hematidrosis 705.89

Hematinuria (*see also* Hemoglobinuria) 791.2
malarial 084.8
paroxysmal 283.2

Hematite miners' lung 503

Hematobilia 576.8

Hematocele (congenital) (diffuse) (idiopathic)
608.83
broad ligament 620.7
canal of Nuck 629.0
cord, male 608.83
fallopian tube 620.8
female NEC 629.0
ischiorectal 569.89
male NEC 608.83
ovary 629.0
pelvis, pelvic
female 629.0
with ectopic pregnancy (*see also*
Pregnancy, ectopic) 633.90
with intrauterine pregnancy 633.91
male 608.83
periuterine 629.0
retrouterine 629.0
scrotum 608.83
spermatic cord (diffuse) 608.83
testis 608.84
traumatic — *see* Injury, internal, pelvis
tunica vaginalis 608.83
uterine ligament 629.0
uterus 621.4
vagina 623.6
vulva 624.5

Hematocephalus 742.4

Hematochezia (*see also* Melena) 578.1

Hematochyluria (*see also* Infestation, filarial)
125.9

Hematocolpos 626.8

Hematocornea 371.12

Hematogenous — *see* condition

Hematoma (skin surface intact) (traumatic) — *see also* Contusion

> *Note* — *Hematomas are coded according to origin and the nature and site of the hematoma or the accompanying injury. Hematomas of unspecified origin are coded as injuries of the sites involved, except:*
>
>   (a) *hematomas of genital organs which are coded as diseases of the organ involved unless they complicate pregnancy or delivery*
>
>   (b) *hematomas of the eye which are coded as diseases of the eye.*
>
>   *For late effect of hematoma classifiable to 920-924 see Late, effect, contusion*

with
    crush injury — *see* Crush
    fracture — *see* Fracture, by site
    injury of internal organs — *see also* Injury,
      internal, by site
      kidney — *see* Hematoma, kidney
        traumatic
      liver — *see* Hematoma, liver, traumatic
      spleen — *see* Hematoma, spleen
    nerve injury — *see* Injury, nerve
    open wound — *see* Wound, open, by site
    skin surface intact — *see* Contusion
abdomen (wall) — *see* Contusion, abdomen
amnion 658.8 ☑
aorta, dissecting 441.00
    abdominal 441.02
    thoracic 441.01
    thoracoabdominal 441.03
arterial (complicating trauma) 904.9
    specified site — *see* Injury, blood vessel, by
      site
auricle (ear) 380.31
birth injury 767.8
    skull 767.19
brain (traumatic) 853.0 ☑

> *Note* — *Use the following fifth-digit subclassification with categories 851-854:*
>
>   *0* *unspecified state of consciousness*
>   *1* *with no loss of consciousness*
>   *2* *with brief [less than one hour] loss of consciousness*
>   *3* *with moderate [1-24 hours] loss of consciousness*
>   *4* *with prolonged [more than 24 hours] loss of consciousness and return to pre-existing conscious level*
>   *5* *with prolonged [more than 24 hours] loss of consciousness, without return to pre-existing conscious level*
>   *Use fifth-digit 5 to designate when a patient is unconscious and dies before regaining consciousness, regardless of the duration of the loss of consciousness*
>   *6* *with loss of consciousness of unspecified duration*
>   *9* *with concussion, unspecified*

  with
    cerebral
      contusion — *see* Contusion, brain
      laceration — *see* Laceration, brain
    open intracranial wound 853.1 ☑
    skull fracture — *see* Fracture, skull, by
      site
  extradural or epidural 852.4 ☑
    with open intracranial wound 852.5 ☑
    fetus or newborn 767.0
    nontraumatic 432.0
  fetus or newborn NEC 767.0
  nontraumatic (*see also* Hemorrhage, brain)
    431
    epidural or extradural 432.0
    newborn NEC 772.8

Hematoma — *see also* Contusion — *continued*
brain — *continued*
  nontraumatic — *continued*
    subarachnoid, arachnoid, or meningeal
      (*see also* Hemorrhage,
      subarachnoid) 430
    subdural (*see also* Hemorrhage,
      subdural) 432.1
  subarachnoid, arachnoid, or meningeal
    852.0 ☑
    with open intracranial wound 852.1 ☑
    fetus or newborn 772.2
    nontraumatic (*see also* Hemorrhage,
      subarachnoid) 430
  subdural 852.2 ☑
    with open intracranial wound 852.3 ☑
    fetus or newborn (localized) 767.0
    nontraumatic (*see also* Hemorrhage,
      subdural) 432.1
breast (nontraumatic) 611.8
broad ligament (nontraumatic) 620.7
  complicating delivery 665.7 ☑
  traumatic — *see* Injury, internal, broad
    ligament
calcified NEC 959.9
capitis 920
  due to birth injury 767.19
  newborn 767.19
cerebral — *see* Hematoma, brain
cesarean section wound 674.3 ☑
chorion — *see* Placenta, abnormal
complicating delivery (perineum) (vulva)
  664.5 ☑
  pelvic 665.7 ☑
  vagina 665.7 ☑
corpus
  cavernosum (nontraumatic) 607.82
  luteum (nontraumatic) (ruptured) 620.1
dura (mater) — *see* Hematoma, brain, subdural
epididymis (nontraumatic) 608.83
epidural (traumatic) — *see also* Hematoma,
  brain, extradural
  spinal — *see* Injury, spinal, by site
episiotomy 674.3 ☑
external ear 380.31
extradural — *see also* Hematoma, brain,
  extradural
  fetus or newborn 767.0
  nontraumatic 432.0
    fetus or newborn 767.0
fallopian tube 620.8
genital organ (nontraumatic)
  female NEC 629.8
  male NEC 608.83
  traumatic (external site) 922.4
    internal — *see* Injury, internal, genital
      organ
graafian follicle (ruptured) 620.0
internal organs (abdomen, chest, or pelvis) —
  see also Injury, internal, by site
  kidney — *see* Hematoma, kidney, traumatic
  liver — *see* Hematoma, liver, traumatic
  spleen — *see* Hematoma, spleen
intracranial — *see* Hematoma, brain
kidney, cystic 593.81
  traumatic 866.01
    with open wound into cavity 866.11
labia (nontraumatic) 624.5
lingual (and other parts of neck, scalp, or face,
  except eye) 920
liver (subcapsular) 573.8
  birth injury 767.8
  fetus or newborn 767.8
  traumatic NEC 864.01
    with
      laceration — *see* Laceration, liver
      open wound into cavity 864.11
mediastinum — *see* Injury, internal,
  mediastinum
meninges, meningeal (brain) — *see also*
  Hematoma, brain, subarachnoid
  spinal — *see* Injury, spinal, by site
mesosalpinx (nontraumatic) 620.8
  traumatic — *see* Injury, internal, pelvis
muscle (traumatic) — *see* Contusion, by site
nasal (septum) (and other part(s) of neck, scalp,
  or face, except eye) 920

Hematoma — *see also* Contusion — *continued*
obstetrical surgical wound 674.3 ☑
orbit, orbital (nontraumatic) 376.32
  traumatic 921.2
ovary (corpus luteum) (nontraumatic) 620.1
  traumatic — *see* Injury, internal, ovary
pelvis (female) (nontraumatic) 629.8
  complicating delivery 665.7 ☑
  male 608.83
  traumatic — *see also* Injury, internal, pelvis
    specified organ NEC (*see also* Injury,
      internal, pelvis) 867.6
penis (nontraumatic) 607.82
pericranial (and neck, or face any part, except
  eye) 920
  due to injury at birth 767.19
perineal wound (obstetrical) 674.3 ☑
  complicating delivery 664.5 ☑
perirenal, cystic 593.81
pinna 380.31
placenta — *see* Placenta, abnormal
postoperative 998.12
retroperitoneal (nontraumatic) 568.81
  traumatic — *see* Injury, internal,
    retroperitoneum
retropubic, male 568.81
scalp (and neck, or face any part, except eye)
  920
  fetus or newborn 767.19
scrotum (nontraumatic) 608.83
  traumatic 922.4
seminal vesicle (nontraumatic) 608.83
  traumatic — *see* Injury, internal, seminal,
    vesicle
spermatic cord — *see also* Injury, internal,
  spermatic cord
  nontraumatic 608.83
spinal (cord) (meninges) — *see also* Injury,
  spinal, by site
  fetus or newborn 767.4
  nontraumatic 336.1
spleen 865.01
  with
    laceration — *see* Laceration, spleen
    open wound into cavity 865.11
sternocleidomastoid, birth injury 767.8
sternomastoid, birth injury 767.8
subarachnoid — *see also* Hematoma, brain,
  subarachnoid
  fetus or newborn 772.2
  nontraumatic (*see also* Hemorrhage,
    subarachnoid) 430
  newborn 772.2
subdural — *see also* Hematoma, brain,
  subdural
  fetus or newborn (localized) 767.0
  nontraumatic (*see also* Hemorrhage,
    subdural) 432.1
subperiosteal (syndrome) 267
  traumatic — *see* Hematoma, by site
superficial, fetus or newborn 772.6
syncytium — *see* Placenta, abnormal
testis (nontraumatic) 608.83
  birth injury 767.8
  traumatic 922.4
tunica vaginalis (nontraumatic) 608.83
umbilical cord 663.6 ☑
  affecting fetus or newborn 762.6
uterine ligament (nontraumatic) 620.7
  traumatic — *see* Injury, internal, pelvis
uterus 621.4
  traumatic — *see* Injury, internal, pelvis
vagina (nontraumatic) (ruptured) 623.6
  complicating delivery 665.7 ☑
  traumatic 922.4
vas deferens (nontraumatic) 608.83
  traumatic — *see* Injury, internal, vas
    deferens
vitreous 379.23
vocal cord 920
vulva (nontraumatic) 624.5
  complicating delivery 664.5 ☑
  fetus or newborn 767.8
  traumatic 922.4

Hematometra 621.4

Hematomyelia 336.1
  with fracture of vertebra (see also Fracture,
      vertebra, by site, with spinal cord injury)
      806.8
  fetus or newborn 767.4
Hematomyelitis 323.9
  late effect — see category 326
Hematoperitoneum (see also Hemoperitoneum)
      568.81
Hematopneumothorax (see also Hemothorax)
      511.8
Hematoporphyria (acquired) (congenital) 277.1
Hematoporphyrinuria (acquired) (congenital)
      277.1
Hematorachis, hematorrhachis 336.1
  fetus or newborn 767.4
Hematosalpinx 620.8
  with
      ectopic pregnancy (see also categories
          633.0-633.9) 639.2
      molar pregnancy (see also categories 630-
          632) 639.2
      infectional (see also Salpingo-oophoritis)
          614.2
Hematospermia 608.82
Hematothorax (see also Hemothorax) 511.8
Hematotympanum 381.03
Hematuria (benign) (essential) (idiopathic) 599.7
  due to S. hematobium 120.0
  endemic 120.0
  intermittent 599.7
  malarial 084.8
  paroxysmal 599.7
  sulfonamide
      correct substance properly administered
          599.7
      overdose or wrong substance given or taken
          961.0
  tropical (bilharziasis) 120.0
  tuberculous (see also Tuberculosis) 016.9 ☑
Hematuric bilious fever 084.8
Hemeralopia 368.10
Hemiabiotrophy 799.89
Hemi-akinesia 781.8
Hemianalgesia (see also Disturbance, sensation)
      782.0
Hemianencephaly 740.0
Hemianesthesia (see also Disturbance, sensation)
      782.0
Hemianopia, hemianopsia (altitudinal)
      (homonymous) 368.46
  binasal 368.47
  bitemporal 368.47
  heteronymous 368.47
  syphilitic 095.8
Hemiasomatognosia 307.9
Hemiathetosis 781.0
Hemiatrophy 799.89
  cerebellar 334.8
  face 349.89
      progressive 349.89
  fascia 728.9
  leg 728.2
  tongue 529.8
Hemiballism(us) 333.5
Hemiblock (cardiac) (heart) (left) 426.2
Hemicardia 746.89
Hemicephalus, hemicephaly 740.0
Hemichorea 333.5
Hemicrania 346.9 ☑
  congenital malformation 740.0
Hemidystrophy — see Hemiatrophy
Hemiectromelia 755.4
Hemihypalgesia (see also Disturbance, sensation)
      782.0
Hemihypertrophy (congenital) 759.89
  cranial 756.0
Hemihypesthesia (see also Disturbance,
      sensation) 782.0
Hemi-inattention 781.8

Hemimelia 755.4
  lower limb 755.30
      paraxial (complete) (incomplete) (intercalary)
          (terminal) 755.32
          fibula 755.37
          tibia 755.36
      transverse (complete) (partial) 755.31
  upper limb 755.20
      paraxial (complete) (incomplete) (intercalary)
          (terminal) 755.22
          radial 755.26
          ulnar 755.27
      transverse (complete) (partial) 755.21
Hemiparalysis (see also Hemiplegia) 342.9 ☑
Hemiparesis (see also Hemiplegia) 342.9 ☑
Hemiparesthesia (see also Disturbance,
      sensation) 782.0
Hemiplegia 342.9 ☑
  acute (see also Disease, cerebrovascular, acute)
      436
  alternans facialis 344.89
  apoplectic (see also Disease, cerebrovascular,
      acute) 436
      late effect or residual
          affecting
              dominant side 438.21
              nondominant side 438.22
              unspecified side 438.20
  arteriosclerotic 437.0
      late effect or residual
          affecting
              dominant side 438.21
              nondominant side 438.22
              unspecified side 438.20
  ascending (spinal) NEC 344.89
  attack (see also Disease, cerebrovascular,
      acute) 436
  brain, cerebral (current episode) 437.8
      congenital 343.1
  cerebral — see Hemiplegia, brain
  congenital (cerebral) (spastic) (spinal) 343.1
  conversion neurosis (hysterical) 300.11
  cortical — see Hemiplegia, brain
  due to
      arteriosclerosis 437.0
          late effect or residual
              affecting
                  dominant side 438.21
                  nondominant side 438.22
                  unspecified side 438.20
      cerebrovascular lesion (see also Disease,
          cerebrovascular, acute) 436
          late effect
              affecting
                  dominant side 438.21
                  nondominant side 438.22
                  unspecified side 438.20
  embolic (current) (see also Embolism, brain)
      434.1 ☑
      late effect
          affecting
              dominant side 438.21
              nondominant side 438.22
              unspecified side 438.20
  flaccid 342.0 ☑
  hypertensive (current episode) 437.8
  infantile (postnatal) 343.4
  late effect
      birth injury, intracranial or spinal 343.4
      cerebrovascular lesion — see Late effect(s)
          (of) cerebrovascular disease
      viral encephalitis 139.0
  middle alternating NEC 344.89
  newborn NEC 767.0
  seizure (current episode) (see also Disease,
      cerebrovascular, acute) 436
  spastic 342.1 ☑
      congenital or infantile 343.1
  specified NEC 342.8 ☑
  thrombotic (current) (see also Thrombosis,
      brain) 434.0 ☑
      late effect — see Late effect(s) (of)
          cerebrovascular disease
Hemisection, spinal cord — see Fracture,
      vertebra, by site, with spinal cord injury

Hemispasm 781.0
  facial 781.0
Hemispatial neglect 781.8
Hemisporosis 117.9
Hemitremor 781.0
Hemivertebra 756.14
Hemobilia 576.8
Hemocholecyst 575.8
Hemochromatosis (acquired) (diabetic)
      (hereditary) (liver) (myocardium) (primary)
      (idiopathic) (secondary) 275.0
  with refractory anemia 238.7   ▲
Hemodialysis V56.0
Hemoglobin — see also condition
  abnormal (disease) — see Disease, hemoglobin
  AS genotype 282.5
  fetal, hereditary persistence 282.7
  high-oxygen-affinity 289.0
  low NEC 285.9
  S (Hb-S), heterozygous 282.5
Hemoglobinemia 283.2
  due to blood transfusion NEC 999.8
      bone marrow 996.85
  paroxysmal 283.2
Hemoglobinopathy (mixed) (see also Disease,
      hemoglobin) 282.7
  with thalassemia 282.49
  sickle-cell 282.60
      with thalassemia (without crisis) 282.41
          with
              crisis 282.42
              vaso-occlusive pain 282.42
Hemoglobinuria, hemoglobinuric 791.2
  with anemia, hemolytic, acquired (chronic)
      NEC 283.2
  cold (agglutinin) (paroxysmal) (with Raynaud's
      syndrome) 283.2
  due to
      exertion 283.2
      hemolysis (from external causes) NEC 283.2
  exercise 283.2
  fever (malaria) 084.8
  infantile 791.2
  intermittent 283.2
  malarial 084.8
  march 283.2
  nocturnal (paroxysmal) 283.2
  paroxysmal (cold) (nocturnal) 283.2
Hemolymphangioma (M9175/0) 228.1
Hemolysis
  fetal — see Jaundice, fetus or newborn
  intravascular (disseminated) NEC 286.6
      with
          abortion — see Abortion, by type, with
              hemorrhage, delayed or excessive
          ectopic pregnancy (see also categories
              633.0-633.9) 639.1
          hemorrhage of pregnancy 641.3 ☑
              affecting fetus or newborn 762.1
          molar pregnancy (see also categories 630-
              632) 639.1
      acute 283.2
      following
          abortion 639.1
          ectopic or molar pregnancy 639.1
  neonatal — see Jaundice, fetus or newborn
  transfusion NEC 999.8
      bone marrow 996.85
Hemolytic — see also condition
  anemia — see Anemia, hemolytic
  uremic syndrome 283.11
Hemometra 621.4
Hemopericardium (with effusion) 423.0
  newborn 772.8
  traumatic (see also Hemothorax, traumatic)
      860.2
      with open wound into thorax 860.3
Hemoperitoneum 568.81
  infectional (see also Peritonitis) 567.29   ▲
  traumatic — see Injury, internal, peritoneum

☑ Additional Digit Required — Refer to the Tabular List (Numeric Code Section) for Additional Digit Selection

Hemophilia (familial) (hereditary) 286.0
  A 286.0
    carrier (asymptomatic) V83.01
      symptomatic V83.02
  acquired 286.5
  B (Leyden) 286.1
  C 286.2
  calcipriva (*see also* Fibrinolysis) 286.7
  classical 286.0
  nonfamilial 286.7
  secondary 286.5
  vascular 286.4
Hemophilus influenzae NEC 041.5
  arachnoiditis (basic) (brain) (spinal) 320.0
    late effect — *see* category 326
  bronchopneumonia 482.2
  cerebral ventriculitis 320.0
    late effect — *see* category 326
  cerebrospinal inflammation 320.0
    late effect — *see* category 326
  infection NEC 041.5
  leptomeningitis 320.0
    late effect — *see* category 326
  meningitis (cerebral) (cerebrospinal) (spinal)
    320.0
    late effect — *see* category 326
  meningomyelitis 320.0
    late effect — *see* category 326
  pachymeningitis (adhesive) (fibrous)
    (hemorrhagic) (hypertrophic) (spinal)
    320.0
    late effect — *see* category 326
  pneumonia (broncho-) 482.2
Hemophthalmos 360.43
Hemopneumothorax (*see also* Hemothorax) 511.8
  traumatic 860.4
    with open wound into thorax 860.5
Hemoptysis 786.3
  due to Paragonimus (westermani) 121.2
  newborn 770.3
  tuberculous (*see also* Tuberculosis, pulmonary)
    011.9 ☑
Hemorrhage, hemorrhagic (nontraumatic) 459.0
  abdomen 459.0
  accidental (antepartum) 641.2 ☑
    affecting fetus or newborn 762.1
  adenoid 474.8
  adrenal (capsule) (gland) (medulla) 255.4
    newborn 772.5
  after labor — *see* Hemorrhage, postpartum
  alveolar
    lung, newborn 770.3
    process 525.8
  alveolus 525.8
  amputation stump (surgical) 998.11
    secondary, delayed 997.69
  anemia (chronic) 280.0
    acute 285.1
  antepartum — *see* Hemorrhage, pregnancy
  anus (sphincter) 569.3
  apoplexy (stroke) 432.9
  arachnoid — *see* Hemorrhage, subarachnoid
  artery NEC 459.0
    brain (*see also* Hemorrhage, brain) 431
    middle meningeal — *see* Hemorrhage,
      subarachnoid
  basilar (ganglion) (*see also* Hemorrhage, brain)
    431
  bladder 596.8
  blood dyscrasia 289.9
  bowel 578.9
    newborn 772.4
  brain (miliary) (nontraumatic) 431
    with
      birth injury 767.0
      arachnoid — *see* Hemorrhage, subarachnoid
    due to
      birth injury 767.0
      rupture of aneurysm (congenital) (*see*
        also Hemorrhage, subarachnoid)
        430
        mycotic 431
        syphilis 094.89
    epidural or extradural — *see* Hemorrhage,
      extradural

Hemorrhage, hemorrhagic — *continued*
  brain — *continued*
    fetus or newborn (anoxic) (hypoxic) (due to
      birth trauma) (nontraumatic) 767.0
      intraventricular 772.10
        grade I 772.11
        grade II 772.12
        grade III 772.13
        grade IV 772.14
    iatrogenic 997.02
    postoperative 997.02
    puerperal, postpartum, childbirth 674.0 ☑
    stem 431
    subarachnoid, arachnoid, or meningeal —
      see Hemorrhage, subarachnoid
    subdural — *see* Hemorrhage, subdural
    traumatic NEC 853.0 ☑

> *Note — Use the following fifth-digit*
> *subclassification with categories 851-854:*
>
> 0   *unspecified state of consciousness*
> 1   *with no loss of consciousness*
> 2   *with brief [less than one hour] loss of*
>   *consciousness*
> 3   *with moderate [1-24 hours] loss of*
>   *consciousness*
> 4   *with prolonged [more than 24 hours]*
>   *loss of consciousness and return to pre-*
>   *existing conscious level*
> 5   *with prolonged [more than 24 hours]*
>   *loss of consciousness, without return to*
>   *pre-existing conscious level*
>   *Use fifth-digit 5 to designate when a patient*
>   *is unconscious and dies before*
>   *regaining consciousness, regardless of*
>   *the duration of the loss of*
>   *consciousness*
> 6   *with loss of consciousness of*
>   *unspecified duration*
> 9   *with concussion, unspecified*

    with
      cerebral
        contusion — *see* Contusion, brain
        laceration — *see* Laceration, brain
      open intracranial wound 853.1 ☑
      skull fracture — *see* Fracture, skull,
        by site
    extradural or epidural 852.4 ☑
      with open intracranial wound 852.5 ☑
    subarachnoid 852.0 ☑
      with open intracranial wound 852.1 ☑
    subdural 852.2 ☑
      with open intracranial wound 852.3 ☑
  breast 611.79
  bronchial tube — *see* Hemorrhage, lung
  bronchopulmonary — *see* Hemorrhage, lung
  bronchus (cause unknown) (*see also*
    Hemorrhage, lung) 786.3
  bulbar (*see also* Hemorrhage, brain) 431
  bursa 727.89
  capillary 448.9
    primary 287.8
  capsular — *see* Hemorrhage, brain
  cardiovascular 429.89
  cecum 578.9
  cephalic (*see also* Hemorrhage, brain) 431
  cerebellar (*see also* Hemorrhage, brain) 431
  cerebellum (*see also* Hemorrhage, brain) 431
  cerebral (*see also* Hemorrhage, brain) 431
    fetus or newborn (anoxic) (traumatic) 767.0
  cerebromeningeal (*see also* Hemorrhage, brain)
    431
  cerebrospinal (*see also* Hemorrhage, brain) 431
  cerebrovascular accident — *see*   ●
    Hemorrhage, brain   ●
  cerebrum (*see also* Hemorrhage, brain) 431
  cervix (stump) (uteri) 622.8
  cesarean section wound 674.3 ☑
  chamber, anterior (eye) 364.41
  childbirth — *see* Hemorrhage, complicating,
    delivery
  choroid 363.61
    expulsive 363.62

Hemorrhage, hemorrhagic — *continued*
  ciliary body 364.41
  cochlea 386.8
  colon — *see* Hemorrhage, intestine
  complicating
    delivery 641.9 ☑
      affecting fetus or newborn 762.1
      associated with
        afibrinogenemia 641.3 ☑
          affecting fetus or newborn 763.89
        coagulation defect 641.3 ☑
          affecting fetus or newborn 763.89
        hyperfibrinolysis 641.3 ☑
          affecting fetus or newborn 763.89
        hypofibrinogenemia 641.3 ☑
          affecting fetus or newborn 763.89
      due to
        low-lying placenta 641.1 ☑
          affecting fetus or newborn 762.0
        placenta previa 641.1 ☑
          affecting fetus or newborn 762.0
        premature separation of placenta
          641.2 ☑
          affecting fetus or newborn 762.1
        retained
          placenta 666.0 ☑
          secundines 666.2 ☑
        trauma 641.8 ☑
          affecting fetus or newborn 763.89
        uterine leiomyoma 641.8 ☑
          affecting fetus or newborn 763.89
    surgical procedure 998.11
  concealed NEC 459.0
  congenital 772.9
  conjunctiva 372.72
    newborn 772.8
  cord, newborn 772.0
    slipped ligature 772.3
    stump 772.3
  corpus luteum (ruptured) 620.1
  cortical (*see also* Hemorrhage, brain) 431
  cranial 432.9
  cutaneous 782.7
    newborn 772.6
  cyst, pancreas 577.2
  cystitis — *see* Cystitis
  delayed
    with
      abortion — *see* Abortion, by type, with
        hemorrhage, delayed or excessive
      ectopic pregnancy (*see also* categories
        633.0-633.9) 639.1
      molar pregnancy (*see also* categories 630-
        632) 639.1
    following
      abortion 639.1
      ectopic or molar pregnancy 639.1
    postpartum 666.2 ☑
  diathesis (familial) 287.9
    newborn 776.0
  disease 287.9
    newborn 776.0
    specified type NEC 287.8
  disorder 287.9
    due to intrinsic circulating anticoagulants
      286.5
    specified type NEC 287.8
  due to
    any device, implant or graft (presence of)
      classifiable to 996.0-996.5 — *see*
      Complications, due to (presence of)
      any device, implant, or graft classified
      to 996.0-996.5 NEC
    intrinsic circulating anticoagulant 286.5
  duodenum, duodenal 537.89
    ulcer — *see* Ulcer, duodenum, with
      hemorrhage
  dura mater — *see* Hemorrhage, subdural
  endotracheal — *see* Hemorrhage, lung
  epicranial subaponeurotic (massive) 767.11
  epidural — *see* Hemorrhage, extradural
  episiotomy 674.3 ☑
  esophagus 530.82
    varix (*see also* Varix, esophagus, bleeding)
      456.0

2006 ICD-9-CM

☑ Additional Digit Required — Refer to the Tabular List (Numeric Code Section) for Additional Digit Selection
▶◀ Revised Text   ● New Line   ▲ Revised Code

October 2005 • Volume 2 — 165

Hemorrhage, hemorrhagic — *continued*
  excessive
    with
      abortion — *see* Abortion, by type, with
          hemorrhage, delayed or excessive
      ectopic pregnancy (*see also* categories
          633.0-633.9) 639.1
      molar pregnancy (*see also* categories 630-
          632) 639.1
    following
      abortion 639.1
      ectopic or molar pregnancy 639.1
  external 459.0
  extradural (traumatic) — *see also* Hemorrhage,
      brain, traumatic, extradural
    birth injury 767.0
    fetus or newborn (anoxic) (traumatic) 767.0
    nontraumatic 432.0
  eye 360.43
    chamber (anterior) (aqueous) 364.41
    fundus 362.81
  eyelid 374.81
  fallopian tube 620.8
  fetomaternal 772.0
    affecting management of pregnancy or
        puerperium 656.0 ☑
  fetus, fetal 772.0
    from
      cut end of co-twin's cord 772.0
      placenta 772.0
      ruptured cord 772.0
      vasa previa 772.0
    into
      co-twin 772.0
      mother's circulation 772.0
        affecting management of pregnancy or
            puerperium 656.0 ☑
  fever (*see also* Fever, hemorrhagic) 065.9
    with renal syndrome 078.6
    arthropod-borne NEC 065.9
    Bangkok 065.4
    Crimean 065.0
    dengue virus 065.4
    epidemic 078.6
    Junin virus 078.7
    Korean 078.6
    Machupo virus 078.7
    mite-borne 065.8
    mosquito-borne 065.4
    Philippine 065.4
    Russian (Yaroslav) 078.6
    Singapore 065.4
    southeast Asia 065.4
    Thailand 065.4
    tick-borne NEC 065.3
  fibrinogenolysis (*see also* Fibrinolysis) 286.6
  fibrinolytic (acquired) (*see also* Fibrinolysis)
      286.6
  fontanel 767.19
  from tracheostomy stoma 519.09
  fundus, eye 362.81
  funis
    affecting fetus or newborn 772.0
    complicating delivery 663.8 ☑
  gastric (*see also* Hemorrhage, stomach) 578.9
  gastroenteric 578.9
    newborn 772.4
  gastrointestinal (tract) 578.9
    newborn 772.4
  genitourinary (tract) NEC 599.89
  gingiva 523.8
  globe 360.43
  gravidarum — *see* Hemorrhage, pregnancy
  gum 523.8
  heart 429.89
  hypopharyngeal (throat) 784.8
  intermenstrual 626.6
    irregular 626.6
    regular 626.5
  internal (organs) 459.0
    capsule (*see also* Hemorrhage, brain) 431
    ear 386.8
    newborn 772.8
  intestine 578.9
    congenital 772.4
    newborn 772.4

Hemorrhage, hemorrhagic — *continued*
  into
    bladder wall 596.7
    bursa 727.89
    corpus luysii (*see also* Hemorrhage, brain)
        431
  intra-abdominal 459.0
    during or following surgery 998.11
  intra-alveolar, newborn (lung) 770.3
  intracerebral (*see also* Hemorrhage, brain) 431
  intracranial NEC 432.9
    puerperal, postpartum, childbirth 674.0 ☑
    traumatic — *see* Hemorrhage, brain,
        traumatic
  intramedullary NEC 336.1
  intraocular 360.43
  intraoperative 998.11
  intrapartum — *see* Hemorrhage, complicating,
      delivery
  intrapelvic
    female 629.8
    male 459.0
  intraperitoneal 459.0
  intrapontine (*see also* Hemorrhage, brain) 431
  intrauterine 621.4
    complicating delivery — *see* Hemorrhage,
        complicating, delivery
    in pregnancy or childbirth — *see*
        Hemorrhage, pregnancy
    postpartum (*see also* Hemorrhage,
        postpartum) 666.1 ☑
  intraventricular (*see also* Hemorrhage, brain)
      431
    fetus or newborn (anoxic) (traumatic) 772.10
      grade I 772.11
      grade II 772.12
      grade III 772.13
      grade IV 772.14
  intravesical 596.7
  iris (postinfectional) (postinflammatory) (toxic)
      364.41
  joint (nontraumatic) 719.10
    ankle 719.17
    elbow 719.12
    foot 719.17
    forearm 719.13
    hand 719.14
    hip 719.15
    knee 719.16
    lower leg 719.16
    multiple sites 719.19
    pelvic region 719.15
    shoulder (region) 719.11
    specified site NEC 719.18
    thigh 719.15
    upper arm 719.12
    wrist 719.13
  kidney 593.81
  knee (joint) 719.16
  labyrinth 386.8
  leg NEC 459.0
  lenticular striate artery (*see also* Hemorrhage,
      brain) 431
  ligature, vessel 998.11
  liver 573.8
  lower extremity NEC 459.0
  lung 786.3
    newborn 770.3
    tuberculous (*see also* Tuberculosis,
        pulmonary) 011.9 ☑
  malaria 084.8
  marginal sinus 641.2 ☑
  massive subaponeurotic, birth injury 767.11
  maternal, affecting fetus or newborn 762.1
  mediastinum 786.3
  medulla (*see also* Hemorrhage, brain) 431
  membrane (brain) (*see also* Hemorrhage,
      subarachnoid) 430
    spinal cord — *see* Hemorrhage, spinal cord
  meninges, meningeal (brain) (middle) (*see also*
      Hemorrhage, subarachnoid) 430
    spinal cord — *see* Hemorrhage, spinal cord
  mesentery 568.81
  metritis 626.8
  midbrain (*see also* Hemorrhage, brain) 431
  mole 631

Hemorrhage, hemorrhagic — *continued*
  mouth 528.9
  mucous membrane NEC 459.0
    newborn 772.8
  muscle 728.89
  nail (subungual) 703.8
  nasal turbinate 784.7
    newborn 772.8
  nasopharynx 478.29
  navel, newborn 772.3
  newborn 772.9
    adrenal 772.5
    alveolar (lung) 770.3
    brain (anoxic) (hypoxic) (due to birth
        trauma) 767.0
    cerebral (anoxic) (hypoxic) (due to birth
        trauma) 767.0
    conjunctiva 772.8
    cutaneous 772.6
    diathesis 776.0
    due to vitamin K deficiency 776.0
    epicranial subaponeurotic (massive) 767.11
    gastrointestinal 772.4
    internal (organs) 772.8
    intestines 772.4
    intra-alveolar (lung) 770.3
    intracranial (from any perinatal cause) 767.0
    intraventricular (from any perinatal cause)
        772.10
      grade I 772.11
      grade II 772.12
      grade III 772.13
      grade IV 772.14
    lung 770.3
    pulmonary (massive) 770.3
    spinal cord, traumatic 767.4
    stomach 772.4
    subaponeurotic (massive) 767.11
    subarachnoid (from any perinatal cause)
        772.2
    subconjunctival 772.8
    subgaleal 767.11
    umbilicus 772.0
      slipped ligature 772.3
      vasa previa 772.0
  nipple 611.79
  nose 784.7
    newborn 772.8
  obstetrical surgical wound 674.3 ☑
  omentum 568.89
    newborn 772.4
  optic nerve (sheath) 377.42
  orbit 376.32
  ovary 620.1
  oviduct 620.8
  pancreas 577.8
  parathyroid (gland) (spontaneous) 252.8
  parturition — *see* Hemorrhage, complicating,
      delivery
  penis 607.82
  pericardium, pericarditis 423.0
  perineal wound (obstetrical) 674.3 ☑
  peritoneum, peritoneal 459.0
  peritonsillar tissue 474.8
    after operation on tonsils 998.11
    due to infection 475
  petechial 782.7
  pituitary (gland) 253.8
  placenta NEC 641.9 ☑
    affecting fetus or newborn 762.1
    from surgical or instrumental damage
        641.8 ☑
      affecting fetus or newborn 762.1
    previa 641.1 ☑
      affecting fetus or newborn 762.0
  pleura — *see* Hemorrhage, lung
  polioencephalitis, superior 265.1
  polymyositis — *see* Polymyositis
  pons (*see also* Hemorrhage, brain) 431
  pontine (*see also* Hemorrhage, brain) 431
  popliteal 459.0
  postcoital 626.7
  postextraction (dental) 998.11
  postmenopausal 627.1
  postnasal 784.7
  postoperative 998.11

☑ Additional Digit Required — Refer to the Tabular List (Numeric Code Section) for Additional Digit Selection

Hemorrhage, hemorrhagic — *continued*
　postpartum (atonic) (following delivery of placenta) 666.1 ☑
　　delayed or secondary (after 24 hours) 666.2 ☑
　　retained placenta 666.0 ☑
　　third stage 666.0 ☑
　pregnancy (concealed) 641.9 ☑
　　accidental 641.2 ☑
　　　affecting fetus or newborn 762.1
　　affecting fetus or newborn 762.1
　　before 22 completed weeks gestation 640.9 ☑
　　　affecting fetus or newborn 762.1
　　due to
　　　abruptio placenta 641.2 ☑
　　　　affecting fetus or newborn 762.1
　　　afibrinogenemia or other coagulation defect (conditions classifiable to 286.0-286.9) 641.3 ☑
　　　　affecting fetus or newborn 762.1
　　　coagulation defect 641.3 ☑
　　　　affecting fetus or newborn 762.1
　　　hyperfibrinolysis 641.3 ☑
　　　　affecting fetus or newborn 762.1
　　　hypofibrinogenemia 641.3 ☑
　　　　affecting fetus or newborn 762.1
　　　leiomyoma, uterus 641.8 ☑
　　　　affecting fetus or newborn 762.1
　　　low-lying placenta 641.1 ☑
　　　　affecting fetus or newborn 762.1
　　　marginal sinus (rupture) 641.2 ☑
　　　　affecting fetus or newborn 762.1
　　　placenta previa 641.1 ☑
　　　　affecting fetus or newborn 762.0
　　　premature separation of placenta (normally implanted) 641.2 ☑
　　　　affecting fetus or newborn 762.1
　　　threatened abortion 640.0 ☑
　　　　affecting fetus or newborn 762.1
　　　trauma 641.8 ☑
　　　　affecting fetus or newborn 762.1
　　early (before 22 completed weeks gestation) 640.9 ☑
　　　affecting fetus or newborn 762.1
　　previous, affecting management of pregnancy or childbirth V23.49
　　unavoidable — *see* Hemorrhage, pregnancy, due to placenta previa
　prepartum (mother) — *see* Hemorrhage, pregnancy
　preretinal, cause unspecified 362.81
　prostate 602.1
　puerperal (*see also* Hemorrhage, postpartum) 666.1 ☑
　pulmonary — *see also* Hemorrhage, lung
　　newborn (massive) 770.3
　　renal syndrome 446.21
　purpura (primary) (*see also* Purpura, thrombocytopenic) 287.39   ▲
　rectum (sphincter) 569.3
　recurring, following initial hemorrhage at time of injury 958.2
　renal 593.81
　　pulmonary syndrome 446.21
　respiratory tract (*see also* Hemorrhage, lung) 786.3
　retina, retinal (deep) (superficial) (vessels) 362.81
　　diabetic 250.5 ☑ *[362.01]*
　　due to birth injury 772.8
　retrobulbar 376.89
　retroperitoneal 459.0
　retroplacental (*see also* Placenta, separation) 641.2 ☑
　scalp 459.0
　　due to injury at birth 767.19
　scrotum 608.83
　secondary (nontraumatic) 459.0
　　following initial hemorrhage at time of injury 958.2
　seminal vesicle 608.83
　skin 782.7
　　newborn 772.6
　spermatic cord 608.83

Hemorrhage, hemorrhagic — *continued*
　spinal (cord) 336.1
　　aneurysm (ruptured) 336.1
　　　syphilitic 094.89
　　due to birth injury 767.4
　　fetus or newborn 767.4
　spleen 289.59
　spontaneous NEC 459.0
　　petechial 782.7
　stomach 578.9
　　newborn 772.4
　　ulcer — *see* Ulcer, stomach, with hemorrhage
　subaponeurotic, newborn 767.11
　　massive (birth injury) 767.11
　subarachnoid (nontraumatic) 430
　　fetus or newborn (anoxic) (traumatic) 772.2
　　puerperal, postpartum, childbirth 674.0 ☑
　　traumatic — *see* Hemorrhage, brain, traumatic, subarachnoid
　subconjunctival 372.72
　　due to birth injury 772.8
　　newborn 772.8
　subcortical (*see also* Hemorrhage, brain) 431
　subcutaneous 782.7
　subdiaphragmatic 459.0
　subdural (nontraumatic) 432.1
　　due to birth injury 767.0
　　fetus or newborn (anoxic) (hypoxic) (due to birth trauma) 767.0
　　puerperal, postpartum, childbirth 674.0 ☑
　　spinal 336.1
　　traumatic — *see* Hemorrhage, brain, traumatic, subdural
　subgaleal 767.11
　subhyaloid 362.81
　subperiosteal 733.99
　subretinal 362.81
　subtentorial (*see also* Hemorrhage, subdural) 432.1
　subungual 703.8
　　due to blood dyscrasia 287.8
　suprarenal (capsule) (gland) 255.4
　　fetus or newborn 772.5
　tentorium (traumatic) — *see also* Hemorrhage, brain, traumatic
　　fetus or newborn 767.0
　　nontraumatic — *see* Hemorrhage, subdural
　testis 608.83
　thigh 459.0
　third stage 666.0 ☑
　thorax — *see* Hemorrhage, lung
　throat 784.8
　thrombocythemia 238.7
　thymus (gland) 254.8
　thyroid (gland) 246.3
　　cyst 246.3
　tongue 529.8
　tonsil 474.8
　　postoperative 998.11
　tooth socket (postextraction) 998.11
　trachea — *see* Hemorrhage, lung
　traumatic — *see also* nature of injury
　　brain — *see* Hemorrhage, brain, traumatic
　　recurring or secondary (following initial hemorrhage at time of injury) 958.2
　tuberculous NEC (*see also* Tuberculosis, pulmonary) 011.9 ☑
　tunica vaginalis 608.83
　ulcer — *see* Ulcer, by site, with hemorrhage
　umbilicus, umbilical cord 772.0
　　after birth, newborn 772.3
　　complicating delivery 663.8 ☑
　　　affecting fetus or newborn 772.0
　　slipped ligature 772.3
　　stump 772.3
　unavoidable (due to placenta previa) 641.1 ☑
　　affecting fetus or newborn 762.0
　upper extremity 459.0
　urethra (idiopathic) 599.84
　uterus, uterine (abnormal) 626.9
　　climacteric 627.0
　　complicating delivery — *see* Hemorrhage, complicating delivery
　　due to
　　　intrauterine contraceptive device 996.76
　　　perforating uterus 996.32

Hemorrhage, hemorrhagic — *continued*
　uterus, uterine — *continued*
　　functional or dysfunctional 626.8
　　in pregnancy — *see* Hemorrhage, pregnancy
　　intermenstrual 626.6
　　　irregular 626.6
　　　regular 626.5
　　postmenopausal 627.1
　　postpartum (*see also* Hemorrhage, postpartum) 666.1 ☑
　　prepubertal 626.8
　　pubertal 626.3
　　puerperal (immediate) 666.1 ☑
　vagina 623.8
　vasa previa 663.5 ☑
　　affecting fetus or newborn 772.0
　vas deferens 608.83
　ventricular (*see also* Hemorrhage, brain) 431
　vesical 596.8
　viscera 459.0
　　newborn 772.8
　vitreous (humor) (intraocular) 379.23
　vocal cord 478.5
　vulva 624.8

Hemorrhoids (anus) (rectum) (without complication) 455.6
　bleeding, prolapsed, strangulated, or ulcerated NEC 455.8
　　external 455.5
　　internal 455.2
　complicated NEC 455.8
　complicating pregnancy and puerperium 671.8 ☑
　external 455.3
　　with complication NEC 455.5
　　bleeding, prolapsed, strangulated, or ulcerated 455.5
　　thrombosed 455.4
　internal 455.0
　　with complication NEC 455.2
　　bleeding, prolapsed, strangulated, or ulcerated 455.2
　　thrombosed 455.1
　residual skin tag 455.9
　sentinel pile 455.9
　thrombosed NEC 455.7
　　external 455.4
　　internal 455.1

Hemosalpinx 620.8

Hemosiderosis 275.0
　dietary 275.0
　pulmonary (idiopathic) 275.0 *[516.1]*
　transfusion NEC 999.8
　　bone marrow 996.85

Hemospermia 608.82

Hemothorax 511.8
　bacterial, nontuberculous 511.1
　newborn 772.8
　nontuberculous 511.8
　　bacterial 511.1
　pneumococcal 511.1
　postoperative 998.11
　staphylococcal 511.1
　streptococcal 511.1
　traumatic 860.2
　　with
　　　open wound into thorax 860.3
　　　pneumothorax 860.4
　　　　with open wound into thorax 860.5
　tuberculous (*see also* Tuberculosis, pleura) 012.0 ☑

Hemotympanum 385.89

Hench-Rosenberg syndrome (palindromic arthritis) (*see also* Rheumatism, palindromic) 719.3 ☑

Henle's warts 371.41

Henoch (-Schönlein)
　disease or syndrome (allergic purpura) 287.0
　purpura (allergic) 287.0

Henpue, henpuye 102.6

Heparitinuria 277.5

Hepar lobatum 095.3

Hepatalgia 573.8

Hepatic — *see also* condition
　flexure syndrome 569.89

☑ Additional Digit Required — Refer to the Tabular List (Numeric Code Section) for Additional Digit Selection
▶◀ Revised Text   ● New Line   ▲ Revised Code

2006 ICD-9-CM   **October 2005 • Volume 2 — 167**

Hepatitis 573.3
  acute (see also Necrosis, liver) 570
    alcoholic 571.1
    infective 070.1
      with hepatic coma 070.0
  alcoholic 571.1
  amebic — see Abscess, liver, amebic
  anicteric (acute) — see Hepatitis, viral
  antigen-associated (HAA) — see Hepatitis, viral,
      type B
  Australian antigen (positive) — see Hepatitis,
      viral, type B
  catarrhal (acute) 070.1
    with hepatic coma 070.0
    chronic 571.40
    newborn 070.1
      with hepatic coma 070.0
  chemical 573.3
  cholangiolitic 573.8
  cholestatic 573.8
  chronic 571.40
    active 571.49
      viral — see Hepatitis, viral
    aggressive 571.49
    persistent 571.41
    viral — see Hepatitis, viral
  cytomegalic inclusion virus 078.5 [573.1]
  diffuse 573.3
  "dirty needle" — see Hepatitis, viral
  drug-induced 573.3
  due to
    Coxsackie 074.8 [573.1]
    cytomegalic inclusion virus 078.5 [573.1]
    infectious mononucleosis 075 [573.1]
    malaria 084.9 [573.2]
    mumps 072.71
    secondary syphilis 091.62
    toxoplasmosis (acquired) 130.5
      congenital (active) 771.2
  epidemic — see Hepatitis, viral, type A
  fetus or newborn 774.4
  fibrous (chronic) 571.49
    acute 570
  from injection, inoculation, or transfusion
      (blood) (other substance) (plasma) (serum)
      (onset within 8 months after
      administration) — see Hepatitis, viral
  fulminant (viral) (see also Hepatitis, viral) 070.9
    with hepatic coma 070.6
    type A 070.1
      with hepatic coma 070.0
    type B — see Hepatitis, viral, type B
  giant cell (neonatal) 774.4
  hemorrhagic 573.8
  history of   ●
    B V12.09   ●
    C V12.09   ●
  homologous serum — see Hepatitis, viral
  hypertrophic (chronic) 571.49
    acute 570
  infectious, infective (acute) (chronic) (subacute)
      070.1
    with hepatic coma 070.0
  inoculation — see Hepatitis, viral
  interstitial (chronic) 571.49
    acute 570
  lupoid 571.49
  malarial 084.9 [573.2]
  malignant (see also Necrosis, liver) 570
  neonatal (toxic) 774.4
  newborn 774.4
  parenchymatous (acute) (see also Necrosis,
      liver) 570
  peliosis 573.3
  persistent, chronic 571.41
  plasma cell 571.49
  postimmunization — see Hepatitis, viral
  postnecrotic 571.49
  posttransfusion — see Hepatitis, viral
  recurrent 571.49
  septic 573.3
  serum — see Hepatitis, viral
    carrier (suspected of) V02.61
  subacute (see also Necrosis, liver) 570
  suppurative (diffuse) 572.0

Hepatitis — continued
  syphilitic (late) 095.3
    congenital (early) 090.0 [573.2]
      late 090.5 [573.2]
    secondary 091.62
  toxic (noninfectious) 573.3
    fetus or newborn 774.4
  tuberculous (see also Tuberculosis) 017.9 ☑
  viral (acute) (anicteric) (cholangiolitic)
      (cholestatic) (chronic) (subacute) 070.9
    with hepatic coma 070.6
    AU-SH type virus — see Hepatitis, viral,
        type B
    Australian antigen — see Hepatitis, viral,
        type B
    B-antigen — see Hepatitis, viral, type B
    Coxsackie 074.8 [573.1]
    cytomegalic inclusion 078.5 [573.1]
    IH (virus) — see Hepatitis, viral, type A
    infectious hepatitis — see Hepatitis, viral,
        type A
    serum hepatitis virus — see Hepatitis, viral,
        type B
    SH — see Hepatitis, viral, type B
    specified type NEC 070.59
      with hepatic coma 070.49
    type A 070.1
      with hepatic coma 070.0
    type B (acute) 070.30
      with
        hepatic coma 070.20
          with hepatitis delta 070.21
        hepatitis delta 070.31
          with hepatic coma 070.21
      carrier status V02.61
      chronic 070.32
        with
          hepatic coma 070.22
            with hepatitis delta 070.23
          hepatitis delta 070.33
            with hepatic coma 070.23
    type C
      acute 070.51
        with hepatic coma 070.41
      carrier status V02.62
      chronic 070.54
        with hepatic coma 070.44
      unspecified 070.70
        with hepatic coma 070.71
    type delta (with hepatitis B carrier state)
        070.52
      with
        active hepatitis B disease — see
            Hepatitis, viral, type B
        hepatic coma 070.42
    type E 070.53
      with hepatic coma 070.43
    vaccination and inoculation (prophylactic)
        V05.3
    Waldenström's (lupoid hepatitis) 571.49

Hepatization, lung (acute) — see also
    Pneumonia, lobar
  chronic (see also Fibrosis, lung) 515
Hepatoblastoma (M8970/3) 155.0
Hepatocarcinoma (M8170/3) 155.0
Hepatocholangiocarcinoma (M8180/3) 155.0
Hepatocholangioma, benign (M8180/0) 211.5
Hepatocholangitis 573.8
Hepatocystitis (see also Cholecystitis) 575.10
Hepatodystrophy 570
Hepatolenticular degeneration 275.1
Hepatolithiasis — see Choledocholithiasis
Hepatoma (malignant) (M8170/3) 155.0
  benign (M8170/0) 211.5
  congenital (M8970/3) 155.0
  embryonal (M8970/3) 155.0
Hepatomegalia glycogenica diffusa 271.0
Hepatomegaly (see also Hypertrophy, liver) 789.1
  congenital 751.69
    syphilitic 090.0
  due to Clonorchis sinensis 121.1
  Gaucher's 272.7
  syphilitic (congenital) 090.0
Hepatoptosis 573.8
Hepatorrhexis 573.8

Hepatosis, toxic 573.8
Hepatosplenomegaly 571.8
  due to S. japonicum 120.2
  hyperlipemic (Bürger-Grutz type) 272.3
Herald patch 696.3
Hereditary — see condition
Heredodegeneration 330.9
  macular 362.70
Heredopathia atactica polyneuritiformis 356.3
Heredosyphilis (see also Syphilis, congenital)
    090.9
Hermaphroditism (true) 752.7
  with specified chromosomal anomaly — see
      Anomaly, chromosomes, sex
Hernia, hernial (acquired) (recurrent) 553.9
  with
    gangrene (obstructed) NEC 551.9
    obstruction NEC 552.9
    and gangrene 551.9
  abdomen (wall) — see Hernia, ventral
  abdominal, specified site NEC 553.8
    with
      gangrene (obstructed) 551.8
      obstruction 552.8
      and gangrene 551.8
  appendix 553.8
    with
      gangrene (obstructed) 551.8
      obstruction 552.8
      and gangrene 551.8
  bilateral (inguinal) — see Hernia, inguinal
  bladder (sphincter)
    congenital (female) (male) 756.71
    female (see also Cystocele, female) 618.01
    male 596.8
  brain 348.4
    congenital 742.0
  broad ligament 553.8
  cartilage, vertebral — see Displacement,
      intervertebral disc
  cerebral 348.4
    congenital 742.0
    endaural 742.0
  ciliary body 364.8
    traumatic 871.1
  colic 553.9
    with
      gangrene (obstructed) 551.9
      obstruction 552.9
      and gangrene 551.9
  colon 553.9
    with
      gangrene (obstructed) 551.9
      obstruction 552.9
      and gangrene 551.9
  colostomy (stoma) 569.69
  Cooper's (retroperitoneal) 553.8
    with
      gangrene (obstructed) 551.8
      obstruction 552.8
      and gangrene 551.8
  crural — see Hernia, femoral
  diaphragm, diaphragmatic 553.3
    with
      gangrene (obstructed) 551.3
      obstruction 552.3
      and gangrene 551.3
    congenital 756.6
    due to gross defect of diaphragm 756.6
    traumatic 862.0
      with open wound into cavity 862.1
  direct (inguinal) — see Hernia, inguinal
  disc, intervertebral — see Displacement,
      intervertebral disc
  diverticulum, intestine 553.9
    with
      gangrene (obstructed) 551.9
      obstruction 552.9
      and gangrene 551.9
  double (inguinal) — see Hernia, inguinal
  due to adhesion with obstruction 560.81   ●
  duodenojejunal 553.8
    with
      gangrene (obstructed) 551.8
      obstruction 552.8
      and gangrene 551.8

☑ Additional Digit Required — Refer to the Tabular List (Numeric Code Section) for Additional Digit Selection

Hernia, hernial — *continued*
  en glissade — *see* Hernia, inguinal
  enterostomy (stoma) 569.69
  epigastric 553.29
    with
      gangrene (obstruction) 551.29
      obstruction 552.29
        and gangrene 551.29
    recurrent 553.21
      with
        gangrene (obstructed) 551.21
        obstruction 552.21
          and gangrene 551.21
  esophageal hiatus (sliding) 553.3
    with
      gangrene (obstructed) 551.3
      obstruction 552.3
        and gangrene 551.3
    congenital 750.6
  external (inguinal) — *see* Hernia, inguinal
  fallopian tube 620.4
  fascia 728.89
  fat 729.30
    eyelid 374.34
    orbital 374.34
    pad 729.30
      eye, eyelid 374.34
      knee 729.31
      orbit 374.34
      popliteal (space) 729.31
      specified site NEC 729.39
  femoral (unilateral) 553.00
    with
      gangrene (obstructed) 551.00
      obstruction 552.00
        with gangrene 551.00
    bilateral 553.02
      gangrenous (obstructed) 551.02
      obstructed 552.02
        with gangrene 551.02
      recurrent 553.03
        gangrenous (obstructed) 551.03
        obstructed 552.03
          with gangrene 551.03
    recurrent (unilateral) 553.01
      bilateral 553.03
        gangrenous (obstructed) 551.03
        obstructed 552.03
          with gangrene 551.03
      gangrenous (obstructed) 551.01
      obstructed 552.01
        with gangrene 551.01
  foramen
    Bochdalek 553.3
      with
        gangrene (obstructed) 551.3
        obstruction 552.3
          and gangrene 551.3
      congenital 756.6
    magnum 348.4
    Morgagni, Morgagnian 553.3
      with
        gangrene 551.3
        obstruction 552.3
          and gangrene 551.3
      congenital 756.6
  funicular (umbilical) 553.1
    with
      gangrene (obstructed) 551.1
      obstruction 552.1
        and gangrene 551.1
    spermatic cord — *see* Hernia, inguinal
  gangrenous — *see* Hernia, by site, with
    gangrene
  gastrointestinal tract 553.9
    with
      gangrene (obstructed) 551.9
      obstruction 552.9
        and gangrene 551.9
  gluteal — *see* Hernia, femoral
  Gruber's (internal mesogastric) 553.8
    with
      gangrene (obstructed) 551.8
      obstruction 552.8
        and gangrene 551.8
  Hesselbach's 553.8
    with
      gangrene (obstructed) 551.8

Hernia, hernial — *continued*
  Hesselbach's — *continued*
    with — *continued*
      obstruction 552.8
        and gangrene 551.8
  hiatal (esophageal) (sliding) 553.3
    with
      gangrene (obstructed) 551.3
      obstruction 552.3
        and gangrene 551.3
    congenital 750.6
  incarcerated (*see also* Hernia, by site, with
    obstruction) 552.9
    gangrenous (*see also* Hernia, by site, with
      gangrene) 551.9
  incisional 553.21
    with
      gangrene (obstructed) 551.21
      obstruction 552.21
        and gangrene 551.21
    lumbar — *see* Hernia, lumbar
    recurrent 553.21
      with
        gangrene (obstructed) 551.21
        obstruction 552.21
          and gangrene 551.21
  indirect (inguinal) — *see* Hernia, inguinal
  infantile — *see* Hernia, inguinal
  infrapatellar fat pad 729.31
  inguinal (direct) (double) (encysted) (external)
    (funicular) (indirect) (infantile) (internal)
    (interstitial) (oblique) (scrotal) (sliding)
    550.9 ☑

> *Note* — *Use the following fifth-digit*
> *subclassification with category 550:*
>
> 0   *unilateral or unspecified (not specified*
>   *as recurrent)*
> 1   *unilateral or unspecified, recurrent*
> 2   *bilateral (not specified as recurrent)*
> 3   *bilateral, recurrent*

    with
      gangrene (obstructed) 550.0 ☑
      obstruction 550.1 ☑
        and gangrene 550.0 ☑
  internal 553.8
    with
      gangrene (obstructed) 551.8
      obstruction 552.8
        and gangrene 551.8
    inguinal — *see* Hernia, inguinal
  interstitial 553.9
    with
      gangrene (obstructed) 551.9
      obstruction 552.9
        and gangrene 551.9
    inguinal — *see* Hernia, inguinal
  intervertebral cartilage or disc — *see*
    Displacement, intervertebral disc
  intestine, intestinal 553.9
    with
      gangrene (obstructed) 551.9
      obstruction 552.9
        and gangrene 551.9
  intra-abdominal 553.9
    with
      gangrene (obstructed) 551.9
      obstruction 552.9
        and gangrene 551.9
  intraparietal 553.9
    with
      gangrene (obstructed) 551.9
      obstruction 552.9
        and gangrene 551.9
  iris 364.8
    traumatic 871.1
  irreducible (*see also* Hernia, by site, with
    obstruction) 552.9
    gangrenous (with obstruction) (*see also*
      Hernia, by site, with gangrene) 551.9
  ischiatic 553.8
    with
      gangrene (obstructed) 551.8
      obstruction 552.8
        and gangrene 551.8

Hernia, hernial — *continued*
  ischiorectal 553.8
    with
      gangrene (obstructed) 551.8
      obstruction 552.8
        and gangrene 551.8
  lens 379.32
    traumatic 871.1
  linea
    alba — *see* Hernia, epigastric
    semilunaris — *see* Hernia, spigelian
  Littre's (diverticular) 553.9
    with
      gangrene (obstructed) 551.9
      obstruction 552.9
        and gangrene 551.9
  lumbar 553.8
    with
      gangrene (obstructed) 551.8
      obstruction 552.8
        and gangrene 551.8
    intervertebral disc 722.10
  lung (subcutaneous) 518.89
    congenital 748.69
  mediastinum 519.3
  mesenteric (internal) 553.8
    with
      gangrene (obstructed) 551.8
      obstruction 552.8
        and gangrene 551.8
  mesocolon 553.8
    with
      gangrene (obstructed) 551.8
      obstruction 552.8
        and gangrene 551.8
  muscle (sheath) 728.89
  nucleus pulposus — *see* Displacement,
    intervertebral disc
  oblique (inguinal) — *see* Hernia, inguinal
  obstructive (*see also* Hernia, by site, with
    obstruction) 552.9
    gangrenous (with obstruction) (*see also*
      Hernia, by site, with gangrene) 551.9
  obturator 553.8
    with
      gangrene (obstructed) 551.8
      obstruction 552.8
        and gangrene 551.8
  omental 553.8
    with
      gangrene (obstructed) 551.8
      obstruction 552.8
        and gangrene 551.8
  orbital fat (pad) 374.34
  ovary 620.4
  oviduct 620.4
  paracolostomy (stoma) 569.69
  paraduodenal 553.8
    with
      gangrene (obstructed) 551.8
      obstruction 552.8
        and gangrene 551.8
  paraesophageal 553.3
    with
      gangrene (obstructed) 551.3
      obstruction 552.3
        and gangrene 551.3
    congenital 750.6
  parahiatal 553.3
    with
      gangrene (obstructed) 551.3
      obstruction 552.3
        and gangrene 551.3
  paraumbilical 553.1
    with
      gangrene (obstructed) 551.1
      obstruction 552.1
        and gangrene 551.1
  parietal 553.9
    with
      gangrene (obstructed) 551.9
      obstruction 552.9
        and gangrene 551.9
  perineal 553.8
    with
      gangrene (obstructed) 551.8

Hernia, hernial — continued
  perineal — continued
    with — continued
      obstruction 552.8
        and gangrene 551.8
  peritoneal sac, lesser 553.8
    with
      gangrene (obstructed) 551.8
      obstruction 552.8
        and gangrene 551.8
  popliteal fat pad 729.31
  postoperative 553.21
    with
      gangrene (obstructed) 551.21
      obstruction 552.21
        and gangrene 551.21
  pregnant uterus 654.4 ☑
  prevesical 596.8
  properitoneal 553.8
    with
      gangrene (obstructed) 551.8
      obstruction 552.8
        and gangrene 551.8
  pudendal 553.8
    with
      gangrene (obstructed) 551.8
      obstruction 552.8
        and gangrene 551.8
  rectovaginal 618.6
  retroperitoneal 553.8
    with
      gangrene (obstructed) 551.8
      obstruction 552.8
        and gangrene 551.8
  Richter's (parietal) 553.9
    with
      gangrene (obstructed) 551.9
      obstruction 552.9
        and gangrene 551.9
  Rieux's, Riex's (retrocecal) 553.8
    with
      gangrene (obstructed) 551.8
      obstruction 552.8
        and gangrene 551.8
  sciatic 553.8
    with
      gangrene (obstructed) 551.8
      obstruction 552.8
        and gangrene 551.8
  scrotum, scrotal — see Hernia, inguinal
  sliding (inguinal) — see also Hernia, inguinal
    hiatus — see Hernia, hiatal
  spigelian 553.29
    with
      gangrene (obstructed) 551.29
      obstruction 552.29
        and gangrene 551.29
  spinal (see also Spina bifida) 741.9 ☑
    with hydrocephalus 741.0 ☑
  strangulated (see also Hernia, by site, with
    obstruction) 552.9
    gangrenous (with obstruction) (see also
      Hernia, by site, with gangrene) 551.9
  supraumbilicus (linea alba) — see Hernia,
    epigastric
  tendon 727.9
  testis (nontraumatic) 550.9 ☑
    meaning
      scrotal hernia 550.9 ☑
      symptomatic late syphilis 095.8
  Treitz's (fossa) 553.8
    with
      gangrene (obstructed) 551.8
      obstruction 552.8
        and gangrene 551.8
  tunica
    albuginea 608.89
    vaginalis 752.89
  umbilicus, umbilical 553.1
    with
      gangrene (obstructed) 551.1
      obstruction 552.1
        and gangrene 551.1
  ureter 593.89
    with obstruction 593.4

Hernia, hernial — continued
  uterus 621.8
    pregnant 654.4 ☑
  vaginal (posterior) 618.6
  Velpeau's (femoral) (see also Hernia, femoral)
    553.00
  ventral 553.20
    with
      gangrene (obstructed) 551.20
      obstruction 552.20
        and gangrene 551.20
    incisional 553.21
    recurrent 553.21
      with
        gangrene (obstructed) 551.21
        obstruction 552.21
          and gangrene 551.21
  vesical
    congenital (female) (male) 756.71
    female (see also Cystocele, female) 618.01
    male 596.8
  vitreous (into anterior chamber) 379.21
    traumatic 871.1

Herniation — see also Hernia
  brain (stem) 348.4
  cerebral 348.4
  gastric mucosa (into duodenal bulb) 537.89
  mediastinum 519.3
  nucleus pulposus — see Displacement,
    intervertebral disc

Herpangina 074.0
Herpes, herpetic 054.9
  auricularis (zoster) 053.71
    simplex 054.73
  blepharitis (zoster) 053.20
    simplex 054.41
  circinate 110.5
  circinatus 110.5
    bullous 694.5
  conjunctiva (simplex) 054.43
    zoster 053.21
  cornea (simplex) 054.43
    disciform (simplex) 054.43
    zoster 053.21
  encephalitis 054.3
  eye (zoster) 053.29
    simplex 054.40
  eyelid (zoster) 053.20
    simplex 054.41
  febrilis 054.9
  fever 054.9
  geniculate ganglionitis 053.11
  genital, genitalis 054.10
    specified site NEC 054.19
  gestationis 646.8 ☑
  gingivostomatitis 054.2
  iridocyclitis (simplex) 054.44
    zoster 053.22
  iris (any site) 695.1
  iritis (simplex) 054.44
  keratitis (simplex) 054.43
    dendritic 054.42
    disciform 054.43
    interstitial 054.43
    zoster 053.21
  keratoconjunctivitis (simplex) 054.43
    zoster 053.21
  labialis 054.9
    meningococcal 036.89
  lip 054.9
  meningitis (simplex) 054.72
    zoster 053.0
  ophthalmicus (zoster) 053.20
    simplex 054.40
  otitis externa (zoster) 053.71
    simplex 054.73
  penis 054.13
  perianal 054.10
  pharyngitis 054.79
  progenitalis 054.10
  scrotum 054.19
  septicemia 054.5
  simplex 054.9
    complicated 054.8
      ophthalmic 054.40
      specified NEC 054.49

Herpes, herpetic — continued
  simplex — continued
    complicated — continued
      specified NEC 054.79
    congenital 771.2
    external ear 054.73
    keratitis 054.43
      dendritic 054.42
    meningitis 054.72
    neuritis 054.79
    specified complication NEC 054.79
      ophthalmic 054.49
    visceral 054.71
  stomatitis 054.2
  tonsurans 110.0
    maculosus (of Hebra) 696.3
  visceral 054.71
  vulva 054.12
  vulvovaginitis 054.11
  whitlow 054.6
  zoster 053.9
    auricularis 053.71
    complicated 053.8
      specified NEC 053.79
    conjunctiva 053.21
    cornea 053.21
    ear 053.71
    eye 053.29
    geniculate 053.11
    keratitis 053.21
      interstitial 053.21
    neuritis 053.10
    ophthalmicus(a) 053.20
    oticus 053.71
    otitis externa 053.71
    specified complication NEC 053.79
    specified site NEC 053.9
  zosteriform, intermediate type 053.9

Herrick's
  anemia (hemoglobin S disease) 282.61
  syndrome (hemoglobin S disease) 282.61
Hers' disease (glycogenosis VI) 271.0
Herter's infantilism (nontropical sprue) 579.0
Herter (-Gee) disease or syndrome (nontropical
  sprue) 579.0
Herxheimer's disease (diffuse idiopathic
  cutaneous atrophy) 701.8
Herxheimer's reaction 995.0
Hesselbach's hernia — see Hernia, Hesselbach's
Heterochromia (congenital) 743.46
  acquired 364.53
  cataract 366.33
  cyclitis 364.21
  hair 704.3
  iritis 364.21
  retained metallic foreign body 360.62
    magnetic 360.52
  uveitis 364.21
Heterophoria 378.40
  alternating 378.45
  vertical 378.43
Heterophyes, small intestine 121.6
Heterophyiasis 121.6
Heteropsia 368.8
Heterotopia, heterotopic — see also Malposition,
  congenital
  cerebralis 742.4
  pancreas, pancreatic 751.7
  spinalis 742.59
Heterotropia 378.30
  intermittent 378.20
    vertical 378.31
  vertical (constant) (intermittent) 378.31
Heubner's disease 094.89
Heubner-Herter disease or syndrome
  (nontropical sprue) 579.0
Hexadactylism 755.0 ☑
Heyd's syndrome (hepatorenal) 572.4
HGSIL (high grade squamous intraepithelial
  lesion) 795.04
Hibernoma (M8880/0) — see Lipoma

☑ Additional Digit Required — Refer to the Tabular List (Numeric Code Section) for Additional Digit Selection

Hiccough 786.8
  epidemic 078.89
  psychogenic 306.1
Hiccup (*see also* Hiccough) 786.8
Hicks (-Braxton) contractures 644.1 ☑
Hidden penis 752.65
Hidradenitis (axillaris) (suppurative) 705.83
Hidradenoma (nodular) (M8400/0) — *see also*
  Neoplasm, skin, benign
  clear cell (M8402/0) — *see* Neoplasm, skin,
    benign
  papillary (M8405/0) — *see* Neoplasm, skin,
    benign
Hidrocystoma (M8404/0) — *see* Neoplasm, skin,
  benign
High
  A₂ anemia 282.49
  altitude effects 993.2
    anoxia 993.2
    on
      ears 993.0
      sinuses 993.1
    polycythemia 289.0
  arch
    foot 755.67
    palate 750.26
  artery (arterial) tension (*see also* Hypertension)
    401.9
    without diagnosis of hypertension 796.2
  basal metabolic rate (BMR) 794.7
  blood pressure (*see also* Hypertension) 401.9
    incidental reading (isolated) (nonspecific), no
      diagnosis of hypertension 796.2
  compliance bladder 596.4
  diaphragm (congenital) 756.6
  frequency deafness (congenital) (regional) 389.8
  head at term 652.5 ☑
    affecting fetus or newborn 763.1
  output failure (cardiac) (*see also* Failure, heart)
    428.9
  oxygen-affinity hemoglobin 289.0
  palate 750.26
  risk
    behavior — *see* Problem
    cervical, human papillomavirus (HPV) DNA
      test positive 795.05
    family situation V61.9
      specified circumstance NEC V61.8
    individual NEC V62.89
    infant NEC V20.1
    patient taking drugs (prescribed) V67.51
      nonprescribed (*see also* Abuse, drugs,
        nondependent) 305.9 ☑
    pregnancy V23.9
      inadequate prenatal care V23.7
      specified problem NEC V23.89
  temperature (of unknown origin) (*see also*
    Pyrexia) 780.6
  thoracic rib 756.3
Hildenbrand's disease (typhus) 081.9
Hilger's syndrome 337.0
Hill diarrhea 579.1
Hilliard's lupus (*see also* Tuberculosis) 017.0 ☑
Hilum — *see* condition
Hip — *see* condition
Hippel's disease (retinocerebral angiomatosis)
  759.6
Hippus 379.49
Hirschfeld's disease (acute diabetes mellitus) (*see*
  also Diabetes) 250.0 ☑
Hirschsprung's disease or megacolon
  (congenital) 751.3
Hirsuties (*see also* Hypertrichosis) 704.1
Hirsutism (*see also* Hypertrichosis) 704.1
Hirudiniasis (external) (internal) 134.2
His-Werner disease (trench fever) 083.1
Hiss-Russell dysentery 004.1
Histamine cephalgia 346.2 ☑
Histidinemia 270.5
Histidinuria 270.5

Histiocytoma (M8832/0) — *see also* Neoplasm,
  skin, benign
  fibrous (M8830/0) — *see also* Neoplasm, skin,
    benign
    atypical (M8830/1) — *see* Neoplasm,
      connective tissue, uncertain behavior
    malignant (M8830/3) — *see* Neoplasm,
      connective tissue, malignant
Histiocytosis (acute) (chronic) (subacute) 277.89
  acute differentiated progressive (M9722/3)
    202.5 ☑
  cholesterol 277.89
  essential 277.89
  lipid, lipoid (essential) 272.7
  lipochrome (familial) 288.1
  malignant (M9720/3) 202.3 ☑
  X (chronic) 277.89
    acute (progressive) (M9722/3) 202.5 ☑
Histoplasmosis 115.90
  with
    endocarditis 115.94
    meningitis 115.91
    pericarditis 115.93
    pneumonia 115.95
    retinitis 115.92
    specified manifestation NEC 115.99
  African (due to Histoplasma duboisii) 115.10
    with
      endocarditis 115.14
      meningitis 115.11
      pericarditis 115.13
      pneumonia 115.15
      retinitis 115.12
      specified manifestation NEC 115.19
  American (due to Histoplasma capsulatum)
    115.00
    with
      endocarditis 115.04
      meningitis 115.01
      pericarditis 115.03
      pneumonia 115.05
      retinitis 115.02
      specified manifestation NEC 115.09
  Darling's — *see* Histoplasmosis, American
  large form (*see also* Histoplasmosis, African)
    115.10
  lung 115.05
  small form (*see also* Histoplasmosis, American)
    115.00
History (personal) **of**
  abuse
    emotional V15.42
    neglect V15.42
    physical V15.41
    sexual V15.41
  affective psychosis V11.1
  alcoholism V11.3
    specified as drinking problem (*see also*
      Abuse, drugs, nondependent) 305.0 ☑
  allergy to
    analgesic agent NEC V14.6
    anesthetic NEC V14.4
    antibiotic agent NEC V14.1
      penicillin V14.0
    anti-infective agent NEC V14.3
    diathesis V15.09
    drug V14.9
      specified type NEC V14.8
    eggs V15.03
    food additives V15.05
    insect bite V15.06
    latex V15.07
    medicinal agents V14.9
      specified type NEC V14.8
    milk products V15.02
    narcotic agent NEC V14.5
    nuts V15.05
      peanuts V15.01
    penicillin V14.0
    radiographic dye V15.08
    seafood V15.04
    serum V14.7
    specified food NEC V15.05
    specified nonmedicinal agents NEC V15.09
    spider bite V15.06
    sulfa V14.2

History (personal) **of** — *continued*
  allergy to — *continued*
    sulfonamides V14.2
    therapeutic agent NEC V15.09
    vaccine V14.7
  anemia V12.3
  arthritis V13.4
  benign neoplasm of brain V12.41
  blood disease V12.3
  calculi, urinary V13.01
  cardiovascular disease V12.50
    myocardial infarction 412
  child abuse V15.41
  cigarette smoking V15.82
  circulatory system disease V12.50
    myocardial infarction 412
  congenital malformation V13.69
  contraception V15.7
  diathesis, allergic V15.09
  digestive system disease V12.70
    peptic ulcer V12.71
    polyps, colonic V12.72
    specified NEC V12.79
  disease (of) V13.9
    blood V12.3
    blood-forming organs V12.3
    cardiovascular system V12.50
    circulatory system V12.50
    digestive system V12.70
      peptic ulcer V12.71
      polyps, colonic V12.72
      specified NEC V12.79
    infectious V12.00
      malaria V12.03
      poliomyelitis V12.02
      specified NEC V12.09
      tuberculosis V12.01
    parasitic V12.00
      specified NEC V12.09
    respiratory system V12.60 ▲
      pneumonia V12.61 ●
      specified NEC V12.69 ●
    skin V13.3
    specified site NEC V13.8
    subcutaneous tissue V13.3
    trophoblastic V13.1
      affecting management of pregnancy V23.1
  disorder (of) V13.9
    endocrine V12.2
    genital system V13.29
    hematological V12.3
    immunity V12.2
    mental V11.9
      affective type V11.1
      manic-depressive V11.1
      neurosis V11.2
      schizophrenia V11.0
      specified type NEC V11.8
    metabolic V12.2
    musculoskeletal NEC V13.5
    nervous system V12.40
      specified type NEC V12.49
    obstetric V13.29
      affecting management of current
        pregnancy V23.49
        pre-term labor V23.41
      pre-term labor V13.21
    sense organs V12.40
      specified type NEC V12.49
    specified site NEC V13.8
    urinary system V13.00
      calculi V13.01
      infection V13.02 ●
      nephrotic syndrome V13.03 ●
      specified NEC V13.09
  drug use
    nonprescribed (*see also* Abuse, drugs,
      nondependent) 305.9 ☑
    patent (*see also* Abuse, drugs,
      nondependent) 305.9 ☑
  effect NEC of external cause V15.89
  embolism (pulmonary) V12.51
  emotional abuse V15.42
  encephalitis V12.42 ●
  endocrine disorder V12.2
  extracorporeal membrane oxygenation (ECMO)
    V15.87

☑ Additional Digit Required — Refer to the Tabular List (Numeric Code Section) for Additional Digit Selection

History (personal) **of** — *continued*
  falling V15.88 ●
  family
    allergy V19.6
    anemia V18.2
    arteriosclerosis V17.4
    arthritis V17.7
    asthma V17.5
    blindness V19.0
    blood disorder NEC V18.3
    cardiovascular disease V17.4
    carrier, genetic disease V18.9 ●
    cerebrovascular disease V17.1
    chronic respiratory condition NEC V17.6
    congenital anomalies V19.5
    consanguinity V19.7
    coronary artery disease V17.3
    cystic fibrosis V18.1
    deafness V19.2
    diabetes mellitus V18.0
    digestive disorders V18.5
    disease or disorder (of)
      allergic V19.6
      blood NEC V18.3
      cardiovascular NEC V17.4
      cerebrovascular V17.1
      coronary artery V17.3
      digestive V18.5
      ear NEC V19.3
      endocrine V18.1
      eye NEC V19.1
      genitourinary NEC V18.7
      hypertensive V17.4
      infectious V18.8
      ischemic heart V17.3
      kidney V18.69
        polycystic V18.61
      mental V17.0
      metabolic V18.1
      musculoskeletal NEC V17.89 ▲
        osteoporosis V17.81 ●
      neurological NEC V17.2
      parasitic V18.8
      psychiatric condition V17.0
      skin condition V19.4
    ear disorder NEC V19.3
    endocrine disease V18.1
    epilepsy V17.2
    eye disorder NEC V19.1
    genetic disease carrier V18.9 ●
    genitourinary disease NEC V18.7
    glomerulonephritis V18.69
    gout V18.1
    hay fever V17.6
    hearing loss V19.2
    hematopoietic neoplasia V16.7
    Hodgkin's disease V16.7
    Huntington's chorea V17.2
    hydrocephalus V19.5
    hypertension V17.4
    hypospadias V13.61
    infectious disease V18.8
    ischemic heart disease V17.3
    kidney disease V18.69
      polycystic V18.61
    leukemia V16.6
    lymphatic malignant neoplasia NEC V16.7
    malignant neoplasm (of) NEC V16.9
      anorectal V16.0
      anus V16.0
      appendix V16.0
      bladder V16.59
      bone V16.8
      brain V16.8
      breast V16.3
        male V16.8
      bronchus V16.1
      cecum V16.0
      cervix V16.49
      colon V16.0
      duodenum V16.0
      esophagus V16.0
      eye V16.8
      gallbladder V16.0
      gastrointestinal tract V16.0
      genital organs V16.40
      hemopoietic NEC V16.7

History (personal) **of** — *continued*
  family — *continued*
    malignant neoplasm (of) — *continued*
      ileum V16.0
      ilium V16.8
      intestine V16.0
      intrathoracic organs NEC V16.2
      kidney V16.51
      larynx V16.2
      liver V16.0
      lung V16.1
      lymphatic NEC V16.7
      ovary V16.41
      oviduct V16.41
      pancreas V16.0
      penis V16.49
      prostate V16.42
      rectum V16.0
      respiratory organs NEC V16.2
      skin V16.8
      specified site NEC V16.8
      stomach V16.0
      testis V16.43
      trachea V16.1
      ureter V16.59
      urethra V16.59
      urinary organs V16.59
      uterus V16.49
      vagina V16.49
      vulva V16.49
    mental retardation V18.4
    metabolic disease NEC V18.1
    mongolism V19.5
    multiple myeloma V16.7
    musculoskeletal disease NEC V17.89 ▲
      osteoporosis V17.81 ●
    nephritis V18.69
    nephrosis V18.69
    osteoporosis V17.81 ●
    parasitic disease V18.8
    polycystic kidney disease V18.61
    psychiatric disorder V17.0
    psychosis V17.0
    retardation, mental V18.4
    retinitis pigmentosa V19.1
    schizophrenia V17.0
    skin conditions V19.4
    specified condition NEC V19.8
    stroke (cerebrovascular) V17.1
    visual loss V19.0
  genital system disorder V13.29
    pre-term labor V13.21
  health hazard V15.9
    falling V15.88 ●
    specified cause NEC V15.89 ●
  hepatitis ●
    B V12.09 ●
    C V12.09 ●
  Hodgkin's disease V10.72
  immunity disorder V12.2
  infection ●
    central nervous system V12.42 ●
    urinary (tract) V13.02 ●
  infectious disease V12.00
    malaria V12.03
    poliomyelitis V12.02
    specified NEC V12.09
    tuberculosis V12.01
  injury NEC V15.5
  insufficient prenatal care V23.7
  irradiation V15.3
  leukemia V10.60
    lymphoid V10.61
    monocytic V10.63
    myeloid V10.62
    specified type NEC V10.69
  little or no prenatal care V23.7
  low birth weight (*see also* Status, low birth weight) V21.30
  lymphosarcoma V10.71
  malaria V12.03
  malignant neoplasm (of) V10.9
    accessory sinus V10.22
    adrenal V10.88
    anus V10.06
    bile duct V10.09
    bladder V10.51

History (personal) **of** — *continued*
  malignant neoplasm (of) — *continued*
    bone V10.81
    brain V10.85
    breast V10.3
    bronchus V10.11
    cervix uteri V10.41
    colon V10.05
    connective tissue NEC V10.89
    corpus uteri V10.42
    digestive system V10.00
      specified part NEC V10.09
    duodenum V10.09
    endocrine gland NEC V10.88
    epididymis V10.48
    esophagus V10.03
    eye V10.84
    fallopian tube V10.44
    female genital organ V10.40
      specified site NEC V10.44
    gallbladder V10.09
    gastrointestinal tract V10.00
    gum V10.02
    hematopoietic NEC V10.79
    hypopharynx V10.02
    ileum V10.09
    intrathoracic organs NEC V10.20
    jejunum V10.09
    kidney V10.52
    large intestine V10.05
    larynx V10.21
    lip V10.02
    liver V10.07
    lung V10.11
    lymphatic NEC V10.79
    lymph glands or nodes NEC V10.79
    male genital organ V10.45
      specified site NEC V10.49
    mediastinum V10.29
    melanoma (of skin) V10.82
    middle ear V10.22
    mouth V10.02
      specified part NEC V10.02
    nasal cavities V10.22
    nasopharynx V10.02
    nervous system NEC V10.86
    nose V10.22
    oropharynx V10.02
    ovary V10.43
    pancreas V10.09
    parathyroid V10.88
    penis V10.49
    pharynx V10.02
    pineal V10.88
    pituitary V10.88
    placenta V10.44
    pleura V10.29
    prostate V10.46
    rectosigmoid junction V10.06
    rectum V10.06
    renal pelvis V10.53
    respiratory organs NEC V10.20
    salivary gland V10.02
    skin V10.83
      melanoma V10.82
    small intestine NEC V10.09
    soft tissue NEC V10.89
    specified site NEC V10.89
    stomach V10.04
    testis V10.47
    thymus V10.29
    thyroid V10.87
    tongue V10.01
    trachea V10.12
    ureter V10.59
    urethra V10.59
    urinary organ V10.50
    uterine adnexa V10.44
    uterus V10.42
    vagina V10.44
    vulva V10.44
  manic-depressive psychosis V11.1
  meningitis V12.42 ●
  mental disorder V11.9
    affective type V11.1
    manic-depressive V11.1
    neurosis V11.2

☑ Additional Digit Required — Refer to the Tabular List (Numeric Code Section) for Additional Digit Selection

History (personal) **of** — *continued*
    mental disorder — *continued*
        schizophrenia V11.0
        specified type NEC V11.8
    metabolic disorder V12.2
    musculoskeletal disorder NEC V13.5
    myocardial infarction 412
    neglect (emotional) V15.42
    nephrotic syndrome V13.03 •
    nervous system disorder V12.40
        specified type NEC V12.49
    neurosis V11.2
    noncompliance with medical treatment V15.81
    nutritional deficiency V12.1
    obstetric disorder V13.29
        affecting management of current pregnancy
            V23.49
            pre-term labor V23.41
        pre-term labor V13.21
    parasitic disease V12.00
        specified NEC V12.09
    perinatal problems V13.7
        low birth weight (*see also* Status, low birth
            weight) V21.30
    physical abuse V15.41
    poisoning V15.6
    poliomyelitis V12.02
    polyps, colonic V12.72
    poor obstetric V13.29
        affecting management of current pregnancy
            V23.49
            pre-term labor V23.41
        pre-term labor V13.21
    psychiatric disorder V11.9
        affective type V11.1
        manic-depressive V11.1
        neurosis V11.2
        schizophrenia V11.0
        specified type NEC V11.8
    psychological trauma V15.49
        emotional abuse V15.42
        neglect V15.42
        physical abuse V15.41
        rape V15.41
    psychoneurosis V11.2
    radiation therapy V15.3
    rape V15.41
    respiratory system disease V12.60 ▲
        pneumonia V12.61 •
        specified NEC V12.69 •
    reticulosarcoma V10.71
    schizophrenia V11.0
    skin disease V13.3
    smoking (tobacco) V15.82
    subcutaneous tissue disease V13.3
    surgery (major) to
        great vessels V15.1
        heart V15.1
        major organs NEC V15.2
    syndrome, nephrotic V13.03 •
    thrombophlebitis V12.52
    thrombosis V12.51
    tobacco use V15.82
    trophoblastic disease V13.1
        affecting management of pregnancy V23.1
    tuberculosis V12.01
    ulcer, peptic V12.71
    urinary system disorder V13.00
        calculi V13.01
        infection V13.02 •
        nephrotic syndrome V13.03 •
        specified NEC V13.09
HIV infection (disease) (illness) — *see* Human
    immunodeficiency virus (disease) (illness)
    (infection)
Hives (bold) (*see also* Urticaria) 708.9
Hoarseness 784.49
Hobnail liver — *see* Cirrhosis, portal
Hobo, hoboism V60.0
Hodgkin's
    disease (M9650/3) 201.9 ☑
        lymphocytic
            depletion (M9653/3) 201.7 ☑
                diffuse fibrosis (M9654/3) 201.7 ☑
                reticular type (M9655/3) 201.7 ☑
            predominance (M9651/3) 201.4 ☑

Hodgkin's — *continued*
    disease — *continued*
        lymphocytic-histiocytic predominance
            (M9651/3) 201.4 ☑
        mixed cellularity (M9652/3) 201.6 ☑
        nodular sclerosis (M9656/3) 201.5 ☑
            cellular phase (M9657/3) 201.5 ☑
        granuloma (M9661/3) 201.1 ☑
        lymphogranulomatosis (M9650/3) 201.9 ☑
        lymphoma (M9650/3) 201.9 ☑
        lymphosarcoma (M9650/3) 201.9 ☑
        paragranuloma (M9660/3) 201.0 ☑
        sarcoma (M9662/3) 201.2 ☑
Hodgson's disease (aneurysmal dilatation of
    aorta) 441.9
    ruptured 441.5
Hodi-potsy 111.0
Hoffa (-Kastert) disease or syndrome
    (liposynovitis prepatellaris) 272.8
Hoffman's syndrome 244.9 [*359.5*]
Hoffmann-Bouveret syndrome (paroxysmal
    tachycardia) 427.2
Hole
    macula 362.54
    optic disc, crater-like 377.22
    retina (macula) 362.54
        round 361.31
            with detachment 361.01
Holla disease (*see also* Spherocytosis) 282.0
Holländer-Simons syndrome (progressive
    lipodystrophy) 272.6
Hollow foot (congenital) 754.71
    acquired 736.73
Holmes' syndrome (visual disorientation) 368.16
Holoprosencephaly 742.2
    due to
        trisomy 13 758.1
        trisomy 18 758.2
Holthouse's hernia — *see* Hernia, inguinal
Homesickness 309.89
Homocystinemia 270.4
Homocystinuria 270.4
Homologous serum jaundice (prophylactic)
    (therapeutic) — *see* Hepatitis, viral
Homosexuality — *omit code*
    ego-dystonic 302.0
    pedophilic 302.2
    problems with 302.0
Homozygous Hb-S disease 282.61
Honeycomb lung 518.89
    congenital 748.4
Hong Kong ear 117.3
HOOD (hereditary osteo-onychodysplasia) 756.89
Hooded
    clitoris 752.49
    penis 752.69
Hookworm (anemia) (disease) (infestation) — *see*
    Ancylostomiasis
Hoppe-Goldflam syndrome 358.00
Hordeolum (external) (eyelid) 373.11
    internal 373.12
Horn
    cutaneous 702.8
        cheek 702.8
        eyelid 702.8
        penis 702.8
    iliac 756.89
    nail 703.8
        congenital 757.5
    papillary 700
Horner's
    syndrome (*see also* Neuropathy, peripheral,
        autonomic) 337.9
        traumatic 954.0
    teeth 520.4
Horseshoe kidney (congenital) 753.3
Horton's
    disease (temporal arteritis) 446.5
    headache or neuralgia 346.2 ☑
Hospice care V66.7
Hospitalism (in children) NEC 309.83

Hourglass contraction, contracture
    bladder 596.8
    gallbladder 575.2
        congenital 751.69
    stomach 536.8
        congenital 750.7
        psychogenic 306.4
    uterus 661.4 ☑
        affecting fetus or newborn 763.7
Household circumstance affecting care V60.9
    specified type NEC V60.8
Housemaid's knee 727.2
Housing circumstance affecting care V60.9
    specified type NEC V60.8
HTLV-I infection 079.51
HTLV-II infection 079.52
HTLV-III (disease) (illness) (infection) — *see*
    Human immunodeficiency virus (disease)
    (illness) (infection)
HTLV-III/LAV (disease) (illness) (infection) — *see*
    Human immunodeficiency virus (disease)
    (illness) (infection)
Huchard's disease (continued arterial
    hypertension) 401.9
Hudson-Stähli lines 371.11
Huguier's disease (uterine fibroma) 218.9
Hum, venous — *omit code*
Human bite (open wound) — *see also* Wound,
    open, by site
    intact skin surface — *see* Contusion
Human immunodeficiency virus (disease)
    (illness) 042
    infection V08
        with symptoms, symptomatic 042
Human immunodeficiency virus-2 infection
    079.53
Human immunovirus (disease) (illness) (infection)
    — *see* Human immunodeficiency virus
    (disease) (illness) (infection)
Human papillomavirus 079.4
    cervical
        high risk, DNA test positive 795.05
        low risk, DNA test positive 795.09
Human T-cell lymphotrophic virus-I infection
    079.51
Human T-cell lymphotrophic virus-II infection
    079.52
Human T-cell lymphotrophic virus-III (disease)
    (illness) (infection) — *see* Human
    immunodeficiency virus (disease) (illness)
    (infection)
Humpback (acquired) 737.9
    congenital 756.19
Hunchback (acquired) 737.9
    congenital 756.19
Hunger 994.2
    air, psychogenic 306.1
    disease 251.1
Hunner's ulcer (*see also* Cystitis) 595.1
Hunt's
    neuralgia 053.11
    syndrome (herpetic geniculate ganglionitis)
        053.11
        dyssynergia cerebellaris myoclonica 334.2
Hunter's glossitis 529.4
Hunter (-Hurler) syndrome
    (mucopolysaccharidosis II) 277.5
Hunterian chancre 091.0
Huntington's
    chorea 333.4
    disease 333.4
Huppert's disease (multiple myeloma) (M9730/3)
    203.0 ☑
Hurler (-Hunter) disease or syndrome
    (mucopolysaccharidosis II) 277.5
Hürthle cell
    adenocarcinoma (M8290/3) 193
    adenoma (M8290/0) 226
    carcinoma (M8290/3) 193
    tumor (M8290/0) 226

Hutchinson's
- disease meaning
  - angioma serpiginosum 709.1
  - cheiropompholyx 705.81
  - prurigo estivalis 692.72
  - summer eruption, or summer prurigo 692.72
- incisors 090.5
- melanotic freckle (M8742/2) — see also Neoplasm, skin, in situ
  - malignant melanoma in (M8742/3) — see Melanoma
- teeth or incisors (congenital syphilis) 090.5

Hutchinson-Boeck disease or syndrome (sarcoidosis) 135

Hutchinson-Gilford disease or syndrome (progeria) 259.8

Hyaline
- degeneration (diffuse) (generalized) 728.9
  - localized — see Degeneration, by site
- membrane (disease) (lung) (newborn) 769

Hyalinosis cutis et mucosae 272.8

Hyalin plaque, sclera, senile 379.16

Hyalitis (asteroid) 379.22
- syphilitic 095.8

Hydatid
- cyst or tumor — see also Echinococcus
  - fallopian tube 752.11
- mole — see Hydatidiform mole
- Morgagni (congenital) 752.89
  - fallopian tube 752.11

Hydatidiform mole (benign) (complicating pregnancy) (delivered) (undelivered) 630
- invasive (M9100/1) 236.1
- malignant (M9100/1) 236.1
- previous, affecting management of pregnancy V23.1

Hydatidosis — see Echinococcus

Hyde's disease (prurigo nodularis) 698.3

Hydradenitis 705.83

Hydradenoma (M8400/0) — see Hidradenoma

Hydralazine lupus or syndrome
- correct substance properly administered 695.4
- overdose or wrong substance given or taken 972.6

Hydramnios 657.0 ☑
- affecting fetus or newborn 761.3

Hydrancephaly 742.3
- with spina bifida (see also Spina bifida) 741.0 ☑

Hydranencephaly 742.3
- with spina bifida (see also Spina bifida) 741.0 ☑

Hydrargyrism NEC 985.0

Hydrarthrosis (see also Effusion, joint) 719.0 ☑
- gonococcal 098.50
- intermittent (see also Rheumatism, palindromic) 719.3 ☑
- of yaws (early) (late) 102.6
- syphilitic 095.8
  - congenital 090.5

Hydremia 285.9

Hydrencephalocele (congenital) 742.0

Hydrencephalomeningocele (congenital) 742.0

Hydroa 694.0
- aestivale 692.72
- gestationis 646.8 ☑
- herpetiformis 694.0
- pruriginosa 694.0
- vacciniforme 692.72

Hydroadenitis 705.83

Hydrocalycosis (see also Hydronephrosis) 591
- congenital 753.29

Hydrocalyx (see also Hydronephrosis) 591

Hydrocele (calcified) (chylous) (idiopathic) (infantile) (inguinal canal) (recurrent) (senile) (spermatic cord) (testis) (tunica vaginalis) 603.9
- canal of Nuck (female) 629.1
  - male 603.9
- congenital 778.6

Hydrocele — continued
- encysted 603.0
  - congenital 778.6
- female NEC 629.8
- infected 603.1
- round ligament 629.8
- specified type NEC 603.8
  - congenital 778.6
- spinalis (see also Spina bifida) 741.9 ☑
- vulva 624.8

Hydrocephalic fetus
- affecting management or pregnancy 655.0 ☑
- causing disproportion 653.6 ☑
  - with obstructed labor 660.1 ☑
    - affecting fetus or newborn 763.1

Hydrocephalus (acquired) (external) (internal) (malignant) (noncommunicating) (obstructive) (recurrent) 331.4
- aqueduct of Sylvius stricture 742.3
  - with spina bifida (see also Spina bifida) 741.0 ☑
- chronic 742.3
  - with spina bifida (see also Spina bifida) 741.0 ☑
- communicating 331.3
- congenital (external) (internal) 742.3
  - with spina bifida (see also Spina bifida) 741.0 ☑
- due to
  - stricture of aqueduct of Sylvius 742.3
    - with spina bifida (see also Spina bifida) 741.0 ☑
  - toxoplasmosis (congenital) 771.2
- fetal affecting management of pregnancy 655.0 ☑
- foramen Magendie block (acquired) 331.3
  - congenital 742.3
    - with spina bifida (see also Spina bifida) 741.0 ☑
- newborn 742.3
  - with spina bifida (see also Spina bifida) 741.0 ☑
- otitic 331.4
- syphilitic, congenital 090.49
- tuberculous (see also Tuberculosis) 013.8 ☑

Hydrocolpos (congenital) 623.8

Hydrocystoma (M8404/0) — see Neoplasm, skin, benign

Hydroencephalocele (congenital) 742.0

Hydroencephalomeningocele (congenital) 742.0

Hydrohematopneumothorax (see also Hemothorax) 511.8

Hydromeningitis — see Meningitis

Hydromeningocele (spinal) (see also Spina bifida) 741.9 ☑
- cranial 742.0

Hydrometra 621.8

Hydrometrocolpos 623.8

Hydromicrocephaly 742.1

Hydromphalus (congenital) (since birth) 757.39

Hydromyelia 742.53

Hydromyelocele (see also Spina bifida) 741.9 ☑

Hydronephrosis 591
- atrophic 591
- congenital 753.29
- due to S. hematobium 120.0
- early 591
- functionless (infected) 591
- infected 591
- intermittent 591
- primary 591
- secondary 591
- tuberculous (see also Tuberculosis) 016.0 ☑

Hydropericarditis (see also Pericarditis) 423.9

Hydropericardium (see also Pericarditis) 423.9

Hydroperitoneum 789.5

Hydrophobia 071

Hydrophthalmos (see also Buphthalmia) 743.20

Hydropneumohemothorax (see also Hemothorax) 511.8

Hydropneumopericarditis (see also Pericarditis) 423.9

Hydropneumopericardium (see also Pericarditis) 423.9

Hydropneumothorax 511.8
- nontuberculous 511.8
  - bacterial 511.1
- pneumococcal 511.1
- staphylococcal 511.1
- streptococcal 511.1
- traumatic 860.0
  - with open wound into thorax 860.1
- tuberculous (see also Tuberculosis, pleura) 012.0 ☑

Hydrops 782.3
- abdominis 789.5
- amnii (complicating pregnancy) (see also Hydramnios) 657.0 ☑
- articulorum intermittens (see also Rheumatism, palindromic) 719.3 ☑
- cardiac (see also Failure, heart) 428.0
- congenital — see Hydrops, fetalis
- endolymphatic (see also Disease, Ménière's) 386.00
- fetal(is) or newborn 778.0
  - due to isoimmunization 773.3
  - not due to isoimmunization 778.0
- gallbladder 575.3
- idiopathic (fetus or newborn) 778.0
- joint (see also Effusion, joint) 719.0 ☑
- labyrinth (see also Disease, Ménière's) 386.00
- meningeal NEC 331.4
- nutritional 262
- pericardium — see Pericarditis
- pleura (see also Hydrothorax) 511.8
- renal (see also Nephrosis) 581.9
- spermatic cord (see also Hydrocele) 603.9

Hydropyonephrosis (see also Pyelitis) 590.80
- chronic 590.00

Hydrorachis 742.53

Hydrorrhea (nasal) 478.1
- gravidarum 658.1 ☑
- pregnancy 658.1 ☑

Hydrosadenitis 705.83

Hydrosalpinx (fallopian tube) (follicularis) 614.1

Hydrothorax (double) (pleural) 511.8
- chylous (nonfilarial) 511.8
  - filaria (see also Infestation, filarial) 125.9
- nontuberculous 511.8
  - bacterial 511.1
- pneumococcal 511.1
- staphylococcal 511.1
- streptococcal 511.1
- traumatic 862.29
  - with open wound into thorax 862.39
- tuberculous (see also Tuberculosis, pleura) 012.0 ☑

Hydroureter 593.5
- congenital 753.22

Hydroureteronephrosis (see also Hydronephrosis) 591

Hydrourethra 599.84

Hydroxykynureninuria 270.2

Hydroxyprolinemia 270.8

Hydroxyprolinuria 270.8

Hygroma (congenital) (cystic) (M9173/0) 228.1
- prepatellar 727.3
- subdural — see Hematoma, subdural

Hymen — see condition

Hymenolepiasis (diminuta) (infection) (infestation) (nana) 123.6

Hymenolepis (diminuta) (infection) (infestation) (nana) 123.6

Hypalgesia (see also Disturbance, sensation) 782.0

Hyperabduction syndrome 447.8

Hyperacidity, gastric 536.8
- psychogenic 306.4

Hyperactive, hyperactivity
- basal cell, uterine cervix 622.10
- bladder 596.51
- bowel (syndrome) 564.9
  - sounds 787.5
- cervix epithelial (basal) 622.10
- child 314.01

Hyperactive, hyperactivity — *continued*
  colon 564.9
  gastrointestinal 536.8
    psychogenic 306.4
  intestine 564.9
  labyrinth (unilateral) 386.51
    with loss of labyrinthine reactivity 386.58
    bilateral 386.52
  nasal mucous membrane 478.1
  stomach 536.8
  thyroid (gland) (*see also* Thyrotoxicosis)
    242.9 ☑
Hyperacusis 388.42
Hyperadrenalism (cortical) 255.3
  medullary 255.6
Hyperadrenocorticism 255.3
  congenital 255.2
  iatrogenic
    correct substance properly administered
      255.3
    overdose or wrong substance given or taken
      962.0
Hyperaffectivity 301.11
Hyperaldosteronism (atypical) (hyperplastic)
    (normoaldosteronal) (normotensive)
    (primary) 255.10
  secondary 255.14
Hyperalgesia (*see also* Disturbance, sensation)
    782.0
Hyperalimentation 783.6
  carotene 278.3
  specified NEC 278.8
  vitamin A 278.2
  vitamin D 278.4
Hyperaminoaciduria 270.9
  arginine 270.6
  citrulline 270.6
  cystine 270.0
  glycine 270.0
  lysine 270.7
  ornithine 270.6
  renal (types I, II, III) 270.0
Hyperammonemia (congenital) 270.6
Hyperamnesia 780.99
Hyperamylasemia 790.5
Hyperaphia 782.0
Hyperazotemia 791.9
Hyperbetalipoproteinemia (acquired) (essential)
    (familial) (hereditary) (primary) (secondary)
    272.0
  with prebetalipoproteinemia 272.2
Hyperbilirubinemia 782.4
  congenital 277.4
  constitutional 277.4
  neonatal (transient) (*see also* Jaundice, fetus or
    newborn) 774.6
  of prematurity 774.2
Hyperbilirubinemica encephalopathia, newborn
    774.7
  due to isoimmunization 773.4
Hypercalcemia, hypercalcemic (idiopathic)
    275.42
  nephropathy 588.89
Hypercalcinuria 275.40
Hypercapnia 786.09
  with mixed acid-base disorder 276.4
  fetal, affecting newborn 770.89
Hypercarotinemia 278.3
Hypercementosis 521.5
Hyperchloremia 276.9
Hyperchlorhydria 536.8
  neurotic 306.4
  psychogenic 306.4
Hypercholesterinemia — *see*
    Hypercholesterolemia
Hypercholesterolemia 272.0
  with hyperglyceridemia, endogenous 272.2
  essential 272.0
  familial 272.0
  hereditary 272.0
  primary 272.0
  pure 272.0

Hypercholesterolosis 272.0
Hyperchylia gastrica 536.8
  psychogenic 306.4
Hyperchylomicronemia (familial) (with
    hyperbetalipoproteinemia) 272.3
Hypercoagulation syndrome (primary) 289.81
  secondary 289.82
Hypercorticosteronism
  correct substance properly administered 255.3
  overdose or wrong substance given or taken
    962.0
Hypercortisonism
  correct substance properly administered 255.3
  overdose or wrong substance given or taken
    962.0
Hyperdynamic beta-adrenergic state or
    syndrome (circulatory) 429.82
Hyperekplexia 759.89
Hyperelectrolytemia 276.9
Hyperemesis 536.2
  arising during pregnancy — *see* Hyperemesis,
    gravidarum
  gravidarum (mild) (before 22 completed weeks
    gestation) 643.0 ☑
    with
      carbohydrate depletion 643.1 ☑
      dehydration 643.1 ☑
      electrolyte imbalance 643.1 ☑
      metabolic disturbance 643.1 ☑
    affecting fetus or newborn 761.8
    severe (with metabolic disturbance) 643.1 ☑
  psychogenic 306.4
Hyperemia (acute) 780.99
  anal mucosa 569.49
  bladder 596.7
  cerebral 437.8
  conjunctiva 372.71
  ear, internal, acute 386.30
  enteric 564.89
  eye 372.71
  eyelid (active) (passive) 374.82
  intestine 564.89
  iris 364.41
  kidney 593.81
  labyrinth 386.30
  liver (active) (passive) 573.8
  lung 514
  ovary 620.8
  passive 780.99
  pulmonary 514
  renal 593.81
  retina 362.89
  spleen 289.59
  stomach 537.89
Hyperesthesia (body surface) (*see also*
    Disturbance, sensation) 782.0
  larynx (reflex) 478.79
    hysterical 300.11
  pharynx (reflex) 478.29
Hyperestrinism 256.0
Hyperestrogenism 256.0
Hyperestrogenosis 256.0
Hyperexplexia 759.89
Hyperextension, joint 718.80
  ankle 718.87
  elbow 718.82
  foot 718.87
  hand 718.84
  hip 718.85
  knee 718.86
  multiple sites 718.89
  pelvic region 718.85
  shoulder (region) 718.81
  specified site NEC 718.88
  wrist 718.83
Hyperfibrinolysis — *see* Fibrinolysis
Hyperfolliculinism 256.0
Hyperfructosemia 271.2
Hyperfunction
  adrenal (cortex) 255.3
    androgenic, acquired benign 255.3
    medulla 255.6
    virilism 255.2

Hyperfunction — *continued*
  corticoadrenal NEC 255.3
  labyrinth — *see* Hyperactive, labyrinth
  medulloadrenal 255.6
  ovary 256.1
    estrogen 256.0
  pancreas 577.8
  parathyroid (gland) 252.00
  pituitary (anterior) (gland) (lobe) 253.1
  testicular 257.0
Hypergammaglobulinemia 289.89
  monoclonal, benign (BMH) 273.1
  polyclonal 273.0
  Waldenström's 273.0
Hyperglobulinemia 273.8
Hyperglycemia 790.6
  maternal
    affecting fetus or newborn 775.0
    manifest diabetes in infant 775.1
  postpancreatectomy (complete) (partial) 251.3
Hyperglyceridemia 272.1
  endogenous 272.1
  essential 272.1
  familial 272.1
  hereditary 272.1
  mixed 272.3
  pure 272.1
Hyperglycinemia 270.7
Hypergonadism
  ovarian 256.1
  testicular (infantile) (primary) 257.0
Hyperheparinemia (*see also* Circulating
    anticoagulants) 286.5
Hyperhidrosis, hyperidrosis 705.21
  axilla 705.21
  face 705.21
  focal (localized) 705.21
    primary 705.21
      axilla 705.21
      face 705.21
      palms 705.21
      soles 705.21
    secondary 705.22
      axilla 705.22
      face 705.22
      palms 705.22
      soles 705.22
  generalized 780.8
  palms 705.21
  psychogenic 306.3
  secondary 780.8
  soles 705.21
Hyperhistidinemia 270.5
Hyperinsulinism (ectopic) (functional) (organic)
    NEC 251.1
  iatrogenic 251.0
  reactive 251.2
  spontaneous 251.2
  therapeutic misadventure (from administration
    of insulin) 962.3
Hyperiodemia 276.9
Hyperirritability (cerebral), in newborn 779.1
Hyperkalemia 276.7
Hyperkeratosis (*see also* Keratosis) 701.1   ▲
  cervix 622.2
  congenital 757.39
  cornea 371.89
  due to yaws (early) (late) (palmar or plantar)
    102.3
  eccentrica 757.39
  figurata centrifuga atrophica 757.39
  follicularis 757.39
    in cutem penetrans 701.1
  limbic (cornea) 371.89
  palmoplantaris climacterica 701.1
  pinta (carate) 103.1
  senile (with pruritus) 702.0
  tongue 528.79
  universalis congenita 757.1
  vagina 623.1
  vocal cord 478.5
  vulva 624.0

Hyperkinesia, hyperkinetic (disease) (reaction) (syndrome) 314.9
- with
  - attention deficit — *see* Disorder, attention deficit
  - conduct disorder 314.2
  - developmental delay 314.1
  - simple disturbance of activity and attention 314.01
  - specified manifestation NEC 314.8
- heart (disease) 429.82
- of childhood or adolescence NEC 314.9

Hyperlacrimation (*see also* Epiphora) 375.20

Hyperlipemia (*see also* Hyperlipidemia) 272.4

Hyperlipidemia 272.4
- carbohydrate-induced 272.1
- combined 272.4
- endogenous 272.1
- exogenous 272.3
- fat-induced 272.3
- group
  - A 272.0
  - B 272.1
  - C 272.2
  - D 272.3
- mixed 272.2
- specified type NEC 272.4

Hyperlipidosis 272.7
- hereditary 272.7

Hyperlipoproteinemia (acquired) (essential) (familial) (hereditary) (primary) (secondary) 272.4
- Fredrickson type
  - I 272.3
  - IIa 272.0
  - IIb 272.2
  - III 272.2
  - IV 272.1
  - V 272.3
- low-density-lipoid-type (LDL) 272.0
- very-low-density-lipoid-type (VLDL) 272.1

Hyperlucent lung, unilateral 492.8

Hyperluteinization 256.1

Hyperlysinemia 270.7

Hypermagnesemia 275.2
- neonatal 775.5

Hypermaturity (fetus or newborn)
- post-term infant 766.21
- prolonged gestation infant 766.22

Hypermenorrhea 626.2

Hypermetabolism 794.7

Hypermethioninemia 270.4

Hypermetropia (congenital) 367.0

Hypermobility
- cecum 564.9
- coccyx 724.71
- colon 564.9
  - psychogenic 306.4
- ileum 564.89
- joint (acquired) 718.80
  - ankle 718.87
  - elbow 718.82
  - foot 718.87
  - hand 718.84
  - hip 718.85
  - knee 718.86
  - multiple sites 718.89
  - pelvic region 718.85
  - shoulder (region) 718.81
  - specified site NEC 718.88
  - wrist 718.83
- kidney, congenital 753.3
- meniscus (knee) 717.5
- scapula 718.81
- stomach 536.8
  - psychogenic 306.4
- syndrome 728.5
- testis, congenital 752.52
- urethral 599.81

Hypermotility
- gastrointestinal 536.8
- intestine 564.9
  - psychogenic 306.4
- stomach 536.8

Hypernasality 784.49

Hypernatremia 276.0
- with water depletion 276.0

Hypernephroma (M8312/3) 189.0

Hyperopia 367.0

Hyperorexia 783.6

Hyperornithinemia 270.6

Hyperosmia (*see also* Disturbance, sensation) 781.1

Hyperosmolality 276.0

Hyperosteogenesis 733.99

Hyperostosis 733.99
- calvarial 733.3
- cortical 733.3
  - infantile 756.59
- frontal, internal of skull 733.3
- interna frontalis 733.3
- monomelic 733.99
- skull 733.3
  - congenital 756.0
- vertebral 721.8
  - with spondylosis — *see* Spondylosis
  - ankylosing 721.6

Hyperovarianism 256.1

Hyperovarism, hyperovaria 256.1

Hyperoxaluria (primary) 271.8

Hyperoxia 987.8

Hyperparathyroidism 252.00
- ectopic 259.3
- other 252.08
- primary 252.01
- secondary (of renal origin) 588.81
  - non-renal 252.02
- tertiary 252.08

Hyperpathia (*see also* Disturbance, sensation) 782.0
- psychogenic 307.80

Hyperperistalsis 787.4
- psychogenic 306.4

Hyperpermeability, capillary 448.9

Hyperphagia 783.6

Hyperphenylalaninemia 270.1

Hyperphoria 378.40
- alternating 378.45

Hyperphosphatemia 275.3

Hyperpiesia (*see also* Hypertension) 401.9

Hyperpiesis (*see also* Hypertension) 401.9

Hyperpigmentation — *see* Pigmentation

Hyperpinealism 259.8

Hyperpipecolatemia 270.7

Hyperpituitarism 253.1

Hyperplasia, hyperplastic
- adenoids (lymphoid tissue) 474.12
  - and tonsils 474.10
- adrenal (capsule) (cortex) (gland) 255.8
  - with
    - sexual precocity (male) 255.2
    - virilism, adrenal 255.2
    - virilization (female) 255.2
  - congenital 255.2
  - due to excess ACTH (ectopic) (pituitary) 255.0
  - medulla 255.8
- alpha cells (pancreatic)
  - with
    - gastrin excess 251.5
    - glucagon excess 251.4
- appendix (lymphoid) 543.0
- artery, fibromuscular NEC 447.8
  - carotid 447.8
  - renal 447.3
- bone 733.99
  - marrow 289.9
- breast (*see also* Hypertrophy, breast) 611.1
- carotid artery 447.8
- cementation, cementum (teeth) (tooth) 521.5
- cervical gland 785.6
- cervix (uteri) 622.10
  - basal cell 622.10
  - congenital 752.49
  - endometrium 622.10
  - polypoid 622.10

Hyperplasia, hyperplastic — *continued*
- chin 524.05
- clitoris, congenital 752.49
- dentin 521.5
- endocervicitis 616.0
- endometrium, endometrial (adenomatous) (atypical) (cystic) (glandular) (polypoid) (uterus) 621.30
  - with atypia 621.33
  - without atypia
    - complex 621.32
    - simple 621.31
- cervix 622.10
- epithelial 709.8
  - focal, oral, including tongue 528.79
  - mouth (focal) 528.79
  - nipple 611.8
  - skin 709.8
  - tongue (focal) 528.79
  - vaginal wall 623.0
- erythroid 289.9
- fascialis ossificans (progressiva) 728.11
- fibromuscular, artery NEC 447.8
  - carotid 447.8
  - renal 447.3
- genital
  - female 629.8
  - male 608.89
- gingiva 523.8
- glandularis
  - cystica uteri 621.30
  - endometrium (uterus) 621.30
  - interstitialis uteri 621.30
- granulocytic 288.8
- gum 523.8
- hymen, congenital 752.49
- islands of Langerhans 251.1
- islet cell (pancreatic) 251.9
  - alpha cells
    - with excess
      - gastrin 251.5
      - glucagon 251.4
  - beta cells 251.1
- juxtaglomerular (complex) (kidney) 593.89
- kidney (congenital) 753.3
- liver (congenital) 751.69
- lymph node (gland) 785.6
- lymphoid (diffuse) (nodular) 785.6
  - appendix 543.0
  - intestine 569.89
- mandibular 524.02
  - alveolar 524.72
  - unilateral condylar 526.89
- Marchand multiple nodular (liver) — *see* Cirrhosis, postnecrotic
- maxillary 524.01
  - alveolar 524.71
- medulla, adrenal 255.8
- myometrium, myometrial 621.2
- nose (lymphoid) (polypoid) 478.1
- oral soft tissue (inflammatory) (irritative) (mucosa) NEC 528.9
  - gingiva 523.8
  - tongue 529.8
- organ or site, congenital NEC — *see* Anomaly, specified type NEC
- ovary 620.8
- palate, papillary 528.9
- pancreatic islet cells 251.9
  - alpha
    - with excess
      - gastrin 251.5
      - glucagon 251.4
  - beta 251.1
- parathyroid (gland) 252.01
- persistent, vitreous (primary) 743.51
- pharynx (lymphoid) 478.29
- prostate 600.90
  - with urinary retention 600.91
  - adenofibromatous 600.20
    - with urinary retention 600.21
  - nodular 600.10
    - with urinary retention 600.11
- renal artery (fibromuscular) 447.3
- reticuloendothelial (cell) 289.9
- salivary gland (any) 527.1
- Schimmelbusch's 610.1

Hyperplasia, hyperplastic — *continued*
  suprarenal (capsule) (gland) 255.8
  thymus (gland) (persistent) 254.0
  thyroid (*see also* Goiter) 240.9
    primary 242.0 ☑
    secondary 242.2 ☑
  tonsil (lymphoid tissue) 474.11
    and adenoids 474.10
  urethrovaginal 599.89
  uterus, uterine (myometrium) 621.2
    endometrium (*see also* Hyperplasia,
      endometrium) 621.30
  vitreous (humor), primary persistent 743.51
  vulva 624.3
  zygoma 738.11
Hyperpnea (*see also* Hyperventilation) 786.01
Hyperpotassemia 276.7
Hyperprebetalipoproteinemia 272.1
  with chylomicronemia 272.3
  familial 272.1
Hyperprolactinemia 253.1
Hyperprolinemia 270.8
Hyperproteinemia 273.8
Hyperprothrombinemia 289.89
Hyperpselaphesia 782.0
Hyperpyrexia 780.6
  heat (effects of) 992.0
  malarial (*see also* Malaria) 084.6
  malignant, due to anesthetic 995.86
  rheumatic — *see* Fever, rheumatic
  unknown origin (*see also* Pyrexia) 780.6
Hyperreactor, vascular 780.2
Hyperreflexia 796.1
  bladder, autonomic 596.54
    with cauda equina 344.61
  detrusor 344.61
Hypersalivation (*see also* Ptyalism) 527.7
Hypersarcosinemia 270.8

Hypersecretion
  ACTH 255.3
  androgens (ovarian) 256.1
  calcitonin 246.0
  corticoadrenal 255.3
  cortisol 255.0
  estrogen 256.0
  gastric 536.8
    psychogenic 306.4
  gastrin 251.5
  glucagon 251.4
  hormone
    ACTH 255.3
    anterior pituitary 253.1
    growth NEC 253.0
    ovarian androgen 256.1
    testicular 257.0
    thyroid stimulating 242.8 ☑
  insulin — *see* Hyperinsulinism
  lacrimal glands (*see also* Epiphora) 375.20
  medulloadrenal 255.6
  milk 676.6 ☑
  ovarian androgens 256.1
  pituitary (anterior) 253.1
  salivary gland (any) 527.7
  testicular hormones 257.0
  thyrocalcitonin 246.0
  upper respiratory 478.9
Hypersegmentation, hereditary 288.2
  eosinophils 288.2
  neutrophil nuclei 288.2
**Hypersensitive, hypersensitiveness,
    hypersensitivity** — *see also* Allergy
  angiitis 446.20
    specified NEC 446.29
  carotid sinus 337.0
  colon 564.9
    psychogenic 306.4
  DNA (deoxyribonucleic acid) NEC 287.2
  drug (*see also* Allergy, drug) 995.2
  esophagus 530.89

**Hypersensitive, hypersensitiveness,
    hypersensitivity** — *see also* Allergy —
    continued
  insect bites — *see* Injury, superficial, by site
  labyrinth 386.58
  pain (*see also* Disturbance, sensation) 782.0
  pneumonitis NEC 495.9
  reaction (*see also* Allergy) 995.3
    upper respiratory tract NEC 478.8
  stomach (allergic) (nonallergic) 536.8
    psychogenic 306.4
Hypersomatotropism (classic) 253.0
Hypersomnia, ▶unspecified◀ 780.54
  with sleep apnea, ▶unspecified◀ 780.53
  alcohol induced 291.82   ●
  drug induced 292.85   ●
  due to   ●
    medical condition classified elsewhere   ●
      327.14   ●
    mental disorder 327.15   ●
  idiopathic   ●
    with long sleep time 327.11   ●
    without long sleep time 327.12   ●
  menstrual related 327.13   ●
  nonorganic origin 307.43
    persistent (primary) 307.44
    transient 307.43
  organic 327.10   ●
    other 327.19   ●
  primary 307.44   ●
  recurrent 327.13   ●
Hypersplenia 289.4
Hypersplenism 289.4
Hypersteatosis 706.3
Hyperstimulation, ovarian 256.1
Hypersuprarenalism 255.3
Hypersusceptibility — *see* Allergy
Hyper-TBG-nemia 246.8
Hypertelorism 756.0
  orbit, orbital 376.41

☑ Additional Digit Required — Refer to the Tabular List (Numeric Code Section) for Additional Digit Selection

Index

Hyperplasia, hyperplastic — Hypertelorism

	Malignant	Benign	Unspecified
Hypertension, hypertensive (arterial) (arteriolar) (crisis) (degeneration) (disease) (essential) (fluctuating) (idiopathic) (intermittent) (labile) (low renin) (orthostatic) (paroxysmal) (primary) (systemic) (uncontrolled) (vascular)	401.0	401.1	401.9
with			
chronic kidney disease	403.01	403.11	403.91 ●
heart involvement (conditions classifiable to 429.0-429.3, 429.8, 429.9 due to hypertension) (see also Hypertension, heart)	402.00	402.10	402.90
with kidney involvement — see Hypertension, cardiorenal			
renal involvement (only conditions classifiable to 585, 586, 587) (excludes conditions classifiable to 584) (see also Hypertension, kidney)	403.00	403.10	403.90
with heart involvement — see Hypertension, cardiorenal			
failure (and sclerosis) (see also Hypertension, kidney)	403.01	403.11	403.91
sclerosis without failure (see also Hypertension, kidney)	403.00	403.10	403.90
accelerated (see also Hypertension, by type, malignant)	401.0	—	—
antepartum — see Hypertension, complicating pregnancy, childbirth, or the puerperium			
cardiorenal (disease)	404.00	404.10	404.90
with			
chronic kidney disease	403.01	403.11	403.91 ●
and heart failure	404.03	404.13	404.93 ●
heart failure	404.01	404.11	404.91
and chronic kidney disease	404.03	404.13	404.93 ●
and renal failure	404.03	404.13	404.93
renal failure	404.02	404.12	404.92
and heart failure	404.03	404.13	404.93
cardiovascular disease (arteriosclerotic) (sclerotic)	402.00	402.10	402.90
with			
heart failure	402.01	402.11	402.91
renal involvement (conditions classifiable to 403) (see also Hypertension, cardiorenal)	404.00	404.10	404.90
cardiovascular renal (disease) (sclerosis) (see also Hypertension, cardiorenal)	404.00	404.10	404.90
cerebrovascular disease NEC	437.2	437.2	437.2
complicating pregnancy, childbirth, or the puerperium	642.2 ✓	642.0 ✓	642.9 ✓
with			
albuminuria (and edema) (mild)	—	—	642.4 ✓
severe	—	—	642.5 ✓
edema (mild)	—	—	642.4 ✓
severe	—	—	642.5 ✓
heart disease	642.2 ✓	642.2 ✓	642.2 ✓
and renal disease	642.2 ✓	642.2 ✓	642.2 ✓
renal disease	642.2 ✓	642.2 ✓	642.2 ✓
and heart disease	642.2 ✓	642.2 ✓	642.2 ✓
chronic	642.2 ✓	642.0 ✓	642.0 ✓
with pre-eclampsia or eclampsia	642.7 ✓	642.7 ✓	642.7 ✓
fetus or newborn	760.0	760.0	760.0
essential	—	642.0 ✓	642.0 ✓
with pre-eclampsia or eclampsia	—	642.7 ✓	642.7 ✓
fetus or newborn	760.0	760.0	760.0
fetus or newborn	760.0	760.0	760.0
gestational	—	—	642.3 ✓
pre-existing	642.2 ✓	642.0 ✓	642.0 ✓
with pre-eclampsia or eclampsia	642.7 ✓	642.7 ✓	642.7 ✓
fetus or newborn	760.0	760.0	760.0
secondary to renal disease	642.1 ✓	642.1 ✓	642.1 ✓
with pre-eclampsia or eclampsia	642.7 ✓	642.7 ✓	642.7 ✓
fetus or newborn	760.0	760.0	760.0
transient	—	—	642.3 ✓
due to			
aldosteronism, primary	405.09	405.19	405.99
brain tumor	405.09	405.19	405.99
bulbar poliomyelitis	405.09	405.19	405.99
calculus			
kidney	405.09	405.19	405.99
ureter	405.09	405.19	405.99
coarctation, aorta	405.09	405.19	405.99
Cushing's disease	405.09	405.19	405.99
glomerulosclerosis (see also Hypertension, kidney)	403.00	403.10	403.90
periarteritis nodosa	405.09	405.19	405.99
pheochromocytoma	405.09	405.19	405.99
polycystic kidney(s)	405.09	405.19	405.99
polycythemia	405.09	405.19	405.99
porphyria	405.09	405.19	405.99
pyelonephritis	405.09	405.19	405.99
renal (artery)			
aneurysm	405.01	405.11	405.91
anomaly	405.01	405.11	405.91
embolism	405.01	405.11	405.91
fibromuscular hyperplasia	405.01	405.11	405.91

✓ Additional Digit Required — Refer to the Tabular List (Numeric Code Section) for Additional Digit Selection

	Malignant	Benign	Unspecified
Hypertension, hypertensive — *continued*			
due to — *continued*			
renal — *continued*			
occlusion	405.01	405.11	405.91
stenosis	405.01	405.11	405.91
thrombosis	405.01	405.11	405.91
encephalopathy	437.2	437.2	437.2
gestational (transient) NEC	—	—	642.3 ☑
Goldblatt's	440.1	440.1	440.1
heart (disease) (conditions classifiable to 429.0-429.3, 429.9 due to hypertension)	402.00	402.10	402.90
with heart failure	402.01	402.11	402.91
hypertensive kidney disease (conditions classifiable to 403) (*see also* Hypertension, cardiorenal)	404.00	404.10	404.90
renal sclerosis (*see also* Hypertension, cardiorenal)	404.00	404.10	404.90
intracranial, benign	—	348.2	—
intraocular	—	—	365.04
kidney	403.00	403.10	403.90
with			
chronic kidney disease	403.01	403.11	403.91 ●
heart involvement (conditions classifiable to 429.0-429.3, 429.8, 429.9 due to hypertension) (*see also* Hypertension, cardiorenal)	404.00	404.10	404.90
hypertensive heart (disease) (conditions classifiable to 402) (*see also* Hypertension, cardiorenal)	404.00	404.10	404.90
lesser circulation	—	—	416.0
necrotizing	401.0	—	—
ocular	—	—	365.04
portal (due to chronic liver disease)	—	—	572.3
postoperative	—	—	997.91
psychogenic	—	—	306.2
puerperal, postpartum — *see* Hypertension, complicating pregnancy, childbirth, or the puerperium			
pulmonary (artery)	—	—	416.8
with cor pulmonale (chronic)	—	—	416.8
acute	—	—	415.0
idiopathic	—	—	416.0
primary	—	—	416.0
of newborn	—	—	747.83
secondary	—	—	416.8
renal (disease) (*see also* Hypertension, kidney)	403.00	403.10	403.90
renovascular NEC	405.01	405.11	405.91
secondary NEC	405.09	405.19	405.99
due to			
aldosteronism, primary	405.09	405.19	405.99
brain tumor	405.09	405.19	405.99
bulbar poliomyelitis	405.09	405.19	405.99
calculus			
kidney	405.09	405.19	405.99
ureter	405.09	405.19	405.99
coarctation, aorta	405.09	405.19	405.99
Cushing's disease	405.09	405.19	405.99
glomerulosclerosis (*see also* Hypertension, kidney)	403.00	403.10	403.90
periarteritis nodosa	405.09	405.19	405.99
pheochromocytoma	405.09	405.19	405.99
polycystic kidney(s)	405.09	405.19	405.99
polycythemia	405.09	405.19	405.99
porphyria	405.09	405.19	405.99
pyelonephritis	405.09	405.19	405.99
renal (artery)			
aneurysm	405.01	405.11	405.91
anomaly	405.01	405.11	405.91
embolism	405.01	405.11	405.91
fibromuscular hyperplasia	405.01	405.11	405.91
occlusion	405.01	405.11	405.91
stenosis	405.01	405.11	405.91
thrombosis	405.01	405.11	405.91
transient	—	—	796.2
of pregnancy	—	—	642.3 ☑
venous, chronic (asymptomatic) (idiopathic)	—	—	459.30
due to			
deep vein thrombosis (*see also* Syndrome, postphlebetic)	—	—	459.10
with			
complication, NEC	—	—	459.39
inflammation	—	—	459.32
with ulcer	—	—	459.33
ulcer	—	—	459.31
with inflammation	—	—	459.33

Hyperthecosis, ovary

Hyperthecosis, ovary 256.8
Hyperthermia (of unknown origin) (*see also*
    Pyrexia) 780.6
  malignant (due to anesthesia) 995.86
  newborn 778.4
Hyperthymergasia (*see also* Psychosis, affective)
  296.0 ☑
  reactive (from emotional stress, psychological
    trauma) 298.1
  recurrent episode 296.1 ☑
  single episode 296.0 ☑
Hyperthymism 254.8
Hyperthyroid (recurrent) — *see* Hyperthyroidism
Hyperthyroidism (latent) (preadult) (recurrent)
  (without goiter) 242.9 ☑

> *Note* — *Use the following fifth-digit
> subclassification with category 242:*
>
> 0   *without mention of thyrotoxic crisis
>   or storm*
>
> 1   *with mention of thyrotoxic crisis or
>   storm*

  with
    goiter (diffuse) 242.0 ☑
      adenomatous 242.3 ☑
        multinodular 242.2 ☑
        uninodular 242.1 ☑
      nodular 242.3 ☑
        multinodular 242.2 ☑
        uninodular 242.1 ☑
    thyroid nodule 242.1 ☑
  complicating pregnancy, childbirth, or
    puerperium 648.1 ☑
  neonatal (transient) 775.3
Hypertonia — *see* Hypertonicity
Hypertonicity
  bladder 596.51
  fetus or newborn 779.89
  gastrointestinal (tract) 536.8
  infancy 779.89
    due to electrolyte imbalance 779.89
  muscle 728.85
  stomach 536.8
    psychogenic 306.4
  uterus, uterine (contractions) 661.4 ☑
    affecting fetus or newborn 763.7
Hypertony — *see* Hypertonicity
Hypertransaminemia 790.4
Hypertrichosis 704.1
  congenital 757.4
  eyelid 374.54
  lanuginosa 757.4
    acquired 704.1
Hypertriglyceridemia, essential 272.1
Hypertrophy, hypertrophic
  adenoids (infectional) 474.12
    and tonsils (faucial) (infective) (lingual)
      (lymphoid) 474.10
  adrenal 255.8
  alveolar process or ridge 525.8
  anal papillae 569.49
  apocrine gland 705.82
  artery NEC 447.8
    carotid 447.8
    congenital (peripheral) NEC 747.60
      gastrointestinal 747.61
      lower limb 747.64
      renal 747.62
      specified NEC 747.69
      spinal 747.82
      upper limb 747.63
    renal 447.3
  arthritis (chronic) (*see also* Osteoarthrosis)
    715.9 ☑
    spine (*see also* Spondylosis) 721.90
  arytenoid 478.79
  asymmetrical (heart) 429.9
  auricular — *see* Hypertrophy, cardiac
  Bartholin's gland 624.8
  bile duct 576.8
  bladder (sphincter) (trigone) 596.8
  blind spot, visual field 368.42
  bone 733.99
  brain 348.8

Hypertrophy, hypertrophic — *continued*
  breast 611.1
    cystic 610.1
    fetus or newborn 778.7
    fibrocystic 610.1
    massive pubertal 611.1
    puerperal, postpartum 676.3 ☑
    senile (parenchymatous) 611.1
  cardiac (chronic) (idiopathic) 429.3
    with
      rheumatic fever (conditions classifiable to
        390)
        active 391.8
          with chorea 392.0
        inactive or quiescent (with chorea)
          398.99
    congenital NEC 746.89
    fatty (*see also* Degeneration, myocardial)
      429.1
    hypertensive (*see also* Hypertension, heart)
      402.90
    rheumatic (with chorea) 398.99
      active or acute 391.8
        with chorea 392.0
    valve (*see also* Endocarditis) 424.90
      congenital NEC 746.89
  cartilage 733.99
  cecum 569.89
  cervix (uteri) 622.6
    congenital 752.49
    elongation 622.6
  clitoris (cirrhotic) 624.2
    congenital 752.49
  colon 569.89
    congenital 751.3
  conjunctiva, lymphoid 372.73
  cornea 371.89
  corpora cavernosa 607.89
  duodenum 537.89
  endometrium (uterus) (*see also* Hyperplasia,
    endometrium) 621.30
    cervix 622.6
  epididymis 608.89
  esophageal hiatus (congenital) 756.6
    with hernia — *see* Hernia, diaphragm
  eyelid 374.30
  falx, skull 733.99
  fat pad 729.30
    infrapatellar 729.31
    knee 729.31
    orbital 374.34
    popliteal 729.31
    prepatellar 729.31
    retropatellar 729.31
    specified site NEC 729.39
  foot (congenital) 755.67
  frenum, frenulum (tongue) 529.8
    linguae 529.8
    lip 528.5
  gallbladder or cystic duct 575.8
  gastric mucosa 535.2 ☑
  gingiva 523.8
  gland, glandular (general) NEC 785.6
  gum (mucous membrane) 523.8
  heart (idiopathic) — *see also* Hypertrophy,
    cardiac
    valve — *see also* Endocarditis
      congenital NEC 746.89
  hemifacial 754.0
  hepatic — *see* Hypertrophy, liver
  hiatus (esophageal) 756.6
  hilus gland 785.6
  hymen, congenital 752.49
  ileum 569.89
  infrapatellar fat pad 729.31
  intestine 569.89
  jejunum 569.89
  kidney (compensatory) 593.1
    congenital 753.3
  labial frenulum 528.5
  labium (majus) (minus) 624.3
  lacrimal gland, chronic 375.03
  ligament 728.9
    spinal 724.8
  linguae frenulum 529.8
  lingual tonsil (infectional) 474.11
  lip (frenum) 528.5

Hypertrophy, hypertrophic — *continued*
  lip — *continued*
    congenital 744.81
  liver 789.1
    acute 573.8
    cirrhotic — *see* Cirrhosis, liver
    congenital 751.69
    fatty — *see* Fatty, liver
  lymph gland 785.6
    tuberculous — *see* Tuberculosis, lymph
      gland
  mammary gland — *see* Hypertrophy, breast
  maxillary frenulum 528.5
  Meckel's diverticulum (congenital) 751.0
  medial meniscus, acquired 717.3
  median bar 600.90
    with urinary retention 600.91
  mediastinum 519.3
  meibomian gland 373.2
  meniscus, knee, congenital 755.64
  metatarsal head 733.99
  metatarsus 733.99
  mouth 528.9
  mucous membrane
    alveolar process 523.8
    nose 478.1
    turbinate (nasal) 478.0
  muscle 728.9
  muscular coat, artery NEC 447.8
    carotid 447.8
    renal 447.3
  myocardium (*see also* Hypertrophy, cardiac)
    429.3
    idiopathic 425.4
  myometrium 621.2
  nail 703.8
    congenital 757.5
  nasal 478.1
    alae 478.1
    bone 738.0
    cartilage 478.1
    mucous membrane (septum) 478.1
    sinus (*see also* Sinusitis) 473.9
    turbinate 478.0
  nasopharynx, lymphoid (infectional) (tissue)
    (wall) 478.29
  neck, uterus 622.6
  nipple 611.1
  normal aperture diaphragm (congenital) 756.6
  nose (*see also* Hypertrophy, nasal) 478.1
  orbit 376.46
  organ or site, congenital NEC — *see* Anomaly,
    specified type NEC
  osteoarthropathy (pulmonary) 731.2
  ovary 620.8
  palate (hard) 526.89
    soft 528.9
  pancreas (congenital) 751.7
  papillae
    anal 569.49
    tongue 529.3
  parathyroid (gland) 252.01
  parotid gland 527.1
  penis 607.89
  phallus 607.89
    female (clitoris) 624.2
  pharyngeal tonsil 474.12
  pharyngitis 472.1
  pharynx 478.29
    lymphoid (infectional) (tissue) (wall) 478.29
  pituitary (fossa) (gland) 253.8
  popliteal fat pad 729.31
  preauricular (lymph) gland (Hampstead) 785.6
  prepuce (congenital) 605
    female 624.2
  prostate (asymptomatic) (early) (recurrent)
    600.90
    with urinary retention 600.91
    adenofibromatous 600.20
      with urinary retention 600.21
    benign 600.00
      with urinary retention 600.01
    congenital 752.89
  pseudoedematous hypodermal 757.0
  pseudomuscular 359.1
  pylorus (muscle) (sphincter) 537.0
    congenital 750.5

Hypertrophy, hypertrophic — *continued*
  pylorus — *continued*
    infantile 750.5
  rectal sphincter 569.49
  rectum 569.49
  renal 593.1
  rhinitis (turbinate) 472.0
  salivary duct or gland 527.1
    congenital 750.26
  scaphoid (tarsal) 733.99
  scar 701.4
  scrotum 608.89
  sella turcica 253.8
  seminal vesicle 608.89
  sigmoid 569.89
  skin condition NEC 701.9
  spermatic cord 608.89
  spinal ligament 724.8
  spleen — *see* Splenomegaly
  spondylitis (spine) (*see also* Spondylosis) 721.90
  stomach 537.89
  subaortic stenosis (idiopathic) 425.1
  sublingual gland 527.1
    congenital 750.26
  submaxillary gland 527.1
  suprarenal (gland) 255.8
  tendon 727.9
  testis 608.89
    congenital 752.89
  thymic, thymus (congenital) (gland) 254.0
  thyroid (gland) (*see also* Goiter) 240.9
    primary 242.0 ☑
    secondary 242.2 ☑
  toe (congenital) 755.65
    acquired 735.8
  tongue 529.8
    congenital 750.15
    frenum 529.8
    papillae (foliate) 529.3
  tonsil (faucial) (infective) (lingual) (lymphoid) 474.11
    with
      adenoiditis 474.01
      tonsillitis 474.00
        and adenoiditis 474.02
      and adenoids 474.10
  tunica vaginalis 608.89
  turbinate (mucous membrane) 478.0
  ureter 593.89
  urethra 599.84
  uterus 621.2
    puerperal, postpartum 674.8 ☑
  uvula 528.9
  vagina 623.8
  vas deferens 608.89
  vein 459.89
  ventricle, ventricular (heart) (left) (right) — *see also* Hypertrophy, cardiac
    congenital 746.89
    due to hypertension (left) (right) (*see also* Hypertension, heart) 402.90
      benign 402.10
      malignant 402.00
    right with ventricular septal defect, pulmonary stenosis or atresia, and dextraposition of aorta 745.2
  verumontanum 599.89
  vesical 596.8
  vocal cord 478.5
  vulva 624.3
    stasis (nonfilarial) 624.3
Hypertropia (intermittent) (periodic) 378.31
Hypertyrosinemia 270.2
Hyperuricemia 790.6
Hypervalinemia 270.3
Hyperventilation (tetany) 786.01
  hysterical 300.11
  psychogenic 306.1
  syndrome 306.1
Hyperviscidosis 277.00
Hyperviscosity (of serum) (syndrome) NEC 273.3
  polycythemic 289.0
  sclerocythemic 282.8

Hypervitaminosis (dietary) NEC 278.8
  A (dietary) 278.2
  D (dietary) 278.4
  from excessive administration or use of vitamin preparations (chronic) 278.8
    reaction to sudden overdose 963.5
    vitamin A 278.2
      reaction to sudden overdose 963.5
    vitamin D 278.4
      reaction to sudden overdose 963.5
    vitamin K
      correct substance properly administered 278.8
      overdose or wrong substance given or taken 964.3
Hypervolemia 276.6
Hypesthesia (*see also* Disturbance, sensation) 782.0
  cornea 371.81
Hyphema (anterior chamber) (ciliary body) (iris) 364.41
  traumatic 921.3
Hyphemia — *see* Hyphema
Hypoacidity, gastric 536.8
  psychogenic 306.4
Hypoactive labyrinth (function) — *see* Hypofunction, labyrinth
Hypoadrenalism 255.4
  tuberculous (*see also* Tuberculosis) 017.6 ☑
Hypoadrenocorticism 255.4
  pituitary 253.4
Hypoalbuminemia 273.8
Hypoalphalipoproteinemia 272.5
Hypobarism 993.2
Hypobaropathy 993.2
Hypobetalipoproteinemia (familial) 272.5
Hypocalcemia 275.41
  cow's milk 775.4
  dietary 269.3
  neonatal 775.4
  phosphate-loading 775.4
Hypocalcification, teeth 520.4
Hypochloremia 276.9
Hypochlorhydria 536.8
  neurotic 306.4
  psychogenic 306.4
Hypocholesteremia 272.5
Hypochondria (reaction) 300.7
Hypochondriac 300.7
Hypochondriasis 300.7
Hypochromasia blood cells 280.9
Hypochromic anemia 280.9
  due to blood loss (chronic) 280.0
    acute 285.1
  microcytic 280.9
Hypocoagulability (*see also* Defect, coagulation) 286.9
Hypocomplementemia 279.8
Hypocythemia (progressive) 284.9
Hypodontia (*see also* Anodontia) 520.0
Hypoeosinophilia 288.8
Hypoesthesia (*see also* Disturbance, sensation) 782.0
  cornea 371.81
  tactile 782.0
Hypoestrinism 256.39
Hypoestrogenism 256.39
Hypoferremia 280.9
  due to blood loss (chronic) 280.0
Hypofertility
  female 628.9
  male 606.1
Hypofibrinogenemia 286.3
  acquired 286.6
  congenital 286.3
Hypofunction
  adrenal (gland) 255.4
    cortex 255.4
    medulla 255.5
    specified NEC 255.5

Hypofunction — *continued*
  cerebral 331.9
  corticoadrenal NEC 255.4
  intestinal 564.89
  labyrinth (unilateral) 386.53
    with loss of labyrinthine reactivity 386.55
    bilateral 386.54
      with loss of labyrinthine reactivity 386.56
  Leydig cell 257.2
  ovary 256.39
    postablative 256.2
  pituitary (anterior) (gland) (lobe) 253.2
    posterior 253.5
  testicular 257.2
    iatrogenic 257.1
    postablative 257.1
    postirradiation 257.1
    postsurgical 257.1
Hypogammaglobulinemia 279.00
  acquired primary 279.06
  non-sex-linked, congenital 279.06
  sporadic 279.06
  transient of infancy 279.09
Hypogenitalism (congenital) (female) (male) 752.89
  penis 752.69
Hypoglycemia (spontaneous) 251.2
  coma 251.0
    diabetic 250.3 ☑
  diabetic 250.8 ☑
  due to insulin 251.0
    therapeutic misadventure 962.3
  familial (idiopathic) 251.2
  following gastrointestinal surgery 579.3
  infantile (idiopathic) 251.2
  in infant of diabetic mother 775.0
  leucine-induced 270.3
  neonatal 775.6
  reactive 251.2
  specified NEC 251.1
Hypoglycemic shock 251.0
  diabetic 250.8 ☑
  due to insulin 251.0
  functional (syndrome) 251.1
Hypogonadism
  female 256.39
  gonadotrophic (isolated) 253.4
  hypogonadotropic (isolated) (with anosmia) 253.4
  isolated 253.4
  male 257.2
    hereditary familial (Reifenstein's syndrome) 259.5   ●●
  ovarian (primary) 256.39
  pituitary (secondary) 253.4
  testicular (primary) (secondary) 257.2
Hypohidrosis 705.0
Hypohidrotic ectodermal dysplasia 757.31
Hypoidrosis 705.0
Hypoinsulinemia, postsurgical 251.3
  postpancreatectomy (complete) (partial) 251.3
Hypokalemia 276.8
Hypokinesia 780.99
Hypoleukia splenica 289.4
Hypoleukocytosis 288.8
Hypolipidemia 272.5
Hypolipoproteinemia 272.5
Hypomagnesemia 275.2
  neonatal 775.4
Hypomania, hypomanic reaction (*see also* Psychosis, affective) 296.0 ☑
  recurrent episode 296.1 ☑
  single episode 296.0 ☑
Hypomastia (congenital) 757.6
Hypomenorrhea 626.1
Hypometabolism 783.9
Hypomotility
  gastrointestinal tract 536.8
    psychogenic 306.4
  intestine 564.89
    psychogenic 306.4
  stomach 536.8
    psychogenic 306.4
Hyponasality 784.49

Hyponatremia 276.1
Hypo-ovarianism 256.39
Hypo-ovarism 256.39
Hypoparathyroidism (idiopathic) (surgically induced) 252.1
   neonatal 775.4
Hypopharyngitis 462
Hypophoria 378.40
Hypophosphatasia 275.3
Hypophosphatemia (acquired) (congenital) (familial) 275.3
   renal 275.3
Hypophyseal, hypophysis — *see also* condition
   dwarfism 253.3
   gigantism 253.0
   syndrome 253.8
Hypophyseothalamic syndrome 253.8
Hypopiesis — *see* Hypotension
Hypopigmentation 709.00
   eyelid 374.53
Hypopinealism 259.8
Hypopituitarism (juvenile) (syndrome) 253.2
   due to
      hormone therapy 253.7
      hypophysectomy 253.7
      radiotherapy 253.7
   postablative 253.7
   postpartum hemorrhage 253.2
Hypoplasia, hypoplasis 759.89
   adrenal (gland) 759.1
   alimentary tract 751.8
      lower 751.2
      upper 750.8
   anus, anal (canal) 751.2
   aorta 747.22
   aortic
      arch (tubular) 747.10
      orifice or valve with hypoplasia of ascending aorta and defective development of left ventricle (with mitral valve atresia) 746.7
   appendix 751.2
   areola 757.6
   arm (*see also* Absence, arm, congenital) 755.20
   artery (congenital) (peripheral) 747.60
      brain 747.81
      cerebral 747.81
      coronary 746.85
      gastrointestinal 747.61
      lower limb 747.64
      pulmonary 747.3
      renal 747.62
      retinal 743.58
      specified NEC 747.69
      spinal 747.82
      umbilical 747.5
      upper limb 747.63
   auditory canal 744.29
      causing impairment of hearing 744.02
   biliary duct (common) or passage 751.61
   bladder 753.8
   bone NEC 756.9
      face 756.0
      malar 756.0
      mandible 524.04
         alveolar 524.74
      marrow 284.9
         acquired (secondary) 284.8
         congenital 284.0
         idiopathic 284.9
      maxilla 524.03
         alveolar 524.73
      skull (*see also* Hypoplasia, skull) 756.0
   brain 742.1
      gyri 742.2
      specified part 742.2
   breast (areola) 757.6
   bronchus (tree) 748.3
   cardiac 746.89
      valve — *see* Hypoplasia, heart, valve
      vein 746.89
   carpus (*see also* Absence, carpal, congenital) 755.28
   cartilaginous 756.9
   cecum 751.2

Hypoplasia, hypoplasis — *continued*
   cementum 520.4
      hereditary 520.5
   cephalic 742.1
   cerebellum 742.2
   cervix (uteri) 752.49
   chin 524.06
   clavicle 755.51
   coccyx 756.19
   colon 751.2
   corpus callosum 742.2
   cricoid cartilage 748.3
   dermal, focal (Goltz) 757.39
   digestive organ(s) or tract NEC 751.8
      lower 751.2
      upper 750.8
   ear 744.29
      auricle 744.23
      lobe 744.29
      middle, except ossicles 744.03
         ossicles 744.04
      ossicles 744.04
   enamel of teeth (neonatal) (postnatal) (prenatal) 520.4
      hereditary 520.5
   endocrine (gland) NEC 759.2
   endometrium 621.8
   epididymis 752.89
   epiglottis 748.3
   erythroid, congenital 284.0
   erythropoietic, chronic acquired 284.8
   esophagus 750.3
   Eustachian tube 744.24
   eye (*see also* Microphthalmos) 743.10
      lid 743.62
   face 744.89
      bone(s) 756.0
   fallopian tube 752.19
   femur (*see also* Absence, femur, congenital) 755.34
   fibula (*see also* Absence, fibula, congenital) 755.37
   finger (*see also* Absence, finger, congenital) 755.29
   focal dermal 757.39
   foot 755.31
   gallbladder 751.69
   genitalia, genital organ(s)
      female 752.89
         external 752.49
         internal NEC 752.89
      in adiposogenital dystrophy 253.8
      male 752.89
         penis 752.69
   glottis 748.3
   hair 757.4
   hand 755.21
   heart 746.89
      left (complex) (syndrome) 746.7
      valve NEC 746.89
         pulmonary 746.01
   humerus (*see also* Absence, humerus, congenital) 755.24
   hymen 752.49
   intestine (small) 751.1
      large 751.2
   iris 743.46
   jaw 524.09
   kidney(s) 753.0
   labium (majus) (minus) 752.49
   labyrinth, membranous 744.05
   lacrimal duct (apparatus) 743.65
   larynx 748.3
   leg (*see also* Absence, limb, congenital, lower) 755.30
   limb 755.4
      lower (*see also* Absence, limb, congenital, lower) 755.30
      upper (*see also* Absence, limb, congenital, upper) 755.20
   liver 751.69
   lung (lobe) 748.5
   mammary (areolar) 757.6
   mandibular 524.04
      alveolar 524.74
      unilateral condylar 526.89

Hypoplasia, hypoplasis — *continued*
   maxillary 524.03
      alveolar 524.73
   medullary 284.9
   megakaryocytic 287.30   ▲
   metacarpus (*see also* Absence, metacarpal, congenital) 755.28
   metatarsus (*see also* Absence, metatarsal, congenital) 755.38
   muscle 756.89
      eye 743.69
   myocardium (congenital) (Uhl's anomaly) 746.84
   nail(s) 757.5
   nasolacrimal duct 743.65
   nervous system NEC 742.8
   neural 742.8
   nose, nasal 748.1
   ophthalmic (*see also* Microphthalmos) 743.10
   organ
      of Corti 744.05
      or site NEC — *see* Anomaly, by site
   osseous meatus (ear) 744.03
   ovary 752.0
   oviduct 752.19
   pancreas 751.7
   parathyroid (gland) 759.2
   parotid gland 750.26
   patella 755.64
   pelvis, pelvic girdle 755.69
   penis 752.69
   peripheral vascular system (congenital) NEC 747.60
      gastrointestinal 747.61
      lower limb 747.64
      renal 747.62
      specified NEC 747.69
      spinal 747.82
      upper limb 747.63
   pituitary (gland) 759.2
   pulmonary 748.5
      arteriovenous 747.3
      artery 747.3
      valve 746.01
   punctum lacrimale 743.65
   radioulnar (*see also* Absence, radius, congenital, with ulna) 755.25
   radius (*see also* Absence, radius, congenital) 755.26
   rectum 751.2
   respiratory system NEC 748.9
   rib 756.3
   sacrum 756.19
   scapula 755.59
   shoulder girdle 755.59
   skin 757.39
   skull (bone) 756.0
      with
         anencephalus 740.0
         encephalocele 742.0
         hydrocephalus 742.3
            with spina bifida (*see also* Spina bifida) 741.0 ☑
         microcephalus 742.1
   spinal (cord) (ventral horn cell) 742.59
      vessel 747.82
   spine 756.19
   spleen 759.0
   sternum 756.3
   tarsus (*see also* Absence, tarsal, congenital) 755.38
   testis, testicle 752.89
   thymus (gland) 279.11
   thyroid (gland) 243
      cartilage 748.3
   tibiofibular (*see also* Absence, tibia, congenital, with fibula) 755.35
   toe (*see also* Absence, toe, congenital) 755.39
   tongue 750.16
   trachea (cartilage) (rings) 748.3
   Turner's (tooth) 520.4
   ulna (*see also* Absence, ulna, congenital) 755.27
   umbilical artery 747.5
   ureter 753.29
   uterus 752.3
   vagina 752.49

Hypoplasia, hypoplasis — *continued*
    vascular (peripheral) NEC (*see also* Hypoplasia,
        peripheral vascular system) 747.60
        brain 747.81
    vein(s) (peripheral) NEC (*see also* Hypoplasia,
        peripheral vascular system) 747.60
        brain 747.81
        cardiac 746.89
        great 747.49
        portal 747.49
        pulmonary 747.49
    vena cava (inferior) (superior) 747.49
    vertebra 756.19
    vulva 752.49
    zonule (ciliary) 743.39
    zygoma 738.12
Hypopotassemia 276.8
Hypoproaccelerinemia (*see also* Defect,
    coagulation) 286.3
Hypoproconvertinemia (congenital) (*see also*
    Defect, coagulation) 286.3
Hypoproteinemia (essential) (hypermetabolic)
    (idiopathic) 273.8
Hypoproteinosis 260
Hypoprothrombinemia (congenital) (hereditary)
    (idiopathic) (*see also* Defect, coagulation)
    286.3
    acquired 286.7
    newborn 776.3
Hypopselaphesia 782.0
Hypopyon (anterior chamber) (eye) 364.05
    iritis 364.05
    ulcer (cornea) 370.04
Hypopyrexia 780.99
Hyporeflex 796.1
Hyporeninemia, extreme 790.99
    in primary aldosteronism 255.10
Hyporesponsive episode 780.09
Hyposecretion
    ACTH 253.4
    ovary 256.39
        postablative 256.2
    salivary gland (any) 527.7
Hyposegmentation of neutrophils, hereditary
    288.2
Hyposiderinemia 280.9
Hyposmolality 276.1
    syndrome 276.1
Hyposomatotropism 253.3
Hyposomnia, ▶unspecified◀ (*see also* Insomnia)
    780.52
    with sleep apnea, unspecified 780.53 ●
Hypospadias (male) 752.61
    female 753.8
Hypospermatogenesis 606.1
Hyposphagma 372.72
Hyposplenism 289.59
Hypostasis, pulmonary 514
Hypostatic — *see* condition
Hyposthenuria 593.89
Hyposuprarenalism 255.4
Hypo-TBG-nemia 246.8
Hypotension (arterial) (constitutional) 458.9
    chronic 458.1
    iatrogenic 458.29
    maternal, syndrome (following labor and
        delivery) 669.2 ☑
    of hemodialysis 458.21
    orthostatic (chronic) 458.0
        dysautonomic-dyskinetic syndrome 333.0
    permanent idiopathic 458.1
    postoperative 458.29
    postural 458.0
    specified type NEC 458.8
    transient 796.3
Hypothermia (accidental) 991.6
    anesthetic 995.89
    newborn NEC 778.3
    not associated with low environmental
        temperature 780.99

Hypothymergasia (*see also* Psychosis, affective)
    296.2 ☑
    recurrent episode 296.3 ☑
    single episode 296.2 ☑
Hypothyroidism (acquired) 244.9
    complicating pregnancy, childbirth, or
        puerperium 648.1 ☑
    congenital 243
    due to
        ablation 244.1
            radioactive iodine 244.1
            surgical 244.0
        iodine (administration) (ingestion) 244.2
            radioactive 244.1
        irradiation therapy 244.1
        p-aminosalicylic acid (PAS) 244.3
        phenylbutazone 244.3
        resorcinol 244.3
        specified cause NEC 244.8
        surgery 244.0
    goitrous (sporadic) 246.1
    iatrogenic NEC 244.3
    iodine 244.2
    pituitary 244.8
    postablative NEC 244.1
    postsurgical 244.0
    primary 244.9
    secondary NEC 244.8
    specified cause NEC 244.8
    sporadic goitrous 246.1
Hypotonia, hypotonicity, hypotony 781.3
    benign congenital 358.8
    bladder 596.4
    congenital 779.89
        benign 358.8
    eye 360.30
        due to
            fistula 360.32
            ocular disorder NEC 360.33
        following loss of aqueous or vitreous 360.33
        primary 360.31
    infantile muscular (benign) 359.0
    muscle 728.9
    uterus, uterine (contractions) — *see* Inertia,
        uterus
Hypotrichosis 704.09
    congenital 757.4
    lid (congenital) 757.4
        acquired 374.55
    postinfectional NEC 704.09
Hypotropia 378.32
Hypoventilation 786.09
    congenital central alveolar syndrome
        327.25 ●
    idiopathic sleep related nonobstructive
        alveolar 327.24 ●
    sleep related, in conditions classifiable
        elsewhere 327.26 ●
Hypovitaminosis (*see also* Deficiency, vitamin)
    269.2
Hypovolemia 276.52 ▲
    surgical shock 998.0
    traumatic (shock) 958.4
Hypoxemia (*see also* Anoxia) 799.02 ▲
    sleep related, in conditions classifiable
        elsewhere 327.26 ●
Hypoxia (*see also* Anoxia) 799.02 ▲
    cerebral 348.1
        during or resulting from a procedure 997.01
        newborn 768.9
            mild or moderate 768.6
            severe 768.5
    fetal, affecting newborn 768.9
    intrauterine — *see* Distress, fetal
    myocardial (*see also* Insufficiency, coronary)
        411.89
        arteriosclerotic — *see* Arteriosclerosis,
            coronary
    newborn 768.9
    sleep related 327.24 ●
Hypsarrhythmia (*see also* Epilepsy) 345.6 ☑
Hysteralgia, pregnant uterus 646.8 ☑
Hysteria, hysterical 300.10
    anxiety 300.20
    Charcôt's gland 300.11

Hysteria, hysterical — *continued*
    conversion (any manifestation) 300.11
    dissociative type NEC 300.15
        psychosis, acute 298.1
Hysteroepilepsy 300.11
Hysterotomy, affecting fetus or newborn 763.89

I

Iatrogenic syndrome of excess cortisol 255.0
Iceland disease (epidemic neuromyasthenia) 049.8
Ichthyosis (congenital) 757.1
    acquired 701.1
    fetalis gravior 757.1
    follicularis 757.1
    hystrix 757.39
    lamellar 757.1
    lingual 528.6
    palmaris and plantaris 757.39
    simplex 757.1
    vera 757.1
    vulgaris 757.1
Ichthyotoxism 988.0
    bacterial (*see also* Poisoning, food) 005.9
Icteroanemia, hemolytic (acquired) 283.9
    congenital (*see also* Spherocytosis) 282.0
Icterus (*see also* Jaundice) 782.4
    catarrhal — *see* Icterus, infectious
    conjunctiva 782.4
        newborn 774.6
    epidemic — *see* Icterus, infectious
    febrilis — *see* Icterus, infectious
    fetus or newborn — *see* Jaundice, fetus or
        newborn
    gravis (*see also* Necrosis, liver) 570
        complicating pregnancy 646.7 ☑
            affecting fetus or newborn 760.8
        fetus or newborn NEC 773.0
        obstetrical 646.7 ☑
            affecting fetus or newborn 760.8
    hematogenous (acquired) 283.9
    hemolytic (acquired) 283.9
        congenital (*see also* Spherocytosis) 282.0
    hemorrhagic (acute) 100.0
        leptospiral 100.0
        newborn 776.0
        spirochetal 100.0
    infectious 070.1
        with hepatic coma 070.0
        leptospiral 100.0
        spirochetal 100.0
    intermittens juvenilis 277.4
    malignant (*see also* Necrosis, liver) 570
    neonatorum (*see also* Jaundice, fetus or
        newborn) 774.6
    pernicious (*see also* Necrosis, liver) 570
    spirochetal 100.0
Ictus solaris, solis 992.0
Ideation ●
    suicidal V62.84 ●
Identity disorder 313.82
    dissociative 300.14
    gender role (child) 302.6
        adult 302.85
    psychosexual (child) 302.6
        adult 302.85
Idioglossia 307.9
Idiopathic — *see* condition
Idiosyncrasy (*see also* Allergy) 995.3
    drug, medicinal substance, and biological —
        see Allergy, drug
Idiot, idiocy (congenital) 318.2
    amaurotic (Bielschowsky) (-Jansky) (family)
        (infantile (late)) (juvenile (late)) (Vogt-
        Spielmeyer) 330.1
    microcephalic 742.1
    Mongolian 758.0
    oxycephalic 756.0
Id reaction (due to bacteria) 692.89
IgE asthma 493.0 ☑

Ileitis (chronic) (*see also* Enteritis) 558.9
  infectious 009.0
  noninfectious 558.9
  regional (ulcerative) 555.0
    with large intestine 555.2
  segmental 555.0
    with large intestine 555.2
  terminal (ulcerative) 555.0
    with large intestine 555.2
Ileocolitis (*see also* Enteritis) 558.9
  infectious 009.0
  regional 555.2
  ulcerative 556.1
Ileostomy status V44.2
  with complication 569.60
Ileotyphus 002.0
Ileum — *see* condition
Ileus (adynamic) (bowel) (colon) (inhibitory) (intestine) (neurogenic) (paralytic) 560.1
  arteriomesenteric duodenal 537.2
  due to gallstone (in intestine) 560.31
  duodenal, chronic 537.2
  following gastrointestinal surgery 997.4
  gallstone 560.31
  mechanical (*see also* Obstruction, intestine) 560.9
  meconium 777.1
    due to cystic fibrosis 277.01
  myxedema 564.89
  postoperative 997.4
  transitory, newborn 777.4
Iliac — *see* condition
Iliotibial band friction syndrome 728.89
Ill, louping 063.1
Illegitimacy V61.6
Illness — *see also* Disease
  factitious 300.19
    with
      combined psychological and physical signs and symptoms 300.19
      predominantly
        physical signs and symptoms 300.19
        psychological symptoms 300.16
  chronic (with physical symptoms) 301.51
  heart — *see* Disease, heart
  manic-depressive (*see also* Psychosis, affective) 296.80
  mental (*see also* Disorder, mental) 300.9
Imbalance 781.2
  autonomic (*see also* Neuropathy, peripheral, autonomic) 337.9
  electrolyte 276.9
    with
      abortion — *see* Abortion, by type, with metabolic disorder
      ectopic pregnancy (*see also* categories 633.0-633.9) 639.4
      hyperemesis gravidarum (before 22 completed weeks gestation) 643.1 ☑
      molar pregnancy (*see also* categories 630-632) 639.4
    following
      abortion 639.4
      ectopic or molar pregnancy 639.4
    neonatal, transitory NEC 775.5
  endocrine 259.9
  eye muscle NEC 378.9
    heterophoria — *see* Heterophoria
  glomerulotubular NEC 593.89
  hormone 259.9
  hysterical (*see also* Hysteria) 300.10
  labyrinth NEC 386.50
  posture 729.9
  sympathetic (*see also* Neuropathy, peripheral, autonomic) 337.9
Imbecile, imbecility 318.0
  moral 301.7
  old age 290.9
  senile 290.9
  specified IQ — *see* IQ
  unspecified IQ 318.0
Imbedding, intrauterine device 996.32
Imbibition, cholesterol (gallbladder) 575.6

Imerslund (-Gräsbeck) syndrome (anemia due to familial selective vitamin B$_{12}$ malabsorption) 281.1
Iminoacidopathy 270.8
Iminoglycinuria, familial 270.8
Immature — *see also* Immaturity
  personality 301.89
Immaturity 765.1 ☑
  extreme 765.0 ☑
  fetus or infant light-for-dates — *see* Light-for-dates
  lung, fetus or newborn 770.4
  organ or site NEC — *see* Hypoplasia
  pulmonary, fetus or newborn 770.4
  reaction 301.89
  sexual (female) (male) 259.0
Immersion 994.1
  foot 991.4
  hand 991.4
Immobile, immobility
  intestine 564.89
  joint — *see* Ankylosis
  syndrome (paraplegic) 728.3
Immunization
  ABO
    affecting management of pregnancy 656.2 ☑
      fetus or newborn 773.1
  complication — *see* Complications, vaccination
  Rh factor
    affecting management of pregnancy 656.1 ☑
      fetus or newborn 773.0
    from transfusion 999.7
Immunodeficiency 279.3
  with
    adenosine-deaminase deficiency 279.2
    defect, predominant
      B-cell 279.00
      T-cell 279.10
    hyperimmunoglobulinemia 279.2
    lymphopenia, hereditary 279.2
    thrombocytopenia and eczema 279.12
    thymic
      aplasia 279.2
      dysplasia 279.2
  autosomal recessive, Swiss-type 279.2
  common variable 279.06
  severe combined (SCID) 279.2
  to Rh factor
    affecting management of pregnancy 656.1 ☑
      fetus or newborn 773.0
  X-linked, with increased IgM 279.05
Immunotherapy, prophylactic V07.2
  antineoplastic V58.12 ●
Impaction, impacted
  bowel, colon, rectum 560.30
    with hernia — *see also* Hernia, by site, with obstruction
      gangrenous — *see* Hernia, by site, with gangrene
    by
      calculus 560.39
      gallstone 560.31
    fecal 560.39
    specified type NEC 560.39
  calculus — *see* Calculus
  cerumen (ear) (external) 380.4
  cuspid 520.6
  dental 520.6
  fecal, feces 560.39
    with hernia — *see also* Hernia, by site, with obstruction
      gangrenous — *see* Hernia, by site, with gangrene
  fracture — *see* Fracture, by site
  gallbladder — *see* Cholelithiasis
  gallstone(s) — *see* Cholelithiasis
    in intestine (any part) 560.31
  intestine(s) 560.30
    with hernia — *see also* Hernia, by site, with obstruction
      gangrenous — *see* Hernia, by site, with gangrene
    by
      calculus 560.39
      gallstone 560.31

Impaction, impacted — *continued*
  intestine(s) — *continued*
    fecal 560.39
    specified type NEC 560.39
  intrauterine device (IUD) 996.32
  molar 520.6
  shoulder 660.4 ☑
    affecting fetus or newborn 763.1
  tooth, teeth 520.6
  turbinate 733.99
Impaired, impairment (function)
  arm V49.1
    movement, involving
      musculoskeletal system V49.1
      nervous system V49.2
  auditory discrimination 388.43
  back V48.3
  body (entire) V49.89
  glucose
    fasting 790.21
    tolerance test (oral) 790.22
  hearing (*see also* Deafness) 389.9
  heart — *see* Disease, heart
  kidney (*see also* Disease, renal) 593.9
    disorder resulting from 588.9
      specified NEC 588.89
  leg V49.1
    movement, involving
      musculoskeletal system V49.1
      nervous system V49.2
  limb V49.1
    movement, involving
      musculoskeletal system V49.1
      nervous system V49.2
  liver 573.8
  mastication 524.9
  mobility
    ear ossicles NEC 385.22
    incostapedial joint 385.22
    malleus 385.21
  myocardium, myocardial (*see also* Insufficiency, myocardial) 428.0
  neuromusculoskeletal NEC V49.89
    back V48.3
    head V48.2
    limb V49.2
    neck V48.3
    spine V48.3
    trunk V48.3
  rectal sphincter 787.99
  renal (*see also* Disease, renal) 593.9
    disorder resulting from 588.9
      specified NEC 588.89
  spine V48.3
  vision NEC 369.9
    both eyes NEC 369.3
    moderate 369.74
      both eyes 369.25
        with impairment of lesser eye (specified as)
          blind, not further specified 369.15
          low vision, not further specified 369.23
          near-total 369.17
          profound 369.18
          severe 369.24
          total 369.16
      one eye 369.74
        with vision of other eye (specified as)
          near-normal 369.75
          normal 369.76
    near-total 369.64
      both eyes 369.04
        with impairment of lesser eye (specified as)
          blind, not further specified 369.02
          total 369.03
      one eye 369.64
        with vision of other eye (specified as)
          near normal 369.65
          normal 369.66
    one eye 369.60
      with low vision of other eye 369.10

Impaired, impairment — *continued*
  vision NEC — *continued*
    profound 369.67
      both eyes 369.08
        with impairment of lesser eye
          (specified as)
          blind, not further specified 369.05
          near-total 369.07
          total 369.06
      one eye 369.67
        with vision of other eye (specified as)
          near-normal 369.68
          normal 369.69
    severe 369.71
      both eyes 369.22
        with impairment of lesser eye
          (specified as)
          blind, not further specified 369.11
          low vision, not further specified
            369.21
          near-total 369.13
          profound 369.14
          total 369.12
      one eye 369.71
        with vision of other eye (specified as)
          near-normal 369.72
          normal 369.73
    total
      both eyes 369.01
      one eye 369.61
        with vision of other eye (specified as)
          near-normal 369.62
          normal 369.63

Impaludism — *see* Malaria

Impediment, speech NEC 784.5
  psychogenic 307.9
  secondary to organic lesion 784.5

Impending
  cerebrovascular accident or attack 435.9
  coronary syndrome 411.1
  delirium tremens 291.0
  myocardial infarction 411.1

Imperception, auditory (acquired) (congenital)
  389.9

Imperfect
  aeration, lung (newborn) 770.5
  closure (congenital)
    alimentary tract NEC 751.8
      lower 751.5
      upper 750.8
    atrioventricular ostium 745.69
    atrium (secundum) 745.5
      primum 745.61
    branchial cleft or sinus 744.41
    choroid 743.59
    cricoid cartilage 748.3
    cusps, heart valve NEC 746.89
      pulmonary 746.09
    ductus
      arteriosus 747.0
      Botalli 747.0
    ear drum 744.29
      causing impairment of hearing 744.03
    endocardial cushion 745.60
    epiglottis 748.3
    esophagus with communication to bronchus
      or trachea 750.3
    Eustachian valve 746.89
    eyelid 743.62
    face, facial (*see also* Cleft, lip) 749.10
    foramen
      Botalli 745.5
      ovale 745.5
    genitalia, genital organ(s) or system
      female 752.89
        external 752.49
        internal NEC 752.89
        uterus 752.3
      male 752.89
        penis 752.69
    glottis 748.3
    heart valve (cusps) NEC 746.89
    interatrial ostium or septum 745.5
    interauricular ostium or septum 745.5
    interventricular ostium or septum 745.4
    iris 743.46
    kidney 753.3

Imperfect — *continued*
  closure — *continued*
    larynx 748.3
    lens 743.36
    lip (*see also* Cleft, lip) 749.10
    nasal septum or sinus 748.1
    nose 748.1
    omphalomesenteric duct 751.0
    optic nerve entry 743.57
    organ or site NEC — *see* Anomaly, specified
      type, by site
    ostium
      interatrial 745.5
      interauricular 745.5
      interventricular 745.4
    palate (*see also* Cleft, palate) 749.00
    preauricular sinus 744.46
    retina 743.56
    roof of orbit 742.0
    sclera 743.47
    septum
      aortic 745.0
      aorticopulmonary 745.0
      atrial (secundum) 745.5
        primum 745.61
      between aorta and pulmonary artery
        745.0
      heart 745.9
      interatrial (secundum) 745.5
        primum 745.61
      interauricular (secundum) 745.5
        primum 745.61
      interventricular 745.4
        with pulmonary stenosis or atresia,
          dextraposition of aorta, and
          hypertrophy of right ventricle
          745.2
        in tetralogy of Fallot 745.2
      nasal 748.1
      ventricular 745.4
        with pulmonary stenosis or atresia,
          dextraposition of aorta, and
          hypertrophy of right ventricle
          745.2
        in tetralogy of Fallot 745.2
    skull 756.0
      with
        anencephalus 740.0
        encephalocele 742.0
        hydrocephalus 742.3
          with spina bifida (*see also* Spina
            bifida) 741.0 ☑
        microcephalus 742.1
    spine (with meningocele) (*see also* Spina
      bifida) 741.90
    thyroid cartilage 748.3
    trachea 748.3
    tympanic membrane 744.29
      causing impairment of hearing 744.03
    uterus (with communication to bladder,
      intestine, or rectum) 752.3
    uvula 749.02
      with cleft lip (*see also* Cleft, palate, with
        cleft lip) 749.20
    vitelline duct 751.0
  development — *see* Anomaly, by site
  erection 607.84
  fusion — *see* Imperfect, closure
  inflation lung (newborn) 770.5
  intestinal canal 751.5
  poise 729.9
  rotation — *see* Malrotation
  septum, ventricular 745.4

Imperfectly descended testis 752.51

Imperforate (congenital) — *see also* Atresia
  anus 751.2
  bile duct 751.61
  cervix (uteri) 752.49
  esophagus 750.3
  hymen 752.42
  intestine (small) 751.1
    large 751.2
  jejunum 751.1
  pharynx 750.29
  rectum 751.2
  salivary duct 750.23
  urethra 753.6

Imperforate — *see also* Atresia — *continued*
  urinary meatus 753.6
  vagina 752.49

Impervious (congenital) — *see also* Atresia
  anus 751.2
  bile duct 751.61
  esophagus 750.3
  intestine (small) 751.1
    large 751.5
  rectum 751.2
  urethra 753.6

Impetiginization of other dermatoses 684

Impetigo (any organism) (any site) (bullous) (circinate)
  (contagiosa) (neonatorum) (simplex) 684
  Bockhart's (superficial folliculitis) 704.8
  external ear 684 *[380.13]*
  eyelid 684 *[373.5]*
  Fox's (contagiosa) 684
  furfuracea 696.5
  herpetiformis 694.3
    nonobstetrical 694.3
  staphylococcal infection 684
  ulcerative 686.8
  vulgaris 684

Impingement, soft tissue between teeth 524.89
  anterior 524.81
  posterior 524.82

Implant, endometrial 617.9

Implantation
  anomalous — *see also* Anomaly, specified type,
    by site
    ureter 753.4
  cyst
    external area or site (skin) NEC 709.8
    iris 364.61
    vagina 623.8
    vulva 624.8
  dermoid (cyst)
    external area or site (skin) NEC 709.8
    iris 364.61
    vagina 623.8
    vulva 624.8
  placenta, low or marginal — *see* Placenta
    previa

Impotence (sexual) 607.84   ▲
  organic origin NEC 607.84
  psychogenic 302.72   ●

Impoverished blood 285.9

Impression, basilar 756.0

Imprisonment V62.5

Improper
  development, infant 764.9 ☑

Improperly tied umbilical cord (causing
  hemorrhage) 772.3

Impulses, obsessional 300.3

Impulsive neurosis 300.3

Inaction, kidney (*see also* Disease, renal) 593.9

Inactive — *see* condition

Inadequate, inadequacy
  biologic 301.6
  cardiac and renal — *see* Hypertension,
    cardiorenal
  constitutional 301.6
  development
    child 783.40
    fetus 764.9 ☑
      affecting management of pregnancy
        656.5 ☑
    genitalia
      after puberty NEC 259.0
      congenital — *see* Hypoplasia, genitalia
    lungs 748.5
    organ or site NEC — *see* Hypoplasia, by site
  dietary 269.9
  distance, interarch 524.28
  education V62.3
  environment
    economic problem V60.2
    household condition NEC V60.1
    poverty V60.2
    unemployment V62.0
  functional 301.6
  household care, due to
    family member
      handicapped or ill V60.4

Inadequate, inadequacy — *continued*
household care, due to — *continued*
family member — *continued*
temporarily away from home V60.4
on vacation V60.5
technical defects in home V60.1
temporary absence from home of person rendering care V60.4
housing (heating) (space) V60.1
interarch distance 524.28
material resources V60.2
mental (*see also* Retardation, mental) 319
nervous system 799.2
personality 301.6
prenatal care in current pregnancy V23.7
pulmonary
function 786.09
newborn 770.89
ventilation, newborn 770.89
respiration 786.09
newborn 770.89
sample, Papanicolaou smear 795.08
social 301.6

Inanition 263.9
with edema 262
due to
deprivation of food 994.2
malnutrition 263.9
fever 780.6

Inappropriate secretion
ACTH 255.0
antidiuretic hormone (ADH) (excessive) 253.6
deficiency 253.5
ectopic hormone NEC 259.3
pituitary (posterior) 253.6

Inattention after or at birth 995.52

Inborn errors of metabolism — *see* Disorder, metabolism

Incarceration, incarcerated
bubonocele — *see also* Hernia, inguinal, with obstruction
gangrenous — *see* Hernia, inguinal, with gangrene
colon (by hernia) — *see also* Hernia, by site with obstruction
gangrenous — *see* Hernia, by site, with gangrene
enterocele 552.9
gangrenous 551.9
epigastrocele 552.29
gangrenous 551.29
epiplocele 552.9
gangrenous 551.9
exomphalos 552.1
gangrenous 551.1
fallopian tube 620.8
hernia — *see also* Hernia, by site, with obstruction
gangrenous — *see* Hernia, by site, with gangrene
iris, in wound 871.1
lens, in wound 871.1
merocele (*see also* Hernia, femoral, with obstruction) 552.00
omentum (by hernia) — *see also* Hernia, by site, with obstruction
gangrenous — *see* Hernia, by site, with gangrene
omphalocele 756.79
rupture (meaning hernia) (*see also* Hernia, by site, with obstruction) 552.9
gangrenous (*see also* Hernia, by site, with gangrene) 551.9
sarcoepiplocele 552.9
gangrenous 551.9
sarcoepiplomphalocele 552.1
with gangrene 551.1
uterus 621.8
gravid 654.3 ☑
causing obstructed labor 660.2 ☑
affecting fetus or newborn 763.1

Incident, cerebrovascular (*see also* Disease, cerebrovascular, acute) 436

Incineration (entire body) (from fire, conflagration, electricity, or lightning) — *see* Burn, multiple, specified sites

Incised wound
external — *see* Wound, open, by site
internal organs (abdomen, chest, or pelvis) — *see* Injury, internal, by site, with open wound

Incision, incisional
hernia — *see* Hernia, incisional
surgical, complication — *see* Complications, surgical procedures
traumatic
external — *see* Wound, open, by site
internal organs (abdomen, chest, or pelvis) — *see* Injury, internal, by site, with open wound

Inclusion
azurophilic leukocytic 288.2
blennorrhea (neonatal) (newborn) 771.6
cyst — *see* Cyst, skin
gallbladder in liver (congenital) 751.69

Incompatibility
ABO
affecting management of pregnancy 656.2 ☑
fetus or newborn 773.1
infusion or transfusion reaction 999.6
blood (group) (Duffy) (E) (K(ell)) (Kidd) (Lewis) (M) (N) (P) (S) NEC
affecting management of pregnancy 656.2 ☑
fetus or newborn 773.2
infusion or transfusion reaction 999.6
marital V61.10
involving divorce or estrangement V61.0
Rh (blood group) (factor)
affecting management of pregnancy 656.1 ☑
fetus or newborn 773.0
infusion or transfusion reaction 999.7
Rhesus — *see* Incompatibility, Rh

Incompetency, incompetence, incompetent
annular
aortic (valve) (*see also* Insufficiency, aortic) 424.1
mitral (valve) — (*see also* Insufficiency, mitral) 424.0
pulmonary valve (heart) (*see also* Endocarditis, pulmonary) 424.3
aortic (valve) (*see also* Insufficiency, aortic) 424.1
syphilitic 093.22
cardiac (orifice) 530.0
valve — *see* Endocarditis
cervix, cervical (os) 622.5
in pregnancy 654.5 ☑
affecting fetus or newborn 761.0
esophagogastric (junction) (sphincter) 530.0
heart valve, congenital 746.89
mitral (valve) — *see* Insufficiency, mitral
papillary muscle (heart) 429.81
pelvic fundus
pubocervical tissue 618.81
rectovaginal tissue 618.82
pulmonary valve (heart) (*see also* Endocarditis, pulmonary) 424.3
congenital 746.09
tricuspid (annular) (rheumatic) (valve) (*see also* Endocarditis, tricuspid) 397.0
valvular — *see* Endocarditis
vein, venous (saphenous) (varicose) (*see also* Varicose, vein) 454.9
velopharyngeal (closure)
acquired 528.9
congenital 750.29

Incomplete — *see also* condition
bladder emptying 788.21
expansion lungs (newborn) 770.5
gestation (liveborn) — *see* Immaturity
rotation — *see* Malrotation

Incontinence 788.30
without sensory awareness 788.34
anal sphincter 787.6
continuous leakage 788.37
feces 787.6
due to hysteria 300.11
nonorganic origin 307.7
hysterical 300.11
mixed (male) (female) (urge and stress) 788.33
overflow 788.38
paradoxical 788.39
rectal 787.6

Incontinence — *continued*
specified NEC 788.39
stress (female) 625.6
male NEC 788.32
urethral sphincter 599.84
urge 788.31
and stress (male) (female) 788.33
urine 788.30
active 788.30
male 788.30
stress 788.32
and urge 788.33
neurogenic 788.39
nonorganic origin 307.6
stress (female) 625.6
male NEC 788.32
urge 788.31
and stress 788.33

Incontinentia pigmenti 757.33

Incoordinate
uterus (action) (contractions) 661.4 ☑
affecting fetus or newborn 763.7

Incoordination
esophageal-pharyngeal (newborn) 787.2
muscular 781.3
papillary muscle 429.81

Increase, increased
abnormal, in development 783.9
androgens (ovarian) 256.1
anticoagulants (antithrombin) (anti-VIIIa) (anti-IXa) (anti-Xa) (anti-XIa) 286.5
postpartum 666.3 ☑
cold sense (*see also* Disturbance, sensation) 782.0
estrogen 256.0
function
adrenal (cortex) 255.3
medulla 255.6
pituitary (anterior) (gland) (lobe) 253.1
posterior 253.6
heat sense (*see also* Disturbance, sensation) 782.0
intracranial pressure 781.99
injury at birth 767.8
light reflex of retina 362.13
permeability, capillary 448.9
pressure
intracranial 781.99
injury at birth 767.8
intraocular 365.00
pulsations 785.9
pulse pressure 785.9
sphericity, lens 743.36
splenic activity 289.4
venous pressure 459.89
portal 572.3

Incrustation, cornea, lead or zinc 930.0

Incyclophoria 378.44

Incyclotropia 378.33

Indeterminate sex 752.7

India rubber skin 756.83

Indicanuria 270.2

Indigestion (bilious) (functional) 536.8
acid 536.8
catarrhal 536.8
due to decomposed food NEC 005.9
fat 579.8
nervous 306.4
psychogenic 306.4

Indirect — *see* condition

Indolent bubo NEC 099.8

Induced
abortion — *see* Abortion, induced
birth, affecting fetus or newborn 763.89
delivery — *see* Delivery
labor — *see* Delivery

Induration, indurated
brain 348.8
breast (fibrous) 611.79
puerperal, postpartum 676.3 ☑
broad ligament 620.8
chancre 091.0
anus 091.1
congenital 090.0
extragenital NEC 091.2

Index

Inadequate, inadequacy — Induration, indurated

Induration, indurated — *continued*
corpora cavernosa (penis) (plastic) 607.89
liver (chronic) 573.8
acute 573.8
lung (black) (brown) (chronic) (fibroid) (*see also*
Fibrosis, lung) 515
essential brown 275.0 *[516.1]*
penile 607.89
phlebitic — *see* Phlebitis
skin 782.8
stomach 537.89

Induratio penis plastica 607.89

Industrial — *see* condition

Inebriety (*see also* Abuse, drugs, nondependent)
305.0 ☑

Inefficiency
kidney (*see also* Disease, renal) 593.9
thyroid (acquired) (gland) 244.9

Inelasticity, skin 782.8

Inequality, leg (acquired) (length) 736.81
congenital 755.30

Inertia
bladder 596.4
neurogenic 596.54
with cauda equina syndrome 344.61
stomach 536.8
psychogenic 306.4
uterus, uterine 661.2 ☑
affecting fetus or newborn 763.7
primary 661.0 ☑
secondary 661.1 ☑
vesical 596.4
neurogenic 596.54
with cauda equina 344.61

Infant — *see also* condition
excessive crying of 780.92
fussy (baby) 780.91
held for adoption V68.89
newborn — *see* Newborn
post-term (gestation period over 40 completed
weeks to 42 completed weeks) 766.21
prolonged gestation of (period over 42
completed weeks) 766.22
syndrome of diabetic mother 775.0

"Infant Hercules" syndrome 255.2

Infantile — *see also* condition
genitalia, genitals 259.0
in pregnancy or childbirth NEC 654.4 ☑
affecting fetus or newborn 763.89
causing obstructed labor 660.2 ☑
affecting fetus or newborn 763.1
heart 746.9
kidney 753.3
lack of care 995.52
macula degeneration 362.75
melanodontia 521.05
os, uterus (*see also* Infantile, genitalia) 259.0
pelvis 738.6
with disproportion (fetopelvic) 653.1 ☑
affecting fetus or newborn 763.1
causing obstructed labor 660.1 ☑
affecting fetus or newborn 763.1
penis 259.0
testis 257.2
uterus (*see also* Infantile, genitalia) 259.0
vulva 752.49

Infantilism 259.9
with dwarfism (hypophyseal) 253.3
Brissaud's (infantile myxedema) 244.9
celiac 579.0
Herter's (nontropical sprue) 579.0
hypophyseal 253.3
hypothalamic (with obesity) 253.8
idiopathic 259.9
intestinal 579.0
pancreatic 577.8
pituitary 253.3
renal 588.0
sexual (with obesity) 259.0

Infants, healthy liveborn — *see* Newborn

Infarct, infarction
adrenal (capsule) (gland) 255.4
amnion 658.8 ☑

Infarct, infarction — *continued*
anterior (with contiguous portion of
intraventricular septum) NEC (*see also*
Infarct, myocardium) 410.1 ☑
appendices epiploicae 557.0
bowel 557.0
brain (stem) 434.91
embolic (*see also* Embolism, brain) 434.11
healed or old without residuals V12.59
iatrogenic 997.02
lacunar 434.91
late effect — *see* Late effect(s) (of)
cerebrovascular disease
postoperative 997.02
puerperal, postpartum, childbirth 674.0 ☑
thrombotic (*see also* Thrombosis, brain)
434.01
breast 611.8
Brewer's (kidney) 593.81
cardiac (*see also* Infarct, myocardium) 410.9 ☑
cerebellar (*see also* Infarct, brain) 434.91
embolic (*see also* Embolism, brain) 434.11
cerebral (*see also* Infarct, brain) 434.91
embolic (*see also* Embolism, brain) 434.11
thrombotic (*see also* Infarct, brain) 434.01
chorion 658.8 ☑
colon (acute) (agnogenic) (embolic)
(hemorrhagic) (nonocclusive)
(nonthrombotic) (occlusive) (segmental)
(thrombotic) (with gangrene) 557.0
coronary artery (*see also* Infarct, myocardium)
410.9 ☑
cortical 434.91
embolic (*see also* Embolism) 444.9
fallopian tube 620.8
gallbladder 575.8
heart (*see also* Infarct, myocardium) 410.9 ☑
hepatic 573.4
hypophysis (anterior lobe) 253.8
impending (myocardium) 411.1
intestine (acute) (agnogenic) (embolic)
(hemorrhagic) (nonocclusive)
(nonthrombotic) (occlusive) (thrombotic)
(with gangrene) 557.0
kidney 593.81
lacunar 434.91
liver 573.4
lung (embolic) (thrombotic) 415.19
with
abortion — *see* Abortion, by type, with,
embolism
ectopic pregnancy (*see also* categories
633.0-633.9) 639.6
molar pregnancy (*see also* categories 630-
632) 639.6
following
abortion 639.6
ectopic or molar pregnancy 639.6
iatrogenic 415.11
in pregnancy, childbirth, or puerperium —
see Embolism, obstetrical
postoperative 415.11
lymph node or vessel 457.8
medullary (brain) — *see* Infarct, brain
meibomian gland (eyelid) 374.85
►mesentery,◄ mesenteric (embolic) (thrombotic)
(with gangrene) 557.0
midbrain — *see* Infarct, brain
myocardium, myocardial (acute or with a
stated duration of 8 weeks or less) (with
hypertension) 410.9 ☑

Note — *Use the following fifth-digit
subclassification with category 410:*

0   episode unspecified

1   initial episode

2   subsequent episode without recurrence

with symptoms after 8 weeks from date of
infarction 414.8
anterior (wall) (with contiguous portion of
intraventricular septum) NEC 410.1 ☑
anteroapical (with contiguous portion of
intraventricular septum) 410.1 ☑

Infarct, infarction — *continued*
myocardium, myocardial — *continued*
anterolateral (wall) 410.0 ☑
anteroseptal (with contiguous portion of
intraventricular septum) 410.1 ☑
apical-lateral 410.5 ☑
atrial 410.8 ☑
basal-lateral 410.5 ☑
chronic (with symptoms after 8 weeks from
date of infarction) 414.8
diagnosed on ECG, but presenting no
symptoms 412
diaphragmatic wall (with contiguous portion
of intraventricular septum) 410.4 ☑
healed or old, currently presenting no
symptoms 412
high lateral 410.5 ☑
impending 411.1
inferior (wall) (with contiguous portion of
intraventricular septum) 410.4 ☑
inferolateral (wall) 410.2 ☑
inferoposterior wall 410.3 ☑
lateral wall 410.5 ☑
non-ST elevation (NSTEMI) 410.7 ☑   ●
nontransmural 410.7 ☑
papillary muscle 410.8 ☑
past (diagnosed on ECG or other special
investigation, but currently presenting
no symptoms) 412
with symptoms NEC 414.8
posterior (strictly) (true) (wall) 410.6 ☑
posterobasal 410.6 ☑
posteroinferior 410.3 ☑
posterolateral 410.5 ☑
previous, currently presenting no symptoms
412
septal 410.8 ☑
specified site NEC 410.8 ☑
ST elevation (STEMI) 410.9 ☑   ●
anterior (wall) 410.1 ☑   ●
anterolateral (wall) 410.0 ☑   ●
inferior (wall) 410.4 ☑   ●
inferolateral (wall) 410.2 ☑   ●
inferoposterior wall 410.3 ☑   ●
lateral wall 410.5 ☑   ●
posterior (strictly) (true) (wall) 410.6 ☑●
specified site NEC 410.8 ☑   ●
subendocardial 410.7 ☑
syphilitic 093.82
non-ST elevation myocardial infarction   ●
(NSTEMI) 410.7 ☑   ●
nontransmural 410.7 ☑
omentum 557.0
ovary 620.8
pancreas 577.8
papillary muscle (*see also* Infarct, myocardium)
410.8 ☑
parathyroid gland 252.8
pituitary (gland) 253.8
placenta (complicating pregnancy) 656.7 ☑
affecting fetus or newborn 762.2
pontine — *see* Infarct, brain
posterior NEC (*see also* Infarct, myocardium)
410.6 ☑
prostate 602.8
pulmonary (artery) (hemorrhagic) (vein) 415.19
with
abortion — *see* Abortion, by type, with
embolism
ectopic pregnancy (*see also* categories
633.0-633.9) 639.6
molar pregnancy (*see also* categories 630-
632) 639.6
following
abortion 639.6
ectopic or molar pregnancy 639.6
iatrogenic 415.11
in pregnancy, childbirth, or puerperium —
see Embolism, obstetrical
postoperative 415.11
renal 593.81
embolic or thrombotic 593.81

Infarct, infarction — *continued*
  retina, retinal 362.84
    with occlusion — *see* Occlusion, retina
  spinal (acute) (cord) (embolic) (nonembolic)
      336.1
  spleen 289.59
    embolic or thrombotic 444.89
  subchorionic — *see* Infarct, placenta
  subendocardial (*see also* Infarct, myocardium)
      410.7 ☑
  suprarenal (capsule) (gland) 255.4
  syncytium — *see* Infarct, placenta
  testis 608.83
  thrombotic (*see also* Thrombosis) 453.9
    artery, arterial — *see* Embolism
  thyroid (gland) 246.3
  ventricle (heart) (*see also* Infarct, myocardium)
      410.9 ☑

Infecting — *see* condition

Infection, infected, infective (opportunistic)
      136.9
  with lymphangitis — *see* Lymphangitis
  abortion — *see* Abortion, by type, with, sepsis
  abscess (skin) — *see* Abscess, by site
  Absidia 117.7
  Acanthocheilonema (perstans) 125.4
    streptocerca 125.6
  accessory sinus (chronic) (*see also* Sinusitis)
      473.9
  Achorion — *see* Dermatophytosis
  Acremonium falciforme 117.4
  acromioclavicular (joint) 711.91
  actinobacillus
    lignieresii 027.8
    mallei 024
    muris 026.1
  actinomadura — *see* Actinomycosis
  Actinomyces (israelii) — *see also* Actinomycosis
    muris-ratti 026.1
  Actinomycetales (actinomadura) (Actinomyces)
      (Nocardia) (Streptomyces) — *see*
      Actinomycosis
  actinomycotic NEC (*see also* Actinomycosis)
      039.9
  adenoid (chronic) 474.01
    acute 463
    and tonsil (chronic) 474.02
      acute or subacute 463
  adenovirus NEC 079.0
    in diseases classified elsewhere — *see*
        category 079 ☑
    unspecified nature or site 079.0
  Aerobacter aerogenes NEC 041.85
    enteritis 008.2
  aerogenes capsulatus (*see also* Gangrene, gas)
      040.0
  aertrycke (*see also* Infection, Salmonella) 003.9
  ajellomyces dermatitidis 116.0
  alimentary canal NEC (*see also* Enteritis, due
      to, by organism) 009.0
  Allescheria boydii 117.6
  Alternaria 118
  alveolus, alveolar (process) (pulpal origin) 522.4
  ameba, amebic (histolytica) (*see also* Amebiasis)
      006.9
    acute 006.0
    chronic 006.1
    free-living 136.2
    hartmanni 007.8
    specified
      site NEC 006.8
      type NEC 007.8
  amniotic fluid or cavity 658.4 ☑
    affecting fetus or newborn 762.7
  anaerobes (cocci) (gram-negative) (gram-
      positive) (mixed) NEC 041.84
  anal canal 569.49
  Ancylostoma braziliense 126.2
  Angiostrongylus cantonensis 128.8
  anisakiasis 127.1
  Anisakis larva 127.1
  anthrax (*see also* Anthrax) 022.9
  antrum (chronic) (*see also* Sinusitis, maxillary)
      473.0
  anus (papillae) (sphincter) 569.49
  arbor virus NEC 066.9
  arbovirus NEC 066.9

Infection, infected, infective — *continued*
  argentophil-rod 027.0
  Ascaris lumbricoides 127.0
  ascomycetes 117.4
  Aspergillus (flavus) (fumigatus) (terreus) 117.3
  atypical
    acid-fast (bacilli) (*see also* Mycobacterium,
        atypical) 031.9
    mycobacteria (*see also* Mycobacterium,
        atypical) 031.9
  auditory meatus (circumscribed) (diffuse)
      (external) (*see also* Otitis, externa) 380.10
  auricle (ear) (*see also* Otitis, externa) 380.10
  axillary gland 683
  Babesiasis 088.82
  Babesiosis 088.82
  Bacillus NEC 041.89
    abortus 023.1
    anthracis (*see also* Anthrax) 022.9
    cereus (food poisoning) 005.89
    coli — *see* Infection, Escherichia coli
    coliform NEC 041.85
    Ducrey's (any location) 099.0
    Flexner's 004.1
    Friedländer's NEC 041.3
    fusiformis 101
    gas (gangrene) (*see also* Gangrene, gas)
        040.0
    mallei 024
    melitensis 023.0
    paratyphoid, paratyphosus 002.9
      A 002.1
      B 002.2
      C 002.3
    Schmorl's 040.3
    Shiga 004.0
    suipestifer (*see also* Infection, Salmonella)
        003.9
    swimming pool 031.1
    typhosa 002.0
    welchii (*see also* Gangrene, gas) 040.0
    Whitmore's 025
  bacterial NEC 041.9
    specified NEC 041.89
      anaerobic NEC 041.84
        gram-negative NEC 041.85
          anaerobic NEC 041.84
  Bacterium
    paratyphosum 002.9
      A 002.1
      B 002.2
      C 002.3
    typhosum 002.0
  Bacteroides (fragilis) (melaninogenicus) (oralis)
      NEC 041.82
  balantidium coli 007.0
  Bartholin's gland 616.8
  Basidiobolus 117.7
  Bedsonia 079.98
    specified NEC 079.88
  bile duct 576.1
  bladder (*see also* Cystitis) 595.9
  Blastomyces, blastomycotic 116.0
    brasiliensis 116.1
    dermatitidis 116.0
    European 117.5
    loboi 116.2
    North American 116.0
    South American 116.1
  blood stream — *see* Septicemia
  bone 730.9 ☑
    specified — *see* Osteomyelitis
  Bordetella 033.9
    bronchiseptica 033.8
    parapertussis 033.1
    pertussis 033.0
  Borrelia
    bergdorfi 088.81
    vincentii (mouth) (pharynx) (tonsil) 101
  brain (*see also* Encephalitis) 323.9
    late effect — *see* category 326
    membranes — (*see also* Meningitis) 322.9
    septic 324.0
      late effect — *see* category 326
    meninges (*see also* Meningitis) 320.9
  branchial cyst 744.42

Infection, infected, infective — *continued*
  breast 611.0
    puerperal, postpartum 675.2 ☑
      with nipple 675.9 ☑
        specified type NEC 675.8 ☑
      nonpurulent 675.2 ☑
      purulent 675.1 ☑
  bronchus (*see also* Bronchitis) 490
    fungus NEC 117.9
  Brucella 023.9
    abortus 023.1
    canis 023.3
    melitensis 023.0
    mixed 023.8
    suis 023.2
  Brugia (Wuchereria) malayi 125.1
  bursa — *see* Bursitis
  buttocks (skin) 686.9
  Candida (albicans) (tropicalis) (*see also*
      Candidiasis) 112.9
    congenital 771.7
  Candiru 136.8
  Capillaria
    hepatica 128.8
    philippinensis 127.5
  cartilage 733.99
  cat liver fluke 121.0
  cellulitis — *see* Cellulitis, by site
  Cephalosporum falciforme 117.4
  Cercomonas hominis (intestinal) 007.3
  cerebrospinal (*see also* Meningitis) 322.9
    late effect — *see* category 326
  cervical gland 683
  cervix (*see also* Cervicitis) 616.0
  cesarean section wound 674.3 ☑
  Chilomastix (intestinal) 007.8
  Chlamydia 079.98
    specified NEC 079.88
  cholera (*see also* Cholera) 001.9
  chorionic plate 658.8 ☑
  Cladosporium
    bantianum 117.8
    carrionii 117.2
    mansoni 111.1
    trichoides 117.8
    wernecki 111.1
  Clonorchis (sinensis) (liver) 121.1
  Clostridium (haemolyticum) (novyi) NEC 041.84
    botulinum 005.1
    histolyticum (*see also* Gangrene, gas) 040.0
    oedematiens (*see also* Gangrene, gas) 040.0
    perfringens 041.83
      due to food 005.2
    septicum (*see also* Gangrene, gas) 040.0
    sordellii (*see also* Gangrene, gas) 040.0
    welchii (*see also* Gangrene, gas) 040.0
      due to food 005.2
  Coccidioides (immitis) (*see also*
      Coccidioidomycosis) 114.9
  coccus NEC 041.89
  colon (*see also* Enteritis, due to, by organism)
      009.0
    bacillus — *see* Infection, Escherichia coli
  colostomy or enterostomy 569.61
  common duct 576.1
  complicating pregnancy, childbirth, or
      puerperium NEC 647.9 ☑
    affecting fetus or newborn 760.2
  Condiobolus 117.7
  congenital NEC 771.89
    Candida albicans 771.7
    chronic 771.2
    cytomegalovirus 771.1
    hepatitis, viral 771.2
    herpes simplex 771.2
    listeriosis 771.2
    malaria 771.2
    poliomyelitis 771.2
    rubella 771.0
    toxoplasmosis 771.2
    tuberculosis 771.2
    urinary (tract) 771.82
    vaccinia 771.2
  coronavirus 079.89
    SARS-associated 079.82
  corpus luteum (*see also* Salpingo-oophoritis)
      614.2

Infection, infected, infective — *continued*
  Corynebacterium diphtheriae — *see* Diphtheria
  Coxsackie (*see also* Coxsackie) 079.2
    endocardium 074.22
    heart NEC 074.20
    in diseases classified elsewhere — *see*
      category 079 ☑
    meninges 047.0
    myocardium 074.23
    pericardium 074.21
    pharynx 074.0
    specified disease NEC 074.8
    unspecified nature or site 079.2
  Cryptococcus neoformans 117.5
  Cryptosporidia 007.4
  Cunninghamella 117.7
  cyst — *see* Cyst
  Cysticercus cellulosae 123.1
  cytomegalovirus 078.5
    congenital 771.1
  dental (pulpal origin) 522.4
  deuteromycetes 117.4
  Dicrocoelium dendriticum 121.8
  Dipetalonema (perstans) 125.4
    streptocerca 125.6
  diphtherial — *see* Diphtheria
  Diphyllobothrium (adult) (latum) (pacificum)
    123.4
    larval 123.5
  Diplogonoporus (grandis) 123.8
  Dipylidium (caninum) 123.8
  Dirofilaria 125.6
  dog tapeworm 123.8
  Dracunculus medinensis 125.7
  Dreschlera 118
    hawaiiensis 117.8
  Ducrey's bacillus (any site) 099.0
  due to or resulting from
    device, implant, or graft (any) (presence of)
      — *see* Complications, infection and
      inflammation, due to (presence of) any
      device, implant, or graft classified to
      996.0-996.5 NEC
    injection, inoculation, infusion, transfusion,
      or vaccination (prophylactic)
      (therapeutic) 999.3
    injury NEC — *see* Wound, open, by site,
      complicated
    surgery 998.59
  duodenum 535.6 ☑
  ear — *see also* Otitis
    external (*see also* Otitis, externa) 380.10
    inner (*see also* Labyrinthitis) 386.30
    middle — *see* Otitis, media
  Eaton's agent NEC 041.81
  Eberthella typhosa 002.0
  Ebola 078.89   ▲
  echinococcosis 122.9
  Echinococcus (*see also* Echinococcus) 122.9
  Echinostoma 121.8
  ECHO virus 079.1
    in diseases classified elsewhere — *see*
      category 079 ☑
    unspecified nature or site 079.1
  Ehrlichiosis 082.40
    chaffeensis 082.41
    specified type NEC 082.49
  Endamoeba — *see* Infection, ameba
  endocardium (*see also* Endocarditis) 421.0
  endocervix (*see also* Cervicitis) 616.0
  Entamoeba — *see* Infection, ameba
  enteric (*see also* Enteritis, due to, by organism)
    009.0
  Enterobacter aerogenes NEC 041.85
  Enterobacter sakazakii 041.85   ●
  Enterobius vermicularis 127.4
  enterococcus NEC 041.04
  enterovirus NEC 079.89
    central nervous system NEC 048
    enteritis 008.67
    meningitis 047.9
  Entomophthora 117.7
  Epidermophyton — *see* Dermatophytosis
  epidermophytosis — *see* Dermatophytosis
  episiotomy 674.3 ☑
  Epstein-Barr virus 075
    chronic 780.79 [139.8]

Infection, infected, infective — *continued*
  erysipeloid 027.1
  Erysipelothrix (insidiosa) (rhusiopathiae) 027.1
  erythema infectiosum 057.0
  Escherichia coli NEC 041.4
    enteritis — *see* Enteritis, E. coli
    generalized 038.42
    intestinal — *see* Enteritis, E. coli
  esophagostomy 530.86
  ethmoidal (chronic) (sinus) (*see also* Sinusitis,
    ethmoidal) 473.2
  Eubacterium 041.84
  Eustachian tube (ear) 381.50
    acute 381.51
    chronic 381.52
  exanthema subitum 057.8
  external auditory canal (meatus) (*see also*
    Otitis, externa) 380.10
  eye NEC 360.00
  eyelid 373.9
    specified NEC 373.8
  fallopian tube (*see also* Salpingo-oophoritis)
    614.2
  fascia 728.89
  Fasciola
    gigantica 121.3
    hepatica 121.3
  Fasciolopsis (buski) 121.4
  fetus (intra-amniotic) — *see* Infection,
    congenital
  filarial — *see* Infestation, filarial
  finger (skin) 686.9
    abscess (with lymphangitis) 681.00
      pulp 681.01
    cellulitis (with lymphangitis) 681.00
    distal closed space (with lymphangitis)
      681.00
    nail 681.02
      fungus 110.1
  fish tapeworm 123.4
    larval 123.5
  flagellate, intestinal 007.9
  fluke — *see* Infestation, fluke
  focal
    teeth (pulpal origin) 522.4
    tonsils 474.00
      and adenoids 474.02
  Fonsecaea
    compactum 117.2
    pedrosoi 117.2
  food (*see also* Poisoning, food) 005.9
  foot (skin) 686.9
    fungus 110.4
  Francisella tularensis (*see also* Tularemia)
    021.9
  frontal sinus (chronic) (*see also* Sinusitis,
    frontal) 473.1
  fungus NEC 117.9
    beard 110.0
    body 110.5
    dermatiacious NEC 117.8
    foot 110.4
    groin 110.3
    hand 110.2
    nail 110.1
    pathogenic to compromised host only 118
    perianal (area) 110.3
    scalp 110.0
    scrotum 110.8
    skin 111.9
      foot 110.4
      hand 110.2
    toenails 110.1
    trachea 117.9
  Fusarium 118
  Fusobacterium 041.84
  gallbladder (*see also* Cholecystitis, acute) 575.0
  Gardnerella vaginalis 041.89
  gas bacillus (*see also* Gas, gangrene) 040.0
  gastric (*see also* Gastritis) 535.5 ☑
  Gastrodiscoides hominis 121.8
  gastroenteric (*see also* Enteritis, due to, by
    organism) 009.0
  gastrointestinal (*see also* Enteritis, due to, by
    organism) 009.0
  gastrostomy 536.41
  generalized NEC (*see also* Septicemia) 038.9

Infection, infected, infective — *continued*
  genital organ or tract NEC
    female 614.9
      with
        abortion — *see* Abortion, by type, with
          sepsis
        ectopic pregnancy (*see also* categories
          633.0-633.9) 639.0
        molar pregnancy (*see also* categories
          630-632) 639.0
      complicating pregnancy 646.6 ☑
        affecting fetus or newborn 760.8
      following
        abortion 639.0
        ectopic or molar pregnancy 639.0
      puerperal, postpartum, childbirth
        670.0 ☑
      minor or localized 646.6 ☑
        affecting fetus or newborn 760.8
    male 608.4
  genitourinary tract NEC 599.0
  Ghon tubercle, primary (*see also* Tuberculosis)
    010.0 ☑
  Giardia lamblia 007.1
  gingival (chronic) 523.1
    acute 523.0
    Vincent's 101
  glanders 024
  Glenosporopsis amazonica 116.2
  Gnathostoma spinigerum 128.1
  Gongylonema 125.6
  gonococcal NEC (*see also* Gonococcus) 098.0
  gram-negative bacilli NEC 041.85
    anaerobic 041.84
  guinea worm 125.7
  gum (*see also* Infection, gingival) 523.1
  Hantavirus 079.81
  heart 429.89
  Helicobacter pylori (H. pylori) 041.86
  helminths NEC 128.9
    intestinal 127.9
      mixed (types classifiable to more than one
        category in 120.0-127.7) 127.8
      specified type NEC 127.7
    specified type NEC 128.8
  Hemophilus influenzae NEC 041.5
    generalized 038.41
  herpes (simplex) (*see also* Herpes, simplex)
    054.9
    congenital 771.2
    zoster (*see also* Herpes, zoster) 053.9
      eye NEC 053.29
  Heterophyes heterophyes 121.6
  Histoplasma (*see also* Histoplasmosis) 115.90
    capsulatum (*see also* Histoplasmosis,
      American) 115.00
    duboisii (*see also* Histoplasmosis, African)
      115.10
  HIV V08
    with symptoms, symptomatic 042
  hookworm (*see also* Ancylostomiasis) 126.9
  human immunodeficiency virus V08
    with symptoms, symptomatic 042
  human papillomavirus 079.4
  hydrocele 603.1
  hydronephrosis 591
  Hymenolepis 123.6
  hypopharynx 478.29
  inguinal glands 683
    due to soft chancre 099.0
  intestine, intestinal (*see also* Enteritis, due to,
    by organism) 009.0
  intrauterine (*see also* Endometritis) 615.9
    complicating delivery 646.6 ☑
  isospora belli or hominis 007.2
  Japanese B encephalitis 062.0
  jaw (bone) (acute) (chronic) (lower) (subacute)
    (upper) 526.4
  joint — *see* Arthritis, infectious or infective
  kidney (cortex) (hematogenous) 590.9
    with
      abortion — *see* Abortion, by type, with
        urinary tract infection
      calculus 592.0
      ectopic pregnancy (*see also* categories
        633.0-633.9) 639.8

☑ Additional Digit Required — Refer to the Tabular List (Numeric Code Section) for Additional Digit Selection

Infection, infected, infective — *continued*
kidney — *continued*
with — *continued*
molar pregnancy (*see also* categories 630-632) 639.8
complicating pregnancy or puerperium 646.6 ☑
affecting fetus or newborn 760.1
following
abortion 639.8
ectopic or molar pregnancy 639.8
pelvis and ureter 590.3
Klebsiella pneumoniae NEC 041.3
knee (skin) NEC 686.9
joint — *see* Arthritis, infectious
Koch's (*see also* Tuberculosis, pulmonary) 011.9 ☑
labia (majora) (minora) (*see also* Vulvitis) 616.10
lacrimal
gland (*see also* Dacryoadenitis) 375.00
passages (duct) (sac) (*see also* Dacryocystitis) 375.30
larynx NEC 478.79
leg (skin) NEC 686.9
Leishmania (*see also* Leishmaniasis) 085.9
braziliensis 085.5
donovani 085.0
Ethiopica 085.3
furunculosa 085.1
infantum 085.0
mexicana 085.4
tropica (minor) 085.1
major 085.2
Leptosphaeria senegalensis 117.4
leptospira (*see also* Leptospirosis) 100.9
Australis 100.89
Bataviae 100.89
pyrogenes 100.89
specified type NEC 100.89
leptospirochetal NEC (*see also* Leptospirosis) 100.9
Leptothrix — *see* Actinomycosis
Listeria monocytogenes (listeriosis) 027.0
congenital 771.2
liver fluke — *see* Infestation, fluke, liver
Loa loa 125.2
eyelid 125.2 [373.6]
Loboa loboi 116.2
local, skin (staphylococcal) (streptococcal) NEC 686.9
abscess — *see* Abscess, by site
cellulitis — *see* Cellulitis, by site
ulcer (*see also* Ulcer, skin) 707.9
Loefflerella
mallei 024
whitmori 025
lung 518.89
atypical Mycobacterium 031.0
tuberculous (*see also* Tuberculosis, pulmonary) 011.9 ☑
basilar 518.89
chronic 518.89
fungus NEC 117.9
spirochetal 104.8
virus — *see* Pneumonia, virus
lymph gland (axillary) (cervical) (inguinal) 683
mesenteric 289.2
lymphoid tissue, base of tongue or posterior pharynx, NEC 474.00
madurella
grisea 117.4
mycetomii 117.4
major
with
abortion — *see* Abortion, by type, with sepsis
ectopic pregnancy (*see also* categories 633.0-633.9) 639.0
molar pregnancy (*see also* categories 630-632) 639.0
following
abortion 639.0
ectopic or molar pregnancy 639.0
puerperal, postpartum, childbirth 670.0 ☑
Malassezia furfur 111.0

Infection, infected, infective — *continued*
Malleomyces
mallei 024
pseudomallei 025
mammary gland 611.0
puerperal, postpartum 675.2 ☑
Mansonella (ozzardi) 125.5
mastoid (suppurative) — *see* Mastoiditis
maxilla, maxillary 526.4
sinus (chronic) (*see also* Sinusitis, maxillary) 473.0
mediastinum 519.2
medina 125.7
meibomian
cyst 373.12
gland 373.12
melioidosis 025
meninges (*see also* Meningitis) 320.9
meningococcal (*see also* condition) 036.9
brain 036.1
cerebrospinal 036.0
endocardium 036.42
generalized 036.2
meninges 036.0
meningococcemia 036.2
specified site NEC 036.89
mesenteric lymph nodes or glands NEC 289.2
Metagonimus 121.5
metatarsophalangeal 711.97
microorganism resistant to drugs — *see* Resistance (to), drugs by microorganisms
Microsporidia 136.8
microsporum, microsporic — *see* Dermatophytosis
Mima polymorpha NEC 041.85
mixed flora NEC 041.89
Monilia (*see also* Candidiasis) 112.9
neonatal 771.7
monkeypox 057.8
Monosporium apiospermum 117.6
mouth (focus) NEC 528.9
parasitic 136.9
Mucor 117.7
muscle NEC 728.89
mycelium NEC 117.9
mycetoma
actinomycotic NEC (*see also* Actinomycosis) 039.9
mycotic NEC 117.4
Mycobacterium, mycobacterial (*see also* Mycobacterium) 031.9
Mycoplasma NEC 041.81
mycotic NEC 117.9
pathogenic to compromised host only 118
skin NEC 111.9
systemic 117.9
myocardium NEC 422.90
nail (chronic) (with lymphangitis) 681.9
finger 681.02
fungus 110.1
ingrowing 703.0
toe 681.11
fungus 110.1
nasal sinus (chronic) (*see also* Sinusitis) 473.9
nasopharynx (chronic) 478.29
acute 460
navel 686.9
newborn 771.4
Neisserian — *see* Gonococcus
Neotestudina rosatii 117.4
newborn, generalized 771.89
nipple 611.0
puerperal, postpartum 675.0 ☑
with breast 675.9 ☑
specified type NEC 675.8 ☑
Nocardia — *see* Actinomycosis
nose 478.1
nostril 478.1
obstetrical surgical wound 674.3 ☑
Oesophagostomum (apiostomum) 127.7
Oestrus ovis 134.0
Oidium albicans (*see also* Candidiasis) 112.9
Onchocerca (volvulus) 125.3
eye 125.3 [360.13]
eyelid 125.3 [373.6]
operation wound 998.59

Infection, infected, infective — *continued*
Opisthorchis (felineus) (tenuicollis) (viverrini) 121.0
orbit 376.00
chronic 376.10
ovary (*see also* Salpingo-oophoritis) 614.2
Oxyuris vermicularis 127.4
pancreas 577.0
Paracoccidioides brasiliensis 116.1
Paragonimus (westermani) 121.2
parainfluenza virus 079.89
parameningococcus NEC 036.9
with meningitis 036.0
parasitic NEC 136.9
paratyphoid 002.9
type A 002.1
type B 002.2
type C 002.3
paraurethral ducts 597.89
parotid gland 527.2
Pasteurella NEC 027.2
multocida (cat-bite) (dog-bite) 027.2
pestis (*see also* Plague) 020.9
pseudotuberculosis 027.2
septica (cat-bite) (dog-bite) 027.2
tularensis (*see also* Tularemia) 021.9
pelvic, female (*see also* Disease, pelvis, inflammatory) 614.9
penis (glans) (retention) NEC 607.2
herpetic 054.13
Peptococcus 041.84
Peptostreptococcus 041.84
periapical (pulpal origin) 522.4
peridental 523.3
perineal wound (obstetrical) 674.3 ☑
periodontal 523.3
periorbital 376.00
chronic 376.10
perirectal 569.49
perirenal (*see also* Infection, kidney) 590.9
peritoneal (*see also* Peritonitis) 567.9
periureteral 593.89
periurethral 597.89
Petriellidium boydii 117.6
pharynx 478.29
Coxsackie virus 074.0
phlegmonous 462
posterior, lymphoid 474.00
Phialophora
gougerotii 117.8
jeanselmei 117.8
verrucosa 117.2
Piedraia hortai 111.3
pinna, acute 380.11
pinta 103.9
intermediate 103.1
late 103.2
mixed 103.3
primary 103.0
pinworm 127.4
pityrosporum furfur 111.0
pleuropneumonia-like organisms NEC (PPLO) 041.81
pneumococcal NEC 041.2
generalized (purulent) 038.2
Pneumococcus NEC 041.2
postoperative wound 998.59
posttraumatic NEC 958.3
postvaccinal 999.3
prepuce NEC 607.1
Proprionibacterium 041.84
prostate (capsule) (*see also* Prostatitis) 601.9
Proteus (mirabilis) (morganii) (vulgaris) NEC 041.6
enteritis 008.3
protozoal NEC 136.8
intestinal NEC 007.9
Pseudomonas NEC 041.7
mallei 024
pneumonia 482.1
pseudomallei 025
psittacosis 073.9
puerperal, postpartum (major) 670.0 ☑
minor 646.6 ☑
pulmonary — *see* Infection, lung
purulent — *see* Abscess
putrid, generalized — *see* Septicemia

Infection, infected, infective — *continued*
pyemic — *see* Septicemia
Pyrenochaeta romeroi 117.4
Q fever 083.0
rabies 071
rectum (sphincter) 569.49
renal (*see also* Infection, kidney) 590.9
   pelvis and ureter 590.3
resistant to drugs — *see* Resistance (to), drugs
   by microorganisms
respiratory 519.8
   chronic 519.8
   influenzal (acute) (upper) 487.1
   lung 518.89
   rhinovirus 460
   syncytial virus 079.6
   upper (acute) (infectious) NEC 465.9
      with flu, grippe, or influenza 487.1
      influenzal 487.1
      multiple sites NEC 465.8
      streptococcal 034.0
      viral NEC 465.9
respiratory syncytial virus (RSV) 079.6
resulting from presence of shunt or other
   internal prosthetic device — *see*
   Complications, infection and
   inflammation, due to (presence of) any
   device, implant, or graft classified to
   996.0-996.5 NEC
● retroperitoneal 567.39
retrovirus 079.50
   human immunodeficiency virus type 2
      [HIV 2] 079.53
   human T-cell lymphotrophic virus type I
      [HTLV-I] 079.51
   human T-cell lymphotrophic virus type II
      [HTLV-II] 079.52
   specified NEC 079.59
Rhinocladium 117.1
Rhinosporidium (*seeberi*) 117.0
rhinovirus
   in diseases classified elsewhere — *see*
      category 079 ☑
   unspecified nature or site 079.3
Rhizopus 117.7
rickettsial 083.9
rickettsialpox 083.2
rubella (*see also* Rubella) 056.9
   congenital 771.0
Saccharomyces (*see also* Candidiasis) 112.9
Saksenaea 117.7
salivary duct or gland (any) 527.2
Salmonella (aertrycke) (callinarum)
   (choleraesuis) (enteritidis) (suipestifer)
   (typhimurium) 003.9
   with
      arthritis 003.23
      gastroenteritis 003.0
      localized infection 003.20
         specified type NEC 003.29
      meningitis 003.21
      osteomyelitis 003.24
      pneumonia 003.22
      septicemia 003.1
      specified manifestation NEC 003.8
   due to food (poisoning) (any serotype) (*see*
      also Poisoning, food, due to,
      Salmonella)
   hirschfeldii 002.3
   localized 003.20
      specified type NEC 003.29
   paratyphi 002.9
      A 002.1
      B 002.2
      C 002.3
   schottmuelleri 002.2
   specified type NEC 003.8
   typhi 002.0
   typhosa 002.0
saprophytic 136.8
Sarcocystis, lindemanni 136.5
SARS-associated coronavirus 079.82
scabies 133.0
Schistosoma — *see* Infestation, Schistosoma
Schmorl's bacillus 040.3
scratch or other superficial injury — *see* Injury,
   superficial, by site

Infection, infected, infective — *continued*
scrotum (acute) NEC 608.4
secondary, burn or open wound (dislocation)
   (fracture) 958.3
seminal vesicle (*see also* Vesiculitis) 608.0
septic
   generalized — *see* Septicemia
   localized, skin (*see also* Abscess) 682.9
septicemic — *see* Septicemia
seroma 998.51
Serratia (marcescens) 041.85
   generalized 038.44
sheep liver fluke 121.3
Shigella 004.9
   boydii 004.2
   dysenteriae 004.0
   flexneri 004.1
   group
      A 004.0
      B 004.1
      C 004.2
      D 004.3
   Schmitz (-Stutzer) 004.0
   schmitzii 004.0
   Shiga 004.0
   sonnei 004.3
   specified type NEC 004.8
Sin Nombre virus 079.81
sinus (*see also* Sinusitis) 473.9
   pilonidal 685.1
      with abscess 685.0
   skin NEC 686.9
Skene's duct or gland (*see also* Urethritis)
   597.89
skin (local) (staphylococcal) (streptococcal)
   NEC 686.9
   abscess — *see* Abscess, by site
   cellulitis — *see* Cellulitis, by site
   due to fungus 111.9
      specified type NEC 111.8
   mycotic 111.9
      specified type NEC 111.8
   ulcer (*see also* Ulcer, skin) 707.9
slow virus 046.9
   specified condition NEC 046.8
Sparganum (mansoni) (proliferum) 123.5
spermatic cord NEC 608.4
sphenoidal (chronic) (sinus) (*see also* Sinusitis,
   sphenoidal) 473.3
Spherophorus necrophorus 040.3
spinal cord NEC (*see also* Encephalitis) 323.9
   abscess 324.1
      late effect — *see* category 326
   late effect — *see* category 326
   meninges — *see* Meningitis
   streptococcal 320.2
Spirillum
   minus or minor 026.0
   morsus muris 026.0
   obermeieri 087.0
spirochetal NEC 104.9
   lung 104.8
   specified nature or site NEC 104.8
spleen 289.59
Sporothrix schenckii 117.1
Sporotrichum (schenckii) 117.1
Sporozoa 136.8
staphylococcal NEC 041.10
   aureus 041.11
   food poisoning 005.0
   generalized (purulent) 038.10
      aureus 038.11
      specified organism NEC 038.19
   pneumonia 482.40
      aureus 482.41
      specified type NEC 482.49
   septicemia 038.10
      aureus 038.11
      specified organism NEC 038.19
   specified NEC 041.19
steatoma 706.2
Stellantchasmus falcatus 121.6
Streptobacillus moniliformis 026.1
streptococcal NEC 041.00
   generalized (purulent) 038.0
   Group
      A 041.01

Infection, infected, infective — *continued*
streptococcal NEC — *continued*
   Group — *continued*
      B 041.02
      C 041.03
      D [enterococcus] 041.04
      G 041.05
   pneumonia — *see* Pneumonia, streptococcal
   septicemia 038.0
   sore throat 034.0
   specified NEC 041.09
Streptomyces — *see* Actinomycosis
streptotrichosis — *see* Actinomycosis
Strongyloides (stercoralis) 127.2
stump (amputation) (posttraumatic) (surgical)
   997.62
   traumatic — *see* Amputation, traumatic, by
      site, complicated
subcutaneous tissue, local NEC 686.9
submaxillary region 528.9
suipestifer (*see also* Infection, Salmonella)
   003.9
swimming pool bacillus 031.1
syphilitic — *see* Syphilis
systemic — *see* Septicemia
Taenia — *see* Infestation, Taenia
Taeniarhynchus saginatus 123.2
tapeworm — *see* Infestation, tapeworm
tendon (sheath) 727.89
Ternidens diminutus 127.7
testis (*see also* Orchitis) 604.90
thigh (skin) 686.9
threadworm 127.4
throat 478.29
   pneumococcal 462
   staphylococcal 462
   streptococcal 034.0
   viral NEC (*see also* Pharyngitis) 462
thumb (skin) 686.9
   abscess (with lymphangitis) 681.00
      pulp 681.01
   cellulitis (with lymphangitis) 681.00
   nail 681.02
thyroglossal duct 529.8
toe (skin) 686.9
   abscess (with lymphangitis) 681.10
   cellulitis (with lymphangitis) 681.10
   nail 681.11
      fungus 110.1
tongue NEC 529.0
   parasitic 112.0
tonsil (faucial) (lingual) (pharyngeal) 474.00
   acute or subacute 463
   and adenoid 474.02
   tag 474.00
tooth, teeth 522.4
   periapical (pulpal origin) 522.4
   peridental 523.3
   periodontal 523.3
   pulp 522.0
   socket 526.5
Torula histolytica 117.5
Toxocara (cani) (cati) (felis) 128.0
Toxoplasma gondii (*see also* Toxoplasmosis)
   130.9
trachea, chronic 491.8
   fungus 117.9
traumatic NEC 958.3
trematode NEC 121.9
trench fever 083.1
Treponema
   denticola 041.84
   macrodenticum 041.84
   pallidum (*see also* Syphilis) 097.9
Trichinella (spiralis) 124
Trichomonas 131.9
   bladder 131.09
   cervix 131.09
   hominis 007.3
   intestine 007.3
   prostate 131.03
   specified site NEC 131.8
   urethra 131.02
   urogenitalis 131.00
   vagina 131.01
   vulva 131.01

☑ Additional Digit Required — Refer to the Tabular List (Numeric Code Section) for Additional Digit Selection

Infection, infected, infective — *continued*
  Trichophyton, trichophytid — *see*
       Dermatophytosis
  Trichosporon (beigelii) cutaneum 111.2
  Trichostrongylus 127.6
  Trichuris (trichiuria) 127.3
  Trombicula (irritans) 133.8
  Trypanosoma (*see also* Trypanosomiasis) 086.9
       cruzi 086.2
  tubal (*see also* Salpingo-oophoritis) 614.2
  tuberculous NEC (*see also* Tuberculosis)
       011.9 ☑
  tubo-ovarian (*see also* Salpingo-oophoritis)
       614.2
  tunica vaginalis 608.4
  tympanic membrane — *see* Myringitis
  typhoid (abortive) (ambulant) (bacillus) 002.0
  typhus 081.9
       flea-borne (endemic) 081.0
       louse-borne (epidemic) 080
       mite-borne 081.2
       recrudescent 081.1
       tick-borne 082.9
            African 082.1
            North Asian 082.2
  umbilicus (septic) 686.9
       newborn NEC 771.4
  ureter 593.89
  urethra (*see also* Urethritis) 597.80
  urinary (tract) NEC 599.0
       with
            abortion — *see* Abortion, by type, with
                 urinary tract infection
            ectopic pregnancy (*see also* categories
                 633.0-633.9) 639.8
            molar pregnancy (*see also* categories 630-
                 632) 639.8
       candidal 112.2
       complicating pregnancy, childbirth, or
            puerperium 646.6 ☑
            affecting fetus or newborn 760.1
       asymptomatic 646.5 ☑
            affecting fetus or newborn 760.1
       diplococcal (acute) 098.0
            chronic 098.2
       due to Trichomonas (vaginalis) 131.00
            following
                 abortion 639.8
                 ectopic or molar pregnancy 639.8
            gonococcal (acute) 098.0
                 chronic or duration of 2 months or
                      over 098.2
            newborn 771.82
       trichomonal 131.00
       tuberculous (*see also* Tuberculosis) 016.3 ☑
  uterus, uterine (*see also* Endometritis) 615.9
  utriculus masculinus NEC 597.89
  vaccination 999.3
  vagina (granulation tissue) (wall) (*see also*
       Vaginitis) 616.10
  varicella 052.9
  varicose veins — *see* Varicose, veins
  variola 050.9
       major 050.0
       minor 050.1
  vas deferens NEC 608.4
  Veillonella 041.84
  verumontanum 597.89
  vesical (*see also* Cystitis) 595.9
  Vibrio
       cholerae 001.0
            El Tor 001.1
       parahaemolyticus (food poisoning) 005.4
       vulnificus 041.85
  Vincent's (gums) (mouth) (tonsil) 101
  virus, viral 079.99
       adenovirus
            in diseases classified elsewhere — *see*
                 category 079 ☑
            unspecified nature or site 079.0
       central nervous system NEC 049.9
            enterovirus 048
                 meningitis 047.9
                      specified type NEC 047.8
            slow virus 046.9
                 specified condition NEC 046.8
       chest 519.8

Infection, infected, infective — *continued*
  virus, viral — *continued*
       conjunctivitis 077.99
            specified type NEC 077.8
       coronavirus 079.89
            SARS-associated 079.82
       Coxsackie (*see also* Infection, Coxsackie)
            079.2
       Ebola 065.8
       ECHO
            in diseases classified elsewhere — *see*
                 category 079 ☑
            unspecified nature or site 079.1
       encephalitis 049.9
            arthropod-borne NEC 064
            tick-borne 063.9
                 specified type NEC 063.8
       enteritis NEC (*see also* Enteritis, viral) 008.8
       exanthem NEC 057.9
       Hantavirus 079.81
       human papilloma 079.4
            in diseases classified elsewhere — *see*
                 category 079 ☑
       intestine (*see also* Enteritis, viral) 008.8
       lung — *see* Pneumonia, viral
       respiratory syncytial (RSV) 079.6
       retrovirus 079.50
       rhinovirus
            in diseases classified elsewhere — *see*
                 category 079 ☑
            unspecified nature or site 079.3
       salivary gland disease 078.5
       slow 046.9
            specified condition NEC 046.8
       specified type NEC 079.89
            in diseases classified elsewhere — *see*
                 category 079 ☑
            unspecified nature or site 079.99
       warts NEC 078.10
       vulva (*see also* Vulvitis) 616.10
  whipworm 127.3
  Whitmore's bacillus 025
  wound (local) (posttraumatic) NEC 958.3
       with
            dislocation — *see* Dislocation, by site,
                 open
            fracture — *see* Fracture, by site, open
            open wound — *see* Wound, open, by site,
                 complicated
       postoperative 998.59
       surgical 998.59
  Wuchereria 125.0
       bancrofti 125.0
       malayi 125.1
  yaws — *see* Yaws
  yeast (*see also* Candidiasis) 112.9
  yellow fever (*see also* Fever, yellow) 060.9
  Yersinia pestis (*see also* Plague) 020.9
  Zeis' gland 373.12
  zoonotic bacterial NEC 027.9
  Zopfia senegalensis 117.4

Infective, infectious — *see* condition

Inferiority complex 301.9
  constitutional psychopathic 301.9

Infertility
  female 628.9
       age related 628.8   ●
       associated with
            adhesions, peritubal 614.6 *[628.2]*
            anomaly
                 cervical mucus 628.4
                 congenital
                      cervix 628.4
                      fallopian tube 628.2
                      uterus 628.3
                      vagina 628.4
            anovulation 628.0
            dysmucorrhea 628.4
            endometritis, tuberculous (*see also*
                 Tuberculosis) 016.7 ☑ *[628.3]*
            Stein-Leventhal syndrome 256.4 *[628.0]*
       due to
            adiposogenital dystrophy 253.8 *[628.1]*
            anterior pituitary disorder NEC
                 253.4 *[628.1]*
                 hyperfunction 253.1 *[628.1]*

Infertility — *continued*
  female — *continued*
       due to — *continued*
            cervical anomaly 628.4
            fallopian tube anomaly 628.2
            ovarian failure 256.39 *[628.0]*
            Stein-Leventhal syndrome 256.4 *[628.0]*
            uterine anomaly 628.3
            vaginal anomaly 628.4
       nonimplantation 628.3
       origin
            cervical 628.4
            pituitary-hypothalamus NEC
                 253.8 *[628.1]*
                 anterior pituitary NEC 253.4 *[628.1]*
                      hyperfunction NEC 253.1 *[628.1]*
                 dwarfism 253.3 *[628.1]*
                 panhypopituitarism 253.2 *[628.1]*
            specified NEC 628.8
            tubal (block) (occlusion) (stenosis) 628.2
                 adhesions 614.6 *[628.2]*
            uterine 628.3
            vaginal 628.4
       previous, requiring supervision of pregnancy
            V23.0
  male 606.9
       absolute 606.0
       due to
            azoospermia 606.0
            drug therapy 606.8
            extratesticular cause NEC 606.8
            germinal cell
                 aplasia 606.0
                 desquamation 606.1
            hypospermatogenesis 606.1
            infection 606.8
            obstruction, afferent ducts 606.8
            oligospermia 606.1
            radiation 606.8
            spermatogenic arrest (complete) 606.0
                 incomplete 606.1
            systemic disease 606.8

Infestation 134.9
  Acanthocheilonema (perstans) 125.4
       streptocerca 125.6
  Acariasis 133.9
       demodex folliculorum 133.8
       Sarcoptes scabiei 133.0
       trombiculae 133.8
  Agamofilaria streptocerca 125.6
  Ancylostoma, Ankylostoma 126.9
       americanum 126.1
       braziliense 126.2
       canium 126.8
       ceylanicum 126.3
       duodenale 126.0
       new world 126.1
       old world 126.0
  Angiostrongylus cantonensis 128.8
  anisakiasis 127.1
  Anisakis larva 127.1
  arthropod NEC 134.1
  Ascaris lumbricoides 127.0
  Bacillus fusiformis 101
  Balantidium coli 007.0
  beef tapeworm 123.2
  Bothriocephalus (latus) 123.4
       larval 123.5
  broad tapeworm 123.4
       larval 123.5
  Brugia malayi 125.1
  Candiru 136.8
  Capillaria
       hepatica 128.8
       philippinensis 127.5
  cat liver fluke 121.0
  Cercomonas hominis (intestinal) 007.3
  cestodes 123.9
       specified type NEC 123.8
  chigger 133.8
  chigoe 134.1
  Chilomastix 007.8
  Clonorchis (sinensis) (liver) 121.1
  coccidia 007.2
  complicating pregnancy, childbirth, or
       puerperium 647.9 ☑
       affecting fetus or newborn 760.8
  Cysticercus cellulosae 123.1

Infestation — continued
Demodex folliculorum 133.8
Dermatobia (hominis) 134.0
Dibothriocephalus (latus) 123.4
  larval 123.5
Dicrocoelium dendriticum 121.8
Diphyllobothrium (adult) (intestinal) (latum)
  (pacificum) 123.4
  larval 123.5
Diplogonoporus (grandis) 123.8
Dipylidium (caninum) 123.8
Distoma hepaticum 121.3
dog tapeworm 123.8
Dracunculus medinensis 125.7
dragon worm 125.7
dwarf tapeworm 123.6
Echinococcus (see also Echinococcus) 122.9
Echinostoma ilocanum 121.8
Embadomonas 007.8
Endamoeba (histolytica) — see Infection,
  ameba
Entamoeba (histolytica) — see Infection, ameba
Enterobius vermicularis 127.4
Epidermophyton — see Dermatophytosis
eyeworm 125.2
Fasciola
  gigantica 121.3
  hepatica 121.3
Fasciolopsis (buski) (small intestine) 121.4
filarial 125.9
  due to
    Acanthocheilonema (perstans) 125.4
      streptocerca 125.6
    Brugia (Wuchereria) malayi 125.1
    Dracunculus medinensis 125.7
    guinea worms 125.7
    Mansonella (ozzardi) 125.5
    Onchocerca volvulus 125.3
      eye 125.3 [360.13]
      eyelid 125.3 [373.6]
    Wuchereria (bancrofti) 125.0
      malayi 125.1
  specified type NEC 125.6
fish tapeworm 123.4
  larval 123.5
fluke 121.9
  blood NEC (see also Schistosomiasis) 120.9
  cat liver 121.0
  intestinal (giant) 121.4
  liver (sheep) 121.3
    cat 121.0
    Chinese 121.1
    clonorchiasis 121.1
    fascioliasis 121.3
    Oriental 121.1
  lung (oriental) 121.2
  sheep liver 121.3
fly larva 134.0
Gasterophilus (intestinalis) 134.0
Gastrodiscoides hominis 121.8
Giardia lamblia 007.1
Gnathostoma (spinigerum) 128.1
Gongylonema 125.6
guinea worm 125.7
helminth NEC 128.9
  intestinal 127.9
    mixed (types classifiable to more than one
      category in 120.0-127.7) 127.8
    specified type NEC 127.7
  specified type NEC 128.8
Heterophyes heterophyes (small intestine)
  121.6
hookworm (see also Infestation, ancylostoma)
  126.9
Hymenolepis (diminuta) (nana) 123.6
intestinal NEC 129
leeches (aquatic) (land) 134.2
Leishmania — see Leishmaniasis
lice (see also Infestation, pediculus) 132.9
Linguatulidae, linguatula (pentastoma) (serrata)
  134.1
Loa loa 125.2
  eyelid 125.2 [373.6]
louse (see also Infestation, pediculus) 132.9
  body 132.1
  head 132.0
  pubic 132.2

Infestation — continued
maggots 134.0
Mansonella (ozzardi) 125.5
medina 125.7
Metagonimus yokogawai (small intestine) 121.5
Microfilaria streptocerca 125.3
  eye 125.3 [360.13]
  eyelid 125.3 [373.6]
Microsporon furfur 111.0
microsporum — see Dermatophytosis
mites 133.9
  scabic 133.0
  specified type NEC 133.8
monilia (albicans) (see also Candidiasis) 112.9
  vagina 112.1
  vulva 112.1
mouth 112.0
Necator americanus 126.1
nematode (intestinal) 127.9
  Ancylostoma (see also Ancylostoma) 126.9
  Ascaris lumbricoides 127.0
  conjunctiva NEC 128.9
  Dioctophyma 128.8
  Enterobius vermicularis 127.4
  Gnathostoma spinigerum 128.1
  Oesophagostomum (apiostomum) 127.7
  Physaloptera 127.4
  specified type NEC 127.7
  Strongyloides stercoralis 127.2
  Ternidens diminutus 127.7
  Trichinella spiralis 124
  Trichostrongylus 127.6
  Trichuris (trichiuria) 127.3
Oesophagostomum (apiostomum) 127.7
Oestrus ovis 134.0
Onchocerca (volvulus) 125.3
  eye 125.3 [360.13]
  eyelid 125.3 [373.6]
Opisthorchis (felineus) (tenuicollis) (viverrini)
  121.0
Oxyuris vermicularis 127.4
Paragonimus (westermani) 121.2
parasite, parasitic NEC 136.9
  eyelid 134.9 [373.6]
  intestinal 129
  mouth 112.0
  orbit 376.13
  skin 134.9
  tongue 112.0
pediculus 132.9
  capitis (humanus) (any site) 132.0
  corporis (humanus) (any site) 132.1
  eyelid 132.0 [373.6]
  mixed (classifiable to more than one
    category in 132.0-132.2) 132.3
  pubis (any site) 132.2
phthirus (pubis) (any site) 132.2
  with any infestation classifiable to 132.0,
    132.1 and 132.3
pinworm 127.4
pork tapeworm (adult) 123.0
protozoal NEC 136.8
pubic louse 132.2
rat tapeworm 123.6
red bug 133.8
roundworm (large) NEC 127.0
sand flea 134.1
saprophytic NEC 136.8
Sarcoptes scabiei 133.0
scabies 133.0
Schistosoma 120.9
  bovis 120.8
  cercariae 120.3
  hematobium 120.0
  intercalatum 120.8
  japonicum 120.2
  mansoni 120.1
  mattheii 120.8
  specified
    site — see Schistosomiasis
    type NEC 120.8
  spindale 120.8
screw worms 134.0
skin NEC 134.9
Sparganum (mansoni) (proliferum) 123.5
  larval 123.5
specified type NEC 134.8

Infestation — continued
Spirometra larvae 123.5
Sporozoa NEC 136.8
Stellantchasmus falcatus 121.6
Strongyloides 127.2
Strongylus (gibsoni) 127.7
Taenia 123.3
  diminuta 123.6
  Echinococcus (see also Echinococcus) 122.9
  mediocanellata 123.2
  nana 123.6
  saginata (mediocanellata) 123.2
  solium (intestinal form) 123.0
    larval form 123.1
Taeniarhynchus saginatus 123.2
tapeworm 123.9
  beef 123.2
  broad 123.4
    larval 123.5
  dog 123.8
  dwarf 123.6
  fish 123.4
    larval 123.5
  pork 123.0
  rat 123.6
Ternidens diminutus 127.7
Tetranychus molestissimus 133.8
threadworm 127.4
tongue 112.0
Toxocara (cani) (cati) (felis) 128.0
trematode(s) NEC 121.9
Trichina spiralis 124
Trichinella spiralis 124
Trichocephalus 127.3
Trichomonas 131.9
  bladder 131.09
  cervix 131.09
  intestine 007.3
  prostate 131.03
  specified site NEC 131.8
  urethra (female) (male) 131.02
  urogenital 131.00
  vagina 131.01
  vulva 131.01
Trichophyton — see Dermatophytosis
Trichostrongylus instabilis 127.6
Trichuris (trichiuria) 127.3
Trombicula (irritans) 133.8
Trypanosoma — see Trypanosomiasis
Tunga penetrans 134.1
Uncinaria americana 126.1
whipworm 127.3
worms NEC 128.9
  intestinal 127.9
Wuchereria 125.0
  bancrofti 125.0
  malayi 125.1

Infiltrate, infiltration
with an iron compound 275.0
amyloid (any site) (generalized) 277.3
calcareous (muscle) NEC 275.49
  localized — see Degeneration, by site
calcium salt (muscle) 275.49
corneal (see also Edema, cornea) 371.20
eyelid 373.9
fatty (diffuse) (generalized) 272.8
  localized — see Degeneration, by site, fatty
glycogen, glycogenic (see also Disease, glycogen
  storage) 271.0
heart, cardiac
  fatty (see also Degeneration, myocardial)
    429.1
  glycogenic 271.0 [425.7]
inflammatory in vitreous 379.29
kidney (see also Disease, renal) 593.9
leukemic (M9800/3) — see Leukemia
liver 573.8
  fatty — see Fatty, liver
  glycogen (see also Disease, glycogen storage)
    271.0
lung (see also Infiltrate, pulmonary) 518.3
  eosinophilic 518.3
  x-ray finding only 793.1

2006 ICD-9-CM

☑ Additional Digit Required — Refer to the Tabular List (Numeric Code Section) for Additional Digit Selection
►◄ Revised Text   ● New Line   ▲ Revised Code

Volume 2 — 193

Infiltrate, infiltration — continued
  lymphatic (see also Leukemia, lymphatic)
    204.9 ☑
    gland, pigmentary 289.3
  muscle, fatty 728.9
  myelogenous (see also Leukemia, myeloid)
    205.9 ☑
  myocardium, myocardial
    fatty (see also Degeneration, myocardial)
      429.1
    glycogenic 271.0 [425.7]
  pulmonary 518.3
    with
      eosinophilia 518.3
      pneumonia — see Pneumonia, by type
    x-ray finding only 793.1
  Ranke's primary (see also Tuberculosis)
    010.0 ☑
  skin, lymphocytic (benign) 709.8
  thymus (gland) (fatty) 254.8
  urine 788.8
  vitreous humor 379.29

Infirmity 799.89
  senile 797

Inflammation, inflamed, inflammatory (with
  exudation)
  abducens (nerve) 378.54
  accessory sinus (chronic) (see also Sinusitis)
    473.9
  adrenal (gland) 255.8
  alimentary canal — see Enteritis
  alveoli (teeth) 526.5
    scorbutic 267
  amnion — see Amnionitis
  anal canal 569.49
  antrum (chronic) (see also Sinusitis, maxillary)
    473.0
  anus 569.49
  appendix (see also Appendicitis) 541
  arachnoid — see Meningitis
  areola 611.0
    puerperal, postpartum 675.0 ☑
  areolar tissue NEC 686.9
  artery — see Arteritis
  auditory meatus (external) (see also Otitis,
    externa) 380.10
  Bartholin's gland 616.8
  bile duct or passage 576.1
  bladder (see also Cystitis) 595.9
  bone — see Osteomyelitis
  bowel (see also Enteritis) 558.9
  brain (see also Encephalitis) 323.9
    late effect — see category 326
    membrane — see Meningitis
  breast 611.0
    puerperal, postpartum 675.2 ☑
  broad ligament (see also Disease, pelvis,
    inflammatory) 614.4
    acute 614.3
  bronchus — see Bronchitis
  bursa — see Bursitis
  capsule
    liver 573.3
    spleen 289.59
  catarrhal (see also Catarrh) 460
    vagina 616.10
  cecum (see also Appendicitis) 541
  cerebral (see also Encephalitis) 323.9
    late effect — see category 326
    membrane — see Meningitis
  cerebrospinal (see also Meningitis) 322.9
    late effect — see category 326
    meningococcal 036.0
    tuberculous (see also Tuberculosis) 013.6 ☑
  cervix (uteri) (see also Cervicitis) 616.0
  chest 519.9
  choroid NEC (see also Choroiditis) 363.20
  cicatrix (tissue) — see Cicatrix
  colon (see also Enteritis) 558.9
    granulomatous 555.1
    newborn 558.9
  connective tissue (diffuse) NEC 728.9
  cornea (see also Keratitis) 370.9
    with ulcer (see also Ulcer, cornea) 370.00
  corpora cavernosa (penis) 607.2
  cranial nerve — see Disorder, nerve, cranial

Inflammation, inflamed, inflammatory —
  continued
  diarrhea — see Diarrhea
  disc (intervertebral) (space) 722.90
    cervical, cervicothoracic 722.91
    lumbar, lumbosacral 722.93
    thoracic, thoracolumbar 722.92
  Douglas' cul-de-sac or pouch (chronic) (see also
    Disease, pelvis, inflammatory) 614.4
    acute 614.3
  due to (presence of) any device, implant, or
    graft classifiable to 996.0-996.5 — see
    Complications, infection and
    inflammation, due to (presence of) any
    device, implant, or graft classified to
    996.0-996.5 NEC
  duodenum 535.6 ☑
  dura mater — see Meningitis
  ear — see also Otitis
    external (see also Otitis, externa) 380.10
    inner (see also Labyrinthitis) 386.30
    middle — see Otitis media
  esophagus 530.10
  ethmoidal (chronic) (sinus) (see also Sinusitis,
    ethmoidal) 473.2
  Eustachian tube (catarrhal) 381.50
    acute 381.51
    chronic 381.52
  extrarectal 569.49
  eye 379.99
  eyelid 373.9
    specified NEC 373.8
  fallopian tube (see also Salpingo-oophoritis)
    614.2
  fascia 728.9
  fetal membranes (acute) 658.4 ☑
    affecting fetus or newborn 762.7
  follicular, pharynx 472.1
  frontal (chronic) (sinus) (see also Sinusitis,
    frontal) 473.1
  gallbladder (see also Cholecystitis, acute) 575.0
  gall duct (see also Cholecystitis) 575.10
  gastrointestinal (see also Enteritis) 558.9
  genital organ (diffuse) (internal)
    female 614.9
      with
        abortion — see Abortion, by type, with
          sepsis
        ectopic pregnancy (see also categories
          633.0-633.9) 639.0
        molar pregnancy (see also categories
          630-632) 639.0
        complicating pregnancy, childbirth, or
          puerperium 646.6 ☑
          affecting fetus or newborn 760.8
      following
        abortion 639.0
        ectopic or molar pregnancy 639.0
      male 608.4
  gland (lymph) (see also Lymphadenitis) 289.3
  glottis (see also Laryngitis) 464.00
    with obstruction 464.01
  granular, pharynx 472.1
  gum 523.1
  heart (see also Carditis) 429.89
  hepatic duct 576.8
  hernial sac — see Hernia, by site
  ileum (see also Enteritis) 558.9
    terminal or regional 555.0
      with large intestine 555.2
  intervertebral disc 722.90
    cervical, cervicothoracic 722.91
    lumbar, lumbosacral 722.93
    thoracic, thoracolumbar 722.92
  intestine (see also Enteritis) 558.9
  jaw (acute) (bone) (chronic) (lower) (suppurative)
    (upper) 526.4
  jejunum — see Enteritis
  joint NEC (see also Arthritis) 716.9 ☑
    sacroiliac 720.2
  kidney (see also Nephritis) 583.9
  knee (joint) 716.66
    tuberculous (active) (see also Tuberculosis)
      015.2 ☑
  labium (majus) (minus) (see also Vulvitis)
    616.10

Inflammation, inflamed, inflammatory —
  continued
  lacrimal
    gland (see also Dacryoadenitis) 375.00
    passages (duct) (sac) (see also
      Dacryocystitis) 375.30
  larynx (see also Laryngitis) 464.00
    with obstruction 464.01
    diphtheritic 032.3
  leg NEC 686.9
  lip 528.5
  liver (capsule) (see also Hepatitis) 573.3
    acute 570
    chronic 571.40
    suppurative 572.0
  lung (acute) (see also Pneumonia) 486
    chronic (interstitial) 518.89
  lymphatic vessel (see also Lymphangitis) 457.2
  lymph node or gland (see also Lymphadenitis)
    289.3
  mammary gland 611.0
    puerperal, postpartum 675.2 ☑
  maxilla, maxillary 526.4
    sinus (chronic) (see also Sinusitis, maxillary)
      473.0
  membranes of brain or spinal cord — see
    Meningitis
  meninges — see Meningitis
  mouth 528.0
  muscle 728.9
  myocardium (see also Myocarditis) 429.0
  nasal sinus (chronic) (see also Sinusitis) 473.9
  nasopharynx — see Nasopharyngitis
  navel 686.9
    newborn NEC 771.4
  nerve NEC 729.2
  nipple 611.0
    puerperal, postpartum 675.0 ☑
  nose 478.1
    suppurative 472.0
  oculomotor nerve 378.51
  optic nerve 377.30
  orbit (chronic) 376.10
    acute 376.00
    chronic 376.10
  ovary (see also Salpingo-oophoritis) 614.2
  oviduct (see also Salpingo-oophoritis) 614.2
  pancreas — see Pancreatitis
  parametrium (chronic) (see also Disease, pelvis,
    inflammatory) 614.4
    acute 614.3
  parotid region 686.9
    gland 527.2
  pelvis, female (see also Disease, pelvis,
    inflammatory) 614.9
  penis (corpora cavernosa) 607.2
  perianal 569.49
  pericardium (see also Pericarditis) 423.9
  perineum (female) (male) 686.9
  perirectal 569.49
  peritoneum (see also Peritonitis) 567.9
  periuterine (see also Disease, pelvis,
    inflammatory) 614.9
  perivesical (see also Cystitis) 595.9
  petrous bone (see also Petrositis) 383.20
  pharynx (see also Pharyngitis) 462
    follicular 472.1
    granular 472.1
  pia mater — see Meningitis
  pleura — see Pleurisy
  postmastoidectomy cavity 383.30
    chronic 383.33
  prostate (see also Prostatitis) 601.9
  rectosigmoid — see Rectosigmoiditis
  rectum (see also Proctitis) 569.49
  respiratory, upper (see also Infection,
    respiratory, upper) 465.9
    chronic, due to external agent — see
      Condition, respiratory, chronic, due to,
      external agent
    due to
      fumes or vapors (chemical) (inhalation)
        506.2
      radiation 508.1
  retina (see also Retinitis) 363.20
  retrocecal (see also Appendicitis) 541
  retroperitoneal (see also Peritonitis) 567.9

Inflammation, inflamed, inflammatory — *continued*
salivary duct or gland (any) (suppurative) 527.2
scorbutic, alveoli, teeth 267
scrotum 608.4
sigmoid — *see* Enteritis
sinus (*see also* Sinusitis) 473.9
Skene's duct or gland (*see also* Urethritis) 597.89
skin 686.9
spermatic cord 608.4
sphenoidal (sinus) (*see also* Sinusitis, sphenoidal) 473.3
spinal
  cord (*see also* Encephalitis) 323.9
    late effect — *see* category 326
  membrane — *see* Meningitis
  nerve — *see* Disorder, nerve
spine (*see also* Spondylitis) 720.9
spleen (capsule) 289.59
stomach — *see* Gastritis
stricture, rectum 569.49
subcutaneous tissue NEC 686.9
suprarenal (gland) 255.8
synovial (fringe) (membrane) — *see* Bursitis
tendon (sheath) NEC 726.90
testis (*see also* Orchitis) 604.90
thigh 686.9
throat (*see also* Sore throat) 462
thymus (gland) 254.8
thyroid (gland) (*see also* Thyroiditis) 245.9
tongue 529.0
tonsil — *see* Tonsillitis
trachea — *see* Tracheitis
trochlear nerve 378.53
tubal (*see also* Salpingo-oophoritis) 614.2
tuberculous NEC (*see also* Tuberculosis) 011.9 ☑
tubo-ovarian (*see also* Salpingo-oophoritis) 614.2
tunica vaginalis 608.4
tympanic membrane — *see* Myringitis
umbilicus, umbilical 686.9
  newborn NEC 771.4
uterine ligament (*see also* Disease, pelvis, inflammatory) 614.4
  acute 614.3
uterus (catarrhal) (*see also* Endometritis) 615.9
uveal tract (anterior) (*see also* Iridocyclitis) 364.3
  posterior — *see* Chorioretinitis
  sympathetic 360.11
vagina (*see also* Vaginitis) 616.10
vas deferens 608.4
vein (*see also* Phlebitis) 451.9
  thrombotic 451.9
    cerebral (*see also* Thrombosis, brain) 434.0 ☑
    leg 451.2
      deep (vessels) NEC 451.19
      superficial (vessels) 451.0
    lower extremity 451.2
      deep (vessels) NEC 451.19
      superficial (vessels) 451.0
vocal cord 478.5
vulva (*see also* Vulvitis) 616.10
Inflation, lung imperfect (newborn) 770.5
Influenza, influenzal 487.1
with
  bronchitis 487.1
  bronchopneumonia 487.0
  cold (any type) 487.1
  digestive manifestations 487.8
  hemoptysis 487.1
  involvement of
    gastrointestinal tract 487.8
    nervous system 487.8
  laryngitis 487.1
  manifestations NEC 487.8
    respiratory 487.1
      pneumonia 487.0
  pharyngitis 487.1
  pneumonia (any form classifiable to 480-483, 485-486) 487.0
  respiratory manifestations NEC 487.1
  sinusitis 487.1
  sore throat 487.1

Influenza, influenzal — *continued*
with — *continued*
  tonsillitis 487.1
  tracheitis 487.1
  upper respiratory infection (acute) 487.1
abdominal 487.8
Asian 487.1
bronchial 487.1
bronchopneumonia 487.0
catarrhal 487.1
epidemic 487.1
gastric 487.8
intestinal 487.8
laryngitis 487.1
maternal affecting fetus or newborn 760.2
  manifest influenza in infant 771.2
pharyngitis 487.1
pneumonia (any form) 487.0
respiratory (upper) 487.1
stomach 487.8
vaccination, prophylactic (against) V04.81
Influenza-like disease 487.1
Infraction, Freiberg's (metatarsal head) 732.5
Infraeruption, teeth 524.34
Infusion complication, misadventure, or reaction — *see* Complication, infusion
Ingestion
chemical — *see* Table of Drugs and Chemicals
drug or medicinal substance
  overdose or wrong substance given or taken 977.9
    specified drug — *see* Table of Drugs and Chemicals
foreign body NEC (*see also* Foreign body) 938
Ingrowing
hair 704.8
nail (finger) (toe) (infected) 703.0
Inguinal — *see* condition
testis 752.51
Inhalation
carbon monoxide 986
flame
  mouth 947.0
  lung 947.1
food or foreign body (*see also* Asphyxia, food or foreign body) 933.1
gas, fumes, or vapor (noxious) 987.9
  specified agent — *see* Table of Drugs and Chemicals
liquid or vomitus (*see also* Asphyxia, food or foreign body) 933.1
  lower respiratory tract NEC 934.9
meconium (fetus or newborn) 770.11 ▲
  with respiratory symptoms 770.12 ●
mucus (*see also* Asphyxia, mucus) 933.1
oil (causing suffocation) (*see also* Asphyxia, food or foreign body) 933.1
pneumonia — *see* Pneumonia, aspiration
smoke 987.9
steam 987.9
stomach contents or secretions (*see also* Asphyxia, food or foreign body) 933.1
  in labor and delivery 668.0 ☑
Inhibition, inhibited
academic as adjustment reaction 309.23
orgasm
  female 302.73
  male 302.74
sexual
  desire 302.71
  excitement 302.72
work as adjustment reaction 309.23
Inhibitor, systemic lupus erythematosus (presence of) 286.5
Iniencephalus, iniencephaly 740.2
Injected eye 372.74

Injury 959.9

> *Note* — For abrasion, insect bite (nonvenomous), blister, or scratch, see Injury, superficial.
>
> *For laceration, traumatic rupture, tear, or penetrating wound of internal organs, such as heart, lung, liver, kidney, pelvic organs, whether or not accompanied by open wound in the same region, see Injury, internal.*
>
> *For nerve injury, see Injury, nerve.*
>
> *For late effect of injuries classifiable to 850-854, 860-869, 900-919, 950-959, see Late, effect, injury, by type.*

abdomen, abdominal (viscera) — *see also* Injury, internal, abdomen
  muscle or wall 959.12
acoustic, resulting in deafness 951.5
adenoid 959.09
adrenal (gland) — *see* Injury, internal, adrenal
alveolar (process) 959.09
ankle (and foot) (and knee) (and leg, except thigh) 959.7
anterior chamber, eye 921.3
anus 959.19
aorta (thoracic) 901.0
  abdominal 902.0
appendix — *see* Injury, internal, appendix
arm, upper (and shoulder) 959.2
artery (complicating trauma) (*see also* Injury, blood vessel, by site) 904.9
  cerebral or meningeal (*see also* Hemorrhage, brain, traumatic, subarachnoid) 852.0 ☑
auditory canal (external) (meatus) 959.09
auricle, auris, ear 959.09
axilla 959.2
back 959.19
bile duct — *see* Injury, internal, bile duct
birth — *see also* Birth, injury
  canal NEC, complicating delivery 665.9 ☑
bladder (sphincter) — *see* Injury, internal, bladder
blast (air) (hydraulic) (immersion) (underwater) NEC 869.0
  with open wound into cavity NEC 869.1
    abdomen or thorax — *see* Injury, internal, by site
  brain — *see* Concussion, brain
  ear (acoustic nerve trauma) 951.5
    with perforation of tympanic membrane — *see* Wound, open, ear, drum
blood vessel NEC 904.9
  abdomen 902.9
    multiple 902.87
    specified NEC 902.89
  aorta (thoracic) 901.0
    abdominal 902.0
  arm NEC 903.9
  axillary 903.00
    artery 903.01
    vein 903.02
  azygos vein 901.89
  basilic vein 903.1
  brachial (artery) (vein) 903.1
  bronchial 901.89
  carotid artery 900.00
    common 900.01
    external 900.02
    internal 900.03
  celiac artery 902.20
    specified branch NEC 902.24
  cephalic vein (arm) 903.1
  colica dextra 902.26
  cystic
    artery 902.24
    vein 902.39
  deep plantar 904.6
  digital (artery) (vein) 903.5
  due to accidental puncture or laceration during procedure 998.2
  extremity
    lower 904.8
      multiple 904.7
      specified NEC 904.7

Injury — *continued*
  blood vessel NEC — *continued*
    extremity — *continued*
      upper 903.9
        multiple 903.8
        specified NEC 903.8
    femoral
      artery (superficial) 904.1
        above profunda origin 904.0
        common 904.0
      vein 904.2
    gastric
      artery 902.21
      vein 902.39
    head 900.9
      intracranial — *see* Injury, intracranial
      multiple 900.82
      specified NEC 900.89
    hemiazygos vein 901.89
    hepatic
      artery 902.22
      vein 902.11
    hypogastric 902.59
      artery 902.51
      vein 902.52
    ileocolic
      artery 902.26
      vein 902.31
    iliac 902.50
      artery 902.53
      specified branch NEC 902.59
      vein 902.54
    innominate
      artery 901.1
      vein 901.3
    intercostal (artery) (vein) 901.81
    jugular vein (external) 900.81
      internal 900.1
    leg NEC 904.8
    mammary (artery) (vein) 901.82
    mesenteric
      artery 902.20
        inferior 902.27
        specified branch NEC 902.29
        superior (trunk) 902.25
          branches, primary 902.26
      vein 902.39
        inferior 902.32
        superior (and primary subdivisions)
          902.31
    neck 900.9
      multiple 900.82
      specified NEC 900.89
    ovarian 902.89
      artery 902.81
      vein 902.82
    palmar artery 903.4
    pelvis 902.9
      multiple 902.87
      specified NEC 902.89
    plantar (deep) (artery) (vein) 904.6
    popliteal 904.40
      artery 904.41
      vein 904.42
    portal 902.33
    pulmonary 901.40
      artery 901.41
      vein 901.42
    radial (artery) (vein) 903.2
    renal 902.40
      artery 902.41
      specified NEC 902.49
      vein 902.42
    saphenous
      artery 904.7
      vein (greater) (lesser) 904.3
    splenic
      artery 902.23
      vein 902.34
    subclavian
      artery 901.1
      vein 901.3
    suprarenal 902.49
    thoracic 901.9
      multiple 901.83
      specified NEC 901.89

Injury — *continued*
  blood vessel NEC — *continued*
    tibial 904.50
      artery 904.50
        anterior 904.51
        posterior 904.53
      vein 904.50
        anterior 904.52
        posterior 904.54
    ulnar (artery) (vein) 903.3
    uterine 902.59
      artery 902.55
      vein 902.56
    vena cava
      inferior 902.10
        specified branches NEC 902.19
      superior 901.2
  brachial plexus 953.4
    newborn 767.6
  brain NEC (*see also* Injury, intracranial)
    854.0 ☑
  breast 959.19
  broad ligament — *see* Injury, internal, broad
    ligament
  bronchus, bronchi — *see* Injury, internal,
    bronchus
  brow 959.09
  buttock 959.19
  canthus, eye 921.1
  cathode ray 990
  cauda equina 952.4
    with fracture, vertebra — *see* Fracture,
      vertebra, sacrum
  cavernous sinus (*see also* Injury, intracranial)
    854.0 ☑
  cecum — *see* Injury, internal, cecum
  celiac ganglion or plexus 954.1
  cerebellum (*see also* Injury, intracranial)
    854.0 ☑
  cervix (uteri) — *see* Injury, internal, cervix
  cheek 959.09
  chest — *see also* Injury, internal, chest
    wall 959.11
  childbirth — *see also* Birth, injury
    maternal NEC 665.9 ☑
  chin 959.09
  choroid (eye) 921.3
  clitoris 959.14
  coccyx 959.19
    complicating delivery 665.6 ☑
  colon — *see* Injury, internal, colon
  common duct — *see* Injury, internal, common
    duct
  conjunctiva 921.1
    superficial 918.2
  cord
    spermatic — *see* Injury, internal, spermatic
      cord
    spinal — *see* Injury, spinal, by site
  cornea 921.3
    abrasion 918.1
    due to contact lens 371.82
    penetrating — *see* Injury, eyeball,
      penetrating
    superficial 918.1
      due to contact lens 371.82
  cortex (cerebral) (*see also* Injury, intracranial)
    854.0 ☑
    visual 950.3
  costal region 959.11
  costochondral 959.11
  cranial
    bones — *see* Fracture, skull, by site
    cavity (*see also* Injury, intracranial) 854.0 ☑
    nerve — *see* Injury, nerve, cranial
  crushing — *see* Crush
  cutaneous sensory nerve
    lower limb 956.4
    upper limb 955.5
  delivery — *see also* Birth, injury
    maternal NEC 665.9 ☑
  Descemet's membrane — *see* Injury, eyeball,
    penetrating
  diaphragm — *see* Injury, internal, diaphragm
  diffuse axonal — *see* Injury, intracranial ●
  duodenum — *see* Injury, internal, duodenum
  ear (auricle) (canal) (drum) (external) 959.09

Injury — *continued*
  elbow (and forearm) (and wrist) 959.3
  epididymis 959.14
  epigastric region 959.12
  epiglottis 959.09
  epiphyseal, current — *see* Fracture, by site
  esophagus — *see* Injury, internal, esophagus
  Eustachian tube 959.09
  extremity (lower) (upper) NEC 959.8
  eye 921.9
    penetrating eyeball — *see* Injury, eyeball,
      penetrating
    superficial 918.9
  eyeball 921.3
    penetrating 871.7
      with
        partial loss (of intraocular tissue)
          871.2
        prolapse or exposure (of intraocular
          tissue) 871.1
        without prolapse 871.0
        foreign body (nonmagnetic) 871.6
          magnetic 871.5
    superficial 918.9
  eyebrow 959.09
  eyelid(s) 921.1
    laceration — *see* Laceration, eyelid
    superficial 918.0
  face (and neck) 959.09
  fallopian tube — *see* Injury, internal, fallopian
    tube
  finger(s) (nail) 959.5
  flank 959.19
  foot (and ankle) (and knee) (and leg, except
    thigh) 959.7
  forceps NEC 767.9
    scalp 767.19
  forearm (and elbow) (and wrist) 959.3
  forehead 959.09
  gallbladder — *see* Injury, internal, gallbladder
  gasserian ganglion 951.2
  gastrointestinal tract — *see* Injury, internal,
    gastrointestinal tract
  genital organ(s)
    with
      abortion — *see* Abortion, by type, with,
        damage to pelvic organs
      ectopic pregnancy (*see also* categories
        633.0-633.9) 639.2
      molar pregnancy (*see also* categories 630-
        632) 639.2
    external 959.14
      fracture of corpus cavernosum penis
        959.13
    following
      abortion 639.2
      ectopic or molar pregnancy 639.2
    internal — *see* Injury, internal, genital
      organs
    obstetrical trauma NEC 665.9 ☑
      affecting fetus or newborn 763.89
  gland
    lacrimal 921.1
      laceration 870.8
    parathyroid 959.09
    salivary 959.09
    thyroid 959.09
  globe (eye) (*see also* Injury, eyeball) 921.3
  grease gun — *see* Wound, open, by site,
    complicated
  groin 959.19
  gum 959.09
  hand(s) (except fingers) 959.4
  head NEC 959.01
    with
      loss of consciousness 850.5
      skull fracture — *see* Fracture, skull, by
        site
  heart — *see* Injury, internal, heart
  heel 959.7
  hip (and thigh) 959.6
  hymen 959.14
  hyperextension (cervical) (vertebra) 847.0
  ileum — *see* Injury, internal, ileum
  iliac region 959.19
  infrared rays NEC 990

☑ Additional Digit Required — Refer to the Tabular List (Numeric Code Section) for Additional Digit Selection

Injury — *continued*
  instrumental (during surgery) 998.2
    birth injury — *see* Birth, injury
    nonsurgical (*see also* Injury, by site) 959.9
    obstetrical 665.9 ☑
      affecting fetus or newborn 763.89
      bladder 665.5 ☑
      cervix 665.3 ☑
      high vaginal 665.4 ☑
      perineal NEC 664.9 ☑
      urethra 665.5 ☑
      uterus 665.5 ☑
    internal 869.0

> **Note** — *For injury of internal organ(s) by foreign body entering through a natural orifice (e.g., inhaled, ingested, or swallowed) — see Foreign body, entering through orifice.*
>
> *For internal injury of any of the following sites with internal injury of any other of the sites — see Injury, internal, multiple.*

    with
      fracture
        pelvis — *see* Fracture, pelvis
        specified site, except pelvis — *see* Injury, internal, by site
      open wound into cavity 869.1
    abdomen, abdominal (viscera) NEC 868.00
      with
        fracture, pelvis — *see* Fracture, pelvis
        open wound into cavity 868.10
      specified site NEC 868.09
        with open wound into cavity 868.19
    adrenal (gland) 868.01
      with open wound into cavity 868.11
    aorta (thoracic) 901.0
      abdominal 902.0
    appendix 863.85
      with open wound into cavity 863.95
    bile duct 868.02
      with open wound into cavity 868.12
    bladder (sphincter) 867.0
      with
        abortion — *see* Abortion, by type, with damage to pelvic organs
        ectopic pregnancy (*see also* categories 633.0-633.9) 639.2
        molar pregnancy (*see also* categories 630-632) 639.2
        open wound into cavity 867.1
      following
        abortion 639.2
        ectopic or molar pregnancy 639.2
      obstetrical trauma 665.5 ☑
        affecting fetus or newborn 763.89
    blood vessel — *see* Injury, blood vessel, by site
    broad ligament 867.6
      with open wound into cavity 867.7
    bronchus, bronchi 862.21
      with open wound into cavity 862.31
    cecum 863.89
      with open wound into cavity 863.99
    cervix (uteri) 867.4
      with
        abortion — *see* Abortion, by type, with damage to pelvic organs
        ectopic pregnancy (*see also* categories 633.0-633.9) 639.2
        molar pregnancy (*see also* categories 630-632) 639.2
        open wound into cavity 867.5
      following
        abortion 639.2
        ectopic or molar pregnancy 639.2
      obstetrical trauma 665.3 ☑
        affecting fetus or newborn 763.89
    chest (*see also* Injury, internal, intrathoracic organs) 862.8
      with open wound into cavity 862.9
    colon 863.40
      with
        open wound into cavity 863.50
      rectum 863.46
        with open wound into cavity 863.56
      ascending (right) 863.41
        with open wound into cavity 863.51

Injury — *continued*
  internal — *continued*
    colon — *continued*
      descending (left) 863.43
        with open wound into cavity 863.53
      multiple sites 863.46
        with open wound into cavity 863.56
      sigmoid 863.44
        with open wound into cavity 863.54
      specified site NEC 863.49
        with open wound into cavity 863.59
      transverse 863.42
        with open wound into cavity 863.52
    common duct 868.02
      with open wound into cavity 868.12
    complicating delivery 665.9 ☑
      affecting fetus or newborn 763.89
    diaphragm 862.0
      with open wound into cavity 862.1
    duodenum 863.21
      with open wound into cavity 863.31
    esophagus (intrathoracic) 862.22
      with open wound into cavity 862.32
      cervical region 874.4
        complicated 874.5
    fallopian tube 867.6
      with open wound into cavity 867.7
    gallbladder 868.02
      with open wound into cavity 868.12
    gastrointestinal tract NEC 863.80
      with open wound into cavity 863.90
    genital organ NEC 867.6
      with open wound into cavity 867.7
    heart 861.00
      with open wound into thorax 861.10
    ileum 863.29
      with open wound into cavity 863.39
    intestine NEC 863.89
      with open wound into cavity 863.99
      large NEC 863.40
        with open wound into cavity 863.50
      small NEC 863.20
        with open wound into cavity 863.30
    intra-abdominal (organ) 868.00
      with open wound into cavity 868.10
      multiple sites 868.09
        with open wound into cavity 868.19
      specified site NEC 868.09
        with open wound into cavity 868.19
    intrathoracic organs (multiple) 862.8
      with open wound into cavity 862.9
      diaphragm (only) — *see* Injury, internal, diaphragm
      heart (only) — *see* Injury, internal, heart
      lung (only) — *see* Injury, internal, lung
      specified site NEC 862.29
        with open wound into cavity 862.39
    intrauterine (*see also* Injury, internal, uterus) 867.4
      with open wound into cavity 867.5
    jejunum 863.29
      with open wound into cavity 863.39
    kidney (subcapsular) 866.00
      with
        disruption of parenchyma (complete) 866.03
          with open wound into cavity 866.13
        hematoma (without rupture of capsule) 866.01
          with open wound into cavity 866.11
        laceration 866.02
          with open wound into cavity 866.12
        open wound into cavity 866.10
    liver 864.00
      with
        contusion 864.01
          with open wound into cavity 864.11
        hematoma 864.01
          with open wound into cavity 864.11
        laceration 864.05
          with open wound into cavity 864.15
          major (disruption of hepatic parenchyma) 864.04
            with open wound into cavity 864.14

Injury — *continued*
  internal — *continued*
    liver — *continued*
      with — *continued*
        laceration — *continued*
          minor (capsule only) 864.02
            with open wound into cavity 864.12
          moderate (involving parenchyma) 864.03
            with open wound into cavity 864.13
          multiple 864.04
          stellate 864.04
            with open wound into cavity 864.14
      open wound into cavity 864.10
    lung 861.20
      with open wound into thorax 861.30
      hemopneumothorax — *see* Hemopneumothorax, traumatic
      hemothorax — *see* Hemothorax, traumatic
      pneumohemothorax — *see* Pneumohemothorax, traumatic
      pneumothorax — *see* Pneumothorax, traumatic
    mediastinum 862.29
      with open wound into cavity 862.39
    mesentery 863.89
      with open wound into cavity 863.99
    mesosalpinx 867.6
      with open wound into cavity 867.7
    multiple 869.0

> **Note** — *Multiple internal injuries of sites classifiable to the same three- or four-digit category should be classified to that category.*
>
> *Multiple injuries classifiable to different fourth-digit subdivisions of 861 (heart and lung injuries) should be dealt with according to coding rules.*

      internal
        with open wound into cavity 869.1
      intra-abdominal organ (sites classifiable to 863-868)
        with
          intrathoracic organ(s) (sites classifiable to 861-862) 869.0
            with open wound into cavity 869.1
          other intra-abdominal organ(s) (sites classifiable to 863-868, except where classifiable to the same three-digit category) 868.09
            with open wound into cavity 868.19
      intrathoracic organ (sites classifiable to 861-862)
        with
          intra-abdominal organ(s) (sites classifiable to 863-868) 869.0
            with open wound into cavity 869.1
          other intrathoracic organ(s) (sites classifiable to 861-862, except where classifiable to the same three-digit category) 862.8
            with open wound into cavity 862.9
    myocardium — *see* Injury, internal, heart
    ovary 867.6
      with open wound into cavity 867.7
    pancreas (multiple sites) 863.84
      with open wound into cavity 863.94
      body 863.82
        with open wound into cavity 863.92
      head 863.81
        with open wound into cavity 863.91
      tail 863.83
        with open wound into cavity 863.93
    pelvis, pelvic (organs) (viscera) 867.8
      with
        fracture, pelvis — *see* Fracture, pelvis
        open wound into cavity 867.9

☑ Additional Digit Required — Refer to the Tabular List (Numeric Code Section) for Additional Digit Selection

▶◀ Revised Text   ● New Line   ▲ Revised Code

Injury — *continued*
  internal — *continued*
    pelvis, pelvic — *continued*
      specified site NEC 867.6
        with open wound into cavity 867.7
    peritoneum 868.03
      with open wound into cavity 868.13
    pleura 862.29
      with open wound into cavity 862.39
    prostate 867.6
      with open wound into cavity 867.7
    rectum 863.45
      with
        colon 863.46
          with open wound into cavity 863.56
        open wound into cavity 863.55
    retroperitoneum 868.04
      with open wound into cavity 868.14
    round ligament 867.6
      with open wound into cavity 867.7
    seminal vesicle 867.6
      with open wound into cavity 867.7
    spermatic cord 867.6
      with open wound into cavity 867.7
      scrotal — *see* Wound, open, spermatic
        cord
    spleen 865.00
      with
        disruption of parenchyma (massive)
          865.04
          with open wound into cavity 865.14
        hematoma (without rupture of capsule)
          865.01
          with open wound into cavity 865.11
        open wound into cavity 865.10
        tear, capsular 865.02
          with open wound into cavity 865.12
          extending into parenchyma 865.03
            with open wound into cavity
              865.13
    stomach 863.0
      with open wound into cavity 863.1
    suprarenal gland (multiple) 868.01
      with open wound into cavity 868.11
    thorax, thoracic (cavity) (organs) (multiple)
      (*see also* Injury, internal, intrathoracic
      organs) 862.8
      with open wound into cavity 862.9
    thymus (gland) 862.29
      with open wound into cavity 862.39
    trachea (intrathoracic) 862.29
      with open wound into cavity 862.39
      cervical region (*see also* Wound, open,
        trachea) 874.02
    ureter 867.2
      with open wound into cavity 867.3
    urethra (sphincter) 867.0
      with
        abortion — *see* Abortion, by type, with
          damage to pelvic organs
        ectopic pregnancy (*see also* categories
          633.0-633.9) 639.2
        molar pregnancy (*see also* categories
          630-632) 639.2
        open wound into cavity 867.1
      following
        abortion 639.2
        ectopic or molar pregnancy 639.2
      obstetrical trauma 665.5 ☑
        affecting fetus or newborn 763.89
    uterus 867.4
      with
        abortion — *see* Abortion, by type, with
          damage to pelvic organs
        ectopic pregnancy (*see also* categories
          633.0-633.9) 639.2
        molar pregnancy (*see also* categories
          630-632) 639.2
        open wound into cavity 867.5
      following
        abortion 639.2
        ectopic or molar pregnancy 639.2
      obstetrical trauma NEC 665.5 ☑
        affecting fetus or newborn 763.89
    vas deferens 867.6
      with open wound into cavity 867.7
    vesical (sphincter) 867.0
      with open wound into cavity 867.1

Injury — *continued*
  internal — *continued*
    viscera (abdominal) (*see also* Injury,
      internal, multiple) 868.00
      with
        fracture, pelvis — *see* Fracture, pelvis
        open wound into cavity 868.10
      thoracic NEC (*see also* Injury, internal,
        intrathoracic organs) 862.8
        with open wound into cavity 862.9
  interscapular region 959.19
  intervertebral disc 959.19
  intestine — *see* Injury, internal, intestine
  intra-abdominal (organs) NEC — *see* Injury,
    internal, intra-abdominal
  intracranial 854.0 ☑

> *Note* — *Use the following fifth-digit*
> *subclassification with categories 851-854:*
>
> 0   *unspecified state of consciousness*
> 1   *with no loss of consciousness*
> 2   *with brief [less than one hour] loss of*
>   *consciousness*
> 3   *with moderate [1-24 hours] loss of*
>   *consciousness*
> 4   *with prolonged [more than 24 hours]*
>   *loss of consciousness and return to pre-*
>   *existing conscious level*
> 5   *with prolonged [more than 24 hours]*
>   *loss of consciousness, without return to*
>   *pre-existing conscious level*
>   *Use fifth-digit 5 to designate when a patient*
>   *is unconscious and dies before*
>   *regaining consciousness, regardless of*
>   *the duration of the loss of*
>   *consciousness*
> 6   *with loss of consciousness of*
>   *unspecified duration*
> 9   *with concussion, unspecified*

    with
      open intracranial wound 854.1 ☑
      skull fracture — *see* Fracture, skull, by
        site
    contusion 851.8 ☑
      with open intracranial wound 851.9 ☑
      brain stem 851.4 ☑
        with open intracranial wound 851.5 ☑
      cerebellum 851.4 ☑
        with open intracranial wound 851.5 ☑
      cortex (cerebral) 851.0 ☑
        with open intracranial wound 851.2 ☑
    hematoma — *see* Injury, intracranial,
      hemorrhage
    hemorrhage 853.0 ☑
      with
        laceration — *see* Injury, intracranial,
          laceration
        open intracranial wound 853.1 ☑
      extradural 852.4 ☑
        with open intracranial wound 852.5 ☑
      subarachnoid 852.0 ☑
        with open intracranial wound 852.1 ☑
      subdural 852.2 ☑
        with open intracranial wound 852.3 ☑
    laceration 851.8 ☑
      with open intracranial wound 851.9 ☑
      brain stem 851.6 ☑
        with open intracranial wound 851.7 ☑
      cerebellum 851.6 ☑
        with open intracranial wound 851.7 ☑
      cortex (cerebral) 851.2 ☑
        with open intracranial wound 851.3 ☑
  intraocular — *see* Injury, eyeball, penetrating
  intrathoracic organs (multiple) — *see* Injury,
    internal, intrathoracic organs
  intrauterine — *see* Injury, internal, intrauterine
  iris 921.3
    penetrating — *see* Injury, eyeball,
      penetrating
  jaw 959.09
  jejunum — *see* Injury, internal, jejunum
  joint NEC 959.9
    old or residual 718.80
      ankle 718.87

Injury — *continued*
  joint NEC — *continued*
    old or residual — *continued*
      elbow 718.82
      foot 718.87
      hand 718.84
      hip 718.85
      knee 718.86
      multiple sites 718.89
      pelvic region 718.85
      shoulder (region) 718.81
      specified site NEC 718.88
      wrist 718.83
  kidney — *see* Injury, internal, kidney
  knee (and ankle) (and foot) (and leg, except
    thigh) 959.7
  labium (majus) (minus) 959.14
  labyrinth, ear 959.09
  lacrimal apparatus, gland, or sac 921.1
    laceration 870.8
  larynx 959.09
  late effect — *see* Late, effects (of), injury
  leg, except thigh (and ankle) (and foot) (and
    knee) 959.7
    upper or thigh 959.6
  lens, eye 921.3
    penetrating — *see* Injury, eyeball,
      penetrating
  lid, eye — *see* Injury, eyelid
  lip 959.09
  liver — *see* Injury, internal, liver
  lobe, parietal — *see* Injury, intracranial
  lumbar (region) 959.19
    plexus 953.5
  lumbosacral (region) 959.19
    plexus 953.5
  lung — *see* Injury, internal, lung
  malar region 959.09
  mastoid region 959.09
  maternal, during pregnancy, affecting fetus or
    newborn 760.5
  maxilla 959.09
  mediastinum — *see* Injury, internal,
    mediastinum
  membrane
    brain (*see also* Injury, intracranial) 854.0 ☑
    tympanic 959.09
  meningeal artery — *see* Hemorrhage, brain,
    traumatic, subarachnoid
  meninges (cerebral) — *see* Injury, intracranial
  mesenteric
    artery — *see* Injury, blood vessel,
      mesenteric, artery
    plexus, inferior 954.1
    vein — *see* Injury, blood vessel, mesenteric,
      vein
  mesentery — *see* Injury, internal, mesentery
  mesosalpinx — *see* Injury, internal,
    mesosalpinx
  middle ear 959.09
  midthoracic region 959.11
  mouth 959.09
  multiple (sites not classifiable to the same four-
    digit category in 959.0-959.7) 959.8
    internal 869.0
      with open wound into cavity 869.1
  musculocutaneous nerve 955.4
  nail
    finger 959.5
    toe 959.7
  nasal (septum) (sinus) 959.09
  nasopharynx 959.09
  neck (and face) 959.09
  nerve 957.9
    abducens 951.3
    abducent 951.3
    accessory 951.6
    acoustic 951.5
    ankle and foot 956.9
    anterior crural, femoral 956.1
    arm (*see also* Injury, nerve, upper limb)
      955.9
    auditory 951.5
    axillary 955.0
    brachial plexus 953.4
    cervical sympathetic 954.0

Injury — *continued*
nerve — *continued*
cranial 951.9
first or olfactory 951.8
second or optic 950.0
third or oculomotor 951.0
fourth or trochlear 951.1
fifth or trigeminal 951.2
sixth or abducens 951.3
seventh or facial 951.4
eighth, acoustic, or auditory 951.5
ninth or glossopharyngeal 951.8
tenth, pneumogastric, or vagus 951.8
eleventh or accessory 951.6
twelfth or hypoglossal 951.7
newborn 767.7
cutaneous sensory
lower limb 956.4
upper limb 955.5
digital (finger) 955.6
toe 956.5
facial 951.4
newborn 767.5
femoral 956.1
finger 955.9
foot and ankle 956.9
forearm 955.9
glossopharyngeal 951.8
hand and wrist 955.9
head and neck, superficial 957.0
hypoglossal 951.7
involving several parts of body 957.8
leg (*see also* Injury, nerve, lower limb) 956.9
lower limb 956.9
multiple 956.8
specified site NEC 956.5
lumbar plexus 953.5
lumbosacral plexus 953.5
median 955.1
forearm 955.1
wrist and hand 955.1
multiple (in several parts of body) (sites not classifiable to the same three-digit category) 957.8
musculocutaneous 955.4
musculospiral 955.3
upper arm 955.3
oculomotor 951.0
olfactory 951.8
optic 950.0
pelvic girdle 956.9
multiple sites 956.8
specified site NEC 956.5
peripheral 957.9
multiple (in several regions) (sites not classifiable to the same three-digit category) 957.8
specified site NEC 957.1
peroneal 956.3
ankle and foot 956.3
lower leg 956.3
plantar 956.5
plexus 957.9
celiac 954.1
mesenteric, inferior 954.1
spinal 953.9
brachial 953.4
lumbosacral 953.5
multiple sites 953.8
sympathetic NEC 954.1
pneumogastric 951.8
radial 955.3
wrist and hand 955.3
sacral plexus 953.5
sciatic 956.0
thigh 956.0
shoulder girdle 955.9
multiple 955.8
specified site NEC 955.7
specified site NEC 957.1
spinal 953.9
plexus — *see* Injury, nerve, plexus, spinal
root 953.9
cervical 953.0
dorsal 953.1
lumbar 953.2
multiple sites 953.8
sacral 953.3

Injury — *continued*
nerve — *continued*
splanchnic 954.1
sympathetic NEC 954.1
cervical 954.0
thigh 956.9
tibial 956.5
ankle and foot 956.2
lower leg 956.5
posterior 956.2
toe 956.9
trigeminal 951.2
trochlear 951.1
trunk, excluding shoulder and pelvic girdles 954.9
specified site NEC 954.8
sympathetic NEC 954.1
ulnar 955.2
forearm 955.2
wrist (and hand) 955.2
upper limb 955.9
multiple 955.8
specified site NEC 955.7
vagus 951.8
wrist and hand 955.9
nervous system, diffuse 957.8
nose (septum) 959.09
obstetrical NEC 665.9 ☑
affecting fetus or newborn 763.89
occipital (region) (scalp) 959.09
lobe (*see also* Injury, intracranial) 854.0 ☑
optic 950.9
chiasm 950.1
cortex 950.3
nerve 950.0
pathways 950.2
orbit, orbital (region) 921.2
penetrating 870.3
with foreign body 870.4
ovary — *see* Injury, internal, ovary
paint-gun — *see* Wound, open, by site, complicated
palate (soft) 959.09
pancreas — *see* Injury, internal, pancreas
parathyroid (gland) 959.09
parietal (region) (scalp) 959.09
lobe — *see* Injury, intracranial
pelvic
floor 959.19
complicating delivery 664.1 ☑
affecting fetus or newborn 763.89
joint or ligament, complicating delivery 665.6 ☑
affecting fetus or newborn 763.89
organs — *see also* Injury, internal, pelvis
with
abortion — *see* Abortion, by type, with damage to pelvic organs
ectopic pregnancy (*see also* categories 633.0-633.9) 639.2
molar pregnancy (*see also* categories 633.0-633.9) 639.2
following
abortion 639.2
ectopic or molar pregnancy 639.2
obstetrical trauma 665.5 ☑
affecting fetus or newborn 763.89
pelvis 959.19
penis 959.14
fracture of corpus cavernosum 959.13
perineum 959.14
peritoneum — *see* Injury, internal, peritoneum
periurethral tissue
with
abortion — *see* Abortion, by type, with damage to pelvic organs
ectopic pregnancy (*see also* categories 633.0-633.9) 639.2
molar pregnancy (*see also* categories 630-632) 639.2
complicating delivery 665.5 ☑
affecting fetus or newborn 763.89
following
abortion 639.2
ectopic or molar pregnancy 639.2
phalanges
foot 959.7
hand 959.5

Injury — *continued*
pharynx 959.09
pleura — *see* Injury, internal, pleura
popliteal space 959.7
prepuce 959.14
prostate — *see* Injury, internal, prostate
pubic region 959.19
pudenda 959.14
radiation NEC 990
radioactive substance or radium NEC 990
rectovaginal septum 959.14
rectum — *see* Injury, internal, rectum
retina 921.3
penetrating — *see* Injury, eyeball, penetrating
retroperitoneal — *see* Injury, internal, retroperitoneum
roentgen rays NEC 990
round ligament — *see* Injury, internal, round ligament
sacral (region) 959.19
plexus 953.5
sacroiliac ligament NEC 959.19
sacrum 959.19
salivary ducts or glands 959.09
scalp 959.09
due to birth trauma 767.19
fetus or newborn 767.19
scapular region 959.2
sclera 921.3
penetrating — *see* Injury, eyeball, penetrating
superficial 918.2
scrotum 959.14
seminal vesicle — *see* Injury, internal, seminal vesicle
shoulder (and upper arm) 959.2
sinus
cavernous (*see also* Injury, intracranial) 854.0 ☑
nasal 959.09
skeleton NEC, birth injury 767.3
skin NEC 959.9
skull — *see* Fracture, skull, by site
soft tissue (of external sites) (severe) — *see* Wound, open, by site
specified site NEC 959.8
spermatic cord — *see* Injury, internal, spermatic cord
spinal (cord) 952.9
with fracture, vertebra — *see* Fracture, vertebra, by site, with spinal cord injury
cervical (C₁-C₄) 952.00
with
anterior cord syndrome 952.02
central cord syndrome 952.03
complete lesion of cord 952.01
incomplete lesion NEC 952.04
posterior cord syndrome 952.04
C₅-C₇ level 952.05
with
anterior cord syndrome 952.07
central cord syndrome 952.08
complete lesion of cord 952.06
incomplete lesion NEC 952.09
posterior cord syndrome 952.09
specified type NEC 952.09
specified type NEC 952.04
dorsal (D₁-D₆) (T₁-T₆) (thoracic) 952.10
with
anterior cord syndrome 952.12
central cord syndrome 952.13
complete lesion of cord 952.11
incomplete lesion NEC 952.14
posterior cord syndrome 952.14
D₇-D₁₂ level (T₇-T₁₂) 952.15
with
anterior cord syndrome 952.17
central cord syndrome 952.18
complete lesion of cord 952.16
incomplete lesion NEC 952.19
posterior cord syndrome 952.19
specified type NEC 952.19
specified type NEC 952.14
lumbar 952.2
multiple sites 952.8

☑ Additional Digit Required — Refer to the Tabular List (Numeric Code Section) for Additional Digit Selection
◄► Revised Text   ● New Line   ▲ Revised Code

2006 ICD-9-CM

Volume 2 — 199

Injury — *continued*
  spinal — *continued*
    nerve (root) NEC — *see* Injury, nerve, spinal, root
    plexus 953.9
      brachial 953.4
      lumbosacral 953.5
      multiple sites 953.8
    sacral 952.3
    thoracic (*see also* Injury, spinal, dorsal) 952.10
  spleen — *see* Injury, internal, spleen
  stellate ganglion 954.1
  sternal region 959.11
  stomach — *see* Injury, internal, stomach
  subconjunctival 921.1
  subcutaneous 959.9
  subdural — *see* Injury, intracranial
  submaxillary region 959.09
  submental region 959.09
  subungual
    fingers 959.5
    toes 959.7
  superficial 919 ☑

Note — *Use the following fourth-digit subdivisions with categories 910-919:*

0	*Abrasion or friction burn without mention of infection*
1	*Abrasion or friction burn, infected*
2	*Blister without mention of infection*
3	*Blister, infected*
4	*Insect bite, nonvenomous, without mention of infection*
5	*Insect bite, nonvenomous, infected*
6	*Superficial foreign body (splinter) without major open wound and without mention of infection*
7	*Superficial foreign body (splinter) without major open wound, infected*
8	*Other and unspecified superficial injury without mention of infection*
9	*Other and unspecified superficial injury, infected*

For late effects of superficial injury, see category 906.2.

---

    abdomen, abdominal (muscle) (wall) (and other part(s) of trunk) 911 ☑
    ankle (and hip, knee, leg, or thigh) 916 ☑
    anus (and other part(s) of trunk) 911 ☑
    arm 913 ☑
      upper (and shoulder) 912 ☑
    auditory canal (external) (meatus) (and other part(s) of face, neck, or scalp, except eye) 910 ☑
    axilla (and upper arm) 912 ☑
    back (and other part(s) of trunk) 911 ☑
    breast (and other part(s) of trunk) 911 ☑
    brow (and other part(s) of face, neck, or scalp, except eye) 910 ☑
    buttock (and other part(s) of trunk) 911 ☑
    canthus, eye 918.0
    cheek(s) (and other part(s) of face, neck, or scalp, except eye) 910 ☑
    chest wall (and other part(s) of trunk) 911 ☑
    chin (and other part(s) of face, neck, or scalp, except eye) 910 ☑
    clitoris (and other part(s) of trunk) 911 ☑
    conjunctiva 918.2
    cornea 918.1
      due to contact lens 371.82
    costal region (and other part(s) of trunk) 911 ☑
    ear(s) (auricle) (canal) (drum) (external) (and other part(s) of face, neck, or scalp, except eye) 910 ☑
    elbow (and forearm) (and wrist) 913 ☑
    epididymis (and other part(s) of trunk) 911 ☑
    epigastric region (and other part(s) of trunk) 911 ☑
    epiglottis (and other part(s) of face, neck, or scalp, except eye) 910 ☑
    eye(s) (and adnexa) NEC 918.9

Injury — *continued*
  superficial — *continued*
    eyelid(s) (and periocular area) 918.0
    face (any part(s), except eye) (and neck or scalp) 910 ☑
    finger(s) (nail) (any) 915 ☑
    flank (and other part(s) of trunk) 911 ☑
    foot (phalanges) (and toe(s)) 917 ☑
    forearm (and elbow) (and wrist) 913 ☑
    forehead (and other part(s) of face, neck, or scalp, except eye) 910 ☑
    globe (eye) 918.9
    groin (and other part(s) of trunk) 911 ☑
    gum(s) (and other part(s) of face, neck, or scalp, except eye) 910 ☑
    hand(s) (except fingers alone) 914 ☑
    head (and other part(s) of face, neck, or scalp, except eye) 910 ☑
    heel (and foot or toe) 917 ☑
    hip (and ankle, knee, leg, or thigh) 916 ☑
    iliac region (and other part(s) of trunk) 911 ☑
    interscapular region (and other part(s) of trunk) 911 ☑
    iris 918.9
    knee (and ankle, hip, leg, or thigh) 916 ☑
    labium (majus) (minus) (and other part(s) of trunk) 911 ☑
    lacrimal (apparatus) (gland) (sac) 918.0
    leg (lower) (upper) (and ankle, hip, knee, or thigh) 916 ☑
    lip(s) (and other part(s) of face, neck, or scalp, except eye) 910 ☑
    lower extremity (except foot) 916 ☑
    lumbar region (and other part(s) of trunk) 911 ☑
    malar region (and other part(s) of face, neck, or scalp, except eye) 910 ☑
    mastoid region (and other part(s) of face, neck, or scalp, except eye) 910 ☑
    midthoracic region (and other part(s) of trunk) 911 ☑
    mouth (and other part(s) of face, neck, or scalp, except eye) 910 ☑
    multiple sites (not classifiable to the same three-digit category) 919 ☑
    nasal (septum) (and other part(s) of face, neck, or scalp, except eye) 910 ☑
    neck (and face or scalp, any part(s), except eye) 910 ☑
    nose (septum) (and other part(s) of face, neck, or scalp, except eye) 910 ☑
    occipital region (and other part(s) of face, neck, or scalp, except eye) 910 ☑
    orbital region 918.0
    palate (soft) (and other part(s) of face, neck, or scalp, except eye) 910 ☑
    parietal region (and other part(s) of face, neck, or scalp, except eye) 910 ☑
    penis (and other part(s) of trunk) 911 ☑
    perineum (and other part(s) of trunk) 911 ☑
    periocular area 918.0
    pharynx (and other part(s) of face, neck, or scalp, except eye) 910 ☑
    popliteal space (and ankle, hip, leg, or thigh) 916 ☑
    prepuce (and other part(s) of trunk) 911 ☑
    pubic region (and other part(s) of trunk) 911 ☑
    pudenda (and other part(s) of trunk) 911 ☑
    sacral region (and other part(s) of trunk) 911 ☑
    salivary (ducts) (glands) (and other part(s) of face, neck, or scalp, except eye) 910 ☑
    scalp (and other part(s) of face or neck, except eye) 910 ☑
    scapular region (and upper arm) 912 ☑
    sclera 918.2
    scrotum (and other part(s) of trunk) 911 ☑
    shoulder (and upper arm) 912 ☑
    skin NEC 919 ☑
    specified site(s) NEC 919 ☑
    sternal region (and other part(s) of trunk) 911 ☑
    subconjunctival 918.2
    subcutaneous NEC 919 ☑

Injury — *continued*
  superficial — *continued*
    submaxillary region (and other part(s) of face, neck, or scalp, except eye) 910 ☑
    submental region (and other part(s) of face, neck, or scalp, except eye) 910 ☑
    supraclavicular fossa (and other part(s) of face, neck or scalp, except eye) 910 ☑
    supraorbital 918.0
    temple (and other part(s) of face, neck, or scalp, except eye) 910 ☑
    temporal region (and other part(s) of face, neck, or scalp, except eye) 910 ☑
    testis (and other part(s) of trunk) 911 ☑
    thigh (and ankle, hip, knee, or leg) 916 ☑
    thorax, thoracic (external) (and other part(s) of trunk) 911 ☑
    throat (and other part(s) of face, neck, or scalp, except eye) 910 ☑
    thumb(s) (nail) 915 ☑
    toe(s) (nail) (subungual) (and foot) 917 ☑
    tongue (and other part(s) of face, neck, or scalp, except eye) 910 ☑
    tooth, teeth (*see also* Abrasion, dental) 521.20
    trunk (any part(s)) 911 ☑
    tunica vaginalis 959.14
    tympanum, tympanic membrane (and other part(s) of face, neck, or scalp, except eye) 910 ☑
    upper extremity NEC 913 ☑
    uvula (and other part(s) of face, neck, or scalp, except eye) 910 ☑
    vagina (and other part(s) of trunk) 911 ☑
    vulva (and other part(s) of trunk) 911 ☑
    wrist (and elbow) (and forearm) 913 ☑
  supraclavicular fossa 959.19
  supraorbital 959.09
  surgical complication (external or internal site) 998.2
  symphysis pubis 959.19
    complicating delivery 665.6 ☑
      affecting fetus or newborn 763.89
  temple 959.09
  temporal region 959.09
  testis 959.14
  thigh (and hip) 959.6
  thorax, thoracic (external) 959.11
    cavity — *see* Injury, internal, thorax
    internal — *see* Injury, internal, intrathoracic organs
  throat 959.09
  thumb(s) (nail) 959.5
  thymus — *see* Injury, internal, thymus
  thyroid (gland) 959.09
  toe (nail) (any) 959.7
  tongue 959.09
  tonsil 959.09
  tooth NEC 873.63
    complicated 873.73
  trachea — *see* Injury, internal, trachea
  trunk 959.19
  tunica vaginalis 959.14
  tympanum, tympanic membrane 959.09
  ultraviolet rays NEC 990
  ureter — *see* Injury, internal, ureter
  urethra (sphincter) — *see* Injury, internal, urethra
  uterus — *see* Injury, internal, uterus
  uvula 959.09
  vagina 959.14
  vascular — *see* Injury, blood vessel
  vas deferens — *see* Injury, internal, vas deferens
  vein (*see also* Injury, blood vessel, by site) 904.9
  vena cava
    inferior 902.10
    superior 901.2
  vesical (sphincter) — *see* Injury, internal, vesical
  viscera (abdominal) — *see* Injury, internal, viscera
    with fracture, pelvis — *see* Fracture, pelvis
  visual 950.9
    cortex 950.3
  vitreous (humor) 871.2

Injury — *continued*
vulva 959.14
whiplash (cervical spine) 847.0
wringer — *see* Crush, by site
wrist (and elbow) (and forearm) 959.3
x-ray NEC 990

Inoculation — *see also* Vaccination
complication or reaction — *see* Complication, vaccination

Insanity, insane (*see also* Psychosis) 298.9
adolescent (*see also* Schizophrenia) 295.9 ☑
alternating (*see also* Psychosis, affective, circular) 296.7
confusional 298.9
acute 293.0
subacute 293.1
delusional 298.9
paralysis, general 094.1
progressive 094.1
paresis, general 094.1
senile 290.20

Insect
bite — *see* Injury, superficial, by site
venomous, poisoning by 989.5

Insemination, artificial V26.1

Insensitivity ●
androgen 259.5 ●
partial 259.5 ●

Insertion
cord (umbilical) lateral or velamentous 663.8 ☑
affecting fetus or newborn 762.6
intrauterine contraceptive device V25.1
placenta, vicious — *see* Placenta, previa
subdermal implantable contraceptive V25.5
velamentous, umbilical cord 663.8 ☑
affecting fetus or newborn 762.6

Insolation 992.0
meaning sunstroke 992.0

Insomnia, ▶unspecified◀ 780.52
with sleep apnea, ▶unspecified◀ 780.51
adjustment 307.41 ●
alcohol induced 291.82 ●
behavioral, of childhood V69.5 ●
drug induced 292.85 ●
due to ●
medical condition classified elsewhere 327.01 ●
mental disorder 327.02 ●
idiopathic 307.42 ●
nonorganic origin 307.41
persistent (primary) 307.42
transient 307.41
organic 327.00 ●
other 327.09 ●
paradoxical 307.42 ●
primary 307.42 ●
psychophysiological 307.42 ●
subjective complaint 307.49

Inspiration
food or foreign body (*see also* Asphyxia, food or foreign body) 933.1
mucus (*see also* Asphyxia, mucus) 933.1

Inspissated bile syndrome, newborn 774.4

Instability
detrusor 596.59
emotional (excessive) 301.3
joint (posttraumatic) 718.80
ankle 718.87
elbow 718.82
foot 718.87
hand 718.84
hip 718.85
knee 718.86
lumbosacral 724.6
multiple sites 718.89
pelvic region 718.85
sacroiliac 724.6
shoulder (region) 718.81
specified site NEC 718.88
wrist 718.83
lumbosacral 724.6
nervous 301.89
personality (emotional) 301.59
thyroid, paroxysmal 242.9 ☑
urethral 599.83
vasomotor 780.2

Insufficiency, insufficient
accommodation 367.4
adrenal (gland) (acute) (chronic) 255.4
medulla 255.5
primary 255.4
specified NEC 255.5
adrenocortical 255.4
anterior guidance 524.54
anus 569.49
aortic (valve) 424.1
with
mitral (valve) disease 396.1
insufficiency, incompetence, or regurgitation 396.3
stenosis or obstruction 396.1
stenosis or obstruction 424.1
with mitral (valve) disease 396.8
congenital 746.4
rheumatic 395.1
with
mitral (valve) disease 396.1
insufficiency, incompetence, or regurgitation 396.3
stenosis or obstruction 396.1
stenosis or obstruction 395.2
with mitral (valve) disease 396.8
specified cause NEC 424.1
syphilitic 093.22
arterial 447.1
basilar artery 435.0
carotid artery 435.8
cerebral 437.1
coronary (acute or subacute) 411.89
mesenteric 557.1
peripheral 443.9
precerebral 435.9
vertebral artery 435.1
vertebrobasilar 435.3
arteriovenous 459.9
basilar artery 435.0
biliary 575.8
cardiac (*see also* Insufficiency, myocardial) 428.0
complicating surgery 997.1
due to presence of (cardiac) prosthesis 429.4
postoperative 997.1
long-term effect of cardiac surgery 429.4
specified during or due to a procedure 997.1
long-term effect of cardiac surgery 429.4
cardiorenal (*see also* Hypertension, cardiorenal) 404.90
cardiovascular (*see also* Disease, cardiovascular) 429.2
renal (*see also* Hypertension, cardiorenal) 404.90
carotid artery 435.8
cerebral (vascular) 437.9
cerebrovascular 437.9
with transient focal neurological signs and symptoms 435.9
acute 437.1
with transient focal neurological signs and symptoms 435.9
circulatory NEC 459.9
fetus or newborn 779.89
convergence 378.83
coronary (acute or subacute) 411.89
chronic or with a stated duration of over 8 weeks 414.8
corticoadrenal 255.4
dietary 269.9
divergence 378.85
food 994.2
gastroesophageal 530.89
gonadal
ovary 256.39
testis 257.2
gonadotropic hormone secretion 253.4
heart — *see also* Insufficiency, myocardial
fetus or newborn 779.89
valve (*see also* Endocarditis) 424.90
congenital NEC 746.89
hepatic 573.8
idiopathic autonomic 333.0
interocclusal distance of teeth (ridge) 524.36
kidney
acute 593.9 ●
chronic 585.9 ●

Insufficiency, insufficient — *continued*
labyrinth, labyrinthine (function) 386.53
bilateral 386.54
unilateral 386.53
lacrimal 375.15
liver 573.8
lung (acute) (*see also* Insufficiency, pulmonary) 518.82
following trauma, surgery, or shock 518.5
newborn 770.89
mental (congenital) (*see also* Retardation, mental) 319
mesenteric 557.1
mitral (valve) 424.0
with
aortic (valve) disease 396.3
insufficiency, incompetence, or regurgitation 396.3
stenosis or obstruction 396.2
obstruction or stenosis 394.2
with aortic valve disease 396.8
congenital 746.6
rheumatic 394.1
with
aortic (valve) disease 396.3
insufficiency, incompetence, or regurgitation 396.3
stenosis or obstruction 396.2
obstruction or stenosis 394.2
with aortic valve disease 396.8
active or acute 391.1
with chorea, rheumatic (Sydenham's) 392.0
specified cause, except rheumatic 424.0
muscle
heart — *see* Insufficiency, myocardial
ocular (*see also* Strabismus) 378.9
myocardial, myocardium (with arteriosclerosis) 428.0
with rheumatic fever (conditions classifiable to 390)
active, acute, or subacute 391.2
with chorea 392.0
inactive or quiescent (with chorea) 398.0
congenital 746.89
due to presence of (cardiac) prosthesis 429.4
fetus or newborn 779.89
following cardiac surgery 429.4
hypertensive (*see also* Hypertension, heart) 402.91
benign 402.11
malignant 402.01
postoperative 997.1
long-term effect of cardiac surgery 429.4
rheumatic 398.0
active, acute, or subacute 391.2
with chorea (Sydenham's) 392.0
syphilitic 093.82
nourishment 994.2
organic 799.89
ovary 256.39
postablative 256.2
pancreatic 577.8
parathyroid (gland) 252.1
peripheral vascular (arterial) 443.9
pituitary (anterior) 253.2
posterior 253.5
placental — *see* Placenta, insufficiency
platelets 287.5
prenatal care in current pregnancy V23.7
progressive pluriglandular 258.9
pseudocholinesterase 289.89
pulmonary (acute) 518.82
following
shock 518.5
surgery 518.5
trauma 518.5
newborn 770.89
valve (*see also* Endocarditis, pulmonary) 424.3
congenital 746.09
pyloric 537.0
renal
acute 593.9 ●
chronic 585.9 ●
due to a procedure 997.5

Insufficiency, insufficient — *continued*
　respiratory 786.09
　　acute 518.82
　　　following shock, surgery, or trauma 518.5
　　newborn 770.89
　rotation — *see* Malrotation
　suprarenal 255.4
　　medulla 255.5
　tarso-orbital fascia, congenital 743.66
　tear film 375.15
　testis 257.2
　thyroid (gland) (acquired) — *see also*
　　　Hypothyroidism
　　congenital 243
　tricuspid (*see also* Endocarditis, tricuspid)
　　　397.0
　　congenital 746.89
　　syphilitic 093.23
　urethral sphincter 599.84
　valve, valvular (heart) (*see also* Endocarditis)
　　　424.90
　vascular 459.9
　　intestine NEC 557.9
　　mesenteric 557.1
　　peripheral 443.9
　　renal (*see also* Hypertension, kidney) 403.90
　velopharyngeal
　　acquired 528.9
　　congenital 750.29
　venous (peripheral) 459.81
　ventricular — *see* Insufficiency, myocardial
　vertebral artery 435.1
　vertebrobasilar artery 435.3
　weight gain during pregnancy 646.8 ☑
　zinc 269.3
Insufflation
　fallopian
　　fertility testing V26.21
　　following sterilization reversal V26.22
　meconium 770.11　　　　　　　　　　　　　▲
　　with respiratory symptoms 770.12　　　●
Insular — *see* condition
Insulinoma (M8151/0)
　malignant (M8151/3)
　　pancreas 157.4
　　specified site — *see* Neoplasm, by site,
　　　malignant
　　unspecified site 157.4
　pancreas 211.7
　specified site — *see* Neoplasm, by site, benign
　unspecified site 211.7
Insuloma — *see* Insulinoma
Insult
　brain 437.9
　　acute 436
　cerebral 437.9
　　acute 436
　cerebrovascular 437.9
　　acute 436
　vascular NEC 437.9
　　acute 436
Insurance examination (certification) V70.3
Intemperance (*see also* Alcoholism) 303.9 ☑
Interception of pregnancy (menstrual extraction)
　　V25.3
Intermenstrual
　bleeding 626.6
　　irregular 626.6
　　regular 626.5
　hemorrhage 626.6
　　irregular 626.6
　　regular 626.5
　pain(s) 625.2
Intermittent — *see* condition
Internal — *see* condition
Interproximal wear 521.10
Interruption
　aortic arch 747.11
　bundle of His 426.50
　fallopian tube (for sterilization) V25.2
　phase-shift, sleep cycle 307.45
　repeated REM-sleep 307.48
　sleep
　　due to perceived environmental disturbances
　　　307.48

Interruption — *continued*
　sleep — *continued*
　　phase-shift, of 24-hour sleep-wake cycle
　　　307.45
　　repeated REM-sleep type 307.48
　vas deferens (for sterilization) V25.2
Intersexuality 752.7
Interstitial — *see* condition
Intertrigo 695.89
　labialis 528.5
Intervertebral disc — *see* condition
Intestine, intestinal — *see also* condition
　flu 487.8
Intolerance
　carbohydrate NEC 579.8
　cardiovascular exercise, with pain (at rest)
　　　(with less than ordinary activity) (with
　　　ordinary activity) V47.2
　cold 780.99
　dissacharide (hereditary) 271.3
　drug
　　correct substance properly administered
　　　995.2
　　wrong substance given or taken in error
　　　977.9
　　　specified drug — *see* Table of Drugs and
　　　　Chemicals
　effort 306.2
　fat NEC 579.8
　foods NEC 579.8
　fructose (hereditary) 271.2
　glucose (-galactose) (congenital) 271.3
　gluten 579.0
　lactose (hereditary) (infantile) 271.3
　lysine (congenital) 270.7
　milk NEC 579.8
　protein (familial) 270.7
　starch NEC 579.8
　sucrose (-isomaltose) (congenital) 271.3
Intoxicated NEC (*see also* Alcoholism) 305.0 ☑
Intoxication
　acid 276.2
　acute
　　alcoholic 305.0 ☑
　　　with alcoholism 303.0 ☑
　　　hangover effects 305.0 ☑
　　caffeine 305.9 ☑
　　hallucinogenic (*see also* Abuse, drugs,
　　　nondependent) 305.3 ☑
　alcohol (acute) 305.0 ☑
　　with alcoholism 303.0 ☑
　　hangover effects 305.0 ☑
　　idiosyncratic 291.4
　　pathological 291.4
　alimentary canal 558.2
　ammonia (hepatic) 572.2
　caffeine 305.9 ☑
　chemical — *see also* Table of Drugs and
　　　Chemicals
　　via placenta or breast milk 760.70
　　　alcohol 760.71
　　　anticonvulsants 760.77　　　　　　　　●
　　　antifungals 760.74　　　　　　　　　　●
　　　anti-infective agents 760.74
　　　antimetabolics 760.78　　　　　　　　●
　　　cocaine 760.75
　　　"crack" 760.75
　　　hallucinogenic agents NEC 760.73
　　　medicinal agents NEC 760.79
　　　narcotics 760.72
　　　obstetric anesthetic or analgesic drug
　　　　763.5
　　　specified agent NEC 760.79
　　　suspected, affecting management of
　　　　pregnancy 655.5 ☑
　cocaine, through placenta or breast milk
　　　760.75
　delirium
　　alcohol 291.0
　　drug 292.81
　drug 292.89　　　　　　　　　　　　　　▲
　　with delirium 292.81
　　correct substance properly administered (*see*
　　　also Allergy, drug) 995.2
　　newborn 779.4

Intoxication — *continued*
　drug — *continued*
　　obstetric anesthetic or sedation 668.9 ☑
　　　affecting fetus or newborn 763.5
　　overdose or wrong substance given or taken
　　　— *see* Table of Drugs and Chemicals
　　pathologic 292.2
　　specific to newborn 779.4
　　via placenta or breast milk 760.70
　　　alcohol 760.71
　　　anticonvulsants 760.77　　　　　　　　●
　　　antifungals 760.74　　　　　　　　　　●
　　　anti-infective agents 760.74
　　　antimetabolics 760.78　　　　　　　　●
　　　cocaine 760.75
　　　"crack" 760.75
　　　hallucinogenic agents 760.73
　　　medicinal agents NEC 760.79
　　　narcotics 760.72
　　　obstetric anesthetic or analgesic drug
　　　　763.5
　　　specified agent NEC 760.79
　　　suspected, affecting management of
　　　　pregnancy 655.5 ☑
　enteric — *see* Intoxication, intestinal
　fetus or newborn, via placenta or breast milk
　　　760.70
　　alcohol 760.71
　　anticonvulsants 760.77　　　　　　　　　●
　　antifungals 760.74　　　　　　　　　　　●
　　anti-infective agents 760.74
　　antimetabolics 760.78　　　　　　　　　●
　　cocaine 760.75
　　"crack" 760.75
　　hallucinogenic agents 760.73
　　medicinal agents NEC 760.79
　　narcotics 760.72
　　obstetric anesthetic or analgesic drug 763.5
　　specified agent NEC 760.79
　　suspected, affecting management of
　　　pregnancy 655.5 ☑
　food — *see* Poisoning, food
　gastrointestinal 558.2
　hallucinogenic (acute) 305.3 ☑
　hepatocerebral 572.2
　idiosyncratic alcohol 291.4
　intestinal 569.89
　　due to putrefaction of food 005.9
　methyl alcohol (*see also* Alcoholism) 305.0 ☑
　　with alcoholism 303.0 ☑
　pathologic 291.4
　　drug 292.2
　potassium (K) 276.7
　septic
　　with
　　　abortion — *see* Abortion, by type, with
　　　　sepsis
　　　ectopic pregnancy (*see also* categories
　　　　633.0-633.9) 639.0
　　　molar pregnancy (*see also* categories 630-
　　　　632) 639.0
　　during labor 659.3 ☑
　　following
　　　abortion 639.0
　　　ectopic or molar pregnancy 639.0
　　generalized — *see* Septicemia
　　puerperal, postpartum, childbirth 670.0 ☑
　serum (prophylactic) (therapeutic) 999.5
　uremic — *see* Uremia
　water 276.6
Intracranial — *see* condition
Intrahepatic gallbladder 751.69
Intraligamentous — *see also* condition
　pregnancy — *see* Pregnancy, cornual
Intraocular — *see also* condition
　sepsis 360.00
Intrathoracic — *see also* condition
　kidney 753.3
　stomach — *see* Hernia, diaphragm
Intrauterine contraceptive device
　checking V25.42
　insertion V25.1
　in situ V45.51
　management V25.42
　prescription V25.02
　　repeat V25.42

Intrauterine contraceptive device — *continued*
  reinsertion V25.42
  removal V25.42
Intraventricular — *see* condition
Intrinsic deformity — *see* Deformity
Intrusion, repetitive, of sleep (due to environmental disturbances) (with atypical polysomnographic features) 307.48
Intumescent, lens (eye) NEC 366.9
  senile 366.12
Intussusception (colon) (enteric) (intestine) (rectum) 560.0
  appendix 543.9
  congenital 751.5
  fallopian tube 620.8
  ileocecal 560.0
  ileocolic 560.0
  ureter (with obstruction) 593.4
Invagination
  basilar 756.0
  colon or intestine 560.0
Invalid (since birth) 799.89
Invalidism (chronic) 799.89
Inversion
  albumin-globulin (A-G) ratio 273.8
  bladder 596.8
  cecum (*see also* Intussusception) 560.0
  cervix 622.8
  nipple 611.79
    congenital 757.6
    puerperal, postpartum 676.3 ☑
  optic papilla 743.57
  organ or site, congenital NEC — *see* Anomaly, specified type NEC
  sleep rhythm 327.39 ▲
    nonorganic origin 307.45
  testis (congenital) 752.51
  uterus (postinfectional) (postpartal, old) 621.7
    chronic 621.7
    complicating delivery 665.2 ☑
      affecting fetus or newborn 763.89
  vagina — *see* Prolapse, vagina
Investigation
  allergens V72.7
  clinical research (control) (normal comparison) (participant) V70.7
Inviability — *see* Immaturity
Involuntary movement, abnormal 781.0
Involution, involutional — *see also* condition
  breast, cystic or fibrocystic 610.1
  depression (*see also* Psychosis, affective) 296.2 ☑
    recurrent episode 296.3 ☑
    single episode 296.2 ☑
  melancholia (*see also* Psychosis, affective) 296.2 ☑
    recurrent episode 296.3 ☑
    single episode 296.2 ☑
  ovary, senile 620.3
  paranoid state (reaction) 297.2
  paraphrenia (climacteric) (menopause) 297.2
  psychosis 298.8
  thymus failure 254.8
IQ
  under 20 318.2
  20-34 318.1
  35-49 318.0
  50-70 317
IRDS 769
Irideremia 743.45
Iridis rubeosis 364.42
  diabetic 250.5 ☑ *[364.42]*
Iridochoroiditis (panuveitis) 360.12
Iridocyclitis NEC 364.3
  acute 364.00
    primary 364.01
    recurrent 364.02
  chronic 364.10
    in
      lepromatous leprosy 030.0 *[364.11]*
      sarcoidosis 135 *[364.11]*
      tuberculosis (*see also* Tuberculosis) 017.3 ☑ *[364.11]*

Iridocyclitis NEC — *continued*
  due to allergy 364.04
  endogenous 364.01
  gonococcal 098.41
  granulomatous 364.10
  herpetic (simplex) 054.44
    zoster 053.22
  hypopyon 364.05
  lens induced 364.23
  nongranulomatous 364.00
  primary 364.01
  recurrent 364.02
  rheumatic 364.10
  secondary 364.04
    infectious 364.03
    noninfectious 364.04
  subacute 364.00
    primary 364.01
    recurrent 364.02
  sympathetic 360.11
  syphilitic (secondary) 091.52
  tuberculous (chronic) (*see also* Tuberculosis) 017.3 ☑ *[364.11]*
Iridocyclochoroiditis (panuveitis) 360.12
Iridodialysis 364.76
Iridodonesis 364.8
Iridoplegia (complete) (partial) (reflex) 379.49
Iridoschisis 364.52
Iris — *see* condition
Iritis 364.3
  acute 364.00
    primary 364.01
    recurrent 364.02
  chronic 364.10
    in
      sarcoidosis 135 *[364.11]*
      tuberculosis (*see also* Tuberculosis) 017.3 ☑ *[364.11]*
  diabetic 250.5 ☑ *[364.42]*
  due to
    allergy 364.04
    herpes simplex 054.44
    leprosy 030.0 *[364.11]*
  endogenous 364.01
  gonococcal 098.41
  gouty 274.89 *[364.11]*
  granulomatous 364.10
  hypopyon 364.05
  lens induced 364.23
  nongranulomatous 364.00
  papulosa 095.8 *[364.11]*
  primary 364.01
  recurrent 364.02
  rheumatic 364.10
  secondary 364.04
    infectious 364.03
    noninfectious 364.04
  subacute 364.00
    primary 364.01
    recurrent 364.02
  sympathetic 360.11
  syphilitic (secondary) 091.52
    congenital 090.0 *[364.11]*
    late 095.8 *[364.11]*
  tuberculous (*see also* Tuberculosis) 017.3 ☑ *[364.11]*
  uratic 274.89 *[364.11]*
Iron
  deficiency anemia 280.9
  metabolism disease 275.0
  storage disease 275.0
Iron-miners' lung 503
Irradiated enamel (tooth, teeth) 521.8
Irradiation
  burn — *see* Burn, by site
  effects, adverse 990
Irreducible, irreducibility — *see* condition
Irregular, irregularity
  action, heart 427.9
  alveolar process 525.8
  bleeding NEC 626.4
  breathing 786.09
  colon 569.89
  contour of cornea 743.41
    acquired 371.70

Irregular, irregularity — *continued*
  dentin in pulp 522.3
  eye movements NEC 379.59
  menstruation (cause unknown) 626.4
  periods 626.4
  prostate 602.9
  pupil 364.75
  respiratory 786.09
  septum (nasal) 470
  shape, organ or site, congenital NEC — *see* Distortion
  sleep-wake rhythm (non-24-hour) 327.39 ▲
    nonorganic origin 307.45
  vertebra 733.99
Irritability (nervous) 799.2
  bladder 596.8
    neurogenic 596.54
      with cauda equina syndrome 344.61
  bowel (syndrome) 564.1
  bronchial (*see also* Bronchitis) 490
  cerebral, newborn 779.1
  colon 564.1
    psychogenic 306.4
  duodenum 564.89
  heart (psychogenic) 306.2
  ileum 564.89
  jejunum 564.89
  myocardium 306.2
  rectum 564.89
  stomach 536.9
    psychogenic 306.4
  sympathetic (nervous system) (*see also* Neuropathy, peripheral, autonomic) 337.9
  urethra 599.84
  ventricular (heart) (psychogenic) 306.2
Irritable — *see* Irritability
Irritation
  anus 569.49
  axillary nerve 353.0
  bladder 596.8
  brachial plexus 353.0
  brain (traumatic) (*see also* Injury, intracranial) 854.0 ☑
    nontraumatic — *see* Encephalitis
  bronchial (*see also* Bronchitis) 490
  cerebral (traumatic) (*see also* Injury, intracranial) 854.0 ☑
    nontraumatic — *see* Encephalitis
  cervical plexus 353.2
  cervix (*see also* Cervicitis) 616.0
  choroid, sympathetic 360.11
  cranial nerve — *see* Disorder, nerve, cranial
  digestive tract 536.9
    psychogenic 306.4
  gastric 536.9
    psychogenic 306.4
  gastrointestinal (tract) 536.9
    functional 536.9
    psychogenic 306.4
  globe, sympathetic 360.11
  intestinal (bowel) 564.9
  labyrinth 386.50
  lumbosacral plexus 353.1
  meninges (traumatic) (*see also* Injury, intracranial) 854.0 ☑
    nontraumatic — *see* Meningitis
  myocardium 306.2
  nerve — *see* Disorder, nerve
  nervous 799.2
  nose 478.1
  penis 607.89
  perineum 709.9
  peripheral
    autonomic nervous system (*see also* Neuropathy, peripheral, autonomic) 337.9
    nerve — *see* Disorder, nerve
  peritoneum (*see also* Peritonitis) 567.9
  pharynx 478.29
  plantar nerve 355.6
  spinal (cord) (traumatic) — *see also* Injury, spinal, by site
    nerve — *see also* Disorder, nerve
      root NEC 724.9
      traumatic — *see* Injury, nerve, spinal
    nontraumatic — *see* Myelitis

☑ Additional Digit Required — Refer to the Tabular List (Numeric Code Section) for Additional Digit Selection
▶◀ Revised Text   ● New Line   ▲ Revised Code

2006 ICD-9-CM

October 2005 • Volume 2 — 203

Index

Intrauterine contraceptive device — Irritation

Irritation — *continued*
stomach 536.9
psychogenic 306.4
sympathetic nerve NEC (*see also* Neuropathy,
peripheral, autonomic) 337.9
ulnar nerve 354.2
vagina 623.9
Isambert's disease 012.3 ☑
Ischemia, ischemic 459.9
basilar artery (with transient neurologic deficit)
435.0
bone NEC 733.40
bowel (transient) 557.9
acute 557.0
chronic 557.1
due to mesenteric artery insufficiency 557.1
brain — *see also* Ischemia, cerebral
recurrent focal 435.9
cardiac (*see also* Ischemia, heart) 414.9
cardiomyopathy 414.8
carotid artery (with transient neurologic deficit)
435.8
cerebral (chronic) (generalized) 437.1
arteriosclerotic 437.0
intermittent (with transient neurologic
deficit) 435.9
puerperal, postpartum, childbirth 674.0 ☑
recurrent focal (with transient neurologic
deficit) 435.9
transient (with transient neurologic deficit)
435.9
colon 557.9
acute 557.0
chronic 557.1
due to mesenteric artery insufficiency 557.1
coronary (chronic) (*see also* Ischemia, heart)
414.9
heart (chronic or with a stated duration of over
8 weeks) 414.9
acute or with a stated duration of 8 weeks
or less (*see also* Infarct, myocardium)
410.9 ☑
without myocardial infarction 411.89
with coronary (artery) occlusion
411.81
subacute 411.89
intestine (transient) 557.9
acute 557.0
chronic 557.1
due to mesenteric artery insufficiency 557.1
kidney 593.81
labyrinth 386.50
muscles, leg 728.89

Ischemia, ischemic — *continued*
myocardium, myocardial (chronic or with a
stated duration of over 8 weeks) 414.8
acute (*see also* Infarct, myocardium)
410.9 ☑
without myocardial infarction 411.89
with coronary (artery) occlusion
411.81
renal 593.81
retina, retinal 362.84
small bowel 557.9
acute 557.0
chronic 557.1
due to mesenteric artery insufficiency 557.1
spinal cord 336.1
subendocardial (*see also* Insufficiency,
coronary) 411.89
vertebral artery (with transient neurologic
deficit) 435.1
Ischialgia (*see also* Sciatica) 724.3
Ischiopagus 759.4
Ischium, ischial — *see* condition
Ischomenia 626.8
Ischuria 788.5
Iselin's disease or osteochondrosis 732.5
Islands of
parotid tissue in
lymph nodes 750.26
neck structures 750.26
submaxillary glands in
fascia 750.26
lymph nodes 750.26
neck muscles 750.26
Islet cell tumor, pancreas (M8150/0) 211.7
Isoimmunization NEC (*see also* Incompatibility)
656.2 ☑
fetus or newborn 773.2
ABO blood groups 773.1
Rhesus (Rh) factor 773.0
Isolation V07.0
social V62.4
Isosporosis 007.2
Issue
medical certificate NEC V68.0
cause of death V68.0
fitness V68.0
incapacity V68.0
repeat prescription NEC V68.1
appliance V68.1

Issue — *continued*
repeat prescription NEC — *continued*
contraceptive V25.40
device NEC V25.49
intrauterine V25.42
specified type NEC V25.49
pill V25.41
glasses V68.1
medicinal substance V68.1
Itch (*see also* Pruritus) 698.9
bakers' 692.89
barbers' 110.0
bricklayers' 692.89
cheese 133.8
clam diggers' 120.3
coolie 126.9
copra 133.8
Cuban 050.1
dew 126.9
dhobie 110.3
eye 379.99
filarial (*see also* Infestation, filarial) 125.9
grain 133.8
grocers' 133.8
ground 126.9
harvest 133.8
jock 110.3
Malabar 110.9
beard 110.0
foot 110.4
scalp 110.0
meaning scabies 133.0
Norwegian 133.0
perianal 698.0
poultrymen's 133.8
sarcoptic 133.0
scrub 134.1
seven year V61.10
meaning scabies 133.0
straw 133.8
swimmers' 120.3
washerwoman's 692.4
water 120.3
winter 698.8
Itsenko-Cushing syndrome (pituitary
basophilism) 255.0
Ivemark's syndrome (asplenia with congenital
heart disease) 759.0
Ivory bones 756.52
Ixodes 134.8
Ixodiasis 134.8

J

Jaccoud's nodular fibrositis, chronic (Jaccoud's syndrome) 714.4

Jackson's
membrane 751.4
paralysis or syndrome 344.89
veil 751.4

Jacksonian
epilepsy (*see also* Epilepsy) 345.5 ☑
seizures (focal) (*see also* Epilepsy) 345.5 ☑

Jacob's ulcer (M8090/3) — *see* Neoplasm, skin, malignant, by site

Jacquet's dermatitis (diaper dermatitis) 691.0

Jadassohn's
blue nevus (M8780/0) — *see* Neoplasm, skin, benign
disease (maculopapular erythroderma) 696.2
intraepidermal epithelioma (M8096/0) — *see* Neoplasm, skin, benign

Jadassohn-Lewandowski syndrome (pachyonychia congenita) 757.5

Jadassohn-Pellizari's disease (anetoderma) 701.3

Jadassohn-Tièche nevus (M8780/0) — *see* Neoplasm, skin, benign

Jaffe-Lichtenstein (-Uehlinger) syndrome 252.01

Jahnke's syndrome (encephalocutaneous angiomatosis) 759.6

Jakob-Creutzfeldt disease ▶(syndrome) (new variant)◀ 046.1
with dementia
with behavioral disturbance 046.1 [294.11]
without behavioral disturbance 046.1 [294.10]

Jaksch (-Luzet) disease or syndrome (pseudoleukemia infantum) 285.8

Jamaican
neuropathy 349.82
paraplegic tropical ataxic-spastic syndrome 349.82

Janet's disease (psychasthenia) 300.89

Janiceps 759.4

Jansky-Bielschowsky amaurotic familial idiocy 330.1

Japanese
B type encephalitis 062.0
river fever 081.2
seven-day fever 100.89

Jaundice (yellow) 782.4
acholuric (familial) (splenomegalic) (*see also* Spherocytosis) 282.0
acquired 283.9
breast milk 774.39
catarrhal (acute) 070.1
with hepatic coma 070.0
chronic 571.9
epidemic — *see* Jaundice, epidemic
cholestatic (benign) 782.4
chronic idiopathic 277.4
epidemic (catarrhal) 070.1
with hepatic coma 070.0
leptospiral 100.0
spirochetal 100.0
febrile (acute) 070.1
with hepatic coma 070.0
leptospiral 100.0
spirochetal 100.0
fetus or newborn 774.6
due to or associated with
ABO
antibodies 773.1
incompatibility, maternal/fetal 773.1
isoimmunization 773.1
absence or deficiency of enzyme system for bilirubin conjugation (congenital) 774.39
blood group incompatibility NEC 773.2
breast milk inhibitors to conjugation 774.39
associated with preterm delivery 774.2
bruising 774.1
Crigler-Najjar syndrome 277.4 [774.31]
delayed conjugation 774.30

Jaundice — *continued*
fetus or newborn — *continued*
due to or associated with — *continued*
delayed conjugation — *continued*
associated with preterm delivery 774.2
development 774.39
drugs or toxins transmitted from mother 774.1
G-6-PD deficiency 282.2 [774.0]
galactosemia 271.1 [774.5]
Gilbert's syndrome 277.4 [774.31]
hepatocellular damage 774.4
hereditary hemolytic anemia (*see also* Anemia, hemolytic) 282.9 [774.0]
hypothyroidism, congenital 243 [774.31]
incompatibility, maternal/fetal NEC 773.2
infection 774.1
inspissated bile syndrome 774.4
isoimmunization NEC 773.2
mucoviscidosis 277.01 [774.5]
obliteration of bile duct, congenital 751.61 [774.5]
polycythemia 774.1
preterm delivery 774.2
red cell defect 282.9 [774.0]
Rh
antibodies 773.0
incompatibility, maternal/fetal 773.0
isoimmunization 773.0
spherocytosis (congenital) 282.0 [774.0]
swallowed maternal blood 774.1
physiological NEC 774.6
from injection, inoculation, infusion, or transfusion (blood) (plasma) (serum) (other substance) (onset within 8 months after administration) — *see* Hepatitis, viral
Gilbert's (familial nonhemolytic) 277.4
hematogenous 283.9
hemolytic (acquired) 283.9
congenital (*see also* Spherocytosis) 282.0
hemorrhagic (acute) 100.0
leptospiral 100.0
newborn 776.0
spirochetal 100.0
hepatocellular 573.8
homologous (serum) — *see* Hepatitis, viral
idiopathic, chronic 277.4
infectious (acute) (subacute) 070.1
with hepatic coma 070.0
leptospiral 100.0
spirochetal 100.0
leptospiral 100.0
malignant (*see also* Necrosis, liver) 570
newborn (physiological) (*see also* Jaundice, fetus or newborn) 774.6
nonhemolytic, congenital familial (Gilbert's) 277.4
nuclear, newborn (*see also* Kernicterus of newborn) 774.7
obstructive NEC (*see also* Obstruction, biliary) 576.8
postimmunization — *see* Hepatitis, viral
posttransfusion — *see* Hepatitis, viral
regurgitation (*see also* Obstruction, biliary) 576.8
serum (homologous) (prophylactic) (therapeutic) — *see* Hepatitis, viral
spirochetal (hemorrhagic) 100.0
symptomatic 782.4
newborn 774.6

Jaw — *see* condition

Jaw-blinking 374.43
congenital 742.8

Jaw-winking phenomenon or syndrome 742.8

Jealousy
alcoholic 291.5
childhood 313.3
sibling 313.3

Jejunitis (*see also* Enteritis) 558.9

Jejunostomy status V44.4

Jejunum, jejunal — *see* condition

Jensen's disease 363.05

Jericho boil 085.1

Jerks, myoclonic 333.2

Jervell-Lange-Nielsen syndrome 426.82 ●

Jeune's disease or syndrome (asphyxiating thoracic dystrophy) 756.4

Jigger disease 134.1

Job's syndrome (chronic granulomatous disease) 288.1

Jod-Basedow phenomenon 242.8 ☑

Johnson-Stevens disease (erythema multiforme exudativum) 695.1

Joint — *see also* condition
Charcôt's 094.0 [713.5]
false 733.82
flail — *see* Flail, joint
mice — *see* Loose, body, joint, by site
sinus to bone 730.9 ☑
von Gies' 095.8

Jordan's anomaly or syndrome 288.2

Josephs-Diamond-Blackfan anemia (congenital hypoplastic) 284.0

Joubert syndrome 759.89

Jumpers' knee 727.2

Jungle yellow fever 060.0

Jüngling's disease (sarcoidosis) 135

Junin virus hemorrhagic fever 078.7

Juvenile — *see also* condition
delinquent 312.9
group (*see also* Disturbance, conduct) 312.2 ☑
neurotic 312.4

K

Kabuki syndrome 759.89

Kahler (-Bozzolo) disease (multiple myeloma) (M9730/3) 203.0 ☑

Kakergasia 300.9

Kakke 265.0

Kala-azar (Indian) (infantile) (Mediterranean) (Sudanese) 085.0

Kalischer's syndrome (encephalocutaneous angiomatosis) 759.6

Kallmann's syndrome (hypogonadotropic hypogonadism with anosmia) 253.4

Kanner's syndrome (autism) (*see also* Psychosis, childhood) 299.0 ☑

Kaolinosis 502

Kaposi's
disease 757.33
lichen ruber 696.4
acuminatus 696.4
moniliformis 697.8
xeroderma pigmentosum 757.33
sarcoma (M9140/3) 176.9
adipose tissue 176.1
aponeurosis 176.1
artery 176.1
blood vessel 176.1
bursa 176.1
connective tissue 176.1
external genitalia 176.8
fascia 176.1
fatty tissue 176.1
fibrous tissue 176.1
gastrointestinal tract NEC 176.3
ligament 176.1
lung 176.4
lymph
gland(s) 176.5
node(s) 176.5
lymphatic(s) NEC 176.1
muscle (skeletal) 176.1
oral cavity NEC 176.8
palate 176.2
scrotum 176.8
skin 176.0
soft tissue 176.1
specified site NEC 176.8
subcutaneous tissue 176.1
synovia 176.1
tendon (sheath) 176.1
vein 176.1

2006 ICD-9-CM

☑ Additional Digit Required — Refer to the Tabular List (Numeric Code Section) for Additional Digit Selection
▶◀ Revised Text   ● New Line   ▲ Revised Code

October 2005 • Volume 2 — 205

Kaposi's — *continued*
  sarcoma — *continued*
    vessel 176.1
    viscera NEC 176.9
    vulva 176.8
  varicelliform eruption 054.0
  vaccinia 999.0
Kartagener's syndrome or triad (sinusitis, bronchiectasis, situs inversus) 759.3
Kasabach-Merritt syndrome (capillary hemangioma associated with thrombocytopenic purpura) 287.39 ▲
Kaschin-Beck disease (endemic polyarthritis) — *see* Disease, Kaschin-Beck
Kast's syndrome (dyschondroplasia with hemangiomas) 756.4
Katatonia — *see* Catatonia
Katayama disease or fever 120.2
Kathisophobia 781.0
Kawasaki disease 446.1
Kayser-Fleischer ring (cornea) (pseudosclerosis) 275.1 [371.14]
Kaznelson's syndrome (congenital hypoplastic anemia) 284.0
Kearns-Sayre syndrome 277.87
Kedani fever 081.2
Kelis 701.4
Kelly (-Patterson) syndrome (sideropenic dysphagia) 280.8
Keloid, cheloid 701.4
  Addison's (morphea) 701.0
  cornea 371.00
  Hawkins' 701.4
  scar 701.4
Keloma 701.4
Kenya fever 082.1
Keratectasia 371.71
  congenital 743.41
Keratitis (nodular) (nonulcerative) (simple) (zonular) NEC 370.9
  with ulceration (*see also* Ulcer, cornea) 370.00
  actinic 370.24
  arborescens 054.42
  areolar 370.22
  bullosa 370.8
  deep — *see* Keratitis, interstitial
  dendritic(a) 054.42
  desiccation 370.34
  diffuse interstitial 370.52
  disciform(is) 054.43
    varicella 052.7 [370.44]
  epithelialis vernalis 372.13 [370.32]
  exposure 370.34
  filamentary 370.23
  gonococcal (congenital) (prenatal) 098.43
  herpes, herpetic (simplex) NEC 054.43
    zoster 053.21
  hypopyon 370.04
  in
    chickenpox 052.7 [370.44]
    exanthema (*see also* Exanthem) 057.9 [370.44]
    paravaccinia (*see also* Paravaccinia) 051.9 [370.44]
    smallpox (*see also* Smallpox) 050.9 [370.44]
    vernal conjunctivitis 372.13 [370.32]
  interstitial (nonsyphilitic) 370.50
    with ulcer (*see also* Ulcer, cornea) 370.00
    diffuse 370.52
    herpes, herpetic (simplex) 054.43
      zoster 053.21
    syphilitic (congenital) (hereditary) 090.3
    tuberculous (*see also* Tuberculosis) 017.3 ☑ [370.59]
  lagophthalmic 370.34
  macular 370.22
  neuroparalytic 370.35
  neurotrophic 370.35
  nummular 370.22
  oyster-shuckers' 370.8
  parenchymatous — *see* Keratitis, interstitial
  petrificans 370.8
  phlyctenular 370.31

Keratitis NEC — *continued*
  postmeasles 055.71
  punctata, punctate 370.21
    leprosa 030.0 [370.21]
    profunda 090.3
    superficial (Thygeson's) 370.21
  purulent 370.8
  pustuliformis profunda 090.3
  rosacea 695.3 [370.49]
  sclerosing 370.54
  specified type NEC 370.8
  stellate 370.22
  striate 370.22
  superficial 370.20
    with conjunctivitis (*see also* Keratoconjunctivitis) 370.40
    punctate (Thygeson's) 370.21
  suppurative 370.8
  syphilitic (congenital) (prenatal) 090.3
  trachomatous 076.1
    late effect 139.1
  tuberculous (phlyctenular) (*see also* Tuberculosis) 017.3 ☑ [370.31]
  ulcerated (*see also* Ulcer, cornea) 370.00
  vesicular 370.8
  welders' 370.24
  xerotic (*see also* Keratomalacia) 371.45
    vitamin A deficiency 264.4
Keratoacanthoma 238.2
Keratocele 371.72
Keratoconjunctivitis (*see also* Keratitis) 370.40
  adenovirus type 8 077.1
  epidemic 077.1
  exposure 370.34
  gonococcal 098.43
  herpetic (simplex) 054.43
    zoster 053.21
  in
    chickenpox 052.7 [370.44]
    exanthema (*see also* Exanthem) 057.9 [370.44]
    paravaccinia (*see also* Paravaccinia) 051.9 [370.44]
    smallpox (*see also* Smallpox) 050.9 [370.44]
  infectious 077.1
  neurotrophic 370.35
  phlyctenular 370.31
  postmeasles 055.71
  shipyard 077.1
  sicca (Sjögren's syndrome) 710.2
    not in Sjögren's syndrome 370.33
  specified type NEC 370.49
  tuberculous (phlyctenular) (*see also* Tuberculosis) 017.3 ☑ [370.31]
Keratoconus 371.60
  acute hydrops 371.62
  congenital 743.41
  stable 371.61
Keratocyst (dental) 526.0
Keratoderma, keratodermia (congenital) (palmaris et plantaris) (symmetrical) 757.39
  acquired 701.1
  blennorrhagica 701.1
    gonococcal 098.81
  climacterium 701.1
  eccentrica 757.39
  gonorrheal 098.81
  punctata 701.1
  tylodes, progressive 701.1
Keratodermatocele 371.72
Keratoglobus 371.70
  congenital 743.41
    associated with buphthalmos 743.22
Keratohemia 371.12
Keratoiritis (*see also* Iridocyclitis) 364.3
  syphilitic 090.3
  tuberculous (*see also* Tuberculosis) 017.3 ☑ [364.11]
Keratolysis exfoliativa (congenital) 757.39
  acquired 695.89
  neonatorum 757.39
Keratoma 701.1
  congenital 757.39
  malignum congenitale 757.1
  palmaris et plantaris hereditarium 757.39

Keratoma — *continued*
  senile 702.0
Keratomalacia 371.45
  vitamin A deficiency 264.4
Keratomegaly 743.41
Keratomycosis 111.1
  nigricans (palmaris) 111.1
Keratopathy 371.40
  band (*see also* Keratitis) 371.43
  bullous (*see also* Keratitis) 371.23
  degenerative (*see also* Degeneration, cornea) 371.40
    hereditary (*see also* Dystrophy, cornea) 371.50
  discrete colliquative 371.49
Keratoscleritis, tuberculous (*see also* Tuberculosis) 017.3 ☑ [370.31]
Keratosis 701.1
  actinic 702.0
  arsenical 692.4
  blennorrhagica 701.1
    gonococcal 098.81
  congenital (any type) 757.39
  ear (middle) (*see also* Cholesteatoma) 385.30
  female genital (external) 629.8
  follicular, vitamin A deficiency 264.8
  follicularis 757.39
    acquired 701.1
    congenital (acneiformis) (Siemens') 757.39
    spinulosa (decalvans) 757.39
    vitamin A deficiency 264.8
  gonococcal 098.81
  larynx, laryngeal 478.79
  male genital (external) 608.89
  middle ear (*see also* Cholesteatoma) 385.30
  nigricans 701.2
    congenital 757.39
  obturans 380.21
  oral epithelium
    residual ridge mucosa
      excessive 528.72
      minimal 528.71
  palmaris et plantaris (symmetrical) 757.39
  penile 607.89
  pharyngeus 478.29
  pilaris 757.39
    acquired 701.1
  punctata (palmaris et plantaris) 701.1
  scrotal 608.89
  seborrheic 702.19
    inflamed 702.11
  senilis 702.0
  solar 702.0
  suprafollicularis 757.39
  tonsillaris 478.29
  vagina 623.1
  vegetans 757.39
  vitamin A deficiency 264.8
Kerato-uveitis (*see also* Iridocyclitis) 364.3
Keraunoparalysis 994.0
Kerion (celsi) 110.0
Kernicterus of newborn (not due to isoimmunization) 774.7
  due to isoimmunization (conditions classifiable to 773.0-773.2) 773.4
Ketoacidosis 276.2
  diabetic 250.1 ☑
Ketonuria 791.6
  branched-chain, intermittent 270.3
Ketosis 276.2
  diabetic 250.1 ☑
Kidney — *see* condition
Kienböck's
  disease 732.3
    adult 732.8
  osteochondrosis 732.3
Kimmelstiel (-Wilson) disease or syndrome (intercapillary glomerulosclerosis) 250.4 ☑ [581.81]
Kink, kinking
  appendix 543.9
  artery 447.1
  cystic duct, congenital 751.61
  hair (acquired) 704.2

Kink, kinking — *continued*
  ileum or intestine (*see also* Obstruction, intestine) 560.9
    Lane's (*see also* Obstruction, intestine) 560.9
  organ or site, congenital NEC — *see* Anomaly, specified type NEC, by site
  ureter (pelvic junction) 593.3
    congenital 753.20
  vein(s) 459.2
    caval 459.2
    peripheral 459.2

Kinnier Wilson's disease (hepatolenticular degeneration) 275.1

Kissing
  osteophytes 721.5
  spine 721.5
  vertebra 721.5

Klauder's syndrome (erythema multiforme, exudativum) 695.1

Klebs' disease (*see also* Nephritis) 583.9

Klein-Waardenburg syndrome (ptosisepicanthus) 270.2

Kleine-Levin syndrome 327.13 ▲

Kleptomania 312.32

Klinefelter's syndrome 758.7

Klinger's disease 446.4

Klippel's disease 723.8

Klippel-Feil disease or syndrome (brevicollis) 756.16

Klippel-Trenaunay syndrome 759.89

Klumpke (-Déjérine) palsy, paralysis (birth) (newborn) 767.6

Klüver-Bucy (-Terzian) syndrome 310.0

Knee — *see* condition

Knifegrinders' rot (*see also* Tuberculosis) 011.4 ☑

Knock-knee (acquired) 736.41
  congenital 755.64

Knot
  intestinal, syndrome (volvulus) 560.2
  umbilical cord (true) 663.2 ☑
    affecting fetus or newborn 762.5

Knots, surfer 919.8
  infected 919.9

Knotting (of)
  hair 704.2
  intestine 560.2

Knuckle pads (Garrod's) 728.79

Köbner's disease (epidermolysis bullosa) 757.39

Koch's
  infection (*see also* Tuberculosis, pulmonary) 011.9 ☑
  relapsing fever 087.9

Koch-Weeks conjunctivitis 372.03

Koenig-Wichman disease (pemphigus) 694.4

Köhler's disease (osteochondrosis) 732.5
  first (osteochondrosis juvenilis) 732.5
  second (Freiburg's infarction, metatarsal head) 732.5
  patellar 732.4
  tarsal navicular (bone) (osteoarthrosis juvenilis) 732.5

Köhler-Mouchet disease (osteoarthrosis juvenilis) 732.5

Köhler-Pellegrini-Stieda disease or syndrome (calcification, knee joint) 726.62

Koilonychia 703.8
  congenital 757.5

Kojevnikov's, Kojewnikoff's epilepsy (*see also* Epilepsy) 345.7 ☑

König's
  disease (osteochondritis dissecans) 732.7
  syndrome 564.89

Koniophthisis (*see also* Tuberculosis) 011.4 ☑

Koplik's spots 055.9

Kopp's asthma 254.8

Korean hemorrhagic fever 078.6

Korsakoff (-Wernicke) disease, psychosis, or syndrome (nonalcoholic) 294.0
  alcoholic 291.1

Korsakov's disease — *see* Korsakoff's disease
Korsakow's disease — *see* Korsakoff's disease

Kostmann's disease or syndrome (infantile genetic agranulocytosis) 288.0

Krabbe's
  disease (leukodystrophy) 330.0
  syndrome
    congenital muscle hypoplasia 756.89
    cutaneocerebral angioma 759.6

Kraepelin-Morel disease (*see also* Schizophrenia) 295.9 ☑

Kraft-Weber-Dimitri disease 759.6

Kraurosis
  ani 569.49
  penis 607.0
  vagina 623.8
  vulva 624.0

Kreotoxism 005.9

Krukenberg's
  spindle 371.13
  tumor (M8490/6) 198.6

Kufs' disease 330.1

Kugelberg-Welander disease 335.11

Kuhnt-Junius degeneration or disease 362.52

Kulchitsky's cell carcinoma (carcinoid tumor of intestine) 259.2

Kümmell's disease or spondylitis 721.7

Kundrat's disease (lymphosarcoma) 200.1 ☑

Kunekune — *see* Dermatophytosis

Kunkel syndrome (lupoid hepatitis) 571.49

Kupffer cell sarcoma (M9124/3) 155.0

Kuru 046.0

Kussmaul's
  coma (diabetic) 250.3 ☑
  disease (polyarteritis nodosa) 446.0
  respiration (air hunger) 786.09

Kwashiorkor (marasmus type) 260

Kyasanur Forest disease 065.2

Kyphoscoliosis, kyphoscoliotic (acquired) (*see also* Scoliosis) 737.30
  congenital 756.19
  due to radiation 737.33
  heart (disease) 416.1
  idiopathic 737.30
    infantile
      progressive 737.32
      resolving 737.31
  late effect of rickets 268.1 *[737.43]*
  specified NEC 737.39
  thoracogenic 737.34
  tuberculous (*see also* Tuberculosis) 015.0 ☑ *[737.43]*

Kyphosis, kyphotic (acquired) (postural) 737.10
  adolescent postural 737.0
  congenital 756.19
  dorsalis juvenilis 732.0
  due to or associated with
    Charcôt-Marie-Tooth disease 356.1 *[737.41]*
    mucopolysaccharidosis 277.5 *[737.41]*
    neurofibromatosis 237.71 *[737.41]*
    osteitis
      deformans 731.0 *[737.41]*
      fibrosa cystica 252.01 *[737.41]*
    osteoporosis (*see also* Osteoporosis) 733.0 ☑ *[737.41]*
    poliomyelitis (*see also* Poliomyelitis) 138 *[737.41]*
    radiation 737.11
    tuberculosis (*see also* Tuberculosis) 015.0 ☑ *[737.41]*
  Kümmell's 721.7
  late effect of rickets 268.1 *[737.41]*
  Morquio-Brailsford type (spinal) 277.5 *[737.41]*
  pelvis 738.6
  postlaminectomy 737.12
  specified cause NEC 737.19
  syphilitic, congenital 090.5 *[737.41]*
  tuberculous (*see also* Tuberculosis) 015.0 ☑ *[737.41]*

Kyrle's disease (hyperkeratosis follicularis in cutem penetrans) 701.1

L

Labia, labium — *see* condition

Labiated hymen 752.49

Labile
  blood pressure 796.2
  emotions, emotionality 301.3
  vasomotor system 443.9

Labioglossal paralysis 335.22

Labium leporinum (*see also* Cleft, lip) 749.10

Labor (*see also* Delivery)
  with complications — *see* Delivery, complicated
  abnormal NEC 661.9 ☑
    affecting fetus or newborn 763.7
  arrested active phase 661.1 ☑
    affecting fetus or newborn 763.7
  desultory 661.2 ☑
    affecting fetus or newborn 763.7
  dyscoordinate 661.4 ☑
    affecting fetus or newborn 763.7
  early onset (22-36 weeks gestation) 644.2 ☑
  failed
    induction 659.1 ☑
      mechanical 659.0 ☑
      medical 659.1 ☑
      surgical 659.0 ☑
    trial (vaginal delivery) 660.6 ☑
  false 644.1 ☑
  forced or induced, affecting fetus or newborn 763.89
  hypertonic 661.4 ☑
    affecting fetus or newborn 763.7
  hypotonic 661.2 ☑
    affecting fetus or newborn 763.7
    primary 661.0 ☑
      affecting fetus or newborn 763.7
    secondary 661.1 ☑
      affecting fetus or newborn 763.7
  incoordinate 661.4 ☑
    affecting fetus or newborn 763.7
  irregular 661.2 ☑
    affecting fetus or newborn 763.7
  long — *see* Labor, prolonged
  missed (at or near term) 656.4 ☑
  obstructed NEC 660.9 ☑
    affecting fetus or newborn 763.1
    due to female genital mutilation 660.8 ☑ ●
    specified cause NEC 660.8 ☑
      affecting fetus or newborn 763.1
  pains, spurious 644.1 ☑
  precipitate 661.3 ☑
    affecting fetus or newborn 763.6
  premature 644.2 ☑
    threatened 644.0 ☑
  prolonged or protracted 662.1 ☑
    affecting fetus or newborn 763.89
    first stage 662.0 ☑
      affecting fetus or newborn 763.89
    second stage 662.2 ☑
      affecting fetus or newborn 763.89
  threatened NEC 644.1 ☑
  undelivered 644.1 ☑

Labored breathing (*see also* Hyperventilation) 786.09

Labyrinthitis (inner ear) (destructive) (latent) 386.30
  circumscribed 386.32
  diffuse 386.31
  focal 386.32
  purulent 386.33
  serous 386.31
  suppurative 386.33
  syphilitic 095.8
  toxic 386.34
  viral 386.35

Laceration — *see also* Wound, open, by site
  accidental, complicating surgery 998.2
  Achilles tendon 845.09
    with open wound 892.2
  anus (sphincter) 879.6
    with
      abortion — *see* Abortion, by type, with damage to pelvic organs
      ectopic pregnancy (*see also* categories 633.0-633.9) 639.2

Laceration — *see also* Wound, open, by site — *continued*
  anus — *continued*
    with — *continued*
      molar pregnancy (*see also* categories 630-632) 639.2
    complicated 879.7
    complicating delivery 664.2 ☑
      with laceration of anal or rectal mucosa 664.3 ☑
    following
      abortion 639.2
      ectopic or molar pregnancy 639.2
    nontraumatic, nonpuerperal 565.0
  bladder (urinary)
    with
      abortion — *see* Abortion, by type, with damage to pelvic organs
      ectopic pregnancy (*see also* categories 633.0-633.9) 639.2
      molar pregnancy (*see also* categories 630-632) 639.2
    following
      abortion 639.2
      ectopic or molar pregnancy 639.2
    obstetrical trauma 665.5 ☑
  blood vessel — *see* Injury, blood vessel, by site
  bowel
    with
      abortion — *see* Abortion, by type, with damage to pelvic organs
      ectopic pregnancy (*see also* categories 633.0-633.9) 639.2
      molar pregnancy (*see also* categories 630-632) 639.2
    following
      abortion 639.2
      ectopic or molar pregnancy 639.2
    obstetrical trauma 665.5 ☑
  brain (cerebral) (membrane) (with hemorrhage) 851.8 ☑

> *Note* — Use the following fifth-digit subclassification with categories 851–854:
> 0 unspecified state of consciousness
> 1 with no loss of consciousness
> 2 with brief [less than one hour] loss of consciousness
> 3 with moderate [1-24 hours] loss of consciousness
> 4 with prolonged [more than 24 hours] loss of consciousness and return to pre-existing conscious level
> 5 with prolonged [more than 24 hours] loss of consciousness, without return to pre-existing conscious level
> Use fifth-digit 5 to designate when a patient is unconscious and dies before regaining consciousness, regardless of the duration of the loss of consciousness
> 6 with loss of consciousness of unspecified duration
> 9 with concussion, unspecified

    with
      open intracranial wound 851.9 ☑
      skull fracture — *see* Fracture, skull, by site
    cerebellum 851.6 ☑
      with open intracranial wound 851.7 ☑
    cortex 851.2 ☑
      with open intracranial wound 851.3 ☑
    during birth 767.0
    stem 851.6 ☑
      with open intracranial wound 851.7 ☑
  broad ligament
    with
      abortion — *see* Abortion, by type, with damage to pelvic organs
      ectopic pregnancy (*see also* categories 633.0-633.9) 639.2
      molar pregnancy (*see also* categories 630-632) 639.2

Laceration — *see also* Wound, open, by site — *continued*
  broad ligament — *continued*
    following
      abortion 639.2
      ectopic or molar pregnancy 639.2
    nontraumatic 620.6
    obstetrical trauma 665.6 ☑
    syndrome (nontraumatic) 620.6
  capsule, joint — *see* Sprain, by site
  cardiac — *see* Laceration, heart
  causing eversion of cervix uteri (old) 622.0
  central, complicating delivery 664.4 ☑
  cerebellum — *see* Laceration, brain, cerebellum
  cerebral — *see also* Laceration, brain
    during birth 767.0
  cervix (uteri)
    with
      abortion — *see* Abortion, by type, with damage to pelvic organs
      ectopic pregnancy (*see also* categories 633.0-633.9) 639.2
      molar pregnancy (*see also* categories 630-632) 639.2
    following
      abortion 639.2
      ectopic or molar pregnancy 639.2
    nonpuerperal, nontraumatic 622.3
    obstetrical trauma (current) 665.3 ☑
    old (postpartal) 622.3
    traumatic — *see* Injury, internal, cervix
  chordae heart 429.5
  complicated 879.9
  cornea — *see* Laceration, eyeball
    superficial 918.1
  cortex (cerebral) — *see* Laceration, brain, cortex
  esophagus 530.89
  eye(s) — *see* Laceration, ocular
  eyeball NEC 871.4
    with prolapse or exposure of intraocular tissue 871.1
    penetrating — *see* Penetrating wound, eyeball
    specified as without prolapse of intraocular tissue 871.0
  eyelid NEC 870.8
    full thickness 870.1
      involving lacrimal passages 870.2
    skin (and periocular area) 870.0
      penetrating — *see* Penetrating wound, orbit
  fourchette
    with
      abortion — *see* Abortion, by type, with damage to pelvic organs
      ectopic pregnancy (*see also* categories 633.0-633.9) 639.2
      molar pregnancy (*see also* categories 630-632) 639.2
    complicating delivery 664.0 ☑
    following
      abortion 639.2
      ectopic or molar pregnancy 639.2
  heart (without penetration of heart chambers) 861.02
    with
      open wound into thorax 861.12
      penetration of heart chambers 861.03
        with open wound into thorax 861.13
  hernial sac — *see* Hernia, by site
  internal organ (abdomen) (chest) (pelvis) NEC — *see* Injury, internal, by site
  kidney (parenchyma) 866.02
    with
      complete disruption of parenchyma (rupture) 866.03
        with open wound into cavity 866.13
      open wound into cavity 866.12
  labia
    complicating delivery 664.0 ☑
  ligament — *see also* Sprain, by site
    with open wound — *see* Wound, open, by site

Laceration — *see also* Wound, open, by site — *continued*
  liver 864.05
    with open wound into cavity 864.15
    major (disruption of hepatic parenchyma) 864.04
      with open wound into cavity 864.14
    minor (capsule only) 864.02
      with open wound into cavity 864.12
    moderate (involving parenchyma without major disruption) 864.03
      with open wound into cavity 864.13
    multiple 864.04
      with open wound into cavity 864.14
    stellate 864.04
      with open wound into cavity 864.14
  lung 861.22
    with open wound into thorax 861.32
  meninges — *see* Laceration, brain
  meniscus (knee) (*see also* Tear, meniscus) 836.2
    old 717.5
    site other than knee — *see also* Sprain, by site
      old NEC (*see also* Disorder, cartilage, articular) 718.0
  muscle — *see also* Sprain, by site
    with open wound — *see* Wound, open, by site
  myocardium — *see* Laceration, heart
  nerve — *see* Injury, nerve, by site
  ocular NEC (*see also* Laceration, eyeball) 871.4
    adnexa NEC 870.8
      penetrating 870.3
        with foreign body 870.4
  orbit (eye) 870.8
    penetrating 870.3
      with foreign body 870.4
  pelvic
    floor (muscles)
      with
        abortion — *see* Abortion, by type, with damage to pelvic organs
        ectopic pregnancy (*see also* categories 633.0-633.9) 639.2
        molar pregnancy (*see also* categories 630-632) 639.2
      complicating delivery 664.1 ☑
      following
        abortion 639.2
        ectopic or molar pregnancy 639.2
      nonpuerperal 618.7
      old (postpartal) 618.7
    organ NEC
      with
        abortion — *see* Abortion, by type, with damage to pelvic organs
        ectopic pregnancy (*see also* categories 633.0-633.9) 639.2
        molar pregnancy (*see also* categories 630-632) 639.2
      complicating delivery 665.5 ☑
        affecting fetus or newborn 763.89
      following
        abortion 639.2
        ectopic or molar pregnancy 639.2
      obstetrical trauma 665.5 ☑
  perineum, perineal (old) (postpartal) 618.7
    with
      abortion — *see* Abortion, by type, with damage to pelvic floor
      ectopic pregnancy (*see also* categories 633.0-633.9) 639.2
      molar pregnancy (*see also* categories 630-632) 639.2
    complicating delivery 664.4 ☑
      first degree 664.0 ☑
      second degree 664.1 ☑
      third degree 664.2 ☑
      fourth degree 664.3 ☑
      central 664.4 ☑
      involving
        anal sphincter 664.2 ☑
        fourchette 664.0 ☑
        hymen 664.0 ☑
        labia 664.0 ☑
        pelvic floor 664.1 ☑
        perineal muscles 664.1 ☑

Laceration — see also Wound, open, by site — continued
  perineum, perineal — continued
    complicating delivery — continued
      involving — continued
        rectovaginal septum 664.2 ☑
          with anal mucosa 664.3 ☑
        skin 664.0 ☑
        sphincter (anal) 664.2 ☑
          with anal mucosa 664.3 ☑
        vagina 664.0 ☑
        vaginal muscles 664.1 ☑
        vulva 664.0 ☑
      secondary 674.2 ☑
    following
      abortion 639.2
      ectopic or molar pregnancy 639.2
    male 879.6
      complicated 879.7
    muscles, complicating delivery 664.1 ☑
    nonpuerperal, current injury 879.6
      complicated 879.7
    secondary (postpartal) 674.2 ☑
  peritoneum
    with
      abortion — see Abortion, by type, with damage to pelvic organs
      ectopic pregnancy (see also categories 633.0-633.9) 639.2
      molar pregnancy (see also categories 630-632) 639.2
    following
      abortion 639.2
      ectopic or molar pregnancy 639.2
    obstetrical trauma 665.5 ☑
  periurethral tissue
    with
      abortion — see Abortion, by type, with damage to pelvic organs
      ectopic pregnancy (see also categories 633.0-633.9) 639.2
      molar pregnancy (see also categories 630-632) 639.2
    following
      abortion 639.2
      ectopic or molar pregnancy 639.2
    obstetrical trauma 665.5 ☑
  rectovaginal (septum)
    with
      abortion — see Abortion, by type, with damage to pelvic organs
      ectopic pregnancy (see also categories 633.0-633.9) 639.2
      molar pregnancy (see also categories 630-632) 639.2
    complicating delivery 665.4 ☑
      with perineum 664.2 ☑
        involving anal or rectal mucosa 664.3 ☑
    following
      abortion 639.2
      ectopic or molar pregnancy 639.2
    nonpuerperal 623.4
    old (postpartal) 623.4
  spinal cord (meninges) — see also Injury, spinal, by site
    due to injury at birth 767.4
    fetus or newborn 767.4
  spleen 865.09
    with
      disruption of parenchyma (massive) 865.04
        with open wound into cavity 865.14
      open wound into cavity 865.19
    capsule (without disruption of parenchyma) 865.02
      with open wound into cavity 865.12
    parenchyma 865.03
      with open wound into cavity 865.13
      massive disruption (rupture) 865.04
        with open wound into cavity 865.14
  tendon 848.9
    with open wound — see Wound, open, by site
    Achilles 845.09
      with open wound 892.2

Laceration — see also Wound, open, by site — continued
  tendon — continued
    lower limb NEC 844.9
      with open wound NEC 894.2
    upper limb NEC 840.9
      with open wound NEC 884.2
  tentorium cerebelli — see Laceration, brain, cerebellum
  tongue 873.64
    complicated 873.74
  urethra
    with
      abortion — see Abortion, by type, with damage to pelvic organs
      ectopic pregnancy (see also categories 633.0-633.9) 639.2
      molar pregnancy (see also categories 630-632) 639.2
    following
      abortion 639.2
      ectopic or molar pregnancy 639.2
    nonpuerperal, nontraumatic 599.84
    obstetrical trauma 665.5 ☑
  uterus
    with
      abortion — see Abortion, by type, with damage to pelvic organs
      ectopic pregnancy (see also categories 633.0-633.9) 639.2
      molar pregnancy (see also categories 630-632) 639.2
    following
      abortion 639.2
      ectopic or molar pregnancy 639.2
    nonpuerperal, nontraumatic 621.8
    obstetrical trauma NEC 665.5 ☑
    old (postpartal) 621.8
  vagina
    with
      abortion — see Abortion, by type, with damage to pelvic organs
      ectopic pregnancy (see also categories 633.0-633.9) 639.2
      molar pregnancy (see also categories 630-632) 639.2
      perineal involvement, complicating delivery 664.0 ☑
    complicating delivery 665.4 ☑
      first degree 664.0 ☑
      second degree 664.1 ☑
      third degree 664.2 ☑
      fourth degree 664.3 ☑
      high 665.4 ☑
      muscles 664.1 ☑
      sulcus 665.4 ☑
      wall 665.4 ☑
    following
      abortion 639.2
      ectopic or molar pregnancy 639.2
    nonpuerperal, nontraumatic 623.4
    old (postpartal) 623.4
  valve, heart — see Endocarditis
  vulva
    with
      abortion — see Abortion, by type, with damage to pelvic organs,
      ectopic pregnancy (see also categories 633.0-633.9) 639.2
      molar pregnancy (see also categories 630-632) 639.2
    complicating delivery 664.0 ☑
    following
      abortion 639.2
      ectopic or molar pregnancy 639.2
    nonpuerperal, nontraumatic 624.4
    old (postpartal) 624.4
Lachrymal — see condition
Lachrymonasal duct — see condition
Lack of
  appetite (see also Anorexia) 783.0
  care
    in home V60.4
    of adult 995.84
    of infant (at or after birth) 995.52
  coordination 781.3

Lack of — continued
  development — see also Hypoplasia
    physiological in childhood 783.40
  education V62.3
  energy 780.79
  financial resources V60.2
  food 994.2
    in environment V60.8
  growth in childhood 783.43
  heating V60.1
  housing (permanent) (temporary) V60.0
    adequate V60.1
  material resources V60.2
  medical attention 799.89
  memory (see also Amnesia) 780.93
    mild, following organic brain damage 310.1
  ovulation 628.0
  person able to render necessary care V60.4
  physical exercise V69.0
  physiologic development in childhood 783.40
  posterior occlusal support 524.57
  prenatal care in current pregnancy V23.7
  shelter V60.0
  sleep V69.4
  water 994.3
Lacrimal — see condition
Lacrimation, abnormal (see also Epiphora) 375.20
Lacrimonasal duct — see condition
Lactation, lactating (breast) (puerperal) (postpartum)
  defective 676.4 ☑
  disorder 676.9 ☑
    specified type NEC 676.8 ☑
  excessive 676.6 ☑
  failed 676.4 ☑
  mastitis NEC 675.2 ☑
  mother (care and/or examination) V24.1
  nonpuerperal 611.6
  suppressed 676.5 ☑
Lacticemia 271.3
  excessive 276.2
Lactosuria 271.3
Lacunar skull 756.0
Laennec's cirrhosis (alcoholic) 571.2
  nonalcoholic 571.5
Lafora's disease 333.2
Lag, lid (nervous) 374.41
Lagleyze-von Hippel disease (retinocerebral angiomatosis) 759.6
Lagophthalmos (eyelid) (nervous) 374.20
  cicatricial 374.23
  keratitis (see also Keratitis) 370.34
  mechanical 374.22
  paralytic 374.21
La grippe — see Influenza
Lahore sore 085.1
Lakes, venous (cerebral) 437.8
Laki-Lorand factor deficiency (see also Defect, coagulation) 286.3
Lalling 307.9
Lambliasis 007.1
Lame back 724.5
Lancereaux's diabetes (diabetes mellitus with marked emaciation) 250.8 ☑ [261]
Landouzy-Déjérine dystrophy (fascioscapulohumeral atrophy) 359.1
Landry's disease or paralysis 357.0
Landry-Guillain-Barré syndrome 357.0
Lane's
  band 751.4
  disease 569.89
  kink (see also Obstruction, intestine) 560.9
Langdon Down's syndrome (mongolism) 758.0
Language abolition 784.69
Lanugo (persistent) 757.4
Laparoscopic surgical procedure converted to open procedure V64.41
Lardaceous
  degeneration (any site) 277.3
  disease 277.3

Lardaceous — continued
  kidney 277.3 [583.81]
  liver 277.3
Large
  baby (regardless of gestational age) 766.1
    exceptionally (weight of 4500 grams or more)
      766.0
    of diabetic mother 775.0
  ear 744.22
  fetus — see also Oversize, fetus
    causing disproportion 653.5 ☑
      with obstructed labor 660.1 ☑
    for dates
      fetus or newborn (regardless of gestational
        age) 766.1
          affecting management of
            pregnancy 656.6 ☑
          exceptionally (weight of 4500 grams or
            more) 766.0
  physiological cup 743.57
  stature 783.9
  waxy liver 277.3
  white kidney — see Nephrosis
Larsen's syndrome (flattened facies and multiple
    congenital dislocations) 755.8
Larsen-Johansson disease (juvenile osteopathia
    patellae) 732.4
Larva migrans
  cutaneous NEC 126.9
    ancylostoma 126.9
  of Diptera in vitreous 128.0
  visceral NEC 128.0
Laryngeal — see also condition
  syncope 786.2
Laryngismus (acute) (infectious) (stridulous) 478.75
  congenital 748.3
  diphtheritic 032.3
Laryngitis (acute) (edematous) (fibrinous)
    (gangrenous) (infective) (infiltrative)
    (malignant) (membranous) (phlegmonous)
    (pneumococcal) (pseudomembranous)
    (septic) (subglottic) (suppurative) (ulcerative)
    (viral) 464.00
  with
    influenza, flu, or grippe 487.1
    obstruction 464.01
    tracheitis (see also Laryngotracheitis) 464.20
      with obstruction 464.21
      acute 464.20
        with obstruction 464.21
      chronic 476.1
  atrophic 476.0
  Borrelia vincentii 101
  catarrhal 476.0
  chronic 476.0
    with tracheitis (chronic) 476.1
    due to external agent — see Condition,
      respiratory, chronic, due to
  diphtheritic (membranous) 032.3
  due to external agent — see Inflammation,
    respiratory, upper, due to
  H. influenzae 464.00
    with obstruction 464.01
  Hemophilus influenzae 464.00
    with obstruction 464.01
  hypertrophic 476.0
  influenzal 487.1
  pachydermic 478.79
  sicca 476.0
  spasmodic 478.75
    acute 464.00
      with obstruction 464.01
  streptococcal 034.0
  stridulous 478.75
  syphilitic 095.8
    congenital 090.5
  tuberculous (see also Tuberculosis, larynx)
    012.3 ☑
  Vincent's 101
Laryngocele (congenital) (ventricular) 748.3
Laryngofissure 478.79
  congenital 748.3
Laryngomalacia (congenital) 748.3

Laryngopharyngitis (acute) 465.0
  chronic 478.9
    due to external agent — see Condition,
      respiratory, chronic, due to
    due to external agent — see Inflammation,
      respiratory, upper, due to
  septic 034.0
Laryngoplegia (see also Paralysis, vocal cord)
    478.30
Laryngoptosis 478.79
Laryngospasm 478.75
  due to external agent — see Condition,
    respiratory, acute, due to
Laryngostenosis 478.74
  congenital 748.3
Laryngotracheitis (acute) (infectional) (viral) (see
    also Laryngitis) 464.20
  with obstruction 464.21
  atrophic 476.1
  Borrelia vincenti 101
  catarrhal 476.1
  chronic 476.1
    due to external agent — see Condition,
      respiratory, chronic, due to
  diphtheritic (membranous) 032.3
  due to external agent — see Inflammation,
    respiratory, upper, due to
  H. influenzae 464.20
    with obstruction 464.21
  hypertrophic 476.1
  influenzal 487.1
  pachydermic 478.75
  sicca 476.1
  spasmodic 478.75
    acute 464.20
      with obstruction 464.21
  streptococcal 034.0
  stridulous 478.75
  syphilitic 095.8
    congenital 090.5
  tuberculous (see also Tuberculosis, larynx)
    012.3 ☑
  Vincent's 101
Laryngotracheobronchitis (see also Bronchitis)
    490
  acute 466.0
  chronic 491.8
  viral 466.0
Laryngotracheobronchopneumonitis — see
    Pneumonia, broncho-
Larynx, laryngeal — see condition
Lasègue's disease (persecution mania) 297.9
Lassa fever 078.89
Lassitude (see also Weakness) 780.79
Late — see also condition
  effect(s) (of) — see also condition
    abscess
      intracranial or intraspinal (conditions
        classifiable to 324) — see category
        326
    adverse effect of drug, medicinal or
      biological substance 909.5
    allergic reaction 909.9
    amputation
      postoperative (late) 997.60
      traumatic (injury classifiable to 885-887
        and 895-897) 905.9
    burn (injury classifiable to 948-949) 906.9
      extremities NEC (injury classifiable to 943
        or 945) 906.7
      hand or wrist (injury classifiable to
        944) 906.6
      eye (injury classifiable to 940) 906.5
      face, head, and neck (injury classifiable
        to 941) 906.5
      specified site NEC (injury classifiable to
        942 and 946-947) 906.8
    cerebrovascular disease (conditions
      classifiable to 430-437) 438.9
      with
        alterations of sensations 438.6
        aphasia 438.11
        apraxia 438.81
        ataxia 438.84

Late — see also condition — continued
  effect(s) (of) — see also condition — continued
    cerebrovascular disease — continued
      with — continued
        cognitive deficits 438.0
        disturbances of vision 438.7
        dysphagia 438.82
        dysphasia 438.12
        facial droop 438.83
        facial weakness 438.83
        hemiplegia/hemiparesis
          affecting
            dominant side 438.21
            nondominant side 438.22
            unspecified side 438.20
        monoplegia of lower limb
          affecting
            dominant side 438.41
            nondominant side 438.42
            unspecified side 438.40
        monoplegia of upper limb
          affecting
            dominant side 438.31
            nondominant side 438.32
            unspecified side 438.30
        paralytic syndrome NEC
          affecting
            bilateral 438.53
            dominant side 438.51
            nondominant side 438.52
            unspecified side 438.50
        speech and language deficit 438.10
        specified type NEC 438.19
        vertigo 438.85
      specified type NEC 438.89
    childbirth complication(s) 677
    complication(s) of
      childbirth 677
      delivery 677
      pregnancy 677
      puerperium 677
      surgical and medical care (conditions
        classifiable to 996-999) 909.3
      trauma (conditions classifiable to 958)
        908.6
    contusion (injury classifiable to 920-924)
      906.3
    crushing (injury classifiable to 925-929)
      906.4
    delivery complication(s) 677
    dislocation (injury classifiable to 830-839)
      905.6
    encephalitis or encephalomyelitis (conditions
      classifiable to 323) — see category 326
      in infectious diseases 139.8
        viral (conditions classifiable to 049.8,
          049.9, 062-064) 139.0
      external cause NEC (conditions classifiable
        to 995) 909.9
        certain conditions classifiable to
          categories 991-994 909.4
    foreign body in orifice (injury classifiable to
      930-939) 908.5
    fracture (multiple) (injury classifiable to 828-
      829) 905.5
      extremity
        lower (injury classifiable to 821-827)
          905.4
          neck of femur (injury classifiable to
            820) 905.3
        upper (injury classifiable to 810-819)
          905.2
      face and skull (injury classifiable to 800-
        804) 905.0
      skull and face (injury classifiable to 800-
        804) 905.0
      spine and trunk (injury classifiable to
        805 and 807-809) 905.1
        with spinal cord lesion (injury
          classifiable to 806) 907.2
    infection
      pyogenic, intracranial — see category 326
    infectious diseases (conditions classifiable to
      001-136) NEC 139.8
    injury (injury classifiable to 959) 908.9
      blood vessel 908.3

Late — *see also* condition — *continued*
  effect(s) (of) — *see also* condition — *continued*
    injury — *continued*
      blood vessel — *continued*
        abdomen and pelvis (injury classifiable to 902) 908.4
        extremity (injury classifiable to 903-904) 908.3
        head and neck (injury classifiable to 900) 908.3
        intracranial (injury classifiable to 850-854) 907.0
          with skull fracture 905.0
        thorax (injury classifiable to 901) 908.4
        internal organ NEC (injury classifiable to 867 and 869) 908.2
        abdomen (injury classifiable to 863-866 and 868) 908.1
        thorax (injury classifiable to 860-862) 908.0
        intracranial (injury classifiable to 850-854) 907.0
          with skull fracture (injury classifiable to 800-801 and 803-804) 905.0
        nerve NEC (injury classifiable to 957) 907.9
          cranial (injury classifiable to 950-951) 907.1
          peripheral NEC (injury classifiable to 957) 907.9
            lower limb and pelvic girdle (injury classifiable to 956) 907.5
            upper limb and shoulder girdle (injury classifiable to 955) 907.4
          roots and plexus(es), spinal (injury classifiable to 953) 907.3
          trunk (injury classifiable to 954) 907.3
        spinal
          cord (injury classifiable to 806 and 952) 907.2
          nerve root(s) and plexus(es) (injury classifiable to 953) 907.3
        superficial (injury classifiable to 910-919) 906.2
        tendon (tendon injury classifiable to 840-848, 880-884 with .2, and 890-894 with .2) 905.8
      meningitis
        bacterial (conditions classifiable to 320) — *see* category 326
        unspecified cause (conditions classifiable to 322) — *see* category 326
      myelitis (*see also* Late, effect(s) (of), encephalitis) — *see* category 326
      parasitic diseases (conditions classifiable to 001-136 NEC) 139.8
      phlebitis or thrombophlebitis of intracranial venous sinuses (conditions classifiable to 325) — *see* category 326
      poisoning due to drug, medicinal or biological substance (conditions classifiable to 960-979) 909.0
      poliomyelitis, acute (conditions classifiable to 045) 138
      pregnancy complication(s) 677
      puerperal complication(s) 677
      radiation (conditions classifiable to 990) 909.2
      rickets 268.1
      sprain and strain without mention of tendon injury (injury classifiable to 840-848, except tendon injury) 905.7
        tendon involvement 905.8
      toxic effect of
        drug, medicinal or biological substance (conditions classifiable to 960-979) 909.0
        nonmedical substance (conditions classifiable to 980-989) 909.1
      trachoma (conditions classifiable to 076) 139.1
      tuberculosis 137.0
        bones and joints (conditions classifiable to 015) 137.3

Late — *see also* condition — *continued*
  effect(s) (of) — *see also* condition — *continued*
    tuberculosis — *continued*
      central nervous system (conditions classifiable to 013) 137.1
      genitourinary (conditions classifiable to 016) 137.2
      pulmonary (conditions classifiable to 010-012) 137.0
      specified organs NEC (conditions classifiable to 014, 017-018) 137.4
      viral encephalitis (conditions classifiable to 049.8, 049.9, 062-064) 139.0
    wound, open
      extremity (injury classifiable to 880-884 and 890-894, except .2) 906.1
      tendon (injury classifiable to 880-884 with .2 and 890-894 with .2) 905.8
      head, neck, and trunk (injury classifiable to 870-879) 906.0
  infant
    post-term (gestation period over 40 completed weeks to 42 completed weeks) 766.21
    prolonged gestation (period over 42 completed weeks) 766.22
Latent — *see* condition
Lateral — *see* condition
Laterocession — *see* Lateroversion
Lateroflexion — *see* Lateroversion
Lateroversion
  cervix — *see* Lateroversion, uterus
  uterus, uterine (cervix) (postinfectional) (postpartal, old) 621.6
    congenital 752.3
    in pregnancy or childbirth 654.4 ☑
      affecting fetus or newborn 763.89
Lathyrism 988.2
Launois' syndrome (pituitary gigantism) 253.0
Launois-Bensaude's lipomatosis 272.8
Launois-Cléret syndrome (adiposogenital dystrophy) 253.8
Laurence-Moon-Biedl syndrome (obesity, polydactyly, and mental retardation) 759.89
LAV (disease) (illness) (infection) — *see* Human immunodeficiency virus (disease) (illness) (infection)
LAV/HTLV-III (disease) (illness) (infection) — *see* Human immunodeficiency virus (disease) (illness) (infection)
Lawford's syndrome (encephalocutaneous angiomatosis) 759.6
Lax, laxity — *see also* Relaxation
  ligament 728.4
  skin (acquired) 701.8
    congenital 756.83
Laxative habit (*see also* Abuse, drugs, nondependent) 305.9 ☑
Lazy leukocyte syndrome 288.0
LCAD (long chain/very long chain acyl CoA dehydrogenase deficiency, VLCAD) 277.85
LCHAD (long chain 3-hydroxyacyl CoA dehydrogenase deficiency) 277.85
Lead — *see also* condition
  exposure to V15.86
  incrustation of cornea 371.15
  poisoning 984.9
    specified type of lead — *see* Table of Drugs and Chemicals
Lead miners' lung 503
Leakage
  amniotic fluid 658.1 ☑
    with delayed delivery 658.2 ☑
    affecting fetus or newborn 761.1
  bile from drainage tube (T tube) 997.4
  blood (microscopic), fetal, into maternal circulation 656.0 ☑
    affecting management of pregnancy or puerperium 656.0 ☑
  device, implant, or graft — *see* Complications, mechanical
  spinal fluid at lumbar puncture site 997.09
  urine, continuous 788.37

Leaky heart — *see* Endocarditis
Learning defect, specific NEC (strephosymbolia) 315.2
Leather bottle stomach (M8142/3) 151.9
Leber's
  congenital amaurosis 362.76
  optic atrophy (hereditary) 377.16
Lederer's anemia or disease (acquired infectious hemolytic anemia) 283.19
Lederer-Brill syndrome (acquired infectious hemolytic anemia) 283.19
Leeches (aquatic) (land) 134.2
Left-sided neglect 781.8
Leg — *see* condition
Legal investigation V62.5
Legg (-Calvé) -Perthes disease or syndrome (osteochondrosis, femoral capital) 732.1
Legionnaires' disease 482.84
Leigh's disease 330.8
Leiner's disease (exfoliative dermatitis) 695.89
Leiofibromyoma (M8890/0) — *see also* Leiomyoma
  uterus (cervix) (corpus) (*see also* Leiomyoma, uterus) 218.9
Leiomyoblastoma (M8891/1) — *see* Neoplasm, connective tissue, uncertain behavior
Leiomyofibroma (M8890/0) — *see also* Neoplasm, connective tissue, benign
  uterus (cervix) (corpus) (*see also* Leiomyoma, uterus) 218.9
Leiomyoma (M8890/0) — *see also* Neoplasm, connective tissue, benign
  bizarre (M8893/0) — *see* Neoplasm, connective tissue, benign
  cellular (M8892/1) — *see* Neoplasm, connective tissue, uncertain behavior
  epithelioid (M8891/1) — *see* Neoplasm, connective tissue, uncertain behavior
  prostate (polypoid) 600.20
    with urinary retention 600.21
  uterus (cervix) (corpus) 218.9
    interstitial 218.1
    intramural 218.1
    submucous 218.0
    subperitoneal 218.2
    subserous 218.2
  vascular (M8894/0) — *see* Neoplasm, connective tissue, benign
Leiomyomatosis (intravascular) (M8890/1) — *see* Neoplasm, connective tissue, uncertain behavior
Leiomyosarcoma (M8890/3) — *see also* Neoplasm, connective tissue, malignant
  epithelioid (M8891/3) — *see* Neoplasm, connective tissue, malignant
Leishmaniasis 085.9
  American 085.5
    cutaneous 085.4
    mucocutaneous 085.5
  Asian desert 085.2
  Brazilian 085.5
  cutaneous 085.9
    acute necrotizing 085.2
    American 085.4
    Asian desert 085.2
    diffuse 085.3
    dry form 085.1
    Ethiopian 085.3
    eyelid 085.5 *[373.6]*
    late 085.1
    lepromatous 085.3
    recurrent 085.1
    rural 085.2
    ulcerating 085.1
    urban 085.1
    wet form 085.2
    zoonotic form 085.2
  dermal — *see also* Leishmaniasis, cutaneous
    post kala-azar 085.0
  eyelid 085.5 *[373.6]*
  infantile 085.0
  Mediterranean 085.0
  mucocutaneous (American) 085.5

2006 ICD-9-CM

☑ Additional Digit Required — Refer to the Tabular List (Numeric Code Section) for Additional Digit Selection
▶◀ Revised Text   ● New Line   ▲ Revised Code

Volume 2 — 211

Leishmaniasis — continued
  naso-oral 085.5
  nasopharyngeal 085.5
  Old World 085.1
  tegumentaria diffusa 085.4
  vaccination, prophylactic (against) V05.2
  visceral (Indian) 085.0
Leishmanoid, dermal — see also Leishmaniasis,
  cutaneous
  post kala-azar 085.0
Leloir's disease 695.4
Lemiere syndrome 451.89
Lenegre's disease 426.0
Lengthening, leg 736.81
Lennox-Gastaut syndrome 345.0 ☑
  with tonic seizures 345.1 ☑
Lennox's syndrome (see also Epilepsy) 345.0 ☑
Lens — see condition
Lenticonus (anterior) (posterior) (congenital)
  743.36
Lenticular degeneration, progressive 275.1
Lentiglobus (posterior) (congenital) 743.36
Lentigo (congenital) 709.09
  juvenile 709.09
  Maligna (M8742/2) — see also Neoplasm, skin,
    in situ
    melanoma (M8742/3) — see Melanoma
  senile 709.09
Leonine leprosy 030.0
Leontiasis
  ossium 733.3
  syphilitic 095.8
    congenital 090.5
Léopold-Lévi's syndrome (paroxysmal thyroid
  instability) 242.9 ☑
Lepore hemoglobin syndrome 282.49
Lepothrix 039.0
Lepra 030.9
  Willan's 696.1
Leprechaunism 259.8
Lepromatous leprosy 030.0
Leprosy 030.9
  anesthetic 030.1
  beriberi 030.1
  borderline (group B) (infiltrated) (neuritic) 030.3
  cornea (see also Leprosy, by type)
    030.9 [371.89]
  dimorphous (group B) (infiltrated) (lepromatous)
    (neuritic) (tuberculoid) 030.3
  eyelid 030.0 [373.4]
  indeterminate (group I) (macular) (neuritic)
    (uncharacteristic) 030.2
  leonine 030.0
  lepromatous (diffuse) (infiltrated) (macular)
    (neuritic) (nodular) (type L) 030.0
  macular (early) (neuritic) (simple) 030.2
  maculoanesthetic 030.1
  mixed 030.0
  neuro 030.1
  nodular 030.0
  primary neuritic 030.3
  specified type or group NEC 030.8
  tubercular 030.1
  tuberculoid (macular) (maculoanesthetic)
    (major) (minor) (neuritic) (type T) 030.1
Leptocytosis, hereditary 282.49
Leptomeningitis (chronic) (circumscribed)
  (hemorrhagic) (nonsuppurative) (see also
  Meningitis) 322.9
  aseptic 047.9
    adenovirus 049.1
    Coxsackie virus 047.0
    ECHO virus 047.1
    enterovirus 047.9
    lymphocytic choriomeningitis 049.0
  epidemic 036.0
  late effect — see category 326
  meningococcal 036.0
  pneumococcal 320.1
  syphilitic 094.2
  tuberculous (see also Tuberculosis, meninges)
    013.0 ☑

Leptomeningopathy (see also Meningitis) 322.9
Leptospiral — see condition
Leptospirochetal — see condition
Leptospirosis 100.9
  autumnalis 100.89
  canicula 100.89
  grippotyphosa 100.89
  hebdomidis 100.89
  icterohemorrhagica 100.0
  nanukayami 100.89
  pomona 100.89
  Weil's disease 100.0
Leptothricosis — see Actinomycosis
Leptothrix infestation — see Actinomycosis
Leptotricosis — see Actinomycosis
Leptus dermatitis 133.8
Léris pleonosteosis 756.89
Léri-Weill syndrome 756.59
Leriche's syndrome (aortic bifurcation occlusion)
  444.0
Lermoyez's syndrome (see also Disease,
  Ménière's) 386.00
Lesbianism — omit code
  ego-dystonic 302.0
  problems with 302.0
Lesch-Nyhan syndrome (hypoxanthine-guanine-
  phosphoribosyltransferase deficiency) 277.2
Lesion
  abducens nerve 378.54
  alveolar process 525.8
  anorectal 569.49
  aortic (valve) — see Endocarditis, aortic
  auditory nerve 388.5
  basal ganglion 333.90
  bile duct (see also Disease, biliary) 576.8
  bladder 596.9
  bone 733.90
  brachial plexus 353.0
  brain 348.8
    congenital 742.9
    vascular (see also Lesion, cerebrovascular)
      437.9
      degenerative 437.1
      healed or old without residuals V12.59
      hypertensive 437.2
      late effect — see Late effect(s) (of)
        cerebrovascular disease
  buccal 528.9
  calcified — see Calcification
  canthus 373.9
  carate — see Pinta, lesions
  cardia 537.89
  cardiac — see also Disease, heart
    congenital 746.9
    valvular — see Endocarditis
  cauda equina 344.60
    with neurogenic bladder 344.61
  cecum 569.89
  cerebral — see Lesion, brain
  cerebrovascular (see also Disease,
    cerebrovascular NEC) 437.9
    degenerative 437.1
      healed or old without residuals V12.59
    hypertensive 437.2
    specified type NEC 437.8
  cervical root (nerve) NEC 353.2
  chiasmal 377.54
    associated with
      inflammatory disorders 377.54
      neoplasm NEC 377.52
        pituitary 377.51
      pituitary disorders 377.51
      vascular disorders 377.53
  chorda tympani 351.8
  coin, lung 793.1
  colon 569.89
  congenital — see Anomaly
  conjunctiva 372.9
  coronary artery (see also Ischemia, heart) 414.9
  cranial nerve 352.9
    first 352.0
    second 377.49
    third
      partial 378.51
      total 378.52

Lesion — continued
  cranial nerve — continued
    fourth 378.53
    fifth 350.9
    sixth 378.54
    seventh 351.9
    eighth 388.5
    ninth 352.2
    tenth 352.3
    eleventh 352.4
    twelfth 352.5
  cystic — see Cyst
  degenerative — see Degeneration
  dermal (skin) 709.9
  Dieulafoy (hemorrhagic)
    of
      duodenum 537.84
      intestine 569.86
      stomach 537.84
  duodenum 537.89
    with obstruction 537.3
  eyelid 373.9
  gasserian ganglion 350.8
  gastric 537.89
  gastroduodenal 537.89
  gastrointestinal 569.89
  glossopharyngeal nerve 352.2
  heart (organic) — see also Disease, heart
    vascular — see Disease, cardiovascular
  helix (ear) 709.9
  hyperchromic, due to pinta (carate) 103.1
  hyperkeratotic (see also Hyperkeratosis) 701.1
  hypoglossal nerve 352.5
  hypopharynx 478.29
  hypothalamic 253.9
  ileocecal coil 569.89
  ileum 569.89
  iliohypogastric nerve 355.79
  ilioinguinal nerve 355.79
  in continuity — see Injury, nerve, by site
  inflammatory — see Inflammation
  intestine 569.89
  intracerebral — see Lesion, brain
  intrachiasmal (optic) (see also Lesion, chiasmal)
    377.54
  intracranial, space-occupying NEC 784.2
  joint 719.90
    ankle 719.97
    elbow 719.92
    foot 719.97
    hand 719.94
    hip 719.95
    knee 719.96
    multiple sites 719.99
    pelvic region 719.95
    sacroiliac (old) 724.6
    shoulder (region) 719.91
    specified site NEC 719.98
    wrist 719.93
  keratotic (see also Keratosis) 701.1
  kidney (see also Disease, renal) 593.9
  laryngeal nerve (recurrent) 352.3
  leonine 030.0
  lip 528.5
  liver 573.8
  lumbosacral
    plexus 353.1
    root (nerve) NEC 353.4
  lung 518.89
    coin 793.1
  maxillary sinus 473.0
  mitral — see Endocarditis, mitral
  motor cortex 348.8
  nerve (see also Disorder, nerve) 355.9
  nervous system 349.9
    congenital 742.9
  nonallopathic NEC 739.9
    in region (of)
      abdomen 739.9
      acromioclavicular 739.7
      cervical, cervicothoracic 739.1
      costochondral 739.8
      costovertebral 739.8
      extremity
        lower 739.6
        upper 739.7
      head 739.0

Lesion — *continued*
  nonallopathic — *continued*
    in region (of) — *continued*
      hip 739.5
      lower extremity 739.6
      lumbar, lumbosacral 739.3
      occipitocervical 739.0
      pelvic 739.5
      pubic 739.5
      rib cage 739.8
      sacral, sacrococcygeal, sacroiliac 739.4
      sternochondral 739.8
      sternoclavicular 739.7
      thoracic, thoracolumbar 739.2
      upper extremity 739.7
  nose (internal) 478.1
  obstructive — *see* Obstruction
  obturator nerve 355.79
  occlusive
    artery — *see* Embolism, artery
  organ or site NEC — *see* Disease, by site
  osteolytic 733.90
  paramacular, of retina 363.32
  peptic 537.89
  periodontal, due to traumatic occlusion 523.8
  perirectal 569.49
  peritoneum (granulomatous) 568.89
  pigmented (skin) 709.00
  pinta — *see* Pinta, lesions
  polypoid — *see* Polyp
  prechiasmal (optic) (*see also* Lesion, chiasmal)
    377.54
  primary — *see also* Syphilis, primary
    carate 103.0
    pinta 103.0
    yaws 102.0
  pulmonary 518.89
    valve (*see also* Endocarditis, pulmonary) 424.3
  pylorus 537.89
  radiation NEC 990
  radium NEC 990
  rectosigmoid 569.89
  retina, retinal — *see also* Retinopathy
    vascular 362.17
  retroperitoneal 568.89
  romanus 720.1
  sacroiliac (joint) 724.6
  salivary gland 527.8
    benign lymphoepithelial 527.8
  saphenous nerve 355.79
  secondary — *see* Syphilis, secondary
  sigmoid 569.89
  sinus (accessory) (nasal) (*see also* Sinusitis)
    473.9
  skin 709.9
    suppurative 686.00
  SLAP (superior glenoid labrum) 840.7
  space-occupying, intracranial NEC 784.2
  spinal cord 336.9
    congenital 742.9
    traumatic (complete) (incomplete)
      (transverse) — *see also* Injury, spinal,
      by site
      with
        broken
          back — *see* Fracture, vertebra, by
            site, with spinal cord injury
          neck — *see* Fracture, vertebra,
            cervical, with spinal cord
            injury
        fracture, vertebra — *see* Fracture,
          vertebra, by site, with spinal
          cord injury
  spleen 289.50
  stomach 537.89
  superior glenoid labrum (SLAP) 840.7
  syphilitic — *see* Syphilis
  tertiary — *see* Syphilis, tertiary
  thoracic root (nerve) 353.3
  tonsillar fossa 474.9
  tooth, teeth 525.8
    white spot 521.01
  traumatic NEC (*see also* nature and site of
    injury) 959.9
  tricuspid (valve) — *see* Endocarditis, tricuspid
  trigeminal nerve 350.9
  ulcerated or ulcerative — *see* Ulcer

Lesion — *continued*
  uterus NEC 621.9
  vagina 623.8
  vagus nerve 352.3
  valvular — *see* Endocarditis
  vascular 459.9
    affecting central nervous system (*see also*
      Lesion, cerebrovascular) 437.9
    following trauma (*see also* Injury, blood
      vessel, by site) 904.9
    retina 362.17
    traumatic — *see* Injury, blood vessel, by site
    umbilical cord 663.6 ☑
      affecting fetus or newborn 762.6
  visual
    cortex NEC (*see also* Disorder, visual, cortex)
      377.73
    pathway NEC (*see also* Disorder, visual,
      pathway) 377.63
  warty — *see* Verruca
  white spot, on teeth 521.01
  x-ray NEC 990
Lethargic — *see* condition
Lethargy 780.79
Letterer-Siwe disease (acute histiocytosis X)
  (M9722/3) 202.5 ☑
Leucinosis 270.3
Leucocoria 360.44
Leucosarcoma (M9850/3) 207.8 ☑
Leukasmus 270.2
Leukemia, leukemic (congenital) (M9800/3)
  208.9 ☑

> Note — *Use the following fifth-digit*
> *subclassification for categories 203–208:*
>
> 0   *without mention of remission*
> 1   *with remission*

  acute NEC (M9801/3) 208.0 ☑
  aleukemic NEC (M9804/3) 208.8 ☑
    granulocytic (M9864/3) 205.8 ☑
  basophilic (M9870/3) 205.1 ☑
  blast (cell) (M9801/3) 208.0 ☑
  blastic (M9801/3) 208.0 ☑
    granulocytic (M9861/3) 205.0 ☑
  chronic NEC (M9803/3) 208.1 ☑
  compound (M9810/3) 207.8 ☑
  eosinophilic (M9880/3) 205.1 ☑
  giant cell (M9910/3) 207.2 ☑
  granulocytic (M9860/3) 205.9 ☑
    acute (M9861/3) 205.0 ☑
    aleukemic (M9864/3) 205.8 ☑
    blastic (M9861/3) 205.0 ☑
    chronic (M9863/3) 205.1 ☑
    subacute (M9862/3) 205.2 ☑
    subleukemic (M9864/3) 205.8 ☑
  hairy cell (M9940/3) 202.4 ☑
  hemoblastic (M9801/3) 208.0 ☑
  histiocytic (M9890/3) 206.9 ☑
  lymphatic (M9820/3) 204.9 ☑
    acute (M9821/3) 204.0 ☑
    aleukemic (M9824/3) 204.8 ☑
    chronic (M9823/3) 204.1 ☑
    subacute (M9822/3) 204.2 ☑
    subleukemic (M9824/3) 204.8 ☑
  lymphoblastic (M9821/3) 204.0 ☑
  lymphocytic (M9820/3) 204.9 ☑
    acute (M9821/3) 204.0 ☑
    aleukemic (M9824/3) 204.8 ☑
    chronic (M9823/3) 204.1 ☑
    subacute (M9822/3) 204.2 ☑
    subleukemic (M9824/3) 204.8 ☑
  lymphogenous (M9820/3) — *see* Leukemia,
    lymphoid
  lymphoid (M9820/3) 204.9 ☑
    acute (M9821/3) 204.0 ☑
    aleukemic (M9824/3) 204.8 ☑
    blastic (M9821/3) 204.0 ☑
    chronic (M9823/3) 204.1 ☑
    subacute (M9822/3) 204.2 ☑
    subleukemic (M9824/3) 204.8 ☑
  lymphosarcoma cell (M9850/3) 207.8 ☑
  mast cell (M9900/3) 207.8 ☑
  megakaryocytic (M9910/3) 207.2 ☑
  megakaryocytoid (M9910/3) 207.2 ☑
  mixed (cell) (M9810/3) 207.8 ☑

Leukemia, leukemic — *continued*
  monoblastic (M9891/3) 206.0 ☑
  monocytic (Schilling-type) (M9890/3) 206.9 ☑
    acute (M9891/3) 206.0 ☑
    aleukemic (M9894/3) 206.8 ☑
    chronic (M9893/3) 206.1 ☑
    Naegeli-type (M9863/3) 205.1 ☑
    subacute (M9892/3) 206.2 ☑
    subleukemic (M9894/3) 206.8 ☑
  monocytoid (M9890/3) 206.9 ☑
    acute (M9891/3) 206.0 ☑
    aleukemic (M9894/3) 206.8 ☑
    chronic (M9893/3) 206.1 ☑
    myelogenous (M9863/3) 205.1 ☑
    subacute (M9892/3) 206.2 ☑
    subleukemic (M9894/3) 206.8 ☑
  monomyelocytic (M9860/3) — *see* Leukemia,
    myelomonocytic
  myeloblastic (M9861/3) 205.0 ☑
  myelocytic (M9863/3) 205.1 ☑
    acute (M9861/3) 205.0 ☑
  myelogenous (M9860/3) 205.9 ☑
    acute (M9861/3) 205.0 ☑
    aleukemic (M9864/3) 205.8 ☑
    chronic (M9863/3) 205.1 ☑
    monocytoid (M9863/3) 205.1 ☑
    subacute (M9862/3) 205.2 ☑
    subleukemic (M9864) 205.8 ☑
  myeloid (M9860/3) 205.9 ☑
    acute (M9861/3) 205.0 ☑
    aleukemic (M9864/3) 205.8 ☑
    chronic (M9863/3) 205.1 ☑
    subacute (M9862/3) 205.2 ☑
    subleukemic (M9864/3) 205.8 ☑
  myelomonocytic (M9860/3) 205.9 ☑
    acute (M9861/3) 205.0 ☑
    chronic (M9863/3) 205.1 ☑
  Naegeli-type monocytic (M9863/3) 205.1 ☑
  neutrophilic (M9865/3) 205.1 ☑
  plasma cell (M9830/3) 203.1 ☑
  plasmacytic (M9830/3) 203.1 ☑
  prolymphocytic (M9825/3) — *see* Leukemia,
    lymphoid
  promyelocytic, acute (M9866/3) 205.0 ☑
  Schilling-type monocytic (M9890/3) — *see*
    Leukemia, monocytic
  stem cell (M9801/3) 208.0 ☑
  subacute NEC (M9802/3) 208.2 ☑
  subleukemic NEC (M9804/3) 208.8 ☑
  thrombocytic (M9910/3) 207.2 ☑
  undifferentiated (M9801/3) 208.0 ☑
Leukemoid reaction (lymphocytic) (monocytic)
  (myelocytic) 288.8
Leukoclastic vasculitis 446.29
Leukocoria 360.44
Leukocythemia — *see* Leukemia
Leukocytosis 288.8
  basophilic 288.8
  eosinophilic 288.3
  lymphocytic 288.8
  monocytic 288.8
  neutrophilic 288.8
Leukoderma 709.09
  syphilitic 091.3
    late 095.8
Leukodermia (*see also* Leukoderma) 709.09
Leukodystrophy (cerebral) (globoid cell)
  (metachromatic) (progressive) (sudanophilic)
  330.0
Leukoedema, mouth or tongue 528.79
Leukoencephalitis
  acute hemorrhagic (postinfectious) NEC
    136.9 *[323.6]*
    postimmunization or postvaccinal 323.5
  subacute sclerosing 046.2
  van Bogaert's 046.2
  van Bogaert's (sclerosing) 046.2
Leukoencephalopathy (*see also* Encephalitis)
  323.9
  acute necrotizing hemorrhagic (postinfectious)
    136.9 *[323.6]*
    postimmunization or postvaccinal 323.5
  metachromatic 330.0
  multifocal (progressive) 046.3
  progressive multifocal 046.3

2006 ICD-9-CM

☑ Additional Digit Required — Refer to the Tabular List (Numeric Code Section) for Additional Digit Selection
▶◀ Revised Text   ● New Line   ▲ Revised Code

Volume 2 — 213

Leukoerythroblastosis 289.0
Leukoerythrosis 289.0
Leukokeratosis (see also Leukoplakia) 702.8
  mouth 528.6
  nicotina palati 528.79
  tongue 528.6
Leukokoria 360.44
Leukokraurosis vulva, vulvae 624.0
Leukolymphosarcoma (M9850/3) 207.8 ☑
Leukoma (cornea) (interfering with central vision) 371.03
  adherent 371.04
Leukomalacia, periventricular 779.7
Leukomelanopathy, hereditary 288.2
Leukonychia (punctata) (striata) 703.8
  congenital 757.5
Leukopathia
  unguium 703.8
    congenital 757.5
Leukopenia 288.0
  cyclic 288.0
  familial 288.0
  malignant 288.0
  periodic 288.0
  transitory neonatal 776.7
Leukopenic — see condition
Leukoplakia 702.8
  anus 569.49
  bladder (postinfectional) 596.8
  buccal 528.6
  cervix (uteri) 622.2
  esophagus 530.83
  gingiva 528.6
  kidney (pelvis) 593.89
  larynx 478.79
  lip 528.6
  mouth 528.6
  oral soft tissue (including tongue) (mucosa) 528.6
  palate 528.6
  pelvis (kidney) 593.89
  penis (infectional) 607.0
  rectum 569.49
  syphilitic 095.8
  tongue 528.6
  tonsil 478.29
  ureter (postinfectional) 593.89
  urethra (postinfectional) 599.84
  uterus 621.8
  vagina 623.1
  vesical 596.8
  vocal cords 478.5
  vulva 624.0
Leukopolioencephalopathy 330.0
Leukorrhea (vagina) 623.5
  due to Trichomonas (vaginalis) 131.00
  trichomonal (Trichomonas vaginalis) 131.00
Leukosarcoma (M9850/3) 207.8 ☑
Leukosis (M9800/3) — see Leukemia
Lev's disease or syndrome (acquired complete heart block) 426.0
Levi's syndrome (pituitary dwarfism) 253.3
Levocardia (isolated) 746.87
  with situs inversus 759.3
Levulosuria 271.2
Lewandowski's disease (primary) (see also Tuberculosis) 017.0 ☑
Lewandowski-Lutz disease (epidermodysplasia verruciformis) 078.19
Lewy body dementia 331.82
Lewy body disease 331.82
Leyden's disease (periodic vomiting) 536.2
Leyden-Möbius dystrophy 359.1
Leydig cell
  carcinoma (M8650/3)
    specified site — see Neoplasm, by site, malignant
    unspecified site
      female 183.0
      male 186.9

Leydig cell — continued
  tumor (M8650/1)
    benign (M8650/0)
      specified site — see Neoplasm, by site, benign
      unspecified site
        female 220
        male 222.0
    malignant (M8650/3)
      specified site — see Neoplasm, by site, malignant
      unspecified site
        female 183.0
        male 186.9
    specified site — see Neoplasm, by site, uncertain behavior
    unspecified site
      female 236.2
      male 236.4
Leydig-Sertoli cell tumor (M8631/0)
  specified site — see Neoplasm, by site, benign
  unspecified site
    female 220
    male 222.0
LGSIL (low grade squamous intraepithelial lesion) 795.03
Liar, pathologic 301.7
Libman-Sacks disease or syndrome 710.0 [424.91]
Lice (infestation) 132.9
  body (pediculus corporis) 132.1
  crab 132.2
  head (pediculus capitis) 132.0
  mixed (classifiable to more than one of the categories 132.0-132.2) 132.3
  pubic (pediculus pubis) 132.2
Lichen 697.9
  albus 701.0
  annularis 695.89
  atrophicus 701.0
  corneus obtusus 698.3
  myxedematous 701.8
  nitidus 697.1
  pilaris 757.39
    acquired 701.1
  planopilaris 697.0
  planus (acute) (chronicus) (hypertrophic) (verrucous) 697.0
    morphoeicus 701.0
    sclerosus (et atrophicus) 701.0
  ruber 696.4
    acuminatus 696.4
    moniliformis 697.8
    obtusus corneus 698.3
    of Wilson 697.0
    planus 697.0
  sclerosus (et atrophicus) 701.0
  scrofulosus (primary) (see also Tuberculosis) 017.0 ☑
  simplex (Vidal's) 698.3
    chronicus 698.3
    circumscriptus 698.3
  spinulosus 757.39
    mycotic 117.9
  striata 697.8
  urticatus 698.2
Lichenification 698.3
  nodular 698.3
Lichenoides tuberculosis (primary) (see also Tuberculosis) 017.0 ☑
Lichtheim's disease or syndrome (subacute combined sclerosis with pernicious anemia) 281.0 [336.2]
Lien migrans 289.59
Lientery (see also Diarrhea) 787.91
  infectious 009.2
Life circumstance problem NEC V62.89
Li-Fraumeni cancer syndrome V84.01
Ligament — see condition
Light-for-dates (infant) 764.0 ☑
  with signs of fetal malnutrition 764.1 ☑
  affecting management of pregnancy 656.5 ☑
Light-headedness 780.4

Lightning (effects) (shock) (stroke) (struck by) 994.0
  burn — see Burn, by site
  foot 266.2
Lightwood's disease or syndrome (renal tubular acidosis) 588.89
Lignac's disease (cystinosis) 270.0
Lignac (-de Toni) (-Fanconi) (-Debré) syndrome (cystinosis) 270.0
Lignac (-Fanconi) syndrome (cystinosis) 270.0
Ligneous thyroiditis 245.3
Likoff's syndrome (angina in menopausal women) 413.9
Limb — see condition
Limitation of joint motion (see also Stiffness, joint) 719.5 ☑
  sacroiliac 724.6
Limit dextrinosis 271.0
Limited
  cardiac reserve — see Disease, heart
  duction, eye NEC 378.63
  mandibular range of motion 524.52
Lindau's disease (retinocerebral angiomatosis) 759.6
Lindau (-von Hippel) disease (angiomatosis retinocerebellosa) 759.6
Linea corneae senilis 371.41
Lines
  Beau's (transverse furrows on fingernails) 703.8
  Harris' 733.91
  Hudson-Stähli 371.11
  Stähli's 371.11
Lingua
  geographical 529.1
  nigra (villosa) 529.3
  plicata 529.5
    congenital 750.13
  tylosis 528.6
Lingual (tongue) — see also condition
  thyroid 759.2
Linitis (gastric) 535.4 ☑
  plastica (M8142/3) 151.9
Lioderma essentialis (cum melanosis et telangiectasia) 757.33
Lip — see also condition
  biting 528.9
Lipalgia 272.8
Lipedema — see Edema
Lipemia (see also Hyperlipidemia) 272.4
  retina, retinalis 272.3
Lipidosis 272.7
  cephalin 272.7
  cerebral (infantile) (juvenile) (late) 330.1
  cerebroretinal 330.1 [362.71]
  cerebroside 272.7
  cerebrospinal 272.7
  chemically-induced 272.7
  cholesterol 272.7
  diabetic 250.8 ☑ [272.7]
  dystopic (hereditary) 272.7
  glycolipid 272.7
  hepatosplenomegalic 272.3
  hereditary, dystopic 272.7
  sulfatide 330.0
Lipoadenoma (M8324/0) — see Neoplasm, by site, benign
Lipoblastoma (M8881/0) — see Lipoma, by site
Lipoblastomatosis (M8881/0) — see Lipoma, by site
Lipochondrodystrophy 277.5
Lipochrome histiocytosis (familial) 288.1
Lipodystrophia progressiva 272.6
Lipodystrophy (progressive) 272.6
  insulin 272.6
  intestinal 040.2
  mesenteric 567.82
Lipofibroma (M8851/0) — see Lipoma, by site
Lipoglycoproteinosis 272.8
Lipogranuloma, sclerosing 709.8

Lipogranulomatosis (disseminated) 272.8
  kidney 272.8
Lipoid — see also condition
  histiocytosis 272.7
    essential 272.7
  nephrosis (see also Nephrosis) 581.3
  proteinosis of Urbach 272.8
Lipoidemia (see also Hyperlipidemia) 272.4
Lipoidosis (see also Lipidosis) 272.7
Lipoma (M8850/0) 214.9
  breast (skin) 214.1
  face 214.0
  fetal (M8881/0) — see also Lipoma, by site
    fat cell (M8880/0) — see Lipoma, by site
  infiltrating (M8856/0) — see Lipoma, by site
  intra-abdominal 214.3
  intramuscular (M8856/0) — see Lipoma, by
    site
  intrathoracic 214.2
  kidney 214.3
  mediastinum 214.2
  muscle 214.8
  peritoneum 214.3
  retroperitoneum 214.3
  skin 214.1
    face 214.0
  spermatic cord 214.4
  spindle cell (M8857/0) — see Lipoma, by site
  stomach 214.3
  subcutaneous tissue 214.1
    face 214.0
  thymus 214.2
  thyroid gland 214.2
Lipomatosis (dolorosa) 272.8
  epidural 214.8
  fetal (M8881/0) — see Lipoma, by site
  Launois-Bensaude's 272.8
Lipomyohemangioma (M8860/0)
  specified site — see Neoplasm, connective
    tissue, benign
  unspecified site 223.0
Lipomyoma (M8860/0)
  specified site — see Neoplasm, connective
    tissue, benign
  unspecified site 223.0
Lipomyxoma (M8852/0) — see Lipoma, by site
Lipomyxosarcoma (M8852/3) — see Neoplasm,
  connective tissue, malignant
Lipophagocytosis 289.89
Lipoproteinemia (alpha) 272.4
  broad-beta 272.2
  floating-beta 272.2
  hyper-pre-beta 272.1
Lipoproteinosis (Rössle-Urbach-Wiethe) 272.8
Liposarcoma (M8850/3) — see also Neoplasm,
  connective tissue, malignant
  differentiated type (M8851/3) — see Neoplasm,
    connective tissue, malignant
  embryonal (M8852/3) — see Neoplasm,
    connective tissue, malignant
  mixed type (M8855/3) — see Neoplasm,
    connective tissue, malignant
  myxoid (M8852/3) — see Neoplasm, connective
    tissue, malignant
  pleomorphic (M8854/3) — see Neoplasm,
    connective tissue, malignant
  round cell (M8853/3) — see Neoplasm,
    connective tissue, malignant
  well differentiated type (M8851/3) — see
    Neoplasm, connective tissue, malignant
Liposynovitis prepatellaris 272.8
Lipping
  cervix 622.0
  spine (see also Spondylosis) 721.90
  vertebra (see also Spondylosis) 721.90
Lip pits (mucus), congenital 750.25
Lipschütz disease or ulcer 616.50
Lipuria 791.1
  bilharziasis 120.0
Liquefaction, vitreous humor 379.21
Lisping 307.9
Lissauer's paralysis 094.1
Lissencephalia, lissencephaly 742.2

Listerellose 027.0
Listeriose 027.0
Listeriosis 027.0
  congenital 771.2
  fetal 771.2
  suspected fetal damage affecting management
    of pregnancy 655.4 ☑
Listlessness 780.79
Lithemia 790.6
Lithiasis — see also Calculus
  hepatic (duct) — see Choledocholithiasis
  urinary 592.9
Lithopedion 779.9
  affecting management of pregnancy 656.8 ☑
Lithosis (occupational) 502
  with tuberculosis — see Tuberculosis,
    pulmonary
Lithuria 791.9
Litigation V62.5
Little
  league elbow 718.82
  stroke syndrome 435.9
Little's disease — see Palsy, cerebral
Littre's
  gland — see condition
  hernia — see Hernia, Littre's
Littritis (see also Urethritis) 597.89
Livedo 782.61
  annularis 782.61
  racemose 782.61
  reticularis 782.61
Live flesh 781.0
Liver — see also condition
  donor V59.6
Livida, asphyxia
  newborn 768.6
Living
  alone V60.3
    with handicapped person V60.4
Lloyd's syndrome 258.1
Loa loa 125.2
Loasis 125.2
Lobe, lobar — see condition
Lobo's disease or blastomycosis 116.2
Lobomycosis 116.2
Lobotomy syndrome 310.0
Lobstein's disease (brittle bones and blue sclera)
  756.51
Lobster-claw hand 755.58
Lobulation (congenital) — see also Anomaly,
  specified type NEC, by site
  kidney, fetal 753.3
  liver, abnormal 751.69
  spleen 759.0
Lobule, lobular — see condition
Local, localized — see condition
Locked bowel or intestine (see also Obstruction,
  intestine) 560.9
Locked-in state 344.81
Locked twins 660.5 ☑
  affecting fetus or newborn 763.1
Locking
  joint (see also Derangement, joint) 718.90
  knee 717.9
Lockjaw (see also Tetanus) 037
Locomotor ataxia (progressive) 094.0
Löffler's
  endocarditis 421.0
  eosinophilia or syndrome 518.3
  pneumonia 518.3
  syndrome (eosinophilic pneumonitis) 518.3
Löfgren's syndrome (sarcoidosis) 135
Loiasis 125.2
  eyelid 125.2 [373.6]
Loneliness V62.89
Lone star fever 082.8
Long labor 662.1 ☑
  affecting fetus or newborn 763.89
  first stage 662.0 ☑

Long labor — continued
  second stage 662.2 ☑
Longitudinal stripes or grooves, nails 703.8
  congenital 757.5
Long-term (current) **drug use** V58.69
  antibiotics V58.62
  anticoagulants V58.61
  anti-inflammatories, non-steroidal (NSAID)
    V58.64
  antiplatelets/antithrombotics V58.63
  aspirin V58.66
  insulin V58.67
  steroids V58.65
Loop
  intestine (see also Volvulus) 560.2
  intrascleral nerve 379.29
  vascular on papilla (optic) 743.57
Loose — see also condition
  body
    in tendon sheath 727.82
    joint 718.10
      ankle 718.17
      elbow 718.12
      foot 718.17
      hand 718.14
      hip 718.15
      knee 717.6
      multiple sites 718.19
      pelvic region 718.15
      prosthetic implant — see Complications,
        mechanical
      shoulder (region) 718.11
      specified site NEC 718.18
      wrist 718.13
    cartilage (joint) (see also Loose, body, joint)
      718.1 ☑
      knee 717.6
    facet (vertebral) 724.9
    prosthetic implant — see Complications,
      mechanical
    sesamoid, joint (see also Loose, body, joint)
      718.1 ☑
    tooth, teeth 525.8
Loosening epiphysis 732.9
Looser (-Debray) -Milkman syndrome
  (osteomalacia with pseudofractures) 268.2
Lop ear (deformity) 744.29
Lorain's disease or syndrome (pituitary
  dwarfism) 253.3
Lorain-Levi syndrome (pituitary dwarfism) 253.3
Lordosis (acquired) (postural) 737.20
  congenital 754.2
  due to or associated with
    Charcôt-Marie-Tooth disease 356.1 [737.42]
    mucopolysaccharidosis 277.5 [737.42]
    neurofibromatosis 237.71 [737.42]
    osteitis
      deformans 731.0 [737.42]
      fibrosa cystica 252.01 [737.42]
    osteoporosis (see also Osteoporosis)
      733.00 [737.42]
    poliomyelitis (see also Poliomyelitis)
      138 [737.42]
    tuberculosis (see also Tuberculosis)
      015.0 ☑ [737.42]
  late effect of rickets 268.1 [737.42]
  postlaminectomy 737.21
  postsurgical NEC 737.22
  rachitic 268.1 [737.42]
  specified NEC 737.29
  tuberculous (see also Tuberculosis)
    015.0 ☑ [737.42]
Loss
  appetite 783.0
    hysterical 300.11
    nonorganic origin 307.59
    psychogenic 307.59
  blood — see Hemorrhage
  central vision 368.41
  consciousness 780.09
    transient 780.2
  control, sphincter, rectum 787.6
    nonorganic origin 307.7
  ear ossicle, partial 385.24
  elasticity, skin 782.8

Lymph
  gland or node — *see* condition
  scrotum (*see also* Infestation, filarial) 125.9
Lymphadenitis 289.3
  with
    abortion — *see* Abortion, by type, with sepsis
    ectopic pregnancy (*see also* categories 633.0-633.9) 639.0
    molar pregnancy (*see also* categories 630-632) 639.0
  acute 683
    mesenteric 289.2
  any site, except mesenteric 289.3
    acute 683
    chronic 289.1
    mesenteric (acute) (chronic) (nonspecific) (subacute) 289.2
    subacute 289.1
      mesenteric 289.2
  breast, puerperal, postpartum 675.2 ☑
  chancroidal (congenital) 099.0
  chronic 289.1
    mesenteric 289.2
  dermatopathic 695.89
  due to
    anthracosis (occupational) 500
    Brugia (Wuchereria) malayi 125.1
    diphtheria (toxin) 032.89
    lymphogranuloma venereum 099.1
    Wuchereria bancrofti 125.0
  following
    abortion 639.0
    ectopic or molar pregnancy 639.0
  generalized 289.3
  gonorrheal 098.89
  granulomatous 289.1
  infectional 683
  mesenteric (acute) (chronic) (nonspecific) (subacute) 289.2
    due to Bacillus typhi 002.0
    tuberculous (*see also* Tuberculosis) 014.8 ☑
  mycobacterial 031.8
  purulent 683
  pyogenic 683
  regional 078.3
  septic 683
  streptococcal 683
  subacute, unspecified site 289.1
  suppurative 683
  syphilitic (early) (secondary) 091.4
    late 095.8
  tuberculous — *see* Tuberculosis, lymph gland
  venereal 099.1
Lymphadenoid goiter 245.2
Lymphadenopathy (general) 785.6
  due to toxoplasmosis (acquired) 130.7
    congenital (active) 771.2
Lymphadenopathy-associated virus (disease) (illness) (infection) — *see* Human immunodeficiency virus (disease) (illness) (infection)
Lymphadenosis 785.6
  acute 075
Lymphangiectasis 457.1
  conjunctiva 372.89
  postinfectional 457.1
  scrotum 457.1
Lymphangiectatic elephantiasis, nonfilarial 457.1
Lymphangioendothelioma (M9170/0) 228.1
  malignant (M9170/3) — *see* Neoplasm, connective tissue, malignant
Lymphangioma (M9170/0) 228.1
  capillary (M9171/0) 228.1
  cavernous (M9172/0) 228.1
  cystic (M9173/0) 228.1
  malignant (M9170/3) — *see* Neoplasm, connective tissue, malignant
Lymphangiomyoma (M9174/0) 228.1
Lymphangiomyomatosis (M9174/1) — *see* Neoplasm, connective tissue, uncertain behavior
Lymphangiosarcoma (M9170/3) — *see* Neoplasm, connective tissue, malignant

Lymphangitis 457.2
  with
    abortion — *see* Abortion, by type, with sepsis
    abscess — *see* Abscess, by site
    cellulitis — *see* Abscess, by site
    ectopic pregnancy (*see also* categories 633.0-633.9) 639.0
    molar pregnancy (*see also* categories 630-632) 639.0
  acute (with abscess or cellulitis) 682.9
    specified site — *see* Abscess, by site
  breast, puerperal, postpartum 675.2 ☑
  chancroidal 099.0
  chronic (any site) 457.2
  due to
    Brugia (Wuchereria) malayi 125.1
    Wuchereria bancrofti 125.0
  following
    abortion 639.0
    ectopic or molar pregnancy 639.0
  gangrenous 457.2
  penis
    acute 607.2
    gonococcal (acute) 098.0
      chronic or duration of 2 months or more 098.2
  puerperal, postpartum, childbirth 670.0 ☑
  strumous, tuberculous (*see also* Tuberculosis) 017.2 ☑
  subacute (any site) 457.2
  tuberculous — *see* Tuberculosis, lymph gland
Lymphatic (vessel) — *see* condition
Lymphatism 254.8
  scrofulous (*see also* Tuberculosis) 017.2 ☑
Lymphectasia 457.1
Lymphedema (*see also* Elephantiasis) 457.1
  acquired (chronic) 457.1
  chronic hereditary 757.0
  congenital 757.0
  idiopathic hereditary 757.0
  praecox 457.1
  secondary 457.1
  surgical NEC 997.99
    postmastectomy (syndrome) 457.0
Lymph-hemangioma (M9120/0) — *see* Hemangioma, by site
Lymphoblastic — *see* condition
Lymphoblastoma (diffuse) (M9630/3) 200.1 ☑
  giant follicular (M9690/3) 202.0 ☑
  macrofollicular (M9690/3) 202.0 ☑
Lymphoblastosis, acute benign 075
Lymphocele 457.8
Lymphocythemia 288.8
Lymphocytic — *see also* condition
  chorioencephalitis (acute) (serous) 049.0
  choriomeningitis (acute) (serous) 049.0
Lymphocytoma (diffuse) (malignant) (M9620/3) 200.1 ☑
Lymphocytomatosis (M9620/3) 200.1 ☑
Lymphocytopenia 288.8
Lymphocytosis (symptomatic) 288.8
  infectious (acute) 078.89
Lymphoepithelioma (M8082/3) — *see* Neoplasm, by site, malignant
Lymphogranuloma (malignant) (M9650/3) 201.9 ☑
  inguinale 099.1
  venereal (any site) 099.1
    with stricture of rectum 099.1
  venereum 099.1
Lymphogranulomatosis (malignant) (M9650/3) 201.9 ☑
  benign (Boeck's sarcoid) (Schaumann's) 135
  Hodgkin's (M9650/3) 201.9 ☑
Lymphoid — *see* condition
Lympholeukoblastoma (M9850/3) 207.8 ☑
Lympholeukosarcoma (M9850/3) 207.8 ☑

Lymphoma (malignant) (M9590/3) 202.8 ☑

> *Note* — Use the following fifth-digit subclassification with categories 200–202:
>
> 0   unspecified site, extranodal and solid organ sites
>
> 1   lymph nodes of head, face, and neck
>
> 2   intrathoracic lymph nodes
>
> 3   intra-abdominal lymph nodes
>
> 4   lymph nodes of axilla and upper limb
>
> 5   lymph nodes of inguinal region and lower limb
>
> 6   intrapelvic lymph nodes
>
> 7   spleen
>
> 8   lymph nodes of multiple sites

  benign (M9590/0) — *see* Neoplasm, by site, benign
  Burkitt's type (lymphoblastic) (undifferentiated) (M9750/3) 200.2 ☑
  Castleman's (mediastinal lymph node hyperplasia) 785.6
  centroblastic-centrocytic
    diffuse (M9614/3) 202.8 ☑
    follicular (M9692/3) 202.0 ☑
  centroblastic type (diffuse) (M9632/3) 202.8 ☑
    follicular (M9697/3) 202.0 ☑
  centrocytic (M9622/3) 202.8 ☑
  compound (M9613/3) 200.8 ☑
  convoluted cell type (lymphoblastic) (M9602/3) 202.8 ☑
  diffuse NEC (M9590/3) 202.8 ☑
  follicular (giant) (M9690/3) 202.0 ☑
    center cell (diffuse) (M9615/3) 202.8 ☑
    cleaved (diffuse) (M9623/3) 202.8 ☑
      follicular (M9695/3) 202.0 ☑
    non-cleaved (diffuse) (M9633/3) 202.8 ☑
      follicular (M9698/3) 202.0 ☑
    centroblastic-centrocytic (M9692/3) 202.0 ☑
    centroblastic type (M9697/3) 202.0 ☑
    lymphocytic
      intermediate differentiation (M9694/3) 202.0 ☑
      poorly differentiated (M9696/3) 202.0 ☑
    mixed (cell type) (lymphocytic-histiocytic) (small cell and large cell) (M9691/3) 202.0 ☑
  germinocytic (M9622/3) 202.8 ☑
  giant, follicular or follicle (M9690/3) 202.0 ☑
  histiocytic (diffuse) (M9640/3) 200.0 ☑
    nodular (M9642/3) 200.0 ☑
    pleomorphic cell type (M9641/3) 200.0 ☑
  Hodgkin's (M9650/3) (*see also* Disease, Hodgkin's) 201.9 ☑
  immunoblastic (type) (M9612/3) 200.8 ☑
  large cell (M9640/3) 200.0 ☑
    nodular (M9642/3) 200.0 ☑
    pleomorphic cell type (M9641/3) 200.0 ☑
  lymphoblastic (diffuse) (M9630/3) 200.1 ☑
    Burkitt's type (M9750/3) 200.2 ☑
    convoluted cell type (M9602/3) 202.8 ☑
  lymphocytic (cell type) (diffuse) (M9620/3) 200.1 ☑
    with plasmacytoid differentiation, diffuse (M9611/3) 200.8 ☑
    intermediate differentiation (diffuse) (M9621/3) 200.1 ☑
      follicular (M9694/3) 202.0 ☑
      nodular (M9694/3) 202.0 ☑
    nodular (M9690/3) 202.0 ☑
    poorly differentiated (diffuse) (M9630/3) 200.1 ☑
      follicular (M9696/3) 202.0 ☑
      nodular (M9696/3) 202.0 ☑
    well differentiated (diffuse) (M9620/3) 200.1 ☑
      follicular (M9693/3) 202.0 ☑
      nodular (M9693/3) 202.0 ☑

Lymphoma — *continued*
lymphocytic-histiocytic, mixed (diffuse)
(M9613/3) 200.8 ☑
follicular (M9691/3) 202.0 ☑
nodular (M9691/3) 202.0 ☑
lymphoplasmacytoid type (M9611/3) 200.8 ☑
lymphosarcoma type (M9610/3) 200.1 ☑
macrofollicular (M9690/3) 202.0 ☑
mixed cell type (diffuse) (M9613/3) 200.8 ☑
follicular (M9691/3) 202.0 ☑
nodular (M9691/3) 202.0 ☑
nodular (M9690/3) 202.0 ☑
histiocytic (M9642/3) 200.0 ☑
lymphocytic (M9690/3) 202.0 ☑
intermediate differentiation (M9694/3)
202.0 ☑
poorly differentiated (M9696/3) 202.0 ☑
mixed (cell type) (lymphocytic-histiocytic)
(small cell and large cell) (M9691/3)
202.0 ☑
non-Hodgkin's type NEC (M9591/3) 202.8 ☑
reticulum cell (type) (M9640/3) 200.0 ☑
small cell and large cell, mixed (diffuse)
(M9613/3) 200.8 ☑
follicular (M9691/3) 202.0 ☑
nodular (9691/3) 202.0 ☑
stem cell (type) (M9601/3) 202.8 ☑
T-cell 202.1 ☑
undifferentiated (cell type) (non-Burkitt's)
(M9600/3) 202.8 ☑
Burkitt's type (M9750/3) 200.2 ☑
Lymphomatosis (M9590/3) — *see also*
Lymphoma
granulomatous 099.1
Lymphopathia
venereum 099.1
veneris 099.1
Lymphopenia 288.8
familial 279.2
Lymphoreticulosis, benign (of inoculation) 078.3
Lymphorrhea 457.8
Lymphosarcoma (M9610/3) 200.1 ☑
diffuse (M9610/3) 200.1 ☑
with plasmacytoid differentiation (M9611/3)
200.8 ☑
lymphoplasmacytic (M9611/3) 200.8 ☑
follicular (giant) (M9690/3) 202.0 ☑
lymphoblastic (M9696/3) 202.0 ☑
lymphocytic, intermediate differentiation
(M9694/3) 202.0 ☑
mixed cell type (M9691/3) 202.0 ☑
giant follicular (M9690/3) 202.0 ☑
Hodgkin's (M9650/3) 201.9 ☑
immunoblastic (M9612/3) 200.8 ☑
lymphoblastic (diffuse) (M9630/3) 200.1 ☑
follicular (M9696/3) 202.0 ☑
nodular (M9696/3) 202.0 ☑
lymphocytic (diffuse) (M9620/3) 200.1 ☑
intermediate differentiation (diffuse)
(M9621/3) 200.1 ☑
follicular (M9694/3) 202.0 ☑
nodular (M9694/3) 202.0 ☑
mixed cell type (diffuse) (M9613/3) 200.8 ☑
follicular (M9691/3) 202.0 ☑
nodular (M9691/3) 202.0 ☑
nodular (M9690/3) 202.0 ☑
lymphoblastic (M9696/3) 202.0 ☑
lymphocytic, intermediate differentiation
(M9694/3) 202.0 ☑
mixed cell type (M9691/3) 202.0 ☑
prolymphocytic (M9631/3) 200.1 ☑
reticulum cell (M9640/3) 200.0 ☑
Lymphostasis 457.8
Lypemania (*see also* Melancholia) 296.2 ☑
Lyssa 071

M

Macacus ear 744.29
Maceration
fetus (cause not stated) 779.9
wet feet, tropical (syndrome) 991.4
Machado-Joseph disease 334.8

Machupo virus hemorrhagic fever 078.7
Macleod's syndrome (abnormal transradiancy,
one lung) 492.8
Macrocephalia, macrocephaly 756.0
Macrocheilia (congenital) 744.81
Macrochilia (congenital) 744.81
Macrocolon (congenital) 751.3
Macrocornea 743.41
associated with buphthalmos 743.22
Macrocytic — *see* condition
Macrocytosis 289.89
Macrodactylia, macrodactylism (fingers)
(thumbs) 755.57
toes 755.65
Macrodontia 520.2
Macroencephaly 742.4
Macrogenia 524.05
Macrogenitosomia (female) (male) (praecox) 255.2
Macrogingivae 523.8
Macroglobulinemia (essential) (idiopathic)
(monoclonal) (primary) (syndrome)
(Waldenström's) 273.3
Macroglossia (congenital) 750.15
acquired 529.8
Macrognathia, macrognathism (congenital)
524.00
mandibular 524.02
alveolar 524.72
maxillary 524.01
alveolar 524.71
Macrogyria (congenital) 742.4
Macrohydrocephalus (*see also* Hydrocephalus)
331.4
Macromastia (*see also* Hypertrophy, breast) 611.1
Macropsia 368.14
Macrosigmoid 564.7
congenital 751.3
Macrospondylitis, acromegalic 253.0
Macrostomia (congenital) 744.83
Macrotia (external ear) (congenital) 744.22
Macula
cornea, corneal
congenital 743.43
interfering with vision 743.42
interfering with central vision 371.03
not interfering with central vision 371.02
degeneration (*see also* Degeneration, macula)
362.50
hereditary (*see also* Dystrophy, retina) 362.70
edema, cystoid 362.53
Maculae ceruleae 132.1
Macules and papules 709.8
Maculopathy, toxic 362.55
Madarosis 374.55
Madelung's
deformity (radius) 755.54
disease (lipomatosis) 272.8
lipomatosis 272.8
Madness (*see also* Psychosis) 298.9
myxedema (acute) 293.0
subacute 293.1
Madura
disease (actinomycotic) 039.9
mycotic 117.4
foot (actinomycotic) 039.4
mycotic 117.4
Maduromycosis (actinomycotic) 039.9
mycotic 117.4
Maffucci's syndrome (dyschondroplasia with
hemangiomas) 756.4
Magenblase syndrome 306.4
Main en griffe (acquired) 736.06
congenital 755.59
Maintenance
chemotherapy regimen or treatment V58.11 ▲
dialysis regimen or treatment
extracorporeal (renal) V56.0
peritoneal V56.8
renal V56.0

Maintenance — *continued*
drug therapy or regimen
chemotherapy, antineoplastic V58.11 ●
immunotherapy, antineoplastic V58.12 ●
external fixation NEC V54.89
radiotherapy V58.0
traction NEC V54.89
Majocchi's
disease (purpura annularis telangiectodes)
709.1
granuloma 110.6
Major — *see* condition
Mal
cerebral (idiopathic) (*see also* Epilepsy) 345.9 ☑
comital (*see also* Epilepsy) 345.9 ☑
de los pintos (*see also* Pinta) 103.9
de Meleda 757.39
de mer 994.6
lie — *see* Presentation, fetal
perforant (*see also* Ulcer, lower extremity)
707.15
Malabar itch 110.9
beard 110.0
foot 110.4
scalp 110.0
Malabsorption 579.9
calcium 579.8
carbohydrate 579.8
disaccharide 271.3
drug-induced 579.8
due to bacterial overgrowth 579.8
fat 579.8
folate, congenital 281.2
galactose 271.1
glucose-galactose (congenital) 271.3
intestinal 579.9
isomaltose 271.3
lactose (hereditary) 271.3
methionine 270.4
monosaccharide 271.8
postgastrectomy 579.3
postsurgical 579.3
protein 579.8
sucrose (-isomaltose) (congenital) 271.3
syndrome 579.9
postgastrectomy 579.3
postsurgical 579.3
Malacia, bone 268.2
juvenile (*see also* Rickets) 268.0
Kienböck's (juvenile) (lunate) (wrist) 732.3
adult 732.8
Malacoplakia
bladder 596.8
colon 569.89
pelvis (kidney) 593.89
ureter 593.89
urethra 599.84
Malacosteon 268.2
juvenile (*see also* Rickets) 268.0
Maladaptation — *see* Maladjustment
Maladie de Roger 745.4
Maladjustment
conjugal V61.10
involving divorce or estrangement V61.0
educational V62.3
family V61.9
specified circumstance NEC V61.8
marital V61.10
involving divorce or estrangement V61.0
occupational V62.2
simple, adult (*see also* Reaction, adjustment)
309.9
situational acute (*see also* Reaction,
adjustment) 309.9
social V62.4
Malaise 780.79
Malakoplakia — *see* Malacoplakia
Malaria, malarial (fever) 084.6
algid 084.9
any type, with
algid malaria 084.9
blackwater fever 084.8

Malaria, malarial — *continued*
  any type, with — *continued*
    fever
      blackwater 084.8
      hemoglobinuric (bilious) 084.8
    hemoglobinuria, malarial 084.8
    hepatitis 084.9 *[573.2]*
    nephrosis 084.9 *[581.81]*
    pernicious complication NEC 084.9
      cardiac 084.9
      cerebral 084.9
  cardiac 084.9
  carrier (suspected) of V02.9
  cerebral 084.9
  complicating pregnancy, childbirth, or
    puerperium 647.4 ☑
  congenital 771.2
  congestion, congestive 084.6
    brain 084.9
  continued 084.0
  estivo-autumnal 084.0
  falciparum (malignant tertian) 084.0
  hematinuria 084.8
  hematuria 084.8
  hemoglobinuria 084.8
  hemorrhagic 084.6
  induced (therapeutically) 084.7
    accidental — *see* Malaria, by type
  liver 084.9 *[573.2]*
  malariae (quartan) 084.2
  malignant (tertian) 084.0
  mixed infections 084.5
  monkey 084.4
  ovale 084.3
  pernicious, acute 084.0
  Plasmodium, P.
    falciparum 084.0
    malariae 084.2
    ovale 084.3
    vivax 084.1
  quartan 084.2
  quotidian 084.0
  recurrent 084.6
    induced (therapeutically) 084.7
      accidental — *see* Malaria, by type
  remittent 084.6
  specified types NEC 084.4
  spleen 084.6
  subtertian 084.0
  tertian (benign) 084.1
    malignant 084.0
  tropical 084.0
  typhoid 084.6
  vivax (benign tertian) 084.1

Malassez's disease (testicular cyst) 608.89

Malassimilation 579.9

Maldescent, testis 752.51

Maldevelopment — *see also* Anomaly, by site
  brain 742.9
  colon 751.5
  hip (joint) 755.63
    congenital dislocation (*see also* Dislocation,
      hip, congenital) 754.30
  mastoid process 756.0
  middle ear, except ossicles 744.03
    ossicles 744.04
  newborn (not malformation) 764.9 ☑
  ossicles, ear 744.04
  spine 756.10
  toe 755.66

Male type pelvis 755.69
  with disproportion (fetopelvic) 653.2 ☑
    affecting fetus or newborn 763.1
    causing obstructed labor 660.1 ☑
      affecting fetus or newborn 763.1

Malformation (congenital) — *see also* Anomaly
  bone 756.9
  bursa 756.9
  circulatory system NEC 747.9
    specified type NEC 747.89
  Chiari
    type I 348.4
    type II (*see also* Spina bifida) 741.0 ☑
    type III 742.0
    type IV 742.2
  cochlea 744.05

Malformation — *see also* Anomaly — *continued*
  digestive system NEC 751.9
    lower 751.5
    specified type NEC 751.8
    upper 750.9
  eye 743.9
  gum 750.9
  heart NEC 746.9
    specified type NEC 746.89
    valve 746.9
  internal ear 744.05
  joint NEC 755.9
    specified type NEC 755.8
  Mondini's (congenital) (malformation, cochlea)
    744.05
  muscle 756.9
  nervous system (central) 742.9
  pelvic organs or tissues
    in pregnancy or childbirth 654.9 ☑
      affecting fetus or newborn 763.89
      causing obstructed labor 660.2 ☑
        affecting fetus or newborn 763.1
  placenta (*see also* Placenta, abnormal) 656.7 ☑
  respiratory organs 748.9
    specified type NEC 748.8
  Rieger's 743.44
  sense organs NEC 742.9
    specified type NEC 742.8
  skin 757.9
    specified type NEC 757.8
  spinal cord 742.9
  teeth, tooth NEC 520.9
  tendon 756.9
  throat 750.9
  umbilical cord (complicating delivery) 663.9 ☑
    affecting fetus or newborn 762.6
  umbilicus 759.9
  urinary system NEC 753.9
    specified type NEC 753.8

Malfunction — *see also* Dysfunction
  arterial graft 996.1
  cardiac pacemaker 996.01
  catheter device — *see* Complications,
    mechanical, catheter
  colostomy 569.62
  cystostomy 997.5
  device, implant, or graft NEC — *see*
    Complications, mechanical
  enteric stoma 569.62
  enterostomy 569.62
  esophagostomy 530.87
  gastroenteric 536.8
  gastrostomy 536.42
  nephrostomy 997.5
  pacemaker — *see* Complications, mechanical,
    pacemaker
  prosthetic device, internal — *see*
    Complications, mechanical
  tracheostomy 519.02
  vascular graft or shunt 996.1

Malgaigne's fracture (closed) 808.43
  open 808.53

Malherbe's
  calcifying epithelioma (M8110/0) — *see*
    Neoplasm, skin, benign
  tumor (M8110/0) — *see* Neoplasm, skin,
    benign

Malibu disease 919.8
  infected 919.9

Malignancy (M8000/3) — *see* Neoplasm, by site,
  malignant

Malignant — *see* condition

Malingerer, malingering V65.2

Mallet, finger (acquired) 736.1
  congenital 755.59
  late effect of rickets 268.1

Malleus 024

Mallory's bodies 034.1

Mallory-Weiss syndrome 530.7

Malnutrition (calorie) 263.9
  complicating pregnancy 648.9 ☑
  degree
    first 263.1
    second 263.0
    third 262

Malnutrition — *continued*
  degree — *continued*
    mild 263.1
    moderate 263.0
    severe 261
      protein-calorie 262
  fetus 764.2 ☑
    "light-for-dates" 764.1 ☑
  following gastrointestinal surgery 579.3
  intrauterine or fetal 764.2 ☑
    fetus or infant "light-for-dates" 764.1 ☑
  lack of care, or neglect (child) (infant) 995.52
    adult 995.84
  malignant 260
  mild 263.1
  moderate 263.0
  protein 260
  protein-calorie 263.9
    severe 262
    specified type NEC 263.8
  severe 261
    protein-calorie NEC 262

Malocclusion (teeth) 524.4
  due to
    abnormal swallowing 524.59
    accessory teeth (causing crowding) 524.31
    dentofacial abnormality NEC 524.89
    impacted teeth (causing crowding) 520.6
    missing teeth 524.30
    mouth breathing 524.59
    sleep postures 524.59
    supernumerary teeth (causing crowding)
      524.31
    thumb sucking 524.59
    tongue, lip, or finger habits 524.59
  temporomandibular (joint) 524.69

Malposition
  cardiac apex (congenital) 746.87
  cervix — *see* Malposition, uterus
  congenital
    adrenal (gland) 759.1
    alimentary tract 751.8
      lower 751.5
      upper 750.8
    aorta 747.21
    appendix 751.5
    arterial trunk 747.29
    artery (peripheral) NEC (*see also*
      Malposition, congenital, peripheral
      vascular system) 747.60
      coronary 746.85
      pulmonary 747.3
    auditory canal 744.29
      causing impairment of hearing 744.02
    auricle (ear) 744.29
      causing impairment of hearing 744.02
      cervical 744.43
    biliary duct or passage 751.69
    bladder (mucosa) 753.8
      exteriorized or extroverted 753.5
    brachial plexus 742.8
    brain tissue 742.4
    breast 757.6
    bronchus 748.3
    cardiac apex 746.87
    cecum 751.5
    clavicle 755.51
    colon 751.5
    digestive organ or tract NEC 751.8
      lower 751.5
      upper 750.8
    ear (auricle) (external) 744.29
      ossicles 744.04
    endocrine (gland) NEC 759.2
    epiglottis 748.3
    Eustachian tube 744.24
    eye 743.8
    facial features 744.89
    fallopian tube 752.19
    finger(s) 755.59
      supernumerary 755.01
    foot 755.67
    gallbladder 751.69
    gastrointestinal tract 751.8

Malposition — *continued*
  congenital — *continued*
    genitalia, genital organ(s) or tract
      female 752.89
        external 752.49
        internal NEC 752.89
      male 752.89
        penis 752.69
        scrotal transposition 752.81
    glottis 748.3
    hand 755.59
    heart 746.87
      dextrocardia 746.87
        with complete transposition of viscera
          759.3
    hepatic duct 751.69
    hip (joint) (*see also* Dislocation, hip,
        congenital) 754.30
    intestine (large) (small) 751.5
      with anomalous adhesions, fixation, or
          malrotation 751.4
    joint NEC 755.8
    kidney 753.3
    larynx 748.3
    limb 755.8
      lower 755.69
      upper 755.59
    liver 751.69
    lung (lobe) 748.69
    nail(s) 757.5
    nerve 742.8
    nervous system NEC 742.8
    nose, nasal (septum) 748.1
    organ or site NEC — *see* Anomaly, specified
        type NEC, by site
    ovary 752.0
    pancreas 751.7
    parathyroid (gland) 759.2
    patella 755.64
    peripheral vascular system 747.60
      gastrointestinal 747.61
      lower limb 747.64
      renal 747.62
      specified NEC 747.69
      spinal 747.82
      upper limb 747.63
    pituitary (gland) 759.2
    respiratory organ or system NEC 748.9
    rib (cage) 756.3
      supernumerary in cervical region 756.2
    scapula 755.59
    shoulder 755.59
    spinal cord 742.59
    spine 756.19
    spleen 759.0
    sternum 756.3
    symphysis pubis 755.69
    testis (undescended) 752.51
    thymus (gland) 759.2
    thyroid (gland) (tissue) 759.2
      cartilage 748.3
    toe(s) 755.66
      supernumerary 755.02
    tongue 750.19
    trachea 748.3
    uterus 752.3
    vein(s) (peripheral) NEC (*see also*
        Malposition, congenital, peripheral
        vascular system) 747.60
      great 747.49
      portal 747.49
      pulmonary 747.49
    vena cava (inferior) (superior) 747.49
  device, implant, or graft — *see* Complications,
      mechanical
  fetus NEC (*see also* Presentation, fetal)
      652.9 ☑
    with successful version 652.1 ☑
    affecting fetus or newborn 763.1
    before labor, affecting fetus or newborn
        761.7
    causing obstructed labor 660.0 ☑
    in multiple gestation (one fetus or more)
        652.6 ☑
      with locking 660.5 ☑
      causing obstructed labor 660.0 ☑

Malposition — *continued*
  gallbladder (*see also* Disease, gallbladder)
      575.8
  gastrointestinal tract 569.89
    congenital 751.8
  heart (*see also* Malposition, congenital, heart)
      746.87
  intestine 569.89
    congenital 751.5
  pelvic organs or tissues
    in pregnancy or childbirth 654.4 ☑
      affecting fetus or newborn 763.89
      causing obstructed labor 660.2 ☑
        affecting fetus or newborn 763.1
  placenta — *see* Placenta, previa
  stomach 537.89
    congenital 750.7
  tooth, teeth 524.30
    with impaction 520.6
  uterus or cervix (acquired) (acute) (adherent)
      (any degree) (asymptomatic)
      (postinfectional) (postpartal, old) 621.6
    anteflexion or anteversion (*see also*
        Anteversion, uterus) 621.6
    congenital 752.3
    flexion 621.6
      lateral (*see also* Lateroversion, uterus)
          621.6
    in pregnancy or childbirth 654.4 ☑
      affecting fetus or newborn 763.89
      causing obstructed labor 660.2 ☑
        affecting fetus or newborn 763.1
    inversion 621.6
    lateral (flexion) (version) (*see also*
        Lateroversion, uterus) 621.6
    lateroflexion (*see also* Lateroversion, uterus)
        621.6
    lateroversion (*see also* Lateroversion, uterus)
        621.6
    retroflexion or retroversion (*see also*
        Retroversion, uterus) 621.6
Malposture 729.9
Malpresentation, fetus (*see also* Presentation,
    fetal) 652.9 ☑
Malrotation
  cecum 751.4
  colon 751.4
  intestine 751.4
  kidney 753.3
Malta fever (*see also* Brucellosis) 023.9
Maltosuria 271.3
Maltreatment (of)
  adult 995.80
    emotional 995.82
    multiple forms 995.85
    neglect (nutritional) 995.84
    physical 995.81
    psychological 995.82
    sexual 995.83
  child 995.50
    emotional 995.51
    multiple forms 995.59
    neglect (nutritional) 995.52
    physical 995.54
      shaken infant syndrome 995.55
    psychological 995.51
    sexual 995.53
  spouse (*see also* Maltreatment, adult) 995.80
Malt workers' lung 495.4
Malum coxae senilis 715.25
Malunion, fracture 733.81
Mammillitis (*see also* Mastitis) 611.0
  puerperal, postpartum 675.2 ☑
Mammitis (*see also* Mastitis) 611.0
  puerperal, postpartum 675.2 ☑
Mammographic microcalcification 793.81
Mammoplasia 611.1
Management
  contraceptive V25.9
    specified type NEC V25.8
  procreative V26.9
    specified type NEC V26.8
Mangled NEC (*see also* nature and site of injury)
    959.9

Mania (monopolar) (*see also* Psychosis, affective)
    296.0 ☑
  alcoholic (acute) (chronic) 291.9
  Bell's — *see* Mania, chronic
  chronic 296.0 ☑
    recurrent episode 296.1 ☑
    single episode 296.0 ☑
  compulsive 300.3
  delirious (acute) 296.0 ☑
    recurrent episode 296.1 ☑
    single episode 296.0 ☑
  epileptic (*see also* Epilepsy) 345.4 ☑
  hysterical 300.10
  inhibited 296.89
  puerperal (after delivery) 296.0 ☑
    recurrent episode 296.1 ☑
    single episode 296.0 ☑
  recurrent episode 296.1 ☑
  senile 290.8
  single episode 296.0 ☑
  stupor 296.89
  stuporous 296.89
  unproductive 296.89
**Manic-depressive insanity, psychosis, reaction,
    or syndrome** (*see also* Psychosis, affective)
    296.80
  circular (alternating) 296.7
    currently
      depressed 296.5 ☑
      episode unspecified 296.7
      hypomanic, previously depressed
          296.4 ☑
      manic 296.4 ☑
      mixed 296.6 ☑
  depressed (type), depressive 296.2 ☑
    atypical 296.82
    recurrent episode 296.3 ☑
    single episode 296.2 ☑
  hypomanic 296.0 ☑
    recurrent episode 296.1 ☑
    single episode 296.0 ☑
  manic 296.0 ☑
    atypical 296.81
    recurrent episode 296.1 ☑
    single episode 296.0 ☑
  mixed NEC 296.89
  perplexed 296.89
  stuporous 296.89
Manifestations, rheumatoid
  lungs 714.81
  pannus — *see* Arthritis, rheumatoid
  subcutaneous nodules — *see* Arthritis,
      rheumatoid
Mankowsky's syndrome (familial dysplastic
    osteopathy) 731.2
Mannoheptulosuria 271.8
Mannosidosis 271.8
Manson's
  disease (schistosomiasis) 120.1
  pyosis (pemphigus contagiosus) 684
  schistosomiasis 120.1
Mansonellosis 125.5
Manual — *see* condition
Maple bark disease 495.6
Maple bark-strippers' lung 495.6
Maple syrup (urine) disease or syndrome 270.3
Marable's syndrome (celiac artery compression)
    447.4
Marasmus 261
  brain 331.9
  due to malnutrition 261
  intestinal 569.89
  nutritional 261
  senile 797
  tuberculous NEC (*see also* Tuberculosis)
      011.9 ☑
Marble
  bones 756.52
  skin 782.61
Marburg disease (virus) 078.89
March
  foot 733.94
  hemoglobinuria 283.2

☑ Additional Digit Required — Refer to the Tabular List (Numeric Code Section) for Additional Digit Selection

Marchand multiple nodular hyperplasia (liver) 571.5

Marchesani (-Weill) syndrome (brachymorphism and ectopia lentis) 759.89

Marchiafava (-Bignami) disease or syndrome 341.8

Marchiafava-Micheli syndrome (paroxysmal nocturnal hemoglobinuria) 283.2

Marcus Gunn's syndrome (jaw-winking syndrome) 742.8

Marfan's
　congenital syphilis 090.49
　disease 090.49
　syndrome (arachnodactyly) 759.82
　　meaning congenital syphilis 090.49
　　　with luxation of lens 090.49 *[379.32]*

Marginal
　implantation, placenta — *see* Placenta, previa
　placenta — *see* Placenta, previa
　sinus (hemorrhage) (rupture) 641.2 ☑
　　affecting fetus or newborn 762.1

Marie's
　cerebellar ataxia 334.2
　syndrome (acromegaly) 253.0

Marie-Bamberger disease or syndrome (hypertrophic) (pulmonary) (secondary) 731.2
　idiopathic (acropachyderma) 757.39
　primary (acropachyderma) 757.39

Marie-Charcôt-Tooth neuropathic atrophy, muscle 356.1

Marie-Strümpell arthritis or disease (ankylosing spondylitis) 720.0

Marihuana, marijuana
　abuse (*see also* Abuse, drugs, nondependent) 305.2 ☑
　dependence (*see also* Dependence) 304.3 ☑

Marion's disease (bladder neck obstruction) 596.0

Marital conflict V61.10

Mark
　port wine 757.32
　raspberry 757.32
　strawberry 757.32
　stretch 701.3
　tattoo 709.09

Maroteaux-Lamy syndrome (mucopolysaccharidosis VI) 277.5

Marriage license examination V70.3

Marrow (bone)
　arrest 284.9
　megakaryocytic 287.30　　　　　　▲
　poor function 289.9

Marseilles fever 082.1

Marsh's disease (exophthalmic goiter) 242.0 ☑

Marshall's (hidrotic) **ectodermal dysplasia** 757.31

Marsh fever (*see also* Malaria) 084.6

Martin's disease 715.27

Martin-Albright syndrome (pseudohypoparathyroidism) 275.49

Martorell-Fabre syndrome (pulseless disease) 446.7

Masculinization, female, with adrenal hyperplasia 255.2

Masculinovoblastoma (M8670/0) 220

Masochism 302.83

Masons' lung 502

Mass
　abdominal 789.3 ☑
　anus 787.99
　bone 733.90
　breast 611.72
　cheek 784.2
　chest 786.6
　cystic — *see* Cyst
　ear 388.8
　epigastric 789.3 ☑
　eye 379.92
　female genital organ 625.8
　gum 784.2

Mass — *continued*
　head 784.2
　intracranial 784.2
　joint 719.60
　　ankle 719.67
　　elbow 719.62
　　foot 719.67
　　hand 719.64
　　hip 719.65
　　knee 719.66
　　multiple sites 719.69
　　pelvic region 719.65
　　shoulder (region) 719.61
　　specified site NEC 719.68
　　wrist 719.63
　kidney (*see also* Disease, kidney) 593.9
　lung 786.6
　lymph node 785.6
　malignant (M8000/3) — *see* Neoplasm, by site, malignant
　mediastinal 786.6
　mouth 784.2
　muscle (limb) 729.89
　neck 784.2
　nose or sinus 784.2
　palate 784.2
　pelvis, pelvic 789.3 ☑
　penis 607.89
　perineum 625.8
　rectum 787.99
　scrotum 608.89
　skin 782.2
　specified organ NEC — *see* Disease of specified organ or site
　splenic 789.2
　substernal 786.6
　　thyroid (*see also* Goiter) 240.9
　superficial (localized) 782.2
　testes 608.89
　throat 784.2
　tongue 784.2
　umbilicus 789.3 ☑
　uterus 625.8
　vagina 625.8
　vulva 625.8

Massive — *see* condition

Mastalgia 611.71
　psychogenic 307.89

Mast cell
　disease 757.33
　　systemic (M9741/3) 202.6 ☑
　leukemia (M9900/3) 207.8 ☑
　sarcoma (M9742/3) 202.6 ☑
　tumor (M9740/1) 238.5
　　malignant (M9740/3) 202.6 ☑

Masters-Allen syndrome 620.6

Mastitis (acute) (adolescent) (diffuse) (interstitial) (lobular) (nonpuerperal) (nonsuppurative) (parenchymatous) (phlegmonous) (simple) (subacute) (suppurative) 611.0
　chronic (cystic) (fibrocystic) 610.1
　cystic 610.1
　　Schimmelbusch's type 610.1
　fibrocystic 610.1
　infective 611.0
　lactational 675.2 ☑
　lymphangitis 611.0
　neonatal (noninfective) 778.7
　　infective 771.5
　periductal 610.4
　plasma cell 610.4
　puerperal, postpartum, (interstitial) (nonpurulent) (parenchymatous) 675.2 ☑
　　purulent 675.1 ☑
　　stagnation 676.2 ☑
　puerperalis 675.2 ☑
　retromammary 611.0
　　puerperal, postpartum 675.1 ☑
　submammary 611.0
　　puerperal, postpartum 675.1 ☑

Mastocytoma (M9740/1) 238.5
　malignant (M9740/3) 202.6 ☑

Mastocytosis 757.33
　malignant (M9741/3) 202.6 ☑
　systemic (M9741/3) 202.6 ☑

Mastodynia 611.71
　psychogenic 307.89

Mastoid — *see* condition

Mastoidalgia (*see also* Otalgia) 388.70

Mastoiditis (coalescent) (hemorrhagic) (pneumococcal) (streptococcal) (suppurative) 383.9
　acute or subacute 383.00
　　with
　　　Gradenigo's syndrome 383.02
　　　petrositis 383.02
　　　specified complication NEC 383.02
　　　subperiosteal abscess 383.01
　chronic (necrotic) (recurrent) 383.1
　tuberculous (*see also* Tuberculosis) 015.6 ☑

Mastopathy, mastopathia 611.9
　chronica cystica 610.1
　diffuse cystic 610.1
　estrogenic 611.8
　ovarian origin 611.8

Mastoplasia 611.1

Masturbation 307.9

Maternal condition, affecting fetus or newborn
　acute yellow atrophy of liver 760.8
　albuminuria 760.1
　anesthesia or analgesia 763.5
　blood loss 762.1
　chorioamnionitis 762.7
　circulatory disease, chronic (conditions classifiable to 390-459, 745-747) 760.3
　congenital heart disease (conditions classifiable to 745-746) 760.3
　cortical necrosis of kidney 760.1
　death 761.6
　diabetes mellitus 775.0
　　manifest diabetes in the infant 775.1
　disease NEC 760.9
　　circulatory system, chronic (conditions classifiable to 390-459, 745-747) 760.3
　　genitourinary system (conditions classifiable to 580-599) 760.1
　　respiratory (conditions classifiable to 490-519, 748) 760.3
　eclampsia 760.0
　hemorrhage NEC 762.1
　hepatitis acute, malignant, or subacute 760.8
　hyperemesis (gravidarum) 761.8
　hypertension (arising during pregnancy) (conditions classifiable to 642) 760.0
　infection
　　disease classifiable to 001-136 760.2
　　genital tract NEC 760.8
　　urinary tract 760.1
　influenza 760.2
　　manifest influenza in the infant 771.2
　injury (conditions classifiable to 800-996) 760.5
　malaria 760.2
　　manifest malaria in infant or fetus 771.2
　malnutrition 760.4
　necrosis of liver 760.8
　nephritis (conditions classifiable to 580-583) 760.1
　nephrosis (conditions classifiable to 581) 760.1
　noxious substance transmitted via breast milk or placenta 760.70
　　alcohol 760.71
　　anticonvulsants 760.77　　　　　　●
　　antifungals 760.74　　　　　　　　●
　　anti-infective agents 760.74
　　antimetabolics 760.78　　　　　　●
　　cocaine 760.75
　　"crack" 760.75
　　diethylstilbestrol [DES] 760.76
　　hallucinogenic agents 760.73
　　medicinal agents NEC 760.79
　　narcotics 760.72
　　obstetric anesthetic or analgesic drug 760.72
　　specified agent NEC 760.79
　nutritional disorder (conditions classifiable to 260-269) 760.4
　operation unrelated to current delivery 760.6
　pre-eclampsia 760.0

Maternal condition, affecting fetus or newborn
— *continued*
  pyelitis or pyelonephritis, arising during
    pregnancy (conditions classifiable to 590)
    760.1
  renal disease or failure 760.1
  respiratory disease, chronic (conditions
    classifiable to 490-519, 748) 760.3
  rheumatic heart disease (chronic) (conditions
    classifiable to 393-398) 760.3
  rubella (conditions classifiable to 056) 760.2
    manifest rubella in the infant or fetus 771.0
  surgery unrelated to current delivery 760.6
    to uterus or pelvic organs 763.89
  syphilis (conditions classifiable to 090-097)
    760.2
    manifest syphilis in the infant or fetus 090.0
  thrombophlebitis 760.3
  toxemia (of pregnancy) 760.0
    pre-eclamptic 760.0
  toxoplasmosis (conditions classifiable to 130)
    760.2
    manifest toxoplasmosis in the infant or fetus
      771.2
  transmission of chemical substance through
    the placenta 760.70
    alcohol 760.71
    anticonvulsants 760.77
    antifungals 760.74
    anti-infective 760.74
    antimetabolics 760.78
    cocaine 760.75
    "crack" 760.75
    diethylstilbestrol [DES] 760.76
    hallucinogenic agents 760.73
    narcotics 760.72
    specified substance NEC 760.79
  uremia 760.1
  urinary tract conditions (conditions classifiable
    to 580-599) 760.1
  vomiting (pernicious) (persistent) (vicious)
    761.8
Maternity — *see* Delivery
Matheiu's disease (leptospiral jaundice) 100.0
Mauclaire's disease or osteochondrosis 732.3
Maxcy's disease 081.0
Maxilla, maxillary — *see* condition
May (-Hegglin) anomaly or syndrome 288.2
Mayaro fever 066.3
Mazoplasia 610.8
MBD (minimal brain dysfunction), child (*see also*
  Hyperkinesia) 314.9
MCAD (medium chain acyl CoA dehydrogenase
  deficiency) 277.85
**McArdle (-Schmid-Pearson) disease or
  syndrome** (glycogenosis V) 271.0
McCune-Albright syndrome (osteitis fibrosa
  disseminata) 756.59
MCLS (mucocutaneous lymph node syndrome)
  446.1
McQuarrie's syndrome (idiopathic familial
  hypoglycemia) 251.2
Measles (black) (hemorrhagic) (suppressed) 055.9
  with
    encephalitis 055.0
    keratitis 055.71
    keratoconjunctivitis 055.71
    otitis media 055.2
    pneumonia 055.1
  complication 055.8
    specified type NEC 055.79
  encephalitis 055.0
  French 056.9
  German 056.9
  keratitis 055.71
  keratoconjunctivitis 055.71
  liberty 056.9
  otitis media 055.2
  pneumonia 055.1
  specified complications NEC 055.79
  vaccination, prophylactic (against) V04.2
Meatitis, urethral (*see also* Urethritis) 597.89
Meat poisoning — *see* Poisoning, food

Meatus, meatal — *see* condition
Meat-wrappers' asthma 506.9
Meckel's
  diverticulitis 751.0
  diverticulum (displaced) (hypertrophic) 751.0
Meconium
  aspiration 770.11   ▲
    with   ●
      pneumonia 770.12   ●
      pneumonitis 770.12   ●
      respiratory symptoms 770.12   ●
    below vocal cords 770.11   ●
      with respiratory symptoms 770.12   ●
    syndrome 770.12   ●
  delayed passage in newborn 777.1
  ileus 777.1
    due to cystic fibrosis 277.01
  in liquor 792.3
    noted during delivery 656.8 ☑
  insufflation 770.11   ▲
    with respiratory symptoms 770.12
  obstruction
    fetus or newborn 777.1
    in mucoviscidosis 277.01
  passage of 792.3
    noted during delivery 763.84   ▲
  peritonitis 777.6
  plug syndrome (newborn) NEC 777.1
  staining 779.84   ●
Median — *see also* condition
  arcuate ligament syndrome 447.4
  bar (prostate) 600.90
    with urinary retention 600.91
  rhomboid glossitis 529.2
  vesical orifice 600.90
    with urinary retention 600.91
Mediastinal shift 793.2
Mediastinitis (acute) (chronic) 519.2
  actinomycotic 039.8
  syphilitic 095.8
  tuberculous (*see also* Tuberculosis) 012.8 ☑
Mediastinopericarditis (*see also* Pericarditis)
  423.9
  acute 420.90
  chronic 423.8
    rheumatic 393
  rheumatic, chronic 393
Mediastinum, mediastinal — *see* condition
Medical services provided for — *see* Health,
  services provided because (of)
Medicine poisoning (by overdose) (wrong
  substance given or taken in error) 977.9
  specified drug or substance — *see* Table of
    Drugs and Chemicals
Medin's disease (poliomyelitis) 045.9 ☑
Mediterranean
  anemia (with other hemoglobinopathy) 282.49
  disease or syndrome (hemipathic) 282.49
  fever (*see also* Brucellosis) 023.9
    familial 277.3
  kala-azar 085.0
  leishmaniasis 085.0
  tick fever 082.1
Medulla — *see* condition
Medullary
  cystic kidney 753.16
  sponge kidney 753.17
Medullated fibers
  optic (nerve) 743.57
  retina 362.85
Medulloblastoma (M9470/3) 191.6
  desmoplastic (M9471/3) 191.6
  specified site — *see* Neoplasm, by site,
    malignant
  unspecified site 191.6
Medulloepithelioma (M9501/3) — *see also*
  Neoplasm, by site, malignant
  teratoid (M9502/3) — *see* Neoplasm, by site,
    malignant
Medullomyoblastoma (M9472/3)
  specified site — *see* Neoplasm, by site,
    malignant
  unspecified site 191.6

Meekeren-Ehlers-Danlos syndrome 756.83
Megacaryocytic — *see* condition
Megacolon (acquired) (functional) (not
  Hirschsprung's disease) 564.7
  aganglionic 751.3
  congenital, congenitum 751.3
  Hirschsprung's (disease) 751.3
  psychogenic 306.4
  toxic (*see also* Colitis, ulcerative) 556.9
Megaduodenum 537.3
Megaesophagus (functional) 530.0
  congenital 750.4
Megakaryocytic — *see* condition
Megalencephaly 742.4
Megalerythema (epidermicum) (infectiosum)
  057.0
Megalia, cutis et ossium 757.39
Megaloappendix 751.5
Megalocephalus, megalocephaly NEC 756.0
Megalocornea 743.41
  associated with buphthalmos 743.22
Megalocytic anemia 281.9
Megalodactylia (fingers) (thumbs) 755.57
  toes 755.65
Megaloduodenum 751.5
Megaloesophagus (functional) 530.0
  congenital 750.4
Megalogastria (congenital) 750.7
Megalomania 307.9
Megalophthalmos 743.8
Megalopsia 368.14
Megalosplenia (*see also* Splenomegaly) 789.2
Megaloureter 593.89
  congenital 753.22
Megarectum 569.49
Megasigmoid 564.7
  congenital 751.3
Megaureter 593.89
  congenital 753.22
Megrim 346.9 ☑
Meibomian
  cyst 373.2
    infected 373.12
  gland — *see* condition
  infarct (eyelid) 374.85
  stye 373.11
Meibomitis 373.12
Meige
  -Milroy disease (chronic hereditary edema)
    757.0
  syndrome (blepharospasm-oromandibular
    dystonia) 333.82
Melalgia, nutritional 266.2
Melancholia (*see also* Psychosis, affective) 296.90
  climacteric 296.2 ☑
    recurrent episode 296.3 ☑
    single episode 296.2 ☑
  hypochondriac 300.7
  intermittent 296.2 ☑
    recurrent episode 296.3 ☑
    single episode 296.2 ☑
  involutional 296.2 ☑
    recurrent episode 296.3 ☑
    single episode 296.2 ☑
  menopausal 296.2 ☑
    recurrent episode 296.3 ☑
    single episode 296.2 ☑
  puerperal 296.2 ☑
  reactive (from emotional stress, psychological
    trauma) 298.0
  recurrent 296.3 ☑
  senile 290.21
  stuporous 296.2 ☑
    recurrent episode 296.3 ☑
    single episode 296.2 ☑
Melanemia 275.0
Melanoameloblastoma (M9363/0) — *see*
  Neoplasm, bone, benign
Melanoblastoma (M8720/3) — *see* Melanoma

☑ Additional Digit Required — Refer to the Tabular List (Numeric Code Section) for Additional Digit Selection

▶◀ Revised Text   ● New Line   ▲ Revised Code

Melanoblastosis
  Block-Sulzberger 757.33
  cutis linearis sive systematisata 757.33
Melanocarcinoma (M8720/3) — *see* Melanoma
Melanocytoma, eyeball (M8726/0) 224.0
Melanoderma, melanodermia 709.09
  Addison's (primary adrenal insufficiency) 255.4
Melanodontia, infantile 521.05
Melanodontoclasia 521.05
Melanoepithelioma (M8720/3) — *see* Melanoma
Melanoma (malignant) (M8720/3) 172.9

> *Note — Except where otherwise indicated,*
> *the morphological varieties of melanoma in*
> *the list below should be coded by site as for*
> *"Melanoma (malignant)". Internal sites*
> *should be coded to malignant neoplasm of*
> *those sites.*

  abdominal wall 172.5
  ala nasi 172.3
  amelanotic (M8730/3) — *see* Melanoma, by site
  ankle 172.7
  anus, anal 154.3
    canal 154.2
  arm 172.6
  auditory canal (external) 172.2
  auricle (ear) 172.2
  auricular canal (external) 172.2
  axilla 172.5
  axillary fold 172.5
  back 172.5
  balloon cell (M8722/3) — *see* Melanoma, by
    site
  benign (M8720/0) — *see* Neoplasm, skin,
    benign
  breast (female) (male) 172.5
  brow 172.3
  buttock 172.5
  canthus (eye) 172.1
  cheek (external) 172.3
  chest wall 172.5
  chin 172.3
  choroid 190.6
  conjunctiva 190.3
  ear (external) 172.2
  epithelioid cell (M8771/3) — *see also*
    Melanoma, by site
    and spindle cell, mixed (M8775/3) — *see*
      Melanoma, by site
  external meatus (ear) 172.2
  eye 190.9
  eyebrow 172.3
  eyelid (lower) (upper) 172.1
  face NEC 172.3
  female genital organ (external) NEC 184.4
  finger 172.6
  flank 172.5
  foot 172.7
  forearm 172.6
  forehead 172.3
  foreskin 187.1
  gluteal region 172.5
  groin 172.5
  hand 172.6
  heel 172.7
  helix 172.2
  hip 172.7
  in
    giant pigmented nevus (M8761/3) — *see*
      Melanoma, by site
    Hutchinson's melanotic freckle (M8742/3) —
      see Melanoma, by site
    junctional nevus (M8740/3) — *see*
      Melanoma, by site
    precancerous melanosis (M8741/3) — *see*
      Melanoma, by site
  interscapular region 172.5
  iris 190.0
  jaw 172.3
  juvenile (M8770/0) — *see* Neoplasm, skin,
    benign
  knee 172.7
  labium
    majus 184.1
    minus 184.2

Melanoma (M8720/3) — *continued*
  lacrimal gland 190.2
  leg 172.7
  lip (lower) (upper) 172.0
  liver 197.7
  lower limb NEC 172.7
  male genital organ (external) NEC 187.9
  meatus, acoustic (external) 172.2
  meibomian gland 172.1
  metastatic
    of or from specified site — *see* Melanoma, by
      site
    site not of skin — *see* Neoplasm, by site,
      malignant, secondary
    to specified site — *see* Neoplasm, by site,
      malignant, secondary
    unspecified site 172.9
  nail 172.9
    finger 172.6
    toe 172.7
  neck 172.4
  nodular (M8721/3) — *see* Melanoma, by site
  nose, external 172.3
  orbit 190.1
  penis 187.4
  perianal skin 172.5
  perineum 172.5
  pinna 172.2
  popliteal (fossa) (space) 172.7
  prepuce 187.1
  pubes 172.5
  pudendum 184.4
  retina 190.5
  scalp 172.4
  scrotum 187.7
  septum nasal (skin) 172.3
  shoulder 172.6
  skin NEC 172.8
  spindle cell (M8772/3) — *see also* Melanoma,
    by site
    type A (M8773/3) 190.0
    type B (M8774/3) 190.0
  submammary fold 172.5
  superficial spreading (M8743/3) — *see*
    Melanoma, by site
  temple 172.3
  thigh 172.7
  toe 172.7
  trunk NEC 172.5
  umbilicus 172.5
  upper limb NEC 172.6
  vagina vault 184.0
  vulva 184.4
Melanoplakia 528.9
Melanosarcoma (M8720/3) — *see also* Melanoma
  epithelioid cell (M8771/3) — *see* Melanoma
Melanosis 709.09
  addisonian (primary adrenal insufficiency)
    255.4
    tuberculous (*see also* Tuberculosis) 017.6 ✔
  adrenal 255.4
  colon 569.89
  conjunctiva 372.55
    congenital 743.49
  corii degenerativa 757.33
  cornea (presenile) (senile) 371.12
    congenital 743.43
      interfering with vision 743.42
  prenatal 743.43
    interfering with vision 743.42
  eye 372.55
    congenital 743.49
  jute spinners' 709.09
  lenticularis progressiva 757.33
  liver 573.8
  precancerous (M8741/2) — *see also* Neoplasm,
    skin, in situ
    malignant melanoma in (M8741/3) — *see*
      Melanoma
  Riehl's 709.09
  sclera 379.19
    congenital 743.47
  suprarenal 255.4
  tar 709.09
  toxic 709.09
Melanuria 791.9

MELAS syndrome (mitochondrial encephalopathy,
  lactic acidosis and stroke-like episodes)
  277.87
Melasma 709.09
  adrenal (gland) 255.4
  suprarenal (gland) 255.4
Melena 578.1
  due to
    swallowed maternal blood 777.3
    ulcer — *see* Ulcer, by site, with hemorrhage
  newborn 772.4
    due to swallowed maternal blood 777.3
Meleney's
  gangrene (cutaneous) 686.09
  ulcer (chronic undermining) 686.09
Melioidosis 025
Melitensis, febris 023.0
Melitococcosis 023.0
Melkersson (-Rosenthal) syndrome 351.8
Mellitus, diabetes — *see* Diabetes
Melorheostosis (bone) (leri) 733.99
Meloschisis 744.83
Melotia 744.29
Membrana
  capsularis lentis posterior 743.39
  epipapillaris 743.57
Membranacea placenta — *see* Placenta,
  abnormal
Membranaceous uterus 621.8
Membrane, membranous — *see also* condition
  folds, congenital — *see* Web
  Jackson's 751.4
  over face (causing asphyxia), fetus or newborn
    768.9
  premature rupture — *see* Rupture,
    membranes, premature
  pupillary 364.74
    persistent 743.46
  retained (complicating delivery) (with
    hemorrhage) 666.2 ✔
    without hemorrhage 667.1 ✔
  secondary (eye) 366.50
  unruptured (causing asphyxia) 768.9
  vitreous humor 379.25
Membranitis, fetal 658.4 ✔
  affecting fetus or newborn 762.7
Memory disturbance, loss or lack (*see also*
  Amnesia) 780.93
  mild, following organic brain damage 310.1
Menadione (vitamin K) **deficiency** 269.0
Menarche, precocious 259.1
Mendacity, pathologic 301.7
Mende's syndrome (ptosis-epicanthus) 270.2
Mendelson's syndrome (resulting from a
  procedure) 997.3
  obstetric 668.0 ✔
Ménétrier's disease or syndrome (hypertrophic
  gastritis) 535.2 ✔
Ménière's disease, syndrome, or vertigo 386.00
  cochlear 386.02
  cochleovestibular 386.01
  inactive 386.04
  in remission 386.04
  vestibular 386.03
Meninges, meningeal — *see* condition
Meningioma (M9530/0) — *see also* Neoplasm,
  meninges, benign
  angioblastic (M9535/0) — *see* Neoplasm,
    meninges, benign
  angiomatous (M9534/0) — *see* Neoplasm,
    meninges, benign
  endotheliomatous (M9531/0) — *see* Neoplasm,
    meninges, benign
  fibroblastic (M9532/0) — *see* Neoplasm,
    meninges, benign
  fibrous (M9532/0) — *see* Neoplasm, meninges,
    benign
  hemangioblastic (M9535/0) — *see* Neoplasm,
    meninges, benign
  hemangiopericytic (M9536/0) — *see* Neoplasm,
    meninges, benign

Meningioma (M9530/0) — *see also* Neoplasm, meninges, benign — *continued*
malignant (M9530/3) — *see* Neoplasm, meninges, malignant
meningiothelial (M9531/0) — *see* Neoplasm, meninges, benign
meningotheliomatous (M9531/0) — *see* Neoplasm, meninges, benign
mixed (M9537/0) — *see* Neoplasm, meninges, benign
multiple (M9530/1) 237.6
papillary (M9538/1) 237.6
psammomatous (M9533/0) — *see* Neoplasm, meninges, benign
syncytial (M9531/0) — *see* Neoplasm, meninges, benign
transitional (M9537/0) — *see* Neoplasm, meninges, benign
Meningiomatosis (diffuse) (M9530/1) 237.6
Meningism (*see also* Meningismus) 781.6
Meningismus (infectional) (pneumococcal) 781.6
due to serum or vaccine 997.09 *[321.8]*
influenzal NEC 487.8
Meningitis (basal) (basic) (basilar) (brain) (cerebral) (cervical) (congestive) (diffuse) (hemorrhagic) (infantile) (membranous) (metastatic) (nonspecific) (pontine) (progressive) (simple) (spinal) (subacute) (sympathetica) (toxic) 322.9
abacterial NEC (*see also* Meningitis, aseptic) 047.9
actinomycotic 039.8 *[320.7]*
adenoviral 049.1
Aerobacter aerogenes 320.82
anaerobes (cocci) (gram-negative) (gram-positive) (mixed) (NEC) 320.81
arbovirus NEC 066.9 *[321.2]*
specified type NEC 066.8 *[321.2]*
aseptic (acute) NEC 047.9
adenovirus 049.1
Coxsackie virus 047.0
due to
adenovirus 049.1
Coxsackie virus 047.0
ECHO virus 047.1
enterovirus 047.9
mumps 072.1
poliovirus (*see also* Poliomyelitis) 045.2 ☑ *[321.2]*
ECHO virus 047.1
herpes (simplex) virus 054.72
zoster 053.0
leptospiral 100.81
lymphocytic choriomeningitis 049.0
noninfective 322.0
Bacillus pyocyaneus 320.89
bacterial NEC 320.9
anaerobic 320.81
gram-negative 320.82
anaerobic 320.81
Bacteroides (fragilis) (oralis) (melaninogenicus) 320.81
cancerous (M8000/6) 198.4
candidal 112.83
carcinomatous (M8010/6) 198.4
caseous (*see also* Tuberculosis, meninges) 013.0 ☑
cerebrospinal (acute) (chronic) (diplococcal) (endemic) (epidemic) (fulminant) (infectious) (malignant) (meningococcal) (sporadic) 036.0
carrier (suspected) of V02.59
chronic NEC 322.2
clear cerebrospinal fluid NEC 322.0
Clostridium (haemolyticum) (novyi) NEC 320.81
coccidioidomycosis 114.2
Coxsackie virus 047.0
cryptococcal 117.5 *[321.0]*
diplococcal 036.0
gram-negative 036.0
gram-positive 320.1
Diplococcus pneumoniae 320.1
due to
actinomycosis 039.8 *[320.7]*
adenovirus 049.1
coccidiomycosis 114.2

Meningitis — *continued*
due to — *continued*
enterovirus 047.9
specified NEC 047.8
histoplasmosis (*see also* Histoplasmosis) 115.91
Listerosis 027.0 *[320.7]*
Lyme disease 088.81 *[320.7]*
moniliasis 112.83
mumps 072.1
neurosyphilis 094.2
nonbacterial organisms NEC 321.8
oidiomycosis 112.83
poliovirus (*see also* Poliomyelitis) 045.2 ☑ *[321.2]*
preventive immunization, inoculation, or vaccination 997.09 *[321.8]*
sarcoidosis 135 *[321.4]*
sporotrichosis 117.1 *[321.1]*
syphilis 094.2
acute 091.81
congenital 090.42
secondary 091.81
trypanosomiasis (*see also* Trypanosomiasis) 086.9 *[321.3]*
whooping cough 033.9 *[320.7]*
E. coli 320.82
ECHO virus 047.1
endothelial-leukocytic, benign, recurrent 047.9
Enterobacter aerogenes 320.82
enteroviral 047.9
specified type NEC 047.8
enterovirus 047.9
specified NEC 047.8
eosinophilic 322.1
epidemic NEC 036.0
Escherichia coli (E. coli) 320.82
Eubacterium 320.81
fibrinopurulent NEC 320.9
specified type NEC 320.89
Friedländer (bacillus) 320.82
fungal NEC 117.9 *[321.1]*
Fusobacterium 320.81
gonococcal 098.82
gram-negative bacteria NEC 320.82
anaerobic 320.81
cocci 036.0
specified NEC 320.82
gram-negative cocci NEC 036.0
specified NEC 320.82
gram-positive cocci NEC 320.9
H. influenzae 320.0
herpes (simplex) virus 054.72
zoster 053.0
infectious NEC 320.9
influenzal 320.0
Klebsiella pneumoniae 320.82
late effect — *see* Late, effect, meningitis
leptospiral (aseptic) 100.81
Listerella (monocytogenes) 027.0 *[320.7]*
Listeria monocytogenes 027.0 *[320.7]*
lymphocytic (acute) (benign) (serous) 049.0
choriomeningitis virus 049.0
meningococcal (chronic) 036.0
Mima polymorpha 320.82
Mollaret's 047.9
monilial 112.83
mumps (virus) 072.1
mycotic NEC 117.9 *[321.1]*
Neisseria 036.0
neurosyphilis 094.2
nonbacterial NEC (*see also* Meningitis, aseptic) 047.9
nonpyogenic NEC 322.0
oidiomycosis 112.83
ossificans 349.2
Peptococcus 320.81
Peptostreptococcus 320.81
pneumococcal 320.1
poliovirus (*see also* Poliomyelitis) 045.2 ☑ *[321.2]*
Proprionibacterium 320.81
Proteus morganii 320.82
Pseudomonas (aeruginosa) (pyocyaneus) 320.82
purulent NEC 320.9
specified organism NEC 320.89

Meningitis — *continued*
pyogenic NEC 320.9
specified organism NEC 320.89
Salmonella 003.21
septic NEC 320.9
specified organism NEC 320.89
serosa circumscripta NEC 322.0
serous NEC (*see also* Meningitis, aseptic) 047.9
lymphocytic 049.0
syndrome 348.2
Serratia (marcescens) 320.82
specified organism NEC 320.89
sporadic cerebrospinal 036.0
sporotrichosis 117.1 *[321.1]*
staphylococcal 320.3
sterile 997.09
streptococcal (acute) 320.2
suppurative 320.9
specified organism NEC 320.89
syphilitic 094.2
acute 091.81
congenital 090.42
secondary 091.81
torula 117.5 *[321.0]*
traumatic (complication of injury) 958.8
Treponema (denticola) (macrodenticum) 320.81
trypanosomiasis 086.1 *[321.3]*
tuberculous (*see also* Tuberculosis, meninges) 013.0 ☑
typhoid 002.0 *[320.7]*
Veillonella 320.81
Vibrio vulnificus 320.82
viral, virus NEC (*see also* Meningitis, aseptic) 047.9
Wallgren's (*see also* Meningitis, aseptic) 047.9
Meningocele (congenital) (spinal) (*see also* Spina bifida) 741.9 ☑
acquired (traumatic) 349.2
cerebral 742.0
cranial 742.0
Meningocerebritis — *see* Meningoencephalitis
Meningococcemia (acute) (chronic) 036.2
Meningococcus, meningococcal (*see also* condition) 036.9
adrenalitis, hemorrhagic 036.3
carditis 036.40
carrier (suspected) of V02.59
cerebrospinal fever 036.0
encephalitis 036.1
endocarditis 036.42
exposure to V01.84
infection NEC 036.9
meningitis (cerebrospinal) 036.0
myocarditis 036.43
optic neuritis 036.81
pericarditis 036.41
septicemia (chronic) 036.2
Meningoencephalitis (*see also* Encephalitis) 323.9
acute NEC 048
bacterial, purulent, pyogenic, or septic — *see* Meningitis
chronic NEC 094.1
diffuse NEC 094.1
diphasic 063.2
due to
actinomycosis 039.8 *[320.7]*
blastomycosis NEC (*see also* Blastomycosis) 116.0 *[323.4]*
free-living amebae 136.2
Listeria monocytogenes 027.0 *[320.7]*
Lyme disease 088.81 *[320.7]*
mumps 072.2
Naegleria (amebae) (gruberi) (organisms) 136.2
rubella 056.01
sporotrichosis 117.1 *[321.1]*
toxoplasmosis (acquired) 130.0
congenital (active) 771.2 *[323.4]*
Trypanosoma 086.1 *[323.2]*
epidemic 036.0
herpes 054.3
herpetic 054.3
H. influenzae 320.0
infectious (acute) 048
influenzal 320.0

Meningoencephalitis (*see also* Encephalitis) — *continued*
late effect — *see* category 326
Listeria monocytogenes 027.0 [320.7]
lymphocytic (serous) 049.0
mumps 072.2
parasitic NEC 123.9 [323.4]
pneumococcal 320.1
primary amebic 136.2
rubella 056.01
serous 048
   lymphocytic 049.0
specific 094.2
staphylococcal 320.3
streptococcal 320.2
syphilitic 094.2
toxic NEC 989.9 [323.7]
   due to
      carbon tetrachloride 987.8 [323.7]
      hydroxyquinoline derivatives poisoning
         961.3 [323.7]
      lead 984.9 [323.7]
      mercury 985.0 [323.7]
      thallium 985.8 [323.7]
toxoplasmosis (acquired) 130.0
trypanosomic 086.1 [323.2]
tuberculous (*see also* Tuberculosis, meninges)
   013.0 ☑
virus NEC 048
Meningoencephalocele 742.0
syphilitic 094.89
   congenital 090.49
Meningoencephalomyelitis (*see also*
   Meningoencephalitis) 323.9
acute NEC 048
   disseminated (postinfectious) 136.9 [323.6]
      postimmunization or postvaccination
         323.5
due to
   actinomycosis 039.8 [320.7]
   torula 117.5 [323.4]
   toxoplasma or toxoplasmosis (acquired)
      130.0
      congenital (active) 771.2 [323.4]
late effect — *see* category 326
Meningoencephalopathy (*see also*
   Meningoencephalomyelitis) 349.9
Meningoencephalopathy (*see also*
   Meningoencephalitis) 348.39
Meningoencephalopoliomyelitis (*see also*
   Poliomyelitis, bulbar) 045.0 ☑
late effect 138
Meningomyelitis (*see also* Meningoencephalitis)
   323.9
blastomycotic NEC (*see also* Blastomycosis)
   116.0 [323.4]
due to
   actinomycosis 039.8 [320.7]
   blastomycosis (*see also* Blastomycosis)
      116.0 [323.4]
   Meningococcus 036.0
   sporotrichosis 117.1 [323.4]
   torula 117.5 [323.4]
late effect — *see* category 326
lethargic 049.8
meningococcal 036.0
syphilitic 094.2
tuberculous (*see also* Tuberculosis, meninges)
   013.0 ☑
Meningomyelocele (*see also* Spina bifida)
   741.9 ☑
syphilitic 094.89
Meningomyeloneuritis — *see*
   Meningoencephalitis
Meningoradiculitis — *see* Meningitis
Meningovascular — *see* condition
Meniscocytosis 282.60
Menkes' syndrome — *see* Syndrome, Menkes'
Menolipsis 626.0
Menometrorrhagia 626.2
Menopause, menopausal (symptoms) (syndrome)
   627.2
arthritis (any site) NEC 716.3 ☑
artificial 627.4
bleeding 627.0

Menopause, menopausal — *continued*
crisis 627.2
depression (*see also* Psychosis, affective)
   296.2 ☑
   agitated 296.2 ☑
      recurrent episode 296.3 ☑
      single episode 296.2 ☑
   psychotic 296.2 ☑
      recurrent episode 296.3 ☑
      single episode 296.2 ☑
   recurrent episode 296.3 ☑
   single episode 296.2 ☑
melancholia (*see also* Psychosis, affective)
   296.2 ☑
   recurrent episode 296.3 ☑
   single episode 296.2 ☑
paranoid state 297.2
paraphrenia 297.2
postsurgical 627.4
premature 256.31
   postirradiation 256.2
   postsurgical 256.2
psychoneurosis 627.2
psychosis NEC 298.8
surgical 627.4
toxic polyarthritis NEC 716.39
Menorrhagia (primary) 626.2
climacteric 627.0
menopausal 627.0
postclimacteric 627.1
postmenopausal 627.1
preclimacteric 627.0
premenopausal 627.0
puberty (menses retained) 626.3
Menorrhalgia 625.3
Menoschesis 626.8
Menostaxis 626.2
Menses, retention 626.8
Menstrual — *see also* Menstruation
cycle, irregular 626.4
disorders NEC 626.9
extraction V25.3
fluid, retained 626.8
molimen 625.4
period, normal V65.5
regulation V25.3
Menstruation
absent 626.0
anovulatory 628.0
delayed 626.8
difficult 625.3
disorder 626.9
   psychogenic 306.52
   specified NEC 626.8
during pregnancy 640.8 ☑
excessive 626.2
frequent 626.2
infrequent 626.1
irregular 626.4
latent 626.8
membranous 626.8
painful (primary) (secondary) 625.3
   psychogenic 306.52
passage of clots 626.2
precocious 626.8
protracted 626.8
retained 626.8
retrograde 626.8
scanty 626.1
suppression 626.8
vicarious (nasal) 625.8
Mentagra (*see also* Sycosis) 704.8
Mental — *see also* condition
deficiency (*see also* Retardation, mental) 319
deterioration (*see also* Psychosis) 298.9
disorder (*see also* Disorder, mental) 300.9
exhaustion 300.5
insufficiency (congenital) (*see also* Retardation,
   mental) 319
observation without need for further medical
   care NEC V71.09
retardation (*see also* Retardation, mental) 319
subnormality (*see also* Retardation, mental)
   319
   mild 317

Mental — *continued*
subnormality — *continued*
   moderate 318.0
   profound 318.2
   severe 318.1
upset (*see also* Disorder, mental) 300.9
Meralgia paresthetica 355.1
Mercurial — *see* condition
Mercurialism NEC 985.0
Merergasia 300.9
Merkel cell tumor — *see* Neoplasm, by site,
   malignant
Merocele (*see also* Hernia, femoral) 553.00
Meromelia 755.4
lower limb 755.30
   intercalary 755.32
      femur 755.34
         tibiofibular (complete) (incomplete)
            755.33
      fibula 755.37
      metatarsal(s) 755.38
      tarsal(s) 755.38
      tibia 755.36
      tibiofibular 755.35
   terminal (complete) (partial) (transverse)
      755.31
   longitudinal 755.32
      metatarsal(s) 755.38
      phalange(s) 755.39
      tarsal(s) 755.38
   transverse 755.31
upper limb 755.20
   intercalary 755.22
      carpal(s) 755.28
      humeral 755.24
         radioulnar (complete) (incomplete)
            755.23
      metacarpal(s) 755.28
      phalange(s) 755.29
      radial 755.26
      radioulnar 755.25
      ulnar 755.27
   terminal (complete) (partial) (transverse)
      755.21
   longitudinal 755.22
      carpal(s) 755.28
      metacarpal(s) 755.28
      phalange(s) 755.29
   transverse 755.21
Merosmia 781.1
MERRF syndrome (myoclonus with epilepsy and
   with ragged red fibers) 277.87
Merycism — *see also* Vomiting
psychogenic 307.53
Merzbacher-Pelizaeus disease 330.0
Mesaortitis — *see* Aortitis
Mesarteritis — *see* Arteritis
Mesencephalitis (*see also* Encephalitis) 323.9
late effect — *see* category 326
Mesenchymoma (M8990/1) — *see also* Neoplasm,
   connective tissue, uncertain behavior
benign (M8990/0) — *see* Neoplasm, connective
   tissue, benign
malignant (M8990/3) — *see* Neoplasm,
   connective tissue, malignant
Mesenteritis   ●
retractile 567.82   ●
sclerosing 567.82   ●
Mesentery, mesenteric — *see* condition
Mesiodens, mesiodentes 520.1
causing crowding 524.31
Mesio-occlusion 524.23
Mesocardia (with asplenia) 746.87
Mesocolon — *see* condition
Mesonephroma (malignant) (M9110/3) — *see also*
   Neoplasm, by site, malignant
benign (M9110/0) — *see* Neoplasm, by site,
   benign
Mesophlebitis — *see* Phlebitis
Mesostromal dysgenesis 743.51

Mesothelioma (malignant) (M9050/3) — *see also* Neoplasm, by site, malignant
  benign (M9050/0) — *see* Neoplasm, by site, benign
  biphasic type (M9053/3) — *see also* Neoplasm, by site, malignant
    benign (M9053/0) — *see* Neoplasm, by site, benign
  epithelioid (M9052/3) — *see also* Neoplasm, by site, malignant
    benign (M9052/0) — *see* Neoplasm, by site, benign
  fibrous (M9051/3) — *see also* Neoplasm, by site, malignant
    benign (M9051/0) — *see* Neoplasm, by site, benign
Metabolic syndrome 277.7
Metabolism disorder 277.9
  specified type NEC 277.89
Metagonimiasis 121.5
Metagonimus infestation (small intestine) 121.5
Metal
  pigmentation (skin) 709.00
  polishers' disease 502
Metalliferous miners' lung 503
Metamorphopsia 368.14
Metaplasia
  bone, in skin 709.3
  breast 611.8
  cervix — *omit code*
  endometrium (squamous) 621.8
  esophagus 530.85
  intestinal, of gastric mucosa 537.89
  kidney (pelvis) (squamous) (*see also* Disease, renal) 593.89
  myelogenous 289.89
  myeloid (agnogenic) (megakaryocytic) 289.89
  spleen 289.59
  squamous cell
    amnion 658.8 ☑
    bladder 596.8
    cervix — *see* condition
    trachea 519.1
    tracheobronchial tree 519.1
    uterus 621.8
      cervix — *see* condition
Metastasis, metastatic
  abscess — *see* Abscess
  calcification 275.40
  cancer, neoplasm, or disease
    from specified site (M8000/3) — *see* Neoplasm, by site, malignant
    to specified site (M8000/6) — *see* Neoplasm, by site, secondary
  deposits (in) (M8000/6) — *see* Neoplasm, by site, secondary
  pneumonia 038.8 *[484.8]*
  spread (to) (M8000/6) — *see* Neoplasm, by site, secondary
Metatarsalgia 726.70
  anterior 355.6
  due to Freiberg's disease 732.5
  Morton's 355.6
Metatarsus, metatarsal — *see also* condition
  abductus valgus (congenital) 754.60
  adductus varus (congenital) 754.53
  primus varus 754.52
  valgus (adductus) (congenital) 754.60
  varus (abductus) (congenital) 754.53
    primus 754.52
Methemoglobinemia 289.7
  acquired (with sulfhemoglobinemia) 289.7
  congenital 289.7
  enzymatic 289.7
  Hb-M disease 289.7
  hereditary 289.7
  toxic 289.7
Methemoglobinuria (*see also* Hemoglobinuria) 791.2
Methicillin-resistant staphylococcus aureus (MRSA) V09.0
Methioninemia 270.4

Metritis (catarrhal) (septic) (suppurative) (*see also* Endometritis) 615.9
  blennorrhagic 098.16
    chronic or duration of 2 months or over 098.36
  cervical (*see also* Cervicitis) 616.0
  gonococcal 098.16
    chronic or duration of 2 months or over 098.36
  hemorrhagic 626.8
  puerperal, postpartum, childbirth 670.0 ☑
  tuberculous (*see also* Tuberculosis) 016.7 ☑
Metropathia hemorrhagica 626.8
Metroperitonitis (*see also* Peritonitis, pelvic, female) 614.5
Metrorrhagia 626.6
  arising during pregnancy — *see* Hemorrhage, pregnancy
  postpartum NEC 666.2 ☑
  primary 626.6
  psychogenic 306.59
  puerperal 666.2 ☑
Metrorrhexis — *see* Rupture, uterus
Metrosalpingitis (*see also* Salpingo-oophoritis) 614.2
Metrostaxis 626.6
Metrovaginitis (*see also* Endometritis) 615.9
  gonococcal (acute) 098.16
    chronic or duration of 2 months or over 098.36
Mexican fever — *see* Typhus, Mexican
Meyenburg-Altherr-Uehlinger syndrome 733.99
Meyer-Schwickerath and Weyers syndrome (dysplasia oculodentodigitalis) 759.89
Meynert's amentia (nonalcoholic) 294.0
  alcoholic 291.1
Mibelli's disease 757.39
Mice, joint (*see also* Loose, body, joint) 718.1 ☑
  knee 717.6
Micheli-Rietti syndrome (thalassemia minor) 282.49
Michotte's syndrome 721.5
Micrencephalon, micrencephaly 742.1
Microalbuminuria 791.0 ●
Microaneurysm, retina 362.14
  diabetic 250.5 ☑ *[362.01]*
Microangiopathy 443.9
  diabetic (peripheral) 250.7 ☑ *[443.81]*
    retinal 250.5 ☑ *[362.01]*
  peripheral 443.9
    diabetic 250.7 ☑ *[443.81]*
  retinal 362.18
    diabetic 250.5 ☑ *[362.01]*
  thrombotic 446.6
    Moschcowitz's (thrombotic thrombocytopenic purpura) 446.6
Microcalcification, mammographic 793.81
Microcephalus, microcephalic, microcephaly 742.1
  due to toxoplasmosis (congenital) 771.2
Microcheilia 744.82
Microcolon (congenital) 751.5
Microcornea (congenital) 743.41
Microcytic — *see* condition
Microdeletions NEC 758.33
Microdontia 520.2
Microdrepanocytosis (thalassemia-Hb-S disease) 282.49
Microembolism
  atherothrombotic — *see* Atheroembolism
  retina 362.33
Microencephalon 742.1
Microfilaria streptocerca infestation 125.3
Microgastria (congenital) 750.7
Microgenia 524.06
Microgenitalia (congenital) 752.89
  penis 752.64
Microglioma (M9710/3)
  specified site — *see* Neoplasm, by site, malignant

Microglioma — *continued*
  unspecified site 191.9
Microglossia (congenital) 750.16
Micrognathia, micrognathism (congenital) 524.00
  mandibular 524.04
    alveolar 524.74
  maxillary 524.03
    alveolar 524.73
Microgyria (congenital) 742.2
Microinfarct, heart (*see also* Insufficiency, coronary) 411.89
Microlithiasis, alveolar, pulmonary 516.2
Micromyelia (congenital) 742.59
Micropenis 752.64
Microphakia (congenital) 743.36
Microphthalmia (congenital) (*see also* Microphthalmos) 743.10
Microphthalmos (congenital) 743.10
  associated with eye and adnexal anomalies NEC 743.12
  due to toxoplasmosis (congenital) 771.2
  isolated 743.11
  simple 743.11
  syndrome 759.89
Micropsia 368.14
Microsporidiosis 136.8
Microsporon furfur infestation 111.0
Microsporosis (*see also* Dermatophytosis) 110.9
  nigra 111.1
Microstomia (congenital) 744.84
Microthelia 757.6
Microthromboembolism — *see* Embolism
Microtia (congenital) (external ear) 744.23
Microtropia 378.34
Micturition
  disorder NEC 788.69
    psychogenic 306.53
  frequency 788.41
    psychogenic 306.53
  nocturnal 788.43
  painful 788.1
    psychogenic 306.53
Middle
  ear — *see* condition
  lobe (right) syndrome 518.0
Midplane — *see* condition
Miescher's disease 709.3
  cheilitis 351.8
  granulomatosis disciformis 709.3
Miescher-Leder syndrome or granulomatosis 709.3
Mieten's syndrome 759.89
Migraine (idiopathic) 346.9 ☑
  with aura 346.0 ☑
  abdominal (syndrome) 346.2 ☑
  allergic (histamine) 346.2 ☑
  atypical 346.1 ☑
  basilar 346.2 ☑
  classical 346.0 ☑
  common 346.1 ☑
  hemiplegic 346.8 ☑
  lower-half 346.2 ☑
  menstrual 625.4
  ophthalmic 346.8 ☑
  ophthalmoplegic 346.8 ☑
  retinal 346.2 ☑
  variant 346.2 ☑
Migrant, social V60.0
Migratory, migrating — *see also* condition
  person V60.0
  testis, congenital 752.52
Mikulicz's disease or syndrome (dryness of mouth, absent or decreased lacrimation) 527.1
Milian atrophia blanche 701.3
Miliaria (crystallina) (rubra) (tropicalis) 705.1
  apocrine 705.82
Miliary — *see* condition
Milium (*see also* Cyst, sebaceous) 706.2
  colloid 709.3

Milium — *continued*
eyelid 374.84
Milk
crust 690.11
excess secretion 676.6 ☑
fever, female 672.0 ☑
poisoning 988.8
retention 676.2 ☑
sickness 988.8
spots 423.1
Milkers' nodes 051.1
Milk-leg (deep vessels) 671.4 ☑
complicating pregnancy 671.3 ☑
nonpuerperal 451.19
puerperal, postpartum, childbirth 671.4 ☑
Milkman (-Looser) disease or syndrome
(osteomalacia with pseudofractures) 268.2
Milky urine (*see also* Chyluria) 791.1
Millar's asthma (laryngismus stridulus) 478.75
Millard-Gubler paralysis or syndrome 344.89
Millard-Gubler-Foville paralysis 344.89
Miller's disease (osteomalacia) 268.2
Miller-Dieker syndrome 758.33
Miller Fisher's syndrome 357.0
Milles' syndrome (encephalocutaneous
angiomatosis) 759.6
Mills' disease 335.29
Millstone makers' asthma or lung 502
Milroy's disease (chronic hereditary edema) 757.0
Miners' — *see also* condition
asthma 500
elbow 727.2
knee 727.2
lung 500
nystagmus 300.89
phthisis (*see also* Tuberculosis) 011.4 ☑
tuberculosis (*see also* Tuberculosis) 011.4 ☑
Minkowski-Chauffard syndrome (*see also*
Spherocytosis) 282.0
Minor — *see* condition
Minor's disease 336.1
Minot's disease (hemorrhagic disease, newborn)
776.0
Minot-von Willebrand (-Jürgens) disease or
syndrome (angiohemophilia) 286.4
Minus (and plus) hand (intrinsic) 736.09
Miosis (persistent) (pupil) 379.42
Mirizzi's syndrome (hepatic duct stenosis) (*see*
also Obstruction, biliary) 576.2
with calculus, cholelithiasis, or stones — *see*
Choledocholithiasis
Mirror writing 315.09
secondary to organic lesion 784.69
Misadventure (prophylactic) (therapeutic) (*see*
also Complications) 999.9
administration of insulin 962.3
infusion — *see* Complications, infusion
local applications (of fomentations, plasters,
etc.) 999.9
burn or scald — *see* Burn, by site
medical care (early) (late) NEC 999.9
adverse effect of drugs or chemicals — *see*
Table of Drugs and Chemicals
burn or scald — *see* Burn, by site
radiation NEC 990
radiotherapy NEC 990
surgical procedure (early) (late) — *see*
Complications, surgical procedure
transfusion — *see* Complications, transfusion
vaccination or other immunological procedure
— *see* Complications, vaccination
Misanthropy 301.7
Miscarriage — *see* Abortion, spontaneous
Mischief, malicious, child (*see also* Disturbance,
conduct) 312.0 ☑
Misdirection
aqueous 365.83
Mismanagement, feeding 783.3
Misplaced, misplacement
kidney (*see also* Disease, renal) 593.0
congenital 753.3

Misplaced, misplacement — *continued*
organ or site, congenital NEC — *see*
Malposition, congenital
Missed
abortion 632
delivery (at or near term) 656.4 ☑
labor (at or near term) 656.4 ☑
Missing — *see also* Absence
teeth (acquired) 525.10
congenital (see also Anodontia) 520.0
due to
caries 525.13
extraction 525.10
periodontal disease 525.12
specified NEC 525.19
trauma 525.11
vertebrae (congenital) 756.13
Misuse of drugs NEC (*see also* Abuse, drug,
nondependent) 305.9 ☑
Mitchell's disease (erythromelalgia) 443.82   ▲
Mite(s)
diarrhea 133.8
grain (itch) 133.8
hair follicle (itch) 133.8
in sputum 133.8
Mitochondrial encephalopathy, lactic acidosis
and stroke-like episodes (MELAS
syndrome) 277.87
Mitochondrial neurogastrointestinal
encephalopathy syndrome (MNGIE) 277.87
Mitral — *see* condition
Mittelschmerz 625.2
Mixed — *see* condition
Mljet disease (mal de Meleda) 757.39
Mobile, mobility
cecum 751.4
coccyx 733.99
excessive — *see* Hypermobility
gallbladder 751.69
kidney 593.0
congenital 753.3
organ or site, congenital NEC — *see*
Malposition, congenital
spleen 289.59
Mobitz heart block (atrioventricular) 426.10
type I (Wenckebach's) 426.13
type II 426.12
Möbius'
disease 346.8 ☑
syndrome
congenital oculofacial paralysis 352.6
ophthalmoplegic migraine 346.8 ☑
Moeller (-Barlow) disease (infantile scurvy) 267
glossitis 529.4
Mohr's syndrome (types I and II) 759.89
Mola destruens (M9100/1) 236.1
Molarization, premolars 520.2
Molar pregnancy 631
hydatidiform (delivered) (undelivered) 630
Mold(s) in vitreous 117.9
Molding, head (during birth) — *omit code*
Mole (pigmented) (M8720/0) — *see also*
Neoplasm, skin, benign
blood 631
Breus' 631
cancerous (M8720/3) — *see* Melanoma
carneous 631
destructive (M9100/1) 236.1
ectopic — *see* Pregnancy, ectopic
fleshy 631
hemorrhagic 631
hydatid, hydatidiform (benign) (complicating
pregnancy) (delivered) (undelivered) (*see*
also Hydatidiform mole) 630
invasive (M9100/1) 236.1
malignant (M9100/1) 236.1
previous, affecting management of
pregnancy V23.1
invasive (hydatidiform) (M9100/1) 236.1

Mole (M8720/0) — *see also* Neoplasm, skin,
benign — *continued*
malignant
meaning
malignant hydatidiform mole (9100/1)
236.1
melanoma (M8720/3) — *see* Melanoma
nonpigmented (M8730/0) — *see* Neoplasm,
skin, benign
pregnancy NEC 631
skin (M8720/0) — *see* Neoplasm, skin, benign
tubal — *see* Pregnancy, tubal
vesicular (*see also* Hydatidiform mole) 630
Molimen, molimina (menstrual) 625.4
Mollaret's meningitis 047.9
Mollities (cerebellar) (cerebral) 437.8
ossium 268.2
Molluscum
contagiosum 078.0
epitheliale 078.0
fibrosum (M8851/0) — *see* Lipoma, by site
pendulum (M8851/0) — *see* Lipoma, by site
Mönckeberg's arteriosclerosis, degeneration,
disease, or sclerosis (*see also*
Arteriosclerosis, extremities) 440.20
Monday fever 504
Monday morning dyspnea or asthma 504
Mondini's malformation (cochlea) 744.05
Mondor's disease (thrombophlebitis of breast)
451.89
Mongolian, mongolianism, mongolism,
mongoloid 758.0
spot 757.33
Monilethrix (congenital) 757.4
Monilia infestation — *see* Candidiasis
Moniliasis — *see also* Candidiasis
neonatal 771.7
vulvovaginitis 112.1
Monkeypox 057.8
Monoarthritis 716.60
ankle 716.67
arm 716.62
lower (and wrist) 716.63
upper (and elbow) 716.62
foot (and ankle) 716.67
forearm (and wrist) 716.63
hand 716.64
leg 716.66
lower 716.66
upper 716.65
pelvic region (hip) (thigh) 716.65
shoulder (region) 716.61
specified site NEC 716.68
Monoblastic — *see* condition
Monochromatism (cone) (rod) 368.54
Monocytic — *see* condition
Monocytosis (symptomatic) 288.8
Monofixation syndrome 378.34
Monomania (*see also* Psychosis) 298.9
Mononeuritis 355.9
cranial nerve — *see* Disorder, nerve, cranial
femoral nerve 355.2
lateral
cutaneous nerve of thigh 355.1
popliteal nerve 355.3
lower limb 355.8
specified nerve NEC 355.79
medial popliteal nerve 355.4
median nerve 354.1
multiplex 354.5
plantar nerve 355.6
posterior tibial nerve 355.5
radial nerve 354.3
sciatic nerve 355.0
ulnar nerve 354.2
upper limb 354.9
specified nerve NEC 354.8
vestibular 388.5
Mononeuropathy (*see also* Mononeuritis) 355.9
diabetic NEC 250.6 ☑ *[355.9]*
lower limb 250.6 ☑ *[355.8]*
upper limb 250.6 ☑ *[354.9]*
iliohypogastric nerve 355.79

Mononeuropathy — *continued*
　ilioinguinal nerve 355.79
　obturator nerve 355.79
　saphenous nerve 355.79
Mononucleosis, infectious 075
　with hepatitis 075 *[573.1]*
Monoplegia 344.5
　brain (current episode) (*see also* Paralysis,
　　brain) 437.8
　　fetus or newborn 767.8
　cerebral (current episode) (*see also* Paralysis,
　　brain) 437.8
　congenital or infantile (cerebral) (spastic)
　　(spinal) 343.3
　embolic (current) (*see also* Embolism, brain)
　　434.1 ☑
　　late effect — *see* Late effect(s) (of)
　　　cerebrovascular disease
　infantile (cerebral) (spastic) (spinal) 343.3
　lower limb 344.30
　　affecting
　　　dominant side 344.31
　　　nondominant side 344.32
　　due to late effect of cerebrovascular accident
　　　— *see* Late effect(s) (of)
　　　cerebrovascular accident
　newborn 767.8
　psychogenic 306.0
　　specified as conversion reaction 300.11
　thrombotic (current) (*see also* Thrombosis,
　　brain) 434.0 ☑
　　late effect — *see* Late effect(s) (of)
　　　cerebrovascular disease
　transient 781.4
　upper limb 344.40
　　affecting
　　　dominant side 344.41
　　　nondominant side 344.42
　　due to late effect of cerebrovascular accident
　　　— *see* Late effect(s) (of)
　　　cerebrovascular accident
Monorchism, monorchidism 752.89
Monteggia's fracture (closed) 813.03
　open 813.13
Mood swings
　brief compensatory 296.99
　rebound 296.99
Moore's syndrome (*see also* Epilepsy) 345.5 ☑
Mooren's ulcer (cornea) 370.07
Mooser-Neill reaction 081.0
Mooser bodies 081.0
Moral
　deficiency 301.7
　imbecility 301.7
Morax-Axenfeld conjunctivitis 372.03
Morbilli (*see also* Measles) 055.9
Morbus
　anglicus, anglorum 268.0
　Beigel 111.2
　caducus (*see also* Epilepsy) 345.9 ☑
　caeruleus 746.89
　celiacus 579.0
　comitialis (see also Epilepsy) 345.9 ☑
　cordis — *see* Disease, heart
　　valvulorum — *see* Endocarditis
　coxae 719.95
　　tuberculous (*see also* Tuberculosis) 015.1 ☑
　hemorrhagicus neonatorum 776.0
　maculosus neonatorum 772.6
　renum 593.0
　senilis (*see also* Osteoarthrosis) 715.9 ☑
Morel-Kraepelin disease (*see also* Schizophrenia)
　295.9 ☑
Morel-Moore syndrome (hyperostosis frontalis
　interna) 733.3
Morel-Morgagni syndrome (hyperostosis frontalis
　interna) 733.3
Morgagni
　cyst, organ, hydatid, or appendage 752.89
　　fallopian tube 752.11
　disease or syndrome (hyperostosis frontalis
　　interna) 733.3

Morgagni-Adams-Stokes syndrome (syncope with
　heart block) 426.9
Morgagni-Stewart-Morel syndrome (hyperostosis
　frontalis interna) 733.3
Moria (*see also* Psychosis) 298.9
Morning sickness 643.0 ☑
Moron 317
Morphea (guttate) (linear) 701.0
Morphine dependence (*see also* Dependence)
　304.0 ☑
Morphinism (*see also* Dependence) 304.0 ☑
Morphinomania (*see also* Dependence) 304.0 ☑
Morphoea 701.0
Morquio (-Brailsford) (-Ullrich) disease or
　syndrome (mucopolysaccharidosis IV) 277.5
　kyphosis 277.5
Morris syndrome (testicular feminization) 259.5 ▲
Morsus humanus (open wound) — *see also*
　Wound, open, by site
　skin surface intact — *see* Contusion
Mortification (dry) (moist) (*see also* Gangrene)
　785.4
Morton's
　disease 355.6
　foot 355.6
　metatarsalgia (syndrome) 355.6
　neuralgia 355.6
　neuroma 355.6
　syndrome (metatarsalgia) (neuralgia) 355.6
　toe 355.6
Morvan's disease 336.0
Mosaicism, mosaic (chromosomal) 758.9
　autosomal 758.5
　sex 758.81
Moschcowitz's syndrome (thrombotic
　thrombocytopenic purpura) 446.6
Mother yaw 102.0
Motion sickness (from travel, any vehicle) (from
　roundabouts or swings) 994.6
Mottled teeth (enamel) (endemic) (nonendemic)
　520.3
Mottling enamel (endemic) (nonendemic) (teeth)
　520.3
Mouchet's disease 732.5
Mould(s) (in vitreous) 117.9
Moulders'
　bronchitis 502
　tuberculosis (*see also* Tuberculosis) 011.4 ☑
Mounier-Kuhn syndrome 748.3　　　　　　　　▲
　with
　　acute exacerbation 494.1　　　　　　　　●
　　bronchiectasis 494.0　　　　　　　　　　●
　　　with (acute) exacerbation 494.1　　　　●
　acquired 519.1　　　　　　　　　　　　　●
　　with bronchiectasis 494.0　　　　　　　●
　　　with (acute) exacerbation 494.1　　　●
Mountain
　fever — *see* Fever, mountain
　sickness 993.2
　　with polycythemia, acquired 289.0
　　acute 289.0
　tick fever 066.1
Mouse, joint (*see also* Loose, body, joint) 718.1 ☑
　knee 717.6
Mouth — *see* condition
Movable
　coccyx 724.71
　kidney (*see also* Disease, renal) 593.0
　　congenital 753.3
　organ or site, congenital NEC — *see*
　　Malposition, congenital
　spleen 289.59
Movement
　abnormal (dystonic) (involuntary) 781.0
　decreased fetal 655.7 ☑
　paradoxical facial 374.43
Moya Moya disease 437.5
Mozart's ear 744.29
MRSA (methicillin-resistant staphylococcus
　aureus) V09.0

Mucha's disease (acute parapsoriasis
　varioliformis) 696.2
Mucha-Haberman syndrome (acute parapsoriasis
　varioliformis) 696.2
Mu-chain disease 273.2
Mucinosis (cutaneous) (papular) 701.8
Mucocele
　appendix 543.9
　buccal cavity 528.9
　gallbladder (*see also* Disease, gallbladder)
　　575.3
　lacrimal sac 375.43
　orbit (eye) 376.81
　salivary gland (any) 527.6
　sinus (accessory) (nasal) 478.1
　turbinate (bone) (middle) (nasal) 478.1
　uterus 621.8
Mucocutaneous lymph node syndrome (acute)
　(febrile) (infantile) 446.1
Mucoenteritis 564.9
Mucolipidosis I, II, III 272.7
Mucopolysaccharidosis (types 1-6) 277.5
　cardiopathy 277.5 *[425.7]*
Mucormycosis (lung) 117.7
Mucositis — *see also* Inflammation, by site
　necroticans agranulocytica 288.0
Mucous — *see also* condition
　patches (syphilitic) 091.3
　　congenital 090.0
Mucoviscidosis 277.00
　with meconium obstruction 277.01
Mucus
　asphyxia or suffocation (*see also* Asphyxia,
　　mucus) 933.1
　　newborn 770.18　　　　　　　　　　　　▲
　in stool 792.1
　plug (*see also* Asphyxia, mucus) 933.1
　　aspiration, of newborn 770.17　　　　　▲
　　tracheobronchial 519.1
　　　newborn 770.18　　　　　　　　　　▲
Muguet 112.0
Mulberry molars 090.5
Mullerian mixed tumor (M8950/3) — *see*
　Neoplasm, by site, malignant
Multicystic kidney 753.19
Multilobed placenta — *see* Placenta, abnormal
Multinodular prostate 600.10
　with urinary retention 600.11
Multiparity V61.5
　affecting
　　fetus or newborn 763.89
　　management of
　　　labor and delivery 659.4 ☑
　　　pregnancy V23.3
　requiring contraceptive management (*see also*
　　Contraception) V25.9
Multipartita placenta — *see* Placenta, abnormal
Multiple, multiplex — *see also* condition
　birth
　　affecting fetus or newborn 761.5
　　healthy liveborn — *see* Newborn, multiple
　digits (congenital) 755.00
　　fingers 755.01
　　toes 755.02
　organ or site NEC — *see* Accessory
　personality 300.14
　renal arteries 747.62
Mumps 072.9
　with complication 072.8
　　specified type NEC 072.79
　encephalitis 072.2
　hepatitis 072.71
　meningitis (aseptic) 072.1
　meningoencephalitis 072.2
　oophoritis 072.79
　orchitis 072.0
　pancreatitis 072.3
　polyneuropathy 072.72
　vaccination, prophylactic (against) V04.6
Mumu (*see also* Infestation, filarial) 125.9
Münchausen syndrome 301.51

Münchmeyer's disease or syndrome (exostosis luxurians) 728.11
Mural — *see* condition
Murmur (cardiac) (heart) (nonorganic) (organic) 785.2
  abdominal 787.5
  aortic (valve) (*see also* Endocarditis, aortic) 424.1
  benign — *omit code*
  cardiorespiratory 785.2
  diastolic — *see* condition
  Flint (*see also* Endocarditis, aortic) 424.1
  functional — *omit code*
  Graham Steell (pulmonic regurgitation) (*see also* Endocarditis, pulmonary) 424.3
  innocent — *omit code*
  insignificant — *omit code*
  midsystolic 785.2
  mitral (valve) — *see* Stenosis, mitral
  physiologic — *see* condition
  presystolic, mitral — *see* Insufficiency, mitral
  pulmonic (valve) (*see also* Endocarditis, pulmonary) 424.3
  Still's (vibratory) — *omit code*
  systolic (valvular) — *see* condition
  tricuspid (valve) — *see* Endocarditis, tricuspid
  undiagnosed 785.2
  valvular — *see* condition
  vibratory — *omit code*
Murri's disease (intermittent hemoglobinuria) 283.2
Muscae volitantes 379.24
Muscle, muscular — *see* condition
Musculoneuralgia 729.1
Mushrooming hip 718.95
Mushroom workers' (pickers') lung 495.5
Mutation
  factor V leiden 289.81
  prothrombin gene 289.81
Mutism (*see also* Aphasia) 784.3
  akinetic 784.3
  deaf (acquired) (congenital) 389.7
  hysterical 300.11
  selective (elective) 313.23   ●
    adjustment reaction 309.83   ●
Myà's disease (congenital dilation, colon) 751.3
Myalgia (intercostal) 729.1
  eosinophilia syndrome 710.5
  epidemic 074.1
    cervical 078.89
  psychogenic 307.89
  traumatic NEC 959.9
Myasthenia 358.00
  cordis — *see* Failure, heart
  gravis 358.00
    with exacerbation (acute) 358.01
    in crisis 358.01
    neonatal 775.2
    pseudoparalytica 358.00
  stomach 536.8
    psychogenic 306.4
  syndrome
    in
      botulism 005.1 *[358.1]*
      diabetes mellitus 250.6 ☑ *[358.1]*
      hypothyroidism (*see also* Hypothyroidism) 244.9 *[358.1]*
      malignant neoplasm NEC 199.1 *[358.1]*
      pernicious anemia 281.0 *[358.1]*
      thyrotoxicosis (*see also* Thyrotoxicosis) 242.9 ☑ *[358.1]*
Myasthenic 728.87
Mycelium infection NEC 117.9
Mycetismus 988.1
Mycetoma (actinomycotic) 039.9
  bone 039.8
    mycotic 117.4
  foot 039.4
    mycotic 117.4
  madurae 039.9
    mycotic 117.4
  maduromycotic 039.9
    mycotic 117.4
  mycotic 117.4

Mycetoma — *continued*
  nocardial 039.9
Mycobacteriosis — *see* Mycobacterium
Mycobacterium, mycobacterial (infection) 031.9
  acid-fast (bacilli) 031.9
  anonymous (*see also* Mycobacterium, atypical) 031.9
  atypical (acid-fast bacilli) 031.9
    cutaneous 031.1
    pulmonary 031.0
      tuberculous (*see also* Tuberculosis, pulmonary) 011.9 ☑
    specified site NEC 031.8
  avium 031.0
    intracellulare complex bacteremia (MAC) 031.2
  balnei 031.1
  Battey 031.0
  cutaneous 031.1
  disseminated 031.2
    avium-intracellulare complex (DMAC) 031.2
  fortuitum 031.0
  intracellulare (battey bacillus) 031.0
  kakerifu 031.8
  kansasii 031.0
  kasongo 031.8
  leprae — *see* Leprosy
  luciflavum 031.0
  marinum 031.1
  pulmonary 031.0
    tuberculous (*see also* Tuberculosis, pulmonary) 011.9 ☑
  scrofulaceum 031.1
  tuberculosis (human, bovine) — *see also* Tuberculosis
    avian type 031.0
  ulcerans 031.1
  xenopi 031.0
Mycosis, mycotic 117.9
  cutaneous NEC 111.9
  ear 111.8 *[380.15]*
  fungoides (M9700/3) 202.1 ☑
  mouth 112.0
  pharynx 117.9
  skin NEC 111.9
  stomatitis 112.0
  systemic NEC 117.9
  tonsil 117.9
  vagina, vaginitis 112.1
Mydriasis (persistent) (pupil) 379.43
Myelatelia 742.59
Myelinoclasis, perivascular, acute (postinfectious) NEC 136.9 *[323.6]*
  postimmunization or postvaccinal 323.5
Myelinosis, central pontine 341.8
Myelitis (acute) (ascending) (cerebellar) (childhood) (chronic) (descending) (diffuse) (disseminated) (pressure) (progressive) (spinal cord) (subacute) (transverse) (*see also* Encephalitis) 323.9
  late effect — *see* category 326
  optic neuritis in 341.0
  postchickenpox 052.7
  postvaccinal 323.5
  syphilitic (transverse) 094.89
  tuberculous (*see also* Tuberculosis) 013.6 ☑
  virus 049.9
Myeloblastic — *see* condition
Myelocele (*see also* Spina bifida) 741.9 ☑
  with hydrocephalus 741.0 ☑
Myelocystocele (*see also* Spina bifida) 741.9 ☑
Myelocytic — *see* condition
Myelocytoma 205.1 ☑
Myelodysplasia (spinal cord) 742.59
  meaning myelodysplastic syndrome — *see* Syndrome, myelodysplastic
Myeloencephalitis — *see* Encephalitis
Myelofibrosis (osteosclerosis) 289.89
Myelogenous — *see* condition
Myeloid — *see* condition
Myelokathexis 288.0
Myeloleukodystrophy 330.0

Myelolipoma (M8870/0) — *see* Neoplasm, by site, benign
Myeloma (multiple) (plasma cell) (plasmacytic) (M9730/3) 203.0 ☑
  monostotic (M9731/1) 238.6
  solitary (M9731/1) 238.6
Myelomalacia 336.8
Myelomata, multiple (M9730/3) 203.0 ☑
Myelomatosis (M9730/3) 203.0 ☑
Myelomeningitis — *see* Meningoencephalitis
Myelomeningocele (spinal cord) (*see also* Spina bifida) 741.9 ☑
  fetal, causing fetopelvic disproportion 653.7 ☑
Myelo-osteo-musculodysplasia hereditaria 756.89
Myelopathic — *see* condition
Myelopathy (spinal cord) 336.9
  cervical 721.1
  diabetic 250.6 ☑ *[336.3]*
  drug-induced 336.8
  due to or with
    carbon tetrachloride 987.8 *[323.7]*
    degeneration or displacement, intervertebral disc 722.70
      cervical, cervicothoracic 722.71
      lumbar, lumbosacral 722.73
      thoracic, thoracolumbar 722.72
    hydroxyquinoline derivatives 961.3 *[323.7]*
    infection — *see* Encephalitis
    intervertebral disc disorder 722.70
      cervical, cervicothoracic 722.71
      lumbar, lumbosacral 722.73
      thoracic, thoracolumbar 722.72
    lead 984.9 *[323.7]*
    mercury 985.0 *[323.7]*
    neoplastic disease (*see also* Neoplasm, by site) 239.9 *[336.3]*
    pernicious anemia 281.0 *[336.3]*
    spondylosis 721.91
      cervical 721.1
      lumbar, lumbosacral 721.42
      thoracic 721.41
    thallium 985.8 *[323.7]*
  lumbar, lumbosacral 721.42
  necrotic (subacute) 336.1
  radiation-induced 336.8
  spondylogenic NEC 721.91
    cervical 721.1
    lumbar, lumbosacral 721.42
    thoracic 721.41
  toxic NEC 989.9 *[323.7]*
  transverse (*see also* Encephalitis) 323.9
  vascular 336.1
Myeloproliferative disease (M9960/1) 238.7
Myeloradiculitis (*see also* Polyneuropathy) 357.0
Myeloradiculodysplasia (spinal) 742.59
Myelosarcoma (M9930/3) 205.3 ☑
Myelosclerosis 289.89
  with myeloid metaplasia (M9961/1) 238.7
  disseminated, of nervous system 340
  megakaryocytic (M9961/1) 238.7
Myelosis (M9860/3) (*see also* Leukemia, myeloid) 205.9 ☑
  acute (M9861/3) 205.0 ☑
  aleukemic (M9864/3) 205.8 ☑
  chronic (M9863/3) 205.1 ☑
  erythremic (M9840/3) 207.0 ☑
    acute (M9841/3) 207.0 ☑
  megakaryocytic (M9920/3) 207.2 ☑
  nonleukemic (chronic) 288.8
  subacute (M9862/3) 205.2 ☑
Myesthenia — *see* Myasthenia
Myiasis (cavernous) 134.0
  orbit 134.0 *[376.13]*
Myoadenoma, prostate 600.20
  with urinary retention 600.21

Myoblastoma
  granular cell (M9580/0) — *see also* Neoplasm, connective tissue, benign
    malignant (M9580/3) — *see* Neoplasm, connective tissue, malignant
  tongue (M9580/0) 210.1
Myocardial — *see* condition
Myocardiopathy (congestive) (constrictive) (familial) (hypertrophic nonobstructive) (idiopathic) (infiltrative) (obstructive) (primary) (restrictive) (sporadic) 425.4
  alcoholic 425.5
  amyloid 277.3 *[425.7]*
  beriberi 265.0 *[425.7]*
  cobalt-beer 425.5
  due to
    amyloidosis 277.3 *[425.7]*
    beriberi 265.0 *[425.7]*
    cardiac glycogenosis 271.0 *[425.7]*
    Chagas' disease 086.0
    Friedreich's ataxia 334.0 *[425.8]*
    influenza 487.8 *[425.8]*
    mucopolysaccharidosis 277.5 *[425.7]*
    myotonia atrophica 359.2 *[425.8]*
    progressive muscular dystrophy 359.1 *[425.8]*
    sarcoidosis 135 *[425.8]*
  glycogen storage 271.0 *[425.7]*
  hypertrophic obstructive 425.1
  metabolic NEC 277.9 *[425.7]*
  nutritional 269.9 *[425.7]*
  obscure (African) 425.2
  peripartum 674.5 ☑
  postpartum 674.5 ☑
  secondary 425.9
  thyrotoxic (*see also* Thyrotoxicosis) 242.9 ☑ *[425.7]*
  toxic NEC 425.9
Myocarditis (fibroid) (interstitial) (old) (progressive) (senile) (with arteriosclerosis) 429.0
  with
    rheumatic fever (conditions classifiable to 390) 398.0
      active (*see also* Myocarditis, acute, rheumatic) 391.2
      inactive or quiescent (with chorea) 398.0
  active (nonrheumatic) 422.90
    rheumatic 391.2
      with chorea (acute) (rheumatic) (Sydenham's) 392.0
  acute or subacute (interstitial) 422.90
    due to Streptococcus (beta-hemolytic) 391.2
    idiopathic 422.91
    rheumatic 391.2
      with chorea (acute) (rheumatic) (Sydenham's) 392.0
    specified type NEC 422.99
  aseptic of newborn 074.23
  bacterial (acute) 422.92
  chagasic 086.0
  chronic (interstitial) 429.0
  congenital 746.89
  constrictive 425.4
  Coxsackie (virus) 074.23
  diphtheritic 032.82
  due to or in
    Coxsackie (virus) 074.23
    diphtheria 032.82
    epidemic louse-borne typhus 080 *[422.0]*
    influenza 487.8 *[422.0]*
    Lyme disease 088.81 *[422.0]*
    scarlet fever 034.1 *[422.0]*
    toxoplasmosis (acquired) 130.3
    tuberculosis (*see also* Tuberculosis) 017.9 ☑ *[422.0]*
    typhoid 002.0 *[422.0]*
    typhus NEC 081.9 *[422.0]*
  eosinophilic 422.91
  epidemic of newborn 074.23
  Fiedler's (acute) (isolated) (subacute) 422.91
  giant cell (acute) (subacute) 422.91
  gonococcal 098.85
  granulomatous (idiopathic) (isolated) (nonspecific) 422.91

Myocarditis — *continued*
  hypertensive (*see also* Hypertension, heart) 402.90
  idiopathic 422.91
    granulomatous 422.91
  infective 422.92
  influenzal 487.8 *[422.0]*
  isolated (diffuse) (granulomatous) 422.91
  malignant 422.99
  meningococcal 036.43
  nonrheumatic, active 422.90
  parenchymatous 422.90
  pneumococcal (acute) (subacute) 422.92
  rheumatic (chronic) (inactive) (with chorea) 398.0
    active or acute 391.2
      with chorea (acute) (rheumatic) (Sydenham's) 392.0
  septic 422.92
  specific (giant cell) (productive) 422.91
  staphylococcal (acute) (subacute) 422.92
  suppurative 422.92
  syphilitic (chronic) 093.82
  toxic 422.93
    rheumatic (*see also* Myocarditis, acute rheumatic) 391.2
  tuberculous (*see also* Tuberculosis) 017.9 ☑ *[422.0]*
  typhoid 002.0 *[422.0]*
  valvular — *see* Endocarditis
  viral, except Coxsackie 422.91
    Coxsackie 074.23
    of newborn (Coxsackie) 074.23
Myocardium, myocardial — *see* condition
Myocardosis (*see also* Cardiomyopathy) 425.4
Myoclonia (essential) 333.2
  epileptica 333.2
  Friedrich's 333.2
  massive 333.2
Myoclonic
  epilepsy, familial (progressive) 333.2
  jerks 333.2
Myoclonus (familial essential) (multifocal) (simplex) 333.2
  with epilepsy and with ragged red fibers (MERRF syndrome) 277.87
  facial 351.8
  massive (infantile) 333.2
  pharyngeal 478.29
Myodiastasis 728.84
Myoendocarditis — *see also* Endocarditis
  acute or subacute 421.9
Myoepithelioma (M8982/0) — *see* Neoplasm, by site, benign
Myofascitis (acute) 729.1
  low back 724.2
Myofibroma (M8890/0) — *see also* Neoplasm, connective tissue, benign
  uterus (cervix) (corpus) (*see also* Leiomyoma) 218.9
Myofibrosis 728.2
  heart (*see also* Myocarditis) 429.0
  humeroscapular region 726.2
  scapulohumeral 726.2
Myofibrositis (*see also* Myositis) 729.1
  scapulohumeral 726.2
Myogelosis (occupational) 728.89
Myoglobinuria 791.3
Myoglobulinuria, primary 791.3
Myokymia — *see also* Myoclonus
  facial 351.8
Myolipoma (M8860/0)
  specified site — *see* Neoplasm, connective tissue, benign
  unspecified site 223.0
Myoma (M8895/0) — *see also* Neoplasm, connective tissue, benign
  cervix (stump) (uterus) (*see also* Leiomyoma) 218.9
  malignant (M8895/3) — *see* Neoplasm, connective tissue, malignant
  prostate 600.20
    with urinary retention 600.21

Myoma — *continued*
  uterus (cervix) (corpus) (*see also* Leiomyoma) 218.9
    in pregnancy or childbirth 654.1 ☑
      affecting fetus or newborn 763.89
      causing obstructed labor 660.2 ☑
        affecting fetus or newborn 763.1
Myomalacia 728.9
  cordis, heart (*see also* Degeneration, myocardial) 429.1
Myometritis (*see also* Endometritis) 615.9
Myometrium — *see* condition
Myonecrosis, clostridial 040.0
Myopathy 359.9
  alcoholic 359.4
  amyloid 277.3 *[359.6]*
  benign congenital 359.0
  central core 359.0
  centronuclear 359.0
  congenital (benign) 359.0
  critical illness 359.81
  distal 359.1
  due to drugs 359.4
  endocrine 259.9 *[359.5]*
    specified type NEC 259.8 *[359.5]*
  extraocular muscles 376.82
  facioscapulohumeral 359.1
  in
    Addison's disease 255.4 *[359.5]*
    amyloidosis 277.3 *[359.6]*
    cretinism 243 *[359.5]*
    Cushing's syndrome 255.0 *[359.5]*
    disseminated lupus erythematosus 710.0 *[359.6]*
    giant cell arteritis 446.5 *[359.6]*
    hyperadrenocorticism NEC 255.3 *[359.5]*
    hyperparathyroidism 252.01 *[359.5]*
    hypopituitarism 253.2 *[359.5]*
    hypothyroidism (*see also* Hypothyroidism) 244.9 *[359.5]*
    malignant neoplasm NEC (M8000/3) 199.1 *[359.6]*
    myxedema (*see also* Myxedema) 244.9 *[359.5]*
    polyarteritis nodosa 446.0 *[359.6]*
    rheumatoid arthritis 714.0 *[359.6]*
    sarcoidosis 135 *[359.6]*
    scleroderma 710.1 *[359.6]*
    Sjögren's disease 710.2 *[359.6]*
    thyrotoxicosis (*see also* Thyrotoxicosis) 242.9 ☑ *[359.5]*
  inflammatory 359.89
  intensive care (ICU) 359.81
  limb-girdle 359.1
  myotubular 359.0
  necrotizing, acute 359.81
  nemaline 359.0
  ocular 359.1
  oculopharyngeal 359.1
  of critical illness 359.81
  primary 359.89
  progressive NEC 359.89
  quadriplegic, acute 359.81
  rod body 359.0
  scapulohumeral 359.1
  specified type NEC 359.89
  toxic 359.4
Myopericarditis (*see also* Pericarditis) 423.9
Myopia (axial) (congenital) (increased curvature or refraction, nucleus of lens) 367.1
  degenerative, malignant 360.21
    malignant 360.21
  progressive high (degenerative) 360.21
Myosarcoma (M8895/3) — *see* Neoplasm, connective tissue, malignant
Myosis (persistent) 379.42
  stromal (endolymphatic) (M8931/1) 236.0
Myositis 729.1
  clostridial 040.0
  due to posture 729.1
  epidemic 074.1
  fibrosa or fibrous (chronic) 728.2
    Volkmann's (complicating trauma) 958.6
  infective 728.0
  interstitial 728.81

Myositis — *continued*
multiple — *see* Polymyositis
occupational 729.1
orbital, chronic 376.12
ossificans 728.12
circumscribed 728.12
progressive 728.11
traumatic 728.12
progressive fibrosing 728.11
purulent 728.0
rheumatic 729.1
rheumatoid 729.1
suppurative 728.0
syphilitic 095.6
traumatic (old) 729.1
Myospasia impulsiva 307.23
Myotonia (acquisita) (intermittens) 728.85
atrophica 359.2
congenita 359.2
dystrophica 359.2
Myotonic pupil 379.46
Myriapodiasis 134.1
Myringitis
with otitis media — *see* Otitis media
acute 384.00
specified type NEC 384.09
bullosa hemorrhagica 384.01
bullous 384.01
chronic 384.1
Mysophobia 300.29
Mytilotoxism 988.0
Myxadenitis labialis 528.5
Myxedema (adult) (idiocy) (infantile) (juvenile)
(thyroid gland) (*see also* Hypothyroidism)
244.9
circumscribed 242.9 ☑
congenital 243
cutis 701.8
localized (pretibial) 242.9 ☑
madness (acute) 293.0
subacute 293.1
papular 701.8
pituitary 244.8
postpartum 674.8 ☑
pretibial 242.9 ☑
primary 244.9
Myxochondrosarcoma (M9220/3) — *see*
Neoplasm, cartilage, malignant
Myxofibroma (M8811/0) — *see also* Neoplasm,
connective tissue, benign
odontogenic (M9320/0) 213.1
upper jaw (bone) 213.0
Myxofibrosarcoma (M8811/3) — *see* Neoplasm,
connective tissue, malignant
Myxolipoma (M8852/0) (*see also* Lipoma, by site)
214.9
Myxoliposarcoma (M8852/3) — *see* Neoplasm,
connective tissue, malignant
Myxoma (M8840/0) — *see also* Neoplasm,
connective tissue, benign
odontogenic (M9320/0) 213.1
upper jaw (bone) 213.0
Myxosarcoma (M8840/3) — *see* Neoplasm,
connective tissue, malignant

N

Naegeli's
disease (hereditary hemorrhagic
thrombasthenia) 287.1
leukemia, monocytic (M9863/3) 205.1 ☑
syndrome (incontinentia pigmenti) 757.33
Naffziger's syndrome 353.0
Naga sore (*see also* Ulcer, skin) 707.9
Nägele's pelvis 738.6
with disproportion (fetopelvic) 653.0 ☑
affecting fetus or newborn 763.1
causing obstructed labor 660.1 ☑
affecting fetus or newborn 763.1
Nager-de Reynier syndrome (dysostosis
mandibularis) 756.0

Nail — *see also* condition
biting 307.9
patella syndrome (hereditary
osteoonychodysplasia) 756.89
Nanism, nanosomia (*see also* Dwarfism) 259.4
hypophyseal 253.3
pituitary 253.3
renis, renalis 588.0
Nanukayami 100.89
Napkin rash 691.0
Narcissism 301.81
Narcolepsy 347.00
with cataplexy 347.01
in conditions classified elsewhere 347.10
with cataplexy 347.11
Narcosis
carbon dioxide (respiratory) 786.09
due to drug
correct substance properly administered
780.09
overdose or wrong substance given or taken
977.9
specified drug — *see* Table of Drugs and
Chemicals
Narcotism (chronic) (*see also* Dependence)
304.9 ☑
acute
correct substance properly administered
349.82
overdose or wrong substance given or taken
967.8
specified drug — *see* Table of Drugs and
Chemicals
NARP (ataxia and retinitis pigmentosa) 277.87
Narrow
anterior chamber angle 365.02
pelvis (inlet) (outlet) — *see* Contraction, pelvis
Narrowing
artery NEC 447.1
auditory, internal 433.8 ☑
basilar 433.0 ☑
with other precerebral artery 433.3 ☑
bilateral 433.3 ☑
carotid 433.1 ☑
with other precerebral artery 433.3 ☑
bilateral 433.3 ☑
cerebellar 433.8 ☑
choroidal 433.8 ☑
communicating posterior 433.8 ☑
coronary — *see also* Arteriosclerosis,
coronary
congenital 746.85
due to syphilis 090.5
hypophyseal 433.8 ☑
pontine 433.8 ☑
precerebral NEC 433.9 ☑
multiple or bilateral 433.3 ☑
specified NEC 433.8 ☑
vertebral 433.2 ☑
with other precerebral artery 433.3 ☑
bilateral 433.3 ☑
auditory canal (external) (*see also* Stricture, ear
canal, acquired) 380.50
cerebral arteries 437.0
cicatricial — *see* Cicatrix
congenital — *see* Anomaly, congenital
coronary artery — *see* Narrowing, artery,
coronary
ear, middle 385.22
Eustachian tube (*see also* Obstruction,
Eustachian tube) 381.60
eyelid 374.46
congenital 743.62
intervertebral disc or space NEC — *see*
Degeneration, intervertebral disc
joint space, hip 719.85
larynx 478.74
lids 374.46
congenital 743.62
mesenteric artery (with gangrene) 557.0
palate 524.89
palpebral fissure 374.46
retinal artery 362.13
ureter 593.3
urethra (*see also* Stricture, urethra) 598.9

Narrowness, abnormal, eyelid 743.62
Nasal — *see* condition
Nasolacrimal — *see* condition
Nasopharyngeal — *see also* condition
bursa 478.29
pituitary gland 759.2
torticollis 723.5
Nasopharyngitis (acute) (infective) (subacute) 460
chronic 472.2
due to external agent — *see* Condition,
respiratory, chronic, due to
due to external agent — *see* Condition,
respiratory, due to
septic 034.0
streptococcal 034.0
suppurative (chronic) 472.2
ulcerative (chronic) 472.2
Nasopharynx, nasopharyngeal — *see* condition
Natal tooth, teeth 520.6
Nausea (*see also* Vomiting) 787.02
with vomiting 787.01
epidemic 078.82
Nausea (*see also* Vomiting)
gravidarum — *see* Hyperemesis, gravidarum
marina 994.6
Navel — *see* condition
Neapolitan fever (*see also* Brucellosis) 023.9
Nearsightedness 367.1
Near-syncope 780.2
Nebécourt's syndrome 253.3
Nebula, cornea (eye) 371.01
congenital 743.43
interfering with vision 743.42
Necator americanus infestation 126.1
Necatoriasis 126.1
Neck — *see* condition
Necrencephalus (*see also* Softening, brain) 437.8
Necrobacillosis 040.3
Necrobiosis 799.89
brain or cerebral (*see also* Softening, brain)
437.8
lipoidica 709.3
diabeticorum 250.8 ☑ [709.3]
Necrodermolysis 695.1
Necrolysis, toxic epidermal 695.1
due to drug
correct substance properly administered
695.1
overdose or wrong substance given or taken
977.9
specified drug — *see* Table of Drugs and
Chemicals
Necrophilia 302.89
Necrosis, necrotic
adrenal (capsule) (gland) 255.8
antrum, nasal sinus 478.1
aorta (hyaline) (*see also* Aneurysm, aorta)
441.9
cystic medial 441.00
abdominal 441.02
thoracic 441.01
thoracoabdominal 441.03
ruptured 441.5
arteritis 446.0
artery 447.5
aseptic, bone 733.40
femur (head) (neck) 733.42
medial condyle 733.43
humoral head 733.41
medial femoral condyle 733.43
specific site NEC 733.49
talus 733.44
avascular, bone NEC (*see also* Necrosis,
aseptic, bone) 733.40
bladder (aseptic) (sphincter) 596.8
bone (*see also* Osteomyelitis) 730.1 ☑
acute 730.0 ☑
aseptic or avascular 733.40
femur (head) (neck) 733.42
medial condyle 733.43
humoral head 733.41
medial femoral condyle 733.43

Necrosis, necrotic — *continued*
   bone — *continued*
      aseptic or avascular — *continued*
         specified site NEC 733.49
            talus 733.44
      ethmoid 478.1
      ischemic 733.40
      jaw 526.4
      marrow 289.89
      Paget's (osteitis deformans) 731.0
      tuberculous — *see* Tuberculosis, bone
   brain (softening) (*see also* Softening, brain)
      437.8
   breast (aseptic) (fat) (segmental) 611.3
   bronchus, bronchi 519.1
   central nervous system NEC (*see also*
      Softening, brain) 437.8
   cerebellar (*see also* Softening, brain) 437.8
   cerebral (softening) (*see also* Softening, brain)
      437.8
   cerebrospinal (softening) (*see also* Softening,
      brain) 437.8
   cornea (*see also* Keratitis) 371.40
   cortical, kidney 583.6
   cystic medial (aorta) 441.00
      abdominal 441.02
      thoracic 441.01
      thoracoabdominal 441.03
   dental 521.09
      pulp 522.1
   due to swallowing corrosive substance — *see*
      Burn, by site
   ear (ossicle) 385.24
   esophagus 530.89
   ethmoid (bone) 478.1
   eyelid 374.50
   fat, fatty (generalized) (*see also* Degeneration,
      fatty) 272.8
      abdominal wall 567.82   ▲
      breast (aseptic) (segmental) 611.3
      intestine 569.89
      localized — *see* Degeneration, by site, fatty
      mesentery 567.82   ▲
      omentum 567.82   ▲
      pancreas 577.8
      peritoneum 567.82   ▲
      skin (subcutaneous) 709.3
         newborn 778.1
   femur (aseptic) (avascular) 733.42
      head 733.42
      medial condyle 733.43
      neck 733.42
   gallbladder (*see also* Cholecystitis, acute) 575.0
   gangrenous 785.4
   gastric 537.89
   glottis 478.79
   heart (myocardium) — *see* Infarct, myocardium
   hepatic (*see also* Necrosis, liver) 570
   hip (aseptic) (avascular) 733.42
   intestine (acute) (hemorrhagic) (massive) 557.0
   ischemic 785.4
   jaw 526.4
   kidney (bilateral) 583.9
      acute 584.9
      cortical 583.6
         acute 584.6
            with
               abortion — *see* Abortion, by type,
                  with renal failure
               ectopic pregnancy (*see also*
                  categories 633.0-633.9) 639.3
               molar pregnancy (*see also*
                  categories 630-632) 639.3
            complicating pregnancy 646.2 ☑
               affecting fetus or newborn 760.1
            following labor and delivery 669.3 ☑
      medullary (papillary) (*see also* Pyelitis)
         590.80
         in
            acute renal failure 584.7
            nephritis, nephropathy 583.7
      papillary (*see also* Pyelitis) 590.80
         in
            acute renal failure 584.7
            nephritis, nephropathy 583.7

Necrosis, necrotic — *continued*
   kidney — *continued*
      tubular 584.5
         with
            abortion — *see* Abortion, by type, with
               renal failure
            ectopic pregnancy (*see also* categories
               633.0-633.9) 639.3
            molar pregnancy (*see also* categories
               630-632) 639.3
         complicating
            abortion 639.3
            ectopic or molar pregnancy 639.3
            pregnancy 646.2 ☑
               affecting fetus or newborn 760.1
         following labor and delivery 669.3 ☑
         traumatic 958.5
   larynx 478.79
   liver (acute) (congenital) (diffuse) (massive)
      (subacute) 570
      with
         abortion — *see* Abortion, by type, with
            specified complication NEC
         ectopic pregnancy (*see also* categories
            633.0-633.9) 639.8
         molar pregnancy (*see also* categories 630-
            632) 639.8
      complicating pregnancy 646.7 ☑
         affecting fetus or newborn 760.8
      following
         abortion 639.8
         ectopic or molar pregnancy 639.8
      obstetrical 646.7 ☑
      postabortal 639.8
      puerperal, postpartum 674.8 ☑
      toxic 573.3
   lung 513.0
   lymphatic gland 683
   mammary gland 611.3
   mastoid (chronic) 383.1
   mesentery 567.0
      fat 567.82   ▲
   mitral valve — *see* Insufficiency, mitral
   myocardium, myocardial — *see* Infarct,
      myocardium
   nose (septum) 478.1
   omentum 557.0
      with mesenteric infarction 557.0
      fat 567.82   ▲
   orbit, orbital 376.10
   ossicles, ear (aseptic) 385.24
   ovary (*see also* Salpingo-oophoritis) 614.2
   pancreas (aseptic) (duct) (fat) 577.8
      acute 577.0
      infective 577.0
   papillary, kidney (*see also* Pyelitis) 590.80
   peritoneum 557.0
      with mesenteric infarction 557.0
      fat 567.82   ▲
   pharynx 462
      in granulocytopenia 288.0
   phosphorus 983.9
   pituitary (gland) (postpartum) (Sheehan) 253.2
   placenta (*see also* Placenta, abnormal) 656.7 ☑
   pneumonia 513.0
   pulmonary 513.0
   pulp (dental) 522.1
   pylorus 537.89
   radiation — *see* Necrosis, by site
   radium — *see* Necrosis, by site
   renal — *see* Necrosis, kidney
   sclera 379.19
   scrotum 608.89
   skin or subcutaneous tissue 709.8
      due to burn — see Burn, by site
      gangrenous 785.4
   spine, spinal (column) 730.18
      acute 730.18
      cord 336.1
   spleen 289.59
   stomach 537.89
   stomatitis 528.1
   subcutaneous fat 709.3
      fetus or newborn 778.1
   subendocardial — *see* Infarct, myocardium
   suprarenal (capsule) (gland) 255.8
   teeth, tooth 521.09

Necrosis, necrotic — *continued*
   testis 608.89
   thymus (gland) 254.8
   tonsil 474.8
   trachea 519.1
   tuberculous NEC — *see* Tuberculosis
   tubular (acute) (anoxic) (toxic) 584.5
      due to a procedure 997.5
   umbilical cord, affecting fetus or newborn
      762.6
   vagina 623.8
   vertebra (lumbar) 730.18
      acute 730.18
      tuberculous (*see also* Tuberculosis)
         015.0 ☑ *[730.8]* ☑
   vesical (aseptic) (bladder) 596.8
   x-ray — *see* Necrosis, by site
Necrospermia 606.0
Necrotizing angiitis 446.0
Negativism 301.7
Neglect (child) (newborn) NEC 995.52
   adult 995.84
   after or at birth 995.52
   hemispatial 781.8
   left-sided 781.8
   sensory 781.8
   visuospatial 781.8
Negri bodies 071
Neill-Dingwall syndrome (microcephaly and
   dwarfism) 759.89
Neisserian infection NEC — *see* Gonococcus
Nematodiasis NEC (*see also* Infestation,
   Nematode) 127.9
   ancylostoma (*see also* Ancylostomiasis) 126.9
Neoformans cryptococcus infection 117.5
Neonatal — *see also* condition
   adrenoleukodystrophy 277.86
   teeth, tooth 520.6
Neonatorum — *see* condition

	Malignant					
	Primary	Secondary	Ca in situ	Benign	Uncertain Behavior	Unspecified
Neoplasm, neoplastic	199.1	199.1	234.9	229.9	238.9	239.9

Notes — 1. The list below gives the code numbers for neoplasms by anatomical site. For each site there are six possible code numbers according to whether the neoplasm in question is malignant, benign, in situ, of uncertain behavior, or of unspecified nature. The description of the neoplasm will often indicate which of the six columns is appropriate; e.g., malignant melanoma of skin, benign fibroadenoma of breast, carcinoma in situ of cervix uteri.

Where such descriptors are not present, the remainder of the Index should be consulted where guidance is given to the appropriate column for each morphological (histological) variety listed; e.g., Mesonephroma — see Neoplasm, malignant; Embryoma — see also Neoplasm, uncertain behavior; Disease, Bowen's — see Neoplasm, skin, in situ. However, the guidance in the Index can be overridden if one of the descriptors mentioned above is present; e.g., malignant adenoma of colon is coded to 153.9 and not to 211.3 as the adjective "malignant" overrides the Index entry "Adenoma — see also Neoplasm, benign."

2. Sites marked with the sign * (e.g., face NEC*) should be classified to malignant neoplasm of skin of these sites if the variety of neoplasm is a squamous cell carcinoma or an epidermoid carcinoma, and to benign neoplasm of skin of these sites if the variety of neoplasm is a papilloma (any type).

	Primary	Secondary	Ca in situ	Benign	Uncertain Behavior	Unspecified
abdomen, abdominal	195.2	198.89	234.8	229.8	238.8	239.8
cavity	195.2	198.89	234.8	229.8	238.8	239.8
organ	195.2	198.89	234.8	229.8	238.8	239.8
viscera	195.2	198.89	234.8	229.8	238.8	239.8
wall	173.5	198.2	232.5	216.5	238.2	239.2
connective tissue	171.5	198.89	—	215.5	238.1	239.2
abdominopelvic	195.8	198.89	234.8	229.8	238.8	239.8
accessory sinus — see Neoplasm, sinus						
acoustic nerve	192.0	198.4	—	225.1	237.9	239.7
acromion (process)	170.4	198.5	—	213.4	238.0	239.2
adenoid (pharynx) (tissue)	147.1	198.89	230.0	210.7	235.1	239.0
adipose tissue (see also Neoplasm, connective tissue)	171.9	198.89	—	215.9	238.1	239.2
adnexa (uterine)	183.9	198.82	233.3	221.8	236.3	239.5
adrenal (cortex) (gland) (medulla)	194.0	198.7	234.8	227.0	237.2	239.7
ala nasi (external)	173.3	198.2	232.3	216.3	238.2	239.2
alimentary canal or tract NEC	159.9	197.8	230.9	211.9	235.5	239.0
alveolar	143.9	198.89	230.0	210.4	235.1	239.0
mucosa	143.9	198.89	230.0	210.4	235.1	239.0
lower	143.1	198.89	230.0	210.4	235.1	239.0
upper	143.0	198.89	230.0	210.4	235.1	239.0
ridge or process	170.1	198.5	—	213.1	238.0	239.2
carcinoma	143.9	—	—	—	—	—
lower	143.1	—	—	—	—	—
upper	143.0	—	—	—	—	—
lower	170.1	198.5	—	213.1	238.0	239.2
mucosa	143.9	198.89	230.0	210.4	235.1	239.0
lower	143.1	198.89	230.0	210.4	235.1	239.0
upper	143.0	198.89	230.0	210.4	235.1	239.0
upper	170.0	198.5	—	213.0	238.0	239.2
sulcus	145.1	198.89	230.0	210.4	235.1	239.0
alveolus	143.9	198.89	230.0	210.4	235.1	239.0
lower	143.1	198.89	230.0	210.4	235.1	239.0
upper	143.0	198.89	230.0	210.4	235.1	239.0
ampulla of Vater	156.2	197.8	230.8	211.5	235.3	239.0
ankle NEC*	195.5	198.89	232.7	229.8	238.8	239.8
anorectum, anorectal (junction)	154.8	197.5	230.7	211.4	235.2	239.0
antecubital fossa or space*	195.4	198.89	232.6	229.8	238.8	239.8
antrum (Highmore) (maxillary)	160.2	197.3	231.8	212.0	235.9	239.1
pyloric	151.2	197.8	230.2	211.1	235.2	239.0
tympanicum	160.1	197.3	231.8	212.0	235.9	239.1
anus, anal	154.3	197.5	230.6	211.4	235.5	239.0
canal	154.2	197.5	230.5	211.4	235.5	239.0
contiguous sites with rectosigmoid junction or rectum	154.8	—	—	—	—	—
margin	173.5	198.2	232.5	216.5	238.2	239.2
skin	173.5	198.2	232.5	216.5	238.2	239.2
sphincter	154.2	197.5	230.5	211.4	235.5	239.0
aorta (thoracic)	171.4	198.89	—	215.4	238.1	239.2
abdominal	171.5	198.89	—	215.5	238.1	239.2

Neoplasm, neoplastic — continued	Primary	Secondary	Ca in situ	Benign	Uncertain Behavior	Unspecified
aortic body	194.6	198.89	—	227.6	237.3	239.7
aponeurosis	171.9	198.89	—	215.9	238.1	239.2
palmar	171.2	198.89	—	215.2	238.1	239.2
plantar	171.3	198.89	—	215.3	238.1	239.2
appendix	153.5	197.5	230.3	211.3	235.2	239.0
arachnoid (cerebral)	192.1	198.4	—	225.2	237.6	239.7
spinal	192.3	198.4	—	225.4	237.6	239.7
areola (female)	174.0	198.81	233.0	217	238.3	239.3
male	175.0	198.81	233.0	217	238.3	239.3
arm NEC*	195.4	198.89	232.6	229.8	238.8	239.8
artery — see Neoplasm, connective tissue						
aryepiglottic fold	148.2	198.89	230.0	210.8	235.1	239.0
hypopharyngeal aspect	148.2	198.89	230.0	210.8	235.1	239.0
laryngeal aspect	161.1	197.3	231.0	212.1	235.6	239.1
marginal zone	148.2	198.89	230.0	210.8	235.1	239.0
arytenoid (cartilage)	161.3	197.3	231.0	212.1	235.6	239.1
fold — see Neoplasm, aryepiglottic						
atlas	170.2	198.5	—	213.2	238.0	239.2
atrium, cardiac	164.1	198.89	—	212.7	238.8	239.8
auditory						
canal (external) (skin)	173.2	198.2	232.2	216.2	238.2	239.2
internal	160.1	197.3	231.8	212.0	235.9	239.1
nerve	192.0	198.4	—	225.1	237.9	239.7
tube	160.1	197.3	231.8	212.0	235.9	239.1
opening	147.2	198.89	230.0	210.7	235.1	239.0
auricle, ear	173.2	198.2	232.2	216.2	238.2	239.2
cartilage	171.0	198.89	—	215.0	238.1	239.2
auricular canal (external)	173.2	198.2	232.2	216.2	238.2	239.2
internal	160.1	197.3	231.8	212.0	235.9	239.1
autonomic nerve or nervous system NEC	171.9	198.89	—	215.9	238.1	239.2
axilla, axillary	195.1	198.89	234.8	229.8	238.8	239.8
fold	173.5	198.2	232.5	216.5	238.2	239.2
back NEC*	195.8	198.89	232.5	229.8	238.8	239.8
Bartholin's gland	184.1	198.82	233.3	221.2	236.3	239.5
basal ganglia	191.0	198.3	—	225.0	237.5	239.6
basis pedunculi	191.7	198.3	—	225.0	237.5	239.6
bile or biliary (tract)	156.9	197.8	230.8	211.5	235.3	239.0
canaliculi (biliferi) (intrahepatic)	155.1	197.8	230.8	211.5	235.3	239.0
canals, interlobular	155.1	197.8	230.8	211.5	235.3	239.0
contiguous sites	156.8	—	—	—	—	—
duct or passage (common) (cystic) (extrahepatic)	156.1	197.8	230.8	211.5	235.3	239.0
contiguous sites with gallbladder	156.8	—	—	—	—	—
interlobular	155.1	197.8	230.8	211.5	235.3	239.0
intrahepatic	155.1	197.8	230.8	211.5	235.3	239.0
and extrahepatic	156.9	197.8	230.8	211.5	235.3	239.0
bladder (urinary)	188.9	198.1	233.7	223.3	236.7	239.4
contiguous sites	188.8	—	—	—	—	—
dome	188.1	198.1	233.7	223.3	236.7	239.4
neck	188.5	198.1	233.7	223.3	236.7	239.4
orifice	188.9	198.1	233.7	223.3	236.7	239.4
ureteric	188.6	198.1	233.7	223.3	236.7	239.4
urethral	188.5	198.1	233.7	223.3	236.7	239.4
sphincter	188.8	198.1	233.7	223.3	236.7	239.4
trigone	188.0	198.1	233.7	223.3	236.7	239.4
urachus	188.7	—	233.7	223.3	236.7	239.4
wall	188.9	198.1	233.7	223.3	236.7	239.4
anterior	188.3	198.1	233.7	223.3	236.7	239.4
lateral	188.2	198.1	233.7	223.3	236.7	239.4
posterior	188.4	198.1	233.7	223.3	236.7	239.4
blood vessel — see Neoplasm, connective tissue						
bone (periosteum)	170.9	198.5	—	213.9	238.0	239.2

Note — Carcinomas and adenocarcinomas, of any type other than intraosseous or odontogenic, of the sites listed under "Neoplasm, bone" should be considered as constituting metastatic spread from an unspecified primary site and coded to 198.5 for morbidity coding and to 199.1 for underlying cause of death coding.

	Primary	Secondary	Ca in situ	Benign	Uncertain Behavior	Unspecified
acetabulum	170.6	198.5	—	213.6	238.0	239.2
acromion (process)	170.4	198.5	—	213.4	238.0	239.2
ankle	170.8	198.5	—	213.8	238.0	239.2
arm NEC	170.4	198.5	—	213.4	238.0	239.2
astragalus	170.8	198.5	—	213.8	238.0	239.2

Neoplasm, neoplastic — *continued*

Site	Malignant Primary	Malignant Secondary	Malignant Ca in situ	Benign	Uncertain Behavior	Unspecified
bone — *continued*						
atlas	170.2	198.5	—	213.2	238.0	239.2
axis	170.2	198.5	—	213.2	238.0	239.2
back NEC	170.2	198.5	—	213.2	238.0	239.2
calcaneus	170.8	198.5	—	213.8	238.0	239.2
calvarium	170.0	198.5	—	213.0	238.0	239.2
carpus (any)	170.5	198.5	—	213.5	238.0	239.2
cartilage NEC	170.9	198.5	—	213.9	238.0	239.2
clavicle	170.3	198.5	—	213.3	238.0	239.2
clivus	170.0	198.5	—	213.0	238.0	239.2
coccygeal vertebra	170.6	198.5	—	213.6	238.0	239.2
coccyx	170.6	198.5	—	213.6	238.0	239.2
costal cartilage	170.3	198.5	—	213.3	238.0	239.2
costovertebral joint	170.3	198.5	—	213.3	238.0	239.2
cranial	170.0	198.5	—	213.0	238.0	239.2
cuboid	170.8	198.5	—	213.8	238.0	239.2
cuneiform	170.9	198.5	—	213.9	238.0	239.2
ankle	170.8	198.5	—	213.8	238.0	239.2
wrist	170.5	198.5	—	213.5	238.0	239.2
digital	170.9	198.5	—	213.9	238.0	239.2
finger	170.5	198.5	—	213.5	238.0	239.2
toe	170.8	198.5	—	213.8	238.0	239.2
elbow	170.4	198.5	—	213.4	238.0	239.2
ethmoid (labyrinth)	170.0	198.5	—	213.0	238.0	239.2
face	170.0	198.5	—	213.0	238.0	239.2
lower jaw	170.1	198.5	—	213.1	238.0	239.2
femur (any part)	170.7	198.5	—	213.7	238.0	239.2
fibula (any part)	170.7	198.5	—	213.7	238.0	239.2
finger (any)	170.5	198.5	—	213.5	238.0	239.2
foot	170.8	198.5	—	213.8	238.0	239.2
forearm	170.4	198.5	—	213.4	238.0	239.2
frontal	170.0	198.5	—	213.0	238.0	239.2
hand	170.5	198.5	—	213.5	238.0	239.2
heel	170.8	198.5	—	213.8	238.0	239.2
hip	170.6	198.5	—	213.6	238.0	239.2
humerus (any part)	170.4	198.5	—	213.4	238.0	239.2
hyoid	170.0	198.5	—	213.0	238.0	239.2
ilium	170.6	198.5	—	213.6	238.0	239.2
innominate	170.6	198.5	—	213.6	238.0	239.2
intervertebral cartilage or disc	170.2	198.5	—	213.2	238.0	239.2
ischium	170.6	198.5	—	213.6	238.0	239.2
jaw (lower)	170.1	198.5	—	213.1	238.0	239.2
upper	170.0	198.5	—	213.0	238.0	239.2
knee	170.7	198.5	—	213.7	238.0	239.2
leg NEC	170.7	198.5	—	213.7	238.0	239.2
limb NEC	170.9	198.5	—	213.9	238.0	239.2
lower (long bones)	170.7	198.5	—	213.7	238.0	239.2
short bones	170.8	198.5	—	213.8	238.0	239.2
upper (long bones)	170.4	198.5	—	213.4	238.0	239.2
short bones	170.5	198.5	—	213.5	238.0	239.2
long	170.9	198.5	—	213.9	238.0	239.2
lower limbs NEC	170.7	198.5	—	213.7	238.0	239.2
upper limbs NEC	170.4	198.5	—	213.4	238.0	239.2
malar	170.0	198.5	—	213.0	238.0	239.2
mandible	170.1	198.5	—	213.1	238.0	239.2
marrow NEC	202.9 ☑	198.5	—	—	—	238.7
mastoid	170.0	198.5	—	213.0	238.0	239.2
maxilla, maxillary (superior)	170.0	198.5	—	213.0	238.0	239.2
inferior	170.1	198.5	—	213.1	238.0	239.2
metacarpus (any)	170.5	198.5	—	213.5	238.0	239.2
metatarsus (any)	170.8	198.5	—	213.8	238.0	239.2
navicular (ankle)	170.8	198.5	—	213.8	238.0	239.2
hand	170.5	198.5	—	213.5	238.0	239.2
nose, nasal	170.0	198.5	—	213.0	238.0	239.2
occipital	170.0	198.5	—	213.0	238.0	239.2
orbit	170.0	198.5	—	213.0	238.0	239.2
parietal	170.0	198.5	—	213.0	238.0	239.2
patella	170.8	198.5	—	213.8	238.0	239.2
pelvic	170.6	198.5	—	213.6	238.0	239.2
phalanges	170.9	198.5	—	213.9	238.0	239.2
foot	170.8	198.5	—	213.8	238.0	239.2
hand	170.5	198.5	—	213.5	238.0	239.2
pubic	170.6	198.5	—	213.6	238.0	239.2
radius (any part)	170.4	198.5	—	213.4	238.0	239.2
rib	170.3	198.5	—	213.3	238.0	239.2
sacral vertebra	170.6	198.5	—	213.6	238.0	239.2

Neoplasm, neoplastic — *continued*

Site	Malignant Primary	Malignant Secondary	Malignant Ca in situ	Benign	Uncertain Behavior	Unspecified
bone — *continued*						
sacrum	170.6	198.5	—	213.6	238.0	239.2
scaphoid (of hand)	170.5	198.5	—	213.5	238.0	239.2
of ankle	170.8	198.5	—	213.8	238.0	239.2
scapula (any part)	170.4	198.5	—	213.4	238.0	239.2
sella turcica	170.0	198.5	—	213.0	238.0	239.2
short	170.9	198.5	—	213.9	238.0	239.2
lower limb	170.8	198.5	—	213.8	238.0	239.2
upper limb	170.5	198.5	—	213.5	238.0	239.2
shoulder	170.4	198.5	—	213.4	238.0	239.2
skeleton, skeletal NEC	170.9	198.5	—	213.9	238.0	239.2
skull	170.0	198.5	—	213.0	238.0	239.2
sphenoid	170.0	198.5	—	213.0	238.0	239.2
spine, spinal (column)	170.2	198.5	—	213.2	238.0	239.2
coccyx	170.6	198.5	—	213.6	238.0	239.2
sacrum	170.6	198.5	—	213.6	238.0	239.2
sternum	170.3	198.5	—	213.3	238.0	239.2
tarsus (any)	170.8	198.5	—	213.8	238.0	239.2
temporal	170.0	198.5	—	213.0	238.0	239.2
thumb	170.5	198.5	—	213.5	238.0	239.2
tibia (any part)	170.7	198.5	—	213.7	238.0	239.2
toe (any)	170.8	198.5	—	213.8	238.0	239.2
trapezium	170.5	198.5	—	213.5	238.0	239.2
trapezoid	170.5	198.5	—	213.5	238.0	239.2
turbinate	170.0	198.5	—	213.0	238.0	239.2
ulna (any part)	170.4	198.5	—	213.4	238.0	239.2
unciform	170.5	198.5	—	213.5	238.0	239.2
vertebra (column)	170.2	198.5	—	213.2	238.0	239.2
coccyx	170.6	198.5	—	213.6	238.0	239.2
sacrum	170.6	198.5	—	213.6	238.0	239.2
vomer	170.0	198.5	—	213.0	238.0	239.2
wrist	170.5	198.5	—	213.5	238.0	239.2
xiphoid process	170.3	198.5	—	213.3	238.0	239.2
zygomatic	170.0	198.5	—	213.0	238.0	239.2
book-leaf (mouth)	145.8	198.89	230.0	210.4	235.1	239.0
bowel — *see* Neoplasm, intestine						
brachial plexus	171.2	198.89	—	215.2	238.1	239.2
brain NEC	191.9	198.3	—	225.0	237.5	239.6
basal ganglia	191.0	198.3	—	225.0	237.5	239.6
cerebellopontine angle	191.6	198.3	—	225.0	237.5	239.6
cerebellum NOS	191.6	198.3	—	225.0	237.5	239.6
cerebrum	191.0	198.3	—	225.0	237.5	239.6
choroid plexus	191.5	198.3	—	225.0	237.5	239.6
contiguous sites	191.8	—	—	—	—	—
corpus callosum	191.8	198.3	—	225.0	237.5	239.6
corpus striatum	191.0	198.3	—	225.0	237.5	239.6
cortex (cerebral)	191.0	198.3	—	225.0	237.5	239.6
frontal lobe	191.1	198.3	—	225.0	237.5	239.6
globus pallidus	191.0	198.3	—	225.0	237.5	239.6
hippocampus	191.2	198.3	—	225.0	237.5	239.6
hypothalamus	191.0	198.3	—	225.0	237.5	239.6
internal capsule	191.0	198.3	—	225.0	237.5	239.6
medulla oblongata	191.7	198.3	—	225.0	237.5	239.6
meninges	192.1	198.4	—	225.2	237.6	239.7
midbrain	191.7	198.3	—	225.0	237.5	239.6
occipital lobe	191.4	198.3	—	225.0	237.5	239.6
parietal lobe	191.3	198.3	—	225.0	237.5	239.6
peduncle	191.7	198.3	—	225.0	237.5	239.6
pons	191.7	198.3	—	225.0	237.5	239.6
stem	191.7	198.3	—	225.0	237.5	239.6
tapetum	191.8	198.3	—	225.0	237.5	239.6
temporal lobe	191.2	198.3	—	225.0	237.5	239.6
thalamus	191.0	198.3	—	225.0	237.5	239.6
uncus	191.2	198.3	—	225.0	237.5	239.6
ventricle (floor)	191.5	198.3	—	225.0	237.5	239.6
branchial (cleft) (vestiges)	146.8	198.89	230.0	210.6	235.1	239.0
breast (connective tissue) (female) (glandular tissue) (soft parts)	174.9	198.81	233.0	217	238.3	239.3
areola	174.0	198.81	233.0	217	238.3	239.3
male	175.0	198.81	233.0	217	238.3	239.3
axillary tail	174.6	198.81	233.0	217	238.3	239.3
central portion	174.1	198.81	233.0	217	238.3	239.3
contiguous sites	174.8	—	—	—	—	—
ectopic sites	174.8	198.81	233.0	217	238.3	239.3
inner	174.8	198.81	233.0	217	238.3	239.3
lower	174.8	198.81	233.0	217	238.3	239.3

Neoplasm, neoplastic — continued	Malignant Primary	Secondary	Ca in situ	Benign	Uncertain Behavior	Unspecified
breast — continued						
lower-inner quadrant	174.3	198.81	233.0	217	238.3	239.3
lower-outer quadrant	174.5	198.81	233.0	217	238.3	239.3
male	175.9	198.81	233.0	217	238.3	239.3
areola	175.0	198.81	233.0	217	238.3	239.3
ectopic tissue	175.9	198.81	233.0	217	238.3	239.3
nipple	175.0	198.81	233.0	217	238.3	239.3
mastectomy site (skin)	173.5	198.2	—	—	—	—
specified as breast tissue	174.8	198.81	—	—	—	—
midline	174.8	198.81	233.0	217	238.3	239.3
nipple	174.0	198.81	233.0	217	238.3	239.3
male	175.0	198.81	233.0	217	238.3	239.3
outer	174.8	198.81	233.0	217	238.3	239.3
skin	173.5	198.2	232.5	216.5	238.2	239.2
tail (axillary)	174.6	198.81	233.0	217	238.3	239.3
upper	174.8	198.81	233.0	217	238.3	239.3
upper-inner quadrant	174.2	198.81	233.0	217	238.3	239.3
upper-outer quadrant	174.4	198.81	233.0	217	238.3	239.3
broad ligament	183.3	198.82	233.3	221.0	236.3	239.5
bronchiogenic, bronchogenic (lung)	162.9	197.0	231.2	212.3	235.7	239.1
bronchiole	162.9	197.0	231.2	212.3	235.7	239.1
bronchus	162.9	197.0	231.2	212.3	235.7	239.1
carina	162.2	197.0	231.2	212.3	235.7	239.1
contiguous sites with lung or trachea	162.8	—	—	—	—	—
lower lobe of lung	162.5	197.0	231.2	212.3	235.7	239.1
main	162.2	197.0	231.2	212.3	235.7	239.1
middle lobe of lung	162.4	197.0	231.2	212.3	235.7	239.1
upper lobe of lung	162.3	197.0	231.2	212.3	235.7	239.1
brow	173.3	198.2	232.3	216.3	238.2	239.2
buccal (cavity)	145.9	198.89	230.0	210.4	235.1	239.0
commissure	145.0	198.89	230.0	210.4	235.1	239.0
groove (lower) (upper)	145.1	198.89	230.0	210.4	235.1	239.0
mucosa	145.0	198.89	230.0	210.4	235.1	239.0
sulcus (lower) (upper)	145.1	198.89	230.0	210.4	235.1	239.0
bulbourethral gland	189.3	198.1	233.9	223.81	236.99	239.5
bursa — see Neoplasm, connective tissue						
buttock NEC*	195.3	198.89	232.5	229.8	238.8	239.8
calf*	195.5	198.89	232.7	229.8	238.8	239.8
calvarium	170.0	198.5	—	213.0	238.0	239.2
calyx, renal	189.1	198.0	233.9	223.1	236.91	239.5
canal						
anal	154.2	197.5	230.5	211.4	235.5	239.0
auditory (external)	173.2	198.2	232.2	216.2	238.2	239.2
auricular (external)	173.2	198.2	232.2	216.2	238.2	239.2
canaliculi, biliary (bilifeiri) (intrahepatic)	155.1	197.8	230.8	211.5	235.3	239.0
canthus (eye) (inner) (outer)	173.1	198.2	232.1	216.1	238.2	239.2
capillary — see Neoplasm, connective tissue						
caput coli	153.4	197.5	230.3	211.3	235.2	239.0
cardia (gastric)	151.0	197.8	230.2	211.1	235.2	239.0
cardiac orifice (stomach)	151.0	197.8	230.2	211.1	235.2	239.0
cardio-esophageal junction	151.0	197.8	230.2	211.1	235.2	239.0
cardio-esophagus	151.0	197.8	230.2	211.1	235.2	239.0
carina (bronchus)	162.2	197.0	231.2	212.3	235.7	239.1
carotid (artery)	171.0	198.89	—	215.0	238.1	239.2
body	194.5	198.89	—	227.5	237.3	239.7
carpus (any bone)	170.5	198.5	—	213.5	238.0	239.2
cartilage (articular) (joint) NEC — see also Neoplasm, bone	170.9	198.5	—	213.9	238.0	239.2
arytenoid	161.3	197.3	231.0	212.1	235.6	239.1
auricular	171.0	198.89	—	215.0	238.1	239.2
bronchi	162.2	197.3	—	212.3	235.7	239.1
connective tissue — see Neoplasm, connective tissue						
costal	170.3	198.5	—	213.3	238.0	239.2
cricoid	161.3	197.3	231.0	212.1	235.6	239.1
cuneiform	161.3	197.3	231.0	212.1	235.6	239.1
ear (external)	171.0	198.89	—	215.0	238.1	239.2
ensiform	170.3	198.5	—	213.3	238.0	239.2
epiglottis	161.1	197.3	231.0	212.1	235.6	239.1
anterior surface	146.4	198.89	230.0	210.6	235.1	239.0
eyelid	171.0	198.89	—	215.0	238.1	239.2
intervertebral	170.2	198.5	—	213.2	238.0	239.2
larynx, laryngeal	161.3	197.3	231.0	212.1	235.6	239.1
nose, nasal	160.0	197.3	231.8	212.0	235.9	239.1
pinna	171.0	198.89	—	215.0	238.1	239.2

Neoplasm, neoplastic — continued	Malignant Primary	Secondary	Ca in situ	Benign	Uncertain Behavior	Unspecified
cartilage NEC — see also Neoplasm, bone — continued						
rib	170.3	198.5	—	213.3	238.0	239.2
semilunar (knee)	170.7	198.5	—	213.7	238.0	239.2
thyroid	161.3	197.3	231.0	212.1	235.6	239.1
trachea	162.0	197.3	231.1	212.2	235.7	239.1
cauda equina	192.2	198.3	—	225.3	237.5	239.7
cavity						
buccal	145.9	198.89	230.0	210.4	235.1	239.0
nasal	160.0	197.3	231.8	212.0	235.9	239.1
oral	145.9	198.89	230.0	210.4	235.1	239.0
peritoneal	158.9	197.6	—	211.8	235.4	239.0
tympanic	160.1	197.3	231.8	212.0	235.9	239.1
cecum	153.4	197.5	230.3	211.3	235.2	239.0
central						
nervous system — see Neoplasm, nervous system						
white matter	191.0	198.3	—	225.0	237.5	239.6
cerebellopontine (angle)	191.6	198.3	—	225.0	237.5	239.6
cerebellum, cerebellar	191.6	198.3	—	225.0	237.5	239.6
cerebrum, cerebral (cortex) (hemisphere) (white matter)	191.0	198.3	—	225.0	237.5	239.6
meninges	192.1	198.4	—	225.2	237.6	239.7
peduncle	191.7	198.3	—	225.0	237.5	239.6
ventricle (any)	191.5	198.3	—	225.0	237.5	239.6
cervical region	195.0	198.89	234.8	229.8	238.8	239.8
cervix (cervical) (uteri) (uterus)	180.9	198.82	233.1	219.0	236.0	239.5
canal	180.0	198.82	233.1	219.0	236.0	239.5
contiguous sites	180.8	—	—	—	—	—
endocervix (canal) (gland)	180.0	198.82	233.1	219.0	236.0	239.5
exocervix	180.1	198.82	233.1	219.0	236.0	239.5
external os	180.1	198.82	233.1	219.0	236.0	239.5
internal os	180.0	198.82	233.1	219.0	236.0	239.5
nabothian gland	180.0	198.82	233.1	219.0	236.0	239.5
squamocolumnar junction	180.8	198.82	233.1	219.0	236.0	239.5
stump	180.8	198.82	233.1	219.0	236.0	239.5
cheek	195.0	198.89	234.8	229.8	238.8	239.8
external	173.3	198.2	232.3	216.3	238.2	239.2
inner aspect	145.0	198.89	230.0	210.4	235.1	239.0
internal	145.0	198.89	230.0	210.4	235.1	239.0
mucosa	145.0	198.89	230.0	210.4	235.1	239.0
chest (wall) NEC	195.1	198.89	234.8	229.8	238.8	239.8
chiasma opticum	192.0	198.4	—	225.1	237.9	239.7
chin	173.3	198.2	232.3	216.3	238.2	239.2
choana	147.3	198.89	230.0	210.7	235.1	239.0
cholangiole	155.1	197.8	230.8	211.5	235.3	239.0
choledochal duct	156.1	197.8	230.8	211.5	235.3	239.0
choroid	190.6	198.4	234.0	224.6	238.8	239.8
plexus	191.5	198.3	—	225.0	237.5	239.6
ciliary body	190.0	198.4	234.0	224.0	238.8	239.8
clavicle	170.3	198.5	—	213.3	238.0	239.2
clitoris	184.3	198.82	233.3	221.2	236.3	239.5
clivus	170.0	198.5	—	213.0	238.0	239.2
cloacogenic zone	154.8	197.5	230.7	211.4	235.5	239.0
coccygeal						
body or glomus	194.6	198.89	—	227.6	237.3	239.7
vertebra	170.6	198.5	—	213.6	238.0	239.2
coccyx	170.6	198.5	—	213.6	238.0	239.2
colon — see also Neoplasm, intestine, large						
and rectum	154.0	197.5	230.4	211.4	235.2	239.0
column, spinal — see Neoplasm, spine						
columnella	173.3	198.2	232.3	216.3	238.2	239.2
commissure						
labial, lip	140.6	198.89	230.0	210.4	235.1	239.0
laryngeal	161.0	197.3	231.0	212.1	235.6	239.1
common (bile) duct	156.1	197.8	230.8	211.5	235.3	239.0
concha	173.2	198.2	232.2	216.2	238.2	239.2
nose	160.0	197.3	231.8	212.0	235.9	239.1
conjunctiva	190.3	198.4	234.0	224.3	238.8	239.8

2006 ICD-9-CM

☑ Additional Digit Required — Refer to the Tabular List (Numeric Code Section) for Additional Digit Selection
▶◀ Revised Text   ● New Line   ▲ Revised Code

Volume 2 — 235

Neoplasm, neoplastic — *continued*	Malignant Primary	Secondary	Ca in situ	Benign	Uncertain Behavior	Unspecified
connective tissue NEC	171.9	198.89	—	215.9	238.1	239.2

Note — *For neoplasms of connective tissue (blood vessel, bursa, fascia, ligament, muscle, peripheral nerves, sympathetic and parasympathetic nerves and ganglia, synovia, tendon, etc.) or of morphological types that indicate connective tissue, code according to the list under "Neoplasm, connective tissue"; for sites that do not appear in this list, code to neoplasm of that site; e.g.,*

> *liposarcoma, shoulder 171.2*
> *leiomyosarcoma, stomach 151.9*
> *neurofibroma, chest wall 215.4*

Morphological types that indicate connective tissue appear in the proper place in the alphabetic index with the instruction "see Neoplasm, connective tissue…"

Neoplasm, neoplastic — *continued*	Malignant Primary	Secondary	Ca in situ	Benign	Uncertain Behavior	Unspecified
abdomen	171.5	198.89	—	215.5	238.1	239.2
abdominal wall	171.5	198.89	—	215.5	238.1	239.2
ankle	171.3	198.89	—	215.3	238.1	239.2
antecubital fossa or space	171.2	198.89	—	215.2	238.1	239.2
arm	171.2	198.89	—	215.2	238.1	239.2
auricle (ear)	171.0	198.89	—	215.0	238.1	239.2
axilla	171.4	198.89	—	215.4	238.1	239.2
back	171.7	198.89	—	215.7	238.1	239.2
breast (female) (*see also* Neoplasm, breast)	174.9	198.81	233.0	217	238.3	239.3
male	175.9	198.81	233.0	217	238.3	239.3
buttock	171.6	198.89	—	215.6	238.1	239.2
calf	171.3	198.89	—	215.3	238.1	239.2
cervical region	171.0	198.89	—	215.0	238.1	239.2
cheek	171.0	198.89	—	215.0	238.1	239.2
chest (wall)	171.4	198.89	—	215.4	238.1	239.2
chin	171.0	198.89	—	215.0	238.1	239.2
contiguous sites	171.8	—		—	—	—
diaphragm	171.4	198.89	—	215.4	238.1	239.2
ear (external)	171.0	198.89	—	215.0	238.1	239.2
elbow	171.2	198.89	—	215.2	238.1	239.2
extrarectal	171.6	198.89	—	215.6	238.1	239.2
extremity	171.8	198.89	—	215.8	238.1	239.2
lower	171.3	198.89	—	215.3	238.1	239.2
upper	171.2	198.89	—	215.2	238.1	239.2
eyelid	171.0	198.89	—	215.0	238.1	239.2
face	171.0	198.89	—	215.0	238.1	239.2
finger	171.2	198.89	—	215.2	238.1	239.2
flank	171.7	198.89	—	215.7	238.1	239.2
foot	171.3	198.89	—	215.3	238.1	239.2
forearm	171.2	198.89	—	215.2	238.1	239.2
forehead	171.0	198.89	—	215.0	238.1	239.2
gastric	171.5	198.89	—	215.5	238.1	—
gastrointestinal	171.5	198.89	—	215.5	238.1	—
gluteal region	171.6	198.89	—	215.6	238.1	239.2
great vessels NEC	171.4	198.89	—	215.4	238.1	239.2
groin	171.6	198.89	—	215.6	238.1	239.2
hand	171.2	198.89	—	215.2	238.1	239.2
head	171.0	198.89	—	215.0	238.1	239.2
heel	171.3	198.89	—	215.3	238.1	239.2
hip	171.3	198.89	—	215.3	238.1	239.2
hypochondrium	171.5	198.89	—	215.5	238.1	239.2
iliopsoas muscle	171.6	198.89	—	215.5	238.1	239.2
infraclavicular region	171.4	198.89	—	215.4	238.1	239.2
inguinal (canal) (region)	171.6	198.89	—	215.6	238.1	239.2
intrathoracic	171.4	198.89	—	215.4	238.1	239.2
intestine	171.5	198.89	—	215.5	238.1	—
ischorectal fossa	171.6	198.89	—	215.6	238.1	239.2
jaw	143.9	198.89	230.0	210.4	235.1	239.0
knee	171.3	198.89	—	215.3	238.1	239.2
leg	171.3	198.89	—	215.3	238.1	239.2
limb NEC	171.9	198.89	—	215.8	238.1	239.2
lower	171.3	198.89	—	215.3	238.1	239.2
upper	171.2	198.89	—	215.2	238.1	239.2
nates	171.6	198.89	—	215.6	238.1	239.2
neck	171.0	198.89	—	215.0	238.1	239.2
orbit	190.1	198.4	234.0	224.1	238.8	239.8
pararectal	171.6	198.89	—	215.6	238.1	239.2
para-urethral	171.6	198.89	—	215.6	238.1	239.2
paravaginal	171.6	198.89	—	215.6	238.1	239.2

Neoplasm, neoplastic — *continued*	Malignant Primary	Secondary	Ca in situ	Benign	Uncertain Behavior	Unspecified
connective tissue NEC — *continued*						
pelvis (floor)	171.6	198.89	—	215.6	238.1	239.2
pelvo-abdominal	171.8	198.89	—	215.8	238.1	239.2
perineum	171.6	198.89	—	215.6	238.1	239.2
perirectal (tissue)	171.6	198.89	—	215.6	238.1	239.2
periurethral (tissue)	171.6	198.89	—	215.6	238.1	239.2
popliteal fossa or space	171.3	198.89	—	215.3	238.1	239.2
presacral	171.6	198.89	—	215.6	238.1	239.2
psoas muscle	171.5	198.89	—	215.5	238.1	239.2
pterygoid fossa	171.0	198.89	—	215.0	238.1	239.2
rectovaginal septum or wall	171.6	198.89	—	215.6	238.1	239.2
rectovesical	171.6	198.89	—	215.6	238.1	239.2
retroperitoneum	158.0	197.6	—	211.8	235.4	239.0
sacrococcygeal region	171.6	198.89	—	215.6	238.1	239.2
scalp	171.0	198.89	—	215.0	238.1	239.2
scapular region	171.4	198.89	—	215.4	238.1	239.2
shoulder	171.2	198.89	—	215.2	238.1	239.2
skin (dermis) NEC	173.9	198.2	232.9	216.9	238.2	239.2
stomach	171.5	198.89	—	215.5	238.1	—
submental	171.0	198.89	—	215.0	238.1	239.2
supraclavicular region	171.0	198.89	—	215.0	238.1	239.2
temple	171.0	198.89	—	215.0	238.1	239.2
temporal region	171.0	198.89	—	215.0	238.1	239.2
thigh	171.3	198.89	—	215.3	238.1	239.2
thoracic (duct) (wall)	171.4	198.89	—	215.4	238.1	239.2
thorax	171.4	198.89	—	215.4	238.1	239.2
thumb	171.2	198.89	—	215.2	238.1	239.2
toe	171.3	198.89	—	215.3	238.1	239.2
trunk	171.7	198.89	—	215.7	238.1	239.2
umbilicus	171.5	198.89	—	215.5	238.1	239.2
vesicorectal	171.6	198.89	—	215.6	238.1	239.2
wrist	171.2	198.89	—	215.2	238.1	239.2
conus medullaris	192.2	198.3	—	225.3	237.5	239.7
cord (true) (vocal)	161.0	197.3	231.0	212.1	235.6	239.1
false	161.1	197.3	231.0	212.1	235.6	239.1
spermatic	187.6	198.82	233.6	222.8	236.6	239.5
spinal (cervical) (lumbar) (thoracic)	192.2	198.3	—	225.3	237.5	239.7
cornea (limbus)	190.4	198.4	234.0	224.4	238.8	239.8
corpus						
albicans	183.0	198.6	233.3	220	236.2	239.5
callosum, brain	191.8	198.3	—	225.0	237.5	239.6
cavernosum	187.3	198.82	233.5	222.1	236.6	239.5
gastric	151.4	197.8	230.2	211.1	235.2	239.0
penis	187.3	198.82	233.5	222.1	236.6	239.5
striatum, cerebrum	191.0	198.3	—	225.0	237.5	239.6
uteri	182.0	198.82	233.2	219.1	236.0	239.5
isthmus	182.1	198.82	233.2	219.1	236.0	239.5
cortex						
adrenal	194.0	198.7	234.8	227.0	237.2	239.7
cerebral	191.0	198.3	—	225.0	237.5	239.6
costal cartilage	170.3	198.5	—	213.3	238.0	239.2
costovertebral joint	170.3	198.5	—	213.3	238.0	239.2
Cowper's gland	189.3	198.1	233.9	223.81	236.99	239.5
cranial (fossa, any)	191.9	198.3	—	225.0	237.5	239.6
meninges	192.1	198.4	—	225.2	237.6	239.7
nerve (any)	192.0	198.4	—	225.1	237.9	239.7
craniobuccal pouch	194.3	198.89	234.8	227.3	237.0	239.7
craniopharyngeal (duct) (pouch)	194.3	198.89	234.8	227.3	237.0	239.7
cricoid	148.0	198.89	230.0	210.8	235.1	239.0
cartilage	161.3	197.3	231.0	212.1	235.6	239.1
cricopharynx	148.0	198.89	230.0	210.8	235.1	239.0
crypt of Morgagni	154.8	197.5	230.7	211.4	235.2	239.0
crystalline lens	190.0	198.4	234.0	224.0	238.8	239.8
cul-de-sac (Douglas')	158.8	197.6	—	211.8	235.4	239.0
cuneiform cartilage	161.3	197.3	231.0	212.1	235.6	239.1
cutaneous — *see* Neoplasm, skin						
cutis — *see* Neoplasm, skin						
cystic (bile) duct (common)	156.1	197.8	230.8	211.5	235.3	239.0
dermis — *see* Neoplasm, skin						
diaphragm	171.4	198.89	—	215.4	238.1	239.2
digestive organs, system, tube, or tract NEC	159.9	197.8	230.9	211.9	235.5	239.0
contiguous sites with peritoneum	159.8	—	—	—	—	—
disc, intervertebral	170.2	198.5	—	213.2	238.0	239.2
disease, generalized	199.0	199.0	234.9	229.9	238.9	199.0
disseminated	199.0	199.0	234.9	229.9	238.9	199.0

☑ Additional Digit Required — Refer to the Tabular List (Numeric Code Section) for Additional Digit Selection
►◄ Revised Text ● New Line ▲ Revised Code

Neoplasm, neoplastic — *continued*	Malignant			Benign	Uncertain Behavior	Unspecified
	Primary	Secondary	Ca in situ			
Douglas' cul-de-sac or pouch	158.8	197.6	—	211.8	235.4	239.0
duodenojejunal junction	152.8	197.4	230.7	211.2	235.2	239.0
duodenum	152.0	197.4	230.7	211.2	235.2	239.0
dura (cranial) (mater)	192.1	198.4	—	225.2	237.6	239.7
cerebral	192.1	198.4	—	225.2	237.6	239.7
spinal	192.3	198.4	—	225.4	237.6	239.7
ear (external)	173.2	198.2	232.2	216.2	238.2	239.2
auricle or auris	173.2	198.2	232.2	216.2	238.2	239.2
canal, external	173.2	198.2	232.2	216.2	238.2	239.2
cartilage	171.0	198.89	—	215.0	238.1	239.2
external meatus	173.2	198.2	232.2	216.2	238.2	239.2
inner	160.1	197.3	231.8	212.0	235.9	239.8
lobule	173.2	198.2	232.2	216.2	238.2	239.2
middle	160.1	197.3	231.8	212.0	235.9	239.8
contiguous sites with accessory sinuses or nasal cavities	160.8	—	—	—	—	—
skin	173.2	198.2	232.2	216.2	238.2	239.2
earlobe	173.2	198.2	232.2	216.2	238.2	239.2
ejaculatory duct	187.8	198.82	233.6	222.8	236.6	239.5
elbow NEC*	195.4	198.89	232.6	229.8	238.8	239.8
endocardium	164.1	198.89	—	212.7	238.8	239.8
endocervix (canal) (gland)	180.0	198.82	233.1	219.0	236.0	239.5
endocrine gland NEC	194.9	198.89	—	227.9	237.4	239.7
pluriglandular NEC	194.8	198.89	234.8	227.8	237.4	239.7
endometrium (gland) (stroma)	182.0	198.82	233.2	219.1	236.0	239.5
ensiform cartilage	170.3	198.5	—	213.3	238.0	239.2
enteric — *see* Neoplasm, intestine						
ependyma (brain)	191.5	198.3	—	225.0	237.5	239.6
epicardium	164.1	198.89	—	212.7	238.8	239.8
epididymis	187.5	198.82	233.6	222.3	236.6	239.5
epidural	192.9	198.4	—	225.9	237.9	239.7
epiglottis	161.1	197.3	231.0	212.1	235.6	239.1
anterior aspect or surface	146.4	198.89	230.0	210.6	235.1	239.0
cartilage	161.3	197.3	231.0	212.1	235.6	239.1
free border (margin)	146.4	198.89	230.0	210.6	235.1	239.0
junctional region	146.5	198.89	230.0	210.6	235.1	239.0
posterior (laryngeal) surface	161.1	197.3	231.0	212.1	235.6	239.1
suprahyoid portion	161.1	197.3	231.0	212.1	235.6	239.1
esophagogastric junction	151.0	197.8	230.2	211.1	235.2	239.0
esophagus	150.9	197.8	230.1	211.0	235.5	239.0
abdominal	150.2	197.8	230.1	211.0	235.5	239.0
cervical	150.0	197.8	230.1	211.0	235.5	239.0
contiguous sites	150.8	—	—	—	—	—
distal (third)	150.5	197.8	230.1	211.0	235.5	239.0
lower (third)	150.5	197.8	230.1	211.0	235.5	239.0
middle (third)	150.4	197.8	230.1	211.0	235.5	239.0
proximal (third)	150.3	197.8	230.1	211.0	235.5	239.0
specified part NEC	150.8	197.8	230.1	211.0	235.5	239.0
thoracic	150.1	197.8	230.1	211.0	235.5	239.0
upper (third)	150.3	197.8	230.1	211.0	235.5	239.0
ethmoid (sinus)	160.3	197.3	231.8	212.0	235.9	239.1
bone or labyrinth	170.0	198.5	—	213.0	238.0	239.2
Eustachian tube	160.1	197.3	231.8	212.0	235.9	239.1
exocervix	180.1	198.82	233.1	219.0	236.0	239.5
external						
meatus (ear)	173.2	198.2	232.2	216.2	238.2	239.2
os, cervix uteri	180.1	198.82	233.1	219.0	236.0	239.5
extradural	192.9	198.4	—	225.9	237.9	239.7
extrahepatic (bile) duct	156.1	197.8	230.8	211.5	235.3	239.0
contiguous sites with gallbladder	156.8	—	—	—	—	—
extraocular muscle	190.1	198.4	234.0	224.1	238.8	239.8
extrarectal	195.3	198.89	234.8	229.8	238.8	239.8
extremity*	195.8	198.89	232.8	229.8	238.8	239.8
lower*	195.5	198.89	232.7	229.8	238.8	239.8
upper*	195.4	198.89	232.6	229.8	238.8	239.8
eye NEC	190.9	198.4	234.0	224.9	238.8	239.8
contiguous sites	190.8	—	—	—	—	—
specified sites NEC	190.8	198.4	234.0	224.8	238.8	239.8
eyeball	190.0	198.4	234.0	224.0	238.8	239.8
eyebrow	173.3	198.2	232.3	216.3	238.2	239.2
eyelid (lower) (skin) (upper)	173.1	198.2	232.1	216.1	238.2	239.2
cartilage	171.0	198.89	—	215.0	238.1	239.2
face NEC*	195.0	198.89	232.3	229.8	238.8	239.8
fallopian tube (accessory)	183.2	198.82	233.3	221.0	236.3	239.5
falx (cerebelli) (cerebri)	192.1	198.4	—	225.2	237.6	239.7

Neoplasm, neoplastic — *continued*	Malignant			Benign	Uncertain Behavior	Unspecified
	Primary	Secondary	Ca in situ			
fascia — *see also* Neoplasm, connective tissue						
palmar	171.2	198.89	—	215.2	238.1	239.2
plantar	171.3	198.89	—	215.3	238.1	239.2
fatty tissue — *see* Neoplasm, connective tissue						
fauces, faucial NEC	146.9	198.89	230.0	210.6	235.1	239.0
pillars	146.2	198.89	230.0	210.6	235.1	239.0
tonsil	146.0	198.89	230.0	210.5	235.1	239.0
femur (any part)	170.7	198.5	—	213.7	238.0	239.2
fetal membrane	181	198.82	233.2	219.8	236.1	239.5
fibrous tissue — *see* Neoplasm, connective tissue						
fibula (any part)	170.7	198.5	—	213.7	238.0	239.2
filum terminale	192.2	198.3	—	225.3	237.5	239.7
finger NEC*	195.4	198.89	232.6	229.8	238.8	239.8
flank NEC*	195.8	198.89	232.5	229.8	238.8	239.8
follicle, nabothian	180.0	198.82	233.1	219.0	236.0	239.5
foot NEC*	195.5	198.89	232.7	229.8	238.8	239.8
forearm NEC*	195.4	198.89	232.6	229.8	238.8	239.8
forehead (skin)	173.3	198.2	232.3	216.3	238.2	239.2
foreskin	187.1	198.82	233.5	222.1	236.6	239.5
fornix						
pharyngeal	147.3	198.89	230.0	210.7	235.1	239.0
vagina	184.0	198.82	233.3	221.1	236.3	239.5
fossa (of)						
anterior (cranial)	191.9	198.3	—	225.0	237.5	239.6
cranial	191.9	198.3	—	225.0	237.5	239.6
ischiorectal	195.3	198.89	234.8	229.8	238.8	239.8
middle (cranial)	191.9	198.3	—	225.0	237.5	239.6
pituitary	194.3	198.89	234.8	227.3	237.0	239.7
posterior (cranial)	191.9	198.3	—	225.0	237.5	239.6
pterygoid	171.0	198.89	—	215.0	238.1	239.2
pyriform	148.1	198.89	230.0	210.8	235.1	239.0
Rosenmüller	147.2	198.89	230.0	210.7	235.1	239.0
tonsillar	146.1	198.89	230.0	210.6	235.1	239.0
fourchette	184.4	198.82	233.3	221.2	236.3	239.5
frenulum						
labii — *see* Neoplasm, lip, internal						
linguae	141.3	198.89	230.0	210.1	235.1	239.0
frontal						
bone	170.0	198.5	—	213.0	238.0	239.2
lobe, brain	191.1	198.3	—	225.0	237.5	239.6
meninges	192.1	198.4	—	225.2	237.6	239.7
pole	191.1	198.3	—	225.0	237.5	239.6
sinus	160.4	197.3	231.8	212.0	235.9	239.1
fundus						
stomach	151.3	197.8	230.2	211.1	235.2	239.0
uterus	182.0	198.82	233.2	219.1	236.0	239.5
gall duct (extrahepatic)	156.1	197.8	230.8	211.5	235.3	239.0
intrahepatic	155.1	197.8	230.8	211.5	235.3	239.0
gallbladder	156.0	197.8	230.8	211.5	235.3	239.0
contiguous sites with extrahepatic bile ducts	156.8	—	—	—	—	—
ganglia (*see also* Neoplasm, connective tissue)	171.9	198.89	—	215.9	238.1	239.2
basal	191.0	198.3	—	225.0	237.5	239.6
ganglion (*see also* Neoplasm, connective tissue)	171.9	198.89	—	215.9	238.1	239.2
cranial nerve	192.0	198.4	—	225.1	237.9	239.7
Gartner's duct	184.0	198.82	233.3	221.1	236.3	239.5
gastric — *see* Neoplasm, stomach						
gastrocolic	159.8	197.8	230.9	211.9	235.5	239.0
gastroesophageal junction	151.0	197.8	230.2	211.1	235.2	239.0
gastrointestinal (tract) NEC	159.9	197.8	230.9	211.9	235.5	239.0
generalized	199.0	199.0	234.9	229.9	238.9	199.0
genital organ or tract						
female NEC	184.9	198.82	233.3	221.9	236.3	239.5
contiguous sites	184.8	—	—	—	—	—
specified site NEC	184.8	198.82	233.3	221.8	236.3	239.5
male NEC	187.9	198.82	233.6	222.9	236.6	239.5
contiguous sites	187.8	—	—	—	—	—
specified site NEC	187.8	198.82	233.6	222.8	236.6	239.5
genitourinary tract						
female	184.9	198.82	233.3	221.9	236.3	239.5
male	187.9	198.82	233.6	222.9	236.6	239.5

☑ Additional Digit Required — Refer to the Tabular List (Numeric Code Section) for Additional Digit Selection

▶◀ Revised Text   ● New Line   ▲ Revised Code

Neoplasm, neoplastic — continued	Malignant Primary	Malignant Secondary	Malignant Ca in situ	Benign	Uncertain Behavior	Unspecified
gingiva (alveolar) (marginal)	143.9	198.89	230.0	210.4	235.1	239.0
lower	143.1	198.89	230.0	210.4	235.1	239.0
mandibular	143.1	198.89	230.0	210.4	235.1	239.0
maxillary	143.0	198.89	230.0	210.4	235.1	239.0
upper	143.0	198.89	230.0	210.4	235.1	239.0
gland, glandular (lymphatic) (system) — see also Neoplasm, lymph gland						
endocrine NEC	194.9	198.89	—	227.9	237.4	239.7
salivary — see Neoplasm, salivary, gland						
glans penis	187.2	198.82	233.5	222.1	236.6	239.5
globus pallidus	191.0	198.3	—	225.0	237.5	239.6
glomus						
coccygeal	194.6	198.89	—	227.6	237.3	239.7
jugularis	194.6	198.89	—	227.6	237.3	239.7
glosso-epiglottic fold(s)	146.4	198.89	230.0	210.6	235.1	239.0
glossopalatine fold	146.2	198.89	230.0	210.6	235.1	239.0
glossopharyngeal sulcus	146.1	198.89	230.0	210.6	235.1	239.0
glottis	161.0	197.3	231.0	212.1	235.6	239.1
gluteal region*	195.3	198.89	232.5	229.8	238.8	239.8
great vessels NEC	171.4	198.89	—	215.4	238.1	239.2
groin NEC	195.3	198.89	232.5	229.8	238.8	239.8
gum	143.9	198.89	230.0	210.4	235.1	239.0
contiguous sites	143.8	—	—	—	—	—
lower	143.1	198.89	230.0	210.4	235.1	239.0
upper	143.0	198.89	230.0	210.4	235.1	239.0
hand NEC*	195.4	198.89	232.6	229.8	238.8	239.8
head NEC*	195.0	198.89	232.4	229.8	238.8	239.8
heart	164.1	198.89	—	212.7	238.8	239.8
contiguous sites with mediastinum or thymus	164.8	—	—	—	—	—
heel NEC*	195.5	198.89	232.7	229.8	238.8	239.8
helix	173.2	198.2	232.2	216.2	238.2	239.2
hematopoietic, hemopoietic tissue NEC	202.8 ☑	198.89	—	—	—	238.7
hemisphere, cerebral	191.0	198.3	—	225.0	237.5	239.6
hemorrhoidal zone	154.2	197.5	230.5	211.4	235.5	239.0
hepatic	155.2	197.7	230.8	211.5	235.3	239.0
duct (bile)	156.1	197.8	230.8	211.5	235.3	239.0
flexure (colon)	153.0	197.5	230.3	211.3	235.2	239.0
primary	155.0	—	—	—	—	—
hilus of lung	162.2	197.0	231.2	212.3	235.7	239.1
hip NEC*	195.5	198.89	232.7	229.8	238.8	239.8
hippocampus, brain	191.2	198.3	—	225.0	237.5	239.6
humerus (any part)	170.4	198.5	—	213.4	238.0	239.2
hymen	184.0	198.82	233.3	221.1	236.3	239.5
hypopharynx, hypopharyngeal NEC	148.9	198.89	230.0	210.8	235.1	239.0
contiguous sites	148.8	—	—	—	—	—
postcricoid region	148.0	198.89	230.0	210.8	235.1	239.0
posterior wall	148.3	198.89	230.0	210.8	235.1	239.0
pyriform fossa (sinus)	148.1	198.89	230.0	210.8	235.1	239.0
specified site NEC	148.8	198.89	230.0	210.8	235.1	239.0
wall	148.9	198.89	230.0	210.8	235.1	239.0
posterior	148.3	198.89	230.0	210.8	235.1	239.0
hypophysis	194.3	198.89	234.8	227.3	237.0	239.7
hypothalamus	191.0	198.3	—	225.0	237.5	239.6
ileocecum, ileocecal (coil) (junction) (valve)	153.4	197.5	230.3	211.3	235.2	239.0
ileum	152.2	197.4	230.7	211.2	235.2	239.0
ilium	170.6	198.5	—	213.6	238.0	239.2
immunoproliferative NEC	203.8 ☑	—	—	—	—	—
infraclavicular (region)*	195.1	198.89	232.5	229.8	238.8	239.8
inguinal (region)*	195.3	198.89	232.5	229.8	238.8	239.8
insula	191.0	198.3	—	225.0	237.5	239.6
insular tissue (pancreas)	157.4	197.8	230.9	211.7	235.5	239.0
brain	191.0	198.3	—	225.0	237.5	239.6
interarytenoid fold	148.2	198.89	230.0	210.8	235.1	239.0
hypopharyngeal aspect	148.2	198.89	230.0	210.8	235.1	239.0
laryngeal aspect	161.1	197.3	231.0	212.1	235.6	239.1
marginal zone	148.2	198.89	230.0	210.8	235.1	239.0
interdental papillae	143.9	198.89	230.0	210.4	235.1	239.0
lower	143.1	198.89	230.0	210.4	235.1	239.0
upper	143.0	198.89	230.0	210.4	235.1	239.0
internal						
capsule	191.0	198.3	—	225.0	237.5	239.6
os (cervix)	180.0	198.82	233.1	219.0	236.0	239.5
intervertebral cartilage or disc	170.2	198.5	—	213.2	238.0	239.2

Neoplasm, neoplastic — continued	Malignant Primary	Malignant Secondary	Malignant Ca in situ	Benign	Uncertain Behavior	Unspecified
intestine, intestinal	159.0	197.8	230.7	211.9	235.2	239.0
large	153.9	197.5	230.3	211.3	235.2	239.0
appendix	153.5	197.5	230.3	211.3	235.2	239.0
caput coli	153.4	197.5	230.3	211.3	235.2	239.0
cecum	153.4	197.5	230.3	211.3	235.2	239.0
colon	153.9	197.5	230.3	211.3	235.2	239.0
and rectum	154.0	197.5	230.4	211.4	235.2	239.0
ascending	153.6	197.5	230.3	211.3	235.2	239.0
caput	153.4	197.5	230.3	211.3	235.2	239.0
contiguous sites	153.8	—	—	—	—	—
descending	153.2	197.5	230.3	211.3	235.2	239.0
distal	153.2	197.5	230.3	211.3	235.2	239.0
left	153.2	197.5	230.3	211.3	235.2	239.0
pelvic	153.3	197.5	230.3	211.3	235.2	239.0
right	153.6	197.5	230.3	211.3	235.2	239.0
sigmoid (flexure)	153.3	197.5	230.3	211.3	235.2	239.0
transverse	153.1	197.5	230.3	211.3	235.2	239.0
contiguous sites	153.8	—	—	—	—	—
hepatic flexure	153.0	197.5	230.3	211.3	235.2	239.0
ileocecum, ileocecal (coil) (valve)	153.4	197.5	230.3	211.3	235.2	239.0
sigmoid flexure (lower) (upper)	153.3	197.5	230.3	211.3	235.2	239.0
splenic flexure	153.7	197.5	230.3	211.3	235.2	239.0
small	152.9	197.4	230.7	211.2	235.2	239.0
contiguous sites	152.8	—	—	—	—	—
duodenum	152.0	197.4	230.7	211.2	235.2	239.0
ileum	152.2	197.4	230.7	211.2	235.2	239.0
jejunum	152.1	197.4	230.7	211.2	235.2	239.0
tract NEC	159.0	197.8	230.7	211.9	235.2	239.0
intra-abdominal	195.2	198.89	234.8	229.8	238.8	239.8
intracranial NEC	191.9	198.3	—	225.0	237.5	239.6
intrahepatic (bile) duct	155.1	197.8	230.8	211.5	235.3	239.0
intraocular	190.0	198.4	234.0	224.0	238.8	239.8
intraorbital	190.1	198.4	234.0	224.1	238.8	239.8
intrasellar	194.3	198.89	234.8	227.3	237.0	239.7
intrathoracic (cavity) (organs NEC)	195.1	198.89	234.8	229.8	238.8	239.8
contiguous sites with respiratory organs	165.8	—	—	—	—	—
iris	190.0	198.4	234.0	224.0	238.8	239.8
ischiorectal (fossa)	195.3	198.89	234.8	229.8	238.8	239.8
ischium	170.6	198.5	—	213.6	238.0	239.2
island of Reil	191.0	198.3	—	225.0	237.5	239.6
islands or islets of Langerhans	157.4	197.8	230.9	211.7	235.5	239.0
isthmus uteri	182.1	198.82	233.2	219.1	236.0	239.5
jaw	195.0	198.89	234.8	229.8	238.8	239.8
bone	170.1	198.5	—	213.1	238.0	239.2
carcinoma	143.9	—	—	—	—	—
lower	143.1	—	—	—	—	—
upper	143.0	—	—	—	—	—
lower	170.1	198.5	—	213.1	238.0	239.2
upper	170.0	198.5	—	213.0	238.0	239.2
carcinoma (any type) (lower) (upper)	195.0	—	—	—	—	—
skin	173.3	198.2	232.3	216.3	238.2	239.2
soft tissues	143.9	198.89	230.0	210.4	235.1	239.0
lower	143.1	198.89	230.0	210.4	235.1	239.0
upper	143.0	198.89	230.0	210.4	235.1	239.0
jejunum	152.1	197.4	230.7	211.2	235.2	239.0
joint NEC (see also Neoplasm, bone)	170.9	198.5	—	213.9	238.0	239.2
acromioclavicular	170.4	198.5	—	213.4	238.0	239.2
bursa or synovial membrane — see Neoplasm, connective tissue						
costovertebral	170.3	198.5	—	213.3	238.0	239.2
sternocostal	170.3	198.5	—	213.3	238.0	239.2
temporomandibular	170.1	198.5	—	213.1	238.0	239.2
junction						
anorectal	154.8	197.5	230.7	211.4	235.5	239.0
cardioesophageal	151.0	197.8	230.2	211.1	235.2	239.0
esophagogastric	151.0	197.8	230.2	211.1	235.2	239.0
gastroesophageal	151.0	197.8	230.2	211.1	235.2	239.0
hard and soft palate	145.5	198.89	230.0	210.4	235.1	239.0
ileocecal	153.4	197.5	230.3	211.3	235.2	239.0
pelvirectal	154.0	197.5	230.4	211.4	235.2	239.0
pelviureteric	189.1	198.0	233.9	223.1	236.91	239.5
rectosigmoid	154.0	197.5	230.4	211.4	235.2	239.0
squamocolumnar, of cervix	180.8	198.82	233.1	219.0	236.0	239.5
kidney (parenchyma)	189.0	198.0	233.9	223.0	236.91	239.5
calyx	189.1	198.0	233.9	223.1	236.91	239.5

☑ Additional Digit Required — Refer to the Tabular List (Numeric Code Section) for Additional Digit Selection

▶◀ Revised Text ● New Line ▲ Revised Code *2006 ICD-9-CM*

Neoplasm, neoplastic — continued	Malignant Primary	Malignant Secondary	Malignant Ca in situ	Benign	Uncertain Behavior	Unspecified
kidney — continued						
hilus	189.1	198.0	233.9	223.1	236.91	239.5
pelvis	189.1	198.0	233.9	223.1	236.91	239.5
knee NEC*	195.5	198.89	232.7	229.8	238.8	239.8
labia (skin)	184.4	198.82	233.3	221.2	236.3	239.5
majora	184.1	198.82	233.3	221.2	236.3	239.5
minora	184.2	198.82	233.3	221.2	236.3	239.5
labial — see also Neoplasm, lip						
sulcus (lower) (upper)	145.1	198.89	230.0	210.4	235.1	239.0
labium (skin)	184.4	198.82	233.3	221.2	236.3	239.5
majus	184.1	198.82	233.3	221.2	236.3	239.5
minus	184.2	198.82	233.3	221.2	236.3	239.5
lacrimal						
canaliculi	190.7	198.4	234.0	224.7	238.8	239.8
duct (nasal)	190.7	198.4	234.0	224.7	238.8	239.8
gland	190.2	198.4	234.0	224.2	238.8	239.8
punctum	190.7	198.4	234.0	224.7	238.8	239.8
sac	190.7	198.4	234.0	224.7	238.8	239.8
Langerhans, islands or islets	157.4	197.8	230.9	211.7	235.5	239.0
laryngopharynx	148.9	198.89	230.0	210.8	235.1	239.0
larynx, laryngeal NEC	161.9	197.3	231.0	212.1	235.6	239.1
aryepiglottic fold	161.1	197.3	231.0	212.1	235.6	239.1
cartilage (arytenoid) (cricoid) (cuneiform) (thyroid)	161.3	197.3	231.0	212.1	235.6	239.1
commissure (anterior) (posterior)	161.0	197.3	231.0	212.1	235.6	239.1
contiguous sites	161.8	—	—	—	—	—
extrinsic NEC	161.1	197.3	231.0	212.1	235.6	239.1
meaning hypopharynx	148.9	198.89	230.0	210.8	235.1	239.0
interarytenoid fold	161.1	197.3	231.0	212.1	235.6	239.1
intrinsic	161.0	197.3	231.0	212.1	235.6	239.1
ventricular band	161.1	197.3	231.0	212.1	235.6	239.1
leg NEC*	195.5	198.89	232.7	229.8	238.8	239.8
lens, crystalline	190.0	198.4	234.0	224.0	238.8	239.8
lid (lower) (upper)	173.1	198.2	232.1	216.1	238.2	239.2
ligament — see also Neoplasm, connective tissue						
broad	183.3	198.82	233.3	221.0	236.3	239.5
Mackenrodt's	183.8	198.82	233.3	221.8	236.3	239.5
non-uterine — see Neoplasm, connective tissue						
round	183.5	198.82	—	221.0	236.3	239.5
sacro-uterine	183.4	198.82	—	221.0	236.3	239.5
uterine	183.4	198.82	—	221.0	236.3	239.5
utero-ovarian	183.8	198.82	233.3	221.8	236.3	239.5
uterosacral	183.4	198.82	—	221.0	236.3	239.5
limb*	195.8	198.89	232.8	229.8	238.8	239.8
lower*	195.5	198.89	232.7	229.8	238.8	239.8
upper*	195.4	198.89	232.6	229.8	238.8	239.8
limbus of cornea	190.4	198.4	234.0	224.4	238.8	239.8
lingual NEC (see also Neoplasm, tongue)	141.9	198.89	230.0	210.1	235.1	239.0
lingula, lung	162.3	197.0	231.2	212.3	235.7	239.1
lip (external) (lipstick area) (vermillion border)	140.9	198.89	230.0	210.0	235.1	239.0
buccal aspect — see Neoplasm, lip, internal						
commissure	140.6	198.89	230.0	210.4	235.1	239.0
contiguous sites	140.8	—	—	—	—	—
with oral cavity or pharynx	149.8	—	—	—	—	—
frenulum — see Neoplasm, lip, internal						
inner aspect — see Neoplasm, lip, internal						
internal (buccal) (frenulum) (mucosa) (oral)	140.5	198.89	230.0	210.0	235.1	239.0
lower	140.4	198.89	230.0	210.0	235.1	239.0
upper	140.3	198.89	230.0	210.0	235.1	239.0
lower	140.1	198.89	230.0	210.0	235.1	239.0
internal (buccal) (frenulum) (mucosa) (oral)	140.4	198.89	230.0	210.0	235.1	239.0
mucosa — see Neoplasm, lip, internal						
oral aspect — see Neoplasm, lip, internal						
skin (commissure) (lower) (upper)	173.0	198.2	232.0	216.0	238.2	239.2
upper	140.0	198.89	230.0	210.0	235.1	239.0
internal (buccal) (frenulum) (mucosa) (oral)	140.3	198.89	230.0	210.0	235.1	239.0

Neoplasm, neoplastic — continued	Malignant Primary	Malignant Secondary	Malignant Ca in situ	Benign	Uncertain Behavior	Unspecified
liver	155.2	197.7	230.8	211.5	235.3	239.0
primary	155.0	—	—	—	—	—
lobe						
azygos	162.3	197.0	231.2	212.3	235.7	239.1
frontal	191.1	198.3	—	225.0	237.5	239.6
lower	162.5	197.0	231.2	212.3	235.7	239.1
middle	162.4	197.0	231.2	212.3	235.7	239.1
occipital	191.4	198.3	—	225.0	237.5	239.6
parietal	191.3	198.3	—	225.0	237.5	239.6
temporal	191.2	198.3	—	225.0	237.5	239.6
upper	162.3	197.0	231.2	212.3	235.7	239.1
lumbosacral plexus	171.6	198.4	—	215.6	238.1	239.2
lung	162.9	197.0	231.2	212.3	235.7	239.1
azygos lobe	162.3	197.0	231.2	212.3	235.7	239.1
carina	162.2	197.0	231.2	212.3	235.7	239.1
contiguous sites with bronchus or trachea	162.8	—	—	—	—	—
hilus	162.2	197.0	231.2	212.3	235.7	239.1
lingula	162.3	197.0	231.2	212.3	235.7	239.1
lobe NEC	162.9	197.0	231.2	212.3	235.7	239.1
lower lobe	162.5	197.0	231.2	212.3	235.7	239.1
main bronchus	162.2	197.0	231.2	212.3	235.7	239.1
middle lobe	162.4	197.0	231.2	212.3	235.7	239.1
upper lobe	162.3	197.0	231.2	212.3	235.7	239.1
lymph, lymphatic						
channel NEC (see also Neoplasm, connective tissue)	171.9	198.89	—	215.9	238.1	239.2
gland (secondary)	—	196.9	—	229.0	238.8	239.8
abdominal	—	196.2	—	229.0	238.8	239.8
aortic	—	196.2	—	229.0	238.8	239.8
arm	—	196.3	—	229.0	238.8	239.8
auricular (anterior) (posterior)	—	196.0	—	229.0	238.8	239.8
axilla, axillary	—	196.3	—	229.0	238.8	239.8
brachial	—	196.3	—	229.0	238.8	239.8
bronchial	—	196.1	—	229.0	238.8	239.8
bronchopulmonary	—	196.1	—	229.0	238.8	239.8
celiac	—	196.2	—	229.0	238.8	239.8
cervical	—	196.0	—	229.0	238.8	239.8
cervicofacial	—	196.0	—	229.0	238.8	239.8
Cloquet	—	196.5	—	229.0	238.8	239.8
colic	—	196.2	—	229.0	238.8	239.8
common duct	—	196.2	—	229.0	238.8	239.8
cubital	—	196.3	—	229.0	238.8	239.8
diaphragmatic	—	196.1	—	229.0	238.8	239.8
epigastric, inferior	—	196.6	—	229.0	238.8	239.8
epitrochlear	—	196.3	—	229.0	238.8	239.8
esophageal	—	196.1	—	229.0	238.8	239.8
face	—	196.0	—	229.0	238.8	239.8
femoral	—	196.5	—	229.0	238.8	239.8
gastric	—	196.2	—	229.0	238.8	239.8
groin	—	196.5	—	229.0	238.8	239.8
head	—	196.0	—	229.0	238.8	239.8
hepatic	—	196.2	—	229.0	238.8	239.8
hilar (pulmonary)	—	196.1	—	229.0	238.8	239.8
splenic	—	196.2	—	229.0	238.8	239.8
hypogastric	—	196.6	—	229.0	238.8	239.8
ileocolic	—	196.2	—	229.0	238.8	239.8
iliac	—	196.6	—	229.0	238.8	239.8
infraclavicular	—	196.3	—	229.0	238.8	239.8
inguina, inguinal	—	196.5	—	229.0	238.8	239.8
innominate	—	196.1	—	229.0	238.8	239.8
intercostal	—	196.1	—	229.0	238.8	239.8
intestinal	—	196.2	—	229.0	238.8	239.8
intra-abdominal	—	196.2	—	229.0	238.8	239.8
intrapelvic	—	196.6	—	229.0	238.8	239.8
intrathoracic	—	196.1	—	229.0	238.8	239.9
jugular	—	196.0	—	229.0	238.8	239.8
leg	—	196.5	—	229.0	238.8	239.8
limb						
lower	—	196.5	—	229.0	238.8	239.8
upper	—	196.3	—	229.0	238.8	239.8
lower limb	—	196.5	—	229.0	238.8	239.9
lumbar	—	196.2	—	229.0	238.8	239.8
mandibular	—	196.0	—	229.0	238.8	239.8
mediastinal	—	196.1	—	229.0	238.8	239.8
mesenteric (inferior) (superior)	—	196.2	—	229.0	238.8	239.8

☑ Additional Digit Required — Refer to the Tabular List (Numeric Code Section) for Additional Digit Selection
►◄ Revised Text　　　● New Line　　　▲ Revised Code

Neoplasm, neoplastic — continued

	Primary	Secondary	Ca in situ	Benign	Uncertain Behavior	Unspecified
		Malignant				
lymph, lymphatic — *continued*						
gland — *continued*						
midcolic	—	196.2	—	229.0	238.8	239.8
multiple sites in categories 196.0-196.6	—	196.8	—	229.0	238.8	239.8
neck	—	196.0	—	229.0	238.8	239.8
obturator	—	196.6	—	229.0	238.8	239.8
occipital	—	196.0	—	229.0	238.8	239.8
pancreatic	—	196.2	—	229.0	238.8	239.8
para-aortic	—	196.2	—	229.0	238.8	239.8
paracervical	—	196.6	—	229.0	238.8	239.8
parametrial	—	196.6	—	229.0	238.8	239.8
parasternal	—	196.1	—	229.0	238.8	239.8
parotid	—	196.0	—	229.0	238.8	239.8
pectoral	—	196.3	—	229.0	238.8	239.8
pelvic	—	196.6	—	229.0	238.8	239.8
peri-aortic	—	196.2	—	229.0	238.8	239.8
peripancreatic	—	196.2	—	229.0	238.8	239.8
popliteal	—	196.5	—	229.0	238.8	239.8
porta hepatis	—	196.2	—	229.0	238.8	239.8
portal	—	196.2	—	229.0	238.8	239.8
preauricular	—	196.0	—	229.0	238.8	239.8
prelaryngeal	—	196.0	—	229.0	238.8	239.8
presymphysial	—	196.6	—	229.0	238.8	239.8
pretracheal	—	196.0	—	229.0	238.8	239.8
primary (any site) NEC	202.9 ✓	—	—	—	—	—
pulmonary (hiler)	—	196.1	—	229.0	238.8	239.8
pyloric	—	196.2	—	229.0	238.8	239.8
retroperitoneal	—	196.2	—	229.0	238.8	239.8
retropharyngeal	—	196.0	—	229.0	238.8	239.8
Rosenmüller's	—	196.5	—	229.0	238.8	239.8
sacral	—	196.6	—	229.0	238.8	239.8
scalene	—	196.0	—	229.0	238.8	239.8
site NEC	—	196.9	—	229.0	238.8	239.8
splenic (hilar)	—	196.2	—	229.0	238.8	239.8
subclavicular	—	196.3	—	229.0	238.8	239.8
subinguinal	—	196.5	—	229.0	238.8	239.8
sublingual	—	196.0	—	229.0	238.8	239.8
submandibular	—	196.0	—	229.0	238.8	239.8
submaxillary	—	196.0	—	229.0	238.8	239.8
submental	—	196.0	—	229.0	238.8	239.8
subscapular	—	196.3	—	229.0	238.8	239.8
supraclavicular	—	196.0	—	229.0	238.8	239.8
thoracic	—	196.1	—	229.0	238.8	239.8
tibial	—	196.5	—	229.0	238.8	239.8
tracheal	—	196.1	—	229.0	238.8	239.8
tracheobronchial	—	196.1	—	229.0	238.8	239.8
upper limb	—	196.3	—	229.0	238.8	239.8
Virchow's	—	196.0	—	229.0	238.8	239.8
node — *see also* Neoplasm, lymph gland						
primary NEC	202.9 ✓	—	—	—	—	—
vessel (*see also* Neoplasm, connective tissue)	171.9	198.89	—	215.9	238.1	239.2
Nackenrodt's ligament	183.8	198.82	233.3	221.8	236.3	239.5
malar	170.0	198.5	—	213.0	238.0	239.2
region — *see* Neoplasm, cheek						
mammary gland — *see* Neoplasm, breast						
mandible	170.1	198.5	—	213.1	238.0	239.2
alveolar						
mucose	143.1	198.89	230.0	210.4	235.1	239.0
ridge or process	170.1	198.5	—	213.1	238.0	239.2
carcinoma	143.1	—	—	—	—	—
carcinoma	143.1	—	—	—	—	—
marrow (bone) NEC	202.9 ✓	198.5	—	—	—	238.7
mastectomy site (skin)	173.5	198.2	—	—	—	—
specified as breast tissue	174.8	198.81	—	—	—	—
mastoid (air cells) (antrum) (cavity)	160.1	197.3	231.8	212.0	235.9	239.1
bone or process	170.0	198.5	—	213.0	238.0	239.2
maxilla, maxillary (superior)	170.0	198.5	—	213.0	238.0	239.2
alveolar						
mucosa	143.0	198.89	230.0	210.4	235.1	239.0
ridge or process	170.0	198.5	—	213.0	238.0	239.2
carcinoma	143.0	—	—	—	—	—
antrum	160.2	197.3	231.8	212.0	235.9	239.1
carcinoma	143.0	—	—	—	—	—

Neoplasm, neoplastic — continued

	Primary	Secondary	Ca in situ	Benign	Uncertain Behavior	Unspecified
		Malignant				
maxilla, maxillary — *continued*						
inferior — *see* Neoplasm, mandible						
sinus	160.2	197.3	231.8	212.0	235.9	239.1
meatus						
external (ear)	173.2	198.2	232.2	216.2	238.2	239.2
Meckel's diverticulum	152.3	197.4	230.7	211.2	235.2	239.0
mediastinum, mediastinal	164.9	197.1	—	212.5	235.8	239.8
anterior	164.2	197.1	—	212.5	235.8	239.8
contiguous sites with heart and thymus	164.8	—	—	—	—	—
posterior	164.3	197.1	—	212.5	235.8	239.8
medulla						
adrenal	194.0	198.7	234.8	227.0	237.2	239.7
oblongata	191.7	198.3	—	225.0	237.5	239.6
meibomian gland	173.1	198.2	232.1	216.1	238.2	239.2
melanoma — *see* Melanoma						
meninges (brain) (cerebral) (cranial) (intracranial)	192.1	198.4	—	225.2	237.6	239.7
spinal (cord)	192.3	198.4	—	225.4	237.6	239.7
meniscus, knee joint (lateral) (medial)	170.7	198.5	—	213.7	238.0	239.2
mesentery, mesenteric	158.8	197.6	—	211.8	235.4	239.0
mesoappendix	158.8	197.6	—	211.8	235.4	239.0
mesocolon	158.8	197.6	—	211.8	235.4	239.0
mesopharynx — *see* Neoplasm, oropharynx						
mesosalpinx	183.3	198.82	233.3	221.0	236.3	239.5
mesovarium	183.3	198.82	233.3	221.0	236.3	239.5
metacarpus (any bone)	170.5	198.5	—	213.5	238.0	239.2
metastatic NEC — *see also* Neoplasm, by site, secondary	—	199.1	—	—	—	—
metatarsus (any bone)	170.8	198.5	—	213.8	238.0	239.2
midbrain	191.7	198.3	—	225.0	237.5	239.6
milk duct — *see* Neoplasm, breast						
mons						
pubis	184.4	198.82	233.3	221.2	236.3	239.5
veneris	184.4	198.82	233.3	221.2	236.3	239.5
motor tract	192.9	198.4	—	225.9	237.9	239.7
brain	191.9	198.3	—	225.0	237.5	239.6
spinal	192.2	198.3	—	225.3	237.5	239.7
mouth	145.9	198.89	230.0	210.4	235.1	239.0
contiguous sites	145.8	—	—	—	—	—
floor	144.9	198.89	230.0	210.3	235.1	239.0
anterior portion	144.0	198.89	230.0	210.3	235.1	239.0
contiguous sites	144.8	—	—	—	—	—
lateral portion	144.1	198.89	230.0	210.3	235.1	239.0
roof	145.5	198.89	230.0	210.4	235.1	239.0
specified part NEC	145.8	198.89	230.0	210.4	235.1	239.0
vestibule	145.1	198.89	230.0	210.4	235.1	239.0
mucosa						
alveolar (ridge or process)	143.9	198.89	230.0	210.4	235.1	239.0
lower	143.1	198.89	230.0	210.4	235.1	239.0
upper	143.0	198.89	230.0	210.4	235.1	239.0
buccal	145.0	198.89	230.0	210.4	235.1	239.0
cheek	145.0	198.89	230.0	210.4	235.1	239.0
lip — *see* Neoplasm, lip, internal						
nasal	160.0	197.3	231.8	212.0	235.9	239.1
oral	145.0	198.89	230.0	210.4	235.1	239.0
Müllerian duct						
female	184.8	198.82	233.3	221.8	236.3	239.5
male	187.8	198.82	233.6	222.8	236.6	239.5
multiple sites NEC	199.0	199.0	234.9	229.9	238.9	199.0
muscle — *see also* Neoplasm, connective tissue						
extraocular	190.1	198.4	234.0	224.1	238.8	239.8
myocardium	164.1	198.89	—	212.7	238.8	239.8
myometrium	182.0	198.82	233.2	219.1	236.0	239.5
myopericardium	164.1	198.89	—	212.7	238.8	239.8
nabothian gland (follicle)	180.0	198.82	233.1	219.0	236.0	239.5
nail	173.9	198.2	232.9	216.9	238.2	239.2
finger	173.6	198.2	232.6	216.6	238.2	239.2
toe	173.7	198.2	232.7	216.7	238.2	239.2
nares, naris (anterior) (posterior)	160.0	197.3	231.8	212.0	235.9	239.1
nasal — *see* Neoplasm, nose						
nasolabial groove	173.3	198.2	232.3	216.3	238.2	239.2
nasolacrimal duct	190.7	198.4	234.0	224.7	238.8	239.8

| | Malignant | | | | |
Neoplasm, neoplastic — *continued*	Primary	Secondary	Ca in situ	Benign	Uncertain Behavior	Unspecified
nasopharynx, nasopharyngeal	147.9	198.89	230.0	210.7	235.1	239.0
contiguous sites	147.8	—	—	—	—	—
floor	147.3	198.89	230.0	210.7	235.1	239.0
roof	147.0	198.89	230.0	210.7	235.1	239.0
specified site NEC	147.8	198.89	230.0	210.7	235.1	239.0
wall	147.9	198.89	230.0	210.7	235.1	239.0
anterior	147.3	198.89	230.0	210.7	235.1	239.0
lateral	147.2	198.89	230.0	210.7	235.1	239.0
posterior	147.1	198.89	230.0	210.7	235.1	239.0
superior	147.0	198.89	230.0	210.7	235.1	239.0
nates	173.5	198.2	232.5	216.5	238.2	239.2
neck NEC*	195.0	198.89	234.8	229.8	238.8	239.8
nerve (autonomic) (ganglion) (parasympathetic) (peripheral) (sympathetic) — *see also* Neoplasm, connective tissue						
abducens	192.0	198.4	—	225.1	237.9	239.7
accessory (spinal)	192.0	198.4	—	225.1	237.9	239.7
acoustic	192.0	198.4	—	225.1	237.9	239.7
auditory	192.0	198.4	—	225.1	237.9	239.7
brachial	171.2	198.89	—	215.2	238.1	239.2
cranial (any)	192.0	198.4	—	225.1	237.9	239.7
facial	192.0	198.4	—	225.1	237.9	239.7
femoral	171.3	198.89	—	215.3	238.1	239.2
glossopharyngeal	192.0	198.4	—	225.1	237.9	239.7
hypoglossal	192.0	198.4	—	225.1	237.9	239.7
intercostal	171.4	198.89	—	215.4	238.1	239.2
lumbar	171.7	198.89	—	215.7	238.1	239.2
median	171.2	198.89	—	215.2	238.1	239.2
obturator	171.3	198.89	—	215.3	238.1	239.2
oculomotor	192.0	198.4	—	225.1	237.9	239.7
olfactory	192.0	198.4	—	225.1	237.9	239.7
optic	192.0	198.4	—	225.1	237.9	239.7
peripheral NEC	171.9	198.89	—	215.9	238.1	239.2
radial	171.2	198.89	—	215.2	238.1	239.2
sacral	171.6	198.89	—	215.6	238.1	239.2
sciatic	171.3	198.89	—	215.3	238.1	239.2
spinal NEC	171.9	198.89	—	215.9	238.1	239.2
trigeminal	192.0	198.4	—	225.1	237.9	239.7
trochlear	192.0	198.4	—	225.1	237.9	239.7
ulnar	171.2	198.89	—	215.2	238.1	239.2
vagus	192.0	198.4	—	225.1	237.9	239.7
nervous system (central) NEC	192.9	198.4	—	225.9	237.9	239.7
autonomic NEC	171.9	198.89	—	215.9	238.1	239.2
brain — *see also* Neoplasm, brain						
membrane or meninges	192.1	198.4	—	225.2	237.6	239.7
contiguous sites	192.8	—	—	—	—	—
parasympathetic NEC	171.9	198.89	—	215.9	238.1	239.2
sympathetic NEC	171.9	198.89	—	215.9	238.1	239.2
nipple (female)	174.0	198.81	233.0	217	238.3	239.3
male	175.0	198.81	233.0	217	238.3	239.3
nose, nasal	195.0	198.89	234.8	229.8	238.8	239.8
ala (external)	173.3	198.2	232.3	216.3	238.2	239.2
bone	170.0	198.5	—	213.0	238.0	239.2
cartilage	160.0	197.3	231.8	212.0	235.9	239.1
cavity	160.0	197.3	231.8	212.0	235.9	239.1
contiguous sites with accessory sinuses or middle ear	160.8	—	—	—	—	—
choana	147.3	198.89	230.0	210.7	235.1	239.0
external (skin)	173.3	198.2	232.3	216.3	238.2	239.2
fossa	160.0	197.3	231.8	212.0	235.9	239.1
internal	160.0	197.3	231.8	212.0	235.9	239.1
mucosa	160.0	197.3	231.8	212.0	235.9	239.1
septum	160.0	197.3	231.8	212.0	235.9	239.1
posterior margin	147.3	198.89	230.0	210.7	235.1	239.0
sinus — *see* Neoplasm, sinus						
skin	173.3	198.2	232.3	216.3	238.2	239.2
turbinate (mucosa)	160.0	197.3	231.8	212.0	235.9	239.1
bone	170.0	198.5	—	213.0	238.0	239.2
vestibule	160.0	197.3	231.8	212.0	235.9	239.1
nostril	160.0	197.3	231.8	212.0	235.9	239.1
nucleus pulposus	170.2	198.5	—	213.2	238.0	239.2
occipital						
bone	170.0	198.5	—	213.0	238.0	239.2
lobe or pole, brain	191.4	198.3	—	225.0	237.5	239.6
odontogenic — *see* Neoplasm, jaw bone						

| | Malignant | | | | |
Neoplasm, neoplastic — *continued*	Primary	Secondary	Ca in situ	Benign	Uncertain Behavior	Unspecified
oesophagus — *see* Neoplasm, esophagus						
olfactory nerve or bulb	192.0	198.4	—	225.1	237.9	239.7
olive (brain)	191.7	198.3	—	225.0	237.5	239.6
omentum	158.8	197.6	—	211.8	235.4	239.0
operculum (brain)	191.0	198.3	—	225.0	237.5	239.6
optic nerve, chiasm, or tract	192.0	198.4	—	225.1	237.9	239.7
oral (cavity)	145.9	198.89	230.0	210.4	235.1	239.0
contiguous sites with lip or pharynx	149.8	—	—	—	—	—
ill-defined	149.9	198.89	230.0	210.4	235.1	239.0
mucosa	145.9	198.89	230.0	210.4	235.1	239.0
orbit	190.1	198.4	234.0	224.1	238.8	239.8
bone	170.0	198.5	—	213.0	238.0	239.2
eye	190.1	198.4	234.0	224.1	238.8	239.8
soft parts	190.1	198.4	234.0	224.1	238.8	239.8
organ of Zuckerkandl	194.6	198.89	—	227.6	237.3	239.7
oropharynx	146.9	198.89	230.0	210.6	235.1	239.0
branchial cleft (vestige)	146.8	198.89	230.0	210.6	235.1	239.0
contiguous sites	146.8	—	—	—	—	—
junctional region	146.5	198.89	230.0	210.6	235.1	239.0
lateral wall	146.6	198.89	230.0	210.6	235.1	239.0
pillars of fauces	146.2	198.89	230.0	210.6	235.1	239.0
posterior wall	146.7	198.89	230.0	210.6	235.1	239.0
specified part NEC	146.8	198.89	230.0	210.6	235.1	239.0
vallecula	146.3	198.89	230.0	210.6	235.1	239.0
os						
external	180.1	198.82	233.1	219.0	236.0	239.5
internal	180.0	198.82	233.1	219.0	236.0	239.5
ovary	183.0	198.6	233.3	220	236.2	239.5
oviduct	183.2	198.82	233.3	221.0	236.3	239.5
palate	145.5	198.89	230.0	210.4	235.1	239.0
hard	145.2	198.89	230.0	210.4	235.1	239.0
junction of hard and soft palate	145.5	198.89	230.0	210.4	235.1	239.0
soft	145.3	198.89	230.0	210.4	235.1	239.0
nasopharyngeal surface	147.3	198.89	230.0	210.7	235.1	239.0
posterior surface	147.3	198.89	230.0	210.7	235.1	239.0
superior surface	147.3	198.89	230.0	210.7	235.1	239.0
palatoglossal arch	146.2	198.89	230.0	210.6	235.1	239.0
palatopharyngeal arch	146.2	198.89	230.0	210.6	235.1	239.0
pallium	191.0	198.3	—	225.0	237.5	239.6
palpebra	173.1	198.2	232.1	216.1	238.2	239.2
pancreas	157.9	197.8	230.9	211.6	235.5	239.0
body	157.1	197.8	230.9	211.6	235.5	239.0
contiguous sites	157.8	—	—	—	—	—
duct (of Santorini) (of Wirsung)	157.3	197.8	230.9	211.6	235.5	239.0
ectopic tissue	157.8	197.8	230.9	211.6	235.5	239.0
head	157.0	197.8	230.9	211.6	235.5	239.0
islet cells	157.4	197.8	230.9	211.7	235.5	239.0
neck	157.8	197.8	230.9	211.6	235.5	239.0
tail	157.2	197.8	230.9	211.6	235.5	239.0
para-aortic body	194.6	198.89	—	227.6	237.3	239.7
paraganglion NEC	194.6	198.89	—	227.6	237.3	239.7
parametrium	183.4	198.82	—	221.0	236.3	239.5
paranephric	158.0	197.6	—	211.8	235.4	239.0
pararectal	195.3	198.89	—	229.8	238.8	239.8
parasagittal (region)	195.0	198.89	234.8	229.8	238.8	239.8
parasellar	192.9	198.4	—	225.9	237.9	239.7
parathyroid (gland)	194.1	198.89	234.8	227.1	237.4	239.7
paraurethral	195.3	198.89	—	229.8	238.8	239.8
gland	189.4	198.1	233.9	223.89	236.99	239.5
paravaginal	195.3	198.89	—	229.8	238.8	239.8
parenchyma, kidney	189.0	198.0	233.9	223.0	236.91	239.5
parietal						
bone	170.0	198.5	—	213.0	238.0	239.2
lobe, brain	191.3	198.3	—	225.0	237.5	239.6
paroophoron	183.3	198.82	233.3	221.0	236.3	239.5
parotid (duct) (gland)	142.0	198.89	230.0	210.2	235.0	239.0
parovarium	183.3	198.82	233.3	221.0	236.3	239.5
patella	170.8	198.5	—	213.8	238.0	239.2
peduncle, cerebral	191.7	198.3	—	225.0	237.5	239.6
pelvirectal junction	154.0	197.5	230.4	211.4	235.2	239.0
pelvis, pelvic	195.3	198.89	234.8	229.8	238.8	239.8
bone	170.6	198.5	—	213.6	238.0	239.2
floor	195.3	198.89	234.8	229.8	238.8	239.8
renal	189.1	198.0	233.9	223.1	236.91	239.5
viscera	195.3	198.89	234.8	229.8	238.8	239.8
wall	195.3	198.89	234.8	229.8	238.8	239.8

☑ Additional Digit Required — Refer to the Tabular List (Numeric Code Section) for Additional Digit Selection

▶◀ Revised Text   ● New Line   ▲ Revised Code

Neoplasm, neoplastic — continued	Malignant Primary	Malignant Secondary	Malignant Ca in situ	Benign	Uncertain Behavior	Unspecified
pelvo-abdominal	195.8	198.89	234.8	229.8	238.8	239.8
penis	187.4	198.82	233.5	222.1	236.6	239.5
body	187.3	198.82	233.5	222.1	236.6	239.5
corpus (cavernosum)	187.3	198.82	233.5	222.1	236.6	239.5
glans	187.2	198.82	233.5	222.1	236.6	239.5
skin NEC	187.4	198.82	233.5	222.1	236.6	239.5
periadrenal (tissue)	158.0	197.6	—	211.8	235.4	239.0
perianal (skin)	173.5	198.2	232.5	216.5	238.2	239.2
pericardium	164.1	198.89	—	212.7	238.8	239.8
perinephric	158.0	197.6	—	211.8	235.4	239.0
perineum	195.3	198.89	234.8	229.8	238.8	239.8
periodontal tissue NEC	143.9	198.89	230.0	210.4	235.1	239.0
periosteum — see Neoplasm, bone						
peripancreatic	158.0	197.6	—	211.8	235.4	239.0
peripheral nerve NEC	171.9	198.89	—	215.9	238.1	239.2
perirectal (tissue)	195.3	198.89	—	229.8	238.8	239.8
perirenal (tissue)	158.0	197.6	—	211.8	235.4	239.0
peritoneum, peritoneal (cavity)	158.9	197.6	—	211.8	235.4	239.0
contiguous sites	158.8	—	—	—	—	—
with digestive organs	159.8	—	—	—	—	—
parietal	158.8	197.6	—	211.8	235.4	239.0
pelvic	158.8	197.6	—	211.8	235.4	239.0
specified part NEC	158.8	197.6	—	211.8	235.4	239.0
peritonsillar (tissue)	195.0	198.89	234.8	229.8	238.8	239.8
periurethral tissue	195.3	198.89	—	229.8	238.8	239.8
phalanges	170.9	198.5	—	213.9	238.0	239.2
foot	170.8	198.5	—	213.8	238.0	239.2
hand	170.5	198.5	—	213.5	238.0	239.2
pharynx, pharyngeal	149.0	198.89	230.0	210.9	235.1	239.0
bursa	147.1	198.89	230.0	210.7	235.1	239.0
fornix	147.3	198.89	230.0	210.7	235.1	239.0
recess	147.2	198.89	230.0	210.7	235.1	239.0
region	149.0	198.89	230.0	210.9	235.1	239.0
tonsil	147.1	198.89	230.0	210.7	235.1	239.0
wall (lateral) (posterior)	149.0	198.89	230.0	210.9	235.1	239.0
pia mater (cerebral) (cranial)	192.1	198.4	—	225.2	237.6	239.7
spinal	192.3	198.4	—	225.4	237.6	239.7
pillars of fauces	146.2	198.89	230.0	210.6	235.1	239.0
pineal (body) (gland)	194.4	198.89	234.8	227.4	237.1	239.7
pinna (ear) NEC	173.2	198.2	232.2	216.2	238.2	239.2
cartilage	171.0	198.89	—	215.0	238.1	239.2
piriform fossa or sinus	148.1	198.89	230.0	210.8	235.1	239.0
pituitary (body) (fossa) (gland) (lobe)	194.3	198.89	234.8	227.3	237.0	239.7
placenta	181	198.82	233.2	219.8	236.1	239.5
pleura, pleural (cavity)	163.9	197.2	—	212.4	235.8	239.1
contiguous sites	163.8	—	—	—	—	—
parietal	163.0	197.2	—	212.4	235.8	239.1
visceral	163.1	197.2	—	212.4	235.8	239.1
plexus						
brachial	171.2	198.89	—	215.2	238.1	239.2
cervical	171.0	198.89	—	215.0	238.1	239.2
choroid	191.5	198.3	—	225.0	237.5	239.6
lumbosacral	171.6	198.89	—	215.6	238.1	239.2
sacral	171.6	198.89	—	215.6	238.1	239.2
pluri-endocrine	194.8	198.89	234.8	227.8	237.4	239.7
pole						
frontal	191.1	198.3	—	225.0	237.5	239.6
occipital	191.4	198.3	—	225.0	237.5	239.6
pons (varolii)	191.7	198.3	—	225.0	237.5	239.6
popliteal fossa or space*	195.5	198.89	234.8	229.8	238.8	239.8
postcricoid (region)	148.0	198.89	230.0	210.8	235.1	239.0
posterior fossa (cranial)	191.9 ▲	198.3	—	225.0	237.5	239.6
postnasal space	147.9	198.89	230.0	210.7	235.1	239.0
prepuce	187.1	198.82	233.5	222.1	236.6	239.5
prepylorus	151.1	197.8	230.2	211.1	235.2	239.0
presacral (region)	195.3	198.89	—	229.8	238.8	239.8
prostate (gland)	185	198.82	233.4	222.2	236.5	239.5
utricle	189.3	198.1	233.9	223.81	236.99	239.5
pterygoid fossa	171.0	198.89	—	215.0	238.1	239.2
pubic bone	170.6	198.5	—	213.6	238.0	239.2
pudenda, pudendum (female)	184.4	198.82	233.3	221.2	236.3	239.5
pulmonary	162.9	197.0	231.2	212.3	235.7	239.1
putamen	191.0	198.3	—	225.0	237.5	239.6
pyloric						
antrum	151.2	197.8	230.2	211.1	235.2	239.0
canal	151.1	197.8	230.2	211.1	235.2	239.0

Neoplasm, neoplastic — continued	Malignant Primary	Malignant Secondary	Malignant Ca in situ	Benign	Uncertain Behavior	Unspecified
pylorus	151.1	197.8	230.2	211.1	235.2	239.0
pyramid (brain)	191.7	198.3	—	225.0	237.5	239.6
pyriform fossa or sinus	148.1	198.89	230.0	210.8	235.1	239.0
radius (any part)	170.4	198.5	—	213.4	238.0	239.2
Rathke's pouch	194.3	198.89	234.8	227.3	237.0	239.7
rectosigmoid (colon) (junction)	154.0	197.5	230.4	211.4	235.2	239.0
contiguous sites with anus or rectum	154.8	—	—	—	—	—
rectouterine pouch	158.8	197.6	—	211.8	235.4	239.0
rectovaginal septum or wall	195.3	198.89	234.8	229.8	238.8	239.8
rectovesical septum	195.3	198.89	234.8	229.8	238.8	239.8
rectum (ampulla)	154.1	197.5	230.4	211.4	235.2	239.0
and colon	154.0	197.5	230.4	211.4	235.2	239.0
contiguous sites with anus or rectosigmoid junction	154.8	—	—	—	—	—
renal	189.0	198.0	233.9	223.0	236.91	239.5
calyx	189.1	198.0	233.9	223.1	236.91	239.5
hilus	189.1	198.0	233.9	223.1	236.91	239.5
parenchyma	189.0	198.0	233.9	223.0	236.91	239.5
pelvis	189.1	198.0	233.9	223.1	236.91	239.5
respiratory						
organs or system NEC	165.9	197.3	231.9	212.9	235.9	239.1
contiguous sites with intrathoracic organs	165.8	—	—	—	—	—
specified sites NEC	165.8	197.3	231.8	212.8	235.9	239.1
tract NEC	165.9	197.3	231.9	212.9	235.9	239.1
upper	165.0	197.3	231.9	212.9	235.9	239.1
retina	190.5	198.4	234.0	224.5	238.8	239.8
retrobulbar	190.1	198.4	—	224.1	238.8	239.8
retrocecal	158.0	197.6	—	211.8	235.4	239.0
retromolar (area) (triangle) (trigone)	145.6	198.89	230.0	210.4	235.1	239.0
retro-orbital	195.0	198.89	234.8	229.8	238.8	239.8
retroperitoneal (space) (tissue)	158.0	197.6	—	211.8	235.4	239.0
contiguous sites	158.8	—	—	—	—	—
retroperitoneum	158.0	197.6	—	211.8	235.4	239.0
contiguous sites	158.8	—	—	—	—	—
retropharyngeal	149.0	198.89	230.0	210.9	235.1	239.0
retrovesical (septum)	195.3	198.89	234.8	229.8	238.8	239.8
rhinencephalon	191.0	198.3	—	225.0	237.5	239.6
rib	170.3	198.5	—	213.3	238.0	239.2
Rosenmüller's fossa	147.2	198.89	230.0	210.7	235.1	239.0
round ligament	183.5	198.82	—	221.0	236.3	239.5
sacrococcyx, sacrococcygeal	170.6	198.5	—	213.6	238.0	239.2
region	195.3	198.89	234.8	229.8	238.8	239.8
sacrouterine ligament	183.4	198.82	—	221.0	236.3	239.5
sacrum, sacral (vertebra)	170.6	198.5	—	213.6	238.0	239.2
salivary gland or duct (major)	142.9	198.89	230.0	210.2	235.0	239.0
contiguous sites	142.8	—	—	—	—	—
minor NEC	145.9	198.89	230.0	210.4	235.1	239.0
parotid	142.0	198.89	230.0	210.2	235.0	239.0
pluriglandular	142.8	198.89	230.0	210.2	235.0	239.0
sublingual	142.2	198.89	230.0	210.2	235.0	239.0
submandibular	142.1	198.89	230.0	210.2	235.0	239.0
submaxillary	142.1	198.89	230.0	210.2	235.0	239.0
salpinx (uterine)	183.2	198.82	233.3	221.0	236.3	239.5
Santorini's duct	157.3	197.8	230.9	211.6	235.5	239.0
scalp	173.4	198.2	232.4	216.4	238.2	239.2
scapula (any part)	170.4	198.5	—	213.4	238.0	239.2
scapular region	195.1	198.89	234.8	229.8	238.8	239.8
scar NEC (see also Neoplasm, skin)	173.9	198.2	232.9	216.9	238.2	239.2
sciatic nerve	171.3	198.89	—	215.3	238.1	239.2
sclera	190.0	198.4	234.0	224.0	238.8	239.8
scrotum (skin)	187.7	198.82	233.6	222.4	236.6	239.5
sebaceous gland — see Neoplasm, skin						
sella turcica	194.3	198.89	234.8	227.3	237.0	239.7
bone	170.0	198.5	—	213.0	238.0	239.2
semilunar cartilage (knee)	170.7	198.5	—	213.7	238.0	239.2
seminal vesicle	187.8	198.82	233.6	222.8	236.6	239.5
septum						
nasal	160.0	197.3	231.8	212.0	235.9	239.1
posterior margin	147.3	198.89	230.0	210.7	235.1	239.0
rectovaginal	195.3	198.89	234.8	229.8	238.8	239.8
rectovesical	195.3	198.89	234.8	229.8	238.8	239.8
urethrovaginal	184.9	198.82	233.3	221.9	236.3	239.5
vesicovaginal	184.9	198.82	233.3	221.9	236.3	239.5
shoulder NEC*	195.4	198.89	232.6	229.8	238.8	239.8
sigmoid flexure (lower) (upper)	153.3	197.5	230.3	211.3	235.2	239.0

Neoplasm, neoplastic — continued	Malignant			Benign	Uncertain Behavior	Unspecified
	Primary	Secondary	Ca in situ			
sinus (accessory)	160.9	197.3	231.8	212.0	235.9	239.1
bone (any)	170.0	198.5	—	213.0	238.0	239.2
contiguous sites with middle ear or nasal cavities	160.8	—	—	—	—	—
ethmoidal	160.3	197.3	231.8	212.0	235.9	239.1
frontal	160.4	197.3	231.8	212.0	235.9	239.1
maxillary	160.2	197.3	231.8	212.0	235.9	239.1
nasal, paranasal NEC	160.9	197.3	231.8	212.0	235.9	239.1
pyriform	148.1	198.89	230.0	210.8	235.1	239.0
sphenoidal	160.5	197.3	231.8	212.0	235.9	239.1
skeleton, skeletal NEC	170.9	198.5	—	213.9	238.0	239.2
Skene's gland	189.4	198.1	233.9	223.89	236.99	239.5
skin NEC	173.9	198.2	232.9	216.9	238.2	239.2
abdominal wall	173.5	198.2	232.5	216.5	238.2	239.2
ala nasi	173.3	198.2	232.3	216.3	238.2	239.2
ankle	173.7	198.2	232.7	216.7	238.2	239.2
antecubital space	173.6	198.2	232.6	216.6	238.2	239.2
anus	173.5	198.2	232.5	216.5	238.2	239.2
arm	173.6	198.2	232.6	216.6	238.2	239.2
auditory canal (external)	173.2	198.2	232.2	216.2	238.2	239.2
auricle (ear)	173.2	198.2	232.2	216.2	238.2	239.2
auricular canal (external)	173.2	198.2	232.2	216.2	238.2	239.2
axilla, axillary fold	173.5	198.2	232.5	216.5	238.2	239.2
back	173.5	198.2	232.5	216.5	238.2	239.2
breast	173.5	198.2	232.5	216.5	238.2	239.2
brow	173.3	198.2	232.3	216.3	238.2	239.2
buttock	173.5	198.2	232.5	216.5	238.2	239.2
calf	173.7	198.2	232.7	216.7	238.2	239.2
canthus (eye) (inner) (outer)	173.1	198.2	232.1	216.1	238.2	239.2
cervical region	173.4	198.2	232.4	216.4	238.2	239.2
cheek (external)	173.3	198.2	232.3	216.3	238.2	239.2
chest (wall)	173.5	198.2	232.5	216.5	238.2	239.2
chin	173.3	198.2	232.3	216.3	238.2	239.2
clavicular area	173.5	198.2	232.5	216.5	238.2	239.2
clitoris	184.3	198.82	233.3	221.2	236.3	239.5
columnella	173.3	198.2	232.3	216.3	238.2	239.2
concha	173.2	198.2	232.2	216.2	238.2	239.2
contiguous sites	173.8	—	—	—	—	—
ear (external)	173.2	198.2	232.2	216.2	238.2	239.2
elbow	173.6	198.2	232.6	216.6	238.2	239.2
eyebrow	173.3	198.2	232.3	216.3	238.2	239.2
eyelid	173.1	198.2	232.1	216.1	238.2	239.2
face NEC	173.3	198.2	232.3	216.3	238.2	239.2
female genital organs (external)	184.4	198.82	233.3	221.2	236.3	239.5
clitoris	184.3	198.82	233.3	221.2	236.3	239.5
labium NEC	184.4	198.82	233.3	221.2	236.3	239.5
majus	184.1	198.82	233.3	221.2	236.3	239.5
minus	184.2	198.82	233.3	221.2	236.3	239.5
pudendum	184.4	198.82	233.3	221.2	236.3	239.5
vulva	184.4	198.82	233.3	221.2	236.3	239.5
finger	173.6	198.2	232.6	216.6	238.2	239.2
flank	173.5	198.2	232.5	216.5	238.2	239.2
foot	173.7	198.2	232.7	216.7	238.2	239.2
forearm	173.6	198.2	232.6	216.6	238.2	239.2
forehead	173.3	198.2	232.3	216.3	238.2	239.2
glabella	173.3	198.2	232.3	216.3	238.2	239.2
gluteal region	173.5	198.2	232.5	216.5	238.2	239.2
groin	173.5	198.2	232.5	216.5	238.2	239.2
hand	173.6	198.2	232.6	216.6	238.2	239.2
head NEC	173.4	198.2	232.4	216.4	238.2	239.2
heel	173.7	198.2	232.7	216.7	238.2	239.2
helix	173.2	198.2	232.2	216.2	238.2	239.2
hip	173.7	198.2	232.7	216.7	238.2	239.2
infraclavicular region	173.5	198.2	232.5	216.5	238.2	239.2
inguinal region	173.5	198.2	232.5	216.5	238.2	239.2
jaw	173.3	198.2	232.3	216.3	238.2	239.2
knee	173.7	198.2	232.7	216.7	238.2	239.2
labia						
majora	184.1	198.82	233.3	221.2	236.3	239.5
minora	184.2	198.82	233.3	221.2	236.3	239.5
leg	173.7	198.2	232.7	216.7	238.2	239.2
lid (lower) (upper)	173.1	198.2	232.1	216.1	238.2	239.2
limb NEC	173.9	198.2	232.9	216.9	238.2	239.5
lower	173.7	198.2	232.7	216.7	238.2	239.2
upper	173.6	198.2	232.6	216.6	238.2	239.2
lip (lower) (upper)	173.0	198.2	232.0	216.0	238.2	239.2

Neoplasm, neoplastic — continued	Malignant			Benign	Uncertain Behavior	Unspecified
	Primary	Secondary	Ca in situ			
skin NEC — continued						
male genital organs	187.9	198.82	233.6	222.9	236.6	239.5
penis	187.4	198.82	233.5	222.1	236.6	239.5
prepuce	187.1	198.82	233.5	222.1	236.6	239.5
scrotum	187.7	198.82	233.6	222.4	236.6	239.5
mastectomy site	173.5	198.2	—	—	—	—
specified as breast tissue	174.8	198.81	—	—	—	—
meatus, acoustic (external)	173.2	198.2	232.2	216.2	238.2	239.2
nates	173.5	198.2	232.5	216.5	238.2	239.0
neck	173.4	198.2	232.4	216.4	238.2	239.2
nose (external)	173.3	198.2	232.3	216.3	238.2	239.2
palm	173.6	198.2	232.6	216.6	238.2	239.2
palpebra	173.1	198.2	232.1	216.1	238.2	239.2
penis NEC	187.4	198.82	233.5	222.1	236.6	239.5
perianal	173.5	198.2	232.5	216.5	238.2	239.2
perineum	173.5	198.2	232.5	216.5	238.2	239.2
pinna	173.2	198.2	232.2	216.2	238.2	239.2
plantar	173.7	198.2	232.7	216.7	238.2	239.2
popliteal fossa or space	173.7	198.2	232.7	216.7	238.2	239.2
prepuce	187.1	198.82	233.5	222.1	236.6	239.5
pubes	173.5	198.2	232.5	216.5	238.2	239.2
sacrococcygeal region	173.5	198.2	232.5	216.5	238.2	239.2
scalp	173.4	198.2	232.4	216.4	238.2	239.2
scapular region	173.5	198.2	232.5	216.5	238.2	239.2
scrotum	187.7	198.82	233.6	222.4	236.6	239.5
shoulder	173.6	198.2	232.6	216.6	238.2	239.2
sole (foot)	173.7	198.2	232.7	216.7	238.2	239.2
specified sites NEC	173.8	198.2	232.8	216.8	238.8	239.2
submammary fold	173.5	198.2	232.5	216.5	238.2	239.2
supraclavicular region	173.4	198.2	232.4	216.4	238.2	239.2
temple	173.3	198.2	232.3	216.3	238.2	239.2
thigh	173.7	198.2	232.7	216.7	238.2	239.2
thoracic wall	173.5	198.2	232.5	216.5	238.2	239.2
thumb	173.6	198.2	232.6	216.6	238.2	239.2
toe	173.7	198.2	232.7	216.7	238.2	239.2
tragus	173.2	198.2	232.2	216.2	238.2	239.2
trunk	173.5	198.2	232.5	216.5	238.2	239.2
umbilicus	173.5	198.2	232.5	216.5	238.2	239.2
vulva	184.4	198.82	233.3	221.2	236.3	239.5
wrist	173.6	198.2	232.6	216.6	238.2	239.2
skull	170.0	198.5	—	213.0	238.0	239.2
soft parts or tissues — see Neoplasm, connective tissue						
specified site NEC	195.8	198.89	234.8	229.8	238.8	239.8
spermatic cord	187.6	198.82	233.6	222.8	236.6	239.5
sphenoid	160.5	197.3	231.8	212.0	235.9	239.1
bone	170.0	198.5	—	213.0	238.0	239.2
sinus	160.5	197.3	231.8	212.0	235.9	239.1
sphincter						
anal	154.2	197.5	230.5	211.4	235.5	239.0
of Oddi	156.1	197.8	230.8	211.5	235.3	239.0
spine, spinal (column)	170.2	198.5	—	213.2	238.0	239.2
bulb	191.7	198.3	—	225.0	237.5	239.6
coccyx	170.6	198.5	—	213.6	238.0	239.2
cord (cervical) (lumbar) (sacral) (thoracic)	192.2	198.3	—	225.3	237.5	239.7
dura mater	192.3	198.4	—	225.4	237.6	239.7
lumbosacral	170.2	198.5	—	213.2	238.0	239.2
membrane	192.3	198.4	—	225.4	237.6	239.7
meninges	192.3	198.4	—	225.4	237.6	239.7
nerve (root)	171.9	198.89	—	215.9	238.1	239.2
pia mater	192.3	198.4	—	225.4	237.6	239.7
root	171.9	198.89	—	215.9	238.1	239.2
sacrum	170.6	198.5	—	213.6	238.0	239.2
spleen, splenic NEC	159.1	197.8	230.9	211.9	235.5	239.0
flexure (colon)	153.7	197.5	230.3	211.3	235.2	239.0
stem, brain	191.7	198.3	—	225.0	237.5	239.6
Stensen's duct	142.0	198.89	230.0	210.2	235.0	239.0
sternum	170.3	198.5	—	213.3	238.0	239.2
stomach	151.9	197.8	230.2	211.1	235.2	239.0
antrum (pyloric)	151.2	197.8	230.2	211.1	235.2	239.0
body	151.4	197.8	230.2	211.1	235.2	239.0
cardia	151.0	197.8	230.2	211.1	235.2	239.0
cardiac orifice	151.0	197.8	230.2	211.1	235.2	239.0
contiguous sites	151.8	—	—	—	—	—

Neoplasm, neoplastic — continued	Malignant — Primary	Malignant — Secondary	Malignant — Ca in situ	Benign	Uncertain Behavior	Unspecified
stomach — continued						
corpus	151.4	197.8	230.2	211.1	235.2	239.0
fundus	151.3	197.8	230.2	211.1	235.2	239.0
greater curvature NEC	151.6	197.8	230.2	211.1	235.2	239.0
lesser curvature NEC	151.5	197.8	230.2	211.1	235.2	239.0
prepylorus	151.1	197.8	230.2	211.1	235.2	239.0
pylorus	151.1	197.8	230.2	211.1	235.2	239.0
wall NEC	151.9	197.8	230.2	211.1	235.2	239.0
anterior NEC	151.8	197.8	230.2	211.1	235.2	239.0
posterior NEC	151.8	197.8	230.2	211.1	235.2	239.0
stroma, endometrial	182.0	198.82	233.2	219.1	236.0	239.5
stump, cervical	180.8	198.82	233.1	219.0	236.0	239.5
subcutaneous (nodule) (tissue) NEC — see Neoplasm, connective tissue						
subdural	192.1	198.4	—	225.2	237.6	239.7
subglottis, subglottic	161.2	197.3	231.0	212.1	235.6	239.1
sublingual	144.9	198.89	230.0	210.3	235.1	239.0
gland or duct	142.2	198.89	230.0	210.2	235.0	239.0
submandibular gland	142.1	198.89	230.0	210.2	235.0	239.0
submaxillary gland or duct	142.1	198.89	230.0	210.2	235.0	239.0
submental	195.0	198.89	234.8	229.8	238.8	239.8
subpleural	162.9	197.0	—	212.3	235.7	239.1
substernal	164.2	197.1	—	212.5	235.8	239.8
sudoriferous, sudoriparous gland, site unspecified	173.9	198.2	232.9	216.9	238.2	239.2
specified site — see Neoplasm, skin						
supraclavicular region	195.0	198.89	234.8	229.8	238.8	239.8
supraglottis	161.1	197.3	231.0	212.1	235.6	239.1
suprarenal (capsule) (cortex) (gland) (medulla)	194.0	198.7	234.8	227.0	237.2	239.7
suprasellar (region)	191.9	198.3	—	225.0	237.5	239.6
sweat gland (apocrine) (eccrine), site unspecified	173.9	198.2	232.9	216.9	238.2	239.2
specified site — see Neoplasm, skin						
sympathetic nerve or nervous system NEC	171.9	198.89	—	215.9	238.1	239.2
symphysis pubis	170.6	198.5	—	213.6	238.0	239.2
synovial membrane — see Neoplasm, connective tissue						
tapetum, brain	191.8	198.3	—	225.0	237.5	239.6
tarsus (any bone)	170.8	198.5	—	213.8	238.0	239.2
temple (skin)	173.3	198.2	232.3	216.3	238.2	239.2
temporal						
bone	170.0	198.5	—	213.0	238.0	239.2
lobe or pole	191.2	198.3	—	225.0	237.5	239.6
region	195.0	198.89	234.8	229.8	238.8	239.8
skin	173.3	198.2	232.3	216.3	238.2	239.2
tendon (sheath) — see Neoplasm, connective tissue						
tentorium (cerebelli)	192.1	198.4	—	225.2	237.6	239.7
testis, testes (descended) (scrotal)	186.9	198.82	233.6	222.0	236.4	239.5
ectopic	186.0	198.82	233.6	222.0	236.4	239.5
retained	186.0	198.82	233.6	222.0	236.4	239.5
undescended	186.0	198.82	233.6	222.0	236.4	239.5
thalamus	191.0	198.3	—	225.0	237.5	239.6
thigh NEC*	195.5	198.89	234.8	229.8	238.8	239.8
thorax, thoracic (cavity) (organs NEC)	195.1	198.89	234.8	229.8	238.8	239.8
duct	171.4	198.89	—	215.4	238.1	239.2
wall NEC	195.1	198.89	234.8	229.8	238.8	239.8
throat	149.0	198.89	230.0	210.9	235.1	239.0
thumb NEC*	195.4	198.89	232.6	229.8	238.8	239.8
thymus (gland)	164.0	198.89	—	212.6	235.8	239.8
contiguous sites with heart and mediastinum	164.8	—	—	—	—	—
thyroglossal duct	193	198.89	234.8	226	237.4	239.7
thyroid (gland)	193	198.89	234.8	226	237.4	239.7
cartilage	161.3	197.3	231.0	212.1	235.6	239.1
tibia (any part)	170.7	198.5	—	213.7	238.0	239.2
toe NEC*	195.5	198.89	232.7	229.8	238.8	239.8
tongue	141.9	198.89	230.0	210.1	235.1	239.0
anterior (two-thirds) NEC	141.4	198.89	230.0	210.1	235.1	239.0
dorsal surface	141.1	198.89	230.0	210.1	235.1	239.0
ventral surface	141.3	198.89	230.0	210.1	235.1	239.0
base (dorsal surface)	141.0	198.89	230.0	210.1	235.1	239.0
border (lateral)	141.2	198.89	230.0	210.1	235.1	239.0
contiguous sites	141.8	—	—	—	—	—

Neoplasm, neoplastic — continued	Malignant — Primary	Malignant — Secondary	Malignant — Ca in situ	Benign	Uncertain Behavior	Unspecified
tongue — continued						
dorsal surface NEC	141.1	198.89	230.0	210.1	235.1	239.0
fixed part NEC	141.0	198.89	230.0	210.1	235.1	239.0
foreamen cecum	141.1	198.89	230.0	210.1	235.1	239.0
frenulum linguae	141.3	198.89	230.0	210.1	235.1	239.0
junctional zone	141.5	198.89	230.0	210.1	235.1	239.0
margin (lateral)	141.2	198.89	230.0	210.1	235.1	239.0
midline NEC	141.1	198.89	230.0	210.1	235.1	239.0
mobile part NEC	141.4	198.89	230.0	210.1	235.1	239.0
posterior (third)	141.0	198.89	230.0	210.1	235.1	239.0
root	141.0	198.89	230.0	210.1	235.1	239.0
surface (dorsal)	141.1	198.89	230.0	210.1	235.1	239.0
base	141.0	198.89	230.0	210.1	235.1	239.0
ventral	141.3	198.89	230.0	210.1	235.1	239.0
tip	141.2	198.89	230.0	210.1	235.1	239.0
tonsil	141.6	198.89	230.0	210.1	235.1	239.0
tonsil	146.0	198.89	230.0	210.5	235.1	239.0
fauces, faucial	146.0	198.89	230.0	210.5	235.1	239.0
lingual	141.6	198.89	230.0	210.1	235.1	239.0
palatine	146.0	198.89	230.0	210.5	235.1	239.0
pharyngeal	147.1	198.89	230.0	210.7	235.1	239.0
pillar (anterior) (posterior)	146.2	198.89	230.0	210.6	235.1	239.0
tonsillar fossa	146.1	198.89	230.0	210.6	235.1	239.0
tooth socket NEC	143.9	198.89	230.0	210.4	235.1	239.0
trachea (cartilage) (mucosa)	162.0	197.3	231.1	212.2	235.7	239.1
contiguous sites with bronchus or lung	162.8	—	—	—	—	—
tracheobronchial	162.8	197.3	231.1	212.2	235.7	239.1
contiguous sites with lung	162.8	—	—	—	—	—
tragus	173.2	198.2	232.2	216.2	238.2	239.2
trunk NEC*	195.8	198.89	232.5	229.8	238.8	239.8
tubo-ovarian	183.8	198.82	233.3	221.8	236.3	239.5
tunica vaginalis	187.8	198.82	233.6	222.8	236.6	239.5
turbinate (bone)	170.0	198.5	—	213.0	238.0	239.2
nasal	160.0	197.3	231.8	212.0	235.9	239.1
tympanic cavity	160.1	197.3	231.8	212.0	235.9	239.1
ulna (any part)	170.4	198.5	—	213.4	238.0	239.2
umbilicus, umbilical	173.5	198.2	232.5	216.5	238.2	239.2
uncus, brain	191.2	198.3	—	225.0	237.5	239.6
unknown site or unspecified	199.1	199.1	234.9	229.9	238.9	239.9
urachus	188.7	198.1	233.7	223.3	236.7	239.4
ureter, ureteral	189.2	198.1	233.9	223.2	236.91	239.5
orifice (bladder)	188.6	198.1	233.7	223.3	236.7	239.4
ureter-bladder (junction)	188.6	198.1	233.7	223.3	236.7	239.4
urethra, urethral (gland)	189.3	198.1	233.9	223.81	236.99	239.5
orifice, internal	188.5	198.1	233.7	223.3	236.7	239.4
urethrovaginal (septum)	184.9	198.82	233.3	221.9	236.3	239.5
urinary organ or system NEC	189.9	198.1	233.9	223.9	236.99	239.5
bladder — see Neoplasm, bladder						
contiguous sites	189.8	—	—	—	—	—
specified sites NEC	189.8	198.1	233.9	223.89	236.99	239.5
utero-ovarian	183.8	198.82	233.3	221.8	236.3	239.5
ligament	183.3	198.82	—	221.0	236.3	239.5
uterosacral ligament	183.4	198.82	—	221.0	236.3	239.5
uterus, uteri, uterine	179	198.82	233.2	219.9	236.0	239.5
adnexa NEC	183.9	198.82	233.3	221.8	236.3	239.5
contiguous sites	183.8	—	—	—	—	—
body	182.0	198.82	233.2	219.1	236.0	239.5
contiguous sites	182.8	—	—	—	—	—
cervix	180.9	198.82	233.1	219.0	236.0	239.5
cornu	182.0	198.82	233.2	219.1	236.0	239.5
corpus	182.0	198.82	233.2	219.1	236.0	239.5
endocervix (canal) (gland)	180.0	198.82	233.1	219.0	236.0	239.5
endometrium	182.0	198.82	233.2	219.1	236.0	239.5
exocervix	180.1	198.82	233.1	219.0	236.0	239.5
external os	180.1	198.82	233.1	219.0	236.0	239.5
fundus	182.0	198.82	233.2	219.1	236.0	239.5
internal os	180.0	198.82	233.1	219.0	236.0	239.5
isthmus	182.1	198.82	233.2	219.1	236.0	239.5
ligament	183.4	198.82	—	221.0	236.3	239.5
broad	183.3	198.82	233.3	221.0	236.3	239.5
round	183.5	198.82	—	221.0	236.3	239.5
lower segment	182.1	198.82	233.2	219.1	236.0	239.5
myometrium	182.0	198.82	233.2	219.1	236.0	239.5
squamocolumnar junction	180.8	198.82	233.1	219.0	236.0	239.5
tube	183.2	198.82	233.3	221.0	236.3	239.5

Neoplasm, neoplastic — continued	Malignant			Benign	Uncertain Behavior	Unspecified
	Primary	Secondary	Ca in situ			
utricle, prostatic	189.3	198.1	233.9	223.81	236.99	239.5
uveal tract	190.0	198.4	234.0	224.0	238.8	239.8
uvula	145.4	198.89	230.0	210.4	235.1	239.0
vagina, vaginal (fornix) (vault) (wall)	184.0	198.82	233.3	221.1	236.3	239.5
vaginovesical	184.9	198.82	233.3	221.9	236.3	239.5
septum	194.9	198.82	233.3	221.9	236.3	239.5
vallecula (epiglottis)	146.3	198.89	230.0	210.6	235.1	239.0
vascular — see Neoplasm, connective tissue						
vas deferens	187.6	198.82	233.6	222.8	236.6	239.5
Vater's ampulla	156.2	197.8	230.8	211.5	235.3	239.0
vein, venous — see Neoplasm, connective tissue						
vena cava (abdominal) (inferior)	171.5	198.89	—	215.5	238.1	239.2
superior	171.4	198.89	—	215.4	238.1	239.2
ventricle (cerebral) (floor) (fourth) (lateral) (third)	191.5	198.3	—	225.0	237.5	239.6
cardiac (left) (right)	164.1	198.89	—	212.7	238.8	239.8
ventricular band of larynx	161.1	197.3	231.0	212.1	235.6	239.1
ventriculus — see Neoplasm, stomach						
vermillion border — see Neoplasm, lip						
vermis, cerebellum	191.6	198.3	—	225.0	237.5	239.6
vertebra (column)	170.2	198.5	—	213.2	238.0	239.2
coccyx	170.6	198.5	—	213.6	238.0	239.2
sacrum	170.6	198.5	—	213.6	238.0	239.2
vesical — see Neoplasm, bladder						
vesicle, seminal	187.8	198.82	233.6	222.8	236.6	239.5
vesicocervical tissue	184.9	198.82	233.3	221.9	236.3	239.5
vesicorectal	195.3	198.89	234.8	229.8	238.8	239.8
vesicovaginal	184.9	198.82	233.3	221.9	236.3	239.5
septum	184.9	198.82	233.3	221.9	236.3	239.5

Neoplasm, neoplastic — continued	Malignant			Benign	Uncertain Behavior	Unspecified
	Primary	Secondary	Ca in situ			
vessel (blood) — see Neoplasm, connective tissue						
vestibular gland, greater	184.1	198.82	233.3	221.2	236.3	239.5
vestibule						
mouth	145.1	198.89	230.0	210.4	235.1	239.0
nose	160.0	197.3	231.8	212.0	235.9	239.1
Virchow's gland	—	196.0	—	229.0	238.8	239.8
viscera NEC	195.8	198.89	234.8	229.8	238.8	239.8
vocal cords (true)	161.0	197.3	231.0	212.1	235.6	239.1
false	161.1	197.3	231.0	212.1	235.6	239.1
vomer	170.0	198.5	—	213.0	238.0	239.2
vulva	184.4	198.82	233.3	221.2	236.3	239.5
vulvovaginal gland	184.4	198.82	233.3	221.2	236.3	239.5
Waldeyer's ring	149.1	198.89	230.0	210.9	235.1	239.0
Wharton's duct	142.1	198.89	230.0	210.2	235.0	239.0
white matter (central) (cerebral)	191.0	198.3	—	225.0	237.5	239.6
windpipe	162.0	197.3	231.1	212.2	235.7	239.1
Wirsung's duct	157.3	197.8	230.9	211.6	235.5	239.0
wolffian (body) (duct)						
female	184.8	198.82	233.3	221.8	236.3	239.5
male	187.8	198.82	233.6	222.8	236.6	239.5
womb — see Neoplasm, uterus						
wrist NEC*	195.4	198.89	232.6	229.8	238.8	239.8
xiphoid process	170.3	198.5	—	213.3	238.0	239.2
Zuckerkandl's organ	194.6	198.89	—	227.6	237.3	239.7

Neovascularization
  choroid 362.16
  ciliary body 364.42
  cornea 370.60
    deep 370.63
    localized 370.61
  iris 364.42
  retina 362.16
  subretinal 362.16

Nephralgia 788.0

Nephritis, nephritic (albuminuric) (azotemic) (congenital) (degenerative) (diffuse) (disseminated) (epithelial) (familial) (focal) (granulomatous) (hemorrhagic) (infantile) (nonsuppurative, excretory) (uremic) 583.9
  with
    edema — see Nephrosis
    lesion of
      glomerulonephritis
        hypocomplementemic persistent 583.2
          with nephrotic syndrome 581.2
            chronic 582.2
        lobular 583.2
          with nephrotic syndrome 581.2
            chronic 582.2
        membranoproliferative 583.2
          with nephrotic syndrome 581.2
            chronic 582.2
        membranous 583.1
          with nephrotic syndrome 581.1
            chronic 582.1
        mesangiocapillary 583.2
          with nephrotic syndrome 581.2
            chronic 582.2
        mixed membranous and proliferative 583.2
          with nephrotic syndrome 581.2
            chronic 582.2
        proliferative (diffuse) 583.0
          with nephrotic syndrome 581.0
            acute 580.0
            chronic 582.0

Nephritis, nephritic — continued
  with — continued
    lesion of — continued
      glomerulonephritis — continued
        rapidly progressive 583.4
          acute 580.4
          chronic 582.4
        interstitial nephritis (diffuse) (focal) 583.89
          with nephrotic syndrome 581.89
          acute 580.89
          chronic 582.89
        necrotizing glomerulitis 583.4
          acute 580.4
          chronic 582.4
        renal necrosis 583.9
          cortical 583.6
          medullary 583.7
        specified pathology NEC 583.89
          with nephrotic syndrome 581.89
          acute 580.89
          chronic 582.89
      necrosis, renal 583.9
        cortical 583.6
        medullary (papillary) 583.7
      nephrotic syndrome (see also Nephrosis) 581.9
      papillary necrosis 583.7
      specified pathology NEC 583.89
  acute 580.9
    extracapillary with epithelial crescents 580.4
    hypertensive (see also Hypertension, kidney) 403.90
    necrotizing 580.4
    poststreptococcal 580.0
    proliferative (diffuse) 580.0
    rapidly progressive 580.4
    specified pathology NEC 580.89
  amyloid 277.3 [583.81]
    chronic 277.3 [582.81]
  arteriolar (see also Hypertension, kidney) 403.90
  arteriosclerotic (see also Hypertension, kidney) 403.90

Nephritis, nephritic — continued
  ascending (see also Pyelitis) 590.80
  atrophic 582.9
  basement membrane NEC 583.89
    with
      pulmonary hemorrhage (Goodpasture's syndrome) 446.21 [583.81]
  calculous, calculus 592.0
  cardiac (see also Hypertension, kidney) 403.90
  cardiovascular (see also Hypertension, kidney) 403.90
  chronic 582.9
    arteriosclerotic (see also Hypertension, kidney) 403.90
    hypertensive (see also Hypertension, kidney) 403.90
  cirrhotic (see also Sclerosis, renal) 587
  complicating pregnancy, childbirth, or puerperium 646.2 ☑
    with hypertension 642.1 ☑
      affecting fetus or newborn 760.0
    affecting fetus or newborn 760.1
  croupous 580.9
  desquamative — see Nephrosis
  due to
    amyloidosis 277.3 [583.81]
      chronic 277.3 [582.81]
    arteriosclerosis (see also Hypertension, kidney) 403.90
    diabetes mellitus 250.4 ☑ [583.81]
      with nephrotic syndrome 250.4 ☑ [581.81]
    diphtheria 032.89 [580.81]
    gonococcal infection (acute) 098.19 [583.81]
      chronic or duration of 2 months or over 098.39 [583.81]
    gout 274.10
    infectious hepatitis 070.9 [580.81]
    mumps 072.79 [580.81]
    specified kidney pathology NEC 583.89
      acute 580.89
      chronic 582.89
    streptotrichosis 039.8 [583.81]
    subacute bacterial endocarditis 421.0 [580.81]

2006 ICD-9-CM

☑ Additional Digit Required — Refer to the Tabular List (Numeric Code Section) for Additional Digit Selection
►◄ Revised Text   ● New Line   ▲ Revised Code

Volume 2 — 245

Index

Nephritis, nephritic — Neuralgia, neuralgic

Nephritis, nephritic — *continued*
  due to — *continued*
    systemic lupus erythematosus
        710.0 *[583.81]*
      chronic 710.0 *[582.81]*
    typhoid fever 002.0 *[580.81]*
  endothelial 582.2
  end stage (chronic) (terminal) NEC 585.6 ▲
  epimembranous 581.1
  exudative 583.89
    with nephrotic syndrome 581.89
    acute 580.89
    chronic 582.89
  gonococcal (acute) 098.19 *[583.81]*
    chronic or duration of 2 months or over
        098.39 *[583.81]*
  gouty 274.10
  hereditary (Alport's syndrome) 759.89
  hydremic — *see* Nephrosis
  hypertensive (*see also* Hypertension, kidney)
        403.90
  hypocomplementemic persistent 583.2
    with nephrotic syndrome 581.2
    chronic 582.2
  immune complex NEC 583.89
  infective (*see also* Pyelitis) 590.80
  interstitial (diffuse) (focal) 583.89
    with nephrotic syndrome 581.89
    acute 580.89
    chronic 582.89
  latent or quiescent — *see* Nephritis, chronic
  lead 984.9
    specified type of lead — *see* Table of Drugs
        and Chemicals
  lobular 583.2
    with nephrotic syndrome 581.2
    chronic 582.2
  lupus 710.0 *[583.81]*
    acute 710.0 *[580.81]*
    chronic 710.0 *[582.81]*
  membranoproliferative 583.2
    with nephrotic syndrome 581.2
    chronic 582.2
  membranous 583.1
    with nephrotic syndrome 581.1
    chronic 582.1
  mesangiocapillary 583.2
    with nephrotic syndrome 581.2
    chronic 582.2
  minimal change 581.3
  mixed membranous and proliferative 583.2
    with nephrotic syndrome 581.2
    chronic 582.2
  necrotic, necrotizing 583.4
    acute 580.4
    chronic 582.4
  nephrotic — *see* Nephrosis
  old — *see* Nephritis, chronic
  parenchymatous 581.89
  polycystic 753.12
    adult type (APKD) 753.13
    autosomal dominant 753.13
    autosomal recessive 753.14
    childhood type (CPKD) 753.14
    infantile type 753.14
  poststreptococcal 580.0
  pregnancy — *see* Nephritis, complicating
        pregnancy
  proliferative 583.0
    with nephrotic syndrome 581.0
    acute 580.0
    chronic 582.0
  purulent (*see also* Pyelitis) 590.80
  rapidly progressive 583.4
    acute 580.4
    chronic 582.4
  salt-losing or salt-wasting (*see also* Disease,
        renal) 593.9
  saturnine 984.9
    specified type of lead — *see* Table of Drugs
        and Chemicals
  septic (*see also* Pyelitis) 590.80
  specified pathology NEC 583.89
    acute 580.89
    chronic 582.89
  staphylococcal (*see also* Pyelitis) 590.80
  streptotrichosis 039.8 *[583.81]*
  subacute (*see also* Nephrosis) 581.9
  suppurative (*see also* Pyelitis) 590.80

Nephritis, nephritic — *continued*
  syphilitic (late) 095.4
    congenital 090.5 *[583.81]*
    early 091.69 *[583.81]*
  terminal (chronic) (end-stage) NEC 585.6   ▲
  toxic — *see* Nephritis, acute
  tubal, tubular — *see* Nephrosis, tubular
  tuberculous (*see also* Tuberculosis)
        016.0 ☑ *[583.81]*
  type II (Ellis) — *see* Nephrosis
  vascular — *see* Hypertension, kidney
  war 580.9
Nephroblastoma (M8960/3) 189.0
  epithelial (M8961/3) 189.0
  mesenchymal (M8962/3) 189.0
Nephrocalcinosis 275.49
Nephrocystitis, pustular (*see also* Pyelitis)
        590.80
Nephrolithiasis (congenital) (pelvis) (recurrent)
        592.0
  uric acid 274.11
Nephroma (M8960/3) 189.0
  mesoblastic (M8960/1) 236.9 ☑
Nephronephritis (*see also* Nephrosis) 581.9
Nephronopthisis 753.16
Nephropathy (*see also* Nephritis) 583.9
  with
    exudative nephritis 583.89
    interstitial nephritis (diffuse) (focal) 583.89
    medullary necrosis 583.7
    necrosis 583.9
      cortical 583.6
      medullary or papillary 583.7
    papillary necrosis 583.7
    specified lesion or cause NEC 583.89
  analgesic 583.89
    with medullary necrosis, acute 584.7
  arteriolar (*see also* Hypertension, kidney)
        403.90
  arteriosclerotic (*see also* Hypertension, kidney)
        403.90
  complicating pregnancy 646.2 ☑
  diabetic 250.4 ☑ *[583.81]*
  gouty 274.10
    specified type NEC 274.19
  hypercalcemic 588.89
  hypertensive (*see also* Hypertension, kidney)
        403.90
  hypokalemic (vacuolar) 588.89
  IgA 583.9
  obstructive 593.89
    congenital 753.20
  phenacetin 584.7
  phosphate-losing 588.0
  potassium depletion 588.89
  proliferative (*see also* Nephritis, proliferative)
        583.0
  protein-losing 588.89
  salt-losing or salt-wasting (*see also* Disease,
        renal) 593.9
  sickle-cell (*see also* Disease, sickle-cell)
        282.60 *[583.81]*
  toxic 584.5
  vasomotor 584.5
  water-losing 588.89
Nephroptosis (*see also* Disease, renal) 593.0
  congenital (displaced) 753.3
Nephropyosis (*see also* Abscess, kidney) 590.2
Nephrorrhagia 593.81
Nephrosclerosis (arteriolar) (arteriosclerotic)
        (chronic) (hyaline) (*see also* Hypertension,
        kidney) 403.90
  gouty 274.10
  hyperplastic (arteriolar) (*see also* Hypertension,
        kidney) 403.90
  senile (*see also* Sclerosis, renal) 587
Nephrosis, nephrotic (Epstein's) (syndrome)
        581.9
  with
    lesion of
      focal glomerulosclerosis 581.1
      glomerulonephritis
        endothelial 581.2
        hypocomplementemic persistent 581.2
        lobular 581.2
        membranoproliferative 581.2
        membranous 581.1

Nephrosis, nephrotic — *continued*
  with — *continued*
    lesion of — *continued*
      glomerulonephritis — *continued*
        mesangiocapillary 581.2
        minimal change 581.3
        mixed membranous and proliferative
              581.2
        proliferative 581.0
      segmental hyalinosis 581.1
      specified pathology NEC 581.89
  acute — *see* Nephrosis, tubular
  anoxic — *see* Nephrosis, tubular
  arteriosclerotic (*see also* Hypertension, kidney)
        403.90
  chemical — *see* Nephrosis, tubular
  cholemic 572.4
  complicating pregnancy, childbirth, or
        puerperium — *see* Nephritis,
        complicating pregnancy
  diabetic 250.4 ☑ *[581.81]*
  hemoglobinuric — *see* Nephrosis, tubular
  in
    amyloidosis 277.3 *[581.81]*
    diabetes mellitus 250.4 ☑ *[581.81]*
    epidemic hemorrhagic fever 078.6
    malaria 084.9 *[581.81]*
    polyarteritis 446.0 *[581.81]*
    systemic lupus erythematosus
          710.0 *[581.81]*
  ischemic — *see* Nephrosis, tubular
  lipoid 581.3
  lower nephron — *see* Nephrosis, tubular
  lupoid 710.0 *[581.81]*
  lupus 710.0 *[581.81]*
  malarial 084.9 *[581.81]*
  minimal change 581.3
  necrotizing — *see* Nephrosis, tubular
  osmotic (sucrose) 588.89
  polyarteritic 446.0 *[581.81]*
  radiation 581.9
  specified lesion or cause NEC 581.89
  syphilitic 095.4
  toxic — *see* Nephrosis, tubular
  tubular (acute) 584.5
    due to a procedure 997.5
    radiation 581.9
Nephrosonephritis hemorrhagic (endemic) 078.6
Nephrostomy status V44.6
  with complication 997.5
Nerve — *see* condition
Nerves 799.2
Nervous (*see also* condition) 799.2
  breakdown 300.9
  heart 306.2
  stomach 306.4
  tension 799.2
Nervousness 799.2
Nesidioblastoma (M8150/0)
  pancreas 211.7
  specified site NEC — *see* Neoplasm, by site,
        benign
  unspecified site 211.7
Netherton's syndrome (ichthyosiform
        erythroderma) 757.1
Nettle rash 708.8
Nettleship's disease (urticaria pigmentosa)
        757.33
Neumann's disease (pemphigus vegetans) 694.4
Neuralgia, neuralgic (acute) (*see also* Neuritis)
        729.2
  accessory (nerve) 352.4
  acoustic (nerve) 388.5
  ankle 355.8
  anterior crural 355.8
  anus 787.99
  arm 723.4
  auditory (nerve) 388.5
  axilla 353.0
  bladder 788.1
  brachial 723.4
  brain — *see* Disorder, nerve, cranial
  broad ligament 625.9
  cerebral — *see* Disorder, nerve, cranial
  ciliary 346.2 ☑
  cranial nerve — *see also* Disorder, nerve,
        cranial

Neuralgia, neuralgic (see also Neuritis) — continued
  fifth or trigeminal (see also Neuralgia, trigeminal) 350.1
  ear 388.71
    middle 352.1
  facial 351.8
  finger 354.9
  flank 355.8
  foot 355.8
  forearm 354.9
  Fothergill's (see also Neuralgia, trigeminal) 350.1
    postherpetic 053.12
  glossopharyngeal (nerve) 352.1
  groin 355.8
  hand 354.9
  heel 355.8
  Horton's 346.2 ☑
  Hunt's 053.11
  hypoglossal (nerve) 352.5
  iliac region 355.8
  infraorbital (see also Neuralgia, trigeminal) 350.1
  inguinal 355.8
  intercostal (nerve) 353.8
    postherpetic 053.19
  jaw 352.1
  kidney 788.0
  knee 355.8
  loin 355.8
  malarial (see also Malaria) 084.6
  mastoid 385.89
  maxilla 352.1
  median thenar 354.1
  metatarsal 355.6
  middle ear 352.1
  migrainous 346.2 ☑
  Morton's 355.6
  nerve, cranial — see Disorder, nerve, cranial
  nose 352.0
  occipital 723.8
  olfactory (nerve) 352.0
  ophthalmic 377.30
    postherpetic 053.19
  optic (nerve) 377.30
  penis 607.9
  perineum 355.8
  pleura 511.0
  postherpetic NEC 053.19
    geniculate ganglion 053.11
    ophthalmic 053.19
    trifacial 053.12
    trigeminal 053.12
  pubic region 355.8
  radial (nerve) 723.4
  rectum 787.99
  sacroiliac joint 724.3
  sciatic (nerve) 724.3
  scrotum 608.9
  seminal vesicle 608.9
  shoulder 354.9
  Sluder's 337.0
  specified nerve NEC — see Disorder, nerve
  spermatic cord 608.9
  sphenopalatine (ganglion) 337.0
  subscapular (nerve) 723.4
  suprascapular (nerve) 723.4
  testis 608.89
  thenar (median) 354.1
  thigh 355.8
  tongue 352.5
  trifacial (nerve) (see also Neuralgia, trigeminal) 350.1
  trigeminal (nerve) 350.1
    postherpetic 053.12
  tympanic plexus 388.71
  ulnar (nerve) 723.4
  vagus 352.3
  wrist 354.9
  writers' 300.89
    organic 333.84
Neurapraxia — see Injury, nerve, by site
Neurasthenia 300.5
  cardiac 306.2
  gastric 306.4
  heart 306.2
  postfebrile 780.79
  postviral 780.79

Neurilemmoma (M9560/0) — see also Neoplasm, connective tissue, benign
  acoustic (nerve) 225.1
  malignant (M9560/3) — see also Neoplasm, connective tissue, malignant
    acoustic (nerve) 192.0
Neurilemmosarcoma (M9560/3) — see Neoplasm, connective tissue, malignant
Neurilemoma — see Neurilemmoma
Neurinoma (M9560/0) — see Neurilemmoma
Neurinomatosis (M9560/1) — see also Neoplasm, connective tissue, uncertain behavior
  centralis 759.5
Neuritis (see also Neuralgia) 729.2
  abducens (nerve) 378.54
  accessory (nerve) 352.4
  acoustic (nerve) 388.5
    syphilitic 094.86
  alcoholic 357.5
    with psychosis 291.1
  amyloid, any site 277.3 [357.4]
  anterior crural 355.8
  arising during pregnancy 646.4 ☑
  arm 723.4
  ascending 355.2
  auditory (nerve) 388.5
  brachial (nerve) NEC 723.4
    due to displacement, intervertebral disc 722.0
  cervical 723.4
  chest (wall) 353.8
  costal region 353.8
  cranial nerve — see also Disorder, nerve, cranial
    first or olfactory 352.0
    second or optic 377.30
    third or oculomotor 378.52
    fourth or trochlear 378.53
    fifth or trigeminal (see also Neuralgia, trigeminal) 350.1
    sixth or abducens 378.54
    seventh or facial 351.8
      newborn 767.5
    eighth or acoustic 388.5
    ninth or glossopharyngeal 352.1
    tenth or vagus 352.3
    eleventh or accessory 352.4
    twelfth or hypoglossal 352.5
  Déjérine-Sottas 356.0
  diabetic 250.6 ☑ [357.2]
  diphtheritic 032.89 [357.4]
  due to
    beriberi 265.0 [357.4]
    displacement, prolapse, protrusion, or rupture of intervertebral disc 722.2
      cervical 722.0
      lumbar, lumbosacral 722.10
      thoracic, thoracolumbar 722.11
    herniation, nucleus pulposus 722.2
      cervical 722.0
      lumbar, lumbosacral 722.10
      thoracic, thoracolumbar 722.11
  endemic 265.0 [357.4]
  facial (nerve) 351.8
    newborn 767.5
  general — see Polyneuropathy
  geniculate ganglion 351.1
    due to herpes 053.11
  glossopharyngeal (nerve) 352.1
  gouty 274.89 [357.4]
  hypoglossal (nerve) 352.5
  ilioinguinal (nerve) 355.8
  in diseases classified elsewhere — see Polyneuropathy, in
  infectious (multiple) 357.0
  intercostal (nerve) 353.8
  interstitial hypertrophic progressive NEC 356.9
  leg 355.8
  lumbosacral NEC 724.4
  median (nerve) 354.1
    thenar 354.1
  multiple (acute) (infective) 356.9
    endemic 265.0 [357.4]
  multiplex endemica 265.0 [357.4]
  nerve root (see also Radiculitis) 729.2
  oculomotor (nerve) 378.52
  olfactory (nerve) 352.0
  optic (nerve) 377.30
    in myelitis 341.0

Neuritis (see also Neuralgia) — continued
  optic — continued
    meningococcal 036.81
  pelvic 355.8
  peripheral (nerve) — see Neuropathy, peripheral
    complicating pregnancy or puerperium 646.4 ☑
    specified nerve NEC — see Mononeuritis
  pneumogastric (nerve) 352.3
  postchickenpox 052.7
  postherpetic 053.19
  progressive hypertrophic interstitial NEC 356.9
  puerperal, postpartum 646.4 ☑
  radial (nerve) 723.4
  retrobulbar 377.32
    syphilitic 094.85
  rheumatic (chronic) 729.2
  sacral region 355.8
  sciatic (nerve) 724.3
    due to displacement of intervertebral disc 722.10
  serum 999.5
  specified nerve NEC — see Disorder, nerve
  spinal (nerve) 355.9
    root (see also Radiculitis) 729.2
  subscapular (nerve) 723.4
  suprascapular (nerve) 723.4
  syphilitic 095.8
  thenar (median) 354.1
  thoracic NEC 724.4
  toxic NEC 357.7
  trochlear (nerve) 378.53
  ulnar (nerve) 723.4
  vagus (nerve) 352.3
Neuroangiomatosis, encephalofacial 759.6
Neuroastrocytoma (M9505/1) — see Neoplasm, by site, uncertain behavior
Neuro-avitaminosis 269.2
Neuroblastoma (M9500/3)
  olfactory (M9522/3) 160.0
  specified site — see Neoplasm, by site, malignant
  unspecified site 194.0
Neurochorioretinitis (see also Chorioretinitis) 363.20
Neurocirculatory asthenia 306.2
Neurocytoma (M9506/0) — see Neoplasm, by site, benign
Neurodermatitis (circumscribed) (circumscripta) (local) 698.3
  atopic 691.8
  diffuse (Brocq) 691.8
  disseminated 691.8
  nodulosa 698.3
Neuroencephalomyelopathy, optic 341.0
Neuroepithelioma (M9503/3) — see also Neoplasm, by site, malignant
  olfactory (M9521/3) 160.0
Neurofibroma (M9540/0) — see also Neoplasm, connective tissue, benign
  melanotic (M9541/0) — see Neoplasm, connective tissue, benign
  multiple (M9540/1) 237.70
    type 1 237.71
    type 2 237.72
  plexiform (M9550/0) — see Neoplasm, connective tissue, benign
Neurofibromatosis (multiple) (M9540/1) 237.70
  acoustic 237.72
  malignant (M9540/3) — see Neoplasm, connective tissue, malignant
  type 1 237.71
  type 2 237.72
  von Recklinghausen's 237.71
Neurofibrosarcoma (M9540/3) — see Neoplasm, connective tissue, malignant
Neurogenic — see also condition
  bladder (atonic) (automatic) (autonomic) (flaccid) (hypertonic) (hypotonic) (inertia) (infranuclear) (irritable) (motor) (nonreflex) (nuclear) (paralysis) (reflex) (sensory) (spastic) (supranuclear) (uninhibited) 596.54
    with cauda equina syndrome 344.61
  bowel 564.81
  heart 306.2

Neuroglioma (M9505/1) — *see* Neoplasm, by site, uncertain behavior

Neurolabyrinthitis (of Dix and Hallpike) 386.12

Neurolathyrism 988.2

Neuroleprosy 030.1

Neuroleptic malignant syndrome 333.92

Neurolipomatosis 272.8

Neuroma (M9570/0) — *see also* Neoplasm, connective tissue, benign
  acoustic (nerve) (M9560/0) 225.1
  amputation (traumatic) — *see also* Injury, nerve, by site
    surgical complication (late) 997.61
  appendix 211.3
  auditory nerve 225.1
  digital 355.6
    toe 355.6
  interdigital (toe) 355.6
  intermetatarsal 355.6
  Morton's 355.6
  multiple 237.70
    type 1 237.71
    type 2 237.72
  nonneoplastic 355.9
    arm NEC 354.9
    leg NEC 355.8
    lower extremity NEC 355.8
    specified site NEC — *see* Mononeuritis, by site
    upper extremity NEC 354.9
  optic (nerve) 225.1
  plantar 355.6
  plexiform (M9550/0) — *see* Neoplasm, connective tissue, benign
  surgical (nonneoplastic) 355.9
    arm NEC 354.9
    leg NEC 355.8
    lower extremity NEC 355.8
    upper extremity NEC 354.9
  traumatic — *see also* Injury, nerve, by site
    old — *see* Neuroma, nonneoplastic

Neuromyalgia 729.1

Neuromyasthenia (epidemic) 049.8

Neuromyelitis 341.8
  ascending 357.0
  optica 341.0

Neuromyopathy NEC 358.9

Neuromyositis 729.1

Neuronevus (M8725/0) — *see* Neoplasm, skin, benign

Neuronitis 357.0
  ascending (acute) 355.2
  vestibular 386.12

Neuroparalytic — *see* condition

Neuropathy, neuropathic (*see also* Disorder, nerve) 355.9
  acute motor 357.82
  alcoholic 357.5
    with psychosis 291.1
  arm NEC 354.9
  ataxia and retinitis pigmentosa (NARP syndrome) 277.87
  autonomic (peripheral) — *see* Neuropathy, peripheral, autonomic
  axillary nerve 353.0
  brachial plexus 353.0
  cervical plexus 353.2
  chronic
    progressive segmentally demyelinating 357.89
    relapsing demyelinating 357.89
  congenital sensory 356.2
  Déjérine-Sottas 356.0
  diabetic 250.6 ☑ *[357.2]*
  entrapment 355.9
    iliohypogastric nerve 355.79
    ilioinguinal nerve 355.79
    lateral cutaneous nerve of thigh 355.1
    median nerve 354.0
    obturator nerve 355.79
    peroneal nerve 355.3
    posterior tibial nerve 355.5
    saphenous nerve 355.79
    ulnar nerve 354.2
  facial nerve 351.9
  hereditary 356.9
    peripheral 356.0
    sensory (radicular) 356.2

Neuropathy, neuropathic (*see also* Disorder, nerve) — *continued*
  hypertrophic
    Charcôt-Marie-Tooth 356.1
    Déjérine-Sottas 356.0
    interstitial 356.9
    Refsum 356.3
  intercostal nerve 354.8
  ischemic — *see* Disorder, nerve
  Jamaican (ginger) 357.7
  leg NEC 355.8
  lower extremity NEC 355.8
  lumbar plexus 353.1
  median nerve 354.1
  motor
    acute 357.82
  multiple (acute) (chronic) (*see also* Polyneuropathy) 356.9
  optic 377.39
    ischemic 377.41
    nutritional 377.33
    toxic 377.34
  peripheral (nerve) (*see also* Polyneuropathy) 356.9
    arm NEC 354.9
    autonomic 337.9
      amyloid 277.3 *[337.1]*
      idiopathic 337.0
      in
        amyloidosis 277.3 *[337.1]*
        diabetes (mellitus) 250.6 ☑ *[337.1]*
        diseases classified elsewhere 337.1
        gout 274.89 *[337.1]*
        hyperthyroidism 242.9 ☑ *[337.1]*
    due to
      antitetanus serum 357.6
      arsenic 357.7
      drugs 357.6
      lead 357.7
      organophosphate compounds 357.7
      toxic agent NEC 357.7
    hereditary 356.0
    idiopathic 356.9
      progressive 356.4
      specified type NEC 356.8
    in diseases classified elsewhere — *see* Polyneuropathy, in
    leg NEC 355.8
    lower extremity NEC 355.8
    upper extremity NEC 354.9
  plantar nerves 355.6
  progressive hypertrophic interstitial 356.9
  radicular NEC 729.2
    brachial 723.4
    cervical NEC 723.4
    hereditary sensory 356.2
    lumbar 724.4
    lumbosacral 724.4
    thoracic NEC 724.4
  sacral plexus 353.1
  sciatic 355.0
  spinal nerve NEC 355.9
    root (*see also* Radiculitis) 729.2
  toxic 357.7
  trigeminal sensory 350.8
  ulnar nerve 354.2
  upper extremity NEC 354.9   ▲
  uremic 585.9 *[357.4]*
  vitamin B$_{12}$ 266.2 *[357.4]*
    with anemia (pernicious) 281.0 *[357.4]*
      due to dietary deficiency 281.1 *[357.4]*

Neurophthisis (*see also* Disorder, nerve)
  diabetic 250.6 ☑ *[357.2]*
  peripheral 356.9

Neuropraxia — *see* Injury, nerve

Neuroretinitis 363.05
  syphilitic 094.85

Neurosarcoma (M9540/3) — *see* Neoplasm, connective tissue, malignant

Neurosclerosis — *see* Disorder, nerve

Neurosis, neurotic 300.9
  accident 300.16
  anancastic, anankastic 300.3
  anxiety (state) 300.00
    generalized 300.02
    panic type 300.01
  asthenic 300.5
  bladder 306.53

Neurosis, neurotic — *continued*
  cardiac (reflex) 306.2
  cardiovascular 306.2
  climacteric, unspecified type 627.2
  colon 306.4
  compensation 300.16
  compulsive, compulsion 300.3
  conversion 300.11
  craft 300.89
  cutaneous 306.3
  depersonalization 300.6
  depressive (reaction) (type) 300.4
  endocrine 306.6
  environmental 300.89
  fatigue 300.5
  functional (*see also* Disorder, psychosomatic) 306.9
  gastric 306.4
  gastrointestinal 306.4
  genitourinary 306.50
  heart 306.2
  hypochondriacal 300.7
  hysterical 300.10
    conversion type 300.11
    dissociative type 300.15
  impulsive 300.3
  incoordination 306.0
    larynx 306.1
    vocal cord 306.1
  intestine 306.4
  larynx 306.1
    hysterical 300.11
    sensory 306.1
  menopause, unspecified type 627.2
  mixed NEC 300.89
  musculoskeletal 306.0
  obsessional 300.3
    phobia 300.3
  obsessive-compulsive 300.3
  occupational 300.89
  ocular 306.7
  oral 307.0
  organ (*see also* Disorder, psychosomatic) 306.9
  pharynx 306.1
  phobic 300.20
  posttraumatic (acute) (situational) 309.81
    chronic 309.81
  psychasthenic (type) 300.89
  railroad 300.16
  rectum 306.4
  respiratory 306.1
  rumination 306.4
  senile 300.89
  sexual 302.70
  situational 300.89
  specified type NEC 300.89
  state 300.9
    with depersonalization episode 300.6
  stomach 306.4
  vasomotor 306.2
  visceral 306.4
  war 300.16

Neurospongioblastosis diffusa 759.5

Neurosyphilis (arrested) (early) (inactive) (late) (latent) (recurrent) 094.9
  with ataxia (cerebellar) (locomotor) (spastic) (spinal) 094.0
  acute meningitis 094.2
  aneurysm 094.89
  arachnoid (adhesive) 094.2
  arteritis (any artery) 094.89
  asymptomatic 094.3
  congenital 090.40
  dura (mater) 094.89
  general paresis 094.1
  gumma 094.9
  hemorrhagic 094.9
  juvenile (asymptomatic) (meningeal) 090.40
  leptomeninges (aseptic) 094.2
  meningeal 094.2
  meninges (adhesive) 094.2
  meningovascular (diffuse) 094.2
  optic atrophy 094.84
  parenchymatous (degenerative) 094.1
  paresis (*see also* Paresis, general) 094.1
  paretic (*see also* Paresis, general) 094.1
  relapse 094.9
  remission in (sustained) 094.9
  serological 094.3

Neurosyphilis — *continued*
  specified nature or site NEC 094.89
  tabes (dorsalis) 094.0
    juvenile 090.40
  tabetic 094.0
    juvenile 090.40
  taboparesis 094.1
    juvenile 090.40
  thrombosis 094.89
  vascular 094.89
Neurotic (*see also* Neurosis) 300.9
  excoriation 698.4
  psychogenic 306.3
Neurotmesis — *see* Injury, nerve, by site
Neurotoxemia — *see* Toxemia
Neutro-occlusion 524.21
Neutropenia, neutropenic (chronic) (cyclic) (drug-induced) (genetic) (idiopathic) (immune) (infantile) (malignant) (periodic) (pernicious) (primary) (splenic) (splenomegaly) (toxic) 288.0
  chronic hypoplastic 288.0
  congenital (nontransient) 288.0
  fever 288.0
  neonatal, transitory (isoimmune) (maternal transfer) 776.7
Neutrophilia, hereditary giant 288.2
Nevocarcinoma (M8720/3) — *see* Melanoma
Nevus (M8720/0) — *see also* Neoplasm, skin, benign

Note — Except where otherwise indicated, varieties of nevus in the list below that are followed by a morphology code number (M---- /0) should be coded by site as for "Neoplasm, skin, benign."

  acanthotic 702.8
  achromic (M8730/0)
  amelanotic (M8730/0)
  anemic, anemicus 709.09
  angiomatous (M9120/0) (*see also* Hemangioma) 228.00
  araneus 448.1
  avasculosus 709.09
  balloon cell (M8722/0)
  bathing trunk (M8761/1) 238.2
  blue (M8780/0)
    cellular (M8790/0)
    giant (M8790/0)
    Jadassohn's (M8780/0)
    malignant (M8780/3) — *see* Melanoma
  capillary (M9131/0) (*see also* Hemangioma) 228.00
  cavernous (M9121/0) (*see also* Hemangioma) 228.00
  cellular (M8720/0)
    blue (M8790/0)
  comedonicus 757.33
  compound (M8760/0)
  conjunctiva (M8720/0) 224.3
  dermal (M8750/0)
    and epidermal (M8760/0)
  epithelioid cell (and spindle cell) (M8770/0)
  flammeus 757.32
    osteohypertrophic 759.89
  hairy (M8720/0)
  halo (M8723/0)
  hemangiomatous (M9120/0) (*see also* Hemangioma) 228.00
  intradermal (M8750/0)
  intraepidermal (M8740/0)
  involuting (M8724/0)
  Jadassohn's (blue) (M8780/0)
  junction, junctional (M8740/0)
    malignant melanoma in (M8740/3) — *see* Melanoma
  juvenile (M8770/0)
  lymphatic (M9170/0) 228.1
  magnocellular (M8726/0)
    specified site — *see* Neoplasm, by site, benign
    unspecified site 224.0
  malignant (M8720/3) — *see* Melanoma
  meaning hemangioma (M9120/0) (*see also* Hemangioma) 228.00
  melanotic (pigmented) (M8720/0)
  multiplex 759.5
  nonneoplastic 448.1

Nevus (M8720/0) — *see also* Neoplasm, skin, benign — *continued*
  nonpigmented (M8730/0)
  nonvascular (M8720/0)
  oral mucosa, white sponge 750.26
  osteohypertrophic, flammeus 759.89
  papillaris (M8720/0)
  papillomatosus (M8720/0)
  pigmented (M8720/0)
    giant (M8761/1) — *see also* Neoplasm, skin, uncertain behavior
      malignant melanoma in (M8761/3) — *see* Melanoma
    systematicus 757.33
  pilosus (M8720/0)
  port wine 757.32
  sanguineous 757.32
  sebaceous (senile) 702.8
  senile 448.1
  spider 448.1
  spindle cell (and epithelioid cell) (M8770/0)
  stellar 448.1
  strawberry 757.32
  syringocystadenomatous papilliferous (M8406/0)
  unius lateris 757.33
  Unna's 757.32
  vascular 757.32
  verrucous 757.33
  white sponge (oral mucosa) 750.26
Newborn (infant) (liveborn)
  affected by maternal abuse of drugs (gestational) (via placenta) (via breast milk) ▶(*see also* Noxious, substances transmitted through placenta or breast milk, affecting fetus or newborn)◀ 760.70
  apnea 770.81 ●
    obstructive 770.82 ●
    specified NEC 770.82 ●
  cardiomyopathy 425.4 ●
    congenital 425.3 ●
  convulsion 779.0 ●
  electrolyte imbalance NEC (transitory) 775.5 ●
  gestation
    24 completed weeks 765.22
    25-26 completed weeks 765.23
    27-28 completed weeks 765.24
    29-30 completed weeks 765.25
    31-32 completed weeks 765.26
    33-34 completed weeks 765.27
    35-36 completed weeks 765.28
    37 or more completed weeks 765.29
    less than 24 completed weeks 765.21
    unspecified completed weeks 765.20
  infection 771.89 ●
    candida 771.7 ●
    mastitis 771.5 ●
    specified NEC 771.89 ●
    urinary tract 771.82 ●
  mastitis 771.5 ●
  multiple NEC
    born in hospital (without mention of cesarean delivery or section) V37.00
      with cesarean delivery or section V37.01
    born outside hospital
      hospitalized V37.1
      not hospitalized V37.2
    mates all liveborn
      born in hospital (without mention of cesarean delivery or section) V34.00
        with cesarean delivery or section V34.01
      born outside hospital
        hospitalized V34.1
        not hospitalized V34.2
    mates all stillborn
      born in hospital (without mention of cesarean delivery or section) V35.00
        with cesarean delivery or section V35.01
      born outside hospital
        hospitalized V35.1
        not hospitalized V35.2
    mates liveborn and stillborn
      born in hospital (without mention of cesarean delivery or section) V36.00
        with cesarean delivery or section V36.01

Newborn (*see also* Noxious, substances transmitted through placenta or breast milk, affecting fetus or newborn) — *continued*
  multiple — *continued*
    mates liveborn and stillborn — *continued*
      born outside hospital
        hospitalized V36.1
        not hospitalized V36.2
  omphalitis 771.4 ●
  seizure 779.0 ●
  sepsis 771.81 ●
  single
    born in hospital (without mention of cesarean delivery or section) V30.00
      with cesarean delivery or section V30.01
    born outside hospital
      hospitalized V30.1
      not hospitalized V30.2
  specified condition NEC 779.89 ●
  twin NEC
    born in hospital (without mention of cesarean delivery or section) V33.00
      with cesarean delivery or section V33.01
    born outside hospital
      hospitalized V33.1
      not hospitalized V33.2
    mate liveborn
      born in hospital V31.0 ☑
      born outside hospital
        hospitalized V31.1
        not hospitalized V31.2
    mate stillborn
      born in hospital V32.0 ☑
      born outside hospital
        hospitalized V32.1
        not hospitalized V32.2
  unspecified as to single or multiple birth
    born in hospital (without mention of cesarean delivery or section) V39.00
      with cesarean delivery or section V39.01
    born outside hospital
      hospitalized V39.1
      not hospitalized V39.2
Newcastle's conjunctivitis or disease 077.8
Nezelof's syndrome (pure alymphocytosis) 279.13
Niacin (amide) **deficiency** 265.2
Nicolas-Durand-Favre disease (climatic bubo) 099.1
Nicolas-Favre disease (climatic bubo) 099.1
Nicotinic acid (amide) **deficiency** 265.2
Niemann-Pick disease (lipid histiocytosis) (splenomegaly) 272.7
Night
  blindness (*see also* Blindness, night) 368.60
    congenital 368.61
    vitamin A deficiency 264.5
  cramps 729.82
  sweats 780.8
  terrors, child 307.46
Nightmare 307.47
  REM-sleep type 307.47
Nipple — *see* condition
Nisbet's chancre 099.0
Nishimoto (-Takeuchi) disease 437.5
Nitritoid crisis or reaction — *see* Crisis, nitritoid
Nitrogen retention, extrarenal 788.9
Nitrosohemoglobinemia 289.89
Njovera 104.0
No
  diagnosis 799.9
  disease (found) V71.9
  room at the inn V65.0
Nocardiasis — *see* Nocardiosis
Nocardiosis 039.9
  with pneumonia 039.1
  lung 039.1
  specified type NEC 039.8
Nocturia 788.43
  psychogenic 306.53
Nocturnal — *see also* condition
  dyspnea (paroxysmal) 786.09
  emissions 608.89
  enuresis 788.36
    psychogenic 307.6
  frequency (micturition) 788.43
    psychogenic 306.53

Nodal rhythm disorder 427.89
Nodding of head 781.0
Node(s) — *see also* Nodule(s)
  Heberden's 715.04
  larynx 478.79
  lymph — *see* condition
  milkers' 051.1
  Osler's 421.0
  rheumatic 729.89
  Schmorl's 722.30
    lumbar, lumbosacral 722.32
    specified region NEC 722.39
    thoracic, thoracolumbar 722.31
  singers' 478.5
  skin NEC 782.2
  tuberculous — *see* Tuberculosis, lymph gland
  vocal cords 478.5
Nodosities, Haygarth's 715.04
Nodule(s), nodular
  actinomycotic (*see also* Actinomycosis) 039.9
  arthritic — *see* Arthritis, nodosa
  cutaneous 782.2
  Haygarth's 715.04
  inflammatory — *see* Inflammation
  juxta-articular 102.7
    syphilitic 095.7
    yaws 102.7
  larynx 478.79
  lung, solitary 518.89
    emphysematous 492.8
  milkers' 051.1
  prostate 600.10
    with urinary retention 600.11
  rheumatic 729.89
  rheumatoid — *see* Arthritis, rheumatoid
  scrotum (inflammatory) 608.4
  singers' 478.5
  skin NEC 782.2
  solitary, lung 518.89
    emphysematous 492.8
  subcutaneous 782.2
  thyroid (gland) (nontoxic) (uninodular) 241.0
    with
      hyperthyroidism 242.1 ☑
      thyrotoxicosis 242.1 ☑
    toxic or with hyperthyroidism 242.1 ☑
  vocal cords 478.5
Noma (gangrenous) (hospital) (infective) 528.1
  auricle (*see also* Gangrene) 785.4
  mouth 528.1
  pudendi (*see also* Vulvitis) 616.10
  vulvae (*see also* Vulvitis) 616.10
Nomadism V60.0
Non-adherence
  artificial skin graft 996.55
  decellularized allodermis graft 996.55
Non-autoimmune hemolytic anemia NEC 283.10
Nonclosure — *see also* Imperfect, closure
  ductus
    arteriosus 747.0
    Botalli 747.0
  Eustachian valve 746.89
  foramen
    Botalli 745.5
    ovale 745.5
Noncompliance with medical treatment V15.81
Nondescent (congenital) — *see also* Malposition, congenital
  cecum 751.4
  colon 751.4
  testis 752.51
Nondevelopment
  brain 742.1
    specified part 742.2
  heart 746.89
  organ or site, congenital NEC — *see* Hypoplasia
Nonengagement
  head NEC 652.5 ☑
    in labor 660.1 ☑
      affecting fetus or newborn 763.1

Nonexanthematous tick fever 066.1
Nonexpansion, lung (newborn) NEC 770.4
Nonfunctioning
  cystic duct (*see also* Disease, gallbladder) 575.8
  gallbladder (*see also* Disease, gallbladder) 575.8
  kidney (*see also* Disease, renal) 593.9
  labyrinth 386.58
Nonhealing
  stump (surgical) 997.69
  wound, surgical 998.83
Nonimplantation of ovum, causing infertility 628.3
Noninsufflation, fallopian tube 628.2
Nonne-Milroy-Meige syndrome (chronic hereditary edema) 757.0
Nonovulation 628.0
Nonpatent fallopian tube 628.2
Nonpneumatization, lung NEC 770.4
Nonreflex bladder 596.54
  with cauda equina 344.61
Nonretention of food — *see* Vomiting
Nonrotation — *see* Malrotation
Nonsecretion, urine (*see also* Anuria) 788.5
  newborn 753.3
Nonunion
  fracture 733.82
  organ or site, congenital NEC — *see* Imperfect, closure
  symphysis pubis, congenital 755.69
  top sacrum, congenital 756.19
Nonviability 765.0 ☑
Nonvisualization, gallbladder 793.3
Nonvitalized tooth 522.9
Non-working side interference 524.56
Normal
  delivery — *see* category 650
  menses V65.5
  state (feared complaint unfounded) V65.5
Normoblastosis 289.89
Normocytic anemia (infectional) 285.9
  due to blood loss (chronic) 280.0
    acute 285.1
Norrie's disease (congenital) (progressive oculoacousticocerebral degeneration) 743.8
North American blastomycosis 116.0
Norwegian itch 133.0
Nose, nasal — *see* condition
Nosebleed 784.7
Nosomania 298.9
Nosophobia 300.29
Nostalgia 309.89
Notch of iris 743.46
Notched lip, congenital (*see also* Cleft, lip) 749.10
Notching nose, congenital (tip) 748.1
Nothnagel's
  syndrome 378.52
  vasomotor acroparesthesia 443.89
Novy's relapsing fever (American) 087.1
Noxious
  foodstuffs, poisoning by
    fish 988.0
    fungi 988.1
    mushrooms 988.1
    plants (food) 988.2
    shellfish 988.0
    specified type NEC 988.8
    toadstool 988.1
  substances transmitted through placenta or breast milk (affecting fetus or newborn) 760.70
    acetretin 760.78 ●
    alcohol 760.71
    aminopterin 760.78 ●
    antiandrogens 760.79 ●
    anticonvulsant 760.77 ●

Noxious — *continued*
  substances transmitted through placenta or breast milk (affecting fetus or newborn) — *continued*
    antifungal 760.74 ●
    anti-infective agents 760.74
    antimetabolic 760.78 ●
    atorvastatin 760.78 ●
    carbamazepine 760.77 ●
    cocaine 760.75
    "crack" 760.75
    diethylstilbestrol (DES) 760.76
    divalproex sodium 760.77 ●
    endocrine disrupting chemicals 760.79 ●
    estrogens 760.79 ●
    etretinate 760.78 ●
    fluconazole 760.74 ●
    fluvastatin 760.78 ●
    hallucinogenic agents NEC 760.73 ●
    hormones 760.79
    lithium 760.79 ●
    lovastatin 760.78 ●
    medicinal agents NEC 760.79
    methotrexate 760.78 ●
    misoprostil 760.79 ●
    narcotics 760.72
    obstetric anesthetic or analgesic 763.5
    phenobarbital 760.77 ●
    phenytoin 760.77 ●
    pravastatin 760.78 ●
    progestins 760.79 ●
    retinoic acid 760.78 ●
    simvastatin 760.78 ●
    solvents 760.79 ●
    specified agent NEC 760.79 ●
    statins 760.78 ●
    suspected, affecting management of pregnancy 655.5 ☑
    tetracycline 760.74 ●
    thalidomide 760.79 ●
    trimethadione 760.77 ●
    valproate 760.77 ●
    valproic acid 760.77 ●
    vitamin A 760.78 ●
Nuchal hitch (arm) 652.8 ☑
Nucleus pulposus — *see* condition
Numbness 782.0
Nuns' knee 727.2
Nursemaid's
  elbow 832.0 ☑
  shoulder 831.0 ☑
Nutmeg liver 573.8
Nutrition, deficient or insufficient (particular kind of food) 269.9
  due to
    insufficient food 994.2
    lack of
      care (child) (infant) 995.52
        adult 995.84
      food 994.2
Nyctalopia (*see also* Blindness, night) 368.60
  vitamin A deficiency 264.5
Nycturia 788.43
  psychogenic 306.53
Nymphomania 302.89
Nystagmus 379.50
  associated with vestibular system disorders 379.54
  benign paroxysmal positional 386.11
  central positional 386.2
  congenital 379.51
  deprivation 379.53
  dissociated 379.55
  latent 379.52
  miners' 300.89
  positional
    benign paroxysmal 386.11
    central 386.2
  specified NEC 379.56
  vestibular 379.54
  visual deprivation 379.53

O

Oasthouse urine disease 270.2
Obermeyer's relapsing fever (European) 087.0
Obesity (constitutional) (exogenous) (familial)
    (nutritional) (simple) 278.00
    adrenal 255.8
    due to hyperalimentation 278.00
    endocrine NEC 259.9
    endogenous 259.9
    Fröhlich's (adiposogenital dystrophy) 253.8
    glandular NEC 259.9
    hypothyroid (see also Hypothyroidism) 244.9
    morbid 278.01
    of pregnancy 646.1 ☑
    pituitary 253.8
    severe 278.01
    thyroid (see also Hypothyroidism) 244.9
Oblique — see also condition
    lie before labor, affecting fetus or newborn
        761.7
Obliquity, pelvis 738.6
Obliteration
    abdominal aorta 446.7
    appendix (lumen) 543.9
    artery 447.1
    ascending aorta 446.7
    bile ducts 576.8
        with calculus, choledocholithiasis, or stones
            — see Choledocholithiasis
        congenital 751.61
            jaundice from 751.61 [774.5]
    common duct 576.8
        with calculus, choledocholithiasis, or stones
            — see Choledocholithiasis
        congenital 751.61
    cystic duct 575.8
        with calculus, choledocholithiasis, or stones
            — see Choledocholithiasis
    disease, arteriolar 447.1
    endometrium 621.8
    eye, anterior chamber 360.34
    fallopian tube 628.2
    lymphatic vessel 457.1
        postmastectomy 457.0
    organ or site, congenital NEC — see Atresia
    placental blood vessels — see Placenta,
        abnormal
    supra-aortic branches 446.7
    ureter 593.89
    urethra 599.84
    vein 459.9
    vestibule (oral) 525.8
Observation (for) V71.9
    without need for further medical care V71.9
    accident NEC V71.4
        at work V71.3
    criminal assault V71.6
    deleterious agent ingestion V71.89
    disease V71.9
        cardiovascular V71.7
            heart V71.7
        mental V71.09
        specified condition NEC V71.89
    foreign body ingestion V71.89
    growth and development variations V21.8
    injuries (accidental) V71.4
        inflicted NEC V71.6
            during alleged rape or seduction V71.5
    malignant neoplasm, suspected V71.1
    postpartum
        immediately after delivery V24.0
        routine follow-up V24.2
    pregnancy
        high-risk V23.9
            specified problem NEC V23.89
        normal (without complication) V22.1
            with nonobstetric complication V22.2
            first V22.0
    rape or seduction, alleged V71.5
        injury during V71.5
    suicide attempt, alleged V71.89
    suspected (undiagnosed) (unproven)
        abuse V71.81
        cardiovascular disease V71.7
        child or wife battering victim V71.6
        concussion (cerebral) V71.6

Observation — continued
    suspected — continued
        condition NEC V71.89
            infant — see Observation, suspected,
                condition, newborn
            newborn V29.9
                cardiovascular disease V29.8
                congenital anomaly V29.8
                genetic V29.3
                infectious V29.0
                ingestion foreign object V29.8
                injury V29.8
                metabolic V29.3
                neoplasm V29.8
                neurological V29.1
                poison, poisoning V29.8
                respiratory V29.2
                specified NEC V29.8
        exposure
            anthrax V71.82
            biologic agent NEC V71.83
                SARS V71.83
        infectious disease not requiring isolation
            V71.89
        malignant neoplasm V71.1
        mental disorder V71.09
        neglect V71.81
        neoplasm
            benign V71.89
            malignant V71.1
            specified condition NEC V71.89
        tuberculosis V71.2
    tuberculosis, suspected V71.2
Obsession, obsessional 300.3
    ideas and mental images 300.3
    impulses 300.3
    neurosis 300.3
    phobia 300.3
    psychasthenia 300.3
    ruminations 300.3
    state 300.3
    syndrome 300.3
Obsessive-compulsive 300.3
    neurosis 300.3
    personality 301.4
    reaction 300.3
Obstetrical trauma NEC (complicating delivery)
    665.9 ☑
    with
        abortion — see Abortion, by type, with
            damage to pelvic organs
        ectopic pregnancy (see also categories
            633.0-633.9) 639.2
        molar pregnancy (see also categories 630-
            632) 639.2
    affecting fetus or newborn 763.89
    following
        abortion 639.2
        ectopic or molar pregnancy 639.2
Obstipation (see also Constipation) 564.00
    psychogenic 306.4
Obstruction, obstructed, obstructive
    airway NEC 519.8
        with
            allergic alveolitis NEC 495.9
            asthma NEC (see also Asthma) 493.9 ☑
            bronchiectasis 494.0
                with acute exacerbation 494.1
            bronchitis (chronic) (see also Bronchitis,
                with, obstruction) 491.20
            emphysema NEC 492.8
        chronic 496
            with
                allergic alveolitis NEC 495.5
                asthma NEC (see also Asthma)
                    493.2 ☑
                bronchiectasis 494.0
                    with acute exacerbation 494.1
                bronchitis (chronic) (see also
                    Bronchitis, with, obstruction)
                    491.20
                emphysema NEC 492.8
        due to
            bronchospasm 519.1
            foreign body 934.9
            inhalation of fumes or vapors 506.9

Obstruction, obstructed, obstructive —
    continued
    airway NEC — continued
        due to — continued
            laryngospasm 478.75
    alimentary canal (see also Obstruction,
        intestine) 560.9
    ampulla of Vater 576.2
        with calculus, cholelithiasis, or stones — see
            Choledocholithiasis
    aortic (heart) (valve) (see also Stenosis, aortic)
        424.1
        rheumatic (see also Stenosis, aortic,
            rheumatic) 395.0
    aortoiliac 444.0
    aqueduct of Sylvius 331.4
        congenital 742.3
            with spina bifida (see also Spina bifida)
                741.0 ☑
    Arnold-Chiari (see also Spina bifida) 741.0 ☑
    artery (see also Embolism, artery) 444.9
        basilar (complete) (partial) (see also
            Occlusion, artery, basilar) 433.0 ☑
        carotid (complete) (partial) (see also
            Occlusion, artery, carotid) 433.1 ☑
        precerebral — see Occlusion, artery,
            precerebral NEC
        retinal (central) (see also Occlusion, retina)
            362.30
        vertebral (complete) (partial) (see also
            Occlusion, artery, vertebral) 433.2 ☑
    asthma (chronic) (with obstructive pulmonary
        disease) 493.2 ☑
    band (intestinal) 560.81
    bile duct or passage (see also Obstruction,
        biliary) 576.2
        congenital 751.61
            jaundice from 751.61 [774.5]
    biliary (duct) (tract) 576.2
        with calculus 574.51
            with cholecystitis (chronic) 574.41
                acute 574.31
        congenital 751.61
            jaundice from 751.61 [774.5]
        gallbladder 575.2
            with calculus 574.21
                with cholecystitis (chronic) 574.11
                    acute 574.01
    bladder neck (acquired) 596.0
        congenital 753.6
    bowel (see also Obstruction, intestine) 560.9
    bronchus 519.1
    canal, ear (see also Stricture, ear canal,
        acquired) 380.50
    cardia 537.89
    caval veins (inferior) (superior) 459.2
    cecum (see also Obstruction, intestine) 560.9
    circulatory 459.9
    colon (see also Obstruction, intestine) 560.9
        sympathicotonic 560.89
    common duct (see also Obstruction, biliary)
        576.2
        congenital 751.61
    coronary (artery) (heart) — see also
        Arteriosclerosis, coronary
        acute (see also Infarct, myocardium)
            410.9 ☑
        without myocardial infarction 411.81
    cystic duct (see also Obstruction, gallbladder)
        575.2
        congenital 751.61
    device, implant, or graft — see Complications,
        due to (presence of) any device, implant,
        or graft classified to 996.0-996.5 NEC
    due to foreign body accidentally left in
        operation wound 998.4
    duodenum 537.3
        congenital 751.1
        due to
            compression NEC 537.3
            cyst 537.3
            intrinsic lesion or disease NEC 537.3
            scarring 537.3
            torsion 537.3
            ulcer 532.91
            volvulus 537.3
    ejaculatory duct 608.89

☑ Additional Digit Required — Refer to the Tabular List (Numeric Code Section) for Additional Digit Selection
▶◀ Revised Text   ● New Line   ▲ Revised Code

2006 ICD-9-CM   **Volume 2 — 251**

Obstruction, obstructed, obstructive — *continued*

endocardium 424.90
  arteriosclerotic 424.99
  specified cause, except rheumatic 424.99
esophagus 530.3
eustachian tube (complete) (partial) 381.60
  cartilaginous
    extrinsic 381.63
    intrinsic 381.62
  due to
    cholesteatoma 381.61
    osseous lesion NEC 381.61
    polyp 381.61
    osseous 381.61
fallopian tube (bilateral) 628.2
fecal 560.39
  with hernia — *see also* Hernia, by site, with obstruction
    gangrenous — *see* Hernia, by site, with gangrene
foramen of Monro (congenital) 742.3
  with spina bifida (*see also* Spina bifida) 741.0 ☑
foreign body — *see* Foreign body
gallbladder 575.2
  with calculus, cholelithiasis, or stones 574.21
    with cholecystitis (chronic) 574.11
      acute 574.01
  congenital 751.69
    jaundice from 751.69 [774.5]
gastric outlet 537.0
gastrointestinal (*see also* Obstruction, intestine) 560.9
glottis 478.79
hepatic 573.8
  duct (*see also* Obstruction, biliary) 576.2
    congenital 751.61
icterus (*see also* Obstruction, biliary) 576.8
  congenital 751.61
ileocecal coil (*see also* Obstruction, intestine) 560.9
ileum (*see also* Obstruction, intestine) 560.9
iliofemoral (artery) 444.81
internal anastomosis — *see* Complications, mechanical, graft
intestine (mechanical) (neurogenic) (paroxysmal) (postinfectional) (reflex) 560.9
  with
    adhesions (intestinal) (peritoneal) 560.81
    hernia — *see also* Hernia, by site, with obstruction
      gangrenous — *see* Hernia, by site, with gangrene
  adynamic (*see also* Ileus) 560.1
  by gallstone 560.31
  congenital or infantile (small) 751.1
    large 751.2
  due to
    Ascaris lumbricoides 127.0
    mural thickening 560.89
    procedure 997.4
      involving urinary tract 997.5
  impaction 560.39
  infantile — *see* Obstruction, intestine, congenital
  newborn
    due to
      fecaliths 777.1
      inspissated milk 777.2
      meconium (plug) 777.1
        in mucoviscidosis 277.01
      transitory 777.4
    specified cause NEC 560.89
    transitory, newborn 777.4
    volvulus 560.2
  intracardiac ball valve prosthesis 996.02
  jaundice (*see also* Obstruction, biliary) 576.8
    congenital 751.61
  jejunum (*see also* Obstruction, intestine) 560.9
  kidney 593.89
  labor 660.9 ☑
    affecting fetus or newborn 763.1

Obstruction, obstructed, obstructive — *continued*

labor — *continued*
  by
    bony pelvis (conditions classifiable to 653.0-653.9) 660.1 ☑
    deep transverse arrest 660.3 ☑
    impacted shoulder 660.4 ☑
    locked twins 660.5 ☑
    malposition (fetus) (conditions classifiable to 652.0-652.9) 660.0 ☑
      head during labor 660.3 ☑
    persistent occipitoposterior position 660.3 ☑
    soft tissue, pelvic (conditions classifiable to 654.0-654.9) 660.2 ☑
lacrimal
  canaliculi 375.53
  congenital 743.65
  punctum 375.52
  sac 375.54
lacrimonasal duct 375.56
  congenital 743.65
  neonatal 375.55
lacteal, with steatorrhea 579.2
laryngitis (*see also* Laryngitis) 464.01
larynx 478.79
  congenital 748.3
liver 573.8
  cirrhotic (*see also* Cirrhosis, liver) 571.5
lung 518.89
  with
    asthma — *see* Asthma
    bronchitis (chronic) 491.20
    emphysema NEC 492.8
  airway, chronic 496
  chronic NEC 496
    with
      asthma (chronic) (obstructive) 493.2 ☑
  disease, chronic 496
    with
      asthma (chronic) (obstructive) 493.2 ☑
  emphysematous 492.8
lymphatic 457.1
meconium
  fetus or newborn 777.1
    in mucoviscidosis 277.01
  newborn due to fecaliths 777.1
mediastinum 519.3
mitral (rheumatic) — *see* Stenosis, mitral
nasal 478.1
  duct 375.56
    neonatal 375.55
  sinus — *see* Sinusitis
nasolacrimal duct 375.56
  congenital 743.65
  neonatal 375.55
nasopharynx 478.29
nose 478.1
organ or site, congenital NEC — *see* Atresia
pancreatic duct 577.8
parotid gland 527.8
pelviureteral junction (*see also* Obstruction, ureter) 593.4
pharynx 478.29
portal (circulation) (vein) 452
prostate 600.90
  with urinary retention 600.91
  valve (urinary) 596.0
pulmonary
  valve (heart) (*see also* Endocarditis, pulmonary) 424.3
  vein, isolated 747.49
pyemic — *see* Septicemia
pylorus (acquired) 537.0
  congenital 750.5
  infantile 750.5
rectosigmoid (*see also* Obstruction, intestine) 560.9
rectum 569.49
renal 593.89
respiratory 519.8
  chronic 496
retinal (artery) (vein) (central) (*see also* Occlusion, retina) 362.30
salivary duct (any) 527.8
  with calculus 527.5

Obstruction, obstructed, obstructive — *continued*

sigmoid (*see also* Obstruction, intestine) 560.9
sinus (accessory) (nasal) (*see also* Sinusitis) 473.9
Stensen's duct 527.8
stomach 537.89
  acute 536.1
  congenital 750.7
submaxillary gland 527.8
  with calculus 527.5
thoracic duct 457.1
thrombotic — *see* Thrombosis
tooth eruption 520.6
trachea 519.1
tracheostomy airway 519.09
tricuspid — *see* Endocarditis, tricuspid
upper respiratory, congenital 748.8
ureter (functional) 593.4
  congenital 753.20
  due to calculus 592.1
ureteropelvic junction, congenital 753.21
ureterovesical junction, congenital 753.22
urethra 599.60 ▲
  congenital 753.6
urinary (moderate) 599.60 ▲
  organ or tract (lower) 599.60 ●
    due to
      benign prostatic hypertrophy (BPH) — *see* category 600 ●
    specified NEC 599.69 ●
      due to
        benign prostatic hypertrophy (BPH) — *see* category 600 ●
  specified NEC 599.69 ●
    due to
      benign prostatic hypertrophy (BPH) — *see* category 600 ●
  prostatic valve 596.0
uropathy 599.60 ▲
uterus 621.8
vagina 623.2
valvular — *see* Endocarditis
vascular graft or shunt 996.1
  atherosclerosis — *see* Arteriosclerosis, coronary
  embolism 996.74
  occlusion NEC 996.74
  thrombus 996.74
vein, venous 459.2
  caval (inferior) (superior) 459.2
  thrombotic — *see* Thrombosis
vena cava (inferior) (superior) 459.2
ventricular shunt 996.2
vesical 596.0
vesicourethral orifice 596.0
vessel NEC 459.9

Obturator — *see* condition

Occlusal

plane deviation 524.76
wear, teeth 521.10

Occlusion

anus 569.49
  congenital 751.2
  infantile 751.2
aortoiliac (chronic) 444.0
aqueduct of Sylvius 331.4
  congenital 742.3
    with spina bifida (*see also* Spina bifida) 741.0 ☑
arteries of extremities, lower 444.22
  without thrombus or embolus (*see also* Arteriosclerosis, extremities) 440.20
  due to stricture or stenosis 447.1
  upper 444.21
    without thrombus or embolus (*see also* Arteriosclerosis, extremities) 440.20
    due to stricture or stenosis 447.1
artery NEC (*see also* Embolism, artery) 444.9
  auditory, internal 433.8 ☑
  basilar 433.0 ☑
    with other precerebral artery 433.3 ☑
    bilateral 433.3 ☑
  brain or cerebral (*see also* Infarct, brain) 434.9 ☑

☑ Additional Digit Required — Refer to the Tabular List (Numeric Code Section) for Additional Digit Selection

Occlusion — *continued*
 artery NEC (*see also* Embolism, artery) —
  continued
  carotid 433.1 ☑
   with other precerebral artery 433.3 ☑
   bilateral 433.3 ☑
  cerebellar (anterior inferior) (posterior
   inferior) (superior) 433.8 ☑
  cerebral (*see also* Infarct, brain) 434.9 ☑
  choroidal (anterior) 433.8 ☑
  communicating posterior 433.8 ☑
  coronary (thrombotic) (*see also* Infarct,
   myocardium) 410.9 ☑
   acute 410.9 ☑
    without myocardial infarction 411.81
   healed or old 412
  hypophyseal 433.8 ☑
  iliac artery 444.81
  mesenteric (embolic) (thrombotic) (with
   gangrene) 557.0
  pontine 433.8 ☑
  precerebral NEC 433.9 ☑
   late effect — *see* Late effect(s) (of)
    cerebrovascular disease
   multiple or bilateral 433.3 ☑
   puerperal, postpartum, childbirth
    674.0 ☑
   specified NEC 433.8 ☑
  renal 593.81
  retinal — *see* Occlusion, retina, artery
  spinal 433.8 ☑
  vertebral 433.2 ☑
   with other precerebral artery 433.3 ☑
   bilateral 433.3 ☑
 basilar (artery) — *see* Occlusion, artery, basilar
 bile duct (any) (*see also* Obstruction, biliary)
  576.2
 bowel (*see also* Obstruction, intestine) 560.9
 brain (artery) (vascular) (*see also* Infarct, brain)
  434.9 ☑
 breast (duct) 611.8
 carotid (artery) (common) (internal) — *see*
  Occlusion, artery, carotid
 cerebellar (anterior inferior) (artery) (posterior
  inferior) (superior) 433.8 ☑
 cerebral (artery) (*see also* Infarct, brain)
  434.9 ☑
 cerebrovascular (*see also* Infarct, brain)
  434.9 ☑
  diffuse 437.0
 cervical canal (*see also* Stricture, cervix) 622.4
  by falciparum malaria 084.0
 cervix (uteri) (*see also* Stricture, cervix) 622.4
 choanal 748.0
 choroidal (artery) 433.8 ☑
 colon (*see also* Obstruction, intestine) 560.9
 communicating posterior artery 433.8 ☑
 coronary (artery) (thrombotic) (*see also* Infarct,
  myocardium) 410.9 ☑
  acute 410.9 ☑
   without myocardial infarction 411.81
  healed or old 412
  without myocardial infarction 411.81
 cystic duct (*see also* Obstruction, gallbladder)
  575.2
  congenital 751.69
 disto
  division I 524.22
  division II 524.22
 embolic — *see* Embolism
 fallopian tube 628.2
  congenital 752.19
 gallbladder (*see also* Obstruction, gallbladder)
  575.2
  congenital 751.69
   jaundice from 751.69 *[774.5]*
 gingiva, traumatic 523.8
 hymen 623.3
  congenital 752.42
 hypophyseal (artery) 433.8 ☑
 iliac artery 444.81
 intestine (*see also* Obstruction, intestine) 560.9
 kidney 593.89
 lacrimal apparatus — *see* Stenosis, lacrimal
 lung 518.89
 lymph or lymphatic channel 457.1
 mammary duct 611.8

Occlusion — *continued*
 mesenteric artery (embolic) (thrombotic) (with
  gangrene) 557.0
 nose 478.1
  congenital 748.0
 organ or site, congenital NEC — *see* Atresia
 oviduct 628.2
  congenital 752.19
 periodontal, traumatic 523.8
 peripheral arteries (lower extremity) 444.22
  without thrombus or embolus (*see also*
   Arteriosclerosis, extremities) 440.20
  due to stricture or stenosis 447.1
  upper extremity 444.21
   without thrombus or embolus (*see also*
    Arteriosclerosis, extremities 440.20
   due to stricture or stenosis 447.1
 pontine (artery) 433.8 ☑
 posterior lingual, of mandibular teeth 524.29
 precerebral artery — *see* Occlusion, artery,
  precerebral NEC
 puncta lacrimalia 375.52
 pupil 364.74
 pylorus (*see also* Stricture, pylorus) 537.0
 renal artery 593.81
 retina, retinal (vascular) 362.30
  artery, arterial 362.30
   branch 362.32
   central (total) 362.31
   partial 362.33
   transient 362.34
   tributary 362.32
  vein 362.30
   branch 362.36
   central (total) 362.35
   incipient 362.37
   partial 362.37
   tributary 362.36
 spinal artery 433.8 ☑
 stent
  coronary 996.72
 teeth (mandibular) (posterior lingual) 524.29
 thoracic duct 457.1
 tubal 628.2
 ureter (complete) (partial) 593.4
  congenital 753.29
 urethra (*see also* Stricture, urethra) 598.9
  congenital 753.6
 uterus 621.8
 vagina 623.2
 vascular NEC 459.9
 vein — *see* Thrombosis
 vena cava (inferior) (superior) 453.2
 ventricle (brain) NEC 331.4
 vertebral (artery) — *see* Occlusion, artery,
  vertebral
 vessel (blood) NEC 459.9
 vulva 624.8

Occlusio pupillae 364.74

Occupational
 problems NEC V62.2
 therapy V57.21

Ochlophobia 300.29

Ochronosis (alkaptonuric) (congenital)
 (endogenous) 270.2
 with chloasma of eyelid 270.2

Ocular muscle — *see also* condition
 myopathy 359.1
 torticollis 781.93

Oculoauriculovertebral dysplasia 756.0

Oculogyric
 crisis or disturbance 378.87
  psychogenic 306.7

Oculomotor syndrome 378.81

Oddi's sphincter spasm 576.5

Odelberg's disease (juvenile osteochondrosis)
 732.1

Odontalgia 525.9

Odontoameloblastoma (M9311/0) 213.1
 upper jaw (bone) 213.0

Odontoclasia 521.05

Odontoclasis 873.63
 complicated 873.73

Odontodysplasia, regional 520.4

Odontogenesis imperfecta 520.5

Odontoma (M9280/0) 213.1
 ameloblastic (M9311/0) 213.1
  upper jaw (bone) 213.0
 calcified (M9280/0) 213.1
  upper jaw (bone) 213.0
 complex (M9282/0) 213.1
  upper jaw (bone) 213.0
 compound (M9281/0) 213.1
  upper jaw (bone) 213.0
 fibroameloblastic (M9290/0) 213.1
  upper jaw (bone) 213.0
 follicular 526.0
  upper jaw (bone) 213.0

Odontomyelitis (closed) (open) 522.0

Odontonecrosis 521.09

Odontorrhagia 525.8

Odontosarcoma, ameloblastic (M9290/3) 170.1
 upper jaw (bone) 170.0

Odynophagia 787.2

Oesophagostomiasis 127.7

Oesophagostomum infestation 127.7

Oestriasis 134.0

Ogilvie's syndrome (sympathicotonic colon
 obstruction) 560.89

Oguchi's disease (retina) 368.61

Ohara's disease (*see also* Tularemia) 021.9

Oidiomycosis (*see also* Candidiasis) 112.9

Oidiomycotic meningitis 112.83

Oidium albicans infection (*see also* Candidiasis)
 112.9

Old age 797
 dementia (of) 290.0

Olfactory — *see* condition

Oligemia 285.9

Oligergasia (*see also* Retardation, mental) 319

Oligoamnios 658.0 ☑
 affecting fetus or newborn 761.2

Oligoastrocytoma, mixed (M9382/3)
 specified site — *see* Neoplasm, by site,
  malignant
 unspecified site 191.9

Oligocythemia 285.9

Oligodendroblastoma (M9460/3)
 specified site — *see* Neoplasm, by site,
  malignant
 unspecified site 191.9

Oligodendroglioma (M9450/3)
 anaplastic type (M9451/3)
  specified site — *see* Neoplasm, by site,
   malignant
  unspecified site 191.9
 specified site — *see* Neoplasm, by site,
  malignant
 unspecified site 191.9

Oligodendroma — *see* Oligodendroglioma

Oligodontia (*see also* Anodontia) 520.0

Oligoencephalon 742.1

Oligohydramnios 658.0 ☑
 affecting fetus or newborn 761.2
 due to premature rupture of membranes
  658.1 ☑
  affecting fetus or newborn 761.2

Oligohydrosis 705.0

Oligomenorrhea 626.1

Oligophrenia (*see also* Retardation, mental) 319
 phenylpyruvic 270.1

Oligospermia 606.1

Oligotrichia 704.09
 congenita 757.4

Oliguria 788.5
 with
  abortion — *see* Abortion, by type, with renal
   failure
  ectopic pregnancy (*see also* categories
   633.0-633.9) 639.3
  molar pregnancy (*see also* categories 630-
   632) 639.3
 complicating
  abortion 639.3

☑ Additional Digit Required — Refer to the Tabular List (Numeric Code Section) for Additional Digit Selection
►◄ Revised Text ● New Line ▲ Revised Code

2006 ICD-9-CM **Volume 2 — 253**

Oliguria — *continued*
  complicating — *continued*
    ectopic or molar pregnancy 639.3
    pregnancy 646.2 ☑
      with hypertension — *see* Toxemia, of
        pregnancy
  due to a procedure 997.5
  following labor and delivery 669.3 ☑
  heart or cardiac — *see* Failure, heart
  puerperal, postpartum 669.3 ☑
  specified due to a procedure 997.5
Ollier's disease (chondrodysplasia) 756.4
Omentitis (*see also* Peritonitis) 567.9
Omentocele (*see also* Hernia, omental) 553.8
Omentum, omental — *see* condition
Omphalitis (congenital) (newborn) 771.4
  not of newborn 686.9
  tetanus 771.3
Omphalocele 756.79
Omphalomesenteric duct, persistent 751.0
Omphalorrhagia, newborn 772.3
Omsk hemorrhagic fever 065.1
Onanism 307.9
Onchocerciasis 125.3
  eye 125.3 *[360.13]*
Onchocercosis 125.3
Oncocytoma (M8290/0) — *see* Neoplasm, by site,
  benign
Ondine's curse 348.8
Oneirophrenia (*see also* Schizophrenia) 295.4 ☑
Onychauxis 703.8
  congenital 757.5
Onychia (with lymphangitis) 681.9
  dermatophytic 110.1
  finger 681.02
  toe 681.11
Onychitis (with lymphangitis) 681.9
  finger 681.02
  toe 681.11
Onychocryptosis 703.0
Onychodystrophy 703.8
  congenital 757.5
Onychogryphosis 703.8
Onychogryposis 703.8
Onycholysis 703.8
Onychomadesis 703.8
Onychomalacia 703.8
Onychomycosis 110.1
  finger 110.1
  toe 110.1
Onycho-osteodysplasia 756.89
Onychophagy 307.9
Onychoptosis 703.8
Onychorrhexis 703.8
  congenital 757.5
Onychoschizia 703.8
Onychotrophia (*see also* Atrophy, nail) 703.8
O'nyong-nyong fever 066.3
Onyxis (finger) (toe) 703.0
Onyxitis (with lymphangitis) 681.9
  finger 681.02
  toe 681.11
Oocyte (egg) (ovum) ●
  donor V59.70 ●
    over age 35 V59.73 ●
      anonymous recipient V59.73 ●
      designated recipient V59.74 ●
    under age 35 V59.71 ●
      anonymous recipient V59.71 ●
      designated recipient V59.72 ●
Oophoritis (cystic) (infectional) (interstitial) (*see
  also* Salpingo-oophoritis) 614.2
  complicating pregnancy 646.6 ☑
  fetal (acute) 752.0
  gonococcal (acute) 098.19
    chronic or duration of 2 months or over
      098.39
  tuberculous (*see also* Tuberculosis) 016.6 ☑

Opacity, opacities
  cornea 371.00
    central 371.03
    congenital 743.43
      interfering with vision 743.42
    degenerative (*see also* Degeneration, cornea)
      371.40
    hereditary (*see also* Dystrophy, cornea)
      371.50
    inflammatory (*see also* Keratitis) 370.9
    late effect of trachoma (healed) 139.1
    minor 371.01
    peripheral 371.02
  enamel (fluoride) (nonfluoride) (teeth) 520.3
  lens (*see also* Cataract) 366.9
  snowball 379.22
  vitreous (humor) 379.24
    congenital 743.51
Opalescent dentin (hereditary) 520.5
Open, opening
  abnormal, organ or site, congenital — *see*
    Imperfect, closure
  angle with
    borderline intraocular pressure 365.01
    cupping of discs 365.01
  bite (anterior) (posterior) 524.29
  false — *see* Imperfect, closure
  wound — *see* Wound, open, by site
Operation
  causing mutilation of fetus 763.89
  destructive, on live fetus, to facilitate birth
    763.89
  for delivery, fetus or newborn 763.89
  maternal, unrelated to current delivery,
    affecting fetus or newborn 760.6
Operational fatigue 300.89
Operative — *see* condition
Operculitis (chronic) 523.4
  acute 523.3
Operculum, retina 361.32
  with detachment 361.01
Ophiasis 704.01
Ophthalmia (*see also* Conjunctivitis) 372.30
  actinic rays 370.24
  allergic (acute) 372.05
    chronic 372.14
  blennorrhagic (neonatorum) 098.40
  catarrhal 372.03
  diphtheritic 032.81
  Egyptian 076.1
  electric, electrica 370.24
  gonococcal (neonatorum) 098.40
  metastatic 360.11
  migraine 346.8 ☑
  neonatorum, newborn 771.6
    gonococcal 098.40
  nodosa 360.14
  phlyctenular 370.31
    with ulcer (*see also* Ulcer, cornea) 370.00
  sympathetic 360.11
Ophthalmitis — *see* Ophthalmia
Ophthalmocele (congenital) 743.66
Ophthalmoneuromyelitis 341.0
**Ophthalmopathy, infiltrative with
  thyrotoxicosis** 242.0 ☑
Ophthalmoplegia (*see also* Strabismus) 378.9
  anterior internuclear 378.86
  ataxia-areflexia syndrome 357.0
  bilateral 378.9
  diabetic 250.5 ☑ *[378.86]*
  exophthalmic 242.0 ☑ *[376.22]*
  external 378.55
    progressive 378.72
    total 378.56
  internal (complete) (total) 367.52
  internuclear 378.86
  migraine 346.8 ☑
  painful 378.55
  Parinaud's 378.81
  progressive external 378.72
  supranuclear, progressive 333.0
  total (external) 378.56
    internal 367.52
  unilateral 378.9

Opisthognathism 524.00
Opisthorchiasis (felineus) (tenuicollis) (viverrini)
  121.0
Opisthotonos, opisthotonus 781.0
Opitz's disease (congestive splenomegaly) 289.51
Opiumism (*see also* Dependence) 304.0 ☑
Oppenheim's disease 358.8
Oppenheim-Urbach disease or syndrome
  (necrobiosis lipoidica diabeticorum)
  250.8 ☑ *[709.3]*
Opsoclonia 379.59
Optic nerve — *see* condition
Orbit — *see* condition
Orchioblastoma (M9071/3) 186.9
Orchitis (nonspecific) (septic) 604.90
  with abscess 604.0
  blennorrhagic (acute) 098.13
    chronic or duration of 2 months or over
      098.33
  diphtheritic 032.89 *[604.91]*
  filarial 125.9 *[604.91]*
  gangrenous 604.99
  gonococcal (acute) 098.13
    chronic or duration of 2 months or over
      098.33
  mumps 072.0
  parotidea 072.0
  suppurative 604.99
  syphilitic 095.8 *[604.91]*
  tuberculous (*see also* Tuberculosis)
    016.5 ☑ *[608.81]*
Orf 051.2
Organic — *see also* condition
  heart — *see* Disease, heart
  insufficiency 799.89
Oriental
  bilharziasis 120.2
  schistosomiasis 120.2
  sore 085.1
Orientation
  ego-dystonic sexual 302.0
Orifice — *see* condition
Origin, both great vessels from right ventricle
  745.11
Ormond's disease or syndrome 593.4
Ornithosis 073.9
  with
    complication 073.8
      specified NEC 073.7
    pneumonia 073.0
    pneumonitis (lobular) 073.0
Orodigitofacial dysostosis 759.89
Oropouche fever 066.3
Orotaciduria, oroticaciduria (congenital)
  (hereditary) (pyrimidine deficiency) 281.4
Oroya fever 088.0
Orthodontics V58.5
  adjustment V53.4
  aftercare V58.5
  fitting V53.4
Orthopnea 786.02
Orthoptic training V57.4
Os, uterus — *see* condition
Osgood-Schlatter
  disease 732.4
  osteochondrosis 732.4
Osler's
  disease (M9950/1) (polycythemia vera) 238.4
  nodes 421.0
Osler-Rendu disease (familial hemorrhagic
  telangiectasia) 448.0
Osler-Vaquez disease (M9950/1) (polycythemia
  vera) 238.4
Osler-Weber-Rendu syndrome (familial
  hemorrhagic telangiectasia) 448.0
Osmidrosis 705.89
Osseous — *see* condition
Ossification
  artery — *see* Arteriosclerosis
  auricle (ear) 380.39

Ossification — *continued*
bronchus 519.1
cardiac (*see also* Degeneration, myocardial) 429.1
cartilage (senile) 733.99
coronary (artery) — *see* Arteriosclerosis, coronary
diaphragm 728.10
ear 380.39
middle (*see also* Otosclerosis) 387.9
falx cerebri 349.2
fascia 728.10
fontanel
defective or delayed 756.0
premature 756.0
heart (*see also* Degeneration, myocardial) 429.1
valve — *see* Endocarditis
larynx 478.79
ligament
posterior longitudinal 724.8
cervical 723.7
meninges (cerebral) 349.2
spinal 336.8
multiple, eccentric centers 733.99
muscle 728.10
heterotopic, postoperative 728.13
myocardium, myocardial (*see also* Degeneration, myocardial) 429.1
penis 607.81
periarticular 728.89
sclera 379.16
tendon 727.82
trachea 519.1
tympanic membrane (*see also* Tympanosclerosis) 385.00
vitreous (humor) 360.44

Osteitis (*see also* Osteomyelitis) 730.2 ☑
acute 730.0 ☑
alveolar 526.5
chronic 730.1 ☑
condensans (ilii) 733.5
deformans (Paget's) 731.0
due to or associated with malignant neoplasm (*see also* Neoplasm, bone, malignant) 170.9 [731.1]
due to yaws 102.6
fibrosa NEC 733.29
cystica (generalisata) 252.01
disseminata 756.59
osteoplastica 252.01
fragilitans 756.51
Garré's (sclerosing) 730.1 ☑
infectious (acute) (subacute) 730.0 ☑
chronic or old 730.1 ☑
jaw (acute) (chronic) (lower) (neonatal) (suppurative) (upper) 526.4
parathyroid 252.01
petrous bone (*see also* Petrositis) 383.20
pubis 733.5
sclerotic, nonsuppurative 730.1 ☑
syphilitic 095.5
tuberculosa
cystica (of Jüngling) 135
multiplex cystoides 135

Osteoarthritica spondylitis (spine) (*see also* Spondylosis) 721.90

Osteoarthritis (*see also* Osteoarthrosis) 715.9 ☑
distal interphalangeal 715.9 ☑
hyperplastic 731.2
interspinalis (*see also* Spondylosis) 721.90
spine, spinal NEC (*see also* Spondylosis) 721.90

Osteoarthropathy (*see also* Osteoarthrosis) 715.9 ☑
chronic idiopathic hypertrophic 757.39
familial idiopathic 757.39
hypertrophic pulmonary 731.2
secondary 731.2
idiopathic hypertrophic 757.39
primary hypertrophic 731.2
pulmonary hypertrophic 731.2
secondary hypertrophic 731.2

Osteoarthrosis (degenerative) (hypertrophic) (rheumatoid) 715.9 ☑

> *Note* — Use the following fifth-digit subclassification with category 715:
>
> 0   *site unspecified*
> 1   *shoulder region*
> 2   *upper arm*
> 3   *forearm*
> 4   *hand*
> 5   *pelvic region and thigh*
> 6   *lower leg*
> 7   *ankle and foot*
> 8   *other specified sites except spine*
> 9   *multiple sites*

Deformans alkaptonurica 270.2
generalized 715.09
juvenilis (Köhler's) 732.5
localized 715.3 ☑
idiopathic 715.1 ☑
primary 715.1 ☑
secondary 715.2 ☑
multiple sites, not specified as generalized 715.89
polyarticular 715.09
spine (*see also* Spondylosis) 721.90
temporomandibular joint 524.69

Osteoblastoma (M9200/0) — *see* Neoplasm, bone, benign

Osteochondritis (*see also* Osteochondrosis) 732.9
dissecans 732.7
hip 732.7
ischiopubica 732.1
multiple 756.59
syphilitic (congenital) 090.0

Osteochondrodermodysplasia 756.59

Osteochondrodystrophy 277.5
deformans 277.5
familial 277.5
fetalis 756.4

Osteochondrolysis 732.7

Osteochondroma (M9210/0) — *see also* Neoplasm, bone, benign
multiple, congenital 756.4

Osteochondromatosis (M9210/1) 238.0
synovial 727.82

Osteochondromyxosarcoma (M9180/3) — *see* Neoplasm, bone, malignant

Osteochondropathy NEC 732.9

Osteochondrosarcoma (M9180/3) — *see* Neoplasm, bone, malignant

Osteochondrosis 732.9
acetabulum 732.1
adult spine 732.8
astragalus 732.5
Blount's 732.4
Buchanan's (juvenile osteochondrosis of iliac crest) 732.1
Buchman's (juvenile osteochondrosis) 732.1
Burns' 732.3
calcaneus 732.5
capitular epiphysis (femur) 732.1
carpal
lunate (wrist) 732.3
scaphoid 732.3
coxae juvenilis 732.1
deformans juvenilis (coxae) (hip) 732.1
Scheuermann's 732.0
spine 732.0
tibia 732.4
vertebra 732.0
Diaz's (astragalus) 732.5
dissecans (knee) (shoulder) 732.7
femoral capital epiphysis 732.1
femur (head) (juvenile) 732.1
foot (juvenile) 732.5
Freiberg's (disease) (second metatarsal) 732.5
Haas' 732.3
Haglund's (os tibiale externum) 732.5
hand (juvenile) 732.3
head of
femur 732.1
humerus (juvenile) 732.3

Osteochondrosis — *continued*
hip (juvenile) 732.1
humerus (juvenile) 732.3
iliac crest (juvenile) 732.1
ilium (juvenile) 732.1
ischiopubic synchondrosis 732.1
Iselin's (osteochondrosis fifth metatarsal) 732.5
juvenile, juvenilis 732.6
arm 732.3
capital femoral epiphysis 732.1
capitellum humeri 732.3
capitular epiphysis 732.1
carpal scaphoid 732.3
clavicle, sternal epiphysis 732.6
coxae 732.1
deformans 732.1
foot 732.5
hand 732.3
hip and pelvis 732.1
lower extremity, except foot 732.4
lunate, wrist 732.3
medial cuneiform bone 732.5
metatarsal (head) 732.5
metatarsophalangeal 732.5
navicular, ankle 732.5
patella 732.4
primary patellar center (of Köhler) 732.4
specified site NEC 732.6
spine 732.0
tarsal scaphoid 732.5
tibia (epiphysis) (tuberosity) 732.4
upper extremity 732.3
vertebra (body) (Calvé) 732.0
epiphyseal plates (of Scheuermann) 732.0
Kienböck's (disease) 732.3
Köhler's (disease) (navicular, ankle) 732.5
patellar 732.4
tarsal navicular 732.5
Legg-Calvé-Perthes (disease) 732.1
lower extremity (juvenile) 732.4
lunate bone 732.3
Mauclaire's 732.3
metacarpal heads (of Mauclaire) 732.3
metatarsal (fifth) (head) (second) 732.5
navicular, ankle 732.5
os calcis 732.5
Osgood-Schlatter 732.4
os tibiale externum 732.5
Panner's 732.3
patella (juvenile) 732.4
patellar center
primary (of Köhler) 732.4
secondary (of Sinding-Larsen) 732.4
pelvis (juvenile) 732.1
Pierson's 732.1
radial head (juvenile) 732.3
Scheuermann's 732.0
Sever's (calcaneum) 732.5
Sinding-Larsen (secondary patellar center) 732.4
spine (juvenile) 732.0
adult 732.8
symphysis pubis (of Pierson) (juvenile) 732.1
syphilitic (congenital) 090.0
tarsal (navicular) (scaphoid) 732.5
tibia (proximal) (tubercle) 732.4
tuberculous — *see* Tuberculosis, bone
ulna 732.3
upper extremity (juvenile) 732.3
van Neck's (juvenile osteochondrosis) 732.1
vertebral (juvenile) 732.0
adult 732.8

Osteoclastoma (M9250/1) 238.0
malignant (M9250/3) — *see* Neoplasm, bone, malignant

Osteocopic pain 733.90

Osteodynia 733.90

Osteodystrophy
azotemic 588.0
chronica deformans hypertrophica 731.0
congenital 756.50
specified type NEC 756.59
deformans 731.0
fibrosa localisata 731.0
parathyroid 252.01
renal 588.0

2006 ICD-9-CM

☑ Additional Digit Required — Refer to the Tabular List (Numeric Code Section) for Additional Digit Selection
►◄ Revised Text   ● New Line   ▲ Revised Code

Volume 2 — 255

Osteofibroma (M9262/0) — *see* Neoplasm, bone, benign

Osteofibrosarcoma (M9182/3) — *see* Neoplasm, bone, malignant

Osteogenesis imperfecta 756.51

Osteogenic — *see* condition

Osteoma (M9180/0) — *see also* Neoplasm, bone, benign
   osteoid (M9191/0) — *see also* Neoplasm, bone, benign
    giant (M9200/0) — *see* Neoplasm, bone, benign

Osteomalacia 268.2
  chronica deformans hypertrophica 731.0
  due to vitamin D deficiency 268.2
  infantile (*see also* Rickets) 268.0
  juvenile (*see also* Rickets) 268.0
  pelvis 268.2
  vitamin D-resistant 275.3

Osteomalacic bone 268.2

Osteomalacosis 268.2

Osteomyelitis (general) (infective) (localized) (neonatal) (purulent) (pyogenic) (septic) (staphylococcal) (streptococcal) (suppurative) (with periostitis) 730.2 ☑

> *Note* — *Use the following fifth-digit subclassification with category 730:*
>
>   *0*   *site unspecified*
>   *1*   *shoulder region*
>   *2*   *upper arm*
>   *3*   *forearm*
>   *4*   *hand*
>   *5*   *pelvic region and thigh*
>   *6*   *lower leg*
>   *7*   *ankle and foot*
>   *8*   *other specified sites*
>   *9*   *multiple sites*

  acute or subacute 730.0 ☑
  chronic or old 730.1 ☑
  due to or associated with
    diabetes mellitus 250.8 ☑ [731.8]
    tuberculosis (*see also* Tuberculosis, bone) 015.9 ☑ [730.8] ☑
      limb bones 015.5 ☑ [730.8] ☑
      specified bones NEC 015.7 ☑ [730.8] ☑
      spine 015.0 ☑ [730.8] ☑
    typhoid 002.0 [730.8] ☑
  Garré's 730.1 ☑
  jaw (acute) (chronic) (lower) (neonatal) (suppurative) (upper) 526.4
  nonsuppurating 730.1 ☑
  orbital 376.03
  petrous bone (*see also* Petrositis) 383.20
  Salmonella 003.24
  sclerosing, nonsuppurative 730.1 ☑
  sicca 730.1 ☑
  syphilitic 095.5
    congenital 090.0 [730.8] ☑
  tuberculous — *see* Tuberculosis, bone
  typhoid 002.0 [730.8] ☑

Osteomyelofibrosis 289.89

Osteomyelosclerosis 289.89

Osteonecrosis 733.40
  meaning osteomyelitis 730.1 ☑

Osteo-onycho-arthro dysplasia 756.89

Osteo-onychodysplasia, hereditary 756.89

Osteopathia
  condensans disseminata 756.53
  hyperostotica multiplex infantilis 756.59
  hypertrophica toxica 731.2
  striata 756.4

Osteopathy resulting from poliomyelitis (*see also* Poliomyelitis) 045.9 ☑ [730.7]
  familial dysplastic 731.2

Osteopecilia 756.53

Osteopenia 733.90

Osteoperiostitis (*see also* Osteomyelitis) 730.2 ☑
  ossificans toxica 731.2
  toxica ossificans 731.2

Osteopetrosis (familial) 756.52

Osteophyte — *see* Exostosis

Osteophytosis — *see* Exostosis

Osteopoikilosis 756.53

Osteoporosis (generalized) 733.00
  circumscripta 731.0
  disuse 733.03
  drug-induced 733.09
  idiopathic 733.02
  postmenopausal 733.01
  posttraumatic 733.7
  screening V82.81
  senile 733.01
  specified type NEC 733.09

Osteoporosis-osteomalacia syndrome 268.2

Osteopsathyrosis 756.51

Osteoradionecrosis, jaw 526.89

Osteosarcoma (M9180/3) — *see also* Neoplasm, bone, malignant
  chondroblastic (M9181/3) — *see* Neoplasm, bone, malignant
  fibroblastic (M9182/3) — *see* Neoplasm, bone, malignant
  in Paget's disease of bone (M9184/3) — *see* Neoplasm, bone, malignant
  juxtacortical (M9190/3) — *see* Neoplasm, bone, malignant
  parosteal (M9190/3) — *see* Neoplasm, bone, malignant
  telangiectatic (M9183/3) — *see* Neoplasm, bone, malignant

Osteosclerosis 756.52
  fragilis (generalisata) 756.52
  myelofibrosis 289.89

Osteosclerotic anemia 289.89

Osteosis
  acromegaloid 757.39
  cutis 709.3
  parathyroid 252.01
  renal fibrocystic 588.0

Österreicher-Turner syndrome 756.89

Ostium
  atrioventriculare commune 745.69
  primum (arteriosum) (defect) (persistent) 745.61
  secundum (arteriosum) (defect) (patent) (persistent) 745.5

Ostrum-Furst syndrome 756.59

Otalgia 388.70
  otogenic 388.71
  referred 388.72

Othematoma 380.31

Otitic hydrocephalus 348.2

Otitis 382.9
  with effusion 381.4
    purulent 382.4
    secretory 381.4
    serous 381.4
    suppurative 382.4
  acute 382.9
  adhesive (*see also* Adhesions, middle ear) 385.10
  chronic 382.9
    with effusion 381.3
    mucoid, mucous (simple) 381.20
    purulent 382.3
    secretory 381.3
    serous 381.10
    suppurative 382.3
  diffuse parasitic 136.8
  externa (acute) (diffuse) (hemorrhagica) 380.10
    actinic 380.22
    candidal 112.82
    chemical 380.22
    chronic 380.23
      mycotic — *see* Otitis, externa, mycotic
      specified type NEC 380.23
    circumscribed 380.10
    contact 380.22
    due to
      erysipelas 035 [380.13]
      impetigo 684 [380.13]
      seborrheic dermatitis 690.10 [380.13]
    eczematoid 380.22
    furuncular 680.0 [380.13]

Otitis — *continued*
  externa — *continued*
    infective 380.10
      chronic 380.16
    malignant 380.14
    mycotic (chronic) 380.15
      due to
        aspergillosis 117.3 [380.15]
        moniliasis 112.82
        otomycosis 111.8 [380.15]
    reactive 380.22
    specified type NEC 380.22
    tropical 111.8 [380.15]
  insidiosa (*see also* Otosclerosis) 387.9
  interna (*see also* Labyrinthitis) 386.30
  media (hemorrhagic) (staphylococcal) (streptococcal) 382.9
    acute 382.9
      with effusion 381.00
      allergic 381.04
        mucoid 381.05
        sanguineous 381.06
        serous 381.04
      catarrhal 381.00
      exudative 381.00
      mucoid 381.02
        allergic 381.05
      necrotizing 382.00
        with spontaneous rupture of ear drum 382.01
        in
          influenza 487.8 [382.02]
          measles 055.2
          scarlet fever 034.1 [382.02]
      nonsuppurative 381.00
      purulent 382.00
        with spontaneous rupture of ear drum 382.01
      sanguineous 381.03
        allergic 381.06
      secretory 381.01
      seromucinous 381.02
      serous 381.01
        allergic 381.04
      suppurative 382.00
        with spontaneous rupture of ear drum 382.01
        due to
          influenza 487.8 [382.02]
          scarlet fever 034.1 [382.02]
      transudative 381.00
    adhesive (*see also* Adhesions, middle ear) 385.10
    allergic 381.4
      acute 381.04
        mucoid 381.05
        sanguineous 381.06
        serous 381.04
      chronic 381.3
    catarrhal 381.4
      acute 381.00
      chronic (simple) 381.10
    chronic 382.9
      with effusion 381.3
      adhesive (*see also* Adhesions, middle ear) 385.10
      allergic 381.3
      atticoantral, suppurative (with posterior or superior marginal perforation of ear drum) 382.2
      benign suppurative (with anterior perforation of ear drum) 382.1
      catarrhal 381.10
      exudative 381.3
      mucinous 381.20
      mucoid, mucous (simple) 381.20
      mucosanguineous 381.29
      nonsuppurative 381.3
      purulent 382.3
      secretory 381.3
      seromucinous 381.3
      serosanguineous 381.19
      serous (simple) 381.10
      suppurative 382.3
        atticoantral (with posterior or superior marginal perforation of ear drum) 382.2

Otitis — continued
  media — continued
    chronic — continued
      suppurative — continued
        benign (with anterior perforation of ear drum) 382.1
        tuberculous (see also Tuberculosis) 017.4 ☑
        tubotympanic 382.1
      transudative 381.3
    exudative 381.4
      acute 381.00
      chronic 381.3
    fibrotic (see also Adhesions, middle ear) 385.10
    mucoid, mucous 381.4
      acute 381.02
      chronic (simple) 381.20
    mucosanguineous, chronic 381.29
    nonsuppurative 381.4
      acute 381.00
      chronic 381.3
    postmeasles 055.2
    purulent 382.4
      acute 382.00
        with spontaneous rupture of ear drum 382.01
      chronic 382.3
    sanguineous, acute 381.03
      allergic 381.06
    secretory 381.4
      acute or subacute 381.01
      chronic 381.3
    seromucinous 381.4
      acute or subacute 381.02
      chronic 381.3
    serosanguineous, chronic 381.19
    serous 381.4
      acute or subacute 381.01
      chronic (simple) 381.10
    subacute — see Otitis, media, acute
    suppurative 382.4
      acute 382.00
        with spontaneous rupture of ear drum 382.01
      chronic 382.3
        atticoantral 382.2
        benign 382.1
        tuberculous (see also Tuberculosis) 017.4 ☑
        tubotympanic 382.1
    transudative 381.4
      acute 381.00
      chronic 381.3
    tuberculous (see also Tuberculosis) 017.4 ☑
  postmeasles 055.2
Otoconia 386.8
Otolith syndrome 386.19
Otomycosis 111.8 *[380.15]*
  in
    aspergillosis 117.3 *[380.15]*
    moniliasis 112.82
Otopathy 388.9
Otoporosis (see also Otosclerosis) 387.9
Otorrhagia 388.69
  traumatic — see nature of injury
Otorrhea 388.60
  blood 388.69
  cerebrospinal (fluid) 388.61
Otosclerosis (general) 387.9
  cochlear (endosteal) 387.2
  involving
    otic capsule 387.2
    oval window
      nonobliterative 387.0
      obliterative 387.1
    round window 387.2
  nonobliterative 387.0
  obliterative 387.1
  specified type NEC 387.8
Otospongiosis (see also Otosclerosis) 387.9
Otto's disease or pelvis 715.35
Outburst, aggressive (see also Disturbance, conduct) 312.0 ☑
  in children or adolescents 313.9

Outcome of delivery
  multiple birth NEC V27.9
    all liveborn V27.5
    all stillborn V27.7
    some liveborn V27.6
    unspecified V27.9
  single V27.9
    liveborn V27.0
    stillborn V27.1
  twins V27.9
    both liveborn V27.2
    both stillborn V27.4
    one liveborn, one stillborn V27.3
Outlet — see also condition
  syndrome (thoracic) 353.0
Outstanding ears (bilateral) 744.29
Ovalocytosis (congenital) (hereditary) (see also Elliptocytosis) 282.1
Ovarian — see also condition
  pregnancy — see Pregnancy, ovarian
  remnant syndrome 620.8
  vein syndrome 593.4
Ovaritis (cystic) (see also Salpingo-oophoritis) 614.2
Ovary, ovarian — see condition
Overactive — see also Hyperfunction
  bladder 596.51
  eye muscle (see also Strabismus) 378.9
  hypothalamus 253.8
  thyroid (see also Thyrotoxicosis) 242.9 ☑
Overactivity, child 314.01
Overbite (deep) (excessive) (horizontal) (vertical) 524.29
Overbreathing (see also Hyperventilation) 786.01
Overconscientious personality 301.4
Overdevelopment — see also Hypertrophy
  breast (female) (male) 611.1
  nasal bones 738.0
  prostate, congenital 752.89
Overdistention — see Distention
Overdose, overdosage (drug) 977.9
  specified drug or substance — see Table of Drugs and Chemicals
Overeating 783.6
  nonorganic origin 307.51
Overexertion (effects) (exhaustion) 994.5
Overexposure (effects) 994.9
  exhaustion 994.4
Overfeeding (see also Overeating) 783.6
Overgrowth, bone NEC 733.99
Overheated (effects) (places) — see Heat
Overinhibited child 313.0
Overjet 524.29
Overlaid, overlying (suffocation) 994.7
Overlap
  excessive horizontal 524.26
Overlapping toe (acquired) 735.8
  congenital (fifth toe) 755.66
Overload
  fluid 276.6
  potassium (K) 276.7
  sodium (Na) 276.0
Overnutrition (see also Hyperalimentation) 783.6
Overproduction — see also Hypersecretion
  ACTH 255.3
  cortisol 255.0
  growth hormone 253.0
  thyroid-stimulating hormone (TSH) 242.8 ☑
Overriding
  aorta 747.21
  finger (acquired) 736.29
    congenital 755.59
  toe (acquired) 735.8
    congenital 755.66
Oversize
  fetus (weight of 4500 grams or more) 766.0
    affecting management of pregnancy 656.6 ☑
    causing disproportion 653.5 ☑
      with obstructed labor 660.1 ☑
        affecting fetus or newborn 763.1

Overstimulation, ovarian 256.1
Overstrained 780.79
  heart — see Hypertrophy, cardiac
Overweight (see also Obesity) 278.02 ▲
Overwork 780.79
Oviduct — see condition
Ovotestis 752.7
Ovulation (cycle)
  failure or lack of 628.0
  pain 625.2
Ovum
  blighted 631
  donor V59.70 ●
    over age 35 V59.73 ●
      anonymous recipient V59.73 ●
      designated recipient V59.74 ●
    under age 35 V59.71 ●
      anonymous recipient V59.71 ●
      designated recipient V59.72 ●
  dropsical 631
  pathologic 631
Owren's disease or syndrome (parahemophilia) (see also Defect, coagulation) 286.3
Oxalosis 271.8
Oxaluria 271.8
Ox heart — see Hypertrophy, cardiac
OX syndrome 758.6
Oxycephaly, oxycephalic 756.0
  syphilitic, congenital 090.0
Oxyuriasis 127.4
Oxyuris vermicularis (infestation) 127.4
Ozena 472.0

P

Pacemaker syndrome 429.4
Pachyderma, pachydermia 701.8
  laryngis 478.5
  laryngitis 478.79
  larynx (verrucosa) 478.79
Pachydermatitis 701.8
Pachydermatocele (congenital) 757.39
  acquired 701.8
Pachydermatosis 701.8
Pachydermoperiostitis
  secondary 731.2
Pachydermoperiostosis
  primary idiopathic 757.39
  secondary 731.2
Pachymeningitis (adhesive) (basal) (brain) (cerebral) (cervical) (chronic) (circumscribed) (external) (fibrous) (hemorrhagic) (hypertrophic) (internal) (purulent) (spinal) (suppurative) (see also Meningitis) 322.9
  gonococcal 098.82
Pachyonychia (congenital) 757.5
  acquired 703.8
Pachyperiosteodermia
  primary or idiopathic 757.39
  secondary 731.2
Pachyperiostosis
  primary or idiopathic 757.39
  secondary 731.2
Pacinian tumor (M9507/0) — see Neoplasm, skin, benign
Pads, knuckle or Garrod's 728.79
Paget's disease (osteitis deformans) 731.0
  with infiltrating duct carcinoma of the breast (M8541/3) — see Neoplasm, breast, malignant
  bone 731.0
    osteosarcoma in (M9184/3) — see Neoplasm, bone, malignant
  breast (M8540/3) 174.0
  extramammary (M8542/3) — see also Neoplasm, skin, malignant
    anus 154.3
    skin 173.5
  malignant (M8540/3)
    breast 174.0

2006 ICD-9-CM

☑ Additional Digit Required — Refer to the Tabular List (Numeric Code Section) for Additional Digit Selection
▶◀ Revised Text   ● New Line   ▲ Revised Code

October 2005 • Volume 2 — 257

Paget's disease

Paget's disease — *continued*
  malignant — *continued*
    specified site NEC (M8542/3) — *see*
      Neoplasm, skin, malignant
    unspecified site 174.0
  mammary (M8540/3) 174.0
  necrosis of bone 731.0
  nipple (M8540/3) 174.0
  osteitis deformans 731.0
Paget-Schroetter syndrome (intermittent venous
    claudication) 453.8
Pain(s)
  abdominal 789.0 ☑
  adnexa (uteri) 625.9
  alimentary, due to vascular insufficiency 557.9
  anginoid (*see also* Pain, precordial) 786.51
  anus 569.42
  arch 729.5
  arm 729.5
  back (postural) 724.5
    low 724.2
    psychogenic 307.89
  bile duct 576.9
  bladder 788.9
  bone 733.90
  breast 611.71
    psychogenic 307.89
  broad ligament 625.9
  cartilage NEC 733.90
  cecum 789.0 ☑
  cervicobrachial 723.3
  chest (central) 786.50
    atypical 786.59
    midsternal 786.51
    musculoskeletal 786.59
    noncardiac 786.59
    substernal 786.51
    wall (anterior) 786.52
  coccyx 724.79
  colon 789.0 ☑
  common duct 576.9
  coronary — *see* Angina
  costochondral 786.52
  diaphragm 786.52
  due to (presence of) any device, implant, or
      graft classifiable to 996.0-996.5 — *see*
      Complications, due to (presence of) any
      device, implant, or graft classified to
      996.0-996.5 NEC
  ear (*see also* Otalgia) 388.70
  epigastric, epigastrium 789.06
  extremity (lower) (upper) 729.5
  eye 379.91
  face, facial 784.0
    atypical 350.2
    nerve 351.8
  false (labor) 644.1 ☑
  female genital organ NEC 625.9
    psychogenic 307.89
  finger 729.5
  flank 789.0 ☑
  foot 729.5
  gallbladder 575.9
  gas (intestinal) 787.3
  gastric 536.8
  generalized 780.99
  genital organ
    female 625.9
    male 608.9
    psychogenic 307.89
  groin 789.0 ☑
  growing 781.99
  hand 729.5
  head (*see also* Headache) 784.0
  heart (see also Pain, precordial) 786.51
  infraorbital (*see also* Neuralgia, trigeminal)
      350.1
  intermenstrual 625.2
  jaw 526.9
  joint 719.40
    ankle 719.47
    elbow 719.42
    foot 719.47
    hand 719.44
    hip 719.45
    knee 719.46

Pain(s) — *continued*
  joint — *continued*
    multiple sites 719.49
    pelvic region 719.45
    psychogenic 307.89
    shoulder (region) 719.41
    specified site NEC 719.48
    wrist 719.43
  kidney 788.0
  labor, false or spurious 644.1 ☑
  laryngeal 784.1
  leg 729.5
  limb 729.5
  low back 724.2
  lumbar region 724.2
  mastoid (*see also* Otalgia) 388.70
  maxilla 526.9
  metacarpophalangeal (joint) 719.44
  metatarsophalangeal (joint) 719.47
  mouth 528.9
  muscle 729.1
    intercostal 786.59
  nasal 478.1
  nasopharynx 478.29
  neck NEC 723.1
    psychogenic 307.89
  nerve NEC 729.2
  neuromuscular 729.1
  nose 478.1
  ocular 379.91
  ophthalmic 379.91
  orbital region 379.91
  osteocopic 733.90
  ovary 625.9
    psychogenic 307.89
  over heart (*see also* Pain, precordial) 786.51
  ovulation 625.2
  pelvic (female) 625.9
    male NEC 789.0 ☑
      psychogenic 307.89
    psychogenic 307.89
  penis 607.9
    psychogenic 307.89
  pericardial (*see also* Pain, precordial) 786.51
  perineum
    female 625.9
    male 608.9
  pharynx 478.29
  pleura, pleural, pleuritic 786.52
  postoperative — *see* Pain, by site
  preauricular 388.70
  precordial (region) 786.51
    psychogenic 307.89
  psychogenic 307.80
    cardiovascular system 307.89
    gastrointestinal system 307.89
    genitourinary system 307.89
    heart 307.89
    musculoskeletal system 307.89
    respiratory system 307.89
    skin 306.3
  radicular (spinal) (*see also* Radiculitis) 729.2
  rectum 569.42
  respiration 786.52
  retrosternal 786.51
  rheumatic NEC 729.0
    muscular 729.1
  rib 786.50
  root (spinal) (*see also* Radiculitis) 729.2
  round ligament (stretch) 625.9
  sacroiliac 724.6
  sciatic 724.3
  scrotum 608.9
    psychogenic 307.89
  seminal vesicle 608.9
  sinus 478.1
  skin 782.0
  spermatic cord 608.9
  spinal root (*see also* Radiculitis) 729.2
  stomach 536.8
    psychogenic 307.89
  substernal 786.51
  temporomandibular (joint) 524.62
  temporomaxillary joint 524.62
  testis 608.9
    psychogenic 307.89

Pain(s) — *continued*
  thoracic spine 724.1
    with radicular and visceral pain 724.4
  throat 784.1
  tibia 733.90
  toe 729.5
  tongue 529.6
  tooth 525.9
  trigeminal (*see also* Neuralgia, trigeminal)
      350.1
  umbilicus 789.05
  ureter 788.0
  urinary (organ) (system) 788.0
  uterus 625.9
    psychogenic 307.89
  vagina 625.9
  vertebrogenic (syndrome) 724.5
  vesical 788.9
  vulva 625.9
  xiphoid 733.90
Painful — *see also* Pain
  arc syndrome 726.19
  coitus
    female 625.0
    male 608.89
    psychogenic 302.76
  ejaculation (semen) 608.89
    psychogenic 302.79
  erection 607.3
  feet syndrome 266.2
  menstruation 625.3
    psychogenic 306.52
  micturition 788.1
  ophthalmoplegia 378.55
  respiration 786.52
  scar NEC 709.2
  urination 788.1
  wire sutures 998.89
Painters' colic 984.9
  specified type of lead — *see* Table of Drugs and
      Chemicals
Palate — *see* condition
Palatoplegia 528.9
Palatoschisis (*see also* Cleft, palate) 749.00
Palilalia 784.69
Palindromic arthritis (*see also* Rheumatism,
    palindromic) 719.3 ☑
Palliative care V66.7
Pallor 782.61
  temporal, optic disc 377.15
Palmar — *see also* condition
  fascia — *see* condition
Palpable
  cecum 569.89
  kidney 593.89
  liver 573.9
  lymph nodes 785.6
  ovary 620.8
  prostate 602.9
  spleen (*see also* Splenomegaly) 789.2
  uterus 625.8
Palpitation (heart) 785.1
  psychogenic 306.2
Palsy (*see also* Paralysis) 344.9
  atrophic diffuse 335.20
  Bell's 351.0
    newborn 767.5
  birth 767.7
  brachial plexus 353.0
    fetus or newborn 767.6
  brain — *see also* Palsy, cerebral
    noncongenital or noninfantile 344.89
      late effect — *see* Late effect(s) (of)
          cerebrovascular disease
    syphilitic 094.89
      congenital 090.49
  bulbar (chronic) (progressive) 335.22
    pseudo NEC 335.23
    supranuclear NEC 344.8 ☑
  cerebral (congenital) (infantile) (spastic) 343.9
    athetoid 333.7

Palsy (see also Paralysis) — continued
  cerebral — continued
    diplegic 343.0
      late effect — see Late effect(s) (of)
        cerebrovascular disease
    hemiplegic 343.1
    monoplegic 343.3
    noncongenital or noninfantile 437.8
      late effect — see Late effect(s) (of)
        cerebrovascular disease
    paraplegic 343.0
    quadriplegic 343.2
    spastic, not congenital or infantile 344.89
    syphilitic 094.89
      congenital 090.49
    tetraplegic 343.2
  cranial nerve — see also Disorder, nerve,
    cranial
    multiple 352.6
  creeping 335.21
  divers' 993.3
  Erb's (birth injury) 767.6
  facial 351.0
    newborn 767.5
  glossopharyngeal 352.2
  Klumpke (-Déjérine) 767.6
  lead 984.9
    specified type of lead — see Table of Drugs
      and Chemicals
  median nerve (tardy) 354.0
  peroneal nerve (acute) (tardy) 355.3
  progressive supranuclear 333.0
  pseudobulbar NEC 335.23
  radial nerve (acute) 354.3
  seventh nerve 351.0
    newborn 767.5
  shaking (see also Parkinsonism) 332.0
  spastic (cerebral) (spinal) 343.9
    hemiplegic 343.1
  specified nerve NEC — see Disorder, nerve
  supranuclear NEC 356.8
    progressive 333.0
  ulnar nerve (tardy) 354.2
  wasting 335.21
Paltauf-Sternberg disease 201.9 ☑
Paludism — see Malaria
Panama fever 084.0
Panaris (with lymphangitis) 681.9
  finger 681.02
  toe 681.11
Panaritium (with lymphangitis) 681.9
  finger 681.02
  toe 681.11
Panarteritis (nodosa) 446.0
  brain or cerebral 437.4
Pancake heart 793.2
  with cor pulmonale (chronic) 416.9
Pancarditis (acute) (chronic) 429.89
  with
    rheumatic
      fever (active) (acute) (chronic) (subacute)
        391.8
        inactive or quiescent 398.99
  rheumatic, acute 391.8
  chronic or inactive 398.99
Pancoast's syndrome or tumor (carcinoma,
  pulmonary apex) (M8010/3) 162.3
Pancoast-Tobias syndrome (M8010/3)
  (carcinoma, pulmonary apex) 162.3
Pancolitis 556.6
Pancreas, pancreatic — see condition
Pancreatitis 577.0
  acute (edematous) (hemorrhagic) (recurrent)
    577.0
  annular 577.0
  apoplectic 577.0
  calcereous 577.0
  chronic (infectious) 577.1
    recurrent 577.1
  cystic 577.2

Pancreatitis — continued
  fibrous 577.8
  gangrenous 577.0
  hemorrhagic (acute) 577.0
  interstitial (chronic) 577.1
    acute 577.0
  malignant 577.0
  mumps 072.3
  painless 577.1
  recurrent 577.1
  relapsing 577.1
  subacute 577.0
  suppurative 577.0
  syphilitic 095.8
Pancreatolithiasis 577.8
Pancytolysis 289.9
Pancytopenia (acquired) 284.8
  with malformations 284.0
  congenital 284.0
Panencephalitis — see also Encephalitis
  subacute, sclerosing 046.2
Panhematopenia 284.8
  congenital 284.0
  constitutional 284.0
  splenic, primary 289.4
Panhemocytopenia 284.8
  congenital 284.0
  constitutional 284.0
Panhypogonadism 257.2
Panhypopituitarism 253.2
  prepubertal 253.3
Panic (attack) (state) 300.01
  reaction to exceptional stress (transient) 308.0
Panmyelopathy, familial constitutional 284.0
Panmyelophthisis 284.9
  acquired (secondary) 284.8
  congenital 284.0
  idiopathic 284.9
Panmyelosis (acute) (M9951/1) 238.7
Panner's disease 732.3
  capitellum humeri 732.3
  head of humerus 732.3
  tarsal navicular (bone) (osteochondrosis) 732.5
Panneuritis endemica 265.0 [357.4]
Panniculitis 729.30
  back 724.8
  knee 729.31
  mesenteric 567.82   ●
  neck 723.6
  nodular, nonsuppurative 729.30
  sacral 724.8
  specified site NEC 729.39
Panniculus adiposus (abdominal) 278.1
Pannus 370.62
  allergic eczematous 370.62
  degenerativus 370.62
  keratic 370.62
  rheumatoid — see Arthritis, rheumatoid
  trachomatosus, trachomatous (active) 076.1
    [370.62]
    late effect 139.1
Panophthalmitis 360.02
Panotitis — see Otitis media
Pansinusitis (chronic) (hyperplastic) (nonpurulent)
  (purulent) 473.8
  acute 461.8
  due to fungus NEC 117.9
  tuberculous (see also Tuberculosis) 012.8 ☑
Panuveitis 360.12
  sympathetic 360.11
Panvalvular disease — see Endocarditis, mitral
Papageienkrankheit 073.9
Papanicolaou smear
  cervix (screening test) V76.2
    as part of gynecological examination V72.31
    for suspected malignant neoplasm V76.2
      no disease found V71.1
    inadequate sample 795.08

Papanicolaou smear — continued
  cervix — continued
    nonspecific abnormal finding 795.00
      with
        atypical squamous cells changes
          cannot exclude high grade
            squamous intraepithelial
            lesion (ASC-H) 795.02
          of undetermined significance (ASC-
            US) 795.01
        high grade squamous intraepithelial
          lesion (HGSIL) 795.04
        low grade squamous intraepithelial
          lesion (LGSIL) 795.03
    nonspecific finding NEC 795.09
    to confirm findings of recent normal
      smear following initial abnormal
      smear V72.32
    unsatisfactory 795.08
  other specified site — see also Screening,
    malignant neoplasm
    for suspected malignant neoplasm — see
      also Screening, malignant neoplasm
      no disease found V71.1
    nonspecific abnormal finding 795.1
  vagina V76.47
    following hysterectomy for malignant
      condition V67.01
Papilledema 377.00
  associated with
    decreased ocular pressure 377.02
    increased intracranial pressure 377.01
    retinal disorder 377.03
  choked disc 377.00
  infectional 377.00
Papillitis 377.31
  anus 569.49
  chronic lingual 529.4
  necrotizing, kidney 584.7
  optic 377.31
  rectum 569.49
  renal, necrotizing 584.7
  tongue 529.0
Papilloma (M8050/0) — see also Neoplasm, by
  site, benign

> Note — Except where otherwise indicated, the
> morphological varieties of papilloma in the list
> below should be coded by site as for "Neoplasm,
> benign."

  acuminatum (female) (male) 078.11
  bladder (urinary) (transitional cell) (M8120/1)
    236.7
    benign (M8120/0) 223.3
  choroid plexus (M9390/0) 225.0
    anaplastic type (M9390/3) 191.5
    malignant (M9390/3) 191.5
  ductal (M8503/0)
  dyskeratotic (M8052/0)
  epidermoid (M8052/0)
  hyperkeratotic (M8052/0)
  intracystic (M8504/0)
  intraductal (M8503/0)
  inverted (M8053/0)
  keratotic (M8052/0)
  parakeratotic (M8052/0)
  pinta (primary) 103.0
  renal pelvis (transitional cell) (M8120/1) 236.99
    benign (M8120/0) 223.1
  Schneiderian (M8121/0)
    specified site — see Neoplasm, by site,
      benign
    unspecified site 212.0
  serous surface (M8461/0)
    borderline malignancy (M8461/1)
      specified site — see Neoplasm, by site,
        uncertain behavior
      unspecified site 236.2
    specified site — see Neoplasm, by site,
      benign
    unspecified site 220
  squamous (cell) (M8052/0)
  transitional (cell) (M8120/0)
    bladder (urinary) (M8120/1) 236.7

Papilloma — *see also* Neoplasm, by site, benign
— *continued*
  transitional — *continued*
    inverted type (M8121/1) — *see* Neoplasm,
      by site, uncertain behavior
    renal pelvis (M8120/1) 236.91
    ureter (M8120/1) 236.91
    ureter (transitional cell) (M8120/1) 236.91
      benign (M8120/0) 223.2
    urothelial (M8120/1) — *see* Neoplasm, by site,
      uncertain behavior
    verrucous (M8051/0)
    villous (M8261/1) — *see* Neoplasm, by site,
      uncertain behavior
    yaws, plantar or palmar 102.1
Papillomata, multiple, of yaws 102.1
Papillomatosis (M8060/0) — *see also* Neoplasm,
  by site, benign
  confluent and reticulate 701.8
  cutaneous 701.8
  ductal, breast 610.1
  Gougerot-Carteaud (confluent reticulate) 701.8
  intraductal (diffuse) (M8505/0) —
    Neoplasm, by site, benign
  subareolar duct (M8506/0) 217
Papillon-Léage and Psaume syndrome
  (orodigitofacial dysostosis) 759.89
Papule 709.8
  carate (primary) 103.0
  fibrous, of nose (M8724/0) 216.3
  pinta (primary) 103.0
Papulosis, malignant 447.8
Papyraceous fetus 779.89
  complicating pregnancy 646.0 ☑
Paracephalus 759.7
Parachute mitral valve 746.5
Paracoccidioidomycosis 116.1
  mucocutaneous-lymphangitic 116.1
  pulmonary 116.1
  visceral 116.1
Paracoccidioidomycosis — *see*
  Paracoccidioidomycosis
Paracusis 388.40
Paradentosis 523.5
Paradoxical facial movements 374.43
Paraffinoma 999.9
Paraganglioma (M8680/1)
  adrenal (M8700/0) 227.0
    malignant (M8700/3) 194.0
  aortic body (M8691/1) 237.3
    malignant (M8691/3) 194.6
  carotid body (M8692/1) 237.3
    malignant (M8692/3) 194.5
  chromaffin (M8700/0) — *see also* Neoplasm, by
    site, benign
    malignant (M8700/3) — *see* Neoplasm, by
      site, malignant
  extra-adrenal (M8693/1)
    malignant (M8693/3)
      specified site — *see* Neoplasm, by site,
        malignant
      unspecified site 194.6
    specified site — *see* Neoplasm, by site,
      uncertain behavior
    unspecified site 237.3
  glomus jugulare (M8690/1) 237.3
    malignant (M8690/3) 194.6
  jugular (M8690/1) 237.3
    malignant (M8680/3)
      specified site — *see* Neoplasm, by site,
        malignant
      unspecified site 194.6
  nonchromaffin (M8693/1)
    malignant (M8693/3)
      specified site — *see* Neoplasm, by site,
        malignant
      unspecified site 194.6
    specified site — *see* Neoplasm, by site,
      uncertain behavior
    unspecified site 237.3
  parasympathetic (M8682/1)
    specified site — *see* Neoplasm, by site,
      uncertain behavior
    unspecified site 237.3

Paraganglioma — *continued*
  specified site — *see* Neoplasm, by site,
    uncertain behavior
  sympathetic (M8681/1)
    specified site — *see* Neoplasm, by site,
      uncertain behavior
    unspecified site 237.3
  unspecified site 237.3
Parageusia 781.1
  psychogenic 306.7
Paragonimiasis 121.2
Paragranuloma, Hodgkin's (M9660/3) 201.0 ☑
Parahemophilia (*see also* Defect, coagulation)
  286.3
Parakeratosis 690.8
  psoriasiformis 696.2
  variegata 696.2
Paralysis, paralytic (complete) (incomplete) 344.9
  with
    broken
      back — *see* Fracture, vertebra, by site,
        with spinal cord injury
      neck — *see* Fracture, vertebra, cervical,
        with spinal cord injury
    fracture, vertebra — *see* Fracture, vertebra,
      by site, with spinal cord injury
    syphilis 094.89
  abdomen and back muscles 355.9
  abdominal muscles 355.9
  abducens (nerve) 378.54
  abductor 355.9
    lower extremity 355.8
    upper extremity 354.9
  accessory nerve 352.4
  accommodation 367.51
    hysterical 300.11
  acoustic nerve 388.5
  agitans 332.0
    arteriosclerotic 332.0
  alternating 344.89
    oculomotor 344.89
  amyotrophic 335.20
  ankle 355.8
  anterior serratus 355.9
  anus (sphincter) 569.49
  apoplectic (current episode) (*see also* Disease,
    cerebrovascular, acute) 436
    late effect — *see* Late effect(s) (of)
      cerebrovascular disease
  arm 344.40
    affecting
      dominant side 344.41
      nondominant side 344.42
    both 344.2
    hysterical 300.11
    late effect — *see* Late effect(s) (of)
      cerebrovascular disease
    psychogenic 306.0
    transient 781.4
    traumatic NEC (*see also* Injury, nerve,
      upper limb) 955.9
  arteriosclerotic (current episode) 437.0
    late effect — *see* Late effect(s) (of)
      cerebrovascular disease
  ascending (spinal), acute 357.0
  associated, nuclear 344.89
  asthenic bulbar 358.00
  ataxic NEC 334.9
    general 094.1
  athetoid 333.7
  atrophic 356.9
    infantile, acute (*see also* Poliomyelitis, with
      paralysis) 045.1 ☑
    muscle NEC 355.9
    progressive 335.21
    spinal (acute) (*see also* Poliomyelitis, with
      paralysis) 045.1 ☑
  attack (*see also* Disease, cerebrovascular,
    acute) 436
  axillary 353.0
  Babinski-Nageotte's 344.89
  Bell's 351.0
    newborn 767.5
  Benedikt's 344.89

Paralysis, paralytic — *continued*
  birth (injury) 767.7
    brain 767.0
    intracranial 767.0
    spinal cord 767.4
  bladder (sphincter) 596.53
    neurogenic 596.54
      with cauda equina syndrome 344.61
    puerperal, postpartum, childbirth 665.5 ☑
    sensory 596.54
      with cauda equina 344.61
    spastic 596.54
      with cauda equina 344.61
  bowel, colon, or intestine (*see also* Ileus) 560.1
  brachial plexus 353.0
    due to birth injury 767.6
    newborn 767.6
  brain
    congenital — *see* Palsy, cerebral
    current episode 437.8
    diplegia 344.2
    hemiplegia 342.9 ☑
      late effect — *see* Late effect(s) (of)
        cerebrovascular disease
    infantile — *see* Palsy, cerebral
    late effect — *see* Late effect(s) (of)
      cerebrovascular disease
    monoplegia — *see also* Monoplegia
      late effect — *see* Late effect(s) (of)
        cerebrovascular disease
    paraplegia 344.1
    quadriplegia — *see* Quadriplegia
    syphilitic, congenital 090.49
    triplegia 344.89
  bronchi 519.1
  Brown-Séquard's 344.89
  bulbar (chronic) (progressive) 335.22
    infantile (*see also* Poliomyelitis, bulbar)
      045.0 ☑
    poliomyelitic (*see also* Poliomyelitis, bulbar)
      045.0 ☑
    pseudo 335.23
    supranuclear 344.89
  bulbospinal 358.00
  cardiac (*see also* Failure, heart) 428.9
  cerebral
    current episode 437.8
    spastic, infantile — *see* Palsy, cerebral
  cerebrocerebellar 437.8
    diplegic infantile 343.0
  cervical
    plexus 353.2
    sympathetic NEC 337.0
  Céstan-Chenais 344.89
  Charcôt-Marie-Tooth type 356.1
  childhood — *see* Palsy, cerebral
  Clark's 343.9
  colon (*see also* Ileus) 560.1
  compressed air 993.3
  compression
    arm NEC 354.9
    cerebral — *see* Paralysis, brain
    leg NEC 355.8
    lower extremity NEC 355.8
    upper extremity NEC 354.9
  congenital (cerebral) (spastic) (spinal) — *see*
    Palsy, cerebral
  conjugate movement (of eye) 378.81
    cortical (nuclear) (supranuclear) 378.81
  convergence 378.83
  cordis (*see also* Failure, heart) 428.9
  cortical (*see also* Paralysis, brain) 437.8
  cranial or cerebral nerve (*see also* Disorder,
    nerve, cranial) 352.9
  creeping 335.21
  crossed leg 344.89
  crutch 953.4
  deglutition 784.9
    hysterical 300.11
  dementia 094.1
  descending (spinal) NEC 335.9

Paralysis, paralytic — continued
  diaphragm (flaccid) 519.4
    due to accidental section of phrenic nerve
      during procedure 998.2
  digestive organs NEC 564.89
  diplegic — see Diplegia
  divergence (nuclear) 378.85
  divers' 993.3
  Duchenne's 335.22
  due to intracranial or spinal birth injury — see
    Palsy, cerebral
  embolic (current episode) (see also Embolism,
    brain) 434.1 ☑
    late effect — see Late effect(s) (of)
      cerebrovascular disease
  enteric (see also Ileus) 560.1
    with hernia — see Hernia, by site, with
      obstruction
  Erb's syphilitic spastic spinal 094.89
  Erb (-Duchenne) (birth) (newborn) 767.6
  esophagus 530.89
  essential, infancy (see also Poliomyelitis)
    045.9 ☑
  extremity
    lower — see Paralysis, leg
    spastic (hereditary) 343.3
      noncongenital or noninfantile 344.1
    transient (cause unknown) 781.4
    upper — see Paralysis, arm
  eye muscle (extrinsic) 378.55
    intrinsic 367.51
  facial (nerve) 351.0
    birth injury 767.5
    congenital 767.5
    following operation NEC 998.2
    newborn 767.5
  familial 359.3
    periodic 359.3
    spastic 334.1
  fauces 478.29
  finger NEC 354.9
  foot NEC 355.8
  gait 781.2
  gastric nerve 352.3
  gaze 378.81
  general 094.1
    ataxic 094.1
    insane 094.1
    juvenile 090.40
    progressive 094.1
    tabetic 094.1
  glossopharyngeal (nerve) 352.2
  glottis (see also Paralysis, vocal cord) 478.30
  gluteal 353.4
  Gubler (-Millard) 344.89
  hand 354.9
    hysterical 300.11
    psychogenic 306.0
  heart (see also Failure, heart) 428.9
  hemifacial, progressive 349.89
  hemiplegic — see Hemiplegia
  hyperkalemic periodic (familial) 359.3
  hypertensive (current episode) 437.8
  hypoglossal (nerve) 352.5
  hypokalemic periodic 359.3
  Hyrtl's sphincter (rectum) 569.49
  hysterical 300.11
  ileus (see also Ileus) 560.1
  infantile (see also Poliomyelitis) 045.9 ☑
    atrophic acute 045.1 ☑
    bulbar 045.0 ☑
    cerebral — see Palsy, cerebral
    paralytic 045.1 ☑
    progressive acute 045.9 ☑
    spastic — see Palsy, cerebral
    spinal 045.9 ☑
  infective (see also Poliomyelitis) 045.9 ☑
  inferior nuclear 344.9
  insane, general or progressive 094.1
  internuclear 378.86
  interosseous 355.9
  intestine (see also Ileus) 560.1
  intracranial (current episode) (see also
    Paralysis, brain) 437.8
    due to birth injury 767.0
  iris 379.49
    due to diphtheria (toxin) 032.81 [379.49]

Paralysis, paralytic — continued
  ischemic, Volkmann's (complicating trauma)
    958.6
  isolated sleep, recurrent 327.43 ●
  Jackson's 344.89
  jake 357.7
  Jamaica ginger (jake) 357.7
  juvenile general 090.40
  Klumpke (-Déjérine) (birth) (newborn) 767.6
  labioglossal (laryngeal) (pharyngeal) 335.22
  Landry's 357.0
  laryngeal nerve (recurrent) (superior) (see also
    Paralysis, vocal cord) 478.30
  larynx (see also Paralysis, vocal cord) 478.30
    due to diphtheria (toxin) 032.3
  late effect
    due to
      birth injury, brain or spinal (cord) — see
        Palsy, cerebral
      edema, brain or cerebral — see Paralysis,
        brain
      lesion
        late effect — see Late effect(s) (of)
          cerebrovascular disease
        spinal (cord) — see Paralysis, spinal
  lateral 335.24
  lead 984.9
    specified type of lead — see Table of Drugs
      and Chemicals
  left side — see Hemiplegia
  leg 344.30
    affecting
      dominant side 344.31
      nondominant side 344.32
    both (see also Paraplegia) 344.1
    crossed 344.89
    hysterical 300.11
    psychogenic 306.0
    transient or transitory 781.4
      traumatic NEC (see also Injury, nerve,
        lower limb) 956.9
  levator palpebrae superioris 374.31
  limb NEC 344.5
    all four — see Quadriplegia
    quadriplegia — see Quadriplegia
  lip 528.5
  Lissauer's 094.1
  local 355.9
  lower limb — see also Paralysis, leg
    both (see also Paraplegia) 344.1
  lung 518.89
    newborn 770.89
  median nerve 354.1
  medullary (tegmental) 344.89
  mesencephalic NEC 344.89
    tegmental 344.89
  middle alternating 344.89
  Millard-Gubler-Foville 344.89
  monoplegic — see Monoplegia
  motor NEC 344.9
    cerebral — see Paralysis, brain
    spinal — see Paralysis, spinal
  multiple
    cerebral — see Paralysis, brain
    spinal — see Paralysis, spinal
  muscle (flaccid) 359.9
    due to nerve lesion NEC 355.9
    eye (extrinsic) 378.55
      intrinsic 367.51
      oblique 378.51
    iris sphincter 364.8
    ischemic (complicating trauma) (Volkmann's)
      958.6
    pseudohypertrophic 359.1
  muscular (atrophic) 359.9
    progressive 335.21
  musculocutaneous nerve 354.9
  musculospiral 354.9
  nerve — see also Disorder, nerve
    third or oculomotor (partial) 378.51
      total 378.52
    fourth or trochlear 378.53
    sixth or abducens 378.54
    seventh or facial 351.0
      birth injury 767.5

Paralysis, paralytic — continued
  nerve — see also Disorder, nerve — continued
    seventh or facial — continued
      due to
        injection NEC 999.9
        operation NEC 997.09
      newborn 767.5
    accessory 352.4
    auditory 388.5
    birth injury 767.7
    cranial or cerebral (see also Disorder, nerve,
      cranial) 352.9
    facial 351.0
      birth injury 767.5
      newborn 767.5
    laryngeal (see also Paralysis, vocal cord)
      478.30
    newborn 767.7
    phrenic 354.8
      newborn 767.7
    radial 354.3
      birth injury 767.6
      newborn 767.6
    syphilitic 094.89
    traumatic NEC (see also Injury, nerve, by
      site) 957.9
    trigeminal 350.9
    ulnar 354.2
  newborn NEC 767.0
  normokalemic periodic 359.3
  obstetrical, newborn 767.7
  ocular 378.9
  oculofacial, congenital 352.6
  oculomotor (nerve) (partial) 378.51
    alternating 344.89
    external bilateral 378.55
    total 378.52
  olfactory nerve 352.0
  palate 528.9
  palatopharyngolaryngeal 352.6
  paratrigeminal 350.9
  periodic (familial) (hyperkalemic) (hypokalemic)
    (normokalemic) (secondary) 359.3
  peripheral
    autonomic nervous system — see
      Neuropathy, peripheral, autonomic
    nerve NEC 355.9
  peroneal (nerve) 355.3
  pharynx 478.29
  phrenic nerve 354.8
  plantar nerves 355.6
  pneumogastric nerve 352.3
  poliomyelitis (current) (see also Poliomyelitis,
    with paralysis) 045.1 ☑
    bulbar 045.0 ☑
  popliteal nerve 355.3
  pressure (see also Neuropathy, entrapment)
    355.9
  progressive 335.21
    atrophic 335.21
    bulbar 335.22
    general 094.1
    hemifacial 349.89
    infantile, acute (see also Poliomyelitis)
      045.9 ☑
    multiple 335.20
  pseudobulbar 335.23
  pseudohypertrophic 359.1
    muscle 359.1
  psychogenic 306.0
  pupil, pupillary 379.49
  quadriceps 355.8
  quadriplegic (see also Quadriplegia) 344.0 ☑
  radial nerve 354.3
    birth injury 767.6
  rectum (sphincter) 569.49
  rectus muscle (eye) 378.55
  recurrent
    isolated sleep 327.43 ●
    laryngeal nerve (see also Paralysis, vocal ●
      cord) 478.30 ●
  respiratory (muscle) (system) (tract) 786.09
    center NEC 344.89
      fetus or newborn 770.89
    congenital 768.9
    newborn 768.9
  right side — see Hemiplegia

2006 ICD-9-CM

☑ Additional Digit Required — Refer to the Tabular List (Numeric Code Section) for Additional Digit Selection
▶◀ Revised Text   ● New Line   ▲ Revised Code

October 2005 • Volume 2 — 261

Paralysis, paralytic — *continued*
Saturday night 354.3
saturnine 984.9
specified type of lead — *see* Table of Drugs
and Chemicals
sciatic nerve 355.0
secondary — *see* Paralysis, late effect
seizure (cerebral) (current episode) (*see also*
Disease, cerebrovascular, acute) 436
late effect — *see* Late effect(s) (of)
cerebrovascular disease
senile NEC 344.9
serratus magnus 355.9
shaking (*see also* Parkinsonism) 332.0
shock (*see also* Disease, cerebrovascular, acute)
436
late effect — *see* Late effect(s) (of)
cerebrovascular disease
shoulder 354.9
soft palate 528.9
spasmodic — *see* Paralysis, spastic
spastic 344.9
cerebral infantile — *see* Palsy, cerebral
congenital (cerebral) — *see* Palsy, cerebral
familial 334.1
hereditary 334.1
infantile 343.9
noncongenital or noninfantile, cerebral
344.9
syphilitic 094.0
spinal 094.89
sphincter, bladder (*see also* Paralysis, bladder)
596.53
spinal (cord) NEC 344.1
accessory nerve 352.4
acute (*see also* Poliomyelitis) 045.9 ☑
ascending acute 357.0
atrophic (acute) (*see also* Poliomyelitis, with
paralysis) 045.1 ☑
spastic, syphilitic 094.89
congenital NEC 343.9
hemiplegic — *see* Hemiplegia
hereditary 336.8
infantile (*see also* Poliomyelitis) 045.9 ☑
late effect NEC 344.89
monoplegic — *see* Monoplegia
nerve 355.9
progressive 335.10
quadriplegic — *see* Quadriplegia
spastic NEC 343.9
traumatic — *see* Injury, spinal, by site
sternomastoid 352.4
stomach 536.3
diabetic 250.6 ☑ *[536.3]*
nerve ▶(nondiabetic)◀ 352.3
stroke (current episode) — *see* Infarct, brain
late effect — *see* Late effect(s) (of)
cerebrovascular disease
subscapularis 354.8
superior nuclear NEC 334.9
supranuclear 356.8
sympathetic
cervical NEC 337.0
nerve NEC (*see also* Neuropathy, peripheral,
autonomic) 337.9
nervous system — *see* Neuropathy,
peripheral, autonomic
syndrome 344.9
specified NEC 344.89
syphilitic spastic spinal (Erb's) 094.89
tabetic general 094.1
thigh 355.8
throat 478.29
diphtheritic 032.0
muscle 478.29
thrombotic (current episode) (*see also*
Thrombosis, brain) 434.0 ☑
late effect — *see* Late effect(s) (of)
cerebrovascular disease
thumb NEC 354.9
tick (-bite) 989.5
Todd's (postepileptic transitory paralysis) 344.89
toe 355.6
tongue 529.8
transient
arm or leg NEC 781.4

Paralysis, paralytic — *continued*
transient — *continued*
traumatic NEC (*see also* Injury, nerve, by
site) 957.9
trapezius 352.4
traumatic, transient NEC (*see also* Injury,
nerve, by site) 957.9
trembling (*see also* Parkinsonism) 332.0
triceps brachii 354.9
trigeminal nerve 350.9
trochlear nerve 378.53
ulnar nerve 354.2
upper limb — *see also* Paralysis, arm
both (*see also* Diplegia) 344.2
uremic — *see* Uremia
uveoparotitic 135
uvula 528.9
hysterical 300.11
postdiphtheritic 032.0
vagus nerve 352.3
vasomotor NEC 337.9
velum palati 528.9
vesical (*see also* Paralysis, bladder) 596.53
vestibular nerve 388.5
visual field, psychic 368.16
vocal cord 478.30
bilateral (partial) 478.33
complete 478.34
complete (bilateral) 478.34
unilateral (partial) 478.31
complete 478.32
Volkmann's (complicating trauma) 958.6
wasting 335.21
Weber's 344.89
wrist NEC 354.9

Paramedial orifice, urethrovesical 753.8

Paramenia 626.9

Parametritis (chronic) (*see also* Disease, pelvis,
inflammatory) 614.4
acute 614.3
puerperal, postpartum, childbirth 670.0 ☑

Parametrium, parametric — *see* condition

Paramnesia (*see also* Amnesia) 780.93

Paramolar 520.1
causing crowding 524.31

Paramyloidosis 277.3

Paramyoclonus multiplex 333.2

Paramyotonia 359.2
congenita 359.2

Paraneoplastic syndrome — *see* condition

Parangi (*see also* Yaws) 102.9

Paranoia 297.1
alcoholic 291.5
querulans 297.8
senile 290.20

Paranoid
dementia (*see also* Schizophrenia) 295.3 ☑
praecox (acute) 295.3 ☑
senile 290.20
personality 301.0
psychosis 297.9
alcoholic 291.5
climacteric 297.2
drug-induced 292.11
involutional 297.2
menopausal 297.2
protracted reactive 298.4
psychogenic 298.4
acute 298.3
senile 290.20
reaction (chronic) 297.9
acute 298.3
schizophrenia (acute) (*see also* Schizophrenia)
295.3 ☑
state 297.9
alcohol-induced 291.5
climacteric 297.2
drug-induced 292.11
due to or associated with
arteriosclerosis (cerebrovascular) 290.42
presenile brain disease 290.12
senile brain disease 290.20
involutional 297.2
menopausal 297.2

Paranoid — *continued*
state — *continued*
senile 290.20
simple 297.0
specified type NEC 297.8
tendencies 301.0
traits 301.0
trends 301.0
type, psychopathic personality 301.0

Paraparesis (*see also* Paralysis) 344.9

Paraphasia 784.3

Paraphilia (*see also* Deviation, sexual) 302.9

Paraphimosis (congenital) 605
chancroidal 099.0

Paraphrenia, paraphrenic (late) 297.2
climacteric 297.2
dementia (*see also* Schizophrenia) 295.3 ☑
involutional 297.2
menopausal 297.2
schizophrenia (acute) (*see also* Schizophrenia)
295.3 ☑

Paraplegia 344.1
with
broken back — *see* Fracture, vertebra, by
site, with spinal cord injury
fracture, vertebra — *see* Fracture, vertebra,
by site, with spinal cord injury
ataxic — *see* Degeneration, combined, spinal
cord
brain (current episode) (*see also* Paralysis,
brain) 437.8
cerebral (current episode) (*see also* Paralysis,
brain) 437.8
congenital or infantile (cerebral) (spastic)
(spinal) 343.0
cortical — *see* Paralysis, brain
familial spastic 334.1
functional (hysterical) 300.11
hysterical 300.11
infantile 343.0
late effect 344.1
Pott's (*see also* Tuberculosis) 015.0 ☑ *[730.88]*
psychogenic 306.0
spastic
Erb's spinal 094.89
hereditary 334.1
not infantile or congenital 344.1
spinal (cord)
traumatic NEC — *see* Injury, spinal, by site
syphilitic (spastic) 094.89
traumatic NEC — *see* Injury, spinal, by site

Paraproteinemia 273.2
benign (familial) 273.1
monoclonal 273.1
secondary to malignant or inflammatory
disease 273.1

Parapsoriasis 696.2
en plaques 696.2
guttata 696.2
lichenoides chronica 696.2
retiformis 696.2
varioliformis (acuta) 696.2

Parascarlatina 057.8

Parasitic — *see also* condition
disease NEC (*see also* Infestation, parasitic)
136.9
contact V01.89
exposure to V01.89
intestinal NEC 129
skin NEC 134.9
stomatitis 112.0
sycosis 110.0
beard 110.0
scalp 110.0
twin 759.4

Parasitism NEC 136.9
intestinal NEC 129
skin NEC 134.9
specified — *see* Infestation

Parasitophobia 300.29

Parasomnia 307.47
alcohol induced 291.82
drug induced 292.85

▲
●
●

Parasomnia — *continued*
  nonorganic origin 307.47
  organic 327.40
    in conditions classified elsewhere 327.44 ●
    other 327.49 ●
Paraspadias 752.69
Paraspasm facialis 351.8
Parathyroid gland — *see* condition
Parathyroiditis (autoimmune) 252.1
Parathyroprival tetany 252.1
Paratrachoma 077.0
Paratyphilitis (*see also* Appendicitis) 541
Paratyphoid (fever) — *see* Fever, paratyphoid
Paratyphus — *see* Fever, paratyphoid
Paraurethral duct 753.8
Para-urethritis 597.89
  gonococcal (acute) 098.0
    chronic or duration of 2 months or over
    098.2
Paravaccinia NEC 051.9
  milkers' node 051.1
Paravaginitis (*see also* Vaginitis) 616.10
Parencephalitis (*see also* Encephalitis) 323.9
  late effect — *see* category 326
Parergasia 298.9
Paresis (*see also* Paralysis) 344.9
  accommodation 367.51
  bladder (spastic) (sphincter) (*see also* Paralysis,
    bladder) 596.53
    tabetic 094.0
  bowel, colon, or intestine (*see also* Ileus) 560.1
  brain or cerebral — *see* Paralysis, brain
  extrinsic muscle, eye 378.55
  general 094.1
    arrested 094.1
    brain 094.1
    cerebral 094.1
    insane 094.1
    juvenile 090.40
      remission 090.49
    progressive 094.1
    remission (sustained) 094.1
    tabetic 094.1
  heart (*see also* Failure, heart) 428.9
  infantile (*see also* Poliomyelitis) 045.9 ☑
  insane 094.1
  juvenile 090.40
  late effect — *see* Paralysis, late effect
  luetic (general) 094.1
  peripheral progressive 356.9
  pseudohypertrophic 359.1
  senile NEC 344.9
  stomach 536.3
    diabetic 250.6 ☑ *[536.3]*
  syphilitic (general) 094.1
    congenital 090.40
  transient, limb 781.4
  vesical (sphincter) NEC 596.53
Paresthesia (*see also* Disturbance, sensation)
  782.0
  Berger's (paresthesia of lower limb) 782.0
  Bernhardt 355.1
  Magnan's 782.0
Paretic — *see* condition
Parinaud's
  conjunctivitis 372.02
  oculoglandular syndrome 372.02
  ophthalmoplegia 378.81
  syndrome (paralysis of conjugate upward gaze)
    378.81
Parkes Weber and Dimitri syndrome
  (encephalocutaneous angiomatosis) 759.6
Parkinson's disease, syndrome, or tremor —
  see Parkinsonism
Parkinsonism (arteriosclerotic) (idiopathic)
  (primary) 332.0
  associated with orthostatic hypotension
    (idiopathic) (symptomatic) 333.0
  due to drugs 332.1
  neuroleptic-induced 332.1 ●
  secondary 332.1
  syphilitic 094.82
Parodontitis 523.4

Parodontosis 523.5
Paronychia (with lymphangitis) 681.9
  candidal (chronic) 112.3
  chronic 681.9
    candidal 112.3
    finger 681.02
    toe 681.11
  finger 681.02
  toe 681.11
  tuberculous (primary) (*see also* Tuberculosis)
    017.0 ☑
Parorexia NEC 307.52
  hysterical 300.11
Parosmia 781.1
  psychogenic 306.7
Parotid gland — *see* condition
Parotiditis (*see also* Parotitis) 527.2
  epidemic 072.9
  infectious 072.9
Parotitis 527.2
  allergic 527.2
  chronic 527.2
  epidemic (*see also* Mumps) 072.9
  infectious (*see also* Mumps) 072.9
  noninfectious 527.2
  nonspecific toxic 527.2
  not mumps 527.2
  postoperative 527.2
  purulent 527.2
  septic 527.2
  suppurative (acute) 527.2
  surgical 527.2
  toxic 527.2
Paroxysmal — *see also* condition
  dyspnea (nocturnal) 786.09
Parrot's disease (syphilitic osteochondritis) 090.0
Parrot fever 073.9
Parry's disease or syndrome (exophthalmic
  goiter) 242.0 ☑
Parry-Romberg syndrome 349.89
Parson's disease (exophthalmic goiter) 242.0 ☑
Parsonage-Aldren-Turner syndrome 353.5
Parsonage-Turner syndrome 353.5
Pars planitis 363.21
Particolored infant 757.39
Parturition — *see* Delivery
Passage
  false, urethra 599.4
  meconium noted during delivery 763.84 ●
  of sounds or bougies (*see also* Attention to
    artificial opening) V55.9
Passive — *see* condition
Pasteurella septica 027.2
Pasteurellosis (*see also* Infection, Pasteurella)
  027.2
PAT (paroxysmal atrial tachycardia) 427.0
Patau's syndrome (trisomy D$_1$) 758.1
Patch
  herald 696.3
Patches
  mucous (syphilitic) 091.3
    congenital 090.0
  smokers' (mouth) 528.6
Patellar — *see* condition
Patellofemoral syndrome 719.46
Patent — *see also* Imperfect closure
  atrioventricular ostium 745.69
  canal of Nuck 752.41
  cervix 622.5
    complicating pregnancy 654.5 ☑
      affecting fetus or newborn 761.0
  ductus arteriosus or Botalli 747.0
  Eustachian
    tube 381.7
    valve 746.89
  foramen
    Botalli 745.5
    ovale 745.5
  interauricular septum 745.5
  interventricular septum 745.4
  omphalomesenteric duct 751.0
  os (uteri) — *see* Patent, cervix

Patent — *see also* Imperfect closure — *continued*
  ostium secundum 745.5
  urachus 753.7
  vitelline duct 751.0
Paternity testing V70.4
Paterson's syndrome (sideropenic dysphagia)
  280.8
Paterson (-Brown) (-Kelly) syndrome (sideropenic
  dysphagia) 280.8
Paterson-Kelly syndrome or web (sideropenic
  dysphagia) 280.8
Pathologic, pathological — *see also* condition
  asphyxia 799.01 ▲
  drunkenness 291.4
  emotionality 301.3
  fracture — *see* Fracture, pathologic
  liar 301.7
  personality 301.9
  resorption, tooth 521.40
    external 521.42
    internal 521.41
    specified NEC 521.49
  sexuality (*see also* Deviation, sexual) 302.9
Pathology (of) — *see* Disease
Patterned motor discharge, idiopathic (*see also*
  Epilepsy) 345.5 ☑
Patulous — *see also* Patent
  anus 569.49
  Eustachian tube 381.7
Pause, sinoatrial 427.81
Pavor nocturnus 307.46
Pavy's disease 593.6
Paxton's disease (white piedra) 111.2
Payr's disease or syndrome (splenic flexure
  syndrome) 569.89
PBA (pseudobulbar affect) 310.8 ●
Pearls
  Elschnig 366.51
  enamel 520.2
Pearl-workers' disease (chronic osteomyelitis)
  (*see also* Osteomyelitis) 730.1 ☑
Pectenitis 569.49
Pectenosis 569.49
Pectoral — *see* condition
Pectus
  carinatum (congenital) 754.82
    acquired 738.3
    rachitic (*see also* Rickets) 268.0
  excavatum (congenital) 754.81
    acquired 738.3
    rachitic (*see also* Rickets) 268.0
  recurvatum (congenital) 754.81
    acquired 738.3
Pedatrophia 261
Pederosis 302.2
Pediculosis (infestation) 132.9
  capitis (head louse) (any site) 132.0
  corporis (body louse) (any site) 132.1
  eyelid 132.0 *[373.6]*
  mixed (classifiable to more than one category in
    132.0-132.2) 132.3
  pubis (pubic louse) (any site) 132.2
  vestimenti 132.1
  vulvae 132.2
Pediculus (infestation) — *see* Pediculosis
Pedophilia 302.2
Peg-shaped teeth 520.2
Pel's crisis 094.0
Pel-Ebstein disease — *see* Disease, Hodgkin's
Pelade 704.01
Pelger-Huät anomaly or syndrome (hereditary
  hyposegmentation) 288.2
Peliosis (rheumatica) 287.0
Pelizaeus-Merzbacher
  disease 330.0
  sclerosis, diffuse cerebral 330.0
Pellagra (alcoholic or with alcoholism) 265.2
  with polyneuropathy 265.2 *[357.4]*
Pellagra-cerebellar-ataxia-renal aminoaciduria
  syndrome 270.0

☑ Additional Digit Required — Refer to the Tabular List (Numeric Code Section) for Additional Digit Selection
▶◀ Revised Text   ● New Line   ▲ Revised Code

Pellegrini's disease (calcification, knee joint) 726.62

Pellegrini (-Stieda) disease or syndrome (calcification, knee joint) 726.62

Pellizzi's syndrome (pineal) 259.8

Pelvic — *see also* condition
   congestion-fibrosis syndrome 625.5
   kidney 753.3

Pelvioectasis 591

Pelviolithiasis 592.0

Pelviperitonitis
   female (*see also* Peritonitis, pelvic, female) 614.5
   male (*see also* Peritonitis) 567.21 ▲

Pelvis, pelvic — *see also* condition or type
   infantile 738.6
   Nägele's 738.6
   obliquity 738.6
   Robert's 755.69

Pemphigoid 694.5
   benign, mucous membrane 694.60
     with ocular involvement 694.61
   bullous 694.5
   cicatricial 694.60
     with ocular involvement 694.61
   juvenile 694.2

Pemphigus 694.4
   benign 694.5
     chronic familial 757.39
   Brazilian 694.4
   circinatus 694.0
   congenital, traumatic 757.39
   conjunctiva 694.61
   contagiosus 684
   erythematodes 694.4
   erythematosus 694.4
   foliaceus 694.4
   frambesiodes 694.4
   gangrenous (*see also* Gangrene) 785.4
   malignant 694.4
   neonatorum, newborn 684
   ocular 694.61
   papillaris 694.4
   seborrheic 694.4
   South American 694.4
   syphilitic (congenital) 090.0
   vegetans 694.4
   vulgaris 694.4
   wildfire 694.4

Pendred's syndrome (familial goiter with deaf-mutism) 243

Pendulous
   abdomen 701.9
     in pregnancy or childbirth 654.4 ☑
       affecting fetus or newborn 763.89
   breast 611.8

Penetrating wound — *see also* Wound, open, by site
   with internal injury — *see* Injury, internal, by site, with open wound
   eyeball 871.7
     with foreign body (nonmagnetic) 871.6
       magnetic 871.5
   ocular (*see also* Penetrating wound, eyeball) 871.7
     adnexa 870.3
       with foreign body 870.4
     orbit 870.3
       with foreign body 870.4

Penetration, pregnant uterus by instrument
   with
     abortion — *see* Abortion, by type, with damage to pelvic organs
     ectopic pregnancy (*see also* categories 633.0-633.9) 639.2
     molar pregnancy (*see also* categories 630-632) 639.2
   complication of delivery 665.1 ☑
     affecting fetus or newborn 763.89
   following
     abortion 639.2
     ectopic or molar pregnancy 639.2

Penfield's syndrome (*see also* Epilepsy) 345.5 ☑

Penicilliosis of lung 117.3

Penis — *see* condition

Penitis 607.2

Penta X syndrome 758.81

Pentalogy (of Fallot) 745.2

Pentosuria (benign) (essential) 271.8

Peptic acid disease 536.8

Peregrinating patient V65.2

Perforated — *see* Perforation

Perforation, perforative (nontraumatic)
   antrum (*see also* Sinusitis, maxillary) 473.0
   appendix 540.0
     with peritoneal abscess 540.1
   atrial septum, multiple 745.5
   attic, ear 384.22
     healed 384.81
   bile duct, except cystic (*see also* Disease, biliary) 576.3
     cystic 575.4
   bladder (urinary) 596.6
     with
       abortion — *see* Abortion, by type, with damage to pelvic organs
       ectopic pregnancy (*see also* categories 633.0-633.9) 639.2
       molar pregnancy (*see also* categories 630-632) 639.2
     following
       abortion 639.2
       ectopic or molar pregnancy 639.2
     obstetrical trauma 665.5 ☑
   bowel 569.83
     with
       abortion — *see* Abortion, by type, with damage to pelvic organs
       ectopic pregnancy (*see also* categories 633.0-633.9) 639.2
       molar pregnancy (*see also* categories 630-632) 639.2
     fetus or newborn 777.6
     following
       abortion 639.2
       ectopic or molar pregnancy 639.2
     obstetrical trauma 665.5 ☑
   broad ligament
     with
       abortion — *see* Abortion, by type, with damage to pelvic organs
       ectopic pregnancy (*see also* categories 633.0-633.9) 639.2
       molar pregnancy (*see also* categories 630-632) 639.2
     following
       abortion 639.2
       ectopic or molar pregnancy 639.2
     obstetrical trauma 665.6 ☑
   by
     device, implant, or graft — *see* Complications, mechanical
     foreign body left accidentally in operation wound 998.4
     instrument (any) during a procedure, accidental 998.2
   cecum 540.0
     with peritoneal abscess 540.1
   cervix (uteri) — *see also* Injury, internal, cervix
     with
       abortion — *see* Abortion, by type, with damage to pelvic organs
       ectopic pregnancy (*see also* categories 633.0-633.9) 639.2
       molar pregnancy (*see also* categories 630-632) 639.2
     following
       abortion 639.2
       ectopic or molar pregnancy 639.2
     obstetrical trauma 665.3 ☑
   colon 569.83
   common duct (bile) 576.3
   cornea (*see also* Ulcer, cornea) 370.00
     due to ulceration 370.06
   cystic duct 575.4
   diverticulum (*see also* Diverticula) 562.10
     small intestine 562.00
   duodenum, duodenal (ulcer) — *see* Ulcer, duodenum, with perforation

Perforation, perforative — *continued*
   ear drum — *see* Perforation, tympanum
   enteritis — *see* Enteritis
   esophagus 530.4
   ethmoidal sinus (*see also* Sinusitis, ethmoidal) 473.2
   foreign body (external site) — *see also* Wound, open, by site, complicated
     internal site, by ingested object — *see* Foreign body
   frontal sinus (*see also* Sinusitis, frontal) 473.1
   gallbladder or duct (*see also* Disease, gallbladder) 575.4
   gastric (ulcer) — *see* Ulcer, stomach, with perforation
   heart valve — *see* Endocarditis
   ileum (*see also* Perforation, intestine) 569.83
   instrumental
     external — *see* Wound, open, by site
     pregnant uterus, complicating delivery 665.9 ☑
     surgical (accidental) (blood vessel) (nerve) (organ) 998.2
   intestine 569.83
     with
       abortion — *see* Abortion, by type, with damage to pelvic organs
       ectopic pregnancy (*see also* categories 633.0-633.9) 639.2
       molar pregnancy (*see also* categories 630-632) 639.2
     fetus or newborn 777.6
     obstetrical trauma 665.5 ☑
     ulcerative NEC 569.83
   jejunum, jejunal 569.83
     ulcer — *see* Ulcer, gastrojejunal, with perforation
   mastoid (antrum) (cell) 383.89
   maxillary sinus (*see also* Sinusitis, maxillary) 473.0
   membrana tympani — *see* Perforation, tympanum
   nasal
     septum 478.1
       congenital 748.1
       syphilitic 095.8
     sinus (*see also* Sinusitis) 473.9
       congenital 748.1
   palate (hard) 526.89
     soft 528.9
       syphilitic 095.8
         syphilitic 095.8
   palatine vault 526.89
     syphilitic 095.8
       congenital 090.5
   pelvic
     floor
       with
         abortion — *see* Abortion, by type, with damage to pelvic organs
         ectopic pregnancy (*see also* categories 633.0-633.9) 639.2
         molar pregnancy (*see also* categories 630-632) 639.2
       obstetrical trauma 664.1 ☑
     organ
       with
         abortion — *see* Abortion, by type, with damage to pelvic organs
         ectopic pregnancy (*see also* categories 633.0-633.9) 639.2
         molar pregnancy (*see also* categories 630-632) 639.2
       following
         abortion 639.2
         ectopic or molar pregnancy 639.2
       obstetrical trauma 665.5 ☑
   perineum — *see* Laceration, perineum
   periurethral tissue
     with
       abortion — *see* Abortion, by type, with damage to pelvic organs
       ectopic pregnancy (*see also* categories 630-632) 639.2
       molar pregnancy (*see also* categories 630-632) 639.2
   pharynx 478.29

☑ Additional Digit Required — Refer to the Tabular List (Numeric Code Section) for Additional Digit Selection

Perforation, perforative — *continued*
pylorus, pyloric (ulcer) — *see* Ulcer, stomach,
with perforation
rectum 569.49
sigmoid 569.83
sinus (accessory) (chronic) (nasal) (*see also*
Sinusitis) 473.9
sphenoidal sinus (*see also* Sinusitis,
sphenoidal) 473.3
stomach (due to ulcer) — *see* Ulcer, stomach,
with perforation
surgical (accidental) (by instrument) (blood
vessel) (nerve) (organ) 998.2
traumatic
external — *see* Wound, open, by site
eye (*see also* Penetrating wound, ocular)
871.7
internal organ — *see* Injury, internal, by site
tympanum (membrane) (persistent
posttraumatic) (postinflammatory) 384.20
with
otitis media — *see* Otitis media
attic 384.22
central 384.21
healed 384.81
marginal NEC 384.23
multiple 384.24
pars flaccida 384.22
total 384.25
traumatic — *see* Wound, open, ear, drum
typhoid, gastrointestinal 002.0
ulcer — *see* Ulcer, by site, with perforation
ureter 593.89
urethra
with
abortion — *see* Abortion, by type, with
damage to pelvic organs
ectopic pregnancy (*see also* categories
633.0-633.9) 639.2
molar pregnancy (*see also* categories 630-
632) 639.2
following
abortion 639.2
ectopic or molar pregnancy 639.2
obstetrical trauma 665.5 ☑
uterus — *see also* Injury, internal, uterus
with
abortion — *see* Abortion, by type, with
damage to pelvic organs
ectopic pregnancy (*see also* categories
633.0-633.9) 639.2
molar pregnancy (*see also* categories 630-
632) 639.2
by intrauterine contraceptive device 996.32
following
abortion 639.2
ectopic or molar pregnancy 639.2
obstetrical trauma — *see* Injury, internal,
uterus, obstetrical trauma
uvula 528.9
syphilitic 095.8
vagina — *see* Laceration, vagina
viscus NEC 799.89
traumatic 868.00
with open wound into cavity 868.10
Periadenitis mucosa necrotica recurrens 528.2
Periangiitis 446.0
Periantritis 535.4 ☑
Periappendicitis (acute) (*see also* Appendicitis)
541
Periarteritis (disseminated) (infectious)
(necrotizing) (nodosa) 446.0
Periarthritis (joint) 726.90
Duplay's 726.2
gonococcal 098.50
humeroscapularis 726.2
scapulohumeral 726.2
shoulder 726.2
wrist 726.4
Periarthrosis (angioneural) — *see* Periarthritis
Peribronchitis 491.9
tuberculous (*see also* Tuberculosis) 011.3 ☑
Pericapsulitis, adhesive (shoulder) 726.0

Pericarditis (granular) (with decompensation)
(with effusion) 423.9
with
rheumatic fever (conditions classifiable to
390)
active (*see also* Pericarditis, rheumatic)
391.0
inactive or quiescent 393
actinomycotic 039.8 *[420.0]*
acute (nonrheumatic) 420.90
with chorea (acute) (rheumatic)
(Sydenham's) 392.0
bacterial 420.99
benign 420.91
hemorrhagic 420.90
idiopathic 420.91
infective 420.90
nonspecific 420.91
rheumatic 391.0
with chorea (acute) (rheumatic)
(Sydenham's) 392.0
sicca 420.90
viral 420.91
adhesive or adherent (external) (internal) 423.1
acute — *see* Pericarditis, acute
rheumatic (external) (internal) 393
amebic 006.8 *[420.0]*
bacterial (acute) (subacute) (with serous or
seropurulent effusion) 420.99
calcareous 423.2
cholesterol (chronic) 423.8
acute 420.90
chronic (nonrheumatic) 423.8
rheumatic 393
constrictive 423.2
Coxsackie 074.21
due to
actinomycosis 039.8 *[420.0]*
amebiasis 006.8 *[420.0]*
Coxsackie (virus) 074.21
histoplasmosis (*see also* Histoplasmosis)
115.93
nocardiosis 039.8 *[420.0]*
tuberculosis (*see also* Tuberculosis)
017.9 ☑ *[420.0]*
fibrinocaseous (*see also* Tuberculosis)
017.9 ☑ *[420.0]*
fibrinopurulent 420.99
fibrinous — *see* Pericarditis, rheumatic
fibropurulent 420.99
fibrous 423.1
gonococcal 098.83
hemorrhagic 423.0
idiopathic (acute) 420.91
infective (acute) 420.90
meningococcal 036.41
neoplastic (chronic) 423.8
acute 420.90
nonspecific 420.91
obliterans, obliterating 423.1
plastic 423.1
pneumococcal (acute) 420.99
postinfarction 411.0
purulent (acute) 420.99
rheumatic (active) (acute) (with effusion) (with
pneumonia) 391.0
with chorea (acute) (rheumatic)
(Sydenham's) 392.0
chronic or inactive (with chorea) 393
septic (acute) 420.99
serofibrinous — *see* Pericarditis, rheumatic
staphylococcal (acute) 420.99
streptococcal (acute) 420.99
suppurative (acute) 420.99
syphilitic 093.81
tuberculous (acute) (chronic) (*see also*
Tuberculosis) 017.9 ☑ *[420.0]*
uremic 585.9 *[420.0]* ▲
viral (acute) 420.91
Pericardium, pericardial — *see* condition
Pericellulitis (*see also* Cellulitis) 682.9
Pericementitis 523.4
acute 523.3
chronic (suppurative) 523.4
Pericholecystitis (*see also* Cholecystitis) 575.10

Perichondritis
auricle 380.00
acute 380.01
chronic 380.02
bronchus 491.9
ear (external) 380.00
acute 380.01
chronic 380.02
larynx 478.71
syphilitic 095.8
typhoid 002.0 *[478.71]*
nose 478.1
pinna 380.00
acute 380.01
chronic 380.02
trachea 478.9
Periclasia 523.5
Pericolitis 569.89
Pericoronitis (chronic) 523.4
acute 523.3
Pericystitis (*see also* Cystitis) 595.9
Pericytoma (M9150/1) — *see also* Neoplasm,
connective tissue, uncertain behavior
benign (M9150/0) — *see* Neoplasm, connective
tissue, benign
malignant (M9150/3) — *see* Neoplasm,
connective tissue, malignant
Peridacryocystitis, acute 375.32
Peridiverticulitis (*see also* Diverticulitis) 562.11
Periduodenitis 535.6 ☑
Periendocarditis (*see also* Endocarditis) 424.90
acute or subacute 421.9
Periepididymitis (*see also* Epididymitis) 604.90
Perifolliculitis (abscedens) 704.8
capitis, abscedens et suffodiens 704.8
dissecting, scalp 704.8
scalp 704.8
superficial pustular 704.8
Perigastritis (acute) 535.0 ☑
Perigastrojejunitis (acute) 535.0 ☑
Perihepatitis (acute) 573.3
chlamydial 099.56
gonococcal 098.86
Peri-ileitis (subacute) 569.89
Perilabyrinthitis (acute) — *see* Labyrinthitis
Perimeningitis — *see* Meningitis
Perimetritis (*see also* Endometritis) 615.9
Perimetrosalpingitis (*see also* Salpingo-
oophoritis) 614.2
Perineocele 618.05
Perinephric — *see* condition
Perinephritic — *see* condition
Perinephritis (*see also* Infection, kidney) 590.9
purulent (*see also* Abscess, kidney) 590.2
Perineum, perineal — *see* condition
Perineuritis NEC 729.2
Periodic — *see also* condition
disease (familial) 277.3
edema 995.1
hereditary 277.6
fever 277.3
limb movement disorder 327.51 ▲
paralysis (familial) 359.3
peritonitis 277.3
polyserositis 277.3
somnolence (*see also* Narcolepsy) 347.00
Periodontal
cyst 522.8
pocket 523.8
Periodontitis (chronic) (complex) (compound)
(local) (simplex) 523.4
acute 523.3
apical 522.6
acute (pulpal origin) 522.4
Periodontoclasia 523.5
Periodontosis 523.5
Periods — *see also* Menstruation
heavy 626.2
irregular 626.4
Perionychia (with lymphangitis) 681.9
finger 681.02
toe 681.11

☑ Additional Digit Required — Refer to the Tabular List (Numeric Code Section) for Additional Digit Selection
▶◀ Revised Text   ● New Line   ▲ Revised Code

2006 ICD-9-CM

October 2005 • Volume 2 — 265

Perioophoritis (see also Salpingo-oophoritis) 614.2
Periorchitis (see also Orchitis) 604.90
Periosteum, periosteal — see condition
Periostitis (circumscribed) (diffuse) (infective) 730.3 ☑

Note — Use the following fifth-digit subclassification with category 730:
0   site unspecified
1   shoulder region
2   upper arm
3   forearm
4   hand
5   pelvic region and thigh
6   lower leg
7   ankle and foot
8   other specified sites
9   multiple sites

with osteomyelitis (see also Osteomyelitis) 730.2 ☑
    acute or subacute 730.0 ☑
    chronic or old 730.1 ☑
albuminosa, albuminosus 730.3 ☑
alveolar 526.5
alveolodental 526.5
dental 526.5
gonorrheal 098.89
hyperplastica, generalized 731.2
jaw (lower) (upper) 526.4
monomelic 733.99
orbital 376.02
syphilitic 095.5
    congenital 090.0 [730.8] ☑
    secondary 091.61
tuberculous (see also Tuberculosis, bone) 015.9 ☑ [730.8] ☑
yaws (early) (hypertrophic) (late) 102.6
Periostosis (see also Periostitis) 730.3 ☑
with osteomyelitis (see also Osteomyelitis) 730.2 ☑
    acute or subacute 730.0 ☑
    chronic or old 730.1 ☑
hyperplastic 756.59
Peripartum cardiomyopathy 674.5 ☑
Periphlebitis (see also Phlebitis) 451.9
lower extremity 451.2
    deep (vessels) 451.19
    superficial (vessels) 451.0
portal 572.1
retina 362.18
superficial (vessels) 451.0
tuberculous (see also Tuberculosis) 017.9 ☑
    retina 017.3 ☑ [362.18]
Peripneumonia — see Pneumonia
Periproctitis 569.49
Periprostatitis (see also Prostatitis) 601.9
Perirectal — see condition
Perirenal — see condition
Perisalpingitis (see also Salpingo-oophoritis) 614.2
Perisigmoiditis 569.89
Perisplenitis (infectional) 289.59
Perispondylitis — see Spondylitis
Peristalsis reversed or visible 787.4
Peritendinitis (see also Tenosynovitis) 726.90
adhesive (shoulder) 726.0
Perithelioma (M9150/1) — see Pericytoma
Peritoneum, peritoneal — see also condition
equilibration test V56.32
Peritonitis (acute) (adhesive) (fibrinous) (hemorrhagic) (idiopathic) (localized) (perforative) (primary) (with adhesions) (with effusion) 567.9
with or following
    abortion — see Abortion, by type, with sepsis
    abscess 567.21   ▲
    appendicitis 540.0
        with peritoneal abscess 540.1

Peritonitis — continued
with or following — continued
    ectopic pregnancy (see also categories 633.0-633.9) 639.0
    molar pregnancy (see also categories 630-632) 639.0
aseptic 998.7
bacterial 567.29   ▲
    spontaneous 567.23   ●
bile, biliary 567.81   ▲
chemical 998.7
chlamydial 099.56
chronic proliferative 567.89   ▲
congenital NEC 777.6
diaphragmatic 567.22   ▲
diffuse NEC 567.29   ▲
diphtheritic 032.83
disseminated NEC 567.29   ▲
due to
    bile 567.81   ▲
    foreign
        body or object accidentally left during a procedure (instrument) (sponge) (swab) 998.4
        substance accidentally left during a procedure (chemical) (powder) (talc) 998.7
    talc 998.7
    urine 567.89   ▲
fibrinopurulent 567.29   ▲
fibrinous 567.29   ▲
fibrocaseous (see also Tuberculosis) 014.0 ☑
fibropurulent 567.29   ▲
general, generalized (acute) 567.21   ▲
gonococcal 098.86
in infective disease NEC 136.9 [567.0]
meconium (newborn) 777.6
pancreatic 577.8
paroxysmal, benign 277.3
pelvic
    female (acute) 614.5
        chronic NEC 614.7
            with adhesions 614.6
        puerperal, postpartum, childbirth 670.0 ☑
    male (acute) 567.21   ▲
periodic (familial) 277.3
phlegmonous 567.29   ▲
pneumococcal 567.1
postabortal 639.0
proliferative, chronic 567.89   ▲
puerperal, postpartum, childbirth 670.0 ☑
purulent 567.29   ▲
septic 567.29   ▲
spontaneous bacterial 567.23   ●
staphylococcal 567.29   ▲
streptococcal 567.29   ▲
subdiaphragmatic 567.29   ▲
subphrenic 567.29   ▲
suppurative 567.29   ▲
syphilitic 095.2
    congenital 090.0 [567.0]
talc 998.7
tuberculous (see also Tuberculosis) 014.0 ☑
urine 567.89   ▲
Peritonsillar — see condition
Peritonsillitis 475
Perityphlitis (see also Appendicitis) 541
Periureteritis 593.89
Periurethral — see condition
Periurethritis (gangrenous) 597.89
Periuterine — see condition
Perivaginitis (see also Vaginitis) 616.10
Perivasculitis, retinal 362.18
Perivasitis (chronic) 608.4
Periventricular leukomalacia 779.7
Perivesiculitis (seminal) (see also Vesiculitis) 608.0
Perlèche 686.8
due to
    moniliasis 112.0
    riboflavin deficiency 266.0
Pernicious — see condition
Pernio, perniosis 991.5

Persecution
delusion 297.9
social V62.4
Perseveration (tonic) 784.69
Persistence, persistent (congenital) 759.89
anal membrane 751.2
arteria stapedia 744.04
atrioventricular canal 745.69
bloody ejaculate 792.2
branchial cleft 744.41
bulbus cordis in left ventricle 745.8
canal of Cloquet 743.51
capsule (opaque) 743.51
cilioretinal artery or vein 743.51
cloaca 751.5
communication — see Fistula, congenital
convolutions
    aortic arch 747.21
    fallopian tube 752.19
    oviduct 752.19
    uterine tube 752.19
double aortic arch 747.21
ductus
    arteriosus 747.0
    Botalli 747.0
fetal
    circulation 747.83
    form of cervix (uteri) 752.49
    hemoglobin (hereditary) ("Swiss variety") 282.7
    pulmonary hypertension 747.83
foramen
    Botalli 745.5
    ovale 745.5
Gartner's duct 752.41   ▲
hemoglobin, fetal (hereditary) (HPFH) 282.7
hyaloid
    artery (generally incomplete) 743.51
    system 743.51
hymen (tag)
    in pregnancy or childbirth 654.8 ☑
        causing obstructed labor 660.2 ☑
lanugo 757.4
left
    posterior cardinal vein 747.49
    root with right arch of aorta 747.21
    superior vena cava 747.49
Meckel's diverticulum 751.0
mesonephric duct 752.89
    fallopian tube 752.11
mucosal disease (middle ear) (with posterior or superior marginal perforation of ear drum) 382.2
nail(s), anomalous 757.5
occiput, anterior or posterior 660.3 ☑
    fetus or newborn 763.1
omphalomesenteric duct 751.0
organ or site NEC — see Anomaly, specified type NEC
ostium
    atrioventriculare commune 745.69
    primum 745.61
    secundum 745.5
ovarian rests in fallopian tube 752.19
pancreatic tissue in intestinal tract 751.5
primary (deciduous)
    teeth 520.6
    vitreous hyperplasia 743.51
pulmonary hypertension 747.83
pupillary membrane 743.46
    iris 743.46
Rhesus (Rh) titer 999.7
right aortic arch 747.21
sinus
    urogenitalis 752.89
    venosus with imperfect incorporation in right auricle 747.49
thymus (gland) 254.8
    hyperplasia 254.0
thyroglossal duct 759.2
thyrolingual duct 759.2
truncus arteriosus or communis 745.0
tunica vasculosa lentis 743.39
umbilical sinus 753.7
urachus 753.7
vegetative state 780.03

Persistence, persistent — *continued*
  vitelline duct 751.0
  wolffian duct 752.89
Person (with)
  admitted for clinical research, as participant or
    control subject V70.7
  awaiting admission to adequate facility
    elsewhere V63.2
    undergoing social agency investigation V63.8
  concern (normal) about sick person in family
    V61.49
  consulting on behalf of another V65.19
    pediatric pre-birth visit for expectant mother
      V65.11
  feared
    complaint in whom no diagnosis was made
      V65.5
    condition not demonstrated V65.5
  feigning illness V65.2
  healthy, accompanying sick person V65.0
  living (in)
    alone V60.3
    boarding school V60.6
    residence remote from hospital or medical
      care facility V63.0
    residential institution V60.6
    without
      adequate
        financial resources V60.2
        housing (heating) (space) V60.1
      housing (permanent) (temporary) V60.0
      material resources V60.2
      person able to render necessary care
        V60.4
      shelter V60.0
  medical services in home not available V63.1
  on waiting list V63.2
    undergoing social agency investigation V63.8
  sick or handicapped in family V61.49
  "worried well" V65.5
Personality
  affective 301.10
  aggressive 301.3
  amoral 301.7
  anancastic, anankastic 301.4
  antisocial 301.7
  asocial 301.7
  asthenic 301.6
  avoidant 301.82
  borderline 301.83
  change 310.1
  compulsive 301.4
  cycloid 301.13
  cyclothymic 301.13
  dependent 301.6
  depressive (chronic) 301.12
  disorder, disturbance NEC 301.9
    with
      antisocial disturbance 301.7
      pattern disturbance NEC 301.9
      sociopathic disturbance 301.7
      trait disturbance 301.9
  dual 300.14
  dyssocial 301.7
  eccentric 301.89
    "haltlose" type 301.89
  emotionally unstable 301.59
  epileptoid 301.3
  explosive 301.3
  fanatic 301.0
  histrionic 301.50
  hyperthymic 301.11
  hypomanic 301.11
  hypothymic 301.12
  hysterical 301.50
  immature 301.89
  inadequate 301.6
  labile 301.59
  masochistic 301.89
  morally defective 301.7
  multiple 300.14
  narcissistic 301.81
  obsessional 301.4
  obsessive-compulsive 301.4
  overconscientious 301.4
  paranoid 301.0

Personality — *continued*
  passive (-dependent) 301.6
  passive-aggressive 301.84
  pathologic NEC 301.9
  pattern defect or disturbance 301.9
  pseudosocial 301.7
  psychoinfantile 301.59
  psychoneurotic NEC 301.89
  psychopathic 301.9
    with
      amoral trend 301.7
      antisocial trend 301.7
      asocial trend 301.7
      pathologic sexuality (*see also* Deviation,
        sexual) 302.9
    mixed types 301.9
  schizoid 301.20
    introverted 301.21
    schizotypal 301.22
    with sexual deviation (*see also* Deviation,
      sexual) 302.9
      antisocial 301.7
      dyssocial 301.7
  type A 301.4
  unstable (emotional) 301.59
Perthes' disease (capital femoral osteochondrosis)
  732.1
Pertussis (*see also* Whooping cough) 033.9
  vaccination, prophylactic (against) V03.6
Peruvian wart 088.0
Perversion, perverted
  appetite 307.52
    hysterical 300.11
  function
    pineal gland 259.8
    pituitary gland 253.9
      anterior lobe
        deficient 253.2
        excessive 253.1
      posterior lobe 253.6
    placenta — *see* Placenta, abnormal
  sense of smell or taste 781.1
    psychogenic 306.7
  sexual (*see also* Deviation, sexual) 302.9
Pervious, congenital — *see also* Imperfect,
  closure
  ductus arteriosus 747.0
Pes (congenital) (*see also* Talipes) 754.70
  abductus (congenital) 754.60
    acquired 736.79
  acquired NEC 736.79
    planus 734
  adductus (congenital) 754.79
    acquired 736.79
  cavus 754.71
    acquired 736.73
  planovalgus (congenital) 754.69
    acquired 736.79
  planus (acquired) (any degree) 734
    congenital 754.61
    rachitic 268.1
  valgus (congenital) 754.61
    acquired 736.79
  varus (congenital) 754.50
    acquired 736.79
Pest (*see also* Plague) 020.9
Pestis (*see also* Plague) 020.9
  bubonica 020.0
  fulminans 020.0
  minor 020.8
  pneumonica — *see* Plague, pneumonic
Petechia, petechiae 782.7
  fetus or newborn 772.6
Petechial
  fever 036.0
  typhus 081.9
Petges-Cléjat or Petges-Clégat syndrome
  (poikilodermatomyositis) 710.3
Petit's
  disease (*see also* Hernia, lumbar) 553.8
Petit mal (idiopathic) (*see also* Epilepsy) 345.0 ☑
  status 345.2
Petrellidosis 117.6

Petrositis 383.20
  acute 383.21
  chronic 383.22
Peutz-Jeghers disease or syndrome 759.6
Peyronie's disease 607.85
Pfeiffer's disease 075
Phacentocele 379.32
  traumatic 921.3
Phacoanaphylaxis 360.19
Phacocele (old) 379.32
  traumatic 921.3
Phaehyphomycosis 117.8
Phagedena (dry) (moist) (*see also* Gangrene) 785.4
  arteriosclerotic 440.24
  geometric 686.09
  penis 607.89
  senile 440.24
  sloughing 785.4
  tropical (*see also* Ulcer, skin) 707.9
  vulva 616.50
Phagedenic — *see also* condition
  abscess — *see also* Abscess
    chancroid 099.0
    bubo NEC 099.8
    chancre 099.0
    ulcer (tropical) (*see also* Ulcer, skin) 707.9
Phagomania 307.52
Phakoma 362.89
Phantom limb (syndrome) 353.6
Pharyngeal — *see also* condition
  arch remnant 744.41
  pouch syndrome 279.11
Pharyngitis (acute) (catarrhal) (gangrenous)
    (infective) (malignant) (membranous)
    (phlegmonous) (pneumococcal)
    (pseudomembranous) (simple)
    (staphylococcal) (subacute) (suppurative)
    (ulcerative) (viral) 462
  with influenza, flu, or grippe 487.1
  aphthous 074.0
  atrophic 472.1
  chronic 472.1
  chlamydial 099.51
  Coxsackie virus 074.0
  diphtheritic (membranous) 032.0
  follicular 472.1
  fusospirochetal 101
  gonococcal 098.6
  granular (chronic) 472.1
  herpetic 054.79
  hypertrophic 472.1
  infectional, chronic 472.1
  influenzal 487.1
  lymphonodular, acute 074.8
  septic 034.0
  streptococcal 034.0
  tuberculous (*see also* Tuberculosis) 012.8 ☑
  vesicular 074.0
Pharyngoconjunctival fever 077.2
Pharyngoconjunctivitis, viral 077.2
Pharyngolaryngitis (acute) 465.0
  chronic 478.9
  septic 034.0
Pharyngoplegia 478.29
Pharyngotonsillitis 465.8
  tuberculous 012.8 ☑
Pharyngotracheitis (acute) 465.8
  chronic 478.9
Pharynx, pharyngeal — *see* condition
Phase of life problem NEC V62.89
Phenomenon
  Arthus' — *see* Arthus' phenomenon
  flashback (drug) 292.89
  jaw-winking 742.8
  Jod-Basedow 242.8 ☑
  L. E. cell 710.0
  lupus erythematosus cell 710.0
  Pelger-Huët (hereditary hyposegmentation)
    288.2
  Raynaud's (paroxysmal digital cyanosis)
    (secondary) 443.0
  Reilly's (*see also* Neuropathy, peripheral,
    autonomic) 337.9
  vasomotor 780.2
  vasospastic 443.9

☑ Additional Digit Required — Refer to the Tabular List (Numeric Code Section) for Additional Digit Selection
◄► Revised Text   ● New Line   ▲ Revised Code

Phenomenon — *continued*
  vasovagal 780.2
  Wenckebach's, heart block (second degree)
    426.13
Phenylketonuria (PKU) 270.1
Phenylpyruvicaciduria 270.1
Pheochromoblastoma (M8700/3)
  specified site — *see* Neoplasm, by site,
    malignant
  unspecified site 194.0
Pheochromocytoma (M8700/0)
  malignant (M8700/3)
    specified site — *see* Neoplasm, by site,
      malignant
    unspecified site 194.0
  specified site — *see* Neoplasm, by site, benign
  unspecified site 227.0
Phimosis (congenital) 605
  chancroidal 099.0
  due to infection 605
Phlebectasia (*see also* Varicose, vein) 454.9
  congenital NEC 747.60
  esophagus (*see also* Varix, esophagus) 456.1
    with hemorrhage (*see also* Varix, esophagus,
      bleeding) 456.0
Phlebitis (infective) (pyemic) (septic) (suppurative)
  451.9
  antecubital vein 451.82
  arm NEC 451.84
    axillary vein 451.89
    basilic vein 451.82
    deep 451.83
    superficial 451.82
  axillary vein 451.89
  basilic vein 451.82
  blue 451.9
  brachial vein 451.83
  breast, superficial 451.89
  cavernous (venous) sinus — *see* Phlebitis,
    intracranial sinus
  cephalic vein 451.82
  cerebral (venous) sinus — *see* Phlebitis,
    intracranial sinus
  chest wall, superficial 451.89
  complicating pregnancy or puerperium
    671.9 ☑
    affecting fetus or newborn 760.3
  cranial (venous) sinus — *see* Phlebitis,
    intracranial sinus
  deep (vessels) 451.19
    femoral vein 451.11
    specified vessel NEC 451.19
  due to implanted device — *see* Complications,
    due to (presence of) any device, implant,
    or graft classified to 996.0-996.5 NEC
  during or resulting from a procedure 997.2
  femoral vein (deep) (superficial) 451.11
  femoropopliteal 451.19
  following infusion, perfusion, or transfusion
    999.2
  gouty 274.89 *[451.9]*
  hepatic veins 451.89
  iliac vein 451.81
  iliofemoral 451.11
  intracranial sinus (any) (venous) 325
    late effect — *see* category 326
    nonpyogenic 437.6
      in pregnancy or puerperium 671.5 ☑
  jugular vein 451.89
  lateral (venous) sinus — *see* Phlebitis,
    intracranial sinus
  leg 451.2
    deep (vessels) 451.19
      femoral vein 451.11
      specified vessel NEC 451.19
    superficial (vessels) 451.0
      femoral vein 451.11
  longitudinal sinus — *see* Phlebitis, intracranial
    sinus
  lower extremity 451.2
    deep (vessels) 451.19
      femoral vein 451.11
      specified vessel NEC 451.19
    superficial (vessels) 451.0
      femoral vein 451.11
  migrans, migrating (superficial) 453.1

Phlebitis — *continued*
  pelvic
    with
      abortion — *see* Abortion, by type, with
        sepsis
      ectopic pregnancy (*see also* categories
        633.0-633.9) 639.0
      molar pregnancy (*see also* categories 630-
        632) 639.0
    following
      abortion 639.0
      ectopic or molar pregnancy 639.0
    puerperal, postpartum 671.4 ☑
  popliteal vein 451.19
  portal (vein) 572.1
  postoperative 997.2
  pregnancy 671.9 ☑
    deep 671.3 ☑
    specified type NEC 671.5 ☑
    superficial 671.2 ☑
  puerperal, postpartum, childbirth 671.9 ☑
    deep 671.4 ☑
    lower extremities 671.2 ☑
    pelvis 671.4 ☑
    specified site NEC 671.5 ☑
    superficial 671.2 ☑
  radial vein 451.83
  retina 362.18
  saphenous (great) (long) 451.0
    accessory or small 451.0
  sinus (meninges) — *see* Phlebitis, intracranial
    sinus
  specified site NEC 451.89
  subclavian vein 451.89
  syphilitic 093.89
  tibial vein 451.19
  ulcer, ulcerative 451.9
    leg 451.2
      deep (vessels) 451.19
        femoral vein 451.11
        specified vessel NEC 451.19
      superficial (vessels) 451.0
        femoral vein 451.11
    lower extremity 451.2
      deep (vessels) 451.19
        femoral vein 451.11
        specified vessel NEC 451.19
      superficial (vessels) 451.0
  ulnar vein 451.83
  umbilicus 451.89
  upper extremity — *see* Phlebitis, arm
    deep (veins) 451.83
      brachial vein 451.83
      radial vein 451.83
      ulnar vein 451.83
    superficial (veins) 451.82
      antecubital vein 451.82
      basilic vein 451.82
      cephalic vein 451.82
  uterus (septic) (*see also* Endometritis) 615.9
  varicose (leg) (lower extremity) (*see also*
    Varicose, vein) 454.1
Phlebofibrosis 459.89
Pheleboliths 459.89
Phlebosclerosis 459.89
Phlebothrombosis — *see* Thrombosis
Phlebotomus fever 066.0
Phlegm, choked on 933.1
Phlegmasia
  alba dolens (deep vessels) 451.19
    complicating pregnancy 671.3 ☑
    nonpuerperal 451.19
    puerperal, postpartum, childbirth 671.4 ☑
  cerulea dolens 451.19
Phlegmon (*see also* Abscess) 682.9
  erysipelatous (*see also* Erysipelas) 035
  iliac 682.2
    fossa 540.1
  throat 478.29
Phlegmonous — *see* condition
Phlyctenulosis (allergic) (keratoconjunctivitis)
  (nontuberculous) 370.31
  cornea 370.31
    with ulcer (*see also* Ulcer, cornea) 370.00
  tuberculous (*see also* Tuberculosis) 017.3 ☑
    [370.31]

Phobia, phobic (reaction) 300.20
  animal 300.29
  isolated NEC 300.29
  obsessional 300.3
  simple NEC 300.29
  social 300.23
  specified NEC 300.29
  state 300.20
Phocas' disease 610.1
Phocomelia 755.4
  lower limb 755.32
    complete 755.33
    distal 755.35
    proximal 755.34
  upper limb 755.22
    complete 755.23
    distal 755.25
    proximal 755.24
Phoria (*see also* Heterophoria) 378.40
Phosphate-losing tubular disorder 588.0
Phosphatemia 275.3
Phosphaturia 275.3
Photoallergic response 692.72
Photocoproporphyria 277.1
Photodermatitis (sun) 692.72
  light other than sun 692.82
Photokeratitis 370.24
Photo-ophthalmia 370.24
Photophobia 368.13
Photopsia 368.15
Photoretinitis 363.31
Photoretinopathy 363.31
Photosensitiveness (sun) 692.72
  light other than sun 692.82
Photosensitization skin (sun) 692.72
  light other than sun 692.82
Phototoxic response 692.72
Phrenitis 323.9
Phrynoderma 264.8
Phthiriasis (pubis) (any site) 132.2
  with any infestation classifiable to 132.0, 132.1
    and 132.3
Phthirus infestation — *see* Phthiriasis
Phthisis (*see also* Tuberculosis) 011.9 ☑
  bulbi (infectional) 360.41
  colliers' 011.4 ☑
  cornea 371.05
  eyeball (due to infection) 360.41
  millstone makers' 011.4 ☑
  miners' 011.4 ☑
  potters' 011.4 ☑
  sandblasters' 011.4 ☑
  stonemasons' 011.4 ☑
Phycomycosis 117.7
Physalopteriasis 127.7
Physical therapy NEC V57.1
  breathing exercises V57.0
Physiological cup, optic papilla
  borderline, glaucoma suspect 365.00
  enlarged 377.14
  glaucomatous 377.14
Phytobezoar 938
  intestine 936
  stomach 935.2
Pian (*see also* Yaws) 102.9
Pianoma 102.1
Piarhemia, piarrhemia (*see also* Hyperlipemia)
  272.4
  bilharziasis 120.9
Pica 307.52
  hysterical 300.11
Pick's
  cerebral atrophy 331.11
    with dementia
      with behavioral disturbance
        331.11 *[294.11]*
      without behavioral disturbance
        331.11 *[294.10]*
  disease
    brain 331.11
    dementia in
      with behavioral disturbance
        331.11 *[294.11]*
      without behavioral disturbance
        331.11 *[294.10]*

Pick's — *continued*
  disease — *continued*
    lipid histiocytosis 272.7
    liver (pericardial pseudocirrhosis of liver) 423.2
    pericardium (pericardial pseudocirrhosis of liver) 423.2
    polyserositis (pericardial pseudocirrhosis of liver) 423.2
    syndrome
      heart (pericardial pseudocirrhosis of liver) 423.2
      liver (pericardial pseudocirrhosis of liver) 423.2
    tubular adenoma (M8640/0)
      specified site — *see* Neoplasm, by site, benign
      unspecified site
        female 220
        male 222.0
Pick-Herxheimer syndrome (diffuse idiopathic cutaneous atrophy) 701.8
Pick-Niemann disease (lipid histiocytosis) 272.7
Pickwickian syndrome (cardiopulmonary obesity) 278.8
Piebaldism, classic 709.09
Piedra 111.2
  beard 111.2
    black 111.3
    white 111.2
  black 111.3
  scalp 111.3
    black 111.3
    white 111.2
  white 111.2
Pierre Marie's syndrome (pulmonary hypertrophic osteoarthropathy) 731.2
Pierre Marie-Bamberger syndrome (hypertrophic pulmonary osteoarthropathy) 731.2
Pierre Mauriac's syndrome (diabetes-dwarfism-obesity) 258.1
Pierre Robin deformity or syndrome (congenital) 756.0
Pierson's disease or osteochondrosis 732.1
Pigeon
  breast or chest (acquired) 738.3
    congenital 754.82
    rachitic (*see also* Rickets) 268.0
  breeders' disease or lung 495.2
  fanciers' disease or lung 495.2
  toe 735.8
Pigmentation (abnormal) 709.00
  anomaly 709.00
    congenital 757.33
    specified NEC 709.09
  conjunctiva 372.55
  cornea 371.10
    anterior 371.11
    posterior 371.13
    stromal 371.12
  lids (congenital) 757.33
    acquired 374.52
  limbus corneae 371.10
  metals 709.00
  optic papilla, congenital 743.57
  retina (congenital) (grouped) (nevoid) 743.53
    acquired 362.74
  scrotum, congenital 757.33
Piles — *see* Hemorrhoids
Pili
  annulati or torti (congenital) 757.4
  incarnati 704.8
Pill roller hand (intrinsic) 736.09
Pilomatrixoma (M8110/0) — *see* Neoplasm, skin, benign
Pilonidal — *see* condition
Pimple 709.8
PIN I (prostatic intraepithelial neoplasia I) 602.3
PIN II (prostatic intraepithelial neoplasia II) 602.3
PIN III (prostatic intraepithelial neoplasia III) 233.4
Pinched nerve — *see* Neuropathy, entrapment
Pineal body or gland — *see* condition
Pinealoblastoma (M9362/3) 194.4

Pinealoma (M9360/1) 237.1
  malignant (M9360/3) 194.4
Pineoblastoma (M9362/3) 194.4
Pineocytoma (M9361/1) 237.1
Pinguecula 372.51
Pinhole meatus (*see also* Stricture, urethra) 598.9
Pink
  disease 985.0
  eye 372.03
  puffer 492.8
Pinkus' disease (lichen nitidus) 697.1
Pinpoint
  meatus (*see also* Stricture, urethra) 598.9
  os uteri (*see also* Stricture, cervix) 622.4
Pinselhaare (congenital) 757.4
Pinta 103.9
  cardiovascular lesions 103.2
  chancre (primary) 103.0
  erythematous plaques 103.1
  hyperchromic lesions 103.1
  hyperkeratosis 103.1
  lesions 103.9
    cardiovascular 103.2
    hyperchromic 103.1
    intermediate 103.1
    late 103.2
    mixed 103.3
    primary 103.0
    skin (achromic) (cicatricial) (dyschromic) 103.2
      hyperchromic 103.1
      mixed (achromic and hyperchromic) 103.3
  papule (primary) 103.0
  skin lesions (achromic) (cicatricial) (dyschromic) 103.2
    hyperchromic 103.1
    mixed (achromic and hyperchromic) 103.3
  vitiligo 103.2
Pintid 103.0
Pinworms (disease) (infection) (infestation) 127.4
Piry fever 066.8
Pistol wound — *see* Gunshot wound
Pit, lip (mucus), **congenital** 750.25
Pitchers' elbow 718.82
Pithecoid pelvis 755.69
  with disproportion (fetopelvic) 653.2 ☑
    affecting fetus or newborn 763.1
    causing obstructed labor 660.1 ☑
Pithiatism 300.11
Pitted — *see also* Pitting
  teeth 520.4
Pitting (edema) (*see also* Edema) 782.3
  lip 782.3
  nail 703.8
    congenital 757.5
Pituitary gland — *see* condition
Pituitary snuff-takers' disease 495.8
Pityriasis 696.5
  alba 696.5
  capitis 690.11
  circinata (et maculata) 696.3
  Hebra's (exfoliative dermatitis) 695.89
  lichenoides et varioliformis 696.2
  maculata (et circinata) 696.3
  nigra 111.1
  pilaris 757.39
    acquired 701.1
    Hebra's 696.4
  rosea 696.3
  rotunda 696.3
  rubra (Hebra) 695.89
    pilaris 696.4
  sicca 690.18
  simplex 690.18
  specified type NEC 696.5
  streptogenes 696.5
  versicolor 111.0
    scrotal 111.0
Placenta, placental
  ablatio 641.2 ☑
    affecting fetus or newborn 762.1

Placenta, placental — *continued*
  abnormal, abnormality 656.7 ☑
    with hemorrhage 641.8 ☑
      affecting fetus or newborn 762.1
    affecting fetus or newborn 762.2
  abruptio 641.2 ☑
    affecting fetus or newborn 762.1
  accessory lobe — *see* Placenta, abnormal
  accreta (without hemorrhage) 667.0 ☑
    with hemorrhage 666.0 ☑
  adherent (without hemorrhage) 667.0 ☑
    with hemorrhage 666.0 ☑
  apoplexy — *see* Placenta, separation
  battledore — *see* Placenta, abnormal
  bilobate — *see* Placenta, abnormal
  bipartita — *see* Placenta, abnormal
  carneous mole 631
  centralis — *see* Placenta, previa
  circumvallata — *see* Placenta, abnormal
  cyst (amniotic) — *see* Placenta, abnormal
  deficiency — *see* Placenta, insufficiency
  degeneration — *see* Placenta, insufficiency
  detachment (partial) (premature) (with hemorrhage) 641.2 ☑
    affecting fetus or newborn 762.1
  dimidiata — *see* Placenta, abnormal
  disease 656.7 ☑
    affecting fetus or newborn 762.2
  duplex — *see* Placenta, abnormal
  dysfunction — *see* Placenta, insufficiency
  fenestrata — *see* Placenta, abnormal
  fibrosis — *see* Placenta, abnormal
  fleshy mole 631
  hematoma — *see* Placenta, abnormal
  hemorrhage NEC — *see* Placenta, separation
  hormone disturbance or malfunction — *see* Placenta, abnormal
  hyperplasia — *see* Placenta, abnormal
  increta (without hemorrhage) 667.0 ☑
    with hemorrhage 666.0 ☑
  infarction 656.7 ☑
    affecting fetus or newborn 762.2
  insertion, vicious — *see* Placenta, previa
  insufficiency
    affecting
      fetus or newborn 762.2
      management of pregnancy 656.5 ☑
  lateral — *see* Placenta, previa
  low implantation or insertion — *see* Placenta, previa
  low-lying — *see* Placenta, previa
  malformation — *see* Placenta, abnormal
  malposition — *see* Placenta, previa
  marginalis, marginata — *see* Placenta, previa
  marginal sinus (hemorrhage) (rupture) 641.2 ☑
    affecting fetus or newborn 762.1
  membranacea — *see* Placenta, abnormal
  multilobed — *see* Placenta, abnormal
  multipartita — *see* Placenta, abnormal
  necrosis — *see* Placenta, abnormal
  percreta (without hemorrhage) 667.0 ☑
    with hemorrhage 666.0 ☑
  polyp 674.4 ☑
  previa (central) (centralis) (complete) (lateral) (marginal) (marginalis) (partial) (partialis) (total) (with hemorrhage) 641.1 ☑
    affecting fetus or newborn 762.0
    noted
      before labor, without hemorrhage (with cesarean delivery) 641.0 ☑
      during pregnancy (without hemorrhage) 641.0 ☑
    without hemorrhage (before labor and delivery) (during pregnancy) 641.0 ☑
  retention (with hemorrhage) 666.0 ☑
    fragments, complicating puerperium (delayed hemorrhage) 666.2 ☑
      without hemorrhage 667.1 ☑
    postpartum, puerperal 666.2 ☑
    without hemorrhage 667.0 ☑
  separation (normally implanted) (partial) (premature) (with hemorrhage) 641.2 ☑
    affecting fetus or newborn 762.1
  septuplex — *see* Placenta, abnormal
  small — *see* Placenta, insufficiency
  softening (premature) — *see* Placenta, abnormal
  spuria — *see* Placenta, abnormal

Pneumonia — *continued*
  aspiration — *continued*
    fetal 770.18 ●
      due to ●
        blood 770.16 ●
        clear amniotic fluid 770.14 ●
        meconium 770.12 ●
        postnatal stomach contents 770.86 ●
    newborn 770.18 ▲
      due to ●
        blood 770.16 ●
        clear amniotic fluid 770.14 ●
        meconium 770.12 ●
        postnatal stomach contents 770.86 ●
  asthenic 514
  atypical (disseminated) (focal) (primary) 486
    with influenza 487.0
  bacillus 482.9
    specified type NEC 482.89
  bacterial 482.9
    specified type NEC 482.89
  Bacteroides (fragilis) (oralis) (melaninogenicus) 482.81
  basal, basic, basilar — *see* Pneumonia, lobar
  broncho-, bronchial (confluent) (croupous) (diffuse) (disseminated) (hemorrhagic) (involving lobes) (lobar) (terminal) 485
    with influenza 487.0
    allergic 518.3
    aspiration (*see also* Pneumonia, aspiration) 507.0
    bacterial 482.9
      specified type NEC 482.89
    capillary 466.19
      with bronchospasm or obstruction 466.19
    chronic (*see also* Fibrosis, lung) 515
    congenital (infective) 770.0
    diplococcal 481
    Eaton's agent 483.0
    Escherichia coli (E. coli) 482.82
    Friedländer's bacillus 482.0
    Hemophilus influenzae 482.2
    hiberno-vernal 083.0 *[484.8]*
    hypostatic 514
    influenzal 487.0
    inhalation (*see also* Pneumonia, aspiration) 507.0
      due to fumes or vapors (chemical) 506.0
    Klebsiella 482.0
    lipid 507.1
      endogenous 516.8
    Mycoplasma (pneumoniae) 483.0
    ornithosis 073.0
    pleuropneumonia-like organisms (PPLO) 483.0
    pneumococcal 481
    Proteus 482.83
    Pseudomonas 482.1
    specified organism NEC 483.8
      bacterial NEC 482.89
    staphylococcal 482.40
      aureus 482.41
      specified type NEC 482.49
    streptococcal — *see* Pneumonia, streptococcal
    typhoid 002.0 *[484.8]*
    viral, virus (*see also* Pneumonia, viral) 480.9
  Butyrivibrio (fibriosolvens) 482.81
  Candida 112.4
  capillary 466.19
    with bronchospasm or obstruction 466.19
  caseous (*see also* Tuberculosis) 011.6 ☑
  catarrhal — *see* Pneumonia, broncho-
  central — *see* Pneumonia, lobar
  Chlamydia, chlamydial 483.1
    pneumoniae 483.1
    psittaci 073.0
    specified type NEC 483.1
    trachomatis 483.1
  cholesterol 516.8
  chronic (*see also* Fibrosis, lung) 515
  cirrhotic (chronic) (*see also* Fibrosis, lung) 515
  Clostridium (haemolyticum) (novyi) NEC 482.81
  confluent — *see* Pneumonia, broncho-
  congenital (infective) 770.0
    aspiration 770.18 ▲
  croupous — *see* Pneumonia, lobar

Pneumonia — *continued*
  cytomegalic inclusion 078.5 *[484.1]*
  deglutition (*see also* Pneumonia, aspiration) 507.0
  desquamative interstitial 516.8
  diffuse — *see* Pneumonia, broncho-
  diplococcal, diplococcus (broncho-) (lobar) 481
  disseminated (focal) — *see* Pneumonia, broncho-
  due to
    adenovirus 480.0
    anaerobes 482.81
    Bacterium anitratum 482.83
    Chlamydia, chlamydial 483.1
      pneumoniae 483.1
      psittaci 073.0
      specified type NEC 483.1
      trachomatis 483.1
    coccidioidomycosis 114.0
    Diplococcus (pneumoniae) 481
    Eaton's agent 483.0
    Escherichia coli (E. coli) 482.82
    Friedländer's bacillus 482.0
    fumes or vapors (chemical) (inhalation) 506.0
    fungus NEC 117.9 *[484.7]*
      coccidioidomycosis 114.0
    Hemophilus influenzae (H. influenzae) 482.2
    Herellea 482.83
    influenza 487.0
    Klebsiella pneumoniae 482.0
    Mycoplasma (pneumoniae) 483.0
    parainfluenza virus 480.2
    pleuropneumonia-like organism (PPLO) 483.0
    Pneumococcus 481
    Pneumocystis carinii 136.3
    Proteus 482.83
    Pseudomonas 482.1
    respiratory syncytial virus 480.1
    rickettsia 083.9 *[484.8]*
    SARS-associated coronavirus 480.3
    specified
      bacteria NEC 482.89
      organism NEC 483.8
      virus NEC 480.8
    Staphylococcus 482.40
      aureus 482.41
      specified type NEC 482.49
    Streptococcus — *see also* Pneumonia, streptococcal
      pneumoniae 481
    virus (*see also* Pneumonia, viral) 480.9
      SARS-associated coronavirus 480.3
  Eaton's agent 483.0
  embolic, embolism (*see* Embolism, pulmonary)
  eosinophilic 518.3
  Escherichia coli (E. coli) 482.82
  Eubacterium 482.81
  fibrinous — *see* Pneumonia, lobar
  fibroid (chronic) (*see also* Fibrosis, lung) 515
  fibrous (*see also* Fibrosis, lung) 515
  Friedländer's bacillus 482.0
  Fusobacterium (nucleatum) 482.81
  gangrenous 513.0
  giant cell (*see also* Pneumonia, viral) 480.9
  gram-negative bacteria NEC 482.83
    anaerobic 482.81
  grippal 487.0
  Hemophilus influenzae (bronchial) (lobar) 482.2
  hypostatic (broncho-) (lobar) 514
  in
    actinomycosis 039.1
    anthrax 022.1 *[484.5]*
    aspergillosis 117.3 *[484.6]*
    candidiasis 112.4
    coccidioidomycosis 114.0
    cytomegalic inclusion disease 078.5 *[484.1]*
    histoplasmosis (*see also* Histoplasmosis) 115.95
    infectious disease NEC 136.9 *[484.8]*
    measles 055.1
    mycosis, systemic NEC 117.9 *[484.7]*
    nocardiasis, nocardiosis 039.1
    ornithosis 073.0
    pneumocystosis 136.3
    psittacosis 073.0
    Q fever 083.0 *[484.8]*

Pneumonia — *continued*
  in — *continued*
    salmonellosis 003.22
    toxoplasmosis 130.4
    tularemia 021.2
    typhoid (fever) 002.0 *[484.8]*
    varicella 052.1
    whooping cough (*see also* Whooping cough) 033.9 *[484.3]*
  infective, acquired prenatally 770.0
  influenzal (broncho) (lobar) (virus) 487.0
  inhalation (*see also* Pneumonia, aspiration) 507.0
    fumes or vapors (chemical) 506.0
  interstitial 516.8
    with influenzal 487.0
    acute 136.3
    chronic (*see also* Fibrosis, lung) 515
    desquamative 516.8
    hypostatic 514
    lipoid 507.1
    lymphoid 516.8
    plasma cell 136.3
    Pseudomonas 482.1
  intrauterine (infective) 770.0
    aspiration 770.18 ▲
      blood 770.16 ●
      clear amniotic fluid 770.14 ●
      meconium 770.12 ●
      postnatal stomach contents 770.86 ●
  Klebsiella pneumoniae 482.0
  Legionnaires' 482.84
  lipid, lipoid (exogenous) (interstitial) 507.1
    endogenous 516.8
  lobar (diplococcal) (disseminated) (double) (interstitial) (pneumococcal, any type) 481
    with influenza 487.0
    bacterial 482.9
      specified type NEC 482.89
    chronic (*see also* Fibrosis, lung) 515
    Escherichia coli (E. coli) 482.82
    Friedländer's bacillus 482.0
    Hemophilus influenzae (H. influenzae) 482.2
    hypostatic 514
    influenzal 487.0
    Klebsiella 482.0
    ornithosis 073.0
    Proteus 482.83
    Pseudomonas 482.1
    psittacosis 073.0
    specified organism NEC 483.8
      bacterial NEC 482.89
    staphylococcal 482.40
      aureus 482.41
      specified type NEC 482.49
    streptococcal — *see* Pneumonia, streptococcal
    viral, virus (*see also* Pneumonia, viral) 480.9
  lobular (confluent) — *see* Pneumonia, broncho-
  Löffler's 518.3
  massive — *see* Pneumonia, lobar
  meconium ►aspiration◄ 770.12 ▲
  metastatic NEC 038.8 *[484.8]*
  Mycoplasma (pneumoniae) 483.0
  necrotic 513.0
  nitrogen dioxide 506.9
  orthostatic 514
  parainfluenza virus 480.2
  parenchymatous (*see also* Fibrosis, lung) 515
  passive 514
  patchy — *see* Pneumonia, broncho-
  Peptococcus 482.81
  Peptostreptococcus 482.81
  plasma cell 136.3
  pleurolobar — *see* Pneumonia, lobar
  pleuropneumonia-like organism (PPLO) 483.0
  pneumococcal (broncho) (lobar) 481
  Pneumocystis (carinii) 136.3
  postinfectional NEC 136.9 *[484.8]*
  postmeasles 055.1
  postoperative 997.3
  primary atypical 486
  Proprionibacterium 482.81
  Proteus 482.83
  Pseudomonas 482.1
  psittacosis 073.0
  radiation 508.0

☑ Additional Digit Required — Refer to the Tabular List (Numeric Code Section) for Additional Digit Selection

Pneumonia — *continued*
  respiratory syncytial virus 480.1
  resulting from a procedure 997.3
  rheumatic 390 *[517.1]*
  Salmonella 003.22
  SARS-associated coronavirus 480.3
  segmented, segmental — *see* Pneumonia,
      broncho-
  Serratia (marcescens) 482.83
  specified
      bacteria NEC 482.89
      organism NEC 483.8
      virus NEC 480.8
  spirochetal 104.8 *[484.8]*
  staphylococcal (broncho) (lobar) 482.40
      aureus 482.41
      specified type NEC 482.49
  static, stasis 514
  streptococcal (broncho) (lobar) NEC 482.30
      Group
          A 482.31
          B 482.32
          specified NEC 482.39
      pneumoniae 481
      specified type NEC 482.39
  Streptococcus pneumoniae 481
  traumatic (complication) (early) (secondary)
      958.8
  tuberculous (any) (*see also* Tuberculosis)
      011.6 ☑
  tularemic 021.2
  TWAR agent 483.1
  varicella 052.1
  Veillonella 482.81
  viral, virus (broncho) (interstitial) (lobar) 480.9
      with influenza, flu, or grippe 487.0
      adenoviral 480.0
      parainfluenza 480.2
      respiratory syncytial 480.1
      SARS-associated coronavirus 480.3
      specified type NEC 480.8
  white (congenital) 090.0
Pneumonic — *see* condition
Pneumonitis (acute) (primary) (*see also*
      Pneumonia) 486
  allergic 495.9
      specified type NEC 495.8
  aspiration 507.0
      due to fumes or gases 506.0
      fetal 770.18   ●
          due to   ●
              blood 770.16   ●
              clear amniotic fluid 770.14   ●
              meconium 770.12   ●
              postnatal stomach contents 770.86   ●
      newborn 770.18   ▲
          due to   ●
              blood 770.16   ●
              clear amniotic fluid 770.14   ●
              meconium 770.12   ●
              postnatal stomach contents 770.86   ●
      obstetric 668.0 ☑
  chemical 506.0
      due to fumes or gases 506.0
  cholesterol 516.8
  chronic (*see also* Fibrosis, lung) 515
  congenital rubella 771.0
  crack 506.0
  due to
      crack (cocaine) 506.0
      fumes or vapors 506.0
      inhalation
          food (regurgitated), milk, vomitus 507.0
          oils, essences 507.1
          saliva 507.0
          solids, liquids NEC 507.8
      toxoplasmosis (acquired) 130.4
          congenital (active) 771.2 *[484.8]*
  eosinophilic 518.3
  fetal aspiration 770.18   ▲
      due to   ●
          blood 770.16   ●
          clear amniotic fluid 770.14   ●
          meconium 770.12   ●
          postnatal stomach contents 770.86   ●

Pneumonitis (*see also* Pneumonia) — *continued*
  hypersensitivity 495.9
  interstitial (chronic) (*see also* Fibrosis, lung)
      515
      lymphoid 516.8
  lymphoid, interstitial 516.8
  meconium ►aspiration◄ 770.12   ▲
  postanesthetic
      correct substance properly administered
          507.0
      obstetric 668.0 ☑
      overdose or wrong substance given 968.4
          specified anesthetic — *see* Table of Drugs
              and Chemicals
  postoperative 997.3
      obstetric 668.0 ☑
  radiation 508.0
  rubella, congenital 771.0
  "ventilation" 495.7
  wood-dust 495.8
Pneumoconiosis — *see* Pneumoconiosis
Pneumoparotid 527.8
Pneumopathy NEC 518.89
  alveolar 516.9
      specified NEC 516.8
  due to dust NEC 504
  parietoalveolar 516.9
      specified condition NEC 516.8
Pneumopericarditis (*see also* Pericarditis) 423.9
  acute 420.90
Pneumopericardium — *see also* Pericarditis
  congenital 770.2
  fetus or newborn 770.2
  traumatic (post) (*see also* Pneumothorax,
      traumatic) 860.0
      with open wound into thorax 860.1
Pneumoperitoneum 568.89
  fetus or newborn 770.2
Pneumophagia (psychogenic) 306.4
Pneumopleurisy, pneumopleuritis (*see also*
      Pneumonia) 486
Pneumopyopericardium 420.99
Pneumopyothorax (*see also* Pyopneumothorax)
      510.9
  with fistula 510.0
Pneumorrhagia 786.3
  newborn 770.3
  tuberculous (*see also* Tuberculosis, pulmonary)
      011.9 ☑
Pneumosiderosis (occupational) 503
Pneumothorax (acute) (chronic) 512.8
  congenital 770.2
  due to operative injury of chest wall or lung
      512.1
      accidental puncture or laceration 512.1
  fetus or newborn 770.2
  iatrogenic 512.1
  postoperative 512.1
  spontaneous 512.8
      fetus or newborn 770.2
      tension 512.0
  sucking 512.8
      iatrogenic 512.1
      postoperative 512.1
  tense valvular, infectional 512.0
  tension 512.0
      iatrogenic 512.1
      postoperative 512.1
      spontaneous 512.0
  traumatic 860.0
      with
          hemothorax 860.4
              with open wound into thorax 860.5
          open wound into thorax 860.1
  tuberculous (*see also* Tuberculosis) 011.7 ☑
Pocket(s)
  endocardial (*see also* Endocarditis) 424.90
  periodontal 523.8
Podagra 274.9
Podencephalus 759.89
Poikilocytosis 790.09
Poikiloderma 709.09
  Civatte's 709.09
  congenital 757.33
  vasculare atrophicans 696.2

Poikilodermatomyositis 710.3
Pointed ear 744.29
Poise imperfect 729.9
Poisoned — *see* Poisoning
Poisoning (acute) — *see also* Table of Drugs and
      Chemicals
  Bacillus, B.
      aertrycke (*see also* Infection, Salmonella) 003.9
      botulinus 005.1
      cholerae (suis) (*see also* Infection,
          Salmonella) 003.9
      paratyphosus (*see also* Infection,
          Salmonella) 003.9
      suipestifer (*see also* Infection, Salmonella)
          003.9
  bacterial toxins NEC 005.9
  berries, noxious 988.2
  blood (general) — *see* Septicemia
  botulism 005.1
  bread, moldy, mouldy — *see* Poisoning, food
  damaged meat — *see* Poisoning, food
  death-cap (Amanita phalloides) (Amanita verna)
      988.1
  decomposed food — *see* Poisoning, food
  diseased food — *see* Poisoning, food
  drug — *see* Table of Drugs and Chemicals
  epidemic, fish, meat, or other food — *see*
      Poisoning, food
  fava bean 282.2
  fish (bacterial) — *see also* Poisoning, food
      noxious 988.0
  food (acute) (bacterial) (diseased) (infected) NEC
      005.9
      due to
          bacillus
              aertrycke (*see also* Poisoning, food,
                  due to Salmonella) 003.9
              botulinus 005.1
              cereus 005.89
              choleraesuis (*see also* Poisoning, food,
                  due to Salmonella) 003.9
              paratyphosus (*see also* Poisoning,
                  food, due to Salmonella) 003.9
              suipestifer (*see also* Poisoning, food,
                  due to Salmonella) 003.9
          Clostridium 005.3
              botulinum 005.1
              perfringens 005.2
              welchii 005.2
          Salmonella (aertrycke) (callinarum)
              (choleraesuis) (enteritidis)
              (paratyphi) (suipestifer) 003.9
              with
                  gastroenteritis 003.0
                  localized infection(s) (*see also*
                      Infection, Salmonella) 003.20
                  septicemia 003.1
                  specified manifestation NEC 003.8
          specified bacterium NEC 005.89
          Staphylococcus 005.0
          Streptococcus 005.89
          Vibrio parahaemolyticus 005.4
          Vibrio vulnificus 005.81
      noxious or naturally toxic 988.0
          berries 988.2
          fish 988.0
          mushroom 988.1
          plants NEC 988.2
  ice cream — *see* Poisoning, food
  ichthyotoxism (bacterial) 005.9
  kreotoxism, food 005.9
  malarial — *see* Malaria
  meat — *see* Poisoning, food
  mushroom (noxious) 988.1
  mussel — *see also* Poisoning, food
      noxious 988.0
  noxious foodstuffs (*see also* Poisoning, food,
      noxious) 988.9
      specified type NEC 988.8
  plants, noxious 988.2
  pork — *see also* Poisoning, food
      specified NEC 988.8
      Trichinosis 124
  ptomaine — *see* Poisoning, food
  putrefaction, food — *see* Poisoning, food
  radiation 508.0

Poisoning — *see also* Table of Drugs and
Chemicals — *continued*
   Salmonella (*see also* Infection, Salmonella)
     003.9
   sausage — *see also* Poisoning, food
     Trichinosis 124
   saxitoxin 988.0
   shellfish — *see also* Poisoning, food
     noxious 988.0
   Staphylococcus, food 005.0
   toxic, from disease NEC 799.89
   truffles — *see* Poisoning, food
   uremic — *see* Uremia
   uric acid 274.9
**Poison ivy, oak, sumac or other plant
   dermatitis** 692.6
Poker spine 720.0
Policeman's disease 729.2
Polioencephalitis (acute) (bulbar) (*see also*
   Poliomyelitis, bulbar) 045.0 ☑
   inferior 335.22
   influenzal 487.8
   superior hemorrhagic (acute) (Wernicke's) 265.1
   Wernicke's (superior hemorrhagic) 265.1
Polioencephalomyelitis (acute) (anterior) (bulbar)
   (*see also* Polioencephalitis) 045.0 ☑
Polioencephalopathy, superior hemorrhagic
   265.1
   with
     beriberi 265.0
     pellagra 265.2
Poliomeningoencephalitis — *see*
   Meningoencephalitis
Poliomyelitis (acute) (anterior) (epidemic)
   045.9 ☑

> *Note* — *Use the following fifth-digit
> subclassification with category 045:*
>
>   *0   poliovirus, unspecified type*
>   *1   poliovirus, type I*
>   *2   poliovirus, type II*
>   *3   poliovirus, type III*

   with
     paralysis 045.1 ☑
       bulbar 045.0 ☑
   abortive 045.2 ☑
   ascending 045.9 ☑
     progressive 045.9 ☑
   bulbar 045.0 ☑
   cerebral 045.0 ☑
   chronic 335.21
   congenital 771.2
   contact V01.2
   deformities 138
   exposure to V01.2
   late effect 138
   nonepidemic 045.9 ☑
   nonparalytic 045.2 ☑
   old with deformity 138
   posterior, acute 053.19
   residual 138
   sequelae 138
   spinal, acute 045.9 ☑
   syphilitic (chronic) 094.89
   vaccination, prophylactic (against) V04.0
Poliosis (eyebrow) (eyelashes) 704.3
   circumscripta (congenital) 757.4
     acquired 704.3
   congenital 757.4
Pollakiuria 788.41
   psychogenic 306.53
Pollinosis 477.0
Pollitzer's disease (hidradenitis suppurativa)
   705.83
Polyadenitis (*see also* Adenitis) 289.3
   malignant 020.0
Polyalgia 729.9
Polyangiitis (essential) 446.0
Polyarteritis (nodosa) (renal) 446.0
Polyarthralgia 719.49
   psychogenic 306.0

Polyarthritis, polyarthropathy NEC 716.59
   due to or associated with other specified
     conditions — *see* Arthritis, due to or
     associated with
   endemic (*see also* Disease, Kaschin-Beck)
     716.0 ☑
   inflammatory 714.9
     specified type NEC 714.89
   juvenile (chronic) 714.30
     acute 714.31
   migratory — *see* Fever, rheumatic
   rheumatic 714.0
     fever (acute) — *see* Fever, rheumatic
Polycarential syndrome of infancy 260
Polychondritis (atrophic) (chronic) (relapsing)
   733.99
Polycoria 743.46
Polycystic (congenital) (disease) 759.89
   degeneration, kidney — *see* Polycystic, kidney
   kidney (congenital) 753.12
     adult type (APKD) 753.13
     autosomal dominant 753.13
     autosomal recessive 753.14
     childhood type (CPKD) 753.14
     infantile type 753.14
   liver 751.62
   lung 518.89
     congenital 748.4
   ovary, ovaries 256.4
   spleen 759.0
Polycythemia (primary) (rubra) (vera) (M9950/1)
   238.4
   acquired 289.0
   benign 289.0
     familial 289.6
   due to
     donor twin 776.4
     fall in plasma volume 289.0
     high altitude 289.0
     maternal-fetal transfusion 776.4
     stress 289.0
   emotional 289.0
   erythropoietin 289.0
   familial (benign) 289.6
   Gaisböck's (hypertonica) 289.0
   high altitude 289.0
   hypertonica 289.0
   hypoxemic 289.0
   neonatorum 776.4
   nephrogenous 289.0
   relative 289.0
   secondary 289.0
   spurious 289.0
   stress 289.0
Polycytosis cryptogenica 289.0
Polydactylism, polydactyly 755.00
   fingers 755.01
   toes 755.02
Polydipsia 783.5
Polydystrophic oligophrenia 277.5
Polyembryoma (M9072/3) — *see* Neoplasm, by
   site, malignant
Polygalactia 676.6 ☑
Polyglandular
   deficiency 258.9
   dyscrasia 258.9
   dysfunction 258.9
   syndrome 258.8
Polyhydramnios (*see also* Hydramnios) 657.0 ☑
Polymastia 757.6
Polymenorrhea 626.2
Polymicrogyria 742.2
Polymyalgia 725
   arteritica 446.5
   rheumatica 725
Polymyositis (acute) (chronic) (hemorrhagic)
   710.4
   with involvement of
     lung 710.4 *[517.8]*
     skin 710.3
   ossificans (generalisata) (progressiva) 728.19
   Wagner's (dermatomyositis) 710.3

Polyneuritis, polyneuritic (*see also*
   Polyneuropathy) 356.9
   alcoholic 357.5
     with psychosis 291.1
   cranialis 352.6
   diabetic 250.6 ☑ *[357.2]*
   demyelinating, chronic inflammatory 357.81
   due to lack of vitamin NEC 269.2 *[357.4]*
   endemic 265.0 *[357.4]*
   erythredema 985.0
   febrile 357.0
   hereditary ataxic 356.3
   idiopathic, acute 357.0
   infective (acute) 357.0
   nutritional 269.9 *[357.4]*
   postinfectious 357.0
Polyneuropathy (peripheral) 356.9
   alcoholic 357.5
   amyloid 277.3 *[357.4]*
   arsenical 357.7
   critical illness 357.82
   diabetic 250.6 ☑ *[357.2]*
   due to
     antitetanus serum 357.6
     arsenic 357.7
     drug or medicinal substance 357.6
       correct substance properly administered
         357.6
       overdose or wrong substance given or
         taken 977.9
       specified drug — *see* Table of Drugs
         and Chemicals
     lack of vitamin NEC 269.2 *[357.4]*
     lead 357.7
     organophosphate compounds 357.7
     pellagra 265.2 *[357.4]*
     porphyria 277.1 *[357.4]*
     serum 357.6
     toxic agent NEC 357.7
   hereditary 356.0
   idiopathic 356.9
     progressive 356.4
   in
     amyloidosis 277.3 *[357.4]*
     avitaminosis 269.2 *[357.4]*
       specified NEC 269.1 *[357.4]*
     beriberi 265.0 *[357.4]*
     collagen vascular disease NEC 710.9 *[357.1]*
     deficiency
       B-complex NEC 266.2 *[357.4]*
       vitamin B 266.9 *[357.4]*
       vitamin B_6 266.1 *[357.4]*
     diabetes 250.6 ☑ *[357.2]*
     diphtheria (*see also* Diphtheria) 032.89
       [357.4]
     disseminated lupus erythematosus 710.0
       [357.1]
     herpes zoster 053.13
     hypoglycemia 251.2 *[357.4]*
     malignant neoplasm (M8000/3) NEC 199.1
       [357.3]
     mumps 072.72
     pellagra 265.2 *[357.4]*
     polyarteritis nodosa 446.0 *[357.1]*
     porphyria 277.1 *[357.4]*
     rheumatoid arthritis 714.0 *[357.1]*
     sarcoidosis 135 *[357.4]*
     uremia 585.9 *[357.4]* ▲
   lead 357.7
   nutritional 269.9 *[357.4]*
     specified NEC 269.8 *[357.4]*
   postherpetic 053.13
   progressive 356.4
   sensory (hereditary) 356.2
Polyonychia 757.5
Polyopia 368.2
   refractive 368.15
Polyorchism, polyorchidism (three testes) 752.89
Polyorrhymenitis (peritoneal) (*see also*
   Polyserositis) 568.82
   pericardial 423.2
Polyostotic fibrous dysplasia 756.54
Polyotia 744.1

Polyp, polypus

Note — Polyps of organs or sites that do not appear in the list below should be coded to the residual category for diseases of the organ or site concerned.

accessory sinus 471.8
adenoid tissue 471.0
adenomatous (M8210/0) — see also Neoplasm, by site, benign
    adenocarcinoma in (M8210/3) — see Neoplasm, by site, malignant
    carcinoma in (M8210/3) — see Neoplasm, by site, malignant
    multiple (M8221/0) — see Neoplasm, by site, benign
antrum 471.8
anus, anal (canal) (nonadenomatous) 569.0
    adenomatous 211.4
Bartholin's gland 624.6
bladder (M8120/1) 236.7
broad ligament 620.8
cervix (uteri) 622.7
    adenomatous 219.0
    in pregnancy or childbirth 654.6 ☑
        affecting fetus or newborn 763.89
        causing obstructed labor 660.2 ☑
    mucous 622.7
    nonneoplastic 622.7
choanal 471.0
cholesterol 575.6
clitoris 624.6
colon (M8210/0) (see also Polyp, adenomatous) 211.3
corpus uteri 621.0
dental 522.0
ear (middle) 385.30
endometrium 621.0
ethmoidal (sinus) 471.8
fallopian tube 620.8
female genital organs NEC 624.8
frontal (sinus) 471.8
gallbladder 575.6
gingiva 523.8
gum 523.8
labia 624.6
larynx (mucous) 478.4
malignant (M8000/3) — see Neoplasm, by site, malignant
maxillary (sinus) 471.8
middle ear 385.30
myometrium 621.0
nares
    anterior 471.9
    posterior 471.0
nasal (mucous) 471.9
    cavity 471.0
    septum 471.9
nasopharyngeal 471.0
neoplastic (M8210/0) — see Neoplasm, by site, benign
nose (mucous) 471.9
oviduct 620.8
paratubal 620.8
pharynx 478.29
    congenital 750.29
placenta, placental 674.4 ☑
prostate 600.20
    with urinary retention 600.21
pudenda 624.6
pulp (dental) 522.0
rectosigmoid 211.4
rectum (nonadenomatous) 569.0
    adenomatous 211.4
septum (nasal) 471.9
sinus (accessory) (ethmoidal) (frontal) (maxillary) (sphenoidal) 471.8
sphenoidal (sinus) 471.8
stomach (M8210/0) 211.1
tube, fallopian 620.8
turbinate, mucous membrane 471.8
ureter 593.89
urethra 599.3
uterine
    ligament 620.8
    tube 620.8

Polyp, polypus — continued
uterus (body) (corpus) (mucous) 621.0
    in pregnancy or childbirth 654.1 ☑
        affecting fetus or newborn 763.89
        causing obstructed labor 660.2 ☑
vagina 623.7
vocal cord (mucous) 478.4
vulva 624.6
Polyphagia 783.6
Polypoid — see condition
Polyposis — see also Polyp
coli (adenomatous) (M8220/0) 211.3
    adenocarcinoma in (M8220/3) 153.9
    carcinoma in (M8220/3) 153.9
familial (M8220/0) 211.3
intestinal (adenomatous) (M8220/0) 211.3
multiple (M8221/0) — see Neoplasm, by site, benign
Polyradiculitis (acute) 357.0
Polyradiculoneuropathy (acute) (segmentally demyelinating) 357.0
Polysarcia 278.00
Polyserositis (peritoneal) 568.82
due to pericarditis 423.2
paroxysmal (familial) 277.3
pericardial 423.2
periodic 277.3
pleural — see Pleurisy
recurrent 277.3
tuberculous (see also Tuberculosis, polyserositis) 018.9 ☑
Polysialia 527.7
Polysplenia syndrome 759.0
Polythelia 757.6
Polytrichia (see also Hypertrichosis) 704.1
Polyunguia (congenital) 757.5
acquired 703.8
Polyuria 788.42
Pompe's disease (glycogenosis II) 271.0
Pompholyx 705.81
Poncet's disease (tuberculous rheumatism) (see also Tuberculosis) 015.9 ☑
Pond fracture — see Fracture, skull, vault
Ponos 085.0
Pons, pontine — see condition
Poor
contractions, labor 661.2 ☑
    affecting fetus or newborn 763.7
fetal growth NEC 764.9 ☑
    affecting management of pregnancy 656.5 ☑
incorporation
    artificial skin graft 996.55
    decellularized allodermis graft 996.55
obstetrical history V13.29
    affecting management of current pregnancy V23.49
        pre-term labor V23.41
    pre-term labor V13.21
sucking reflex (newborn) 796.1
vision NEC 369.9
Poradenitis, nostras 099.1
Porencephaly (congenital) (developmental) (true) 742.4
acquired 348.0
nondevelopmental 348.0
traumatic (post) 310.2
Porocephaliasis 134.1
Porokeratosis 757.39
disseminated superficial actinic (DSAP) 692.75
Poroma, eccrine (M8402/0) — see Neoplasm, skin, benign
Porphyria (acute) (congenital) (constitutional) (erythropoietic) (familial) (hepatica) (idiopathic) (idiosyncratic) (intermittent) (latent) (mixed hepatic) (photosensitive) (South African genetic) (Swedish) 277.1
acquired 277.1
cutaneatarda
    hereditaria 277.1
    symptomatica 277.1

Porphyria — continued
due to drugs
    correct substance properly administered 277.1
    overdose or wrong substance given or taken 977.9
        specified drug — see Table of Drugs and Chemicals
secondary 277.1
toxic NEC 277.1
variegata 277.1
Porphyrinuria (acquired) (congenital) (secondary) 277.1
Porphyruria (acquired) (congenital) 277.1
Portal — see condition
Port wine nevus or mark 757.32
Posadas-Wernicke disease 114.9
Position
fetus, abnormal (see also Presentation, fetal) 652.9 ☑
teeth, faulty (see also Anomaly, position tooth) 524.30
Positive
culture (nonspecific) 795.39
    AIDS virus V08
    blood 790.7
    HIV V08
    human immunodeficiency virus V08
    nose 795.39
    skin lesion NEC 795.39
    spinal fluid 792.0
    sputum 795.39
    stool 792.1
    throat 795.39
    urine 791.9
    wound 795.39
findings, anthrax 795.31
HIV V08
human immunodeficiency virus (HIV) V08
PPD 795.5
serology
    AIDS virus V08
        inconclusive 795.71
    HIV V08
        inconclusive 795.71
    human immunodeficiency virus (HIV) V08
        inconclusive 795.71
    syphilis 097.1
        with signs or symptoms — see Syphilis, by site and stage
        false 795.6
    skin test 795.7 ☑
        tuberculin (without active tuberculosis) 795.5
    VDRL 097.1
        with signs or symptoms — see Syphilis, by site and stage
        false 795.6
    Wassermann reaction 097.1
        false 795.6
Postcardiotomy syndrome 429.4
Postcaval ureter 753.4
Postcholecystectomy syndrome 576.0
Postclimacteric bleeding 627.1
Postcommissurotomy syndrome 429.4
Postconcussional syndrome 310.2
Postcontusional syndrome 310.2
Postcricoid region — see condition
Post-dates (pregnancy) — see Pregnancy
Postencephalitic — see also condition
syndrome 310.8
Posterior — see condition
Posterolateral sclerosis (spinal cord) — see Degeneration, combined
Postexanthematous — see condition
Postfebrile — see condition
Postgastrectomy dumping syndrome 564.2
Posthemiplegic chorea 344.89
Posthemorrhagic anemia (chronic) 280.0
acute 285.1
newborn 776.5
Posthepatitis syndrome 780.79

Postherpetic neuralgia (intercostal) (syndrome)
(zoster) 053.19
geniculate ganglion 053.11
ophthalmica 053.19
trigeminal 053.12

Posthitis 607.1

Postimmunization complication or reaction —
see Complications, vaccination

Postinfectious — see condition

Postinfluenzal syndrome 780.79

Postlaminectomy syndrome 722.80
cervical, cervicothoracic 722.81
kyphosis 737.12
lumbar, lumbosacral 722.83
thoracic, thoracolumbar 722.82

Postleukotomy syndrome 310.0

Postlobectomy syndrome 310.0

Postmastectomy lymphedema (syndrome) 457.0

Postmaturity, postmature (fetus or newborn)
(gestation period over 42 completed weeks)
766.22
affecting management of pregnancy
post-term pregnancy 645.1 ☑
prolonged pregnancy 645.2 ☑
syndrome 766.22

Postmeasles — see also condition
complication 055.8
specified NEC 055.79

Postmenopausal
endometrium (atrophic) 627.8
suppurative (see also Endometritis) 615.9
hormone replacement therapy V07.4
status (age related) (natural) V49.81

Postnasal drip — see Sinusitis

Postnatal — see condition

Postoperative — see also condition
confusion state 293.9
psychosis 293.9
status NEC (see also Status (post)) V45.89

Postpancreatectomy hyperglycemia 251.3

Postpartum — see also condition
anemia 648.2 ☑
cardiomyopathy 674.5 ☑
observation
immediately after delivery V24.0
routine follow-up V24.2

Postperfusion syndrome NEC 999.8
bone marrow 996.85

Postpoliomyelitic — see condition

Postsurgery status NEC (see also Status (post))
V45.89

Post-term (pregnancy) 645.1 ☑
infant (gestation period over 40 completed
weeks to 42 completed weeks) 766.21

Posttraumatic — see condition

Posttraumatic brain syndrome, nonpsychotic
310.2

Post-typhoid abscess 002.0

Postures, hysterical 300.11

Postvaccinal reaction or complication — see
Complications, vaccination

Postvagotomy syndrome 564.2

Postvalvulotomy syndrome 429.4

Postvasectomy sperm count V25.8

Potain's disease (pulmonary edema) 514

Potain's syndrome (gastrectasis with dyspepsia)
536.1

Pott's
curvature (spinal) (see also Tuberculosis)
015.0 ☑ [737.43]
disease or paraplegia (see also Tuberculosis)
015.0 ☑ [730.88]
fracture (closed) 824.4
open 824.5
gangrene 440.24
osteomyelitis (see also Tuberculosis)
015.0 ☑ [730.88]
spinal curvature (see also Tuberculosis)
015.0 ☑ [737.43]
tumor, puffy (see also Osteomyelitis) 730.2 ☑

Potter's
asthma 502
disease 753.0
facies 754.0
lung 502
syndrome (with renal agenesis) 753.0

Pouch
bronchus 748.3
Douglas' — see condition
esophagus, esophageal (congenital) 750.4
acquired 530.6
gastric 537.1
Hartmann's (abnormal sacculation of
gallbladder neck) 575.8
of intestine V44.3
attention to V55.3
pharynx, pharyngeal (congenital) 750.27

Poulet's disease 714.2

Poultrymen's itch 133.8

Poverty V60.2

Prader-Labhart-Willi-Fanconi syndrome
(hypogenital dystrophy with diabetic
tendency) 759.81

Prader-Willi syndrome (hypogenital dystrophy
with diabetic tendency) 759.81

Preachers' voice 784.49

Pre-AIDS — see Human immunodeficiency virus
(disease) (illness) (infection)

Preauricular appendage 744.1

Prebetalipoproteinemia (acquired) (essential)
(familial) (hereditary) (primary) (secondary)
272.1
with chylomicronemia 272.3

Precipitate labor 661.3 ☑
affecting fetus or newborn 763.6

Preclimacteric bleeding 627.0
menorrhagia 627.0

Precocious
adrenarche 259.1
menarche 259.1
menstruation 626.8
pubarche 259.1
puberty NEC 259.1
sexual development NEC 259.1
thelarche 259.1

Precocity, sexual (constitutional) (cryptogenic)
(female) (idiopathic) (male) NEC 259.1
with adrenal hyperplasia 255.2

Precordial pain 786.51
psychogenic 307.89

Predeciduous teeth 520.2

Prediabetes, prediabetic 790.29
complicating pregnancy, childbirth, or
puerperium 648.8 ☑
fetus or newborn 775.8

Predislocation status of hip, at birth (see also
Subluxation, congenital, hip) 754.32

Preeclampsia (mild) 642.4 ☑
with pre-existing hypertension 642.7 ☑
affecting fetus or newborn 760.0
severe 642.5 ☑
superimposed on pre-existing hypertensive
disease 642.7 ☑

Preeruptive color change, teeth, tooth 520.8

Preexcitation 426.7
atrioventricular conduction 426.7
ventricular 426.7

Preglaucoma 365.00

Pregnancy (single) (uterine) (without sickness)
V22.2

Note — Use the following fifth-digit
subclassification with categories 640-648, 651-
676:

0 unspecified as to episode of care

1 delivered, with or without mention of
antepartum condition

2 delivered, with mention of postpartum
complication

3 antepartum condition or complication

4 postpartum condition or complication

Pregnancy — continued
abdominal (ectopic) 633.00
with intrauterine pregnancy 633.01
affecting fetus or newborn 761.4
abnormal NEC 646.9 ☑
ampullar — see Pregnancy, tubal
broad ligament — see Pregnancy, cornual
cervical — see Pregnancy, cornual
combined (extrauterine and intrauterine) — see
Pregnancy, cornual
complicated (by) 646.9 ☑
abnormal, abnormality NEC 646.9 ☑
cervix 654.6 ☑
cord (umbilical) 663.9 ☑
glucose tolerance (conditions classifiable
to 790.21-790.29) 648.8 ☑
pelvic organs or tissues NEC 654.9 ☑
pelvis (bony) 653.0 ☑
perineum or vulva 654.8 ☑
placenta, placental (vessel) 656.7 ☑
position
cervix 654.4 ☑
placenta 641.1 ☑
without hemorrhage 641.0 ☑
uterus 654.4 ☑
size, fetus 653.5 ☑
uterus (congenital) 654.0 ☑
abscess or cellulitis
bladder 646.6 ☑
genitourinary tract (conditions classifiable
to 590, 595, 597, 599.0, 614.0-
614.5, 614.7-614.9, 615) 646.6 ☑
kidney 646.6 ☑
urinary tract NEC 646.6 ☑
adhesion, pelvic peritoneal 648.9 ☑
air embolism 673.0 ☑
albuminuria 646.2 ☑
with hypertension — see Toxemia, of
pregnancy
amnionitis 658.4 ☑
amniotic fluid embolism 673.1 ☑
anemia (conditions classifiable to 280-285)
648.2 ☑
atrophy, yellow (acute) (liver) (subacute)
646.7 ☑
bacilluria, asymptomatic 646.5 ☑
bacteriuria, asymptomatic 646.5 ☑
bicornis or bicornuate uterus 654.0 ☑
biliary problems 646.8 ☑
bone and joint disorders (conditions
classifiable to 720-724 or conditions
affecting lower limbs classifiable to
711-719, 725-738) 648.7 ☑
breech presentation (buttocks) (complete)
(frank) 652.2 ☑
with successful version 652.1 ☑
cardiovascular disease (conditions
classifiable to 390-398, 410-429)
648.6 ☑
congenital (conditions classifiable to 745-
747) 648.5 ☑
cerebrovascular disorders (conditions
classifiable to 430-434, 436-437)
674.0 ☑
cervicitis (conditions classifiable to 616.0)
646.6 ☑
chloasma (gravidarum) 646.8 ☑
chorea (gravidarum) — see Eclampsia,
pregnancy
cholelithiasis 646.8 ☑
contraction, pelvis (general) 653.1 ☑
inlet 653.2 ☑
outlet 653.3 ☑
convulsions (eclamptic) (uremic) 642.6 ☑
with pre-existing hypertension 642.7 ☑
current disease or condition (nonobstetric)
abnormal glucose tolerance 648.8 ☑
anemia 648.2 ☑
bone and joint (lower limb) 648.7 ☑
cardiovascular 648.6 ☑
congenital 648.5 ☑
cerebrovascular 674.0 ☑
diabetic 648.0 ☑
drug dependence 648.3 ☑
female genital mutilation 648.9 ☑ ●

Pregnancy — *continued*
  complicated (by) — *continued*
    current disease or condition — *continued*
      genital organ or tract 646.6 ☑
      gonorrheal 647.1 ☑
      hypertensive 642.2 ☑
        renal 642.1 ☑
      infectious 647.9 ☑
        specified type NEC 647.8 ☑
      liver 646.7 ☑
      malarial 647.4 ☑
      nutritional deficiency 648.9 ☑
      parasitic NEC 647.8 ☑
      periodontal disease 648.9 ☑
      renal 646.2 ☑
        hypertensive 642.1 ☑
      rubella 647.5 ☑
      specified condition NEC 648.9 ☑
      syphilitic 647.0 ☑
      thyroid 648.1 ☑
      tuberculous 647.3 ☑
      urinary 646.6 ☑
      venereal 647.2 ☑
      viral NEC 647.6 ☑
    cystitis 646.6 ☑
    cystocele 654.4 ☑
    death of fetus (near term) 656.4 ☑
      early pregnancy (before 22 completed
        weeks gestation) 632
    deciduitis 646.6 ☑
    decreased fetal movements 655.7 ☑
    diabetes (mellitus) (conditions classifiable to
      250) 648.0 ☑
    disorders of liver 646.7 ☑
    displacement, uterus NEC 654.4 ☑
    disproportion — *see* Disproportion
    double uterus 654.0 ☑
    drug dependence (conditions classifiable to
      304) 648.3 ☑
    dysplasia, cervix 654.6 ☑
    early onset of delivery (spontaneous)
      644.2 ☑
    eclampsia, eclamptic (coma) (convulsions)
      (delirium) (nephritis) (uremia) 642.6 ☑
      with pre-existing hypertension 642.7 ☑
    edema 646.1 ☑
      with hypertension — *see* Toxemia, of
        pregnancy
    effusion, amniotic fluid 658.1 ☑
      delayed delivery following 658.2 ☑
    embolism
      air 673.0 ☑
      amniotic fluid 673.1 ☑
      blood-clot 673.2 ☑
      cerebral 674.0 ☑
      pulmonary NEC 673.2 ☑
      pyemic 673.3 ☑
      septic 673.3 ☑
    emesis (gravidarum) — *see* Pregnancy,
      complicated, vomiting
    endometritis (conditions classifiable to
      615.0-615.9) 646.6 ☑
      decidual 646.6 ☑
    excessive weight gain NEC 646.1 ☑
    face presentation 652.4 ☑
    failure, fetal head to enter pelvic brim
      652.5 ☑
    false labor (pains) 644.1 ☑
    fatigue 646.8 ☑
    fatty metamorphosis of liver 646.7 ☑
    female genital mutilation 648.9 ☑   ●
    fetal
      death (near term) 656.4 ☑
        early (before 22 completed weeks
          gestation) 632
      deformity 653.7 ☑
      distress 656.8 ☑
      reduction of multiple fetuses reduced ●
        to single fetus 651.7 ☑   ●
    fibroid (tumor) (uterus) 654.1 ☑
    footling presentation 652.8 ☑
      with successful version 652.1 ☑
    gallbladder disease 646.8 ☑
    goiter 648.1 ☑
    gonococcal infection (conditions classifiable
      to 098) 647.1 ☑

Pregnancy — *continued*
  complicated (by) — *continued*
    gonorrhea (conditions classifiable to 098)
      647.1 ☑
    hemorrhage 641.9 ☑
      accidental 641.2 ☑
      before 22 completed weeks gestation NEC
        640.9 ☑
      cerebrovascular 674.0 ☑
      due to
        afibrinogenemia or other coagulation
          defect (conditions classifiable to
          286.0-286.9) 641.3 ☑
        leiomyoma, uterine 641.8 ☑
        marginal sinus (rupture) 641.2 ☑
        premature separation, placenta
          641.2 ☑
        trauma 641.8 ☑
      early (before 22 completed weeks
        gestation) 640.9 ☑
      threatened abortion 640.0 ☑
      unavoidable 641.1 ☑
    hepatitis (acute) (malignant) (subacute)
      646.7 ☑
      viral 647.6 ☑
    herniation of uterus 654.4 ☑
    high head at term 652.5 ☑
    hydatidiform mole (delivered) (undelivered)
      630
    hydramnios 657.0 ☑
    hydrocephalic fetus 653.6 ☑
    hydrops amnii 657.0 ☑
    hydrorrhea 658.1 ☑
    hyperemesis (gravidarum) — *see*
      Hyperemesis, gravidarum
    hypertension — *see* Hypertension,
      complicating pregnancy
    hypertensive
      heart and renal disease 642.2 ☑
      heart disease 642.2 ☑
      renal disease 642.2 ☑
    hyperthyroidism 648.1 ☑
    hypothyroidism 648.1 ☑
    hysteralgia 646.8 ☑
    icterus gravis 646.7 ☑
    incarceration, uterus 654.3 ☑
    incompetent cervix (os) 654.5 ☑
    infection 647.9 ☑
      amniotic fluid 658.4 ☑
      bladder 646.6 ☑
      genital organ (conditions classifiable to
        614.0-614.5, 614.7-614.9, 615)
        646.6 ☑
      kidney (conditions classifiable to 590.0-
        590.9) 646.6 ☑
      urinary (tract) 646.6 ☑
        asymptomatic 646.5 ☑
    infective and parasitic diseases NEC
      647.8 ☑
    inflammation
      bladder 646.6 ☑
      genital organ (conditions classifiable to
        614.0-614.5, 614.7-614.9, 615)
        646.6 ☑
      urinary tract NEC 646.6 ☑
    injury 648.9 ☑
    insufficient weight gain 646.8 ☑
    intrauterine fetal death (near term) NEC
      656.4 ☑
      early (before 22 completed weeks'
        gestation) 632
    malaria (conditions classifiable to 084)
      647.4 ☑
    malformation, uterus (congenital) 654.0 ☑
    malnutrition (conditions classifiable to 260-
      269) 648.9 ☑
    malposition
      fetus — *see* Pregnancy, complicated,
        malpresentation
      uterus or cervix 654.4 ☑
    malpresentation 652.9 ☑
      with successful version 652.1 ☑
      in multiple gestation 652.6 ☑
      specified type NEC 652.8 ☑
    marginal sinus hemorrhage or rupture
      641.2 ☑
    maternal obesity syndrome 646.1 ☑
    menstruation 640.8 ☑

Pregnancy — *continued*
  complicated (by) — *continued*
    mental disorders (conditions classifiable to
      290-303, 305-316, 317-319) 648.4 ☑
    mentum presentation 652.4 ☑
    missed
      abortion 632
      delivery (at or near term) 656.4 ☑
      labor (at or near term) 656.4 ☑
    necrosis
      genital organ or tract (conditions
        classifiable to 614.0-614.5, 614.7-
        614.9, 615) 646.6 ☑
      liver (conditions classifiable to 570)
        646.7 ☑
      renal, cortical 646.2 ☑
    nephritis or nephrosis (conditions
      classifiable to 580-589) 646.2 ☑
      with hypertension 642.1 ☑
    nephropathy NEC 646.2 ☑
    neuritis (peripheral) 646.4 ☑
    nutritional deficiency (conditions classifiable
      to 260-269) 648.9 ☑
    oblique lie or presentation 652.3 ☑
      with successful version 652.1 ☑
    obstetrical trauma NEC 665.9 ☑
    oligohydramnios NEC 658.0 ☑
    onset of contractions before 37 weeks
      644.0 ☑
    oversize fetus 653.5 ☑
    papyraceous fetus 646.0 ☑
    patent cervix 654.5 ☑
    pelvic inflammatory disease (conditions
      classifiable to 614.0-614.5, 614.7-
      614.9, 615) 646.6 ☑
    pelvic peritoneal adhesion 648.9 ☑
    placenta, placental
      abnormality 656.7 ☑
      abruptio or ablatio 641.2 ☑
      detachment 641.2 ☑
      disease 656.7 ☑
      infarct 656.7 ☑
      low implantation 641.1 ☑
        without hemorrhage 641.0 ☑
      malformation 656.7 ☑
      malposition 641.1 ☑
        without hemorrhage 641.0 ☑
      marginal sinus hemorrhage 641.2 ☑
      previa 641.1 ☑
        without hemorrhage 641.0 ☑
      separation (premature) (undelivered)
        641.2 ☑
    placentitis 658.4 ☑
    polyhydramnios 657.0 ☑
    postmaturity
      post-term 645.1 ☑
      prolonged 645.2 ☑
    prediabetes 648.8 ☑
    pre-eclampsia (mild) 642.4 ☑
      severe 642.5 ☑
      superimposed on pre-existing
        hypertensive disease 642.7 ☑
    premature rupture of membranes 658.1 ☑
      with delayed delivery 658.2 ☑
    previous
      infertility V23.0
      nonobstetric condition V23.89
      poor obstetrical history V23.49
      premature delivery V23.41
      trophoblastic disease (conditions
        classifiable to 630) V23.1
    prolapse, uterus 654.4 ☑
    proteinuria (gestational) 646.2 ☑
      with hypertension — *see* Toxemia, of
        pregnancy
    pruritus (neurogenic) 646.8 ☑
    psychosis or psychoneurosis 648.4 ☑
    ptyalism 646.8 ☑
    pyelitis (conditions classifiable to 590.0-
      590.9) 646.6 ☑
    renal disease or failure NEC 646.2 ☑
      with secondary hypertension 642.1 ☑
      hypertensive 642.2 ☑
    retention, retained dead ovum 631
    retroversion, uterus 654.3 ☑
    Rh immunization, incompatibility, or
      sensitization 656.1 ☑

Pregnancy — *continued*
  complicated (by) — *continued*
    rubella (conditions classifiable to 056)
      647.5 ☑
    rupture
      amnion (premature) 658.1 ☑
        with delayed delivery 658.2 ☑
      marginal sinus (hemorrhage) 641.2 ☑
      membranes (premature) 658.1 ☑
        with delayed delivery 658.2 ☑
      uterus (before onset of labor) 665.0 ☑
    salivation (excessive) 646.8 ☑
    salpingo-oophoritis (conditions classifiable to
      614.0-614.2) 646.6 ☑
    septicemia (conditions classifiable to 038.0-
      038.9) 647.8 ☑
      postpartum 670.0 ☑
      puerperal 670.0 ☑
    spasms, uterus (abnormal) 646.8 ☑
    specified condition NEC 646.8 ☑
    spurious labor pains 644.1 ☑
    superfecundation 651.9 ☑
    superfetation 651.9 ☑
    syphilis (conditions classifiable to 090-097)
      647.0 ☑
    threatened
      abortion 640.0 ☑
      premature delivery 644.2 ☑
      premature labor 644.0 ☑
    thrombophlebitis (superficial) 671.2 ☑
      deep 671.3 ☑
    thrombosis 671.9 ☑
      venous (superficial) 671.2 ☑
        deep 671.3 ☑
    thyroid dysfunction (conditions classifiable
      to 240-246) 648.1 ☑
    thyroiditis 648.1 ☑
    thyrotoxicosis 648.1 ☑
    torsion of uterus 654.4 ☑
    toxemia — *see* Toxemia, of pregnancy
    transverse lie or presentation 652.3 ☑
      with successful version 652.1 ☑
    trauma 648.9 ☑
      obstetrical 665.9 ☑
    tuberculosis (conditions classifiable to 010-
      018) 647.3 ☑
    tumor
      cervix 654.6 ☑
      ovary 654.4 ☑
      pelvic organs or tissue NEC 654.4 ☑
      uterus (body) 654.1 ☑
        cervix 654.6 ☑
      vagina 654.7 ☑
      vulva 654.8 ☑
    unstable lie 652.0 ☑
    uremia — *see* Pregnancy, complicated, renal
      disease
    urethritis 646.6 ☑
    vaginitis or vulvitis (conditions classifiable to
      616.1) 646.6 ☑
    varicose
      placental vessels 656.7 ☑
      veins (legs) 671.0 ☑
        perineum 671.1 ☑
        vulva 671.1 ☑
    varicosity, labia or vulva 671.1 ☑
    venereal disease NEC (conditions classifiable
      to 099) 647.2 ☑
    viral disease NEC (conditions classifiable to
      042, 050-055, 057-079) 647.6 ☑
    vomiting (incoercible) (pernicious)
      (persistent) (uncontrollable) (vicious)
      643.9 ☑
      due to organic disease or other cause
        643.8 ☑
      early — *see* Hyperemesis, gravidarum
      late (after 22 completed weeks gestation)
        643.2 ☑
    young maternal age 659.8 ☑
  complications NEC 646.9 ☑
  cornual 633.80
    with intrauterine pregnancy 633.81
    affecting fetus or newborn 761.4
  death, maternal NEC 646.9 ☑
  delivered — *see* Delivery
  ectopic (ruptured) NEC 633.90
    with intrauterine pregnancy 633.91
    abdominal — *see* Pregnancy, abdominal

Pregnancy — *continued*
  ectopic NEC — *continued*
    affecting fetus or newborn 761.4
    combined (extrauterine and intrauterine) —
      see Pregnancy, cornual
    ovarian — *see* Pregnancy, ovarian
    specified type NEC 633.80
      with intrauterine pregnancy 633.81
      affecting fetus or newborn 761.4
    tubal — *see* Pregnancy, tubal
  examination, pregnancy
    negative result V72.41
    not confirmed V72.40
    positive result V72.42   ●
  extrauterine — *see* Pregnancy, ectopic
  fallopian — *see* Pregnancy, tubal
  false 300.11
    labor (pains) 644.1 ☑
  fatigue 646.8 ☑
  illegitimate V61.6
  incidental finding V22.2
  in double uterus 654.0 ☑
  interstitial — *see* Pregnancy, cornual
  intraligamentous — *see* Pregnancy, cornual
  intramural — *see* Pregnancy, cornual
  intraperitoneal — *see* Pregnancy, abdominal
  isthmian — *see* Pregnancy, tubal
  management affected by
    abnormal, abnormality
      fetus (suspected) 655.9 ☑
        specified NEC 655.8 ☑
      placenta 656.7 ☑
    advanced maternal age NEC 659.6 ☑
      multigravida 659.6 ☑
      primigravida 659.5 ☑
    antibodies (maternal)
      anti-c 656.1 ☑
      anti-d 656.1 ☑
      anti-e 656.1 ☑
      blood group (ABO) 656.2 ☑
        Rh(esus) 656.1 ☑
    elderly multigravida 659.6 ☑
    elderly primigravida 659.5 ☑
    fetal (suspected)
      abnormality 655.9 ☑
        acid-base balance 656.8 ☑
        heart rate or rhythm 659.7 ☑
        specified NEC 655.8 ☑
      acidemia 656.3 ☑
      anencephaly 655.0 ☑
      bradycardia 659.7 ☑
      central nervous system malformation
        655.0 ☑
      chromosomal abnormalities (conditions
        classifiable to 758.0-758.9) 655.1 ☑
      damage from
        drugs 655.5 ☑
          obstetric, anesthetic, or sedative
          655.5 ☑
        environmental toxins 655.8 ☑
        intrauterine contraceptive device
          655.8 ☑
        maternal
          alcohol addiction 655.4 ☑
          disease NEC 655.4 ☑
          drug use 655.5 ☑
          listeriosis 655.4 ☑
          rubella 655.3 ☑
          toxoplasmosis 655.4 ☑
          viral infection 655.3 ☑
        radiation 655.6 ☑
      death (near term) 656.4 ☑
        early (before 22 completed weeks'
          gestation) 632
      distress 656.8 ☑
      excessive growth 656.6 ☑
      growth retardation 656.5 ☑
      hereditary disease 655.2 ☑
      hydrocephalus 655.0 ☑
      intrauterine death 656.4 ☑
      poor growth 656.5 ☑
      spina bifida (with myelomeningocele)
        655.0 ☑
    fetal-maternal hemorrhage 656.0 ☑
    hereditary disease in family (possibly)
      affecting fetus 655.2 ☑
    incompatibility, blood groups (ABO)
      656.2 ☑

Pregnancy — *continued*
  management affected by — *continued*
    fetal — *continued*
      Rh(esus) 656.1 ☑
    insufficient prenatal care V23.7
    intrauterine death 656.4 ☑
    isoimmunization (ABO) 656.2 ☑
      Rh(esus) 656.1 ☑
    large-for-dates fetus 656.6 ☑
    light-for-dates fetus 656.5 ☑
    meconium in liquor 656.8 ☑
    mental disorder (conditions classifiable to
      290-303, 305-316, 317-319) 648.4 ☑
    multiparity (grand) 659.4 ☑
    poor obstetric history V23.49
      pre-term labor V23.41
    postmaturity
      post-term 645.1 ☑
      prolonged 645.2 ☑
    post-term pregnancy 645.1 ☑
    previous
      abortion V23.2
        habitual 646.3 ☑
      cesarean delivery 654.2 ☑
      difficult delivery V23.49
      forceps delivery V23.49
      habitual abortions 646.3 ☑
      hemorrhage, antepartum or postpartum
        V23.49
      hydatidiform mole V23.1
      infertility V23.0
      malignancy NEC V23.89
      nonobstetrical conditions V23.89
      premature delivery V23.41
      trophoblastic disease (conditions in 630)
        V23.1
      vesicular mole V23.1
    prolonged pregnancy 645.2 ☑
    small-for-dates fetus 656.5 ☑
    young maternal age 659.8 ☑
  maternal death NEC 646.9 ☑
  mesometric (mural) — *see* Pregnancy, cornual
  molar 631
    hydatidiform (*see also* Hydatidiform mole)
      630
      previous, affecting management of
        pregnancy V23.1
    previous, affecting management of
      pregnancy V23.49
  multiple NEC 651.9 ☑
    with fetal loss and retention of one or more
      fetus(es) 651.6 ☑
    affecting fetus or newborn 761.5
    following (elective) fetal reduction   ●
      651.7 ☑   ●
    specified type NEC 651.8 ☑
      with fetal loss and retention of one or
        more fetus(es) 651.6 ☑
      following (elective) fetal reduction   ●
        651.7 ☑   ●
  mural — *see* Pregnancy, cornual
  observation NEC V22.1
    first pregnancy V22.0
    high-risk V23.9
      specified problem NEC V23.89
  ovarian 633.20
    with intrauterine pregnancy 633.21
    affecting fetus or newborn 761.4
  possible, not (yet) confirmed V72.40
  postmature
    post-term 645.1 ☑
    prolonged 645.2 ☑
  post-term 645.1 ☑
  prenatal care only V22.1
    first pregnancy V22.0
    high-risk V23.9
      specified problem NEC V23.89
  prolonged 645.2 ☑
  quadruplet NEC 651.2 ☑
    with fetal loss and retention of one or more
      fetus(es) 651.5 ☑
    affecting fetus or newborn 761.5
    following (elective) fetal reduction   ●
      651.7 ☑   ●
  quintuplet NEC 651.8 ☑
    with fetal loss and retention of one or more
      fetus(es) 651.6 ☑

☑ Additional Digit Required — Refer to the Tabular List (Numeric Code Section) for Additional Digit Selection

Pregnancy — *continued*
  quintuplet NEC — *continued*
    affecting fetus or newborn 761.5
    following (elective) fetal reduction ●
      651.7 ☑ ●
  sextuplet NEC 651.8 ☑
    with fetal loss and retention of one or more
      fetus(es) 651.6 ☑
    affecting fetus or newborn 761.5
    following (elective) fetal reduction ●
      651.7 ☑ ●
  spurious 300.11
  superfecundation NEC 651.9 ☑
    with fetal loss and retention of one or more
      fetus(es) 651.6 ☑
    following (elective) fetal reduction ●
      651.7 ☑ ●
  superfetation NEC 651.9 ☑
    with fetal loss and retention of one or more
      fetus(es) 651.6 ☑
    following (elective) fetal reduction ●
      651.7 ☑ ●
  supervision (of) (for) — *see also* Pregnancy,
      management affected by
    elderly
      multigravida V23.82
      primigravida V23.81
    high-risk V23.9
      insufficient prenatal care V23.7
      specified problem NEC V23.89
    multiparity V23.3
    normal NEC V22.1
      first V22.0
    poor
      obstetric history V23.49
        pre-term labor V23.41
      reproductive history V23.5
    previous
      abortion V23.2
      hydatidiform mole V23.1
      infertility V23.0
      neonatal death V23.5
      stillbirth V23.5
      trophoblastic disease V23.1
      vesicular mole V23.1
    specified problem NEC V23.89
    young
      multigravida V23.84
      primigravida V23.83
  triplet NEC 651.1 ☑
    with fetal loss and retention of one or more
      fetus(es) 651.4 ☑
    affecting fetus or newborn 761.5
    following (elective) fetal reduction ●
      651.7 ☑ ●
  tubal (with rupture) 633.10
    with intrauterine pregnancy 633.11
    affecting fetus or newborn 761.4
  twin NEC 651.0 ☑
    with fetal loss and retention of one fetus
      651.3 ☑
    affecting fetus or newborn 761.5
    following (elective) fetal reduction ●
      651.7 ☑ ●
  unconfirmed V72.40
  undelivered (no other diagnosis) V22.2
    with false labor 644.1 ☑
    high-risk V23.9
      specified problem NEC V23.89
  unwanted NEC V61.7
Pregnant uterus — *see* condition
Preiser's disease (osteoporosis) 733.09
Prekwashiorkor 260
Preleukemia 238.7
Preluxation of hip, congenital (*see also*
      Subluxation, congenital, hip) 754.32
Premature — *see also* condition
  beats (nodal) 427.60
    atrial 427.61
    auricular 427.61
    postoperative 997.1
    specified type NEC 427.69
    supraventricular 427.61
    ventricular 427.69
  birth NEC 765.1 ☑

Premature — *see also* condition — *continued*
  closure
    cranial suture 756.0
    fontanel 756.0
    foramen ovale 745.8
  contractions 427.60
    atrial 427.61
    auricular 427.61
    auriculoventricular 427.61
    heart (extrasystole) 427.60
    junctional 427.60
    nodal 427.60
    postoperative 997.1
    ventricular 427.69
  ejaculation 302.75
  infant NEC 765.1 ☑
    excessive 765.0 ☑
    light-for-dates — *see* Light-for-dates
  labor 644.2 ☑
    threatened 644.0 ☑
  lungs 770.4
  menopause 256.31
  puberty 259.1
  rupture of membranes or amnion 658.1 ☑
    affecting fetus or newborn 761.1
    delayed delivery following 658.2 ☑
  senility (syndrome) 259.8
  separation, placenta (partial) — *see* Placenta,
      separation
  ventricular systole 427.69
Prematurity NEC 765.1 ☑
  extreme 765.0 ☑
Premenstrual syndrome 625.4
Premenstrual tension 625.4
Premolarization, cuspids 520.2
Premyeloma 273.1
Prenatal
  care, normal pregnancy V22.1
    first V22.0
  death, cause unknown — *see* Death, fetus
  screening — *see* Antenatal, screening
Prepartum — *see* condition
Preponderance, left or right ventricular 429.3
Prepuce — *see* condition
Presbycardia 797
  hypertensive (*see also* Hypertension, heart)
      402.90
Presbycusis 388.01
Presbyesophagus 530.89
Presbyophrenia 310.1
Presbyopia 367.4
Prescription of contraceptives NEC V25.02
  diaphragm V25.02
  oral (pill) V25.01
    emergency V25.03
    postcoital V25.03
    repeat V25.41
  repeat V25.40
    oral (pill) V25.41
Presenile — *see also* condition
  aging 259.8
  dementia (*see also* Dementia, presenile) 290.10
Presenility 259.8
Presentation, fetal
  abnormal 652.9 ☑
    with successful version 652.1 ☑
    before labor, affecting fetus or newborn
      761.7
    causing obstructed labor 660.0 ☑
      affecting fetus or newborn, any, except
        breech 763.1
    in multiple gestation (one or more) 652.6 ☑
    specified NEC 652.8 ☑
  arm 652.7 ☑
    causing obstructed labor 660.0 ☑
  breech (buttocks) (complete) (frank) 652.2 ☑
    with successful version 652.1 ☑
      before labor, affecting fetus or newborn
        761.7
    before labor, affecting fetus or newborn
      761.7
  brow 652.4 ☑
    causing obstructed labor 660.0 ☑

Presentation, fetal — *continued*
  buttocks 652.2 ☑
  chin 652.4 ☑
  complete 652.2 ☑
  compound 652.8 ☑
  cord 663.0 ☑
  extended head 652.4 ☑
  face 652.4 ☑
    to pubes 652.8 ☑
  footling 652.8 ☑
  frank 652.2 ☑
  hand, leg, or foot NEC 652.8 ☑
  incomplete 652.8 ☑
  mentum 652.4 ☑
  multiple gestation (one fetus or more) 652.6 ☑
  oblique 652.3 ☑
    with successful version 652.1 ☑
  shoulder 652.8 ☑
    affecting fetus or newborn 763.1
  transverse 652.3 ☑
    with successful version 652.1 ☑
  umbilical cord 663.0 ☑
  unstable 652.0 ☑
Prespondylolisthesis (congenital) (lumbosacral)
      756.11
Pressure
  area, skin ulcer (*see also* Decubitus) 707.00
  atrophy, spine 733.99
  birth, fetus or newborn NEC 767.9
  brachial plexus 353.0
  brain 348.4
    injury at birth 767.0
  cerebral — *see* Pressure, brain
  chest 786.59
  cone, tentorial 348.4
    injury at birth 767.0
  funis — *see* Compression, umbilical cord
  hyposystolic (*see also* Hypotension) 458.9
  increased
    intracranial 781.99
      due to
        benign intracranial hypertension 348.2
        hydrocephalus — *see* hydrocephalus
        injury at birth 767.8
      intraocular 365.00
  lumbosacral plexus 353.1
  mediastinum 519.3
  necrosis (chronic) (skin) (*see also* Decubitus)
      707.00
  nerve — *see* Compression, nerve
  paralysis (*see also* Neuropathy, entrapment)
      355.9
  sore (chronic) (*see also* Decubitus) 707.00
  spinal cord 336.9
  ulcer (chronic) (*see also* Decubitus) 707.00
  umbilical cord — *see* Compression, umbilical
      cord
  venous, increased 459.89
Pre-syncope 780.2
Preterm infant NEC 765.1 ☑
  extreme 765.0 ☑
Priapism (penis) 607.3
Prickling sensation (*see also* Disturbance,
      sensation) 782.0
Prickly heat 705.1
Primary — *see* condition
Primigravida, elderly
  affecting
    fetus or newborn 763.89
    management of pregnancy, labor, and
      delivery 659.5 ☑
Primipara, old
  affecting
    fetus or newborn 763.89
    management of pregnancy, labor, and
      delivery 659.5 ☑
Primula dermatitis 692.6
Primus varus (bilateral) (metatarsus) 754.52
P.R.I.N.D. 436
Pringle's disease (tuberous sclerosis) 759.5
Prinzmetal's angina 413.1
Prinzmetal-Massumi syndrome (anterior chest
      wall) 786.52
Prizefighter ear 738.7

Problem (with) V49.9
  academic V62.3
  acculturation V62.4
  adopted child V61.29
  aged
    in-law V61.3
    parent V61.3
    person NEC V61.8
  alcoholism in family V61.41
  anger reaction (*see also* Disturbance, conduct)
      312.0 ☑
  behavior, child 312.9
  behavioral V40.9
    specified NEC V40.3
  betting V69.3
  cardiorespiratory NEC V47.2
  care of sick or handicapped person in family or
      household V61.49
  career choice V62.2
  communication V40.1
  conscience regarding medical care V62.6
  delinquency (juvenile) 312.9
  diet, inappropriate V69.1
  digestive NEC V47.3
  ear NEC V41.3
  eating habits, inappropriate V69.1
  economic V60.2
    affecting care V60.9
      specified type NEC V60.8
  educational V62.3
  enuresis, child 307.6
  exercise, lack of V69.0
  eye NEC V41.1
  family V61.9
    specified circumstance NEC V61.8
  fear reaction, child 313.0
  feeding (elderly) (infant) 783.3
    newborn 779.3
    nonorganic 307.59   ▲
  fetal, affecting management of pregnancy
      656.9 ☑
    specified type NEC 656.8 ☑
  financial V60.2
  foster child V61.29
    specified NEC V41.8
  functional V41.9
    specified type NEC V41.8
  gambling V69.3
  genital NEC V47.5
  head V48.9
    deficiency V48.0
    disfigurement V48.6
    mechanical V48.2
    motor V48.2
    movement of V48.2
    sensory V48.4
    specified condition NEC V48.8
  hearing V41.2
  high-risk sexual behavior V69.2
  identity 313.82
  influencing health status NEC V49.89
  internal organ NEC V47.9
    deficiency V47.0
    mechanical or motor V47.1
  interpersonal NEC V62.81
  jealousy, child 313.3
  learning V40.0
  legal V62.5
  life circumstance NEC V62.89
  lifestyle V69.9
    specified NEC V69.8
  limb V49.9
    deficiency V49.0
    disfigurement V49.4
    mechanical V49.1
    motor V49.2
    movement, involving
      musculoskeletal system V49.1
      nervous system V49.2
    sensory V49.3
    specified condition NEC V49.5
  litigation V62.5
  living alone V60.3
  loneliness NEC V62.89
  marital V61.10
    involving
      divorce V61.0

Problem (with) — *continued*
  marital — *continued*
    involving — *continued*
      estrangement V61.0
      psychosexual disorder 302.9
      sexual function V41.7
    relationship V61.10   ●
  mastication V41.6
  medical care, within family V61.49
  mental V40.9
    specified NEC V40.2
  mental hygiene, adult V40.9
  multiparity V61.5
  nail biting, child 307.9
  neck V48.9
    deficiency V48.1
    disfigurement V48.7
    mechanical V48.3
    motor V48.3
    movement V48.3
    sensory V48.5
    specified condition NEC V48.8
  neurological NEC 781.99
  none (feared complaint unfounded) V65.5
  occupational V62.2
  parent-child V61.20
    relationship V61.20   ●
  partner V61.10
    relationship V61.10   ●
  personal NEC V62.89
    interpersonal conflict NEC V62.81
  personality (*see also* Disorder, personality) 301.9
  phase of life V62.89
  placenta, affecting management of pregnancy
      656.9 ☑
    specified type NEC 656.8 ☑
  poverty V60.2
  presence of sick or handicapped person in
      family or household V61.49
  psychiatric 300.9
  psychosocial V62.9
    specified type NEC V62.89
  relational NEC V62.81
  relationship, childhood 313.3
  religious or spiritual belief
    other than medical care V62.89
    regarding medical care V62.6
  self-damaging behavior V69.8
  sexual
    behavior, high-risk V69.2
    function NEC V41.7
  sibling
    relational V61.8   ●
    relationship V61.8   ●
  sight V41.0
  sleep, lack of V69.4
  sleep disorder, child 307.40
  smell V41.5
  speech V40.1
  spite reaction, child (*see also* Disturbance,
      conduct) 312.0 ☑
  spoiled child reaction (*see also* Disturbance,
      conduct) 312.1 ☑
  swallowing V41.6
  tantrum, child (*see also* Disturbance, conduct)
      312.1 ☑
  taste V41.5
  thumb sucking, child 307.9
  tic (child) 307.21
  trunk V48.9
    deficiency V48.1
    disfigurement V48.7
    mechanical V48.3
    motor V48.3
    movement V48.3
    sensory V48.5
    specified condition NEC V48.8
  unemployment V62.0
  urinary NEC V47.4
  voice production V41.4
Procedure (surgical) **not done** NEC V64.3
  because of
    contraindication V64.1
    patient's decision V64.2
      for reasons of conscience or religion
          V62.6
    specified reason NEC V64.3

Procidentia
  anus (sphincter) 569.1
  rectum (sphincter) 569.1
  stomach 537.89
  uteri 618.1
Proctalgia 569.42
  fugax 564.6
  spasmodic 564.6
    psychogenic 307.89
Proctitis 569.49
  amebic 006.8
  chlamydial 099.52
  gonococcal 098.7
  granulomatous 555.1
  idiopathic 556.2
    with ulcerative sigmoiditis 556.3
  tuberculous (*see also* Tuberculosis) 014.8 ☑
  ulcerative (chronic) (nonspecific) 556.2
    with ulcerative sigmoiditis 556.3
Proctocele
  female (without uterine prolapse) 618.04
    with uterine prolapse 618.4
      complete 618.3
      incomplete 618.2
  male 569.49
Proctocolitis, idiopathic 556.2
  with ulcerative sigmoiditis 556.3
Proctoptosis 569.1
Proctosigmoiditis 569.89
  ulcerative (chronic) 556.3
Proctospasm 564.6
  psychogenic 306.4
Prodromal-AIDS — *see* Human immunodeficiency
      virus (disease) (illness) (infection)
Profichet's disease or syndrome 729.9
Progeria (adultorum) (syndrome) 259.8
Prognathism (mandibular) (maxillary) 524.10
Progonoma (melanotic) (M9363/0) — *see*
      Neoplasm, by site, benign
Progressive — *see* condition
Prolapse, prolapsed
  anus, anal (canal) (sphincter) 569.1
  arm or hand, complicating delivery 652.7 ☑
    causing obstructed labor 660.0 ☑
      affecting fetus or newborn 763.1
    fetus or newborn 763.1
  bladder (acquired) (mucosa) (sphincter)
    congenital (female) (male) 756.71
    female (*see also* Cystocele, female) 618.01
    male 596.8
  breast implant (prosthetic) 996.54
  cecostomy 569.69
  cecum 569.89
  cervix, cervical (stump) (hypertrophied) 618.1
    anterior lip, obstructing labor 660.2 ☑
      affecting fetus or newborn 763.1
    congenital 752.49
    postpartal (old) 618.1
  ciliary body 871.1
  colon (pedunculated) 569.89
  colostomy 569.69
  conjunctiva 372.73
  cord — *see* Prolapse, umbilical cord
  disc (intervertebral) — *see* Displacement,
      intervertebral disc
  duodenum 537.89
  eye implant (orbital) 996.59
    lens (ocular) 996.53
  fallopian tube 620.4
  fetal extremity, complicating delivery 652.8 ☑
    causing obstructed labor 660.0 ☑
    fetus or newborn 763.1
  funis — *see* Prolapse, umbilical cord
  gastric (mucosa) 537.89
  genital, female 618.9
    specified NEC 618.89
  globe 360.81
  ileostomy bud 569.69
  intervertebral disc — *see* Displacement,
      intervertebral disc
  intestine (small) 569.89
  iris 364.8
    traumatic 871.1

Prolapse, prolapsed — *continued*
  kidney (*see also* Disease, renal) 593.0
    congenital 753.3
  laryngeal muscles or ventricle 478.79
  leg, complicating delivery 652.8 ☑
    causing obstructed labor 660.0 ☑
    fetus or newborn 763.1
  liver 573.8
  meatus urinarius 599.5
  mitral valve 424.0
  ocular lens implant 996.53
  organ or site, congenital NEC — *see*
    Malposition, congenital
  ovary 620.4
  pelvic (floor), female 618.89
  perineum, female 618.89
  pregnant uterus 654.4 ☑
  rectum (mucosa) (sphincter) 569.1
    due to Trichuris trichiuria 127.3
  spleen 289.59
  stomach 537.89
  umbilical cord
    affecting fetus or newborn 762.4
    complicating delivery 663.0 ☑
  ureter 593.89
    with obstruction 593.4
  ureterovesical orifice 593.89
  urethra (acquired) (infected) (mucosa) 599.5
    congenital 753.8
  uterovaginal 618.4
    complete 618.3
    incomplete 618.2
    specified NEC 618.89
  uterus (first degree) (second degree) (third
      degree) (complete) (without vaginal wall
      prolapse) 618.1
    with mention of vaginal wall prolapse — *see*
      Prolapse, uterovaginal
    congenital 752.3
    in pregnancy or childbirth 654.4 ☑
      affecting fetus or newborn 763.1
      causing obstructed labor 660.2 ☑
        affecting fetus or newborn 763.1
    postpartal (old) 618.1
  uveal 871.1
  vagina (anterior) (posterior) (vault) (wall)
      (without uterine prolapse) 618.00
    with uterine prolapse 618.4
      complete 618.3
      incomplete 618.2
    paravaginal 618.02
    posthysterectomy 618.5
    specified NEC 618.09
  vitreous (humor) 379.26
    traumatic 871.1
  womb — *see* Prolapse, uterus
Prolapsus, female 618.9
Proliferative — *see* condition
Prolinemia 270.8
Prolinuria 270.8
Prolonged, prolongation
  bleeding time (*see also* Defect, coagulation)
      790.92
    "idiopathic" (in von Willebrand's disease)
      286.4
  coagulation time (*see also* Defect, coagulation)
      790.92
  gestation syndrome 766.22
  labor 662.1 ☑
    affecting fetus or newborn 763.89
    first stage 662.0 ☑
    second stage 662.2 ☑
  pregnancy 645.2 ☑
  PR interval 426.11
  prothrombin time (*see also* Defect, coagulation)
      790.92
  QT interval 794.31 ●
    syndrome 426.82 ●
  rupture of membranes (24 hours or more prior
      to onset of labor) 658.2 ☑
  uterine contractions in labor 661.4 ☑
    affecting fetus or newborn 763.7
Prominauris 744.29
Prominence
  auricle (ear) (congenital) 744.29
    acquired 380.32

Prominence — *continued*
  ischial spine or sacral promontory
    with disproportion (fetopelvic) 653.3 ☑
      affecting fetus or newborn 763.1
      causing obstructed labor 660.1 ☑
        affecting fetus or newborn 763.1
  nose (congenital) 748.1
    acquired 738.0
Pronation
  ankle 736.79
  foot 736.79
    congenital 755.67
Prophylactic
  administration of
    antibiotics V07.39
    antitoxin, any V07.2
    antivenin V07.2
    chemotherapeutic agent NEC V07.39
      fluoride V07.31
    diphtheria antitoxin V07.2
    gamma globulin V07.2
    immune sera (gamma globulin) V07.2
    RhoGAM V07.2
    tetanus antitoxin V07.2
  chemotherapy NEC V07.39
    fluoride V07.31
  hormone replacement (postmenopausal) V07.4
  immunotherapy V07.2
  measure V07.9
    specified type NEC V07.8
  postmenopausal hormone replacement V07.4
  sterilization V25.2
Proptosis (ocular) (*see also* Exophthalmos) 376.30
  thyroid 242.0 ☑
Propulsion
  eyeball 360.81
Prosecution, anxiety concerning V62.5
Prostate, prostatic — *see* condition
Prostatism 600.90
  with urinary retention 600.91
Prostatitis (congestive) (suppurative) 601.9
  acute 601.0
  cavitary 601.8
  chlamydial 099.54
  chronic 601.1
  diverticular 601.8
  due to Trichomonas (vaginalis) 131.03
  fibrous 600.90
    with urinary retention 600.91
  gonococcal (acute) 098.12
    chronic or duration of 2 months or over
      098.32
  granulomatous 601.8
  hypertrophic 600.00
    with urinary retention 600.01
  specified type NEC 601.8
  subacute 601.1
  trichomonal 131.03
  tuberculous (*see also* Tuberculosis)
    016.5 ☑ [601.4]
Prostatocystitis 601.3
Prostatorrhea 602.8
Prostatoseminovesiculitis, trichomonal 131.03
Prostration 780.79
  heat 992.5
    anhydrotic 992.3
    due to
      salt (and water) depletion 992.4
      water depletion 992.3
  nervous 300.5
  newborn 779.89
  senile 797
Protanomaly 368.51
Protanopia (anomalous trichromat) (complete)
    (incomplete) 368.51
Protein
  deficiency 260
  malnutrition 260
  sickness (prophylactic) (therapeutic) 999.5
Proteinemia 790.99
Proteinosis
  alveolar, lung or pulmonary 516.0
  lipid 272.8

Proteinosis — *continued*
  lipoid (of Urbach) 272.8
Proteinuria (*see also* Albuminuria) 791.0
  Bence-Jones NEC 791.0
  gestational 646.2 ☑
    with hypertension — *see* Toxemia, of
      pregnancy
  orthostatic 593.6
  postural 593.6
Proteolysis, pathologic 286.6
Protocoproporphyria 277.1
Protoporphyria (erythrohepatic) (erythropoietic)
    277.1
Protrusio acetabuli 718.65
Protrusion
  acetabulum (into pelvis) 718.65
  device, implant, or graft — *see* Complications,
    mechanical
  ear, congenital 744.29
  intervertebral disc — *see* Displacement,
    intervertebral disc
  nucleus pulposus — *see* Displacement,
    intervertebral disc
Proud flesh 701.5
Prune belly (syndrome) 756.71
Prurigo (ferox) (gravis) (Hebra's) (hebrae) (mitis)
    (simplex) 698.2
  agria 698.3
  asthma syndrome 691.8
  Besnier's (atopic dermatitis) (infantile eczema)
    691.8
  eczematodes allergicum 691.8
  estivalis (Hutchinson's) 692.72
  Hutchinson's 692.72
  nodularis 698.3
  psychogenic 306.3
Pruritus, pruritic 698.9
  ani 698.0
    psychogenic 306.3
  conditions NEC 698.9
    psychogenic 306.3
  due to Onchocerca volvulus 125.3
  ear 698.9
  essential 698.9
  genital organ(s) 698.1
    psychogenic 306.3
  gravidarum 646.8 ☑
  hiemalis 698.8
  neurogenic (any site) 306.3
  perianal 698.0
  psychogenic (any site) 306.3
  scrotum 698.1
    psychogenic 306.3
  senile, senilis 698.8
  Trichomonas 131.9
  vulva, vulvae 698.1
    psychogenic 306.3
Psammocarcinoma (M8140/3) — *see* Neoplasm,
    by site, malignant
Pseudarthrosis, pseudoarthrosis (bone) 733.82
  joint following fusion V45.4
Pseudoacanthosis
  nigricans 701.8
Pseudoaneurysm — *see* Aneurysm
Pseudoangina (pectoris) — *see* Angina
Pseudoangioma 452
Pseudo-Argyll-Robertson pupil 379.45
Pseudoarteriosus 747.89
Pseudoarthrosis — *see* Pseudarthrosis
Pseudoataxia 799.89
Pseudobulbar affect (PBA) 310.8 ●
Pseudobursa 727.89
Pseudocholera 025
Pseudochromidrosis 705.89
Pseudocirrhosis, liver, pericardial 423.2
Pseudocoarctation 747.21
Pseudocowpox 051.1
Pseudocoxalgia 732.1
Pseudocroup 478.75
Pseudocyesis 300.11
Pseudocyst
  lung 518.89

Pseudocyst — *continued*
  pancreas 577.2
  retina 361.19
Pseudodementia 300.16
Pseudoelephantiasis neuroarthritica 757.0
Pseudoemphysema 518.89
Pseudoencephalitis
  superior (acute) hemorrhagic 265.1
Pseudoerosion cervix, congenital 752.49
Pseudoexfoliation, lens capsule 366.11
Pseudofracture (idiopathic) (multiple)
  (spontaneous) (symmetrical) 268.2
Pseudoglanders 025
Pseudoglioma 360.44
Pseudogout — *see* Chondrocalcinosis
Pseudohallucination 780.1
Pseudohemianesthesia 782.0
Pseudohemophilia (Bernuth's) (hereditary)
  (type B) 286.4
  type A 287.8
  vascular 287.8
Pseudohermaphroditism 752.7
  with chromosomal anomaly — *see* Anomaly,
    chromosomal
  adrenal 255.2
  female (without adrenocortical disorder) 752.7
    with adrenocortical disorder 255.2
    adrenal 255.2
  male (without gonadal disorder) 752.7
    with
      adrenocortical disorder 255.2
      cleft scrotum 752.7
      feminizing testis 259.5   ▲
      gonadal disorder 257.9
      adrenal 255.2
Pseudohole, macula 362.54
Pseudo-Hurler's disease (mucolipidosis III) 272.7
Pseudohydrocephalus 348.2
Pseudohypertrophic muscular dystrophy (Erb's)
  359.1
Pseudohypertrophy, muscle 359.1
Pseudohypoparathyroidism 275.49
Pseudoinfluenza 487.1
Pseudoinsomnia 307.49
Pseudoleukemia 288.8
  infantile 285.8
Pseudomembranous — *see* condition
Pseudomeningocele (cerebral) (infective) 349.2
  postprocedural 997.01   ●
  spinal 349.2
Pseudomenstruation 626.8
Pseudomucinous
  cyst (ovary) (M8470/0) 220
  peritoneum 568.89
Pseudomyeloma 273.1
Pseudomyxoma peritonei (M8480/6) 197.6
Pseudoneuritis optic (nerve) 377.24
  papilla 377.24
    congenital 743.57
Pseudoneuroma — *see* Injury, nerve, by site
Pseudo-obstruction
  intestine (chronic) (idiopathic) (intermittent
    secondary) (primary) 564.89
    acute 560.89
Pseudopapilledema 377.24
Pseudoparalysis
  arm or leg 781.4
  atonic, congenital 358.8
Pseudopelade 704.09
Pseudophakia V43.1
Pseudopolycythemia 289.0
Pseudopolyposis, colon 556.4
Pseudoporencephaly 348.0
Pseudopseudohypoparathyroidism 275.49
Pseudopsychosis 300.16
Pseudopterygium 372.52
Pseudoptosis (eyelid) 374.34
Pseudorabies 078.89

Pseudoretinitis, pigmentosa 362.65
Pseudorickets 588.0
  senile (Pozzi's) 731.0
Pseudorubella 057.8
Pseudoscarlatina 057.8
Pseudosclerema 778.1
Pseudosclerosis (brain)
  Jakob's 046.1
  of Westphal (-Strümpell) (hepatolenticular
    degeneration) 275.1
  spastic 046.1
    with dementia
      with behavioral disturbance 046.1
        [294.11]
      without behavioral disturbance 046.1
        [294.10]
Pseudoseizure 780.39
  non-psychiatric 780.39
  psychiatric 300.11
Pseudotabes 799.89
  diabetic 250.6 ☑ *[337.1]*
Pseudotetanus (*see also* Convulsions) 780.39
Pseudotetany 781.7
  hysterical 300.11
Pseudothalassemia 285.0
Pseudotrichinosis 710.3
Pseudotruncus arteriosus 747.29
Pseudotuberculosis, pasteurella (infection) 027.2
Pseudotumor
  cerebri 348.2
  orbit (inflammatory) 376.11
Pseudo-Turner's syndrome 759.89
Pseudoxanthoma elasticum 757.39
Psilosis (sprue) (tropical) 579.1
  Monilia 112.89
  nontropical 579.0
  not sprue 704.00
Psittacosis 073.9
Psoitis 728.89
Psora NEC 696.1
Psoriasis 696.1
  any type, except arthropathic 696.1
  arthritic, arthropathic 696.0
  buccal 528.6
  flexural 696.1
  follicularis 696.1
  guttate 696.1
  inverse 696.1
  mouth 528.6
  nummularis 696.1
  psychogenic 316 *[696.1]*
  punctata 696.1
  pustular 696.1
  rupioides 696.1
  vulgaris 696.1
Psorospermiasis 136.4
Psorospermosis 136.4
  follicularis (vegetans) 757.39
Psychalgia 307.80
Psychasthenia 300.89
  compulsive 300.3
  mixed compulsive states 300.3
  obsession 300.3
Psychiatric disorder or problem NEC 300.9
Psychogenic — *see also* condition
  factors associated with physical conditions 316
Psychoneurosis, psychoneurotic (*see also*
  Neurosis) 300.9
  anxiety (state) 300.00
  climacteric 627.2
  compensation 300.16
  compulsion 300.3
  conversion hysteria 300.11
  depersonalization 300.6
  depressive type 300.4
  dissociative hysteria 300.15
  hypochondriacal 300.7
  hysteria 300.10
    conversion type 300.11
    dissociative type 300.15
  mixed NEC 300.89
  neurasthenic 300.5

Psychoneurosis, psychoneurotic — *continued*
  obsessional 300.3
  obsessive-compulsive 300.3
  occupational 300.89
  personality NEC 301.89
  phobia 300.20
  senile NEC 300.89
Psychopathic — *see also* condition
  constitution, posttraumatic 310.2
    with psychosis 293.9
  personality 301.9
    amoral trends 301.7
    antisocial trends 301.7
    asocial trends 301.7
    mixed types 301.7
  state 301.9
Psychopathy, sexual (*see also* Deviation, sexual)
  302.9
**Psychophysiologic, psychophysiological
  condition** — *see* Reaction,
  psychophysiologic
Psychose passionelle 297.8
Psychosexual identity disorder 302.6
  adult-life 302.85
  childhood 302.6
Psychosis 298.9
  acute hysterical 298.1
  affecting management of pregnancy, childbirth,
    or puerperium 648.4 ☑
  affective (*see also* Disorder, mood) 296.90

> *Note* — Use the following *fifth-digit
> subclassification with categories 296.0-296.6:*
>
> 0   *unspecified*
> 1   *mild*
> 2   *moderate*
> 3   *severe, without mention of psychotic
>   behavior*
> 4   *severe, specified as with psychotic
>   behavior*
> 5   *in partial or unspecified remission*
> 6   *in full remission*

    drug-induced 292.84
    due to or associated with physical condition
      293.83
    involutional 296.2 ☑
      recurrent episode 296.3 ☑
      single episode 296.2 ☑
    manic-depressive 296.80
      circular (alternating) 296.7
        currently depressed 296.5 ☑
        currently manic 296.4 ☑
      depressed type 296.2 ☑
        atypical 296.82
        recurrent episode 296.3 ☑
        single episode 296.2 ☑
      manic 296.0 ☑
        atypical 296.81
        recurrent episode 296.1 ☑
        single episode 296.0 ☑
      mixed type NEC 296.89
      specified type NEC 296.89
    senile 290.21
    specified type NEC 296.99
  alcoholic 291.9
    with
      anxiety 291.89
      delirium tremens 291.0
      delusions 291.5
      dementia 291.2
      hallucinosis 291.3
      mood disturbance 291.89
      jealousy 291.5
      paranoia 291.5
      persisting amnesia 291.1
      sexual dysfunction 291.89
      sleep disturbance 291.89
    amnestic confabulatory 291.1
    delirium tremens 291.0
    hallucinosis 291.3
    Korsakoff's, Korsakov's, Korsakow's 291.1
    paranoid type 291.5
    pathological intoxication 291.4

Psychosis — *continued*
  alcoholic — *continued*
    polyneuritic 291.1
    specified type NEC 291.89
  alternating (*see also* Psychosis, manic-depressive, circular) 296.7
  anergastic (*see also* Psychosis, organic) 294.9
  arteriosclerotic 290.40
    with
      acute confusional state 290.41
      delirium 290.41
      delusions 290.42
      depressed mood 290.43
    depressed type 290.43
    paranoid type 290.42
    simple type 290.40
    uncomplicated 290.40
  atypical 298.9
    depressive 296.82
    manic 296.81
  borderline (schizophrenia) (*see also* Schizophrenia) 295.5 ☑
    of childhood (*see also* Psychosis, childhood) 299.8 ☑
    prepubertal 299.8 ☑
  brief reactive 298.8
  childhood, with origin specific to 299.9 ☑

> Note — Use the following fifth-digit subclassification with category 299:
>
> 0   current or active state
> 1   residual state

    atypical 299.8 ☑
    specified type NEC 299.8 ☑
  circular (*see also* Psychosis, manic-depressive, circular) 296.7
  climacteric (*see also* Psychosis, involutional) 298.8
  confusional 298.9
    acute 293.0
    reactive 298.2
    subacute 293.1
  depressive (*see also* Psychosis, affective) 296.2 ☑
    atypical 296.82
    involutional 296.2 ☑
      with hypomania (bipolar II) 296.89
      recurrent episode 296.3 ☑
      single episode 296.2 ☑
    psychogenic 298.0
    reactive (emotional stress) (psychological trauma) 298.0
    recurrent episode 296.3 ☑
      with hypomania (bipolar II) 296.89
    single episode 296.2 ☑
  disintegrative, childhood (*see also* Psychosis, childhood) 299.1 ☑
  drug 292.9
    with
      affective syndrome 292.84
      amnestic syndrome 292.83
      anxiety 292.89
      delirium 292.81
        withdrawal 292.0
      delusions 292.11
      dementia 292.82
      depressive state 292.84
      hallucinations 292.12
      hallucinosis 292.12
      mood disorder 292.84
      mood disturbance 292.84
      organic personality syndrome NEC 292.89
      sexual dysfunction 292.89
      sleep disturbance 292.89
      withdrawal syndrome (and delirium) 292.0
    affective syndrome 292.84
    delusions 292.11
    hallucinatory state 292.12
    hallucinosis 292.12
    paranoid state 292.11
    specified type NEC 292.89
    withdrawal syndrome (and delirium) 292.0
  due to or associated with physical condition (*see also* Psychosis, organic) 293.9

Psychosis — *continued*
  epileptic NEC 294.8
  excitation (psychogenic) (reactive) 298.1
  exhaustive (*see also* Reaction, stress, acute) 308.9
  hypomanic (*see also* Psychosis, affective) 296.0 ☑
    recurrent episode 296.1 ☑
    single episode 296.0 ☑
  hysterical 298.8
    acute 298.1
  incipient 298.8
    schizophrenic (*see also* Schizophrenia) 295.5 ☑
  induced 297.3
  infantile (*see also* Psychosis, childhood) 299.0 ☑
  infective 293.9
    acute 293.0
    subacute 293.1
  in
    conditions classified elsewhere
      with
        delusions 293.81
        hallucinations 293.82
    pregnancy, childbirth, or puerperium 648.4 ☑
  interactional (childhood) (*see also* Psychosis, childhood) 299.1 ☑
  involutional 298.8
    depressive (*see also* Psychosis, affective) 296.2 ☑
      recurrent episode 296.3 ☑
      single episode 296.2 ☑
    melancholic 296.2 ☑
      recurrent episode 296.3 ☑
      single episode 296.2 ☑
    paranoid state 297.2
    paraphrenia 297.2
  Korsakoff's, Korakov's, Korsakow's (nonalcoholic) 294.0
    alcoholic 291.1
  mania (phase) (*see also* Psychosis, affective) 296.0 ☑
    recurrent episode 296.1 ☑
    single episode 296.0 ☑
  manic (*see also* Psychosis, affective) 296.0 ☑
    atypical 296.81
    recurrent episode 296.1 ☑
    single episode 296.0 ☑
  manic-depressive 296.80
    circular 296.7
      currently
        depressed 296.5 ☑
        manic 296.4 ☑
      mixed 296.6 ☑
    depressive 296.2 ☑
      recurrent episode 296.3 ☑
        with hypomania (bipolar II) 296.89
      single episode 296.2 ☑
    hypomanic 296.0 ☑
      recurrent episode 296.1 ☑
      single episode 296.0 ☑
    manic 296.0 ☑
      atypical 296.81
      recurrent episode 296.1 ☑
      single episode 296.0 ☑
    mixed NEC 296.89
    perplexed 296.89
    stuporous 296.89
  menopausal (*see also* Psychosis, involutional) 298.8
  mixed schizophrenic and affective (*see also* Schizophrenia) 295.7 ☑
  multi-infarct (cerebrovascular) (*see also* Psychosis, arteriosclerotic) 290.40
  organic NEC 294.9
    due to or associated with
      addiction
        alcohol (*see also* Psychosis, alcoholic) 291.9
        drug (*see also* Psychosis, drug) 292.9
      alcohol intoxication, acute (*see also* Psychosis, alcoholic) 291.9
      alcoholism (*see also* Psychosis, alcoholic) 291.9
      arteriosclerosis (cerebral) (*see also* Psychosis, arteriosclerotic) 290.40

Psychosis — *continued*
  organic NEC — *continued*
    due to or associated with — *continued*
      cerebrovascular disease
        acute (psychosis) 293.0
        arteriosclerotic (*see also* Psychosis, arteriosclerotic) 290.40
      childbirth — *see* Psychosis, puerperal
      dependence
        alcohol (*see also* Psychosis, alcoholic) 291.9
        drug 292.9
      disease
        alcoholic liver (*see also* Psychosis, alcoholic) 291.9
        brain
          arteriosclerotic (*see also* Psychosis, arteriosclerotic) 290.40
        cerebrovascular
          acute (psychosis) 293.0
          arteriosclerotic (*see also* Psychosis, arteriosclerotic) 290.40
        endocrine or metabolic 293.9
          acute (psychosis) 293.0
          subacute (psychosis) 293.1
        Jakob-Creutzfeldt ▶(new variant)◀
          with behavioral disturbance 046.1 *[294.11]*
          without behavioral disturbance 046.1 *[294.10]*
        liver, alcoholic (*see also* Psychosis, alcoholic) 291.9
      disorder
        cerebrovascular
          acute (psychosis) 293.0
        endocrine or metabolic 293.9
          acute (psychosis) 293.0
          subacute (psychosis) 293.1
      epilepsy
        with behavioral disturbance 345.9 ☑ *[294.11]*
        without behavioral disturbance 345.9 ☑ *[294.10]*
        transient (acute) 293.0
      Huntington's chorea
        with behavioral disturbance 333.4 *[294.11]*
        without behavioral disturbance 333.4 *[294.10]*
      infection
        brain 293.9
          acute (psychosis) 293.0
          chronic 294.8
          subacute (psychosis) 293.1
        intracranial NEC 293.9
          acute (psychosis) 293.0
          chronic 294.8
          subacute (psychosis) 293.1
      intoxication
        alcoholic (acute) (*see also* Psychosis, alcoholic) 291.9
        pathological 291.4
        drug (*see also* Psychosis, drug) 292.2
      ischemia
        cerebrovascular (generalized) (*see also* Psychosis, arteriosclerotic) 290.40
      Jakob-Creutzfeldt disease ▶(syndrome) (new variant)◀
        with behavioral disturbance 046.1 *[294.11]*
        without behavioral disturbance 046.1 *[294.10]*
      multiple sclerosis
        with behavioral disturbance 340 *[294.11]*
        without behavioral disturbance 340 *[294.10]*
      physical condition NEC 293.9
        with
          delusions 293.81
          hallucinations 293.82
      presenility 290.10
      puerperium — *see* Psychosis, puerperal
      sclerosis, multiple
        with behavioral disturbance 340 *[294.11]*

Psychosis — *continued*
  organic NEC — *continued*
    due to or associated with — *continued*
      sclerosis, multiple — *continued*
        without behavioral disturbance
          340 *[294.10]*
      senility 290.20
      status epilepticus
        with behavioral disturbance
          345.3 *[294.11]*
        without behavioral disturbance
          345.3 *[294.10]*
    trauma
      brain (birth) (from electrical current)
        (surgical) 293.9
        acute (psychosis) 293.0
        chronic 294.8
        subacute (psychosis) 293.1
        unspecified physical condition
          293.9
          with
            delusions 293.81
            hallucinations 293.82
    infective 293.9
      acute (psychosis) 293.0
      subacute 293.1
    posttraumatic 293.9
      acute 293.0
      subacute 293.1
    specified type NEC 294.8
    transient 293.9
      with
        anxiety 293.84
        delusions 293.81
        depression 293.83
        hallucinations 293.82
      depressive type 293.83
      hallucinatory type 293.82
      paranoid type 293.81
      specified type NEC 293.89
  paranoic 297.1
  paranoid (chronic) 297.9
    alcoholic 291.5
    chronic 297.1
    climacteric 297.2
    involutional 297.2
    menopausal 297.2
    protracted reactive 298.4
    psychogenic 298.4
      acute 298.3
    schizophrenic (*see also* Schizophrenia)
      295.3 ☑
    senile 290.20
  paroxysmal 298.9
    senile 290.20
  polyneuritic, alcoholic 291.1
  postoperative 293.9
  postpartum — *see* Psychosis, puerperal
  prepsychotic (*see also* Schizophrenia) 295.5 ☑
  presbyophrenic (type) 290.8
  presenile (*see also* Dementia, presenile) 290.10
  prison 300.16
  psychogenic 298.8
    depressive 298.0
    paranoid 298.4
      acute 298.3
  puerperal
    specified type — *see* categories 295-298 ☑
    unspecified type 293.89
      acute 293.0
      chronic 293.89
      subacute 293.1
  reactive (emotional stress) (psychological
    trauma) 298.8
    brief 298.8
    confusion 298.2
    depressive 298.0
    excitation 298.1
  schizo-affective (depressed) (excited) (*see also*
    Schizophrenia) 295.7 ☑
  schizophrenia, schizophrenic (*see also*
    Schizophrenia) 295.9 ☑
    borderline type 295.5 ☑
      of childhood (*see also* Psychosis,
        childhood) 299.8 ☑
    catatonic (excited) (withdrawn) 295.2 ☑
    childhood type (*see also* Psychosis,
      childhood) 299.9 ☑

Psychosis — *continued*
  schizophrenia, schizophrenic — *continued*
    hebephrenic 295.1 ☑
    incipient 295.5 ☑
    latent 295.5 ☑
    paranoid 295.3 ☑
    prepsychotic 295.5 ☑
    prodromal 295.5 ☑
    pseudoneurotic 295.5 ☑
    pseudopsychopathic 295.5 ☑
    schizophreniform 295.4 ☑
    simple 295.0 ☑
    undifferentiated type 295.9 ☑
  schizophreniform 295.4 ☑
  senile NEC 290.20
    with
      delusional features 290.20
      depressive features 290.21
    depressed type 290.21
    paranoid type 290.20
    simple deterioration 290.20
    specified type — *see* categories 295-298 ☑
  shared 297.3
  situational (reactive) 298.8
  symbiotic (childhood) (*see also* Psychosis,
    childhood) 299.1 ☑
  toxic (acute) 293.9
Psychotic (*see also* condition) 298.9
  episode 298.9
    due to or associated with physical
      conditions (*see also* Psychosis,
      organic) 293.9
Pterygium (eye) 372.40
  central 372.43
  colli 744.5
  double 372.44
  peripheral (stationary) 372.41
    progressive 372.42
  recurrent 372.45
Ptilosis 374.55
Ptomaine (poisoning) (*see also* Poisoning, food)
  005.9
Ptosis (adiposa) 374.30
  breast 611.8
  cecum 569.89
  colon 569.89
  congenital (eyelid) 743.61
    specified site NEC — *see* Anomaly, specified
      type NEC
  epicanthus syndrome 270.2
  eyelid 374.30
    congenital 743.61
    mechanical 374.33
    myogenic 374.32
    paralytic 374.31
  gastric 537.5
  intestine 569.89
  kidney (*see also* Disease, renal) 593.0
    congenital 753.3
  liver 573.8
  renal (*see also* Disease, renal) 593.0
    congenital 753.3
  splanchnic 569.89
  spleen 289.59
  stomach 537.5
  viscera 569.89
Ptyalism 527.7
  hysterical 300.11
  periodic 527.2
  pregnancy 646.8 ☑
  psychogenic 306.4
Ptyalolithiasis 527.5
Pubalgia 848.8
Pubarche, precocious 259.1
Pubertas praecox 259.1
Puberty V21.1
  abnormal 259.9
  bleeding 626.3
  delayed 259.0
  precocious (constitutional) (cryptogenic)
    (idiopathic) NEC 259.1
    due to
      adrenal
        cortical hyperfunction 255.2
        hyperplasia 255.2
      cortical hyperfunction 255.2

Puberty — *continued*
  precocious — *continued*
    due to — *continued*
      ovarian hyperfunction 256.1
        estrogen 256.0
      pineal tumor 259.8
      testicular hyperfunction 257.0
    premature 259.1
      due to
        adrenal cortical hyperfunction 255.2
        pineal tumor 259.8
        pituitary (anterior) hyperfunction 253.1
Puckering, macula 362.56
Pudenda, pudendum — *see* condition
Puente's disease (simple glandular cheilitis)
  528.5
Puerperal
  abscess
    areola 675.1 ☑
    Bartholin's gland 646.6 ☑
    breast 675.1 ☑
    cervix (uteri) 670.0 ☑
    fallopian tube 670.0 ☑
    genital organ 670.0 ☑
    kidney 646.6 ☑
    mammary 675.1 ☑
    mesosalpinx 670.0 ☑
    nabothian 646.6 ☑
    nipple 675.0 ☑
    ovary, ovarian 670.0 ☑
    oviduct 670.0 ☑
    parametric 670.0 ☑
    para-uterine 670.0 ☑
    pelvic 670.0 ☑
    perimetric 670.0 ☑
    periuterine 670.0 ☑
    retro-uterine 670.0 ☑
    subareolar 675.1 ☑
    suprapelvic 670.0 ☑
    tubal (ruptured) 670.0 ☑
    tubo-ovarian 670.0 ☑
    urinary tract NEC 646.6 ☑
    uterine, uterus 670.0 ☑
    vagina (wall) 646.6 ☑
    vaginorectal 646.6 ☑
    vulvovaginal gland 646.6 ☑
  accident 674.9 ☑
  adnexitis 670.0 ☑
  afibrinogenemia, or other coagulation defect
    666.3 ☑
  albuminuria (acute) (subacute) 646.2 ☑
    pre-eclamptic 642.4 ☑
  anemia (conditions classifiable to 280-285)
    648.2 ☑
  anuria 669.3 ☑
  apoplexy 674.0 ☑
  asymptomatic bacteriuria 646.5 ☑
  atrophy, breast 676.3 ☑
  blood dyscrasia 666.3 ☑
  caked breast 676.2 ☑
  cardiomyopathy 674.5 ☑
  cellulitis — *see* Puerperal, abscess
  cerebrovascular disorder (conditions
    classifiable to 430-434, 436-437) 674.0 ☑
  cervicitis (conditions classifiable to 616.0)
    646.6 ☑
  coagulopathy (any) 666.3 ☑
  complications 674.9 ☑
    specified type NEC 674.8 ☑
  convulsions (eclamptic) (uremic) 642.6 ☑
    with pre-existing hypertension 642.7 ☑
  cracked nipple 676.1 ☑
  cystitis 646.6 ☑
  cystopyelitis 646.6 ☑
  deciduitis (acute) 670.0 ☑
  delirium NEC 293.9
  diabetes (mellitus) (conditions classifiable to
    250) 648.0 ☑
  disease 674.9 ☑
    breast NEC 676.3 ☑
    cerebrovascular (acute) 674.0 ☑
    nonobstetric NEC (*see also* Pregnancy,
      complicated, current disease or
      condition) 648.9 ☑
    pelvis inflammatory 670.0 ☑
    renal NEC 646.2 ☑

Puerperal — *continued*
  disease — *continued*
    tubo-ovarian 670.0 ☑
    Valsuani's (progressive pernicious anemia) 648.2 ☑
  disorder
    lactation 676.9 ☑
      specified type NEC 676.8 ☑
    nonobstetric NEC (*see also* Pregnancy, complicated, current disease or condition) 648.9 ☑
  disruption
    cesarean wound 674.1 ☑
    episiotomy wound 674.2 ☑
    perineal laceration wound 674.2 ☑
  drug dependence (conditions classifiable to 304) 648.3 ☑
  eclampsia 642.6 ☑
    with pre-existing hypertension 642.7 ☑
  embolism (pulmonary) 673.2 ☑
    air 673.0 ☑
    amniotic fluid 673.1 ☑
    blood-clot 673.2 ☑
    brain or cerebral 674.0 ☑
    cardiac 674.8 ☑
    fat 673.8 ☑
    intracranial sinus (venous) 671.5 ☑
    pyemic 673.3 ☑
    septic 673.3 ☑
    spinal cord 671.5 ☑
  endometritis (conditions classifiable to 615.0-615.9) 670.0 ☑
  endophlebitis — *see* Puerperal, phlebitis
  endotrachelitis 646.6 ☑
  engorgement, breasts 676.2 ☑
  erysipelas 670.0 ☑
  failure
    lactation 676.4 ☑
    renal, acute 669.3 ☑
  fever 670.0 ☑
    meaning pyrexia (of unknown origin) 672.0 ☑
    meaning sepsis 670.0 ☑
  fissure, nipple 676.1 ☑
  fistula
    breast 675.1 ☑
    mammary gland 675.1 ☑
    nipple 675.0 ☑
  galactophoritis 675.2 ☑
  galactorrhea 676.6 ☑
  gangrene
    gas 670.0 ☑
    uterus 670.0 ☑
  gonorrhea (conditions classifiable to 098) 647.1 ☑
  hematoma, subdural 674.0 ☑
  hematosalpinx, infectional 670.0 ☑
  hemiplegia, cerebral 674.0 ☑
  hemorrhage 666.1 ☑
    brain 674.0 ☑
    bulbar 674.0 ☑
    cerebellar 674.0 ☑
    cerebral 674.0 ☑
    cortical 674.0 ☑
    delayed (after 24 hours) (uterine) 666.2 ☑
    extradural 674.0 ☑
    internal capsule 674.0 ☑
    intracranial 674.0 ☑
    intrapontine 674.0 ☑
    meningeal 674.0 ☑
    pontine 674.0 ☑
    subarachnoid 674.0 ☑
    subcortical 674.0 ☑
    subdural 674.0 ☑
    uterine, delayed 666.2 ☑
    ventricular 674.0 ☑
  hemorrhoids 671.8 ☑
  hepatorenal syndrome 674.8 ☑
  hypertrophy
    breast 676.3 ☑
    mammary gland 676.3 ☑
  induration breast (fibrous) 676.3 ☑
  infarction
    lung — *see* Puerperal, embolism
    pulmonary — *see* Puerperal, embolism

Puerperal — *continued*
  infection
    Bartholin's gland 646.6 ☑
    breast 675.2 ☑
      with nipple 675.9 ☑
        specified type NEC 675.8 ☑
    cervix 646.6 ☑
    endocervix 646.6 ☑
    fallopian tube 670.0 ☑
    generalized 670.0 ☑
    genital tract (major) 670.0 ☑
      minor or localized 646.6 ☑
    kidney (bacillus coli) 646.6 ☑
    mammary gland 675.2 ☑
      with nipple 675.9 ☑
        specified type NEC 675.8 ☑
    nipple 675.0 ☑
      with breast 675.9 ☑
        specified type NEC 675.8 ☑
    ovary 670.0 ☑
    pelvic 670.0 ☑
    peritoneum 670.0 ☑
    renal 646.6 ☑
    tubo-ovarian 670.0 ☑
    urinary (tract) NEC 646.6 ☑
      asymptomatic 646.5 ☑
    uterus, uterine 670.0 ☑
    vagina 646.6 ☑
  inflammation — *see also* Puerperal, infection
    areola 675.1 ☑
    Bartholin's gland 646.6 ☑
    breast 675.2 ☑
    broad ligament 670.0 ☑
    cervix (uteri) 646.6 ☑
    fallopian tube 670.0 ☑
    genital organs 670.0 ☑
      localized 646.6 ☑
    mammary gland 675.2 ☑
    nipple 675.0 ☑
    ovary 670.0 ☑
    oviduct 670.0 ☑
    pelvis 670.0 ☑
    periuterine 670.0 ☑
    tubal 670.0 ☑
    vagina 646.6 ☑
    vein — *see* Puerperal, phlebitis
  inversion, nipple 676.3 ☑
  ischemia, cerebral 674.0 ☑
  lymphangitis 670.0 ☑
    breast 675.2 ☑
  malaria (conditions classifiable to 084) 647.4 ☑
  malnutrition 648.9 ☑
  mammillitis 675.0 ☑
  mammitis 675.2 ☑
  mania 296.0 ☑
    recurrent episode 296.1 ☑
    single episode 296.0 ☑
  mastitis 675.2 ☑
    purulent 675.1 ☑
    retromammary 675.1 ☑
    submammary 675.1 ☑
  melancholia 296.2 ☑
    recurrent episode 296.3 ☑
    single episode 296.2 ☑
  mental disorder (conditions classifiable to 290-303, 305-316, 317-319) 648.4 ☑
  metritis (septic) (suppurative) 670.0 ☑
  metroperitonitis 670.0 ☑
  metrorrhagia 666.2 ☑
  metrosalpingitis 670.0 ☑
  metrovaginitis 670.0 ☑
  milk leg 671.4 ☑
  monoplegia, cerebral 674.0 ☑
  necrosis
    kidney, tubular 669.3 ☑
    liver (acute) (subacute) (conditions classifiable to 570) 674.8 ☑
    ovary 670.0 ☑
    renal cortex 669.3 ☑
  nephritis or nephrosis (conditions classifiable to 580-589) 646.2 ☑
    with hypertension 642.1 ☑
  nutritional deficiency (conditions classifiable to 260-269) 648.9 ☑
  occlusion, precerebral artery 674.0 ☑
  oliguria 669.3 ☑
  oophoritis 670.0 ☑

Puerperal — *continued*
  ovaritis 670.0 ☑
  paralysis
    bladder (sphincter) 665.5 ☑
    cerebral 674.0 ☑
  paralytic stroke 674.0 ☑
  parametritis 670.0 ☑
  paravaginitis 646.6 ☑
  pelviperitonitis 670.0 ☑
  perimetritis 670.0 ☑
  perimetrosalpingitis 670.0 ☑
  perinephritis 646.6 ☑
  perioophoritis 670.0 ☑
  periphlebitis — *see* Puerperal, phlebitis
  perisalpingitis 670.0 ☑
  peritoneal infection 670.0 ☑
  peritonitis (pelvic) 670.0 ☑
  perivaginitis 646.6 ☑
  phlebitis 671.9 ☑
    deep 671.4 ☑
    intracranial sinus (venous) 671.5 ☑
    pelvic 671.4 ☑
    specified site NEC 671.5 ☑
    superficial 671.2 ☑
  phlegmasia alba dolens 671.4 ☑
  placental polyp 674.4 ☑
  pneumonia, embolic — *see* Puerperal, embolism
  prediabetes 648.8 ☑
  pre-eclampsia (mild) 642.4 ☑
    with pre-existing hypertension 642.7 ☑
    severe 642.5 ☑
  psychosis, unspecified (*see also* Psychosis, puerperal) 293.89
  pyelitis 646.6 ☑
  pyelocystitis 646.6 ☑
  pyelohydronephrosis 646.6 ☑
  pyelonephritis 646.6 ☑
  pyelonephrosis 646.6 ☑
  pyemia 670.0 ☑
  pyocystitis 646.6 ☑
  pyohemia 670.0 ☑
  pyometra 670.0 ☑
  pyonephritis 646.6 ☑
  pyonephrosis 646.6 ☑
  pyo-oophoritis 670.0 ☑
  pyosalpingitis 670.0 ☑
  pyosalpinx 670.0 ☑
  pyrexia (of unknown origin) 672.0 ☑
  renal
    disease NEC 646.2 ☑
    failure, acute 669.3 ☑
  retention
    decidua (fragments) (with delayed hemorrhage) 666.2 ☑
      without hemorrhage 667.1 ☑
    placenta (fragments) (with delayed hemorrhage) 666.2 ☑
      without hemorrhage 667.1 ☑
    secundines (fragments) (with delayed hemorrhage) 666.2 ☑
      without hemorrhage 667.1 ☑
  retracted nipple 676.0 ☑
  rubella (conditions classifiable to 056) 647.5 ☑
  salpingitis 670.0 ☑
  salpingo-oophoritis 670.0 ☑
  salpingo-ovaritis 670.0 ☑
  salpingoperitonitis 670.0 ☑
  sapremia 670.0 ☑
  secondary perineal tear 674.2 ☑
  sepsis (pelvic) 670.0 ☑
  septicemia 670.0 ☑
  subinvolution (uterus) 674.8 ☑
  sudden death (cause unknown) 674.9 ☑
  suppuration — *see* Puerperal, abscess
  syphilis (conditions classifiable to 090-097) 647.0 ☑
  tetanus 670.0 ☑
  thelitis 675.0 ☑
  thrombocytopenia 666.3 ☑
  thrombophlebitis (superficial) 671.2 ☑
    deep 671.4 ☑
    pelvic 671.4 ☑
    specified site NEC 671.5 ☑
  thrombosis (venous) — *see* Thrombosis, puerperal

Puerperal — *continued*
  thyroid dysfunction (conditions classifiable to
      240-246) 648.1 ☑
  toxemia (*see also* Toxemia, of pregnancy)
      642.4 ☑
    eclamptic 642.6 ☑
      with pre-existing hypertension 642.7 ☑
    pre-eclamptic (mild) 642.4 ☑
      with
        convulsions 642.6 ☑
        pre-existing hypertension 642.7 ☑
      severe 642.5 ☑
  tuberculosis (conditions classifiable to 010-018)
      647.3 ☑
  uremia 669.3 ☑
  vaginitis (conditions classifiable to 616.1)
      646.6 ☑
  varicose veins (legs) 671.0 ☑
    vulva or perineum 671.1 ☑
  vulvitis (conditions classifiable to 616.1)
      646.6 ☑
  vulvovaginitis (conditions classifiable to 616.1)
      646.6 ☑
  white leg 671.4 ☑
Pulled muscle — *see* Sprain, by site
Pulmolithiasis 518.89
Pulmonary — *see* condition
Pulmonitis (unknown etiology) 486
Pulpitis (acute) (anachoretic) (chronic)
      (hyperplastic) (putrescent) (suppurative)
      (ulcerative) 522.0
Pulpless tooth 522.9
Pulse
  alternating 427.89
    psychogenic 306.2
  bigeminal 427.89
  fast 785.0
  feeble, rapid, due to shock following injury
      958.4
  rapid 785.0
  slow 427.89
  strong 785.9
  trigeminal 427.89
  water-hammer (*see also* Insufficiency, aortic)
      424.1
  weak 785.9
Pulseless disease 446.7
Pulsus
  alternans or trigeminy 427.89
    psychogenic 306.2
Punch drunk 310.2
Puncta lacrimalia occlusion 375.52
Punctiform hymen 752.49
Puncture (traumatic) — *see also* Wound, open, by
      site
  accidental, complicating surgery 998.2
  bladder, nontraumatic 596.6
  by
    device, implant, or graft — *see*
        Complications, mechanical
    foreign body
      internal organs — *see also* Injury,
          internal, by site
        by ingested object — *see* Foreign body
      left accidentally in operation wound
          998.4
    instrument (any) during a procedure,
        accidental 998.2
  internal organs, abdomen, chest, or pelvis —
      see Injury, internal, by site
  kidney, nontraumatic 593.89
Pupil — *see* condition
Pupillary membrane 364.74
  persistent 743.46
Pupillotonia 379.46
  pseudotabetic 379.46
Purpura 287.2
  abdominal 287.0
  allergic 287.0
  anaphylactoid 287.0
  annularis telangiectodes 709.1
  arthritic 287.0
  autoerythrocyte sensitization 287.2
  autoimmune 287.0

Purpura — *continued*
  bacterial 287.0
  Bateman's (senile) 287.2
  capillary fragility (hereditary) (idiopathic) 287.8
  cryoglobulinemic 273.2
  devil's pinches 287.2
  fibrinolytic (*see also* Fibrinolysis) 286.6
  fulminans, fulminous 286.6
  gangrenous 287.0
  hemorrhagic (*see also* Purpura,
      thrombocytopenic) 287.39   ▲
    nodular 272.7
    nonthrombocytopenic 287.0
    thrombocytopenic 287.39   ▲
  Henoch's (purpura nervosa) 287.0
  Henoch-Schönlein (allergic) 287.0
  hypergammaglobulinemic (benign primary)
      (Waldenström's) 273.0
  idiopathic 287.31   ▲
    nonthrombocytopenic 287.0
    thrombocytopenic 287.31   ▲
  immune thrombocytopenic 287.31   ●
  infectious 287.0
  malignant 287.0
  neonatorum 772.6
  nervosa 287.0
  newborn NEC 772.6
  nonthrombocytopenic 287.2
    hemorrhagic 287.0
    idiopathic 287.0
  nonthrombopenic 287.2
  peliosis rheumatica 287.0
  pigmentaria, progressiva 709.09
  posttransfusion 287.4
  primary 287.0
  primitive 287.0
  red cell membrane sensitivity 287.2
  rheumatica 287.0
  Schönlein (-Henoch) (allergic) 287.0
  scorbutic 267
  senile 287.2
  simplex 287.2
  symptomatica 287.0
  telangiectasia annularis 709.1
  thrombocytopenic (*see also* Thrombocytopenia)
      287.30   ▲
    congenital 287.33   ●
    essential 287.30   ●
    hereditary 287.31   ●
    idiopathic 287.31   ●
    immune 287.31   ●
    neonatal, transitory (*see also*
        Thrombocytopenia, neonatal
        transitory) 776.1
    primary 287.30   ●
    puerperal, postpartum 666.3 ☑
    thrombotic 446.6
  thrombohemolytic (*see also* Fibrinolysis) 286.6
  thrombopenic (*see also* Thrombocytopenia)
      287.30   ▲
    congenital 287.33   ●
    essential 287.30   ●
    thrombotic 446.6
      thrombocytic 446.6
      thrombocytopenic 446.6
  toxic 287.0
  variolosa 050.0
  vascular 287.0
  visceral symptoms 287.0
  Werlhof's (*see also* Purpura, thrombocytopenic)
      287.39   ▲
Purpuric spots 782.7
Purulent — *see* condition
Pus
  absorption, general — *see* Septicemia
  in
    stool 792.1
    urine 791.9
  tube (rupture) (*see also* Salpingo-oophoritis)
      614.2
Pustular rash 782.1
Pustule 686.9
  malignant 022.0
  nonmalignant 686.9
Putnam's disease (subacute combined sclerosis
      with pernicious anemia) 281.0 [*336.2*]

Putnam-Dana syndrome (subacute combined
      sclerosis with pernicious anemia) 281.0
      [*336.2*]
Putrefaction, intestinal 569.89
Putrescent pulp (dental) 522.1
Pyarthritis — *see* Pyarthrosis
Pyarthrosis (*see also* Arthritis, pyogenic) 711.0 ☑
  tuberculous — *see* Tuberculosis, joint
Pycnoepilepsy, pycnolepsy (idiopathic) (*see also*
      Epilepsy) 345.0 ☑
Pyelectasia 593.89
Pyelectasis 593.89
Pyelitis (congenital) (uremic) 590.80
  with
    abortion — *see* Abortion, by type, with
        specified complication NEC
    contracted kidney 590.00
    ectopic pregnancy (*see also* categories
        633.0-633.9) 639.8
    molar pregnancy (*see also* categories 630-
        632) 639.8
  acute 590.10
    with renal medullary necrosis 590.11
  chronic 590.00
    with
      renal medullary necrosis 590.01
  complicating pregnancy, childbirth, or
      puerperium 646.6 ☑
    affecting fetus or newborn 760.1
  cystica 590.3
    following
      abortion 639.8
      ectopic or molar pregnancy 639.8
  gonococcal 098.19
    chronic or duration of 2 months or over
        098.39
  tuberculous (*see also* Tuberculosis) 016.0 ☑
      [*590.81*]
Pyelocaliectasis 593.89
Pyelocystitis (*see also* Pyelitis) 590.80
Pyelohydronephrosis 591
Pyelonephritis (*see also* Pyelitis) 590.80
  acute 590.10
    with renal medullary necrosis 590.11
  chronic 590.00
  syphilitic (late) 095.4
  tuberculous (*see also* Tuberculosis) 016.0 ☑
      [*590.81*]
Pyelonephrosis (*see also* Pyelitis) 590.80
  chronic 590.00
Pyelophlebitis 451.89
Pyelo-ureteritis cystica 590.3
Pyemia, pyemic (purulent) (*see also* Septicemia)
      038.9
  abscess — *see* Abscess
  arthritis (*see also* Arthritis, pyogenic) 711.0 ☑
  Bacillus coli 038.42
  embolism — *see* Embolism, pyemic
  fever 038.9
  infection 038.9
  joint (*see also* Arthritis, pyogenic) 711.0 ☑
  liver 572.1
  meningococcal 036.2
  newborn 771.81
  phlebitis — *see* Phlebitis
  pneumococcal 038.2
  portal 572.1
  postvaccinal 999.3
  specified organism NEC 038.8
  staphylococcal 038.10
    aureus 038.11
    specified organism NEC 038.19
  streptococcal 038.0
  tuberculous — *see* Tuberculosis, miliary
Pygopagus 759.4
Pykno-epilepsy, pyknolepsy (idiopathic) (*see also*
      Epilepsy) 345.0 ☑
Pyle (-Cohn) disease (craniometaphyseal
      dysplasia) 756.89
Pylephlebitis (suppurative) 572.1
Pylethrombophlebitis 572.1
Pylethrombosis 572.1
Pyloritis (*see also* Gastritis) 535.5 ☑
Pylorospasm (reflex) 537.81
  congenital or infantile 750.5

☑ Additional Digit Required — Refer to the Tabular List (Numeric Code Section) for Additional Digit Selection
▶◀ Revised Text   ● New Line   ▲ Revised Code

Pylorospasm — *continued*
  neurotic 306.4
  newborn 750.5
  psychogenic 306.4
Pylorus, pyloric — *see* condition
Pyoarthrosis — *see* Pyarthrosis
Pyocele
  mastoid 383.00
  sinus (accessory) (nasal) (*see also* Sinusitis) 473.9
  turbinate (bone) 473.9
  urethra (*see also* Urethritis) 597.0
Pyococcal dermatitis 686.00
Pyococcide, skin 686.00
Pyocolpos (*see also* Vaginitis) 616.10
Pyocyaneus dermatitis 686.09
Pyocystitis (*see also* Cystitis) 595.9
Pyoderma, pyodermia 686.00
  gangrenosum 686.01
  specified type NEC 686.09
  vegetans 686.8
Pyodermatitis 686.00
  vegetans 686.8
Pyogenic — *see* condition
Pyohemia — *see* Septicemia
Pyohydronephrosis (*see also* Pyelitis) 590.80
Pyometra 615.9
Pyometritis (*see also* Endometritis) 615.9
Pyometrium (*see also* Endometritis) 615.9
Pyomyositis 728.0
  ossificans 728.19
  tropical (bungpagga) 040.81
Pyonephritis (*see also* Pyelitis) 590.80
  chronic 590.00
Pyonephrosis (congenital) (*see also* Pyelitis) 590.80
  acute 590.10
Pyo-oophoritis (*see also* Salpingo-oophoritis) 614.2
Pyo-ovarium (*see also* Salpingo-oophoritis) 614.2
Pyopericarditis 420.99
Pyopericardium 420.99
Pyophlebitis — *see* Phlebitis
Pyopneumopericardium 420.99
Pyopneumothorax (infectional) 510.9
  with fistula 510.0
  subdiaphragmatic (*see also* Peritonitis) 567.29 ▲
  subphrenic (*see also* Peritonitis) 567.29 ▲
  tuberculous (*see also* Tuberculosis, pleura) 012.0 ☑
Pyorrhea (alveolar) (alveolaris) 523.4
  degenerative 523.5
Pyosalpingitis (*see also* Salpingo-oophoritis) 614.2
Pyosalpinx (*see also* Salpingo-oophoritis) 614.2
Pyosepticemia — *see* Septicemia
Pyosis
  Corlett's (impetigo) 684
  Manson's (pemphigus contagiosus) 684
Pyothorax 510.9
  with fistula 510.0
  tuberculous (*see also* Tuberculosis, pleura) 012.0 ☑
Pyoureter 593.89
  tuberculous (*see also* Tuberculosis) 016.2 ☑
Pyramidopallidonigral syndrome 332.0
Pyrexia (of unknown origin) (P.U.O.) 780.6
  atmospheric 992.0
  during labor 659.2 ☑
  environmentally-induced newborn 778.4
  heat 992.0
  newborn, environmentally-induced 778.4
  puerperal 672.0 ☑
Pyroglobulinemia 273.8
Pyromania 312.33
Pyrosis 787.1
Pyrroloporphyria 277.1
Pyuria (bacterial) 791.9

Q

Q fever 083.0
  with pneumonia 083.0 [484.8]
Quadricuspid aortic valve 746.89
Quadrilateral fever 083.0
Quadriparesis — *see* Quadriplegia
  meaning muscle weakness 728.87 ●
Quadriplegia 344.00
  with fracture, vertebra (process) — *see* Fracture, vertebra, cervical, with spinal cord injury
  brain (current episode) 437.8
  C1-C4
    complete 344.01
    incomplete 344.02
  C5-C7
    complete 344.03
    incomplete 344.04
  cerebral (current episode) 437.8
  congenital or infantile (cerebral) (spastic) (spinal) 343.2
  cortical 437.8
  embolic (current episode) (*see also* Embolism, brain) 434.1 ☑
  infantile (cerebral) (spastic) (spinal) 343.2
  newborn NEC 767.0
  specified NEC 344.09
  thrombotic (current episode) (*see also* Thrombosis, brain) 434.0 ☑
  traumatic — *see* Injury, spinal, cervical
Quadruplet
  affected by maternal complications of pregnancy 761.5
  healthy liveborn — *see* Newborn, multiple
  pregnancy (complicating delivery) NEC 651.8 ☑
    with fetal loss and retention of one or more fetus(es) 651.5 ☑
    following (elective) fetal reduction 651.7 ☑ ●
Quarrelsomeness 301.3
Quartan
  fever 084.2
  malaria (fever) 084.2
Queensland fever 083.0
  coastal 083.0
  seven-day 100.89
Quervain's disease 727.04
  thyroid (subacute granulomatous thyroiditis) 245.1
Queyrat's erythroplasia (M8080/2)
  specified site — *see* Neoplasm, skin, in situ
  unspecified site 233.5
Quincke's disease or edema — *see* Edema, angioneurotic
Quinquaud's disease (acne decalvans) 704.09
Quinsy (gangrenous) 475
Quintan fever 083.1
Quintuplet
  affected by maternal complications of pregnancy 761.5
  healthy liveborn — *see* Newborn, multiple
  pregnancy (complicating delivery) NEC 651.2 ☑
    with fetal loss and retention of one or more fetus(es) 651.6 ☑
    following (elective) fetal reduction 651.7 ☑ ●
Quotidian
  fever 084.0
  malaria (fever) 084.0

R

Rabbia 071
Rabbit fever (*see also* Tularemia) 021.9
Rabies 071
  contact V01.5
  exposure to V01.5
  inoculation V04.5
    reaction — *see* Complications, vaccination
  vaccination, prophylactic (against) V04.5
Rachischisis (*see also* Spina bifida) 741.9 ☑

Rachitic — *see also* condition
  deformities of spine 268.1
  pelvis 268.1
    with disproportion (fetopelvic) 653.2 ☑
      affecting fetus or newborn 763.1
      causing obstructed labor 660.1 ☑
        affecting fetus or newborn 763.1
Rachitis, rachitism — *see also* Rickets
  acute 268.0
  fetalis 756.4
  renalis 588.0
  tarda 268.0
Racket nail 757.5
Radial nerve — *see* condition
Radiation effects or sickness — *see also* Effect, adverse, radiation
  cataract 366.46
  dermatitis 692.82
  sunburn (*see also* Sunburn) 692.71
Radiculitis (pressure) (vertebrogenic) 729.2
  accessory nerve 723.4
  anterior crural 724.4
  arm 723.4
  brachial 723.4
  cervical NEC 723.4
  due to displacement of intervertebral disc — *see* Neuritis, due to, displacement intervertebral disc
  leg 724.4
  lumbar NEC 724.4
  lumbosacral 724.4
  rheumatic 729.2
  syphilitic 094.89
  thoracic (with visceral pain) 724.4
Radiculomyelitis 357.0
  toxic, due to
    Clostridium tetani 037
    Corynebacterium diphtheriae 032.89
Radiculopathy (*see also* Radiculitis) 729.2
Radioactive substances, adverse effect — *see* Effect, adverse, radioactive substance
Radiodermal burns (acute) (chronic) (occupational) — *see* Burn, by site
Radiodermatitis 692.82
Radionecrosis — *see* Effect, adverse, radiation
Radiotherapy session V58.0
Radium, adverse effect — *see* Effect, adverse, radioactive substance
Raeder-Harbitz syndrome (pulseless disease) 446.7
Rage (*see also* Disturbance, conduct) 312.0 ☑
  meaning rabies 071
Rag sorters' disease 022.1
Raillietiniasis 123.8
Railroad neurosis 300.16
Railway spine 300.16
Raised — *see* Elevation
Raiva 071
Rake teeth, tooth 524.39
Rales 786.7
Ramifying renal pelvis 753.3
Ramsay Hunt syndrome (herpetic geniculate ganglionitis) 053.11
  meaning dyssynergia cerebellaris myoclonica 334.2
Ranke's primary infiltration (*see also* Tuberculosis) 010.0 ☑
Ranula 527.6
  congenital 750.26
Rape
  adult 995.83 ●
  alleged, observation or examination V71.5
  child 995.53 ●
Rapid
  feeble pulse, due to shock, following injury 958.4
  heart (beat) 785.0
    psychogenic 306.2
  respiration 786.06
    psychogenic 306.1

Rapid — *continued*
 second stage (delivery) 661.3 ☑
  affecting fetus or newborn 763.6
 time-zone change syndrome 327.35 ▲
Rarefaction, bone 733.99
Rash 782.1
 canker 034.1
 diaper 691.0
 drug (internal use) 693.0
  contact 692.3
 ECHO 9 virus 078.89
 enema 692.89
 food (*see also* Allergy, food) 693.1
 heat 705.1
 napkin 691.0
 nettle 708.8
 pustular 782.1
 rose 782.1
  epidemic 056.9
  of infants 057.8
 scarlet 034.1
 serum (prophylactic) (therapeutic) 999.5
 toxic 782.1
 wandering tongue 529.1
Rasmussen's aneurysm (*see also* Tuberculosis)
  011.2 ☑
Rat-bite fever 026.9
 due to Streptobacillus moniliformis 026.1 ☑
 spirochetal (morsus muris) 026.0 ☑
Rathke's pouch tumor (M9350/1) 237.0
Raymond (-Céstan) syndrome 433.8 ☑
Raynaud's
 disease or syndrome (paroxysmal digital
  cyanosis) 443.0
 gangrene (symmetric) 443.0 *[785.4]*
 phenomenon (paroxysmal digital cyanosis)
  (secondary) 443.0
RDS 769
Reaction
 acute situational maladjustment (*see also*
  Reaction, adjustment) 309.9
 adaptation (*see also* Reaction, adjustment)
  309.9
 adjustment 309.9
  with
   anxious mood 309.24
    with depressed mood 309.28
   conduct disturbance 309.3
    combined with disturbance of
     emotions 309.4
   depressed mood 309.0
    brief 309.0
     with anxious mood 309.28
    prolonged 309.1
   elective mutism 309.83
   mixed emotions and conduct 309.4
   mutism, elective 309.83
   physical symptoms 309.82
   predominant disturbance (of)
    conduct 309.3
    emotions NEC 309.29
     mixed 309.28
    mixed, emotions and conduct 309.4
    specified type NEC 309.89
   specific academic or work inhibition
    309.23
   withdrawal 309.83
  depressive 309.0
   with conduct disturbance 309.4
   brief 309.0
   prolonged 309.1
  specified type NEC 309.89
 adverse food NEC 995.7
 affective (*see also* Psychosis, affective) 296.90
  specified type NEC 296.99
 aggressive 301.3
  unsocialized (*see also* Disturbance, conduct)
   312.0 ☑
 allergic (*see also* Allergy) 995.3
  drug, medicinal substance, and biological —
   see Allergy, drug
  food — *see* Allergy, food
  serum 999.5
 anaphylactic — *see* Shock, anaphylactic
 anesthesia — *see* Anesthesia, complication

Reaction — *continued*
 anger 312.0 ☑
 antisocial 301.7
 antitoxin (prophylactic) (therapeutic) — *see*
  Complications, vaccination
 anxiety 300.00
 asthenic 300.5
 compulsive 300.3
 conversion (anesthetic) (autonomic)
  (hyperkinetic) (mixed paralytic)
  (paresthetic) 300.11
 deoxyribonuclease (DNA) (DNase)
  hypersensitivity NEC 287.2
 depressive 300.4
  acute 309.0
  affective (*see also* Psychosis, affective)
   296.2 ☑
   recurrent episode 296.3 ☑
   single episode 296.2 ☑
  brief 309.0
  manic (*see also* Psychosis, affective) 296.80
  neurotic 300.4
  psychoneurotic 300.4
  psychotic 298.0
 dissociative 300.15
 drug NEC (*see also* Table of Drugs and
  Chemicals) 995.2
  allergic — *see* Allergy, drug
  correct substance properly administered
   995.2
  obstetric anesthetic or analgesic NEC
   668.9 ☑
   affecting fetus or newborn 763.5
   specified drug — *see* Table of Drugs and
    Chemicals
  overdose or poisoning 977.9
   specified drug — *see* Table of Drugs and
    Chemicals
  specific to newborn 779.4
  transmitted via placenta or breast milk —
   see Absorption, drug, through
   placenta
  withdrawal NEC 292.0
   infant of dependent mother 779.5
  wrong substance given or taken in error
   977.9
   specified drug — *see* Table of Drugs and
    Chemicals
 dyssocial 301.7
 erysipeloid 027.1
 fear 300.20
  child 313.0
 fluid loss, cerebrospinal 349.0
 food — *see also* Allergy, food
  adverse NEC 995.7
  anaphylactic shock — *see* Anaphylactic
   shock, due to, food
 foreign
  body NEC 728.82
   in operative wound (inadvertently left)
    998.4
   due to surgical material intentionally
    left — *see* Complications, due to
    (presence of) any device, implant,
    or graft classified to 996.0-996.5
    NEC
  substance accidentally left during a
   procedure (chemical) (powder) (talc)
   998.7
   body or object (instrument) (sponge)
    (swab) 998.4
 graft-versus-host (GVH) 996.85
 grief (acute) (brief) 309.0
  prolonged 309.1
 gross stress (*see also* Reaction, stress, acute)
  308.9
 group delinquent (*see also* Disturbance,
  conduct) 312.2 ☑
 Herxheimer's 995.0
 hyperkinetic (*see also* Hyperkinesia) 314.9
 hypochondriacal 300.7
 hypoglycemic, due to insulin 251.0
  therapeutic misadventure 962.3
 hypomanic (*see also* Psychosis, affective)
  296.0 ☑
  recurrent episode 296.1 ☑
  single episode 296.0 ☑

Reaction — *continued*
 hysterical 300.10
  conversion type 300.11
  dissociative 300.15
 id (bacterial cause) 692.89
 immaturity NEC 301.89
  aggressive 301.3
  emotional instability 301.59
 immunization — *see* Complications,
  vaccination
 incompatibility
  blood group (ABO) (infusion) (transfusion)
   999.6
  Rh (factor) (infusion) (transfusion) 999.7
 inflammatory — *see* Infection
 infusion — *see* Complications, infusion
 inoculation (immune serum) — *see*
  Complications, vaccination
 insulin 995.2
 involutional
  paranoid 297.2
  psychotic (*see also* Psychosis, affective,
   depressive) 296.2 ☑
 leukemoid (lymphocytic) (monocytic)
  (myelocytic) 288.8
 LSD (*see also* Abuse, drugs, nondependent)
  305.3 ☑
 lumbar puncture 349.0
 manic-depressive (*see also* Psychosis, affective)
  296.80
  depressed 296.2 ☑
   recurrent episode 296.3 ☑
   single episode 296.2 ☑
  hypomanic 296.0 ☑
 neurasthenic 300.5
 neurogenic (*see also* Neurosis) 300.9
 neurotic NEC 300.9
 neurotic-depressive 300.4
 nitritoid — *see* Crisis, nitritoid
 obsessive ►compulsive◄ 300.3
 organic 293.9
  acute 293.0
  subacute 293.1
 overanxious, child or adolescent 313.0
 paranoid (chronic) 297.9
  acute 298.3
  climacteric 297.2
  involutional 297.2
  menopausal 297.2
  senile 290.20
  simple 297.0
 passive
  aggressive 301.84
  dependency 301.6
 personality (*see also* Disorder, personality)
  301.9
 phobic 300.20
 postradiation — *see* Effect, adverse, radiation
 psychogenic NEC 300.9
 psychoneurotic (*see also* Neurosis) 300.9
  anxiety 300.00
  compulsive 300.3
  conversion 300.11
  depersonalization 300.6
  depressive 300.4
  dissociative 300.15
  hypochondriacal 300.7
  hysterical 300.10
   conversion type 300.11
   dissociative type 300.15
  neurasthenic 300.5
  obsessive 300.3
  obsessive-compulsive 300.3
  phobic 300.20
  tension state 300.9
 psychophysiologic NEC (*see also* Disorder,
  psychosomatic) 306.9
  cardiovascular 306.2
  digestive 306.4
  endocrine 306.6
  gastrointestinal 306.4
  genitourinary 306.50
  heart 306.2
  hemic 306.8
  intestinal (large) (small) 306.4
  laryngeal 306.1
  lymphatic 306.8

Reaction — continued
  psychophysiologic NEC (see also Disorder,
    psychosomatic) — continued
    musculoskeletal 306.0
    pharyngeal 306.1
    respiratory 306.1
    skin 306.3
    special sense organs 306.7
  psychosomatic (see also Disorder,
    psychosomatic) 306.9
  psychotic (see also Psychosis) 298.9
    depressive 298.0
    due to or associated with physical condition
      (see also Psychosis, organic) 293.9
    involutional (see also Psychosis, affective)
      296.2 ☑
      recurrent episode 296.3 ☑
      single episode 296.2 ☑
  pupillary (myotonic) (tonic) 379.46
  radiation — see Effect, adverse, radiation
  runaway — see also Disturbance, conduct
    socialized 312.2 ☑
    undersocialized, unsocialized 312.1 ☑
  scarlet fever toxin — see Complications,
    vaccination
  schizophrenic (see also Schizophrenia) 295.9 ☑
    latent 295.5 ☑
  serological for syphilis — see Serology for
    syphilis
  serum (prophylactic) (therapeutic) 999.5
    immediate 999.4
  situational (see also Reaction, adjustment)
    309.9
    acute, to stress 308.3
    adjustment (see also Reaction, adjustment)
      309.9
  somatization (see also Disorder, psychosomatic)
    306.9
  spinal puncture 349.0
  spite, child (see also Disturbance, conduct)
    312.0 ☑
  stress, acute 308.9
    with predominant disturbance (of)
      consciousness 308.1
      emotions 308.0
      mixed 308.4
      psychomotor 308.2
      specified type NEC 308.3
    bone or cartilage — see Fracture, stress
  surgical procedure — see Complications,
    surgical procedure
  tetanus antitoxin — see Complications,
    vaccination
  toxin-antitoxin — see Complications,
    vaccination
  transfusion (blood) (bone marrow)
    (lymphocytes) (allergic) — see
    Complications, transfusion
  tuberculin skin test, nonspecific (without active
    tuberculosis) 795.5
    positive (without active tuberculosis) 795.5
  ultraviolet — see Effect, adverse, ultraviolet
  undersocialized, unsocialized — see also
    Disturbance, conduct
    aggressive (type) 312.0 ☑
    unaggressive (type) 312.1 ☑
  vaccination (any) — see Complications,
    vaccination
  white graft (skin) 996.52
  withdrawing, child or adolescent 313.22
  x-ray — see Effect, adverse, x-rays

Reactive depression (see also Reaction,
  depressive) 300.4
  neurotic 300.4
  psychoneurotic 300.4
  psychotic 298.0

Rebound tenderness 789.6 ☑

Recalcitrant patient V15.81

Recanalization, thrombus — see Thrombosis

Recession, receding
  chamber angle (eye) 364.77
  chin 524.06
  gingival (postinfective) (postoperative) 523.20
    generalized 523.25
    localized 523.24
    minimal 523.21

Recession, receding — continued
  gingival — continued
    moderate 523.22
    severe 523.23

Recklinghausen's disease (M9540/1) 237.71
  bones (osteitis fibrosa cystica) 252.01

Recklinghausen-Applebaum disease
  (hemochromatosis) 275.0

Reclus' disease (cystic) 610.1

Recrudescent typhus (fever) 081.1

Recruitment, auditory 388.44

Rectalgia 569.42

Rectitis 569.49

Rectocele
  female (without uterine prolapse) 618.04
    with uterine prolapse 618.4
      complete 618.3
      incomplete 618.2
  in pregnancy or childbirth 654.4 ☑
    causing obstructed labor 660.2 ☑
      affecting fetus or newborn 763.1
  male 569.49
  vagina, vaginal (outlet) 618.04

Rectosigmoiditis 569.89
  ulcerative (chronic) 556.3

Rectosigmoid junction — see condition

Rectourethral — see condition

Rectovaginal — see condition

Rectovesical — see condition

Rectum, rectal — see condition

Recurrent — see condition

Red bugs 133.8

Red cedar asthma 495.8

Redness
  conjunctiva 379.93
  eye 379.93
  nose 478.1

Reduced ventilatory or vital capacity 794.2

Reduction
  function
    kidney (see also Disease, renal) 593.9
    liver 573.8
  ventilatory capacity 794.2
  vital capacity 794.2

Redundant, redundancy
  abdomen 701.9
  anus 751.5
  cardia 537.89
  clitoris 624.2
  colon (congenital) 751.5
  foreskin (congenital) 605
  intestine 751.5
  labia 624.3
  organ or site, congenital NEC — see Accessory
  panniculus (abdominal) 278.1
  prepuce (congenital) 605
  pylorus 537.89
  rectum 751.5
  scrotum 608.89
  sigmoid 751.5
  skin (of face) 701.9
    eyelids 374.30
  stomach 537.89
  uvula 528.9
  vagina 623.8

Reduplication — see Duplication

Referral
  adoption (agency) V68.89
  nursing care V63.8
  patient without examination or treatment
    V68.81
  social services V63.8

Reflex — see also condition
  blink, deficient 374.45
  hyperactive gag 478.29
  neurogenic bladder NEC 596.54
    atonic 596.54
      with cauda equina syndrome 344.61
  vasoconstriction 443.9
  vasovagal 780.2

Reflux
  esophageal 530.81
    with esophagitis 530.11

Reflux — continued
  esophagitis 530.11
  gastroesophageal 530.81
  mitral — see Insufficiency, mitral
  ureteral — see Reflux, vesicoureteral
  vesicoureteral 593.70
    with
      reflux nephropathy 593.73
        bilateral 593.72
        unilateral 593.71

Reformed gallbladder 576.0

Reforming, artificial openings (see also
  Attention to, artificial, opening) V55.9

Refractive error (see also Error, refractive) 367.9

Refsum's disease or syndrome (heredopathia
  atactica polyneuritiformis) 356.3

Refusal of
  food 307.59
    hysterical 300.11
  treatment because of, due to
    patient's decision NEC V64.2
    reason of conscience or religion V62.6

Regaud
  tumor (M8082/3) — see Neoplasm,
    nasopharynx, malignant
  type carcinoma (M8082/3) — see Neoplasm,
    nasopharynx, malignant

Regional — see condition

Regulation feeding (elderly) (infant) 783.3
  newborn 779.3

Regurgitated
  food, choked on 933.1
  stomach contents, choked on 933.1

Regurgitation
  aortic (valve) (see also Insufficiency, aortic)
    424.1
    congenital 746.4
    syphilitic 093.22
  food — see also Vomiting
    with reswallowing — see Rumination
    newborn 779.3
  gastric contents — see Vomiting
  heart — see Endocarditis
  mitral (valve) — see also Insufficiency, mitral
    congenital 746.6
  myocardial — see Endocarditis
  pulmonary (heart) (valve) (see also
    Endocarditis, pulmonary) 424.3
  stomach — see Vomiting
  tricuspid — see Endocarditis, tricuspid
  valve, valvular — see Endocarditis
  vesicoureteral — see Reflux, vesicoureteral

Rehabilitation V57.9
  multiple types V57.89
  occupational V57.21
  specified type NEC V57.89
  speech V57.3
  vocational V57.22

Reichmann's disease or syndrome
  (gastrosuccorrhea) 536.8

Reifenstein's syndrome (hereditary familial
  hypogonadism, male) 259.5 ▲

Reilly's syndrome or phenomenon (see also
  Neuropathy, peripheral, autonomic) 337.9

Reimann's periodic disease 277.3

Reinsertion, contraceptive device V25.42

Reiter's disease, syndrome, or urethritis
  099.3 [711.1] ☑

Rejection
  food, hysterical 300.11
  transplant 996.80
    bone marrow 996.85
    corneal 996.51
    organ (immune or nonimmune cause)
      996.80
      bone marrow 996.85
      heart 996.83
      intestines 996.87
      kidney 996.81
      liver 996.82
      lung 996.84
      pancreas 996.86

Rejection — *continued*
  transplant — *continued*
    organ — *continued*
      specified NEC 996.89
      skin 996.52
        artificial 996.55
        decellularized allodermis 996.55

Relapsing fever 087.9
  Carter's (Asiatic) 087.0
  Dutton's (West African) 087.1
  Koch's 087.9
  louse-borne (epidemic) 087.0
  Novy's (American) 087.1
  Obermeyer's (European) 087.0
  Spirillum 087.9
  tick-borne (endemic) 087.1

Relaxation
  anus (sphincter) 569.49
    due to hysteria 300.11
  arch (foot) 734
    congenital 754.61
  back ligaments 728.4
  bladder (sphincter) 596.59
  cardio-esophageal 530.89
  cervix (*see also* Incompetency, cervix) 622.5
  diaphragm 519.4
  inguinal rings — *see* Hernia, inguinal
  joint (capsule) (ligament) (paralytic) (*see also* Derangement, joint) 718.90
    congenital 755.8
  lumbosacral joint 724.6
  pelvic floor 618.89
  pelvis 618.89
  perineum 618.89
  posture 729.9
  rectum (sphincter) 569.49
  sacroiliac (joint) 724.6
  scrotum 608.89
  urethra (sphincter) 599.84
  uterus (outlet) 618.89
  vagina (outlet) 618.89
  vesical 596.59

Remains
  canal of Cloquet 743.51
  capsule (opaque) 743.51

Remittent fever (malarial) 084.6

Remnant
  canal of Cloquet 743.51
  capsule (opaque) 743.51
  cervix, cervical stump (acquired) (postoperative) 622.8
  cystic duct, postcholecystectomy 576.0
  fingernail 703.8
    congenital 757.5
  meniscus, knee 717.5
  thyroglossal duct 759.2
  tonsil 474.8
    infected 474.00
  urachus 753.7

Remote effect of cancer — *see* condition

Removal (of)
  catheter (urinary) (indwelling) V53.6
    from artificial opening — *see* Attention to, artificial, opening
    non-vascular V58.82
    vascular V58.81
  cerebral ventricle (communicating) shunt V53.01
  device — *see also* Fitting (of)
    contraceptive V25.42
    fixation
      external V54.89
      internal V54.01
      traction V54.89
  dressing V58.3
  ileostomy V55.2
  Kirschner wire V54.89
  nonvascular catheter V58.82
  pin V54.01
  plaster cast V54.89
  plate (fracture) V54.01
  rod V54.01
  screw V54.01
  splint, external V54.89
  subdermal implantable contraceptive V25.43

Removal (of) — *continued*
  suture V58.3
  traction device, external V54.89
  vascular catheter V58.81

Ren
  arcuatus 753.3
  mobile, mobilis (*see also* Disease, renal) 593.0
    congenital 753.3
  unguliformis 753.3

Renal — *see also* condition
  glomerulohyalinosis-diabetic syndrome 250.4 ☑ *[581.81]*

Rendu-Osler-Weber disease or syndrome
  (familial hemorrhagic telangiectasia) 448.0

Reninoma (M8361/1) 236.91

Rénon-Delille syndrome 253.8

Repair
  pelvic floor, previous, in pregnancy or childbirth 654.4 ☑
    affecting fetus or newborn 763.89
  scarred tissue V51

Replacement by artificial or mechanical device or prosthesis of (*see also* Fitting (of))
  artificial skin V43.83
  bladder V43.5
  blood vessel V43.4
  breast V43.82
  eye globe V43.0
  heart
    with
      assist device V43.21
      fully implantable artificial heart V43.22
    valve V43.3
  intestine V43.89
  joint V43.60
    ankle V43.66
    elbow V43.62
    finger V43.69
    hip (partial) (total) V43.64
    knee V43.65
    shoulder V43.61
    specified NEC V43.69
    wrist V43.63
  kidney V43.89
  larynx V43.81
  lens V43.1
  limb(s) V43.7
  liver V43.89
  lung V43.89
  organ NEC V43.89
  pancreas V43.89
  skin (artificial) V43.83
  tissue NEC V43.89

Reprogramming
  cardiac pacemaker V53.31

Request for expert evidence V68.2

Reserve, decreased or low
  cardiac — *see* Disease, heart
  kidney (*see also* Disease, renal) 593.9

Residual — *see also* condition
  bladder 596.8
  foreign body — *see* Retention, foreign body
  state, schizophrenic (*see also* Schizophrenia) 295.6 ☑
  urine 788.69

Resistance, resistant (to)
  activated protein C 289.81

Note — use the following subclassification for categories V09.5, V09.7, V09.8, V09.9:

0	*without mention of resistance to multiple drugs*
1	*with resistance to multiple drugs*
	V09.5 *quinolones and fluoroquinolones*
	V09.7 *antimycobacterial agents*
	V09.8 *specified drugs NEC*
	V09.9 *unspecified drugs*

  drugs by microorganisms V09.9 ☑
    Amikacin V09.4
    aminoglycosides V09.4
    Amodiaquine V09.5 ☑

Resistance, resistant — *continued*
  drugs by microorganisms — *continued*
    Amoxicillin V09.0
    Ampicillin V09.0
    antimycobacterial agents V09.7 ☑
    Azithromycin V09.2
    Azlocillin V09.0
    Aztreonam V09.1
    B-lactam antibiotics V09.1
    Bacampicillin V09.0
    Bacitracin V09.8 ☑
    Benznidazole V09.8 ☑
    Capreomycin V09.7 ☑
    Carbenicillin V09.0
    Cefaclor V09.1
    Cefadroxil V09.1
    Cefamandole V09.1
    Cefatetan V09.1
    Cefazolin V09.1
    Cefixime V09.1
    Cefonicid V09.1
    Cefoperazone V09.1
    Ceforanide V09.1
    Cefotaxime V09.1
    Cefoxitin V09.1
    Ceftazidime V09.1
    Ceftizoxime V09.1
    Ceftriaxone V09.1
    Cefuroxime V09.1
    Cephalexin V09.1
    Cephaloglycin V09.1
    Cephaloridine V09.1
    Cephalosporins V09.1
    Cephalothin V09.1
    Cephapirin V09.1
    Cephradine V09.1
    Chloramphenicol V09.8 ☑
    Chloraquine V09.5 ☑
    Chlorguanide V09.8 ☑
    Chlorproguanil V09.8 ☑
    Chlortetracycline V09.3
    Cinoxacin V09.5 ☑
    Ciprofloxacin V09.5 ☑
    Clarithromycin V09.2
    Clindamycin V09.8 ☑
    Clioquinol V09.5 ☑
    Clofazimine V09.7 ☑
    Cloxacillin V09.0
    Cyclacillin V09.0
    Cycloserine V09.7 ☑
    Dapsone [DZ] V09.7 ☑
    Demeclocycline V09.3
    Dicloxacillin V09.0
    Doxycycline V09.3
    Enoxacin V09.5 ☑
    Erythromycin V09.2
    Ethambutol [EMB] V09.7 ☑
    Ethionamide [ETA] V09.7 ☑
    fluoroquinolones V09.5 ☑
    Gentamicin V09.4
    Halofantrine V09.8 ☑
    Imipenem V09.1
    Iodoquinol V09.5 ☑
    Isoniazid [INH] V09.7 ☑
    Kanamycin V09.4
    macrolides V09.2
    Mafenide V09.6
    MDRO (multiple drug resistant organisms) NOS V09.91 ☑
    Mefloquine V09.8 ☑
    Melasoprol V09.8 ☑
    Methacycline V09.3
    Methenamine V09.8 ☑
    Methicillin V09.0
    Metronidazole V09.8 ☑
    Mezlocillin V09.0
    Minocycline V09.3
    multiple drug resistant organisms NOS V09.91
    Nafcillin V09.0
    Nalidixic acid V09.5 ☑
    Natamycin V09.2
    Neomycin V09.4
    Netilmicin V09.4
    Nimorazole V09.8 ☑
    Nitrofurantoin V09.8 ☑

Resistance, resistant — *continued*
   drugs by microorganisms — *continued*
      Nitrofurtimox V09.8 ☑
      Norfloxacin V09.5 ☑
      Nystatin V09.2
      Ofloxacin V09.5 ☑
      Oleandomycin V09.2
      Oxacillin V09.0
      Oxytetracycline V09.3
      Para-amino salicylic acid [PAS] V09.7 ☑
      Paromomycin V09.4
      Penicillin (G) (V) (VK) V09.0
      penicillins V09.0
      Pentamidine V09.8 ☑
      Piperacillin V09.0
      Primaquine V09.5 ☑
      Proguanil V09.8 ☑
      Pyrazinamide [PZA] V09.7 ☑
      Pyrimethamine/Sulfalene V09.8 ☑
      Pyrimethamine/Sulfodoxine V09.8 ☑
      Quinacrine V09.5 ☑
      Quinidine V09.8 ☑
      Quinine V09.8 ☑
      quinolones V09.5 ☑
      Rifabutin V09.7 ☑
      Rifampin [RIF] V09.7 ☑
      Rifamycin V09.7 ☑
      Rolitetracycline V09.3
      specified drugs NEC V09.8 ☑
      Spectinomycin V09.8 ☑
      Spiramycin V09.2
      Streptomycin [SM] V09.4
      Sulfacetamide V09.6
      Sulfacytine V09.6
      Sulfadiazine V09.6
      Sulfadoxine V09.6
      Sulfamethoxazole V09.6
      Sulfapyridine V09.6
      Sulfasalizine V09.6
      Sulfasoxazone V09.6
      sulfonamides V09.6
      Sulfasoxazole V09.7 ☑
      tetracycline V09.3
      tetracyclines V09.3
      Thiamphenicol V09.8 ☑
      Ticarcillin V09.0
      Tinidazole V09.8 ☑
      Tobramycin V09.4
      Triamphenicol V09.8 ☑
      Trimethoprim V09.8 ☑
      Vancomycin V09.8 ☑
   insulin 277.7
Resorption
   biliary 576.8
      purulent or putrid (*see also* Cholecystitis)
         576.8
   dental (roots) 521.40
      alveoli 525.8
      pathological
         external 521.42
         internal 521.41
         specified NEC 521.49
   septic — *see* Septicemia
   teeth (roots) 521.40
      pathological
         external 521.42
         internal 521.41
         specified NEC 521.49
Respiration
   asymmetrical 786.09
   bronchial 786.09
   Cheyne-Stokes (periodic respiration) 786.04
   decreased, due to shock following injury 958.4
   disorder of 786.00
      psychogenic 306.1
      specified NEC 786.09
   failure 518.81
      acute 518.81
      acute and chronic 518.84
      chronic 518.83
      newborn 770.84
   insufficiency 786.09
      acute 518.82
      newborn NEC 770.89
   Kussmaul (air hunger) 786.09
   painful 786.52

Respiration — *continued*
   periodic 786.09
      high altitude 327.22   ●
   poor 786.09
      newborn NEC 770.89
   sighing 786.7
      psychogenic 306.1
   wheezing 786.07
Respiratory — *see also* condition
   distress 786.09
      acute 518.82
      fetus or newborn NEC 770.89
      syndrome (newborn) 769
         adult (following shock, surgery, or
            trauma) 518.5
            specified NEC 518.82
   failure 518.81
      acute 518.81
      acute and chronic 518.84
      chronic 518.83
Respiratory syncytial virus (RSV) 079.6
   bronchiolitis 466.11
   pneumonia 480.1
   vaccination, prophylactic (against) V04.82
Response
   photoallergic 692.72
   phototoxic 692.72
Rest, rests
   mesonephric duct 752.89
      fallopian tube 752.11
   ovarian, in fallopian tubes 752.19
   wolffian duct 752.89
Restless leg (syndrome) 333.99
Restlessness 799.2
**Restoration of organ continuity from previous
   sterilization** (tuboplasty) (vasoplasty) V26.0
Restriction of housing space V60.1
Restzustand, schizophrenic (*see also*
   Schizophrenia) 295.6 ☑
Retained — *see* Retention
Retardation
   development, developmental, specific (*see also*
      Disorder, development, specific) 315.9
      learning, specific 315.2
         arithmetical 315.1
         language (skills) 315.31
            expressive 315.31
            mixed receptive-expressive 315.32
         mathematics 315.1
         reading 315.00
            phonological 315.39
            written expression 315.2
         motor 315.4
   endochondral bone growth 733.91
   growth (physical) in childhood 783.43
      due to malnutrition 263.2
      fetal (intrauterine) 764.9 ☑
         affecting management of pregnancy
            656.5 ☑
   intrauterine growth 764.9 ☑
      affecting management of pregnancy 656.5 ☑
   mental 319
      borderline V62.89
      mild, IQ 50-70 317
      moderate, IQ 35-49 318.0
      profound, IQ under 20 318.2
      severe, IQ 20-34 318.1
   motor, specific 315.4
   physical 783.43
      child 783.43
      due to malnutrition 263.2
      fetus (intrauterine) 764.9 ☑
         affecting management of pregnancy
            656.5 ☑
   psychomotor NEC 307.9
   reading 315.00
Retching — *see* Vomiting
Retention, retained
   bladder (*see also* Retention, urine) 788.20
      psychogenic 306.53
   carbon dioxide 276.2
   cyst — *see* Cyst

Retention, retained — *continued*
   dead
      fetus (after 22 completed weeks gestation)
         656.4 ☑
         early fetal death (before 22 completed
            weeks gestation) 632
      ovum 631
   decidua (following delivery) (fragments) (with
      hemorrhage) 666.2 ☑
      without hemorrhage 667.1 ☑
   deciduous tooth 520.6
   dental root 525.3
   fecal (*see also* Constipation) 564.00
   fluid 276.6
   foreign body — *see also* Foreign body, retained
      bone 733.99
      current trauma — *see* Foreign body, by site
         or type
      middle ear 385.83
      muscle 729.6
      soft tissue NEC 729.6
   gastric 536.8
   membranes (following delivery) (with
      hemorrhage) 666.2 ☑
      with abortion — *see* Abortion, by type
      without hemorrhage 667.1 ☑
   menses 626.8
   milk (puerperal) 676.2 ☑
   nitrogen, extrarenal 788.9
   placenta (total) (with hemorrhage) 666.0 ☑
      with abortion — *see* Abortion, by type
      portions or fragments 666.2 ☑
         without hemorrhage 667.1 ☑
      without hemorrhage 667.0 ☑
   products of conception
      early pregnancy (fetal death before 22
         completed weeks gestation) 632
      following
         abortion — *see* Abortion, by type
         delivery 666.2 ☑
            with hemorrhage 666.2 ☑
            without hemorrhage 667.1 ☑
   secundines (following delivery) (with
      hemorrhage) 666.2 ☑
      with abortion — *see* Abortion, by type
      complicating puerperium (delayed
         hemorrhage) 666.2 ☑
      without hemorrhage 667.1 ☑
   smegma, clitoris 624.8
   urine NEC 788.20
      bladder, incomplete emptying 788.21
         due to   ●
            benign prostatic hypertrophy   ●
               (BPH) — *see* category 600   ●
         due to   ●
            benign prostatic hypertrophy (BPH)   ●
               — *see* category 600   ●
      psychogenic 306.53
      specified NEC 788.29
   water (in tissue) (*see also* Edema) 782.3
Reticulation, dust (occupational) 504
Reticulocytosis NEC 790.99
Reticuloendotheliosis
   acute infantile (M9722/3) 202.5 ☑
   leukemic (M9940/3) 202.4 ☑
   malignant (M9720/3) 202.3 ☑
   nonlipid (M9722/3) 202.5 ☑
Reticulohistiocytoma (giant cell) 277.89
Reticulohistiocytosis, multicentric 272.8
Reticulolymphosarcoma (diffuse) (M9613/3)
   200.8 ☑
   follicular (M9691/3) 202.0 ☑
   nodular (M9691/3) 202.0 ☑
Reticulosarcoma (M9640/3) 200.0 ☑
   nodular (M9642/3) 200.0 ☑
   pleomorphic cell type (M9641/3) 200.0 ☑
Reticulosis (skin)
   acute of infancy (M9722/3) 202.5 ☑
   histiocytic medullary (M9721/3) 202.3 ☑
   lipomelanotic 695.89
   malignant (M9720/3) 202.3 ☑
   Sézary's (M9701/3) 202.2 ☑
Retina, retinal — *see* condition

Retinitis (*see also* Chorioretinitis) 363.20
  albuminurica 585.9 *[363.10]* ▲
  arteriosclerotic 440.8 *[362.13]*
  central angiospastic 362.41
  Coat's 362.12
  diabetic 250.5 ☑ *[362.01]*
  disciformis 362.52
  disseminated 363.10
    metastatic 363.14
    neurosyphilitic 094.83
    pigment epitheliopathy 363.15
  exudative 362.12
  focal 363.00
    in histoplasmosis 115.92
      capsulatum 115.02
      duboisii 115.12
    juxtapapillary 363.05
    macular 363.06
    paramacular 363.06
    peripheral 363.08
    posterior pole NEC 363.07
  gravidarum 646.8 ☑
  hemorrhagica externa 362.12
  juxtapapillary (Jensen's) 363.05
  luetic — *see* Retinitis, syphilitic
  metastatic 363.14
  pigmentosa 362.74
  proliferans 362.29
  proliferating 362.29
  punctata albescens 362.76
  renal 585.9 *[363.13]* ▲
  syphilitic (secondary) 091.51
    congenital 090.0 *[363.13]*
    early 091.51
    late 095.8 *[363.13]*
  syphilitica, central, recurrent 095.8 *[363.13]*
  tuberculous (*see also* Tuberculous)
    017.3 ☑ *[363.13]*
Retinoblastoma (M9510/3) 190.5
  differentiated type (M9511/3) 190.5
  undifferentiated type (M9512/3) 190.5
Retinochoroiditis (*see also* Chorioretinitis)
  363.20
  central angiospastic 362.41
  disseminated 363.10
    metastatic 363.14
    neurosyphilitic 094.83
    pigment epitheliopathy 363.15
    syphilitic 094.83
  due to toxoplasmosis (acquired) (focal) 130.2
  focal 363.00
    in histoplasmosis 115.92
      capsulatum 115.02
      duboisii 115.12
    juxtapapillary (Jensen's) 363.05
    macular 363.06
    paramacular 363.06
    peripheral 363.08
    posterior pole NEC 363.07
  juxtapapillaris 363.05
  syphilitic (disseminated) 094.83
Retinopathy (background) 362.10
  arteriosclerotic 440.8 *[362.13]*
  atherosclerotic 440.8 *[362.13]*
  central serous 362.41
  circinate 362.10
  Coat's 362.12
  diabetic 250.5 ☑ *[362.01]*
    nonproliferative 250.5 ☑ *[362.03]* ●
      mild 250.5 ☑ *[362.04]* ●
      moderate 250.5 ☑ *[362.05]* ●
      severe 250.5 ☑ *[362.06]* ●
    proliferative 250.5 ☑ *[362.02]* ●
  exudative 362.12
  hypertensive 362.11
  nonproliferative ●
    diabetic 250.5 ☑ *[362.03]* ●
      mild 250.5 ☑ *[362.04]* ●
      moderate 250.5 ☑ *[362.05]* ●
      severe 250.5 ☑ *[362.06]* ●
  of prematurity 362.21
  pigmentary, congenital 362.74
  proliferative 362.29
    diabetic 250.5 ☑ *[362.02]*
    sickle-cell 282.60 *[362.29]*
  solar 363.31

Retinoschisis 361.10
  bullous 361.12
  congenital 743.56
  flat 361.11
  juvenile 362.73
Retractile testis 752.52
Retraction
  cervix (*see also* Retroversion, uterus) 621.6
  drum (membrane) 384.82
  eyelid 374.41
  finger 736.29
  head 781.0
  lid 374.41
  lung 518.89
  mediastinum 519.3
  nipple 611.79
    congenital 757.6
    puerperal, postpartum 676.0 ☑
  palmar fascia 728.6
  pleura (*see also* Pleurisy) 511.0
  ring, uterus (Bandl's) (pathological) 661.4 ☑
    affecting fetus or newborn 763.7
  sternum (congenital) 756.3
    acquired 738.3
    during respiration 786.9
  substernal 738.3
  supraclavicular 738.8
  syndrome (Duane's) 378.71
  uterus (*see also* Retroversion, uterus) 621.6
  valve (heart) — *see* Endocarditis
Retrobulbar — *see* condition
Retrocaval ureter 753.4
Retrocecal — *see also* condition
  appendix (congenital) 751.5
Retrocession — *see* Retroversion
Retrodisplacement — *see* Retroversion
Retroflection, retroflexion — *see* Retroversion
Retrognathia, retrognathism (mandibular)
  (maxillary) 524.10
Retrograde
  ejaculation 608.87
  menstruation 626.8
Retroiliac ureter 753.4
Retroperineal — *see* condition
Retroperitoneal — *see* condition
Retroperitonitis (*see also* Peritonitis) 567.9
Retropharyngeal — *see* condition
Retroplacental — *see* condition
Retroposition — *see* Retroversion
Retrosternal thyroid (congenital) 759.2
Retroversion, retroverted
  cervix (*see also* Retroversion, uterus) 621.6
  female NEC (*see also* Retroversion, uterus)
    621.6
  iris 364.70
  testis (congenital) 752.51
  uterus, uterine (acquired) (acute) (adherent)
    (any degree) (asymptomatic) (cervix)
    (postinfectional) (postpartal, old) 621.6
    congenital 752.3
    in pregnancy or childbirth 654.3 ☑
      affecting fetus or newborn 763.89
      causing obstructed labor 660.2 ☑
        affecting fetus or newborn 763.1
Retrusion, premaxilla (developmental) 524.04
Rett's syndrome 330.8
Reverse, reversed
  peristalsis 787.4
Reye's syndrome 331.81
Reye-Sheehan syndrome (postpartum pituitary
  necrosis) 253.2
Rh (factor)
  hemolytic disease 773.0
  incompatibility, immunization, or sensitization
    affecting management of pregnancy 656.1 ☑
    fetus or newborn 773.0
    transfusion reaction 999.7
    negative mother, affecting fetus or newborn
      773.0
    titer elevated 999.7
    transfusion reaction 999.7
Rhabdomyolysis (idiopathic) 728.88

Rhabdomyoma (M8900/0) — *see also* Neoplasm,
  connective tissue, benign
  adult (M8904/0) — *see* Neoplasm, connective
    tissue, benign
  fetal (M8903/0) — *see* Neoplasm, connective
    tissue, benign
  glycogenic (M8904/0) — *see* Neoplasm,
    connective tissue, benign
Rhabdomyosarcoma (M8900/3) — *see also*
  Neoplasm, connective tissue, malignant
  alveolar (M8920/3) — *see* Neoplasm,
    connective tissue, malignant
  embryonal (M8910/3) — *see* Neoplasm,
    connective tissue, malignant
  mixed type (M8902/3) — *see* Neoplasm,
    connective tissue, malignant
  pleomorphic (M8901/3) — *see* Neoplasm,
    connective tissue, malignant
Rhabdosarcoma (M8900/3) — *see*
  Rhabdomyosarcoma
Rhesus (factor) (Rh) incompatibility — *see* Rh,
  incompatibility
Rheumaticosis — *see* Rheumatism
Rheumatism, rheumatic (acute NEC) 729.0
  adherent pericardium 393
  arthritis
    acute or subacute — *see* Fever, rheumatic
    chronic 714.0
      spine 720.0
  articular (chronic) NEC (*see also* Arthritis)
    716.9 ☑
    acute or subacute — *see* Fever, rheumatic
  back 724.9
  blennorrhagic 098.59
  carditis — *see* Disease, heart, rheumatic
  cerebral — *see* Fever, rheumatic
  chorea (acute) — *see* Chorea, rheumatic
  chronic NEC 729.0
  coronary arteritis 391.9
    chronic 398.99
  degeneration, myocardium (*see also*
    Degeneration, myocardium, with
    rheumatic fever) 398.0
  desert 114.0
  febrile — *see* Fever, rheumatic
  fever — *see* Fever, rheumatic
  gonococcal 098.59
  gout 274.0
  heart
    disease (*see also* Disease, heart, rheumatic)
      398.90
    failure (chronic) (congestive) (inactive)
      398.91
  hemopericardium — *see* Rheumatic,
    pericarditis
  hydropericardium — *see* Rheumatic,
    pericarditis
  inflammatory (acute) (chronic) (subacute) — *see*
    Fever, rheumatic
  intercostal 729.0
    meaning Tietze's disease 733.6
  joint (chronic) NEC (*see also* Arthritis) 716.9 ☑
    acute — *see* Fever, rheumatic
  mediastinopericarditis — *see* Rheumatic,
    pericarditis
  muscular 729.0
  myocardial degeneration (*see also*
    Degeneration, myocardium, with
    rheumatic fever) 398.0
  myocarditis (chronic) (inactive) (with chorea)
    398.0
    active or acute 391.2
      with chorea (acute) (rheumatic)
      (Sydenham's) 392.0
  myositis 729.1
  neck 724.9
  neuralgic 729.0
  neuritis (acute) (chronic) 729.2
  neuromuscular 729.0
  nodose — *see* Arthritis, nodosa
  nonarticular 729.0
  palindromic 719.30
    ankle 719.37
    elbow 719.32
    foot 719.37
    hand 719.34

Rheumatism, rheumatic — *continued*
  palindromic — *continued*
    hip 719.35
    knee 719.36
    multiple sites 719.39
    pelvic region 719.35
    shoulder (region) 719.31
    specified site NEC 719.38
    wrist 719.33
  pancarditis, acute 391.8
    with chorea (acute) (rheumatic)
      (Sydenham's) 392.0
    chronic or inactive 398.99
  pericarditis (active) (acute) (with effusion) (with
    pneumonia) 391.0
    with chorea (acute) (rheumatic)
      (Sydenham's) 392.0
    chronic or inactive 393
  pericardium — *see* Rheumatic, pericarditis
  pleuropericarditis — *see* Rheumatic,
    pericarditis
  pneumonia 390 [517.1]
  pneumonitis 390 [517.1]
  pneumopericarditis — *see* Rheumatic,
    pericarditis
  polyarthritis
    acute or subacute — *see* Fever, rheumatic
    chronic 714.0
  polyarticular NEC (*see also* Arthritis) 716.9 ☑
  psychogenic 306.0
  radiculitis 729.2
  sciatic 724.3
  septic — *see* Fever, rheumatic
  spine 724.9
  subacute NEC 729.0
  torticollis 723.5
  tuberculous NEC (*see also* Tuberculosis)
    015.9 ☑
  typhoid fever 002.0
Rheumatoid — *see also* condition
  lungs 714.81
Rhinitis (atrophic) (catarrhal) (chronic) (croupous)
  (fibrinous) (hyperplastic) (hypertrophic)
  (membranous) (purulent) (suppurative)
  (ulcerative) 472.0
  with
    hay fever (*see also* Fever, hay) 477.9
      with asthma (bronchial) 493.0 ☑
    sore throat — *see* Nasopharyngitis
  acute 460
  allergic (nonseasonal) (seasonal) (*see also* Fever,
    hay) 477.9
    with asthma (*see also* Asthma) 493.0 ☑
    due to food 477.1
  granulomatous 472.0
  infective 460
  obstructive 472.0
  pneumococcal 460
  syphilitic 095.8
    congenital 090.0
  tuberculous (*see also* Tuberculosis) 012.8 ☑
  vasomotor (*see also* Fever, hay) 477.9
Rhinoantritis (chronic) 473.0
  acute 461.0
Rhinodacryolith 375.57
Rhinolalia (aperta) (clausa) (open) 784.49
Rhinolith 478.1
  nasal sinus (*see also* Sinusitis) 473.9
Rhinomegaly 478.1
Rhinopharyngitis (acute) (subacute) (*see also*
  Nasopharyngitis) 460
  chronic 472.2
  destructive ulcerating 102.5
  mutilans 102.5
Rhinophyma 695.3
Rhinorrhea 478.1
  cerebrospinal (fluid) 349.81
  paroxysmal (*see also* Fever, hay) 477.9
  spasmodic (*see also* Fever, hay) 477.9
Rhinosalpingitis 381.50
  acute 381.51
  chronic 381.52
Rhinoscleroma 040.1
Rhinosporidiosis 117.0

Rhinovirus infection 079.3
Rhizomelic chrondrodysplasia punctata 277.86
Rhizomelique, pseudopolyarthritic 446.5
Rhoads and Bomford anemia (refractory)
  238.7 ▲
Rhus
  diversiloba dermatitis 692.6
  radicans dermatitis 692.6
  toxicodendron dermatitis 692.6
  venenata dermatitis 692.6
  verniciflua dermatitis 692.6
Rhythm
  atrioventricular nodal 427.89
  disorder 427.9
    coronary sinus 427.89
    ectopic 427.89
    nodal 427.89
  escape 427.89
  heart, abnormal 427.9
    fetus or newborn — *see* Abnormal, heart
      rate
  idioventricular 426.89
    accelerated 427.89
  nodal 427.89
  sleep, inversion 327.39 ▲
    nonorganic origin 307.45
Rhytidosis facialis 701.8
Rib — *see also* condition
  cervical 756.2
Riboflavin deficiency 266.0
Rice bodies (*see also* Loose, body, joint) 718.1 ☑
  knee 717.6
Richter's hernia — *see* Hernia, Richter's
Ricinism 988.2
Rickets (active) (acute) (adolescent) (adult) (chest
  wall) (congenital) (current) (infantile)
  (intestinal) 268.0
  celiac 579.0
  fetal 756.4
  hemorrhagic 267
  hypophosphatemic with nephrotic-glycosuric
    dwarfism 270.0
  kidney 588.0
  late effect 268.1
  renal 588.0
  scurvy 267
  vitamin D-resistant 275.3
Rickettsial disease 083.9
  specified type NEC 083.8
Rickettsialpox 083.2
Rickettsiosis NEC 083.9
  specified type NEC 083.8
  tick-borne 082.9
    specified type NEC 082.8
  vesicular 083.2
Ricord's chancre 091.0
Riddoch's syndrome (visual disorientation)
  368.16
Rider's
  bone 733.99
  chancre 091.0
Ridge, alveolus — *see also* condition
  edentulous
    atrophy 525.20
      mandible 525.20
        minimal 525.21
        moderate 525.22
        severe 525.23
      maxilla 525.20
        minimal 525.24
        moderate 525.25
        severe 525.26
    flabby 525.20
Ridged ear 744.29
Riedel's
  disease (ligneous thyroiditis) 245.3
  lobe, liver 751.69
  struma (ligneous thyroiditis) 245.3
  thyroiditis (ligneous) 245.3
Rieger's anomaly or syndrome (mesodermal
  dysgenesis, anterior ocular segment) 743.44
Riehl's melanosis 709.09

Rietti-Greppi-Micheli anemia or syndrome
  282.49
Rieux's hernia — *see* Hernia, Rieux's
Rift Valley fever 066.3
Riga's disease (cachectic aphthae) 529.0
Riga-Fede disease (cachectic aphthae) 529.0
Riggs' disease (compound periodontitis) 523.4
Right middle lobe syndrome 518.0
Rigid, rigidity — *see also* condition
  abdominal 789.4 ☑
  articular, multiple congenital 754.89
  back 724.8
  cervix uteri
    in pregnancy or childbirth 654.6 ☑
      affecting fetus or newborn 763.89
      causing obstructed labor 660.2 ☑
        affecting fetus or newborn 763.1
  hymen (acquired) (congenital) 623.3
  nuchal 781.6
  pelvic floor
    in pregnancy or childbirth 654.4 ☑
      affecting fetus or newborn 763.89
      causing obstructed labor 660.2 ☑
        affecting fetus or newborn 763.1
  perineum or vulva
    in pregnancy or childbirth 654.8 ☑
      affecting fetus or newborn 763.89
      causing obstructed labor 660.2 ☑
        affecting fetus or newborn 763.1
  spine 724.8
  vagina
    in pregnancy or childbirth 654.7 ☑
      affecting fetus or newborn 763.89
      causing obstructed labor 660.2 ☑
        affecting fetus or newborn 763.1
Rigors 780.99
Riley-Day syndrome (familial dysautonomia)
  742.8
Ring(s)
  aorta 747.21
  Bandl's, complicating delivery 661.4 ☑
    affecting fetus or newborn 763.7
  contraction, complicating delivery 661.4 ☑
    affecting fetus or newborn 763.7
  esophageal (congenital) 750.3
  Fleischer (-Kayser) (cornea) 275.1 [371.14]
  hymenal, tight (acquired) (congenital) 623.3
  Kayser-Fleischer (cornea) 275.1 [371.14]
  retraction, uterus, pathological 661.4 ☑
    affecting fetus or newborn 763.7
  Schatzki's (esophagus) (congenital) (lower)
    750.3
    acquired 530.3
  Soemmering's 366.51
  trachea, abnormal 748.3
  vascular (congenital) 747.21
  Vossius' 921.3
    late effect 366.21
Ringed hair (congenital) 757.4
Ringing in the ear (*see also* Tinnitus) 388.30
Ringworm 110.9
  beard 110.0
  body 110.5
  Burmese 110.9
  corporeal 110.5
  foot 110.4
  groin 110.3
  hand 110.2
  honeycomb 110.0
  nails 110.1
  perianal (area) 110.3
  scalp 110.0
  specified site NEC 110.8
  Tokelau 110.5
Rise, venous pressure 459.89
Risk
  factor — *see* Problem
  falling V15.88 ●
  suicidal 300.9
Ritter's disease (dermatitis exfoliativa
  neonatorum) 695.81
Rivalry, sibling 313.3

Rivalta's disease (cervicofacial actinomycosis) 039.3

River blindness 125.3 *[360.13]*

Robert's pelvis 755.69
  with disproportion (fetopelvic) 653.0 ☑
    affecting fetus or newborn 763.1
    causing obstructed labor 660.1 ☑
      affecting fetus or newborn 763.1

Robin's syndrome 756.0

Robinson's (hidrotic) **ectodermal dysplasia** 757.31

Robles' disease (onchocerciasis) 125.3 *[360.13]*

Rochalimea — *see* Rickettsial disease

Rocky Mountain fever (spotted) 082.0

Rodent ulcer (M8090/3) — *see also* Neoplasm, skin, malignant
  cornea 370.07

Roentgen ray, adverse effect — *see* Effect, adverse, x-ray

Roetheln 056.9

Roger's disease (congenital interventricular septal defect) 745.4

Rokitansky's
  disease (*see also* Necrosis, liver) 570
  tumor 620.2

Rokitansky-Aschoff sinuses (mucosal outpouching of gallbladder) (*see also* Disease, gallbladder) 575.8

Rokitansky-Kuster-Hauser syndrome (congenital absence vagina) 752.49

Rollet's chancre (syphilitic) 091.0

Rolling of head 781.0

Romano-Ward syndrome ▶(prolonged QT interval syndrome)◀ 426.82   ▲

Romanus lesion 720.1

Romberg's disease or syndrome 349.89

Roof, mouth — *see* condition

Rosacea 695.3
  acne 695.3
  keratitis 695.3 *[370.49]*

Rosary, rachitic 268.0

Rose
  cold 477.0
  fever 477.0
  rash 782.1
    epidemic 056.9
    of infants 057.8

Rosen-Castleman-Liebow syndrome (pulmonary proteinosis) 516.0

Rosenbach's erysipelatoid or erysipeloid 027.1

Rosenthal's disease (factor XI deficiency) 286.2

Roseola 057.8
  infantum, infantilis 057.8

Rossbach's disease (hyperchlorhydria) 536.8
  psychogenic 306.4

Rössle-Urbach-Wiethe lipoproteinosis 272.8

Ross river fever 066.3

Rostan's asthma (cardiac) (*see also* Failure, ventricular, left) 428.1

Rot
  Barcoo (*see also* Ulcer, skin) 707.9
  knife-grinders' (*see also* Tuberculosis) 011.4 ☑

Rot-Bernhardt disease 355.1

Rotation
  anomalous, incomplete or insufficient — *see* Malrotation
  cecum (congenital) 751.4
  colon (congenital) 751.4
  manual, affecting fetus or newborn 763.89
  spine, incomplete or insufficient 737.8
  tooth, teeth 524.35
  vertebra, incomplete or insufficient 737.8

Röteln 056.9

Roth's disease or meralgia 355.1

Roth-Bernhardt disease or syndrome 355.1

Rothmund (-Thomson) syndrome 757.33

Rotor's disease or syndrome (idiopathic hyperbilirubinemia) 277.4

Rotundum ulcus — *see* Ulcer, stomach

Round
  back (with wedging of vertebrae) 737.10
    late effect of rickets 268.1
  hole, retina 361.31
    with detachment 361.01
  ulcer (stomach) — *see* Ulcer, stomach
  worms (infestation) (large) NEC 127.0

Roussy-Lévy syndrome 334.3

Routine postpartum follow-up V24.2

Roy (-Jutras) syndrome (acropachyderma) 757.39

Rubella (German measles) 056.9
  complicating pregnancy, childbirth, or puerperium 647.5 ☑
  complication 056.8
    neurological 056.00
      encephalomyelitis 056.01
      specified type NEC 056.09
    specified type NEC 056.79
  congenital 771.0
  contact V01.4
  exposure to V01.4
  maternal
    with suspected fetal damage affecting management of pregnancy 655.3 ☑
    affecting fetus or newborn 760.2
      manifest rubella in infant 771.0
  specified complications NEC 056.79
  vaccination, prophylactic (against) V04.3

Rubeola (measles) (*see also* Measles) 055.9
  complicated 055.8
  meaning rubella (*see also* Rubella) 056.9
  scarlatinosis 057.8

Rubeosis iridis 364.42
  diabetica 250.5 ☑ *[364.42]*

Rubinstein-Taybi's syndrome (brachydactylia, short stature and mental retardation) 759.89

Rud's syndrome (mental deficiency, epilepsy, and infantilism) 759.89

Rudimentary (congenital) — *see also* Agenesis
  arm 755.22
  bone 756.9
  cervix uteri 752.49
  eye (*see also* Microphthalmos) 743.10
  fallopian tube 752.19
  leg 755.32
  lobule of ear 744.21
  patella 755.64
  respiratory organs in thoracopagus 759.4
  tracheal bronchus 748.3
  uterine horn 752.3
  uterus 752.3
    in male 752.7
    solid or with cavity 752.3
  vagina 752.49

Ruiter-Pompen (-Wyers) syndrome (angiokeratoma corporis diffusum) 272.7

Ruled out condition (*see also* Observation, suspected) V71.9

Rumination — *see also* Vomiting
  disorder 307.53
  neurotic 300.3
  obsessional 300.3
  psychogenic 307.53

Runaway reaction — *see also* Disturbance, conduct
  socialized 312.2 ☑
  undersocialized, unsocialized 312.1 ☑

Runeberg's disease (progressive pernicious anemia) 281.0

Runge's syndrome (postmaturity) 766.22

Rupia 091.3
  congenital 090.0
  tertiary 095.9

Rupture, ruptured 553.9
  abdominal viscera NEC 799.89
    obstetrical trauma 665.5 ☑
  abscess (spontaneous) — *see* Abscess, by site
  amnion — *see* Rupture, membranes
  aneurysm — *see* Aneurysm
  anus (sphincter) — *see* Laceration, anus
  aorta, aortic 441.5
    abdominal 441.3

Rupture, ruptured — *continued*
  aorta, aortic — *continued*
    arch 441.1
    ascending 441.1
    descending 441.5
      abdominal 441.3
      thoracic 441.1
    syphilitic 093.0
    thoracoabdominal 441.6
    thorax, thoracic 441.1
    transverse 441.1
    traumatic (thoracic) 901.0
      abdominal 902.0
    valve or cusp (*see also* Endocarditis, aortic) 424.1
  appendix (with peritonitis) 540.0
    with peritoneal abscess 540.1
    traumatic — *see* Injury, internal, gastrointestinal tract
  arteriovenous fistula, brain (congenital) 430
  artery 447.2
    brain (*see also* Hemorrhage, brain) 431
    coronary (*see also* Infarct, myocardium) 410.9 ☑
    heart (*see also* Infarct, myocardium) 410.9 ☑
    pulmonary 417.8
    traumatic (complication) (*see also* Injury, blood vessel, by site) 904.9
  bile duct, except cystic (*see also* Disease, biliary) 576.3
    cystic 575.4
    traumatic — *see* Injury, internal, intra-abdominal
  bladder (sphincter) 596.6
    with
      abortion — *see* Abortion, by type, with damage to pelvic organs
      ectopic pregnancy (*see also* categories 633.0-633.9) 639.2
      molar pregnancy (*see also* categories 630-632) 639.2
    following
      abortion 639.2
      ectopic or molar pregnancy 639.2
    nontraumatic 596.6
    obstetrical trauma 665.5 ☑
    spontaneous 596.6
    traumatic — *see* Injury, internal, bladder
  blood vessel (*see also* Hemorrhage) 459.0
    brain (*see also* Hemorrhage, brain) 431
    heart (*see also* Infarct, myocardium) 410.9 ☑
    traumatic (complication) (*see also* Injury, blood vessel, by site) 904.9
  bone — *see* Fracture, by site
  bowel 569.89
    traumatic — *see* Injury, internal, intestine
  Bowman's membrane 371.31
  brain
    aneurysm (congenital) (*see also* Hemorrhage, subarachnoid) 430
      late effect — *see* Late effect(s) (of) cerebrovascular disease
      syphilitic 094.87
    hemorrhagic (*see also* Hemorrhage, brain) 431
    injury at birth 767.0
    syphilitic 094.89
  capillaries 448.9
  cardiac (*see also* Infarct, myocardium) 410.9 ☑
  cartilage (articular) (current) — *see also* Sprain, by site
    knee — *see* Tear, meniscus
    semilunar — *see* Tear, meniscus
  cecum (with peritonitis) 540.0
    with peritoneal abscess 540.1
    traumatic 863.89
      with open wound into cavity 863.99
  cerebral aneurysm (congenital) (*see also* Hemorrhage, subarachnoid) 430
    late effect — *see* Late effect(s) (of) cerebrovascular disease
  cervix (uteri)
    with
      abortion — *see* Abortion, by type, with damage to pelvic organs

2006 ICD-9-CM   ☑ Additional Digit Required — Refer to the Tabular List (Numeric Code Section) for Additional Digit Selection   October 2005 • Volume 2 — **293**

▶◀ Revised Text   ● New Line   ▲ Revised Code

Rupture, ruptured — *continued*
  cervix — *continued*
    with — *continued*
      ectopic pregnancy (*see also* categories 633.0-633.9) 639.2
      molar pregnancy (*see also* categories 630-632) 639.2
    following
      abortion 639.2
      ectopic or molar pregnancy 639.2
    obstetrical trauma 665.3 ☑
    traumatic — *see* Injury, internal, cervix
  chordae tendineae 429.5
  choroid (direct) (indirect) (traumatic) 363.63
  circle of Willis (*see also* Hemorrhage, subarachnoid) 430
    late effect — *see* Late effect(s) (of) cerebrovascular disease
  colon 569.89
    traumatic — *see* Injury, internal, colon
  cornea (traumatic) — *see also* Rupture, eye
    due to ulcer 370.00
  coronary (artery) (thrombotic) (*see also* Infarct, myocardium) 410.9 ☑
  corpus luteum (infected) (ovary) 620.1
  cyst — *see* Cyst
  cystic duct (*see also* Disease, gallbladder) 575.4
  Descemet's membrane 371.33
    traumatic — *see* Rupture, eye
  diaphragm — *see also* Hernia, diaphragm
    traumatic — *see* Injury, internal, diaphragm
  diverticulum
    bladder 596.3
    intestine (large) (*see also* Diverticula) 562.10
      small 562.00
  duodenal stump 537.89
  duodenum (ulcer) — *see* Ulcer, duodenum, with perforation
  ear drum (*see also* Perforation, tympanum) 384.20
    with otitis media — *see* Otitis media
    traumatic — *see* Wound, open, ear
  esophagus 530.4
    traumatic 862.22
      with open wound into cavity 862.32
      cervical region — *see* Wound, open, esophagus
  eye (without prolapse of intraocular tissue) 871.0
    with
      exposure of intraocular tissue 871.1
      partial loss of intraocular tissue 871.2
      prolapse of intraocular tissue 871.1
    due to burn 940.5
  fallopian tube 620.8
    due to pregnancy — *see* Pregnancy, tubal
    traumatic — *see* Injury, internal, fallopian tube
  fontanel 767.3
  free wall (ventricle) (*see also* Infarct, myocardium) 410.9 ☑
  gallbladder or duct (*see also* Disease, gallbladder) 575.4
    traumatic — *see* Injury, internal, gallbladder
  gastric (*see also* Rupture, stomach) 537.89
    vessel 459.0
  globe (eye) (traumatic) — *see* Rupture, eye
  graafian follicle (hematoma) 620.0
  heart (auricle) (ventricle) (*see also* Infarct, myocardium) 410.9 ☑
    infectional 422.90
    traumatic — *see* Rupture, myocardium, traumatic
  hymen 623.8
  internal
    organ, traumatic — *see also* Injury, internal, by site
      heart — *see* Rupture, myocardium, traumatic
      kidney — *see* Rupture, kidney
      liver — *see* Rupture, liver
      spleen — *see* Rupture, spleen, traumatic
    semilunar cartilage — *see* Tear, meniscus
  intervertebral disc — *see* Displacement, intervertebral disc
    traumatic (current) — *see* Dislocation, vertebra

Rupture, ruptured — *continued*
  intestine 569.89
    traumatic — *see* Injury, internal, intestine
  intracranial, birth injury 767.0
  iris 364.76
    traumatic — *see* Rupture, eye
  joint capsule — *see* Sprain, by site
  kidney (traumatic) 866.03
    with open wound into cavity 866.13
    due to birth injury 767.8
    nontraumatic 593.89
  lacrimal apparatus (traumatic) 870.2
  lens (traumatic) 366.20
  ligament — *see also* Sprain, by site
    with open wound — *see* Wound, open, by site
    old (*see also* Disorder, cartilage, articular) 718.0 ☑
  liver (traumatic) 864.04
    with open wound into cavity 864.14
    due to birth injury 767.8
    nontraumatic 573.8
  lymphatic (node) (vessel) 457.8
  marginal sinus (placental) (with hemorrhage) 641.2 ☑
    affecting fetus or newborn 762.1
  meaning hernia — *see* Hernia
  membrana tympani (*see also* Perforation, tympanum) 384.20
    with otitis media — *see* Otitis media
    traumatic — *see* Wound, open, ear
  membranes (spontaneous)
    artificial
      delayed delivery following 658.3 ☑
        affecting fetus or newborn 761.1
      fetus or newborn 761.1
    delayed delivery following 658.2 ☑
      affecting fetus or newborn 761.1
    premature (less than 24 hours prior to onset of labor) 658.1 ☑
      affecting fetus or newborn 761.1
    delayed delivery following 658.2 ☑
      affecting fetus or newborn 761.1
  meningeal artery (*see also* Hemorrhage, subarachnoid) 430
    late effect — *see* Late effect(s) (of) cerebrovascular disease
  meniscus (knee) — *see also* Tear, meniscus
    old (*see also* Derangement, meniscus) 717.5
      site other than knee — *see* Disorder, cartilage, articular
    site other than knee — *see* Sprain, by site
  mesentery 568.89
    traumatic — *see* Injury, internal, mesentery
  mitral — *see* Insufficiency, mitral
  muscle (traumatic) NEC — *see also* Sprain, by site
    with open wound — *see* Wound, open, by site
    nontraumatic 728.83
  musculotendinous cuff (nontraumatic) (shoulder) 840.4
  mycotic aneurysm, causing cerebral hemorrhage (*see also* Hemorrhage, subarachnoid) 430
    late effect — *see* Late effect(s) (of) cerebrovascular disease
  myocardium, myocardial (*see also* Infarct, myocardium) 410.9 ☑
    traumatic 861.03
      with open wound into thorax 861.13
  nontraumatic (meaning hernia) (*see also* Hernia, by site) 553.9
  obstructed (*see also* Hernia, by site, with obstruction) 552.9
    gangrenous (*see also* Hernia, by site, with gangrene) 551.9
  operation wound 998.32
    internal 998.31
  ovary, ovarian 620.8
    corpus luteum 620.1
    follicle (graafian) 620.0
  oviduct 620.8
    due to pregnancy — *see* Pregnancy, tubal
  pancreas 577.8
    traumatic — *see* Injury, internal, pancreas
  papillary muscle (ventricular) 429.6

Rupture, ruptured — *continued*
  pelvic
    floor, complicating delivery 664.1 ☑
    organ NEC — *see* Injury, pelvic, organs
  penis (traumatic) — *see* Wound, open, penis
  perineum 624.8
    during delivery (*see also* Laceration, perineum, complicating delivery) 664.4 ☑
  pharynx (nontraumatic) (spontaneous) 478.29
  pregnant uterus (before onset of labor) 665.0 ☑
  prostate (traumatic) — *see* Injury, internal, prostate
  pulmonary
    artery 417.8
    valve (heart) (*see also* Endocarditis, pulmonary) 424.3
    vein 417.8
    vessel 417.8
  pupil, sphincter 364.75
  pus tube (*see also* Salpingo-oophoritis) 614.2
  pyosalpinx (*see also* Salpingo-oophoritis) 614.2
  rectum 569.49
    traumatic — *see* Injury, internal, rectum
  retina, retinal (traumatic) (without detachment) 361.30
    with detachment (*see also* Detachment, retina, with retinal defect) 361.00
  rotator cuff (capsule) (traumatic) 840.4
    nontraumatic, complete 727.61
  sclera 871.0
  semilunar cartilage, knee (*see also* Tear, meniscus) 836.2
    old (*see also* Derangement, meniscus) 717.5
  septum (cardiac) 410.8 ☑
  sigmoid 569.89
    traumatic — *see* Injury, internal, colon, sigmoid
  sinus of Valsalva 747.29
  spinal cord — *see also* Injury, spinal, by site
    due to injury at birth 767.4
    fetus or newborn 767.4
    syphilitic 094.89
    traumatic — *see also* Injury, spinal, by site
      with fracture — *see* Fracture, vertebra, by site, with spinal cord injury
  spleen 289.59
    congenital 767.8
    due to injury at birth 767.8
    malarial 084.9
    nontraumatic 289.59
    spontaneous 289.59
    traumatic 865.04
      with open wound into cavity 865.14
  splenic vein 459.0
  stomach 537.89
    due to injury at birth 767.8
    traumatic — *see* Injury, internal, stomach
    ulcer — *see* Ulcer, stomach, with perforation
  synovium 727.50
    specified site NEC 727.59
  tendon (traumatic) — *see also* Sprain, by site
    with open wound — *see* Wound, open, by site
    Achilles 845.09
      nontraumatic 727.67
    ankle 845.09
      nontraumatic 727.68
    biceps (long head) 840.8
      nontraumatic 727.62
    foot 845.10
      interphalangeal (joint) 845.13
      metatarsophalangeal (joint) 845.12
      nontraumatic 727.68
      specified site NEC 845.19
      tarsometatarsal (joint) 845.11
    hand 842.10
      carpometacarpal (joint) 842.11
      interphalangeal (joint) 842.13
      metacarpophalangeal (joint) 842.12
      nontraumatic 727.63
        extensors 727.63
        flexors 727.64
      specified site NEC 842.19
    nontraumatic 727.60
      specified site NEC 727.69

Rupture, ruptured — *continued*
  tendon — *see also* Sprain, by site — *continued*
    patellar 844.8
      nontraumatic 727.66
    quadriceps 844.8
      nontraumatic 727.65
    rotator cuff (capsule) 840.4
      nontraumatic, complete 727.61
    wrist 842.00
      carpal (joint) 842.01
      nontraumatic 727.63
        extensors 727.63
        flexors 727.64
      radiocarpal (joint) (ligament) 842.02
      radioulnar (joint), distal 842.09
      specified site NEC 842.09
  testis (traumatic) 878.2
    complicated 878.3
    due to syphilis 095.8
  thoracic duct 457.8
  tonsil 474.8
  traumatic
    with open wound — *see* Wound, open, by site
    aorta — *see* Rupture, aorta, traumatic
    ear drum — *see* Wound, open, ear, drum
    external site — *see* Wound, open, by site
    eye 871.2
    globe (eye) — *see* Wound, open, eyeball
    internal organ (abdomen, chest, or pelvis) — *see also* Injury, internal, by site
      heart — *see* Rupture, myocardium, traumatic
      kidney — *see* Rupture, kidney
      liver — *see* Rupture, liver
      spleen — *see* Rupture, spleen, traumatic
    ligament, muscle, or tendon — *see also* Sprain, by site
      with open wound — *see* Wound, open, by site

Rupture, ruptured — *continued*
  traumatic — *continued*
    meaning hernia — *see* Hernia
  tricuspid (heart) (valve) — *see* Endocarditis, tricuspid
  tube, tubal 620.8
    abscess (*see also* Salpingo-oophoritis) 614.2
    due to pregnancy — *see* Pregnancy, tubal
  tympanum, tympanic (membrane) (*see also* Perforation, tympanum) 384.20
    with otitis media — *see* Otitis media
    traumatic — *see* Wound, open, ear, drum
  umbilical cord 663.8 ☑
    fetus or newborn 772.0
  ureter (traumatic) (*see also* Injury, internal, ureter) 867.2
    nontraumatic 593.89
  urethra 599.84
    with
      abortion — *see* Abortion, by type, with damage to pelvic organs
      ectopic pregnancy (*see also* categories 633.0-633.9) 639.2
      molar pregnancy (*see also* categories 630-632) 639.2
    following
      abortion 639.2
      ectopic or molar pregnancy 639.2
    obstetrical trauma 665.5 ☑
    traumatic — *see* Injury, internal urethra
  uterosacral ligament 620.8
  uterus (traumatic) — *see also* Injury, internal uterus
    affecting fetus or newborn 763.89
    during labor 665.1 ☑
    nonpuerperal, nontraumatic 621.8
    nontraumatic 621.8
    pregnant (during labor) 665.1 ☑
      before labor 665.0 ☑

Rupture, ruptured — *continued*
  vagina 878.6
    complicated 878.7
    complicating delivery — *see* Laceration, vagina, complicating delivery
  valve, valvular (heart) — *see* Endocarditis
  varicose vein — *see* Varicose, vein
  varix — *see* Varix
  vena cava 459.0
  ventricle (free wall) (left) (*see also* Infarct, myocardium) 410.9 ☑
  vesical (urinary) 596.6
    traumatic — *see* Injury, internal, bladder
  vessel (blood) 459.0
    pulmonary 417.8
  viscus 799.89
  vulva 878.4
    complicated 878.5
    complicating delivery 664.0 ☑
Russell's dwarf (uterine dwarfism and craniofacial dysostosis) 759.89
Russell's dysentery 004.8
Russell (-Silver) syndrome (congenital hemihypertrophy and short stature) 759.89
Russian spring-summer type encephalitis 063.0
Rust's disease (tuberculous spondylitis) 015.0 ☑ *[720.81]*
Rustitskii's disease (multiple myeloma) (M9730/3) 203.0 ☑
Ruysch's disease (Hirschsprung's disease) 751.3
Rytand-Lipsitch syndrome (complete atrioventricular block) 426.0

S

Saber
shin 090.5
tibia 090.5
Sac, lacrimal — *see* condition
Saccharomyces infection (*see also* Candidiasis)
112.9
Saccharopinuria 270.7
Saccular — *see* condition
Sacculation
aorta (nonsyphilitic) (*see also* Aneurysm, aorta)
441.9
ruptured 441.5
syphilitic 093.0
bladder 596.3
colon 569.89
intralaryngeal (congenital) (ventricular) 748.3
larynx (congenital) (ventricular) 748.3
organ or site, congenital — *see* Distortion
pregnant uterus, complicating delivery 654.4 ☑
affecting fetus or newborn 763.1
causing obstructed labor 660.2 ☑
affecting fetus or newborn 763.1
rectosigmoid 569.89
sigmoid 569.89
ureter 593.89
urethra 599.2
vesical 596.3
Sachs (-Tay) disease (amaurotic familial idiocy)
330.1
Sacks-Libman disease 710.0 *[424.91]*
Sacralgia 724.6
Sacralization
fifth lumbar vertebra 756.15
incomplete (vertebra) 756.15
Sacrodynia 724.6
Sacroiliac joint — *see* condition
Sacroiliitis NEC 720.2
Sacrum — *see* condition
Saddle
back 737.8
embolus, aorta 444.0
nose 738.0
congenital 754.0
due to syphilis 090.5
Sadism (sexual) 302.84
Saemisch's ulcer 370.04
Saenger's syndrome 379.46
Sago spleen 277.3
Sailors' skin 692.74
Saint
Anthony's fire (*see also* Erysipelas) 035
Guy's dance — *see* Chorea
Louis-type encephalitis 062.3
triad (*see also* Hernia, diaphragm) 553.3
Vitus' dance — *see* Chorea
Salicylism
correct substance properly administered
535.4 ☑
overdose or wrong substance given or taken
965.1
Salivary duct or gland — *see also* condition
virus disease 078.5
Salivation (excessive) (*see also* Ptyalism) 527.7
Salmonella (aertrycke) (choleraesuis) (enteritidis)
(gallinarum) (suipestifer) (typhimurium) (*see
also* Infection, Salmonella) 003.9
arthritis 003.23
carrier (suspected) of V02.3
meningitis 003.21
osteomyelitis 003.24
pneumonia 003.22
septicemia 003.1
typhosa 002.0
carrier (suspected) of V02.1
Salmonellosis 003.0
with pneumonia 003.22
Salpingitis (catarrhal) (fallopian tube) (nodular)
(pseudofollicular) (purulent) (septic) (*see also*
Salpingo-oophoritis) 614.2

Salpingitis (*see also* Salpingo-oophoritis) —
continued
ear 381.50
acute 381.51
chronic 381.52
Eustachian (tube) 381.50
acute 381.51
chronic 381.52
follicularis 614.1
gonococcal (chronic) 098.37
acute 098.17
interstitial, chronic 614.1
isthmica nodosa 614.1
old — *see* Salpingo-oophoritis, chronic
puerperal, postpartum, childbirth 670.0 ☑
specific (chronic) 098.37
acute 098.17
tuberculous (acute) (chronic) (*see also*
Tuberculosis) 016.6 ☑
venereal (chronic) 098.37
acute 098.17
Salpingocele 620.4
Salpingo-oophoritis (catarrhal) (purulent)
(ruptured) (septic) (suppurative) 614.2
acute 614.0
with
abortion — *see* Abortion, by type, with
sepsis
ectopic pregnancy (*see also* categories
633.0-633.9) 639.0
molar pregnancy (*see also* categories 630-
632) 639.0
following
abortion 639.0
ectopic or molar pregnancy 639.0
gonococcal 098.17
puerperal, postpartum, childbirth 670.0 ☑
tuberculous (*see also* Tuberculosis) 016.6 ☑
chronic 614.1
gonococcal 098.37
tuberculous (*see also* Tuberculosis) 016.6 ☑
complicating pregnancy 646.6 ☑
affecting fetus or newborn 760.8
gonococcal (chronic) 098.37
acute 098.17
old — *see* Salpingo-oophoritis, chronic
puerperal 670.0 ☑
specific — *see* Salpingo-oophoritis, gonococcal
subacute (*see also* Salpingo-oophoritis, acute)
614.0
tuberculous (acute) (chronic) (*see also*
Tuberculosis) 016.6 ☑
venereal — *see* Salpingo-oophoritis, gonococcal
Salpingo-ovaritis (*see also* Salpingo-oophoritis)
614.2
Salpingoperitonitis (*see also* Salpingo-oophoritis)
614.2
Salt-losing
nephritis (*see also* Disease, renal) 593.9
syndrome (*see also* Disease, renal) 593.9
Salt-rheum (*see also* Eczema) 692.9
Salzmann's nodular dystrophy 371.46
Sampson's cyst or tumor 617.1
Sandblasters'
asthma 502
lung 502
Sander's disease (paranoia) 297.1
Sandfly fever 066.0
Sandhoff's disease 330.1
Sanfilippo's syndrome (mucopolysaccharidosis
III) 277.5
Sanger-Brown's ataxia 334.2
San Joaquin Valley fever 114.0
Sao Paulo fever or typhus 082.0
Saponification, mesenteric 567.89 ▲
Sapremia — *see* Septicemia
Sarcocele (benign)
syphilitic 095.8
congenital 090.5
Sarcoepiplocele (*see also* Hernia) 553.9

Sarcoepiplomphalocele (*see also* Hernia,
umbilicus) 553.1
Sarcoid (any site) 135
with lung involvement 135 *[517.8]*
Boeck's 135
Darier-Roussy 135
Spiegler-Fendt 686.8
Sarcoidosis 135
cardiac 135 *[425.8]*
lung 135 *[517.8]*
Sarcoma (M8800/3) — *see also* Neoplasm,
connective tissue, malignant
alveolar soft part (M9581/3) — *see* Neoplasm,
connective tissue, malignant
ameloblastic (M9330/3) 170.1
upper jaw (bone) 170.0
botryoid (M8910/3) — *see* Neoplasm,
connective tissue, malignant
botryoides (M8910/3) — *see* Neoplasm,
connective tissue, malignant
cerebellar (M9480/3) 191.6
circumscribed (arachnoidal) (M9471/3)
191.6
circumscribed (arachnoidal) cerebellar
(M9471/3) 191.6
clear cell, of tendons and aponeuroses
(M9044/3) — *see* Neoplasm, connective
tissue, malignant
embryonal (M8991/3) — *see* Neoplasm,
connective tissue, malignant
endometrial (stromal) (M8930/3) 182.0
isthmus 182.1
endothelial (M9130/3) — *see also* Neoplasm,
connective tissue, malignant
bone (M9260/3) — *see* Neoplasm, bone,
malignant
epithelioid cell (M8804/3) — *see* Neoplasm,
connective tissue, malignant
Ewing's (M9260/3) — *see* Neoplasm, bone,
malignant
follicular dendritic cell 202.9 ☑
germinoblastic (diffuse) (M9632/3) 202.8 ☑
follicular (M9697/3) 202.0 ☑
giant cell (M8802/3) — *see also* Neoplasm,
connective tissue, malignant
bone (M9250/3) — *see* Neoplasm, bone,
malignant
glomoid (M8710/3) — *see* Neoplasm,
connective tissue, malignant
granulocytic (M9930/3) 205.3 ☑
hemangioendothelial (M9130/3) — *see*
Neoplasm, connective tissue, malignant
hemorrhagic, multiple (M9140/3) — *see*
Kaposi's, sarcoma
Hodgkin's (M9662/3) 201.2 ☑
immunoblastic (M9612/3) 200.8 ☑
interdigitating dendritic cell 202.9 ☑
Kaposi's (M9140/3) — *see* Kaposi's, sarcoma
Kupffer cell (M9124/3) 155.0
Langerhans cell 202.9 ☑
leptomeningeal (M9530/3) — *see* Neoplasm,
meninges, malignant
lymphangioendothelial (M9170/3) — *see*
Neoplasm, connective tissue, malignant
lymphoblastic (M9630/3) 200.1 ☑
lymphocytic (M9620/3) 200.1 ☑
mast cell (M9740/3) 202.6 ☑
melanotic (M8720/3) — *see* Melanoma
meningeal (M9530/3) — *see* Neoplasm,
meninges, malignant
meningothelial (M9530/3) — *see* Neoplasm,
meninges, malignant
mesenchymal (M8800/3) — *see also* Neoplasm,
connective tissue, malignant
mixed (M8990/3) — *see* Neoplasm,
connective tissue, malignant
mesothelial (M9050/3) — *see* Neoplasm, by
site, malignant
monstrocellular (M9481/3)
specified site — *see* Neoplasm, by site,
malignant
unspecified site 191.9
myeloid (M9930/3) 205.3 ☑
neurogenic (M9540/3) — *see* Neoplasm,
connective tissue, malignant

☑ Additional Digit Required — Refer to the Tabular List (Numeric Code Section) for Additional Digit Selection

2006 ICD-9-CM
▶◀ Revised Text
● New Line
▲ Revised Code
October 2005 • Volume 2 — 297

Sarcoma (M8800/3) — *see also* Neoplasm, connective tissue, malignant — *continued*
  odontogenic (M9270/3) 170.1
    upper jaw (bone) 170.0
  osteoblastic (M9180/3) — *see* Neoplasm, bone, malignant
  osteogenic (M9180/3) — *see also* Neoplasm, bone, malignant
    juxtacortical (M9190/3) — *see* Neoplasm, bone, malignant
      periosteal (M9190/3) — *see* Neoplasm, bone, malignant
  periosteal (M8812/3) — *see also* Neoplasm, bone, malignant
    osteogenic (M9190/3) — *see* Neoplasm, bone, malignant
  plasma cell (M9731/3) 203.8 ☑
  pleomorphic cell (M8802/3) — *see* Neoplasm, connective tissue, malignant
  reticuloendothelial (M9720/3) 202.3 ☑
  reticulum cell (M9640/3) 200.0 ☑
    nodular (M9642/3) 200.0 ☑
    pleomorphic cell type (M9641/3) 200.0 ☑
  round cell (M8803/3) — *see* Neoplasm, connective tissue, malignant
  small cell (M8803/3) — *see* Neoplasm, connective tissue, malignant
  spindle cell (M8801/3) — *see* Neoplasm, connective tissue, malignant
  stromal (endometrial) (M8930/3) 182.0
    isthmus 182.1
  synovial (M9040/3) — *see also* Neoplasm, connective tissue, malignant
    biphasic type (M9043/3) — *see* Neoplasm, connective tissue, malignant
    epithelioid cell type (M9042/3) — *see* Neoplasm, connective tissue, malignant
    spindle cell type (M9041/3) — *see* Neoplasm, connective tissue, malignant

Sarcomatosis
  meningeal (M9539/3) — *see* Neoplasm, meninges, malignant
  specified site NEC (M8800/3) — *see* Neoplasm, connective tissue, malignant
  unspecified site (M8800/6) 171.9

Sarcosinemia 270.8
Sarcosporidiosis 136.5
Satiety, early 780.94
Saturnine — *see* condition
Saturnism 984.9
  specified type of lead — *see* Table of Drugs and Chemicals
Satyriasis 302.89
Sauriasis — *see* Ichthyosis
Sauriderma 757.39
Sauriosis — *see* Ichthyosis
Savill's disease (epidemic exfoliative dermatitis) 695.89
SBE (subacute bacterial endocarditis) 421.0
Scabies (any site) 133.0
Scabs 782.8
Scaglietti-Dagnini syndrome (acromegalic macrospondylitis) 253.0
Scald, scalded — *see also* Burn, by site
  skin syndrome 695.1
Scalenus anticus (anterior) syndrome 353.0
Scales 782.8
Scalp — *see* condition
Scaphocephaly 756.0
Scaphoiditis, tarsal 732.5
Scapulalgia 733.90
Scapulohumeral myopathy 359.1
Scar, scarring (*see also* Cicatrix) 709.2
  adherent 709.2
  atrophic 709.2
  cervix
    in pregnancy or childbirth 654.6 ☑
      affecting fetus or newborn 763.89
      causing obstructed labor 660.2 ☑
        affecting fetus or newborn 763.1

Scar, scarring (*see also* Cicatrix) — *continued*
  cheloid 701.4
  chorioretinal 363.30
    disseminated 363.35
    macular 363.32
    peripheral 363.34
    posterior pole NEC 363.33
  choroid (*see also* Scar, chorioretinal) 363.30
  compression, pericardial 423.9
  congenital 757.39
  conjunctiva 372.64
  cornea 371.00
    xerophthalmic 264.6
  due to previous cesarean delivery, complicating pregnancy or childbirth 654.2 ☑
    affecting fetus or newborn 763.89
  duodenal (bulb) (cap) 537.3
  hypertrophic 701.4
  keloid 701.4
  labia 624.4
  lung (base) 518.89
  macula 363.32
    disseminated 363.35
    peripheral 363.34
  muscle 728.89
  myocardium, myocardial 412
  painful 709.2
  papillary muscle 429.81
  posterior pole NEC 363.33
    macular — *see* Scar, macula
  postnecrotic (hepatic) (liver) 571.9
  psychic V15.49
  retina (*see also* Scar, chorioretinal) 363.30
  trachea 478.9
  uterus 621.8
    in pregnancy or childbirth NEC 654.9 ☑
      affecting fetus or newborn 763.89
      due to previous cesarean delivery 654.2 ☑
  vulva 624.4
Scarabiasis 134.1
Scarlatina 034.1
  anginosa 034.1
  maligna 034.1
  myocarditis, acute 034.1 *[422.0]*
    old (*see also* Myocarditis) 429.0
  otitis media 034.1 *[382.02]*
  ulcerosa 034.1
Scarlatinella 057.8
Scarlet fever (albuminuria) (angina) (convulsions) (lesions of lid) (rash) 034.1
Schamberg's disease, dermatitis, or dermatosis (progressive pigmentary dermatosis) 709.09
Schatzki's ring (esophagus) (lower) (congenital) 750.3
  acquired 530.3
Schaufenster krankheit 413.9
Schaumann's
  benign lymphogranulomatosis 135
  disease (sarcoidosis) 135
  syndrome (sarcoidosis) 135
Scheie's syndrome (mucopolysaccharidosis IS) 277.5
Schenck's disease (sporotrichosis) 117.1
Scheuermann's disease or osteochondrosis 732.0
Scheuthauer-Marie-Sainton syndrome (cleidocranialis dysostosis) 755.59
Schilder (-Flatau) disease 341.1
Schilling-type monocytic leukemia (M9890/3) 206.9 ☑
Schimmelbusch's disease, cystic mastitis, or hyperplasia 610.1
Schirmer's syndrome (encephalocutaneous angiomatosis) 759.6
Schistocelia 756.79
Schistoglossia 750.13
Schistosoma infestation — *see* Infestation, Schistosoma
Schistosomiasis 120.9
  Asiatic 120.2
  bladder 120.0
  chestermani 120.8

Schistosomiasis — *continued*
  colon 120.1
  cutaneous 120.3
  due to
    S. hematobium 120.0
    S. japonicum 120.2
    S. mansoni 120.1
    S. mattheii 120.8
  eastern 120.2
  genitourinary tract 120.0
  intestinal 120.1
  lung 120.2
  Manson's (intestinal) 120.1
  Oriental 120.2
  pulmonary 120.2
  specified type NEC 120.8
  vesical 120.0
Schizencephaly 742.4
Schizo-affective psychosis (*see also* Schizophrenia) 295.7 ☑
Schizodontia 520.2
Schizoid personality 301.20
  introverted 301.21
  schizotypal 301.22
Schizophrenia, schizophrenic (reaction) 295.9 ☑

> *Note* — Use the following fifth-digit subclassification with category 295:
>
> 0   unspecified
> 1   subchronic
> 2   chronic
> 3   subchronic with acute exacerbation
> 4   chronic with acute exacerbation
> 5   in remission

  acute (attack) NEC 295.8 ☑
    episode 295.4 ☑
  atypical form 295.8 ☑
  borderline 295.5 ☑
  catalepsy 295.2 ☑
  catatonic (type) (acute) (excited) (withdrawn) 295.2 ☑
  childhood (type) (*see also* Psychosis, childhood) 299.9 ☑
  chronic NEC 295.6 ☑
  coenesthesiopathic 295.8 ☑
  cyclic (type) 295.7 ☑
  disorganized (type) 295.1 ☑
  flexibilitas cerea 295.2 ☑
  hebephrenic (type) (acute) 295.1 ☑
  incipient 295.5 ☑
  latent 295.5 ☑
  paranoid (type) (acute) 295.3 ☑
  paraphrenic (acute) 295.3 ☑
  prepsychotic 295.5 ☑
  primary (acute) 295.0 ☑
  prodromal 295.5 ☑
  pseudoneurotic 295.5 ☑
  pseudopsychopathic 295.5 ☑
  reaction 295.9 ☑
  residual type (state) 295.6 ☑
  restzustand 295.6 ☑
  schizo-affective (type) (depressed) (excited) 295.7 ☑
  schizophreniform type 295.4 ☑
  simple (type) (acute) 295.0 ☑
  simplex (acute) 295.0 ☑
  specified type NEC 295.8 ☑
  syndrome of childhood NEC (*see also* Psychosis, childhood) 299.9 ☑
  undifferentiated type 295.9 ☑
    acute 295.8 ☑
    chronic 295.6 ☑
Schizothymia 301.20
  introverted 301.21
  schizotypal 301.22
Schlafkrankheit 086.5
Schlatter's tibia (osteochondrosis) 732.4
Schlatter-Osgood disease (osteochondrosis, tibial tubercle) 732.4
Schloffer's tumor (*see also* Peritonitis) 567.29 ▲
Schmidt's syndrome
  sphallo-pharyngo-laryngeal hemiplegia 352.6

Schmidt's syndrome — *continued*
  thyroid-adrenocortical insufficiency 258.1
  vagoaccessory 352.6
Schmincke
  carcinoma (M8082/3) — *see* Neoplasm,
    nasopharynx, malignant
  tumor (M8082/3) — *see* Neoplasm,
    nasopharynx, malignant
Schmitz (-Stutzer) dysentery 004.0
Schmorl's disease or nodes 722.30
  lumbar, lumbosacral 722.32
  specified region NEC 722.39
  thoracic, thoracolumbar 722.31
Schneider's syndrome 047.9
Schneiderian
  carcinoma (M8121/3)
    specified site — *see* Neoplasm, by site,
      malignant
    unspecified site 160.0
  papilloma (M8121/0)
    specified site — *see* Neoplasm, by site,
      benign
    unspecified site 212.0
Schnitzler syndrome 273.1
Schoffer's tumor (*see also* Peritonitis) 567.29 ▲
Scholte's syndrome (malignant carcinoid) 259.2
Scholz's disease 330.0
Scholz (-Bielschowsky-Henneberg) syndrome
  330.0
Schönlein (-Henoch) disease (primary) (purpura)
  (rheumatic) 287.0
School examination V70.3
Schottmüller's disease (*see also* Fever,
  paratyphoid) 002.9
Schroeder's syndrome (endocrine-hypertensive)
  255.3
Schüller-Christian disease or syndrome (chronic
  histiocytosis X) 277.89
Schultz's disease or syndrome (agranulocytosis)
  288.0
Schultze's acroparesthesia, simple 443.89
Schwalbe-Ziehen-Oppenheimer disease 333.6
Schwannoma (M9560/0) — *see also* Neoplasm,
  connective tissue, benign
  malignant (M9560/3) — *see* Neoplasm,
    connective tissue, malignant
Schwartz (-Jampel) syndrome 756.89
Schwartz-Bartter syndrome (inappropriate
  secretion of antidiuretic hormone) 253.6
Schweninger-Buzzi disease (macular atrophy)
  701.3
Sciatic — *see* condition
Sciatica (infectional) 724.3
  due to
    displacement of intervertebral disc 722.10
    herniation, nucleus pulposus 722.10
  wallet 724.3   ●
Scimitar syndrome (anomalous venous drainage,
  right lung to inferior vena cava) 747.49
Sclera — *see* condition
Sclerectasia 379.11
Scleredema
  adultorum 710.1
  Buschke's 710.1
  newborn 778.1
Sclerema
  adiposum (newborn) 778.1
  adultorum 710.1
  edematosum (newborn) 778.1
  neonatorum 778.1
  newborn 778.1
Scleriasis — *see* Scleroderma
Scleritis 379.00
  with corneal involvement 379.05
  anterior (annular) (localized) 379.03
  brawny 379.06
  granulomatous 379.09
  posterior 379.07
  specified NEC 379.09
  suppurative 379.09
  syphilitic 095.0

Scleritis — *continued*
  tuberculous (nodular) (*see also* Tuberculosis)
    017.3 ☑ [379.09]
Sclerochoroiditis (*see also* Scleritis) 379.00
Scleroconjunctivitis (*see also* Scleritis) 379.00
Sclerocystic ovary (syndrome) 256.4
Sclerodactylia 701.0
Scleroderma, sclerodermia (acrosclerotic)
  (diffuse) (generalized) (progressive)
  (pulmonary) 710.1
  circumscribed 701.0
  linear 701.0
  localized (linear) 701.0
  newborn 778.1
Sclerokeratitis 379.05
  meaning sclerosing keratitis 370.54
  tuberculous (*see also* Tuberculosis)
    017.3 ☑ [379.09]
Scleroma, trachea 040.1
Scleromalacia
  multiple 731.0
  perforans 379.04
Scleromyxedema 701.8
Scleroperikeratitis 379.05
Sclerose en plaques 340
Sclerosis, sclerotic
  adrenal (gland) 255.8
  Alzheimer's 331.0
    with dementia — *see* Alzheimer's, dementia
  amyotrophic (lateral) 335.20
  annularis fibrosi
    aortic 424.1
    mitral 424.0
  aorta, aortic 440.0
    valve (*see also* Endocarditis, aortic) 424.1
  artery, arterial, arteriolar, arteriovascular —
    see Arteriosclerosis
  ascending multiple 340
  Baló's (concentric) 341.1
  basilar — *see* Sclerosis, brain
  bone (localized) NEC 733.99
  brain (general) (lobular) 341.9
    Alzheimer's — *see* Alzheimer's, dementia
    artery, arterial 437.0
    atrophic lobar 331.0
      with dementia
        with behavioral disturbance 331.0
          [294.11]
        without behavioral disturbance 331.0
          [294.10]
    diffuse 341.1
      familial (chronic) (infantile) 330.0
      infantile (chronic) (familial) 330.0
      Pelizaeus-Merzbacher type 330.0
    disseminated 340
    hereditary 334.2
    infantile (degenerative) (diffuse) 330.0
    insular 340
    Krabbe's 330.0
    miliary 340
    multiple 340
    Pelizaeus-Merzbacher 330.0
    progressive familial 330.0
    senile 437.0
    tuberous 759.5
  bulbar, progressive 340
  bundle of His 426.50
    left 426.3
    right 426.4
  cardiac — *see* Arteriosclerosis, coronary
  cardiorenal (*see also* Hypertension, cardiorenal)
    404.90
  cardiovascular (*see also* Disease,
    cardiovascular) 429.2
    renal (*see also* Hypertension, cardiorenal)
      404.90
  centrolobar, familial 330.0
  cerebellar — *see* Sclerosis, brain
  cerebral — *see* Sclerosis, brain
  cerebrospinal 340
    disseminated 340
    multiple 340
  cerebrovascular 437.0

Sclerosis, sclerotic — *continued*
  choroid 363.40
    diffuse 363.56
  combined (spinal cord) — *see also*
    Degeneration, combined
    multiple 340
  concentric, Baló's 341.1
  cornea 370.54
  coronary (artery) — *see* Arteriosclerosis,
    coronary
  corpus cavernosum
    female 624.8
    male 607.89
  Dewitzky's
    aortic 424.1
    mitral 424.0
  diffuse NEC 341.1
  disease, heart — *see* Arteriosclerosis, coronary
  disseminated 340
  dorsal 340
  dorsolateral (spinal cord) — *see* Degeneration,
    combined
  endometrium 621.8
  extrapyramidal 333.90
  eye, nuclear (senile) 366.16
  Friedreich's (spinal cord) 334.0
  funicular (spermatic cord) 608.89
  gastritis 535.4 ☑
  general (vascular) — *see* Arteriosclerosis
  gland (lymphatic) 457.8
  hepatic 571.9
  hereditary
    cerebellar 334.2
    spinal 334.0
  idiopathic cortical (Garré's) (*see also*
    Osteomyelitis) 730.1 ☑
  ilium, piriform 733.5
  insular 340
    pancreas 251.8
  Islands of Langerhans 251.8
  kidney — *see* Sclerosis, renal
  larynx 478.79
  lateral 335.24
    amyotrophic 335.20
    descending 335.24
    primary 335.24
    spinal 335.24
  liver 571.9
  lobar, atrophic (of brain) 331.0
    with dementia
      with behavioral disturbance 331.0
        [294.11]
      without behavioral disturbance 331.0
        [294.10]
  lung (*see also* Fibrosis, lung) 515
  mastoid 383.1
  mitral — *see* Endocarditis, mitral
  Mönckeberg's (medial) (*see also*
    Arteriosclerosis, extremities) 440.20
  multiple (brain stem) (cerebral) (generalized)
    (spinal cord) 340
  myocardium, myocardial — *see*
    Arteriosclerosis, coronary
  nuclear (senile), eye 366.16
  ovary 620.8
  pancreas 577.8
  penis 607.89
  peripheral arteries (*see also* Arteriosclerosis,
    extremities) 440.20
  plaques 340
  pluriglandular 258.8
  polyglandular 258.8
  posterior (spinal cord) (syphilitic) 094.0
  posterolateral (spinal cord) — *see* Degeneration,
    combined
  prepuce 607.89
  primary lateral 335.24
  progressive systemic 710.1
  pulmonary (*see also* Fibrosis, lung) 515
    artery 416.0
    valve (heart) (*see also* Endocarditis,
      pulmonary) 424.3
  renal 587
    with
      cystine storage disease 270.0
      hypertension (*see also* Hypertension,
        kidney) 403.90

2006 ICD-9-CM

☑ Additional Digit Required — Refer to the Tabular List (Numeric Code Section) for Additional Digit Selection
▶◀ Revised Text   ● New Line   ▲ Revised Code

October 2005 • Volume 2 — 299

Sclerosis, sclerotic — continued

renal — continued
  with — continued
    hypertensive heart disease (conditions
        classifiable to 402) (see also
        Hypertension, cardiorenal) 404.90
    arteriolar (hyaline) (see also Hypertension,
        kidney) 403.90
    hyperplastic (see also Hypertension,
        kidney) 403.90
  retina (senile) (vascular) 362.17
  rheumatic
    aortic valve 395.9
    mitral valve 394.9
  Schilder's 341.1
  senile — see Arteriosclerosis
  spinal (cord) (general) (progressive) (transverse)
      336.8
    ascending 357.0
    combined — see also Degeneration,
        combined
      multiple 340
      syphilitic 094.89
    disseminated 340
    dorsolateral — see Degeneration, combined
    hereditary (Friedreich's) (mixed form) 334.0
    lateral (amyotrophic) 335.24
    multiple 340
    posterior (syphilitic) 094.0
  stomach 537.89
  subendocardial, congenital 425.3
  systemic (progressive) 710.1
    with lung involvement 710.1 [517.2]
  tricuspid (heart) (valve) — see Endocarditis,
      tricuspid
  tuberous (brain) 759.5
  tympanic membrane (see also
      Tympanosclerosis) 385.00
  valve, valvular (heart) — see Endocarditis
  vascular — see Arteriosclerosis
  vein 459.89

Sclerotenonitis 379.07

Sclerotitis (see also Scleritis) 379.00
  syphilitic 095.0
  tuberculous (see also Tuberculosis)
      017.3 ☑ [379.09]

Scoliosis (acquired) (postural) 737.30
  congenital 754.2
  due to or associated with
    Charcôt-Marie-Tooth disease 356.1 [737.43]
    mucopolysaccharidosis 277.5 [737.43]
    neurofibromatosis 237.71 [737.43]
    osteitis
      deformans 731.0 [737.43]
      fibrosa cystica 252.01 [737.43]
    osteoporosis (see also Osteoporosis) 733.00
        [737.43]
    poliomyelitis 138 [737.43]
    radiation 737.33
    tuberculosis (see also Tuberculosis)
        015.0 ☑ [737.43]
  idiopathic 737.30
    infantile
      progressive 737.32
      resolving 737.31
  paralytic 737.39
  rachitic 268.1
  sciatic 724.3
  specified NEC 737.39
  thoracogenic 737.34
  tuberculous (see also Tuberculosis)
      015.0 ☑ [737.43]

Scoliotic pelvis 738.6
  with disproportion (fetopelvic) 653.0 ☑
    affecting fetus or newborn 763.1
    causing obstructed labor 660.1 ☑
      affecting fetus or newborn 763.1

Scorbutus, scorbutic 267
  anemia 281.8

Scotoma (ring) 368.44
  arcuate 368.43
  Bjerrum 368.43
  blind spot area 368.42
  central 368.41
  centrocecal 368.41
  paracecal 368.42

Scotoma — continued

paracentral 368.41
scintillating 368.12
Seidel 368.43

Scratch — see Injury, superficial, by site

Screening (for) V82.9
  alcoholism V79.1
  anemia, deficiency NEC V78.1
    iron V78.0
  anomaly, congenital V82.89
  antenatal V28.9
    alphafetoprotein levels, raised V28.1
    based on amniocentesis V28.2
      chromosomal anomalies V28.0
      raised alphafetoprotein levels V28.1
    fetal growth retardation using ultrasonics
        V28.4
    isoimmunization V28.5
    malformations using ultrasonics V28.3
    raised alphafetoprotein levels V28.1
    specified condition NEC V28.8
    Streptococcus B V28.6
  arterial hypertension V81.1
  arthropod-borne viral disease NEC V73.5
  asymptomatic bacteriuria V81.5
  bacterial
    conjunctivitis V74.4
    disease V74.9
      specified condition NEC V74.8
  bacteriuria, asymptomatic V81.5
  blood disorder NEC V78.9
    specified type NEC V78.8
  bronchitis, chronic V81.3
  brucellosis V74.8
  cancer — see Screening, malignant neoplasm
  cardiovascular disease NEC V81.2
  cataract V80.2
  Chagas' disease V75.3
  chemical poisoning V82.5
  cholera V74.0
  cholesterol level V77.91
  chromosomal
    anomalies
      by amniocentesis, antenatal V28.0
      maternal postnatal V82.4
    athletes V70.3
  condition
    cardiovascular NEC V81.2
    eye NEC V80.2
    genitourinary NEC V81.6
    neurological V80.0
    respiratory NEC V81.4
    skin V82.0
    specified NEC V82.89
  congenital
    anomaly V82.89
      eye V80.2
    dislocation of hip V82.3
    eye condition or disease V80.2
  conjunctivitis, bacterial V74.4
  contamination NEC (see also Poisoning) V82.5
  coronary artery disease V81.0
  cystic fibrosis V77.6
  deficiency anemia NEC V78.1
    iron V78.0
  dengue fever V73.5
  depression V79.0
  developmental handicap V79.9
    in early childhood V79.3
    specified type NEC V79.8
  diabetes mellitus V77.1
  diphtheria V74.3
  disease or disorder V82.9
    bacterial V74.9
      specified NEC V74.8
    blood V78.9
      specified type NEC V78.8
    blood-forming organ V78.9
      specified type NEC V78.8
    cardiovascular NEC V81.2
      hypertensive V81.1
      ischemic V81.0
    Chagas' V75.3
    chlamydial V73.98
      specified NEC V73.88
    ear NEC V80.3

Screening (for) — continued

disease or disorder — continued
  endocrine NEC V77.99
  eye NEC V80.2
  genitourinary NEC V81.6
  heart NEC V81.2
    hypertensive V81.1
    ischemic V81.0
  immunity NEC V77.99
  infectious NEC V75.9
  lipoid NEC V77.91
  mental V79.9
    specified type NEC V79.8
  metabolic NEC V77.99
    inborn NEC V77.7
  neurological V80.0
  nutritional NEC V77.99
  rheumatic NEC V82.2
  rickettsial V75.0
  sickle-cell V78.2
    trait V78.2
  specified type NEC V82.89
  thyroid V77.0
  vascular NEC V81.2
    ischemic V81.0
  venereal V74.5
  viral V73.99
    arthropod-borne NEC V73.5
    specified type NEC V73.89
dislocation of hip, congenital V82.3
drugs in athletes V70.3
emphysema (chronic) V81.3
encephalitis, viral (mosquito or tick borne)
    V73.5
endocrine disorder NEC V77.99
eye disorder NEC V80.2
  congenital V80.2
fever
  dengue V73.5
  hemorrhagic V73.5
  yellow V73.4
filariasis V75.6
galactosemia V77.4
genitourinary condition NEC V81.6
glaucoma V80.1
gonorrhea V74.5
gout V77.5
Hansen's disease V74.2
heart disease NEC V81.2
  hypertensive V81.1
  ischemic V81.0
heavy metal poisoning V82.5
helminthiasis, intestinal V75.7
hematopoietic malignancy V76.89
hemoglobinopathies NEC V78.3
hemorrhagic fever V73.5
Hodgkin's disease V76.89
hormones in athletes V70.3
hypercholesterolemia V77.91
hyperlipdemia V77.91
hypertension V81.1
immunity disorder NEC V77.99
inborn errors of metabolism NEC V77.7
infection
  bacterial V74.9
    specified type NEC V74.8
  mycotic V75.4
  parasitic NEC V75.8
infectious disease V75.9
  specified type NEC V75.8
ingestion of radioactive substance V82.5
intestinal helminthiasis V75.7
iron deficiency anemia V78.0
ischemic heart disease V81.0
lead poisoning V82.5
leishmaniasis V75.2
leprosy V74.2
leptospirosis V74.8
leukemia V76.89
lipoid disorder NEC V77.91
lymphoma V76.89
malaria V75.1
malignant neoplasm (of) V76.9
  bladder V76.3
  blood V76.89

Screening (for) — *continued*
malignant neoplasm (of) — *continued*
breast V76.10
mammogram NEC V76.12
for high-risk patient V76.11
specified type NEC V76.19
cervix V76.2
colon V76.51
colorectal V76.51
hematopoietic system V76.89
intestine V76.50
colon V76.51
small V76.52
lung V76.0
lymph (glands) V76.89
nervous system V76.81
oral cavity V76.42
other specified neoplasm NEC V76.89
ovary V76.46
prostate V76.44
rectum V76.41
respiratory organs V76.0
skin V76.43
specified sites NEC V76.49
testis V76.45
vagina V76.47
following hysterectomy for malignant
condition V67.01
maternal postnatal chromosomal anomalies
V82.4
malnutrition V77.2
mammogram NEC V76.12
for high-risk patient V76.11
measles V73.2
mental
disorder V79.9
specified type NEC V79.8
retardation V79.2
metabolic disorder NEC V77.99
metabolic errors, inborn V77.7
mucoviscidosis V77.6
multiphasic V82.6
mycosis V75.4
mycotic infection V75.4
nephropathy V81.5
neurological condition V80.0
nutritional disorder V77.99
obesity V77.8
osteoporosis V82.81
parasitic infection NEC V75.8
phenylketonuria V77.3
plague V74.8
poisoning
chemical NEC V82.5
contaminated water supply V82.5
heavy metal V82.5
poliomyelitis V73.0
postnatal chromosomal anomalies, maternal
V82.4
prenatal — *see* Screening, antenatal
pulmonary tuberculosis V74.1
radiation exposure V82.5
renal disease V81.5
respiratory condition NEC V81.4
rheumatic disorder NEC V82.2
rheumatoid arthritis V82.1
rickettsial disease V75.0
rubella V73.3
schistosomiasis V75.5
senile macular lesions of eye V80.2
sickle-cell anemia, disease, or trait V78.2
skin condition V82.0
sleeping sickness V75.3
smallpox V73.1
special V82.9
specified condition NEC V82.89
specified type NEC V82.89
spirochetal disease V74.9
specified type NEC V74.8
stimulants in athletes V70.3
syphilis V74.5
tetanus V74.8
thyroid disorder V77.0
trachoma V73.6
trypanosomiasis V75.3
tuberculosis, pulmonary V74.1
venereal disease V74.5

Screening (for) — *continued*
viral encephalitis
mosquito-borne V73.5
tick-borne V73.5
whooping cough V74.8
worms, intestinal V75.7
yaws V74.6
yellow fever V73.4
Scrofula (*see also* Tuberculosis) 017.2 ☑
Scrofulide (primary) (*see also* Tuberculosis)
017.0 ☑
Scrofuloderma, scrofulodermia (any site)
(primary) (*see also* Tuberculosis) 017.0 ☑
Scrofulosis (universal) (*see also* Tuberculosis)
017.2 ☑
Scrofulosis lichen (primary) (*see also*
Tuberculosis) 017.0 ☑
Scrofulous — *see* condition
Scrotal tongue 529.5
congenital 750.13
Scrotum — *see* condition
Scurvy (gum) (infantile) (rickets) (scorbutic) 267
Sea-blue histiocyte syndrome 272.7
Seabright-Bantam syndrome
(pseudohypoparathyroidism) 275.49
Seasickness 994.6
Seatworm 127.4
Sebaceous
cyst (*see also* Cyst, sebaceous) 706.2
gland disease NEC 706.9
Sebocystomatosis 706.2
Seborrhea, seborrheic 706.3
adiposa 706.3
capitis 690.11
congestiva 695.4
corporis 706.3
dermatitis 690.10
infantile 690.12
diathesis in infants 695.89
eczema 690.18
infantile 690.12
keratosis 702.19
inflamed 702.11
nigricans 705.89
sicca 690.18
wart 702.19
inflamed 702.11
Seckel's syndrome 759.89
Seclusion pupil 364.74
Seclusiveness, child 313.22
Secondary — *see also* condition
neoplasm — *see* Neoplasm, by site, malignant,
secondary
Secretan's disease or syndrome (posttraumatic
edema) 782.3
Secretion
antidiuretic hormone, inappropriate (syndrome)
253.6
catecholamine, by pheochromocytoma 255.6
hormone
antidiuretic, inappropriate (syndrome) 253.6
by
carcinoid tumor 259.2
pheochromocytoma 255.6
ectopic NEC 259.3
urinary
excessive 788.42
suppression 788.5
Section
cesarean
affecting fetus or newborn 763.4
post mortem, affecting fetus or newborn
761.6
previous, in pregnancy or childbirth
654.2 ☑
affecting fetus or newborn 763.89
nerve, traumatic — *see* Injury, nerve, by site
Seeligmann's syndrome (ichthyosis congenita)
757.1
Segmentation, incomplete (congenital) — *see*
also Fusion
bone NEC 756.9

Segmentation, incomplete — *see also* Fusion —
continued
lumbosacral (joint) 756.15
vertebra 756.15
lumbosacral 756.15
Seizure 780.39
akinetic (idiopathic) (*see also* Epilepsy) 345.0 ☑
psychomotor 345.4 ☑
apoplexy, apoplectic (*see also* Disease,
cerebrovascular, acute) 436
atonic (*see also* Epilepsy) 345.0 ☑
autonomic 300.11
brain or cerebral (*see also* Disease,
cerebrovascular, acute) 436
convulsive (*see also* Convulsions) 780.39
cortical (focal) (motor) (*see also* Epilepsy)
345.5 ☑
epilepsy, epileptic (cryptogenic) (*see also*
Epilepsy) 345.9 ☑
epileptiform, epileptoid 780.39
focal (*see also* Epilepsy) 345.5 ☑
febrile 780.31
with status epilepticus 345.3   ●
heart — *see* Disease, heart
hysterical 300.11
Jacksonian (focal) (*see also* Epilepsy) 345.5 ☑
motor type 345.5 ☑
sensory type 345.5 ☑
newborn 779.0
paralysis (*see also* Disease, cerebrovascular,
acute) 436
recurrent 780.39
epileptic — *see* Epilepsy
repetitive 780.39
epileptic — *see* Epilepsy
salaam (*see also* Epilepsy) 345.6 ☑
uncinate (*see also* Epilepsy) 345.4 ☑
Self-mutilation 300.9
Semicoma 780.09
Semiconsciousness 780.09
Seminal
vesicle — *see* condition
vesiculitis (*see also* Vesiculitis) 608.0
Seminoma (M9061/3)
anaplastic type (M9062/3)
specified site — *see* Neoplasm, by site,
malignant
unspecified site 186.9
specified site — *see* Neoplasm, by site,
malignant
spermatocytic (M9063/3)
specified site — *see* Neoplasm, by site,
malignant
unspecified site 186.9
unspecified site 186.9
Semliki Forest encephalitis 062.8
Senear-Usher disease or syndrome (pemphigus
erythematosus) 694.4
Senecio jacobae dermatitis 692.6
Senectus 797
Senescence 797
Senile (*see also* condition) 797
cervix (atrophic) 622.8
degenerative atrophy, skin 701.3
endometrium (atrophic) 621.8
fallopian tube (atrophic) 620.3
heart (failure) 797
lung 492.8
ovary (atrophic) 620.3
syndrome 259.8
vagina, vaginitis (atrophic) 627.3
wart 702.0
Senility 797
with
acute confusional state 290.3
delirium 290.3
mental changes 290.9
psychosis NEC (*see also* Psychosis, senile)
290.20
premature (syndrome) 259.8
Sensation
burning (*see also* Disturbance, sensation)
782.0
tongue 529.6

☑ Additional Digit Required — Refer to the Tabular List (Numeric Code Section) for Additional Digit Selection
▶◀ Revised Text   ● New Line   ▲ Revised Code

Sensation — continued
  choking 784.9
  loss of (see also Disturbance, sensation) 782.0
  prickling (see also Disturbance, sensation) 782.0
  tingling (see also Disturbance, sensation) 782.0
Sense loss (touch) (see also Disturbance, sensation) 782.0
  smell 781.1
  taste 781.1
Sensibility disturbance NEC (cortical) (deep) (vibratory) (see also Disturbance, sensation) 782.0
Sensitive dentine 521.8
Sensitiver Beziehungswahn 297.8
Sensitivity, sensitization — see also Allergy
  autoerythrocyte 287.2
  carotid sinus 337.0
  child (excessive) 313.21
  cold, autoimmune 283.0
  methemoglobin 289.7
  suxamethonium 289.89
  tuberculin, without clinical or radiological symptoms 795.5
Sensory
  extinction 781.8
  neglect 781.8
Separation
  acromioclavicular — see Dislocation, acromioclavicular
  anxiety, abnormal 309.21
  apophysis, traumatic — see Fracture, by site
  choroid 363.70
    hemorrhagic 363.72
    serous 363.71
  costochondral (simple) (traumatic) — see Dislocation, costochondral
  delayed
    umbilical cord 779.83
  epiphysis, epiphyseal
    nontraumatic 732.9
      upper femoral 732.2
    traumatic — see Fracture, by site
  fracture — see Fracture, by site
  infundibulum cardiac from right ventricle by a partition 746.83
  joint (current) (traumatic) — see Dislocation, by site
  placenta (normally implanted) — see Placenta, separation
  pubic bone, obstetrical trauma 665.6 ☑
  retina, retinal (see also Detachment, retina) 361.9
    layers 362.40
      sensory (see also Retinoschisis) 361.10
    pigment epithelium (exudative) 362.42
      hemorrhagic 362.43
  sternoclavicular (traumatic) — see Dislocation, sternoclavicular
  symphysis pubis, obstetrical trauma 665.6 ☑
  tracheal ring, incomplete (congenital) 748.3
Sepsis (generalized) 995.91
  with
    abortion — see Abortion, by type, with sepsis
    ectopic pregnancy (see also categories 633.0-633.9) 639.0
    molar pregnancy (see also categories 630-632) 639.0
  buccal 528.3
  complicating labor 659.3 ☑
  dental (pulpal origin) 522.4
  female genital organ NEC 614.9
  fetus (intrauterine) 771.81
  following
    abortion 639.0
    ectopic or molar pregnancy 639.0
    infusion, perfusion, or transfusion 999.3
  Friedländer's 038.49
  intraocular 360.00
  localized
    in operation wound 998.59
    skin (see also Abscess) 682.9
  malleus 024

Sepsis — continued
  nadir 038.9
  newborn (organism unspecified) NEC 771.81
  oral 528.3
  puerperal, postpartum, childbirth (pelvic) 670.0 ☑
  resulting from infusion, injection, transfusion, or vaccination 999.3
  severe 995.92
  skin, localized (see also Abscess) 682.9
  umbilical (newborn) (organism unspecified) 771.89
    tetanus 771.3
  urinary 599.0
    meaning sepsis 995.91
    meaning urinary tract infection 599.0
Septate — see also Septum
Septic — see also condition
  adenoids 474.01
    and tonsils 474.02
  arm (with lymphangitis) 682.3
  embolus — see Embolism
  finger (with lymphangitis) 681.00
  foot (with lymphangitis) 682.7
  gallbladder (see also Cholecystitis) 575.8
  hand (with lymphangitis) 682.4
  joint (see also Arthritis, septic) 711.0 ☑
  kidney (see also Infection, kidney) 590.9
  leg (with lymphangitis) 682.6
  mouth 528.3
  nail 681.9
    finger 681.02
    toe 681.11
  shock (endotoxic) 785.52
  sore (see also Abscess) 682.9
    throat 034.0
      milk-borne 034.0
      streptococcal 034.0
  spleen (acute) 289.59
  teeth (pulpal origin) 522.4
  throat 034.0
  thrombus — see Thrombosis
  toe (with lymphangitis) 681.10
  tonsils 474.00
    and adenoids 474.02
  umbilical cord (newborn) (organism unspecified) 771.89
  uterus (see also Endometritis) 615.9
Septicemia, septicemic (generalized) (suppurative) 038.9
  with
    abortion — see Abortion, by type, with sepsis
    ectopic pregnancy (see also categories 633.0-633.9) 639.0
    molar pregnancy (see also categories 630-632) 639.0
  Aerobacter aerogenes 038.49
  anaerobic 038.3
  anthrax 022.3
  Bacillus coli 038.42
  Bacteroides 038.3
  Clostridium 038.3
  complicating labor 659.3 ☑
  cryptogenic 038.9
  enteric gram-negative bacilli 038.40
  Enterobacter aerogenes 038.49
  Erysipelothrix (insidiosa) (rhusiopathiae) 027.1
  Escherichia coli 038.42
  following
    abortion 639.0
    ectopic or molar pregnancy 639.0
    infusion, injection, transfusion, or vaccination 999.3
  Friedländer's (bacillus) 038.49
  gangrenous 038.9
  gonococcal 098.89
  gram-negative (organism) 038.40
    anaerobic 038.3
  Hemophilus influenzae 038.41
  herpes (simplex) 054.5
  herpetic 054.5
  Listeria monocytogenes 027.0
  meningeal — see Meningitis
  meningococcal (chronic) (fulminating) 036.2
  navel, newborn (organism unspecified) 771.89

Septicemia, septicemic — continued
  newborn (organism unspecified) 771.81
  plague 020.2
  pneumococcal 038.2
  postabortal 639.0
  postoperative 998.59
  Proteus vulgaris 038.49
  Pseudomonas (aeruginosa) 038.43
  puerperal, postpartum 670.0 ☑
  Salmonella (aertrycke) (callinarum) (choleraesuis) (enteritidis) (suipestifer) 003.1
  Serratia 038.44
  Shigella (see also Dysentery, bacillary) 004.9
  specified organism NEC 038.8
  staphylococcal 038.10
    aureus 038.11
    specified organism NEC 038.19
  streptococcal (anaerobic) 038.0
  Streptococcus pneumoniae 038.2
  suipestifer 003.1
  umbilicus, newborn (organism unspecified) 771.89
  viral 079.99
  Yersinia enterocolitica 038.49
Septum, septate (congenital) — see also Anomaly, specified type NEC
  anal 751.2
  aqueduct of Sylvius 742.3
    with spina bifida (see also Spina bifida) 741.0 ☑
  hymen 752.49
  uterus (see also Double, uterus) 752.2
  vagina 752.49
    in pregnancy or childbirth 654.7 ☑
      affecting fetus or newborn 763.89
      causing obstructed labor 660.2 ☑
        affecting fetus or newborn 763.1
Sequestration
  lung (congenital) (extralobar) (intralobar) 748.5
  orbit 376.10
  pulmonary artery (congenital) 747.3
  splenic 289.52
Sequestrum
  bone (see also Osteomyelitis) 730.1 ☑
    jaw 526.4
  dental 525.8
  jaw bone 526.4
  sinus (accessory) (nasal) (see also Sinusitis) 473.9
    maxillary 473.0
Sequoiosis asthma 495.8
Serology for syphilis
  doubtful
    with signs or symptoms — see Syphilis, by site and stage
    follow-up of latent syphilis — see Syphilis, latent
  false positive 795.6
  negative, with signs or symptoms — see Syphilis, by site and stage
  positive 097.1
    with signs or symptoms — see Syphilis, by site and stage
    false 795.6
    follow-up of latent syphilis — see Syphilis, latent
    only finding — see Syphilis, latent
  reactivated 097.1
Seroma (postoperative) (non-infected) 998.13
  infected 998.51
Seropurulent — see condition
Serositis, multiple 569.89
  pericardial 423.2
  peritoneal 568.82
  pleural — see Pleurisy
Serotonin syndrome 333.99
Serous — see condition
Sertoli cell
  adenoma (M8640/0)
    specified site — see Neoplasm, by site, benign
    unspecified site
      female 220
      male 222.0

Sertoli cell — *continued*
carcinoma (M8640/3)
specified site — *see* Neoplasm, by site, malignant
unspecified site 186.9
syndrome (germinal aplasia) 606.0
tumor (M8640/0)
with lipid storage (M8641/0)
specified site — *see* Neoplasm, by site, benign
unspecified site
female 220
male 222.0
specified site — *see* Neoplasm, by site, benign
unspecified site
female 220
male 222.0

Sertoli-Leydig cell tumor (M8631/0)
specified site — *see* Neoplasm, by site, benign
unspecified site
female 220
male 222.0

Serum
allergy, allergic reaction 999.5
shock 999.4
arthritis 999.5 *[713.6]*
complication or reaction NEC 999.5
disease NEC 999.5
hepatitis 070.3 ☑
intoxication 999.5
jaundice (homologous) — *see* Hepatitis, viral, type B
neuritis 999.5
poisoning NEC 999.5
rash NEC 999.5
reaction NEC 999.5
sickness NEC 999.5

Sesamoiditis 733.99

Seven-day fever 061
of
Japan 100.89
Queensland 100.89

Sever's disease or osteochondrosis (calcaneum) 732.5

Sex chromosome mosaics 758.81

Sextuplet
affected by maternal complications of pregnancy 761.5
healthy liveborn — *see* Newborn, multiple
pregnancy (complicating delivery) NEC 651.8 ☑
with fetal loss and retention of one or more fetus(es) 651.6 ☑
following (elective) fetal reduction 651.7 ☑ ●

Sexual
anesthesia 302.72
deviation (*see also* Deviation, sexual) 302.9
disorder (*see also* Deviation, sexual) 302.9
frigidity (female) 302.72
function, disorder of (psychogenic) 302.70
specified type NEC 302.79
immaturity (female) (male) 259.0
impotence 607.84 ▲
organic origin NEC 607.84
psychogenic 302.72 ●
precocity (constitutional) (cryptogenic) (female) (idiopathic) (male) NEC 259.1
with adrenal hyperplasia 255.2
sadism 302.84

Sexuality, pathological (*see also* Deviation, sexual) 302.9

Sézary's disease, reticulosis, or syndrome (M9701/3) 202.2 ☑

Shadow, lung 793.1

Shaken infant syndrome 995.55

Shaking
head (tremor) 781.0
palsy or paralysis (*see also* Parkinsonism) 332.0

Shallowness, acetabulum 736.39

Shaver's disease or syndrome (bauxite pneumoconiosis) 503

Shearing
artificial skin graft 996.55

Shearing — *continued*
decellularized allodermis graft 996.55

Sheath (tendon) — *see* condition

Shedding
nail 703.8
teeth, premature, primary (deciduous) 520.6

Sheehan's disease or syndrome (postpartum pituitary necrosis) 253.2

Shelf, rectal 569.49

Shell
shock (current) (*see also* Reaction, stress, acute) 308.9
lasting state 300.16
teeth 520.5

Shield kidney 753.3

Shift, mediastinal 793.2

Shifting
pacemaker 427.89
sleep-work schedule (affecting sleep) 327.36 ▲

Shiga's
bacillus 004.0
dysentery 004.0

Shigella (dysentery) (*see also* Dysentery, bacillary) 004.9
carrier (suspected) of V02.3

Shigellosis (*see also* Dysentery, bacillary) 004.9

Shingles (*see also* Herpes, zoster) 053.9
eye NEC 053.29

Shin splints 844.9

Shipyard eye or disease 077.1

Shirodkar suture, in pregnancy 654.5 ☑

Shock 785.50
with
abortion — *see* Abortion, by type, with shock
ectopic pregnancy (*see also* categories 633.0-633.9) 639.5
molar pregnancy (*see also* categories 630-632) 639.5
allergic — *see* Shock, anaphylactic
anaclitic 309.21
anaphylactic 995.0
chemical — *see* Table of Drugs and Chemicals
correct medicinal substance properly administered 995.0
drug or medicinal substance
correct substance properly administered 995.0
overdose or wrong substance given or taken 977.9
specified drug — *see* Table of Drugs and Chemicals
following sting(s) 989.5
food — *see* Anaphylactic shock, due to, food
immunization 999.4
serum 999.4
anaphylactoid — *see* Shock, anaphylactic
anesthetic
correct substance properly administered 995.4
overdose or wrong substance given 968.4
specified anesthetic — *see* Table of Drugs and Chemicals
birth, fetus or newborn NEC 779.89
cardiogenic 785.51
chemical substance — *see* Table of Drugs and Chemicals
circulatory 785.59
complicating
abortion — *see* Abortion, by type, with shock
ectopic pregnancy (*see also* categories 633.0-633.9) 639.5
labor and delivery 669.1 ☑
molar pregnancy (*see also* categories 630-632) 639.5
culture 309.29
due to
drug 995.0
correct substance properly administered 995.0
overdose or wrong substance given or taken 977.9
specified drug — *see* Table of Drugs and Chemicals

Shock — *continued*
due to — *continued*
food — *see* Anaphylactic shock, due to, food
during labor and delivery 669.1 ☑
electric 994.8
endotoxic 785.52
due to surgical procedure 998.0
following
abortion 639.5
ectopic or molar pregnancy 639.5
injury (immediate) (delayed) 958.4
labor and delivery 669.1 ☑
gram-negative 785.52
hematogenic 785.59
hemorrhagic
due to
disease 785.59
surgery (intraoperative) (postoperative) 998.0
trauma 958.4
hypovolemic NEC 785.59
surgical 998.0
traumatic 958.4
insulin 251.0
therapeutic misadventure 962.3
kidney 584.5
traumatic (following crushing) 958.5
lightning 994.0
lung 518.5
nervous (*see also* Reaction, stress, acute) 308.9
obstetric 669.1 ☑
with
abortion — *see* Abortion, by type, with shock
ectopic pregnancy (*see also* categories 633.0-633.9) 639.5
molar pregnancy (*see also* categories 630-632) 639.5
following
abortion 639.5
ectopic or molar pregnancy 639.5
paralysis, paralytic (*see also* Disease, cerebrovascular, acute) 436
late effect — *see* Late effect(s) (of) cerebrovascular disease
pleural (surgical) 998.0
due to trauma 958.4
postoperative 998.0
with
abortion — *see* Abortion, by type, with shock
ectopic pregnancy (*see also* categories 633.0-633.9) 639.5
molar pregnancy (*see also* categories 630-632) 639.5
following
abortion 639.5
ectopic or molar pregnancy 639.5
psychic (*see also* Reaction, stress, acute) 308.9
past history (of) V15.49
psychogenic (*see also* Reaction, stress, acute) 308.9
septic 785.52
with
abortion — *see* Abortion, by type, with shock
ectopic pregnancy (*see also* categories 633.0-633.9) 639.5
molar pregnancy (*see also* categories 630-632) 639.5
due to
surgical procedure 998.0
transfusion NEC 999.8
bone marrow 996.85
following
abortion 639.5
ectopic or molar pregnancy 639.5
surgical procedure 998.0
transfusion NEC 999.8
bone marrow 996.85
spinal — *see also* Injury, spinal, by site
with spinal bone injury — *see* Fracture, vertebra, by site, with spinal cord injury
surgical 998.0
therapeutic misadventure NEC (*see also* Complications) 998.89

2006 ICD-9-CM

☑ Additional Digit Required — Refer to the Tabular List (Numeric Code Section) for Additional Digit Selection
▶◀ Revised Text ● New Line ▲ Revised Code

October 2005 • Volume 2 — 303

Shock — *continued*
  thyroxin 962.7
  toxic 040.82
  transfusion — *see* Complications, transfusion
  traumatic (immediate) (delayed) 958.4
Shoemakers' chest 738.3
Short, shortening, shortness
  Achilles tendon (acquired) 727.81
  arm 736.89
    congenital 755.20
  back 737.9
  bowel syndrome 579.3
  breath 786.05
  chain acyl CoA dehydrogenase deficiency
      (SCAD) 277.85
  common bile duct, congenital 751.69
  cord (umbilical) 663.4 ☑
    affecting fetus or newborn 762.6
  cystic duct, congenital 751.69
  esophagus (congenital) 750.4
  femur (acquired) 736.81
    congenital 755.34
  frenulum linguae 750.0
  frenum, lingual 750.0
  hamstrings 727.81
  hip (acquired) 736.39
    congenital 755.63
  leg (acquired) 736.81
    congenital 755.30
  metatarsus (congenital) 754.79
    acquired 736.79
  organ or site, congenital NEC — *see* Distortion
  palate (congenital) 750.26
  P-R interval syndrome 426.81
  radius (acquired) 736.09
    congenital 755.26
  round ligament 629.8
  sleeper 307.49
  stature, constitutional (hereditary) 783.43
  tendon 727.81
    Achilles (acquired) 727.81
      congenital 754.79
    congenital 756.89
  thigh (acquired) 736.81
    congenital 755.34
  tibialis anticus 727.81
  umbilical cord 663.4 ☑
    affecting fetus or newborn 762.6
  urethra 599.84
  uvula (congenital) 750.26
  vagina 623.8
Shortsightedness 367.1
Shoshin (acute fulminating beriberi) 265.0
Shoulder — *see* condition
Shovel-shaped incisors 520.2
Shower, thromboembolic — *see* Embolism
Shunt (status)
  aortocoronary bypass V45.81
  arterial-venous (dialysis) V45.1
  arteriovenous, pulmonary (acquired) 417.0
    congenital 747.3
      traumatic (complication) 901.40
  cerebral ventricle (communicating) in situ
      V45.2
  coronary artery bypass V45.81
  surgical, prosthetic, with complications — *see*
      Complications, shunt
  vascular NEC V45.89
Shutdown
  renal 586
    with
      abortion — *see* Abortion, by type, with
          renal failure
      ectopic pregnancy (*see also* categories
          633.0-633.9) 639.3
      molar pregnancy (*see also* categories 630-
          632) 639.3
    complicating
      abortion 639.3
      ectopic or molar pregnancy 639.3
    following labor and delivery 669.3 ☑
Shwachman's syndrome 288.0
Shy-Drager syndrome (orthostatic hypotension
    with multisystem degeneration) 333.0

Sialadenitis (any gland) (chronic) (suppurative)
    527.2
  epidemic — *see* Mumps
Sialadenosis, periodic 527.2
Sialaporia 527.7
Sialectasia 527.8
Sialitis 527.2
Sialoadenitis (*see also* Sialadenitis) 527.2
Sialoangitis 527.2
Sialodochitis (fibrinosa) 527.2
Sialodocholithiasis 527.5
Sialolithiasis 527.5
Sialorrhea (*see also* Ptyalism) 527.7
  periodic 527.2
Sialosis 527.8
  rheumatic 710.2
Siamese twin 759.4
Sicard's syndrome 352.6
Sicca syndrome (keratoconjunctivitis) 710.2
Sick 799.9
  cilia syndrome 759.89
  or handicapped person in family V61.49
Sickle-cell
  anemia (see also Disease, sickle-cell) 282.60
  disease (see also Disease, sickle-cell) 282.60
  hemoglobin
    C disease (without crisis) 282.63
      with
        crisis 282.64
          vaso-occlusive pain 282.64
    D disease (without crisis) 282.68
      with crisis 282.69
    E disease (without crisis) 282.68
      with crisis 282.69
  thalassemia (without crisis) 282.41
    with
      crisis 282.42
        vaso-occlusive pain 282.42
  trait 282.5
Sicklemia (*see also* Disease, sickle-cell) 282.60
  trait 282.5
Sickness
  air (travel) 994.6
  airplane 994.6
  alpine 993.2
  altitude 993.2
  Andes 993.2
  aviators' 993.2
  balloon 993.2
  car 994.6
  compressed air 993.3
  decompression 993.3
  green 280.9
  harvest 100.89
  milk 988.8
  morning 643.0 ☑
  motion 994.6
  mountain 993.2
    acute 289.0
  protein (*see also* Complications, vaccination)
      999.5
  radiation NEC 990
  roundabout (motion) 994.6
  sea 994.6
  serum NEC 999.5
  sleeping (African) 086.5
    by Trypanosoma 086.5
      gambiense 086.3
      rhodesiense 086.4
    Gambian 086.3
    late effect 139.8
    Rhodesian 086.4
  sweating 078.2
  swing (motion) 994.6
  train (railway) (travel) 994.6
  travel (any vehicle) 994.6
Sick sinus syndrome 427.81
Sideropenia (*see also* Anemia, iron deficiency)
    280.9
Siderosis (lung) (occupational) 503
  cornea 371.15
  eye (bulbi) (vitreous) 360.23
  lens 360.23

Siegal-Cattan-Mamou disease (periodic) 277.3
Siemens' syndrome
  ectodermal dysplasia 757.31
  keratosis follicularis spinulosa (decalvans)
      757.39
Sighing respiration 786.7
Sigmoid
  flexure — *see* condition
  kidney 753.3
Sigmoiditis — *see* Enteritis
Silfverskiöld's syndrome 756.50
Silicosis, silicotic (complicated) (occupational)
    (simple) 502
  fibrosis, lung (confluent) (massive)
      (occupational) 502
  non-nodular 503
  pulmonum 502
Silicotuberculosis (*see also* Tuberculosis)
    011.4 ☑
Silo fillers' disease 506.9
Silver's syndrome (congenital hemihypertrophy
    and short stature) 759.89
Silver wire arteries, retina 362.13
Silvestroni-Bianco syndrome (thalassemia
    minima) 282.49
Simian crease 757.2
Simmonds' cachexia or disease (pituitary
    cachexia) 253.2
Simons' disease or syndrome (progressive
    lipodystrophy) 272.6
Simple, simplex — *see* condition
Sinding-Larsen disease (juvenile osteopathia
    patellae) 732.4
Singapore hemorrhagic fever 065.4
Singers' node or nodule 478.5
Single
  atrium 745.69
  coronary artery 746.85
  umbilical artery 747.5
  ventricle 745.3
Singultus 786.8
  epidemicus 078.89
Sinus — *see also* Fistula
  abdominal 569.81
  arrest 426.6
  arrhythmia 427.89
  bradycardia 427.89
    chronic 427.81
  branchial cleft (external) (internal) 744.41
  coccygeal (infected) 685.1
    with abscess 685.0
  dental 522.7
  dermal (congenital) 685.1
    with abscess 685.0
  draining — *see* Fistula
  infected, skin NEC 686.9
  marginal, ruptured or bleeding 641.2 ☑
    affecting fetus or newborn 762.1
  pause 426.6
  pericranii 742.0
  pilonidal (infected) (rectum) 685.1
    with abscess 685.0
  preauricular 744.46
  rectovaginal 619.1
  sacrococcygeal (dermoid) (infected) 685.1
    with abscess 685.0
  skin
    infected NEC 686.9
    noninfected — *see* Ulcer, skin
  tachycardia 427.89
  tarsi syndrome 726.79
  testis 608.89
  tract (postinfectional) — *see* Fistula
  urachus 753.7
Sinuses, Rokitansky-Aschoff (*see also* Disease,
    gallbladder) 575.8
Sinusitis (accessory) (nasal) (hyperplastic)
    (nonpurulent) (purulent) (chronic) 473.9
  with influenza, flu, or grippe 487.1
  acute 461.9
    ethmoidal 461.2
    frontal 461.1
    maxillary 461.0
    specified type NEC 461.8

Sinusitis — *continued*
  acute — *continued*
    sphenoidal 461.3
  allergic (*see also* Fever, hay) 477.9
  antrum — *see* Sinusitis, maxillary
  due to
    fungus, any sinus 117.9
    high altitude 993.1
  ethmoidal 473.2
    acute 461.2
  frontal 473.1
    acute 461.1
  influenzal 478.1
  maxillary 473.0
    acute 461.0
  specified site NEC 473.8
  sphenoidal 473.3
    acute 461.3
  syphilitic, any sinus 095.8
  tuberculous, any sinus (*see also* Tuberculosis)
    012.8 ☑

Sinusitis-bronchiectasis-situs inversus
  (syndrome) (triad) 759.3
Sipple's syndrome (medullary thyroid carcinoma-
  pheochromocytoma) 193
Sirenomelia 759.89
Siriasis 992.0
Sirkari's disease 085.0
SIRS (systemic inflammatory response syndrome)
  995.90
  due to
    infectious process 995.91
      with organ dysfunction 995.92
    non-infectious process 995.93
      with organ dysfunction 995.94
Siti 104.0
Sitophobia 300.29
Situation, psychiatric 300.9
Situational
  disturbance (transient) (*see also* Reaction,
    adjustment) 309.9
    acute 308.3
  maladjustment, acute (*see also* Reaction,
    adjustment) 309.9
  reaction (*see also* Reaction, adjustment) 309.9
    acute 308.3
Situs inversus or transversus 759.3
  abdominalis 759.3
  thoracis 759.3
Sixth disease 057.8
Sjögren (-Gougerot) syndrome or disease
  (keratoconjunctivitis sicca) 710.2
  with lung involvement 710.2 [517.8]
Sjögren-Larsson syndrome (ichthyosis congenita)
  757.1
Skeletal — *see* condition
Skene's gland — *see* condition
Skenitis (*see also* Urethritis) 597.89
  gonorrheal (acute) 098.0
    chronic or duration of 2 months or over
      098.2
Skerljevo 104.0
Skevas-Zerfus disease 989.5
Skin — *see also* condition
  donor V59.1
  hidebound 710.9
SLAP lesion (superior glenoid labrum) 840.7
Slate-dressers' lung 502
Slate-miners' lung 502
Sleep
  deprivation V69.4
  disorder 780.50
    with apnea — *see* Apnea, sleep
    child 307.40
    movement, ►unspecified◄ 780.58
    nonorganic origin 307.40
      specified type NEC 307.49
  disturbance 780.50
    with apnea — *see* Apnea, sleep
    nonorganic origin 307.40
      specified type NEC 307.49
  drunkenness 307.47
  movement disorder, ►unspecified◄ 780.58

Sleep — *continued*
  paroxysmal (*see also* Narcolepsy) 347.00
  related movement disorder, ►unspecified◄
    780.58
  rhythm inversion 327.39
    nonorganic origin 307.45
  walking 307.46
    hysterical 300.13
Sleeping sickness 086.5
  late effect 139.8
Sleeplessness (*see also* Insomnia) 780.52
  menopausal 627.2
  nonorganic origin 307.41
Slipped, slipping
  epiphysis (postinfectional) 732.9
    traumatic (old) 732.9
      current — *see* Fracture, by site
    upper femoral (nontraumatic) 732.2
  intervertebral disc — *see* Displacement,
    intervertebral disc
  ligature, umbilical 772.3
  patella 717.89
  rib 733.99
  sacroiliac joint 724.6
  tendon 727.9
  ulnar nerve, nontraumatic 354.2
  vertebra NEC (*see also* Spondylolisthesis)
    756.12
Slocumb's syndrome 255.3
Sloughing (multiple) (skin) 686.9
  abscess — *see* Abscess, by site
  appendix 543.9
  bladder 596.8
  fascia 728.9
  graft — *see* Complications, graft
  phagedena (*see also* Gangrene) 785.4
  reattached extremity (*see also* Complications,
    reattached extremity) 996.90
  rectum 569.49
  scrotum 608.89
  tendon 727.9
  transplanted organ (*see also* Rejection,
    transplant, organ, by site) 996.80
  ulcer (*see also* Ulcer, skin) 707.9
Slow
  feeding newborn 779.3
  fetal, growth NEC 764.9 ☑
    affecting management of pregnancy 656.5 ☑
Slowing
  heart 427.89
  urinary stream 788.62
Sluder's neuralgia or syndrome 337.0
Slurred, slurring, speech 784.5
Small, smallness
  cardiac reserve — *see* Disease, heart
  for dates
    fetus or newborn 764.0 ☑
      with malnutrition 764.1 ☑
      affecting management of pregnancy
        656.5 ☑
  infant, term 764.0 ☑
    with malnutrition 764.1 ☑
    affecting management of pregnancy 656.5 ☑
  introitus, vagina 623.3
  kidney, unknown cause 589.9
    bilateral 589.1
    unilateral 589.0
  ovary 620.8
  pelvis
    with disproportion (fetopelvic) 653.1 ☑
      affecting fetus or newborn 763.1
    causing obstructed labor 660.1 ☑
      affecting fetus or newborn 763.1
  placenta — *see* Placenta, insufficiency
  uterus 621.8
  white kidney 582.9
Small-for-dates (*see also* Light-for-dates) 764.0 ☑
  affecting management of pregnancy 656.5 ☑
Smallpox 050.9
  contact V01.3
  exposure to V01.3
  hemorrhagic (pustular) 050.0
  malignant 050.0
  modified 050.2

▲

Smallpox — *continued*
  vaccination
    complications — *see* Complications,
      vaccination
    prophylactic (against) V04.1
Smith's fracture (separation) (closed) 813.41
  open 813.51
Smith-Lemli Opitz syndrome
  (cerebrohepatorenal syndrome) 759.89
Smith-Magenis syndrome 758.33
Smith-Strang disease (oasthouse urine) 270.2
Smokers'
  bronchitis 491.0
  cough 491.0
  syndrome (*see also* Abuse, drugs,
    nondependent) 305.1
  throat 472.1
  tongue 528.6
Smothering spells 786.09
Snaggle teeth, tooth 524.39
Snapping
  finger 727.05
  hip 719.65
  jaw 524.69
    temporomandibular joint sounds on opening
      or closing 524.64
  knee 717.9
  thumb 727.05
Sneddon-Wilkinson disease or syndrome
  (subcorneal pustular dermatosis) 694.1
Sneezing 784.9
  intractable 478.1
Sniffing
  cocaine (*see also* Dependence) 304.2 ☑
  ether (*see also* Dependence) 304.6 ☑
  glue (airplane) (*see also* Dependence) 304.6 ☑
Snoring 786.09
Snow blindness 370.24
Snuffles (nonsyphilitic) 460
  syphilitic (infant) 090.0
Social migrant V60.0
Sodoku 026.0
Soemmering's ring 366.51
Soft — *see also* condition
  enlarged prostate 600.00
    with urinary retention 600.01
  nails 703.8
Softening
  bone 268.2
  brain (necrotic) (progressive) 434.9 ☑
    arteriosclerotic 437.0
    congenital 742.4
    embolic (*see also* Embolism, brain) 434.1 ☑
    hemorrhagic (*see also* Hemorrhage, brain)
      431
    occlusive 434.9 ☑
    thrombotic (*see also* Thrombosis, brain)
      434.0 ☑
  cartilage 733.92
  cerebellar — *see* Softening, brain
  cerebral — *see* Softening, brain
  cerebrospinal — *see* Softening, brain
  myocardial, heart (*see also* Degeneration,
    myocardial) 429.1
  nails 703.8
  spinal cord 336.8
  stomach 537.89
Solar fever 061
Soldier's
  heart 306.2
  patches 423.1
Solitary
  cyst
    bone 733.21
    kidney 593.2
  kidney (congenital) 753.0
  tubercle, brain (*see also* Tuberculosis, brain)
    013.2 ☑
  ulcer, bladder 596.8
Somatization reaction, somatic reaction (*see
  also* Disorder, psychosomatic) 306.9
  disorder 300.81

2006 ICD-9-CM

☑ Additional Digit Required — Refer to the Tabular List (Numeric Code Section) for Additional Digit Selection
►◄ Revised Text   ● New Line   ▲ Revised Code

October 2005 • Volume 2 — 305

Somatoform disorder

Somatoform disorder 300.82
  atypical 300.82
  severe 300.81
  undifferentiated 300.82
Somnambulism 307.46
  hysterical 300.13
Somnolence 780.09
  nonorganic origin 307.43
  periodic 349.89
Sonne dysentery 004.3
Soor 112.0
Sore
  Delhi 085.1
  desert (see also Ulcer, skin) 707.9
  eye 379.99
  Lahore 085.1
  mouth 528.9
    canker 528.2
    due to dentures 528.9
  muscle 729.1
  Naga (see also Ulcer, skin) 707.9
  oriental 085.1
  pressure (see also Decubitus) 707.00
    with gangrene (see also Decubitus)
      707.00 [785.4]
  skin NEC 709.9
  soft 099.0
  throat 462
    with influenza, flu, or grippe 487.1
    acute 462
    chronic 472.1
    clergyman's 784.49
    coxsackie (virus) 074.0
    diphtheritic 032.0
    epidemic 034.0
    gangrenous 462
    herpetic 054.79
    influenzal 487.1
    malignant 462
    purulent 462
    putrid 462
    septic 034.0
    streptococcal (ulcerative) 034.0
    ulcerated 462
    viral NEC 462
      Coxsackie 074.0
  tropical (see also Ulcer, skin) 707.9
  veldt (see also Ulcer, skin) 707.9
Sotos' syndrome (cerebral gigantism) 253.0
Sounds
  friction, pleural 786.7
  succussion, chest 786.7
  temporomandibular joint
    on opening or closing 524.64
South African cardiomyopathy syndrome 425.2
South American
  blastomycosis 116.1
  trypanosomiasis — see Trypanosomiasis
Southeast Asian hemorrhagic fever 065.4
Spacing, teeth, abnormal 524.30
  excessive 524.32
Spade-like hand (congenital) 754.89
Spading nail 703.8
  congenital 757.5
Spanemia 285.9
Spanish collar 605
Sparganosis 123.5
Spasm, spastic, spasticity (see also condition)
  781.0
  accommodation 367.53
  ampulla of Vater (see also Disease, gallbladder)
    576.8
  anus, ani (sphincter) (reflex) 564.6
    psychogenic 306.4
  artery NEC 443.9
    basilar 435.0
    carotid 435.8
    cerebral 435.9
      specified artery NEC 435.8
    retinal (see also Occlusion, retinal, artery)
      362.30
    vertebral 435.1
    vertebrobasilar 435.3
  Bell's 351.0

Spasm, spastic, spasticity (see also condition) —
  continued
  bladder (sphincter, external or internal) 596.8
  bowel 564.9
    psychogenic 306.4
  bronchus, bronchiole 519.1
  cardia 530.0
  cardiac — see Angina
  carpopedal (see also Tetany) 781.7
  cecum 564.9
    psychogenic 306.4
  cerebral (arteries) (vascular) 435.9
    specified artery NEC 435.8
  cerebrovascular 435.9
  cervix, complicating delivery 661.4 ☑
    affecting fetus or newborn 763.7
  ciliary body (of accommodation) 367.53
  colon 564.1
    psychogenic 306.4
  common duct (see also Disease, biliary) 576.8
  compulsive 307.22
  conjugate 378.82
  convergence 378.84
  coronary (artery) — see Angina
  diaphragm (reflex) 786.8
    psychogenic 306.1
  duodenum, duodenal (bulb) 564.89
  esophagus (diffuse) 530.5
    psychogenic 306.4
  facial 351.8
  fallopian tube 620.8
  gait 781.2
  gastrointestinal (tract) 536.8
    psychogenic 306.4
  glottis 478.75
    hysterical 300.11
    psychogenic 306.1
      specified as conversion reaction 300.11
    reflex through recurrent laryngeal nerve
      478.75
  habit 307.20
    chronic 307.22
    transient (of childhood) 307.21
  heart — see Angina
  hourglass — see Contraction, hourglass
  hysterical 300.11
  infantile (see also Epilepsy) 345.6 ☑
  internal oblique, eye 378.51
  intestinal 564.9
    psychogenic 306.4
  larynx, laryngeal 478.75
    hysterical 300.11
    psychogenic 306.1
      specified as conversion reaction 300.11
  levator palpebrae superioris 333.81
  lightning (see also Epilepsy) 345.6 ☑
  mobile 781.0
  muscle 728.85
    back 724.8
    psychogenic 306.0
  nerve, trigeminal 350.1
  nervous 306.0
  nodding 307.3
    infantile (see also Epilepsy) 345.6 ☑
  occupational 300.89
  oculogyric 378.87
  ophthalmic artery 362.30
  orbicularis 781.0
  perineal 625.8
  peroneo-extensor (see also Flat, foot) 734
  pharynx (reflex) 478.29
    hysterical 300.11
    psychogenic 306.1
      specified as conversion reaction 300.11
  pregnant uterus, complicating delivery 661.4 ☑
  psychogenic 306.0
  pylorus 537.81
    adult hypertrophic 537.0
    congenital or infantile 750.5
    psychogenic 306.4
  rectum (sphincter) 564.6
    psychogenic 306.4
  retinal artery NEC (see also Occlusion, retina,
    artery) 362.30
  sacroiliac 724.6
  salaam (infantile) (see also Epilepsy) 345.6 ☑
  saltatory 781.0

Spasm, spastic, spasticity (see also condition) —
  continued
  sigmoid 564.9
    psychogenic 306.4
  sphincter of Oddi (see also Disease,
    gallbladder) 576.5
  stomach 536.8
    neurotic 306.4
  throat 478.29
    hysterical 300.11
    psychogenic 306.1
      specified as conversion reaction 300.11
  tic 307.20
    chronic 307.22
    transient (of childhood) 307.21
  tongue 529.8
  torsion 333.6
  trigeminal nerve 350.1
    postherpetic 053.12
  ureter 593.89
  urethra (sphincter) 599.84
  uterus 625.8
    complicating labor 661.4 ☑
      affecting fetus or newborn 763.7
  vagina 625.1
    psychogenic 306.51
  vascular NEC 443.9
  vasomotor NEC 443.9
  vein NEC 459.89
  vesical (sphincter, external or internal) 596.8
  viscera 789.0 ☑
Spasmodic — see condition
Spasmophilia (see also Tetany) 781.7
Spasmus nutans 307.3
Spastic — see also Spasm
  child 343.9
Spasticity — see also Spasm
  cerebral, child 343.9
Speakers' throat 784.49
Specific, specified — see condition
Speech
  defect, disorder, disturbance, impediment NEC
    784.5
    psychogenic 307.9
  therapy V57.3
Spells 780.39
  breath-holding 786.9
Spencer's disease (epidemic vomiting) 078.82
Spens' syndrome (syncope with heart block)
  426.9
Spermatic cord — see condition
Spermatocele 608.1
  congenital 752.89
Spermatocystitis 608.4
Spermatocytoma (M9063/3)
  specified site — see Neoplasm, by site,
    malignant
  unspecified site 186.9
Spermatorrhea 608.89
Sperm counts
  fertility testing V26.21
  following sterilization reversal V26.22
  postvasectomy V25.8
Sphacelus (see also Gangrene) 785.4
Sphenoidal — see condition
Sphenoiditis (chronic) (see also Sinusitis,
  sphenoidal) 473.3
Sphenopalatine ganglion neuralgia 337.0
Sphericity, increased, lens 743.36
Spherocytosis (congenital) (familial) (hereditary)
  282.0
  hemoglobin disease 282.7
  sickle-cell (disease) 282.60
Spherophakia 743.36
Sphincter — see condition
Sphincteritis, sphincter of Oddi (see also
  Cholecystitis) 576.8
Sphingolipidosis 272.7
Sphingolipodystrophy 272.7
Sphingomyelinosis 272.7
Spicule tooth 520.2

☑ Additional Digit Required — Refer to the Tabular List (Numeric Code Section) for Additional Digit Selection

◄► Revised Text   ● New Line   ▲ Revised Code

Spider
finger 755.59
nevus 448.1
vascular 448.1
Spiegler-Fendt sarcoid 686.8
Spielmeyer-Stock disease 330.1
Spielmeyer-Vogt disease 330.1
Spina bifida (aperta) 741.9 ☑

> *Note — Use the following fifth-digit*
> *subclassification with category 741:*
>
> *0   unspecified region*
> *1   cervical region*
> *2   dorsal [thoracic] region*
> *3   lumbar region*

with hydrocephalus 741.0 ☑
fetal (suspected), affecting management of
pregnancy 655.0 ☑
occulta 756.17
Spindle, Krukenberg's 371.13
Spine, spinal — *see* condition
Spiradenoma (eccrine) (M8403/0) — *see*
Neoplasm, skin, benign
Spirillosis NEC (*see also* Fever, relapsing) 087.9
Spirillum minus 026.0
Spirillum obermeieri infection 087.0
Spirochetal — *see* condition
Spirochetosis 104.9
arthritic, arthritica 104.9 *[711.8]* ☑
bronchopulmonary 104.8
icterohemorrhagica 100.0
lung 104.8
Spitting blood (*see also* Hemoptysis) 786.3
Splanchnomegaly 569.89
Splanchnoptosis 569.89
Spleen, splenic — *see also* condition
agenesis 759.0
flexure syndrome 569.89
neutropenia syndrome 288.0
sequestration syndrome 289.52
Splenectasis (*see also* Splenomegaly) 789.2
Splenitis (interstitial) (malignant) (nonspecific)
289.59
malarial (*see also* Malaria) 084.6
tuberculous (*see also* Tuberculosis) 017.7 ☑
Splenocele 289.59
Splenomegalia — *see* Splenomegaly
Splenomegalic — *see* condition
Splenomegaly 789.2
Bengal 789.2
cirrhotic 289.51
congenital 759.0
congestive, chronic 289.51
cryptogenic 789.2
Egyptian 120.1
Gaucher's (cerebroside lipidosis) 272.7
idiopathic 789.2
malarial (*see also* Malaria) 084.6
neutropenic 288.0
Niemann-Pick (lipid histiocytosis) 272.7
siderotic 289.51
syphilitic 095.8
congenital 090.0
tropical (Bengal) (idiopathic) 789.2
Splenopathy 289.50
Splenopneumonia — *see* Pneumonia
Splenoptosis 289.59
Splinter — *see* Injury, superficial, by site
Split, splitting
heart sounds 427.89
lip, congenital (*see also* Cleft, lip) 749.10
nails 703.8
urinary stream 788.61
Spoiled child reaction (*see also* Disturbance,
conduct) 312.1 ☑
Spondylarthritis (*see also* Spondylosis) 721.90
Spondylarthrosis (*see also* Spondylosis) 721.90
Spondylitis 720.9
ankylopoietica 720.0
ankylosing (chronic) 720.0
atrophic 720.9
ligamentous 720.9

Spondylitis — *continued*
chronic (traumatic) (*see also* Spondylosis)
721.90
deformans (chronic) (*see also* Spondylosis)
721.90
gonococcal 098.53
gouty 274.0
hypertrophic (*see also* Spondylosis) 721.90
infectious NEC 720.9
juvenile (adolescent) 720.0
Kümmell's 721.7
Marie-Strümpell (ankylosing) 720.0
muscularis 720.9
ossificans ligamentosa 721.6
osteoarthritica (*see also* Spondylosis) 721.90
posttraumatic 721.7
proliferative 720.0
rheumatoid 720.0
rhizomelica 720.0
sacroiliac NEC 720.2
senescent (*see also* Spondylosis) 721.90
senile (*see also* Spondylosis) 721.90
static (*see also* Spondylosis) 721.90
traumatic (chronic) (*see also* Spondylosis)
721.90
tuberculous (*see also* Tuberculosis)
015.0 ☑ *[720.81]*
typhosa 002.0 *[720.81]*
Spondyloarthrosis (*see also* Spondylosis) 721.90
Spondylolisthesis (congenital) (lumbosacral)
756.12
with disproportion (fetopelvic) 653.3 ☑
affecting fetus or newborn 763.1
causing obstructed labor 660.1 ☑
affecting fetus or newborn 763.1
acquired 738.4
degenerative 738.4
traumatic 738.4
acute (lumbar) — *see* Fracture, vertebra,
lumbar
site other than lumbosacral — *see*
Fracture, vertebra, by site
Spondylolysis (congenital) 756.11
acquired 738.4
cervical 756.19
lumbosacral region 756.11
with disproportion (fetopelvic) 653.3 ☑
affecting fetus or newborn 763.1
causing obstructed labor 660.1 ☑
affecting fetus or newborn 763.1
Spondylopathy
inflammatory 720.9
specified type NEC 720.89
traumatic 721.7
Spondylose rhizomelique 720.0
Spondylosis 721.90
with
disproportion 653.3 ☑
affecting fetus or newborn 763.1
causing obstructed labor 660.1 ☑
affecting fetus or newborn 763.1
myelopathy NEC 721.91
cervical, cervicodorsal 721.0
with myelopathy 721.1
inflammatory 720.9
lumbar, lumbosacral 721.3
with myelopathy 721.42
sacral 721.3
with myelopathy 721.42
thoracic 721.2
with myelopathy 721.41
traumatic 721.7
Sponge
divers' disease 989.5
inadvertently left in operation wound 998.4
kidney (medullary) 753.17
Spongioblastoma (M9422/3)
multiforme (M9440/3)
specified site — *see* Neoplasm, by site,
malignant
unspecified site 191.9
polare (M9423/3)
specified site — *see* Neoplasm, by site,
malignant
unspecified site 191.9

Spongioblastoma (M9422/3) — *continued*
primitive polar (M9443/3)
specified site — *see* Neoplasm, by site,
malignant
unspecified site 191.9
specified site — *see* Neoplasm, by site,
malignant
unspecified site 191.9
Spongiocytoma (M9400/3)
specified site — *see* Neoplasm, by site,
malignant
unspecified site 191.9
Spongioneuroblastoma (M9504/3) — *see*
Neoplasm, by site, malignant
Spontaneous — *see also* condition
fracture — *see* Fracture, pathologic
Spoon nail 703.8
congenital 757.5
Sporadic — *see* condition
Sporotrichosis (bones) (cutaneous) (disseminated)
(epidermal) (lymphatic) (lymphocutaneous)
(mucous membranes) (pulmonary) (skeletal)
(visceral) 117.1
Sporotrichum schenckii infection 117.1
Spots, spotting
atrophic (skin) 701.3
Bitôt's (in the young child) 264.1
café au lait 709.09
cayenne pepper 448.1
cotton wool (retina) 362.83
de Morgan's (senile angiomas) 448.1
Fúchs' black (myopic) 360.21
intermenstrual
irregular 626.6
regular 626.5
interpalpebral 372.53
Koplik's 055.9
liver 709.09
Mongolian (pigmented) 757.33
of pregnancy 641.9 ☑
purpuric 782.7
ruby 448.1
Spotted fever — *see* Fever, spotted
Sprain, strain (joint) (ligament) (muscle) (tendon)
848.9
abdominal wall (muscle) 848.8
Achilles tendon 845.09
acromioclavicular 840.0
ankle 845.00
and foot 845.00
anterior longitudinal, cervical 847.0
arm 840.9
upper 840.9
and shoulder 840.9
astragalus 845.00
atlanto-axial 847.0
atlanto-occipital 847.0
atlas 847.0
axis 847.0
back (*see also* Sprain, spine) 847.9
breast bone 848.40
broad ligament — *see* Injury, internal, broad
ligament
calcaneofibular 845.02
carpal 842.01
carpometacarpal 842.11
cartilage
costal, without mention of injury to sternum
848.3
involving sternum 848.42
ear 848.8
knee 844.9
with current tear (*see also* Tear,
meniscus) 836.2
semilunar (knee) 844.8
with current tear (*see also* Tear,
meniscus) 836.2
septal, nose 848.0
thyroid region 848.2
xiphoid 848.49
cervical, cervicodorsal, cervicothoracic 847.0
chondrocostal, without mention of injury to
sternum 848.3
involving sternum 848.42
chondrosternal 848.42

2006 ICD-9-CM

☑ Additional Digit Required — Refer to the Tabular List (Numeric Code Section) for Additional Digit Selection
►◄ Revised Text   ● New Line   ▲ Revised Code

Volume 2 — 307

Sprain, strain — *continued*
chronic (joint) — *see* Derangement, joint
clavicle 840.9
coccyx 847.4
collar bone 840.9
collateral, knee (medial) (tibial) 844.1
   lateral (fibular) 844.0
   recurrent or old 717.89
      lateral 717.81
      medial 717.82
coracoacromial 840.8
coracoclavicular 840.1
coracohumeral 840.2
coracoid (process) 840.9
coronary, knee 844.8
costal cartilage, without mention of injury to sternum 848.3
   involving sternum 848.42
cricoarytenoid articulation 848.2
cricothyroid articulation 848.2
cruciate
   knee 844.2
   old 717.89
      anterior 717.83
      posterior 717.84
deltoid
   ankle 845.01
   shoulder 840.8
dorsal (spine) 847.1
ear cartilage 848.8
elbow 841.9
   and forearm 841.9
   specified site NEC 841.8
femur (proximal end) 843.9
   distal end 844.9
fibula (proximal end) 844.9
   distal end 845.00
fibulocalcaneal 845.02
finger(s) 842.10
foot 845.10
   and ankle 845.00
forearm 841.9
   and elbow 841.9
   specified site NEC 841.8
glenoid (shoulder) (*see also* SLAP lesion) 840.8
hand 842.10
hip 843.9
   and thigh 843.9
humerus (proximal end) 840.9
   distal end 841.9
iliofemoral 843.0
infraspinatus 840.3
innominate
   acetabulum 843.9
   pubic junction 848.5
   sacral junction 846.1
internal
   collateral, ankle 845.01
   semilunar cartilage 844.8
      with current tear (*see also* Tear, meniscus) 836.2
      old 717.5
interphalangeal
   finger 842.13
   toe 845.13
ischiocapsular 843.1
jaw (cartilage) (meniscus) 848.1
   old 524.69
knee 844.9
   and leg 844.9
   old 717.5
      collateral
         lateral 717.81
         medial 717.82
      cruciate
         anterior 717.83
         posterior 717.84
late effect — *see* Late, effects (of), sprain
lateral collateral, knee 844.0
   old 717.81
leg 844.9
   and knee 844.9
ligamentum teres femoris 843.8
low back 846.9
lumbar (spine) 847.2
lumbosacral 846.0
   chronic or old 724.6

Sprain, strain — *continued*
mandible 848.1
   old 524.69
maxilla 848.1
medial collateral, knee 844.1
   old 717.82
meniscus
   jaw 848.1
      old 524.69
   knee 844.8
      with current tear (*see also* Tear, meniscus) 836.2
      old 717.5
   mandible 848.1
      old 524.69
   specified site NEC 848.8
metacarpal 842.10
   distal 842.12
   proximal 842.11
metacarpophalangeal 842.12
metatarsal 845.10
metatarsophalangeal 845.12
midcarpal 842.19
midtarsal 845.19
multiple sites, except fingers alone or toes alone 848.8
neck 847.0
nose (septal cartilage) 848.0
occiput from atlas 847.0
old — *see* Derangement, joint
orbicular, hip 843.8
patella(r) 844.8
   old 717.89
pelvis 848.5
phalanx
   finger 842.10
   toe 845.10
radiocarpal 842.02
radiohumeral 841.2
radioulnar 841.9
   distal 842.09
radius, radial (proximal end) 841.9
   and ulna 841.9
      distal 842.09
   collateral 841.0
   distal end 842.00
recurrent — *see* Sprain, by site
rib (cage), without mention of injury to sternum 848.3
   involving sternum 848.42
rotator cuff (capsule) 840.4
round ligament — *see also* Injury, internal, round ligament
   femur 843.8
sacral (spine) 847.3
sacrococcygeal 847.3
sacroiliac (region) 846.9
   chronic or old 724.6
   ligament 846.1
   specified site NEC 846.8
sacrospinatus 846.2
sacrospinous 846.2
sacrotuberous 846.3
scaphoid bone, ankle 845.00
scapula(r) 840.9
semilunar cartilage (knee) 844.8
   with current tear (*see also* Tear, meniscus) 836.2
   old 717.5
septal cartilage (nose) 848.0
shoulder 840.9
   and arm, upper 840.9
   blade 840.9
specified site NEC 848.8
spine 847.9
   cervical 847.0
   coccyx 847.4
   dorsal 847.1
   lumbar 847.2
   lumbosacral 846.0
      chronic or old 724.6
   sacral 847.3
   sacroiliac (*see also* Sprain, sacroiliac) 846.9
      chronic or old 724.6
   thoracic 847.1
sternoclavicular 848.41
sternum 848.40

Sprain, strain — *continued*
subglenoid (*see also* SLAP lesion) 840.8
subscapularis 840.5
supraspinatus 840.6
symphysis
   jaw 848.1
      old 524.69
   mandibular 848.1
      old 524.69
   pubis 848.5
talofibular 845.09
tarsal 845.10
tarsometatarsal 845.11
temporomandibular 848.1
   old 524.69
teres
   ligamentum femoris 843.8
   major or minor 840.8
thigh (proximal end) 843.9
   and hip 843.9
   distal end 844.9
thoracic (spine) 847.1
thorax 848.8
thumb 842.10
thyroid cartilage or region 848.2
tibia (proximal end) 844.9
   distal end 845.00
tibiofibular
   distal 845.03
   superior 844.3
toe(s) 845.10
trachea 848.8
trapezoid 840.8
ulna, ulnar (proximal end) 841.9
   collateral 841.1
   distal end 842.00
ulnohumeral 841.3
vertebrae (*see also* Sprain, spine) 847.9
   cervical, cervicodorsal, cervicothoracic 847.0
wrist (cuneiform) (scaphoid) (semilunar) 842.00
xiphoid cartilage 848.49
Sprengel's deformity (congenital) 755.52
Spring fever 309.23
Sprue 579.1
   celiac 579.0
   idiopathic 579.0
   meaning thrush 112.0
   nontropical 579.0
   tropical 579.1
Spur — *see also* Exostosis
   bone 726.91
      calcaneal 726.73
   calcaneal 726.73
   iliac crest 726.5
   nose (septum) 478.1
      bone 726.91
   septal 478.1
Spuria placenta — *see* Placenta, abnormal
Spurway's syndrome (brittle bones and blue sclera) 756.51
Sputum, abnormal (amount) (color) (excessive) (odor) (purulent) 786.4
   bloody 786.3
Squamous — *see also* condition
   cell metaplasia
      bladder 596.8
      cervix — *see* condition
   epithelium in
      cervical canal (congenital) 752.49
      uterine mucosa (congenital) 752.3
   metaplasia
      bladder 596.8
      cervix — *see* condition
Squashed nose 738.0
   congenital 754.0
Squeeze, divers' 993.3
Squint (*see also* Strabismus) 378.9
   accommodative (*see also* Esotropia) 378.00
   concomitant (*see also* Heterotropia) 378.30
Stab — *see also* Wound, open, by site
   internal organs — *see* Injury, internal, by site, with open wound
Staggering gait 781.2
   hysterical 300.11

Staghorn calculus 592.0

Stälh's
ear 744.29
pigment line (cornea) 371.11

Stälhi's pigment lines (cornea) 371.11

Stain, ▶**staining**◄
meconium 779.84
port wine 757.32
tooth, teeth (hard tissues) 521.7
  due to
    accretions 523.6
    deposits (betel) (black) (green) (materia
      alba) (orange) (tobacco) 523.6
    metals (copper) (silver) 521.7
    nicotine 523.6
    pulpal bleeding 521.7
    tobacco 523.6

Stammering 307.0

Standstill
atrial 426.6
auricular 426.6
cardiac (see also Arrest, cardiac) 427.5
sinoatrial 426.6
sinus 426.6
ventricular (see also Arrest, cardiac) 427.5

Stannosis 503

Stanton's disease (melioidosis) 025

Staphylitis (acute) (catarrhal) (chronic)
(gangrenous) (membranous) (suppurative)
(ulcerative) 528.3

Staphylococcemia 038.10
aureus 038.11
specified organism NEC 038.19

Staphylococcus, staphylococcal — see condition

Staphyloderma (skin) 686.00

Staphyloma 379.11
anterior, localized 379.14
ciliary 379.11
cornea 371.73
equatorial 379.13
posterior 379.12
posticum 379.12
ring 379.15
sclera NEC 379.11

Starch eating 307.52

Stargardt's disease 362.75

Starvation (inanition) (due to lack of food) 994.2
edema 262
voluntary NEC 307.1

Stasis
bile (duct) (see also Disease, biliary) 576.8
bronchus (see also Bronchitis) 490
cardiac (see also Failure, heart) 428.0
cecum 564.89
colon 564.89
dermatitis (see also Varix, with stasis
  dermatitis) 454.1
duodenal 536.8
eczema (see also Varix, with stasis dermatitis)
  454.1
edema (see also Hypertension, venous) 459.30
foot 991.4
gastric 536.3
ileocecal coil 564.89
ileum 564.89
intestinal 564.89
jejunum 564.89
kidney 586
liver 571.9
  cirrhotic — see Cirrhosis, liver
lymphatic 457.8
pneumonia 514
portal 571.9
pulmonary 514
rectal 564.89
renal 586
  tubular 584.5
stomach 536.3
ulcer
  with varicose veins 454.0
  without varicose veins 459.81
urine NEC (see also Retention, urine) 788.20
venous 459.81

State
affective and paranoid, mixed, organic
  psychotic 294.8
agitated 307.9
  acute reaction to stress 308.2
anxiety (neurotic) (see also Anxiety) 300.00
  specified type NEC 300.09
apprehension (see also Anxiety) 300.00
  specified type NEC 300.09
climacteric, female 627.2
  following induced menopause 627.4
clouded
  epileptic (see also Epilepsy) 345.9 ☑
  paroxysmal (idiopathic) (see also Epilepsy)
    345.9 ☑
compulsive (mixed) (with obsession) 300.3
confusional 298.9
  acute 293.0
    with
      arteriosclerotic dementia 290.41
      presenile brain disease 290.11
      senility 290.3
    alcoholic 291.0
    drug-induced 292.81
  epileptic 293.0
  postoperative 293.9
  reactive (emotional stress) (psychological
    trauma) 298.2
  subacute 293.1
constitutional psychopathic 301.9
convulsive (see also Convulsions) 780.39
depressive NEC 311
  induced by drug 292.84
  neurotic 300.4
dissociative 300.15
hallucinatory 780.1
  induced by drug 292.12
hypercoagulable (primary) 289.81
  secondary 289.82
hyperdynamic beta-adrenergic circulatory
  429.82
locked-in 344.81
menopausal 627.2
  artificial 627.4
  following induced menopause 627.4
neurotic NEC 300.9
  with depersonalization episode 300.6
obsessional 300.3
oneiroid (see also Schizophrenia) 295.4 ☑
panic 300.01
paranoid 297.9
  alcohol-induced 291.5
  arteriosclerotic 290.42
  climacteric 297.2
  drug-induced 292.11
  in
    presenile brain disease 290.12
    senile brain disease 290.20
  involutional 297.2
  menopausal 297.2
  senile 290.20
  simple 297.0
postleukotomy 310.0
pregnant (see also Pregnancy) V22.2
psychogenic, twilight 298.2
psychotic, organic (see also Psychosis, organic)
  294.9
  mixed paranoid and affective 294.8
  senile or presenile NEC 290.9
  transient NEC 293.9
    with
      anxiety 293.84
      delusions 293.81
      depression 293.83
      hallucinations 293.82
residual schizophrenic (see also Schizophrenia)
  295.6 ☑
tension (see also Anxiety) 300.9
transient organic psychotic 293.9
  anxiety type 293.84
  depressive type 293.83
  hallucinatory type 293.83
  paranoid type 293.81
  specified type NEC 293.89
twilight
  epileptic 293.0
  psychogenic 298.2

State — continued
vegetative (persistent) 780.03

Status (post)
absence
  epileptic (see also Epilepsy) 345.2
  of organ, acquired (postsurgical) — see
    Absence, by site, acquired
anastomosis of intestine (for bypass) V45.3
angioplasty, percutaneous transluminal
  coronary V45.82
anginosus 413.9
ankle prosthesis V43.66
aortocoronary bypass or shunt V45.81
arthrodesis V45.4
artificially induced condition NEC V45.89
artificial opening (of) V44.9
  gastrointestinal tract NEC V44.4
  specified site NEC V44.8
  urinary tract NEC V44.6
  vagina V44.7
aspirator V46.0
awaiting organ transplant V49.83
asthmaticus (see also Asthma) 493.9 ☑
bed confinement V49.84
breast implant removal V45.83
cardiac
  device (in situ) V45.00
    carotid sinus V45.09
      fitting or adjustment V53.39
    defibrillator, automatic implantable
      V45.02
    pacemaker V45.01
      fitting or adjustment V53.31
carotid sinus stimulator V45.09
cataract extraction V45.61
chemotherapy V66.2
  current V58.69
circumcision, female 629.20
clitorectomy (female genital mutilation type I)
  629.21
  with excision of labia minora (female genital
    mutilation type II) 629.22
colostomy V44.3
contraceptive device V45.59
  intrauterine V45.51
  subdermal V45.52
convulsivus idiopathicus (see also Epilepsy)
  345.3
coronary artery bypass or shunt V45.81
cystostomy V44.50
  appendico-vesicostomy V44.52
  cutaneous-vesicostomy V44.51
  specified type NEC V44.59
defibrillator, automatic implantable cardiac
  V45.02
dental crowns V45.84
dental fillings V45.84
dental restoration V45.84
dental sealant V49.82
dialysis ▶(hemo) (peritoneal)◄ V45.1
donor V59.9
drug therapy or regimen V67.59
  high-risk medication NEC V67.51
elbow prosthesis V43.62
enterostomy V44.4
epileptic, epilepticus (absence) (grand mal) (see
  also Epilepsy) 345.3
  focal motor 345.7 ☑
  partial 345.7 ☑
  petit mal 345.2
  psychomotor 345.7 ☑
  temporal lobe 345.7 ☑
eye (adnexa) surgery V45.69
female genital mutilation 629.20
  type I 629.21
  type II 629.22
  type III 629.23
filtering bleb (eye) (postglaucoma) V45.69
  with rupture or complication 997.99
  postcataract extraction (complication)
    997.99
finger joint prosthesis V43.69
gastrostomy V44.1
grand mal 345.3
heart valve prosthesis V43.3
hemodialysis V45.1

2006 ICD-9-CM

☑ Additional Digit Required — Refer to the Tabular List (Numeric Code Section) for Additional Digit Selection
▶◄ Revised Text   ● New Line   ▲ Revised Code

October 2005 • Volume 2 — 309

Status — *continued*
  hip prosthesis (joint) (partial) (total) V43.64
  ileostomy V44.2
  infibulation (female genital mutilation type III)
        629.23
  insulin pump V45.85
  intestinal bypass V45.3
  intrauterine contraceptive device V45.51
  jejunostomy V44.4
  knee joint prosthesis V43.65
  lacunaris 437.8
  lacunôsis 437.8
  low birth weight V21.30
        less than 500 grams V21.31
        500-999 grams V21.32
        1000-1499 grams V21.33
        1500-1999 grams V21.34
        2000-2500 grams V21.35
  lymphaticus 254.8
  malignant neoplasm, ablated or excised — *see*
        History, malignant neoplasm
  marmoratus 333.7
  mutilation, female 629.20
        type I 629.21
        type II 629.22
        type III 629.23
  nephrostomy V44.6
  neuropacemaker NEC V45.89
        brain V45.89
        carotid sinus V45.09
        neurologic NEC V45.89
  organ replacement
        by artificial or mechanical device or
              prosthesis of
              artery V43.4
              artificial skin V43.83
              bladder V43.5
              blood vessel V43.4
              breast V43.82
              eye globe V43.0
              heart
        ·   assist device V43.21
                    fully implantable artificial heart
                          V43.22
                    valve V43.3
              intestine V43.89
              joint V43.60
                    ankle V43.66
                    elbow V43.62
                    finger V43.69
                    hip (partial) (total) V43.64
                    knee V43.65
                    shoulder V43.61
                    specified NEC V43.69
                    wrist V43.63
              kidney V43.89
              larynx V43.81
              lens V43.1
              limb(s) V43.7
              liver V43.89
              lung V43.89
              organ NEC V43.89
              pancreas V43.89
              skin (artificial) V43.83
              tissue NEC V43.89
              vein V43.4
        by organ transplant (heterologous)
              (homologous) — *see* Status, transplant
  pacemaker
        brain V45.89
        cardiac V45.01
        carotid sinus V45.09
        neurologic NEC V45.89
        specified site.NEC V45.89
  percutaneous transluminal coronary
        angioplasty V45.82
  peritoneal dialysis V45.1
  petit mal 345.2
  postcommotio cerebri 310.2
  postmenopausal (age related) (natural) V49.81
  postoperative NEC V45.89
  postpartum NEC V24.2
        care immediately following delivery V24.0
        routine follow-up V24.2
  postsurgical NEC V45.89
  renal dialysis V45.1

Status — *continued*
  respirator ▶[ventilator]◀ V46.11
        encounter
              during
                    mechanical failure V46.14   ●
                    power failure V46.12   ●
              for weaning V46.13   ●
  reversed jejunal transposition (for bypass)
        V45.3
  shoulder prosthesis V43.61
  shunt
        aortocoronary bypass V45.81
        arteriovenous (for dialysis) V45.1
        cerebrospinal fluid V45.2
        vascular NEC V45.89
              aortocoronary (bypass) V45.81
        ventricular (communicating) (for drainage)
              V45.2
  sterilization
        tubal ligation V26.51
        vasectomy V26.52
  subdermal contraceptive device V45.52
  thymicolymphaticus 254.8
  thymicus 254.8
  thymolymphaticus 254.8
  tooth extraction 525.10
  tracheostomy V44.0
  transplant
        blood vessel V42.89
        bone V42.4
              marrow V42.81
        cornea V42.5
        heart V42.1
              valve V42.2
        intestine V42.84
        kidney V42.0
        liver V42.7
        lung V42.6
        organ V42.9
              specified site NEC V42.89
        pancreas V42.83
        peripheral stem cells V42.82
        skin V42.3
        stem cells, peripheral V42.82
        tissue V42.9
              specified type NEC V42.89
        vessel, blood V42.89
  tubal ligation V26.51
  ureterostomy V44.6
  urethrostomy V44.6
  vagina, artificial V44.7
  vascular shunt NEC V45.89
        aortocoronary (bypass) V45.81
  vasectomy V26.52
  ventilator ▶[respirator]◀ V46.11
        encounter
              during
                    mechanical failure V46.14   ●
                    power failure V46.12   ●
              for weaning V46.13   ●
  wrist prosthesis V43.63
Stave fracture — *see* Fracture, metacarpus,
        metacarpal bone(s)
Steal
  subclavian artery 435.2
  vertebral artery 435.1
Stealing, solitary, child problem (*see also*
        Disturbance, conduct) 312.1 ☑
Steam burn — *see* Burn, by site
Steatocystoma multiplex 706.2
Steatoma (infected) 706.2
  eyelid (cystic) 374.84
        infected 373.13
Steatorrhea (chronic) 579.8
  with lacteal obstruction 579.2
  idiopathic 579.0
        adult 579.0
        infantile 579.0
  pancreatic 579.4
  primary 579.0
  secondary 579.8
  specified cause NEC 579.8
  tropical 579.1
Steatosis 272.8
  heart (*see also* Degeneration, myocardial) 429.1
  kidney 593.89
  liver 571.8

Steele-Richardson (-Olszewski) Syndrome 333.0
Stein's syndrome (polycystic ovary) 256.4
Stein-Leventhal syndrome (polycystic ovary)
        256.4
Steinbrocker's syndrome (*see also* Neuropathy,
        peripheral, autonomic) 337.9
Steinert's disease 359.2
Stenocardia (*see also* Angina) 413.9
Stenocephaly 756.0
Stenosis (cicatricial) — *see also* Stricture
  ampulla of Vater 576.2
        with calculus, cholelithiasis, or stones — *see*
              Choledocholithiasis
  anus, anal (canal) (sphincter) 569.2
        congenital 751.2
  aorta (ascending) 747.22
        arch 747.10
        arteriosclerotic 440.0
        calcified 440.0
  aortic (valve) 424.1
        with
              mitral (valve)
                    insufficiency or incompetence 396.2
                    stenosis or obstruction 396.0
        atypical 396.0
        congenital 746.3
        rheumatic 395.0
              with
                    insufficiency, incompetency or
                          regurgitation 395.2
                          with mitral (valve) disease 396.8
                    mitral (valve)
                          disease (stenosis) 396.0
                          insufficiency or incompetence 396.2
                          stenosis or obstruction 396.0
        specified cause, except rheumatic 424.1
        syphilitic 093.22
  aqueduct of Sylvius (congenital) 742.3
        with spina bifida (*see also* Spina bifida)
              741.0 ☑
        acquired 331.4
  artery NEC 447.1
        basilar — *see* Narrowing, artery, basilar
        carotid (common) (internal) — *see*
              Narrowing, artery, carotid
        celiac 447.4
        cerebral 437.0
              due to
                    embolism (*see also* Embolism, brain)
                          434.1 ☑
                    thrombus (*see also* Thrombosis, brain)
                          434.0 ☑
        precerebral — *see* Narrowing, artery,
              precerebral
        pulmonary (congenital) 747.3
              acquired 417.8
        renal 440.1
        vertebral — *see* Narrowing, artery, vertebral
  bile duct or biliary passage (*see also*
        Obstruction, biliary) 576.2
        congenital 751.61
  bladder neck (acquired) 596.0
        congenital 753.6
  brain 348.8
  bronchus 519.1
        syphilitic 095.8
  cardia (stomach) 537.89
        congenital 750.7
  cardiovascular (*see also* Disease,
        cardiovascular) 429.2
  carotid artery — *see* Narrowing, artery, carotid
  cervix, cervical (canal) 622.4
        congenital 752.49
        in pregnancy or childbirth 654.6 ☑
              affecting fetus or newborn 763.89
              causing obstructed labor 660.2 ☑
                    affecting fetus or newborn 763.1
  colon (*see also* Obstruction, intestine) 560.9
        congenital 751.2
  colostomy 569.62
  common bile duct (*see also* Obstruction,
        biliary) 576.2
        congenital 751.61
  coronary (artery) — *see* Arteriosclerosis,
        coronary

Stenosis — *see also* Stricture — *continued*
  cystic duct (*see also* Obstruction, gallbladder)
      575.2
    congenital 751.61
  due to (presence of) any device, implant, or
      graft classifiable to 996.0-996.5 — *see*
      Complications, due to (presence of) any
      device, implant, or graft classified to
      996.0-996.5 NEC
  duodenum 537.3
    congenital 751.1
  ejaculatory duct NEC 608.89
  endocervical os — *see* Stenosis, cervix
  enterostomy 569.62
  esophagostomy 530.87
  esophagus 530.3
    congenital 750.3
    syphilitic 095.8
      congenital 090.5
  external ear canal 380.50
    secondary to
      inflammation 380.53
      surgery 380.52
      trauma 380.51
  gallbladder (*see also* Obstruction, gallbladder)
      575.2
  glottis 478.74
  heart valve (acquired) — *see also* Endocarditis
    congenital NEC 746.89
      aortic 746.3
      mitral 746.5
      pulmonary 746.02
      tricuspid 746.1
  hepatic duct (*see also* Obstruction, biliary)
      576.2
  hymen 623.3
  hypertrophic subaortic (idiopathic) 425.1
  infundibulum cardiac 746.83
  intestine (*see also* Obstruction, intestine) 560.9
    congenital (small) 751.1
      large 751.2
  lacrimal
    canaliculi 375.53
    duct 375.56
      congenital 743.65
    punctum 375.52
      congenital 743.65
    sac 375.54
      congenital 743.65
  lacrimonasal duct 375.56
    congenital 743.65
    neonatal 375.55
  larynx 478.74
    congenital 748.3
    syphilitic 095.8
      congenital 090.5
  mitral (valve) (chronic) (inactive) 394.0
    with
      aortic (valve)
        disease (insufficiency) 396.1
        insufficiency or incompetence 396.1
        stenosis or obstruction 396.0
      incompetency, insufficiency or
        regurgitation 394.2
        with aortic valve disease 396.8
    active or acute 391.1
      with chorea (acute) (rheumatic)
        (Sydenham's) 392.0
    congenital 746.5
    specified cause, except rheumatic 424.0
    syphilitic 093.21
  myocardium, myocardial (*see also*
      Degeneration, myocardial) 429.1
    hypertrophic subaortic (idiopathic) 425.1
  nares (anterior) (posterior) 478.1
    congenital 748.0
  nasal duct 375.56
    congenital 743.65
  nasolacrimal duct 375.56
    congenital 743.65
    neonatal 375.55
  organ or site, congenital NEC — *see* Atresia
  papilla of Vater 576.2
    with calculus, cholelithiasis, or stones — *see*
        Choledocholithiasis

Stenosis — *see also* Stricture — *continued*
  pulmonary (artery) (congenital) 747.3
    with ventricular septal defect, dextraposition
        of aorta and hypertrophy of right
        ventricle 745.2
    acquired 417.8
    infundibular 746.83
    in tetralogy of Fallot 745.2
    subvalvular 746.83
    valve (*see also* Endocarditis, pulmonary)
        424.3
      congenital 746.02
    vein 747.49
      acquired 417.8
    vessel NEC 417.8
  pulmonic (congenital) 746.02
    infundibular 746.83
    subvalvular 746.83
  pylorus (hypertrophic) 537.0
    adult 537.0
    congenital 750.5
    infantile 750.5
  rectum (sphincter) (*see also* Stricture, rectum)
      569.2
  renal artery 440.1
  salivary duct (any) 527.8
  sphincter of Oddi (*see also* Obstruction, biliary)
      576.2
  spinal 724.00
    cervical 723.0
    lumbar, lumbosacral 724.02
    nerve (root) NEC 724.9
    specified region NEC 724.09
    thoracic, thoracolumbar 724.01
  stomach, hourglass 537.6
  subaortic 746.81
    hypertrophic (idiopathic) 425.1
  supra (valvular)-aortic 747.22
  trachea 519.1
    congenital 748.3
    syphilitic 095.8
    tuberculous (*see also* Tuberculosis) 012.8 ☑
  tracheostomy 519.02
  tricuspid (valve) (*see also* Endocarditis,
      tricuspid) 397.0
    congenital 746.1
    nonrheumatic 424.2
  tubal 628.2
  ureter (*see also* Stricture, ureter) 593.3
    congenital 753.29
  urethra (*see also* Stricture, urethra) 598.9
  vagina 623.2
    congenital 752.49
    in pregnancy or childbirth 654.7 ☑
      affecting fetus or newborn 763.89
      causing obstructed labor 660.2 ☑
        affecting fetus or newborn 763.1
  valve (cardiac) (heart) (*see also* Endocarditis)
      424.90
    congenital NEC 746.89
      aortic 746.3
      mitral 746.5
      pulmonary 746.02
      tricuspid 746.1
      urethra 753.6
  valvular (*see also* Endocarditis) 424.90
    congenital NEC 746.89
      urethra 753.6
  vascular graft or shunt 996.1
    atherosclerosis — *see* Arteriosclerosis,
        extremities
    embolism 996.74
    occlusion NEC 996.74
    thrombus 996.74
  vena cava (inferior) (superior) 459.2
    congenital 747.49
  ventricular shunt 996.2
  vulva 624.8
Stercolith (*see also* Fecalith) 560.39
  appendix 543.9
Stercoraceous, stercoral ulcer 569.82
  anus or rectum 569.41
Stereopsis, defective
  with fusion 368.33
  without fusion 368.32
Stereotypes NEC 307.3

Sterility
  female — *see* Infertility, female
  male (*see also* Infertility, male) 606.9
Sterilization, admission for V25.2
  status
    tubal ligation V26.51
    vasectomy V26.52
Sternalgia (*see also* Angina) 413.9
Sternopagus 759.4
Sternum bifidum 756.3
Sternutation 784.9
Steroid
  effects (adverse) (iatrogenic)
    cushingoid
      correct substance properly administered
          255.0
      overdose or wrong substance given or
          taken 962.0
    diabetes
      correct substance properly administered
          251.8
      overdose or wrong substance given or
          taken 962.0
    due to
      correct substance properly administered
          255.8
      overdose or wrong substance given or
          taken 962.0
    fever
      correct substance properly administered
          780.6
      overdose or wrong substance given or
          taken 962.0
    withdrawal
      correct substance properly administered
          255.4
      overdose or wrong substance given or
          taken 962.0
  responder 365.03
Stevens-Johnson disease or syndrome
    (erythema multiforme exudativum) 695.1
Stewart-Morel syndrome (hyperostosis frontalis
    interna) 733.3
Sticker's disease (erythema infectiosum) 057.0
Stickler syndrome 759.89   ●
Sticky eye 372.03
Stieda's disease (calcification, knee joint) 726.62
Stiff
  back 724.8
  neck (*see also* Torticollis) 723.5
Stiff-baby 759.89
Stiff-man syndrome 333.91
Stiffness, joint NEC 719.50
  ankle 719.57
  back 724.8
  elbow 719.52
  finger 719.54
  hip 719.55
  knee 719.56
  multiple sites 719.59
  sacroiliac 724.6
  shoulder 719.51
  specified site NEC 719.58
  spine 724.9
  surgical fusion V45.4
  wrist 719.53
Stigmata, congenital syphilis 090.5
Still's disease or syndrome 714.30
Still-Felty syndrome (rheumatoid arthritis with
    splenomegaly and leukopenia) 714.1
Stillbirth, stillborn NEC 779.9
Stiller's disease (asthenia) 780.79
Stilling-Türk-Duane syndrome (ocular retraction
    syndrome) 378.71
Stimulation, ovary 256.1
Sting (animal) (bee) (fish) (insect) (jellyfish)
    (Portuguese man-o-war) (wasp) (venomous)
    989.5
  anaphylactic shock or reaction 989.5
  plant 692.6
Stippled epiphyses 756.59

☑ Additional Digit Required — Refer to the Tabular List (Numeric Code Section) for Additional Digit Selection
▶◀ Revised Text   ● New Line   ▲ Revised Code

2006 ICD-9-CM

October 2005 • Volume 2 — **311**

Stitch
abscess 998.59
burst (in external operation wound) 998.32
internal 998.31
in back 724.5
Stojano's (subcostal) **syndrome** 098.86
Stokes' disease (exophthalmic goiter) 242.0 ☑
Stokes-Adams syndrome (syncope with heart
block) 426.9
Stokvis' (-Talma) disease (enterogenous cyanosis)
289.7
Stomach — *see* condition
Stoma malfunction
colostomy 569.62
cystostomy 997.5
enterostomy 569.62
esophagostomy 530.87
gastrostomy 536.42
ileostomy 569.62
nephrostomy 997.5
tracheostomy 519.02
ureterostomy 997.5
Stomatitis 528.0
angular 528.5
due to dietary or vitamin deficiency 266.0
aphthous 528.2
candidal 112.0
catarrhal 528.0
denture 528.9
diphtheritic (membranous) 032.0
due to
dietary deficiency 266.0
thrush 112.0
vitamin deficiency 266.0
epidemic 078.4
epizootic 078.4
follicular 528.0
gangrenous 528.1
herpetic 054.2
herpetiformis 528.2
malignant 528.0
membranous acute 528.0
monilial 112.0
mycotic 112.0
necrotic 528.1
ulcerative 101
necrotizing ulcerative 101
parasitic 112.0
septic 528.0
spirochetal 101
suppurative (acute) 528.0
ulcerative 528.0
necrotizing 101
ulceromembranous 101
vesicular 528.0
with exanthem 074.3
Vincent's 101
Stomatocytosis 282.8
Stomatomycosis 112.0
Stomatorrhagia 528.9
Stone(s) — *see also* Calculus
bladder 594.1
diverticulum 594.0
cystine 270.0
heart syndrome (*see also* Failure, ventricular,
left) 428.1
kidney 592.0
prostate 602.0
pulp (dental) 522.2
renal 592.0
salivary duct or gland (any) 527.5
ureter 592.1
urethra (impacted) 594.2
urinary (duct) (impacted) (passage) 592.9
bladder 594.1
diverticulum 594.0
lower tract NEC 594.9
specified site 594.8
xanthine 277.2
Stonecutters' lung 502
tuberculous (*see also* Tuberculosis) 011.4 ☑
Stonemasons'
asthma, disease, or lung 502
tuberculous (*see also* Tuberculosis) 011.4 ☑
phthisis (*see also* Tuberculosis) 011.4 ☑

Stoppage
bowel (*see also* Obstruction, intestine) 560.9
heart (*see also* Arrest, cardiac) 427.5
intestine (*see also* Obstruction, intestine) 560.9
urine NEC (*see also* Retention, urine) 788.20
Storm, thyroid (apathetic) (*see also*
Thyrotoxicosis) 242.9 ☑
Strabismus (alternating) (congenital)
(nonparalytic) 378.9
concomitant (*see also* Heterotropia) 378.30
convergent (*see also* Esotropia) 378.00
divergent (*see also* Exotropia) 378.10
convergent (*see also* Esotropia) 378.00
divergent (*see also* Exotropia) 378.10
due to adhesions, scars — *see* Strabismus,
mechanical
in neuromuscular disorder NEC 378.73
intermittent 378.20
vertical 378.31
latent 378.40
convergent (esophoria) 378.41
divergent (exophoria) 378.42
vertical 378.43
mechanical 378.60
due to
Brown's tendon sheath syndrome 378.61
specified musculofascial disorder NEC
378.62
paralytic 378.50
third or oculomotor nerve (partial) 378.51
total 378.52
fourth or trochlear nerve 378.53
sixth or abducens nerve 378.54
specified type NEC 378.73
vertical (hypertropia) 378.31
Strain — *see also* Sprain, by site
eye NEC 368.13
heart — *see* Disease, heart
meaning gonorrhea — *see* Gonorrhea
physical NEC V62.89
postural 729.9
psychological NEC V62.89
Strands
conjunctiva 372.62
vitreous humor 379.25
Strangulation, strangulated 994.7
appendix 543.9
asphyxiation or suffocation by 994.7
bladder neck 596.0
bowel — *see* Strangulation, intestine
colon — *see* Strangulation, intestine
cord (umbilical) — *see* Compression, umbilical
cord
due to birth injury 767.8
food or foreign body (*see also* Asphyxia, food)
933.1
hemorrhoids 455.8
external 455.5
internal 455.2
hernia — *see also* Hernia, by site, with
obstruction
gangrenous — *see* Hernia, by site, with
gangrene
intestine (large) (small) 560.2
with hernia — *see also* Hernia, by site, with
obstruction
gangrenous — *see* Hernia, by site, with
gangrene
congenital (small) 751.1
large 751.2
mesentery 560.2
mucus (*see also* Asphyxia, mucus) 933.1
newborn 770.18 ▲
omentum 560.2
organ or site, congenital NEC — *see* Atresia
ovary 620.8
due to hernia 620.4
penis 607.89
foreign body 939.3
rupture (*see also* Hernia, by site, with
obstruction) 552.9
gangrenous (*see also* Hernia, by site, with
gangrene) 551.9
stomach, due to hernia (*see also* Hernia, by
site, with obstruction) 552.9
with gangrene (*see also* Hernia, by site, with
gangrene) 551.9

Strangulation, strangulated — *continued*
umbilical cord — *see* Compression, umbilical
cord
vesicourethral orifice 596.0
Strangury 788.1
Strawberry
gallbladder (*see also* Disease, gallbladder)
575.6
mark 757.32
tongue (red) (white) 529.3
Straw itch 133.8
Streak, ovarian 752.0
Strephosymbolia 315.01
secondary to organic lesion 784.69
Streptobacillary fever 026.1
Streptobacillus moniliformis 026.1
Streptococcemia 038.0
Streptococcicosis — *see* Infection, streptococcal
Streptococcus, streptococcal — *see* condition
Streptoderma 686.00
Streptomycosis — *see* Actinomycosis
Streptothricosis — *see* Actinomycosis
Streptothrix — *see* Actinomycosis
Streptotrichosis — *see* Actinomycosis
Stress
fracture — *see* Fracture, stress
polycythemia 289.0
reaction (gross) (*see also* Reaction, stress,
acute) 308.9
Stretching, nerve — *see* Injury, nerve, by site
Striae (albicantes) (atrophicae) (cutis distensae)
(distensae) 701.3
Striations of nails 703.8
Stricture (*see also* Stenosis) 799.89
ampulla of Vater 576.2
with calculus, cholelithiasis, or stones — *see*
Choledocholithiasis
anus (sphincter) 569.2
congenital 751.2
infantile 751.2
aorta (ascending) 747.22
arch 747.10
arteriosclerotic 440.0
calcified 440.0
aortic (valve) (*see also* Stenosis, aortic) 424.1
congenital 746.3
aqueduct of Sylvius (congenital) 742.3
with spina bifida (*see also* Spina bifida)
741.0 ☑
acquired 331.4
artery 447.1
basilar — *see* Narrowing, artery, basilar
carotid (common) (internal) — *see*
Narrowing, artery, carotid
celiac 447.4
cerebral 437.0
congenital 747.81
due to
embolism (*see also* Embolism, brain)
434.1 ☑
thrombus (*see also* Thrombosis, brain)
434.0 ☑
congenital (peripheral) 747.60
cerebral 747.81
coronary 746.85
gastrointestinal 747.61
lower limb 747.64
renal 747.62
retinal 743.58
specified NEC 747.69
spinal 747.82
umbilical 747.5
upper limb 747.63
coronary — *see* Arteriosclerosis, coronary
congenital 746.85
precerebral — *see* Narrowing, artery,
precerebral NEC
pulmonary (congenital) 747.3
acquired 417.8
renal 440.1
vertebral — *see* Narrowing, artery, vertebral
auditory canal (congenital) (external) 744.02
acquired (*see also* Stricture, ear canal,
acquired) 380.50

Stricture (*see also* Stenosis) — *continued*
  bile duct or passage (any) (postoperative) (*see also* Obstruction, biliary) 576.2
    congenital 751.61
  bladder 596.8
    congenital 753.6
    neck 596.0
      congenital 753.6
  bowel (*see also* Obstruction, intestine) 560.9
  brain 348.8
  bronchus 519.1
    syphilitic 095.8
  cardia (stomach) 537.89
    congenital 750.7
  cardiac — *see also* Disease, heart
    orifice (stomach) 537.89
  cardiovascular (*see also* Disease, cardiovascular) 429.2
  carotid artery — *see* Narrowing, artery, carotid
  cecum (*see also* Obstruction, intestine) 560.9
  cervix, cervical (canal) 622.4
    congenital 752.49
    in pregnancy or childbirth 654.6 ☑
      affecting fetus or newborn 763.89
      causing obstructed labor 660.2 ☑
        affecting fetus or newborn 763.1
  colon (*see also* Obstruction, intestine) 560.9
    congenital 751.2
  colostomy 569.62
  common bile duct (*see also* Obstruction, biliary) 576.2
    congenital 751.61
  coronary (artery) — *see* Arteriosclerosis, coronary
    congenital 746.85
  cystic duct (*see also* Obstruction, gallbladder) 575.2
    congenital 751.61
  cystostomy 997.5
  digestive organs NEC, congenital 751.8
  duodenum 537.3
    congenital 751.1
  ear canal (external) (congenital) 744.02
    acquired 380.50
      secondary to
        inflammation 380.53
        surgery 380.52
        trauma 380.51
  ejaculatory duct 608.85
  enterostomy 569.62
  esophagostomy 530.87
  esophagus (corrosive) (peptic) 530.3
    congenital 750.3
    syphilitic 095.8
      congenital 090.5
  eustachian tube (*see also* Obstruction, Eustachian tube) 381.60
    congenital 744.24
  fallopian tube 628.2
    gonococcal (chronic) 098.37
      acute 098.17
    tuberculous (*see also* Tuberculosis) 016.6 ☑
  gallbladder (*see also* Obstruction, gallbladder) 575.2
    congenital 751.69
  glottis 478.74
  heart — *see also* Disease, heart
    congenital NEC 746.89
    valve — *see also* Endocarditis
      congenital NEC 746.89
        aortic 746.3
        mitral 746.5
        pulmonary 746.02
        tricuspid 746.1
  hepatic duct (*see also* Obstruction, biliary) 576.2
  hourglass, of stomach 537.6
  hymen 623.3
  hypopharynx 478.29
  intestine (*see also* Obstruction, intestine) 560.9
    congenital (small) 751.1
      large 751.2
    ischemic 557.1
  lacrimal
    canaliculi 375.53
      congenital 743.65

Stricture (*see also* Stenosis) — *continued*
  lacrimal — *continued*
    punctum 375.52
      congenital 743.65
    sac 375.54
      congenital 743.65
  lacrimonasal duct 375.56
    congenital 743.65
    neonatal 375.55
  larynx 478.79
    congenital 748.3
    syphilitic 095.8
      congenital 090.5
  lung 518.89
  meatus
    ear (congenital) 744.02
      acquired (*see also* Stricture, ear canal, acquired) 380.50
    osseous (congenital) (ear) 744.03
      acquired (*see also* Stricture, ear canal, acquired) 380.50
    urinarius (*see also* Stricture, urethra) 598.9
      congenital 753.6
  mitral (valve) (*see also* Stenosis, mitral) 394.0
    congenital 746.5
    specified cause, except rheumatic 424.0
  myocardium, myocardial (*see also* Degeneration, myocardial) 429.1
    hypertrophic subaortic (idiopathic) 425.1
  nares (anterior) (posterior) 478.1
    congenital 748.0
  nasal duct 375.56
    congenital 743.65
    neonatal 375.55
  nasolacrimal duct 375.56
    congenital 743.65
    neonatal 375.55
  nasopharynx 478.29
    syphilitic 095.8
  nephrostomy 997.5
  nose 478.1
    congenital 748.0
  nostril (anterior) (posterior) 478.1
    congenital 748.0
  organ or site, congenital NEC — *see* Atresia
  osseous meatus (congenital) (ear) 744.03
    acquired (*see also* Stricture, ear canal, acquired) 380.50
  os uteri (*see also* Stricture, cervix) 622.4
  oviduct — *see* Stricture, fallopian tube
  pelviureteric junction 593.3
  pharynx (dilation) 478.29
  prostate 602.8
  pulmonary, pulmonic
    artery (congenital) 747.3
      acquired 417.8
      noncongenital 417.8
    infundibulum (congenital) 746.83
    valve (*see also* Endocarditis, pulmonary) 424.3
      congenital 746.02
    vein (congenital) 747.49
      acquired 417.8
    vessel NEC 417.8
  punctum lacrimale 375.52
    congenital 743.65
  pylorus (hypertrophic) 537.0
    adult 537.0
    congenital 750.5
    infantile 750.5
  rectosigmoid 569.89
  rectum (sphincter) 569.2
    congenital 751.2
    due to
      chemical burn 947.3
      irradiation 569.2
      lymphogranuloma venereum 099.1
    gonococcal 098.7
    inflammatory 099.1
    syphilitic 095.8
    tuberculous (*see also* Tuberculosis) 014.8 ☑
  renal artery 440.1
  salivary duct or gland (any) 527.8
  sigmoid (flexure) (*see also* Obstruction, intestine) 560.9
  spermatic cord 608.85

Stricture (*see also* Stenosis) — *continued*
  stoma (following) (of)
    colostomy 569.62
    cystostomy 997.5
    enterostomy 569.62
    esophagostomy 530.87
    gastrostomy 536.42
    ileostomy 569.62
    nephrostomy 997.5
    tracheostomy 519.02
    ureterostomy 997.5
  stomach 537.89
    congenital 750.7
    hourglass 537.6
  subaortic 746.81
    hypertrophic (acquired) (idiopathic) 425.1
  subglottic 478.74
  syphilitic NEC 095.8
  tendon (sheath) 727.81
  trachea 519.1
    congenital 748.3
    syphilitic 095.8
    tuberculous (*see also* Tuberculosis) 012.8 ☑
  tracheostomy 519.02
  tricuspid (valve) (*see also* Endocarditis, tricuspid) 397.0
    congenital 746.1
    nonrheumatic 424.2
  tunica vaginalis 608.85
  ureter (postoperative) 593.3
    congenital 753.29
    tuberculous (*see also* Tuberculosis) 016.2 ☑
  ureteropelvic junction 593.3
    congenital 753.21
  ureterovesical orifice 593.3
    congenital 753.22
  urethra (anterior) (meatal) (organic) (posterior) (spasmodic) 598.9
    associated with schistosomiasis (*see also* Schistosomiasis) 120.9 [598.01]
    congenital (valvular) 753.6
    due to
      infection 598.00
        syphilis 095.8 [598.01]
      trauma 598.1
    gonococcal 098.2 [598.01]
    gonorrheal 098.2 [598.01]
    infective 598.00
    late effect of injury 598.1
    postcatheterization 598.2
    postobstetric 598.1
    postoperative 598.2
    specified cause NEC 598.8
    syphilitic 095.8 [598.01]
    traumatic 598.1
    valvular, congenital 753.6
  urinary meatus (*see also* Stricture, urethra) 598.9
    congenital 753.6
  uterus, uterine 621.5
    os (external) (internal) — *see* Stricture, cervix
  vagina (outlet) 623.2
    congenital 752.49
  valve (cardiac) (heart) (*see also* Endocarditis) 424.90
    congenital (cardiac) (heart) NEC 746.89
      aortic 746.3
      mitral 746.5
      pulmonary 746.02
      tricuspid 746.1
    urethra 753.6
  valvular (*see also* Endocarditis) 424.90
  vascular graft or shunt 996.1
    atherosclerosis — *see* Arteriosclerosis, extremities
    embolism 996.74
    occlusion NEC 996.74
    thrombus 996.74
  vas deferens 608.85
    congenital 752.89
  vein 459.2
  vena cava (inferior) (superior) NEC 459.2
    congenital 747.49
  ventricular shunt 996.2
  vesicourethral orifice 596.0
    congenital 753.6
  vulva (acquired) 624.8

Stridor 786.1
  congenital (larynx) 748.3
Stridulous — *see* condition
Strippling of nails 703.8
Stroke 434.91
  apoplectic (*see also* Disease, cerebrovascular, acute) 436
  brain — *see* Infarct, brain
  embolic 434.11
  epileptic — *see* Epilepsy
  healed or old V12.59
  heart — *see* Disease, heart
  heat 992.0
  hemorrhagic — *see* Hemorrhage, brain ●
  iatrogenic 997.02
  in evolution 435.9
  ischemic 434.91
  late effect — *see* Late effect(s) (of) cerebrovascular disease
  lightning 994.0
  paralytic — *see* Infarct, brain
  postoperative 997.02
  progressive 435.9
  thrombotic 434.01
Stromatosis, endometrial (M8931/1) 236.0
Strong pulse 785.9
Strongyloides stercoralis infestation 127.2
Strongyloidiasis 127.2
Strongyloidosis 127.2
Strongylus (gibsoni) infestation 127.7
Strophulus (newborn) 779.89
  pruriginosus 698.2
Struck by lightning 994.0
Struma (*see also* Goiter) 240.9
  fibrosa 245.3
  Hashimoto (struma lymphomatosa) 245.2
  lymphomatosa 245.2
  nodosa (simplex) 241.9
    endemic 241.9
    multinodular 241.1
    sporadic 241.9
    toxic or with hyperthyroidism 242.3 ☑
      multinodular 242.2 ☑
      uninodular 242.1 ☑
    toxicosa 242.3 ☑
      multinodular 242.2 ☑
      uninodular 242.1 ☑
    uninodular 241.0
  ovarii (M9090/0) 220
    and carcinoid (M9091/1) 236.2
    malignant (M9090/3) 183.0
  Riedel's (ligneous thyroiditis) 245.3
  scrofulous (*see also* Tuberculosis) 017.2 ☑
  tuberculous (*see also* Tuberculosis) 017.2 ☑
    abscess 017.2 ☑
    adenitis 017.2 ☑
    lymphangitis 017.2 ☑
    ulcer 017.2 ☑
Strumipriva cachexia (*see also* Hypothyroidism) 244.9
Strümpell-Marie disease or spine (ankylosing spondylitis) 720.0
Strümpell-Westphal pseudosclerosis (hepatolenticular degeneration) 275.1
Stuart's disease (congenital factor X deficiency) (*see also* Defect, coagulation) 286.3
Stuart-Prower factor deficiency (congenital factor X deficiency) (*see also* Defect, coagulation) 286.3
Students' elbow 727.2
Stuffy nose 478.1
Stump — *see also* Amputation
  cervix, cervical (healed) 622.8
Stupor 780.09
  catatonic (*see also* Schizophrenia) 295.2 ☑
  circular (*see also* Psychosis, manic-depressive, circular) 296.7
  manic 296.89
  manic-depressive (*see also* Psychosis, affective) 296.89
  mental (anergic) (delusional) 298.9
  psychogenic 298.8
  reaction to exceptional stress (transient) 308.2

Stupor — *continued*
  traumatic NEC — *see also* Injury, intracranial
    with spinal (cord)
      lesion — *see* Injury, spinal, by site
      shock — *see* Injury, spinal, by site
Sturge (-Weber) (-Dimitri) disease or syndrome (encephalocutaneous angiomatosis) 759.6
Sturge-Kalischer-Weber syndrome (encephalocutaneous angiomatosis) 759.6
Stuttering 307.0
Sty, stye 373.11
  external 373.11
  internal 373.12
  meibomian 373.12
Subacidity, gastric 536.8
  psychogenic 306.4
Subacute — *see* condition
Subarachnoid — *see* condition
Subclavian steal syndrome 435.2
Subcortical — *see* condition
Subcostal syndrome 098.86
  nerve compression 354.8
Subcutaneous, subcuticular — *see* condition
Subdelirium 293.1
Subdural — *see* condition
Subendocardium — *see* condition
Subependymoma (M9383/1) 237.5
Suberosis 495.3
Subglossitis — *see* Glossitis
Subhemophilia 286.0
Subinvolution (uterus) 621.1
  breast (postlactational) (postpartum) 611.8
  chronic 621.1
  puerperal, postpartum 674.8 ☑
Sublingual — *see* condition
Sublinguitis 527.2
Subluxation — *see also* Dislocation, by site
  congenital NEC — *see also* Malposition, congenital
    hip (unilateral) 754.32
      with dislocation of other hip 754.35
      bilateral 754.33
    joint
      lower limb 755.69
      shoulder 755.59
      upper limb 755.59
    lower limb (joint) 755.69
    shoulder (joint) 755.59
    upper limb (joint) 755.59
  lens 379.32
    anterior 379.33
    posterior 379.34
  rotary, cervical region of spine — *see* Fracture, vertebra, cervical
Submaxillary — *see* condition
Submersion (fatal) (nonfatal) 994.1
Submissiveness (undue), in child 313.0
Submucous — *see* condition
Subnormal, subnormality
  accommodation (*see also* Disorder, accommodation) 367.9
  mental (*see also* Retardation, mental) 319
    mild 317
    moderate 318.0
    profound 318.2
    severe 318.1
  temperature (accidental) 991.6
    not associated with low environmental temperature 780.99
Subphrenic — *see* condition
Subscapular nerve — *see* condition
Subseptus uterus 752.3
Subsiding appendicitis 542
Substernal thyroid (*see also* Goiter) 240.9
  congenital 759.2
Substitution disorder 300.11
Subtentorial — *see* condition
Subtertian
  fever 084.0
  malaria (fever) 084.0

Subthyroidism (acquired) (*see also* Hypothyroidism) 244.9
  congenital 243
Succenturiata placenta — *see* Placenta, abnormal
Succussion sounds, chest 786.7
Sucking thumb, child 307.9
Sudamen 705.1
Sudamina 705.1
Sudanese kala-azar 085.0
Sudden
  death, cause unknown (less than 24 hours) 798.1
    during childbirth 669.9 ☑
    infant 798.0
    puerperal, postpartum 674.9 ☑
  hearing loss NEC 388.2
  heart failure (*see also* Failure, heart) 428.9
  infant death syndrome 798.0
Sudeck's atrophy, disease, or syndrome 733.7
SUDS (sudden unexplained death) 798.2
Suffocation (*see also* Asphyxia) 799.01 ▲
  by
    bed clothes 994.7
    bunny bag 994.7
    cave-in 994.7
    constriction 994.7
    drowning 994.1
    inhalation
      food or foreign body (*see also* Asphyxia, food or foreign body) 933.1
      oil or gasoline (*see also* Asphyxia, food or foreign body) 933.1
    overlying 994.7
    plastic bag 994.7
    pressure 994.7
    strangulation 994.7
  during birth 768.1
  mechanical 994.7
Sugar
  blood
    high 790.29
    low 251.2
  in urine 791.5
Suicide, suicidal (attempted)
  by poisoning — *see* Table of Drugs and Chemicals
  ideation V62.84 ●
  risk 300.9
  tendencies 300.9
  trauma NEC (*see also* nature and site of injury) 959.9
Suipestifer infection (*see also* Infection, Salmonella) 003.9
Sulfatidosis 330.0
Sulfhemoglobinemia, sulphemoglobinemia (acquired) (congenital) 289.7
Sumatran mite fever 081.2
Summer — *see* condition
Sunburn 692.71
  dermatitis 692.71
  due to
    other ultraviolet radiation 692.82
    tanning bed 692.82
  first degree 692.71
  second degree 692.76
  third degree 692.77
Sunken
  acetabulum 718.85
  fontanels 756.0
Sunstroke 992.0
Superfecundation 651.9 ☑
  with fetal loss and retention of one or more fetus(es) 651.6 ☑
  following (elective) fetal reduction 651.7 ☑ ●
Superfetation 651.9 ☑
  with fetal loss and retention of one or more fetus(es) 651.6 ☑
  following (elective) fetal reduction 651.7 ☑ ●
Superinvolution uterus 621.8
Supernumerary (congenital)
  aortic cusps 746.89

Supernumerary — *continued*
auditory ossicles 744.04
bone 756.9
breast 757.6
carpal bones 755.56
cusps, heart valve NEC 746.89
mitral 746.5
pulmonary 746.09
digit(s) 755.00
finger 755.01
toe 755.02
ear (lobule) 744.1
fallopian tube 752.19
finger 755.01
hymen 752.49
kidney 753.3
lacrimal glands 743.64
lacrimonasal duct 743.65
lobule (ear) 744.1
mitral cusps 746.5
muscle 756.82
nipples 757.6
organ or site NEC — *see* Accessory
ossicles, auditory 744.04
ovary 752.0
oviduct 752.19
pulmonic cusps 746.09
rib 756.3
cervical or first 756.2
syndrome 756.2
roots (of teeth) 520.2
spinal vertebra 756.19
spleen 759.0
tarsal bones 755.67
teeth 520.1
causing crowding 524.31
testis 752.89
thumb 755.01
toe 755.02
uterus 752.2
vagina 752.49
vertebra 756.19
Supervision (of)
contraceptive method previously prescribed
V25.40
intrauterine device V25.42
oral contraceptive (pill) V25.41
specified type NEC V25.49
subdermal implantable contraceptive V25.43
dietary (for) V65.3
allergy (food) V65.3
colitis V65.3
diabetes mellitus V65.3
food allergy intolerance V65.3
gastritis V65.3
hypercholesterolemia V65.3
hypoglycemia V65.3
intolerance (food) V65.3
obesity V65.3
specified NEC V65.3
lactation V24.1
pregnancy — *see* Pregnancy, supervision of
Supplemental teeth 520.1
causing crowding 524.31
Suppression
binocular vision 368.31
lactation 676.5 ☑
menstruation 626.8
ovarian secretion 256.39
renal 586
urinary secretion 788.5
urine 788.5
Suppuration, suppurative — *see also* condition
accessory sinus (chronic) (*see also* Sinusitis)
473.9
adrenal gland 255.8
antrum (chronic) (*see also* Sinusitis, maxillary)
473.0
bladder (*see also* Cystitis) 595.89
bowel 569.89
brain 324.0
late effect 326
breast 611.0
puerperal, postpartum 675.1 ☑
dental periosteum 526.5
diffuse (skin) 686.00

Suppuration, suppurative — *see also* condition
— *continued*
ear (middle) (*see also* Otitis media) 382.4
external (*see also* Otitis, externa) 380.10
internal 386.33
ethmoidal (sinus) (chronic) (*see also* Sinusitis,
ethmoidal) 473.2
fallopian tube (*see also* Salpingo-oophoritis)
614.2
frontal (sinus) (chronic) (*see also* Sinusitis,
frontal) 473.1
gallbladder (*see also* Cholecystitis, acute) 575.0
gum 523.3
hernial sac — *see* Hernia, by site
intestine 569.89
joint (*see also* Arthritis, suppurative) 711.0 ☑
labyrinthine 386.33
lung 513.0
mammary gland 611.0
puerperal, postpartum 675.1 ☑
maxilla, maxillary 526.4
sinus (chronic) (*see also* Sinusitis, maxillary)
473.0
muscle 728.0
nasal sinus (chronic) (*see also* Sinusitis) 473.9
pancreas 577.0
parotid gland 527.2
pelvis, pelvic
female (*see also* Disease, pelvis,
inflammatory) 614.4
acute 614.3
male (*see also* Peritonitis) 567.21 ▲
pericranial (*see also* Osteomyelitis) 730.2 ☑
salivary duct or gland (any) 527.2
sinus (nasal) (*see also* Sinusitis) 473.9
sphenoidal (sinus) (chronic) (*see also* Sinusitis,
sphenoidal) 473.3
thymus (gland) 254.1
thyroid (gland) 245.0
tonsil 474.8
uterus (*see also* Endometritis) 615.9
vagina 616.10
wound — *see also* Wound, open, by site,
complicated
dislocation — *see* Dislocation, by site,
compound
fracture — *see* Fracture, by site, open
scratch or other superficial injury — *see*
Injury, superficial, by site
Supraeruption, teeth 524.34
Supraglottitis 464.50
with obstruction 464.51
Suprapubic drainage 596.8
Suprarenal (gland) — *see* condition
Suprascapular nerve — *see* condition
Suprasellar — *see* condition
Supraspinatus syndrome 726.10
Surfer knots 919.8
infected 919.9
Surgery
cosmetic NEC V50.1
following healed injury or operation V51
hair transplant V50.0
elective V50.9
breast augmentation or reduction V50.1
circumcision, ritual or routine (in absence of
medical indication) V50.2
cosmetic NEC V50.1
ear piercing V50.3
face-lift V50.1
following healed injury or operation V51
hair transplant V50.0
not done because of
contraindication V64.1
patient's decision V64.2
specified reason NEC V64.3
plastic
breast augmentation or reduction V50.1
cosmetic V50.1
face-lift V50.1
following healed injury or operation V51
repair of scarred tissue (following healed
injury or operation) V51
specified type NEC V50.8

Surgery — *continued*
previous, in pregnancy or childbirth
cervix 654.6 ☑
affecting fetus or newborn 763.89
causing obstructed labor 660.2 ☑
affecting fetus or newborn 763.1
pelvic soft tissues NEC 654.9 ☑
affecting fetus or newborn 763.89
causing obstructed labor 660.2 ☑
affecting fetus or newborn 763.1
perineum or vulva 654.8 ☑
uterus NEC 654.9 ☑
affecting fetus or newborn 763.89
causing obstructed labor 660.2 ☑
affecting fetus or newborn 763.1
due to previous cesarean delivery
654.2 ☑
vagina 654.7 ☑
Surgical
abortion — *see* Abortion, legal
emphysema 998.81
kidney (*see also* Pyelitis) 590.80
operation NEC 799.9
procedures, complication or misadventure —
see Complications, surgical procedure
shock 998.0
Susceptibility
genetic
to
neoplasm
malignant, of
breast V84.01
endometrium V84.04
other V84.09
ovary V84.02
prostate V84.03
other disease V84.8
Suspected condition, ruled out (*see also*
Observation, suspected) V71.9
specified condition NEC V71.89
Suspended uterus, in pregnancy or childbirth
654.4 ☑
affecting fetus or newborn 763.89
causing obstructed labor 660.2 ☑
affecting fetus or newborn 763.1
Sutton's disease 709.09
Sutton and Gull's disease (arteriolar
nephrosclerosis) (*see also* Hypertension,
kidney) 403.90
Suture
burst (in external operation wound) 998.32
internal 998.31
inadvertently left in operation wound 998.4
removal V58.3
Shirodkar, in pregnancy (with or without
cervical incompetence) 654.5 ☑
Swab inadvertently left in operation wound
998.4
Swallowed, swallowing
difficulty (*see also* Dysphagia) 787.2
foreign body NEC (*see also* Foreign body) 938
Swamp fever 100.89
Swan neck hand (intrinsic) 736.09
Sweat(s), sweating
disease or sickness 078.2
excessive (*see also* Hyperhidrosis) 780.8
fetid 705.89
fever 078.2
gland disease 705.9
specified type NEC 705.89
miliary 078.2
night 780.8
Sweeley-Klionsky disease (angiokeratoma
corporis diffusum) 272.7
Sweet's syndrome (acute febrile neutrophilic
dermatosis) 695.89
Swelling
abdominal (not referable to specific organ)
789.3 ☑
adrenal gland, cloudy 255.8
ankle 719.07
anus 787.99
arm 729.81
breast 611.72

☑ Additional Digit Required — Refer to the Tabular List (Numeric Code Section) for Additional Digit Selection
►◄ Revised Text   ● New Line   ▲ Revised Code

2006 ICD-9-CM

October 2005 • Volume 2 — 315

Supernumerary — Swelling

Index

Swelling — Syndrome

Swelling — *continued*
Calabar 125.2
cervical gland 785.6
cheek 784.2
chest 786.6
ear 388.8
epigastric 789.3 ☑
extremity (lower) (upper) 729.81
eye 379.92
female genital organ 625.8
finger 729.81
foot 729.81
glands 785.6
gum 784.2
hand 729.81
head 784.2
inflammatory — *see* Inflammation
joint (*see also* Effusion, joint) 719.0 ☑
    tuberculous — *see* Tuberculosis, joint
kidney, cloudy 593.89
leg 729.81
limb 729.81
liver 573.8
lung 786.6
lymph nodes 785.6
mediastinal 786.6
mouth 784.2
muscle (limb) 729.81
neck 784.2
nose or sinus 784.2
palate 784.2
pelvis 789.3 ☑
penis 607.83
perineum 625.8
rectum 787.99
scrotum 608.86
skin 782.2
splenic (*see also* Splenomegaly) 789.2
substernal 786.6
superficial, localized (skin) 782.2
testicle 608.86
throat 784.2
toe 729.81
tongue 784.2
tubular (*see also* Disease, renal) 593.9
umbilicus 789.3 ☑
uterus 625.8
vagina 625.8
vulva 625.8
wandering, due to Gnathostoma (spinigerum) 128.1
white — *see* Tuberculosis, arthritis
Swift's disease 985.0
Swimmers'
ear (acute) 380.12
itch 120.3
Swimming in the head 780.4
Swollen — *see also* Swelling
glands 785.6
Swyer-James syndrome (unilateral hyperlucent lung) 492.8
Swyer's syndrome (XY pure gonadal dysgenesis) 752.7
Sycosis 704.8
barbae (not parasitic) 704.8
contagiosa 110.0
lupoid 704.8
mycotic 110.0
parasitic 110.0
vulgaris 704.8
Sydenham's chorea — *see* Chorea, Sydenham's
Sylvatic yellow fever 060.0
Sylvest's disease (epidemic pleurodynia) 074.1
Symblepharon 372.63
congenital 743.62
Symonds' syndrome 348.2
Sympathetic — *see* condition
Sympatheticotonia (*see also* Neuropathy, peripheral, autonomic) 337.9
Sympathicoblastoma (M9500/3)
specified site — *see* Neoplasm, by site, malignant
unspecified site 194.0

Sympathicogonioma (M9500/3) — *see* Sympathicoblastoma
Sympathoblastoma (M9500/3) — *see* Sympathicoblastoma
Sympathogonioma (M9500/3) — *see* Sympathicoblastoma
Symphalangy (*see also* Syndactylism) 755.10
Symptoms, specified (general) NEC 780.99
abdomen NEC 789.9
bone NEC 733.90
breast NEC 611.79
cardiac NEC 785.9
cardiovascular NEC 785.9
chest NEC 786.9
development NEC 783.9
digestive system NEC 787.99
eye NEC 379.99
gastrointestinal tract NEC 787.99
genital organs NEC
    female 625.9
    male 608.9
head and neck NEC 784.9
heart NEC 785.9
joint NEC 719.60
    ankle 719.67
    elbow 719.62
    foot 719.67
    hand 719.64
    hip 719.65
    knee 719.66
    multiple sites 719.69
    pelvic region 719.65
    shoulder (region) 719.61
    specified site NEC 719.68
    wrist 719.63
larynx NEC 784.9
limbs NEC 729.89
lymphatic system NEC 785.9
menopausal 627.2
metabolism NEC 783.9
mouth NEC 528.9
muscle NEC 728.9
musculoskeletal NEC 781.99
    limbs NEC 729.89
nervous system NEC 781.99
neurotic NEC 300.9
nutrition, metabolism, and development NEC 783.9
pelvis NEC 789.9
    female 625.9
peritoneum NEC 789.9
respiratory system NEC 786.9
skin and integument NEC 782.9
subcutaneous tissue NEC 782.9
throat NEC 784.9
tonsil NEC 784.9
urinary system NEC 788.9
vascular NEC 785.9
Sympus 759.89
Synarthrosis 719.80
ankle 719.87
elbow 719.82
foot 719.87
hand 719.84
hip 719.85
knee 719.86
multiple sites 719.89
pelvic region 719.85
shoulder (region) 719.81
specified site NEC 719.88
wrist 719.83
Syncephalus 759.4
Synchondrosis 756.9
abnormal (congenital) 756.9
ischiopubic (van Neck's) 732.1
Synchysis (senile) (vitreous humor) 379.21
scintillans 379.22
Syncope (near) (pre-) 780.2
anginosa 413.9
bradycardia 427.89
cardiac 780.2
carotid sinus 337.0
complicating delivery 669.2 ☑
due to lumbar puncture 349.0
fatal 798.1

Syncope — *continued*
heart 780.2
heat 992.1
laryngeal 786.2
tussive 786.2
vasoconstriction 780.2
vasodepressor 780.2
vasomotor 780.2
vasovagal 780.2
Syncytial infarct — *see* Placenta, abnormal
Syndactylism, syndactyly (multiple sites) 755.10
fingers (without fusion of bone) 755.11
    with fusion of bone 755.12
toes (without fusion of bone) 755.13
    with fusion of bone 755.14
Syndrome — *see also* Disease
abdominal
    acute 789.0 ☑
    migraine 346.2 ☑
    muscle deficiency 756.79
Abercrombie's (amyloid degeneration) 277.3
abnormal innervation 374.43
abstinence
    alcohol 291.81
    drug 292.0
Abt-Letterer-Siwe (acute histiocytosis X) (M9722/3) 202.5 ☑
Achard-Thiers (adrenogenital) 255.2
acid pulmonary aspiration 997.3
    obstetric (Mendelson's) 668.0 ☑
acquired immune deficiency 042
acquired immunodeficiency 042
acrocephalosyndactylism 755.55
acute abdominal 789.0 ☑
acute chest 517.3
acute coronary 411.1
Adair-Dighton (brittle bones and blue sclera, deafness) 756.51
Adams-Stokes (-Morgagni) (syncope with heart block) 426.9
addisonian 255.4
Adie (-Holmes) (pupil) 379.46
adiposogenital 253.8
adrenal
    hemorrhage 036.3
    meningococcic 036.3
adrenocortical 255.3
adrenogenital (acquired) (congenital) 255.2
    feminizing 255.2
    iatrogenic 760.79
    virilism (acquired) (congenital) 255.2
affective organic NEC 293.89
    drug-induced 292.84
afferent loop NEC 537.89
African macroglobulinemia 273.3
Ahumada-Del Castillo (nonpuerperal galactorrhea and amenorrhea) 253.1
air blast concussion — *see* Injury, internal, by site
Alagille 759.89   ●
Albright (-Martin) (pseudohypoparathyroidism) 275.49
Albright-McCune-Sternberg (osteitis fibrosa disseminata) 756.59
alcohol withdrawal 291.81
Alder's (leukocyte granulation anomaly) 288.2
Aldrich (-Wiskott) (eczema-thrombocytopenia) 279.12
Alibert-Bazin (mycosis fungoides) (M9700/3) 202.1 ☑
Alice in Wonderland 293.89
Allen-Masters 620.6
Alligator baby (ichthyosis congenita) 757.1
Alport's (hereditary hematuria-nephropathy-deafness) 759.89
Alvarez (transient cerebral ischemia) 435.9
alveolar capillary block 516.3
Alzheimer's 331.0
    with dementia — *see* Alzheimer's, dementia
amnestic (confabulatory) 294.0
    alcohol-induced persisting 291.1
    drug-induced 292.83
    posttraumatic 294.0
amotivational 292.89
amyostatic 275.1
amyotrophic lateral sclerosis 335.20

Syndrome — *see also* Disease — *continued*
  androgen insensitivity 259.5 ●
  Angelman 759.89
  angina (*see also* Angina) 413.9
  ankyloglossia superior 750.0
  anterior
    chest wall 786.52
    compartment (tibial) 958.8
    spinal artery 433.8 ☑
      compression 721.1
    tibial (compartment) 958.8
  antibody deficiency 279.00
    agammaglobulinemic 279.00
    congenital 279.04
    hypogammaglobulinemic 279.00
  anticardiolipin antibody 795.79
  antimongolism 758.39
  antiphospholipid antibody 795.79
  Anton (-Babinski) (hemiasomatognosia) 307.9
  anxiety (*see also* Anxiety) 300.00
    organic 293.84
  aortic
    arch 446.7
    bifurcation (occlusion) 444.0
    ring 747.21
  Apert's (acrocephalosyndactyly) 755.55
  Apert-Gallais (adrenogenital) 255.2
  aphasia-apraxia-alexia 784.69
  apical ballooning 429.89 ●
  "approximate answers" 300.16
  arcuate ligament (-celiac axis) 447.4
  arcus aortae 446.7
  arc welders' 370.24
  argentaffin, argintaffinoma 259.2
  Argonz-Del Castillo (nonpuerperal galactorrhea and amenorrhea) 253.1
  Argyll Robertson's (syphilitic) 094.89
    nonsyphilitic 379.45
  arm-shoulder (*see also* Neuropathy, peripheral, autonomic) 337.9
  Arnold-Chiari (*see also* Spina bifida) 741.0 ☑
    type I 348.4
    type II 741.0 ☑
    type III 742.0
    type IV 742.2
  Arrillaga-Ayerza (pulmonary artery sclerosis with pulmonary hypertension) 416.0
  arteriomesenteric duodenum occlusion 537.89
  arteriovenous steal 996.73
  arteritis, young female (obliterative brachiocephalic) 446.7
  aseptic meningitis — *see* Meningitis, aseptic
  Asherman's 621.5
  Asperger's 299.8 ☑
  asphyctic (*see also* Anxiety) 300.00
  aspiration, of newborn (massive) 770.18 ▲
    meconium 770.12 ●
  ataxia-telangiectasia 334.8
  Audry's (acropachyderma) 757.39
  auriculotemporal 350.8
  autosomal — *see also* Abnormal, autosomes NEC
    deletion 758.39
      5p 758.31
      22q11.2 758.32
  Avellis' 344.89
  Axenfeld's 743.44
  Ayerza (-Arrillaga) (pulmonary artery sclerosis with pulmonary hypertension) 416.0
  Baader's (erythema multiforme exudativum) 695.1
  Baastrup's 721.5
  Babinski (-Vaquez) (cardiovascular syphilis) 093.89
  Babinski-Fröhlich (adiposogenital dystrophy) 253.8
  Babinski-Nageotte 344.89
  Bagratuni's (temporal arteritis) 446.5
  Bakwin-Krida (craniometaphyseal dysplasia) 756.89
  Balint's (psychic paralysis of visual disorientation) 368.16
  Ballantyne (-Runge) (postmaturity) 766.22
  ballooning posterior leaflet 424.0
  Banti's — *see* Cirrhosis, liver
  Bard-Pic's (carcinoma, head of pancreas) 157.0

Syndrome — *see also* Disease — *continued*
  Bardet-Biedl (obesity, polydactyly, and mental retardation) 759.89
  Barlow's (mitral valve prolapse) 424.0
  Barlow (-Möller) (infantile scurvy) 267
  Baron Munchausen's 301.51
  Barré-Guillain 357.0
  Barré-Liéou (posterior cervical sympathetic) 723.2
  Barrett's (chronic peptic ulcer of esophagus) 530.85
  Bársony-Polgár (corkscrew esophagus) 530.5
  Bársony-Teschendorf (corkscrew esophagus) 530.5
  Barth 759.89 ●
  Bartter's (secondary hyperaldosteronism with juxtaglomerular hyperplasia) 255.13
  Basedow's (exophthalmic goiter) 242.0 ☑
  basilar artery 435.0
  basofrontal 377.04
  Bassen-Kornzweig (abetalipoproteinemia) 272.5
  Batten-Steinert 359.2
  battered
    adult 995.81
    baby or child 995.54
    spouse 995.81
  Baumgarten-Cruveilhier (cirrhosis of liver) 571.5
  Beals 759.82
  Bearn-Kunkel (-Slater) (lupoid hepatitis) 571.49
  Beau's (*see also* Degeneration, myocardial) 429.1
  Bechterew-Strümpell-Marie (ankylosing spondylitis) 720.0
  Beck's (anterior spinal artery occlusion) 433.8 ☑
  Beckwith (-Wiedemann) 759.89
  Behçet's 136.1
  Bekhterev-Strümpell-Marie (ankylosing spondylitis) 720.0
  Benedikt's 344.89
  Béquez César (-Steinbrinck-Chédiak-Higashi) (congenital gigantism of peroxidase granules) 288.2
  Bernard-Horner (*see also* Neuropathy, peripheral, autonomic) 337.9
  Bernard-Sergent (acute adrenocortical insufficiency) 255.4
  Bernhardt-Roth 355.1
  Bernheim's (*see also* Failure, heart) 428.0
  Bertolotti's (sacralization of fifth lumbar vertebra) 756.15
  Besnier-Boeck-Schaumann (sarcoidosis) 135
  Bianchi's (aphasia-apraxia-alexia syndrome) 784.69
  Biedl-Bardet (obesity, polydactyly, and mental retardation) 759.89
  Biemond's (obesity, polydactyly, and mental retardation) 759.89
  big spleen 289.4
  bilateral polycystic ovarian 256.4
  Bing-Horton's 346.2 ☑
  Biörck (-Thorson) (malignant carcinoid) 259.2
  Blackfan-Diamond (congenital hypoplastic anemia) 284.0
  black lung 500
  black widow spider bite 989.5
  bladder neck (*see also* Incontinence, urine) 788.30
  blast (concussion) — *see* Blast, injury
  blind loop (postoperative) 579.2
  Bloch-Siemens (incontinentia pigmenti) 757.33
  Bloch-Sulzberger (incontinentia pigmenti) 757.33
  Bloom (-Machacek) (-Torre) 757.39
  Blount-Barber (tibia vara) 732.4
  blue
    bloater 491.20
      with
        acute bronchitis 491.22
        exacerbation (acute) 491.21
    diaper 270.0
    drum 381.02
    sclera 756.51
    toe 445.02
  Boder-Sedgwick (ataxia-telangiectasia) 334.8

Syndrome — *see also* Disease — *continued*
  Boerhaave's (spontaneous esophageal rupture) 530.4
  Bonnevie-Ullrich 758.6
  Bonnier's 386.19
  Bouillaud's (rheumatic heart disease) 391.9
  Bourneville (-Pringle) (tuberous sclerosis) 759.5
  Bouveret (-Hoffmann) (paroxysmal tachycardia) 427.2
  brachial plexus 353.0
  Brachman-de Lange (Amsterdam dwarf, mental retardation, and brachycephaly) 759.89
  bradycardia-tachycardia 427.81
  Brailsford-Morquio (dystrophy) (mucopolysaccharidosis IV) 277.5
  brain (acute) (chronic) (nonpsychotic) (organic) (with behavioral reaction) (with neurotic reaction) 310.9
    with
      presenile brain disease (*see also* Dementia, presenile) 290.10
      psychosis, psychotic reaction (*see also* Psychosis, organic) 294.9
    chronic alcoholic 291.2
    congenital (*see also* Retardation, mental) 319
    postcontusional 310.2
    posttraumatic
      nonpsychotic 310.2
      psychotic 293.9
        acute 293.0
        chronic (*see also* Psychosis, organic) 294.8
        subacute 293.1
    psycho-organic (*see also* Syndrome, psycho-organic) 310.9
    psychotic (*see also* Psychosis, organic) 294.9
    senile (*see also* Dementia, senile) 290.0
  branchial arch 744.41
  Brandt's (acrodermatitis enteropathica) 686.8
  Brennemann's 289.2
  Briquet's 300.81
  Brissaud-Meige (infantile myxedema) 244.9
  broad ligament laceration 620.6
  Brock's (atelectasis due to enlarged lymph nodes) 518.0
  Brown's tendon sheath 378.61
  Brown-Séquard 344.89
  brown spot 756.59
  Brugada 746.89
  Brugsch's (acropachyderma) 757.39
  bubbly lung 770.7
  Buchem's (hyperostosis corticalis) 733.3
  Budd-Chiari (hepatic vein thrombosis) 453.0
  Büdinger-Ludloff-Läwen 717.89
  bulbar 335.22
    lateral (*see also* Disease, cerebrovascular, acute) 436
  Bullis fever 082.8
  bundle of Kent (anomalous atrioventricular excitation) 426.7
  Bürger-Grütz (essential familial hyperlipemia) 272.3
  Burke's (pancreatic insufficiency and chronic neutropenia) 577.8
  Burnett's (milk-alkali) 275.42
  Burnier's (hypophyseal dwarfism) 253.3
  burning feet 266.2
  Bywaters' 958.5
  Caffey's (infantile cortical hyperostosis) 756.59
  Calvé-Legg-Perthes (osteochondrosis, femoral capital) 732.1
  Caplan (-Colinet) syndrome 714.81
  capsular thrombosis (*see also* Thrombosis, brain) 434.0 ☑
  carbohydrate-deficient glycoprotein (CDGS) ● 271.8 ●
  carcinogenic thrombophlebitis 453.1
  carcinoid 259.2
  cardiac asthma (*see also* Failure, ventricular, left) 428.1
  cardiacos negros 416.0
  cardiopulmonary obesity 278.8
  cardiorenal (*see also* Hypertension, cardiorenal) 404.90
  cardiorespiratory distress (idiopathic), newborn 769

☑ Additional Digit Required — Refer to the Tabular List (Numeric Code Section) for Additional Digit Selection
▶◀ Revised Text   ● New Line   ▲ Revised Code

Syndrome — *see also* Disease — *continued*
Eisenmenger's (ventricular septal defect) 745.4
Ekbom's (restless legs) 333.99
Ekman's (brittle bones and blue sclera) 756.51
electric feet 266.2
Elephant man 237.71
Ellison-Zollinger (gastric hypersecretion with pancreatic islet cell tumor) 251.5
Ellis-van Creveld (chondroectodermal dysplasia) 756.55
embryonic fixation 270.2
empty sella (turcica) 253.8
endocrine-hypertensive 255.3
Engel-von Recklinghausen (osteitis fibrosa cystica) 252.01
enteroarticular 099.3
entrapment — *see* Neuropathy, entrapment
eosinophilia myalgia 710.5
epidemic vomiting 078.82
Epstein's — *see* Nephrosis
Erb (-Oppenheim)-Goldflam 358.00
Erdheim's (acromegalic macrospondylitis) 253.0
Erlacher-Blount (tibia vara) 732.4
erythrocyte fragmentation 283.19
euthyroid sick 790.94
Evans' (thrombocytopenic purpura) 287.32 ▲
excess cortisol, iatrogenic 255.0
exhaustion 300.5
extrapyramidal 333.90
eyelid-malar-mandible 756.0
eye retraction 378.71
Faber's (achlorhydric anemia) 280.9
Fabry (-Anderson) (angiokeratoma corporis diffusum) 272.7
facet 724.8
Fallot's 745.2
falx (*see also* Hemorrhage, brain) 431
familial eczema-thrombocytopenia 279.12
Fanconi's (anemia) (congenital pancytopenia) 284.0
Fanconi (-de Toni) (-Debré) (cystinosis) 270.0
Farber (-Uzman) (disseminated lipogranulomatosis) 272.8
fatigue NEC 300.5
chronic 780.71
faulty bowel habit (idiopathic megacolon) 564.7
FDH (focal dermal hypoplasia) 757.39
fecal reservoir 560.39
Feil-Klippel (brevicollis) 756.16
Felty's (rheumatoid arthritis with splenomegaly and leukopenia) 714.1
fertile eunuch 257.2
fetal alcohol 760.71
late effect 760.71
fibrillation-flutter 427.32
fibrositis (periarticular) 729.0
Fiedler's (acute isolated myocarditis) 422.91
Fiessinger-Leroy (-Reiter) 099.3
Fiessinger-Rendu (erythema multiforme exudativum) 695.1
first arch 756.0
Fisher's 357.0
Fitz's (acute hemorrhagic pancreatitis) 577.0
Fitz-Hugh and Curtis 098.86
due to
Chlamydia trachomatis 099.56
Neisseria gonorrhoeae (gonococcal peritonitis) 098.86
Flajani (-Basedow) (exophthalmic goiter) 242.0 ☑
floppy
infant 781.99
valve (mitral) 424.0
flush 259.2
Foix-Alajouanine 336.1
Fong's (hereditary osteo-onychodysplasia) 756.89
foramen magnum 348.4
Forbes-Albright (nonpuerperal amenorrhea and lactation associated with pituitary tumor) 253.1
Foster-Kennedy 377.04
Foville's (peduncular) 344.89
fragile X 759.83
Franceschetti's (mandibulofacial dysostosis) 756.0
Fraser's 759.89

Syndrome — *see also* Disease — *continued*
Freeman-Sheldon 759.89
Frey's (auriculotemporal) 705.22
Friderichsen-Waterhouse 036.3
Friedrich-Erb-Arnold (acropachyderma) 757.39
Fröhlich's (adiposogenital dystrophy) 253.8
Froin's 336.8
Frommel-Chiari 676.6 ☑
frontal lobe 310.0
Fukuhara 277.87
Fuller Albright's (osteitis fibrosa disseminata) 756.59
functional
bowel 564.9
prepubertal castrate 752.89
Gaisböck's (polycythemia hypertonica) 289.0
ganglion (basal, brain) 333.90
geniculi 351.1
Ganser's, hysterical 300.16
Gardner-Diamond (autoerythrocyte sensitization) 287.2
gastroesophageal junction 530.0
gastroesophageal laceration-hemorrhage 530.7
gastrojejunal loop obstruction 537.89
Gayet-Wernicke's (superior hemorrhagic polioencephalitis) 265.1
Gee-Herter-Heubner (nontropical sprue) 579.0
Gélineau's (*see also* Narcolepsy) 347.00
genito-anorectal 099.1
Gerhardt's (vocal cord paralysis) 478.30
Gerstmann's (finger agnosia) 784.69
Gianotti Crosti 057.8 ●
due to known virus — *see* Infection, virus ●
due to unknown virus 057.8 ●
Gilbert's 277.4
Gilford (-Hutchinson) (progeria) 259.8
Gilles de la Tourette's 307.23
Gillespie's (dysplasia oculodentodigitalis) 759.89
Glénard's (enteroptosis) 569.89
Glinski-Simmonds (pituitary cachexia) 253.2
glucuronyl transferase 277.4
glue ear 381.20
Goldberg (-Maxwell) (-Morris) (testicular feminization) 259.5 ▲
Goldenhar's (oculoauriculovertebral dysplasia) 756.0
Goldflam-Erb 358.00
Goltz-Gorlin (dermal hypoplasia) 757.39
Good's 279.06
Goodpasture's (pneumorenal) 446.21
Gopalan's (burning feet) 266.2
Gorlin-Chaudhry-Moss 759.89
Gougerot (-Houwer)-Sjögren (keratoconjunctivitis sicca) 710.2
Gougerot-Blum (pigmented purpuric lichenoid dermatitis) 709.1
Gougerot-Carteaud (confluent reticulate papillomatosis) 701.8
Gouley's (constrictive pericarditis) 423.2
Gowers' (vasovagal attack) 780.2
Gowers-Paton-Kennedy 377.04
Gradenigo's 383.02
gray or grey (chloramphenicol) (newborn) 779.4
Greig's (hypertelorism) 756.0
Gubler-Millard 344.89
Guérin-Stern (arthrogryposis multiplex congenita) 754.89
Guillain-Barré (-Strohl) 357.0
Gunn's (jaw-winking syndrome) 742.8
Günther's (congenital erythropoietic porphyria) 277.1
gustatory sweating 350.8
H₃O 759.81
Hadfield-Clarke (pancreatic infantilism) 577.8
Haglund-Läwen-Fründ 717.89
hair tourniquet — *see also* Injury, superficial, by site
finger 915.8
infected 915.9
penis 911.8
infected 911.9
toe 917.8
infected 917.9
hairless women 257.8
Hallermann-Streiff 756.0

Syndrome — *see also* Disease — *continued*
Hallervorden-Spatz 333.0
Hamman's (spontaneous mediastinal emphysema) 518.1
Hamman-Rich (diffuse interstitial pulmonary fibrosis) 516.3
Hand-Schüller-Christian (chronic histiocytosis X) 277.89
hand-foot 282.61
Hanot-Chauffard (-Troisier) (bronze diabetes) 275.0
Harada's 363.22
Hare's (M8010/3) (carcinoma, pulmonary apex) 162.3
Harkavy's 446.0
harlequin color change 779.89
Harris' (organic hyperinsulinism) 251.1
Hart's (pellagra-cerebellar ataxia-renal aminoaciduria) 270.0
Hayem-Faber (achlorhydric anemia) 280.9
Hayem-Widal (acquired hemolytic jaundice) 283.9
Heberden's (angina pectoris) 413.9
Hedinger's (malignant carcinoid) 259.2
Hegglin's 288.2
Heller's (infantile psychosis) (*see also* Psychosis, childhood) 299.1 ☑
H.E.L.L.P 642.5 ☑
hemolytic-uremic (adult) (child) 283.11
Hench-Rosenberg (palindromic arthritis) (*see also* Rheumatism, palindromic) 719.3 ☑
Henoch-Schönlein (allergic purpura) 287.0
hepatic flexure 569.89
hepatorenal 572.4
due to a procedure 997.4
following delivery 674.8 ☑
hepatourologic 572.4
Herrick's (hemoglobin S disease) 282.61
Herter (-Gee) (nontropical sprue) 579.0
Heubner-Herter (nontropical sprue) 579.0
Heyd's (hepatorenal) 572.4
HHHO 759.81
Hilger's 337.0
Hoffa (-Kastert) (liposynovitis prepatellaris) 272.8
Hoffmann's 244.9 *[359.5]*
Hoffmann-Bouveret (paroxysmal tachycardia) 427.2
Hoffmann-Werdnig 335.0
Holländer-Simons (progressive lipodystrophy) 272.6
Holmes' (visual disorientation) 368.16
Holmes-Adie 379.46
Hoppe-Goldflam 358.00
Horner's (*see also* Neuropathy, peripheral, autonomic) 337.9
traumatic — *see* Injury, nerve, cervical sympathetic
hospital addiction 301.51
Hunt's (herpetic geniculate ganglionitis) 053.11
dyssynergia cerebellaris myoclonica 334.2
Hunter (-Hurler) (mucopolysaccharidosis II) 277.5
hunterian glossitis 529.4
Hurler (-Hunter) (mucopolysaccharidosis II) 277.5
Hutchinson's incisors or teeth 090.5
Hutchinson-Boeck (sarcoidosis) 135
Hutchinson-Gilford (progeria) 259.8
hydralazine
correct substance properly administered 695.4
overdose or wrong substance given or taken 972.6
hydraulic concussion (abdomen) (*see also* Injury, internal, abdomen) 868.00
hyperabduction 447.8
hyperactive bowel 564.9
hyperaldosteronism with hypokalemic alkalosis (Bartter's) 255.13
hypercalcemic 275.42
hypercoagulation NEC 289.89
hypereosinophilic (idiopathic) 288.3
hyperkalemic 276.7
hyperkinetic — *see also* Hyperkinesia
heart 429.82
hyperlipemia-hemolytic anemia-icterus 571.1

☑ Additional Digit Required — Refer to the Tabular List (Numeric Code Section) for Additional Digit Selection
▶◀ Revised Text   ● New Line   ▲ Revised Code

2006 ICD-9-CM   **October 2005 • Volume 2 — 319**

Syndrome — *see also* Disease — *continued*
hypermobility 728.5
hypernatremia 276.0
hyperosmolarity 276.0
hypersomnia-bulimia 349.89
hypersplenic 289.4
hypersympathetic (*see also* Neuropathy,
   peripheral, autonomic) 337.9
hypertransfusion, newborn 776.4
hyperventilation, psychogenic 306.1
hyperviscosity (of serum) NEC 273.3
   polycythemic 289.0
   sclerothymic 282.8
hypoglycemic (familial) (neonatal) 251.2
   functional 251.1
hypokalemic 276.8
hypophyseal 253.8
hypophyseothalamic 253.8
hypopituitarism 253.2
hypoplastic left heart 746.7
hypopotassemia 276.8
hyposmolality 276.1
hypotension, maternal 669.2 ☑
hypotonia-hypomentia-hypogonadism-obesity
   759.81
ICF (intravascular coagulation-fibrinolysis) (*see*
   also Fibrinolysis) 286.6
idiopathic cardiorespiratory distress, newborn
   769
idiopathic nephrotic (infantile) 581.9
iliotibial band 728.89
Imerslund (-Gräsbeck) (anemia due to familial
   selective vitamin B$_{12}$ malabsorption)
   281.1
immobility (paraplegic) 728.3
immunity deficiency, combined 279.2
impending coronary 411.1
impingement
   shoulder 726.2
   vertebral bodies 724.4
inappropriate secretion of antidiuretic hormone
   (ADH) 253.6
incomplete
   mandibulofacial 756.0
infant
   death, sudden (SIDS) 798.0
   Hercules 255.2
   of diabetic mother 775.0
   shaken 995.55
infantilism 253.3
inferior vena cava 459.2
influenza-like 487.1
inspissated bile, newborn 774.4
insufficient sleep 307.44   ●
intermediate coronary (artery) 411.1
internal carotid artery (*see also* Occlusion,
   artery, carotid) 433.1 ☑
interspinous ligament 724.8
intestinal
   carcinoid 259.2
   gas 787.3
   knot 560.2
intravascular
   coagulation-fibrinolysis (ICF) (*see also*
      Fibrinolysis) 286.6
   coagulopathy (*see also* Fibrinolysis) 286.6
inverted Marfan's 759.89
IRDS (idiopathic respiratory distress, newborn)
   769
irritable
   bowel 564.1
   heart 306.2
   weakness 300.5
ischemic bowel (transient) 557.9
   chronic 557.1
   due to mesenteric artery insufficiency 557.1
Itsenko-Cushing (pituitary basophilism) 255.0
IVC (intravascular coagulopathy) (*see also*
   Fibrinolysis) 286.6
Ivemark's (asplenia with congenital heart
   disease) 759.0
Jaccoud's 714.4
Jackson's 344.89
Jadassohn-Lewandowski (pachyonchia
   congenita) 757.5
Jaffe-Lichtenstein (-Uehlinger) 252.01
Jahnke's (encephalocutaneous angiomatosis)
   759.6

Syndrome — *see also* Disease — *continued*
Jakob-Creutzfeldt ►(new variant)◄ 046.1
   with dementia
      with behavioral disturbance 046.1
         [294.11]
      without behavioral disturbance 046.1
         [294.10]
Jaksch's (pseudoleukemia infantum) 285.8
Jaksch-Hayem (-Luzet) (pseudoleukemia
   infantum) 285.8
jaw-winking 742.8
jejunal 564.2
Jervell-Lange-Nielsen 426.82   ●
jet lag 327.35   ▲
Jeune's (asphyxiating thoracic dystrophy of
   newborn) 756.4
Job's (chronic granulomatous disease) 288.1
Jordan's 288.2
Joseph-Diamond-Blackfan (congenital
   hypoplastic anemia) 284.0
Joubert 759.89
jugular foramen 352.6
Kabuki 759.89
Kahler's (multiple myeloma) (M9730/3)
   203.0 ☑
Kalischer's (encephalocutaneous angiomatosis)
   759.6
Kallmann's (hypogonadotropic hypogonadism
   with anosmia) 253.4
Kanner's (autism) (*see also* Psychosis,
   childhood) 299.0 ☑
Kartagener's (sinusitis, bronchiectasis, situs
   inversus) 759.3
Kasabach-Merritt (capillary hemangioma
   associated with thrombocytopenic
   purpura) 287.39   ▲
Kast's (dyschondroplasia with hemangiomas)
   756.4
Kaznelson's (congenital hypoplastic anemia)
   284.0
Kearns-Sayre 277.87
Kelly's (sideropenic dysphagia) 280.8
Kimmelstiel-Wilson (intercapillary
   glomerulosclerosis) 250.4 ☑ [581.81]
Klauder's (erythema multiforme exudativum)
   695.1
Klein-Waardenburg (ptosis-epicanthus) 270.2
Kleine-Levin 327.13   ▲
Klinefelter's 758.7
Klippel-Feil (brevicollis) 756.16
Klippel-Trenaunay 759.89
Klumpke (-Déjérine) (injury to brachial plexus
   at birth) 767.6
Klüver-Bucy (-Terzian) 310.0
Köhler-Pellegrini-Stieda (calcification, knee
   joint) 726.62
König's 564.89
Korsakoff's (nonalcoholic) 294.0
   alcoholic 291.1
Korsakoff (-Wernicke) (nonalcoholic) 294.0
   alcoholic 291.1
Kostmann's (infantile genetic agranulocytosis)
   288.0
Krabbe's
   congenital muscle hypoplasia 756.89
   cutaneocerebral angioma 759.6
Kunkel (lupoid hepatitis) 571.49
labyrinthine 386.50
laceration, broad ligament 620.6
Langdon Down (mongolism) 758.0
Larsen's (flattened facies and multiple
   congenital dislocations) 755.8
lateral
   cutaneous nerve of thigh 355.1
   medullary (*see also* Disease, cerebrovascular
      acute) 436
Launois' (pituitary gigantism) 253.0
Launois-Cléret (adiposogenital dystrophy) 253.8
Laurence-Moon (-Bardet)-Biedl (obesity,
   polydactyly, and mental retardation)
   759.89
Lawford's (encephalocutaneous angiomatosis)
   759.6
lazy
   leukocyte 288.0
   posture 728.3

Syndrome — *see also* Disease — *continued*
Lederer-Brill (acquired infectious hemolytic
   anemia) 283.19
Legg-Calvé-Perthes (osteochondrosis capital
   femoral) 732.1
Lemiere 451.89
Lennox-Gastaut syndrome 345.0 ☑
   with tonic seizures 345.1 ☑
Lennox's (*see also* Epilepsy) 345.0 ☑
lenticular 275.1
Léopold-Lévi's (paroxysmal thyroid instability)
   242.9 ☑
Lepore hemoglobin 282.49
Léri-Weill 756.59
Leriche's (aortic bifurcation occlusion) 444.0
Lermoyez's (*see also* Disease, Ménière's) 386.00
Lesch-Nyhan (hypoxanthine-guanine-
   phosphoribosyltransferase deficiency)
   277.2
Lev's (acquired complete heart block) 426.0
Levi's (pituitary dwarfism) 253.3
Lévy-Roussy 334.3
Lichtheim's (subacute combined sclerosis with
   pernicious anemia) 281.0 [336.2]
Li-Fraumeni V84.01
Lightwood's (renal tubular acidosis) 588.89
Lignac (-de Toni) (-Fanconi) (-Debré) (cystinosis)
   270.0
Likoff's (angina in menopausal women) 413.9
liver-kidney 572.4
Lloyd's 258.1
lobotomy 310.0
Löffler's (eosinophilic pneumonitis) 518.3
Löfgren's (sarcoidosis) 135
long arm 18 or 21 deletion 758.39
Looser (-Debray)-Milkman (osteomalacia with
   pseudofractures) 268.2
Lorain-Levi (pituitary dwarfism) 253.3
Louis-Bar (ataxia-telangiectasia) 334.8
low
   atmospheric pressure 993.2
   back 724.2
      psychogenic 306.0
   output (cardiac) (*see also* Failure, heart)
      428.9
Lowe's (oculocerebrorenal dystrophy) 270.8
Lowe-Terrey-MacLachlan (oculocerebrorenal
   dystrophy) 270.8
lower radicular, newborn 767.4
Lown (-Ganong)-Levine (short P-R interval,
   normal QRS complex, and
   supraventricular tachycardia) 426.81
Lucey-Driscoll (jaundice due to delayed
   conjugation) 774.30
Luetscher's (dehydration) 276.51   ▲
lumbar vertebral 724.4
Lutembacher's (atrial septal defect with mitral
   stenosis) 745.5
Lyell's (toxic epidermal necrolysis) 695.1
   due to drug
      correct substance properly administered
         695.1
      overdose or wrong substance given or
         taken 977.9
      specified drug — *see* Table of Drugs
         and Chemicals
MacLeod's 492.8
macrogenitosomia praecox 259.8
macroglobulinemia 273.3
Maffucci's (dyschondroplasia with
   hemangiomas) 756.4
Magenblase 306.4
magnesium-deficiency 781.7
Mal de Debarquement 780.4
malabsorption 579.9
   postsurgical 579.3
   spinal fluid 331.3
malignant carcinoid 259.2
Mallory-Weiss 530.7
mandibulofacial dysostosis 756.0
manic-depressive (*see also* Psychosis, affective)
   296.80
Mankowsky's (familial dysplastic osteopathy)
   731.2
maple syrup (urine) 270.3
Marable's (celiac artery compression) 447.4

☑ Additional Digit Required — Refer to the Tabular List (Numeric Code Section) for Additional Digit Selection
►◄ Revised Text   ● New Line   ▲ Revised Code

320 — Volume 2 • October 2005   *2006 ICD-9-CM*

Syndrome — *see also* Disease — *continued*
Marchesani (-Weill) (brachymorphism and
        ectopia lentis) 759.89
Marchiafava-Bignami 341.8
Marchiafava-Micheli (paroxysmal nocturnal
        hemoglobinuria) 283.2
Marcus Gunn's (jaw-winking syndrome) 742.8
Marfan's (arachnodactyly) 759.82
        meaning congenital syphilis 090.49
        with luxation of lens 090.49 *[379.32]*
Marie's (acromegaly) 253.0
        primary or idiopathic (acropachyderma)
            757.39
        secondary (hypertrophic pulmonary
            osteoarthropathy) 731.2
Markus-Adie 379.46
Maroteaux-Lamy (mucopolysaccharidosis VI)
        277.5
Martin's 715.27
Martin-Albright (pseudohypoparathyroidism)
        275.49
Martorell-Fabré (pulseless disease) 446.7
massive aspiration of newborn 770.18   ▲
Masters-Allen 620.6
mastocytosis 757.33
maternal hypotension 669.2 ☑
maternal obesity 646.1 ☑
May (-Hegglin) 288.2
McArdle (-Schmid) (-Pearson) (glycogenosis V)
        271.0
McCune-Albright (osteitis fibrosa disseminata)
        756.59
McQuarrie's (idiopathic familial hypoglycemia)
        251.2
meconium
        aspiration 770.12   ▲
        plug (newborn) NEC 777.1
median arcuate ligament 447.4
mediastinal fibrosis 519.3
Meekeren-Ehlers-Danlos 756.83
Meige (blepharospasm-oromandibular dystonia)
        333.82
        -Milroy (chronic hereditary edema) 757.0
MELAS (mitochondrial encephalopathy, lactic
        acidosis and stroke-like episodes) 277.87
Melkersson (-Rosenthal) 351.8
Mende's (ptosis-epicanthus) 270.2
Mendelson's (resulting from a procedure) 997.3
        during labor 668.0 ☑
        obstetric 668.0 ☑
Ménétrier's (hypertrophic gastritis) 535.2 ☑
Ménière's (*see also* Disease, Ménière's) 386.00
meningo-eruptive 047.1
Menkes' 759.89
        glutamic acid 759.89
        maple syrup (urine) disease 270.3
menopause 627.2
        postartificial 627.4
menstruation 625.4
MERRF (myoclonus with epilepsy and with
        ragged red fibers) 277.87
mesenteric
        artery, superior 557.1
        vascular insufficiency (with gangrene) 557.1
metabolic 277.7
metastatic carcinoid 259.2
Meyenburg-Altherr-Uehlinger 733.99
Meyer-Schwickerath and Weyers (dysplasia
        oculodentodigitalis) 759.89
Micheli-Rietti (thalassemia minor) 282.49
Michotte's 721.5
micrognathia-glossoptosis 756.0
microphthalmos (congenital) 759.89
midbrain 348.8
middle
        lobe (lung) (right) 518.0
        radicular 353.0
Miescher's
        familial acanthosis nigricans 701.2
        granulomatosis disciformis 709.3
Mieten's 759.89
migraine 346.0 ☑
Mikity-Wilson (pulmonary dysmaturity) 770.7
Mikulicz's (dryness of mouth, absent or
        decreased lacrimation) 527.1
milk alkali (milk drinkers') 275.42

Syndrome — *see also* Disease — *continued*
Milkman (-Looser) (osteomalacia with
        pseudofractures) 268.2
Millard-Gubler 344.89
Miller-Dieker 758.33
Miller Fisher's 357.0
Milles' (encephalocutaneous angiomatosis)
        759.6
Minkowski-Chauffard (*see also* Spherocytosis)
        282.0
Mirizzi's (hepatic duct stenosis) 576.2
        with calculus, cholelithiasis, or stones — *see*
            Choledocholithiasis
mitochondrial neurogastrointestinal
        encephalopathy (MNGIE) 277.87
mitral
        click (-murmur) 785.2
        valve prolapse 424.0
MNGIE (mitochondrial neurogastrointestinal
        encephalopathy) 277.87
Möbius'
        congenital oculofacial paralysis 352.6
        ophthalmoplegic migraine 346.8 ☑
Mohr's (types I and II) 759.89
monofixation 378.34
Moore's (*see also* Epilepsy) 345.5 ☑
Morel-Moore (hyperostosis frontalis interna)
        733.3
Morel-Morgagni (hyperostosis frontalis interna)
        733.3
Morgagni (-Stewart-Morel) (hyperostosis
        frontalis interna) 733.3
Morgagni-Adams-Stokes (syncope with heart
        block) 426.9
Morquio (-Brailsford) (-Ullrich)
        (mucopolysaccharidosis IV) 277.5   ▲
Morris (testicular feminization) 259.5   ▲
Morton's (foot) (metatarsalgia) (metatarsal
        neuralgia) (neuralgia) (neuroma) (toe)
        355.6
Moschcowitz (-Singer-Symmers) (thrombotic
        thrombocytopenic purpura) 446.6
Mounier-Kuhn 748.3   ▲
        with
            acute exacerbation 494.1   ●
            bronchiectasis 494.0   ●
                with (acute) exacerbation 494.1   ●
        acquired 519.1   ●
            with bronchiectasis 494.0   ●
                with (acute) exacerbation 494.1   ●
Mucha-Haberman (acute parapsoriasis
        varioliformis) 696.2
mucocutaneous lymph node (acute) (febrile)
        (infantile) (MCLS) 446.1
multiple
        deficiency 260
        operations 301.51
Munchausen's 301.51
Münchmeyer's (exostosis luxurians) 728.11
Murchison-Sanderson — *see* Disease,
        Hodgkin's
myasthenic — *see* Myasthenia, syndrome
myelodysplastic 238.7
myeloproliferative (chronic) (M9960/1) 238.7
myofascial pain NEC 729.1
Naffziger's 353.0
Nager-de Reynier (dysostosis mandibularis)
        756.0
nail-patella (hereditary osteo-onychodysplasia)
        756.89
NARP (neuropathy, ataxia and retinitis
        pigmentosa) 277.87
Nebécourt's 253.3
Neill-Dingwall (microencephaly and dwarfism)
        759.89
nephrotic (*see also* Nephrosis) 581.9
        diabetic 250.4 ☑ *[581.81]*
Netherton's (ichthyosiform erythroderma) 757.1
neurocutaneous 759.6
neuroleptic malignant 333.92
Nezelof's (pure alymphocytosis) 279.13
Niemann-Pick (lipid histiocytosis) 272.7
Nonne-Milroy-Meige (chronic hereditary edema)
        757.0
nonsense 300.16
Noonan's 759.89

Syndrome — *see also* Disease — *continued*
Nothnagel's
        ophthalmoplegia-cerebellar ataxia 378.52
        vasomotor acroparesthesia 443.89
nucleus ambiguous-hypoglossal 352.6
OAV (oculoauriculovertebral dysplasia) 756.0
obsessional 300.3
oculocutaneous 364.24
oculomotor 378.81
oculourethroarticular 099.3
Ogilvie's (sympathicotonic colon obstruction)
        560.89
ophthalmoplegia-cerebellar ataxia 378.52
Oppenheim-Urbach (necrobiosis lipoidica
        diabeticorum) 250.8 ☑ *[709.3]*
oral-facial-digital 759.89
organic
        affective NEC 293.83
            drug-induced 292.84
        anxiety 293.84
        delusional 293.81
            alcohol-induced 291.5
            drug-induced 292.11
            due to or associated with
                arteriosclerosis 290.42
                presenile brain disease 290.12
                senility 290.20
        depressive 293.83
            drug-induced 292.84
            due to or associated with
                arteriosclerosis 290.43
                presenile brain disease 290.13
                senile brain disease 290.21
        hallucinosis 293.82
            drug-induced 292.84
organic affective 293.83
        induced by drug 292.84
organic personality 310.1
        induced by drug 292.89
Ormond's 593.4
orodigitofacial 759.89
orthostatic hypotensive-dysautonomic
        dyskinetic 333.0
Osler-Weber-Rendu (familial hemorrhagic
        telangiectasia) 448.0
osteodermopathic hyperostosis 757.39
osteoporosis-osteomalacia 268.2
Österreicher-Turner (hereditary osteo-
        onychodysplasia) 756.89
Ostrum-Furst 756.59
otolith 386.19
otopalatodigital 759.89
outlet (thoracic) 353.0
ovarian remnant 620.8
ovarian vein 593.4
Owren's (*see also* Defect, coagulation) 286.3
OX 758.6
pacemaker 429.4
Paget-Schroetter (intermittent venous
        claudication) 453.8
pain — *see* Pain
painful
        apicocostal vertebral (M8010/3) 162.3
        arc 726.19
        bruising 287.2
        feet 266.2
Pancoast's (carcinoma, pulmonary apex)
        (M8010/3) 162.3
panhypopituitary (postpartum) 253.2
papillary muscle 429.81
        with myocardial infarction 410.8 ☑
Papillon-Léage and Psaume (orodigitofacial
        dysostosis) 759.89
parabiotic (transfusion)
        donor (twin) 772.0
        recipient (twin) 776.4
paralysis agitans 332.0
paralytic 344.9
        specified type NEC 344.89
paraneoplastic — *see* condition
Parinaud's (paralysis of conjugate upward gaze)
        378.81
        oculoglandular 372.02
Parkes Weber and Dimitri (encephalocutaneous
        angiomatosis) 759.6
Parkinson's (*see also* Parkinsonism) 332.0
parkinsonian (*see also* Parkinsonism) 332.0

☑ Additional Digit Required — Refer to the Tabular List (Numeric Code Section) for Additional Digit Selection

Syndrome — *see also* Disease — *continued*
Parry's (exophthalmic goiter) 242.0 ☑
Parry-Romberg 349.89
Parsonage-Aldren-Turner 353.5
Parsonage-Turner 353.5
Patau's (trisomy D₁) 758.1
patellofemoral 719.46
Paterson (-Brown) (-Kelly) (sideropenic dysphagia) 280.8
Payr's (splenic flexure syndrome) 569.89
pectoral girdle 447.8
pectoralis minor 447.8
Pelger-Huët (hereditary hyposegmentation) 288.2
pellagra-cerebellar ataxia-renal aminoaciduria 270.0
Pellegrini-Stieda 726.62
pellagroid 265.2
Pellizzi's (pineal) 259.8
pelvic congestion (-fibrosis) 625.5
Pendred's (familial goiter with deaf-mutism) 243
Penfield's (*see also* Epilepsy) 345.5 ☑
Penta X 758.81
peptic ulcer — *see* Ulcer, peptic 533.9 ☑
perabduction 447.8
periodic 277.3
periurethral fibrosis 593.4
persistent fetal circulation 747.83
Petges-Cléjat (poikilodermatomyositis) 710.3
Peutz-Jeghers 759.6
Pfeiffer (acrocephalosyndactyly) 755.55
phantom limb 353.6
pharyngeal pouch 279.11
Pick's (pericardial pseudocirrhosis of liver) 423.2
    heart 423.2
    liver 423.2
Pick-Herxheimer (diffuse idiopathic cutaneous atrophy) 701.8
Pickwickian (cardiopulmonary obesity) 278.8
PIE (pulmonary infiltration with eosinophilia) 518.3
Pierre Marie-Bamberger (hypertrophic pulmonary osteoarthropathy) 731.2
Pierre Mauriac's (diabetes-dwarfism-obesity) 258.1
Pierre Robin 756.0
pigment dispersion, iris 364.53
pineal 259.8
pink puffer 492.8
pituitary 253.0
placental
    dysfunction 762.2
    insufficiency 762.2
    transfusion 762.3
plantar fascia 728.71
plica knee 727.83
Plummer-Vinson (sideropenic dysphagia) 280.8
pluricarential of infancy 260
plurideficiency of infancy 260
pluriglandular (compensatory) 258.8
polycarential of infancy 260
polyglandular 258.8
polysplenia 759.0
pontine 433.8 ☑
popliteal
    artery entrapment 447.8
    web 756.89
postartificial menopause 627.4
postcardiotomy 429.4
postcholecystectomy 576.0
postcommissurotomy 429.4
postconcussional 310.2
postcontusional 310.2
postencephalitic 310.8
posterior
    cervical sympathetic 723.2
    fossa compression 348.4
    inferior cerebellar artery (*see also* Disease, cerebrovascular, acute) 436
postgastrectomy (dumping) 564.2
post-gastric surgery 564.2
posthepatitis 780.79
postherpetic (neuralgia) (zoster) 053.19
    geniculate ganglion 053.11
    ophthalmica 053.19

Syndrome — *see also* Disease — *continued*
postimmunization — *see* Complications, vaccination
postinfarction 411.0
postinfluenza (asthenia) 780.79
postirradiation 990
postlaminectomy 722.80
    cervical, cervicothoracic 722.81
    lumbar, lumbosacral 722.83
    thoracic, thoracolumbar 722.82
postleukotomy 310.0
postlobotomy 310.0
postmastectomy lymphedema 457.0
postmature (of newborn) 766.22
postmyocardial infarction 411.0
postoperative NEC 998.9
    blind loop 579.2
postpartum panhypopituitary 253.2
postperfusion NEC 999.8
    bone marrow 996.85
postpericardiotomy 429.4
postphlebitic (asymptomatic) 459.10
    with
        complications NEC 459.19
        inflammation 459.12
            and ulcer 459.13
        stasis dermatitis 459.12
            with ulcer 459.13
        ulcer 459.11
            with inflammation 459.13
postpolio (myelitis) 138
postvagotomy 564.2
postvalvulotomy 429.4
postviral (asthenia) NEC 780.79
Potain's (gastrectasis with dyspepsia) 536.1
potassium intoxication 276.7
Potter's 753.0
Prader (-Labhart) -Willi (-Fanconi) 759.81
preinfarction 411.1
preleukemic 238.7
premature senility 259.8
premenstrual 625.4
premenstrual tension 625.4
pre ulcer 536.9
Prinzmetal-Massumi (anterior chest wall syndrome) 786.52
Profichet's 729.9
progeria 259.8
progressive pallidal degeneration 333.0
prolonged gestation 766.22
Proteus (dermal hypoplasia) 757.39
prune belly 756.71
prurigo-asthma 691.8
pseudocarpal tunnel (sublimis) 354.0
pseudohermaphroditism-virilism-hirsutism 255.2
pseudoparalytica 358.00
pseudo-Turner's 759.89
psycho-organic 293.9
    acute 293.0
    anxiety type 293.84
    depressive type 293.83
    hallucinatory type 293.82
    nonpsychotic severity 310.1
        specified focal (partial) NEC 310.8
    paranoid type 293.81
    specified type NEC 293.89
    subacute 293.1
pterygolymphangiectasia 758.6
ptosis-epicanthus 270.2
pulmonary
    arteriosclerosis 416.0
    hypoperfusion (idiopathic) 769
    renal (hemorrhagic) 446.21
pulseless 446.7
Putnam-Dana (subacute combined sclerosis with pernicious anemia) 281.0 [336.2]
pyloroduodenal 537.89
pyramidopallidonigral 332.0
pyriformis 355.0
▶QT◀ interval prolongation 426.82   ▲
radicular NEC 729.2
    lower limbs 724.4
    upper limbs 723.4
        newborn 767.4
Raeder-Harbitz (pulseless disease) 446.7

Syndrome — *see also* Disease — *continued*
Ramsay Hunt's
    dyssynergia cerebellaris myoclonica 334.2
    herpetic geniculate ganglionitis 053.11
rapid time-zone change 327.35   ▲
Raymond (-Céstan) 433.8 ☑
Raynaud's (paroxysmal digital cyanosis) 443.0
RDS (respiratory distress syndrome, newborn) 769
Refsum's (heredopathia atactica polyneuritiformis) 356.3
Reichmann's (gastrosuccorrhea) 536.8
Reifenstein's (hereditary familial hypogonadism, male) 259.5   ▲
Reilly's (*see also* Neuropathy, peripheral, autonomic) 337.9
Reiter's 099.3
renal glomerulohyalinosis-diabetic 250.4 ☑ [581.81]
Rendu-Osler-Weber (familial hemorrhagic telangiectasia) 448.0
renofacial (congenital biliary fibroangiomatosis) 753.0
Rénon-Delille 253.8
respiratory distress (idiopathic) (newborn) 769
    adult (following shock, surgery, or trauma) 518.5
        specified NEC 518.82
restless leg 333.99
retinoblastoma (familial) 190.5
retraction (Duane's) 378.71
retroperitoneal fibrosis 593.4
Rett's 330.8
Reye's 331.81
Reye-Sheehan (postpartum pituitary necrosis) 253.2
Riddoch's (visual disorientation) 368.16
Ridley's (*see also* Failure, ventricular, left) 428.1
Rieger's (mesodermal dysgenesis, anterior ocular segment) 743.44
Rietti-Greppi-Micheli (thalassemia minor) 282.49
right ventricular obstruction — *see* Failure, heart
Riley-Day (familial dysautonomia) 742.8
Robin's 756.0
Rokitansky-Kuster-Hauser (congenital absence, vagina) 752.49
Romano-Ward ▶(prolonged QT interval syndrome)◀ 426.82   ▲
Romberg's 349.89
Rosen-Castleman-Liebow (pulmonary proteinosis) 516.0
rotator cuff, shoulder 726.10
Roth's 355.1
Rothmund's (congenital poikiloderma) 757.33
Rotor's (idiopathic hyperbilirubinemia) 277.4
Roussy-Lévy 334.3
Roy (-Jutras) (acropachyderma) 757.39
rubella (congenital) 771.0
Rubinstein-Taybi's (brachydactylia, short stature, and mental retardation) 759.89
Rud's (mental deficiency, epilepsy, and infantilism) 759.89
Ruiter-Pompen (-Wyers) (angiokeratoma corporis diffusum) 272.7
Runge's (postmaturity) 766.22
Russell (-Silver) (congenital hemihypertrophy and short stature) 759.89
Rytand-Lipsitch (complete atrioventricular block) 426.0
sacralization-scoliosis-sciatica 756.15
sacroiliac 724.6
Saenger's 379.46
salt
    depletion (*see also* Disease, renal) 593.9
        due to heat NEC 992.8
            causing heat exhaustion or prostration 992.4
    low (*see also* Disease, renal) 593.9
salt-losing (*see also* Disease, renal) 593.9
Sanfilippo's (mucopolysaccharidosis III) 277.5
Scaglietti-Dagnini (acromegalic macrospondylitis) 253.0
scalded skin 695.1
scalenus anticus (anterior) 353.0

Syndrome — *see also* Disease — *continued*
scapulocostal 354.8
scapuloperoneal 359.1
scapulovertebral 723.4
Schaumann's (sarcoidosis) 135
Scheie's (mucopolysaccharidosis IS) 277.5
Scheuthauer-Marie-Sainton (cleidocranialis
   dysostosis) 755.59
Schirmer's (encephalocutaneous angiomatosis)
   759.6
schizophrenic, of childhood NEC (*see also*
   Psychosis, childhood) 299.9 ☑
Schmidt's
   sphallo-pharyngo-laryngeal hemiplegia 352.6
   thyroid-adrenocortical insufficiency 258.1
   vagoaccessory 352.6
Schneider's 047.9
Schnitzler 273.1
Scholte's (malignant carcinoid) 259.2
Scholz (-Bielschowsky-Henneberg) 330.0
Schroeder's (endocrine-hypertensive) 255.3
Schüller-Christian (chronic histiocytosis X)
   277.89
Schultz's (agranulocytosis) 288.0
Schwartz (-Jampel) 756.89
Schwartz-Bartter (inappropriate secretion of
   antidiuretic hormone) 253.6
Scimitar (anomalous venous drainage, right
   lung to inferior vena cava) 747.49
sclerocystic ovary 256.4
sea-blue histiocyte 272.7
Seabright-Bantam
   (pseudohypoparathyroidism) 275.49
Seckel's 759.89
Secretan's (posttraumatic edema) 782.3
secretoinhibitor (keratoconjunctivitis sicca)
   710.2
Seeligmann's (ichthyosis congenita) 757.1
Senear-Usher (pemphigus erythematosus)
   694.4
senilism 259.8
serotonin 333.99
serous meningitis 348.2
Sertoli cell (germinal aplasia) 606.0
sex chromosome mosaic 758.81
Sézary's (reticulosis) (M9701/3) 202.2 ☑
shaken infant 995.55
Shaver's (bauxite pneumoconiosis) 503
Sheehan's (postpartum pituitary necrosis)
   253.2
shock (traumatic) 958.4
   kidney 584.5
      following crush injury 958.5
   lung 518.5
   neurogenic 308.9
   psychic 308.9
short
   bowel 579.3
   P-R interval 426.81
shoulder-arm (*see also* Neuropathy, peripheral,
   autonomic) 337.9
shoulder-girdle 723.4
shoulder-hand (*see also* Neuropathy,
   peripheral, autonomic) 337.9
Shwachman's 288.0
Shy-Drager (orthostatic hypotension with
   multisystem degeneration) 333.0
Sicard's 352.6
sicca (keratoconjunctivitis) 710.2
sick
   cell 276.1
   cilia 759.89
   sinus 427.81
sideropenic 280.8
Siemens'
   ectodermal dysplasia 757.31
   keratosis follicularis spinulosa (decalvans)
      757.39
Silfverskiöld's (osteochondrodystrophy,
   extremities) 756.50
Silver's (congenital hemihypertrophy and short
   stature) 759.89
Silvestroni-Bianco (thalassemia minima) 282.49
Simons' (progressive lipodystrophy) 272.6
sinus tarsi 726.79
sinusitis-bronchiectasis-situs inversus 759.3

Syndrome — *see also* Disease — *continued*
Sipple's (medullary thyroid carcinoma-
   pheochromocytoma) 193
Sjögren (-Gougerot) (keratoconjunctivitis sicca)
   710.2
   with lung involvement 710.2 [517.8]
Sjögren-Larsson (ichthyosis congenita) 757.1
Slocumb's 255.3
Sluder's 337.0
Smith-Lemli-Opitz (cerebrohepatorenal
   syndrome) 759.89
Smith-Magenis 758.33
smokers' 305.1
Sneddon-Wilkinson (subcorneal pustular
   dermatosis) 694.1
Sotos' (cerebral gigantism) 253.0
South African cardiomyopathy 425.2
spasmodic
   upward movement, eye(s) 378.82
   winking 307.20
Spens' (syncope with heart block) 426.9
spherophakia-brachymorphia 759.89
spinal cord injury — *see also* Injury, spinal, by
   site
   with fracture, vertebra — *see* Fracture,
      vertebra, by site, with spinal cord
      injury
   cervical — *see* Injury, spinal, cervical
   fluid malabsorption (acquired) 331.3
splenic
   agenesis 759.0
   flexure 569.89
   neutropenia 288.0
   sequestration 289.52
Spurway's (brittle bones and blue sclera)
   756.51
staphylococcal scalded skin 695.1
Stein's (polycystic ovary) 256.4
Stein-Leventhal (polycystic ovary) 256.4
Steinbrocker's (*see also* Neuropathy,
   peripheral, autonomic) 337.9
Stevens-Johnson (erythema multiforme
   exudativum) 695.1
Stewart-Morel (hyperostosis frontalis interna)
   733.3
Stickler 759.89   ●
stiff-baby 759.89
stiff-man 333.91
Still's (juvenile rheumatoid arthritis) 714.30
Still-Felty (rheumatoid arthritis with
   splenomegaly and leukopenia) 714.1
Stilling-Türk-Duane (ocular retraction
   syndrome) 378.71
Stojano's (subcostal) 098.86
Stokes (-Adams) (syncope with heart block)
   426.9
Stokvis-Talma (enterogenous cyanosis) 289.7
stone heart (*see also* Failure, ventricular, left)
   428.1
straight-back 756.19
stroke (*see also* Disease, cerebrovascular,
   acute) 436
   little 435.9
Sturge-Kalischer-Weber (encephalotrigeminal
   angiomatosis) 759.6
Sturge-Weber (-Dimitri) (encephalocutaneous
   angiomatosis) 759.6
subclavian-carotid obstruction (chronic) 446.7
subclavian steal 435.2
subcoracoid-pectoralis minor 447.8
subcostal 098.86
   nerve compression 354.8
subperiosteal hematoma 267
subphrenic interposition 751.4
sudden infant death (SIDS) 798.0
Sudeck's 733.7
Sudeck-Leriche 733.7
superior
   cerebellar artery (*see also* Disease,
      cerebrovascular, acute) 436
   mesenteric artery 557.1
   pulmonary sulcus (tumor) (M8010/3) 162.3
   vena cava 459.2
suprarenal cortical 255.3
supraspinatus 726.10
swallowed blood 777.3
sweat retention 705.1

Syndrome — *see also* Disease — *continued*
Sweet's (acute febrile neutrophilic dermatosis)
   695.89
Swyer-James (unilateral hyperlucent lung)
   492.8
Swyer's (XY pure gonadal dysgenesis) 752.7
Symonds' 348.2
sympathetic
   cervical paralysis 337.0
   pelvic 625.5
syndactylic oxycephaly 755.55
syphilitic-cardiovascular 093.89
systemic
   fibrosclerosing 710.8
   inflammatory response (SIRS) 995.90
      due to
         infectious process 995.91
            with organ dysfunction 995.92
         non-infectious process 995.93
            with organ dysfunction 995.94
systolic click (-murmur) 785.2
Tabagism 305.1
tachycardia-bradycardia 427.81
Takayasu (-Onishi) (pulseless disease) 446.7
Tapia's 352.6
tarsal tunnel 355.5
Taussig-Bing (transposition, aorta and
   overriding pulmonary artery) 745.11
Taybi's (otopalatodigital) 759.89
Taylor's 625.5
teething 520.7
tegmental 344.89
telangiectasis-pigmentation-cataract 757.33
temporal 383.02
   lobectomy behavior 310.0
temporomandibular joint-pain-dysfunction
   [TMJ] NEC 524.60
   specified NEC 524.69
Terry's 362.21
testicular feminization 259.5   ▲
testis, nonvirilizing 257.8
tethered (spinal) cord 742.59
thalamic 348.8
Thibierge-Weissenbach (cutaneous systemic
   sclerosis) 710.1
Thiele 724.6
thoracic outlet (compression) 353.0
thoracogenous rheumatic (hypertrophic
   pulmonary osteoarthropathy) 731.2
Thorn's (*see also* Disease, renal) 593.9
Thorson-Biörck (malignant carcinoid) 259.2
thrombopenia-hemangioma 287.39   ▲
thyroid-adrenocortical insufficiency 258.1
Tietze's 733.6
time-zone (rapid) 327.35   ▲
Tobias' (carcinoma, pulmonary apex)
   (M8010/3) 162.3
toilet seat 926.0
Tolosa-Hunt 378.55
Toni-Fanconi (cystinosis) 270.0
Touraine's (hereditary osteo-onychodysplasia)
   756.89
Touraine-Solente-Golé (acropachyderma)
   757.39
toxic
   oil 710.5
   shock 040.82
transfusion
   fetal-maternal 772.0
   twin
      donor (infant) 772.0
      recipient (infant) 776.4
Treacher Collins' (incomplete mandibulofacial
   dysostosis) 756.0
trigeminal plate 259.8
triple X female 758.81
trisomy NEC 758.5
   13 or D₁ 758.1
   16-18 or E 758.2
   18 or E₃ 758.2
   20 758.5
   21 or G (mongolism) 758.0
   22 or G (mongolism) 758.0
   G 758.0
Troisier-Hanot-Chauffard (bronze diabetes)
   275.0
tropical wet feet 991.4

☑ Additional Digit Required — Refer to the Tabular List (Numeric Code Section) for Additional Digit Selection

Syndrome — *see also* Disease — *continued*
- Trousseau's (thrombophlebitis migrans visceral cancer) 453.1
- Türk's (ocular retraction syndrome) 378.71
- Turner's 758.6
- Turner-Varny 758.6
- twin-to-twin transfusion 762.3
  - recipient twin 776.4
- Uehlinger's (acropachyderma) 757.39
- Ullrich (-Bonnevie) (-Turner) 758.6
- Ullrich-Feichtiger 759.89
- underwater blast injury (abdominal) (*see also* Injury, internal, abdomen) 868.00
- universal joint, cervix 620.6
- Unverricht (-Lundborg) 333.2
- Unverricht-Wagner (dermatomyositis) 710.3
- upward gaze 378.81
- Urbach-Oppenheim (necrobiosis lipoidica diabeticorum) 250.8 ☑ *[709.3]*
- Urbach-Wiethe (lipoid proteinosis) 272.8 ▲
- uremia, chronic 585.9
- urethral 597.81
- urethro-oculoarticular 099.3
- urethro-oculosynovial 099.3
- urohepatic 572.4
- uveocutaneous 364.24
- uveomeningeal, uveomeningitis 363.22
- vagohypoglossal 352.6
- vagovagal 780.2
- van Buchem's (hyperostosis corticalis) 733.3
- van der Hoeve's (brittle bones and blue sclera, deafness) 756.51
- van der Hoeve-Halbertsma-Waardenburg (ptosis-epicanthus) 270.2
- van der Hoeve-Waardenburg-Gualdi (ptosis-epicanthus) 270.2
- van Neck-Odelberg (juvenile osteochondrosis) 732.1
- vanishing twin 651.33
- vascular splanchnic 557.0
- vasomotor 443.9
- vasovagal 780.2
- VATER 759.89
- Velo-cardio-facial 758.32
- vena cava (inferior) (superior) (obstruction) 459.2
- Verbiest's (claudicatio intermittens spinalis) 435.1
- Vernet's 352.6
- vertebral
  - artery 435.1
    - compression 721.1
    - lumbar 724.4
    - steal 435.1
- vertebrogenic (pain) 724.5
- vertiginous NEC 386.9
- video display tube 723.8
- Villaret's 352.6
- Vinson-Plummer (sideropenic dysphagia) 280.8
- virilizing adrenocortical hyperplasia, congenital 255.2
- virus, viral 079.99
- visceral larval migrans 128.0
- visual disorientation 368.16
- vitamin B₆ deficiency 266.1
- vitreous touch 997.99
- Vogt's (corpus striatum) 333.7
- Vogt-Koyanagi 364.24
- Volkmann's 958.6
- von Bechterew-Strümpell (ankylosing spondylitis) 720.0
- von Graefe's 378.72
- von Hippel-Lindau (angiomatosis retinocerebellosa) 759.6
- von Schroetter's (intermittent venous claudication) 453.8
- von Willebrand (-Jürgens) (angiohemophilia) 286.4
- Waardenburg-Klein (ptosis epicanthus) 270.2
- Wagner (-Unverricht) (dermatomyositis) 710.3
- Waldenström's (macroglobulinemia) 273.3
- Waldenström-Kjellberg (sideropenic dysphagia) 280.8
- Wallenberg's (posterior inferior cerebellar artery) (*see also* Disease, cerebrovascular, acute) 436
- Waterhouse (-Friderichsen) 036.3

Syndrome — *see also* Disease — *continued*
- water retention 276.6
- Weber's 344.89
- Weber-Christian (nodular nonsuppurative panniculitis) 729.30
- Weber-Cockayne (epidermolysis bullosa) 757.39
- Weber-Dimitri (encephalocutaneous angiomatosis) 759.6
- Weber-Gubler 344.89
- Weber-Leyden 344.89
- Weber-Osler (familial hemorrhagic telangiectasia) 448.0
- Wegener's (necrotizing respiratory granulomatosis) 446.4
- Weill-Marchesani (brachymorphism and ectopia lentis) 759.89
- Weingarten's (tropical eosinophilia) 518.3
- Weiss-Baker (carotid sinus syncope) 337.0
- Weissenbach-Thibierge (cutaneous systemic sclerosis) 710.1
- Werdnig-Hoffmann 335.0
- Werlhof-Wichmann (*see also* Purpura, thrombocytopenic) 287.39 ▲
- Werner's (polyendocrine adenomatosis) 258.0
- Werner's (progeria adultorum) 259.8
- Wernicke's (nonalcoholic) (superior hemorrhagic polioencephalitis) 265.1
- Wernicke-Korsakoff (nonalcoholic) 294.0
  - alcoholic 291.1
- Westphal-Strümpell (hepatolenticular degeneration) 275.1
- wet
  - brain (alcoholic) 303.9 ☑
  - feet (maceration) (tropical) 991.4
  - lung
    - adult 518.5
    - newborn 770.6
- whiplash 847.0
- Whipple's (intestinal lipodystrophy) 040.2
- "whistling face" (craniocarpotarsal dystrophy) 759.89
- Widal (-Abrami) (acquired hemolytic jaundice) 283.9
- Wilkie's 557.1
- Wilkinson-Sneddon (subcorneal pustular dermatosis) 694.1
- Willan-Plumbe (psoriasis) 696.1
- Willebrand (-Jürgens) (angiohemophilia) 286.4
- Willi-Prader (hypogenital dystrophy with diabetic tendency) 759.81
- Wilson's (hepatolenticular degeneration) 275.1
- Wilson-Mikity 770.7
- Wiskott-Aldrich (eczema-thrombocytopenia) 279.12
- withdrawal
  - alcohol 291.81
  - drug 292.0
    - infant of dependent mother 779.5
- Woakes' (ethmoiditis) 471.1
- Wolff-Parkinson-White (anomalous atrioventricular excitation) 426.7
- Wright's (hyperabduction) 447.8
- X
  - cardiac 413.9
  - dysmetabolic 277.7
- xiphoidalgia 733.99
- XO 758.6
- XXX 758.81
- XXXXY 758.81
- XXY 758.7
- yellow vernix (placental dysfunction) 762.2
- Zahorsky's 074.0
- Zellweger 277.86
- Zieve's (jaundice, hyperlipemia and hemolytic anemia) 571.1
- Zollinger-Ellison (gastric hypersecretion with pancreatic islet cell tumor) 251.5
- Zuelzer-Ogden (nutritional megaloblastic anemia) 281.2

Synechia (iris) (pupil) 364.70
- anterior 364.72
  - peripheral 364.73
- intrauterine (traumatic) 621.5
- posterior 364.71
- vulvae, congenital 752.49

Synesthesia (*see also* Disturbance, sensation) 782.0

Synodontia 520.2

Synophthalmus 759.89

Synorchidism 752.89

Synorchism 752.89

Synostosis (congenital) 756.59
- astragaloscaphoid 755.67
- radioulnar 755.53
- talonavicular (bar) 755.67
- tarsal 755.67

Synovial — *see* condition

Synovioma (M9040/3) — *see also* Neoplasm, connective tissue, malignant
- benign (M9040/0) — *see* Neoplasm, connective tissue, benign

Synoviosarcoma (M9040/3) — *see* Neoplasm, connective tissue, malignant

Synovitis 727.00
- chronic crepitant, wrist 727.2
- due to crystals — *see* Arthritis, due to crystals
- gonococcal 098.51
- gouty 274.0
- syphilitic 095.7
  - congenital 090.0
- traumatic, current — *see* Sprain, by site
- tuberculous — *see* Tuberculosis, synovitis
- villonodular 719.20
  - ankle 719.27
  - elbow 719.22
  - foot 719.27
  - hand 719.24
  - hip 719.25
  - knee 719.26
  - multiple sites 719.29
  - pelvic region 719.25
  - shoulder (region) 719.21
  - specified site NEC 719.28
  - wrist 719.23

Syphilide 091.3
- congenital 090.0
- newborn 090.0
- tubercular 095.8
  - congenital 090.0

Syphilis, syphilitic (acquired) 097.9
- with lung involvement 095.1
- abdomen (late) 095.2
- acoustic nerve 094.86
- adenopathy (secondary) 091.4
- adrenal (gland) 095.8
  - with cortical hypofunction 095.8
- age under 2 years NEC (*see also* Syphilis, congenital) 090.9
  - acquired 097.9
- alopecia (secondary) 091.82
- anemia 095.8
- aneurysm (artery) (ruptured) 093.89
  - aorta 093.0
  - central nervous system 094.89
  - congenital 090.5
- anus 095.8
  - primary 091.1
  - secondary 091.3
- aorta, aortic (arch) (abdominal) (insufficiency) (pulmonary) (regurgitation) (stenosis) (thoracic) 093.89
  - aneurysm 093.0
- arachnoid (adhesive) 094.2
- artery 093.89
  - cerebral 094.89
  - spinal 094.89
- arthropathy (neurogenic) (tabetic) 094.0 *[713.5]*
- asymptomatic — *see* Syphilis, latent
- ataxia, locomotor (progressive) 094.0
- atrophoderma maculatum 091.3
- auricular fibrillation 093.89
- Bell's palsy 094.89
- bladder 095.8
- bone 095.5
  - secondary 091.61
- brain 094.89
- breast 095.8
- bronchus 095.8
- bubo 091.0
- bulbar palsy 094.89
- bursa (late) 095.7

Syphilis, syphilitic — *continued*
cardiac decompensation 093.89
cardiovascular (early) (late) (primary)
(secondary) (tertiary) 093.9
specified type and site NEC 093.89
causing death under 2 years of age (*see also*
Syphilis, congenital) 090.9
stated to be acquired NEC 097.9
central nervous system (any site) (early) (late)
(latent) (primary) (recurrent) (relapse)
(secondary) (tertiary) 094.9
with
ataxia 094.0
paralysis, general 094.1
juvenile 090.40
paresis (general) 094.1
juvenile 090.40
tabes (dorsalis) 094.0
juvenile 090.40
taboparesis 094.1
juvenile 090.40
aneurysm (ruptured) 094.87
congenital 090.40
juvenile 090.40
remission in (sustained) 094.9
serology doubtful, negative, or positive 094.9
specified nature or site NEC 094.89
vascular 094.89
cerebral 094.89
meningovascular 094.2
nerves 094.89
sclerosis 094.89
thrombosis 094.89
cerebrospinal 094.89
tabetic 094.0
cerebrovascular 094.89
cervix 095.8
chancre (multiple) 091.0
extragenital 091.2
Rollet's 091.2
Charcôt's joint 094.0 [713.5]
choked disc 094.89 [377.00]
chorioretinitis 091.51
congenital 090.0 [363.13]
late 094.83
choroiditis 091.51
congenital 090.0 [363.13]
late 094.83
prenatal 090.0 [363.13]
choroidoretinitis (secondary) 091.51
congenital 090.0 [363.13]
late 094.83
ciliary body (secondary) 091.52
late 095.8 [364.11]
colon (late) 095.8
combined sclerosis 094.89
complicating pregnancy, childbirth or
puerperium 647.0 ☑
affecting fetus or newborn 760.2
condyloma (latum) 091.3
congenital 090.9
with
encephalitis 090.41
paresis (general) 090.40
tabes (dorsalis) 090.40
taboparesis 090.40
chorioretinitis, choroiditis 090.0 [363.13]
early or less than 2 years after birth NEC
090.2
with manifestations 090.0
latent (without manifestations) 090.1
negative spinal fluid test 090.1
serology, positive 090.1
symptomatic 090.0
interstitial keratitis 090.3
juvenile neurosyphilis 090.40
late or 2 years or more after birth NEC
090.7
chorioretinitis, choroiditis 090.5 [363.13]
interstitial keratitis 090.3
juvenile neurosyphilis NEC 090.40
latent (without manifestations) 090.6
negative spinal fluid test 090.6
serology, positive 090.6
symptomatic or with manifestations NEC
090.5
interstitial keratitis 090.3

Syphilis, syphilitic — *continued*
conjugal 097.9
tabes 094.0
conjunctiva 095.8 [372.10]
contact V01.6
cord, bladder 094.0
cornea, late 095.8 [370.59]
coronary (artery) 093.89
sclerosis 093.89
coryza 095.8
congenital 090.0
cranial nerve 094.89
cutaneous — *see* Syphilis, skin
dacryocystitis 095.8
degeneration, spinal cord 094.89
d'emblée 095.8
dementia 094.1
paralytica 094.1
juvenilis 090.40
destruction of bone 095.5
dilatation, aorta 093.0
due to blood transfusion 097.9
dura mater 094.89
ear 095.8
inner 095.8
nerve (eighth) 094.86
neurorecurrence 094.86
early NEC 091.0
cardiovascular 093.9
central nervous system 094.9
paresis 094.1
tabes 094.0
latent (without manifestations) (less than 2
years after infection) 092.9
negative spinal fluid test 092.9
serological relapse following treatment
092.0
serology positive 092.9
paresis 094.1
relapse (treated, untreated) 091.7
skin 091.3
symptomatic NEC 091.89
extragenital chancre 091.2
primary, except extragenital chancre
091.0
secondary (*see also* Syphilis, secondary)
091.3
relapse (treated, untreated) 091.7
tabes 094.0
ulcer 091.3
eighth nerve 094.86
endemic, nonvenereal 104.0
endocarditis 093.20
aortic 093.22
mitral 093.21
pulmonary 093.24
tricuspid 093.23
epididymis (late) 095.8
epiglottis 095.8
epiphysitis (congenital) 090.0
esophagus 095.8
Eustachian tube 095.8
exposure to V01.6
eye 095.8 [363.13]
neuromuscular mechanism 094.85
eyelid 095.8 [373.5]
with gumma 095.8 [373.5]
ptosis 094.89
fallopian tube 095.8
fracture 095.5
gallbladder (late) 095.8
gastric 095.8
crisis 094.0
polyposis 095.8
general 097.9
paralysis 094.1
juvenile 090.40
genital (primary) 091.0
glaucoma 095.8
gumma (late) NEC 095.9
cardiovascular system 093.9
central nervous system 094.9
congenital 090.5
heart or artery 093.89
heart 093.89
block 093.89
decompensation 093.89

Syphilis, syphilitic — *continued*
heart — *continued*
disease 093.89
failure 093.89
valve (*see also* Syphilis, endocarditis) 093.20
hemianesthesia 094.89
hemianopsia 095.8
hemiparesis 094.89
hemiplegia 094.89
hepatic artery 093.89
hepatitis 095.3
hepatomegaly 095.3
congenital 090.0
hereditaria tarda (*see also* Syphilis, congenital,
late) 090.7
hereditary (*see also* Syphilis, congenital) 090.9
interstitial keratitis 090.3
Hutchinson's teeth 090.5
hyalitis 095.8
inactive — *see* Syphilis, latent
infantum NEC (*see also* Syphilis, congenital)
090.9
inherited — *see* Syphilis, congenital
internal ear 095.8
intestine (late) 095.8
iris, iritis (secondary) 091.52
late 095.8 [364.11]
joint (late) 095.8
keratitis (congenital) (early) (interstitial) (late)
(parenchymatous) (punctata profunda)
090.3
kidney 095.4
lacrimal apparatus 095.8
laryngeal paralysis 095.8
larynx 095.8
late 097.0
cardiovascular 093.9
central nervous system 094.9
latent or 2 years or more after infection
(without manifestations) 096
negative spinal fluid test 096
serology positive 096
paresis 094.1
specified site NEC 095.8
symptomatic or with symptoms 095.9
tabes 094.0
latent 097.1
central nervous system 094.9
date of infection unspecified 097.1
early or less than 2 years after infection
092.9
late or 2 years or more after infection 096
serology
doubtful
follow-up of latent syphilis 097.1
central nervous system 094.9
date of infection unspecified 097.1
early or less than 2 years after
infection 092.9
late or 2 years or more after
infection 096
positive, only finding 097.1
date of infection unspecified 097.1
early or less than 2 years after
infection 097.1
late or 2 years or more after infection
097.1
lens 095.8
leukoderma 091.3
late 095.8
lienis 095.8
lip 091.3
chancre 091.2
late 095.8
primary 091.2
Lissauer's paralysis 094.1
liver 095.3
secondary 091.62
locomotor ataxia 094.0
lung 095.1
lymphadenitis (secondary) 091.4
lymph gland (early) (secondary) 091.4
late 095.8
macular atrophy of skin 091.3
striated 095.8

Syphilis, syphilitic — *continued*

maternal, affecting fetus or newborn 760.2
  manifest syphilis in newborn — *see* Syphilis, congenital
mediastinum (late) 095.8
meninges (adhesive) (basilar) (brain) (spinal cord) 094.2
meningitis 094.2
  acute 091.81
  congenital 090.42
meningoencephalitis 094.2
meningovascular 094.2
  congenital 090.49
mesarteritis 093.89
  brain 094.89
  spine 094.89
middle ear 095.8
mitral stenosis 093.21
monoplegia 094.89
mouth (secondary) 091.3
  late 095.8
mucocutaneous 091.3
  late 095.8
mucous
  membrane 091.3
    late 095.8
  patches 091.3
    congenital 090.0
mulberry molars 090.5
muscle 095.6
myocardium 093.82
myositis 095.6
nasal sinus 095.8
neonatorum NEC (*see also* Syphilis, congenital) 090.9
nerve palsy (any cranial nerve) 094.89
nervous system, central 094.9
neuritis 095.8
  acoustic nerve 094.86
neurorecidive of retina 094.83
neuroretinitis 094.85
newborn (*see also* Syphilis, congenital) 090.9
nodular superficial 095.8
nonvenereal, endemic 104.0
nose 095.8
  saddle back deformity 090.5
  septum 095.8
    perforated 095.8
occlusive arterial disease 093.89
ophthalmic 095.8 [363.13]
ophthalmoplegia 094.89
optic nerve (atrophy) (neuritis) (papilla) 094.84
orbit (late) 095.8
orchitis 095.8
organic 097.9
osseous (late) 095.5
osteochondritis (congenital) 090.0
osteoporosis 095.5
ovary 095.8
oviduct 095.8
palate 095.8
  gumma 095.8
  perforated 090.5
pancreas (late) 095.8
pancreatitis 095.8
paralysis 094.89
  general 094.1
  juvenile 090.40
paraplegia 094.89
paresis (general) 094.1
  juvenile 090.40
paresthesia 094.89
Parkinson's disease or syndrome 094.82
paroxysmal tachycardia 093.89
pemphigus (congenital) 090.0
penis 091.0
  chancre 091.0
  late 095.8
pericardium 093.81
perichondritis, larynx 095.8
periosteum 095.5
  congenital 090.0
  early 091.61
  secondary 091.61
peripheral nerve 095.8
petrous bone (late) 095.5

pharynx 095.8
  secondary 091.3
pituitary (gland) 095.8
placenta 095.8
pleura (late) 095.8
pneumonia, white 090.0
pontine (lesion) 094.89
portal vein 093.89
primary NEC 091.2
  anal 091.1
  and secondary (*see also* Syphilis, secondary) 091.9
  cardiovascular 093.9
  central nervous system 094.9
  extragenital chancre NEC 091.2
  fingers 091.2
  genital 091.0
  lip 091.2
  specified site NEC 091.2
  tonsils 091.2
prostate 095.8
psychosis (intracranial gumma) 094.89
ptosis (eyelid) 094.89
pulmonary (late) 095.1
  artery 093.89
pulmonum 095.1
pyelonephritis 095.4
recently acquired, symptomatic NEC 091.89
rectum 095.8
respiratory tract 095.8
retina
  late 094.83
  neurorecidive 094.83
retrobulbar neuritis 094.85
salpingitis 095.8
sclera (late) 095.0
sclerosis
  cerebral 094.89
  coronary 093.89
  multiple 094.89
  subacute 094.89
scotoma (central) 095.8
scrotum 095.8
secondary (and primary) 091.9
  adenopathy 091.4
  anus 091.3
  bone 091.61
  cardiovascular 093.9
  central nervous system 094.9
  chorioretinitis, choroiditis 091.51
  hepatitis 091.62
  liver 091.62
  lymphadenitis 091.4
  meningitis, acute 091.81
  mouth 091.3
  mucous membranes 091.3
  periosteum 091.61
  periostitis 091.61
  pharynx 091.3
  relapse (treated) (untreated) 091.7
  skin 091.3
  specified form NEC 091.89
  tonsil 091.3
  ulcer 091.3
  viscera 091.69
  vulva 091.3
seminal vesicle (late) 095.8
seronegative
  with signs or symptoms — *see* Syphilis, by site or stage
seropositive
  with signs or symptoms — *see* Syphilis, by site or stage
  follow-up of latent syphilis — *see* Syphilis, latent
  only finding — *see* Syphilis, latent
seventh nerve (paralysis) 094.89
sinus 095.8
sinusitis 095.8
skeletal system 095.5
skin (early) (secondary) (with ulceration) 091.3
  late or tertiary 095.8
small intestine 095.8
spastic spinal paralysis 094.0
spermatic cord (late) 095.8

spinal (cord) 094.89
  with
    paresis 094.1
    tabes 094.0
spleen 095.8
splenomegaly 095.8
spondylitis 095.5
staphyloma 095.8
stigmata (congenital) 090.5
stomach 095.8
synovium (late) 095.7
tabes dorsalis (early) (late) 094.0
  juvenile 090.40
tabetic type 094.0
  juvenile 090.40
taboparesis 094.1
  juvenile 090.40
tachycardia 093.89
tendon (late) 095.7
tertiary 097.0
  with symptoms 095.8
  cardiovascular 093.9
  central nervous system 094.9
  multiple NEC 095.8
  specified site NEC 095.8
testis 095.8
thorax 095.8
throat 095.8
thymus (gland) 095.8
thyroid (late) 095.8
tongue 095.8
tonsil (lingual) 095.8
  primary 091.2
  secondary 091.3
trachea 095.8
tricuspid valve 093.23
tumor, brain 094.89
tunica vaginalis (late) 095.8
ulcer (any site) (early) (secondary) 091.3
  late 095.9
  perforating 095.9
    foot 094.0
urethra (stricture) 095.8
urogenital 095.8
uterus 095.8
uveal tract (secondary) 091.50
  late 095.8 [363.13]
uveitis (secondary) 091.50
  late 095.8 [363.13]
uvula (late) 095.8
  perforated 095.8
vagina 091.0
  late 095.8
valvulitis NEC 093.20
vascular 093.89
  brain or cerebral 094.89
vein 093.89
  cerebral 094.89
ventriculi 095.8
vesicae urinariae 095.8
viscera (abdominal) 095.2
  secondary 091.69
vitreous (hemorrhage) (opacities) 095.8
vulva 091.0
  late 095.8
  secondary 091.3

Syphiloma 095.9
cardiovascular system 093.9
central nervous system 094.9
circulatory system 093.9
congenital 090.5

Syphilophobia 300.29

Syringadenoma (M8400/0) — *see also* Neoplasm, skin, benign
papillary (M8406/0) — *see* Neoplasm, skin, benign

Syringobulbia 336.0

Syringocarcinoma (M8400/3) — *see* Neoplasm, skin, malignant

Syringocystadenoma (M8400/0) — *see also* Neoplasm, skin, benign
papillary (M8406/0) — *see* Neoplasm, skin, benign

Syringocystoma (M8407/0) — *see* Neoplasm, skin, benign

Syringoma (M8407/0) — *see also* Neoplasm, skin, benign

chondroid (M8940/0) — *see* Neoplasm, by site, benign

Syringomyelia 336.0

Syringomyelitis 323.9

late effect — *see* category 326

Syringomyelocele (*see also* Spina bifida) 741.9 ☑

Syringopontia 336.0

System, systemic — *see also* condition

disease, combined — *see* Degeneration, combined

fibrosclerosing syndrome 710.8

inflammatory response syndrome (SIRS) 995.90

due to

infectious process 995.91

with organ dysfunction 995.92

non-infectious process 995.93

with organ dysfunction 995.94

lupus erythematosus 710.0

inhibitor 286.5

T

Tab — *see* Tag

Tabacism 989.84

Tabacosis 989.84

Tabardillo 080

flea-borne 081.0

louse-borne 080

Tabes, tabetic

with

central nervous system syphilis 094.0

Charcôt's joint 094.0 [713.5]

cord bladder 094.0

crisis, viscera (any) 094.0

paralysis, general 094.1

paresis (general) 094.1

perforating ulcer 094.0

arthropathy 094.0 [713.5]

bladder 094.0

bone 094.0

cerebrospinal 094.0

congenital 090.40

conjugal 094.0

dorsalis 094.0

neurosyphilis 094.0

early 094.0

juvenile 090.40

latent 094.0

mesenterica (*see also* Tuberculosis) 014.8 ☑

paralysis insane, general 094.1

peripheral (nonsyphilitic) 799.89

spasmodic 094.0

not dorsal or dorsalis 343.9

syphilis (cerebrospinal) 094.0

Taboparalysis 094.1

Taboparesis (remission) 094.1

with

Charcôt's joint 094.1 [713.5]

cord bladder 094.1

perforating ulcer 094.1

juvenile 090.40

Tachyalimentation 579.3

Tachyarrhythmia, tachyrhythmia — *see also* Tachycardia

paroxysmal with sinus bradycardia 427.81

Tachycardia 785.0

atrial 427.89

auricular 427.89

AV nodal re-entry (re-entrant) 427.89 ●

newborn 779.82

nodal 427.89

nonparoxysmal atrioventricular 426.89

nonparoxysmal atrioventricular (nodal) 426.89

paroxysmal 427.2

with sinus bradycardia 427.81

atrial (PAT) 427.0

psychogenic 316 [427.0]

atrioventricular (AV) 427.0

psychogenic 316 [427.0]

essential 427.2

junctional 427.0

nodal 427.0

Tachycardia — *continued*

paroxysmal — *continued*

psychogenic 316 [427.2]

atrial 316 [427.0]

supraventricular 316 [427.0]

ventricular 316 [427.1]

supraventricular 427.0

psychogenic 316 [427.0]

ventricular 427.1

psychogenic 316 [427.1]

postoperative 997.1

psychogenic 306.2

sick sinus 427.81

sinoauricular 427.89

sinus 427.89

supraventricular 427.89

ventricular (paroxysmal) 427.1

psychogenic 316 [427.1]

Tachypnea 786.06

hysterical 300.11

newborn (idiopathic) (transitory) 770.6

psychogenic 306.1

transitory, of newborn 770.6

Taenia (infection) (infestation) (*see also* Infestation, taenia) 123.3

diminuta 123.6

echinococcal infestation (*see also* Echinococcus) 122.9

nana 123.6

saginata infestation 123.2

solium (intestinal form) 123.0

larval form 123.1

Taeniasis (intestine) (*see also* Infestation, taenia) 123.3

saginata 123.2

solium 123.0

Taenzer's disease 757.4

Tag (hypertrophied skin) (infected) 701.9

adenoid 474.8

anus 455.9

endocardial (*see also* Endocarditis) 424.90

hemorrhoidal 455.9

hymen 623.8

perineal 624.8

preauricular 744.1

rectum 455.9

sentinel 455.9

skin 701.9

accessory 757.39

anus 455.9

congenital 757.39

preauricular 744.1

rectum 455.9

tonsil 474.8

urethra, urethral 599.84

vulva 624.8

Tahyna fever 062.5

Takayasu (-Onishi) disease or syndrome (pulseless disease) 446.7

Talc granuloma 728.82

in operation wound 998.7 ●

Talcosis 502

Talipes (congenital) 754.70

acquired NEC 736.79

planus 734

asymmetric 754.79

acquired 736.79

calcaneovalgus 754.62

acquired 736.76

calcaneovarus 754.59

acquired 736.76

calcaneus 754.79

acquired 736.76

cavovarus 754.59

acquired 736.75

cavus 754.71

acquired 736.73

equinovalgus 754.69

acquired 736.72

equinovarus 754.51

acquired 736.71

equinus 754.79

acquired, NEC 736.72

percavus 754.71

acquired 736.73

Talipes — *continued*

planovalgus 754.69

acquired 736.79

planus (acquired) (any degree) 734

congenital 754.61

due to rickets 268.1

valgus 754.60

acquired 736.79

varus 754.50

acquired 736.79

Talma's disease 728.85

Tamponade heart (Rose's) (*see also* Pericarditis) 423.9

Tanapox 078.89

Tangier disease (familial high-density lipoprotein deficiency) 272.5

Tank ear 380.12

Tantrum (childhood) (*see also* Disturbance, conduct) 312.1 ☑

Tapeworm (infection) (infestation) (*see also* Infestation, tapeworm) 123.9

Tapia's syndrome 352.6

Tarantism 297.8

Target-oval cell anemia 282.49

Tarlov's cyst 355.9

Tarral-Besnier disease (pityriasis rubra pilaris) 696.4

Tarsalgia 729.2

Tarsal tunnel syndrome 355.5

Tarsitis (eyelid) 373.00

syphilitic 095.8 [373.00]

tuberculous (*see also* Tuberculosis) 017.0 ☑ [373.4]

Tartar (teeth) 523.6

Tattoo (mark) 709.09

Taurodontism 520.2

Taussig-Bing defect, heart, or syndrome (transposition, aorta and overriding pulmonary artery) 745.11

Tay's choroiditis 363.41

Tay-Sachs

amaurotic familial idiocy 330.1

disease 330.1

Taybi's syndrome (otopalatodigital) 759.89

Taylor's

disease (diffuse idiopathic cutaneous atrophy) 701.8

syndrome 625.5

Tear, torn (traumatic) — *see also* Wound, open, by site

anus, anal (sphincter) 863.89

with open wound in cavity 863.99

complicating delivery 664.2 ☑

with mucosa 664.3 ☑

nontraumatic, nonpuerperal 565.0

articular cartilage, old (*see also* Disorder, cartilage, articular) 718.0 ☑

bladder

with

abortion — *see* Abortion, by type, with damage to pelvic organs

ectopic pregnancy (*see also* categories 633.0-633.9) 639.2

molar pregnancy (*see also* categories 630-632) 639.2

following

abortion 639.2

ectopic or molar pregnancy 639.2

obstetrical trauma 665.5 ☑

bowel

with

abortion — *see* Abortion, by type, with damage to pelvic organs

ectopic pregnancy (*see also* categories 633.0-633.9) 639.2

molar pregnancy (*see also* categories 630-632) 639.2

following

abortion 639.2

ectopic or molar pregnancy 639.2

obstetrical trauma 665.5 ☑

Tear, torn — *see also* Wound, open, by site —
  continued
  broad ligament
    with
      abortion — *see* Abortion, by type, with
        damage to pelvic organs
      ectopic pregnancy (*see also* categories
        633.0-633.9) 639.2
      molar pregnancy (*see also* categories 630-
        632) 639.2
    following
      abortion 639.2
      ectopic or molar pregnancy 639.2
    obstetrical trauma 665.6 ☑
  bucket handle (knee) (meniscus) — *see* Tear,
    meniscus
  capsule
    joint — *see* Sprain, by site
    spleen — *see* Laceration, spleen, capsule
  cartilage — *see also* Sprain, by site
    articular, old (*see also* Disorder, cartilage,
      articular) 718.0 ☑
    knee — *see* Tear, meniscus
    semilunar (knee) (current injury) — *see*
      Tear, meniscus
  cervix
    with
      abortion — *see* Abortion, by type, with
        damage to pelvic organs
      ectopic pregnancy (*see also* categories
        633.0-633.9) 639.2
      molar pregnancy (*see also* categories 630-
        632) 639.2
    following
      abortion 639.2
      ectopic or molar pregnancy 639.2
    obstetrical trauma (current) 665.3 ☑
    old 622.3
  internal organ (abdomen, chest, or pelvis) —
    see Injury, internal, by site
  ligament — *see also* Sprain, by site
    with open wound — *see* Wound, open by
      site
  meniscus (knee) (current injury) 836.2
    bucket handle 836.0
      old 717.0
    lateral 836.1
      anterior horn 836.1
        old 717.42
      bucket handle 836.1
        old 717.41
        old 717.40
      posterior horn 836.1
        old 717.43
      specified site NEC 836.1
        old 717.49
    medial 836.0
      anterior horn 836.0
        old 717.1
      bucket handle 836.0
        old 717.0
        old 717.3
      posterior horn 836.0
        old 717.2
    old NEC 717.5
    site other than knee — *see* Sprain, by site
  muscle — *see also* Sprain, by site
    with open wound — *see* Wound, open by
      site
  pelvic
    floor, complicating delivery 664.1 ☑
    organ NEC
      with
        abortion — *see* Abortion, by type, with
          damage to pelvic organs
        ectopic pregnancy (*see also* categories
          633.0-633.9) 639.2
        molar pregnancy (*see also* categories
          630-632) 639.2
      following
        abortion 639.2
        ectopic or molar pregnancy 639.2
      obstetrical trauma 665.5 ☑
  perineum — *see also* Laceration, perineum
    obstetrical trauma 665.5 ☑

Tear, torn — *see also* Wound, open, by site —
  continued
  periurethral tissue
    with
      abortion — *see* Abortion, by type, with
        damage to pelvic organs
      ectopic pregnancy (*see also* categories
        633.0-633.9) 639.2
      molar pregnancy (*see also* categories 630-
        632) 639.2
    following
      abortion 639.2
      ectopic or molar pregnancy 639.2
    obstetrical trauma 665.5 ☑
  rectovaginal septum — *see* Laceration,
    rectovaginal septum
  retina, retinal (recent) (with detachment)
    361.00
    without detachment 361.30
    dialysis (juvenile) (with detachment) 361.04
    giant (with detachment) 361.03
    horseshoe (without detachment) 361.32
    multiple (with detachment) 361.02
      without detachment 361.33
    old
      delimited (partial) 361.06
      partial 361.06
      total or subtotal 361.07
    partial (without detachment)
      giant 361.03
      multiple defects 361.02
      old (delimited) 361.06
      single defect 361.01
    round hole (without detachment) 361.31
    single defect (with detachment) 361.01
    total or subtotal (recent) 361.05
      old 361.07
  rotator cuff (traumatic) 840.4
    current injury 840.4
    degenerative 726.10
    nontraumatic 727.61
  semilunar cartilage, knee (*see also* Tear,
    meniscus) 836.2
    old 717.5
  tendon — *see also* Sprain, by site
    with open wound — *see* Wound, open by
      site
  tentorial, at birth 767.0
  umbilical cord
    affecting fetus or newborn 772.0
    complicating delivery 663.8 ☑
  urethra
    with
      abortion — *see* Abortion, by type, with
        damage to pelvic organs
      ectopic pregnancy (*see also* categories
        633.0-633.9) 639.2
      molar pregnancy (*see also* categories 630-
        632) 639.2
    following
      abortion 639.2
      ectopic or molar pregnancy 639.2
    obstetrical trauma 665.5 ☑
  uterus — *see* Injury, internal, uterus
  vagina — *see* Laceration, vagina
  vessel, from catheter 998.2
  vulva, complicating delivery 664.0 ☑

Tear stone 375.57

Teeth, tooth — *see also* condition
  grinding 306.8

Teething 520.7
  syndrome 520.7

Tegmental syndrome 344.89

Telangiectasia, telangiectasis (verrucous) 448.9
  ataxic (cerebellar) 334.8
  familial 448.0
  hemorrhagic, hereditary (congenital) (senile)
    448.0
  hereditary hemorrhagic 448.0
  retina 362.15
  spider 448.1

Telecanthus (congenital) 743.63

Telescoped bowel or intestine (*see also*
  Intussusception) 560.0

Teletherapy, adverse effect NEC 990

Telogen effluvium 704.02

Temperature
  body, high (of unknown origin) (*see also*
    Pyrexia) 780.6
  cold, trauma from 991.9
    newborn 778.2
    specified effect NEC 991.8
  high
    body (of unknown origin) (*see also* Pyrexia)
      780.6
    trauma from — *see* Heat

Temper tantrum (childhood) (*see also*
  Disturbance, conduct) 312.1 ☑

Temple — *see* condition

Temporal — *see also* condition
  lobe syndrome 310.0

Temporomandibular joint-pain-dysfunction
  syndrome 524.60

Temporosphenoidal — *see* condition

Tendency
  bleeding (*see also* Defect, coagulation) 286.9
  homosexual, ego-dystonic 302.0
  paranoid 301.0
  suicide 300.9

Tenderness
  abdominal (generalized) (localized) 789.6 ☑
  rebound 789.6 ☑
  skin 782.0

Tendinitis, tendonitis (*see also* Tenosynovitis)
  726.90
  Achilles 726.71
  adhesive 726.90
    shoulder 726.0
  calcific 727.82
    shoulder 726.11
  gluteal 726.5
  patellar 726.64
  peroneal 726.79
  pes anserinus 726.61
  psoas 726.5
  tibialis (anterior) (posterior) 726.72
  trochanteric 726.5

Tendon — *see* condition

Tendosynovitis — *see* Tenosynovitis

Tendovaginitis — *see* Tenosynovitis

Tenesmus 787.99
  rectal 787.99
  vesical 788.9

Tenia — *see* Taenia

Teniasis — *see* Taeniasis

Tennis elbow 726.32

Tenonitis — *see also* Tenosynovitis
  eye (capsule) 376.04

Tenontosynovitis — *see* Tenosynovitis

Tenontothecitis — *see* Tenosynovitis

Tenophyte 727.9

Tenosynovitis 727.00
  adhesive 726.90
    shoulder 726.0
  ankle 727.06
  bicipital (calcifying) 726.12
  buttock 727.09
  due to crystals — *see* Arthritis, due to crystals
  elbow 727.09
  finger 727.05
  foot 727.06
  gonococcal 098.51
  hand 727.05
  hip 727.09
  knee 727.09
  radial styloid 727.04
  shoulder 726.10
    adhesive 726.0
  spine 720.1
  supraspinatus 726.10
  toe 727.06
  tuberculous — *see* Tuberculosis, tenosynovitis
  wrist 727.05

Tenovaginitis — *see* Tenosynovitis

Tension
  arterial, high (*see also* Hypertension) 401.9
    without diagnosis of hypertension 796.2

☑ Additional Digit Required — Refer to the Tabular List (Numeric Code Section) for Additional Digit Selection

Tension — *continued*
  headache 307.81
  intraocular (elevated) 365.00
  nervous 799.2
  ocular (elevated) 365.00
  pneumothorax 512.0
    iatrogenic 512.1
    postoperative 512.1
    spontaneous 512.0
  premenstrual 625.4
  state 300.9

Tentorium — *see* condition

Teratencephalus 759.89

Teratism 759.7

Teratoblastoma (malignant) (M9080/3) — *see* Neoplasm, by site, malignant

Teratocarcinoma (M9081/3) — *see also* Neoplasm, by site, malignant
  liver 155.0

Teratoma (solid) (M9080/1) — *see also* Neoplasm, by site, uncertain behavior
  adult (cystic) (M9080/0) — *see* Neoplasm, by site, benign
  and embryonal carcinoma, mixed (M9081/3) — *see* Neoplasm, by site, malignant
  benign (M9080/0) — *see* Neoplasm, by site, benign
  combined with choriocarcinoma (M9101/3) — *see* Neoplasm, by site, malignant
  cystic (adult) (M9080/0) — *see* Neoplasm, by site, benign
  differentiated type (M9080/0) — *see* Neoplasm, by site, benign
  embryonal (M9080/3) — *see also* Neoplasm, by site, malignant
    liver 155.0
  fetal
    sacral, causing fetopelvic disproportion 653.7 ☑
  immature (M9080/3) — *see* Neoplasm, by site, malignant
  liver (M9080/3) 155.0
    adult, benign, cystic, differentiated type or mature (M9080/0) 211.5
  malignant (M9080/3) — *see also* Neoplasm, by site, malignant
    anaplastic type (M9082/3) — *see* Neoplasm, by site, malignant
    intermediate type (M9083/3) — *see* Neoplasm, by site, malignant
    liver (M9080/3) 155.0
    trophoblastic (M9102/3)
      specified site — *see* Neoplasm, by site, malignant
      unspecified site 186.9
    undifferentiated type (M9082/3) — *see* Neoplasm, by site, malignant
  mature (M9080/0) — *see* Neoplasm, by site, benign
  ovary (M9080/0) 220
    embryonal, immature, or malignant (M9080/3) 183.0
  suprasellar (M9080/3) — *see* Neoplasm, by site, malignant
  testis (M9080/3) 186.9
    adult, benign, cystic, differentiated type or mature (M9080/0) 222.0
    undescended 186.0

Terminal care V66.7

Termination
  anomalous — *see also* Malposition, congenital
    portal vein 747.49
    right pulmonary vein 747.42
  pregnancy (legal) (therapeutic) (*see* Abortion, legal) 635.9 ☑
    fetus NEC 779.6
    illegal (*see also* Abortion, illegal) 636.9 ☑

Ternidens diminutus infestation 127.7

Terrors, night (child) 307.46

Terry's syndrome 362.21

Tertiary — *see* condition

Tessellated fundus, retina (tigroid) 362.89

Test(s)
  AIDS virus V72.6

Test(s) — *continued*
  adequacy
    hemodialysis V56.31
    peritoneal dialysis V56.32
  allergen V72.7
  bacterial disease NEC (*see also* Screening, by name of disease) V74.9
  basal metabolic rate V72.6
  blood-alcohol V70.4
  blood-drug V70.4
    for therapeutic drug monitoring V58.83
  blood typing V72.86   ●
  developmental, infant or child V20.2
  Dick V74.8
  fertility V26.21
  genetic V26.32   ▲
    for genetic disease carrier status V26.31 ●
  hearing V72.1
  HIV V72.6
  human immunodeficiency virus V72.6
  Kveim V82.89
  laboratory V72.6
    for medicolegal reason V70.4
  Mantoux (for tuberculosis) V74.1
  mycotic organism V75.4
  parasitic agent NEC V75.8
  paternity V70.4
  peritoneal equilibration V56.32
  pregnancy
    negative result V72.41
    positive ►result◄ V72.42   ▲
      first pregnancy V72.42   ▲
    unconfirmed V72.40
  preoperative V72.84
    cardiovascular V72.81
    respiratory V72.82
    specified NEC V72.83
  procreative management NEC V26.29
  sarcoidosis V82.89
  Schick V74.3
  Schultz-Charlton V74.8
  skin, diagnostic
    allergy V72.7
    bacterial agent NEC (*see also* Screening, by name of disease) V74.9
    Dick V74.8
    hypersensitivity V72.7
    Kveim V82.89
    Mantoux V74.1
    mycotic organism V75.4
    parasitic agent NEC V75.8
    sarcoidosis V82.89
    Schick V74.3
    Schultz-Charlton V74.8
    tuberculin V74.1
  specified type NEC V72.85
  tuberculin V74.1
  vision V72.0
  Wassermann
    positive (*see also* Serology for syphilis, positive) 097.1
    false 795.6

Testicle, testicular, testis — *see also* condition
  feminization (syndrome) 259.5   ▲

Tetanus, tetanic (cephalic) (convulsions) 037
  with
    abortion — *see* Abortion, by type, with sepsis
    ectopic pregnancy (*see also* categories 633.0-633.9) 639.0
    molar pregnancy (*see* categories 630-632) 639.0
  following
    abortion 639.0
    ectopic or molar pregnancy 639.0
  inoculation V03.7
    reaction (due to serum) — *see* Complications, vaccination
  neonatorum 771.3
  puerperal, postpartum, childbirth 670.0 ☑

Tetany, tetanic 781.7
  alkalosis 276.3
  associated with rickets 268.0
  convulsions 781.7
    hysterical 300.11
  functional (hysterical) 300.11

Tetany, tetanic — *continued*
  hyperkinetic 781.7
    hysterical 300.11
  hyperpnea 786.01
    hysterical 300.11
    psychogenic 306.1
  hyperventilation 786.01
    hysterical 300.11
    psychogenic 306.1
  hypocalcemic, neonatal 775.4
  hysterical 300.11
  neonatal 775.4
  parathyroid (gland) 252.1
  parathyroprival 252.1
  postoperative 252.1
  postthyroidectomy 252.1
  pseudotetany 781.7
    hysterical 300.11
  psychogenic 306.1
    specified as conversion reaction 300.11

Tetralogy of Fallot 745.2

Tetraplegia — *see* Quadriplegia

Thailand hemorrhagic fever 065.4

Thalassanemia 282.49

Thalassemia (alpha) (beta) (disease) (Hb-C) (Hb-D) (Hb-E) (Hb-H) (Hb-I) (high fetal gene) (high fetal hemoglobin) (intermedia) (major) (minima) (minor) (mixed) (trait) (with other hemoglobinopathy) 282.49
  Hb-S (without crisis) 282.41
    with
      crisis 282.42
      vaso-occlusive pain 282.42
  sickle-cell (without crisis) 282.41
    with
      crisis 282.42
      vaso-occlusive pain 282.42

Thalassemic variants 282.49

Thaysen-Gee disease (nontropical sprue) 579.0

Thecoma (M8600/0) 220
  malignant (M8600/3) 183.0

Thelarche, precocious 259.1

Thelitis 611.0
  puerperal, postpartum 675.0 ☑

Therapeutic — *see* condition

Therapy V57.9
  blood transfusion, without reported diagnosis V58.2
  breathing V57.0
  chemotherapy, ►antineoplastic◄ V58.11   ▲
    fluoride V07.31
    prophylactic NEC V07.39
  dialysis (intermittent) (treatment)
    extracorporeal V56.0
    peritoneal V56.8
    renal V56.0
    specified type NEC V56.8
  exercise NEC V57.1
    breathing V57.0
  extracorporeal dialysis (renal) V56.0
  fluoride prophylaxis V07.31
  hemodialysis V56.0
  hormone replacement (postmenopausal) V07.4
  immunotherapy antineoplastic V58.12   ●
  long term oxygen therapy V46.2
  occupational V57.21
  orthoptic V57.4
  orthotic V57.81
  peritoneal dialysis V56.8
  physical NEC V57.1
  postmenopausal hormone replacement V07.4
  radiation V58.0
  speech V57.3
  vocational V57.22

Thermalgesia 782.0

Thermalgia 782.0

Thermanalgesia 782.0

Thermanesthesia 782.0

Thermic — *see* condition

Thermography (abnormal) 793.9
  breast 793.89

Thermoplegia 992.0

Thesaurismosis
amyloid 277.3
bilirubin 277.4
calcium 275.40
cystine 270.0
glycogen (see also Disease, glycogen storage) 271.0
kerasin 272.7
lipoid 272.7
melanin 255.4
phosphatide 272.7
urate 274.9

Thiaminic deficiency 265.1
with beriberi 265.0

Thibierge-Weissenbach syndrome (cutaneous systemic sclerosis) 710.1

Thickened endometrium 793.5

Thickening
bone 733.99
extremity 733.99
breast 611.79
hymen 623.3
larynx 478.79
nail 703.8
congenital 757.5
periosteal 733.99
pleura (see also Pleurisy) 511.0
skin 782.8
subepiglottic 478.79
tongue 529.8
valve, heart — see Endocarditis

Thiele syndrome 724.6

Thigh — see condition

Thinning vertebra (see also Osteoporosis) 733.00

Thirst, excessive 783.5
due to deprivation of water 994.3

Thomsen's disease 359.2

Thomson's disease (congenital poikiloderma) 757.33

Thoracic — see also condition
kidney 753.3
outlet syndrome 353.0
stomach — see Hernia, diaphragm

Thoracogastroschisis (congenital) 759.89

Thoracopagus 759.4

Thoracoschisis 756.3

Thoracoscopic surgical procedure converted to open procedure V64.42

Thorax — see condition

Thorn's syndrome (see also Disease, renal) 593.9

Thornwaldt's, Tornwaldt's
bursitis (pharyngeal) 478.29
cyst 478.26
disease (pharyngeal bursitis) 478.29

Thorson-Biörck syndrome (malignant carcinoid) 259.2

Threadworm (infection) (infestation) 127.4

Threatened
abortion or miscarriage 640.0 ☑
with subsequent abortion (see also Abortion, spontaneous) 634.9 ☑
affecting fetus 762.1
labor 644.1 ☑
affecting fetus or newborn 761.8
premature 644.0 ☑
miscarriage 640.0 ☑
affecting fetus 762.1
premature
delivery 644.2 ☑
affecting fetus or newborn 761.8
labor 644.0 ☑
before 22 completed weeks gestation 640.0 ☑

Three-day fever 066.0

Threshers' lung 495.0

Thrix annulata (congenital) 757.4

Throat — see condition

Thrombasthenia (Glanzmann's) (hemorrhagic) (hereditary) 287.1

Thromboangiitis 443.1
obliterans (general) 443.1
cerebral 437.1

Thromboangiitis — continued
obliterans — continued
vessels
brain 437.1
spinal cord 437.1

Thromboarteritis — see Arteritis

Thromboasthenia (Glanzmann's) (hemorrhagic) (hereditary) 287.1

Thrombocytasthenia (Glanzmann's) 287.1

Thrombocythemia (essential) (hemorrhagic) (primary) (M9962/1) 238.7
idiopathic (M9962/1) 238.7

Thrombocytopathy (dystrophic) (granulopenic) 287.1

Thrombocytopenia, thrombocytopenic 287.5
with
absent radii (TAR) syndrome 287.33 ●
giant hemangioma 287.39 ●
amegakaryocytic, congenital 287.33 ▲
congenital 287.33 ▲
cyclic 287.39 ▲
dilutional 287.4
due to
drugs 287.4
extracorporeal circulation of blood 287.4
massive blood transfusion 287.4
platelet alloimmunization 287.4
essential 287.30 ▲
hereditary 287.33 ▲
Kasabach-Merritt 287.39 ▲
neonatal, transitory 776.1
due to
exchange transfusion 776.1
idiopathic maternal thrombocytopenia 776.1
isoimmunization 776.1
primary 287.30 ▲
puerperal, postpartum 666.3 ☑
purpura (see also Purpura, thrombocytopenic) 287.30 ▲
thrombotic 446.6
secondary 287.4
sex-linked 287.39 ▲

Thrombocytosis, essential 289.9

Thromboembolism — see Embolism

Thrombopathy (Bernard-Soulier) 287.1
constitutional 286.4
Willebrand-Jürgens (angiohemophilia) 286.4

Thrombopenia (see also Thrombocytopenia) 287.5

Thrombophlebitis 451.9
antecubital vein 451.82
antepartum (superficial) 671.2 ☑
affecting fetus or newborn 760.3
deep 671.3 ☑
arm 451.89
deep 451.83
superficial 451.82
breast, superficial 451.89
cavernous (venous) sinus — see
Thrombophlebitis, intracranial venous sinus
cephalic vein 451.82
cerebral (sinus) (vein) 325
late effect — see category 326
nonpyogenic 437.6
in pregnancy or puerperium 671.5 ☑
late effect — see Late effect(s) (of) cerebrovascular disease
due to implanted device — see Complications, due to (presence of) any device, implant or graft classified to 996.0-996.5 NEC
during or resulting from a procedure NEC 997.2
femoral 451.11
femoropopliteal 451.19
following infusion, perfusion, or transfusion 999.2
hepatic (vein) 451.89
idiopathic, recurrent 453.1
iliac vein 451.81
iliofemoral 451.11
intracranial venous sinus (any) 325
late effect — see category 326
nonpyogenic 437.6
in pregnancy or puerperium 671.5 ☑

Thrombophlebitis — continued
intracranial venous sinus — continued
nonpyogenic — continued
late effect — see Late effect(s) (of) cerebrovascular disease
jugular vein 451.89
lateral (venous) sinus — see Thrombophlebitis, intracranial venous sinus
leg 451.2
deep (vessels) 451.19
femoral vein 451.11
specified vessel NEC 451.19
superficial (vessels) 451.0
femoral vein 451.11
longitudinal (venous) sinus — see
Thrombophlebitis, intracranial venous sinus
lower extremity 451.2
deep (vessels) 451.19
femoral vein 451.11
specified vessel NEC 451.19
superficial (vessels) 451.0
migrans, migrating 453.1
pelvic
with
abortion — see Abortion, by type, with sepsis
ectopic pregnancy (see also categories 633.0-633.9) 639.0
molar pregnancy (see also categories 630-632) 639.0
following
abortion 639.0
ectopic or molar pregnancy 639.0
puerperal 671.4 ☑
popliteal vein 451.19
portal (vein) 572.1
postoperative 997.2
pregnancy (superficial) 671.2 ☑
affecting fetus or newborn 760.3
deep 671.3 ☑
puerperal, postpartum, childbirth (extremities) (superficial) 671.2 ☑
deep 671.4 ☑
pelvic 671.4 ☑
specified site NEC 671.5 ☑
radial vein 451.83
saphenous (greater) (lesser) 451.0
sinus (intracranial) — see Thrombophlebitis, intracranial venous sinus
specified site NEC 451.89
tibial vein 451.19

Thrombosis, thrombotic (marantic) (multiple) (progressive) (septic) (vein) (vessel) 453.9
with childbirth or during the puerperium — see
Thrombosis, puerperal, postpartum
antepartum — see Thrombosis, pregnancy
aorta, aortic 444.1
abdominal 444.0
bifurcation 444.0
saddle 444.0
terminal 444.0
thoracic 444.1
valve — see Endocarditis, aortic
apoplexy (see also Thrombosis, brain) 434.0 ☑
late effect — see Late effect(s) (of) cerebrovascular disease
appendix, septic — see Appendicitis, acute
arteriolar-capillary platelet, disseminated 446.6
artery, arteries (postinfectional) 444.9
auditory, internal 433.8 ☑
basilar (see also Occlusion, artery, basilar) 433.0 ☑
carotid (common) (internal) (see also Occlusion, artery, carotid) 433.1 ☑
with other precerebral artery 433.3 ☑
cerebellar (anterior inferior) (posterior inferior) (superior) 433.8 ☑
cerebral (see also Thrombosis, brain) 434.0 ☑
choroidal (anterior) 433.8 ☑
communicating posterior 433.8 ☑
coronary (see also Infarct, myocardium) 410.9 ☑
without myocardial infarction 411.81
due to syphilis 093.89

Thrombophlebitis — *continued*
  artery, arteries — *continued*
    coronary (*see also* Infarct, myocardium) — *continued*
      healed or specified as old 412
    extremities 444.22
      lower 444.22
      upper 444.21
    femoral 444.22
    hepatic 444.89
    hypophyseal 433.8 ☑
    meningeal, anterior or posterior 433.8 ☑
    mesenteric (with gangrene) 557.0
    ophthalmic (*see also* Occlusion, retina) 362.30
    pontine 433.8 ☑
    popliteal 444.22
    precerebral — *see* Occlusion, artery, precerebral NEC
    pulmonary 415.19
      iatrogenic 415.11
      postoperative 415.11
    renal 593.81
    retinal (*see also* Occlusion, retina) 362.30
    specified site NEC 444.89
    spinal, anterior or posterior 433.8 ☑
    traumatic (complication) (early) (*see also* Injury, blood vessel, by site) 904.9
    vertebral (*see also* Occlusion, artery, vertebral) 433.2 ☑
      with other precerebral artery 433.3 ☑
  atrial (endocardial) 424.90
    due to syphilis 093.89
  auricular (*see also* Infarct, myocardium) 410.9 ☑
  axillary (vein) 453.8
  basilar (artery) (*see also* Occlusion, artery, basilar) 433.0 ☑
  bland NEC 453.9
  brain (artery) (stem) 434.0 ☑
    due to syphilis 094.89
    iatrogenic 997.02
    late effect — *see* Late effect(s) (of) cerebrovascular disease
    postoperative 997.02
    puerperal, postpartum, childbirth 674.0 ☑
    sinus (*see also* Thrombosis, intracranial venous sinus) 325
  capillary 448.9
    arteriolar, generalized 446.6
  cardiac (*see also* Infarct, myocardium) 410.9 ☑
    due to syphilis 093.89
    healed or specified as old 412
    valve — *see* Endocarditis
  carotid (artery) (common) (internal) (*see also* Occlusion, artery, carotid) 433.1 ☑
    with other precerebral artery 433.3 ☑
  cavernous sinus (venous) — *see* Thrombosis, intracranial venous sinus
  cerebellar artery (anterior inferior) (posterior inferior) (superior) 433.8 ☑
    late effect — *see* Late effect(s) (of) cerebrovascular disease
  cerebral (arteries) (*see also* Thrombosis, brain) 434.0 ☑
    late effect — *see* Late effect(s) (of) cerebrovascular disease
  coronary (artery) (*see also* Infarct, myocardium) 410.9 ☑
    without myocardial infarction 411.81
    due to syphilis 093.89
    healed or specified as old 412
  corpus cavernosum 607.82
  cortical (*see also* Thrombosis, brain) 434.0 ☑
  due to (presence of) any device, implant, or graft classifiable to 996.0-996.5 — *see* Complications, due to (presence of) any device, implant, or graft classifiable to 996.0-996.5 NEC
  effort 453.8
  endocardial — *see* Infarct, myocardium
  eye (*see also* Occlusion, retina) 362.30
  femoral (vein) 453.8
    with inflammation or phlebitis 451.11
    artery 444.22
    deep 453.41
  genital organ, male 608.83

Thrombosis, thrombotic — *continued*
  heart (chamber) (*see also* Infarct, myocardium) 410.9 ☑
  hepatic (vein) 453.0
    artery 444.89
    infectional or septic 572.1
  iliac (vein) 453.8
    with inflammation or phlebitis 451.81
    artery (common) (external) (internal) 444.81
  inflammation, vein — *see* Thrombophlebitis
  internal carotid artery (*see also* Occlusion, artery, carotid) 433.1 ☑
    with other precerebral artery 433.3 ☑
  intestine (with gangrene) 557.0
  intracranial (*see also* Thrombosis, brain) 434.0 ☑
    venous sinus (any) 325
      nonpyogenic origin 437.6
        in pregnancy or puerperium 671.5 ☑
  intramural (*see also* Infarct, myocardium) 410.9 ☑
    without
      cardiac condition 429.89
      coronary artery disease 429.89
      myocardial infarction 429.89
    healed or specified as old 412
  jugular (bulb) 453.8
  kidney 593.81
    artery 593.81
  lateral sinus (venous) — *see* Thrombosis, intracranial venous sinus
  leg 453.8
    with inflammation or phlebitis — *see* Thrombophlebitis
    deep (vessels) 453.40
      lower (distal) 453.42
      upper (proximal) 453.41
    superficial (vessels) 453.8
  liver (venous) 453.0
    artery 444.89
    infectional or septic 572.1
    portal vein 452
  longitudinal sinus (venous) — *see* Thrombosis, intracranial venous sinus
  lower extremity 453.8
    deep vessels 453.40
      calf 453.42
      distal (lower leg) 453.42
      femoral 453.41
      iliac 453.41
      lower leg 453.42
      peroneal 453.42
      popliteal 453.41
      proximal (upper leg) 453.41
      thigh 453.41
      tibial 453.42
  lung 415.19
    iatrogenic 415.11
    postoperative 415.11
  marantic, dural sinus 437.6
  meninges (brain) (*see also* Thrombosis, brain) 434.0 ☑
  mesenteric (artery) (with gangrene) 557.0
    vein (inferior) (superior) 557.0
  mitral — *see* Insufficiency, mitral
  mural (heart chamber) (*see also* Infarct, myocardium) 410.9 ☑
    without
      cardiac condition 429.89
      coronary artery disease 429.89
      myocardial infarction 429.89
    due to syphilis 093.89
    following myocardial infarction 429.79
    healed or specified as old 412
  omentum (with gangrene) 557.0
  ophthalmic (artery) (*see also* Occlusion, retina) 362.30
  pampiniform plexus (male) 608.83
    female 620.8
  parietal (*see also* Infarct, myocardium) 410.9 ☑
  penis, penile 607.82
  peripheral arteries 444.22
    lower 444.22
    upper 444.21
  platelet 446.6
  portal 452
    due to syphilis 093.89

Thrombosis, thrombotic — *continued*
  portal — *continued*
    infectional or septic 572.1
  precerebral artery — *see also* Occlusion, artery, precerebral NEC
  pregnancy 671.9 ☑
    deep (vein) 671.3 ☑
    superficial (vein) 671.2 ☑
  puerperal, postpartum, childbirth 671.9 ☑
    brain (artery) 674.0 ☑
      venous 671.5 ☑
    cardiac 674.8 ☑
    cerebral (artery) 674.0 ☑
      venous 671.5 ☑
    deep (vein) 671.4 ☑
    intracranial sinus (nonpyogenic) (venous) 671.5 ☑
    pelvic 671.4 ☑
    pulmonary (artery) 673.2 ☑
    specified site NEC 671.5 ☑
    superficial 671.2 ☑
  pulmonary (artery) (vein) 415.19
    iatrogenic 415.11
    postoperative 415.11
  renal (artery) 593.81
    vein 453.3
  resulting from presence of shunt or other internal prosthetic device — *see* Complications, due to (presence of) any device, implant, or graft classifiable to 996.0-996.5 NEC
  retina, retinal (artery) 362.30
    arterial branch 362.32
    central 362.31
    partial 362.33
    vein
      central 362.35
      tributary (branch) 362.36
  scrotum 608.83
  seminal vesicle 608.83
  sigmoid (venous) sinus (*see* Thrombosis, intracranial venous sinus) 325
  silent NEC 453.9
  sinus, intracranial (venous) (any) (*see also* Thrombosis, intracranial venous sinus) 325
  softening, brain (*see also* Thrombosis, brain) 434.0 ☑
  specified site NEC 453.8
  spermatic cord 608.83
  spinal cord 336.1
    due to syphilis 094.89
    in pregnancy or puerperium 671.5 ☑
    pyogenic origin 324.1
      late effect — *see* category 326
  spleen, splenic 289.59
    artery 444.89
  testis 608.83
  traumatic (complication) (early) (*see also* Injury, blood vessel, by site) 904.9
  tricuspid — *see* Endocarditis, tricuspid
  tumor — *see* Neoplasm, by site ●
  tunica vaginalis 608.83
  umbilical cord (vessels) 663.6 ☑
    affecting fetus or newborn 762.6
  vas deferens 608.83
  vein
    deep 453.40 ▲
    lower extremity — *see* Thrombosis, lower extremity
  vena cava (inferior) (superior) 453.2

Thrombus — *see* Thrombosis

Thrush 112.0
  newborn 771.7

Thumb — *see also* condition
  gamekeeper's 842.12
  sucking (child problem) 307.9

Thygeson's superficial punctate keratitis 370.21

Thymergasia (*see also* Psychosis, affective) 296.80

Thymitis 254.8

Thymoma (benign) (M8580/0) 212.6
  malignant (M8580/3) 164.0

Thymus, thymic (gland) — *see* condition

Thyrocele (*see also* Goiter) 240.9
Thyroglossal — *see also* condition
   cyst 759.2
   duct, persistent 759.2
Thyroid (body) (gland) — *see also* condition
   lingual 759.2
Thyroiditis 245.9
   acute (pyogenic) (suppurative) 245.0
      nonsuppurative 245.0
   autoimmune 245.2
   chronic (nonspecific) (sclerosing) 245.8
      fibrous 245.3
      lymphadenoid 245.2
      lymphocytic 245.2
      lymphoid 245.2
   complicating pregnancy, childbirth, or
      puerperium 648.1 ☑
   de Quervain's (subacute granulomatous) 245.1
   fibrous (chronic) 245.3
   giant (cell) (follicular) 245.1
   granulomatous (de Quervain's) (subacute)
      245.1
   Hashimoto's (struma lymphomatosa) 245.2
   iatrogenic 245.4
   invasive (fibrous) 245.3
   ligneous 245.3
   lymphocytic (chronic) 245.2
   lymphoid 245.2
   lymphomatous 245.2
   pseudotuberculous 245.1
   pyogenic 245.0
   radiation 245.4
   Riedel's (ligneous) 245.3
   subacute 245.1
   suppurative 245.0
   tuberculous (*see also* Tuberculosis) 017.5 ☑
   viral 245.1
   woody 245.3
Thyrolingual duct, persistent 759.2
Thyromegaly 240.9
Thyrotoxic
   crisis or storm (*see also* Thyrotoxicosis)
      242.9 ☑
   heart failure (*see also* Thyrotoxicosis)
      242.9 ☑ [425.7]
Thyrotoxicosis 242.9 ☑

> *Note* — Use the following fifth-digit
> subclassification with category 242:
>
>   0   *without mention of thyrotoxic crisis or*
>   *storm*
>
>   1   *with mention of thyrotoxic crisis or*
>   *storm*

   with
      goiter (diffuse) 242.0 ☑
         adenomatous 242.3 ☑
            multinodular 242.2 ☑
            uninodular 242.1 ☑
         nodular 242.3 ☑
            multinodular 242.2 ☑
            uninodular 242.1 ☑
      infiltrative
         dermopathy 242.0 ☑
         ophthalmopathy 242.0 ☑
      thyroid acropachy 242.0 ☑
   complicating pregnancy, childbirth, or
      puerperium 648.1 ☑
   due to
      ectopic thyroid nodule 242.4 ☑
      ingestion of (excessive) thyroid material
         242.8 ☑
      specified cause NEC 242.8 ☑
   factitia 242.8 ☑
   heart 242.9 ☑ *[425.7]*
   neonatal (transient) 775.3
TIA (transient ischemic attack) 435.9
   with transient neurologic deficit 435.9
   late effect — *see* Late effect(s) (of)
      cerebrovascular disease
Tibia vara 732.4
Tic 307.20
   breathing 307.20
   child problem 307.21

Tic — *continued*
   compulsive 307.22
   convulsive 307.20
   degenerative (generalized) (localized) 333.3
      facial 351.8
   douloureux (*see also* Neuralgia, trigeminal)
      350.1
      atypical 350.2
   habit 307.20
      chronic (motor or vocal) 307.22
      transient (of childhood) 307.21
   lid 307.20
      transient (of childhood) 307.21
   motor-verbal 307.23
   occupational 300.89
   orbicularis 307.20
      transient (of childhood) 307.21
   organic origin 333.3
   postchoreic — *see* Chorea
   psychogenic 307.20
      compulsive 307.22
   salaam 781.0
   spasm 307.20
      chronic (motor or vocal) 307.22
      transient (of childhood) 307.21
Tick (-borne) fever NEC 066.1
   American mountain 066.1
   Colorado 066.1
   hemorrhagic NEC 065.3
      Crimean 065.0
      Kyasanur Forest 065.2
      Omsk 065.1
   mountain 066.1
   nonxanthematous 066.1
Tick-bite fever NEC 066.1
   African 087.1
   Colorado (virus) 066.1
   Rocky Mountain 082.0
Tick paralysis 989.5
Tics and spasms, compulsive 307.22
Tietze's disease or syndrome 733.6
Tight, tightness
   anus 564.89
   chest 786.59
   fascia (lata) 728.9
   foreskin (congenital) 605
   hymen 623.3
   introitus (acquired) (congenital) 623.3
   rectal sphincter 564.89
   tendon 727.81
      Achilles (heel) 727.81
   urethral sphincter 598.9
Tilting vertebra 737.9
Timidity, child 313.21
Tinea (intersecta) (tarsi) 110.9
   amiantacea 110.0
   asbestina 110.0
   barbae 110.0
   beard 110.0
   black dot 110.0
   blanca 111.2
   capitis 110.0
   corporis 110.5
   cruris 110.3
   decalvans 704.09
   flava 111.0
   foot 110.4
   furfuracea 111.0
   imbricata (Tokelau) 110.5
   lepothrix 039.0
   manuum 110.2
   microsporic (*see also* Dermatophytosis) 110.9
   nigra 111.1
   nodosa 111.2
   pedis 110.4
   scalp 110.0
   specified site NEC 110.8
   sycosis 110.0
   tonsurans 110.0
   trichophytic (*see also* Dermatophytosis) 110.9
   unguium 110.1
   versicolor 111.0
Tingling sensation (*see also* Disturbance,
      sensation) 782.0
Tin-miners' lung 503

Tinnitus (aurium) 388.30
   audible 388.32
   objective 388.32
   subjective 388.31
Tipping
   pelvis 738.6
      with disproportion (fetopelvic) 653.0 ☑
         affecting fetus or newborn 763.1
         causing obstructed labor 660.1 ☑
            affecting fetus or newborn 763.1
   teeth 524.33
Tiredness 780.79
Tissue — *see* condition
Tobacco
   abuse (affecting health) NEC (*see also* Abuse,
      drugs, nondependent) 305.1
   heart 989.84
Tobias' syndrome (carcinoma, pulmonary apex)
      (M8010/3) 162.3
Tocopherol deficiency 269.1
Todd's
   cirrhosis — *see* Cirrhosis, biliary
   paralysis (postepileptic transitory paralysis)
      344.89
Toe — *see* condition
Toilet, artificial opening (*see also* Attention to,
      artificial, opening) V55.9
Tokelau ringworm 110.5
Tollwut 071
Tolosa-Hunt syndrome 378.55
Tommaselli's disease
   correct substance properly administered 599.7
   overdose or wrong substance given or taken
      961.4
Tongue — *see also* condition
   worms 134.1
Tongue tie 750.0
Toni-Fanconi syndrome (cystinosis) 270.0
Tonic pupil 379.46
Tonsil — *see* condition
Tonsillitis (acute) (catarrhal) (croupous)
      (follicular) (gangrenous) (infective) (lacunar)
      (lingual) (malignant) (membranous)
      (phlegmonous) (pneumococcal)
      (pseudomembranous) (purulent) (septic)
      (staphylococcal) (subacute) (suppurative)
      (toxic) (ulcerative) (vesicular) (viral) 463
   with influenza, flu, or grippe 487.1
   chronic 474.00
   diphtheritic (membranous) 032.0
   hypertrophic 474.00
   influenzal 487.1
   parenchymatous 475
   streptococcal 034.0
   tuberculous (*see also* Tuberculosis) 012.8 ☑
   Vincent's 101
Tonsillopharyngitis 465.8
Tooth, teeth — *see* condition
Toothache 525.9
Topagnosis 782.0
Tophi (gouty) 274.0
   ear 274.81
   heart 274.82
   specified site NEC 274.82
Torn — *see* Tear, torn
Tornwaldt's bursitis (disease) (pharyngeal
      bursitis) 478.29
   cyst 478.26
Torpid liver 573.9
Torsion
   accessory tube 620.5
   adnexa (female) 620.5
   aorta (congenital) 747.29
      acquired 447.1
   appendix epididymis 608.2
   bile duct 576.8
      with calculus, choledocholithiasis or stones
         — *see* Choledocholithiasis
      congenital 751.69
   bowel, colon, or intestine 560.2
   cervix (*see also* Malposition, uterus) 621.6
   duodenum 537.3

Torsion — *continued*
  dystonia — *see* Dystonia, torsion
  epididymis 608.2
    appendix 608.2
  fallopian tube 620.5
  gallbladder (*see also* Disease, gallbladder)
      575.8
    congenital 751.69
  gastric 537.89
  hydatid of Morgagni (female) 620.5
  kidney (pedicle) 593.89
  Meckel's diverticulum (congenital) 751.0
  mesentery 560.2
  omentum 560.2
  organ or site, congenital NEC — *see* Anomaly,
      specified type NEC
  ovary (pedicle) 620.5
    congenital 752.0
  oviduct 620.5
  penis 607.89
    congenital 752.69
  renal 593.89
  spasm — *see* Dystonia, torsion
  spermatic cord 608.2
  spleen 289.59
  testicle, testis 608.2
  tibia 736.89
  umbilical cord — *see* Compression, umbilical
      cord
  uterus (*see also* Malposition, uterus) 621.6
Torticollis (intermittent) (spastic) 723.5
  congenital 754.1
    sternomastoid 754.1
  due to birth injury 767.8
  hysterical 300.11
  ocular 781.93
  psychogenic 306.0
    specified as conversion reaction 300.11
  rheumatic 723.5
  rheumatoid 714.0
  spasmodic 333.83
  traumatic, current NEC 847.0
Tortuous
  artery 447.1
  fallopian tube 752.19
  organ or site, congenital NEC — *see* Distortion
  renal vessel (congenital) 747.62
  retina vessel (congenital) 743.58
    acquired 362.17
  ureter 593.4
  urethra 599.84
  vein — *see* Varicose, vein
Torula, torular (infection) 117.5
  histolytica 117.5
  lung 117.5
Torulosis 117.5
Torus
  fracture
    fibula 823.41
      with tibia 823.42
    radius 813.45
    tibia 823.40
      with fibula 823.42
  mandibularis 526.81
  palatinus 526.81
Touch, vitreous 997.99
Touraine's syndrome (hereditary osteo-
    onychodysplasia) 756.89
Touraine-Solente-Golé syndrome
    (acropachyderma) 757.39
Tourette's disease (motor-verbal tic) 307.23
Tower skull 756.0
  with exophthalmos 756.0
Toxemia 799.89
  with
    abortion — *see* Abortion, by type, with
        toxemia
  bacterial — *see* Septicemia
  biliary (*see also* Disease, biliary) 576.8
  burn — *see* Burn, by site
  congenital NEC 779.89
  eclamptic 642.6 ☑
    with pre-existing hypertension 642.7 ☑
  erysipelatous (*see also* Erysipelas) 035
  fatigue 799.89

Toxemia — *continued*
  fetus or newborn NEC 779.89
  food (*see also* Poisoning, food) 005.9
  gastric 537.89
  gastrointestinal 558.2
  intestinal 558.2
  kidney (*see also* Disease, renal) 593.9
  lung 518.89
  malarial NEC (*see also* Malaria) 084.6
  maternal (of pregnancy), affecting fetus or
      newborn 760.0
  myocardial — *see* Myocarditis, toxic
  of pregnancy (mild) (pre-eclamptic) 642.4 ☑
    with
      convulsions 642.6 ☑
      pre-existing hypertension 642.7 ☑
    affecting fetus or newborn 760.0
    severe 642.5 ☑
  pre-eclamptic — *see* Toxemia, of pregnancy
  puerperal, postpartum — *see* Toxemia, of
      pregnancy
  pulmonary 518.89
  renal (*see also* Disease, renal) 593.9
  septic (*see also* Septicemia) 038.9
  small intestine 558.2
  staphylococcal 038.10
    aureus 038.11
    due to food 005.0
    specified organism NEC 038.19
  stasis 799.89
  stomach 537.89
  uremic (*see also* Uremia) 586
  urinary 586
Toxemica cerebropathia psychica (nonalcoholic)
    294.0
  alcoholic 291.1
Toxic (poisoning) — *see also* condition
  from drug or poison — *see* Table of Drugs and
      Chemicals
  oil syndrome 710.5
  shock syndrome 040.82
  thyroid (gland) (*see also* Thyrotoxicosis)
      242.9 ☑
Toxicemia — *see* Toxemia
Toxicity
  dilantin
    asymptomatic 796.0
    symptomatic — *see* Table of Drugs and
        Chemicals
  drug
    asymptomatic 796.0
    symptomatic — *see* Table of Drugs and
        Chemicals
  fava bean 282.2
  from drug or poison
    asymptomatic 796.0
    symptomatic — *see* Table of Drugs and
        Chemicals
Toxicosis (*see also* Toxemia) 799.89
  capillary, hemorrhagic 287.0
Toxinfection 799.89
  gastrointestinal 558.2
Toxocariasis 128.0
Toxoplasma infection, generalized 130.9
Toxoplasmosis (acquired) 130.9
  with pneumonia 130.4
  congenital, active 771.2
  disseminated (multisystemic) 130.8
  maternal
    with suspected damage to fetus affecting
        management of pregnancy 655.4 ☑
    affecting fetus or newborn 760.2
      manifest toxoplasmosis in fetus or
          newborn 771.2
  multiple sites 130.8
  multisystemic disseminated 130.8
  specified site NEC 130.7
Trabeculation, bladder 596.8
Trachea — *see* condition
Tracheitis (acute) (catarrhal) (infantile)
    (membranous) (plastic) (pneumococcal)
    (septic) (suppurative) (viral) 464.10
  with
    bronchitis 490

Tracheitis — *continued*
  with — *continued*
    bronchitis — *continued*
      acute or subacute 466.0
      chronic 491.8
      tuberculosis — *see* Tuberculosis,
          pulmonary
    laryngitis (acute) 464.20
      with obstruction 464.21
      chronic 476.1
      tuberculous (*see also* Tuberculosis,
          larynx) 012.3 ☑
    obstruction 464.11
  chronic 491.8
    with
      bronchitis (chronic) 491.8
      laryngitis (chronic) 476.1
    due to external agent — *see* Condition,
        respiratory, chronic, due to
  diphtheritic (membranous) 032.3
  due to external agent — *see* Inflammation,
      respiratory, upper, due to
  edematous 464.11
  influenzal 487.1
  streptococcal 034.0
  syphilitic 095.8
  tuberculous (*see also* Tuberculosis) 012.8 ☑
Trachelitis (nonvenereal) (*see also* Cervicitis)
    616.0
  trichomonal 131.09
Tracheobronchial — *see* condition
Tracheobronchitis (*see also* Bronchitis) 490
  acute or subacute 466.0
    with bronchospasm or obstruction 466.0
  chronic 491.8
  influenzal 487.1
  senile 491.8
Tracheobronchomegaly (congenital) 748.3 ●
  with bronchiectasis 494.0   ●
    with (acute) exacerbation 494.1   ●
  acquired 519.1   ●
    with bronchiectasis 494.0   ●
      with (acute) exacerbation 494.1   ●
Tracheobronchopneumonitis — *see* Pneumonia,
    broncho
Tracheocele (external) (internal) 519.1
  congenital 748.3
Tracheomalacia 519.1
  congenital 748.3
Tracheopharyngitis (acute) 465.8
  chronic 478.9
    due to external agent — *see* Condition,
        respiratory, chronic, due to
  due to external agent — *see* Inflammation,
      respiratory, upper, due to
Tracheostenosis 519.1
  congenital 748.3
Tracheostomy
  attention to V55.0
  complication 519.00
  hemorrhage 519.09
  infection 519.01
  malfunctioning 519.02
  obstruction 519.09
  sepsis 519.01
  status V44.0
  stenosis 519.02
Trachoma, trachomatous 076.9
  active (stage) 076.1
  contraction of conjunctiva 076.1
  dubium 076.0
  healed or late effect 139.1
  initial (stage) 076.0
  Türck's (chronic catarrhal laryngitis) 476.0
Trachyphonia 784.49
Training
  insulin pump V65.46
  orthoptic V57.4
  orthotic V57.81
Train sickness 994.6
Trait
  hemoglobin
    abnormal NEC 282.7
      with thalassemia 282.49

Trait — *continued*
  hemoglobin — *continued*
    C (*see also* Disease, hemoglobin, C) 282.7
      with elliptocytosis 282.7
    S (Hb-S) 282.5
    Lepore 282.49
      with other abnormal hemoglobin NEC 282.49
  paranoid 301.0
  sickle-cell 282.5
    with
      elliptocytosis 282.5
      spherocytosis 282.5
Traits, paranoid 301.0
Tramp V60.0
Trance 780.09
  hysterical 300.13
Transaminasemia 790.4
Transfusion, blood
  donor V59.01
    stem cells V59.02
  incompatible 999.6
  reaction or complication — *see* Complications, transfusion
  syndrome
    fetomaternal 772.0
    twin-to-twin
      blood loss (donor twin) 772.0
      recipient twin 776.4
  without reported diagnosis V58.2
Transient — *see also* condition
  alteration of awareness 780.02
  blindness 368.12
  deafness (ischemic) 388.02
  global amnesia 437.7
  person (homeless) NEC V60.0
Transitional, lumbosacral joint of vertebra 756.19
Translocation
  autosomes NEC 758.5
    13-15 758.1
    16-18 758.2
    21 or 22 758.0
    balanced in normal individual 758.4
    D₁ 758.1
    E₃ 758.2
    G 758.0
  balanced autosomal in normal individual 758.4
  chromosomes NEC 758.89
  Down's syndrome 758.0
Translucency, iris 364.53
Transmission of chemical substances through the placenta (affecting fetus or newborn) 760.70
  alcohol 760.71
  anticonvulsants 760.77 ●
  antifungals 760.74 ●
  anti-infective agents 760.74
  antimetabolics 760.78 ●
  cocaine 760.75
  "crack" 760.75
  diethylstilbestrol [DES] 760.76
  hallucinogenic agents 760.73
  medicinal agents NEC 760.79
  narcotics 760.72
  obstetric anesthetic or analgesic drug 763.5
  specified agent NEC 760.79
  suspected, affecting management of pregnancy 655.5 ☑
Transplant(ed)
  bone V42.4
    marrow V42.81
  complication — *see also* Complications, due to (presence of) any device, implant, or graft classified to 996.0-996.5 NEC
    bone marrow 996.85
    corneal graft NEC 996.79
      infection or inflammation 996.69
      reaction 996.51
      rejection 996.51
    organ (failure) (immune or nonimmune cause) (infection) (rejection) 996.80
      bone marrow 996.85
      heart 996.83
      intestines 996.87

Transplant(ed) — *continued*
  complication — *see also* Complications, due to (presence of) any device, implant, or graft classified to 996.0-996.5 NEC — *continued*
    organ — *continued*
      kidney 996.81
      liver 996.82
      lung 996.84
      pancreas 996.86
      specified NEC 996.89
    skin NEC 996.79
      infection or inflammation 996.69
      rejection 996.52
        artificial 996.55
        decellularized allodermis 996.55
  cornea V42.5
  hair V50.0
  heart V42.1
    valve V42.2
  intestine V42.84
  kidney V42.0
  liver V42.7
  lung V42.6
  organ V42.9
    specified NEC V42.89
  pancreas V42.83
  peripheral stem cells V42.82
  skin V42.3
  stem cells, peripheral V42.82
  tissue V42.9
    specified NEC V42.89
Transplants, ovarian, endometrial 617.1
Transposed — *see* Transposition
Transposition (congenital) — *see also* Malposition, congenital
  abdominal viscera 759.3
  aorta (dextra) 745.11
  appendix 751.5
  arterial trunk 745.10
  colon 751.5
  great vessels (complete) 745.10
    both originating from right ventricle 745.11
    corrected 745.12
    double outlet right ventricle 745.11
    incomplete 745.11
    partial 745.11
    specified type NEC 745.19
  heart 746.87
    with complete transposition of viscera 759.3
  intestine (large) (small) 751.5
  pulmonary veins 747.49
  reversed jejunal (for bypass) (status) V45.3
  scrotal 752.81
  stomach 750.7
    with general transposition of viscera 759.3
  teeth, tooth 524.30
  vessels (complete) 745.10
    partial 745.11
  viscera (abdominal) (thoracic) 759.3
Trans-sexualism 302.50
  with
    asexual history 302.51
    heterosexual history 302.53
    homosexual history 302.52
Transverse — *see also* condition
  arrest (deep), in labor 660.3 ☑
    affecting fetus or newborn 763.1
  lie 652.3 ☑
    before labor, affecting fetus or newborn 761.7
    causing obstructed labor 660.0 ☑
      affecting fetus or newborn 763.1
    during labor, affecting fetus or newborn 763.1
Transvestism, transvestitism (transvestic fetishism) 302.3
Trapped placenta (with hemorrhage) 666.0 ☑
  without hemorrhage 667.0 ☑
Trauma, traumatism (*see also* Injury, by site) 959.9
  birth — *see* Birth, injury NEC
  causing hemorrhage of pregnancy or delivery 641.8 ☑

Trauma, traumatism (*see also* Injury, by site) — *continued*
  complicating
    abortion — *see* Abortion, by type, with damage to pelvic organs
    ectopic pregnancy (*see also* categories 633.0-633.9) 639.2
    molar pregnancy (*see also* categories 630-632) 639.2
  during delivery NEC 665.9 ☑
  following
    abortion 639.2
    ectopic or molar pregnancy 639.2
  maternal, during pregnancy, affecting fetus or newborn 760.5
  neuroma — *see* Injury, nerve, by site
  previous major, affecting management of pregnancy, childbirth, or puerperium V23.89
  psychic (current) — *see also* Reaction, adjustment
    previous (history) V15.49
  psychologic, previous (affecting health) V15.49
  transient paralysis — *see* Injury, nerve, by site
Traumatic — *see* condition
Treacher Collins' syndrome (incomplete facial dysostosis) 756.0
Treitz's hernia — *see* Hernia, Treitz's
Trematode infestation NEC 121.9
Trematodiasis NEC 121.9
Trembles 988.8
Trembling paralysis (*see also* Parkinsonism) 332.0
Tremor 781.0
  essential (benign) 333.1
  familial 333.1
  flapping (liver) 572.8
  hereditary 333.1
  hysterical 300.11
  intention 333.1
  medication-induced postural 333.1 ●
  mercurial 985.0
  muscle 728.85
  Parkinson's (*see also* Parkinsonism) 332.0
  psychogenic 306.0
    specified as conversion reaction 300.11
  senilis 797
  specified type NEC 333.1
Trench
  fever 083.1
  foot 991.4
  mouth 101
  nephritis — *see* Nephritis, acute
Treponema pallidum infection (*see also* Syphilis) 097.9
Treponematosis 102.9
  due to
    T. pallidum — *see* Syphilis
    T. pertenue (yaws) (*see also* Yaws) 102.9
Triad
  Kartagener's 759.3
  Reiter's (complete) (incomplete) 099.3
  Saint's (*see also* Hernia, diaphragm) 553.3
Trichiasis 704.2
  cicatricial 704.2
  eyelid 374.05
    with entropion (*see also* Entropion) 374.00
Trichinella spiralis (infection) (infestation) 124
Trichinelliasis 124
Trichinellosis 124
Trichiniasis 124
Trichinosis 124
Trichobezoar 938
  intestine 936
  stomach 935.2
Trichocephaliasis 127.3
Trichocephalosis 127.3
Trichocephalus infestation 127.3
Trichoclasis 704.2
Trichoepithelioma (M8100/0) — *see also* Neoplasm, skin, benign
  breast 217

Trichoepithelioma (M8100/0) — *see also* Neoplasm, skin, benign — *continued*
genital organ NEC — *see* Neoplasm, by site, benign
malignant (M8100/3) — *see* Neoplasm, skin, malignant
Trichofolliculoma (M8101/0) — *see* Neoplasm, skin, benign
Tricholemmoma (M8102/0) — *see* Neoplasm, skin, benign
Trichomatosis 704.2
Trichomoniasis 131.9
bladder 131.09
cervix 131.09
intestinal 007.3
prostate 131.03
seminal vesicle 131.09
specified site NEC 131.8
urethra 131.02
urogenitalis 131.00
vagina 131.01
vulva 131.01
vulvovaginal 131.01
Trichomycosis 039.0
axillaris 039.0
nodosa 111.2
nodularis 111.2
rubra 039.0
Trichonocardiosis (axillaris) (palmellina) 039.0
Trichonodosis 704.2
Trichophytid, trichophyton infection (*see also* Dermatophytosis) 110.9
Trichophytide — *see* Dermatophytosis
Trichophytobezoar 938
intestine 936
stomach 935.2
Trichophytosis — *see* Dermatophytosis
Trichoptilosis 704.2
Trichorrhexis (nodosa) 704.2
Trichosporosis nodosa 111.2
Trichostasis spinulosa (congenital) 757.4
Trichostrongyliasis (small intestine) 127.6
Trichostrongylosis 127.6
Trichostrongylus (instabilis) infection 127.6
Trichotillomania 312.39
Trichromat, anomalous (congenital) 368.59
Trichromatopsia, anomalous (congenital) 368.59
Trichuriasis 127.3
Trichuris trichiuria (any site) (infection) (infestation) 127.3
Tricuspid (valve) — *see* condition
Trifid — *see also* Accessory
kidney (pelvis) 753.3
tongue 750.13
Trigeminal neuralgia (*see also* Neuralgia, trigeminal) 350.1
Trigeminoencephaloangiomatosis 759.6
Trigeminy 427.89
postoperative 997.1
Trigger finger (acquired) 727.03
congenital 756.89
Trigonitis (bladder) (chronic) (pseudomembranous) 595.3
tuberculous (*see also* Tuberculosis) 016.1 ☑
Trigonocephaly 756.0
Trihexosidosis 272.7
Trilobate placenta — *see* Placenta, abnormal
Trilocular heart 745.8
Tripartita placenta — *see* Placenta, abnormal
Triple — *see also* Accessory
kidneys 753.3
uteri 752.2
X female 758.81
Triplegia 344.89
congenital or infantile 343.8
Triplet
affected by maternal complications of pregnancy 761.5
healthy liveborn — *see* Newborn, multiple

Triplet — *continued*
pregnancy (complicating delivery) NEC 651.1 ☑
with fetal loss and retention of one or more fetus(es) 651.4 ☑
following (elective) fetal reduction 651.7 ☑ ●
Triplex placenta — *see* Placenta, abnormal
Triplication — *see* Accessory
Trismus 781.0
neonatorum 771.3
newborn 771.3
Trisomy (syndrome) NEC 758.5
13 (partial) 758.1
16-18 758.2
18 (partial) 758.2
21 (partial) 758.0
22 758.0
autosomes NEC 758.5
D₁ 758.1
E₃ 758.2
G (group) 758.0
group D₁ 758.1
group E 758.2
group G 758.0
Tritanomaly 368.53
Tritanopia 368.53
Troisier-Hanot-Chauffard syndrome (bronze diabetes) 275.0
Trombidiosis 133.8
Trophedema (hereditary) 757.0
congenital 757.0
Trophoblastic disease (*see also* Hydatidiform mole) 630
previous, affecting management of pregnancy V23.1
Tropholymphedema 757.0
Trophoneurosis NEC 356.9
arm NEC 354.9
disseminated 710.1
facial 349.89
leg NEC 355.8
lower extremity NEC 355.8
upper extremity NEC 354.9
Tropical — *see also* condition
maceration feet (syndrome) 991.4
wet foot (syndrome) 991.4
Trouble — *see also* Disease
bowel 569.9
heart — *see* Disease, heart
intestine 569.9
kidney (*see also* Disease, renal) 593.9
nervous 799.2
sinus (*see also* Sinusitis) 473.9
Trousseau's syndrome (thrombophlebitis migrans) 453.1
Truancy, childhood — *see also* Disturbance, conduct
socialized 312.2 ☑
undersocialized, unsocialized 312.1 ☑
Truncus
arteriosus (persistent) 745.0
common 745.0
communis 745.0
Trunk — *see* condition
Trychophytide — *see* Dermatophytosis
Trypanosoma infestation — *see* Trypanosomiasis
Trypanosomiasis 086.9
with meningoencephalitis 086.9 [323.2]
African 086.5
due to Trypanosoma 086.5
gambiense 086.3
rhodesiense 086.4
American 086.2
with
heart involvement 086.0
other organ involvement 086.1
without mention of organ involvement 086.2
Brazilian — *see* Trypanosomiasis, American
Chagas' — *see* Trypanosomiasis, American
due to Trypanosoma
cruzi — *see* Trypanosomiasis, American
gambiense 086.3

Trypanosomiasis — *continued*
due to Trypanosoma — *continued*
rhodesiense 086.4
gambiense, Gambian 086.3
North American — *see* Trypanosomiasis, American
rhodesiensis, Rhodesian 086.4
South American — *see* Trypanosomiasis, American
T-shaped incisors 520.2
Tsutsugamushi fever 081.2
Tube, tubal, tubular — *see also* condition
ligation, admission for V25.2
Tubercle — *see also* Tuberculosis
brain, solitary 013.2 ☑
Darwin's 744.29
epithelioid noncaseating 135
Ghon, primary infection 010.0 ☑
Tuberculid, tuberculide (indurating) (lichenoid) (miliary) (papulonecrotic) (primary) (skin) (subcutaneous) (*see also* Tuberculosis) 017.0 ☑
Tuberculoma — *see also* Tuberculosis
brain (any part) 013.2 ☑
meninges (cerebral) (spinal) 013.1 ☑
spinal cord 013.4 ☑
Tuberculosis, tubercular, tuberculous (calcification) (calcified) (caseous) (chromogenic acid-fast bacilli) (congenital) (degeneration) (disease) (fibrocaseous) (fistula) (gangrene) (interstitial) (isolated circumscribed lesions) (necrosis) (parenchymatous) (ulcerative) 011.9 ☑

Note — Use the following fifth-digit subclassification with categories 010-018:

0   unspecified
1   bacteriological or histological examination not done
2   bacteriological or histological examination unknown (at present)
3   tubercle bacilli found (in sputum) by microscopy
4   tubercle bacilli not found (in sputum) by microscopy, but found by bacterial culture
5   tubercle bacilli not found by bacteriological examination, but tuberculosis confirmed histologically
6   tubercle bacilli not found by bacteriological or histological examination, but tuberculosis confirmed by other methods [inoculation of animals]

For tuberculous conditions specified as late effects or sequelae, see category 137.

abdomen 014.8 ☑
lymph gland 014.8 ☑
abscess 011.9 ☑
arm 017.9 ☑
bone (*see also* Osteomyelitis, due to, tuberculosis) 015.9 ☑ [730.8]
hip 015.1 ☑ [730.85]
knee 015.2 ☑ [730.86]
sacrum 015.0 ☑ [730.88]
specified site NEC 015.7 ☑ [730.88]
spinal 015.0 ☑ [730.88]
vertebra 015.0 ☑ [730.88]
brain 013.3 ☑
breast 017.9 ☑
Cowper's gland 016.5 ☑
dura (mater) 013.8 ☑
brain 013.3 ☑
spinal cord 013.5 ☑
epidural 013.8 ☑
brain 013.3 ☑
spinal cord 013.5 ☑
frontal sinus — *see* Tuberculosis, sinus
genital organs NEC 016.9 ☑
female 016.7 ☑
male 016.5 ☑
genitourinary NEC 016.9 ☑

☑ Additional Digit Required — Refer to the Tabular List (Numeric Code Section) for Additional Digit Selection
▶◀ Revised Text   ● New Line   ▲ Revised Code

2006 ICD-9-CM

October 2005 • Volume 2 — **335**

Tuberculosis, tubercular, tuberculous — *continued*

abscess — *continued*

gland (lymphatic) — *see* Tuberculosis, lymph gland

hip 015.1 ☑

iliopsoas 015.0 ☑ *[730.88]*

intestine 014.8 ☑

ischiorectal 014.8 ☑

joint 015.9 ☑

   hip 015.1 ☑

   knee 015.2 ☑

   specified joint NEC 015.8 ☑

   vertebral 015.0 ☑ *[730.88]*

kidney 016.0 ☑ *[590.81]*

knee 015.2 ☑

lumbar 015.0 ☑ *[730.88]*

lung 011.2 ☑

   primary, progressive 010.8 ☑

meninges (cerebral) (spinal) 013.0 ☑

pelvic 016.9 ☑

   female 016.7 ☑

   male 016.5 ☑

perianal 014.8 ☑

   fistula 014.8 ☑

perinephritic 016.0 ☑ *[590.81]*

perineum 017.9 ☑

perirectal 014.8 ☑

psoas 015.0 ☑ *[730.88]*

rectum 014.8 ☑

retropharyngeal 012.8 ☑

sacrum 015.0 ☑ *[730.88]*

scrofulous 017.2 ☑

scrotum 016.5 ☑

skin 017.0 ☑

   primary 017.0 ☑

spinal cord 013.5 ☑

spine or vertebra (column) 015.0 ☑ *[730.88]*

strumous 017.2 ☑

subdiaphragmatic 014.8 ☑

testis 016.5 ☑

thigh 017.9 ☑

urinary 016.3 ☑

   kidney 016.0 ☑ *[590.81]*

uterus 016.7 ☑

accessory sinus — *see* Tuberculosis, sinus

Addison's disease 017.6 ☑

adenitis (*see also* Tuberculosis, lymph gland) 017.2 ☑

adenoids 012.8 ☑

adenopathy (*see also* Tuberculosis, lymph gland) 017.2 ☑

   tracheobronchial 012.1 ☑

      primary progressive 010.8 ☑

adherent pericardium 017.9 ☑ *[420.0]*

adnexa (uteri) 016.7 ☑

adrenal (capsule) (gland) 017.6 ☑

air passage NEC 012.8 ☑

alimentary canal 014.8 ☑

anemia 017.9 ☑

ankle (joint) 015.8 ☑

   bone 015.5 ☑ *[730.87]*

anus 014.8 ☑

apex (*see also* Tuberculosis, pulmonary) 011.9 ☑

apical (*see also* Tuberculosis, pulmonary) 011.9 ☑

appendicitis 014.8 ☑

appendix 014.8 ☑

arachnoid 013.0 ☑

artery 017.9 ☑

arthritis (chronic) (synovial) 015.9 ☑ *[711.40]*

   ankle 015.8 ☑ *[730.87]*

   hip 015.1 ☑ *[711.45]*

   knee 015.2 ☑ *[711.46]*

   specified site NEC 015.8 ☑ *[711.48]*

   spine or vertebra (column) 015.0 ☑ *[720.81]*

   wrist 015.8 ☑ *[730.83]*

articular — *see* Tuberculosis, joint

ascites 014.0 ☑

asthma (*see also* Tuberculosis, pulmonary) 011.9 ☑

axilla, axillary 017.2 ☑

   gland 017.2 ☑

bilateral (*see also* Tuberculosis, pulmonary) 011.9 ☑

bladder 016.1 ☑

Tuberculosis, tubercular, tuberculous — *continued*

bone (*see also* Osteomyelitis, due to, tuberculosis) 015.9 ☑ *[730.8]* ☑

   hip 015.1 ☑ *[730.85]*

   knee 015.2 ☑ *[730.86]*

   limb NEC 015.5 ☑ *[730.88]*

   sacrum 015.0 ☑ *[730.88]*

   specified site NEC 015.7 ☑ *[730.88]*

   spinal or vertebral column 015.0 ☑ *[730.88]*

bowel 014.8 ☑

   miliary 018.9 ☑

brain 013.2 ☑

breast 017.9 ☑

broad ligament 016.7 ☑

bronchi, bronchial, bronchus 011.3 ☑

   ectasia, ectasis 011.5 ☑

   fistula 011.3 ☑

      primary, progressive 010.8 ☑

   gland 012.1 ☑

      primary, progressive 010.8 ☑

   isolated 012.2 ☑

   lymph gland or node 012.1 ☑

      primary, progressive 010.8 ☑

bronchiectasis 011.5 ☑

bronchitis 011.3 ☑

bronchopleural 012.0 ☑

bronchopneumonia, bronchopneumonic 011.6 ☑

bronchorrhagia 011.3 ☑

bronchotracheal 011.3 ☑

   isolated 012.2 ☑

bronchus — *see* Tuberculosis, bronchi

bronze disease (Addison's) 017.6 ☑

buccal cavity 017.9 ☑

bulbourethral gland 016.5 ☑

bursa (*see also* Tuberculosis, joint) 015.9 ☑

cachexia NEC (*see also* Tuberculosis, pulmonary) 011.9 ☑

cardiomyopathy 017.9 ☑ *[425.8]*

caries (*see also* Tuberculosis, bone) 015.9 ☑ *[730.8]*

cartilage (*see also* Tuberculosis, bone) 015.9 ☑ *[730.8]*

   intervertebral 015.0 ☑ *[730.88]*

catarrhal (*see also* Tuberculosis, pulmonary) 011.9 ☑

cecum 014.8 ☑

cellular tissue (primary) 017.0 ☑

cellulitis (primary) 017.0 ☑

central nervous system 013.9 ☑

   specified site NEC 013.8 ☑

cerebellum (current) 013.2 ☑

cerebral (current) 013.2 ☑

   meninges 013.0 ☑

cerebrospinal 013.6 ☑

   meninges 013.0 ☑

cerebrum (current) 013.2 ☑

cervical 017.2 ☑

   gland 017.2 ☑

   lymph nodes 017.2 ☑

cervicitis (uteri) 016.7 ☑

cervix 016.7 ☑

chest (*see also* Tuberculosis, pulmonary) 011.9 ☑

childhood type or first infection 010.0 ☑

choroid 017.3 ☑ *[363.13]*

choroiditis 017.3 ☑ *[363.13]*

ciliary body 017.3 ☑ *[364.11]*

colitis 014.8 ☑

colliers' 011.4 ☑

colliquativa (primary) 017.0 ☑

colon 014.8 ☑

   ulceration 014.8 ☑

complex, primary 010.0 ☑

complicating pregnancy, childbirth, or puerperium 647.3 ☑

   affecting fetus or newborn 760.2

congenital 771.2

conjunctiva 017.3 ☑ *[370.31]*

connective tissue 017.9 ☑

   bone — *see* Tuberculosis, bone

contact V01.1

converter (tuberculin skin test) (without disease) 795.5

cornea (ulcer) 017.3 ☑ *[370.31]*

Cowper's gland 016.5 ☑

Tuberculosis, tubercular, tuberculous — *continued*

coxae 015.1 ☑ *[730.85]*

coxalgia 015.1 ☑ *[730.85]*

cul-de-sac of Douglas 014.8 ☑

curvature, spine 015.0 ☑ *[737.40]*

cutis (colliquativa) (primary) 017.0 ☑

cyst, ovary 016.6 ☑

cystitis 016.1 ☑

dacryocystitis 017.3 ☑ *[375.32]*

dactylitis 015.5 ☑

diarrhea 014.8 ☑

diffuse (*see also* Tuberculosis, miliary) 018.9 ☑

   lung — *see* Tuberculosis, pulmonary

   meninges 013.0 ☑

digestive tract 014.8 ☑

disseminated (*see also* Tuberculosis, miliary) 018.9 ☑

   meninges 013.0 ☑

duodenum 014.8 ☑

dura (mater) 013.9 ☑

   abscess 013.8 ☑

      cerebral 013.3 ☑

      spinal 013.5 ☑

dysentery 014.8 ☑

ear (inner) (middle) 017.4 ☑

   bone 015.6 ☑

   external (primary) 017.0 ☑

   skin (primary) 017.0 ☑

elbow 015.8 ☑

emphysema — *see* Tuberculosis, pulmonary

empyema 012.0 ☑

encephalitis 013.6 ☑

endarteritis 017.9 ☑

endocarditis (any valve) 017.9 ☑ *[424.91]*

endocardium (any valve) 017.9 ☑ *[424.91]*

endocrine glands NEC 017.9 ☑

endometrium 016.7 ☑

enteric, enterica 014.8 ☑

enteritis 014.8 ☑

enterocolitis 014.8 ☑

epididymis 016.4 ☑

epididymitis 016.4 ☑

epidural abscess 013.8 ☑

   brain 013.3 ☑

   spinal cord 013.5 ☑

epiglottis 012.3 ☑

episcleritis 017.3 ☑ *[379.00]*

erythema (induratum) (nodosum) (primary) 017.1 ☑

esophagus 017.8 ☑

Eustachian tube 017.4 ☑

exposure to V01.1

exudative 012.0 ☑

   primary, progressive 010.1 ☑

eye 017.3 ☑

   glaucoma 017.3 ☑ *[365.62]*

eyelid (primary) 017.0 ☑

   lupus 017.0 ☑ *[373.4]*

fallopian tube 016.6 ☑

fascia 017.9 ☑

fauces 012.8 ☑

finger 017.9 ☑

first infection 010.0 ☑

fistula, perirectal 014.8 ☑

Florida 011.6 ☑

foot 017.9 ☑

funnel pelvis 137.3

gallbladder 017.9 ☑

galloping (*see also* Tuberculosis, pulmonary) 011.9 ☑

ganglionic 015.9 ☑

gastritis 017.9 ☑

gastrocolic fistula 014.8 ☑

gastroenteritis 014.8 ☑

gastrointestinal tract 014.8 ☑

general, generalized 018.9 ☑

   acute 018.0 ☑

   chronic 018.8 ☑

genital organs NEC 016.9 ☑

   female 016.7 ☑

   male 016.5 ☑

genitourinary NEC 016.9 ☑

genu 015.2 ☑

glandulae suprarenalis 017.6 ☑

glandular, general 017.2 ☑

glottis 012.3 ☑

☑ Additional Digit Required — Refer to the Tabular List (Numeric Code Section) for Additional Digit Selection

►◄ Revised Text   ● New Line   ▲ Revised Code

Tuberculosis, tubercular, tuberculous —
continued
grinders' 011.4 ☑
groin 017.2 ☑
gum 017.9 ☑
hand 017.9 ☑
heart 017.9 ☑ *[425.8]*
hematogenous — *see* Tuberculosis, miliary
hemoptysis (*see also* Tuberculosis, pulmonary) 011.9 ☑
hemorrhage NEC (*see also* Tuberculosis, pulmonary) 011.9 ☑
hemothorax 012.0 ☑
hepatitis 017.9 ☑
hilar lymph nodes 012.1 ☑
primary, progressive 010.8 ☑
hip (disease) (joint) 015.1 ☑
bone 015.1 ☑ *[730.85]*
hydrocephalus 013.8 ☑
hydropneumothorax 012.0 ☑
hydrothorax 012.0 ☑
hypoadrenalism 017.6 ☑
hypopharynx 012.8 ☑
ileocecal (hyperplastic) 014.8 ☑
ileocolitis 014.8 ☑
ileum 014.8 ☑
iliac spine (superior) 015.0 ☑ *[730.88]*
incipient NEC (*see also* Tuberculosis, pulmonary) 011.9 ☑
indurativa (primary) 017.1 ☑
infantile 010.0 ☑
infection NEC 011.9 ☑
without clinical manifestation 010.0 ☑
infraclavicular gland 017.2 ☑
inguinal gland 017.2 ☑
inguinalis 017.2 ☑
intestine (any part) 014.8 ☑
iris 017.3 ☑ *[364.11]*
iritis 017.3 ☑ *[364.11]*
ischiorectal 014.8 ☑
jaw 015.7 ☑ *[730.88]*
jejunum 014.8 ☑
joint 015.9 ☑
hip 015.1 ☑
knee 015.2 ☑
specified site NEC 015.8 ☑
vertebral 015.0 ☑ *[730.88]*
keratitis 017.3 ☑ *[370.31]*
interstitial 017.3 ☑ *[370.59]*
keratoconjunctivitis 017.3 ☑ *[370.31]*
kidney 016.0 ☑
knee (joint) 015.2 ☑
kyphoscoliosis 015.0 ☑ *[737.43]*
kyphosis 015.0 ☑ *[737.41]*
lacrimal apparatus, gland 017.3 ☑
laryngitis 012.3 ☑
larynx 012.3 ☑
leptomeninges, leptomeningitis (cerebral) (spinal) 013.0 ☑
lichenoides (primary) 017.0 ☑
linguae 017.9 ☑
lip 017.9 ☑
liver 017.9 ☑
lordosis 015.0 ☑ *[737.42]*
lung — *see* Tuberculosis, pulmonary
luposa 017.0 ☑
eyelid 017.0 ☑ *[373.4]*
lymphadenitis — *see* Tuberculosis, lymph gland
lymphangitis — *see* Tuberculosis, lymph gland
lymphatic (gland) (vessel) — *see* Tuberculosis, lymph gland
lymph gland or node (peripheral) 017.2 ☑
abdomen 014.8 ☑
bronchial 012.1 ☑
primary, progressive 010.8 ☑
cervical 017.2 ☑
hilar 012.1 ☑
primary, progressive 010.8 ☑
intrathoracic 012.1 ☑
primary, progressive 010.8 ☑
mediastinal 012.1 ☑
primary, progressive 010.8 ☑
mesenteric 014.8 ☑
peripheral 017.2 ☑
retroperitoneal 014.8 ☑
tracheobronchial 012.1 ☑
primary, progressive 010.8 ☑

Tuberculosis, tubercular, tuberculous —
continued
malignant NEC (*see also* Tuberculosis, pulmonary) 011.9 ☑
mammary gland 017.9 ☑
marasmus NEC (*see also* Tuberculosis, pulmonary) 011.9 ☑
mastoiditis 015.6 ☑
maternal, affecting fetus or newborn 760.2
mediastinal (lymph) gland or node 012.1 ☑
primary, progressive 010.8 ☑
mediastinitis 012.8 ☑
primary, progressive 010.8 ☑
mediastinopericarditis 017.9 ☑ *[420.0]*
mediastinum 012.8 ☑
primary, progressive 010.8 ☑
medulla 013.9 ☑
brain 013.2 ☑
spinal cord 013.4 ☑
melanosis, Addisonian 017.6 ☑
membrane, brain 013.0 ☑
meninges (cerebral) (spinal) 013.0 ☑
meningitis (basilar) (brain) (cerebral) (cerebrospinal) (spinal) 013.0 ☑
meningoencephalitis 013.0 ☑
mesentery, mesenteric 014.8 ☑
lymph gland or node 014.8 ☑
miliary (any site) 018.9 ☑
acute 018.0 ☑
chronic 018.8 ☑
specified type NEC 018.8 ☑
millstone makers' 011.4 ☑
miners' 011.4 ☑
moulders' 011.4 ☑
mouth 017.9 ☑
multiple 018.9 ☑
acute 018.0 ☑
chronic 018.8 ☑
muscle 017.9 ☑
myelitis 013.6 ☑
myocarditis 017.9 ☑ *[422.0]*
myocardium 017.9 ☑ *[422.0]*
nasal (passage) (sinus) 012.8 ☑
nasopharynx 012.8 ☑
neck gland 017.2 ☑
nephritis 016.0 ☑ *[583.81]*
nerve 017.9 ☑
nose (septum) 012.8 ☑
ocular 017.3 ☑
old NEC 137.0
without residuals V12.01
omentum 014.8 ☑
oophoritis (acute) (chronic) 016.6 ☑
optic 017.3 ☑ *[377.39]*
nerve trunk 017.3 ☑ *[377.39]*
papilla, papillae 017.3 ☑ *[377.39]*
orbit 017.3 ☑
orchitis 016.5 ☑ *[608.81]*
organ, specified NEC 017.9 ☑
orificialis (primary) 017.0 ☑
osseous (*see also* Tuberculosis, bone) 015.9 ☑ *[730.8]*
osteitis (*see also* Tuberculosis, bone) 015.9 ☑ *[730.8]*
osteomyelitis (*see also* Tuberculosis, bone) 015.9 ☑ *[730.8]*
otitis (media) 017.4 ☑
ovaritis (acute) (chronic) 016.6 ☑
ovary (acute) (chronic) 016.6 ☑
oviducts (acute) (chronic) 016.6 ☑
pachymeningitis 013.0 ☑
palate (soft) 017.9 ☑
pancreas 017.9 ☑
papulonecrotic (primary) 017.0 ☑
parathyroid glands 017.9 ☑
paronychia (primary) 017.0 ☑
parotid gland or region 017.9 ☑
pelvic organ NEC 016.9 ☑
female 016.7 ☑
male 016.5 ☑
pelvis (bony) 015.7 ☑ *[730.85]*
penis 016.5 ☑
peribronchitis 011.3 ☑
pericarditis 017.9 ☑ *[420.0]*
pericardium 017.9 ☑ *[420.0]*
perichondritis, larynx 012.3 ☑
perineum 017.9 ☑

Tuberculosis, tubercular, tuberculous —
continued
periostitis (*see also* Tuberculosis, bone) 015.9 ☑ *[730.8]*
periphlebitis 017.9 ☑
eye vessel 017.3 ☑ *[362.18]*
retina 017.3 ☑ *[362.18]*
perirectal fistula 014.8 ☑
peritoneal gland 014.8 ☑
peritoneum 014.0 ☑
peritonitis 014.0 ☑
pernicious NEC (*see also* Tuberculosis, pulmonary) 011.9 ☑
pharyngitis 012.8 ☑
pharynx 012.8 ☑
phlyctenulosis (conjunctiva) 017.3 ☑ *[370.31]*
phthisis NEC (*see also* Tuberculosis, pulmonary) 011.9 ☑
pituitary gland 017.9 ☑
placenta 016.7 ☑
pleura, pleural, pleurisy, pleuritis (fibrinous) (obliterative) (purulent) (simple plastic) (with effusion) 012.0 ☑
primary, progressive 010.1 ☑
pneumonia, pneumonic 011.6 ☑
pneumothorax 011.7 ☑
polyserositis 018.9 ☑
acute 018.0 ☑
chronic 018.8 ☑
potters' 011.4 ☑
prepuce 016.5 ☑
primary 010.9 ☑
complex 010.0 ☑
complicated 010.8 ☑
with pleurisy or effusion 010.1 ☑
progressive 010.8 ☑
with pleurisy or effusion 010.1 ☑
skin 017.0 ☑
proctitis 014.8 ☑
prostate 016.5 ☑ *[601.4]*
prostatitis 016.5 ☑ *[601.4]*
pulmonaris (*see also* Tuberculosis, pulmonary) 011.9 ☑
pulmonary (artery) (incipient) (malignant) (multiple round foci) (pernicious) (reinfection stage) 011.9 ☑
cavitated or with cavitation 011.2 ☑
primary, progressive 010.8 ☑
childhood type or first infection 010.0 ☑
chromogenic acid-fast bacilli 795.39
fibrosis or fibrotic 011.4 ☑
infiltrative 011.0 ☑
primary, progressive 010.9 ☑
nodular 011.1 ☑
specified NEC 011.8 ☑
sputum positive only 795.39
status following surgical collapse of lung NEC 011.9 ☑
pyelitis 016.0 ☑ *[590.81]*
pyelonephritis 016.0 ☑ *[590.81]*
pyemia — *see* Tuberculosis, miliary
pyonephrosis 016.0 ☑
pyopneumothorax 012.0 ☑
pyothorax 012.0 ☑
rectum (with abscess) 014.8 ☑
fistula 014.8 ☑
reinfection stage (*see also* Tuberculosis, pulmonary) 011.9 ☑
renal 016.0 ☑
renis 016.0 ☑
reproductive organ 016.7 ☑
respiratory NEC (*see also* Tuberculosis, pulmonary) 011.9 ☑
specified site NEC 012.8 ☑
retina 017.3 ☑ *[363.13]*
retroperitoneal (lymph gland or node) 014.8 ☑
gland 014.8 ☑
retropharyngeal abscess 012.8 ☑
rheumatism 015.9 ☑
rhinitis 012.8 ☑
sacroiliac (joint) 015.8 ☑
sacrum 015.0 ☑ *[730.88]*
salivary gland 017.9 ☑
salpingitis (acute) (chronic) 016.6 ☑
sandblasters' 011.4 ☑
sclera 017.3 ☑ *[379.09]*
scoliosis 015.0 ☑ *[737.43]*

☑ Additional Digit Required — Refer to the Tabular List (Numeric Code Section) for Additional Digit Selection

▶◀ Revised Text   ● New Line   ▲ Revised Code

Tuberculosis, tubercular, tuberculous — *continued*

scrofulous 017.2 ☑
scrotum 016.5 ☑
seminal tract or vesicle 016.5 ☑ *[608.81]*
senile NEC (*see also* Tuberculosis, pulmonary) 011.9 ☑
septic NEC (*see also* Tuberculosis, miliary) 018.9 ☑
shoulder 015.8 ☑
  blade 015.7 ☑ *[730.8]* ☑
sigmoid 014.8 ☑
sinus (accessory) (nasal) 012.8 ☑
  bone 015.7 ☑ *[730.88]*
  epididymis 016.4 ☑
skeletal NEC (*see also* Osteomyelitis, due to tuberculosis) 015.9 ☑ *[730.8]* ☑
skin (any site) (primary) 017.0 ☑
small intestine 014.8 ☑
soft palate 017.9 ☑
spermatic cord 016.5 ☑
spinal
  column 015.0 ☑ *[730.88]*
  cord 013.4 ☑
  disease 015.0 ☑ *[730.88]*
  medulla 013.4 ☑
  membrane 013.0 ☑
  meninges 013.0 ☑
spine 015.0 ☑ *[730.88]*
spleen 017.7 ☑
splenitis 017.7 ☑
spondylitis 015.0 ☑ *[720.81]*
spontaneous pneumothorax — *see* Tuberculosis, pulmonary
sternoclavicular joint 015.8 ☑
stomach 017.9 ☑
stonemasons' 011.4 ☑
struma 017.2 ☑
subcutaneous tissue (cellular) (primary) 017.0 ☑
subcutis (primary) 017.0 ☑
subdeltoid bursa 017.9 ☑
submaxillary 017.9 ☑
  region 017.9 ☑
supraclavicular gland 017.2 ☑
suprarenal (capsule) (gland) 017.6 ☑
swelling, joint (*see also* Tuberculosis, joint) 015.9 ☑
symphysis pubis 015.7 ☑ *[730.88]*
synovitis 015.9 ☑ *[727.01]*
  hip 015.1 ☑ *[727.01]*
  knee 015.2 ☑ *[727.01]*
  specified site NEC 015.8 ☑ *[727.01]*
  spine or vertebra 015.0 ☑ *[727.01]*
systemic — *see* Tuberculosis, miliary
tarsitis (eyelid) 017.0 ☑ *[373.4]*
  ankle (bone) 015.5 ☑ *[730.87]*
tendon (sheath) — *see* Tuberculosis, tenosynovitis
tenosynovitis 015.9 ☑ *[727.01]*
  hip 015.1 ☑ *[727.01]*
  knee 015.2 ☑ *[727.01]*
  specified site NEC 015.8 ☑ *[727.01]*
  spine or vertebra 015.0 ☑ *[727.01]*
testis 016.5 ☑ *[608.81]*
throat 012.8 ☑
thymus gland 017.9 ☑
thyroid gland 017.5 ☑
toe 017.9 ☑
tongue 017.9 ☑
tonsil (lingual) 012.8 ☑
tonsillitis 012.8 ☑
trachea, tracheal 012.8 ☑
  gland 012.1 ☑
    primary, progressive 010.8 ☑
  isolated 012.2 ☑
tracheobronchial 011.3 ☑
  glandular 012.1 ☑
    primary, progressive 010.8 ☑
  isolated 012.2 ☑
  lymph gland or node 012.1 ☑
    primary, progressive 010.8 ☑
tubal 016.6 ☑
tunica vaginalis 016.5 ☑
typhlitis 014.8 ☑
ulcer (primary) (skin) 017.0 ☑
  bowel or intestine 014.8 ☑

Tuberculosis, tubercular, tuberculous — *continued*

ulcer — *continued*
  specified site NEC — *see* Tuberculosis, by site
  unspecified site — *see* Tuberculosis, pulmonary
ureter 016.2 ☑
urethra, urethral 016.3 ☑
urinary organ or tract 016.3 ☑
  kidney 016.0 ☑
uterus 016.7 ☑
uveal tract 017.3 ☑ *[363.13]*
uvula 017.9 ☑
vaccination, prophylactic (against) V03.2
vagina 016.7 ☑
vas deferens 016.5 ☑
vein 017.9 ☑
verruca (primary) 017.0 ☑
verrucosa (cutis) (primary) 017.0 ☑
vertebra (column) 015.0 ☑ *[730.88]*
vesiculitis 016.5 ☑ *[608.81]*
viscera NEC 014.8 ☑
vulva 016.7 ☑ *[616.51]*
wrist (joint) 015.8 ☑
  bone 015.5 ☑ *[730.83]*

Tuberculum
auriculae 744.29
occlusal 520.2
paramolare 520.2

Tuberous sclerosis (brain) 759.5

Tubo-ovarian — *see* condition

Tuboplasty, after previous sterilization V26.0

Tubotympanitis 381.10

Tularemia 021.9
with
  conjunctivitis 021.3
  pneumonia 021.2
bronchopneumonic 021.2
conjunctivitis 021.3
cryptogenic 021.1
disseminated 021.8
enteric 021.1
generalized 021.8
glandular 021.8
intestinal 021.1
oculoglandular 021.3
ophthalmic 021.3
pneumonia 021.2
pulmonary 021.2
specified NEC 021.8
typhoidal 021.1
ulceroglandular 021.0
vaccination, prophylactic (against) V03.4

Tularensis conjunctivitis 021.3

Tumefaction — *see also* Swelling
liver (*see also* Hypertrophy, liver) 789.1

Tumor (M8000/1) — *see also* Neoplasm, by site, unspecified nature
Abrikossov's (M9580/0) — *see also* Neoplasm, connective tissue, benign
  malignant (M9580/3) — *see* Neoplasm, connective tissue, malignant
acinar cell (M8550/1) — *see* Neoplasm, by site, uncertain behavior
acinic cell (M8550/1) — *see* Neoplasm, by site, uncertain behavior
adenomatoid (M9054/0) — *see also* Neoplasm, by site, benign
  odontogenic (M9300/0) 213.1
    upper jaw (bone) 213.0
adnexal (skin) (M8390/0) — *see* Neoplasm, skin, benign
adrenal
  cortical (benign) (M8370/0) 227.0
    malignant (M8370/3) 194.0
  rest (M8671/0) — *see* Neoplasm, by site, benign
alpha cell (M8152/0)
  malignant (M8152/3)
    pancreas 157.4
    specified site NEC — *see* Neoplasm, by site, malignant
    unspecified site 157.4
  pancreas 211.7

Tumor (M8000/1) — *see also* Neoplasm, by site, unspecified nature — *continued*
alpha cell (M8152/0) — *continued*
  specified site NEC — *see* Neoplasm, by site, benign
  unspecified site 211.7
aneurysmal (*see also* Aneurysm) 442.9
aortic body (M8691/1) 237.3
  malignant (M8691/3) 194.6
argentaffin (M8241/1) — *see* Neoplasm, by site, uncertain behavior
basal cell (M8090/1) — *see also* Neoplasm, skin, uncertain behavior
benign (M8000/0) — *see* Neoplasm, by site, benign
beta cell (M8151/0)
  malignant (M8151/3)
    pancreas 157.4
    specified site — *see* Neoplasm, by site, malignant
    unspecified site 157.4
  pancreas 211.7
  specified site NEC — *see* Neoplasm, by site, benign
  unspecified site 211.7
blood — *see* Hematoma
Brenner (M9000/0) 220
  borderline malignancy (M9000/1) 236.2
  malignant (M9000/3) 183.0
  proliferating (M9000/1) 236.2
Brooke's (M8100/0) — *see* Neoplasm, skin, benign
brown fat (M8880/0) — *see* Lipoma, by site
Burkitt's (M9750/3) 200.2 ☑
calcifying epithelial odontogenic (M9340/0) 213.1
  upper jaw (bone) 213.0
carcinoid (M8240/1) — *see* Carcinoid
carotid body (M8692/1) 237.3
  malignant (M8692/3) 194.5
Castleman's (mediastinal lymph node hyperplasia) 785.6
cells (M8001/1) — *see also* Neoplasm, by site, unspecified nature
  benign (M8001/0) — *see* Neoplasm, by site, benign
  malignant (M8001/3) — *see* Neoplasm, by site, malignant
  uncertain whether benign or malignant (M8001/1) — *see* Neoplasm, by site, uncertain nature
cervix
  in pregnancy or childbirth 654.6 ☑
    affecting fetus or newborn 763.89
    causing obstructed labor 660.2 ☑
      affecting fetus or newborn 763.1
chondromatous giant cell (M9230/0) — *see* Neoplasm, bone, benign
chromaffin (M8700/0) — *see also* Neoplasm, by site, benign
  malignant (M8700/3) — *see* Neoplasm, by site, malignant
Cock's peculiar 706.2
Codman's (benign chondroblastoma) (M9230/0) — *see* Neoplasm, bone, benign
dentigerous, mixed (M9282/0) 213.1
  upper jaw (bone) 213.0
dermoid (M9084/0) — *see* Neoplasm, by site, benign
  with malignant transformation (M9084/3) 183.0
desmoid (extra-abdominal) (M8821/1) — *see also* Neoplasm, connective tissue, uncertain behavior
  abdominal (M8822/1) — *see* Neoplasm, connective tissue, uncertain behavior
embryonal (mixed) (M9080/1) — *see also* Neoplasm, by site, uncertain behavior
  liver (M9080/3) 155.0
endodermal sinus (M9071/3)
  specified site — *see* Neoplasm, by site, malignant
  unspecified site
    female 183.0
    male 186.9

Tumor (M8000/1) — *see also* Neoplasm, by site, unspecified nature — *continued*
  epithelial
    benign (M8010/0) — *see* Neoplasm, by site, benign
    malignant (M8010/3) — *see* Neoplasm, by site, malignant
  Ewing's (M9260/3) — *see* Neoplasm, bone, malignant
  fatty — *see* Lipoma
  fetal, causing disproportion 653.7 ☑
    causing obstructed labor 660.1 ☑
  fibroid (M8890/0) — *see* Leiomyoma
  G cell (M8153/1)
    malignant (M8153/3)
      pancreas 157.4
      specified site NEC — *see* Neoplasm, by site, malignant
      unspecified site 157.4
    specified site — *see* Neoplasm, by site, uncertain behavior
    unspecified site 235.5
  giant cell (type) (M8003/1) — *see also* Neoplasm, by site, unspecified nature
    bone (M9250/1) 238.0
      malignant (M9250/3) — *see* Neoplasm, bone, malignant
    chondromatous (M9230/0) — *see* Neoplasm, bone, benign
    malignant (M8003/3) — *see* Neoplasm, by site, malignant
    peripheral (gingiva) 523.8
    soft parts (M9251/1) — *see also* Neoplasm, connective tissue, uncertain behavior
      malignant (M9251/3) — *see* Neoplasm, connective tissue, malignant
    tendon sheath 727.02
  glomus (M8711/0) — *see also* Hemangioma, by site
    jugulare (M8690/1) 237.3
    malignant (M8690/3) 194.6
  gonadal stromal (M8590/1) — *see* Neoplasm, by site, uncertain behavior
  granular cell (M9580/0) — *see also* Neoplasm, connective tissue, benign
    malignant (M9580/3) — *see* Neoplasm, connective tissue, malignant
  granulosa cell (M8620/1) 236.2
    malignant (M8620/3) 183.0
  granulosa cell-theca cell (M8621/1) 236.2
    malignant (M8621/3) 183.0
  Grawitz's (hypernephroma) (M8312/3) 189.0
  hazard-crile (M8350/3) 193
  hemorrhoidal — *see* Hemorrhoids
  hilar cell (M8660/0) 220
  Hürthle cell (benign) (M8290/0) 226
    malignant (M8290/3) 193
  hydatid (*see also* Echinococcus) 122.9
  hypernephroid (M8311/1) — *see also* Neoplasm, by site, uncertain behavior
  interstitial cell (M8650/1) — *see also* Neoplasm, by site, uncertain behavior
    benign (M8650/0) — *see* Neoplasm, by site, benign
    malignant (M8650/3) — *see* Neoplasm, by site, malignant
  islet cell (M8150/0)
    malignant (M8150/3)
      pancreas 157.4
      specified site — *see* Neoplasm, by site, malignant
      unspecified site 157.4
    pancreas 211.7
    specified site NEC — *see* Neoplasm, by site, benign
    unspecified site 211.7
  juxtaglomerular (M8361/1) 236.91
  Krukenberg's (M8490/6) 198.6
  Leydig cell (M8650/1)
    benign (M8650/0)
      specified site — *see* Neoplasm, by site, benign

Tumor (M8000/1) — *see also* Neoplasm, by site, unspecified nature — *continued*
  Leydig cell (M8650/1) — *continued*
    benign (M8650/0) — *continued*
      unspecified site
        female 220
        male 222.0
    malignant (M8650/3)
      specified site — *see* Neoplasm, by site, malignant
      unspecified site
        female 183.0
        male 186.9
    specified site — *see* Neoplasm, by site, uncertain behavior
    unspecified site
      female 236.2
      male 236.4
  lipid cell, ovary (M8670/0) 220
  lipoid cell, ovary (M8670/0) 220
  lymphomatous, benign (M9590/0) — *see also* Neoplasm, by site, benign
  Malherbe's (M8110/0) — *see* Neoplasm, skin, benign
  malignant (M8000/3) — *see also* Neoplasm, by site, malignant
    fusiform cell (type) (M8004/3) — *see* Neoplasm, by site, malignant
    giant cell (type) (M8003/3) — *see* Neoplasm, by site, malignant
    mixed NEC (M8940/3) — *see* Neoplasm, by site, malignant
    small cell (type) (M8002/3) — *see* Neoplasm, by site, malignant
    spindle cell (type) (M8004/3) — *see* Neoplasm, by site, malignant
  mast cell (M9740/1) 238.5
    malignant (M9740/3) 202.6 ☑
  melanotic, neuroectodermal (M9363/0) — *see* Neoplasm, by site, benign
  Merkel cell — *see* Neoplasm, by site, malignant
  mesenchymal
    malignant (M8800/3) — *see* Neoplasm, connective tissue, malignant
    mixed (M8990/1) — *see* Neoplasm, connective tissue, uncertain behavior
  mesodermal, mixed (M8951/3) — *see also* Neoplasm, by site, malignant
    liver 155.0
  mesonephric (M9110/1) — *see also* Neoplasm, by site, uncertain behavior
    malignant (M9110/3) — *see* Neoplasm, by site, malignant
  metastatic
    from specified site (M8000/3) — *see* Neoplasm, by site, malignant
    to specified site (M8000/6) — *see* Neoplasm, by site, malignant, secondary
  mixed NEC (M8940/0) — *see also* Neoplasm, by site, benign
    malignant (M8940/3) — *see* Neoplasm, by site, malignant
  mucocarcinoid, malignant (M8243/3) — *see* Neoplasm, by site, malignant
  mucoepidermoid (M8430/1) — *see* Neoplasm, by site, uncertain behavior
  Mullerian, mixed (M8950/3) — *see* Neoplasm, by site, malignant
  myoepithelial (M8982/0) — *see* Neoplasm, by site, benign
  neurogenic olfactory (M9520/3) 160.0
  nonencapsulated sclerosing (M8350/3) 193
  odontogenic (M9270/1) 238.0
    adenomatoid (M9300/0) 213.1
      upper jaw (bone) 213.0
    benign (M9270/0) 213.1
      upper jaw (bone) 213.0
    calcifying epithelial (M9340/0) 213.1
      upper jaw (bone) 213.0
    malignant (M9270/3) 170.1
      upper jaw (bone) 170.0
    squamous (M9312/0) 213.1
      upper jaw (bone) 213.0
  ovarian stromal (M8590/1) 236.2
  ovary
    in pregnancy or childbirth 654.4 ☑
      affecting fetus or newborn 763.89

Tumor (M8000/1) — *see also* Neoplasm, by site, unspecified nature — *continued*
  ovary — *continued*
    in pregnancy or childbirth — *continued*
      causing obstructed labor 660.2 ☑
        affecting fetus or newborn 763.1
  pacinian (M9507/0) — *see* Neoplasm, skin, benign
  Pancoast's (M8010/3) 162.3
  papillary — *see* Papilloma
  pelvic, in pregnancy or childbirth 654.9 ☑
    affecting fetus or newborn 763.89
    causing obstructed labor 660.2 ☑
      affecting fetus or newborn 763.1
  phantom 300.11
  plasma cell (M9731/1) 238.6
    benign (M9731/0) — *see* Neoplasm, by site, benign
    malignant (M9731/3) 203.8 ☑
  polyvesicular vitelline (M9071/3)
    specified site — *see* Neoplasm, by site, malignant
    unspecified site
      female 183.0
      male 186.9
  Pott's puffy (*see also* Osteomyelitis) 730.2 ☑
  Rathke's pouch (M9350/1) 237.0
  regaud's (M8082/3) — *see* Neoplasm, nasopharynx, malignant
  rete cell (M8140/0) 222.0
  retinal anlage (M9363/0) — *see* Neoplasm, by site, benign
  Rokitansky's 620.2
  salivary gland type, mixed (M8940/0) — *see also* Neoplasm, by site, benign
    malignant (M8940/3) — *see* Neoplasm, by site, malignant
  Sampson's 617.1
  Schloffer's (*see also* Peritonitis) 567.29 ▲
  Schmincke (M8082/3) — *see* Neoplasm, nasopharynx, malignant
  sebaceous (*see also* Cyst, sebaceous) 706.2
  secondary (M8000/6) — *see* Neoplasm, by site, secondary
  Sertoli cell (M8640/0)
    with lipid storage (M8641/0)
      specified site — *see* Neoplasm, by site, benign
      unspecified site
        female 220
        male 222.0
    specified site — *see* Neoplasm, by site, benign
    unspecified site
      female 220
      male 222.0
  Sertoli-Leydig cell (M8631/0)
    specified site, — *see* Neoplasm, by site, benign
    unspecified site
      female 220
      male 222.0
  sex cord (-stromal) (M8590/1) — *see* Neoplasm, by site, uncertain behavior
  skin appendage (M8390/0) — *see* Neoplasm, skin, benign
  soft tissue
    benign (M8800/0) — *see* Neoplasm, connective tissue, benign
    malignant (M8800/3) — *see* Neoplasm, connective tissue, malignant
  sternomastoid 754.1
  stromal
    gastric 238.1
      benign 215.5
      malignant 171.5
      uncertain behavior 238.1
    gastrointestinal 238.1
      benign 215.5
      malignant 171.5
      uncertain behavior 238.1
    intestine 238.1
      benign 215.5
      malignant 171.5
      uncertain behavior 238.1

Tumor (M8000/1) — *see also* Neoplasm, by site, unspecified nature — *continued*
  stromal — *continued*
    stomach 238.1
      benign 215.5
      malignant 171.5
      uncertain behavior 238.1
    superior sulcus (lung) (pulmonary) (syndrome) (M8010/3) 162.3
    suprasulcus (M8010/3) 162.3
    sweat gland (M8400/1) — *see also* Neoplasm, skin, uncertain behavior
      benign (M8400/0) — *see* Neoplasm, skin, benign
      malignant (M8400/3) — *see* Neoplasm, skin, malignant
    syphilitic brain 094.89
      congenital 090.49
    testicular stromal (M8590/1) 236.4
    theca cell (M8600/0) 220
    theca cell-granulosa cell (M8621/1) 236.2
    theca-lutein (M8610/0) 220
    turban (M8200/0) 216.4
    uterus
      in pregnancy or childbirth 654.1 ☑
        affecting fetus or newborn 763.89
        causing obstructed labor 660.2 ☑
          affecting fetus or newborn 763.1
    vagina
      in pregnancy or childbirth 654.7 ☑
        affecting fetus or newborn 763.89
        causing obstructed labor 660.2 ☑
          affecting fetus or newborn 763.1
    varicose (*see also* Varicose, vein) 454.9
    von Recklinghausen's (M9540/1) 237.71
    vulva
      in pregnancy or childbirth 654.8 ☑
        affecting fetus or newborn 763.89
        causing obstructed labor 660.2 ☑
          affecting fetus or newborn 763.1
    Warthin's (salivary gland) (M8561/0) 210.2
    white — *see also* Tuberculosis, arthritis
    White-Darier 757.39
    Wilms' (nephroblastoma) (M8960/3) 189.0
    yolk sac (M9071/3)
      specified site — *see* Neoplasm, by site, malignant
      unspecified site
        female 183.0
        male 186.9
Tumorlet (M8040/1) — *see* Neoplasm, by site, uncertain behavior
Tungiasis 134.1
Tunica vasculosa lentis 743.39
Tunnel vision 368.45
Turban tumor (M8200/0) 216.4
Türck's trachoma (chronic catarrhal laryngitis) 476.0
Türk's syndrome (ocular retraction syndrome) 378.71
Turner's
  hypoplasia (tooth) 520.4
  syndrome 758.6
  tooth 520.4
Turner-Kieser syndrome (hereditary osteo-onychodysplasia) 756.89
Turner-Varny syndrome 758.6
Turricephaly 756.0
Tussis convulsiva (*see also* Whooping cough) 033.9
Twin
  affected by maternal complications of pregnancy 761.5
  conjoined 759.4
  healthy liveborn — *see* Newborn, twin
  pregnancy (complicating delivery) NEC 651.0 ☑
    with fetal loss and retention of one fetus 651.3 ☑
    following (elective) fetal reduction 651.7 ☑ ●
Twinning, teeth 520.2
Twist, twisted
  bowel, colon, or intestine 560.2
  hair (congenital) 757.4

Twist, twisted — *continued*
  mesentery 560.2
  omentum 560.2
  organ or site, congenital NEC — *see* Anomaly, specified type NEC
  ovarian pedicle 620.5
    congenital 752.0
  umbilical cord — *see* Compression, umbilical cord
Twitch 781.0
Tylosis 700
  buccalis 528.6
  gingiva 523.8
  linguae 528.6
  palmaris et plantaris 757.39
Tympanism 787.3
Tympanites (abdominal) (intestine) 787.3
Tympanitis — *see* Myringitis
Tympanosclerosis 385.00
  involving
    combined sites NEC 385.09
      with tympanic membrane 385.03
    tympanic membrane 385.01
      with ossicles 385.02
        and middle ear 385.03
Tympanum — *see* condition
Tympany
  abdomen 787.3
  chest 786.7
Typhlitis (*see also* Appendicitis) 541
Typhoenteritis 002.0
Typhogastric fever 002.0
Typhoid (abortive) (ambulant) (any site) (fever) (hemorrhagic) (infection) (intermittent) (malignant) (rheumatic) 002.0
  with pneumonia 002.0 [484.8]
  abdominal 002.0
  carrier (suspected) of V02.1
  cholecystitis (current) 002.0
  clinical (Widal and blood test negative) 002.0
  endocarditis 002.0 [421.1]
  inoculation reaction — *see* Complications, vaccination
  meningitis 002.0 [320.7]
  mesenteric lymph nodes 002.0
  myocarditis 002.0 [422.0]
  osteomyelitis (*see also* Osteomyelitis, due to, typhoid) 002.0 [730.8] ☑
  perichondritis, larynx 002.0 [478.71]
  pneumonia 002.0 [484.8]
  spine 002.0 [720.81]
  ulcer (perforating) 002.0
  vaccination, prophylactic (against) V03.1
  Widal negative 002.0
Typhomalaria (fever) (*see also* Malaria) 084.6
Typhomania 002.0
Typhoperitonitis 002.0
Typhus (fever) 081.9
  abdominal, abdominalis 002.0
  African tick 082.1
  amarillic (*see also* Fever, Yellow) 060.9
  brain 081.9
  cerebral 081.9
  classical 080
  endemic (flea-borne) 081.0
  epidemic (louse-borne) 080
  exanthematic NEC 080
  exanthematicus SAI 080
    brillii SAI 081.1
    Mexicanus SAI 081.0
    pediculo vestimenti causa 080
    typhus murinus 081.0
  flea-borne 081.0
  Indian tick 082.1
  Kenya tick 082.1
  louse-borne 080
  Mexican 081.0
    flea-borne 081.0
    louse-borne 080
    tabardillo 080
  mite-borne 081.2
  murine 081.0
  North Asian tick-borne 082.2
  petechial 081.9

Typhus — *continued*
  Queensland tick 082.3
  rat 081.0
  recrudescent 081.1
  recurrent (*see also* Fever, relapsing) 087.9
  São Paulo 082.0
  scrub (China) (India) (Malaya) (New Guinea) 081.2
  shop (of Malaya) 081.0
  Siberian tick 082.2
  tick-borne NEC 082.9
  tropical 081.2
  vaccination, prophylactic (against) V05.8
Tyrosinemia 270.2
  neonatal 775.8
Tyrosinosis (Medes) (Sakai) 270.2
Tyrosinuria 270.2
Tyrosyluria 270.2

U

Uehlinger's syndrome (acropachyderma) 757.39
Uhl's anomaly or disease (hypoplasia of myocardium, right ventricle) 746.84
Ulcer, ulcerated, ulcerating, ulceration, ulcerative 707.9
  with gangrene 707.9 [785.4]
  abdomen (wall) (*see also* Ulcer, skin) 707.8
  ala, nose 478.1
  alveolar process 526.5
  amebic (intestine) 006.9
    skin 006.6
  anastomotic — *see* Ulcer, gastrojejunal
  anorectal 569.41
  antral — *see* Ulcer, stomach
  anus (sphincter) (solitary) 569.41
    varicose — *see* Varicose, ulcer, anus
  aphthous (oral) (recurrent) 528.2
    genital organ(s)
      female 616.8
      male 608.89
    mouth 528.2
  arm (*see also* Ulcer, skin) 707.8
  arteriosclerotic plaque — *see* Arteriosclerosis, by site
  artery NEC 447.2
    without rupture 447.8
  atrophic NEC — *see* Ulcer, skin
  Barrett's (chronic peptic ulcer of esophagus) 530.85
  bile duct 576.8
  bladder (solitary) (sphincter) 596.8
    bilharzial (*see also* Schistosomiasis) 120.9 [595.4]
    submucosal (*see also* Cystitis) 595.1
    tuberculous (*see also* Tuberculosis) 016.1 ☑
  bleeding NEC — *see* Ulcer, peptic, with hemorrhage
  bone 730.9 ☑
  bowel (*see also* Ulcer, intestine) 569.82
  breast 611.0
  bronchitis 491.8
  bronchus 519.1
  buccal (cavity) (traumatic) 528.9
  burn (acute) — *see* Ulcer, duodenum
  Buruli 031.1
  buttock (*see also* Ulcer, skin) 707.8
    decubitus (*see also* Ulcer, decubitus) 707.00
  cancerous (M8000/3) — *see* Neoplasm, by site, malignant
  cardia — *see* Ulcer, stomach
  cardio-esophageal (peptic) 530.20
    with bleeding 530.21
  cecum (*see also* Ulcer, intestine) 569.82
  cervix (uteri) (trophic) 622.0
    with mention of cervicitis 616.0
  chancroidal 099.0
  chest (wall) (*see also* Ulcer, skin) 707.8
  Chiclero 085.4
  chin (pyogenic) (*see also* Ulcer, skin) 707.8
  chronic (cause unknown) — *see also* Ulcer, skin
    penis 607.89
  Cochin-China 085.1
  colitis — *see* Colitis, ulcerative

Ulcer, ulcerated, ulcerating, ulceration, ulcerative — *continued*
colon (*see also* Ulcer, intestine) 569.82
conjunctiva (acute) (postinfectional) 372.00
cornea (infectional) 370.00
with perforation 370.06
annular 370.02
catarrhal 370.01
central 370.03
dendritic 054.42
marginal 370.01
mycotic 370.05
phlyctenular, tuberculous (*see also* Tuberculosis) 017.3 ☑ [370.31]
ring 370.02
rodent 370.07
serpent, serpiginous 370.04
superficial marginal 370.01
tuberculous (*see also* Tuberculosis) 017.3 ☑ [370.31]
corpus cavernosum (chronic) 607.89
crural — *see* Ulcer, lower extremity
Curling's — *see* Ulcer, duodenum
Cushing's — *see* Ulcer, peptic
cystitis (interstitial) 595.1
decubitus (unspecified site) 707.00
with gangrene 707.00 [785.4]
ankle 707.06
back
lower 707.03
upper 707.02
buttock 707.05
elbow 707.01
head 707.09
heel 707.07
hip 707.04
other site 707.09
sacrum 707.03
shoulder blades 707.02
dendritic 054.42
diabetes, diabetic (mellitus) 250.8 ☑ [707.9]
lower limb 250.8 ☑ [707.10]
ankle 250.8 ☑ [707.13]
calf 250.8 ☑ [707.12]
foot 250.8 ☑ [707.15]
heel 250.8 ☑ [707.14]
knee 250.8 ☑ [707.19]
specified site NEC 250.8 ☑ [707.19]
thigh 250.8 ☑ [707.11]
toes 250.8 ☑ [707.15]
specified site NEC 250.8 ☑ [707.8]
Dieulafoy — *see* Lesion, Dieulafoy
due to
infection NEC — *see* Ulcer, skin
radiation, radium — *see* Ulcer, by site
trophic disturbance (any region) — *see* Ulcer, skin
x-ray — *see* Ulcer, by site
duodenum, duodenal (eroded) (peptic) 532.9 ☑

Note — *Use the following fifth-digit subclassification with categories 531-534:*

0   *without mention of obstruction*
1   *with obstruction*

with
hemorrhage (chronic) 532.4 ☑
and perforation 532.6 ☑
perforation (chronic) 532.5 ☑
and hemorrhage 532.6 ☑
acute 532.3 ☑
with
hemorrhage 532.0 ☑
and perforation 532.2 ☑
perforation 532.1 ☑
and hemorrhage 532.2 ☑
bleeding (recurrent) — *see* Ulcer, duodenum, with hemorrhage
chronic 532.7 ☑
with
hemorrhage 532.4 ☑
and perforation 532.6 ☑
perforation 532.5 ☑
and hemorrhage 532.6 ☑
penetrating — *see* Ulcer, duodenum, with perforation

Ulcer, ulcerated, ulcerating, ulceration, ulcerative — *continued*
duodenum, duodenal — *continued*
perforating — *see* Ulcer, duodenum, with perforation
dysenteric NEC 009.0
elusive 595.1
endocarditis (any valve) (acute) (chronic) (subacute) 421.0
enteritis — *see* Colitis, ulcerative
enterocolitis 556.0
epiglottis 478.79
esophagus (peptic) 530.20
with bleeding 530.21
due to ingestion
aspirin 530.20
chemicals 530.20
medicinal agents 530.20
fungal 530.20
infectional 530.20
varicose (*see also* Varix, esophagus) 456.1
bleeding (*see also* Varix, esophagus, bleeding) 456.0
eye NEC 360.00
dendritic 054.42
eyelid (region) 373.01
face (*see also* Ulcer, skin) 707.8
fauces 478.29
Fenwick (-Hunner) (solitary) (*see also* Cystitis) 595.1
fistulous NEC — *see* Ulcer, skin
foot (indolent) (*see also* Ulcer, lower extremity) 707.15
perforating 707.15
leprous 030.1
syphilitic 094.0
trophic 707.15
varicose 454.0
inflamed or infected 454.2
frambesial, initial or primary 102.0
gallbladder or duct 575.8
gall duct 576.8
gangrenous (*see also* Gangrene) 785.4
gastric — *see* Ulcer, stomach
gastrocolic — *see* Ulcer, gastrojejunal
gastroduodenal — *see* Ulcer, peptic
gastroesophageal — *see* Ulcer, stomach
gastrohepatic — *see* Ulcer, stomach
gastrointestinal — *see* Ulcer, gastrojejunal
gastrojejunal (eroded) (peptic) 534.9 ☑

Note — *Use the following fifth-digit subclassification with categories 531-534:*

0   *without mention of obstruction*
1   *with obstruction*

with
hemorrhage (chronic) 534.4 ☑
and perforation 534.6 ☑
perforation 534.5 ☑
and hemorrhage 534.6 ☑
acute 534.3 ☑
with
hemorrhage 534.0 ☑
and perforation 534.2 ☑
perforation 534.1 ☑
and hemorrhage 534.2 ☑
bleeding (recurrent) — *see* Ulcer, gastrojejunal, with hemorrhage
chronic 534.7 ☑
with
hemorrhage 534.4 ☑
and perforation 534.6 ☑
perforation 534.5 ☑
and hemorrhage 534.6 ☑
penetrating — *see* Ulcer, gastrojejunal, with perforation
perforating — *see* Ulcer, gastrojejunal, with perforation
gastrojejunocolic — *see* Ulcer, gastrojejunal
genital organ
female 629.8
male 608.89
gingiva 523.8
gingivitis 523.1
glottis 478.79

Ulcer, ulcerated, ulcerating, ulceration, ulcerative — *continued*
granuloma of pudenda 099.2
groin (*see also* Ulcer, skin) 707.8
gum 523.8
gumma, due to yaws 102.4
hand (*see also* Ulcer, skin) 707.8
hard palate 528.9
heel (*see also* Ulcer, lower extremity) 707.14
decubitus (*see also* Ulcer, decubitus) 707.07
hemorrhoids 455.8
external 455.5
internal 455.2
hip (*see also* Ulcer, skin) 707.8
decubitus (*see also* Ulcer, decubitus) 707.04
Hunner's 595.1
hypopharynx 478.29
hypopyon (chronic) (subacute) 370.04
hypostaticum — *see* Ulcer, varicose
ileocolitis 556.1
ileum (*see also* Ulcer, intestine) 569.82
intestine, intestinal 569.82
with perforation 569.83
amebic 006.9
duodenal — *see* Ulcer, duodenum
granulocytopenic (with hemorrhage) 288.0
marginal 569.82
perforating 569.83
small, primary 569.82
stercoraceous 569.82
stercoral 569.82
tuberculous (*see also* Tuberculosis) 014.8 ☑
typhoid (fever) 002.0
varicose 456.8
ischemic 707.9
lower extremity (*see also* Ulcer, lower extremity) 707.10
ankle 707.13
calf 707.12
foot 707.15
heel 707.14
knee 707.19
specified site NEC 707.19
thigh 707.11
toes 707.15
jejunum, jejunal — *see* Ulcer, gastrojejunal
keratitis (*see also* Ulcer, cornea) 370.00
knee — *see* Ulcer, lower extremity
labium (majus) (minus) 616.50
laryngitis (*see also* Laryngitis) 464.00
with obstruction 464.01
larynx (aphthous) (contact) 478.79
diphtheritic 032.3
leg — *see* Ulcer, lower extremity
lip 528.5
Lipschütz's 616.50
lower extremity (atrophic) (chronic) (neurogenic) (perforating) (pyogenic) (trophic) (tropical) 707.10
with gangrene (*see also* Ulcer, lower extremity) 707.10 [785.4]
arteriosclerotic 440.24
ankle 707.13
arteriosclerotic 440.23
with gangrene 440.24
calf 707.12
decubitus 707.00
with gangrene 707.00 [785.4]
ankle 707.06
buttock 707.05
heel 707.07
hip 707.04
foot 707.15
heel 707.14
knee 707.19
specified site NEC 707.19
thigh 707.11
toes 707.15
varicose 454.0
inflamed or infected 454.2
luetic — *see* Ulcer, syphilitic
lung 518.89
tuberculous (*see also* Tuberculosis) 011.2 ☑
malignant (M8000/3) — *see* Neoplasm, by site, malignant
marginal NEC — *see* Ulcer, gastrojejunal
meatus (urinarius) 597.89
Meckel's diverticulum 751.0

☑ Additional Digit Required — Refer to the Tabular List (Numeric Code Section) for Additional Digit Selection
▶◀ Revised Text   ● New Line   ▲ Revised Code

2006 ICD-9-CM   **Volume 2 — 341**

Ulcer, ulcerated, ulcerating, ulceration, ulcerative — *continued*
Meleney's (chronic undermining) 686.09
Mooren's (cornea) 370.07
mouth (traumatic) 528.9
mycobacterial (skin) 031.1
nasopharynx 478.29
navel cord (newborn) 771.4
neck (*see also* Ulcer, skin) 707.8
 uterus 622.0
neurogenic NEC — *see* Ulcer, skin
nose, nasal (infectional) (passage) 478.1
 septum 478.1
  varicose 456.8
 skin — *see* Ulcer, skin
 spirochetal NEC 104.8
oral mucosa (traumatic) 528.9
palate (soft) 528.9
penetrating NEC — *see* Ulcer, peptic, with
 perforation
penis (chronic) 607.89
peptic (site unspecified) 533.9 ☑

Note — *Use the following fifth-digit*
subclassification with categories 531-534:

0 *without mention of obstruction*
1 *with obstruction*

---

 with
  hemorrhage 533.4 ☑
   and perforation 533.6 ☑
  perforation (chronic) 533.5 ☑
   and hemorrhage 533.6 ☑
 acute 533.3 ☑
  with
   hemorrhage 533.0 ☑
    and perforation 533.2 ☑
   perforation 533.1 ☑
    and hemorrhage 533.2 ☑
 bleeding (recurrent) — *see* Ulcer, peptic,
  with hemorrhage
 chronic 533.7 ☑
  with
   hemorrhage 533.4 ☑
    and perforation 533.6 ☑
   perforation 533.5 ☑
    and hemorrhage 533.6 ☑
 penetrating — *see* Ulcer, peptic, with
  perforation
perforating NEC (*see also* Ulcer, peptic, with
 perforation) 533.5 ☑
 skin 707.9
perineum (*see also* Ulcer, skin) 707.8
peritonsillar 474.8
phagedenic (tropical) NEC — *see* Ulcer, skin
pharynx 478.29
phlebitis — *see* Phlebitis
plaster (*see also* Ulcer, decubitus) 707.00
popliteal space — *see* Ulcer, lower extremity
postpyloric — *see* Ulcer, duodenum
prepuce 607.89
prepyloric — *see* Ulcer, stomach
pressure (*see also* Ulcer, decubitus) 707.00
primary of intestine 569.82
 with perforation 569.83
proctitis 556.2
 with ulcerative sigmoiditis 556.3
prostate 601.8
pseudopeptic — *see* Ulcer, peptic
pyloric — *see* Ulcer, stomach
rectosigmoid 569.82
 with perforation 569.83
rectum (sphincter) (solitary) 569.41
 stercoraceous, stercoral 569.41
 varicose — *see* Varicose, ulcer, anus
retina (*see also* Chorioretinitis) 363.20
rodent (M8090/3) — *see also* Neoplasm, skin,
 malignant
 cornea 370.07
round — *see* Ulcer, stomach
sacrum (region) (*see also* Ulcer, skin) 707.8
Saemisch's 370.04
scalp (*see also* Ulcer, skin) 707.8
sclera 379.09
scrofulous (*see also* Tuberculosis) 017.2 ☑
scrotum 608.89
 tuberculous (*see also* Tuberculosis) 016.5 ☑

Ulcer, ulcerated, ulcerating, ulceration, ulcerative — *continued*
scrotum — *continued*
 varicose 456.4
seminal vesicle 608.89
sigmoid 569.82
 with perforation 569.83
skin (atrophic) (chronic) (neurogenic) (non-
 healing) (perforating) (pyogenic) (trophic)
 707.9
 with gangrene 707.9 *[785.4]*
 amebic 006.6
 decubitus (*see also* Ulcer, decubitus) 707.00
  with gangrene 707.00 *[785.4]*
 in granulocytopenia 288.0
 lower extremity (*see also* Ulcer, lower
  extremity) 707.10
  with gangrene 707.10 *[785.4]*
   arteriosclerotic 440.24
  ankle 707.13
  arteriosclerotic 440.23
   with gangrene 440.24
  calf 707.12
  foot 707.15
  heel 707.14
  knee 707.19
  specified site NEC 707.19
  thigh 707.11
  toes 707.15
 mycobacterial 031.1
 syphilitic (early) (secondary) 091.3
 tuberculous (primary) (*see also*
  Tuberculosis) 017.0 ☑
 varicose — *see* Ulcer, varicose
sloughing NEC — *see* Ulcer, skin
soft palate 528.9
solitary, anus or rectum (sphincter) 569.41
sore throat 462
 streptococcal 034.0
spermatic cord 608.89
spine (tuberculous) 015.0 ☑ *[730.88]*
stasis (leg) (venous) 454.0
 with varicose veins 454.0
 without varicose veins 459.81
 inflamed or infected 454.2
stercoral, stercoraceous 569.82
 with perforation 569.83
 anus or rectum 569.41
stoma, stomal — *see* Ulcer, gastrojejunal
stomach (eroded) (peptic) (round) 531.9 ☑

Note — *Use the following fifth-digit*
subclassification with categories 531-534:

0 *without mention of obstruction*
1 *with obstruction*

---

 with
  hemorrhage 531.4 ☑
   and perforation 531.6 ☑
  perforation (chronic) 531.5 ☑
   and hemorrhage 531.6 ☑
 acute 531.3 ☑
  with
   hemorrhage 531.0 ☑
    and perforation 531.2 ☑
   perforation 531.1 ☑
    and hemorrhage 531.2 ☑
 bleeding (recurrent) — *see* Ulcer, stomach,
  with hemorrhage
 chronic 531.7 ☑
  with
   hemorrhage 531.4 ☑
    and perforation 531.6 ☑
   perforation 531.5 ☑
    and hemorrhage 531.6 ☑
 penetrating — *see* Ulcer, stomach, with
  perforation
 perforating — *see* Ulcer, stomach, with
  perforation
stomatitis 528.0
stress — *see* Ulcer, peptic
strumous (tuberculous) (*see also* Tuberculosis)
 017.2 ☑
submental (*see also* Ulcer, skin) 707.8
submucosal, bladder 595.1

Ulcer, ulcerated, ulcerating, ulceration, ulcerative — *continued*
syphilitic (any site) (early) (secondary) 091.3
 late 095.9
 perforating 095.9
  foot 094.0
testis 608.89
thigh — *see* Ulcer, lower extremity
throat 478.29
 diphtheritic 032.0
toe — *see* Ulcer, lower extremity
tongue (traumatic) 529.0
tonsil 474.8
 diphtheritic 032.0
trachea 519.1
trophic — *see* Ulcer, skin
tropical NEC (*see also* Ulcer, skin) 707.9
tuberculous — *see* Tuberculosis, ulcer
tunica vaginalis 608.89
turbinate 730.9 ☑
typhoid (fever) 002.0
 perforating 002.0
umbilicus (newborn) 771.4
unspecified site NEC — *see* Ulcer, skin
urethra (meatus) (*see also* Urethritis) 597.89
uterus 621.8
 cervix 622.0
  with mention of cervicitis 616.0
 neck 622.0
  with mention of cervicitis 616.0
vagina 616.8
valve, heart 421.0
varicose (lower extremity, any part) 454.0
 anus — *see* Varicose, ulcer, anus
 broad ligament 456.5
 esophagus (*see also* Varix, esophagus) 456.1
  bleeding (*see also* Varix, esophagus,
   bleeding) 456.0
 inflamed or infected 454.2
 nasal septum 456.8
 perineum 456.6
 rectum — *see* Varicose, ulcer, anus
 scrotum 456.4
 specified site NEC 456.8
 sublingual 456.3
 vulva 456.6
vas deferens 608.89
vesical (*see also* Ulcer, bladder) 596.8
vulva (acute) (infectional) 616.50
 Behçet's syndrome 136.1 *[616.51]*
 herpetic 054.12
 tuberculous 016.7 ☑ *[616.51]*
vulvobuccal, recurring 616.50
x-ray — *see* Ulcer, by site
yaws 102.4
Ulcerosa scarlatina 034.1
Ulcus — *see also* Ulcer
cutis tuberculosum (*see also* Tuberculosis)
 017.0 ☑
duodeni — *see* Ulcer, duodenum
durum 091.0
 extragenital 091.2
gastrojejunale — *see* Ulcer, gastrojejunal
hypostaticum — *see* Ulcer, varicose
molle (cutis) (skin) 099.0
serpens corneae (pneumococcal) 370.04
ventriculi — *see* Ulcer, stomach
Ulegyria 742.4
Ulerythema
acneiforma 701.8
centrifugum 695.4
ophryogenes 757.4
Ullrich (-Bonnevie) (-Turner) syndrome 758.6
Ullrich-Feichtiger syndrome 759.89
Ulnar — *see* condition
Ulorrhagia 523.8
Ulorrhea 523.8
Umbilicus, umbilical — *see also* condition
cord necrosis, affecting fetus or newborn 762.6
Unavailability of medical facilities (at) V63.9
due to
 investigation by social service agency V63.8
 lack of services at home V63.1
 remoteness from facility V63.0
 waiting list V63.2

Unavailability of medical facilities — *continued*
  home V63.1
  outpatient clinic V63.0
  specified reason NEC V63.8
Uncinaria americana infestation 126.1
Uncinariasis (*see also* Ancylostomiasis) 126.9
Unconscious, unconsciousness 780.09
Underdevelopment — *see also* Undeveloped
  sexual 259.0
Undernourishment 269.9
Undernutrition 269.9
Under observation — *see* Observation
Underweight 783.22
  for gestational age — *see* Light-for-dates
Underwood's disease (sclerema neonatorum)
  778.1
Undescended — *see also* Malposition, congenital
  cecum 751.4
  colon 751.4
  testis 752.51
Undetermined diagnosis or cause 799.9
Undeveloped, undevelopment — *see also*
  Hypoplasia
  brain (congenital) 742.1
  cerebral (congenital) 742.1
  fetus or newborn 764.9 ☑
  heart 746.89
  lung 748.5
  testis 257.2
  uterus 259.0
Undiagnosed (disease) 799.9
Undulant fever (*see also* Brucellosis) 023.9
Unemployment, anxiety concerning V62.0
Unequal leg (acquired) (length) 736.81
  congenital 755.30
Unerupted teeth, tooth 520.6
Unextracted dental root 525.3
Unguis incarnatus 703.0
Unicornis uterus 752.3
Unicorporeus uterus 752.3
Uniformis uterus 752.3
Unilateral — *see also* condition
  development, breast 611.8
  organ or site, congenital NEC — *see* Agenesis
  vagina 752.49
Unilateralis uterus 752.3
Unilocular heart 745.8
Uninhibited bladder 596.54
  with cauda equina syndrome 344.61
  neurogenic (*see also* Neurogenic, bladder) 596.54
Union, abnormal — *see also* Fusion
  divided tendon 727.89
  larynx and trachea 748.3
Universal
  joint, cervix 620.6
  mesentery 751.4
Unknown
  cause of death 799.9
  diagnosis 799.9
Unna's disease (seborrheic dermatitis) 690.10
Unresponsiveness, adrenocorticotropin (ACTH)
  255.4
Unsatisfactory smear 795.08
Unsoundness of mind (*see also* Psychosis) 298.9
Unspecified cause of death 799.9
Unstable
  back NEC 724.9
  colon 569.89
  joint — *see* Instability, joint
  lie 652.0 ☑
    affecting fetus or newborn (before labor)
      761.7
    causing obstructed labor 660.0 ☑
      affecting fetus or newborn 763.1
  lumbosacral joint (congenital) 756.19
    acquired 724.6
  sacroiliac 724.6
  spine NEC 724.9
Untruthfulness, child problem (*see also*
  Disturbance, conduct) 312.0 ☑

**Unverricht (-Lundborg) disease, syndrome, or
  epilepsy** 333.2
Unverricht-Wagner syndrome (dermatomyositis)
  710.3
Upper respiratory — *see* condition
Upset
  gastric 536.8
    psychogenic 306.4
  gastrointestinal 536.8
    psychogenic 306.4
    virus (*see also* Enteritis, viral) 008.8
  intestinal (large) (small) 564.9
    psychogenic 306.4
  menstruation 626.9
  mental 300.9
  stomach 536.8
    psychogenic 306.4
Urachus — *see also* condition
  patent 753.7
  persistent 753.7
Uratic arthritis 274.0
Urbach's lipoid proteinosis 272.8
Urbach-Oppenheim disease or syndrome
  (necrobiosis lipoidica diabeticorum)
  250.8 ☑ *[709.3]*
Urbach-Wiethe disease or syndrome (lipoid
  proteinosis) 272.8
Urban yellow fever 060.1
Urea, blood, high — *see* Uremia
Uremia, uremic (absorption) (amaurosis)
  (amblyopia) (aphasia) (apoplexy) (coma)
  (delirium) (dementia) (dropsy) (dyspnea)
  (fever) (intoxication) (mania) (paralysis)
  (poisoning) (toxemia) (vomiting) 586
  with
    abortion — *see* Abortion, by type, with renal
      failure
    ectopic pregnancy (*see also* categories
      633.0-633.9) 639.3
    hypertension (*see also* Hypertension, kidney)
      403.91
    molar pregnancy (*see also* categories 630-
      632) 639.3
  chronic 585.9   ▲
  complicating
    abortion 639.3
    ectopic or molar pregnancy 639.3
    hypertension (*see also* Hypertension, kidney)
      403.91
    labor and delivery 669.3 ☑
  congenital 779.89
  extrarenal 788.9
  hypertensive (chronic) (*see also* Hypertension,
    kidney) 403.91
  maternal NEC, affecting fetus or newborn
    760.1
  neuropathy 585.9 *[357.4]*   ▲
  pericarditis 585.9 *[420.0]*   ▲
  prerenal 788.9
  pyelitic (*see also* Pyelitis) 590.80
Ureter, ureteral — *see* condition
Ureteralgia 788.0
Ureterectasis 593.89
Ureteritis 593.89
  cystica 590.3
  due to calculus 592.1
  gonococcal (acute) 098.19
    chronic or duration of 2 months or over
      098.39
  nonspecific 593.89
Ureterocele (acquired) 593.89
  congenital 753.23
Ureterolith 592.1
Ureterolithiasis 592.1
Ureterostomy status V44.6
  with complication 997.5
Urethra, urethral — *see* condition
Urethralgia 788.9
Urethritis (abacterial) (acute) (allergic) (anterior)
  (chronic) (nonvenereal) (posterior) (recurrent)
  (simple) (subacute) (ulcerative)
  (undifferentiated) 597.80

Urethritis — *continued*
  diplococcal (acute) 098.0
    chronic or duration of 2 months or over
      098.2
  due to Trichomonas (vaginalis) 131.02
  gonococcal (acute) 098.0
    chronic or duration of 2 months or over
      098.2
  nongonococcal (sexually transmitted) 099.40
    Chlamydia trachomatis 099.41
    Reiter's 099.3
    specified organism NEC 099.49
  nonspecific (sexually transmitted) (*see also*
    Urethritis, nongonococcal) 099.40
  not sexually transmitted 597.80
  Reiter's 099.3
  trichomonal or due to Trichomonas (vaginalis)
    131.02
  tuberculous (*see also* Tuberculosis) 016.3 ☑
  venereal NEC (*see also* Urethritis,
    nongonococcal) 099.40
Urethrocele
  female 618.03
    with uterine prolapse 618.4
      complete 618.3
      incomplete 618.2
  male 599.5
Urethrolithiasis 594.2
Urethro-oculoarticular syndrome 099.3
Urethro-oculosynovial syndrome 099.3
Urethrorectal — *see* condition
Urethrorrhagia 599.84
Urethrorrhea 788.7
Urethrostomy status V44.6
  with complication 997.5
Urethrotrigonitis 595.3
Urethrovaginal — *see* condition
Urhidrosis, uridrosis 705.89
Uric acid
  diathesis 274.9
  in blood 790.6
Uricacidemia 790.6
Uricemia 790.6
Uricosuria 791.9
Urination
  frequent 788.41
  painful 788.1
  urgency 788.63
Urine, urinary — *see also* condition
  abnormality NEC 788.69
  blood in (*see also* Hematuria) 599.7
  discharge, excessive 788.42
  enuresis 788.30
    nonorganic origin 307.6
  extravasation 788.8
  frequency 788.41
  incontinence 788.30
    active 788.30
    female 788.30
      stress 625.6
        and urge 788.33
    male 788.30
      stress 788.32
        and urge 788.33
    mixed (stress and urge) 788.33
    neurogenic 788.39
    nonorganic origin 307.6
    overflow 788.38
    stress (female) 625.6
      male NEC 788.32
  intermittent stream 788.61
  pus in 791.9
  retention or stasis NEC 788.20
    bladder, incomplete emptying 788.21
    psychogenic 306.53
    specified NEC 788.29
  secretion
    deficient 788.5
    excessive 788.42
    frequency 788.41
  stream
    intermittent 788.61
    slowing 788.62
    splitting 788.61

☑ Additional Digit Required — Refer to the Tabular List (Numeric Code Section) for Additional Digit Selection
▶◀ Revised Text   ● New Line   ▲ Revised Code

Urine, urinary — *see also* condition — *continued*
  stream — *continued*
    weak 788.62
    urgency 788.63
Urinemia — *see* Uremia
Urinoma NEC 599.9
  bladder 596.8
  kidney 593.89
  renal 593.89
  ureter 593.89
  urethra 599.84
Uroarthritis, infectious 099.3
Urodialysis 788.5
Urolithiasis 592.9
Uronephrosis 593.89
Uropathy 599.9
  obstructive 599.60   ▲
Urosepsis 599.0
  meaning sepsis 995.91
  meaning urinary tract infection 599.0
Urticaria 708.9
  with angioneurotic edema 995.1
    hereditary 277.6
  allergic 708.0
  cholinergic 708.5
  chronic 708.8
  cold, familial 708.2
  dermatographic 708.3
  due to
    cold or heat 708.2
    drugs 708.0
    food 708.0
    inhalants 708.0
    plants 708.8
    serum 999.5
  factitial 708.3
  giant 995.1
    hereditary 277.6

Urticaria — *continued*
  gigantea 995.1
    hereditary 277.6
  idiopathic 708.1
  larynx 995.1
    hereditary 277.6
  neonatorum 778.8
  nonallergic 708.1
  papulosa (Hebra) 698.2
  perstans hemorrhagica 757.39
  pigmentosa 757.33
  recurrent periodic 708.8
  serum 999.5
  solare 692.72
  specified type NEC 708.8
  thermal (cold) (heat) 708.2
  vibratory 708.4
Urticarioides acarodermatitis 133.9
Use of
  nonprescribed drugs (*see also* Abuse, drugs,
    nondependent) 305.9 ☑
  patent medicines (*see also* Abuse, drugs,
    nondependent) 305.9 ☑
Usher-Senear disease (pemphigus erythematosus)
  694.4
Uta 085.5
Uterine size-date discrepancy 646.8 ☑
Uteromegaly 621.2
Uterovaginal — *see* condition
Uterovesical — *see* condition
Uterus — *see* condition
Utriculitis (utriculus prostaticus) 597.89
Uveal — *see* condition
Uveitis (anterior) (*see also* Iridocyclitis) 364.3
  acute or subacute 364.00
    due to or associated with
      gonococcal infection 098.41
      herpes (simplex) 054.44
        zoster 053.22

Uveitis (*see also* Iridocyclitis) — *continued*
  acute or subacute — *continued*
    primary 364.01
    recurrent 364.02
    secondary (noninfectious) 364.04
      infectious 364.03
  allergic 360.11
  chronic 364.10
    due to or associated with
      sarcoidosis 135 *[364.11]*
      tuberculosis (*see also* Tuberculosis)
        017.3 ☑ *[364.11]*
  due to
    operation 360.11
    toxoplasmosis (acquired) 130.2
      congenital (active) 771.2
  granulomatous 364.10
  heterochromic 364.21
  lens-induced 364.23
  nongranulomatous 364.00
  posterior 363.20
    disseminated — *see* Chorioretinitis,
      disseminated
    focal — *see* Chorioretinitis, focal
  recurrent 364.02
  sympathetic 360.11
  syphilitic (secondary) 091.50
    congenital 090.0 *[363.13]*
    late 095.8 *[363.13]*
  tuberculous (*see also* Tuberculosis)
    017.3 ☑ *[364.11]*
Uveoencephalitis 363.22
Uveokeratitis (*see also* Iridocyclitis) 364.3
Uveoparotid fever 135
Uveoparotitis 135
Uvula — *see* condition
Uvulitis (acute) (catarrhal) (chronic) (gangrenous)
  (membranous) (suppurative) (ulcerative)
  528.3

☑ Additional Digit Required — Refer to the Tabular List (Numeric Code Section) for Additional Digit Selection

▶◀ Revised Text   ● New Line   ▲ Revised Code

V

Vaccination
complication or reaction — *see* Complications, vaccination
not ►carried out◄ V64.00 ▲
  because of
    acute illness V64.01 ●
    allergy to vaccine or component V64.04 ●
    caregiver refusal V64.05 ●
    chronic illness V64.02 ●
    immune compromised state V64.03 ●
    patient had disease being vaccinated against V64.08 ●
    patient refusal V64.06 ●
    reason NEC V64.09 ●
    religious reasons V64.07 ●
prophylactic (against) V05.9
  arthropod-borne viral
    disease NEC V05.1
    encephalitis V05.0
  chickenpox V05.4
  cholera (alone) V03.0
    with typhoid-paratyphoid (cholera + TAB) V06.0
  common cold V04.7
  diphtheria (alone) V03.5
    with
      poliomyelitis (DTP+ polio) V06.3
      tetanus V06.5
        pertussis combined (DTP) (DTaP) V06.1
      typhoid-paratyphoid (DTP + TAB) V06.2
  disease (single) NEC V05.9
    bacterial NEC V03.9
      specified type NEC V03.89
    combination NEC V06.9
      specified type NEC V06.8
    specified type NEC V05.8
  encephalitis, viral, arthropod-borne V05.0
  Hemophilus influenzae, type B [Hib] V03.81
  hepatitis, viral V05.3
  influenza V04.81
    with
      Streptococcus pneumoniae [pneumococcus] V06.6
  leishmaniasis V05.2
  measles (alone) V04.2
    with mumps-rubella (MMR) V06.4
  mumps (alone) V04.6
    with measles and rubella (MMR) V06.4
  pertussis alone V03.6
  plague V03.3
  poliomyelitis V04.0
    with diphtheria-tetanus-pertussis (DTP + polio) V06.3
  rabies V04.5
  respiratory syncytial virus (RSV) V04.82
  rubella (alone) V04.3
    with measles and mumps (MMR) V06.4
  smallpox V04.1
  Streptococcus pneumoniae [pneumococcus] V03.82
    with
      influenza V06.6
  tetanus toxoid (alone) V03.7
    with diphtheria [Td] [DT] V06.5
      with
        pertussis (DTP) (DTaP) V06.1
          with poliomyelitis (DTP+polio) V06.3
  tuberculosis (BCG) V03.2
  tularemia V03.4
  typhoid-paratyphoid (TAB) (alone) V03.1
    with diphtheria-tetanus-pertussis (TAB + DTP) V06.2
  varicella V05.4
  viral
    disease NEC V04.89
    encephalitis, arthropod-borne V05.0
    hepatitis V05.3
  yellow fever V04.4
Vaccinia (generalized) 999.0
congenital 771.2
conjunctiva 999.3

Vaccinia — continued
eyelids 999.0 *[373.5]*
localized 999.3
nose 999.3
not from vaccination 051.0
  eyelid 051.0 *[373.5]*
sine vaccinatione 051.0
without vaccination 051.0
Vacuum
extraction of fetus or newborn 763.3
in sinus (accessory) (nasal) (*see also* Sinusitis) 473.9
Vagabond V60.0
Vagabondage V60.0
Vagabonds' disease 132.1
Vagina, vaginal — *see* condition
Vaginalitis (tunica) 608.4
Vaginismus (reflex) 625.1
functional 306.51
hysterical 300.11
psychogenic 306.51
Vaginitis (acute) (chronic) (circumscribed) (diffuse) (emphysematous) (Hemophilus vaginalis) (nonspecific) (nonvenereal) (ulcerative) 616.10
with
  abortion — *see* Abortion, by type, with sepsis
  ectopic pregnancy (*see also* categories 633.0-633.9) 639.0
  molar pregnancy (*see also* categories 630-632) 639.0
adhesive, congenital 752.49
atrophic, postmenopausal 627.3
bacterial 616.10
blennorrhagic (acute) 098.0
  chronic or duration of 2 months or over 098.2
candidal 112.1
chlamydial 099.53
complicating pregnancy or puerperium 646.6 ☑
  affecting fetus or newborn 760.8
congenital (adhesive) 752.49
due to
  C. albicans 112.1
  Trichomonas (vaginalis) 131.01
following
  abortion 639.0
  ectopic or molar pregnancy 639.0
gonococcal (acute) 098.0
  chronic or duration of 2 months or over 098.2
granuloma 099.2
Monilia 112.1
mycotic 112.1
pinworm 127.4 *[616.11]*
postirradiation 616.10
postmenopausal atrophic 627.3
senile (atrophic) 627.3
syphilitic (early) 091.0
  late 095.8
trichomonal 131.01
tuberculous (*see also* Tuberculosis) 016.7 ☑
venereal NEC 099.8
Vaginosis — *see* Vaginitis
Vagotonia 352.3
Vagrancy V60.0
Vallecula — *see* condition
Valley fever 114.0
Valsuani's disease (progressive pernicious anemia, puerperal) 648.2 ☑
Valve, valvular (formation) — *see also* condition
cerebral ventricle (communicating) in situ V45.2
cervix, internal os 752.49
colon 751.5
congenital NEC — *see* Atresia
formation, congenital NEC — *see* Atresia
heart defect — *see* Anomaly, heart, valve
ureter 753.29
  pelvic junction 753.21
  vesical orifice 753.22
urethra 753.6

Valvulitis (chronic) (*see also* Endocarditis) 424.90
rheumatic (chronic) (inactive) (with chorea) 397.9
  active or acute (aortic) (mitral) (pulmonary) (tricuspid) 391.1
syphilitic NEC 093.20
  aortic 093.22
  mitral 093.21
  pulmonary 093.24
  tricuspid 093.23
Valvulopathy — *see* Endocarditis
van Bogaert's leukoencephalitis (sclerosing) (subacute) 046.2
van Bogaert-Nijssen (-Peiffer) disease 330.0
van Buchem's syndrome (hyperostosis corticalis) 733.3
van Creveld-von Gierke disease (glycogenosis I) 271.0
van den Bergh's disease (enterogenous cyanosis) 289.7
van der Hoeve's syndrome (brittle bones and blue sclera, deafness) 756.51
van der Hoeve-Halbertsma-Waardenburg syndrome (ptosis-epicanthus) 270.2
van der Hoeve-Waardenburg-Gualdi syndrome (ptosis epicanthus) 270.2
Vancomycin (glycopeptide)
intermediate staphylococcus aureus (VISA/GISA) V09.8
resistant
  enterococcus (VRE) V09.8
  staphylococcus aureus (VRSA/GRSA) V09.8
Vanillism 692.89
Vanishing lung 492.0
van Neck (-Odelberg) disease or syndrome (juvenile osteochondrosis) 732.1
Vanishing twin 651.33
Vapor asphyxia or suffocation NEC 987.9
specified agent — *see* Table of Drugs and Chemicals
Vaquez's disease (M9950/1) 238.4
Vaquez-Osler disease (polycythemia vera) (M9950/1) 238.4
Variance, lethal ball, prosthetic heart valve 996.02
Variants, thalassemic 282.49
Variations in hair color 704.3
Varicella 052.9
with
  complication 052.8
    specified NEC 052.7
  pneumonia 052.1
  vaccination and inoculation (against) (prophylactic) V05.4
exposure to V01.71
Varices — *see* Varix
Varicocele (scrotum) (thrombosed) 456.4
ovary 456.5
perineum 456.6
spermatic cord (ulcerated) 456.4
Varicose
aneurysm (ruptured) (*see also* Aneurysm) 442.9
dermatitis (lower extremity) — *see* Varicose, vein, inflamed or infected
eczema — *see* Varicose, vein
phlebitis — *see* Varicose, vein, inflamed or infected
placental vessel — *see* Placenta, abnormal
tumor — *see* Varicose, vein
ulcer (lower extremity, any part) 454.0
  anus 455.8
    external 455.5
    internal 455.2
  esophagus (*see also* Varix, esophagus) 456.1
    bleeding (*see also* Varix, esophagus, bleeding) 456.0
  inflamed or infected 454.2
  nasal septum 456.8
  perineum 456.6
  rectum — *see* Varicose, ulcer, anus
  scrotum 456.4
  specified site NEC 456.8

☑ Additional Digit Required — Refer to the Tabular List (Numeric Code Section) for Additional Digit Selection
►◄ Revised Text ● New Line ▲ Revised Code

2006 ICD-9-CM October 2005 • Volume 2 — 345

Varicose — continued
  vein (lower extremity) (ruptured) (see also Varix)
      454.9
    with
      complications NEC 454.8
      edema 454.8
      inflammation or infection 454.1
        ulcerated 454.2
      pain 454.8
      stasis dermatitis 454.1
        with ulcer 454.2
      swelling 454.8
      ulcer 454.0
        inflamed or infected 454.2
    anus — see Hemorrhoids
    broad ligament 456.5
    congenital (peripheral) 747.60
      gastrointestinal 747.61
      lower limb 747.64
      renal 747.62
      specified NEC 747.69
      upper limb 747.63
    esophagus (ulcerated) (see also Varix,
        esophagus) 456.1
      bleeding (see also Varix, esophagus,
        bleeding) 456.0
    inflamed or infected 454.1
      with ulcer 454.2
    in pregnancy or puerperium 671.0 ☑
      vulva or perineum 671.1 ☑
    nasal septum (with ulcer) 456.8
    pelvis 456.5
    perineum 456.6
      in pregnancy, childbirth, or puerperium
        671.1 ☑
    rectum — see Hemorrhoids
    scrotum (ulcerated) 456.4
    specified site NEC 456.8
    sublingual 456.3
    ulcerated 454.0
      inflamed or infected 454.2
    umbilical cord, affecting fetus or newborn
        762.6
    urethra 456.8
    vulva 456.6
      in pregnancy, childbirth, or puerperium
        671.1 ☑
  vessel — see also Varix
    placenta — see Placenta, abnormal
Varicosis, varicosities, varicosity (see also Varix)
    454.9
Variola 050.9
  hemorrhagic (pustular) 050.0
  major 050.0
  minor 050.1
  modified 050.2
Varioloid 050.2
Variolosa, purpura 050.0
Varix (lower extremity) (ruptured) 454.9
  with
    complications NEC 454.8
    edema 454.8
    inflammation or infection 454.1
      with ulcer 454.2
    pain 454.8
    stasis dermatitis 454.1
      with ulcer 454.2
    swelling 454.8
    ulcer 454.0
      with inflammation or infection 454.2
  aneurysmal (see also Aneurysm) 442.9
  anus — see Hemorrhoids
  arteriovenous (congenital) (peripheral) NEC
      747.60
    gastrointestinal 747.61
    lower limb 747.64
    renal 747.62
    specified NEC 747.69
    spinal 747.82
    upper limb 747.63
  bladder 456.5
  broad ligament 456.5
  congenital (peripheral) 747.60

Varix — continued
  esophagus (ulcerated) 456.1
    bleeding 456.0
      in
        cirrhosis of liver 571.5 [456.20]
        portal hypertension 572.3 [456.20]
      congenital 747.69
        in
          cirrhosis of liver 571.5 [456.21]
            with bleeding 571.5 [456.20]
          portal hypertension 572.3 [456.21]
            with bleeding 572.3 [456.20]
  gastric 456.8
  inflamed or infected 454.1
    ulcerated 454.2
  in pregnancy or puerperium 671.0 ☑
    perineum 671.1 ☑
    vulva 671.1 ☑
  labia (majora) 456.6
  orbit 456.8
    congenital 747.69
  ovary 456.5
  papillary 448.1
  pelvis 456.5
  perineum 456.6
    in pregnancy or puerperium 671.1 ☑
  pharynx 456.8
  placenta — see Placenta, abnormal
  prostate 456.8
  rectum — see Hemorrhoids
  renal papilla 456.8
  retina 362.17
  scrotum (ulcerated) 456.4
  sigmoid colon 456.8
  specified site NEC 456.8
  spinal (cord) (vessels) 456.8
  spleen, splenic (vein) (with phlebolith) 456.8
  sublingual 456.3
  ulcerated 454.0
    inflamed or infected 454.2
  umbilical cord, affecting fetus or newborn
      762.6
  uterine ligament 456.5
  vocal cord 456.8
  vulva 456.6
    in pregnancy, childbirth, or puerperium
      671.1 ☑
Vasa previa 663.5 ☑
  affecting fetus or newborn 762.6
  hemorrhage from, affecting fetus or newborn
      772.0
Vascular — see also condition
  loop on papilla (optic) 743.57
  sheathing, retina 362.13
  spasm 443.9
  spider 448.1
Vascularity, pulmonary, congenital 747.3
Vascularization
  choroid 362.16
  cornea 370.60
    deep 370.63
    localized 370.61
  retina 362.16
  subretinal 362.16
Vasculitis 447.6
  allergic 287.0
  cryoglobulinemic 273.2
  disseminated 447.6
  kidney 447.8
  leukocytoclastic 446.29
  nodular 695.2
  retinal 362.18
  rheumatic — see Fever, rheumatic
Vasculopathy
  cardiac allograft 996.83
Vas deferens — see condition
Vas deferentitis 608.4
Vasectomy, admission for V25.2
Vasitis 608.4
  nodosa 608.4
  scrotum 608.4
  spermatic cord 608.4
  testis 608.4
  tuberculous (see also Tuberculosis) 016.5 ☑
  tunica vaginalis 608.4
  vas deferens 608.4

Vasodilation 443.9
Vasomotor — see condition
Vasoplasty, after previous sterilization V26.0
Vasoplegia, splanchnic (see also Neuropathy,
    peripheral, autonomic) 337.9
Vasospasm 443.9
  cerebral (artery) 435.9
    with transient neurologic deficit 435.9
  nerve
    arm NEC 354.9
    autonomic 337.9
    brachial plexus 353.0
    cervical plexus 353.2
    leg NEC 355.8
    lower extremity NEC 355.8
    peripheral NEC 355.9
    spinal NEC 355.9
    sympathetic 337.9
    upper extremity NEC 354.9
  peripheral NEC 443.9
  retina (artery) (see also Occlusion, retinal,
      artery) 362.30
Vasospastic — see condition
Vasovagal attack (paroxysmal) 780.2
  psychogenic 306.2
Vater's ampulla — see condition
VATER syndrome 759.89
Vegetation, vegetative
  adenoid (nasal fossa) 474.2
  consciousness (persistent) 780.03
  endocarditis (acute) (any valve) (chronic)
      (subacute) 421.0
  heart (mycotic) (valve) 421.0
  state (persistent) 780.03
Veil
  Jackson's 751.4
  over face (causing asphyxia) 768.9
Vein, venous — see condition
Veldt sore (see also Ulcer, skin) 707.9
Velo-cardio-facial syndrome 758.32
Velpeau's hernia — see Hernia, femoral
Venereal
  balanitis NEC 099.8
  bubo 099.1
  disease 099.9
    specified nature or type NEC 099.8
  granuloma inguinale 099.2
  lymphogranuloma (Durand-Nicolas-Favre), any
      site 099.1
  salpingitis 098.37
  urethritis (see also Urethritis, nongonococcal)
      099.40
  vaginitis NEC 099.8
  warts 078.19
Vengefulness, in child (see also Disturbance,
    conduct) 312.0 ☑
Venofibrosis 459.89
Venom, venomous
  bite or sting (animal or insect) 989.5
  poisoning 989.5
Venous — see condition
Ventouse delivery NEC 669.5 ☑
  affecting fetus or newborn 763.3
Ventral — see condition
Ventricle, ventricular — see also condition
  escape 427.69
  standstill (see also Arrest, cardiac) 427.5
Ventriculitis, cerebral (see also Meningitis) 322.9
Ventriculostomy status V45.2
Verbiest's syndrome (claudicatio intermittens
    spinalis) 435.1
Vernet's syndrome 352.6
Verneuil's disease (syphilitic bursitis) 095.7
Verruca (filiformis) 078.10
  acuminata (any site) 078.11
  necrogenica (primary) (see also Tuberculosis)
      017.0 ☑
  plana (juvenilis) 078.19
  peruana 088.0

☑ Additional Digit Required — Refer to the Tabular List (Numeric Code Section) for Additional Digit Selection

Verruca — *continued*
peruviana 088.0
plantaris 078.19
seborrheica 702.19
inflamed 702.11
senilis 702.0
tuberculosa (primary) (*see also* Tuberculosis)
017.0 ☑
venereal 078.19
viral NEC 078.10
Verrucosities (*see also* Verruca) 078.10
Verrucous endocarditis (acute) (any valve)
(chronic) (subacute) 710.0 *[424.91]*
nonbacterial 710.0 *[424.91]*
Verruga
peruana 088.0
peruviana 088.0
Verse's disease (calcinosis intervertebralis)
275.49 *[722.90]*
Version
before labor, affecting fetus or newborn 761.7
cephalic (correcting previous malposition)
652.1 ☑
affecting fetus or newborn 763.1
cervix (*see also* Malposition, uterus) 621.6
uterus (postinfectional) (postpartal, old) (*see
also* Malposition, uterus) 621.6
forward — *see* Anteversion, uterus
lateral — *see* Lateroversion, uterus
Vertebra, vertebral — *see* condition
Vertigo 780.4
auditory 386.19
aural 386.19
benign paroxysmal positional 386.11
central origin 386.2
cerebral 386.2
Dix and Hallpike (epidemic) 386.12
endemic paralytic 078.81
epidemic 078.81
Dix and Hallpike 386.12
Gerlier's 078.81
Pedersen's 386.12
vestibular neuronitis 386.12
epileptic — *see* Epilepsy
Gerlier's (epidemic) 078.81
hysterical 300.11
labyrinthine 386.10
laryngeal 786.2
malignant positional 386.2
Ménière's (*see also* Disease, Ménière's) 386.00
menopausal 627.2
otogenic 386.19
paralytic 078.81
paroxysmal positional, benign 386.11
Pedersen's (epidemic) 386.12
peripheral 386.10
specified type NEC 386.19
positional
benign paroxysmal 386.11
malignant 386.2
Verumontanitis (chronic) (*see also* Urethritis)
597.89
Vesania (*see also* Psychosis) 298.9
Vesical — *see* condition
Vesicle
cutaneous 709.8
seminal — *see* condition
skin 709.8
Vesicocolic — *see* condition
Vesicoperineal — *see* condition
Vesicorectal — *see* condition
Vesicourethrorectal — *see* condition
Vesicovaginal — *see* condition
Vesicular — *see* condition
Vesiculitis (seminal) 608.0
amebic 006.8
gonorrheal (acute) 098.14
chronic or duration of 2 months or over
098.34
trichomonal 131.09
tuberculous (*see also* Tuberculosis)
016.5 ☑ *[608.81]*

Vestibulitis (ear) (*see also* Labyrinthitis) 386.30
nose (external) 478.1
vulvar 616.10
Vestibulopathy, acute peripheral (recurrent)
386.12
Vestige, vestigial — *see also* Persistence
branchial 744.41
structures in vitreous 743.51
Vibriosis NEC 027.9
Vidal's disease (lichen simplex chronicus) 698.3
Video display tube syndrome 723.8
Vienna-type encephalitis 049.8
Villaret's syndrome 352.6
Villous — *see* condition
VIN I (vulvar intraepithelial neoplasia I) 624.8
VIN II (vulvar intraepithelial neoplasia II) 624.8
VIN III (vulvar intraepithelial neoplasia III) 233.3
Vincent's
angina 101
bronchitis 101
disease 101
gingivitis 101
infection (any site) 101
laryngitis 101
stomatitis 101
tonsillitis 101
Vinson-Plummer syndrome (sideropenic
dysphagia) 280.8
Viosterol deficiency (*see also* Deficiency,
calciferol) 268.9
Virchow's disease 733.99
Viremia 790.8
Virilism (adrenal) (female) NEC 255.2
with
3-beta-hydroxysteroid dehydrogenase defect
255.2
11-hydroxylase defect 255.2
21-hydroxylase defect 255.2
adrenal
hyperplasia 255.2
insufficiency (congenital) 255.2
cortical hyperfunction 255.2
Virilization (female) (suprarenal) (*see also*
Virilism) 255.2
isosexual 256.4
Virulent bubo 099.0
Virus, viral — *see also* condition
infection NEC (*see also* Infection, viral) 079.99
septicemia 079.99
VISA (vancomycin intermediate staphylococcus
aureus) V09.8
Viscera, visceral — *see* condition
Visceroptosis 569.89
Visible peristalsis 787.4
Vision, visual
binocular, suppression 368.31
blurred, blurring 368.8
hysterical 300.11
defect, defective (*see also* Impaired, vision)
369.9
disorientation (syndrome) 368.16
disturbance NEC (*see also* Disturbance, vision)
368.9
hysterical 300.11
examination V72.0
field, limitation 368.40
fusion, with defective steropsis 368.33
hallucinations 368.16
halos 368.16
loss 369.9
both eyes (*see also* Blindness, both eyes)
369.3
complete (*see also* Blindness, both eyes)
369.00
one eye 369.8
sudden 368.16
low (both eyes) 369.20
one eye (other eye normal) (*see also*
Impaired, vision) 369.70
blindness, other eye 369.10
perception, simultaneous without fusion
368.32
tunnel 368.45

Vitality, lack or want of 780.79
newborn 779.89
Vitamin deficiency NEC (*see also* Deficiency,
vitamin) 269.2
Vitelline duct, persistent 751.0
Vitiligo 709.01
due to pinta (carate) 103.2
eyelid 374.53
vulva 624.8
Vitium cordis — *see* Disease, heart
Vitreous — *see also* condition
touch syndrome 997.99
VLCAD (long chain/very long chain acyl CoA
dehydrogenase deficiency, LCAD) 277.85
Vocal cord — *see* condition
Vocational rehabilitation V57.22
Vogt's (Cecile) disease or syndrome 333.7
Vogt-Koyanagi syndrome 364.24
Vogt-Spielmeyer disease (amaurotic familial
idiocy) 330.1
Voice
change (*see also* Dysphonia) 784.49
loss (*see also* Aphonia) 784.41
Volhard-Fahr disease (malignant nephrosclerosis)
403.00
Volhynian fever 083.1
Volkmann's ischemic contracture or paralysis
(complicating trauma) 958.6
Voluntary starvation 307.1
Volvulus (bowel) (colon) (intestine) 560.2
with
hernia — *see also* Hernia, by site, with
obstruction
gangrenous — *see* Hernia, by site, with
gangrene
perforation 560.2
congenital 751.5
duodenum 537.3
fallopian tube 620.5
oviduct 620.5
stomach (due to absence of gastrocolic
ligament) 537.89
Vomiting 787.03
with nausea 787.01
allergic 535.4 ☑
asphyxia 933.1
bilious (cause unknown) 787.0 ☑
following gastrointestinal surgery 564.3
blood (*see also* Hematemesis) 578.0
causing asphyxia, choking, or suffocation (*see
also* Asphyxia, food) 933.1
cyclical 536.2
psychogenic 306.4
epidemic 078.82
fecal matter 569.89
following gastrointestinal surgery 564.3
functional 536.8
psychogenic 306.4
habit 536.2
hysterical 300.11
nervous 306.4
neurotic 306.4
newborn 779.3
of or complicating pregnancy 643.9 ☑
due to
organic disease 643.8 ☑
specific cause NEC 643.8 ☑
early — *see* Hyperemesis, gravidarum
late (after 22 completed weeks of gestation)
643.2 ☑
pernicious or persistent 536.2
complicating pregnancy — *see* Hyperemesis,
gravidarum
psychogenic 306.4
physiological 787.0 ☑
psychic 306.4
psychogenic 307.54
stercoral 569.89
uncontrollable 536.2
psychogenic 306.4
uremic — *see* Uremia
winter 078.82

2006 ICD-9-CM

☑ Additional Digit Required — Refer to the Tabular List (Numeric Code Section) for Additional Digit Selection
▶◀ Revised Text ● New Line ▲ Revised Code

Volume 2 — 347

Verruca — Vomiting

von Bechterew (-Strumpell) disease or syndrome (ankylosing spondylitis) 720.0

von Bezold's abscess 383.01

von Economo's disease (encephalitis lethargica) 049.8

von Eulenburg's disease (congenital paramyotonia) 359.2

von Gierke's disease (glycogenosis I) 271.0

von Gies' joint 095.8

von Graefe's disease or syndrome 378.72

von Hippel (-Lindau) disease or syndrome (retinocerebral angiomatosis) 759.6

von Jaksch's anemia or disease (pseudoleukemia infantum) 285.8

von Recklinghausen's
  disease or syndrome (nerves) (skin) (M9540/1) 237.71
    bones (osteitis fibrosa cystica) 252.01
  tumor (M9540/1) 237.71

von Recklinghausen-Applebaum disease (hemochromatosis) 275.0

von Schroetter's syndrome (intermittent venous claudication) 453.8

von Willebrand (-Jürgens) (-Minot) disease or syndrome (angiohemophilia) 286.4

von Zambusch's disease (lichen sclerosus et atrophicus) 701.0

Voorhoeve's disease or dyschondroplasia 756.4

Vossius' ring 921.3
  late effect 366.21

Voyeurism 302.82

VRE (vancomycin resistant enterococcus) V09.8

Vrolik's disease (osteogenesis imperfecta) 756.51

VRSA (vancomycin resistant staphylococcus aureus) V09.8

Vulva — *see* condition

Vulvismus 625.1

Vulvitis (acute) (allergic) (aphthous) (chronic) (gangrenous) (hypertrophic) (intertriginous) 616.10
  with
    abortion — *see* Abortion, by type, with sepsis
    ectopic pregnancy (*see also* categories 633.0-633.9) 639.0
    molar pregnancy (*see also* categories 630-632) 639.0
  adhesive, congenital 752.49
  blennorrhagic (acute) 098.0
    chronic or duration of 2 months or over 098.2
  chlamydial 099.53
  complicating pregnancy or puerperium 646.6 ☑
  due to Ducrey's bacillus 099.0
  following
    abortion 639.0
    ectopic or molar pregnancy 639.0
  gonococcal (acute) 098.0
    chronic or duration of 2 months or over 098.2
  herpetic 054.11
  leukoplakic 624.0
  monilial 112.1
  puerperal, postpartum, childbirth 646.6 ☑
  syphilitic (early) 091.0
    late 095.8
  trichomonal 131.01

Vulvodynia 625.9

Vulvorectal — *see* condition

Vulvovaginitis (*see also* Vulvitis) 616.10
  amebic 006.8
  chlamydial 099.53
  gonococcal (acute) 098.0
    chronic or duration of 2 months or over 098.2
  herpetic 054.11
  monilial 112.1
  trichomonal (Trichomonas vaginalis) 131.01

W

Waardenburg's syndrome 756.89
  meaning ptosis-epicanthus 270.2

Waardenburg-Klein syndrome (ptosis-epicanthus) 270.2

Wagner's disease (colloid milium) 709.3

Wagner (-Unverricht) syndrome (dermatomyositis) 710.3

Waiting list, person on V63.2
  undergoing social agency investigation V63.8

Wakefulness disorder (*see also* Hypersomnia) 780.54
  nonorganic origin 307.43

Waldenström's
  disease (osteochondrosis, capital femoral) 732.1
  hepatitis (lupoid hepatitis) 571.49
  hypergammaglobulinemia 273.0
  macroglobulinemia 273.3
  purpura, hypergammaglobulinemic 273.0
  syndrome (macroglobulinemia) 273.3

Waldenström-Kjellberg syndrome (sideropenic dysphagia) 280.8

Walking
  difficulty 719.7
    psychogenic 307.9
  sleep 307.46
    hysterical 300.13

Wall, abdominal — *see* condition

Wallenberg's syndrome (posterior inferior cerebellar artery) (*see also* Disease, cerebrovascular, acute) 436

Wallgren's
  disease (obstruction of splenic vein with collateral circulation) 459.89
  meningitis (*see also* Meningitis, aseptic) 047.9

Wandering
  acetabulum 736.39
  gallbladder 751.69
  kidney, congenital 753.3
  organ or site, congenital NEC — *see* Malposition, congenital
  pacemaker (atrial) (heart) 427.89
  spleen 289.59

Wardrop's disease (with lymphangitis) 681.9
  finger 681.02
  toe 681.11

War neurosis 300.16

Wart (common) (digitate) (filiform) (infectious) (viral) 078.10
  external genital organs (venereal) 078.19
  fig 078.19
  Hassall-Henle's (of cornea) 371.41
  Henle's (of cornea) 371.41
  juvenile 078.19
  moist 078.10
  Peruvian 088.0
  plantar 078.19
  prosector (*see also* Tuberculosis) 017.0 ☑
  seborrheic 702.19
    inflamed 702.11
  senile 702.0
  specified NEC 078.19
  syphilitic 091.3
  tuberculous (*see also* Tuberculosis) 017.0 ☑
  venereal (female) (male) 078.19

Warthin's tumor (salivary gland) (M8561/0) 210.2

Washerwoman's itch 692.4

Wassilieff's disease (leptospiral jaundice) 100.0

Wasting
  disease 799.4
    due to malnutrition 261
  extreme (due to malnutrition) 261
  muscular NEC 728.2
  palsy, paralysis 335.21
  pelvic muscle 618.83

Water
  clefts 366.12
  deprivation of 994.3
  in joint (*see also* Effusion, joint) 719.0 ☑
  intoxication 276.6
  itch 120.3
  lack of 994.3

Water — *continued*
  loading 276.6
  on
    brain — *see* Hydrocephalus
    chest 511.8
  poisoning 276.6

Waterbrash 787.1

Water-hammer pulse (*see also* Insufficiency, aortic) 424.1

Waterhouse (-Friderichsen) disease or syndrome 036.3

Water-losing nephritis 588.89

Wax in ear 380.4

Waxy
  degeneration, any site 277.3
  disease 277.3
  kidney 277.3 [583.81]
  liver (large) 277.3
  spleen 277.3

Weak, weakness (generalized) 780.79
  arches (acquired) 734
    congenital 754.61
  bladder sphincter 596.59
  congenital 779.89
  eye muscle — *see* Strabismus
  facial 781.94
  foot (double) — *see* Weak, arches
  heart, cardiac (*see also* Failure, heart) 428.9
    congenital 746.9
  mind 317
  muscle ►(generalized)◄ 728.87
  myocardium (*see also* Failure, heart) 428.9
  newborn 779.89
  pelvic fundus
    pubocervical tissue 618.81
    rectovaginal tissue 618.82
  pulse 785.9
  senile 797
  urinary stream 788.62
  valvular — *see* Endocarditis

Wear, worn, tooth, teeth (approximal) (hard tissues) (interproximal) (occlusal) — *see also* Attrition, teeth 521.10

Weather, weathered
  effects of
    cold NEC 991.9
      specified effect NEC 991.8
    hot (*see also* Heat) 992.9
  skin 692.74

Web, webbed (congenital) — *see also* Anomaly, specified type NEC
  canthus 743.63
  digits (*see also* Syndactylism) 755.10
  duodenal 751.5
  esophagus 750.3
  fingers (*see also* Syndactylism, fingers) 755.11
  larynx (glottic) (subglottic) 748.2
  neck (pterygium colli) 744.5
  Paterson-Kelly (sideropenic dysphagia) 280.8
  popliteal syndrome 756.89
  toes (*see also* Syndactylism, toes) 755.13

Weber's paralysis or syndrome 344.89

Weber-Christian disease or syndrome (nodular nonsuppurative panniculitis) 729.30

Weber-Cockayne syndrome (epidermolysis bullosa) 757.39

Weber-Dimitri syndrome 759.6

Weber-Gubler syndrome 344.89

Weber-Leyden syndrome 344.89

Weber-Osler syndrome (familial hemorrhagic telangiectasia) 448.0

Wedge-shaped or wedging vertebra (*see also* Osteoporosis) 733.00

Wegener's granulomatosis or syndrome 446.4

Wegner's disease (syphilitic osteochondritis) 090.0

Weight
  gain (abnormal) (excessive) 783.1
    during pregnancy 646.1 ☑
      insufficient 646.8 ☑
  less than 1000 grams at birth 765.0 ☑
  loss (cause unknown) 783.21

Weightlessness 994.9

Note — For fracture with open wound, see Fracture.

For laceration, traumatic rupture, tear or penetrating wound of internal organs, such as heart, lung, liver, kidney, pelvic organs, etc., whether or not accompanied by open wound or fracture in the same region, see Injury, internal.

For contused wound, see Contusion. For crush injury, see Crush. For abrasion, insect bite (nonvenomous), blister, or scratch, see Injury, superficial.

Complicated includes wounds with:
  delayed healing
  delayed treatment
  foreign body
  primary infection
For late effect of open wound, see Late, effect, wound, open, by site.

2006 ICD-9-CM

☑ Additional Digit Required — Refer to the Tabular List (Numeric Code Section) for Additional Digit Selection
▶◀ Revised Text ● New Line ▲ Revised Code

October 2005 • Volume 2 — 349

Index

Wound, open — Wound, open

Wound, open — *continued*
  brain — *see* Injury, intracranial, with open
    intracranial wound
  breast 879.0
    complicated 879.1
  brow 873.42
    complicated 873.52
  buccal mucosa 873.61
    complicated 873.71
  buttock 877.0
    complicated 877.1
  calf 891.0
    with tendon involvement 891.2
    complicated 891.1
  canaliculus lacrimalis 870.8
    with laceration of eyelid 870.2
  canthus, eye 870.8
    laceration — *see* Laceration, eyelid
  cavernous sinus — *see* Injury, intracranial
  cerebellum — *see* Injury, intracranial
  cervical esophagus 874.4
    complicated 874.5
  cervix — *see* Injury, internal, cervix
  cheek(s) (external) 873.41
    complicated 873.51
    internal 873.61
      complicated 873.71
  chest (wall) (external) 875.0
    complicated 875.1
  chin 873.44
    complicated 873.54
  choroid 363.63
  ciliary body (eye) (*see also* Wound, open,
      intraocular) 871.9
  clitoris 878.8
    complicated 878.9
  cochlea 872.64
    complicated 872.74
  complicated 879.9
  conjunctiva — *see* Wound, open, intraocular
  cornea (nonpenetrating) (*see also* Wound, open,
      intraocular) 871.9
  costal region 875.0
    complicated 875.1
  Descemet's membrane (*see also* Wound, open,
      intraocular) 871.9
  digit(s)
    foot 893.0
      with tendon involvement 893.2
      complicated 893.1
    hand 883.0
      with tendon involvement 883.2
      complicated 883.1
  drumhead, ear 872.61
    complicated 872.71
  ear 872.8
    canal 872.02
      complicated 872.12
    complicated 872.9
    drum 872.61
      complicated 872.71
    external 872.00
      complicated 872.10
    multiple sites 872.69
      complicated 872.79
    ossicles (incus) (malleus) (stapes) 872.62
      complicated 872.72
    specified part NEC 872.69
      complicated 872.79
  elbow 881.01
    with tendon involvement 881.21
    complicated 881.11
  epididymis 878.2
    complicated 878.3
  epigastric region 879.2
    complicated 879.3
  epiglottis 874.01
    complicated 874.11
  esophagus (cervical) 874.4
    complicated 874.5
    thoracic — *see* Injury, internal, esophagus
  Eustachian tube 872.63
    complicated 872.73
  extremity
    lower (multiple) NEC 894.0
      with tendon involvement 894.2
      complicated 894.1

Wound, open — *continued*
  extremity — *continued*
    upper (multiple) NEC 884.0
      with tendon involvement 884.2
      complicated 884.1
  eye(s) (globe) — *see* Wound, open, intraocular
  eyeball NEC 871.9
    laceration (*see also* Laceration, eyeball)
      871.4
    penetrating (*see also* Penetrating wound,
      eyeball) 871.7
  eyebrow 873.42
    complicated 873.52
  eyelid NEC 870.8
    laceration — *see* Laceration, eyelid
  face 873.40
    complicated 873.50
    multiple sites 873.49
      complicated 873.59
    specified part NEC 873.49
      complicated 873.59
  fallopian tube — *see* Injury, internal, fallopian
    tube
  finger(s) (nail) (subungual) 883.0
    with tendon involvement 883.2
    complicated 883.1
  flank 879.4
    complicated 879.5
  foot (any part except toe(s) alone) 892.0
    with tendon involvement 892.2
    complicated 892.1
  forearm 881.00
    with tendon involvement 881.20
    complicated 881.10
  forehead 873.42
    complicated 873.52
  genital organs (external) NEC 878.8
    complicated 878.9
    internal — *see* Injury, internal, by site
  globe (eye) (*see also* Wound, open, eyeball)
      871.9
  groin 879.4
    complicated 879.5
  gum(s) 873.62
    complicated 873.72
  hand (except finger(s) alone) 882.0
    with tendon involvement 882.2
    complicated 882.1
  head NEC 873.8
    with intracranial injury — *see* Injury,
        intracranial
      due to or associated with skull fracture —
          see Fracture, skull
    complicated 873.9
    scalp — *see* Wound, open, scalp
  heel 892.0
    with tendon involvement 892.2
    complicated 892.1
  high-velocity (grease gun) — *see* Wound, open,
    complicated, by site
  hip 890.0
    with tendon involvement 890.2
    complicated 890.1
  hymen 878.6
    complicated 878.7
  hypochondrium 879.4
    complicated 879.5
  hypogastric region 879.2
    complicated 879.3
  iliac (region) 879.4
    complicated 879.5
  incidental to
    dislocation — *see* Dislocation, open, by site
    fracture — *see* Fracture, open, by site
    intracranial injury — *see* Injury,
        intracranial, with open intracranial
        wound
    nerve injury — *see* Injury, nerve, by site
  inguinal region 879.4
    complicated 879.5
  instep 892.0
    with tendon involvement 892.2
    complicated 892.1
  interscapular region 876.0
    complicated 876.1
  intracranial — *see* Injury, intracranial, with
    open intracranial wound

Wound, open — *continued*
  intraocular 871.9
    with
      partial loss (of intraocular tissue) 871.2
      prolapse or exposure (of intraocular
          tissue) 871.1
    laceration (*see also* Laceration, eyeball) 871.4
    penetrating 871.7
      with foreign body (nonmagnetic) 871.6
        magnetic 871.5
      without prolapse (of intraocular tissue)
          871.0
  iris (*see also* Wound, open, eyeball) 871.9
  jaw (fracture not involved) 873.44
    with fracture — *see* Fracture, jaw
    complicated 873.54
  knee 891.0
    with tendon involvement 891.2
    complicated 891.1
  labium (majus) (minus) 878.4
    complicated 878.5
  lacrimal apparatus, gland, or sac 870.8
    with laceration of eyelid 870.2
  larynx 874.01
    with trachea 874.00
      complicated 874.10
    complicated 874.11
  leg (multiple) 891.0
    with tendon involvement 891.2
    complicated 891.1
    lower 891.0
      with tendon involvement 891.2
      complicated 891.1
    thigh 890.0
      with tendon involvement 890.2
      complicated 890.1
    upper 890.0
      with tendon involvement 890.2
      complicated 890.1
  lens (eye) (alone) (*see also* Cataract, traumatic)
      366.20
    with involvement of other eye structures —
        see Wound, open, eyeball
  limb
    lower (multiple) NEC 894.0
      with tendon involvement 894.2
      complicated 894.1
    upper (multiple) NEC 884.0
      with tendon involvement 884.2
      complicated 884.1
  lip 873.43
    complicated 873.53
  loin 876.0
    complicated 876.1
  lumbar region 876.0
    complicated 876.1
  malar region 873.41
    complicated 873.51
  mastoid region 873.49
    complicated 873.59
  mediastinum — *see* Injury, internal,
      mediastinum
  midthoracic region 875.0
    complicated 875.1
  mouth 873.60
    complicated 873.70
    floor 873.64
      complicated 873.74
    multiple sites 873.69
      complicated 873.79
    specified site NEC 873.69
      complicated 873.79
  multiple, unspecified site(s) 879.8

> *Note — Multiple open wounds of sites
> classifiable to the same four-digit category
> should be classified to that category unless
> they are in different limbs.*
>
> *Multiple open wounds of sites classifiable to
> different four-digit categories, or to different
> limbs, should be coded separately.*

    complicated 879.9
    lower limb(s) (one or both) (sites classifiable
        to more than one three-digit category
        in 890 to 893) 894.0

Wound, open — *continued*
  multiple, unspecified site(s) — *continued*
    lower limb(s) — *continued*
      with tendon involvement 894.2
      complicated 894.1
    upper limb(s) (one or both) (sites classifiable
      to more than one three-digit category
      in 880 to 883) 884.0
      with tendon involvement 884.2
      complicated 884.1
  muscle — *see* Sprain, by site
  nail
    finger(s) 883.0
      complicated 883.1
    thumb 883.0
      complicated 883.1
    toe(s) 893.0
      complicated 893.1
  nape (neck) 874.8
    complicated 874.9
    specified part NEC 874.8
      complicated 874.9
  nasal — *see also* Wound, open, nose
    cavity 873.22
      complicated 873.32
    septum 873.21
      complicated 873.31
    sinuses 873.23
      complicated 873.33
  nasopharynx 873.22
    complicated 873.32
  neck 874.8
    complicated 874.9
    nape 874.8
      complicated 874.9
    specified part NEC 874.8
      complicated 874.9
  nerve — *see* Injury, nerve, by site
  non-healing surgical 998.83
  nose 873.20
    complicated 873.30
    multiple sites 873.29
      complicated 873.39
    septum 873.21
      complicated 873.31
    sinuses 873.23
      complicated 873.33
  occipital region — *see* Wound, open, scalp
  ocular NEC 871.9
    adnexa 870.9
      specified region NEC 870.8
    laceration (*see also* Laceration, ocular) 871.4
    muscle (extraocular) 870.3
      with foreign body 870.4
    eyelid 870.1
    intraocular — *see* Wound, open, eyeball
    penetrating (*see also* Penetrating wound,
      ocular) 871.7
  orbit 870.8
    penetrating 870.3
      with foreign body 870.4
  orbital region 870.9
  ovary — *see* Injury, internal, pelvic organs
  palate 873.65
    complicated 873.75
  palm 882.0
    with tendon involvement 882.2
    complicated 882.1
  parathyroid (gland) 874.2
    complicated 874.3
  parietal region — *see* Wound, open, scalp
  pelvic floor or region 879.6
    complicated 879.7
  penis 878.0
    complicated 878.1
  perineum 879.6
    complicated 879.7
  periocular area 870.8
    laceration of skin 870.0
  pharynx 874.4
    complicated 874.5
  pinna 872.01
    complicated 872.11
  popliteal space 891.0
    with tendon involvement 891.2
    complicated 891.1

Wound, open — *continued*
  prepuce 878.0
    complicated 878.1
  pubic region 879.2
    complicated 879.3
  pudenda 878.8
    complicated 878.9
  rectovaginal septum 878.8
    complicated 878.9
  sacral region 877.0
    complicated 877.1
  sacroiliac region 877.0
    complicated 877.1
  salivary (ducts) (glands) 873.69
    complicated 873.79
  scalp 873.0
    complicated 873.1
  scalpel, fetus or newborn 767.8
  scapular region 880.01
    with tendon involvement 880.21
    complicated 880.11
    involving other sites of upper arm 880.09
      with tendon involvement 880.29
      complicated 880.19
  sclera — (*see also* Wound, open, intraocular)
    871.9
  scrotum 878.2
    complicated 878.3
  seminal vesicle — *see* Injury, internal, pelvic
    organs
  shin 891.0
    with tendon involvement 891.2
    complicated 891.1
  shoulder 880.00
    with tendon involvement 880.20
    complicated 880.10
    involving other sites of upper arm 880.09
      with tendon involvement 880.29
      complicated 880.19
  skin NEC 879.8
    complicated 879.9
  skull — *see also* Injury, intracranial, with open
    intracranial wound
    with skull fracture — *see* Fracture, skull
  spermatic cord (scrotal) 878.2
    complicated 878.3
    pelvic region — *see* Injury, internal,
      spermatic cord
  spinal cord — *see* Injury, spinal
  sternal region 875.0
    complicated 875.1
  subconjunctival — *see* Wound, open,
    intraocular
  subcutaneous NEC 879.8
    complicated 879.9
  submaxillary region 873.44
    complicated 873.54
  submental region 873.44
    complicated 873.54
  subungual
    finger(s) (thumb) — *see* Wound, open, finger
    toe(s) — *see* Wound, open, toe
  supraclavicular region 874.8
    complicated 874.9
  supraorbital 873.42
    complicated 873.52
  surgical, non-healing 998.83
  temple 873.49
    complicated 873.59
  temporal region 873.49
    complicated 873.59
  testis 878.2
    complicated 878.3
  thigh 890.0
    with tendon involvement 890.2
    complicated 890.1
  thorax, thoracic (external) 875.0
    complicated 875.1
  throat 874.8
    complicated 874.9
  thumb (nail) (subungual) 883.0
    with tendon involvement 883.2
    complicated 883.1
  thyroid (gland) 874.2
    complicated 874.3

Wound, open — *continued*
  toe(s) (nail) (subungual) 893.0
    with tendon involvement 893.2
    complicated 893.1
  tongue 873.64
    complicated 873.74
  tonsil — *see* Wound, open, neck
  trachea (cervical region) 874.02
    with larynx 874.00
      complicated 874.10
    complicated 874.12
    intrathoracic — *see* Injury, internal, trachea
  trunk (multiple) NEC 879.6
    complicated 879.7
    specified site NEC 879.6
      complicated 879.7
  tunica vaginalis 878.2
    complicated 878.3
  tympanic membrane 872.61
    complicated 872.71
  tympanum 872.61
    complicated 872.71
  umbilical region 879.2
    complicated 879.3
  ureter — *see* Injury, internal, ureter
  urethra — *see* Injury, internal, urethra
  uterus — *see* Injury, internal, uterus
  uvula 873.69
    complicated 873.79
  vagina 878.6
    complicated 878.7
  vas deferens — *see* Injury, internal, vas
    deferens
  vitreous (humor) 871.2
  vulva 878.4
    complicated 878.5
  wrist 881.02
    with tendon involvement 881.22
    complicated 881.12

Wright's syndrome (hyperabduction) 447.8
  pneumonia 390 [517.1]

Wringer injury — *see* Crush injury, by site

Wrinkling of skin 701.8

Wrist — *see also* condition
  drop (acquired) 736.05

Wrong drug (given in error) NEC 977.9
  specified drug or substance — *see* Table of
    Drugs and Chemicals

Wry neck — *see also* Torticollis
  congenital 754.1

Wuchereria infestation 125.0
  bancrofti 125.0
  Brugia malayi 125.1
  malayi 125.1

Wuchereriasis 125.0

Wuchereriosis 125.0

Wuchernde struma langhans (M8332/3) 193

X

Xanthelasma 272.2
  eyelid 272.2 [374.51]
  palpebrarum 272.2 [374.51]

Xanthelasmatosis (essential) 272.2

Xanthelasmoidea 757.33

Xanthine stones 277.2

Xanthinuria 277.2

Xanthofibroma (M8831/0) — *see* Neoplasm,
  connective tissue, benign

Xanthoma(s), xanthomatosis 272.2
  with
    hyperlipoproteinemia
      type I 272.3
      type III 272.2
      type IV 272.1
      type V 272.3
  bone 272.7
  craniohypophyseal 277.89
  cutaneotendinous 272.7
  diabeticorum 250.8 ☑ [272.2]
  disseminatum 272.7
  eruptive 272.2

☑ Additional Digit Required — Refer to the Tabular List (Numeric Code Section) for Additional Digit Selection
▶◀ Revised Text   ● New Line   ▲ Revised Code

2006 ICD-9-CM

Volume 2 — 351

Xanthoma(s), xanthomatosis — *continued*
eyelid 272.2 *[374.51]*
familial 272.7
hereditary 272.7
hypercholesterinemic 272.0
hypercholesterolemic 272.0
hyperlipemic 272.4
hyperlipidemic 272.4
infantile 272.7
joint 272.7
juvenile 272.7
multiple 272.7
multiplex 272.7
primary familial 272.7
tendon (sheath) 272.7
tuberosum 272.2
tuberous 272.2
tubo-eruptive 272.2
Xanthosis 709.09
surgical 998.81
Xenophobia 300.29
Xeroderma (congenital) 757.39
acquired 701.1
eyelid 373.33
eyelid 373.33
pigmentosum 757.33
vitamin A deficiency 264.8
Xerophthalmia 372.53
vitamin A deficiency 264.7
Xerosis
conjunctiva 372.53
with Bitôt's spot 372.53
vitamin A deficiency 264.1
vitamin A deficiency 264.0
cornea 371.40
with corneal ulceration 370.00
vitamin A deficiency 264.3
vitamin A deficiency 264.2
cutis 706.8
skin 706.8
Xerostomia 527.7
Xiphodynia 733.90
Xiphoidalgia 733.90
Xiphoiditis 733.99
Xiphopagus 759.4
XO syndrome 758.6

X-ray
effects, adverse, NEC 990
of chest
for suspected tuberculosis V71.2
routine V72.5
XXX syndrome 758.81
XXXXY syndrome 758.81
XXY syndrome 758.7
Xyloketosuria 271.8
Xylosuria 271.8
Xylulosuria 271.8
XYY syndrome 758.81

Y

Yawning 786.09
psychogenic 306.1
Yaws 102.9
bone or joint lesions 102.6
butter 102.1
chancre 102.0
cutaneous, less than five years after infection 102.2
early (cutaneous) (macular) (maculopapular) (micropapular) (papular) 102.2
frambeside 102.2
skin lesions NEC 102.2
eyelid 102.9 *[373.4]*
ganglion 102.6
gangosis, gangosa 102.5
gumma, gummata 102.4
bone 102.6
gummatous
frambeside 102.4
osteitis 102.6
periostitis 102.6
hydrarthrosis 102.6
hyperkeratosis (early) (late) (palmar) (plantar) 102.3
initial lesions 102.0
joint lesions 102.6
juxta-articular nodules 102.7
late nodular (ulcerated) 102.4
latent (without clinical manifestations) (with positive serology) 102.8
mother 102.0

Yaws — *continued*
mucosal 102.7
multiple papillomata 102.1
nodular, late (ulcerated) 102.4
osteitis 102.6
papilloma, papillomata (palmar) (plantar) 102.1
periostitis (hypertrophic) 102.6
ulcers 102.4
wet crab 102.1
Yeast infection (*see also* Candidiasis) 112.9
Yellow
atrophy (liver) 570
chronic 571.8
resulting from administration of blood, plasma, serum, or other biological substance (within 8 months of administration) — *see* Hepatitis, viral
fever — *see* Fever, yellow
jack (*see also* Fever, yellow) 060.9
jaundice (*see also* Jaundice) 782.4
Yersinia septica 027.8

Z

Zagari's disease (xerostomia) 527.7
Zahorsky's disease (exanthema subitum) 057.8
syndrome (herpangina) 074.0
Zellweger syndrome 277.86
Zenker's diverticulum (esophagus) 530.6
Ziehen-Oppenheim disease 333.6
Zieve's syndrome (jaundice, hyperlipemia, and hemolytic anemia) 571.1
Zika fever 066.3
Zollinger-Ellison syndrome (gastric hypersecretion with pancreatic islet cell tumor) 251.5
Zona (*see also* Herpes, zoster) 053.9
Zoophilia (erotica) 302.1
Zoophobia 300.29
Zoster (herpes) (*see also* Herpes, zoster) 053.9
Zuelzer (-Ogden) anemia or syndrome (nutritional megaloblastic anemia) 281.2
Zygodactyly (*see also* Syndactylism) 755.10
Zygomycosis 117.7
Zymotic — *see* condition

SECTION 2

Alphabetic Index to Poisoning and External Causes of Adverse Effects of Drugs and Other Chemical Substances
TABLE OF DRUGS AND CHEMICALS

This table contains a classification of drugs and other chemical substances to identify poisoning states and external causes of adverse effects.

Each of the listed substances in the table is assigned a code according to the poisoning classification (960-989). These codes are used when there is a statement of poisoning, overdose, wrong substance given or taken, or intoxication.

The table also contains a listing of external causes of adverse effects. An adverse effect is a pathologic manifestation due to ingestion or exposure to drugs or other chemical substances (e.g., dermatitis, hypersensitivity reaction, aspirin gastritis). The adverse effect is to be identified by the appropriate code found in Section 1, Index to Diseases and Injuries. An external cause code can then be used to identify the circumstances involved. The table headings pertaining to external causes are defined below:

Accidental poisoning (E850-E869) — accidental overdose of drug, wrong substance given or taken, drug taken inadvertently, accidents in the usage of drugs and biologicals in medical and surgical procedures, and to show external causes of poisonings classifiable to 980-989.

Therapeutic use (E930-E949) — a correct substance properly administered in therapeutic or prophylactic dosage as the external cause of adverse effects.

Suicide attempt (E950-E952) — instances in which self-inflicted injuries or poisonings are involved.

Assault (E961-E962) — injury or poisoning inflicted by another person with the intent to injure or kill.

Undetermined (E980-E982) — to be used when the intent of the poisoning or injury cannot be determined whether it was intentional or accidental.

The American Hospital Formulary Service list numbers are included in the table to help classify new drugs not identified in the table by name. The AHFS list numbers are keyed to the continually revised American Hospital Formulary Service (AHFS).* These listings are found in the table under the main term **Drug.**

Excluded from the table are radium and other radioactive substances. The classification of adverse effects and complications pertaining to these substances will be found in Section 1, Index to Diseases and Injuries, and Section 3, Index to External Causes of Injuries.

Although certain substances are indexed with one or more subentries, the majority are listed according to one use or state. It is recognized that many substances may be used in various ways, in medicine and in industry, and may cause adverse effects whatever the state of the agent (solid, liquid, or fumes arising from a liquid). In cases in which the reported data indicates a use or state not in the table, or which is clearly different from the one listed, an attempt should be made to classify the substance in the form which most nearly expresses the reported facts.

*American Hospital Formulary Service, 2 vol. (Washington, D.C.: American Society of Hospital Pharmacists, 1959-)

	Poisoning	External Cause (E-Code)				
		Accident	Therapeutic Use	Suicide Attempt	Assault	Undetermined
1-propanol	980.3	E860.4	—	E950.9	E962.1	E980.9
2-propanol	980.2	E860.3	—	E950.9	E962.1	E980.9
2, 4-D (dichlorophenoxyacetic acid)	989.4	E863.5	—	E950.6	E962.1	E980.7
2, 4-toluene diisocyanate	983.0	E864.0	—	E950.7	E962.1	E980.6
2, 4, 5-T (trichlorophenoxyacetic acid)	989.2	E863.5	—	E950.6	E962.1	E980.7
14-hydroxydihydromorph- inone	965.09	E850.2	E935.2	E950.0	E962.0	E980.0
ABOB	961.7	E857	E931.7	E950.4	E962.0	E980.4
Abrus (seed)	988.2	E865.3	—	E950.9	E962.1	E980.9
Absinthe	980.0	E860.1	—	E950.9	E962.1	E980.9
beverage	980.0	E860.0	—	E950.9	E962.1	E980.9
Acenocoumarin, acenocoumarol	964.2	E858.2	E934.2	E950.4	E962.0	E980.4
Acepromazine	969.1	E853.0	E939.1	E950.3	E962.0	E980.3
Acetal	982.8	E862.4	—	E950.9	E962.1	E980.9
Acetaldehyde (vapor)	987.8	E869.8	—	E952.8	E962.2	E982.8
liquid	989.89	E866.8	—	E950.9	E962.1	E980.9
Acetaminophen	965.4	E850.4	E935.4	E950.0	E962.0	E980.0
Acetaminosalol	965.1	E850.3	E935.3	E950.0	E962.0	E980.0
Acetanilid(e)	965.4	E850.4	E935.4	E950.0	E962.0	E980.0
Acetarsol, acetarsone	961.1	E857	E931.1	E950.4	E962.0	E980.4
Acetazolamide	974.2	E858.5	E944.2	E950.4	E962.0	E980.4
Acetic						
acid	983.1	E864.1	—	E950.7	E962.1	E980.6
with sodium acetate (ointment)	976.3	E858.7	E946.3	E950.4	E962.0	E980.4
irrigating solution	974.5	E858.5	E944.5	E950.4	E962.0	E980.4
lotion	976.2	E858.7	E946.2	E950.4	E962.0	E980.4
anhydride	983.1	E864.1	—	E950.7	E962.1	E980.6
ether (vapor)	982.8	E862.4	—	E950.9	E962.1	E980.9
Acetohexamide	962.3	E858.0	E932.3	E950.4	E962.0	E980.4
Acetomenaphthone	964.3	E858.2	E934.3	E950.4	E962.0	E980.4
Acetomorphine	965.01	E850.0	E935.0	E950.0	E962.0	E980.0
Acetone (oils) (vapor)	982.8	E862.4	—	E950.9	E962.1	E980.9
Acetophenazine (maleate)	969.1	E853.0	E939.1	E950.3	E962.0	E980.3
Acetophenetidin	965.4	E850.4	E935.4	E950.0	E962.0	E980.0
Acetophenone	982.0	E862.4	—	E950.9	E962.1	E980.9

	Poisoning	External Cause (E-Code)				
		Accident	Therapeutic Use	Suicide Attempt	Assault	Undetermined
Acetorphine	965.09	E850.2	E935.2	E950.0	E962.0	E980.0
Acetosulfone (sodium)	961.8	E857	E931.8	E950.4	E962.0	E980.4
Acetrizoate (sodium)	977.8	E858.8	E947.8	E950.4	E962.0	E980.4
Acetylcarbromal	967.3	E852.2	E937.3	E950.2	E962.0	E980.2
Acetylcholine (chloride)	971.0	E855.3	E941.0	E950.4	E962.0	E980.4
Acetylcysteine	975.5	E858.6	E945.5	E950.4	E962.0	E980.4
Acetyldigitoxin	972.1	E858.3	E942.1	E950.4	E962.0	E980.4
Acetyldihydrocodeine	965.09	E850.2	E935.2	E950.0	E962.0	E980.0
Acetyldihydrocodeinone	965.09	E850.2	E935.2	E950.0	E962.0	E980.0
Acetylene (gas) (industrial)	987.1	E868.1	—	E951.8	E962.2	E981.8
incomplete combustion of — see Carbon monoxide, fuel, utility						
tetrachloride (vapor)	982.3	E862.4	—	E950.9	E962.1	E980.9
Acetyliodosalicylic acid	965.1	E850.3	E935.3	E950.0	E962.0	E980.0
Acetylphenylhydrazine	965.8	E850.8	E935.8	E950.0	E962.0	E980.0
Acetylsalicylic acid	965.1	E850.3	E935.3	E950.0	E962.0	E980.0
Achromycin	960.4	E856	E930.4	E950.4	E962.0	E980.4
ophthalmic preparation	976.5	E858.7	E946.5	E950.4	E962.0	E980.4
topical NEC	976.0	E858.7	E946.0	E950.4	E962.0	E980.4
Acidifying agents	963.2	E858.1	E933.2	E950.4	E962.0	E980.4
Acids (corrosive) NEC	983.1	E864.1	—	E950.7	E962.1	E980.6
Aconite (wild)	988.2	E865.4	—	E950.9	E962.1	E980.9
Aconitine (liniment)	976.8	E858.7	E946.8	E950.4	E962.0	E980.4
Aconitum ferox	988.2	E865.4	—	E950.9	E962.1	E980.9
Acridine	983.0	E864.0	—	E950.7	E962.1	E980.6
vapor	987.8	E869.8	—	E952.8	E962.2	E982.8
Acriflavine	961.9	E857	E931.9	E950.4	E962.0	E980.4
Acrisorcin	976.0	E858.7	E946.0	E950.4	E962.0	E980.4
Acrolein (gas)	987.8	E869.8	—	E952.8	E962.2	E982.8
liquid	989.89	E866.8	—	E950.9	E962.1	E980.9
Actaea spicata	988.2	E865.4	—	E950.9	E962.1	E980.9
Acterol	961.5	E857	E931.5	E950.4	E962.0	E980.4
ACTH	962.4	E858.0	E932.4	E950.4	E962.0	E980.4
Acthar	962.4	E858.0	E932.4	E950.4	E962.0	E980.4
Actinomycin (C)(D)	960.7	E856	E930.7	E950.4	E962.0	E980.4
Adalin (acetyl)	967.3	E852.2	E937.3	E950.2	E962.0	E980.2
Adenosine (phosphate)	977.8	E858.8	E947.8	E950.4	E962.0	E980.4
Adhesives	989.89	E866.6	—	E950.9	E962.1	E980.9

☑ Additional Digit Required — Refer to the Tabular List (Numeric Code Section) for Additional Digit Selection
►◄ Revised Text   ● New Line   ▲ Revised Code

	Poisoning	Accident	Therapeutic Use	Suicide Attempt	Assault	Undetermined
ADH	962.5	E858.0	E932.5	E950.4	E962.0	E980.4
Adicillin	960.0	E856	E930.0	E950.4	E962.0	E980.4
Adiphenine	975.1	E855.6	E945.1	E950.4	E962.0	E980.4
Adjunct, pharmaceutical	977.4	E858.8	E947.4	E950.4	E962.0	E980.4
Adrenal (extract, cortex or medulla) (glucocorticoids) (hormones) (mineralocorticoids)	962.0	E858.0	E932.0	E950.4	E962.0	E980.4
ENT agent	976.6	E858.7	E946.6	E950.4	E962.0	E980.4
ophthalmic preparation	976.5	E858.7	E946.5	E950.4	E962.0	E980.4
topical NEC	976.0	E858.7	E946.0	E950.4	E962.0	E980.4
Adrenalin	971.2	E855.5	E941.2	E950.4	E962.0	E980.4
Adrenergic blocking agents	971.3	E855.6	E941.3	E950.4	E962.0	E980.4
Adrenergics	971.2	E855.5	E941.2	E950.4	E962.0	E980.4
Adrenochrome (derivatives)	972.8	E858.3	E942.8	E950.4	E962.0	E980.4
Adrenocorticotropic hormone	962.4	E858.0	E932.4	E950.4	E962.0	E980.4
Adrenocorticotropin	962.4	E858.0	E932.4	E950.4	E962.0	E980.4
Adriamycin	960.7	E856	E930.7	E950.4	E962.0	E980.4
Aerosol spray — see Sprays						
Aerosporin	960.8	E856	E930.8	E950.4	E962.0	E980.4
ENT agent	976.6	E858.7	E946.6	E950.4	E962.0	E980.4
ophthalmic preparation	976.5	E858.7	E946.5	E950.4	E962.0	E980.4
topical NEC	976.0	E858.7	E946.0	E950.4	E962.0	E980.4
Aethusa cynapium	988.2	E865.4	—	E950.9	E962.1	E980.9
Afghanistan black	969.6	E854.1	E939.6	E950.3	E962.0	E980.3
Aflatoxin	989.7	E865.9	—	E950.9	E962.1	E980.9
African boxwood	988.2	E865.4	—	E950.9	E962.1	E980.9
Agar (-agar)	973.3	E858.4	E943.3	E950.4	E962.0	E980.4
Agricultural agent NEC	989.89	E863.9	—	E950.6	E962.1	E980.7
Agrypnal	967.0	E851	E937.0	E950.1	E962.0	E980.1
Air contaminant(s), source or type not specified	987.9	E869.9	—	E952.9	E962.2	E982.9
specified type — see specific substance						
Akee	988.2	E865.4	—	E950.9	E962.1	E980.9
Akrinol	976.0	E858.7	E946.0	E950.4	E962.0	E980.4
Alantolactone	961.6	E857	E931.6	E950.4	E962.0	E980.4
Albamycin	960.8	E856	E930.8	E950.4	E962.0	E980.4
Albumin (normal human serum)	964.7	E858.2	E934.7	E950.4	E962.0	E980.4
Albuterol	975.7	E858.6	E945.7	E950.4	E962.0	E980.4
Alcohol	980.9	E860.9	—	E950.9	E962.1	E980.9
absolute	980.0	E860.1	—	E950.9	E962.1	E980.9
beverage	980.0	E860.0	E947.8	E950.9	E962.1	E980.9
amyl	980.3	E860.4	—	E950.9	E962.1	E980.9
antifreeze	980.1	E860.2	—	E950.9	E962.1	E980.9
butyl	980.3	E860.4	—	E950.9	E962.1	E980.9
dehydrated	980.0	E860.1	—	E950.9	E962.1	E980.9
beverage	980.0	E860.0	E947.8	E950.9	E962.1	E980.9
denatured	980.0	E860.1	—	E950.9	E962.1	E980.9
deterrents	977.3	E858.8	E947.3	E950.4	E962.0	E980.4
diagnostic (gastric function)	977.8	E858.8	E947.8	E950.4	E962.0	E980.4
ethyl	980.0	E860.1	—	E950.9	E962.1	E980.9
beverage	980.0	E860.0	E947.8	E950.9	E962.1	E980.9
grain	980.0	E860.1	—	E950.9	E962.1	E980.9
beverage	980.0	E860.0	E947.8	E950.9	E962.1	E980.9
industrial	980.9	E860.9	—	E950.9	E962.1	E980.9
isopropyl	980.2	E860.3	—	E950.9	E962.1	E980.9
methyl	980.1	E860.2	—	E950.9	E962.1	E980.9
preparation for consumption	980.0	E860.0	E947.8	E950.9	E962.1	E980.9
propyl	980.3	E860.4	—	E950.9	E962.1	E980.9
secondary	980.2	E860.3	—	E950.9	E962.1	E980.9
radiator	980.1	E860.2	—	E950.9	E962.1	E980.9
rubbing	980.2	E860.3	—	E950.9	E962.1	E980.9
specified type NEC	980.8	E860.8	—	E950.9	E962.1	E980.9
surgical	980.9	E860.9	—	E950.9	E962.1	E980.9
vapor (from any type of alcohol)	987.8	E869.8	—	E952.8	E962.2	E982.8
wood	980.1	E860.2	—	E950.9	E962.1	E980.9
Alcuronium chloride	975.2	E858.6	E945.2	E950.4	E962.0	E980.4
Aldactone	974.4	E858.5	E944.4	E950.4	E962.0	E980.4
Aldicarb	989.3	E863.2	—	E950.6	E962.1	E980.7
Aldomet	972.6	E858.3	E942.6	E950.4	E962.0	E980.4
Aldosterone	962.0	E858.0	E932.0	E950.4	E962.0	E980.4
Aldrin (dust)	989.2	E863.0	—	E950.6	E962.1	E980.7
Algeldrate	973.0	E858.4	E943.0	E950.4	E962.0	E980.4
Alidase	963.4	E858.1	E933.4	E950.4	E962.0	E980.4

	Poisoning	Accident	Therapeutic Use	Suicide Attempt	Assault	Undetermined
Aliphatic thiocyanates	989.0	E866.8	—	E950.9	E962.1	E980.9
Alkaline antiseptic solution (aromatic)	976.6	E858.7	E946.6	E950.4	E962.0	E980.4
Alkalinizing agents (medicinal)	963.3	E858.1	E933.3	E950.4	E962.0	E980.4
Alkalis, caustic	983.2	E864.2	—	E950.7	E962.1	E980.6
Alkalizing agents (medicinal)	963.3	E858.1	E933.3	E950.4	E962.0	E980.4
Alka-seltzer	965.1	E850.3	E935.3	E950.0	E962.0	E980.0
Alkavervir	972.6	E858.3	E942.6	E950.4	E962.0	E980.4
Allegron	969.0	E854.0	E939.0	E950.3	E962.0	E980.3
Alleve — see Naproxen						
Allobarbital, allobarbitone	967.0	E851	E937.0	E950.1	E962.0	E980.1
Allopurinol	974.7	E858.5	E944.7	E950.4	E962.0	E980.4
Allylestrenol	962.2	E858.0	E932.2	E950.4	E962.0	E980.4
Allylisopropylacetylurea	967.8	E852.8	E937.8	E950.2	E962.0	E980.2
Allylisopropylmalonylurea	967.0	E851	E937.0	E950.1	E962.0	E980.1
Allyltribromide	967.3	E852.2	E937.3	E950.2	E962.0	E980.2
Aloe, aloes, aloin	973.1	E858.4	E943.1	E950.4	E962.0	E980.4
Alosetron	973.8	E858.4	E943.8	E950.4	E962.0	E980.4
Aloxidone	966.0	E855.0	E936.0	E950.4	E962.0	E980.4
Aloxiprin	965.1	E850.3	E935.3	E950.0	E962.0	E980.0
Alpha amylase	963.4	E858.1	E933.4	E950.4	E962.0	E980.4
Alphaprodine (hydrochloride)	965.09	E850.2	E935.2	E950.0	E962.0	E980.0
Alpha tocopherol	963.5	E858.1	E933.5	E950.4	E962.0	E980.4
Alseroxylon	972.6	E858.3	E942.6	E950.4	E962.0	E980.4
Alum (ammonium) (potassium)	983.2	E864.2	—	E950.7	E962.1	E980.6
medicinal (astringent) NEC	976.2	E858.7	E946.2	E950.4	E962.0	E980.4
Aluminium, aluminum (gel) (hydroxide)	973.0	E858.4	E943.0	E950.4	E962.0	E980.4
acetate solution	976.2	E858.7	E946.2	E950.4	E962.0	E980.4
aspirin	965.1	E850.3	E935.3	E950.0	E962.0	E980.0
carbonate	973.0	E858.4	E943.0	E950.4	E962.0	E980.4
glycinate	973.0	E858.4	E943.0	E950.4	E962.0	E980.4
nicotinate	972.2	E858.3	E942.2	E950.4	E962.0	E980.4
ointment (surgical) (topical)	976.3	E858.7	E946.3	E950.4	E962.0	E980.4
phosphate	973.0	E858.4	E943.0	E950.4	E962.0	E980.4
subacetate	976.2	E858.7	E946.2	E950.4	E962.0	E980.4
topical NEC	976.3	E858.7	E946.3	E950.4	E962.0	E980.4
Alurate	967.0	E851	E937.0	E950.1	E962.0	E980.1
Alverine (citrate)	975.1	E858.6	E945.1	E950.4	E962.0	E980.4
Alvodine	965.09	E850.2	E935.2	E950.0	E962.0	E980.0
Amanita phalloides	988.1	E865.5	—	E950.9	E962.1	E980.9
Amantadine (hydrochloride)	966.4	E855.0	E936.4	E950.4	E962.0	E980.4
Ambazone	961.9	E857	E931.9	E950.4	E962.0	E980.4
Ambenonium	971.0	E855.3	E941.0	E950.4	E962.0	E980.4
Ambutonium bromide	971.1	E855.4	E941.1	E950.4	E962.0	E980.4
Ametazole	977.8	E858.8	E947.8	E950.4	E962.0	E980.4
Amethocaine (infiltration) (topical)	968.5	E855.2	E938.5	E950.4	E962.0	E980.4
nerve block (peripheral) (plexus)	968.6	E855.2	E938.6	E950.4	E962.0	E980.4
spinal	968.7	E855.2	E938.7	E950.4	E962.0	E980.4
Amethopterin	963.1	E858.1	E933.1	E950.4	E962.0	E980.4
Amfepramone	977.0	E858.8	E947.0	E950.4	E962.0	E980.4
Amidon	965.02	E850.1	E935.1	E950.0	E962.0	E980.0
Amidopyrine	965.5	E850.5	E935.5	E950.0	E962.0	E980.0
Aminacrine	976.0	E858.7	E946.0	E950.4	E962.0	E980.4
Aminitrozole	961.5	E857	E931.5	E950.4	E962.0	E980.4
Aminoacetic acid	974.5	E858.5	E944.5	E950.4	E962.0	E980.4
Amino acids	974.5	E858.5	E944.5	E950.4	E962.0	E980.4
Aminocaproic acid	964.4	E858.2	E934.4	E950.4	E962.0	E980.4
Aminoethylisothiourium	963.8	E858.1	E933.8	E950.4	E962.0	E980.4
Aminoglutethimide	966.3	E855.0	E936.3	E950.4	E962.0	E980.4
Aminometradine	974.3	E858.5	E944.3	E950.4	E962.0	E980.4
Aminopentamide	971.1	E855.4	E941.1	E950.4	E962.0	E980.4
Aminophenazone	965.5	E850.5	E935.5	E950.0	E962.0	E980.0
Aminophenol	983.0	E864.0	—	E950.7	E962.1	E980.6
Aminophenylpyridone	969.5	E853.8	E939.5	E950.3	E962.0	E980.3
Aminophylline	975.7	E858.6	E945.7	E950.4	E962.0	E980.4
Aminopterin	963.1	E858.1	E933.1	E950.4	E962.0	E980.4
Aminopyrine	965.5	E850.5	E935.5	E950.0	E962.0	E980.0
Aminosalicylic acid	961.8	E857	E931.8	E950.4	E962.0	E980.4
Amiphenazole	970.1	E854.3	E940.1	E950.4	E962.0	E980.4
Amiquinsin	972.6	E858.3	E942.6	E950.4	E962.0	E980.4
Amisometradine	974.3	E858.5	E944.3	E950.4	E962.0	E980.4
Amitriptyline	969.0	E854.0	E939.0	E950.3	E962.0	E980.3
Ammonia (fumes) (gas) (vapor)	987.8	E869.8	—	E952.8	E962.2	E982.8
liquid (household) NEC	983.2	E861.4	—	E950.7	E962.1	E980.6
spirit, aromatic	970.8	E854.3	E940.8	E950.4	E962.0	E980.4

☑ Additional Digit Required — Refer to the Tabular List (Numeric Code Section) for Additional Digit Selection

◄► Revised Text   ● New Line   ▲ Revised Code

	Poisoning	Accident	Therapeutic Use	Suicide Attempt	Assault	Undeter-mined
Ammoniated mercury	976.0	E858.7	E946.0	E950.4	E962.0	E980.4
Ammonium						
carbonate	983.2	E864.2	—	E950.7	E962.1	E980.6
chloride (acidifying agent)	963.2	E858.1	E933.2	E950.4	E962.0	E980.4
expectorant	975.5	E858.6	E945.5	E950.4	E962.0	E980.4
compounds (household)						
NEC	983.2	E861.4	—	E950.7	E962.1	E980.6
fumes (any usage)	987.8	E869.8	—	E952.8	E962.2	E982.8
industrial	983.2	E864.2	—	E950.7	E962.1	E980.6
ichthyosulfonate	976.4	E858.7	E946.4	E950.4	E962.0	E980.4
mandelate	961.9	E857	E931.9	E950.4	E962.0	E980.4
Amobarbital	967.0	E851	E937.0	E950.1	E962.0	E980.1
Amodiaquin(e)	961.4	E857	E931.4	E950.4	E962.0	E980.4
Amopyroquin(e)	961.4	E857	E931.4	E950.4	E962.0	E980.4
Amphenidone	969.5	E853.8	E939.5	E950.3	E962.0	E980.3
Amphetamine	969.7	E854.2	E939.7	E950.3	E962.0	E980.3
Amphomycin	960.8	E856	E930.8	E950.4	E962.0	E980.4
Amphotericin B	960.1	E856	E930.1	E950.4	E962.0	E980.4
topical	976.0	E858.7	E946.0	E950.4	E962.0	E980.4
Ampicillin	960.0	E856	E930.0	E950.4	E962.0	E980.4
Amprotropine	971.1	E855.4	E941.1	E950.4	E962.0	E980.4
Amygdalin	977.8	E858.8	E947.8	E950.4	E962.0	E980.4
Amyl						
acetate (vapor)	982.8	E862.4	—	E950.9	E962.1	E980.9
alcohol	980.3	E860.4	—	E950.9	E962.1	E980.9
nitrite (medicinal)	972.4	E858.3	E942.4	E950.4	E962.0	E980.4
Amylase (alpha)	963.4	E858.1	E933.4	E950.4	E962.0	E980.4
Amylene hydrate	980.8	E860.8	—	E950.9	E962.1	E980.9
Amylobarbitone	967.0	E851	E937.0	E950.1	E962.0	E980.1
Amylocaine	968.9	E855.2	E938.9	E950.4	E962.0	E980.4
infiltration (subcutaneous)	968.5	E855.2	E938.5	E950.4	E962.0	E980.4
nerve block (peripheral)						
(plexus)	968.6	E855.2	E938.6	E950.4	E962.0	E980.4
spinal	968.7	E855.2	E938.7	E950.4	E962.0	E980.4
topical (surface)	968.5	E855.2	E938.5	E950.4	E962.0	E980.4
Amytal (sodium)	967.0	E851	E937.0	E950.1	E962.0	E980.1
Analeptics	970.0	E854.3	E940.0	E950.4	E962.0	E980.4
Analgesics	965.9	E850.9	E935.9	E950.0	E962.0	E980.0
aromatic NEC	965.4	E850.4	E935.4	E950.0	E962.0	E980.0
non-narcotic NEC	965.7	E850.7	E935.7	E950.0	E962.0	E980.0
specified NEC	965.8	E850.8	E935.8	E950.0	E962.0	E980.0
Anamirta cocculus	988.2	E865.3	—	E950.9	E962.1	E980.9
Ancillin	960.0	E856	E930.0	E950.4	E962.0	E980.4
Androgens (anabolic						
congeners)	962.1	E858.0	E932.1	E950.4	E962.0	E980.4
Androstalone	962.1	E858.0	E932.1	E950.4	E962.0	E980.4
Androsterone	962.1	E858.0	E932.1	E950.4	E962.0	E980.4
Anemone pulsatilla	988.2	E865.4	—	E950.9	E962.1	E980.9
Anesthesia, anesthetic						
(general) NEC	968.4	E855.1	E938.4	E950.4	E962.0	E980.4
block (nerve) (plexus)	968.6	E855.2	E938.6	E950.4	E962.0	E980.4
gaseous NEC	968.2	E855.1	E938.2	E950.4	E962.0	E980.4
halogenated hydrocarbon						
derivatives NEC	968.2	E855.1	E938.2	E950.4	E962.0	E980.4
infiltration (intradermal)						
(subcutaneous)						
(submucosal)	968.5	E855.2	E938.5	E950.4	E962.0	E980.4
intravenous	968.3	E855.1	E938.3	E950.4	E962.0	E980.4
local NEC	968.9	E855.2	E938.9	E950.4	E962.0	E980.4
nerve blocking (peripheral)						
(plexus)	968.6	E855.2	E938.6	E950.4	E962.0	E980.4
rectal NEC	968.3	E855.1	E938.3	E950.4	E962.0	E980.4
spinal	968.7	E855.2	E938.7	E950.4	E962.0	E980.4
surface	968.5	E855.2	E938.5	E950.4	E962.0	E980.4
topical	968.5	E855.2	E938.5	E950.4	E962.0	E980.4
Aneurine	963.5	E858.1	E933.5	E950.4	E962.0	E980.4
Anginine — *see* Glyceryl trinitrate						
Angio-Conray	977.8	E858.8	E947.8	E950.4	E962.0	E980.4
Angiotensin	971.2	E855.5	E941.2	E950.4	E962.0	E980.4
Anhydrohydroxypro-						
gesterone	962.2	E858.0	E932.2	E950.4	E962.0	E980.4
Anhydron	974.3	E858.5	E944.3	E950.4	E962.0	E980.4
Anileridine	965.09	E850.2	E935.2	E950.0	E962.0	E980.0
Aniline (dye) (liquid)	983.0	E864.0	—	E950.7	E962.1	E980.6
analgesic	965.4	E850.4	E935.4	E950.0	E962.0	E980.0
derivatives, therapeutic						
NEC	965.4	E850.4	E935.4	E950.0	E962.0	E980.0
vapor	987.8	E869.8	—	E952.8	E962.2	E982.8
Anisindione	964.2	E858.2	E934.2	E950.4	E962.0	E980.4
Aniscoropine	971.1	E855.4	E941.1	E950.4	E962.0	E980.4
Anorexic agents	977.0	E858.8	E947.0	E950.4	E962.0	E980.4
Ant (bite) (sting)	989.5	E905.5	—	E950.9	E962.1	E980.9

	Poisoning	Accident	Therapeutic Use	Suicide Attempt	Assault	Undeter-mined
Antabuse	977.3	E858.8	E947.3	E950.4	E962.0	E980.4
Antacids	973.0	E858.4	E943.0	E950.4	E962.0	E980.4
Antazoline	963.0	E858.1	E933.0	E950.4	E962.0	E980.4
Anthelmintics	961.6	E857	E931.6	E950.4	E962.0	E980.4
Anthralin	976.4	E858.7	E946.4	E950.4	E962.0	E980.4
Anthramycin	960.7	E856	E930.7	E950.4	E962.0	E980.4
Antiadrenergics	971.3	E855.6	E941.3	E950.4	E962.0	E980.4
Antiallergic agents	963.0	E858.1	E933.0	E950.4	E962.0	E980.4
Antianemic agents NEC	964.1	E858.2	E934.1	E950.4	E962.0	E980.4
Antiaris toxicaria	988.2	E865.4	—	E950.9	E962.1	E980.9
Antiarteriosclerotic agents	972.2	E858.3	E942.2	E950.4	E962.0	E980.4
Antiasthmatics	975.7	E858.6	E945.7	E950.4	E962.0	E980.4
Antibiotics	960.9	E856	E930.9	E950.4	E962.0	E980.4
antifungal	960.1	E856	E930.1	E950.4	E962.0	E980.4
antimycobacterial	960.6	E856	E930.6	E950.4	E962.0	E980.4
antineoplastic	960.7	E856	E930.7	E950.4	E962.0	E980.4
cephalosporin (group)	960.5	E856	E930.5	E950.4	E962.0	E980.4
chloramphenicol (group)	960.2	E856	E930.2	E950.4	E962.0	E980.4
macrolides	960.3	E856	E930.3	E950.4	E962.0	E980.4
specified NEC	960.8	E856	E930.8	E950.4	E962.0	E980.4
tetracycline (group)	960.4	E856	E930.4	E950.4	E962.0	E980.4
Anticancer agents NEC	963.1	E858.1	E933.1	E950.4	E962.0	E980.4
antibiotics	960.7	E856	E930.7	E950.4	E962.0	E980.4
Anticholinergics	971.1	E855.4	E941.1	E950.4	E962.0	E980.4
Anticholinesterase						
(organophosphorus)						
(reversible)	971.0	E855.3	E941.0	E950.4	E962.0	E980.4
Anticoagulants	964.2	E858.2	E934.2	E950.4	E962.0	E980.4
antagonists	964.5	E858.2	E934.5	E950.4	E962.0	E980.4
Anti-common cold						
agents NEC	975.6	E858.6	E945.6	E950.4	E962.0	E980.4
Anticonvulsants NEC	966.3	E855.0	E936.3	E950.4	E962.0	E980.4
Antidepressants	969.0	E854.0	E939.0	E950.3	E962.0	E980.3
Antidiabetic agents	962.3	E858.0	E932.3	E950.4	E962.0	E980.4
Antidiarrheal agents	973.5	E858.4	E943.5	E950.4	E962.0	E980.4
Antidiuretic hormone	962.5	E858.0	E932.5	E950.4	E962.0	E980.4
Antidotes NEC	977.2	E858.8	E947.2	E950.4	E962.0	E980.4
Antiemetic agents	963.0	E858.1	E933.0	E950.4	E962.0	E980.4
Antiepilepsy agent NEC	966.3	E855.0	E936.3	E950.4	E962.0	E980.4
Antifertility pills	962.2	E858.0	E932.2	E950.4	E962.0	E980.4
Antiflatulents	973.8	E858.4	E943.8	E950.4	E962.0	E980.4
Antifreeze	989.89	E866.8	—	E950.9	E962.1	E980.9
alcohol	980.1	E860.2	—	E950.9	E962.1	E980.9
ethylene glycol	982.8	E862.4	—	E950.9	E962.1	E980.9
Antifungals (nonmedicinal)						
(sprays)	989.4	E863.6	—	E950.6	E962.1	E980.7
medicinal NEC	961.9	E857	E931.9	E950.4	E962.0	E980.4
antibiotic	960.1	E856	E930.1	E950.4	E962.0	E980.4
topical	976.0	E858.7	E946.0	E950.4	E962.0	E980.4
Antigastric secretion						
agents	973.0	E858.4	E943.0	E950.4	E962.0	E980.4
Antihelmintics	961.6	E857	E931.6	E950.4	E962.0	E980.4
Antihemophilic factor						
(human)	964.7	E858.2	E934.7	E950.4	E962.0	E980.4
Antihistamine	963.0	E858.1	E933.0	E950.4	E962.0	E980.4
Antihypertensive agents						
NEC	972.6	E858.3	E942.6	E950.4	E962.0	E980.4
Anti-infectives NEC	961.9	E857	E931.9	E950.4	E962.0	E980.4
antibiotics	960.9	E856	E930.9	E950.4	E962.0	E980.4
specified NEC	960.8	E856	E930.8	E950.4	E962.0	E980.4
antihelmintic	961.6	E857	E931.6	E950.4	E962.0	E980.4
antimalarial	961.4	E857	E931.4	E950.4	E962.0	E980.4
antimycobacterial NEC	961.8	E857	E931.8	E950.4	E962.0	E980.4
antibiotics	960.6	E856	E930.6	E950.4	E962.0	E980.4
antiprotozoal NEC	961.5	E857	E931.5	E950.4	E962.0	E980.4
blood	961.4	E857	E931.4	E950.4	E962.0	E980.4
antiviral	961.7	E857	E931.7	E950.4	E962.0	E980.4
arsenical	961.1	E857	E931.1	E950.4	E962.0	E980.4
ENT agents	976.6	E858.7	E946.6	E950.4	E962.0	E980.4
heavy metals NEC	961.2	E857	E931.2	E950.4	E962.0	E980.4
local	976.0	E858.7	E946.0	E950.4	E962.0	E980.4
ophthalmic preparation	976.5	E858.7	E946.5	E950.4	E962.0	E980.4
topical NEC	976.0	E858.7	E946.0	E950.4	E962.0	E980.4
Anti-inflammatory agents						
(topical)	976.0	E858.7	E946.0	E950.4	E962.0	E980.4
Antiknock (tetraethyl lead)	984.1	E862.1	—	E950.9	E962.1	E980.9
Antilipemics	972.2	E858.3	E942.2	E950.4	E962.0	E980.4
Antimalarials	961.4	E857	E931.4	E950.4	E962.0	E980.4
Antimony (compounds) (vapor)						
NEC	985.4	E866.2	—	E950.9	E962.1	E980.9
anti-infectives	961.2	E857	E931.2	E950.4	E962.0	E980.4

		External Cause (E-Code)				
	Poisoning	Accident	Therapeutic Use	Suicide Attempt	Assault	Undetermined
Antimony — *continued*						
pesticides (vapor)	985.4	E863.4	—	E950.6	E962.2	E980.7
potassium tartrate	961.2	E857	E931.2	E950.4	E962.0	E980.4
tartrated	961.2	E857	E931.2	E950.4	E962.0	E980.4
Antimuscarinic agents	971.1	E855.4	E941.1	E950.4	E962.0	E980.4
Antimycobacterials NEC	961.8	E857	E931.8	E950.4	E962.0	E980.4
antibiotics	960.6	E856	E930.6	E950.4	E962.0	E980.4
Antineoplastic agents	963.1	E858.1	E933.1	E950.4	E962.0	E980.4
antibiotics	960.7	E856	E930.7	E950.4	E962.0	E980.4
Anti-Parkinsonism agents	966.4	E855.0	E936.4	E950.4	E962.0	E980.4
Antiphlogistics	965.69	E850.6	E935.6	E950.0	E962.0	E980.0
Antiprotozoals NEC	961.5	E857	E931.5	E950.4	E962.0	E980.4
blood	961.4	E857	E931.4	E950.4	E962.0	E980.4
Antipruritics (local)	976.1	E858.7	E946.1	E950.4	E962.0	E980.4
Antipsychotic agents NEC	969.3	E853.8	E939.3	E950.3	E962.0	E980.3
Antipyretics	965.9	E850.9	E935.9	E950.0	E962.0	E980.0
specified NEC	965.8	E850.8	E935.8	E950.0	E962.0	E980.0
Antipyrine	965.5	E850.5	E935.5	E950.0	E962.0	E980.0
Antirabies serum (equine)	979.9	E858.8	E949.9	E950.4	E962.0	E980.4
Antirheumatics	965.69	E850.6	E935.6	E950.0	E962.0	E980.0
Antiseborrheics	976.4	E858.7	E946.4	E950.4	E962.0	E980.4
Antiseptics (external) (medicinal)	976.0	E858.7	E946.0	E950.4	E962.0	E980.4
Antistine	963.0	E858.1	E933.0	E950.4	E962.0	E980.4
Antithyroid agents	962.8	E858.0	E932.8	E950.4	E962.0	E980.4
Antitoxin, any	979.9	E858.8	E949.9	E950.4	E962.0	E980.4
Antituberculars	961.8	E857	E931.8	E950.4	E962.0	E980.4
antibiotics	960.6	E856	E930.6	E950.4	E962.0	E980.4
Antitussives	975.4	E858.6	E945.4	E950.4	E962.0	E980.4
Antivaricose agents (sclerosing)	972.7	E858.3	E942.7	E950.4	E962.0	E980.4
Antivenin (crotaline) (spider-bite)	979.9	E858.8	E949.9	E950.4	E962.0	E980.4
Antivert	963.0	E858.1	E933.0	E950.4	E962.0	E980.4
Antivirals NEC	961.7	E857	E931.7	E950.4	E962.0	E980.4
Ant poisons — *see* Pesticides						
Antrol	989.4	E863.4	—	E950.6	E962.1	E980.7
fungicide	989.4	E863.6	—	E950.6	E962.1	E980.7
Apomorphine hydrochloride (emetic)	973.6	E858.4	E943.6	E950.4	E962.0	E980.4
Appetite depressants, central	977.0	E858.8	E947.0	E950.4	E962.0	E980.4
Apresoline	972.6	E858.3	E942.6	E950.4	E962.0	E980.4
Aprobarbital, aprobarbitone	967.0	E851	E937.0	E950.1	E962.0	E980.1
Apronalide	967.8	E852.8	E937.8	E950.2	E962.0	E980.2
Aqua fortis	983.1	E864.1	—	E950.7	E962.1	E980.6
Arachis oil (topical)	976.3	E858.7	E946.3	E950.4	E962.0	E980.4
cathartic	973.2	E858.4	E943.2	E950.4	E962.0	E980.4
Aralen	961.4	E857	E931.4	E950.4	E962.0	E980.4
Arginine salts	974.5	E858.5	E944.5	E950.4	E962.0	E980.4
Argyrol	976.0	E858.7	E946.0	E950.4	E962.0	E980.4
ENT agent	976.6	E858.7	E946.6	E950.4	E962.0	E980.4
ophthalmic preparation	976.5	E858.7	E946.5	E950.4	E962.0	E980.4
Aristocort	962.0	E858.0	E932.0	E950.4	E962.0	E980.4
ENT agent	976.6	E858.7	E946.6	E950.4	E962.0	E980.4
ophthalmic preparation	976.5	E858.7	E946.5	E950.4	E962.0	E980.4
topical NEC	976.0	E858.7	E946.0	E950.4	E962.0	E980.4
Aromatics, corrosive	983.0	E864.0	—	E950.7	E962.1	E980.6
disinfectants	983.0	E861.4	—	E950.7	E962.1	E980.6
Arsenate of lead (insecticide)	985.1	E863.4	—	E950.8	E962.1	E980.8
herbicide	985.1	E863.5	—	E950.8	E962.1	E980.8
Arsenic, arsenicals (compounds) (dust) (fumes) (vapor) NEC	985.1	E866.3	—	E950.8	E962.1	E980.8
anti-infectives	961.1	E857	E931.1	E950.4	E962.0	E980.4
pesticide (dust) (fumes)	985.1	E863.4	—	E950.8	E962.1	E980.8
Arsine (gas)	985.1	E866.3	—	E950.8	E962.1	E980.8
Arsphenamine (silver)	961.1	E857	E931.1	E950.4	E962.0	E980.4
Arsthinol	961.1	E857	E931.1	E950.4	E962.0	E980.4
Artane	971.1	E855.4	E941.1	E950.4	E962.0	E980.4
Arthropod (venomous) NEC	989.5	E905.5	—	E950.9	E962.1	E980.9
Asbestos	989.81	E866.8	—	E950.9	E962.1	E980.9
Ascaridole	961.6	E857	E931.6	E950.4	E962.0	E980.4
Ascorbic acid	963.5	E858.1	E933.5	E950.4	E962.0	E980.4
Asiaticoside	976.0	E858.7	E946.0	E950.4	E962.0	E980.4
Aspidium (oleoresin)	961.6	E857	E931.6	E950.4	E962.0	E980.4
Aspirin	965.1	E850.3	E935.3	E950.0	E962.0	E980.0
Astringents (local)	976.2	E858.7	E946.2	E950.4	E962.0	E980.4
Atabrine	961.3	E857	E931.3	E950.4	E962.0	E980.4
Ataractics	969.5	E853.8	E939.5	E950.3	E962.0	E980.3
Atonia drug, intestinal	973.3	E858.4	E943.3	E950.4	E962.0	E980.4

	Poisoning	Accident	Therapeutic Use	Suicide Attempt	Assault	Undetermined
Atophan	974.7	E858.5	E944.7	E950.4	E962.0	E980.4
Atropine	971.1	E855.4	E941.1	E950.4	E962.0	E980.4
Attapulgite	973.5	E858.4	E943.5	E950.4	E962.0	E980.4
Attenuvax	979.4	E858.8	E949.4	E950.4	E962.0	E980.4
Aureomycin	960.4	E856	E930.4	E950.4	E962.0	E980.4
ophthalmic preparation	976.5	E858.7	E946.5	E950.4	E962.0	E980.4
topical NEC	976.0	E858.7	E946.0	E950.4	E962.0	E980.4
Aurothioglucose	965.69	E850.6	E935.6	E950.0	E962.0	E980.0
Aurothioglycanide	965.69	E850.6	E935.6	E950.0	E962.0	E980.0
Aurothiomalate	965.69	E850.6	E935.6	E950.0	E962.0	E980.0
Automobile fuel	981	E862.1	—	E950.9	E962.1	E980.9
Autonomic nervous system agents NEC	971.9	E855.9	E941.9	E950.4	E962.0	E980.4
Avlosulfon	961.8	E857	E931.8	E950.4	E962.0	E980.4
Avomine	967.8	E852.8	E937.8	E950.2	E962.0	E980.2
Azacyclonol	969.5	E853.8	E939.5	E950.3	E962.0	E980.3
Azapetine	971.3	E855.6	E941.3	E950.4	E962.0	E980.4
Azaribine	963.1	E858.1	E933.1	E950.4	E962.0	E980.4
Azaserine	960.7	E856	E930.7	E950.4	E962.0	E980.4
Azathioprine	963.1	E858.1	E933.1	E950.4	E962.0	E980.4
Azosulfamide	961.0	E857	E931.0	E950.4	E962.0	E980.4
Azulfidine	961.0	E857	E931.0	E950.4	E962.0	E980.4
Azuresin	977.8	E858.8	E947.8	E950.4	E962.0	E980.4
Bacimycin	976.0	E858.7	E946.0	E950.4	E962.0	E980.4
ophthalmic preparation	976.5	E858.7	E946.5	E950.4	E962.0	E980.4
Bacitracin	960.8	E856	E930.8	E950.4	E962.0	E980.4
ENT agent	976.6	E858.7	E946.6	E950.4	E962.0	E980.4
ophthalmic preparation	976.5	E858.7	E946.5	E950.4	E962.0	E980.4
topical NEC	976.0	E858.7	E946.0	E950.4	E962.0	E980.4
Baking soda	963.3	E858.1	E933.3	E950.4	E962.0	E980.4
BAL	963.8	E858.1	E933.8	E950.4	E962.0	E980.4
Bamethan (sulfate)	972.5	E858.3	E942.5	E950.4	E962.0	E980.4
Bamipine	963.0	E858.1	E933.0	E950.4	E962.0	E980.4
Baneberry	988.2	E865.4	—	E950.9	E962.1	E980.9
Banewort	988.2	E865.4	—	E950.9	E962.1	E980.9
Barbenyl	967.0	E851	E937.0	E950.1	E962.0	E980.1
Barbital, barbitone	967.0	E851	E937.0	E950.1	E962.0	E980.1
Barbiturates, barbituric acid	967.0	E851	E937.0	E950.1	E962.0	E980.1
anesthetic (intravenous)	968.3	E855.1	E938.3	E950.4	E962.0	E980.4
Barium (carbonate) (chloride) (sulfate)	985.8	E866.4	—	E950.9	E962.1	E980.9
diagnostic agent	977.8	E858.8	E947.8	E950.4	E962.0	E980.4
pesticide	985.8	E863.4	—	E950.6	E962.1	E980.7
rodenticide	985.8	E863.7	—	E950.6	E962.1	E980.7
Barrier cream	976.3	E858.7	E946.3	E950.4	E962.0	E980.4
Battery acid or fluid	983.1	E864.1	—	E950.7	E962.1	E980.6
Bay rum	980.8	E860.8	—	E950.9	E962.1	E980.9
BCG vaccine	978.0	E858.8	E948.0	E950.4	E962.0	E980.4
Bearsfoot	988.2	E865.4	—	E950.9	E962.1	E980.9
Beclamide	966.3	E855.0	E936.3	E950.4	E962.0	E980.4
Bee (sting) (venom)	989.5	E905.3	—	E950.9	E962.1	E980.9
Belladonna (alkaloids)	971.1	E855.4	E941.1	E950.4	E962.0	E980.4
Bemegride	970.0	E854.3	E940.0	E950.4	E962.0	E980.4
Benactyzine	969.8	E855.8	E939.8	E950.3	E962.0	E980.3
Benadryl	963.0	E858.1	E933.0	E950.4	E962.0	E980.4
Bendrofluazide	974.3	E858.5	E944.3	E950.4	E962.0	E980.4
Bendroflumethiazide	974.3	E858.5	E944.3	E950.4	E962.0	E980.4
Benemid	974.7	E858.5	E944.7	E950.4	E962.0	E980.4
Benethamine penicillin G	960.0	E856	E930.0	E950.4	E962.0	E980.4
Benisone	976.0	E858.7	E946.0	E950.4	E962.0	E980.4
Benoquin	976.8	E858.7	E946.8	E950.4	E962.0	E980.4
Benoxinate	968.5	E855.2	E938.5	E950.4	E962.0	E980.4
Bentonite	976.3	E858.7	E946.3	E950.4	E962.0	E980.4
Benzalkonium (chloride)	976.0	E858.7	E946.0	E950.4	E962.0	E980.4
ophthalmic preparation	976.5	E858.7	E946.5	E950.4	E962.0	E980.4
Benzamidosalicylate (calcium)	961.8	E857	E931.8	E950.4	E962.0	E980.4
Benzathine penicillin	960.0	E856	E930.0	E950.4	E962.0	E980.4
Benzcarbimine	963.1	E858.1	E933.1	E950.4	E962.0	E980.4
Benzedrex	971.2	E855.5	E941.2	E950.4	E962.0	E980.4
Benzedrine (amphetamine)	969.7	E854.2	E939.7	E950.3	E962.0	E980.3
Benzene (acetyl) (dimethyl) (methyl) (solvent) (vapor)	982.0	E862.4	—	E950.9	E962.1	E980.9
hexachloride (gamma) (insecticide) (vapor)	989.2	E863.0	—	E950.6	E962.1	E980.7
Benzethonium	976.0	E858.7	E946.0	E950.4	E962.0	E980.4
Benzhexol (chloride)	966.4	E855.0	E936.4	E950.4	E962.0	E980.4
Benzilonium	971.1	E855.4	E941.1	E950.4	E962.0	E980.4
Benzin(e) — *see* Ligroin						

☑ Additional Digit Required — Refer to the Tabular List (Numeric Code Section) for Additional Digit Selection
▶◀ Revised Text ● New Line ▲ Revised Code

	Poisoning	External Cause (E-Code)				
		Accident	Therapeutic Use	Suicide Attempt	Assault	Undetermined
Benziodarone	972.4	E858.3	E942.4	E950.4	E962.0	E980.4
Benzocaine	968.5	E855.2	E938.5	E950.4	E962.0	E980.4
Benzodiapin	969.4	E853.2	E939.4	E950.3	E962.0	E980.3
Benzodiazepines (tranquilizers) NEC	969.4	E853.2	E939.4	E950.3	E962.0	E980.3
Benzoic acid (with salicylic acid) (anti-infective)	976.0	E858.7	E946.0	E950.4	E962.0	E980.4
Benzoin	976.3	E858.7	E946.3	E950.4	E962.0	E980.4
Benzol (vapor)	982.0	E862.4	—	E950.9	E962.1	E980.9
Benzomorphan	965.09	E850.2	E935.2	E950.0	E962.0	E980.0
Benzonatate	975.4	E858.6	E945.4	E950.4	E962.0	E980.4
Benzothiadiazides	974.3	E858.5	E944.3	E950.4	E962.0	E980.4
Benzoylpas	961.8	E857	E931.8	E950.4	E962.0	E980.4
Benzperidol	969.5	E853.8	E939.5	E950.3	E962.0	E980.3
Benzphetamine	977.0	E858.8	E947.0	E950.4	E962.0	E980.4
Benzpyrinium	971.0	E855.3	E941.0	E950.4	E962.0	E980.4
Benzquinamide	963.0	E858.1	E933.0	E950.4	E962.0	E980.4
Benzthiazide	974.3	E858.5	E944.3	E950.4	E962.0	E980.4
Benztropine	971.1	E855.4	E941.1	E950.4	E962.0	E980.4
Benzyl						
acetate	982.8	E862.4	—	E950.9	E962.1	E980.9
benzoate (anti-infective)	976.0	E858.7	E946.0	E950.4	E962.0	E980.4
morphine	965.09	E850.2	E935.2	E950.0	E962.0	E980.0
penicillin	960.0	E856	E930.0	E950.4	E962.0	E980.4
Bephenium						
hydroxynapthoate	961.6	E857	E931.6	E950.4	E962.0	E980.4
Bergamot oil	989.89	E866.8	—	E950.9	E962.1	E980.9
Berries, poisonous	988.2	E865.3	—	E950.9	E962.1	E980.9
Beryllium (compounds) (fumes)	985.3	E866.4	—	E950.9	E962.1	E980.9
Beta-carotene	976.3	E858.7	E946.3	E950.4	E962.0	E980.4
Beta-Chlor	967.1	E852.0	E937.1	E950.2	E962.0	E980.2
Betamethasone	962.0	E858.0	E932.0	E950.4	E962.0	E980.4
topical	976.0	E858.7	E946.0	E950.4	E962.0	E980.4
Betazole	977.8	E858.8	E947.8	E950.4	E962.0	E980.4
Bethanechol	971.0	E855.3	E941.0	E950.4	E962.0	E980.4
Bethanidine	972.6	E858.3	E942.6	E950.4	E962.0	E980.4
Betula oil	976.3	E858.7	E946.3	E950.4	E962.0	E980.4
Bhang	969.6	E854.1	E939.6	E950.3	E962.0	E980.3
Bialamicol	961.5	E857	E931.5	E950.4	E962.0	E980.4
Bichloride of mercury —						
see Mercury, chloride						
Bichromates (calcium) (crystals) (potassium) (sodium)	983.9	E864.3	—	E950.7	E962.1	E980.6
fumes	987.8	E869.8	—	E952.8	E962.2	E982.8
Biguanide derivatives, oral	962.3	E858.0	E932.3	E950.4	E962.0	E980.4
Biligrafin	977.8	E858.8	E947.8	E950.4	E962.0	E980.4
Bilopaque	977.8	E858.8	E947.8	E950.4	E962.0	E980.4
Bioflavonoids	972.8	E858.3	E942.8	E950.4	E962.0	E980.4
Biological substance NEC	979.9	E858.8	E949.9	E950.4	E962.0	E980.4
Biperiden	966.4	E855.0	E936.4	E950.4	E962.0	E980.4
Bisacodyl	973.1	E858.4	E943.1	E950.4	E962.0	E980.4
Bishydroxycoumarin	964.2	E858.2	E934.2	E950.4	E962.0	E980.4
Bismarsen	961.1	E857	E931.1	E950.4	E962.0	E980.4
Bismuth (compounds) NEC	985.8	E866.4	—	E950.9	E962.1	E980.9
anti-infectives	961.2	E857	E931.2	E950.4	E962.0	E980.4
subcarbonate	973.5	E858.4	E943.5	E950.4	E962.0	E980.4
sulfarsphenamine	961.1	E857	E931.1	E950.4	E962.0	E980.4
Bithionol	961.6	E857	E931.6	E950.4	E962.0	E980.4
Bitter almond oil	989.0	E866.8	—	E950.9	E962.1	E980.9
Bittersweet	988.2	E865.4	—	E950.9	E962.1	E930.9
Black						
flag	989.4	E863.4	—	E950.6	E962.1	E980.7
henbane	988.2	E865.4	—	E950.9	E962.1	E980.9
leaf (40)	989.4	E863.4	—	E950.6	E962.1	E980.7
widow spider (bite)	989.5	E905.1	—	E950.9	E962.1	E980.9
antivenin	979.9	E858.8	E949.9	E950.4	E962.0	E980.4
Blast furnace gas (carbon monoxide from)	986	E868.8	—	E952.1	E962.2	E982.1
Bleach NEC	983.9	E864.3	—	E950.7	E962.1	E980.6
Bleaching solutions	983.9	E864.3	—	E950.7	E962.1	E980.6
Bleomycin (sulfate)	960.7	E856	E930.7	E950.4	E962.0	E980.4
Blockain	968.9	E855.2	E938.9	E950.4	E962.0	E980.4
infiltration (subcutaneous)	968.5	E855.2	E938.5	E950.4	E962.0	E980.4
nerve block (peripheral) (plexus)	968.6	E855.2	E938.6	E950.4	E962.0	E980.4
topical (surface)	968.5	E855.2	E938.5	E950.4	E962.0	E980.4
Blood (derivatives) (natural) (plasma) (whole)	964.7	E858.2	E934.7	E950.4	E962.0	E980.4
affecting agent	964.9	E858.2	E934.9	E950.4	E962.0	E980.4
specified NEC	964.8	E858.2	E934.8	E950.4	E962.0	E980.4

	Poisoning	External Cause (E-Code)				
		Accident	Therapeutic Use	Suicide Attempt	Assault	Undetermined
Blood — continued						
substitute (macromolecular)	964.8	E858.2	E934.8	E950.4	E962.0	E980.4
Blue velvet	965.09	E850.2	E935.2	E950.0	E962.0	E980.0
Bone meal	989.89	E866.5	—	E950.9	E962.1	E980.9
Bonine	963.0	E858.1	E933.0	E950.4	E962.0	E980.4
Boracic acid	976.0	E858.7	E946.0	E950.4	E962.0	E980.4
ENT agent	976.6	E858.7	E946.6	E950.4	E962.0	E980.4
ophthalmic preparation	976.5	E858.7	E946.5	E950.4	E962.0	E980.4
Borate (cleanser) (sodium)	989.6	E861.3	—	E950.9	E962.1	E980.9
Borax (cleanser)	989.6	E861.3	—	E950.9	E962.1	E980.9
Boric acid	976.0	E858.7	E946.0	E950.4	E962.0	E980.4
ENT agent	976.6	E858.7	E946.6	E950.4	E962.0	E980.4
ophthalmic preparation	976.5	E858.7	E946.5	E950.4	E962.0	E980.4
Boron hydride NEC	989.89	E866.8	—	E950.9	E962.1	E980.9
fumes or gas	987.8	E869.8	—	E952.8	E962.2	E982.8
Botox	975.3	E858.6	E945.3	E950.4	E962.0	E980.4
Brake fluid vapor	987.8	E869.8	—	E952.8	E962.2	E982.8
Brass (compounds) (fumes)	985.8	E866.4	—	E950.9	E962.1	E980.9
Brasso	981	E861.3	—	E950.9	E962.1	E980.9
Bretylium (tosylate)	972.6	E858.3	E942.6	E950.4	E962.0	E980.4
Brevital (sodium)	968.3	E855.1	E938.3	E950.4	E962.0	E980.4
British antilewisite	963.8	E858.1	E933.8	E950.4	E962.0	E980.4
Bromal (hydrate)	967.3	E852.2	E937.3	E950.2	E962.0	E980.2
Bromelains	963.4	E858.1	E933.4	E950.4	E962.0	E980.4
Bromides NEC	967.3	E852.2	E937.3	E950.2	E962.0	E980.2
Bromine (vapor)	987.8	E869.8	—	E952.8	E962.2	E982.8
compounds (medicinal)	967.3	E852.2	E937.3	E950.2	E962.0	E980.2
Bromisovalum	967.3	E852.2	E937.3	E950.2	E962.0	E980.2
Bromobenzyl cyanide	987.5	E869.3	—	E952.8	E962.2	E982.8
Bromodiphenhydramine	963.0	E858.1	E933.0	E950.4	E962.0	E980.4
Bromoform	967.3	E852.2	E937.3	E950.2	E962.0	E980.2
Bromophenol blue reagent	977.8	E858.8	E947.8	E950.4	E962.0	E980.4
Bromosalicylhydroxamic acid	961.8	E857	E931.8	E950.4	E962.0	E980.4
Bromo-seltzer	965.4	E850.4	E935.4	E950.0	E962.0	E980.0
Brompheniramine	963.0	E858.1	E933.0	E950.4	E962.0	E980.4
Bromural	967.3	E852.2	E937.3	E950.2	E962.0	E980.2
Brown spider (bite) (venom)	989.5	E905.1	—	E950.9	E962.1	E980.9
Brucia	988.2	E865.3	—	E950.9	E962.1	E980.9
Brucine	989.1	E863.7	—	E950.6	E962.1	E980.7
Brunswick green — see Copper						
Bruten — see Ibuprofen						
Bryonia (alba) (dioica)	988.2	E865.4	—	E950.9	E962.1	E980.9
Buclizine	969.5	E853.8	E939.5	E950.3	E962.0	E980.3
Bufferin	965.1	E850.3	E935.3	E950.0	E962.0	E980.0
Bufotenine	969.6	E854.1	E939.6	E950.3	E962.0	E980.3
Buphenine	971.2	E855.5	E941.2	E950.4	E962.0	E980.4
Bupivacaine	968.9	E855.2	E938.9	E950.4	E962.0	E980.4
infiltration (subcutaneous)	968.5	E855.2	E938.5	E950.4	E962.0	E980.4
nerve block (peripheral) (plexus)	968.6	E855.2	E938.6	E950.4	E962.0	E980.4
Busulfan	963.1	E858.1	E933.1	E950.4	E962.0	E980.4
Butabarbital (sodium)	967.0	E851	E937.0	E950.1	E962.0	E980.1
Butabarbitone	967.0	E851	E937.0	E950.1	E962.0	E980.1
Butabarpal	967.0	E851	E937.0	E950.1	E962.0	E980.1
Butacaine	968.5	E855.2	E938.5	E950.4	E962.0	E980.4
Butallylonal	967.0	E851	E937.0	E950.1	E962.0	E980.1
Butane (distributed in mobile container)	987.0	E868.0	—	E951.1	E962.2	E981.1
distributed through pipes	987.0	E867	—	E951.0	E962.2	E981.0
incomplete combustion of — see Carbon monoxide, butane						
Butanol	980.3	E860.4	—	E950.9	E962.1	E980.9
Butanone	982.8	E862.4	—	E950.9	E962.1	E980.9
Butaperazine	969.1	E853.0	E939.1	E950.3	E962.0	E980.3
Butazolidin	965.5	E850.5	E935.5	E950.0	E962.0	E980.0
Butethal	967.0	E851	E937.0	E950.1	E962.0	E980.1
Butethamate	971.1	E855.4	E941.1	E950.4	E962.0	E980.4
Buthalitone (sodium)	968.3	E855.1	E938.3	E950.4	E962.0	E980.4
Butisol (sodium)	967.0	E851	E937.0	E950.1	E962.0	E980.1
Butobarbital, butobarbitone	967.0	E851	E937.0	E950.1	E962.0	E980.1
Butriptyline	969.0	E854.0	E939.0	E950.3	E962.0	E980.3
Buttercups	988.2	E865.4	—	E950.9	E962.1	E980.9
Butter of antimony — see Antimony						
Butyl						
acetate (secondary)	982.8	E862.4	—	E950.9	E962.1	E980.9
alcohol	980.3	E860.4	—	E950.9	E962.1	E980.9
carbinol	980.8	E860.8	—	E950.9	E962.1	E980.9
carbitol	982.8	E862.4	—	E950.9	E962.1	E980.9
cellosolve	982.8	E862.4	—	E950.9	E962.1	E980.9

☑ Additional Digit Required — Refer to the Tabular List (Numeric Code Section) for Additional Digit Selection

▶◀ Revised Text   ● New Line   ▲ Revised Code

	Poisoning	Accident	Therapeutic Use	Suicide Attempt	Assault	Undetermined
Butyl — *continued*						
chloral (hydrate)	967.1	E852.0	E937.1	E950.2	E962.0	E980.2
formate	982.8	E862.4	—	E950.9	E962.1	E980.9
scopolammonium bromide	971.1	E855.4	E941.1	E950.4	E962.0	E980.4
Butyn	968.5	E855.2	E938.5	E950.4	E962.0	E980.4
Butyrophenone (-based tranquilizers)	969.2	E853.1	E939.2	E950.3	E962.0	E980.3
Cacodyl, cacodylic acid — *see* Arsenic						
Cactinomycin	960.7	E856	E930.7	E950.4	E962.0	E980.4
Cade oil	976.4	E858.7	E946.4	E950.4	E962.0	E980.4
Cadmium (chloride) (compounds) (dust) (fumes) (oxide)	985.5	E866.4	—	E950.9	E962.1	E980.9
sulfide (medicinal) NEC	976.4	E858.7	E946.4	E950.4	E962.0	E980.4
Caffeine	969.7	E854.2	E939.7	E950.3	E962.0	E980.3
Calabar bean	988.2	E865.4	—	E950.9	E962.1	E980.9
Caladium seguinum	988.2	E865.4	—	E950.9	E962.1	E980.9
Calamine (liniment) (lotion)	976.3	E858.7	E946.3	E950.4	E962.0	E980.4
Calciferol	963.5	E858.1	E933.5	E950.4	E962.0	E980.4
Calcium (salts) NEC	974.5	E858.5	E944.5	E950.4	E962.0	E980.4
acetylsalicylate	965.1	E850.3	E935.3	E950.0	E962.0	E980.0
benzamidosalicylate	961.8	E857	E931.8	E950.4	E962.0	E980.4
carbaspirin	965.1	E850.3	E935.3	E950.0	E962.0	E980.0
carbimide (citrated)	977.3	E858.8	E947.3	E950.4	E962.0	E980.4
carbonate (antacid)	973.0	E858.4	E943.0	E950.4	E962.0	E980.4
cyanide (citrated)	977.3	E858.8	E947.3	E950.4	E962.0	E980.4
dioctyl sulfosuccinate	973.2	E858.4	E943.2	E950.4	E962.0	E980.4
disodium edathamil	963.8	E858.1	E933.8	E950.4	E962.0	E980.4
disodium edetate	963.8	E858.1	E933.8	E950.4	E962.0	E980.4
EDTA	963.8	E858.1	E933.8	E950.4	E962.0	E980.4
hydrate, hydroxide	983.2	E864.2	—	E950.7	E962.1	E980.6
mandelate	961.9	E857	E931.9	E950.4	E962.0	E980.4
oxide	983.2	E864.2	—	E950.7	E962.1	E980.6
Calomel — *see* Mercury, chloride						
Caloric agents NEC	974.5	E858.5	E944.5	E950.4	E962.0	E980.4
Calusterone	963.1	E858.1	E933.1	E950.4	E962.0	E980.4
Camoquin	961.4	E857	E931.4	E950.4	E962.0	E980.4
Camphor (oil)	976.1	E858.7	E946.1	E950.4	E962.0	E980.4
Candeptin	976.0	E858.7	E946.0	E950.4	E962.0	E980.4
Candicidin	976.0	E858.7	E946.0	E950.4	E962.0	E980.4
Cannabinols	969.6	E854.1	E939.6	E950.3	E962.0	E980.3
Cannabis (derivatives) (indica) (sativa)	969.6	E854.1	E939.6	E950.3	E962.0	E980.3
Canned heat	980.1	E860.2	—	E950.9	E962.1	E980.9
Cantharides, cantharidin, cantharis	976.8	E858.7	E946.8	E950.4	E962.0	E980.4
Capillary agents	972.8	E858.3	E942.8	E950.4	E962.0	E980.4
Capreomycin	960.6	E856	E930.6	E950.4	E962.0	E980.4
Captodiame, captodiamine	969.5	E853.8	E939.5	E950.3	E962.0	E980.3
Caramiphen (hydrochloride)	971.1	E855.4	E941.1	E950.4	E962.0	E980.4
Carbachol	971.0	E855.3	E941.0	E950.4	E962.0	E980.4
Carbacrylamine resins	974.5	E858.5	E944.5	E950.4	E962.0	E980.4
Carbamate (sedative)	967.8	E852.8	E937.8	E950.2	E962.0	E980.2
herbicide	989.3	E863.5	—	E950.6	E962.1	E980.7
insecticide	989.3	E863.2	—	E950.6	E962.1	E980.7
Carbamazepine	966.3	E855.0	E936.3	E950.4	E962.0	E980.4
Carbamic esters	967.8	E852.8	E937.8	E950.2	E962.0	E980.2
Carbamide	974.4	E858.5	E944.4	E950.4	E962.0	E980.4
topical	976.8	E858.7	E946.8	E950.4	E962.0	E980.4
Carbamylcholine chloride	971.0	E855.3	E941.0	E950.4	E962.0	E980.4
Carbarsone	961.1	E857	E931.1	E950.4	E962.0	E980.4
Carbaryl	989.3	E863.2	—	E950.6	E962.1	E980.7
Carbaspirin	965.1	E850.3	E935.3	E950.0	E962.0	E980.0
Carbazochrome	972.8	E858.3	E942.8	E950.4	E962.0	E980.4
Carbenicillin	960.0	E856	E930.0	E950.4	E962.0	E980.4
Carbenoxolone	973.8	E858.4	E943.8	E950.4	E962.0	E980.4
Carbetapentane	975.4	E858.6	E945.4	E950.4	E962.0	E980.4
Carbimazole	962.8	E858.0	E932.8	E950.4	E962.0	E980.4
Carbinol	980.1	E860.2	—	E950.9	E962.1	E980.9
Carbinoxamine	963.0	E858.1	E933.0	E950.4	E962.0	E980.4
Carbitol	982.8	E862.4	—	E950.9	E962.1	E980.9
Carbocaine	968.9	E855.2	E938.9	E950.4	E962.0	E980.4
infiltration (subcutaneous)	968.5	E855.2	E938.5	E950.4	E962.0	E980.4
nerve block (peripheral) (plexus)	968.6	E855.2	E938.6	E950.4	E962.0	E980.4
topical (surface)	968.5	E855.2	E938.5	E950.4	E962.0	E980.4
Carbol-fuchsin solution	976.0	E858.7	E946.0	E950.4	E962.0	E980.4
Carbolic acid (*see also* Phenol)	983.0	E864.0	—	E950.7	E962.1	E980.6
Carbomycin	960.8	E856	E930.8	E950.4	E962.0	E980.4

	Poisoning	Accident	Therapeutic Use	Suicide Attempt	Assault	Undetermined
Carbon						
bisulfide (liquid) (vapor)	982.2	E862.4	—	E950.9	E962.1	E980.9
dioxide (gas)	987.8	E869.8	—	E952.8	E962.2	E982.8
disulfide (liquid) (vapor)	982.2	E862.4	—	E950.9	E962.1	E980.9
monoxide (from incomplete combustion of) (in)						
NEC	986	E868.9	—	E952.1	E962.2	E982.1
blast furnace gas	986	E868.8	—	E952.1	E962.2	E982.1
butane (distributed in mobile container)	986	E868.0	—	E951.1	E962.2	E981.1
distributed through pipes	986	E867	—	E951.0	E962.2	E981.0
charcoal fumes	986	E868.3	—	E952.1	E962.2	E982.1
coal						
gas (piped)	986	E867	—	E951.0	E962.2	E981.0
solid (in domestic stoves, fireplaces)	986	E868.3	—	E952.1	E962.2	E982.1
coke (in domestic stoves, fireplaces)	986	E868.3	—	E952.1	E962.2	E982.1
exhaust gas (motor) not in transit	986	E868.2	—	E952.0	E962.2	E982.0
combustion engine, any not in watercraft	986	E868.2	—	E952.0	E962.2	E982.0
farm tractor, not in transit	986	E868.2	—	E952.0	E962.2	E982.0
gas engine	986	E868.2	—	E952.0	E962.2	E982.0
motor pump	986	E868.2	—	E952.0	E962.2	E982.0
motor vehicle, not in transit	986	E868.2	—	E952.0	E962.2	E982.0
fuel (in domestic use)	986	E868.3	—	E952.1	E962.2	E982.1
gas (piped)	986	E867	—	E951.0	E962.2	E981.0
in mobile container	986	E868.0	—	E951.1	E962.2	E981.1
utility	986	E868.1	—	E951.8	E962.2	E981.1
in mobile container	986	E868.0	—	E951.1	E962.2	E981.1
piped (natural)	986	E867	—	E951.0	E962.2	E981.0
illuminating gas	986	E868.1	—	E951.8	E962.2	E981.8
industrial fuels or gases, any	986	E868.8	—	E952.1	E962.2	E982.1
kerosene (in domestic stoves, fireplaces)	986	E868.3	—	E952.1	E962.2	E982.1
kiln gas or vapor	986	E868.8	—	E952.1	E962.2	E982.1
motor exhaust gas, not in transit	986	E868.2	—	E952.0	E962.2	E982.0
piped gas (manufactured) (natural)	986	E867	—	E951.0	E962.2	E981.0
producer gas	986	E868.8	—	E951.2	E962.2	E982.1
propane (distributed in mobile container)	986	E868.0	—	E951.1	E962.2	E981.1
distributed through pipes	986	E867	—	E951.0	E962.2	E981.0
specified source NEC	986	E868.8	—	E952.1	E962.2	E982.1
stove gas	986	E868.1	—	E951.8	E962.2	E981.8
piped	986	E867	—	E951.0	E962.2	E981.0
utility	986	E868.1	—	E951.8	E962.2	E981.8
piped	986	E867	—	E951.0	E962.2	E981.0
water gas	986	E868.1	—	E951.8	E962.2	E981.8
wood (in domestic stoves, fireplaces)	986	E868.3	—	E952.1	E962.2	E982.1
tetrachloride (vapor) NEC	987.8	E869.8	—	E952.8	E962.2	E982.8
liquid (cleansing agent) NEC	982.1	E861.3	—	E950.9	E962.1	E980.9
solvent	982.1	E862.4	—	E950.9	E962.1	E980.9
Carbonic acid (gas)	987.8	E869.8	—	E952.8	E962.2	E982.8
anhydrase inhibitors	974.2	E858.5	E944.2	E950.4	E962.0	E980.4
Carbowax	976.3	E858.7	E946.3	E950.4	E962.0	E980.4
Carbrital	967.0	E851	E937.0	E950.1	E962.0	E980.1
Carbromal (derivatives)	967.3	E852.2	E937.3	E950.2	E962.0	E980.2
Cardiac						
depressants	972.0	E858.3	E942.0	E950.4	E962.0	E980.4
rhythm regulators	972.0	E858.3	E942.0	E950.4	E962.0	E980.4

☑ Additional Digit Required — Refer to the Tabular List (Numeric Code Section) for Additional Digit Selection

▶◀ Revised Text ● New Line ▲ Revised Code

Parasomnia — *continued*
  nonorganic origin 307.47
  organic 327.40 ●
    in conditions classified elsewhere 327.44 ●
    other 327.49 ●
Paraspadias 752.69
Paraspasm facialis 351.8
Parathyroid gland — *see* condition
Parathyroiditis (autoimmune) 252.1
Parathyroprival tetany 252.1
Paratrachoma 077.0
Paratyphilitis (*see also* Appendicitis) 541
Paratyphoid (fever) — *see* Fever, paratyphoid
Paratyphus — *see* Fever, paratyphoid
Paraurethral duct 753.8
Para-urethritis 597.89
  gonococcal (acute) 098.0
    chronic or duration of 2 months or over 098.2
Paravaccinia NEC 051.9
  milkers' node 051.1
Paravaginitis (*see also* Vaginitis) 616.10
Parencephalitis (*see also* Encephalitis) 323.9
  late effect — *see* category 326
Parergasia 298.9
Paresis (*see also* Paralysis) 344.9
  accommodation 367.51
  bladder (spastic) (sphincter) (*see also* Paralysis, bladder) 596.53
    tabetic 094.0
  bowel, colon, or intestine (*see also* Ileus) 560.1
  brain or cerebral — *see* Paralysis, brain
  extrinsic muscle, eye 378.55
  general 094.1
    arrested 094.1
    brain 094.1
    cerebral 094.1
    insane 094.1
    juvenile 090.40
      remission 090.49
    progressive 094.1
    remission (sustained) 094.1
    tabetic 094.1
  heart (*see also* Failure, heart) 428.9
  infantile (*see also* Poliomyelitis) 045.9 ☑
  insane 094.1
  juvenile 090.40
  late effect — *see* Paralysis, late effect
  luetic (general) 094.1
  peripheral progressive 356.9
  pseudohypertrophic 359.1
  senile NEC 344.9
  stomach 536.3
    diabetic 250.6 ☑ [536.3]
  syphilitic (general) 094.1
    congenital 090.40
  transient, limb 781.4
  vesical (sphincter) NEC 596.53
Paresthesia (*see also* Disturbance, sensation) 782.0
  Berger's (paresthesia of lower limb) 782.0
  Bernhardt 355.1
  Magnan's 782.0
Paretic — *see* condition
Parinaud's
  conjunctivitis 372.02
  oculoglandular syndrome 372.02
  ophthalmoplegia 378.81
  syndrome (paralysis of conjugate upward gaze) 378.81
Parkes Weber and Dimitri syndrome (encephalocutaneous angiomatosis) 759.6
Parkinson's disease, syndrome, or tremor — *see* Parkinsonism
Parkinsonism (arteriosclerotic) (idiopathic) (primary) 332.0
  associated with orthostatic hypotension (idiopathic) (symptomatic) 333.0
  due to drugs 332.1
  neuroleptic-induced 332.1 ●
  secondary 332.1
  syphilitic 094.82
Parodontitis 523.4

Parodontosis 523.5
Paronychia (with lymphangitis) 681.9
  candidal (chronic) 112.3
  chronic 681.9
    candidal 112.3
    finger 681.02
    toe 681.11
  finger 681.02
  toe 681.11
  tuberculous (primary) (*see also* Tuberculosis) 017.0 ☑
Parorexia NEC 307.52
  hysterical 300.11
Parosmia 781.1
  psychogenic 306.7
Parotid gland — *see* condition
Parotiditis (*see also* Parotitis) 527.2
  epidemic 072.9
  infectious 072.9
Parotitis 527.2
  allergic 527.2
  chronic 527.2
  epidemic (*see also* Mumps) 072.9
  infectious (*see also* Mumps) 072.9
  noninfectious 527.2
  nonspecific toxic 527.2
  not mumps 527.2
  postoperative 527.2
  purulent 527.2
  septic 527.2
  suppurative (acute) 527.2
  surgical 527.2
  toxic 527.2
Paroxysmal — *see also* condition
  dyspnea (nocturnal) 786.09
Parrot's disease (syphilitic osteochondritis) 090.0
Parrot fever 073.9
Parry's disease or syndrome (exophthalmic goiter) 242.0 ☑
Parry-Romberg syndrome 349.89
Parson's disease (exophthalmic goiter) 242.0 ☑
Parsonage-Aldren-Turner syndrome 353.5
Parsonage-Turner syndrome 353.5
Pars planitis 363.21
Particolored infant 757.39
Parturition — *see* Delivery
Passage
  false, urethra 599.4
  meconium noted during delivery 763.84 ●
  of sounds or bougies (*see also* Attention to artificial opening) V55.9
Passive — *see* condition
Pasteurella septica 027.2
Pasteurellosis (*see also* Infection, Pasteurella) 027.2
PAT (paroxysmal atrial tachycardia) 427.0
Patau's syndrome (trisomy D₁) 758.1
Patch
  herald 696.3
Patches
  mucous (syphilitic) 091.3
    congenital 090.0
  smokers' (mouth) 528.6
Patellar — *see* condition
Patellofemoral syndrome 719.46
Patent — *see also* Imperfect closure
  atrioventricular ostium 745.69
  canal of Nuck 752.41
  cervix 622.5
    complicating pregnancy 654.5 ☑
      affecting fetus or newborn 761.0
  ductus arteriosus or Botalli 747.0
  Eustachian
    tube 381.7
    valve 746.89
  foramen
    Botalli 745.5
    ovale 745.5
  interauricular septum 745.5
  interventricular septum 745.4
  omphalomesenteric duct 751.0
  os (uteri) — *see* Patent, cervix

Patent — *see also* Imperfect closure — *continued*
    ostium secundum 745.5
  urachus 753.7
  vitelline duct 751.0
Paternity testing V70.4
Paterson's syndrome (sideropenic dysphagia) 280.8
Paterson (-Brown) (-Kelly) syndrome (sideropenic dysphagia) 280.8
Paterson-Kelly syndrome or web (sideropenic dysphagia) 280.8
Pathologic, pathological — *see also* condition
  asphyxia 799.01 ▲
  drunkenness 291.4
  emotionality 301.3
  fracture — *see* Fracture, pathologic
  liar 301.7
  personality 301.9
  resorption, tooth 521.40
    external 521.42
    internal 521.41
    specified NEC 521.49
  sexuality (*see also* Deviation, sexual) 302.9
Pathology (of) — *see* Disease
Patterned motor discharge, idiopathic (*see also* Epilepsy) 345.5 ☑
Patulous — *see also* Patent
  anus 569.49
  Eustachian tube 381.7
Pause, sinoatrial 427.81
Pavor nocturnus 307.46
Pavy's disease 593.6
Paxton's disease (white piedra) 111.2
Payr's disease or syndrome (splenic flexure syndrome) 569.89
PBA (pseudobulbar affect) 310.8 ●
Pearls
  Elschnig 366.51
  enamel 520.2
Pearl-workers' disease (chronic osteomyelitis) (*see also* Osteomyelitis) 730.1 ☑
Pectenitis 569.49
Pectenosis 569.49
Pectoral — *see* condition
Pectus
  carinatum (congenital) 754.82
    acquired 738.3
    rachitic (*see also* Rickets) 268.0
  excavatum (congenital) 754.81
    acquired 738.3
    rachitic (*see also* Rickets) 268.0
  recurvatum (congenital) 754.81
    acquired 738.3
Pedatrophia 261
Pederosis 302.2
Pediculosis (infestation) 132.9
  capitis (head louse) (any site) 132.0
  corporis (body louse) (any site) 132.1
  eyelid 132.0 [373.6]
  mixed (classifiable to more than one category in 132.0-132.2) 132.3
  pubis (pubic louse) (any site) 132.2
  vestimenti 132.1
  vulvae 132.2
Pediculus (infestation) — *see* Pediculosis
Pedophilia 302.2
Peg-shaped teeth 520.2
Pel's crisis 094.0
Pel-Ebstein disease — *see* Disease, Hodgkin's
Pelade 704.01
Pelger-Huët anomaly or syndrome (hereditary hyposegmentation) 288.2
Peliosis (rheumatica) 287.0
Pelizaeus-Merzbacher
  disease 330.0
  sclerosis, diffuse cerebral 330.0
Pellagra (alcoholic or with alcoholism) 265.2
  with polyneuropathy 265.2 [357.4]
Pellagra-cerebellar-ataxia-renal aminoaciduria syndrome 270.0

2006 ICD-9-CM

☑ Additional Digit Required — Refer to the Tabular List (Numeric Code Section) for Additional Digit Selection
▶◀ Revised Text   ● New Line   ▲ Revised Code

October 2005 • Volume 2 — 263

Pellegrini's disease (calcification, knee joint) 726.62

Pellegrini (-Stieda) disease or syndrome (calcification, knee joint) 726.62

Pellizzi's syndrome (pineal) 259.8

Pelvic — *see also* condition
   congestion-fibrosis syndrome 625.5
   kidney 753.3

Pelvioectasis 591

Pelviolithiasis 592.0

Pelviperitonitis
   female (*see also* Peritonitis, pelvic, female) 614.5
   male (*see also* Peritonitis) 567.21 ▲

Pelvis, pelvic — *see also* condition or type
   infantile 738.6
   Nägele's 738.6
   obliquity 738.6
   Robert's 755.69

Pemphigoid 694.5
   benign, mucous membrane 694.60
      with ocular involvement 694.61
   bullous 694.5
   cicatricial 694.60
      with ocular involvement 694.61
   juvenile 694.2

Pemphigus 694.4
   benign 694.5
      chronic familial 757.39
   Brazilian 694.4
   circinatus 694.0
   congenital, traumatic 757.39
   conjunctiva 694.61
   contagiosus 684
   erythematodes 694.4
   erythematosus 694.4
   foliaceus 694.4
   frambesiodes 694.4
   gangrenous (*see also* Gangrene) 785.4
   malignant 694.4
   neonatorum, newborn 684
   ocular 694.61
   papillaris 694.4
   seborrheic 694.4
   South American 694.4
   syphilitic (congenital) 090.0
   vegetans 694.4
   vulgaris 694.4
   wildfire 694.4

Pendred's syndrome (familial goiter with deaf-mutism) 243

Pendulous
   abdomen 701.9
      in pregnancy or childbirth 654.4 ☑
         affecting fetus or newborn 763.89
   breast 611.8

Penetrating wound — *see also* Wound, open, by site
   with internal injury — *see* Injury, internal, by site, with open wound
   eyeball 871.7
      with foreign body (nonmagnetic) 871.6
         magnetic 871.5
   ocular (*see also* Penetrating wound, eyeball) 871.7
   adnexa 870.3
      with foreign body 870.4
   orbit 870.3
      with foreign body 870.4

Penetration, pregnant uterus by instrument
   with
      abortion — *see* Abortion, by type, with damage to pelvic organs
      ectopic pregnancy (*see also* categories 633.0-633.9) 639.2
      molar pregnancy (*see also* categories 630-632) 639.2
   complication of delivery 665.1 ☑
      affecting fetus or newborn 763.89
   following
      abortion 639.2
      ectopic or molar pregnancy 639.2

Penfield's syndrome (*see also* Epilepsy) 345.5 ☑

Penicilliosis of lung 117.3

Penis — *see* condition

Penitis 607.2

Penta X syndrome 758.81

Pentalogy (of Fallot) 745.2

Pentosuria (benign) (essential) 271.8

Peptic acid disease 536.8

Peregrinating patient V65.2

Perforated — *see* Perforation

Perforation, perforative (nontraumatic)
   antrum (*see also* Sinusitis, maxillary) 473.0
   appendix 540.0
      with peritoneal abscess 540.1
   atrial septum, multiple 745.5
   attic, ear 384.22
      healed 384.81
   bile duct, except cystic (*see also* Disease, biliary) 576.3
      cystic 575.4
   bladder (urinary) 596.6
      with
         abortion — *see* Abortion, by type, with damage to pelvic organs
         ectopic pregnancy (*see also* categories 633.0-633.9) 639.2
         molar pregnancy (*see also* categories 630-632) 639.2
      following
         abortion 639.2
         ectopic or molar pregnancy 639.2
      obstetrical trauma 665.5 ☑
   bowel 569.83
      with
         abortion — *see* Abortion, by type, with damage to pelvic organs
         ectopic pregnancy (*see also* categories 633.0-633.9) 639.2
         molar pregnancy (*see also* categories 630-632) 639.2
      fetus or newborn 777.6
      following
         abortion 639.2
         ectopic or molar pregnancy 639.2
      obstetrical trauma 665.5 ☑
   broad ligament
      with
         abortion — *see* Abortion, by type, with damage to pelvic organs
         ectopic pregnancy (*see also* categories 633.0-633.9) 639.2
         molar pregnancy (*see also* categories 630-632) 639.2
      following
         abortion 639.2
         ectopic or molar pregnancy 639.2
      obstetrical trauma 665.6 ☑
   by
      device, implant, or graft — *see* Complications, mechanical
      foreign body left accidentally in operation wound 998.4
      instrument (any) during a procedure, accidental 998.2
   cecum 540.0
      with peritoneal abscess 540.1
   cervix (uteri) — *see also* Injury, internal, cervix
      with
         abortion — *see* Abortion, by type, with damage to pelvic organs
         ectopic pregnancy (*see also* categories 633.0-633.9) 639.2
         molar pregnancy (*see also* categories 630-632) 639.2
      following
         abortion 639.2
         ectopic or molar pregnancy 639.2
      obstetrical trauma 665.3 ☑
   colon 569.83
   common duct (bile) 576.3
   cornea (*see also* Ulcer, cornea) 370.00
      due to ulceration 370.06
   cystic duct 575.4
   diverticulum (*see also* Diverticula) 562.10
      small intestine 562.00
   duodenum, duodenal (ulcer) — *see* Ulcer, duodenum, with perforation

Perforation, perforative — *continued*
   ear drum — *see* Perforation, tympanum
   enteritis — *see* Enteritis
   esophagus 530.4
   ethmoidal sinus (*see also* Sinusitis, ethmoidal) 473.2
   foreign body (external site) — *see also* Wound, open, by site, complicated
      internal site, by ingested object — *see* Foreign body
   frontal sinus (*see also* Sinusitis, frontal) 473.1
   gallbladder or duct (*see also* Disease, gallbladder) 575.4
   gastric (ulcer) — *see* Ulcer, stomach, with perforation
   heart valve — *see* Endocarditis
   ileum (*see also* Perforation, intestine) 569.83
   instrumental
      external — *see* Wound, open, by site
      pregnant uterus, complicating delivery 665.9 ☑
      surgical (accidental) (blood vessel) (nerve) (organ) 998.2
   intestine 569.83
      with
         abortion — *see* Abortion, by type, with damage to pelvic organs
         ectopic pregnancy (*see also* categories 633.0-633.9) 639.2
         molar pregnancy (*see also* categories 630-632) 639.2
      fetus or newborn 777.6
      obstetrical trauma 665.5 ☑
      ulcerative NEC 569.83
   jejunum, jejunal 569.83
      ulcer — *see* Ulcer, gastrojejunal, with perforation
   mastoid (antrum) (cell) 383.89
   maxillary sinus (*see also* Sinusitis, maxillary) 473.0
   membrana tympani — *see* Perforation, tympanum
   nasal
      septum 478.1
         congenital 748.1
         syphilitic 095.8
      sinus (*see also* Sinusitis) 473.9
         congenital 748.1
   palate (hard) 526.89
      soft 528.9
         syphilitic 095.8
            syphilitic 095.8
   palatine vault 526.89
      syphilitic 095.8
         congenital 090.5
   pelvic
      floor
         with
            abortion — *see* Abortion, by type, with damage to pelvic organs
            ectopic pregnancy (*see also* categories 633.0-633.9) 639.2
            molar pregnancy (*see also* categories 630-632) 639.2
         obstetrical trauma 664.1 ☑
      organ
         with
            abortion — *see* Abortion, by type, with damage to pelvic organs
            ectopic pregnancy (*see also* categories 633.0-633.9) 639.2
            molar pregnancy (*see also* categories 630-632) 639.2
         following
            abortion 639.2
            ectopic or molar pregnancy 639.2
         obstetrical trauma 665.5 ☑
   perineum — *see* Laceration, perineum
   periurethral tissue
      with
         abortion — *see* Abortion, by type, with damage to pelvic organs
         ectopic pregnancy (*see also* categories 630-632) 639.2
         molar pregnancy (*see also* categories 630-632) 639.2
   pharynx 478.29

☑ Additional Digit Required — Refer to the Tabular List (Numeric Code Section) for Additional Digit Selection

Perforation, perforative — *continued*
  pylorus, pyloric (ulcer) — *see* Ulcer, stomach,
      with perforation
  rectum 569.49
  sigmoid 569.83
  sinus (accessory) (chronic) (nasal) (*see also*
      Sinusitis) 473.9
  sphenoidal sinus (*see also* Sinusitis,
      sphenoidal) 473.3
  stomach (due to ulcer) — *see* Ulcer, stomach,
      with perforation
  surgical (accidental) (by instrument) (blood
      vessel) (nerve) (organ) 998.2
  traumatic
      external — *see* Wound, open, by site
      eye (*see also* Penetrating wound, ocular)
          871.7
      internal organ — *see* Injury, internal, by site
  tympanum (membrane) (persistent
      posttraumatic) (postinflammatory) 384.20
      with
          otitis media — *see* Otitis media
      attic 384.22
      central 384.21
      healed 384.81
      marginal NEC 384.23
      multiple 384.24
      pars flaccida 384.22
      total 384.25
      traumatic — *see* Wound, open, ear, drum
  typhoid, gastrointestinal 002.0
  ulcer — *see* Ulcer, by site, with perforation
  ureter 593.89
  urethra
      with
          abortion — *see* Abortion, by type, with
              damage to pelvic organs
          ectopic pregnancy (*see also* categories
              633.0-633.9) 639.2
          molar pregnancy (*see also* categories 630-
              632) 639.2
      following
          abortion 639.2
          ectopic or molar pregnancy 639.2
      obstetrical trauma 665.5 ☑
  uterus — *see* Injury, internal, uterus
      with
          abortion — *see* Abortion, by type, with
              damage to pelvic organs
          ectopic pregnancy (*see also* categories
              633.0-633.9) 639.2
          molar pregnancy (*see also* categories 630-
              632) 639.2
      by intrauterine contraceptive device 996.32
      following
          abortion 639.2
          ectopic or molar pregnancy 639.2
      obstetrical trauma — *see* Injury, internal,
          uterus, obstetrical trauma
  uvula 528.9
      syphilitic 095.8
  vagina — *see* Laceration, vagina
  viscus NEC 799.89
      traumatic 868.00
          with open wound into cavity 868.10
Periadenitis mucosa necrotica recurrens 528.2
Periangiitis 446.0
Periantritis 535.4 ☑
Periappendicitis (acute) (*see also* Appendicitis)
    541
Periarteritis (disseminated) (infectious)
    (necrotizing) (nodosa) 446.0
Periarthritis (joint) 726.90
    Duplay's 726.2
    gonococcal 098.50
    humeroscapularis 726.2
    scapulohumeral 726.2
    shoulder 726.2
    wrist 726.4
Periarthrosis (angioneural) — *see* Periarthritis
Peribronchitis 491.9
    tuberculous (*see also* Tuberculosis) 011.3 ☑
Pericapsulitis, adhesive (shoulder) 726.0

Pericarditis (granular) (with decompensation)
    (with effusion) 423.9
    with
        rheumatic fever (conditions classifiable to
            390)
            active (*see also* Pericarditis, rheumatic)
                391.0
            inactive or quiescent 393
    actinomycotic 039.8 *[420.0]*
    acute (nonrheumatic) 420.90
        with chorea (acute) (rheumatic)
            (Sydenham's) 392.0
        bacterial 420.99
        benign 420.91
        hemorrhagic 420.90
        idiopathic 420.91
        infective 420.90
        nonspecific 420.91
        rheumatic 391.0
            with chorea (acute) (rheumatic)
                (Sydenham's) 392.0
        sicca 420.90
        viral 420.91
    adhesive or adherent (external) (internal) 423.1
        acute — *see* Pericarditis, acute
        rheumatic (external) (internal) 393
    amebic 006.8 *[420.0]*
    bacterial (acute) (subacute) (with serous or
        seropurulent effusion) 420.99
    calcareous 423.2
    cholesterol (chronic) 423.8
        acute 420.90
    chronic (nonrheumatic) 423.8
        rheumatic 393
    constrictive 423.2
    Coxsackie 074.21
    due to
        actinomycosis 039.8 *[420.0]*
        amebiasis 006.8 *[420.0]*
        Coxsackie (virus) 074.21
        histoplasmosis (*see also* Histoplasmosis)
            115.93
        nocardiosis 039.8 *[420.0]*
        tuberculosis (*see also* Tuberculosis)
            017.9 ☑ *[420.0]*
    fibrinocaseous (*see also* Tuberculosis)
        017.9 ☑ *[420.0]*
    fibrinopurulent 420.99
    fibrinous — *see* Pericarditis, rheumatic
    fibropurulent 420.99
    fibrous 423.1
    gonococcal 098.83
    hemorrhagic 423.0
    idiopathic (acute) 420.91
    infective (acute) 420.90
    meningococcal 036.41
    neoplastic (chronic) 423.8
        acute 420.90
    nonspecific 420.91
    obliterans, obliterating 423.1
    plastic 423.1
    pneumococcal (acute) 420.99
    postinfarction 411.0
    purulent (acute) 420.99
    rheumatic (active) (acute) (with effusion) (with
        pneumonia) 391.0
        with chorea (acute) (rheumatic)
            (Sydenham's) 392.0
        chronic or inactive (with chorea) 393
    septic (acute) 420.99
    serofibrinous — *see* Pericarditis, rheumatic
    staphylococcal (acute) 420.99
    streptococcal (acute) 420.99
    suppurative (acute) 420.99
    syphilitic 093.81
    tuberculous (acute) (chronic) (*see also*
        Tuberculosis) 017.9 ☑ *[420.0]*
    uremic 585.9 *[420.0]*   ▲
    viral (acute) 420.91
Pericardium, pericardial — *see* condition
Pericellulitis (*see also* Cellulitis) 682.9
Pericementitis 523.4
    acute 523.3
    chronic (suppurative) 523.4
Pericholecystitis (*see also* Cholecystitis) 575.10

Perichondritis
    auricle 380.00
        acute 380.01
        chronic 380.02
    bronchus 491.9
    ear (external) 380.00
        acute 380.01
        chronic 380.02
    larynx 478.71
        syphilitic 095.8
        typhoid 002.0 *[478.71]*
    nose 478.1
    pinna 380.00
        acute 380.01
        chronic 380.02
    trachea 478.9
Periclasia 523.5
Pericolitis 569.89
Pericoronitis (chronic) 523.4
    acute 523.3
Pericystitis (*see also* Cystitis) 595.9
Pericytoma (M9150/1) — *see also* Neoplasm,
    connective tissue, uncertain behavior
    benign (M9150/0) — *see* Neoplasm, connective
        tissue, benign
    malignant (M9150/3) — *see* Neoplasm,
        connective tissue, malignant
Peridacryocystitis, acute 375.32
Periduverticulitis (*see also* Diverticulitis) 562.11
Periduodenitis 535.6 ☑
Periendocarditis (*see also* Endocarditis) 424.90
    acute or subacute 421.9
Periepididymitis (*see also* Epididymitis) 604.90
Perifolliculitis (abscedens) 704.8
    capitis, abscedens et suffodiens 704.8
    dissecting, scalp 704.8
    scalp 704.8
    superficial pustular 704.8
Perigastritis (acute) 535.0 ☑
Perigastrojejunitis (acute) 535.0 ☑
Perihepatitis (acute) 573.3
    chlamydial 099.56
    gonococcal 098.86
Peri-ileitis (subacute) 569.89
Perilabyrinthitis (acute) — *see* Labyrinthitis
Perimeningitis — *see* Meningitis
Perimetritis (*see also* Endometritis) 615.9
Perimetrosalpingitis (*see also* Salpingo-
    oophoritis) 614.2
Perineocele 618.05
Perinephric — *see* condition
Perinephritic — *see* condition
Perinephritis (*see also* Infection, kidney) 590.9
    purulent (*see also* Abscess, kidney) 590.2
Perineum, perineal — *see* condition
Perineuritis NEC 729.2
Periodic — *see also* condition
    disease (familial) 277.3
    edema 995.1
        hereditary 277.6
    fever 277.3
    limb movement disorder 327.51   ▲
    paralysis (familial) 359.3
    peritonitis 277.3
    polyserositis 277.3
    somnolence (*see also* Narcolepsy) 347.00
Periodontal
    cyst 522.8
    pocket 523.8
Periodontitis (chronic) (complex) (compound)
    (local) (simplex) 523.4
    acute 523.3
    apical 522.6
        acute (pulpal origin) 522.4
Periodontoclasia 523.5
Periodontosis 523.5
Periods — *see also* Menstruation
    heavy 626.2
    irregular 626.4
Perionychia (with lymphangitis) 681.9
    finger 681.02
    toe 681.11

2006 ICD-9-CM

☑ Additional Digit Required — Refer to the Tabular List (Numeric Code Section) for Additional Digit Selection
▶◀ Revised Text   ● New Line   ▲ Revised Code

October 2005 • Volume 2 — 265

Perioophoritis (*see also* Salpingo-oophoritis) 614.2

Periorchitis (*see also* Orchitis) 604.90

Periosteum, periosteal — *see* condition

Periostitis (circumscribed) (diffuse) (infective) 730.3 ☑

> *Note* — *Use the following fifth-digit subclassification with category 730:*
>
> 0   *site unspecified*
> 1   *shoulder region*
> 2   *upper arm*
> 3   *forearm*
> 4   *hand*
> 5   *pelvic region and thigh*
> 6   *lower leg*
> 7   *ankle and foot*
> 8   *other specified sites*
> 9   *multiple sites*

  with osteomyelitis (*see also* Osteomyelitis) 730.2 ☑
    acute or subacute 730.0 ☑
    chronic or old 730.1 ☑
  albuminosa, albuminosus 730.3 ☑
  alveolar 526.5
  alveolodental 526.5
  dental 526.5
  gonorrheal 098.89
  hyperplastica, generalized 731.2
  jaw (lower) (upper) 526.4
  monomelic 733.99
  orbital 376.02
  syphilitic 095.5
    congenital 090.0 [730.8] ☑
    secondary 091.61
  tuberculous (*see also* Tuberculosis, bone) 015.9 ☑ [730.8] ☑
  yaws (early) (hypertrophic) (late) 102.6

Periostosis (*see also* Periostitis) 730.3 ☑
  with osteomyelitis (*see also* Osteomyelitis) 730.2 ☑
    acute or subacute 730.0 ☑
    chronic or old 730.1 ☑
  hyperplastic 756.59

Peripartum cardiomyopathy 674.5 ☑

Periphlebitis (*see also* Phlebitis) 451.9
  lower extremity 451.2
    deep (vessels) 451.19
    superficial (vessels) 451.0
  portal 572.1
  retina 362.18
  superficial (vessels) 451.0
  tuberculous (*see also* Tuberculosis) 017.9 ☑
    retina 017.3 ☑ [362.18]

Peripneumonia — *see* Pneumonia

Periproctitis 569.49

Periprostatitis (*see also* Prostatitis) 601.9

Perirectal — *see* condition

Perirenal — *see* condition

Perisalpingitis (*see also* Salpingo-oophoritis) 614.2

Perisigmoiditis 569.89

Perisplenitis (infectional) 289.59

Perispondylitis — *see* Spondylitis

Peristalsis reversed or visible 787.4

Peritendinitis (*see also* Tenosynovitis) 726.90
  adhesive (shoulder) 726.0

Perithelioma (M9150/1) — *see* Pericytoma

Peritoneum, peritoneal — *see also* condition
  equilibration test V56.32

Peritonitis (acute) (adhesive) (fibrinous) (hemorrhagic) (idiopathic) (localized) (perforative) (primary) (with adhesions) (with effusion) 567.9
  with or following
    abortion — *see* Abortion, by type, with sepsis
    abscess 567.21 ▲
    appendicitis 540.0
      with peritoneal abscess 540.1

Peritonitis — *continued*
  with or following — *continued*
    ectopic pregnancy (*see also* categories 633.0-633.9) 639.0
    molar pregnancy (*see also* categories 630-632) 639.0
  aseptic 998.7
  bacterial 567.29 ▲
    spontaneous 567.23 ●
  bile, biliary 567.81 ▲
  chemical 998.7
  chlamydial 099.56
  chronic proliferative 567.89 ▲
  congenital NEC 777.6
  diaphragmatic 567.22 ▲
  diffuse NEC 567.29 ▲
  diphtheritic 032.83
  disseminated NEC 567.29 ▲
  due to
    bile 567.81 ▲
    foreign
      body or object accidentally left during a procedure (instrument) (sponge) (swab) 998.4
      substance accidentally left during a procedure (chemical) (powder) (talc) 998.7
    talc 998.7
    urine 567.89 ▲
  fibrinopurulent 567.29 ▲
  fibrinous 567.29 ▲
  fibrocaseous (*see also* Tuberculosis) 014.0 ☑
  fibropurulent 567.29 ▲
  general, generalized (acute) 567.21 ▲
  gonococcal 098.86
  in infective disease NEC 136.9 [567.0]
  meconium (newborn) 777.6
  pancreatic 577.8
  paroxysmal, benign 277.3
  pelvic
    female (acute) 614.5
      chronic NEC 614.7
        with adhesions 614.6
    puerperal, postpartum, childbirth 670.0 ☑
    male (acute) 567.21 ▲
  periodic (familial) 277.3
  phlegmonous 567.29 ▲
  pneumococcal 567.1
  postabortal 639.0
  proliferative, chronic 567.89 ▲
  puerperal, postpartum, childbirth 670.0 ☑
  purulent 567.29 ▲
  septic 567.29 ▲
  spontaneous bacterial 567.23 ●
  staphylococcal 567.29 ▲
  streptococcal 567.29 ▲
  subdiaphragmatic 567.29 ▲
  subphrenic 567.29 ▲
  suppurative 567.29 ▲
  syphilitic 095.2
    congenital 090.0 [567.0]
  talc 998.7
  tuberculous (*see also* Tuberculosis) 014.0 ☑
  urine 567.89 ▲

Peritonsillar — *see* condition

Peritonsillitis 475

Perityphlitis (*see also* Appendicitis) 541

Periureteritis 593.89

Periurethral — *see* condition

Periurethritis (gangrenous) 597.89

Periuterine — *see* condition

Perivaginitis (*see also* Vaginitis) 616.10

Perivasculitis, retinal 362.18

Perivasitis (chronic) 608.4

Periventricular leukomalacia 779.7

Perivesiculitis (seminal) (*see also* Vesiculitis) 608.0

Perlèche 686.8
  due to
    moniliasis 112.0
    riboflavin deficiency 266.0

Pernicious — *see* condition

Pernio, perniosis 991.5

Persecution
  delusion 297.9
  social V62.4

Perseveration (tonic) 784.69

Persistence, persistent (congenital) 759.89
  anal membrane 751.2
  arteria stapedia 744.04
  atrioventricular canal 745.69
  bloody ejaculate 792.2
  branchial cleft 744.41
  bulbus cordis in left ventricle 745.8
  canal of Cloquet 743.51
  capsule (opaque) 743.51
  cilioretinal artery or vein 743.51
  cloaca 751.5
  communication — *see* Fistula, congenital
  convolutions
    aortic arch 747.21
    fallopian tube 752.19
    oviduct 752.19
    uterine tube 752.19
  double aortic arch 747.21
  ductus
    arteriosus 747.0
    Botalli 747.0
  fetal
    circulation 747.83
    form of cervix (uteri) 752.49
    hemoglobin (hereditary) ("Swiss variety") 282.7
    pulmonary hypertension 747.83
  foramen
    Botalli 745.5
    ovale 745.5
  Gartner's duct 752.41 ▲
  hemoglobin, fetal (hereditary) (HPFH) 282.7
  hyaloid
    artery (generally incomplete) 743.51
    system 743.51
  hymen (tag)
    in pregnancy or childbirth 654.8 ☑
      causing obstructed labor 660.2 ☑
  lanugo 757.4
  left
    posterior cardinal vein 747.49
    root with right arch of aorta 747.21
    superior vena cava 747.49
  Meckel's diverticulum 751.0
  mesonephric duct 752.89
    fallopian tube 752.11
  mucosal disease (middle ear) (with posterior or superior marginal perforation of ear drum) 382.2
  nail(s), anomalous 757.5
  occiput, anterior or posterior 660.3 ☑
    fetus or newborn 763.1
  omphalomesenteric duct 751.0
  organ or site NEC — *see* Anomaly, specified type NEC
  ostium
    atrioventriculare commune 745.69
    primum 745.61
    secundum 745.5
  ovarian rests in fallopian tube 752.19
  pancreatic tissue in intestinal tract 751.5
  primary (deciduous)
    teeth 520.6
    vitreous hyperplasia 743.51
  pulmonary hypertension 747.83
  pupillary membrane 743.46
    iris 743.46
  Rhesus (Rh) titer 999.7
  right aortic arch 747.21
  sinus
    urogenitalis 752.89
    venosus with imperfect incorporation in right auricle 747.49
  thymus (gland) 254.8
    hyperplasia 254.0
  thyroglossal duct 759.2
  thyrolingual duct 759.2
  truncus arteriosus or communis 745.0
  tunica vasculosa lentis 743.39
  umbilical sinus 753.7
  urachus 753.7
  vegetative state 780.03

Persistence, persistent — *continued*
  vitelline duct 751.0
  wolffian duct 752.89
Person (with)
  admitted for clinical research, as participant or
    control subject V70.7
  awaiting admission to adequate facility
    elsewhere V63.2
    undergoing social agency investigation V63.8
  concern (normal) about sick person in family
    V61.49
  consulting on behalf of another V65.19
    pediatric pre-birth visit for expectant mother
      V65.11
  feared
    complaint in whom no diagnosis was made
      V65.5
    condition not demonstrated V65.5
  feigning illness V65.2
  healthy, accompanying sick person V65.0
  living (in)
    alone V60.3
    boarding school V60.6
    residence remote from hospital or medical
      care facility V63.0
    residential institution V60.6
    without
      adequate
        financial resources V60.2
        housing (heating) (space) V60.1
      housing (permanent) (temporary) V60.0
      material resources V60.2
      person able to render necessary care
        V60.4
      shelter V60.0
  medical services in home not available V63.1
  on waiting list V63.2
    undergoing social agency investigation V63.8
  sick or handicapped in family V61.49
  "worried well" V65.5
Personality
  affective 301.10
  aggressive 301.3
  amoral 301.7
  anancastic, anankastic 301.4
  antisocial 301.7
  asocial 301.7
  asthenic 301.6
  avoidant 301.82
  borderline 301.83
  change 310.1
  compulsive 301.4
  cycloid 301.13
  cyclothymic 301.13
  dependent 301.6
  depressive (chronic) 301.12
  disorder, disturbance NEC 301.9
    with
      antisocial disturbance 301.7
      pattern disturbance NEC 301.9
      sociopathic disturbance 301.7
      trait disturbance 301.9
  dual 300.14
  dyssocial 301.7
  eccentric 301.89
    "haltlose" type 301.89
  emotionally unstable 301.59
  epileptoid 301.3
  explosive 301.3
  fanatic 301.0
  histrionic 301.50
  hyperthymic 301.11
  hypomanic 301.11
  hypothymic 301.12
  hysterical 301.50
  immature 301.89
  inadequate 301.6
  labile 301.59
  masochistic 301.89
  morally defective 301.7
  multiple 300.14
  narcissistic 301.81
  obsessional 301.4
  obsessive-compulsive 301.4
  overconscientious 301.4
  paranoid 301.0

Personality — *continued*
  passive (-dependent) 301.6
  passive-aggressive 301.84
  pathologic NEC 301.9
  pattern defect or disturbance 301.9
  pseudosocial 301.7
  psychoinfantile 301.59
  psychoneurotic NEC 301.89
  psychopathic 301.9
    with
      amoral trend 301.7
      antisocial trend 301.7
      asocial trend 301.7
      pathologic sexuality (*see also* Deviation,
        sexual) 302.9
    mixed types 301.9
  schizoid 301.20
    introverted 301.21
    schizotypal 301.22
    with sexual deviation (*see also* Deviation,
      sexual) 302.9
      antisocial 301.7
      dyssocial 301.7
  type A 301.4
  unstable (emotional) 301.59
Perthes' disease (capital femoral osteochondrosis)
  732.1
Pertussis (*see also* Whooping cough) 033.9
  vaccination, prophylactic (against) V03.6
Peruvian wart 088.0
Perversion, perverted
  appetite 307.52
    hysterical 300.11
  function
    pineal gland 259.8
    pituitary gland 253.9
      anterior lobe
        deficient 253.2
        excessive 253.1
      posterior lobe 253.6
    placenta — *see* Placenta, abnormal
  sense of smell or taste 781.1
    psychogenic 306.7
  sexual (*see also* Deviation, sexual) 302.9
Pervious, congenital — *see also* Imperfect,
  closure
  ductus arteriosus 747.0
Pes (congenital) (*see also* Talipes) 754.70
  abductus (congenital) 754.60
    acquired 736.79
  acquired NEC 736.79
    planus 734
  adductus (congenital) 754.79
    acquired 736.79
  cavus 754.71
    acquired 736.73
  planovalgus (congenital) 754.69
    acquired 736.79
  planus (acquired) (any degree) 734
    congenital 754.61
    rachitic 268.1
  valgus (congenital) 754.61
    acquired 736.79
  varus (congenital) 754.50
    acquired 736.79
Pest (*see also* Plague) 020.9
Pestis (*see also* Plague) 020.9
  bubonica 020.0
  fulminans 020.0
  minor 020.8
  pneumonica — *see* Plague, pneumonic
Petechia, petechiae 782.7
  fetus or newborn 772.6
Petechial
  fever 036.0
  typhus 081.9
Petges-Cléjat or Petges-Clégat syndrome
  (poikilodermatomyositis) 710.3
Petit's
  disease (*see also* Hernia, lumbar) 553.8
Petit mal (idiopathic) (*see also* Epilepsy) 345.0 ☑
  status 345.2
Petrellidosis 117.6

Petrositis 383.20
  acute 383.21
  chronic 383.22
Peutz-Jeghers disease or syndrome 759.6
Peyronie's disease 607.85
Pfeiffer's disease 075
Phacentocele 379.32
  traumatic 921.3
Phacoanaphylaxis 360.19
Phacocele (old) 379.32
  traumatic 921.3
Phaehyphomycosis 117.8
Phagedena (dry) (moist) (*see also* Gangrene) 785.4
  arteriosclerotic 440.24
  geometric 686.09
  penis 607.89
  senile 440.24
  sloughing 785.4
  tropical (*see also* Ulcer, skin) 707.9
  vulva 616.50
Phagedenic — *see also* condition
  abscess — *see also* Abscess
    chancroid 099.0
  bubo NEC 099.8
  chancre 099.0
  ulcer (tropical) (*see also* Ulcer, skin) 707.9
Phagomania 307.52
Phakoma 362.89
Phantom limb (syndrome) 353.6
Pharyngeal — *see also* condition
  arch remnant 744.41
  pouch syndrome 279.11
Pharyngitis (acute) (catarrhal) (gangrenous)
  (infective) (malignant) (membranous)
  (phlegmonous) (pneumococcal)
  (pseudomembranous) (simple)
  (staphylococcal) (subacute) (suppurative)
  (ulcerative) (viral) 462
  with influenza, flu, or grippe 487.1
  aphthous 074.0
  atrophic 472.1
  chronic 472.1
  chlamydial 099.51
  Coxsackie virus 074.0
  diphtheritic (membranous) 032.0
  follicular 472.1
  fusospirochetal 101
  gonococcal 098.6
  granular (chronic) 472.1
  herpetic 054.79
  hypertrophic 472.1
  infectional, chronic 472.1
  influenzal 487.1
  lymphonodular, acute 074.8
  septic 034.0
  streptococcal 034.0
  tuberculous (*see also* Tuberculosis) 012.8 ☑
  vesicular 074.0
Pharyngoconjunctival fever 077.2
Pharyngoconjunctivitis, viral 077.2
Pharyngolaryngitis (acute) 465.0
  chronic 478.9
  septic 034.0
Pharyngoplegia 478.29
Pharyngotonsillitis 465.8
  tuberculous 012.8 ☑
Pharyngotracheitis (acute) 465.8
  chronic 478.9
Pharynx, pharyngeal — *see* condition
Phase of life problem NEC V62.89
Phenomenon
  Arthus' — *see* Arthus' phenomenon
  flashback (drug) 292.89
  jaw-winking 742.8
  Jod-Basedow 242.8 ☑
  L. E. cell 710.0
  lupus erythematosus cell 710.0
  Pelger-Huët (hereditary hyposegmentation)
    288.2
  Raynaud's (paroxysmal digital cyanosis)
    (secondary) 443.0
  Reilly's (*see also* Neuropathy, peripheral,
    autonomic) 337.9
  vasomotor 780.2
  vasospastic 443.9

☑ Additional Digit Required — Refer to the Tabular List (Numeric Code Section) for Additional Digit Selection

Phenomenon — *continued*
vasovagal 780.2
Wenckebach's, heart block (second degree)
426.13
Phenylketonuria (PKU) 270.1
Phenylpyruvicaciduria 270.1
Pheochromoblastoma (M8700/3)
specified site — *see* Neoplasm, by site,
malignant
unspecified site 194.0
Pheochromocytoma (M8700/0)
malignant (M8700/3)
specified site — *see* Neoplasm, by site,
malignant
unspecified site 194.0
specified site — *see* Neoplasm, by site, benign
unspecified site 227.0
Phimosis (congenital) 605
chancroidal 099.0
due to infection 605
Phlebectasia (*see also* Varicose, vein) 454.9
congenital NEC 747.60
esophagus (*see also* Varix, esophagus) 456.1
with hemorrhage (*see also* Varix, esophagus,
bleeding) 456.0
Phlebitis (infective) (pyemic) (septic) (suppurative)
451.9
antecubital vein 451.82
arm NEC 451.84
axillary vein 451.89
basilic vein 451.82
deep 451.83
superficial 451.82
axillary vein 451.89
basilic vein 451.82
blue 451.9
brachial vein 451.83
breast, superficial 451.89
cavernous (venous) sinus — *see* Phlebitis,
intracranial sinus
cephalic vein 451.82
cerebral (venous) sinus — *see* Phlebitis,
intracranial sinus
chest wall, superficial 451.89
complicating pregnancy or puerperium
671.9 ☑
affecting fetus or newborn 760.3
cranial (venous) sinus — *see* Phlebitis,
intracranial sinus
deep (vessels) 451.19
femoral vein 451.11
specified vessel NEC 451.19
due to implanted device — *see* Complications,
due to (presence of) any device, implant,
or graft classified to 996.0-996.5 NEC
during or resulting from a procedure 997.2
femoral vein (deep) (superficial) 451.11
femoropopliteal 451.19
following infusion, perfusion, or transfusion
999.2
gouty 274.89 [451.9]
hepatic veins 451.89
iliac vein 451.81
iliofemoral 451.11
intracranial sinus (any) (venous) 325
late effect — *see* category 326
nonpyogenic 437.6
in pregnancy or puerperium 671.5 ☑
jugular vein 451.89
lateral (venous) sinus — *see* Phlebitis,
intracranial sinus
leg 451.2
deep (vessels) 451.19
femoral vein 451.11
specified vessel NEC 451.19
superficial (vessels) 451.0
femoral vein 451.11
longitudinal sinus — *see* Phlebitis, intracranial
sinus
lower extremity 451.2
deep (vessels) 451.19
femoral vein 451.11
specified vessel NEC 451.19
superficial (vessels) 451.0
femoral vein 451.11
migrans, migrating (superficial) 453.1

Phlebitis — *continued*
pelvic
with
abortion — *see* Abortion, by type, with
sepsis
ectopic pregnancy (*see also* categories
633.0-633.9) 639.0
molar pregnancy (*see also* categories 630-
632) 639.0
following
abortion 639.0
ectopic or molar pregnancy 639.0
puerperal, postpartum 671.4 ☑
popliteal vein 451.19
portal (vein) 572.1
postoperative 997.2
pregnancy 671.9 ☑
deep 671.3 ☑
specified type NEC 671.5 ☑
superficial 671.2 ☑
puerperal, postpartum, childbirth 671.9 ☑
deep 671.4 ☑
lower extremities 671.2 ☑
pelvis 671.4 ☑
specified site NEC 671.5 ☑
superficial 671.2 ☑
radial vein 451.83
retina 362.18
saphenous (great) (long) 451.0
accessory or small 451.0
sinus (meninges) — *see* Phlebitis, intracranial
sinus
specified site NEC 451.89
subclavian vein 451.89
syphilitic 093.89
tibial vein 451.19
ulcer, ulcerative 451.9
leg 451.2
deep (vessels) 451.19
femoral vein 451.11
specified vessel NEC 451.19
superficial (vessels) 451.0
femoral vein 451.11
lower extremity 451.2
deep (vessels) 451.19
femoral vein 451.11
specified vessel NEC 451.19
superficial (vessels) 451.0
ulnar vein 451.83
umbilicus 451.89
upper extremity — *see* Phlebitis, arm
deep (veins) 451.83
brachial vein 451.83
radial vein 451.83
ulnar vein 451.83
superficial (veins) 451.82
antecubital vein 451.82
basilic vein 451.82
cephalic vein 451.82
uterus (septic) (*see also* Endometritis) 615.9
varicose (leg) (lower extremity) (*see also*
Varicose, vein) 454.1
Phlebofibrosis 459.89
Phleboliths 459.89
Phlebosclerosis 459.89
Phlebothrombosis — *see* Thrombosis
Phlebotomus fever 066.0
Phlegm, choked on 933.1
Phlegmasia
alba dolens (deep vessels) 451.19
complicating pregnancy 671.3 ☑
nonpuerperal 451.19
puerperal, postpartum, childbirth 671.4 ☑
cerulea dolens 451.19
Phlegmon (*see also* Abscess) 682.9
erysipelatous (*see also* Erysipelas) 035
iliac 682.2
fossa 540.1
throat 478.29
Phlegmonous — *see* condition
Phlyctenulosis (allergic) (keratoconjunctivitis)
(nontuberculous) 370.31
cornea 370.31
with ulcer (*see also* Ulcer, cornea) 370.00
tuberculous (*see also* Tuberculosis) 017.3 ☑
[370.31]

Phobia, phobic (reaction) 300.20
animal 300.29
isolated NEC 300.29
obsessional 300.3
simple NEC 300.29
social 300.23
specified NEC 300.29
state 300.20
Phocas' disease 610.1
Phocomelia 755.4
lower limb 755.32
complete 755.33
distal 755.35
proximal 755.34
upper limb 755.22
complete 755.23
distal 755.25
proximal 755.24
Phoria (*see also* Heterophoria) 378.40
Phosphate-losing tubular disorder 588.0
Phosphatemia 275.3
Phosphaturia 275.3
Photoallergic response 692.72
Photocoproporphyria 277.1
Photodermatitis (sun) 692.72
light other than sun 692.82
Photokeratitis 370.24
Photo-ophthalmia 370.24
Photophobia 368.13
Photopsia 368.15
Photoretinitis 363.31
Photoretinopathy 363.31
Photosensitiveness (sun) 692.72
light other than sun 692.82
Photosensitization skin (sun) 692.72
light other than sun 692.82
Phototoxic response 692.72
Phrenitis 323.9
Phrynoderma 264.8
Phthiriasis (pubis) (any site) 132.2
with any infestation classifiable to 132.0, 132.1
and 132.3
Phthirus infestation — *see* Phthiriasis
Phthisis (*see also* Tuberculosis) 011.9 ☑
bulbi (infectional) 360.41
colliers' 011.4 ☑
cornea 371.05
eyeball (due to infection) 360.41
millstone makers' 011.4 ☑
miners' 011.4 ☑
potters' 011.4 ☑
sandblasters' 011.4 ☑
stonemasons' 011.4 ☑
Phycomycosis 117.7
Physalopteriasis 127.7
Physical therapy NEC V57.1
breathing exercises V57.0
Physiological cup, optic papilla
borderline, glaucoma suspect 365.00
enlarged 377.14
glaucomatous 377.14
Phytobezoar 938
intestine 936
stomach 935.2
Pian (*see also* Yaws) 102.9
Pianoma 102.1
Piarhemia, piarrhemia (*see also* Hyperlipemia)
272.4
bilharziasis 120.9
Pica 307.52
hysterical 300.11
Pick's
cerebral atrophy 331.11
with dementia
with behavioral disturbance
331.11 [294.11]
without behavioral disturbance
331.11 [294.10]
disease
brain 331.11
dementia in
with behavioral disturbance
331.11 [294.11]
without behavioral disturbance
331.11 [294.10]

☑ Additional Digit Required — Refer to the Tabular List (Numeric Code Section) for Additional Digit Selection
▶◀ Revised Text   ● New Line   ▲ Revised Code

2006 ICD-9-CM   **Volume 2 — 269**

Placenta, placental — *continued*
  succenturiata — *see* Placenta, abnormal
  syphilitic 095.8
  transfusion syndromes 762.3
  transmission of chemical substance — *see*
    Absorption, chemical, through placenta
  trapped (with hemorrhage) 666.0 ☑
    without hemorrhage 667.0 ☑
  trilobate — *see* Placenta, abnormal
  tripartita — *see* Placenta, abnormal
  triplex — *see* Placenta, abnormal
  varicose vessel — *see* Placenta, abnormal
  vicious insertion — *see* Placenta, previa

Placentitis
  affecting fetus or newborn 762.7
  complicating pregnancy 658.4 ☑

Plagiocephaly (skull) 754.0

Plague 020.9
  abortive 020.8
  ambulatory 020.8
  bubonic 020.0
  cellulocutaneous 020.1
  lymphatic gland 020.0
  pneumonic 020.5
    primary 020.3
    secondary 020.4
  pulmonary — *see* Plague, pneumonic
  pulmonic — *see* Plague, pneumonic
  septicemic 020.2
  tonsillar 020.9
    septicemic 020.2
  vaccination, prophylactic (against) V03.3

Planning, family V25.09
  contraception V25.9
  procreation V26.4

Plaque
  artery, arterial — *see* Arteriosclerosis
  calcareous — *see* Calcification
  Hollenhorst's (retinal) 362.33
  tongue 528.6

Plasma cell myeloma 203.0 ☑

Plasmacytoma, plasmocytoma (solitary)
  (M9731/1) 238.6
  benign (M9731/0) — *see* Neoplasm, by site,
    benign
  malignant (M9731/3) 203.8 ☑

Plasmacytosis 288.8

Plaster ulcer (*see also* Decubitus) 707.00

Platybasia 756.0

Platyonychia (congenital) 757.5
  acquired 703.8

Platypelloid pelvis 738.6
  with disproportion (fetopelvic) 653.2 ☑
    affecting fetus or newborn 763.1
    causing obstructed labor 660.1 ☑
      affecting fetus or newborn 763.1
  congenital 755.69

Platyspondylia 756.19

Plethora 782.62
  newborn 776.4

Pleura, pleural — *see* condition

Pleuralgia 786.52

Pleurisy (acute) (adhesive) (chronic) (costal)
  (diaphragmatic) (double) (dry) (fetid)
  (fibrinous) (fibrous) (interlobar) (latent) (lung)
  (old) (plastic) (primary) (residual) (sicca)
  (sterile) (subacute) (unresolved) (with
  adherent pleura) 511.0
  with
    effusion (without mention of cause) 511.9
      bacterial, nontuberculous 511.1
      nontuberculous NEC 511.9
        bacterial 511.1
      pneumococcal 511.1
      specified type NEC 511.8
      staphylococcal 511.1
      streptococcal 511.1
      tuberculous (*see also* Tuberculosis,
        pleura) 012.0 ☑
        primary, progressive 010.1 ☑
    influenza, flu, or grippe 487.1
  tuberculosis — *see* Pleurisy, tuberculous
  encysted 511.8

Pleurisy — *continued*
  exudative (*see also* Pleurisy, with effusion)
    511.9
    bacterial, nontuberculous 511.1
  fibrinopurulent 510.9
    with fistula 510.0
  fibropurulent 510.9
    with fistula 510.0
  hemorrhagic 511.8
  influenzal 487.1
  pneumococcal 511.0
    with effusion 511.1
  purulent 510.9
    with fistula 510.0
  septic 510.9
    with fistula 510.0
  serofibrinous (*see also* Pleurisy, with effusion)
    511.9
    bacterial, nontuberculous 511.1
  seropurulent 510.9
    with fistula 510.0
  serous (*see also* Pleurisy, with effusion) 511.9
    bacterial, nontuberculous 511.1
  staphylococcal 511.0
    with effusion 511.1
  streptococcal 511.0
    with effusion 511.1
  suppurative 510.9
    with fistula 510.0
  traumatic (post) (current) 862.29
    with open wound into cavity 862.39
  tuberculous (with effusion) (*see also*
    Tuberculosis, pleura) 012.0 ☑
    primary, progressive 010.1 ☑

Pleuritis sicca — *see* Pleurisy

Pleurobronchopneumonia (*see also* Pneumonia,
  broncho-) 485

Pleurodynia 786.52
  epidemic 074.1
  viral 074.1

Pleurohepatitis 573.8

Pleuropericarditis (*see also* Pericarditis) 423.9
  acute 420.90

Pleuropneumonia (acute) (bilateral) (double)
  (septic) (*see also* Pneumonia) 486
  chronic (*see also* Fibrosis, lung) 515

Pleurorrhea (*see also* Hydrothorax) 511.8

Plexitis, brachial 353.0

Plica
  knee 727.83
  polonica 132.0
  tonsil 474.8

Plicae dysphonia ventricularis 784.49

Plicated tongue 529.5
  congenital 750.13

Plug
  bronchus NEC 519.1
  meconium (newborn) NEC 777.1
  mucus — *see* Mucus, plug

Plumbism 984.9
  specified type of lead — *see* Table of Drugs and
    Chemicals

Plummer's disease (toxic nodular goiter) 242.3 ☑

Plummer-Vinson syndrome (sideropenic
  dysphagia) 280.8

Pluricarential syndrome of infancy 260

Plurideficiency syndrome of infancy 260

Plus (and minus) hand (intrinsic) 736.09

PMDD (premenstrual dysphoric disorder) 625.4

PMS 625.4

Pneumathemia — *see* Air, embolism, by type

Pneumatic drill or hammer disease 994.9

Pneumatocele (lung) 518.89
  intracranial 348.8
  tension 492.0

Pneumatosis
  cystoides intestinalis 569.89
  peritonei 568.89
  pulmonum 492.8

Pneumaturia 599.84

Pneumoblastoma (M8981/3) — *see* Neoplasm,
  lung, malignant

Pneumocephalus 348.8

Pneumococcemia 038.2

Pneumococcus, pneumococcal — *see* condition

Pneumoconiosis (due to) (inhalation of) 505
  aluminum 503
  asbestos 501
  bagasse 495.1
  bauxite 503
  beryllium 503
  carbon electrode makers' 503
  coal
    miners' (simple) 500
    workers' (simple) 500
  cotton dust 504
  diatomite fibrosis 502
  dust NEC 504
    inorganic 503
    lime 502
    marble 502
    organic NEC 504
  fumes or vapors (from silo) 506.9
  graphite 503
  hard metal 503
  mica 502
  moldy hay 495.0
  rheumatoid 714.81
  silica NEC 502
    and carbon 500
  silicate NEC 502
  talc 502

Pneumocystis carinii pneumonia 136.3

Pneumocystosis 136.3
  with pneumonia 136.3

Pneumoenteritis 025

Pneumohemopericardium (*see also* Pericarditis)
  423.9

Pneumohemothorax (*see also* Hemothorax) 511.8
  traumatic 860.4
    with open wound into thorax 860.5

Pneumohydropericardium (*see also* Pericarditis)
  423.9

Pneumohydrothorax (*see also* Hydrothorax)
  511.8

Pneumomediastinum 518.1
  congenital 770.2
  fetus or newborn 770.2

Pneumomycosis 117.9

Pneumonia (acute) (Alpenstich) (benign) (bilateral)
  (brain) (cerebral) (circumscribed) (congestive)
  (creeping) (delayed resolution) (double)
  (epidemic) (fever) (flash) (fulminant) (fungoid)
  (granulomatous) (hemorrhagic) (incipient)
  (infantile) (infectious) (infiltration) (insular)
  (intermittent) (latent) (lobe) (migratory)
  (newborn) (organized) (overwhelming)
  (primary) (progressive) (pseudolobar)
  (purulent) (resolved) (secondary) (senile)
  (septic) (suppurative) (terminal) (true)
  (unresolved) (vesicular) 486
  with influenza, flu, or grippe 487.0
  adenoviral 480.0
  adynamic 514
  alba 090.0
  allergic 518.3
  alveolar — *see* Pneumonia, lobar
  anaerobes 482.81
  anthrax 022.1 [484.5]
  apex, apical — *see* Pneumonia, lobar
  ascaris 127.0 [484.8]
  aspiration 507.0
    due to
      aspiration of microorganisms
        bacterial 482.9
          specified type NEC 482.89
        specified organism NEC 483.8
          bacterial NEC 482.89
        viral 480.9
          specified type NEC 480.8
      food (regurgitated) 507.0
      gastric secretions 507.0
      milk 507.0
      oils, essences 507.1
      solids, liquids NEC 507.8
      vomitus 507.0

☑ Additional Digit Required — Refer to the Tabular List (Numeric Code Section) for Additional Digit Selection

▶◀ Revised Text   ● New Line   ▲ Revised Code

Pneumonia — *continued*
  aspiration — *continued*
    fetal 770.18 ●
      due to ●
        blood 770.16 ●
        clear amniotic fluid 770.14 ●
        meconium 770.12 ●
        postnatal stomach contents 770.86 ●
    newborn 770.18 ▲
      due to ●
        blood 770.16 ●
        clear amniotic fluid 770.14 ●
        meconium 770.12 ●
        postnatal stomach contents 770.86 ●
  asthenic 514
  atypical (disseminated) (focal) (primary) 486
    with influenza 487.0
  bacillus 482.9
    specified type NEC 482.89
  bacterial 482.9
    specified type NEC 482.89
  Bacteroides (fragilis) (oralis) (melaninogenicus) 482.81
  basal, basic, basilar — *see* Pneumonia, lobar
  broncho-, bronchial (confluent) (croupous) (diffuse) (disseminated) (hemorrhagic) (involving lobes) (lobar) (terminal) 485
    with influenza 487.0
    allergic 518.3
    aspiration (*see also* Pneumonia, aspiration) 507.0
    bacterial 482.9
      specified type NEC 482.89
    capillary 466.19
      with bronchospasm or obstruction 466.19
    chronic (*see also* Fibrosis, lung) 515
    congenital (infective) 770.0
    diplococcal 481
    Eaton's agent 483.0
    Escherichia coli (E. coli) 482.82
    Friedländer's bacillus 482.0
    Hemophilus influenzae 482.2
    hiberno-vernal 083.0 *[484.8]*
    hypostatic 514
    influenzal 487.0
    inhalation (*see also* Pneumonia, aspiration) 507.0
      due to fumes or vapors (chemical) 506.0
    Klebsiella 482.0
    lipid 507.1
      endogenous 516.8
    Mycoplasma (pneumoniae) 483.0
    ornithosis 073.0
    pleuropneumonia-like organisms (PPLO) 483.0
    pneumococcal 481
    Proteus 482.83
    Pseudomonas 482.1
    specified organism NEC 483.8
      bacterial NEC 482.89
    staphylococcal 482.40
      aureus 482.41
      specified type NEC 482.49
    streptococcal — *see* Pneumonia, streptococcal
    typhoid 002.0 *[484.8]*
    viral, virus (*see also* Pneumonia, viral) 480.9
  Butyrivibrio (fibriosolvens) 482.81
  Candida 112.4
  capillary 466.19
    with bronchospasm or obstruction 466.19
  caseous (*see also* Tuberculosis) 011.6 ☑
  catarrhal — *see* Pneumonia, broncho-
  central — *see* Pneumonia, lobar
  Chlamydia, chlamydial 483.1
    pneumoniae 483.1
    psittaci 073.0
    specified type NEC 483.1
    trachomatis 483.1
  cholesterol 516.8
  chronic (*see also* Fibrosis, lung) 515
  cirrhotic (chronic) (*see also* Fibrosis, lung) 515
  Clostridium (haemolyticum) (novyi) NEC 482.81
  confluent — *see* Pneumonia, broncho-
  congenital (infective) 770.0
    aspiration 770.18 ▲
  croupous — *see* Pneumonia, lobar

Pneumonia — *continued*
  cytomegalic inclusion 078.5 *[484.1]*
  deglutition (*see also* Pneumonia, aspiration) 507.0
  desquamative interstitial 516.8
  diffuse — *see* Pneumonia, broncho-
  diplococcal, diplococcus (broncho-) (lobar) 481
  disseminated (focal) — *see* Pneumonia, broncho-
  due to
    adenovirus 480.0
    anaerobes 482.81
    Bacterium anitratum 482.83
    Chlamydia, chlamydial 483.1
      pneumoniae 483.1
      psittaci 073.0
      specified type NEC 483.1
      trachomatis 483.1
    coccidioidomycosis 114.0
    Diplococcus (pneumoniae) 481
    Eaton's agent 483.0
    Escherichia coli (E. coli) 482.82
    Friedländer's bacillus 482.0
    fumes or vapors (chemical) (inhalation) 506.0
    fungus NEC 117.9 *[484.7]*
      coccidioidomycosis 114.0
    Hemophilus influenzae (H. influenzae) 482.2
    Herellea 482.83
    influenza 487.0
    Klebsiella pneumoniae 482.0
    Mycoplasma (pneumoniae) 483.0
    parainfluenza virus 480.2
    pleuropneumonia-like organism (PPLO) 483.0
    Pneumococcus 481
    Pneumocystis carinii 136.3
    Proteus 482.83
    Pseudomonas 482.1
    respiratory syncytial virus 480.1
    rickettsia 083.9 *[484.8]*
    SARS-associated coronavirus 480.3
    specified
      bacteria NEC 482.89
      organism NEC 483.8
      virus NEC 480.8
    Staphylococcus 482.40
      aureus 482.41
      specified type NEC 482.49
    Streptococcus — *see also* Pneumonia, streptococcal
      pneumoniae 481
    virus (*see also* Pneumonia, viral) 480.9
      SARS-associated coronavirus 480.3
  Eaton's agent 483.0
  embolic, embolism (*see* Embolism, pulmonary)
  eosinophilic 518.3
  Escherichia coli (E. coli) 482.82
  Eubacterium 482.81
  fibrinous — *see* Pneumonia, lobar
  fibroid (chronic) (*see also* Fibrosis, lung) 515
  fibrous (*see also* Fibrosis, lung) 515
  Friedländer's bacillus 482.0
  Fusobacterium (nucleatum) 482.81
  gangrenous 513.0
  giant cell (*see also* Pneumonia, viral) 480.9
  gram-negative bacteria NEC 482.83
    anaerobic 482.81
  grippal 487.0
  Hemophilus influenzae (bronchial) (lobar) 482.2
  hypostatic (broncho-) (lobar) 514
  in
    actinomycosis 039.1
    anthrax 022.1 *[484.5]*
    aspergillosis 117.3 *[484.6]*
    candidiasis 112.4
    coccidioidomycosis 114.0
    cytomegalic inclusion disease 078.5 *[484.1]*
    histoplasmosis (*see also* Histoplasmosis) 115.95
    infectious disease NEC 136.9 *[484.8]*
    measles 055.1
    mycosis, systemic NEC 117.9 *[484.7]*
    nocardiasis, nocardiosis 039.1
    ornithosis 073.0
    pneumocystosis 136.3
    psittacosis 073.0
    Q fever 083.0 *[484.8]*

Pneumonia — *continued*
  in — *continued*
    salmonellosis 003.22
    toxoplasmosis 130.4
    tularemia 021.2
    typhoid (fever) 002.0 *[484.8]*
    varicella 052.1
    whooping cough (*see also* Whooping cough) 033.9 *[484.3]*
  infective, acquired prenatally 770.0
  influenzal (broncho) (lobar) (virus) 487.0
  inhalation (*see also* Pneumonia, aspiration) 507.0
    fumes or vapors (chemical) 506.0
  interstitial 516.8
    with influenzal 487.0
    acute 136.3
    chronic (*see also* Fibrosis, lung) 515
    desquamative 516.8
    hypostatic 514
    lipoid 507.1
    lymphoid 516.8
    plasma cell 136.3
    Pseudomonas 482.1
  intrauterine (infective) 770.0
    aspiration 770.18 ▲
      blood 770.16 ●
      clear amniotic fluid 770.14 ●
      meconium 770.12 ●
      postnatal stomach contents 770.86 ●
  Klebsiella pneumoniae 482.0
  Legionnaires' 482.84
  lipid, lipoid (exogenous) (interstitial) 507.1
    endogenous 516.8
  lobar (diplococcal) (disseminated) (double) (interstitial) (pneumococcal, any type) 481
    with influenza 487.0
    bacterial 482.9
      specified type NEC 482.89
    chronic (*see also* Fibrosis, lung) 515
    Escherichia coli (E. coli) 482.82
    Friedländer's bacillus 482.0
    Hemophilus influenzae (H. influenzae) 482.2
    hypostatic 514
    influenzal 487.0
    Klebsiella 482.0
    ornithosis 073.0
    Proteus 482.83
    Pseudomonas 482.1
    psittacosis 073.0
    specified organism NEC 483.8
      bacterial NEC 482.89
    staphylococcal 482.40
      aureus 482.41
      specified type NEC 482.49
    streptococcal — *see* Pneumonia, streptococcal
    viral, virus (*see also* Pneumonia, viral) 480.9
  lobular (confluent) — *see* Pneumonia, broncho-
  Löffler's 518.3
  massive — *see* Pneumonia, lobar
  meconium ▶aspiration◀ 770.12 ▲
  metastatic NEC 038.8 *[484.8]*
  Mycoplasma (pneumoniae) 483.0
  necrotic 513.0
  nitrogen dioxide 506.9
  orthostatic 514
  parainfluenza virus 480.2
  parenchymatous (*see also* Fibrosis, lung) 515
  passive 514
  patchy — *see* Pneumonia, broncho-
  Peptococcus 482.81
  Peptostreptococcus 482.81
  plasma cell 136.3
  pleurolobar — *see* Pneumonia, lobar
  pleuropneumonia-like organism (PPLO) 483.0
  pneumococcal (broncho) (lobar) 481
  Pneumocystis (carinii) 136.3
  postinfectional NEC 136.9 *[484.8]*
  postmeasles 055.1
  postoperative 997.3
  primary atypical 486
  Proprionibacterium 482.81
  Proteus 482.83
  Pseudomonas 482.1
  psittacosis 073.0
  radiation 508.0

Index

Pneumonia — Poisoning

Pneumonia — *continued*
  respiratory syncytial virus 480.1
  resulting from a procedure 997.3
  rheumatic 390 *[517.1]*
  Salmonella 003.22
  SARS-associated coronavirus 480.3
  segmented, segmental — *see* Pneumonia,
    broncho-
  Serratia (marcescens) 482.83
  specified
    bacteria NEC 482.89
    organism NEC 483.8
    virus NEC 480.8
  spirochetal 104.8 *[484.8]*
  staphylococcal (broncho) (lobar) 482.40
    aureus 482.41
    specified type NEC 482.49
  static, stasis 514
  streptococcal (broncho) (lobar) NEC 482.30
    Group
      A 482.31
      B 482.32
      specified NEC 482.39
    pneumoniae 481
    specified type NEC 482.39
  Streptococcus pneumoniae 481
  traumatic (complication) (early) (secondary)
    958.8
  tuberculous (any) (*see also* Tuberculosis)
    011.6 ☑
  tularemic 021.2
  TWAR agent 483.1
  varicella 052.1
  Veillonella 482.81
  viral, virus (broncho) (interstitial) (lobar) 480.9
    with influenza, flu, or grippe 487.0
    adenoviral 480.0
    parainfluenza 480.2
    respiratory syncytial 480.1
    SARS-associated coronavirus 480.3
    specified type NEC 480.8
  white (congenital) 090.0
Pneumonic — *see* condition
Pneumonitis (acute) (primary) (*see also*
  Pneumonia) 486
  allergic 495.9
    specified type NEC 495.8
  aspiration 507.0
    due to fumes or gases 506.0
    fetal 770.18 ●
      due to ●
        blood 770.16 ●
        clear amniotic fluid 770.14 ●
        meconium 770.12 ●
        postnatal stomach contents 770.86 ●
    newborn 770.18 ▲
      due to ●
        blood 770.16 ●
        clear amniotic fluid 770.14 ●
        meconium 770.12 ●
        postnatal stomach contents 770.86 ●
    obstetric 668.0 ☑
  chemical 506.0
    due to fumes or gases 506.0
  cholesterol 516.8
  chronic (*see also* Fibrosis, lung) 515
  congenital rubella 771.0
  crack 506.0
  due to
    crack (cocaine) 506.0
    fumes or vapors 506.0
    inhalation
      food (regurgitated), milk, vomitus 507.0
      oils, essences 507.1
      saliva 507.0
      solids, liquids NEC 507.8
    toxoplasmosis (acquired) 130.4
      congenital (active) 771.2 *[484.8]*
  eosinophilic 518.3
  fetal aspiration 770.18 ▲
    due to ●
      blood 770.16 ●
      clear amniotic fluid 770.14 ●
      meconium 770.12 ●
      postnatal stomach contents 770.86 ●

Pneumonitis (*see also* Pneumonia) — *continued*
  hypersensitivity 495.9
  interstitial (chronic) (*see also* Fibrosis, lung)
    515
    lymphoid 516.8
  lymphoid, interstitial 516.8
  meconium ▶aspiration◀ 770.12 ▲
  postanesthetic
    correct substance properly administered
      507.0
    obstetric 668.0 ☑
    overdose or wrong substance given 968.4
      specified anesthetic — *see* Table of Drugs
        and Chemicals
  postoperative 997.3
    obstetric 668.0 ☑
  radiation 508.0
  rubella, congenital 771.0
  "ventilation" 495.7
  wood-dust 495.8
Pneumoconiosis — *see* Pneumoconiosis
Pneumoparotid 527.8
Pneumopathy NEC 518.89
  alveolar 516.9
    specified NEC 516.8
  due to dust NEC 504
  parietoalveolar 516.9
    specified condition NEC 516.8
Pneumopericarditis (*see also* Pericarditis) 423.9
  acute 420.90
Pneumopericardium — *see also* Pericarditis
  congenital 770.2
  fetus or newborn 770.2
  traumatic (post) (*see also* Pneumothorax,
    traumatic) 860.0
    with open wound into thorax 860.1
Pneumoperitoneum 568.89
  fetus or newborn 770.2
Pneumophagia (psychogenic) 306.4
Pneumopleurisy, pneumopleuritis (*see also*
  Pneumonia) 486
Pneumopyopericardium 420.99
Pneumopyothorax (*see also* Pyopneumothorax)
  510.9
  with fistula 510.0
Pneumorrhagia 786.3
  newborn 770.3
  tuberculous (*see also* Tuberculosis, pulmonary)
    011.9 ☑
Pneumosiderosis (occupational) 503
Pneumothorax (acute) (chronic) 512.8
  congenital 770.2
  due to operative injury of chest wall or lung
    512.1
    accidental puncture or laceration 512.1
  fetus or newborn 770.2
  iatrogenic 512.1
  postoperative 512.1
  spontaneous 512.8
    fetus or newborn 770.2
    tension 512.0
  sucking 512.8
    iatrogenic 512.1
    postoperative 512.1
  tense valvular, infectional 512.0
  tension 512.0
    iatrogenic 512.1
    postoperative 512.1
    spontaneous 512.0
  traumatic 860.0
    with
      hemothorax 860.4
        with open wound into thorax 860.5
      open wound into thorax 860.1
  tuberculous (*see also* Tuberculosis) 011.7 ☑
Pocket(s)
  endocardial (*see also* Endocarditis) 424.90
  periodontal 523.8
Podagra 274.9
Podencephalus 759.89
Poikilocytosis 790.09
Poikiloderma 709.09
  Civatte's 709.09
  congenital 757.33
  vasculare atrophicans 696.2

Poikilodermatomyositis 710.3
Pointed ear 744.29
Poise imperfect 729.9
Poisoned — *see* Poisoning
Poisoning (acute) — *see also* Table of Drugs and
  Chemicals
  Bacillus, B.
    aertrycke (*see also* Infection, Salmonella) 003.9
    botulinus 005.1
    cholerae (suis) (*see also* Infection,
      Salmonella) 003.9
    paratyphosus (*see also* Infection,
      Salmonella) 003.9
    suipestifer (*see also* Infection, Salmonella)
      003.9
  bacterial toxins NEC 005.9
  berries, noxious 988.2
  blood (general) — *see* Septicemia
  botulism 005.1
  bread, moldy, mouldy — *see* Poisoning, food
  damaged meat — *see* Poisoning, food
  death-cap (Amanita phalloides) (Amanita verna)
    988.1
  decomposed food — *see* Poisoning, food
  diseased food — *see* Poisoning, food
  drug — *see* Table of Drugs and Chemicals
  epidemic, fish, meat, or other food — *see*
    Poisoning, food
  fava bean 282.2
  fish (bacterial) — *see also* Poisoning, food
    noxious 988.0
  food (acute) (bacterial) (diseased) (infected) NEC
    005.9
    due to
      bacillus
        aertrycke (*see also* Poisoning, food,
          due to Salmonella) 003.9
        botulinus 005.1
        cereus 005.89
        choleraesuis (*see also* Poisoning, food,
          due to Salmonella) 003.9
        paratyphosus (*see also* Poisoning,
          food, due to Salmonella) 003.9
        suipestifer (*see also* Poisoning, food,
          due to Salmonella) 003.9
      Clostridium 005.3
        botulinum 005.1
        perfringens 005.2
        welchii 005.2
      Salmonella (aertrycke) (callinarum)
        (choleraesuis) (enteritidis)
        (paratyphi) (suipestifer) 003.9
        with
          gastroenteritis 003.0
          localized infection(s) (*see also*
            Infection, Salmonella) 003.20
          septicemia 003.1
          specified manifestation NEC 003.8
      specified bacterium NEC 005.89
      Staphylococcus 005.0
      Streptococcus 005.89
      Vibrio parahaemolyticus 005.4
      Vibrio vulnificus 005.81
    noxious or naturally toxic 988.0
      berries 988.2
      fish 988.0
      mushroom 988.1
      plants NEC 988.2
  ice cream — *see* Poisoning, food
  ichthyotoxism (bacterial) 005.9
  kreotoxism, food 005.9
  malarial — *see* Malaria
  meat — *see* Poisoning, food
  mushroom (noxious) 988.1
  mussel — *see also* Poisoning, food
    noxious 988.0
  noxious foodstuffs (*see also* Poisoning, food,
    noxious) 988.9
    specified type NEC 988.8
  plants, noxious 988.2
  pork — *see also* Poisoning, food
    specified NEC 988.8
    Trichinosis 124
  ptomaine — *see* Poisoning, food
  putrefaction, food — *see* Poisoning, food
  radiation 508.0

☑ Additional Digit Required — Refer to the Tabular List (Numeric Code Section) for Additional Digit Selection

Poisoning — *see also* Table of Drugs and
     Chemicals — *continued*
     Salmonella (*see also* Infection, Salmonella)
       003.9
     sausage — *see also* Poisoning, food
       Trichinosis 124
     saxitoxin 988.0
     shellfish — *see also* Poisoning, food
       noxious 988.0
     Staphylococcus, food 005.0
     toxic, from disease NEC 799.89
     truffles — *see* Poisoning, food
     uremic — *see* Uremia
     uric acid 274.9

Poison ivy, oak, sumac or other plant
     dermatitis 692.6

Poker spine 720.0

Policeman's disease 729.2

Polioencephalitis (acute) (bulbar) (*see also*
     Poliomyelitis, bulbar) 045.0 ☑
     inferior 335.22
     influenzal 487.8
     superior hemorrhagic (acute) (Wernicke's) 265.1
     Wernicke's (superior hemorrhagic) 265.1

Polioencephalomyelitis (acute) (anterior) (bulbar)
     (*see also* Polioencephalitis) 045.0 ☑

Polioencephalopathy, superior hemorrhagic
     265.1
     with
       beriberi 265.0
       pellagra 265.2

Poliomeningoencephalitis — *see*
     Meningoencephalitis

Poliomyelitis (acute) (anterior) (epidemic)
     045.9 ☑

> *Note* — *Use the following fifth-digit
> subclassification with category 045:*
>
> 0   *poliovirus, unspecified type*
> 1   *poliovirus, type I*
> 2   *poliovirus, type II*
> 3   *poliovirus, type III*

     with
       paralysis 045.1 ☑
         bulbar 045.0 ☑
     abortive 045.2 ☑
     ascending 045.9 ☑
       progressive 045.9 ☑
     bulbar 045.0 ☑
     cerebral 045.0 ☑
     chronic 335.21
     congenital 771.2
     contact V01.2
     deformities 138
     exposure to V01.2
     late effect 138
     nonepidemic 045.9 ☑
     nonparalytic 045.2 ☑
     old with deformity 138
     posterior, acute 053.19
     residual 138
     sequelae 138
     spinal, acute 045.9 ☑
     syphilitic (chronic) 094.89
     vaccination, prophylactic (against) V04.0

Poliosis (eyebrow) (eyelashes) 704.3
     circumscripta (congenital) 757.4
       acquired 704.3
     congenital 757.4

Pollakiuria 788.41
     psychogenic 306.53

Pollinosis 477.0

Pollitzer's disease (hidradenitis suppurativa)
     705.83

Polyadenitis (*see also* Adenitis) 289.3
     malignant 020.0

Polyalgia 729.9

Polyangiitis (essential) 446.0

Polyarteritis (nodosa) (renal) 446.0

Polyarthralgia 719.49
     psychogenic 306.0

Polyarthritis, polyarthropathy NEC 716.59
     due to or associated with other specified
       conditions — *see* Arthritis, due to or
       associated with
     endemic (*see also* Disease, Kaschin-Beck)
       716.0
     inflammatory 714.9
       specified type NEC 714.89
     juvenile (chronic) 714.30
       acute 714.31
     migratory — *see* Fever, rheumatic
     rheumatic 714.0
       fever (acute) — *see* Fever, rheumatic

Polycarential syndrome of infancy 260

Polychondritis (atrophic) (chronic) (relapsing)
     733.99

Polycoria 743.46

Polycystic (congenital) (disease) 759.89
     degeneration, kidney — *see* Polycystic, kidney
     kidney (congenital) 753.12
       adult type (APKD) 753.13
       autosomal dominant 753.13
       autosomal recessive 753.14
       childhood type (CPKD) 753.14
       infantile type 753.14
     liver 751.62
     lung 518.89
       congenital 748.4
     ovary, ovaries 256.4
     spleen 759.0

Polycythemia (primary) (rubra) (vera) (M9950/1)
     238.4
     acquired 289.0
     benign 289.0
       familial 289.6
     due to
       donor twin 776.4
       fall in plasma volume 289.0
       high altitude 289.0
       maternal-fetal transfusion 776.4
       stress 289.0
     emotional 289.0
     erythropoietin 289.0
     familial (benign) 289.6
     Gaisböck's (hypertonica) 289.0
     high altitude 289.0
     hypertonica 289.0
     hypoxemic 289.0
     neonatorum 776.4
     nephrogenous 289.0
     relative 289.0
     secondary 289.0
     spurious 289.0
     stress 289.0

Polycytosis cryptogenica 289.0

Polydactylism, polydactyly 755.00
     fingers 755.01
     toes 755.02

Polydipsia 783.5

Polydystrophic oligophrenia 277.5

Polyembryoma (M9072/3) — *see* Neoplasm, by
     site, malignant

Polygalactia 676.6 ☑

Polyglandular
     deficiency 258.9
     dyscrasia 258.9
     dysfunction 258.9
     syndrome 258.8

Polyhydramnios (*see also* Hydramnios) 657.0 ☑

Polymastia 757.6

Polymenorrhea 626.2

Polymicrogyria 742.2

Polymyalgia 725
     arteritica 446.5
     rheumatica 725

Polymyositis (acute) (chronic) (hemorrhagic)
     710.4
     with involvement of
       lung 710.4 [517.8]
       skin 710.3
     ossificans (generalisata) (progressiva) 728.19
     Wagner's (dermatomyositis) 710.3

Polyneuritis, polyneuritic (*see also*
     Polyneuropathy) 356.9
     alcoholic 357.5
       with psychosis 291.1
     cranialis 352.6
     diabetic 250.6 ☑ [357.2]
     demyelinating, chronic inflammatory 357.81
     due to lack of vitamin NEC 269.2 [357.4]
     endemic 265.0 [357.4]
     erythredema 985.0
     febrile 357.0
     hereditary ataxic 356.3
     idiopathic, acute 357.0
     infective (acute) 357.0
     nutritional 269.9 [357.4]
     postinfectious 357.0

Polyneuropathy (peripheral) 356.9
     alcoholic 357.5
     amyloid 277.3 [357.4]
     arsenical 357.7
     critical illness 357.82
     diabetic 250.6 ☑ [357.2]
     due to
       antitetanus serum 357.6
       arsenic 357.7
       drug or medicinal substance 357.6
         correct substance properly administered
           357.6
         overdose or wrong substance given or
           taken 977.9
         specified drug — *see* Table of Drugs
           and Chemicals
       lack of vitamin NEC 269.2 [357.4]
       lead 357.7
       organophosphate compounds 357.7
       pellagra 265.2 [357.4]
       porphyria 277.1 [357.4]
       serum 357.6
       toxic agent NEC 357.7
     hereditary 356.0
     idiopathic 356.9
       progressive 356.4
     in
       amyloidosis 277.3 [357.4]
       avitaminosis 269.2 [357.4]
         specified NEC 269.1 [357.4]
       beriberi 265.0 [357.4]
       collagen vascular disease NEC 710.9 [357.1]
       deficiency
         B-complex NEC 266.2 [357.4]
         vitamin B 266.9 [357.4]
         vitamin B_6 266.1 [357.4]
       diabetes 250.6 ☑ [357.2]
       diphtheria (*see also* Diphtheria) 032.89
         [357.4]
       disseminated lupus erythematosus 710.0
         [357.1]
       herpes zoster 053.13
       hypoglycemia 251.2 [357.4]
       malignant neoplasm (M8000/3) NEC 199.1
         [357.3]
       mumps 072.72
       pellagra 265.2 [357.4]
       polyarteritis nodosa 446.0 [357.1]
       porphyria 277.1 [357.4]
       rheumatoid arthritis 714.0 [357.1]
       sarcoidosis 135 [357.4]
       uremia 585.9 [357.4]   ▲
     lead 357.7
     nutritional 269.9 [357.4]
       specified NEC 269.8 [357.4]
     postherpetic 053.13
     progressive 356.4
     sensory (hereditary) 356.2

Polyonychia 757.5

Polyopia 368.2
     refractive 368.15

Polyorchism, polyorchidism (three testes) 752.89

Polyorrhymenitis (peritoneal) (*see also*
     Polyserositis) 568.82
     pericardial 423.2

Polyostotic fibrous dysplasia 756.54

Polyotia 744.1

Index

Polyp, polypus — Posthepatitis syndrome

Polyp, polypus

Note — Polyps of organs or sites that do not appear in the list below should be coded to the residual category for diseases of the organ or site concerned.

accessory sinus 471.8
adenoid tissue 471.0
adenomatous (M8210/0) — *see also* Neoplasm, by site, benign
  adenocarcinoma in (M8210/3) — *see* Neoplasm, by site, malignant
  carcinoma in (M8210/3) — *see* Neoplasm, by site, malignant
  multiple (M8221/0) — *see* Neoplasm, by site, benign
antrum 471.8
anus, anal (canal) (nonadenomatous) 569.0
  adenomatous 211.4
Bartholin's gland 624.6
bladder (M8120/1) 236.7
broad ligament 620.8
cervix (uteri) 622.7
  adenomatous 219.0
  in pregnancy or childbirth 654.6 ☑
    affecting fetus or newborn 763.89
    causing obstructed labor 660.2 ☑
  mucous 622.7
  nonneoplastic 622.7
choanal 471.0
cholesterol 575.6
clitoris 624.6
colon (M8210/0) (*see also* Polyp, adenomatous) 211.3
corpus uteri 621.0
dental 522.0
ear (middle) 385.30
endometrium 621.0
ethmoidal (sinus) 471.8
fallopian tube 620.8
female genital organs NEC 624.8
frontal (sinus) 471.8
gallbladder 575.6
gingiva 523.8
gum 523.8
labia 624.6
larynx (mucous) 478.4
malignant (M8000/3) — *see* Neoplasm, by site, malignant
maxillary (sinus) 471.8
middle ear 385.30
myometrium 621.0
nares
  anterior 471.9
  posterior 471.0
nasal (mucous) 471.9
  cavity 471.0
  septum 471.9
nasopharyngeal 471.0
neoplastic (M8210/0) — *see* Neoplasm, by site, benign
nose (mucous) 471.9
oviduct 620.8
paratubal 620.8
pharynx 478.29
  congenital 750.29
placenta, placental 674.4 ☑
prostate 600.20
  with urinary retention 600.21
pudenda 624.6
pulp (dental) 522.0
rectosigmoid 211.4
rectum (nonadenomatous) 569.0
  adenomatous 211.4
septum (nasal) 471.9
sinus (accessory) (ethmoidal) (frontal) (maxillary) (sphenoidal) 471.8
sphenoidal (sinus) 471.8
stomach (M8210/0) 211.1
tube, fallopian 620.8
turbinate, mucous membrane 471.8
ureter 593.89
urethra 599.3
uterine
  ligament 620.8
  tube 620.8

Polyp, polypus — *continued*
uterus (body) (corpus) (mucous) 621.0
  in pregnancy or childbirth 654.1 ☑
    affecting fetus or newborn 763.89
    causing obstructed labor 660.2 ☑
vagina 623.7
vocal cord (mucous) 478.4
vulva 624.6
Polyphagia 783.6
Polypoid — *see* condition
Polyposis — *see also* Polyp
coli (adenomatous) (M8220/0) 211.3
  adenocarcinoma in (M8220/3) 153.9
  carcinoma in (M8220/3) 153.9
familial (M8220/0) 211.3
intestinal (adenomatous) (M8220/0) 211.3
multiple (M8221/0) — *see* Neoplasm, by site, benign
Polyradiculitis (acute) 357.0
Polyradiculoneuropathy (acute) (segmentally demyelinating) 357.0
Polysarcia 278.00
Polyserositis (peritoneal) 568.82
due to pericarditis 423.2
paroxysmal (familial) 277.3
pericardial 423.2
periodic 277.3
pleural — *see* Pleurisy
recurrent 277.3
tuberculous (*see also* Tuberculosis, polyserositis) 018.9 ☑
Polysialia 527.7
Polysplenia syndrome 759.0
Polythelia 757.6
Polytrichia (*see also* Hypertrichosis) 704.1
Polyunguia (congenital) 757.5
acquired 703.8
Polyuria 788.42
Pompe's disease (glycogenosis II) 271.0
Pompholyx 705.81
Poncet's disease (tuberculous rheumatism) (*see also* Tuberculosis) 015.9 ☑
Pond fracture — *see* Fracture, skull, vault
Ponos 085.0
Pons, pontine — *see* condition
Poor
contractions, labor 661.2 ☑
  affecting fetus or newborn 763.7
fetal growth NEC 764.9 ☑
  affecting management of pregnancy 656.5 ☑
incorporation
  artificial skin graft 996.55
  decellularized allodermis graft 996.55
obstetrical history V13.29
  affecting management of current pregnancy V23.49
    pre-term labor V23.41
  pre-term labor V13.21
sucking reflex (newborn) 796.1
vision NEC 369.9
Poradenitis, nostras 099.1
Porencephaly (congenital) (developmental) (true) 742.4
acquired 348.0
nondevelopmental 348.0
traumatic (post) 310.2
Porocephaliasis 134.1
Porokeratosis 757.39
disseminated superficial actinic (DSAP) 692.75
Poroma, eccrine (M8402/0) — *see* Neoplasm, skin, benign
Porphyria (acute) (congenital) (constitutional) (erythropoietic) (familial) (hepatica) (idiopathic) (idiosyncratic) (intermittent) (latent) (mixed hepatic) (photosensitive) (South African genetic) (Swedish) 277.1
acquired 277.1
cutaneatarda
  hereditaria 277.1
  symptomatica 277.1

Porphyria — *continued*
due to drugs
  correct substance properly administered 277.1
  overdose or wrong substance given or taken 977.9
    specified drug — *see* Table of Drugs and Chemicals
secondary 277.1
toxic NEC 277.1
variegata 277.1
Porphyrinuria (acquired) (congenital) (secondary) 277.1
Porphyruria (acquired) (congenital) 277.1
Portal — *see* condition
Port wine nevus or mark 757.32
Posadas-Wernicke disease 114.9
Position
fetus, abnormal (*see also* Presentation, fetal) 652.9 ☑
teeth, faulty (*see also* Anomaly, position tooth) 524.30
Positive
culture (nonspecific) 795.39
  AIDS virus V08
  blood 790.7
  HIV V08
  human immunodeficiency virus V08
  nose 795.39
  skin lesion NEC 795.39
  spinal fluid 792.0
  sputum 795.39
  stool 792.1
  throat 795.39
  urine 791.9
  wound 795.39
findings, anthrax 795.31
HIV V08
human immunodeficiency virus (HIV) V08
PPD 795.5
serology
  AIDS virus V08
    inconclusive 795.71
  HIV V08
    inconclusive 795.71
  human immunodeficiency virus (HIV) V08
    inconclusive 795.71
  syphilis 097.1
    with signs or symptoms — *see* Syphilis, by site and stage
    false 795.6
skin test 795.7 ☑
  tuberculin (without active tuberculosis) 795.5
VDRL 097.1
  with signs or symptoms — *see* Syphilis, by site and stage
  false 795.6
Wassermann reaction 097.1
  false 795.6
Postcardiotomy syndrome 429.4
Postcaval ureter 753.4
Postcholecystectomy syndrome 576.0
Postclimacteric bleeding 627.1
Postcommissurotomy syndrome 429.4
Postconcussional syndrome 310.2
Postcontusional syndrome 310.2
Postcricoid region — *see* condition
Post-dates (pregnancy) — *see* Pregnancy
Postencephalitic — *see also* condition
syndrome 310.8
Posterior — *see* condition
Posterolateral sclerosis (spinal cord) — *see* Degeneration, combined
Postexanthematous — *see* condition
Postfebrile — *see* condition
Postgastrectomy dumping syndrome 564.2
Posthemiplegic chorea 344.89
Posthemorrhagic anemia (chronic) 280.0
acute 285.1
newborn 776.5
Posthepatitis syndrome 780.79

Postherpetic neuralgia (intercostal) (syndrome) (zoster) 053.19
  geniculate ganglion 053.11
  ophthalmica 053.19
  trigeminal 053.12
Posthitis 607.1
Postimmunization complication or reaction — see Complications, vaccination
Postinfectious — see condition
Postinfluenzal syndrome 780.79
Postlaminectomy syndrome 722.80
  cervical, cervicothoracic 722.81
  kyphosis 737.12
  lumbar, lumbosacral 722.83
  thoracic, thoracolumbar 722.82
Postleukotomy syndrome 310.0
Postlobectomy syndrome 310.0
Postmastectomy lymphedema (syndrome) 457.0
Postmaturity, postmature (fetus or newborn) (gestation period over 42 completed weeks) 766.22
  affecting management of pregnancy
    post-term pregnancy 645.1 ☑
    prolonged pregnancy 645.2 ☑
  syndrome 766.22
Postmeasles — see also condition
  complication 055.8
    specified NEC 055.79
Postmenopausal
  endometrium (atrophic) 627.8
    suppurative (see also Endometritis) 615.9
  hormone replacement therapy V07.4
  status (age related) (natural) V49.81
Postnasal drip — see Sinusitis
Postnatal — see condition
Postoperative — see also condition
  confusion state 293.9
  psychosis 293.9
  status NEC (see also Status (post)) V45.89
Postpancreatectomy hyperglycemia 251.3
Postpartum — see also condition
  anemia 648.2 ☑
  cardiomyopathy 674.5 ☑
  observation
    immediately after delivery V24.0
    routine follow-up V24.2
Postperfusion syndrome NEC 999.8
  bone marrow 996.85
Postpoliomyelitic — see condition
Postsurgery status NEC (see also Status (post)) V45.89
Post-term (pregnancy) 645.1 ☑
  infant (gestation period over 40 completed weeks to 42 completed weeks) 766.21
Posttraumatic — see condition
Posttraumatic brain syndrome, nonpsychotic 310.2
Post-typhoid abscess 002.0
Postures, hysterical 300.11
Postvaccinal reaction or complication — see Complications, vaccination
Postvagotomy syndrome 564.2
Postvalvulotomy syndrome 429.4
Postvasectomy sperm count V25.8
Potain's disease (pulmonary edema) 514
Potain's syndrome (gastrectasis with dyspepsia) 536.1
Pott's
  curvature (spinal) (see also Tuberculosis) 015.0 *[737.43]*
  disease or paraplegia (see also Tuberculosis) 015.0 *[730.88]*
  fracture (closed) 824.4
    open 824.5
  gangrene 440.24
  osteomyelitis (see also Tuberculosis) 015.0 *[730.88]*
  spinal curvature (see also Tuberculosis) 015.0 *[737.43]*
  tumor, puffy (see also Osteomyelitis) 730.2 ☑

Potter's
  asthma 502
  disease 753.0
  facies 754.0
  lung 502
  syndrome (with renal agenesis) 753.0
Pouch
  bronchus 748.3
  Douglas' — see condition
  esophagus, esophageal (congenital) 750.4
    acquired 530.6
  gastric 537.1
  Hartmann's (abnormal sacculation of gallbladder neck) 575.8
    of intestine V44.3
      attention to V55.3
  pharynx, pharyngeal (congenital) 750.27
Poulet's disease 714.2
Poultrymen's itch 133.8
Poverty V60.2
Prader-Labhart-Willi-Fanconi syndrome (hypogenital dystrophy with diabetic tendency) 759.81
Prader-Willi syndrome (hypogenital dystrophy with diabetic tendency) 759.81
Preachers' voice 784.49
Pre-AIDS — see Human immunodeficiency virus (disease) (illness) (infection)
Preauricular appendage 744.1
Prebetalipoproteinemia (acquired) (essential) (familial) (hereditary) (primary) (secondary) 272.1
  with chylomicronemia 272.3
Precipitate labor 661.3 ☑
  affecting fetus or newborn 763.6
Preclimacteric bleeding 627.0
  menorrhagia 627.0
Precocious
  adrenarche 259.1
  menarche 259.1
  menstruation 626.8
  pubarche 259.1
  puberty NEC 259.1
  sexual development NEC 259.1
  thelarche 259.1
Precocity, sexual (constitutional) (cryptogenic) (female) (idiopathic) (male) NEC 259.1
  with adrenal hyperplasia 255.2
Precordial pain 786.51
  psychogenic 307.89
Predeciduous teeth 520.2
Prediabetes, prediabetic 790.29
  complicating pregnancy, childbirth, or puerperium 648.8 ☑
  fetus or newborn 775.8
Predislocation status of hip, at birth (see also Subluxation, congenital, hip) 754.32
Preeclampsia (mild) 642.4 ☑
  with pre-existing hypertension 642.7 ☑
  affecting fetus or newborn 760.0
  severe 642.5 ☑
  superimposed on pre-existing hypertensive disease 642.7 ☑
Preeruptive color change, teeth, tooth 520.8
Preexcitation 426.7
  atrioventricular conduction 426.7
  ventricular 426.7
Preglaucoma 365.00
Pregnancy (single) (uterine) (without sickness) V22.2

> *Note — Use the following fifth-digit subclassification with categories 640-648, 651-676:*
>
> 0   *unspecified as to episode of care*
> 1   *delivered, with or without mention of antepartum condition*
> 2   *delivered, with mention of postpartum complication*
> 3   *antepartum condition or complication*
> 4   *postpartum condition or complication*

Pregnancy — continued
  abdominal (ectopic) 633.00
    with intrauterine pregnancy 633.01
    affecting fetus or newborn 761.4
  abnormal NEC 646.9 ☑
  ampullar — see Pregnancy, tubal
  broad ligament — see Pregnancy, cornual
  cervical — see Pregnancy, cornual
  combined (extrauterine and intrauterine) — see Pregnancy, cornual
  complicated (by) 646.9 ☑
    abnormal, abnormality NEC 646.9 ☑
      cervix 654.6 ☑
      cord (umbilical) 663.9 ☑
      glucose tolerance (conditions classifiable to 790.21-790.29) 648.8 ☑
      pelvic organs or tissues NEC 654.9 ☑
      pelvis (bony) 653.0 ☑
      perineum or vulva 654.8 ☑
      placenta, placental (vessel) 656.7 ☑
      position
        cervix 654.4 ☑
        placenta 641.1 ☑
          without hemorrhage 641.0 ☑
        uterus 654.4 ☑
      size, fetus 653.5 ☑
      uterus (congenital) 654.0 ☑
    abscess or cellulitis
      bladder 646.6 ☑
      genitourinary tract (conditions classifiable to 590, 595, 597, 599.0, 614.0-614.5, 614.7-614.9, 615) 646.6 ☑
      kidney 646.6 ☑
      urinary tract NEC 646.6 ☑
    adhesion, pelvic peritoneal 648.9 ☑
    air embolism 673.0 ☑
    albuminuria 646.2 ☑
      with hypertension — see Toxemia, of pregnancy
    amnionitis 658.4 ☑
    amniotic fluid embolism 673.1 ☑
    anemia (conditions classifiable to 280-285) 648.2 ☑
    atrophy, yellow (acute) (liver) (subacute) 646.7 ☑
    bacilluria, asymptomatic 646.5 ☑
    bacteriuria, asymptomatic 646.5 ☑
    bicornis or bicornuate uterus 654.0 ☑
    biliary problems 646.8 ☑
    bone and joint disorders (conditions classifiable to 720-724 or conditions affecting lower limbs classifiable to 711-719, 725-738) 648.7 ☑
    breech presentation (buttocks) (complete) (frank) 652.2 ☑
      with successful version 652.1 ☑
    cardiovascular disease (conditions classifiable to 390-398, 410-429) 648.6 ☑
      congenital (conditions classifiable to 745-747) 648.5 ☑
    cerebrovascular disorders (conditions classifiable to 430-434, 436-437) 674.0 ☑
    cervicitis (conditions classifiable to 616.0) 646.6 ☑
    chloasma (gravidarum) 646.8 ☑
    chorea (gravidarum) — see Eclampsia, pregnancy
    cholelithiasis 646.8 ☑
    contraction, pelvis (general) 653.1 ☑
      inlet 653.2 ☑
      outlet 653.3 ☑
    convulsions (eclamptic) (uremic) 642.6 ☑
      with pre-existing hypertension 642.7 ☑
    current disease or condition (nonobstetric)
      abnormal glucose tolerance 648.8 ☑
      anemia 648.2 ☑
      bone and joint (lower limb) 648.7 ☑
      cardiovascular 648.6 ☑
        congenital 648.5 ☑
      cerebrovascular 674.0 ☑
      diabetic 648.0 ☑
      drug dependence 648.3 ☑
      female genital mutilation 648.9 ☑   ●

Pregnancy — *continued*
  complicated (by) — *continued*
    current disease or condition — *continued*
      genital organ or tract 646.6 ☑
      gonorrheal 647.1 ☑
      hypertensive 642.2 ☑
        renal 642.1 ☑
      infectious 647.9 ☑
        specified type NEC 647.8 ☑
      liver 646.7 ☑
      malarial 647.4 ☑
      nutritional deficiency 648.9 ☑
      parasitic NEC 647.8 ☑
      periodontal disease 648.9 ☑
      renal 646.2 ☑
        hypertensive 642.1 ☑
      rubella 647.5 ☑
      specified condition NEC 648.9 ☑
      syphilitic 647.0 ☑
      thyroid 648.1 ☑
      tuberculous 647.3 ☑
      urinary 646.6 ☑
      venereal 647.2 ☑
      viral NEC 647.6 ☑
    cystitis 646.6 ☑
    cystocele 654.4 ☑
    death of fetus (near term) 656.4 ☑
      early pregnancy (before 22 completed weeks gestation) 632
    deciduitis 646.6 ☑
    decreased fetal movements 655.7 ☑
    diabetes (mellitus) (conditions classifiable to 250) 648.0 ☑
    disorders of liver 646.7 ☑
    displacement, uterus NEC 654.4 ☑
    disproportion — *see* Disproportion
    double uterus 654.0 ☑
    drug dependence (conditions classifiable to 304) 648.3 ☑
    dysplasia, cervix 654.6 ☑
    early onset of delivery (spontaneous) 644.2 ☑
    eclampsia, eclamptic (coma) (convulsions) (delirium) (nephritis) (uremia) 642.6 ☑
      with pre-existing hypertension 642.7 ☑
    edema 646.1 ☑
      with hypertension — *see* Toxemia, of pregnancy
    effusion, amniotic fluid 658.1 ☑
      delayed delivery following 658.2 ☑
    embolism
      air 673.0 ☑
      amniotic fluid 673.1 ☑
      blood-clot 673.2 ☑
      cerebral 674.0 ☑
      pulmonary NEC 673.2 ☑
      pyemic 673.3 ☑
      septic 673.3 ☑
    emesis (gravidarum) — *see* Pregnancy, complicated, vomiting
    endometritis (conditions classifiable to 615.0-615.9) 646.6 ☑
      decidual 646.6 ☑
    excessive weight gain NEC 646.1 ☑
    face presentation 652.4 ☑
    failure, fetal head to enter pelvic brim 652.5 ☑
    false labor (pains) 644.1 ☑
    fatigue 646.8 ☑
    fatty metamorphosis of liver 646.7 ☑
    female genital mutilation 648.9 ☑ ●
    fetal
      death (near term) 656.4 ☑
        early (before 22 completed weeks gestation) 632
      deformity 653.7 ☑
      distress 656.8 ☑
      reduction of multiple fetuses reduced ●
        to single fetus 651.7 ☑ ●
    fibroid (tumor) (uterus) 654.1 ☑
    footling presentation 652.8 ☑
      with successful version 652.1 ☑
    gallbladder disease 646.8 ☑
    goiter 648.1 ☑
    gonococcal infection (conditions classifiable to 098) 647.1 ☑

Pregnancy — *continued*
  complicated (by) — *continued*
    gonorrhea (conditions classifiable to 098) 647.1 ☑
    hemorrhage 641.9 ☑
      accidental 641.2 ☑
      before 22 completed weeks gestation NEC 640.9 ☑
      cerebrovascular 674.0 ☑
      due to
        afibrinogenemia or other coagulation defect (conditions classifiable to 286.0-286.9) 641.3 ☑
        leiomyoma, uterine 641.8 ☑
        marginal sinus (rupture) 641.2 ☑
        premature separation, placenta 641.2 ☑
        trauma 641.8 ☑
      early (before 22 completed weeks gestation) 640.9 ☑
      threatened abortion 640.0 ☑
      unavoidable 641.1 ☑
    hepatitis (acute) (malignant) (subacute) 646.7 ☑
      viral 647.6 ☑
    herniation of uterus 654.4 ☑
    high head at term 652.5 ☑
    hydatidiform mole (delivered) (undelivered) 630
    hydramnios 657.0 ☑
    hydrocephalic fetus 653.6 ☑
    hydrops amnii 657.0 ☑
    hydrorrhea 658.1 ☑
    hyperemesis (gravidarum) — *see* Hyperemesis, gravidarum
    hypertension — *see* Hypertension, complicating pregnancy
    hypertensive
      heart and renal disease 642.2 ☑
      heart disease 642.2 ☑
      renal disease 642.2 ☑
    hyperthyroidism 648.1 ☑
    hypothyroidism 648.1 ☑
    hysteralgia 646.8 ☑
    icterus gravis 646.7 ☑
    incarceration, uterus 654.3 ☑
    incompetent cervix (os) 654.5 ☑
    infection 647.9 ☑
      amniotic fluid 658.4 ☑
      bladder 646.6 ☑
      genital organ (conditions classifiable to 614.0-614.5, 614.7-614.9, 615) 646.6 ☑
      kidney (conditions classifiable to 590.0-590.9) 646.6 ☑
      urinary (tract) 646.6 ☑
        asymptomatic 646.5 ☑
    infective and parasitic diseases NEC 647.8 ☑
    inflammation
      bladder 646.6 ☑
      genital organ (conditions classifiable to 614.0-614.5, 614.7-614.9, 615) 646.6 ☑
      urinary tract NEC 646.6 ☑
    injury 648.9 ☑
    insufficient weight gain 646.8 ☑
    intrauterine fetal death (near term) NEC 656.4 ☑
      early (before 22 completed weeks' gestation) 632
    malaria (conditions classifiable to 084) 647.4 ☑
    malformation, uterus (congenital) 654.0 ☑
    malnutrition (conditions classifiable to 260-269) 648.9 ☑
    malposition
      fetus — *see* Pregnancy, complicated, malpresentation
      uterus or cervix 654.4 ☑
    malpresentation 652.9 ☑
      with successful version 652.1 ☑
      in multiple gestation 652.6 ☑
      specified type NEC 652.8 ☑
    marginal sinus hemorrhage or rupture 641.2 ☑
    maternal obesity syndrome 646.1 ☑
    menstruation 640.8 ☑

Pregnancy — *continued*
  complicated (by) — *continued*
    mental disorders (conditions classifiable to 290-303, 305-316, 317-319) 648.4 ☑
    mentum presentation 652.4 ☑
    missed
      abortion 632
      delivery (at or near term) 656.4 ☑
      labor (at or near term) 656.4 ☑
    necrosis
      genital organ or tract (conditions classifiable to 614.0-614.5, 614.7-614.9, 615) 646.6 ☑
      liver (conditions classifiable to 570) 646.7 ☑
      renal, cortical 646.2 ☑
    nephritis or nephrosis (conditions classifiable to 580-589) 646.2 ☑
      with hypertension 642.1 ☑
    nephropathy NEC 646.2 ☑
    neuritis (peripheral) 646.4 ☑
    nutritional deficiency (conditions classifiable to 260-269) 648.9 ☑
    oblique lie or presentation 652.3 ☑
      with successful version 652.1 ☑
    obstetrical trauma NEC 665.9 ☑
    oligohydramnios NEC 658.0 ☑
    onset of contractions before 37 weeks 644.0 ☑
    oversize fetus 653.5 ☑
    papyraceous fetus 646.0 ☑
    patent cervix 654.5 ☑
    pelvic inflammatory disease (conditions classifiable to 614.0-614.5, 614.7-614.9, 615) 646.6 ☑
    pelvic peritoneal adhesion 648.9 ☑
    placenta, placental
      abnormality 656.7 ☑
      abruptio or ablatio 641.2 ☑
      detachment 641.2 ☑
      disease 656.7 ☑
      infarct 656.7 ☑
      low implantation 641.1 ☑
        without hemorrhage 641.0 ☑
      malformation 656.7 ☑
      malposition 641.1 ☑
        without hemorrhage 641.0 ☑
      marginal sinus hemorrhage 641.2 ☑
      previa 641.1 ☑
        without hemorrhage 641.0 ☑
      separation (premature) (undelivered) 641.2 ☑
    placentitis 658.4 ☑
    polyhydramnios 657.0 ☑
    postmaturity
      post-term 645.1 ☑
      prolonged 645.2 ☑
    prediabetes 648.8 ☑
    pre-eclampsia (mild) 642.4 ☑
      severe 642.5 ☑
      superimposed on pre-existing hypertensive disease 642.7 ☑
    premature rupture of membranes 658.1 ☑
      with delayed delivery 658.2 ☑
    previous
      infertility V23.0
      nonobstetric condition V23.89
      poor obstetrical history V23.49
      premature delivery V23.41
      trophoblastic disease (conditions classifiable to 630) V23.1
    prolapse, uterus 654.4 ☑
    proteinuria (gestational) 646.2 ☑
      with hypertension — *see* Toxemia, of pregnancy
    pruritus (neurogenic) 646.8 ☑
    psychosis or psychoneurosis 648.4 ☑
    ptyalism 646.8 ☑
    pyelitis (conditions classifiable to 590.0-590.9) 646.6 ☑
    renal disease or failure NEC 646.2 ☑
      with secondary hypertension 642.1 ☑
      hypertensive 642.2 ☑
    retention, retained dead ovum 631
    retroversion, uterus 654.3 ☑
    Rh immunization, incompatibility, or sensitization 656.1 ☑

☑ Additional Digit Required — Refer to the Tabular List (Numeric Code Section) for Additional Digit Selection

Pregnancy — *continued*
  complicated (by) — *continued*
    rubella (conditions classifiable to 056) 647.5 ☑
    rupture
      amnion (premature) 658.1 ☑
        with delayed delivery 658.2 ☑
      marginal sinus (hemorrhage) 641.2 ☑
      membranes (premature) 658.1 ☑
        with delayed delivery 658.2 ☑
      uterus (before onset of labor) 665.0 ☑
    salivation (excessive) 646.8 ☑
    salpingo-oophoritis (conditions classifiable to 614.0-614.2) 646.6 ☑
    septicemia (conditions classifiable to 038.0-038.9) 647.8 ☑
      postpartum 670.0 ☑
      puerperal 670.0 ☑
    spasms, uterus (abnormal) 646.8 ☑
    specified condition NEC 646.8 ☑
    spurious labor pains 644.1 ☑
    superfecundation 651.9 ☑
    superfetation 651.9 ☑
    syphilis (conditions classifiable to 090-097) 647.0 ☑
    threatened
      abortion 640.0 ☑
      premature delivery 644.2 ☑
      premature labor 644.0 ☑
    thrombophlebitis (superficial) 671.2 ☑
      deep 671.3 ☑
    thrombosis 671.9 ☑
      venous (superficial) 671.2 ☑
      deep 671.3 ☑
    thyroid dysfunction (conditions classifiable to 240-246) 648.1 ☑
    thyroiditis 648.1 ☑
    thyrotoxicosis 648.1 ☑
    torsion of uterus 654.4 ☑
    toxemia — *see* Toxemia, of pregnancy
    transverse lie or presentation 652.3 ☑
      with successful version 652.1 ☑
    trauma 648.9 ☑
      obstetrical 665.9 ☑
    tuberculosis (conditions classifiable to 010-018) 647.3 ☑
    tumor
      cervix 654.6 ☑
      ovary 654.4 ☑
      pelvic organs or tissue NEC 654.4 ☑
      uterus (body) 654.1 ☑
        cervix 654.6 ☑
      vagina 654.7 ☑
      vulva 654.8 ☑
    unstable lie 652.0 ☑
    uremia — *see* Pregnancy, complicated, renal disease
    urethritis 646.6 ☑
    vaginitis or vulvitis (conditions classifiable to 616.1) 646.6 ☑
    varicose
      placental vessels 656.7 ☑
      veins (legs) 671.0 ☑
        perineum 671.1 ☑
        vulva 671.1 ☑
    varicosity, labia or vulva 671.1 ☑
    venereal disease NEC (conditions classifiable to 099) 647.2 ☑
    viral disease NEC (conditions classifiable to 042, 050-055, 057-079) 647.6 ☑
    vomiting (incoercible) (pernicious) (persistent) (uncontrollable) (vicious) 643.9 ☑
      due to organic disease or other cause 643.8 ☑
      early — *see* Hyperemesis, gravidarum
      late (after 22 completed weeks gestation) 643.2 ☑
    young maternal age 659.8 ☑
  complications NEC 646.9 ☑
  cornual 633.80
    with intrauterine pregnancy 633.81
    affecting fetus or newborn 761.4
  death, maternal NEC 646.9 ☑
  delivered — *see* Delivery
  ectopic (ruptured) NEC 633.90
    with intrauterine pregnancy 633.91
    abdominal — *see* Pregnancy, abdominal

Pregnancy — *continued*
  ectopic NEC — *continued*
    affecting fetus or newborn 761.4
    combined (extrauterine and intrauterine) — *see* Pregnancy, cornual
    ovarian — *see* Pregnancy, ovarian
    specified type NEC 633.80
      with intrauterine pregnancy 633.81
      affecting fetus or newborn 761.4
    tubal — *see* Pregnancy, tubal
  examination, pregnancy
    negative result V72.41
    not confirmed V72.40
    positive result V72.42   ●
  extrauterine — *see* Pregnancy, ectopic
  fallopian — *see* Pregnancy, tubal
  false 300.11
    labor (pains) 644.1 ☑
  fatigue 646.8 ☑
  illegitimate V61.6
  incidental finding V22.2
  in double uterus 654.0 ☑
  interstitial — *see* Pregnancy, cornual
  intraligamentous — *see* Pregnancy, cornual
  intramural — *see* Pregnancy, cornual
  intraperitoneal — *see* Pregnancy, abdominal
  isthmian — *see* Pregnancy, tubal
  management affected by
    abnormal, abnormality
      fetus (suspected) 655.9 ☑
        specified NEC 655.8 ☑
      placenta 656.7 ☑
    advanced maternal age NEC 659.6 ☑
      multigravida 659.6 ☑
      primigravida 659.5 ☑
    antibodies (maternal)
      anti-c 656.1 ☑
      anti-d 656.1 ☑
      anti-e 656.1 ☑
      blood group (ABO) 656.2 ☑
      Rh(esus) 656.1 ☑
    elderly multigravida 659.6 ☑
    elderly primigravida 659.5 ☑
    fetal (suspected)
      abnormality 655.9 ☑
        acid-base balance 656.8 ☑
        heart rate or rhythm 659.7 ☑
        specified NEC 655.8 ☑
      acidemia 656.3 ☑
      anencephaly 655.0 ☑
      bradycardia 659.7 ☑
      central nervous system malformation 655.0 ☑
      chromosomal abnormalities (conditions classifiable to 758.0-758.9) 655.1 ☑
      damage from
        drugs 655.5 ☑
          obstetric, anesthetic, or sedative 655.5 ☑
        environmental toxins 655.8 ☑
        intrauterine contraceptive device 655.8 ☑
        maternal
          alcohol addiction 655.4 ☑
          disease NEC 655.4 ☑
          drug use 655.5 ☑
          listeriosis 655.4 ☑
          rubella 655.3 ☑
          toxoplasmosis 655.4 ☑
          viral infection 655.3 ☑
        radiation 655.6 ☑
      death (near term) 656.4 ☑
        early (before 22 completed weeks' gestation) 632
      distress 656.8 ☑
      excessive growth 656.6 ☑
      growth retardation 656.5 ☑
      hereditary disease 655.2 ☑
      hydrocephalus 655.0 ☑
      intrauterine death 656.4 ☑
      poor growth 656.5 ☑
      spina bifida (with myelomeningocele) 655.0 ☑
      fetal-maternal hemorrhage 656.0 ☑
      hereditary disease in family (possibly) affecting fetus 655.2 ☑
      incompatibility, blood groups (ABO) 656.2 ☑

Pregnancy — *continued*
  management affected by — *continued*
    fetal — *continued*
      Rh(esus) 656.1 ☑
    insufficient prenatal care V23.7
    intrauterine death 656.4 ☑
    isoimmunization (ABO) 656.2 ☑
      Rh(esus) 656.1 ☑
    large-for-dates fetus 656.6 ☑
    light-for-dates fetus 656.5 ☑
    meconium in liquor 656.8 ☑
    mental disorder (conditions classifiable to 290-303, 305-316, 317-319) 648.4 ☑
    multiparity (grand) 659.4 ☑
    poor obstetric history V23.49
      pre-term labor V23.41
    postmaturity
      post-term 645.1 ☑
      prolonged 645.2 ☑
    post-term pregnancy 645.1 ☑
    previous
      abortion V23.2
        habitual 646.3 ☑
      cesarean delivery 654.2 ☑
      difficult delivery V23.49
      forceps delivery V23.49
      habitual abortions 646.3 ☑
      hemorrhage, antepartum or postpartum V23.49
      hydatidiform mole V23.1
      infertility V23.0
      malignancy NEC V23.89
      nonobstetrical conditions V23.89
      premature delivery V23.41
      trophoblastic disease (conditions in 630) V23.1
      vesicular mole V23.1
    prolonged pregnancy 645.2 ☑
    small-for-dates fetus 656.5 ☑
    young maternal age 659.8 ☑
  maternal death NEC 646.9 ☑
  mesometric (mural) — *see* Pregnancy, cornual
  molar 631
    hydatidiform (*see also* Hydatidiform mole) 630
      previous, affecting management of pregnancy V23.1
    previous, affecting management of pregnancy V23.49
  multiple NEC 651.9 ☑
    with fetal loss and retention of one or more fetus(es) 651.6 ☑
    affecting fetus or newborn 761.5
    following (elective) fetal reduction 651.7 ☑   ● ●
    specified type NEC 651.8 ☑
      with fetal loss and retention of one or more fetus(es) 651.6 ☑
      following (elective) fetal reduction 651.7 ☑   ● ●
  mural — *see* Pregnancy, cornual
  observation NEC V22.1
    first pregnancy V22.0
    high-risk V23.9
      specified problem NEC V23.89
  ovarian 633.20
    with intrauterine pregnancy 633.21
    affecting fetus or newborn 761.4
  possible, not (yet) confirmed V72.40
  postmature
    post-term 645.1 ☑
    prolonged 645.2 ☑
  post-term 645.1 ☑
  prenatal care only V22.1
    first pregnancy V22.0
    high-risk V23.9
      specified problem NEC V23.89
  prolonged 645.2 ☑
  quadruplet NEC 651.2 ☑
    with fetal loss and retention of one or more fetus(es) 651.5 ☑
    affecting fetus or newborn 761.5
    following (elective) fetal reduction 651.7 ☑   ● ●
  quintuplet NEC 651.8 ☑
    with fetal loss and retention of one or more fetus(es) 651.6 ☑

Pregnancy — *continued*
  quintuplet NEC — *continued*
    affecting fetus or newborn 761.5
    following (elective) fetal reduction ●
      651.7 ☑ ●
  sextuplet NEC 651.8 ☑
    with fetal loss and retention of one or more
      fetus(es) 651.6 ☑
    affecting fetus or newborn 761.5
    following (elective) fetal reduction ●
      651.7 ☑ ●
  spurious 300.11
  superfecundation NEC 651.9 ☑
    with fetal loss and retention of one or more
      fetus(es) 651.6 ☑
    following (elective) fetal reduction ●
      651.7 ☑ ●
  superfetation NEC 651.9 ☑
    with fetal loss and retention of one or more
      fetus(es) 651.6 ☑
    following (elective) fetal reduction ●
      651.7 ☑ ●
  supervision (of) (for) — *see also* Pregnancy,
      management affected by
    elderly
      multigravida V23.82
      primigravida V23.81
    high-risk V23.9
      insufficient prenatal care V23.7
      specified problem NEC V23.89
    multiparity V23.3
    normal NEC V22.1
      first V22.0
    poor
      obstetric history V23.49
        pre-term labor V23.41
      reproductive history V23.5
    previous
      abortion V23.2
      hydatidiform mole V23.1
      infertility V23.0
      neonatal death V23.5
      stillbirth V23.5
      trophoblastic disease V23.1
      vesicular mole V23.1
    specified problem NEC V23.89
    young
      multigravida V23.84
      primigravida V23.83
  triplet NEC 651.1 ☑
    with fetal loss and retention of one or more
      fetus(es) 651.4 ☑
    affecting fetus or newborn 761.5
    following (elective) fetal reduction ●
      651.7 ☑ ●
  tubal (with rupture) 633.10
    with intrauterine pregnancy 633.11
    affecting fetus or newborn 761.4
  twin NEC 651.0 ☑
    with fetal loss and retention of one fetus
      651.3 ☑
    affecting fetus or newborn 761.5
    following (elective) fetal reduction ●
      651.7 ☑ ●
  unconfirmed V72.40
  undelivered (no other diagnosis) V22.2
    with false labor 644.1 ☑
    high-risk V23.9
      specified problem NEC V23.89
  unwanted NEC V61.7

Pregnant uterus — *see* condition
Preiser's disease (osteoporosis) 733.09
Prekwashiorkor 260
Preleukemia 238.7
Preluxation of hip, congenital (*see also*
    Subluxation, congenital, hip) 754.32
Premature — *see also* condition
  beats (nodal) 427.60
    atrial 427.61
    auricular 427.61
    postoperative 997.1
    specified type NEC 427.69
    supraventricular 427.61
    ventricular 427.69
  birth NEC 765.1 ☑

Premature — *see also* condition — *continued*
  closure
    cranial suture 756.0
    fontanel 756.0
    foramen ovale 745.8
  contractions 427.60
    atrial 427.61
    auricular 427.61
    auriculoventricular 427.61
    heart (extrasystole) 427.60
    junctional 427.60
    nodal 427.60
    postoperative 997.1
    ventricular 427.69
  ejaculation 302.75
  infant NEC 765.1 ☑
    excessive 765.0 ☑
    light-for-dates — *see* Light-for-dates
  labor 644.2 ☑
    threatened 644.0 ☑
  lungs 770.4
  menopause 256.31
  puberty 259.1
  rupture of membranes or amnion 658.1 ☑
    affecting fetus or newborn 761.1
    delayed delivery following 658.2 ☑
  senility (syndrome) 259.8
  separation, placenta (partial) — *see* Placenta,
      separation
  ventricular systole 427.69
Prematurity NEC 765.1 ☑
  extreme 765.0 ☑
Premenstrual syndrome 625.4
Premenstrual tension 625.4
Premolarization, cuspids 520.2
Premyeloma 273.1
Prenatal
  care, normal pregnancy V22.1
    first V22.0
  death, cause unknown — *see* Death, fetus
  screening — *see* Antenatal, screening
Prepartum — *see* condition
Preponderance, left or right ventricular 429.3
Prepuce — *see* condition
Presbycardia 797
  hypertensive (*see also* Hypertension, heart)
    402.90
Presbycusis 388.01
Presbyesophagus 530.89
Presbyophrenia 310.1
Presbyopia 367.4
Prescription of contraceptives NEC V25.02
  diaphragm V25.02
  oral (pill) V25.01
    emergency V25.03
    postcoital V25.03
    repeat V25.41
  repeat V25.40
    oral (pill) V25.41
Presenile — *see also* condition
  aging 259.8
  dementia (*see also* Dementia, presenile) 290.10
Presenility 259.8
Presentation, fetal
  abnormal 652.9 ☑
    with successful version 652.1 ☑
    before labor, affecting fetus or newborn
      761.7
    causing obstructed labor 660.0 ☑
      affecting fetus or newborn, any, except
        breech 763.1
    in multiple gestation (one or more) 652.6 ☑
    specified NEC 652.8 ☑
  arm 652.7 ☑
    causing obstructed labor 660.0 ☑
  breech (buttocks) (complete) (frank) 652.2 ☑
    with successful version 652.1 ☑
    before labor, affecting fetus or newborn
      761.7
    before labor, affecting fetus or newborn
      761.7
  brow 652.4 ☑
    causing obstructed labor 660.0 ☑

Presentation, fetal — *continued*
  buttocks 652.2 ☑
  chin 652.4 ☑
  complete 652.2 ☑
  compound 652.8 ☑
  cord 663.0 ☑
  extended head 652.4 ☑
  face 652.4 ☑
    to pubes 652.8 ☑
  footling 652.8 ☑
  frank 652.2 ☑
  hand, leg, or foot NEC 652.8 ☑
  incomplete 652.8 ☑
  mentum 652.4 ☑
  multiple gestation (one fetus or more) 652.6 ☑
  oblique 652.3 ☑
    with successful version 652.1 ☑
  shoulder 652.8 ☑
    affecting fetus or newborn 763.1
  transverse 652.3 ☑
    with successful version 652.1 ☑
  umbilical cord 663.0 ☑
  unstable 652.0 ☑
Prespondylolisthesis (congenital) (lumbosacral)
    756.11
Pressure
  area, skin ulcer (*see also* Decubitus) 707.00
  atrophy, spine 733.99
  birth, fetus or newborn NEC 767.9
  brachial plexus 353.0
  brain 348.4
    injury at birth 767.0
  cerebral — *see* Pressure, brain
  chest 786.59
  cone, tentorial 348.4
    injury at birth 767.0
  funis — *see* Compression, umbilical cord
  hyposystolic (*see also* Hypotension) 458.9
  increased
    intracranial 781.99
      due to
        benign intracranial hypertension 348.2
        hydrocephalus — *see* hydrocephalus
        injury at birth 767.8
      intraocular 365.00
  lumbosacral plexus 353.1
  mediastinum 519.3
  necrosis (chronic) (skin) (*see also* Decubitus)
    707.00
  nerve — *see* Compression, nerve
  paralysis (*see also* Neuropathy, entrapment)
    355.9
  sore (chronic) (*see also* Decubitus) 707.00
  spinal cord 336.9
  ulcer (chronic) (*see also* Decubitus) 707.00
  umbilical cord — *see* Compression, umbilical
    cord
  venous, increased 459.89
Pre-syncope 780.2
Preterm infant NEC 765.1 ☑
  extreme 765.0 ☑
Priapism (penis) 607.3
Prickling sensation (*see also* Disturbance,
    sensation) 782.0
Prickly heat 705.1
Primary — *see* condition
Primigravida, elderly
  affecting
    fetus or newborn 763.89
    management of pregnancy, labor, and
      delivery 659.5 ☑
Primipara, old
  affecting
    fetus or newborn 763.89
    management of pregnancy, labor, and
      delivery 659.5 ☑
Primula dermatitis 692.6
Primus varus (bilateral) (metatarsus) 754.52
P.R.I.N.D. 436
Pringle's disease (tuberous sclerosis) 759.5
Prinzmetal's angina 413.1
Prinzmetal-Massumi syndrome (anterior chest
    wall) 786.52
Prizefighter ear 738.7

Problem (with) V49.9
  academic V62.3
  acculturation V62.4
  adopted child V61.29
  aged
    in-law V61.3
    parent V61.3
    person NEC V61.8
  alcoholism in family V61.41
  anger reaction (*see also* Disturbance, conduct)
    312.0 ☑
  behavior, child 312.9
  behavioral V40.9
    specified NEC V40.3
  betting V69.3
  cardiorespiratory NEC V47.2
  care of sick or handicapped person in family or
    household V61.49
  career choice V62.2
  communication V40.1
  conscience regarding medical care V62.6
  delinquency (juvenile) 312.9
  diet, inappropriate V69.1
  digestive NEC V47.3
  ear NEC V41.3
  eating habits, inappropriate V69.1
  economic V60.2
    affecting care V60.9
      specified type NEC V60.8
  educational V62.3
  enuresis, child 307.6
  exercise, lack of V69.0
  eye NEC V41.1
  family V61.9
    specified circumstance NEC V61.8
  fear reaction, child 313.0
  feeding (elderly) (infant) 783.3
    newborn 779.3
    nonorganic 307.59 ▲
  fetal, affecting management of pregnancy
    656.9 ☑
    specified type NEC 656.8 ☑
  financial V60.2
  foster child V61.29
    specified NEC V41.8
  functional V41.9
    specified type NEC V41.8
  gambling V69.3
  genital NEC V47.5
  head V48.9
    deficiency V48.0
    disfigurement V48.6
    mechanical V48.2
    motor V48.2
    movement of V48.2
    sensory V48.4
    specified condition NEC V48.8
  hearing V41.2
  high-risk sexual behavior V69.2
  identity 313.82
  influencing health status NEC V49.89
  internal organ NEC V47.9
    deficiency V47.0
    mechanical or motor V47.1
  interpersonal NEC V62.81
  jealousy, child 313.3
  learning V40.0
  legal V62.5
  life circumstance NEC V62.89
  lifestyle V69.9
    specified NEC V69.8
  limb V49.9
    deficiency V49.0
    disfigurement V49.4
    mechanical V49.1
    motor V49.2
    movement, involving
      musculoskeletal system V49.1
      nervous system V49.2
    sensory V49.3
    specified condition NEC V49.5
  litigation V62.5
  living alone V60.3
  loneliness NEC V62.89
  marital V61.10
    involving
      divorce V61.0

Problem (with) — *continued*
  marital — *continued*
    involving — *continued*
      estrangement V61.0
      psychosexual disorder 302.9
      sexual function V41.7
    relationship V61.10 ●
  mastication V41.6
  medical care, within family V61.49
  mental V40.9
    specified NEC V40.2
  mental hygiene, adult V40.9
  multiparity V61.5
  nail biting, child 307.9
  neck V48.9
    deficiency V48.1
    disfigurement V48.7
    mechanical V48.3
    motor V48.3
    movement V48.3
    sensory V48.5
    specified condition NEC V48.8
  neurological NEC 781.99
  none (feared complaint unfounded) V65.5
  occupational V62.2
  parent-child V61.20
    relationship V61.20 ●
  partner V61.10
    relationship V61.10 ●
  personal NEC V62.89
    interpersonal conflict NEC V62.81
  personality (*see also* Disorder, personality) 301.9
  phase of life V62.89
  placenta, affecting management of pregnancy
    656.9 ☑
    specified type NEC 656.8 ☑
  poverty V60.2
  presence of sick or handicapped person in
    family or household V61.49
  psychiatric 300.9
  psychosocial V62.9
    specified type NEC V62.89
  relational NEC V62.81
  relationship, childhood 313.3
  religious or spiritual belief
    other than medical care V62.89
    regarding medical care V62.6
  self-damaging behavior V69.8
  sexual
    behavior, high-risk V69.2
    function NEC V41.7
  sibling
    relational V61.8 ●
    relationship V61.8 ●
  sight V41.0
  sleep, lack of V69.4
  sleep disorder, child 307.40
  smell V41.5
  speech V40.1
  spite reaction, child (*see also* Disturbance,
    conduct) 312.0 ☑
  spoiled child reaction (*see also* Disturbance,
    conduct) 312.1 ☑
  swallowing V41.6
  tantrum, child (*see also* Disturbance, conduct)
    312.1 ☑
  taste V41.5
  thumb sucking, child 307.9
  tic (child) 307.21
  trunk V48.9
    deficiency V48.1
    disfigurement V48.7
    mechanical V48.3
    motor V48.3
    movement V48.3
    sensory V48.5
    specified condition NEC V48.8
  unemployment V62.0
  urinary NEC V47.4
  voice production V41.4
Procedure (surgical) **not done** NEC V64.3
  because of
    contraindication V64.1
    patient's decision V64.2
      for reasons of conscience or religion
        V62.6
    specified reason NEC V64.3

Procidentia
  anus (sphincter) 569.1
  rectum (sphincter) 569.1
  stomach 537.89
  uteri 618.1
Proctalgia 569.42
  fugax 564.6
  spasmodic 564.6
    psychogenic 307.89
Proctitis 569.49
  amebic 006.8
  chlamydial 099.52
  gonococcal 098.7
  granulomatous 555.1
  idiopathic 556.2
    with ulcerative sigmoiditis 556.3
  tuberculous (*see also* Tuberculosis) 014.8 ☑
  ulcerative (chronic) (nonspecific) 556.2
    with ulcerative sigmoiditis 556.3
Proctocele
  female (without uterine prolapse) 618.04
    with uterine prolapse 618.4
      complete 618.3
      incomplete 618.2
  male 569.49
Proctocolitis, idiopathic 556.2
  with ulcerative sigmoiditis 556.3
Proctoptosis 569.1
Proctosigmoiditis 569.89
  ulcerative (chronic) 556.3
Proctospasm 564.6
  psychogenic 306.4
Prodromal-AIDS — *see* Human immunodeficiency
  virus (disease) (illness) (infection)
Profichet's disease or syndrome 729.9
Progeria (adultorum) (syndrome) 259.8
Prognathism (mandibular) (maxillary) 524.10
Prognoma (melanotic) (M9363/0) — *see*
  Neoplasm, by site, benign
Progressive — *see* condition
Prolapse, prolapsed
  anus, anal (canal) (sphincter) 569.1
  arm or hand, complicating delivery 652.7 ☑
    causing obstructed labor 660.0 ☑
      affecting fetus or newborn 763.1
    fetus or newborn 763.1
  bladder (acquired) (mucosa) (sphincter)
    congenital (female) (male) 756.71
    female (*see also* Cystocele, female) 618.01
    male 596.8
  breast implant (prosthetic) 996.54
  cecostomy 569.69
  cecum 569.89
  cervix, cervical (stump) (hypertrophied) 618.1
    anterior lip, obstructing labor 660.2 ☑
      affecting fetus or newborn 763.1
    congenital 752.49
    postpartal (old) 618.1
  ciliary body 871.1
  colon (pedunculated) 569.89
  colostomy 569.69
  conjunctiva 372.73
  cord — *see* Prolapse, umbilical cord
  disc (intervertebral) — *see* Displacement,
    intervertebral disc
  duodenum 537.89
  eye implant (orbital) 996.59
    lens (ocular) 996.53
  fallopian tube 620.4
  fetal extremity, complicating delivery 652.8 ☑
    causing obstructed labor 660.0 ☑
    fetus or newborn 763.1
  funis — *see* Prolapse, umbilical cord
  gastric (mucosa) 537.89
  genital, female 618.9
    specified NEC 618.89
  globe 360.81
  ileostomy bud 569.69
  intervertebral disc — *see* Displacement,
    intervertebral disc
  intestine (small) 569.89
  iris 364.8
    traumatic 871.1

Index

Prolapse, prolapsed — Pseudocyst

Prolapse, prolapsed — *continued*
kidney (*see also* Disease, renal) 593.0
  congenital 753.3
laryngeal muscles or ventricle 478.79
leg, complicating delivery 652.8 ☑
  causing obstructed labor 660.0 ☑
  fetus or newborn 763.1
liver 573.8
meatus urinarius 599.5
mitral valve 424.0
ocular lens implant 996.53
organ or site, congenital NEC — *see*
  Malposition, congenital
ovary 620.4
pelvic (floor), female 618.89
perineum, female 618.89
pregnant uterus 654.4 ☑
rectum (mucosa) (sphincter) 569.1
  due to Trichuris trichiuria 127.3
spleen 289.59
stomach 537.89
umbilical cord
  affecting fetus or newborn 762.4
  complicating delivery 663.0 ☑
ureter 593.89
  with obstruction 593.4
ureterovesical orifice 593.89
urethra (acquired) (infected) (mucosa) 599.5
  congenital 753.8
uterovaginal 618.4
  complete 618.3
  incomplete 618.2
  specified NEC 618.89
uterus (first degree) (second degree) (third
  degree) (complete) (without vaginal wall
  prolapse) 618.1
  with mention of vaginal wall prolapse — *see*
    Prolapse, uterovaginal
  congenital 752.3
  in pregnancy or childbirth 654.4 ☑
    affecting fetus or newborn 763.1
    causing obstructed labor 660.2 ☑
      affecting fetus or newborn 763.1
  postpartal (old) 618.1
uveal 871.1
vagina (anterior) (posterior) (vault) (wall)
  (without uterine prolapse) 618.00
  with uterine prolapse 618.4
    complete 618.3
    incomplete 618.2
  paravaginal 618.02
  posthysterectomy 618.5
  specified NEC 618.09
vitreous (humor) 379.26
  traumatic 871.1
womb — *see* Prolapse, uterus
Prolapsus, female 618.9
Proliferative — *see* condition
Prolinemia 270.8
Prolinuria 270.8
Prolonged, prolongation
bleeding time (*see also* Defect, coagulation)
  790.92
  "idiopathic" (in von Willebrand's disease)
    286.4
coagulation time (*see also* Defect, coagulation)
  790.92
gestation syndrome 766.22
labor 662.1 ☑
  affecting fetus or newborn 763.89
  first stage 662.0 ☑
  second stage 662.2 ☑
  pregnancy 645.2 ☑
PR interval 426.11
prothrombin time (*see also* Defect, coagulation)
  790.92
QT interval 794.31
  syndrome 426.82
rupture of membranes (24 hours or more prior
  to onset of labor) 658.2 ☑
uterine contractions in labor 661.4 ☑
  affecting fetus or newborn 763.7
Prominauris 744.29
Prominence
auricle (ear) (congenital) 744.29
  acquired 380.32

Prominence — *continued*
ischial spine or sacral promontory
  with disproportion (fetopelvic) 653.3 ☑
    affecting fetus or newborn 763.1
    causing obstructed labor 660.1 ☑
      affecting fetus or newborn 763.1
nose (congenital) 748.1
  acquired 738.0
Pronation
ankle 736.79
foot 736.79
  congenital 755.67
Prophylactic
administration of
  antibiotics V07.39
  antitoxin, any V07.2
  antivenin V07.2
  chemotherapeutic agent NEC V07.39
    fluoride V07.31
  diphtheria antitoxin V07.2
  gamma globulin V07.2
  immune sera (gamma globulin) V07.2
  RhoGAM V07.2
  tetanus antitoxin V07.2
chemotherapy NEC V07.39
  fluoride V07.31
hormone replacement (postmenopausal) V07.4
immunotherapy V07.2
measure V07.9
  specified type NEC V07.8
postmenopausal hormone replacement V07.4
sterilization V25.2
Proptosis (ocular) (*see also* Exophthalmos) 376.30
thyroid 242.0 ☑
Propulsion
eyeball 360.81
Prosecution, anxiety concerning V62.5
Prostate, prostatic — *see* condition
Prostatism 600.90
with urinary retention 600.91
Prostatitis (congestive) (suppurative) 601.9
acute 601.0
cavitary 601.8
chlamydial 099.54
chronic 601.1
diverticular 601.8
due to Trichomonas (vaginalis) 131.03
fibrous 600.90
  with urinary retention 600.91
gonococcal (acute) 098.12
  chronic or duration of 2 months or over
    098.32
granulomatous 601.8
hypertrophic 600.00
  with urinary retention 600.01
specified type NEC 601.8
subacute 601.1
trichomonal 131.03
tuberculous (*see also* Tuberculosis)
  016.5 ☑ [601.4]
Prostatocystitis 601.3
Prostatorrhea 602.8
Prostatoseminovesiculitis, trichomonal 131.03
Prostration 780.79
heat 992.5
  anhydrotic 992.3
  due to
    salt (and water) depletion 992.4
    water depletion 992.3
nervous 300.5
newborn 779.89
senile 797
Protanomaly 368.51
Protanopia (anomalous trichromat) (complete)
  (incomplete) 368.51
Protein
deficiency 260
malnutrition 260
sickness (prophylactic) (therapeutic) 999.5
Proteinemia 790.99
Proteinosis
alveolar, lung or pulmonary 516.0
lipid 272.8

Proteinosis — *continued*
lipoid (of Urbach) 272.8
Proteinuria (*see also* Albuminuria) 791.0
Bence-Jones NEC 791.0
gestational 646.2 ☑
  with hypertension — *see* Toxemia, of
    pregnancy
orthostatic 593.6
postural 593.6
Proteolysis, pathologic 286.6
Protocoproporphyria 277.1
Protoporphyria (erythrohepatic) (erythropoietic)
  277.1
Protrusio acetabuli 718.65
Protrusion
acetabulum (into pelvis) 718.65
device, implant, or graft — *see* Complications,
  mechanical
ear, congenital 744.29
intervertebral disc — *see* Displacement,
  intervertebral disc
nucleus pulposus — *see* Displacement,
  intervertebral disc
Proud flesh 701.5
Prune belly (syndrome) 756.71
Prurigo (ferox) (gravis) (Hebra's) (hebrae) (mitis)
  (simplex) 698.2
agria 698.3
asthma syndrome 691.8
Besnier's (atopic dermatitis) (infantile eczema)
  691.8
eczematodes allergicum 691.8
estivalis (Hutchinson's) 692.72
Hutchinson's 692.72
nodularis 698.3
psychogenic 306.3
Pruritus, pruritic 698.9
ani 698.0
  psychogenic 306.3
conditions NEC 698.9
  psychogenic 306.3
due to Onchocerca volvulus 125.3
ear 698.9
essential 698.9
genital organ(s) 698.1
  psychogenic 306.3
gravidarum 646.8 ☑
hiemalis 698.8
neurogenic (any site) 306.3
perianal 698.0
psychogenic (any site) 306.3
scrotum 698.1
  psychogenic 306.3
senile, senilis 698.8
Trichomonas 131.9
vulva, vulvae 698.1
  psychogenic 306.3
Psammocarcinoma (M8140/3) — *see* Neoplasm,
  by site, malignant
Pseudarthrosis, pseudoarthrosis (bone) 733.82
joint following fusion V45.4
Pseudoacanthosis
nigricans 701.8
Pseudoaneurysm — *see* Aneurysm
Pseudoangina (pectoris) — *see* Angina
Pseudoangioma 452
Pseudo-Argyll-Robertson pupil 379.45
Pseudoarteriosus 747.89
Pseudoarthrosis — *see* Pseudarthrosis
Pseudoataxia 799.89
Pseudobulbar affect (PBA) 310.8 ●
Pseudobursa 727.89
Pseudocholera 025
Pseudochromidrosis 705.89
Pseudocirrhosis, liver, pericardial 423.2
Pseudocoarctation 747.21
Pseudocowpox 051.1
Pseudocoxalgia 732.1
Pseudocroup 478.75
Pseudocyesis 300.11
Pseudocyst
lung 518.89

Pseudocyst — *continued*
  pancreas 577.2
  retina 361.19
Pseudodementia 300.16
Pseudoelephantiasis neuroarthritica 757.0
Pseudoemphysema 518.89
Pseudoencephalitis
  superior (acute) hemorrhagic 265.1
Pseudoerosion cervix, congenital 752.49
Pseudoexfoliation, lens capsule 366.11
Pseudofracture (idiopathic) (multiple)
  (spontaneous) (symmetrical) 268.2
Pseudoglanders 025
Pseudoglioma 360.44
Pseudogout — *see* Chondrocalcinosis
Pseudohallucination 780.1
Pseudohemianesthesia 782.0
Pseudohemophilia (Bernuth's) (hereditary)
  (type B) 286.4
  type A 287.8
  vascular 287.8
Pseudohermaphroditism 752.7
  with chromosomal anomaly — *see* Anomaly,
    chromosomal
  adrenal 255.2
  female (without adrenocortical disorder) 752.7
    with adrenocortical disorder 255.2
    adrenal 255.2
  male (without gonadal disorder) 752.7
    with
      adrenocortical disorder 255.2
      cleft scrotum 752.7
      feminizing testis 259.5   ▲
      gonadal disorder 257.9
    adrenal 255.2
Pseudohole, macula 362.54
Pseudo-Hurler's disease (mucolipidosis III) 272.7
Pseudohydrocephalus 348.2
Pseudohypertrophic muscular dystrophy (Erb's)
  359.1
Pseudohypertrophy, muscle 359.1
Pseudohypoparathyroidism 275.49
Pseudoinfluenza 487.1
Pseudoinsomnia 307.49
Pseudoleukemia 288.8
  infantile 285.8
Pseudomembranous — *see* condition
Pseudomeningocele (cerebral) (infective) 349.2
  postprocedural 997.01   ●
  spinal 349.2
Pseudomenstruation 626.8
Pseudomucinous
  cyst (ovary) (M8470/0) 220
  peritoneum 568.89
Pseudomyeloma 273.1
Pseudomyxoma peritonei (M8480/6) 197.6
Pseudoneuritis optic (nerve) 377.24
  papilla 377.24
  congenital 743.57
Pseudoneuroma — *see* Injury, nerve, by site
Pseudo-obstruction
  intestine (chronic) (idiopathic) (intermittent
    secondary) (primary) 564.89
  acute 560.89
Pseudopapilledema 377.24
Pseudoparalysis
  arm or leg 781.4
  atonic, congenital 358.8
Pseudopelade 704.09
Pseudophakia V43.1
Pseudopolycythemia 289.0
Pseudopolyposis, colon 556.4
Pseudoporencephaly 348.0
Pseudopseudohypoparathyroidism 275.49
Pseudopsychosis 300.16
Pseudopterygium 372.52
Pseudoptosis (eyelid) 374.34
Pseudorabies 078.89

Pseudoretinitis, pigmentosa 362.65
Pseudorickets 588.0
  senile (Pozzi's) 731.0
Pseudorubella 057.8
Pseudoscarlatina 057.8
Pseudosclerema 778.1
Pseudosclerosis (brain)
  Jakob's 046.1
  of Westphal (-Strümpell) (hepatolenticular
    degeneration) 275.1
  spastic 046.1
    with dementia
      with behavioral disturbance 046.1
        [294.11]
      without behavioral disturbance 046.1
        [294.10]
Pseudoseizure 780.39
  non-psychiatric 780.39
  psychiatric 300.11
Pseudotabes 799.89
  diabetic 250.6 ☑ *[337.1]*
Pseudotetanus (*see also* Convulsions) 780.39
Pseudotetany 781.7
  hysterical 300.11
Pseudothalassemia 285.0
Pseudotrichinosis 710.3
Pseudotruncus arteriosus 747.29
Pseudotuberculosis, pasteurella (infection) 027.2
Pseudotumor
  cerebri 348.2
  orbit (inflammatory) 376.11
Pseudo-Turner's syndrome 759.89
Pseudoxanthoma elasticum 757.39
Psilosis (sprue) (tropical) 579.1
  Monilia 112.89
  nontropical 579.0
  not sprue 704.00
Psittacosis 073.9
Psoitis 728.89
Psora NEC 696.1
Psoriasis 696.1
  any type, except arthropathic 696.1
  arthritic, arthropathic 696.0
  buccal 528.6
  flexural 696.1
  follicularis 696.1
  guttate 696.1
  inverse 696.1
  mouth 528.6
  nummularis 696.1
  psychogenic 316 *[696.1]*
  punctata 696.1
  pustular 696.1
  rupioides 696.1
  vulgaris 696.1
Psorospermiasis 136.4
Psorospermosis 136.4
  follicularis (vegetans) 757.39
Psychalgia 307.80
Psychasthenia 300.89
  compulsive 300.3
  mixed compulsive states 300.3
  obsession 300.3
Psychiatric disorder or problem NEC 300.9
Psychogenic — *see also* condition
  factors associated with physical conditions 316
Psychoneurosis, psychoneurotic (*see also*
  Neurosis) 300.9
  anxiety (state) 300.00
  climacteric 627.2
  compensation 300.16
  compulsion 300.3
  conversion hysteria 300.11
  depersonalization 300.6
  depressive type 300.4
  dissociative hysteria 300.15
  hypochondriacal 300.7
  hysteria 300.10
    conversion type 300.11
    dissociative type 300.15
  mixed NEC 300.89
  neurasthenic 300.5

Psychoneurosis, psychoneurotic — *continued*
  obsessional 300.3
  obsessive-compulsive 300.3
  occupational 300.89
  personality NEC 301.89
  phobia 300.20
  senile NEC 300.89
Psychopathic — *see also* condition
  constitution, posttraumatic 310.2
    with psychosis 293.9
  personality 301.9
    amoral trends 301.7
    antisocial trends 301.7
    asocial trends 301.7
    mixed types 301.7
  state 301.9
Psychopathy, sexual (*see also* Deviation, sexual)
  302.9
Psychophysiologic, psychophysiological
  condition — *see* Reaction,
  psychophysiologic
Psychose passionelle 297.8
Psychosexual identity disorder 302.6
  adult-life 302.85
  childhood 302.6
Psychosis 298.9
  acute hysterical 298.1
  affecting management of pregnancy, childbirth,
    or puerperium 648.4 ☑
  affective (*see also* Disorder, mood) 296.90

Note — Use the following fifth-digit subclassification with categories 296.0-296.6:
0   unspecified
1   mild
2   moderate
3   severe, without mention of psychotic behavior
4   severe, specified as with psychotic behavior
5   in partial or unspecified remission
6   in full remission

  drug-induced 292.84
  due to or associated with physical condition
    293.83
  involutional 296.2 ☑
    recurrent episode 296.3 ☑
    single episode 296.2 ☑
  manic-depressive 296.80
    circular (alternating) 296.7
      currently depressed 296.5 ☑
      currently manic 296.4 ☑
    depressed type 296.2 ☑
      atypical 296.82
      recurrent episode 296.3 ☑
      single episode 296.2 ☑
    manic 296.0 ☑
      atypical 296.81
      recurrent episode 296.1 ☑
      single episode 296.0 ☑
    mixed type NEC 296.89
    specified type NEC 296.89
  senile 290.21
  specified type NEC 296.99
  alcoholic 291.9
    with
      anxiety 291.89
      delirium tremens 291.0
      delusions 291.5
      dementia 291.2
      hallucinosis 291.3
      mood disturbance 291.89
      jealousy 291.5
      paranoia 291.5
      persisting amnesia 291.1
      sexual dysfunction 291.89
      sleep disturbance 291.89
    amnestic confabulatory 291.1
    delirium tremens 291.0
    hallucinosis 291.3
    Korsakoff's, Korsakov's, Korsakow's 291.1
    paranoid type 291.5
    pathological intoxication 291.4

☑ Additional Digit Required — Refer to the Tabular List (Numeric Code Section) for Additional Digit Selection

Psychosis — *continued*
alcoholic — *continued*
polyneuritic 291.1
specified type NEC 291.89
alternating (*see also* Psychosis, manic-depressive, circular) 296.7
anergastic (*see also* Psychosis, organic) 294.9
arteriosclerotic 290.40
with
acute confusional state 290.41
delirium 290.41
delusions 290.42
depressed mood 290.43
depressed type 290.43
paranoid type 290.42
simple type 290.40
uncomplicated 290.40
atypical 298.9
depressive 296.82
manic 296.81
borderline (schizophrenia) (*see also* Schizophrenia) 295.5 ☑
of childhood (*see also* Psychosis, childhood) 299.8 ☑
prepubertal 299.8 ☑
brief reactive 298.8
childhood, with origin specific to 299.9 ☑

Note — Use the following fifth-digit subclassification with category 299:

0   current or active state
1   residual state

atypical 299.8 ☑
specified type NEC 299.8 ☑
circular (*see also* Psychosis, manic-depressive, circular) 296.7
climacteric (*see also* Psychosis, involutional) 298.8
confusional 298.9
acute 293.0
reactive 298.2
subacute 293.1
depressive (*see also* Psychosis, affective) 296.2 ☑
atypical 296.82
involutional 296.2 ☑
with hypomania (bipolar II) 296.89
recurrent episode 296.3 ☑
single episode 296.2 ☑
psychogenic 298.0
reactive (emotional stress) (psychological trauma) 298.0
recurrent episode 296.3 ☑
with hypomania (bipolar II) 296.89
single episode 296.2 ☑
disintegrative, childhood (*see also* Psychosis, childhood) 299.1 ☑
drug 292.9
with
affective syndrome 292.84
amnestic syndrome 292.83
anxiety 292.89
delirium 292.81
withdrawal 292.0
delusions 292.11
dementia 292.82
depressive state 292.84
hallucinations 292.12
hallucinosis 292.12
mood disorder 292.84
mood disturbance 292.84
organic personality syndrome NEC 292.89
sexual dysfunction 292.89
sleep disturbance 292.89
withdrawal syndrome (and delirium) 292.0
affective syndrome 292.84
delusions 292.11
hallucinatory state 292.12
hallucinosis 292.12
paranoid state 292.11
specified type NEC 292.89
withdrawal syndrome (and delirium) 292.0
due to or associated with physical condition (*see also* Psychosis, organic) 293.9

Psychosis — *continued*
epileptic NEC 294.8
excitation (psychogenic) (reactive) 298.1
exhaustive (*see also* Reaction, stress, acute) 308.9
hypomanic (*see also* Psychosis, affective) 296.0 ☑
recurrent episode 296.1 ☑
single episode 296.0 ☑
hysterical 298.8
acute 298.1
incipient 298.8
schizophrenic (*see also* Schizophrenia) 295.5 ☑
induced 297.3
infantile (*see also* Psychosis, childhood) 299.0 ☑
infective 293.9
acute 293.0
subacute 293.1
in
conditions classified elsewhere
with
delusions 293.81
hallucinations 293.82
pregnancy, childbirth, or puerperium 648.4 ☑
interactional (childhood) (*see also* Psychosis, childhood) 299.1 ☑
involutional 298.8
depressive (*see also* Psychosis, affective) 296.2 ☑
recurrent episode 296.3 ☑
single episode 296.2 ☑
melancholic 296.2 ☑
recurrent episode 296.3 ☑
single episode 296.2 ☑
paranoid state 297.2
paraphrenia 297.2
Korsakoff's, Korakov's, Korsakow's (nonalcoholic) 294.0
alcoholic 291.1
mania (phase) (*see also* Psychosis, affective) 296.0 ☑
recurrent episode 296.1 ☑
single episode 296.0 ☑
manic (*see also* Psychosis, affective) 296.0 ☑
atypical 296.81
recurrent episode 296.1 ☑
single episode 296.0 ☑
manic-depressive 296.80
circular 296.7
currently
depressed 296.5 ☑
manic 296.4 ☑
mixed 296.6 ☑
depressive 296.2 ☑
recurrent episode 296.3 ☑
with hypomania (bipolar II) 296.89
single episode 296.2 ☑
hypomanic 296.0 ☑
recurrent episode 296.1 ☑
single episode 296.0 ☑
manic 296.0 ☑
atypical 296.81
recurrent episode 296.1 ☑
single episode 296.0 ☑
mixed NEC 296.89
perplexed 296.89
stuporous 296.89
menopausal (*see also* Psychosis, involutional) 298.8
mixed schizophrenic and affective (*see also* Schizophrenia) 295.7 ☑
multi-infarct (cerebrovascular) (*see also* Psychosis, arteriosclerotic) 290.40
organic NEC 294.9
due to or associated with
addiction
alcohol (*see also* Psychosis, alcoholic) 291.9
drug (*see also* Psychosis, drug) 292.9
alcohol intoxication, acute (*see also* Psychosis, alcoholic) 291.9
alcoholism (*see also* Psychosis, alcoholic) 291.9
arteriosclerosis (cerebral) (*see also* Psychosis, arteriosclerotic) 290.40

Psychosis — *continued*
organic NEC — *continued*
due to or associated with — *continued*
cerebrovascular disease
acute (psychosis) 293.0
arteriosclerotic (*see also* Psychosis, arteriosclerotic) 290.40
childbirth — *see* Psychosis, puerperal
dependence
alcohol (*see also* Psychosis, alcoholic) 291.9
drug 292.9
disease
alcoholic liver (*see also* Psychosis, alcoholic) 291.9
brain
arteriosclerotic (*see also* Psychosis, arteriosclerotic) 290.40
cerebrovascular
acute (psychosis) 293.0
arteriosclerotic (*see also* Psychosis, arteriosclerotic) 290.40
endocrine or metabolic 293.9
acute (psychosis) 293.0
subacute (psychosis) 293.1
Jakob-Creutzfeldt ►(new variant)◄
with behavioral disturbance 046.1 [294.11]
without behavioral disturbance 046.1 [294.10]
liver, alcoholic (*see also* Psychosis, alcoholic) 291.9
disorder
cerebrovascular
acute (psychosis) 293.0
endocrine or metabolic 293.9
acute (psychosis) 293.0
subacute (psychosis) 293.1
epilepsy
with behavioral disturbance 345.9 ☑ [294.11]
without behavioral disturbance 345.9 ☑ [294.10]
transient (acute) 293.0
Huntington's chorea
with behavioral disturbance 333.4 [294.11]
without behavioral disturbance 333.4 [294.10]
infection
brain 293.9
acute (psychosis) 293.0
chronic 294.8
subacute (psychosis) 293.1
intracranial NEC 293.9
acute (psychosis) 293.0
chronic 294.8
subacute (psychosis) 293.1
intoxication
alcoholic (acute) (*see also* Psychosis, alcoholic) 291.9
pathological 291.4
drug (*see also* Psychosis, drug) 292.2
ischemia
cerebrovascular (generalized) (*see also* Psychosis, arteriosclerotic) 290.40
Jakob-Creutzfeldt disease ►(syndrome) (new variant)◄
with behavioral disturbance 046.1 [294.11]
without behavioral disturbance 046.1 [294.10]
multiple sclerosis
with behavioral disturbance 340 [294.11]
without behavioral disturbance 340 [294.10]
physical condition NEC 293.9
with
delusions 293.81
hallucinations 293.82
presenility 290.10
puerperium — *see* Psychosis, puerperal
sclerosis, multiple
with behavioral disturbance 340 [294.11]

Psychosis — *continued*
  organic NEC — *continued*
    due to or associated with — *continued*
      sclerosis, multiple — *continued*
        without behavioral disturbance
          340 *[294.10]*
      senility 290.20
      status epilepticus
        with behavioral disturbance
          345.3 *[294.11]*
        without behavioral disturbance
          345.3 *[294.10]*
      trauma
        brain (birth) (from electrical current)
          (surgical) 293.9
          acute (psychosis) 293.0
          chronic 294.8
          subacute (psychosis) 293.1
          unspecified physical condition
            293.9
            with
              delusions 293.81
              hallucinations 293.82
  infective 293.9
    acute (psychosis) 293.0
    subacute 293.1
  posttraumatic 293.9
    acute 293.0
    subacute 293.1
  specified type NEC 294.8
  transient 293.9
    with
      anxiety 293.84
      delusions 293.81
      depression 293.83
      hallucinations 293.82
    depressive type 293.83
    hallucinatory type 293.82
    paranoid type 293.81
    specified type NEC 293.89
 paranoic 297.1
 paranoid (chronic) 297.9
  alcoholic 291.5
  chronic 297.1
  climacteric 297.2
  involutional 297.2
  menopausal 297.2
  protracted reactive 298.4
  psychogenic 298.4
    acute 298.3
  schizophrenic (*see also* Schizophrenia)
    295.3 ☑
  senile 290.20
 paroxysmal 298.9
  senile 290.20
 polyneuritic, alcoholic 291.1
 postoperative 293.9
 postpartum — *see* Psychosis, puerperal
 prepsychotic (*see also* Schizophrenia) 295.5 ☑
 presbyophrenic (type) 290.8
 presenile (*see also* Dementia, presenile) 290.10
 prison 300.16
 psychogenic 298.8
  depressive 298.0
  paranoid 298.4
    acute 298.3
 puerperal
  specified type — *see* categories 295-298 ☑
  unspecified type 293.89
    acute 293.0
    chronic 293.89
    subacute 293.1
 reactive (emotional stress) (psychological
    trauma) 298.8
  brief 298.8
  confusion 298.2
  depressive 298.0
  excitation 298.1
 schizo-affective (depressed) (excited) (*see also*
    Schizophrenia) 295.7 ☑
 schizophrenia, schizophrenic (*see also*
    Schizophrenia) 295.9 ☑
  borderline type 295.5 ☑
    of childhood (*see also* Psychosis,
      childhood) 299.8 ☑
  catatonic (excited) (withdrawn) 295.2 ☑
  childhood type (*see also* Psychosis,
    childhood) 299.9 ☑

Psychosis — *continued*
 schizophrenia, schizophrenic — *continued*
  hebephrenic 295.1 ☑
  incipient 295.5 ☑
  latent 295.5 ☑
  paranoid 295.3 ☑
  prepsychotic 295.5 ☑
  prodromal 295.5 ☑
  pseudoneurotic 295.5 ☑
  pseudopsychopathic 295.5 ☑
  schizophreniform 295.4 ☑
  simple 295.0 ☑
  undifferentiated type 295.9 ☑
 schizophreniform 295.4 ☑
 senile NEC 290.20
  with
    delusional features 290.20
    depressive features 290.21
  depressed type 290.21
  paranoid type 290.20
  simple deterioration 290.20
  specified type — *see* categories 295-298 ☑
 shared 297.3
 situational (reactive) 298.8
 symbiotic (childhood) (*see also* Psychosis,
    childhood) 299.1 ☑
 toxic (acute) 293.9
Psychotic (*see also* condition) 298.9
 episode 298.9
  due to or associated with physical
    conditions (*see also* Psychosis,
    organic) 293.9
Pterygium (eye) 372.40
 central 372.43
 colli 744.5
 double 372.44
 peripheral (stationary) 372.41
  progressive 372.42
 recurrent 372.45
Ptilosis 374.55
Ptomaine (poisoning) (*see also* Poisoning, food)
    005.9
Ptosis (adiposa) 374.30
 breast 611.8
 cecum 569.89
 colon 569.89
 congenital (eyelid) 743.61
  specified site NEC — *see* Anomaly, specified
    type NEC
 epicanthus syndrome 270.2
 eyelid 374.30
  congenital 743.61
  mechanical 374.33
  myogenic 374.32
  paralytic 374.31
 gastric 537.5
 intestine 569.89
 kidney (*see also* Disease, renal) 593.0
  congenital 753.3
 liver 573.8
 renal (*see also* Disease, renal) 593.0
  congenital 753.3
 splanchnic 569.89
 spleen 289.59
 stomach 537.5
 viscera 569.89
Ptyalism 527.7
 hysterical 300.11
 periodic 527.2
 pregnancy 646.8 ☑
 psychogenic 306.4
Ptyalolithiasis 527.5
Pubalgia 848.8
Pubarche, precocious 259.1
Pubertas praecox 259.1
Puberty V21.1
 abnormal 259.9
 bleeding 626.3
 delayed 259.0
 precocious (constitutional) (cryptogenic)
    (idiopathic) NEC 259.1
  due to
    adrenal
      cortical hyperfunction 255.2
      hyperplasia 255.2
    cortical hyperfunction 255.2

Puberty — *continued*
 precocious — *continued*
  due to — *continued*
    ovarian hyperfunction 256.1
      estrogen 256.0
    pineal tumor 259.8
    testicular hyperfunction 257.0
  premature 259.1
    due to
      adrenal cortical hyperfunction 255.2
      pineal tumor 259.8
      pituitary (anterior) hyperfunction 253.1
Puckering, macula 362.56
Pudenda, pudendum — *see* condition
Puente's disease (simple glandular cheilitis)
    528.5
Puerperal
 abscess
  areola 675.1 ☑
  Bartholin's gland 646.6 ☑
  breast 675.1 ☑
  cervix (uteri) 670.0 ☑
  fallopian tube 670.0 ☑
  genital organ 670.0 ☑
  kidney 646.6 ☑
  mammary 675.1 ☑
  mesosalpinx 670.0 ☑
  nabothian 646.6 ☑
  nipple 675.0 ☑
  ovary, ovarian 670.0 ☑
  oviduct 670.0 ☑
  parametric 670.0 ☑
  para-uterine 670.0 ☑
  pelvic 670.0 ☑
  perimetric 670.0 ☑
  periuterine 670.0 ☑
  retro-uterine 670.0 ☑
  subareolar 675.1 ☑
  suprapelvic 670.0 ☑
  tubal (ruptured) 670.0 ☑
  tubo-ovarian 670.0 ☑
  urinary tract NEC 646.6 ☑
  uterine, uterus 670.0 ☑
  vagina (wall) 646.6 ☑
  vaginorectal 646.6 ☑
  vulvovaginal gland 646.6 ☑
 accident 674.9 ☑
 adnexitis 670.0 ☑
 afibrinogenemia, or other coagulation defect
    666.3 ☑
 albuminuria (acute) (subacute) 646.2 ☑
  pre-eclamptic 642.4 ☑
 anemia (conditions classifiable to 280-285)
    648.2 ☑
 anuria 669.3 ☑
 apoplexy 674.0 ☑
 asymptomatic bacteriuria 646.5 ☑
 atrophy, breast 676.3 ☑
 blood dyscrasia 666.3 ☑
 caked breast 676.2 ☑
 cardiomyopathy 674.5 ☑
 cellulitis — *see* Puerperal, abscess
 cerebrovascular disorder (conditions
    classifiable to 430-434, 436-437) 674.0 ☑
 cervicitis (conditions classifiable to 616.0)
    646.6 ☑
 coagulopathy (any) 666.3 ☑
 complications 674.9 ☑
  specified type NEC 674.8 ☑
 convulsions (eclamptic) (uremic) 642.6 ☑
  with pre-existing hypertension 642.7 ☑
 cracked nipple 676.1 ☑
 cystitis 646.6 ☑
 cystopyelitis 646.6 ☑
 deciduitis (acute) 670.0 ☑
 delirium NEC 293.9
 diabetes (mellitus) (conditions classifiable to
    250) 648.0 ☑
 disease 674.9 ☑
  breast NEC 676.3 ☑
  cerebrovascular (acute) 674.0 ☑
  nonobstetric NEC (*see also* Pregnancy,
    complicated, current disease or
    condition) 648.9 ☑
  pelvis inflammatory 670.0 ☑
  renal NEC 646.2 ☑

☑ Additional Digit Required — Refer to the Tabular List (Numeric Code Section) for Additional Digit Selection

Puerperal — *continued*
disease — *continued*
   tubo-ovarian 670.0 ☑
   Valsuani's (progressive pernicious anemia)
       648.2 ☑
disorder
   lactation 676.9 ☑
      specified type NEC 676.8 ☑
   nonobstetric NEC (*see also* Pregnancy,
       complicated, current disease or
       condition) 648.9 ☑
disruption
   cesarean wound 674.1 ☑
   episiotomy wound 674.2 ☑
   perineal laceration wound 674.2 ☑
drug dependence (conditions classifiable to
       304) 648.3 ☑
eclampsia 642.6 ☑
   with pre-existing hypertension 642.7 ☑
embolism (pulmonary) 673.2 ☑
   air 673.0 ☑
   amniotic fluid 673.1 ☑
   blood-clot 673.2 ☑
   brain or cerebral 674.0 ☑
   cardiac 674.8 ☑
   fat 673.8 ☑
   intracranial sinus (venous) 671.5 ☑
   pyemic 673.3 ☑
   septic 673.3 ☑
   spinal cord 671.5 ☑
endometritis (conditions classifiable to 615.0-
       615.9) 670.0 ☑
endophlebitis — *see* Puerperal, phlebitis
endotrachelitis 646.6 ☑
engorgement, breasts 676.2 ☑
erysipelas 670.0 ☑
failure
   lactation 676.4 ☑
   renal, acute 669.3 ☑
fever 670.0 ☑
   meaning pyrexia (of unknown origin)
       672.0 ☑
   meaning sepsis 670.0 ☑
fissure, nipple 676.1 ☑
fistula
   breast 675.1 ☑
   mammary gland 675.1 ☑
   nipple 675.0 ☑
galactophoritis 675.2 ☑
galactorrhea 676.6 ☑
gangrene
   gas 670.0 ☑
   uterus 670.0 ☑
gonorrhea (conditions classifiable to 098)
       647.1 ☑
hematoma, subdural 674.0 ☑
hematosalpinx, infectional 670.0 ☑
hemiplegia, cerebral 674.0 ☑
hemorrhage 666.1 ☑
   brain 674.0 ☑
   bulbar 674.0 ☑
   cerebellar 674.0 ☑
   cerebral 674.0 ☑
   cortical 674.0 ☑
   delayed (after 24 hours) (uterine) 666.2 ☑
   extradural 674.0 ☑
   internal capsule 674.0 ☑
   intracranial 674.0 ☑
   intrapontine 674.0 ☑
   meningeal 674.0 ☑
   pontine 674.0 ☑
   subarachnoid 674.0 ☑
   subcortical 674.0 ☑
   subdural 674.0 ☑
   uterine, delayed 666.2 ☑
   ventricular 674.0 ☑
hemorrhoids 671.8 ☑
hepatorenal syndrome 674.8 ☑
hypertrophy
   breast 676.3 ☑
   mammary gland 676.3 ☑
induration breast (fibrous) 676.3 ☑
infarction
   lung — *see* Puerperal, embolism
   pulmonary — *see* Puerperal, embolism

Puerperal — *continued*
infection
   Bartholin's gland 646.6 ☑
   breast 675.2 ☑
      with nipple 675.9 ☑
         specified type NEC 675.8 ☑
   cervix 646.6 ☑
   endocervix 646.6 ☑
   fallopian tube 670.0 ☑
   generalized 670.0 ☑
   genital tract (major) 670.0 ☑
      minor or localized 646.6 ☑
   kidney (bacillus coli) 646.6 ☑
   mammary gland 675.2 ☑
      with nipple 675.9 ☑
         specified type NEC 675.8 ☑
   nipple 675.0 ☑
      with breast 675.9 ☑
         specified type NEC 675.8 ☑
   ovary 670.0 ☑
   pelvic 670.0 ☑
   peritoneum 670.0 ☑
   renal 646.6 ☑
   tubo-ovarian 670.0 ☑
   urinary (tract) NEC 646.6 ☑
      asymptomatic 646.5 ☑
   uterus, uterine 670.0 ☑
   vagina 646.6 ☑
inflammation — *see also* Puerperal, infection
   areola 675.1 ☑
   Bartholin's gland 646.6 ☑
   breast 675.2 ☑
   broad ligament 670.0 ☑
   cervix (uteri) 646.6 ☑
   fallopian tube 670.0 ☑
   genital organs 670.0 ☑
      localized 646.6 ☑
   mammary gland 675.2 ☑
   nipple 675.0 ☑
   ovary 670.0 ☑
   oviduct 670.0 ☑
   pelvis 670.0 ☑
   periuterine 670.0 ☑
   tubal 670.0 ☑
   vagina 646.6 ☑
   vein — *see* Puerperal, phlebitis
inversion, nipple 676.3 ☑
ischemia, cerebral 674.0 ☑
lymphangitis 670.0 ☑
   breast 675.2 ☑
malaria (conditions classifiable to 084) 647.4 ☑
malnutrition 648.9 ☑
mammillitis 675.0 ☑
mammitis 675.2 ☑
mania 296.0 ☑
   recurrent episode 296.1 ☑
   single episode 296.0 ☑
mastitis 675.2 ☑
   purulent 675.1 ☑
   retromammary 675.1 ☑
   submammary 675.1 ☑
melancholia 296.2 ☑
   recurrent episode 296.3 ☑
   single episode 296.2 ☑
mental disorder (conditions classifiable to 290-
       303, 305-316, 317-319) 648.4 ☑
metritis (septic) (suppurative) 670.0 ☑
metroperitonitis 670.0 ☑
metrorrhagia 666.2 ☑
metrosalpingitis 670.0 ☑
metrovaginitis 670.0 ☑
milk leg 671.4 ☑
monoplegia, cerebral 674.0 ☑
necrosis
   kidney, tubular 669.3 ☑
   liver (acute) (subacute) (conditions
       classifiable to 570) 674.8 ☑
   ovary 670.0 ☑
   renal cortex 669.3 ☑
nephritis or nephrosis (conditions classifiable
       to 580-589) 646.2 ☑
   with hypertension 642.1 ☑
nutritional deficiency (conditions classifiable to
       260-269) 648.9 ☑
occlusion, precerebral artery 674.0 ☑
oliguria 669.3 ☑
oophoritis 670.0 ☑

Puerperal — *continued*
ovaritis 670.0 ☑
paralysis
   bladder (sphincter) 665.5 ☑
   cerebral 674.0 ☑
paralytic stroke 674.0 ☑
parametritis 670.0 ☑
paravaginitis 646.6 ☑
pelviperitonitis 670.0 ☑
perimetritis 670.0 ☑
perimetrosalpingitis 670.0 ☑
perinephritis 646.6 ☑
perioophoritis 670.0 ☑
periphlebitis — *see* Puerperal, phlebitis
perisalpingitis 670.0 ☑
peritoneal infection 670.0 ☑
peritonitis (pelvic) 670.0 ☑
perivaginitis 646.6 ☑
phlebitis 671.9 ☑
   deep 671.4 ☑
   intracranial sinus (venous) 671.5 ☑
   pelvic 671.4 ☑
   specified site NEC 671.5 ☑
   superficial 671.2 ☑
phlegmasia alba dolens 671.4 ☑
placental polyp 674.4 ☑
pneumonia, embolic — *see* Puerperal,
       embolism
prediabetes 648.8 ☑
pre-eclampsia (mild) 642.4 ☑
   with pre-existing hypertension 642.7 ☑
   severe 642.5 ☑
psychosis, unspecified (*see also* Psychosis,
       puerperal) 293.89
pyelitis 646.6 ☑
pyelocystitis 646.6 ☑
pyelohydronephrosis 646.6 ☑
pyelonephritis 646.6 ☑
pyelonephrosis 646.6 ☑
pyemia 670.0 ☑
pyocystitis 646.6 ☑
pyohemia 670.0 ☑
pyometra 670.0 ☑
pyonephritis 646.6 ☑
pyonephrosis 646.6 ☑
pyo-oophoritis 670.0 ☑
pyosalpingitis 670.0 ☑
pyosalpinx 670.0 ☑
pyrexia (of unknown origin) 672.0 ☑
renal
   disease NEC 646.2 ☑
   failure, acute 669.3 ☑
retention
   decidua (fragments) (with delayed
       hemorrhage) 666.2 ☑
      without hemorrhage 667.1 ☑
   placenta (fragments) (with delayed
       hemorrhage) 666.2 ☑
      without hemorrhage 667.1 ☑
   secundines (fragments) (with delayed
       hemorrhage) 666.2 ☑
      without hemorrhage 667.1 ☑
retracted nipple 676.0 ☑
rubella (conditions classifiable to 056) 647.5 ☑
salpingitis 670.0 ☑
salpingo-oophoritis 670.0 ☑
salpingo-ovaritis 670.0 ☑
salpingoperitonitis 670.0 ☑
sapremia 670.0 ☑
secondary perineal tear 674.2 ☑
sepsis (pelvic) 670.0 ☑
septicemia 670.0 ☑
subinvolution (uterus) 674.8 ☑
sudden death (cause unknown) 674.9 ☑
suppuration — *see* Puerperal, abscess
syphilis (conditions classifiable to 090-097)
       647.0 ☑
tetanus 670.0 ☑
thelitis 675.0 ☑
thrombocytopenia 666.3 ☑
thrombophlebitis (superficial) 671.2 ☑
   deep 671.4 ☑
   pelvic 671.4 ☑
   specified site NEC 671.5 ☑
thrombosis (venous) — *see* Thrombosis,
       puerperal

Puerperal — *continued*
  thyroid dysfunction (conditions classifiable to 240-246) 648.1 ☑
  toxemia (*see also* Toxemia, of pregnancy) 642.4 ☑
    eclamptic 642.6 ☑
      with pre-existing hypertension 642.7 ☑
    pre-eclamptic (mild) 642.4 ☑
      with
        convulsions 642.6 ☑
        pre-existing hypertension 642.7 ☑
      severe 642.5 ☑
  tuberculosis (conditions classifiable to 010-018) 647.3 ☑
  uremia 669.3 ☑
  vaginitis (conditions classifiable to 616.1) 646.6 ☑
  varicose veins (legs) 671.0 ☑
    vulva or perineum 671.1 ☑
  vulvitis (conditions classifiable to 616.1) 646.6 ☑
  vulvovaginitis (conditions classifiable to 616.1) 646.6 ☑
  white leg 671.4 ☑
Pulled muscle — *see* Sprain, by site
Pulmolithiasis 518.89
Pulmonary — *see* condition
Pulmonitis (unknown etiology) 486
Pulpitis (acute) (anachoretic) (chronic) (hyperplastic) (putrescent) (suppurative) (ulcerative) 522.0
Pulpless tooth 522.9
Pulse
  alternating 427.89
    psychogenic 306.2
  bigeminal 427.89
  fast 785.0
  feeble, rapid, due to shock following injury 958.4
  rapid 785.0
  slow 427.89
  strong 785.9
  trigeminal 427.89
  water-hammer (*see also* Insufficiency, aortic) 424.1
  weak 785.9
Pulseless disease 446.7
Pulsus
  alternans or trigeminy 427.89
    psychogenic 306.2
Punch drunk 310.2
Puncta lacrimalia occlusion 375.52
Punctiform hymen 752.49
Puncture (traumatic) — *see also* Wound, open, by site
  accidental, complicating surgery 998.2
  bladder, nontraumatic 596.6
  by
    device, implant, or graft — *see* Complications, mechanical
    foreign body
      internal organs — *see also* Injury, internal, by site
        by ingested object — *see* Foreign body
      left accidentally in operation wound 998.4
    instrument (any) during a procedure, accidental 998.2
  internal organs, abdomen, chest, or pelvis — *see* Injury, internal, by site
  kidney, nontraumatic 593.89
Pupil — *see* condition
Pupillary membrane 364.74
  persistent 743.46
Pupillotonia 379.46
  pseudotabetic 379.46
Purpura 287.2
  abdominal 287.0
  allergic 287.0
  anaphylactoid 287.0
  annularis telangiectodes 709.1
  arthritic 287.0
  autoerythrocyte sensitization 287.2
  autoimmune 287.0

Purpura — *continued*
  bacterial 287.0
  Bateman's (senile) 287.2
  capillary fragility (hereditary) (idiopathic) 287.8
  cryoglobulinemic 273.2
  devil's pinches 287.2
  fibrinolytic (*see also* Fibrinolysis) 286.6
  fulminans, fulminous 286.6
  gangrenous 287.0
  hemorrhagic (*see also* Purpura, thrombocytopenic) 287.39   ▲
    nodular 272.7
    nonthrombocytopenic 287.0
    thrombocytopenic 287.39   ▲
  Henoch's (purpura nervosa) 287.0
  Henoch-Schönlein (allergic) 287.0
  hypergammaglobulinemic (benign primary) (Waldenström's) 273.0
  idiopathic 287.31   ▲
    nonthrombocytopenic 287.0
    thrombocytopenic 287.31   ▲
  immune thrombocytopenic 287.31   ●
  infectious 287.0
  malignant 287.0
  neonatorum 772.6
  nervosa 287.0
  newborn NEC 772.6
  nonthrombocytopenic 287.2
    hemorrhagic 287.0
    idiopathic 287.0
  nonthrombopenic 287.2
  peliosis rheumatica 287.0
  pigmentaria, progressiva 709.09
  posttransfusion 287.4
  primary 287.0
  primitive 287.0
  red cell membrane sensitivity 287.2
  rheumatica 287.0
  Schönlein (-Henoch) (allergic) 287.0
  scorbutic 267
  senile 287.2
  simplex 287.2
  symptomatica 287.0
  telangiectasia annularis 709.1
  thrombocytopenic (*see also* Thrombocytopenia) 287.30   ▲
    congenital 287.33   ●
    essential 287.30   ●
    hereditary 287.31   ●
    idiopathic 287.31   ●
    immune 287.31   ●
    neonatal, transitory (*see also* Thrombocytopenia, neonatal transitory) 776.1
    primary 287.30   ●
    puerperal, postpartum 666.3 ☑
    thrombotic 446.6
  thrombohemolytic (*see also* Fibrinolysis) 286.6
  thrombopenic (*see also* Thrombocytopenia) 287.30   ▲
    congenital 287.33   ●
    essential 287.30   ●
    thrombotic 446.6
      thrombocytic 446.6
      thrombocytopenic 446.6
  toxic 287.0
  variolosa 050.0
  vascular 287.0
  visceral symptoms 287.0
  Werlhof's (*see also* Purpura, thrombocytopenic) 287.39   ▲
Purpuric spots 782.7
Purulent — *see* condition
Pus
  absorption, general — *see* Septicemia
  in
    stool 792.1
    urine 791.9
  tube (rupture) (*see also* Salpingo-oophoritis) 614.2
Pustular rash 782.1
Pustule 686.9
  malignant 022.0
  nonmalignant 686.9
Putnam's disease (subacute combined sclerosis with pernicious anemia) 281.0 *[336.2]*

Putnam-Dana syndrome (subacute combined sclerosis with pernicious anemia) 281.0 *[336.2]*
Putrefaction, intestinal 569.89
Putrescent pulp (dental) 522.1
Pyarthritis — *see* Pyarthrosis
Pyarthrosis (*see also* Arthritis, pyogenic) 711.0 ☑
  tuberculous — *see* Tuberculosis, joint
Pycnoepilepsy, pycnolepsy (idiopathic) (*see also* Epilepsy) 345.0 ☑
Pyelectasia 593.89
Pyelectasis 593.89
Pyelitis (congenital) (uremic) 590.80
  with
    abortion — *see* Abortion, by type, with specified complication NEC
    contracted kidney 590.00
    ectopic pregnancy (*see also* categories 633.0-633.9) 639.8
    molar pregnancy (*see also* categories 630-632) 639.8
  acute 590.10
    with renal medullary necrosis 590.11
  chronic 590.00
    with
      renal medullary necrosis 590.01
  complicating pregnancy, childbirth, or puerperium 646.6 ☑
    affecting fetus or newborn 760.1
  cystica 590.3
    following
      abortion 639.8
      ectopic or molar pregnancy 639.8
  gonococcal 098.19
    chronic or duration of 2 months or over 098.39
  tuberculous (*see also* Tuberculosis) 016.0 ☑ *[590.81]*
Pyelocaliectasis 593.89
Pyelocystitis (*see also* Pyelitis) 590.80
Pyelohydronephrosis 591
Pyelonephritis (*see also* Pyelitis) 590.80
  acute 590.10
    with renal medullary necrosis 590.11
  chronic 590.00
  syphilitic (late) 095.4
  tuberculous (*see also* Tuberculosis) 016.0 ☑ *[590.81]*
Pyelonephrosis (*see also* Pyelitis) 590.80
  chronic 590.00
Pyelophlebitis 451.89
Pyelo-ureteritis cystica 590.3
Pyemia, pyemic (purulent) (*see also* Septicemia) 038.9
  abscess — *see* Abscess
  arthritis (*see also* Arthritis, pyogenic) 711.0 ☑
  Bacillus coli 038.42
  embolism — *see* Embolism, pyemic
  fever 038.9
  infection 038.9
  joint (*see also* Arthritis, pyogenic) 711.0 ☑
  liver 572.1
  meningococcal 036.2
  newborn 771.81
  phlebitis — *see* Phlebitis
  pneumococcal 038.2
  portal 572.1
  postvaccinal 999.3
  specified organism NEC 038.8
  staphylococcal 038.10
    aureus 038.11
    specified organism NEC 038.19
  streptococcal 038.0
  tuberculous — *see* Tuberculosis, miliary
Pygopagus 759.4
Pykno-epilepsy, pyknolepsy (idiopathic) (*see also* Epilepsy) 345.0 ☑
Pyle (-Cohn) disease (craniometaphyseal dysplasia) 756.89
Pylephlebitis (suppurative) 572.1
Pylethrombophlebitis 572.1
Pylethrombosis 572.1
Pyloritis (*see also* Gastritis) 535.5 ☑
Pylorospasm (reflex) 537.81
  congenital or infantile 750.5

Pylorospasm — *continued*
  neurotic 306.4
  newborn 750.5
  psychogenic 306.4
Pylorus, pyloric — *see* condition
Pyoarthrosis — *see* Pyarthrosis
Pyocele
  mastoid 383.00
  sinus (accessory) (nasal) (*see also* Sinusitis) 473.9
  turbinate (bone) 473.9
  urethra (*see also* Urethritis) 597.0
Pyococcal dermatitis 686.00
Pyococcide, skin 686.00
Pyocolpos (*see also* Vaginitis) 616.10
Pyocyaneus dermatitis 686.09
Pyocystitis (*see also* Cystitis) 595.9
Pyoderma, pyodermia 686.00
  gangrenosum 686.01
  specified type NEC 686.09
  vegetans 686.8
Pyodermatitis 686.00
  vegetans 686.8
Pyogenic — *see* condition
Pyohemia — *see* Septicemia
Pyohydronephrosis (*see also* Pyelitis) 590.80
Pyometra 615.9
Pyometritis (*see also* Endometritis) 615.9
Pyometrium (*see also* Endometritis) 615.9
Pyomyositis 728.0
  ossificans 728.19
  tropical (bungpagga) 040.81
Pyonephritis (*see also* Pyelitis) 590.80
  chronic 590.00
Pyonephrosis (congenital) (*see also* Pyelitis) 590.80
  acute 590.10
Pyo-oophoritis (*see also* Salpingo-oophoritis) 614.2
Pyo-ovarium (*see also* Salpingo-oophoritis) 614.2
Pyopericarditis 420.99
Pyopericardium 420.99
Pyophlebitis — *see* Phlebitis
Pyopneumopericardium 420.99
Pyopneumothorax (infectional) 510.9
  with fistula 510.0
  subdiaphragmatic (*see also* Peritonitis) 567.29 ▲
  subphrenic (*see also* Peritonitis) 567.29 ▲
  tuberculous (*see also* Tuberculosis, pleura) 012.0 ☑
Pyorrhea (alveolar) (alveolaris) 523.4
  degenerative 523.5
Pyosalpingitis (*see also* Salpingo-oophoritis) 614.2
Pyosalpinx (*see also* Salpingo-oophoritis) 614.2
Pyosepticemia — *see* Septicemia
Pyosis
  Corlett's (impetigo) 684
  Manson's (pemphigus contagiosus) 684
Pyothorax 510.9
  with fistula 510.0
  tuberculous (*see also* Tuberculosis, pleura) 012.0 ☑
Pyoureter 593.89
  tuberculous (*see also* Tuberculosis) 016.2 ☑
Pyramidopallidonigral syndrome 332.0
Pyrexia (of unknown origin) (P.U.O.) 780.6
  atmospheric 992.0
  during labor 659.2 ☑
  environmentally-induced newborn 778.4
  heat 992.0
  newborn, environmentally-induced 778.4
  puerperal 672.0 ☑
Pyroglobulinemia 273.8
Pyromania 312.33
Pyrosis 787.1
Pyrroloporphyria 277.1
Pyuria (bacterial) 791.9

Q

Q fever 083.0
  with pneumonia 083.0 *[484.8]*
Quadricuspid aortic valve 746.89
Quadrilateral fever 083.0
Quadriparesis — *see* Quadriplegia
  meaning muscle weakness 728.87 ●
Quadriplegia 344.00
  with fracture, vertebra (process) — *see* Fracture, vertebra, cervical, with spinal cord injury
  brain (current episode) 437.8
  C1-C4
    complete 344.01
    incomplete 344.02
  C5-C7
    complete 344.03
    incomplete 344.04
  cerebral (current episode) 437.8
  congenital or infantile (cerebral) (spastic) (spinal) 343.2
  cortical 437.8
  embolic (current episode) (*see also* Embolism, brain) 434.1 ☑
  infantile (cerebral) (spastic) (spinal) 343.2
  newborn NEC 767.0
  specified NEC 344.09
  thrombotic (current episode) (*see also* Thrombosis, brain) 434.0 ☑
  traumatic — *see* Injury, spinal, cervical
Quadruplet
  affected by maternal complications of pregnancy 761.5
  healthy liveborn — *see* Newborn, multiple
  pregnancy (complicating delivery) NEC 651.8 ☑
    with fetal loss and retention of one or more fetus(es) 651.5 ☑
    following (elective) fetal reduction 651.7 ☑ ●
       ●
Quarrelsomeness 301.3
Quartan
  fever 084.2
  malaria (fever) 084.2
Queensland fever 083.0
  coastal 083.0
  seven-day 100.89
Quervain's disease 727.04
  thyroid (subacute granulomatous thyroiditis) 245.1
Queyrat's erythroplasia (M8080/2)
  specified site — *see* Neoplasm, skin, in situ
  unspecified site 233.5
Quincke's disease or edema — *see* Edema, angioneurotic
Quinquaud's disease (acne decalvans) 704.09
Quinsy (gangrenous) 475
Quintan fever 083.1
Quintuplet
  affected by maternal complications of pregnancy 761.5
  healthy liveborn — *see* Newborn, multiple
  pregnancy (complicating delivery) NEC 651.2 ☑
    with fetal loss and retention of one or more fetus(es) 651.6 ☑
    following (elective) fetal reduction 651.7 ☑ ●
       ●
Quotidian
  fever 084.0
  malaria (fever) 084.0

R

Rabbia 071
Rabbit fever (*see also* Tularemia) 021.9
Rabies 071
  contact V01.5
  exposure to V01.5
  inoculation V04.5
    reaction — *see* Complications, vaccination
  vaccination, prophylactic (against) V04.5
Rachischisis (*see also* Spina bifida) 741.9 ☑

Rachitic — *see also* condition
  deformities of spine 268.1
  pelvis 268.1
    with disproportion (fetopelvic) 653.2 ☑
      affecting fetus or newborn 763.1
      causing obstructed labor 660.1 ☑
        affecting fetus or newborn 763.1
Rachitis, rachitism — *see also* Rickets
  acute 268.0
  fetalis 756.4
  renalis 588.0
  tarda 268.0
Racket nail 757.5
Radial nerve — *see* condition
Radiation effects or sickness — *see also* Effect, adverse, radiation
  cataract 366.46
  dermatitis 692.82
  sunburn (*see also* Sunburn) 692.71
Radiculitis (pressure) (vertebrogenic) 729.2
  accessory nerve 723.4
  anterior crural 724.4
  arm 723.4
  brachial 723.4
  cervical NEC 723.4
  due to displacement of intervertebral disc — *see* Neuritis, due to, displacement intervertebral disc
  leg 724.4
  lumbar NEC 724.4
  lumbosacral 724.4
  rheumatic 729.2
  syphilitic 094.89
  thoracic (with visceral pain) 724.4
Radiculomyelitis 357.0
  toxic, due to
    Clostridium tetani 037
    Corynebacterium diphtheriae 032.89
Radiculopathy (*see also* Radiculitis) 729.2
Radioactive substances, adverse effect — *see* Effect, adverse, radioactive substance
Radiodermal burns (acute) (chronic) (occupational) — *see* Burn, by site
Radiodermatitis 692.82
Radionecrosis — *see* Effect, adverse, radiation
Radiotherapy session V58.0
Radium, adverse effect — *see* Effect, adverse, radioactive substance
Raeder-Harbitz syndrome (pulseless disease) 446.7
Rage (*see also* Disturbance, conduct) 312.0 ☑
  meaning rabies 071
Rag sorters' disease 022.1
Raillietiniasis 123.8
Railroad neurosis 300.16
Railway spine 300.16
Raised — *see* Elevation
Raiva 071
Rake teeth, tooth 524.39
Rales 786.7
Ramifying renal pelvis 753.3
Ramsay Hunt syndrome (herpetic geniculate ganglionitis) 053.11
  meaning dyssynergia cerebellaris myoclonica 334.2
Ranke's primary infiltration (*see also* Tuberculosis) 010.0 ☑
Ranula 527.6
  congenital 750.26
Rape
  adult 995.83 ●
  alleged, observation or examination V71.5
  child 995.53 ●
Rapid
  feeble pulse, due to shock, following injury 958.4
  heart (beat) 785.0
    psychogenic 306.2
  respiration 786.06
    psychogenic 306.1

Rapid — *continued*
    second stage (delivery) 661.3 ☑
        affecting fetus or newborn 763.6
    time-zone change syndrome 327.35 ▲

Rarefaction, bone 733.99

Rash 782.1
    canker 034.1
    diaper 691.0
    drug (internal use) 693.0
        contact 692.3
    ECHO 9 virus 078.89
    enema 692.89
    food (*see also* Allergy, food) 693.1
    heat 705.1
    napkin 691.0
    nettle 708.8
    pustular 782.1
    rose 782.1
        epidemic 056.9
        of infants 057.8
    scarlet 034.1
    serum (prophylactic) (therapeutic) 999.5
    toxic 782.1
    wandering tongue 529.1

Rasmussen's aneurysm (*see also* Tuberculosis)
    011.2 ☑

Rat-bite fever 026.9
    due to Streptobacillus moniliformis 026.1 ☑
    spirochetal (morsus muris) 026.0 ☑

Rathke's pouch tumor (M9350/1) 237.0

Raymond (-Céstan) syndrome 433.8 ☑

Raynaud's
    disease or syndrome (paroxysmal digital
        cyanosis) 443.0
    gangrene (symmetric) 443.0 *[785.4]*
    phenomenon (paroxysmal digital cyanosis)
        (secondary) 443.0

RDS 769

Reaction
    acute situational maladjustment (*see also*
        Reaction, adjustment) 309.9
    adaptation (*see also* Reaction, adjustment)
        309.9
    adjustment 309.9
        with
            anxious mood 309.24
                with depressed mood 309.28
            conduct disturbance 309.3
                combined with disturbance of
                    emotions 309.4
            depressed mood 309.0
                brief 309.0
                    with anxious mood 309.28
                prolonged 309.1
            elective mutism 309.83
            mixed emotions and conduct 309.4
            mutism, elective 309.83
            physical symptoms 309.82
            predominant disturbance (of)
                conduct 309.3
                emotions NEC 309.29
                    mixed 309.28
                mixed, emotions and conduct 309.4
                specified type NEC 309.89
            specific academic or work inhibition
                309.23
            withdrawal 309.83
        depressive 309.0
            with conduct disturbance 309.4
            brief 309.0
            prolonged 309.1
        specified type NEC 309.89
    adverse food NEC 995.7
    affective (*see also* Psychosis, affective) 296.90
        specified type NEC 296.99
    aggressive 301.3
        unsocialized (*see also* Disturbance, conduct)
            312.0 ☑
    allergic (*see also* Allergy) 995.3
        drug, medicinal substance, and biological —
            see Allergy, drug
        food — *see* Allergy, food
        serum 999.5
    anaphylactic — *see* Shock, anaphylactic
    anesthesia — *see* Anesthesia, complication

Reaction — *continued*
    anger 312.0 ☑
    antisocial 301.7
    antitoxin (prophylactic) (therapeutic) — *see*
        Complications, vaccination
    anxiety 300.00
    asthenic 300.5
    compulsive 300.3
    conversion (anesthetic) (autonomic)
        (hyperkinetic) (mixed paralytic)
        (paresthetic) 300.11
    deoxyribonuclease (DNA) (DNase)
        hypersensitivity NEC 287.2
    depressive 300.4
        acute 309.0
        affective (*see also* Psychosis, affective)
            296.2 ☑
            recurrent episode 296.3 ☑
            single episode 296.2 ☑
        brief 309.0
        manic (*see also* Psychosis, affective) 296.80
        neurotic 300.4
        psychoneurotic 300.4
        psychotic 298.0
    dissociative 300.15
    drug NEC (*see also* Table of Drugs and
        Chemicals) 995.2
        allergic — *see* Allergy, drug
        correct substance properly administered
            995.2
        obstetric anesthetic or analgesic NEC
            668.9 ☑
            affecting fetus or newborn 763.5
            specified drug — *see* Table of Drugs and
                Chemicals
        overdose or poisoning 977.9
            specified drug — *see* Table of Drugs and
                Chemicals
        specific to newborn 779.4
        transmitted via placenta or breast milk —
            see Absorption, drug, through
            placenta
        withdrawal NEC 292.0
            infant of dependent mother 779.5
        wrong substance given or taken in error
            977.9
            specified drug — *see* Table of Drugs and
                Chemicals
    dyssocial 301.7
    erysipeloid 027.1
    fear 300.20
        child 313.0
    fluid loss, cerebrospinal 349.0
    food — *see also* Allergy, food
        adverse NEC 995.7
        anaphylactic shock — *see* Anaphylactic
            shock, due to, food
    foreign
        body NEC 728.82
            in operative wound (inadvertently left)
                998.4
                due to surgical material intentionally
                    left — *see* Complications, due to
                    (presence of) any device, implant,
                    or graft classified to 996.0-996.5
                    NEC
            substance accidentally left during a
                procedure (chemical) (powder) (talc)
                998.7
                body or object (instrument) (sponge)
                    (swab) 998.4
    graft-versus-host (GVH) 996.85
    grief (acute) (brief) 309.0
        prolonged 309.1
    gross stress (*see also* Reaction, stress, acute)
        308.9
    group delinquent (*see also* Disturbance,
        conduct) 312.2 ☑
    Herxheimer's 995.0
    hyperkinetic (*see also* Hyperkinesia) 314.9
    hypochondriacal 300.7
    hypoglycemic, due to insulin 251.0
        therapeutic misadventure 962.3
    hypomanic (*see also* Psychosis, affective)
        296.0 ☑
        recurrent episode 296.1 ☑
        single episode 296.0 ☑

Reaction — *continued*
    hysterical 300.10
        conversion type 300.11
        dissociative 300.15
    id (bacterial cause) 692.89
    immaturity NEC 301.89
        aggressive 301.3
        emotional instability 301.59
    immunization — *see* Complications,
        vaccination
    incompatibility
        blood group (ABO) (infusion) (transfusion)
            999.6
        Rh (factor) (infusion) (transfusion) 999.7
    inflammatory — *see* Infection
    infusion — *see* Complications, infusion
    inoculation (immune serum) — *see*
        Complications, vaccination
    insulin 995.2
    involutional
        paranoid 297.2
        psychotic (*see also* Psychosis, affective,
            depressive) 296.2 ☑
    leukemoid (lymphocytic) (monocytic)
        (myelocytic) 288.8
    LSD (*see also* Abuse, drugs, nondependent)
        305.3 ☑
    lumbar puncture 349.0
    manic-depressive (*see also* Psychosis, affective)
        296.80
        depressed 296.2 ☑
            recurrent episode 296.3 ☑
            single episode 296.2 ☑
        hypomanic 296.0 ☑
    neurasthenic 300.5
    neurogenic (*see also* Neurosis) 300.9
    neurotic NEC 300.9
    neurotic-depressive 300.4
    nitritoid — *see* Crisis, nitritoid
    obsessive ▶compulsive◀ 300.3
    organic 293.9
        acute 293.0
        subacute 293.1
    overanxious, child or adolescent 313.0
    paranoid (chronic) 297.9
        acute 298.3
        climacteric 297.2
        involutional 297.2
        menopausal 297.2
        senile 290.20
        simple 297.0
    passive
        aggressive 301.84
        dependency 301.6
    personality (*see also* Disorder, personality)
        301.9
    phobic 300.20
    postradiation — *see* Effect, adverse, radiation
    psychogenic NEC 300.9
    psychoneurotic (*see also* Neurosis) 300.9
        anxiety 300.00
        compulsive 300.3
        conversion 300.11
        depersonalization 300.6
        depressive 300.4
        dissociative 300.15
        hypochondriacal 300.7
        hysterical 300.10
            conversion type 300.11
            dissociative type 300.15
        neurasthenic 300.5
        obsessive 300.3
        obsessive-compulsive 300.3
        phobic 300.20
        tension state 300.9
    psychophysiologic NEC (*see also* Disorder,
        psychosomatic) 306.9
        cardiovascular 306.2
        digestive 306.4
        endocrine 306.6
        gastrointestinal 306.4
        genitourinary 306.50
        heart 306.2
        hemic 306.8
        intestinal (large) (small) 306.4
        laryngeal 306.1
        lymphatic 306.8

Reaction — continued
  psychophysiologic NEC (see also Disorder,
      psychosomatic) — continued
    musculoskeletal 306.0
    pharyngeal 306.1
    respiratory 306.1
    skin 306.3
    special sense organs 306.7
  psychosomatic (see also Disorder,
      psychosomatic) 306.9
  psychotic (see also Psychosis) 298.9
    depressive 298.0
    due to or associated with physical condition
        (see also Psychosis, organic) 293.9
    involutional (see also Psychosis, affective)
        296.2 ☑
      recurrent episode 296.3 ☑
      single episode 296.2 ☑
  pupillary (myotonic) (tonic) 379.46
  radiation — see Effect, adverse, radiation
  runaway — see also Disturbance, conduct
    socialized 312.2 ☑
    undersocialized, unsocialized 312.1 ☑
  scarlet fever toxin — see Complications,
      vaccination
  schizophrenic (see also Schizophrenia) 295.9 ☑
    latent 295.5 ☑
  serological for syphilis — see Serology for
      syphilis
  serum (prophylactic) (therapeutic) 999.5
    immediate 999.4
  situational (see also Reaction, adjustment)
      309.9
    acute, to stress 308.3
    adjustment (see also Reaction, adjustment)
        309.9
  somatization (see also Disorder, psychosomatic)
      306.9
  spinal puncture 349.0
  spite, child (see also Disturbance, conduct)
      312.0 ☑
  stress, acute 308.9
    with predominant disturbance (of)
      consciousness 308.1
      emotions 308.0
      mixed 308.4
      psychomotor 308.2
      specified type NEC 308.3
    bone or cartilage — see Fracture, stress
  surgical procedure — see Complications,
      surgical procedure
  tetanus antitoxin — see Complications,
      vaccination
  toxin-antitoxin — see Complications,
      vaccination
  transfusion (blood) (bone marrow)
      (lymphocytes) (allergic) — see
      Complications, transfusion
  tuberculin skin test, nonspecific (without active
      tuberculosis) 795.5
    positive (without active tuberculosis) 795.5
  ultraviolet — see Effect, adverse, ultraviolet
  undersocialized, unsocialized — see also
      Disturbance, conduct
    aggressive (type) 312.0 ☑
    unaggressive (type) 312.1 ☑
  vaccination (any) — see Complications,
      vaccination
  white graft (skin) 996.52
  withdrawing, child or adolescent 313.22
  x-ray — see Effect, adverse, x-rays
Reactive depression (see also Reaction,
    depressive) 300.4
  neurotic 300.4
  psychoneurotic 300.4
  psychotic 298.0
Rebound tenderness 789.6 ☑
Recalcitrant patient V15.81
Recanalization, thrombus — see Thrombosis
Recession, receding
  chamber angle (eye) 364.77
  chin 524.06
  gingival (postinfective) (postoperative) 523.20
    generalized 523.25
    localized 523.24
    minimal 523.21

Recession, receding — continued
  gingival — continued
    moderate 523.22
    severe 523.23
Recklinghausen's disease (M9540/1) 237.71
  bones (osteitis fibrosa cystica) 252.01
Recklinghausen-Applebaum disease
    (hemochromatosis) 275.0
Reclus' disease (cystic) 610.1
Recrudescent typhus (fever) 081.1
Recruitment, auditory 388.44
Rectalgia 569.42
Rectitis 569.49
Rectocele
  female (without uterine prolapse) 618.04
    with uterine prolapse 618.4
      complete 618.3
      incomplete 618.2
  in pregnancy or childbirth 654.4 ☑
    causing obstructed labor 660.2 ☑
      affecting fetus or newborn 763.1
  male 569.49
  vagina, vaginal (outlet) 618.04
Rectosigmoiditis 569.89
  ulcerative (chronic) 556.5
Rectosigmoid junction — see condition
Rectourethral — see condition
Rectovaginal — see condition
Rectovesical — see condition
Rectum, rectal — see condition
Recurrent — see condition
Red bugs 133.8
Red cedar asthma 495.8
Redness
  conjunctiva 379.93
  eye 379.93
  nose 478.1
Reduced ventilatory or vital capacity 794.2
Reduction
  function
    kidney (see also Disease, renal) 593.9
    liver 573.8
  ventilatory capacity 794.2
  vital capacity 794.2
Redundant, redundancy
  abdomen 701.9
  anus 751.5
  cardia 537.89
  clitoris 624.2
  colon (congenital) 751.5
  foreskin (congenital) 605
  intestine 751.5
  labia 624.3
  organ or site, congenital NEC — see Accessory
  panniculus (abdominal) 278.1
  prepuce (congenital) 605
  pylorus 537.89
  rectum 751.5
  scrotum 608.89
  sigmoid 751.5
  skin (of face) 701.9
    eyelids 374.30
  stomach 537.89
  uvula 528.9
  vagina 623.8
Reduplication — see Duplication
Referral
  adoption (agency) V68.89
  nursing care V63.8
  patient without examination or treatment
      V68.81
  social services V63.8
Reflex — see also condition
  blink, deficient 374.45
  hyperactive gag 478.29
  neurogenic bladder NEC 596.54
    atonic 596.54
      with cauda equina syndrome 344.61
  vasoconstriction 443.9
  vasovagal 780.2
Reflux
  esophageal 530.81
    with esophagitis 530.11

Reflux — continued
  esophagitis 530.11
  gastroesophageal 530.81
  mitral — see Insufficiency, mitral
  ureteral — see Reflux, vesicoureteral
  vesicoureteral 593.70
    with
      reflux nephropathy 593.73
        bilateral 593.72
        unilateral 593.71
Reformed gallbladder 576.0
Reforming, artificial openings (see also
    Attention to, artificial, opening) V55.9
Refractive error (see also Error, refractive) 367.9
Refsum's disease or syndrome (heredopathia
    atactica polyneuritiformis) 356.3
Refusal of
  food 307.59
    hysterical 300.11
  treatment because of, due to
    patient's decision NEC V64.2
    reason of conscience or religion V62.6
Regaud
  tumor (M8082/3) — see Neoplasm,
      nasopharynx, malignant
  type carcinoma (M8082/3) — see Neoplasm,
      nasopharynx, malignant
Regional — see condition
Regulation feeding (elderly) (infant) 783.3
  newborn 779.3
Regurgitated
  food, choked on 933.1
  stomach contents, choked on 933.1
Regurgitation
  aortic (valve) (see also Insufficiency, aortic)
      424.1
    congenital 746.4
    syphilitic 093.22
  food — see also Vomiting
    with reswallowing — see Rumination
    newborn 779.3
  gastric contents — see Vomiting
  heart — see Endocarditis
  mitral (valve) — see also Insufficiency, mitral
    congenital 746.6
  myocardial — see Endocarditis
  pulmonary (heart) (valve) (see also
      Endocarditis, pulmonary) 424.3
  stomach — see Vomiting
  tricuspid — see Endocarditis, tricuspid
  valve, valvular — see Endocarditis
  vesicoureteral — see Reflux, vesicoureteral
Rehabilitation V57.9
  multiple types V57.89
  occupational V57.21
  specified type NEC V57.89
  speech V57.3
  vocational V57.22
Reichmann's disease or syndrome
    (gastrosuccorrhea) 536.8
Reifenstein's syndrome (hereditary familial
    hypogonadism, male) 259.5   ▲
Reilly's syndrome or phenomenon (see also
    Neuropathy, peripheral, autonomic) 337.9
Reimann's periodic disease 277.3
Reinsertion, contraceptive device V25.42
Reiter's disease, syndrome, or urethritis
    099.3 [711.1] ☑
Rejection
  food, hysterical 300.11
  transplant 996.80
    bone marrow 996.85
    corneal 996.51
    organ (immune or nonimmune cause)
        996.80
      bone marrow 996.85
      heart 996.83
      intestines 996.87
      kidney 996.81
      liver 996.82
      lung 996.84
      pancreas 996.86

Rejection — *continued*
transplant — *continued*
organ — *continued*
specified NEC 996.89
skin 996.52
artificial 996.55
decellularized allodermis 996.55

Relapsing fever 087.9
Carter's (Asiatic) 087.0
Dutton's (West African) 087.1
Koch's 087.9
louse-borne (epidemic) 087.0
Novy's (American) 087.1
Obermeyer's (European) 087.0
Spirillum 087.9
tick-borne (endemic) 087.1

Relaxation
anus (sphincter) 569.49
due to hysteria 300.11
arch (foot) 734
congenital 754.61
back ligaments 728.4
bladder (sphincter) 596.59
cardio-esophageal 530.89
cervix (*see also* Incompetency, cervix) 622.5
diaphragm 519.4
inguinal rings — *see* Hernia, inguinal
joint (capsule) (ligament) (paralytic) (*see also* Derangement, joint) 718.90
congenital 755.8
lumbosacral joint 724.6
pelvic floor 618.89
pelvis 618.89
perineum 618.89
posture 729.9
rectum (sphincter) 569.49
sacroiliac (joint) 724.6
scrotum 608.89
urethra (sphincter) 599.84
uterus (outlet) 618.89
vagina (outlet) 618.89
vesical 596.59

Remains
canal of Cloquet 743.51
capsule (opaque) 743.51

Remittent fever (malarial) 084.6

Remnant
canal of Cloquet 743.51
capsule (opaque) 743.51
cervix, cervical stump (acquired) (postoperative) 622.8
cystic duct, postcholecystectomy 576.0
fingernail 703.8
congenital 757.5
meniscus, knee 717.5
thyroglossal duct 759.2
tonsil 474.8
infected 474.00
urachus 753.7

Remote effect of cancer — *see* condition

Removal (of)
catheter (urinary) (indwelling) V53.6
from artificial opening — *see* Attention to, artificial, opening
non-vascular V58.82
vascular V58.81
cerebral ventricle (communicating) shunt V53.01
device — *see also* Fitting (of)
contraceptive V25.42
fixation
external V54.89
internal V54.01
traction V54.89
dressing V58.3
ileostomy V55.2
Kirschner wire V54.89
nonvascular catheter V58.82
pin V54.01
plaster cast V54.89
plate (fracture) V54.01
rod V54.01
screw V54.01
splint, external V54.89
subdermal implantable contraceptive V25.43

Removal (of) — *continued*
suture V58.3
traction device, external V54.89
vascular catheter V58.81

Ren
arcuatus 753.3
mobile, mobilis (*see also* Disease, renal) 593.0
congenital 753.3
unguliformis 753.3

Renal — *see also* condition
glomerulohyalinosis-diabetic syndrome 250.4 ☑ *[581.81]*

Rendu-Osler-Weber disease or syndrome (familial hemorrhagic telangiectasia) 448.0

Reninoma (M8361/1) 236.91

Rénon-Delille syndrome 253.8

Repair
pelvic floor, previous, in pregnancy or childbirth 654.4 ☑
affecting fetus or newborn 763.89
scarred tissue V51

Replacement by artificial or mechanical device or prosthesis of (*see also* Fitting (of))
artificial skin V43.83
bladder V43.5
blood vessel V43.4
breast V43.82
eye globe V43.0
heart
with
assist device V43.21
fully implantable artificial heart V43.22
valve V43.3
intestine V43.89
joint V43.60
ankle V43.66
elbow V43.62
finger V43.69
hip (partial) (total) V43.64
knee V43.65
shoulder V43.61
specified NEC V43.69
wrist V43.63
kidney V43.89
larynx V43.81
lens V43.1
limb(s) V43.7
liver V43.89
lung V43.89
organ NEC V43.89
pancreas V43.89
skin (artificial) V43.83
tissue NEC V43.89

Reprogramming
cardiac pacemaker V53.31

Request for expert evidence V68.2

Reserve, decreased or low
cardiac — *see* Disease, heart
kidney (*see also* Disease, renal) 593.9

Residual — *see also* condition
bladder 596.8
foreign body — *see* Retention, foreign body
state, schizophrenic (*see also* Schizophrenia) 295.6 ☑
urine 788.69

Resistance, resistant (to)
activated protein C 289.81

> *Note — use the following subclassification for categories V09.5, V09.7, V09.8, V09.9:*
>
> 0   *without mention of resistance to multiple drugs*
> 1   *with resistance to multiple drugs*
>   V09.5   *quinolones and fluoroquinolones*
>   V09.7   *antimycobacterial agents*
>   V09.8   *specified drugs NEC*
>   V09.9   *unspecified drugs*

drugs by microorganisms V09.9 ☑
Amikacin V09.4
aminoglycosides V09.4
Amodiaquine V09.5 ☑

Resistance, resistant — *continued*
drugs by microorganisms — *continued*
Amoxicillin V09.0
Ampicillin V09.0
antimycobacterial agents V09.7 ☑
Azithromycin V09.2
Azlocillin V09.0
Aztreonam V09.1
B-lactam antibiotics V09.1
Bacampicillin V09.0
Bacitracin V09.8 ☑
Benznidazole V09.8 ☑
Capreomycin V09.7 ☑
Carbenicillin V09.0
Cefaclor V09.1
Cefadroxil V09.1
Cefamandole V09.1
Cefatetan V09.1
Cefazolin V09.1
Cefixime V09.1
Cefonicid V09.1
Cefoperazone V09.1
Ceforanide V09.1
Cefotaxime V09.1
Cefoxitin V09.1
Ceftazidime V09.1
Ceftizoxime V09.1
Ceftriaxone V09.1
Cefuroxime V09.1
Cephalexin V09.1
Cephaloglycin V09.1
Cephaloridine V09.1
Cephalosporins V09.1
Cephalothin V09.1
Cephapirin V09.1
Cephradine V09.1
Chloramphenicol V09.8 ☑
Chloraquine V09.5 ☑
Chlorguanide V09.8 ☑
Chlorproguanil V09.8 ☑
Chlortetracycline V09.3
Cinoxacin V09.5 ☑
Ciprofloxacin V09.5 ☑
Clarithromycin V09.2
Clindamycin V09.8 ☑
Clioquinol V09.5 ☑
Clofazimine V09.7 ☑
Cloxacillin V09.0
Cyclacillin V09.0
Cycloserine V09.7 ☑
Dapsone [DZ] V09.7 ☑
Demeclocycline V09.3
Dicloxacillin V09.0
Doxycycline V09.3
Enoxacin V09.5 ☑
Erythromycin V09.2
Ethambutol [EMB] V09.7 ☑
Ethionamide [ETA] V09.7 ☑
fluoroquinolones V09.5 ☑
Gentamicin V09.4
Halofantrine V09.8 ☑
Imipenem V09.1
Iodoquinol V09.5 ☑
Isoniazid [INH] V09.7 ☑
Kanamycin V09.4
macrolides V09.2
Mafenide V09.6
MDRO (multiple drug resistant organisms) NOS V09.91
Mefloquine V09.8 ☑
Melasoprol V09.8 ☑
Methacycline V09.3
Methenamine V09.8 ☑
Methicillin V09.0
Metronidazole V09.8 ☑
Mezlocillin V09.0
Minocycline V09.3
multiple drug resistant organisms NOS V09.91
Nafcillin V09.0
Nalidixic acid V09.5 ☑
Natamycin V09.2
Neomycin V09.4
Netilmicin V09.4
Nimorazole V09.8 ☑
Nitrofurantoin V09.8 ☑

Resistance, resistant — *continued*
  drugs by microorganisms — *continued*
    Nitrofurtimox V09.8 ☑
    Norfloxacin V09.5 ☑
    Nystatin V09.2
    Ofloxacin V09.5 ☑
    Oleandomycin V09.2
    Oxacillin V09.0
    Oxytetracycline V09.3
    Para-amino salicylic acid [PAS] V09.7 ☑
    Paromomycin V09.4
    Penicillin (G) (V) (VK) V09.0
    penicillins V09.0
    Pentamidine V09.8 ☑
    Piperacillin V09.0
    Primaquine V09.5 ☑
    Proguanil V09.8 ☑
    Pyrazinamide [PZA] V09.7 ☑
    Pyrimethamine/Sulfalene V09.8 ☑
    Pyrimethamine/Sulfodoxine V09.8 ☑
    Quinacrine V09.5 ☑
    Quinidine V09.8 ☑
    Quinine V09.8 ☑
    quinolones V09.5 ☑
    Rifabutin V09.7 ☑
    Rifampin [RIF] V09.7 ☑
    Rifamycin V09.7 ☑
    Rolitetracycline V09.3
    specified drugs NEC V09.8 ☑
    Spectinomycin V09.8 ☑
    Spiramycin V09.2
    Streptomycin [SM] V09.4
    Sulfacetamide V09.6
    Sulfacytine V09.6
    Sulfadiazine V09.6
    Sulfadoxine V09.6
    Sulfamethoxazole V09.6
    Sulfapyridine V09.6
    Sulfasalizine V09.6
    Sulfasoxazone V09.6
    sulfonamides V09.6
    Sulfasoxazole V09.7 ☑
    tetracycline V09.3
    tetracyclines V09.3
    Thiamphenicol V09.8 ☑
    Ticarcillin V09.0
    Tinidazole V09.8 ☑
    Tobramycin V09.4
    Triamphenicol V09.8 ☑
    Trimethoprim V09.8 ☑
    Vancomycin V09.8 ☑
  insulin 277.7

Resorption
  biliary 576.8
    purulent or putrid (*see also* Cholecystitis)
      576.8
  dental (roots) 521.40
    alveoli 525.8
    pathological
      external 521.42
      internal 521.41
      specified NEC 521.49
  septic — *see* Septicemia
  teeth (roots) 521.40
    pathological
      external 521.42
      internal 521.41
      specified NEC 521.49

Respiration
  asymmetrical 786.09
  bronchial 786.09
  Cheyne-Stokes (periodic respiration) 786.04
  decreased, due to shock following injury 958.4
  disorder of 786.00
    psychogenic 306.1
    specified NEC 786.09
  failure 518.81
    acute 518.81
    acute and chronic 518.84
    chronic 518.83
    newborn 770.84
  insufficiency 786.09
    acute 518.82
    newborn NEC 770.89
  Kussmaul (air hunger) 786.09
  painful 786.52

Respiration — *continued*
  periodic 786.09
    high altitude 327.22
  poor 786.09
    newborn NEC 770.89
  sighing 786.7
    psychogenic 306.1
  wheezing 786.07
Respiratory — *see also* condition
  distress 786.09
    acute 518.82
    fetus or newborn NEC 770.89
    syndrome (newborn) 769
      adult (following shock, surgery, or
        trauma) 518.5
      specified NEC 518.82
  failure 518.81
    acute 518.81
    acute and chronic 518.84
    chronic 518.83
Respiratory syncytial virus (RSV) 079.6
  bronchiolitis 466.11
  pneumonia 480.1
  vaccination, prophylactic (against) V04.82
Response
  photoallergic 692.72
  phototoxic 692.72
Rest, rests
  mesonephric duct 752.89
    fallopian tube 752.11
  ovarian, in fallopian tubes 752.19
  wolffian duct 752.89
Restless leg (syndrome) 333.99
Restlessness 799.2
**Restoration of organ continuity from previous
    sterilization** (tuboplasty) (vasoplasty) V26.0
Restriction of housing space V60.1
Restzustand, schizophrenic (*see also*
    Schizophrenia) 295.6 ☑
Retained — *see* Retention
Retardation
  development, developmental, specific (*see also*
    Disorder, development, specific) 315.9
  learning, specific 315.2
    arithmetical 315.1
    language (skills) 315.31
      expressive 315.31
      mixed receptive-expressive 315.32
    mathematics 315.1
    reading 315.00
      phonological 315.39
      written expression 315.2
    motor 315.4
  endochondral bone growth 733.91
  growth (physical) in childhood 783.43
    due to malnutrition 263.2
    fetal (intrauterine) 764.9 ☑
      affecting management of pregnancy
        656.5 ☑
  intrauterine growth 764.9 ☑
    affecting management of pregnancy 656.5 ☑
  mental 319
    borderline V62.89
    mild, IQ 50-70 317
    moderate, IQ 35-49 318.0
    profound, IQ under 20 318.2
    severe, IQ 20-34 318.1
  motor, specific 315.4
  physical 783.43
    child 783.43
    due to malnutrition 263.2
    fetus (intrauterine) 764.9 ☑
      affecting management of pregnancy
        656.5 ☑
  psychomotor NEC 307.9
  reading 315.00
Retching — *see* Vomiting
Retention, retained
  bladder (*see also* Retention, urine) 788.20
    psychogenic 306.53
  carbon dioxide 276.2
  cyst — *see* Cyst

Retention, retained — *continued*
  dead
    fetus (after 22 completed weeks gestation)
      656.4 ☑
      early fetal death (before 22 completed
        weeks gestation) 632
    ovum 631
  decidua (following delivery) (fragments) (with
    hemorrhage) 666.2 ☑
    without hemorrhage 667.1 ☑
  deciduous tooth 520.6
  dental root 525.3
  fecal (*see also* Constipation) 564.00
  fluid 276.6
  foreign body — *see also* Foreign body, retained
    bone 733.99
    current trauma — *see* Foreign body, by site
      or type
    middle ear 385.83
    muscle 729.6
    soft tissue NEC 729.6
  gastric 536.8
  membranes (following delivery) (with
    hemorrhage) 666.2 ☑
    with abortion — *see* Abortion, by type
    without hemorrhage 667.1 ☑
  menses 626.8
  milk (puerperal) 676.2 ☑
  nitrogen, extrarenal 788.9
  placenta (total) (with hemorrhage) 666.0 ☑
    with abortion — *see* Abortion, by type
    portions or fragments 666.2 ☑
      without hemorrhage 667.1 ☑
    without hemorrhage 667.0 ☑
  products of conception
    early pregnancy (fetal death before 22
      completed weeks gestation) 632
    following
      abortion — *see* Abortion, by type
      delivery 666.2 ☑
        with hemorrhage 666.2 ☑
        without hemorrhage 667.1 ☑
  secundines (following delivery) (with
    hemorrhage) 666.2 ☑
    with abortion — *see* Abortion, by type
    complicating puerperium (delayed
      hemorrhage) 666.2 ☑
    without hemorrhage 667.1 ☑
  smegma, clitoris 624.8
  urine NEC 788.20
    bladder, incomplete emptying 788.21
      due to ●
        benign prostatic hypertrophy ●
          (BPH) — *see* category 600 ●
      due to ●
        benign prostatic hypertrophy (BPH) ●
          — *see* category 600 ●
    psychogenic 306.53
    specified NEC 788.29
  water (in tissue) (*see also* Edema) 782.3
Reticulation, dust (occupational) 504
Reticulocytosis NEC 790.99
Reticuloendotheliosis
  acute infantile (M9722/3) 202.5 ☑
  leukemic (M9940/3) 202.4 ☑
  malignant (M9720/3) 202.3 ☑
  nonlipid (M9722/3) 202.5 ☑
Reticulohistiocytoma (giant cell) 277.89
Reticulohistiocytosis, multicentric 272.8
Reticulolymphosarcoma (diffuse) (M9613/3)
  200.8 ☑
  follicular (M9691/3) 202.0 ☑
  nodular (M9691/3) 202.0 ☑
Reticulosarcoma (M9640/3) 200.0 ☑
  nodular (M9642/3) 200.0 ☑
  pleomorphic cell type (M9641/3) 200.0 ☑
Reticulosis (skin)
  acute of infancy (M9722/3) 202.5 ☑
  histiocytic medullary (M9721/3) 202.3 ☑
  lipomelanotic 695.89
  malignant (M9720/3) 202.3 ☑
  Sézary's (M9701/3) 202.2 ☑
Retina, retinal — *see* condition

Retinitis (*see also* Chorioretinitis) 363.20
  albuminurica 585.9 *[363.10]* ▲
  arteriosclerotic 440.8 *[362.13]*
  central angiospastic 362.41
  Coat's 362.12
  diabetic 250.5 ☑ *[362.01]*
  disciformis 362.52
  disseminated 363.10
    metastatic 363.14
    neurosyphilitic 094.83
    pigment epitheliopathy 363.15
  exudative 362.12
  focal 363.00
    in histoplasmosis 115.92
      capsulatum 115.02
      duboisii 115.12
    juxtapapillary 363.05
    macular 363.06
    paramacular 363.06
    peripheral 363.08
    posterior pole NEC 363.07
  gravidarum 646.8 ☑
  hemorrhagica externa 362.12
  juxtapapillary (Jensen's) 363.05
  luetic — *see* Retinitis, syphilitic
  metastatic 363.14
  pigmentosa 362.74
  proliferans 362.29
  proliferating 362.29
  punctata albescens 362.76
  renal 585.9 *[363.13]* ▲
  syphilitic (secondary) 091.51
    congenital 090.0 *[363.13]*
    early 091.51
    late 095.8 *[363.13]*
  syphilitica, central, recurrent 095.8 *[363.13]*
  tuberculous (*see also* Tuberculous)
    017.3 ☑ *[363.13]*
Retinoblastoma (M9510/3) 190.5
  differentiated type (M9511/3) 190.5
  undifferentiated type (M9512/3) 190.5
Retinochoroiditis (*see also* Chorioretinitis)
    363.20
  central angiospastic 362.41
  disseminated 363.10
    metastatic 363.14
    neurosyphilitic 094.83
    pigment epitheliopathy 363.15
    syphilitic 094.83
  due to toxoplasmosis (acquired) (focal) 130.2
  focal 363.00
    in histoplasmosis 115.92
      capsulatum 115.02
      duboisii 115.12
    juxtapapillary (Jensen's) 363.05
    macular 363.06
    paramacular 363.06
    peripheral 363.08
    posterior pole NEC 363.07
  juxtapapillaris 363.05
  syphilitic (disseminated) 094.83
Retinopathy (background) 362.10
  arteriosclerotic 440.8 *[362.13]*
  atherosclerotic 440.8 *[362.13]*
  central serous 362.41
  circinate 362.10
  Coat's 362.12
  diabetic 250.5 ☑ *[362.01]*
    nonproliferative 250.5 ☑ *[362.03]* ●
      mild 250.5 ☑ *[362.04]* ●
      moderate 250.5 ☑ *[362.05]* ●
      severe 250.5 ☑ *[362.06]* ●
    proliferative 250.5 ☑ *[362.02]* ●
  exudative 362.12
  hypertensive 362.11
  nonproliferative ●
    diabetic 250.5 ☑ *[362.03]* ●
      mild 250.5 ☑ *[362.04]* ●
      moderate 250.5 ☑ *[362.05]* ●
      severe 250.5 ☑ *[362.06]* ●
  of prematurity 362.21
  pigmentary, congenital 362.74
  proliferative 362.29
    diabetic 250.5 ☑ *[362.02]* ●
    sickle-cell 282.60 *[362.29]*
  solar 363.31

Retinoschisis 361.10
  bullous 361.12
  congenital 743.56
  flat 361.11
  juvenile 362.73
Retractile testis 752.52
Retraction
  cervix (*see also* Retroversion, uterus) 621.6
  drum (membrane) 384.82
  eyelid 374.41
  finger 736.29
  head 781.0
  lid 374.41
  lung 518.89
  mediastinum 519.3
  nipple 611.79
    congenital 757.6
    puerperal, postpartum 676.0 ☑
  palmar fascia 728.6
  pleura (*see also* Pleurisy) 511.0
  ring, uterus (Bandl's) (pathological) 661.4 ☑
    affecting fetus or newborn 763.7
  sternum (congenital) 756.3
    acquired 738.3
    during respiration 786.9
  substernal 738.3
  supraclavicular 738.8
  syndrome (Duane's) 378.71
  uterus (*see also* Retroversion, uterus) 621.6
  valve (heart) — *see* Endocarditis
Retrobulbar — *see* condition
Retrocaval ureter 753.4
Retrocecal — *see also* condition
  appendix (congenital) 751.5
Retrocession — *see* Retroversion
Retrodisplacement — *see* Retroversion
Retroflection, retroflexion — *see* Retroversion
Retrognathia, retrognathism (mandibular)
    (maxillary) 524.10
Retrograde
  ejaculation 608.87
  menstruation 626.8
Retroiliac ureter 753.4
Retroperineal — *see* condition
Retroperitoneal — *see* condition
Retroperitonitis (*see also* Peritonitis) 567.9
Retropharyngeal — *see* condition
Retroplacental — *see* condition
Retroposition — *see* Retroversion
Retrosternal thyroid (congenital) 759.2
Retroversion, retroverted
  cervix (*see also* Retroversion, uterus) 621.6
  female NEC (*see also* Retroversion, uterus)
    621.6
  iris 364.70
  testis (congenital) 752.51
  uterus, uterine (acquired) (acute) (adherent)
    (any degree) (asymptomatic) (cervix)
    (postinfectional) (postpartal, old) 621.6
    congenital 752.3
    in pregnancy or childbirth 654.3 ☑
      affecting fetus or newborn 763.89
      causing obstructed labor 660.2 ☑
        affecting fetus or newborn 763.1
Retrusion, premaxilla (developmental) 524.04
Rett's syndrome 330.8
Reverse, reversed
  peristalsis 787.4
Reye's syndrome 331.81
Reye-Sheehan syndrome (postpartum pituitary
    necrosis) 253.2
Rh (factor)
  hemolytic disease 773.0
  incompatibility, immunization, or sensitization
    affecting management of pregnancy 656.1 ☑
    fetus or newborn 773.0
    transfusion reaction 999.7
  negative mother, affecting fetus or newborn
    773.0
  titer elevated 999.7
  transfusion reaction 999.7
Rhabdomyolysis (idiopathic) 728.88

Rhabdomyoma (M8900/0) — *see also* Neoplasm,
    connective tissue, benign
  adult (M8904/0) — *see* Neoplasm, connective
    tissue, benign
  fetal (M8903/0) — *see* Neoplasm, connective
    tissue, benign
  glycogenic (M8904/0) — *see* Neoplasm,
    connective tissue, benign
Rhabdomyosarcoma (M8900/3) — *see also*
    Neoplasm, connective tissue, malignant
  alveolar (M8920/3) — *see* Neoplasm,
    connective tissue, malignant
  embryonal (M8910/3) — *see* Neoplasm,
    connective tissue, malignant
  mixed type (M8902/3) — *see* Neoplasm,
    connective tissue, malignant
  pleomorphic (M8901/3) — *see* Neoplasm,
    connective tissue, malignant
Rhabdosarcoma (M8900/3) — *see*
    Rhabdomyosarcoma
Rhesus (factor) (Rh) incompatibility — *see* Rh,
    incompatibility
Rheumaticosis — *see* Rheumatism
Rheumatism, rheumatic (acute NEC) 729.0
  adherent pericardium 393
  arthritis
    acute or subacute — *see* Fever, rheumatic
    chronic 714.0
      spine 720.0
  articular (chronic) NEC (*see also* Arthritis)
    716.9 ☑
    acute or subacute — *see* Fever, rheumatic
  back 724.9
  blennorrhagic 098.59
  carditis — *see* Disease, heart, rheumatic
  cerebral — *see* Fever, rheumatic
  chorea (acute) — *see* Chorea, rheumatic
  chronic NEC 729.0
  coronary arteritis 391.9
    chronic 398.99
  degeneration, myocardium (*see also*
    Degeneration, myocardium, with
    rheumatic fever) 398.0
  desert 114.0
  febrile — *see* Fever, rheumatic
  fever — *see* Fever, rheumatic
  gonococcal 098.59
  gout 274.0
  heart
    disease (*see also* Disease, heart, rheumatic)
      398.90
    failure (chronic) (congestive) (inactive)
      398.91
  hemopericardium — *see* Rheumatic,
    pericarditis
  hydropericardium — *see* Rheumatic,
    pericarditis
  inflammatory (acute) (chronic) (subacute) — *see*
    Fever, rheumatic
  intercostal 729.0
    meaning Tietze's disease 733.6
  joint (chronic) NEC (*see also* Arthritis) 716.9 ☑
    acute — *see* Fever, rheumatic
  mediastinopericarditis — *see* Rheumatic,
    pericarditis
  muscular 729.0
  myocardial degeneration (*see also*
    Degeneration, myocardium, with
    rheumatic fever) 398.0
  myocarditis (chronic) (inactive) (with chorea)
    398.0
    active or acute 391.2
      with chorea (acute) (rheumatic)
        (Sydenham's) 392.0
  myositis 729.1
  neck 724.9
  neuralgic 729.0
  neuritis (acute) (chronic) 729.2
  neuromuscular 729.0
  nodose — *see* Arthritis, nodosa
  nonarticular 729.0
  palindromic 719.30
    ankle 719.37
    elbow 719.32
    foot 719.37
    hand 719.34

☑ Additional Digit Required — Refer to the Tabular List (Numeric Code Section) for Additional Digit Selection

Rheumatism, rheumatic — *continued*
  palindromic — *continued*
    hip 719.35
    knee 719.36
    multiple sites 719.39
    pelvic region 719.35
    shoulder (region) 719.31
    specified site NEC 719.38
    wrist 719.33
  pancarditis, acute 391.8
    with chorea (acute) (rheumatic)
      (Sydenham's) 392.0
    chronic or inactive 398.99
  pericarditis (active) (acute) (with effusion) (with
    pneumonia) 391.0
    with chorea (acute) (rheumatic)
      (Sydenham's) 392.0
    chronic or inactive 393
  pericardium — *see* Rheumatic, pericarditis
  pleuropericarditis — *see* Rheumatic,
    pericarditis
  pneumonia 390 *[517.1]*
  pneumonitis 390 *[517.1]*
  pneumopericarditis — *see* Rheumatic,
    pericarditis
  polyarthritis
    acute or subacute — *see* Fever, rheumatic
    chronic 714.0
  polyarticular NEC (*see also* Arthritis) 716.9 ☑
  psychogenic 306.0
  radiculitis 729.2
  sciatic 724.3
  septic — *see* Fever, rheumatic
  spine 724.9
  subacute NEC 729.0
  torticollis 723.5
  tuberculous NEC (*see also* Tuberculosis)
    015.9 ☑
  typhoid fever 002.0

Rheumatoid — *see also* condition
  lungs 714.81

Rhinitis (atrophic) (catarrhal) (chronic) (croupous)
  (fibrinous) (hyperplastic) (hypertrophic)
  (membranous) (purulent) (suppurative)
  (ulcerative) 472.0
  with
    hay fever (*see also* Fever, hay) 477.9
      with asthma (bronchial) 493.0 ☑
    sore throat — *see* Nasopharyngitis
  acute 460
  allergic (nonseasonal) (seasonal) (*see also* Fever,
    hay) 477.9
    with asthma (*see also* Asthma) 493.0 ☑
    due to food 477.1
  granulomatous 472.0
  infective 460
  obstructive 472.0
  pneumococcal 460
  syphilitic 095.8
    congenital 090.0
  tuberculous (*see also* Tuberculosis) 012.8 ☑
  vasomotor (*see also* Fever, hay) 477.9

Rhinoantritis (chronic) 473.0
  acute 461.0

Rhinodacryolith 375.57

Rhinolalia (aperta) (clausa) (open) 784.49

Rhinolith 478.1
  nasal sinus (*see also* Sinusitis) 473.9

Rhinomegaly 478.1

Rhinopharyngitis (acute) (subacute) (*see also*
  Nasopharyngitis) 460
  chronic 472.2
  destructive ulcerating 102.5
  mutilans 102.5

Rhinophyma 695.3

Rhinorrhea 478.1
  cerebrospinal (fluid) 349.81
  paroxysmal (*see also* Fever, hay) 477.9
  spasmodic (*see also* Fever, hay) 477.9

Rhinosalpingitis 381.50
  acute 381.51
  chronic 381.52

Rhinoscleroma 040.1

Rhinosporidiosis 117.0

Rhinovirus infection 079.3

Rhizomelic chrondrodysplasia punctata 277.86

Rhizomelique, pseudopolyarthritic 446.5

Rhoads and Bomford anemia (refractory)
  238.7   ▲

Rhus
  diversiloba dermatitis 692.6
  radicans dermatitis 692.6
  toxicodendron dermatitis 692.6
  venenata dermatitis 692.6
  verniciflua dermatitis 692.6

Rhythm
  atrioventricular nodal 427.89
  disorder 427.9
    coronary sinus 427.89
    ectopic 427.89
    nodal 427.89
  escape 427.89
  heart, abnormal 427.9
    fetus or newborn — *see* Abnormal, heart
      rate
  idioventricular 426.89
    accelerated 427.89
  nodal 427.89
  sleep, inversion 327.39   ▲
    nonorganic origin 307.45

Rhytidosis facialis 701.8

Rib — *see also* condition
  cervical 756.2

Riboflavin deficiency 266.0

Rice bodies (*see also* Loose, body, joint) 718.1 ☑
  knee 717.6

Richter's hernia — *see* Hernia, Richter's

Ricinism 988.2

Rickets (active) (acute) (adolescent) (adult) (chest
  wall) (congenital) (current) (infantile)
  (intestinal) 268.0
  celiac 579.0
  fetal 756.4
  hemorrhagic 267
  hypophosphatemic with nephrotic-glycosuric
    dwarfism 270.0
  kidney 588.0
  late effect 268.1
  renal 588.0
  scurvy 267
  vitamin D-resistant 275.3

Rickettsial disease 083.9
  specified type NEC 083.8

Rickettsialpox 083.2

Rickettsiosis NEC 083.9
  specified type NEC 083.8
  tick-borne 082.9
    specified type NEC 082.8
  vesicular 083.2

Ricord's chancre 091.0

Riddoch's syndrome (visual disorientation)
  368.16

Rider's
  bone 733.99
  chancre 091.0

Ridge, alveolus — *see also* condition
  edentulous
    atrophy 525.20
      mandible 525.20
        minimal 525.21
        moderate 525.22
        severe 525.23
      maxilla 525.20
        minimal 525.24
        moderate 525.25
        severe 525.26
    flabby 525.20

Ridged ear 744.29

Riedel's
  disease (ligneous thyroiditis) 245.3
  lobe, liver 751.69
  struma (ligneous thyroiditis) 245.3
  thyroiditis (ligneous) 245.3

Rieger's anomaly or syndrome (mesodermal
  dysgenesis, anterior ocular segment) 743.44

Riehl's melanosis 709.09

Rietti-Greppi-Micheli anemia or syndrome
  282.49

Rieux's hernia — *see* Hernia, Rieux's

Rift Valley fever 066.3

Riga's disease (cachectic aphthae) 529.0

Riga-Fede disease (cachectic aphthae) 529.0

Riggs' disease (compound periodontitis) 523.4

Right middle lobe syndrome 518.0

Rigid, rigidity — *see also* condition
  abdominal 789.4 ☑
  articular, multiple congenital 754.89
  back 724.8
  cervix uteri
    in pregnancy or childbirth 654.6 ☑
      affecting fetus or newborn 763.89
      causing obstructed labor 660.2 ☑
        affecting fetus or newborn 763.1
  hymen (acquired) (congenital) 623.3
  nuchal 781.6
  pelvic floor
    in pregnancy or childbirth 654.4 ☑
      affecting fetus or newborn 763.89
      causing obstructed labor 660.2 ☑
        affecting fetus or newborn 763.1
  perineum or vulva
    in pregnancy or childbirth 654.8 ☑
      affecting fetus or newborn 763.89
      causing obstructed labor 660.2 ☑
        affecting fetus or newborn 763.1
  spine 724.8
  vagina
    in pregnancy or childbirth 654.7 ☑
      affecting fetus or newborn 763.89
      causing obstructed labor 660.2 ☑
        affecting fetus or newborn 763.1

Rigors 780.99

Riley-Day syndrome (familial dysautonomia)
  742.8

Ring(s)
  aorta 747.21
  Bandl's, complicating delivery 661.4 ☑
    affecting fetus or newborn 763.7
  contraction, complicating delivery 661.4 ☑
    affecting fetus or newborn 763.7
  esophageal (congenital) 750.3
  Fleischer (-Kayser) (cornea) 275.1 *[371.14]*
  hymenal, tight (acquired) (congenital) 623.3
  Kayser-Fleischer (cornea) 275.1 *[371.14]*
  retraction, uterus, pathological 661.4 ☑
    affecting fetus or newborn 763.7
  Schatzki's (esophagus) (congenital) (lower)
    750.3
    acquired 530.3
  Soemmering's 366.51
  trachea, abnormal 748.3
  vascular (congenital) 747.21
  Vossius' 921.3
    late effect 366.21

Ringed hair (congenital) 757.4

Ringing in the ear (*see also* Tinnitus) 388.30

Ringworm 110.9
  beard 110.0
  body 110.5
  Burmese 110.9
  corporeal 110.5
  foot 110.4
  groin 110.3
  hand 110.2
  honeycomb 110.0
  nails 110.1
  perianal (area) 110.3
  scalp 110.0
  specified site NEC 110.8
  Tokelau 110.5

Rise, venous pressure 459.89

Risk
  factor — *see* Problem
  falling V15.88   ●
  suicidal 300.9

Ritter's disease (dermatitis exfoliativa
  neonatorum) 695.81

Rivalry, sibling 313.3

Rivalta's disease (cervicofacial actinomycosis) 039.3
River blindness 125.3 [360.13]
Robert's pelvis 755.69
  with disproportion (fetopelvic) 653.0 ☑
    affecting fetus or newborn 763.1
    causing obstructed labor 660.1 ☑
      affecting fetus or newborn 763.1
Robin's syndrome 756.0
Robinson's (hidrotic) **ectodermal dysplasia** 757.31
Robles' disease (onchocerciasis) 125.3 [360.13]
Rochalimea — see Rickettsial disease
Rocky Mountain fever (spotted) 082.0
Rodent ulcer (M8090/3) — see also Neoplasm, skin, malignant
  cornea 370.07
Roentgen ray, adverse effect — see Effect, adverse, x-ray
Roetheln 056.9
Roger's disease (congenital interventricular septal defect) 745.4
Rokitansky's
  disease (see also Necrosis, liver) 570
  tumor 620.2
Rokitansky-Aschoff sinuses (mucosal outpouching of gallbladder) (see also Disease, gallbladder) 575.8
Rokitansky-Kuster-Hauser syndrome (congenital absence vagina) 752.49
Rollet's chancre (syphilitic) 091.0
Rolling of head 781.0
Romano-Ward syndrome ▶(prolonged QT interval syndrome)◀ 426.82   ▲
Romanus lesion 720.1
Romberg's disease or syndrome 349.89
Roof, mouth — see condition
Rosacea 695.3
  acne 695.3
  keratitis 695.3 [370.49]
Rosary, rachitic 268.0
Rose
  cold 477.0
  fever 477.0
  rash 782.1
    epidemic 056.9
    of infants 057.8
Rosen-Castleman-Liebow syndrome (pulmonary proteinosis) 516.0
Rosenbach's erysipelatoid or erysipeloid 027.1
Rosenthal's disease (factor XI deficiency) 286.2
Roseola 057.8
  infantum, infantilis 057.8
Rossbach's disease (hyperchlorhydria) 536.8
  psychogenic 306.4
Rössle-Urbach-Wiethe lipoproteinosis 272.8
Ross river fever 066.3
Rostan's asthma (cardiac) (see also Failure, ventricular, left) 428.1
Rot
  Barcoo (see also Ulcer, skin) 707.9
  knife-grinders' (see also Tuberculosis) 011.4 ☑
Rot-Bernhardt disease 355.1
Rotation
  anomalous, incomplete or insufficient — see Malrotation
  cecum (congenital) 751.4
  colon (congenital) 751.4
  manual, affecting fetus or newborn 763.89
  spine, incomplete or insufficient 737.8
  tooth, teeth 524.35
  vertebra, incomplete or insufficient 737.8
Röteln 056.9
Roth's disease or meralgia 355.1
Roth-Bernhardt disease or syndrome 355.1
Rothmund (-Thomson) syndrome 757.33
Rotor's disease or syndrome (idiopathic hyperbilirubinemia) 277.4
Rotundum ulcus — see Ulcer, stomach

Round
  back (with wedging of vertebrae) 737.10
    late effect of rickets 268.1
  hole, retina 361.31
    with detachment 361.01
  ulcer (stomach) — see Ulcer, stomach
  worms (infestation) (large) NEC 127.0
Roussy-Lévy syndrome 334.3
Routine postpartum follow-up V24.2
Roy (-Jutras) syndrome (acropachyderma) 757.39
Rubella (German measles) 056.9
  complicating pregnancy, childbirth, or puerperium 647.5 ☑
  complication 056.8
    neurological 056.00
      encephalomyelitis 056.01
      specified type NEC 056.09
    specified type NEC 056.79
  congenital 771.0
  contact V01.4
  exposure to V01.4
  maternal
    with suspected fetal damage affecting management of pregnancy 655.3 ☑
    affecting fetus or newborn 760.2
      manifest rubella in infant 771.0
  specified complications NEC 056.79
  vaccination, prophylactic (against) V04.3
Rubeola (measles) (see also Measles) 055.9
  complicated 055.8
  meaning rubella (see also Rubella) 056.9
  scarlatinosa 057.8
Rubeosis iridis 364.42
  diabetica 250.5 ☑ [364.42]
Rubinstein-Taybi's syndrome (brachydactylia, short stature and mental retardation) 759.89
Rud's syndrome (mental deficiency, epilepsy, and infantilism) 759.89
Rudimentary (congenital) — see also Agenesis
  arm 755.22
  bone 756.9
  cervix uteri 752.49
  eye (see also Microphthalmos) 743.10
  fallopian tube 752.19
  leg 755.32
  lobule of ear 744.21
  patella 755.64
  respiratory organs in thoracopagus 759.4
  tracheal bronchus 748.3
  uterine horn 752.3
  uterus 752.3
    in male 752.7
    solid or with cavity 752.3
  vagina 752.49
Ruiter-Pompen (-Wyers) syndrome (angiokeratoma corporis diffusum) 272.7
Ruled out condition (see also Observation, suspected) V71.9
Rumination — see also Vomiting
  disorder 307.53
  neurotic 300.3
  obsessional 300.3
  psychogenic 307.53
Runaway reaction — see also Disturbance, conduct
  socialized 312.2 ☑
  undersocialized, unsocialized 312.1 ☑
Runeberg's disease (progressive pernicious anemia) 281.0
Runge's syndrome (postmaturity) 766.22
Rupia 091.3
  congenital 090.0
  tertiary 095.9
Rupture, ruptured 553.9
  abdominal viscera NEC 799.89
    obstetrical trauma 665.5 ☑
  abscess (spontaneous) — see Abscess, by site
  amnion — see Rupture, membranes
  aneurysm — see Aneurysm
  anus (sphincter) — see Laceration, anus
  aorta, aortic 441.5
    abdominal 441.3

Rupture, ruptured — continued
  aorta, aortic — continued
    arch 441.1
    ascending 441.1
    descending 441.5
      abdominal 441.3
      thoracic 441.1
    syphilitic 093.0
    thoracoabdominal 441.6
    thorax, thoracic 441.1
    transverse 441.1
    traumatic (thoracic) 901.0
      abdominal 902.0
    valve or cusp (see also Endocarditis, aortic) 424.1
  appendix (with peritonitis) 540.0
    with peritoneal abscess 540.1
    traumatic — see Injury, internal, gastrointestinal tract
  arteriovenous fistula, brain (congenital) 430
  artery 447.2
    brain (see also Hemorrhage, brain) 431
    coronary (see also Infarct, myocardium) 410.9 ☑
    heart (see also Infarct, myocardium) 410.9 ☑
    pulmonary 417.8
    traumatic (complication) (see also Injury, blood vessel, by site) 904.9
  bile duct, except cystic (see also Disease, biliary) 576.3
    cystic 575.4
    traumatic — see Injury, internal, intra-abdominal
  bladder (sphincter) 596.6
    with
      abortion — see Abortion, by type, with damage to pelvic organs
      ectopic pregnancy (see also categories 633.0-633.9) 639.2
      molar pregnancy (see also categories 630-632) 639.2
    following
      abortion 639.2
      ectopic or molar pregnancy 639.2
    nontraumatic 596.6
    obstetrical trauma 665.5 ☑
    spontaneous 596.6
    traumatic — see Injury, internal, bladder
  blood vessel (see also Hemorrhage) 459.0
    brain (see also Hemorrhage, brain) 431
    heart (see also Infarct, myocardium) 410.9 ☑
    traumatic (complication) (see also Injury, blood vessel, by site) 904.9
  bone — see Fracture, by site
  bowel 569.89
    traumatic — see Injury, internal, intestine
  Bowman's membrane 371.31
  brain
    aneurysm (congenital) (see also Hemorrhage, subarachnoid) 430
      late effect — see Late effect(s) (of) cerebrovascular disease
      syphilitic 094.87
    hemorrhagic (see also Hemorrhage, brain) 431
    injury at birth 767.0
    syphilitic 094.89
  capillaries 448.9
  cardiac (see also Infarct, myocardium) 410.9 ☑
  cartilage (articular) (current) — see also Sprain, by site
    knee — see Tear, meniscus
    semilunar — see Tear, meniscus
  cecum (with peritonitis) 540.0
    with peritoneal abscess 540.1
    traumatic 863.89
      with open wound into cavity 863.99
  cerebral aneurysm (congenital) (see also Hemorrhage, subarachnoid) 430
    late effect — see Late effect(s) (of) cerebrovascular disease
  cervix (uteri)
    with
      abortion — see Abortion, by type, with damage to pelvic organs

---

Rupture, ruptured — *continued*
    cervix — *continued*
        with — *continued*
            ectopic pregnancy (*see also* categories 633.0-633.9) 639.2
            molar pregnancy (*see also* categories 630-632) 639.2
        following
            abortion 639.2
            ectopic or molar pregnancy 639.2
        obstetrical trauma 665.3 ☑
        traumatic — *see* Injury, internal, cervix
    chordae tendineae 429.5
    choroid (direct) (indirect) (traumatic) 363.63
    circle of Willis (*see also* Hemorrhage, subarachnoid) 430
        late effect — *see* Late effect(s) (of) cerebrovascular disease
    colon 569.89
        traumatic — *see* Injury, internal, colon
    cornea (traumatic) — *see also* Rupture, eye
        due to ulcer 370.00
    coronary (artery) (thrombotic) (*see also* Infarct, myocardium) 410.9 ☑
    corpus luteum (infected) (ovary) 620.1
    cyst — *see* Cyst
    cystic duct (*see also* Disease, gallbladder) 575.4
    Descemet's membrane 371.33
        traumatic — *see* Rupture, eye
    diaphragm — *see also* Hernia, diaphragm
        traumatic — *see* Injury, internal, diaphragm
    diverticulum
        bladder 596.3
        intestine (large) (*see also* Diverticula) 562.10
            small 562.00
    duodenal stump 537.89
    duodenum (ulcer) — *see* Ulcer, duodenum, with perforation
    ear drum (*see also* Perforation, tympanum) 384.20
        with otitis media — *see* Otitis media
        traumatic — *see* Wound, open, ear
    esophagus 530.4
        traumatic 862.22
            with open wound into cavity 862.32
            cervical region — *see* Wound, open, esophagus
    eye (without prolapse of intraocular tissue) 871.0
        with
            exposure of intraocular tissue 871.1
            partial loss of intraocular tissue 871.2
            prolapse of intraocular tissue 871.1
        due to burn 940.5
    fallopian tube 620.8
        due to pregnancy — *see* Pregnancy, tubal
        traumatic — *see* Injury, internal, fallopian tube
    fontanel 767.3
    free wall (ventricle) (*see also* Infarct, myocardium) 410.9 ☑
    gallbladder or duct (*see also* Disease, gallbladder) 575.4
        traumatic — *see* Injury, internal, gallbladder
    gastric (*see also* Rupture, stomach) 537.89
        vessel 459.0
    globe (eye) (traumatic) — *see* Rupture, eye
    graafian follicle (hematoma) 620.0
    heart (auricle) (ventricle) (*see also* Infarct, myocardium) 410.9 ☑
        infectional 422.90
        traumatic — *see* Rupture, myocardium, traumatic
    hymen 623.8
    internal
        organ, traumatic — *see also* Injury, internal, by site
            heart — *see* Rupture, myocardium, traumatic
            kidney — *see* Rupture, kidney
            liver — *see* Rupture, liver
            spleen — *see* Rupture, spleen, traumatic
        semilunar cartilage — *see* Tear, meniscus
    intervertebral disc — *see* Displacement, intervertebral disc
        traumatic (current) — *see* Dislocation, vertebra

Rupture, ruptured — *continued*
    intestine 569.89
        traumatic — *see* Injury, internal, intestine
    intracranial, birth injury 767.0
    iris 364.76
        traumatic — *see* Rupture, eye
    joint capsule — *see* Sprain, by site
    kidney (traumatic) 866.03
        with open wound into cavity 866.13
        due to birth injury 767.8
        nontraumatic 593.89
    lacrimal apparatus (traumatic) 870.2
    lens (traumatic) 366.20
    ligament — *see also* Sprain, by site
        with open wound — *see* Wound, open, by site
        old (*see also* Disorder, cartilage, articular) 718.0 ☑
    liver (traumatic) 864.04
        with open wound into cavity 864.14
        due to birth injury 767.8
        nontraumatic 573.8
    lymphatic (node) (vessel) 457.8
    marginal sinus (placental) (with hemorrhage) 641.2 ☑
        affecting fetus or newborn 762.1
    meaning hernia — *see* Hernia
    membrana tympani (*see also* Perforation, tympanum) 384.20
        with otitis media — *see* Otitis media
        traumatic — *see* Wound, open, ear
    membranes (spontaneous)
        artificial
            delayed delivery following 658.3 ☑
                affecting fetus or newborn 761.1
                fetus or newborn 761.1
            delayed delivery following 658.2 ☑
                affecting fetus or newborn 761.1
            premature (less than 24 hours prior to onset of labor) 658.1 ☑
                affecting fetus or newborn 761.1
            delayed delivery following 658.2 ☑
                affecting fetus or newborn 761.1
    meningeal artery (*see also* Hemorrhage, subarachnoid) 430
        late effect — *see* Late effect(s) (of) cerebrovascular disease
    meniscus (knee) — *see also* Tear, meniscus
        old (*see also* Derangement, meniscus) 717.5
            site other than knee — *see* Disorder, cartilage, articular
        site other than knee — *see* Sprain, by site
    mesentery 568.89
        traumatic — *see* Injury, internal, mesentery
    mitral — *see* Insufficiency, mitral
    muscle (traumatic) NEC — *see also* Sprain, by site
        with open wound — *see* Wound, open, by site
        nontraumatic 728.83
    musculotendinous cuff (nontraumatic) (shoulder) 840.4
    mycotic aneurysm, causing cerebral hemorrhage (*see also* Hemorrhage, subarachnoid) 430
        late effect — *see* Late effect(s) (of) cerebrovascular disease
    myocardium, myocardial (*see also* Infarct, myocardium) 410.9 ☑
        traumatic 861.03
            with open wound into thorax 861.13
    nontraumatic (meaning hernia) (*see also* Hernia, by site) 553.9
    obstructed (*see also* Hernia, by site, with obstruction) 552.9
        gangrenous (*see also* Hernia, by site, with gangrene) 551.9
    operation wound 998.32
        internal 998.31
    ovary, ovarian 620.8
        corpus luteum 620.1
        follicle (graafian) 620.0
    oviduct 620.8
        due to pregnancy — *see* Pregnancy, tubal
    pancreas 577.8
        traumatic — *see* Injury, internal, pancreas
    papillary muscle (ventricular) 429.6

Rupture, ruptured — *continued*
    pelvic
        floor, complicating delivery 664.1 ☑
        organ NEC — *see* Injury, pelvic, organs
    penis (traumatic) — *see* Wound, open, penis
    perineum 624.8
        during delivery (*see also* Laceration, perineum, complicating delivery) 664.4 ☑
    pharynx (nontraumatic) (spontaneous) 478.29
    pregnant uterus (before onset of labor) 665.0 ☑
    prostate (traumatic) — *see* Injury, internal, prostate
    pulmonary
        artery 417.8
        valve (heart) (*see also* Endocarditis, pulmonary) 424.3
        vein 417.8
        vessel 417.8
    pupil, sphincter 364.75
    pus tube (*see also* Salpingo-oophoritis) 614.2
    pyosalpinx (*see also* Salpingo-oophoritis) 614.2
    rectum 569.49
        traumatic — *see* Injury, internal, rectum
    retina, retinal (traumatic) (without detachment) 361.30
        with detachment (*see also* Detachment, retina, with retinal defect) 361.00
    rotator cuff (capsule) (traumatic) 840.4
        nontraumatic, complete 727.61
    sclera 871.0
    semilunar cartilage, knee (*see also* Tear, meniscus) 836.2
        old (*see also* Derangement, meniscus) 717.5
    septum (cardiac) 410.8 ☑
    sigmoid 569.89
        traumatic — *see* Injury, internal, colon, sigmoid
    sinus of Valsalva 747.29
    spinal cord — *see* Injury, spinal, by site
        due to injury at birth 767.4
        fetus or newborn 767.4
        syphilitic 094.89
        traumatic — *see also* Injury, spinal, by site
            with fracture — *see* Fracture, vertebra, by site, with spinal cord injury
    spleen 289.59
        congenital 767.8
        due to injury at birth 767.8
        malarial 084.9
        nontraumatic 289.59
        spontaneous 289.59
        traumatic 865.04
            with open wound into cavity 865.14
    splenic vein 459.0
    stomach 537.89
        due to injury at birth 767.8
        traumatic — *see* Injury, internal, stomach
        ulcer — *see* Ulcer, stomach, with perforation
    synovium 727.50
        specified site NEC 727.59
    tendon (traumatic) — *see also* Sprain, by site
        with open wound — *see* Wound, open, by site
        Achilles 845.09
            nontraumatic 727.67
        ankle 845.09
            nontraumatic 727.68
        biceps (long head) 840.8
            nontraumatic 727.62
        foot 845.10
            interphalangeal (joint) 845.13
            metatarsophalangeal (joint) 845.12
            nontraumatic 727.68
            specified site NEC 845.19
            tarsometatarsal (joint) 845.11
        hand 842.10
            carpometacarpal (joint) 842.11
            interphalangeal (joint) 842.13
            metacarpophalangeal (joint) 842.12
            nontraumatic 727.63
                extensors 727.63
                flexors 727.64
            specified site NEC 842.19
        nontraumatic 727.60
            specified site NEC 727.69

Rupture, ruptured — *continued*
  tendon — *see also* Sprain, by site — *continued*
    patellar 844.8
      nontraumatic 727.66
    quadriceps 844.8
      nontraumatic 727.65
    rotator cuff (capsule) 840.4
      nontraumatic, complete 727.61
    wrist 842.00
      carpal (joint) 842.01
        nontraumatic 727.63
          extensors 727.63
          flexors 727.64
      radiocarpal (joint) (ligament) 842.02
      radioulnar (joint), distal 842.09
      specified site NEC 842.09
  testis (traumatic) 878.2
    complicated 878.3
    due to syphilis 095.8
  thoracic duct 457.8
  tonsil 474.8
  traumatic
    with open wound — *see* Wound, open, by
      site
    aorta — *see* Rupture, aorta, traumatic
    ear drum — *see* Wound, open, ear, drum
    external site — *see* Wound, open, by site
    eye 871.2
    globe (eye) — *see* Wound, open, eyeball
    internal organ (abdomen, chest, or pelvis) —
      see also Injury, internal, by site
      heart — *see* Rupture, myocardium,
        traumatic
      kidney — *see* Rupture, kidney
      liver — *see* Rupture, liver
      spleen — *see* Rupture, spleen, traumatic
    ligament, muscle, or tendon — *see also*
      Sprain, by site
      with open wound — *see* Wound, open, by
        site

Rupture, ruptured — *continued*
  traumatic — *continued*
    meaning hernia — *see* Hernia
  tricuspid (heart) (valve) — *see* Endocarditis,
    tricuspid
  tube, tubal 620.8
    abscess (*see also* Salpingo-oophoritis) 614.2
    due to pregnancy — *see* Pregnancy, tubal
  tympanum, tympanic (membrane) (*see also*
    Perforation, tympanum) 384.20
    with otitis media — *see* Otitis media
    traumatic — *see* Wound, open, ear, drum
  umbilical cord 663.8 ☑
    fetus or newborn 772.0
  ureter (traumatic) (*see also* Injury, internal,
    ureter) 867.2
    nontraumatic 593.89
  urethra 599.84
    with
      abortion — *see* Abortion, by type, with
        damage to pelvic organs
      ectopic pregnancy (*see also* categories
        633.0-633.9) 639.2
      molar pregnancy (*see also* categories 630-
        632) 639.2
    following
      abortion 639.2
      ectopic or molar pregnancy 639.2
    obstetrical trauma 665.5 ☑
    traumatic — *see* Injury, internal urethra
  uterosacral ligament 620.8
  uterus (traumatic) — *see also* Injury, internal
    uterus
    affecting fetus or newborn 763.89
    during labor 665.1 ☑
    nonpuerperal, nontraumatic 621.8
    nontraumatic 621.8
    pregnant (during labor) 665.1 ☑
      before labor 665.0 ☑

Rupture, ruptured — *continued*
  vagina 878.6
    complicated 878.7
    complicating delivery — *see* Laceration,
      vagina, complicating delivery
  valve, valvular (heart) — *see* Endocarditis
  varicose vein — *see* Varicose, vein
  varix — *see* Varix
  vena cava 459.0
  ventricle (free wall) (left) (*see also* Infarct,
    myocardium) 410.9 ☑
  vesical (urinary) 596.6
    traumatic — *see* Injury, internal, bladder
  vessel (blood) 459.0
    pulmonary 417.8
  viscus 799.89
  vulva 878.4
    complicated 878.5
    complicating delivery 664.0 ☑

Russell's dwarf (uterine dwarfism and
  craniofacial dysostosis) 759.89
Russell's dysentery 004.8
Russell (-Silver) syndrome (congenital
  hemihypertrophy and short stature) 759.89
Russian spring-summer type encephalitis 063.0
Rust's disease (tuberculous spondylitis)
  015.0 ☑ *[720.81]*
Rustitskii's disease (multiple myeloma)
  (M9730/3) 203.0 ☑
Ruysch's disease (Hirschsprung's disease) 751.3
Rytand-Lipsitch syndrome (complete
  atrioventricular block) 426.0

S

Saber
  shin 090.5
  tibia 090.5
Sac, lacrimal — *see* condition
Saccharomyces infection (*see also* Candidiasis) 112.9
Saccharopinuria 270.7
Saccular — *see* condition
Sacculation
  aorta (nonsyphilitic) (*see also* Aneurysm, aorta) 441.9
    ruptured 441.5
    syphilitic 093.0
  bladder 596.3
  colon 569.89
  intralaryngeal (congenital) (ventricular) 748.3
  larynx (congenital) (ventricular) 748.3
  organ or site, congenital — *see* Distortion
  pregnant uterus, complicating delivery 654.4 ☑
    affecting fetus or newborn 763.1
      causing obstructed labor 660.2 ☑
        affecting fetus or newborn 763.1
  rectosigmoid 569.89
  sigmoid 569.89
  ureter 593.89
  urethra 599.2
  vesical 596.3
Sachs (-Tay) disease (amaurotic familial idiocy) 330.1
Sacks-Libman disease 710.0 *[424.91]*
Sacralgia 724.6
Sacralization
  fifth lumbar vertebra 756.15
  incomplete (vertebra) 756.15
Sacrodynia 724.6
Sacroiliac joint — *see* condition
Sacroiliitis NEC 720.2
Sacrum — *see* condition
Saddle
  back 737.8
  embolus, aorta 444.0
  nose 738.0
    congenital 754.0
    due to syphilis 090.5
Sadism (sexual) 302.84
Saemisch's ulcer 370.04
Saenger's syndrome 379.46
Sago spleen 277.3
Sailors' skin 692.74
Saint
  Anthony's fire (*see also* Erysipelas) 035
  Guy's dance — *see* Chorea
  Louis-type encephalitis 062.3
  triad (*see also* Hernia, diaphragm) 553.3
  Vitus' dance — *see* Chorea
Salicylism
  correct substance properly administered 535.4 ☑
  overdose or wrong substance given or taken 965.1
Salivary duct or gland — *see also* condition
  virus disease 078.5
Salivation (excessive) (*see also* Ptyalism) 527.7
Salmonella (aertrycke) (choleraesuis) (enteritidis) (gallinarum) (suipestifer) (typhimurium) (*see also* Infection, Salmonella) 003.9
  arthritis 003.23
  carrier (suspected) of V02.3
  meningitis 003.21
  osteomyelitis 003.24
  pneumonia 003.22
  septicemia 003.1
  typhosa 002.0
    carrier (suspected) of V02.1
Salmonellosis 003.0
  with pneumonia 003.22
Salpingitis (catarrhal) (fallopian tube) (nodular) (pseudofollicular) (purulent) (septic) (*see also* Salpingo-oophoritis) 614.2

Salpingitis (*see also* Salpingo-oophoritis) — *continued*
  ear 381.50
    acute 381.51
    chronic 381.52
  Eustachian (tube) 381.50
    acute 381.51
    chronic 381.52
  follicularis 614.1
  gonococcal (chronic) 098.37
    acute 098.17
  interstitial, chronic 614.1
  isthmica nodosa 614.1
  old — *see* Salpingo-oophoritis, chronic
  puerperal, postpartum, childbirth 670.0 ☑
  specific (chronic) 098.37
    acute 098.17
  tuberculous (acute) (chronic) (*see also* Tuberculosis) 016.6 ☑
  venereal (chronic) 098.37
    acute 098.17
Salpingocele 620.4
Salpingo-oophoritis (catarrhal) (purulent) (ruptured) (septic) (suppurative) 614.2
  acute 614.0
    with
      abortion — *see* Abortion, by type, with sepsis
      ectopic pregnancy (*see also* categories 633.0-633.9) 639.0
      molar pregnancy (*see also* categories 630-632) 639.0
    following
      abortion 639.0
      ectopic or molar pregnancy 639.0
    gonococcal 098.17
    puerperal, postpartum, childbirth 670.0 ☑
    tuberculous (*see also* Tuberculosis) 016.6 ☑
  chronic 614.1
    gonococcal 098.37
    tuberculous (see also Tuberculosis) 016.6 ☑
  complicating pregnancy 646.6 ☑
    affecting fetus or newborn 760.8
  gonococcal (chronic) 098.37
    acute 098.17
  old — *see* Salpingo-oophoritis, chronic
  puerperal 670.0 ☑
  specific — *see* Salpingo-oophoritis, gonococcal
  subacute (*see also* Salpingo-oophoritis, acute) 614.0
  tuberculous (acute) (chronic) (*see also* Tuberculosis) 016.6 ☑
  venereal — *see* Salpingo-oophoritis, gonococcal
Salpingo-ovaritis (*see also* Salpingo-oophoritis) 614.2
Salpingoperitonitis (*see also* Salpingo-oophoritis) 614.2
Salt-losing
  nephritis (*see also* Disease, renal) 593.9
  syndrome (*see also* Disease, renal) 593.9
Salt-rheum (*see also* Eczema) 692.9
Salzmann's nodular dystrophy 371.46
Sampson's cyst or tumor 617.1
Sandblasters'
  asthma 502
  lung 502
Sander's disease (paranoia) 297.1
Sandfly fever 066.0
Sandhoff's disease 330.1
Sanfilippo's syndrome (mucopolysaccharidosis III) 277.5
Sanger-Brown's ataxia 334.2
San Joaquin Valley fever 114.0
Sao Paulo fever or typhus 082.0
Saponification, mesenteric 567.89   ▲
Sapremia — *see* Septicemia
Sarcocele (benign)
  syphilitic 095.8
    congenital 090.5
Sarcoepiplocele (*see also* Hernia) 553.9

Sarcoepiplomphalocele (*see also* Hernia, umbilicus) 553.1
Sarcoid (any site) 135
  with lung involvement 135 *[517.8]*
  Boeck's 135
  Darier-Roussy 135
  Spiegler-Fendt 686.8
Sarcoidosis 135
  cardiac 135 *[425.8]*
  lung 135 *[517.8]*
Sarcoma (M8800/3) — *see also* Neoplasm, connective tissue, malignant
  alveolar soft part (M9581/3) — *see* Neoplasm, connective tissue, malignant
  ameloblastic (M9330/3) 170.1
    upper jaw (bone) 170.0
  botryoid (M8910/3) — *see* Neoplasm, connective tissue, malignant
  botryoides (M8910/3) — *see* Neoplasm, connective tissue, malignant
  cerebellar (M9480/3) 191.6
    circumscribed (arachnoidal) (M9471/3) 191.6
  circumscribed (arachnoidal) cerebellar (M9471/3) 191.6
  clear cell, of tendons and aponeuroses (M9044/3) — *see* Neoplasm, connective tissue, malignant
  embryonal (M8991/3) — *see* Neoplasm, connective tissue, malignant
  endometrial (stromal) (M8930/3) 182.0
    isthmus 182.1
  endothelial (M9130/3) — *see also* Neoplasm, connective tissue, malignant
    bone (M9260/3) — *see* Neoplasm, bone, malignant
  epithelioid cell (M8804/3) — *see* Neoplasm, connective tissue, malignant
  Ewing's (M9260/3) — *see* Neoplasm, bone, malignant
  follicular dendritic cell 202.9 ☑
  germinoblastic (diffuse) (M9632/3) 202.8 ☑
    follicular (M9697/3) 202.0 ☑
  giant cell (M8802/3) — *see also* Neoplasm, connective tissue, malignant
    bone (M9250/3) — *see* Neoplasm, bone, malignant
  glomoid (M8710/3) — *see* Neoplasm, connective tissue, malignant
  granulocytic (M9930/3) 205.3 ☑
  hemangioendothelial (M9130/3) — *see* Neoplasm, connective tissue, malignant
  hemorrhagic, multiple (M9140/3) — *see* Kaposi's, sarcoma
  Hodgkin's (M9662/3) 201.2 ☑
  immunoblastic (M9612/3) 200.8 ☑
  interdigitating dendritic cell 202.9 ☑
  Kaposi's (M9140/3) — *see* Kaposi's, sarcoma
  Kupffer cell (M9124/3) 155.0
  Langerhans cell 202.9 ☑
  leptomeningeal (M9530/3) — *see* Neoplasm, meninges, malignant
  lymphangioendothelial (M9170/3) — *see* Neoplasm, connective tissue, malignant
  lymphoblastic (M9630/3) 200.1 ☑
  lymphocytic (M9620/3) 200.1 ☑
  mast cell (M9740/3) 202.6 ☑
  melanotic (M8720/3) — *see* Melanoma
  meningeal (M9530/3) — *see* Neoplasm, meninges, malignant
  meningothelial (M9530/3) — *see* Neoplasm, meninges, malignant
  mesenchymal (M8800/3) — *see also* Neoplasm, connective tissue, malignant
    mixed (M8990/3) — *see* Neoplasm, connective tissue, malignant
  mesothelial (M9050/3) — *see* Neoplasm, by site, malignant
  monstrocellular (M9481/3)
    specified site — *see* Neoplasm, by site, malignant
    unspecified site 191.9
  myeloid (M9930/3) 205.3 ☑
  neurogenic (M9540/3) — *see* Neoplasm, connective tissue, malignant

Sarcoma (M8800/3) — *see also* Neoplasm, connective tissue, malignant — *continued*
  odontogenic (M9270/3) 170.1
    upper jaw (bone) 170.0
  osteoblastic (M9180/3) — *see* Neoplasm, bone, malignant
  osteogenic (M9180/3) — *see also* Neoplasm, bone, malignant
    juxtacortical (M9190/3) — *see* Neoplasm, bone, malignant
    periosteal (M9190/3) — *see* Neoplasm, bone, malignant
  periosteal (M8812/3) — *see also* Neoplasm, bone, malignant
    osteogenic (M9190/3) — *see* Neoplasm, bone, malignant
  plasma cell (M9731/3) 203.8 ☑
  pleomorphic cell (M8802/3) — *see* Neoplasm, connective tissue, malignant
  reticuloendothelial (M9720/3) 202.3 ☑
  reticulum cell (M9640/3) 200.0 ☑
    nodular (M9642/3) 200.0 ☑
    pleomorphic cell type (M9641/3) 200.0 ☑
  round cell (M8803/3) — *see* Neoplasm, connective tissue, malignant
  small cell (M8803/3) — *see* Neoplasm, connective tissue, malignant
  spindle cell (M8801/3) — *see* Neoplasm, connective tissue, malignant
  stromal (endometrial) (M8930/3) 182.0
    isthmus 182.1
  synovial (M9040/3) — *see also* Neoplasm, connective tissue, malignant
    biphasic type (M9043/3) — *see* Neoplasm, connective tissue, malignant
    epithelioid cell type (M9042/3) — *see* Neoplasm, connective tissue, malignant
    spindle cell type (M9041/3) — *see* Neoplasm, connective tissue, malignant
Sarcomatosis
  meningeal (M9539/3) — *see* Neoplasm, meninges, malignant
  specified site NEC (M8800/3) — *see* Neoplasm, connective tissue, malignant
  unspecified site (M8800/6) 171.9
Sarcosinemia 270.8
Sarcosporidiosis 136.5
Satiety, early 780.94
Saturnine — *see* condition
Saturnism 984.9
  specified type of lead — *see* Table of Drugs and Chemicals
Satyriasis 302.89
Sauriasis — *see* Ichthyosis
Sauriderma 757.39
Sauriosis — *see* Ichthyosis
Savill's disease (epidemic exfoliative dermatitis) 695.89
SBE (subacute bacterial endocarditis) 421.0
Scabies (any site) 133.0
Scabs 782.8
Scaglietti-Dagnini syndrome (acromegalic macrospondylitis) 253.0
Scald, scalded — *see also* Burn, by site
  skin syndrome 695.1
Scalenus anticus (anterior) syndrome 353.0
Scales 782.8
Scalp — *see* condition
Scaphocephaly 756.0
Scaphoiditis, tarsal 732.5
Scapulalgia 733.90
Scapulohumeral myopathy 359.1
Scar, scarring (*see also* Cicatrix) 709.2
  adherent 709.2
  atrophic 709.2
  cervix
    in pregnancy or childbirth 654.6 ☑
      affecting fetus or newborn 763.89
      causing obstructed labor 660.2 ☑
        affecting fetus or newborn 763.1

Scar, scarring (*see also* Cicatrix) — *continued*
  cheloid 701.4
  chorioretinal 363.30
    disseminated 363.35
    macular 363.32
    peripheral 363.34
    posterior pole NEC 363.33
  choroid (*see also* Scar, chorioretinal) 363.30
  compression, pericardial 423.9
  congenital 757.39
  conjunctiva 372.64
  cornea 371.00
    xerophthalmic 264.6
  due to previous cesarean delivery, complicating pregnancy or childbirth 654.2 ☑
    affecting fetus or newborn 763.89
  duodenal (bulb) (cap) 537.3
  hypertrophic 701.4
  keloid 701.4
  labia 624.4
  lung (base) 518.89
  macula 363.32
    disseminated 363.35
    peripheral 363.34
  muscle 728.89
  myocardium, myocardial 412
  painful 709.2
  papillary muscle 429.81
  posterior pole NEC 363.33
    macular — *see* Scar, macula
  postnecrotic (hepatic) (liver) 571.9
  psychic V15.49
  retina (*see also* Scar, chorioretinal) 363.30
  trachea 478.9
  uterus 621.8
    in pregnancy or childbirth NEC 654.9 ☑
      affecting fetus or newborn 763.89
      due to previous cesarean delivery 654.2 ☑
  vulva 624.4
Scarabiasis 134.1
Scarlatina 034.1
  anginosa 034.1
  maligna 034.1
  myocarditis, acute 034.1 *[422.0]*
    old (*see also* Myocarditis) 429.0
  otitis media 034.1 *[382.02]*
  ulcerosa 034.1
Scarlatinella 057.8
Scarlet fever (albuminuria) (angina) (convulsions) (lesions of lid) (rash) 034.1
Schamberg's disease, dermatitis, or dermatosis (progressive pigmentary dermatosis) 709.09
Schatzki's ring (esophagus) (lower) (congenital) 750.3
  acquired 530.3
Schaufenster krankheit 413.9
Schaumann's
  benign lymphogranulomatosis 135
  disease (sarcoidosis) 135
  syndrome (sarcoidosis) 135
Scheie's syndrome (mucopolysaccharidosis IS) 277.5
Schenck's disease (sporotrichosis) 117.1
Scheuermann's disease or osteochondrosis 732.0
Scheuthauer-Marie-Sainton syndrome (cleidocranialis dysostosis) 755.59
Schilder (-Flatau) disease 341.1
Schilling-type monocytic leukemia (M9890/3) 206.9 ☑
Schimmelbusch's disease, cystic mastitis, or hyperplasia 610.1
Schirmer's syndrome (encephalocutaneous angiomatosis) 759.6
Schistocelia 756.79
Schistoglossia 750.13
Schistosoma infestation — *see* Infestation, Schistosoma
Schistosomiasis 120.9
  Asiatic 120.2
  bladder 120.0
  chestermani 120.8

Schistosomiasis — *continued*
  colon 120.1
  cutaneous 120.3
  due to
    S. hematobium 120.0
    S. japonicum 120.2
    S. mansoni 120.1
    S. mattheii 120.8
  eastern 120.2
  genitourinary tract 120.0
  intestinal 120.1
  lung 120.2
  Manson's (intestinal) 120.1
  Oriental 120.2
  pulmonary 120.2
  specified type NEC 120.8
  vesical 120.0
Schizencephaly 742.4
Schizo-affective psychosis (*see also* Schizophrenia) 295.7 ☑
Schizodontia 520.2
Schizoid personality 301.20
  introverted 301.21
  schizotypal 301.22
Schizophrenia, schizophrenic (reaction) 295.9 ☑

> *Note* — Use the following fifth-digit subclassification with category 295:
>
>   0   *unspecified*
>   1   *subchronic*
>   2   *chronic*
>   3   *subchronic with acute exacerbation*
>   4   *chronic with acute exacerbation*
>   5   *in remission*

  acute (attack) NEC 295.8 ☑
    episode 295.4 ☑
  atypical form 295.8 ☑
  borderline 295.5 ☑
  catalepsy 295.2 ☑
  catatonic (type) (acute) (excited) (withdrawn) 295.2 ☑
  childhood (type) (*see also* Psychosis, childhood) 299.9 ☑
  chronic NEC 295.6 ☑
  coenesthesiopathic 295.8 ☑
  cyclic (type) 295.7 ☑
  disorganized (type) 295.1 ☑
  flexibilitas cerea 295.2 ☑
  hebephrenic (type) (acute) 295.1 ☑
  incipient 295.5 ☑
  latent 295.5 ☑
  paranoid (type) (acute) 295.3 ☑
  paraphrenic (acute) 295.3 ☑
  prepsychotic 295.5 ☑
  primary (acute) 295.0 ☑
  prodromal 295.5 ☑
  pseudoneurotic 295.5 ☑
  pseudopsychopathic 295.5 ☑
  reaction 295.9 ☑
  residual type (state) 295.6 ☑
  restzustand 295.6 ☑
  schizo-affective (type) (depressed) (excited) 295.7 ☑
  schizophreniform type 295.4 ☑
  simple (type) (acute) 295.0 ☑
  simplex (acute) 295.0 ☑
  specified type NEC 295.8 ☑
  syndrome of childhood NEC (*see also* Psychosis, childhood) 299.9 ☑
  undifferentiated type 295.9 ☑
    acute 295.8 ☑
    chronic 295.6 ☑
Schizothymia 301.20
  introverted 301.21
  schizotypal 301.22
Schlafkrankheit 086.5
Schlatter's tibia (osteochondrosis) 732.4
Schlatter-Osgood disease (osteochondrosis, tibial tubercle) 732.4
Schloffer's tumor (*see also* Peritonitis) 567.29 ▲
Schmidt's syndrome
  sphallo-pharyngo-laryngeal hemiplegia 352.6

Schmidt's syndrome — *continued*
  thyroid-adrenocortical insufficiency 258.1
  vagoaccessory 352.6
Schmincke
  carcinoma (M8082/3) — *see* Neoplasm,
    nasopharynx, malignant
  tumor (M8082/3) — *see* Neoplasm,
    nasopharynx, malignant
Schmitz (-Stutzer) dysentery 004.0
Schmorl's disease or nodes 722.30
  lumbar, lumbosacral 722.32
  specified region NEC 722.39
  thoracic, thoracolumbar 722.31
Schneider's syndrome 047.9
Schneiderian
  carcinoma (M8121/3)
    specified site — *see* Neoplasm, by site,
      malignant
    unspecified site 160.0
  papilloma (M8121/0)
    specified site — *see* Neoplasm, by site,
      benign
    unspecified site 212.0
Schnitzler syndrome 273.1
Schoffer's tumor (*see also* Peritonitis) 567.29 ▲
Scholte's syndrome (malignant carcinoid) 259.2
Scholz's disease 330.0
Scholz (-Bielschowsky-Henneberg) syndrome
  330.0
Schönlein (-Henoch) disease (primary) (purpura)
  (rheumatic) 287.0
School examination V70.3
Schottmüller's disease (*see also* Fever,
  paratyphoid) 002.9
Schroeder's syndrome (endocrine-hypertensive)
  255.3
Schüller-Christian disease or syndrome (chronic
  histiocytosis X) 277.89
Schultz's disease or syndrome (agranulocytosis)
  288.0
Schultze's acroparesthesia, simple 443.89
Schwalbe-Ziehen-Oppenheimer disease 333.6
Schwannoma (M9560/0) — *see also* Neoplasm,
  connective tissue, benign
  malignant (M9560/3) — *see* Neoplasm,
    connective tissue, malignant
Schwartz (-Jampel) syndrome 756.89
Schwartz-Bartter syndrome (inappropriate
  secretion of antidiuretic hormone) 253.6
Schweninger-Buzzi disease (macular atrophy)
  701.3
Sciatic — *see* condition
Sciatica (infectional) 724.3
  due to
    displacement of intervertebral disc 722.10
    herniation, nucleus pulposus 722.10
  wallet 724.3 ●
Scimitar syndrome (anomalous venous drainage,
  right lung to inferior vena cava) 747.49
Sclera — *see* condition
Sclerectasia 379.11
Scleredema
  adultorum 710.1
  Buschke's 710.1
  newborn 778.1
Sclerema
  adiposum (newborn) 778.1
  adultorum 710.1
  edematosum (newborn) 778.1
  neonatorum 778.1
  newborn 778.1
Scleriasis — *see* Scleroderma
Scleritis 379.00
  with corneal involvement 379.05
  anterior (annular) (localized) 379.03
  brawny 379.06
  granulomatous 379.09
  posterior 379.07
  specified NEC 379.09
  suppurative 379.09
  syphilitic 095.0

Scleritis — *continued*
  tuberculous (nodular) (*see also* Tuberculosis)
    017.3 ☑ *[379.09]*
Sclerochoroiditis (*see also* Scleritis) 379.00
Scleroconjunctivitis (*see also* Scleritis) 379.00
Sclerocystic ovary (syndrome) 256.4
Sclerodactylia 701.0
Scleroderma, sclerodermia (acrosclerotic)
  (diffuse) (generalized) (progressive)
  (pulmonary) 710.1
  circumscribed 701.0
  linear 701.0
  localized (linear) 701.0
  newborn 778.1
Sclerokeratitis 379.05
  meaning sclerosing keratitis 370.54
  tuberculous (*see also* Tuberculosis)
    017.3 ☑ *[379.09]*
Scleroma, trachea 040.1
Scleromalacia
  multiple 731.0
  perforans 379.04
Scleromyxedema 701.8
Scleroperikeratitis 379.05
Sclerose en plaques 340
Sclerosis, sclerotic
  adrenal (gland) 255.8
  Alzheimer's 331.0
    with dementia — *see* Alzheimer's, dementia
  amyotrophic (lateral) 335.20
  annularis fibrosi
    aortic 424.1
    mitral 424.0
  aorta, aortic 440.0
    valve (*see also* Endocarditis, aortic) 424.1
  artery, arterial, arteriolar, arteriovascular —
    see Arteriosclerosis
  ascending multiple 340
  Baló's (concentric) 341.1
  basilar — *see* Sclerosis, brain
  bone (localized) NEC 733.99
  brain (general) (lobular) 341.9
    Alzheimer's — *see* Alzheimer's, dementia
    artery, arterial 437.0
    atrophic lobar 331.0
      with dementia
        with behavioral disturbance 331.0
          [294.11]
        without behavioral disturbance 331.0
          [294.10]
    diffuse 341.1
      familial (chronic) (infantile) 330.0
      infantile (chronic) (familial) 330.0
      Pelizaeus-Merzbacher type 330.0
    disseminated 340
    hereditary 334.2
    infantile (degenerative) (diffuse) 330.0
    insular 340
    Krabbe's 330.0
    miliary 340
    multiple 340
    Pelizaeus-Merzbacher 330.0
    progressive familial 330.0
    senile 437.0
    tuberous 759.5
  bulbar, progressive 340
  bundle of His 426.50
    left 426.3
    right 426.4
  cardiac — *see* Arteriosclerosis, coronary
  cardiorenal (*see also* Hypertension, cardiorenal)
    404.90
  cardiovascular (*see also* Disease,
    cardiovascular) 429.2
    renal (*see also* Hypertension, cardiorenal)
      404.90
  centrolobar, familial 330.0
  cerebellar — *see* Sclerosis, brain
  cerebral — *see* Sclerosis, brain
  cerebrospinal 340
    disseminated 340
    multiple 340
  cerebrovascular 437.0

Sclerosis, sclerotic — *continued*
  choroid 363.40
    diffuse 363.56
  combined (spinal cord) — *see also*
    Degeneration, combined
    multiple 340
  concentric, Baló's 341.1
  cornea 370.54
  coronary (artery) — *see* Arteriosclerosis,
    coronary
  corpus cavernosum
    female 624.8
    male 607.89
  Dewitzky's
    aortic 424.1
    mitral 424.0
  diffuse NEC 341.1
  disease, heart — *see* Arteriosclerosis, coronary
  disseminated 340
  dorsal 340
  dorsolateral (spinal cord) — *see* Degeneration,
    combined
  endometrium 621.8
  extrapyramidal 333.90
  eye, nuclear (senile) 366.16
  Friedreich's (spinal cord) 334.0
  funicular (spermatic cord) 608.89
  gastritis 535.4 ☑
  general (vascular) — *see* Arteriosclerosis
  gland (lymphatic) 457.8
  hepatic 571.9
  hereditary
    cerebellar 334.2
    spinal 334.0
  idiopathic cortical (Garré's) (*see also*
    Osteomyelitis) 730.1 ☑
  ilium, piriform 733.5
  insular 340
    pancreas 251.8
  Islands of Langerhans 251.8
  kidney — *see* Sclerosis, renal
  larynx 478.79
  lateral 335.24
    amyotrophic 335.20
    descending 335.24
    primary 335.24
    spinal 335.24
  liver 571.9
  lobar, atrophic (of brain) 331.0
    with dementia
      with behavioral disturbance 331.0
        [294.11]
      without behavioral disturbance 331.0
        [294.10]
  lung (*see also* Fibrosis, lung) 515
  mastoid 383.1
  mitral — *see* Endocarditis, mitral
  Mönckeberg's (medial) (*see also*
    Arteriosclerosis, extremities) 440.20
  multiple (brain stem) (cerebral) (generalized)
    (spinal cord) 340
  myocardium, myocardial — *see*
    Arteriosclerosis, coronary
  nuclear (senile), eye 366.16
  ovary 620.8
  pancreas 577.8
  penis 607.89
  peripheral arteries (*see also* Arteriosclerosis,
    extremities) 440.20
  plaques 340
  pluriglandular 258.8
  polyglandular 258.8
  posterior (spinal cord) (syphilitic) 094.0
  posterolateral (spinal cord) — *see* Degeneration,
    combined
  prepuce 607.89
  primary lateral 335.24
  progressive systemic 710.1
  pulmonary (*see also* Fibrosis, lung) 515
    artery 416.0
    valve (heart) (*see also* Endocarditis,
      pulmonary) 424.3
  renal 587
    with
      cystine storage disease 270.0
      hypertension (*see also* Hypertension,
        kidney) 403.90

Sclerosis, sclerotic — *continued*
  renal — *continued*
    with — *continued*
      hypertensive heart disease (conditions classifiable to 402) (*see also* Hypertension, cardiorenal) 404.90
      arteriolar (hyaline) (*see also* Hypertension, kidney) 403.90
      hyperplastic (*see also* Hypertension, kidney) 403.90
  retina (senile) (vascular) 362.17
  rheumatic
    aortic valve 395.9
    mitral valve 394.9
  Schilder's 341.1
  senile — *see* Arteriosclerosis
  spinal (cord) (general) (progressive) (transverse) 336.8
    ascending 357.0
    combined — *see also* Degeneration, combined
      multiple 340
      syphilitic 094.89
    disseminated 340
    dorsolateral — *see* Degeneration, combined
    hereditary (Friedreich's) (mixed form) 334.0
    lateral (amyotrophic) 335.24
    multiple 340
    posterior (syphilitic) 094.0
  stomach 537.89
  subendocardial, congenital 425.3
  systemic (progressive) 710.1
    with lung involvement 710.1 [517.2]
  tricuspid (heart) (valve) — *see* Endocarditis, tricuspid
  tuberous (brain) 759.5
  tympanic membrane (*see also* Tympanosclerosis) 385.00
  valve, valvular (heart) — *see* Endocarditis
  vascular — *see* Arteriosclerosis
  vein 459.89

Sclerotenonitis 379.07

Sclerotitis (*see also* Scleritis) 379.00
  syphilitic 095.0
  tuberculous (*see also* Tuberculosis) 017.3 ☑ [379.09]

Scoliosis (acquired) (postural) 737.30
  congenital 754.2
  due to or associated with
    Charcôt-Marie-Tooth disease 356.1 [737.43]
    mucopolysaccharidosis 277.5 [737.43]
    neurofibromatosis 237.71 [737.43]
    osteitis
      deformans 731.0 [737.43]
      fibrosa cystica 252.01 [737.43]
    osteoporosis (*see also* Osteoporosis) 733.00 [737.43]
    poliomyelitis 138 [737.43]
    radiation 737.33
    tuberculosis (*see also* Tuberculosis) 015.0 ☑ [737.43]
  idiopathic 737.30
    infantile
      progressive 737.32
      resolving 737.31
  paralytic 737.39
  rachitic 268.1
  sciatic 724.3
  specified NEC 737.39
  thoracogenic 737.34
  tuberculous (*see also* Tuberculosis) 015.0 ☑ [737.43]

Scoliotic pelvis 738.6
  with disproportion (fetopelvic) 653.0 ☑
    affecting fetus or newborn 763.1
    causing obstructed labor 660.1 ☑
      affecting fetus or newborn 763.1

Scorbutus, scorbutic 267
  anemia 281.8

Scotoma (ring) 368.44
  arcuate 368.43
  Bjerrum 368.43
  blind spot area 368.42
  central 368.41
  centrocecal 368.41
  paracecal 368.42

Scotoma — *continued*
  paracentral 368.41
  scintillating 368.12
  Seidel 368.43

Scratch — *see* Injury, superficial, by site

Screening (for) V82.9
  alcoholism V79.1
  anemia, deficiency NEC V78.1
    iron V78.0
  anomaly, congenital V82.89
  antenatal V28.9
    alphafetoprotein levels, raised V28.1
    based on amniocentesis V28.2
      chromosomal anomalies V28.0
      raised alphafetoprotein levels V28.1
    fetal growth retardation using ultrasonics V28.4
    isoimmunization V28.5
    malformations using ultrasonics V28.3
    raised alphafetoprotein levels V28.1
    specified condition NEC V28.8
    Streptococcus B V28.6
  arterial hypertension V81.1
  arthropod-borne viral disease NEC V73.5
  asymptomatic bacteriuria V81.5
  bacterial
    conjunctivitis V74.4
    disease V74.9
      specified condition NEC V74.8
  bacteriuria, asymptomatic V81.5
  blood disorder NEC V78.9
    specified type NEC V78.8
  bronchitis, chronic V81.3
  brucellosis V74.8
  cancer — *see* Screening, malignant neoplasm
  cardiovascular disease NEC V81.2
  cataract V80.2
  Chagas' disease V75.3
  chemical poisoning V82.5
  cholera V74.0
  cholesterol level V77.91
  chromosomal
    anomalies
      by amniocentesis, antenatal V28.0
      maternal postnatal V82.4
    athletes V70.3
  condition
    cardiovascular NEC V81.2
    eye NEC V80.2
    genitourinary NEC V81.6
    neurological V80.0
    respiratory NEC V81.4
    skin V82.0
    specified NEC V82.89
  congenital
    anomaly V82.89
      eye V80.2
    dislocation of hip V82.3
    eye condition or disease V80.2
  conjunctivitis, bacterial V74.4
  contamination NEC (*see also* Poisoning) V82.5
  coronary artery disease V81.0
  cystic fibrosis V77.6
  deficiency anemia NEC V78.1
    iron V78.0
  dengue fever V73.5
  depression V79.0
  developmental handicap V79.9
    in early childhood V79.3
    specified type NEC V79.8
  diabetes mellitus V77.1
  diphtheria V74.3
  disease or disorder V82.9
    bacterial V74.9
      specified NEC V74.8
    blood V78.9
      specified type NEC V78.8
    blood-forming organ V78.9
      specified type NEC V78.8
    cardiovascular NEC V81.2
      hypertensive V81.1
      ischemic V81.0
    Chagas' V75.3
    chlamydial V73.98
      specified NEC V73.88
    ear NEC V80.3

Screening (for) — *continued*
  disease or disorder — *continued*
    endocrine NEC V77.99
    eye NEC V80.2
    genitourinary NEC V81.6
    heart NEC V81.2
      hypertensive V81.1
      ischemic V81.0
    immunity NEC V77.99
    infectious NEC V75.9
    lipoid NEC V77.91
    mental V79.9
      specified type NEC V79.8
    metabolic NEC V77.99
      inborn NEC V77.7
    neurological V80.0
    nutritional NEC V77.99
    rheumatic NEC V82.2
    rickettsial V75.0
    sickle-cell V78.2
      trait V78.2
    specified type NEC V82.89
    thyroid V77.0
    vascular NEC V81.2
      ischemic V81.0
    venereal V74.5
    viral V73.99
      arthropod-borne NEC V73.5
      specified type NEC V73.89
  dislocation of hip, congenital V82.3
  drugs in athletes V70.3
  emphysema (chronic) V81.3
  encephalitis, viral (mosquito or tick borne) V73.5
  endocrine disorder NEC V77.99
  eye disorder NEC V80.2
    congenital V80.2
  fever
    dengue V73.5
    hemorrhagic V73.5
    yellow V73.4
  filariasis V75.6
  galactosemia V77.4
  genitourinary condition NEC V81.6
  glaucoma V80.1
  gonorrhea V74.5
  gout V77.5
  Hansen's disease V74.2
  heart disease NEC V81.2
    hypertensive V81.1
    ischemic V81.0
  heavy metal poisoning V82.5
  helminthiasis, intestinal V75.7
  hematopoietic malignancy V76.89
  hemoglobinopathies NEC V78.3
  hemorrhagic fever V73.5
  Hodgkin's disease V76.89
  hormones in athletes V70.3
  hypercholesterolemia V77.91
  hyperlipdemia V77.91
  hypertension V81.1
  immunity disorder NEC V77.99
  inborn errors of metabolism NEC V77.7
  infection
    bacterial V74.9
      specified type NEC V74.8
    mycotic V75.4
    parasitic NEC V75.8
  infectious disease V75.9
    specified type NEC V75.8
  ingestion of radioactive substance V82.5
  intestinal helminthiasis V75.7
  iron deficiency anemia V78.0
  ischemic heart disease V81.0
  lead poisoning V82.5
  leishmaniasis V75.2
  leprosy V74.2
  leptospirosis V74.8
  leukemia V76.89
  lipoid disorder NEC V77.91
  lymphoma V76.89
  malaria V75.1
  malignant neoplasm (of) V76.9
    bladder V76.3
    blood V76.89

Screening (for) — *continued*
  malignant neoplasm (of) — *continued*
    breast V76.10
      mammogram NEC V76.12
        for high-risk patient V76.11
      specified type NEC V76.19
    cervix V76.2
    colon V76.51
    colorectal V76.51
    hematopoietic system V76.89
    intestine V76.50
      colon V76.51
      small V76.52
    lung V76.0
    lymph (glands) V76.89
    nervous system V76.81
    oral cavity V76.42
    other specified neoplasm NEC V76.89
    ovary V76.46
    prostate V76.44
    rectum V76.41
    respiratory organs V76.0
    skin V76.43
    specified sites NEC V76.49
    testis V76.45
    vagina V76.47
      following hysterectomy for malignant condition V67.01
  maternal postnatal chromosomal anomalies V82.4
  malnutrition V77.2
  mammogram NEC V76.12
    for high-risk patient V76.11
  measles V73.2
  mental
    disorder V79.9
      specified type NEC V79.8
    retardation V79.2
  metabolic disorder NEC V77.99
  metabolic errors, inborn V77.7
  mucoviscidosis V77.6
  multiphasic V82.6
  mycosis V75.4
  mycotic infection V75.4
  nephropathy V81.5
  neurological condition V80.0
  nutritional disorder V77.99
  obesity V77.8
  osteoporosis V82.81
  parasitic infection NEC V75.8
  phenylketonuria V77.3
  plague V74.8
  poisoning
    chemical NEC V82.5
    contaminated water supply V82.5
      heavy metal V82.5
  poliomyelitis V73.0
  postnatal chromosomal anomalies, maternal V82.4
  prenatal — *see* Screening, antenatal
  pulmonary tuberculosis V74.1
  radiation exposure V82.5
  renal disease V81.5
  respiratory condition NEC V81.4
  rheumatic disorder NEC V82.2
  rheumatoid arthritis V82.1
  rickettsial disease V75.0
  rubella V73.3
  schistosomiasis V75.5
  senile macular lesions of eye V80.2
  sickle-cell anemia, disease, or trait V78.2
  skin condition V82.0
  sleeping sickness V75.3
  smallpox V73.1
  special V82.9
    specified condition NEC V82.89
  specified type NEC V82.89
  spirochetal disease V74.9
    specified type NEC V74.8
  stimulants in athletes V70.3
  syphilis V74.5
  tetanus V74.8
  thyroid disorder V77.0
  trachoma V73.6
  trypanosomiasis V75.3
  tuberculosis, pulmonary V74.1
  venereal disease V74.5

Screening (for) — *continued*
  viral encephalitis
    mosquito-borne V73.5
    tick-borne V73.5
  whooping cough V74.8
  worms, intestinal V75.7
  yaws V74.6
  yellow fever V73.4
Scrofula (*see also* Tuberculosis) 017.2 ☑
Scrofulide (primary) (*see also* Tuberculosis) 017.0 ☑
Scrofuloderma, scrofulodermia (any site) (primary) (*see also* Tuberculosis) 017.0 ☑
Scrofulosis (universal) (*see also* Tuberculosis) 017.2 ☑
Scrofulosis lichen (primary) (*see also* Tuberculosis) 017.0 ☑
Scrofulous — *see* condition
Scrotal tongue 529.5
  congenital 750.13
Scrotum — *see* condition
Scurvy (gum) (infantile) (rickets) (scorbutic) 267
Sea-blue histiocyte syndrome 272.7
Seabright-Bantam syndrome (pseudohypoparathyroidism) 275.49
Seasickness 994.6
Seatworm 127.4
Sebaceous
  cyst (*see also* Cyst, sebaceous) 706.2
  gland disease NEC 706.9
Sebocystomatosis 706.2
Seborrhea, seborrheic 706.3
  adiposa 706.3
  capitis 690.11
  congestiva 695.4
  corporis 706.3
  dermatitis 690.10
    infantile 690.12
  diathesis in infants 695.89
  eczema 690.18
    infantile 690.12
  keratosis 702.19
    inflamed 702.11
  nigricans 705.89
  sicca 690.18
  wart 702.19
    inflamed 702.11
Seckel's syndrome 759.89
Seclusion pupil 364.74
Seclusiveness, child 313.22
Secondary — *see also* condition
  neoplasm — *see* Neoplasm, by site, malignant, secondary
Secretan's disease or syndrome (posttraumatic edema) 782.3
Secretion
  antidiuretic hormone, inappropriate (syndrome) 253.6
  catecholamine, by pheochromocytoma 255.6
  hormone
    antidiuretic, inappropriate (syndrome) 253.6
    by
      carcinoid tumor 259.2
      pheochromocytoma 255.6
    ectopic NEC 259.3
  urinary
    excessive 788.42
    suppression 788.5
Section
  cesarean
    affecting fetus or newborn 763.4
    post mortem, affecting fetus or newborn 761.6
    previous, in pregnancy or childbirth 654.2 ☑
      affecting fetus or newborn 763.89
  nerve, traumatic — *see* Injury, nerve, by site
Seeligmann's syndrome (ichthyosis congenita) 757.1
Segmentation, incomplete (congenital) — *see also* Fusion
  bone NEC 756.9

Segmentation, incomplete — *see also* Fusion — *continued*
  lumbosacral (joint) 756.15
  vertebra 756.15
    lumbosacral 756.15
Seizure 780.39
  akinetic (idiopathic) (*see also* Epilepsy) 345.0 ☑
    psychomotor 345.4 ☑
  apoplexy, apoplectic (*see also* Disease, cerebrovascular, acute) 436
  atonic (*see also* Epilepsy) 345.0 ☑
  autonomic 300.11
  brain or cerebral (*see also* Disease, cerebrovascular, acute) 436
  convulsive (*see also* Convulsions) 780.39
  cortical (focal) (motor) (*see also* Epilepsy) 345.5 ☑
  epilepsy, epileptic (cryptogenic) (*see also* Epilepsy) 345.9 ☑
  epileptiform, epileptoid 780.39
    focal (*see also* Epilepsy) 345.5 ☑
  febrile 780.31
    with status epilepticus 345.3   ●
  heart — *see* Disease, heart
  hysterical 300.11
  Jacksonian (focal) (*see also* Epilepsy) 345.5 ☑
    motor type 345.5 ☑
    sensory type 345.5 ☑
  newborn 779.0
  paralysis (*see also* Disease, cerebrovascular, acute) 436
  recurrent 780.39
    epileptic — *see* Epilepsy
  repetitive 780.39
    epileptic — *see* Epilepsy
  salaam (*see also* Epilepsy) 345.6 ☑
  uncinate (*see also* Epilepsy) 345.4 ☑
Self-mutilation 300.9
Semicoma 780.09
Semiconsciousness 780.09
Seminal
  vesicle — *see* condition
  vesiculitis (*see also* Vesiculitis) 608.0
Seminoma (M9061/3)
  anaplastic type (M9062/3)
    specified site — *see* Neoplasm, by site, malignant
    unspecified site 186.9
  specified site — *see* Neoplasm, by site, malignant
  spermatocytic (M9063/3)
    specified site — *see* Neoplasm, by site, malignant
    unspecified site 186.9
  unspecified site 186.9
Semliki Forest encephalitis 062.8
Senear-Usher disease or syndrome (pemphigus erythematosus) 694.4
Senecio jacobae dermatitis 692.6
Senectus 797
Senescence 797
Senile (*see also* condition) 797
  cervix (atrophic) 622.8
  degenerative atrophy, skin 701.3
  endometrium (atrophic) 621.8
  fallopian tube (atrophic) 620.3
  heart (failure) 797
  lung 492.8
  ovary (atrophic) 620.3
  syndrome 259.8
  vagina, vaginitis (atrophic) 627.3
  wart 702.0
Senility 797
  with
    acute confusional state 290.3
    delirium 290.3
    mental changes 290.9
    psychosis NEC (*see also* Psychosis, senile) 290.20
  premature (syndrome) 259.8
Sensation
  burning (*see also* Disturbance, sensation) 782.0
    tongue 529.6

☑ Additional Digit Required — Refer to the Tabular List (Numeric Code Section) for Additional Digit Selection
▶◀ Revised Text   ● New Line   ▲ Revised Code

2006 ICD-9-CM

October 2005 • Volume 2 — **301**

Sensation — *continued*
 choking 784.9
 loss of (*see also* Disturbance, sensation) 782.0
 prickling (*see also* Disturbance, sensation)
  782.0
 tingling (*see also* Disturbance, sensation) 782.0
Sense loss (touch) (*see also* Disturbance,
  sensation) 782.0
 smell 781.1
 taste 781.1
Sensibility disturbance NEC (cortical) (deep)
  (vibratory) (*see also* Disturbance, sensation)
  782.0
Sensitive dentine 521.8
Sensitiver Beziehungswahn 297.8
Sensitivity, sensitization — *see also* Allergy
 autoerythrocyte 287.2
 carotid sinus 337.0
 child (excessive) 313.21
 cold, autoimmune 283.0
 methemoglobin 289.7
 suxamethonium 289.89
 tuberculin, without clinical or radiological
  symptoms 795.5
Sensory
 extinction 781.8
 neglect 781.8
Separation
 acromioclavicular — *see* Dislocation,
  acromioclavicular
 anxiety, abnormal 309.21
 apophysis, traumatic — *see* Fracture, by site
 choroid 363.70
  hemorrhagic 363.72
  serous 363.71
 costochondral (simple) (traumatic) — *see*
  Dislocation, costochondral
 delayed
  umbilical cord 779.83
 epiphysis, epiphyseal
  nontraumatic 732.9
   upper femoral 732.2
  traumatic — *see* Fracture, by site
 fracture — *see* Fracture, by site
 infundibulum cardiac from right ventricle by a
  partition 746.83
 joint (current) (traumatic) — *see* Dislocation, by
  site
 placenta (normally implanted) — *see* Placenta,
  separation
 pubic bone, obstetrical trauma 665.6 ☑
 retina, retinal (*see also* Detachment, retina)
  361.9
  layers 362.40
   sensory (*see also* Retinoschisis) 361.10
  pigment epithelium (exudative) 362.42
   hemorrhagic 362.43
 sternoclavicular (traumatic) — *see* Dislocation,
  sternoclavicular
 symphysis pubis, obstetrical trauma 665.6 ☑
 tracheal ring, incomplete (congenital) 748.3
Sepsis (generalized) 995.91
 with
  abortion — *see* Abortion, by type, with
   sepsis
  ectopic pregnancy (*see also* categories
   633.0-633.9) 639.0
  molar pregnancy (*see also* categories 630-
   632) 639.0
 buccal 528.3
 complicating labor 659.3 ☑
 dental (pulpal origin) 522.4
 female genital organ NEC 614.9
 fetus (intrauterine) 771.81
 following
  abortion 639.0
  ectopic or molar pregnancy 639.0
  infusion, perfusion, or transfusion 999.3
 Friedländer's 038.49
 intraocular 360.00
 localized
  in operation wound 998.59
  skin (*see also* Abscess) 682.9
 malleus 024

Sepsis — *continued*
 nadir 038.9
 newborn (organism unspecified) NEC 771.81
 oral 528.3
 puerperal, postpartum, childbirth (pelvic)
  670.0 ☑
 resulting from infusion, injection, transfusion,
  or vaccination 999.3
 severe 995.92
 skin, localized (*see also* Abscess) 682.9
 umbilical (newborn) (organism unspecified)
  771.89
  tetanus 771.3
 urinary 599.0
  meaning sepsis 995.91
  meaning urinary tract infection 599.0
Septate — *see also* Septum
Septic — *see also* condition
 adenoids 474.01
  and tonsils 474.02
 arm (with lymphangitis) 682.3
 embolus — *see* Embolism
 finger (with lymphangitis) 681.00
 foot (with lymphangitis) 682.7
 gallbladder (*see also* Cholecystitis) 575.8
 hand (with lymphangitis) 682.4
 joint (*see also* Arthritis, septic) 711.0 ☑
 kidney (*see also* Infection, kidney) 590.9
 leg (with lymphangitis) 682.6
 mouth 528.3
 nail 681.9
  finger 681.02
  toe 681.11
 shock (endotoxic) 785.52
 sore (*see also* Abscess) 682.9
  throat 034.0
   milk-borne 034.0
   streptococcal 034.0
 spleen (acute) 289.59
 teeth (pulpal origin) 522.4
 throat 034.0
 thrombus — *see* Thrombosis
 toe (with lymphangitis) 681.10
 tonsils 474.00
  and adenoids 474.02
 umbilical cord (newborn) (organism
  unspecified) 771.89
 uterus (*see also* Endometritis) 615.9
Septicemia, septicemic (generalized)
  (suppurative) 038.9
 with
  abortion — *see* Abortion, by type, with
   sepsis
  ectopic pregnancy (*see also* categories
   633.0-633.9) 639.0
  molar pregnancy (*see also* categories 630-
   632) 639.0
 Aerobacter aerogenes 038.49
 anaerobic 038.3
 anthrax 022.3
 Bacillus coli 038.42
 Bacteroides 038.3
 Clostridium 038.3
 complicating labor 659.3 ☑
 cryptogenic 038.9
 enteric gram-negative bacilli 038.40
 Enterobacter aerogenes 038.49
 Erysipelothrix (insidiosa) (rhusiopathiae) 027.1
 Escherichia coli 038.42
 following
  abortion 639.0
  ectopic or molar pregnancy 639.0
  infusion, injection, transfusion, or
   vaccination 999.3
 Friedländer's (bacillus) 038.49
 gangrenous 038.9
 gonococcal 098.89
 gram-negative (organism) 038.40
  anaerobic 038.3
 Hemophilus influenzae 038.41
 herpes (simplex) 054.5
 herpetic 054.5
 Listeria monocytogenes 027.0
 meningeal — *see* Meningitis
 meningococcal (chronic) (fulminating) 036.2
 navel, newborn (organism unspecified) 771.89

Septicemia, septicemic — *continued*
 newborn (organism unspecified) 771.81
 plague 020.2
 pneumococcal 038.2
 postabortal 639.0
 postoperative 998.59
 Proteus vulgaris 038.49
 Pseudomonas (aeruginosa) 038.43
 puerperal, postpartum 670.0 ☑
 Salmonella (aertrycke) (callinarum)
  (choleraesuis) (enteritidis) (suipestifer)
  003.1
 Serratia 038.44
 Shigella (*see also* Dysentery, bacillary) 004.9
 specified organism NEC 038.8
 staphylococcal 038.10
  aureus 038.11
  specified organism NEC 038.19
 streptococcal (anaerobic) 038.0
 Streptococcus pneumoniae 038.2
 suipestifer 003.1
 umbilicus, newborn (organism unspecified)
  771.89
 viral 079.99
 Yersinia enterocolitica 038.49
Septum, septate (congenital) — *see also*
  Anomaly, specified type NEC
 anal 751.2
 aqueduct of Sylvius 742.3
  with spina bifida (*see also* Spina bifida)
   741.0 ☑
 hymen 752.49
 uterus (*see also* Double, uterus) 752.2
 vagina 752.49
  in pregnancy or childbirth 654.7 ☑
   affecting fetus or newborn 763.89
   causing obstructed labor 660.2 ☑
    affecting fetus or newborn 763.1
Sequestration
 lung (congenital) (extralobar) (intralobar) 748.5
 orbit 376.10
 pulmonary artery (congenital) 747.3
 splenic 289.52
Sequestrum
 bone (*see also* Osteomyelitis) 730.1 ☑
  jaw 526.4
 dental 525.8
 jaw bone 526.4
 sinus (accessory) (nasal) (*see also* Sinusitis) 473.9
  maxillary 473.0
Sequoiosis asthma 495.8
Serology for syphilis
 doubtful
  with signs or symptoms — *see* Syphilis, by
   site and stage
  follow-up of latent syphilis — *see* Syphilis,
   latent
 false positive 795.6
 negative, with signs or symptoms — *see*
  Syphilis, by site and stage
 positive 097.1
  with signs or symptoms — *see* Syphilis, by
   site and stage
  false 795.6
  follow-up of latent syphilis — *see* Syphilis,
   latent
  only finding — *see* Syphilis, latent
 reactivated 097.1
Seroma (postoperative) (non-infected) 998.13
 infected 998.51
Seropurulent — *see* condition
Serositis, multiple 569.89
 pericardial 423.2
 peritoneal 568.82
 pleural — *see* Pleurisy
Serotonin syndrome 333.99
Serous — *see* condition
Sertoli cell
 adenoma (M8640/0)
  specified site — *see* Neoplasm, by site,
   benign
  unspecified site
   female 220
   male 222.0

☑ Additional Digit Required — Refer to the Tabular List (Numeric Code Section) for Additional Digit Selection
▶◀ Revised Text ● New Line ▲ Revised Code

Sertoli cell — *continued*
  carcinoma (M8640/3)
    specified site — *see* Neoplasm, by site,
      malignant
    unspecified site 186.9
  syndrome (germinal aplasia) 606.0
  tumor (M8640/0)
    with lipid storage (M8641/0)
      specified site — *see* Neoplasm, by site,
        benign
      unspecified site
        female 220
        male 222.0
    specified site — *see* Neoplasm, by site,
      benign
    unspecified site
      female 220
      male 222.0
Sertoli-Leydig cell tumor (M8631/0)
  specified site — *see* Neoplasm, by site, benign
  unspecified site
    female 220
    male 222.0
Serum
  allergy, allergic reaction 999.5
    shock 999.4
  arthritis 999.5 *[713.6]*
  complication or reaction NEC 999.5
  disease NEC 999.5
  hepatitis 070.3 ☑
  intoxication 999.5
  jaundice (homologous) — *see* Hepatitis, viral,
    type B
  neuritis 999.5
  poisoning NEC 999.5
  rash NEC 999.5
  reaction NEC 999.5
  sickness NEC 999.5
Sesamoiditis 733.99
Seven-day fever 061
  of
    Japan 100.89
    Queensland 100.89
Sever's disease or osteochondrosis (calcaneum)
  732.5
Sex chromosome mosaics 758.81
Sextuplet
  affected by maternal complications of
    pregnancy 761.5
  healthy liveborn — *see* Newborn, multiple
  pregnancy (complicating delivery) NEC 651.8 ☑
    with fetal loss and retention of one or more
      fetus(es) 651.6 ☑
    following (elective) fetal reduction   ●
      651.7 ☑   ●
Sexual
  anesthesia 302.72
  deviation (*see also* Deviation, sexual) 302.9
  disorder (*see also* Deviation, sexual) 302.9
  frigidity (female) 302.72
  function, disorder of (psychogenic) 302.70
    specified type NEC 302.79
  immaturity (female) (male) 259.0
  impotence 607.84   ▲
    organic origin NEC 607.84
    psychogenic 302.72   ●
  precocity (constitutional) (cryptogenic) (female)
    (idiopathic) (male) NEC 259.1
    with adrenal hyperplasia 255.2
  sadism 302.84
Sexuality, pathological (*see also* Deviation,
  sexual) 302.9
Sézary's disease, reticulosis, or syndrome
  (M9701/3) 202.2 ☑
Shadow, lung 793.1
Shaken infant syndrome 995.55
Shaking
  head (tremor) 781.0
  palsy or paralysis (*see also* Parkinsonism)
    332.0
Shallowness, acetabulum 736.39
Shaver's disease or syndrome (bauxite
  pneumoconiosis) 503
Shearing
  artificial skin graft 996.55

Shearing — *continued*
  decellularized allodermis graft 996.55
Sheath (tendon) — *see* condition
Shedding
  nail 703.8
  teeth, premature, primary (deciduous) 520.6
Sheehan's disease or syndrome (postpartum
  pituitary necrosis) 253.2
Shelf, rectal 569.49
Shell
  shock (current) (*see also* Reaction, stress,
    acute) 308.9
    lasting state 300.16
  teeth 520.5
Shield kidney 753.3
Shift, mediastinal 793.2
Shifting
  pacemaker 427.89
  sleep-work schedule (affecting sleep) 327.36 ▲
Shiga's
  bacillus 004.0
  dysentery 004.0
Shigella (dysentery) (*see also* Dysentery, bacillary)
  004.9
  carrier (suspected) of V02.3
Shigellosis (*see also* Dysentery, bacillary) 004.9
Shingles (*see also* Herpes, zoster) 053.9
  eye NEC 053.29
Shin splints 844.9
Shipyard eye or disease 077.1
Shirodkar suture, in pregnancy 654.5 ☑
Shock 785.50
  with
    abortion — *see* Abortion, by type, with
      shock
    ectopic pregnancy (*see also* categories
      633.0-633.9) 639.5
    molar pregnancy (*see also* categories 630-
      632) 639.5
  allergic — *see* Shock, anaphylactic
  anaclitic 309.21
  anaphylactic 995.0
    chemical — *see* Table of Drugs and
      Chemicals
    correct medicinal substance properly
      administered 995.0
    drug or medicinal substance
      correct substance properly administered
        995.0
      overdose or wrong substance given or
        taken 977.9
        specified drug — *see* Table of Drugs
          and Chemicals
    following sting(s) 989.5
    food — *see* Anaphylactic shock, due to, food
    immunization 999.4
    serum 999.4
  anaphylactoid — *see* Shock, anaphylactic
  anesthetic
    correct substance properly administered
      995.4
    overdose or wrong substance given 968.4
      specified anesthetic — *see* Table of Drugs
        and Chemicals
  birth, fetus or newborn NEC 779.89
  cardiogenic 785.51
  chemical substance — *see* Table of Drugs and
    Chemicals
  circulatory 785.59
  complicating
    abortion — *see* Abortion, by type, with
      shock
    ectopic pregnancy (*see also* categories
      633.0-633.9) 639.5
    labor and delivery 669.1 ☑
    molar pregnancy (*see also* categories 630-
      632) 639.5
  culture 309.29
  due to
    drug 995.0
      correct substance properly administered
        995.0
      overdose or wrong substance given or
        taken 977.9
      specified drug — *see* Table of Drugs
        and Chemicals

Shock — *continued*
  due to — *continued*
    food — *see* Anaphylactic shock, due to, food
  during labor and delivery 669.1 ☑
  electric 994.8
  endotoxic 785.52
    due to surgical procedure 998.0
  following
    abortion 639.5
    ectopic or molar pregnancy 639.5
    injury (immediate) (delayed) 958.4
    labor and delivery 669.1 ☑
  gram-negative 785.52
  hematogenic 785.59
  hemorrhagic
    due to
      disease 785.59
      surgery (intraoperative) (postoperative)
        998.0
      trauma 958.4
  hypovolemic NEC 785.59
    surgical 998.0
    traumatic 958.4
  insulin 251.0
    therapeutic misadventure 962.3
  kidney 584.5
    traumatic (following crushing) 958.5
  lightning 994.0
  lung 518.5
  nervous (*see also* Reaction, stress, acute) 308.9
  obstetric 669.1 ☑
    with
      abortion — *see* Abortion, by type, with
        shock
      ectopic pregnancy (*see also* categories
        633.0-633.9) 639.5
      molar pregnancy (*see also* categories 630-
        632) 639.5
    following
      abortion 639.5
      ectopic or molar pregnancy 639.5
  paralysis, paralytic (*see also* Disease,
    cerebrovascular, acute) 436
    late effect — *see* Late effect(s) (of)
      cerebrovascular disease
  pleural (surgical) 998.0
    due to trauma 958.4
  postoperative 998.0
    with
      abortion — *see* Abortion, by type, with
        shock
      ectopic pregnancy (*see also* categories
        633.0-633.9) 639.5
      molar pregnancy (*see also* categories 630-
        632) 639.5
    following
      abortion 639.5
      ectopic or molar pregnancy 639.5
  psychic (*see also* Reaction, stress, acute) 308.9
    past history (of) V15.49
  psychogenic (*see also* Reaction, stress, acute)
    308.9
  septic 785.52
    with
      abortion — *see* Abortion, by type, with
        shock
      ectopic pregnancy (*see also* categories
        633.0-633.9) 639.5
      molar pregnancy (*see also* categories 630-
        632) 639.5
    due to
      surgical procedure 998.0
      transfusion NEC 999.8
        bone marrow 996.85
    following
      abortion 639.5
      ectopic or molar pregnancy 639.5
      surgical procedure 998.0
      transfusion NEC 999.8
        bone marrow 996.85
  spinal — *see also* Injury, spinal, by site
    with spinal bone injury — *see* Fracture,
      vertebra, by site, with spinal cord
      injury
  surgical 998.0
  therapeutic misadventure NEC (*see also*
    Complications) 998.89

☑ Additional Digit Required — Refer to the Tabular List (Numeric Code Section) for Additional Digit Selection
▶◀ Revised Text   ● New Line   ▲ Revised Code

2006 ICD-9-CM   **October 2005 • Volume 2 — 303**

Sertoli cell — Shock

Shock — *continued*
  thyroxin 962.7
  toxic 040.82
  transfusion — *see* Complications, transfusion
  traumatic (immediate) (delayed) 958.4

Shoemakers' chest 738.3

Short, shortening, shortness
  Achilles tendon (acquired) 727.81
  arm 736.89
    congenital 755.20
  back 737.9
  bowel syndrome 579.3
  breath 786.05
  chain acyl CoA dehydrogenase deficiency
    (SCAD) 277.85
  common bile duct, congenital 751.69
  cord (umbilical) 663.4 ☑
    affecting fetus or newborn 762.6
  cystic duct, congenital 751.69
  esophagus (congenital) 750.4
  femur (acquired) 736.81
    congenital 755.34
  frenulum linguae 750.0
  frenum, lingual 750.0
  hamstrings 727.81
  hip (acquired) 736.39
    congenital 755.63
  leg (acquired) 736.81
    congenital 755.30
  metatarsus (congenital) 754.79
    acquired 736.79
  organ or site, congenital NEC — *see* Distortion
  palate (congenital) 750.26
  P-R interval syndrome 426.81
  radius (acquired) 736.09
    congenital 755.26
  round ligament 629.8
  sleeper 307.49
  stature, constitutional (hereditary) 783.43
  tendon 727.81
    Achilles (acquired) 727.81
      congenital 754.79
    congenital 756.89
  thigh (acquired) 736.81
    congenital 755.34
  tibialis anticus 727.81
  umbilical cord 663.4 ☑
    affecting fetus or newborn 762.6
  urethra 599.84
  uvula (congenital) 750.26
  vagina 623.8

Shortsightedness 367.1

Shoshin (acute fulminating beriberi) 265.0

Shoulder — *see* condition

Shovel-shaped incisors 520.2

Shower, thromboembolic — *see* Embolism

Shunt (status)
  aortocoronary bypass V45.81
  arterial-venous (dialysis) V45.1
  arteriovenous, pulmonary (acquired) 417.0
    congenital 747.3
    traumatic (complication) 901.40
  cerebral ventricle (communicating) in situ
    V45.2
  coronary artery bypass V45.81
  surgical, prosthetic, with complications — *see*
    Complications, shunt
  vascular NEC V45.89

Shutdown
  renal 586
    with
      abortion — *see* Abortion, by type, with
        renal failure
      ectopic pregnancy (*see also* categories
        633.0-633.9) 639.3
      molar pregnancy (*see also* categories 630-
        632) 639.3
    complicating
      abortion 639.3
      ectopic or molar pregnancy 639.3
    following labor and delivery 669.3 ☑

Shwachman's syndrome 288.0

Shy-Drager syndrome (orthostatic hypotension
  with multisystem degeneration) 333.0

Sialadenitis (any gland) (chronic) (suppurative)
  527.2
  epidemic — *see* Mumps

Sialadenosis, periodic 527.2

Sialaporia 527.7

Sialectasia 527.8

Sialitis 527.2

Sialoadenitis (*see also* Sialadenitis) 527.2

Sialoangitis 527.2

Sialodochitis (fibrinosa) 527.2

Sialodocholithiasis 527.5

Sialolithiasis 527.5

Sialorrhea (*see also* Ptyalism) 527.7
  periodic 527.2

Sialosis 527.8
  rheumatic 710.2

Siamese twin 759.4

Sicard's syndrome 352.6

Sicca syndrome (keratoconjunctivitis) 710.2

Sick 799.9
  cilia syndrome 759.89
  or handicapped person in family V61.49

Sickle-cell
  anemia (*see also* Disease, sickle-cell) 282.60
  disease (*see also* Disease, sickle-cell) 282.60
  hemoglobin
    C disease (without crisis) 282.63
      with
        crisis 282.64
        vaso-occlusive pain 282.64
    D disease (without crisis) 282.68
      with crisis 282.69
    E disease (without crisis) 282.68
      with crisis 282.69
    thalassemia (without crisis) 282.41
      with
        crisis 282.42
        vaso-occlusive pain 282.42
  trait 282.5

Sicklemia (*see also* Disease, sickle-cell) 282.60
  trait 282.5

Sickness
  air (travel) 994.6
  airplane 994.6
  alpine 993.2
  altitude 993.2
  Andes 993.2
  aviators' 993.2
  balloon 993.2
  car 994.6
  compressed air 993.3
  decompression 993.3
  green 280.9
  harvest 100.89
  milk 988.8
  morning 643.0 ☑
  motion 994.6
  mountain 993.2
    acute 289.0
  protein (*see also* Complications, vaccination)
    999.5
  radiation NEC 990
  roundabout (motion) 994.6
  sea 994.6
  serum NEC 999.5
  sleeping (African) 086.5
    by Trypanosoma 086.5
      gambiense 086.3
      rhodesiense 086.4
    Gambian 086.3
    late effect 139.8
    Rhodesian 086.4
  sweating 078.2
  swing (motion) 994.6
  train (railway) (travel) 994.6
  travel (any vehicle) 994.6

Sick sinus syndrome 427.81

Sideropenia (*see also* Anemia, iron deficiency)
  280.9

Siderosis (lung) (occupational) 503
  cornea 371.15
  eye (bulbi) (vitreous) 360.23
  lens 360.23

Siegal-Cattan-Mamou disease (periodic) 277.3

Siemens' syndrome
  ectodermal dysplasia 757.31
  keratosis follicularis spinulosa (decalvans)
    757.39

Sighing respiration 786.7

Sigmoid
  flexure — *see* condition
  kidney 753.3

Sigmoiditis — *see* Enteritis

Silfverskiöld's syndrome 756.50

Silicosis, silicotic (complicated) (occupational)
  (simple) 502
  fibrosis, lung (confluent) (massive)
    (occupational) 502
  non-nodular 503
  pulmonum 502

Silicotuberculosis (*see also* Tuberculosis)
  011.4 ☑

Silo fillers' disease 506.9

Silver's syndrome (congenital hemihypertrophy
  and short stature) 759.89

Silver wire arteries, retina 362.13

Silvestroni-Bianco syndrome (thalassemia
  minima) 282.49

Simian crease 757.2

Simmonds' cachexia or disease (pituitary
  cachexia) 253.2

Simons' disease or syndrome (progressive
  lipodystrophy) 272.6

Simple, simplex — *see* condition

Sinding-Larsen disease (juvenile osteopathia
  patellae) 732.4

Singapore hemorrhagic fever 065.4

Singers' node or nodule 478.5

Single
  atrium 745.69
  coronary artery 746.85
  umbilical artery 747.5
  ventricle 745.3

Singultus 786.8
  epidemicus 078.89

Sinus — *see also* Fistula
  abdominal 569.81
  arrest 426.6
  arrhythmia 427.89
  bradycardia 427.89
    chronic 427.81
  branchial cleft (external) (internal) 744.41
  coccygeal (infected) 685.1
    with abscess 685.0
  dental 522.7
  dermal (congenital) 685.1
    with abscess 685.0
  draining — *see* Fistula
  infected, skin NEC 686.9
  marginal, ruptured or bleeding 641.2 ☑
    affecting fetus or newborn 762.1
  pause 426.6
  pericranii 742.0
  pilonidal (infected) (rectum) 685.1
    with abscess 685.0
  preauricular 744.46
  rectovaginal 619.1
  sacrococcygeal (dermoid) (infected) 685.1
    with abscess 685.0
  skin
    infected NEC 686.9
    noninfected — *see* Ulcer, skin
  tachycardia 427.89
  tarsi syndrome 726.79
  testis 608.89
  tract (postinfectional) — *see* Fistula
  urachus 753.7

Sinuses, Rokitansky-Aschoff (*see also* Disease,
  gallbladder) 575.8

Sinusitis (accessory) (nasal) (hyperplastic)
  (nonpurulent) (purulent) (chronic) 473.9
  with influenza, flu, or grippe 487.1
  acute 461.9
    ethmoidal 461.2
    frontal 461.1
    maxillary 461.0
    specified type NEC 461.8

☑ Additional Digit Required — Refer to the Tabular List (Numeric Code Section) for Additional Digit Selection
◄► Revised Text   ● New Line   ▲ Revised Code

Sinusitis — continued
  acute — continued
    sphenoidal 461.3
  allergic (see also Fever, hay) 477.9
  antrum — see Sinusitis, maxillary
  due to
    fungus, any sinus 117.9
    high altitude 993.1
  ethmoidal 473.2
    acute 461.2
  frontal 473.1
    acute 461.1
  influenzal 478.1
  maxillary 473.0
    acute 461.0
  specified site NEC 473.8
  sphenoidal 473.3
    acute 461.3
  syphilitic, any sinus 095.8
  tuberculous, any sinus (see also Tuberculosis) 012.8 ☑

Sinusitis-bronchiectasis-situs inversus (syndrome) (triad) 759.3

Sipple's syndrome (medullary thyroid carcinoma-pheochromocytoma) 193

Sirenomelia 759.89

Siriasis 992.0

Sirkari's disease 085.0

SIRS (systemic inflammatory response syndrome) 995.90
  due to
    infectious process 995.91
      with organ dysfunction 995.92
    non-infectious process 995.93
      with organ dysfunction 995.94

Siti 104.0

Sitophobia 300.29

Situation, psychiatric 300.9

Situational
  disturbance (transient) (see also Reaction, adjustment) 309.9
    acute 308.3
  maladjustment, acute (see also Reaction, adjustment) 309.9
  reaction (see also Reaction, adjustment) 309.9
    acute 308.3

Situs inversus or transversus 759.3
  abdominalis 759.3
  thoracis 759.3

Sixth disease 057.8

Sjögren (-Gougerot) syndrome or disease (keratoconjunctivitis sicca) 710.2
  with lung involvement 710.2 [517.8]

Sjögren-Larsson syndrome (ichthyosis congenita) 757.1

Skeletal — see condition

Skene's gland — see condition

Skenitis (see also Urethritis) 597.89
  gonorrheal (acute) 098.0
    chronic or duration of 2 months or over 098.2

Skerljevo 104.0

Skevas-Zerfus disease 989.5

Skin — see also condition
  donor V59.1
  hidebound 710.9

SLAP lesion (superior glenoid labrum) 840.7

Slate-dressers' lung 502

Slate-miners' lung 502

Sleep
  deprivation V69.4
  disorder 780.50
    with apnea — see Apnea, sleep
    child 307.40
    movement, ▶unspecified◀ 780.58
    nonorganic origin 307.40
      specified type NEC 307.49
  disturbance 780.50
    with apnea — see Apnea, sleep
    nonorganic origin 307.40
      specified type NEC 307.49
  drunkenness 307.47
  movement disorder, ▶unspecified◀ 780.58

Sleep — continued
  paroxysmal (see also Narcolepsy) 347.00
  related movement disorder, ▶unspecified◀ 780.58
  rhythm inversion 327.39 ▲
    nonorganic origin 307.45
  walking 307.46
    hysterical 300.13

Sleeping sickness 086.5
  late effect 139.8

Sleeplessness (see also Insomnia) 780.52
  menopausal 627.2
  nonorganic origin 307.41

Slipped, slipping
  epiphysis (postinfectional) 732.9
    traumatic (old) 732.9
      current — see Fracture, by site
    upper femoral (nontraumatic) 732.2
  intervertebral disc — see Displacement, intervertebral disc
  ligature, umbilical 772.3
  patella 717.89
  rib 733.99
  sacroiliac joint 724.6
  tendon 727.9
  ulnar nerve, nontraumatic 354.2
  vertebra NEC (see also Spondylolisthesis) 756.12

Slocumb's syndrome 255.3

Sloughing (multiple) (skin) 686.9
  abscess — see Abscess, by site
  appendix 543.9
  bladder 596.8
  fascia 728.9
  graft — see Complications, graft
  phagedena (see also Gangrene) 785.4
  reattached extremity (see also Complications, reattached extremity) 996.90
  rectum 569.49
  scrotum 608.89
  tendon 727.9
  transplanted organ (see also Rejection, transplant, organ, by site) 996.80
  ulcer (see also Ulcer, skin) 707.9

Slow
  feeding newborn 779.3
  fetal, growth NEC 764.9 ☑
    affecting management of pregnancy 656.5 ☑

Slowing
  heart 427.89
  urinary stream 788.62

Sluder's neuralgia or syndrome 337.0

Slurred, slurring, speech 784.5

Small, smallness
  cardiac reserve — see Disease, heart
  for dates
    fetus or newborn 764.0 ☑
      with malnutrition 764.1 ☑
      affecting management of pregnancy 656.5 ☑
    infant, term 764.0 ☑
      with malnutrition 764.1 ☑
      affecting management of pregnancy 656.5 ☑
  introitus, vagina 623.3
  kidney, unknown cause 589.9
    bilateral 589.1
    unilateral 589.0
  ovary 620.8
  pelvis
    with disproportion (fetopelvic) 653.1 ☑
      affecting fetus or newborn 763.1
    causing obstructed labor 660.1 ☑
      affecting fetus or newborn 763.1
  placenta — see Placenta, insufficiency
  uterus 621.8
  white kidney 582.9

Small-for-dates (see also Light-for-dates) 764.0 ☑
  affecting management of pregnancy 656.5 ☑

Smallpox 050.9
  contact V01.3
  exposure to V01.3
  hemorrhagic (pustular) 050.0
  malignant 050.0
  modified 050.2

Smallpox — continued
  vaccination
    complications — see Complications, vaccination
    prophylactic (against) V04.1

Smith's fracture (separation) (closed) 813.41
  open 813.51

Smith-Lemli Opitz syndrome (cerebrohepatorenal syndrome) 759.89

Smith-Magenis syndrome 758.33

Smith-Strang disease (oasthouse urine) 270.2

Smokers'
  bronchitis 491.0
  cough 491.0
  syndrome (see also Abuse, drugs, nondependent) 305.1
  throat 472.1
  tongue 528.6

Smothering spells 786.09

Snaggle teeth, tooth 524.39

Snapping
  finger 727.05
  hip 719.65
  jaw 524.69
    temporomandibular joint sounds on opening or closing 524.64
  knee 717.9
  thumb 727.05

Sneddon-Wilkinson disease or syndrome (subcorneal pustular dermatosis) 694.1

Sneezing 784.9
  intractable 478.1

Sniffing
  cocaine (see also Dependence) 304.2 ☑
  ether (see also Dependence) 304.6 ☑
  glue (airplane) (see also Dependence) 304.6 ☑

Snoring 786.09

Snow blindness 370.24

Snuffles (nonsyphilitic) 460
  syphilitic (infant) 090.0

Social migrant V60.0

Sodoku 026.0

Soemmering's ring 366.51

Soft — see also condition
  enlarged prostate 600.00
    with urinary retention 600.01
  nails 703.8

Softening
  bone 268.2
  brain (necrotic) (progressive) 434.9 ☑
    arteriosclerotic 437.0
    congenital 742.4
    embolic (see also Embolism, brain) 434.1 ☑
    hemorrhagic (see also Hemorrhage, brain) 431
    occlusive 434.9 ☑
    thrombotic (see also Thrombosis, brain) 434.0 ☑
  cartilage 733.92
  cerebellar — see Softening, brain
  cerebral — see Softening, brain
  cerebrospinal — see Softening, brain
  myocardial, heart (see also Degeneration, myocardial) 429.1
  nails 703.8
  spinal cord 336.8
  stomach 537.89

Solar fever 061

Soldier's
  heart 306.2
  patches 423.1

Solitary
  cyst
    bone 733.21
    kidney 593.2
  kidney (congenital) 753.0
  tubercle, brain (see also Tuberculosis, brain) 013.2 ☑
  ulcer, bladder 596.8

Somatization reaction, somatic reaction (see also Disorder, psychosomatic) 306.9
  disorder 300.81

☑ Additional Digit Required — Refer to the Tabular List (Numeric Code Section) for Additional Digit Selection
▶◀ Revised Text   ● New Line   ▲ Revised Code

2006 ICD-9-CM   October 2005 • Volume 2 — 305

☑ Additional Digit Required — Refer to the Tabular List (Numeric Code Section) for Additional Digit Selection

Spider
 finger 755.59
 nevus 448.1
 vascular 448.1
Spiegler-Fendt sarcoid 686.8
Spielmeyer-Stock disease 330.1
Spielmeyer-Vogt disease 330.1
Spina bifida (aperta) 741.9 ☑

> Note — Use the following fifth-digit
> subclassification with category 741:
>
> 0   unspecified region
> 1   cervical region
> 2   dorsal [thoracic] region
> 3   lumbar region

 with hydrocephalus 741.0 ☑
  fetal (suspected), affecting management of
   pregnancy 655.0 ☑
 occulta 756.17
Spindle, Krukenberg's 371.13
Spine, spinal — see condition
Spiradenoma (eccrine) (M8403/0) — see
  Neoplasm, skin, benign
Spirillosis NEC (see also Fever, relapsing) 087.9
Spirillum minus 026.0
Spirillum obermeieri infection 087.0
Spirochetal — see condition
Spirochetosis 104.9
 arthritic, arthritica 104.9 [711.8] ☑
 bronchopulmonary 104.8
 icterohemorrhagica 100.0
 lung 104.8
Spitting blood (see also Hemoptysis) 786.3
Splanchnomegaly 569.89
Splanchnoptosis 569.89
Spleen, splenic — see also condition
 agenesis 759.0
 flexure syndrome 569.89
 neutropenia syndrome 288.0
 sequestration syndrome 289.52
Splenectasis (see also Splenomegaly) 789.2
Splenitis (interstitial) (malignant) (nonspecific)
  289.59
 malarial (see also Malaria) 084.6
 tuberculous (see also Tuberculosis) 017.7 ☑
Splenocele 289.59
Splenomegalia — see Splenomegaly
Splenomegalic — see condition
Splenomegaly 789.2
 Bengal 789.2
 cirrhotic 289.51
 congenital 759.0
 congestive, chronic 289.51
 cryptogenic 789.2
 Egyptian 120.1
 Gaucher's (cerebroside lipidosis) 272.7
 idiopathic 789.2
 malarial (see also Malaria) 084.6
 neutropenic 288.0
 Niemann-Pick (lipid histiocytosis) 272.7
 siderotic 289.51
 syphilitic 095.8
  congenital 090.0
 tropical (Bengal) (idiopathic) 789.2
Splenopathy 289.50
Splenopneumonia — see Pneumonia
Splenoptosis 289.59
Splinter — see Injury, superficial, by site
Split, splitting
 heart sounds 427.89
 lip, congenital (see also Cleft, lip) 749.10
 nails 703.8
 urinary stream 788.61
Spoiled child reaction (see also Disturbance,
  conduct) 312.1 ☑
Spondylarthritis (see also Spondylosis) 721.90
Spondylarthrosis (see also Spondylosis) 721.90
Spondylitis 720.9
 ankylopoietica 720.0
 ankylosing (chronic) 720.0
 atrophic 720.9
  ligamentous 720.9

Spondylitis — continued
 chronic (traumatic) (see also Spondylosis)
   721.90
 deformans (chronic) (see also Spondylosis)
   721.90
 gonococcal 098.53
 gouty 274.0
 hypertrophic (see also Spondylosis) 721.90
 infectious NEC 720.9
 juvenile (adolescent) 720.0
 Kümmell's 721.7
 Marie-Strümpell (ankylosing) 720.0
 muscularis 720.9
 ossificans ligamentosa 721.6
 osteoarthritica (see also Spondylosis) 721.90
 posttraumatic 721.7
 proliferative 720.0
 rheumatoid 720.0
 rhizomelica 720.0
 sacroiliac NEC 720.2
 senescent (see also Spondylosis) 721.90
 senile (see also Spondylosis) 721.90
 static (see also Spondylosis) 721.90
 traumatic (chronic) (see also Spondylosis)
   721.90
 tuberculous (see also Tuberculosis)
   015.0 ☑ [720.81]
 typhosa 002.0 [720.81]
Spondyloarthrosis (see also Spondylosis) 721.90
Spondylolisthesis (congenital) (lumbosacral)
  756.12
 with disproportion (fetopelvic) 653.3 ☑
  affecting fetus or newborn 763.1
  causing obstructed labor 660.1 ☑
   affecting fetus or newborn 763.1
 acquired 738.4
 degenerative 738.4
 traumatic 738.4
  acute (lumbar) — see Fracture, vertebra,
    lumbar
  site other than lumbosacral — see
    Fracture, vertebra, by site
Spondylolysis (congenital) 756.11
 acquired 738.4
 cervical 756.19
 lumbosacral region 756.11
  with disproportion (fetopelvic) 653.3 ☑
   affecting fetus or newborn 763.1
   causing obstructed labor 660.1 ☑
    affecting fetus or newborn 763.1
Spondylopathy
 inflammatory 720.9
  specified type NEC 720.89
 traumatic 721.7
Spondylose rhizomelique 720.0
Spondylosis 721.90
 with
  disproportion 653.3 ☑
   affecting fetus or newborn 763.1
   causing obstructed labor 660.1 ☑
    affecting fetus or newborn 763.1
  myelopathy NEC 721.91
 cervical, cervicodorsal 721.0
  with myelopathy 721.1
 inflammatory 720.9
 lumbar, lumbosacral 721.3
  with myelopathy 721.42
 sacral 721.3
  with myelopathy 721.42
 thoracic 721.2
  with myelopathy 721.41
 traumatic 721.7
Sponge
 divers' disease 989.5
 inadvertently left in operation wound 998.4
 kidney (medullary) 753.17
Spongioblastoma (M9422/3)
 multiforme (M9440/3)
  specified site — see Neoplasm, by site,
    malignant
  unspecified site 191.9
 polare (M9423/3)
  specified site — see Neoplasm, by site,
    malignant
  unspecified site 191.9

Spongioblastoma (M9422/3) — continued
 primitive polar (M9443/3)
  specified site — see Neoplasm, by site,
    malignant
  unspecified site 191.9
  specified site — see Neoplasm, by site,
    malignant
  unspecified site 191.9
Spongiocytoma (M9400/3)
 specified site — see Neoplasm, by site,
   malignant
 unspecified site 191.9
Spongioneuroblastoma (M9504/3) — see
  Neoplasm, by site, malignant
Spontaneous — see also condition
 fracture — see Fracture, pathologic
Spoon nail 703.8
 congenital 757.5
Sporadic — see condition
Sporotrichosis (bones) (cutaneous) (disseminated)
  (epidermal) (lymphatic) (lymphocutaneous)
  (mucous membranes) (pulmonary) (skeletal)
  (visceral) 117.1
Sporotrichum schenckii infection 117.1
Spots, spotting
 atrophic (skin) 701.3
 Bitôt's (in the young child) 264.1
 café au lait 709.09
 cayenne pepper 448.1
 cotton wool (retina) 362.83
 de Morgan's (senile angiomas) 448.1
 Fúchs' black (myopic) 360.21
 intermenstrual
  irregular 626.6
  regular 626.5
 interpalpebral 372.53
 Koplik's 055.9
 liver 709.09
 Mongolian (pigmented) 757.33
 of pregnancy 641.9 ☑
 purpuric 782.7
 ruby 448.1
Spotted fever — see Fever, spotted
Sprain, strain (joint) (ligament) (muscle) (tendon)
  848.9
 abdominal wall (muscle) 848.8
 Achilles tendon 845.09
 acromioclavicular 840.0
 ankle 845.00
  and foot 845.00
 anterior longitudinal, cervical 847.0
 arm 840.9
  upper 840.9
   and shoulder 840.9
 astragalus 845.00
 atlanto-axial 847.0
 atlanto-occipital 847.0
 atlas 847.0
 axis 847.0
 back (see also Sprain, spine) 847.9
 breast bone 848.40
 broad ligament — see Injury, internal, broad
   ligament
 calcaneofibular 845.02
 carpal 842.01
 carpometacarpal 842.11
 cartilage
  costal, without mention of injury to sternum
    848.3
   involving sternum 848.42
  ear 848.8
  knee 844.9
   with current tear (see also Tear,
     meniscus) 836.2
  semilunar (knee) 844.8
   with current tear (see also Tear,
     meniscus) 836.2
  septal, nose 848.0
  thyroid region 848.2
  xiphoid 848.49
 cervical, cervicodorsal, cervicothoracic 847.0
 chondrocostal, without mention of injury to
   sternum 848.3
  involving sternum 848.42
 chondrosternal 848.42

2006 ICD-9-CM

☑ Additional Digit Required — Refer to the Tabular List (Numeric Code Section) for Additional Digit Selection
▶◀ Revised Text   ● New Line   ▲ Revised Code

Volume 2 — 307

Sprain, strain — Staggering gait

n — continued
joint) — *see* Derangement, joint
840.9
847.4
bone 840.9
lateral, knee (medial) (tibial) 844.1
lateral (fibular) 844.0
recurrent or old 717.89
lateral 717.81
medial 717.82
coracoacromial 840.8
coracoclavicular 840.1
coracohumeral 840.2
coracoid (process) 840.9
coronary, knee 844.8
costal cartilage, without mention of injury to
sternum 848.3
involving sternum 848.42
cricoarytenoid articulation 848.2
cricothyroid articulation 848.2
cruciate
knee 844.2
old 717.89
anterior 717.83
posterior 717.84
deltoid
ankle 845.01
shoulder 840.8
dorsal (spine) 847.1
ear cartilage 848.8
elbow 841.9
and forearm 841.9
specified site NEC 841.8
femur (proximal end) 843.9
distal end 844.9
fibula (proximal end) 844.9
distal end 845.00
fibulocalcaneal 845.02
finger(s) 842.10
foot 845.10
and ankle 845.00
forearm 841.9
and elbow 841.9
specified site NEC 841.8
glenoid (shoulder) (*see also* SLAP lesion) 840.8
hand 842.10
hip 843.9
and thigh 843.9
humerus (proximal end) 840.9
distal end 841.9
iliofemoral 843.0
infraspinatus 840.3
innominate
acetabulum 843.9
pubic junction 848.5
sacral junction 846.1
internal
collateral, ankle 845.01
semilunar cartilage 844.8
with current tear (*see also* Tear,
meniscus) 836.2
old 717.5
interphalangeal
finger 842.13
toe 845.13
ischiocapsular 843.1
jaw (cartilage) (meniscus) 848.1
old 524.69
knee 844.9
and leg 844.9
old 717.5
collateral
lateral 717.81
medial 717.82
cruciate
anterior 717.83
posterior 717.84
late effect — *see* Late, effects (of), sprain
lateral collateral, knee 844.0
old 717.81
leg 844.9
and knee 844.9
ligamentum teres femoris 843.8
low back 846.9
lumbar (spine) 847.2
lumbosacral 846.0
chronic or old 724.6

Sprain, strain — *continued*
mandible 848.1
old 524.69
maxilla 848.1
medial collateral, knee 844.1
old 717.82
meniscus
jaw 848.1
old 524.69
knee 844.8
with current tear (*see also* Tear,
meniscus) 836.2
old 717.5
mandible 848.1
old 524.69
specified site NEC 848.8
metacarpal 842.10
distal 842.12
proximal 842.11
metacarpophalangeal 842.12
metatarsal 845.10
metatarsophalangeal 845.12
midcarpal 842.19
midtarsal 845.19
multiple sites, except fingers alone or toes
alone 848.8
neck 847.0
nose (septal cartilage) 848.0
occiput from atlas 847.0
old — *see* Derangement, joint
orbicular, hip 843.8
patella(r) 844.8
old 717.89
pelvis 848.5
phalanx
finger 842.10
toe 845.10
radiocarpal 842.02
radiohumeral 841.2
radioulnar 841.9
distal 842.09
radius, radial (proximal end) 841.9
and ulna 841.9
distal 842.09
collateral 841.0
distal end 842.00
recurrent — *see* Sprain, by site
rib (cage), without mention of injury to sternum
848.3
involving sternum 848.42
rotator cuff (capsule) 840.4
round ligament — *see also* Injury, internal,
round ligament
femur 843.8
sacral (spine) 847.3
sacrococcygeal 847.3
sacroiliac (region) 846.9
chronic or old 724.6
ligament 846.1
specified site NEC 846.8
sacrospinatus 846.2
sacrospinous 846.2
sacrotuberous 846.3
scaphoid bone, ankle 845.00
scapula(r) 840.9
semilunar cartilage (knee) 844.8
with current tear (*see also* Tear, meniscus)
836.2
old 717.5
septal cartilage (nose) 848.0
shoulder 840.9
and arm, upper 840.9
blade 840.9
specified site NEC 848.8
spine 847.9
cervical 847.0
coccyx 847.4
dorsal 847.1
lumbar 847.2
lumbosacral 846.0
chronic or old 724.6
sacral 847.3
sacroiliac (*see also* Sprain, sacroiliac) 846.9
chronic or old 724.6
thoracic 847.1
sternoclavicular 848.41
sternum 848.40

Sprain, strain — *continued*
subglenoid (*see also* SLAP lesion) 840.8
subscapularis 840.5
supraspinatus 840.6
symphysis
jaw 848.1
old 524.69
mandibular 848.1
old 524.69
pubis 848.5
talofibular 845.09
tarsal 845.10
tarsometatarsal 845.11
temporomandibular 848.1
old 524.69
teres
ligamentum femoris 843.8
major or minor 840.8
thigh (proximal end) 843.9
and hip 843.9
distal end 844.9
thoracic (spine) 847.1
thorax 848.8
thumb 842.10
thyroid cartilage or region 848.2
tibia (proximal end) 844.9
distal end 845.00
tibiofibular
distal 845.03
superior 844.3
toe(s) 845.10
trachea 848.8
trapezoid 840.8
ulna, ulnar (proximal end) 841.9
collateral 841.1
distal end 842.00
ulnohumeral 841.3
vertebrae (*see also* Sprain, spine) 847.9
cervical, cervicodorsal, cervicothoracic 847.0
wrist (cuneiform) (scaphoid) (semilunar) 842.00
xiphoid cartilage 848.49
Sprengel's deformity (congenital) 755.52
Spring fever 309.23
Sprue 579.1
celiac 579.0
idiopathic 579.0
meaning thrush 112.0
nontropical 579.0
tropical 579.1
Spur — *see also* Exostosis
bone 726.91
calcaneal 726.73
calcaneal 726.73
iliac crest 726.5
nose (septum) 478.1
bone 726.91
septal 478.1
Spuria placenta — *see* Placenta, abnormal
Spurway's syndrome (brittle bones and blue
sclera) 756.51
Sputum, abnormal (amount) (color) (excessive)
(odor) (purulent) 786.4
bloody 786.3
Squamous — *see also* condition
cell metaplasia
bladder 596.8
cervix — *see* condition
epithelium in
cervical canal (congenital) 752.49
uterine mucosa (congenital) 752.3
metaplasia
bladder 596.8
cervix — *see* condition
Squashed nose 738.0
congenital 754.0
Squeeze, divers' 993.3
Squint (*see also* Strabismus) 378.9
accommodative (*see also* Esotropia) 378.00
concomitant (*see also* Heterotropia) 378.30
Stab — *see also* Wound, open, by site
internal organs — *see* Injury, internal, by site,
with open wound
Staggering gait 781.2
hysterical 300.11

Staghorn calculus — Status

2006 ICD-9-CM
☑ Additional Digit Required — Refer to the Tabular List (Numeric Code Section) for Additional Digit Selection
▶◀ Revised Text   ● New Line   ▲ Revised Code   **October 2005 • Volume 2 — 309**

...inued
...esis (joint) (partial) (total) V43.64
...y V44.2
...tion (female genital mutilation type III)
  ...329.23
...in pump V45.85
...stinal bypass V45.3
...rauterine contraceptive device V45.51
...junostomy V44.4
knee joint prosthesis V43.65
lacunaris 437.8
lacunosis 437.8
low birth weight V21.30
  less than 500 grams V21.31
  500-999 grams V21.32
  1000-1499 grams V21.33
  1500-1999 grams V21.34
  2000-2500 grams V21.35
lymphaticus 254.8
malignant neoplasm, ablated or excised — see
    History, malignant neoplasm
marmoratus 333.7
mutilation, female 629.20
  type I 629.21
  type II 629.22
  type III 629.23
nephrostomy V44.6
neuropacemaker NEC V45.89
  brain V45.89
  carotid sinus V45.09
  neurologic NEC V45.89
organ replacement
  by artificial or mechanical device or
      prosthesis of
    artery V43.4
    artificial skin V43.83
    bladder V43.5
    blood vessel V43.4
    breast V43.82
    eye globe V43.0
    heart
      assist device V43.21
      fully implantable artificial heart
          V43.22
      valve V43.3
    intestine V43.89
    joint V43.60
      ankle V43.66
      elbow V43.62
      finger V43.69
      hip (partial) (total) V43.64
      knee V43.65
      shoulder V43.61
      specified NEC V43.69
      wrist V43.63
    kidney V43.89
    larynx V43.81
    lens V43.1
    limb(s) V43.7
    liver V43.89
    lung V43.89
    organ NEC V43.89
    pancreas V43.89
    skin (artificial) V43.83
    tissue NEC V43.89
    vein V43.4
  by organ transplant (heterologous)
      (homologous) — see Status, transplant
pacemaker
  brain V45.89
  cardiac V45.01
  carotid sinus V45.09
  neurologic NEC V45.89
  specified site NEC V45.89
percutaneous transluminal coronary
    angioplasty V45.82
peritoneal dialysis V45.1
petit mal 345.2
postcommotio cerebri 310.2
postmenopausal (age related) (natural) V49.81
postoperative NEC V45.89
postpartum NEC V24.2
  care immediately following delivery V24.0
  routine follow-up V24.2
postsurgical NEC V45.89
renal dialysis V45.1

Status — continued
  respirator ▶[ventilator]◀ V46.11
    encounter
      during
        mechanical failure V46.14
        power failure V46.12
      for weaning V46.13
  reversed jejunal transposition (for bypass)
      V45.3
  shoulder prosthesis V43.61
  shunt
    aortocoronary bypass V45.81
    arteriovenous (for dialysis) V45.1
    cerebrospinal fluid V45.2
    vascular NEC V45.89
      aortocoronary (bypass) V45.81
    ventricular (communicating) (for drainage)
        V45.2
  sterilization
    tubal ligation V26.51
    vasectomy V26.52
  subdermal contraceptive device V45.52
  thymicolymphaticus 254.8
  thymicus 254.8
  thymolymphaticus 254.8
  tooth extraction 525.10
  tracheostomy V44.0
  transplant
    blood vessel V42.89
    bone V42.4
      marrow V42.81
    cornea V42.5
    heart V42.1
      valve V42.2
    intestine V42.84
    kidney V42.0
    liver V42.7
    lung V42.6
    organ V42.9
      specified site NEC V42.89
    pancreas V42.83
    peripheral stem cells V42.82
    skin V42.3
    stem cells, peripheral V42.82
    tissue V42.9
      specified type NEC V42.89
    vessel, blood V42.89
  tubal ligation V26.51
  ureterostomy V44.6
  urethrostomy V44.6
  vagina, artificial V44.7
  vascular shunt NEC V45.89
    aortocoronary (bypass) V45.81
  vasectomy V26.52
  ventilator ▶[respirator]◀ V46.11
    encounter
      during
        mechanical failure V46.14
        power failure V46.12
      for weaning V46.13
  wrist prosthesis V43.63
Stave fracture — see Fracture, metacarpus,
    metacarpal bone(s)
Steal
  subclavian artery 435.2
  vertebral artery 435.1
Stealing, solitary, child problem (see also
    Disturbance, conduct) 312.1 ☑
Steam burn — see Burn, by site
Steatocystoma multiplex 706.2
Steatoma (infected) 706.2
  eyelid (cystic) 374.84
    infected 373.13
Steatorrhea (chronic) 579.8
  with lacteal obstruction 579.2
  idiopathic 579.0
    adult 579.0
    infantile 579.0
  pancreatic 579.4
  primary 579.0
  secondary 579.8
  specified cause NEC 579.8
  tropical 579.1
Steatosis 272.8
  heart (see also Degeneration, myocardial) 429.1
  kidney 593.89
  liver 571.8

Steele-Richardson (-Olszewski) Syndrome 333.0
Stein's syndrome (polycystic ovary) 256.4
Stein-Leventhal syndrome (polycystic ovary)
    256.4
Steinbrocker's syndrome (see also Neuropathy,
    peripheral, autonomic) 337.9
Steinert's disease 359.2
Stenocardia (see also Angina) 413.9
Stenocephaly 756.0
Stenosis (cicatricial) — see also Stricture
  ampulla of Vater 576.2
    with calculus, cholelithiasis, or stones — see
        Choledocholithiasis
  anus, anal (canal) (sphincter) 569.2
    congenital 751.2
  aorta (ascending) 747.22
    arch 747.10
    arteriosclerotic 440.0
    calcified 440.0
  aortic (valve) 424.1
    with
      mitral (valve)
        insufficiency or incompetence 396.2
        stenosis or obstruction 396.0
    atypical 396.0
    congenital 746.3
    rheumatic 395.0
      with
        insufficiency, incompetency or
            regurgitation 395.2
          with mitral (valve) disease 396.8
        mitral (valve)
          disease (stenosis) 396.0
          insufficiency or incompetence 396.2
          stenosis or obstruction 396.0
    specified cause, except rheumatic 424.1
    syphilitic 093.22
  aqueduct of Sylvius (congenital) 742.3
    with spina bifida (see also Spina bifida)
        741.0 ☑
    acquired 331.4
  artery NEC 447.1
    basilar — see Narrowing, artery, basilar
    carotid (common) (internal) — see
        Narrowing, artery, carotid
    celiac 447.4
    cerebral 437.0
      due to
        embolism (see also Embolism, brain)
            434.1 ☑
        thrombus (see also Thrombosis, brain)
            434.0 ☑
    precerebral — see Narrowing, artery,
        precerebral
    pulmonary (congenital) 747.3
      acquired 417.8
    renal 440.1
    vertebral — see Narrowing, artery, vertebral
  bile duct or biliary passage (see also
      Obstruction, biliary) 576.2
    congenital 751.61
  bladder neck (acquired) 596.0
    congenital 753.6
  brain 348.8
  bronchus 519.1
    syphilitic 095.8
  cardia (stomach) 537.89
    congenital 750.7
  cardiovascular (see also Disease,
      cardiovascular) 429.2
  carotid artery — see Narrowing, artery, carotid
  cervix, cervical (canal) 622.4
    congenital 752.49
    in pregnancy or childbirth 654.6 ☑
      affecting fetus or newborn 763.89
      causing obstructed labor 660.2 ☑
        affecting fetus or newborn 763.1
  colon (see also Obstruction, intestine) 560.9
    congenital 751.2
  colostomy 569.62
  common bile duct (see also Obstruction,
      biliary) 576.2
    congenital 751.61
  coronary (artery) — see Arteriosclerosis,
      coronary

1. INFECTIOUS AND PARASITIC DISEASES (001-139)

Note: Categories for "late effects" of infectious and parasitic diseases are to be found at 137-139.

INCLUDES   diseases generally recognized as communicable or transmissible as well as a few diseases of unknown but possibly infectious origin

EXCLUDES   *acute respiratory infections (460-466)*
carrier or suspected carrier of infectious organism (V02.0-V02.9)
certain localized infections
influenza (487.0-487.8)

INTESTINAL INFECTIOUS DISEASES (001-009)

EXCLUDES   *helminthiases (120.0-129)*

✓4th **001 Cholera**

DEF: An acute infectious enteritis caused by a potent enterotoxin elaborated by *Vibrio cholerae*; the vibrio produces a toxin in the intestinal tract that changes the permeability of the mucosa leading to diarrhea and dehydration.

001.0   Due to Vibrio cholerae

001.1   Due to Vibrio cholerae el tor

001.9   Cholera, unspecified

✓4th **002 Typhoid and paratyphoid fevers**

DEF: Typhoid fever: an acute generalized illness caused by *Salmonella typhi*; notable clinical features are fever, headache, abdominal pain, cough, toxemia, leukopenia, abnormal pulse, rose spots on the skin, bacteremia, hyperplasia of intestinal lymph nodes, mesenteric lymphadenopathy, and Peyer's patches in the intestines.

DEF: Paratyphoid fever: a prolonged febrile illness, much like typhoid but usually less severe; caused by salmonella serotypes other than *S. typhi*, especially *S. enteritidis* serotypes paratyphi A and B and *S. choleraesuis*.

002.0   Typhoid fever
Typhoid (fever) (infection) [any site]

002.1   Paratyphoid fever A

002.2   Paratyphoid fever B

002.3   Paratyphoid fever C

002.9   Paratyphoid fever, unspecified

✓4th **003 Other salmonella infections**

INCLUDES   infection or food poisoning by Salmonella [any serotype]

DEF: Infections caused by a genus of gram-negative, anaerobic bacteria of the family *Enterobacteriaceae*; affecting warm-blooded animals, like humans; major symptoms are enteric fevers, acute gastroenteritis and septicemia.

003.0   Salmonella gastroenteritis
Salmonellosis

003.1   Salmonella septicemia

✓5th **003.2   Localized salmonella infections**

    003.20   Localized salmonella infection, unspecified

    003.21   Salmonella meningitis

    003.22   Salmonella pneumonia

    003.23   Salmonella arthritis

    003.24   Salmonella osteomyelitis

    003.29   Other

003.8   Other specified salmonella infections

003.9   Salmonella infection, unspecified

✓4th **004 Shigellosis**

INCLUDES   bacillary dysentery

DEF: Acute infectious dysentery caused by the genus *Shigella*, of the family *Enterobacteriaceae*; affecting the colon causing the release of blood-stained stools with accompanying tenesmus, abdominal cramps and fever.

004.0   Shigella dysenteriae
Infection by group A Shigella (Schmitz) (Shiga)

004.1   Shigella flexneri
Infection by group B Shigella

004.2   Shigella boydii
Infection by group C Shigella

004.3   Shigella sonnei
Infection by group D Shigella

004.8   Other specified Shigella infections

004.9   Shigellosis, unspecified

✓4th **005 Other food poisoning (bacterial)**

EXCLUDES   *salmonella infections (003.0-003.9)*
toxic effect of:
food contaminants (989.7)
noxious foodstuffs (988.0-988.9)

DEF: Enteritis caused by ingesting contaminated foods and characterized by diarrhea, abdominal pain, vomiting; symptoms may be mild or life threatening.

005.0   Staphylococcal food poisoning
Staphylococcal toxemia specified as due to food

005.1   Botulism
Food poisoning due to Clostridium botulinum

005.2   Food poisoning due to Clostridium perfringens [C. welchii]
Enteritis necroticans

005.3   Food poisoning due to other Clostridia

005.4   Food poisoning due to Vibrio parahaemolyticus

✓5th **005.8   Other bacterial food poisoning**

EXCLUDES   *salmonella food poisoning (003.0-003.9)*

    005.81   Food poisoning due to Vibrio vulnificus

    005.89   Other bacterial food poisoning
Food poisoning due to Bacillus cereus

005.9   Food poisoning, unspecified

✓4th **006 Amebiasis**

INCLUDES   infection due to Entamoeba histolytica

EXCLUDES   *amebiasis due to organisms other than Entamoeba histolytica (007.8)*

DEF: Infection of the large intestine caused by *Entamoeba histolytica*; usually asymptomatic but symptoms may range from mild diarrhea to profound life-threatening dysentery. Extraintestinal complications include hepatic abscess, which may rupture into the lung, pericardium or abdomen, causing life-threatening infections.

006.0   Acute amebic dysentery without mention of abscess
Acute amebiasis
DEF: Sudden, severe *Entamoeba histolytica* infection causing bloody stools.

006.1   Chronic intestinal amebiasis without mention of abscess
Chronic:
  amebiasis
  amebic dysentery

006.2   Amebic nondysenteric colitis
DEF: *Entamoeba histolytica* infection with inflamed colon but no dysentery.

006.3   Amebic liver abscess
Hepatic amebiasis

006.4   Amebic lung abscess
Amebic abscess of lung (and liver)

006.5   Amebic brain abscess
Amebic abscess of brain (and liver) (and lung)

006.6   Amebic skin ulceration
Cutaneous amebiasis

006.8   Amebic infection of other sites
Amebic: Ameboma
  appendicitis
  balanitis
EXCLUDES   *specific infections by free-living amebae (136.2)*

006.9   Amebiasis, unspecified
Amebiasis NOS

✓4th ✓5th Additional Digit Required   RUG III Special Care Dx   RUG III Clinically Complex Dx   Hospice Non-cancer Dx   **CD PDx** Clinical Dimension PDx   **CD SDx** Clinical Dimension SDx

2006 ICD•9•CM   **Volume 1 — 1**

Infectious and Parasitic Diseases

007–009.0

√4ᵗʰ **007 Other protozoal intestinal diseases**

INCLUDES   protozoal:
     colitis
     diarrhea
     dysentery

007.0 Balantidiasis
     Infection by Balantidium coli

007.1 Giardiasis
     Infection by Giardia lamblia   Lambliasis

007.2 Coccidiosis
     Infection by Isospora belli and Isospora hominis
     Isosporiasis

007.3 Intestinal trichomoniasis

DEF: Colitis, diarrhea, or dysentery caused by the protozoa *Trichomonas*.

007.4 Cryptosporidiosis

AHA: 4Q, '97, 30

DEF: An intestinal infection by protozoan parasites causing intractable diarrhea in patients with AIDS and other immunosuppressed individuals.

007.5 Cyclosporiasis

AHA: 4Q, '00, 38

DEF: An infection of the small intestine by the protozoal organism, *Cyclospora caytenanesis*, spread to humans though ingestion of contaminated water or food. Symptoms include watery diarrhea with frequent explosive bowel movements, loss of appetite, loss of weight, bloating, increased gas, stomach cramps, nausea, vomiting, muscle aches, low grade fever, and fatigue.

007.8 Other specified protozoal intestinal diseases
     Amebiasis due to organisms other than Entamoeba histolytica

007.9 Unspecified protozoal intestinal disease
     Flagellate diarrhea   Protozoal dysentery NOS

√4ᵗʰ **008 Intestinal infections due to other organisms**

INCLUDES   any condition classifiable to 009.0-009.3 with mention of the responsible organisms

EXCLUDES   *food poisoning by these organisms (005.0-005.9)*

√5ᵗʰ **008.0 Escherichia coli [E. coli]**

AHA: 4Q, '92, 17

008.00 E. coli, unspecified
     E. coli enteritis NOS

008.01 Enteropathogenic E. coli

DEF: *E. coli* causing inflammation of intestines.

008.02 Enterotoxigenic E. coli

DEF: A toxic reaction to *E. coli* of the intestinal mucosa, causing voluminous watery secretions.

008.03 Enteroinvasive E. coli

DEF: *E. coli* infection penetrating intestinal mucosa.

008.04 Enterohemorrhagic E. coli

DEF: *E. coli* infection penetrating the intestinal mucosa, producing microscopic ulceration and bleeding.

008.09 Other intestinal E. coli infections

008.1 Arizona group of paracolon bacilli

008.2 Aerobacter aerogenes
     Enterobacter aeogenes

008.3 Proteus (mirabilis) (morganii)

√5ᵗʰ **008.4 Other specified bacteria**

AHA: 4Q, '92, 18

008.41 Staphylococcus
     Staphylococcal enterocolitis

008.42 Pseudomonas

AHA: 2Q, '89, 10

008.43 Campylobacter

008.44 Yersinia enterocolitica

008.45 Clostridium difficile
     Pseudomembranous colitis

DEF: An overgrowth of a species of bacterium that is a part of the normal colon flora in human infants and sometimes in adults; produces a toxin that causes pseudomembranous enterocolitis.; typically is seen in patients undergoing antibiotic therapy.

008.46 Other anaerobes
     Anaerobic enteritis NOS
     Bacteroides (fragilis)
     Gram-negative anaerobes

008.47 Other gram-negative bacteria
     Gram-negative enteritis NOS

EXCLUDES   *gram-negative anaerobes (008.46)*

008.49 Other

AHA: 2Q, '89, 10; 1Q, '88, 6

008.5 Bacterial enteritis, unspecified

√5ᵗʰ **008.6 Enteritis due to specified virus**

AHA: 4Q, '92, 18

008.61 Rotavirus

008.62 Adenovirus

008.63 Norwalk virus
     Norwalk-like agent

008.64 Other small round viruses [SRVs]
     Small round virus NOS

008.65 Calicivirus

DEF: Enteritis due to a subgroup of *Picornaviruses*.

008.66 Astrovirus

008.67 Enterovirus NEC
     Coxsackie virus   Echovirus

EXCLUDES   *poliovirus (045.0-045.9)*

008.69 Other viral enteritis
     Torovirus

AHA: 1Q, '03, 10

008.8 Other organism, not elsewhere classified
     Viral: Viral:
       enteritis NOS   gastroenteritis

EXCLUDES   *influenza with involvement of gastrointestinal tract (487.8)*

√4ᵗʰ **009 Ill-defined intestinal infections**

EXCLUDES   *diarrheal disease or intestinal infection due to specified organism (001.0-008.8)*
     diarrhea following gastrointestinal surgery (564.4)
     intestinal malabsorption (579.0-579.9)
     ischemic enteritis (557.0-557.9)
     other noninfectious gastroenteritis and colitis (558.1-558.9)
     regional enteritis (555.0-555.9)
     ulcerative colitis (556)

009.0 Infectious colitis, enteritis, and gastroenteritis
     Colitis
     Enteritis   } septic
     Gastroenteritis

     Dysentery: Dysentery:
       NOS   hemorrhagic
       catarrhal

AHA: 3Q, '99, 4

DEF: Colitis: An inflammation of mucous membranes of the colon.

DEF: Enteritis: An inflammation of mucous membranes of the small intestine.

DEF: Gastroenteritis: An inflammation of mucous membranes of stomach and intestines.

N Newborn Age: 0   P Pediatric Age: 0-17   M Maternity Age: 12-55   A Adult Age: 15-124   Manifestation Code   ◄ Revised Text   ● New Code   ▲ Revised Code Title

009.1 Colitis, enteritis, and gastroenteritis of presumed infectious origin

> EXCLUDES   *colitis NOS (558.9)*
> *enteritis NOS (558.9)*
> *gastroenteritis NOS (558.9)*

AHA: 3Q, '99, 6

009.2 Infectious diarrhea
Diarrhea:
   dysenteric
   epidemic
Infectious diarrheal disease NOS

009.3 Diarrhea of presumed infectious origin

> EXCLUDES   *diarrhea NOS (787.91)*

AHA: N-D, '87, 7

TUBERCULOSIS (010–018)

> INCLUDES   infection by Mycobacterium tuberculosis (human) (bovine)
> EXCLUDES   *congenital tuberculosis (771.2)*
> *late effects of tuberculosis (137.0-137.4)*

The following fifth-digit subclassification is for use with categories 010-018:

  0 unspecified
  1 bacteriological or histological examination not done
  2 bacteriological or histological examination unknown (at present)
  3 tubercle bacilli found (in sputum) by microscopy
  4 tubercle bacilli not found (in sputum) by microscopy, but found by bacterial culture
  5 tubercle bacilli not found by bacteriological examination, but tuberculosis confirmed histologically
  6 tubercle bacilli not found by bacteriological or histological examination but tuberculosis confirmed by other methods [inoculation of animals]

DEF: An infection by *Mycobacterium tuberculosis* causing the formation of small, rounded nodules, called tubercles, that can disseminate throughout the body via lymph and blood vessels. Localized tuberculosis is most often seen in the lungs.

010 Primary tuberculous infection
DEF: Tuberculosis of the lungs occurring when the patient is first infected.

§ ✓5ᵗʰ **010.0 Primary tuberculous infection**

> EXCLUDES   *nonspecific reaction to tuberculin skin test without active tuberculosis (795.5)*
> *positive PPD (795.5)*
> *positive tuberculin skin test without active tuberculosis (795.5)*

DEF: Hilar or paratracheal lymph node enlargement in pulmonary tuberculosis.

§ ✓5ᵗʰ **010.1 Tuberculous pleurisy in primary progressive tuberculosis**
DEF: Inflammation and exudation in the lining of the tubercular lung.

§ ✓5ᵗʰ **010.8 Other primary progressive tuberculosis**

> EXCLUDES   *tuberculous erythema nodosum (017.1)*

§ ✓5ᵗʰ **010.9 Primary tuberculous infection, unspecified**

011 Pulmonary tuberculosis
Use additional code to identify any associated silicosis (502)

§ ✓5ᵗʰ **011.0 Tuberculosis of lung, infiltrative**
§ ✓5ᵗʰ **011.1 Tuberculosis of lung, nodular**
§ ✓5ᵗʰ **011.2 Tuberculosis of lung with cavitation**

§ ✓5ᵗʰ **011.3 Tuberculosis of bronchus**

> EXCLUDES   *isolated bronchial tuberculosis (012.2)*

§ ✓5ᵗʰ **011.4 Tuberculous fibrosis of lung**
§ ✓5ᵗʰ **011.5 Tuberculous bronchiectasis**
§ ✓5ᵗʰ **011.6 Tuberculous pneumonia [any form]**
DEF: Inflammatory pulmonary reaction to tuberculous cells.

§ ✓5ᵗʰ **011.7 Tuberculous pneumothorax**
DEF: Spontaneous rupture of damaged tuberculous pulmonary tissue.

§ ✓5ᵗʰ **011.8 Other specified pulmonary tuberculosis**
§ ✓5ᵗʰ **011.9 Pulmonary tuberculosis, unspecified**
Respiratory tuberculosis NOS
Tuberculosis of lung NOS

012 Other respiratory tuberculosis

> EXCLUDES   *respiratory tuberculosis, unspecified (011.9)*

§ ✓5ᵗʰ **012.0 Tuberculous pleurisy**
Tuberculosis of pleura
Tuberculous empyema
Tuberculous hydrothorax

> EXCLUDES   *pleurisy with effusion without mention of cause (511.9)*
> *tuberculous pleurisy in primary progressive tuberculosis (010.1)*

DEF: Inflammation and exudation in the lining of the tubercular lung.

§ ✓5ᵗʰ **012.1 Tuberculosis of intrathoracic lymph nodes**
Tuberculosis of lymph nodes:
   hilar
   mediastinal
   tracheobronchial
Tuberculous tracheobronchial adenopathy

> EXCLUDES   *that specified as primary (010.0-010.9)*

§ ✓5ᵗʰ **012.2 Isolated tracheal or bronchial tuberculosis**
§ ✓5ᵗʰ **012.3 Tuberculous laryngitis**
Tuberculosis of glottis

§ ✓5ᵗʰ **012.8 Other specified respiratory tuberculosis**
Tuberculosis of: Tuberculosis of:
   mediastinum   nose (septum)
   nasopharynx   sinus [any nasal]

013 Tuberculosis of meninges and central nervous system

§ ✓5ᵗʰ **013.0 Tuberculous meningitis**   `CD PDx`
Tuberculosis of meninges (cerebral) (spinal)
Tuberculous:
   leptomeningitis
   meningoencephalitis

> EXCLUDES   *tuberculoma of meninges (013.1)*

§ ✓5ᵗʰ **013.1 Tuberculoma of meninges**   `CD PDx`
§ ✓5ᵗʰ **013.2 Tuberculoma of brain**   `CD PDx`
Tuberculosis of brain (current disease)
§ ✓5ᵗʰ **013.3 Tuberculous abscess of brain**   `CD PDx`
§ ✓5ᵗʰ **013.4 Tuberculoma of spinal cord**   `CD PDx`
§ ✓5ᵗʰ **013.5 Tuberculous abscess of spinal cord**   `CD PDx`
§ ✓5ᵗʰ **013.6 Tuberculous encephalitis or myelitis**   `CD PDx`
§ ✓5ᵗʰ **013.8 Other specified tuberculosis of central nervous system**   `CD PDx`
§ ✓5ᵗʰ **013.9 Unspecified tuberculosis of central nervous system**   `CD PDx`
Tuberculosis of central nervous system NOS

014 Tuberculosis of intestines, peritoneum, and mesenteric glands

§ ✓5ᵗʰ **014.0 Tuberculous peritonitis**
Tuberculous ascites
DEF: Tuberculous inflammation of the membrane lining the abdomen.

---

§   Requires fifth-digit. See beginning of section 010-018 for codes and definitions.

✓4ᵗʰ / ✓5ᵗʰ Additional Digit Required   RUG III Special Care Dx   RUG III Clinically Complex Dx   Hospice Non-cancer Dx   `CD PDx` Clinical Dimension PDx   `CD SDx` Clinical Dimension SDx

2006 ICD•9•CM   Volume 1 — 3

§ ✓5ᵗʰ **014.8**   **Other**
    Tuberculosis (of):
      anus
      intestine (large) (small)
      mesenteric glands
      rectum
      retroperitoneal (lymph nodes)
    Tuberculous enteritis

✓4ᵗʰ **015**   **Tuberculosis of bones and joints**
    Use additional code to identify manifestation, as:
    tuberculous:
      arthropathy (711.4)
      necrosis of bone (730.8)
      osteitis (730.8)
      osteomyelitis (730.8)
      synovitis (727.01)
      tenosynovitis (727.01)

§ ✓5ᵗʰ **015.0**   **Vertebral column**
    Pott's disease
    Use additional code to identify manifestation, as:
      curvature of spine [Pott's] (737.4)
      kyphosis (737.4)
      spondylitis (720.81)

§ ✓5ᵗʰ **015.1**   **Hip**

§ ✓5ᵗʰ **015.2**   **Knee**

§ ✓5ᵗʰ **015.5**   **Limb bones**
    Tuberculous dactylitis

§ ✓5ᵗʰ **015.6**   **Mastoid**
    Tuberculous mastoiditis

§ ✓5ᵗʰ **015.7**   **Other specified bone**

§ ✓5ᵗʰ **015.8**   **Other specified joint**

§ ✓5ᵗʰ **015.9**   **Tuberculosis of unspecified bones and joints**

✓4ᵗʰ **016**   **Tuberculosis of genitourinary system**

§ ✓5ᵗʰ **016.0**   **Kidney**
    Renal tuberculosis
    Use additional code to identify manifestation, as:
    tuberculous:
      nephropathy (583.81)
      pyelitis (590.81)
      pyelonephritis (590.81)

§ ✓5ᵗʰ **016.1**   **Bladder**

§ ✓5ᵗʰ **016.2**   **Ureter**

§ ✓5ᵗʰ **016.3**   **Other urinary organs**

§ ✓5ᵗʰ **016.4**   **Epididymis**   ♂

§ ✓5ᵗʰ **016.5**   **Other male genital organs**   ♂
    Use additional code to identify manifestation, as:
    tuberculosis of:
      prostate (601.4)
      seminal vesicle (608.81)
      testis (608.81)

§ ✓5ᵗʰ **016.6**   **Tuberculous oophoritis and salpingitis**   ♀

§ ✓5ᵗʰ **016.7**   **Other female genital organs**   ♀
    Tuberculous:
      cervicitis
      endometritis

§ ✓5ᵗʰ **016.9**   **Genitourinary tuberculosis, unspecified**

✓4ᵗʰ **017**   **Tuberculosis of other organs**

§ ✓5ᵗʰ **017.0**   **Skin and subcutaneous cellular tissue**

Lupus:	Tuberculosis:
exedens	cutis
vulgaris	lichenoides
Scrofuloderma	papulonecrotica
Tuberculosis:	verrucosa cutis
colliquativa	

    EXCLUDES   lupus erythematosus (695.4)
      disseminated (710.0)
    lupus NOS (710.0)
    nonspecific reaction to tuberculin skin
      test without active tuberculosis
      (795.5)
    positive PPD (795.5)
    positive tuberculin skin test without
      active tuberculosis (795.5)

§ ✓5ᵗʰ **017.1**   **Erythema nodosum with hypersensitivity reaction in tuberculosis**

Bazin's disease	Erythema:
Erythema:	nodosum, tuberculous
induratum	Tuberculosis indurativa

    EXCLUDES   erythema nodosum NOS (695.2)
DEF: Tender, inflammatory, bilateral nodules appearing on the shins and thought to be an allergic reaction to tuberculotoxin.

§ ✓5ᵗʰ **017.2**   **Peripheral lymph nodes**

Scrofula	Tuberculous adenitis
Scrofulous abscess	

    EXCLUDES   tuberculosis of lymph nodes:
      bronchial and mediastinal (012.1)
      mesenteric and retroperitoneal
       (014.8)
      tuberculous tracheobronchial
       adenopathy (012.1)
DEF: Scrofula: Old name for tuberculous cervical lymphadenitis.

§ ✓5ᵗʰ **017.3**   **Eye**
    Use additional code to identify manifestation, as:
    tuberculous:
      chorioretinitis, disseminated (363.13)
      episcleritis (379.09)
      interstitial keratitis (370.59)
      iridocyclitis, chronic (364.11)
      keratoconjunctivitis (phlyctenular) (370.31)

§ ✓5ᵗʰ **017.4**   **Ear**
    Tuberculosis of ear
    Tuberculous otitis media
    EXCLUDES   tuberculous mastoiditis (015.6)

§ ✓5ᵗʰ **017.5**   **Thyroid gland**

§ ✓5ᵗʰ **017.6**   **Adrenal glands**
    Addison's disease, tuberculous

§ ✓5ᵗʰ **017.7**   **Spleen**

§ ✓5ᵗʰ **017.8**   **Esophagus**

§ ✓5ᵗʰ **017.9**   **Other specified organs**
    Use additional code to identify manifestation, as:
    tuberculosis of:
      endocardium [any valve] (424.91)
      myocardium (422.0)
      pericardium (420.0)

✓4ᵗʰ **018**   **Miliary tuberculosis**
    INCLUDES   tuberculosis:
      disseminated
      generalized
      miliary, whether of a single specified site,
       multiple sites, or unspecified site
      polyserositis
DEF: A form of tuberculosis caused by caseous material carried through the bloodstream planting seedlike tubercles in various body organs.

§ ✓5ᵗʰ **018.0**   **Acute miliary tuberculosis**

§ ✓5ᵗʰ **018.8**   **Other specified miliary tuberculosis**

§ ✓5ᵗʰ **018.9**   **Miliary tuberculosis, unspecified**

---

§   Requires fifth-digit. See beginning of section 010-018 for codes and definitions.

N Newborn Age: 0   **P** Pediatric Age: 0-17   **M** Maternity Age: 12-55   **A** Adult Age: 15-124   Manifestation Code   ►◄ Revised Text   ● New Code   ▲ Revised Code Title

ZOONOTIC BACTERIAL DISEASES (020-027)

✓4ᵗʰ 020 Plague

INCLUDES   infection by Yersinia [Pasteurella] pestis

020.0 Bubonic

DEF: Most common acute and severe form of plague characterized by lymphadenopathy (buboes), chills, fever and headache.

020.1 Cellulocutaneous

DEF: Plague characterized by inflammation and necrosis of skin.

020.2 Septicemic

DEF: Plague characterized by massive infection in the bloodstream.

020.3 Primary pneumonic

DEF: Plague characterized by massive pulmonary infection.

020.4 Secondary pneumonic

DEF: Lung infection as a secondary complication of plague.

020.5 Pneumonic, unspecified

020.8 Other specified types of plague

Abortive plague   Pestis minor
Ambulatory plague

020.9 Plague, unspecified

✓4ᵗʰ 021 Tularemia

INCLUDES   deerfly fever
infection by Francisella [Pasteurella] tularensis
rabbit fever

DEF: A febrile disease transmitted by the bites of deer flies, fleas and ticks, by inhalations of aerosolized *F. tularensis* or by ingestion of contaminated food or water; patients quickly develop fever, chills, weakness, headache, backache and malaise.

021.0 Ulceroglandular tularemia

DEF: Lesions occur at the site *Francisella tularensis* organism enters body, usually the fingers or hands.

021.1 Enteric tularemia

Tularemia: Tularemia:
  cryptogenic   typhoidal
  intestinal

021.2 Pulmonary tularemia

Bronchopneumonic tularemia

021.3 Oculoglandular tularemia

DEF: Painful conjunctival infection by *Francisella tularensis* organism with possible corneal, preauricular lymph, or lacrimal involvement.

021.8 Other specified tularemia

Tularemia: Tularemia:
  generalized or disseminated   glandular

021.9 Unspecified tularemia

✓4ᵗʰ 022 Anthrax

AHA: 4Q, '02, 70

DEF: An infectious bacterial disease usually transmitted by contact with infected animals or their discharges or products; it is classified by primary routes of inoculation as cutaneous, gastrointestinal and by inhalation.

022.0 Cutaneous anthrax

Malignant pustule

022.1 Pulmonary anthrax

Respiratory anthrax
Wool-sorters' disease

022.2 Gastrointestinal anthrax

022.3 Anthrax septicemia

022.8 Other specified manifestations of anthrax

022.9 Anthrax, unspecified

✓4ᵗʰ 023 Brucellosis

INCLUDES   fever:
        Malta
        Mediterranean
        undulant

DEF: An infectious disease caused by gram-negative, aerobic coccobacilli organisms; it is transmitted to humans through contact with infected tissue or dairy products; fever, sweating, weakness and aching are symptoms.

023.0 Brucella melitensis

DEF: Infection from direct or indirect contact with infected sheep or goats.

023.1 Brucella abortus

DEF: Infection from direct or indirect contact with infected cattle.

023.2 Brucella suis

DEF: Infection from direct or indirect contact with infected swine.

023.3 Brucella canis

DEF: Infection from direct or indirect contact with infected dogs.

023.8 Other brucellosis

Infection by more than one organism

023.9 Brucellosis, unspecified

024 Glanders

Infection by:
    Actinobacillus mallei   Farcy
    Malleomyces mallei   Malleus
    Pseudomonas mallei

DEF: Equine infection causing mucosal inflammation and skin ulcers in humans.

025 Melioidosis

Infection by: Infection by:
   Malleomyces pseudomallei   Pseudoglanders
   Pseudomonas pseudomallei   Whitmore's bacillus

DEF: Rare infection caused by *Pseudomonas pseudomallei*; clinical symptoms range from localized infection to fatal septicemia.

✓4ᵗʰ 026 Rat-bite fever

026.0 Spirillary fever

Rat-bite fever due to Spirillum minor [S. minus]
Sodoku

026.1 Streptobacillary fever

Epidemic arthritic erythema
Haverhill fever
Rat-bite fever due to Streptobacillus moniliformis

026.9 Unspecified rat-bite fever

✓4ᵗʰ 027 Other zoonotic bacterial diseases

027.0 Listeriosis

Infection   ⎫
Septicemia ⎬ by Listeria monocytogenes
          ⎭

Use additional code to identify manifestation, as meningitis (320.7)

EXCLUDES   congenital listeriosis (771.2)

027.1 Erysipelothrix infection

Erysipeloid (of Rosenbach)
Infection   ⎫ by Erysipelothrix insidiosa
Septicemia ⎬   [E. rhusiopathiae]

DEF: Usually associated with handling of fish, meat, or poultry; symptoms range from localized inflammation to septicemia.

027.2 Pasteurellosis

Pasteurella pseudotuberculosis infection
Mesenteric adenitis   ⎫ by Pasteurella multocida
Septic infection (cat   ⎬   [P. septica]
  bite) (dog bite)   ⎭

EXCLUDES   infection by:
      Francisella [Pasteurella] tularensis
       (021.0-021.9)
      Yersinia [Pasteurella] pestis (020.0-
       020.9)

DEF: Swelling, abscesses, or septicemia from *Pasteurella multocida*, commonly transmitted to humans by a dog or cat scratch.

027.8 Other specified zoonotic bacterial diseases

027.9 Unspecified zoonotic bacterial disease

✓4ᵗʰ ✓5ᵗʰ Additional Digit Required   RUG III Special Care Dx   RUG III Clinically Complex Dx   Hospice Non-cancer Dx   CD PDx Clinical Dimension PDx   CD SDx Clinical Dimension SDx

2006 ICD•9•CM   **Volume 1 — 5**

OTHER BACTERIAL DISEASES (030-041)

EXCLUDES *bacterial venereal diseases (098.0-099.9)*
bartonellosis (088.0)

✓4ᵗʰ **030 Leprosy**
INCLUDES Hansen's disease
infection by Mycobacterium leprae

030.0 Lepromatous [type L]
Lepromatous leprosy (macular) (diffuse) (infiltrated) (nodular) (neuritic)

DEF: Infectious, disseminated leprosy bacilli with lesions and deformities.

030.1 Tuberculoid [type T]
Tuberculoid leprosy (macular) (maculoanesthetic) (major) (minor) (neuritic)

DEF: Relatively benign, self-limiting leprosy with neuralgia and scales.

030.2 Indeterminate [group I]
Indeterminate [uncharacteristic] leprosy (macular) (neuritic)

DEF: Uncharacteristic leprosy, frequently an early manifestation.

030.3 Borderline [group B]
Borderline or dimorphous leprosy (infiltrated) (neuritic)

DEF: Transitional form of leprosy, neither lepromatous nor tuberculoid.

030.8 Other specified leprosy
030.9 Leprosy, unspecified

✓4ᵗʰ **031 Diseases due to other mycobacteria**
031.0 Pulmonary
Battey disease
Infection by Mycobacterium:
avium
intracellulare [Battey bacillus]
kansasii

031.1 Cutaneous
Buruli ulcer
Infection by Mycobacterium:
marinum [M. balnei]
ulcerans

031.2 Disseminated
Disseminated mycobacterium avium-intracellulare complex (DMAC)
Mycobacterium avium-intracellulare complex (MAC) bacteremia

AHA: 4Q, '97, 31

DEF: Disseminated mycobacterium avium-intracellulare complex (DMAC): A serious systemic form of MAC commonly observed in patients in the late course of AIDS.

DEF: Mycobacterium avium-intracellulare complex (MAC) bacterium: Human pulmonary disease, lymphadenitis in children and systemic disease in immunocompromised individuals caused by a slow growing, gram-positive, aerobic organism.

031.8 Other specified mycobacterial diseases
031.9 Unspecified diseases due to mycobacteria
Atypical mycobacterium infection NOS

✓4ᵗʰ **032 Diphtheria**
INCLUDES infection by Corynebacterium diphtheriae

032.0 Faucial diphtheria
Membranous angina, diphtheritic
DEF: Diphtheria of the throat.

032.1 Nasopharyngeal diphtheria
032.2 Anterior nasal diphtheria
032.3 Laryngeal diphtheria
Laryngotracheitis, diphtheritic

✓5ᵗʰ **032.8 Other specified diphtheria**
032.81 Conjunctival diphtheria
Pseudomembranous diphtheritic conjunctivitis
032.82 Diphtheritic myocarditis

032.83 Diphtheritic peritonitis
032.84 Diphtheritic cystitis
032.85 Cutaneous diphtheria
032.89 Other
032.9 Diphtheria, unspecified

✓4ᵗʰ **033 Whooping cough**
INCLUDES pertussis
Use additional code to identify any associated pneumonia (484.3)

DEF: An acute, highly contagious respiratory tract infection caused by *Bordetella pertussis* and *B. bronchiseptica*; characteristic paroxysmal cough.

033.0 Bordetella pertussis [B. pertussis]
033.1 Bordetella parapertussis [B. parapertussis]
033.8 Whooping cough due to other specified organism
Bordetella bronchiseptica [B. bronchiseptica]
033.9 Whooping cough, unspecified organism

✓4ᵗʰ **034 Streptococcal sore throat and scarlet fever**
034.0 Streptococcal sore throat

Septic:	Streptococcal:
angina	laryngitis
sore throat	pharyngitis
Streptococcal:	tonsillitis
angina	

034.1 Scarlet fever
Scarlatina
EXCLUDES *parascarlatina (057.8)*

DEF: Streptococcal infection and fever with red rash spreading from trunk.

035 Erysipelas
EXCLUDES *postpartum or puerperal erysipelas (670)*

DEF: An acute superficial cellulitis involving the dermal lymphatics; it is often caused by group A streptococci.

✓4ᵗʰ **036 Meningococcal infection**
036.0 Meningococcal meningitis
Cerebrospinal fever (meningococcal)
Meningitis:
cerebrospinal
epidemic

036.1 Meningococcal encephalitis
036.2 Meningococcemia
Meningococcal septicemia

036.3 Waterhouse-Friderichsen syndrome, meningococcal
Meningococcal hemorrhagic adrenalitis
Meningococcic adrenal syndrome
Waterhouse-Friderichsen syndrome NOS

✓5ᵗʰ **036.4 Meningococcal carditis**
036.40 Meningococcal carditis, unspecified
036.41 Meningococcal pericarditis
DEF: Meningococcal infection of the outer membrane of the heart.

036.42 Meningococcal endocarditis
DEF: Meningococcal infection of the membranes lining the cavities of the heart.

036.43 Meningococcal myocarditis
DEF: Meningococcal infection of the muscle of the heart.

✓5ᵗʰ **036.8 Other specified meningococcal infections**
036.81 Meningococcal optic neuritis
036.82 Meningococcal arthropathy
036.89 Other
036.9 Meningococcal infection, unspecified
Meningococcal infection NOS

N Newborn Age: 0   P Pediatric Age: 0-17   M Maternity Age: 12-55   A Adult Age: 15-124   Manifestation Code   ▶◀ Revised Text   ● New Code   ▲ Revised Code Title

037 Tetanus

> EXCLUDES   tetanus:
> complicating:
> abortion (634-638 with .0, 639.0)
> ectopic or molar pregnancy (639.0)
> neonatorum (771.3)
> puerperal (670)

DEF: An acute, often fatal, infectious disease caused by the anaerobic, spore-forming bacillus *Clostridium tetani*; the bacillus most often enters the body through a contaminated wound, burns, surgical wounds, or cutaneous ulcers. Symptoms include lockjaw, spasms, seizures, and paralysis.

√4ᵗʰ 038 Septicemia

Use additional code for systemic inflammatory response syndrome (SIRS) (995.91-995.92)

> EXCLUDES   bacteremia (790.7)
> during labor (659.3)
> following ectopic or molar pregnancy (639.0)
> following infusion, injection, transfusion, or vaccination (999.3)
> postpartum, puerperal (670)
> septicemia (sepsis) of newborn (771.81)
> that complicating abortion (634-638 with .0, 639.0)

AHA: 2Q, '04, 16; 4Q, '88, 10; 3Q, '88, 12

DEF: A systemic disease associated with the presence and persistence of pathogenic microorganisms or their toxins in the blood.

038.0 Streptococcal septicemia

AHA: 4Q, '03, 79; 2Q, '96, 5

√5ᵗʰ **038.1 Staphylococcal septicemia**

AHA: 4Q, '97, 32

038.10 Staphylococcal septicemia, unspecified

038.11 Staphylococcus aureus septicemia

AHA: ▶1Q, '05, 7;◀ 2Q, '00, 5; 4Q, '98, 42

038.19 Other staphylococcal septicemia

AHA: 2Q, '00, 5

038.2 Pneumococcal septicemia [Streptococcus pneumoniae septicemia]

AHA: 2Q, '96, 5; 1Q, '91, 13

038.3 Septicemia due to anaerobes

Septicemia due to bacteroides

> EXCLUDES   gas gangrene (040.0)
> that due to anaerobic streptococci (038.0)

DEF: Infection of blood by microorganisms that thrive without oxygen.

√5ᵗʰ **038.4 Septicemia due to other gram-negative organisms**

DEF: Infection of blood by microorganisms categorized as gram-negative by Gram's method of staining for identification of bacteria.

038.40 Gram-negative organism, unspecified

Gram-negative septicemia NOS

038.41 Hemophilus influenzae [H. influenzae]

038.42 Escherichia coli [E. coli]

AHA: 4Q, '03, 73

038.43 Pseudomonas

038.44 Serratia

038.49 Other

038.8 Other specified septicemias

> EXCLUDES   septicemia (due to):
> anthrax (022.3)
> gonococcal (098.89)
> herpetic (054.5)
> meningococcal (036.2)
> septicemic plague (020.2)

038.9 Unspecified septicemia

Septicemia NOS

> EXCLUDES   bacteremia NOS (790.7)

AHA: 2Q, '04, 16; 4Q, '03, 79; 2Q, '00, 3; 3Q, '99, 5, 9; 1Q, '98, 5; 3Q, '96, 16; 2Q, '96, 6

√4ᵗʰ 039 Actinomycotic infections

> INCLUDES   actinomycotic mycetoma
> infection by Actinomycetales, such as species of Actinomyces, Actinomadura, Nocardia, Streptomyces
> maduromycosis (actinomycotic)
> schizomycetoma (actinomycotic)

DEF: Inflammatory lesions and abscesses at site of infection by *Actinomyces israelii.*

039.0 Cutaneous

Erythrasma   Trichomycosis axillaris

039.1 Pulmonary

Thoracic actinomycosis

039.2 Abdominal

039.3 Cervicofacial

039.4 Madura foot

> EXCLUDES   madura foot due to mycotic infection (117.4)

039.8 Of other specified sites

039.9 Of unspecified site

Actinomycosis NOS   Nocardiosis NOS
Maduromycosis NOS

√4ᵗʰ 040 Other bacterial diseases

> EXCLUDES   bacteremia NOS (790.7)
> bacterial infection NOS (041.9)

040.0 Gas gangrene

Gas bacillus infection or gangrene
Infection by Clostridium:
  histolyticum
  oedematiens
  perfringens [welchii]
  septicum
  sordellii
Malignant edema
Myonecrosis, clostridial
Myositis, clostridial

AHA: 1Q, '95, 11

040.1 Rhinoscleroma

DEF: Growths on the nose and nasopharynx caused by *Klebsiella rhinoscleromatis.*

040.2 Whipple's disease

Intestinal lipodystrophy

040.3 Necrobacillosis

DEF: Infection with *Fusobacterium necrophorum* causing abscess or necrosis.

√5ᵗʰ **040.8 Other specified bacterial diseases**

040.81 Tropical pyomyositis

040.82 Toxic shock syndrome

Use additional code to identify the organism

AHA: 4Q, '02, 44

DEF: Syndrome caused by staphylococcal exotoxin that may rapidly progress to severe and intractable shock; symptoms include characteristic sunburn-like rash with peeling of skin on palms and soles, sudden onset high fever, vomiting, diarrhea, myalgia, and hypotension.

040.89 Other

AHA: N-D, '86, 7

√4ᵗʰ 041 Bacterial infection in conditions classified elsewhere and of unspecified site

Note: This category is provided to be used as an additional code to identify the bacterial agent in diseases classified elsewhere. This category will also be used to classify bacterial infections of unspecified nature or site.

> EXCLUDES   bacteremia NOS (790.7)
> septicemia (038.0-038.9)

AHA: 2Q, '01, 12; J-A, '84, 19

√5ᵗʰ **041.0 Streptococcus**

041.00 Streptococcus, unspecified

041.01 Group A

AHA: 1Q, '02, 3

√4ᵗʰ / √5ᵗʰ Additional Digit Required   RUG III Special Care Dx   RUG III Clinically Complex Dx   Hospice Non-cancer Dx   CD PDx Clinical Dimension PDx   CD SDx Clinical Dimension SDx

041.02 **Group B**

041.03 **Group C**

041.04 **Group D [Enterococcus]**

041.05 **Group G**

041.09 **Other Streptococcus**

√5ᵗʰ 041.1 **Staphylococcus**

041.10 **Staphylococcus, unspecified**

041.11 **Staphylococcus aureus**

AHA: 4Q, '03, 104, 106; 2Q, '01, 11; 4Q, '98, 42, 54; 4Q, '97, 32

041.19 **Other Staphylococcus**

041.2 **Pneumococcus**

041.3 **Friedländer's bacillus**

Infection by Klebsiella pneumoniae

041.4 **Escherichia coli [E. coli]**

041.5 **Hemophilus influenzae [H. influenzae]**

041.6 **Proteus (mirabilis) (morganii)**

041.7 **Pseudomonas**

AHA: 4Q, '02, 45

√5ᵗʰ 041.8 **Other specified bacterial infections**

041.81 **Mycoplasma**

Eaton's agent

Pleuropneumonia-like organisms [PPLO]

041.82 **Bacteroides fragilis**

DEF: Anaerobic gram-negative bacilli of the gastrointestinal tract; frequently implicated in intra-abdominal infection; commonly resistant to antibiotics.

041.83 **Clostridium perfringens**

041.84 **Other anaerobes**

Gram-negative anaerobes

EXCLUDES *Helicobacter pylori (041.86)*

041.85 **Other gram-negative organisms**

Aerobacter aerogenes

Gram-negative bacteria NOS

Mima polymorpha

Serratia

EXCLUDES *gram-negative anaerobes (041.84)*

AHA: 1Q, '95, 18

041.86 **Helicobacter pylori (H. pylori)**

AHA: 4Q, '95, 60

041.89 **Other specified bacteria**

AHA: 2Q, '03, 7

041.9 **Bacterial infection, unspecified**

AHA: 2Q, '91, 9

HUMAN IMMUNODEFICIENCY VIRUS (HIV) INFECTION (042)

042 **Human immunodeficiency virus [HIV] disease**

Acquired immune deficiency syndrome

Acquired immunodeficiency syndrome

AIDS

AIDS-like syndrome

AIDS-related complex

ARC

HIV infection, symptomatic

Use additional code(s) to identify all manifestations of HIV

Use additional code to identify HIV-2 infection (079.53)

EXCLUDES *asymptomatic HIV infection status (V08)*
exposure to HIV virus (V01.79)
nonspecific serologic evidence of HIV (795.71)

AHA: ▶1Q, '05, 7;◀2Q, '04, 11; 1Q, '04, 5; 1Q, '03, 15; 1Q, '99, 14; 4Q, '97, 30, 31; 1Q, '93, 21; 2Q, '92, 11; 3Q, '90, 17; J-A, '87, 8

POLIOMYELITIS AND OTHER NON-ARTHROPOD-BORNE VIRAL DISEASES OF CENTRAL NERVOUS SYSTEM (045-049)

√4ᵗʰ 045 **Acute poliomyelitis**

EXCLUDES *late effects of acute poliomyelitis (138)*

The following fifth-digit subclassification is for use with category 045:

0 **poliovirus, unspecified type**

1 **poliovirus type I**

2 **poliovirus type II**

3 **poliovirus type III**

√5ᵗʰ 045.0 **Acute paralytic poliomyelitis specified as bulbar** `CD PDx`

Infantile paralysis (acute) ⎫
Poliomyelitis (acute) ⎬ specified as bulbar
(anterior) ⎭

Polioencephalitis (acute) (bulbar)
Polioencephalomyelitis (acute) (anterior) (bulbar)

DEF: Acute paralytic infection occurring where the brain merges with the spinal cord; affecting breathing, swallowing, and heart rate.

√5ᵗʰ 045.1 **Acute poliomyelitis with other paralysis** `CD PDx`

Paralysis: Paralysis:
  acute atrophic, spinal   infantile, paralytic
Poliomyelitis (acute): ⎫
  anterior   ⎬ with paralysis except
  epidemic   ⎭   bulbar

DEF: Paralytic infection affecting peripheral or spinal nerves.

√5ᵗʰ 045.2 **Acute nonparalytic poliomyelitis** `CD PDx`

Poliomyelitis (acute) ⎫
  anterior   ⎬ specified as nonparalytic
  epidemic ⎭

DEF: Nonparalytic infection causing pain, stiffness, and paresthesias.

√5ᵗʰ 045.9 **Acute poliomyelitis, unspecified** `CD PDx`

Infantile paralysis ⎫
Poliomyelitis (acute) ⎬ unspecified whether
  anterior   ⎪   paralytic or
  epidemic ⎭   nonparalytic

√4ᵗʰ 046 **Slow virus infection of central nervous system**

046.0 **Kuru** `CD PDx`

DEF: A chronic, progressive, fatal nervous system disorder; clinical symptoms include cerebellar ataxia, trembling, spasticity and progressive dementia.

046.1 **Jakob-Creutzfeldt disease** `CD PDx`

Subacute spongiform encephalopathy

DEF: Communicable, progressive spongiform encephalopathy thought to be caused by an infectious particle known as a "prion" (proteinaceous infection particle). This is a progressive, fatal disease manifested principally by mental deterioration.

046.2 **Subacute sclerosing panencephalitis** `CD PDx`

Dawson's inclusion body encephalitis

Van Bogaert's sclerosing leukoencephalitis

DEF: Progressive viral infection causing cerebral dysfunction, blindness, dementia, and death (SSPE).

046.3 **Progressive multifocal leukoencephalopathy** `CD PDx`

Multifocal leukoencephalopathy NOS

DEF: Infection affecting cerebral cortex in patients with weakened immune systems.

046.8 **Other specified slow virus infection of central nervous system** `CD PDx`

046.9 **Unspecified slow virus infection of central nervous system** `CD PDx`

Ⓝ Newborn Age: 0   Ⓟ Pediatric Age: 0-17   Ⓜ Maternity Age: 12-55   Ⓐ Adult Age: 15-124   Manifestation Code   ►◄ Revised Text   ● New Code   ▲ Revised Code Title

✓4th **047 Meningitis due to enterovirus**

INCLUDES	meningitis:	meningitis:
	abacterial	viral
	aseptic	

EXCLUDES *meningitis due to:*
adenovirus (049.1)
arthropod-borne virus (060.0-066.9)
leptospira (100.81)
virus of:
   herpes simplex (054.72)
   herpes zoster (053.0)
   lymphocytic choriomeningitis (049.0)
   mumps (072.1)
   poliomyelitis (045.0-045.9)
any other infection specifically classified
   elsewhere

AHA: J-F, '87, 6

047.0 Coxsackie virus `CD PDx`

047.1 ECHO virus `CD PDx`
   Meningo-eruptive syndrome

047.8 Other specified viral meningitis `CD PDx`

047.9 Unspecified viral meningitis `CD PDx`
   Viral meningitis NOS

048 Other enterovirus diseases of central nervous `CD PDx`
system
   Boston exanthem

✓4th **049 Other non-arthropod-borne viral diseases of central nervous**
system

EXCLUDES *late effects of viral encephalitis (139.0)*

049.0 Lymphocytic choriomeningitis `CD PDx`
   Lymphocytic:
      meningitis (serous) (benign)
      meningoencephalitis (serous) (benign)

049.1 Meningitis due to adenovirus `CD PDx`

DEF: Inflammation of lining of brain caused by Arenaviruses and usually occurring in adults in fall and winter months.

049.8 Other specified non-arthropod-borne `CD PDx`
viral diseases of central nervous system

Encephalitis:	Encephalitis:
acute:	lethargica
inclusion body	Rio Bravo
necrotizing	von Economo's disease
epidemic	

049.9 Unspecified non-arthropod-borne viral `CD PDx`
diseases of central nervous system
   Viral encephalitis NOS

VIRAL DISEASES ACCOMPANIED BY EXANTHEM (050-057)

EXCLUDES *arthropod-borne viral diseases (060.0-066.9)*
Boston exanthem (048)

✓4th **050 Smallpox**

050.0 Variola major
   Hemorrhagic (pustular) smallpox
   Malignant smallpox
   Purpura variolosa

DEF: Form of smallpox known for its high mortality; exists only in laboratories.

050.1 Alastrim
   Variola minor

DEF: Mild form of smallpox known for its low mortality rate.

050.2 Modified smallpox
   Varioloid

DEF: Mild form occurring in patients with history of infection or vaccination.

050.9 Smallpox, unspecified

✓4th **051 Cowpox and paravaccinia**

051.0 Cowpox
   Vaccinia not from vaccination

EXCLUDES *vaccinia (generalized) (from vaccination)*
   (999.0)

DEF: A disease contracted by milking infected cows; vesicles usually appear on the fingers, may spread to hands and adjacent areas and usually disappear without scarring; other associated features of the disease may include local edema, lymphangitis and regional lymphadenitis with or without fever.

051.1 Pseudocowpox
   Milkers' node

DEF: Hand lesions and mild fever in dairy workers caused by exposure to paravaccinia.

051.2 Contagious pustular dermatitis
   Ecthyma contagiosum
   Orf

DEF: Skin eruptions caused by exposure to poxvirus-infected sheep or goats.

051.9 Paravaccinia, unspecified

✓4th **052 Chickenpox**

DEF: Contagious infection by *Varicella-zoster* virus causing rash with pustules and fever.

052.0 Postvaricella encephalitis
   Postchickenpox encephalitis

052.1 Varicella (hemorrhagic) pneumonitis

052.7 With other specified complications
   AHA: 1Q, '02, 3

052.8 With unspecified complication

052.9 Varicella without mention of complication
   Chickenpox NOS   Varicella NOS

✓4th **053 Herpes zoster**

INCLUDES	shingles
	zona

DEF: Self-limiting infection by *varicella-zoster* virus causing unilateral eruptions and neuralgia along affected nerves.

053.0 With meningitis

DEF: *Varicella-zoster* virus infection causing inflammation of the lining of the brain and/or spinal cord.

✓5th **053.1 With other nervous system complications**

053.10 With unspecified nervous system
complication

053.11 Geniculate herpes zoster
   Herpetic geniculate ganglionitis

DEF: Unilateral eruptions and neuralgia along the facial nerve geniculum affecting face and outer and middle ear.

053.12 Postherpetic trigeminal neuralgia

DEF: Severe oral or nasal pain following a herpes zoster infection.

053.13 Postherpetic polyneuropathy

DEF: Multiple areas of pain following a herpes zoster infection.

053.19 Other

✓5th **053.2 With ophthalmic complications**

053.20 Herpes zoster dermatitis of eyelid
   Herpes zoster ophthalmicus

053.21 Herpes zoster keratoconjunctivitis

053.22 Herpes zoster iridocyclitis

053.29 Other

✓5th **053.7 With other specified complications**

053.71 Otitis externa due to herpes zoster

053.79 Other

053.8 With unspecified complication

053.9 Herpes zoster without mention of complication
   Herpes zoster NOS

✓4th Additional Digit Required   RUG III Special Care Dx   RUG III Clinically Complex Dx   Hospice Non-cancer Dx   `CD PDx` Clinical Dimension PDx   `CD SDx` Clinical Dimension SDx
✓5th

Infectious and Parasitic Diseases

054–062.4

√4ᵗʰ **054 Herpes simplex**

INCLUDES EXCLUDES congenital herpes simplex (771.2)

054.0 Eczema herpeticum
Kaposi's varicelliform eruption
DEF: Herpes simplex virus invading site of preexisting skin inflammation.

√5ᵗʰ **054.1 Genital herpes**
AHA: J-F, '87, 15, 16
054.10 Genital herpes, unspecified
Herpes progenitalis
054.11 Herpetic vulvovaginitis ♀
054.12 Herpetic ulceration of vulva ♀
054.13 Herpetic infection of penis ♂
054.19 Other
054.2 Herpetic gingivostomatitis
054.3 Herpetic meningoencephalitis
Herpes encephalitis   Simian B disease
DEF: Inflammation of the brain and its lining, caused by infection of herpes simplex 1 in adults and simplex 2 in newborns.

√5ᵗʰ **054.4 With ophthalmic complications**
054.40 With unspecified ophthalmic complication
054.41 Herpes simplex dermatitis of eyelid
054.42 Dendritic keratitis
054.43 Herpes simplex disciform keratitis
054.44 Herpes simplex iridocyclitis
054.49 Other
054.5 Herpetic septicemia
AHA: 2Q, '00, 5
054.6 Herpetic whitlow
Herpetic felon
DEF: A primary infection of the terminal segment of a finger by herpes simplex; intense itching and pain start the disease, vesicles form, and tissue ultimately is destroyed.

√5ᵗʰ **054.7 With other specified complications**
054.71 Visceral herpes simplex
054.72 Herpes simplex meningitis
054.73 Herpes simplex otitis externa
054.79 Other
054.8 With unspecified complication
054.9 Herpes simplex without mention of complication

√4ᵗʰ **055 Measles**
INCLUDES morbilli   rubeola
055.0 Postmeasles encephalitis
055.1 Postmeasles pneumonia
055.2 Postmeasles otitis media
√5ᵗʰ **055.7 With other specified complications**
055.71 Measles keratoconjunctivitis
Measles keratitis
055.79 Other
055.8 With unspecified complication
055.9 Measles without mention of complication

√4ᵗʰ **056 Rubella**
INCLUDES German measles
EXCLUDES congenital rubella (771.0)
DEF: Acute but usually benign togavirus infection causing fever, sore throat, and rash; associated with complications to fetus as a result of maternal infection.

√5ᵗʰ **056.0 With neurological complications**
056.00 With unspecified neurological complication
056.01 Encephalomyelitis due to rubella
Encephalitis   ⎱
Meningoencephalitis   ⎰ due to rubella
056.09 Other

√5ᵗʰ **056.7 With other specified complications**
056.71 Arthritis due to rubella
056.79 Other
056.8 With unspecified complications
056.9 Rubella without mention of complication

√4ᵗʰ **057 Other viral exanthemata**
DEF: Skin eruptions or rashes and fever caused by viruses, including poxviruses.

057.0 Erythema infectiosum [fifth disease]
DEF: A moderately contagious, benign, epidemic disease, usually seen in children, and of probable viral etiology; a red macular rash appears on the face and may spread to the limbs and trunk.

057.8 Other specified viral exanthemata
Dukes (-Filatow) disease
Exanthema subitum [sixth disease]
Fourth disease
Parascarlatina
Pseudoscarlatina
Roseola infantum

057.9 Viral exanthem, unspecified

ARTHROPOD-BORNE VIRAL DISEASES (060-066)
Use additional code to identify any associated meningitis (321.2)
EXCLUDES late effects of viral encephalitis (139.0)

√4ᵗʰ **060 Yellow fever**
DEF: Fever and jaundice from infection by mosquito-borne virus of genus *Flavivirus*.

060.0 Sylvatic
Yellow fever: Yellow fever:
  jungle   sylvan
DEF: Yellow fever transmitted from animal to man, via mosquito.

060.1 Urban
DEF: Yellow fever transmitted from man to man, via mosquito.

060.9 Yellow fever, unspecified

061 Dengue
Breakbone fever
EXCLUDES hemorrhagic fever caused by dengue virus (065.4)
DEF: Acute, self-limiting infection by mosquito-borne virus characterized by fever and generalized aches.

√4ᵗʰ **062 Mosquito-borne viral encephalitis**
062.0 Japanese encephalitis
Japanese B encephalitis
DEF: Flavivirus causing inflammation of the brain, with a wide range of clinical manifestations.

062.1 Western equine encephalitis
DEF: Alphavirus WEE infection causing inflammation of the brain, found in areas west of the Mississippi; transmitted horse to mosquito to man.

062.2 Eastern equine encephalitis
EXCLUDES Venezuelan equine encephalitis (066.2)
DEF: Alphavirus EEE causing inflammation of the brain and spinal cord, found as far north as Canada and south into South America and Mexico; transmitted horse to mosquito to man.

062.3 St. Louis encephalitis
DEF: Epidemic form caused by Flavivirus and transmitted by mosquito, and characterized by fever, difficulty in speech, and headache.

062.4 Australian encephalitis
Australian arboencephalitis   Murray Valley
Australian X disease   encephalitis
DEF: Flavivirus causing inflammation of the brain, occurring in Australia and New Guinea.

N Newborn Age: 0   P Pediatric Age: 0-17   M Maternity Age: 12-55   A Adult Age: 15-124   Manifestation Code   ►◄ Revised Text   ● New Code   ▲ Revised Code Title

10 — Volume 1   2006 ICD•9•CM

062.5 California virus encephalitis
Encephalitis: Tahyna fever
   California
   La Crosse
> DEF: Bunyamwere virus causing inflammation of the brain.

062.8 Other specified mosquito-borne viral encephalitis
Encephalitis by Ilheus virus
> **EXCLUDES**   West Nile virus (066.40-066.49)

062.9 Mosquito-borne viral encephalitis, unspecified

✓4th **063 Tick-borne viral encephalitis**
> **INCLUDES**   diphasic meningoencephalitis

063.0 Russian spring-summer [taiga] encephalitis

063.1 Louping ill
> DEF: Inflammation of brain caused by virus transmitted sheep to tick to man; incidence usually limited to British Isles.

063.2 Central European encephalitis
> DEF: Inflammation of brain caused by virus transmitted by tick; limited to central Europe and presenting with two distinct phases.

063.8 Other specified tick-borne viral encephalitis
Langat encephalitis   Powassan encephalitis

063.9 Tick-borne viral encephalitis, unspecified

064 Viral encephalitis transmitted by other and unspecified arthropods
Arthropod-borne viral encephalitis, vector unknown
Negishi virus encephalitis
> **EXCLUDES**   viral encephalitis NOS (049.9)

✓4th **065 Arthropod-borne hemorrhagic fever**

065.0 Crimean hemorrhagic fever [CHF Congo virus]
Central Asian hemorrhagic fever

065.1 Omsk hemorrhagic fever

065.2 Kyasanur Forest disease

065.3 Other tick-borne hemorrhagic fever

065.4 Mosquito-borne hemorrhagic fever
Chikungunya hemorrhagic fever
Dengue hemorrhagic fever
> **EXCLUDES**   Chikungunya fever (066.3)
>   dengue (061)
>   yellow fever (060.0-060.9)

065.8 Other specified arthropod-borne hemorrhagic fever
Mite-borne hemorrhagic fever

065.9 Arthropod-borne hemorrhagic fever, unspecified
Arbovirus hemorrhagic fever NOS

✓4th **066 Other arthropod-borne viral diseases**

066.0 Phlebotomus fever
Changuinola fever
Sandfly fever
> DEF: Sandfly-borne viral infection occurring in Asia, Mideast and South America.

066.1 Tick-borne fever
Nairobi sheep disease   Tick fever:
Tick fever: Kemerovo
   American mountain   Quaranfil
   Colorado

066.2 Venezuelan equine fever
Venezuelan equine encephalitis
> DEF: Alphavirus VEE infection causing inflammation of the brain, usually limited to South America, Mexico, and Florida; transmitted horse to mosquito to man

066.3 Other mosquito-borne fever
Fever (viral):   Fever (viral):
   Bunyamwera   Oropouche
   Bwamba   Pixuna
   Chikungunya   Rift valley
   Guama   Ross river
   Mayaro   Wesselsbron
   Mucambo   Zika
   O'Nyong-Nyong
> **EXCLUDES**   dengue (061)
>   yellow fever (060.0-060.9)

✓5th **066.4 West Nile fever**
> AHA: 4Q, '02, 44
> DEF: Mosquito-borne fever causing fatal inflammation of the brain, the lining of the brain, or of the lining of the brain and spinal cord.

066.40 West Nile fever, unspecified
West Nile fever NOS
West Nile fever without complications
West Nile virus NOS

066.41 West Nile fever with encephalitis
West Nile encephalitis
West Nile encephalomyelitis
> AHA: ▶4Q, '04, 51◀

066.42 West Nile fever with other neurologic manifestation
Use additional code to specify the neurologic manifestation
> AHA: ▶4Q, '04, 51◀

066.49 West Nile fever with other complications
Use additional code to specify the other conditions

066.8 Other specified arthropod-borne viral diseases
Chandipura fever   Piry fever

066.9 Arthropod-borne viral disease, unspecified
Arbovirus infection NOS

OTHER DISEASES DUE TO VIRUSES AND CHLAMYDIAE (070-079)

✓4th **070 Viral hepatitis**
> **INCLUDES**   viral hepatitis (acute) (chronic)
> **EXCLUDES**   cytomegalic inclusion virus hepatitis (078.5)

> The following fifth-digit subclassification is for use with categories 070.2 and 070.3:
>   **0** acute or unspecified, without mention of hepatitis delta
>   **1** acute or unspecified, with hepatitis delta
>   **2** chronic, without mention of hepatitis delta
>   **3** chronic, with hepatitis delta

> DEF: Hepatitis A : HAV infection is self-limiting with flulike symptoms; transmission, fecal-oral.
> DEF: Hepatitis B: HBV infection can be chronic and systemic; transmission, bodily fluids.
> DEF: Hepatitis C: HCV infection can be chronic and systemic; transmission, blood transfusion and unidentified agents.
> DEF: Hepatitis D (delta): HDV occurs only in the presence of hepatitis B virus.
> DEF: Hepatitis E: HEV is epidemic form; transmission and nature under investigation.

070.0 Viral hepatitis A with hepatic coma

070.1 Viral hepatitis A without mention of hepatic coma
Infectious hepatitis

✓5th **070.2 Viral hepatitis B with hepatic coma**
> AHA: 4Q, '91, 28

✓5th **070.3 Viral hepatitis B without mention of hepatic coma**
Serum hepatitis
> AHA: 1Q, '93, 28; 4Q, '91, 28

✓5th **070.4 Other specified viral hepatitis with hepatic coma**
> AHA: 4Q, '91, 28

070.41 Acute hepatitis C with hepatic coma

070.42 Hepatitis delta without mention of active hepatitis B disease with hepatic coma
Hepatitis delta with hepatitis B carrier state

070.43 Hepatitis E with hepatic coma

070.44 Chronic hepatitis C with hepatic coma

070.49 Other specified viral hepatitis with hepatic coma

✓5th **070.5 Other specified viral hepatitis without mention of hepatic coma**
> AHA: 4Q, '91, 28

070.51 Acute hepatitis C without mention of hepatic coma

✓4th ✓5th Additional Digit Required   **RUG III Special Care Dx**   **RUG III Clinically Complex Dx**   **Hospice Non-cancer Dx**   **CD PDx** Clinical Dimension PDx   **CD SDx** Clinical Dimension SDx

2006 ICD•9•CM   **February 2005 • Volume 1 — 11**

070.52 Hepatitis delta without mention of active hepatititis B disease or hepatic coma

070.53 Hepatitis E without mention of hepatic coma

070.54 Chronic hepatitis C without mention of hepatic coma

070.59 Other specified viral hepatitis without mention of hepatic coma

070.6 Unspecified viral hepatitis with hepatic coma

> EXCLUDES *unspecified viral hepatitis C with hepatic coma (070.71)*

✓5th **070.7 Unspecified viral hepatitis C**

070.70 Unspecified viral hepatitis C without hepatic coma

Unspecified viral hepatitis C NOS

AHA: ▶4Q, '04, 52◀

070.71 Unspecified viral hepatitis C with hepatic coma

AHA: ▶4Q, '04, 52◀

070.9 Unspecified viral hepatitis without mention of hepatic coma

Viral hepatitis NOS

> EXCLUDES *unspecified viral hepatitis C without hepatic coma (070.70)*

071 Rabies

Hydrophobia   Lyssa

DEF: Acute infectious disease of the CNS caused by a rhabdovirus; usually spread by virus-laden saliva from bites by infected animals; it progresses from fever, restlessness, and extreme excitability, to hydrophobia, seizures, confusion and death.

✓4th **072 Mumps**

DEF: Acute infectious disease caused by paramyxovirus; usually seen in children less than 15 years of age; salivary glands are typically enlarged, and other organs, such as testes, pancreas and meninges, are often involved.

072.0 Mumps orchitis   ♂

072.1 Mumps meningitis

072.2 Mumps encephalitis

Mumps meningoencephalitis

072.3 Mumps pancreatitis

✓5th **072.7 Mumps with other specified complications**

072.71 Mumps hepatitis

072.72 Mumps polyneuropathy

072.79 Other

072.8 Mumps with unspecified complication

072.9 Mumps without mention of complication

Epidemic parotitis   Infectious parotitis

✓4th **073 Ornithosis**

> INCLUDES parrot fever
> psittacosis

DEF: *Chlamydia psittaci* infection often transmitted from birds to humans.

073.0 With pneumonia

Lobular pneumonitis due to ornithosis

073.7 With other specified complications

073.8 With unspecified complication

073.9 Ornithosis, unspecified

✓4th **074 Specific diseases due to Coxsackie virus**

> EXCLUDES *Coxsackie virus:*
> *infection NOS (079.2)*
> *meningitis (047.0)*

074.0 Herpangina

Vesicular pharyngitis

DEF: Acute infectious coxsackie virus infection causing throat lesions, fever, and vomiting; generally affects children in summer.

074.1 Epidemic pleurodynia

Bornholm disease   Epidemic:
Devil's grip   myalgia
          myositis

DEF: Paroxysmal pain in chest, accompanied by fever and usually limited to children and young adults; caused by coxsackie virus.

✓5th **074.2 Coxsackie carditis**

074.20 Coxsackie carditis, unspecified

074.21 Coxsackie pericarditis

DEF: Coxsackie infection of the outer lining of the heart.

074.22 Coxsackie endocarditis

DEF: Coxsackie infection within the heart's cavities.

074.23 Coxsackie myocarditis

Aseptic myocarditis of newborn

DEF: Coxsackie infection of the muscle of the heart.

074.3 Hand, foot, and mouth disease

Vesicular stomatitis and exanthem

DEF: Mild coxsackie infection causing lesions on hands, feet and oral mucosa, most commonly seen in preschool children.

074.8 Other specified diseases due to Coxsackie virus

Acute lymphonodular pharyngitis

075 Infectious mononucleosis

Glandular fever   Pfeiffer's disease
Monocytic angina

AHA: 3Q, '01, 13; M-A, '87, 8

DEF: Acute infection by Epstein-Barr virus causing fever, sore throat, enlarged lymph glands and spleen, and fatigue; usually seen in teens and young adults.

✓4th **076 Trachoma**

> EXCLUDES *late effect of trachoma (139.1)*

DEF: A chronic infectious disease of the cornea and conjunctiva caused by a strain of the bacteria *Chlamydia trachomatis*; the infection can cause photophobia, pain, excessive tearing and sometimes blindness.

076.0 Initial stage

Trachoma dubium

076.1 Active stage

Granular conjunctivitis (trachomatous)
Trachomatous:
          follicular conjunctivitis
          pannus

076.9 Trachoma, unspecified

Trachoma NOS

✓4th **077 Other diseases of conjunctiva due to viruses and Chlamydiae**

> EXCLUDES *ophthalmic complications of viral diseases classified elsewhere*

077.0 Inclusion conjunctivitis

Paratrachoma   Swimming pool conjunctivitis

> EXCLUDES *inclusion blennorrhea (neonatal) (771.6)*

DEF: Pus in conjunctiva caused by *Chlamydiae trachomatis.*

077.1 Epidemic keratoconjunctivitis

Shipyard eye

DEF: Highly contagious corneal or conjunctival infection caused by adenovirus type 8; symptoms include inflammation and corneal infiltrates.

077.2 Pharyngoconjunctival fever

Viral pharyngoconjunctivitis

077.3 Other adenoviral conjunctivitis

Acute adenoviral follicular conjunctivitis

077.4 Epidemic hemorrhagic conjunctivitis

Apollo:
          conjunctivitis
          disease
Conjunctivitis due to enterovirus type 70
Hemorrhagic conjunctivitis (acute) (epidemic)

077.8 Other viral conjunctivitis

Newcastle conjunctivitis

✓5th **077.9 Unspecified diseases of conjunctiva due to viruses and Chlamydiae**

077.98 Due to Chlamydiae

077.99 Due to viruses

Viral conjunctivitis NOS

✓4th **078 Other diseases due to viruses and Chlamydiae**

> EXCLUDES *viral infection NOS (079.0-079.9)*
> *viremia NOS (790.8)*

078.0 Molluscum contagiosum

DEF: Benign poxvirus infection causing small bumps on the skin or conjunctiva; transmitted by close contact.

N Newborn Age: 0   P Pediatric Age: 0-17   M Maternity Age: 12-55   A Adult Age: 15-124   Manifestation Code   ▶◀ Revised Text   ● New Code   ▲ Revised Code Title

12 — Volume 1 • February 2005   *2006 ICD•9•CM*

√5th **078.1 Viral warts**

Viral warts due to human papilloma virus

AHA: 2Q, '97, 9; 3Q, '93, 22

DEF: A keratotic papilloma of the epidermis caused by the human papilloma virus; the superficial vegetative lesions last for varying durations and eventually regress spontaneously.

078.10 Viral warts, unspecified

Condyloma NOS   Verruca:
Verruca: Vulgaris
  NOS   Warts (infectious)

078.11 Condyloma acuminatum

DEF: Clusters of mucosa or epidermal lesions on external genitalia; viral infection is sexually transmitted.

078.19 Other specified viral warts

Genital warts NOS   Verruca:
Verruca: plantaris
  plana

078.2 Sweating fever

Miliary fever   Sweating disease

DEF: A viral infection characterized by profuse sweating; various papular, vesicular and other eruptions cause the blockage of sweat glands.

078.3 Cat-scratch disease

Benign lymphoreticulosis (of inoculation)
Cat-scratch fever

078.4 Foot and mouth disease

Aphthous fever   Epizootic:
Epizootic: stomatitis
  aphthae

DEF: Ulcers on oral mucosa, legs, and feet after exposure to infected animal.

078.5 Cytomegaloviral disease

Cytomegalic inclusion disease
Salivary gland virus disease
Use additional code to identify manifestation, as:
  cytomegalic inclusion virus:
    hepatitis (573.1)
    pneumonia (484.1)
    EXCLUDES *congenital cytomegalovirus infection*
                (771.1)

AHA: 1Q, '03, 10; 3Q, '98, 4; 2Q, '93, 11; 1Q, '89, 9

DEF: A herpes virus inclusion associated with serious disease morbidity including fever, leukopenia, pneumonia, retinitis, hepatitis and organ transplant; often leads to syndromes such as hepatomegaly, splenomegaly and thrombocytopenia; a common post-transplant complication for organ transplant recipients.

078.6 Hemorrhagic nephrosonephritis

Hemorrhagic fever: Hemorrhagic fever:
  epidemic   Russian
  Korean   with renal syndrome

DEF: Viral infection causing kidney dysfunction and bleeding disorders.

078.7 Arenaviral hemorrhagic fever

Hemorrhagic fever: Hemorrhagic fever:
  Argentine   Junin virus
  Bolivian   Machupo virus

√5th **078.8 Other specified diseases due to viruses and Chlamydiae**

EXCLUDES *epidemic diarrhea (009.2)*
           lymphogranuloma venereum (099.1)

078.81 Epidemic vertigo

078.82 Epidemic vomiting syndrome

Winter vomiting disease

078.88 Other specified diseases due to Chlamydiae

AHA: 4Q, '96, 22

078.89 Other specified diseases due to viruses

Epidemic cervical myalgia
Marburg disease
Tanapox

√4th **079 Viral and chlamydial infection in conditions classified elsewhere and of unspecified site**

Note: This category is provided to be used as an additional code to identify the viral agent in diseases classifiable elsewhere. This category will also be used to classify virus infection of unspecified nature or site.

079.0 Adenovirus

079.1 ECHO virus

DEF: An "orphan" enteric RNA virus, certain serotypes of which are associated with human disease, especially aseptic meningitis.

079.2 Coxsackie virus

DEF: A heterogenous group of viruses associated with aseptic meningitis, myocarditis, pericarditis, and acute onset juvenile diabetes.

079.3 Rhinovirus

DEF: Rhinoviruses affect primarily the upper respiratory tract. Over 100 distinct types infect humans.

079.4 Human papillomavirus

AHA: 2Q, '97, 9; 4Q, '93, 22

DEF: Viral infection caused by the genus *Papillomavirus* causing cutaneous and genital warts, including verruca vulgaris and condyloma acuminatum; certain types are associated with cervical dysplasia, cancer and other genital malignancies.

√5th **079.5 Retrovirus**

EXCLUDES *human immunodeficiency virus, type 1*
[HIV-1] (042)
human T-cell lymphotrophic virus,
type III [HTLV-III] (042)
lymphadenopathy-associated virus
[LAV] (042)

AHA: 4Q, '93, 22, 23

DEF: A large group of RNA viruses that carry reverse transcriptase and include the leukoviruses and lentiviruses.

079.50 Retrovirus, unspecified

079.51 Human T-cell lymphotrophic virus, type I [HTLV-I]

079.52 Human T-cell lymphotrophic virus, type II [HTLV-II]

079.53 Human immunodeficiency virus, type 2 [HIV-2]

079.59 Other specified retrovirus

079.6 Respiratory syncytial virus (RSV)

AHA: 4Q, '96, 27, 28

DEF: The major respiratory pathogen of young children, causing severe bronchitis and bronchopneumonia, and minor infection in adults.

√5th **079.8 Other specified viral and chlamydial infections**

AHA: 1Q, '88, 12

079.81 Hantavirus

AHA: 4Q, '95, 60

DEF: An infection caused by the Muerto Canyon virus whose primary rodent reservoir is the deer mouse *Peromyscus maniculatus*; commonly characterized by fever, myalgias, headache, cough and rapid decline.

079.82 SARS-associated coronavirus

AHA: 4Q, '03, 4

DEF: A life-threatening respiratory disease described as severe acute respiratory syndrome (SARS); etiology coronavirus; most common presenting symptoms may range from mild to more severe forms of flu-like conditions; fever, chills, cough, headache, myalgia; diagnosis of SARS is based upon clinical, laboratory, and epidemiological criteria.

079.88 Other specified chlamydial infection

079.89 Other specified viral infection

√4th   Additional Digit Required   RUG III Special Care Dx   RUG III Clinically Complex Dx   Hospice Non-cancer Dx   **CD PDx** Clinical Dimension PDx   **CD SDx** Clinical Dimension SDx
√5th

☑5ᵗʰ 079.9 Unspecified viral and chlamydial infections

> **EXCLUDES** *viremia NOS (790.8)*

AHA: 2Q, '91, 8

079.98 Unspecified chlamydial infection
Chlamydial infections NOS

079.99 Unspecified viral infection
Viral infections NOS

RICKETTSIOSES AND OTHER ARTHROPOD-BORNE DISEASES (080-088)

> **EXCLUDES** *arthropod-borne viral diseases (060.0-066.9)*

080 Louse-borne [epidemic] typhus

Typhus (fever):   Typhus (fever):
  classical   exanthematic NOS
  epidemic   louse-borne

> **DEF:** *Rickettsia prowazekii;* causes severe headache, rash, high fever.

☑4ᵗʰ 081 Other typhus

081.0 Murine [endemic] typhus

Typhus (fever):   Typhus (fever):
  endemic   flea-borne

> **DEF:** Milder typhus caused by *Rickettsia typhi (mooseri);* transmitted by rat flea.

081.1 Brill's disease
Brill-Zinsser disease
Recrudescent typhus (fever)

081.2 Scrub typhus

Japanese river fever   Mite-borne typhus
Kedani fever   Tsutsugamushi

081.9 Typhus, unspecified
Typhus (fever) NOS

☑4ᵗʰ 082 Tick-borne rickettsioses

082.0 Spotted fevers
Rocky mountain spotted fever
Sao Paulo fever

082.1 Boutonneuse fever

African tick typhus   Marseilles fever
India tick typhus   Mediterranean tick fever
Kenya tick typhus

082.2 North Asian tick fever
Siberian tick typhus

082.3 Queensland tick typhus

☑5ᵗʰ 082.4 Ehrlichiosis

AHA: 4Q, '00, 38

082.40 Ehrlichiosis, unspecified

082.41 Ehrlichiosis chaffeensis [E. chaffeensis]

> **DEF:** A febrile illness caused by bacterial infection, also called human monocytic ehrlichiosis (HME). Causal organism is *Ehrlichia chaffeensis,* transmitted by the Lone Star tick, *Amblyomma americanum.* Symptoms include fever, chills, myalgia, nausea, vomiting, diarrhea, confusion, and severe headache occurring one week after a tick bite. Clinical findings are lymphadenopathy, rash, thrombocytopenia, leukopenia, and abnormal liver function tests.

082.49 Other ehrlichiosis

082.8 Other specified tick-borne rickettsioses
Lone star fever

AHA: 4Q, '99, 19

082.9 Tick-borne rickettsiosis, unspecified
Tick-borne typhus NOS

☑4ᵗʰ 083 Other rickettsioses

083.0 Q fever

> **DEF:** Infection of *Coxiella burnettii* usually acquired through airborne organisms.

083.1 Trench fever

Quintan fever   Wolhynian fever

083.2 Rickettsialpox
Vesicular rickettsiosis

> **DEF:** Infection of Rickettsia akari usually acquired through a mite bite.

083.8 Other specified rickettsioses

083.9 Rickettsiosis, unspecified

☑4ᵗʰ 084 Malaria

> Note: Subcategories 084.0-084.6 exclude the listed conditions with mention of pernicious complications (084.8-084.9).

> **EXCLUDES** *congenital malaria (771.2)*

> **DEF:** Mosquito-borne disease causing high fever and prostration and cataloged by species of *Plasmodium: P. falciparum, P. malariae, P. ovale,* and *P. vivax.*

084.0 Falciparum malaria [malignant tertian]

Malaria (fever):
  by Plasmodium falciparum
  subtertian

084.1 Vivax malaria [benign tertian]
Malaria (fever) by Plasmodium vivax

084.2 Quartan malaria
Malaria (fever) by Plasmodium malariae
Malariae malaria

084.3 Ovale malaria
Malaria (fever) by Plasmodium ovale

084.4 Other malaria
Monkey malaria

084.5 Mixed malaria
Malaria (fever) by more than one parasite

084.6 Malaria, unspecified
Malaria (fever) NOS

084.7 Induced malaria
Therapeutically induced malaria

> **EXCLUDES** *accidental infection from syringe, blood transfusion, etc. (084.0-084.6, above, according to parasite species)*
> *transmission from mother to child during delivery (771.2)*

084.8 Blackwater fever

Hemoglobinuric: Malarial hemoglobinuria
  fever (bilious)
  malaria

> **DEF:** Severe hemic and renal complication of *Plasmodium falciparum* infection.

084.9 Other pernicious complications of malaria

Algid malaria
Cerebral malaria
Use additional code to identify complication, as:
  malarial:
    hepatitis (573.2)
    nephrosis (581.81)

☑4ᵗʰ 085 Leishmaniasis

085.0 Visceral [kala-azar]

Dumdum fever   Leishmaniasis:
Infection by Leishmania: dermal, post-kala-azar
  donovani   Mediterranean
  infantum   visceral (Indian)

085.1 Cutaneous, urban

Aleppo boil   Leishmaniasis, cutaneous:
Baghdad boil   dry form
Delhi boil   late
Infection by Leishmania   recurrent
  tropica (minor)   ulcerating
                           Oriental sore

085.2 Cutaneous, Asian desert

Infection by Leishmania tropica major
Leishmaniasis, cutaneous:
  acute necrotizing
  rural
  wet form
  zoonotic form

085.3 Cutaneous, Ethiopian

Infection by Leishmania ethiopica
Leishmaniasis, cutaneous:
  diffuse
  lepromatous

Ⓝ Newborn Age: 0   Ⓟ Pediatric Age: 0-17   Ⓜ Maternity Age: 12-55   Ⓐ Adult Age: 15-124   ▐ Manifestation Code   ▶◀ Revised Text   ● New Code   ▲ Revised Code Title

14 — Volume 1   *2006 ICD•9•CM*

085.4　Cutaneous, American
Chiclero ulcer
Infection by Leishmania mexicana
Leishmaniasis tegumentaria diffusa

085.5　Mucocutaneous (American)
Espundia
Infection by Leishmania braziliensis
Uta

085.9　Leishmaniasis, unspecified

✓4ᵗʰ **086　Trypanosomiasis**
Use additional code to identify manifestations, as:
trypanosomiasis:
encephalitis (323.2)
meningitis (321.3)

086.0　Chagas' disease with heart involvement
American trypanosomiasis
Infection by Trypanosoma cruzi ⎫ with heart involvement
Any condition classifiable to 086.2 with heart involvement

086.1　Chagas' disease with other organ involvement
American trypanosomiasis
Infection by Trypanosoma cruzi ⎫ with involvement of organ other than heart
Any condition classifiable to 086.2 with involvement of organ other than heart

086.2　Chagas' disease without mention of organ involvement
American trypanosomiasis
Infection by Trypanosoma cruzi

086.3　Gambian trypanosomiasis
Gambian sleeping sickness
Infection by Trypanosoma gambiense

086.4　Rhodesian trypanosomiasis
Infection by Trypanosoma rhodesiense
Rhodesian sleeping sickness

086.5　African trypanosomiasis, unspecified
Sleeping sickness NOS

086.9　Trypanosomiasis, unspecified

✓4ᵗʰ **087　Relapsing fever**
INCLUDES　recurrent fever
DEF: Infection of *Borrelia;* symptoms are episodic and include fever and arthralgia.

087.0　Louse-borne

087.1　Tick-borne

087.9　Relapsing fever, unspecified

✓4ᵗʰ **088　Other arthropod-borne diseases**

088.0　Bartonellosis
Carrión's disease　　Verruga peruana
Oroya fever

✓5ᵗʰ **088.8　Other specified arthropod-borne diseases**

088.81　Lyme disease
Erythema chronicum migrans
AHA: 4Q, '91, 15; 3Q, '90, 14; 2Q, '89, 10
DEF: A recurrent multisystem disorder caused by the spirochete *Borrelia burgdorferi* with the carrier being the tick *Ixodes dammini;* the disease begins with lesions of erythema chronicum migrans; it is followed by arthritis of the large joints, myalgia, malaise, and neurological and cardiac manifestations.

088.82　Babesiosis
Babesiasis
AHA: 4Q, '93, 23
DEF: A tick-borne disease caused by infection of *Babesia,* characterized by fever, malaise, listlessness, severe anemia and hemoglobinuria.

088.89　Other

088.9　Arthropod-borne disease, unspecified

SYPHILIS AND OTHER VENEREAL DISEASES (090-099)
EXCLUDES　nonvenereal endemic syphilis (104.0)
urogenital trichomoniasis (131.0)

✓4ᵗʰ **090　Congenital syphilis**
DEF: Infection by spirochete *Treponema pallidum* acquired in utero from the infected mother.

090.0　Early congenital syphilis, symptomatic
Congenital syphilitic:　Congenital syphilitic:
choroiditis　　　　　splenomegaly
coryza (chronic)　　Syphilitic (congenital):
hepatomegaly　　　　epiphysitis
mucous patches　　　osteochondritis
periostitis　　　　　pemphigus
Any congenital syphilitic condition specified as early or manifest less than two years after birth

090.1　Early congenital syphilis, latent
Congenital syphilis without clinical manifestations, with positive serological reaction and negative spinal fluid test, less than two years after birth

090.2　Early congenital syphilis, unspecified
Congenital syphilis NOS, less than two years after birth

090.3　Syphilitic interstitial keratitis
Syphilitic keratitis:　Syphilitic keratitis:
parenchymatous　　punctata profunda
EXCLUDES　interstitial keratitis NOS (370.50)

✓5ᵗʰ **090.4　Juvenile neurosyphilis**
Use additional code to identify any associated mental disorder
DEF: *Treponema pallidum* infection involving the nervous system.

090.40　Juvenile neurosyphilis, unspecified
Congenital neurosyphilis
Dementia paralytica juvenilis
Juvenile:
general paresis
tabes
taboparesis

090.41　Congenital syphilitic encephalitis
DEF: Congenital *Treponema pallidum* infection involving the brain.

090.42　Congenital syphilitic meningitis
DEF: Congenital *Treponema pallidum* infection involving the lining of the brain and/or spinal cord.

090.49　Other

090.5　Other late congenital syphilis, symptomatic
Gumma due to congenital syphilis
Hutchinson's teeth
Syphilitic saddle nose
Any congenital syphilitic condition specified as late or manifest two years or more after birth

090.6　Late congenital syphilis, latent
Congenital syphilis without clinical manifestations, with positive serological reaction and negative spinal fluid test, two years or more after birth

090.7　Late congenital syphilis, unspecified
Congenital syphilis NOS, two years or more after birth

090.9　Congenital syphilis, unspecified

✓4ᵗʰ **091　Early syphilis, symptomatic**
EXCLUDES　early cardiovascular syphilis (093.0-093.9)
early neurosyphilis (094.0-094.9)

091.0　Genital syphilis (primary)
Genital chancre
DEF: Genital lesion at the site of initial infection by *Treponema pallidum.*

091.1　Primary anal syphilis
DEF: Anal lesion at the site of initial infection by *Treponema pallidum.*

✓4ᵗʰ ✓5ᵗʰ Additional Digit Required　　RUG III Special Care Dx　　　RUG III Clinically Complex Dx　　Hospice Non-cancer Dx　　CD PDx Clinical Dimension PDx　　CD SDx Clinical Dimension SDx

2006 ICD•9•CM　　　　　　　　　　　　　　　　　　　　　　　　　　　　　　　　　　　Volume 1 — 15

Infectious and Parasitic Diseases

091.2–095.3

091.2 Other primary syphilis
Primary syphilis of: Primary syphilis of:
   breast   lip
   fingers   tonsils
DEF: Lesion at the site of initial infection by *Treponema pallidum*.

091.3 Secondary syphilis of skin or mucous membranes
Condyloma latum   Secondary syphilis of:
Secondary syphilis of: skin
   anus   tonsils
   mouth   vulva
   pharynx
DEF: Transitory or chronic lesions following initial syphilis infection.

091.4 Adenopathy due to secondary syphilis
Syphilitic adenopathy (secondary)
Syphilitic lymphadenitis (secondary)

√5ᵗʰ **091.5 Uveitis due to secondary syphilis**
091.50 Syphilitic uveitis, unspecified
091.51 Syphilitic chorioretinitis (secondary)
DEF: Inflammation of choroid and retina as a secondary infection.
091.52 Syphilitic iridocyclitis (secondary)
DEF: Inflammation of iris and ciliary body as a secondary infection.

√5ᵗʰ **091.6 Secondary syphilis of viscera and bone**
091.61 Secondary syphilitic periostitis
DEF: Inflammation of outer layers of bone as a secondary infection.
091.62 Secondary syphilitic hepatitis
Secondary syphilis of liver
091.69 Other viscera

091.7 Secondary syphilis, relapse
Secondary syphilis, relapse (treated) (untreated)
DEF: Return of symptoms of syphilis following asymptomatic period.

√5ᵗʰ **091.8 Other forms of secondary syphilis**
091.81 Acute syphilitic meningitis (secondary)
DEF: Sudden, severe inflammation of the lining of the brain and/or spinal cord as a secondary infection.
091.82 Syphilitic alopecia
DEF: Hair loss following initial syphilis infection.
091.89 Other

091.9 Unspecified secondary syphilis

√4ᵗʰ **092 Early syphilis, latent**
INCLUDES   syphilis (acquired) without clinical manifestations, with positive serological reaction and negative spinal fluid test, less than two years after infection

092.0 Early syphilis, latent, serological relapse after treatment
092.9 Early syphilis, latent, unspecified

√4ᵗʰ **093 Cardiovascular syphilis**
093.0 Aneurysm of aorta, specified as syphilitic
Dilatation of aorta, specified as syphilitic
093.1 Syphilitic aortitis
DEF: Inflammation of the aorta – the main artery leading from the heart.

√5ᵗʰ **093.2 Syphilitic endocarditis**
DEF: Inflammation of the tissues lining the cavities of the heart.
093.20 Valve, unspecified
Syphilitic ostial coronary disease
093.21 Mitral valve
093.22 Aortic valve
Syphilitic aortic incompetence or stenosis
093.23 Tricuspid valve
093.24 Pulmonary valve

√5ᵗʰ **093.8 Other specified cardiovascular syphilis**
093.81 Syphilitic pericarditis
DEF: Inflammation of the outer lining of the heart.
093.82 Syphilitic myocarditis
DEF: Inflammation of the muscle of the heart.
093.89 Other
093.9 Cardiovascular syphilis, unspecified

√4ᵗʰ **094 Neurosyphilis**
Use additional code to identify any associated mental disorder
094.0 Tabes dorsalis
Locomotor ataxia (progressive)
Posterior spinal sclerosis (syphilitic)
Tabetic neurosyphilis
Use additional code to identify manifestation, as: neurogenic arthropathy [Charcot's joint disease] (713.5)
DEF: Progressive degeneration of nerves associated with long-term syphilis; causing pain, wasting away, incontinence, and ataxia.
094.1 General paresis
Dementia paralytica
General paralysis (of the insane) (progressive)
Paretic neurosyphilis
Taboparesis
DEF: Degeneration of brain associated with long-term syphilis, causing loss of brain function, progressive dementia, and paralysis.
094.2 Syphilitic meningitis
Meningovascular syphilis
EXCLUDES   *acute syphilitic meningitis (secondary) (091.81)*
DEF: Inflammation of the lining of the brain and/or spinal cord.
094.3 Asymptomatic neurosyphilis
√5ᵗʰ **094.8 Other specified neurosyphilis**
094.81 Syphilitic encephalitis
094.82 Syphilitic Parkinsonism
DEF: Decreased motor function, tremors, and muscular rigidity.
094.83 Syphilitic disseminated retinochoroiditis
DEF: Inflammation of retina and choroid due to neurosyphilis.
094.84 Syphilitic optic atrophy
DEF: Degeneration of the eye and its nerves due to neurosyphilis.
094.85 Syphilitic retrobulbar neuritis
DEF: Inflammation of the posterior optic nerve to neurosyphilis.
094.86 Syphilitic acoustic neuritis
DEF: Inflammation of acoustic nerve due to neurosyphilis.
094.87 Syphilitic ruptured cerebral aneurysm
094.89 Other
094.9 Neurosyphilis, unspecified
Gumma (syphilitic)
Syphilis (early) (late) } of central nervous system
Syphiloma   NOS

√4ᵗʰ **095 Other forms of late syphilis, with symptoms**
INCLUDES   gumma (syphilitic)
syphilis, late, tertiary, or unspecified stage
095.0 Syphilitic episcleritis
095.1 Syphilis of lung
095.2 Syphilitic peritonitis
095.3 Syphilis of liver

Ⓝ Newborn Age: 0   Ⓟ Pediatric Age: 0-17   Ⓜ Maternity Age: 12-55   Ⓐ Adult Age: 15-124   Manifestation Code   ►◄ Revised Text   ● New Code   ▲ Revised Code Title

16 — Volume 1   *2006 ICD•9•CM*

095.4   **Syphilis of kidney**

095.5   **Syphilis of bone**

095.6   **Syphilis of muscle**
     Syphilitic myositis

095.7   **Syphilis of synovium, tendon, and bursa**
     Syphilitic: Syphilitic:
       bursitis   synovitis

095.8   **Other specified forms of late symptomatic syphilis**
     EXCLUDES   *cardiovascular syphilis (093.0-093.9)*
                  neurosyphilis (094.0-094.9)

095.9   **Late symptomatic syphilis, unspecified**

096 Late syphilis, latent
     Syphilis (acquired) without clinical manifestations, with
       positive serological reaction and negative spinal fluid
       test, two years or more after infection

√4ᵗʰ **097 Other and unspecified syphilis**

097.0   **Late syphilis, unspecified**

097.1   **Latent syphilis, unspecified**
     Positive serological reaction for syphilis

097.9   **Syphilis, unspecified**
     Syphilis (acquired) NOS
     EXCLUDES   *syphilis NOS causing death under two*
                  years of age (090.9)

√4ᵗʰ **098 Gonococcal infections**
     DEF: *Neisseria gonorrhoeae* infection generally acquired in utero or in
     sexual congress.

098.0   **Acute, of lower genitourinary tract**
     Gonococcal: Gonorrhea (acute):
       Bartholinitis (acute)   NOS
       urethritis (acute)   genitourinary (tract) NOS
       vulvovaginitis (acute)

√5ᵗʰ **098.1**   **Acute, of upper genitourinary tract**

098.10 Gonococcal infection (acute) of upper genitourinary tract, site unspecified

098.11 Gonococcal cystitis (acute)
     Gonorrhea (acute) of bladder

098.12 Gonococcal prostatitis (acute)   ♂

098.13 Gonococcal epididymo-orchitis (acute)   ♂
     Gonococcal orchitis (acute)
     DEF: Acute inflammation of the testes.

098.14 Gonococcal seminal vesiculitis (acute)   ♂
     Gonorrhea (acute) of seminal vesicle

098.15 Gonococcal cervicitis (acute)   ♀
     Gonorrhea (acute) of cervix

098.16 Gonococcal endometritis (acute)   ♀
     Gonorrhea (acute) of uterus

098.17 Gonococcal salpingitis, specified as acute   ♀
     DEF: Acute inflammation of the fallopian tubes.

098.19 Other

098.2   **Chronic, of lower genitourinary tract**
     Gonococcal:
       Bartholinitis   ⎫ specified as chronic
       urethritis   ⎪ or with
       vulvovaginitis   ⎬ duration of
     Gonorrhea: ⎪ two months
       NOS   ⎪ or more
       genitourinary (tract)   ⎭

     Any condition classifiable to 098.0 specified as
       chronic or with duration of two months or more

√5ᵗʰ **098.3**   **Chronic, of upper genitourinary tract**
     INCLUDES   any condition classifiable to 098.1
               stated as chronic or with a
               duration of two months or more

098.30 Chronic gonococcal infection of upper genitourinary tract, site unspecified

098.31 Gonococcal cystitis, chronic
     Any condition classifiable to 098.11,
       specified as chronic
     Gonorrhea of bladder, chronic

098.32 Gonococcal prostatitis, chronic   ♂
     Any condition classifiable to 098.12,
       specified as chronic

098.33 Gonococcal epididymo-orchitis, chronic   ♂
     Any condition classifiable to 098.13,
       specified as chronic
     Chronic gonococcal orchitis
     DEF: Chronic inflammation of the testes.

098.34 Gonococcal seminal vesiculitis, chronic   ♂
     Any condition classifiable to 098.14,
       specified as chronic
     Gonorrhea of seminal vesicle, chronic

098.35 Gonococcal cervicitis, chronic   ♀
     Any condition classifiable to 098.15,
       specified as chronic
     Gonorrhea of cervix, chronic

098.36 Gonococcal endometritis, chronic   ♀
     Any condition classifiable to 098.16,
       specified as chronic
     DEF: Chronic inflammation of the uterus.

098.37 Gonococcal salpingitis (chronic)   ♀
     DEF: Chronic inflammation of the fallopian tubes.

098.39 Other

√5ᵗʰ **098.4**   **Gonococcal infection of eye**

098.40 Gonococcal conjunctivitis (neonatorum)
     Gonococcal ophthalmia (neonatorum)
     DEF: Infection of conjunctiva present at birth.

098.41 Gonococcal iridocyclitis
     DEF: Inflammation and infection of iris and ciliary body.

098.42 Gonococcal endophthalmia
     DEF: Inflammation and infection of contents of eyeball.

098.43 Gonococcal keratitis
     DEF: Inflammation and infection of the cornea.

098.49 Other

√5ᵗʰ **098.5**   **Gonococcal infection of joint**

098.50 Gonococcal arthritis
     Gonococcal infection of joint NOS

098.51 Gonococcal synovitis and tenosynovitis

098.52 Gonococcal bursitis
     DEF: Inflammation of the sac-like cavities in a joint.

098.53 Gonococcal spondylitis

098.59 Other
     Gonococcal rheumatism

098.6   **Gonococcal infection of pharynx**

098.7   **Gonococcal infection of anus and rectum**
     Gonococcal proctitis

√5ᵗʰ **098.8**   **Gonococcal infection of other specified sites**

098.81 Gonococcal keratosis (blennorrhagica)
     DEF: Pustular skin lesions caused by *Neisseria*
     gonorrhoeae.

098.82 Gonococcal meningitis
     DEF: Inflammation of lining of brain and/or spinal cord.

098.83 Gonococcal pericarditis
     DEF: Inflammation of the outer lining of the heart.

098.84 Gonococcal endocarditis
     DEF: Inflammation of tissues lining the cavities of heart.

098.85 Other gonococcal heart disease

098.86 Gonococcal peritonitis
     DEF: Inflammation of the membrane lining the abdomen.

√4ᵗʰ
√5ᵗʰ   Additional Digit Required   RUG III Special Care Dx   RUG III Clinically Complex Dx   Hospice Non-cancer Dx   **CD PDx** Clinical Dimension PDx   **CD SDx** Clinical Dimension SDx

2006 ICD•9•CM   **Volume 1 — 17**

098.89 Other
Gonococcemia

✓4ᵗʰ **099 Other venereal diseases**

  099.0 Chancroid

Bubo (inguinal):	Chancre:
chancroidal	Ducrey's
due to Hemophilus	simple
ducreyi	soft
	Ulcus molle (cutis) (skin)

DEF: A sexually transmitted disease caused by *Haemophilus ducreyi*; it is identified by a painful primary ulcer at the site of inoculation (usually external genitalia) with related lymphadenitis.

  099.1 Lymphogranuloma venereum
Climatic or tropical bubo
(Durand-) Nicolas-Favre disease
Esthiomene
Lymphogranuloma inguinale

DEF: Sexually transmitted infection of *Chlamydia trachomatis* causing skin lesions.

  099.2 Granuloma inguinale

Donovanosis	Granuloma venereum
Granuloma pudendi	Pudendal ulcer
(ulcerating)	

DEF: Chronic, sexually transmitted infection of *Calymmatobacterium granulomatis* causing progressive, anogenital skin ulcers.

  099.3 Reiter's disease
Reiter's syndrome
Use additional code for associated:
  arthropathy (711.1)
  conjunctivitis (372.33)

DEF: A symptom complex of unknown etiology consisting of urethritis, conjunctivitis, arthritis and myocutaneous lesions. It occurs most commonly in young men and patients with HIV and may precede or follow AIDS. Also a form of reactive arthritis.

✓5ᵗʰ **099.4 Other nongonococcal urethritis [NGU]**
  099.40 Unspecified
    Nonspecific urethritis
  099.41 Chlamydia trachomatis
  099.49 Other specified organism

✓5ᵗʰ **099.5 Other venereal diseases due to Chlamydia trachomatis**
  EXCLUDES   *Chlamydia trachomatis infection of conjunctiva (076.0-076.9, 077.0, 077.9)*
    Lymphogranuloma venereum (099.1)

DEF: Venereal diseases caused by *Chlamydia trachomatis* at other sites besides the urethra (e.g., pharynx, anus and rectum, conjunctiva and peritoneum).

  099.50 Unspecified site
  099.51 Pharynx
  099.52 Anus and rectum
  099.53 Lower genitourinary sites
    EXCLUDES   *urethra (099.41)*
    Use additional code to specify site of infection, such as:
      bladder (595.4)
      cervix (616.0)
      vagina and vulva (616.11)
  099.54 Other genitourinary sites
    Use additional code to specify site of infection, such as:
      pelvic inflammatory disease NOS (614.9)
      testis and epididymis (604.91)
  099.55 Unspecified genitourinary site
  099.56 Peritoneum
    Perihepatitis
  099.59 Other specified site

  099.8 Other specified venereal diseases
  099.9 Venereal disease, unspecified

OTHER SPIROCHETAL DISEASES (100-104)

✓4ᵗʰ **100 Leptospirosis**

DEF: An infection of any spirochete of the genus Leptospire in blood. This zoonosis is transmitted to humans most often by exposure with contaminated animal tissues or water and less often by contact with urine. Patients present with flulike symptoms, the most common being muscle aches involving the thighs and low back. Treatment is with hydration and antibiotics.

  100.0 Leptospirosis icterohemorrhagica
Leptospiral or spirochetal jaundice (hemorrhagic)
Weil's disease

✓5ᵗʰ **100.8 Other specified leptospiral infections**
  100.81 Leptospiral meningitis (aseptic)
  100.89 Other

Fever:	Infection by Leptospira:
Fort Bragg	australis
pretibial	bataviae
swamp	pyrogenes

  100.9 Leptospirosis, unspecified

101 Vincent's angina

Acute necrotizing ulcerative:	Trench mouth
gingivitis	Vincent's:
stomatitis	gingivitis
Fusospirochetal pharyngitis	infection [any site]
Spirochetal stomatitis	

DEF: Painful ulceration with edema and hypermic patches of the oropharyngeal and throat membranes; it is caused by spreading of acute ulcerative gingivitis.

✓4ᵗʰ **102 Yaws**
  INCLUDES   frambesia
              pian

DEF: An infectious, endemic, tropical disease caused by *Treponema pertenue*; it usually affects persons 15 years old or younger; a primary cutaneous lesion develops, then a granulomatous skin eruption, and occasionally lesions that destroy skin and bone.

  102.0 Initial lesions
Chancre of yaws
Frambesia, initial or primary
Initial frambesial ulcer
Mother yaw

  102.1 Multiple papillomata and wet crab yaws

Butter yaws	Plantar or palmar
Frambesioma	papilloma of yaws
Pianoma	

  102.2 Other early skin lesions
Cutaneous yaws, less than five years after infection
Early yaws (cutaneous) (macular) (papular)
  (maculopapular) (micropapular)
Frambeside of early yaws

  102.3 Hyperkeratosis
Ghoul hand
Hyperkeratosis, palmar or plantar (early) (late) due
  to yaws
Worm-eaten soles

DEF: Overgrowth of skin of palm of bottoms of feet, due to yaws.

  102.4 Gummata and ulcers
Gummatous frambeside
Nodular late yaws (ulcerated)

DEF: Rubbery lesions and areas of dead skin caused by yaws.

  102.5 Gangosa
Rhinopharyngitis mutilans

DEF: Massive, mutilating lesions of the nose and oral cavity caused by yaws.

N Newborn Age: 0   P Pediatric Age: 0-17   M Maternity Age: 12-55   A Adult Age: 15-124   Manifestation Code   ◄ Revised Text   ● New Code   ▲ Revised Code Title

18 — Volume 1   *2006 ICD•9•CM*

102.6   Bone and joint lesions
Goundou
Gumma, bone   } of yaws (late)
Gummatous osteitis or
periostitis

Hydrarthrosis
Osteitis   } of yaws (early) (late)
Periostitis (hypertrophic)

102.7   Other manifestations
Juxta-articular nodules of yaws
Mucosal yaws

102.8   Latent yaws
Yaws without clinical manifestations, with positive
serology

102.9   Yaws, unspecified

✓4ᵗʰ **103   Pinta**

DEF: A chronic form of treponematosis, endemic in areas of tropical
America; it is identified by the presence of red, violet, blue, coffee-colored
or white spots on the skin.

103.0   Primary lesions
Chancre (primary)
Papule (primary)   } of pinta [carate]
Pintid

103.1   Intermediate lesions
Erythematous plaques
Hyperchromic lesions } of pinta [carate]
Hyperkeratosis

103.2   Late lesions
Cardiovascular lesions
Skin lesions:
achromic
cicatricial   } of pinta [carate]
dyschromic
Vitiligo

103.3   Mixed lesions
Achromic and hyperchromic skin lesions of pinta
[carate]

103.9   Pinta, unspecified

✓4ᵗʰ **104   Other spirochetal infection**

104.0   Nonvenereal endemic syphilis
Bejel   Njovera

DEF: *Treponema pallidum, T. pertenue,* or *T. caroteum* infection
transmitted non-sexually, causing lesions on mucosa and skin.

104.8   Other specified spirochetal infections
EXCLUDES   *relapsing fever (087.0-087.9)*
            syphilis (090.0-097.9)

104.9   Spirochetal infection, unspecified

MYCOSES (110-118)

Use additional code to identify manifestation as:
arthropathy (711.6)
meningitis (321.0-321.1)
otitis externa (380.15)
EXCLUDES   *infection by Actinomycetales, such as species of
            Actinomyces, Actinomadura, Nocardia,
            Streptomyces (039.0-039.9)*

✓4ᵗʰ **110   Dermatophytosis**
INCLUDES   infection by species of Epidermophyton,
            Microsporum, and Trichophyton
            tinea, any type except those in 111

DEF: Superficial infection of the skin caused by a parasitic fungus.

110.0   Of scalp and beard
Kerion   Trichophytic tinea
Sycosis, mycotic   [black dot tinea], scalp

110.1   Of nail
Dermatophytic onychia   Tinea unguium
Onychomycosis

110.2   Of hand
Tinea manuum

110.3   Of groin and perianal area
Dhobie itch   Tinea cruris
Eczema marginatum

110.4   Of foot
Athlete's foot   Tinea pedis

110.5   Of the body
Herpes circinatus   Tinea imbricata [Tokelau]

110.6   Deep seated dermatophytosis
Granuloma trichophyticum
Majocchi's granuloma

110.8   Of other specified sites

110.9   Of unspecified site
Favus NOS   Ringworm NOS
Microsporic tinea NOS

✓4ᵗʰ **111   Dermatomycosis, other and unspecified**

111.0   Pityriasis versicolor
Infection by Malassezia [Pityrosporum] furfur
Tinea flava
Tinea versicolor

111.1   Tinea nigra
Infection by Cladosporium species
Keratomycosis nigricans
Microsporosis nigra
Pityriasis nigra
Tinea palmaris nigra

111.2   Tinea blanca
Infection by Trichosporon (beigelii) cutaneum
White piedra

111.3   Black piedra
Infection by Piedraia hortai

111.8   Other specified dermatomycoses

111.9   Dermatomycosis, unspecified

✓4ᵗʰ **112   Candidiasis**
INCLUDES   infection by Candida species
            moniliasis
EXCLUDES   *neonatal monilial infection (771.7)*

DEF: Fungal infection caused by Candida; usually seen in mucous membranes
or skin.

112.0   Of mouth
Thrush (oral)

112.1   Of vulva and vagina   ♀
Candidal vulvovaginitis   Monilial vulvovaginitis

112.2   Of other urogenital sites
Candidal balanitis
AHA: 4Q, '03, 105; 4Q, '96, 33

112.3   Of skin and nails
Candidal intertrigo
Candidal onychia
Candidal perionyxis [paronychia]

112.4   Of lung
Candidal pneumonia
AHA: 2Q, '98, 7

112.5   Disseminated
Systemic candidiasis
AHA: 2Q, '00, 5; 2Q, '89, 10

✓5ᵗʰ **112.8   Of other specified sites**

112.81   Candidal endocarditis

112.82   Candidal otitis externa
Otomycosis in moniliasis

112.83   Candidal meningitis

112.84   Candidal esophagitis
AHA: 4Q, '92, 19

112.85   Candidal enteritis
AHA: 4Q, '92, 19

112.89   Other
AHA: 1Q, '92, 17; 3Q, '91, 20

112.9   Of unspecified site

✓4ᵗʰ
✓5ᵗʰ Additional Digit Required   RUG III Special Care Dx   RUG III Clinically Complex Dx   Hospice Non-cancer Dx   CD PDx Clinical Dimension PDx   CD SDx Clinical Dimension SDx

2006 ICD•9•CM   Volume 1 — 19

Infectious and Parasitic Diseases

114–120.2

✓4ᵗʰ 114 Coccidioidomycosis

INCLUDES   infection by Coccidioides (immitis)
Posada-Wernicke disease

AHA: 4Q, '93, 23

DEF: A fungal disease caused by inhalation of dust particles containing arthrospores of *Coccidioides immitis*; a self-limited respiratory infection; the primary form is known as San Joaquin fever, desert fever or valley fever.

114.0   Primary coccidioidomycosis (pulmonary)
Acute pulmonary coccidioidomycosis
Coccidioidomycotic pneumonitis
Desert rheumatism
Pulmonary coccidioidomycosis
San Joaquin Valley fever
DEF: Acute, self-limiting *Coccidioides immitis* infection of the lung.

114.1   Primary extrapulmonary coccidioidomycosis
Chancriform syndrome
Primary cutaneous coccidioidomycosis
DEF: Acute, self-limiting *Coccidioides immitis* infection in nonpulmonary site.

114.2   Coccidioidal meningitis
DEF: *Coccidioides immitis* infection of the lining of the brain and/or spinal cord.

114.3   Other forms of progressive coccidioidomycosis
Coccidioidal granuloma
Disseminated coccidioidomycosis

114.4   Chronic pulmonary coccidioidomycosis
114.5   Pulmonary coccidioidomycosis, unspecified
114.9   Coccidioidomycosis, unspecified

✓4ᵗʰ 115 Histoplasmosis

The following fifth-digit subclassification is for use with category 115:
   0   **without mention of manifestation**
   1   **meningitis**
   2   **retinitis**
   3   **pericarditis**
   4   **endocarditis**
   5   **pneumonia**
   9   **other**

✓5ᵗʰ 115.0   Infection by Histoplasma capsulatum
American histoplasmosis
Darling's disease
Reticuloendothelial cytomycosis
Small form histoplasmosis

✓5ᵗʰ 115.1   Infection by Histoplasma duboisii
African histoplasmosis
Large form histoplasmosis

✓5ᵗʰ 115.9   Histoplasmosis, unspecified
Histoplasmosis NOS

✓4ᵗʰ 116 Blastomycotic infection

116.0   Blastomycosis
Blastomycotic dermatitis
Chicago disease
Cutaneous blastomycosis
Disseminated blastomycosis
Gilchrist's disease
Infection by Blastomyces [Ajellomyces] dermatitidis
North American blastomycosis
Primary pulmonary blastomycosis

116.1   Paracoccidioidomycosis
Brazilian blastomycosis
Infection by Paracoccidioides [Blastomyces] brasiliensis
Lutz-Splendore-Almeida disease
Mucocutaneous-lymphangitic paracoccidioidomycosis
Pulmonary paracoccidioidomycosis
South American blastomycosis
Visceral paracoccidioidomycosis

116.2   Lobomycosis
Infections by Loboa [Blastomyces] loboi
Keloidal blastomycosis
Lobo's disease

✓4ᵗʰ 117 Other mycoses

117.0   Rhinosporidiosis
Infection by Rhinosporidium seeberi

117.1   Sporotrichosis
Cutaneous sporotrichosis
Disseminated sporotrichosis
Infection by Sporothrix [Sporotrichum] schenckii
Lymphocutaneous sporotrichosis
Pulmonary sporotrichosis
Sporotrichosis of the bones

117.2   Chromoblastomycosis
Chromomycosis
Infection by Cladosporium carrionii, Fonsecaea compactum, Fonsecaea pedrosoi, Phialophora verrucosa

117.3   Aspergillosis
Infection by Aspergillus species, mainly A. fumigatus, A. flavus group, A. terreus group

AHA: 4Q, '97, 40

117.4   Mycotic mycetomas
Infection by various genera and species of Ascomycetes and Deuteromycetes, such as Acremonium [Cephalosporium] falciforme, Neotestudina rosatii, Madurella grisea, Madurella mycetomii, Pyrenochaeta romeroi, Zopfia [Leptosphaeria] senegalensis
Madura foot, mycotic
Maduromycosis, mycotic
EXCLUDES   actinomycotic mycetomas (039.0-039.9)

117.5   Cryptococcosis
Busse-Buschke's disease
European cryptococcosis
Infection by Cryptococcus neoformans
Pulmonary cryptococcosis
Systemic cryptococcosis
Torula

117.6   Allescheriosis [Petriellidosis]
Infections by Allescheria [Petriellidium] boydii [Monosporium apiospermum]
EXCLUDES   mycotic mycetoma (117.4)

117.7   Zygomycosis [Phycomycosis or Mucormycosis]
Infection by species of Absidia, Basidiobolus, Conidiobolus, Cunninghamella, Entomophthora, Mucor, Rhizopus, Saksenaea

117.8   Infection by dematiacious fungi, [Phaehyphomycosis]
Infection by dematiacious fungi, such as Cladosporium trichoides [bantianum], Dreschlera hawaiiensis, Phialophora gougerotii, Phialophora jeanselmi

117.9   Other and unspecified mycoses

118 Opportunistic mycoses
Infection of skin, subcutaneous tissues, and/or organs by a wide variety of fungi generally considered to be pathogenic to compromised hosts only (e.g., infection by species of Alternaria, Dreschlera, Fusarium)

HELMINTHIASES (120-129)

✓4ᵗʰ 120 Schistosomiasis [bilharziasis]

DEF: Infection caused by *Schistosoma*, a genus of flukes or trematode parasites.

120.0   Schistosoma haematobium
Vesical schistosomiasis NOS

120.1   Schistosoma mansoni
Intestinal schistosomiasis NOS

120.2   Schistosoma japonicum
Asiatic schistosomiasis NOS
Katayama disease or fever

N Newborn Age: 0   P Pediatric Age: 0-17   M Maternity Age: 12-55   A Adult Age: 15-124   Manifestation Code   ◄► Revised Text   ● New Code   ▲ Revised Code Title

20 — Volume 1   *2006 ICD•9•CM*

120.3　Cutaneous
　　Cercarial dermatitis
　　Infection by cercariae of Schistosoma
　　Schistosome dermatitis
　　Swimmers' itch

120.8　Other specified schistosomiasis
　　Infection by Schistosoma:
　　　bovis
　　　intercalatum
　　　mattheii
　　　spindale
　　Schistosomiasis chestermani

120.9　Schistosomiasis, unspecified
　　Blood flukes NOS
　　Hemic distomiasis

√4ᵗʰ **121　Other trematode infections**

121.0　Opisthorchiasis
　　Infection by:
　　　cat liver fluke
　　　Opisthorchis (felineus) (tenuicollis) (viverrini)

121.1　Clonorchiasis
　　Biliary cirrhosis due to clonorchiasis
　　Chinese liver fluke disease
　　Hepatic distomiasis due to Clonorchis sinensis
　　Oriental liver fluke disease

121.2　Paragonimiasis
　　Infection by Paragonimus
　　Lung fluke disease (oriental)
　　Pulmonary distomiasis

121.3　Fascioliasis
　　Infection by Fasciola:
　　　gigantica
　　　hepatica
　　Liver flukes NOS
　　Sheep liver fluke infection

121.4　Fasciolopsiasis
　　Infection by Fasciolopsis (buski)
　　Intestinal distomiasis

121.5　Metagonimiasis
　　Infection by Metagonimus yokogawai

121.6　Heterophyiasis
　　Infection by:
　　　Heterophyes heterophyes
　　　Stellantchasmus falcatus

121.8　Other specified trematode infections
　　Infection by:
　　　Dicrocoelium dendriticum
　　　Echinostoma ilocanum
　　　Gastrodiscoides hominis

121.9　Trematode infection, unspecified
　　Distomiasis NOS
　　Fluke disease NOS

√4ᵗʰ **122　Echinococcosis**
　　INCLUDES　echinococciasis
　　　　　　　hydatid disease
　　　　　　　hydatidosis

　DEF: Infection caused by larval forms of tapeworms of the genus *Echinococcus.*

122.0　Echinococcus granulosus infection of liver
122.1　Echinococcus granulosus infection of lung
122.2　Echinococcus granulosus infection of thyroid
122.3　Echinococcus granulosus infection, other
122.4　Echinococcus granulosus infection, unspecified
122.5　Echinococcus multilocularis infection of liver
122.6　Echinococcus multilocularis infection, other
122.7　Echinococcus multilocularis infection, unspecified
122.8　Echinococcosis, unspecified, of liver
122.9　Echinococcosis, other and unspecified

√4ᵗʰ **123　Other cestode infection**

123.0　Taenia solium infection, intestinal form
　　Pork tapeworm (adult) (infection)

123.1　Cysticercosis
　　Cysticerciasis
　　Infection by Cysticercus cellulosae [larval form of Taenia solium]

　AHA: 2Q, '97, 8

123.2　Taenia saginata infection
　　Beef tapeworm (infection)
　　Infection by Taeniarhynchus saginatus

123.3　Taeniasis, unspecified

123.4　Diphyllobothriasis, intestinal
　　Diphyllobothrium (adult) (latum) (pacificum) infection
　　Fish tapeworm (infection)

123.5　Sparganosis [larval diphyllobothriasis]
　　Infection by:
　　　Diphyllobothrium larvae
　　　Sparganum (mansoni) (proliferum)
　　　Spirometra larvae

123.6　Hymenolepiasis
　　Dwarf tapeworm (infection)
　　Hymenolepis (diminuta) (nana) infection
　　Rat tapeworm (infection)

123.8　Other specified cestode infection
　　Diplogonoporus (grandis)　⎫
　　Dipylidium (caninum)　　 ⎬ infection
　　　　　　　　　　　　　　⎭
　　Dog tapeworm (infection)

123.9　Cestode infection, unspecified
　　Tapeworm (infection) NOS

124　Trichinosis
　　Trichinella spiralis infection　　　Trichiniasis
　　Trichinellosis

　DEF: Infection by *Trichinella spiralis*, the smallest of the parasitic nematodes.

√4ᵗʰ **125　Filarial infection and dracontiasis**

125.0　Bancroftian filariasis
　　Chyluria　　　⎫
　　Elephantiasis　⎪
　　Infection　　　⎬ due to Wuchereria bancrofti
　　Lymphadenitis　⎪
　　Lymphangitis　 ⎭
　　Wuchereriasis

125.1　Malayan filariasis
　　Brugia filariasis　⎫
　　Chyluria　　　　⎪
　　Elephantiasis　　⎬ due to Brugia
　　Infection　　　　⎪　 [Wuchereria]
　　Lymphadenitis　⎪　　 malayi
　　Lymphangitis　 ⎭

125.2　Loiasis
　　Eyeworm disease of Africa　　Loa loa infection

125.3　Onchocerciasis
　　Onchocerca volvulus infection
　　Onchocercosis

125.4　Dipetalonemiasis
　　Infection by:
　　　Acanthocheilonema perstans
　　　Dipetalonema perstans

125.5　Mansonella ozzardi infection
　　Filariasis ozzardi

125.6　Other specified filariasis
　　Dirofilaria infection
　　Infection by:
　　　Acanthocheilonema streptocerca
　　　Dipetalonema streptocerca

125.7　Dracontiasis
　　Guinea-worm infection
　　Infection by Dracunculus medinensis

125.9　Unspecified filariasis

√4ᵗʰ / √5ᵗʰ Additional Digit Required　　RUG III Special Care Dx　　RUG III Clinically Complex Dx　　Hospice Non-cancer Dx　　CD PDx Clinical Dimension PDx　　CD SDx Clinical Dimension SDx

2006 ICD•9•CM　　　　　　　　　　　　　　　　　　　　　　　　　　　　　　　　　　Volume 1 — 21

Infectious and Parasitic Diseases

126–134.0

✓4ᵗʰ **126 Ancylostomiasis and necatoriasis**

INCLUDES cutaneous larva migrans due to Ancylostoma
hookworm (disease) (infection)
uncinariasis

126.0 Ancylostoma duodenale

126.1 Necator americanus

126.2 Ancylostoma braziliense

126.3 Ancylostoma ceylanicum

126.8 Other specified Ancylostoma

126.9 Ancylostomiasis and necatoriasis, unspecified
Creeping eruption NOS
Cutaneous larva migrans NOS

✓4ᵗʰ **127 Other intestinal helminthiases**

127.0 Ascariasis
Ascaridiasis
Infection by Ascaris lumbricoides
Roundworm infection

127.1 Anisakiasis
Infection by Anisakis larva

127.2 Strongyloidiasis
Infection by Strongyloides stercoralis
EXCLUDES *trichostrongyliasis (127.6)*

127.3 Trichuriasis
Infection by Trichuris trichiura
Trichocephaliasis
Whipworm (disease) (infection)

127.4 Enterobiasis
Infection by Enterobius vermicularis
Oxyuriasis
Oxyuris vermicularis infection
Pinworm (disease) (infection)
Threadworm infection

127.5 Capillariasis
Infection by Capillaria philippinensis
EXCLUDES *infection by Capillaria hepatica (128.8)*

127.6 Trichostrongyliasis
Infection by Trichostrongylus species

127.7 Other specified intestinal helminthiasis
Infection by:
Oesophagostomum apiostomum and related
species
Ternidens diminutus
other specified intestinal helminth
Physalopteriasis

127.8 Mixed intestinal helminthiasis
Infection by intestinal helminths classified to more
than one of the categories 120.0-127.7
Mixed helminthiasis NOS

127.9 Intestinal helminthiasis, unspecified

✓4ᵗʰ **128 Other and unspecified helminthiases**

128.0 Toxocariasis
Larva migrans visceralis
Toxocara (canis) (cati) infection
Visceral larva migrans syndrome

128.1 Gnathostomiasis
Infection by Gnathostoma spinigerum and related
species

128.8 Other specified helminthiasis
Infection by:
Angiostrongylus cantonensis
Capillaria hepatica
other specified helminth

128.9 Helminth infection, unspecified
Helminthiasis NOS   Worms NOS

129 Intestinal parasitism, unspecified

OTHER INFECTIOUS AND PARASITIC DISEASES (130–136)

✓4ᵗʰ **130 Toxoplasmosis**

INCLUDES infection by toxoplasma gondii
toxoplasmosis (acquired)
EXCLUDES *congenital toxoplasmosis (771.2)*

130.0 Meningoencephalitis due to toxoplasmosis
Encephalitis due to acquired toxoplasmosis

130.1 Conjunctivitis due to toxoplasmosis

130.2 Chorioretinitis due to toxoplasmosis
Focal retinochoroiditis due to acquired
toxoplasmosis

130.3 Myocarditis due to toxoplasmosis

130.4 Pneumonitis due to toxoplasmosis

130.5 Hepatitis due to toxoplasmosis

130.7 Toxoplasmosis of other specified sites

130.8 Multisystemic disseminated toxoplasmosis
Toxoplasmosis of multiple sites

130.9 Toxoplasmosis, unspecified

✓4ᵗʰ **131 Trichomoniasis**

INCLUDES infection due to Trichomonas (vaginalis)

✓5ᵗʰ **131.0 Urogenital trichomoniasis**

131.00 Urogenital trichomoniasis, unspecified
Fluor (vaginalis)   trichomonal or due to
Leukorrhea   }   Trichomonas
(vaginalis)   (vaginalis)

DEF: *Trichomonas vaginalis* infection of reproductive
and urinary organs, transmitted through coitus.

131.01 Trichomonal vulvovaginitis ♀
Vaginitis, trichomonal or due to
Trichomonas (vaginalis)

DEF: *Trichomonas vaginalis* infection of vulva and
vagina; often asymptomatic, transmitted through coitus.

131.02 Trichomonal urethritis
DEF: *Trichomonas vaginalis* infection of the urethra.

131.03 Trichomonal prostatitis ♂
DEF: *Trichomonas vaginalis* infection of the prostate.

131.09 Other

131.8 Other specified sites
EXCLUDES *intestinal (007.3)*

131.9 Trichomoniasis, unspecified

✓4ᵗʰ **132 Pediculosis and phthirus infestation**

132.0 Pediculus capitis [head louse]

132.1 Pediculus corporis [body louse]

132.2 Phthirus pubis [pubic louse]
Pediculus pubis

132.3 Mixed infestation
Infestation classifiable to more than one of the
categories 132.0-132.2

132.9 Pediculosis, unspecified

✓4ᵗʰ **133 Acariasis**

133.0 Scabies
Infestation by Sarcoptes scabiei   Sarcoptic itch
Norwegian scabies

133.8 Other acariasis
Chiggers   Infestation by:
Infestation by: Trombicula
Demodex folliculorum

133.9 Acariasis, unspecified
Infestation by mites NOS

✓4ᵗʰ **134 Other infestation**

134.0 Myiasis
Infestation by: Infestation by:
Dermatobia (hominis)   maggots
fly larvae   Oestrus ovis
Gasterophilus (intestinalis)

 Newborn Age: 0   P Pediatric Age: 0-17   M Maternity Age: 12-55   A Adult Age: 15-124   Manifestation Code   ▶◀ Revised Text   ● New Code   ▲ Revised Code Title

134.1　Other arthropod infestation

Infestation by:　　　Jigger disease
　chigoe　　　　　　Scarabiasis
　sand flea　　　　　Tungiasis
　Tunga penetrans

134.2　Hirudiniasis

Hirudiniasis (external) (internal)
Leeches (aquatic) (land)

134.8　Other specified infestations

134.9　Infestation, unspecified

Infestation (skin) NOS　　　Skin parasites NOS

135　Sarcoidosis

Besnier-Boeck-Schaumann disease
Lupoid (miliary) of Boeck
Lupus pernio (Besnier)
Lymphogranulomatosis, benign (Schaumann's)
Sarcoid (any site):
　NOS
　Boeck
　Darier-Roussy
Uveoparotid fever

DEF: A chronic, granulomatous reticulosis (abnormal increase in cells), affecting any organ or tissue; acute form has high rate of remission; chronic form is progressive.

✓4ᵗʰ　136　Other and unspecified infectious and parasitic diseases

136.0　Ainhum

Dactylolysis spontanea

DEF: A disease affecting the toes, especially the fifth digit, and sometimes the fingers, especially seen in black adult males; it is characterized by a linear constriction around the affected digit leading to spontaneous amputation of the distal part of the digit.

136.1　Behçet's syndrome

DEF: A chronic inflammatory disorder of unknown etiology involving the small blood vessels; it is characterized by recurrent aphthous ulceration of the oral and pharyngeal mucous membranes and the genitalia, skin lesions, severe uvetis, retinal vascularitis and optic atrophy.

136.2　Specific infections by free-living amebae

Meningoencephalitis due to Naegleria

136.3　Pneumocystosis

Pneumonia due to Pneumocystis carinii

AHA: ▶1Q, '05, 7;◀ 1Q, '03, 15; N-D, '87, 5, 6

DEF: *Pneumocystis carinii* fungus causing pneumonia in immunocompromised patients; a leading cause of death among AIDS patients.

136.4　Psorospermiasis

136.5　Sarcosporidiosis

Infection by Sarcocystis lindemanni

DEF: *Sarcocystis* infection causing muscle cysts of intestinal inflammation.

136.8　Other specified infectious and parasitic diseases

Candiru infestation

136.9　Unspecified infectious and parasitic diseases

Infectious disease NOS　　Parasitic disease NOS

AHA: 2Q, '91, 8

LATE EFFECTS OF INFECTIOUS AND PARASITIC DISEASES (137-139)

✓4ᵗʰ　137　Late effects of tuberculosis

Note: This category is to be used to indicate conditions classifiable to 010-018 as the cause of late effects, which are themselves classified elsewhere. The "late effects" include those specified as such, as sequelae, or as due to old or inactive tuberculosis, without evidence of active disease.

137.0　Late effects of respiratory or unspecified tuberculosis

137.1　Late effects of central nervous system tuberculosis

137.2　Late effects of genitourinary tuberculosis

137.3　Late effects of tuberculosis of bones and joints

137.4　Late effects of tuberculosis of other specified organs

138　Late effects of acute poliomyelitis

Note: This category is to be used to indicate conditions classifiable to 045 as the cause of late effects, which are themselves classified elsewhere. The "late effects" include conditions specified as such, or as sequelae, or as due to old or inactive poliomyelitis, without evidence of active disease.

✓4ᵗʰ　139　Late effects of other infectious and parasitic diseases

Note: This category is to be used to indicate conditions classifiable to categories 001-009, 020-041, 046-136 as the cause of late effects, which are themselves classified elsewhere. The "late effects" include conditions specified as such; they also include sequela of diseases classifiable to the above categories if there is evidence that the disease itself is no longer present.

139.0　Late effects of viral encephalitis

Late effects of conditions classifiable to 049.8-049.9, 062-064

139.1　Late effects of trachoma

Late effects of conditions classifiable to 076

139.8　Late effects of other and unspecified infectious and parasitic diseases

AHA: 4Q, '91, 15; 3Q, '90, 14; M-A, '87, 8

✓4ᵗʰ
✓5ᵗʰ Additional Digit Required　　RUG III Special Care Dx　　RUG III Clinically Complex Dx　　Hospice Non-cancer Dx　　**CD PDx** Clinical Dimension PDx　　**CD SDx** Clinical Dimension SDx

2006 ICD•9•CM　　　　　　　　　　　　　　　　　　　　　　　　　　　　　　　　　　　**October 2005 • Volume 1 — 23**

2. NEOPLASMS (140-239)

Notes:

1. Content

This chapter contains the following broad groups:

140-195	Malignant neoplasms, stated or presumed to be primary, of specified sites, except of lymphatic and hematopoietic tissue
196-198	Malignant neoplasms, stated or presumed to be secondary, of specified sites
199	Malignant neoplasms, without specification of site
200-208	Malignant neoplasms, stated or presumed to be primary, of lymphatic and hematopoietic tissue
210-229	Benign neoplasms
230-234	Carcinoma in situ
235-238	Neoplasms of uncertain behavior [see Note, above category 235]
239	Neoplasms of unspecified nature

2. Functional activity

All neoplasms are classified in this chapter, whether or not functionally active. An additional code from Chapter 3 may be used to identify such functional activity associated with any neoplasm, e.g.:

catecholamine-producing malignant pheochromocytoma of adrenal:

code 194.0, additional code 255.6

basophil adenoma of pituitary with Cushing's syndrome:

code 227.3, additional code 255.0

3. Morphology [Histology]

For those wishing to identify the histological type of neoplasms, a comprehensive coded nomenclature, which comprises the morphology rubrics of the ICD-Oncology, is given in Appendix A.

4. Malignant neoplasms overlapping site boundaries

Categories 140-195 are for the classification of primary malignant neoplasms according to their point of origin. A malignant neoplasm that overlaps two or more subcategories within a three-digit rubric and whose point of origin cannot be determined should be classified to the subcategory .8 "Other."

For example, "carcinoma involving tip and ventral surface of tongue" should be assigned to 141.8. On the other hand, "carcinoma of tip of tongue, extending to involve the ventral surface" should be coded to 141.2, as the point of origin, the tip, is known. Three subcategories (149.8, 159.8, 165.8) have been provided for malignant neoplasms that overlap the boundaries of three-digit rubrics within certain systems.

Overlapping malignant neoplasms that cannot be classified as indicated above should be assigned to the appropriate subdivision of category 195 (Malignant neoplasm of other and ill-defined sites).

AHA: 2Q, '90, 7

DEF: An abnormal growth, such as a tumor. Morphology determines behavior, i.e., whether it will remain intact (benign) or spread to adjacent tissue (malignant). The term mass is not synonymous with neoplasm, as it is often used to describe cysts and thickenings such as those occurring with hematoma or infection.

MALIGNANT NEOPLASM OF LIP, ORAL CAVITY, AND PHARYNX (140-149)

> **EXCLUDES**   carcinoma in situ (230.0)

√4ᵗʰ **140 Malignant neoplasm of lip**

> **EXCLUDES**   skin of lip (173.0)

140.0   **Upper lip, vermilion border**

Upper lip:	Upper lip:
NOS	lipstick area
external	

Lip

140.1   **Lower lip, vermilion border**

Lower lip:	Lower lip:
NOS	lipstick area
external	

140.3   **Upper lip, inner aspect**

Upper lip:	Upper lip:
buccal aspect	mucosa
frenulum	oral aspect

140.4   **Lower lip, inner aspect**

Lower lip:	Lower lip:
buccal aspect	mucosa
frenulum	oral aspect

140.5   **Lip, unspecified, inner aspect**

Lip, not specified whether upper or lower:
buccal aspect
frenulum
mucosa
oral aspect

140.6   **Commissure of lip**

Labial commissure

140.8   **Other sites of lip**

Malignant neoplasm of contiguous or overlapping sites of lip whose point of origin cannot be determined

140.9   **Lip, unspecified, vermilion border**

Lip, not specified as upper or lower:
NOS
external
lipstick area

√4ᵗʰ **141 Malignant neoplasm of tongue**

141.0   **Base of tongue**

Dorsal surface of base of tongue
Fixed part of tongue NOS

141.1   **Dorsal surface of tongue**

Anterior two-thirds of tongue, dorsal surface
Dorsal tongue NOS
Midline of tongue

> **EXCLUDES**   dorsal surface of base of tongue (141.0)

141.2   **Tip and lateral border of tongue**

141.3   **Ventral surface of tongue**

Anterior two-thirds of tongue, ventral surface
Frenulum linguae

141.4   **Anterior two-thirds of tongue, part unspecified**

Mobile part of tongue NOS

141.5   **Junctional zone**

Border of tongue at junction of fixed and mobile parts at insertion of anterior tonsillar pillar

141.6   **Lingual tonsil**

141.8   **Other sites of tongue**

Malignant neoplasm of contiguous or overlapping sites of tongue whose point of origin cannot be determined

141.9   **Tongue, unspecified**

Tongue NOS

√4ᵗʰ √5ᵗʰ Additional Digit Required   RUG III Special Care Dx   RUG III Clinically Complex Dx   Hospice Non-cancer Dx   **CD PDx** Clinical Dimension PDx   **CD SDx** Clinical Dimension SDx

2006 ICD•9•CM   **Volume 1 — 25**

Neoplasms

142–146.9

Tongue

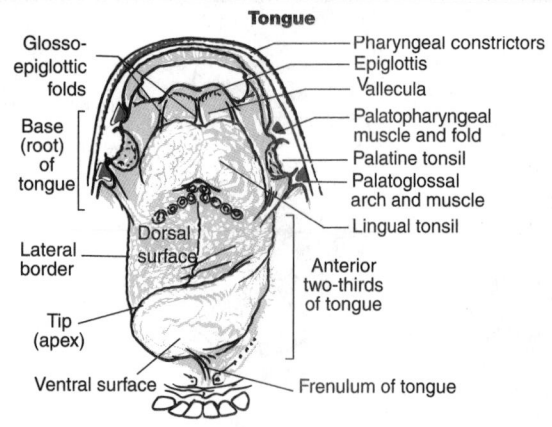

- Glosso-epiglottic folds
- Pharyngeal constrictors
- Epiglottis
- Vallecula
- Palatopharyngeal muscle and fold
- Palatine tonsil
- Palatoglossal arch and muscle
- Lingual tonsil
- Base (root) of tongue
- Dorsal surface
- Lateral border
- Anterior two-thirds of tongue
- Tip (apex)
- Ventral surface
- Frenulum of tongue

☑4ᵗʰ **142 Malignant neoplasm of major salivary glands**

    INCLUDES   salivary ducts

    EXCLUDES   *malignant neoplasm of minor salivary glands:*
                       NOS (145.9)
                       buccal mucosa (145.0)
                       soft palate (145.3)
                       tongue (141.0-141.9)
                       tonsil, palatine (146.0)

   142.0   **Parotid gland**

   142.1   **Submandibular gland**
            Submaxillary gland

   142.2   **Sublingual gland**

   142.8   **Other major salivary glands**
            Malignant neoplasm of contiguous or overlapping sites of salivary glands and ducts whose point of origin cannot be determined

   142.9   **Salivary gland, unspecified**
            Salivary gland (major) NOS

☑4ᵗʰ **143 Malignant neoplasm of gum**

    INCLUDES   alveolar (ridge) mucosa
                     gingiva (alveolar) (marginal)
                     interdental papillae

    EXCLUDES   *malignant odontogenic neoplasms (170.0-170.1)*

   143.0   **Upper gum**

   143.1   **Lower gum**

   143.8   **Other sites of gum**
            Malignant neoplasm of contiguous or overlapping sites of gum whose point of origin cannot be determined

   143.9   **Gum, unspecified**

☑4ᵗʰ **144 Malignant neoplasm of floor of mouth**

   144.0   **Anterior portion**
            Anterior to the premolar-canine junction

   144.1   **Lateral portion**

   144.8   **Other sites of floor of mouth**
            Malignant neoplasm of contiguous or overlapping sites of floor of mouth whose point of origin cannot be determined

   144.9   **Floor of mouth, part unspecified**

☑4ᵗʰ **145 Malignant neoplasm of other and unspecified parts of mouth**

    EXCLUDES   *mucosa of lips (140.0-140.9)*

   145.0   **Cheek mucosa**
            Buccal mucosa
            Cheek, inner aspect

   145.1   **Vestibule of mouth**
            Buccal sulcus (upper) (lower)
            Labial sulcus (upper) (lower)

   145.2   **Hard palate**

   145.3   **Soft palate**
      EXCLUDES   *nasopharyngeal [posterior] [superior] surface of soft palate (147.3)*

   145.4   **Uvula**

   145.5   **Palate, unspecified**
            Junction of hard and soft palate   Roof of mouth

   145.6   **Retromolar area**

   145.8   **Other specified parts of mouth**
            Malignant neoplasm of contiguous or overlapping sites of mouth whose point of origin cannot be determined

   145.9   **Mouth, unspecified**
            Buccal cavity NOS
            Minor salivary gland, unspecified site
            Oral cavity NOS

☑4ᵗʰ **146 Malignant neoplasm of oropharynx**

   146.0   **Tonsil**
            Tonsil:
               NOS
               faucial
               palatine
      EXCLUDES   *lingual tonsil (141.6)*
                         pharyngeal tonsil (147.1)

        AHA: S-O, '87, 8

   146.1   **Tonsillar fossa**

   146.2   **Tonsillar pillars (anterior) (posterior)**
            Faucial pillar   Palatoglossal arch
            Glossopalatine fold   Palatopharyngeal arch

   146.3   **Vallecula**
            Anterior and medial surface of the pharyngoepiglottic fold

   146.4   **Anterior aspect of epiglottis**
            Epiglottis, free border [margin]
            Glossoepiglottic fold(s)
      EXCLUDES   *epiglottis:*
                      NOS (161.1)
                      suprahyoid portion (161.1)

   146.5   **Junctional region**
            Junction of the free margin of the epiglottis, the aryepiglottic fold, and the pharyngoepiglottic fold

   146.6   **Lateral wall of oropharynx**

   146.7   **Posterior wall of oropharynx**

   146.8   **Other specified sites of oropharynx**
            Branchial cleft
            Malignant neoplasm of contiguous or overlapping sites of oropharynx whose point of origin cannot be determined

   146.9   **Oropharynx, unspecified**
        AHA: 2Q, '02, 6

Mouth

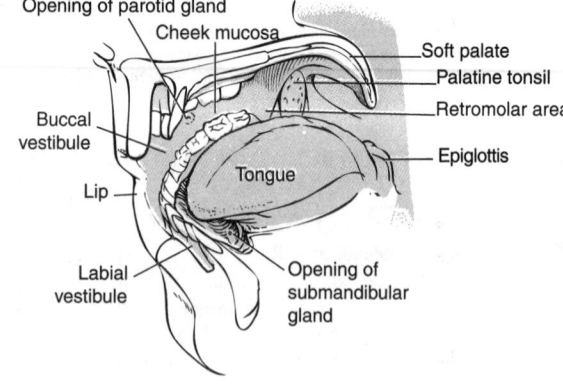

- Opening of parotid gland
- Cheek mucosa
- Soft palate
- Palatine tonsil
- Retromolar area
- Buccal vestibule
- Epiglottis
- Lip
- Tongue
- Labial vestibule
- Opening of submandibular gland

N Newborn Age: 0   P Pediatric Age: 0-17   M Maternity Age: 12-55   A Adult Age: 15-124   Manifestation Code   ◄ Revised Text   ● New Code   ▲ Revised Code Title

26 — Volume 1   *2006 ICD•9•CM*

Main Salivary Glands

Nasopharynx

Oropharynx

Hypopharynx

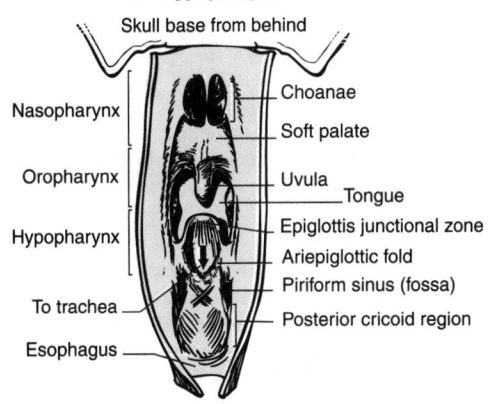

√4th **147 Malignant neoplasm of nasopharynx**

    147.0   **Superior wall**
        Roof of nasopharynx

    147.1   **Posterior wall**
        Adenoid   Pharyngeal tonsil

    147.2   **Lateral wall**
        Fossa of Rosenmüller   Pharyngeal recess
        Opening of auditory tube

    147.3   **Anterior wall**
        Floor of nasopharynx
        Nasopharyngeal [posterior] [superior] surface of soft
          palate
        Posterior margin of nasal septum and choanae

    147.8   **Other specified sites of nasopharynx**
        Malignant neoplasm of contiguous or overlapping
          sites of nasopharynx whose point of origin
          cannot be determined

    147.9   **Nasopharynx, unspecified**
        Nasopharyngeal wall NOS

√4th **148 Malignant neoplasm of hypopharynx**

    148.0   **Postcricoid region**

    148.1   **Pyriform sinus**
        Pyriform fossa

    148.2   **Aryepiglottic fold, hypopharyngeal aspect**
        Aryepiglottic fold or interarytenoid fold:
          NOS
          marginal zone
        EXCLUDES *aryepiglottic fold or interarytenoid fold,*
              laryngeal aspect (161.1)

    148.3   **Posterior hypopharyngeal wall**

    148.8   **Other specified sites of hypopharynx**
        Malignant neoplasm of contiguous or overlapping
          sites of hypopharynx whose point of origin
          cannot be determined

    148.9   **Hypopharynx, unspecified**
        Hypopharyngeal wall NOS
        Hypopharynx NOS

√4th **149 Malignant neoplasm of other and ill-defined sites within the lip, oral cavity, and pharynx**

    149.0   **Pharynx, unspecified**

    149.1   **Waldeyer's ring**

    149.8   **Other**
        Malignant neoplasms of lip, oral cavity, and pharynx
          whose point of origin cannot be assigned to
          any one of the categories 140-148
        EXCLUDES *"book leaf" neoplasm [ventral surface*
              of tongue and floor of mouth]
              (145.8)

    149.9   **Ill-defined**

MALIGNANT NEOPLASM OF DIGESTIVE ORGANS AND PERITONEUM (150-159)

    EXCLUDES *carcinoma in situ (230.1-230.9)*

√4th **150 Malignant neoplasm of esophagus**

    150.0   **Cervical esophagus**

    150.1   **Thoracic esophagus**

    150.2   **Abdominal esophagus**
        EXCLUDES *adenocarcinoma (151.0)*
              cardio-esophageal junction (151.0)

    150.3   **Upper third of esophagus**
        Proximal third of esophagus

    150.4   **Middle third of esophagus**

    150.5   **Lower third of esophagus**
        Distal third of esophagus
        EXCLUDES *adenocarcinoma (151.0)*
              cardio-esophageal junction (151.0)

    150.8   **Other specified part**
        Malignant neoplasm of contiguous or overlapping
          sites of esophagus whose point of origin cannot
          be determined

    150.9   **Esophagus, unspecified**

√4th √5th Additional Digit Required   RUG III Special Care Dx   RUG III Clinically Complex Dx   Hospice Non-cancer Dx   **CD PDx** Clinical Dimension PDx   **CD SDx** Clinical Dimension SDx

✓4th 151 Malignant neoplasm of stomach

151.0 Cardia
Cardiac orifice
Cardio-esophageal junction
> EXCLUDES   *squamous cell carcinoma (150.2, 150.5)*

151.1 Pylorus
Prepylorus   Pyloric canal

151.2 Pyloric antrum
Antrum of stomach NOS

151.3 Fundus of stomach

151.4 Body of stomach

151.5 Lesser curvature, unspecified
Lesser curvature, not classifiable to 151.1-151.4

151.6 Greater curvature, unspecified
Greater curvature, not classifiable to 151.0-151.4

151.8 Other specified sites of stomach
Anterior wall, not classifiable to 151.0-151.4
Posterior wall, not classifiable to 151.0-151.4
Malignant neoplasm of contiguous or overlapping
sites of stomach whose point of origin cannot
be determined

151.9 Stomach, unspecified
Carcinoma ventriculi   Gastric cancer

✓4th 152 Malignant neoplasm of small intestine, including duodenum

152.0 Duodenum

152.1 Jejunum

152.2 Ileum
> EXCLUDES   *ileocecal valve (153.4)*

152.3 Meckel's diverticulum

152.8 Other specified sites of small intestine
Duodenojejunal junction
Malignant neoplasm of contiguous or overlapping
sites of small intestine whose point of origin
cannot be determined

152.9 Small intestine, unspecified

✓4th 153 Malignant neoplasm of colon

153.0 Hepatic flexure

153.1 Transverse colon

153.2 Descending colon
Left colon

153.3 Sigmoid colon
Sigmoid (flexure)
> EXCLUDES   *rectosigmoid junction (154.0)*

153.4 Cecum
Ileocecal valve

153.5 Appendix

153.6 Ascending colon
Right colon

153.7 Splenic flexure

153.8 Other specified sites of large intestine
Malignant neoplasm of contiguous or overlapping
sites of colon whose point of origin cannot be
determined
> EXCLUDES   *ileocecal valve (153.4)*
>   *rectosigmoid junction (154.0)*

153.9 Colon, unspecified
Large intestine NOS

✓4th 154 Malignant neoplasm of rectum, rectosigmoid junction, and anus

154.0 Rectosigmoid junction
Colon with rectum
Rectosigmoid (colon)

154.1 Rectum
Rectal ampulla

154.2 Anal canal
Anal sphincter
> EXCLUDES   *skin of anus (172.5, 173.5)*
> **AHA:** 1Q, '01, 8

Colon

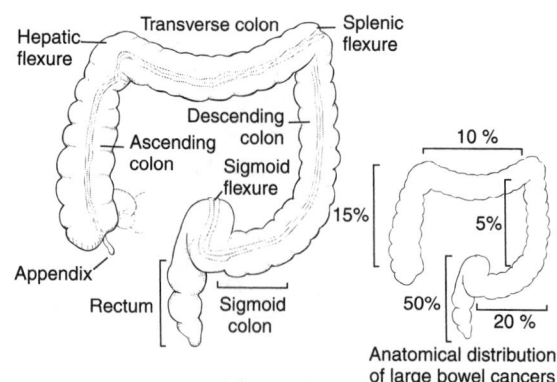

Anatomical distribution
of large bowel cancers

154.3 Anus, unspecified
> EXCLUDES   *anus:*
>   *margin (172.5, 173.5)*
>   *skin (172.5, 173.5)*
>   *perianal skin (172.5, 173.5)*

154.8 Other
Anorectum
Cloacogenic zone
Malignant neoplasm of contiguous or overlapping
sites of rectum, rectosigmoid junction, and
anus whose point of origin cannot be
determined

✓4th 155 Malignant neoplasm of liver and intrahepatic bile ducts

155.0 Liver, primary
Carcinoma:
   liver, specified as primary
   hepatocellular
   liver cell
Hepatoblastoma

155.1 Intrahepatic bile ducts
Canaliculi biliferi   Intrahepatic:
Interlobular: biliary passages
   bile ducts   canaliculi
   biliary canals   gall duct
> EXCLUDES   *hepatic duct (156.1)*

155.2 Liver, not specified as primary or secondary

✓4th 156 Malignant neoplasm of gallbladder and extrahepatic bile ducts

156.0 Gallbladder

156.1 Extrahepatic bile ducts
Biliary duct or passage NOS
Common bile duct
Cystic duct
Hepatic duct
Sphincter of Oddi

156.2 Ampulla of Vater
> **DEF:** Malignant neoplasm in the area of dilation at the juncture of
> the common bile and pancreatic ducts near the opening into the
> lumen of the duodenum.

156.8 Other specified sites of gallbladder and extrahepatic bile ducts
Malignant neoplasm of contiguous or overlapping
sites of gallbladder and extrahepatic bile ducts
whose point of origin cannot be determined

156.9 Biliary tract, part unspecified
Malignant neoplasm involving both intrahepatic and
extrahepatic bile ducts

✓4th 157 Malignant neoplasm of pancreas

157.0 Head of pancreas
> **AHA:** 4Q, '00, 40

157.1 Body of pancreas

157.2 Tail of pancreas

N Newborn Age: 0   P Pediatric Age: 0-17   M Maternity Age: 12-55   A Adult Age: 15-124   Manifestation Code   ►◄ Revised Text   ● New Code   ▲ Revised Code Title

157.3   **Pancreatic duct**
Duct of:
Santorini
Wirsung

157.4   **Islets of Langerhans**
Islets of Langerhans, any part of pancreas
Use additional code to identify any functional
activity

DEF: Malignant neoplasm within the structures of the pancreas that
produce insulin, somatostatin and glucagon.

157.8   **Other specified sites of pancreas**
Ectopic pancreatic tissue
Malignant neoplasm of contiguous or overlapping
sites of pancreas whose point of origin cannot
be determined

157.9   **Pancreas, part unspecified**
AHA: 4Q, '89, 11

√4ᵗʰ **158 Malignant neoplasm of retroperitoneum and peritoneum**

158.0   **Retroperitoneum**
Periadrenal tissue   Perirenal tissue
Perinephric tissue   Retrocecal tissue

158.8   **Specified parts of peritoneum**
Cul-de-sac (of Douglas)
Mesentery
Mesocolon
Omentum
Peritoneum:
parietal
pelvic
Rectouterine pouch
Malignant neoplasm of contiguous or overlapping
sites of retroperitoneum and peritoneum whose
point of origin cannot be determined

158.9   **Peritoneum, unspecified**

√4ᵗʰ **159 Malignant neoplasm of other and ill-defined sites within the
digestive organs and peritoneum**

159.0   **Intestinal tract, part unspecified**
Intestine NOS

159.1   **Spleen, not elsewhere classified**
Angiosarcoma ⎫
Fibrosarcoma ⎬ of spleen

> EXCLUDES   *Hodgkin's disease (201.0-201.9)*
> *lymphosarcoma (200.1)*
> *reticulosarcoma (200.0)*

159.8   **Other sites of digestive system and intra-abdominal
organs**
Malignant neoplasm of digestive organs and
peritoneum whose point of origin cannot be
assigned to any one of the categories 150-158

> EXCLUDES   *anus and rectum (154.8)*
> *cardio-esophageal junction (151.0)*
> *colon and rectum (154.0)*

Retroperitoneum and Peritoneum

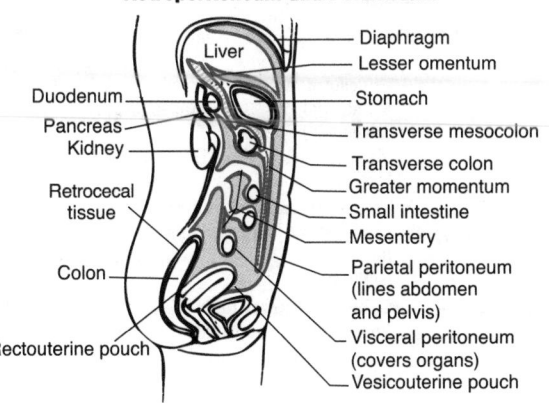

159.9   **Ill-defined**
Alimentary canal or tract NOS
Gastrointestinal tract NOS

> EXCLUDES   *abdominal NOS (195.2)*
> *intra-abdominal NOS (195.2)*

MALIGNANT NEOPLASM OF RESPIRATORY AND INTRATHORACIC ORGANS (160-165)

> EXCLUDES   *carcinoma in situ (231.0-231.9)*

√4ᵗʰ **160 Malignant neoplasm of nasal cavities, middle ear, and
accessory sinuses**

160.0   **Nasal cavities**
Cartilage of nose   Septum of nose
Conchae, nasal   Vestibule of nose
Internal nose

> EXCLUDES   *nasal bone (170.0)*
> *nose NOS (195.0)*
> *olfactory bulb (192.0)*
> *posterior margin of septum and
> choanae (147.3)*
> *skin of nose (172.3, 173.3)*
> *turbinates (170.0)*

160.1   **Auditory tube, middle ear, and mastoid air cells**
Antrum tympanicum   Tympanic cavity
Eustachian tube

> EXCLUDES   *auditory canal (external) (172.2, 173.2)*
> *bone of ear (meatus) (170.0)*
> *cartilage of ear (171.0)*
> *ear (external) (skin) (172.2, 173.2)*

160.2   **Maxillary sinus**
Antrum (Highmore) (maxillary)

160.3   **Ethmoidal sinus**

160.4   **Frontal sinus**

160.5   **Sphenoidal sinus**

160.8   **Other**
Malignant neoplasm of contiguous or overlapping
sites of nasal cavities, middle ear, and
accessory sinuses whose point of origin cannot
be determined

160.9   **Accessory sinus, unspecified**

√4ᵗʰ **161 Malignant neoplasm of larynx**

161.0   **Glottis**
Intrinsic larynx
Laryngeal commissure (anterior) (posterior)
True vocal cord
Vocal cord NOS

161.1   **Supraglottis**
Aryepiglottic fold or interarytenoid fold, laryngeal
aspect
Epiglottis (suprahyoid portion) NOS
Extrinsic larynx
False vocal cords
Posterior (laryngeal) surface of epiglottis
Ventricular bands

> EXCLUDES   *anterior aspect of epiglottis (146.4)*
> *aryepiglottic fold or interarytenoid fold:*
> *NOS (148.2)*
> *hypopharyngeal aspect (148.2)*
> *marginal zone (148.2)*

161.2   **Subglottis**

161.3   **Laryngeal cartilages**
Cartilage: Cartilage:
arytenoid   cuneiform
cricoid   thyroid

161.8   **Other specified sites of larynx**
Malignant neoplasm of contiguous or overlapping
sites of larynx whose point of origin cannot be
determined

161.9   **Larynx, unspecified**

√4ᵗʰ √5ᵗʰ Additional Digit Required   **RUG III Special Care Dx**   **RUG III Clinically Complex Dx**   Hospice Non-cancer Dx   **CD PDx** Clinical Dimension PDx   **CD SDx** Clinical Dimension SDx

2006 ICD•9•CM   **Volume 1 — 29**

Neoplasms

162–170.7

√4ᵗʰ **162 Malignant neoplasm of trachea, bronchus, and lung**

162.0   Trachea

Cartilage } of trachea
Mucosa

162.2   Main bronchus
Carina
Hilus of lung

162.3   Upper lobe, bronchus or lung
AHA: 1Q, '04, 4

162.4   Middle lobe, bronchus or lung

162.5   Lower lobe, bronchus or lung

162.8   Other parts of bronchus or lung
Malignant neoplasm of contiguous or overlapping
sites of bronchus or lung whose point of origin
cannot be determined

162.9   Bronchus and lung, unspecified
AHA: 2Q, '97, 3; 4Q, '96, 48

√4ᵗʰ **163 Malignant neoplasm of pleura**

163.0   Parietal pleura

163.1   Visceral pleura

163.8   Other specified sites of pleura
Malignant neoplasm of contiguous or overlapping
sites of pleura whose point of origin cannot be
determined

163.9   Pleura, unspecified

√4ᵗʰ **164 Malignant neoplasm of thymus, heart, and mediastinum**

164.0   Thymus

164.1   Heart
Endocardium   Myocardium
Epicardium   Pericardium
EXCLUDES   *great vessels (171.4)*

164.2   Anterior mediastinum

164.3   Posterior mediastinum

164.8   Other
Malignant neoplasm of contiguous or overlapping
sites of thymus, heart, and mediastinum
whose point of origin cannot be determined

164.9   Mediastinum, part unspecified

√4ᵗʰ **165 Malignant neoplasm of other and ill-defined sites within the respiratory system and intrathoracic organs**

165.0   Upper respiratory tract, part unspecified

165.8   Other
Malignant neoplasm of respiratory and intrathoracic
organs whose point of origin cannot be
assigned to any one of the categories 160-164

165.9   Ill-defined sites within the respiratory system
Respiratory tract NOS
EXCLUDES   *intrathoracic NOS (195.1)*
           thoracic NOS (195.1)

MALIGNANT NEOPLASM OF BONE, CONNECTIVE TISSUE, SKIN, AND BREAST (170-176)

EXCLUDES   *carcinoma in situ: carcinoma in situ:*
           breast (233.0)   skin (232.0-232.9)

√4ᵗʰ **170 Malignant neoplasm of bone and articular cartilage**
INCLUDES   cartilage (articular) (joint)
           periosteum
EXCLUDES   *bone marrow NOS (202.9)*
           cartilage:
             ear (171.0)
             eyelid (171.0)
             larynx (161.3)
             nose (160.0)
           synovia (171.0-171.9)

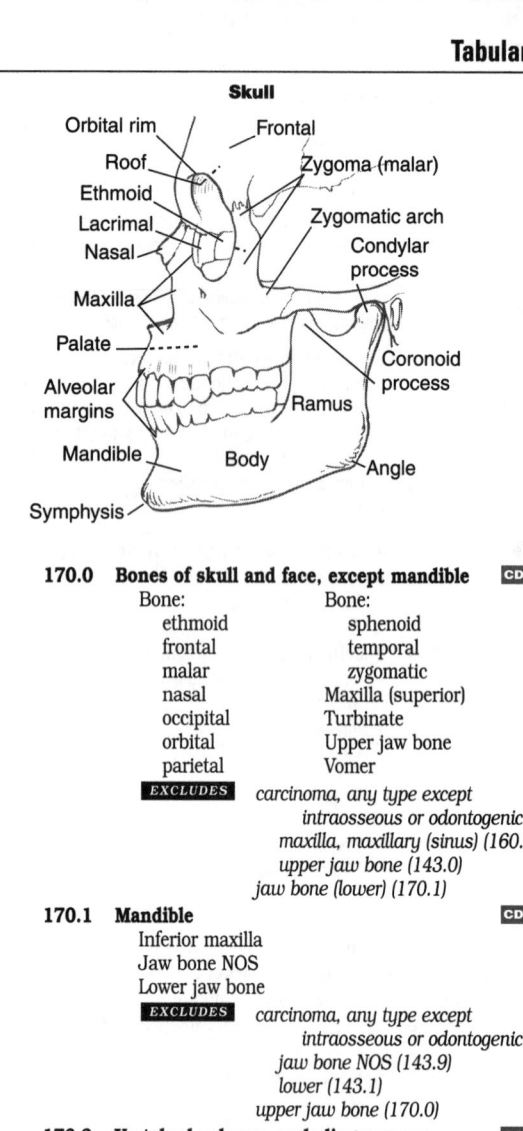

Skull

Orbital rim · Frontal · Roof · Zygoma (malar) · Ethmoid · Zygomatic arch · Lacrimal · Condylar process · Nasal · Maxilla · Palate · Coronoid process · Alveolar margins · Ramus · Mandible · Body · Angle · Symphysis

170.0   Bones of skull and face, except mandible   `CD PDx`

Bone: Bone:
 ethmoid   sphenoid
 frontal   temporal
 malar   zygomatic
 nasal   Maxilla (superior)
 occipital   Turbinate
 orbital   Upper jaw bone
 parietal   Vomer
EXCLUDES   *carcinoma, any type except*
             intraosseous or odontogenic:
             maxilla, maxillary (sinus) (160.2)
             upper jaw bone (143.0)
             jaw bone (lower) (170.1)

170.1   Mandible   `CD PDx`
Inferior maxilla
Jaw bone NOS
Lower jaw bone
EXCLUDES   *carcinoma, any type except*
             intraosseous or odontogenic:
             jaw bone NOS (143.9)
             lower (143.1)
             upper jaw bone (170.0)

170.2   Vertebral column, excluding sacrum and coccyx   `CD PDx`
Spinal column   Vertebra
Spine
EXCLUDES   *sacrum and coccyx (170.6)*

170.3   Ribs, sternum, and clavicle   `CD PDx`
Costal cartilage
Costovertebral joint
Xiphoid process

170.4   Scapula and long bones of upper limb   `CD PDx`
Acromion   Radius
Bones NOS of upper limb   Ulna
Humerus
AHA: 2Q, '99, 9

170.5   Short bones of upper limb   `CD PDx`
Carpal   Scaphoid (of hand)
Cuneiform, wrist   Semilunar or lunate
Metacarpal   Trapezium
Navicular, of hand Trapezoid
Phalanges of hand   Unciform
Pisiform

170.6   Pelvic bones, sacrum, and coccyx   `CD PDx`
Coccygeal vertebra   Pubic bone
Ilium   Sacral vertebra
Ischium

170.7   Long bones of lower limb   `CD PDx`
Bones NOS of lower limb
Femur
Fibula
Tibia

Ⓝ Newborn Age: 0   Ⓟ Pediatric Age: 0-17   Ⓜ Maternity Age: 12-55   Ⓐ Adult Age: 15-124   `Manifestation Code`   ▶◀ Revised Text   ● New Code   ▲ Revised Code Title

170.8 **Short bones of lower limb** `CD PDx`
　　Astragalus [talus]　　Navicular (of ankle)
　　Calcaneus　　Patella
　　Cuboid　　Phalanges of foot
　　Cuneiform, ankle　　Tarsal
　　Metatarsal

170.9 **Bone and articular cartilage,** `CD PDx`
　　site unspecified

✓4th **171 Malignant neoplasm of connective and other soft tissue**

　　INCLUDES　blood vessel　　muscle
　　　　　　bursa　　peripheral, sympathetic,
　　　　　　fascia　　　and parasympathetic
　　　　　　fat　　　nerves and ganglia
　　　　　　ligament, except　synovia
　　　　　　　uterine　　tendon (sheath)

　　EXCLUDES　*cartilage (of):*
　　　　　　articular (170.0-170.9)
　　　　　　larynx (161.3)
　　　　　　nose (160.0)
　　　　　connective tissue:
　　　　　　breast (174.0-175.9)
　　　　　　internal organs—code to malignant neoplasm
　　　　　　　of the site [e.g., leiomyosarcoma of
　　　　　　　stomach, 151.9]
　　　　　heart (164.1)
　　　　　uterine ligament (183.4)

171.0 **Head, face, and neck** `CD PDx`
　　Cartilage of:　　Cartilage of:
　　　ear　　　eyelid
　　AHA: 2Q, '99, 6

171.2 **Upper limb, including shoulder** `CD PDx`
　　Arm　　Forearm
　　Finger　　Hand

171.3 **Lower limb, including hip** `CD PDx`
　　Foot　　Thigh
　　Leg　　Toe
　　Popliteal space

171.4 **Thorax** `CD PDx`
　　Axilla　　　Great vessels
　　Diaphragm
　　　EXCLUDES　*heart (164.1)*
　　　　　　mediastinum (164.2-164.9)
　　　　　　thymus (164.0)

171.5 **Abdomen** `CD PDx`
　　Abdominal wall　　Hypochondrium
　　　EXCLUDES　*peritoneum (158.8)*
　　　　　　retroperitoneum (158.0)

171.6 **Pelvis** `CD PDx`
　　Buttock　　Inguinal region
　　Groin　　Perineum
　　　EXCLUDES　*pelvic peritoneum (158.8)*
　　　　　　retroperitoneum (158.0)
　　　　　　uterine ligament, any (183.3-183.5)

171.7 **Trunk, unspecified** `CD PDx`
　　Back NOS
　　Flank NOS

171.8 **Other specified sites of connective and** `CD PDx`
　　other soft tissue
　　Malignant neoplasm of contiguous or overlapping
　　　sites of connective tissue whose point of origin
　　　cannot be determined

171.9 **Connective and other soft tissue,** `CD PDx`
　　site unspecified

✓4th **172 Malignant melanoma of skin**
　　INCLUDES　melanocarcinoma
　　　　　　melanoma (skin) NOS
　　EXCLUDES　*skin of genital organs (184.0-184.9, 187.1-*
　　　　　　187.9)
　　　　　sites other than skin—code to malignant
　　　　　　neoplasm of the site

　　DEF: Malignant neoplasm of melanocytes; most common in skin, may involve
　　oral cavity, esophagus, anal canal, vagina, leptomeninges, or conjunctiva.

172.0 **Lip**
　　　EXCLUDES　*vermilion border of lip (140.0-140.1,*
　　　　　　140.9)

172.1 **Eyelid, including canthus**

172.2 **Ear and external auditory canal**
　　Auricle (ear)
　　Auricular canal, external
　　External [acoustic] meatus
　　Pinna

172.3 **Other and unspecified parts of face**
　　Cheek (external)　　Forehead
　　Chin　　Nose, external
　　Eyebrow　　Temple

172.4 **Scalp and neck**

172.5 **Trunk, except scrotum**
　　Axilla　　Perianal skin
　　Breast　　Perineum
　　Buttock　　Umbilicus
　　Groin
　　　EXCLUDES　*anal canal (154.2)*
　　　　　　anus NOS (154.3)
　　　　　　scrotum (187.7)

172.6 **Upper limb, including shoulder**
　　Arm　　Forearm
　　Finger　　Hand

172.7 **Lower limb, including hip**
　　Ankle　　Leg
　　Foot　　Popliteal area
　　Heel　　Thigh
　　Knee　　Toe

172.8 **Other specified sites of skin**
　　Malignant melanoma of contiguous or overlapping
　　　sites of skin whose point of origin cannot be
　　　determined

172.9 **Melanoma of skin, site unspecified**

✓4th **173 Other malignant neoplasm of skin**
　　INCLUDES　malignant neoplasm of:
　　　　　　sebaceous glands
　　　　　　sudoriferous, sudoriparous glands
　　　　　　sweat glands
　　EXCLUDES　*Kaposi's sarcoma (176.0-176.9)*
　　　　　malignant melanoma of skin (172.0-172.9)
　　　　　skin of genital organs (184.0-184.9,
　　　　　　187.1-187.9)

　　AHA: 1Q, '00, 18; 2Q, '96, 12

173.0 **Skin of lip**
　　　EXCLUDES　*vermilion border of lip (140.0-140.1,*
　　　　　　140.9)

173.1 **Eyelid, including canthus**
　　　EXCLUDES　*cartilage of eyelid (171.0)*

173.2 **Skin of ear and external auditory canal**
　　Auricle (ear)　　　External meatus
　　Auricular canal, external　　Pinna
　　　EXCLUDES　*cartilage of ear (171.0)*

173.3 **Skin of other and unspecified parts of face**
　　Cheek, external　　Forehead
　　Chin　　Nose, external
　　Eyebrow　　Temple
　　AHA: 1Q, '00, 3

173.4 **Scalp and skin of neck**

173.5 **Skin of trunk, except scrotum**
　　Axillary fold　　Skin of:
　　Perianal skin　　　buttock
　　Skin of:　　　chest wall
　　　abdominal wall　　groin
　　　anus　　　perineum
　　　back　　Umbilicus
　　　breast
　　　EXCLUDES　*anal canal (154.2)*
　　　　　　anus NOS (154.3)
　　　　　　skin of scrotum (187.7)

　　AHA: 1Q, '01, 8

✓4th
✓5th Additional Digit Required　　RUG III Special Care Dx　　RUG III Clinically Complex Dx　　Hospice Non-cancer Dx　　`CD PDx` Clinical Dimension PDx　　`CD SDx` Clinical Dimension SDx

2006 ICD•9•CM　　　　　　　　　　　　　　　　　　　　　　　　　　　　　　　　　Volume 1 — 31

Neoplasms

173.6–184.1

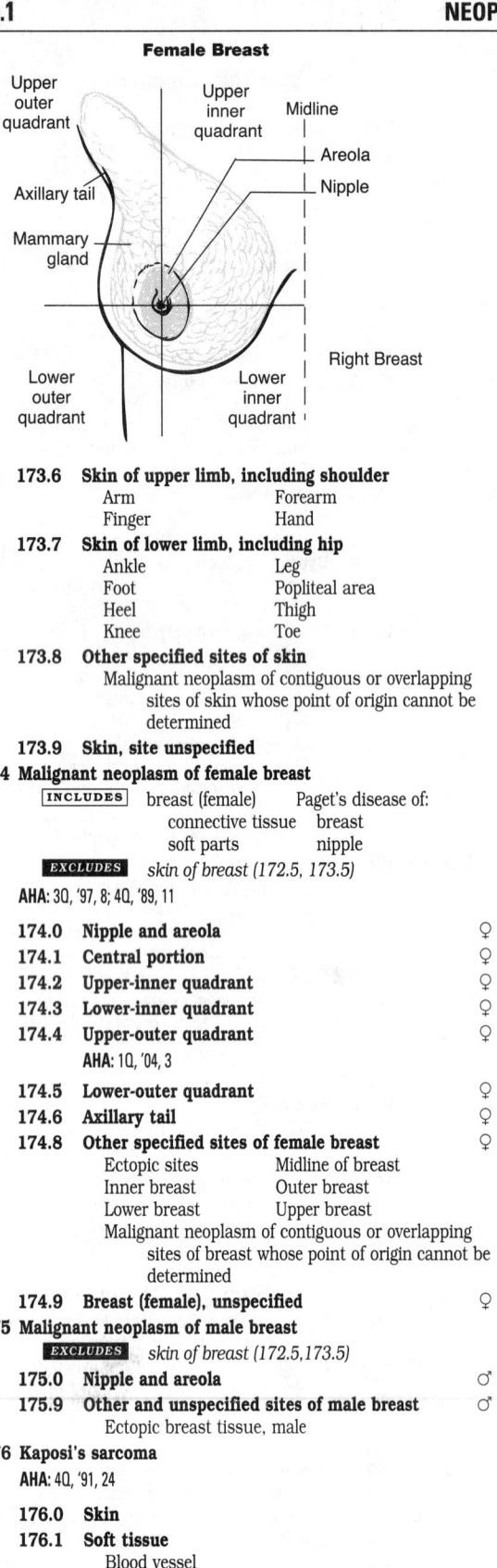

Female Breast

Upper outer quadrant
Upper inner quadrant
Midline
Areola
Nipple
Axillary tail
Mammary gland
Right Breast
Lower outer quadrant
Lower inner quadrant

173.6 Skin of upper limb, including shoulder
Arm   Forearm
Finger   Hand

173.7 Skin of lower limb, including hip
Ankle   Leg
Foot   Popliteal area
Heel   Thigh
Knee   Toe

173.8 Other specified sites of skin
Malignant neoplasm of contiguous or overlapping sites of skin whose point of origin cannot be determined

173.9 Skin, site unspecified

✓4ᵗʰ **174 Malignant neoplasm of female breast**
INCLUDES   breast (female)   Paget's disease of:
connective tissue   breast
soft parts   nipple
EXCLUDES   skin of breast (172.5, 173.5)
AHA: 3Q, '97, 8; 4Q, '89, 11

174.0 Nipple and areola   ♀
174.1 Central portion   ♀
174.2 Upper-inner quadrant   ♀
174.3 Lower-inner quadrant   ♀
174.4 Upper-outer quadrant   ♀
AHA: 1Q, '04, 3
174.5 Lower-outer quadrant   ♀
174.6 Axillary tail   ♀
174.8 Other specified sites of female breast   ♀
Ectopic sites   Midline of breast
Inner breast   Outer breast
Lower breast   Upper breast
Malignant neoplasm of contiguous or overlapping sites of breast whose point of origin cannot be determined
174.9 Breast (female), unspecified   ♀

✓4ᵗʰ **175 Malignant neoplasm of male breast**
EXCLUDES   skin of breast (172.5,173.5)
175.0 Nipple and areola   ♂
175.9 Other and unspecified sites of male breast ♂
Ectopic breast tissue, male

✓4ᵗʰ **176 Kaposi's sarcoma**
AHA: 4Q, '91, 24
176.0 Skin
176.1 Soft tissue
Blood vessel
Connective tissue
Fascia
Ligament
Lymphatic(s) NEC
Muscle
EXCLUDES   lymph glands and nodes (176.5)
176.2 Palate

176.3 Gastrointestinal sites
176.4 Lung
176.5 Lymph nodes
176.8 Other specified sites
Oral cavity NEC
176.9 Unspecified
Viscera NOS

MALIGNANT NEOPLASM OF GENITOURINARY ORGANS (179-189)
EXCLUDES   carcinoma in situ (233.1-233.9)

179 Malignant neoplasm of uterus, part unspecified   ♀
✓4ᵗʰ **180 Malignant neoplasm of cervix uteri**
INCLUDES   invasive malignancy [carcinoma]
EXCLUDES   carcinoma in situ (233.1)
180.0 Endocervix   ♀
Cervical canal NOS   Endocervical gland
Endocervical canal
180.1 Exocervix   ♀
180.8 Other specified sites of cervix   ♀
Cervical stump
Squamocolumnar junction of cervix
Malignant neoplasm of contiguous or overlapping sites of cervix uteri whose point of origin cannot be determined
180.9 Cervix uteri, unspecified   ♀
181 Malignant neoplasm of placenta   ♀
Choriocarcinoma NOS
Chorioepithelioma NOS
EXCLUDES   chorioadenoma (destruens) (236.1)
hydatidiform mole (630)
malignant (236.1)
invasive mole (236.1)
male choriocarcinoma NOS (186.0-186.9)

✓4ᵗʰ **182 Malignant neoplasm of body of uterus**
EXCLUDES   carcinoma in situ (233.2)
182.0 Corpus uteri, except isthmus   ♀
Cornu   Fundus
Endometrium   Myometrium
182.1 Isthmus   ♀
Lower uterine segment
182.8 Other specified sites of body of uterus   ♀
Malignant neoplasm of contiguous or overlapping sites of body of uterus whose point of origin cannot be determined
EXCLUDES   uterus NOS (179)

✓4ᵗʰ **183 Malignant neoplasm of ovary and other uterine adnexa**
EXCLUDES   Douglas' cul-de-sac (158.8)
183.0 Ovary   ♀
Use additional code to identify any functional activity
183.2 Fallopian tube   ♀
Oviduct   Uterine tube
183.3 Broad ligament   ♀
Mesovarium   Parovarian region
183.4 Parametrium   ♀
Uterine ligament NOS Uterosacral ligament
183.5 Round ligament   ♀
AHA: 3Q, '99, 5
183.8 Other specified sites of uterine adnexa   ♀
Tubo-ovarian
Utero-ovarian
Malignant neoplasm of contiguous or overlapping sites of ovary and other uterine adnexa whose point of origin cannot be determined
183.9 Uterine adnexa, unspecified   ♀

✓4ᵗʰ **184 Malignant neoplasm of other and unspecified female genital organs**
EXCLUDES   carcinoma in situ (233.3)
184.0 Vagina   ♀
Gartner's duct   Vaginal vault
184.1 Labia majora   ♀
Greater vestibular [Bartholin's] gland

N Newborn Age: 0   P Pediatric Age: 0-17   M Maternity Age: 12-55   A Adult Age: 15-124   Manifestation Code   ◄► Revised Text   ● New Code   ▲ Revised Code Title

| 184.2 | Labia minora | ♀ |

184.2 **Labia minora** ♀
184.3 **Clitoris** ♀
184.4 **Vulva, unspecified** ♀
   External female genitalia NOS
   Pudendum
184.8 **Other specified sites of female genital organs** ♀
   Malignant neoplasm of contiguous or overlapping
      sites of female genital organs whose point of
      origin cannot be determined
184.9 **Female genital organ, site unspecified** ♀
   Female genitourinary tract NOS

185 **Malignant neoplasm of prostate** ♂
   EXCLUDES *seminal vesicles (187.8)*
   AHA: 3Q, '03, 13; 3Q, '99, 5; 3Q, '92, 7

✓4ᵗʰ 186 **Malignant neoplasm of testis**
   Use additional code to identify any functional activity
186.0 **Undescended testis** ♂
   Ectopic testis   Retained testis
186.9 **Other and unspecified testis** ♂
   Testis: Testis:
      NOS   scrotal
      descended

✓4ᵗʰ 187 **Malignant neoplasm of penis and other male genital organs**
187.1 **Prepuce** ♂
   Foreskin
187.2 **Glans penis** ♂
187.3 **Body of penis** ♂
   Corpus cavernosum
187.4 **Penis, part unspecified** ♂
   Skin of penis NOS
187.5 **Epididymis** ♂
187.6 **Spermatic cord** ♂
   Vas deferens
187.7 **Scrotum** ♂
   Skin of scrotum
187.8 **Other specified sites of male genital organs** ♂
   Seminal vesicle
   Tunica vaginalis
   Malignant neoplasm of contiguous or overlapping
      sites of penis and other male genital organs
      whose point of origin cannot be determined
187.9 **Male genital organ, site unspecified** ♂
   Male genital organ or tract NOS

✓4ᵗʰ 188 **Malignant neoplasm of bladder**
   EXCLUDES *carcinoma in situ (233.7)*
188.0 **Trigone of urinary bladder**
188.1 **Dome of urinary bladder**
188.2 **Lateral wall of urinary bladder**
188.3 **Anterior wall of urinary bladder**
188.4 **Posterior wall of urinary bladder**
188.5 **Bladder neck**
   Internal urethral orifice
188.6 **Ureteric orifice**
188.7 **Urachus**
188.8 **Other specified sites of bladder**
   Malignant neoplasm of contiguous or overlapping
      sites of bladder whose point of origin cannot
      be determined
188.9 **Bladder, part unspecified**
   Bladder wall NOS
   AHA: 1Q, '00, 5

✓4ᵗʰ 189 **Malignant neoplasm of kidney and other and unspecified urinary organs**
189.0 **Kidney, except pelvis**
   Kidney NOS   Kidney parenchyma
   AHA: ▶2Q, '04, 4◀
189.1 **Renal pelvis**
   Renal calyces   Ureteropelvic junction

189.2 **Ureter**
   EXCLUDES *ureteric orifice of bladder (188.6)*
189.3 **Urethra**
   EXCLUDES *urethral orifice of bladder (188.5)*
189.4 **Paraurethral glands**
189.8 **Other specified sites of urinary organs**
   Malignant neoplasm of contiguous or overlapping
      sites of kidney and other urinary organs whose
      point of origin cannot be determined
189.9 **Urinary organ, site unspecified**
   Urinary system NOS

MALIGNANT NEOPLASM OF OTHER AND UNSPECIFIED SITES (190-199)
   EXCLUDES *carcinoma in situ (234.0-234.9)*

✓4ᵗʰ 190 **Malignant neoplasm of eye**
   EXCLUDES *carcinoma in situ (234.0)*
         eyelid (skin) (172.1, 173.1)
            cartilage (171.0)
         optic nerve (192.0)
         orbital bone (170.0)
190.0 **Eyeball, except conjunctiva, cornea, retina, and choroid**
   Ciliary body   Sclera
   Crystalline lens   Uveal tract
   Iris
190.1 **Orbit**
   Connective tissue of orbit
   Extraocular muscle
   Retrobulbar
   EXCLUDES *bone of orbit (170.0)*
190.2 **Lacrimal gland**
190.3 **Conjunctiva**
190.4 **Cornea**
190.5 **Retina**
190.6 **Choroid**
190.7 **Lacrimal duct**
   Lacrimal sac   Nasolacrimal duct
190.8 **Other specified sites of eye**
   Malignant neoplasm of contiguous or overlapping
      sites of eye whose point of origin cannot be
      determined
190.9 **Eye, part unspecified**

✓4ᵗʰ 191 **Malignant neoplasm of brain**
   EXCLUDES *cranial nerves (192.0)*
         retrobulbar area (190.1)
191.0 **Cerebrum, except lobes and ventricles**   `CD PDx`
   Basal ganglia   Globus pallidus
   Cerebral cortex   Hypothalamus
   Corpus striatum   Thalamus
191.1 **Frontal lobe**   `CD PDx`
191.2 **Temporal lobe**   `CD PDx`
   Hippocampus   Uncus
191.3 **Parietal lobe**   `CD PDx`

Brain and Meninges

Fourth ventricle — Cerebrum — Corpus callosum — Thalamus — Hypothalamus — Hypophysis — Cerebellum — Pons — Medulla oblongata

Midsagittal Section (between hemispheres)

✓4ᵗʰ ✓5ᵗʰ Additional Digit Required   RUG III Special Care Dx   RUG III Clinically Complex Dx   Hospice Non-cancer Dx   `CD PDx` Clinical Dimension PDx   `CD SDx` Clinical Dimension SDx

2006 ICD•9•CM   **February 2005 • Volume 1 — 33**

Neoplasms

191.4–196.3

191.4 Occipital lobe `CD PDx`

191.5 Ventricles `CD PDx`
Choroid plexus   Floor of ventricle

191.6 Cerebellum NOS `CD PDx`
Cerebellopontine angle

191.7 Brain stem `CD PDx`
Cerebral peduncle   Midbrain
Medulla oblongata   Pons

191.8 Other parts of brain `CD PDx`
Corpus callosum
Tapetum
Malignant neoplasm of contiguous or overlapping
    sites of brain whose point of origin cannot be
    determined

191.9 Brain, unspecified `CD PDx`
Cranial fossa NOS

✓4th **192 Malignant neoplasm of other and unspecified parts of
nervous system**
> EXCLUDES *peripheral, sympathetic, and parasympathetic
> nerves and ganglia (171.0-171.9)*

192.0 Cranial nerves `CD PDx`
Olfactory bulb

192.1 Cerebral meninges `CD PDx`
Dura (mater)   Meninges NOS
Falx (cerebelli) (cerebri)   Tentorium

192.2 Spinal cord `CD PDx`
Cauda equina

192.3 Spinal meninges `CD PDx`

192.8 Other specified sites of nervous system `CD PDx`
Malignant neoplasm of contiguous or overlapping
    sites of other parts of nervous system whose
    point of origin cannot be determined

192.9 Nervous system, part unspecified `CD PDx`
Nervous system (central) NOS
> EXCLUDES *meninges NOS (192.1)*

193 Malignant neoplasm of thyroid gland
Sipple's syndrome
Thyroglossal duct
Use additional code to identify any functional activity

✓4th **194 Malignant neoplasm of other endocrine glands and related
structures**
Use additional code to identify any functional activity
> EXCLUDES *islets of Langerhans (157.4)*
> *ovary (183.0)*
> *testis (186.0-186.9)*
> *thymus (164.0)*

194.0 Adrenal gland
Adrenal cortex   Suprarenal gland
Adrenal medulla

194.1 Parathyroid gland

194.3 Pituitary gland and craniopharyngeal duct
Craniobuccal pouch   Rathke's pouch
Hypophysis   Sella turcica
AHA: J-A, '85, 9

194.4 Pineal gland

194.5 Carotid body

194.6 Aortic body and other paraganglia
Coccygeal body   Para-aortic body
Glomus jugulare

194.8 Other
Pluriglandular involvement NOS
Note: If the sites of multiple involvements are known,
    they should be coded separately.

194.9 Endocrine gland, site unspecified

✓4th **195 Malignant neoplasm of other and ill-defined sites**
> INCLUDES   malignant neoplasms of contiguous sites, not
> elsewhere classified, whose point of
> origin cannot be determined
> EXCLUDES *malignant neoplasm:*
> *lymphatic and hematopoietic tissue (200.0-
> 208.9)*
> *secondary sites (196.0-198.8)*
> *unspecified site (199.0-199.1)*

195.0 Head, face, and neck
Cheek NOS   Nose NOS
Jaw NOS   Supraclavicular region NOS
AHA: 4Q, '03, 107

195.1 Thorax
Axilla   Intrathoracic NOS
Chest (wall) NOS

195.2 Abdomen
Intra-abdominal NOS
AHA: 2Q, '97, 3

195.3 Pelvis
Groin
Inguinal region NOS
Presacral region
Sacrococcygeal region
Sites overlapping systems within pelvis, as:
    rectovaginal (septum)
    rectovesical (septum)

195.4 Upper limb

195.5 Lower limb

195.8 Other specified sites
Back NOS   Trunk NOS
Flank NOS

✓4th **196 Secondary and unspecified malignant neoplasm of lymph
nodes**
> EXCLUDES *any malignant neoplasm of lymph nodes,*
> *specified as primary (200.0-202.9)*
> *Hodgkin's disease (201.0-201.9)*
> *lymphosarcoma (200.1)*
> *other forms of lymphoma (202.0-202.9)*
> *reticulosarcoma (200.0)*

AHA: 2Q, '92, 3; M-J, '85, 3

196.0 Lymph nodes of head, face, and neck
Cervical   Scalene
Cervicofacial   Supraclavicular

196.1 Intrathoracic lymph nodes
Bronchopulmonary   Mediastinal
Intercostal   Tracheobronchial

196.2 Intra-abdominal lymph nodes
Intestinal   Retroperitoneal
Mesenteric
AHA: 4Q, '03, 111

196.3 Lymph nodes of axilla and upper limb
Brachial   Infraclavicular
Epitrochlear   Pectoral

Lymph Nodes

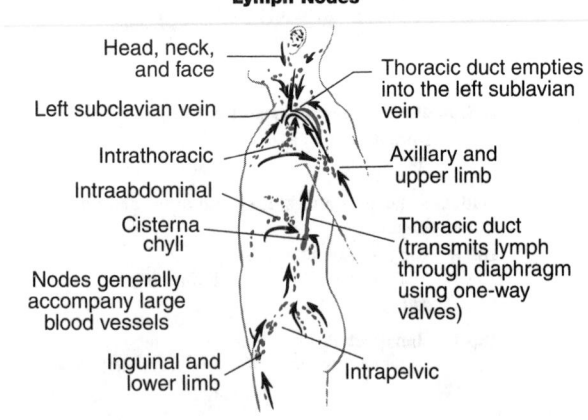

Head, neck, and face
Left subclavian vein
Intrathoracic
Intraabdominal
Cisterna chyli
Nodes generally accompany large blood vessels
Inguinal and lower limb
Thoracic duct empties into the left sublavian vein
Axillary and upper limb
Thoracic duct (transmits lymph through diaphragm using one-way valves)
Intrapelvic

 Newborn Age: 0   P Pediatric Age: 0-17   M Maternity Age: 12-55   A Adult Age: 15-124   Manifestation Code   ►◄ Revised Text   ● New Code   ▲ Revised Code Title

34 — Volume 1   *2006 ICD•9•CM*

196.5 Lymph nodes of inguinal region and lower limb
Femoral   Popliteal
Groin   Tibial

196.6 Intrapelvic lymph nodes
Hypogastric   Obturator
Iliac   Parametrial

196.8 Lymph nodes of multiple sites

196.9 Site unspecified
Lymph nodes NOS

✓4th **197 Secondary malignant neoplasm of respiratory and digestive systems**
EXCLUDES *lymph node metastasis (196.0-196.9)*
AHA: M-J, '85, 3

197.0 Lung
Bronchus
AHA: 2Q, '99, 9

197.1 Mediastinum

197.2 Pleura
AHA: 4Q, '03, 110; 4Q, '89, 11

197.3 Other respiratory organs
Trachea

197.4 Small intestine, including duodenum

197.5 Large intestine and rectum

197.6 Retroperitoneum and peritoneum
AHA: ▶2Q, '04, 4;◀ 4Q, '89, 11

197.7 Liver, specified as secondary

197.8 Other digestive organs and spleen
AHA: 2Q, '97, 3; 2Q, '92, 3

✓4th **198 Secondary malignant neoplasm of other specified sites**
EXCLUDES *lymph node metastasis (196.0-196.9)*
AHA: M-J, '85, 3

198.0 Kidney

198.1 Other urinary organs

198.2 Skin
Skin of breast

198.3 Brain and spinal cord
AHA: 3Q, '99, 7

198.4 Other parts of nervous system
Meninges (cerebral) (spinal)
AHA: J-F, '87, 7

198.5 Bone and bone marrow
AHA: 4Q, '03, 110; 3Q, '99, 5; 2Q, '92, 3; 1Q, '91, 16; 4Q, '89, 10

198.6 Ovary   ♀

198.7 Adrenal gland
Suprarenal gland

✓5th **198.8 Other specified sites**
198.81 Breast
EXCLUDES *skin of breast (198.2)*
198.82 Genital organs
198.89 Other
EXCLUDES *retroperitoneal lymph nodes (196.2)*
AHA: 2Q, '97, 4

✓4th **199 Malignant neoplasm without specification of site**
199.0 Disseminated
Carcinomatosis
Generalized: ⎫ unspecified site
  cancer   ⎬ (primary)
  malignancy   ⎪ (secondary)
Multiple cancer ⎭
AHA: 4Q, '89, 10

199.1 Other
Cancer   ⎫ unspecified site
Carcinoma ⎬ (primary)
Malignancy ⎭ (secondary)

MALIGNANT NEOPLASM OF LYMPHATIC AND HEMATOPOIETIC TISSUE (200-208)

EXCLUDES *secondary neoplasm of:*
bone marrow (198.5)
spleen (197.8)
secondary and unspecified neoplasm of lymph nodes (196.0-196.9)

The following fifth-digit subclassification is for use with categories 200-202:
0 unspecified site, extranodal and solid organ sites
1 lymph nodes of head, face, and neck
2 intrathoracic lymph nodes
3 intra-abdominal lymph nodes
4 lymph nodes of axilla and upper limb
5 lymph nodes of inguinal region and lower limb
6 intrapelvic lymph nodes
7 spleen
8 lymph nodes of multiple sites

✓4th **200 Lymphosarcoma and reticulosarcoma**
AHA: 2Q, '92, 3; N-D, '86, 5

✓5th **200.0 Reticulosarcoma**
Lymphoma (malignant):
  histiocytic (diffuse):
    nodular
    pleomorphic cell type
    reticulum cell type
Reticulum cell sarcoma:
  NOS
  pleomorphic cell type
AHA: For code 200.03: 3Q, '01, 12

DEF: Malignant lymphoma of primarily histolytic cells; commonly originates in reticuloendothelium of lymph nodes.

✓5th **200.1 Lymphosarcoma**
Lymphoblastoma (diffuse)   Lymphosarcoma:
Lymphoma (malignant):   NOS
  lymphoblastic (diffuse)   diffuse NOS
  lymphocytic (cell type)   lymphoblastic (diffuse)
    (diffuse)   lymphocytic (diffuse)
  lymphosarcoma type   prolymphocytic
EXCLUDES *lymphosarcoma:*
follicular or nodular (202.0)
mixed cell type (200.8)
lymphosarcoma cell leukemia (207.8)

DEF: Malignant lymphoma created from anaplastic lymphoid cells resembling lymphocytes or lymphoblasts.

✓5th **200.2 Burkitt's tumor or lymphoma**
Malignant lymphoma, Burkitt's type

DEF: Large osteolytic lesion most common in jaw or as abdominal mass; usually found in central Africa but reported elsewhere.

✓5th **200.8 Other named variants**
Lymphoma (malignant):
  lymphoplasmacytoid type
  mixed lymphocytic-histiocytic (diffuse)
Lymphosarcoma, mixed cell type (diffuse)
Reticulolymphosarcoma (diffuse)

✓4th **201 Hodgkin's disease**
AHA: 2Q, '92, 3; N-D, '86, 5

DEF: Painless, progressive enlargement of lymph nodes, spleen and general lymph tissue; symptoms include anorexia, lassitude, weight loss, fever, pruritis, night sweats, anemia.

✓5th **201.0 Hodgkin's paragranuloma**
✓5th **201.1 Hodgkin's granuloma**
AHA: 2Q, '99, 7

✓4th ✓5th Additional Digit Required   RUG III Special Care Dx   RUG III Clinically Complex Dx   Hospice Non-cancer Dx   CD PDx Clinical Dimension PDx   CD SDx Clinical Dimension SDx

2006 ICD•9•CM   **February 2005 • Volume 1 — 35**

§ ✓5ᵗʰ **201.2 Hodgkin's sarcoma**

§ ✓5ᵗʰ **201.4 Lymphocytic-histiocytic predominance**

§ ✓5ᵗʰ **201.5 Nodular sclerosis**
Hodgkin's disease, nodular sclerosis:
NOS
cellular phase

§ ✓5ᵗʰ **201.6 Mixed cellularity**

§ ✓5ᵗʰ **201.7 Lymphocytic depletion**
Hodgkin's disease, lymphocytic depletion:
NOS
diffuse fibrosis
reticular type

§ ✓5ᵗʰ **201.9 Hodgkin's disease, unspecified**
Hodgkin's: Malignant:
disease NOS   lymphogranuloma
lymphoma NOS   lymphogranulomatosis

✓4ᵗʰ **202 Other malignant neoplasms of lymphoid and histiocytic tissue**
AHA: 2Q, '92, 3; N-D, '86, 5

§ ✓5ᵗʰ **202.0 Nodular lymphoma**
Brill-Symmers disease   Lymphosarcoma:
Lymphoma: follicular (giant)
   follicular (giant)   nodular
   lymphocytic, nodular   Reticulosarcoma, follicular
                    or nodular
DEF: Lymphomatous cells clustered into nodules within the lymph node; usually occurs in older adults and may involve all nodes and possibly extranodal sites.

§ ✓5ᵗʰ **202.1 Mycosis fungoides**
AHA: 2Q, '92, 4
DEF: Type of cutaneous T-cell lymphoma; may evolve into generalized lymphoma; formerly thought to be of fungoid origin.

§ ✓5ᵗʰ **202.2 Sézary's disease**
AHA: 2Q, '99, 7
DEF: Type of cutaneous T-cell lymphoma with erythroderma, intense pruritus, peripheral lymphadenopathy, abnormal hyperchromatic mononuclear cells in skin, lymph nodes and peripheral blood.

§ ✓5ᵗʰ **202.3 Malignant histiocytosis**
Histiocytic medullary reticulosis
Malignant:
   reticuloendotheliosis
   reticulosis

§ ✓5ᵗʰ **202.4 Leukemic reticuloendotheliosis**
Hairy-cell leukemia
DEF: Chronic leukemia with large, mononuclear cells with "hairy" appearance in marrow, spleen, liver, blood.

§ ✓5ᵗʰ **202.5 Letterer-Siwe disease**
Acute:
   differentiated progressive histiocytosis
   histiocytosis X (progressive)
   infantile reticuloendotheliosis
   reticulosis of infancy
     EXCLUDES   Hand-Schüller-Christian disease (277.89)
                histiocytosis (acute) (chronic) (277.89)
                histiocytosis X (chronic) (277.89)
DEF: A recessive reticuloendotheliosis of early childhood, with a hemorrhagic tendency, eczema-like skin eruption, hepatosplenomegaly, including lymph node enlargement, and progressive anemia; it is often a fatal disease with no established cause.

§ ✓5ᵗʰ **202.6 Malignant mast cell tumors**
Malignant: Mast cell sarcoma
   mastocytoma   Systemic tissue mast
   mastocytosis   cell disease
     EXCLUDES   mast cell leukemia (207.8)

§ ✓5ᵗʰ **202.8 Other lymphomas**
Lymphoma (malignant):
NOS
diffuse
     EXCLUDES   benign lymphoma (229.0)
AHA: 2Q, '92, 4

§ ✓5ᵗʰ **202.9 Other and unspecified malignant neoplasms of lymphoid and histiocytic tissue**
Follicular dendritic cell sarcoma
Interdigitating dendritic cell sarcoma
Langerhans cell sarcoma
Malignant neoplasm of bone marrow NOS

✓4ᵗʰ **203 Multiple myeloma and immunoproliferative neoplasms**
The following fifth-digit subclassification is for use with category 203:
   0 without mention of remission
   1 in remission

✓5ᵗʰ **203.0 Multiple myeloma**
Kahler's disease   Myelomatosis
     EXCLUDES   solitary myeloma (238.6)
AHA: 1Q, '96, 16; 4Q, '91, 26

✓5ᵗʰ **203.1 Plasma cell leukemia**
Plasmacytic leukemia
AHA: 4Q, '90, 26; S-O, '86, 12

✓5ᵗʰ **203.8 Other immunoproliferative neoplasms**
AHA: 4Q, '90, 26; S-O, '86, 12

✓4ᵗʰ **204 Lymphoid leukemia**
INCLUDES   leukemia:
              lymphatic
              lymphoblastic
              lymphocytic
              lymphogenous
AHA: 3Q, '93, 4

The following fifth-digit subclassification is for use with category 204:
   0 without mention of remission
   1 in remission

✓5ᵗʰ **204.0 Acute**
     EXCLUDES   acute exacerbation of chronic lymphoid leukemia (204.1)
AHA: 3Q, '99, 6

✓5ᵗʰ **204.1 Chronic**

✓5ᵗʰ **204.2 Subacute**

✓5ᵗʰ **204.8 Other lymphoid leukemia**
Aleukemic leukemia: Aleukemic leukemia:
   lymphatic   lymphoid
   lymphocytic

✓5ᵗʰ **204.9 Unspecified lymphoid leukemia**

✓4ᵗʰ **205 Myeloid leukemia**
INCLUDES   leukemia: leukemia:
      granulocytic   myelomonocytic
      myeloblastic   myelosclerotic
      myelocytic   myelosis
      myelogenous
AHA: 3Q, '93, 3; 4Q, '91, 26; 4Q, '90, 3; M-J, '85, 18

The following fifth-digit subclassification is for use with category 205:
   0 without mention of remission
   1 in remission

✓5ᵗʰ **205.0 Acute**
Acute promyelocytic leukemia
     EXCLUDES   acute exacerbation of chronic myeloid leukemia (205.1)

§ Requires fifth-digit. See beginning of section 200-208 for codes and definitions

N Newborn Age: 0   P Pediatric Age: 0-17   M Maternity Age: 12-55   A Adult Age: 15-124   Manifestation Code   ◄► Revised Text   ● New Code   ▲ Revised Code Title

36 — Volume 1   *2006 ICD•9•CM*

Neoplasms

205.1–211.0

√5th **205.1 Chronic**
    Eosinophilic leukemia   Neutrophilic leukemia
    AHA: 1Q, '00, 6; J-A, '85, 13

√5th **205.2 Subacute**

√5th **205.3 Myeloid sarcoma**
    Chloroma   Granulocytic sarcoma

√5th **205.8 Other myeloid leukemia**
    Aleukemic leukemia: Aleukemic leukemia:
       granulocytic   myeloid
       myelogenous   Aleukemic myelosis

√5th **205.9 Unspecified myeloid leukemia**

√4th **206 Monocytic leukemia**
    INCLUDES   leukemia:
                histiocytic
                monoblastic
                monocytoid

The following fifth-digit subclassification is for use with category 206:
    0 without mention of remission
    1 in remission

√5th **206.0 Acute**
    EXCLUDES   *acute exacerbation of chronic monocytic leukemia (206.1)*

√5th **206.1 Chronic**

√5th **206.2 Subacute**

√5th **206.8 Other monocytic leukemia**
    Aleukemic:
       monocytic leukemia
       monocytoid leukemia

√5th **206.9 Unspecified monocytic leukemia**

√4th **207 Other specified leukemia**
    EXCLUDES   *leukemic reticuloendotheliosis (202.4)*
                  plasma cell leukemia (203.1)

The following fifth-digit subclassification is for use with category 207:
    0 without mention of remission
    1 in remission

√5th **207.0 Acute erythremia and erythroleukemia**
    Acute erythremic myelosis
    Di Guglielmo's disease
    Erythremic myelosis

    DEF: Erythremia: polycythemia vera.

    DEF: Erythroleukemia: a malignant blood dyscrasia (a myeloproliferative disorder).

√5th **207.1 Chronic erythremia**
    Heilmeyer-Schöner disease

√5th **207.2 Megakaryocytic leukemia**
    Megakaryocytic myelosis   Thrombocytic leukemia

√5th **207.8 Other specified leukemia**
    Lymphosarcoma cell leukemia

√4th **208 Leukemia of unspecified cell type**
The following fifth-digit subclassification is for use with category 208:
    0 without mention of remission
    1 in remission

√5th **208.0 Acute**
    Acute leukemia NOS   Stem cell leukemia
    Blast cell leukemia
         EXCLUDES   *acute exacerbation of chronic unspecified leukemia (208.1)*

√5th **208.1 Chronic**
    Chronic leukemia NOS

√5th **208.2 Subacute**
    Subacute leukemia NOS

√5th **208.8 Other leukemia of unspecified cell type**

√5th **208.9 Unspecified leukemia**
    Leukemia NOS

BENIGN NEOPLASMS (210-229)

√4th **210 Benign neoplasm of lip, oral cavity, and pharynx**
    EXCLUDES   *cyst (of):*
                  jaw (526.0-526.2,526.89)
                  oral soft tissue (528.4)
                  radicular (522.8)

210.0 Lip
    Frenulum labii
    Lip (inner aspect) (mucosa) (vermilion border)
         EXCLUDES   *labial commissure (210.4)*
                    skin of lip (216.0)

210.1 Tongue
    Lingual tonsil

210.2 Major salivary glands
    Gland: Gland:
       parotid   submandibular
       sublingual
         EXCLUDES   *benign neoplasms of minor salivary glands:*
                    NOS (210.4)
                    buccal mucosa (210.4)
                    lips (210.0)
                    palate (hard) (soft) (210.4)
                    tongue (210.1)
                    tonsil, palatine (210.5)

210.3 Floor of mouth

210.4 Other and unspecified parts of mouth
    Gingiva   Oral mucosa
    Gum (upper) (lower)   Palate (hard) (soft)
    Labial commissure   Uvula
    Oral cavity NOS
         EXCLUDES   *benign odontogenic neoplasms of bone (213.0-213.1)*
                    developmental odontogenic cysts (526.0)
                    mucosa of lips (210.0)
                    nasopharyngeal [posterior] [superior] surface of soft palate (210.7)

210.5 Tonsil
    Tonsil (faucial) (palatine)
         EXCLUDES   *lingual tonsil (210.1)*
                    pharyngeal tonsil (210.7)
                    tonsillar:
                       fossa (210.6)
                       pillars (210.6)

210.6 Other parts of oropharynx
    Branchial cleft or vestiges   Tonsillar:
    Epiglottis, anterior aspect   fossa
    Fauces NOS   pillars
    Mesopharynx NOS   Vallecula
         EXCLUDES   *epiglottis:*
                    NOS (212.1)
                    suprahyoid portion (212.1)

210.7 Nasopharynx
    Adenoid tissue   Pharyngeal tonsil
    Lymphadenoid tissue   Posterior nasal septum

210.8 Hypopharynx
    Arytenoid fold   Postcricoidregion
    Laryngopharynx   Pyriform fossa

210.9 Pharynx, unspecified
    Throat NOS

√4th **211 Benign neoplasm of other parts of digestive system**
211.0 Esophagus

Neoplasms

211.1 Stomach
Body
Cardia } of stomach
Fundus

Cardiac orifice
Pylorus

211.2 Duodenum, jejunum, and ileum
Small intestine NOS
> **EXCLUDES** ampulla of Vater (211.5)
> ileocecal valve (211.3)

211.3 Colon
Appendix   Ileocecal valve
Cecum   Large intestine NOS
> **EXCLUDES** rectosigmoid junction (211.4)

AHA: 4Q, '01, 56

211.4 Rectum and anal canal
Anal canal or sphincter   Rectosigmoid junction
Anus NOS
> **EXCLUDES** anus:
> margin (216.5)
> skin (216.5)
> perianal skin (216.5)

211.5 Liver and biliary passages
Ampulla of Vater   Gallbladder
Common bile duct   Hepatic duct
Cystic duct   Sphincter of Oddi

211.6 Pancreas, except islets of Langerhans

211.7 Islets of Langerhans
Islet cell tumor
Use additional code to identify any functional
    activity

211.8 Retroperitoneum and peritoneum
Mesentery   Omentum
Mesocolon   Retroperitoneal tissue

211.9 Other and unspecified site
Alimentary tract NOS
Digestive system NOS
Gastrointestinal tract NOS
Intestinal tract NOS
Intestine NOS
Spleen, not elsewhere classified

✓4ᵗʰ **212 Benign neoplasm of respiratory and intrathoracic organs**

212.0 Nasal cavities, middle ear, and accessory sinuses
Cartilage of nose   Sinus:
Eustachian tube   ethmoidal
Nares   frontal
Septum of nose   maxillary
                    sphenoidal
> **EXCLUDES** auditory canal (external) (216.2)
> bone of:
> ear (213.0)
> nose [turbinates] (213.0)
> cartilage of ear (215.0)
> ear (external) (skin) (216.2)
> nose NOS (229.8)
> skin (216.3)
> olfactory bulb (225.1)
> polyp of:
> accessory sinus (471.8)
> ear (385.30-385.35)
> nasal cavity (471.0)
> posterior margin of septum and
> choanae (210.7)

212.1 Larynx
Cartilage: Epiglottis (suprahyoid portion) NOS
arytenoid   Glottis
cricoid   Vocal cords (false) (true)
cuneiform
thyroid
> **EXCLUDES** epiglottis, anterior aspect (210.6)
> polyp of vocal cord or larynx (478.4)

212.2 Trachea

212.3 Bronchus and lung
Carina   Hilus of lung

212.4 Pleura

212.5 Mediastinum

212.6 Thymus

212.7 Heart
> **EXCLUDES** great vessels (215.4)

212.8 Other specified sites

212.9 Site unspecified
Respiratory organ NOS
Upper respiratory tract NOS
> **EXCLUDES** intrathoracic NOS (229.8)
> thoracic NOS (229.8)

✓4ᵗʰ **213 Benign neoplasm of bone and articular cartilage**
> **INCLUDES** cartilage (articular) (joint)
> periosteum
> **EXCLUDES** cartilage of: cartilage of:
> ear (215.0)   nose (212.0)
> eyelid (215.0)   exostosis NOS (726.91)
> larynx (212.1)   synovia (215.0-215.9)

213.0 Bones of skull and face `CD PDx`
> **EXCLUDES** lower jaw bone (213.1)

213.1 Lower jaw bone `CD PDx`

213.2 Vertebral column, excluding sacrum `CD PDx`
and coccyx

213.3 Ribs, sternum, and clavicle `CD PDx`

213.4 Scapula and long bones of upper limb `CD PDx`

213.5 Short bones of upper limb `CD PDx`

213.6 Pelvic bones, sacrum, and coccyx `CD PDx`

213.7 Long bones of lower limb `CD PDx`

213.8 Short bones of lower limb `CD PDx`

213.9 Bone and articular cartilage, `CD PDx`
site unspecified

✓4ᵗʰ **214 Lipoma**
> **INCLUDES** angiolipoma
> fibrolipoma
> hibernoma
> lipoma (fetal) (infiltrating) (intramuscular)
> myelolipoma
> myxolipoma

DEF: Benign tumor frequently composed of mature fat cells; may occasionally be composed of fetal fat cells.

214.0 Skin and subcutaneous tissue of face

214.1 Other skin and subcutaneous tissue

214.2 Intrathoracic organs

214.3 Intra-abdominal organs

214.4 Spermatic cord ♂

214.8 Other specified sites
AHA: 3Q, '94, 7

214.9 Lipoma, unspecified site

✓4ᵗʰ **215 Other benign neoplasm of connective and other soft tissue**
> **INCLUDES** blood vessel
> bursa
> fascia
> ligament
> muscle
> peripheral, sympathetic, and parasympathetic
> nerves and ganglia
> synovia
> tendon (sheath)
> **EXCLUDES** cartilage:
> articular (213.0-213.9)
> larynx (212.1)
> nose (212.0)
> connective tissue of:
> breast (217)
> internal organ, except lipoma and
> hemangioma—code to benign neoplasm
> of the site
> lipoma (214.0-214.9)

 Newborn Age: 0   ▣ Pediatric Age: 0-17   Ⓜ Maternity Age: 12-55   Ⓐ Adult Age: 15-124   ▮Manifestation Code   ◄► Revised Text   ● New Code   ▲ Revised Code Title

38 — Volume 1   *2006 ICD•9•CM*

215.0   **Head, face, and neck**

215.2   **Upper limb, including shoulder**

215.3   **Lower limb, including hip**

215.4   **Thorax**

> EXCLUDES   *heart (212.7)*
> *mediastinum (212.5)*
> *thymus (212.6)*

215.5   **Abdomen**

Abdominal wall   Hypochondrium

215.6   **Pelvis**

Buttock   Inguinal region
Groin   Perineum

> EXCLUDES   *uterine:*
> *leiomyoma (218.0-218.9)*
> *ligament, any (221.0)*

215.7   **Trunk, unspecified**

Back NOS   Flank NOS

215.8   **Other specified sites**

215.9   **Site unspecified**

√4ᵗʰ **216 Benign neoplasm of skin**

> INCLUDES   blue nevus   pigmented nevus
> dermatofibroma   syringoadenoma
> hydrocystoma   syringoma

> EXCLUDES   *skin of genital organs (221.0-222.9)*

AHA: 1Q, '00, 21

216.0   **Skin of lip**

> EXCLUDES   *vermilion border of lip (210.0)*

216.1   **Eyelid, including canthus**

> EXCLUDES   *cartilage of eyelid (215.0)*

216.2   **Ear and external auditory canal**

Auricle (ear)   External meatus
Auricular canal, external   Pinna

> EXCLUDES   *cartilage of ear (215.0)*

216.3   **Skin of other and unspecified parts of face**

Cheek, external   Nose, external
Eyebrow   Temple

216.4   **Scalp and skin of neck**

216.5   **Skin of trunk, except scrotum**

Axillary fold   Skin of:
Perianal skin   buttock
Skin of: chest wall
  abdominal wall   groin
  anus   perineum
  back   Umbilicus
  breast

> EXCLUDES   *anal canal (211.4)*
> *anus NOS (211.4)*
> *skin of scrotum (222.4)*

216.6   **Skin of upper limb, including shoulder**

216.7   **Skin of lower limb, including hip**

216.8   **Other specified sites of skin**

216.9   **Skin, site unspecified**

217 Benign neoplasm of breast

Breast (male) (female):   Breast (male) (female):
  connective tissue   soft parts
  glandular tissue

> EXCLUDES   *adenofibrosis (610.2)*
> *benign cyst of breast (610.0)*
> *fibrocystic disease (610.1)*
> *skin of breast (216.5)*

AHA: 1Q, '00, 4

√4ᵗʰ **218 Uterine leiomyoma**

> INCLUDES   fibroid (bleeding) (uterine)
> uterine:
>   fibromyoma
>   myoma

DEF: Benign tumor primarily derived from uterine smooth muscle tissue; may contain fibrous, fatty, or epithelial tissue; also called uterine fibroid or myoma.

218.0   **Submucous leiomyoma of uterus**   ♀

Types of Uterine Fibroids

218.1   **Intramural leiomyoma of uterus**   ♀
Interstitial leiomyoma of uterus

218.2   **Subserous leiomyoma of uterus**   ♀

218.9   **Leiomyoma of uterus, unspecified**   ♀

AHA: 1Q, '03, 4

√4ᵗʰ **219 Other benign neoplasm of uterus**

219.0   **Cervix uteri**   ♀

219.1   **Corpus uteri**   ♀

Endometrium   Myometrium
Fundus

219.8   **Other specified parts of uterus**   ♀

219.9   **Uterus, part unspecified**   ♀

220 Benign neoplasm of ovary

Use additional code to identify any functional activity (256.0-256.1)

> EXCLUDES   *cyst:*
> *corpus albicans (620.2)*
> *corpus luteum (620.1)*
> *endometrial (617.1)*
> *follicular (atretic) (620.0)*
> *graafian follicle (620.0)*
> *ovarian NOS (620.2)*
> *retention (620.2)*

√4ᵗʰ **221 Benign neoplasm of other female genital organs**

> INCLUDES   adenomatous polyp
> benign teratoma

> EXCLUDES   *cyst:*
> *epoophoron (752.11)*
> *fimbrial (752.11)*
> *Gartner's duct (752.11)*
> *parovarian (752.11)*

221.0   **Fallopian tube and uterine ligaments**   ♀

Oviduct
Parametruim
Uterine ligament (broad) (round) (uterosacral)
Uterine tube

221.1   **Vagina**   ♀

221.2   **Vulva**   ♀

Clitoris
External female genitalia NOS
Greater vestibular [Bartholin's] gland
Labia (majora) (minora)
Pudendum

> EXCLUDES   *Bartholin's (duct) (gland) cyst (616.2)*

221.8   **Other specified sites of female genital organs**   ♀

221.9   **Female genital organ, site unspecified**   ♀
Female genitourinary tract NOS

√4ᵗʰ **222 Benign neoplasm of male genital organs**

222.0   **Testis**   ♂
Use additional code to identify any functional activity

222.1   **Penis**   ♂
Corpus cavernosum
Glans penis
Prepuce

√4ᵗʰ / √5ᵗʰ Additional Digit Required   **RUG III** Special Care Dx   **RUG III** Clinically Complex Dx   Hospice Non-cancer Dx   **CD PDx** Clinical Dimension PDx   **CD SDx** Clinical Dimension SDx

222.2 **Prostate** ♂
    EXCLUDES *adenomatous hyperplasia of prostate*
        (600.20-600.21)
      prostatic:
        adenoma (600.20-600.21)
        enlargement (600.00-600.01)
        hypertrophy (600.00-600.01)

222.3 **Epididymis** ♂
222.4 **Scrotum** ♂
    Skin of scrotum
222.8 **Other specified sites of male genital organs** ♂
    Seminal vesicle
    Spermatic cord
222.9 **Male genital organ, site unspecified** ♂
    Male genitourinary tract NOS

✓4ᵗʰ 223 **Benign neoplasm of kidney and other urinary organs**
223.0 **Kidney, except pelvis**
    Kidney NOS
    EXCLUDES *renal:*
        calyces (223.1)
        pelvis (223.1)
223.1 **Renal pelvis**
223.2 **Ureter**
    EXCLUDES *ureteric orifice of bladder (223.3)*
223.3 **Bladder**
✓5ᵗʰ 223.8 **Other specified sites of urinary organs**
    223.81 **Urethra**
        EXCLUDES *urethral orifice of bladder*
            (223.3)
    223.89 **Other**
        Paraurethral glands
223.9 **Urinary organ, site unspecified**
    Urinary system NOS

✓4ᵗʰ 224 **Benign neoplasm of eye**
    EXCLUDES *cartilage of eyelid (215.0)*
        eyelid (skin) (216.1)
        optic nerve (225.1)
        orbital bone (213.0)
224.0 **Eyeball, except conjunctiva, cornea, retina, and choroid**
    Ciliary body   Sclera
    Iris   Uveal tract
224.1 **Orbit**
    EXCLUDES *bone of orbit (213.0)*
224.2 **Lacrimal gland**
224.3 **Conjunctiva**
224.4 **Cornea**
224.5 **Retina**
    EXCLUDES *hemangioma of retina (228.03)*
224.6 **Choroid**
224.7 **Lacrimal duct**
    Lacrimal sac   Nasolacrimal duct
224.8 **Other specified parts of eye**
224.9 **Eye, part unspecified**

Eyeball

Posterior segment
Vitreous
Optic nerve
Conjunctiva
Sclera
Optic disc
Lens
Cornea
Choroid
Sclera
Retina
Iris
Anterior chamber
Pars plana

✓4ᵗʰ 225 **Benign neoplasm of brain and other parts of nervous system**
    EXCLUDES *hemangioma (228.02)*
        neurofibromatosis (237.7)
        peripheral, sympathetic, and parasympathetic
            nerves and ganglia (215.0-215.9)
        retrobulbar (224.1)
225.0 **Brain** `CD PDx`
225.1 **Cranial nerves** `CD PDx`
    AHA: ▶4Q, '04, 113◀
225.2 **Cerebral meninges** `CD PDx`
    Meninges NOS   Meningioma (cerebral)
225.3 **Spinal cord** `CD PDx`
    Cauda equina
225.4 **Spinal meninges** `CD PDx`
    Spinal meningioma
225.8 **Other specified sites of nervous system** `CD PDx`
225.9 **Nervous system, part unspecified** `CD PDx`
    Nervous system (central) NOS
    EXCLUDES *meninges NOS (225.2)*

226 **Benign neoplasm of thyroid glands**
    Use additional code to identify any functional activity

✓4ᵗʰ 227 **Benign neoplasm of other endocrine glands and related structures**
    Use additional code to identify any functional activity
    EXCLUDES *ovary (220)*   *testis (222.0)*
        pancreas (211.6)
227.0 **Adrenal gland**
    Suprarenal gland
227.1 **Parathyroid gland**
227.3 **Pituitary gland and craniopharyngeal duct (pouch)**
    Craniobuccal pouch   Rathke's pouch
    Hypophysis   Sella turcica
227.4 **Pineal gland**
    Pineal body
227.5 **Carotid body**
227.6 **Aortic body and other paraganglia**
    Coccygeal body   Para-aortic body
    Glomus jugulare
    AHA: N-D, '84, 17
227.8 **Other**
227.9 **Endocrine gland, site unspecified**

✓4ᵗʰ 228 **Hemangioma and lymphangioma, any site**
    INCLUDES angioma (benign) (cavernous) (congenital) NOS
        cavernous nevus
        glomus tumor
        hemangioma (benign) (congenital)
    EXCLUDES *benign neoplasm of spleen, except hemangioma*
            and lymphangioma (211.9)
        glomus jugulare (227.6)
        nevus:
            NOS (216.0-216.9)
            blue or pigmented (216.0-216.9)
            vascular (757.32)
    AHA: 1Q, '00, 21

✓5ᵗʰ 228.0 **Hemangioma, any site**
    AHA: J-F, '85, 19

    DEF: A common benign tumor usually occurring in infancy; composed of newly formed blood vessels due to malformation of angioblastic tissue.

    228.00 **Of unspecified site**
    228.01 **Of skin and subcutaneous tissue**
    228.02 **Of intracranial structures**
    228.03 **Of retina**
    228.04 **Of intra-abdominal structures**
        Peritoneum   Retroperitoneal tissue
    228.09 **Of other sites**
        Systemic angiomatosis
        AHA: 3Q, '91, 20

N Newborn Age: 0   P Pediatric Age: 0-17   M Maternity Age: 12-55   A Adult Age: 15-124   Manifestation Code   ◄► Revised Text   ● New Code   ▲ Revised Code Title

40 — Volume 1 • February 2005   2006 ICD•9•CM

228.1 **Lymphangioma, any site**
Congenital lymphangioma
Lymphatic nevus

✓4th 229 **Benign neoplasm of other and unspecified sites**

229.0 **Lymph nodes**
EXCLUDES   *lymphangioma (228.1)*

229.8 **Other specified sites**
Intrathoracic NOS   Thoracic NOS

229.9 **Site unspecified**

CARCINOMA IN SITU (230-234)

INCLUDES   Bowen's disease
erythroplasia
Queyrat's erythroplasia

EXCLUDES   *leukoplakia—see Alphabetic Index*

DEF: A neoplastic type; with tumor cells confined to epithelium of origin; without further invasion.

✓4th 230 **Carcinoma in situ of digestive organs**

230.0 **Lip, oral cavity, and pharynx**
Gingiva   Oropharynx
Hypopharynx   Salivary gland or duct
Mouth [any part]   Tongue
Nasopharynx

EXCLUDES   *aryepiglottic fold or interarytenoid fold,
laryngeal aspect (231.0)
epiglottis:
NOS (231.0)
suprahyoid portion (231.0)
skin of lip (232.0)*

230.1 **Esophagus**

230.2 **Stomach**
Body
Cardia } of stomach
Fundus

Cardiac orifice   Pylorus

230.3 **Colon**
Appendix   Ileocecal valve
Cecum   Large intestine NOS

EXCLUDES   *rectosigmoid junction (230.4)*

230.4 **Rectum**
Rectosigmoid junction

230.5 **Anal canal**
Anal sphincter

230.6 **Anus, unspecified**
EXCLUDES   *anus:
margin (232.5)
skin (232.5)
perianal skin (232.5)*

230.7 **Other and unspecified parts of intestine**
Duodenum   Jejunum
Ileum   Small intestine NOS

EXCLUDES   *ampulla of Vater (230.8)*

230.8 **Liver and biliary system**
Ampulla of Vater   Gallbladder
Common bile duct   Hepatic duct
Cystic duct   Sphincter of Oddi

230.9 **Other and unspecified digestive organs**
Digestive organ NOS   Pancreas
Gastrointestinal tract NOS   Spleen

✓4th 231 **Carcinoma in situ of respiratory system**

231.0 **Larynx**
Cartilage: Epiglottis:
arytenoid   NOS
cricoid   posterior surface
cuneiform   suprahyoid portion
thyroid   Vocal cords (false) (true)

EXCLUDES   *aryepiglottic fold or interarytenoid fold:
NOS (230.0)
hypopharyngeal aspect (230.0)
marginal zone (230.0)*

231.1 **Trachea**

231.2 **Bronchus and lung**
Carina
Hilus of lung

231.8 **Other specified parts of respiratory system**
Accessory sinuses   Nasal cavities
Middle ear   Pleura

EXCLUDES   *ear (external) (skin) (232.2)
nose NOS (234.8)
skin (232.3)*

231.9 **Respiratory system, part unspecified**
Respiratory organ NOS

✓4th 232 **Carcinoma in situ of skin**
INCLUDES   pigment cells

232.0 **Skin of lip**
EXCLUDES   *vermilion border of lip (230.0)*

232.1 **Eyelid, including canthus**

232.2 **Ear and external auditory canal**

232.3 **Skin of other and unspecified parts of face**

232.4 **Scalp and skin of neck**

232.5 **Skin of trunk, except scrotum**
Anus, margin   Skin of:
Axillary fold   breast
Perianal skin   buttock
Skin of: chest wall
abdominal wall   groin
anus   perineum
back   Umbilicus

EXCLUDES   *anal canal (230.5)
anus NOS (230.6)
skin of genital organs (233.3, 233.5-
233.6)*

232.6 **Skin of upper limb, including shoulder**

232.7 **Skin of lower limb, including hip**

232.8 **Other specified sites of skin**

232.9 **Skin, site unspecified**

✓4th 233 **Carcinoma in situ of breast and genitourinary system**

233.0 **Breast**
EXCLUDES   *Paget's disease (174.0-174.9)
skin of breast (232.5)*

233.1 **Cervix uteri**   ♀
Cervical intraepithelial neoplasia III [CIN III]
Severe dysplasia of cervix

EXCLUDES   *cervical intraepithelial neoplasia II [CIN
II] (622.12)
cytologic evidence of malignancy
without histologic confirmation
(795.04)
high grade squamous intraepithelial
lesion (HGSIL) (795.04)
moderate dysplasia of cervix (622.12)*

AHA: 3Q, '92, 7; 3Q, '92, 8; 1Q, '91, 11

233.2 **Other and unspecified parts of uterus**   ♀

233.3 **Other and unspecified female genital organs** ♀

233.4 **Prostate**   ♂

233.5 **Penis**   ♂

233.6 **Other and unspecified male genital organs**   ♂

233.7 **Bladder**

233.9 **Other and unspecified urinary organs**

✓4th 234 **Carcinoma in situ of other and unspecified sites**

234.0 **Eye**
EXCLUDES   *cartilage of eyelid (234.8)
eyelid (skin) (232.1)
optic nerve (234.8)
orbital bone (234.8)*

234.8 **Other specified sites**
Endocrine gland [any]

234.9 **Site unspecified**
Carcinoma in situ NOS

✓4th
✓5th   Additional Digit Required   RUG III Special Care Dx   RUG III Clinically Complex Dx   Hospice Non-cancer Dx   CD PDx Clinical Dimension PDx   CD SDx Clinical Dimension SDx

2006 ICD•9•CM   Volume 1 — 41

228.1–234.9

Neoplasms

235–238.5

NEOPLASMS OF UNCERTAIN BEHAVIOR (235-238)

Note: Categories 235–238 classify by site certain histomorphologically well-defined neoplasms, the subsequent behavior of which cannot be predicted from the present appearance.

✓4th **235 Neoplasm of uncertain behavior of digestive and respiratory systems**

235.0 Major salivary glands

Gland: Gland:
   parotid   submandibular
   sublingual

EXCLUDES   *minor salivary glands (235.1)*

235.1 Lip, oral cavity, and pharynx

Gingiva   Nasopharynx
Hypopharynx   Oropharynx
Minor salivary glands   Tongue
Mouth

EXCLUDES   *aryepiglottic fold or interarytenoid fold, laryngeal aspect (235.6)*
        epiglottis:
          NOS (235.6)
          suprahyoid portion (235.6)
        skin of lip (238.2)

235.2 Stomach, intestines, and rectum

235.3 Liver and biliary passages

Ampulla of Vater   Gallbladder
Bile ducts [any]   Liver

235.4 Retroperitoneum and peritoneum

235.5 Other and unspecified digestive organs

Anal: Esophagus
   canal   Pancreas
   sphincter   Spleen
Anus NOS

EXCLUDES   *anus:*
        margin (238.2)
        skin (238.2)
      perianal skin (238.2)

235.6 Larynx

EXCLUDES   *aryepiglottic fold or interarytenoid fold:*
        NOS (235.1)
        hypopharyngeal aspect (235.1)
        marginal zone (235.1)

235.7 Trachea, bronchus, and lung

235.8 Pleura, thymus, and mediastinum

235.9 Other and unspecified respiratory organs

Accessory sinuses   Nasal cavities
Middle ear   Respiratory organ NOS

EXCLUDES   *ear (external) (skin) (238.2)*
        nose (238.8)
        skin (238.2)

✓4th **236 Neoplasm of uncertain behavior of genitourinary organs**

236.0 Uterus   ♀

236.1 Placenta   ♀

Chorioadenoma (destruens)
Invasive mole
Malignant hydatid(iform) mole

236.2 Ovary   ♀

Use additional code to identify any functional activity

236.3 Other and unspecified female genital organs   ♀

236.4 Testis   ♂

Use additional code to identify any functional activity

236.5 Prostate   ♂

236.6 Other and unspecified male genital organs   ♂

236.7 Bladder

✓5th **236.9 Other and unspecified urinary organs**

236.90 Urinary organ, unspecified

236.91 Kidney and ureter

236.99 Other

✓4th **237 Neoplasm of uncertain behavior of endocrine glands and nervous system**

237.0 Pituitary gland and craniopharyngeal duct

Use additional code to identify any functional activity

237.1 Pineal gland

237.2 Adrenal gland

Suprarenal gland
Use additional code to identify any functional activity

237.3 Paraganglia

Aortic body   Coccygeal body
Carotid body   Glomus jugulare

AHA: N-D, '84, 17

237.4 Other and unspecified endocrine glands

Parathyroid gland   Thyroid gland

237.5 Brain and spinal cord

237.6 Meninges

Meninges: Meninges:
   NOS   spinal
   cerebral

✓5th **237.7 Neurofibromatosis**

von Recklinghausen's disease

DEF: An inherited condition with developmental changes in the nervous system, muscles, bones and skin; multiple soft tumors (neurofibromas) distributed over the entire body.

237.70 Neurofibromatosis, unspecified

237.71 Neurofibromatosis, type 1 [von Recklinghausen's disease]

237.72 Neurofibromatosis, type 2 [acoustic neurofibromatosis]

DEF: Inherited condition with cutaneous lesions, benign tumors of peripheral nerves and bilateral 8th nerve masses.

237.9 Other and unspecified parts of nervous system

Cranial nerves

EXCLUDES   *peripheral, sympathetic, and parasympathetic nerves and ganglia (238.1)*

✓4th **238 Neoplasm of uncertain behavior of other and unspecified sites and tissues**

238.0 Bone and articular cartilage

EXCLUDES   *cartilage:*
        ear (238.1)
        eyelid (238.1)
        larynx (235.6)
        nose (235.9)
        synovia (238.1)

AHA: ▶4Q, '04, 128◀

238.1 Connective and other soft tissue

Peripheral, sympathetic, and parasympathetic nerves and ganglia

EXCLUDES   *cartilage (of):*
        articular (238.0)
        larynx (235.6)
        nose (235.9)
      connective tissue of breast (238.3)

238.2 Skin

EXCLUDES   *anus NOS (235.5)*
      skin of genital organs (236.3, 236.6)
      vermilion border of lip (235.1)

238.3 Breast

EXCLUDES   *skin of breast (238.2)*

238.4 Polycythemia vera

DEF: Abnormal proliferation of all bone marrow elements, increased red cell mass and total blood volume; unknown etiology, frequently associated with splenomegaly, leukocytosis, and thrombocythemia.

238.5 Histiocytic and mast cells

Mast cell tumor NOS   Mastocytoma NOS

N Newborn Age: 0   P Pediatric Age: 0-17   M Maternity Age: 12-55   A Adult Age: 15-124   Manifestation Code   ◄► Revised Text   ● New Code   ▲ Revised Code Title

42 — Volume 1 • February 2005   *2006 ICD•9•CM*

238.6   **Plasma cells**

Plasmacytoma NOS   Solitary myeloma

238.7   **Other lymphatic and hematopoietic tissues**

Disease:

    lymphoproliferative (chronic) NOS

    myeloproliferative (chronic) NOS

Idiopathic thrombocythemia

Megakaryocytic myelosclerosis

Myelodysplastic syndrome

Myelosclerosis with myeloid metaplasia

Panmyelosis (acute)

►Refractory anemia◄

   EXCLUDES   myelofibrosis (289.89)

                  myelosclerosis NOS (289.89)

                  myelosis:

                      NOS (205.9)

                      megakaryocytic (207.2)

AHA: 3Q, '01, 13; 1Q, '97, 5; 2Q, '89, 8

238.8   **Other specified sites**

Eye   Heart

   EXCLUDES   eyelid (skin) (238.2)

                  cartilage (238.1)

238.9   **Site unspecified**

NEOPLASMS OF UNSPECIFIED NATURE (239)

√4ᵗʰ **239 Neoplasms of unspecified nature**

Note: Category 239 classifies by site neoplasms of unspecified morphology and behavior. The term "mass,"unless otherwise stated, is not to be regarded as a neoplastic growth.

   INCLUDES   "growth" NOS   new growth NOS

                 neoplasm NOS   tumor NOS

239.0   **Digestive system**

   EXCLUDES   anus:

                  margin (239.2)

                  skin (239.2)

              perianal skin (239.2)

239.1   **Respiratory system**

239.2   **Bone, soft tissue, and skin**

   EXCLUDES   anal canal (239.0)

                  anus NOS (239.0)

                  bone marrow (202.9)

                  cartilage:

                      larynx (239.1)

                      nose (239.1)

                  connective tissue of breast (239.3)

                  skin of genital organs (239.5)

                  vermilion border of lip (239.0)

239.3   **Breast**

   EXCLUDES   skin of breast (239.2)

239.4   **Bladder**

239.5   **Other genitourinary organs**

239.6   **Brain**

   EXCLUDES   cerebral meninges (239.7)

                  cranial nerves (239.7)

239.7   **Endocrine glands and other parts of nervous system**

   EXCLUDES   peripheral, sympathetic, and

                    parasympathetic nerves and

                    ganglia (239.2)

239.8   **Other specified sites**

   EXCLUDES   eyelid (skin) (239.2)

                  cartilage (239.2)

                  great vessels (239.2)

                  optic nerve (239.7)

239.9   **Site unspecified**

√4ᵗʰ
√5ᵗʰ   Additional Digit Required   RUG III Special Care Dx   RUG III Clinically Complex Dx   Hospice Non-cancer Dx   **CD PDx** Clinical Dimension PDx   **CD SDx** Clinical Dimension SDx

2006 ICD•9•CM   **October 2005 • Volume 1 — 43**

3. ENDOCRINE, NUTRITIONAL AND METABOLIC DISEASES, AND IMMUNITY DISORDERS (240-279)

> **EXCLUDES** *endocrine and metabolic disturbances specific to the fetus and newborn (775.0-775.9)*

Note: All neoplasms, whether functionally active or not, are classified in Chapter 2. Codes in Chapter 3 (i.e., 242.8, 246.0, 251-253, 255-259) may be used to identify such functional activity associated with any neoplasm, or by ectopic endocrine tissue.

DISORDERS OF THYROID GLAND (240-246)

✓4th 240 Simple and unspecified goiter

DEF: An enlarged thyroid gland often caused by an inadequate dietary intake of iodine.

240.0 Goiter, specified as simple
Any condition classifiable to 240.9, specified as simple

240.9 Goiter, unspecified
Enlargement of thyroid
Goiter or struma:
  NOS
  diffuse colloid
  endemic
Goiter or struma:
  hyperplastic
  nontoxic (diffuse)
  parenchymatous
  sporadic

> **EXCLUDES** *congenital (dyshormonogenic) goiter (246.1)*

✓4th 241 Nontoxic nodular goiter

> **EXCLUDES** *adenoma of thyroid (226)*
> *cystadenoma of thyroid (226)*

241.0 Nontoxic uninodular goiter
Thyroid nodule   Uninodular goiter (nontoxic)
DEF: Enlarged thyroid, commonly due to decreased thyroid production, with single nodule; no clinical hypothyroidism.

241.1 Nontoxic multinodular goiter
Multinodular goiter (nontoxic)
DEF: Enlarged thyroid, commonly due to decreased thyroid production with multiple nodules; no clinical hypothyroidism.

241.9 Unspecified nontoxic nodular goiter
Adenomatous goiter
Nodular goiter (nontoxic) NOS
Struma nodosa (simplex)

✓4th 242 Thyrotoxicosis with or without goiter

> **EXCLUDES** *neonatal thyrotoxicosis (775.3)*

DEF: A condition caused by excess quantities of thyroid hormones being introduced into the tissues

The following fifth-digit subclassification is for use with category 242:
  0 without mention of thyrotoxic crisis or storm
  1 with mention of thyrotoxic crisis or storm

The Endocrine System

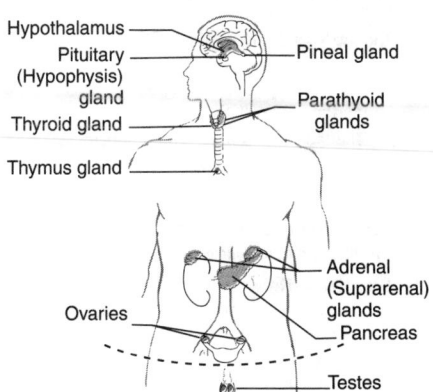

Hypothalamus
Pituitary (Hypophysis) gland
Thyroid gland
Thymus gland
Pineal gland
Parathyroid glands
Ovaries
Adrenal (Suprarenal) glands
Pancreas
Testes

✓5th 242.0 Toxic diffuse goiter
Basedow's disease
Exophthalmic or toxic goiter NOS
Graves' disease
Primary thyroid hyperplasia
CC Excl: 017.50-017.56, 017.90-017.96, 240.0, 240.9, 241.0-241.9, 242.00-242.91,243, 244.0-244.9, 245.0-245.9, 246.0-246.9, 259.8-259.9

DEF: Diffuse thyroid enlargement accompanied by hyperthyroidism, bulging eyes, and dermopathy.

✓5th 242.1 Toxic uninodular goiter
Thyroid nodule ⎫ toxic or with
Uninodular goiter ⎬ hyperthyroidism

DEF: Symptomatic hyperthyroidism with a single nodule on the enlarged thyroid gland. Abrupt onset of symptoms; including extreme nervousness, insomnia, weight loss, tremors, and psychosis or coma.

✓5th 242.2 Toxic multinodular goiter
Secondary thyroid hyperplasia

DEF: Symptomatic hyperthyroidism with multiple nodules on the enlarged thyroid gland. Abrupt onset of symptoms; including extreme nervousness, insomnia, weight loss, tremors, and psychosis or coma

✓5th 242.3 Toxic nodular goiter, unspecified
Adenomatous goiter ⎫
Nodular goiter ⎬ toxic or with
Struma nodosa ⎭ hyperthyroidism

Any condition classifiable to 241.9 specified as toxic or with hyperthyroidism

✓5th 242.4 Thyrotoxicosis from ectopic thyroid nodule

✓5th 242.8 Thyrotoxicosis of other specified origin
Overproduction of thyroid-stimulating hormone [TSH]
Thyrotoxicosis:
  factitia from ingestion of excessive thyroid material
Use additional E code to identify cause, if drug-induced

✓5th 242.9 Thyrotoxicosis without mention of goiter or other cause
Hyperthyroidism NOS
Thyrotoxicosis NOS

243 Congenital hypothyroidism
Congenital thyroid insufficiency
Cretinism (athyrotic) (endemic)
Use additional code to identify associated mental retardation

> **EXCLUDES** *congenital (dyshormonogenic) goiter (246.1)*

DEF: Underproduction of thyroid hormone present from birth.

✓4th 244 Acquired hypothyroidism

> **INCLUDES** athyroidism (acquired)
> hypothyroidism (acquired)
> myxedema (adult) (juvenile)
> thyroid (gland) insufficiency (acquired)

244.0 Postsurgical hypothyroidism
DEF: Underproduction of thyroid hormone due to surgical removal of all or part of the thyroid gland.

244.1 Other postablative hypothyroidism
Hypothyroidism following therapy, such as irradiation

244.2 Iodine hypothyroidism
Hypothyroidism resulting from administration or ingestion of iodide
Use additional E code to identify drug

244.3 Other iatrogenic hypothyroidism
Hypothyroidism resulting from:
  P-aminosalicylic acid [PAS]
  Phenylbutazone
  Resorcinol
Iatrogenic hypothyroidism NOS
Use additional E code to identify drug

✓4th ✓5th Additional Digit Required   RUG III Special Care Dx   RUG III Clinically Complex Dx   Hospice Non-cancer Dx   **CD PDx** Clinical Dimension PDx   **CD SDx** Clinical Dimension SDx

2006 ICD•9•CM   **Volume 1 — 45**

Endocrine, Nutritional and Metabolic, Immunity   244.8–250.4

244.8   **Other specified acquired hypothyroidism**
Secondary hypothyroidism NEC

AHA: J-A, '85, 9

244.9   **Unspecified hypothyroidism**
Hypothyroidism ⎱
Myxedema   ⎰ primary or NOS

AHA: 3Q, '99, 19; 4Q, '96, 29

✓4ᵗʰ **245 Thyroiditis**

245.0   **Acute thyroiditis**
Abscess of thyroid   Thyroiditis:
Thyroiditis: pyogenic
   nonsuppurative, acute   suppurative
Use additional code to identify organism

DEF: Inflamed thyroid caused by infection, with abscess and liquid puris.

245.1   **Subacute thyroiditis**
Thyroiditis: Thyroiditis:
   de Quervain's   granulomatous
   giant cell   viral

DEF: Inflammation of the thyroid, characterized by fever and painful enlargement of the thyroid gland, with granulomas in the gland.

245.2   **Chronic lymphocytic thyroiditis**
Hashimoto's disease
Struma lymphomatosa
Thyroiditis:
   autoimmune
   lymphocytic (chronic)

DEF: Autoimmune disease of thyroid; lymphocytes infiltrate the gland and thyroid antibodies are produced; women more often affected.

245.3   **Chronic fibrous thyroiditis**
Struma fibrosa   Thyroiditis:
Thyroiditis: ligneous
   invasive (fibrous)   Riedel's

DEF: Persistent fibrosing inflammation of thyroid with adhesions to nearby structures; rare condition

245.4   **Iatrogenic thyroiditis**
Use additional code to identify cause

DEF: Thyroiditis resulting from treatment or intervention by physician or in a patient intervention setting.

245.8   **Other and unspecified chronic thyroiditis**
Chronic thyroiditis:
   NOS
   nonspecific

245.9   **Thyroiditis, unspecified**
Thyroiditis NOS

✓4ᵗʰ **246 Other disorders of thyroid**

246.0   **Disorders of thyrocalcitonin secretion**
Hypersecretion of calcitonin or thyrocalcitonin

246.1   **Dyshormonogenic goiter**
Congenital (dyshormonogenic) goiter
Goiter due to enzyme defect in synthesis of thyroid
     hormone
Goitrous cretinism (sporadic)

246.2   **Cyst of thyroid**
EXCLUDES   cystadenoma of thyroid (226)

246.3   **Hemorrhage and infarction of thyroid**

246.8   **Other specified disorders of thyroid**
Abnormality of thyroid-binding globulin
Atrophy of thyroid
Hyper-TBG-nemia
Hypo-TBG-nemia

246.9   **Unspecified disorder of thyroid**

DISEASES OF OTHER ENDOCRINE GLANDS (250-259)

✓4ᵗʰ **250 Diabetes mellitus**

EXCLUDES   gestational diabetes (648.8)
hyperglycemia NOS (790.6)
neonatal diabetes mellitus (775.1)
nonclinical diabetes (790.29)

The following fifth-digit subclassification is for use with category 250:

0 type II or unspecified type, not stated as uncontrolled
Fifth-digit 0 is for use for type II patients, even if the patient requires insulin
Use additional code, if applicable, for associated long-term (current) insulin use V58.67x

1 type I [juvenile type], not stated as uncontrolled

2 type II or unspecified type, uncontrolled
Fifth-digit 2 is for use for type II patients, even if the patient requires insulin
Use additional code, if applicable, for associated long-term (current) insulin use V58.67x

3 type I [juvenile type], uncontrolled

AHA: 4Q, '04, 56; 2Q, '04, 17; 2Q, '02, 13; 2Q,'01, 16; 2Q,'98, 15; 4Q, '97, 32; 2Q, '97, 14; 3Q, '96, 5; 4Q, '93, 19; 2Q, '92, 5; 3Q, '91, 3; 2Q, '90, 22; N-D, '85, 11

DEF: Diabetes mellitus: Inability to metabolize carbohydrates, proteins, and fats with insufficient secretion of insulin. Symptoms may be unremarkable, with long-term complications, involving kidneys, nerves, blood vessels, and eyes.

DEF: Uncontrolled diabetes: A nonspecific term indicating that the current treatment regimen does not keep the blood sugar level of a patient within acceptable levels.

✓5ᵗʰ **250.0**   **Diabetes mellitus without mention of complication**   `CD PDx`
Diabetes mellitus without mention of complication or manifestation classifiable to 250.1-250.9
Diabetes (mellitus) NOS

AHA: 4Q, '97, 32; N-D, '85, 11; **For code 250.00:** 4Q, '04, 55; 4Q, '03, 105, 108; 2Q, '03, 16; 1Q, '02, 7, 11; **For code 250.01:** ▶1Q, '05, 15;◀ 4Q, '04, 55; 4Q, '03, 110; 2Q, '03, 6; **For code 250.02:** 1Q, '03, 5

✓5ᵗʰ **250.1**   **Diabetes with ketoacidosis**   `CD PDx`
Diabetic:
   acidosis ⎱
   ketosis   ⎰ without mention of coma

AHA: 3Q, '91, 6; **For code 250.11:** 4Q, '03, 82

DEF: Diabetic hyperglycemic crisis causing ketone presence in body fluids.

✓5ᵗʰ **250.2**   **Diabetes with hyperosmolarity**   `CD PDx`
Hyperosmolar (nonketotic) coma

AHA: 4Q, '93, 19; 3Q, '91, 7

✓5ᵗʰ **250.3**   **Diabetes with other coma**   `CD PDx`
Diabetic coma (with ketoacidosis)
Diabetic hypoglycemic coma
Insulin coma NOS
EXCLUDES   diabetes with hyperosmolar coma (250.2)

AHA: 3Q, '91, 7, 12

DEF: Coma (not hyperosmolar) caused by hyperglycemia or hypoglycemia as complication of diabetes.

✓5ᵗʰ **250.4**   **Diabetes with renal manifestations**   `CD PDx`
Use additional code to identify manifestation, as:
▶chronic kidney disease (585.1-585.9)◀
diabetic:
   nephropathy NOS (583.81)
   nephrosis (581.81)
   intercapillary glomerulosclerosis (581.81)
   Kimmelstiel-Wilson syndrome (581.81)

AHA: 3Q, '91, 8, 12; S-O, '87, 9; S-O, '84, 3; **For code 250.40:** 1Q, '03, 20

Ⓝ Newborn Age: 0   Ⓟ Pediatric Age: 0-17   Ⓜ Maternity Age: 12-55   Ⓐ Adult Age: 15-124   `Manifestation Code`   ▶◀ Revised Text   ● New Code   ▲ Revised Code Title

√5ᵗʰ **250.5** **Diabetes with ophthalmic manifestations** `CD PDx`
  Use additional code to identify manifestation, as:
  diabetic:
  blindness (369.00-369.9)
  cataract (366.41)
  glaucoma (365.44)
  ▶macular edema (362.07)◀
  retinal edema ▶(362.07)◀
  retinopathy ▶(362.01-362.07)◀
  AHA: 3Q, '91, 8; S-O, '85, 11

√5ᵗʰ **250.6** **Diabetes with neurological manifestations** `CD PDx`
  Use additional code to identify manifestation, as:
  diabetic:
  amyotrophy (358.1)
  gastroparalysis (536.3)
  gastroparesis (536.3)
  mononeuropathy (354.0-355.9)
  neurogenic arthropathy (713.5)
  peripheral autonomic neuropathy (337.1)
  polyneuropathy (357.2)
  AHA: 2Q, '93, 6; 2Q, '92, 15; 3Q, '91, 9; N-D, '84, 9 ;
  For code 250.60: 4Q, '03, 105; **For code 250.61:** 2Q, '04, 7

√5ᵗʰ **250.7** **Diabetes with peripheral circulatory disorders** `CD PDx`
  Use additional code to identify manifestation, as:
  diabetic:
  gangrene (785.4)
  peripheral angiopathy (443.81)
  AHA: 1Q, '96, 10; 3Q, '94, 5; 2Q, '94, 17; 3Q, '91, 10; 3Q, '90, 15;
  For code 250.70: 1Q, '04, 14

  DEF: Blood vessel damage or disease, usually in the feet, legs, or hands, as a complication of diabetes.

√5ᵗʰ **250.8** **Diabetes with other specified manifestations** `CD PDx`
  Diabetic hypoglycemia
  Hypoglycemic shock
  Use additional code to identify manifestation, as:
  any associated ulceration (707.10-707.9)
  diabetic bone changes (731.8)
  Use additional E code to identify cause, if drug-induced
  AHA: 4Q, '00, 44; 4Q, '97, 43; 2Q, '97, 16; 4Q, '93, 20; 3Q, '91, 10;
  For code 250.80: 1Q, '04, 14

√5ᵗʰ **250.9** **Diabetes with unspecified complication** `CD PDx`
  AHA: 2Q, '92, 15; 3Q, '91, 7, 12

√4ᵗʰ **251** **Other disorders of pancreatic internal secretion**
  251.0 **Hypoglycemic coma**
  Iatrogenic hyperinsulinism
  Non-diabetic insulin coma
  Use additional E code to identify cause, if drug-induced
  EXCLUDES *hypoglycemic coma in diabetes mellitus (250.3)*
  DEF: Coma induced by low blood sugar in non-diabetic patient.

  251.1 **Other specified hypoglycemia**
  Hyperinsulinism: Hyperplasia of pancreatic
  NOS   islet beta cells NOS
  ectopic
  functional
  EXCLUDES *hypoglycemia:*
          in diabetes mellitus (250.8)
          in infant of diabetic mother (775.0)
        hypoglycemic coma (251.0)
        neonatal hypoglycemia (775.6)
  Use additional E code to identify cause, if drug-induced.
  AHA: 1Q, '03, 10

  DEF: Excessive production of insulin by the pancreas; associated with obesity and insulin-producing tumors.

Dorsal View of Parathyroid Glands

Parathyroid glands
↓
Parathyroid hormone (PTH)
↓
Calcium in bones ———————→ Calcium in blood

251.2 **Hypoglycemia, unspecified**
  Hypoglycemia: Hypoglycemia:
  NOS   spontaneous
  reactive
  EXCLUDES *hypoglycemia:*
          with coma (251.0)
          in diabetes mellitus (250.8)
          leucine-induced (270.3)
  AHA: M-A, '85, 8

251.3 **Postsurgical hypoinsulinemia**
  Hypoinsulinemia following complete or partial pancreatectomy
  Postpancreatectomy hyperglycemia
  AHA: 3Q, '91, 6

251.4 **Abnormality of secretion of glucagon**
  Hyperplasia of pancreatic islet alpha cells with glucagon excess
  DEF: Production malfunction of a pancreatic hormone secreted by cells of the islets of Langerhans.

251.5 **Abnormality of secretion of gastrin**
  Hyperplasia of pancreatic alpha cells with gastrin excess
  Zollinger-Ellison syndrome

251.8 **Other specified disorders of pancreatic internal secretion**
  AHA: 2Q, '98, 15; 3Q, '91, 6

251.9 **Unspecified disorder of pancreatic internal secretion**
  Islet cell hyperplasia NOS

√4ᵗʰ **252** **Disorders of parathyroid gland**
√5ᵗʰ **252.0** **Hyperparathyroidism**
  EXCLUDES *ectopic hyperparathyroidism (259.3)*
  DEF: Abnormally high secretion of parathyroid hormones causing bone deterioration, reduced renal function, kidney stones.

  252.00 **Hyperparathyroidism, unspecified**
  252.01 **Primary hyperparathyroidism**
  Hyperplasia of parathyroid
  DEF: Parathyroid dysfunction commonly caused by hyperplasia of two or more glands; characteristic hypercalcemia and increased parathyroid hormone levels.

  252.02 **Secondary hyperparathyroidism, non-renal**
  EXCLUDES *secondary hyperparathyroidism (of renal origin) (588.81)*
  AHA: 4Q, '04, 57-59
  DEF: Underlying disease of nonrenal origin decreases blood levels of calcium causing the parathyroid to release increased levels of parathyroid hormone; parathyroid hormone levels return to normal once underlying condition is treated and blood calcium levels are normal.

  252.08 **Other hyperparathyroidism**
  Tertiary hyperparathyroidism
  DEF: Tertiary hyperparathyroidism: chronic secondary hyperparathyroidism leads to adenomatous parathyroid causing irreversible abnormal production of parathyroid hormone (PTH); PTH remains high after the serum calcium levels are brought under control.

√4ᵗʰ / √5ᵗʰ Additional Digit Required   RUG III Special Care Dx   RUG III Clinically Complex Dx   Hospice Non-cancer Dx   `CD PDx` Clinical Dimension PDx   `CD SDx` Clinical Dimension SDx

Endocrine, Nutritional and Metabolic, Immunity

252.1–255.11

252.1 Hypoparathyroidism

Parathyroiditis   Tetany:
(autoimmune)   parathyroid
                        parathyroprival

EXCLUDES   pseudohypoparathyroidism (275.4)
            pseudopseudohypoparathyroidism
            (275.4)
            tetany NOS (781.7)
            transitory neonatal
            hypoparathyroidism (775.4)

DEF: Abnormally low secretion of parathyroid hormones which causes decreased calcium and increased phosphorus in the blood. Resulting in muscle cramps, tetany, urinary frequency and cataracts.

252.8 Other specified disorders of parathyroid gland

Cyst
Hemorrhage   } of parathyroid gland

252.9 Unspecified disorder of parathyroid gland

✓4ᵗʰ **253 Disorders of the pituitary gland and its hypothalamic control**

INCLUDES   the listed conditions whether the disorder is in the pituitary or the hypothalamus

EXCLUDES   Cushing's syndrome (255.0)

253.0 Acromegaly and gigantism

Overproduction of growth hormone

DEF: Acromegaly: chronic, beginning in middle age; caused by hypersecretion of the pituitary growth hormone; produces enlarged parts of skeleton, especially the nose, ears, jaws, fingers and toes.

DEF: Gigantism: pituitary gigantism caused by excess growth of short flat bones; men may grow 78 to 80 inches tall.

253.1 Other and unspecified anterior pituitary hyperfunction

Forbes-Albright syndrome

EXCLUDES   overproduction of:
            ACTH (255.3)
            thyroid-stimulating hormone [TSH]
            (242.8)

AHA: J-A, '85, 9

DEF: Spontaneous galactorrhea-amenorrhea syndrome unrelated to pregnancy; usually related to presence of pituitary tumor.

253.2 Panhypopituitarism

Cachexia, pituitary
Necrosis of pituitary (postpartum)
Pituitary insufficiency NOS
Sheehan's syndrome
Simmonds' disease

EXCLUDES   iatrogenic hypopituitarism (253.7)

DEF: Damage to or absence of pituitary gland leading to impaired sexual function, weight loss, fatigue, bradycardia, hypotension, pallor, depression, and impaired growth in children; called Simmonds' disease if cachexia is prominent.

253.3 Pituitary dwarfism

Isolated deficiency of (human) growth hormone [HGH]
Lorain-Levi dwarfism

DEF: Dwarfism with infantile physical characteristics due to abnormally low secretion of growth hormone and gonadotropin deficiency.

253.4 Other anterior pituitary disorders

Isolated or partial deficiency of an anterior pituitary hormone, other than growth hormone
Prolactin deficiency

AHA: J-A, '85, 9

253.5 Diabetes insipidus

Vasopressin deficiency

EXCLUDES   nephrogenic diabetes insipidus (588.1)

DEF: Metabolic disorder causing insufficient antidiuretic hormone release; symptoms include frequent urination, thirst, ravenous hunger, loss of weight, fatigue.

253.6 Other disorders of neurohypophysis

Syndrome of inappropriate secretion of antidiuretic hormone [ADH]

EXCLUDES   ectopic antidiuretic hormone secretion
            (259.3)

253.7 Iatrogenic pituitary disorders

Hypopituitarism: Hypopituitarism:
  hormone-induced   postablative
  hypophysectomy-induced   radiotherapy-induced
Use additional E code to identify cause

DEF: Pituitary dysfunction that results from drug therapy, radiation therapy, or surgery, causing mild to severe symptoms.

253.8 Other disorders of the pituitary and other syndromes of diencephalohypophyseal origin

Abscess of pituitary   Cyst of Rathke's pouch
Adiposogenital dystrophy   Fröhlich's syndrome

EXCLUDES   craniopharyngioma (237.0)

253.9 Unspecified

Dyspituitarism

✓4ᵗʰ **254 Diseases of thymus gland**

EXCLUDES   aplasia or dysplasia with immunodeficiency
            (279.2)
            hypoplasia with immunodeficiency (279.2)
            myasthenia gravis (358.00-358.01)

254.0 Persistent hyperplasia of thymus

Hypertrophy of thymus

DEF: Continued abnormal growth of the twin lymphoid lobes that produce T lymphocytes.

254.1 Abscess of thymus

254.8 Other specified diseases of thymus gland

Atrophy
Cyst   } of thymus

EXCLUDES   thymoma (212.6)

254.9 Unspecified disease of thymus gland

✓4ᵗʰ **255 Disorders of adrenal glands**

INCLUDES   the listed conditions whether the basic disorder is in the adrenals or is pituitary-induced

255.0 Cushing's syndrome

Adrenal hyperplasia due to excess ACTH
Cushing's syndrome:
  NOS
  iatrogenic
  idiopathic
  pituitary-dependent
Ectopic ACTH syndrome
Iatrogenic syndrome of excess cortisol
Overproduction of cortisol
Use additional E code to identify cause, if drug-induced

EXCLUDES   congenital adrenal hyperplasia (255.2)

DEF: Due to adrenal cortisol oversecretion or glucocorticoid medications; may cause fatty tissue of the face, neck and body; osteoporosis and curvature of spine, hypertension, diabetes mellitus, female genitourinary problems, male impotence, degeneration of muscle tissues, weakness.

✓5ᵗʰ **255.1 Hyperaldosteronism**

AHA: 4Q, '03, 48

DEF: Oversecretion of aldosterone causing fluid retention, hypertension.

255.10 Primary aldosteronism

Aldosteronism NOS
Hyperaldosteronism, unspecified

EXCLUDES   Conn's syndrome (255.12)

255.11 Glucocorticoid-remediable aldosteronism

Familial aldosteronism type I

EXCLUDES   Conn's syndrome (255.12)

DEF: A rare autosomal dominant familial form of primary aldosteronism in which the secretion of aldosterone is under the influence of adrenocortiotrophic hormone (ACTH) rather than the renin-angiotensin mechanism; characterized by moderate hypersecretion of aldosterone and suppressed plasma renin activity rapidly reversed by administration of glucosteroids; symptoms include hypertension and mild hypokalemia.

N Newborn Age: 0   P Pediatric Age: 0-17   M Maternity Age: 12-55   A Adult Age: 15-124   Manifestation Code   ◄► Revised Text   ● New Code   ▲ Revised Code Title

48 — Volume 1   *2006 ICD•9•CM*

255.12 Conn's syndrome
DEF: A type of primary aldosteronism caused by an adenoma of the glomerulosa cells in the adrenal cortex; presence of hypertension.

255.13 Bartter's syndrome
DEF: A cluster of symptoms caused by a defect in the ability of the kidney to reabsorb potassium; signs include alkalosis (hypokalemic alkalosis), increased aldosterone, increased plasma renin, and normal blood pressure; symptoms include muscle cramping, weakness, constipation, frequency of urination, and failure to grow; also known as urinary potassium wasting or juxtaglomerular cell hyperplasia.

255.14 Other secondary aldosteronism

255.2 Adrenogenital disorders
Achard-Thiers syndrome
Adrenogenital syndromes, virilizing or feminizing, whether acquired or associated with congenital adrenal hyperplasia consequent on inborn enzyme defects in hormone synthesis
Congenital adrenal hyperplasia
Female adrenal pseudohermaphroditism
Male:
   macrogenitosomia praecox
   sexual precocity with adrenal hyperplasia
Virilization (female) (suprarenal)
   EXCLUDES   *adrenal hyperplasia due to excess ACTH (255.0)*
        isosexual virilization (256.4)

255.3 Other corticoadrenal overactivity
Acquired benign adrenal androgenic overactivity
Overproduction of ACTH

255.4 Corticoadrenal insufficiency
Addisonian crisis   Adrenal:
Addison's disease NOS   crisis
Adrenal: hemorrhage
  atrophy (autoimmune)   infarction
  calcification   insufficiency NOS
   EXCLUDES   *tuberculous Addison's disease (017.6)*
DEF: Underproduction of adrenal hormones causing low blood pressure.

255.5 Other adrenal hypofunction
Adrenal medullary insufficiency
   EXCLUDES   *Waterhouse-Friderichsen syndrome (meningococcal) (036.3)*

255.6 Medulloadrenal hyperfunction
Catecholamine secretion by pheochromocytoma

255.8 Other specified disorders of adrenal glands
Abnormality of cortisol-binding globulin

255.9 Unspecified disorder of adrenal glands

√4ᵗʰ **256 Ovarian dysfunction**
AHA: 4Q, '00, 51

256.0 Hyperestrogenism   ♀
DEF: Excess secretion of estrogen by the ovaries; characterized by ovaries containing multiple follicular cysts filled with serous fluid.

256.1 Other ovarian hyperfunction   ♀
Hypersecretion of ovarian androgens
AHA: 3Q, '95, 15

256.2 Postablative ovarian failure   ♀
Ovarian failure: Ovarian failure:
  iatrogenic   postsurgical
  postirradiation
Use additional code for states associated with artificial menopause (627.4)
   EXCLUDES   *acquired absence of ovary (V45.77)*
        asymptomatic age-related (natural) postmenopausal status (V49.81)
AHA: 2Q, '02, 12
DEF: Failed ovarian function after medical or surgical intervention.

√5ᵗʰ **256.3 Other ovarian failure**
Use additional code for states associated with natural menopause (627.2)
   EXCLUDES   *asymptomatic age-related (natural) postmenopausal status (V49.81)*
AHA: 4Q, '01, 41

256.31 Premature menopause   A   ♀
DEF: Permanent cessation of ovarian function before the age of 40 occuring naturally of unknown cause.

256.39 Other ovarian failure   ♀
Delayed menarche
Ovarian hypofunction
Primary ovarian failure NOS

256.4 Polycystic ovaries   ♀
Isosexual virilization   Stein-Leventhal syndrome
DEF: Multiple serous filled cysts of ovary; symptoms of infertility, hirsutism, oligomenorrhea or amenorrhea.

256.8 Other ovarian dysfunction   ♀

256.9 Unspecified ovarian dysfunction   ♀

√4ᵗʰ **257 Testicular dysfunction**

257.0 Testicular hyperfunction   ♂
Hypersecretion of testicular hormones

257.1 Postablative testicular hypofunction   ♂
Testicular hypofunction:
  iatrogenic
  postirradiation
  postsurgical

257.2 Other testicular hypofunction
Defective biosynthesis of testicular androgen
Eunuchoidism:
  NOS
  hypogonadotropic
Failure:
  Leydig's cell, adult
  seminiferous tubule, adult
Testicular hypogonadism
   EXCLUDES   *azoospermia (606.0)*

257.8 Other testicular dysfunction
   EXCLUDES ▶ *androgen insensitivity syndrome (259.5)*◀

257.9 Unspecified testicular dysfunction   ♂

√4ᵗʰ **258 Polyglandular dysfunction and related disorders**

258.0 Polyglandular activity in multiple endocrine adenomatosis
Wermer's syndrome
DEF: Wermer's syndrome: A rare hereditary condition characterized by the presence of adenomas or hyperplasia in more than one endocrine gland causing premature aging.

258.1 Other combinations of endocrine dysfunction
Lloyd's syndrome   Schmidt's syndrome

258.8 Other specified polyglandular dysfunction

258.9 Polyglandular dysfunction, unspecified

√4ᵗʰ **259 Other endocrine disorders**

259.0 Delay in sexual development and puberty, not elsewhere classified
Delayed puberty

259.1 Precocious sexual development and puberty, not elsewhere classified   P
Sexual precocity: Sexual precocity:
  NOS   cryptogenic
  constitutional   idiopathic

259.2 Carcinoid syndrome
Hormone secretion by carcinoid tumors
DEF: Presence of carcinoid tumors that spread to liver; characterized by cyanotic flushing of skin, diarrhea, bronchospasm, acquired tricuspid and pulmonary stenosis, sudden drops in blood pressure, edema, ascites.

√4ᵗʰ / √5ᵗʰ Additional Digit Required   RUG III Special Care Dx   RUG III Clinically Complex Dx   Hospice Non-cancer Dx   **CD PDx** Clinical Dimension PDx   **CD SDx** Clinical Dimension SDx

2006 ICD•9•CM   **October 2005 • Volume 1 — 49**

Endocrine, Nutritional and Metabolic, Immunity

259.3–267

259.3 **Ectopic hormone secretion, not elsewhere classified**
Ectopic:
    antidiuretic hormone secretion [ADH]
    hyperparathyroidism
    EXCLUDES *ectopic ACTH syndrome (255.0)*
AHA: N-D, '85, 4

259.4 **Dwarfism, not elsewhere classified**
Dwarfism: Dwarfism:
    NOS   constitutional
    EXCLUDES *dwarfism:*
        achondroplastic (756.4)
        intrauterine (759.7)
        nutritional (263.2)
        pituitary (253.3)
        renal (588.0)
        progeria (259.8)

259.5 **Androgen insensitivity syndrome**
Partial androgen insensitivity
Reifenstein syndrome

259.8 **Other specified endocrine disorders**
Pineal gland dysfunction
Progeria
Werner's syndrome

259.9 **Unspecified endocrine disorder**
Disturbance: Infantilism NOS
    endocrine NOS
    hormone NOS

NUTRITIONAL DEFICIENCIES (260-269)
EXCLUDES *deficiency anemias (280.0-281.9)*

260 Kwashiorkor
Nutritional edema with dyspigmentation of skin and hair
DEF: Syndrome, particularly of children; excessive carbohydrate with inadequate protein intake, inhibited growth potential, anomalies in skin and hair pigmentation, edema and liver disease.

261 Nutritional marasmus
Nutritional atrophy   Severe malnutrition NOS
Severe calorie deficiency
DEF: Protein-calorie malabsorption or malnutrition of children; characterized by tissue wasting, dehydration, and subcutaneous fat depletion; may occur with infectious disease; also called infantile atrophy.

262 Other severe, protein-calorie malnutrition
Nutritional edema without mention of dyspigmentation of skin and hair
AHA: 4Q, '92, 24; J-A, '85, 12

✓4ᵗʰ 263 Other and unspecified protein-calorie malnutrition
AHA: 4Q, '92, 24

263.0 **Malnutrition of moderate degree**
AHA: J-A, '85, 1
DEF: Malnutrition characterized by biochemical changes in electrolytes, lipids, blood plasma.

263.1 **Malnutrition of mild degree**
AHA: J-A, '85, 1

263.2 **Arrested development following protein-calorie malnutrition**
Nutritional dwarfism
Physical retardation due to malnutrition

263.8 **Other protein-calorie malnutrition**

263.9 **Unspecified protein-calorie malnutrition**
Dystrophy due to malnutrition
Malnutrition (calorie) NOS
    EXCLUDES *nutritional deficiency NOS (269.9)*
AHA: 4Q, '03, 109; N-D, '84, 19

✓4ᵗʰ 264 Vitamin A deficiency
264.0 **With conjunctival xerosis**
DEF: Vitamin A deficiency with conjunctival dryness.

264.1 **With conjunctival xerosis and Bitot's spot**
Bitot's spot in the young child
DEF: Vitamin A deficiency with conjunctival dryness, superficial spots of keratinized epithelium.

264.2 **With corneal xerosis**
DEF: Vitamin A deficiency with corneal dryness.

264.3 **With corneal ulceration and xerosis**
DEF: Vitamin A deficiency with corneal dryness, epithelial ulceration.

264.4 **With keratomalacia**
DEF: Vitamin A deficiency creating corneal dryness; progresses to corneal insensitivity, softness, necrosis; usually bilateral.

264.5 **With night blindness**
DEF: Vitamin A deficiency causing vision failure in dim light.

264.6 **With xerophthalmic scars of cornea**
DEF: Vitamin A deficiency with corneal scars from dryness.

264.7 **Other ocular manifestations of vitamin A deficiency**
Xerophthalmia due to vitamin A deficiency

264.8 **Other manifestations of vitamin A deficiency**
Follicular keratosis ⎫ due to vitamin A
Xeroderma   ⎬ deficiency

264.9 **Unspecified vitamin A deficiency**
Hypovitaminosis A NOS

✓4ᵗʰ 265 Thiamine and niacin deficiency states
265.0 **Beriberi**
DEF: Inadequate vitamin B_1 (thiamine) intake, affects heart and peripheral nerves; individual may become edematous and develop cardiac disease due to the excess fluid; alcoholics and people with a diet of excessive polished rice prone to the disease.

265.1 **Other and unspecified manifestations of thiamine deficiency**
Other vitamin B_1 deficiency states

265.2 **Pellagra**
Deficiency: Deficiency:
    niacin (-tryptophan)   vitamin PP
    nicotinamide   Pellagra (alcoholic)
    nicotinic acid
DEF: Niacin deficiency causing dermatitis, inflammation of mucous membranes, diarrhea, and psychic disturbances.

✓4ᵗʰ 266 Deficiency of B-complex components
266.0 **Ariboflavinosis**
Riboflavin [vitamin B_2] deficiency
AHA: S-O, '86, 10
DEF: Vitamin B_2 (riboflavin) deficiency marked by swollen lips and tongue fissures, corneal vascularization, scaling lesions, and anemia.

266.1 **Vitamin B_6 deficiency**
Deficiency: Deficiency:
    pyridoxal   pyridoxine
    pyridoxamine   Vitamin B_6 deficiency
                            syndrome
    EXCLUDES *vitamin B_6-responsive sideroblastic anemia (285.0)*
DEF: Vitamin B_6 deficiency causing skin, lip, and tongue disturbances, peripheral neuropathy; and convulsions in infants.

266.2 **Other B-complex deficiencies**
Deficiency: Deficiency:
    cyanocobalamin   vitamin B_{12}
    folic acid
    EXCLUDES *combined system disease with anemia (281.0-281.1)*
        deficiency anemias (281.0-281.9)
        subacute degeneration of spinal cord with anemia (281.0-281.1)

266.9 **Unspecified vitamin B deficiency**

267 Ascorbic acid deficiency
Deficiency of vitamin C
Scurvy
    EXCLUDES *scorbutic anemia (281.8)*
DEF: Vitamin C deficiency causing swollen gums, myalgia, weight loss, and weakness.

Ⓝ Newborn Age: 0   Ⓟ Pediatric Age: 0-17   Ⓜ Maternity Age: 12-55   Ⓐ Adult Age: 15-124   ▮Manifestation Code▮   ◄► Revised Text   ● New Code   ▲ Revised Code Title

✓4th **268 Vitamin D deficiency**

> EXCLUDES   *vitamin D-resistant:*
> *osteomalacia (275.3)*
> *rickets (275.3)*

268.0 Rickets, active

> EXCLUDES   *celiac rickets (579.0)*
> *renal rickets (588.0)*

DEF: Inadequate vitamin D intake, usually in pediatrics, that affects bones most involved with muscular action; may cause nodules on ends and sides of bones; delayed closure of fontanels in infants; symptoms may include muscle soreness, and profuse sweating.

268.1 Rickets, late effect

> Any condition specified as due to rickets and stated to be a late effect or sequela of rickets
> Use additional code to identify the nature of late effect

DEF: Distorted or demineralized bones as a result of vitamin D deficiency.

268.2 Osteomalacia, unspecified

DEF: Softening of bones due to decrease in calcium; marked by pain, tenderness, muscular weakness, anorexia, and weight loss.

268.9 Unspecified vitamin D deficiency

> Avitaminosis D

✓4th **269 Other nutritional deficiencies**

269.0 Deficiency of vitamin K

> EXCLUDES   *deficiency of coagulation factor due to vitamin K deficiency (286.7)*
> *vitamin K deficiency of newborn (776.0)*

269.1 Deficiency of other vitamins

> Deficiency: Deficiency:
> vitamin E   vitamin P

269.2 Unspecified vitamin deficiency

> Multiple vitamin deficiency NOS

269.3 Mineral deficiency, not elsewhere classified

> Deficiency: Deficiency:
> calcium, dietary   iodine

> EXCLUDES   *deficiency:*
> *calcium NOS (275.4)*
> *potassium (276.8)*
> *sodium (276.1)*

269.8 Other nutritional deficiency

> EXCLUDES   *adult failure to thrive (783.7)*
> *failure to thrive in childhood (783.41)*
> *feeding problems (783.3)*
> *newborn (779.3)*

269.9 Unspecified nutritional deficiency

OTHER METABOLIC AND IMMUNITY DISORDERS (270-279)

> Use additional code to identify any associated mental retardation

✓4th **270 Disorders of amino-acid transport and metabolism**

> EXCLUDES   *abnormal findings without manifest disease (790.0-796.9)*
> *disorders of purine and pyrimidine metabolism (277.1-277.2)*
> *gout (274.0-274.9)*

270.0 Disturbances of amino-acid transport

> Cystinosis   Glycinuria (renal)
> Cystinuria   Hartnup disease
> Fanconi (-de Toni) (-Debré) syndrome

270.1 Phenylketonuria [PKU]

> Hyperphenylalaninemia

DEF: Inherited metabolic condition causing excess phenylpyruvic and other acids in urine; results in mental retardation, neurological manifestations, including spasticity and tremors, light pigmentation, eczema, and mousy odor.

270.2 Other disturbances of aromatic amino-acid metabolism

> Albinism   Hypertyrosinemia
> Alkaptonuria   Indicanuria
> Alkaptonuric ochronosis   Kynureninase defects
> Disturbances of metabolism   Oasthouse urine disease
>   of tyrosine and   Ochronosis
>   tryptophan   Tyrosinosis
> Homogentisic acid defects   Tyrosinuria
> Hydroxykynureninuria   Waardenburg syndrome

> EXCLUDES   *vitamin B₆-deficiency syndrome (266.1)*

AHA: 3Q, '99, 20

270.3 Disturbances of branched-chain amino-acid metabolism

> Disturbances of metabolism of leucine, isoleucine, and valine
> Hypervalinemia
> Intermittent branched-chain ketonuria
> Leucine-induced hypoglycemia
> Leucinosis
> Maple syrup urine disease

AHA: 3Q, '00, 8

270.4 Disturbances of sulphur-bearing amino-acid metabolism

> Cystathioninemia
> Cystathioninuria
> Disturbances of metabolism of methionine, homocystine, and cystathionine
> Homocystinuria
> Hypermethioninemia
> Methioninemia

AHA: 1Q, '04, 6

270.5 Disturbances of histidine metabolism

> Carnosinemia
> Histidinemia
> Hyperhistidinemia
> Imidazole aminoaciduria

270.6 Disorders of urea cycle metabolism

> Argininosuccinic aciduria
> Citrullinemia
> Disorders of metabolism of ornithine, citrulline, argininosuccinic acid, arginine, and ammonia
> Hyperammonemia
> Hyperomithinemia

270.7 Other disturbances of straight-chain amino-acid metabolism

> Glucoglycinuria
> Glycinemia (with methyl-malonic acidemia)
> Hyperglycinemia
> Hyperlysinemia
> Other disturbances of metabolism of glycine, threonine, serine, glutamine, and lysine
> Pipecolic acidemia
> Saccharopinuria

AHA: 3Q, '00, 8

270.8 Other specified disorders of amino-acid metabolism

> Alaninemia   Iminoacidopathy
> Ethanolaminuria   Prolinemia
> Glycoprolinuria   Prolinuria
> Hydroxyprolinemia   Sarcosinemia
> Hyperprolinemia

270.9 Unspecified disorder of amino-acid metabolism

✓4th ✓5th **Additional Digit Required**   RUG III Special Care Dx   RUG III Clinically Complex Dx   Hospice Non-cancer Dx   **CD PDx** Clinical Dimension PDx   **CD SDx** Clinical Dimension SDx

2006 ICD•9•CM   Volume 1 — 51

Lipid Metabolism

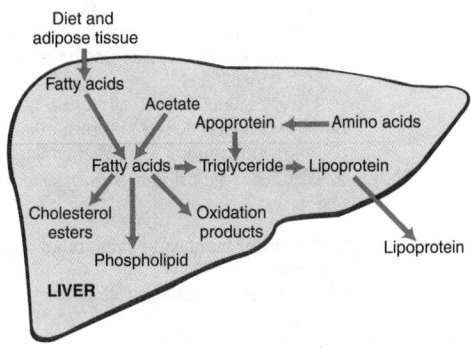

✓4ᵗʰ **271 Disorders of carbohydrate transport and metabolism**

> EXCLUDES   *abnormality of secretion of glucagon (251.4)*
> *diabetes mellitus (250.0-250.9)*
> *hypoglycemia NOS (251.2)*
> *mucopolysaccharidosis (277.5)*

271.0 Glycogenosis
Amylopectinosis
Glucose-6-phosphatase deficiency
Glycogen storage disease
McArdle's disease
Pompe's disease
von Gierke's disease

AHA: 1Q, '98, 5

271.1 Galactosemia
Galactose-1-phosphate uridyl transferase deficiency
Galactosuria

DEF: Any of three genetic disorders due to defective galactose metabolism; symptoms include failure to thrive in infancy, jaundice, liver and spleen damage, cataracts, and mental retardation.

271.2 Hereditary fructose intolerance
Essential benign fructosuria   Fructosemia

DEF: Chromosome recessive disorder of carbohydrate metabolism; in infants, occurs after dietary sugar introduced; characterized by enlarged spleen, yellowish cast to skin, and progressive inability to thrive.

271.3 Intestinal disaccharidase deficiencies and disaccharide malabsorption
Intolerance or malabsorption (congenital) (of):
   glucose-galactose
   lactose
   sucrose-isomaltose

271.4 Renal glycosuria
Renal diabetes

DEF: Persistent abnormal levels of glucose in urine, with normal blood glucose levels; caused by failure of the renal tubules to reabsorb glucose.

271.8 Other specified disorders of carbohydrate transport and metabolism
Essential benign pentosuria   Mannosidosis
Fucosidosis   Oxalosis
Glycolic aciduria   Xylosuria
Hyperoxaluria (primary)   Xylulosuria

271.9 Unspecified disorder of carbohydrate transport and metabolism

✓4ᵗʰ **272 Disorders of lipoid metabolism**

> EXCLUDES   *localized cerebral lipidoses (330.1)*

272.0 Pure hypercholesterolemia
Familial hypercholesterolemia
Fredrickson Type IIa hyperlipoproteinemia
Hyperbetalipoproteinemia
Hyperlipidemia, Group A
Low-density-lipoid-type [LDL] hyperlipoproteinemia

272.1 Pure hyperglyceridemia
Endogenous hyperglyceridemia
Fredrickson Type IV hyperlipoproteinemia
Hyperlipidemia, Group B
Hyperprebetalipoproteinemia
Hypertriglyceridemia, essential
Very-low-density-lipoid-type [VLDL]
   hyperlipoproteinemia

272.2 Mixed hyperlipidemia
Broad- or floating-betalipoproteinemia
Fredrickson Type IIb or III hyperlipoproteinemia
Hypercholesterolemia with endogenous
   hyperglyceridemia
Hyperbetalipoproteinemia with
   prebetalipoproteinemia
Tubo-eruptive xanthoma
Xanthoma tuberosum

DEF: Elevated levels of lipoprotein, a complex of fats and proteins, in blood due to inherited metabolic disorder.

272.3 Hyperchylomicronemia
Bûrger-Grütz syndrome
Fredrickson type I or V hyperlipoproteinemia
Hyperlipidemia, Group D
Mixed hyperglyceridemia

272.4 Other and unspecified hyperlipidemia
Alpha-lipoproteinemia
Combined hyperlipidemia
Hyperlipidemia NOS
Hyperlipoproteinemia NOS

AHA: ▶1Q, '05, 17◀

DEF: Hyperlipoproteinemia: elevated levels of transient chylomicrons in the blood which are a form of lipoproteins which transport dietary cholesterol and triglycerides from the small intestine to the blood.

272.5 Lipoprotein deficiencies
Abetalipoproteinemia
Bassen-Kornzweig syndrome
High-density lipoid deficiency
Hypoalphalipoproteinemia
Hypobetalipoproteinemia (familial)

DEF: Abnormally low levels of lipoprotein, a complex of fats and protein, in the blood.

272.6 Lipodystrophy
Barraquer-Simons disease
Progressive lipodystrophy
Use additional E code to identify cause, if iatrogenic

> EXCLUDES   *intestinal lipodystrophy (040.2)*

DEF: Disturbance of fat metabolism resulting in loss of fatty tissue in some areas of the body.

272.7 Lipidoses
Chemically-induced lipidosis
Disease:
   Anderson's
   Fabry's
   Gaucher's
   I cell [mucolipidosis I]
   lipoid storage NOS
   Niemann-Pick
   pseudo-Hurler's or mucolipdosis III
   triglyceride storage, Type I or II
   Wolman's or triglyceride storage, Type III
Mucolipidosis II
Primary familial xanthomatosis

> EXCLUDES   *cerebral lipidoses (330.1)*
> *Tay-Sachs disease (330.1)*

DEF: Lysosomal storage diseases marked by an abnormal amount of lipids in reticuloendothelial cells.

272.8 Other disorders of lipoid metabolism
Hoffa's disease or liposynovitis prepatellaris
Launois-Bensaude's lipomatosis
Lipoid dermatoarthritis

272.9 Unspecified disorder of lipoid metabolism

N Newborn Age: 0   P Pediatric Age: 0-17   M Maternity Age: 12-55   A Adult Age: 15-124   Manifestation Code   ▶◀ Revised Text   ● New Code   ▲ Revised Code Title

✓4ᵗʰ 273 Disorders of plasma protein metabolism

> **EXCLUDES** *agammaglobulinemia and hypogammaglobulinemia (279.0-279.2)*
> *coagulation defects (286.0-286.9)*
> *hereditary hemolytic anemias (282.0-282.9)*

273.0 Polyclonal hypergammaglobulinemia

Hypergammaglobulinemic purpura:
benign primary
Waldenström's

DEF: Elevated blood levels of gamma globulins, frequently found in patients with chronic infectious diseases.

273.1 Monoclonal paraproteinemia

Benign monoclonal hypergammaglobulinemia [BMH]
Monoclonal gammopathy:
NOS
associated with lymphoplasmacytic dyscrasias
benign
Paraproteinemia:
benign (familial)
secondary to malignant or inflammatory disease

273.2 Other paraproteinemias

Cryoglobulinemic: Mixed cryoglobulinemia
purpura
vasculitis

273.3 Macroglobulinemia

Macroglobulinemia (idiopathic) (primary)
Waldenström's macroglobulinemia

DEF: Elevated blood levels of macroglobulins (plasma globulins of high weight); characterized by malignant neoplasms of bone marrow, spleen, liver, or lymph nodes; symptoms include weakness, fatigue, bleeding disorders, and vision problems.

273.4 Alpha-1-antitrypsin deficiency

AAT deficiency

DEF: ▶Disorder of plasma protein metabolism that results in a deficiency of Alpha-1-antitrypsin, an acute-phase reactive protein, released into the blood in response to infection or injury to protect tissue against the harmful effect of enzymes.◀

273.8 Other disorders of plasma protein metabolism

Abnormality of transport protein
Bisalbuminemia

AHA: 2Q, '98, 11

273.9 Unspecified disorder of plasma protein metabolism

✓4ᵗʰ 274 Gout

> **EXCLUDES** *lead gout (984.0-984.9)*

AHA: 2Q, '95, 4

DEF: Purine and pyrimidine metabolic disorders; manifested by hyperuricemia and recurrent acute inflammatory arthritis; monosodium urate or monohydrate crystals may be deposited in and around the joints, leading to joint destruction, and severe crippling.

274.0 Gouty arthropathy   `CD PDx`

✓5ᵗʰ 274.1 Gouty nephropathy

274.10 Gouty nephropathy, unspecified   `CD PDx`

AHA: N-D, '85, 15

274.11 Uric acid nephrolithiasis   `CD PDx`

DEF: Sodium urate stones in the kidney.

274.19 Other   `CD PDx`

✓5ᵗʰ 274.8 Gout with other specified manifestations

274.81 Gouty tophi of ear   `CD PDx`

DEF: Chalky sodium urate deposit in the ear due to gout; produces chronic inflammation of external ear.

274.82 Gouty tophi of other sites   `CD PDx`

Gouty tophi of heart

274.89 Other   `CD PDx`

Use additional code to identify manifestations, as:
gouty:
iritis (364.11)
neuritis (357.4)

274.9 Gout, unspecified   `CD PDx`

✓4ᵗʰ 275 Disorders of mineral metabolism

> **EXCLUDES** *abnormal findings without manifest disease (790.0-796.9)*

275.0 Disorders of iron metabolism

Bronzed diabetes   Pigmentary cirrhosis (of liver)
Hemochromatosis

> **EXCLUDES** *anemia:*
> *iron deficiency (280.0-280.9)*
> *sideroblastic (285.0)*

AHA: 2Q, '97, 11

275.1 Disorders of copper metabolism

Hepatolenticular degeneration
Wilson's disease

275.2 Disorders of magnesium metabolism

Hypermagnesemia   Hypomagnesemia

275.3 Disorders of phosphorus metabolism

Familial hypophosphatemia Vitamin D-resistant:
Hypophosphatasia   osteomalacia
rickets

✓5ᵗʰ 275.4 Disorders of calcium metabolism

> **EXCLUDES** *parathyroid disorders (252.00-252.9)*
> *vitamin D deficiency (268.0-268.9)*

AHA: 4Q, '97, 33

275.40 Unspecified disorder of calcium metabolism

275.41 Hypocalcemia

DEF: Abnormally decreased blood calcium level; symptoms include hyperactive deep tendon reflexes, muscle, abdominal cramps, and carpopedal spasm.

275.42 Hypercalcemia

AHA: 4Q, '03, 110

DEF: Abnormally increased blood calcium level; symptoms include muscle weakness, fatigue, nausea, depression, and constipation.

275.49 Other disorders of calcium metabolism

Nephrocalcinosis
Pseudohypoparathyroidism
Pseudopseudohypoparathyroidism

DEF: Nephrocalcinosis: calcium phosphate deposits in the tubules of the kidney with resultant renal insufficiency.

DEF: Pseudohypoparathyroidism: inherited disorder with signs and symptoms of hypoparathyroidism; caused by inadequate response to parathyroid hormone, not hormonal deficiency. Symptoms include muscle cramps, tetany, urinary frequency, blurred vision due to cataracts, and dry scaly skin.

DEF: Pseudopseudohypoparathyroidism: clinical manifestations of hypoparathyroidism without affecting blood calcium levels.

275.8 Other specified disorders of mineral metabolism

275.9 Unspecified disorder of mineral metabolism

✓4ᵗʰ 276 Disorders of fluid, electrolyte, and acid-base balance

> **EXCLUDES** *diabetes insipidus (253.5)*
> *familial periodic paralysis (359.3)*

276.0 Hyperosmolality and/or hypernatremia

Sodium [Na] excess   Sodium [Na] overload

276.1 Hyposmolality and/or hyponatremia

Sodium [Na] deficiency

276.2 Acidosis

Acidosis: Acidosis:
NOS   metabolic
lactic   respiratory

> **EXCLUDES** *diabetic acidosis (250.1)*

AHA: J-F, '87, 15

DEF: Disorder involves decrease of pH (hydrogen ion) concentration in blood and cellular tissues; caused by increase in acid and decrease in bicarbonate.

✓4ᵗʰ ✓5ᵗʰ Additional Digit Required   RUG III Special Care Dx   RUG III Clinically Complex Dx   Hospice Non-cancer Dx   `CD PDx` Clinical Dimension PDx   `CD SDx` Clinical Dimension SDx

276.3 Alkalosis

Alkalosis: Alkalosis:
  NOS   respiratory
  metabolic

DEF: Accumulation of base (non-acid part of salt), or loss of acid without relative loss of base in body fluids; caused by increased arterial plasma bicarbonate concentration or loss of carbon dioxide due to hyperventilation.

276.4 Mixed acid-base balance disorder

Hypercapnia with mixed acid-base disorder

√5ᵗʰ 276.5 Volume depletion

EXCLUDES   hypovolemic shock:
                 postoperative (998.0)
                 traumatic (958.4)

AHA: 1Q, '03, 5, 22; 3Q, '02, 21; 4Q, '97, 30; 2Q, '88, 9

● **276.50 Volume depletion, unspecified**

● **276.51 Dehydration**

● **276.52 Hypovolemia**

Depletion of volume of plasma

276.6 Fluid overload

Fluid retention

EXCLUDES   ascites (789.5)
                 localized edema (782.3)

276.7 Hyperpotassemia

Hyperkalemia   Potassium [K]:
Potassium [K]:   intoxication
  excess   overload

AHA: ▶1Q, '05, 9;◀ 2Q, '01, 12

DEF: Elevated blood levels of potassium; symptoms include abnormal EKG readings, weakness; related to defective renal excretion.

276.8 Hypopotassemia

Hypokalemia   Potassium [K] deficiency

DEF: Decreased blood levels of potassium; symptoms include neuromuscular disorders.

276.9 Electrolyte and fluid disorders not elsewhere classified

Electrolyte imbalance Hypochloremia
Hyperchloremia

EXCLUDES   electrolyte imbalance:
                 associated with hyperemesis
                   gravidarum (643.1)
                 complicating labor and delivery
                   (669.0)
                 following abortion and ectopic or
                   molar pregnancy (634-638
                   with .4, 639.4)

AHA: J-F, '87, 15

√4ᵗʰ 277 Other and unspecified disorders of metabolism

√5ᵗʰ 277.0 Cystic fibrosis

Fibrocystic disease of the pancreas
Mucoviscidosis

AHA: 4Q, '90, 16; 3Q, '90, 18

DEF: Generalized, genetic disorder of infants, children, and young adults marked by exocrine gland dysfunction; characterized by chronic pulmonary disease with excess mucus production, pancreatic deficiency, high levels of electrolytes in the sweat.

277.00 Without mention of meconium ileus

Cystic fibrosis NOS

AHA: 2Q, '03, 12

277.01 With meconium ileus   N

Meconium:
  ileus (of newborn)
  obstruction of intestine in mucoviscidosis

277.02 With pulmonary manifestations

Cystic fibrosis with pulmonary exacerbation
Use additional code to identify any
  infectious organism present, such as:
  pseudomonas (041.7)

AHA: 4Q, '02, 45-46

277.03 With gastrointestinal manifestations

EXCLUDES   with meconium ileus (277.01)

AHA: 4Q, '02, 45

277.09 With other manifestations

277.1 Disorders of porphyrin metabolism

Hematoporphyria   Porphyrinuria
Hematoporphyrinuria   Protocoproporphyria
Hereditary coproporphyria Protoporphyria
Porphyria   Pyrroloporphyria

277.2 Other disorders of purine and pyrimidine metabolism

Hypoxanthine-guanine-phosphoribosyltransferase
  deficiency [HG-PRT deficiency]
Lesch-Nyhan syndrome
Xanthinuria

EXCLUDES   gout (274.0-274.9)
                 orotic aciduric anemia (281.4)

277.3 Amyloidosis

Amyloidosis: Benign paroxysmal peritonitis
  NOS   Familial Mediterranean fever
  inherited systemic   Hereditary cardiac
  nephropathic   amyloidosis
  neuropathic (Portuguese) (Swiss)
  secondary

AHA: 1Q, '96, 16

DEF: Conditions of diverse etiologies characterized by the accumulation of insoluble fibrillar proteins (amyloid) in various organs and tissues of the body, compromising vital functions.

277.4 Disorders of bilirubin excretion

Hyperbilirubinemia: Syndrome:
  congenital   Dubin-Johnson
  constitutional   Gilbert's
Syndrome: Rotor's
  Crigler-Najjar

EXCLUDES   hyperbilirubinemias specific to the
                 perinatal period (774.0-774.7)

277.5 Mucopolysaccharidosis

Gargoylism   Morquio-Brailsford disease
Hunter's syndrome   Osteochondrodystrophy
Hurler's syndrome   Sanfilippo's syndrome
Lipochondrodystrophy   Scheie's syndrome
Maroteaux-Lamy syndrome

DEF: Metabolism disorders evidenced by excretion of various mucopolysaccharides in urine and infiltration of these substances into connective tissue, with resulting various defects of bone, cartilage and connective tissue.

277.6 Other deficiencies of circulating enzymes

Hereditary angioedema

277.7 Dysmetabolic syndrome X

Use additional code for associated manifestation,
  such as:
  cardiovascular disease (414.00-414.07)
  obesity (278.00-278.01)

AHA: 4Q, '01, 42

DEF: A specific group of metabolic disorders that are related to the state of insulin resistance (decreased cellular response to insulin) without elevated blood sugars; often related to elevated cholesterol and triglycerides, obesity, cardiovascular disease, and high blood pressure.

√5ᵗʰ 277.8 Other specified disorders of metabolism

AHA: 4Q, '03, 50; 2Q, '01, 18; S-O, '87, 9

277.81 Primary carnitine deficiency

277.82 Carnitine deficiency due to inborn errors of metabolism

277.83 Iatrogenic carnitine deficiency

Carnitine deficiency due to:
  hemodialysis
  valproic acid therapy

277.84 Other secondary carnitine deficiency

N Newborn Age: 0   P Pediatric Age: 0-17   M Maternity Age: 12-55   A Adult Age: 15-124   Manifestation Code   ▶◀ Revised Text   ● New Code   ▲ Revised Code Title

277.85 Disorders of fatty acid oxidation
Carnitine palmitoyltransferase deficiencies
(CPT1, CPT2)
Glutaric aciduria type II (type IIA, IIB, IIC)
Long chain 3-hydroxyacyl CoA
dehydrogenase deficiency (LCHAD)
Long chain/very long chain acyl CoA dehy-
drogenase deficiency (LCAD, VLCAD)
Medium chain acyl CoA dehydrogenase
deficiency (MCAD)
Short chain acyl CoA dehydrogenase
deficiency (SCAD)

> **EXCLUDES** *primary carnitine deficiency
> (277.81)*

277.86 Peroxisomal disorders
Adrenomyeloneuropathy
Neonatal adrenoleukodystrophy
Rhizomelic chrondrodysplasia punctata
X-linked adrenoleukodystrophy
Zellweger syndrome

> **EXCLUDES** *infantile Refsum disease
> (356.3)*

277.87 Disorders of mitochondrial metabolism
Kearns-Sayre syndrome
Mitochondrial Encephalopathy, Lactic
Acidosis and Stroke-like episodes
(MELAS syndrome)
Mitochondrial Neurogastrointestinal
Encephalopathy syndrome (MNGIE)
Myoclonus with Epilepsy and with Ragged
Red Fibers (MERRF syndrome)
Neuropathy, Ataxia and Retinitis
Pigmentosa (NARP syndrome)
Use additional code for associated conditions

> **EXCLUDES** *disorders of pyruvate
> metabolism (271.8)
> Leber's optic atrophy (377.16)
> Leigh's subacute necrotizing
> encephalopathy (330.8)
> Reye's syndrome (331.81)*

AHA: 4Q, '04, 62

277.89 Other specified disorders of metabolism
Hand-Schüller-Christian disease
Histiocytosis (acute) (chronic)
Histiocytosis X (chronic)

> **EXCLUDES** *histiocytosis:
> acute differentiated
> progressive (202.5)
> X, acute (progressive) (202.5)*

277.9 Unspecified disorder of metabolism
Enzymopathy NOS

▲ √4ᵗʰ **278 Overweight, obesity and other hyperalimentation**

> **EXCLUDES** *hyperalimentation NOS (783.6)
> poisoning by vitamins NOS (963.5)
> polyphagia (783.6)*

▲ √5ᵗʰ **278.0 Overweight and obesity**
▶Use additional code to identify Body Mass Index
(BMI), if known (V85.21- V85.4)◀

> **EXCLUDES** *adiposogenital dystrophy (253.8)
> obesity of endocrine origin NOS (259.9)*

278.00 Obesity, unspecified
Obesity NOS

AHA: 4Q, '01, 42; 1Q, '99, 5, 6

278.01 Morbid obesity
Severe obesity

AHA: 3Q, '03, 6-8

DEF: Increased weight beyond limits of skeletal and
physical requirements (125 percent or more over ideal
body weight), as a result of excess fat in subcutaneous
connective tissues.

● **278.02 Overweight**

278.1 Localized adiposity
Fat pad

278.2 Hypervitaminosis A

278.3 Hypercarotinemia
DEF: Elevated blood carotene level due to ingesting excess
carotenoids or the inability to convert carotenoids to vitamin A.

278.4 Hypervitaminosis D
DEF: Weakness, fatigue, loss of weight, and other symptoms
resulting from ingesting excessive amounts of vitamin D.

278.8 Other hyperalimentation

√4ᵗʰ **279 Disorders involving the immune mechanism**

√5ᵗʰ **279.0 Deficiency of humoral immunity**
DEF: Inadequate immune response to bacterial infections with
potential reinfection by viruses due to lack of circulating
immunoglobulins (acquired antibodies).

279.00 Hypogammaglobulinemia, unspecified
Agammaglobulinemia NOS

279.01 Selective IgA immunodeficiency

279.02 Selective IgM immunodeficiency

**279.03 Other selective immunoglobulin
deficiencies**
Selective deficiency of IgG

279.04 Congenital hypogammaglobulinemia
Agammaglobulinemia:
Bruton's type
X-linked

279.05 Immunodeficiency with increased IgM
Immunodeficiency with hyper-IgM:
autosomal recessive
X-linked

279.06 Common variable immunodeficiency
Dysgammaglobulinemia (acquired)
(congenital) (primary)
Hypogammaglobulinemia:
acquired primary
congenital non-sex-linked
sporadic

279.09 Other
Transient hypogammaglobulinemia of
infancy

√5ᵗʰ **279.1 Deficiency of cell-mediated immunity**

**279.10 Immunodeficiency with predominant
T-cell defect, unspecified**
AHA: S-O, '87, 10

279.11 DiGeorge's syndrome
Pharyngeal pouch syndrome
Thymic hypoplasia

DEF: Congenital disorder due to defective development of
the third and fourth pharyngeal pouches; results in
hypoplasia or aplasia of the thymus, parathyroid glands;
related to congenital heart defects, anomalies of the
great vessels, esophageal atresia, and abnormalities of
facial structures.

279.12 Wiskott-Aldrich syndrome
DEF: A disease characterized by chronic conditions, such
as eczema, suppurative otitis media and anemia; it
results from an X-linked recessive gene and is classified
as an immune deficiency syndrome.

279.13 Nezelof's syndrome
Cellular immunodeficiency with abnormal
immunoglobulin deficiency

DEF: Immune system disorder characterized by a
pathological deficiency in cellular immunity and humoral
antibodies resulting in inability to fight infectious
diseases.

279.19 Other

> **EXCLUDES** *ataxia-telangiectasia (334.8)*

√4ᵗʰ **Additional Digit Required** | RUG III Special Care Dx | RUG III Clinically Complex Dx | Hospice Non-cancer Dx | **CD PDx** Clinical Dimension PDx | **CD SDx** Clinical Dimension SDx
√5ᵗʰ

279.2   Combined immunity deficiency

Agammaglobulinemia:
   autosomal recessive
   Swiss-type
   x-linked recessive
Severe combined immunodeficiency [SCID]
Thymic:
   alymphoplasia
   aplasia or dysplasia with immunodeficiency

   EXCLUDES   *thymic hypoplasia (279.11)*

DEF: Agammaglobulinemia: No immunoglobulins in the blood.

DEF: Thymic alymphoplasia: Severe combined immunodeficiency; result of failed lymphoid tissue development.

279.3   Unspecified immunity deficiency

279.4   Autoimmune disease, not elsewhere classified

Autoimmune disease NOS

   EXCLUDES   *transplant failure or rejection (996.80-996.89)*

279.8   Other specified disorders involving the immune mechanism

Single complement $[C_1-C_9]$ deficiency or dysfunction

279.9   Unspecified disorder of immune mechanism

AHA: 3Q, '92, 13

N Newborn Age: 0   P Pediatric Age: 0-17   M Maternity Age: 12-55   A Adult Age: 15-124   Manifestation Code   ►◄ Revised Text   ● New Code   ▲ Revised Code Title

56 — Volume 1   2006 ICD•9•CM

4. DISEASES OF THE BLOOD AND BLOOD-FORMING ORGANS (280-289)

EXCLUDES *anemia complicating pregnancy or the puerperium (648.2)*

✓4ᵗʰ **280 Iron deficiency anemias**

INCLUDES anemia:
asiderotic
hypochromic-microcytic
sideropenic

EXCLUDES *familial microcytic anemia (282.49)*

280.0 Secondary to blood loss (chronic)
Normocytic anemia due to blood loss
EXCLUDES *acute posthemorrhagic anemia (285.1)*
AHA: 4Q, '93, 34

280.1 Secondary to inadequate dietary iron intake

280.8 Other specified iron deficiency anemias
Paterson-Kelly syndrome
Plummer-Vinson syndrome
Sideropenic dysphagia

280.9 Iron deficiency anemia, unspecified
Anemia:
achlorhydric
chlorotic
idiopathic hypochromic
iron [Fe] deficiency NOS

✓4ᵗʰ **281 Other deficiency anemias**

281.0 Pernicious anemia
Anemia:
Addison's
Biermer's
congenital pernicious
Congenital intrinsic factor [Castle's] deficiency
EXCLUDES *combined system disease without mention of anemia (266.2)*
subacute degeneration of spinal cord without mention of anemia (266.2)
AHA: N-D, '84, 1; S-O, '84, 16

DEF: Chronic progressive anemia due to Vitamin B_{12} malabsorption; caused by lack of a secretion known as intrinsic factor, which is produced by the gastric mucosa of the stomach.

281.1 Other vitamin B_{12} deficiency anemia
Anemia:
vegan's
vitamin B_{12} deficiency (dietary)
due to selective vitamin B_{12} malabsorption with proteinuria
Syndrome:
Imerslund's
Imerslund-Gräsbeck
EXCLUDES *combined system disease without mention of anemia (266.2)*
subacute degeneration of spinal cord without mention of anemia (266.2)

281.2 Folate-deficiency anemia
Congenital folate malabsorption
Folate or folic acid deficiency anemia:
NOS
dietary
drug-induced
Goat's milk anemia
Nutritional megaloblastic anemia (of infancy)
Use additional E code to identify drug

DEF: Macrocytic anemia resembles pernicious anemia but without absence of hydrochloric acid secretions; responsive to folic acid therapy.

281.3 Other specified megaloblastic anemias not elsewhere classified
Combined B_{12} and folate-deficiency anemia
Refractory megaloblastic anemia

DEF: Megaloblasts predominant in bone marrow with few normoblasts; rare familial type associated with proteinuria and genitourinary tract anomalies.

281.4 Protein-deficiency anemia
Amino-acid-deficiency anemia

281.8 Anemia associated with other specified nutritional deficiency
Scorbutic anemia

281.9 Unspecified deficiency anemia
Anemia: Anemia:
dimorphic   nutritional NOS
macrocytic   simple chronic
megaloblastic NOS

✓4ᵗʰ **282 Hereditary hemolytic anemias**

DEF: Escalated rate of erythrocyte destruction; similar to all anemias, occurs when imbalance exists between blood loss and blood production.

282.0 Hereditary spherocytosis
Acholuric (familial) jaundice
Congenital hemolytic anemia (spherocytic)
Congenital spherocytosis
Minkowski-Chauffard syndrome
Spherocytosis (familial)
EXCLUDES *hemolytic anemia of newborn (773.0-773.5)*

DEF: Hereditary, chronic illness marked by abnormal red blood cell membrane; symptoms include enlarged spleen, jaundice; and anemia in severe cases.

282.1 Hereditary elliptocytosis
Elliptocytosis (congenital)
Ovalocytosis (congenital) (hereditary)

DEF: Genetic hemolytic anemia characterized by malformed, elliptical erythrocytes; there is increased destruction of red cells with resulting anemia.

282.2 Anemias due to disorders of glutathione metabolism
Anemia:
6-phosphogluconic dehydrogenase deficiency
enzyme deficiency, drug-induced
erythrocytic glutathione deficiency
glucose-6-phosphate dehydrogenase [G-6-PD] deficiency
glutathione-reductase deficiency
hemolytic nonspherocytic (hereditary), type I
Disorder of pentose phosphate pathway
Favism

282.3 Other hemolytic anemias due to enzyme deficiency
Anemia:
hemolytic nonspherocytic (hereditary), type II
hexokinase deficiency
pyruvate kinase [PK] deficiency
triosephosphate isomerase deficiency

✓5ᵗʰ **282.4 Thalassemias**
EXCLUDES *sickle-cell:*
disease (282.60-282.69)
trait (282.5)
AHA: 4Q, '03, 51

DEF: A group of inherited hemolytic disorders characterized by decreased production of at least one of the four polypeptide globin chains which results in defective hemoglobin synthesis; symptoms include severe anemia, expanded marrow spaces, transfusional and absorptive iron overload, impaired growth rate, thickened cranial bones, and pathologic fractures.

282.41 Sickle-cell thalassemia without crisis
Sickle-cell thalassemia NOS
Thalassemia Hb-S disease without crisis

✓4ᵗʰ
✓5ᵗʰ Additional Digit Required   **RUG III Special Care Dx**   **RUG III Clinically Complex Dx**   Hospice Non-cancer Dx   **CD PDx** Clinical Dimension PDx   **CD SDx** Clinical Dimension SDx

2006 ICD•9•CM   Volume 1 — 57

Blood and Blood-Forming Organs

282.42–283.19

282.42　Sickle-cell thalassemia with crisis
Sickle-cell thalassemia with vaso-occlusive pain
Thalassemia Hb-S disease with crisis
Use additional code for type of crisis, such as:
acute chest syndrome (517.3)
splenic sequestration (289.52)

282.49　Other thalassemia
Cooley's anemia
▶Hb-Bart's disease◀
Hereditary leptocytosis
Mediterranean anemia (with other hemoglobinopathy)
Microdrepanocytosis
Thalassemia (alpha) (beta) (intermedia) (major) (minima) (minor) (mixed) (trait) (with other hemoglobinopathy)
Thalassemia NOS

282.5　Sickle-cell trait
Hb-AS genotype　　　Heterozygous:
Hemoglobin S [Hb-S] trait　　hemoglobin S
　　　　　　　　　　　　　　Hb-S

EXCLUDES　*that with other hemoglobinopathy (282.60-282.69)*
that with thalassemia (282.49)

DEF: Heterozygous genetic makeup characterized by one gene for normal hemoglobin and one for sickle-cell hemoglobin; clinical disease rarely present.

√5ᵗʰ　282.6　Sickle-cell disease
Sickle-cell anemia

EXCLUDES　*sickle-cell thalassemia (282.41-282.42)*
sickle-cell trait (282.5)

DEF: Inherited blood disorder; sickle-shaped red blood cells are hard and pointed, clogging blood flow; anemia characterized by periodic episodes of pain, acute abdominal discomfort, skin ulcerations of the legs, increased infections; occurs primarily in persons of African descent.

282.60　Sickle-cell disease, unspecified
Sickle-cell anemia NOS
AHA: 2Q, '97, 11

282.61　Hb-SS disease without crisis

282.62　Hb-SS disease with crisis
Hb-SS disease with vaso-occlusive pain
Sickle-cell crisis NOS
Use additional code for type of crisis, such as:
acute chest syndrome (517.3)
splenic sequestration (289.52)
AHA: 4Q, '03, 56; 2Q, '98, 8; 2Q, '91, 15

282.63　Sickle-cell/Hb-C disease without crisis
Hb-S/Hb-C disease without crisis

282.64　Sickle-cell/Hb-C disease with crisis
Hb-S/Hb-C disease with crisis
Sickle-cell/Hb-C disease with vaso-occlusive pain
Use additional code for type of crisis, such as:
acute chest syndrome (517.3)
splenic sequestration (289.52)
AHA: 4Q, '03, 51

282.68　Other sickle-cell disease without crisis
Hb-S/Hb-D
Hb-S/Hb-E } disease without
Sickle-cell/Hb-D　　crisis
Sickle-cell/Hb-E

AHA: 4Q, '03, 51

282.69　Other sickle-cell disease with crisis
Hb-S/Hb-D
Hb-S/Hb-E } disease with crisis
Sickle-cell/Hb-D
Sickle-cell/Hb-E

Other sickle-cell disease with vaso-occlusive pain
Use additional code for type of crisis, such as:
acute chest syndrome (517.3)
splenic sequestration (289.52)

282.7　Other hemoglobinopathies
Abnormal hemoglobin NOS
Congenital Heinz-body anemia
Disease:
hemoglobin C [Hb-C]
hemoglobin D [Hb-D]
hemoglobin E [Hb-E]
hemoglobin Zurich [Hb-Zurich]
Hemoglobinopathy NOS
Hereditary persistence of fetal hemoglobin[HPFH]
Unstable hemoglobin hemolytic disease

EXCLUDES　*familial polycythemia (289.6)*
hemoglobin M [Hb-M] disease (289.7)
high-oxygen-affinity hemoglobin (289.0)

DEF: Any disorder of hemoglobin due to alteration of molecular structure; may include overt anemia.

282.8　Other specified hereditary hemolytic anemias
Stomatocytosis

282.9　Hereditary hemolytic anemia, unspecified
Hereditary hemolytic anemia NOS

√4ᵗʰ　283　Acquired hemolytic anemias

DEF: Non-hereditary anemia characterized by premature destruction of red blood cells; caused by infectious organisms, poisons, and physical agents

AHA: N-D, '84, 1

283.0　Autoimmune hemolytic anemias
Autoimmune hemolytic disease (cold type) (warm type)
Chronic cold hemagglutinin disease
Cold agglutinin disease or hemoglobinuria
Hemolytic anemia:
cold type (secondary) (symptomatic)
drug-induced
warm type (secondary) (symptomatic)
Use additional E code to identify cause, if drug-induced

EXCLUDES　*Evans' syndrome ▶(287.32)◀*
hemolytic disease of newborn (773.0-773.5)

√5ᵗʰ　283.1　Non-autoimmune hemolytic anemias
Use additional E code to identify cause

DEF: Hemolytic anemia and thrombocytopenia with acute renal failure; relatively rare condition; 50 percent of patients require renal dialysis.

AHA: 4Q, '93, 25

283.10　Non-autoimmune hemolytic anemia, unspecified

283.11　Hemolytic-uremic syndrome

283.19　Other non-autoimmune hemolytic anemias
Hemolytic anemia:
mechanical
microangiopathic
toxic

Ⓝ Newborn Age: 0　　Ⓟ Pediatric Age: 0-17　　Ⓜ Maternity Age: 12-55　　Ⓐ Adult Age: 15-124　　│Manifestation Code│　　▶◀ Revised Text　　● New Code　　▲ Revised Code Title

283.2 Hemoglobinuria due to hemolysis from external causes
Acute intravascular hemolysis
Hemoglobinuria:
  from exertion
  march
  paroxysmal (cold) (nocturnal)
  due to other hemolysis
Marchiafava-Micheli syndrome
Use additional E code to identify cause

283.9 Acquired hemolytic anemia, unspecified
Acquired hemolytic anemia NOS
Chronic idiopathic hemolytic anemia

✓4th 284 Aplastic anemia
AHA: 1Q, '91, 14; N-D, '84, 1; S-O, '84, 16

DEF: Bone marrow failure to produce the normal amount of blood components; generally non-responsive to usual therapy.

284.0 Constitutional aplastic anemia

Aplasia, (pure) red cell:
  congenital
  of infants
  primary
Blackfan-Diamond syndrome
Familial hypoplastic anemia
Fanconi's anemia
Pancytopenia with malformations
AHA: 1Q, '91, 14

284.8 Other specified aplastic anemias
Aplastic anemia (due to):
  chronic systemic disease
  drugs
  infection
  radiation
  toxic (paralytic)
Pancytopenia (acquired)
Red cell aplasia (acquired) (adult) (pure) (with thymoma)
Use additional E code to identify cause
AHA: 1Q, '97, 5; 1Q, '92, 15; 1Q, '91, 14

284.9 Aplastic anemia, unspecified
Anemia: Anemia:
  aplastic (idiopathic) NOS nonregenerative
  aregenerative   Medullary hypoplasia
  hypoplastic NOS
    EXCLUDES ► refractory anemia (238.7)◄

DEF: Group of hereditary anemias occurring in the Mediterranean and Southeast Asia; characterized by impaired hemoglobin synthesis; homozygous form may cause death in utero; mild red blood cell anomalies in heterozygous.

✓4th 285 Other and unspecified anemias
AHA: 1Q, '91, 14; N-D, '84, 1

285.0 Sideroblastic anemia
Anemia:
  hypochromic with iron loading
  sideroachrestic
  sideroblastic: sideroblastic:
    acquired   secondary (drug-induced)
    congenital   (due to disease)
    hereditary   sex-linked hypochromic
    primary   vitamin B_6-responsive
Pyridoxine-responsive (hypochromic) anemia
Use additional E code to identify cause, if drug induced
    EXCLUDES ► refractory sideroblastic anemia (238.7)◄

DEF: Characterized by a disruption of final heme synthesis; results in iron overload of reticuloendothelial tissues.

285.1 Acute posthemorrhagic anemia
Anemia due to acute blood loss
  EXCLUDES anemia due to chronic blood loss (280.0)
        blood loss anemia NOS (280.0)

AHA: 2Q, '92, 15

✓5th 285.2 Anemia in chronic illness
AHA: 4Q, '00, 39

285.21 Anemia in chronic kidney disease
►Anemia in end stage renal disease◄
Erythropoietin-resistant anemia (EPO resistant anemia)

285.22 Anemia in neoplastic disease

285.29 Anemia of other chronic illness

285.8 Other specified anemias
Anemia:
  dyserythropoietic (congenital)
  dyshematopoietic (congenital)
  leukoerythroblastic
  von Jaksch's
Infantile pseudoleukemia
AHA: 1Q, '91, 16

285.9 Anemia, unspecified
Anemia: Anemia:
  NOS   profound
  essential   progressive
  normocytic, not due secondary
    to blood loss Oligocythemia
    EXCLUDES anemia (due to):
        blood loss:
          acute (285.1)
          chronic or unspecified (280.0)
          iron deficiency (280.0-280.9)
AHA: 1Q, '02, 14; 2Q, '92, 16; M-A, '85, 13; N-D, '84, 1

✓4th 286 Coagulation defects
286.0 Congenital factor VIII disorder
Antihemophilic globulin Hemophilia:
  [AHG] deficiency   A
Factor VIII (functional)   classical
  deficiency   familial
Hemophilia: hereditary
  NOS   Subhemophilia
    EXCLUDES factor VIII deficiency with vascular defect (286.4)

DEF: Hereditary, sex-linked, results in missing antihemophilic globulin (AHG) (factor VIII); causes abnormal coagulation characterized by increased tendency to bleeding, large bruises of skin, soft tissue; may also be bleeding in mouth, nose, gastrointestinal tract; after childhood, hemorrhages in joints, resulting in swelling and impaired function.

286.1 Congenital factor IX disorder
Christmas disease
Deficiency:
  factor IX (functional)
  plasma thromboplastin component [PTC]
Hemophilia B

DEF: Deficiency of plasma thromboplastin component (PTC) (factor IX) and plasma thromboplastin antecedent (PTA); PTC deficiency clinically indistinguishable from classical hemophilia; PTA deficiency found in both sexes.

286.2 Congenital factor XI deficiency
Hemophilia C
Plasma thromboplastin antecedent [PTA] deficiency
Rosenthal's disease

286.3 Congenital deficiency of other clotting factors

Congenital afibrinogenemia
Deficiency:
AC globulin factor:
I [fibrinogen]
II [prothrombin]
V [labile]
VII [stable]
X [Stuart-Prower]
XII [Hageman]
XIII [fibrin stabilizing]
Laki-Lorand factor
proaccelerin
Disease:
Owren's
Stuart-Prower
Dysfibrinogenemia (congenital)
Dysprothrombinemia (constitutional)
Hypoproconvertinemia
Hypoprothrmbinemia (hereditary)
Parahemophilia

286.4 von Willebrand's disease

Angiohemophilia (A) (B)
Constitutional thrombopathy
Factor VIII deficiency with vascular defect
Pseudohemophilia type B
Vascular hemophilia
von Willebrand's (-Jürgens') disease

> **EXCLUDES**   *factor VIII deficiency:*
> *NOS (286.0)*
> *with functional defect (286.0)*
> *hereditary capillary fragility (287.8)*

DEF: Abnormal blood coagulation caused by deficient blood Factor VII; congenital; symptoms include excess or prolonged bleeding, such as hemorrhage during menstruation, following birthing, or after surgical procedure.

286.5 Hemorrhagic disorder due to intrinsic circulating anticoagulants

Antithrombinemia
Antithromboplastinemia
Antithromboplastino-genemia
Hyperheparinemia
Increase in:
anti-VIIIa
anti-IXa
anti-Xa
anti-XIa
antithrombin
Secondary hemophilia
Systemic lupus erythematosus [SLE] inhibitor

AHA: 3Q, '92, 15; 3Q, '90, 14

286.6 Defibrination syndrome

Afibrinogenemia, acquired
Consumption coagulopathy
Diffuse or disseminated intravascular coagulation
[DIC syndrome]
Fibrinolytic hemorrhage, acquired
Hemorrhagic fibrinogenolysis
Pathologic fibrinolysis
Purpura:
fibrinolytic
fulminans

> **EXCLUDES**   *that complicating:*
> *abortion (634-638 with .1, 639.1)*
> *pregnancy or the puerperium (641.3, 666.3)*
> *disseminated intravascular coagulation in newborn (776.2)*

AHA: 4Q, '93, 29

DEF: Characterized by destruction of circulating fibrinogen; often precipitated by other conditions, such as injury, causing release of thromboplastic particles in blood stream.

286.7 Acquired coagulation factor deficiency

Deficiency of coagulation factor due to:
liver disease
vitamin K deficiency
Hypoprothrombinemia, acquired
Use additional E code to identify cause, if drug induced

> **EXCLUDES**   *vitamin K deficiency of newborn (776.0)*

AHA: 4Q, '93, 29

286.9 Other and unspecified coagulation defects

Defective coagulation NOS
Deficiency, coagulation factor NOS
Delay, coagulation
Disorder:
coagulation
hemostasis

> **EXCLUDES**   *abnormal coagulation profile (790.92)*
> *hemorrhagic disease of newborn (776.0)*
> *that complicating:*
> *abortion (634-638 with .1, 639.1)*
> *pregnancy or the puerperium (641.3, 666.3)*

AHA: 4Q, '99, 22; 4Q, '93, 29

✓4ᵗʰ 287 Purpura and other hemorrhagic conditions

> **EXCLUDES**   *hemorrhagic thrombocythemia (238.7)*
> *purpura fulminans (286.6)*

AHA: 1Q, '91, 14

287.0 Allergic purpura

Peliosis rheumatica   Purpura:
Purpura: rheumatica
anaphylactoid   Schönlein-Henoch
autoimmune   vascular
Henoch's   Vasculitis, allergic
nonthrombocytopenic:
hemorrhagic
idiopathic

> **EXCLUDES**   *hemorrhagic purpura ▶(287.39)◄*
> *purpura annularis telangiectodes (709.1)*

DEF: Any hemorrhagic condition, thrombocytic or nonthrombocytopenic in origin, caused by a presumed allergic reaction.

287.1 Qualitative platelet defects

Thrombasthenia (hemorrhagic) (hereditary)
Thrombocytasthenia
Thrombocytopathy (dystrophic)
Thrombopathy (Bernard-Soulier)

> **EXCLUDES**   *von Willebrand's disease (286.4)*

287.2 Other nonthrombocytopenic purpuras

Purpura: Purpura:
NOS   simplex
senile

✓5ᵗʰ 287.3 Primary thrombocytopenia

> **EXCLUDES**   *thrombotic thrombocytopenic purpura (446.6)*
> *transient thrombocytopenia of newborn (776.1)*

DEF: Decrease in number of blood platelets in circulating blood and purpural skin hemorrhages.

● 287.30 Primary thrombocytopenia, unspecified
Megakaryocytic hypoplasia

● 287.31 Immune thrombocytopenic purpura
Idiopathic thrombocytopenic purpura
Tidal platelet dysgenesis

● 287.32 Evans' syndrome

Ⓝ Newborn Age: 0   Ⓟ Pediatric Age: 0-17   Ⓜ Maternity Age: 12-55   Ⓐ Adult Age: 15-124   Manifestation Code   ▶◀ Revised Text   ● New Code   ▲ Revised Code Title

● **287.33 Congenital and hereditary thrombocytopenic purpura**

Congenital and hereditary thrombocytopenia

Thrombocytopenia with absent radii (TAR) syndrome

EXCLUDES *Wiskott-Aldrich syndrome (279.12)*

● **287.39 Other primary thrombocytopenia**

287.4   Secondary thrombocytopenia

Posttransfusion purpura

Thrombocytopenia (due to):

dilutional

drugs

extracorporeal circulation of blood

massive blood transfusion

platelet alloimmunization

Use additional E code to identify cause

EXCLUDES *transient thrombocytopenia of newborn (776.1)*

AHA: M-A, '85, 14

DEF: Reduced number of platelets in circulating blood as consequence of an underlying disease or condition.

287.5   Thrombocytopenia, unspecified

287.8   Other specified hemorrhagic conditions

Capillary fragility (hereditary)

Vascular pseudohemophilia

287.9   Unspecified hemorrhagic conditions

Hemorrhagic diathesis (familial)

✓4th **288 Diseases of white blood cells**

EXCLUDES *leukemia (204.0-208.9)*

AHA: 1Q, '91, 14

288.0   Agranulocytosis

Infantile genetic agranulocytosis   Neutropenia:

Kostmann's syndrome   immune

Neutropenia: periodic

NOS   toxic

cyclic   Neutropenic

drug-induced   splenomegaly

Use additional E code to identify drug or other cause

EXCLUDES *transitory neonatal neutropenia (776.7)*

AHA: 3Q, '99, 6; 2Q, '99, 9; 3Q, '96, 16; 2Q, '96, 6

DEF: Sudden, severe condition characterized by reduced number of white blood cells; results in sores in the throat, stomach or skin; symptoms include chills, fever; some drugs can bring on condition.

288.1   Functional disorders of polymorphonuclear neutrophils

Chronic (childhood) granulomatous disease

Congenital dysphagocytosis

Job's syndrome

Lipochrome histiocytosis (familial)

Progressive septic granulomatosis

288.2   Genetic anomalies of leukocytes

Anomaly (granulation) (granulocyte) or syndrome:

Alder's (-Reilly)

Chédiak-Steinbrinck (-Higashi)

Jordan's

May-Hegglin

Pelger-Huet

Hereditary:

hypersegmentation

hyposegmentation

leukomelanopathy

288.3   Eosinophilia

Eosinophilia: Eosinophilia:

allergic   secondary

hereditary   Eosinophilic leukocytosis

idiopathic

EXCLUDES *Löffler's syndrome (518.3)*
pulmonary eosinophilia (518.3)

AHA: 3Q, '00, 11

DEF: Elevated number of eosinophils in the blood; characteristic of allergic states and various parasitic infections.

288.8   Other specified disease of white blood cells

Leukemoid reaction: Lymphocytopenia

lymphocytic   Lymphocytosis (symptomatic)

monocytic   Lymphopenia

myelocytic   Monocytosis (symptomatic)

Leukocytosis   Plasmacytosis

EXCLUDES *immunity disorders (279.0-279.9)*

AHA: M-A, '87, 12

288.9   Unspecified disease of white blood cells

✓4th **289 Other diseases of blood and blood-forming organs**

289.0   Polycythemia, secondary

High-oxygen-affinity hemoglobin

Polycythemia:

acquired

benign

due to:

fall in plasma volume

high altitude

emotional

erythropoietin

hypoxemic

nephrogenous

relative

spurious

stress

EXCLUDES *polycythemia:*
neonatal (776.4)
primary (238.4)
vera (238.4)

DEF: Elevated number of red blood cells in circulating blood as result of reduced oxygen supply to the tissues.

289.1   Chronic lymphadenitis

Chronic:

adenitis ⎤ any lymph node, except
lymphadenitis ⎦   mesenteric

EXCLUDES *acute lymphadenitis (683)*
mesenteric (289.2)
enlarged glands NOS (785.6)

DEF: Persistent inflammation of lymph node tissue; origin of infection is usually elsewhere.

289.2   Nonspecific mesenteric lymphadenitis

Mesenteric lymphadenitis (acute) (chronic)

DEF: Inflammation of the lymph nodes in peritoneal fold that encases abdominal organs; disease resembles acute appendicitis; unknown etiology.

289.3   Lymphadenitis, unspecified, except mesenteric

AHA: 2Q, '92, 8

289.4   Hypersplenism

"Big spleen" syndrome   Hypersplenia

Dyssplenism

EXCLUDES *primary splenic neutropenia (288.0)*

DEF: An overactive spleen; it causes a deficiency of the peripheral blood components, an increase in bone marrow cells and sometimes a notable increase in the size of the spleen.

✓5th **289.5   Other diseases of spleen**

289.50 Disease of spleen, unspecified

289.51 Chronic congestive splenomegaly

289.52 Splenic sequestration

Code first sickle-cell disease in crisis (282.42, 282.62, 282.64, 282.69)

AHA: 4Q, '03, 51

DEF: Blood is entrapped in the spleen due to vessel occlusion; most often associated with sickle-cell disease; spleen becomes enlarged and there is a sharp drop in hemoglobin.

✓4th ✓5th Additional Digit Required   RUG III Special Care Dx   RUG III Clinically Complex Dx   Hospice Non-cancer Dx   **CD PDx** Clinical Dimension PDx   **CD SDx** Clinical Dimension SDx

Blood and Blood-Forming Organs

289.59–289.9

289.59 Other

Lien migrans	Splenic:
Perisplenitis	fibrosis
Splenic:	infarction
abscess	rupture, nontraumatic
atrophy	Splenitis
cyst	Wandering spleen

EXCLUDES   *bilharzial splenic fibrosis (120.0-120.9)*
hepatolienal fibrosis (571.5)
splenomegaly NOS (789.2)

289.6 Familial polycythemia
Familial:
   benign polycythemia
   erythrocytosis

DEF: Elevated number of red blood cells.

289.7 Methemoglobinemia
Congenital NADH [DPNH]-methemoglobin-reductase
   deficiency
Hemoglobin M [Hb-M] disease
Methemoglobinemia:
   NOS
   acquired (with sulfhemoglobinemia)
   hereditary
   toxic
Stokvis' disease
Sulfhemoglobinemia
Use additional E code to identify cause

DEF: Presence in the blood of methemoglobin, a chemically altered form of hemoglobin; causes cyanosis, headache, dizziness, ataxia dyspnea, tachycardia, nausea, stupor, coma, and, rarely, death.

√5ᵗʰ 289.8 Other specified diseases of blood and blood-forming organs
AHA: 4Q, '03, 56; 1Q, '02, 16; 2Q, '89, 8; M-A, '87, 12

DEF: Hypercoagulable states: a group of inherited or acquired abnormalities of specific proteins and anticoagulant factors; also called thromboembolic states or thrombotic disorders, these disorders result in the abnormal development of blood clots.

289.81 Primary hypercoagulable state
Activated protein C resistance
Antithrombin III deficiency
Factor V Leiden mutation
Lupus anticoagulant
Protein C deficiency
Protein S deficiency
Prothrombin gene mutation

DEF: Activated protein C resistance: decreased effectiveness of protein C to degrade factor V, necessary to inhibit clotting cascade; also called Factor V Leiden mutation.

DEF: Antithrombin III deficiency: deficiency in plasma antithrombin III one of six naturally occurring antithrombins that limit coagulation.

DEF: Factor V Leiden mutation: also called activated protein C resistance.

DEF: Lupus anticoagulant: deficiency in a circulating anticoagulant that inhibits the conversion of prothrombin into thrombin; autoimmune antibodies induce procoagulant surfaces in platelets; also called anti-phospholipid syndrome.

DEF: Protein C deficiency: deficiency of activated protein C which functions to bring the blood-clotting process into balance; same outcome as factor V Leiden mutation.

DEF: Protein S deficiency: similar to protein C deficiency; protein S is a vitamin K dependent cofactor in the activation of protein C.

DEF: Prothrombin gene mutation: increased levels of prothrombin, or factor II, a plasma protein that is converted to thrombin, which acts upon fibrinogen to form the fibrin.

289.82 Secondary hypercoagulable state
289.89 Other specified diseases of blood and blood-forming organs
Hypergammaglobulinemia
Myelofibrosis
Pseudocholinesterase deficiency

289.9 Unspecified diseases of blood and blood-forming organs
Blood dyscrasia NOS
Erythroid hyperplasia

AHA: M-A, '85, 14

Ⓝ Newborn Age: 0   Ⓟ Pediatric Age: 0-17   Ⓜ Maternity Age: 12-55   Ⓐ Adult Age: 15-124   Manifestation Code   ►◄ Revised Text   ● New Code   ▲ Revised Code Title

62 — Volume 1   *2006 ICD•9•CM*

5. MENTAL DISORDERS (290-319)

PSYCHOSES (290-299)

> **EXCLUDES**   mental retardation (317-319)

ORGANIC PSYCHOTIC CONDITIONS (290-294)

> **INCLUDES**   psychotic organic brain syndrome
>
> **EXCLUDES**   nonpsychotic syndromes of organic etiology (310.0-310.9)
> psychoses classifiable to 295-298 and without impairment of orientation, comprehension, calculation, learning capacity, and judgment, but associated with physical disease, injury, or condition affecting the brain [eg., following childbirth] (295.0-298.8)

✓4ᵗʰ **290 Dementias**

Code first the associated neurological condition

> **EXCLUDES**   dementia due to alcohol (291.0-291.2)
> dementia due to drugs (292.82)
> dementia not classified as senile, presenile, or arteriosclerotic (294.10-294.11)
> psychoses classifiable to 295-298 occurring in the senium without dementia or delirium (295.0-298.8)
> senility with mental changes of nonpsychotic severity (310.1)
> transient organic psychotic conditions (293.0-293.9)

290.0   **Senile dementia, uncomplicated**   A

Senile dementia:
    NOS
    simple type

> **EXCLUDES**   mild memory disturbances, not amounting to dementia, associated with senile brain disease (310.1)
> senile dementia with:
>   delirium or confusion (290.3)
>   delusional [paranoid] features (290.20)
>   depressive features (290.21)

AHA: 4Q, '99, 4

✓5ᵗʰ **290.1**   **Presenile dementia**

Brain syndrome with presenile brain disease

> **EXCLUDES**   arteriosclerotic dementia (290.40-290.43)
> dementia associated with other cerebral conditions (294.10-294.11)

AHA: N-D, '84, 20

290.10   **Presenile dementia, uncomplicated**   A

Presenile dementia: Presenile dementia:
   NOS   simple type

290.11   **Presenile dementia with delirium**   A

Presenile dementia with acute confusional state

AHA: 1Q, '88, 3

290.12   **Presenile dementia with delusional features**   A

Presenile dementia, paranoid type

290.13   **Presenile dementia with depressive features**   A

Presenile dementia, depressed type

✓5ᵗʰ **290.2**   **Senile dementia with delusional or depressive features**

> **EXCLUDES**   senile dementia:
>   NOS (290.0)
>   with delirium and/or confusion (290.3)

290.20   **Senile dementia with delusional features**   A

Senile dementia, paranoid type
Senile psychosis NOS

290.21   **Senile dementia with depressive features**   A

290.3   **Senile dementia with delirium**   A

Senile dementia with acute confusional state

> **EXCLUDES**   senile:
>   dementia NOS (290.0)
>   psychosis NOS (290.20)

✓5ᵗʰ **290.4**   **Vascular dementia**

Multi-infarct dementia or psychosis
Use additional code to identify cerebral atherosclerosis (437.0)

> **EXCLUDES**   suspected cases with no clear evidence of arteriosclerosis (290.9)

AHA: 1Q, '88, 3

290.40   **Vascular dementia, uncomplicated**   A

Arteriosclerotic dementia:
   NOS
   simple type

290.41   **Vascular dementia with delirium**   A

Arteriosclerotic dementia with acute confusional state

290.42   **Vascular dementia with delusions**   A

Arteriosclerotic dementia, paranoid type

290.43   **Vascular dementia with depressed mood**   A

Arteriosclerotic dementia, depressed type

290.8   **Other specified senile psychotic conditions**

Presbyophrenic psychosis

290.9   **Unspecified senile psychotic condition**   A

✓4ᵗʰ **291 Alcohol induced mental disorders**

> **EXCLUDES**   alcoholism without psychosis (303.0-303.9)

AHA: 1Q, '88, 3; S-O, '86, 3

291.0   **Alcohol withdrawal delirium**

Alcoholic delirium   Delirium tremens

> **EXCLUDES**   alcohol withdrawal (291.81)

AHA: 2Q, '91, 11

291.1   **Alcohol induced persisting amnestic disorder**

Alcoholic polyneuritic psychosis
Korsakoff's psychosis, alcoholic
Wernicke-Korsakoff syndrome (alcoholic)

AHA: 1Q, '88, 3

DEF: Prominent and lasting reduced memory span, disordered time appreciation and confabulation, occurring in alcoholics, as sequel to acute alcoholic psychosis.

291.2   **Alcohol induced persisting dementia**

Alcoholic dementia NOS
Alcoholism associated with dementia NOS
Chronic alcoholic brain syndrome

291.3   **Alcohol induced psychotic disorder with hallucinations**

Alcoholic: Alcoholic:
   hallucinosis (acute)   psychosis with hallucinosis

> **EXCLUDES**   alcohol withdrawal with delirium (291.0)
> schizophrenia (295.0-295.9) and paranoid states (297.0-297.9) taking the form of chronic hallucinosis with clear consciousness in an alcoholic

AHA: 2Q, '91, 11

DEF: Psychosis lasting less than six months with slight or no clouding of consciousness in which auditory hallucinations predominate.

✓4ᵗʰ✓5ᵗʰ Additional Digit Required   RUG III Special Care Dx   RUG III Clinically Complex Dx   Hospice Non-cancer Dx   **CD PDx** Clinical Dimension PDx   **CD SDx** Clinical Dimension SDx

291.4 Idiosyncratic alcohol intoxication

Pathologic: Pathologic:
   alcohol intoxication   drunkenness

EXCLUDES   *acute alcohol intoxication (305.0)*
      in alcoholism (303.0)
     simple drunkenness (305.0)

DEF: Unique behavioral patterns, like belligerence, after intake of relatively small amounts of alcohol; behavior not due to excess consumption.

291.5 Alcohol induced psychotic disorder with delusions

Alcoholic: Alcoholic:
   paranoia   psychosis, paranoid type

EXCLUDES   *nonalcoholic paranoid states (297.0-297.9)*
     schizophrenia, paranoid type (295.3)

√5ᵗʰ **291.8 Other specified alcohol induced mental disorders**

AHA: 3Q, '94, 13; J-A, '85, 10

291.81 Alcohol withdrawal

Alcohol:
   abstinence syndrome or symptoms
   withdrawal syndrome or symptoms

EXCLUDES   *alcohol withdrawal:*
     delirium (291.0)
     hallucinosis (291.3)
     delirium tremens (291.0)

AHA: 4Q, '96, 28; 2Q, '91, 11

291.82 Alcohol induced sleep disorders

Alcohol induced circadian rhythm sleep disorders
Alcohol induced hypersomnia
Alcohol induced insomnia
Alcohol induced parasomnia

291.89 Other

Alcohol induced anxiety disorder
Alcohol induced mood disorder
Alcohol induced sexual dysfunction

291.9 Unspecified alcohol induced mental disorders

Alcoholic:
   mania NOS
   psychosis NOS
Alcoholism (chronic) with psychosis
Alcohol related disorder NOS

√4ᵗʰ **292 Drug induced mental disorders**

INCLUDES   organic brain syndrome associated with consumption of drugs

Use additional code for any associated drug dependence (304.0-304.9)
Use additional E code to identify drug

AHA: 3Q, '04, 8; 2Q, '91, 11; S-O, '86, 3

292.0 Drug withdrawal

Drug:
   abstinence syndrome or symptoms
   withdrawal syndrome or symptoms

AHA: 1Q, '97, 12; 1Q, '88, 3

√5ᵗʰ **292.1 Drug induced psychotic disorders**

292.11 Drug induced psychotic disorder with delusions

Paranoid state induced by drugs

292.12 Drug induced psychotic disorder with hallucinations

Hallucinatory state induced by drugs

EXCLUDES   *states following LSD or other hallucinogens, lasting only a few days or less ["bad trips"] (305.3)*

292.2 Pathological drug intoxication

Drug reaction:
   NOS   } resulting in brief
   idiosyncratic   psychotic states
   pathologic

EXCLUDES   *expected brief psychotic reactions to hallucinogens ["bad trips"] (305.3)*
   physiological side-effects of drugs (e.g., dystonias)

√5ᵗʰ **292.8 Other specified drug induced mental disorders**

292.81 Drug induced delirium

AHA: 1Q, '88, 3

292.82 Drug induced persisting dementia

292.83 Drug induced persisting amnestic disorder

292.84 Drug induced mood disorder

Depressive state induced by drugs

292.85 Drug induced sleep disorders

Drug induced circadian rhythm sleep disorder
Drug induced hypersomnia
Drug induced insomnia
Drug induced parasomnia

292.89 Other

Drug induced anxiety disorder
Drug induced organic personality syndrome
Drug induced sexual dysfunction
Drug intoxication

292.9 Unspecified drug induced mental disorder

Drug related disorder NOS
Organic psychosis NOS due to or associated with drugs

√4ᵗʰ **293 Transient mental disorders due to conditions classified elsewhere**

INCLUDES   transient organic mental disorders not associated with alcohol or drugs

Code first the associated physical or neurological condition

EXCLUDES   *confusional state or delirium superimposed on senile dementia (290.3)*
   dementia due to:
     alcohol (291.0-291.9)
     arteriosclerosis (290.40-290.43)
     drugs (292.82)
     senility (290.0)

293.0 Delirium due to conditions classified elsewhere

Acute:
   confusional state
   infective psychosis
   organic reaction
   posttraumatic organic psychosis
   psycho-organic syndrome
Acute psychosis associated with endocrine, metabolic, or cerebrovascular disorder
Epileptic:
   confusional state
   twilight state

AHA: 1Q, '88, 3

293.1 Subacute delirium

Subacute:
   confusional state
   infective psychosis
   organic reaction
   posttraumatic organic psychosis
   psycho-organic syndrome
   psychosis associated with endocrine or metabolic disorder

√5ᵗʰ **293.8 Other specified transient mental disorders due to conditions classified elsewhere**

293.81 Psychotic disorder with delusions in conditions classified elsewhere

Transient organic psychotic condition, paranoid type

293.82 Psychotic disorder with hallucinations in conditions classified elsewhere

Transient organic psychotic condition, hallucinatory type

293.83 Mood disorder in conditions classified elsewhere

Transient organic psychotic condition, depressive type

293.84 Anxiety disorder in conditions classified elsewhere

AHA: 4Q, '96, 29

| N Newborn Age: 0 | P Pediatric Age: 0-17 | M Maternity Age: 12-55 | A Adult Age: 15-124 | Manifestation Code | ►◄ Revised Text | ● New Code | ▲ Revised Code Title |

293.89 Other
Catatonic disorder in conditions classified elsewhere

293.9 Unspecified transient mental disorder in conditions classified elsewhere
Organic psychosis: Organic psychosis:
  infective NOS   transient NOS
  posttraumatic NOS   Psycho-organic syndrome

√4th **294 Persistent mental disorders due to conditions classified elsewhere**
INCLUDES organic psychotic brain syndromes (chronic), not elsewhere classified

AHA: M-A, '85, 12

294.0 Amnestic disorder in conditions classified elsewhere
Korsakoff's psychosis or syndrome (nonalcoholic)
Code first underlying condition
EXCLUDES alcoholic:
                amnestic syndrome (291.1)
                Korsakoff's psychosis (291.1)

√5th **294.1 Dementia in conditions classified elsewhere**
Dementia of the Alzheimer's type
Code first any underlying physical condition, as:
  dementia in:
    Alzheimer's disease (331.0)
    cerebral lipidoses (330.1)
    dementia with Lewy bodies (331.82)
    dementia with Parkinsonism (331.82)
    epilepsy (345.0-345.9)
    frontal dementia (331.19)
    frontotemporal dementia (331.19)
    general paresis [syphilis] (094.1)
    hepatolenticular degeneration (275.1)
    Huntington's chorea (333.4)
    Jakob-Creutzfeldt disease (046.1)
    multiple sclerosis (340)
    Pick's disease of the brain (331.11)
    polyarteritis nodosa (446.0)
    syphilis (094.1)
EXCLUDES dementia:
                arteriosclerotic (290.40-290.43)
                presenile (290.10-290.13)
                senile (290.0)
              epileptic psychosis NOS (294.8)

AHA: 4Q, '00, 40; 1Q, '99, 14; N-D, '85, 5

294.10 Dementia in conditions classified elsewhere without behavioral disturbance
Dementia in conditions classified elsewhere NOS

294.11 Dementia in conditions classified elsewhere with behavioral disturbance
Aggressive behavior
Combative behavior
Violent behavior
Wandering off

AHA: 4Q, '00, 41

294.8 Other persistent mental disorders due to conditions classified elsewhere
Amnestic disorder NOS
Dementia NOS
Epileptic psychosis NOS
Mixed paranoid and affective organic psychotic states
Use additional code for associated epilepsy (345.0-345.9)
EXCLUDES mild memory disturbances, not amounting to dementia (310.1)

AHA: 3Q, '03, 14; 1Q, '88, 5

294.9 Unspecified persistent mental disorders due to conditions classified elsewhere
Cognitive disorder NOS
Organic psychosis (chronic)

OTHER PSYCHOSES (295-299)
Use additional code to identify any associated physical disease, injury, or condition affecting the brain with psychoses classifiable to 295-298

√4th **295 Schizophrenic disorders**
INCLUDES schizophrenia of the types described in 295.0-295.9 occurring in children
EXCLUDES childhood type schizophrenia (299.9)
              infantile autism (299.0)

The following fifth-digit subclassification is for use with category 295:
0 unspecified
1 subchronic
2 chronic
3 subchronic with acute exacerbation
4 chronic with acute exacerbation
5 in remission

DEF: Group of disorders with disturbances in thought (delusions, hallucinations), mood (blunted, flattened, inappropriate affect), sense of self, relationship to world; also bizarre, purposeless behavior, repetitive activity, or inactivity.

√5th **295.0 Simple type**
Schizophrenia simplex
EXCLUDES latent schizophrenia (295.5)

√5th **295.1 Disorganized type**
Hebephrenia
Hebephrenic type schizophrenia

DEF: Inappropriate behavior; results in extreme incoherence and disorganization of time, place and sense of social appropriateness; withdrawal from routine social interaction may occur.

√5th **295.2 Catatonic type**
Catatonic (schizophrenia):   Schizophrenic:
  agitation   catalepsy
  excitation   catatonia
  excited type   flexibilitas cerea
  stupor
  withdrawn type

DEF: Extreme changes in motor activity; one extreme is decreased response or reaction to the environment and the other is spontaneous activity.

√5th **295.3 Paranoid type**
Paraphrenic schizophrenia
EXCLUDES involutional paranoid state (297.2)
              paranoia (297.1)
              paraphrenia (297.2)

DEF: Preoccupied with delusional suspicions and auditory hallucinations related to single theme; usually hostile, grandiose, overly religious, occasionally hypochondriacal.

√5th **295.4 Schizophreniform disorder**
Oneirophrenia   Schizophreniform:
Schizophreniform: psychosis, confusional type
  attack
EXCLUDES acute forms of schizophrenia of:
                catatonic type (295.2)
                hebephrenic type (295.1)
                paranoid type (295.3)
                simple type (295.0)
                undifferentiated type (295.8)

√5th **295.5 Latent schizophrenia**
Latent schizophrenic reaction
Schizophrenia:
  borderline
  incipient
  prepsychotic
  prodromal
  pseudoneurotic
  pseudopsychopathic
EXCLUDES schizoid personality (301.20-301.22)

√4th √5th Additional Digit Required   RUG III Special Care Dx   RUG III Clinically Complex Dx   Hospice Non-cancer Dx   CD PDx Clinical Dimension PDx   CD SDx Clinical Dimension SDx

2006 ICD•9•CM   **Volume 1 — 65**

Mental Disorders

295.6–296.99

§ ✓5ᵗʰ **295.6 Residual type**
Chronic undifferentiated schizophrenia
Restzustand (schizophrenic)
Schizophrenic residual state

§ ✓5ᵗʰ **295.7 Schizoaffective disorder**
Cyclic schizophrenia
Mixed schizophrenic and affective psychosis
Schizo-affective psychosis
Schizophreniform psychosis, affective type

§ ✓5ᵗʰ **295.8 Other specified types of schizophrenia**
Acute (undifferentiated) schizophrenia
Atypical schizophrenia
Cenesthopathic schizophrenia
EXCLUDES *infantile autism (299.0)*

§ ✓5ᵗʰ **295.9 Unspecified schizophrenia**
Schizophrenia:
NOS
mixed NOS
undifferentiated NOS
undifferentiated type
Schizophrenic reaction NOS
Schizophreniform psychosis NOS
AHA: 3Q, '95, 6

✓4ᵗʰ **296 Episodic mood disorders**
INCLUDES episodic affective disorders
EXCLUDES *neurotic depression (300.4)*
reactive depressive psychosis (298.0)
reactive excitation (298.1)

The following fifth-digit subclassification is for use with categories 296.0-296.6:
0 unspecified
1 mild
2 moderate
3 severe, without mention of psychotic behavior
4 severe, specified as with psychotic behavior
5 in partial or unspecified remission
6 in full remission

AHA: M-A, '85, 14

✓5ᵗʰ **296.0 Bipolar I disorder, single manic episode**
Hypomania (mild) NOS
Hypomanic psychosis
Mania (monopolar) NOS } single episode or unspecified
Manic-depressive psychosis
or reaction:
hypomanic
manic

EXCLUDES *circular type, if there was a previous attack of depression (296.4)*

DEF: Mood disorder identified by hyperactivity; may show extreme agitation or exaggerated excitability; speech and thought processes may be accelerated.

✓5ᵗʰ **296.1 Manic disorder, recurrent episode**
Any condition classifiable to 296.0, stated to be recurrent
EXCLUDES *circular type, if there was a previous attack of depression (296.4)*

✓5ᵗʰ **296.2 Major depressive disorder, single episode**
Depressive psychosis
Endogenous depression
Involutional melancholia
Manic-depressive psychosis or } single episode or unspecified
reaction, depressed type
Monopolar depression
Psychotic depression

EXCLUDES *circular type, if previous attack was of manic type (296.5)*
depression NOS (311)
reactive depression (neurotic) (300.4)
psychotic (298.0)

DEF: Mood disorder that produces depression; may exhibit as sadness, low self-esteem, or guilt feelings; other manifestations may be withdrawal from friends and family; interrupted sleep.

✓5ᵗʰ **296.3 Major depressive disorder, recurrent episode**
Any condition classifiable to 296.2, stated to be recurrent
EXCLUDES *circular type, if previous attack was of manic type (296.5)*
depression NOS (311)
reactive depression (neurotic) (300.4)
psychotic (298.0)

✓5ᵗʰ **296.4 Bipolar I disorder, most recent episode (or current) manic**
Bipolar disorder, now manic
Manic-depressive psychosis, circular type but currently manic
EXCLUDES *brief compensatory or rebound mood swings (296.99)*

✓5ᵗʰ **296.5 Bipolar I disorder, most recent episode (or current) depressed**
Bipolar disorder, now depressed
Manic-depressive psychosis, circular type but currently depressed
EXCLUDES *brief compensatory or rebound mood swings (296.99)*

✓5ᵗʰ **296.6 Bipolar I disorder, most recent episode (or current) mixed**
Manic-depressive psychosis, circular type, mixed

296.7 Bipolar I disorder, most recent episode (or current) unspecified
Atypical bipolar affective disorder NOS
Manic-depressive psychosis, circular type, current condition not specified as either manic or depressive

DEF: Manic-depressive disorder referred to as bipolar because of the mood range from manic to depressive.

✓5ᵗʰ **296.8 Other and unspecified bipolar disorders**
296.80 Bipolar disorder, unspecified
Bipolar disorder NOS
Manic-depressive:
reaction NOS
syndrome NOS

296.81 Atypical manic disorder
296.82 Atypical depressive disorder
296.89 Other
Bipolar II disorder
Manic-depressive psychosis, mixed type

✓5ᵗʰ **296.9 Other and unspecified episodic mood disorder**
EXCLUDES *psychogenic affective psychoses (298.0-298.8)*

296.90 Unspecified episodic mood disorder
Affective psychosis NOS
Melancholia NOS
Mood disorder NOS
AHA: M-A, '85, 14

296.99 Other specified episodic mood disorder
Mood swings: Mood swings:
brief compensatory   rebound

---

§ Requires fifth-digit. See category 295 for codes and definitions.

N Newborn Age: 0   P Pediatric Age: 0-17   M Maternity Age: 12-55   A Adult Age: 15-124   Manifestation Code   ▶◀ Revised Text   ● New Code   ▲ Revised Code Title

✓4ᵗʰ **297 Delusional disorders**
> INCLUDES paranoid disorders
> EXCLUDES *acute paranoid reaction (298.3)*
> *alcoholic jealousy or paranoid state (291.5)*
> *paranoid schizophrenia (295.3)*

297.0 Paranoid state, simple

297.1 Delusional disorder
> Chronic paranoid psychosis
> Sander's disease
> Systematized delusions
> EXCLUDES *paranoid personality disorder (301.0)*

297.2 Paraphrenia
> Involutional paranoid state
> Late paraphrenia
> Paraphrenia (involutional)
>
> DEF: Paranoid schizophrenic disorder that persists over a prolonged period but does not distort personality despite persistent delusions.

297.3 Shared psychotic disorder
> Folie à deux
> Induced psychosis or paranoid disorder
>
> DEF: Mental disorder two people share; first person with the delusional disorder convinces second person because of a close relationship and shared experiences to accept the delusions.

297.8 Other specified paranoid states
> Paranoia querulans
> Sensitiver Beziehungswahn
> EXCLUDES *acute paranoid reaction or state (298.3)*
> *senile paranoid state (290.20)*

297.9 Unspecified paranoid state
> Paranoid: Paranoid:
>   disorder NOS   reaction NOS
>   psychosis NOS   state NOS
>
> AHA: J-A, '85, 9

✓4ᵗʰ **298 Other nonorganic psychoses**
> INCLUDES psychotic conditions due to or provoked by:
>   emotional stress
>   environmental factors as major part of etiology

298.0 Depressive type psychosis
> Psychogenic depressive psychosis
> Psychotic reactive depression
> Reactive depressive psychosis
> EXCLUDES *manic-depressive psychosis, depressed type (296.2-296.3)*
> *neurotic depression (300.4)*
> *reactive depression NOS (300.4)*

298.1 Excitative type psychosis
> Acute hysterical psychosis   Reactive excitation
> Psychogenic excitation
> EXCLUDES *manic-depressive psychosis, manic type (296.0-296.1)*
>
> DEF: Affective disorder similar to manic-depressive psychosis, in the manic phase, seemingly brought on by stress.

298.2 Reactive confusion
> Psychogenic confusion   Psychogenic twilight state
> EXCLUDES *acute confusional state (293.0)*
>
> DEF: Confusion, disorientation, cloudiness in consciousness; brought on by severe emotional upheaval.

298.3 Acute paranoid reaction
> Acute psychogenic paranoid psychosis
> Bouffée délirante
> EXCLUDES *paranoid states (297.0-297.9)*

298.4 Psychogenic paranoid psychosis
> Protracted reactive paranoid psychosis

298.8 Other and unspecified reactive psychosis
> Brief psychotic disorder
> Brief reactive psychosis NOS
> Hysterical psychosis
> Psychogenic psychosis NOS
> Psychogenic stupor
> EXCLUDES *acute hysterical psychosis (298.1)*

298.9 Unspecified psychosis
> Atypical psychosis
> Psychosis NOS
> Psychotic disorder NOS

✓4ᵗʰ **299 Pervasive developmental disorders**
> EXCLUDES *adult type psychoses occurring in childhood, as:*
> *affective disorders (296.0-296.9)*
> *manic-depressive disorders (296.0-296.9)*
> *schizophrenia (295.0-295.9)*

The following fifth-digit subclassification is for use with category 299:
> **0 current or active state**
> **1 residual state**

✓5ᵗʰ **299.0 Autistic disorder**
> Childhood autism   Kanner's syndrome
> Infantile psychosis
> EXCLUDES *disintegrative psychosis (299.1)*
> *Heller's syndrome (299.1)*
> *schizophrenic syndrome of childhood (299.9)*
>
> DEF: Severe mental disorder of children, results in impaired social behavior; abnormal development of communicative skills, appears to be unaware of the need for emotional support and offers little emotional response to family members.

✓5ᵗʰ **299.1 Childhood disintegrative disorder**
> Heller's syndrome
> Use additional code to identify any associated neurological disorder
> EXCLUDES *infantile autism (299.0)*
> *schizophrenic syndrome of childhood (299.9)*
>
> DEF: Mental disease of children identified by impaired development of reciprocal social skills, verbal and nonverbal communication skills, imaginative play.

✓5ᵗʰ **299.8 Other specified pervasive developmental disorders**
> Asperger's disorder
> Atypical childhood psychosis
> Borderline psychosis of childhood
> EXCLUDES *simple stereotypes without psychotic disturbance (307.3)*

✓5ᵗʰ **299.9 Unspecified pervasive developmental disorder**
> Child psychosis NOS
> Pervasive developmental disorder NOS
> Schizophrenia, childhood type NOS
> Schizophrenic syndrome of childhood NOS
> EXCLUDES *schizophrenia of adult type occurring in childhood (295.0-295.9)*

NEUROTIC DISORDERS, PERSONALITY DISORDERS, AND OTHER NONPSYCHOTIC MENTAL DISORDERS (300-316)

✓4ᵗʰ **300 Anxiety, dissociative and somatoform disorders**

✓5ᵗʰ **300.0 Anxiety states**
> EXCLUDES *anxiety in:*
> *acute stress reaction (308.0)*
> *transient adjustment reaction (309.24)*
> *neurasthenia (300.5)*
> *psychophysiological disorders (306.0-306.9)*
> *separation anxiety (309.21)*
>
> DEF: Mental disorder characterized by anxiety and avoidance behavior not particularly related to any specific situation or stimulus; symptoms include emotional instability, apprehension, fatigue.

✓4ᵗʰ ✓5ᵗʰ
Additional Digit Required   RUG III Special Care Dx   RUG III Clinically Complex Dx   Hospice Non-cancer Dx   **CD PDx** Clinical Dimension PDx   **CD SDx** Clinical Dimension SDx

2006 ICD•9•CM   **Volume 1 — 67**

Mental Disorders

300.00–300.5

300.00 Anxiety state, unspecified

Anxiety: Anxiety:
  neurosis   state (neurotic)
  reaction   Atypical anxiety disorder

AHA: 1Q, '02, 6

300.01 Panic disorder without agoraphobia

Panic: Panic:
  attack   state

  EXCLUDES *panic disorder with agoraphobia (300.21)*

DEF: Neurotic disorder characterized by recurrent panic or anxiety, apprehension, fear or terror; symptoms include shortness of breath, palpitations, dizziness, faintness or shakiness; fear of dying may persist or fear of other morbid consequences.

300.02 Generalized anxiety disorder

300.09 Other

✓5th 300.1 Dissociative, conversion and factitious disorders

  EXCLUDES *adjustment reaction (309.0-309.9)*
  anorexia nervosa (307.1)
  gross stress reaction (308.0-308.9)
  hysterical personality (301.50-301.59)
  psychophysiologic disorders (306.0-306.9)

300.10 Hysteria, unspecified

300.11 Conversion disorder

Astasia-abasia,   Hysterical
  hysterical   blindness
Conversion hysteria   deafness
  or reaction   paralysis

AHA: N-D, '85, 15

DEF: Mental disorder that impairs physical functions with no physiological basis; sensory motor symptoms include seizures, paralysis, temporary blindness; increase in stress or avoidance of unpleasant responsibilities may precipitate.

300.12 Dissociative amnesia

Hysterical amnesia

300.13 Dissociative fugue

Hysterical fugue

DEF: Dissociative hysteria; identified by loss of memory, flight from familiar surroundings; conscious activity is not associated with perception of surroundings, no later memory of episode.

300.14 Dissociative identity disorder

300.15 Dissociative disorder or reaction, unspecified

DEF: Hysterical neurotic episode; sudden but temporary changes in perceived identity, memory, consciousness; segregated memory patterns exist separate from dominant personality.

300.16 Factitious disorder with predominantly psychological signs and symptoms

  Compensation neurosis
  Ganser's syndrome, hysterical

DEF: A disorder characterized by the purposeful assumption of mental illness symptoms; the symptoms are not real, possibly representing what the patient imagines mental illness to be like, and are acted out more often when another person is present.

300.19 Other and unspecified factitious illness

  Factitious disorder (with combined psychological and physical signs and symptoms) (with predominantly physical signs and symptoms) NOS

  EXCLUDES *multiple operations or hospital addiction syndrome (301.51)*

✓5th 300.2 Phobic disorders

  EXCLUDES *anxiety state not associated with a specific situation or object (300.00-300.09)*
  obsessional phobias (300.3)

300.20 Phobia, unspecified

Anxiety-hysteria NOS
Phobia NOS

300.21 Agoraphobia with panic disorder

Fear of:
  open spaces ⎫
  streets ⎬ with panic attacks
  travel ⎭

Panic disorder with agoraphobia

  EXCLUDES *agoraphobia without panic disorder (300.22)*
  panic disorder without agoraphobia (300.01)

300.22 Agoraphobia without mention of panic attacks

Any condition classifiable to 300.21 without mention of panic attacks

300.23 Social phobia

Fear of: Fear of:
  eating in public   washing in public
  public speaking

300.29 Other isolated or specific phobias

Acrophobia   Claustrophobia
Animal phobias   Fear of crowds

300.3 Obsessive-compulsive disorders

Anancastic neurosis   Obsessional phobia [any]
Compulsive neurosis

  EXCLUDES *obsessive-compulsive symptoms occurring in:*
  endogenous depression (296.2-296.3)
  organic states (eg., encephalitis)
  schizophrenia (295.0-295.9)

300.4 Dysthymic disorder

Anxiety depression   Neurotic depressive state
Depression with anxiety   Reactive depression
Depressive reaction

  EXCLUDES *adjustment reaction with depressive symptoms (309.0-309.1)*
  depression NOS (311)
  manic-depressive psychosis, depressed type (296.2-296.3)
  reactive depressive psychosis (298.0)

DEF: Depression without psychosis; less severe depression related to personal change or unexpected circumstances; also referred to as "reactional depression."

300.5 Neurasthenia

Fatigue neurosis   Psychogenic:
Nervous debility   general fatigue
Psychogenic:
  asthenia

Use additional code to identify any associated physical disorder

  EXCLUDES *anxiety state (300.00-300.09)*
  neurotic depression (300.4)
  psychophysiological disorders (306.0-306.9)
  specific nonpsychotic mental disorders following organic brain damage (310.0-310.9)

DEF: Physical and mental symptoms caused primarily by what is known as mental exhaustion; symptoms include chronic weakness, fatigue.

N Newborn Age: 0   P Pediatric Age: 0-17   M Maternity Age: 12-55   A Adult Age: 15-124   Manifestation Code   ►◄ Revised Text   ● New Code   ▲ Revised Code Title

68 — Volume 1   *2006 ICD•9•CM*

300.6 Depersonalization disorder
Derealization (neurotic)
Neurotic state with depersonalization episode
> **EXCLUDES**   *depersonalization associated with:*
> *anxiety (300.00-300.09)*
> *depression (300.4)*
> *manic-depressive disorder or*
> *psychosis (296.0-296.9)*
> *schizophrenia (295.0-295.9)*

DEF: Dissociative disorder characterized by feelings of strangeness about self or body image; symptoms include dizziness, anxiety, fear of insanity, loss of reality of surroundings.

300.7 Hypochondriasis
Body dysmorphic disorder
> **EXCLUDES**   *hypochondriasis in:*
> *hysteria (300.10-300.19)*
> *manic-depressive psychosis,*
> *depressed type (296.2-296.3)*
> *neurasthenia (300.5)*
> *obsessional disorder (300.3)*
> *schizophrenia (295.0-295.9)*

√5th **300.8 Somatoform disorders**

300.81 Somatization disorder
Briquet's disorder
Severe somatoform disorder

300.82 Undifferentiated somatoform disorder
Atypical somatoform disorder
Somatoform disorder NOS

AHA: 4Q, '96, 29

DEF: Disorders in which patients have symptoms that suggest an organic disease but no evidence of physical disorder after repeated testing.

300.89 Other somatoform disorders
Occupational neurosis, including writers' cramp
Psychasthenia
Psychasthenic neurosis

300.9 Unspecified nonpsychotic mental disorder
Psychoneurosis NOS

√4th **301 Personality disorders**
> **INCLUDES**   character neurosis

Use additional code to identify any associated neurosis or psychosis, or physical condition
> **EXCLUDES**   *nonpsychotic personality disorder associated*
> *with organic brain syndromes (310.0-*
> *310.9)*

301.0 Paranoid personality disorder
Fanatic personality
Paranoid personality (disorder)
Paranoid traits
> **EXCLUDES**   *acute paranoid reaction (298.3)*
> *alcoholic paranoia (291.5)*
> *paranoid schizophrenia (295.3)*
> *paranoid states (297.0-297.9)*

AHA: J-A, '85, 9

√5th **301.1 Affective personality disorder**
> **EXCLUDES**   *affective psychotic disorders (296.0-*
> *296.9)*
> *neurasthenia (300.5)*
> *neurotic depression (300.4)*

301.10 Affective personality disorder, unspecified

301.11 Chronic hypomanic personality disorder
Chronic hypomanic disorder
Hypomanic personality

301.12 Chronic depressive personality disorder
Chronic depressive disorder
Depressive character or personality

301.13 Cyclothymic disorder
Cycloid personality
Cyclothymia
Cyclothymic personality

√5th **301.2 Schizoid personality disorder**
> **EXCLUDES**   *schizophrenia (295.0-295.9)*

301.20 Schizoid personality disorder, unspecified

301.21 Introverted personality

301.22 Schizotypal personality disorder

301.3 Explosive personality disorder
Aggressive: Emotional instability
   personality   (excessive)
   reaction   Pathological emotionality
Aggressiveness   Quarrelsomeness
> **EXCLUDES**   *dyssocial personality (301.7)*
> *hysterical neurosis (300.10-300.19)*

301.4 Obsessive-compulsive personality disorder
Anancastic personality
Obsessional personality
> **EXCLUDES**   *obsessive-compulsive disorder (300.3)*
> *phobic state (300.20-300.29)*

√5th **301.5 Histrionic personality disorder**
> **EXCLUDES**   *hysterical neurosis (300.10-300.19)*

DEF: Extreme emotional behavior, often theatrical; often concerned about own appeal; may demand attention, exhibit seductive behavior.

301.50 Histrionic personality disorder, unspecified
Hysterical personality NOS

301.51 Chronic factitious illness with physical symptoms
Hospital addiction syndrome
Multiple operations syndrome
Munchausen syndrome

301.59 Other histrionic personality disorder
Personality: Personality:
   emotionally unstable   psychoinfantile
   labile

301.6 Dependent personality disorder
Asthenic personality   Passive personality
Inadequate personality
> **EXCLUDES**   *neurasthenia (300.5)*
> *passive-aggressive personality (301.84)*

DEF: Overwhelming feeling of helplessness; fears of abandonment may persist; difficulty in making personal decisions without confirmation by others; low self-esteem due to irrational sensitivity to criticism.

301.7 Antisocial personality disorder
Amoral personality
Asocial personality
Dyssocial personality
Personality disorder with predominantly sociopathic or asocial manifestation
> **EXCLUDES**   *disturbance of conduct without*
> *specifiable personality disorder*
> *(312.0-312.9)*
> *explosive personality (301.3)*

AHA: S-O, '84, 16

DEF: Continuous antisocial behavior that violates rights of others; social traits include extreme aggression, total disregard for traditional social rules.

√5th **301.8 Other personality disorders**

301.81 Narcissistic personality disorder

DEF: Grandiose fantasy or behavior, lack of social empathy, hypersensitive to the lack of others' judgment, exploits others; also sense of entitlement to have expectations met, need for continual admiration.

301.82 Avoidant personality disorder

DEF: Personality disorder marked by feelings of social inferiority; sensitivity to criticism, emotionally restrained due to fear of rejection.

√4th √5th Additional Digit Required   RUG III Special Care Dx   RUG III Clinically Complex Dx   Hospice Non-cancer Dx   **CD PDx** Clinical Dimension PDx   **CD SDx** Clinical Dimension SDx

2006 ICD•9•CM   **Volume 1 — 69**

Mental Disorders

301.83–302.9

301.83 Borderline personality disorder

DEF: Personality disorder characterized by unstable moods, self-image, and interpersonal relationships; uncontrolled anger, impulsive and self-destructive acts, fears of abandonment, feelings of emptiness and boredom, recurrent suicide threats or self-mutilation.

301.84 Passive-aggressive personality

DEF: Pattern of procrastination and refusal to meet standards; introduce own obstacles to success and exploit failure.

301.89 Other

Personality: Personality:
eccentric   masochistic
"haltlose" type   psychoneurotic
immature

EXCLUDES   psychoinfantile personality (301.59)

301.9 Unspecified personality disorder

Pathological personality NOS
Personality disorder NOS
Psychopathic:
    constitutional state
    personality (disorder)

√4ᵗʰ **302 Sexual and gender identity disorders**

EXCLUDES   sexual disorder manifest in:
     organic brain syndrome (290.0-294.9, 310.0-310.9)
     psychosis (295.0-298.9)

302.0 Ego-dystonic sexual orientation

Ego-dystonic lesbianism
Sexual orientation conflict disorder

EXCLUDES   homosexual pedophilia (302.2)

302.1 Zoophilia

Bestiality

DEF: A sociodeviant disorder marked by engaging in sexual intercourse with animals.

302.2 Pedophilia

DEF: A sociodeviant condition of adults characterized by sexual activity with children.

302.3 Transvestic fetishism

EXCLUDES   trans-sexualism (302.5)

DEF: The desire to dress in clothing of opposite sex.

302.4 Exhibitionism

DEF: Sexual deviant behavior; exposure of genitals to strangers; behavior prompted by intense sexual urges and fantasies.

√5ᵗʰ **302.5 Trans-sexualism**

EXCLUDES   transvestism (302.3)

DEF: Gender identity disturbance; overwhelming desire to change anatomic sex, due to belief that individual is a member of the opposite sex.

302.50 With unspecified sexual history

302.51 With asexual history

302.52 With homosexual history

302.53 With heterosexual history

302.6 Gender identity disorder in children

Feminism in boys
Gender identity disorder NOS

EXCLUDES   gender identity disorder in adult (302.85)
     trans-sexualism (302.50-302.53)
     transvestism (302.3)

√5ᵗʰ **302.7 Psychosexual dysfunction**

EXCLUDES   impotence of organic origin (607.84)
     normal transient symptoms from ruptured hymen
     transient or occasional failures of erection due to fatigue, anxiety, alcohol, or drugs

302.70 Psychosexual dysfunction, unspecified

Sexual dysfunction NOS

302.71 Hypoactive sexual desire disorder

EXCLUDES   decreased sexual desire NOS (799.81)

302.72 With inhibited sexual excitement

Female sexual arousal disorder
Frigidity
Impotence
Male erectile disorder

302.73 Female orgasmic disorder   ♀

302.74 Male orgasmic disorder   ♂

302.75 Premature ejaculation   ♂

302.76 Dyspareunia, psychogenic   ♀

DEF: Difficult or painful sex due to psychosomatic state.

302.79 With other specified psychosexual dysfunctions

Sexual aversion disorder

√5ᵗʰ **302.8 Other specified psychosexual disorders**

302.81 Fetishism

DEF: Psychosexual disorder noted for intense sexual urges and arousal precipitated by fantasies; use of inanimate objects, such as clothing, to stimulate sexual arousal, orgasm.

302.82 Voyeurism

DEF: Psychosexual disorder characterized by uncontrollable impulse to observe others, without their knowledge, who are nude or engaged in sexual activity.

302.83 Sexual masochism

DEF: Psychosexual disorder noted for need to achieve sexual gratification through humiliating or hurtful acts inflicted on self.

302.84 Sexual sadism

DEF: Psychosexual disorder noted for need to achieve sexual gratification through humiliating or hurtful acts inflicted on someone else.

302.85 Gender identity disorder in adolescents or adults

EXCLUDES   gender identity disorder NOS (302.6)
     gender identity disorder in children (302.6)

302.89 Other

Frotteurism
Nymphomania
Satyriasis

302.9 Unspecified psychosexual disorder

Paraphilia NOS
Pathologic sexuality NOS
Sexual deviation NOS
Sexual disorder NOS

N Newborn Age: 0   P Pediatric Age: 0-17   M Maternity Age: 12-55   A Adult Age: 15-124   Manifestation Code   ►◄ Revised Text   ● New Code   ▲ Revised Code Title

✓4th **303 Alcohol dependence syndrome**

Use additional code to identify any associated condition, as:
alcoholic psychoses (291.0-291.9)
drug dependence (304.0-304.9)
physical complications of alcohol, such as:
cerebral degeneration (331.7)
cirrhosis of liver (571.2)
epilepsy (345.0-345.9)
gastritis (535.3)
hepatitis (571.1)
liver damage NOS (571.3)

EXCLUDES *drunkenness NOS (305.0)*

The following fifth-digit subclassification is for use with category 303:

    0 unspecified
    1 continuous
    2 episodic
    3 in remission

AHA: 3Q, '95, 6; 2Q, '91, 9; 4Q, '88, 8; S-O, '86, 3

✓5th **303.0 Acute alcoholic intoxication**
Acute drunkenness in alcoholism

✓5th **303.9 Other and unspecified alcohol dependence**
Chronic alcoholism   Dipsomania

AHA: 2Q, '02, 4; 2Q, '89, 9

✓4th **304 Drug dependence**

EXCLUDES *nondependent abuse of drugs (305.1-305.9)*

The following fifth-digit subclassification is for use with category 304:

    0 unspecified
    1 continuous
    2 episodic
    3 in remission

AHA: 2Q, '91, 10; 4Q, '88, 8; S-O, '86, 3

✓5th **304.0 Opioid type dependence**
Heroin   Opium alkaloids and their
Meperidine   derivatives
Methadone   Synthetics with morphine-like
Morphine   effects
Opium

✓5th **304.1 Sedative, hypnotic or anxiolytic dependence**
Barbiturates
Nonbarbiturate sedatives and tranquilizers with a
similar effect:
chlordiazepoxide   meprobamate
diazepam   methaqualone
glutethimide

✓5th **304.2 Cocaine dependence**
Coca leaves and derivatives

✓5th **304.3 Cannabis dependence**
Hashish   Marihuana
Hemp

✓5th **304.4 Amphetamine and other psychostimulant
dependence**
Methylphenidate   Phenmetrazine

✓5th **304.5 Hallucinogen dependence**
Dimethyltryptamine [DMT]
Lysergic acid diethylamide [LSD] and derivatives
Mescaline
Psilocybin

✓5th **304.6 Other specified drug dependence**
Absinthe addiction
Glue sniffing
Inhalant dependence
Phencyclidine dependence
EXCLUDES *tobacco dependence (305.1)*

✓5th **304.7 Combinations of opioid type drug with
any other**
AHA: M-A, '86, 12

✓5th **304.8 Combinations of drug dependence
excluding opioid type drug**
AHA: M-A, '86, 12

✓5th **304.9 Unspecified drug dependence**
Drug addiction NOS   Drug dependence NOS
AHA: For code 304.90: 4Q, '03, 103

✓4th **305 Nondependent abuse of drugs**

Note: Includes cases where a person, for whom no other
diagnosis is possible, has come under medical care
because of the maladaptive effect of a drug on which he is
not dependent and that he has taken on his own initiative
to the detriment of his health or social functioning.

EXCLUDES *alcohol dependence syndrome (303.0-303.9)*
drug dependence (304.0-304.9)
drug withdrawal syndrome (292.0)
*poisoning by drugs or medicinal substances
(960.0-979.9)*

The following fifth-digit subclassification is for use with codes
305.0, 305.2-305.9:

    0 unspecified
    1 continuous
    2 episodic
    3 in remission

AHA: 2Q, '91, 10; 4Q, '88, 8; S-O, '86, 3

✓5th **305.0 Alcohol abuse**
Drunkenness NOS
Excessive drinking of alcohol NOS
"Hangover" (alcohol)
Inebriety NOS
EXCLUDES *acute alcohol intoxication in alcoholism
(303.0)*
alcoholic psychoses (291.0-291.9)
AHA: 3Q, '96, 16

305.1 Tobacco use disorder
Tobacco dependence
EXCLUDES *history of tobacco use (V15.82)*
AHA: 2Q, '96, 10; N-D, '84, 12

✓5th **305.2 Cannabis abuse**

✓5th **305.3 Hallucinogen abuse**
Acute intoxication from hallucinogens ["bad trips"]
LSD reaction

✓5th **305.4 Sedative, hypnotic or anxiolytic abuse**

✓5th **305.5 Opioid abuse**

✓5th **305.6 Cocaine abuse**
AHA: 1Q, '93, 25; ▶**For code 305.60:** 1Q, '05, 6◀

✓5th **305.7 Amphetamine or related acting
sympathomimetic abuse**
AHA: For code 305.70: 2Q, '03, 10-11

✓5th **305.8 Antidepressant type abuse**

✓5th **305.9 Other, mixed, or unspecified drug abuse**
Caffeine intoxication
Inhalant abuse
"Laxative habit"
Misuse of drugs NOS
Nonprescribed use of drugs or patent medicinals
Phencyclidine abuse
AHA: 3Q, '99, 20

✓4th
✓5th Additional Digit Required   RUG III Special Care Dx   RUG III Clinically Complex Dx   Hospice Non-cancer Dx   **CD PDx** Clinical Dimension PDx   **CD SDx** Clinical Dimension SDx

2006 ICD•9•CM   **October 2005 • Volume 1 — 71**

✓4ᵗʰ 306 Physiological malfunction arising from mental factors

INCLUDES psychogenic:

physical symptoms ⎫ not involving
physiological ⎬ tissue
manifestations ⎭ damage

EXCLUDES hysteria (300.11-300.19)
physical symptoms secondary to a psychiatric
disorder classified elsewhere
psychic factors associated with physical
conditions involving tissue damage
classified elsewhere (316)
specific nonpsychotic mental disorders following
organic brain damage (310.0-310.9)

DEF: Functional disturbances or interruptions due to mental or psychological
causes; no tissue damage sustained in these conditions.

306.0 Musculoskeletal
Psychogenic paralysis
Psychogenic torticollis
EXCLUDES Gilles de la Tourette's syndrome
(307.23)
paralysis as hysterical or conversion
reaction (300.11)
tics (307.20-307.22)

306.1 Respiratory
Psychogenic: Psychogenic:
air hunger   hyperventilation
cough   yawning
hiccough
EXCLUDES psychogenic asthma (316 and 493.9)

306.2 Cardiovascular
Cardiac neurosis
Cardiovascular neurosis
Neurocirculatory asthenia
Psychogenic cardiovascular disorder
EXCLUDES psychogenic paroxysmal tachycardia
(316 and 427.2)

AHA: J-A, '85, 14

DEF: Neurocirculatory asthenia: functional nervous and circulatory
irregularities with palpitations, dyspnea, fatigue, rapid pulse,
precordial pain, fear of effort, discomfort during exercise, anxiety;
also called DaCosta's syndrome, Effort syndrome, Irritable or
Soldier's Heart.

306.3 Skin
Psychogenic pruritus
EXCLUDES psychogenic:
alopecia (316 and 704.00)
dermatitis (316 and 692.9)
eczema (316 and 691.8 or 692.9)
urticaria (316 and 708.0-708.9)

306.4 Gastrointestinal
Aerophagy
Cyclical vomiting, psychogenic
Diarrhea, psychogenic
Nervous gastritis
Psychogenic dyspepsia
EXCLUDES cyclical vomiting NOS (536.2)
globus hystericus (300.11)
mucous colitis (316 and 564.9)
psychogenic:
cardiospasm (316 and 530.0)
duodenal ulcer (316 and 532.0-
532.9)
gastric ulcer (316 and 531.0-531.9)
peptic ulcer NOS (316 and 533.0-
533.9)
vomiting NOS (307.54)

AHA: 2Q, '89, 11

DEF: Aerophagy: excess swallowing of air, usually unconscious;
related to anxiety; results in distended abdomen or belching, often
interpreted by the patient as a physical disorder.

✓5ᵗʰ 306.5 Genitourinary
EXCLUDES enuresis, psychogenic (307.6)
frigidity (302.72)
impotence (302.72)
psychogenic dyspareunia (302.76)

**306.50 Psychogenic genitourinary malfunction,
unspecified**
306.51 Psychogenic vaginismus ♀
Functional vaginismus

DEF: Psychogenic response resulting in painful
contractions of vaginal canal muscles; can be severe
enough to prevent sexual intercourse.

306.52 Psychogenic dysmenorrhea ♀
306.53 Psychogenic dysuria
306.59 Other
AHA: M-A, '87, 11

306.6 Endocrine
306.7 Organs of special sense
EXCLUDES hysterical blindness or deafness
(300.11)
psychophysical visual disturbances
(368.16)

306.8 Other specified psychophysiological malfunction
Bruxism   Teeth grinding
306.9 Unspecified psychophysiological malfunction
Psychophysiologic disorder NOS
Psychosomatic disorder NOS

✓4ᵗʰ 307 Special symptoms or syndromes, not elsewhere classified
Note: This category is intended for use if the psychopathology is
manifested by a single specific symptom or group of
symptoms which is not part of an organic illness or other
mental disorder classifiable elsewhere.
EXCLUDES those due to mental disorders classified
elsewhere
those of organic origin

307.0 Stuttering
EXCLUDES dysphasia (784.5)
lisping or lalling (307.9)
retarded development of speech
(315.31-315.39)

307.1 Anorexia nervosa
EXCLUDES eating disturbance NOS (307.50)
feeding problem (783.3)
of nonorganic origin (307.59)
loss of appetite (783.0)
of nonorganic origin (307.59)

AHA: 4Q, '89, 11

✓5ᵗʰ 307.2 Tics
EXCLUDES nail-biting or thumb-sucking (307.9)
stereotypes occurring in isolation
(307.3)
tics of organic origin (333.3)

DEF: Involuntary muscle response usually confined to the face,
shoulders.

307.20 Tic disorder, unspecified
Tic disorder NOS
307.21 Transient tic disorder
307.22 Chronic motor or vocal tic disorder
307.23 Tourette's disorder
Motor-verbal tic disorder

DEF: Syndrome of facial and vocal tics in childhood;
progresses to spontaneous or involuntary jerking,
obscene utterances, other uncontrollable actions
considered inappropriate.

307.3 Stereotypic movement disorder
Body-rocking   Spasmus nutans
Head banging   Stereotypes NOS
EXCLUDES tics (307.20-307.23)
of organic origin (333.3)

Ⓝ Newborn Age: 0   Ⓟ Pediatric Age: 0-17   Ⓜ Maternity Age: 12-55   Ⓐ Adult Age: 15-124   Manifestation Code   ◄► Revised Text   ● New Code   ▲ Revised Code Title

√5ᵗʰ **307.4 Specific disorders of sleep of nonorganic origin**
> EXCLUDES   *narcolepsy (347.00-347.11)*
> ▶*organic hypersomnia (327.10-327.19)*
> *organic insomnia (327.00-327.09)*◀
> *those of unspecified cause (780.50-780.59)*

307.40 Nonorganic sleep disorder, unspecified

307.41 Transient disorder of initiating or maintaining sleep
> ▶Adjustment insomnia◀
> Hyposomnia ⎤ associated with inter-
> Insomnia   ⎟ mittent emotional
> Sleeplessness ⎦ reactions or conflicts

307.42 Persistent disorder of initiating or maintaining sleep
> Hyposomnia, insomnia, or sleeplessness associated with:
> anxiety
> conditioned arousal
> depression (major) (minor)
> psychosis
> ▶Idiopathic insomnia
> Paradoxical insomnia
> Primary insomnia
> Psychophysiological insomnia◀

307.43 Transient disorder of initiating or maintaining wakefulness
> Hypersomnia associated with acute or intermittent emotional reactions or conflicts

307.44 Persistent disorder of initiating or maintaining wakefulness
> Hypersomnia associated with depression (major) (minor)
> ▶Insufficient sleep syndrome
> Primary hypersomnia◀
> EXCLUDES ▶ *sleep deprivation (V69.4)*◀

307.45 Circadian rhythm sleep disorder of nonorganic origin

307.46 Sleep arousal disorder
> Night terror disorder   Sleepwalking
> Night terrors   Somnambulism
> Sleep terror disorder
>
> DEF: Sleepwalking marked by extreme terror, panic, screaming, confusion; no recall of event upon arousal; term may refer to simply the act of sleepwalking.

307.47 Other dysfunctions of sleep stages or arousal from sleep
> Nightmare disorder
> Nightmares:
> NOS
> REM-sleep type
> Sleep drunkenness

307.48 Repetitive intrusions of sleep
> Repetitive intrusion of sleep with:
> atypical polysomnographic features
> environmental disturbances
> repeated REM-sleep interruptions

307.49 Other
> "Short-sleeper"
> Subjective insomnia complaint

√5ᵗʰ **307.5 Other and unspecified disorders of eating**
> EXCLUDES   *anorexia:*
> *nervosa (307-1)*
> *of unspecified cause (783.0)*
> *overeating, of unspecified cause (783.6)*
> *vomiting:*
> *NOS (787.0)*
> *cyclical (536.2)*
> *psychogenic (306.4)*

307.50 Eating disorder, unspecified
> Eating disorder NOS

307.51 Bulimia nervosa
> Overeating of nonorganic origin
> DEF: Mental disorder commonly characterized by binge eating followed by self-induced vomiting; perceptions of being fat; and fear the inability to stop eating voluntarily.

307.52 Pica
> Perverted appetite of nonorganic origin
> DEF: Compulsive eating disorder characterized by craving for substances, other than food; such as paint chips or dirt.

307.53 Rumination disorder
> Regurgitation, of nonorganic origin, of food with reswallowing
> EXCLUDES   *obsessional rumination (300.3)*

307.54 Psychogenic vomiting

307.59 Other
> ▶Feeding disorder of infancy or early childhood of nonorganic origin◀
> Infantile feeding ⎤
>   disturbances ⎟ of nonorganic
> Loss of appetite ⎦ origin

307.6 Enuresis
> Enuresis (primary) (secondary) of nonorganic origin
> EXCLUDES   *enuresis of unspecified cause (788.3)*
>
> DEF: Involuntary urination past age of normal control; also called bedwetting; no trace to biological problem; focus on psychological issues.

307.7 Encopresis
> Encopresis (continuous) (discontinuous) of nonorganic origin
> EXCLUDES   *encopresis of unspecified cause (787.6)*
>
> DEF: Inability to control bowel movements; cause traced to psychological, not biological, problems.

√5ᵗʰ **307.8 Pain disorders related to psychological factors**

307.80 Psychogenic pain, site unspecified

307.81 Tension headache
> EXCLUDES   *headache:*
> *NOS (784.0)*
> *migraine (346.0-346.9)*
>
> AHA: N-D, '85, 16

307.89 Other
> Code first to site of pain
> EXCLUDES   *pain disorder exclusively attributed to psychological factors (307.80)*
> *psychogenic pain (307.80)*

307.9 Other and unspecified special symptoms or syndromes, not elsewhere classified
> Communication   Lisping
>   disorder NOS   Masturbation
> Hair plucking   Nail-biting
> Lalling   Thumb-sucking

√4ᵗʰ **308 Acute reaction to stress**
> INCLUDES   catastrophic stress
> combat fatigue
> gross stress reaction (acute)
> transient disorders in response to exceptional physical or mental stress which usually subside within hours or days
>
> EXCLUDES   *adjustment reaction or disorder (309.0-309.9)*
> *chronic stress reaction (309.1-309.9)*

308.0 Predominant disturbance of emotions
> Anxiety ⎤
> Emotional crisis ⎟ as acute reaction to
> Panic state ⎦ exceptional [gross] stress

308.1 Predominant disturbance of consciousness
> Fugues as acute reaction to exceptional [gross] stress

308.2 Predominant psychomotor disturbance
> Agitation states ⎤ as acute reaction to exceptional
> Stupor ⎦ [gross] stress

√4ᵗʰ √5ᵗʰ Additional Digit Required   RUG III Special Care Dx   RUG III Clinically Complex Dx   Hospice Non-cancer Dx   CD PDx Clinical Dimension PDx   CD SDx Clinical Dimension SDx

2006 ICD•9•CM   October 2005 • Volume 1 — 73

Mental Disorders

308.3–311

308.3   **Other acute reactions to stress**
Acute situational disturbance
Acute stress disorder
> **EXCLUDES**   *prolonged posttraumatic emotional disturbance (309.81)*

308.4   **Mixed disorders as reaction to stress**

308.9   **Unspecified acute reaction to stress**

√4th **309 Adjustment reaction**
> **INCLUDES**   adjustment disorders
> reaction (adjustment) to chronic stress
> **EXCLUDES**   *acute reaction to major stress (308.0-308.9)*
> *neurotic disorders (300.0-300.9)*

309.0   **Adjustment disorder with depressed mood**
Grief reaction
> **EXCLUDES**   *affective psychoses (296.0-296.9)*
> *neurotic depression (300.4)*
> *prolonged depressive reaction (309.1)*
> *psychogenic depressive psychosis (298.0)*

309.1   **Prolonged depressive reaction**
> **EXCLUDES**   *affective psychoses (296.0-296.9)*
> *brief depressive reaction (309.0)*
> *neurotic depression (300.4)*
> *psychogenic depressive psychosis (298.0)*

√5th **309.2**   **With predominant disturbance of other emotions**

309.21   **Separation anxiety disorder**
DEF: Abnormal apprehension by a child when physically separated from support environment; byproduct of abnormal symbiotic child-parent relationship.

309.22   **Emancipation disorder of adolescence and early adult life**
DEF: Adjustment reaction of late adolescence; conflict over independence from parental supervision; symptoms include difficulty in making decisions, increased reliance on parental advice, deliberate adoption of values in opposition of parents.

309.23   **Specific academic or work inhibition**

309.24   **Adjustment disorder with anxiety**

309.28   **Adjustment disorder with mixed anxiety and depressed mood**
Adjustment reaction with anxiety and depression

309.29   **Other**
Culture shock

309.3   **Adjustment disorder with disturbance of conduct**
Conduct disturbance ⎫
Destructiveness   ⎬ as adjustment reaction
> **EXCLUDES**   *destructiveness in child (312.9)*
> *disturbance of conduct NOS (312.9)*
> *dyssocial behavior without manifest psychiatric disorder (V71.01-V71.02)*
> *personality disorder with predominantly sociopathic or asocial manifestations (301.7)*

309.4   **Adjustment disorder with mixed disturbance of emotions and conduct**

√5th **309.8**   **Other specified adjustment reactions**

309.81   **Posttraumatic stress disorder**
Chronic posttraumatic stress disorder
Concentration camp syndrome
Posttraumatic stress disorder NOS
> **EXCLUDES**   *acute stress disorder (308.3)*
> *posttraumatic brain syndrome: nonpsychotic (310.2) psychotic (293.0-293.9)*

DEF: Preoccupation with traumatic events beyond normal experience; events such as rape, personal assault, combat, natural disasters, accidents, torture precipitate disorder; also recurring flashbacks of trauma; symptoms include difficulty remembering, sleeping, or concentrating, and guilt feelings for surviving.

309.82   **Adjustment reaction with physical symptoms**

309.83   **Adjustment reaction with withdrawal**
Elective mutism as adjustment reaction
Hospitalism (in children) NOS

309.89   **Other**

309.9   **Unspecified adjustment reaction**
Adaptation reaction NOS
Adjustment reaction NOS

√4th **310 Specific nonpsychotic mental disorders due to brain damage**
> **EXCLUDES**   *neuroses, personality disorders, or other nonpsychotic conditions occurring in a form similar to that seen with functional disorders but in association with a physical condition (300.0-300.9, 301.0-301.9)*

310.0   **Frontal lobe syndrome**
Lobotomy syndrome
Postleucotomy syndrome [state]
> **EXCLUDES**   *postcontusion syndrome (310.2)*

310.1   **Personality change due to conditions classified elsewhere**
Cognitive or personality change of other type, of nonpsychotic severity
Organic psychosyndrome of nonpsychotic severity
Presbyophrenia NOS
Senility with mental changes of nonpsychotic severity
> **EXCLUDES**   *memory loss of unknown cause (780.93)*

DEF: Personality disorder caused by organic factors, such as brain lesions, head trauma, or cerebrovascular accident (CVA).

310.2   **Postconcussion syndrome**
Postcontusion syndrome or encephalopathy
Posttraumatic brain syndrome, nonpsychotic
Status postcommotio cerebri
> **EXCLUDES**   *frontal lobe syndrome (310.0)*
> *postencephalitic syndrome (310.8)*
> *any organic psychotic conditions following head injury (293.0-294.0)*

AHA: 4Q, '90, 24

DEF: Nonpsychotic disorder due to brain trauma, causes symptoms unrelated to any disease process; symptoms include amnesia, serial headaches, rapid heartbeat, fatigue, disrupted sleep patterns, inability to concentrate.

310.8   **Other specified nonpsychotic mental disorders following organic brain damage**
Mild memory disturbance
Postencephalitic syndrome
Other focal (partial) organic psychosyndromes

310.9   **Unspecified nonpsychotic mental disorder following organic brain damage**
AHA: 4Q, '03, 103

311 Depressive disorder, not elsewhere classified
Depressive disorder NOS   Depression NOS
Depressive state NOS
> **EXCLUDES**   *acute reaction to major stress with depressive symptoms (308.0)*
> *affective personality disorder (301.10-301.13)*
> *affective psychoses (296.0-296.9)*
> *brief depressive reaction (309.0)*
> *depressive states associated with stressful events (309.0-309.1)*
> *disturbance of emotions specific to childhood and adolescence, with misery and unhappiness (313.1)*
> *mixed adjustment reaction with depressive symptoms (309.4)*
> *neurotic depression (300.4)*
> *prolonged depressive adjustment reaction (309.1)*
> *psychogenic depressive psychosis (298.0)*

AHA: 4Q, '03, 75

N Newborn Age: 0   P Pediatric Age: 0-17   M Maternity Age: 12-55   A Adult Age: 15-124   Manifestation Code   ▶◀ Revised Text   ● New Code   ▲ Revised Code Title

✓4ᵗʰ **312 Disturbance of conduct, not elsewhere classified**

> EXCLUDES   *adjustment reaction with disturbance of conduct (309.3)*
> *drug dependence (304.0-304.9)*
> *dyssocial behavior without manifest psychiatric disorder (V71.01-V71.02)*
> *personality disorder with predominantly sociopathic or asocial manifestations (301.7)*
> *sexual deviations (302.0-302.9)*

The following fifth-digit subclassification is for use with categories 312.0-312.2:

    0 unspecified
    1 mild
    2 moderate
    3 severe

✓5ᵗʰ **312.0 Undersocialized conduct disorder, aggressive type**
Aggressive outburst   Unsocialized aggressive
Anger reaction   disorder

DEF: Mental condition identified by behaviors disrespectful of others' rights and of age-appropriate social norms or rules; symptoms include bullying, vandalism, verbal and physical abusiveness, lying, stealing, defiance.

✓5ᵗʰ **312.1 Undersocialized conduct disorder, unaggressive type**
Childhood truancy, unsocialized
Solitary stealing
Tantrums

✓5ᵗʰ **312.2 Socialized conduct disorder**
Childhood truancy, socialized   Group delinquency

> EXCLUDES   *gang activity without manifest psychiatric disorder (V71.01)*

✓5ᵗʰ **312.3 Disorders of impulse control, not elsewhere classified**
  312.30 Impulse control disorder, unspecified
  312.31 Pathological gambling
  312.32 Kleptomania
  312.33 Pyromania
  312.34 Intermittent explosive disorder
  312.35 Isolated explosive disorder
  312.39 Other
        Trichotillomania

312.4 Mixed disturbance of conduct and emotions
Neurotic delinquency

> EXCLUDES   *compulsive conduct disorder (312.3)*

✓5ᵗʰ **312.8 Other specified disturbances of conduct, not elsewhere classified**
  312.81 Conduct disorder, childhood onset type
  312.82 Conduct disorder, adolescent onset type
  312.89 Other conduct disorder
        Conduct disorder of unspecified onset

312.9 Unspecified disturbance of conduct
Delinquency (juvenile)
Disruptive behavior disorder NOS

✓4ᵗʰ **313 Disturbance of emotions specific to childhood and adolescence**

> EXCLUDES   *adjustment reaction (309.0-309.9)*
> *emotional disorder of neurotic type (300.0-300.9)*
> *masturbation, nail-biting, thumbsucking, and other isolated symptoms (307.0-307.9)*

313.0 Overanxious disorder
Anxiety and fearfulness ⎫ of childhood and
Overanxious disorder   ⎬ adolescence

> EXCLUDES   *abnormal separation anxiety (309.21)*
> *anxiety states (300.00-300.09)*
> *hospitalism in children (309.83)*
> *phobic state (300.20-300.29)*

313.1 Misery and unhappiness disorder

> EXCLUDES   *depressive neurosis (300.4)*

✓5ᵗʰ **313.2 Sensitivity, shyness, and social withdrawal disorder**

> EXCLUDES   *infantile autism (299.0)*
> *schizoid personality (301.20-301.22)*
> *schizophrenia (295.0-295.9)*

  313.21 Shyness disorder of childhood
        Sensitivity reaction of childhood or adolescence
  313.22 Introverted disorder of childhood
        Social withdrawal ⎫ of childhood or
        Withdrawal   ⎬ adolescence
        reaction
  313.23 Selective mutism

> EXCLUDES   *elective mutism as adjustment reaction (309.83)*

313.3 Relationship problems
Sibling jealousy

> EXCLUDES   *relationship problems associated with aggression, destruction, or other forms of conduct disturbance (312.0-312.9)*

✓5ᵗʰ **313.8 Other or mixed emotional disturbances of childhood or adolescence**
  313.81 Oppositional defiant disorder
        DEF: Mental disorder of children noted for pervasive opposition, defiance of authority.
  313.82 Identity disorder
        Identity problem
        DEF: Distress of adolescents caused by inability to form acceptable self-identity; uncertainty about career choice, sexual orientation, moral values.
  313.83 Academic underachievement disorder
  313.89 Other   P
        Reactive attachment disorder of infancy or early childhood

313.9 Unspecified emotional disturbance of   P
childhood or adolescence
Mental disorder of infancy, childhood or adolescence NOS

✓4ᵗʰ **314 Hyperkinetic syndrome of childhood**

> EXCLUDES   *hyperkinesis as symptom of underlying disorder—code the underlying disorder*

✓5ᵗʰ **314.0 Attention deficit disorder**
Adult
Child

DEF: A behavioral disorder usually diagnosed at an early age; characterized by the inability to focus attention for a normal period of time.

  314.00 Without mention of hyperactivity
        Predominantly inattentive type
        AHA: 1Q, '97, 8

  314.01 With hyperactivity
        Combined type
        Overactivity NOS
        Predominantly hyperactive/impulsive type
        Simple disturbance of attention with overactivity
        AHA: 1Q, '97, 8

314.1 Hyperkinesis with developmental delay
Developmental disorder of hyperkinesis
Use additional code to identify any associated neurological disorder

314.2 Hyperkinetic conduct disorder
Hyperkinetic conduct disorder without developmental delay

> EXCLUDES   *hyperkinesis with significant delays in specific skills (314.1)*

314.8 Other specified manifestations of hyperkinetic syndrome

---

✓4ᵗʰ
✓5ᵗʰ **Additional Digit Required**   **RUG III Special Care Dx**   **RUG III Clinically Complex Dx**   Hospice Non-cancer Dx   **CD PDx** Clinical Dimension PDx   **CD SDx** Clinical Dimension SDx

2006 ICD•9•CM   **Volume 1 — 75**

Mental Disorders

314.9–319

314.9   **Unspecified hyperkinetic syndrome**
Hyperkinetic reaction of childhood or adolescence NOS
Hyperkinetic syndrome NOS

✓4ᵗʰ **315 Specific delays in development**
> EXCLUDES   *that due to a neurological disorder (320.0-389.9)*

✓5ᵗʰ **315.0**   **Specific reading disorder**

315.00   **Reading disorder, unspecified**

315.01   **Alexia**
DEF: Lack of ability to understand written language; manifestation of aphasia.

315.02   **Developmental dyslexia**
DEF: Serious impairment of reading skills unexplained in relation to general intelligence and teaching processes; it can be inherited or congenital.

315.09   **Other**
Specific spelling difficulty

315.1   **Mathematics disorder**
Dyscalculia

315.2   **Other specific learning difficulties**
Disorder of written expression
> EXCLUDES   *specific arithmetical disorder (315.1)*
> *specific reading disorder (315.00-315.09)*

✓5ᵗʰ **315.3**   **Developmental speech or language disorder**

315.31   **Expressive language disorder**
Developmental aphasia
Word deafness
> EXCLUDES   *acquired aphasia (784.3)*
> *elective mutism (309.83, 313.0, 313.23)*

315.32   **Mixed receptive-expressive language disorder**
AHA: 4Q, '96, 30

315.39   **Other**
Developmental articulation disorder
Dyslalia
Phonological disorder
> EXCLUDES   *lisping and lalling (307.9)*
> *stammering and stuttering (307.0)*

315.4   **Developmental coordination disorder**
Clumsiness syndrome   Specific motor development
Dyspraxia syndrome   disorder

315.5   **Mixed development disorder**
AHA: 2Q, '02, 11

315.8   **Other specified delays in development**

315.9   **Unspecified delay in development**
Developmental disorder NOS
Learning disorder NOS

316 Psychic factors associated with diseases classified elsewhere
Psychologic factors in physical conditions classified elsewhere
Use additional code to identify the associated physical condition, as:
psychogenic:
asthma (493.9)
dermatitis (692.9)
duodenal ulcer (532.0-532.9)
eczema (691.8, 692.9)
gastric ulcer (531.0-531.9)
mucous colitis (564.9)
paroxysmal tachycardia (427.2)
ulcerative colitis (556)
urticaria (708.0-708.9)
psychosocial dwarfism (259.4)
> EXCLUDES   *physical symptoms and physiological malfunctions, not involving tissue damage, of mental origin (306.0-306.9)*

MENTAL RETARDATION (317-319)
Use additional code(s) to identify any associated psychiatric or physical condition(s)

317 Mild mental retardation
High-grade defect
IQ 50-70
Mild mental subnormality

✓4ᵗʰ **318 Other specified mental retardation**

318.0   **Moderate mental retardation**
IQ 35-49
Moderate mental subnormality

318.1   **Severe mental retardation**
IQ 20-34   Severe mental subnormality

318.2   **Profound mental retardation**
IQ under 20   Profound mental subnormality

319 Unspecified mental retardation
Mental deficiency NOS   Mental subnormality NOS

Ⓝ Newborn Age: 0   Ⓟ Pediatric Age: 0-17   Ⓜ Maternity Age: 12-55   Ⓐ Adult Age: 15-124   Manifestation Code   ▶◀ Revised Text   ● New Code   ▲ Revised Code Title

76 — Volume 1   *2006 ICD•9•CM*

6. DISEASES OF THE NERVOUS SYSTEM AND SENSE ORGANS (320-389)

INFLAMMATORY DISEASES OF THE CENTRAL NERVOUS SYSTEM (320-326)

√4th **320 Bacterial meningitis**

INCLUDES arachnoiditis
leptomeningitis
meningitis   } bacterial
meningoencephalitis
meningomyelitis
pachymeningitis

AHA: J-F, '87, 6

DEF: Bacterial infection causing inflammation of the lining of the brain and/or spinal cord.

320.0 Hemophilus meningitis `CD PDx`
Meningitis due to Hemophilus influenzae [H. influenzae]

320.1 Pneumococcal meningitis `CD PDx`

320.2 Streptococcal meningitis `CD PDx`

320.3 Staphylococcal meningitis `CD PDx`

320.7 *Meningitis in other bacterial diseases classified elsewhere* `CD SDx`
Code first underlying disease, as:
actinomycosis (039.8)
listeriosis (027.0)
typhoid fever (002.0)
whooping cough (033.0-033.9)
EXCLUDES meningitis (in):
epidemic (036.0)
gonococcal (098.82)
meningococcal (036.0)
salmonellosis (003.21)
syphilis:
NOS (094.2)
congenital (090.42)
meningovascular (094.2)
secondary (091.81)
tuberculous (013.0)

√5th **320.8 Meningitis due to other specified bacteria**

320.81 Anaerobic meningitis `CD PDx`
Bacteroides (fragilis)
Gram-negative anaerobes

320.82 Meningitis due to gram-negative bacteria, not elsewhere classified `CD PDx`
Aerobacter aerogenespneumoniae
Escherichia coli [E. coli]
Friedländer bacillus
Klebsiella
Proteus morganii
Pseudomonas
EXCLUDES gram-negative anaerobes (320.81)

320.89 Meningitis due to other specified bacteria `CD PDx`
Bacillus pyocyaneus

320.9 Meningitis due to unspecified bacterium `CD PDx`
Meningitis: Meningitis:
bacterial NOS   pyogenic NOS
purulent NOS   suppurative NOS

√4th **321 Meningitis due to other organisms**
AHA: J-F, '87, 6

DEF: Infection causing inflammation of the lining of the brain and/or spinal cord, due to organisms other than bacteria.

321.0 *Cryptococcal meningitis* `CD SDx`
Code first underlying disease (117.5)

321.1 *Meningitis in other fungal diseases* `CD SDx`
Code first underlying disease (110.0-118)
EXCLUDES meningitis in:
candidiasis (112.83)
coccidioidomycosis (114.2)
histoplasmosis (115.01, 115.11, 115.91)

321.2 *Meningitis due to viruses not elsewhere classified* `CD SDx`
Code first underlying disease, as:
meningitis due to arbovirus (060.0-066.9)
EXCLUDES meningitis (due to):
abacterial (047.0-047.9)
adenovirus (049.1)
aseptic NOS (047.9)
Coxsackie (virus)(047.0)
ECHO virus (047.1)
enterovirus (047.0-047.9)
herpes simplex virus (054.72)
herpes zoster virus (053.0)
lymphocytic choriomeningitis virus (049.0)
mumps (072.1)
viral NOS (047.9)
meningo-eruptive syndrome (047.1)

AHA: ▶4Q, '04, 51◀

321.3 *Meningitis due to trypanosomiasis* `CD SDx`
Code first underlying disease (086.0-086.9)

321.4 *Meningitis in sarcoidosis* `CD SDx`
Code first underlying disease (135)

321.8 *Meningitis due to other nonbacterial organisms classified elsewhere* `CD SDx`
Code first underlying disease
EXCLUDES leptospiral meningitis (100.81)

√4th **322 Meningitis of unspecified cause**

INCLUDES arachnoiditis
leptomeningitis   } with no organism
meningitis   specified as
pachymeningitis   cause

AHA: J-F, '87, 6

DEF: Infection causing inflammation of the lining of the brain and/or spinal cord, due to unspecified cause.

322.0 Nonpyogenic meningitis `CD PDx`
Meningitis with clear cerebrospinal fluid

322.1 Eosinophilic meningitis `CD PDx`

322.2 Chronic meningitis `CD PDx`

322.9 Meningitis, unspecified `CD PDx`

√4th **323 Encephalitis, myelitis, and encephalomyelitis**

INCLUDES acute disseminated encephalomyelitis
meningoencephalitis, except bacterial
meningomyelitis, except bacterial
myelitis (acute):
ascending
transverse
EXCLUDES bacterial:
meningoencephalitis (320.0-320.9)
meningomyelitis (320.0-320.9)

DEF: Encephalitis: inflammation of brain tissues.
DEF: Myelitis: inflammation of the spinal cord.
DEF: Encephalomyelitis: inflammation of brain and spinal cord.

323.0 *Encephalitis in viral diseases classified elsewhere* `CD SDx`
Code first underlying disease, as:
cat-scratch disease (078.3)
infectious mononucleosis (075)
ornithosis (073.7)
EXCLUDES encephalitis (in):
arthropod-borne viral (062.0-064)
herpes simplex (054.3)
mumps (072.2)
poliomyelitis (045.0-045.9)
rubella (056.01)
slow virus infections of central nervous system (046.0-046.9)
other viral diseases of central nervous system (049.8-049.9)
viral NOS (049.9)

√4th Additional Digit Required   RUG III Special Care Dx   RUG III Clinically Complex Dx   Hospice Non-cancer Dx   `CD PDx` Clinical Dimension PDx   `CD SDx` Clinical Dimension SDx

323.1 Encephalitis in rickettsial diseases classified elsewhere `CD SDx`

Code first underlying disease (080-083.9)

DEF: Inflammation of the brain caused by rickettsial disease carried by louse, tick, or mite.

323.2 Encephalitis in protozoal diseases classified elsewhere `CD SDx`

Code first underlying disease, as:
malaria (084.0-084.9)
trypanosomiasis (086.0-086.9)

DEF: Inflammation of the brain caused by protozoal disease carried by mosquitoes and flies.

323.4 Other encephalitis due to infection classified elsewhere `CD SDx`

Code first underlying disease

> EXCLUDES encephalitis (in):
> meningococcal (036.1)
> syphilis:
> NOS (094.81)
> congenital (090.41)
> toxoplasmosis (130.0)
> tuberculosis (013.6)
> meningoencephalitis due to free-living
> ameba [Naegleria] (136.2)

323.5 Encephalitis following immunization procedures `CD PDx`

Encephalitis ⎱ postimmunization or
Encephalomyelitis ⎰ postvaccinal

Use additional E code to identify vaccine

323.6 Postinfectious encephalitis `CD SDx`

▶Infectious acute disseminated encephalomyelitis (ADEM)◀

Code first underlying disease

> EXCLUDES encephalitis:
> postchickenpox (052.0)
> postmeasles (055.0)

DEF: Infection, inflammation of brain several weeks following the outbreak of a systemic infection.

323.7 Toxic encephalitis `CD SDx`

Code first underlying cause, as:
carbon tetrachloride (982.1)
hydroxyquinoline derivatives (961.3)
lead (984.0-984.9)
mercury (985.0)
thallium (985.8)

AHA: 2Q, '97, 8

323.8 Other causes of encephalitis `CD PDx`

▶Noninfectious acute disseminated encephalomyelitis (ADEM)◀

323.9 Unspecified cause of encephalitis `CD PDx`

`✓4ᵗʰ` **324 Intracranial and intraspinal abscess**

324.0 Intracranial abscess `CD PDx`

Abscess (embolic): Abscess (embolic) of brain
cerebellar [any part]:
cerebral epidural
extradural
otogenic
subdural

> EXCLUDES tuberculous (013.3)

324.1 Intraspinal abscess `CD PDx`

Abscess (embolic) of spinal cord [any part]:
epidural
extradural
subdural

> EXCLUDES tuberculous (013.5)

324.9 Of unspecified site `CD PDx`

Extradural or subdural abscess NOS

325 Phlebitis and thrombophlebitis of intracranial venous sinuses `CD PDx`

Embolism ⎫ of cavernous, lateral, or
Endophlebitis ⎪ other intracranial
Phlebitis, septic or suppurative ⎬ or unspecified
Thrombophlebitis ⎪ intracranial
Thrombosis ⎭ venous sinus

> EXCLUDES that specified as:
> complicating pregnancy, childbirth, or the
> puerperium (671.5)
> of nonpyogenic origin (437.6)

DEF: Inflammation and formation of blood clot in a vein within the brain or its lining.

326 Late effects of intracranial abscess or pyogenic infection `CD PDx`

Note: This category is to be used to indicate conditions whose primary classification is to 320-325 [excluding 320.7, 321.0-321.8, 323.0-323.4, 323.6-323.7] as the cause of late effects, themselves classifiable elsewhere. The "late effects" include conditions specified as such, or as sequelae, which may occur at any time after the resolution of the causal condition.

Use additional code to identify condition, as:
hydrocephalus (331.4)
paralysis (342.0-342.9, 344.0-344.9)

`✓4ᵗʰ` **327 Organic sleep disorders**

`✓5ᵗʰ` **327.0 Organic disorders of initiating and maintaining sleep [Organic insomnia]**

> EXCLUDES insomnia NOS (780.52)
> insomnia not due to a substance or
> known physiological condition
> (307.41-307.42)
> insomnia with sleep apnea NOS
> (780.51)

327.00 Organic insomnia, unspecified

327.01 Insomnia due to medical condition classified elsewhere

Code first underlying condition

> EXCLUDES insomnia due to mental
> disorder (327.02)

327.02 Insomnia due to mental disorder

Code first mental disorder

> EXCLUDES alcohol induced insomnia
> (291.82)
> drug induced insomnia (292.85)

327.09 Other organic insomnia

`✓5ᵗʰ` **327.1 Organic disorder of excessive somnolence [Organic hypersomnia]**

> EXCLUDES hypersomnia NOS (780.54)
> hypersomnia not due to a substance or
> known physiological condition
> (307.43-307.44)
> hypersomnia with sleep apnea NOS
> (780.53)

327.10 Organic hypersomnia, unspecified

327.11 Idiopathic hypersomnia with long sleep time

327.12 Idiopathic hypersomnia without long sleep time

327.13 Recurrent hypersomnia

Kleine-Levin syndrome
Menstrual related hypersomnia

327.14 Hypersomnia due to medical condition classified elsewhere

Code first underlying condition

> EXCLUDES hypersomnia due to mental
> disorder (327.15)

327.15 Hypersomnia due to mental disorder

Code first mental disorder

> EXCLUDES alcohol induced hypersomnia
> (291.82)
> drug induced hypersomnia
> (292.85)

N Newborn Age: 0   P Pediatric Age: 0-17   M Maternity Age: 12-55   A Adult Age: 15-124   Manifestation Code   ▶◀ Revised Text   ● New Code   ▲ Revised Code Title

78 — Volume 1 • October 2005

2006 ICD•9•CM

● 　　　　327.19 **Other organic hypersomnia**

● ✓5ᵗʰ 327.2 **Organic sleep apnea**

EXCLUDES　*Cheyne-Stokes breathing (786.04)*
*hypersomnia with sleep apnea NOS
(780.53)*
*insomnia with sleep apnea NOS
(780.51)*
*sleep apnea in newborn (770.81-
770.82)*
sleep apnea NOS (780.57)

● 　　　　327.20 **Organic sleep apnea, unspecified**

● 　　　　327.21 **Primary central sleep apnea**

● 　　　　327.22 **High altitude periodic breathing**

● 　　　　327.23 **Obstructive sleep apnea (adult) (pediatric)**

● 　　　　327.24 **Idiopathic sleep related nonobstructive
alveolar hypoventilation**
Sleep related hypoxia

● 　　　　327.25 **Congenital central alveolar hypoventilation
syndrome**

● 　　　　327.26 **Sleep related hypoventilation/hypoxemia in
conditions classifiable elsewhere**
Code first underlying condition

● 　　　　327.27 **Central sleep apnea in conditions classified
elsewhere**
Code first underlying condition

● 　　　　327.29 **Other organic sleep apnea**

● ✓5ᵗʰ 327.3 **Circadian rhythm sleep disorder**
Organic disorder of sleep wake cycle
Organic disorder of sleep wake schedule

EXCLUDES　*alcohol induced circadian rhythm sleep
disorder (291.82)*
*circadian rhythm sleep disorder of
nonorganic origin (307.45)*
*disruption of 24 hour sleep wake cycle
NOS (780.55)*
*drug induced circadian rhythm sleep
disorder (292.85)*

● 　　　　327.30 **Circadian rhythm sleep disorder,
unspecified**

● 　　　　327.31 **Circadian rhythm sleep disorder, delayed
sleep phase type**

● 　　　　327.32 **Circadian rhythm sleep disorder, advanced
sleep phase type**

● 　　　　327.33 **Circadian rhythm sleep disorder, irregular
sleep-wake type**

● 　　　　327.34 **Circadian rhythm sleep disorder, free-
running type**

● 　　　　327.35 **Circadian rhythm sleep disorder, jet lag
type**

● 　　　　327.36 **Circadian rhythm sleep disorder, shift work
type**

● 　　　　327.37 **Circadian rhythm sleep disorder in
conditions classified elsewhere**
Code first underlying condition

● 　　　　327.39 **Other circadian rhythm sleep disorder**

● ✓5ᵗʰ 327.4 **Organic parasomnia**

EXCLUDES　*alcohol induced parasomnia (291.82)*
drug induced parasomnia (292.85)
*parasomnia not due to a known
physiological condition (307.47)*

● 　　　　327.40 **Organic parasomnia, unspecified**

● 　　　　327.41 **Confusional arousals**

● 　　　　327.42 **REM sleep behavior disorder**

● 　　　　327.43 **Recurrent isolated sleep paralysis**

● 　　　　327.44 **Parasomnia in conditions classified
elsewhere**
Code first underlying condition

● 　　　　327.49 **Other organic parasomnia**

● ✓5ᵗʰ 327.5 **Organic sleep related movement disorders**

EXCLUDES　*restless leg syndrome (333.99)*
*sleep related movement disorder NOS
(780.58)*

● 　　　　327.51 **Periodic limb movement disorder**
Periodic limb movement sleep disorder

● 　　　　327.52 **Sleep related leg cramps**

● 　　　　327.53 **Sleep related bruxism**

● 　　　　327.59 **Other organic sleep related movement
disorders**

● 　　　327.8 **Other organic sleep disorders**

HEREDITARY AND DEGENERATIVE DISEASES OF THE CENTRAL NERVOUS SYSTEM (330-337)

EXCLUDES　*hepatolenticular degeneration (275.1)*
multiple sclerosis (340)
*other demyelinating diseases of central nervous
system (341.0-341.9)*

✓4ᵗʰ 330 **Cerebral degenerations usually manifest in childhood**
Use additional code to identify associated mental retardation

330.0 **Leukodystrophy**　　　　`CD PDx`
Krabbe's disease
Leukodystrophy
NOS
globoid cell
metachromatic
sudanophilic
Pelizaeus-Merzbacher
disease
Sulfatide lipidosis

DEF: Hereditary disease of arylsulfatase or cerebroside sulfatase;
characterized by a diffuse loss of myelin in CNS; infantile form
causes blindness, motor disturbances, rigidity, mental deterioration
and, occasionally, convulsions.

330.1 **Cerebral lipidoses**　　　　`CD PDx`
Amaurotic (familial) idiocy
Disease:
Batten
Jansky-Bielschowsky
Kufs'
Disease:
Spielmeyer-Vogt
Tay-Sachs
Gangliosidosis

DEF: Genetic disorder causing abnormal lipid accumulation in the
reticuloendothelial cells of the brain.

330.2 *Cerebral degeneration in generalized
lipidoses*　　　　`CD SDx`
Code first underlying disease, as:
Fabry's disease (272.7)
Gaucher's disease (272.7)
Niemann-Pick disease (272.7)
sphingolipidosis (272.7)

330.3 *Cerebral degeneration of childhood in
other diseases classified elsewhere*　　　　`CD SDx`
Code first underlying disease, as:
Hunter's disease (277.5)
mucopolysaccharidosis (277.5)

330.8 **Other specified cerebral degenerations
in childhood**　　　　`CD PDx`
Alpers' disease or gray-matter degeneration
Infantile necrotizing encephalomyelopathy
Leigh's disease
Subacute necrotizing encephalopathy or
encephalomyelopathy

AHA: N-D, '85, 5

330.9 **Unspecified cerebral degeneration in
childhood**　　　　`CD PDx`

✓4ᵗʰ 331 **Other cerebral degenerations**

331.0 **Alzheimer's disease**　　　　`CD PDx`

AHA: 4Q, '00, 41; 4Q, '99, 7; N-D, '84, 20

DEF: Diffuse atrophy of cerebral cortex; causing a progressive
decline in intellectual and physical functions, including memory
loss, personality changes and profound dementia.

✓5ᵗʰ 331.1 **Frontotemporal dementia**
Use additional code for associated behavioral
disturbance (294.10-294.11)

AHA: 4Q, '03, 57

DEF: Rare, progressive degenerative brain disease, similar to
Alzheimer's; cortical atrophy affects the frontal and temporal lobes.

✓4ᵗʰ ✓5ᵗʰ　Additional Digit Required　　RUG III Special Care Dx　　RUG III Clinically Complex Dx　　Hospice Non-cancer Dx　　`CD PDx` Clinical Dimension PDx　`CD SDx` Clinical Dimension SDx

2006 ICD•9•CM　　　　　　　　　　　　　　　　　　　　　　　　　　　　　　**October 2005 • Volume 1 — 79**

331.11 Pick's disease `CD PDx`

DEF: A less common form of progressive frontotemporal dementia with asymmetrical atrophy of the frontal and temporal regions of the cerebral cortex including abnormal rounded brain cells called Pick cells together with the presence of abnormal staining of protein (called tau) within the cells, called Pick bodies; symptoms include prominent apathy, deterioration of social skills, behavioral changes such as disinhibition and restlessness, echolalia, impairment of language, memory, and intellect, increased carelessness, poor personal hygiene, and decreased attention span.

331.19 Other frontotemporal dementia `CD PDx`
Frontal dementia

331.2 Senile degeneration of brain `CD PDx`
    EXCLUDES   senility NOS (797)

331.3 Communicating hydrocephalus `CD PDx`
    EXCLUDES   congenital hydrocephalus (741.0, 742.3)

AHA: S-O, '85, 12

DEF: Subarachnoid hemorrhage and meningitis causing excess buildup of cerebrospinal fluid in cavities due to nonabsorption of fluid back through fluid pathways.

331.4 Obstructive hydrocephalus `CD PDx`
Acquired hydrocephalus NOS
    EXCLUDES   congenital hydrocephalus (741.0, 742.3)

AHA: 4Q, '03, 106; 1Q, '99, 9

DEF: Obstruction of cerebrospinal fluid passage from brain into spinal canal.

331.7 *Cerebral degeneration in diseases classified elsewhere* `CD SDx`
Code first underlying disease, as:
    alcoholism (303.0-303.9)
    beriberi (265.0)
    cerebrovascular disease (430-438)
    congenital hydrocephalus (741.0, 742.3)
    myxedema (244.0-244.9)
    neoplastic disease (140.0-239.9)
    vitamin B_{12} deficiency (266.2)
    EXCLUDES   cerebral degeneration in:
        Jakob-Creutzfeldt disease (046.1)
        progressive multifocal
            leukoencephalopathy (046.3)
        subacute spongiform
            encephalopathy (046.1)

☑5th **331.8 Other cerebral degeneration**

331.81 Reye's syndrome `CD PDx` `P`
DEF: Rare childhood illness, often developed after a bout of viral upper respiratory infection; characterized by vomiting, elevated serum transaminase, changes in liver and other viscera; symptoms may be followed by an encephalopathic phase with brain swelling, disturbances of consciousness and seizures; can be fatal.

331.82 Dementia with Lewy bodies `CD PDx`
Dementia with Parkinsonism
Lewy body dementia
Lewy body disease
Use additional code for associated behavioral disturbances (294.10-294.11)

AHA: 4Q, '03, 57

DEF: A cerebral dementia with neurophysiologic changes including increased hippocampal volume, hypoperfusion in the occipital lobes, and beta amyloid deposits with neurofibrillarity tangles, atrophy of cortex and brainstem, hallmark neuropsychologic characteristics are fluctuating cognition with pronounced variation in attention and alertness; recurrent hallucinations; and parkinsonism.

331.89 Other `CD PDx`
Cerebral ataxia

331.9 Cerebral degeneration, unspecified `CD PDx`

☑4th **332 Parkinson's disease**
    EXCLUDES   dementia with Parkinsonism (331.82)

332.0 Paralysis agitans `CD PDx`
Parkinsonism or Parkinson's disease:
    NOS   primary
    idiopathic
AHA: M-A, '87, 7

DEF: Form of parkinsonism; progressive, occurs in senior years; characterized by masklike facial expression; condition affects ability to stand erect, walk smoothly; weakened muscles, also tremble and involuntarily movement.

332.1 Secondary Parkinsonism `CD PDx`
▶Neuroleptic-induced Parkinsonism◀
Parkinsonism due to drugs
Use additional E code to identify drug, if drug-induced
    EXCLUDES   Parkinsonism (in):
        Huntington's disease (333.4)
        progressive supranuclear palsy
            (333.0)
        Shy-Drager syndrome (333.0)
        syphilitic (094.82)

☑4th **333 Other extrapyramidal disease and abnormal movement disorders**
    INCLUDES   other forms of extrapyramidal, basal ganglia, or striatopallidal disease
    EXCLUDES   abnormal movements of head NOS (781.0)
        ▶sleep related movement disorders (327.51-327.59)◀

333.0 Other degenerative diseases of the basal ganglia `CD PDx`
Atrophy or degeneration:
    olivopontocerebellar [Déjérine-Thomas syndrome]
    pigmentary pallidal [Hallervorden-Spatz disease]
    striatonigral
Parkinsonian syndrome associated with:
    idiopathic orthostatic hypotension
    symptomatic orthostatic hypotension
Progressive supranuclear ophthalmoplegia
Shy-Drager syndrome
AHA: 3Q, '96, 8

333.1 Essential and other specified forms of tremor `CD PDx`
Benign essential tremor
Familial tremor
▶Medication-induced postural tremor◀
Use additional E code to identify drug, if drug-induced
    EXCLUDES   tremor NOS (781.0)

333.2 Myoclonus `CD PDx`
Familial essential myoclonus
Progressive myoclonic epilepsy
Unverricht-Lundborg disease
Use additional E code to identify drug, if drug-induced
AHA: 3Q, '97, 4; M-A, '87, 12

DEF: Spontaneous movements or contractions of muscles.

333.3 Tics of organic origin `CD PDx`
Use additional E code to identify drug, if drug-induced
    EXCLUDES   Gilles de la Tourette's syndrome
        (307.23)
        habit spasm (307.22)
        tic NOS (307.20)

333.4 Huntington's chorea `CD PDx`
DEF: Genetic disease characterized by chronic progressive mental deterioration; dementia and death within 15 years of onset.

333.5 Other choreas `CD PDx`
Hemiballism(us)
Paroxysmal choreo-athetosis
Use additional E code to identify drug, if drug-induced
    EXCLUDES   Sydenham's or rheumatic chorea
        (392.0-392.9)

N Newborn Age: 0   P Pediatric Age: 0-17   M Maternity Age: 12-55   A Adult Age: 15-124   Manifestation Code   ▶◀ Revised Text   ● New Code   ▲ Revised Code Title

333.6 Idiopathic torsion dystonia `CD PDx`
Dystonia:
deformans progressiva
musculorum deformans
(Schwalbe-) Ziehen-Oppenheim disease
DEF: Sustained muscular contractions, causing twisting and
repetitive movements that result in abnormal postures of trunk and
limbs; etiology unknown.

333.7 Symptomatic torsion dystonia `CD PDx`
Athetoid cerebral palsy [Vogt's disease]
Double athetosis (syndrome)
▶Neuroleptic-induced acute dystonia◀
Use additional E code to identify drug, if drug-induced

√5th **333.8 Fragments of torsion dystonia**
Use additional E code to identify drug, if drug-induced

333.81 Blepharospasm `CD PDx`
DEF: Uncontrolled winking or blinking due to orbicularis
oculi muscle spasm.

333.82 Orofacial dyskinesia `CD PDx`
▶Neuroleptic-induced tardive dyskinesia◀
DEF: Uncontrolled movement of mouth or facial muscles.

333.83 Spasmodic torticollis `CD PDx`
`EXCLUDES`   torticollis:
NOS (723.5)
hysterical (300.11)
psychogenic (306.0)
DEF: Uncontrolled movement of head due to spasms of
neck muscle.

333.84 Organic writers' cramp `CD PDx`
`EXCLUDES`   psychogenic (300.89)

333.89 Other `CD PDx`

√5th **333.9 Other and unspecified extrapyramidal
diseases and abnormal movement disorders**

333.90 Unspecified extrapyramidal disease `CD PDx`
and abnormal movement disorder
▶Medication-induced movement disorders
NOS
Use additional E code to identify drug, if
drug-induced◀

333.91 Stiff-man syndrome `CD PDx`

333.92 Neuroleptic malignant syndrome `CD PDx`
Use additional E code to identify drug
AHA: 4Q, '94, 37

333.93 Benign shuddering attacks `CD PDx`
AHA: 4Q, '94, 37

333.99 Other `CD PDx`
▶Neuroleptic-induced acute akathisia◀
Restless legs
▶Use additional E code to identify drug, if
drug-induced◀
AHA: 4Q, '04, 95; 2Q, '04, 12; 4Q, '94, 37

√4th **334 Spinocerebellar disease**
`EXCLUDES`   olivopontocerebellar degeneration (333.0)
peroneal muscular atrophy (356.1)

334.0 Friedreich's ataxia `CD PDx`
DEF: Genetic recessive disease of children; sclerosis of dorsal,
lateral spinal cord columns; characterized by ataxia, speech
impairment, swaying and irregular movements, with muscle
paralysis, especially of lower limbs.

334.1 Hereditary spastic paraplegia `CD PDx`

334.2 Primary cerebellar degeneration `CD PDx`
Cerebellar ataxia:
Marie's
Sanger-Brown
Dyssynergia cerebellaris myoclonica
Primary cerebellar degeneration:
NOS
hereditary
sporadic

334.3 Other cerebellar ataxia `CD PDx`
Cerebellar ataxia NOS
Use additional E code to identify drug, if drug-induced

334.4 Cerebellar ataxia in diseases classified `CD SDx`
elsewhere
Code first underlying disease, as:
alcoholism (303.0-303.9)
myxedema (244.0-244.9)
neoplastic disease (140.0-239.9)

334.8 Other spinocerebellar diseases `CD PDx`
Ataxia-telangiectasia [Louis-Bar syndrome]
Corticostriatal-spinal degeneration

334.9 Spinocerebellar disease, unspecified `CD PDx`

√4th **335 Anterior horn cell disease**

335.0 Werdnig-Hoffmann disease `CD PDx`
Infantile spinal muscular atrophy
Progressive muscular atrophy of infancy
DEF: Spinal muscle atrophy manifested in prenatal period or shortly
after birth; symptoms include hypotonia, atrophy of skeletal muscle;
death occurs in infancy.

√5th **335.1 Spinal muscular atrophy**

**335.10 Spinal muscular atrophy,
unspecified** `CD PDx`

335.11 Kugelberg-Welander disease `CD PDx`
Spinal muscular atrophy:
familial
juvenile
DEF: Hereditary; juvenile muscle atrophy; appears during
first two decades of life; due to lesions of anterior horns
of spinal cord; includes wasting, diminution of lower
body muscles and twitching.

335.19 Other `CD PDx`
Adult spinal muscular atrophy

√5th **335.2 Motor neuron disease**

335.20 Amyotrophic lateral sclerosis `CD PDx` `A`
Motor neuron disease (bulbar) (mixed type)
AHA: 4Q, '95, 81

335.21 Progressive muscular atrophy `CD PDx`
Duchenne-Aran muscular atrophy
Progressive muscular atrophy (pure)

335.22 Progressive bulbar palsy `CD PDx`

335.23 Pseudobulbar palsy `CD PDx`

335.24 Primary lateral sclerosis `CD PDx`

335.29 Other `CD PDx`

335.8 Other anterior horn cell diseases `CD PDx`

335.9 Anterior horn cell disease, unspecified `CD PDx`

√4th **336 Other diseases of spinal cord**

336.0 Syringomyelia and syringobulbia `CD PDx`
AHA: 1Q, '89, 10

336.1 Vascular myelopathies `CD PDx`
Acute infarction of spinal cord (embolic)
(nonembolic)
Arterial thrombosis of spinal cord
Edema of spinal cord
Hematomyelia
Subacute necrotic myelopathy

336.2 Subacute combined degeneration of spinal `CD SDx`
cord in diseases classified elsewhere
Code first underlying disease, as:
pernicious anemia (281.0)
other vitamin B_{12} deficiency anemia (281.1)
vitamin B_{12} deficiency (266.2)

336.3 Myelopathy in other diseases classified `CD SDx`
elsewhere
Code first underlying disease, as:
myelopathy in neoplastic disease (140.0-239.9)
`EXCLUDES`   myelopathy in:
intervertebral disc disorder (722.70-
722.73)
spondylosis (721.1, 721.41-721.42,
721.91)
AHA: 3Q, '99, 5

336.8 Other myelopathy `CD PDx`
Myelopathy: Myelopathy:
drug-induced   radiation-induced
Use additonal E code to identify cause

√4th √5th Additional Digit Required   RUG III Special Care Dx   RUG III Clinically Complex Dx   Hospice Non-cancer Dx   `CD PDx` Clinical Dimension PDx   `CD SDx` Clinical Dimension SDx

336.9   **Unspecified disease of spinal cord**   `CD PDx`
Cord compression NOS   Myelopathy NOS
EXCLUDES   myelitis (323.0-323.9)
spinal (canal) stenosis (723.0, 724.00-724.09)

✓4th **337 Disorders of the autonomic nervous system**
INCLUDES   disorders of peripheral autonomic, sympathetic, parasympathetic, or vegetative system
EXCLUDES   familial dysautonomia [Riley-Day syndrome] (742.8)

337.0   **Idiopathic peripheral autonomic neuropathy**   `CD PDx`
Carotid sinus syncope or syndrome
Cervical sympathetic dystrophy or paralysis

337.1   *Peripheral autonomic neuropathy in disorders classified elsewhere*   `CD SDx`
Code first underlying disease, as:
amyloidosis (277.3)
diabetes (250.6)
AHA: 2Q, '93, 6; N-D, '84, 9

✓5th **337.2**   **Reflex sympathetic dystrophy**
AHA: 4Q, '93, 24
DEF: Disturbance of the sympathetic nervous system evidenced by sweating, pain, pallor and edema following injury to nerves or blood vessels.

337.20   **Reflex sympathetic dystrophy, unspecified**   `CD PDx`

337.21   **Reflex sympathetic dystrophy of the upper limb**   `CD PDx`

337.22   **Reflex sympathetic dystrophy of the lower limb**   `CD PDx`

337.29   **Reflex sympathetic dystrophy of other specified site**   `CD PDx`

337.3   **Autonomic dysreflexia**   `CD PDx`
Use additional code to identify the cause, such as:
decubitus ulcer (707.00-707.09)
fecal impaction (560.39)
urinary tract infection (599.0)
AHA: 4Q, '98, 37
DEF: Noxious stimuli evokes paroxysmal hypertension, bradycardia, excess sweating, headache, pilomotor responses, facial flushing, and nasal congestion due to uncontrolled parasympathetic nerve response; usually occurs in patients with spinal cord injury above major sympathetic outflow tract (T$_6$).

337.9   **Unspecified disorder of autonomic nervous system**   `CD PDx`

OTHER DISORDERS OF THE CENTRAL NERVOUS SYSTEM (340-349)

340 Multiple sclerosis   `CD PDx`
Disseminated or multiple sclerosis:
NOS
brain stem
cord
generalized

✓4th **341 Other demyelinating diseases of central nervous system**

341.0   **Neuromyelitis optica**   `CD PDx`

341.1   **Schilder's disease**   `CD PDx`
Baló's concentric sclerosis   Encephalitis periaxialis:
Encephalitis periaxialis: diffusa [Schilder's]
concentrica [Baló's]
DEF: Chronic leukoencephalopathy of children and adolescents; symptoms include blindness, deafness, bilateral spasticity and progressive mental deterioration.

341.8   **Other demyelinating diseases of central nervous system**   `CD PDx`
Central demyelination of corpus callosum
Central pontine myelinosis
Marchiafava (-Bignami) disease
AHA: N-D, '87, 6

341.9   **Demyelinating disease of central nervous system, unspecified**   `CD PDx`

✓4th **342 Hemiplegia and hemiparesis**
Note: This category is to be used when hemiplegia (complete) (incomplete) is reported without further specification, or is stated to be old or long-standing but of unspecified cause. The category is also for use in multiple coding to identify these types of hemiplegia resulting from any cause.
EXCLUDES   congenital (343.1)
hemiplegia due to late effect of cerebrovascular accident (438.20-438.22)
infantile NOS (343.4)

The following fifth-digits are for use with codes 342.0-342.9:
  0   **affecting unspecified side**
  1   **affecting dominant side**
  2   **affecting nondominant side**
AHA: 4Q, '94, 38

✓5th **342.0**   **Flaccid hemiplegia**   `CD PDx`
✓5th **342.1**   **Spastic hemiplegia**   `CD PDx`
✓5th **342.8**   **Other specified hemiplegia**   `CD PDx`
✓5th **342.9**   **Hemiplegia, unspecified**   `CD PDx`
AHA: 4Q, '98, 87

✓4th **343 Infantile cerebral palsy**
INCLUDES   cerebral:
palsy NOS
spastic infantile paralysis
congenital spastic paralysis (cerebral)
Little's disease
paralysis (spastic) due to birth injury:
intracranial
spinal
EXCLUDES   hereditary cerebral paralysis, such as:
hereditary spastic paraplegia (334.1)
Vogt's disease (333.7)
spastic paralysis specified as noncongenital or noninfantile (344.0-344.9)

343.0   **Diplegic**   `CD PDx`
Congenital diplegia   Congenital paraplegia
DEF: Paralysis affecting both sides of the body simultaneously.

343.1   **Hemiplegic**   `CD PDx`
Congenital hemiplegia
EXCLUDES   infantile hemiplegia NOS (343.4)

343.2   **Quadriplegic**   `CD PDx`
Tetraplegic

343.3   **Monoplegic**   `CD PDx`

343.4   **Infantile hemiplegia**   `CD PDx`
Infantile hemiplegia (postnatal) NOS

343.8   **Other specified infantile cerebral palsy**   `CD PDx`

343.9   **Infantile cerebral palsy, unspecified**   `CD PDx`
Cerebral palsy NOS

✓4th **344 Other paralytic syndromes**
Note: This category is to be used when the listed conditions are reported without further specification or are stated to be old or long-standing but of unspecified cause. The category is also for use in multiple coding to identify these conditions resulting from any cause.
INCLUDES   paralysis (complete) (incomplete), except as classifiable to 342 and 343
EXCLUDES   congenital or infantile cerebral palsy (343.0-343.9)
hemiplegia (342.0-342.9)
congenital or infantile (343.1, 343.4)

✓5th **344.0**   **Quadriplegia and quadriparesis**

344.00   **Quadriplegia unspecified**   `CD PDx`
AHA: 4Q, '03, 103; 4Q, '98, 38

344.01   **C$_1$-C$_4$ complete**   `CD PDx`
344.02   **C$_1$-C$_4$ incomplete**   `CD PDx`
344.03   **C$_5$-C$_7$ complete**   `CD PDx`
344.04   **C$_5$-C$_7$ incomplete**   `CD PDx`
344.09   **Other**   `CD PDx`
AHA: 1Q, '01, 12; 4Q, '98, 39

344.1   **Paraplegia**   `CD PDx`
Paralysis of both lower limbs   Paraplegia (lower)
AHA: 4Q, '03, 110; M-A, '87, 10

N Newborn Age: 0   **P** Pediatric Age: 0-17   **M** Maternity Age: 12-55   **A** Adult Age: 15-124   `Manifestation Code`   ◄► Revised Text   ● New Code   ▲ Revised Code Title

82 — Volume 1   *2006 ICD•9•CM*

344.2 Diplegia of upper limbs `CD PDx`
    Diplegia (upper)   Paralysis of both upper limbs

√5th **344.3 Monoplegia of lower limb**
    Paralysis of lower limb
        EXCLUDES   *monoplegia of lower limb due to late effect of cerebrovascular accident (438.40-438.42)*

    344.30 Affecting unspecified side `CD PDx`
    344.31 Affecting dominant side `CD PDx`
    344.32 Affecting nondominant side `CD PDx`

√5th **344.4 Monoplegia of upper limb**
    Paralysis of upper limb
        EXCLUDES   *monoplegia of upper limb due to late effect of cerebrovascular accident (438.30-438.32)*

    344.40 Affecting unspecified side `CD PDx`
    344.41 Affecting dominant side `CD PDx`
    344.42 Affecting nondominant side `CD PDx`

344.5 Unspecified monoplegia `CD PDx`

√5th **344.6 Cauda equina syndrome**
    DEF: Dull pain and paresthesias in sacrum, perineum and bladder due to compression of spinal nerve roots; pain radiates down buttocks, back of thigh, calf of leg and into foot with prickling, burning sensations.

    344.60 Without mention of neurogenic `CD PDx`
            bladder
    344.61 With neurogenic bladder `CD PDx`
        Acontractile bladder
        Autonomic hyperreflexia of bladder
        Cord bladder
        Detrusor hyperreflexia
        AHA: M-J, '87, 12; M-A, '87, 10

√5th **344.8 Other specified paralytic syndromes**
    344.81 Locked-in state `CD PDx`
        AHA: 4Q, '93, 24
        DEF: State of consciousness where patients are paralyzed and unable to respond to environmental stimuli; patients have eye movements, and stimuli can enter the brain but patients cannot respond to stimuli.

    344.89 Other specified paralytic syndrome `CD PDx`
        AHA: 2Q, '99, 4

344.9 Paralysis, unspecified `CD PDx`

√4th **345 Epilepsy**

The following fifth-digit subclassification is for use with categories 345.0, .1, .4-.9:
    0 without mention of intractable epilepsy
    1 with intractable epilepsy

    EXCLUDES   *progressive myoclonic epilepsy (333.2)*
AHA: 1Q, '93, 24; 2Q, '92, 8; 4Q, '92, 23

DEF: Brain disorder characterized by electrical-like disturbances; may include occasional impairment or loss of consciousness, abnormal motor phenomena and psychic or sensory disturbances.

√5th **345.0 Generalized nonconvulsive epilepsy**
    Absences: Pykno-epilepsy
      atonic   Seizures:
      typical   akinetic
    Minor epilepsy   atonic
    Petit mal
    AHA: For code 345.00: 1Q, '04, 18

√5th **345.1 Generalized convulsive epilepsy**
    Epileptic seizures: Epileptic seizures:
      clonic   tonic-clonic
      myoclonic   Grand mal
      tonic   Major epilepsy
        EXCLUDES   *convulsions:*
              NOS (780.3)
              infantile (780.3)
              newborn (779.0)
           infantile spasms (345.6)
    AHA: 3Q, '97, 4

    DEF: Convulsive seizures with tension of limbs (tonic) or rhythmic contractions (clonic).

345.2 Petit mal status
    Epileptic absence status
    DEF: Minor myoclonic spasms and sudden momentary loss of consciousness in epilepsy.

345.3 Grand mal status
    Status epilepticus NOS
        EXCLUDES   *epilepsia partialis continua (345.7)*
           status:
             psychomotor (345.7)
             temporal lobe (345.7)
    DEF: Sudden loss of consciousness followed by generalized convulsions in epilepsy.

√5th **345.4 Partial epilepsy, with impairment of consciousness**
    Epilepsy:
      limbic system
      partial:
        secondarily generalized
        with memory and ideational disturbances
      psychomotor
      psychosensory
      temporal lobe
    Epileptic automatism

√5th **345.5 Partial epilepsy, without mention of impairment of consciousness**
    Epilepsy: Epilepsy:
      Bravais-Jacksonian NOS   sensory-induced
      focal (motor) NOS   somatomotor
      Jacksonian NOS   somatosensory
      motor partial   visceral
      partial NOS   visual

√5th **345.6 Infantile spasms**
    Hypsarrhythmia   Salaam attacks
    Lightning spasms
        EXCLUDES   *salaam tic (781.0)*
    AHA: N-D, '84, 12

√5th **345.7 Epilepsia partialis continua**
    Kojevnikov's epilepsy
    DEF: Continuous muscle contractions and relaxation; result of abnormal neural discharge.

√5th **345.8 Other forms of epilepsy**
    Epilepsy: Epilepsy:
      cursive [running]   gelastic

√5th **345.9 Epilepsy, unspecified**
    Epileptic convulsions, fits, or seizures NOS
        EXCLUDES   *convulsive seizure or fit NOS (780.3)*
    AHA: N-D, '87, 12

√4th **346 Migraine**
    DEF: Benign vascular headache of extreme pain; commonly associated with irritability, nausea, vomiting and often photophobia; premonitory visual hallucination of a crescent in the visual field (scotoma).

The following fifth-digit subclassification is for use with category 346:
    0 without mention of intractable migraine
    1 with intractable migraine, so stated

√5th **346.0 Classical migraine**
    Migraine preceded or accompanied by transient focal neurological phenomena
    Migraine with aura

√5th **346.1 Common migraine**
    Atypical migraine   Sick headache

√5th **346.2 Variants of migraine**
    Cluster headache   Migraine:
    Histamine cephalgia   lower half
    Horton's neuralgia   retinal
    Migraine: Neuralgia:
      abdominal   ciliary
      basilar   migrainous

√5th **346.8 Other forms of migraine**
    Migraine: Migraine:
      hemiplegic   ophthalmoplegic

√5th **346.9 Migraine, unspecified**
    AHA: N-D, '85, 16

√4th √5th **Additional Digit Required**   RUG III Special Care Dx   RUG III Clinically Complex Dx   Hospice Non-cancer Dx   `CD PDx` Clinical Dimension PDx   `CD SDx` Clinical Dimension SDx

√4ᵗʰ **347 Cataplexy and narcolepsy**

DEF: Cataplexy: Sudden onset of muscle weakness with loss of tone and strength; caused by aggressive or spontaneous emotions.

DEF: Narcolepsy: Brief, recurrent, uncontrollable episodes of sound sleep.

√5ᵗʰ **347.0 Narcolepsy**

347.00 Without cataplexy `CD PDx`
Narcolepsy NOS

347.01 With cataplexy `CD PDx`

√5ᵗʰ **347.1 Narcolepsy in conditions classified elsewhere**
Code first underlying condition

347.10 Without cataplexy `CD PDx`

347.11 With cataplexy `CD PDx`

√4ᵗʰ **348 Other conditions of brain**

348.0 Cerebral cysts `CD PDx`
Arachnoid cyst   Porencephaly, acquired
Porencephalic cyst   Pseudoporencephaly
EXCLUDES *porencephaly (congenital) (742.4)*

348.1 Anoxic brain damage `CD PDx`
EXCLUDES *that occurring in:*
abortion (634-638 with .7, 639.8)
ectopic or molar pregnancy (639.8)
labor or delivery (668.2, 669.4)
that of newborn (767.0, 768.0-768.9,
772.1-772.2)
Use additional E code to identify cause
DEF: Brain injury due to lack of oxygen, other than birth trauma.

348.2 Benign intracranial hypertension `CD PDx`
Pseudotumor cerebri
EXCLUDES *hypertensive encephalopathy (437.2)*
DEF: Elevated pressure in brain due to fluid retention in brain cavities.

√5ᵗʰ **348.3 Encephalopathy, not elsewhere classified**
AHA: 4Q, '03, 58; 3Q, '97, 4

348.30 Encephalopathy, unspecified `CD PDx`

348.31 Metabolic encephalopathy `CD PDx`
Septic encephalopathy

348.39 Other encephalopathy `CD PDx`
EXCLUDES *encephalopathy:*
alcoholic (291.2)
hepatic (572.2)
hypertensive (437.2)
toxic (349.82)

348.4 Compression of brain `CD PDx`
Compression } brain (stem)
Herniation
Posterior fossa compression syndrome
AHA: 4Q, '94, 37
DEF: Elevated pressure in brain due to blood clot, tumor, fracture, abscess, other condition.

348.5 Cerebral edema `CD PDx`
DEF: Elevated pressure in the brain due to fluid retention in brain tissues.

348.8 Other conditions of brain `CD PDx`
Cerebral: Cerebral:
calcification   fungus
AHA: S-O, '87, 9

348.9 Unspecified condition of brain `CD PDx`

√4ᵗʰ **349 Other and unspecified disorders of the nervous system**

349.0 Reaction to spinal or lumbar puncture `CD PDx`
Headache following lumbar puncture
AHA: 2Q, '99, 9; 3Q, '90, 18

349.1 Nervous system complications from surgically implanted device `CD PDx`
EXCLUDES *immediate postoperative complications (997.00-997.09)*
mechanical complications of nervous system device (996.2)

349.2 Disorders of meninges, not elsewhere classified `CD PDx`
Adhesions, meningeal (cerebral) (spinal)
Cyst, spinal meninges
Meningocele, acquired
Pseudomeningocele, acquired
AHA: 2Q, '98, 18; 3Q, '94, 4

√5ᵗʰ **349.8 Other specified disorders of nervous system**

349.81 Cerebrospinal fluid rhinorrhea `CD PDx`
EXCLUDES *cerebrospinal fluid otorrhea (388.61)*
DEF: Cerebrospinal fluid discharging from the nose; caused by fracture of frontal bone with tearing of dura mater and arachnoid.

349.82 Toxic encephalopathy `CD PDx`
Use additional E code to identify cause
AHA: 4Q, '93, 29
DEF: Brain tissue degeneration due to toxic substance.

349.89 Other `CD PDx`

349.9 Unspecified disorders of nervous system `CD PDx`
Disorder of nervous system (central) NOS

DISORDERS OF THE PERIPHERAL NERVOUS SYSTEM (350-359)

EXCLUDES *diseases of:*
acoustic [8th] nerve (388.5)
oculomotor [3rd, 4th, 6th] nerves (378.0-378.9)
optic [2nd] nerve (377.0-377.9)
peripheral autonomic nerves (337.0-337.9)
neuralgia
neuritis } *NOS or "rheumatic" (729.2)*
radiculitis
peripheral neuritis in pregnancy (646.4)

√4ᵗʰ **350 Trigeminal nerve disorders**
INCLUDES disorders of 5th cranial nerve

350.1 Trigeminal neuralgia
Tic douloureux   Trigeminal neuralgia NOS
Trifacial neuralgia
EXCLUDES *postherpetic (053.12)*

350.2 Atypical face pain

350.8 Other specified trigeminal nerve disorders

350.9 Trigeminal nerve disorder, unspecified

√4ᵗʰ **351 Facial nerve disorders**
INCLUDES disorders of 7th cranial nerve
EXCLUDES *that in newborn (767.5)*

351.0 Bell's palsy
Facial palsy
DEF: Unilateral paralysis of face due to lesion on facial nerve; produces facial distortion.

351.1 Geniculate ganglionitis
Geniculate ganglionitis NOS
EXCLUDES *herpetic (053.11)*
DEF: Inflammation of tissue at bend in facial nerve.

351.8 Other facial nerve disorders
Facial myokymia   Melkersson's syndrome
AHA: 3Q, '02, 13

351.9 Facial nerve disorder, unspecified

√4ᵗʰ **352 Disorders of other cranial nerves**

352.0 Disorders of olfactory [lst] nerve `CD PDx`

352.1 Glossopharyngeal neuralgia `CD PDx`
AHA: 2Q, '02, 8
DEF: Pain between throat and ear along petrosal and jugular ganglia.

352.2 Other disorders of glossopharyngeal [9th] nerve `CD PDx`

352.3 Disorders of pneumogastric [10th] nerve `CD PDx`
Disorders of vagal nerve
EXCLUDES *paralysis of vocal cords or larynx (478.30-478.34)*
DEF: Nerve disorder affecting ear, tongue, pharynx, larynx, esophagus, viscera and thorax.

N Newborn Age: 0   P Pediatric Age: 0-17   M Maternity Age: 12-55   A Adult Age: 15-124   Manifestation Code   ◄ Revised Text   ● New Code   ▲ Revised Code Title

Peripheral Nervous System

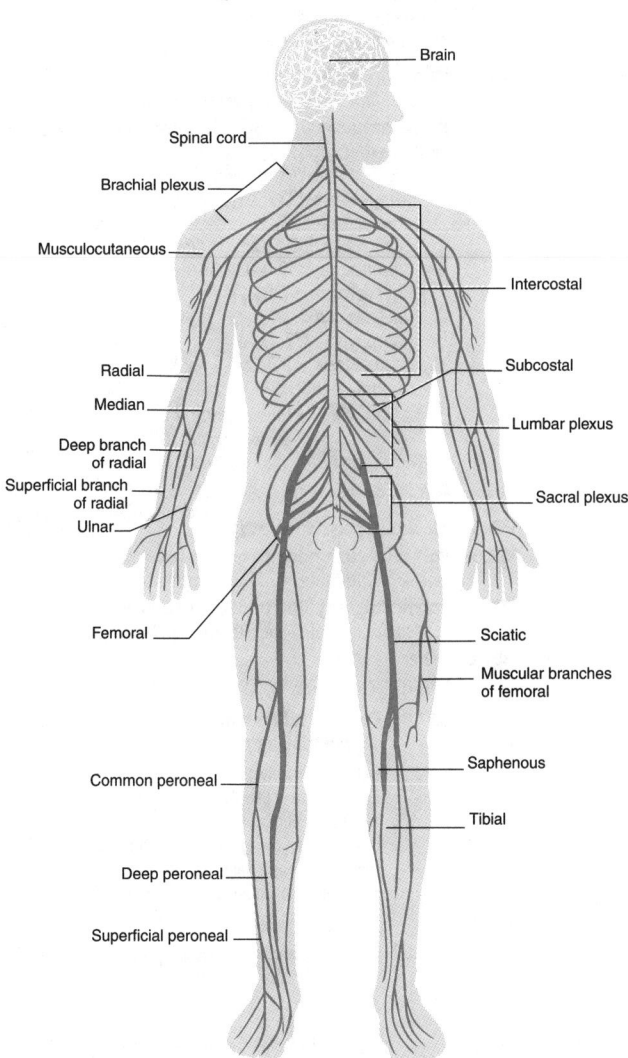

Trigeminal and Facial Nerve Branches

352.4 **Disorders of accessory [11th] nerve** `CD PDx`

DEF: Nerve disorder affecting palate, pharynx, larynx, thoracic viscera, sternocleidomastoid and trapezius muscles.

352.5 **Disorders of hypoglossal [12th] nerve** `CD PDx`

DEF: Nerve disorder affecting tongue muscles.

352.6 **Multiple cranial nerve palsies** `CD PDx`
Collet-Sicard syndrome
Polyneuritis cranialis

352.9 **Unspecified disorder of cranial nerves** `CD PDx`

√4ᵗʰ **353 Nerve root and plexus disorders**

EXCLUDES conditions due to:
intervertebral disc disorders (722.0-722.9)
spondylosis (720.0-721.9)
vertebrogenic disorders (723.0-724.9)

353.0 **Brachial plexus lesions**
Cervical rib syndrome
Costoclavicular syndrome
Scalenus anticus syndrome
Thoracic outlet syndrome
EXCLUDES brachial neuritis or radiculitis NOS
(723.4)
that in newborn (767.6)\

DEF: Acquired disorder in tissue along nerves in shoulder; causes corresponding motor and sensory dysfunction.

353.1 **Lumbosacral plexus lesions**
DEF: Acquired disorder in tissue along nerves in lower back; causes corresponding motor and sensory dysfunction.

353.2 **Cervical root lesions, not elsewhere classified**

353.3 **Thoracic root lesions, not elsewhere classified**

353.4 **Lumbosacral root lesions, not elsewhere classified**

353.5 **Neuralgic amyotrophy**
Parsonage-Aldren-Turner syndrome

353.6 **Phantom limb (syndrome)**
DEF: Abnormal tingling or a burning sensation, transient aches, and intermittent or continuous pain perceived as originating in the absent limb.

353.8 **Other nerve root and plexus disorders**

353.9 **Unspecified nerve root and plexus disorder**

√4ᵗʰ **354 Mononeuritis of upper limb and mononeuritis multiplex**
DEF: Inflammation of a single nerve; known as mononeuritis multiplex when several nerves in unrelated body areas are affected.

354.0 **Carpal tunnel syndrome**
Median nerve entrapment
Partial thenar atrophy
DEF: Compression of median nerve by tendons; causes pain, tingling, numbness and burning sensation in hand.

354.1 **Other lesion of median nerve**
Median nerve neuritis

354.2 **Lesion of ulnar nerve**
Cubital tunnel syndrome   Tardy ulnar nerve palsy

354.3 **Lesion of radial nerve**
Acute radial nerve palsy
AHA: N-D, '87, 6

354.4 **Causalgia of upper limb**
EXCLUDES causalgia:
NOS (355.9)
lower limb (355.71)

DEF: Peripheral nerve damage, upper limb; usually due to injury; causes burning sensation and trophic skin changes.

354.5 **Mononeuritis multiplex**
Combinations of single conditions classifiable to 354
or 355

354.8 **Other mononeuritis of upper limb**

354.9 **Mononeuritis of upper limb, unspecified**

√4ᵗʰ **355 Mononeuritis of lower limb**

355.0 **Lesion of sciatic nerve**
EXCLUDES sciatica NOS (724.3)
AHA: 2Q, '89, 12

DEF: Acquired disorder of sciatic nerve; causes motor and sensory dysfunction in back, buttock and leg.

355.1 **Meralgia paresthetica**
Lateral cutaneous femoral nerve of thigh
compression or syndrome
DEF: Inguinal ligament entraps lateral femoral cutaneous nerve; causes tingling, pain and numbness along outer thigh.

355.2 **Other lesion of femoral nerve**

355.3 **Lesion of lateral popliteal nerve**
Lesion of common peroneal nerve

355.4 **Lesion of medial popliteal nerve**

355.5 **Tarsal tunnel syndrome**
DEF: Compressed, entrapped posterior tibial nerve; causes tingling, pain and numbness in sole of foot.

√4ᵗʰ / √5ᵗʰ Additional Digit Required   **RUG III Special Care Dx**   **RUG III Clinically Complex Dx**   **Hospice Non-cancer Dx**   `CD PDx` Clinical Dimension PDx   `CD SDx` Clinical Dimension SDx

2006 ICD•9•CM   **Volume 1 — 85**

Nervous System and Sense Organs

355.6–358.1

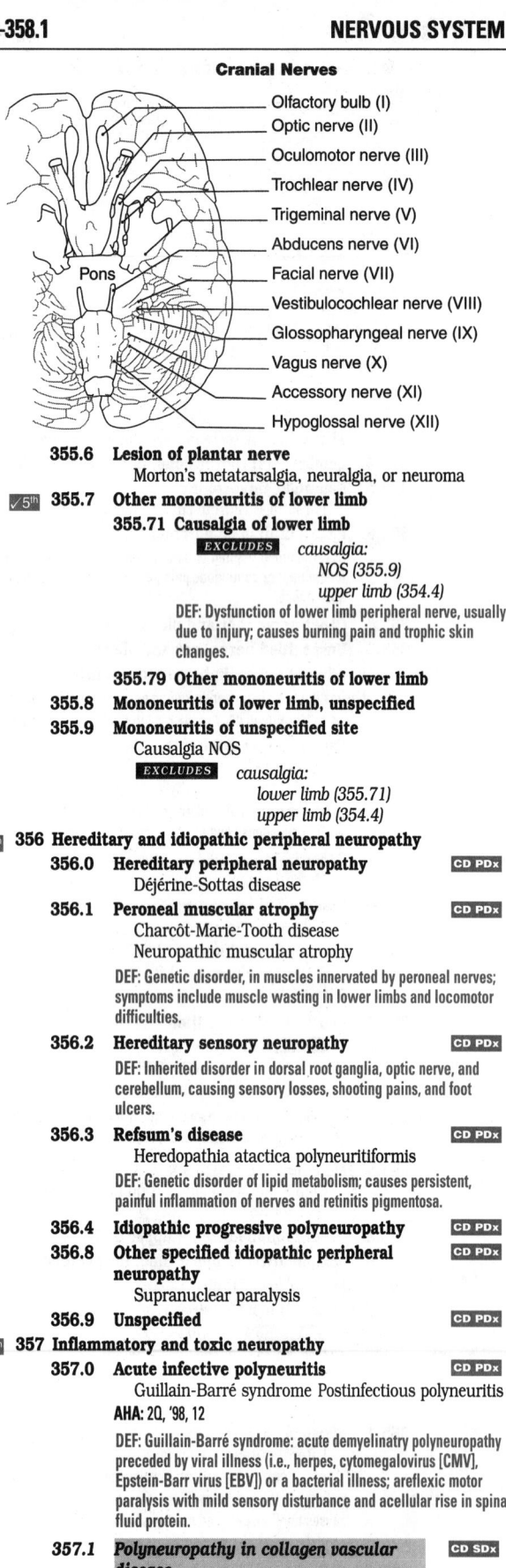

Cranial Nerves

Olfactory bulb (I)
Optic nerve (II)
Oculomotor nerve (III)
Trochlear nerve (IV)
Trigeminal nerve (V)
Abducens nerve (VI)
Facial nerve (VII)
Vestibulocochlear nerve (VIII)
Glossopharyngeal nerve (IX)
Vagus nerve (X)
Accessory nerve (XI)
Hypoglossal nerve (XII)

Pons

355.6 Lesion of plantar nerve
Morton's metatarsalgia, neuralgia, or neuroma

√5th **355.7 Other mononeuritis of lower limb**

355.71 Causalgia of lower limb

EXCLUDES   causalgia:
NOS (355.9)
upper limb (354.4)

DEF: Dysfunction of lower limb peripheral nerve, usually due to injury; causes burning pain and trophic skin changes.

355.79 Other mononeuritis of lower limb

355.8 Mononeuritis of lower limb, unspecified

355.9 Mononeuritis of unspecified site
Causalgia NOS

EXCLUDES   causalgia:
lower limb (355.71)
upper limb (354.4)

√4th **356 Hereditary and idiopathic peripheral neuropathy**

356.0 Hereditary peripheral neuropathy   CD PDx
Déjérine-Sottas disease

356.1 Peroneal muscular atrophy   CD PDx
Charcôt-Marie-Tooth disease
Neuropathic muscular atrophy

DEF: Genetic disorder, in muscles innervated by peroneal nerves; symptoms include muscle wasting in lower limbs and locomotor difficulties.

356.2 Hereditary sensory neuropathy   CD PDx

DEF: Inherited disorder in dorsal root ganglia, optic nerve, and cerebellum, causing sensory losses, shooting pains, and foot ulcers.

356.3 Refsum's disease   CD PDx
Heredopathia atactica polyneuritiformis

DEF: Genetic disorder of lipid metabolism; causes persistent, painful inflammation of nerves and retinitis pigmentosa.

356.4 Idiopathic progressive polyneuropathy   CD PDx

356.8 Other specified idiopathic peripheral neuropathy   CD PDx
Supranuclear paralysis

356.9 Unspecified   CD PDx

√4th **357 Inflammatory and toxic neuropathy**

357.0 Acute infective polyneuritis   CD PDx
Guillain-Barré syndrome Postinfectious polyneuritis
AHA: 2Q, '98, 12

DEF: Guillain-Barré syndrome: acute demyelinatry polyneuropathy preceded by viral illness (i.e., herpes, cytomegalovirus [CMV], Epstein-Barr virus [EBV]) or a bacterial illness; areflexic motor paralysis with mild sensory disturbance and acellular rise in spinal fluid protein.

357.1 Polyneuropathy in collagen vascular disease   CD SDx
Code first underlying disease, as:
disseminated lupus erythematosus (710.0)
polyarteritis nodosa (446.0)
rheumatoid arthritis (714.0)

357.2 Polyneuropathy in diabetes   CD SDx
Code first underlying disease (250.6)
AHA: 4Q, '03, 105; 2Q, '92, 15

357.3 Polyneuropathy in malignant disease   CD SDx
Code first underlying disease (140.0-208.9)

357.4 Polyneuropathy in other diseases classified elsewhere   CD SDx
Code first underlying disease, as:
amyloidosis (277.3)
beriberi (265.0)
deficiency of B vitamins (266.0-266.9)
diphtheria (032.0-032.9)
hypoglycemia (251.2)
pellagra (265.2)
porphyria (277.1)
sarcoidosis (135)
uremia ▶(585.9)◀

EXCLUDES   polyneuropathy in:
herpes zoster (053.13)
mumps (072.72)

AHA: 2Q, '98, 152

357.5 Alcoholic polyneuropathy   CD PDx

357.6 Polyneuropathy due to drugs   CD PDx
Use additional E code to identify drug

357.7 Polyneuropathy due to other toxic agents   CD PDx
Use additional E code to identify toxic agent

√5th **357.8 Other**
AHA: 4Q, '02, 47; 2Q, '98, 12

357.81 Chronic inflammatory demyelinating polyneuritis   CD PDx

DEF: Chronic inflammatory demyelinating polyneuritis: inflammation of peripheral nerves resulting in destruction of myelin sheath; associated with diabetes mellitus, dysproteinemias, renal failure and malnutrition; symptoms include tingling, numbness, burning pain, diminished tendon reflexes, weakness, and atrophy in lower extremities.

357.82 Critical illness polyneuropathy   CD PDx
Acute motor neuropathy
AHA: 4Q, '03, 111

DEF: An acute axonal neuropathy, both sensory and motor, that is associated with Systemic Inflammatory Response Syndrome (SIRS).

357.89 Other inflammatory and toxic neuropathy   CD PDx

357.9 Unspecified   CD PDx

√4th **358 Myoneural disorders**

√5th **358.0 Myasthenia gravis**
AHA: 4Q, '03, 59

DEF: Autoimmune disorder of acetylcholine at neuromuscular junction; causing fatigue of voluntary muscles.

358.00 Myasthenia gravis without (acute) exacerbation   CD PDx
Myasthenia gravis NOS

358.01 Myasthenia gravis with (acute) exacerbation   CD PDx
Myasthenia gravis in crisis
AHA: ▶1Q, '05, 4;◀ 4Q, '04, 139

358.1 Myasthenic syndromes in diseases classified elsewhere   CD SDx

Amyotrophy
Eaton-Lambert syndrome } from stated cause classified elsewhere

Code first underlying disease, as:
botulism (005.1)
diabetes mellitus (250.6)
hypothyroidism (244.0-244.9)
malignant neoplasm (140.0-208.9)
pernicious anemia (281.0)
thyrotoxicosis (242.0-242.9)

N Newborn Age: 0   P Pediatric Age: 0-17   M Maternity Age: 12-55   A Adult Age: 15-124   Manifestation Code   ▶◀ Revised Text   ● New Code   ▲ Revised Code Title

358.2 **Toxic myoneural disorders** `CD PDx`
     Use additional E code to identify toxic agent

358.8 **Other specified myoneural disorders** `CD PDx`

358.9 **Myoneural disorders, unspecified** `CD PDx`
     AHA: 2Q, '02, 16

√4th **359 Muscular dystrophies and other myopathies**
     EXCLUDES   idiopathic polymyositis (710.4)

359.0 **Congenital hereditary muscular dystrophy**
     Benign congenital myopathy   Myotubular myopathy
     Central core disease   Nemaline body disease
     Centronuclear myopathy
        EXCLUDES   arthrogryposis multiplex congenita
                   (754.89)

     DEF: Genetic disorder; causing progressive or nonprogressive
     muscle weakness.

359.1 **Hereditary progressive muscular dystrophy**
     Muscular dystrophy: Muscular dystrophy:
       NOS   Gower's
       distal   Landouzy-Déjérine
       Duchenne   limb-girdle
       Erb's   ocular
       fascioscapulohumeral   oculopharyngeal

     DEF: Genetic degenerative, muscle disease; causes progressive
     weakness, wasting of muscle with no nerve involvement.

359.2 **Myotonic disorders**
     Dystrophia myotonica   Paramyotonia congenita
     Eulenburg's disease   Steinert's disease
     Myotonia congenita   Thomsen's disease

     DEF: Impaired movement due to spasmatic, rigid muscles.

359.3 **Familial periodic paralysis**
     Hypokalemic familial periodic paralysis

     DEF: Genetic disorder; characterized by rapidly progressive flaccid
     paralysis; attacks often occur after exercise or exposure to cold or
     dietary changes.

359.4 **Toxic myopathy**
     Use additional E code to identify toxic agent
     AHA: 1Q, '88, 5

     DEF: Muscle disorder caused by toxic agent.

359.5 *Myopathy in endocrine diseases classified*
elsewhere
     Code first underlying disease, as:
       Addison's disease (255.4)
       Cushing's syndrome (255.0)
       hypopituitarism (253.2)
       myxedema (244.0-244.9)
       thyrotoxicosis (242.0-242.9)

     DEF: Muscle disorder secondary to dysfunction in hormone
     secretion.

359.6 *Symptomatic inflammatory myopathy in diseases*
classified elsewhere
     Code first underlying disease, as:
       amyloidosis (277.3)
       disseminated lupus erythematosus (710.0)
       malignant neoplasm (140.0-208.9)
       polyarteritis nodosa (446.0)
       rheumatoid arthritis (714.0)
       sarcoidosis (135)
       scleroderma (710.1)
       Sjögren's disease (710.2)

√5th **359.8** **Other myopathies**
     AHA: 4Q, '02, 47; 3Q, '90, 17

     359.81 **Critical illness myopathy**
       Acute necrotizing myopathy
       Acute quadriplegic myopathy
       Intensive care (ICU) myopathy
       Myopathy of critical illness

     359.89 **Other myopathies**

359.9 **Myopathy, unspecified**

DISORDERS OF THE EYE AND ADNEXA (360-379)

√4th **360 Disorders of the globe**
     INCLUDES   disorders affecting multiple structures of eye

√5th **360.0** **Purulent endophthalmitis**

     360.00 **Purulent endophthalmitis, unspecified**

     360.01 **Acute endophthalmitis**

     360.02 **Panophthalmitis**

     360.03 **Chronic endophthalmitis**

     360.04 **Vitreous abscess**

√5th **360.1** **Other endophthalmitis**

     360.11 **Sympathetic uveitis**
       DEF: Inflammation of vascular layer of uninjured eye;
       follows injury to other eye.

     360.12 **Panuveitis**
       DEF: Inflammation of entire vascular layer of eye,
       including choroid, iris and ciliary body.

     360.13 **Parasitic endophthalmitis NOS**
       DEF: Parasitic infection causing inflammation of the
       entire eye.

     360.14 **Ophthalmia nodosa**
       DEF: Conjunctival inflammation caused by embedded
       hairs.

     360.19 **Other**
       Phacoanaphylactic endophthalmitis

√5th **360.2** **Degenerative disorders of globe**
     AHA: 3Q, '91, 3

     360.20 **Degenerative disorder of globe, unspecified**

     360.21 **Progressive high (degenerative) myopia**
       Malignant myopia
       DEF: Severe, progressive nearsightedness in adults,
       complicated by serious disease of the choroid; leads to
       retinal detachment and blindness.

     360.23 **Siderosis**
       DEF: Iron pigment deposits within tissue of eyeball;
       caused by high iron content of blood.

     360.24 **Other metallosis**
       Chalcosis
       DEF: Metal deposits, other than iron, within eyeball
       tissues.

     360.29 **Other**
       EXCLUDES   xerophthalmia (264.7)

Eye

Sclera, Cornea, Iris, Pupil, Anterior chamber, Posterior chamber, Ciliary body, Conjunctiva, Vitreous body, Lens, Hyaloid canal, Choroid (uvea), Lamina cribosa, Optic nerve, Optic disk, Fovea, Retina, Globe (Eyeball)

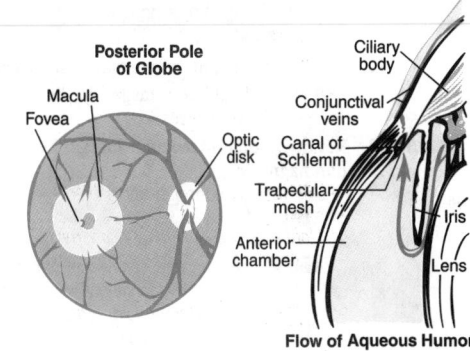

Posterior Pole of Globe — Macula, Fovea, Optic disk, Anterior chamber, Ciliary body, Conjunctival veins, Canal of Schlemm, Trabecular mesh, Iris, Lens

Flow of Aqueous Humor

√4th √5th **Additional Digit Required**   **RUG III Special Care Dx**   **RUG III Clinically Complex Dx**   **Hospice Non-cancer Dx**   `CD PDx` Clinical Dimension PDx   `CD SDx` Clinical Dimension SDx

2006 ICD•9•CM   **Volume 1 — 87**

Adnexa

Upper eyelid
Orbicularis oculi muscle
Orbital septum
Tarsal plate (cartilage)
Müller's muscle
Conjunctival fornix
Globe (eyeball)
Lower eyelid
Tarsal plate
Fascia bulbi (Tenon's capsule)
Orbital septum
Orbital floor
Orbital roof
Levator palpebri muscle
Optic nerve
Retrobulbar space
Extraocular muscle

✓5th 360.3 Hypotony of eye

360.30 Hypotony, unspecified
DEF: Low osmotic pressure causing lack of tone, tension and strength.

360.31 Primary hypotony

360.32 Ocular fistula causing hypotony
DEF: Low intraocular pressure due to leak through abnormal passage.

360.33 Hypotony associated with other ocular disorders

360.34 Flat anterior chamber
DEF: Low pressure behind cornea, causing compression.

✓5th 360.4 Degenerated conditions of globe

360.40 Degenerated globe or eye, unspecified

360.41 Blind hypotensive eye
Atrophy of globe Phthisis bulbi
DEF: Vision loss due to extremely low intraocular pressure.

360.42 Blind hypertensive eye
Absolute glaucoma
DEF: Vision loss due to painful, high intraocular pressure.

360.43 Hemophthalmos, except current injury
EXCLUDES traumatic (871.0-871.9, 921.0-921.9)
DEF: Pool of blood within eyeball, not from current injury.

360.44 Leucocoria
DEF: Whitish mass or reflex in the pupil behind lens; also called cat's eye reflex; often indicative of retinoblastoma.

✓5th 360.5 Retained (old) intraocular foreign body, magnetic
EXCLUDES current penetrating injury with magnetic foreign body (871.5)
retained (old) foreign body of orbit (376.6)

360.50 Foreign body, magnetic, intraocular, unspecified

360.51 Foreign body, magnetic, in anterior chamber

360.52 Foreign body, magnetic, in iris or ciliary body

360.53 Foreign body, magnetic, in lens

360.54 Foreign body, magnetic, in vitreous

360.55 Foreign body, magnetic, in posterior wall

360.59 Foreign body, magnetic, in other or multiple sites

✓5th 360.6 Retained (old) intraocular foreign body, nonmagnetic
Retained (old) foreign body:
NOS
nonmagnetic
EXCLUDES current penetrating injury with (nonmagnetic) foreign body (871.6)
retained (old) foreign body in orbit (376.6)

360.60 Foreign body, intraocular, unspecified

360.61 Foreign body in anterior chamber

360.62 Foreign body in iris or ciliary body

360.63 Foreign body in lens

360.64 Foreign body in vitreous

360.65 Foreign body in posterior wall

360.69 Foreign body in other or multiple sites

✓5th 360.8 Other disorders of globe

360.81 Luxation of globe
DEF: Displacement of eyeball.

360.89 Other

360.9 Unspecified disorder of globe

✓4th 361 Retinal detachments and defects
DEF: Light-sensitive layer at back of eye, separates from blood supply; disrupting vision.

✓5th 361.0 Retinal detachment with retinal defect
Rhegmatogenous retinal detachment
EXCLUDES detachment of retinal pigment epithelium (362.42-362.43)
retinal detachment (serous) (without defect) (361.2)

361.00 Retinal detachment with retinal defect, unspecified

361.01 Recent detachment, partial, with single defect

361.02 Recent detachment, partial, with multiple defects

361.03 Recent detachment, partial, with giant tear

361.04 Recent detachment, partial, with retinal dialysis
Dialysis (juvenile) of retina (with detachment)

361.05 Recent detachment, total or subtotal

361.06 Old detachment, partial
Delimited old retinal detachment

361.07 Old detachment, total or subtotal

✓5th 361.1 Retinoschisis and retinal cysts
EXCLUDES juvenile retinoschisis (362.73)
microcystoid degeneration of retina (362.62)
parasitic cyst of retina (360.13)

361.10 Retinoschisis, unspecified
DEF: Separation of retina due to degenerative process of aging; should not be confused with acute retinal detachment.

361.11 Flat retinoschisis
DEF: Slow, progressive split of retinal sensory layers.

361.12 Bullous retinoschisis
DEF: Fluid retention between split retinal sensory layers.

361.13 Primary retinal cysts

361.14 Secondary retinal cysts

361.19 Other
Pseudocyst of retina

361.2 Serous retinal detachment
Retinal detachment without retinal defect
EXCLUDES central serous retinopathy (362.41)
retinal pigment epithelium detachment (362.42-362.43)

✓5th 361.3 Retinal defects without detachment
EXCLUDES chorioretinal scars after surgery for detachment (363.30-363.35)
peripheral retinal degeneration without defect (362.60-362.66)

361.30 Retinal defect, unspecified
Retinal break(s) NOS

361.31 Round hole of retina without detachment

361.32 Horseshoe tear of retina without detachment
Operculum of retina without mention of detachment

361.33 Multiple defects of retina without detachment

N Newborn Age: 0　　P Pediatric Age: 0-17　　M Maternity Age: 12-55　　A Adult Age: 15-124　　Manifestation Code　　►◄ Revised Text　　● New Code　　▲ Revised Code Title

88 — Volume 1　　　2006 ICD•9•CM

✓5th　**361.8**　**Other forms of retinal detachment**

361.81 **Traction detachment of retina**
Traction detachment with vitreoretinal organization

361.89 **Other**
AHA: 3Q, '99, 12

361.9 **Unspecified retinal detachment**
AHA: N-D, '87, 10

✓4th　**362**　**Other retinal disorders**
　　EXCLUDES　chorioretinal scars (363.30-363.35)
　　　　chorioretinitis (363.0-363.2)

✓5th　**362.0**　*Diabetic retinopathy*
Code first diabetes (250.5)
DEF: Retinal changes in diabetes of long duration; causes hemorrhages, microaneurysms, waxy deposits and proliferative noninflammatory degenerative disease of retina.

362.01 *Background diabetic retinopathy*
Diabetic retinal microaneurysms
Diabetic retinopathy NOS

362.02 *Proliferative diabetic retinopathy*
AHA: 3Q, '96, 5

● **362.03** *Nonproliferative diabetic retinopathy NOS*
● **362.04** *Mild nonproliferative diabetic retinopathy*
● **362.05** *Moderate nonproliferative diabetic retinopathy*
● **362.06** *Severe nonproliferative diabetic retinopathy*
● **362.07** *Diabetic macular edema*
Note: Code 362.07 must be used with a code for diabetic retinopathy (362.01-362.06)
Diabetic retinal edema

✓5th　**362.1**　**Other background retinopathy and retinal vascular changes**

362.10 **Background retinopathy, unspecified**

362.11 **Hypertensive retinopathy**
AHA: 3Q, '90, 3
DEF: Retinal irregularities caused by systemic hypertension.

362.12 **Exudative retinopathy**
Coats' syndrome
AHA: 3Q, '99, 12

362.13 **Changes in vascular appearance**
Vascular sheathing of retina
Use additional code for any associated atherosclerosis (440.8)

362.14 **Retinal microaneurysms NOS**
DEF: Microscopic dilation of retinal vessels in nondiabetic.

362.15 **Retinal telangiectasia**
DEF: Dilation of blood vessels of the retina.

362.16 **Retinal neovascularization NOS**
Neovascularization:　Neovascularization:
choroidal　　　　　subretinal
DEF: New and abnormal vascular growth in the retina.

362.17 **Other intraretinal microvascular abnormalities**
Retinal varices

362.18 **Retinal vasculitis**
Eales' disease　　Retinal:
Retinal:　　　　　perivasculitis
arteritis　　　　phlebitis
endarteritis
DEF: Inflammation of retinal blood vessels.

✓5th　**362.2**　**Other proliferative retinopathy**

362.21 **Retrolental fibroplasia**
DEF: Fibrous tissue in vitreous, from retina to lens, causing blindness; associated with premature infants requiring high amounts of oxygen.

362.29 **Other nondiabetic proliferative retinopathy**

✓5th　**362.3**　**Retinal vascular occlusion**
DEF: Obstructed blood flow to and from retina.

362.30 **Retinal vascular occlusion, unspecified**

362.31 **Central retinal artery occlusion**

362.32 **Arterial branch occlusion**

362.33 **Partial arterial occlusion**
Hollenhorst plaque
Retinal microembolism

362.34 **Transient arterial occlusion**
Amaurosis fugax
AHA: 1Q, '00, 16

362.35 **Central retinal vein occlusion**
AHA: 2Q, '93, 6

362.36 **Venous tributary (branch) occlusion**

362.37 **Venous engorgement**
Occlusion:
incipient ⎫ of retinal vein
partial　 ⎭

✓5th　**362.4**　**Separation of retinal layers**
　　EXCLUDES　retinal detachment (serous) (361.2)
　　　　rhegmatogenous (361.00-361.07)

362.40 **Retinal layer separation, unspecified**

362.41 **Central serous retinopathy**
DEF: Serous-filled blister causing detachment of retina from pigment epithelium.

362.42 **Serous detachment of retinal pigment epithelium**
Exudative detachment of retinal pigment epithelium
DEF: Blister of fatty fluid causing detachment of retina from pigment epithelium.

362.43 **Hemorrhagic detachment of retinal pigment epithelium**
DEF: Blood-filled blister causing detachment of retina from pigment epithelium.

✓5th　**362.5**　**Degeneration of macula and posterior pole**
　　EXCLUDES　degeneration of optic disc (377.21-377.24)
　　　　hereditary retinal degeneration [dystrophy] (362.70-362.77)

362.50 **Macular degeneration (senile), unspecified**

362.51 **Nonexudative senile macular degeneration**
Senile macular degeneration:
atrophic
dry

362.52 **Exudative senile macular degeneration**
Kuhnt-Junius degeneration
Senile macular degeneration:
disciform
wet
DEF: Leakage in macular blood vessels with loss of visual acuity.

362.53 **Cystoid macular degeneration**
Cystoid macular edema
DEF: Retinal swelling and cyst formation in macula.

362.54 **Macular cyst, hole, or pseudohole**

362.55 **Toxic maculopathy**
Use additional E code to identify drug, if drug induced

362.56 **Macular puckering**
Preretinal fibrosis

362.57 **Drusen (degenerative)**
DEF: White, hyaline deposits on Bruch's membrane (lamina basalis choroideae).

✓5th　**362.6**　**Peripheral retinal degenerations**
　　EXCLUDES　hereditary retinal degeneration [dystrophy] (362.70-362.77)
　　　　retinal degeneration with retinal defect (361.00-361.07)

362.60 **Peripheral retinal degeneration, unspecified**

✓4th ✓5th Additional Digit Required　　RUG III Special Care Dx　　　RUG III Clinically Complex Dx　　　Hospice Non-cancer Dx　　　CD PDx Clinical Dimension PDx　　CD SDx Clinical Dimension SDx

2006 ICD•9•CM　　　　　　　　　　　　　　　　　　　　　　　　　　　　October 2005 • Volume 1 — 89

362.61 Paving stone degeneration
DEF: Degeneration of peripheral retina; causes thinning through which choroid is visible.

362.62 Microcystoid degeneration
Blessig's cysts   Iwanoff's cysts

362.63 Lattice degeneration
Palisade degeneration of retina
DEF: Degeneration of retina; often bilateral, usually benign; characterized by lines intersecting at irregular intervals in peripheral retina; retinal thinning and retinal holes may occur.

362.64 Senile reticular degeneration
DEF: Net-like appearance of retina; sign of degeneration.

362.65 Secondary pigmentary degeneration
Pseudoretinitis pigmentosa

362.66 Secondary vitreoretinal degenerations

√5ᵗʰ **362.7 Hereditary retinal dystrophies**
DEF: Genetically induced progressive changes in retina.

362.70 Hereditary retinal dystrophy, unspecified

362.71 *Retinal dystrophy in systemic or cerebroretinal lipidoses*
Code first underlying disease, as:
cerebroretinal lipidoses (330.1)
systemic lipidoses (272.7)

362.72 *Retinal dystrophy in other systemic disorders and syndromes*
Code first underlying disease, as:
Bassen-Kornzweig syndrome (272.5)
Refsum's disease (356.3)

362.73 Vitreoretinal dystrophies
Juvenile retinoschisis

362.74 Pigmentary retinal dystrophy
Retinal dystrophy, albipunctate
Retinitis pigmentosa

362.75 Other dystrophies primarily involving the sensory retina
Progressive cone(-rod) dystrophy
Stargardt's disease

362.76 Dystrophies primarily involving the retinal pigment epithelium
Fundus flavimaculatus
Vitelliform dystrophy

362.77 Dystrophies primarily involving Bruch's membrane
Dystrophy:
hyaline
pseudoinflammatory foveal
Hereditary drusen

√5ᵗʰ **362.8 Other retinal disorders**
EXCLUDES   chorioretinal inflammations (363.0-363.2)
chorioretinal scars (363.30-363.35)

362.81 Retinal hemorrhage
Hemorrhage:
preretinal
retinal (deep) (superficial)
subretinal
AHA: 4Q, '96, 43

362.82 Retinal exudates and deposits

362.83 Retinal edema
Retinal:
cotton wool spots
edema (localized) (macular) (peripheral)
DEF: Retinal swelling due to fluid accumulation.

362.84 Retinal ischemia
DEF: Reduced retinal blood supply.

362.85 Retinal nerve fiber bundle defects

362.89 Other retinal disorders

362.9 Unspecified retinal disorder

√4ᵗʰ **363 Chorioretinal inflammations, scars, and other disorders of choroid**

√5ᵗʰ **363.0 Focal chorioretinitis and focal retinochoroiditis**
EXCLUDES   focal chorioretinitis or retinochoroiditis in:
histoplasmosis (115.02, 115.12, 115.92)
toxoplasmosis (130.2)
congenital infection (771.2)

363.00 Focal chorioretinitis, unspecified
Focal:
choroiditis or chorioretinitis NOS
retinitis or retinochoroiditis NOS

363.01 Focal choroiditis and chorioretinitis, juxtapapillary

363.03 Focal choroiditis and chorioretinitis of other posterior pole

363.04 Focal choroiditis and chorioretinitis, peripheral

363.05 Focal retinitis and retinochoroiditis, juxtapapillary
Neuroretinitis

363.06 Focal retinitis and retinochoroiditis, macular or paramacular

363.07 Focal retinitis and retinochoroiditis of other posterior pole

363.08 Focal retinitis and retinochoroiditis, peripheral

√5ᵗʰ **363.1 Disseminated chorioretinitis and disseminated retinochoroiditis**
EXCLUDES   disseminated choroiditis or chorioretinitis in secondary syphilis (091.51)
neurosyphilitic disseminated retinitis or retinochoroiditis (094.83)
retinal (peri)vasculitis (362.18)

363.10 Disseminated chorioretinitis, unspecified
Disseminated:
choroiditis or chorioretinitis NOS
retinitis or retinochoroiditis NOS

363.11 Disseminated choroiditis and chorioretinitis, posterior pole

363.12 Disseminated choroiditis and chorioretinitis, peripheral

363.13 Disseminated choroiditis and chorioretinitis, generalized
Code first any underlying disease, as:
tuberculosis (017.3)

363.14 Disseminated retinitis and retinochoroiditis, metastatic

363.15 Disseminated retinitis and retinochoroiditis, pigment epitheliopathy
Acute posterior multifocal placoid pigment epitheliopathy
DEF: Widespread inflammation of retina and choroid; characterized by pigmented epithelium involvement.

√5ᵗʰ **363.2 Other and unspecified forms of chorioretinitis and retinochoroiditis**
EXCLUDES   panophthalmitis (360.02)
sympathetic uveitis (360.11)
uveitis NOS (364.3)

363.20 Chorioretinitis, unspecified
Choroiditis NOS   Uveitis, posterior NOS
Retinitis NOS

363.21 Pars planitis
Posterior cyclitis
DEF: Inflammation of peripheral retina and ciliary body; characterized by bands of white cells.

363.22 Harada's disease
DEF: Retinal detachment and bilateral widespread exudative choroiditis; symptoms include headache, vomiting, increased lymphocytes in cerebrospinal fluid; and temporary or permanent deafness may occur.

√5ᵗʰ **363.3 Chorioretinal scars**
Scar (postinflammatory) (postsurgical) (posttraumatic):
choroid
retina

| N Newborn Age: 0 | P Pediatric Age: 0-17 | M Maternity Age: 12-55 | A Adult Age: 15-124 | Manifestation Code | ◄ Revised Text | ● New Code | ▲ Revised Code Title |

363.30 Chorioretinal scar, unspecified

363.31 Solar retinopathy
DEF: Retinal scarring caused by solar radiation.

363.32 Other macular scars

363.33 Other scars of posterior pole

363.34 Peripheral scars

363.35 Disseminated scars

√5th **363.4 Choroidal degenerations**

363.40 Choroidal degeneration, unspecified
Choroidal sclerosis NOS

363.41 Senile atrophy of choroid
DEF: Wasting away of choroid; due to aging.

363.42 Diffuse secondary atrophy of choroid
DEF: Wasting away of choroid in systemic disease.

363.43 Angioid streaks of choroid
DEF: Degeneration of choroid; characterized by dark brown steaks radiating from optic disk; occurs with pseudoxanthoma, elasticum or Paget's disease.

√5th **363.5 Hereditary choroidal dystrophies**
Hereditary choroidal atrophy:
partial [choriocapillaris]
total [all vessels]

363.50 Hereditary choroidal dystrophy or atrophy, unspecified

363.51 Circumpapillary dystrophy of choroid, partial

363.52 Circumpapillary dystrophy of choroid, total
Helicoid dystrophy of choroid

363.53 Central dystrophy of choroid, partial
Dystrophy, choroidal:
central areolar
circinate

363.54 Central choroidal atrophy, total
Dystrophy, choroidal:
central gyrate
serpiginous

363.55 Choroideremia
DEF: Hereditary choroid degeneration, occurs in first decade; characterized by constricted visual field and ultimately blindness in males; less debilitating in females.

363.56 Other diffuse or generalized dystrophy, partial
Diffuse choroidal sclerosis

363.57 Other diffuse or generalized dystrophy, total
Generalized gyrate atrophy, choroid

√5th **363.6 Choroidal hemorrhage and rupture**

363.61 Choroidal hemorrhage, unspecified

363.62 Expulsive choroidal hemorrhage

363.63 Choroidal rupture

√5th **363.7 Choroidal detachment**

363.70 Choroidal detachment, unspecified

363.71 Serous choroidal detachment
DEF: Detachment of choroid from sclera; due to blister of serous fluid.

363.72 Hemorrhagic choroidal detachment
DEF: Detachment of choroid from sclera; due to blood-filled blister.

363.8 Other disorders of choroid

363.9 Unspecified disorder of choroid

√4th **364 Disorders of iris and ciliary body**

√5th **364.0 Acute and subacute iridocyclitis**
Anterior uveitis
Cyclitis   acute,
Iridocyclitis   subacute
Iritis

EXCLUDES   gonococcal (098.41)
herpes simplex (054.44)
herpes zoster (053.22)

364.00 Acute and subacute iridocyclitis, unspecified

364.01 Primary iridocyclitis

364.02 Recurrent iridocyclitis

364.03 Secondary iridocyclitis, infectious

364.04 Secondary iridocyclitis, noninfectious
Aqueous: Aqueous:
cells   flare
fibrin

364.05 Hypopyon
DEF: Accumulation of white blood cells between cornea and lens.

√5th **364.1 Chronic iridocyclitis**
EXCLUDES   posterior cyclitis (363.21)

364.10 Chronic iridocyclitis, unspecified

364.11 Chronic iridocyclitis in diseases classified elsewhere
Code first underlying disease, as:
sarcoidosis (135)
tuberculosis (017.3)
EXCLUDES   syphilitic iridocyclitis (091.52)
DEF: Persistent inflammation of iris and ciliary body; due to underlying disease or condition.

√5th **364.2 Certain types of iridocyclitis**
EXCLUDES   posterior cyclitis (363.21)
sympathetic uveitis (360.11)

364.21 Fuchs' heterochromic cyclitis
DEF: Chronic cyclitis characterized by differences in the color of the two irises; the lighter iris appears in the inflamed eye.

364.22 Glaucomatocyclitic crises
DEF: One-sided form of secondary open angle glaucoma; recurrent, uncommon and of short duration; causes high intraocular pressure, rarely damage.

364.23 Lens-induced iridocyclitis
DEF: Inflammation of iris; due to immune reaction to proteins in lens following trauma or other lens abnormality.

364.24 Vogt-Koyanagi syndrome
DEF: Uveomeningitis with exudative iridocyclitis and choroiditis; causes depigmentation of hair and skin, detached retina; tinnitus and loss of hearing may occur.

364.3 Unspecified iridocyclitis
Uveitis NOS

√5th **364.4 Vascular disorders of iris and ciliary body**

364.41 Hyphema
Hemorrhage of iris or ciliary body
DEF: Hemorrhage in anterior chamber; also called hyphemia or "blood shot" eyes.

364.42 Rubeosis iridis
Neovascularization of iris or ciliary body
DEF: Blood vessel and connective tissue formation on surface of iris; symptomatic of diabetic retinopathy, central retinal vein occlusion and retinal detachment.

√5th **364.5 Degenerations of iris and ciliary body**

364.51 Essential or progressive iris atrophy

364.52 Iridoschisis
DEF: Splitting of the iris into two layers.

364.53 Pigmentary iris degeneration
Acquired heterochromia
Pigment dispersion syndrome } of iris
Translucency

364.54 Degeneration of pupillary margin
Atrophy of sphincter
Ectropion of pigment epithelium } of iris

364.55 Miotic cysts of pupillary margin
DEF: Serous-filled sacs in pupillary margin of iris.

364.56 Degenerative changes of chamber angle

364.57 Degenerative changes of ciliary body

364.59 Other iris atrophy
Iris atrophy (generalized) (sector shaped)

√4th √5th   Additional Digit Required   RUG III Special Care Dx   RUG III Clinically Complex Dx   Hospice Non-cancer Dx   CD PDx Clinical Dimension PDx   CD SDx Clinical Dimension SDx

2006 ICD•9•CM   **Volume 1 — 91**

Nervous System and Sense Organs

364.6–365.61

√5ᵗʰ **364.6 Cysts of iris, ciliary body, and anterior chamber**
> **EXCLUDES** *miotic pupillary cyst (364.55)*
> *parasitic cyst (360.13)*

364.60 Idiopathic cysts
> DEF: Fluid-filled sacs in iris or ciliary body; unknown etiology.

364.61 Implantation cysts
> Epithelial down-growth, anterior chamber
> Implantation cysts (surgical) (traumatic)

364.62 Exudative cysts of iris or anterior chamber

364.63 Primary cyst of pars plana
> DEF: Fluid-filled sacs of outermost ciliary ring.

364.64 Exudative cyst of pars plana
> DEF: Protein, fatty-filled sacs of outermost ciliary ring; due to fluid lead from blood vessels.

√5ᵗʰ **364.7 Adhesions and disruptions of iris and ciliary body**
> **EXCLUDES** *flat anterior chamber (360.34)*

364.70 Adhesions of iris, unspecified
> Synechiae (iris) NOS

364.71 Posterior synechiae
> DEF: Adhesion binding iris to lens.

364.72 Anterior synechiae
> DEF: Adhesion binding the iris to cornea.

364.73 Goniosynechiae
> Peripheral anterior synechiae
> DEF: Adhesion binding the iris to cornea at the angle of the anterior chamber.

364.74 Pupillary membranes
> Iris bombé   Pupillary:
> Pupillary: seclusion
>   occlusion
> DEF: Membrane traversing the pupil and blocking vision.

364.75 Pupillary abnormalities
> Deformed pupil   Rupture of sphincter, pupil
> Ectopic pupil

364.76 Iridodialysis
> DEF: Separation of the iris from the ciliary body base; due to trauma or surgical accident.

364.77 Recession of chamber angle
> DEF: Receding of anterior chamber angle of the eye; restricts vision.

364.8 Other disorders of iris and ciliary body
> Prolapse of iris NOS
> **EXCLUDES** *prolapse of iris in recent wound (871.1)*

364.9 Unspecified disorder of iris and ciliary body

√4ᵗʰ **365 Glaucoma**
> **EXCLUDES** *blind hypertensive eye [absolute glaucoma] (360.42)*
> *congenital glaucoma (743.20-743.22)*
> DEF: Rise in intraocular pressure which restricts blood flow; multiple causes.

√5ᵗʰ **365.0 Borderline glaucoma [glaucoma suspect]**
> AHA: 1Q, '90, 8

365.00 Preglaucoma, unspecified

365.01 Open angle with borderline findings
> Open angle with:
>   borderline intraocular pressure
>   cupping of optic discs
> DEF: Minor block of aqueous outflow from eye.

365.02 Anatomical narrow angle

365.03 Steroid responders

365.04 Ocular hypertension
> DEF: High fluid pressure within eye; no apparent cause.

√5ᵗʰ **365.1 Open-angle glaucoma**

365.10 Open-angle glaucoma, unspecified
> Wide-angle glaucoma NOS

365.11 Primary open angle glaucoma
> Chronic simple glaucoma
> DEF: High intraocular pressure, despite free flow of aqueous.

365.12 Low tension glaucoma

365.13 Pigmentary glaucoma
> DEF: High intraocular pressure; due to iris pigment granules blocking aqueous flow.

365.14 Glaucoma of childhood
> Infantile or juvenile glaucoma

365.15 Residual stage of open angle glaucoma

√5ᵗʰ **365.2 Primary angle-closure glaucoma**

365.20 Primary angle-closure glaucoma, unspecified

365.21 Intermittent angle-closure glaucoma
> Angle-closure glaucoma:
>   interval   subacute
> DEF: Recurring attacks of high intraocular pressure; due to blocked aqueous flow.

365.22 Acute angle-closure glaucoma
> DEF: Sudden, severe rise in intraocular pressure due to blockage in aqueous drainage.

365.23 Chronic angle-closure glaucoma
> AHA: 2Q, '98, 16

365.24 Residual stage of angle-closure glaucoma

√5ᵗʰ **365.3 Corticosteroid-induced glaucoma**
> DEF: Elevated intraocular pressure; due to long-term corticosteroid therapy.

365.31 Glaucomatous stage

365.32 Residual stage

√5ᵗʰ **365.4 Glaucoma associated with congenital anomalies, dystrophies, and systemic syndromes**

365.41 *Glaucoma associated with chamber angle anomalies*
> *Code first associated disorder, as:*
>   Axenfeld's anomaly (743.44)
>   Rieger's anomaly or syndrome (743.44)

365.42 *Glaucoma associated with anomalies of iris*
> *Code first associated disorder, as:*
>   aniridia (743.45)
>   essential iris atrophy (364.51)

365.43 *Glaucoma associated with other anterior segment anomalies*
> *Code first associated disorder, as:*
>   microcornea (743.41)'

365.44 *Glaucoma associated with systemic syndromes*
> *Code first associated disease, as*
>   neurofibromatosis (237.7)
>   Sturge-Weber (-Dimitri) syndrome (759.6)

√5ᵗʰ **365.5 Glaucoma associated with disorders of the lens**

365.51 Phacolytic glaucoma
> Use additional code for associated
>   hypermature cataract (366.18)
> DEF: Elevated intraocular pressure; due to lens protein blocking aqueous flow.

365.52 Pseudoexfoliation glaucoma
> Use additional code for associated
>   pseudoexfoliation of capsule (366.11)
> DEF: Glaucoma characterized by small grayish particles deposited on the lens.

365.59 Glaucoma associated with other lens disorders
> Use additional code for associated disorder, as:
>   dislocation of lens (379.33-379.34)
>   spherophakia (743.36)

√5ᵗʰ **365.6 Glaucoma associated with other ocular disorders**

365.60 Glaucoma associated with unspecified ocular disorder

365.61 Glaucoma associated with pupillary block
> Use additional code for associated disorder, as:
>   seclusion of pupil [iris bombé] (364.74)
> DEF: Acute, open-angle glaucoma caused by mature cataract; aqueous flow is blocked by lens material and macrophages.

N Newborn Age: 0   P Pediatric Age: 0-17   M Maternity Age: 12-55   A Adult Age: 15-124   Manifestation Code   ▶◀ Revised Text   ● New Code   ▲ Revised Code Title

365.62 Glaucoma associated with ocular inflammations
Use additional code for associated disorder, as:
glaucomatocyclitic crises (364.22)
iridocyclitis (364.0-364.3)

365.63 Glaucoma associated with vascular disorders
Use additional code for associated disorder, as:
central retinal vein occlusion (362.35)
hyphema (364.41)

365.64 Glaucoma associated with tumors or cysts
Use additional code for associated disorder, as:
benign neoplasm (224.0-224.9)
epithelial down-growth (364.61)
malignant neoplasm (190.0-190.9)

365.65 Glaucoma associated with ocular trauma
Use additional code for associated condition, as:
contusion of globe (921.3)
recession of chamber angle (364.77)

√5th **365.8 Other specified forms of glaucoma**

365.81 Hypersecretion glaucoma

365.82 Glaucoma with increased episcleral venous pressure

365.83 Aqueous misdirection
Malignant glaucoma
AHA: 4Q, '02, 48
DEF: A form of glaucoma that occurs when aqueous humor flows into the posterior chamber of the eye (vitreous) rather than through the normal recycling channels into the anterior chamber.

365.89 Other specified glaucoma
AHA: 2Q, '98, 16

365.9 Unspecified glaucoma
AHA: 3Q, '03, 14; 2Q, '01, 16

√4th **366 Cataract**
DEF: A variety of conditions that create a cloudy, or calcified lens that obstructs vision.

EXCLUDES congenital cataract (743.30-743.34)

√5th **366.0 Infantile, juvenile, and presenile cataract**

366.00 Nonsenile cataract, unspecified

366.01 Anterior subcapsular polar cataract
DEF: Defect within the front, center lens surface.

366.02 Posterior subcapsular polar cataract
DEF: Defect within the rear, center lens surface.

366.03 Cortical, lamellar, or zonular cataract
DEF: Opacities radiating from center to edge of lens; appear as thin, concentric layers of lens.

366.04 Nuclear cataract

366.09 Other and combined forms of nonsenile cataract

Aqueous Misdirection Syndrome

Cataract

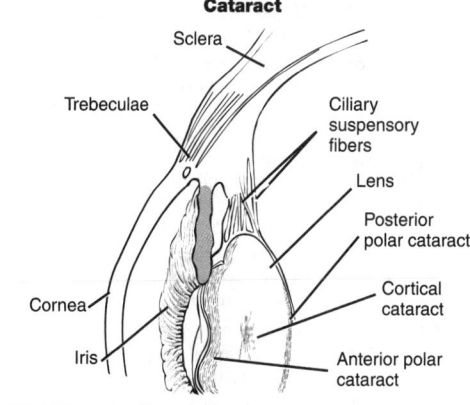

√5th **366.1 Senile cataract**
AHA: 3Q, '91, 3; S-O, '85, 10

366.10 Senile cataract, unspecified   A
AHA: 1Q, '03, 5

366.11 Pseudoexfoliation of lens capsule   A

366.12 Incipient cataract   A
Cataract: Cataract:
coronary   punctate
immature NOS   Water clefts
DEF: Minor disorders of lens not affecting vision; due to aging.

366.13 Anterior subcapsular polar senile cataract   A

366.14 Posterior subcapsular polar senile cataract   A

366.15 Cortical senile cataract   A

366.16 Nuclear sclerosis   A
Cataracta brunescens
Nuclear cataract

366.17 Total or mature cataract   A

366.18 Hypermature cataract   A
Morgagni cataract

366.19 Other and combined forms of senile cataract   A

√5th **366.2 Traumatic cataract**

366.20 Traumatic cataract, unspecified

366.21 Localized traumatic opacities
Vossius' ring

366.22 Total traumatic cataract

366.23 Partially resolved traumatic cataract

√5th **366.3 Cataract secondary to ocular disorders**

366.30 Cataracta complicata, unspecified

366.31 Glaucomatous flecks (subcapsular)
Code first underlying glaucoma (365.0-365.9)

366.32 Cataract in inflammatory disorders
Code first underlying condition, as:
chronic choroiditis (363.0-363.2)

366.33 Cataract with neovascularization
Code first underlying condition, as:
chronic iridocyclitis (364.10)

366.34 Cataract in degenerative disorders
Sunflower cataract
Code first underlying condition, as:
chalcosis (360.24)
degenerative myopia (360.21)
pigmentary retinal dystrophy (362.74)

√5th **366.4 Cataract associated with other disorders**

366.41 Diabetic cataract
Code first diabetes (250.5)
AHA: 3Q, '91, 3; S-O, '85, 11

366.42 Tetanic cataract
Code first underlying disease, as:
calcinosis (275.4)
hypoparathyroidism (252.1)

√4th
√5th Additional Digit Required   RUG III Special Care Dx   RUG III Clinically Complex Dx   Hospice Non-cancer Dx   **CD PDx** Clinical Dimension PDx   **CD SDx** Clinical Dimension SDx

2006 ICD•9•CM   Volume 1 — 93

Nervous System and Sense Organs

366.43–368.47

366.43 Myotonic cataract
Code first underlying disorder (359.2)

366.44 Cataract associated with other syndromes
Code first underlying condition, as:
craniofacial dysostosis (756.0)
galactosemia (271.1)

366.45 Toxic cataract
Drug-induced cataract
Use additional E code to identify drug or
other toxic substance

**366.46 Cataract associated with radiation and
other physical influences**
Use additional E code to identify cause

✓5th **366.5 After-cataract**

366.50 After-cataract, unspecified
Secondary cataract NOS

366.51 Soemmering's ring
DEF: A donut-shaped lens remnant and a capsule behind
the pupil as a result of cataract surgery or trauma.

366.52 Other after-cataract, not obscuring vision

366.53 After-cataract, obscuring vision

366.8 Other cataract
Calcification of lens

366.9 Unspecified cataract

✓4th **367 Disorders of refraction and accommodation**

367.0 Hypermetropia
Far-sightedness   Hyperopia
DEF: Refraction error, called also hyperopia, focal point is posterior
to retina; abnormally short anteroposterior diameter or subnormal
refractive power; causes farsightedness.

367.1 Myopia
Near-sightedness
DEF: Refraction error, focal point is anterior to retina; causes near-
sightedness.

✓5th **367.2 Astigmatism**

367.20 Astigmatism, unspecified

367.21 Regular astigmatism

367.22 Irregular astigmatism

✓5th **367.3 Anisometropia and aniseikonia**

367.31 Anisometropia
DEF: Eyes with refractive powers that differ by at least
one diopter.

367.32 Aniseikonia
DEF: Eyes with unequal retinal imaging; usually due to
refractive error.

367.4 Presbyopia
DEF: Loss of crystalline lens elasticity; causes errors of
accommodation; due to aging.

✓5th **367.5 Disorders of accommodation**

367.51 Paresis of accommodation
Cycloplegia
DEF: Partial paralysis of ciliary muscle; causing focus
problems.

367.52 Total or complete internal ophthalmoplegia
DEF: Total paralysis of ciliary muscle; large pupil
incapable of focus.

367.53 Spasm of accommodation
DEF: Abnormal contraction of ciliary muscle; causes
focus problems.

✓5th **367.8 Other disorders of refraction and accommodation**

367.81 Transient refractive change

367.89 Other
Drug-induced ⎱ disorders of refraction
Toxic ⎰ and accommodation

**367.9 Unspecified disorder of refraction and
accommodation**

✓4th **368 Visual disturbances**
EXCLUDES   electrophysiological disturbances (794.11-794.14)

✓5th **368.0 Amblyopia ex anopsia**
DEF: Vision impaired due to disuse; esotropia often cause.

368.00 Amblyopia, unspecified

368.01 Strabismic amblyopia
Suppression amblyopia

368.02 Deprivation amblyopia
DEF: Decreased vision associated with suppressed
retinal image of one eye.

368.03 Refractive amblyopia

✓5th **368.1 Subjective visual disturbances**

368.10 Subjective visual disturbance, unspecified

368.11 Sudden visual loss

368.12 Transient visual loss
Concentric fading   Scintillating scotoma

368.13 Visual discomfort
Asthenopia   Photophobia
Eye strain

368.14 Visual distortions of shape and size
Macropsia   Micropsia
Metamorphopsia

**368.15 Other visual distortions and entoptic
phenomena**
Photopsia   Refractive:
Refractive: polyopia
diplopia   Visual halos

368.16 Psychophysical visual disturbances
Visual: Visual:
agnosia   hallucinations
disorientation syndrome

368.2 Diplopia
Double vision

✓5th **368.3 Other disorders of binocular vision**

368.30 Binocular vision disorder, unspecified

368.31 Suppression of binocular vision

**368.32 Simultaneous visual perception without
fusion**

368.33 Fusion with defective stereopsis
DEF: Faulty depth perception though normal ability to
focus.

368.34 Abnormal retinal correspondence

✓5th **368.4 Visual field defects**

368.40 Visual field defect, unspecified

368.41 Scotoma involving central area
Scotoma: Scotoma:
central   paracentral
centrocecal
DEF: Vision loss (blind spot) in central five degrees of
visual field.

368.42 Scotoma of blind spot area
Enlarged: Paracecal scotoma
angioscotoma
blind spot

368.43 Sector or arcuate defects
Scotoma: Scotoma:
arcuate   Seidel
Bjerrum
DEF: Arc-shaped blind spot caused by retinal nerve
damage.

368.44 Other localized visual field defect
Scotoma: Visual field defect:
NOS   nasal step
ring   peripheral

368.45 Generalized contraction or constriction

368.46 Homonymous bilateral field defects
Hemianopsia (altitudinal) (homonymous)
Quadrant anopia
DEF: Disorders found in the corresponding vertical
halves of the visual fields of both eyes.

368.47 Heteronymous bilateral field defects
Hemianopsia: Hemianopsia:
binasal   bitemporal
DEF: Disorders in the opposite halves of the visual fields
of both eyes.

N Newborn Age: 0   P Pediatric Age: 0-17   M Maternity Age: 12-55   A Adult Age: 15-124   Manifestation Code   ▶◀ Revised Text   ● New Code   ▲ Revised Code Title

√5ᵗʰ **368.5 Color vision deficiencies**
Color blindness

368.51 Protan defect
Protanomaly   Protanopia
DEF: Mild difficulty distinguishing green and red hues with shortened spectrum; sex-linked affecting one percent of males.

368.52 Deutan defect
Deuteranomaly   Deuteranopia
DEF: Male-only disorder; difficulty in distinguishing green and red, no shortened spectrum.

368.53 Tritan defect
Tritanomaly   Tritanopia
DEF: Difficulty in distinguishing blue and yellow; occurs often due to drugs, retinal detachment and central nervous system diseases.

368.54 Achromatopsia
Monochromatism (cone) (rod)
DEF: Complete color blindness; caused by disease, injury to retina, optic nerve or pathway.

368.55 Acquired color vision deficiencies

368.59 Other color vision deficiencies

√5ᵗʰ **368.6 Night blindness**
Nyctalopia
DEF: Nyctalopia: disorder of vision in dim light or night blindness.

368.60 Night blindness, unspecified

368.61 Congenital night blindness
Hereditary night blindness
Oguchi's disease

368.62 Acquired night blindness
EXCLUDES   *that due to vitamin A deficiency (264.5)*

368.63 Abnormal dark adaptation curve
Abnormal threshold
Delayed adaptation } of cones or rods

368.69 Other night blindness

368.8 Other specified visual disturbances
Blurred vision NOS
AHA: 4Q, '02, 56

368.9 Unspecified visual disturbance
AHA: ▶1Q, '04, 15◀

√4ᵗʰ **369 Blindness and low vision**
Note: Visual impairment refers to a functional limitation of the eye (e.g., limited visual acuity or visual field). It should be distinguished from visual disability, indicating a limitation of the abilities of the individual (e.g., limited reading skills, vocational skills), and from visual handicap, indicating a limitation of personal and socioeconomic independence (e.g., limited mobility, limited employability).

The levels of impairment defined in the table on this page are based on the recommendations of the WHO Study Group on Prevention of Blindness (Geneva, November 6–10, 1972; WHO Technical Report Series 518), and of the International Council of Ophthalmology (1976).

Note that definitions of blindness vary in different settings.

For international reporting WHO defines blindness as profound impairment. This definition can be applied to blindness of one eye (369.1, 369.6) and to blindness of the individual (369.0).

For determination of benefits in the U.S.A., the definition of legal blindness as severe impairment is often used. This definition applies to blindness of the individual only.

EXCLUDES   *correctable impaired vision due to refractive errors (367.0-367.9)*

√5ᵗʰ **369.0 Profound impairment, both eyes**

369.00 Impairment level not further specified
Blindness:
NOS according to WHO definition
both eyes

369.01 Better eye: total impairment; lesser eye: total impairment

369.02 Better eye: near-total impairment; lesser eye: not further specified

369.03 Better eye: near-total impairment; lesser eye: total impairment

369.04 Better eye: near-total impairment; lesser eye: near-total impairment

369.05 Better eye: profound impairment; lesser eye: not further specified

369.06 Better eye: profound impairment; lesser eye: total impairment

369.07 Better eye: profound impairment; lesser eye: near-total impairment

369.08 Better eye: profound impairment; lesser eye: profound impairment

√5ᵗʰ **369.1 Moderate or severe impairment, better eye, profound impairment lesser eye**

369.10 Impairment level not further specified
Blindness, one eye, low vision other eye

369.11 Better eye: severe impairment; lesser eye: blind, not further specified

369.12 Better eye: severe impairment; lesser eye: total impairment

369.13 Better eye: severe impairment; lesser eye: near-total impairment

369.14 Better eye: severe impairment; lesser eye: profound impairment

Classification		LEVELS OF VISUAL IMPAIRMENT	Additional descriptors which may be encountered
"legal"	WHO	Visual acuity and/or visual field limitation (whichever is worse)	
LEGAL BLINDNESS (U.S.A.) both eyes	(NEAR-) NORMAL VISION	RANGE OF NORMAL VISION 20/10 20/13 20/16 20/20 20/25 2.0 1.6 1.25 1.0 0.8	
		NEAR-NORMAL VISION 20/30 20/40 20/50 20/60 0.7 0.6 0.5 0.4 0.3	
	LOW VISION	MODERATE VISUAL IMPAIRMENT 20/70 20/80 20/100 20/125 20/160 0.25 0.20 0.16 0.12	Moderate low vision
		SEVERE VISUAL IMPAIRMENT 20/200 20/250 20/320 20/400 0.10 0.08 0.06 0.05 Visual field: 20 degrees or less	Severe low vision, "Legal" blindness
	BLINDNESS (WHO) one or both eyes	PROFOUND VISUAL IMPAIRMENT 20/500 20/630 20/800 20/1000 0.04 0.03 0.025 0.02 Count fingers at: less than 3m (10 ft.) Visual field: 10 degrees or less	Profound low vision, Moderate blindness
		NEAR-TOTAL VISUAL IMPAIRMENT Visual acuity: less than 0.02 (20/1000) Count fingers at: 1m (3 ft.) or less Hand movements: 5m (15 ft.) or less Light projection, light perception Visual field: 5 degrees or less	Severe blindness, Near-total blindness
		TOTAL VISUAL IMPAIRMENT No light perception (NLP)	Total blindness

Visual acuity refers to best achievable acuity with correction.

Non-listed Snellen fractions may be classified by converting to the nearest decimal equivalent, e.g. 10/200 = 0.05, 6/30 = 0.20.

CF (count fingers) without designation of distance, may be classified to profound impairment.

HM (hand motion) without designation of distance, may be classified to near-total impairment.

Visual field measurements refer to the largest field diameter for a 1/100 white test object.

√4ᵗʰ √5ᵗʰ Additional Digit Required   RUG III Special Care Dx   RUG III Clinically Complex Dx   Hospice Non-cancer Dx   **CD PDx** Clinical Dimension PDx   **CD SDx** Clinical Dimension SDx

369.15 Better eye: moderate impairment; lesser eye: blind, not further specified

369.16 Better eye: moderate impairment; lesser eye: total impairment

369.17 Better eye: moderate impairment; lesser eye: near-total impairment

369.18 Better eye: moderate impairment; lesser eye: profound impairment

√5ᵗʰ **369.2** Moderate or severe impairment, both eyes

369.20 Impairment level not further specified
Low vision, both eyes NOS

369.21 Better eye: severe impairment; lesser eye: not further specified

369.22 Better eye: severe impairment; lesser eye: severe impairment

369.23 Better eye: moderate impairment; lesser eye: not further specified

369.24 Better eye: moderate impairment; lesser eye: severe impairment

369.25 Better eye: moderate impairment; lesser eye: moderate impairment

369.3 Unqualified visual loss, both eyes
EXCLUDES   blindness NOS:
legal [U.S.A. definition] (369.4)
WHO definition (369.00)

369.4 Legal blindness, as defined in U.S.A.
Blindness NOS according to U.S.A. definition
EXCLUDES   legal blindness with specification of impairment level (369.01-369.08, 369.11-369.14, 369.21-369.22)

√5ᵗʰ **369.6** Profound impairment, one eye

369.60 Impairment level not further specified
Blindness, one eye

369.61 One eye: total impairment; other eye: not specified

369.62 One eye: total impairment; other eye: near-normal vision

369.63 One eye: total impairment; other eye: normal vision

369.64 One eye: near-total impairment; other eye: not specified

369.65 One eye: near-total impairment; other eye: near-normal vision

369.66 One eye: near-total impairment; other eye: normal vision

369.67 One eye: profound impairment; other eye: not specified

369.68 One eye: profound impairment; other eye: near-normal vision

369.69 One eye: profound impairment; other eye: normal vision

√5ᵗʰ **369.7** Moderate or severe impairment, one eye

369.70 Impairment level not further specified
Low vision, one eye

369.71 One eye: severe impairment; other eye: not specified

369.72 One eye: severe impairment; other eye: near-normal vision

369.73 One eye: severe impairment; other eye: normal vision

369.74 One eye: moderate impairment; other eye: not specified

369.75 One eye: moderate impairment; other eye: near-normal vision

369.76 One eye: moderate impairment; other eye: normal vision

369.8 Unqualified visual loss, one eye

369.9 Unspecified visual loss
AHA: 4Q, '02, 114; 3Q, '02, 20

√4ᵗʰ **370 Keratitis**

√5ᵗʰ **370.0 Corneal ulcer**
EXCLUDES   that due to vitamin A deficiency (264.3)

370.00 Corneal ulcer, unspecified

370.01 Marginal corneal ulcer

370.02 Ring corneal ulcer

370.03 Central corneal ulcer

370.04 Hypopyon ulcer
Serpiginous ulcer
DEF: Corneal ulcer with an accumulation of pus in the eye's anterior chamber.

370.05 Mycotic corneal ulcer
DEF: Fungal infection causing corneal tissue loss.

370.06 Perforated corneal ulcer
DEF: Tissue loss through all layers of cornea.

370.07 Mooren's ulcer
DEF: Tissue loss, with chronic inflammation, at junction of cornea and sclera; seen in elderly.

√5ᵗʰ **370.2 Superficial keratitis without conjunctivitis**
EXCLUDES   dendritic [herpes simplex] keratitis (054.42)

370.20 Superficial keratitis, unspecified

370.21 Punctate keratitis
Thygeson's superficial punctate keratitis
DEF: Formation of cellular and fibrinous deposits (keratic precipitates) on posterior surface; deposits develop after injury or iridocyclitis.

370.22 Macular keratitis
Keratitis: Keratitis:
   areolar   stellate
   nummular   striate

370.23 Filamentary keratitis
DEF: Keratitis characterized by twisted filaments of mucoid material on the cornea's surface.

370.24 Photokeratitis
Snow blindness   Welders' keratitis
AHA: 3Q, '96, 6
DEF: Painful, inflamed cornea; due to extended exposure to ultraviolet light.

√5ᵗʰ **370.3 Certain types of keratoconjunctivitis**

370.31 Phlyctenular keratoconjunctivitis
Phlyctenulosis
Use additional code for any associated tuberculosis (017.3)
DEF: Miniature blister on conjunctiva or cornea; associated with tuberculosis and malnutrition disorders.

370.32 Limbar and corneal involvement in vernal conjunctivitis
Use additional code for vernal conjunctivitis (372.13)
DEF: Corneal itching and inflammation in conjunctivitis; often limited to lining of eyelids.

370.33 Keratoconjunctivitis sicca, not specified as Sjögren's
EXCLUDES   Sjögren's syndrome (710.2)
DEF: Inflammation of conjunctiva and cornea; characterized by "horny" looking tissue and excess blood in these areas; decreased flow of lacrimal (tear) is a contributing factor.

370.34 Exposure keratoconjunctivitis
AHA: 3Q, '96, 6
DEF: Incomplete closure of eyelid causing dry, inflamed eye.

370.35 Neurotrophic keratoconjunctivitis

√5ᵗʰ **370.4 Other and unspecified keratoconjunctivitis**

370.40 Keratoconjunctivitis, unspecified
Superficial keratitis with conjunctivitis NOS

370.44 *Keratitis or keratoconjunctivitis in exanthema*
Code first underlying condition (050.0-052.9)
EXCLUDES   herpes simplex (054.43)
herpes zoster (053.21)
measles (055.71)

Ⓝ Newborn Age: 0   Ⓟ Pediatric Age: 0-17   Ⓜ Maternity Age: 12-55   Ⓐ Adult Age: 15-124   ⬛ Manifestation Code   ▶◀ Revised Text   ● New Code   ▲ Revised Code Title

Nervous System and Sense Organs   *369.15–370.44*

370.49 Other

> EXCLUDES   *epidemic keratoconjunctivitis (077.1)*

√5th **370.5 Interstitial and deep keratitis**

370.50 Interstitial keratitis, unspecified

370.52 Diffuse interstitial keratitis

> Cogan's syndrome
>
> DEF: Inflammation of cornea; with deposits in middle corneal layers; may obscure vision.

370.54 Sclerosing keratitis

> DEF: Chronic corneal inflammation leading to opaque scarring.

370.55 Corneal abscess

> DEF: Pocket of pus and inflammation on the cornea.

370.59 Other

> EXCLUDES   *disciform herpes simplex keratitis (054.43)*
> *syphilitic keratitis (090.3)*

√5th **370.6 Corneal neovascularization**

370.60 Corneal neovascularization, unspecified

370.61 Localized vascularization of cornea

> DEF: Limited infiltration of cornea by new blood vessels.

370.62 Pannus (corneal)

> AHA: 3Q, '02, 20
>
> DEF: Buildup of superficial vascularization and granulated tissue under epithelium of cornea.

370.63 Deep vascularization of cornea

> DEF: Deep infiltration of cornea by new blood vessels.

370.64 Ghost vessels (corneal)

370.8 Other forms of keratitis

> AHA: 3Q, '94, 5

370.9 Unspecified keratitis

√4th **371 Corneal opacity and other disorders of cornea**

√5th **371.0 Corneal scars and opacities**

> EXCLUDES   *that due to vitamin A deficiency (264.6)*

371.00 Corneal opacity, unspecified

> Corneal scar NOS

371.01 Minor opacity of cornea

> Corneal nebula

371.02 Peripheral opacity of cornea

> Corneal macula not interfering with central vision

371.03 Central opacity of cornea

> Corneal:
>
> leucoma ⎫ interfering with central
> macula ⎬ vision

371.04 Adherent leucoma

> DEF: Dense, opaque corneal growth adhering to the iris; also spelled as leukoma.

371.05 Phthisical cornea

> Code first underlying tuberculosis (017.3)

√5th **371.1 Corneal pigmentations and deposits**

371.10 Corneal deposit, unspecified

371.11 Anterior pigmentations

> Stähli's lines

371.12 Stromal pigmentations

> Hematocornea

371.13 Posterior pigmentations

> Krukenberg spindle

371.14 Kayser-Fleischer ring

> DEF: Copper deposits forming ring at outer edge of cornea; seen in Wilson's disease and other liver disorders.

371.15 Other deposits associated with metabolic disorders

371.16 Argentous deposits

> DEF: Silver deposits in cornea.

√5th **371.2 Corneal edema**

371.20 Corneal edema, unspecified

371.21 Idiopathic corneal edema

> DEF: Corneal swelling and fluid retention of unknown cause.

371.22 Secondary corneal edema

> DEF: Corneal swelling and fluid retention caused by an underlying disease, injury, or condition.

371.23 Bullous keratopathy

> DEF: Corneal degeneration; characterized by recurring, rupturing epithelial "blisters;" ruptured blebs expose corneal nerves, cause great pain; occurs in glaucoma, iridocyclitis and Fuchs' epithelial dystrophy.

371.24 Corneal edema due to wearing of contact lenses

√5th **371.3 Changes of corneal membranes**

371.30 Corneal membrane change, unspecified

371.31 Folds and rupture of Bowman's membrane

371.32 Folds in Descemet's membrane

371.33 Rupture in Descemet's membrane

√5th **371.4 Corneal degenerations**

371.40 Corneal degeneration, unspecified

371.41 Senile corneal changes

> Arcus senilis   Hassall-Henle bodies

371.42 Recurrent erosion of cornea

> EXCLUDES   *Mooren's ulcer (370.07)*

371.43 Band-shaped keratopathy

> DEF: Horizontal bands of superficial corneal calcium deposits.

371.44 Other calcerous degenerations of cornea

371.45 Keratomalacia NOS

> EXCLUDES   *that due to vitamin A deficiency (264.4)*
>
> DEF: Destruction of the cornea by keratinization of the epithelium with ulceration and perforation of the cornea; seen in cases of vitamin A deficiency.

371.46 Nodular degeneration of cornea

> Salzmann's nodular dystrophy

371.48 Peripheral degenerations of cornea

> Marginal degeneration of cornea [Terrien's]

371.49 Other

> Discrete colliquative keratopathy

√5th **371.5 Hereditary corneal dystrophies**

> DEF: Genetic disorder; leads to opacities, edema or lesions of cornea.

371.50 Corneal dystrophy, unspecified

371.51 Juvenile epithelial corneal dystrophy

371.52 Other anterior corneal dystrophies

> Corneal dystrophy: Corneal dystrophy:
> microscopic cystic   ring-like

371.53 Granular corneal dystrophy

371.54 Lattice corneal dystrophy

371.55 Macular corneal dystrophy

371.56 Other stromal corneal dystrophies

> Crystalline corneal dystrophy

371.57 Endothelial corneal dystrophy

> Combined corneal dystrophy
> Cornea guttata
> Fuchs' endothelial dystrophy

371.58 Other posterior corneal dystrophies

> Polymorphous corneal dystrophy

√5th **371.6 Keratoconus**

> DEF: Bilateral bulging protrusion of anterior cornea; often due to noninflammatory thinning.

371.60 Keratoconus, unspecified

371.61 Keratoconus, stable condition

371.62 Keratoconus, acute hydrops

√4th
√5th Additional Digit Required   RUG III Special Care Dx   RUG III Clinically Complex Dx   Hospice Non-cancer Dx   **CD PDx** Clinical Dimension PDx   **CD SDx** Clinical Dimension SDx

Nervous System and Sense Organs

371.7–372.64

√5th **371.7** **Other corneal deformities**

371.70 **Corneal deformity, unspecified**

371.71 **Corneal ectasia**

DEF: Bulging protrusion of thinned, scarred cornea.

371.72 **Descemetocele**

DEF: Protrusion of Descemet's membrane into cornea.

371.73 **Corneal staphyloma**

DEF: Protrusion of cornea into adjacent tissue.

√5th **371.8** **Other corneal disorders**

371.81 **Corneal anesthesia and hypoesthesia**

DEF: Decreased or absent sensitivity of cornea..

371.82 **Corneal disorder due to contact lens**

EXCLUDES corneal edema due to contact lens (371.24)

DEF: Contact lens wear causing cornea disorder, excluding swelling.

371.89 **Other**

AHA: 3Q, '99, 12

371.9 **Unspecified corneal disorder**

√4th **372 Disorders of conjunctiva**

EXCLUDES keratoconjunctivitis (370.3-370.4)

√5th **372.0** **Acute conjunctivitis**

372.00 **Acute conjunctivitis, unspecified**

372.01 **Serous conjunctivitis, except viral**

EXCLUDES viral conjunctivitis NOS (077.9)

372.02 **Acute follicular conjunctivitis**

Conjunctival folliculosis NOS

EXCLUDES conjunctivitis:
adenoviral (acute follicular) (077.3)
epidemic hemorrhagic (077.4)
inclusion (077.0)
Newcastle (077.8)
epidemic keratoconjunctivitis (077.1)
pharyngoconjunctival fever (077.2)

DEF: Severe conjunctival inflammation with dense infiltrations of lymphoid tissues of inner eyelids; may be traced to a viral or chlamydial etiology.

372.03 **Other mucopurulent conjunctivitis**

Catarrhal conjunctivitis

EXCLUDES blennorrhea neonatorum (gonococcal) (098.40)
neonatal conjunctivitis(771.6)
ophthalmia neonatorum NOS (771.6)

372.04 **Pseudomembranous conjunctivitis**

Membranous conjunctivitis

EXCLUDES diphtheritic conjunctivitis (032.81)

DEF: Severe inflammation of conjunctiva; false membrane develops on inner surface of eyelid; membrane can be removed without harming epithelium, due to bacterial infections, toxic and allergic factors, and viral infections.

372.05 **Acute atopic conjunctivitis**

DEF: Sudden, severe conjunctivitis due to allergens.

√5th **372.1** **Chronic conjunctivitis**

372.10 **Chronic conjunctivitis, unspecified**

372.11 **Simple chronic conjunctivitis**

372.12 **Chronic follicular conjunctivitis**

DEF: Persistent conjunctival inflammation with dense, localized infiltrations of lymphoid tissues of inner eyelids.

372.13 **Vernal conjunctivitis**

AHA: 3Q, '96, 8

372.14 **Other chronic allergic conjunctivitis**

AHA: 3Q, '96, 8

372.15 *Parasitic conjunctivitis*

Code first underlying disease, as:
filariasis (125.0-125.9)
mucocutaneous leishmaniasis (085.5)

√5th **372.2** **Blepharoconjunctivitis**

372.20 **Blepharoconjunctivitis, unspecified**

372.21 **Angular blepharoconjunctivitis**

DEF: Inflammation at junction of upper and lower eyelids; may block lacrimal secretions.

372.22 **Contact blepharoconjunctivitis**

√5th **372.3** **Other and unspecified conjunctivitis**

372.30 **Conjunctivitis, unspecified**

372.31 *Rosacea conjunctivitis*

Code first underlying rosacea dermatitis (695.3)

372.33 *Conjunctivitis in mucocutaneous disease*

Code first underlying disease, as:
erythema multiforme (695.1)
Reiter's disease (099.3)

EXCLUDES ocular pemphigoid (694.61)

372.39 **Other**

√5th **372.4** **Pterygium**

EXCLUDES pseudopterygium (372.52)

DEF: Wedge-shaped, conjunctival thickening that advances from the inner corner of the eye toward the cornea.

372.40 **Pterygium, unspecified**

372.41 **Peripheral pterygium, stationary**

372.42 **Peripheral pterygium, progressive**

372.43 **Central pterygium**

372.44 **Double pterygium**

372.45 **Recurrent pterygium**

√5th **372.5** **Conjunctival degenerations and deposits**

372.50 **Conjunctival degeneration, unspecified**

372.51 **Pinguecula**

DEF: Proliferative spot on the bulbar conjunctiva located near the sclerocorneal junction, usually on the nasal side; it is seen in elderly people.

372.52 **Pseudopterygium**

DEF: Conjunctival scar joined to the cornea; it looks like a pterygium but is not attached to the tissue.

372.53 **Conjunctival xerosis**

EXCLUDES conjunctival xerosis due to vitamin A deficiency (264.0, 264.1, 264.7)

DEF: Dry conjunctiva due to vitamin A deficiency; related to Bitot's spots; may develop into xerophthalmia and keratomalacia.

372.54 **Conjunctival concretions**

DEF: Calculus or deposit on conjunctiva.

372.55 **Conjunctival pigmentations**

Conjunctival argyrosis

DEF: Color deposits in conjunctiva.

372.56 **Conjunctival deposits**

√5th **372.6** **Conjunctival scars**

372.61 **Granuloma of conjunctiva**

372.62 **Localized adhesions and strands of conjunctiva**

DEF: Abnormal fibrous connections in conjunctiva.

372.63 **Symblepharon**

Extensive adhesions of conjunctiva

DEF: Adhesion of the eyelids to the eyeball.

372.64 **Scarring of conjunctiva**

Contraction of eye socket (after enucleation)

N Newborn Age: 0   P Pediatric Age: 0-17   M Maternity Age: 12-55   A Adult Age: 15-124   Manifestation Code   ▶◀ Revised Text   ● New Code   ▲ Revised Code Title

√5ᵗʰ 372.7　Conjunctival vascular disorders and cysts

372.71　Hyperemia of conjunctiva
>　DEF:　Conjunctival blood vessel congestion causing eye redness.

372.72　Conjunctival hemorrhage
>　HyposphagmaSubconjunctival hemorrhage

372.73　Conjunctival edema
>　Chemosis of conjunctiva
>　Subconjunctival edema
>　DEF:　Fluid retention and swelling in conjunctival tissue.

372.74　Vascular abnormalities of conjunctiva
>　Aneurysm(ata) of conjunctiva

372.75　Conjunctival cysts
>　DEF:　Abnormal sacs of fluid in conjunctiva.

√5ᵗʰ 372.8　Other disorders of conjunctiva

372.81　Conjunctivochalasis
>　AHA: 4Q, '00, 41
>　DEF:　Bilateral condition of redundant conjunctival tissue between globe and lower eyelid margin; may cover lower punctum, interferring with normal tearing.

372.89　Other disorders of conjunctiva

372.9　Unspecified disorder of conjunctiva

√4ᵗʰ 373　Inflammation of eyelids

√5ᵗʰ 373.0　Blepharitis
>　**EXCLUDES**　blepharoconjunctivitis (372.20-372.22)

373.00　Blepharitis, unspecified

373.01　Ulcerative blepharitis

373.02　Squamous blepharitis

√5ᵗʰ 373.1　Hordeolum and other deep inflammation of eyelid
>　DEF:　Purulent, localized, staphylococcal infection in sebaceous glands of eyelids.

373.11　Hordeolum externum
>　Hordeolum NOS Stye
>　DEF:　Infection of the oil glands in the eyelash follicles.

373.12　Hordeolum internum
>　Infection of meibomian gland
>　DEF:　Infection of the oil gland of the eyelid margin.

373.13　Abscess of eyelid
>　Furuncle of eyelid
>　DEF:　Inflamed pocket of pus on the eyelid.

373.2　Chalazion
>　Meibomian (gland) cyst
>　**EXCLUDES**　infected meibomian gland (373.12)
>　DEF:　Chronic inflammation of the meibomian gland, causing an eyelid mass.

√5ᵗʰ 373.3　Noninfectious dermatoses of eyelid

373.31　Eczematous dermatitis of eyelid

373.32　Contact and allergic dermatitis of eyelid

373.33　Xeroderma of eyelid

373.34　Discoid lupus erythematosus of eyelid

373.4　*Infective dermatitis of eyelid of types resulting in deformity*
>　*Code first underlying disease, as:*
>　leprosy (030.0-030.9)
>　lupus vulgaris (tuberculous) (017.0)
>　yaws (102.0-102.9)

373.5　*Other infective dermatitis of eyelid*
>　*Code first underlying disease, as:*
>　actinomycosis (039.3)
>　impetigo (684)
>　mycotic dermatitis (110.0-111.9)
>　vaccinia (051.0)
>　postvaccination (999.0)
>　**EXCLUDES**　herpes:
>　　　simplex (054.41)
>　　　zoster (053.20)

373.6　*Parasitic infestation of eyelid*
>　*Code first underlying disease, as:*
>　leishmaniasis (085.0-085.9)
>　loiasis (125.2)
>　onchocerciasis (125.3)
>　pediculosis (132.0)

373.8　Other inflammations of eyelids

373.9　Unspecified inflammation of eyelid

√4ᵗʰ 374　Other disorders of eyelids

√5ᵗʰ 374.0　Entropion and trichiasis of eyelid
>　DEF: Entropion: turning inward of eyelid edge toward eyeball.
>　DEF: Trichiasis: ingrowing eyelashes marked by irritation with possible distortion of sight.

374.00　Entropion, unspecified

374.01　Senile entropion　　　　　A

374.02　Mechanical entropion

374.03　Spastic entropion

374.04　Cicatricial entropion

374.05　Trichiasis without entropion

√5ᵗʰ 374.1　Ectropion
>　DEF: Turning outward (eversion) of eyelid edge; exposes palpebral conjunctiva; dryness irritation result.

374.10　Ectropion, unspecified

374.11　Senile ectropion　　　　　A

374.12　Mechanical ectropion

374.13　Spastic ectropion

374.14　Cicatricial ectropion

√5ᵗʰ 374.2　Lagophthalmos
>　DEF: Incomplete closure of eyes; causes dry eye and other complications.

374.20　Lagophthalmos, unspecified

374.21　Paralytic lagophthalmos

374.22　Mechanical lagophthalmos

374.23　Cicatricial lagophthalmos

√5ᵗʰ 374.3　Ptosis of eyelid

374.30　Ptosis of eyelid, unspecified
>　AHA: 2Q, '96, 11

374.31　Paralytic ptosis
>　DEF: Drooping of upper eyelid due to nerve disorder.

374.32　Myogenic ptosis
>　DEF: Drooping of upper eyelid due to muscle disorder.

374.33　Mechanical ptosis
>　DEF: Outside force causes drooping of upper eyelid.

374.34　Blepharochalasis
>　Pseudoptosis
>　DEF:　Loss of elasticity, thickened or indurated skin of eyelids associated with recurrent episodes of idiopathic edema causing intracellular tissue atrophy.

Entropion and Ectropion

Normal eyelashes　　　Entropion　　　Ectropion

 Additional Digit Required　　**RUG III Special Care Dx**　　　**RUG III Clinically Complex Dx**　　**Hospice Non-cancer Dx**　　**CD PDx** Clinical Dimension PDx　　**CD SDx** Clinical Dimension SDx

2006 ICD•9•CM　　　　　　　　　　　　　　　　　　　　　　　　　　　　　　　　　　　　　**Volume 1 — 99**

Nervous System and Sense Organs

374.4–375.54

√5th **374.4 Other disorders affecting eyelid function**

    EXCLUDES   *blepharoclonus (333.81)*
        blepharospasm (333.81)
        facial nerve palsy (351.0)
        third nerve palsy or paralysis (378.51-378.52)
        tic (psychogenic) (307.20-307.23)
        organic (333.3)

    374.41 Lid retraction or lag

    374.43 Abnormal innervation syndrome
        Jaw-blinking
        Paradoxical facial movements

    374.44 Sensory disorders

    374.45 Other sensorimotor disorders
        Deficient blink reflex

    374.46 Blepharophimosis
        Ankyloblepharon
        DEF: Narrowing of palpebral fissure horizontally; caused by laterally displaced inner canthi; either acquired or congenital.

√5th **374.5 Degenerative disorders of eyelid and periocular area**

    374.50 Degenerative disorder of eyelid, unspecified

    374.51 Xanthelasma
        Xanthoma (planum) (tuberosum) of eyelid
        Code first underlying condition (272.0-272.9)
        DEF: Fatty tumors of the eyelid linked to high fat content of blood.

    374.52 Hyperpigmentation of eyelid
        Chloasma   Dyspigmentation
        DEF: Excess pigment of eyelid.

    374.53 Hypopigmentation of eyelid
        Vitiligo of eyelid
        DEF: Lack of color pigment of the eyelid.

    374.54 Hypertrichosis of eyelid
        DEF: Excessive eyelash growth.

    374.55 Hypotrichosis of eyelid
        Madarosis of eyelid
        DEF: Less than normal, or absent, eyelashes.

    374.56 Other degenerative disorders of skin affecting eyelid

√5th **374.8 Other disorders of eyelid**

    374.81 Hemorrhage of eyelid
        EXCLUDES   *black eye (921.0)*

    374.82 Edema of eyelid
        Hyperemia of eyelid
        DEF: Swelling and fluid retention in eyelid.

    374.83 Elephantiasis of eyelid
        DEF: Filarial disease causing dermatitis and enlargement of eyelid.

    374.84 Cysts of eyelids
        Sebaceous cyst of eyelid

    374.85 Vascular anomalies of eyelid

    374.86 Retained foreign body of eyelid

    374.87 Dermatochalasis
        DEF: Acquired form of connective tissue disorder associated with decreased elastic tissue and abnormal elastin formation resulting in loss of elasticity of the skin of the eyelid, generally associated with aging.

    374.89 Other disorders of eyelid

    374.9 Unspecified disorder of eyelid

√4th **375 Disorders of lacrimal system**

√5th **375.0 Dacryoadenitis**

    375.00 Dacryoadenitis, unspecified

    375.01 Acute dacryoadenitis
        DEF: Severe, sudden inflammation of the lacrimal gland.

Lacrimal System

Superior and inferior lobes of lacrimal gland

Medial angle

Lacrimal ducts

Lacrimal canaliculi

Nasolacrimal sac

Lacrimal caruncle

Superior, inferior lacrimal puncta

Superior, inferior lacrimal puncta

Left eye

    375.02 Chronic dacryoadenitis
        DEF: Persistent inflammation of the lacrimal gland.

    375.03 Chronic enlargement of lacrimal gland

√5th **375.1 Other disorders of lacrimal gland**

    375.11 Dacryops
        DEF: Overproduction and constant flow of tears; may cause distended lacrimal duct.

    375.12 Other lacrimal cysts and cystic degeneration

    375.13 Primary lacrimal atrophy

    375.14 Secondary lacrimal atrophy
        DEF: Wasting away of the lacrimal gland due to another disease.

    375.15 Tear film insufficiency, unspecified
        Dry eye syndrome
        AHA: 3Q, '96, 6
        DEF: Eye dryness and irritation from insufficient tear production.

    375.16 Dislocation of lacrimal gland

√5th **375.2 Epiphora**
    DEF: Abnormal development of tears due to stricture of lacrimal passages.

    375.20 Epiphora, unspecified as to cause

    375.21 Epiphora due to excess lacrimation
        DEF: Tear overflow due to overproduction.

    375.22 Epiphora due to insufficient drainage
        DEF: Tear overflow due to blocked drainage.

√5th **375.3 Acute and unspecified inflammation of lacrimal passages**
        EXCLUDES   *neonatal dacryocystitis (771.6)*

    375.30 Dacryocystitis, unspecified

    375.31 Acute canaliculitis, lacrimal

    375.32 Acute dacryocystitis
        Acute peridacryocystitis

    375.33 Phlegmonous dacryocystitis
        DEF: Infection of the tear sac with pockets of pus.

√5th **375.4 Chronic inflammation of lacrimal passages**

    375.41 Chronic canaliculitis

    375.42 Chronic dacryocystitis

    375.43 Lacrimal mucocele

√5th **375.5 Stenosis and insufficiency of lacrimal passages**

    375.51 Eversion of lacrimal punctum
        DEF: Abnormal turning outward of the tear duct.

    375.52 Stenosis of lacrimal punctum
        DEF: Abnormal narrowing of the tear duct.

    375.53 Stenosis of lacrimal canaliculi

    375.54 Stenosis of lacrimal sac
        DEF: Abnormal narrowing of the tear sac.

N Newborn Age: 0   P Pediatric Age: 0-17   M Maternity Age: 12-55   A Adult Age: 15-124   Manifestation Code   ◄► Revised Text   ● New Code   ▲ Revised Code Title

375.55 Obstruction of nasolacrimal duct, neonatal

> **EXCLUDES**   *congenital anomaly of nasolacrimal duct (743.65)*

> DEF: Acquired, abnormal obstruction of tear drainage system from the eye to the nose; in an infant.

375.56 Stenosis of nasolacrimal duct, acquired

375.57 Dacryolith

> DEF: Concretion or stone anywhere in lacrimal system.

√5th **375.6 Other changes of lacrimal passages**

375.61 Lacrimal fistula

> DEF: Abnormal communication from the lacrimal system.

375.69 Other

√5th **375.8 Other disorders of lacrimal system**

375.81 Granuloma of lacrimal passages

> DEF: Abnormal nodules within lacrimal system.

375.89 Other

375.9 Unspecified disorder of lacrimal system

√4th **376 Disorders of the orbit**

√5th **376.0 Acute inflammation of orbit**

376.00 Acute inflammation of orbit, unspecified

376.01 Orbital cellulitis

> Abscess of orbit

> DEF: Infection of tissue between the orbital bone and eyeball.

376.02 Orbital periostitis

> DEF: Inflammation of connective tissue covering the orbital bone.

376.03 Orbital osteomyelitis

> DEF: Inflammation of the orbital bone.

376.04 Tenonitis

√5th **376.1 Chronic inflammatory disorders of orbit**

376.10 Chronic inflammation of orbit, unspecified

376.11 Orbital granuloma

> Pseudotumor (inflammatory) of orbit

> DEF: Abnormal nodule between orbital bone and eyeball.

376.12 Orbital myositis

> DEF: Painful inflammation of the muscles of the eye

376.13 Parasitic infestation of orbit

> Code first underlying disease, as:
> hydatid infestation of orbit (122.3, 122.6, 122.9)
> myiasis of orbit (134.0)

√5th **376.2 Endocrine exophthalmos**

> Code first underlying thyroid disorder (242.0-242.9)

376.21 Thyrotoxic exophthalmos

> DEF: Painful inflammation of eye muscles.

376.22 Exophthalmic ophthalmoplegia

> DEF: Inability to rotate eye as a result of bulging eyes.

√5th **376.3 Other exophthalmic conditions**

376.30 Exophthalmos, unspecified

> DEF: Abnormal protrusion of eyeball.

376.31 Constant exophthalmos

> DEF: Continuous, abnormal protrusion or bulging of eyeball.

376.32 Orbital hemorrhage

> DEF: Bleeding behind the eyeball, causing it to bulge forward.

376.33 Orbital edema or congestion

> DEF: Fluid retention behind eyeball, causing forward bulge.

376.34 Intermittent exophthalmos

376.35 Pulsating exophthalmos

> DEF: Bulge or protrusion; associated with a carotid-cavernous fistula.

376.36 Lateral displacement of globe

> DEF: Abnormal displacement of the eyeball away from nose, toward temple.

√5th **376.4 Deformity of orbit**

376.40 Deformity of orbit, unspecified

376.41 Hypertelorism of orbit

> DEF: Abnormal increase in interorbital distance; associated with congenital facial deformities; may be accompanied by mental deficiency.

376.42 Exostosis of orbit

> DEF: Abnormal bony growth of orbit.

376.43 Local deformities due to bone disease

> DEF: Acquired abnormalities of orbit; due to bone disease.

376.44 Orbital deformities associated with craniofacial deformities

376.45 Atrophy of orbit

> DEF: Wasting away of bone tissue of orbit.

376.46 Enlargement of orbit

376.47 Deformity due to trauma or surgery

√5th **376.5 Enophthalmos**

> DEF: Recession of eyeball deep into eye socket.

376.50 Enophthalmos, unspecified as to cause

376.51 Enophthalmos due to atrophy of orbital tissue

376.52 Enophthalmos due to trauma or surgery

376.6 Retained (old) foreign body following penetrating wound of orbit

> Retrobulbar foreign body

√5th **376.8 Other orbital disorders**

376.81 Orbital cysts

> Encephalocele of orbit

> **AHA:** 3Q, '99, 13

376.82 Myopathy of extraocular muscles

> DEF: Disease in the muscles that control eyeball movement.

376.89 Other

376.9 Unspecified disorder of orbit

√4th **377 Disorders of optic nerve and visual pathways**

√5th **377.0 Papilledema**

377.00 Papilledema, unspecified

377.01 Papilledema associated with increased intracranial pressure

377.02 Papilledema associated with decreased ocular pressure

> **CC Excl:** see Code 377.00

377.03 Papilledema associated with retinal disorder

377.04 Foster-Kennedy syndrome

> DEF: Retrobulbar optic neuritis, central scotoma and optic atrophy; caused by tumors in frontal lobe of brain that press downward.

√5th **377.1 Optic atrophy**

377.10 Optic atrophy, unspecified

377.11 Primary optic atrophy

> **EXCLUDES**   *neurosyphilitic optic atrophy (094.84)*

377.12 Postinflammatory optic atrophy

> DEF: Adverse effect of inflammation causing wasting away of eye.

377.13 Optic atrophy associated with retinal dystrophies

> DEF: Progressive changes in retinal tissue due to metabolic disorder causing wasting away of eye.

√4th Additional Digit Required   **RUG III Special Care Dx**   **RUG III Clinically Complex Dx**   Hospice Non-cancer Dx   **CD PDx** Clinical Dimension PDx   **CD SDx** Clinical Dimension SDx

Nervous System and Sense Organs

377.14–378.2

377.14 Glaucomatous atrophy [cupping] of optic disc

377.15 Partial optic atrophy
Temporal pallor of optic disc

377.16 Hereditary optic atrophy
Optic atrophy: Optic atrophy:
  dominant hereditary   Leber's

√5th **377.2 Other disorders of optic disc**

377.21 Drusen of optic disc

377.22 Crater-like holes of optic disc

377.23 Coloboma of optic disc
DEF: Ocular malformation caused by the failure of fetal fissure of optic stalk to close.

377.24 Pseudopapilledema

√5th **377.3 Optic neuritis**
EXCLUDES   *meningococcal optic neuritis (036.81)*

377.30 Optic neuritis, unspecified

377.31 Optic papillitis
DEF: Swelling and inflammation of the optic disc.

377.32 Retrobulbar neuritis (acute)
EXCLUDES   *syphilitic retrobulbar neuritis (094.85)*
DEF: Inflammation of optic nerve immediately behind the eyeball.

377.33 Nutritional optic neuropathy
DEF: Malnutrition causing optic nerve disorder.

377.34 Toxic optic neuropathy
Toxic amblyopia
DEF: Toxic substance causing optic nerve disorder.

377.39 Other
EXCLUDES   *ischemic optic neuropathy (377.41)*

√5th **377.4 Other disorders of optic nerve**

377.41 Ischemic optic neuropathy
DEF: Decreased blood flow affecting optic nerve.

377.42 Hemorrhage in optic nerve sheaths
DEF: Bleeding in meningeal lining of optic nerve.

377.49 Other
Compression of optic nerve

√5th **377.5 Disorders of optic chiasm**

377.51 Associated with pituitary neoplasms and disorders
DEF: Abnormal pituitary growth causing disruption in nerve chain from retina to brain.

377.52 Associated with other neoplasms
DEF: Abnormal growth, other than pituitary, causing disruption in nerve chain from retina to brain.

377.53 Associated with vascular disorders
DEF: Vascular disorder causing disruption in nerve chain from retina to brain.

377.54 Associated with inflammatory disorders
DEF: Inflammatory disease causing disruption in nerve chain from retina to brain.

√5th **377.6 Disorders of other visual pathways**

377.61 Associated with neoplasms

377.62 Associated with vascular disorders

377.63 Associated with inflammatory disorders

√5th **377.7 Disorders of visual cortex**
EXCLUDES   *visual:*
agnosia (368.16)
hallucinations (368.16)
halos (368.15)

377.71 Associated with neoplasms

377.72 Associated with vascular disorders

377.73 Associated with inflammatory disorders

Eye Musculature

Superior rectus   Superior oblique
Lateral rectus   Medial rectus
Inferior oblique   Inferior rectus
Muscles and actions (right eye)

R.   L.
Monocular (one eye only) esotropia (inward)

Monocular exotropia (outward)

Monocular hypertropia (upward)

377.75 Cortical blindness
DEF: Blindness due to brain disorder, rather than eye disorder.

377.9 Unspecified disorder of optic nerve and visual pathways

√4th **378 Strabismus and other disorders of binocular eye movements**
EXCLUDES   *nystagmus and other irregular eye movements (379.50-379.59)*
DEF: Misalignment of the eyes due to imbalance in extraocular muscles.

√5th **378.0 Esotropia**
Convergent concomitant strabismus
EXCLUDES   *intermittent esotropia (378.20-378.22)*
DEF: Visual axis deviation created by one eye fixing upon an image and the other eye deviating inward.

378.00 Esotropia, unspecified

378.01 Monocular esotropia

378.02 Monocular esotropia with A pattern

378.03 Monocular esotropia with V pattern

378.04 Monocular esotropia with other noncomitancies
Monocular esotropia with X or Y pattern

378.05 Alternating esotropia

378.06 Alternating esotropia with A pattern

378.07 Alternating esotropia with V pattern

378.08 Alternating esotropia with other noncomitancies
Alternating esotropia with X or Y pattern

√5th **378.1 Exotropia**
Divergent concomitant strabismus
EXCLUDES   *intermittent exotropia (378.20, 378.23-378.24)*
DEF: Visual axis deviation created by one eye fixing upon an image and the other eye deviating outward.

378.10 Exotropia, unspecified

378.11 Monocular exotropia

378.12 Monocular exotropia with A pattern

378.13 Monocular exotropia with V pattern

378.14 Monocular exotropia with other noncomitancies
Monocular exotropia with X or Y pattern

378.15 Alternating exotropia

378.16 Alternating exotropia with A pattern

378.17 Alternating exotropia with V pattern

378.18 Alternating exotropia with other noncomitancies
Alternating exotropia with X or Y pattern

√5th **378.2 Intermittent heterotropia**
EXCLUDES   *vertical heterotropia (intermittent) (378.31)*
DEF: Deviation of eyes seen only at intervals; it is also called strabismus.

N Newborn Age: 0   P Pediatric Age: 0-17   M Maternity Age: 12-55   A Adult Age: 15-124   Manifestation Code   ►◄ Revised Text   ● New Code   ▲ Revised Code Title

102 — Volume 1   *2006 ICD•9•CM*

378.20 Intermittent heterotropia, unspecified
Intermittent: Intermittent:
esotropia NOS   exotropia NOS

378.21 Intermittent esotropia, monocular

378.22 Intermittent esotropia, alternating

378.23 Intermittent exotropia, monocular

378.24 Intermittent exotropia, alternating

√5th **378.3 Other and unspecified heterotropia**

378.30 Heterotropia, unspecified

378.31 Hypertropia
Vertical heterotropia (constant) (intermittent)

378.32 Hypotropia

378.33 Cyclotropia

378.34 Monofixation syndrome
Microtropia

378.35 Accommodative component in esotropia

√5th **378.4 Heterophoria**
DEF: Deviation occurring only when the other eye is covered..

378.40 Heterophoria, unspecified

378.41 Esophoria

378.42 Exophoria

378.43 Vertical heterophoria

378.44 Cyclophoria

378.45 Alternating hyperphoria

√5th **378.5 Paralytic strabismus**
DEF: Deviation of the eye due to nerve paralysis affecting muscle.

378.50 Paralytic strabismus, unspecified

378.51 Third or oculomotor nerve palsy, partial
AHA: 3Q, '91, 9

378.52 Third or oculomotor nerve palsy, total
AHA: 2Q, '89, 12

378.53 Fourth or trochlear nerve palsy
AHA: 2Q, '01, 21

378.54 Sixth or abducens nerve palsy
AHA: 2Q, '89, 12

378.55 External ophthalmoplegia

378.56 Total ophthalmoplegia

√5th **378.6 Mechanical strabismus**
DEF: Deviation of the eye due to an outside force upon the extraocular muscles.

378.60 Mechanical strabismus, unspecified

378.61 Brown's (tendon) sheath syndrome
DEF: Congenital or acquired shortening of the anterior sheath of the superior oblique muscle; the eye is unable to move upward and inward; it is usually unilateral.

378.62 Mechanical strabismus from other musculofascial disorders

378.63 Limited duction associated with other conditions

√5th **378.7 Other specified strabismus**

378.71 Duane's syndrome
DEF: Congenital, affects one eye; due to abnormal fibrous bands attached to rectus muscle; inability to abduct affected eye with retraction of globe.

378.72 Progressive external ophthalmoplegia
DEF: Paralysis progressing from one eye muscle to another.

378.73 Strabismus in other neuromuscular disorders

√5th **378.8 Other disorders of binocular eye movements**
EXCLUDES nystagmus (379.50-379.56)

378.81 Palsy of conjugate gaze
DEF: Paralysis progressing from one eye muscle to another.

378.82 Spasm of conjugate gaze
DEF: Muscle contractions impairing parallel movement of eye.

378.83 Convergence insufficiency or palsy

378.84 Convergence excess or spasm

378.85 Anomalies of divergence

378.86 Internuclear ophthalmoplegia
DEF: Eye movement anomaly due to brainstem lesion.

378.87 Other dissociated deviation of eye movements
Skew deviation

378.9 Unspecified disorder of eye movements
Ophthalmoplegia NOS   Strabismus NOS
AHA: 2Q, '01, 21

√4th **379 Other disorders of eye**

√5th **379.0 Scleritis and episcleritis**
EXCLUDES syphilitic episcleritis (095.0)

379.00 Scleritis, unspecified
Episcleritis NOS

379.01 Episcleritis periodica fugax
DEF: Hyperemia (engorgement) of the sclera and overlying conjunctiva characterized by a sudden onset and short duration.

379.02 Nodular episcleritis
DEF: Inflammation of the outermost layer of the sclera, with formation of nodules.

379.03 Anterior scleritis

379.04 Scleromalacia perforans
DEF: Scleral thinning, softening and degeneration; seen with rheumatoid arthritis.

379.05 Scleritis with corneal involvement
Scleroperikeratitis

379.06 Brawny scleritis
DEF: Severe scleral inflammation with thickening corneal margins.

379.07 Posterior scleritis
Sclerotenonitis

379.09 Other
Scleral abscess

√5th **379.1 Other disorders of sclera**
EXCLUDES blue sclera (743.47)

379.11 Scleral ectasia
Scleral staphyloma NOS
DEF: Protrusion of the contents of the eyeball where the sclera has thinned.

379.12 Staphyloma posticum
DEF: Ring-shaped protrusion or bulging of sclera and uveal tissue at posterior pole of eye.

379.13 Equatorial staphyloma
DEF: Ring-shaped protrusion or bulging of sclera and uveal tissue midway between front and back of eye.

379.14 Anterior staphyloma, localized

379.15 Ring staphyloma

379.16 Other degenerative disorders of sclera

379.19 Other

√5th **379.2 Disorders of vitreous body**
DEF: Disorder of clear gel that fills space between retina and lens.

379.21 Vitreous degeneration
Vitreous: Vitreous:
cavitation   liquefaction
detachment

379.22 Crystalline deposits in vitreous
Asteroid hyalitis   Synchysis scintillans

379.23 Vitreous hemorrhage
AHA: 3Q, '91, 15

379.24 Other vitreous opacities
Vitreous floaters

379.25 Vitreous membranes and strands

√4th √5th Additional Digit Required   RUG III Special Care Dx   RUG III Clinically Complex Dx   Hospice Non-cancer Dx   **CD PDx** Clinical Dimension PDx   **CD SDx** Clinical Dimension SDx

2006 ICD•9•CM   Volume 1 — 103

379.26 Vitreous prolapse

DEF: Slipping of vitreous from normal position.

379.29 Other disorders of vitreous

EXCLUDES *vitreous abscess (360.04)*

AHA: 1Q, '99, 11

✓5th **379.3 Aphakia and other disorders of lens**

EXCLUDES *after-cataract (366.50-366.53)*

379.31 Aphakia

EXCLUDES *cataract extraction status (V45.61)*

DEF: Absence of eye's crystalline lens.

379.32 Subluxation of lens

379.33 Anterior dislocation of lens

DEF: Lens displaced toward iris.

379.34 Posterior dislocation of lens

DEF: Lens displaced backward toward vitreous.

379.39 Other disorders of lens

✓5th **379.4 Anomalies of pupillary function**

379.40 Abnormal pupillary function, unspecified

379.41 Anisocoria

DEF: Unequal pupil diameter.

379.42 Miosis (persistent), not due to miotics

DEF: Abnormal contraction of pupil less than 2 millimeters.

379.43 Mydriasis (persistent), not due to mydriatics

DEF: Morbid dilation of pupil.

379.45 Argyll Robertson pupil, atypical

Argyll Robertson phenomenon or pupil, nonsyphilitic

EXCLUDES *Argyll Robertson pupil (syphilitic) (094.89)*

DEF: Failure of pupil to respond to light; affects both eyes; may be caused by diseases such as syphilis of the central nervous system or miosis.

379.46 Tonic pupillary reaction

Adie's pupil or syndrome

379.49 Other

Hippus   Pupillary paralysis

✓5th **379.5 Nystagmus and other irregular eye movements**

379.50 Nystagmus, unspecified

AHA: 4Q, '02, 68; 2Q, '01, 21

DEF: Involuntary, rapid, rhythmic movement of eyeball; vertical, horizontal, rotatory or mixed; cause may be congenital, acquired, physiological, neurological, myopathic, or due to ocular diseases.

379.51 Congenital nystagmus

379.52 Latent nystagmus

379.53 Visual deprivation nystagmus

379.54 Nystagmus associated with disorders of the vestibular system

379.55 Dissociated nystagmus

379.56 Other forms of nystagmus

379.57 Deficiencies of saccadic eye movements

Abnormal optokinetic response

DEF: Saccadic eye movements; small, rapid, involuntary movements by both eyes simultaneously, due to changing point of fixation on visualized object.

379.58 Deficiencies of smooth pursuit movements

379.59 Other irregularities of eye movements

Opsoclonus

379.8 Other specified disorders of eye and adnexa

✓5th **379.9 Unspecified disorder of eye and adnexa**

379.90 Disorder of eye, unspecified

379.91 Pain in or around eye

379.92 Swelling or mass of eye

Ear and Mastoid Process

Helix · External auditory meatus · Antihelix · Concha · Tragus · Mastoid process · Antitragus

379.93 Redness or discharge of eye

379.99 Other ill-defined disorders of eye

EXCLUDES *blurred vision NOS (368.8)*

DISEASES OF THE EAR AND MASTOID PROCESS (380-389)

✓4th **380 Disorders of external ear**

✓5th **380.0 Perichondritis and chondritis of pinna**

Chondritis of auricle

Perichondritis of auricle

380.00 Perichondritis of pinna, unspecified

380.01 Acute perichondritis of pinna

380.02 Chronic perichondritis of pinna

380.03 Chondritis of pinna

DEF: ►Infection that has progressed into the cartilage; presents as indurated and edematous skin over the pinna; vascular compromise occurs with tissue necrosis and deformity.◄

AHA: ►4Q, '04, 76◄

✓5th **380.1 Infective otitis externa**

380.10 Infective otitis externa, unspecified

Otitis externa (acute):   Otitis externa (acute):
NOS   hemorrhagica
circumscribed   infective NOS
diffuse

380.11 Acute infection of pinna

EXCLUDES *furuncular otitis externa (680.0)*

380.12 Acute swimmers' ear

Beach ear   Tank ear

DEF: Otitis externa due to swimming.

380.13 Other acute infections of external ear

Code first underlying disease, as:
erysipelas (035)
impetigo (684)
seborrheic dermatitis (690.10-690.18)

EXCLUDES *herpes simplex (054.73)*
herpes zoster (053.71)

380.14 Malignant otitis externa

DEF: Severe necrotic otitis externa; due to bacteria.

380.15 Chronic mycotic otitis externa

Code first underlying disease, as:
aspergillosis (117.3)
otomycosis NOS (111.9)

EXCLUDES *candidal otitis externa (112.82)*

380.16 Other chronic infective otitis externa

Chronic infective otitis externa NOS

✓5th **380.2 Other otitis externa**

380.21 Cholesteatoma of external ear

Keratosis obturans of external ear (canal)

EXCLUDES *cholesteatoma NOS (385.30-385.35)*
postmastoidectomy (383.32)

DEF: Cystlike mass filled with debris, including cholesterol; rare, congenital condition.

380.22 Other acute otitis externa

Acute otitis externa: Acute otitis externa:
actinic   eczematoid
chemical   reactive
contact

N Newborn Age: 0   P Pediatric Age: 0-17   M Maternity Age: 12-55   A Adult Age: 15-124 | Manifestation Code | ►◄ Revised Text   ● New Code   ▲ Revised Code Title

380.23 Other chronic otitis externa
Chronic otitis externa NOS

√5ᵗʰ **380.3 Noninfectious disorders of pinna**

380.30 Disorder of pinna, unspecified

380.31 Hematoma of auricle or pinna

380.32 Acquired deformities of auricle or pinna
> EXCLUDES   *cauliflower ear (738.7)*
>
> **AHA:** 3Q, '03, 12

380.39 Other
> EXCLUDES   *gouty tophi of ear (274.81)*

380.4 Impacted cerumen
Wax in ear

√5ᵗʰ **380.5 Acquired stenosis of external ear canal**
Collapse of external ear canal

380.50 Acquired stenosis of external ear canal, unspecified as to cause

380.51 Secondary to trauma
> DEF: Narrowing of the external ear canal; due to trauma.

380.52 Secondary to surgery
> DEF: Postsurgical narrowing of the external ear canal.

380.53 Secondary to inflammation
> DEF: Narrowing of the external ear canal; due to chronic inflammation.

√5ᵗʰ **380.8 Other disorders of external ear**

380.81 Exostosis of external ear canal

380.89 Other

380.9 Unspecified disorder of external ear

√4ᵗʰ **381 Nonsuppurative otitis media and Eustachian tube disorders**

√5ᵗʰ **381.0 Acute nonsuppurative otitis media**
Acute tubotympanic catarrh
Otitis media, acute or subacute:
   catarrhal
   exudative
   transudative
   with effusion
> EXCLUDES   *otitic barotrauma (993.0)*

381.00 Acute nonsuppurative otitis media, unspecified

381.01 Acute serous otitis media
Acute or subacute secretory otitis media
> DEF: Sudden, severe infection of the middle ear.

381.02 Acute mucoid otitis media
Acute or subacute seromucinous otitis media
Blue drum syndrome
> DEF: Sudden, severe infection of the middle ear, with mucous.

381.03 Acute sanguinous otitis media
> DEF: Sudden, severe infection of the middle ear, with blood.

381.04 Acute allergic serous otitis media

381.05 Acute allergic mucoid otitis media

381.06 Acute allergic sanguinous otitis media

√5ᵗʰ **381.1 Chronic serous otitis media**
Chronic tubotympanic catarrh

381.10 Chronic serous otitis media, simple or unspecified
> DEF: Persistent infection of the middle ear, without pus.

381.19 Other
Serosanguinous chronic otitis media

√5ᵗʰ **381.2 Chronic mucoid otitis media**
Glue ear
> EXCLUDES   *adhesive middle ear disease (385.10-385.19)*
>
> DEF: Chronic condition; characterized by viscous fluid in middle ear; due to obstructed Eustachian tube.

381.20 Chronic mucoid otitis media, simple or unspecified

381.29 Other
Mucosanguinous chronic otitis media

381.3 Other and unspecified chronic nonsuppurative otitis media
Otitis media, chronic: Otitis media, chronic:
   allergic   seromucinous
   exudative   transudative
   secretory   with effusion

381.4 Nonsuppurative otitis media, not specified as acute or chronic
Otitis media: Otitis media:
   allergic   seromucinous
   catarrhal   serous
   exudative   transudative
   mucoid   with effusion
   secretory

√5ᵗʰ **381.5 Eustachian salpingitis**

381.50 Eustachian salpingitis, unspecified

381.51 Acute Eustachian salpingitis
> DEF: Sudden, severe inflammation of the Eustachian tube.

381.52 Chronic Eustachian salpingitis
> DEF: Persistent inflammation of the Eustachian tube.

√5ᵗʰ **381.6 Obstruction of Eustachian tube**
Stenosis   } of Eustachian tube
Stricture

381.60 Obstruction of Eustachian tube, unspecified

381.61 Osseous obstruction of Eustachian tube
Obstruction of Eustachian tube from cholesteatoma, polyp, or other osseous lesion

381.62 Intrinsic cartilagenous obstruction of Eustachian tube
> DEF: Blockage of Eustachian tube; due to cartilage overgrowth.

381.63 Extrinsic cartilagenous obstruction of Eustachian tube
Compression of Eustachian tube

381.7 Patulous Eustachian tube
> DEF: Distended, oversized Eustachian tube.

√5ᵗʰ **381.8 Other disorders of Eustachian tube**

381.81 Dysfunction of Eustachian tube

381.89 Other

381.9 Unspecified Eustachian tube disorder

√4ᵗʰ **382 Suppurative and unspecified otitis media**

√5ᵗʰ **382.0 Acute suppurative otitis media**
Otitis media, acute: Otitis media, acute:
   necrotizing NOS   purulent

382.00 Acute suppurative otitis media without spontaneous rupture of ear drum
> DEF: Sudden, severe inflammation of middle ear, with pus.

382.01 Acute suppurative otitis media with spontaneous rupture of ear drum
> DEF: Sudden, severe inflammation of middle ear, with pressure tearing ear drum tissue.

382.02 *Acute suppurative otitis media in diseases classified elsewhere*
> *Code first underlying disease, as:*
>   influenza (487.8)
>   scarlet fever (034.1)
> EXCLUDES   *postmeasles otitis (055.2)*

382.1 Chronic tubotympanic suppurative otitis media
Benign chronic   } (with anterior
  suppurative otitis media   perforation
Chronic tubotympanic disease } of ear drum)
> DEF: Inflammation of tympanic cavity and auditory tube; with pus formation.

√4ᵗʰ
√5ᵗʰ Additional Digit Required   RUG III Special Care Dx   RUG III Clinically Complex Dx   Hospice Non-cancer Dx   **CD PDx** Clinical Dimension PDx   **CD SDx** Clinical Dimension SDx

2006 ICD•9•CM   **Volume 1 — 105**

Nervous System and Sense Organs

382.2–385.02

Middle and Inner Ear

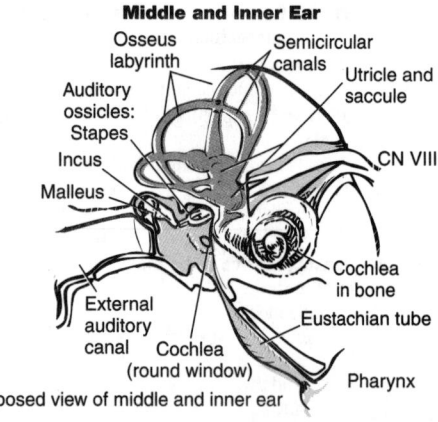

Osseus labyrinth
Semicircular canals
Utricle and saccule
Auditory ossicles:
Stapes
Incus
Malleus
CN VIII
Cochlea in bone
External auditory canal
Cochlea (round window)
Eustachian tube
Pharynx

Exposed view of middle and inner ear

382.2 Chronic atticoantral suppurative otitis media

Chronic atticoantral disease   } (with posterior or superior marginal perforation of ear drum)

Persistent mucosal disease

382.3 Unspecified chronic suppurative otitis media
Chronic purulent otitis media

EXCLUDES   *tuberculous otitis media (017.4)*

DEF: Inflammation of upper tympanic membrane and mastoid antrum; with pus formation.

382.4 Unspecified suppurative otitis media
Purulent otitis media NOS

382.9 Unspecified otitis media

Otitis media: Otitis media:
   NOS   chronic NOS
   acute NOS

AHA: N-D, '84, 16

√4ᵗʰ **383 Mastoiditis and related conditions**

√5ᵗʰ **383.0 Acute mastoiditis**
Abscess of mastoid   Empyema of mastoid

383.00 Acute mastoiditis without complications
DEF: Sudden, severe inflammation of mastoid air cells.

383.01 Subperiosteal abscess of mastoid
DEF: Pocket of pus within the mastoid bone.

383.02 Acute mastoiditis with other complications
Gradenigo's syndrome

383.1 Chronic mastoiditis
Caries of mastoid
Fistula of mastoid

EXCLUDES   *tuberculous mastoiditis (015.6)*

DEF: Persistent inflammation of the mastoid air cells.

√5ᵗʰ **383.2 Petrositis**

Coalescing osteitis
Inflammation   } of petrous bone
Osteomyelitis

383.20 Petrositis, unspecified
383.21 Acute petrositis
DEF: Sudden, severe inflammation of dense bone behind the ear.

383.22 Chronic petrositis
DEF: Persistent inflammation of dense bone behind the ear.

√5ᵗʰ **383.3 Complications following mastoidectomy**
383.30 Postmastoidectomy complication, unspecified
383.31 Mucosal cyst of postmastoidectomy cavity
DEF: Mucous-lined cyst cavity following removal of mastoid bone.

383.32 Recurrent cholesteatoma of postmastoidectomy cavity
DEF: Cystlike mass of cell debris in cavity following removal of mastoid bone.

383.33 Granulations of postmastoidectomy cavity
Chronic inflammation of postmastoidectomy cavity
DEF: Granular tissue in cavity following removal of mastoid bone.

√5ᵗʰ **383.8 Other disorders of mastoid**
383.81 Postauricular fistula
DEF: Abnormal passage behind mastoid cavity.

383.89 Other
383.9 Unspecified mastoiditis

√4ᵗʰ **384 Other disorders of tympanic membrane**
√5ᵗʰ **384.0 Acute myringitis without mention of otitis media**
384.00 Acute myringitis, unspecified
Acute tympanitis NOS
DEF: Sudden, severe inflammation of ear drum.

384.01 Bullous myringitis
Myringitis bullosa hemorrhagica
DEF: Type of viral otitis media characterized by the appearance of serous or hemorrhagic blebs on the tympanic membrane.

384.09 Other
384.1 Chronic myringitis without mention of otitis media
Chronic tympanitis
DEF: Persistent inflammation of ear drum; with no evidence of middle ear infection.

√5ᵗʰ **384.2 Perforation of tympanic membrane**
Perforation of ear drum: Perforation of ear drum:
   NOS   postinflammatory
   persistent   posttraumatic

EXCLUDES   *otitis media with perforation of tympanic membrane (382.00-382.9)*
traumatic perforation [current injury] (872.61)

384.20 Perforation of tympanic membrane, unspecified
384.21 Central perforation of tympanic membrane
384.22 Attic perforation of tympanic membrane
Pars flaccida
384.23 Other marginal perforation of tympanic membrane
384.24 Multiple perforations of tympanic membrane
384.25 Total perforation of tympanic membrane

√5ᵗʰ **384.8 Other specified disorders of tympanic membrane**
384.81 Atrophic flaccid tympanic membrane
Healed perforation of ear drum
384.82 Atrophic nonflaccid tympanic membrane

384.9 Unspecified disorder of tympanic membrane

√4ᵗʰ **385 Other disorders of middle ear and mastoid**
EXCLUDES   *mastoiditis (383.0-383.9)*

√5ᵗʰ **385.0 Tympanosclerosis**
385.00 Tympanosclerosis, unspecified as to involvement
385.01 Tympanosclerosis involving tympanic membrane only
DEF: Tough, fibrous tissue impeding functions of ear drum.

385.02 Tympanosclerosis involving tympanic membrane and ear ossicles
DEF: Tough, fibrous tissue impeding functions of middle ear bones (stapes, malleus, incus).

Ⓝ Newborn Age: 0   Ⓟ Pediatric Age: 0-17   Ⓜ Maternity Age: 12-55   Ⓐ Adult Age: 15-124   Manifestation Code   ◄ Revised Text   ● New Code   ▲ Revised Code Title

106 — Volume 1   *2006 ICD•9•CM*

385.03 Tympanosclerosis involving tympanic membrane, ear ossicles, and middle ear

DEF: Tough, fibrous tissue impeding functions of ear drum, middle ear bones and middle ear canal.

385.09 Tympanosclerosis involving other combination of structures

√5ᵗʰ **385.1 Adhesive middle ear disease**

Adhesive otitis   Otitis media:
Otitis media: fibrotic
  chronic adhesive

EXCLUDES   *glue ear (381.20-381.29)*

DEF: Adhesions of middle ear structures.

385.10 Adhesive middle ear disease, unspecified as to involvement

385.11 Adhesions of drum head to incus

385.12 Adhesions of drum head to stapes

385.13 Adhesions of drum head to promontorium

385.19 Other adhesions and combinations

√5ᵗʰ **385.2 Other acquired abnormality of ear ossicles**

385.21 Impaired mobility of malleus

Ankylosis of malleus

385.22 Impaired mobility of other ear ossicles

Ankylosis of ear ossicles, except malleus

385.23 Discontinuity or dislocation of ear ossicles

DEF: Disruption in auditory chain; created by malleus, incus and stapes.

385.24 Partial loss or necrosis of ear ossicles

DEF: Tissue loss in malleus, incus and stapes.

√5ᵗʰ **385.3 Cholesteatoma of middle ear and mastoid**

Cholesterosis
Epidermosis   } of (middle) ear
Keratosis
Polyp

EXCLUDES   *cholesteatoma:*
      external ear canal (380.21)
      recurrent of postmastoidectomy cavity (383.32)

DEF: Cystlike mass of middle ear and mastoid antrum filled with debris, including cholesterol.

385.30 Cholesteatoma, unspecified

385.31 Cholesteatoma of attic

385.32 Cholesteatoma of middle ear

385.33 Cholesteatoma of middle ear and mastoid

AHA: 3Q, '00, 10

DEF: Cystlike mass of cell debris in middle ear and mastoid air cells behind ear.

385.35 Diffuse cholesteatosis

√5ᵗʰ **385.8 Other disorders of middle ear and mastoid**

385.82 Cholesterin granuloma

DEF: Granuloma formed of fibrotic tissue; contains cholesterol crystals surrounded by foreign-body cells; found in the middle ear and mastoid area.

Cholesteatoma

Middle ear chamber

Cholesteatoma   Ear drum
sac

385.83 Retained foreign body of middle ear

AHA: 3Q, '94, 7; N-D, '87, 9

385.89 Other

385.9 Unspecified disorder of middle ear and mastoid

√4ᵗʰ **386 Vertiginous syndromes and other disorders of vestibular system**

EXCLUDES   *vertigo NOS (780.4)*

AHA: M-A, '85, 12

√5ᵗʰ **386.0 Ménière's disease**

Endolymphatic hydrops
Lermoyez's syndrome
Ménière's syndrome or vertigo

DEF: Distended membranous labyrinth of middle ear from endolymphatic hydrops; causes ischemia, failure of nerve function; hearing and balance dysfunction; symptoms include fluctuating deafness, ringing in ears and dizziness.

386.00 Ménière's disease, unspecified

Ménière's disease (active)

386.01 Active Ménière's disease, cochleovestibular

386.02 Active Ménière's disease, cochlear

386.03 Active Ménière's disease, vestibular

386.04 Inactive Ménière's disease

Ménière's disease in remission

√5ᵗʰ **386.1 Other and unspecified peripheral vertigo**

EXCLUDES   *epidemic vertigo (078.81)*

386.10 Peripheral vertigo, unspecified

386.11 Benign paroxysmal positional vertigo

Benign paroxysmal positional nystagmus

386.12 Vestibular neuronitis

Acute (and recurrent) peripheral vestibulopathy

DEF: Transient benign vertigo, unknown cause; characterized by response to caloric stimulation on one side, nystagmus with rhythmic movement of eyes; normal auditory function present; occurs in young adults.

386.19 Other

Aural vertigo
Otogenic vertigo

386.2 Vertigo of central origin

Central positional nystagmus
Malignant positional vertigo

√5ᵗʰ **386.3 Labyrinthitis**

386.30 Labyrinthitis, unspecified

386.31 Serous labyrinthitis

Diffuse labyrinthitis

DEF: Inflammation of labyrinth; with fluid buildup.

386.32 Circumscribed labyrinthitis

Focal labyrinthitis

386.33 Suppurative labyrinthitis

Purulent labyrinthitis

DEF: Inflammation of labyrinth; with pus.

386.34 Toxic labyrinthitis

DEF: Inflammation of labyrinth; due to toxic reaction.

386.35 Viral labyrinthitis

√5ᵗʰ **386.4 Labyrinthine fistula**

386.40 Labyrinthine fistula, unspecified

386.41 Round window fistula

386.42 Oval window fistula

386.43 Semicircular canal fistula

386.48 Labyrinthine fistula of combined sites

√5ᵗʰ **386.5 Labyrinthine dysfunction**

386.50 Labyrinthine dysfunction, unspecified

386.51 Hyperactive labyrinth, unilateral

DEF: Abnormal increased sensitivity of labyrinth to stimuli such as sound, pressure or gravitational change, affecting one ear.

√4ᵗʰ
√5ᵗʰ Additional Digit Required   **RUG III Special Care Dx**   **RUG III Clinically Complex Dx**   Hospice Non-cancer Dx   **CD PDx** Clinical Dimension PDx   **CD SDx** Clinical Dimension SDx

2006 ICD•9•CM   Volume 1 — 107

Nervous System and Sense Organs

386.52–389.9

386.52 Hyperactive labyrinth, bilateral

DEF: Abnormal increased sensitivity of labyrinth to stimuli such as sound, pressure or gravitational change, affecting both ears.

386.53 Hypoactive labyrinth, unilateral

DEF: Abnormal decreased sensitivity of labyrinth to stimuli such as sound, pressure or gravitational change, affecting one ear.

386.54 Hypoactive labyrinth, bilateral

Abnormal decreased sensitivity of labyrinth to stimuli such as sound, pressure or gravitational change, affecting both ears.

386.55 Loss of labyrinthine reactivity, unilateral

DEF: Decreased function of the labyrinth sensors, affecting one ear.

386.56 Loss of labyrinthine reactivity, bilateral

DEF: Decreased function of the labyrinth sensors, affecting both ears.

386.58 Other forms and combinations

386.8 Other disorders of labyrinth

386.9 Unspecified vertiginous syndromes and labyrinthine disorders

√4th **387 Otosclerosis**

INCLUDES   otospongiosis

DEF: Synonym for otospongiosis, spongy bone formation in the labyrinth bones of the ear; it causes progressive hearing impairment.

387.0 Otosclerosis involving oval window, nonobliterative

DEF: Tough, fibrous tissue impeding functions of oval window.

387.1 Otosclerosis involving oval window, obliterative

DEF: Tough, fibrous tissue blocking oval window.

387.2 Cochlear otosclerosis

Otosclerosis involving: Otosclerosis involving:
  otic capsule   round window

DEF: Tough, fibrous tissue impeding functions of cochlea.

387.8 Other otosclerosis

387.9 Otosclerosis, unspecified

√4th **388 Other disorders of ear**

√5th **388.0 Degenerative and vascular disorders of ear**

388.00 Degenerative and vascular disorders, unspecified

388.01 Presbyacusis

DEF: Progressive, bilateral perceptive hearing loss caused by advancing age; it is also known as presbycusis.

388.02 Transient ischemic deafness

DEF: Restricted blood flow to auditory organs causing temporary hearing loss.

√5th **388.1 Noise effects on inner ear**

388.10 Noise effects on inner ear, unspecified

388.11 Acoustic trauma (explosive) to ear

Otitic blast injury

388.12 Noise-induced hearing loss

388.2 Sudden hearing loss, unspecified

√5th **388.3 Tinnitus**

DEF: Abnormal noises in ear; may be heard by others beside the affected individual; noises include ringing, clicking, roaring and buzzing.

388.30 Tinnitus, unspecified

388.31 Subjective tinnitus

388.32 Objective tinnitus

√5th **388.4 Other abnormal auditory perception**

388.40 Abnormal auditory perception, unspecified

388.41 Diplacusis

DEF: Perception of a single auditory sound as two sounds at two different levels of intensity.

388.42 Hyperacusis

DEF: Exceptionally acute sense of hearing caused by such conditions as Bell's palsy; this term may also refer to painful sensitivity to sounds.

388.43 Impairment of auditory discrimination

DEF: Impaired ability to distinguish tone of sound.

388.44 Recruitment

DEF: Perception of abnormally increased loudness caused by a slight increase in sound intensity; it is a term used in audiology.

388.5 Disorders of acoustic nerve

Acoustic neuritis
Degeneration   } of acoustic or eighth nerve
Disorder

EXCLUDES   acoustic neuroma (225.1)
     syphilitic acoustic neuritis (094.86)

AHA: M-A, '87, 8

√5th **388.6 Otorrhea**

388.60 Otorrhea, unspecified

Discharging ear NOS

388.61 Cerebrospinal fluid otorrhea

EXCLUDES   cerebrospinal fluid rhinorrhea (349.81)

DEF: Spinal fluid leakage from ear.

388.69 Other

Otorrhagia

√5th **388.7 Otalgia**

388.70 Otalgia, unspecified

Earache NOS

388.71 Otogenic pain

388.72 Referred pain

388.8 Other disorders of ear

388.9 Unspecified disorder of ear

√4th **389 Hearing loss**

√5th **389.0 Conductive hearing loss**

Conductive deafness

AHA: 4Q, '89, 5

DEF: Dysfunction in sound-conducting structures of external or middle ear causing hearing loss.

389.00 Conductive hearing loss, unspecified

389.01 Conductive hearing loss, external ear

389.02 Conductive hearing loss, tympanic membrane

389.03 Conductive hearing loss, middle ear

389.04 Conductive hearing loss, inner ear

389.08 Conductive hearing loss of combined types

√5th **389.1 Sensorineural hearing loss**

Perceptive hearing loss or deafness

EXCLUDES   abnormal auditory perception (388.40-388.44)
     psychogenic deafness (306.7)

AHA: 4Q, '89, 5

DEF: Nerve conduction causing hearing loss.

389.10 Sensorineural hearing loss, unspecified

AHA: 1Q, '93, 29

389.11 Sensory hearing loss

389.12 Neural hearing loss

389.14 Central hearing loss

389.18 Sensorineural hearing loss of combined types

389.2 Mixed conductive and sensorineural hearing loss

Deafness or hearing loss of type classifiable to 389.0 with type classifiable to 389.1

389.7 Deaf mutism, not elsewhere classifiable

Deaf, nonspeaking

389.8 Other specified forms of hearing loss

389.9 Unspecified hearing loss

Deafness NOS

AHA: ▶1Q, '04, 15◀

N Newborn Age: 0   P Pediatric Age: 0-17   M Maternity Age: 12-55   A Adult Age: 15-124 | Manifestation Code | ▶◀ Revised Text   ● New Code   ▲ Revised Code Title

7. DISEASES OF THE CIRCULATORY SYSTEM (390-459)

ACUTE RHEUMATIC FEVER (390-392)

DEF: Febrile disease occurs mainly in children or young adults following throat infection by group A *streptococci*; symptoms include fever, joint pain, lesions of heart, blood vessels and joint connective tissue, abdominal pain, skin changes, and chorea.

390 Rheumatic fever without mention of heart involvement

Arthritis, rheumatic, acute or subacute

Rheumatic fever (active) (acute)

Rheumatism, articular, acute or subacute

EXCLUDES *that with heart involvement (391.0-391.9)*

√4ᵗʰ 391 Rheumatic fever with heart involvement

EXCLUDES *chronic heart diseases of rheumatic origin (398.0-398.9) unless rheumatic fever is also present or there is evidence of recrudescence or activity of the rheumatic process*

391.0 Acute rheumatic pericarditis

Rheumatic:

  fever (active) (acute) with pericarditis

  pericarditis (acute)

Any condition classifiable to 390 with pericarditis

EXCLUDES *that not specified as rheumatic (420.0-420.9)*

DEF: Sudden, severe inflammation of heart lining due to rheumatic fever.

391.1 Acute rheumatic endocarditis

Rheumatic:

  endocarditis, acute

  fever (active) (acute) with endocarditis or valvulitis

  valvulitis acute

Any condition classifiable to 390 with endocarditis or valvulitis

DEF: Sudden, severe inflammation of heart cavities due to rheumatic fever.

391.2 Acute rheumatic myocarditis

Rheumatic fever (active) (acute) with myocarditis

Any condition classifiable to 390 with myocarditis

DEF: Sudden, severe inflammation of heart muscles due to rheumatic fever.

391.8 Other acute rheumatic heart disease

Rheumatic:

  fever (active) (acute) with other or multiple types of heart involvement

  pancarditis, acute

Any condition classifiable to 390 with other or multiple types of heart involvement

391.9 Acute rheumatic heart disease, unspecified

Rheumatic:

  carditis, acute

  fever (active) (acute) with unspecified type of heart involvement

  heart disease, active or acute

Any condition classifiable to 390 with unspecified type of heart involvement

√4ᵗʰ 392 Rheumatic chorea

INCLUDES Sydenham's chorea

EXCLUDES chorea:

  NOS (333.5)

  Huntington's (333.4)

DEF: Childhood disease linked with rheumatic fever and streptococcal infections; symptoms include spasmodic, involuntary movements of limbs or facial muscles, psychic symptoms, and irritability.

392.0 With heart involvement   **CD PDx**

Rheumatic chorea with heart involvement of any type classifiable to 391

392.9 Without mention of heart involvement   **CD PDx**

CHRONIC RHEUMATIC HEART DISEASE (393-398)

393 Chronic rheumatic pericarditis

Adherent pericardium, rheumatic

Chronic rheumatic:

  mediastinopericarditis   myopericarditis

EXCLUDES *pericarditis NOS or not specified as rheumatic (423.0-423.9)*

DEF: Persistent inflammation of heart lining due to rheumatic heart disease.

√4ᵗʰ 394 Diseases of mitral valve

EXCLUDES *that with aortic valve involvement (396.0-396.9)*

394.0 Mitral stenosis

Mitral (valve):   Mitral (valve):

  obstruction (rheumatic)   stenosis NOS

DEF: Narrowing, of mitral valve between left atrium and left ventricle; due to rheumatic heart disease.

394.1 Rheumatic mitral insufficiency

Rheumatic mitral: Rheumatic mitral:

  incompetence   regurgitation

EXCLUDES *that not specified as rheumatic (424.0)*

DEF: Malfunction of mitral valve between left atrium and left ventricle; due to rheumatic heart disease.

394.2 Mitral stenosis with insufficiency

Mitral stenosis with incompetence or regurgitation

DEF: A narrowing or stricture of the mitral valve situated between the left atrium and left ventricle. The stenosis interferes with blood flow from the atrium into the ventricle. If the valve does not completely close, it becomes insufficient (inadequate) and cannot prevent regurgitation (abnormal backward flow) into the atrium when the left ventricle contracts. This abnormal function is also called incompetence.

394.9 Other and unspecified mitral valve diseases

Mitral (valve):   Mitral (valve):

  disease (chronic)   failure

√4ᵗʰ 395 Diseases of aortic valve

EXCLUDES *that not specified as rheumatic (424.1)*

          that with mitral valve involvement (396.0-396.9)

395.0 Rheumatic aortic stenosis

Rheumatic aortic (valve) obstruction

AHA: 4Q, '88, 8

DEF: Narrowing of the aortic valve; results in backflow into ventricle; due to rheumatic heart disease.

395.1 Rheumatic aortic insufficiency

Rheumatic aortic: Rheumatic aortic:

  incompetence   regurgitation

DEF: Malfunction of the aortic valve; results in backflow into left ventricle; due to rheumatic heart disease.

395.2 Rheumatic aortic stenosis with insufficiency

Rheumatic aortic stenosis with incompetence or regurgitation

DEF: Malfunction and narrowing, of the aortic valve; results in backflow into left ventricle; due to rheumatic heart disease.

395.9 Other and unspecified rheumatic aortic diseases

Rheumatic aortic (valve) disease

√4ᵗʰ 396 Diseases of mitral and aortic valves

INCLUDES involvement of both mitral and aortic valves, whether specified as rheumatic or not

AHA: N-D, '87, 8

396.0 Mitral valve stenosis and aortic valve stenosis

Atypical aortic (valve) stenosis

Mitral and aortic (valve) obstruction (rheumatic)

396.1 Mitral valve stenosis and aortic valve insufficiency

396.2 Mitral valve insufficiency and aortic valve stenosis

AHA: 2Q, '00, 16

396.3 Mitral valve insufficiency and aortic valve insufficiency

Mitral and aortic (valve):   Mitral and aortic (valve):

  incompetence   regurgitation

√4ᵗʰ √5ᵗʰ Additional Digit Required   **RUG III Special Care Dx**   **RUG III Clinically Complex Dx**   Hospice Non-cancer Dx   **CD PDx** Clinical Dimension PDx   **CD SDx** Clinical Dimension SDx

2006 ICD•9•CM   Volume 1 — 109

396.8   **Multiple involvement of mitral and aortic valve**
Stenosis and insufficiency of mitral or aortic valve with stenosis or insufficiency, or both, of the other valve

396.9   **Mitral and aortic valve diseases, unspecified**

✓4ᵗʰ **397 Diseases of other endocardial structures**

397.0   **Diseases of tricuspid valve**

Tricuspid (valve)   Tricuspid (valve)
(rheumatic):   (rheumatic):
disease   regurgitation
insufficiency   stenosis
obstruction

AHA: 2Q, '00, 16

DEF: Malfunction of the valve between right atrium and right ventricle; due to rheumatic heart disease.

397.1   **Rheumatic diseases of pulmonary valve**
EXCLUDES   *that not specified as rheumatic (424.3)*

397.9   **Rheumatic diseases of endocardium, valve unspecified**

Rheumatic: Rheumatic:
endocarditis (chronic)   valvulitis (chronic)
EXCLUDES   *that not specified as rheumatic (424.90-424.99)*

✓4ᵗʰ **398 Other rheumatic heart disease**

398.0   **Rheumatic myocarditis**
Rheumatic degeneration of myocardium
EXCLUDES   *myocarditis not specified as rheumatic (429.0)*

DEF: Chronic inflammation of heart muscle; due to rheumatic heart disease.

✓5ᵗʰ **398.9**   **Other and unspecified rheumatic heart diseases**

398.90 Rheumatic heart disease, unspecified
Rheumatic: Rheumatic:
carditis   heart disease NOS
EXCLUDES   *carditis not specified as rheumatic (429.89)*
heart disease NOS not specified as rheumatic (429.9)

398.91 Rheumatic heart failure (congestive)
Rheumatic left ventricular failure
AHA: 1Q, '95, 6; 3Q, '88, 3
DEF: Decreased cardiac output, edema and hypertension; due to rheumatic heart disease.

398.99 Other

HYPERTENSIVE DISEASE (401-405)

EXCLUDES   *that complicating pregnancy, childbirth, or the puerperium (642.0-642.9)*
that involving coronary vessels (410.00-414.9)
AHA:: 3Q, '90, 3; 2Q, '89, 12; S-O, '87, 9; J-A, '84, 11

✓4ᵗʰ **401 Essential hypertension**
INCLUDES   high blood pressure
hyperpiesia
hyperpiesis
hypertension (arterial) (essential) (primary) (systemic)
hypertensive vascular:
degeneration   disease
EXCLUDES   *elevated blood pressure without diagnosis of hypertension (796.2)*
pulmonary hypertension (416.0-416.9)
that involving vessels of:
brain (430-438)
eye (362.11)
AHA: 2Q, '92, 5
DEF: Hypertension that occurs without apparent organic cause; idiopathic.

401.0   **Malignant**
AHA: 4Q, '97, 37; M-J, '85, 19
DEF: Severe high arterial blood pressure; results in necrosis in kidney, retina, etc.; hemorrhages occur and death commonly due to uremia or rupture of cerebral vessel.

401.1   **Benign**
DEF: Mildly elevated arterial blood pressure.

401.9   **Unspecified**
AHA: 4Q, '04, 78; 4Q, '03, 105, 108, 111; 3Q, 03, 14; 2Q, '03, 16; 4Q, '97, 37

✓4ᵗʰ **402 Hypertensive heart disease**
INCLUDES   hypertensive: hypertensive:
cardiomegaly   cardiovascular disease
cardiopathy   heart (disease) (failure)
any condition classifiable to 429.0-429.3, 429.8, 429.9 due to hypertension
Use additional code to specify type of heart failure ▶(428.0-428.43), if known◀
AHA: 4Q, '02, 49; 2Q, '93, 9; N-D, '84, 18

✓5ᵗʰ **402.0**   **Malignant**
402.00 Without heart failure
402.01 With heart failure

✓5ᵗʰ **402.1**   **Benign**
402.10 Without heart failure
402.11 With heart failure

✓5ᵗʰ **402.9**   **Unspecified**
402.90 Without heart failure
402.91 With heart failure
AHA: 4Q, '02, 52; 1Q, '93, 19; 2Q, '89, 12

▲ ✓4ᵗʰ **403 Hypertensive kidney disease**
INCLUDES   arteriolar nephritis
arteriosclerosis of:
kidney
renal arterioles
arteriosclerotic nephritis (chronic) (interstitial)
hypertensive:
nephropathy
renal failure
uremia (chronic)
nephrosclerosis
renal sclerosis with hypertension
any condition classifiable to 585, 586, or 587 with any condition classifiable to 401
EXCLUDES   *acute renal failure (584.5-584.9)*
renal disease stated as not due to hypertension
renovascular hypertension (405.0-405.9 with fifth-digit 1)
▶Use additional code to identify the stage of chronic kidney disease (585.1-585.6), if known◀

The following fifth-digit subclassification is for use with category 403:
▲   **0**   **without chronic kidney disease**
▲   **1**   **with chronic kidney disease**

AHA: 4Q, '92, 22; 2Q, '92, 5

▲ ✓5ᵗʰ **403.0**   **Malignant**
▲ ✓5ᵗʰ **403.1**   **Benign**
▲ ✓5ᵗʰ **403.9**   **Unspecified**
AHA: For code 403.91: 1Q, '04, 14; 1Q, '03, 20; 2Q, '01, 11; 3Q, '91, 8

▲ ✓4ᵗʰ **404 Hypertensive heart and kidney disease**
INCLUDES   disease:
cardiorenal
cardiovascular renal
any condition classifiable to 402 with any condition classifiable to 403
Use additional code to specify type of heart failure ▶(428.0-428.43), if known◀
▶Use additional code to identify the stage of chronic kidney disease (585.1-585.6), if known◀

The following fifth-digit subclassification is for use with category 404:
▲   **0**   **without heart failure or chronic kidney disease**
   1   **with heart failure**
▲   **2**   **with chronic kidney disease**
▲   **3**   **with heart failure and chronic kidney disease**

AHA: 4Q, '02, 49; 3Q, '90, 3; J-A, '84, 14

▲ ✓5ᵗʰ **404.0**   **Malignant**
▲ ✓5ᵗʰ **404.1**   **Benign**

Ⓝ Newborn Age: 0   Ⓟ Pediatric Age: 0-17   Ⓜ Maternity Age: 12-55   Ⓐ Adult Age: 15-124   Manifestation Code   ▶◀ Revised Text   ● New Code   ▲ Revised Code Title

▲ ✓5ᵗʰ **404.9** **Unspecified**

✓4ᵗʰ **405 Secondary hypertension**
     AHA: 3Q, '90, 3; S-O, '87, 9, 11; J-A, '84,14

DEF: High arterial blood pressure due to or with a variety of primary diseases, such as renal disorders, CNS disorders, endocrine, and vascular diseases.

✓5ᵗʰ **405.0** **Malignant**
     405.01 Renovascular
     405.09 Other

✓5ᵗʰ **405.1** **Benign**
     405.11 Renovascular
     405.19 Other

✓5ᵗʰ **405.9** **Unspecified**
     405.91 Renovascular
     405.99 Other
     AHA: 3Q, '00, 4

ISCHEMIC HEART DISEASE (410-414)

INCLUDES   that with mention of hypertension
Use additional code to identify presence of hypertension
(401.0-405.9)
AHA: J-A, '84, 5

✓4ᵗʰ **410 Acute myocardial infarction**
     INCLUDES   cardiac infarction
       coronary (artery):
         embolism
         occlusion
         rupture
         thrombosis
       infarction of heart, myocardium, or ventricle
       rupture of heart, myocardium, or ventricle
       ▶ST elevation (STEMI) and non-ST elevation
         (NSTEMI) myocardial infarction◀
       any condition classifiable to 414.1-414.9
         specified as acute or with a stated
         duration of 8 weeks or less

The following fifth-digit subclassification is for use with
category 410:
   0 episode of care unspecified
     Use when the source document does not contain
     sufficient information for the assignment of
     fifth digit 1 or 2.
   1 initial episode of care
     Use fifth-digit 1 to designate the first episode of
     care (regardless of facility site) for a newly
     diagnosed myocardial infarction. The fifth-
     digit 1 is assigned regardless of the number
     of times a patient may be transferred during
     the initial episode of care.
   2 subsequent episode of care
     Use fifth-digit 2 to designate an episode of care
     following the initial episode when the patient
     is admitted for further observation,
     evaluation or treatment for a myocardial
     infarction that has received initial treatment,
     but is still less than 8 weeks old.

AHA : 3Q, '01, 21; 3Q, '98, 15; 4Q, '97, 37; 3Q, '95, 9; 4Q, '92, 24; 1Q, '92,10; 3Q, '91, 18; 1Q, '91, 14; 3Q, '89, 3

DEF: A sudden insufficiency of blood supply to an area of the heart muscle; usually due to a coronary artery occlusion.

✓5ᵗʰ **410.0** **Of anterolateral wall**
     ▶ST elevation myocardial infarction (STEMI) of
       anterolateral wall◀

✓5ᵗʰ **410.1** **Of other anterior wall**
     Infarction:
     anterior (wall) NOS ⎤ (with contiguous portion
     anteroapical   ⎥ of intraventricular
     anteroseptal   ⎦ septum)
     ▶ST elevation myocardial infarction (STEMI) of other
       anterior wall◀
     AHA: For code 410.11: 3Q, '03, 10

✓5ᵗʰ **410.2** **Of inferolateral wall**
     ▶ST elevation myocardial infarction (STEMI) of
       inferolateral wall◀

Acute Myocardial Infarction

Anatomic Sites

Anterolateral 410.0 | Other lateral 410.5 | Posterobasal 410.6
Anteroseptal 410.1 | Postero-lateral 410.5
Inferoposterior 410.3 | Atrium only 410.8
Apical 410.1 | Other and septum 410.4 | Septum only / Papillary muscle

✓5ᵗʰ **410.3** **Of inferoposterior wall**
     ▶ST elevation myocardial infarction (STEMI) of
       inferoposterior wall◀

✓5ᵗʰ **410.4** **Of other inferior wall**
     Infarction:
     diaphragmatic wall ⎤ (with contiguous portion
     NOS   ⎥ of intraventricular
     inferior (wall) NOS ⎦ septum)
     ▶ST elevation myocardial infarction (STEMI) of other
       inferior wall◀
     AHA: 1Q, '00, 7, 26; 4Q, '99, 9; 3Q, '97, 10; **For code 410.41:** 2Q, '01, 8, 9

✓5ᵗʰ **410.5** **Of other lateral wall**
     Infarction: Infarction:
     apical-lateral   high lateral
     basal-lateral   posterolateral
     ▶ST elevation myocardial infarction (STEMI) of other
       lateral wall◀

✓5ᵗʰ **410.6** **True posterior wall infarction**
     Infarction:
     posterobasal
     strictly posterior
     ▶ST elevation myocardial infarction (STEMI) of true
       posterior wall◀

✓5ᵗʰ **410.7** **Subendocardial infarction**
     ▶Non-ST elevation myocardial infarction (NSTEMI)◀
     Nontransmural infarction
     AHA: 1Q, '00, 7

✓5ᵗʰ **410.8** **Of other specified sites**
     Infarction of:
     atrium
     papillary muscle
     septum alone
     ▶ST elevation myocardial infarction (STEMI) of other
       specified sites◀

✓5ᵗʰ **410.9** **Unspecified site**
     Acute myocardial infarction NOS
     Coronary occlusion NOS
     ▶Myocardial infarction NOS◀
     AHA: 1Q, '96, 17; 1Q, '92, 9; **For code 410.91:** 3Q '02, 5

✓4ᵗʰ **411 Other acute and subacute forms of ischemic heart disease**
     AHA: 4Q, '94, 55; 3Q, '91, 24

     411.0 **Postmyocardial infarction syndrome**
       Dressler's syndrome

DEF: Complication developing several days/weeks after myocardial infarction; symptoms include fever, leukocytosis, chest pain, evidence of pericarditis, pleurisy, and pneumonitis; tendency to recur.

     411.1 **Intermediate coronary syndrome**
       Impending infarction   Preinfarction syndrome
       Preinfarction angina   Unstable angina
       EXCLUDES   angina (pectoris) (413.9)
            decubitus (413.0)
       AHA: 2Q, '04, 3; 1Q, '03, 12; 3Q, '01, 15; 2Q, '01, 7, 9; 4Q, '98, 86; 2Q, '96, 10; 3Q, '91, 24; 1Q, '91, 14; 3Q, '90, 6; 4Q, '89, 10

DEF: A condition representing an intermediate stage between angina of effort and acute myocardial infarction. It is often documented by the physician as "unstable angina."

✓4ᵗʰ / ✓5ᵗʰ Additional Digit Required   RUG III Special Care Dx   RUG III Clinically Complex Dx   Hospice Non-cancer Dx   CD PDx Clinical Dimension PDx   CD SDx Clinical Dimension SDx

Circulatory System

411.8–414.19

✓5ᵗʰ **411.8 Other**
AHA: 3Q, '91, 18; 3Q, '89, 4

411.81 Acute coronary occlusion without myocardial infarction

Acute coronary (artery):

embolism	without or not
obstruction	resulting in
occlusion	myocardial
thrombosis	infarction

EXCLUDES obstruction without infarction due to atherosclerosis (414.00-414.07)
occlusion without infarction due to atherosclerosis (414.00-414.07)

AHA: 3Q, '91, 24; 1Q, '91, 14

DEF: Interrupted blood flow to a portion of the heart; without tissue death.

411.89 Other

Coronary insufficiency (acute)
Subendocardial ischemia

AHA: 3Q, '01, 14; 1Q, '92, 9

412 Old myocardial infarction

Healed myocardial infarction
Past myocardial infarction diagnosed on ECG [EKG] or other special investigation, but currently presenting no symptoms

AHA: 2Q, '03, 10; 2Q, '01, 9; 3Q, '98, 15; 2Q, '91, 22; 3Q, '90, 7

✓4ᵗʰ **413 Angina pectoris**

DEF: Severe constricting pain in the chest, often radiating from the precordium to the left shoulder and down the arm, due to ischemia of the heart muscle; usually caused by coronary disease; pain is often precipitated by effort or excitement.

413.0 Angina decubitus

Nocturnal angina

DEF: Angina occurring only in the recumbent position.

413.1 Prinzmetal angina

Variant angina pectoris

DEF Angina occurring when patient is recumbent; associated with ST-segment elevations.

413.9 Other and unspecified angina pectoris

Angina:	Anginal syndrome
NOS	Status anginosus
cardiac	Stenocardia
of effort	Syncope anginosa

EXCLUDES preinfarction angina (411.1)

AHA: 3Q, '02, 4; 3Q, '91, 16; 3Q, '90, 6

✓4ᵗʰ **414 Other forms of chronic ischemic heart disease**

EXCLUDES arteriosclerotic cardiovascular disease [ASCVD] (429.2)
cardiovascular:
arteriosclerosis or sclerosis (429.2)
degeneration or disease (429.2)

✓5ᵗʰ **414.0 Coronary atherosclerosis**

Arteriosclerotic heart disease [ASHD]
Atherosclerotic heart disease
Coronary (artery):
arteriosclerosis
arteritis or endarteritis
atheroma
sclerosis
stricture

EXCLUDES embolism of graft (996.72)
occlusion NOS of graft (996.72)
thrombus of graft (996.72)

AHA: 2Q, '97, 13; 2Q, '95, 17; 4Q, '94, 49; 2Q, '94, 13; 1Q, '94, 6; 3Q, '90, 7

DEF: A chronic condition marked by thickening and loss of elasticity of the coronary artery; caused by deposits of plaque containing cholesterol, lipoid material and lipophages.

Arteries of the Heart

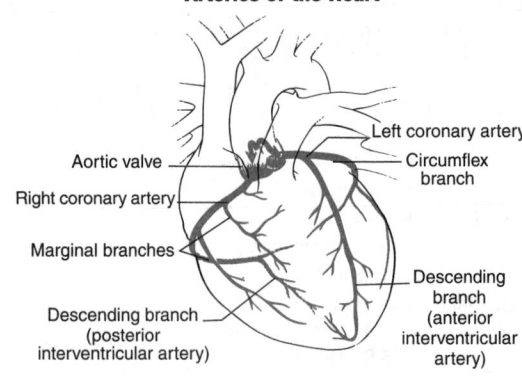

414.00 Of unspecified type of vessel, native or graft [A]
AHA: 1Q, '04, 24; 2Q, '03, 16; 3Q, '01, 15; 4Q, '99, 4; 3Q, '97, 15; 4Q, '96, 31

414.01 Of native coronary artery [A]
AHA: ▶2Q, '04, 3;◀ 4Q, '03, 105, 108; 3Q,'03, 9, 14; 3Q, '02, 4-9; 3Q, '01, 15; 2Q, '01, 8, 9; 3Q, '97, 15; 2Q, '96, 10; 4Q, '96, 31

DEF: Plaque deposits in natural heart vessels.

414.02 Of autologous vein bypass graft [A]
DEF: Plaque deposit in grafted vein originating within patient.

414.03 Of nonautologous biological bypass graft [A]
DEF: Plaque deposits in grafted vessel originating outside patient.

414.04 Of artery bypass graft [A]
Internal mammary artery
AHA: 4Q, '96, 31
DEF: Plaque deposits in grafted artery originating within patient.

414.05 Of unspecified type of bypass graft [A]
Bypass graft NOS
AHA: 3Q, '97, 15; 4Q, '96, 31

414.06 Of native coronary artery of transplanted heart
AHA: 4Q, '03, 60; 4Q, '02, 53

414.07 Of bypass graft (artery) (vein) of transplanted heart [A]

✓5ᵗʰ **414.1 Aneurysm and dissection of heart**
AHA: 4Q, '02, 54

414.10 Aneurysm of heart (wall)
Aneurysm (arteriovenous):
mural
ventricular

414.11 Aneurysm of coronary vessels
Aneurysm (arteriovenous) of coronary vessels
AHA: 3Q, '03, 10; 1Q, '99, 17
DEF: Dilatation of all three-vessel wall layers forming a sac filled with blood.

414.12 Dissection of coronary artery
DEF: A tear in the intimal arterial wall of a coronary artery resulting in the sudden intrusion of blood within the layers of the wall.

414.19 Other aneurysm of heart
Arteriovenous fistula, acquired, of heart

[N] Newborn Age: 0   [P] Pediatric Age: 0-17   [M] Maternity Age: 12-55   [A] Adult Age: 15-124   Manifestation Code   ▶◀ Revised Text   ● New Code   ▲ Revised Code Title

414.8 Other specified forms of chronic ischemic heart disease
Chronic coronary insufficiency
Ischemia, myocardial (chronic)
Any condition classifiable to 410 specified as chronic, or presenting with symptoms after 8 weeks from date of infarction
EXCLUDES *coronary insufficiency (acute) (411.89)*
AHA: 3Q, '01, 15; 1Q, '92, 10; 3Q, '90, 7; 3Q, '90, 15; 2Q, '90, 19

414.9 Chronic ischemic heart disease, unspecified
Ischemic heart disease NOS

DISEASES OF PULMONARY CIRCULATION (415-417)

√4ᵗʰ **415 Acute pulmonary heart disease**
415.0 Acute cor pulmonale
EXCLUDES *cor pulmonale NOS (416.9)*
DEF: A heart-lung disease marked by dilation and failure of the right side of heart; due to pulmonary embolism; ventilatory function is impaired and pulmonary hypertension results within hours.

√5ᵗʰ **415.1 Pulmonary embolism and infarction**
Pulmonary (artery) (vein):
apoplexy   infarction (hemorrhagic)
embolism   thrombosis
EXCLUDES *that complicating:*
abortion (634-638 with .6, 639.6)
ectopic or molar pregnancy (639.6)
pregnancy, childbirth, or the puerperium (673.0-673.8)

AHA: 4Q, '90, 25

DEF: Embolism: closure of the pulmonary artery or branch; due to thrombosis (blood clot).

DEF: Infarction: necrosis of lung tissue; due to obstructed arterial blood supply, most often by pulmonary embolism.

415.11 Iatrogenic pulmonary embolism and infarction
AHA: 4Q, '95, 58

415.19 Other

√4ᵗʰ **416 Chronic pulmonary heart disease**
416.0 Primary pulmonary hypertension
Idiopathic pulmonary arteriosclerosis
Pulmonary hypertension (essential) (idiopathic) (primary)
DEF: A rare increase in pulmonary circulation, often resulting in right ventricular failure or fatal syncope.

416.1 Kyphoscoliotic heart disease
DEF: High blood pressure within the lungs as a result of curvature of the spine.

416.8 Other chronic pulmonary heart diseases
Pulmonary hypertension, secondary

416.9 Chronic pulmonary heart disease, unspecified
Chronic cardiopulmonary disease
Cor pulmonale (chronic) NOS

√4ᵗʰ **417 Other diseases of pulmonary circulation**
417.0 Arteriovenous fistula of pulmonary vessels
EXCLUDES *congenital arteriovenous fistula (747.3)*
DEF: Abnormal communication between blood vessels within lung.

417.1 Aneurysm of pulmonary artery
EXCLUDES *congenital aneurysm (747.3)*

417.8 Other specified diseases of pulmonary circulation
Pulmonary: Pulmonary:
arteritis   endarteritis
Rupture ⎱ of pulmonary vessel
Stricture ⎰

417.9 Unspecified disease of pulmonary circulation

Anatomy

Superior vena cava
Aorta
Pulmonary artery
Pulmonary vein
Aortic valve
Pulmonary valve
Right atrium
Left atrium
Mitral valve
Tricuspid valve
Right ventricle
Chorda tendinae
Inferior vena cava
Left ventricle

Blood Flow

OTHER FORMS OF HEART DISEASE (420-429)

√4ᵗʰ **420 Acute pericarditis**
INCLUDES acute:
mediastinopericarditis
myopericarditis
pericardial effusion
pleuropericarditis
pneumopericarditis
EXCLUDES *acute rheumatic pericarditis (391.0)*
postmyocardial infarction syndrome [Dressler's] (411.0)
DEF: Inflammation of the pericardium (heart sac); pericardial friction rub results from this inflammation and is heard as a scratchy or leathery sound.

420.0 Acute pericarditis in diseases classified elsewhere
Code first underlying disease, as:
actinomycosis (039.8)
amebiasis (006.8)
nocardiosis (039.8)
tuberculosis (017.9)
uremia ▶(585.9)◀
EXCLUDES *pericarditis (acute) (in):*
Coxsackie (virus) (074.21)
gonococcal (098.83)
histoplasmosis (115.0-115.9 with fifth-digit 3)
meningococcal infection (036.41)
syphilitic (093.81)

√5ᵗʰ **420.9 Other and unspecified acute pericarditis**
420.90 Acute pericarditis, unspecified
Pericarditis (acute):   Pericarditis (acute):
NOS   sicca
infective NOS
AHA: 2Q, '89, 12

420.91 Acute idiopathic pericarditis
Pericarditis, acute: Pericarditis, acute:
benign   viral
nonspecific

√4ᵗʰ
√5ᵗʰ Additional Digit Required   RUG III Special Care Dx   RUG III Clinically Complex Dx   Hospice Non-cancer Dx   CD PDx Clinical Dimension PDx   CD SDx Clinical Dimension SDx

2006 ICD•9•CM   October 2005 • Volume 1 — 113

Circulatory System

420.99–424.0

420.99 Other

Pericarditis (acute):   Pericarditis (acute):
pneumococcal   suppurative
purulent   Pneumopyopericardium
staphylococcal   Pyopericardium
streptococcal

> **EXCLUDES** *pericarditis in diseases classified elsewhere (420.0)*

✓4ᵗʰ **421 Acute and subacute endocarditis**

DEF: Bacterial inflammation of the endocardium (intracardiac area); major symptoms include fever, fatigue, heart murmurs, splenomegaly, embolic episodes and areas of infarction.

421.0 Acute and subacute bacterial endocarditis

Endocarditis (acute)   Endocarditis (acute)
(chronic) (subacute):   (chronic) (subacute):
bacterial   ulcerative
infective NOS   vegetative
lenta   Infective aneurysm
malignant   Subacute bacterial
purulent   endocarditis [SBE]
septic

Use additional code to identify infectious organism [e.g., Streptococcus 041.0, Staphylococcus 041.1]

AHA: 1Q, '99, 12; 1Q, '91, 15

421.1 Acute and subacute infective endocarditis in diseases classified elsewhere

Code first underlying disease, as:
blastomycosis (116.0)
Q fever (083.0)
typhoid (fever) (002.0)

> **EXCLUDES** *endocarditis (in):*
> *Coxsackie (virus) (074.22)*
> *gonococcal (098.84)*
> *histoplasmosis (115.0-115.9 with fifth-digit 4)*
> *meningococcal infection (036.42)*
> *monilial (112.81)*

421.9 Acute endocarditis, unspecified

Endocarditis ⎫
Myoendocarditis ⎬ acute or subacute
Periendocarditis ⎭

> **EXCLUDES** *acute rheumatic endocarditis (391.1)*

✓4ᵗʰ **422 Acute myocarditis**

> **EXCLUDES** *acute rheumatic myocarditis (391.2)*

DEF: Acute inflammation of the muscular walls of the heart (myocardium).

422.0 Acute myocarditis in diseases classified elsewhere

Code first underlying disease, as:
myocarditis (acute):
influenzal (487.8)
tuberculous (017.9)

> **EXCLUDES** *myocarditis (acute) (due to):*
> *aseptic, of newborn (074.23)*
> *Coxsackie (virus) (074.23)*
> *diphtheritic (032.82)*
> *meningococcal infection (036.43)*
> *syphilitic (093.82)*
> *toxoplasmosis (130.3)*

✓5ᵗʰ **422.9 Other and unspecified acute myocarditis**

422.90 Acute myocarditis, unspecified

Acute or subacute (interstitial) myocarditis

422.91 Idiopathic myocarditis

Myocarditis (acute or subacute):
Fiedler's
giant cell
isolated (diffuse) (granulomatous)
nonspecific granulomatous

422.92 Septic myocarditis

Myocarditis, acute or subacute:
pneumococcal
staphylococcal

Use additional code to identify infectious organism [e.g., Staphylococcus 041.1]

> **EXCLUDES** *myocarditis, acute or subacute:*
> *in bacterial diseases classified elsewhere (422.0)*
> *streptococcal (391.2)*

422.93 Toxic myocarditis

DEF: Inflammation of the heart muscle due to an adverse reaction to certain drugs or chemicals reaching the heart through the bloodstream.

422.99 Other

✓4ᵗʰ **423 Other diseases of pericardium**

> **EXCLUDES** *that specified as rheumatic (393)*

423.0 Hemopericardium

DEF: Blood in the pericardial sac (pericardium).

423.1 Adhesive pericarditis

Adherent pericardium   Pericarditis:
Fibrosis of pericardium   adhesive
Milk spots   obliterative
                         Soldiers' patches

DEF: Two layers of serous pericardium adhere to each other by fibrous adhesions.

423.2 Constrictive pericarditis

Concato's disease   Pick's disease of heart (and liver)

DEF: Inflammation identified by a rigid, thickened and sometimes calcified pericardium; ventricles of the heart cannot be adequately filled and congestive heart failure may result.

423.8 Other specified diseases of pericardium

Calcification ⎫
Fistula   ⎬ of pericardium

AHA: 2Q, '89, 12

423.9 Unspecified disease of pericardium

✓4ᵗʰ **424 Other diseases of endocardium**

> **EXCLUDES** *bacterial endocarditis (421.0-421.9)*
> *rheumatic endocarditis (391.1, 394.0-397.9)*
> *syphilitic endocarditis (093.20-093.24)*

424.0 Mitral valve disorders

Mitral (valve):
incompetence ⎫
insufficiency ⎬ NOS of specified cause,
regurgitation ⎭   except rheumatic

> **EXCLUDES** *mitral (valve):*
> *disease (394.9)*
> *failure (394.9)*
> *stenosis (394.0)*
> *the listed conditions:*
> *specified as rheumatic (394.1)*
> *unspecified as to cause but with mention of:*
> *diseases of aortic valve (396.0-396.9)*
> *mitral stenosis or obstruction (394.2)*

AHA: 2Q, '00, 16; 3Q, '98, 11; N-D, '87, 8; N-D, '84, 8

Ⓝ Newborn Age: 0   Ⓟ Pediatric Age: 0-17   Ⓜ Maternity Age: 12-55   Ⓐ Adult Age: 15-124   Manifestation Code   ►◄ Revised Text   ● New Code   ▲ Revised Code Title

114 — Volume 1   *2006 ICD•9•CM*

424.1 Aortic valve disorders

Aortic (valve):

incompetence
insufficiency } NOS of specified
regurgitation   cause, except
stenosis   rheumatic

EXCLUDES *hypertrophic subaortic stenosis (425.1)*
that specified as rheumatic (395.0-395.9)
that of unspecified cause but with mention of diseases of mitral valve (396.0-396.9)

AHA: 4Q, '88, 8; N-D, '87, 8

424.2 Tricuspid valve disorders, specified as nonrheumatic

Tricuspid valve:

incompetence
insufficiency } of specified cause,
regurgitation   except
stenosis   rheumatic

EXCLUDES *rheumatic or of unspecified cause (397.0)*

424.3 Pulmonary valve disorders

Pulmonic: Pulmonic:
incompetence NOS   regurgitation NOS
insufficiency NOS   stenosis NOS

EXCLUDES *that specified as rheumatic (397.1)*

✓5th **424.9 Endocarditis, valve unspecified**

424.90 Endocarditis, valve unspecified, unspecified cause

Endocarditis (chronic):
NOS
nonbacterial thrombotic

Valvular:

incompetence
insufficiency } of unspecified
regurgitation   valve,
stenosis   unspecified
                 cause

Valvulitis (chronic)

424.91 *Endocarditis in diseases classified elsewhere*

Code first underlying disease as:
atypical verrucous endocarditis [Libman-Sacks] (710.0)
disseminated lupus erythematosus (710.0)
tuberculosis (017.9)

EXCLUDES *syphilitic (093.20-093.24)*

424.99 Other

Any condition classifiable to 424.90 with specified cause, except rheumatic

EXCLUDES *endocardial fibroelastosis (425.3)*
that specified as rheumatic (397.9)

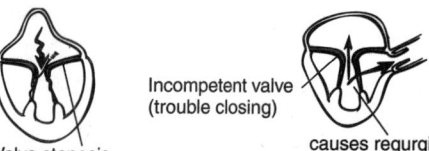

Heart Valve Disorders

Valve stenosis (trouble opening)
Incompetent valve (trouble closing)
causes regurgitation (backflow of blood)
Insuficient valve (unable to close completely)
Shortened, fused chorda tendinae
Ventricular hypertrophy

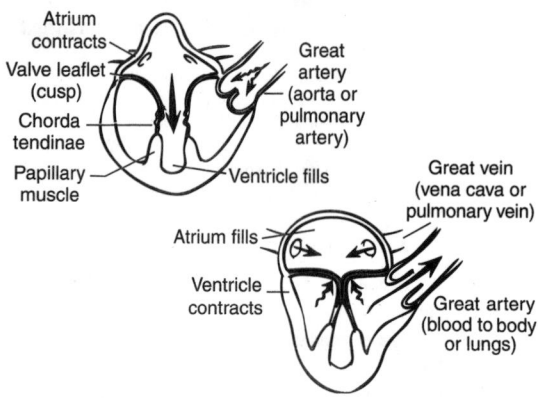

Normal Heart Valve Function

Atrium contracts
Valve leaflet (cusp)
Chorda tendinae
Papillary muscle
Great artery (aorta or pulmonary artery)
Ventricle fills
Atrium fills
Great vein (vena cava or pulmonary vein)
Ventricle contracts
Great artery (blood to body or lungs)

✓4th **425 Cardiomyopathy**

INCLUDES myocardiopathy

AHA: J-A, '85, 15

425.0 Endomyocardial fibrosis

425.1 Hypertrophic obstructive cardiomyopathy

Hypertrophic subaortic stenosis (idiopathic)

DEF: Cardiomyopathy marked by left ventricle hypertrophy, enlarged septum; results in obstructed blood flow.

425.2 Obscure cardiomyopathy of Africa

Becker's disease
Idiopathic mural endomyocardial disease

425.3 Endocardial fibroelastosis

Elastomyofibrosis

DEF: A condition marked by left ventricle hypertrophy and conversion of the endocardium into a thick fibroelastic coat; capacity of the ventricle may be reduced, but is often increased.

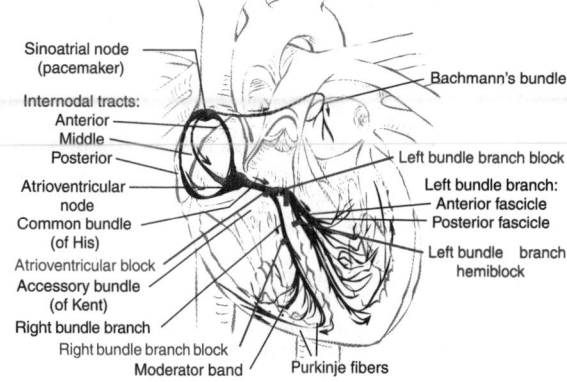

Nerve Conduction of the Heart

Sinoatrial node (pacemaker)
Internodal tracts:
Anterior
Middle
Posterior
Atrioventricular node
Common bundle (of His)
Atrioventricular block
Accessory bundle (of Kent)
Right bundle branch
Right bundle branch block
Moderator band
Bachmann's bundle
Left bundle branch block
Left bundle branch:
Anterior fascicle
Posterior fascicle
Left bundle branch hemiblock
Purkinje fibers

✓4th
✓5th Additional Digit Required   RUG III Special Care Dx   RUG III Clinically Complex Dx   Hospice Non-cancer Dx   **CD PDx** Clinical Dimension PDx   **CD SDx** Clinical Dimension SDx

2006 ICD•9•CM   **Volume 1 — 115**

Circulatory System

425.4–427.32

425.4 Other primary cardiomyopathies

Cardiomyopathy:
NOS
congestive
constrictive
familial
hypertrophic

Cardiomyopathy:
idiopathic
nonobstructive
obstructive
restrictive
Cardiovascular collagenosis

AHA: 1Q, '00, 22; 4Q, '97, 55; 2Q, '90, 19

425.5 Alcoholic cardiomyopathy

AHA: S-O, '85, 15

DEF: Heart disease as result of excess alcohol consumption.

425.7 *Nutritional and metabolic cardiomyopathy*

Code first underlying disease, as:
amyloidosis (277.3)
beriberi (265.0)
cardiac glycogenosis (271.0)
mucopolysaccharidosis (277.5)
thyrotoxicosis (242.0-242.9)

EXCLUDES   gouty tophi of heart (274.82)

425.8 *Cardiomyopathy in other diseases classified elsewhere*

Code first underlying disease, as:
Friedreich's ataxia (334.0)
myotonia atrophica (359.2)
progressive muscular dystrophy (359.1)
sarcoidosis (135)

EXCLUDES   cardiomyopathy in Chagas' disease (086.0)

AHA: 2Q, '93, 9

425.9 Secondary cardiomyopathy, unspecified

√4ᵗʰ 426 Conduction disorders

DEF: Disruption or disturbance in the electrical impulses that regulate heartbeats.

426.0 Atrioventricular block, complete

Third degree atrioventricular block

√5ᵗʰ 426.1 Atrioventricular block, other and unspecified

426.10 Atrioventricular block, unspecified
Atrioventricular [AV] block (incomplete) (partial)

426.11 First degree atrioventricular block
Incomplete atrioventricular block, first degree
Prolonged P-R interval NOS

426.12 Mobitz (type) II atrioventricular block
Incomplete atrioventricular block:
Mobitz (type) II
second degree, Mobitz (type) II

DEF: Impaired conduction of excitatory impulse from cardiac atrium to ventricle through AV node.

426.13 Other second degree atrioventricular block
Incomplete atrioventricular block:
Mobitz (type) I [Wenckebach's]
second degree:
NOS
Mobitz (type) I
with 2:1 atrioventricular response [block]
Wenckebach's phenomenon

DEF: Wenckebach's phenomenon: impulses generated at constant rate to sinus node, P-R interval lengthens; results in cycle of ventricular inadequacy and shortened P-R interval; second-degree A-V block commonly called "Mobitz type 1."

426.2 Left bundle branch hemiblock

Block:
left anterior fascicular
left posterior fascicular

426.3 Other left bundle branch block

Left bundle branch block:
NOS
anterior fascicular with posterior fascicular
complete
main stem

426.4 Right bundle branch block

AHA: 3Q, '00, 3

√5ᵗʰ 426.5 Bundle branch block, other and unspecified

426.50 Bundle branch block, unspecified

426.51 Right bundle branch block and left posterior fascicular block

426.52 Right bundle branch block and left anterior fascicular block

426.53 Other bilateral bundle branch block
Bifascicular block NOS
Bilateral bundle branch block NOS
Right bundle branch with left bundle branch block (incomplete) (main stem)

426.54 Trifascicular block

426.6 Other heart block

Intraventricular block:
NOS
diffuse
myofibrillar

Sinoatrial block
Sinoauricular block

426.7 Anomalous atrioventricular excitation

Atrioventricular conduction:
accelerated
accessory
pre-excitation
Ventricular pre-excitation
Wolff-Parkinson-White syndrome

DEF: Wolff-Parkinson-White: normal conduction pathway is bypassed; results in short P-R interval on EKG; tendency to supraventricular tachycardia.

√5ᵗʰ 426.8 Other specified conduction disorders

426.81 Lown-Ganong-Levine syndrome
Syndrome of short P-R interval, normal QRS complexes, and supraventricular tachycardias

426.82 Long QT syndrome

426.89 Other
Dissociation:
atrioventricular [AV]
interference
isorhythmic
Nonparoxysmal AV nodal tachycardia

426.9 Conduction disorder, unspecified

Heart block NOS   Stokes-Adams syndrome

√4ᵗʰ 427 Cardiac dysrhythmias

EXCLUDES   that complicating:
abortion (634-638 with .7, 639.8)
ectopic or molar pregnancy (639.8)
labor or delivery (668.1, 669.4)

AHA: J-A, '85, 15

DEF: Disruption or disturbance in the rhythm of heartbeats.

427.0 Paroxysmal supraventricular tachycardia

Paroxysmal tachycardia:
atrial [PAT]
atrioventricular [AV]

Paroxysmal tachycardia:
junctional
nodal

DEF: Rapid atrial rhythm.

427.1 Paroxysmal ventricular tachycardia

Ventricular tachycardia (paroxysmal)

AHA: 3Q, '95, 9; M-A, '86, 11

DEF: Rapid ventricular rhythm.

427.2 Paroxysmal tachycardia, unspecified

Bouveret-Hoffmann syndrome
Paroxysmal tachycardia:
essential
NOS

√5ᵗʰ 427.3 Atrial fibrillation and flutter

427.31 Atrial fibrillation
AHA: 4Q, '04, 78, 121; 3Q, '04, 7; 4Q, '03, 95, 105; 1Q, '03, 8; 2Q, '99, 17; 3Q, '95, 8

DEF: Irregular, rapid atrial contractions.

427.32 Atrial flutter
AHA: 4Q, '03, 94

DEF: Regular, rapid atrial contractions.

N Newborn Age: 0   **P** Pediatric Age: 0-17   **M** Maternity Age: 12-55   **A** Adult Age: 15-124   **Manifestation Code**   ►◄ Revised Text   ● New Code   ▲ Revised Code Title

✓5ᵗʰ 427.4 Ventricular fibrillation and flutter

427.41 Ventricular fibrillation

AHA: 3Q, '02, 5

DEF: Irregular, rapid ventricular contractions.

427.42 Ventricular flutter

DEF: Regular, rapid, ventricular contractions.

427.5 Cardiac arrest

Cardiorespiratory arrest

AHA: 3Q,'02, 5; 2Q, '00, 12; 3Q, '95, 8; 2Q, '88, 8

✓5ᵗʰ 427.6 Premature beats

427.60 Premature beats, unspecified

Ectopic beats   Premature contractions
Extrasystoles   or systoles NOS
Extrasystolic arrhythmia

427.61 Supraventricular premature beats

Atrial premature beats, contractions, or systoles

427.69 Other

Ventricular premature beats, contractions, or systoles

AHA: 4Q, '93, 42

✓5ᵗʰ 427.8 Other specified cardiac dysrhythmias

427.81 Sinoatrial node dysfunction

Sinus bradycardia: Syndrome:
   persistent   sick sinus
   severe   tachycardia-
           bradycardia

> EXCLUDES   sinus bradycardia NOS
>   (427.89)

AHA: 3Q, '00, 8

DEF: Complex cardiac arrhythmia; appears as severe sinus bradycardia, sinus bradycardia with tachycardia, or sinus bradycardia with atrioventricular block.

427.89 Other

Rhythm disorder: Rhythm disorder:
   coronary sinus   nodal
   ectopic   Wandering (atrial)
           pacemaker

> EXCLUDES   carotid sinus syncope (337.0)
>   neonatal bradycardia (779.81)
>   neonatal tachycardia (779.82)
>   reflex bradycardia (337.0)
>   tachycardia NOS (785.0)

427.9 Cardiac dysrhythmia, unspecified

Arrhythmia (cardiac) NOS

AHA: 2Q, '89, 10

✓4ᵗʰ 428 Heart failure

Code, if applicable, heart failure due to hypertension first (402.0-402.9, with fifth-digit 1 or 404.0-404.9 with fifth-digit 1 or 3)

> EXCLUDES   following cardiac surgery (429.4)
>   rheumatic (398.91)
>   that complicating:
>   abortion (634-638 with .7, 639.8)
>   ectopic or molar pregnancy (639.8)
>   labor or delivery (668.1, 669.4)

AHA: 4Q, '02, 49; 3Q, '98, 5; 2Q, '90, 16; 2Q, '90, 19; 2Q, '89, 10; 3Q, '88, 3

428.0 Congestive heart failure, unspecified

Congestive heart disease
Right heart failure (secondary to left heart failure)

> EXCLUDES   fluid overload NOS (276.6)

AHA:▶1Q, '05, 5, 9;◀ 4Q, '04, 140; 3Q, '04, 7; 4Q, '03, 109; 1Q, '03, 9; 4Q, '02, 52; 2Q, '01, 13; 4Q, '00, 48; 2Q, '00, 16; 1Q, '00, 22; 4Q, '99, 4; 1Q, '99, 11; 4Q, '97, 55; 3Q, '97, 10; 3Q, '96, 9; 3Q, '91, 18; 3Q, '91, 19; 2Q, '89, 12

DEF: Mechanical inadequacy; caused by inability of heart to pump and circulate blood; results in fluid collection in lungs, hypertension, congestion and edema of tissue.

428.1 Left heart failure

Acute edema of lung   ⎫ with heart disease NOS
Acute pulmonary edema ⎬ or heart failure
             ⎭
Cardiac asthma   Left ventricular failure

DEF: Mechanical inadequacy of left ventricle; causing fluid in lungs.

✓5ᵗʰ 428.2 Systolic heart failure

> EXCLUDES   combined systolic and diastolic heart
>   failure (428.40-428.43)

DEF: Heart failure due to a defect in expulsion of blood caused by an abnormality in systolic function, or ventricular contractile dysfunction.

428.20 Unspecified

428.21 Acute

428.22 Chronic

428.23 Acute on chronic

AHA: 1Q, '03, 9

✓5ᵗʰ 428.3 Diastolic heart failure

> EXCLUDES   combined systolic and diastolic heart
>   failure (428.40-428.43)

DEF: Heart failure due to resistance to ventricular filling caused by an abnormality in the diastolic function.

428.30 Unspecified

AHA: 4Q, '02, 52

428.31 Acute

428.32 Chronic

428.33 Acute on chronic

✓5ᵗʰ 428.4 Combined systolic and diastolic heart failure

428.40 Unspecified

428.41 Acute

AHA: 4Q, '04, 140

428.42 Chronic

428.43 Acute on chronic

AHA: 4Q, '02, 52

428.9 Heart failure, unspecified

Cardiac failure NOS   Myocardial failure NOS
Heart failure NOS   Weak heart

AHA: 2Q, '89, 10; N-D, '85, 14

✓4ᵗʰ 429 Ill-defined descriptions and complications of heart disease

429.0 Myocarditis, unspecified

Myocarditis:
   NOS   ⎫
   chronic (interstitial) ⎬ (with mention of
   fibroid   arteriosclerosis)
   senile   ⎭

Use additional code to identify presence of arteriosclerosis

> EXCLUDES   acute or subacute (422.0-422.9)
>   rheumatic (398.0)
>   acute (391.2)
>   that due to hypertension (402.0-402.9)

Echocardiography of Heart Failure

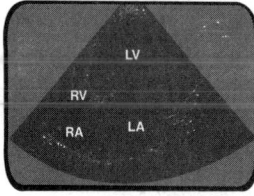

Four-chamber echocardiograms, two-dimensional views.
LV: Left ventricle
RV: Right ventricle
RA: Right atrium
LA: Left atrium

Systolic dysfunction with dilated LV

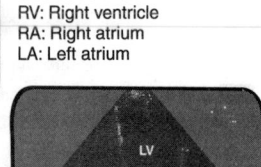

Diastolic dysfunction with LV hypertrophy

▱4ᵗʰ
▱5ᵗʰ Additional Digit Required   RUG III Special Care Dx   RUG III Clinically Complex Dx   Hospice Non-cancer Dx   **CD PDx** Clinical Dimension PDx   **CD SDx** Clinical Dimension SDx

2006 ICD•9•CM   **October 2005 • Volume 1 — 117**

Circulatory System

429.1 Myocardial degeneration
Degeneration of heart or myocardium:
  fatty
  mural
  muscular   (with mention of arteriosclerosis)
Myocardial:
  degeneration
  disease
Use additional code to identify presence of arteriosclerosis
  EXCLUDES   *that due to hypertension (402.0-402.9)*

429.2 Cardiovascular disease, unspecified
Arteriosclerotic cardiovascular disease [ASCVD]
Cardiovascular arteriosclerosis
Cardiovascular:
  degeneration
  disease   (with mention of arteriosclerosis)
  sclerosis
Use additional code to identify presence of arteriosclerosis
  EXCLUDES   *that due to hypertension (402.0-402.9)*

429.3 Cardiomegaly
Cardiac: Ventricular dilatation
  dilatation
  hypertrophy
  EXCLUDES   *that due to hypertension (402.0-402.9)*

429.4 Functional disturbances following cardiac surgery
Cardiac insufficiency   following cardiac surgery
Heart failure   or due to prosthesis
Postcardiotomy syndrome
Postvalvulotomy syndrome
  EXCLUDES   *cardiac failure in the immediate postoperative period (997.1)*
AHA: 2Q, '02, 12; N-D, '85, 6

429.5 Rupture of chordae tendineae
DEF: Torn tissue, between heart valves and papillary muscles.

429.6 Rupture of papillary muscle
DEF: Torn muscle, between chordae tendineae and heart wall.

√5ᵗʰ **429.7 Certain sequelae of myocardial infarction, not elsewhere classified**
Use additional code to identify the associated myocardial infarction:
  with onset of 8 weeks or less (410.00-410.92)
  with onset of more than 8 weeks (414.8)
  EXCLUDES   *congenital defects of heart (745, 746)*
    coronary aneurysm (414.11)
    disorders of papillary muscle (429.6, 429.81)
    postmyocardial infarction syndrome (411.0)
    rupture of chordae tendineae (429.5)
AHA: 3Q, '89, 5

429.71 Acquired cardiac septal defect   **A**
  EXCLUDES   *acute septal infarction (410.00-410.92)*
DEF: Abnormal communication, between opposite heart chambers; due to defect of septum; not present at birth.

429.79 Other   **A**
Mural thrombus (atrial) (ventricular), acquired, following myocardial infarction
AHA: 1Q, '92, 10

√5ᵗʰ **429.8 Other ill-defined heart diseases**
429.81 Other disorders of papillary muscle
Papillary muscle: Papillary muscle:
  atrophy   incompetence
  degeneration   incoordination
  dysfunction   scarring

429.82 Hyperkinetic heart disease
DEF: Condition of unknown origin in young adults; marked by increased cardiac output at rest, increased rate of ventricular ejection; may lead to heart failure.

Berry Aneurysms

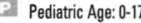

429.89 Other
Carditis
  EXCLUDES   *that due to hypertension (402.0-402.9)*
AHA: 1Q, '92, 10

429.9 Heart disease, unspecified
Heart disease (organic) NOS   Morbus cordis NOS
  EXCLUDES   *that due to hypertension (402.0-402.9)*
AHA: 1Q, '93, 19

CEREBROVASCULAR DISEASE (430-438)
  INCLUDES   with mention of hypertension (conditions classifiable to 401-405)
Use additional code to identify presence of hypertension
  EXCLUDES   *any condition classifiable to 430-434, 436, 437 occurring during pregnancy, childbirth, or the puerperium, or specified as puerperal (674.0)*
    iatrogenic cerebrovascular infarction or hemorrhage (997.02)
AHA: 1Q, '93, 27; 3Q, '90, 3; 2Q, '89, 8; M-A, '85, 6

430 **Subarachnoid hemorrhage**   **CD PDx**
Meningeal hemorrhage   Ruptured:
Ruptured: (congenital) cerebral
  berry aneurysm   aneurysm NOS
  EXCLUDES   *syphilitic ruptured cerebral aneurysm (094.87)*
DEF: Bleeding in space between brain and lining.
AHA: ▶4Q, '04, 77◀

431 **Intracerebral hemorrhage**   **CD PDx**
Hemorrhage (of):   Hemorrhage (of):
  basilar   internal capsule
  bulbar   intrapontine
  cerebellar   pontine
  cerebral   subcortical
  cerebromeningeal ventricular
  cortical   Rupture of blood vessel in brain
DEF: Bleeding within the brain.
AHA: ▶4Q, '04, 77◀

√4ᵗʰ 432 **Other and unspecified intracranial hemorrhage**
AHA: ▶4Q, '04, 77◀

432.0 Nontraumatic extradural hemorrhage   **CD PDx**
Nontraumatic epidural hemorrhage
DEF: Bleeding, nontraumatic, between skull and brain lining.

432.1 Subdural hemorrhage   **CD PDx**
Subdural hematoma, nontraumatic
DEF: Bleeding, between outermost and other layers of brain lining.

432.9 Unspecified intracranial hemorrhage   **CD PDx**
Intracranial hemorrhage NOS

N Newborn Age: 0   **P** Pediatric Age: 0-17   **M** Maternity Age: 12-55   **A** Adult Age: 15-124   **Manifestation Code**   ▶◀ Revised Text   ● New Code   ▲ Revised Code Title

√4th **433 Occlusion and stenosis of precerebral arteries**

INCLUDES   embolism
     narrowing   } of basilar, carotid, and
     obstruction   vertebral arteries
     thrombosis

EXCLUDES   *insufficiency NOS of
precerebral arteries (435.0-435.9)*

The following fifth-digit subclassification is for use with
category 433:
    0   without mention of cerebral infarction
    1   with cerebral infarction

AHA: 2Q, '95, 14; 3Q, '90, 16

DEF: Blockage, stricture, arteries branching into brain.

√5th **433.0 Basilar artery**   CD PDx

√5th **433.1 Carotid artery**   CD PDx
    AHA: 1Q, '00, 16; For code 433.10: 1Q, '02, 7, 10

√5th **433.2 Vertebral artery**   CD PDx

√5th **433.3 Multiple and bilateral**   CD PDx
    AHA: 2Q, '02, 19

√5th **433.8 Other specified precerebral artery**   CD PDx

√5th **433.9 Unspecified precerebral artery**   CD PDx
    Precerebral artery NOS

√4th **434 Occlusion of cerebral arteries**

The following fifth-digit subclassification is for use with
category 434:
    0   without mention of cerebral infarction
    1   with cerebral infarction

AHA: 2Q, '95, 14

√5th **434.0 Cerebral thrombosis**   CD PDx
    Thrombosis of cerebral arteries
    AHA: For code 434.01: ▶4Q, '04, 77◀

√5th **434.1 Cerebral embolism**   CD PDx
    AHA: 3Q, '97, 11; For code 434.11: ▶4Q, '04, 77◀

√5th **434.9 Cerebral artery occlusion, unspecified**   CD PDx
    AHA: 4Q, '98, 87; For code 434.91: ▶4Q, '04, 77-78◀

√4th **435 Transient cerebral ischemia**

INCLUDES   cerebrovascular insufficiency (acute) with trans-
     ient focal neurological signs and symptoms
     insufficiency of basilar, carotid, and vertebral
     arteries
     spasm of cerebral arteries

EXCLUDES   *acute cerebrovascular insufficiency NOS (437.1)
that due to any condition classifiable to 433
(433.0-433.9)*

DEF: Temporary restriction of blood flow, to arteries branching into brain.

435.0 Basilar artery syndrome   CD PDx

435.1 Vertebral artery syndrome   CD PDx

435.2 Subclavian steal syndrome   CD PDx
    DEF: Cerebrovascular insufficiency, due to occluded subclavian
    artery; symptoms include pain in mastoid and posterior head
    regions, flaccid paralysis of arm and diminished or absent radial
    pulse on affected side.

435.3 Vertebrobasilar artery syndrome   CD PDx
    AHA: 4Q, '95, 60

    DEF: Transient ischemic attack; due to brainstem dysfunction;
    symptoms include confusion, vertigo, binocular blindness, diplopia,
    unilateral or bilateral weakness and paresthesis of extremities.

435.8 Other specified transient cerebral   CD PDx
    ischemias

435.9 Unspecified transient cerebral ischemia   CD PDx
    Impending cerebrovascular accident
    Intermittent cerebral ischemia
    Transient ischemic attack [TIA]
    AHA: N-D, '85, 12

Cerebrovascular Arteries

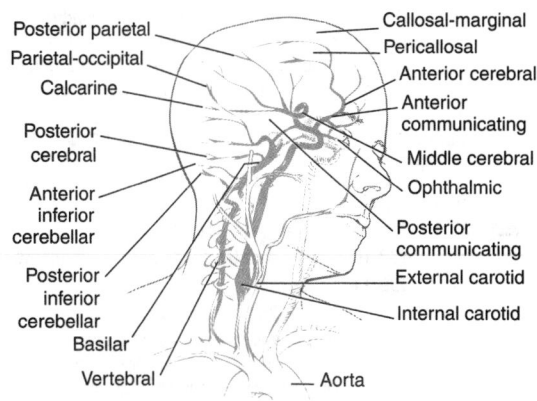

436 Acute, but ill-defined, cerebrovascular disease   CD PDx
    Apoplexy, apoplectic: Apoplexy, apoplectic:
     NOS   seizure
     attack   Cerebral seizure
     cerebral

EXCLUDES   *any condition classifiable to categories 430-435
cerebrovascular accident (434.91)
CVA (ischemic) (434.91)
   embolic (434.11)
   hemorrhagic (430, 431, 432.0-432.9)
   thrombotic (434.01)
postoperative cerebrovascular accident (997.02)
stroke (ischemic) (434.91)
   embolic (434.11)
   hemorrhagic (430, 431, 432.0-432.9)
   thrombotic (434.01)*

AHA: ▶4Q, '04, 77;◀ 4Q, '99, 3

√4th **437 Other and ill-defined cerebrovascular disease**

437.0 Cerebral atherosclerosis   A   CD PDx
    Atheroma of cerebral arteries
    Cerebral arteriosclerosis

437.1 Other generalized ischemic cerebrovascular   CD PDx
    disease
    Acute cerebrovascular insufficiency NOS
    Cerebral ischemia (chronic)

437.2 Hypertensive encephalopathy   CD PDx
    AHA: J-A, '84, 14

    DEF: Cerebral manifestations (such as visual disturbances and
    headache) due to high blood pressure.

437.3 Cerebral aneurysm, nonruptured   CD PDx
    Internal carotid artery, intracranial portion
    Internal carotid artery NOS
    EXCLUDES   *congenital cerebral aneurysm,
nonruptured (747.81)
internal carotid artery, extracranial
portion (442.81)*

437.4 Cerebral arteritis   CD PDx
    AHA: 4Q, '99, 21

    DEF: Inflammation of a cerebral artery or arteries.

437.5 Moyamoya disease   CD PDx
    DEF: Cerebrovascular ischemia; vessels occlude and rupture
    causing tiny hemorrhages at base of brain; predominantly affects
    Japanese.

437.6 Nonpyogenic thrombosis of intracranial   CD PDx
    venous sinus
    EXCLUDES   *pyogenic (325)*

437.7 Transient global amnesia   CD PDx
    AHA: 4Q, '92, 20

    DEF: Episode of short-term memory loss, not often recurrent;
    pathogenesis unknown; with no signs or symptoms of neurological
    disorder.

437.8 Other   CD PDx

437.9 Unspecified   CD PDx
    Cerebrovascular disease or lesion NOS

√4th √5th Additional Digit Required   RUG III Special Care Dx   RUG III Clinically Complex Dx   Hospice Non-cancer Dx   CD PDx Clinical Dimension PDx   CD SDx Clinical Dimension SDx

√4ᵗʰ **438 Late effects of cerebrovascular disease**

Note: This category is to be used to indicate conditions in 430-437 as the cause of late effects. The "late effects" include conditions specified as such, as sequelae, which may occur at any time after the onset of the causal condition.

AHA: 4Q, '99, 4, 6, 7; 4Q, '98, 39, 88; 4Q, '97, 35, 37; 4Q, '92, 21;N-D,'86, 12; M-A, '86, 7

438.0 Cognitive deficits

√5ᵗʰ **438.1 Speech and language deficits**

438.10 Speech and language deficit, unspecified

438.11 Aphasia

AHA: 4Q, '03, 105; 4Q, '97, 36

DEF: Impairment or absence of the ability to communicate by speech, writing or signs or to comprehend the spoken or written language due to disease or injury to the brain. Total aphasia is the loss of function of both sensory and motor areas of the brain.

438.12 Dysphasia

AHA: 4Q, '99, 3, 9

DEF: Impaired speech; marked by inability to sequence language.

438.19 Other speech and language deficits

√5ᵗʰ **438.2 Hemiplegia/hemiparesis**

DEF: Paralysis of one side of the body.

438.20 Hemiplegia affecting unspecified side

AHA: 4Q, '03, 105; 4Q, '99, 3, 9

438.21 Hemiplegia affecting dominant side

438.22 Hemiplegia affecting nondominant side

AHA: 4Q, '03, 105; 1Q, '02, 16

√5ᵗʰ **438.3 Monoplegia of upper limb**

DEF: Paralysis of one limb or one muscle group.

438.30 Monoplegia of upper limb affecting unspecified side

438.31 Monoplegia of upper limb affecting dominant side

438.32 Monoplegia of upper limb affecting nondominant side

√5ᵗʰ **438.4 Monoplegia of lower limb**

438.40 Monoplegia of lower limb affecting unspecified side

438.41 Monoplegia of lower limb affecting dominant side

438.42 Monoplegia of lower limb affecting nondominant side

√5ᵗʰ **438.5 Other paralytic syndrome**

Use additional code to identify type of paralytic syndrome, such as:
locked-in state (344.81)
quadriplegia (344.00-344.09)

EXCLUDES late effects of cerebrovascular accident with:
hemiplegia/hemiparesis (438.20-438.22)
monoplegia of lower limb (438.40-438.42)
monoplegia of upper limb (438.30-438.32)

438.50 Other paralytic syndrome affecting unspecified side

438.51 Other paralytic syndrome affecting dominant side

438.52 Other paralytic syndrome affecting nondominant side

438.53 Other paralytic syndrome, bilateral

AHA: 4Q, '98, 39

438.6 Alterations of sensations

Use additional code to identify the altered sensation

438.7 Disturbances of vision

Use additional code to identify the visual disturbance

AHA: 4Q, '02, 56

√5ᵗʰ **438.8 Other late effects of cerebrovascular disease**

438.81 Apraxia

DEF: Inability to activate learned movements; no known sensory or motor impairment.

438.82 Dysphagia

DEF: Inability or difficulty in swallowing.

438.83 Facial weakness

Facial droop

438.84 Ataxia

AHA: 4Q, '02, 56

438.85 Vertigo

438.89 Other late effects of cerebrovascular disease

Use additional code to identify the late effect

AHA: ▶1Q, '05, 13;◄ 4Q, '98, 39

438.9 Unspecified late effects of cerebrovascular disease

DISEASES OF ARTERIES, ARTERIOLES, AND CAPILLARIES (440-448)

√4ᵗʰ **440 Atherosclerosis**

INCLUDES arteriolosclerosis
arteriosclerosis (obliterans) (senile)
arteriosclerotic vascular disease
atheroma
degeneration:
arterial
arteriovascular
vascular
endarteritis deformans or obliterans
senile:
arteritis
endarteritis

EXCLUDES atheroembolism (445.01-445.89)
atherosclerosis of bypass graft of the extremities (440.30-440.32)

DEF: Stricture and reduced elasticity of an artery; due to plaque deposits.

440.0 Of aorta A

AHA: 2Q, '93, 7; 2Q, '93, 8; 4Q, '88, 8

440.1 Of renal artery A

EXCLUDES atherosclerosis of renal arterioles (403.00-403.91)

√5ᵗʰ **440.2 Of native arteries of the extremities**

EXCLUDES atherosclerosis of bypass graft of the extremities (440.30-440.32)

AHA: 4Q, '94, 49; 4Q, '93, 27; 4Q, '92, 25; 3Q, '90, 15; M-A, '87, 6

440.20 Atherosclerosis of the extremities, unspecified A

440.21 Atherosclerosis of the extremities with intermittent claudication A

DEF: Atherosclerosis; marked by pain, tension and weakness after walking; no symptoms while at rest.

440.22 Atherosclerosis of the extremities with rest pain A

INCLUDES any condition classifiable to 440.21

DEF: Atherosclerosis, marked by pain, tension and weakness while at rest.

440.23 Atherosclerosis of the extremities with ulceration A

Use additional code for any associated ulceration (707.10-707.9)

INCLUDES any condition classifiable to 440.21 and 440.22

AHA: 4Q, '00, 44

N Newborn Age: 0   P Pediatric Age: 0-17   M Maternity Age: 12-55   A Adult Age: 15-124   Manifestation Code   ▶◀ Revised Text   ● New Code   ▲ Revised Code Title

120 — Volume 1 • October 2005

2006 ICD•9•CM

Map of Major Arteries

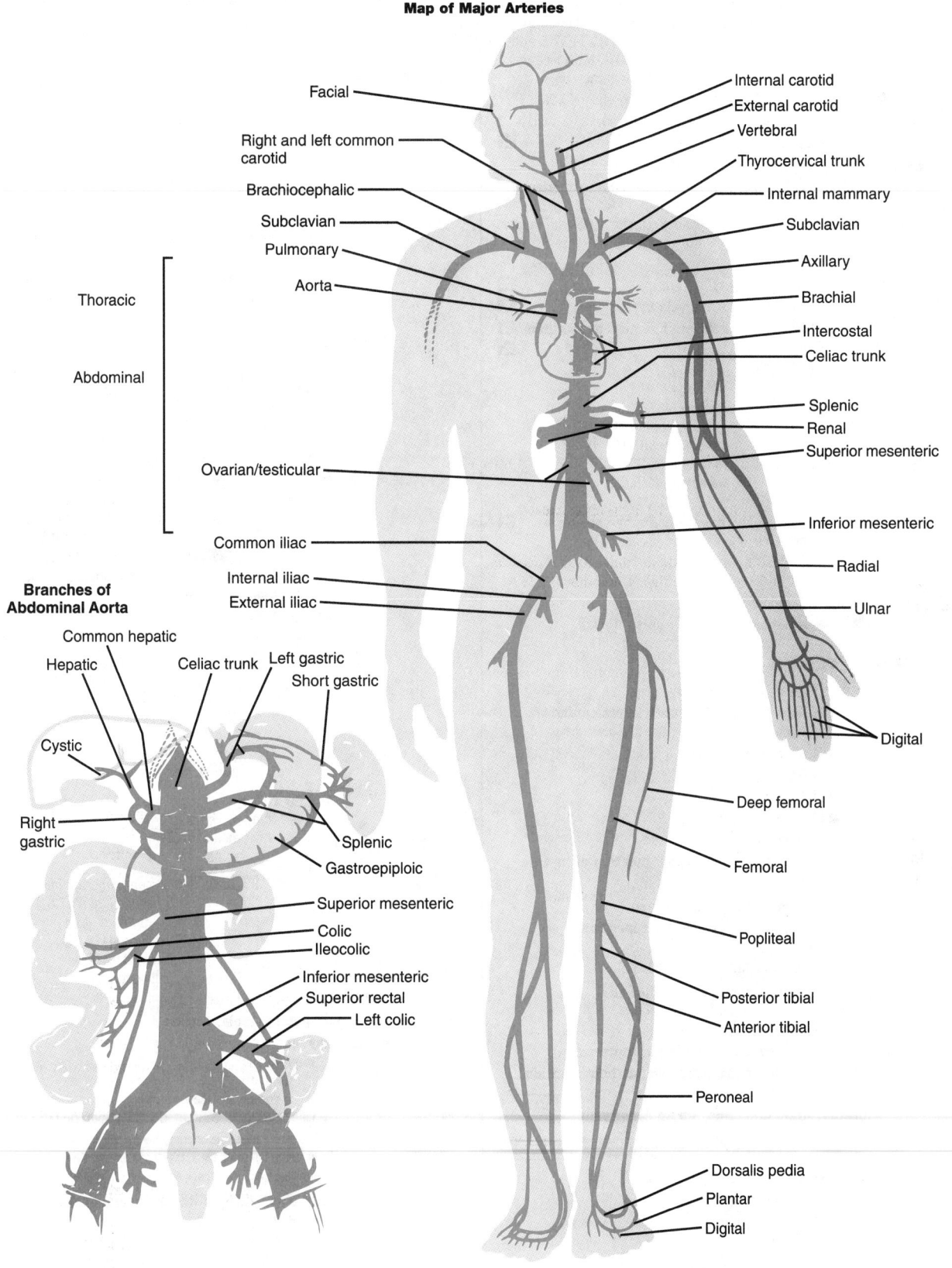

Facial

Right and left common carotid

Brachiocephalic

Subclavian

Pulmonary

Aorta

Thoracic

Abdominal

Ovarian/testicular

Common iliac

Internal iliac

External iliac

Internal carotid

External carotid

Vertebral

Thyrocervical trunk

Internal mammary

Subclavian

Axillary

Brachial

Intercostal

Celiac trunk

Splenic

Renal

Superior mesenteric

Inferior mesenteric

Radial

Ulnar

Digital

Deep femoral

Femoral

Popliteal

Posterior tibial

Anterior tibial

Peroneal

Dorsalis pedia

Plantar

Digital

Branches of Abdominal Aorta

Common hepatic

Hepatic

Cystic

Right gastric

Celiac trunk

Left gastric

Short gastric

Splenic

Gastroepiploic

Superior mesenteric

Colic

Ileocolic

Inferior mesenteric

Superior rectal

Left colic

Additional Digit Required · RUG III Special Care Dx · RUG III Clinically Complex Dx · Hospice Non-cancer Dx · CD PDx Clinical Dimension PDx · CD SDx Clinical Dimension SDx

2006 ICD•9•CM

Volume 1 — 121

440.24 Atherosclerosis of the extremities with gangrene

INCLUDES   any condition classifiable to 440.21, 440.22, and 440.23 with ischemic gangrene 785.4

EXCLUDES   gas gangrene (040.0)

AHA: 4Q, '03, 109; 3Q, '03, 14; 4Q, '95, 54; 1Q, '95, 11

440.29 Other A

✓5ᵗʰ **440.3 Of bypass graft of extremities**

EXCLUDES   atherosclerosis of native arteries of the extremities (440.21-440.24)
embolism [occlusion NOS] [thrombus] of graft (996.74)

AHA: 4Q, '94, 49

440.30 Of unspecified graft A
440.31 Of autologous vein bypass graft A
440.32 Of nonautologous biological bypass graft A

440.8 Of other specified arteries A

EXCLUDES   basilar (433.0)
carotid (433.1)
cerebral (437.0)
coronary (414.00-414.07)
mesenteric (557.1)
precerebral (433.0-433.9)
pulmonary (416.0)
vertebral (433.2)

440.9 Generalized and unspecified atherosclerosis A

Arteriosclerotic vascular disease NOS

EXCLUDES   arteriosclerotic cardiovascular disease [ASCVD] (429.2)

✓4ᵗʰ **441 Aortic aneurysm and dissection**

EXCLUDES   syphilitic aortic aneurysm (093.0)
traumatic aortic aneurysm (901.0, 902.0)

✓5ᵗʰ **441.0 Dissection of aorta**

AHA: 4Q, '89, 10

DEF: Dissection or splitting of wall of the aorta; due to blood entering through intimal tear or interstitial hemorrhage.

441.00 Unspecified site
441.01 Thoracic
441.02 Abdominal
441.03 Thoracoabdominal

441.1 Thoracic aneurysm, ruptured

441.2 Thoracic aneurysm without mention of rupture

AHA: 3Q, '92, 10

441.3 Abdominal aneurysm, ruptured

441.4 Abdominal aneurysm without mention of rupture

AHA: 4Q, '00, 64; 1Q, '99, 15, 16, 17; 3Q, '92, 10

441.5 Aortic aneurysm of unspecified site, ruptured

Rupture of aorta NOS

441.6 Thoracoabdominal aneurysm, ruptured

441.7 Thoracoabdominal aneurysm, without mention of rupture

Thoracic, Abdominal and Aortic Aneurysm

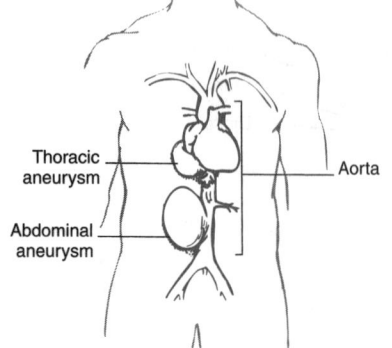

Thoracic aneurysm

Abdominal aneurysm

Aorta

441.9 Aortic aneurysm of unspecified site without mention of rupture

Aneurysm
Dilatation   } of aorta
Hyaline necrosis

✓4ᵗʰ **442 Other aneurysm**

INCLUDES   aneurysm (ruptured) (cirsoid) (false) (varicose)
aneurysmal varix

EXCLUDES   arteriovenous aneurysm or fistula:
acquired (447.0)
congenital (747.60-747.69)
traumatic (900.0-904.9)

DEF: Dissection or splitting of arterial wall; due to blood entering through intimal tear or interstitial hemorrhage.

442.0 Of artery of upper extremity
442.1 Of renal artery
442.2 Of iliac artery

AHA: 1Q, '99, 16, 17

442.3 Of artery of lower extremity

Aneurysm:
femoral   } artery
popliteal

AHA: 3Q, '02, 24-26; 1Q, '99, 16

✓5ᵗʰ **442.8 Of other specified artery**

442.81 Artery of neck

Aneurysm of carotid artery (common) (external) (internal, extracranial portion)

EXCLUDES   internal carotid artery, intra-cranial portion (437.3)

442.82 Subclavian artery
442.83 Splenic artery
442.84 Other visceral artery

Aneurysm:
celiac
gastroduodenal
gastroepiploic   } artery
hepatic
pancreaticoduodenal
superior mesenteric

442.89 Other

Aneurysm:
mediastinal   } artery
spinal

EXCLUDES   cerebral (nonruptured) (437.3)
congenital (747.81)
ruptured (430)
coronary (414.11)
heart (414.10)
pulmonary (417.1)

442.9 Of unspecified site

✓4ᵗʰ **443 Other peripheral vascular disease**

443.0 Raynaud's syndrome

Raynaud's:
disease
phenomenon (secondary)

Use additional code to identify gangrene (785.4)

DEF: Constriction of the arteries, due to cold or stress; bilateral ischemic attacks of fingers, toes, nose or ears; symptoms include pallor, paresthesia and pain; more common in females.

443.1 Thromboangiitis obliterans [Buerger's disease]

Presenile gangrene

DEF: Inflammatory disease of extremity blood vessels, mainly the lower; occurs primarily in young men and leads to tissue ischemia and gangrene.

✓5ᵗʰ **443.2 Other arterial dissection**

EXCLUDES   dissection of aorta (441.00-441.03)
dissection of coronary arteries (414.12)

AHA: 4Q, '02, 54

443.21 Dissection of carotid artery

N Newborn Age: 0   P Pediatric Age: 0-17   M Maternity Age: 12-55   A Adult Age: 15-124   Manifestation Code   ►◄ Revised Text   ● New Code   ▲ Revised Code Title

443.22 Dissection of iliac artery

443.23 Dissection of renal artery

443.24 Dissection of vertebral artery

443.29 Dissection of other artery

√5ᵗʰ **443.8 Other specified peripheral vascular diseases**

　443.81 *Peripheral angiopathy in diseases classified elsewhere*

　　Code first underlying disease, as:
　　diabetes mellitus (250.7)
　　AHA: 1Q, '04, 14; 3Q, '91, 10

● 　**443.82 Erythromelalgia**

　443.89 Other

　　Acrocyanosis　　　　Erythrocyanosis
　　Acroparesthesia:
　　　simple [Schultze's type]
　　　vasomotor [Nothnagel's type]
　　　　EXCLUDES　*chilblains (991.5)*
　　　　　frostbite (991.0-991.3)
　　　　　immersion foot (991.4)

443.9 Peripheral vascular disease, unspecified

　Intermittent claudication NOS
　Peripheral:
　　angiopathy NOS
　　vascular disease NOS
　Spasm of artery
　　EXCLUDES　*atherosclerosis of the arteries of the extremities (440.20-440.22)*
　　　spasm of cerebral artery (435.0-435.9)
　　AHA: 4Q, '92, 25; 3Q, '91, 10

√4ᵗʰ **444 Arterial embolism and thrombosis**

　INCLUDES　infarction:
　　　embolic
　　　thrombotic
　　occlusion
　　EXCLUDES　*atheroembolism (445.01-445.89)*
　　　that complicating:
　　　　abortion (634-638 with .6, 639.6)
　　　　ectopic or molar pregnancy (639.6)
　　　　pregnancy, childbirth, or the pueperium (673.0-673.8)

　AHA: 2Q, '92, 11; 4Q, '90, 27

444.0 Of abdominal aorta

　Aortic bifurcation syndrome　　Leriche's syndrome
　Aortoiliac obstruction　　　　Saddle embolus
　AHA: 2Q, '93, 7; 4Q, '90, 27

444.1 Of thoracic aorta

　Embolism or thrombosis of aorta (thoracic)

√5ᵗʰ **444.2 Of arteries of the extremities**

　AHA: M-A, '87, 6

　444.21 Upper extremity

　444.22 Lower extremity

　　Arterial embolism or thrombosis:
　　　femoral
　　　peripheral NOS
　　　popliteal
　　　　EXCLUDES　*iliofemoral (444.81)*
　　AHA: 3Q, '03, 10; 1Q, '03, 17; 3Q, '90, 16

Arterial Diseases and Disorders

Lipids
Calcium deposits

Intimal proliferation

Atherosclerosis narrowing lumen

Thrombus (clot) forming in lumen

Organization of thrombus and recanalization

Embolus (from elsewhere) occluding lumen

Aneurysm bypasses lumen or...

...bulges from arterial wall

Arteriovenous fistula

√5ᵗʰ **444.8 Of other specified artery**

　444.81 Iliac artery

　　AHA: 1Q, '03, 16

　444.89 Other

　　EXCLUDES　*basilar (433.0)*
　　　carotid (433.1)
　　　cerebral (434.0-434.9)
　　　coronary (410.00-410.92)
　　　mesenteric (557.0)
　　　ophthalmic (362.30-362.34)
　　　precerebral (433.0-433.9)
　　　pulmonary (415.19)
　　　renal (593.81)
　　　retinal (362.30-362.34)
　　　vertebral (433.2)

444.9 Of unspecified artery

√4ᵗʰ **445 Atheroembolism**

　INCLUDES　atherothrombotic microembolism
　　　cholesterol embolism

　AHA: 4Q, '02, 57

√5ᵗʰ **445.0 Of extremities**

　445.01 Upper extremity

　445.02 Lower extremity

√5ᵗʰ **445.8 Of other sites**

　445.81 Kidney

　　Use additional code for any associated
　　kidney failure (584, 585)

　445.89 Other site

√4ᵗʰ **446 Polyarteritis nodosa and allied conditions**

　446.0 Polyarteritis nodosa

　　Disseminated necrotizing periarteritis
　　Necrotizing angiitis
　　Panarteritis (nodosa)
　　Periarteritis (nodosa)

　　DEF: Inflammation of small and mid-size arteries; symptoms related to involved arteries in kidneys, muscles, gastrointestinal tract and heart; results in tissue death.

　446.1 Acute febrile mucocutaneous lymph node syndrome [MCLS]

　　Kawasaki disease

　　DEF: Acute febrile disease of children; marked by erythema of conjunctiva and mucous membranes of upper respiratory tract, skin eruptions and edema.

√5ᵗʰ **446.2 Hypersensitivity angiitis**

　　EXCLUDES　*antiglomerular basement membrane disease without pulmonary hemorrhage (583.89)*

　446.20 Hypersensitivity angiitis, unspecified

　446.21 Goodpasture's syndrome

　　Antiglomerular basement membrane antibody-mediated nephritis with pulmonary hemorrhage
　　Use additional code to identify renal disease (583.81)

　　DEF: Glomerulonephritis associated with hematuria, progresses rapidly; results in death from renal failure.

　446.29 Other specified hypersensitivity angiitis

　　AHA: 1Q, '95, 13

　446.3 Lethal midline granuloma

　　Malignant granuloma of face

　　DEF: Granulomatous lesion; in nose or paranasal sinuses; often fatal; occurs chiefly in males.

　446.4 Wegener's granulomatosis

　　Necrotizing respiratory granulomatosis
　　Wegener's syndrome
　　AHA: 3Q, '00, 11

　　DEF: A disease occurring mainly in men; marked by necrotizing granulomas and ulceration of the upper respiratory tract; underlying condition is a vasculitis affecting small vessels and is possibly due to an immune disorder.

√4ᵗʰ √5ᵗʰ **Additional Digit Required**　RUG III Special Care Dx　RUG III Clinically Complex Dx　Hospice Non-cancer Dx　CD PDx Clinical Dimension PDx　CD SDx Clinical Dimension SDx

2006 ICD•9•CM　　　　　　　　　　　　　　　　**October 2005 • Volume 1 — 123**

Circulatory System

443.22–446.4

446.5   Giant cell arteritis
Cranial arteritis   Temporal arteritis
Horton's disease
DEF: Inflammation of arteries; due to giant cells affecting carotid
artery branches, resulting in occlusion; symptoms include fever,
headache and neurological problems; occurs in elderly.

446.6   Thrombotic microangiopathy
Moschcowitz's syndrome
Thrombotic thrombocytopenic purpura
DEF: Blockage of small blood vessels; due to hyaline deposits;
symptoms include purpura, CNS disorders; results in protracted
disease or rapid death.

446.7   Takayasu's disease
Aortic arch arteritis
Pulseless disease
DEF: Progressive obliterative arteritis of brachiocephalic trunk, left
subclavian, and left common carotid arteries above aortic arch;
results in ischemia in brain, heart and arm; pulses impalpable in
head, neck and arms; more common in young adult females.

✓4ᵗʰ **447   Other disorders of arteries and arterioles**

447.0   Arteriovenous fistula, acquired
Arteriovenous aneurysm, acquired
> **EXCLUDES**   *cerebrovascular (437.3)*
> *coronary (414.19)*
> *pulmonary (417.0)*
> *surgically created arteriovenous shunt*
>   *or fistula:*
>   *complication (996.1, 996.61-996.62)*
>   *status or presence (V45.1)*
> *traumatic (900.0-904.9)*

DEF: Communication between an artery and vein caused by error in
healing.

447.1   Stricture of artery
AHA: 2Q, '93, 8; M-A, '87, 6

447.2   Rupture of artery
Erosion
Fistula, except arteriovenous } of artery
Ulcer
> **EXCLUDES**   *traumatic rupture of artery (900.0-*
> *904.9)*

447.3   Hyperplasia of renal artery
Fibromuscular hyperplasia of renal artery
DEF: Overgrowth of cells in muscular lining of renal artery.

447.4   Celiac artery compression syndrome
Celiac axis syndrome
Marable's syndrome

447.5   Necrosis of artery

447.6   Arteritis, unspecified
Aortitis NOS
Endarteritis NOS
> **EXCLUDES**   *arteritis, endarteritis:*
>   *aortic arch (446.7)*
>   *cerebral (437.4)*
>   *coronary (414.00-414.07)*
>   *deformans (440.0-440.9)*
>   *obliterans (440.0-440.9)*
>   *pulmonary (417.8)*
>   *senile (440.0-440.9)*
> *polyarteritis NOS (446.0)*
> *syphilitic aortitis (093.1)*

AHA: 1Q, '95, 3

447.8   Other specified disorders of arteries and arterioles
Fibromuscular hyperplasia of arteries, except renal

447.9   Unspecified disorders of arteries and arterioles

✓4ᵗʰ **448   Disease of capillaries**

448.0   Hereditary hemorrhagic telangiectasia
Rendu-Osler-Weber disease
DEF: Genetic disease with onset after puberty; results in multiple
telangiectases, dilated venules on skin and mucous membranes;
recurrent bleeding may occur.

448.1   Nevus, non-neoplastic
Nevus:
araneus
senile
spider
stellar
> **EXCLUDES**   *neoplastic (216.0-216.9)*
> *port wine (757.32)*
> *strawberry (757.32)*

DEF: Enlarged or malformed blood vessels of skin; results in
reddish swelling, skin patch, or birthmark.

448.9   Other and unspecified capillary diseases
Capillary:
hemorrhage
hyperpermeability
thrombosis
> **EXCLUDES**   *capillary fragility (hereditary) (287.8)*

DISEASES OF VEINS AND LYMPHATICS, AND OTHER DISEASES OF CIRCULATORY SYSTEM (451-459)

✓4ᵗʰ **451   Phlebitis and thrombophlebitis**
> **INCLUDES**   endophlebitis   periphlebitis
> inflammation, vein   suppurative phlebitis

Use additional E code to identify drug, if drug-induced
> **EXCLUDES**   *that complicating:*
>   *abortion (634-638 with .7, 639.8)*
>   *ectopic or molar pregnancy (639.8)*
>   *pregnancy, childbirth, or the puerperium*
>   *(671.0-671.9)*
> *that due to or following:*
>   *implant or catheter device (996.61-996.62)*
>   *infusion, perfusion, or transfusion (999.2)*

AHA: 1Q, '92, 16
DEF: Inflammation of a vein (phlebitis) with formation of a thrombus
(thrombophlebitis).

451.0   Of superficial vessels of lower extremities
Saphenous vein (greater) (lesser)
AHA: 3Q, '91, 16

✓5ᵗʰ **451.1   Of deep vessels of lower extremities**
AHA: 3Q, '91, 16

451.11 Femoral vein (deep) (superficial)
451.19 Other
Femoropopliteal vein   Tibial vein
Popliteal vein

451.2   Of lower extremities, unspecified
AHA: ▶4Q, '04, 80◀

✓5ᵗʰ **451.8   Of other sites**
> **EXCLUDES**   *intracranial venous sinus (325)*
> *nonpyogenic (437.6)*
> *portal (vein) (572.1)*

451.81 Iliac vein
451.82 Of superficial veins of upper extremities
Antecubital vein   Cephalic vein
Basilic vein
451.83 Of deep veins of upper extremities
Brachial vein   Ulnar vein
Radial vein
451.84 Of upper extremities, unspecified
451.89 Other
Axillary vein   Thrombophlebitis of
Jugular vein   breast (Mondor's
Subclavian vein   disease)

451.9   Of unspecified site

452   Portal vein thrombosis
Portal (vein) obstruction
> **EXCLUDES**   *hepatic vein thrombosis (453.0)*
> *phlebitis of portal vein (572.1)*

DEF: Formation of a blood clot in main vein of liver.

Ⓝ Newborn Age: 0   Ⓟ Pediatric Age: 0-17   Ⓜ Maternity Age: 12-55   Ⓐ Adult Age: 15-124   Manifestation Code   ▶◀ Revised Text   ● New Code   ▲ Revised Code Title

Map of Major Veins

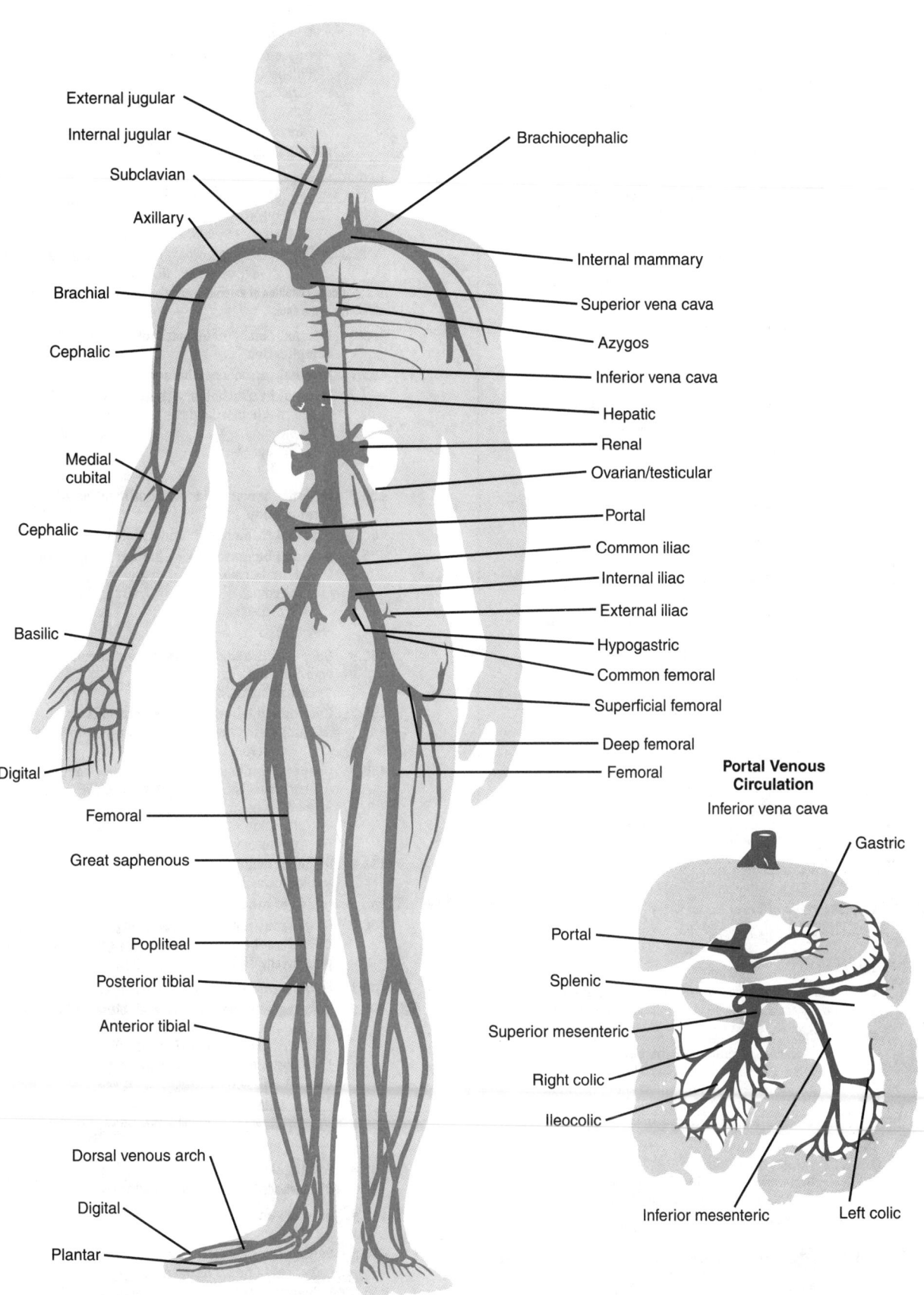

External jugular

Internal jugular

Subclavian

Axillary

Brachial

Cephalic

Medial cubital

Cephalic

Basilic

Digital

Femoral

Great saphenous

Popliteal

Posterior tibial

Anterior tibial

Dorsal venous arch

Digital

Plantar

Brachiocephalic

Internal mammary

Superior vena cava

Azygos

Inferior vena cava

Hepatic

Renal

Ovarian/testicular

Portal

Common iliac

Internal iliac

External iliac

Hypogastric

Common femoral

Superficial femoral

Deep femoral

Femoral

Portal Venous Circulation

Inferior vena cava

Gastric

Portal

Splenic

Superior mesenteric

Right colic

Ileocolic

Inferior mesenteric

Left colic

✓4ᵗʰ ✓5ᵗʰ   Additional Digit Required   RUG III Special Care Dx   RUG III Clinically Complex Dx   Hospice Non-cancer Dx   **CD PDx** Clinical Dimension PDx   **CD SDx** Clinical Dimension SDx

2006 ICD•9•CM   **Volume 1 — 125**

Circulatory System

453–456.6

✓4th **453 Other venous embolism and thrombosis**

> EXCLUDES   *that complicating:*
> *abortion (634-638 with .7, 639.8)*
> *ectopic or molar pregnancy (639.8)*
> *pregnancy, childbirth, or the puerperium*
> *(671.0-671.9)*
> *that with inflammation, phlebitis, and*
> *thrombophlebitis (451.0-451.9)*

AHA: 1Q, '92, 16

453.0 Budd-Chiari syndrome
Hepatic vein thrombosis
DEF: Thrombosis or other obstruction of hepatic vein; symptoms include enlarged liver, extensive collateral vessels, intractable ascites and severe portal hypertension.

453.1 Thrombophlebitis migrans
DEF: Slow, advancing thrombophlebitis; appearing first in one vein then another.

453.2 Of vena cava

453.3 Of renal vein

✓5th **453.4 Venous embolism and thrombosis of deep vessels of lower extremity**

> **453.40 Venous embolism and thrombosis of unspecified deep vessels of lower extremity**
> Deep vein thrombosis NOS
> DVT NOS

> **453.41 Venous embolism and thrombosis of deep vessels of proximal lower extremity**
> Femoral   Thigh
> Iliac   Upper leg NOS
> Popliteal
> **AHA: ▶4Q, '04, 79◀**

> **453.42 Venous embolism and thrombosis of deep vessels of distal lower extremity**
> Calf   Peroneal
> Lower leg NOS   Tibial

453.8 Of other specified veins

> EXCLUDES   *cerebral (434.0-434.9)*
> *coronary (410.00-410.92)*
> *intracranial venous sinus (325)*
>   *nonpyogenic (437.6)*
> *mesenteric (557.0)*
> *portal (452)*
> *precerebral (433.0-433.9)*
> *pulmonary (415.19)*

AHA: 3Q, '91, 16; M-A, '87, 6

453.9 Of unspecified site
Embolism of vein   Thrombosis (vein)

✓4th **454 Varicose veins of lower extremities**

> EXCLUDES   *that complicating pregnancy, childbirth, or the puerperium (671.0)*

AHA: 2Q, '91, 20

DEF: Dilated leg veins; due to incompetent vein valves that allow reversed blood flow and cause tissue erosion or weakness of wall; may be painful.

454.0 With ulcer   A
Varicose ulcer (lower extremity, any part)
Varicose veins with ulcer of lower extremity [any part] or of unspecified site
Any condition classifiable to 454.9 with ulcer or specified as ulcerated

454.1 With inflammation   A
Stasis dermatitis
Varicose veins with inflammation of lower extremity [any part] or of unspecified site
Any condition classifiable to 454.9 with inflammation or specified as inflamed

454.2 With ulcer and inflammation   A
Varicose veins with ulcer and inflammation of lower extremity [any part] or of unspecified site
Any condition classifiable to 454.9 with ulcer and inflammation

454.8 With other complications
Edema   Swelling
Pain
AHA: 4Q, '02, 58

454.9 Asymptomatic varicose veins   A
Phlebectasia   }
Varicose veins   }   of lower extremity [any part]
Varix   }   or of unspecified site
Varicose veins NOS
AHA: 4Q, '02, 58

✓4th **455 Hemorrhoids**

> INCLUDES   hemorrhoids (anus) (rectum)
> piles
> varicose veins, anus or rectum

> EXCLUDES   *that complicating pregnancy, childbirth, or the puerperium (671.8)*

DEF: Varicose condition of external hemorrhoidal veins causing painful swellings at the anus.

455.0 Internal hemorrhoids without mention of complication

455.1 Internal thrombosed hemorrhoids

455.2 Internal hemorrhoids with other complication
Internal hemorrhoids: Internal hemorrhoids:
   bleeding   strangulated
   prolapsed   ulcerated
AHA: 1Q, '03, 8

455.3 External hemorrhoids without mention of complication

455.4 External thrombosed hemorrhoids

455.5 External hemorrhoids with other complication
External hemorrhoids: External hemorrhoids:
   bleeding   strangulated
   prolapsed   ulcerated
AHA: 1Q, '03, 8

455.6 Unspecified hemorrhoids without mention of complication
Hemorrhoids NOS

455.7 Unspecified thrombosed hemorrhoids
Thrombosed hemorrhoids, unspecified whether internal or external

455.8 Unspecified hemorrhoids with other complication
Hemorrhoids, unspecified whether internal or external:
   bleeding   strangulated
   prolapsed   ulcerated

455.9 Residual hemorrhoidal skin tags
Skin tags, anus or rectum

✓4th **456 Varicose veins of other sites**

456.0 Esophageal varices with bleeding
DEF: Distended, tortuous, veins of lower esophagus, usually due to portal hypertension.

456.1 Esophageal varices without mention of bleeding

✓5th **456.2 Esophageal varices in diseases classified elsewhere**
Code first underlying cause, as:
cirrhosis of liver (571.0-571.9)
portal hypertension (572.3)

> **456.20 With bleeding**
> **AHA: N-D, '85, 14**

> **456.21 Without mention of bleeding**
> **AHA: 2Q, '02, 4**

456.3 Sublingual varices
DEF: Distended, tortuous veins beneath tongue.

456.4 Scrotal varices   ♂
Varicocele

456.5 Pelvic varices
Varices of broad ligament

456.6 Vulval varices   ♀
Varices of perineum

> EXCLUDES   *that complicating pregnancy, childbirth, or the puerperium (671.1)*

N Newborn Age: 0   P Pediatric Age: 0-17   M Maternity Age: 12-55   A Adult Age: 15-124   Manifestation Code   ▶◀ Revised Text   ● New Code   ▲ Revised Code Title

456.8 Varices of other sites
Varicose veins of nasal septum (with ulcer)

EXCLUDES   *placental varices (656.7)*
retinal varices (362.17)
varicose ulcer of unspecified site (454.0)
varicose veins of unspecified site (454.9)

AHA: 2Q, '02, 4

✓4ᵗʰ **457 Noninfectious disorders of lymphatic channels**

457.0 Postmastectomy lymphedema syndrome   A

Elephantiasis
Obliteration of lymphatic vessel   } due to mastectomy

AHA: 2Q, '02, 12

DEF: Reduced lymphatic circulation following mastectomy; symptoms include swelling of the arm on the operative side.

457.1 Other lymphedema
Elephantiasis   Lymphedema:
   (nonfilarial) NOS   praecox
Lymphangiectasis   secondary
Lymphedema: Obliteration, lymphatic vessel
   acquired (chronic)

EXCLUDES   *elephantiasis (nonfilarial):*
congenital (757.0)
eyelid (374.83)
vulva (624.8)

AHA: ▶3Q, '04, 5◀

DEF: Fluid retention due to reduced lymphatic circulation; due to other than mastectomy.

457.2 Lymphangitis
Lymphangitis: Lymphangitis:
   NOS   subacute
   chronic

EXCLUDES   *acute lymphangitis (682.0-682.9)*

457.8 Other noninfectious disorders of lymphatic channels
Chylocele (nonfilarial)   Lymph node or vessel:
Chylous: fistula
   ascites   infarction
   cyst   rupture

EXCLUDES   *chylocele:*
filarial (125.0-125.9)
tunica vaginalis (nonfilarial) (608.84)

AHA: 1Q, '04, 5; 3Q, '03, 17

457.9 Unspecified noninfectious disorder of lymphatic channels

✓4ᵗʰ **458 Hypotension**

INCLUDES   hypopiesis

EXCLUDES   *cardiovascular collapse (785.50)*
maternal hypotension syndrome (669.2)
shock (785.50-785.59)
Shy-Drager syndrome (333.0)

458.0 Orthostatic hypotension
Hypotension: Hypotension:
   orthostatic (chronic)   postural

AHA: 3Q, '00, 8

DEF: Low blood pressure; occurs when standing.

458.1 Chronic hypotension
Permanent idiopathic hypotension
DEF: Persistent low blood pressure.

✓5ᵗʰ **458.2 Iatrogenic hypotension**
AHA: 4Q. '03, 60; 3Q, '02, 12; 4Q, '95, 57

DEF: Abnormally low blood pressure; due to medical treatment.

458.21 Hypotension of hemodialysis
Intra-dialytic hypotension
AHA: 4Q. '03, 61

458.29 Other iatrogenic hypotension
Postoperative hypotension

458.8 Other specified hypotension
AHA: 4Q, '97, 37

458.9 Hypotension, unspecified
Hypotension (arterial) NOS

✓4ᵗʰ **459 Other disorders of circulatory system**
459.0 Hemorrhage, unspecified
Rupture of blood vessel NOS
Spontaneous hemorrhage NEC

EXCLUDES   *hemorrhage:*
gastrointestinal NOS (578.9)
in newborn NOS (772.9)
secondary or recurrent following trauma (958.2)
traumatic rupture of blood vessel (900.0-904.9)

AHA: 4Q, '90, 26

459.1 Postphlebitic syndrome
Chronic venous hypertension due to deep vein thrombosis

EXCLUDES   *chronic venous hypertension without deep vein thrombosis (459.30-459.39)*

AHA: 4Q, '02, 58; 2Q, '91, 20

DEF: Various conditions following deep vein thrombosis; including edema, pain, stasis dermatitis, cellulitis, varicose veins and ulceration of the lower leg.

459.10 Postphlebitic syndrome without complications
Asymptomatic postphlebitic syndrome
Postphlebitic syndrome NOS

459.11 Postphlebitic syndrome with ulcer

459.12 Postphlebitic syndrome with inflammation

459.13 Postphlebitic syndrome with ulcer and inflammation

459.19 Postphlebitic syndrome with other complication

459.2 Compression of vein
Stricture of vein
Vena cava syndrome (inferior) (superior)

✓5ᵗʰ **459.3 Chronic venous hypertension (idiopathic)**
Stasis edema

EXCLUDES   *chronic venous hypertension due to deep vein thrombosis (459.10-459.19)*
varicose veins (454.0-454.9)

AHA: 4Q, '02, 59

459.30 Chronic venous hypertension without complications
Asymptomatic chronic venous hypertension
Chronic venous hypertension NOS

459.31 Chronic venous hypertension with ulcer
AHA: 4Q, '02, 43

459.32 Chronic venous hypertension with inflammation

459.33 Chronic venous hypertension with ulcer and inflammation

459.39 Chronic venous hypertension with other complication

✓5ᵗʰ **459.8 Other specified disorders of circulatory system**

459.81 Venous (peripheral) insufficiency, unspecified
Chronic venous insufficiency NOS
Use additional code for any associated ulceration (707.10-707.9)
AHA: ▶3Q, '04, 5;◀ 2Q, '91, 20; M-A, '87, 6

DEF: Insufficient drainage, venous blood, any part of body, results in edema or dermatosis.

459.89 Other
Collateral circulation (venous), any site
Phlebosclerosis
Venofibrosis

459.9 Unspecified circulatory system disorder

✓4ᵗʰ✓5ᵗʰ Additional Digit Required   RUG III Special Care Dx   RUG III Clinically Complex Dx   Hospice Non-cancer Dx   CD PDx Clinical Dimension PDx   CD SDx Clinical Dimension SDx

8. DISEASES OF THE RESPIRATORY SYSTEM (460-519)

Use additional code to identify infectious organism

ACUTE RESPIRATORY INFECTIONS (460-466)

> **EXCLUDES** *pneumonia and influenza (480.0-487.8)*

460 Acute nasopharyngitis [common cold]

Coryza (acute)
Nasal catarrh, acute
Nasopharyngitis:
  NOS
  acute

Nasopharyngitis:
  infective NOS
Rhinitis:
  acute
  infective

> **EXCLUDES** *nasopharyngitis, chronic (472.2)*
> *pharyngitis:*
>   *acute or unspecified (462)*
>   *chronic (472.1)*
> *rhinitis:*
>   *allergic (477.0-477.9)*
>   *chronic or unspecified (472.0)*
> *sore throat:*
>   *acute or unspecified (462)*
>   *chronic (472.1)*

AHA: 1Q, '88, 12

DEF: Acute inflammation of mucous membranes; extends from nares to pharynx.

√4th 461 Acute sinusitis

> **INCLUDES**
> abscess
> empyema   acute, of sinus
> infection   (accessory)
> inflammation   (nasal)
> suppuration

> **EXCLUDES** *chronic or unspecified sinusitis (473.0-473.9)*

461.0 Maxillary
  Acute antritis

461.1 Frontal

461.2 Ethmoidal

461.3 Sphenoidal

461.8 Other acute sinusitis
  Acute pansinusitis

461.9 Acute sinusitis, unspecified
  Acute sinusitis NOS

462 Acute pharyngitis

Acute sore throat NOS
Pharyngitis (acute):
  NOS
  gangrenous
  infective
  phlegmonous
  pneumococcal

Pharyngitis (acute):
  staphylococcal
  suppurative
  ulcerative
Sore throat (viral) NOS
Viral pharyngitis

> **EXCLUDES** *absce*
> *peritonsillar [quinsy] (475)*
> *pharyngeal NOS (478.29)*
> *retropharyngeal (478.24)*
> *chronic pharyngitis (472.1)*
> *infectious mononucleosis (075)*
> *that specified as (due to):*
>   *Coxsackie (virus) (074.0)*
>   *gonococcus (098.6)*
>   *herpes simplex (054.79)*
>   *influenza (487.1)*
>   *septic (034.0)*
>   *streptococcal (034.0)*

AHA: 4Q, '99, 26; S-O, '85, 8

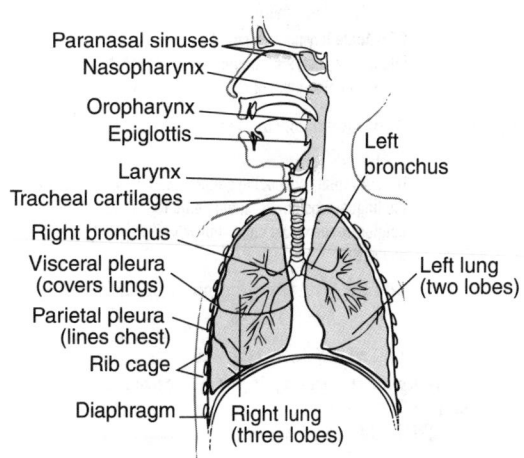

Respiratory System

(Labels: Paranasal sinuses, Nasopharynx, Oropharynx, Epiglottis, Larynx, Tracheal cartilages, Right bronchus, Visceral pleura (covers lungs), Parietal pleura (lines chest), Rib cage, Diaphragm, Left bronchus, Left lung (two lobes), Right lung (three lobes))

463 Acute tonsillitis

Tonsillitis (acute):
  NOS
  follicular
  gangrenous
  infective
  pneumococcal

Tonsillitis (acute):
  septic
  staphylococcal
  suppurative
  ulcerative
  viral

> **EXCLUDES** *chronic tonsillitis (474.0)*
> *hypertrophy of tonsils (474.1)*
> *peritonsillar abscess [quinsy] (475)*
> *sore throat:*
>   *acute or NOS (462)*
>   *septic (034.0)*
> *streptococcal tonsillitis (034.0)*

AHA: N-D, '84, 16

√4th 464 Acute laryngitis and tracheitis

> **EXCLUDES** *that associated with influenza (487.1)*
> *that due to Streptococcus (034.0)*

√5th 464.0 Acute laryngitis

Laryngitis (acute):
  NOS
  edematous
  Hemophilus influenzae [H. influenzae]
  pneumococcal
  septic
  suppurative
  ulcerative

> **EXCLUDES** *chronic laryngitis (476.0-476.1)*
> *influenzal laryngitis (487.1)*

AHA: 4Q, '01, 42

464.00 Without mention of obstruction

464.01 With obstruction

√5th 464.1 Acute tracheitis

Tracheitis (acute):
  NOS
  catarrhal

Tracheitis (acute):
  viral

> **EXCLUDES** *chronic tracheitis (491.8)*

464.10 Without mention of obstruction

464.11 With obstruction

√5th 464.2 Acute laryngotracheitis

Laryngotracheitis (acute)
Tracheitis (acute) with laryngitis (acute)

> **EXCLUDES** *chronic laryngotracheitis (476.1)*

464.20 Without mention of obstruction

464.21 With obstruction

√5th 464.3 Acute epiglottitis

Viral epiglottitis

> **EXCLUDES** *epiglottitis, chronic (476.1)*

464.30 Without mention of obstruction

464.31 With obstruction

√4th √5th Additional Digit Required   RUG III Special Care Dx   RUG III Clinically Complex Dx   Hospice Non-cancer Dx   **CD PDx** Clinical Dimension PDx   **CD SDx** Clinical Dimension SDx

2006 ICD•9•CM   **Volume 1 — 129**

Respiratory System

464.4–473.3

464.4 Croup

Croup syndrome

DEF: Acute laryngeal obstruction due to allergy, foreign body or infection; symptoms include barking cough, hoarseness and harsh, persistent high-pitched respiratory sound.

√5ᵗʰ **464.5 Supraglottitis, unspecified**

AHA: 4Q, '01, 42

DEF: A rapidly advancing generalized upper respiratory infection of the lingual tonsillar area, epiglottic folds, false vocal cords, and the epiglottis; seen most commonly in children, but can affect people of any age.

464.50 Without mention of obstruction

AHA: 4Q, '01, 43

464.51 With obstruction

√4ᵗʰ **465 Acute upper respiratory infections of multiple or unspecified sites**

EXCLUDES   upper respiratory infection due to:
       influenza (487.1)
       Streptococcus (034.0)

465.0 Acute laryngopharyngitis

DEF: Acute infection of the vocal cords and pharynx.

465.8 Other multiple sites

Multiple URI

465.9 Unspecified site

Acute URI NOS
Upper respiratory infection (acute)

√4ᵗʰ **466 Acute bronchitis and bronchiolitis**

INCLUDES   that with:
       bronchospasm
       obstruction

AHA: 4Q, '04, 137; 4Q, '96, 28; 4Q, '91, 24

466.0 Acute bronchitis

Bronchitis, acute or subacute:	Bronchitis, acute or subacute:
fibrinous	viral
membranous	with tracheitis
pneumococcal	Croupous bronchitis
purulent	Tracheobronchitis, acute
septic	

EXCLUDES   acute bronchitis with chronic obstructive pulmonary disease (491.22)

AHA: 1Q, '04, 3; 1Q, '88, 12

DEF: Acute inflammation of main branches of bronchial tree due to infectious or irritant agents; symptoms include cough with a varied production of sputum, fever, substernal soreness, and lung rales.

√5ᵗʰ **466.1 Acute bronchiolitis**

Bronchiolitis (acute)   Capillary pneumonia

DEF: Acute inflammation of finer subdivisions of bronchial tree due to infectious or irritant agents; symptoms include cough with a varied production of sputum, fever, substernal soreness, and lung rales.

466.11 Acute bronchiolitis due to respiratory syncytial virus (RSV)

AHA: ▶1Q, '05, 10;◀ 4Q, '96, 27

466.19 Acute bronchiolitis due to other infectious organisms

Use additional code to identify organism

Upper Respiratory System

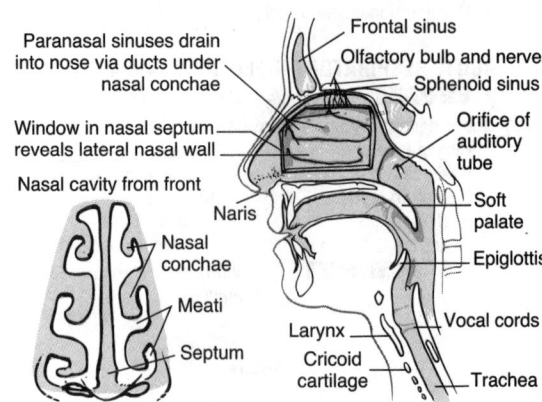

OTHER DISEASES OF THE UPPER RESPIRATORY TRACT (470-478)

470 Deviated nasal septum

Deflected septum (nasal) (acquired)

EXCLUDES   congenital (754.0)

√4ᵗʰ **471 Nasal polyps**

EXCLUDES   adenomatous polyps (212.0)

471.0 Polyp of nasal cavity

Polyp:	Polyp:
choanal	nasopharyngeal

471.1 Polypoid sinus degeneration

Woakes' syndrome or ethmoiditis

471.8 Other polyp of sinus

Polyp of sinus:
   accessory
   ethmoidal
   maxillary
   sphenoidal

471.9 Unspecified nasal polyp

Nasal polyp NOS

√4ᵗʰ **472 Chronic pharyngitis and nasopharyngitis**

472.0 Chronic rhinitis

Ozena	Rhinitis:
Rhinitis:	hypertrophic
NOS	obstructive
atrophic	purulent
granulomatous	ulcerative

EXCLUDES   allergic rhinitis (477.0-477.9)

DEF: Persistent inflammation of mucous membranes of nose.

472.1 Chronic pharyngitis

Chronic sore throat	Pharyngitis:
Pharyngitis:	granular (chronic)
atrophic	hypertrophic

472.2 Chronic nasopharyngitis

EXCLUDES   acute or unspecified nasopharyngitis (460)

DEF: Persistent inflammation of mucous membranes extending from nares to pharynx.

√4ᵗʰ **473 Chronic sinusitis**

INCLUDES   abscess
     empyema   (chronic) of sinus
     infection   (accessory) (nasal)
     suppuration

EXCLUDES   acute sinusitis (461.0-461.9)

473.0 Maxillary

Antritis (chronic)

473.1 Frontal

473.2 Ethmoidal

EXCLUDES   Woakes' ethmoiditis (471.1)

473.3 Sphenoidal

N Newborn Age: 0   P Pediatric Age: 0-17   M Maternity Age: 12-55   A Adult Age: 15-124   Manifestation Code   ▶◀ Revised Text   ● New Code   ▲ Revised Code Title

Paranasal Sinuses

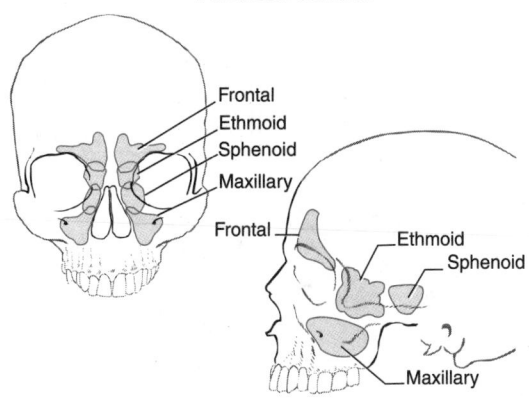

Frontal
Ethmoid
Sphenoid
Maxillary

Frontal

Ethmoid
Sphenoid

Maxillary

473.8   Other chronic sinusitis
Pansinusitis (chronic)

473.9   Unspecified sinusitis (chronic)
Sinusitis (chronic) NOS

√4ᵗʰ 474   Chronic disease of tonsils and adenoids

√5ᵗʰ 474.0   Chronic tonsillitis and adenoiditis

> **EXCLUDES** *acute or unspecified tonsillitis (463)*

AHA: 4Q, '97, 38

474.00   Chronic tonsillitis

474.01   Chronic adenoiditis

474.02   Chronic tonsillitis and adenoiditis

√5ᵗʰ 474.1   Hypertrophy of tonsils and adenoids
Enlargement
Hyperplasia   } of tonsils or adenoids
Hypertrophy

> **EXCLUDES** *that with:*
> *adenoiditis (474.01)*
> *adenoiditis and tonsillitis (474.02)*
> *tonsillitis (474.00)*

474.10   Tonsils with adenoids

474.11   Tonsils alone

474.12   Adenoids alone

474.2   Adenoid vegetations
DEF: Fungus-like growth of lymph tissue between the nares and pharynx.

474.8   Other chronic disease of tonsils and adenoids
Amygdalolith   Tonsillar tag
Calculus, tonsil   Ulcer, tonsil
Cicatrix of tonsil (and adenoid)

474.9   Unspecified chronic disease of tonsils and adenoids
Disease (chronic) of tonsils (and adenoids)

475 Peritonsillar abscess
Abscess of tonsil   Quinsy
Peritonsillar cellulitis

> **EXCLUDES** *tonsillitis:*
> *acute or NOS (463)*
> *chronic (474.0)*

√4ᵗʰ 476   Chronic laryngitis and laryngotracheitis

476.0   Chronic laryngitis
Laryngitis: Laryngitis:
catarrhal   sicca
hypertrophic

476.1   Chronic laryngotracheitis
Laryngitis, chronic, with tracheitis (chronic)
Tracheitis, chronic, with laryngitis

> **EXCLUDES** *chronic tracheitis (491.8)*
> *laryngitis and tracheitis, acute or*
> *unspecified (464.00-464.51)*

√4ᵗʰ 477   Allergic rhinitis

> **INCLUDES** allergic rhinitis (nonseasonal) (seasonal)
> hay fever
> spasmodic rhinorrhea

> **EXCLUDES** *allergic rhinitis with asthma (bronchial) (493.0)*

DEF: True immunoglobulin E (IgE)-mediated allergic reaction of nasal mucosa; seasonal (typical hay fever) or perennial (year-round allergens: dust, food, dander).

477.0   Due to pollen
Pollinosis

477.1   Due to food
AHA: 4Q, '00, 42

477.2   Due to animal (cat) (dog) hair and dander

477.8   Due to other allergen

477.9   Cause unspecified
AHA: 2Q, '97, 9

√4ᵗʰ 478   Other diseases of upper respiratory tract

478.0   Hypertrophy of nasal turbinates
DEF: Overgrowth, enlargement of shell-shaped bones, in nasal cavity.

478.1   Other diseases of nasal cavity and sinuses
Abscess
Necrosis   } of nose (septum)
Ulcer

Cyst or mucocele of sinus (nasal)
Rhinolith

> **EXCLUDES** *varicose ulcer of nasal septum (456.8)*

√5ᵗʰ 478.2   Other diseases of pharynx, not elsewhere classified

478.20   Unspecified disease of pharynx

478.21   Cellulitis of pharynx or nasopharynx

478.22   Parapharyngeal abscess

478.24   Retropharyngeal abscess
DEF: Purulent infection, behind pharynx and front of precerebral fascia.

478.25   Edema of pharynx or nasopharynx

478.26   Cyst of pharynx or nasopharynx

478.29   Other
Abscess of pharynx or nasopharynx

> **EXCLUDES** *ulcerative pharyngitis (462)*

√5ᵗʰ 478.3   Paralysis of vocal cords or larynx
DEF: Loss of motor ability of vocal cords or larynx; due to nerve or muscle damage.

478.30   Paralysis, unspecified
Laryngoplegia   Paralysis of glottis

478.31   Unilateral, partial

478.32   Unilateral, complete

478.33   Bilateral, partial

478.34   Bilateral, complete

478.4   Polyp of vocal cord or larynx

> **EXCLUDES** *adenomatous polyps (212.1)*

478.5   Other diseases of vocal cords
Abscess
Cellulitis
Granuloma   } of vocal cords
Leukoplakia

Chorditis (fibrinous) (nodosa) (tuberosa)
Singers' nodes

478.6   Edema of larynx
Edema (of):   Edema (of):
glottis   supraglottic
subglottic

√5ᵗʰ 478.7   Other diseases of larynx, not elsewhere classified

478.70   Unspecified disease of larynx

478.71   Cellulitis and perichondritis of larynx
DEF: Inflammation of deep soft tissues or lining of bone of the larynx.

√4ᵗʰ
√5ᵗʰ Additional Digit Required   RUG III Special Care Dx   RUG III Clinically Complex Dx   Hospice Non-cancer Dx   **CD PDx** Clinical Dimension PDx   **CD SDx** Clinical Dimension SDx

2006 ICD•9•CM   **Volume 1 — 131**

478.74 Stenosis of larynx

478.75 Laryngeal spasm

Laryngismus (stridulus)

DEF: Involuntary muscle contraction of the larynx.

478.79 Other

Abscess
Necrosis
Obstruction } of larynx
Pachyderma
Ulcer

> **EXCLUDES** ulcerative laryngitis (464.00-464.01)

AHA: 3Q, '91, 20

478.8 Upper respiratory tract hypersensitivity reaction, site unspecified

> **EXCLUDES** hypersensitivity reaction of lower respiratory tract, as:
> extrinsic allergic alveolitis (495.0-495.9)
> pneumoconiosis (500-505)

478.9 Other and unspecified diseases of upper respiratory tract

Abscess } of trachea
Cicatrix

PNEUMONIA AND INFLUENZA (480-487)

> **EXCLUDES** pneumonia:
> allergic or eosinophilic (518.3)
> aspiration:
> NOS (507.0)
> newborn ▶(770.18)◀
> solids and liquids (507.0-507.8)
> congenital (770.0)
> lipoid (507.1)
> passive (514)
> rheumatic (390)

✓4ᵗʰ **480 Viral pneumonia**

480.0 Pneumonia due to adenovirus

480.1 Pneumonia due to respiratory syncytial virus

AHA: 4Q, '96, 28; 1Q, '88, 12

480.2 Pneumonia due to parainfluenza virus

480.3 Pneumonia due to SARS-associated coronavirus

AHA: 4Q, '03, 46-47

DEF: A severe adult respiratory syndrome caused by the coronavirus, specified as inflammation of the lungs with consolidation.

480.8 Pneumonia due to other virus not elsewhere classified

> **EXCLUDES** congenital rubella pneumonitis (771.0)
> influenza with pneumonia, any form (487.0)
> pneumonia complicating viral diseases classified elsewhere (484.1-484.8)

480.9 Viral pneumonia, unspecified

AHA: 3Q, '98, 5

481 Pneumococcal pneumonia [Streptococcus pneumoniae pneumonia]

Lobar pneumonia, organism unspecified

AHA: 2Q, '98, 7; 4Q, '92, 19; 1Q, '92, 18; 1Q, '91, 13; 1Q, '88, 13; M-A, '85, 6

✓4ᵗʰ **482 Other bacterial pneumonia**

AHA: 4Q, '93, 39

482.0 Pneumonia due to Klebsiella pneumoniae

482.1 Pneumonia due to Pseudomonas

482.2 Pneumonia due to Hemophilus influenzae [H. influenzae]

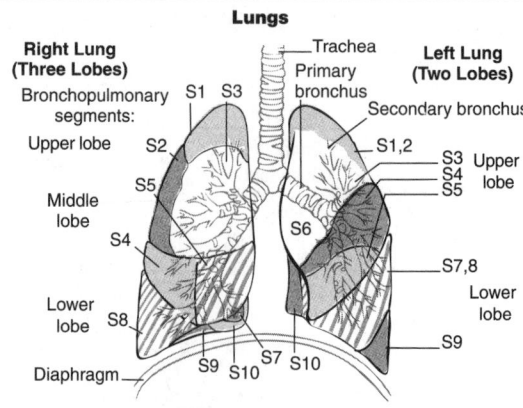

Lungs

Right Lung (Three Lobes) — Trachea — Left Lung (Two Lobes)

Primary bronchus
Bronchopulmonary segments:
Upper lobe — S1 S3 — Secondary bronchus
S2 — S1,2
S5 — S3 Upper lobe
Middle lobe — S4 S5
S4 — S6
Lower lobe — S8 — S7,8 — Lower lobe
S9 — S9
Diaphragm — S9 S10 S7 S10

✓5ᵗʰ **482.3 Pneumonia due to Streptococcus**

> **EXCLUDES** Streptococcus pneumoniae (481)

AHA: 1Q, '88, 13

482.30 Streptococcus, unspecified

482.31 Group A

482.32 Group B

482.39 Other Streptococcus

✓5ᵗʰ **482.4 Pneumonia due to Staphylococcus**

AHA: 3Q, '91, 16

482.40 Pneumonia due to Staphylococcus, unspecified

482.41 Pneumonia due to Staphylococcus aureus

482.49 Other Staphylococcus pneumonia

✓5ᵗʰ **482.8 Pneumonia due to other specified bacteria**

> **EXCLUDES** pneumonia, complicating infectious disease classified elsewhere (484.1-484.8)

AHA: 3Q, '88, 11

482.81 Anaerobes

Bacteroides (melaninogenicus)
Gram-negative anaerobes

482.82 Escherichia coli [E. coli]

482.83 Other gram-negative bacteria

Gram-negative pneumonia NOS
Proteus
Serratia marcescens

> **EXCLUDES** gram-negative anaerobes (482.81)
> Legionnaires' disease (482.84)

AHA: 2Q, '98, 5; 3Q, '94, 9

482.84 Legionnaires' disease

AHA: 4Q, '97, 40

DEF: Severe and often fatal infection by Legionella pneumophilia; symptoms include high fever, gastrointestinal pain, headache, myalgia, dry cough, and pneumonia; transmitted airborne via air conditioning systems, humidifiers, water faucets, shower heads; not person-to-person contact.

482.89 Other specified bacteria

AHA: 2Q, '97, 6

482.9 Bacterial pneumonia unspecified

AHA: 2Q, '98, 6; 2Q, '97, 6; 1Q, '94, 17

✓4ᵗʰ **483 Pneumonia due to other specified organism**

AHA: N-D, '87, 5

483.0 Mycoplasma pneumoniae

Eaton's agent
Pleuropneumonia-like organism [PPLO]

483.1 Chlamydia

AHA: 4Q, '96, 3

483.8 Other specified organism

Ⓝ Newborn Age: 0 　Ⓟ Pediatric Age: 0-17 　Ⓜ Maternity Age: 12-55 　Ⓐ Adult Age: 15-124 　Manifestation Code 　▶◀ Revised Text 　● New Code 　▲ Revised Code Title

√4ᵗʰ **484 Pneumonia in infectious diseases classified elsewhere**

> EXCLUDES *influenza with pneumonia, any form (487.0)*

484.1 Pneumonia in cytomegalic inclusion disease
Code first underlying disease (078.5)

484.3 Pneumonia in whooping cough
Code first underlying disease (033.0-033.9)

484.5 Pneumonia in anthrax
Code first underlying disease (022.1)

484.6 Pneumonia in aspergillosis
Code first underlying disease (117.3)

AHA: 4Q, '97, 40

484.7 Pneumonia in other systemic mycoses
Code first underlying disease
> EXCLUDES *pneumonia in:*
> *candidiasis (112.4)*
> *coccidioidomycosis (114.0)*
> *histoplasmosis (115.0-115.9 with*
> *fifth-digit 5)*

484.8 Pneumonia in other infectious diseases classified elsewhere
Code first underlying disease, as:
Q fever (083.0)
typhoid fever (002.0)
> EXCLUDES *pneumonia in:*
> *actinomycosis (039.1)*
> *measles (055.1)*
> *nocardiosis (039.1)*
> *ornithosis (073.0)*
> *Pneumocystis carinii (136.3)*
> *salmonellosis (003.22)*
> *toxoplasmosis (130.4)*
> *tuberculosis (011.6)*
> *tularemia (021.2)*
> *varicella (052.1)*

485 Bronchopneumonia, organism unspecified
Bronchopneumonia: Pneumonia:
    hemorrhagic   lobular
    terminal   segmental
Pleurobronchopneumonia
> EXCLUDES *bronchiolitis (acute) (466.11-466.19)*
> *chronic (491.8)*
> *lipoid pneumonia (507.1)*

486 Pneumonia, organism unspecified
> EXCLUDES *hypostatic or passive pneumonia (514)*
> *influenza with pneumonia, any form (487.0)*
> *inhalation or aspiration pneumonia due to*
> *foreign materials (507.0-507.8)*
> *pneumonitis due to fumes and vapors (506.0)*

AHA: 4Q, '99, 6; 3Q, '99, 9; 3Q, '98, 7; 2Q, '98, 4, 5; 1Q, '98, 8; 3Q, '97, 9;
3Q, '94, 10; 3Q, '88, 11

√4ᵗʰ **487 Influenza**
> EXCLUDES *Hemophilus influenzae [H. influenzae]:*
> *infection NOS (041.5)*
> *laryngitis (464.00-464.01)*
> *meningitis (320.0)*

487.0 With pneumonia
Influenza with pneumonia, any form
Influenzal:
    bronchopneumonia
    pneumonia
▶Use additional code to identify the type of
pneumonia (480.0-480.9, 481, 482.0-482.9,
483.0-483.8, 485)◀

487.1 With other respiratory manifestations
Influenza NOS
Influenzal:
    laryngitis
    pharyngitis
    respiratory infection (upper) (acute)
AHA: 4Q, '99, 26

Bronchioli and Alveoli

To trachea
Pulmonary arteriole
Terminal bronchiolus
Elastic fibers
Capillary
network
over all
alveioli
Alveoli
Alveolus

487.8 With other manifestations
Encephalopathy due to influenza
Influenza with involvement of gastrointestinal tract
> EXCLUDES *"intestinal flu" [viral gastroenteritis]*
> *(008.8)*

CHRONIC OBSTRUCTIVE PULMONARY DISEASE AND ALLIED CONDITIONS (490-496)

AHA: 3Q, '88, 5

490 Bronchitis, not specified as acute or chronic
Bronchitis NOS: Tracheobronchitis NOS
    catarrhal
    with tracheitis NOS
> EXCLUDES *bronchitis:*
> *allergic NOS (493.9)*
> *due to fumes and vapors (506.0)*

√4ᵗʰ **491 Chronic bronchitis**
> EXCLUDES *chronic obstructive asthma (493.2)*

491.0 Simple chronic bronchitis
Catarrhal bronchitis, chronic
Smokers' cough

491.1 Mucopurulent chronic bronchitis
Bronchitis (chronic) (recurrent):
    fetid
    mucopurulent
    purulent
AHA: 3Q, '88, 12

DEF: Chronic bronchial infection characterized by both mucus and
pus secretions in the bronchial tree; recurs after asymptomatic
periods; signs are coughing, expectoration and secondary changes
in the lung.

√5ᵗʰ **491.2 Obstructive chronic bronchitis**
Bronchitis:
    emphysematous
    obstructive (chronic) (diffuse)
Bronchitis with:
    chronic airway obstruction
    emphysema
> EXCLUDES *asthmatic bronchitis (acute) NOS*
> *(493.9)*
> *chronic obstructive asthma (493.2)*

AHA: 3Q, '97, 9; 4Q, '91, 25; 2Q, '91, 21

491.20 Without exacerbation
Emphysema with chronic bronchitis
AHA: 3Q, '97, 9

√4ᵗʰ
√5ᵗʰ Additional Digit Required   RUG III Special Care Dx   RUG III Clinically Complex Dx   Hospice Non-cancer Dx   CD PDx Clinical Dimension PDx   CD SDx Clinical Dimension SDx

2006 ICD•9•CM   **October 2005 • Volume 1 — 133**

Respiratory System

491.21–494.1

Interrelationship Between Chronic Airway Obstruction, Chronic Bronchitis and Emphysema

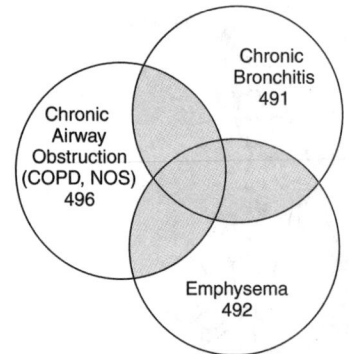

Shaded area:
Obstructive Chronic
Bronchitis (Chronic Bronchitis
with COPD) 491.20-491.21

491.21 With (acute) exacerbation
Acute exacerbation of chronic obstructive
pulmonary disease [COPD]
Decompensated chronic obstructive
pulmonary disease [COPD]
Decompensated chronic obstructive
pulmonary disease [COPD] with
exacerbation
> **EXCLUDES**   chronic obstructive asthma
> with acute exacerbation
> (493.22)

AHA: 1Q, '04, 3; 3Q, '02, 18, 19; 4Q, '01, 43; 2Q, '96, 10

491.22 With acute bronchitis
AHA: 4Q, '04, 82

491.8 Other chronic bronchitis

Chronic:
tracheitis
tracheobronchitis
AHA: 1Q, '92, 12

491.9 Unspecified chronic bronchitis
✓4ᵗʰ 492 Emphysema
492.0 Emphysematous bleb
Giant bullous emphysema
Ruptured emphysematous bleb
Tension pneumatocele
Vanishing lung
AHA: 2Q, '93, 3

DEF: Formation of vesicle or bulla in emphysematous lung, more
than one millimeter; contains serum or blood.

492.8 Other emphysema
Emphysema (lung or   Emphysema (lung or
    pulmonary):   pulmonary):
    NOS   unilateral
    centriacinar   vesicular
    centrilobular   MacLeod's syndrome
    obstructive   Swyer-James syndrome
    panacinar   Unilateral hyperlucent lung
    panlobular
> **EXCLUDES**   emphysema:
> with chronic bronchitis (491.20-
> 491.22)
> compensatory (518.2)
> due to fumes and vapors (506.4)
> interstitial (518.1)
> newborn (770.2)
> mediastinal (518.1)
> surgical (subcutaneous) (998.81)
> traumatic (958.7)

AHA: ▶1Q, '05, 4;◀ 4Q, '93, 41; J-A, '84, 17

✓4ᵗʰ 493 Asthma
> **EXCLUDES**   wheezing NOS (786.07)

The following fifth-digit subclassification is for use with codes
493.0-493.2, 493.9:
   0   **unspecified**
   1   **with status asthmaticus**
   2   **with (acute) exacerbation**

AHA: 4Q, '04, 137; 4Q, '03, 62; 4Q, '01,43; 4Q, '00, 42; 1Q, '91, 13; 3Q, '88, 9;
J-A, '85, 8; N-D, '84, 17

DEF: Status asthmaticus: severe, intractable episode of asthma unresponsive
to normal therapeutic measures.

✓5ᵗʰ 493.0 Extrinsic asthma
Asthma: Asthma:
   allergic with   hay
      stated cause   platinum
   atopic   Hay fever with asthma
   childhood
> **EXCLUDES**   asthma:
> allergic NOS (493.9)
> detergent (507.8)
> miners' (500)
> wood (495.8)

DEF: Transient stricture of airway diameters of bronchi; due to
environmental factor; also called allergic (bronchial) asthma.

✓5ᵗʰ 493.1 Intrinsic asthma
Late-onset asthma
AHA: 3Q, '88, 9; M-A, '85, 7

DEF: Transient stricture, of airway diameters of bronchi; due to
pathophysiological disturbances.

✓5ᵗʰ 493.2 Chronic obstructive asthma
Asthma with chronic obstructive pulmonary disease
[COPD]
Chronic asthmatic bronchitis
> **EXCLUDES**   acute bronchitis (466.0)
> chronic obstructive bronchitis (491.20-
> 491.22)

AHA: 2Q, '91, 21; 2Q, '90, 20; **For code 493.20:** 4Q, '03, 108

DEF: Persistent narrowing of airway diameters in the bronchial
tree, restricting airflow and causing constant labored breathing.

✓5ᵗʰ 493.8 Other forms of asthma
AHA: 4Q, '03, 62

493.81 Exercise induced bronchospasm
493.82 Cough variant asthma

✓5ᵗʰ 493.9 Asthma, unspecified
Asthma (bronchial) (allergic NOS)
Bronchitis:
   allergic
   asthmatic
AHA: 4Q, '97, 40, **For code 493.90:** 4Q, '04, 137; 4Q, '03, 108; 4Q, '99,
25; 1Q, '97, 7; ▶**For code 493.91:** 1Q, '05, 5;◀ **For code 493.92:**
1Q, '03, 9

✓4ᵗʰ 494 Bronchiectasis
Bronchiectasis (fusiform) (postinfectious) (recurrent)
Bronchiolectasis
> **EXCLUDES**   congenital (748.61)
> tuberculous bronchiectasis (current disease)
> (011.5)

AHA: 4Q, '00, 42

DEF: Dilation of bronchi; due to infection or chronic conditions; causes
decreased lung capacity and recurrent infections of lungs.

494.0 Bronchiectasis without acute exacerbation
494.1 Bronchiectasis with acute exacerbation

Ⓝ Newborn Age: 0   Ⓟ Pediatric Age: 0-17   Ⓜ Maternity Age: 12-55   Ⓐ Adult Age: 15-124   Manifestation Code   ▶◀ Revised Text   ● New Code   ▲ Revised Code Title

Respiratory System

495–508.9

✓4ᵗʰ **495 Extrinsic allergic alveolitis**

> INCLUDES   allergic alveolitis and pneumonitis due to inhaled organic dust particles of fungal, thermophilic actinomycete, or other origin

> DEF: Pneumonitis due to particles inhaled into lung, often at workplace; symptoms include cough, chills, fever, increased heart and respiratory rates; develops within hours of exposure.

     495.0 Farmers' lung

     495.1 Bagassosis

     495.2 Bird-fanciers' lung
> Budgerigar-fanciers' disease or lung
> Pigeon-fanciers' disease or lung

     495.3 Suberosis
> Cork-handlers' disease or lung

     495.4 Malt workers' lung
> Alveolitis due to Aspergillus clavatus

     495.5 Mushroom workers' lung

     495.6 Maple bark-strippers' lung
> Alveolitis due to Cryptostroma corticale

     495.7 "Ventilation" pneumonitis
> Allergic alveolitis due to fungal, thermophilic actinomycete, and other organisms growing in ventilation [air conditioning] systems

     495.8 Other specified allergic alveolitis and pneumonitis
> Cheese-washers' lung
> Coffee workers' lung
> Fish-meal workers' lung
> Furriers' lung
> Grain-handlers' disease or lung
> Pituitary snuff-takers' disease
> Sequoiosis or red-cedar asthma
> Wood asthma

     495.9 Unspecified allergic alveolitis and pneumonitis
> Alveolitis, allergic (extrinsic)
> Hypersensitivity pneumonitis

496 Chronic airway obstruction, not elsewhere classified

> Note: This code is not to be used with any code from categories 491-493
> Chronic:
>   nonspecific lung disease
>   obstructive lung disease
>   obstructive pulmonary disease [COPD] NOS

> EXCLUDES   chronic obstructive lung disease [COPD] specified (as) (with):
>   allergic alveolitis (495.0-495.9)
>   asthma (493.20-493.22)
>   bronchiectasis (494.0-494.1)
>   bronchitis (491.20-491.22)
>   with emphysema (491.20-491.22)
>   emphysema (492.0-492.8)

> AHA: 4Q, '03, 109; 2Q, '00, 15; 2Q, '92, 16; 2Q, '91, 21; 3Q, '88, 56

PNEUMOCONIOSES AND OTHER LUNG DISEASES DUE TO EXTERNAL AGENTS (500-508)

> DEF: Permanent deposits of particulate matter, within lungs; due to occupational or environmental exposure; results in chronic induration and fibrosis. (See specific listings in 500-508 code range)

500 Coal workers' pneumoconiosis   A
> Anthracosilicosis   Coal workers' lung
> Anthracosis   Miner's asthma
> Black lung disease

501 Asbestosis   A

502 Pneumoconiosis due to other silica or silicates
> Pneumoconiosis due to talc
> Silicotic fibrosis (massive) of lung
> Silicosis (simple) (complicated)

503 Pneumoconiosis due to other inorganic dust
> Aluminosis (of lung)   Graphite fibrosis (of lung)
> Bauxite fibrosis (of lung)   Siderosis
> Berylliosis   Stannosis

504 Pneumonopathy due to inhalation of other dust
> Byssinosis   Flax-dressers' disease
> Cannabinosis

> EXCLUDES   allergic alveolitis (495.0-495.9)
>   asbestosis (501)
>   bagassosis (495.1)
>   farmers' lung (495.0)

505 Pneumoconiosis, unspecified

✓4ᵗʰ **506 Respiratory conditions due to chemical fumes and vapors**
> Use additional E code to identify cause

     506.0 Bronchitis and pneumonitis due to fumes and vapors
> Chemical bronchitis (acute)

     506.1 Acute pulmonary edema due to fumes and vapors
> Chemical pulmonary edema (acute)
> EXCLUDES   acute pulmonary edema NOS (518.4)
>   chronic or unspecified pulmonary edema (514)

> AHA: 3Q, '88, 4

     506.2 Upper respiratory inflammation due to fumes and vapors

     506.3 Other acute and subacute respiratory conditions due to fumes and vapors

     506.4 Chronic respiratory conditions due to fumes and vapors
> Emphysema (diffuse) (chronic)
> Obliterative bronchiolitis (chronic) (subacute)   } due to inhalation of chemical fumes and vapors
> Pulmonary fibrosis (chronic)

     506.9 Unspecified respiratory conditions due to fumes and vapors
> Silo-fillers' disease

✓4ᵗʰ **507 Pneumonitis due to solids and liquids**
> EXCLUDES   fetal aspiration pneumonitis ▶(770.18)◄

> AHA: 3Q, '91, 16

     507.0 Due to inhalation of food or vomitus
> Aspiration pneumonia (due to):
>   NOS
>   food (regurgitated)
>   gastric secretions
>   milk
>   saliva
>   vomitus

> AHA: 1Q, '89, 10

     507.1 Due to inhalation of oils and essences
> Lipoid pneumonia (exogenous)
> EXCLUDES   endogenous lipoid pneumonia (516.8)

     507.8 Due to other solids and liquids
> Detergent asthma

✓4ᵗʰ **508 Respiratory conditions due to other and unspecified external agents**
> Use additional E code to identify cause

     508.0 Acute pulmonary manifestations due to radiation
> Radiation pneumonitis

> AHA: 2Q, '88, 4

     508.1 Chronic and other pulmonary manifestations due to radiation
> Fibrosis of lung following radiation

     508.8 Respiratory conditions due to other specified external agents

     508.9 Respiratory conditions due to unspecified external agent

---

✓4ᵗʰ / ✓5ᵗʰ **Additional Digit Required**   **RUG III Special Care Dx**   **RUG III Clinically Complex Dx**   **Hospice Non-cancer Dx**   **CD PDx** Clinical Dimension PDx   **CD SDx** Clinical Dimension SDx

Respiratory System

510–516.3

OTHER DISEASES OF RESPIRATORY SYSTEM (510-519)

✓4ᵗʰ 510 Empyema
Use additional code to identify infectious organism (041.0-041.9)

EXCLUDES abscess of lung (513.0)

DEF: Purulent infection, within pleural space.

510.0 With fistula
Fistula:
  bronchocutaneous
  bronchopleural
  hepatopleural
  mediastinal
  pleural
  thoracic
Any condition classifiable to 510.9 with fistula

DEF: Purulent infection of respiratory cavity; with communication from cavity to another structure.

510.9 Without mention of fistula
Abscess: Pleurisy:
  pleura   septic
  thorax   seropurulent
Empyema (chest) (lung)   suppurative
  (pleura)   Pyopneumothorax
Fibrinopurulent pleurisy Pyothorax
Pleurisy:
  purulent

AHA: 3Q, '94, 6

✓4ᵗʰ 511 Pleurisy

EXCLUDES malignant pleural effusion (197.2)
pleurisy with mention of tuberculosis, current disease (012.0)

DEF: Inflammation of serous membrane of lungs and lining of thoracic cavity; causes exudation in cavity or membrane surface.

511.0 Without mention of effusion or current tuberculosis
Adhesion, lung or pleura Pleurisy:
Calcification of pleura   NOS
Pleurisy (acute) (sterile): pneumococcal
  diaphragmatic   staphylococcal
  fibrinous   streptococcal
  interlobar   Thickening of pleura

AHA: 3Q, '94, 5

511.1 With effusion, with mention of a bacterial cause other than tuberculosis
Pleurisy with effusion (exudative) (serous):
  pneumococcal
  staphylococcal
  streptococcal
  other specified nontuberculous bacterial cause

511.8 Other specified forms of effusion, except tuberculous
Encysted pleurisy
Hemopneumothorax
Hemothorax
Hydropneumothorax
Hydrothorax

EXCLUDES traumatic (860.2-860.5, 862.29, 862.39)

AHA: 1Q, '97, 10

511.9 Unspecified pleural effusion
Pleural effusion NOS
Pleurisy:
  exudative
  serofibrinous
  serous
  with effusion NOS

AHA: 2Q, '03, 7; 3Q, '91, 19; 4Q, '89, 11

✓4ᵗʰ 512 Pneumothorax
DEF: Collapsed lung; due to gas or air in pleural space.

512.0 Spontaneous tension pneumothorax
AHA: 3Q, '94, 5

DEF: Leaking air from lung into lining causing collapse.

512.1 Iatrogenic pneumothorax
Postoperative pneumothorax

AHA: 4Q, '94, 40

DEF: Air trapped in the lining of the lung following surgery.

512.8 Other spontaneous pneumothorax
Pneumothorax:
  NOS
  acute
  chronic

EXCLUDES pneumothorax:
  congenital (770.2)
  traumatic (860.0-860.1, 860.4-860.5)
  tuberculous, current disease (011.7)

AHA: 2Q, '93, 3

✓4ᵗʰ 513 Abscess of lung and mediastinum
513.0 Abscess of lung
Abscess (multiple) of lung
Gangrenous or necrotic pneumonia
Pulmonary gangrene or necrosis

AHA: 2Q, '98, 7

513.1 Abscess of mediastinum

514 Pulmonary congestion and hypostasis
Hypostatic: Pulmonary edema:
  bronchopneumonia   NOS
  pneumonia   chronic
Passive pneumonia
Pulmonary congestion
  (chronic) (passive)

EXCLUDES acute pulmonary edema:
  NOS (518.4)
  with mention of heart disease or failure (428.1)

AHA: 2Q, '98, 6; 3Q, '88, 5

DEF: Excessive retention of interstitial fluid in the lungs and pulmonary vessels; due to poor circulation.

515 Postinflammatory pulmonary fibrosis
Cirrhosis of lung
Fibrosis of lung (atrophic)
  (confluent) (massive)   ⎫
  (perialveolar)   ⎬ chronic or unspecified
  (peribronchial)   ⎭
Induration of lung

DEF: Fibrosis and scarring of the lungs due to inflammatory reaction.

✓4ᵗʰ 516 Other alveolar and parietoalveolar pneumonopathy
516.0 Pulmonary alveolar proteinosis

DEF: Reduced ventilation; due to proteinaceous deposits on alveoli; symptoms include dyspnea, cough, chest pain, weakness, weight loss, and hemoptysis.

516.1 Idiopathic pulmonary hemosiderosis
Code first underlying disease (275.0)
Essential brown induration of lung

DEF: Fibrosis of alveolar walls; marked by abnormal amounts hemosiderin in lungs; primarily affects children; symptoms include anemia, fluid in lungs, and blood in sputum; etiology unknown.

516.2 Pulmonary alveolar microlithiasis

DEF: Small calculi in pulmonary alveoli resembling sand-like particles on x-ray.

516.3 Idiopathic fibrosing alveolitis
Alveolar capillary block
Diffuse (idiopathic) (interstitial) pulmonary fibrosis
Hamman-Rich syndrome

N Newborn Age: 0   P Pediatric Age: 0-17   M Maternity Age: 12-55   A Adult Age: 15-124   Manifestation Code   ►◄ Revised Text   ● New Code   ▲ Revised Code Title

136 — Volume 1   *2006 ICD•9•CM*

516.8   Other specified alveolar and parietoalveolar pneumonopathies
    Endogenous lipoid pneumonia
    Interstitial pneumonia (desquamative) (lymphoid)
        EXCLUDES   lipoid pneumonia, exogenous or
                unspecified (507.1)

    AHA: 1Q, '92, 12

516.9   Unspecified alveolar and parietoalveolar pneumonopathy

√4ᵗʰ **517   Lung involvement in conditions classified elsewhere**
        EXCLUDES   rheumatoid lung (714.81)

517.1   *Rheumatic pneumonia*
        Code first underlying disease (390)

517.2   *Lung involvement in systemic sclerosis*
        Code first underlying disease (710.1)

517.3   *Acute chest syndrome*
        *Code first sickle-cell disease in crisis (282.42, 282.62,
            282.64, 282.69)*

    AHA: 4Q, '03, 51, 56

517.8   *Lung involvement in other diseases classified elsewhere*
        Code first underlying disease, as:
            amyloidosis (277.3)
            polymyositis (710.4)
            sarcoidosis (135)
            Sjögren's disease (710.2)
            systemic lupus erythematosus (710.0)
            EXCLUDES   syphilis (095.1)

    AHA: 2Q, '03, 7

√4ᵗʰ **518   Other diseases of lung**

518.0   Pulmonary collapse
    Atelectasis
    Collapse of lung
    Middle lobe syndrome
        EXCLUDES   atelectasis:
                congenital (partial) (770.5)
                primary (770.4)
                tuberculous, current disease (011.8)

    AHA: 4Q, '90, 25

518.1   Interstitial emphysema
    Mediastinal emphysema
        EXCLUDES   surgical (subcutaneous) emphysema
                (998.81)
                that in fetus or newborn (770.2)
                traumatic emphysema (958.7)

    AHA: 4Q, '90, 25

    DEF: Escaped air from the alveoli trapped in the interstices of the
    lung; trauma or cough may cause the disease.

518.2   Compensatory emphysema

    DEF: Distention of all or part of the lung caused by disease
    processes or surgical intervention that decreased volume in
    another part of the lung; overcompensation reaction to the loss of
    capacity in another part of the lung.

518.3   Pulmonary eosinophilia
    Eosinophilic asthma
    Löffler's syndrome
    Pneumonia:
        allergic
        eosinophilic
    Tropical eosinophilia

    DEF: Infiltration, into pulmonary parenchyma of eosinophilia;
    results in cough, fever, and dyspnea.

518.4   Acute edema of lung, unspecified
    Acute pulmonary edema NOS
    Pulmonary edema, postoperative
        EXCLUDES   pulmonary edema:
                acute, with mention of heart disease
                    or failure (428.1)
                chronic or unspecified (514)
                due to external agents (506.0-508.9)

    DEF: Severe, sudden fluid retention within lung tissues.

518.5   Pulmonary insufficiency following trauma and surgery
    Adult respiratory distress syndrome
    Pulmonary insufficiency following:
        shock
        surgery
        trauma
    Shock lung
        EXCLUDES   adult respiratory distress syndrome
                associated with other conditions
                (518.82)
                pneumonia:
                    aspiration (507.0)
                    hypostatic (514)
                respiratory failure in other conditions
                    (518.81, 518.83-518.84)

    AHA: 4Q, '04, 139; 3Q, '88, 3; 3Q, '88, 7; S-O, '87, 1

518.6   Allergic bronchopulmonary aspergillosis

    AHA: 4Q, '97, 40

    DEF: Noninvasive hypersensitive reaction; due to allergic reaction
    to *Aspergillus fumigatus* (mold).

√5ᵗʰ **518.8   Other diseases of lung**

518.81   Acute respiratory failure
    Respiratory failure NOS
        EXCLUDES   acute and chronic respiratory
                failure (518.84)
                acute respiratory distress
                (518.82)
                chronic respiratory failure
                (518.83)
                respiratory arrest (799.1)
                respiratory failure, newborn
                (770.84)

    AHA: ▶1Q, '05, 3-8;◀ 4Q, '04, 139; 1Q, '03, 15; 4Q, '98, 41; 3Q, '91, 14;
            2Q, '91, 3; 2Q, '90, 20; 3Q, '88, 7; 3Q, '88, 10; S-
            O, '87, 17

518.82   Other pulmonary insufficiency, not elsewhere classified
    Acute respiratory distress
    Acute respiratory insufficiency
    Adult respiratory distress syndrome NEC
        EXCLUDES   adult respiratory distress
                syndrome associated
                with trauma and surgery
                (518.5)
                pulmonary insufficiency
                    following trauma and
                    surgery (518.5)
                respiratory distress:
                    NOS (786.09)
                    newborn (770.89)
                    syndrome, newborn (769)
                shock lung (518.5)

    AHA: 4Q, '03, 105; 2Q, '91, 21; 3Q, '88, 7

518.83   Chronic respiratory failure
    AHA: 4Q, '03, 103, 111

518.84   Acute and chronic respiratory failure
    Acute on chronic respiratory failure

√4ᵗʰ
√5ᵗʰ Additional Digit Required   **RUG III Special Care Dx**   **RUG III Clinically Complex Dx**   **Hospice Non-cancer Dx**   **CD PDx** Clinical Dimension PDx   **CD SDx** Clinical Dimension SDx

518.89 Other diseases of lung, not elsewhere classified

Broncholithiasis   Lung disease NOS
Calcification of lung   Pulmolithiasis

AHA: 3Q, '90, 18; 4Q, '88, 6

DEF: Broncholithiasis: calculi in lumen of transbronchial tree.

DEF: Pulmolithiasis: calculi in lung.

√4ᵗʰ **519 Other diseases of respiratory system**

√5ᵗʰ **519.0 Tracheostomy complications**

519.00 Tracheostomy complication, unspecified

519.01 Infection of tracheostomy

Use additional code to identify type of infection, such as:
abscess or cellulitis of neck (682.1)
septicemia (038.0-038.9)
Use additional code to identify organism (041.00-041.9)

AHA: 4Q, '98, 41

519.02 Mechanical complication of tracheostomy

Tracheal stenosis due to tracheostomy

519.09 Other tracheostomy complications

Hemorrhage due to tracheostomy
Tracheoesophageal fistula due to tracheostomy

519.1 Other diseases of trachea and bronchus, not elsewhere classified

Calcification ⎤
Stenosis   ⎬ of bronchus or trachea
Ulcer   ⎦

AHA: 3Q, '02, 18; 3Q, '88, 6

519.2 Mediastinitis

DEF: Inflammation of tissue between organs behind sternum.

519.3 Other diseases of mediastinum, not elsewhere classified

Fibrosis ⎤
Hernia   ⎬ of mediastinum
Retraction ⎦

519.4 Disorders of diaphragm

Diaphragmitis   Relaxation of diaphragm
Paralysis of diaphragm

EXCLUDES *congenital defect of diaphragm (756.6)*
diaphragmatic hernia (551-553 with .3)
congenital (756.6)

519.8 Other diseases of respiratory system, not elsewhere classified

AHA: 4Q, '89, 12

519.9 Unspecified disease of respiratory system

Respiratory disease (chronic) NOS

N Newborn Age: 0   P Pediatric Age: 0-17   M Maternity Age: 12-55   A Adult Age: 15-124   Manifestation Code   ▶◀ Revised Text   ● New Code   ▲ Revised Code Title

138 — Volume 1   *2006 ICD•9•CM*

9. DISEASES OF THE DIGESTIVE SYSTEM (520-579)

DISEASES OF ORAL CAVITY, SALIVARY GLANDS, AND JAWS (520-529)

√4ᵗʰ 520 Disorders of tooth development and eruption

520.0 Anodontia
Absence of teeth (complete) (congenital) (partial)
fHypodontia
Oligodontia
> **EXCLUDES** *acquired absence of teeth (525.10-525.19)*

520.1 Supernumerary teeth
Distomolar   Paramolar
Fourth molar   Supplemental teeth
Mesiodens
> **EXCLUDES** *supernumerary roots (520.2)*

520.2 Abnormalities of size and form
Concrescence ⎫
Fusion   ⎬ of teeth
Gemination   ⎭

Dens evaginatus   Microdontia
Dens in dente   Peg-shaped [conical] teeth
Dens invaginatus   Supernumerary roots
Enamel pearls   Taurodontism
Macrodontia   Tuberculum paramolare
> **EXCLUDES** *that due to congenital syphilis (090.5) tuberculum Carabelli, which is regarded as a normal variation*

520.3 Mottled teeth
Mottling of enamel
Dental fluorosis   Nonfluoride enamel opacities

Digestive System

The Oral Cavity

Teeth

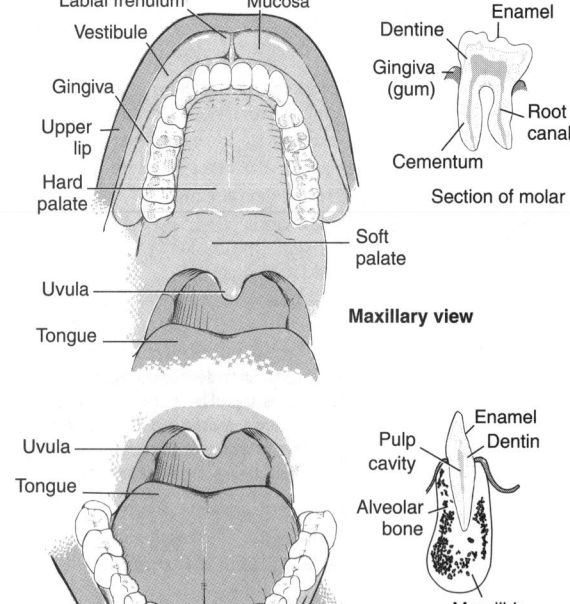

Maxillary view

Mandibulary view

Section of molar

Section of incisor

520.4 Disturbances of tooth formation
Aplasia and hypoplasia of cementum
Dilaceration of tooth
Enamel hypoplasia (neonatal) (postnatal) (prenatal)
Horner's teeth
Hypocalcification of teeth
Regional odontodysplasia
Turner's tooth
> **EXCLUDES** *Hutchinson's teeth and mulberry molars in congenital syphilis (090.5)*
> *mottled teeth (520.3)*

520.5 Hereditary disturbances in tooth structure, not elsewhere classified
Amelogenesis   ⎫
Dentinogenesis ⎬ imperfecta
Odontogenesis ⎭

Dentinal dysplasia
Shell teeth

520.6 Disturbances in tooth eruption
Teeth: Tooth eruption:
  embedded   late
  impacted   obstructed
  natal   premature
  neonatal
  primary [deciduous]:
    persistent
    shedding, premature
> **EXCLUDES** *exfoliation of teeth (attributable to disease of surrounding tissues) (525.0-525.19)*

520.7 Teething syndrome

520.8 Other specified disorders of tooth development and eruption
Color changes during tooth formation
Pre-eruptive color changes
> **EXCLUDES** *posteruptive color changes (521.7)*

520.9 Unspecified disorder of tooth development and eruption

√4ᵗʰ
√5ᵗʰ Additional Digit Required   RUG III Special Care Dx   RUG III Clinically Complex Dx   Hospice Non-cancer Dx   **CD PDx** Clinical Dimension PDx   **CD SDx** Clinical Dimension SDx

2006 ICD•9•CM   Volume 1 — 139

√4th **521 Diseases of hard tissues of teeth**

√5th **521.0 Dental caries**

521.00 Dental caries, unspecified
AHA: 4Q, '01,44

521.01 Dental caries limited to enamel
Initial caries   White spot lesion

521.02 Dental caries extending into dentine

521.03 Dental caries extending into pulp

521.04 Arrested dental caries

521.05 Odontoclasia
Infantile melanodontia
Melanodontoclasia
EXCLUDES internal and external resorption of teeth (521.40-521.49)

DEF: A pathological dental condition described as stained areas, loss of tooth substance, and hypoplasia linked to nutritional deficiencies during tooth development and to cariogenic oral conditions; synonyms are melanodontoclasia and infantile melanodontia.

521.06 Dental caries pit and fissure

521.07 Dental caries of smooth surface

521.08 Dental caries of root surface

521.09 Other dental caries
AHA: 3Q, '02, 14

√5th **521.1 Excessive attrition (approximal wear) (occlusal wear)**

521.10 Excessive attrition, unspecified

521.11 Excessive attrition, limited to enamel

521.12 Excessive attrition, extending into dentine

521.13 Excessive attrition, extending into pulp

521.14 Excessive attrition, localized

521.15 Excessive attrition, generalized

√5th **521.2 Abrasion**
Abrasion:
dentifrice
habitual
occupational } of teeth
ritual
traditional
Wedge defect NOS

521.20 Abrasion, unspecified

521.21 Abrasion, limited to enamel

521.22 Abrasion, extending into dentine

521.23 Abrasion, extending into pulp

521.24 Abrasion, localized

521.25 Abrasion, generalized

√5th **521.3 Erosion**
Erosion of teeth: Erosion of teeth:
NOS   idiopathic
due to: occupational
medicine
persistent vomiting

521.30 Erosion, unspecified

521.31 Erosion, limited to enamel

521.32 Erosion, extending into dentine

521.33 Erosion, extending into pulp

521.34 Erosion, localized

521.35 Erosion, generalized

√5th **521.4 Pathological resorption**
DEF: Loss of dentin and cementum due to disease process.

521.40 Pathological resorption, unspecified

521.41 Pathological resorption, internal

521.42 Pathological resorption, external

521.49 Other pathological resorption
Internal granuloma of pulp

521.5 Hypercementosis
Cementation hyperplasia
DEF: Excess deposits of cementum, on tooth root.

521.6 Ankylosis of teeth
DEF: Adhesion of tooth to surrounding bone.

521.7 Intrinsic posteruptive color changes
Staining [discoloration] of teeth:
NOS
due to:
drugs
metals
pulpal bleeding
EXCLUDES accretions [deposits] on teeth (523.6)
extrinsic color changes (523.6)
pre-eruptive color changes (520.8)

521.8 Other specified diseases of hard tissues of teeth
Irradiated enamel   Sensitive dentin

521.9 Unspecified disease of hard tissues of teeth

√4th **522 Diseases of pulp and periapical tissues**

522.0 Pulpitis
Pulpal:
abscess
polyp
Pulpitis:
acute
chronic (hyperplastic) (ulcerative)
suppurative

522.1 Necrosis of the pulp
Pulp gangrene
DEF: Death of pulp tissue.

522.2 Pulp degeneration
Denticles   Pulp stones
Pulp calcifications

522.3 Abnormal hard tissue formation in pulp
Secondary or irregular dentin

522.4 Acute apical periodontitis of pulpal origin
DEF: Severe inflammation of periodontal ligament due to pulpal inflammation or necrosis.

522.5 Periapical abscess without sinus
Abscess: Abscess:
dental   dentoalveolar
EXCLUDES periapical abscess with sinus (522.7)

522.6 Chronic apical periodontitis
Apical or periapical granuloma
Apical periodontitis NOS

522.7 Periapical abscess with sinus
Fistula: Fistula:
alveolar process   dental

522.8 Radicular cyst
Cyst: Cyst:
apical (periodontal)   residual radicular
periapical
radiculodental
EXCLUDES lateral developmental or lateral periodontal cyst (526.0)
DEF: Cyst in tissue around tooth apex due to chronic infection of granuloma around root.

522.9 Other and unspecified diseases of pulp and periapical tissues

√4th **523 Gingival and periodontal diseases**

523.0 Acute gingivitis
EXCLUDES acute necrotizing ulcerative gingivitis (101)
herpetic gingivostomatitis (054.2)

523.1 Chronic gingivitis
Gingivitis (chronic):   Gingivitis (chronic):
NOS   simple marginal
desquamative   ulcerative
hyperplastic   Gingivostomatitis
EXCLUDES herpetic gingivostomatitis (054.2)

√5th **523.2 Gingival recession**
Gingival recession (postinfective) (postoperative)

523.20 Gingival recession, unspecified

523.21 Gingival recession, minimal

523.22 Gingival recession, moderate

N Newborn Age: 0   P Pediatric Age: 0-17   M Maternity Age: 12-55   A Adult Age: 15-124   Manifestation Code   ▶◀ Revised Text   ● New Code   ▲ Revised Code Title

523.23 Gingival recession, severe

523.24 Gingival recession, localized

523.25 Gingival recession, generalized

523.3 Acute periodontitis

Acute: Paradontal abscess
  pericementitis   Periodontal abscess
  pericoronitis

EXCLUDES acute apical periodontitis (522.4)
periapical abscess (522.5, 522.7)

DEF: Severe inflammation, of tissues supporting teeth.

523.4 Chronic periodontitis

Alveolar pyorrhea   Periodontitis:
Chronic pericoronitis   complex
Pericementitis (chronic)   simplex
Periodontitis:
  NOS

EXCLUDES chronic apical periodontitis (522.6)

523.5 Periodontosis

523.6 Accretions on teeth

Dental calculus:
  subgingival
  supragingival
Deposits on teeth:
  betel
  materia alba
  soft
  tartar
  tobacco
Extrinsic discoloration of teeth

EXCLUDES intrinsic discoloration of teeth (521.7)

DEF: Foreign material on tooth surface, usually plaque or calculus.

523.8 Other specified periodontal diseases

Giant cell: Gingival polyp
  epulis   Periodontal lesions due to
  peripheral granuloma   traumatic occlusion
Gingival: Peripheral giant cell
  cysts   granuloma
  enlargement NOS
  fibromatosis

EXCLUDES leukoplakia of gingiva (528.6)

523.9 Unspecified gingival and periodontal disease

AHA: 3Q, '02, 14

✓4th 524 Dentofacial anomalies, including malocclusion

✓5th 524.0 Major anomalies of jaw size

EXCLUDES hemifacial atrophy or hypertrophy
(754.0)
unilateral condylar hyperplasia or
hypoplasia of mandible (526.89)

524.00 Unspecified anomaly

DEF: Unspecified deformity of jaw size.

524.01 Maxillary hyperplasia

DEF: Overgrowth or over development of upper jaw bone.

524.02 Mandibular hyperplasia

DEF: Overgrowth or over development of lower jaw bone.

524.03 Maxillary hypoplasia

DEF: Incomplete or underdeveloped, upper jaw bone.

524.04 Mandibular hypoplasia

DEF: Incomplete or underdeveloped, lower jaw bone.

524.05 Macrogenia

DEF: Enlarged, jaw, especially chin; affects bone, soft tissue, or both.

524.06 Microgenia

DEF: Underdeveloped mandible, characterized by an extremely small chin.

524.07 Excessive tuberosity of jaw

524.09 Other specified anomaly

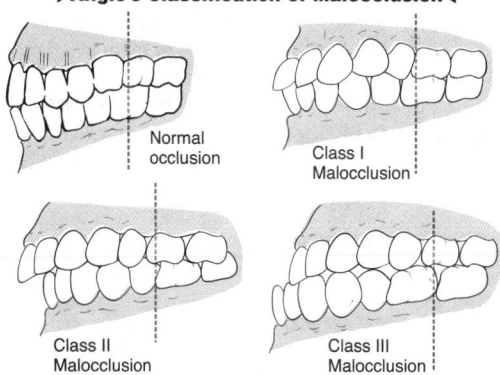

▶**Angle's Classification of Malocclusion**◀

Normal occlusion

Class I Malocclusion

Class II Malocclusion

Class III Malocclusion

✓5th 524.1 Anomalies of relationship of jaw to cranial base

524.10 Unspecified anomaly

Prognathism   Retrognathism

DEF: Prognathism: protrusion of lower jaw.

DEF: Retrognathism: jaw is located posteriorly to a normally positioned jaw; backward position of mandible.

524.11 Maxillary asymmetry

DEF: Absence of symmetry of maxilla.

524.12 Other jaw asymmetry

524.19 Other specified anomaly

✓5th 524.2 Anomalies of dental arch relationship

EXCLUDES hemifacial atrophy or hypertrophy
(754.0)
soft tissue impingement (524.81-
524.82)
unilateral condylar hyperplasia or
hypoplasia of mandible (526.89)

524.20 Unspecified anomaly of dental arch relationship

524.21 Angle's class I

Neutro-occlusion

524.22 Angle's class II

Disto-occlusion Division I
Disto-occlusion Division II

524.23 Angle's class III

Mesio-occlusion

524.24 Open anterior occlusal relationship

524.25 Open posterior occlusal relationship

524.26 Excessive horizontal overlap

524.27 Reverse articulation

Anterior articulation
Posterior articulation

524.28 Anomalies of interarch distance

Excessive interarch distance
Inadequate interarch distance

524.29 Other anomalies of dental arch relationship

✓5th 524.3 Anomalies of tooth position of fully erupted teeth

EXCLUDES impacted or embedded teeth with
abnormal position of such teeth
or adjacent teeth (520.6)

524.30 Unspecified anomaly of tooth position

Diastema of teeth NOS
Displacement of teeth NOS
Transposition of teeth NOS

524.31 Crowding of teeth

524.32 Excessive spacing of teeth

524.33 Horizontal displacement of teeth

Tipping of teeth

524.34 Vertical displacement of teeth

Infraeruption of teeth
Supraeruption of teeth

524.35 Rotation of teeth

524.36 Insufficient interocclusal distance of teeth (ridge)

✓4th
✓5th Additional Digit Required   RUG III Special Care Dx   RUG III Clinically Complex Dx   Hospice Non-cancer Dx   CD PDx Clinical Dimension PDx   CD SDx Clinical Dimension SDx

2006 ICD•9•CM

February 2005 • Volume 1 — 141

Digestive System

524.37–526.4

524.37 Excessive interocclusal distance of teeth
Loss of occlusal vertical dimension

524.39 Other anomalies of tooth position

524.4 Malocclusion, unspecified
DEF: Malposition of top and bottom teeth; interferes with chewing.

√5th **524.5 Dentofacial functional abnormalities**

524.50 Dentofacial functional abnormality, unspecified

524.51 Abnormal jaw closure

524.52 Limited mandibular range of motion

524.53 Deviation in opening and closing of the mandible

524.54 Insufficient anterior guidance

524.55 Centric occlusion maximum intercuspation discrepancy

524.56 Non-working side interference

524.57 Lack of posterior occlusal support

524.59 Other dentofacial functional abnormalities
Abnormal swallowing Sleep postures
Mouth breathing Tongue, lip, or finger
habits

√5th **524.6 Temporomandibular joint disorders**
EXCLUDES current temporomandibular joint:
dislocation (830.0-830.1)
strain (848.1)

524.60 Temporomandibular joint disorders, unspecified
Temporomandibular joint-pain-dysfunction syndrome [TMJ]

524.61 Adhesions and ankylosis (bony or fibrous)
DEF: Stiffening or union of temporomandibular joint due to bony or fibrous union across joint.

524.62 Arthralgia of temporomandibular joint
DEF: Pain in temporomandibular joint; not inflammatory in nature.

524.63 Articular disc disorder (reducing or non-reducing)

524.64 Temporomandibular joint sounds on opening and/or closing the jaw

524.69 Other specified temporomandibular joint disorders

√5th **524.7 Dental alveolar anomalies**

524.70 Unspecified alveolar anomaly

524.71 Alveolar maxillary hyperplasia
DEF: Excessive tissue formation in the dental alveoli of upper jaw.

524.72 Alveolar mandibular hyperplasia
DEF: Excessive tissue formation in the dental alveoli of lower jaw.

524.73 Alveolar maxillary hypoplasia
DEF: Incomplete or underdeveloped, alveolar tissue of upper jaw.

524.74 Alveolar mandibular hypoplasia
DEF: Incomplete or underdeveloped, alveolar tissue of lower jaw.

524.75 Vertical displacement of alveolus and teeth
Extrusion of alveolus and teeth

524.76 Occlusal plane deviation

524.79 Other specified alveolar anomaly

√5th **524.8 Other specified dentofacial anomalies**

524.81 Anterior soft tissue impingement

524.82 Posterior soft tissue impingement

524.89 Other specified dentofacial anomalies

524.9 Unspecified dentofacial anomalies

√4th **525 Other diseases and conditions of the teeth and supporting structures**

525.0 Exfoliation of teeth due to systemic causes
DEF: Deterioration of teeth and surrounding structures due to systemic disease.

√5th **525.1 Loss of teeth due to trauma, extraction, or periodontal disease**
►Code first class of edentulism (525.40-525.44, 525.50-525.54)◄
AHA: 4Q, '01, 44

525.10 Acquired absence of teeth, unspecified
Tooth extraction status, NOS

525.11 Loss of teeth due to trauma

525.12 Loss of teeth due to periodontal disease

525.13 Loss of teeth due to caries

525.19 Other loss of teeth

√5th **525.2 Atrophy of edentulous alveolar ridge**

525.20 Unspecified atrophy of edentulous alveolar ridge
Atrophy of the mandible NOS
Atrophy of the maxilla NOS

525.21 Minimal atrophy of the mandible

525.22 Moderate atrophy of the mandible

525.23 Severe atrophy of the mandible

525.24 Minimal atrophy of the maxilla

525.25 Moderate atrophy of the maxilla

525.26 Severe atrophy of the maxilla

525.3 Retained dental root

● √5th **525.4 Complete edentulism**
Use additional code to identify cause of edentulism (525.10-525.19)

● **525.40 Complete edentulism, unspecified**
Edentulism NOS

● **525.41 Complete edentulism, class I**

● **525.42 Complete edentulism, class II**

● **525.43 Complete edentulism, class III**

● **525.44 Complete edentulism, class IV**

● √5th **525.5 Partial edentulism**
Use additional code to identify cause of edentulism (525.10-525.19)

● **525.50 Partial edentulism, unspecified**

● **525.51 Partial edentulism, class I**

● **525.52 Partial edentulism, class II**

● **525.53 Partial edentulism, class III**

● **525.54 Partial edentulism, class IV**

525.8 Other specified disorders of the teeth and supporting structures
Enlargement of alveolar ridge NOS
Irregular alveolar process

525.9 Unspecified disorder of the teeth and supporting structures

√4th **526 Diseases of the jaws**

526.0 Developmental odontogenic cysts
Cyst: Cyst:
dentigerous lateral periodontal
eruption primordial
follicular Keratocyst
lateral developmental
EXCLUDES radicular cyst (522.8)

526.1 Fissural cysts of jaw
Cyst: Cyst:
globulomaxillary median palatal
incisor canal nasopalatine
median anterior maxillary palatine of papilla
EXCLUDES cysts of oral soft tissues (528.4)

526.2 Other cysts of jaws
Cyst of jaw: Cyst of jaw:
NOS hemorrhagic
aneurysmal traumatic

526.3 Central giant cell (reparative) granuloma
EXCLUDES peripheral giant cell granuloma (523.8)

526.4 Inflammatory conditions
Abscess
Osteitis ⎫ of jaw (acute) (chronic)
Osteomyelitis (neonatal) ⎬ (suppurative)
Periostitis ⎭
Sequestrum of jaw bone
EXCLUDES alveolar osteitis (526.5)

N Newborn Age: 0 P Pediatric Age: 0-17 M Maternity Age: 12-55 A Adult Age: 15-124 Manifestation Code ►◄ Revised Text ● New Code ▲ Revised Code Title

526.5 Alveolitis of jaw
Alveolar osteitis   Dry socket
DEF: Inflammation, of alveoli or tooth socket.

√5th **526.8 Other specified diseases of the jaws**
526.81 Exostosis of jaw
Torus mandibularis   Torus palatinus
DEF: Spur or bony outgrowth on the jaw.

526.89 Other
Cherubism
Fibrous dysplasia } of jaw(s)
Latent bone cyst
Osteoradionecrosis

Unilateral condylar hyperplasia or
hypoplasia of mandible

526.9 Unspecified disease of the jaws

√4th **527 Diseases of the salivary glands**

527.0 Atrophy
DEF: Wasting away, necrosis of salivary gland tissue.

527.1 Hypertrophy
DEF: Overgrowth or overdeveloped salivary gland tissue.

527.2 Sialoadenitis
Parotitis: Sialoangitis
  NOS   Sialodochitis
  allergic
  toxic
> EXCLUDES   epidemic or infectious parotitis (072.0-
> 072.9)
> uveoparotid fever (135)

DEF: Inflammation of salivary gland.

527.3 Abscess

527.4 Fistula
> EXCLUDES   congenital fistula of salivary gland
> (750.24)

527.5 Sialolithiasis
Calculus } of salivary gland or duct
Stone
Sialodocholithiasis

527.6 Mucocele
Mucous:
  extravasation cyst of salivary gland
  retention cyst of salivary gland
Ranula
DEF: Dilated salivary gland cavity filled with mucous.

527.7 Disturbance of salivary secretion
Hyposecretion   Sialorrhea
Ptyalism   Xerostomia

527.8 Other specified diseases of the salivary glands
Benign lymphoepithelial lesion of salivary gland
Sialectasia
Sialosis
Stenosis } of salivary duct
Stricture

527.9 Unspecified disease of the salivary glands

√4th **528 Diseases of the oral soft tissues, excluding lesions specific for gingiva and tongue**

528.0 Stomatitis
Stomatitis: Vesicular stomatitis
  NOS
  ulcerative
> EXCLUDES   stomatitis:
> acute necrotizing ulcerative (101)
> aphthous (528.2)
> gangrenous (528.1)
> herpetic (054.2)
> Vincent's (101)

AHA: 2Q, '99, 9
DEF: Inflammation of oral mucosa; labial and buccal mucosa, tongue, plate, floor of the mouth, and gingivae.

528.1 Cancrum oris
Gangrenous stomatitis   Noma
DEF: A severely gangrenous lesion of mouth due to fusospirochetal infection; destroys buccal, labial and facial tissues; can be fatal; found primarily in debilitated and malnourished children.

528.2 Oral aphthae
Aphthous stomatitis
Canker sore
Periadenitis mucosa necrotica recurrens
Recurrent aphthous ulcer
Stomatitis herpetiformis
> EXCLUDES   herpetic stomatitis (054.2)

DEF: Small oval or round ulcers of the mouth marked by a grayish exudate and a red halo effect.

528.3 Cellulitis and abscess
Cellulitis of mouth (floor)   Oral fistula
Ludwig's angina
> EXCLUDES   abscess of tongue (529.0)
> cellulitis or abscess of lip (528.5)
> fistula (of):
> dental (522.7)
> lip (528.5)
> gingivitis (523.0-523.1)

528.4 Cysts
Dermoid cyst
Epidermoid cyst
Epstein's pearl
Lymphoepithelial cyst } of mouth
Nasoalveolar cyst
Nasolabial cyst
> EXCLUDES   cyst:
> gingiva (523.8)
> tongue (529.8)

528.5 Diseases of lips
Abscess
Cellulitis } of lip(s)
Fistula
Hypertrophy

Cheilitis: Cheilodynia
  NOS   Cheilosis
  angular
> EXCLUDES   actinic cheilitis (692.79)
> congenital fistula of lip (750.25)
> leukoplakia of lips (528.6)

AHA: S-O, '86, 10

528.6 Leukoplakia of oral mucosa, including tongue
Leukokeratosis of oral   Leukoplakia of:
  mucosa   lips
Leukoplakia of: tongue
  gingiva
> EXCLUDES   carcinoma in situ (230.0, 232.0)
> leukokeratosis nicotina palati (528.79)

DEF: Thickened white patches of epithelium on mucous membranes of mouth.

√5th **528.7 Other disturbances of oral epithelium, including tongue**
> EXCLUDES   carcinoma in situ (230.0, 232.0)
> leukokeratosis NOS (702)

528.71 Minimal keratinized residual ridge mucosa

528.72 Excessive keratinized residual ridge mucosa

528.79 Other disturbances of oral epithelium, including tongue
Erythroplakia of mouth or tongue
Focal epithelial hyperplasia of mouth or
  tongue
Leukoedema of mouth or tongue
Leukokeratosis nicotina palate

528.8 Oral submucosal fibrosis, including of tongue

528.9 Other and unspecified diseases of the oral soft tissues
Cheek and lip biting
Denture sore mouth
Denture stomatitis
Melanoplakia
Papillary hyperplasia of palate
Eosinophilic granuloma
Irritative hyperplasia } of oral mucosa
Pyogenic granuloma
Ulcer (traumatic)

√4th √5th Additional Digit Required   RUG III Special Care Dx   RUG III Clinically Complex Dx   Hospice Non-cancer Dx   CD PDx Clinical Dimension PDx   CD SDx Clinical Dimension SDx

2006 ICD•9•CM   **Volume 1 — 143**

✓4ᵗʰ **529 Diseases and other conditions of the tongue**

529.0 Glossitis

Abscess
Ulceration (traumatic) } of tongue

> **EXCLUDES** glossitis:
> benign migratory (529.1)
> Hunter's (529.4)
> median rhomboid (529.2)
> Moeller's (529.4)

529.1 Geographic tongue

Benign migratory glossitis   Glossitis areata
exfoliativa
DEF: Chronic glossitis; marked by filiform papillae atrophy and
inflammation; no known etiology.

529.2 Median rhomboid glossitis

DEF: A noninflammatory, congenital disease characterized by
rhomboid-like lesions at the middle third of the tongue's dorsal
surface.

529.3 Hypertrophy of tongue papillae

Black hairy tongue   Hypertrophy of foliate papillae
Coated tongue   Lingua villosa nigra

529.4 Atrophy of tongue papillae

Bald tongue   Glossitis:
Glazed tongue   Moeller's
Glossitis: Glossodynia exfoliativa
Hunter's   Smooth atrophic tongue

529.5 Plicated tongue

Fissured
Furrowed } tongue
Scrotal

> **EXCLUDES** fissure of tongue, congenital (750.13)

DEF: Cracks, fissures or furrows, on dorsal surface of tongue.

529.6 Glossodynia

Glossopyrosis   Painful tongue
> **EXCLUDES** glossodynia exfoliativa (529.4)

529.8 Other specified conditions of the tongue

Atrophy
Crenated
Enlargement } (of) tongue
Hypertrophy

Glossocele
Glossoptosis

> **EXCLUDES** erythroplasia of tongue (528.79)
> leukoplakia of tongue (528.6)
> macroglossia (congenital) (750.15)
> microglossia (congenital) (750.16)
> oral submucosal fibrosis (528.8)

529.9 Unspecified condition of the tongue

DISEASES OF ESOPHAGUS, STOMACH, AND DUODENUM (530-537)

✓4ᵗʰ **530 Diseases of esophagus**

> **EXCLUDES** esophageal varices (456.0-456.2)

530.0 Achalasia and cardiospasm

Achalasia (of cardia)   Megaesophagus
Aperistalsis of esophagus
> **EXCLUDES** congenital cardiospasm (750.7)

DEF: Failure of smooth muscle fibers to relax, at gastrointestinal
junctures; such as esophagogastric sphincter when swallowing.

✓5ᵗʰ **530.1 Esophagitis**

Abscess of esophagus   Esophagitis:
Esophagitis: peptic
NOS   postoperative
chemical   regurgitant
Use additional E code to identify cause, if induced
by chemical
> **EXCLUDES** tuberculous esophagitis (017.8)

AHA: 4Q, '93, 27; 1Q, '92, 17; 3Q, '91, 20

530.10 Esophagitis, unspecified

530.11 Reflux esophagitis

AHA: 4Q, '95, 82

DEF: Inflammation of lower esophagus; due to
regurgitated gastric acid.

Esophagus

530.12 Acute esophagitis

AHA: 4Q, '01, 45

DEF: An acute inflammation of the mucous lining or
submucosal coat of the esophagus.

530.19 Other esophagitis

AHA: 3Q, '01, 10

✓5ᵗʰ **530.2 Ulcer of esophagus**

Ulcer of esophagus: Ulcer of esophagus:
fungal   peptic
Ulcer of esophagus due to ingestion of:
aspirin   chemicals
medicines
Use additional E code to identify cause, if induced
by chemical or drug

AHA: 4Q, '03, 63

530.20 Ulcer of esophagus without bleeding

Ulcer of esophagus NOS

530.21 Ulcer of esophagus with bleeding

> **EXCLUDES** bleeding esophageal varices
> (456.0, 456.20)

530.3 Stricture and stenosis of esophagus

Compression of esophagus
Obstruction of esophagus
> **EXCLUDES** congenital stricture of esophagus (750.3)

AHA: 2Q, '01, 4; 2Q, '97, 3; 1Q, '88, 13

530.4 Perforation of esophagus

Rupture of esophagus
> **EXCLUDES** traumatic perforation of esophagus
> (862.22, 862.32, 874.4-874.5)

530.5 Dyskinesia of esophagus

Corkscrew esophagus   Esophagospasm
Curling esophagus   Spasm of esophagus
> **EXCLUDES** cardiospasm (530.0)

AHA: 1Q, '88, 13; N-D, '84, 19

DEF: Difficulty performing voluntary esophageal movements.

530.6 Diverticulum of esophagus, acquired

Diverticulum, acquired: Diverticulum, acquired:
epiphrenic   traction
pharyngoesophageal   Zenker's
pulsion   (hypopharyngeal)
subdiaphragmatic   Esophageal pouch, acquired
Esophagocele, acquired
> **EXCLUDES** congenital diverticulum of esophagus
> (750.4)

AHA: J-F, '85, 3

530.7 Gastroesophageal laceration-hemorrhage syndrome

Mallory-Weiss syndrome
DEF: Laceration of distal esophagus and proximal stomach due to
vomiting, hiccups or other sustained activity.

✓5ᵗʰ **530.8 Other specified disorders of esophagus**

530.81 Esophageal reflux

Gastroesophageal reflux
> **EXCLUDES** reflux esophagitis (530.11)

AHA: 2Q, '01, 4; 1Q, '95, 7; 4Q, '92, 27

DEF: Regurgitation of the gastric contents into esophagus
and possibly pharynx; where aspiration may occur
between the vocal cords and down into the trachea.

N Newborn Age: 0   P Pediatric Age: 0-17   M Maternity Age: 12-55   A Adult Age: 15-124   Manifestation Code   ▶◀ Revised Text   ● New Code   ▲ Revised Code Title

530.82 Esophageal hemorrhage

> EXCLUDES   hemorrhage due to esophageal varices (456.0-456.2)

AHA: ▶1Q, '05, 17;◀ 4Q, '03, 63

530.83 Esophageal leukoplakia

530.84 Tracheoesophageal fistula

> EXCLUDES   congenital tracheoesophageal fistula (750.3)

530.86 Infection of esophagostomy

> Use additional code to specify infection

530.87 Mechanical complication of esophagostomy

> Malfunction of esophagostomy

530.85 Barrett's esophagus

AHA 4Q, '03, 63

DEF: A metaplastic disorder in which specialized columnar epithelial cells replace the normal squamous epithelial cells; an acquired condition secondary to chronic gastroesophageal reflux damage to the mucosa; associated with increased risk of developing adenocarcinoma.

530.89 Other

> EXCLUDES   Paterson-Kelly syndrome (280.8)

530.9 Unspecified disorder of esophagus

√4th **531 Gastric ulcer**

> INCLUDES   ulcer (peptic):
> prepyloric
> pylorus
> stomach

Use additional E code to identify drug, if drug-induced

> EXCLUDES   peptic ulcer NOS (533.0-533.9)

The following fifth-digit subclassification is for use with category 531:

0 without mention of obstruction
1 with obstruction

AHA: 1Q, '91, 15; 4Q, '90, 27

DEF: Destruction of tissue in lumen of stomach due to action of gastric acid and pepsin on gastric mucosa decreasing resistance to ulcers.

√5th **531.0 Acute with hemorrhage**
AHA: N-D, '84, 15

√5th **531.1 Acute with perforation**

√5th **531.2 Acute with hemorrhage and perforation**

√5th **531.3 Acute without mention of hemorrhage or perforation**

√5th **531.4 Chronic or unspecified with hemorrhage**
AHA: 4Q, '90, 22

√5th **531.5 Chronic or unspecified with perforation**

√5th **531.6 Chronic or unspecified with hemorrhage and perforation**

√5th **531.7 Chronic without mention of hemorrhage or perforation**

√5th **531.9 Unspecified as acute or chronic, without mention of hemorrhage or perforation**

√4th **532 Duodenal ulcer**

> INCLUDES   erosion (acute) of duodenum
> ulcer (peptic):
> duodenum
> postpyloric

Use additional E code to identify drug, if drug-induced

> EXCLUDES   peptic ulcer NOS (533.0-533.9)

The following fifth-digit subclassification is for use with category 532:

0 without mention of obstruction
1 with obstruction

AHA: 4Q, '90, 27; 1Q, '91, 15

DEF: Ulcers in duodenum due to action of gastric acid and pepsin on mucosa decreasing resistance to ulcers.

√5th **532.0 Acute with hemorrhage**
AHA: 4Q, '90, 22

√5th **532.1 Acute with perforation**

Stomach

√5th **532.2 Acute with hemorrhage and perforation**

√5th **532.3 Acute without mention of hemorrhage or perforation**

√5th **532.4 Chronic or unspecified with hemorrhage**

√5th **532.5 Chronic or unspecified with perforation**

√5th **532.6 Chronic or unspecified with hemorrhage and perforation**

√5th **532.7 Chronic without mention of hemorrhage or perforation**

√5th **532.9 Unspecified as acute or chronic, without mention of hemorrhage or perforation**

√4th **533 Peptic ulcer, site unspecified**

> INCLUDES   gastroduodenal ulcer NOS
> peptic ulcer NOS
> stress ulcer NOS

Use additional E code to identify drug, if drug-induced

> EXCLUDES   peptic ulcer:
> duodenal (532.0-532.9)
> gastric (531.0-531.9)

The following fifth-digit subclassification is for use with category 533:

0 without mention of obstruction
1 with obstruction

AHA: 1Q, '91, 15; 4Q, '90, 27

DEF: Ulcer of mucous membrane of esophagus, stomach or duodenum due to gastric acid secretion.

√5th **533.0 Acute with hemorrhage**

√5th **533.1 Acute with perforation**

√5th **533.2 Acute with hemorrhage and perforation**
AHA: For code 533.20: 3Q, '03, 6

√5th **533.3 Acute without mention of hemorrhage and perforation**

√5th **533.4 Chronic or unspecified with hemorrhage**

√5th **533.5 Chronic or unspecified with perforation**

√5th **533.6 Chronic or unspecified with hemorrhage and perforation**

√5th **533.7 Chronic without mention of hemorrhage or perforation**
AHA: 2Q, '89, 16

√5th **533.9 Unspecified as acute or chronic, without mention of hemorrhage or perforation**

√4th **534 Gastrojejunal ulcer**

> INCLUDES   ulcer (peptic) or erosion: ulcer (peptic) or erosion:
> anastomotic   jejunal
> gastrocolic   marginal
> gastrointestinal   stomal
> gastrojejunal

> EXCLUDES   primary ulcer of small intestine (569.82)

The following fifth-digit subclassification is for use with category 534:

0 without mention of obstruction
1 with obstruction

AHA: 1Q, '91, 15; 4Q, '90, 27

√5th **534.0 Acute with hemorrhage**

√4th √5th Additional Digit Required   **RUG III Special Care Dx**   **RUG III Clinically Complex Dx**   **Hospice Non-cancer Dx**   **CD PDx** Clinical Dimension PDx   **CD SDx** Clinical Dimension SDx

2006 ICD•9•CM

October 2005 • Volume 1 — 145

§ ✓5ᵗʰ **534.1** Acute with perforation

§ ✓5ᵗʰ **534.2** Acute with hemorrhage and perforation

§ ✓5ᵗʰ **534.3** Acute without mention of hemorrhage or perforation

§ ✓5ᵗʰ **534.4** Chronic or unspecified with hemorrhage

§ ✓5ᵗʰ **534.5** Chronic or unspecified with perforation

§ ✓5ᵗʰ **534.6** Chronic or unspecified with hemorrhage and perforation

§ ✓5ᵗʰ **534.7** Chronic without mention of hemorrhage or perforation

§ ✓5ᵗʰ **534.9** Unspecified as acute or chronic, without mention of hemorrhage or perforation

✓4ᵗʰ **535 Gastritis and duodenitis**

The following fifth-digit subclassification is for use with category 535:

0 without mention of hemorrhage

1 with hemorrhage

AHA: 2Q, '92, 9; 4Q, '91, 25

✓5ᵗʰ **535.0 Acute gastritis**
AHA: 2Q, '92, 8; N-D, '86, 9

✓5ᵗʰ **535.1 Atrophic gastritis**
Gastritis: Gastritis:
atrophic-hyperplastic   chronic (atrophic)
AHA: 1Q, '94, 18
DEF: Inflammation of stomach, with mucous membrane atrophy and peptic gland destruction.

✓5ᵗʰ **535.2 Gastric mucosal hypertrophy**
Hypertrophic gastritis

✓5ᵗʰ **535.3 Alcoholic gastritis**

✓5ᵗʰ **535.4 Other specified gastritis**
Gastritis: Gastritis:
allergic   superficial
bile induced   toxic
irritant
AHA: 4Q, '90, 27

✓5ᵗʰ **535.5 Unspecified gastritis and gastroduodenitis**
AHA: For code 535.50: 4Q, '99, 25

✓5ᵗʰ **535.6 Duodenitis**
DEF: Inflammation of intestine, between pylorus and jejunum.

✓4ᵗʰ **536 Disorders of function of stomach**
EXCLUDES *functional disorders of stomach specified as psychogenic (306.4)*

536.0 Achlorhydria
DEF: Absence of gastric acid due to gastric mucosa atrophy; unresponsive to histamines; also known as gastric anacidity.

536.1 Acute dilatation of stomach
Acute distention of stomach

536.2 Persistent vomiting
Habit vomiting   Uncontrollable vomiting
Persistent vomiting [not of pregnancy]
EXCLUDES *excessive vomiting in pregnancy (643.0-643.9)*
vomiting NOS (787.0)

536.3 Gastroparesis
Gastroparalysis
AHA: ▶2Q, '04, 7;◀ 2Q, '01, 4; 4Q, '94, 42
DEF: Slight degree of paralysis within muscular coat of stomach.

✓5ᵗʰ **536.4 Gastrostomy complications**
AHA: 4Q, '98, 42

536.40 Gastrostomy complication,unspecified

536.41 Infection of gastrostomy
Use additional code to specify type of infection, such as:
abscess or cellulitis of abdomen (682.2)
septicemia (038.0-038.9)
Use additional code to identify organism (041.00-041.9)
AHA: 4Q, '98, 42

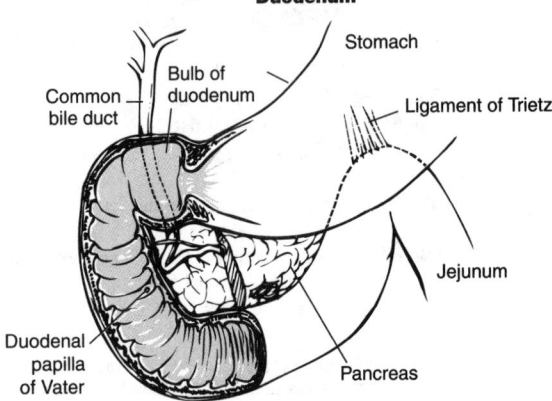

Duodenum

Stomach

Bulb of duodenum

Ligament of Trietz

Common bile duct

Jejunum

Duodenal papilla of Vater

Pancreas

536.42 Mechanical complication of gastrostomy

536.49 Other gastrostomy complications
AHA: 4Q, '98, 42

536.8 Dyspepsia and other specified disorders of function of stomach
Achylia gastrica   Hyperchlorhydria
Hourglass contraction   Hypochlorhydria
of stomach   Indigestion
Hyperacidity
EXCLUDES *achlorhydria (536.0)*
heartburn (787.1)
AHA: 2Q, '93, 6; 2Q, '89, 16; N-D, '84, 9

536.9 Unspecified functional disorder of stomach
Functional gastrointestinal:
disorder
disturbance
irritation

✓4ᵗʰ **537 Other disorders of stomach and duodenum**

537.0 Acquired hypertrophic pyloric stenosis
Constriction
Obstruction } of pylorus, acquired or adult
Stricture
EXCLUDES *congenital or infantile pyloric stenosis (750.5)*
AHA: 2Q, '01, 4; J-F, '85, 14

537.1 Gastric diverticulum
EXCLUDES *congenital diverticulum of stomach (750.7)*
AHA: J-F, '85, 4
DEF: Herniated sac or pouch, within stomach or duodenum.

537.2 Chronic duodenal ileus
DEF: Persistent obstruction between pylorus and jejunum.

537.3 Other obstruction of duodenum
Cicatrix
Stenosis
Stricture } of duodenum
Volvulus
EXCLUDES *congenital obstruction of duodenum (751.1)*

537.4 Fistula of stomach or duodenum
Gastrocolic fistula   Gastrojejunocolic fistula

537.5 Gastroptosis
DEF: Downward displacement of stomach.

537.6 Hourglass stricture or stenosis of stomach
Cascade stomach
EXCLUDES *congenital hourglass stomach (750.7)*
hourglass contraction of stomach (536.8)

✓5ᵗʰ **537.8 Other specified disorders of stomach and duodenum**
AHA: 4Q, '91, 25

§ Requires fifth-digit. See category 534 for codes and definitions.

Ⓝ Newborn Age: 0   Ⓟ Pediatric Age: 0-17   Ⓜ Maternity Age: 12-55   Ⓐ Adult Age: 15-124   Manifestation Code   ▶◀ Revised Text   ● New Code   ▲ Revised Code Title

537.81 Pylorospasm

EXCLUDES *congenital pylorospasm (750.5)*

DEF: Spasm of the pyloric sphincter.

537.82 Angiodysplasia of stomach and duodenum (without mention of hemorrhage)

AHA: 3Q, '96, 10; 4Q, '90, 4

537.83 Angiodysplasia of stomach and duodenum with hemorrhage

DEF: Bleeding of stomach and duodenum due to vascular abnormalities.

537.84 Dieulafoy lesion (hemorrhagic) of stomach and duodenum

AHA: 4Q, '02, 60

DEF: An abnormally large and convoluted submucosal artery protruding through a defect in the mucosa in the stomach or intestines that can erode the epithelium causing hemorrhaging; also called Dieulafoy's vascular malformation.

537.89 Other

Gastric or duodenal:
    prolapse
    rupture
Intestinal metaplasia of gastric mucosa
Passive congestion of stomach

EXCLUDES *diverticula of duodenum (562.00-562.01)*
gastrointestinal hemorrhage (578.0-578.9)

AHA: N-D, '84, 7

537.9 Unspecified disorder of stomach and duodenum

APPENDICITIS (540-543)

✓4th 540 Acute appendicitis

AHA: N-D, '84, 19

DEF: Inflammation of vermiform appendix due to fecal obstruction, neoplasm or foreign body of appendiceal lumen; causes infection, edema and infarction of appendiceal wall; may result in mural necrosis, and perforation.

540.0 With generalized peritonitis

Appendicitis (acute):
    fulminating
    gangrenous   with:
    obstructive   perforation
Cecitis (acute)   peritonitis (generalized)
                           rupture

Rupture of appendix

EXCLUDES *acute appendicitis with peritoneal abscess (540.1)*

540.1 With peritoneal abscess

With generalized peritonitis
Abscess of appendix

AHA: N-D, '84, 19

540.9 Without mention of peritonitis

Acute:
    appendicitis:
        fulminating   without mention of
        gangrenous   perforation,
        inflamed   peritonitis, or rupture
        obstructive
        cecitis

AHA: 1Q, '01, 15; 4Q, '97, 52

541 Appendicitis, unqualified

AHA: 2Q, '90, 26

542 Other appendicitis

Appendicitis: Appendicitis:
    chronic   relapsing
    recurrent   subacute

EXCLUDES *hyperplasia (lymphoid) of appendix (543.0)*

AHA: 1Q, '01, 15

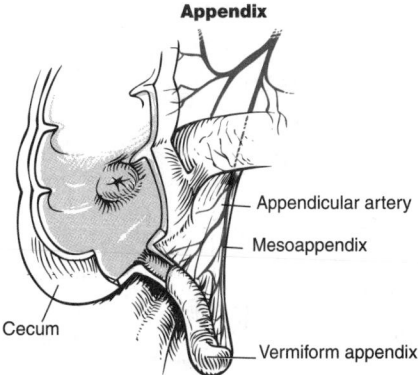

Appendix

Appendicular artery
Mesoappendix
Cecum
Vermiform appendix

✓4th 543 Other diseases of appendix

543.0 Hyperplasia of appendix (lymphoid)

DEF: Proliferation of cells in appendix tissue.

543.9 Other and unspecified diseases of appendix

Appendicular or appendiceal:
    colic
    concretion
    fistula
Diverticulum
Fecalith
Intussusception   of appendix
Mucocele
Stercolith

HERNIA OF ABDOMINAL CAVITY (550-553)

INCLUDES hernia:
    acquired
    congenital, except diaphragmatic or hiatal

✓4th 550 Inguinal hernia

INCLUDES bubonocele
    inguinal hernia (direct) (double) (indirect)
        (oblique) (sliding)
    scrotal hernia

The following fifth-digit subclassification is for use with category 550:

0 unilateral or unspecified (not specified as recurrent)
    Unilateral NOS
1 unilateral or unspecified, recurrent
2 bilateral (not specified as recurrent)
    Bilateral NOS
3 bilateral, recurrent

AHA: N-D, '85, 12

DEF: Hernia protrusion of an abdominal organ or tissue through inguinal canal.
DEF: Indirect inguinal hernia: (external or oblique) leaves abdomen through deep inguinal ring, passes through inguinal canal lateral to the inferior epigastric artery.
DEF: Direct inguinal hernia: (internal) emerges between inferior epigastric artery and rectus muscle edge.

✓5th 550.0 Inguinal hernia, with gangrene

Inguinal hernia with gangrene (and obstruction)

✓5th 550.1 Inguinal hernia, with obstruction, without mention of gangrene

Inguinal hernia with mention of incarceration, irreducibility, or strangulation

✓5th 550.9 Inguinal hernia, without mention of obstruction or gangrene

Inguinal hernia NOS

AHA: For code: 550.91: 3Q, '03, 10; 1Q, '03, 4

✓4th 551 Other hernia of abdominal cavity, with gangrene

INCLUDES that with gangrene (and obstruction)

✓5th 551.0 Femoral hernia with gangrene

551.00 Unilateral or unspecified (not specified as recurrent)

Femoral hernia NOS with gangrene

✓4th/✓5th Additional Digit Required   RUG III Special Care Dx   RUG III Clinically Complex Dx   Hospice Non-cancer Dx   CD PDx Clinical Dimension PDx   CD SDx Clinical Dimension SDx

Digestive System

551.01–553

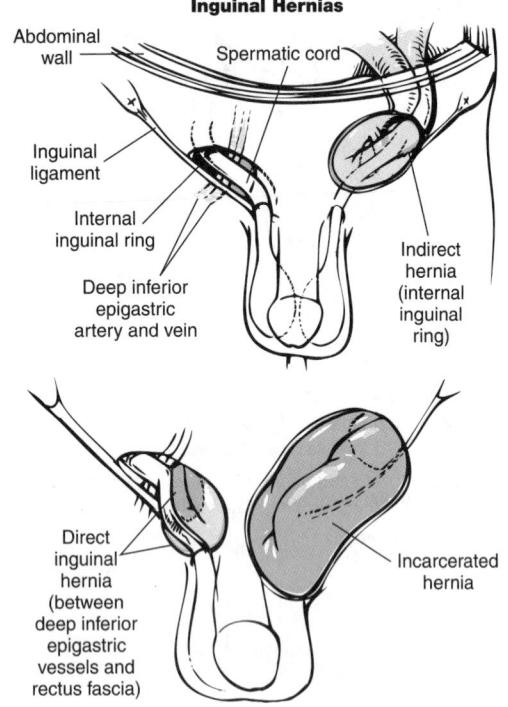

Inguinal Hernias

Abdominal wall
Spermatic cord
Inguinal ligament
Internal inguinal ring
Deep inferior epigastric artery and vein
Indirect hernia (internal inguinal ring)

Direct inguinal hernia (between deep inferior epigastric vessels and rectus fascia)
Incarcerated hernia

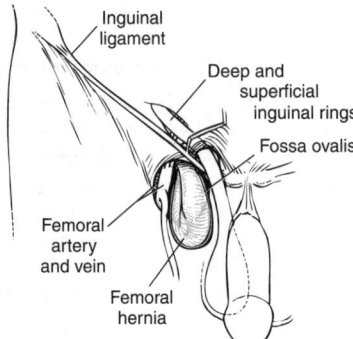

Femoral Hernia

Inguinal ligament
Deep and superficial inguinal rings
Fossa ovalis
Femoral artery and vein
Femoral hernia

Hernias of Abdominal Cavity

Hiatal hernia
Diaphragm
Epigastric hernia
Incisional hernia
Umbilical hernia
Inguinal hernia

551.01 Unilateral or unspecified, recurrent
551.02 Bilateral (not specified as recurrent)
551.03 Bilateral, recurrent
551.1 Umbilical hernia with gangrene
     Parumbilical hernia specified as gangrenous
✓5ᵗʰ **551.2 Ventral hernia with gangrene**
551.20 Ventral, unspecified, with gangrene
551.21 Incisional, with gangrene
     Hernia:
        postoperative ⎫
        recurrent, ventral ⎬ specified as
                    ⎭ gangrenous
551.29 Other
     Epigastric hernia specified as gangrenous
551.3 Diaphragmatic hernia with gangrene
     Hernia:
        hiatal (esophageal) (sliding) ⎫
        paraesophageal ⎬ specified as
        Thoracic stomach ⎭ gangrenous
       EXCLUDES *congenital diaphragmatic hernia (756.6)*
551.8 Hernia of other specified sites, with gangrene
     Any condition classifiable to 553.8 if specified as gangrenous
551.9 Hernia of unspecified site, with gangrene
     Any condition classifiable to 553.9 if specified as gangrenous
✓4ᵗʰ **552 Other hernia of abdominal cavity, with obstruction, but without mention of gangrene**
       EXCLUDES *that with mention of gangrene (551.0-551.9)*
✓5ᵗʰ **552.0 Femoral hernia with obstruction**
     Femoral hernia specified as incarcerated, irreducible, strangulated, or causing obstruction
552.00 Unilateral or unspecified (not specified as recurrent)
552.01 Unilateral or unspecified, recurrent
552.02 Bilateral (not specified as recurrent)
552.03 Bilateral, recurrent
552.1 Umbilical hernia with obstruction
     Parumbilical hernia specified as incarcerated, irreducible, strangulated, or causing obstruction

✓5ᵗʰ **552.2 Ventral hernia with obstruction**
     Ventral hernia specified as incarcerated, irreducible, strangulated, or causing obstruction
552.20 Ventral, unspecified, with obstruction
552.21 Incisional, with obstruction
     Hernia:
        postoperative ⎫ specified as incarcer-
        recurrent, ⎬ ated, irreducible,
        ventral ⎭ strangulated, or causing obstruction
       AHA: 3Q.'03, 11
552.29 Other
     Epigastric hernia specified as incarcerated, irreducible, strangulated, or causing obstruction
552.3 Diaphragmatic hernia with obstruction
     Hernia:
        hiatal (esophageal) ⎫ specified as incarcerated,
        (sliding) ⎬ irreducible,
        paraesophageal ⎬ strangulated, or
        Thoracic stomach ⎭ causing obstruction
       EXCLUDES *congenital diaphragmatic hernia (756.6)*
552.8 Hernia of other specified sites, with obstruction
     Any condition classifiable to 553.8 if specified as incarcerated, irreducible, strangulated, or causing obstruction
       EXCLUDES ▶ *hernia due to adhesion with obstruction (560.81)*◀
       AHA: 1Q, '04, 10
552.9 Hernia of unspecified site, with obstruction
     Any condition classifiable to 553.9 if specified as incarcerated, irreducible, strangulated, or causing obstruction
✓4ᵗʰ **553 Other hernia of abdominal cavity without mention of obstruction or gangrene**
       EXCLUDES *the listed conditions with mention of:*
                        gangrene (and obstruction) (551.0-551.9)
                        obstruction (552.0-552.9)

Ⓝ Newborn Age: 0   Ⓟ Pediatric Age: 0-17   Ⓜ Maternity Age: 12-55   Ⓐ Adult Age: 15-124   Manifestation Code   ▶◀ Revised Text   ● New Code   ▲ Revised Code Title

Diaphragmatic Hernias

- Esophagus
- Gastroesophageal junction (remains in place)
- Stomach
- Diaphragm
- Gastroesophageal junction (slides up and down)
- Paraesophageal Hiatal Hernia
- Sliding Hiatal Hernia

√5th **553.0 Femoral hernia**

553.00 Unilateral or unspecified (not specified as recurrent)
Femoral hernia NOS

553.01 Unilateral or unspecified, recurrent

553.02 Bilateral (not specified as recurrent)

553.03 Bilateral, recurrent

553.1 Umbilical hernia
Parumbilical hernia

√5th **553.2 Ventral hernia**

553.20 Ventral, unspecified
AHA: 3Q, '03, 6

553.21 Incisional
Hernia: Hernia:
postoperative   recurrent, ventral
AHA: 3Q, '03, 6

553.29 Other
Hernia: Hernia:
epigastric   spigelian

553.3 Diaphragmatic hernia
Hernia: Thoracic stomach
hiatal (esophageal)
(sliding)
paraesophageal
EXCLUDES   congenital:
diaphragmatic hernia (756.6)
hiatal hernia (750.6)
esophagocele (530.6)
AHA: 2Q, '01, 6; 1Q, '00, 6

553.8 Hernia of other specified sites
Hernia:
ischiatic
ischiorectal
lumbar
obturator
pudendal
retroperitoneal
sciatic
Other abdominal hernia of specified site
EXCLUDES   vaginal enterocele (618.6)

553.9 Hernia of unspecified site
Enterocele   Hernia:
Epiplocele   intestinal
Hernia: intra-abdominal
NOS   Rupture (nontraumatic)
interstitial   Sarcoepiplocele

NONINFECTIOUS ENTERITIS AND COLITIS (555-558)

√4th **555 Regional enteritis**
INCLUDES   Crohn's disease
Granulomatous enteritis
EXCLUDES   ulcerative colitis (556)
DEF: Inflammation of intestine; classified to site.

555.0 Small intestine
Ileitis: Regional enteritis or
regional   Crohn's disease of:
segmental   duodenum
terminal   ileum
                jejunum

555.1 Large intestine
Colitis: Regional enteritis or
granulmatous   Crohn's disease of:
regional   colon
transmural   large bowel
                rectum
AHA: 3Q, '99, 8

555.2 Small intestine with large intestine
Regional ileocolitis
AHA: 1Q, '03, 18

555.9 Unspecified site
Crohn's disease NOS
Regional enteritis NOS
AHA: 3Q, '99, 8; 4Q, '97, 42; 2Q, '97, 3

√4th **556 Ulcerative colitis**
AHA: 3Q, '99, 8

DEF: Chronic inflammation of mucosal lining of intestinal tract; may be single area or entire colon.

556.0 Ulcerative (chronic) enterocolitis

556.1 Ulcerative (chronic) ileocolitis

556.2 Ulcerative (chronic) proctitis

556.3 Ulcerative (chronic) proctosigmoiditis

556.4 Pseudopolyposis of colon

556.5 Left-sided ulcerative (chronic) colitis

556.6 Universal ulcerative (chronic) colitis
Pancolitis

556.8 Other ulcerative colitis

556.9 Ulcerative colitis, unspecified
Ulcerative enteritis NOS
AHA: 1Q, '03, 10

√4th **557 Vascular insufficiency of intestine**
EXCLUDES   necrotizing enterocolitis of the newborn (777.5)
DEF: Inadequacy of intestinal vessels.

557.0 Acute vascular insufficiency of intestine
Acute:
hemorrhagic enterocolitis
ischemic colitis, enteritis, or enterocolitis
massive necrosis of intestine
Bowel infarction
Embolism of mesenteric artery
Fulminant enterocolitis
Hemorrhagic necrosis of intestine
Infarction of appendices epiploicae
Intestinal gangrene
Intestinal infarction (acute) (agnogenic)
(hemorrhagic) (nonocclusive)
Mesenteric infarction (embolic) (thrombotic)
Necrosis of intestine
Terminal hemorrhagic enteropathy
Thrombosis of mesenteric artery
AHA: 4Q, '01, 53

557.1 Chronic vascular insufficiency of intestine
Angina, abdominal
Chronic ischemic colitis, enteritis, or enterocolitis
Ischemic stricture of intestine
Mesenteric:
angina
artery syndrome (superior)
vascular insufficiency
AHA: 3Q, '96, 9; 4Q, '90, 4; N-D, '86, 11; N-D, '84, 7

√4th
√5th Additional Digit Required   **RUG III Special Care Dx**   **RUG III Clinically Complex Dx**   **Hospice Non-cancer Dx**   **CD PDx** Clinical Dimension PDx   **CD SDx** Clinical Dimension SDx

2006 ICD•9•CM   **Volume 1 — 149**

Large Intestine

Volvulus and Diverticulitis

557.9 Unspecified vascular insufficiency of intestine
Alimentary pain due to vascular insufficiency
Ischemic colitis, enteritis, or enterocolitis NOS

✓4ᵗʰ **558 Other and unspecified noninfectious gastroenteritis and colitis**

> **EXCLUDES** *infectious:*
> *colitis, enteritis, or gastroenteritis (009.0-009.1)*
> *diarrhea (009.2-009.3)*

558.1 Gastroenteritis and colitis due to radiation
Radiation enterocolitis

558.2 Toxic gastroenteritis and colitis
Use additional E code to identify cause

558.3 Allergic gastroenteritis and colitis
Use additional code to identify type of food allergy (V15.01-V15.05)

AHA: 1Q, '03, 12; 4Q, '00, 42

DEF: True immunoglobulin E (IgE)-mediated allergic reaction of the lining of the stomach, intestines, or colon to food proteins; causes nausea, vomiting, diarrhea, and abdominal cramping.

558.9 Other and unspecified noninfectious gastroenteritis and colitis

Colitis
Enteritis
Gastroenteritis } NOS, dietetic, or
Ileitis   noninfectious
Jejunitis
Sigmoiditis

AHA: 3Q, '99, 4, 6; N-D, '87, 7

OTHER DISEASES OF INTESTINES AND PERITONEUM (560-569)

✓4ᵗʰ **560 Intestinal obstruction without mention of hernia**

> **EXCLUDES** *duodenum (537.2-537.3)*
> *inguinal hernia with obstruction (550.1)*
> *intestinal obstruction complicating hernia (552.0-552.9)*
> *mesenteric:*
> *embolism (557.0)*
> *infarction (557.0)*
> *thrombosis (557.0)*
> *neonatal intestinal obstruction (277.01, 777.1-777.2, 777.4)*

560.0 Intussusception
Intussusception (colon) (intestine) (rectum)
Invagination of intestine or colon

> **EXCLUDES** *intussusception of appendix (543.9)*

AHA: 4Q, '98, 82

DEF: Prolapse of a bowel section into adjacent section; occurs primarily in children; symptoms include paroxysmal pain, vomiting, presence of lower abdominal tumor and blood, and mucous passage from rectum.

560.1 Paralytic ileus
Adynamic ileus
Ileus (of intestine) (of bowel) (of colon)
Paralysis of intestine or colon

> **EXCLUDES** *gallstone ileus (560.31)*

AHA: J-F, '87, 13

DEF: Obstruction of ileus due to inhibited bowel motility.

560.2 Volvulus
Knotting
Strangulation } of intestine, bowel, or
Torsion   colon
Twist

DEF: Entanglement of bowel; causes obstruction; may compromise bowel circulation.

✓5ᵗʰ **560.3 Impaction of intestine**

560.30 Impaction of intestine, unspecified
Impaction of colon

560.31 Gallstone ileus
Obstruction of intestine by gallstone

560.39 Other
Concretion of intestine
Enterolith
Fecal impaction

AHA: 4Q, '98, 38

✓5ᵗʰ **560.8 Other specified intestinal obstruction**

560.81 Intestinal or peritoneal adhesions with obstruction (postoperative) (postinfection)

> **EXCLUDES** *adhesions without obstruction (568.0)*

AHA: 4Q, '95, 55; 3Q, '95, 6; N-D, '87, 9

DEF: Obstruction of peritoneum or intestine due to abnormal union of tissues.

560.89 Other
Acute pseudo-obstruction of intestine
Mural thickening causing obstruction

> **EXCLUDES** *ischemic stricture of intestine (557.1)*

AHA: 2Q, '97, 3; 1Q, '88, 6

560.9 Unspecified intestinal obstruction
Enterostenosis
Obstruction
Occlusion
Stenosis } of intestine or colon
Stricture

> **EXCLUDES** *congenital stricture or stenosis of intestine (751.1-751.2)*

N Newborn Age: 0   P Pediatric Age: 0-17   M Maternity Age: 12-55   A Adult Age: 15-124   Manifestation Code   ◄► Revised Text   ● New Code   ▲ Revised Code Title

150 — Volume 1   *2006 ICD•9•CM*

✓4ᵗʰ **562 Diverticula of intestine**

Use additional code to identify any associated:
peritonitis (567.0-567.9)

> **EXCLUDES**   congenital diverticulum of colon (751.5)
> diverticulum of appendix (543.9)
> Meckel's diverticulum (751.0)

AHA: 4Q, '91, 25; J-F, '85, 1

✓5ᵗʰ **562.0 Small intestine**

562.00 Diverticulosis of small intestine (without mention of hemorrhage)

Diverticulosis:

duodenum
ileum   } without mention of diverticulitis
jejunum

> DEF: Saclike herniations of mucous lining of small intestine.

562.01 Diverticulitis of small intestine (without mention of hemorrhage)

Diverticulitis (with diverticulosis):
duodenum
ileum
jejunum
small intestine

> DEF: Inflamed saclike herniations of mucous lining of small intestine.

562.02 Diverticulosis of small intestine with hemorrhage

562.03 Diverticulitis of small intestine with hemorrhage

✓5ᵗʰ **562.1 Colon**

562.10 Diverticulosis of colon (without mention of hemorrhage)

Diverticulosis:
NOS
intestine (large)   } without mention of diverticulitis
Diverticular disease (colon)

AHA: 3Q, '02, 15; 4Q, '90, 21; J-F, '85, 5

> DEF: Saclike herniations of mucous lining of large intestine

562.11 Diverticulitis of colon (without mention of hemorrhage)

Diverticulitis (with diverticulosis):
NOS
colon
intestine (large)

AHA: 1Q, '96, 14; J-F, '85, 5

> DEF: Inflamed saclike herniations of mucosal lining of large intestine.

562.12 Diverticulosis of colon with hemorrhage

562.13 Diverticulitis of colon with hemorrhage

✓4ᵗʰ **564 Functional digestive disorders, not elsewhere classified**

> **EXCLUDES**   functional disorders of stomach (536.0-536.9)
> those specified as psychogenic (306.4)

✓5ᵗʰ **564.0 Constipation**

AHA: 4Q, '01, 45

564.00 Constipation, unspecified

564.01 Slow transit constipation

> DEF: Delay in the transit of fecal material through the colon secondary to smooth muscle dysfunction or decreased peristaltic contractions along the colon: also called colonic inertia or delayed transit.

564.02 Outlet dysfunction constipation

> DEF: Failure to relax the paradoxical contractions of the striated pelvic floor muscles during the attempted defecation.

564.09 Other constipation

564.1 Irritable bowel syndrome

Irritable colon
Spastic colon

AHA: 1Q, '88, 6

> DEF: Functional gastrointestinal disorder (FGID); symptoms following meals include diarrhea, constipation, abdominal pain; other symptoms include bloating, gas, distended abdomen, nausea, vomiting, appetite loss, emotional distress, and depression.

564.2 Postgastric surgery syndromes

Dumping syndrome   Postgastrectomy syndrome
Jejunal syndrome   Postvagotomy syndrome

> **EXCLUDES**   malnutrition following gastrointestinal surgery (579.3)
> postgastrojejunostomy ulcer (534.0-534.9)

AHA: 1Q, '95, 11

564.3 Vomiting following gastrointestinal surgery

Vomiting (bilious) following gastrointestinal surgery

564.4 Other postoperative functional disorders

Diarrhea following gastrointestinal surgery

> **EXCLUDES**   colostomy and enterostomy complications (569.60-569.69)

564.5 Functional diarrhea

> **EXCLUDES**   diarrhea:
> NOS (787.91)
> psychogenic (306.4)

> DEF: Diarrhea with no detectable organic cause.

564.6 Anal spasm

Proctalgia fugax

564.7 Megacolon, other than Hirschsprung's

Dilatation of colon

> **EXCLUDES**   megacolon:
> congenital [Hirschsprung's] (751.3)
> toxic (556)

> DEF: Enlarged colon; congenital or acquired; can occur acutely or become chronic.

✓5ᵗʰ **564.8 Other specified functional disorders of intestine**

> **EXCLUDES**   malabsorption (579.0-579.9)

AHA: 1Q, '88, 6

564.81 Neurogenic bowel

AHA: 1Q, '01, 12; 4Q, '98, 45

> DEF: Disorder of bowel due to spinal cord lesion above conus medullaris; symptoms include precipitous micturition, nocturia, catheter intolerance, headache, sweating, nasal obstruction and spastic contractions.

564.89 Other functional disorders of intestine

Atony of colon

564.9 Unspecified functional disorder of intestine

✓4ᵗʰ **565 Anal fissure and fistula**

565.0 Anal fissure

Tear of anus, nontraumatic

> **EXCLUDES**   traumatic (863.89, 863.99)

> DEF: Ulceration of cleft at anal mucosa; causes pain, itching, bleeding, infection, and sphincter spasm; may occur with hemorrhoids.

565.1 Anal fistula

Fistula:
anorectal
rectal
rectum to skin

> **EXCLUDES**   fistula of rectum to internal organs—
> see Alphabetic Index
> ischiorectal fistula (566)
> rectovaginal fistula (619.1)

> DEF: Abnormal opening on cutaneous surface near anus; may lack connection with rectum.

Digestive System

566–569.49

Anal Fistula and Abscess

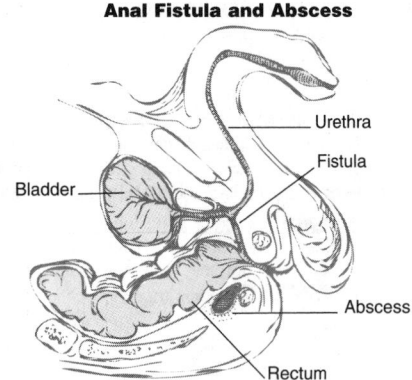

- Urethra
- Fistula
- Bladder
- Abscess
- Rectum

566 Abscess of anal and rectal regions

Abscess:
- ischiorectal
- perianal
- perirectal

Cellulitis:
- anal
- perirectal
- rectal
- Ischiorectal fistula

▲ ✓4ᵗʰ **567 Peritonitis and retroperitoneal infections**

EXCLUDES   peritonitis:
- benign paroxysmal (277.3)
- pelvic, female (614.5, 614.7)
- periodic familial (277.3)
- puerperal (670)
- with or following:
  - abortion (634-638 with .0, 639.0)
  - appendicitis (540.0-540.1)
  - ectopic or molar pregnancy (639.0)

DEF: Inflammation of the peritoneal cavity.

567.0 Peritonitis in infectious diseases classified elsewhere

Code first underlying disease

EXCLUDES   peritonitis:
- gonococcal (098.86)
- syphilitic (095.2)
- tuberculous (014.0)

567.1 Pneumococcal peritonitis

✓5ᵗʰ **567.2 Other suppurative peritonitis**

AHA: 2Q, '01, 11, 12; 3Q, '99, 9; 2Q, '98, 19

- **567.21 Peritonitis (acute) generalized**
  Pelvic peritonitis, male

- **567.22 Peritoneal abscess**

  Abscess (of):
  - abdominopelvic
  - mesenteric
  - omentum
  - peritoneum

  Abscess (of):
  - retrocecal
  - subdiaphragmatic
  - subhepatic
  - subphrenic

- **567.23 Spontaneous bacterial peritonitis**

- **567.29 Other suppurative peritonitis**
  Subphrenic peritonitis

- ✓5ᵗʰ **567.3 Retroperitoneal infections**

  - **567.31 Psoas muscle abscess**

  - **567.38 Other retroperitoneal abscess**

  - **567.39 Other retroperitoneal infections**

Rectum and Anus

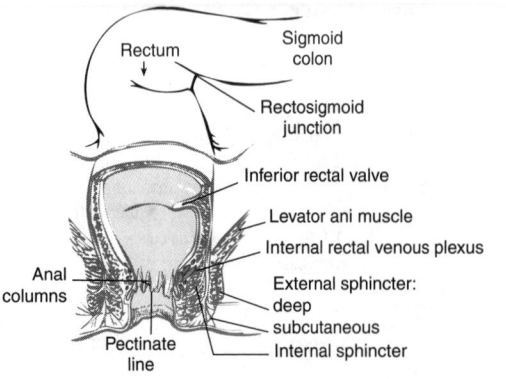

- Rectum
- Sigmoid colon
- Rectosigmoid junction
- Inferior rectal valve
- Levator ani muscle
- Internal rectal venous plexus
- Anal columns
- External sphincter:
  - deep
  - subcutaneous
  - Internal sphincter
- Pectinate line

✓5ᵗʰ **567.8 Other specified peritonitis**

- **567.81 Choleperitonitis**
  Peritonitis due to bile

- **567.82 Sclerosing mesenteritis**
  Fat necrosis of peritoneum
  (Idiopathic) sclerosing mesenteric fibrosis
  Mesenteric lipodystrophy
  Mesenteric panniculitis
  Retractile mesenteritis

- **567.89 Other specified peritonitis**
  Chronic proliferative peritonitis
  Mesenteric saponification
  Peritonitis due to urine

567.9 Unspecified peritonitis
  Peritonitis NOS
  Peritonitis of unspecified cause
  AHA: 1Q, '04, 10

✓4ᵗʰ **568 Other disorders of peritoneum**

568.0 Peritoneal adhesions (postoperative) (postinfection)

Adhesions (of):
- abdominal (wall)
- diaphragm
- intestine
- male pelvis

Adhesions (of):
- mesenteric
- omentum
- stomach
- Adhesive bands

EXCLUDES   adhesions:
- pelvic, female (614.6)
- with obstruction:
  - duodenum (537.3)
  - intestine (560.81)

AHA: 3Q. '03, 7, 11; 4Q, '95, 55; 3Q, '95, 7; S-O, '85, 11

DEF: Abnormal union of tissues in peritoneum.

✓5ᵗʰ **568.8 Other specified disorders of peritoneum**

- **568.81 Hemoperitoneum (nontraumatic)**

- **568.82 Peritoneal effusion (chronic)**
  EXCLUDES   ascites NOS (789.5)
  DEF: Persistent leakage of fluid within peritoneal cavity.

- **568.89 Other**
  Peritoneal:
  - cyst
  Peritoneal:
  - granuloma

568.9 Unspecified disorder of peritoneum

✓4ᵗʰ **569 Other disorders of intestine**

569.0 Anal and rectal polyp
  Anal and rectal polyp NOS
  EXCLUDES   adenomatous anal and rectal polyp (211.4)

569.1 Rectal prolapse
  Procidentia:
  - anus (sphincter)
  - rectum (sphincter)
  Proctoptosis
  Prolapse:
  - anal canal
  - rectal mucosa
  EXCLUDES   prolapsed hemorrhoids (455.2, 455.5)

569.2 Stenosis of rectum and anus
  Stricture of anus (sphincter)

569.3 Hemorrhage of rectum and anus
  EXCLUDES   gastrointestinal bleeding NOS (578.9)
  melena (578.1)

✓5ᵗʰ **569.4 Other specified disorders of rectum and anus**

569.41 Ulcer of anus and rectum
  Solitary ulcer ⎤ of anus (sphincter) or
  Stercoral ulcer ⎦   rectum (sphincter)

569.42 Anal or rectal pain
  AHA: 1Q, '03, 8; 1Q, '96, 13

569.49 Other
  Granuloma ⎤ of rectum (sphincter)
  Rupture ⎦
  Hypertrophy of anal papillae
  Proctitis NOS
  EXCLUDES   fistula of rectum to:
  - internal organs—see Alphabetic Index
  - skin (565.1)
  hemorrhoids (455.0-455.9)
  incontinence of sphincter ani (787.6)

N   Newborn Age: 0   P   Pediatric Age: 0-17   M   Maternity Age: 12-55   A   Adult Age: 15-124   Manifestation Code   ▶◀ Revised Text   ● New Code   ▲ Revised Code Title

569.5 Abscess of intestine
> EXCLUDES   appendiceal abscess (540.1)

✓5ᵗʰ **569.6 Colostomy and enterostomy complications**
AHA: 4Q, '95, 58

DEF: Complication in a surgically created opening, from intestine to surface skin.

569.60 Colostomy and enterostomy complication, unspecified

569.61 Infection of colostomy or enterostomy
Use additional code to identify organism (041.00-041.9)
Use additional code to specify type of infection, such as:
abscess or cellulitis of abdomen (682.2)
septicemia (038.0-038.9)

569.62 Mechanical complication of colostomy and enterostomy
Malfunction of colostomy and enterostomy
AHA: 1Q, '03, 10; 4Q, '98, 44

569.69 Other complication
Fistula   Prolapse
Hernia
AHA: 3Q, '98, 16

✓5ᵗʰ **569.8 Other specified disorders of intestine**
AHA: 4Q, '91, 25

569.81 Fistula of intestine, excluding rectum and anus
Fistula: Fistula:
abdominal wall   enteroenteric
enterocolic   ileorectal
> EXCLUDES   fistula of intestine to internal organs—see Alphabetic Index
> persistent postoperative fistula (998.6)

AHA: 3Q, '99, 8

569.82 Ulceration of intestine
Primary ulcer of intestine
Ulceration of colon
> EXCLUDES   that with perforation (569.83)

569.83 Perforation of intestine

569.84 Angiodysplasia of intestine (without mention of hemorrhage)
AHA: 3Q, '96, 10; 4Q, '90, 4; 4Q, '90, 21

DEF: Small vascular abnormalities of the intestinal tract without bleeding problems.

569.85 Angiodysplasia of intestine with hemorrhage
AHA: 3Q, '96, 9

DEF: Small vascular abnormalities of the intestinal tract with bleeding problems.

569.86 Dieulafoy lesion (hemorrhagic) of intestine
AHA: 4Q, '02, 60-61

569.89 Other
Enteroptosis
Granuloma   } of intestine
Prolapse
Pericolitis
Perisigmoiditis
Visceroptosis
> EXCLUDES   gangrene of intestine, mesentery, or omentum (557.0)
> hemorrhage of intestine NOS (578.9)
> obstruction of intestine (560.0-560.9)

AHA: 3Q, '96, 9

569.9 Unspecified disorder of intestine

OTHER DISEASES OF DIGESTIVE SYSTEM (570-579)

570 Acute and subacute necrosis of liver
Acute hepatic failure
Acute or subacute hepatitis, not specified as infective
Necrosis of liver (acute) (diffuse) (massive) (subacute)
Parenchymatous degeneration of liver
Yellow atrophy (liver) (acute) (subacute)
> EXCLUDES   icterus gravis of newborn (773.0-773.2)
> serum hepatitis (070.2-070.3)
> that with:
> abortion (634-638 with .7, 639.8)
> ectopic or molar pregnancy (639.8)
> pregnancy, childbirth, or the puerperium (646.7)
> viral hepatitis (070.0-070.9)

AHA: 1Q, '00, 22

✓4ᵗʰ **571 Chronic liver disease and cirrhosis**

571.0 Alcoholic fatty liver   A

571.1 Acute alcoholic hepatitis   A
Acute alcoholic liver disease
AHA: 2Q, '02, 4

571.2 Alcoholic cirrhosis of liver   A
Florid cirrhosis
Laennec's cirrhosis (alcoholic)
AHA: 2Q, '02, 4; 1Q, '02, 3; N-D, '85, 14

DEF: Fibrosis and dysfunction, of liver; due to alcoholic liver disease.

571.3 Alcoholic liver damage, unspecified   A

✓5ᵗʰ **571.4 Chronic hepatitis**
> EXCLUDES   viral hepatitis (acute) (chronic) (070.0-070.9)

571.40 Chronic hepatitis, unspecified

571.41 Chronic persistent hepatitis

571.49 Other
Chronic hepatitis:
active
aggressive
Recurrent hepatitis
AHA: 3Q, '99, 19; N-D, '85, 14

571.5 Cirrhosis of liver without mention of alcohol
Cirrhosis of liver: Cirrhosis of liver:
NOS   postnecrotic
cryptogenic   Healed yellow atrophy
macronodular   (liver)
micronodular   Portal cirrhosis
posthepatitic

DEF: Fibrosis and dysfunction of liver; not alcohol related.

571.6 Biliary cirrhosis
Chronic nonsuppurative destructive cholangitis
Cirrhosis:
cholangitic
cholestatic

Liver

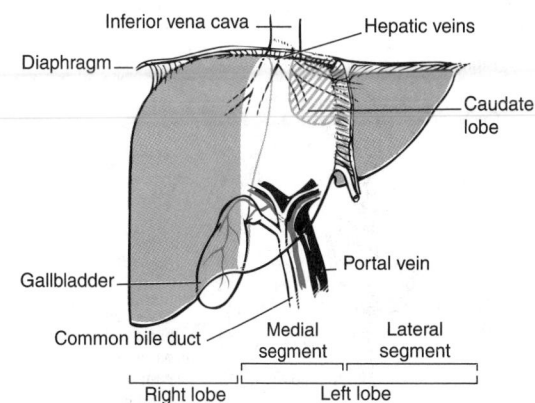

570 Acute and subacute necrosis of liver (diagram labels:)
Inferior vena cava — Hepatic veins
Diaphragm —
Caudate lobe
Portal vein
Gallbladder —
Common bile duct —
Medial segment — Lateral segment
Right lobe — Left lobe

✓4ᵗʰ ✓5ᵗʰ Additional Digit Required   RUG III Special Care Dx   RUG III Clinically Complex Dx   Hospice Non-cancer Dx   CD PDx Clinical Dimension PDx   CD SDx Clinical Dimension SDx

2006 ICD•9•CM   Volume 1 — 153

571.8 **Other chronic nonalcoholic liver disease**
Chronic yellow atrophy (liver)
Fatty liver, without mention of alcohol
AHA: 2Q, '96, 12

571.9 **Unspecified chronic liver disease without mention of alcohol**

✓4th **572 Liver abscess and sequelae of chronic liver disease**

572.0 **Abscess of liver**
EXCLUDES   *amebic liver abscess (006.3)*

572.1 **Portal pyemia**
Phlebitis of portal vein   Pylephlebitis
Portal thrombophlebitis   Pylethrombophlebitis

DEF: Inflammation of portal vein or branches; may be due to intestinal disease; symptoms include fever, chills, jaundice, sweating, and abscess in various body parts.

572.2 **Hepatic coma**
Hepatic encephalopathy
Hepatocerebral intoxication
Portal-systemic encephalopathy
AHA: 1Q, '02, 3; 3Q, '95, 14

572.3 **Portal hypertension**
DEF: Abnormally high blood pressure in the portal vein.

572.4 **Hepatorenal syndrome**
EXCLUDES   *that following delivery (674.8)*

DEF: Hepatic and renal failure characterized by cirrhosis with ascites or obstructive jaundice, oliguria, and low sodium concentration.

572.8 **Other sequelae of chronic liver disease**

✓4th **573 Other disorders of liver**
EXCLUDES   *amyloid or lardaceous degeneration of liver (277.3)*
congenital cystic disease of liver (751.62)
glycogen infiltration of liver (271.0)
hepatomegaly NOS (789.1)
portal vein obstruction (452)

573.0 **Chronic passive congestion of liver**
DEF: Blood accumulation in liver tissue.

573.1 *Hepatitis in viral diseases classified elsewhere*
Code first underlying disease as:
Coxsackie virus disease (074.8)
cytomegalic inclusion virus disease (078.5)
infectious mononucleosis (075)
EXCLUDES   *hepatitis (in):*
mumps (072.71)
viral (070.0-070.9)
yellow fever (060.0-060.9)

573.2 *Hepatitis in other infectious diseases classified elsewhere*
Code first underlying disease, as:
malaria (084.9)
EXCLUDES   *hepatitis in:*
late syphilis (095.3)
secondary syphilis (091.62)
toxoplasmosis (130.5)

Gallbladder and Bile Ducts

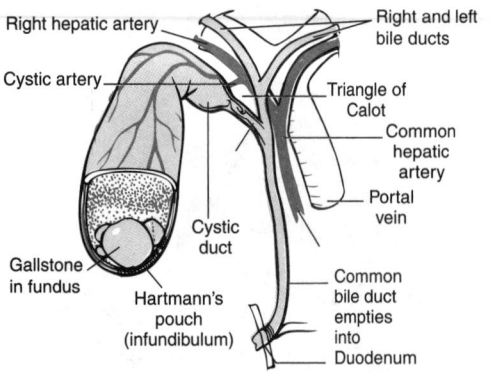

573.3 **Hepatitis, unspecified**
Toxic (noninfectious) hepatitis
Use additional E code to identify cause
AHA: 3Q, '98, 3, 4; 4Q, '90, 26

573.4 **Hepatic infarction**

573.8 **Other specified disorders of liver**
Hepatoptosis

573.9 **Unspecified disorder of liver**

✓4th **574 Cholelithiasis**

The following fifth-digit subclassification is for use with category 574:
0 without mention of obstruction
1 with obstruction

✓5th **574.0** **Calculus of gallbladder with acute cholecystitis**
Biliary calculus
Calculus of cystic duct } with acute cholecystitis
Cholelithiasis

Any condition classifiable to 574.2 with acute cholecystitis
AHA: 4Q, '96, 32

✓5th **574.1** **Calculus of gallbladder with other cholecystitis**
Biliary calculus
Calculus of cystic duct } with cholecystitis
Cholelithiasis

Cholecystitis with cholelithiasis NOS
Any condition classifiable to 574.2 with cholecystitis (chronic)
AHA: 3Q, '99, 9; 4Q, '96, 32, 69; 2Q, '96, 13;
For code 574.10: 1Q, '03, 5

✓5th **574.2** **Calculus of gallbladder without mention of cholecystitis**
Biliary: Cholelithiasis NOS
  calculus NOS   Colic (recurrent) of
  colic NOS   gallbladder
Calculus of cystic duct   Gallstone (impacted)
AHA: For code 574.20: 1Q, '88, 14

✓5th **574.3** **Calculus of bile duct with acute cholecystitis**
Calculus of bile
  duct [any] } with acute
Choledocholithiasis } cholecystitis

Any condition classifiable to 574.5 with acute cholecystitis

✓5th **574.4** **Calculus of bile duct with other cholecystitis**
Calculus of bile duct
  [any] } with cholecystitis
Choledocholithiasis } (chronic)

Any condition classifiable to 574.5 with cholecystitis (chronic)

✓5th **574.5** **Calculus of bile duct without mention of cholecystitis**
Calculus of: Choledocholithiasis
  bile duct [any]   Hepatic:
  common duct   colic (recurrent)
  hepatic duct   lithiasis
AHA: 3Q, '94, 11

✓5th **574.6** **Calculus of gallbladder and bile duct with acute cholecystitis**
Any condition classifiable to 574.0 and 574.3
AHA: 4Q, '96, 32

✓5th **574.7** **Calculus of gallbladder and bile duct with other cholecystitis**
Any condition classifiable to 574.1 and 574.4
AHA: 4Q, '96, 32

N Newborn Age: 0   P Pediatric Age: 0-17   M Maternity Age: 12-55   A Adult Age: 15-124   Manifestation Code   ►◄ Revised Text   ● New Code   ▲ Revised Code Title

√5th 574.8 Calculus of gallbladder and bile duct with acute and chronic cholecystitis
Any condition classifiable to 574.6 and 574.7
AHA: 4Q, '96, 32

√5th 574.9 Calculus of gallbladder and bile duct without cholecystitis
Any condition classifiable to 574.2 and 574.5
AHA: 4Q, '96, 32

√4th 575 Other disorders of gallbladder

575.0 Acute cholecystitis
Abscess of gallbladder
Angiocholecystitis
Cholecystitis:
  emphysematous (acute)
  gangrenous   } without mention
  suppurative   of calculus
Empyema of gallbladder
Gangrene of gallbladder

EXCLUDES   *that with:*
    acute and chronic cholecystitis
      (575.12)
    choledocholithiasis (574.3)
    choledocholithiasis and
      cholelithiasis (574.6)
    cholelithiasis (574.0)

AHA: 3Q, '91, 17

√5th 575.1 Other cholecystitis
Cholecystitis:
  NOS   } without mention
  chronic   of calculus

EXCLUDES   *that with:*
    choledocholithiasis (574.4)
    choledocholithiasis and
      cholelithiasis (574.8)
    cholelithiasis (574.1)

AHA: 4Q, '96, 32

575.10 Cholecystitis, unspecified
Cholecystitis NOS

575.11 Chronic cholecystitis

575.12 Acute and chronic cholecystitis
AHA: 4Q, '97, 52; 4Q, '96, 32

575.2 Obstruction of gallbladder
Occlusion
Stenosis   } of cystic duct or gallbladder without
Stricture   mention of calculus

EXCLUDES   *that with calculus (574.0-574.2 with*
    fifth-digit 1)

575.3 Hydrops of gallbladder
Mucocele of gallbladder
AHA: 2Q, '89, 13
DEF: Serous fluid accumulation in bladder.

575.4 Perforation of gallbladder
Rupture of cystic duct or gallbladder

575.5 Fistula of gallbladder
Fistula: Fistula:
  cholecystoduodenal   cholecystoenteric

575.6 Cholesterolosis of gallbladder
Strawberry gallbladder
AHA: 4Q, '90, 17
DEF: Cholesterol deposits in gallbladder tissue.

575.8 Other specified disorders of gallbladder
Adhesions
Atrophy
Cyst   } (of) cystic duct or
Hypertrophy   gallbladder
Nonfunctioning
Ulcer

Biliary dyskinesia
EXCLUDES   *Hartmann's pouch of intestine (V44.3)*
    nonvisualization of gallbladder (793.3)

AHA: 4Q, '90, 26; 2Q, '89, 13

575.9 Unspecified disorder of gallbladder

√4th 576 Other disorders of biliary tract
EXCLUDES   *that involving the:*
    cystic duct (575.0-575.9)
    gallbladder (575.0-575.9)

576.0 Postcholecystectomy syndrome
AHA: 1Q, '88, 10
DEF: Jaundice or abdominal pain following cholecystectomy.

576.1 Cholangitis
Cholangitis: Cholangitis:
  NOS   recurrent
  acute   sclerosing
  ascending   secondary
  chronic   stenosing
  primary   suppurative
AHA: 2Q, '99, 13

576.2 Obstruction of bile duct
Occlusion   } of bile duct, except cystic
Stenosis   duct, without mention
Stricture   of calculus

EXCLUDES   *congenital (751.61)*
    that with calculus (574.3-574.5 with
      fifth-digit 1)

AHA: 3Q, '03, 17-18; 1Q, '01, 8; 2Q, '99, 13

576.3 Perforation of bile duct
Rupture of bile duct, except cystic duct

576.4 Fistula of bile duct
Choledochoduodenal fistula

576.5 Spasm of sphincter of Oddi

576.8 Other specified disorders of biliary tract
Adhesions
Atrophy
Cyst
Hypertrophy   } of bile duct [any]
Stasis
Ulcer

EXCLUDES   *congenital choledochal cyst (751.69)*
AHA: 3Q, '03, 17; 2Q, '99, 14

576.9 Unspecified disorder of biliary tract

√4th 577 Diseases of pancreas

577.0 Acute pancreatitis
Abscess of pancreas   Pancreatitis:
Necrosis of pancreas: acute (recurrent)
  acute   apoplectic
  infective   hemorrhagic
Pancreatitis: subacute
  NOS   suppurative
EXCLUDES   *mumps pancreatitis (072.3)*
AHA: 3Q, '99, 9; 2Q, '98, 19; 2Q, '96, 13; 2Q, '89, 9

577.1 Chronic pancreatitis
Chronic pancreatitis: Pancreatitis:
  NOS   painless
  infectious   recurrent
  interstitial   relapsing
AHA: 1Q, '01, 8; 2Q, '96, 13; 3Q, '94, 11

577.2 Cyst and pseudocyst of pancreas

√4th √5th Additional Digit Required   RUG III Special Care Dx   RUG III Clinically Complex Dx   Hospice Non-cancer Dx   **CD PDx** Clinical Dimension PDx   **CD SDx** Clinical Dimension SDx

Digestive System

577.8–579.9

577.8 Other specified diseases of pancreas

Atrophy
Calculus } of pancreas
Cirrhosis
Fibrosis

Pancreatic: Pancreatolithiasis
  infantilism
  necrosis:
    NOS
    aseptic
    fat

> **EXCLUDES** fibrocystic disease of pancreas
> (277.00-277.09)
> islet cell tumor of pancreas (211.7)
> pancreatic steatorrhea (579.4)

AHA: 1Q, '01, 8

577.9 Unspecified disease of pancreas

✓4ᵗʰ **578 Gastrointestinal hemorrhage**

> **EXCLUDES** that with mention of:
> angiodysplasia of stomach and duodenum
> (537.83)
> angiodysplasia of intestine (569.85)
> diverticulitis, intestine:
>   large (562.13)
>   small (562.03)
> diverticulosis, intestine:
>   large (562.12)
>   small (562.02)
> gastritis and duodenitis (535.0-535.6)
> ulcer:
>   duodenal, gastric, gastrojejunal or peptic
>   (531.00-534.91)

AHA: 2Q, '92, 9; 4Q, '90, 20

578.0 Hematemesis
Vomiting of blood
AHA: 2Q, '02, 4

578.1 Blood in stool
Melena
> **EXCLUDES** melena of the newborn (772.4, 777.3)
> occult blood (792.1)

AHA: 2Q, '92, 8

578.9 Hemorrhage of gastrointestinal tract, unspecified
Gastric hemorrhage
Intestinal hemorrhage
AHA: N-D, '86, 9

✓4ᵗʰ **579 Intestinal malabsorption**

579.0 Celiac disease
Celiac: Gee (-Herter) disease
  crisis   Gluten enteropathy
  infantilism   Idiopathic steatorrhea
  rickets   Nontropical sprue

DEF: Malabsorption syndrome due to gluten consumption; symptoms include fetid, bulky, frothy, oily stools; distended abdomen, gas, weight loss, asthenia, electrolyte depletion and vitamin B, D and K deficiency.

579.1 Tropical sprue
Sprue: Tropical steatorrhea
  NOS
  tropical

DEF: Diarrhea, occurs in tropics; may be due to enteric infection and malnutrition.

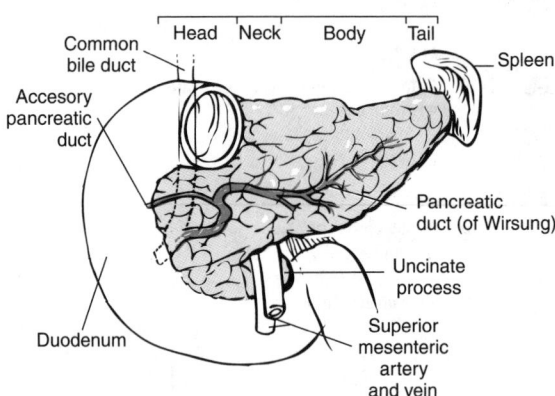

Pancreas

579.2 Blind loop syndrome
Postoperative blind loop syndrome
DEF: Obstruction or impaired passage in small intestine due to alterations, from strictures or surgery; causes stasis, abnormal bacterial flora, diarrhea, weight loss, multiple vitamin deficiency, and megaloblastic anemia.

579.3 Other and unspecified postsurgical nonabsorption
Hypoglycemia } following gastrointestinal
Malnutrition } surgery
AHA: 4Q, '03, 104

579.4 Pancreatic steatorrhea
DEF: Excess fat in feces due to absence of pancreatic juice in intestine.

579.8 Other specified intestinal malabsorption
Enteropathy: Steatorrhea (chronic)
  exudative
  protein-losing
AHA: 1Q, '88, 6

579.9 Unspecified intestinal malabsorption
Malabsorption syndrome NOS
AHA: ▶4Q, '04, 59◀

Ⓝ Newborn Age: 0   Ⓟ Pediatric Age: 0-17   Ⓜ Maternity Age: 12-55   Ⓐ Adult Age: 15-124   Manifestation Code   ▶◀ Revised Text   ● New Code   ▲ Revised Code Title

10. DISEASES OF THE GENITOURINARY SYSTEM (580-629)

Kidney

Nephron

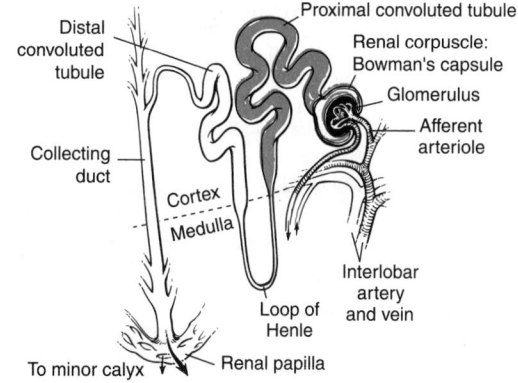

NEPHRITIS, NEPHROTIC SYNDROME, AND NEPHROSIS (580-589)

> **EXCLUDES** hypertensive renal disease (403.00-403.91)

✓4ᵗʰ **580 Acute glomerulonephritis**

> **INCLUDES** acute nephritis

DEF: Acute, severe inflammation in tuft of capillaries that filter the kidneys.

580.0 With lesion of proliferative glomerulonephritis
Acute (diffuse) proliferative glomerulonephritis
Acute poststreptococcal glomerulonephritis

580.4 With lesion of rapidly progressive glomerulonephritis
Acute nephritis with lesion of necrotizing glomerulitis

DEF: Acute glomerulonephritis; progresses to ESRD with diffuse epithelial proliferation.

✓5ᵗʰ **580.8 With other specified pathological lesion in kidney**

580.81 Acute glomerulonephritis in diseases classified elsewhere
Code first underlying disease, as:
infectious hepatitis (070.0-070.9)
mumps (072.79)
subacute bacterial endocarditis (421.0)
typhoid fever (002.0)

580.89 Other
Glomerulonephritis, acute, with lesion of:
exudative nephritis
interstitial (diffuse) (focal) nephritis

580.9 Acute glomerulonephritis with unspecified pathological lesion in kidney
Glomerulonephritis:
NOS
hemorrhagic   } specified as acute
Nephritis
Nephropathy

✓4ᵗʰ **581 Nephrotic syndrome**

DEF: Disease process marked by symptoms such as; extensive edema, notable proteinuria, hypoalbuminemia, and susceptibility to intercurrent infections.

581.0 With lesion of proliferative glomerulonephritis

581.1 With lesion of membranous glomerulonephritis
Epimembranous nephritis
Idiopathic membranous glomerular disease
Nephrotic syndrome with lesion of:
focal glomerulosclerosis
sclerosing membranous glomerulonephritis
segmental hyalinosis

581.2 With lesion of membranoproliferative glomerulonephritis
Nephrotic syndrome with lesion (of):
endothelial
hypocomplementemic
persistent
lobular   } glomerulonephritis
mesangiocapillary
mixed membranous and
proliferative

DEF: Glomerulonephritis combined with clinical features of nephrotic syndrome; characterized by uneven thickening of glomerular capillary walls and mesangial cell increase; slowly progresses to ESRD.

581.3 With lesion of minimal change glomerulonephritis
Foot process disease   Minimal change:
Lipoid nephrosis   glomerulitis
Minimal change: nephrotic syndrome
glomerular disease

✓5ᵗʰ **581.8 With other specified pathological lesion in kidney**

581.81 Nephrotic syndrome in diseases classified elsewhere
Code first underlying disease, as:
amyloidosis (277.3)
diabetes mellitus (250.4)
malaria (084.9)
polyarteritis (446.0)
systemic lupus erythematosus (710.0)
> **EXCLUDES** nephrosis in epidemic hemorr-
hagic fever (078.6)

AHA: 3Q, '91, 3; S-O, '85, 3

581.89 Other
Glomerulonephritis with edema and lesion of:
exudative nephritis
interstitial (diffuse) (focal) nephritis

581.9 Nephrotic syndrome with unspecified pathological lesion in kidney
Glomerulonephritis with edema NOS
Nephritis:
nephrotic NOS
with edema NOS
Nephrosis NOS
Renal disease with edema NOS

✓4ᵗʰ **582 Chronic glomerulonephritis**

> **INCLUDES** chronic nephritis

DEF: Slow progressive type of nephritis characterized by inflammation of the capillary loops in the glomeruli of the kidney, which leads to renal failure.

582.0 With lesion of proliferative glomerulonephritis
Chronic (diffuse) proliferative glomerulonephritis

582.1 With lesion of membranous glomerulonephritis
Chronic glomerulonephritis:
membranous
sclerosing
Focal glomerulosclerosis
Segmental hyalinosis

AHA: S-O, '84, 16

582.2 With lesion of membranoproliferative glomerulonephritis
Chronic glomerulonephritis:
endothelial
hypocomplementemic persistent
lobular
membranoproliferative
mesangiocapillary
mixed membranous and proliferative

DEF: Chronic glomerulonephritis with mesangial cell proliferation.

✓4ᵗʰ
✓5ᵗʰ Additional Digit Required   RUG III Special Care Dx   RUG III Clinically Complex Dx   Hospice Non-cancer Dx   **CD PDx** Clinical Dimension PDx   **CD SDx** Clinical Dimension SDx

2006 ICD•9•CM   Volume 1 — 157

Genitourinary System

582.4–585

582.4　With lesion of rapidly progressive glomerulonephritis

Chronic nephritis with lesion of necrotizing glomerulitis

DEF: Chronic glomerulonephritisrapidly progresses to ESRD; marked by diffuse epithelial proliferation.

√5ᵗʰ **582.8　With other specified pathological lesion in kidney**

582.81　Chronic glomerulonephritis in diseases classified elsewhere

Code first underlying disease, as:
amyloidosis (277.3)
systemic lupus erythematosus (710.0)

582.89　Other

Chronic glomerulonephritis with lesion of:
exudative nephritis
interstitial (diffuse) (focal) nephritis

582.9　Chronic glomerulonephritis with unspecified pathological lesion in kidney

Glomerulonephritis:
NOS
hemorrhagic } specified as chronic
Nephritis
Nephropathy

AHA: 2Q, '01, 12

√4ᵗʰ **583　Nephritis and nephropathy, not specified as acute or chronic**

INCLUDES　"renal disease" so stated, not specified as acute or chronic but with stated pathology or cause

583.0　With lesion of proliferative glomerulonephritis

Proliferative:　　　　　Proliferative
　glomerulonephritis　　nephritis NOS
　(diffuse) NOS　　　　nephropathy NOS

583.1　With lesion of membranous glomerulonephritis

Membranous:
　glomerulonephritis NOS
　nephritis NOS
Membranous nephropathy NOS

DEF: Kidney inflammation or dysfunction with deposits on glomerular capillary basement membranes.

583.2　With lesion of membranoproliferative glomerulonephritis

Membranoproliferative:
　glomerulonephritis NOS　　nephropathy NOS
　nephritis NOS
Nephritis NOS, with lesion of:
　hypocomplementemic
　persistent
　lobular
　mesangiocapillary　　} glomerulonephritis
　mixed membranous and
　proliferative

DEF: Kidney inflammation or dysfunction with mesangial cell proliferation.

583.4　With lesion of rapidly progressive glomerulonephritis

Necrotizing or rapidly progressive:
　glomerulitis NOS　　　nephritis NOS
　glomerulonephritis NOS　nephropathy NOS
Nephritis, unspecified, with lesion of necrotizing glomerulitis

DEF: Kidney inflammation or dysfunction; rapidly progresses to ESRD marked by diffuse epithelial proliferation.

583.6　With lesion of renal cortical necrosis

Nephritis NOS　　} with (renal) cortical
Nephropathy NOS　} necrosis

Renal cortical necrosis NOS

583.7　With lesion of renal medullary necrosis

Nephritis NOS　　} with (renal) medullary
Nephropathy NOS　} [papillary] necrosis

√5ᵗʰ **583.8　With other specified pathological lesion in kidney**

583.81　Nephritis and nephropathy, not specified as acute or chronic, in diseases classified elsewhere

Code first underlying disease, as:
amyloidosis (277.3)
diabetes mellitus (250.4)
gonococcal infection (098.19)
Goodpasture's syndrome (446.21)
systemic lupus erythematosus (710.0)
tuberculosis (016.0)

EXCLUDES　*gouty nephropathy (274.10)*
syphilitic nephritis (095.4)

AHA: 2Q, '03, 7; 3Q, '91, 3; S-O, '85, 3

583.89　Other

Glomerulitis　　　　} with lesion of:
Glomerulonephritis　　exudative
Nephritis　　　　　　} nephritis
Nephropathy　　　　interstitial
Renal disease　　　　nephritis

583.9　With unspecified pathological lesion in kidney

Glomerulitis
Glomerulonephritis　} NOS
Nephritis
Nephropathy

EXCLUDES　*nephropathy complicating pregnancy, labor, or the puerperium (642.0-642.9, 646.2)*
renal disease NOS with no stated cause (593.9)

√4ᵗʰ **584　Acute renal failure**

EXCLUDES　*following labor and delivery (669.3)*
posttraumatic (958.5)
that complicating:
　abortion (634-638 with .3, 639.3)
　ectopic or molar pregnancy (639.3)

AHA: 1Q, '93, 18; 2Q, '92, 5; 4Q, '92, 22

DEF: State resulting from increasing urea and related substances from the blood (azotemia), often with urine output of less than 500 ml per day.

584.5　With lesion of tubular necrosis

Lower nephron nephrosis
Renal failure with (acute) tubular necrosis
Tubular necrosis:
　NOS
　acute

DEF: Acute decline in kidney efficiency with destruction of tubules.

584.6　With lesion of renal cortical necrosis

DEF: Acute decline in kidney efficiency with destruction of renal tissues that filter blood.

584.7　With lesion of renal medullary [papillary] necrosis

Necrotizing renal papillitis

DEF: Acute decline in kidney efficiency with destruction of renal tissues that collect urine.

584.8　With other specified pathological lesion in kidney

AHA: N-D, '85, 1

584.9　Acute renal failure, unspecified

AHA: 2Q , '03, 7; 1Q, '03, 22; 3Q, '02, 21, 28; 2Q, '01, 14; 1Q, '00, 22; 3Q, '96, 9; 4Q, '88, 1

▲ √4ᵗʰ **585　Chronic kidney disease (CKD)**

Chronic uremia
►Use additional code to identify kidney transplant status, if applicable (V42.0)◄
Use additional code to identify manifestation as:
uremic:
　neuropathy (357.4)
　pericarditis (420.0)

EXCLUDES　*that with any condition classifiable to 401 (403.0-403.9 with fifth-digit 1)*

AHA: 1Q, '04, 5; 4Q, '03, 61, 111; 2Q, '03, 7; 2Q, '01, 12, 13; 1Q, '01, 3; 4Q, '98, 55; 3Q, '98, 6, 7; 2Q, '98, 20; 3Q, '96, 9; 1Q, '93, 18; 3Q, '91, 8; 4Q, '89, 1; N-D, '85, 15; S-O, '84, 3

N Newborn Age: 0　　P Pediatric Age: 0-17　　M Maternity Age: 12-55　　A Adult Age: 15-124　　Manifestation Code　　►◄ Revised Text　　● New Code　　▲ Revised Code Title

- **585.1 Chronic kidney disease, Stage I**
- **585.2 Chronic kidney disease, Stage II (mild)**
- **585.3 Chronic kidney disease, Stage III (moderate)**
- **585.4 Chronic kidney disease, Stage IV (severe)**
- **585.5 Chronic kidney disease, Stage V**
- **585.6 End stage renal disease**
- **585.9 Chronic kidney disease, unspecified**
  Chronic renal disease
  Chronic renal failure NOS
  Chronic renal insufficiency

586 Renal failure, unspecified
  Uremia NOS
  EXCLUDES *following labor and delivery (669.3)*
    posttraumatic renal failure (958.5)
    that complicating:
      abortion (634-638 with .3, 639.3)
      ectopic or molar pregnancy (639.3)
    uremia:
      extrarenal (788.9)
      prerenal (788.9)
    with any condition classifiable to 401 (403.0-
      403.9 with fifth-digit 1)
  AHA: 3Q, '98, 6; 1Q, '93, 18; 1Q, '88. 3
  DEF: Renal failure: kidney functions cease; malfunction may be due to inability to excrete metabolized substances or retain level of electrolytes.
  DEF: Uremia: excess urea, creatinine and other nitrogenous products of protein and amino acid metabolism in blood due to reduced excretory function in bilateral kidney disease; also called azotemia.

587 Renal sclerosis, unspecified
  Atrophy of kidney   Renal:
  Contracted kidney   cirrhosis
                             fibrosis
  EXCLUDES *nephrosclerosis (arteriolar) (arteriosclerotic)*
    (403.00-403.91)
    with hypertension (403.00-403.91)

✓4ᵗʰ **588 Disorders resulting from impaired renal function**
  588.0 Renal osteodystrophy
    Azotemic osteodystrophy
    Phosphate-losing tubular disorders
    Renal:
      dwarfism   infantilism
      rickets
    DEF: Bone disorder that results in various bone diseases such as osteomalacia, osteoporosis or osteosclerosis; caused by impaired renal function, an abnormal level of phosphorus in the blood and impaired stimulation of the parathyroid.

  588.1 Nephrogenic diabetes insipidus
    EXCLUDES *diabetes insipidus NOS (253.5)*
    DEF: Type of diabetes due to renal tubules inability to reabsorb water; not responsive to vasopressin; may develop into chronic renal insufficiency.

✓5ᵗʰ **588.8 Other specified disorders resulting from impaired renal function**
    EXCLUDES *secondary hypertension (405.0-405.9)*
    588.81 Secondary hyperparathyroidism (of renal origin)
      Secondary hyperparathyroidism NOS
      AHA: 4Q, '04, 58-59
      DEF: Parathyroid dysfunction caused by chronic renal failure; phosphate clearance is impaired, phosphate is released from bone, vitamin D is not produced, intestinal calcium absorption is low, and blood levels of calcium are lowered causing excessive production of parathyroid hormone.

    588.89 Other specified disorders resulting from impaired renal function
      Hypokalemic nephropathy
  588.9 Unspecified disorder resulting from impaired renal function

✓4ᵗʰ **589 Small kidney of unknown cause**
  589.0 Unilateral small kidney
  589.1 Bilateral small kidneys
  589.9 Small kidney, unspecified

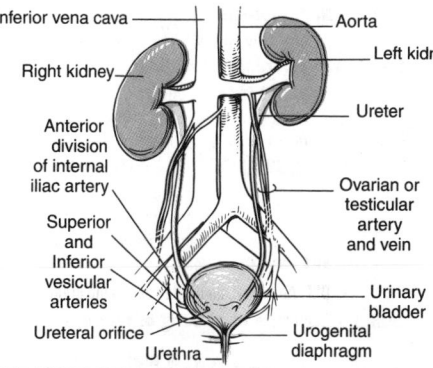
Genitourinary System

Inferior vena cava · Aorta · Right kidney · Left kidney · Anterior division of internal iliac artery · Ureter · Superior and Inferior vesicular arteries · Ovarian or testicular artery and vein · Ureteral orifice · Urethra · Urinary bladder · Urogenital diaphragm

OTHER DISEASES OF URINARY SYSTEM (590-599)

✓4ᵗʰ **590 Infections of kidney**
  Use additional code to identify organism, such as Escherichia coli [E. coli] (041.4)

✓5ᵗʰ **590.0 Chronic pyelonephritis**
    Chronic pyelitis
    Chronic pyonephrosis
    Code, if applicable, any causal condition first
    590.00 Without lesion of renal medullary necrosis
    590.01 With lesion of renal medullary necrosis

✓5ᵗʰ **590.1 Acute pyelonephritis**
    Acute pyelitis   Acute pyonephrosis
    590.10 Without lesion of renal medullary necrosis
    590.11 With lesion of renal medullary necrosis

  590.2 Renal and perinephric abscess
    Abscess: Abscess:
      kidney   perirenal
      nephritic   Carbuncle of kidney

  590.3 Pyeloureteritis cystica
    Infection of renal pelvis and ureter
    Ureteritis cystica
    DEF: Inflammation and formation of submucosal cysts in the kidney, pelvis, and ureter.

✓5ᵗʰ **590.8 Other pyelonephritis or pyonephrosis, not specified as acute or chronic**
    590.80 Pyelonephritis, unspecified
      Pyelitis NOS
      Pyelonephritis NOS
      AHA: 1Q, '98, 10; 4Q, '97, 40

    590.81 *Pyelitis or pyelonephritis in diseases classified elsewhere*
      Code first underlying disease, as:
        tuberculosis (016.0)

  590.9 Infection of kidney, unspecified
    EXCLUDES *urinary tract infection NOS (599.0)*

591 Hydronephrosis
  Hydrocalycosis   Hydroureteronephrosis
  Hydronephrosis
  EXCLUDES *congenital hydronephrosis (753.29)*
    hydroureter (593.5)
  AHA: 2Q, '98, 9
  DEF: Distention of kidney and pelvis, with urine build-up due to ureteral obstruction; pyonephrosis may result.

✓4ᵗʰ **592 Calculus of kidney and ureter**
  EXCLUDES *nephrocalcinosis (275.4)*
  592.0 Calculus of kidney
    Nephrolithiasis NOS   Staghorn calculus
    Renal calculus or stone   Stone in kidney
    EXCLUDES *uric acid nephrolithiasis (274.11)*
    AHA: 1Q, '00, 4

  592.1 Calculus of ureter
    Ureteric stone   Ureterolithiasis
    AHA: 2Q, '98, 9; 4Q, '97, 40' 1Q, '91, 11

  592.9 Urinary calculus, unspecified
    AHA: 1Q, '98, 10; 4Q, '97, 40

✓4ᵗʰ ✓5ᵗʰ Additional Digit Required RUG III Special Care Dx RUG III Clinically Complex Dx Hospice Non-cancer Dx **CD PDx** Clinical Dimension PDx **CD SDx** Clinical Dimension SDx

2006 ICD•9•CM **October 2005 • Volume 1 — 159**

Genitourinary System

585.1–592.9

Genitourinary System

593–595.3

✓4ᵗʰ **593 Other disorders of kidney and ureter**

593.0 Nephroptosis

Floating kidney   Mobile kidney

593.1 Hypertrophy of kidney

593.2 Cyst of kidney, acquired

Cyst (multiple) (solitary) of kidney, not congenital

Peripelvic (lymphatic) cyst

> **EXCLUDES**   calyceal or pyelogenic cyst of kidney
> (591)
> congenital cyst of kidney (753.1)
> polycystic (disease of) kidney (753.1)

AHA: 4Q, '90, 3

DEF: Abnormal, fluid-filled sac in the kidney, not present at birth.

593.3 Stricture or kinking of ureter

Angulation ⎱
Constriction ⎰ of ureter (post-operative)

Stricture of pelviureteric junction

AHA: 2Q, '98, 9

DEF: Stricture or knot in tube connecting kidney to bladder.

593.4 Other ureteric obstruction

Idiopathic retroperitoneal fibrosis

Occlusion NOS of ureter

> **EXCLUDES**   that due to calculus (592.1)

AHA: 2Q, '97, 4

593.5 Hydroureter

> **EXCLUDES**   congenital hydroureter (753.22)
> hydroureteronephrosis (591)

593.6 Postural proteinuria

Benign postural proteinuria   Orthostatic proteinuria

> **EXCLUDES**   proteinuria NOS (791.0)3

DEF: Excessive amounts of serum protein in the urine caused by the body position, e.g., orthostatic and lordotic.

✓5ᵗʰ **593.7 Vesicoureteral reflux**

AHA: 4Q, '94, 42

DEF: Backflow of urine, from bladder into ureter due to obstructed bladder neck.

593.70 Unspecified or without reflux nephropathy

593.71 With reflux nephropathy, unilateral

593.72 With reflux nephropathy, bilateral

593.73 With reflux nephropathy NOS

Bladder

Anterior View

Fundus   Left ureter

Right ureter

Lateral wall

Ureteral orifice

Trigone

Uvula of bladder

Urethra

Lateral View

Urachus

Left ureter

Peritoneum

Pubic bone

Urogenital diaphragm

✓5ᵗʰ **593.8 Other specified disorders of kidney and ureter**

593.81 Vascular disorders of kidney

Renal (artery):   Renal (artery):
   embolism   thrombosis
   hemorrhage   Renal infarction

593.82 Ureteral fistula

Intestinoureteral fistula

> **EXCLUDES**   fistula between ureter and
> female genital tract
> (619.0)

DEF: Abnormal communication, between tube connecting kidney to bladder and another structure.

593.89 Other

Adhesions, kidney   Polyp of ureter
   or ureter   Pyelectasia
Periureteritis   Ureterocele

> **EXCLUDES**   tuberculosis of ureter (016.2)
> ureteritis cystica (590.3)

593.9 Unspecified disorder of kidney and ureter

▶Acute renal disease
Acute renal insufficiency
Renal disease NOS◀
Salt-losing nephritis or syndrome

> **EXCLUDES** ▶ chronic renal insufficiency (585.9)◀
> cystic kidney disease (753.1)
> nephropathy, so stated (583.0-583.9)
> renal disease:
>   arising in pregnancy or the
>   puerperium (642.1-642.2,
>   642.4-642.7, 646.2)
>   not specified as acute or chronic, but
>   with stated pathology or cause
>   (583.0-583.9)

AHA: 1Q, '93, 17

✓4ᵗʰ **594 Calculus of lower urinary tract**

594.0 Calculus in diverticulum of bladder

DEF: Stone or mineral deposit in abnormal sac on the bladder wall.

594.1 Other calculus in bladder

Urinary bladder stone

> **EXCLUDES**   staghorn calculus (592.0)

DEF: Stone or mineral deposit in bladder.

594.2 Calculus in urethra

DEF: Stone or mineral deposit in tube that empties urine from bladder.

594.8 Other lower urinary tract calculus

AHA: J-F, '85, 16

594.9 Calculus of lower urinary tract, unspecified

> **EXCLUDES**   calculus of urinary tract NOS (592.9)

✓4ᵗʰ **595 Cystitis**

> **EXCLUDES**   prostatocystitis (601.3)

Use additional code to identify organism, such as Escherichia coli [E. coli] (041.4)

595.0 Acute cystitis

> **EXCLUDES**   trigonitis (595.3)

AHA: 2Q, '99, 15

DEF: Acute inflammation of bladder.

595.1 Chronic interstitial cystitis

Hunner's ulcer
Panmural fibrosis of bladder
Submucous cystitis

DEF: Inflamed lesion affecting bladder wall; symptoms include urinary frequency, pain on bladder filling, nocturia, and distended bladder.

595.2 Other chronic cystitis

Chronic cystitis NOS   Subacute cystitis

> **EXCLUDES**   trigonitis (595.3)

DEF: Persistent inflammation of bladder.

595.3 Trigonitis

Follicular cystitis   Urethrotrigonitis
Trigonitis (acute) (chronic)

DEF: Inflammation of the triangular area of the bladder called the trigonum vesicae.

N Newborn Age: 0   P Pediatric Age: 0-17   M Maternity Age: 12-55   A Adult Age: 15-124   **Manifestation Code**   ▶◀ Revised Text   ● New Code   ▲ Revised Code Title

595.4 Cystitis in diseases classified elsewhere
Code first underlying disease, as:
actinomycosis (039.8)
amebiasis (006.8)
bilharziasis (120.0-120.9)
Echinococcus infestation (122.3, 122.6)
EXCLUDES   cystitis:
diphtheritic (032.84)
gonococcal (098.11, 098.31)
monilial (112.2)
trichomonal (131.09)
tuberculous (016.1)

√5th **595.8 Other specified types of cystitis**

595.81 Cystitis cystica
DEF: Inflammation of the bladder characterized by formation of multiple cysts.

595.82 Irradiation cystitis
Use additional E code to identify cause
DEF: Inflammation of the bladder due to effects of radiation.

595.89 Other
Abscess of bladder   Cystitis:
Cystitis: emphysematous
bullous   glandularis

595.9 Cystitis, unspecified

√4th **596 Other disorders of bladder**
Use additional code to identify urinary incontinence (625.6, 788.30-788.39)
AHA: M-A, '87, 10

596.0 Bladder neck obstruction
Contracture (acquired) ⎫ of bladder neck or
Obstruction (acquired) ⎬ vesicourethral
Stenosis (acquired)   ⎭ orifice
EXCLUDES   congenital (753.6)
AHA: 3Q, '02, 28; 2Q, '01, 14; N-D, '86, 10
DEF: Bladder outlet and vesicourethral obstruction; occurs more often in males as a consequence of benign prostatic hypertrophy or prostatic cancer; may also occur in either sex due to strictures, following radiation, cystoscopy, catheterization, injury, infection, blood clots, bladder cancer, impaction or disease compressing bladder neck.

596.1 Intestinovesical fistula
Fistula: Fistula:
enterovesical   vesicoenteric
vesicocolic   vesicorectal
DEF: Abnormal communication, between intestine and bladder.

596.2 Vesical fistula, not elsewhere classified
Fistula: Fistula:
bladder NOS   vesicocutaneous
urethrovesical   vesicoperineal
EXCLUDES   fistula between bladder and female genital tract (619.0)
DEF: Abnormal communication between bladder and another structure.

596.3 Diverticulum of bladder
Diverticulitis   ⎫ of bladder
Diverticulum (acquired) (false) ⎭
EXCLUDES   that with calculus in diverticulum of bladder (594.0)
DEF: Abnormal pouch in bladder wall.

596.4 Atony of bladder
High compliance bladder
Hypotonicity ⎫ of bladder
Inertia   ⎭
EXCLUDES   neurogenic bladder (596.54)
DEF: Distended, bladder with loss of expulsive force; linked to CNS disease.

√5th **596.5 Other functional disorders of bladder**
EXCLUDES   cauda equina syndrome with neurogenic bladder (344.61)

596.51 Hypertonicity of bladder
Hyperactivity   Overactive bladder
DEF: Abnormal tension of muscular wall of bladder; may appear after surgery of voluntary nerve.

596.52 Low bladder compliance
DEF: Low bladder capacity; causes increased pressure and frequent urination.

596.53 Paralysis of bladder
DEF: Impaired bladder motor function due to nerve or muscle damage.

596.54 Neurogenic bladder NOS
AHA: 1Q, '01, 12
DEF: Unspecified dysfunctional bladder due to lesion of central, peripheral nervous system; may result in incontinence, residual urine retention, urinary infection, stones and renal failure.

596.55 Detrusor sphincter dyssynergia
DEF: Instability of the urinary bladder sphincter muscle associated with urinary incontinence..

596.59 Other functional disorder of bladder
Detrusor instability
DEF: Detrusor instability: instability of bladder; marked by uninhibited contractions often leading to incontinence.

596.6 Rupture of bladder, nontraumatic

596.7 Hemorrhage into bladder wall
Hyperemia of bladder
EXCLUDES   acute hemorrhagic cystitis (595.0)

596.8 Other specified disorders of bladder
Bladder: Bladder:
calcified   hemorrhage
contracted   hypertrophy
EXCLUDES   cystocele, female (618.01-618.02, 618.09, 618.2-618.4)
hernia or prolapse of bladder, female (618.01-618.02, 618.09, 618.2-618.4)
AHA: J-F, '85, 8

596.9 Unspecified disorder of bladder
AHA: J-F, '85, 8

√4th **597 Urethritis, not sexually transmitted, and urethral syndrome**
EXCLUDES   nonspecific urethritis, so stated (099.4)

597.0 Urethral abscess
Abscess: Abscess of:
periurethral   Cowper's gland
urethral (gland)   Littré's gland
Abscess of: Periurethral cellulitis
bulbourethral gland
EXCLUDES   urethral caruncle (599.3)
DEF: Pocket of pus in tube that empties urine from the bladder.

√5th **597.8 Other urethritis**

597.80 Urethritis, unspecified

597.81 Urethral syndrome NOS

597.89 Other
Adenitis, Skene's glands
Cowperitis
Meatitis, urethral
Ulcer, urethra (meatus)
Verumontanitis
EXCLUDES   trichomonal (131.02)

√4th **598 Urethral stricture**
Use additional code to identify urinary incontinence (625.6, 788.30-788.39)
INCLUDES   pinhole meatus
stricture of urinary meatus
EXCLUDES   congenital stricture of urethra and urinary meatus (753.6)
DEF: Narrowing of tube that empties urine from bladder.

√5th **598.0 Urethral stricture due to infection**

598.00 Due to unspecified infection

598.01 Due to infective diseases classified elsewhere
Code first underlying disease, as:
gonococcal infection (098.2)
schistosomiasis (120.0-120.9)
syphilis (095.8)

√4th √5th Additional Digit Required   RUG III Special Care Dx   RUG III Clinically Complex Dx   Hospice Non-cancer Dx   CD PDx Clinical Dimension PDx   CD SDx Clinical Dimension SDx

2006 ICD•9•CM   **Volume 1 — 161**

Genitourinary System

598.1–600.9

598.1 Traumatic urethral stricture
Stricture of urethra: Stricture of urethra:
late effect of injury   postobstetric
EXCLUDES *postoperative following surgery on genitourinary tract (598.2)*

598.2 Postoperative urethral stricture
Postcatheterization stricture of urethra
AHA: 3Q, '97, 6

598.8 Other specified causes of urethral stricture
AHA: N-D, '84, 9

598.9 Urethral stricture, unspecified

✓4ᵗʰ **599 Other disorders of urethra and urinary tract**

599.0 Urinary tract infection, site not specified
EXCLUDES *candidiasis of urinary tract (112.2)*
urinary tract infection of newborn (771.82)
Use additional code to identify organism, such as Escherichia coli [E. coli] (041.4)
AHA: 2Q, '04, 13; 4Q, '03, 79; 4Q, '99, 6; 2Q, '99, 15;1Q, '98, 5; 2Q, '96, 7; 4Q, '96, 33; 2Q, '95, 7; 1Q, '92, 13

599.1 Urethral fistula
Fistula: Urinary fistula NOS
urethroperineal
urethrorectal
EXCLUDES *fistula:*
urethroscrotal (608.89)
urethrovaginal (619.0)
urethrovesicovaginal (619.0)
AHA: 3Q, '97, 6

599.2 Urethral diverticulum
DEF: Abnormal pouch in urethral wall.

599.3 Urethral caruncle
Polyp of urethra

599.4 Urethral false passage
DEF: Abnormal opening in urethra due to surgery; trauma or disease.

599.5 Prolapsed urethral mucosa
Prolapse of urethra   Urethrocele
EXCLUDES *urethrocele, female (618.03, 618.09, 618.2-618.4)*

▲ ✓5ᵗʰ **599.6 Urinary obstruction**
Use additional code to identify urinary incontinence (625.6, 788.30-788.39)
EXCLUDES *obstructive nephropathy NOS (593.89)*
▶*urinary obstruction due to hyperplasia of prostate (600.0-600.9 with fifth-digit 1)*◀

● **599.60 Urinary obstruction, unspecified**
Obstructive uropathy NOS
Urinary (tract) obstruction NOS

● **599.69 Urinary obstruction, not elsewhere classified**

599.7 Hematuria
Hematuria (benign) (essential)
EXCLUDES *hemoglobinuria (791.2)*
AHA: 1Q, '00, 5; 3Q, '95, 8
DEF: Blood in urine.

✓5ᵗʰ **599.8 Other specified disorders of urethra and urinary tract**
Use additional code to identify urinary incontinence (625.6, 788.30-788.39), if present
EXCLUDES *symptoms and other conditions classifiable to 788.0-788.2, 788.4-788.9, 791.0-791.9*

599.81 Urethral hypermobility
DEF: Hyperactive urethra.

599.82 Intrinsic (urethral) spincter deficiency [ISD]
AHA: 2Q, '96, 15
DEF: Malfunctioning urethral sphincter.

599.83 Urethral instability
DEF: Inconsistent functioning of urethra.

599.84 Other specified disorders of urethra
Rupture of urethra (nontraumatic)
Urethral:
cyst   granuloma
DEF: Rupture of urethra due to herniation or breaking down of tissue; not due to trauma.
DEF: Urethral cyst: abnormal sac in urethra; usually fluid filled.
DEF: Granuloma: inflammatory cells forming small nodules in urethra.

599.89 Other specified disorders of urinary tract

599.9 Unspecified disorder of urethra and urinary tract

DISEASES OF MALE GENITAL ORGANS (600-608)

✓4ᵗʰ **600 Hyperplasia of prostate**
Use additional code to identify urinary incontinence (788.30-788.39)
AHA: 3Q, '94, 12; 3Q, '92, 7; N-D, '86, 10
DEF: Fibrostromal proliferation in periurethral glands, causes blood in urine; etiology unknown.

✓5ᵗʰ **600.0 Hypertrophy (benign) of prostate**
Benign prostatic hypertrophy
Enlargement of prostate
Smooth enlarged prostate
Soft enlarged prostate
AHA: 4Q, '03, 63; 1Q, '03, 6; 3Q, '02, 28; 2Q, '01, 14

600.00 Hypertrophy (benign) of prostate without urinary obstruction Ⓐ ♂
Hypertrophy (benign) of prostate NOS

600.01 Hypertrophy (benign) of prostate with urinary obstruction Ⓐ ♂
Hypertrophy (benign) of prostate with urinary retention
AHA: 4Q, '03, 64

✓5ᵗʰ **600.1 Nodular prostate**
Hard, firm prostate   Multinodular prostate
EXCLUDES *malignant neoplasm of prostate (185)*
AHA: 4Q, '03, 63
DEF: Hard, firm nodule in prostate.

600.10 Nodular prostate without urinary obstruction Ⓐ ♂
Nodular prostate NOS

600.11 Nodular prostate with urinary obstruction Ⓐ ♂
Nodular prostate with urinary retention

✓5ᵗʰ **600.2 Benign localized hyperplasia of prostate**
Adenofibromatous   Fibroma of prostate
hypertrophy of prostate   Myoma of prostate
Adenoma of prostate   Polyp of prostate
Fibroadenoma of prostate
EXCLUDES *benign neoplasms of prostate (222.2)*
hypertrophy of prostate (600.00-600.01)
malignant neoplasm of prostate (185)
AHA: 4Q, '03, 63
DEF: Benign localized hyperplasia is a clearly defined epithelial tumor. Other terms used for this condition are adenofibromatous hypertrophy of prostate, adenoma of prostate, fibroadenoma of prostate, fibroma of prostate, myoma of prostate, and polyp of prostate.

600.20 Benign localized hyperplasia of prostate without urinary obstruction Ⓐ ♂
Benign localized hyperplasia of prostate NOS

600.21 Benign localized hyperplasia of prostate with urinary obstruction Ⓐ ♂
Benign localized hyperplasia of prostate with urinary retention

600.3 Cyst of prostate Ⓐ ♂
DEF: Sacs of fluid, which differentiate this from either nodular or adenomatous tumors.

✓5ᵗʰ **600.9 Hyperplasia of prostate, unspecified**
Median bar   Prostatic obstruction NOS
AHA: 4Q, '03, 63

Ⓝ Newborn Age: 0   Ⓟ Pediatric Age: 0-17   Ⓜ Maternity Age: 12-55   Ⓐ Adult Age: 15-124   Manifestation Code   ▶◀ Revised Text   ● New Code   ▲ Revised Code Title

Male Pelvic Organs

Common Inguinal Canal Anomalies

600.90 Hyperplasia of prostate, unspecified, [A] ♂ without urinary obstruction
> Hyperplasia of prostate NOS

600.91 Hyperplasia of prostate, unspecified, [A] ♂ with urinary obstruction
> Hyperplasia of prostate, unspecified, with urinary retention

✓4th **601 Inflammatory diseases of prostate**
> Use additional code to identify organism, such as Staphylococcus (041.1), or Streptococcus (041.0)

601.0 Acute prostatitis [A] ♂

601.1 Chronic prostatitis [A] ♂

601.2 Abscess of prostate [A] ♂

601.3 Prostatocystitis [A] ♂

601.4 *Prostatitis in diseases classified elsewhere* [A] ♂
> Code first underlying disease, as:
> actinomycosis (039.8)
> blastomycosis (116.0)
> syphilis (095.8)
> tuberculosis (016.5)
> EXCLUDES prostatitis:
> gonococcal (098.12, 098.32)
> monilial (112.2)
> trichomonal (131.03)

601.8 Other specified inflammatory diseases of prostate [A] ♂
> Prostatitis: Prostatitis:
> cavitary granulomatous
> diverticular

601.9 Prostatitis, unspecified [A] ♂
> Prostatitis NOS

✓4th **602 Other disorders of prostate**

602.0 Calculus of prostate [A] ♂
> Prostatic stone
> DEF: Stone or mineral deposit in prostate.

602.1 Congestion or hemorrhage of prostate [A] ♂
> DEF: Bleeding or fluid collection in prostate.

602.2 Atrophy of prostate [A] ♂

602.3 Dysplasia of prostate ♂
> Prostatic intraepithelial neoplasia I (PIN I)
> Prostatic intraepithelial neoplasia II (PIN II)
> EXCLUDES prostatic intraepithelial neoplasia III (PIN III) (233.4)

> **AHA:** 4Q, '01, 46

> DEF: Abnormality of shape and size of the intraepithelial tissues of the prostate; pre-malignant condition characteristized by stalks and absence of a basilar cell layer; synonyms are intraductal dysplasia, large acinar atypical hyperplasia, atypical primary hyperplasia, hyperplasia with malignant changes, marked atypia, or duct-acinar dysplasia.

602.8 Other specified disorders of prostate [A] ♂
> Fistula
> Infarction } of prostate
> Stricture
> Periprostatic adhesions

602.9 Unspecified disorder of prostate [A] ♂

✓4th **603 Hydrocele**
> INCLUDES hydrocele of spermatic cord, testis, or tunica vaginalis
> EXCLUDES congenital (778.6)
> DEF: Circumscribed collection of fluid in tunica vaginalis, spermatic cord or testis.

603.0 Encysted hydrocele

603.1 Infected hydrocele
> Use additional code to identify organism

603.8 Other specified types of hydrocele

603.9 Hydrocele, unspecified

✓4th **604 Orchitis and epididymitis**
> Use additional code to identify organism, such as Escherichia coli [E. coli] (041.4), Staphylococcus (041.1), or Streptococcus (041.0)

604.0 Orchitis, epididymitis, and epididymo-orchitis, with abscess ♂
> Abscess of epididymis or testis

✓5th **604.9 Other orchitis, epididymitis, and epididymo-orchitis, without mention of abscess**

604.90 Orchitis and epididymitis, unspecified ♂

604.91 *Orchitis and epididymitis in diseases classified elsewhere* ♂
> Code first underlying disease, as:
> diphtheria (032.89)
> filariasis (125.0-125.9)
> syphilis (095.8)
> EXCLUDES orchitis:
> gonococcal (098.13, 098.33)
> mumps (072.0)
> tuberculous (016.5)
> tuberculous epididymitis (016.4)

604.99 Other ♂

605 Redundant prepuce and phimosis ♂
> Adherent prepuce Phimosis (congenital)
> Paraphimosis Tight foreskin
> DEF: Constriction of preputial orifice causing inability of the prepuce to be drawn back over the glans; it may be congenital or caused by infection.

✓4th **606 Infertility, male**
> **AHA:** 2Q, '96, 9

606.0 Azoospermia [A] ♂
> Absolute infertility Infertility due to:
> Infertility due to: spermatogenic arrest
> germinal (cell) aplasia (complete)
> DEF: Absence of spermatozoa in the semen or inability to produce spermatozoa.

606.1 Oligospermia [A] ♂
> Infertility due to:
> germinal cell desquamation
> hypospermatogenesis
> incomplete spermatogenic arrest
> DEF: Insufficient number of sperm in semen.

606.8 Infertility due to extratesticular causes [A] ♂
> Infertility due to: Infertility due to:
> drug therapy radiation
> infection systemic disease
> obstruction of efferent
> ducts

606.9 Male infertility, unspecified [A] ♂

✓4th
✓5th Additional Digit Required   RUG III Special Care Dx   RUG III Clinically Complex Dx   Hospice Non-cancer Dx   CD PDx Clinical Dimension PDx   CD SDx Clinical Dimension SDx

2006 ICD•9•CM   **Volume 1 — 163**

Genitourinary System

607–610.2

✓4ᵗʰ **607 Disorders of penis**
> EXCLUDES   *phimosis (605)*

607.0 Leukoplakia of penis   ♂
Kraurosis of penis
> EXCLUDES   *carcinoma in situ of penis (233.5)*
> *erythroplasia of Queyrat (233.5)*

DEF: White, thickened patches on glans penis.

607.1 Balanoposthitis   ♂
Balanitis
Use additional code to identify organism
DEF: Inflammation of glans penis and prepuce.

607.2 Other inflammatory disorders of penis   ♂
Abscess ⎫
Boil ⎬ of corpus cavernosum
Carbuncle ⎪   or penis
Cellulitis ⎭
Cavernitis (penis)
Use additional code to identify organism
> EXCLUDES   *herpetic infection (054.13)*

607.3 Priapism   ♂
Painful erection
DEF: Prolonged penile erection without sexual stimulation.

✓5ᵗʰ **607.8 Other specified disorders of penis**

607.81 Balanitis xerotica obliterans   ♂
Induratio penis plastica
DEF: Inflammation of the glans penis, caused by stricture of the opening of the prepuce.

607.82 Vascular disorders of penis   ♂
Embolism ⎫
Hematoma ⎪
  (nontraumatic) ⎬ of corpus
Hemorrhage ⎪ cavernosum
Thrombosis ⎭ or penis

607.83 Edema of penis   ♂
DEF: Fluid retention within penile tissues.

607.84 Impotence of organic origin   🄰 ♂
> EXCLUDES   ▶ *nonorganic (302.72)* ◀

AHA: 3Q, '91, 11
DEF: Physiological cause interfering with erection.

607.85 Peyronie's disease   ♂
AHA: 4Q, '03, 64
DEF: A severe curvature of the erect penis due to fibrosis of the cavernous sheaths.

607.89 Other   ♂
Atrophy ⎫
Fibrosis ⎬ of corpus cavernosum
Hypertrophy ⎪ or penis
Ulcer (chronic) ⎭

607.9 Unspecified disorder of penis   ♂

✓4ᵗʰ **608 Other disorders of male genital organs**

608.0 Seminal vesiculitis   ♂
Abscess ⎫
Cellulitis ⎬ of seminal vesicle
Vesiculitis (seminal)
Use additional code to identify organism
> EXCLUDES   *gonococcal infection (098.14, 098.34)*

DEF: Inflammation of seminal vesicle.

608.1 Spermatocele   ♂
DEF: Cystic enlargement of the epididymis or the testis; the cysts contain spermatozoa.

Torsion of Testes

Torsion of testis

Testes after correction showing bilateral fixation

608.2 Torsion of testis   ♂
Torsion of: Torsion of:
epididymis   testicle
spermatic cord
DEF: Twisted or rotated testis; may compromise blood flow.

608.3 Atrophy of testis   ♂

608.4 Other inflammatory disorders of male genital organs   ♂
Abscess ⎫
Boil ⎬ of scrotum, spermatic cord, testis
Carbuncle ⎪ [except abscess], tunica
Cellulitis ⎭ vaginalis, or vas deferens
Vasitis
Use additional code to identify organism
> EXCLUDES   *abscess of testis (604.0)*

✓5ᵗʰ **608.8 Other specified disorders of male genital organs**

608.81 Disorders of male genital organs in diseases classified elsewhere   ♂
Code first underlying disease, as:
filariasis (125.0-125.9)
tuberculosis (016.5)

608.82 Hematospermia   ♂
AHA: 4Q, '01, 46
DEF: Presence of blood in the ejaculate; relatively common, affecting men of any age after puberty; cause is often difficult to determine since the semen originates in several organs, often the result of a viral bacterial infection and inflammation.

608.83 Vascular disorders   ♂
Hematoma ⎫ of seminal vesicle,
  (nontraumatic) ⎪ spermatic cord,
Hemorrhage ⎬ testis, scrotum,
Thrombosis ⎪ tunica vaginalis,
   ⎭ or vas deferens
Hematocele NOS, male
AHA: 4Q, '03, 110

608.84 Chylocele of tunica vaginalis   ♂
DEF: Chylous effusion into tunica vaginalis; due to infusion of lymphatic fluids.

608.85 Stricture   ♂
Stricture of: Stricture of:
spermatic cord   vas deferens
tunica vaginalis

608.86 Edema   ♂

608.87 Retrograde ejaculation   ♂
AHA: 4Q, '01, 46
DEF: Condition where the semen travels to the bladder rather than out through the urethra due to damaged nerves causing the bladder neck to remain open during ejaculation.

608.89 Other   ♂
Atrophy ⎫ of seminal vesicle, sperm-
Fibrosis ⎪ atic cord, testis, scro-
Hypertrophy ⎬ tum, tunica vaginalis,
Ulcer ⎭ or vas deferens
> EXCLUDES   *atrophy of testis (608.3)*

608.9 Unspecified disorder of male genital organs   ♂

DISORDERS OF BREAST (610-611)

✓4ᵗʰ **610 Benign mammary dysplasias**

610.0 Solitary cyst of breast
Cyst (solitary) of breast

610.1 Diffuse cystic mastopathy   🄰
Chronic cystic mastitis   Fibrocystic disease of
Cystic breast   breast
DEF: Extensive formation of nodular cysts in breast tissue; symptoms include tenderness, change in size and hyperplasia of ductal epithelium.

610.2 Fibroadenosis of breast
Fibroadenosis of breast: Fibroadenosis of breast:
NOS   diffuse
chronic   periodic
cystic   segmental
DEF: Non-neoplastic nodular condition of breast.

🄽 Newborn Age: 0   🄿 Pediatric Age: 0-17   🄼 Maternity Age: 12-55   🄰 Adult Age: 15-124   Manifestation Code   ▶◀ Revised Text   ● New Code   ▲ Revised Code Title

164 — Volume 1 • October 2005   *2006 ICD•9•CM*

610.3 **Fibrosclerosis of breast**
DEF: Fibrous tissue in breast.

610.4 **Mammary duct ectasia**
    Comedomastitis   Mastitis:
    Duct ectasia   periductal
                        plasma cell
DEF: Atrophy of duct epithelium; causes distended collecting ducts of mammary gland; drying up of breast secretion, intraductal inflammation and periductal and interstitial chronic inflammatory reaction.

610.8 **Other specified benign mammary dysplasias**
    Mazoplasia   Sebaceous cyst of breast

610.9 **Benign mammary dysplasia, unspecified**

√4th **611 Other disorders of breast**
> EXCLUDES   *that associated with lactation or the puerperium (675.0-676.9)*

611.0 **Inflammatory disease of breast**
    Abscess (acute) (chronic)   Mastitis (acute) (subacute)
      (nonpuerperal) of: (nonpuerperal):
       areola   NOS
       breast   infective
       Mammillary fistula   retromammary
                           submammary
> EXCLUDES   *carbuncle of breast (680.2)*
> *chronic cystic mastitis (610.1)*
> *neonatal infective mastitis (771.5)*
> *thrombophlebitis of breast [Mondor's disease] (451.89)*

611.1 **Hypertrophy of breast**
    Gynecomastia   Hypertrophy of breast:
    Hypertrophy of breast: massive pubertal
      NOS

611.2 **Fissure of nipple**

611.3 **Fat necrosis of breast**
    Fat necrosis (segmental) of breast
DEF: Splitting of neutral fats in adipose tissue cells as a result of trauma; a firm circumscribed mass is then formed in the breast.

611.4 **Atrophy of breast**

611.5 **Galactocele**

611.6 **Galactorrhea not associated with childbirth**

√5th **611.7** **Signs and symptoms in breast**

     611.71 Mastodynia
         Pain in breast

     611.72 Lump or mass in breast
         AHA: 2Q, '03, 4-5

     611.79 Other
         Induration of breast   Nipple discharge
         Inversion of nipple   Retraction of nipple

611.8 **Other specified disorders of breast**
    Hematoma (nontraumatic) ⎫
    Infarction   ⎬ of breast
                          ⎭
    Occlusion of breast duct
    Subinvolution of breast (postlactational) (postpartum)

611.9 **Unspecified breast disorder**

INFLAMMATORY DISEASE OF FEMALE PELVIC ORGANS (614-616)
    Use additional code to identify organism, such as
    Staphylococcus (041.1), or Streptococcus (041.0)
> EXCLUDES   *that associated with pregnancy, abortion, childbirth, or the puerperium (630-676.9)*

√4th **614 Inflammatory disease of ovary, fallopian tube, pelvic cellular tissue, and peritoneum**
> EXCLUDES   *endometritis (615.0-615.9)*
> *major infection following delivery (670)*
> *that complicating:*
> *abortion (634-638 with .0, 639.0)*
> *ectopic or molar pregnancy (639.0)*
> *pregnancy or labor (646.6)*

614.0 **Acute salpingitis and oophoritis**   ♀
    Any condition classifiable to 614.2, specified as acute or subacute
DEF: Acute inflammation, of ovary and fallopian tube.

614.1 **Chronic salpingitis and oophoritis**   ♀
    Hydrosalpinx
    Salpingitis:
      follicularis
      isthmica nodosa
    Any condition classifiable to 614.2, specified as chronic
DEF: Persistent inflammation of ovary and fallopian tube.

614.2 **Salpingitis and oophoritis not specified as acute, subacute, or chronic**   ♀
    Abscess (of):   Pyosalpinx
      fallopian tube   Perisalpingitis
      ovary   Salpingitis
      tubo-ovarian   Salpingo-oophoritis
    Oophoritis   Tubo-ovarian inflammatory
    Periophoritis   disease
> EXCLUDES   *gonococcal infection (chronic) (098.37)*
> *acute (098.17)*
> *tuberculous (016.6)*

AHA: 2Q, '91, 5

614.3 **Acute parametritis and pelvic cellulitis**   ♀
    Acute inflammatory pelvic disease
    Any condition classifiable to 614.4, specified as acute
DEF: Parametritis: inflammation of the parametrium; pelvic cellulitis is a synonym for parametritis.

614.4 **Chronic or unspecified parametritis and pelvic cellulitis**   ♀
    Abscess (of):
      broad ligament ⎫
      parametrium   ⎬ chronic or NOS
      pelvis, female   ⎬
      pouch of Douglas ⎭
    Chronic inflammatory pelvic disease
    Pelvic cellulitis, female
> EXCLUDES   *tuberculous (016.7)*

614.5 **Acute or unspecified pelvic peritonitis, female**   ♀

614.6 **Pelvic peritoneal adhesions, female (postoperative) (postinfection)**   ♀
    Adhesions: Adhesions:
      peritubal   tubo-ovarian
    Use additional code to identify any associated infertility (628.2)
AHA: 3Q, '03, 6; 1Q, '03, 4; 3Q, '95, 7; 3Q, '94, 12
DEF: Fibrous scarring abnormally joining structures within abdomen.

614.7 **Other chronic pelvic peritonitis, female**   ♀
> EXCLUDES   *tuberculous (016.7)*

614.8 **Other specified inflammatory disease of female pelvic organs and tissues**   ♀

614.9 **Unspecified inflammatory disease of female pelvic organs and tissues**   ♀
    Pelvic infection or inflammation, female NOS
    Pelvic inflammatory disease [PID]

√4th **615 Inflammatory diseases of uterus, except cervix**
> EXCLUDES   *following delivery (670)*
> *hyperplastic endometritis (621.30-621.33)*
> *that complicating:*
> *abortion (634-638 with .0, 639.0)*
> *ectopic or molar pregnancy (639.0)*
> *pregnancy or labor (646.6)*

615.0 **Acute**   ♀
    Any condition classifiable to 615.9, specified as acute or subacute

615.1 **Chronic**   ♀
    Any condition classifiable to 615.9, specified as chronic

615.9 **Unspecified inflammatory disease of uterus**   ♀
    Endometritis   Perimetritis
    Endomyometritis   Pyometra
    Metritis   Uterine abscess
    Myometritis

√4th √5th Additional Digit Required   RUG III Special Care Dx   RUG III Clinically Complex Dx   Hospice Non-cancer Dx   CD PDx Clinical Dimension PDx   CD SDx Clinical Dimension SDx

2006 ICD•9•CM   Volume 1 — 165

Genitourinary System

616–618

✓4th **616 Inflammatory disease of cervix, vagina, and vulva**

> EXCLUDES   *that complicating:*
> *abortion (634-638 with .0, 639.0)*
> *ectopic or molar pregnancy (639.0)*
> *pregnancy, childbirth, or the puerperium (646.6)*

616.0 Cervicitis and endocervicitis ♀

> Cervicitis ⎱ with or without mention of
> Endocervicitis ⎰   erosion or ectropion
> Nabothian (gland) cyst or follicle
>
> > EXCLUDES   *erosion or ectropion without mention of cervicitis (622.0)*

✓5th **616.1 Vaginitis and vulvovaginitis**

> **DEF:** Inflammation or infection of vagina or external female genitalia.

> **616.10 Vaginitis and vulvovaginitis, unspecified** ♀
>
> > Vaginitis:
> >   NOS
> >   postirradiation
> > Vulvitis NOS
> > Vulvovaginitis NOS
> > Use additional code to identify organism, such as Escherichia coli [E. coli] (041.4), Staphylococcus (041.1), or Streptococcus (041.0)
> >
> > > EXCLUDES   *noninfective leukorrhea (623.5)*
> > > *postmenopausal or senile vaginitis (627.3)*

> **616.11 Vaginitis and vulvovaginitis in diseases classified elsewhere** ♀
>
> > *Code first underlying disease, as:*
> > pinwurm vaginitis (127.4)
> >
> > > EXCLUDES   *herpetic vulvovaginitis (054.11)*
> > > *monilial vulvotaginitis (112.1)*
> > > *trichomonal vaginitis or vulvovaginitis (131.01)*

616.2 Cyst of Bartholin's gland ♀

> Bartholin's duct cyst
> **DEF:** Fluid-filled sac within gland of vaginal orifice.

616.3 Abscess of Bartholin's gland ♀

> Vulvovaginal gland abscess

616.4 Other abscess of vulva ♀

> Abscess ⎫
> Carbuncle ⎬ of vulva
> Furuncle ⎭

✓5th **616.5 Ulceration of vulva**

> **616.50 Ulceration of vulva, unspecified** ♀
>
> > Ulcer NOS of vulva

> **616.51 Ulceration of vulva in diseases classified elsewhere** ♀
>
> > *Code first underlying disease, as:*
> > Behçet's syndrome (136.1)
> > tuberculosis (016.7)
> >
> > > EXCLUDES   *vulvar ulcer (in):*
> > > *gonococcal (098.0)*
> > > *herpes simplex (054.12)*
> > > *syphilitic (091.0)*

616.8 Other specified inflammatory diseases of cervix, vagina, and vulva ♀

> Caruncle, vagina or labium
> Ulcer, vagina
>
> > EXCLUDES   *noninflammatory disorders of:*
> > *cervix (622.0-622.9)*
> > *vagina (623.0-623.9)*
> > *vulva (624.0-624.9)*

616.9 Unspecified inflammatory disease of cervix, vagina, and vulva ♀

OTHER DISORDERS OF FEMALE GENITAL TRACT (617-629)

✓4th **617 Endometriosis**

617.0 Endometriosis of uterus ♀

> Adenomyosis   Endometriosis:
> Endometriosis: internal
>   cervix   myometrium
>
> > EXCLUDES   *stromal endometriosis (236.0)*
>
> **AHA:** 3Q, '92, 7
>
> **DEF:** Aberrant uterine mucosal tissue; creating products of menses and inflamed uterine tissues.

617.1 Endometriosis of ovary ♀

> Chocolate cyst of ovary
> Endometrial cystoma of ovary
> **DEF:** Aberrant uterine tissue; creating products of menses and inflamed ovarian tissues.

617.2 Endometriosis of fallopian tube ♀

> **DEF:** Aberrant uterine tissue; creating products of menses and inflamed tissues of fallopian tubes.

617.3 Endometriosis of pelvic peritoneum ♀

> Endometriosis: Endometriosis:
>   broad ligament   parametrium
>   cul-de-sac (Douglas')   round ligament
> **DEF:** Aberrant uterine tissue; creating products of menses and inflamed peritoneum tissues.

617.4 Endometriosis of rectovaginal septum and vagina ♀

> **DEF:** Aberrant uterine tissue; creating products of menses and inflamed tissues in and behind vagina.

617.5 Endometriosis of intestine ♀

> Endometriosis: Endometriosis:
>   appendix   rectum
>   colon
> **DEF:** Aberrant uterine tissue; creating products of menses and inflamed intestinal tissues.

617.6 Endometriosis in scar of skin ♀

617.8 Endometriosis of other specified sites ♀

> Endometriosis: Endometriosis:
>   bladder   umbilicus
>   lung   vulva

617.9 Endometriosis, site unspecified ♀

✓4th **618 Genital prolapse**

> Use additional code to identify urinary incontinence (625.6, 788.31, 788.33-788.39)
>
> > EXCLUDES   *that complicating pregnancy, labor, or delivery (654.4)*

Female Genitourinary System

Skull base from behind

Nasopharynx

Oropharynx

Hypopharynx

To trachea

Esophagus

Choanae
Soft palate
Uvula
Tongue
Epiglottis junctional zone
Ariepiglottic fold
Piriform sinus (fossa)
Posterior cricoid region

Common Sites of Endometriosis

Common sites of endometriosis, in descending order of frequency:
(1) ovary
(2) cul de sac
(3) utersacral ligaments
(4) broad ligaments
(5) fallopian tube
(6) uterovesical fold
(7) round ligament
(8) vermiform appedix
(9) vagina
(10) rectovaginal septum

 Newborn Age: 0   Pediatric Age: 0-17   Maternity Age: 12-55   Adult Age: 15-124   Manifestation Code   ▶◀ Revised Text   ● New Code   ▲ Revised Code Title

166 — Volume 1   *2006 ICD•9•CM*

Types of Vaginal Hernias

Urethrocele — Uterus, Bladder, Rectum, Urethra, Vaginal canal, Urethrocele

Cystocele — Uterus, Bladder, Rectum, Urethra, Cystocele, Vaginal canal

Rectocele — Uterus, Bladder, Rectum, Urethra, Rectocele, Vaginal canal

Enterocele — Uterus, Bladder, Rectum, Urethra, Terminal ileum, Vaginal canal

▶Vaginal Midline Cystocele◀

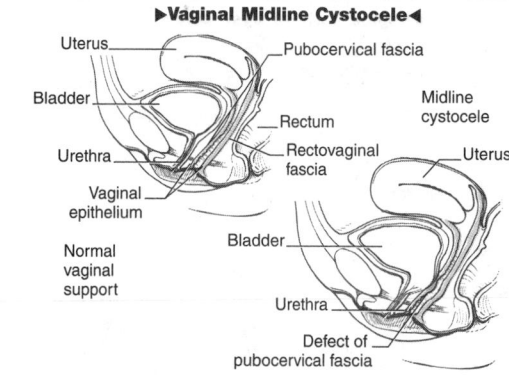

Uterus, Bladder, Urethra, Vaginal epithelium, Normal vaginal support, Pubocervical fascia, Rectum, Rectovaginal fascia, Midline cystocele

Uterus, Bladder, Urethra, Defect of pubocervical fascia

✓5ᵗʰ **618.0 Prolapse of vaginal walls without mention of uterine prolapse**

> **EXCLUDES** *that with uterine prolapse (618.2-618.4)*
> *enterocele (618.6)*
> *vaginal vault prolapse following hysterectomy (618.5)*

618.00 Unspecified prolapse of vaginal walls ♀
Vaginal prolapse NOS

618.01 Cystocele, midline ♀
Cystocele NOS
DEF: ▶ Defect in the pubocervical fascia, the supportive layer of the bladder, causing bladder drop and herniated into the vagina along the midline.◀

618.02 Cystocele, lateral ♀
Paravaginal
DEF: ▶ Loss of support of the lateral attachment of the vagina at the arcus tendinous results in bladder drop; bladder herniates into the vagina laterally; also called paravaginal defect.◀

618.03 Urethrocele ♀
618.04 Rectocele ♀
Proctocele
618.05 Perineocele ♀
618.09 Other prolapse of vaginal walls without mention of uterine prolapse ♀
Cystourethrocele

618.1 Uterine prolapse without mention of vaginal wall prolapse ♀
Descensus uteri   Uterine prolapse:
Uterine prolapse: first degree
NOS   second degree
complete   third degree
> **EXCLUDES** *that with mention of cystocele, ureth-rocele, or rectocele (618.2-618.4)*

618.2 Uterovaginal prolapse, incomplete ♀
DEF: Downward displacement of uterus downward into vagina.

618.3 Uterovaginal prolapse, complete ♀
DEF: Downward displacement of uterus exposed within external genitalia.

618.4 Uterovaginal prolapse, unspecified ♀
618.5 Prolapse of vaginal vault after hysterectomy ♀
618.6 Vaginal enterocele, congenital or acquired ♀
Pelvic enterocele, congenital or acquired
DEF: Vaginal vault hernia formed by the loop of the small intestine protruding into the rectal vaginal pouch; can also accompany uterine prolapse or follow hysterectomy.

618.7 Old laceration of muscles of pelvic floor ♀
✓5ᵗʰ **618.8 Other specified genital prolapse**
618.81 Incompetence or weakening of pubocervical tissue ♀
618.82 Incompetence or weakening of rectovaginal tissue ♀
618.83 Pelvic muscle wasting ♀
Disuse atrophy of pelvic muscles and anal sphincter
618.89 Other specified genital prolapse ♀
618.9 Unspecified genital prolapse ♀

✓4ᵗʰ **619 Fistula involving female genital tract**
> **EXCLUDES** *vesicorectal and intestinovesical fistula (596.1)*

619.0 Urinary-genital tract fistula, female ♀
Fistula: Fistula:
cervicovesical   uteroureteric
ureterovaginal   uterovesical
urethrovaginal   vesicocervicovaginal
urethrovesicovaginal   vesicovaginal

619.1 Digestive-genital tract fistula, female ♀
Fistula: Fistula:
intestinouterine   rectovulval
intestinovaginal   sigmoidovaginal
rectovaginal   uterorectal

619.2 Genital tract-skin fistula, female ♀
Fistula: Fistula:
uterus to abdominal wall   vaginoperineal

619.8 Other specified fistulas involving female genital tract ♀
Fistula: Fistula:
cervix   uterus
cul-de-sac (Douglas')   vagina

619.9 Unspecified fistula involving female genital tract ♀

✓4ᵗʰ **620 Noninflammatory disorders of ovary, fallopian tube, and broad ligament**
> **EXCLUDES** *hydrosalpinx (614.1)*

620.0 Follicular cyst of ovary ♀
Cyst of graafian follicle
DEF: Fluid-filled, encapsulated cyst due to occluded follicle duct that secretes hormones into ovaries.

620.1 Corpus luteum cyst or hematoma ♀
Corpus luteum hemorrhage or rupture
Lutein cyst
DEF: Fluid-filled cyst due to serous developing from corpus luteum or clotted blood.

620.2 Other and unspecified ovarian cyst ♀
Cyst:
NOS
corpus albicans
retention NOS   } of ovary
serous
theca-lutein
Simple cystoma of ovary
> **EXCLUDES** *cystadenoma (benign) (serous) (220)*
> *developmental cysts (752.0)*
> *neoplastic cysts (220)*
> *polycystic ovaries (256.4)*
> *Stein-Leventhal syndrome (256.4)*

620.3 Acquired atrophy of ovary and fallopian tube ♀
Senile involution of ovary

620.4 Prolapse or hernia of ovary and fallopian tube ♀
Displacement of ovary and fallopian tube
Salpingocele

620.5 Torsion of ovary, ovarian pedicle, or fallopian tube ♀
Torsion: Torsion:
accessory tube   hydatid of Morgagni

620.6 Broad ligament laceration syndrome ♀
Masters-Allen syndrome

✓4ᵗʰ ✓5ᵗʰ Additional Digit Required   RUG III Special Care Dx   RUG III Clinically Complex Dx   Hospice Non-cancer Dx   **CD PDx** Clinical Dimension PDx   **CD SDx** Clinical Dimension SDx

2006 ICD•9•CM   February 2005 • Volume 1 — 167

Genitourinary System

620.7–622.4

▶Vaginal Lateral Cystocele◀

Symphysis pubis
Cooper's ligament
Arcus tendineus
Bladder
Pubocervical fascia
Normal vaginal support
Lateral cystocele
Fascial defects

Uterus and Ovaries

Fundus of uterus
Mesosalpinx
Mesovarium
Suspensory ligaments
Uterine (fallopian tube)
Body
Ligament of ovary
Ovary
Uterosacral ligament
Cervix
Vagina
Fimbria
Ovary
Broad ligament

620.7 Hematoma of broad ligament ♀
Hematocele, broad ligament
DEF: Blood within peritoneal fold that supports uterus.

620.8 Other noninflammatory disorders of ovary, fallopian tube, and broad ligament ♀
Cyst
Polyp } of broad ligament or fallopian tube

Infarction
Rupture } of ovary or fallopian tube

Hematosalpinx
EXCLUDES hematosalpinx in ectopic pregnancy (639.2)
peritubal adhesions (614.6)
torsion of ovary, ovarian pedicle, or fallopian tube (620.5)

620.9 Unspecified noninflammatory disorder of ovary, fallopian tube, and broad ligament ♀

✓4ᵗʰ **621 Disorders of uterus, not elsewhere classified**

621.0 Polyp of corpus uteri ♀
Polyp: Polyp:
endometrium   uterus NOS
EXCLUDES cervical polyp NOS (622.7)

621.1 Chronic subinvolution of uterus ♀
EXCLUDES puerperal (674.8)
AHA: 1Q, '91, 11
DEF: Abnormal size of uterus after delivery; the uterus does not return to its normal size after the birth of a child.

621.2 Hypertrophy of uterus ♀
Bulky or enlarged uterus
EXCLUDES puerperal (674.8)

✓5ᵗʰ **621.3 Endometrial hyperplasia**
Hyperplasia (adenomatous) (cystic) (glandular) of endometrium
DEF: Abnormal cystic overgrowth of endometrial tissue.

621.30 Endometrial hyperplasia, unspecified ♀
Endometrial hyperplasia NOS

621.31 Simple endometrial hyperplasia without atypia ♀

621.32 Complex endometrial hyperplasia without atypia ♀

621.33 Endometrial hyperplasia with atypia ♀

621.4 Hematometra ♀
Hemometra
EXCLUDES that in congenital anomaly (752.2-752.3)
DEF: Accumulated blood in uterus.

621.5 Intrauterine synechiae ♀
Adhesions of uterus   Band(s) of uterus

621.6 Malposition of uterus ♀
Anteversion
Retroflexion } of uterus
Retroversion
EXCLUDES malposition complicating pregnancy, labor, or delivery (654.3-654.4)

621.7 Chronic inversion of uterus ♀
EXCLUDES current obstetrical trauma (665.2)
prolapse of uterus (618.1-618.4)

621.8 Other specified disorders of uterus, not elsewhere classified ♀
Atrophy, acquired
Cyst
Fibrosis NOS } of uterus
Old laceration (postpartum)
Ulcer
EXCLUDES bilharzial fibrosis (120.0-120.9)
endometriosis (617.0)
fistulas (619.0-619.8)
inflammatory diseases (615.0-615.9)

621.9 Unspecified disorder of uterus ♀

✓4ᵗʰ **622 Noninflammatory disorders of cervix**
EXCLUDES abnormality of cervix complicating pregnancy, labor, or delivery (654.5-654.6)
fistula (619.0-619.8)

622.0 Erosion and ectropion of cervix ♀
Eversion
Ulcer } of cervix
EXCLUDES that in chronic cervicitis (616.0)
DEF: Ulceration or turning outward of uterine cervix.

✓5ᵗʰ **622.1 Dysplasia of cervix (uteri)**
EXCLUDES abnormal results from cervical cytologic examination without histologic confirmation (795.00-795.09)
carcinoma in situ of cervix (233.1)
cervical intraepithelial neoplasia III [CIN III] (233.1)
AHA: 1Q, '91, 11
DEF: Abnormal cell structures in portal between uterus and vagina.

622.10 Dysplasia of cervix, unspecified ♀
Anaplasia of cervix   Cervical dysplasia
Cervical atypism   NOS

622.11 Mild dysplasia of cervix ♀
Cervical intraepithelial neoplasia I [CIN I]

622.12 Moderate dysplasia of cervix ♀
Cervical intraepithelial neoplasia II [CIN II]
EXCLUDES carcinoma in situ of cervix (233.1)
cervical intraepithelial neoplasia III [CIN III] (233.1)
severe dysplasia (233.1)

622.2 Leukoplakia of cervix (uteri) ♀
EXCLUDES carcinoma in situ of cervix (233.1)
DEF: Thickened, white patches on portal between uterus and vagina.

622.3 Old laceration of cervix ♀
Adhesions
Band(s) } of cervix
Cicatrix (postpartum)
EXCLUDES current obstetrical trauma (665.3)
DEF: Scarring or other evidence of old wound on cervix.

622.4 Stricture and stenosis of cervix ♀
Atresia (acquired)
Contracture } of cervix
Occlusion
Pinpoint os uteri
EXCLUDES congenital (752.49)
that complicating labor (654.6)

N Newborn Age: 0   P Pediatric Age: 0-17   M Maternity Age: 12-55   A Adult Age: 15-124   Manifestation Code   ▶◀ Revised Text   ● New Code   ▲ Revised Code Title

622.5 Incompetence of cervix ♀
> **EXCLUDES** *complicating pregnancy (654.5)*
> *that affecting fetus or newborn (761.0)*

DEF: Inadequate functioning of cervix; marked by abnormal widening during pregnancy; causing miscarriage.

622.6 Hypertrophic elongation of cervix ♀

DEF: Overgrowth of cervix tissues extending down into vagina.

622.7 Mucous polyp of cervix ♀
Polyp NOS of cervix
> **EXCLUDES** *adenomatous polyp of cervix (219.0)*

622.8 Other specified noninflammatory disorders of ♀
cervix

Atrophy (senile) ⎤
Cyst ⎟ of cervix
Fibrosis ⎟
Hemorrhage ⎦

> **EXCLUDES** *endometriosis (617.0)*
> *fistula (619.0-619.8)*
> *inflammatory diseases (616.0)*

622.9 Unspecified noninflammatory disorder of cervix ♀

✓4ᵗʰ **623 Noninflammatory disorders of vagina**
> **EXCLUDES** *abnormality of vagina complicating pregnancy,*
> *labor, or delivery (654.7)*
> *congenital absence of vagina (752.49)*
> *congenital diaphragm or bands (752.49)*
> *fistulas involving vagina (619.0-619.8)*

623.0 Dysplasia of vagina ♀
> **EXCLUDES** *carcinoma in situ of vagina (233.3)*

623.1 Leukoplakia of vagina ♀

DEF: Thickened white patches on vaginal canal.

623.2 Stricture or atresia of vagina ♀
Adhesions (postoperative) (postradiation) of vagina
Occlusion of vagina
Stenosis, vagina
Use additional E code to identify any external cause
> **EXCLUDES** *congenital atresia or stricture (752.49)*

623.3 Tight hymenal ring ♀
Rigid hymen ⎤
Tight hymenal ring ⎟ acquired or congenital
Tight introitus ⎦
> **EXCLUDES** *imperforate hymen (752.42)*

623.4 Old vaginal laceration ♀
> **EXCLUDES** *old laceration involving muscles of*
> *pelvic floor (618.7)*

DEF: Scarring or other evidence of old wound on vagina.

623.5 Leukorrhea, not specified as infective ♀
Leukorrhea NOS of vagina
Vaginal discharge NOS
> **EXCLUDES** *trichomonal (131.00)*

DEF: Viscid whitish discharge, from vagina.

623.6 Vaginal hematoma ♀
> **EXCLUDES** *current obstetrical trauma (665.7)*

623.7 Polyp of vagina ♀

623.8 Other specified noninflammatory disorders of ♀
vagina
Cyst ⎤
Hemorrhage ⎦ of vagina

623.9 Unspecified noninflammatory disorder of vagina ♀

✓4ᵗʰ **624 Noninflammatory disorders of vulva and perineum**
> **EXCLUDES** *abnormality of vulva and perineum complicating*
> *pregnancy, labor, or delivery (654.8)*
> *condyloma acuminatum (078.1)*
> *fistulas involving:*
> *perineum — see Alphabetic Index*
> *vulva (619.0-619.8)*
> *vulval varices (456.6)*
> *vulvar involvement in skin conditions (690-709.9)*

624.0 Dystrophy of vulva ♀
Kraurosis ⎤
Leukoplakia ⎦ of vulva
> **EXCLUDES** *carcinoma in situ of vulva (233.3)*

624.1 Atrophy of vulva ♀

624.2 Hypertrophy of clitoris ♀
> **EXCLUDES** *that in endocrine disorders (255.2, 256.1)*

624.3 Hypertrophy of labia ♀
Hypertrophy of vulva NOS

DEF: Overgrowth of fleshy folds on either side of vagina.

624.4 Old laceration or scarring of vulva ♀

DEF: Scarring or other evidence of old wound on external female genitalia.

624.5 Hematoma of vulva ♀
> **EXCLUDES** *that complicating delivery (664.5)*

DEF: Blood in tissue of external genitalia.

624.6 Polyp of labia and vulva ♀

624.8 Other specified noninflammatory disorders of ♀
vulva and perineum
Cyst ⎤
Edema ⎟ of vulva
Stricture ⎦

AHA: 1Q, '03, 13; 1Q, '95, 8

624.9 Unspecified noninflammatory disorder of vulva ♀
and perineum

✓4ᵗʰ **625 Pain and other symptoms associated with female genital**
organs

625.0 Dyspareunia ♀
> **EXCLUDES** *psychogenic dyspareunia (302.76)*

DEF: Difficult or painful sexual intercourse.

625.1 Vaginismus ♀
Colpospasm   Vulvismus
> **EXCLUDES** *psychogenic vaginismus (306.51)*

DEF: Vaginal spasms; due to involuntary contraction of musculature; prevents intercourse.

625.2 Mittelschmerz ♀
Intermenstrual pain   Ovulation pain

DEF: Pain occurring between menstrual periods.

625.3 Dysmenorrhea ♀
Painful menstruation
> **EXCLUDES** *psychogenic dysmenorrhea (306.52)*

AHA: 2Q, '94, 12

625.4 Premenstrual tension syndromes ♀
Menstrual: Premenstrual dysphoric disorder
   migraine   Premenstrual syndrome
   molimen   Premenstrual tension NOS

AHA: 4Q, '03, 116

625.5 Pelvic congestion syndrome ♀
Congestion-fibrosis syndrome   Taylor's syndrome

DEF: Excessive accumulated of blood in vessels of pelvis; may occur after orgasm; causes abnormal menstruation, lower back pain and vaginal discharge.

625.6 Stress incontinence, female ♀
> **EXCLUDES** *mixed incontinence (788.33)*
> *stress incontinence, male (788.32)*

DEF: Involuntary leakage of urine due to insufficient sphincter control; occurs upon sneezing, laughing, coughing, sudden movement or lifting.

625.8 Other specified symptoms associated with ♀
female genital organs

AHA: N-D, '85, 16

625.9 Unspecified symptom associated with female ♀
genital organs

✓4ᵗʰ **626 Disorders of menstruation and other abnormal bleeding**
from female genital tract
> **EXCLUDES** *menopausal and premenopausal bleeding (627.0)*
> *pain and other symptoms associated with*
> *menstrual cycle (625.2-625.4)*
> *postmenopausal bleeding (627.1)*

626.0 Absence of menstruation ♀
Amenorrhea (primary) (secondary)

626.1 Scanty or infrequent menstruation ♀
Hypomenorrhea   Oligomenorrhea

✓4ᵗʰ
✓5ᵗʰ Additional Digit Required   RUG III Special Care Dx   RUG III Clinically Complex Dx   Hospice Non-cancer Dx   **CD PDx** Clinical Dimension PDx   **CD SDx** Clinical Dimension SDx

2006 ICD•9•CM   **Volume 1 — 169**

Genitourinary System

626.2–629.9

626.2 Excessive or frequent menstruation ♀

Heavy periods   Menorrhagia
Menometrorrhagia   Plymenorrhea

EXCLUDES   premenopausal (627.0)
                  that in puberty (626.3)

626.3 Puberty bleeding ♀

Excessive bleeding associated with onset of
     menstrual periods
Pubertal menorrhagia

626.4 Irregular menstrual cycle ♀

Irregular: Irregular:
   bleeding NOS   periods
   menstruation

626.5 Ovulation bleeding ♀

Regular intermenstrual bleeding

626.6 Metrorrhagia ♀

Bleeding unrelated to menstrual cycle
Irregular intermenstrual bleeding

626.7 Postcoital bleeding ♀

DEF: Bleeding from vagina after sexual intercourse.

626.8 Other ♀

Dysfunctional or functional uterine hemorrhage NOS
Menstruation:
   retained
   suppression of

626.9 Unspecified ♀

√4ᵗʰ **627 Menopausal and postmenopausal disorders**

EXCLUDES   asymptomatic age-related (natural)
                postmenopausal status (V49.81)

627.0 Premenopausal menorrhagia ♀

Excessive bleeding associated with onset of
     menopause
Menorrhagia:
   climacteric
   menopausal
   preclimacteric

627.1 Postmenopausal bleeding ♀

627.2 Symptomatic menopausal or female climacteric ♀
states

Symptoms, such as flushing, sleeplessness,
     headache, lack of concentration, associated
     with the menopause

627.3 Postmenopausal atrophic vaginitis ♀

Senile (atrophic) vaginitis

627.4 Symptomatic states associated with artificial ♀
menopause

Postartificial menopause syndromes
Any condition classifiable to 627.1, 627.2, or 627.3
     which follows induced menopause

DEF: Conditions arising after hysterectomy.

627.8 Other specified menopausal and ♀
postmenopausal disorders

EXCLUDES   premature menopause NOS (256.31)

627.9 Unspecified menopausal and postmenopausal ♀
disorder

√4ᵗʰ **628 Infertility, female**

INCLUDES   primary and secondary sterility

AHA: 2Q, '96, 9; 1Q, '95, 7

DEF: Infertility: inability to conceive for at least one year with regular
intercourse.

DEF: Primary infertility: occurring in patients who have never conceived.

DEF: Secondary infertility: occurring in patients who have previously
conceived.

628.0 Associated with anovulation ♀

Anovulatory cycle
Use additional code for any associated Stein-
     Leventhal syndrome (256.4)

628.1 Of pituitary-hypothalamic origin ♀

Code first underlying cause, as:
   adiposogenital dystrophy (253.8)
   anterior pituitary disorder (253.0-253.4)

628.2 Of tubal origin ♀

Infertility associated with congenital anomaly of tube
Tubal:
   block
   occlusion
   stenosis
Use additional code for any associated peritubal
     adhesions (614.6)

AHA: ▶4Q, '04, 88◀

628.3 Of uterine origin ♀

Infertility associated with congenital anomaly of
     uterus
Nonimplantation
Use additional code for any associated tuberculous
     endometritis (016.7)

628.4 Of cervical or vaginal origin ♀

Infertility associated with:
   anomaly of cervical mucus
   congenital structural anomaly
   dysmucorrhea

628.8 Of other specified origin ♀

628.9 Of unspecified origin ♀

√4ᵗʰ **629 Other disorders of female genital organs**

629.0 Hematocele, female, not elsewhere classified ♀

EXCLUDES   hematocele or hematoma:
               broad ligament (620.7)
               fallopian tube (620.8)
               that associated with ectopic
                  pregnancy (633.00-633.91)
               uterus (621.4)
               vagina (623.6)
               vulva (624.5)

629.1 Hydrocele, canal of Nuck ♀

Cyst of canal of Nuck (acquired)

EXCLUDES   congenital (752.41)

√5ᵗʰ **629.2 Female genital mutilation status** ♀

Female circumcision status

629.20 Female genital mutilation status, ♀
unspecified

Female genital mutilation status NOS

629.21 Female genital mutilation Type I ♀
status

Clitorectomy status

DEF: ▶ Female genital mutilation involving clitorectomy,
with part or all of the clitoris removed◀

629.22 Female genital mutilation Type II ♀
status

Clitorectomy with excision of labia minora
     status

AHA: ▶4Q, '04, 90◀

DEF: ▶ Female genital mutilation involving clitoris and
the labia minora amputation◀

629.23 Female genital mutilation Type III ♀
status

Infibulation status

AHA: ▶4Q, '04, 90◀

DEF: ▶ Female genital mutilation involving removal, most
or all of the labia minora excised, labia majora incised
which is then made into a hood of skin over the urethral
and vaginal opening◀

629.8 Other specified disorders of female genital ♀
organs

629.9 Unspecified disorder of female genital organs ♀

Habitual aborter without current pregnancy

N Newborn Age: 0   P Pediatric Age: 0-17   M Maternity Age: 12-55   A Adult Age: 15-124   Manifestation Code   ▶◀ Revised Text   ● New Code   ▲ Revised Code Title

11. COMPLICATIONS OF PREGNANCY, CHILDBIRTH, AND THE PUERPERIUM (630-677)

ECTOPIC AND MOLAR PREGNANCY (630-633)

Use additional code from category 639 to identify any complications

630 Hydatidiform mole   M ♀

Trophoblastic disease NOS   Vesicularmole

EXCLUDES   *chorioadenoma (destruens) (236.1)*
chorionepithelioma (181)
malignant hydatidiform mole (236.1)

DEF: Abnormal product of pregnancy; marked by mass of cysts resembling bunch of grapes due to chorionic villi proliferation, and dissolution; must be surgically removed.

631 Other abnormal product of conception   M ♀

Blighted ovum   Mole:
Mole: fleshy
    NOS   stone
    carneous

632 Missed abortion   M ♀

Early fetal death before completion of 22 weeks' gestation with retention of dead fetus

Retained products of conception, not following spontaneous or induced abortion or delivery

EXCLUDES   *failed induced abortion (638.0-638.9)*
fetal death (intrauterine) (late) (656.4)
missed delivery (656.4)
that with abnormal product of conception (630, 631)

AHA: 1Q, '01, 5

✓4ᵗʰ 633 Ectopic pregnancy

INCLUDES   ruptured ectopic pregnancy

AHA: 4Q, '02, 61

DEF: Fertilized egg develops outside uterus.

633.0 Abdominal pregnancy

Intraperitoneal pregnancy

633.00 Abdominal pregnancy without intrauterine pregnancy   M ♀

633.01 Abdominal pregnancy with intrauterine pregnancy   M ♀

633.1 Tubal pregnancy

Fallopian pregnancy
Rupture of (fallopian) tube due to pregnancy
Tubal abortion

AHA: 2Q, '90, 27

633.10 Tubal pregnancy without intrauterine pregnancy   M ♀

633.11 Tubal pregnancy with intrauterine pregnancy   M ♀

633.2 Ovarian pregnancy

633.20 Ovarian pregnancy without intrauterine pregnancy   M ♀

633.21 Ovarian pregnancy with intrauterine pregnancy   M ♀

633.8 Other ectopic pregnancy

Pregnancy: Pregnancy:
    cervical   intraligamentous
    combined   mesometric
    cornual   mural

633.80 Other ectopic pregnancy without intrauterine pregnancy   M ♀

633.81 Other ectopic pregnancy with intrauterine pregnancy   M ♀

633.9 Unspecified ectopic pregnancy

633.90 Unspecified ectopic pregnancy without intrauterine pregnancy   M ♀

633.91 Unspecified ectopic pregnancy with intrauterine pregnancy   M ♀

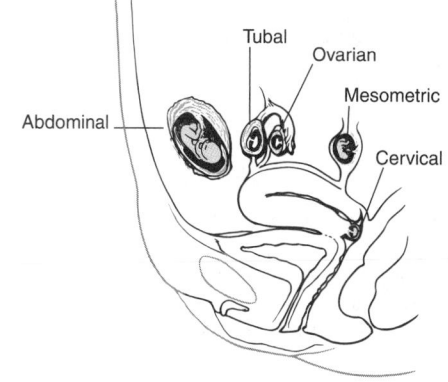

Ectopic Pregnancy Sites

Tubal — Ovarian — Mesometric — Abdominal — Cervical

OTHER PREGNANCY WITH ABORTIVE OUTCOME (634-639)

The following fourth-digit subdivisions are for use with categories 634-638:

.0 Complicated by genital tract and pelvic infection

Endometritis
Salpingo-oophoritis
Sepsis NOS
Septicemia NOS
Any condition classifiable to 639.0, with condition classifiable to 634-638

EXCLUDES   *urinary tract infection (634-638 with .7)*

.1 Complicated by delayed or excessive hemorrhage

Afibrinogenemia
Defibrination syndrome
Intravascular hemolysis
Any condition classifiable to 639.1, with condition classifiable to 634-638
uterus

.2 Complicated by damage to pelvic organs and tissues

Laceration, perforation, or tear of:
    bladder
Any condition classifiable to 639.2, with condition classifiable to 634-638

.3 Complicated by renal failure

Oliguria
Uremia
Any condition classifiable to 639.3, with condition classifiable to 634-638

.4 Complicated by metabolic disorder

Electrolyte imbalance with conditions classifiable to 634-638

.5 Complicated by shock

Circulatory collapse
Shock (postoperative) (septic)
Any condition classifiable to 639.5, with condition classifiable to 634-638

.6 Complicated by embolism

Embolism:
    NOS
    amniotic fluid
    pulmonary
Any condition classifiable to 639.6, with condition classifiable to 634-638

.7 With other specified complications

Cardiac arrest or failure
Urinary tract infection
Any condition classifiable to 639.8, with condition classifiable to 634-638

.8 With unspecified complication

.9 Without mention of complication

✓4ᵗʰ ✓5ᵗʰ Additional Digit Required   **RUG III Special Care Dx**   **RUG III Clinically Complex Dx**   Hospice Non-cancer Dx   **CD PDx** Clinical Dimension PDx   **CD SDx** Clinical Dimension SDx

2006 ICD•9•CM   **Volume 1 — 171**

Complications of Pregnancy, Childbirth & Puerperium

634–639

§ ✓4ᵗʰ **634 Spontaneous abortion**

Requires fifth-digit to identify stage:
  0 unspecified
  1 incomplete
  2 complete

INCLUDES   miscarriage
          spontaneous abortion

AHA: 2Q, '91, 16

DEF: Spontaneous premature expulsion of the products of conception from the uterus

✓5ᵗʰ **634.0 Complicated by genital tract and pelvic infection**   M♀

✓5ᵗʰ **634.1 Complicated by delayed or excessive hemorrhage**   M♀
AHA: For code 634.11: 1Q, '03, 6

✓5ᵗʰ **634.2 Complicated by damage to pelvic organs or tissues**   M♀

✓5ᵗʰ **634.3 Complicated by renal failure**   M♀

✓5ᵗʰ **634.4 Complicated by metabolic disorder**   M♀

✓5ᵗʰ **634.5 Complicated by shock**   M♀

✓5ᵗʰ **634.6 Complicated by embolism**   M♀

✓5ᵗʰ **634.7 With other specified complications**   M♀

✓5ᵗʰ **634.8 With unspecified complication**   M♀

✓5ᵗʰ **634.9 Without mention of complication**   M♀

§ ✓4ᵗʰ **635 Legally induced abortion**

Requires fifth-digit to identify stage:
  0 unspecified
  1 incomplete
  2 complete

INCLUDES   abortion or termination of pregnancy:
          elective
          legal
          therapeutic
EXCLUDES   menstrual extraction or regulation (V25.3)

AHA: 2Q, '94, 14

DEF: Intentional expulsion of products of conception from uterus performed by medical professionals inside boundaries of law.

✓5ᵗʰ **635.0 Complicated by genital tract and pelvic infection**   M♀

✓5ᵗʰ **635.1 Complicated by delayed or excessive hemorrhage**   M♀

✓5ᵗʰ **635.2 Complicated by damage to pelvic organs or tissues**   M♀

✓5ᵗʰ **635.3 Complicated by renal failure**   M♀

✓5ᵗʰ **635.4 Complicated by metabolic disorder**   M♀

✓5ᵗʰ **635.5 Complicated by shock**   M♀

✓5ᵗʰ **635.6 Complicated by embolism**   M♀

✓5ᵗʰ **635.7 With other specified complications**   M♀

✓5ᵗʰ **635.8 With unspecified complication**   M♀

✓5ᵗʰ **635.9 Without mention of complication**   M♀

§ ✓4ᵗʰ **636 Illegally induced abortion**

Requires fifth-digit to identify stage:
  0 unspecified
  1 incomplete
  2 complete

INCLUDES   abortion:
          criminal
          illegal
          self-induced

AHA: 2Q, '91, 16

DEF: Intentional expulsion of products of conception from uterus; outside boundaries of law.

✓5ᵗʰ **636.0 Complicated by genital tract and pelvic infection**   M♀

✓5ᵗʰ **636.1 Complicated by delayed or excessive hemorrhage**   M♀

✓5ᵗʰ **636.2 Complicated by damage to pelvic organs or tissues**   M♀

✓5ᵗʰ **636.3 Complicated by renal failure**   M♀

✓5ᵗʰ **636.4 Complicated by metabolic disorder**   M♀

✓5ᵗʰ **636.5 Complicated by shock**   M♀

✓5ᵗʰ **636.6 Complicated by embolism**   M♀

✓5ᵗʰ **636.7 With other specified complications**   M♀

✓5ᵗʰ **636.8 With unspecified complication**   M♀

✓5ᵗʰ **636.9 Without mention of complication**   M♀

§ ✓4ᵗʰ **637 Unspecified abortion**

Requires fifth-digit to identify stage:
  0 unspecified
  1 incomplete
  2 complete

INCLUDES   abortion NOS
          retained products of conception following abortion, not classifiable elsewhere

AHA: 2Q, '94, 14; 2Q, '91, 16

✓5ᵗʰ **637.0 Complicated by genital tract and pelvic infection**   M♀

✓5ᵗʰ **637.1 Complicated by delayed or excessive hemorrhage**   M♀

✓5ᵗʰ **637.2 Complicated by damage to pelvic organs or tissues**   M♀

✓5ᵗʰ **637.3 Complicated by renal failure**   M♀

✓5ᵗʰ **637.4 Complicated by metabolic disorder**   M♀

✓5ᵗʰ **637.5 Complicated by shock**   M♀

✓5ᵗʰ **637.6 Complicated by embolism**   M♀

✓5ᵗʰ **637.7 With other specified complications**   M♀

✓5ᵗʰ **637.8 With unspecified complication**   M♀

✓5ᵗʰ **637.9 Without mention of complication**   M♀

§ ✓4ᵗʰ **638 Failed attempted abortion**

INCLUDES   failure of attempted induction of (legal) abortion
EXCLUDES   incomplete abortion (634.0-637.9)

DEF: Continued pregnancy despite an attempted legal abortion.

638.0 Complicated by genital tract and pelvic infection   M♀

638.1 Complicated by delayed or excessive hemorrhage   M♀

638.2 Complicated by damage to pelvic organs or tissues   M♀

638.3 Complicated by renal failure   M♀

638.4 Complicated by metabolic disorder   M♀

638.5 Complicated by shock   M♀

638.6 Complicated by embolism   M♀

638.7 With other specified complications   M♀

638.8 With unspecified complication   M♀

638.9 Without mention of complication   M♀

✓4ᵗʰ **639 Complications following abortion and ectopic and molar pregnancies**

Note: This category is provided for use when it is required to classify separately the complications classifiable to the fourth-digit level in categories 634-638; for example:

a)   when the complication itself was responsible for an episode of medical care, the abortion, ectopic or molar pregnancy itself having been dealt with at a previous episode

b)   when these conditions are immediate complications of ectopic or molar pregnancies classifiable to 630-633 where they cannot be identified at fourth-digit level.

§   See beginning of section 634-639 for fourth-digit definitions.

N Newborn Age: 0   P Pediatric Age: 0-17   M Maternity Age: 12-55   A Adult Age: 15-124   Manifestation Code   ◄► Revised Text   ● New Code   ▲ Revised Code Title

639.0 Genital tract and pelvic infection   M ♀

Endometritis
Parametritis
Pelvic peritonitis
Salpingitis   } following conditions classifiable to 630-638
Salpingo-oophoritis
Sepsis NOS
Septicemia NOS

        EXCLUDES *urinary tract infection (639.8)*

AHA 2Q, '91, 5

639.1 Delayed or excessive hemorrhage   M ♀

Afibrinogenemia
Defibrination syndrome   } following conditions classifiable to 630-638
Intravascular hemolysis

639.2 Damage to pelvic organs and tissues   M ♀

Laceration, perforation, or
   tear of:
    bladder
    bowel
    broad ligament   } following conditions classifiable to 630-638
    cervix
    periurethral tissue
    uterus
    vagina

639.3 Renal failure   M ♀

Oliguria
Renal:
   failure (acute)
   shutdown   } following conditions classifiable to 630-638
   tubular necrosis
Uremia

639.4 Metabolic disorders   M ♀

Electrolyte imbalance following conditions classifiable to 630-638

639.5 Shock   M ♀

Circulatory collapse
Shock (postoperative)   } following conditions classifiable to 630-638
   (septic)

639.6 Embolism   M ♀

Embolism:
   NOS
   air
   amniotic fluid
   blood-clot   } following conditions classifiable to 630-638
   fat
   pulmonary
   pyemic
   septic
   soap

639.8 Other specified complications following abortion or ectopic and molar pregnancy   M ♀

Acute yellow atrophy or
   necrosis of liver
Cardiac arrest or failure   } following conditions classifiable to 630-638
Cerebral anoxia
Urinary tract infection

639.9 Unspecified complication following abortion or ectopic and molar pregnancy   M ♀

Complication(s) not further specified following conditions classifiable to 630-638

COMPLICATIONS MAINLY RELATED TO PREGNANCY (640-648)

INCLUDES   the listed conditions even if they arose or were present during labor, delivery, or the puerperium

AHA: 2Q, '90, 11

The following fifth-digit subclassification is for use with categories 640-648 to denote the current episode of care. Valid fifth-digits are in [brackets] under each code.

0 unspecified as to episode of care or not applicable
1 delivered, with or without mention of antepartum condition
   Antepartum condition with delivery
   Delivery NOS (with mention of antepartum complication during current episode of care)
   Intrapartum obstetric condition (with mention of antepartum complication during current episode of care)
   Pregnancy, delivered (with mention of antepartum complication during current episode of care)
2 delivered, with mention of postpartum complication
   Delivery with mention of puerperal complication during current episode of care
3 antepartum condition or complication
   Antepartum obstetric condition, not delivered during the current episode of care
4 postpartum condition or complication
   Postpartum or puerperal obstetric condition or complication following delivery that occurred:
    during previous episode of care
    outside hospital, with subsequent admission for observation or care

✓4ᵗʰ 640 Hemorrhage in early pregnancy
   INCLUDES hemorrhage before completion of 22 weeks' gestation

§ **✓5ᵗʰ 640.0 Threatened abortion**   M ♀
[0,1,3]   **CC Excl:** 640.00-640.93, 641.00-641.13, 646.80-646.93, 648.90-648.94, 650, 669.40-669.44, 669.80-669.94
   DEF: Bloody discharge during pregnancy; cervix may be dilated and pregnancy is threatened, but the pregnancy is not terminated.

§ **✓5ᵗʰ 640.8 Other specified hemorrhage in early**   M ♀
[0,1,3] **pregnancy**

§ **✓5ᵗʰ 640.9 Unspecified hemorrhage in early pregnancy**   M ♀
[0,1,3] **CC Excl:** see Code 640.0

✓4ᵗʰ 641 Antepartum hemorrhage, abruptio placentae, and placenta previa

Placenta Previa

| Low (marginal) implantation | Partial placenta previa | Total placenta previa |

§ Requires fifth-digit. Valid digits are in [brackets] under each code. See beginning of section 640-648 for codes and definitions.

✓4ᵗʰ
✓5ᵗʰ Additional Digit Required   RUG III Special Care Dx   RUG III Clinically Complex Dx   Hospice Non-cancer Dx   **CD PDx** Clinical Dimension PDx   **CD SDx** Clinical Dimension SDx

2006 ICD•9•CM   **Volume 1 — 173**

§ ✓5ᵗʰ **641.0 Placenta previa without hemorrhage**   Ⓜ♀
  [0,1,3]

Low impantation of placenta
Placenta previa noted:
  during pregnancy   } without
  before labor (and delivered   hemorrhage
  by caesarean delivery.)

DEF: Placenta implanted in lower segment of uterus; commonly causes hemorrhage in the last trimester of pregnancy.

§ ✓5ᵗʰ **641.1 Hemorrhage from placenta previa**   Ⓜ♀
  [0,1,3]

Low-lying placenta   }
Placenta previa   } NOS or with
  incomplete   }   hemorrhage
  marginal   }   (intrapartum)
  partial   }
  total   }

EXCLUDES *hemorrhage from vasa previa (663.5)*

§ ✓5ᵗʰ **641.2 Premature separation of placenta**   Ⓜ♀
  [0,1,3]

Ablatio placentae
Abruptio placentae
Accidental antepartum hemorrhage
Couvelaire uterus
Detachment of placenta (premature)
Premature separation of normally implanted
  placenta

DEF: Abruptio placentae: premature detachment of the placenta, characterized by shock, oliguria and decreased fibrinogen.

§ ✓5ᵗʰ **641.3 Antepartum hemorrhage associated with coagulation defects**   Ⓜ♀
  [0,1,3]

Antepartum or intrapartum hemorrhage associated with:
  afibrinogenemia
  hyperfibrinolysis
  hypofibrinogenemia

DEF: Uterine hemorrhage prior to delivery.

§ ✓5ᵗʰ **641.8 Other antepartum hemorrhage**   Ⓜ♀
  [0,1,3]

Antepartum or intrapartum hemorrhage associated with:
  trauma
  uterine leiomyoma

§ ✓5ᵗʰ **641.9 Unspecified antepartum hemorrhage**   Ⓜ♀
  [0,1,3]

Hemorrhage: Hemorrhage:
  antepartum NOS   of pregnancy NOS
  intrapartum NOS

✓4ᵗʰ **642 Hypertension complicating pregnancy, childbirth, and the puerperium**

Abruptio Placentae

Partial separation   Partial separation   Complete separation
  (concealed   (apparent   (concealed
  bleeding)   hemorrhage)   hemorrhage)

§ ✓5ᵗʰ **642.0 Benign essential hypertension complicating pregnancy, childbirth, and the puerperium**   Ⓜ♀
  [0-4]

Hypertension: specified as complicating,
  benign essential   or as a reason for
  chronic NOS   obstetric care during
  essential   pregnancy, childbirth,
  pre-existing NOS   or the puerperium

§ ✓5ᵗʰ **642.1 Hypertension secondary to renal disease, complicating pregnancy, childbirth, and the puerperium**   Ⓜ♀
  [0-4]

Hypertension secondary to renal disease, specified as complicating, or as a reason for obstetric care during pregnancy, childbirth, or the puerperium

§ ✓5ᵗʰ **642.2 Other pre-existing hypertension complicating pregnancy, childbirth, and the puerperium**   Ⓜ♀
  [0-4]

Hypertensive: specified as complicating,
  heart and renal   or as a reason for
    disease   obstetric care
  heart disease   during pregnancy,
  renal disease   childbirth, or the
  Malignant   puerperium
    hypertension

§ ✓5ᵗʰ **642.3 Transient hypertension of pregnancy**   Ⓜ♀
  [0-4]

Gestational hypertension
Transient hypertension, so described, in pregnancy, childbirth, or the puerperium

AHA: 3Q, '90, 4

§ ✓5ᵗʰ **642.4 Mild or unspecified pre-eclampsia**   Ⓜ♀
  [0-4]

Hypertension in pregnancy, childbirth, or the puerperium, not specified as pre-existing, with either albuminuria or edema, or both; mild or unspecified

Pre-eclampsia: Toxemia (pre-eclamptic):
  NOS   NOS
  mild   mild

EXCLUDES *albuminuria in pregnancy, without mention of hypertension (646.2) edema in pregnancy, without mention of hypertension (646.1)*

§ ✓5ᵗʰ **642.5 Severe pre-eclampsia**   Ⓜ♀
  [0-4]

Hypertension in pregnancy, childbirth, or the puerperium, not specified as pre-existing, with either albuminuria or edema, or both; specified as severe

Pre-eclampsia, severe
Toxemia (pre-eclamptic), severe

AHA: N-D, '85, 3

§ ✓5ᵗʰ **642.6 Eclampsia**   Ⓜ♀
  [0-4]

Toxemia:
  eclamptic
  with convulsions

§ ✓5ᵗʰ **642.7 Pre-eclampsia or eclampsia superimposed on pre-existing hypertension**   Ⓜ♀
  [0-4]

Conditions classifiable to 642.4-642.6, with conditions classifiable to 642.0-642.2

§ ✓5ᵗʰ **642.9 Unspecified hypertension complicating pregnancy, childbirth, or the puerperium**   Ⓜ♀
  [0-4]

Hypertension NOS, without mention of albuminuria or edema, complicating pregnancy, childbirth, or the puerperium

✓4ᵗʰ **643 Excessive vomiting in pregnancy**

INCLUDES hyperemesis   }
vomiting: } arising during
  persistent   }   pregnancy
  vicious   }

hyperemesis gravidarum

§ Requires fifth-digit. Valid digits are in [brackets] under each code. See beginning of section 640-648 for codes and definitions.

Ⓝ Newborn Age: 0   Ⓟ Pediatric Age: 0-17   Ⓜ Maternity Age: 12-55   Ⓐ Adult Age: 15-124   Manifestation Code   ►◄ Revised Text   ● New Code   ▲ Revised Code Title

§ ✓5th **643.0 Mild hyperemesis gravidarum** M ♀
[0,1,3]
    Hyperemesis gravidarum, mild or unspecified, starting before the end of the 22nd week of gestation
    DEF: Detrimental vomiting and nausea.

§ ✓5th **643.1 Hyperemesis gravidarum with metabolic** M ♀
[0,1,3] **disturbance**
    Hyperemesis gravidarum, starting before the end of the 22nd week of gestation, with metabolic disturbance, such as:
      carbohydrate depletion
      dehydration
      electrolyte imbalance

§ ✓5th **643.2 Late vomiting of pregnancy** M ♀
[0,1,3]
    Excessive vomiting starting after 22 completed weeks of gestation

§ ✓5th **643.8 Other vomiting complicating pregnancy** M ♀
[0,1,3]
    Vomiting due to organic disease or other cause, specified as complicating pregnancy, or as a reason for obstetric care during pregnancy
    Use additional code to specify cause

§ ✓5th **643.9 Unspecified vomiting of pregnancy** M ♀
[0,1,3]
    Vomiting as a reason for care during pregnancy, length of gestation unspecified

✓4th **644 Early or threatened labor**

§ ✓5th **644.0 Threatened premature labor** M ♀
[0,3]
    Premature labor after 22 weeks, but before 37 completed weeks of gestation without delivery
    EXCLUDES *that occurring before 22 completed weeks of gestation (640.0)*

§ ✓5th **644.1 Other threatened labor** M ♀
[0,3]
    False labor:
      NOS
      after 37 completed weeks of gestation } without delivery
      Threatened labor NOS

§ ✓5th **644.2 Early onset of delivery** M ♀
[0,1]
    Onset (spontaneous) of delivery } before 37 completed weeks of gestation
    Premature labor with onset of delivery
    AHA: 2Q, '91, 16

✓4th **645 Late pregnancy**
    AHA: 4Q, '91, 26

§ ✓5th **645.1 Post term pregnancy** M ♀
[0,1,3]
    Pregnancy over 40 completed weeks to 42 completed weeks gestation

§ ✓5th **645.2 Prolonged pregnancy** M ♀
[0,1,3]
    Pregnancy which has advanced beyond 42 completed weeks gestation

✓4th **646 Other complications of pregnancy, not elsewhere classified**
    Use additional code(s) to further specify complication
    AHA: 4Q, '95, 59

§ ✓5th **646.0 Papyraceous fetus** M ♀
[0,1,3]
    DEF: Fetus retained in the uterus beyond natural term, exhibits parchment-like skin.

§ ✓5th **646.1 Edema or excessive weight gain in pregnancy,** M ♀
[0-4] **without mention of hypertension**
    Gestational edema
    Maternal obesity syndrome
    EXCLUDES *that with mention of hypertension (642.0-642.9)*

§ ✓5th **646.2 Unspecified renal disease in pregnancy,** M ♀
[0-4] **without mention of hypertension**
    Albuminuria } in pregnancy or the puerperium, without mention of hypertension
    Nephropathy NOS
    Renal disease NOS
    Uremia
    Gestational proteinuria
    EXCLUDES *that with mention of hypertension (642.0-642.9)*

§ ✓5th **646.3 Habitual aborter** M ♀
[0,1,3]
    EXCLUDES *with current abortion (634.0-634.9)*
        without current pregnancy (629.9)
    DEF: Three or more consecutive spontaneous abortions.

§ ✓5th **646.4 Peripheral neuritis in pregnancy** M ♀
[0-4]

§ ✓5th **646.5 Asymptomatic bacteriuria in pregnancy** M ♀
[0-4]

§ ✓5th **646.6 Infections of genitourinary tract in** M ♀
[0-4] **pregnancy**
    Conditions classifiable to 590, 595, 597, 599.0, 616 complicating pregnancy, childbirth, or the puerperium
    Conditions classifiable to 614.0-614.5, 614.7-614.9, 615 complicating pregnancy or labor
    EXCLUDES *major puerperal infection (670)*
    AHA: For code 646.63: ▶4Q, '04, 90◀

§ ✓5th **646.7 Liver disorders in pregnancy** M ♀
[0,1,3]
    Acute yellow atrophy of liver (obstetric) (true) } of pregnancy
    Icterus gravis
    Necrosis of liver
    EXCLUDES *hepatorenal syndrome following delivery (674.8)*
        viral hepatitis (647.6)

§ ✓5th **646.8 Other specified complications of pregnancy** M ♀
[0-4]
    Fatigue during pregnancy
    Herpes gestationis
    Insufficient weight gain of pregnancy
    Uterine size-date discrepancy
    AHA: 3Q, '98, 16, J-F, '85, 15

§ ✓5th **646.9 Unspecified complication of pregnancy** M ♀
[0,1,3]

✓4th **647 Infectious and parasitic conditions in the mother classifiable elsewhere, but complicating pregnancy, childbirth, or the puerperium**
    INCLUDES the listed conditions when complicating the pregnant state, aggravated by the pregnancy, or when a main reason for obstetric care
    EXCLUDES *those conditions in the mother known or suspected to have affected the fetus (655.0-655.9)*
    Use additional code(s) to further specify complication

§ ✓5th **647.0 Syphilis** M ♀
[0-4]
    Conditions classifiable to 090-097

§ ✓5th **647.1 Gonorrhea** M ♀
[0-4]
    Conditions classifiable to 098

§ ✓5th **647.2 Other venereal diseases** M ♀
[0-4]
    Conditions classifiable to 099

§ ✓5th **647.3 Tuberculosis** M ♀
[0-4]
    Conditions classifiable to 010-018

§ ✓5th **647.4 Malaria** M ♀
[0-4]
    Conditions classifiable to 084

§ ✓5th **647.5 Rubella** M ♀
[0-4]
    Conditions classifiable to 056

§ ✓5th **647.6 Other viral diseases** M ♀
[0-4]
    Conditions classifiable to 042 and 050-079, except 056
    AHA: J-F, '85, 15

---

§ Requires fifth-digit. Valid digits are in [brackets] under each code. See beginning of section 640-648 for codes and definitions.

✓4th / ✓5th Additional Digit Required   RUG III Special Care Dx   RUG III Clinically Complex Dx   Hospice Non-cancer Dx   **CD PDx** Clinical Dimension PDx   **CD SDx** Clinical Dimension SDx

Complications of Pregnancy, Childbirth & Puerperium

647.8–652.3

§ ✓5ᵗʰ **647.8** **Other specified infectious and parasitic** Ⓜ♀
[0-4]   **diseases**

§ ✓5ᵗʰ **647.9** **Unspecified infection or infestation** Ⓜ♀
[0-4]

✓4ᵗʰ **648** **Other current conditions in the mother classifiable elsewhere, but complicating pregnancy, childbirth, or the puerperium**

INCLUDES   the listed conditions when complicating the pregnant state, aggravated by the pregnancy, or when a main reason for obstetric care

EXCLUDES   *those conditions in the mother known or suspected to have affected the fetus (655.0-665.9)*

Use additional code(s) to identify the condition

§ ✓5ᵗʰ **648.0** **Diabetes mellitus** Ⓜ♀
[0-4]   Conditions classifiable to 250

EXCLUDES   *gestational diabetes (648.8)*

AHA: 3Q, '91, 5

§ ✓5ᵗʰ **648.1** **Thyroid dysfunction** Ⓜ♀
[0-4]   Conditions classifiable to 240-246

§ ✓5ᵗʰ **648.2** **Anemia** Ⓜ♀
[0-4]   Conditions classifiable to 280-285

AHA: For code **648.22**: 1Q, '02, 14

§ ✓5ᵗʰ **648.3** **Drug dependence** Ⓜ♀
[0-4]   Conditions classifiable to 304

AHA: 2Q, '98, 13; 4Q, '88, 8

§ ✓5ᵗʰ **648.4** **Mental disorders** Ⓜ♀
[0-4]   Conditions classifiable to 290-303, 305-316, 317-319

AHA: 2Q, '98, 13; 4Q, '95, 63

§ ✓5ᵗʰ **648.5** **Congenital cardiovascular disorders** Ⓜ♀
[0-4]   Conditions classifiable to 745-747

§ ✓5ᵗʰ **648.6** **Other cardiovascular diseases** Ⓜ♀
[0-4]   Conditions classifiable to 390-398, 410-429

EXCLUDES   *cerebrovascular disorders in the puerperium (674.0)*
peripartum cardiomyopathy (674.5)
venous complications (671.0-671.9)

AHA: 3Q, '98, 11

§ ✓5ᵗʰ **648.7** **Bone and joint disorders of back, pelvis, and** Ⓜ♀
[0-4]   **lower limbs**
Conditions classifiable to 720-724, and those classifiable to 711-719 or 725-738, specified as affecting the lower limbs

§ ✓5ᵗʰ **648.8** **Abnormal glucose tolerance** Ⓜ♀
[0-4]   Conditions classifiable to ▶790.21-790.29◀
Gestational diabetes
▶Use additional code, if applicable, for associated long-term (current) insulin use (V58.67)◀

AHA: 3Q, '91, 5; For code **648.83**: 4Q, '04, 56

DEF: Glucose intolerance arising in pregnancy, resolving at end of pregnancy.

§ ✓5ᵗʰ **648.9** **Other current conditions classifiable elsewhere** Ⓜ♀
[0-4]   Conditions classifiable to 440-459
Nutritional deficiencies [conditions classifiable to 260-269]

AHA: 4Q, '04, 88; N-D, '87, 10; For code **648.91**: 1Q, '02, 14; For code **648.93**: 4Q, '04, 90

NORMAL DELIVERY, AND OTHER INDICATIONS FOR CARE IN PREGNANCY, LABOR, AND DELIVERY (650-659)

The following fifth-digit subclassification is for use with categories 651-659 to denote the current episode of care. Valid fifth-digits are in [brackets] under each code.

0 **unspecified as to episode of care or not applicable**
1 **delivered, with or without mention of antepartum condition**
2 **delivered, with mention of postpartum complication**
3 **antepartum condition or complication**
4 **postpartum condition or complication**

650 **Normal delivery** Ⓜ♀
Delivery requiring minimal or no assistance, with or without episiotomy, without fetal manipulation [e.g., rotation version] or instrumentation [forceps] of spontaneous, cephalic, vaginal, full-term, single, live-born infant. This code is for use as a single diagnosis code and is not to be used with any other code in the range 630-676.

EXCLUDES   *breech delivery (assisted) (spontaneous) NOS (652.2)*
delivery by vacuum extractor, forceps, cesarean section, or breech extraction, without specified complication (669.5-669.7)

Use additional code to indicate outcome of delivery (V27.0)

AHA: 2Q, '02, 10; 3Q, '01, 12; 3Q, '00, 5; 4Q, '95, 28, 59

✓4ᵗʰ **651** **Multiple gestation**

§ ✓5ᵗʰ **651.0** **Twin pregnancy** Ⓜ♀
[0,1,3]

§ ✓5ᵗʰ **651.1** **Triplet pregnancy** Ⓜ♀
[0,1,3]

§ ✓5ᵗʰ **651.2** **Quadruplet pregnancy** Ⓜ♀
[0,1,3]

§ ✓5ᵗʰ **651.3** **Twin pregnancy with fetal loss and retention** Ⓜ♀
[0,1,3]   **of one fetus**

§ ✓5ᵗʰ **651.4** **Triplet pregnancy with fetal loss and** Ⓜ♀
[0,1,3]   **retention of one or more fetus(es)**

§ ✓5ᵗʰ **651.5** **Quadruplet pregnancy with fetal loss and** Ⓜ♀
[0,1,3]   **retention of one or more fetus(es)**

§ ✓5ᵗʰ **651.6** **Other multiple pregnancy with fetal loss and** Ⓜ♀
[0,1,3]   **retention of one or more fetus(es)**

● § ✓5ᵗʰ **651.7** **Multiple gestation following (elective) fetal** Ⓜ♀
[0,1,3]   **reduction**
Fetal reduction of multiple fetuses reduced to single fetus

§ ✓5ᵗʰ **651.8** **Other specified multiple gestation** Ⓜ♀
[0,1,3]

§ ✓5ᵗʰ **651.9** **Unspecified multiple gestation** Ⓜ♀
[0,1,3]

✓4ᵗʰ **652** **Malposition and malpresentation of fetus**
Code first any associated obstructed labor (660.0)

§ ✓5ᵗʰ **652.0** **Unstable lie** Ⓜ♀
[0,1,3]   DEF: Changing fetal position.

§ ✓5ᵗʰ **652.1** **Breech or other malpresentation successfully** Ⓜ♀
[0,1,3]   **converted to cephalic presentation**
Cephalic version NOS

§ ✓5ᵗʰ **652.2** **Breech presentation without mention of** Ⓜ♀
[0,1,3]   **version**
Breech delivery (assisted) (spontaneous) NOS
Buttocks presentation
Complete breech
Frank breech

EXCLUDES   *footling presentation (652.8)*
incomplete breech (652.8)

DEF: Fetal presentation of buttocks or feet at birth canal.

§ ✓5ᵗʰ **652.3** **Transverse or oblique presentation** Ⓜ♀
[0,1,3]   Oblique lie   Transverse lie

EXCLUDES   *transverse arrest of fetal head (660.3)*

§ Requires fifth-digit. Valid digits are in [brackets] under each code. See beginning of section 640-648 for codes and definitions.

Ⓝ Newborn Age: 0   Ⓟ Pediatric Age: 0-17   Ⓜ Maternity Age: 12-55   Ⓐ Adult Age: 15-124   Manifestation Code   ▶◀ Revised Text   ● New Code   ▲ Revised Code Title

Malposition and Malpresentation

Cephalopelvic Disproportion

§ ✓5ᵗʰ **652.4** **Face or brow presentation** M ♀
[0,1,3]   Mentum presentation

§ ✓5ᵗʰ **652.5** **High head at term** M ♀
[0,1,3]   Failure of head to enter pelvic brim

§ ✓5ᵗʰ **652.6** **Multiple gestation with malpresentation of** M ♀
[0,1,3] **one fetus or more**

§ ✓5ᵗʰ **652.7** **Prolapsed arm** M ♀
[0,1,3]

§ ✓5ᵗʰ **652.8** **Other specified malposition or** M ♀
[0,1,3] **malpresentation**
     Compound presentation

§ ✓5ᵗʰ **652.9** **Unspecified malposition or malpresentation** M ♀
[0,1,3]

✓4ᵗʰ **653 Disproportion**
     Code first any associated obstructed labor (660.1)

§ ✓5ᵗʰ **653.0** **Major abnormality of bony pelvis, not further** M ♀
[0,1,3] **specified**
     Pelvic deformity NOS

§ ✓5ᵗʰ **653.1** **Generally contracted pelvis** M ♀
[0,1,3]   Contracted pelvis NOS

§ ✓5ᵗʰ **653.2** **Inlet contraction of pelvis** M ♀
[0,1,3]   Inlet contraction (pelvis)

§ ✓5ᵗʰ **653.3** **Outlet contraction of pelvis** M ♀
[0,1,3]   Outlet contraction (pelvis)

§ ✓5ᵗʰ **653.4** **Fetopelvic disproportion** M ♀
[0,1,3]   Cephalopelvic disproportion NOS
     Disproportion of mixed maternal and fetal origin,
       with normally formed fetus

§ ✓5ᵗʰ **653.5** **Unusually large fetus causing disproportion** M ♀
[0,1,3]   Disproportion of fetal origin with normally formed
       fetus
     Fetal disproportion NOS
     EXCLUDES *that when the reason for medical care*
*   was concern for the fetus (656.6)*

§ ✓5ᵗʰ **653.6** **Hydrocephalic fetus causing disproportion** M ♀
[0,1,3]   **EXCLUDES** *that when the reason for medical care*
*   was concern for the fetus (655.0)*

§ ✓5ᵗʰ **653.7** **Other fetal abnormality causing disproportion** M ♀
[0,1,3]   Conjoined twins   Fetal:
     Fetal: myelomeningocele
       ascites   sacral teratoma
       hydrops   tumor

§ ✓5ᵗʰ **653.8** **Disproportion of other origin** M ♀
[0,1,3]   **EXCLUDES** *shoulder (girdle) dystocia (660.4)*

§ ✓5ᵗʰ **653.9** **Unspecified disproportion** M ♀
[0,1,3]

✓4ᵗʰ **654 Abnormality of organs and soft tissues of pelvis**
     INCLUDES the listed conditions during pregnancy,
             childbirth, or the puerperium
     Code first any associated obstructed labor (660.2)

§ ✓5ᵗʰ **654.0** **Congenital abnormalities of uterus** M ♀
[0-4]   Double uterus   Uterus bicornis

§ ✓5ᵗʰ **654.1** **Tumors of body of uterus** M ♀
[0-4]   Uterine fibroids

§ ✓5ᵗʰ **654.2** **Previous cesarean delivery** M ♀
[0,1,3]   Uterine scar from previous cesarean delivery
     AHA: 1Q, '92, 8

§ ✓5ᵗʰ **654.3** **Retroverted and incarcerated gravid uterus** M ♀
[0-4]

     DEF: Retroverted: tilted back uterus; no change in angle of
     longitudinal axis.

     DEF: Incarcerated: immobile, fixed uterus.

§ ✓5ᵗʰ **654.4** **Other abnormalities in shape or position of** M ♀
[0-4] **gravid uterus and of neighboring structures**
     Cystocele   Prolapse of gravid uterus
     Pelvic floor repair   Rectocele
     Pendulous abdomen   Rigid pelvic floor

§ ✓5ᵗʰ **654.5** **Cervical incompetence** M ♀
[0-4]   Presence of Shirodkar suture with or without
           mention of cervical incompetence
     DEF: Abnormal cervix; tendency to dilate in second trimester;
     causes premature fetal expulsion.

     DEF: Shirodkar suture: purse-string suture used to artificially close
     incompetent cervix.

§ ✓5ᵗʰ **654.6** **Other congenital or acquired abnormality of** M ♀
[0-4] **cervix**
     Cicatricial cervix   Rigid cervix (uteri)
     Polyp of cervix   Stenosis or stricture of
     Previous surgery to cervix   cervix
                          Tumor of cervix

§ ✓5ᵗʰ **654.7** **Congenital or acquired abnormality of vagina** M ♀
[0-4]   Previous surgery to vagina   Stricture of vagina
     Septate vagina   Tumor of vagina
     Stenosis of vagina (acquired) (congenital)

§ ✓5ᵗʰ **654.8** **Congenital or acquired abnormality of vulva** M ♀
[0-4]   Fibrosis of perineum   Rigid perineum
     Persistent hymen   Tumor of vulva
     Previous surgery to
        perineum or vulva
     EXCLUDES *varicose veins of vulva (671.1)*
     AHA: 1Q, '03, 14

§ ✓5ᵗʰ **654.9** **Other and unspecified** M ♀
[0-4]   Uterine scar NEC

✓4ᵗʰ **655 Known or suspected fetal abnormality affecting**
   management of mother
     INCLUDES the listed conditions in the fetus as a reason
             for observation or obstetrical care of the
             mother, or for termination of pregnancy
     AHA: 3Q, '90, 4

§ ✓5ᵗʰ **655.0** **Central nervous system malformation in fetus** M ♀
[0,1,3]   Fetal or suspected fetal:
     anencephaly
     hydrocephalus
     spina bifida (with myelomeningocele)

§ Requires fifth-digit. Valid digits are in [brackets] under each code. See beginning of section 640-648 for codes and definitions.

✓4ᵗʰ / ✓5ᵗʰ Additional Digit Required   **RUG III Special Care Dx**   **RUG III Clinically Complex Dx**   **Hospice Non-cancer Dx**   **CD PDx** Clinical Dimension PDx   **CD SDx** Clinical Dimension SDx

2006 ICD•9•CM   **Volume 1 — 177**

§ ✓5ᵗʰ **655.1 Chromosomal abnormality in fetus** Ⓜ ♀
[0,1,3]

§ ✓5ᵗʰ **655.2 Hereditary disease in family possibly** Ⓜ ♀
[0,1,3] **affecting fetus**

§ ✓5ᵗʰ **655.3 Suspected damage to fetus from viral** Ⓜ ♀
[0,1,3] **disease in the mother**
　　Suspected damage to fetus from maternal rubella

§ ✓5ᵗʰ **655.4 Suspected damage to fetus from other** Ⓜ ♀
[0,1,3] **disease in the mother**
　　Suspected damage to fetus from maternal:
　　　alcohol addiction
　　　listeriosis
　　　toxoplasmosis

§ ✓5ᵗʰ **655.5 Suspected damage to fetus from drugs** Ⓜ ♀
[0,1,3]

§ ✓5ᵗʰ **655.6 Suspected damage to fetus from radiation** Ⓜ ♀
[0,1,3]

§ ✓5ᵗʰ **655.7 Decreased fetal movements** Ⓜ ♀
[0,1,3]

AHA: 4Q, '97, 41

§ ✓5ᵗʰ **655.8 Other known or suspected fetal abnormality,** Ⓜ ♀
[0,1,3] **not elsewhere classified**
　　Suspected damage to fetus from:
　　　environmental toxins
　　　intrauterine contraceptive device

§ ✓5ᵗʰ **655.9 Unspecified** Ⓜ ♀
[0,1,3]

✓4ᵗʰ **656 Other fetal and placental problems affecting**
management of mother

§ ✓5ᵗʰ **656.0 Fetal-maternal hemorrhage** Ⓜ ♀
[0,1,3] 　Leakage (microscopic) of fetal blood into maternal
　　　circulation

§ ✓5ᵗʰ **656.1 Rhesus isoimmunization** Ⓜ ♀
[0,1,3] 　Anti-D [Rh] antibodies
　　Rh incompatibility
DEF: Antibodies developing against Rh factor; mother with Rh negative develops antibodies against Rh positive fetus.

§ ✓5ᵗʰ **656.2 Isoimmunization from other and unspecified** Ⓜ ♀
[0,1,3] **blood-group incompatibility**
　　ABO isoimmunization.

§ ✓5ᵗʰ **656.3 Fetal distress** Ⓜ ♀
[0,1,3] 　Fetal metabolic acidemia
　　EXCLUDES abnormal fetal acid-base balance
　　　　　　(656.8)
　　　　　abnormality in fetal heart rate or
　　　　　　rhythm (659.7)
　　　　　fetal bradycardia (659.7)
　　　　　fetal distress NOS (656.8)
　　　　　fetal tachycardia (659.7)
　　　　　meconium in liquor (656.8)

AHA: N-D, '86, 4

DEF: Life-threatening disorder; fetal anoxia, hemolytic disease and other miscellaneous diseases cause fetal distress.

§ ✓5ᵗʰ **656.4 Intrauterine death** Ⓜ ♀
[0,1,3] 　Fetal death:
　　　NOS
　　　after completion of 22 weeks' gestation
　　　late
　　Missed delivery
　　EXCLUDES missed abortion (632)

§ ✓5ᵗʰ **656.5 Poor fetal growth** Ⓜ ♀
[0,1,3] 　"Light-for-dates"
　　"Placental insufficiency"
　　"Small-for-dates"

§ ✓5ᵗʰ **656.6 Excessive fetal growth** Ⓜ ♀
[0,1,3] 　"Large-for-dates"

§ ✓5ᵗʰ **656.7 Other placental conditions** Ⓜ ♀
[0,1,3] 　Abnormal placenta
　　Placental infarct
　　EXCLUDES placental polyp (674.4)
　　　　　placentitis (658.4)

§ ✓5ᵗʰ **656.8 Other specified fetal and placental problems** Ⓜ ♀
[0,1,3] 　Abnormal acid-base balance
　　Intrauterine acidosis
　　Lithopedian
　　Meconium in liquor
DEF: Lithopedion: Calcified fetus; not expelled by mother.

§ ✓5ᵗʰ **656.9 Unspecified fetal and placental problem** Ⓜ ♀
[0,1,3]

✓4ᵗʰ **657 Polyhydramnios** Ⓜ ♀
[0,1,3]

§ ✓5ᵗʰ Use 0 as fourth-digit for this category
　　Hydramnios
AHA: 4Q, '91, 26

DEF: Excess amniotic fluid.

✓4ᵗʰ **658 Other problems associated with amniotic cavity and**
membranes
　EXCLUDES amniotic fluid embolism (673.1)

§ ✓5ᵗʰ **658.0 Oligohydramnios** Ⓜ ♀
[0,1,3] 　Oligohydramnios without mention of rupture of
　　　membranes
DEF: Deficient amount of amniotic fluid.

§ ✓5ᵗʰ **658.1 Premature rupture of membranes** Ⓜ ♀
[0,1,3] 　Rupture of amniotic sac less than 24 hours prior to
　　　the onset of labor
AHA: For code 658.13: 1Q, '01, 5; 4Q, '98, 77

§ ✓5ᵗʰ **658.2 Delayed delivery after spontaneous or** Ⓜ ♀
[0,1,3] **unspecified rupture of membranes**
　　Prolonged rupture of membranes NOS
　　Rupture of amniotic sac 24 hours or more prior to
　　　the onset of labor

§ ✓5ᵗʰ **658.3 Delayed delivery after artificial rupture of** Ⓜ ♀
[0,1,3] **membranes**

§ ✓5ᵗʰ **658.4 Infection of amniotic cavity** Ⓜ ♀
[0,1,3] 　Amnionitis　　　　Membranitis
　　Chorioamnionitis　　Placentitis

§ ✓5ᵗʰ **658.8 Other** Ⓜ ♀
[0,1,3] 　Amnion nodosum　　Amniotic cyst

§ ✓5ᵗʰ **658.9 Unspecified** Ⓜ ♀
[0,1,3]

✓4ᵗʰ **659 Other indications for care or intervention related to labor**
and delivery, not elsewhere classified

§ ✓5ᵗʰ **659.0 Failed mechanical induction** Ⓜ ♀
[0,1,3] 　Failure of induction of labor by surgical or other
　　　instrumental methods

§ ✓5ᵗʰ **659.1 Failed medical or unspecified induction** Ⓜ ♀
[0,1,3] 　Failed induction NOS
　　Failure of induction of labor by medical methods,
　　　such as oxytocic drugs

§ ✓5ᵗʰ **659.2 Maternal pyrexia during labor, unspecified** Ⓜ ♀
[0,1,3] 　**DEF:** Fever during labor.

§ ✓5ᵗʰ **659.3 Generalized infection during labor** Ⓜ ♀
[0,1,3] 　Septicemia during labor

§ ✓5ᵗʰ **659.4 Grand multiparity** Ⓜ ♀
[0,1,3] 　**EXCLUDES** supervision only, in pregnancy (V23.3)
　　　　　without current pregnancy (V61.5)
DEF: Having borne six or more children previously.

§ ✓5ᵗʰ **659.5 Elderly primigravida** Ⓜ ♀
[0,1,3] 　First pregnancy in a woman who will be 35 years of
　　　age or older at expected date of delivery
　　EXCLUDES supervision only, in pregnancy (V23.81)
AHA: 3Q, '01, 12

§ ✓5ᵗʰ **659.6 Elderly multigravida** Ⓜ ♀
[0,1,3] 　Second or more pregnancy in a woman who will
　　　be 35 years of age or older at expected date
　　　of delivery
　　EXCLUDES elderly primigravida 659.5
　　　　　supervision only, in pregnancy (V23.82)
AHA: 3Q, '01, 12

§ Requires fifth-digit. Valid digits are in [brackets] under each code. See beginning of section 640-648 for codes and definitions.

Ⓝ Newborn Age: 0　Ⓟ Pediatric Age: 0-17　Ⓜ Maternity Age: 12-55　Ⓐ Adult Age: 15-124　Manifestation Code　▶◀ Revised Text　● New Code　▲ Revised Code Title

178 — Volume 1

2006 ICD•9•CM

§ ✓5ᵗʰ **659.7** **Abnormality in fetal heart rate or rhythm** Ⓜ♀
[0,1,3]   Depressed fetal heart tones
Fetal:
    bradycardia
    tachycardia
Fetal heart rate decelerations
Non-reassuring fetal heart rate or rhythm
AHA: 4Q, '98, 48

§ ✓5ᵗʰ **659.8** **Other specified indications for care or** Ⓜ♀
[0,1,3] **intervention related to labor and delivery**
    Pregnancy in a female less than 16 years old at
       expected date of delivery
Very young maternal age
AHA: 3Q, '01, 12

§ ✓5ᵗʰ **659.9** **Unspecified indication for care or intervention** Ⓜ♀
[0,1,3] **related to labor and delivery**

COMPLICATIONS OCCURRING MAINLY IN THE COURSE OF LABOR AND DELIVERY (660-669)

The following fifth-digit subclassification is for use with categories 660-669 to denote the current episode of care. Valid fifth-digits are in [brackets] under each code.

   0   unspecified as to episode of care or not applicable
   1   delivered, with or without mention of antepartum condition
   2   delivered, with mention of postpartum complication
   3   antepartum condition or complication
   4   postpartum condition or complication

✓4ᵗʰ **660 Obstructed labor**
AHA: 3Q, '95, 10

§ ✓5ᵗʰ **660.0** **Obstruction caused by malposition of fetus** Ⓜ♀
[0,1,3] **at onset of labor**
    Any condition classifiable to 652, causing
       obstruction during labor
Use additional code from 652.0-652.9 to identify
       condition

§ ✓5ᵗʰ **660.1** **Obstruction by bony pelvis** Ⓜ♀
[0,1,3]   Any condition classifiable to 653, causing
       obstruction during labor
Use additional code from 653.0-653.9 to identify
       condition

§ ✓5ᵗʰ **660.2** **Obstruction by abnormal pelvic soft tissues** Ⓜ♀
[0,1,3]   Prolapse of anterior lip of cervix
Any condition classifiable to 654, causing
       obstruction during labor
Use additional code from 654.0-654.9 to identify
       condition

§ ✓5ᵗʰ **660.3** **Deep transverse arrest and persistent** Ⓜ♀
[0,1,3] **occipitoposterior position**

§ ✓5ᵗʰ **660.4** **Shoulder (girdle) dystocia** Ⓜ♀
[0,1,3]   Impacted shoulders
DEF: Obstructed labor due to impacted fetal shoulders.

§ ✓5ᵗʰ **660.5** **Locked twins** Ⓜ♀
[0,1,3]

§ ✓5ᵗʰ **660.6** **Failed trial of labor, unspecified** Ⓜ♀
[0,1,3]   Failed trial of labor, without mention of condition or
       suspected condition

§ ✓5ᵗʰ **660.7** **Failed forceps or vacuum extractor,** Ⓜ♀
[0,1,3] **unspecified**
    Application of ventouse or forceps, without mention
       of condition

§ ✓5ᵗʰ **660.8** **Other causes of obstructed labor** Ⓜ♀
[0,1,3]   ▶Use additional code to identify condition◀
AHA: 4Q, '04, 88

§ ✓5ᵗʰ **660.9** **Unspecified obstructed labor** Ⓜ♀
[0,1,3]   Dystocia:
      NOS
      fetal NOS
      maternal NOS

✓4ᵗʰ **661 Abnormality of forces of labor**

§ ✓5ᵗʰ **661.0** **Primary uterine inertia** Ⓜ♀
[0,1,3]   Failure of cervical dilation
Hypotonic uterine dysfunction, primary
Prolonged latent phase of labor
DEF: Lack of efficient contractions during labor causing prolonged labor.

§ ✓5ᵗʰ **661.1** **Secondary uterine inertia** Ⓜ♀
[0,1,3]   Arrested active phase of labor
Hypotonic uterine dysfunction, secondary

§ ✓5ᵗʰ **661.2** **Other and unspecified uterine inertia** Ⓜ♀
[0,1,3]   Desultory labor
Irregular labor
Poor contractions
Slow slope active phase of labor

§ ✓5ᵗʰ **661.3** **Precipitate labor** Ⓜ♀
[0,1,3]   **DEF:** Rapid labor and delivery.

§ ✓5ᵗʰ **661.4** **Hypertonic, incoordinate, or prolonged** Ⓜ♀
[0,1,3] **uterine contractions**
    Cervical spasm
Contraction ring (dystocia)
Dyscoordinate labor
Hourglass contraction of uterus
Hypertonic uterine dysfunction
Incoordinate uterine action
Retraction ring (Bandl's) (pathological)
Tetanic contractions
Uterine dystocia NOS
Uterine spasm

§ ✓5ᵗʰ **661.9** **Unspecified abnormality of labor** Ⓜ♀
[0,1,3]

✓4ᵗʰ **662 Long labor**

§ ✓5ᵗʰ **662.0** **Prolonged first stage** Ⓜ♀
[0,1,3]

§ ✓5ᵗʰ **662.1** **Prolonged labor, unspecified** Ⓜ♀
[0,1,3]

§ ✓5ᵗʰ **662.2** **Prolonged second stage** Ⓜ♀
[0,1,3]

§ ✓5ᵗʰ **662.3** **Delayed delivery of second twin, triplet, etc.** Ⓜ♀
[0,1,3]

✓4ᵗʰ **663 Umbilical cord complications**

§ ✓5ᵗʰ **663.0** **Prolapse of cord** Ⓜ♀
[0,1,3]   Presentation of cord
DEF: Abnormal presentation of fetus; marked by protruding umbilical cord during labor; can cause fetal death.

§ ✓5ᵗʰ **663.1** **Cord around neck, with compression** Ⓜ♀
[0,1,3]   Cord tightly around neck

§ ✓5ᵗʰ **663.2** **Other and unspecified cord entanglement,** Ⓜ♀
[0,1,3] **with compression**
    Entanglement of cords of twins in mono-amniotic
       sac
Knot in cord (with compression)

§ ✓5ᵗʰ **663.3** **Other and unspecified cord entanglement,** Ⓜ♀
[0,1,3] **without mention of compression**
AHA: For code 663.31: 2Q, '03, 9

§ ✓5ᵗʰ **663.4** **Short cord** Ⓜ♀
[0,1,3]

§ ✓5ᵗʰ **663.5** **Vasa previa** Ⓜ♀
[0,1,3]
DEF: Abnormal presentation of fetus marked by blood vessels of umbilical cord in front of fetal head.

§ ✓5ᵗʰ **663.6** **Vascular lesions of cord** Ⓜ♀
[0,1,3]   Bruising of cord
Hematoma of cord
Thrombosis of vessels of cord

---

§ Requires fifth-digit. Valid digits are in [brackets] under each code. See beginning of section 640-648 for codes and definitions.

✓4ᵗʰ
✓5ᵗʰ Additional Digit Required   **RUG III Special Care Dx**   **RUG III Clinically Complex Dx**   **Hospice Non-cancer Dx**   **CD PDx** Clinical Dimension PDx   **CD SDx** Clinical Dimension SDx

Complications of Pregnancy, Childbirth & Puerperium

663.8–668

Perineal Lacerations

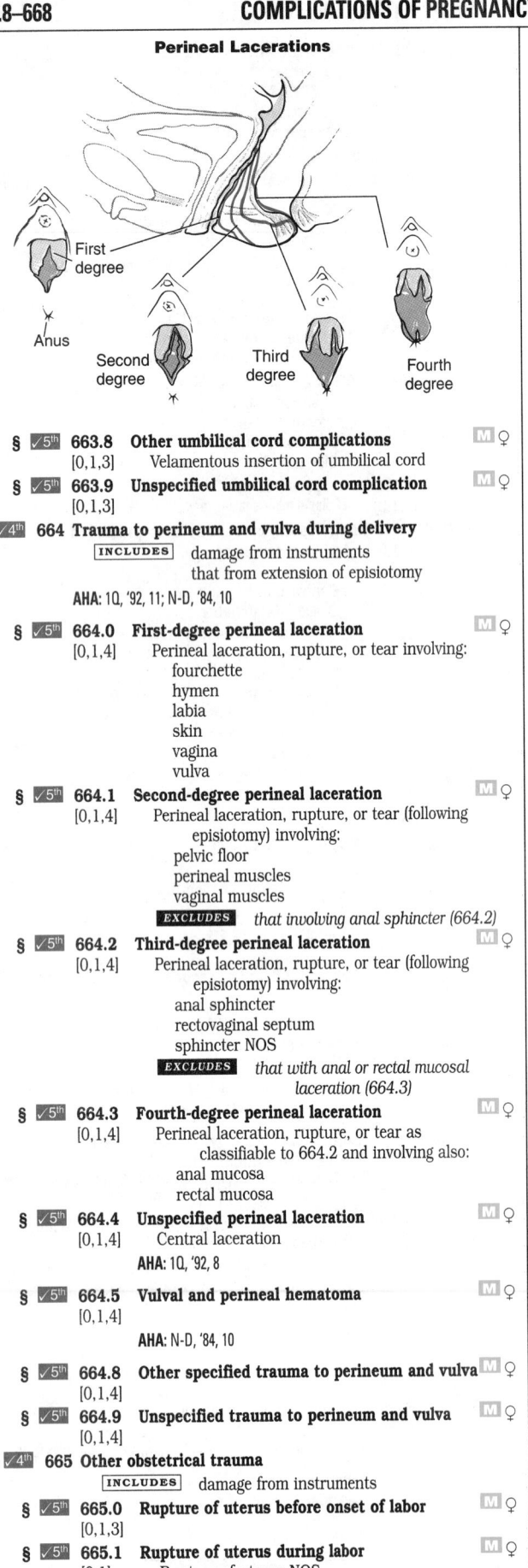

First degree

Anus

Second degree

Third degree

Fourth degree

§ ✓5ᵗʰ **663.8 Other umbilical cord complications**   M ♀
[0,1,3]   Velamentous insertion of umbilical cord

§ ✓5ᵗʰ **663.9 Unspecified umbilical cord complication**   M ♀
[0,1,3]

✓4ᵗʰ **664 Trauma to perineum and vulva during delivery**
INCLUDES damage from instruments
that from extension of episiotomy

AHA: 1Q, '92, 11; N-D, '84, 10

§ ✓5ᵗʰ **664.0 First-degree perineal laceration**   M ♀
[0,1,4]   Perineal laceration, rupture, or tear involving:
fourchette
hymen
labia
skin
vagina
vulva

§ ✓5ᵗʰ **664.1 Second-degree perineal laceration**   M ♀
[0,1,4]   Perineal laceration, rupture, or tear (following
episiotomy) involving:
pelvic floor
perineal muscles
vaginal muscles
EXCLUDES that involving anal sphincter (664.2)

§ ✓5ᵗʰ **664.2 Third-degree perineal laceration**   M ♀
[0,1,4]   Perineal laceration, rupture, or tear (following
episiotomy) involving:
anal sphincter
rectovaginal septum
sphincter NOS
EXCLUDES that with anal or rectal mucosal
laceration (664.3)

§ ✓5ᵗʰ **664.3 Fourth-degree perineal laceration**   M ♀
[0,1,4]   Perineal laceration, rupture, or tear as
classifiable to 664.2 and involving also:
anal mucosa
rectal mucosa

§ ✓5ᵗʰ **664.4 Unspecified perineal laceration**   M ♀
[0,1,4]   Central laceration
AHA: 1Q, '92, 8

§ ✓5ᵗʰ **664.5 Vulval and perineal hematoma**   M ♀
[0,1,4]
AHA: N-D, '84, 10

§ ✓5ᵗʰ **664.8 Other specified trauma to perineum and vulva**   M ♀
[0,1,4]

§ ✓5ᵗʰ **664.9 Unspecified trauma to perineum and vulva**   M ♀
[0,1,4]

✓4ᵗʰ **665 Other obstetrical trauma**
INCLUDES damage from instruments

§ ✓5ᵗʰ **665.0 Rupture of uterus before onset of labor**   M ♀
[0,1,3]

§ ✓5ᵗʰ **665.1 Rupture of uterus during labor**   M ♀
[0,1]   Rupture of uterus NOS

§ ✓5ᵗʰ **665.2 Inversion of uterus**   M ♀
[0,2,4]

§ ✓5ᵗʰ **665.3 Laceration of cervix**   M ♀
[0,1,4]

§ ✓5ᵗʰ **665.4 High vaginal laceration**   M ♀
[0,1,4]   Laceration of vaginal wall or sulcus without mention
of perineal laceration

§ ✓5ᵗʰ **665.5 Other injury to pelvic organs**   M ♀
[0,1,4]   Injury to: Injury to:
bladder   urethra
AHA: M-A, '87, 10

§ ✓5ᵗʰ **665.6 Damage to pelvic joints and ligaments**   M ♀
[0,1,4]   Avulsion of inner symphyseal cartilage
Damage to coccyx
Separation of symphysis (pubis)
AHA: N-D, '84, 12

§ ✓5ᵗʰ **665.7 Pelvic hematoma**   M ♀
[0,1,2,4]   Hematoma of vagina

§ ✓5ᵗʰ **665.8 Other specified obstetrical trauma**   M ♀
[0-4]

§ ✓5ᵗʰ **665.9 Unspecified obstetrical trauma**   M ♀
[0-4]

✓4ᵗʰ **666 Postpartum hemorrhage**
AHA: 1Q, '88, 14

§ ✓5ᵗʰ **666.0 Third-stage hemorrhage**   M ♀
[0,2,4]   Hemorrhage associated with retained, trapped,
or adherent placenta
Retained placenta NOS

§ ✓5ᵗʰ **666.1 Other immediate postpartum hemorrhage**   M ♀
[0,2,4]   Atony of uterus
Hemorrhage within the first 24 hours following
delivery of placenta
Postpartum hemorrhage (atonic) NOS

§ ✓5ᵗʰ **666.2 Delayed and secondary postpartum**   M ♀
[0,2,4]   **hemorrhage**
Hemorrhage:
after the first 24 hours following delivery
associated with retained portions of placenta or
membranes
Postpartum hemorrhage specified as delayed or
secondary
Retained products of conception NOS, following
delivery

§ ✓5ᵗʰ **666.3 Postpartum coagulation defects**   M ♀
[0,2,4]   Postpartum: Postpartum:
afibrinogenemia   fibrinolysis

✓4ᵗʰ **667 Retained placenta or membranes, without hemorrhage**
AHA: 1Q, '88, 14

DEF: Postpartum condition resulting from failure to expel placental membrane
tissues due to failed contractions of uterine wall.

§ ✓5ᵗʰ **667.0 Retained placenta without hemorrhage**   M ♀
[0,2,4]   Placenta accreta
Retained placenta: } without
NOS   hemorrhage
total

§ ✓5ᵗʰ **667.1 Retained portions of placenta or membranes,**   M ♀
[0,2,4]   **without hemorrhage**
Retained products of conception following delivery,
without hemorrhage

✓4ᵗʰ **668 Complications of the administration of anesthetic or other
sedation in labor and delivery**
INCLUDES complications arising from the administration
of a general or local anesthetic, analgesic,
or other sedation in labor and delivery
EXCLUDES reaction to spinal or lumbar puncture (349.0)
spinal headache (349.0)
Use additional code(s) to further specify complication

§ Requires fifth-digit. Valid digits are in [brackets] under each code. See beginning of section 640-648 for codes and definitions.

N Newborn Age: 0   P Pediatric Age: 0-17   M Maternity Age: 12-55   A Adult Age: 15-124   Manifestation Code   ◄► Revised Text   ● New Code   ▲ Revised Code Title

§ ✓5ᵗʰ **668.0 Pulmonary complications** Ⓜ♀
[0-4]

Inhalation [aspiration] of stomach contents or secretions ⎫
Mendelson's syndrome ⎬ following anesthesia or other sedation in labor or delivery
Pressure collapse of lung ⎭

§ ✓5ᵗʰ **668.1 Cardiac complications** Ⓜ♀
[0-4]   Cardiac arrest or failure following anesthesia or other sedation in labor and delivery

§ ✓5ᵗʰ **668.2 Central nervous system complications** Ⓜ♀
[0-4]   Cerebral anoxia following anesthesia or other sedation in labor and delivery

§ ✓5ᵗʰ **668.8 Other complications of anesthesia or other sedation in labor and delivery** Ⓜ♀
[0-4]
AHA: 2Q, '99, 9

§ ✓5ᵗʰ **668.9 Unspecified complication of anesthesia and other sedation** Ⓜ♀
[0-4]

✓4ᵗʰ **669 Other complications of labor and delivery, not elsewhere classified**

§ ✓5ᵗʰ **669.0 Maternal distress** Ⓜ♀
[0-4]   Metabolic disturbance in labor and delivery

§ ✓5ᵗʰ **669.1 Shock during or following labor and delivery** Ⓜ♀
[0-4]   Obstetric shock

§ ✓5ᵗʰ **669.2 Maternal hypotension syndrome** Ⓜ♀
[0-4]

DEF: Low arterial blood pressure, in mother, during labor and delivery.

§ ✓5ᵗʰ **669.3 Acute renal failure following labor and delivery** Ⓜ♀
[0,2,4]

§ ✓5ᵗʰ **669.4 Other complications of obstetrical surgery and procedures** Ⓜ♀
[0-4]

Cardiac: ⎫
arrest ⎬ following cesarean or other obstetrical surgery or procedure, including delivery NOS
failure ⎭
Cerebral anoxia

EXCLUDES complications of obstetrical surgical wounds (674.1-674.3)

§ ✓5ᵗʰ **669.5 Forceps or vacuum extractor delivery without mention of indication** Ⓜ♀
[0,1]   Delivery by ventouse, without mention of indication

§ ✓5ᵗʰ **669.6 Breech extraction, without mention of indication** Ⓜ♀
[0,1]
EXCLUDES breech delivery NOS (652.2)

§ ✓5ᵗʰ **669.7 Cesarean delivery, without mention of indication** Ⓜ♀
[0,1]
AHA: For code 699.71: 1Q, '01, 11

§ ✓5ᵗʰ **669.8 Other complications of labor and delivery** Ⓜ♀
[0-4]

§ ✓5ᵗʰ **669.9 Unspecified complication of labor and delivery** Ⓜ♀
[0-4]

COMPLICATIONS OF THE PUERPERIUM (670-677)

Note: Categories 671 and 673-676 include the listed conditions even if they occur during pregnancy or childbirth.

The following fifth-digit subclassification is for use with categories 670-676 to denote the current episode of care. Valid fifth-digits are in [brackets] under each code.

0 **unspecified as to episode of care or not applicable**

1 **delivered, with or without mention of antepartum condition**

2 **delivered, with mention of postpartum complication**

3 **antepartum condition or complication**

4 **postpartum condition or complication**

✓4ᵗʰ **670 Major puerperal infection** Ⓜ♀
[0,2,4]

§ ✓5ᵗʰ   Use 0 as fourth-digit for this category

Puerperal: Puerperal:
endometritis   peritonitis
fever (septic)   pyemia
pelvic: salpingitis
cellulitis   septicemia
sepsis

EXCLUDES infection following abortion (639.0)
minor genital tract infection following delivery (646.6)
puerperal pyrexia NOS (672)
puerperal fever NOS (672)
puerperal pyrexia of unknown origin (672)
urinary tract infection following delivery (646.6)

AHA: 4Q, '91, 26; 2Q, '91, 5

DEF: Infection and inflammation, following childbirth.

✓4ᵗʰ **671 Venous complications in pregnancy and the puerperium**

§ ✓5ᵗʰ **671.0 Varicose veins of legs** Ⓜ♀
[0-4]   Varicose veins NOS

DEF: Distended, tortuous veins on legs associated with pregnancy.

§ ✓5ᵗʰ **671.1 Varicose veins of vulva and perineum** Ⓜ♀
[0-4]

DEF: Distended, tortuous veins on external female genitalia associated with pregnancy.

§ ✓5ᵗʰ **671.2 Superficial thrombophlebitis** Ⓜ♀
[0-4]   Thrombophlebitis (superficial)

§ ✓5ᵗʰ **671.3 Deep phlebothrombosis, antepartum** Ⓜ♀
[0,1,3]   Deep-vein thrombosis, antepartum

§ ✓5ᵗʰ **671.4 Deep phlebothrombosis, postpartum** Ⓜ♀
[0,2,4]   Deep-vein thrombosis, postpartum
Pelvic thrombophlebitis, postpartum
Phlegmasia alba dolens (puerperal)

§ ✓5ᵗʰ **671.5 Other phlebitis and thrombosis** Ⓜ♀
[0-4]   Cerebral venous thrombosis
Thrombosis of intracranial venous sinus

§ ✓5ᵗʰ **671.8 Other venous complications** Ⓜ♀
[0-4]   Hemorrhoids

§ ✓5ᵗʰ **671.9 Unspecified venous complication** Ⓜ♀
[0-4]   Phlebitis NOS
Thrombosis NOS

✓4ᵗʰ **672 Pyrexia of unknown origin during the puerperium** Ⓜ♀
[0,2,4]

§ ✓5ᵗʰ   Use 0 as fourth-digit for this category

Postpartum fever NOS
Puerperal fever NOS
Puerperal pyrexia NOS

AHA: 4Q, '91, 2

DEF: Fever of unknown origin experienced by the mother after childbirth.

✓4ᵗʰ **673 Obstetrical pulmonary embolism**
INCLUDES pulmonary emboli in pregnancy, childbirth, or the puerperium, or specified as puerperal
EXCLUDES embolism following abortion (639.6)

§ ✓5ᵗʰ **673.0 Obstetrical air embolism** Ⓜ♀
[0-4]

DEF: Sudden blocking of pulmonary artery with air or nitrogen bubbles during puerperium.

§ ✓5ᵗʰ **673.1 Amniotic fluid embolism** Ⓜ♀
[0-4]

DEF: Sudden onset of pulmonary artery blockage from amniotic fluid entering the mother's circulation near the end of pregnancy due to strong uterine contractions.

§ ✓5ᵗʰ **673.2 Obstetrical blood-clot embolism** Ⓜ♀
[0-4]   Puerperal pulmonary embolism NOS
AHA: ▶For code 673.24: 1Q, '05, 6◀

DEF: Blood clot blocking artery in the lung; associated with pregnancy.

§ ✓5ᵗʰ **673.3 Obstetrical pyemic and septic embolism** Ⓜ♀
[0-4]

---

§ Requires fifth-digit. Valid digits are in [brackets] under each code. See beginning of section 640-648 for codes and definitions.

✓4ᵗʰ
✓5ᵗʰ Additional Digit Required   RUG III Special Care Dx   RUG III Clinically Complex Dx   Hospice Non-cancer Dx   **CD PDx** Clinical Dimension PDx   **CD SDx** Clinical Dimension SDx

§ ✓5ᵗʰ **673.8**   **Other pulmonary embolism**   Ⓜ ♀
[0-4]   Fat embolism

✓4ᵗʰ **674**   **Other and unspecified complications of the puerperium, not elsewhere classified**

§ ✓5ᵗʰ **674.0**   **Cerebrovascular disorders in the**   Ⓜ ♀
[0-4]   **puerperium**
       Any condition classifiable to 430-434, 436-437 occurring during pregnancy, childbirth, or the puerperium, or specified as puerperal
       EXCLUDES   *intracranial venous sinus thrombosis (671.5)*

§ ✓5ᵗʰ **674.1**   **Disruption of cesarean wound**   Ⓜ ♀
[0,2,4]   Dehiscence or disruption of uterine wound
       EXCLUDES   *uterine rupture before onset of labor (665.0)*
           uterine rupture during labor (665.1)

§ ✓5ᵗʰ **674.2**   **Disruption of perineal wound**   Ⓜ ♀
[0,2,4]   Breakdown of perineum   Disruption of wound of:
       Disruption of wound of: perineal laceration
          episiotomy   Secondary perineal tear
       AHA: For code 674.24: 1Q, '97, 9

§ ✓5ᵗʰ **674.3**   **Other complications of obstetrical surgical**   Ⓜ ♀
[0,2,4]   **wounds**
       Hematoma
       Hemorrhage } of cesarean section or perineal wound
       Infection
       EXCLUDES   *damage from instruments in delivery (664.0-665.9)*
       AHA: 2Q, '91, 5

§ ✓5ᵗʰ **674.4**   **Placental polyp**   Ⓜ ♀
[0,2,4]

§ ✓5ᵗʰ **674.5**   **Peripartum cardiomyopathy**   Ⓜ ♀
[0-4]   Postpartum cardiomyopathy
       AHA: 4Q, '03, 65

       DEF: Any structural or functional abnormality of the ventricular myocardium, non-inflammatory disease of obscure or unknown etiology with onset during the postpartum period.

§ ✓5ᵗʰ **674.8**   **Other**   Ⓜ ♀
[0,2,4]   Hepatorenal syndrome, following delivery
       Postpartum:
          subinvolution of uterus
          uterine hypertrophy
       AHA: 3Q, '98, 16

§ ✓5ᵗʰ **674.9**   **Unspecified**   Ⓜ ♀
[0,2,4]   Sudden death of unknown cause during the puerperium

✓4ᵗʰ **675**   **Infections of the breast and nipple associated with childbirth**
       INCLUDES   the listed conditions during pregnancy, childbirth, or the puerperium

§ ✓5ᵗʰ **675.0**   **Infections of nipple**   Ⓜ ♀
[0-4]   Abscess of nipple

§ ✓5ᵗʰ **675.1**   **Abscess of breast**   Ⓜ ♀
[0-4]   Abscess:
          mammary
          purulent
          retromammary
          subareolar
          submammary

§ ✓5ᵗʰ **675.2**   **Nonpurulent mastitis**   Ⓜ ♀
[0-4]   Lymphangitis of breast
       Mastitis:
          NOS
          interstitial
          parenchymatous

§ ✓5ᵗʰ **675.8**   **Other specified infections of the breast and**   Ⓜ ♀
[0-4]   **nipple**

§ ✓5ᵗʰ **675.9**   **Unspecified infection of the breast and nipple**   Ⓜ ♀
[0-4]

Lactation Process: Ejection Reflex Arc

§ ✓4ᵗʰ **676**   **Other disorders of the breast associated with childbirth and disorders of lactation**
       INCLUDES   the listed conditions during pregnancy, the puerperium, or lactation

§ ✓5ᵗʰ **676.0**   **Retracted nipple**   Ⓜ ♀
[0-4]

§ ✓5ᵗʰ **676.1**   **Cracked nipple**   Ⓜ ♀
[0-4]   Fissure of nipple

§ ✓5ᵗʰ **676.2**   **Engorgement of breasts**   Ⓜ ♀
[0-4]

       DEF: Abnormal accumulation of milk in ducts of breast.

§ ✓5ᵗʰ **676.3**   **Other and unspecified disorder of breast**   Ⓜ ♀
[0-4]

§ ✓5ᵗʰ **676.4**   **Failure of lactation**   Ⓜ ♀
[0-4]   Agalactia

       DEF: Abrupt ceasing of milk secretion by breast.

§ ✓5ᵗʰ **676.5**   **Suppressed lactation**   Ⓜ ♀
[0-4]

§ ✓5ᵗʰ **676.6**   **Galactorrhea**   Ⓜ ♀
[0-4]   **EXCLUDES**   *galactorrhea not associated with childbirth (611.6)*

       DEF: Excessive or persistent milk secretion by breast; may be in absence of nursing.

§ ✓5ᵗʰ **676.8**   **Other disorders of lactation**   Ⓜ ♀
[0-4]   Galactocele

       DEF: Galactocele: Obstructed mammary gland, creating retention cyst, results in milk-filled cysts enlarging mammary gland.

§ ✓5ᵗʰ **676.9**   **Unspecified disorder of lactation**   Ⓜ ♀
[0-4]

677   **Late effect of complication of pregnancy, childbirth,**   ♀
       and the puerperium
       Note: This category is to be used to indicate conditions in 632-648.9 and 651-676.9 as the cause of the late effect, themselves classifiable elsewhere. The "late effects" include conditions specified as such, or as sequelae, which may occur at any time after puerperium.
       Code first any sequelae
       AHA: 1Q, '97, 9; 4Q, '94, 42

---

§   Requires fifth-digit. Valid digits are in [brackets] under each code.   See beginning of section 640-648 for codes and definitions.

Ⓝ Newborn Age: 0   Ⓟ Pediatric Age: 0-17   Ⓜ Maternity Age: 12-55   Ⓐ Adult Age: 15-124   Manifestation Code   ►◄ Revised Text   ● New Code   ▲ Revised Code Title

12. DISEASES OF THE SKIN AND SUBCUTANEOUS TISSUE
(680-709)

Skin and Subcutaneous Layer

- Hair follicle
- Epidermis
- Dermis
- Hypodermis (subcutaneous layer)
- Bulb
- Sebaceous gland
- Arrector pili muscle
- Thick-skin epidermis
- Hair shaft
- Pacinian corpuscle
- Hair matrix
- Sweat (eccrine gland)
- Sensory nerve
- Blood vessels

INFECTIONS OF SKIN AND SUBCUTANEOUS TISSUE (680-686)

EXCLUDES   *certain infections of skin classified under "Infectious and Parasitic Diseases," such as:*
erysipelas (035)
erysipeloid of Rosenbach (027.1)
herpes:
    simplex (054.0-054.9)
    zoster (053.0-053.9)
molluscum contagiosum (078.0)
viral warts (078.1)

✔4ᵗʰ **680 Carbuncle and furuncle**

INCLUDES   boil
furunculosis

DEF: Carbuncle: necrotic boils in skin and subcutaneous tissue of neck or back mainly due to staphylococcal infection.

DEF: Furuncle: circumscribed inflammation of corium and subcutaneous tissue due to staphylococcal infection.

680.0   Face
Ear [any part]   Nose (septum)
Face [any part, except eye]   Temple (region)

EXCLUDES   *eyelid (373.13)*
lacrimal apparatus (375.31)
orbit (376.01)

680.1   Neck
680.2   Trunk
Abdominal wall   Flank
Back [any part, except Groin
    buttocks]   Pectoral region
Breast   Perineum
Chest wall   Umbilicus

EXCLUDES   *buttocks (680.5)*
external genital organs:
    female (616.4)
    male (607.2, 608.4)

680.3   Upper arm and forearm
Arm [any part,   Axilla
    except hand]   Shoulder

680.4   Hand
Finger [any]   Wrist
Thumb

680.5   Buttock
Anus   Gluteal region

680.6   Leg, except foot
Ankle   Knee
Hip   Thigh

680.7   Foot
Heel   Toe

680.8   Other specified sites
Head [any part, except face]
Scalp

EXCLUDES   *external genital organs:*
    female (616.4)
    male (607.2, 608.4)

680.9   Unspecified site
Boil NOS   Furuncle NOS
Carbuncle NOS

✔4ᵗʰ **681 Cellulitis and abscess of finger and toe**

INCLUDES   that with lymphangitis
Use additional code to identify organism, such as Staphylococcus (041.1)

AHA: 2Q, '91, 5; J-F, '87, 12

DEF: Acute suppurative inflammation and edema in subcutaneous tissue or muscle of finger or toe.

✔5ᵗʰ **681.0   Finger**

681.00 Cellulitis and abscess, unspecified
681.01 Felon
Pulp abscess   Whitlow
EXCLUDES   *herpetic whitlow (054.6)*

DEF: Painful abscess of fingertips caused by infection in the closed space of terminal phalanx.

681.02 Onychia and paronychia of finger
Panaritium } of finger
Perionychia

DEF: Onychia: inflammation of nail matrix; causes nail loss.

DEF: Paronychia: inflammation of tissue folds around nail.

✔5ᵗʰ **681.1   Toe**

681.10 Cellulitis and abscess, unspecified
AHA: ▶1Q, '05, 14◀

681.11 Onychia and paronychia of toe
Panaritium } of toe
Perionychia

681.9   Cellulitis and abscess of unspecified digit
Infection of nail NOS

✔4ᵗʰ **682 Other cellulitis and abscess**

INCLUDES   abscess (acute)   } (with lymphangitis)
cellulitis (diffuse)   except of
lymphangitis, acute }   finger or toe

Use additional code to identify organism, such as Staphylococcus (041.1)

EXCLUDES   *lymphangitis (chronic) (subacute) (457.2)*

AHA: 2Q, '91, 5; 2Q, '89, 13; J-F, '87, 12; S-O, '85, 10

DEF: Cellulitis: Acute suppurative inflammation of deep subcutaneous tissue and sometimes muscle due to infection of wound, burn or other lesion.

682.0   Face
Cheek, external   Nose, external
Chin   Submandibular
Forehead   Temple (region)

EXCLUDES   *ear [any part] (380.10-380.16)*
eyelid (373.13)
lacrimal apparatus (375.31)
lip (528.5)
mouth (528.3)
nose (internal) (478.1)
orbit (376.01)

682.1   Neck
682.2   Trunk
Abdominal wall   Groin
Back [any part, except   Pectoral region
    buttock]   Perineum
Chest wall   Umbilicus, except newborn
Flank

EXCLUDES   *anal and rectal regions (566)*
breast:
    NOS (611.0)
    puerperal (675.1)
external genital organs:
    female (616.3-616.4)
    male (604.0, 607.2, 608.4)
umbilicus, newborn (771.4)

AHA: 4Q, '98, 42

✔4ᵗʰ
✔5ᵗʰ **Additional Digit Required**   RUG III Special Care Dx   RUG III Clinically Complex Dx   Hospice Non-cancer Dx   CD PDx Clinical Dimension PDx   CD SDx Clinical Dimension SDx

2006 ICD•9•CM   **October 2005 • Volume 1 — 183**

Lymphatic System of Head and Neck

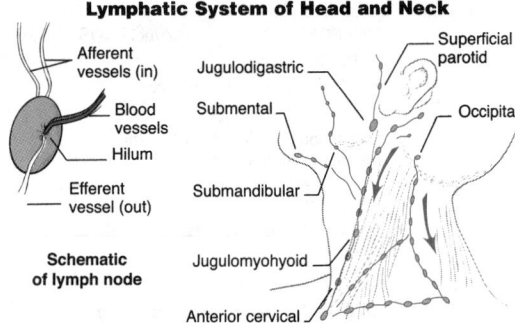

Schematic of lymph node

Afferent vessels (in)
Blood vessels
Hilum
Efferent vessel (out)

Jugulodigastric
Submental
Submandibular
Jugulomyohyoid
Anterior cervical
Superficial parotid
Occipital

Lymphatic drainage of the head, neck, and face

682.3   Upper arm and forearm
Arm [any part, except hand]
Axilla
Shoulder
> **EXCLUDES**   hand (682.4)

AHA: 2Q, '03, 7

682.4   Hand, except fingers and thumb
Wrist
> **EXCLUDES**   finger and thumb (681.00-681.02)

682.5   Buttock
Gluteal region
> **EXCLUDES**   anal and rectal regions (566)

682.6   Leg, except foot
Ankle   Knee
Hip   Thigh

AHA: ▶3Q, '04, 5;◀ 4Q, '03, 108

682.7   Foot, except toes
Heel
> **EXCLUDES**   toe (681.10-681.11)

682.8   Other specified sites
Head [except face]   Scalp
> **EXCLUDES**   face (682.0)

682.9   Unspecified site
Abscess NOS   Lymphangitis, acute NOS
Cellulitis NOS
> **EXCLUDES**   lymphangitis NOS (457.2)

683 Acute lymphadenitis
Abscess (acute)
Adenitis, acute   }   lymph gland or node,
Lymphadenitis, acute   except mesenteric

Use additional code to identify organism, such as Staphylococcus (041.1)
> **EXCLUDES**   enlarged glands NOS (785.6)
> lymphadenitis:
>   chronic or subacute, except mesenteric (289.1)
>   mesenteric (acute) (chronic) (subacute) (289.2)
>   unspecified (289.3)

DEF: Acute inflammation of lymph nodes due to primary infection located elsewhere in the body.

684 Impetigo
Impetiginization of other dermatoses
Impetigo (contagiosa) [any site] [any organism]:
    bullous
    circinate
    neonatorum
    simplex
Pemphigus neonatorum
> **EXCLUDES**   impetigo herpetiformis (694.3)

DEF: Infectious skin disease commonly occurring in children; caused by group A streptococci or *Staphylococcus aureus*; skin lesions usually appear on the face and consist of subcorneal vesicles and bullae that burst and form yellow crusts.

√4ᵗʰ 685 Pilonidal cyst
> **INCLUDES**   fistula
>   sinus   } coccygeal or pilonidal

DEF: Hair-containing cyst or sinus in the tissues of the sacrococcygeal area; often drains through opening at the postanal dimple.

Stages of Pilonidal Disease

Normal follicle
Stretched follicle
Infected follicle
Acute abscess
Chronic abscess
Epithelial tube

685.0   With abscess
685.1   Without mention of abscess

√4ᵗʰ 686 Other local infections of skin and subcutaneous tissue
Use additional code to identify any infectious organism (041.0-041.8)

√5ᵗʰ 686.0   Pyoderma
Dermatitis: Dermatitis:
   purulent   suppurative
   septic

DEF: Nonspecific purulent skin disease related most to furuncles, pustules, or possibly carbuncles.

686.00   Pyoderma, unspecified
686.01   Pyoderma gangrenosum
AHA: 4Q, '97, 42

DEF: Persistent debilitating skin disease, characterized by irregular, boggy, blue-red ulcerations, with central healing and undermined edges.

686.09   Other pyoderma

686.1   Pyogenic granuloma
Granuloma:
   septic
   suppurative
   telangiectaticum
> **EXCLUDES**   pyogenic granuloma of oral mucosa (528.9)

DEF: Solitary polypoid capillary hemangioma often associated with local irritation, trauma, and superimposed inflammation; located on the skin and gingival or oral mucosa.

686.8   Other specified local infections of skin and subcutaneous tissue
Bacterid (pustular)   Ecthyma
Dermatitis vegetans   Perlèche
> **EXCLUDES**   dermatitis infectiosa eczematoides (690.8)
> panniculitis (729.30-729.39)

686.9   Unspecified local infection of skin and subcutaneous tissue
Fistula of skin NOS   Skin infection NOS
> **EXCLUDES**   fistula to skin from internal organs — see Alphabetic Index

OTHER INFLAMMATORY CONDITIONS OF SKIN AND SUBCUTANEOUS TISSUE (690-698)
> **EXCLUDES**   panniculitis (729.30-729.39)

√4ᵗʰ 690 Erythematosquamous dermatosis
> **EXCLUDES**   eczematous dermatitis of eyelid (373.31)
> parakeratosis variegata (696.2)
> psoriasis (696.0-696.1)
> seborrheic keratosis (702.11-702.19)

√5ᵗʰ 690.1   Seborrheic dermatitis

690.10   Seborrheic dermatitis, unspecified
Seborrheic dermatitis NOS

690.11   Seborrhea capitis   ▣P
Cradle cap

690.12   Seborrheic infantile dermatitis   ▣P

690.18   Other seborrheic dermatitis

Ⓝ Newborn Age: 0   Ⓟ Pediatric Age: 0-17   Ⓜ Maternity Age: 12-55   Ⓐ Adult Age: 15-124   ⬛ Manifestation Code   ▶◀ Revised Text   ● New Code   ▲ Revised Code Title

184 — Volume 1 • February 2005   *2006 ICD•9•CM*

690.8　Other erythematosquamous dermatosis

√4ᵗʰ 691 Atopic dermatitis and related conditions

DEF: Atopic dermatitis: chronic, pruritic, inflammatory skin disorder found on the face and antecubital and popliteal fossae; noted in persons with a hereditary predisposition to pruritus, and often accompanied by allergic rhinitis, hay fever, asthma, and extreme itching; also called allergic dermatitis, allergic or atopic eczema, or disseminated neurodermatitis.

691.0　Diaper or napkin rash

Ammonia dermatitis　　Diaper or napkin:
Diaper or napkin:　　　rash
　dermatitis　　　　　　Psoriasiform napkin eruption
　erythema

691.8　Other atopic dermatitis and related conditions

Atopic dermatitis　　　Eczema:
Besnier's prurigo　　　　intrinsic (allergic)
Eczema:　　　　　　　　Neurodermatitis:
　atopic　　　　　　　　　atopic
　flexural　　　　　　　　diffuse (of Brocq)

√4ᵗʰ 692 Contact dermatitis and other eczema

INCLUDES	dermatitis:　　　　eczema (acute) (chronic):
	NOS　　　　　　　NOS
	contact　　　　　　allergic
	occupational　　　erythematous
	venenata　　　　　occupational

EXCLUDES　allergy NOS (995.3)
　　　　　　contact dermatitis of eyelids (373.32)
　　　　　　dermatitis due to substances taken internally
　　　　　　　(693.0-693.9)
　　　　　　eczema of external ear (380.22)
　　　　　　perioral dermatitis (695.3)
　　　　　　urticarial reactions (708.0-708.9, 995.1)

DEF: Contact dermatitis: acute or chronic dermatitis caused by initial irritant effect of a substance, or by prior sensitization to a substance coming once again in contact with skin.

692.0　Due to detergents

692.1　Due to oils and greases

692.2　Due to solvents

Dermatitis due to solvents of:
　chlorocompound ⎤
　cyclohexane　　 ⎟
　ester　　　　　　⎬ group
　glycol　　　　　 ⎟
　hydrocarbon　　 ⎟
　ketone　　　　　⎦

692.3　Due to drugs and medicines in contact with skin

Dermatitis (allergic)　Dermatitis (allergic)
　(contact) due to:　　　(contact) due to:
　arnica　　　　　　　neomycin
　fungicides　　　　　pediculocides
　iodine　　　　　　　phenols
　keratolytics　　　　scabicides
　mercurials　　　　　any drug applied to skin
Dermatitis medicamentosa due to drug applied to
　skin
Use additional E code to identify drug
　　EXCLUDES　allergy NOS due to drugs (995.2)
　　　　　　　　dermatitis due to ingested drugs (693.0)
　　　　　　　　dermatitis medicamentosa NOS (693.0)

692.4　Due to other chemical products

Dermatitis due to:
　acids　　　　　　　insecticide
　adhesive plaster　　nylon
　alkalis　　　　　　plastic
　caustics　　　　　　rubber
　dichromate
AHA: 2Q, '89, 16

692.5　Due to food in contact with skin

Dermatitis, contact,　Dermatitis, contact,
　due to:　　　　　　　due to:
　cereals　　　　　　　fruit
　fish　　　　　　　　meat
　flour　　　　　　　　milk
　　EXCLUDES　dermatitis due to:
　　　　　　　　dyes (692.89)
　　　　　　　　ingested foods (693.1)
　　　　　　　　preservatives (692.89)

692.6　Due to plants [except food]

Dermatitis due to:
　lacquer tree [Rhus verniciflua]
　poison:
　　ivy [Rhus toxicodendron]
　　oak [Rhus diversiloba]
　　sumac [Rhus venenata]
　　vine [Rhus radicans]
　primrose [Primula]
　ragweed [Senecio jacobae]
　other plants in contact with the skin
　　EXCLUDES　allergy NOS due to pollen (477.0)
　　　　　　　　nettle rash (708.8)

√5ᵗʰ 692.7 Due to solar radiation

　　EXCLUDES　sunburn due to other ultraviolet
　　　　　　　　　radiation exposure (692.82)

692.70 Unspecified dermatitis due to sun

692.71 Sunburn

First degree sunburn　　Sunburn NOS
AHA: 4Q, '01, 47

692.72 Acute dermatitis due to solar radiation

Berlogue dermatitis
Photoallergic response
Phototoxic response
Polymorphus light eruption
Acute solar skin damage NOS
　　EXCLUDES　sunburn (692.71, 692.76-
　　　　　　　　　692.77)
Use additional E code to identify drug, if
　drug induced

DEF: Berloque dermatitis: Phytophotodermatitis due to sun exposure after use of a product containing bergamot oil; causes red patches, which may turn brown.

DEF: Photoallergic response: Dermatitis due to hypersensitivity to the sun; causes papulovesicular, eczematous or exudative eruptions.

DEF: Phototoxic response: Chemically induced sensitivity to sun causes burn-like reaction, occasionally vesiculation and subsequent hyperpigmentation.

DEF: Polymorphous light eruption: Inflammatory skin eruptions due to sunlight exposure; eruptions differ in size and shape.

DEF: Acute solar skin damage (NOS): Rapid, unspecified injury to skin from sun.

692.73 Actinic reticuloid and actinic granuloma

DEF: Actinic reticuloid: Dermatosis aggravated by light, causes chronic eczema-like eruption on exposed skin which extends to other unexposed surfaces; occurs in the eldery.

DEF: Actinic granuloma: Inflammatory response of skin to sun causing small nodule of microphages.

692.74 Other chronic dermatitis due to solar radiation

Chronic solar skin damage NOS
Solar elastosis
　　EXCLUDES　actinic [solar] keratosis (702.0)
DEF: Solar elastosis: Premature aging of skin of light-skinned people; causes inelasticity, thinning or thickening, wrinkling, dryness, scaling and hyperpigmentation.

DEF: Chronic solar skin damage (NOS): Chronic skin impairment due to exposure to the sun, not otherwise specified.

√4ᵗʰ
√5ᵗʰ Additional Digit Required　　RUG III Special Care Dx　　RUG III Clinically Complex Dx　　Hospice Non-cancer Dx　　CD PDx Clinical Dimension PDx　　CD SDx Clinical Dimension SDx

2006 ICD•9•CM　　　　　　　　　　　　　　　　　　　　　　　　　　　　　　　　　　　　　**Volume 1 — 185**

692.75 Disseminated superficial actinic porokeratosis (DSAP)

DEF: Autosomal dominant skin condition occurring in skin that has been overexposed to the sun. Primarily affects women over the age of 16; characterized by numerous superficial annular, keratotic, brownish-red spots or thickenings with depressed centers and sharp, ridged borders. High risk that condition will evolve into squamous cell carcinoma.

692.76 Sunburn of second degree

AHA: 4Q, '01, 47

692.77 Sunburn of third degree

AHA: 4Q, '01, 47

692.79 Other dermatitis due to solar radiation

Hydroa aestivale
Photodermatitis
Photosensitiveness } (due to sun)

Solar skin damage NOS

✓5th **692.8 Due to other specified agents**

692.81 Dermatitis due to cosmetics

692.82 Dermatitis due to other radiation

Infrared rays   Tanning bed
Light, except   Ultraviolet rays, except
    from sun   from sun
Radiation NOS   X-rays

EXCLUDES   solar radiation (692.70-692.79)

AHA: 4Q, '01, 47

692.83 Dermatitis due to metals

Jewelry

692.84 Due to animal (cat) (dog) dander

Due to animal (cat) (dog) hair

692.89 Other

Dermatitis due to: Dermatitis due to:
cold weather   hot weather
dyes   preservatives

EXCLUDES   allergy (NOS) (rhinitis) due to animal hair or dander (477.2)
allergy to dust (477.8)
sunburn (692.71, 692.76-692.77)

692.9 Unspecified cause

Dermatitis:
NOS
contact NOS
venenata NOS
Eczema NOS

✓4th **693 Dermatitis due to substances taken internally**

EXCLUDES   adverse effect NOS of drugs and medicines (995.2)
allergy NOS (995.3)
contact dermatitis (692.0-692.9)
urticarial reactions (708.0-708.9, 995.1)

DEF: Inflammation of skin due to ingested substance.

693.0 Due to drugs and medicines

Dermatitis medicamentosa NOS
Use additional E code to identify drug

EXCLUDES   that due to drugs in contact with skin (692.3)

693.1 Due to food

693.8 Due to other specified substances taken internally

693.9 Due to unspecified substance taken internally

EXCLUDES   dermatitis NOS (692.9)

✓4th **694 Bullous dermatoses**

694.0 Dermatitis herpetiformis

Dermatosis herpetiformis   Hydroa herpetiformis
Duhring's disease

EXCLUDES   herpes gestationis (646.8)
dermatitis herpetiformis:
juvenile (694.2)
senile (694.5)

DEF: Chronic, relapsing multisystem disease manifested most in the cutaneous system; seen as an extremely pruritic eruption of various combinations of lesions that frequently heal leaving hyperpigmentation or hypopigmentation and occasionally scarring; usually associated with an asymptomatic gluten-sensitive enteropathy, and immunogenic factors are believed to play a role in its origin.

694.1 Subcorneal pustular dermatosis

Sneddon-Wilkinson disease or syndrome

DEF: Chronic relapses of sterile pustular blebs beneath the horny skin layer of the trunk and skin folds; resembles dermatitis herpetiformis.

694.2 Juvenile dermatitis herpetiformis

Juvenile pemphigoid

694.3 Impetigo herpetiformis

DEF: Rare dermatosis associated with pregnancy; marked by itching pustules in third trimester, hypocalcemia, tetany, fever and lethargy; may result in maternal or fetal death.

694.4 Pemphigus

Pemphigus: Pemphigus:
NOS   malignant
erythematosus   vegetans
foliaceus   vulgaris

EXCLUDES   pemphigus neonatorum (684)

DEF: Chronic, relapsing, sometimes fatal skin diseases; causes vesicles, bullae; autoantibodies against intracellular connections cause acantholysis.

694.5 Pemphigoid

Benign pemphigus NOS
Bullous pemphigoid
Herpes circinatus bullosus
Senile dermatitis herpetiformis

✓5th **694.6 Benign mucous membrane pemphigoid**

Cicatricial pemphigoid
Mucosynechial atrophic bullous dermatitis

694.60 Without mention of ocular involvement

694.61 With ocular involvement

Ocular pemphigus

DEF: Mild self-limiting, subepidermal blistering of mucosa including the conjunctiva, seen predominantly in the elderly. It produces adhesions and scarring.

694.8 Other specified bullous dermatoses

EXCLUDES   herpes gestationis (646.8)

694.9 Unspecified bullous dermatoses

✓4th **695 Erythematous conditions**

695.0 Toxic erythema

Erythema venenatum

695.1 Erythema multiforme

Erythema iris   Scalded skin syndrome
Herpes iris   Stevens-Johnson syndrome
Lyell's syndrome   Toxic epidermal necrolysis

DEF: Symptom complex with a varied skin eruption pattern of macular, bullous, papular, nodose, or vesicular lesions on the neck, face, and legs; gastritis and rheumatic pains are also noticeable, first-seen symptoms; complex is secondary to a number of factors, including infections, ingestants, physical agents, malignancy and pregnancy.

695.2 Erythema nodosum

EXCLUDES   tuberculous erythema nodosum (017.1)

DEF: Panniculitis (an inflammatory reaction of the subcutaneous fat) of women, usually seen as a hypersensitivity reaction to various infections, drugs, sarcoidosis, and specific enteropathies; the acute stage is often associated with other symptoms, including fever, malaise, and arthralgia; the lesions are pink to blue in color, appear in crops as tender nodules and are found on the front of the legs below the knees.

N Newborn Age: 0   P Pediatric Age: 0-17   M Maternity Age: 12-55   A Adult Age: 15-124   Manifestation Code   ▶◀ Revised Text   ● New Code   ▲ Revised Code Title

186 — Volume 1   2006 ICD•9•CM

695.3 Rosacea
Acne:
erythematosa
rosacea
Perioral dermatitis
Rhinophyma

DEF: Chronic skin disease, usually of the face, characterized by persistent erythema and sometimes by telangiectasis with acute episodes of edema, engorgement papules, and pustules.

695.4 Lupus erythematosus
Lupus:
erythematodes (discoid)
erythematosus (discoid), not disseminated
EXCLUDES lupus (vulgaris) NOS (017.0)
systemic [disseminated] lupus
erythematosus (710.0)

DEF: Group of connective tissue disorders occurring as various cutaneous diseases of unknown origin; it primarily affects women between the ages of 20 and 40.

√5th **695.8 Other specified erythematous conditions**
695.81 Ritter's disease
Dermatitis exfoliativa neonatorum

DEF: Infectious skin disease of infants and young children marked by eruptions ranging from a localized bullous type to widespread development of easily ruptured fine vesicles and bullae; results in exfoliation of large planes of skin and leaves raw areas; also called staphylococcal scalded skin syndrome.

695.89 Other
Erythema intertrigo
Intertrigo
Pityriasis rubra (Hebra)
EXCLUDES mycotic intertrigo (111.0-111.9)

AHA: S-O, '86, 10

695.9 Unspecified erythematous condition
Erythema NOS   Erythroderma (secondary)

√4th **696 Psoriasis and similar disorders**
696.0 Psoriatic arthropathy

DEF: Psoriasis associated with inflammatory arthritis; often involves interphalangeal joints.

696.1 Other psoriasis
Acrodermatitis continua Psoriasis:
Dermatitis repens   any type, except
Psoriasis: arthropathic
NOS
EXCLUDES psoriatic arthropathy (696.0)

696.2 Parapsoriasis
Parakeratosis variegata
Parapsoriasis lichenoides chronica
Pityriasis lichenoides et varioliformis

DEF: Erythrodermas similar to lichen, planus and psoriasis; symptoms include redness and itching; resistant to treatment.

696.3 Pityriasis rosea
Pityriasis circinata (et maculata)

DEF: Common, self-limited rash of unknown etiology marked by a solitary erythematous, salmon or fawn-colored herald plaque on the trunk, arms or thighs; followed by development of papular or macular lesions that tend to peel and form a scaly collarette.

696.4 Pityriasis rubra pilaris
Devergie's disease   Lichen ruber acuminatus
EXCLUDES pityriasis rubra (Hebra) (695.89)

DEF: Inflammatory disease of hair follicles; marked by firm, red lesions topped by horny plugs; may form patches; occurs on fingers elbows, knees.

696.5 Other and unspecified pityriasis
Pityriasis: Pityriasis:
NOS   streptogenes
alba
EXCLUDES pityriasis:
simplex (690.18)
versicolor (111.0)

696.8 Other

√4th **697 Lichen**
EXCLUDES lichen:
obtusus corneus (698.3)
pilaris (congenital) (757.39)
ruber acuminatus (696.4)
sclerosus et atrophicus (701.0)
scrofulosus (017.0)
simplex chronicus (698.3)
spinulosus (congenital) (757.39)
urticatus (698.2)

697.0 Lichen planus
Lichen: Lichen:
planopilaris   ruber planus

DEF: Inflammatory, pruritic skin disease; marked by angular, flat-top, violet-colored papules; may be acute and widespread or chronic and localized.

697.1 Lichen nitidus
Pinkus' disease

DEF: Chronic, inflammatory, usually asymptomatic skin disorder, characterized by numerous glistening, flat-topped, discrete, smooth, skin-colored micropapules most often on penis, lower abdomen, inner thighs, wrists, forearms, breasts and buttocks.

697.8 Other lichen, not elsewhere classified
Lichen: Lichen:
ruber moniliforme striata

697.9 Lichen, unspecified

√4th **698 Pruritus and related conditions**
EXCLUDES pruritus specified as psychogenic (306.3)

DEF: Pruritus: Intense, persistent itching due to irritation of sensory nerve endings from organic or psychogenic causes.

698.0 Pruritus ani
Perianal itch

698.1 Pruritus of genital organs

698.2 Prurigo
Lichen urticatus   Prurigo:
Prurigo: mitis
NOS   simplex
Hebra's   Urticaria papulosa (Hebra)
EXCLUDES prurigo nodularis (698.3)

698.3 Lichenification and lichen simplex chronicus
Hyde's disease
Neurodermatitis (circumscripta) (local)
Prurigo nodularis
EXCLUDES neurodermatitis, diffuse (of Brocq)
(691.8)

DEF: Lichenification: thickening of skin due to prolonged rubbing or scratching.

DEF: Lichen simplex chronicus: eczematous dermatitis, of face, neck, extremities, scrotum, vulva, and perianal region due to repeated itching, rubbing and scratching; spontaneous or evolves with other dermatoses.

698.4 Dermatitis factitia [artefacta]
Dermatitis ficta
Neurotic excoriation
Use additional code to identify any associated
mental disorder

DEF: Various types of self-inflicted skin lesions characterized in appearance as an erythema to a gangrene.

698.8 Other specified pruritic conditions
Pruritus: Winter itch
hiemalis
senilis

698.9 Unspecified pruritic disorder
Itch NOS   Pruritus NOS

√4th √5th Additional Digit Required   RUG III Special Care Dx   RUG III Clinically Complex Dx   Hospice Non-cancer Dx   CD PDx Clinical Dimension PDx   CD SDx Clinical Dimension SDx

2006 ICD•9•CM   Volume 1 — 187

Skin and Subcutaneous Tissue

700–704.3

OTHER DISEASES OF SKIN AND SUBCUTANEOUS TISSUE (700-709)

> **EXCLUDES**   conditions confined to eyelids (373.0-374.9)
> congenital conditions of skin, hair, and nails
> (757.0-757.9)

700 Corns and callosities

Callus   Clavus

DEF: Corns: Conical or horny thickening of skin on toes, due to friction, pressure from shoes and hosiery; pain and inflammation may develop.

DEF: Callosities: Localized overgrowth (hyperplasia) of the horny epidermal layer due to pressure or friction.

✓4th 701 Other hypertrophic and atrophic conditions of skin

> **EXCLUDES**   dermatomyositis (710.3)
> hereditary edema of legs (757.0)
> scleroderma (generalized) (710.1)

701.0 Circumscribed scleroderma

Addison's keloid   Morphea
Dermatosclerosis, localized   Scleroderma, circum-
Lichen sclerosus   scribed or localized
    et atrophicus

DEF: Thickened, hardened, skin and subcutaneous tissue; may involve musculoskeletal system.

701.1 Keratoderma, acquired

Acquired:
   ichthyosis
   keratoderma palmaris et plantaris
Elastosis perforans serpiginosa
Hyperkeratosis:
   NOS
   follicularis in cutem penetrans
   palmoplantaris climacterica
Keratoderma:
   climactericum
   tylodes, progressive
Keratosis (blennorrhagica)

> **EXCLUDES**   Darier's disease [keratosis follicularis]
> (congenital) (757.39)
> keratosis:
>   arsenical (692.4)
>   gonococcal (098.81)

AHA: 4Q, '94, 48

701.2 Acquired acanthosis nigricans

Keratosis nigricans

DEF: Diffuse velvety hyperplasia of the spinous skin layer of the axilla and other body folds marked by gray, brown, or black pigmentation; in adult form it is often associated with an internal carcinoma (malignant acanthosis nigricans) in a benign, nevoid form it is relatively generalized; benign juvenile form with obesity is sometimes caused by an endocrine disturbance.

701.3 Striae atrophicae

Atrophic spots of skin
Atrophoderma maculatum
Atrophy blanche (of Milian)
Degenerative colloid atrophy
Senile degenerative atrophy
Striae distensae

DEF: Bands of atrophic, depressed, wrinkled skin associated with stretching of skin from pregnancy, obesity, or rapid growth during puberty.

701.4 Keloid scar

Cheloid   Keloid
Hypertrophic scar

DEF: Overgrowth of scar tissue due to excess amounts of collagen during connective tissue repair; occurs mainly on upper trunk, face.

701.5 Other abnormal granulation tissue

Excessive granulation

701.8 Other specified hypertrophic and atrophic conditions of skin

Acrodermatitis atrophicans chronica
Atrophia cutis senilis
Atrophoderma neuriticum
Confluent and reticulate papillomatosis
Cutis laxa senilis
Elastosis senilis
Folliculitis ulerythematosa reticulata
Gougerot-Carteaud syndrome or disease

701.9 Unspecified hypertrophic and atrophic conditions of skin

Atrophoderma

✓4th 702 Other dermatoses

> **EXCLUDES**   carcinoma in situ (232.0-232.9)

702.0 Actinic keratosis

AHA: 1Q, '92, 18

DEF: Wart-like growth, red or skin-colored; may form a cutaneous horn.

✓5th 702.1 Seborrheic keratosis

DEF: Common, benign, lightly pigmented, warty growth composed of basaloid cells.

702.11 Inflamed seborrheic keratosis

702.19 Other seborrheic keratosis

Seborrheic keratosis NOS

702.8 Other specified dermatoses

✓4th 703 Diseases of nail

> **EXCLUDES**   congenital anomalies (757.5)
> onychia and paronychia (681.02, 681.11)

703.0 Ingrowing nail

Ingrowing nail with infection
Unguis incarnatus

> **EXCLUDES**   infection, nail NOS (681.9)

703.8 Other specified diseases of nail

Dystrophia unguium   Onychauxis
Hypertrophy of nail   Onychogryposis
Koilonychia   Onycholysis
Leukonychia (punctata) (striata)

703.9 Unspecified disease of nail

✓4th 704 Diseases of hair and hair follicles

> **EXCLUDES**   congenital anomalies (757.4)

✓5th 704.0 Alopecia

> **EXCLUDES**   madarosis (374.55)
> syphilitic alopecia (091.82)

DEF: Lack of hair, especially on scalp; often called baldness; may be partial or total; occurs at any age.

704.00 Alopecia, unspecified

Baldness   Loss of hair

704.01 Alopecia areata

Ophiasis

DEF: Alopecia areata: usually reversible, inflammatory, patchy hair loss found in beard or scalp.

DEF: Ophiasis: alopecia areata of children; marked by band around temporal and occipital scalp margins.

704.02 Telogen effluvium

DEF: Shedding of hair from premature telogen development in follicles due to stress, including shock, childbirth, surgery, drugs or weight loss.

704.09 Other

Folliculitis decalvans
Hypotrichosis:
   NOS
   postinfectional NOS
Pseudopelade

704.1 Hirsutism

Hypertrichosis: Polytrichia
   NOS
   lanuginosa, acquired

> **EXCLUDES**   hypertrichosis of eyelid (374.54)

DEF: Excess hair growth; often in unexpected places and amounts.

704.2 Abnormalities of the hair

Atrophic hair   Trichiasis:
Clastothrix   NOS
Fragilitas crinium   cicatrical
              Trichorrhexis (nodosa)

> **EXCLUDES**   trichiasis of eyelid (374.05)

704.3 Variations in hair color

Canities (premature)   Poliosis:
Grayness, hair (premature)   NOS
Heterochromia of hair   circumscripta, acquired

N Newborn Age: 0   P Pediatric Age: 0-17   M Maternity Age: 12-55   A Adult Age: 15-124   Manifestation Code   ►◄ Revised Text   ● New Code   ▲ Revised Code Title

704.8 **Other specified diseases of hair and hair follicles**

Folliculitis: Sycosis:
    NOS   NOS
    abscedens et suffodiens   barbae [not parasitic]
    pustular   lupoid
Perifolliculitis: vulgaris
    NOS
    capitis abscedens et suffodiens
    scalp

704.9 **Unspecified disease of hair and hair follicles**

√4th **705** **Disorders of sweat glands**

705.0 **Anhidrosis**

Hypohidrosis   Oligohidrosis
DEF: Lack or deficiency of ability to sweat.

705.1 **Prickly heat**

Heat rash   Sudamina
Miliaria rubra (tropicalis)

√5th **705.2** **Focal hyperhidrosis**

EXCLUDES   *generalized (secondary) hyperhidrosis (780.8)*

705.21 **Primary focal hyperhidrosis**

Focal hyperhidrosis NOS
Hyperhidrosis NOS
Hyperhidrosis of:
    axilla
    face
    palms
    soles

AHA: 4Q, '04, 91

DEF: A rare condition that is a disorders of the sweat glands resulting in excessive production of sweat; occurs in the absence of any underlying or causative condition and is almost always focal, confined to one or more specific areas of the body.

705.22 **Secondary focal hyperhidrosis**

Frey's syndrome

AHA: 4Q, '04, 91

DEF: Secondary focal hyperhidrosis: a symptom of an underlying disease process resulting in excessive sweating beyond what the body requires to maintain thermal control, confined to one or more specific areas of the body.

DEF: Frey's syndrome: an auriculotemporal syndrome due to lesion on the parotid gland; characteristic redness and excessive sweating on the cheek in connection with eating.

√5th **705.8** **Other specified disorders of sweat glands**

705.81 **Dyshidrosis**

Cheiropompholyx   Pompholyx
DEF: Vesicular eruption, on hands, feet causing itching and burning.

705.82 **Fox-Fordyce disease**

DEF: Chronic, usually pruritic disease chiefly of women evidenced by small follicular papular eruptions, especially in the axillary and pubic areas; develops from the closure and rupture of the affected apocrine glands' intraepidermal portion of the ducts.

705.83 **Hidradenitis**

Hidradenitis suppurativa
DEF: Inflamed sweat glands.

705.89 **Other**

Bromhidrosis   Granulosis rubra nasi
Chromhidrosis   Urhidrosis
EXCLUDES   *generalized hyperhidrosis (780.8)*
                hidrocystoma (216.0-216.9)
DEF: Bromhidrosis: foul-smelling axillary sweat due to decomposed bacteria.
DEF: Chromhidrosis: secretion of colored sweat.
DEF: Granulosis rubra nasi: ideopathic condition of children; causes redness, sweating around nose, face and chin; tends to end by puberty.
DEF: Urhidrosis: urinous substance, such as uric acid, in sweat; occurs in uremia.

705.9 **Unspecified disorder of sweat glands**

Disorder of sweat glands NOS

√4th **706** **Diseases of sebaceous glands**

706.0 **Acne varioliformis**

Acne: Acne:
    frontalis   necrotica
DEF: Rare form of acne characterized by persistent brown papulo-pustules usually on the brow and temporoparietal part of the scalp.

706.1 **Other acne**

Acne: Acne:
    NOS   vulgaris
    conglobata   Blackhead
    cystic   Comedo
    pustular
EXCLUDES   *acne rosacea (695.3)*

706.2 **Sebaceous cyst**

Atheroma, skin   Wen
Keratin cyst
DEF: Benign epidermal cyst, contains sebum and keratin; presents as firm, circumscribed nodule.

706.3 **Seborrhea**

EXCLUDES   *seborrhea:*
         capitis (690.11)
         sicca (690.18)
      seborrheic
         dermatitis (690.10)
         keratosis (702.11-702.19)
DEF: Seborrheic dermatitis marked by excessive secretion of sebum; the sebum forms an oily coating, crusts, or scales on the skin; it is also called hypersteatosis.

706.8 **Other specified diseases of sebaceous glands**

Asteatosis (cutis)   Xerosis cutis

706.9 **Unspecified disease of sebaceous glands**

√4th **707** **Chronic ulcer of skin**

INCLUDES   non-infected sinus of skin
             non-healing ulcer
EXCLUDES   *specific infections classified under "Infectious and Parasitic Diseases" (001.0-136.9)*
             varicose ulcer (454.0, 454.2)
AHA: 4Q, '04, 92

√5th **707.0** **Decubitus ulcer**

Bed sore   Plaster ulcer
Decubitus ulcer [any site]   Pressure ulcer
AHA: 1Q, '04, 14; 4Q, '03, 110; 4Q, '99, 20; 1Q, '96, 15; 3Q, '90, 15; N-D, '87, 9

707.00 Unspecified site

707.01 Elbow

707.02 Upper back

Shoulder blades

707.03 Lower back

Sacrum
AHA: ▶1Q, '05, 16◄

707.04 Hip

707.05 Buttock

707.06 Ankle

707.07 Heel

AHA: ▶1Q, '05, 16◄

707.09 Other site

Head

√4th √5th Additional Digit Required   RUG III Special Care Dx   RUG III Clinically Complex Dx   Hospice Non-cancer Dx   CD PDx Clinical Dimension PDx   CD SDx Clinical Dimension SDx

2006 ICD•9•CM   October 2005 • Volume 1 — 189

Skin and Subcutaneous Tissue

707.1–709.9

Four Stages of Decubitus Ulcers

First Stage
Nonblanchable erythema

Second Stage
Partial thickness skin loss involving epidermis, dermis, or both

Third Stage
Full thickness skin loss extending through subcutaneous tissue

Fourth Stage
Full thickness skin loss extending to muscle and bone

Cutaneous Lesions

Surface Lesions

Fissure   Polyp growth   Ulcer

Solid Lesions

Flat macule   Slightly elevated wheal   Solid papule

Sac Lesions

Cyst   Clear fluid vesicle   Pustule

✓5ᵗʰ **707.1 Ulcer of lower limbs, except decubitus**
Ulcer, chronic:
   neurogenic ⎫
   trophic   ⎬ of lower limb

Code, if applicable, any causal condition first:
  atherosclerosis of the extremities with ulceration (440.23)
  chronic venous hypertension with ulcer (459.31)
  chronic venous hypertension with ulcer and inflammation (459.33)
  diabetes mellitus (250.80-250.83)
  postphlebitic syndrome with ulcer (459.11)
  postphlebitic syndrome with ulcer and inflammation (459.13)

AHA: 4Q, '01, 44; 4Q, '99, 15

707.10 Ulcer of lower limb, unspecified
AHA: ▶3Q, '04, 5;◀ 4Q, '02, 43

707.11 Ulcer of thigh
707.12 Ulcer of calf
707.13 Ulcer of ankle
707.14 Ulcer of heel and midfoot
Plantar surface of midfoot

707.15 Ulcer of other part of foot
Toes

707.19 Ulcer of other part of lower limb

707.8 Chronic ulcer of other specified sites
Ulcer, chronic:
   neurogenic ⎫
   trophic   ⎬ of other specified sites

707.9 Chronic ulcer of unspecified site
Chronic ulcer NOS   Tropical ulcer NOS
Trophic ulcer NOS   Ulcer of skin NOS

✓4ᵗʰ **708 Urticaria**
EXCLUDES   edema:
   angioneurotic (995.1)
   Quincke's (995.1)
   hereditary angioedema (277.6)
  urticaria:
   giant (995.1)
   papulosa (Hebra) (698.2)
   pigmentosa (juvenile) (congenital) (757.33)

DEF: Skin disorder marked by raised edematous patches of skin or mucous membrane with intense itching; also called hives.

708.0 Allergic urticaria
708.1 Idiopathic urticaria
708.2 Urticaria due to cold and heat
Thermal urticaria
708.3 Dermatographic urticaria
Dermatographia   Factitial urticaria
708.4 Vibratory urticaria
708.5 Cholinergic urticaria

708.8 Other specified urticaria
Nettle rash   Urticaria:
Urticaria: recurrent periodic
  chronic

708.9 Urticaria, unspecified
Hives NOS

✓4ᵗʰ **709 Other disorders of skin and subcutaneous tissue**

✓5ᵗʰ **709.0 Dyschromia**
EXCLUDES   albinism (270.2)
   pigmented nevus (216.0-216.9)
   that of eyelid (374.52-374.53)

DEF: Pigment disorder of skin or hair.

709.00 Dyschromia, unspecified
709.01 Vitiligo
DEF: Persistent, progressive development of nonpigmented white patches on otherwise normal skin

709.09 Other

709.1 Vascular disorders of skin
Angioma serpiginosum
Purpura (primary) annularis telangiectodes

709.2 Scar conditions and fibrosis of skin
Adherent scar (skin)   Fibrosis, skin NOS
Cicatrix   Scar NOS
Disfigurement (due to scar)
EXCLUDES   keloid scar (701.4)

AHA: N-D, '84, 19

709.3 Degenerative skin disorders
Calcinosis: Degeneration, skin
  circumscripta   Deposits, skin
  cutis   Senile dermatosis NOS
Colloid milium   Subcutaneous calcification

709.4 Foreign body granuloma of skin and subcutaneous tissue
EXCLUDES   residual foreign body without granuloma of skin and subcutaneous tissue (729.6)
   that of muscle (728.82)

709.8 Other specified disorders of skin
Epithelial hyperplasia
Menstrual dermatosis
Vesicular eruption

AHA: N-D, '87, 6

DEF: Epithelial hyperplasia: increased number of epitheleal cells.

DEF: Vesicular eruption: liquid-filled structures appearing through skin.

709.9 Unspecified disorder of skin and subcutaneous tissue
Dermatosis NOS

Ⓝ Newborn Age: 0   Ⓟ Pediatric Age: 0-17   Ⓜ Maternity Age: 12-55   Ⓐ Adult Age: 15-124   Manifestation Code   ▶◀ Revised Text   ● New Code   ▲ Revised Code Title

13. DISEASES OF THE MUSCULOSKELETAL SYSTEM AND CONNECTIVE TISSUE (710-739)

Joint Structures

The following fifth-digit subclassification is for use with categories 711-712, 715-716, 718-719, and 730:

0 site unspecified

1 shoulder region
    Acromioclavicular joint(s)
    Clavicle
    Glenohumeral joint(s)
    Scapula
    Sternoclavicular joint(s)

2 upper arm
    Elbow joint
    Humerus

3 forearm
    Radius
    Ulna
    Wrist joint

4 hand
    Carpus
    Metacarpus
    Phalanges [fingers]

5 pelvic region and thigh
    Buttock
    Femur
    Hip (joint)

6 lower leg
    Fibula   Patella
    Knee joint   Tibia

7 ankle and foot
    Ankle joint   Phalanges, foot
    Digits [toes]   Tarsus
    Metatarsus   Other joints in foot

8 other specified sites
    Head   Skull
    Neck   Trunk
    Ribs   Vertebral column

9 multiple sites

ARTHROPATHIES AND RELATED DISORDERS (710-719)

EXCLUDES *disorders of spine (720.0-724.9)*

√4ᵗʰ **710 Diffuse diseases of connective tissue**

INCLUDES all collagen diseases whose effects are not mainly confined to a single system

EXCLUDES *those affecting mainly the cardiovascular system, i.e., polyarteritis nodosa and allied conditions (446.0-446.7)*

710.0 Systemic lupus erythematosus   `CD PDx`
    Disseminated lupus erythematosus
    Libman-Sacks disease
    Use additional code to identify manifestation, as:
       endocarditis (424.91)
       nephritis (583.81)
         chronic (582.81)
       nephrotic syndrome (581.81)
    EXCLUDES *lupus erythematosus (discoid) NOS (695.4)*

AHA: 2Q, '03, 7-8; 2Q, '97, 8

DEF: A chronic multisystemic inflammatory disease affecting connective tissue; marked by anemia, leukopenia, muscle and joint pains, fever, rash of a butterfly pattern around cheeks and forehead area; of unknown etiology.

710.1 Systemic sclerosis   `CD PDx`
    Acrosclerosis   Progressive systemic sclerosis
    CRST syndrome   Scleroderma
    Use additional code to identify manifestation, as:
       lung involvement (517.2)
       myopathy (359.6)
    EXCLUDES *circumscribed scleroderma (701.0)*

AHA: 1Q, '88, 6

DEF: Systemic disease, involving excess fibrotic collagen build-up; symptoms include thickened skin; fibrotic degenerative changes in various organs; and vascular abnormalities; condition occurs more often in females.

710.2 Sicca syndrome   `CD PDx`
    Keratoconjunctivitis sicca   Sjögren's disease

DEF: Autoimmune disease; associated with keratoconjunctivitis, laryngopharyngitis, rhinitis, dry mouth, enlarged parotid gland, and chronic polyarthritis.

710.3 Dermatomyositis   `CD PDx`
    Poikilodermatomyositis
    Polymyositis with skin involvement

DEF: Polymyositis associated with flat-top purple papules on knuckles; marked by upper eyelid rash, edema of eyelids and orbit area, red rash on forehead, neck, shoulders, trunk and arms; symptoms include fever, weight loss aching muscles; visceral cancer (in individuals older than 40).

710.4 Polymyositis   `CD PDx`

DEF: Chronic, progressive, inflammatory skeletal muscle disease; causes weakness of limb girdles, neck, pharynx; may precede or follow scleroderma, Sjogren's disease, systemic lupus erythematosus, arthritis, or malignancy.

710.5 Eosinophilia myalgia syndrome   `CD PDx`
    Toxic oil syndrome
    Use additional E code to identify drug, if drug induced

CC Excl: 292.0-292.9, 293.0-293.7, 293.84, 293.9, 710.5

AHA: 4Q, '92, 21

DEF: Eosinophilia myalgia syndrome (EMS): inflammatory, multisystem fibrosis; associated with ingesting elemetary L-tryptophan; symptoms include myalgia, weak limbs and bulbar muscles, distal sensory loss, areflexia, arthralgia, cough, fever, fatigue, skin rashes, myopathy, and eosinophil counts greater than 1000/microliter.

DEF: Toxic oil syndrome: syndrome similar to EMS due to ingesting contaminated cooking oil.

710.8 Other specified diffuse diseases of connective tissue   `CD PDx`
    Multifocal fibrosclerosis (idiopathic) NEC
    Systemic fibrosclerosing syndrome

AHA: M-A, '87, 12

710.9 Unspecified diffuse connective tissue disease `CD PDx`
    Collagen disease NOS

√4ᵗʰ √5ᵗʰ Additional Digit Required   RUG III Special Care Dx   RUG III Clinically Complex Dx   Hospice Non-cancer Dx   `CD PDx` Clinical Dimension PDx   `CD SDx` Clinical Dimension SDx

√4ᵗʰ **711 Arthropathy associated with infections**

> INCLUDES   arthritis
> arthropathy
> polyarthritis
> polyarthropathy
>
> } associated with conditions classifiable below

> EXCLUDES   rheumatic fever (390)

The following fifth-digit subclassification is for use with category 711; valid digits are in [brackets] under each code. See list at beginning of chapter for definitions.

    0   site unspecified
    1   shoulder region
    2   upper arm
    3   forearm
    4   hand
    5   pelvic region and thigh
    6   lower leg
    7   ankle and foot
    8   other specified sites
    9   multiple sites

AHA: 1Q, '92, 17

§ √5ᵗʰ **711.0 Pyogenic arthritis**   CD PDx
[0-9]   Arthritis or polyarthritis (due to):
      coliform [Escherichia coli]
      Hemophilus influenzae [H. influenzae]
      pneumococcal
      Pseudomonas
      staphylococcal
      streptococcal
    Pyarthrosis
    Use additional code to identify infectious organism (041.0-041.8)

AHA: 1Q, '92, 16; 1Q, '91, 15

DEF: Infectious arthritis caused by various bacteria; marked by inflamed synovial membranes, and purulent effusion in joints.

§ √5ᵗʰ **711.1 Arthropathy associated with Reiter's disease and nonspecific urethritis**   CD SDx
[0-9]   Code first underlying disease as:
      nonspecific urethritis (099.4)
      Reiter's disease (099.3)

DEF: Reiter's disease: joint disease marked by diarrhea, urethritis, conjunctivitis, keratosis and arthritis; of unknown etiology; affects young males.

DEF: Urethritis: inflamed urethra.

§ √5ᵗʰ **711.2 Arthropathy in Behçet's syndrome**   CD SDx
[0-9]   Code first underlying disease (136.1)

DEF: Behçet's syndrome: Chronic inflammatory disorder, of unknown etiology; affects small blood vessels; causes ulcers of oral and pharyngeal mucous membranes and genitalia, skin lesions, retinal vasculitis, optic atrophy and severe uveitis.

§ √5ᵗʰ **711.3 Postdysenteric arthropathy**   CD SDx
[0-9]   Code first underlying disease as:
      dysentery (009.0)
      enteritis, infectious (008.0-009.3)
      paratyphoid fever (002.1-002.9)
      typhoid fever (002.0)
      EXCLUDES   salmonella arthritis (003.23)

§ √5ᵗʰ **711.4 Arthropathy associated with other bacterial diseases**   CD SDx
[0-9]   Code first underlying disease as:
      diseases classifiable to 010-040, 090-099, except as in 711.1, 711.3, and 713.5
      leprosy (030.0-030.9)
      tuberculosis (015.0-015.9)
      EXCLUDES   gonococcal arthritis (098.50)
                   meningococcal arthritis (036.82)

§ √5ᵗʰ **711.5 Arthropathy associated with other viral diseases**   CD SDx
[0-9]   Code first underlying disease as:
      diseases classifiable to 045-049, 050-079, 480, 487
      O'nyong nyong (066.3)
      EXCLUDES   that due to rubella (056.71)

§ √5ᵗʰ **711.6 Arthropathy associated with mycoses**   CD SDx
[0-9]   Code first underlying disease (110.0-118)

§ √5ᵗʰ **711.7 Arthropathy associated with helminthiasis**   CD SDx
[0-9]   Code first underlying disease as:
      filariasis (125.0-125.9)

§ √5ᵗʰ **711.8 Arthropathy associated with other infectious and parasitic diseases**   CD SDx
[0-9]   Code first underlying disease as:
      diseases classifiable to 080-088, 100-104, 130-136
      EXCLUDES   arthropathy associated with sarcoidosis (713.7)

AHA: 4Q, '91, 15; 3Q, '90, 14

√5ᵗʰ **711.9 Unspecified infective arthritis**   CD PDx
[0-9]   Infective arthritis or polyarthritis (acute) (chronic) (subacute) NOS

√4ᵗʰ **712 Crystal arthropathies**
> INCLUDES   crystal-induced arthritis and synovitis
> EXCLUDES   gouty arthropathy (274.0)

DEF: Joint disease due to urate crystal deposit in joints or synovial membranes.

The following fifth-digit subclassification is for use with category 712; valid digits are in [brackets] under each code. See list at beginning of chapter for definitions.

    0   site unspecified
    1   shoulder region
    2   upper arm
    3   forearm
    4   hand
    5   pelvic region and thigh
    6   lower leg
    7   ankle and foot
    8   other specified sites
    9   multiple sites

§ √5ᵗʰ **712.1 Chondrocalcinosis due to dicalcium phosphate crystals**   CD SDx
[0-9]   Chondrocalcinosis due to dicalcium phosphate crystals (with other crystals)
    Code first underlying disease (275.4)

§ √5ᵗʰ **712.2 Chondrocalcinosis due to pyrophosphate crystals**   CD SDx
[0-9]   Code first underlying disease (275.4)

§ √5ᵗʰ **712.3 Chondrocalcinosis, unspecified**   CD SDx
[0-9]   Code first underlying disease (275.4)

§ √5ᵗʰ **712.8 Other specified crystal arthropathies**   CD PDx
[0-9]

§ √5ᵗʰ **712.9 Unspecified crystal arthropathy**   CD PDx
[0-9]

---

§   Requires fifth-digit. Valid digits are in [brackets] under each code. See beginning of section 710-739 for codes and definitions.

N Newborn Age: 0   P Pediatric Age: 0-17   M Maternity Age: 12-55   A Adult Age: 15-124   Manifestation Code   ◄ Revised Text   ● New Code   ▲ Revised Code Title

✓4ᵗʰ **713 Arthropathy associated with other disorders classified elsewhere**

INCLUDES arthritis / arthropathy / polyarthritis / polyarthropathy } associated with conditions classifiable below

713.0 Arthropathy associated with other endocrine and metabolic disorders `CD SDx`
Code first underlying disease as:
  acromegaly (253.0)
  hemochromatosis (275.0)
  hyperparathyroidism (252.00-252.08)
  hypogammaglobulinemia (279.00-279.09)
  hypothyroidism (243-244.9)
  lipoid metabolism disorder (272.0-272.9)
  ochronosis (270.2)
  EXCLUDES arthropathy associated with:
    amyloidosis (713.7)
    crystal deposition disorders, except gout (712.1-712.9)
    diabetic neuropathy (713.5)
    gouty arthropathy (274.0)

713.1 Arthropathy associated with gastro-intestinal conditions other than infections `CD SDx`
Code first underlying disease as:
  regional enteritis (555.0-555.9)
  ulcerative colitis (556)

713.2 Arthropathy associated with hematological disorders `CD SDx`
Code first underlying disease as:
  hemoglobinopathy (282.4-282.7)
  hemophilia (286.0-286.2)
  leukemia (204.0-208.9)
  malignant reticulosis (202.3)
  multiple myelomatosis (203.0)
  EXCLUDES arthropathy associated with Henoch-Schönlein purpura (713.6)

713.3 Arthropathy associated with dermatological disorders `CD SDx`
Code first underlying disease as:
  erythema multiforme (695.1)
  erythema nodosum (695.2)
  EXCLUDES psoriatic arthropathy (696.0)

713.4 Arthropathy associated with respiratory disorders `CD SDx`
Code first underlying disease as:
  diseases classifiable to 490-519
  EXCLUDES arthropathy associated with respiratory infections (711.0, 711.4-711.8)

713.5 Arthropathy associated with neurological disorders `CD SDx`
Charcôt's arthropathy / Neuropathic arthritis } associated with diseases classifiable elsewhere

Code first underlying disease as:
  neuropathic joint disease [Charcôt's joints]:
    NOS (094.0)
    diabetic (250.6)
    syringomyelic (336.0)
    tabetic [syphilitic] (094.0)

713.6 Arthropathy associated with hypersensitivity reaction `CD SDx`
Code first underlying disease as:
  Henoch (-Schönlein) purpura (287.0)
  serum sickness (999.5)
  EXCLUDES allergic arthritis NOS (716.2)

713.7 Other general diseases with articular involvement `CD SDx`
Code first underlying disease as:
  amyloidosis (277.3)
  familial Mediterranean fever (277.3)
  sarcoidosis (135)
AHA: 2Q, '97, 12

713.8 Arthropathy associated with other conditions classifiable elsewhere `CD SDx`
Code first underlying disease as:
  conditions classifiable elsewhere except as in 711.1-711.8, 712, and 713.0-713.7

✓4ᵗʰ **714 Rheumatoid arthritis and other inflammatory polyarthropathies**
  EXCLUDES rheumatic fever (390)
    rheumatoid arthritis of spine NOS (720.0)
AHA: 2Q, '95, 3

714.0 Rheumatoid arthritis `CD PDx`
Arthritis or polyarthritis:
  atrophic
  rheumatic (chronic)
Use additional code to identify manifestation, as:
  myopathy (359.6)
  polyneuropathy (357.1)
  EXCLUDES juvenile rheumatoid arthritis NOS (714.30)
AHA: 1Q, '90, 5
DEF: Chronic systemic disease principally of joints, manifested by inflammatory changes in articular structures and synovial membranes, atrophy, and loss in bone density.

714.1 Felty's syndrome `CD PDx`
Rheumatoid arthritis with splenoadenomegaly and leukopenia
DEF: Syndrome marked by rheumatoid arthritis, splenomegaly, leukopenia, pigmented spots on lower extremity skin, anemia, and thrombocytopenia.

714.2 Other rheumatoid arthritis with visceral or systemic involvement `CD PDx`
Rheumatoid carditis

✓5ᵗʰ **714.3 Juvenile chronic polyarthritis**
DEF: Rheumatoid arthritis of more than one joint; lasts longer than six weeks in age 17 or younger; symptoms include fever, erythematous rash, weight loss, lymphadenopathy, hepatosplenomegaly and pericarditis.

  714.30 Polyarticular juvenile rheumatoid arthritis, chronic or unspecified `CD PDx`
    Juvenile rheumatoid arthritis NOS
    Still's disease
  714.31 Polyarticular juvenile rheumatoid arthritis, acute `CD PDx`
  714.32 Pauciarticular juvenile rheumatoid arthritis `CD PDx`
  714.33 Monoarticular juvenile rheumatoid arthritis `CD PDx`

714.4 Chronic postrheumatic arthropathy `CD PDx`
  Chronic rheumatoid nodular fibrositis
  Jaccoud's syndrome
DEF: Persistent joint disorder; follows previous rheumatic infection.

✓5ᵗʰ **714.8 Other specified inflammatory polyarthropathies**
  714.81 Rheumatoid lung `CD PDx`
    Caplan's syndrome
    Diffuse interstitial rheumatoid disease of lung
    Fibrosing alveolitis, rheumatoid
    DEF: Lung disorders associated with rheumatoid arthritis.
  714.89 Other `CD PDx`

714.9 Unspecified inflammatory polyarthropathy `CD PDx`
  Inflammatory polyarthropathy or polyarthritis NOS
  EXCLUDES polyarthropathy NOS (716.5)

✓4ᵗʰ / ✓5ᵗʰ Additional Digit Required | RUG III Special Care Dx | RUG III Clinically Complex Dx | Hospice Non-cancer Dx | `CD PDx` Clinical Dimension PDx | `CD SDx` Clinical Dimension SDx

√4ᵗʰ **715 Osteoarthrosis and allied disorders**

Note: Localized, in the subcategories below, includes bilateral involvement of the same site.

INCLUDES   arthritis or polyarthritis:
      degenerative
      hypertrophic
     degenerative joint disease
     osteoarthritis

EXCLUDES   *Marie-Strümpell spondylitis (720.0)*
     osteoarthrosis [osteoarthritis] of spine (721.0-721.9)

The following fifth-digit subclassification is for use with category 715; valid digits are in [brackets] under each code. See list at beginning of chapter for definitions.

   0   site unspecified
   1   shoulder region
   2   upper arm
   3   forearm
   4   hand
   5   pelvic region and thigh
   6   lower leg
   7   ankle and foot
   8   other specified sites
   9   multiple sites

§ √5ᵗʰ **715.0 Osteoarthrosis, generalized**
[0,4,9]   Degenerative joint disease, involving multiple joints
     Primary generalized hypertrophic osteoarthrosis

DEF: Chronic noninflammatory arthritis; marked by degenerated articular cartilage and enlarged bone; symptoms include pain and stiffness with activity; occurs among elderly.

§ √5ᵗʰ **715.1 Osteoarthrosis, localized, primary**
[0-8]   Localized osteoarthropathy, idiopathic

§ √5ᵗʰ **715.2 Osteoarthrosis, localized, secondary**
[0-8]   Coxae malum senilis

§ √5ᵗʰ **715.3 Osteoarthrosis, localized, not specified whether primary or secondary**
[0-8]   Otto's pelvis

AHA: For code 715.35: ▶3Q, '04, 12; 2Q, '04, 15;◀
For code 715.36: 4Q, '03, 118; 2Q, '95, 5

§ √5ᵗʰ **715.8 Osteoarthrosis involving, or with mention of more than one site, but not specified as generalized**
[0,9]

§ √5ᵗʰ **715.9 Osteoarthrosis, unspecified whether generalized or localized**
[0-8]

AHA: For code 715.90: 2Q, '97, 12

√4ᵗʰ **716 Other and unspecified arthropathies**
EXCLUDES   *cricoarytenoid arthropathy (478.79)*

The following fifth-digit subclassification is for use with category 716; valid digits are in [brackets] under each code. See list at beginning of chapter for definitions.

   0   site unspecified
   1   shoulder region
   2   upper arm
   3   forearm
   4   hand
   5   pelvic region and thigh
   6   lower leg
   7   ankle and foot
   8   other specified sites
   9   multiple sites

AHA: 2Q, '95, 3

§ √5ᵗʰ **716.0 Kaschin-Beck disease**   CD PDx
[0-9]   Endemic polyarthritis

DEF: Chronic degenerative disease of spine and peripheral joints; occurs in eastern Siberian, northern Chinese, and Korean youth; may be a mycotoxicosis caused by eating cereals infected with fungus.

§ √5ᵗʰ **716.1 Traumatic arthropathy**   CD PDx
[0-9]   AHA: For code 711.16: 1Q, '02, 9

§ √5ᵗʰ **716.2 Allergic arthritis**   CD PDx
[0-9]   EXCLUDES   *arthritis associated with Henoch-Schönlein purpura or serum sickness (713.6)*

§ √5ᵗʰ **716.3 Climacteric arthritis**   CD PDx ♀
[0-9]   Menopausal arthritis

DEF: Ovarian hormone deficiency; causes pain in small joints, shoulders, elbows or knees; affects females at menopause; also called arthropathia ovaripriva.

§ √5ᵗʰ **716.4 Transient arthropathy**   CD PDx
[0-9]   EXCLUDES   *palindromic rheumatism (719.3)*

§ √5ᵗʰ **716.5 Unspecified polyarthropathy or polyarthritis**   CD PDx
[0-9]

§ √5ᵗʰ **716.6 Unspecified monoarthritis**   CD PDx
[0-8]   Coxitis

§ √5ᵗʰ **716.8 Other specified arthropathy**   CD PDx
[0-9]

§ √5ᵗʰ **716.9 Arthropathy, unspecified**   CD PDx
[0-9]   Arthritis
    Arthropathy } (acute) (chronic) (subacute)

     Articular rheumatism (chronic)
     Inflammation of joint NOS

√4ᵗʰ **717 Internal derangement of knee**
INCLUDES   degeneration
    rupture, old } of articular cartilage or
    tear, old   meniscus of knee

EXCLUDES   *acute derangement of knee (836.0-836.6)*
    ankylosis (718.5)
    contracture (718.4)
    current injury (836.0-836.6)
    deformity (736.4-736.6)
    recurrent dislocation (718.3)

717.0 Old bucket handle tear of medial meniscus   CD PDx
   Old bucket handle tear of unspecified cartilage

717.1 Derangement of anterior horn of medial meniscus   CD PDx

717.2 Derangement of posterior horn of medial meniscus   CD PDx

717.3 Other and unspecified derangement of medial meniscus   CD PDx
   Degeneration of internal semilunar cartilage

√5ᵗʰ **717.4 Derangement of lateral meniscus**

   717.40 Derangement of lateral meniscus, unspecified   CD PDx

   717.41 Bucket handle tear of lateral meniscus   CD PDx

   717.42 Derangement of anterior horn of lateral meniscus   CD PDx

   717.43 Derangement of posterior horn of lateral meniscus   CD PDx

   717.49 Other   CD PDx

717.5 Derangement of meniscus, not elsewhere classified   CD PDx
   Congenital discoid meniscus
   Cyst of semilunar cartilage
   Derangement of semilunar cartilage NOS

717.6 Loose body in knee   CD PDx
   Joint mice, knee
   Rice bodies, knee (joint)

DEF: The presence in the joint synovial area of a small, frequently calcified, loose body created from synovial membrane, organized fibrin fragments of articular cartilage or arthritis osteophytes.

717.7 Chondromalacia of patella   CD PDx
   Chondromalacia patellae
   Degeneration [softening] of articular cartilage of patella

AHA: M-A, '85, 14; N-D, '84, 9

DEF: Softened patella cartilage.

§ Requires fifth-digit. Valid digits are in [brackets] under each code. See beginning of section 710-739 for codes and definitions.

N Newborn Age: 0   P Pediatric Age: 0-17   M Maternity Age: 12-55   A Adult Age: 15-124   Manifestation Code   ▶◀ Revised Text   ● New Code   ▲ Revised Code Title

Disruption and Tears of Meniscus

Bucket-handle   Flap-type   Peripheral / Radial

Horizontal cleavage   Vertical   Congenital discoid meniscus

Internal Derangements of Knee

Disruptions of Cruciate Ligament

Chondromalacia of Patella

Anterior

Posterior

"Kissing" lesion of fermur

✓5ᵗʰ **717.8**   **Other internal derangement of knee**

    717.81 Old disruption of lateral collateral ligament `CD PDx`

    717.82 Old disruption of medial collateral ligament `CD PDx`

    717.83 Old disruption of anterior cruciate ligament `CD PDx`

    717.84 Old disruption of posterior cruciate ligament `CD PDx`

    717.85 Old disruption of other ligaments of knee `CD PDx`
       Capsular ligament of knee

    717.89 Other `CD PDx`
       Old disruption of ligaments NOS

   717.9 Unspecified internal derangement of knee `CD PDx`
       Derangement NOS of knee

✓4ᵗʰ **718 Other derangement of joint**
    EXCLUDES   jaw (524.60-524.69)

The following fifth-digit subclassification is for use with category 718; valid digits are in [brackets] under each code. See list at beginning of chapter for definitions.

    0 site unspecified
    1 shoulder region
    2 upper arm
    3 forearm
    4 hand
    5 pelvic region and thigh
    6 lower leg
    7 ankle and foot
    8 other specified sites
    9 multiple sites

§ ✓5ᵗʰ **718.0 Articular cartilage disorder** `CD PDx`
[0-5,7-9]   Meniscus: Meniscus:
      disorder   tear, old
      rupture, old   Old rupture of ligament(s) of joint NOS

      EXCLUDES   articular cartilage disorder:
          in ochronosis (270.2)
          knee (717.0-717.9)
          chondrocalcinosis (275.4)
          metastatic calcification (275.4)

§ ✓5ᵗʰ **718.1 Loose body in joint** `CD PDx`
[0-5,7-9]   Joint mice
      EXCLUDES   knee (717.6)

    AHA: For code 718.17: 2Q, '01, 15

    DEF: Calcified loose bodies in synovial fluid; due to arthritic osteophytes.

§ ✓5ᵗʰ **718.2 Pathological dislocation** `CD PDx`
[0-9]   Dislocation or displacement of joint, not recurrent and not current injury
      Spontaneous dislocation (joint)

§ ✓5ᵗʰ **718.3 Recurrent dislocation of joint** `CD PDx`
[0-9]   **AHA:** N-D, '87, 7

§ ✓5ᵗʰ **718.4 Contracture of joint** `CD PDx`
[0-9]   **AHA:** 4Q, '98, 40

§ ✓5ᵗʰ **718.5 Ankylosis of joint** `CD PDx`
[0-9]   Ankylosis of joint (fibrous) (osseous)
      EXCLUDES   spine (724.9)
          stiffness of joint without mention of ankylosis (719.5)

    DEF: Immobility and solidification, of joint; due to disease, injury or surgical procedure.

§ ✓5ᵗʰ **718.6 Unspecified intrapelvic protrusion of acetabulum** `CD PDx`
[0,5]   Protrusio acetabuli, unspecified

    DEF: Sinking of the floor of acetabulum; causing femoral head to protrude, limits hip movement; of unknown etiology.

§ ✓5ᵗʰ **718.7 Developmental dislocation of joint** `CD PDx`
[0-9]   *EXCLUDES*   congenital dislocation of joint (754.0-755.8)
          traumatic dislocation of joint (830-839)

    AHA: 4Q, '01, 48

§ ✓5ᵗʰ **718.8 Other joint derangement, not elsewhere classified** `CD PDx`
[0-9]   Flail joint (paralytic)   Instability of joint
      EXCLUDES   deformities classifiable to 736 (736.0-736.9)

§ ✓5ᵗʰ **718.9 Unspecified derangement of joint** `CD PDx`
[0-5,7-9]   *EXCLUDES*   knee (717.9)

✓4ᵗʰ **719 Other and unspecified disorders of joint**
    EXCLUDES   jaw (524.60-524.69)

The following fifth-digit subclassification is for use with codes 719.0-719.6, 719.8-719.9; valid digits are in [brackets] under each code. See list at beginning of chapter for definitions.

    0 site unspecified
    1 shoulder region
    2 upper arm
    3 forearm
    4 hand
    5 pelvic region and thigh
    6 lower leg
    7 ankle and foot
    8 other specified sites
    9 multiple sites

§ ✓5ᵗʰ **719.0 Effusion of joint**
[0-9]   Hydrarthrosis
      Swelling of joint, with or without pain
      EXCLUDES   intermittent hydrarthrosis (719.3)

§ ✓5ᵗʰ **719.1 Hemarthrosis**
[0-9]   *EXCLUDES*   current injury (840.0-848.9)

§ ✓5ᵗʰ **719.2 Villonodular synovitis**
[0-9]

    DEF: Overgrowth of synovial tissue, especially at knee joint; due to macrophage infiltration of giant cells in synovial villi and fibrous nodules.

---

§   Requires fifth-digit. Valid digits are in [brackets] under each code. See beginning of section 710-739 for codes and definitions.

✓4ᵗʰ / ✓5ᵗʰ **Additional Digit Required**   RUG III Special Care Dx   RUG III Clinically Complex Dx   Hospice Non-cancer Dx   `CD PDx` Clinical Dimension PDx   `CD SDx` Clinical Dimension SDx

2006 ICD•9•CM   **Volume 1 — 195**

Joint Derangements and Disorders

Loose body in joint

Dislocation of joint

Joint contracture

Ankylosis of joint

Synovial effusion (fluid)

Hemarthrosis (blood)

§ ✓5ᵗʰ **719.3 Palindromic rheumatism**
[0-9]   Hench-Rosenberg syndrome
    Intermittent hydrarthrosis
DEF: Recurrent episodes of afebrile arthritis and periarthritis marked by their complete disappearance after a few days or hours; causes swelling, redness, and disability usually affecting only one joint; no known cause; affects adults of either sex.

§ ✓5ᵗʰ **719.4 Pain in joint**
[0-9]   Arthralgia
AHA: For code 719.46: 1Q, '01, 3

§ ✓5ᵗʰ **719.5 Stiffness of joint, not elsewhere classified**
[0-9]

§ ✓5ᵗʰ **719.6 Other symptoms referable to joint**
[0-9]   Joint crepitus   Snapping hip
AHA: 1Q, '94, 15

719.7 Difficulty in walking
    EXCLUDES   *abnormality of gait (781.2)*
AHA: ▶2Q, '04, 15;◀ 4Q, '03, 66

§ ✓5ᵗʰ **719.8 Other specified disorders of joint**
[0-9]   Calcification of joint   Fistula of joint
    EXCLUDES   *temporomandibular joint pain-*
        dysfunction syndrome [Costen's
        syndrome] (524.60)

§ ✓5ᵗʰ **719.9 Unspecified disorder of joint**
[0-9]

DORSOPATHIES (720-724)
    EXCLUDES   *curvature of spine (737.0-737.9)*
        osteochondrosis of spine (juvenile) (732.0)
        adult (732.8)

✓4ᵗʰ **720 Ankylosing spondylitis and other inflammatory spondylopathies**

720.0 Ankylosing spondylitis   `CD PDx`
    Rheumatoid arthritis of spine NOS
    Spondylitis:
      Marie-Strümpell
      rheumatoid
DEF: Rheumatoid arthritis of spine and sacroiliac joints; fusion and deformity in spine follows; affects mainly males; cause unknown.

720.1 Spinal enthesopathy   `CD PDx`
    Disorder of peripheral ligamentous or muscular
      attachments of spine
    Romanus lesion
DEF: Tendinous or muscular vertebral bone attachment abnormality.

720.2 Sacroiliitis, not elsewhere classified   `CD PDx`
    Inflammation of sacroiliac joint NOS
DEF: Pain due to inflammation in joint, at juncture of sacrum and hip.

✓5ᵗʰ **720.8 Other inflammatory spondylopathies**
720.81 Inflammatory spondylopathies in   `CD SDx`
    diseases classified elsewhere
    Code first underlying disease as:
      tuberculosis (015.0)

720.89 Other   `CD PDx`
720.9 Unspecified inflammatory spondylopathy   `CD PDx`
    Spondylitis NOS

✓4ᵗʰ **721 Spondylosis and allied disorders**
AHA: 2Q, '89, 14

DEF: Degenerative changes in spinal joint.

721.0 Cervical spondylosis without myelopathy   `CD PDx`
    Cervical or cervicodorsal:
      arthritis
      osteoarthritis
      spondylarthritis

721.1 Cervical spondylosis with myelopathy   `CD PDx`
    Anterior spinal artery compression syndrome
    Spondylogenic compression of cervical spinal cord
    Vertebral artery compression syndrome

721.2 Thoracic spondylosis without myelopathy   `CD PDx`
    Thoracic: Thoracic:
      arthritis   spondylarthritis
      osteoarthritis

721.3 Lumbosacral spondylosis without   `CD PDx`
myelopathy
    Lumbar or lumbosacral: Lumbar or lumbosacral:
      arthritis   spondylarthritis
      osteoarthritis
AHA: 4Q, '02, 107

✓5ᵗʰ **721.4 Thoracic or lumbar spondylosis with myelopathy**
721.41 Thoracic region   `CD PDx`
    Spondylogenic compression of thoracic
      spinal cord
721.42 Lumbar region   `CD PDx`
    Spondylogenic compression of lumbar
      spinal cord

721.5 Kissing spine   `CD PDx`
    Baastrup's syndrome
DEF: Compression of spinous processes of adjacent vertebrae; due to mutual contact.

721.6 Ankylosing vertebral hyperostosis   `CD PDx`
721.7 Traumatic spondylopathy   `CD PDx`
    Kümmell's disease or spondylitis
721.8 Other allied disorders of spine   `CD PDx`
✓5ᵗʰ **721.9 Spondylosis of unspecified site**
721.90 Without mention of myelopathy   `CD PDx`
    Spinal:
      arthritis (deformans) (degenerative)
        (hypertrophic)
      osteoarthritis NOS
    Spondylarthrosis NOS

721.91 With myelopathy   `CD PDx`
    Spondylogenic compression of spinal cord
      NOS

✓4ᵗʰ **722 Intervertebral disc disorders**
AHA: 1Q, '88, 10

722.0 Displacement of cervical intervertebral   `CD PDx`
disc without myelopathy
    Neuritis (brachial) or radiculitis due to displacement
      or rupture of cervical intervertebral disc
    Any condition classifiable to 722.2 of the cervical or
      cervicothoracic intervertebral disc

§   Requires fifth-digit. Valid digits are in [brackets] under each code. See beginning of section 710-739 for codes and definitions.

N Newborn Age: 0   **P** Pediatric Age: 0-17   **M** Maternity Age: 12-55   **A** Adult Age: 15-124   `Manifestation Code`   ▶◀ Revised Text   ● New Code   ▲ Revised Code Title

Normal Anatomy of Vertebral Disc

Normal Top View

Normal Side View

Derangement of Vertebral Disc

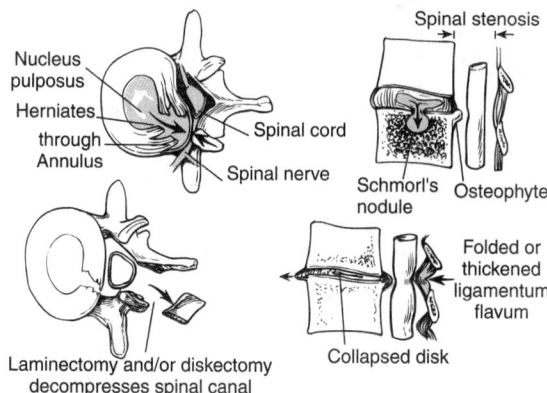

Laminectomy and/or diskectomy decompresses spinal canal

Collapsed disk

√5th **722.1 Displacement of thoracic or lumbar intervertebral disc without myelopathy**

722.10 Lumbar intervertebral disc without myelopathy `CD PDx`

Lumbago or sciatica due to displacement of intervertebral disc

Neuritis or radiculitis due to displacement or rupture of lumbar intervertebral disc

Any condition classifiable to 722.2 of the lumbar or lumbosacral intervertebral disc

AHA: 3Q, '03, 12; 1Q, '03, 7; 4Q, '02, 107

722.11 Thoracic intervertebral disc without myelopathy `CD PDx`

Any condition classifiable to 722.2 of thoracic intervertebral disc

722.2 Displacement of intervertebral disc, site unspecified, without myelopathy `CD PDx`

Discogenic syndrome NOS

Herniation of nucleus pulposus NOS

Intervertebral disc NOS:

extrusion

prolapse

protrusion

rupture

Neuritis or radiculitis due to displacement or rupture of intervertebral disc

√5th **722.3 Schmorl's nodes**

DEF: Irregular bone defect in the margin of the vertebral body; causes herniation into end plate of vertebral body.

722.30 Unspecified region `CD PDx`
722.31 Thoracic region `CD PDx`
722.32 Lumbar region `CD PDx`
722.39 Other `CD PDx`

722.4 Degeneration of cervical intervertebral disc `CD PDx`

Degeneration of cervicothoracic intervertebral disc

√5th **722.5 Degeneration of thoracic or lumbar intervertebral disc**

722.51 Thoracic or thoracolumbar intervertebral disc `CD PDx`

722.52 Lumbar or lumbosacral intervertebral disc `CD PDx`

AHA: 4Q, '04, 133

722.6 Degeneration of intervertebral disc, site unspecified `CD PDx`

Degenerative disc disease NOS

Narrowing of intervertebral disc or space NOS

√5th **722.7 Intervertebral disc disorder with myelopathy**

722.70 Unspecified region `CD PDx`
722.71 Cervical region `CD PDx`
722.72 Thoracic region `CD PDx`
722.73 Lumbar region `CD PDx`

√5th **722.8 Postlaminectomy syndrome**

AHA: J-F, '87, 7

DEF: Spinal disorder due to spinal laminectomy surgery.

722.80 Unspecified region `CD PDx`
722.81 Cervical region `CD PDx`
722.82 Thoracic region `CD PDx`
722.83 Lumbar region `CD PDx`

AHA: 2Q, '97, 15

√5th **722.9 Other and unspecified disc disorder**

Calcification of intervertebral cartilage or disc

Discitis

722.90 Unspecified region `CD PDx`

AHA: N-D, '84, 19

722.91 Cervical region `CD PDx`
722.92 Thoracic region `CD PDx`
722.93 Lumbar region `CD PDx`

√4th **723 Other disorders of cervical region**

EXCLUDES conditions due to:

intervertebral disc disorders (722.0-722.9)

spondylosis (721.0-721.9)

AHA: 3Q, '94, 14; 2Q, '89, 14

723.0 Spinal stenosis in cervical region `CD PDx`

AHA: 4Q, '03, 101

723.1 Cervicalgia `CD PDx`

Pain in neck

DEF: Pain in cervical spine or neck region.

723.2 Cervicocranial syndrome `CD PDx`

Barré-Liéou syndrome

Posterior cervical sympathetic syndrome

DEF: Neurologic disorder of upper cervical spine and nerve roots.

AHA: N-D, '85, 12

723.3 Cervicobrachial syndrome (diffuse) `CD PDx`

DEF: Complex of symptoms due to scalenus anterior muscle compressing the brachial plexus; pain radiates from shoulder to arm or back of neck.

723.4 Brachial neuritis or radiculitis NOS `CD PDx`

Cervical radiculitis

Radicular syndrome of upper limbs

723.5 Torticollis, unspecified `CD PDx`

Contracture of neck

EXCLUDES congenital (754.1)

due to birth injury (767.8)

hysterical (300.11)

ocular torticollis (781.93)

psychogenic (306.0)

spasmodic (333.83)

traumatic, current (847.0)

AHA: ▶1Q, '95, 7;◄ 2Q, '01, 21

DEF: Abnormally positioned neck relative to head; due to cervical muscle or fascia contractions; also called wryneck.

√4th √5th **Additional Digit Required** | RUG III Special Care Dx | RUG III Clinically Complex Dx | Hospice Non-cancer Dx | `CD PDx` Clinical Dimension PDx | `CD SDx` Clinical Dimension SDx

Spinal Stenosis in Cervical Region

Spinal cord in fluid-filled
Dural sac

Old displacement/dislocation of C₁ on C₂

Posterior longitudinal ligament

Spinal cord

Vertebral body

Spinal canal

Torticollis

723.6 **Panniculitis specified as affecting neck** `CD PDx`

DEF: Inflammation of the panniculus adiposus (subcutaneous fat) in the neck.

723.7 **Ossification of posterior longitudinal ligament in cervical region** `CD PDx`

723.8 **Other syndromes affecting cervical region** `CD PDx`
Cervical syndrome NEC
Klippel's disease
Occipital neuralgia
AHA: 1Q, '00, 7

723.9 **Unspecified musculoskeletal disorders and symptoms referable to neck** `CD PDx`
Cervical (region) disorder NOS

√4th **724 Other and unspecified disorders of back**
EXCLUDES collapsed vertebra (code to cause, e.g.,
osteoporosis, 733.00-733.09)
conditions due to:
intervertebral disc disorders (722.0-722.9)
spondylosis (721.0-721.9)
AHA: 2Q, '89, 14

√5th **724.0** **Spinal stenosis, other than cervical**
724.00 **Spinal stenosis, unspecified region** `CD PDx`
724.01 **Thoracic region** `CD PDx`
724.02 **Lumbar region** `CD PDx`
AHA: 4Q, '99, 13

724.09 **Other** `CD PDx`
724.1 **Pain in thoracic spine** `CD PDx`
724.2 **Lumbago** `CD PDx`
Low back pain   Lumbalgia
Low back syndrome
AHA: N-D, '85, 12

724.3 **Sciatica** `CD PDx`
Neuralgia or neuritis of sciatic nerve
EXCLUDES specified lesion of sciatic nerve (355.0)
AHA: 2Q, '89, 12

724.4 **Thoracic or lumbosacral neuritis or radiculitis, unspecified** `CD PDx`
Radicular syndrome of lower limbs
AHA: 2Q, '99, 3

724.5 **Backache, unspecified** `CD PDx`
Vertebrogenic (pain) syndrome NOS

724.6 **Disorders of sacrum** `CD PDx`
Ankylosis } lumbosacral or sacroiliac (joint)
Instability

√5th **724.7** **Disorders of coccyx**
724.70 **Unspecified disorder of coccyx** `CD PDx`
724.71 **Hypermobility of coccyx** `CD PDx`
724.79 **Other** `CD PDx`
Coccygodynia

724.8 **Other symptoms referable to back** `CD PDx`
Ossification of posterior longitudinal ligament NOS
Panniculitis specified as sacral or affecting back

724.9 **Other unspecified back disorders** `CD PDx`
Ankylosis of spine NOS
Compression of spinal nerve root NEC
Spinal disorder NOS
EXCLUDES sacroiliitis (720.2)

RHEUMATISM, EXCLUDING THE BACK (725-729)

INCLUDES disorders of muscles and tendons and their attachments, and of other soft tissues

725 Polymyalgia rheumatica `CD PDx`
DEF: Joint and muscle pain, pelvis, and shoulder girdle stiffness, high sedimentation rate and temporal arteritis; occurs in elderly.

√4th **726 Peripheral enthesopathies and allied syndromes**
Note: Enthesopathies are disorders of peripheral ligamentous or muscular attachments.
EXCLUDES spinal enthesopathy (720.1)

726.0 **Adhesive capsulitis of shoulder**

√5th **726.1** **Rotator cuff syndrome of shoulder and allied disorders**
726.10 **Disorders of bursae and tendons in shoulder region, unspecified**
Rotator cuff syndrome NOS
Supraspinatus syndrome NOS
AHA: 2Q, '01, 11

726.11 **Calcifying tendinitis of shoulder**
726.12 **Bicipital tenosynovitis**
726.19 **Other specified disorders**
EXCLUDES complete rupture of rotator cuff, nontraumatic (727.61)

726.2 **Other affections of shoulder region, not elsewhere classified**
Periarthritis of shoulder
Scapulohumeral fibrositis

√5th **726.3** **Enthesopathy of elbow region**
726.30 **Enthesopathy of elbow, unspecified**
726.31 **Medial epicondylitis**
726.32 **Lateral epicondylitis**
Epicondylitis NOS   Tennis elbow
Golfers' elbow
726.33 **Olecranon bursitis**
Bursitis of elbow
726.39 **Other**

726.4 **Enthesopathy of wrist and carpus**
Bursitis of hand or wrist
Periarthritis of wrist

726.5 **Enthesopathy of hip region**
Bursitis of hip   Psoas tendinitis
Gluteal tendinitis   Trochanteric tendinitis
Iliac crest spur

√5th **726.6** **Enthesopathy of knee**
726.60 **Enthesopathy of knee, unspecified**
Bursitis of knee NOS
726.61 **Pes anserinus tendinitis or bursitis**
DEF: Inflamed tendons of sartorius, gracilis and semitendinosus muscles of medial aspect of knee.
726.62 **Tibial collateral ligament bursitis**
Pellegrini-Stieda syndrome
726.63 **Fibular collateral ligament bursitis**
726.64 **Patellar tendinitis**
726.65 **Prepatellar bursitis**
726.69 **Other**
Bursitis:
infrapatellar
subpatellar

N Newborn Age: 0   P Pediatric Age: 0-17   M Maternity Age: 12-55   A Adult Age: 15-124   Manifestation Code   ◄► Revised Text   ● New Code   ▲ Revised Code Title

√5ᵗʰ **726.7 Enthesopathy of ankle and tarsus**

726.70 Enthesopathy of ankle and tarsus, unspecified
Metatarsalgia NOS
EXCLUDES *Morton's metatarsalgia (355.6)*

726.71 Achilles bursitis or tendinitis

726.72 Tibialis tendinitis
Tibialis (anterior) (posterior) tendinitis

726.73 Calcaneal spur
DEF: Overgrowth of calcaneous bone; causes pain on walking; due to chronic avulsion injury of plantar fascia from calcaneus.

726.79 Other
Peroneal tendinitis

726.8 Other peripheral enthesopathies

√5ᵗʰ **726.9 Unspecified enthesopathy**

726.90 Enthesopathy of unspecified site
Capsulitis NOS
Periarthritis NOS
Tendinitis NOS

726.91 Exostosis of unspecified site
Bone spur NOS
AHA: 2Q, '01, 15

√4ᵗʰ **727 Other disorders of synovium, tendon, and bursa**

√5ᵗʰ **727.0 Synovitis and tenosynovitis**

727.00 Synovitis and tenosynovitis, unspecified
Synovitis NOS
Tenosynovitis NOS

727.01 *Synovitis and tenosynovitis in diseases classified elsewhere*
Code first underlying disease as:
tuberculosis (015.0-015.9)
EXCLUDES *crystal-induced (275.4)*
gonococcal (098.51)
gouty (274.0)
syphilitic (095.7)

Bunion

Normal metatarsophalangeal joint

Exostosis

Ganglia

Extensor tendon sheaths

Ganglion of wrist (fluid-filled sac)

Baker's cyst connected to knee joint synovial cavity

727.02 Giant cell tumor of tendon sheath

727.03 Trigger finger (acquired)
DEF: Stenosing tenosynovitis or nodule in flexor tendon; cessation of flexion or extension movement in finger, followed by snapping into place.

727.04 Radial styloid tenosynovitis
de Quervain's disease

727.05 Other tenosynovitis of hand and wrist

727.06 Tenosynovitis of foot and ankle

727.09 Other

727.1 Bunion
DEF: Enlarged first metatarsal head due to inflamed bursa; results in laterally displaced great toe.

727.2 Specific bursitides often of occupational origin
Beat: Miners':
   elbow   elbow
   hand   knee
   knee
Chronic crepitant synovitis of wrist

727.3 Other bursitis
Bursitis NOS
EXCLUDES *bursitis:*
gonococcal (098.52)
subacromial (726.19)
subcoracoid (726.19)
subdeltoid (726.19)
syphilitic (095.7)
"frozen shoulder" (726.0)

√5ᵗʰ **727.4 Ganglion and cyst of synovium, tendon, and bursa**

727.40 Synovial cyst, unspecified
EXCLUDES *that of popliteal space (727.51)*
AHA: 2Q, '97, 6

727.41 Ganglion of joint

727.42 Ganglion of tendon sheath

727.43 Ganglion, unspecified

727.49 Other
Cyst of bursa

√5ᵗʰ **727.5 Rupture of synovium**

727.50 Rupture of synovium, unspecified

727.51 Synovial cyst of popliteal space
Baker's cyst (knee)

727.59 Other

√5ᵗʰ **727.6 Rupture of tendon, nontraumatic**

727.60 Nontraumatic rupture of unspecified tendon

727.61 Complete rupture of rotator cuff

727.62 Tendons of biceps (long head)

727.63 Extensor tendons of hand and wrist

727.64 Flexor tendons of hand and wrist

727.65 Quadriceps tendon

727.66 Patellar tendon

727.67 Achilles tendon

727.68 Other tendons of foot and ankle

727.69 Other

√5ᵗʰ **727.8 Other disorders of synovium, tendon, and bursa**

727.81 Contracture of tendon (sheath)
Short Achilles tendon (acquired)

727.82 Calcium deposits in tendon and bursa
Calcification of tendon NOS
Calcific tendinitis NOS
EXCLUDES *peripheral ligamentous or muscular attachments (726.0-726.9)*

√4ᵗʰ √5ᵗʰ Additional Digit Required   RUG III Special Care Dx   RUG III Clinically Complex Dx   Hospice Non-cancer Dx   **CD PDx** Clinical Dimension PDx   **CD SDx** Clinical Dimension SDx

2006 ICD•9•CM   **Volume 1 — 199**

Musculoskeletal System and Connective Tissue

727.83–729.0

727.83 Plica syndrome
Plica knee

DEF: A fold in the synovial tissue that begins to form before birth, creating a septum between two pockets of synovial tissue; two most common plicae are the medial patellar plica and the suprapatellar plica. Plica syndrome, or plica knee, refers to symptomatic plica. Experienced by females more commonly than males.

727.89 Other
Abscess of bursa or tendon
> EXCLUDES *xanthomatosis localized to tendons (272.7)*

AHA: 2Q, '89, 15

727.9 Unspecified disorder of synovium, tendon, and bursa

√4ᵗʰ **728 Disorders of muscle, ligament, and fascia**
> EXCLUDES *enthesopathies (726.0-726.9)*
> *muscular dystrophies (359.0-359.1)*
> *myoneural disorders (358.00-358.9)*
> *myopathies (359.2-359.9)*
> *old disruption of ligaments of knee (717.81-717.89)*

728.0 Infective myositis `CD PDx`
Myositis:
  purulent
  suppurative
> EXCLUDES *myositis:*
> *epidemic (074.1)*
> *interstitial (728.81)*
> *syphilitic (095.6)*
> *tropical (040.81)*

DEF: Inflamed connective septal tissue of muscle.

√5ᵗʰ **728.1 Muscular calcification and ossification**
728.10 Calcification and ossification, unspecified `CD PDx`
Massive calcification (paraplegic)

728.11 Progressive myositis ossificans `CD PDx`
DEF: Progressive myositic disease; marked by bony tissue formed by voluntary muscle; occurs among very young.

728.12 Traumatic myositis ossificans `CD PDx`
Myositis ossificans (circumscripta)

728.13 Postoperative heterotopic calcification `CD PDx`
DEF: Abnormal formation of calcium deposits in muscular tissue after surgery, marked by a corresponding loss of muscle tone and tension.

728.19 Other `CD PDx`
Polymyositis ossificans

728.2 Muscular wasting and disuse atrophy, not elsewhere classified `CD PDx`
Amyotrophia NOS Myofibrosis
> EXCLUDES *neuralgic amyotrophy (353.5)*
> *pelvic muscle wasting and disuse atrophy (618.83)*
> *progressive muscular atrophy (335.0-335.9)*

728.3 Other specific muscle disorders `CD PDx`
Arthrogryposis
Immobility syndrome (paraplegic)
> EXCLUDES *arthrogryposis multiplex congenita (754.89)*
> *stiff-man syndrome (333.91)*

728.4 Laxity of ligament `CD PDx`
728.5 Hypermobility syndrome `CD PDx`
728.6 Contracture of palmar fascia `CD PDx` `A`
Dupuytren's contracture

DEF: Dupuytren's contracture: flexion deformity of finger, due to shortened, thickened fibrosing of palmar fascia; cause unknown; associated with long-standing epilepsy; occurs more often in males.

√5ᵗʰ **728.7 Other fibromatoses**
728.71 Plantar fascial fibromatosis `CD PDx`
Contracture of plantar fascia
Plantar fasciitis (traumatic)

DEF: Plantar fascia fibromatosis; causes nodular swelling and pain; not associated with contractures.

728.79 Other `CD PDx`
Garrod's or knuckle pads
Nodular fasciitis
Pseudosarcomatous fibromatosis (proliferative) (subcutaneous)

DEF: Knuckle pads: Pea-size nodules on dorsal surface of interphalangeal joints; new growth of fibrous tissue with thickened dermis and epidermis.

√5ᵗʰ **728.8 Other disorders of muscle, ligament, and fascia**
728.81 Interstitial myositis `CD PDx`
DEF: Inflammation of septal connective parts of muscle tissue.

728.82 Foreign body granuloma of muscle `CD PDx`
Talc granuloma of muscle

728.83 Rupture of muscle, nontraumatic `CD PDx`
728.84 Diastasis of muscle `CD PDx`
Diastasis recti (abdomen)
> EXCLUDES *diastasis recti complicating pregnancy, labor, and delivery (665.8)*

DEF: Muscle separation, such as recti abdominis after repeated pregnancies.

728.85 Spasm of muscle `CD PDx`
728.86 Necrotizing fasciitis `CD PDx`
Use additional code to identify:
  infectious organism (041.00-041.89)
  gangrene (785.4), if applicable

DEF: Fulminating infection begins with extensive cellulitis, spreads to superficial and deep fascia; causes thrombosis of subcutaneous vessels, and gangrene of underlying tissue.

728.87 Muscle weakness (generalized) `CD PDx`
> EXCLUDES *generalized weakness (780.79)*

AHA: ▶1Q, '05, 13;◀ 4Q, '03, 66

728.88 Rhabdomyolysis `CD PDx`
AHA: 4Q, '03, 66

DEF: A disintegration or destruction of muscle; an acute disease characterized by the excretion of myoglobin into the urine.

728.89 Other `CD PDx`
Eosinophilic fasciitis
Use additional E code to identify drug, if drug induced
AHA: 3Q, '02, 28; 2Q, '01, 14, 15

DEF: Eosinophilic fasciitis: inflammation of fascia of extremities associated with eosinophilia, edema, and swelling; occurs alone or as part of myalgia syndrome.

728.9 Unspecified disorder of muscle, ligament, and fascia `CD PDx`
AHA: 4Q, '88, 11

√4ᵗʰ **729 Other disorders of soft tissues**
> EXCLUDES *acroparesthesia (443.89)*
> *carpal tunnel syndrome (354.0)*
> *disorders of the back (720.0-724.9)*
> *entrapment syndromes (354.0-355.9)*
> *palindromic rheumatism (719.3)*
> *periarthritis (726.0-726.9)*
> *psychogenic rheumatism (306.0)*

729.0 Rheumatism, unspecified and fibrositis
DEF: General term describes diseases of muscle, tendon, nerve, joint, or bone; symptoms include pain and stiffness.

`N` Newborn Age: 0   `P` Pediatric Age: 0-17   `M` Maternity Age: 12-55   `A` Adult Age: 15-124   `Manifestation Code`   ▶◀ Revised Text   ● New Code   ▲ Revised Code Title

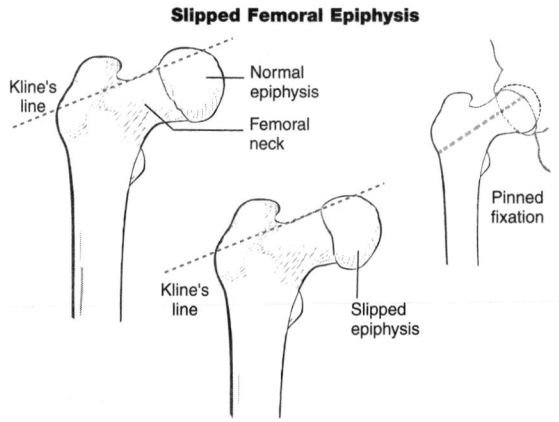

Slipped Femoral Epiphysis

Kline's line — Normal epiphysis

Femoral neck

Pinned fixation

Kline's line

Slipped epiphysis

729.1 Myalgia and myositis, unspecified
Fibromyositis NOS
DEF: Myalgia: muscle pain.
DEF: Myositis: inflamed voluntary muscle.
DEF: Fibromyositis: inflamed fibromuscular tissue.

729.2 Neuralgia, neuritis, and radiculitis, unspecified
> EXCLUDES brachial radiculitis (723.4)
> cervical radiculitis (723.4)
> lumbosacral radiculitis (724.4)
> mononeuritis (354.0-355.9)
> radiculitis due to intervertebral disc
> involvement (722.0-722.2, 722.7)
> sciatica (724.3)

DEF: Neuralgia: paroxysmal pain along nerve; symptoms include brief pain and tenderness at point nerve exits.

DEF: Neuritis: inflamed nerve, symptoms include paresthesia, paralysis and loss of reflexes at nerve site.

DEF: Radiculitis: inflamed nerve root.

√5ᵗʰ 729.3 Panniculitis, unspecified
DEF: Inflammatory reaction of subcutaneous fat; causes nodules; often develops in abdominal region.

  729.30 Panniculitis, unspecified site
  Weber-Christian disease
  DEF: Febrile, nodular, nonsuppurative, relapsing inflammation of subcutaneous fat.

  729.31 Hypertrophy of fat pad, knee
  Hypertrophy of infrapatellar fat pad
  729.39 Other site
  > EXCLUDES panniculitis specified as
  > (affecting):
  > back (724.8)
  > neck (723.6)
  > sacral (724.8)

729.4 Fasciitis, unspecified
> EXCLUDES necrotizing fasciitis (728.86)
> nodular fasciitis (728.79)

AHA: 2Q, '94, 13

729.5 Pain in limb
729.6 Residual foreign body in soft tissue
> EXCLUDES foreign body granuloma:
> muscle (728.82)
> skin and subcutaneous tissue
> (709.4)

√5ᵗʰ 729.8 Other musculoskeletal symptoms referable to limbs
  729.81 Swelling of limb
    AHA: 4Q, '88, 6

  729.82 Cramp

729.89 Other
> EXCLUDES abnormality of gait (781.2)
> tetany (781.7)
> transient paralysis of limb
> (781.4)

AHA: 4Q, '88, 12

729.9 Other and unspecified disorders of soft tissue
Polyalgia

OSTEOPATHIES, CHONDROPATHIES, AND ACQUIRED MUSCULOSKELETAL DEFORMITIES (730-739)

√4ᵗʰ 730 Osteomyelitis, periostitis, and other infections involving bone
> EXCLUDES jaw (526.4-526.5)
> petrous bone (383.2)

Use additional code to identify organism, such as Staphylococcus (041.1)

The following fifth-digit subclassification is for use with category 730; valid digits are in [brackets] under each code. See list at beginning of chapter for definitions.
  0 site unspecified
  1 shoulder region
  2 upper arm
  3 forearm
  4 hand
  5 pelvic region and thigh
  6 lower leg
  7 ankle and foot
  8 other specified sites
  9 multiple sites

AHA: 4Q, '97, 43

DEF: Osteomyelitis: bacterial inflammation of bone tissue and marrow.

DEF: Periostitis: inflammation of specialized connective tissue; causes swelling of bone and aching pain.

§ √5ᵗʰ 730.0 Acute osteomyelitis   `CD PDx`
[0-9]
Abscess of any bone except accessory sinus, jaw, or mastoid
Acute or subacute osteomyelitis, with or without mention of periostitis
AHA: For code 730.06: 1Q, '02, 4; For code 730.07: 1Q, '04, 14

§ √5ᵗʰ 730.1 Chronic osteomyelitis   `CD PDx`
[0-9]
Brodie's abscess
Chronic or old osteomyelitis, with or without mention of periostitis
Sclerosing osteomyelitis of Garré
> EXCLUDES aseptic necrosis of bone (733.40-733.49)

§ √5ᵗʰ 730.2 Unspecified osteomyelitis   `CD PDx`
[0-9]
Osteitis or osteomyelitis NOS, with or without mention of periostitis

§ √5ᵗʰ 730.3 Periostitis without mention of osteomyelitis `CD PDx`
[0-9]
Abscess of periosteum ⎫ without mention of
Periostosis   ⎬ osteomyelitis
> EXCLUDES that in secondary syphilis (091.61)

§ √5ᵗʰ 730.7 Osteopathy resulting from poliomyelitis   `CD SDx`
[0-9]
Code first underlying disease (045.0-045.9)

§ √5ᵗʰ 730.8 Other infections involving bone in diseases `CD SDx`
[0-9] **classified elsewhere**
Code first underlying disease as:
tuberculosis (015.0-015.9)
typhoid fever (002.0)
> EXCLUDES syphilis of bone NOS (095.5)
AHA: 2Q, '97, 16; 3Q, '91, 10

§ √5ᵗʰ 730.9 Unspecified infection of bone   `CD PDx`
[0-9]

---

§ Requires fifth-digit. Valid digits are in [brackets] under each code. See beginning of section 710-739 for codes and definitions

√4ᵗʰ / √5ᵗʰ Additional Digit Required | RUG III Special Care Dx | | RUG III Clinically Complex Dx | Hospice Non-cancer Dx   `CD PDx` Clinical Dimension PDx   `CD SDx` Clinical Dimension SDx

✓4ᵗʰ **731 Osteitis deformans and osteopathies associated with other disorders classified elsewhere**

DEF: Osteitis deformans: Bone disease marked by episodes of increased bone loss, excessive repair attempts follow; causes weakened, deformed bones with increased mass, bowed long bones, deformed flat bones, pain and pathological fractures; may be fatal if associated with congestive heart failure, giant cell tumors or bone sarcoma; also called Paget's disease.

731.0 Osteitis deformans without mention of bone tumor `CD PDx`
    Paget's disease of bone

731.1 Osteitis deformans in diseases classified elsewhere `CD SDx`
    Code first underlying disease as:
        malignant neoplasm of bone (170.0-170.9)

731.2 Hypertrophic pulmonary osteoarthropathy `CD PDx`
    Bamberger-Marie disease
    DEF: Clubbing, of fingers and toes; related to enlarged ends of long bones; due to chronic lung and heart disease.

731.8 Other bone involvement in diseases classified elsewhere `CD SDx`
    Code first underlying disease as:
        diabetes mellitus (250.8)
    Use additional code to specify bone condition, such as:
        acute osteomyelitis (730.00-730.09)
    AHA: 1Q, '04, 14; 4Q, '97, 43; 2Q, '97, 16

✓4ᵗʰ **732 Osteochondropathies**

DEF: Conditions related to both bone and cartilage, or conditions in which cartilage is converted to bone (enchondral ossification).

732.0 Juvenile osteochondrosis of spine `CD PDx`
    Juvenile osteochondrosis (of)
        marginal or vertebral epiphysis (of Scheuermann)
        spine NOS
    Vertebral epiphysitis
    `EXCLUDES` adolescent postural kyphosis (737.0)

732.1 Juvenile osteochondrosis of hip and pelvis `CD PDx`
    Coxa plana
    Ischiopubic synchondrosis (of van Neck)
    Osteochondrosis (juvenile) of:
        acetabulum
        head of femur (of Legg-Calvé-Perthes)
        iliac crest (of Buchanan)
        symphysis pubis (of Pierson)
    Pseudocoxalgia

732.2 Nontraumatic slipped upper femoral epiphysis `CD PDx`
    Slipped upper femoral epiphysis NOS

732.3 Juvenile osteochondrosis of upper extremity `CD PDx`
    Osteochondrosis (juvenile) of:
        capitulum of humerus (of Panner)
        carpal lunate (of Kienbock)
        hand NOS
        head of humerus (of Haas)
        heads of metacarpals (of Mauclaire)
        lower ulna (of Burns)
        radial head (of Brailsford)
        upper extremity NOS

732.4 Juvenile osteochondrosis of lower extremity, excluding foot `CD PDx`
    Osteochondrosis (juvenile) of:
        lower extremity NOS
        primary patellar center (of Köhler)
        proximal tibia (of Blount)
        secondary patellar center (of Sinding-Larsen)
        tibial tubercle (of Osgood-Schlatter)
    Tibia vara

732.5 Juvenile osteochondrosis of foot `CD PDx`
    Calcaneal apophysitis
    Epiphysitis, os calcis
    Osteochondrosis (juvenile) of:
        astragalus (of Diaz)
        calcaneum (of Sever)
        foot NOS
        metatarsal
            second (of Freiberg)
            fifth (of Iselin)
        os tibiale externum (of Haglund)
        tarsal navicular (of Köhler)

732.6 Other juvenile osteochondrosis `CD PDx`
    Apophysitis ⎫
    Epiphysitis ⎬ specified as juvenile, of
    Osteochondritis ⎪ other site,
    Osteochondrosis ⎭ or site NOS

732.7 Osteochondritis dissecans `CD PDx`
732.8 Other specified forms of osteochondropathy `CD PDx`
    Adult osteochondrosis of spine

732.9 Unspecified osteochondropathy `CD PDx`
    Apophysitis ⎫ NOS
    Epiphysitis ⎬ not specified as adult
    Osteochondritis ⎪ or juvenile, of
    Osteochondrosis ⎭ unspecified site

✓4ᵗʰ **733 Other disorders of bone and cartilage**
    `EXCLUDES` bone spur (726.91)
        cartilage of, or loose body in, joint (717.0-717.9, 718.0-718.9)
        giant cell granuloma of jaw (526.3)
        osteitis fibrosa cystica generalisata (252.01)
        osteomalacia (268.2)
        polyostotic fibrous dysplasia of bone (756.54)
        prognathism, retrognathism (524.1)
        xanthomatosis localized to bone (272.7)

✓5ᵗʰ **733.0 Osteoporosis**

DEF: Bone mass reduction that ultimately results in fractures after minimal trauma; dorsal kyphosis or loss of height often occur.

733.00 Osteoporosis, unspecified
    Wedging of vertebra NOS
    AHA: 3Q, '01,19; 2Q, '98, 12

733.01 Senile osteoporosis
    Postmenopausal osteoporosis

733.02 Idiopathic osteoporosis

733.03 Disuse osteoporosis

733.09 Other
    Drug-induced osteoporosis
    Use additional E code to identify drug
    AHA: 4Q, '03, 108

✓5ᵗʰ **733.1 Pathologic fracture**
    Spontaneous fracture
    `EXCLUDES` stress fracture (733.93-733.95)
        traumatic fracture (800-829)
    AHA: 4Q, '93, 25; N-D, '86, 10; N-D, '85, 16
    DEF: Fracture due to bone structure weakening by pathological processes (e.g., osteoporosis, neoplasms and osteomalacia).

733.10 Pathologic fracture, unspecified site

733.11 Pathologic fracture of humerus

733.12 Pathologic fracture of distal radius and ulna
    Wrist NOS

733.13 Pathologic fracture of vertebrae
    Collapse of vertebra NOS
    AHA: 3Q, '99, 5

733.14 Pathologic fracture of neck of femur
    Femur NOS   Hip NOS
    AHA: 1Q, '01, 1; 1Q, '96, 16

Ⓝ Newborn Age: 0   Ⓟ Pediatric Age: 0-17   Ⓜ Maternity Age: 12-55   Ⓐ Adult Age: 15-124   `Manifestation Code`   ◄ Revised Text   ● New Code   ▲ Revised Code Title

733.15 Pathologic fracture of other specified part of femur
AHA: 2Q, '98, 12

733.16 Pathologic fracture of tibia or fibula
Ankle NOS

733.19 Pathologic fracture of other specified site

✓4th **733.2 Cyst of bone**

733.20 Cyst of bone (localized), unspecified

733.21 Solitary bone cyst
Unicameral bone cyst

733.22 Aneurysmal bone cyst

DEF: Solitary bone lesion, bulges into periosteum; marked by calcified rim.

733.29 Other
Fibrous dysplasia (monostotic)
EXCLUDES   *cyst of jaw (526.0-526.2, 526.89)*
osteitis fibrosa cystica (252.01)
polyostotic fibrousdyplasia of bone (756.54)

733.3 Hyperostosis of skull
Hyperostosis interna frontalis
Leontiasis ossium

DEF: Abnormal bone growth on inner aspect of cranial bones.

✓5th **733.4 Aseptic necrosis of bone**
EXCLUDES   *osteochondropathies (732.0-732.9)*

DEF: Infarction of bone tissue due to a nonfectious etiology, such as a fracture, ischemic disorder or administration of immunosuppressive drugs; leads to degenerative joint disease or nonunion of fractures.

733.40 Aseptic necrosis of bone, site unspecified

733.41 Head of humerus

733.42 Head and neck of femur
Femur NOS
EXCLUDES   *Legg-Calvé-Perthes disease (732.1)*

733.43 Medial femoral condyle

733.44 Talus

733.49 Other

733.5 Osteitis condensans
Piriform sclerosis of ilium

DEF: Idiopathic condition marked by low back pain; associated with oval or triangular sclerotic, opaque bone next to sacroiliac joints in the ileum.

733.6 Tietze's disease
Costochondral junction syndrome
Costochondritis

DEF: Painful, idiopathic, nonsuppurative, swollen costal cartilage sometimes confused with cardiac symptoms because the anterior chest pain resembles that of coronary artery disease.

Acquired Deformities of Toe

Hallux valgus

Hallux varus

Hallux malleus (hammer of big toe)

Hammertoe

733.7 Algoneurodystrophy
Disuse atrophy of bone   Sudeck's atrophy
DEF: Painful, idiopathic.

✓5th **733.8 Malunion and nonunion of fracture**
AHA: 2Q, '94, 5

733.81 Malunion of fracture

733.82 Nonunion of fracture
Pseudoarthrosis (bone)

✓5th **733.9 Other and unspecified disorders of bone and cartilage**

733.90 Disorder of bone and cartilage, unspecified

733.91 Arrest of bone development or growth
Epiphyseal arrest

733.92 Chondromalacia
Chondromalacia:
NOS
localized, except patella
systemic
tibial plateau
EXCLUDES   *chondromalacia of patella (717.7)*

DEF: Articular cartilage softening.

733.93 Stress fracture of tibia or fibula
Stress reaction of tibia or fibula
AHA: 4Q, '01,48

733.94 Stress fracture of the metatarsals
Stress reaction of metatarsals
AHA: 4Q, '01,48

733.95 Stress fracture of other bone
Stress reaction of other bone
AHA: 4Q, '01,48

733.99 Other
Diaphysitis
Hypertrophy of bone
Relapsing polychondritis
AHA: J-F, '87, 14

734 Flat foot
Pes planus (acquired)
Talipes planus (acquired)
EXCLUDES   *congenital (754.61)*
rigid flat foot (754.61)
spastic (everted) flat foot (754.61)

✓4th **735 Acquired deformities of toe**
EXCLUDES   *congenital (754.60-754.69, 755.65-755.66)*

735.0 Hallux valgus (acquired)
DEF: Angled displacement of the great toe, causing it to ride over or under other toes.

735.1 Hallux varus (acquired)
DEF: Angled displacement of the great toe toward the body midline, away from the other toes.

735.2 Hallux rigidus
DEF: Limited flexion movement at metatarsophalangeal joint of great toe; due to degenerative joint disease.

735.3 Hallux malleus
DEF: Extended proximal phalanx, flexed distal phalanges, of great toe; foot resembles claw or hammer.

735.4 Other hammer toe (acquired)

735.5 Claw toe (acquired)
DEF: Hyperextended proximal phalanges, flexed middle and distal phalanges.

735.8 Other acquired deformities of toe

735.9 Unspecified acquired deformity of toe

✓4th ✓5th Additional Digit Required   RUG III Special Care Dx   RUG III Clinically Complex Dx   Hospice Non-cancer Dx   CD PDx Clinical Dimension PDx   CD SDx Clinical Dimension SDx

Musculoskeletal System and Connective Tissue

736–736.71

Acquired Deformities of Forearm

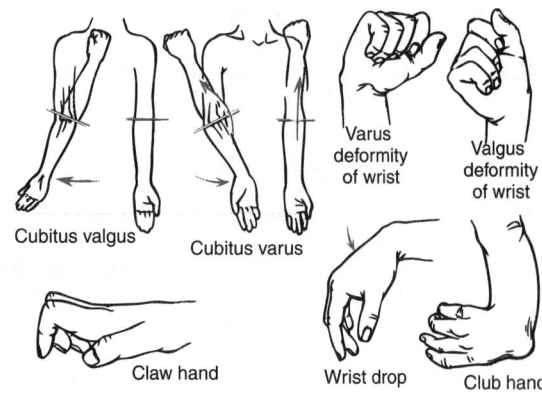

Cubitus valgus   Cubitus varus

Varus deformity of wrist

Valgus deformity of wrist

Claw hand   Wrist drop   Club hand

√4ᵗʰ **736 Other acquired deformities of limbs**

EXCLUDES   *congenital (754.3-755.9)*

√5ᵗʰ **736.0 Acquired deformities of forearm, excluding fingers**

736.00 Unspecified deformity

Deformity of elbow, forearm, hand, or wrist (acquired) NOS

736.01 Cubitus valgus (acquired)

DEF: Deviation of the elbow away from the body midline upon extension; it occurs when the palm is turning outward.

736.02 Cubitus varus (acquired)

DEF: Elbow joint displacement angled laterally; when the forearm is extended, it is deviated toward the midline of the body; also called "gun stock" deformity.

736.03 Valgus deformity of wrist (acquired)

DEF: Abnormal angulation away from the body midline.

736.04 Varus deformity of wrist (acquired)

DEF: Abnormal angulation toward the body midline.

736.05 Wrist drop (acquired)

DEF: Inability to extend the hand at the wrist due to extensor muscle paralysis

736.06 Claw hand (acquired)

DEF: Flexion and atrophy of the hand and fingers; found in ulnar nerve lesions, syringomyelia, and leprosy.

736.07 Club hand, acquired

DEF: Twisting of the hand out of shape or position; caused by the congenital absence of the ulna or radius.

736.09 Other

736.1 Mallet finger

DEF: Permanently flexed distal phalanx.

√5ᵗʰ **736.2 Other acquired deformities of finger**

736.20 Unspecified deformity

Deformity of finger (acquired) NOS

736.21 Boutonniere deformity

DEF: A deformity of the finger caused by flexion of the proximal interphalangeal joint and hyperextension of the distal joint; also called buttonhole deformity.

736.22 Swan-neck deformity

DEF: Flexed distal and hyperextended proximal interphalangeal joint.

736.29 Other

EXCLUDES   *trigger finger (727.03)*

AHA: 2Q, '89, 13

Acquired Deformities of Hip

Genu valga (knock-knee)

Genu vara (bowleg)

Normal angle   Coxa valga   Coxa vara

Acquired Deformities of Lower Limb

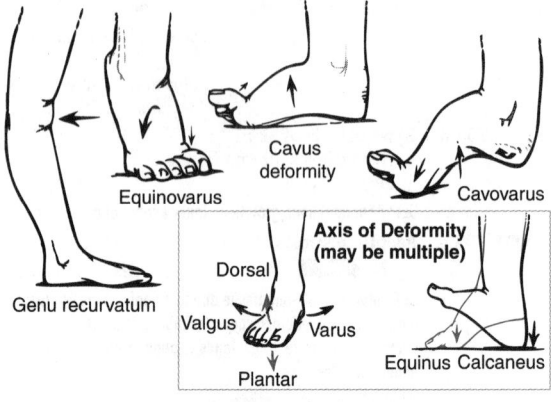

Equinovarus

Cavus deformity

Cavovarus

Genu recurvatum

Axis of Deformity (may be multiple)

Dorsal

Valgus   Varus

Plantar

Equinus Calcaneus

√5ᵗʰ **736.3 Acquired deformities of hip**

736.30 Unspecified deformity

Deformity of hip (acquired) NOS

736.31 Coxa valga (acquired)

DEF: Increase of at least 140 degrees in the angle formed by the axis of the head and the neck of the femur, and the axis of its shaft.

736.32 Coxa vara (acquired)

DEF: The bending downward of the neck of the femur: causing difficulty in movement; a right angle or less may be formed by the axis of the head and neck of the femur, and the axis of its shaft.

736.39 Other

AHA: 2Q, '91, 18

√5ᵗʰ **736.4 Genu valgum or varum (acquired)**

736.41 Genu valgum (acquired)

DEF: Abnormally close together and an abnormally large space between the ankles; also called "knock-knees."

736.42 Genu varum (acquired)

DEF: Abnormally separated knees and the inward bowing of the legs; it is also called "bowlegs."

736.5 Genu recurvatum (acquired)

DEF: Hyperextended knees; also called "backknee."

736.6 Other acquired deformities of knee

Deformity of knee (acquired) NOS

√5ᵗʰ **736.7 Other acquired deformities of ankle and foot**

EXCLUDES   *deformities of toe (acquired) (735.0-735.9)*

pes planus (acquired) (734)

736.70 Unspecified deformity of ankle and foot, acquired

736.71 Acquired equinovarus deformity

Clubfoot, acquired

EXCLUDES   *clubfoot not specified as acquired (754.5-754.7)*

N Newborn Age: 0   P Pediatric Age: 0-17   M Maternity Age: 12-55   A Adult Age: 15-124   Manifestation Code   ►◄ Revised Text   ● New Code   ▲ Revised Code Title

Kyphosis and Lordosis

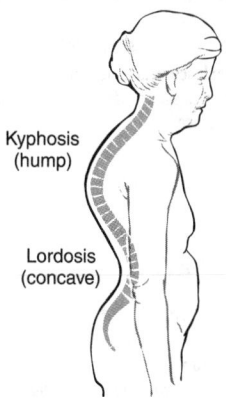

Kyphosis (hump)

Lordosis (concave)

Scoliosis and Kyphoscoliosis

Scoliosis

Kyphoscoliosis

736.72 Equinus deformity of foot, acquired
DEF: A plantar flexion deformity that forces people to walk on their toes.

736.73 Cavus deformity of foot
> **EXCLUDES** that with claw foot (736.74)

DEF: Abnormally high longitudinal arch of the foot.

736.74 Claw foot, acquired
DEF: High foot arch with hyperextended toes at metatarsophalangeal joint and flexed toes at distal joints; also called "main en griffe."

736.75 Cavovarus deformity of foot, acquired
DEF: Inward turning of the heel from the midline of the leg and an abnormally high longitudinal arch.

736.76 Other calcaneus deformity
736.79 Other
Acquired:
pes }
talipes } not elsewhere classified

✓5ᵗʰ **736.8 Acquired deformities of other parts of limbs**
736.81 Unequal leg length (acquired)
736.89 Other
Deformity (acquired):
arm or leg, not elsewhere classified
shoulder

736.9 Acquired deformity of limb, site unspecified

✓4ᵗʰ **737 Curvature of spine**
> **EXCLUDES** congenital (754.2)

737.0 Adolescent postural kyphosis
> **EXCLUDES** osteochondrosis of spine (juvenile) (732.0)
> adult (732.8)

✓5ᵗʰ **737.1 Kyphosis (acquired)**
737.10 Kyphosis (acquired) (postural)
737.11 Kyphosis due to radiation
737.12 Kyphosis, postlaminectomy
AHA: J-F, '87, 7

737.19 Other
> **EXCLUDES** that associated with conditions classifiable elsewhere (737.41)

✓5ᵗʰ **737.2 Lordosis (acquired)**
DEF: Swayback appearance created by an abnormally increased spinal curvature; it is also referred to as "hollow back" or "saddle back."

737.20 Lordosis (acquired) (postural)
737.21 Lordosis, postlaminectomy
737.22 Other postsurgical lordosis
737.29 Other
> **EXCLUDES** that associated with conditions classifiable elsewhere (737.42)

✓5ᵗʰ **737.3 Kyphoscoliosis and scoliosis**
DEF: Kyphoscoliosis: backward and lateral curvature of the spinal column; it is found in vertebral osteochondrosis.

DEF: Scoliosis: an abnormal deviation of the spine to the left or right of the midline

737.30 Scoliosis [and kyphoscoliosis], idiopathic
AHA: 3Q, '03, 19

737.31 Resolving infantile idiopathic scoliosis
737.32 Progressive infantile idiopathic scoliosis
AHA: 3Q, '02, 12

737.33 Scoliosis due to radiation
737.34 Thoracogenic scoliosis
737.39 Other
> **EXCLUDES** that associated with conditions classifiable elsewhere (737.43)
> that in kyphoscoliotic heart disease (416.1)

AHA: 2Q, '02, 16

✓5ᵗʰ **737.4 Curvature of spine associated with other conditions**
Code first associated condition as:
Charcôt-Marie-Tooth disease (356.1)
mucopolysaccharidosis (277.5)
neurofibromatosis (237.7)
osteitis deformans (731.0)
osteitis fibrosa cystica (252.01)
osteoporosis (733.00-733.09)
poliomyelitis (138)
tuberculosis [Pott's curvature] (015.0)

737.40 Curvature of spine, unspecified
737.41 Kyphosis
737.42 Lordosis
737.43 Scoliosis
737.8 Other curvatures of spine
737.9 Unspecified curvature of spine
Curvature of spine (acquired) (idiopathic) NOS
Hunchback, acquired
> **EXCLUDES** deformity of spine NOS (738.5)

✓4ᵗʰ **738 Other acquired deformity**
> **EXCLUDES** congenital (754.0-756.9, 758.0-759.9)
> dentofacial anomalies (524.0-524.9)

738.0 Acquired deformity of nose
Deformity of nose (acquired)
Overdevelopment of nasal bones
> **EXCLUDES** deflected or deviated nasal septum (470)

✓5ᵗʰ **738.1 Other acquired deformity of head**
738.10 Unspecified deformity
738.11 Zygomatic hyperplasia
DEF: Abnormal enlargement of the zygoma (processus zygomaticus temporalis).

✓4ᵗʰ / ✓5ᵗʰ Additional Digit Required | **RUG III Special Care Dx** | **RUG III Clinically Complex Dx** | Hospice Non-cancer Dx | **CD PDx** Clinical Dimension PDx | **CD SDx** Clinical Dimension SDx

2006 ICD•9•CM | Volume 1 — 205

738.12 Zygomatic hypoplasia

DEF: Underdevelopment of the zygoma (processus zygomaticus temporalis).

738.19 Other specified deformity

AHA: 2Q, '03, 13

738.2 Acquired deformity of neck

738.3 Acquired deformity of chest and rib

Deformity: Pectus:
    chest (acquired)   carinatum, acquired
    rib (acquired)   excavatum, acquired

738.4 Acquired spondylolisthesis

Degenerative spondylolisthesis
Spondylolysis, acquired
    EXCLUDES   congenital (756.12)

DEF: Vertebra displaced forward over another; due to bilateral defect in vertebral arch, eroded articular surface of posterior facts and elongated pedicle between fifth lumbar vertebra and sacrum.

738.5 Other acquired deformity of back or spine

Deformity of spine NOS
    EXCLUDES   curvature of spine (737.0-737.9)

738.6 Acquired deformity of pelvis

Pelvic obliquity
    EXCLUDES   intrapelvic protrusion of acetabulum (718.6)
    that in relation to labor and delivery (653.0-653.4, 653.8-653.9)

DEF: Pelvic obliquity: slanting or inclination of the pelvis at an angle between 55 and 60 degrees between the plane of the pelvis and the horizontal plane.

738.7 Cauliflower ear

DEF: Abnormal external ear; due to injury, subsequent perichondritis.

738.8 Acquired deformity of other specified site

Deformity of clavicle

AHA: 2Q, '01, 15

738.9 Acquired deformity of unspecified site

√4ᵗʰ **739 Nonallopathic lesions, not elsewhere classified**

    INCLUDES   segmental dysfunction
    somatic dysfunction

DEF: Disability, loss of function or abnormality of a body part that is neither classifiable to a particular system nor brought about therapeutically to counteract another disease.

739.0 Head region

Occipitocervical region

739.1 Cervical region

Cervicothoracic region

739.2 Thoracic region

Thoracolumbar region

739.3 Lumbar region

Lumbosacral region

739.4 Sacral region

Sacrococcygeal region   Sacroiliac region

739.5 Pelvic region

Hip region   Pubic region

739.6 Lower extremities

739.7 Upper extremities

Acromioclavicular region
Sternoclavicular region

739.8 Rib cage

Costochondral region   Sternochondral region
Costovertebral region

739.9 Abdomen and other

AHA: 2Q, '89, 14

14. CONGENITAL ANOMALIES (740-759)

√4ᵗʰ **740 Anencephalus and similar anomalies**

740.0   Anencephalus

Acrania   Hemicephaly
Amyelencephalus   Hemianencephaly

DEF: Fetus without cerebrum, cerebellum and flat bones of skull.

740.1   Craniorachischisis

DEF: Congenital slit in cranium and vertebral column

740.2   Iniencephaly

DEF: Spinal cord passes through enlarged occipital bone (foramen magnum); absent vertebral bone layer and spinal processes; resulting in both reduction in number and proper fusion of the vertebrae.

√4ᵗʰ **741 Spina bifida**

EXCLUDES   *spina bifida occulta (756.17)*

The following fifth-digit subclassification is for use with category 741:

   0   unspecified region
   1   cervical region
   2   dorsal [thoracic] region
   3   lumbar region

AHA: 3Q, '94, 7

DEF: Lack of closure of spinal cord's bony encasement; marked by cord protrusion into lumbosacral area; evident by elevated alpha-fetoprotein of amniotic fluid

√5ᵗʰ **741.0   With hydrocephalus**   **CD PDx**

Arnold-Chiari syndrome, type II
Any condition classifiable to 741.9 with any condition classifiable to 742.3
Chiari malformation, type II

AHA: 4Q, '97, 51; 4Q, '94, 37; S-O, '87, 10

√5ᵗʰ **741.9   Without mention of hydrocephalus**   **CD PDx**

Hydromeningocele (spinal)   Myelocystocele
Hydromyelocele   Rachischisis
Meningocele (spinal)   Spina bifida (aperta)
Meningomyelocele   Syringomyelocele
Myelocele

√4ᵗʰ **742 Other congenital anomalies of nervous system**

EXCLUDES ▶ *congenital central alveolar hypoventilation syndrome (327.25)*◀

742.0   Encephalocele   **CD PDx**

Encephalocystocele
Encephalomyelocele
Hydroencephalocele
Hydromeningocele, cranial
Meningocele, cerebral
Meningoencephalocele

AHA: 4Q, '94, 37

DEF: Brain tissue protrudes through skull defect.

Spina Bifida

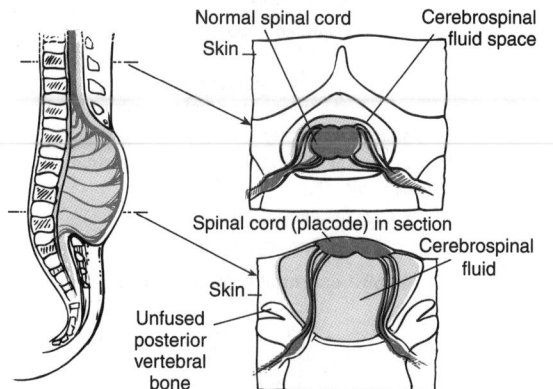

Normal spinal cord
Skin
Cerebrospinal fluid space
Spinal cord (placode) in section
Cerebrospinal fluid
Skin
Unfused posterior vertebral bone

Normal Ventricles and Hydrocephalus

Cerebrospinal fluid in ventricles
Normal Ventricles
Third ventricle (III)
Choroid plexus produces Cerebrospinal fluid (CSF)
Lateral ventricles (I and II)
Fourth ventricle (IV)
Foramen of Monro
Foramen of Luschka
Cerebral aqueduct (Sylvius)
Foramen of Magendie

Hydrocephalus

Enlarged ventricles
Blockage of any CSF passage increases pressure in skull, which may push tissue through the Incisura tentorii or through the Foramen magnum

742.1   Microcephalus   **CD PDx**

Hydromicrocephaly
Micrencephaly

DEF: Extremely small head or brain.

742.2   Reduction deformities of brain   **CD PDx**

Absence   ⎫
Agenesis   ⎬ of part of brain
Aplasia   ⎮
Hypoplasia   ⎭

Agyria   Holoprosencephaly
Arhinencephaly   Microgyria

AHA: 3Q, '03, 15; 4Q, '94, 37

742.3   Congenital hydrocephalus   **CD PDx**

Aqueduct of Sylvius:
   anomaly
   obstruction, congenital
   stenosis
Atresia of foramina of Magendie and Luschka
Hydrocephalus in newborn

EXCLUDES   *hydrocephalus:*
   acquired (331.3-331.4)
   due to congenital toxoplasmosis (771.2)
   with any condition classifiable to 741.9 (741.0)

DEF: Fluid accumulation within the skull; involves subarachnoid (external) or ventricular (internal) brain spaces.

742.4   Other specified anomalies of brain   **CD PDx**

Congenital cerebral cyst   Multiple anomalies of brain
Macroencephaly   NOS
Macrogyria   Porencephaly
Megalencephaly   Ulegyria

AHA: 1Q, '99, 9; 3Q, '92, 12

√5ᵗʰ **742.5   Other specified anomalies of spinal cord**

742.51 Diastematomyelia   **CD PDx**

DEF: Congenital anomaly often associated with spina bifida; the spinal cord is separated into halves by bony tissue resembling a "spike" (spicule), each half surrounded by a dural sac.

√4ᵗʰ √5ᵗʰ **Additional Digit Required**   **RUG III Special Care Dx**   **RUG III Clinically Complex Dx**   **Hospice Non-cancer Dx**   **CD PDx** Clinical Dimension PDx   **CD SDx** Clinical Dimension SDx

Congenital Anomalies

742.53–743.62

742.53 Hydromyelia `CD PDx`
Hydrorhachis

DEF: Dilated central spinal cord canal; characterized by increased fluid accumulation.

742.59 Other `CD PDx`
Amyelia
Atelomyelia
Congenital anomaly of spinal meninges
Defective development of cauda equina
Hypoplasia of spinal cord
Myelatelia
Myelodysplasia
AHA: 2Q, '91, 14; 1Q, '89, 10

742.8 Other specified anomalies of nervous system `CD PDx`
Agenesis of nerve
Displacement of brachial plexus
Familial dysautonomia
Jaw-winking syndrome
Marcus-Gunn syndrome
Riley-Day syndrome
EXCLUDES neurofibromatosis (237.7)

742.9 Unspecified anomaly of brain, spinal cord, and nervous system `CD PDx`
Anomaly
Congenital: } of: { brain
  disease   nervous system
  lesion   spinal cord
Deformity

✓4ᵗʰ **743 Congenital anomalies of eye**
✓5ᵗʰ **743.0 Anophthalmos**

DEF: Complete absence of the eyes or the presence of vestigial eyes.

743.00 Clinical anophthalmos, unspecified
Agenesis } of eye
Congenital absence
Anophthalmos NOS

743.03 Cystic eyeball, congenital

743.06 Cryptophthalmos
DEF: Eyelids continue over eyeball, results in apparent absence of eyelids.

✓5ᵗʰ **743.1 Microphthalmos**
Dysplasia } of eye
Hypoplasia
Rudimentary eye
DEF: Abnormally small eyeballs, may be opacities of cornea and lens, scarring of choroid and retina.

743.10 Microphthalmos, unspecified

743.11 Simple microphthalmos

743.12 Microphthalmos associated with other anomalies of eye and adnexa

✓5ᵗʰ **743.2 Buphthalmos**
Glaucoma: Hydrophthalmos
  congenital
  newborn
EXCLUDES glaucoma of childhood (365.14)
  traumatic glaucoma due to birth injury (767.8)
DEF: Distended, enlarged fibrous coats of eye; due to intraocular pressure of congenital glaucoma.

743.20 Buphthalmos, unspecified

743.21 Simple buphthalmos

743.22 Buphthalmos associated with other ocular anomalies
Keratoglobus, congenital } associated with
Megalocornea   buphthalmos

✓5ᵗʰ **743.3 Congenital cataract and lens anomalies**
EXCLUDES infantile cataract (366.00-366.09)
DEF: Opaque eye lens.

743.30 Congenital cataract, unspecified

743.31 Capsular and subcapsular cataract

743.32 Cortical and zonular cataract

743.33 Nuclear cataract

743.34 Total and subtotal cataract, congenital

743.35 Congenital aphakia
Congenital absence of lens

743.36 Anomalies of lens shape
Microphakia   Spherophakia

743.37 Congenital ectopic lens

743.39 Other

✓5ᵗʰ **743.4 Coloboma and other anomalies of anterior segment**
DEF: Coloboma: ocular tissue defect associated with defect of ocular fetal intraocular fissure; may cause small pit on optic disk, major defects of iris, ciliary body, choroid, and retina.

743.41 Anomalies of corneal size and shape
Microcornea
EXCLUDES that associated with buphthalmos (743.22)

743.42 Corneal opacities, interfering with vision, congenital

743.43 Other corneal opacities, congenital

743.44 Specified anomalies of anterior chamber, chamber angle, and related structures
Anomaly: Anomaly:
  Axenfeld's   Rieger's
  Peters'

743.45 Aniridia
AHA: 3Q, '02, 20
DEF: Incompletely formed or absent iris; affects both eyes; dominant trait; also called congenital hyperplasia of iris.

743.46 Other specified anomalies of iris and ciliary body
Anisocoria, congenital   Coloboma of iris
Atresia of pupil   Corectopia

743.47 Specified anomalies of sclera

743.48 Multiple and combined anomalies of anterior segment

743.49 Other

✓5ᵗʰ **743.5 Congenital anomalies of posterior segment**
743.51 Vitreous anomalies
Congenital vitreous opacity

743.52 Fundus coloboma
DEF: Absent retinal and choroidal tissue; occurs in lower fundus; a bright white ectatic zone of exposed sclera extends into and changes the optic disk.

743.53 Chorioretinal degeneration, congenital

743.54 Congenital folds and cysts of posterior segment

743.55 Congenital macular changes

743.56 Other retinal changes, congenital
AHA: 3Q, '99, 12

743.57 Specified anomalies of optic disc
Coloboma of optic disc (congenital)

743.58 Vascular anomalies
Congenital retinal aneurysm

743.59 Other

✓5ᵗʰ **743.6 Congenital anomalies of eyelids, lacrimal system, and orbit**
743.61 Congenital ptosis
DEF: Drooping of eyelid.

743.62 Congenital deformities of eyelids
Ablepharon   Congenital:
Absence of eyelid   ectropion
Accessory eyelid   entropion
AHA: 1Q, '00, 22

N Newborn Age: 0   P Pediatric Age: 0-17   M Maternity Age: 12-55   A Adult Age: 15-124   Manifestation Code   ◄► Revised Text   ● New Code   ▲ Revised Code Title

743.63 Other specified congenital anomalies of eyelid
Absence, agenesis, of cilia

743.64 Specified congenital anomalies of lacrimal gland

743.65 Specified congenital anomalies of lacrimal passages
Absence, agenesis of:
    lacrimal apparatus
    punctum lacrimale
    Accessory lacrimal canal

743.66 Specified congenital anomalies of orbit

743.69 Other
Accessory eye muscles

743.8 Other specified anomalies of eye
> EXCLUDES   *congenital nystagmus (379.51)*
>   *ocular albinism (270.2)*
>   *retinitis pigmentosa (362.74)*

743.9 Unspecified anomaly of eye
Congenital:
  anomaly NOS   } of eye [any part]
  deformity NOS

✓4th **744 Congenital anomalies of ear, face, and neck**
> EXCLUDES   *anomaly of:*
>   *cervical spine (754.2, 756.10-756.19)*
>   *larynx (748.2-748.3)*
>   *nose (748.0-748.1)*
>   *parathyroid gland (759.2)*
>   *thyroid gland (759.2)*
>   *cleft lip (749.10-749.25)*

✓5th **744.0 Anomalies of ear causing impairment of hearing**
> EXCLUDES   *congenital deafness without mention of*
>   *cause (389.0-389.9)*

744.00 Unspecified anomaly of ear with impairment of hearing

744.01 Absence of external ear
Absence of:
  auditory canal (external)
  auricle (ear) (with stenosis or atresia of auditory canal)

744.02 Other anomalies of external ear with impairment of hearing
Atresia or stricture of auditory canal (external)

744.03 Anomaly of middle ear, except ossicles
Atresia or stricture of osseous meatus (ear)

744.04 Anomalies of ear ossicles
Fusion of ear ossicles

744.05 Anomalies of inner ear
Congenital anomaly of:
  membranous labyrinth
  organ of Corti

744.09 Other
Absence of ear, congenital

744.1 Accessory auricle
Accessory tragus   Supernumerary:
Polyotia   ear
Preauricular appendage   lobule

DEF: Redundant tissue or structures of ear.

✓5th **744.2 Other specified anomalies of ear**
> EXCLUDES   *that with impairment of hearing*
>   *(744.00-744.09)*

744.21 Absence of ear lobe, congenital

744.22 Macrotia
DEF: Abnormally large pinna of ear.

744.23 Microtia
DEF: Hypoplasia of pinna; associated with absent or closed auditory canal.

744.24 Specified anomalies of Eustachian tube
Absence of Eustachian tube

744.29 Other
Bat ear   Prominence of auricle
Darwin's tubercle   Ridge ear
Pointed ear
> EXCLUDES   *preauricular sinus (744.46)*

744.3 Unspecified anomaly of ear
Congenital:
  anomaly NOS   } of ear, not elsewhere
  deformity NOS   classified

✓5th **744.4 Branchial cleft cyst or fistula; preauricular sinus**
744.41 Branchial cleft sinus or fistula
Branchial:
  sinus (external) (internal)
  vestige

DEF: Cyst due to failed closure of embryonic branchial cleft.

744.42 Branchial cleft cyst

744.43 Cervical auricle

744.46 Preauricular sinus or fistula

744.47 Preauricular cyst

744.49 Other
Fistula (of):   Fistula (of):
  auricle, congenital   cervicoaural

744.5 Webbing of neck
Pterygium colli

DEF: Thick, triangular skinfold, stretches from lateral side of neck across shoulder; associated with Turner's and Noonan's syndromes.

✓5th **744.8 Other specified anomalies of face and neck**
744.81 Macrocheilia
Hypertrophy of lip, congenital
DEF: Abnormally large lips.

744.82 Microcheilia
DEF: Abnormally small lips.

744.83 Macrostomia
DEF: Bilateral or unilateral anomaly, of mouth due to malformed maxillary and mandibular processes; results in mouth extending toward ear.

744.84 Microstomia
DEF: Abnormally small mouth.

744.89 Other
> EXCLUDES   *congenital fistula of lip*
>   *(750.25)*
>   *musculoskeletal anomalies*
>   *(754.0-754.1, 756.0)*

744.9 Unspecified anomalies of face and neck
Congenital:
  anomaly NOS   } of face [any part] or
  deformity NOS   neck [any part]

✓4th **745 Bulbus cordis anomalies and anomalies of cardiac septal closure**
745.0 Common truncus
Absent septum   } between aorta and
Communication (abnormal) }   pulmonary artery

Aortic septal defect
Common aortopulmonary trunk
Persistent truncus arteriosus

✓5th **745.1 Transposition of great vessels**
745.10 Complete transposition of great vessels
Transposition of great vessels:
  NOS
  classical

✓4th
✓5th   Additional Digit Required   RUG III Special Care Dx   RUG III Clinically Complex Dx   Hospice Non-cancer Dx   CD PDx Clinical Dimension PDx   CD SDx Clinical Dimension SDx

2006 ICD•9•CM   **Volume 1 — 209**

Heart Defects

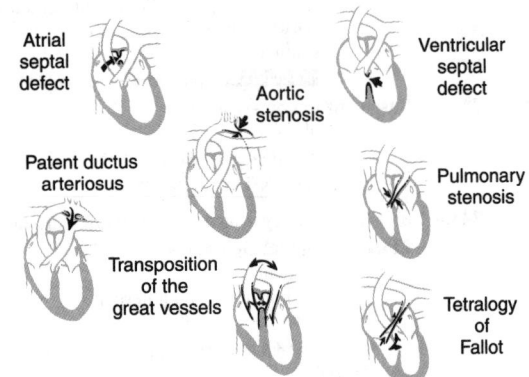

Atrial septal defect

Ventricular septal defect

Aortic stenosis

Patent ductus arteriosus

Pulmonary stenosis

Transposition of the great vessels

Tetralogy of Fallot

745.11 Double outlet right ventricle
Dextratransposition of aorta
Incomplete transposition of great vessels
Origin of both great vessels from right ventricle
Taussig-Bing syndrome or defect

745.12 Corrected transposition of great vessels

745.19 Other

745.2 Tetralogy of Fallot
Fallot's pentalogy
Ventricular septal defect with pulmonary stenosis or atresia, dextraposition of aorta, and hypertrophy of right ventricle
EXCLUDES *Fallot's triad (746.09)*

DEF: Obstructed cardiac outflow causes pulmonary stenosis, interventricular septal defect and right ventricular hypertrophy.

745.3 Common ventricle
Cor triloculare biatriatum
Single ventricle

745.4 Ventricular septal defect
Eisenmenger's defect or complex
Gerbo dedefect
Interventricular septal defect
Left ventricular-right atrial communication
Roger's disease
EXCLUDES *common atrioventricular canal type (745.69)*
single ventricle (745.3)

745.5 Ostium secundum type atrial septal defect
Defect: Patent or persistent:
 atrium secundum   foramen ovale
 fossa ovalis   ostium secundum
Lutembacher's syndrome

DEF: Opening in atrial septum due to failure of the septum secundum and the endocardial cushions to fuse; there is a rim of septum surrounding the defect.

✓5ᵗʰ **745.6 Endocardial cushion defects**
DEF: Atrial and/or ventricular septa defects causing abnormal fusion of cushions in atrioventricular canal.

745.60 Endocardial cushion defect, unspecified type
DEF: Septal defect due to imperfect fusion of endocardial cushions.

745.61 Ostium primum defect
Persistent ostium primum

DEF: Opening in low, posterior septum primum; causes cleft in basal portion of atrial septum; associated with cleft mitral valve.

745.69 Other
Absence of atrial septum
Atrioventricular canal type ventricular septal defect
Common atrioventricular canal
Common atrium

745.7 Cor biloculare
Absence of atrial and ventricular septa

DEF: Atrial and ventricular septal defect; marked by heart with two cardiac chambers (one atrium, one ventricle), and one atrioventricular valve.

745.8 Other

745.9 Unspecified defect of septal closure
Septal defect NOS

✓4ᵗʰ **746 Other congenital anomalies of heart**
EXCLUDES *endocardial fibroelastosis (425.3)*

✓5ᵗʰ **746.0 Anomalies of pulmonary valve**
EXCLUDES *infundibular or subvalvular pulmonic stenosis (746.83)*
tetralogy of Fallot (745.2)

746.00 Pulmonary valve anomaly, unspecified

746.01 Atresia, congenital
Congenital absence of pulmonary valve

746.02 Stenosis, congenital
AHA: 1Q, '04, 16

DEF: Stenosis of opening between pulmonary artery and right ventricle; causes obstructed blood outflow from right ventricle.

746.09 Other
Congenital insufficiency of pulmonary valve
Fallot's triad or trilogy

746.1 Tricuspid atresia and stenosis, congenital
Absence of tricuspid valve

746.2 Ebstein's anomaly
DEF: Malformation of the tricuspid valve characterized by septal and posterior leaflets attaching to the wall of the right ventricle; causing the right ventricle to fuse with the atrium producing a large right atrium and a small ventricle; causes a malfunction of the right ventricle with accompanying complications such as heart failure and abnormal cardiac rhythm.

746.3 Congenital stenosis of aortic valve
Congenital aortic stenosis
EXCLUDES *congenital:*
subaortic stenosis (746.81)
supravalvular aortic stenosis (747.22)

AHA: 4Q, '88, 8

DEF: Stenosis of orifice of aortic valve; obstructs blood outflow from left ventricle.

746.4 Congenital insufficiency of aortic valve
Bicuspid aortic valve
Congenital aortic insufficiency

DEF: Impaired functioning of aortic valve due to incomplete closure; causes backflow (regurgitation) of blood from aorta to left ventricle.

746.5 Congenital mitral stenosis
Fused commissure   ⎫
Parachute deformity ⎬ of mitral valve
Supernumerary cusps ⎭

DEF: Stenosis of left atrioventricular orifice.

746.6 Congenital mitral insufficiency
DEF: Impaired functioning of mitral valve due to incomplete closure; causes backflow of blood from left ventricle to left atrium.

746.7 Hypoplastic left heart syndrome
Atresia, or marked hypoplasia, of aortic orifice or valve, with hypoplasia of ascending aorta and defective development of left ventricle (with mitral valve atresia)

✓5ᵗʰ **746.8 Other specified anomalies of heart**
746.81 Subaortic stenosis
DEF: Stenosis, of left ventricular outflow tract due to fibrous tissue ring or septal hypertrophy below aortic valve.

Ⓝ Newborn Age: 0   Ⓟ Pediatric Age: 0-17   Ⓜ Maternity Age: 12-55   Ⓐ Adult Age: 15-124   ▮Manifestation Code▮   ►◄ Revised Text   ● New Code   ▲ Revised Code Title

746.82 Cor triatriatum

DEF: Transverse septum divides left atrium due to failed resorption of embryonic common pulmonary vein; results in three atrial chambers.

746.83 Infundibular pulmonic stenosis

Subvalvular pulmonic stenosis

DEF: Stenosis of right ventricle outflow tract within infundibulum due to fibrous diaphragm below valve or long, narrow fibromuscular channel.

746.84 Obstructive anomalies of heart, not elsewhere classified

Uhl's disease

746.85 Coronary artery anomaly

Anomalous origin or communication of coronary artery
Arteriovenous malformation of coronary artery
Coronary artery:
　absence
　arising from aorta or pulmonary trunk
　single

AHA: N-D, '85, 3

746.86 Congenital heart block

Complete or incomplete atrioventricular [AV] block

DEF: Impaired conduction of electrical impulses; due to maldeveloped junctional tissue.

746.87 Malposition of heart and cardiac apex

Abdominal heart　　Levocardia (isolated)
Dextrocardia　　　Mesocardia
Ectopia cordis

EXCLUDES　dextrocardia with complete transposition of viscera (759.3)

746.89 Other

Atresia
Hypoplasia } of cardiac vein

Congenital:　　　Congenital:
　cardiomegaly　　pericardial defect
　diverticulum, left ventricle

AHA: 3Q, '00, 3; 1Q, '99, 11; J-F, '85, 3

746.9 Unspecified anomaly of heart

Congenital:
　anomaly of heart NOS
　heart disease NOS

√4ᵗʰ 747 Other congenital anomalies of circulatory system

747.0 Patent ductus arteriosus

Patent ductus Botalli
Persistent ductus arteriosus

DEF: Open lumen in ductus arteriosus causes arterial blood recirculation in lungs; inhibits blood supply to aorta; symptoms such as shortness of breath more noticeable upon activity.

√5ᵗʰ 747.1 Coarctation of aorta

DEF: Localized deformity of aortic media seen as a severe constriction of the vessel lumen; major symptom is high blood pressure in the arms and low pressure in the legs; a CVA, rupture of the aorta, bacterial endocarditis or congestive heart failure can follow if left untreated.

747.10 Coarctation of aorta (preductal) (postductal)

Hypoplasia of aortic arch

AHA: 1Q, '99, 11; 4Q, '88, 8

747.11 Interruption of aortic arch

√5ᵗʰ 747.2 Other anomalies of aorta

747.20 Anomaly of aorta, unspecified

747.21 Anomalies of aortic arch

Anomalous origin, right subclavian artery
Dextraposition of aorta
Double aortic arch
Kommerell's diverticulum
Overriding aorta
Persistent:
　convolutions, aortic arch
　right aortic arch
Vascular ring

EXCLUDES　hypoplasia of aortic arch (747.10)

AHA: 1Q, '03, 15

747.22 Atresia and stenosis of aorta

Absence
Aplasia
Hypoplasia } of aorta
Stricture

Supra (valvular)-aortic stenosis

EXCLUDES　congenital aortic (valvular) stenosis or stricture, so stated (746.3)
　hypoplasia of aorta in hypoplastic left heart syndrome (746.7)

747.29 Other

Aneurysm of sinus of Valsalva
Congenital:
　aneurysm
　dilation } of aorta

747.3 Anomalies of pulmonary artery

Agenesis
Anomaly
Atresia
Coarctation } of pulmonary artery
Hypoplasia
Stenosis

Pulmonary arteriovenous aneurysm

AHA: 1Q, '04, 16; 1Q, '94, 15; 4Q, '88, 8

√5ᵗʰ 747.4 Anomalies of great veins

747.40 Anomaly of great veins, unspecified

Anomaly NOS of:　　Anomaly NOS of:
　pulmonary veins　　vena cava

747.41 Total anomalous pulmonary venous connection

Total anomalous pulmonary venous return [TAPVR]:
　subdiaphragmatic
　supradiaphragmatic

747.42 Partial anomalous pulmonary venous connection

Partial anomalous pulmonary venous return

747.49 Other anomalies of great veins

Absence
Congenital stenosis } of vena cava (inferior) (superior)

Persistent:
　left posterior cardinal vein
　left superior vena cava
Scimitar syndrome
Transposition of pulmonary veins NOS

747.5 Absence or hypoplasia of umbilical artery

Single umbilical artery

√4ᵗʰ
√5ᵗʰ Additional Digit Required　　**RUG III Special Care Dx**　　　**RUG III Clinically Complex Dx**　　　**Hospice Non-cancer Dx**　　　**CD PDx** Clinical Dimension PDx　　**CD SDx** Clinical Dimension SDx

2006 ICD•9•CM　　　**Volume 1 — 211**

Congenital Anomalies

747.6–748.9

√5th **747.6 Other anomalies of peripheral vascular system**

Absence
Anomaly } of artery or vein, NEC
Atresia

Arteriovenous aneurysm (peripheral)
Arteriovenous malformation of the peripheral
     vascular system
Congenital:
     aneurysm (peripheral)   stricture, artery
     phlebectasia   varix
Multiple renal arteries

EXCLUDES *anomalies of:*
     cerebral vessels (747.81)
     pulmonary artery (747.3)
     congenital retinal aneurysm (743.58)
     hemangioma (228.00-228.09)
     lymphangioma (228.1)

**747.60 Anomaly of the peripheral vascular system,
unspecified site**

747.61 Gastrointestinal vessel anomaly

AHA: 3Q '96, 10

747.62 Renal vessel anomaly

747.63 Upper limb vessel anomaly

747.64 Lower limb vessel anomaly

**747.69 Anomalies of other specified sites of
peripheral vascular system**

√5th **747.8 Other specified anomalies of circulatory system**

747.81 Anomalies of cerebrovascular system
Arteriovenous malformation of brain
Cerebral arteriovenous aneurysm,
     congenital
Congenital anomalies of cerebral vessels

EXCLUDES *ruptured cerebral
     (arteriovenous)
     aneurysm (430)*

747.82 Spinal vessel anomaly
Arteriovenous malformation of spinal vessel

AHA: 3Q, '95, 5

747.83 Persistent fetal circulation   N
Persistent pulmonary hypertension
Primary pulmonary hypertension of
     newborn

AHA: 4Q, '02, 62

DEF: A return to fetal-type circulation due to constriction
of pulmonary arterioles and opening of the ductus
arteriosus and foramen ovale, right-to-left shunting
occurs, oxygenation of the blood does not occur, and the
lungs remain constricted after birth; PFC is seen in term
or post-term infants causes include asphyxiation,
meconium aspiration syndrome, acidosis, sepsis, and
developmental immaturity.

747.89 Other
Aneurysm, congenital, specified site not
     elsewhere classified

EXCLUDES *congenital aneurysm:
     coronary (746.85)
     peripheral (747.6)
     pulmonary (747.3)
     retinal (743.58)*

AHA: 4Q, '02, 63

747.9 Unspecified anomaly of circulatory system

√4th **748 Congenital anomalies of respiratory system**

EXCLUDES ► *congenital central alveolar hypoventilation
     syndrome (327.25)* ◄
     congenital defect of diaphragm (756.6)

748.0 Choanal atresia

Atresia   } of nares (anterior)
Congenital stenosis }   (posterior)

DEF: Occluded posterior nares (choana), bony or membranous due
to failure of embryonic bucconasal membrane to rupture.

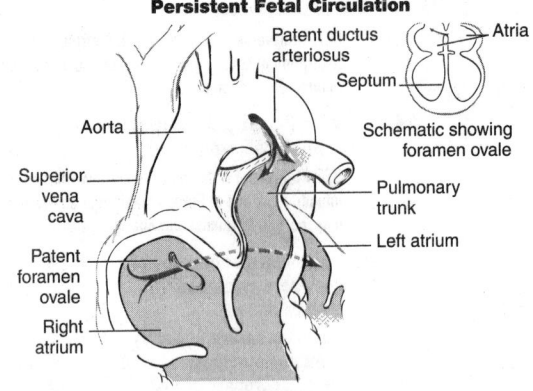

Persistent Fetal Circulation

Patent ductus arteriosus — Atria

Septum

Schematic showing
foramen ovale

Aorta

Superior
vena
cava

Pulmonary
trunk

Patent
foramen
ovale

Left atrium

Right
atrium

748.1 Other anomalies of nose
Absent nose   Congenital:
Accessory nose   notching of tip of nose
Cleft nose   perforation of wall of
Congenital: nasal sinus
   deformity of nose   Deformity of wall of nasal sinus

EXCLUDES *congenital deviation of nasal septum
     (754.0)*

748.2 Web of larynx
Web of larynx: Web of larynx:
   NOS   subglottic
   glottic

DEF: Malformed larynx; marked by thin, translucent, or thick,
fibrotic spread between vocal folds; affects speech.

748.3 Other anomalies of larynx, trachea, and bronchus
Absence or agenesis of: Congenital:
   bronchus   dilation, trachea
   larynx   stenosis:
   trachea   larynx
Anomaly(of):   trachea
   cricoid cartilage   tracheocele
   epiglottis   Diverticulum:
   thyroid cartilage   bronchus
   tracheal cartilage   trachea
Atresia (of):   Fissure of epiglottis
   epiglottis   Laryngocele
   glottis   Posterior cleft of cricoid
   larynx   cartilage (congenital)
   trachea   Rudimentary tracheal
Cleft thyroid, cartilage,   bronchus
   congenital   Stridor, laryngeal, congenital

AHA: 1Q, '99, 14

748.4 Congenital cystic lung
Disease, lung: Honeycomb lung, congenital
   cystic, congenital
   polycystic, congenital

EXCLUDES *acquired or unspecified cystic lung
     (518.89)*

DEF: Enlarged air spaces of lung parenchyma.

748.5 Agenesis, hypoplasia, and dysplasia of lung
Absence of lung (fissures) (lobe)
   (lobe)   Hypoplasia of lung
Aplasia of lung   Sequestration of lung

√5th **748.6 Other anomalies of lung**

748.60 Anomaly of lung, unspecified

748.61 Congenital bronchiectasis

748.69 Other
Accessory lung (lobe)
Azygos lobe (fissure), lung

748.8 Other specified anomalies of respiratory system
Abnormal communication between pericardial and
     pleural sacs
Anomaly, pleural folds
Atresia of nasopharynx
Congenital cyst of mediastinum

748.9 Unspecified anomaly of respiratory system
Anomaly of respiratory system NOS

N Newborn Age: 0   P Pediatric Age: 0-17   M Maternity Age: 12-55   A Adult Age: 15-124   Manifestation Code   ►◄ Revised Text   ● New Code   ▲ Revised Code Title

Cleft Lip and Palate

Unilateral cleft lip

No cleft palate

Cleft lip with cleft alveolar ridge

No cleft palate

Unilateral cleft lip and cleft palate

Alveolar ridge

Cleft palate

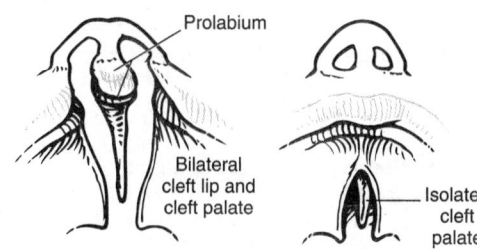

Prolabium

Bilateral cleft lip and cleft palate

Isolated cleft palate

☑4ᵗʰ **749 Cleft palate and cleft lip**

☑5ᵗʰ **749.0 Cleft palate**

749.00 Cleft palate, unspecified

749.01 Unilateral, complete

749.02 Unilateral, incomplete
Cleft uvula

749.03 Bilateral, complete

749.04 Bilateral, incomplete

☑5ᵗʰ **749.1 Cleft lip**
Cheiloschisis   Harelip
Congenital fissure of lip   Labium leporinum

749.10 Cleft lip, unspecified

749.11 Unilateral, complete

749.12 Unilateral, incomplete

749.13 Bilateral, complete

749.14 Bilateral, incomplete

☑5ᵗʰ **749.2 Cleft palate with cleft lip**
Cheilopalatoschisis

749.20 Cleft palate with cleft lip, unspecified

749.21 Unilateral, complete

749.22 Unilateral, incomplete

749.23 Bilateral, complete
AHA: 1Q, '96, 14

749.24 Bilateral, incomplete

749.25 Other combinations

☑4ᵗʰ **750 Other congenital anomalies of upper alimentary tract**
EXCLUDES   dentofacial anomalies (524.0-524.9)

750.0 Tongue tie
Ankyloglossia
DEF: Restricted tongue movement due to lingual frenum extending toward tip of tongue. Tongue may be fused to mouth floor affecting speech.

☑5ᵗʰ **750.1 Other anomalies of tongue**

750.10 Anomaly of tongue, unspecified

750.11 Aglossia
DEF: Absence of tongue.

750.12 Congenital adhesions of tongue

750.13 Fissure of tongue
Bifid tongue   Double tongue

750.15 Macroglossia
Congenital hypertrophy of tongue

750.16 Microglossia
Hypoplasia of tongue

750.19 Other

☑5ᵗʰ **750.2 Other specified anomalies of mouth and pharynx**

750.21 Absence of salivary gland

750.22 Accessory salivary gland

750.23 Atresia, salivary duct
Imperforate salivary duct

750.24 Congenital fistula of salivary gland

750.25 Congenital fistula of lip
Congenital (mucus) lip pits

750.26 Other specified anomalies of mouth
Absence of uvula

750.27 Diverticulum of pharynx
Pharyngeal pouch

750.29 Other specified anomalies of pharynx
Imperforate pharynx

750.3 Tracheoesophageal fistula, esophageal atresia and stenosis
Absent esophagus   Congenital fistula:
Atresia of esophagus   esophagobronchial
Congenital: esophagotracheal
 esophageal ring   Imperforate esophagus
 stenosis of esophagus   Webbed esophagus
 stricture of esophagus

750.4 Other specified anomalies of esophagus
Dilatation, congenital
Displacement, congenital
Diverticulum   } (of) esophagus
Duplication
Giant
Esophageal pouch
EXCLUDES   congenital hiatus hernia (750.6)
AHA: J-F, '85, 3

750.5 Congenital hypertrophic pyloric stenosis
Congenital or infantile:
 constriction
 hypertrophy
 spasm   } of pylorus
 stenosis
 stricture

DEF: Obstructed pylorus due to overgrowth of pyloric muscle.

750.6 Congenital hiatus hernia
Displacement of cardia through esophageal hiatus
EXCLUDES   congenital diaphragmatic hernia (756.6)

750.7 Other specified anomalies of stomach
Congenital:
 cardiospasm
 hourglass stomach
Displacement of stomach
Diverticulum of stomach, congenital
Duplication of stomach
Megalogastria
Microgastria
Transposition of stomach

750.8 Other specified anomalies of upper alimentary tract

750.9 Unspecified anomaly of upper alimentary tract
Congenital:
 anomaly NOS   } of upper alimentary tract [any
 deformity NOS }   part, except tongue]

☑4ᵗʰ **751 Other congenital anomalies of digestive system**

751.0 Meckel's diverticulum
Meckel's diverticulum (displaced) (hypertrophic)
Persistent:
 omphalomesenteric duct
 vitelline duct
AHA: 1Q, '04, 10

DEF: Malformed sacs or appendages of ileum of small intestine; can cause strangulation, volvulus and intussusception.

☑4ᵗʰ
☑5ᵗʰ Additional Digit Required   RUG III Special Care Dx   RUG III Clinically Complex Dx   Hospice Non-cancer Dx   **CD PDx** Clinical Dimension PDx   **CD SDx** Clinical Dimension SDx

2006 ICD•9•CM   **Volume 1 — 213**

Congenital Anomalies

751.1 **Atresia and stenosis of small intestine** [P]

Atresia of: Atresia of:
  duodenum   intestine NOS
  ileum
Congenital:
  absence
  obstruction   } of small intestine or
  stenosis   intestine NOS
  stricture

Imperforate jejunum

751.2 **Atresia and stenosis of large intestine, rectum, and anal canal** [P]

Absence: Congenital or infantile:
  anus (congenital)   obstruction of large
  appendix, congenital   intestine
  large intestine, congenital occlusion of anus
  rectum   stricture of anus
Atresia of: Imperforate:
  anus   anus
  colon   rectum
  rectum   Stricture of rectum,
             congenital

AHA: 2Q, '98, 16

751.3 **Hirschsprung's disease and other congenital functional disorders of colon**

Aganglionosis   Congenital megacolon
Congenital dilation of colon Macrocolon

DEF: Hirschsprung's disease: enlarged or dilated colon (megacolon), with absence of ganglion cells in the narrowed wall distally; causes inability to defecate.

751.4 **Anomalies of intestinal fixation**

Congenital adhesions: Rotation of cecum or colon:
  omental, anomalous   failure of
  peritoneal   incomplete
  Jackson's membrane   insufficient
  Malrotation of colon   Universal mesentery

751.5 **Other anomalies of intestine**

Congenital diverticulum, colon Megaloappendix
Dolichocolon   Megaloduodenum
Duplication of: Microcolon
  anus   Persistent cloaca
  appendix   Transposition of:
  cecum   appendix
  intestine   colon
Ectopic anus   intestine

AHA: 3Q, '02, 11; 3Q, '01, 8

√5th **751.6** **Anomalies of gallbladder, bile ducts, and liver**

  751.60 **Unspecified anomaly of gallbladder, bile ducts, and liver**

  751.61 **Biliary atresia** [P]

Congenital:
  absence
  hypoplasia } of bile duct (common)
  obstruction   or passage
  stricture

AHA: S-O, '87, 8

  751.62 **Congenital cystic disease of liver**

Congenital polycystic disease of liver
Fibrocystic disease of liver

  751.69 **Other anomalies of gallbladder, bile ducts, and liver**

Absence of: Duplication of:
  gallbladder, congenital biliary duct
  liver (lobe)   cystic duct
Accessory: gallbladder
  hepatic ducts   liver
  liver   Floating:
Congenital: gallbladder
  choledochal cyst   liver
  hepatomegaly   Intrahepatic
            gallbladder

AHA: S-O, '87, 8

751.7 **Anomalies of pancreas**

Absence
Accessory
Agenesis } (of) pancreas
Annular
Hypoplasia

Ectopic pancreatic tissue   Pancreatic heterotopia

EXCLUDES *diabetes mellitus:*
    congenital (250.0-250.9)
    neonatal (775.1)
  fibrocystic disease of pancreas
    (277.00-277.09)

751.8 **Other specified anomalies of digestive system**

Absence (complete) (partial) of alimentary tract NOS
Duplication
Malposition, congenital } of digestive organs NOS

EXCLUDES *congenital diaphragmatic hernia (756.6)*
  congenital hiatus hernia (750.6)

751.9 **Unspecified anomaly of digestive system**

Congenital:
  anomaly NOS } of digestive system NOS
  deformity NOS

√4th **752 Congenital anomalies of genital organs**

EXCLUDES *syndromes associated with anomalies in the number and form of chromosomes (758.0-758.9)*
  testicular feminization syndrome ▶*(259.5)*◄

752.0 **Anomalies of ovaries** ♀

Absence, congenital
Accessory   } (of) ovary
Ectopic
Streak

√5th **752.1** **Anomalies of fallopian tubes and broad ligaments**

  752.10 **Unspecified anomaly of fallopian tubes and broad ligaments** ♀

  752.11 **Embryonic cyst of fallopian tubes and broad ligaments** ♀

Cyst: Cyst:
  epoophoron   parovarian
  fimbrial

AHA: S-O, '85, 13

  752.19 **Other** ♀

Absence
Accessory } (of) fallopian tube or
Atresia   broad ligament

752.2 **Doubling of uterus** ♀

Didelphic uterus
Doubling of uterus [any degree] (associated with doubling of cervix and vagina)

752.3 **Other anomalies of uterus** ♀

Absence, congenital
Agenesis   } (of) uterus
Aplasia
Bicornuate

Uterus unicornis
Uterus with only one functioning horn

√5th **752.4** **Anomalies of cervix, vagina, and external female genitalia**

  752.40 **Unspecified anomaly of cervix, vagina, and external female genitalia** ♀

  752.41 **Embryonic cyst of cervix, vagina, and external female genitalia** ♀

Cyst of:
  canal of Nuck, congenital
  ▶Gartner's duct◄
  vagina, embryonal
  vulva, congenital

DEF: Embryonic fluid-filled cysts, of cervix, vagina or external female genitalia.

  752.42 **Imperforate hymen** ♀

DEF: Complete closure of membranous fold around external opening of vagina.

[N] Newborn Age: 0 [P] Pediatric Age: 0-17 [M] Maternity Age: 12-55 [A] Adult Age: 15-124 Manifestation Code ▶◄ Revised Text ● New Code ▲ Revised Code Title

752.49 Other anomalies of cervix, vagina, and external female genitalia ♀

Absence } of cervix, clitoris,
Agenesis }   vagina, or vulva

Congenital stenosis or stricture of:
  cervical canal
  vagina

EXCLUDES *double vagina associated with total duplication (752.2)*

✓5th **752.5 Undescended and retractile testicle**
AHA: 4Q, '96, 33

752.51 Undescended testis ♂
Cryptorchism   Ectopic testis

752.52 Retractile testis ♂

✓5th **752.6 Hypospadias and epispadias and other penile anomalies**
AHA: 4Q, '96, 34, 35

752.61 Hypospadias ♂
AHA: 4Q, '03, 67-68; 3Q, '97, 6

DEF: Abnormal opening of urethra on the ventral surface of the penis or perineum; also a rare defect of vagina.

752.62 Epispadias ♂
Anaspadias

DEF: Urethra opening on dorsal surface of penis; in females appears as a slit in the upper wall of urethra.

752.63 Congenital chordee ♂
DEF: Ventral bowing of penis due to fibrous band along corpus spongiosum; occurs with hypospadias.

752.64 Micropenis ♂
752.65 Hidden penis ♂
752.69 Other penile anomalies ♂

752.7 Indeterminate sex and pseudohermaphroditism
Gynandrism   Pseudohermaphroditism
Hermaphroditism   (male) (female)
Ovotestis   Pure gonadal dysgenesis

EXCLUDES *pseudohermaphroditism:*
female, with adrenocortical disorder (255.2)
male, with gonadal disorder (257.8)
with specified chromosomal anomaly (758.0-758.9)
testicular feminization syndrome ▶(259.5)◀

DEF: Pseudohermaphroditism: presence of gonads of one sex and external genitalia of other sex.

✓5th **752.8 Other specified anomalies of genital organs**
EXCLUDES *congenital hydrocele (778.6)*
penile anomalies (752.61-752.69)
phimosis or paraphimosis (605)

752.81 Scrotal transposition ♂
AHA: 4Q, '03, 67-68

752.89 Other specified anomalies of genital organs
Absence of: Fusion of testes
  prostate   Hypoplasia of testis
  spermatic cord   Monorchism
  vas deferens   Polyorchism
Anorchism
Aplasia (congenital) of:
  prostate
  round ligament
  testicle
Atresia of:
  ejaculatory duct
  vas deferens

752.9 Unspecified anomaly of genital organs
Congenital:
  anomaly NOS } of genital organ,
  deformity NOS }   not elsewhere classified

Hypospadias and Epispadias

Glans penis
Glandular hypospadias
Penile hypospadias
Scrotal hypospadias
Penile raphe
Scrotum
Scrotal raphe

Normal external urethral orifice
Glans penis
Foreskin (retracted)
Epispadias

Hypospadias (ventral view)
Epispadias (dorsal view)

✓4th **753 Congenital anomalies of urinary system**
753.0 Renal agenesis and dysgenesis
Atrophy of kidney:
  congenital   Congenital absence of kidney(s)
  infantile   Hypoplasia of kidney(s)

✓5th **753.1 Cystic kidney disease**
EXCLUDES *acquired cyst of kidney (593.2)*
AHA: 4Q, '90. 3

753.10 Cystic kidney disease, unspecified
753.11 Congenital single renal cyst
753.12 Polycystic kidney, unspecified type
753.13 Polycystic kidney, autosomal dominant
DEF: Slow progressive disease characterized by bilateral cysts causing increased kidney size and impaired function.

753.14 Polycystic kidney, autosomal recessive
DEF: Rare disease characterized by multiple cysts involving kidneys and liver, producing renal and hepatic failure in childhood or adolescence.

753.15 Renal dysplasia
753.16 Medullary cystic kidney
Nephronopthisis
DEF: Diffuse kidney disease results in uremia onset prior to age 20.

753.17 Medullary sponge kidney
DEF: Dilated collecting tubules; usually asymptomatic but calcinosis in tubules may cause renal insufficiency.

753.19 Other specified cystic kidney disease
Multicystic kidney

✓5th **753.2 Obstructive defects of renal pelvis and ureter**
AHA: 4Q, '96, 35

753.20 Unspecified obstructive defect of renal pelvis and ureter
753.21 Congenital obstruction of ureteropelvic junction
DEF: Stricture at junction of ureter and renal pelvis.

753.22 Congenital obstruction of ureterovesical junction
Adynamic ureter   Congenital hydroureter
DEF: Stricture at junction of ureter and bladder.

753.23 Congenital ureterocele
753.29 Other
753.3 Other specified anomalies of kidney
Accessory kidney   Fusion of kidneys
Congenital: Giant kidney
  calculus of kidney   Horseshoe kidney
  displaced kidney   Hyperplasia of kidney
Discoid kidney   Lobulation of kidney
Double kidney with   Malrotation of kidney
  double pelvis   Trifid kidney (pelvis)
Ectopic kidney

✓4th ✓5th Additional Digit Required   RUG III Special Care Dx   RUG III Clinically Complex Dx   Hospice Non-cancer Dx   **CD PDx** Clinical Dimension PDx   **CD SDx** Clinical Dimension SDx

2006 ICD•9•CM   October 2005 • Volume 1 — 215

Congenital Anomalies

753.4–755.02

753.4   **Other specified anomalies of ureter**
Absent ureter   Double ureter
Accessory ureter   Ectopic ureter
Deviation of ureter   Implantation, anomalous
Displaced ureteric
    orifice of ureter

753.5   **Exstrophy of urinary bladder**
Ectopia vesicae   Extroversion of bladder
DEF: Absence of lower abdominal and anterior bladder walls with posterior bladder wall protrusion.

753.6   **Atresia and stenosis of urethra and bladder neck**
Congenital obstruction: Imperforate urinary
   bladder neck   meatus
   urethra   Impervious urethra
Congenital stricture of: Urethral valve formation
   urethra (valvular)
   urinary meatus
   vesicourethral orifice

753.7   **Anomalies of urachus**
Cyst
Fistula } (of) urachussinus
Patent
Persistent umbilical sinus

753.8   **Other specified anomalies of bladder and urethra**
Absence, congenital of: Congenital urethrorectal
   bladder   fistula
   urethra   Congenital prolapse of:
Accessory: bladder (mucosa)
   bladder   urethra
   urethra   Double:
Congenital: urethra
   diverticulum of bladder   urinary meatus
   hernia of bladder

753.9   **Unspecified anomaly of urinary system**
Congenital:
   anomaly NOS } of urinary system [any part,
   deformity NOS   except urachus]

√4ᵗʰ **754**   **Certain congenital musculoskeletal deformities**
INCLUDES   nonteratogenic deformities which are
          considered to be due to intrauterine
          malposition and pressure

754.0   **Of skull, face, and jaw**
Asymmetry of face   Dolichocephaly
Compression facies   Plagiocephaly
Depressions in skull   Potter's facies
Deviation of nasal   Squashed or bent nose,
   septum, congenital   congenital
EXCLUDES   *dentofacial anomalies (524.0-524.9)*
          syphilitic saddle nose (090.5)

754.1   **Of sternocleidomastoid muscle**
Congenital sternomastoid torticollis
Congenital wryneck
Contracture of sternocleidomastoid (muscle)
Sternomastoid tumor

754.2   **Of spine**
Congenital postural: Congenital postural:
   lordosis   scoliosis

√5ᵗʰ **754.3**   **Congenital dislocation of hip**
754.30   **Congenital dislocation of hip, unilateral**
Congenital dislocation of hip NOS
754.31   **Congenital dislocation of hip, bilateral**
754.32   **Congenital subluxation of hip, unilateral**
Congenital flexion deformity, hip or thigh
Predislocation status of hip at birth
Preluxation of hip, congenital
754.33   **Congenital subluxation of hip, bilateral**
754.35   **Congenital dislocation of one hip with subluxation of other hip**

√5ᵗʰ **754.4**   **Congenital genu recurvatum and bowing of long bones of leg**
754.40   **Genu recurvatum**
DEF: Backward curving of knee joint.

754.41   **Congenital dislocation of knee (with genu recurvatum)**
754.42   **Congenital bowing of femur**
754.43   **Congenital bowing of tibia and fibula**
754.44   **Congenital bowing of unspecified long bones of leg**

√5ᵗʰ **754.5**   **Varus deformities of feet**
EXCLUDES   *acquired (736.71, 736.75, 736.79)*
754.50   **Talipes varus**
Congenital varus deformity of foot, unspecified
Pes varus
DEF: Inverted foot marked by outer sole resting on ground.
754.51   **Talipes equinovarus**
Equinovarus (congenital)
DEF: Elevated, outward rotation of heel; also called clubfoot.
754.52   **Metatarsus primus varus**
DEF: Malformed first metatarsal bone, with bone angled toward body.
754.53   **Metatarsus varus**
754.59   **Other**
Talipes calcaneovarus

√5ᵗʰ **754.6**   **Valgus deformities of feet**
EXCLUDES   *valgus deformity of foot (acquired) (736.79)*
754.60   **Talipes valgus**
Congenital valgus deformity of foot, unspecified
754.61   **Congenital pes planus**
Congenital rocker bottom flat foot
Flat foot, congenital
EXCLUDES   *pes planus (acquired) (734)*
754.62   **Talipes calcaneovalgus**
754.69   **Other**
Talipes: Talipes:
   equinovalgus   planovalgus

√5ᵗʰ **754.7**   **Other deformities of feet**
EXCLUDES   *acquired (736.70-736.79)*
754.70   **Talipes, unspecified**
Congenital deformity of foot NOS
754.71   **Talipes cavus**
Cavus foot (congenital)
754.79   **Other**
Asymmetric talipes   Talipes:
Talipes: equinus
   calcaneus

√5ᵗʰ **754.8**   **Other specified nonteratogenic anomalies**
754.81   **Pectus excavatum**
Congenital funnel chest
754.82   **Pectus carinatum**
Congenital pigeon chest [breast]
754.89   **Other**
Club hand (congenital)
Congenital:
   deformity of chest wall
   dislocation of elbow
Generalized flexion contractures of lower
   limb joints, congenital
Spade-like hand (congenital)

√4ᵗʰ **755**   **Other congenital anomalies of limbs**
EXCLUDES   *those deformities classifiable to 754.0-754.8*

√5ᵗʰ **755.0**   **Polydactyly**
755.00   **Polydactyly, unspecified digits**
Supernumerary digits
755.01   **Of fingers**
Accessory fingers
755.02   **Of toes**
Accessory toes

N Newborn Age: 0   P Pediatric Age: 0-17   M Maternity Age: 12-55   A Adult Age: 15-124   Manifestation Code   ►◄ Revised Text   ● New Code   ▲ Revised Code Title

√5ᵗʰ **755.1 Syndactyly**

    Symphalangy   Webbing of digits

755.10 Of multiple and unspecified sites

755.11 Of fingers without fusion of bone

755.12 Of fingers with fusion of bone

755.13 Of toes without fusion of bone

755.14 Of toes with fusion of bone

√5ᵗʰ **755.2 Reduction deformities of upper limb**

755.20 Unspecified reduction deformity of upper limb

    Ectromelia NOS ⎱ of upper limb
    Hemimelia NOS ⎰

    Shortening of arm, congenital

755.21 Transverse deficiency of upper limb

    Amelia of upper limb
    Congenital absence of:
      fingers, all (complete or partial)
      forearm, including hand and fingers
      upper limb, complete
    Congenital amputation of upper limb
    Transverse hemimelia of upper limb

755.22 Longitudinal deficiency of upper limb, not elsewhere classified

    Phocomelia NOS of upper limb
    Rudimentary arm

755.23 Longitudinal deficiency, combined, involving humerus, radius, and ulna (complete or incomplete)

    Congenital absence of arm and forearm (complete or incomplete) with or without metacarpal deficiency and/or phalangeal deficiency, incomplete
    Phocomelia, complete, of upper limb

755.24 Longitudinal deficiency, humeral, complete or partial (with or without distal deficiencies, incomplete)

    Congenital absence of humerus (with or without absence of some [but not all] distal elements)
    Proximal phocomelia of upper limb

755.25 Longitudinal deficiency, radioulnar, complete or partial (with or without distal deficiencies, incomplete)

    Congenital absence of radius and ulna (with or without absence of some [but not all] distal elements)
    Distal phocomelia of upper limb

755.26 Longitudinal deficiency, radial, complete or partial (with or without distal deficiencies, incomplete)

    Agenesis of radius
    Congenital absence of radius (with or without absence of some [but not all] distal elements)

755.27 Longitudinal deficiency, ulnar, complete or partial (with or without distal deficiencies, incomplete)

    Agenesis of ulna
    Congenital absence of ulna (with or without absence of some [but not all] distal elements)

755.28 Longitudinal deficiency, carpals or metacarpals, complete or partial (with or without incomplete phalangeal deficiency)

755.29 Longitudinal deficiency, phalanges, complete or partial

    Absence of finger, congenital
    Aphalangia of upper limb, terminal, complete or partial

    EXCLUDES   *terminal deficiency of all five digits (755.21)*
                 transverse deficiency of phalanges (755.21)

√5ᵗʰ **755.3 Reduction deformities of lower limb**

755.30 Unspecified reduction deformity of lower limb

    Ectromelia NOS ⎱ of lower limb
    Hemimelia NOS ⎰

    Shortening of leg, congenital

755.31 Transverse deficiency of lower limb

    Amelia of lower limb
    Congenital absence of:
      foot
      leg, including foot and toes
      lower limb, complete
      toes, all, complete
    Transverse hemimelia of lower limb

755.32 Longitudinal deficiency of lower limb, not elsewhere classified

    Phocomelia NOS of lower limb

755.33 Longitudinal deficiency, combined, involving femur, tibia, and fibula (complete or incomplete)

    Congenital absence of thigh and (lower) leg (complete or incomplete) with or without metacarpal deficiency and/or phalangeal deficiency, incomplete
    Phocomelia, complete, of lower limb

755.34 Longitudinal deficiency, femoral, complete or partial (with or without distal deficiencies, incomplete)

    Congenital absence of femur (with or without absence of some [but not all] distal elements)
    Proximal phocomelia of lower limb

755.35 Longitudinal deficiency, tibiofibular, complete or partial (with or without distal deficiencies, incomplete)

    Congenital absence of tibia and fibula (with or without absence of some [but not all] distal elements)
    Distal phocomelia of lower limb

755.36 Longitudinal deficiency, tibia, complete or partial (with or without distal deficiencies, incomplete)

    Agenesis of tibia
    Congenital absence of tibia (with or without absence of some [but not all] distal elements)

755.37 Longitudinal deficiency, fibular, complete or partial (with or without distal deficiencies, incomplete)

    Agenesis of fibula
    Congenital absence of fibula (with or without absence of some [but not all] distal elements)

755.38 Longitudinal deficiency, tarsals or metatarsals, complete or partial (with or without incomplete phalangeal deficiency)

755.39 Longitudinal deficiency, phalanges, complete or partial

    Absence of toe, congenital
    Aphalangia of lower limb, terminal, complete or partial

    EXCLUDES   *terminal deficiency of all five digits (755.31)*
                 transverse deficiency of phalanges (755.31)

755.4 Reduction deformities, unspecified limb

    Absence, congenital (complete or partial) of limb NOS
    Amelia ⎱
    Ectromelia ⎱ of unspecified limb
    Hemimelia ⎰
    Phocomelia ⎰

√5ᵗʰ **755.5 Other anomalies of upper limb, including shoulder girdle**

755.50 Unspecified anomaly of upper limb

⊿4ᵗʰ
⊿5ᵗʰ Additional Digit Required   **RUG III Special Care Dx**   **RUG III Clinically Complex Dx**   Hospice Non-cancer Dx   **CD PDx** Clinical Dimension PDx   **CD SDx** Clinical Dimension SDx

2006 ICD•9•CM   Volume 1 — 217

Congenital Anomalies

755.51–756.3

755.51 Congenital deformity of clavicle

755.52 Congenital elevation of scapula
Sprengel's deformity

755.53 Radioulnar synostosis
DEF: Osseous adhesion of radius and ulna.

755.54 Madelung's deformity
DEF: Distal ulnar overgrowth or radial shortening; also called carpus curvus.

755.55 Acrocephalosyndactyly
Apert's syndrome
DEF: Premature cranial suture fusion (craniostenosis); marked by cone-shaped or pointed (acrocephaly) head and webbing of the fingers (syndactyly); it is very similar to craniofacial dysostosis.

755.56 Accessory carpal bones

755.57 Macrodactylia (fingers)
DEF: Abnormally large fingers, toes.

755.58 Cleft hand, congenital
Lobster-claw hand
DEF: Extended separation between fingers into metacarpus; also may refer to large fingers and absent middle fingers of hand.

755.59 Other
Cleidocranial dysostosis
Cubitus:
    valgus, congenital
    varus, congenital
EXCLUDES   club hand (congenital) (754.89)
              congenital dislocation of elbow (754.89)

√5ᵗʰ **755.6 Other anomalies of lower limb, including pelvic girdle**

755.60 Unspecified anomaly of lower limb

755.61 Coxa valga, congenital
DEF: Abnormally wide angle between the neck and shaft of the femur.

755.62 Coxa vara, congenital
DEF: Diminished angle between neck and shaft of femur.

755.63 Other congenital deformity of hip (joint)
Congenital anteversion of femur (neck)
EXCLUDES   congenital dislocation of hip (754.30-754.35)
AHA: 1Q, '94, 15; S-O, '84, 15

755.64 Congenital deformity of knee (joint)
Congenital:
    absence of patella
    genu valgum [knock-knee]
    genu varum [bowleg]
    Rudimentary patella

755.65 Macrodactylia of toes
DEF: Abnormally large toes.

755.66 Other anomalies of toes
Congenital: Congenital:
    hallux valgus   hammer toe
    hallux varus

755.67 Anomalies of foot, not elsewhere classified
Astragaloscaphoid synostosis
Calcaneonavicular bar
Coalition of calcaneus
Talonavicular synostosis
Tarsal coalitions

755.69 Other
Congenital:
    angulation of tibia
    deformity (of):
        ankle (joint)
        sacroiliac (joint)
    fusion of sacroiliac joint

755.8 Other specified anomalies of unspecified limb

755.9 Unspecified anomaly of unspecified limb
Congenital:
    anomaly NOS } of unspecified limb
    deformity NOS
EXCLUDES   reduction deformity of unspecified limb (755.4)

√4ᵗʰ **756 Other congenital musculoskeletal anomalies**
EXCLUDES   those deformities classifiable to 754.0-754.8

756.0 Anomalies of skull and face bones
Absence of skull bones   Imperfect fusion of skull
Acrocephaly   Oxycephaly
Congenital deformity   Platybasia
   of forehead   Premature closure of
Craniosynostosis   cranial sutures
Crouzon's disease   Tower skull
Hypertelorism   Trigonocephaly
EXCLUDES   acrocephalosyndactyly [Apert's syndrome] (755.55)
        dentofacial anomalies (524.0-524.9)
        skull defects associated with brain anomalies, such as:
          anencephalus (740.0)
          encephalocele (742.0)
          hydrocephalus (742.3)
          microcephalus (742.1)
AHA: 3Q, '98, 9; 3Q, '96, 15

√5ᵗʰ **756.1 Anomalies of spine**

756.10 Anomaly of spine, unspecified

756.11 Spondylolysis, lumbosacral region
Prespondylolisthesis (lumbosacral)
DEF: Bilateral or unilateral defect through the pars interarticularis of a vertebra causes spondylolisthesis.

756.12 Spondylolisthesis
DEF: Downward slipping of lumbar vertebra over next vertebra; usually related to pelvic deformity.

756.13 Absence of vertebra, congenital

756.14 Hemivertebra
DEF: Incomplete development of one side of a vertebra.

756.15 Fusion of spine [vertebra], congenital

756.16 Klippel-Feil syndrome
DEF: Short, wide neck; limits range of motion due to abnormal number of cervical vertebra or fused hemivertebrae.

756.17 Spina bifida occulta
EXCLUDES   spina bifida (aperta) (741.0-741.9)
DEF: Spina bifida marked by a bony spinal canal defect without a protrusion of the cord or meninges; it is diagnosed by radiography and has no symptoms.

756.19 Other
Platyspondylia
Supernumerary vertebra

756.2 Cervical rib
Supernumerary rib in the cervical region
DEF: Costa cervicalis: extra rib attached to cervical vertebra.

756.3 Other anomalies of ribs and sternum
Congenital absence of: Congenital:
    rib   fissure of sternum
    sternum   fusion of ribs
                  Sternum bifidum
EXCLUDES   nonteratogenic deformity of chest wall (754.81-754.89)

N Newborn Age: 0   P Pediatric Age: 0-17   M Maternity Age: 12-55   A Adult Age: 15-124   Manifestation Code   ►◄ Revised Text   ● New Code   ▲ Revised Code Title

756.4 Chondrodystrophy

Achondroplasia   Enchondromatosis
Chondrodystrophia (fetalis)   Ollier's disease
Dyschondroplasia

| EXCLUDES | lipochondrodystrophy [Hurler's syndrome] (277.5) |
| | Morquio's disease (277.5) |

AHA: 2Q, '02, 16; S-O, '87, 10

DEF: Abnormal development of cartilage.

√5ᵗʰ 756.5 Osteodystrophies

756.50 Osteodystrophy, unspecified

756.51 Osteogenesis imperfecta

Fragilitas ossium
Osteopsathyrosis

DEF: A collagen disorder commonly characterized by brittle, osteoporotic, easily fractured bones, hypermobility of joints, blue sclerae, and a tendency to hemorrhage.

756.52 Osteopetrosis

DEF: Abnormally dense bone, optic atrophy, hepatosplenomegaly, deafness; sclerosing depletes bone marrow and nerve foramina of skull; often fatal.

756.53 Osteopoikilosis

DEF: Multiple sclerotic foci on ends of long bones, stippling in round, flat bones; identified by x-ray.

756.54 Polyostotic fibrous dysplasia of bone

DEF: Fibrous tissue displaces bone results in segmented ragged-edge café-au-lait spots; occurs in girls of early puberty.

756.55 Chondroectodermal dysplasia

Ellis-van Creveld syndrome

DEF: Inadequate enchondral bone formation; impaired development of hair and teeth, polydactyly, and cardiac septum defects.

756.56 Multiple epiphyseal dysplasia

756.59 Other

Albright (-McCune)-Sternberg syndrome

756.6 Anomalies of diaphragm

Absence of diaphragm
Congenital hernia:
    diaphragmatic
    foramen of Morgagni
Eventration of diaphragm

| EXCLUDES | congenital hiatus hernia (750.6) |

√5ᵗʰ 756.7 Anomalies of abdominal wall

756.70 Anomaly of abdominal wall, unspecified

756.71 Prune belly syndrome

Eagle-Barrett syndrome
Prolapse of bladder mucosa

AHA: 4Q, '97, 44

DEF: Prune belly syndrome: absence of lower rectus abdominis muscle and lower and medial oblique muscles; results in dilated bladder and ureters, dysplastic kidneys and hydronephrosis; more common in male infants with undescended testicles.

756.79 Other congenital anomalies of abdominal wall

Exomphalos
Gastroschisis
Omphalocele

| EXCLUDES | umbilical hernia (551-553 with .1) |

DEF: Exomphalos: umbilical hernia prominent navel.

DEF: Gastroschisis: fissure of abdominal wall, results in protruding small or large intestine.

DEF: Omphalocele: hernia of umbilicus due to impaired abdominal wall; results in membrane-covered intestine protruding through peritoneum and amnion.

√5ᵗʰ 756.8 Other specified anomalies of muscle, tendon, fascia, and connective tissue

756.81 Absence of muscle and tendon

Absence of muscle (pectoral)

756.82 Accessory muscle

756.83 Ehlers-Danlos syndrome

DEF: Danlos syndrome: connective tissue disorder causes hyperextended skin and joints; results in fragile blood vessels with bleeding, poor wound healing and subcutaneous pseudotumors.

756.89 Other

Amyotrophia congenita
Congenital shortening of tendon

AHA: 3Q, '99, 16

756.9 Other and unspecified anomalies of musculoskeletal system

Congenital:
    anomaly NOS   } of musculoskeletal system,
    deformity NOS }   not elsewhere classified

√4ᵗʰ 757 Congenital anomalies of the integument

| INCLUDES | anomalies of skin, subcutaneous tissue, hair, nails, and breast |

| EXCLUDES | hemangioma (228.00-228.09) |
| | pigmented nevus (216.0-216.9) |

757.0 Hereditary edema of legs

Congenital lymphedema
Hereditary trophedema
Milroy's disease

757.1 Ichthyosis congenita

Congenital ichthyosis
Harlequin fetus
Ichthyosiform erythroderma

DEF: Overproduction of skin cells causes scaling of skin; may result in stillborn fetus or death soon after birth.

757.2 Dermatoglyphic anomalies

Abnormal palmar creases

DEF: Abnormal skin-line patterns of fingers, palms, toes and soles; initial finding of possible chromosomal abnormalities.

√5ᵗʰ 757.3 Other specified anomalies of skin

757.31 Congenital ectodermal dysplasia

DEF: Tissues and structures originate in embryonic ectoderm; includes anhidrotic and hidrotic ectodermal dysplasia and EEC syndrome.

757.32 Vascular hamartomas

Birthmarks   Strawberry nevus
Port-wine stain

DEF: Benign tumor of blood vessels; due to malformed angioblastic tissues.

757.33 Congenital pigmentary anomalies of skin

Congenital poikiloderma
Urticaria pigmentosa
Xeroderma pigmentosum

| EXCLUDES | albinism (270.2) |

√4ᵗʰ Additional Digit Required   RUG III Special Care Dx   RUG III Clinically Complex Dx   Hospice Non-cancer Dx   **CD PDx** Clinical Dimension PDx   **CD SDx** Clinical Dimension SDx
√5ᵗʰ

2006 ICD•9•CM   **Volume 1 — 219**

Congenital Anomalies

757.39–759.4

757.39 Other

Accessory skin tags, congenital
Congenital scar
Epidermolysis bullosa
Keratoderma (congenital)
> EXCLUDES   *pilonidal cyst (685.0-685.1)*

757.4 Specified anomalies of hair

Congenital:
  alopecia
  atrichosis
  beaded hair

Congenital:
  hypertrichosis
  monilethrix
  Persistent lanugo

757.5 Specified anomalies of nails

Anonychia
Congenital:
  clubnail
  koilonychia

Congenital:
  leukonychia
  onychauxis
  pachyonychia

757.6 Specified anomalies of breast

Absent
Accessory } breast or nipple
Supernumerary

Hypoplasia of breast
> EXCLUDES   *absence of pectoral muscle (756.81)*

757.8 Other specified anomalies of the integument

757.9 Unspecified anomaly of the integument

Congenital:
  anomaly NOS } of integument
  deformity NOS

✓4th 758 Chromosomal anomalies

> INCLUDES   syndromes associated with anomalies in the number and form of chromosomes

Use additional codes for conditions associated with the chromosomal anomalies

758.0 Down's syndrome

Mongolism
Translocation Down's syndrome

Trisomy:
  21 or 22
  G

758.1 Patau's syndrome

Trisomy:
  13

Trisomy:
  D_1

DEF: Trisomy of 13th chromosome; characteristic failure to thrive, severe mental impairment, seizures, abnormal eyes, low-set ears and sloped forehead.

758.2 Edwards' syndrome

Trisomy:
  18
  E_3

DEF: Trisomy of 18th chromosome; characteristic mental and physical impairments; mainly affects females.

✓5th 758.3 Autosomal deletion syndromes

758.31 Cri-du-chat syndrome

Deletion 5p
DEF: Hereditary congenital syndrome caused by a microdeletion of short arm of chromosome 5; characterized by catlike cry in newborn, microcephaly, severe mental deficiency, and hypertelorism.

758.32 Velo-cardio-facial syndrome

Deletion 22q11.2
DEF:▶ Microdeletion syndrome affecting multiple organs; characteristic cleft palate, heart defects, elongated face with almond-shaped eyes, wide nose, small ears, weak immune systems, weak musculature, hypothyroidism, short stature, and scoliosis; deletion at q11.2 on the long arm of the chromosome 22.◄

758.33 Other microdeletions

Miller-Dieker syndrome
Smith-Magenis syndrome
DEF:▶ Miller-Dieker syndrome: deletion from the short arm of chromosome 17; characteristic mental retardation, speech and motor development delays, neurological complications, and multiple abnormalities affecting the kidneys, heart, gastrointestinal tract, and other organ; death in infancy or early childhood◄

DEF:▶ Smith-Magenis syndrome: deletion in a certain area of chromosome 17 that results in craniofacial changes, speech delay, hoarse voice, hearing loss in many, and behavioral problems, such as self-destructive head banging, wrist biting, and tearing at nails.◄

758.39 Other autosomal deletions

758.4 Balanced autosomal translocation in normal individual

758.5 Other conditions due to autosomal anomalies

Accessory autosomes NEC

758.6 Gonadal dysgenesis

Ovarian dysgenesis
Turner's syndrome
XO syndrome
> EXCLUDES   *pure gonadal dysgenesis (752.7)*

758.7 Klinefelter's syndrome   ♂

XXY syndrome
DEF: Impaired embryonic development of seminiferous tubes; results in small testes, azoospermia, infertility and enlarged mammary glands.

✓5th 758.8 Other conditions due to chromosome anomalies

758.81 Other conditions due to sex chromosome anomalies

758.89 Other

758.9 Conditions due to anomaly of unspecified chromosome

✓4th 759 Other and unspecified congenital anomalies

759.0 Anomalies of spleen

Aberrant
Absent } spleen
Accessory

Congenital splenomegaly
Ectopic spleen
Lobulation of spleen

759.1 Anomalies of adrenal gland

Aberrant
Absent } adrenal gland
Accessory

> EXCLUDES   *adrenogenital disorders (255.2)*
> *congenital disorders of steroid metabolism (255.2)*

759.2 Anomalies of other endocrine glands

Absent parathyroid gland
Accessory thyroid gland
Persistent thyroglossal or thyrolingual duct
Thyroglossal (duct) cyst
> EXCLUDES   *congenital:*
> *goiter (246.1)*
> *hypothyroidism (243)*

759.3 Situs inversus

Situs inversus or transversus:
  abdominalis
  thoracis

Transposition of viscera:
  abdominal
  thoracic

> EXCLUDES   *dextrocardia without mention of complete transposition (746.87)*

DEF: Laterally transposed thoracic and abdominal viscera.

759.4 Conjoined twins

Craniopagus
Dicephalus
Pygopagus

Thoracopagus
Xiphopagus

N Newborn Age: 0   P Pediatric Age: 0-17   M Maternity Age: 12-55   A Adult Age: 15-124   Manifestation Code   ▶◀ Revised Text   ● New Code   ▲ Revised Code Title

220 — Volume 1 • February 2005   *2006 ICD•9•CM*

759.5   Tuberous sclerosis
Bourneville's disease   Epiloia

DEF: Hamartomas of brain, retina and viscera, impaired mental ability, seizures and adenoma sebaceum.

759.6   Other hamartoses, not elsewhere classified
Syndrome: Syndrome:
Peutz-Jeghers   von Hippel-Lindau
Sturge-Weber (-Dimitri)

EXCLUDES   neurofibromatosis (237.7)

AHA: 3Q, '92, 12

DEF: Peutz-Jeghers: hereditary syndrome characterized by hamartomas of small intestine.

DEF: Sturge-Weber: congenital syndrome characterized by unilateral port-wine stain over trigeminal nerve, underlying meninges and cerebral cortex.

DEF: von Hipple-Lindau: hereditary syndrome of congenital angiomatosis of the retina and cerebellum.

759.7   Multiple congenital anomalies, so described
Congenital:
anomaly, multiple NOS
deformity, multiple NOS

√5ᵗʰ **759.8   Other specified anomalies**
AHA: S-O, '87, 9; S-O, '85, 11

759.81 Prader-Willi syndrome
759.82 Marfan syndrome
AHA: 3Q, '93, 11

759.83 Fragile X syndrome
AHA: 4Q, '94, 41

759.89 Other
Congenital malformation syndromes affecting multiple systems, not elsewhere classified
Laurence-Moon-Biedl syndrome

AHA: ▶2Q, '04, 12;◄ 1Q, '01, 3; 3Q, '99, 17, 18; 3Q, '98, 8

759.9   Congenital anomaly, unspecified

√4ᵗʰ
√5ᵗʰ   Additional Digit Required   RUG III Special Care Dx   RUG III Clinically Complex Dx   Hospice Non-cancer Dx   **CD PDx** Clinical Dimension PDx   **CD SDx** Clinical Dimension SDx

2006 ICD•9•CM   **February 2005 • Volume 1 — 221**

15. CERTAIN CONDITIONS ORIGINATING IN THE PERINATAL PERIOD (760-779)

INCLUDES ► conditions which have their origin in the perinatal period, before birth through the first 28 days after birth, even though death or morbidity occurs later ◄

Use additional code(s) to further specify condition

MATERNAL CAUSES OF PERINATAL MORBIDITY AND MORTALITY (760-763)

AHA: 2Q, '89, 14; 3Q, '90, 5

✓4th **760 Fetus or newborn affected by maternal conditions which may be unrelated to present pregnancy**

INCLUDES the listed maternal conditions only when specified as a cause of mortality or morbidity of the fetus or newborn

EXCLUDES *maternal endocrine and metabolic disorders affecting fetus or newborn (775.0-775.9)*

AHA: 1Q, '94, 8; 2Q, '92, 12; N-D, '84, 11

760.0 Maternal hypertensive disorders
Fetus or newborn affected by maternal conditions classifiable to 642

760.1 Maternal renal and urinary tract diseases
Fetus or newborn affected by maternal conditions classifiable to 580-599

760.2 Maternal infections
Fetus or newborn affected by maternal infectious disease classifiable to 001-136 and 487, but fetus or newborn not manifesting that disease

EXCLUDES *congenital infectious diseases (771.0-771.8)*
maternal genital tract and other localized infections (760.8)

760.3 Other chronic maternal circulatory and respiratory diseases
Fetus or newborn affected by chronic maternal conditions classifiable to 390-459, 490-519, 745-748

760.4 Maternal nutritional disorders
Fetus or newborn affected by:
maternal disorders classifiable to 260-269
maternal malnutrition NOS
EXCLUDES *fetal malnutrition (764.10-764.29)*

760.5 Maternal injury
Fetus or newborn affected by maternal conditions classifiable to 800-995

760.6 Surgical operation on mother
EXCLUDES *cesarean section for present delivery (763.4)*
damage to placenta from amniocentesis, cesarean section, or surgical induction (762.1)
previous surgery to uterus or pelvic organs (763.89)

✓5th **760.7 Noxious influences affecting fetus or newborn via placenta or breast milk**
Fetus or newborn affected by noxious substance transmitted via placenta or breast milk
EXCLUDES *anesthetic and analgesic drugs administered during labor and delivery (763.5)*
drug withdrawal syndrome in newborn (779.5)

AHA: 3Q, '91, 21

760.70 Unspecified noxious substance
Fetus or newborn affected by:
Drug NEC

760.71 Alcohol
Fetal alcohol syndrome

760.72 Narcotics

760.73 Hallucinogenic agents

760.74 Anti-infectives
Antibiotics
►Antifungals◄

760.75 Cocaine
AHA: 3Q, '94, 6; 2Q, '92, 12; 4Q, '91, 26

760.76 Diethylstilbestrol [DES]
AHA: 4Q, '94, 45

● **760.77 Anticonvulsants**
Carbamazepine   Phenytoin
Phenobarbital   Valproic acid

● **760.78 Antimetabolic agents**
Methotrexate   Statins
Retinoic acid

760.79 Other
Fetus or newborn affected by:
immune sera
medicinal agents   transmitted via
NEC   placenta or
toxic substance   breast milk
NEC

760.8 Other specified maternal conditions affecting fetus or newborn
Maternal genital tract and other localized infection affecting fetus or newborn, but fetus or newborn not manifesting that disease
EXCLUDES *maternal urinary tract infection affecting fetus or newborn (760.1)*

760.9 Unspecified maternal condition affecting fetus or newborn

✓4th **761 Fetus or newborn affected by maternal complications of pregnancy**
INCLUDES the listed maternal conditions only when specified as a cause of mortality or morbidity of the fetus or newborn

761.0 Incompetent cervix
DEF: Inadequate functioning of uterine cervix.

761.1 Premature rupture of membranes

761.2 Oligohydramnios
EXCLUDES *that due to premature rupture of membranes (761.1)*
DEF: Deficient amniotic fluid.

761.3 Polyhydramnios
Hydramnios (acute) (chronic)
DEF: Excess amniotic fluid.

761.4 Ectopic pregnancy
Pregnancy: Pregnancy:
abdominal   tubal
intraperitoneal

761.5 Multiple pregnancy
Triplet (pregnancy)   Twin (pregnancy)

761.6 Maternal death

761.7 Malpresentation before labor
Breech presentation
External version
Oblique lie   before labor
Transverse lie
Unstable lie

761.8 Other specified maternal complications of pregnancy affecting fetus or newborn
Spontaneous abortion, fetus

761.9 Unspecified maternal complication of pregnancy affecting fetus or newborn

✓4th **762 Fetus or newborn affected by complications of placenta, cord, and membranes**
INCLUDES the listed maternal conditions only when specified as a cause of mortality or morbidity in the fetus or newborn

AHA: 1Q, '94, 8

762.0 Placenta previa N
DEF: Place\nta developed in lower segment of uterus; causes hemorrhaging in last trimester.

✓4th ✓5th Additional Digit Required   RUG III Special Care Dx   RUG III Clinically Complex Dx   Hospice Non-cancer Dx   CD PDx Clinical Dimension PDx   CD SDx Clinical Dimension SDx

762.1 **Other forms of placental separation and hemorrhage** N
Abruptio placentae
Antepartum hemorrhage
Damage to placenta from amniocentesis, cesarean section, or surgical induction
Maternal blood loss
Premature separation of placenta
Rupture of marginal sinus

762.2 **Other and unspecified morphological and functional abnormalities of placenta** N
Placental: Placental:
dysfunction   insufficiency
infarction

762.3 **Placental transfusion syndromes** N
Placental and cord abnormality resulting in twin-to-twin or other transplacental transfusion
Use additional code to indicate resultant condition in fetus or newborn:
fetal blood loss (772.0)
polycythemia neonatorum (776.4)

762.4 **Prolapsed cord** N
Cord presentation

762.5 **Other compression of umbilical cord** N
Cord around neck   Knot in cord
Entanglement of cord   Torsion of cord
AHA: 2Q, '03, 9

762.6 **Other and unspecified conditions of umbilical cord** N
Short cord
Thrombosis
Varices } of umbilical cord
Velamentous insertion
Vasa previa
EXCLUDES   *infection of umbilical cord (771.4)*
single umbilical artery (747.5)

762.7 **Chorioamnionitis** N
Amnionitis   Placentitis
Membranitis
DEF: Inflamed fetal membrane.

762.8 **Other specified abnormalities of chorion and amnion** N

762.9 **Unspecified abnormality of chorion and amnion** N

√4th **763 Fetus or newborn affected by other complications of labor and delivery**
INCLUDES   the listed conditions only when specified as a cause of mortality or morbidity in the fetus or newborn
AHA: 1Q, '94, 8

763.0 **Breech delivery and extraction** N

763.1 **Other malpresentation, malposition, and disproportion during labor and delivery** N
Fetus or newborn affected by:
abnormality of bony pelvis
contracted pelvis
persistent occipitoposterior position
shoulder presentation
transverse lie
conditions classifiable to 652, 653, and 660

763.2 **Forceps delivery** N
Fetus or newborn affected by forceps extraction

763.3 **Delivery by vacuum extractor** N

763.4 **Cesarean delivery** N
EXCLUDES   *placental separation or hemorrhage from cesarean section (762.1)*

763.5 **Maternal anesthesia and analgesia** N
Reactions and intoxications from maternal opiates and tranquilizers during labor and delivery
EXCLUDES   *drug withdrawal syndrome in newborn (779.5)*

763.6 **Precipitate delivery** N
Rapid second stage

763.7 **Abnormal uterine contractions** N
Fetus or newborn affected by:
contraction ring
hypertonic labor
hypotonic uterine dysfunction
uterine inertia or dysfunction
conditions classifiable to 661, except 661.3

√5th **763.8** **Other specified complications of labor and delivery affecting fetus or newborn**
AHA: 4Q, '98, 46

763.81 **Abnormality in fetal heart rate or rhythm before the onset of labor** N

763.82 **Abnormality in fetal heart rate or rhythm during labor** N
AHA: 4Q, '98, 46

763.83 **Abnormality in fetal heart rate or rhythm, unspecified as to time of onset** N

● **763.84** **Meconium passage during delivery** N
EXCLUDES   *meconium aspiration (770.11, 770.12)*
meconium staining (779.84)

763.89 **Other specified complications of labor and delivery affecting fetus or newborn** N
Fetus or newborn affected by:
abnormality of maternal soft tissues
destructive operation on live fetus to facilitate delivery
induction of labor (medical)
previous surgery to uterus or pelvic organs
other conditions classifiable to 650-669
other procedures used in labor and delivery

763.9 **Unspecified complication of labor and delivery affecting fetus or newborn** N

OTHER CONDITIONS ORIGINATING IN THE PERINATAL PERIOD (764-779)

The following fifth-digit subclassification is for use with category 764 and codes 765.0-765.1 to denote birthweight:

0   **unspecified [weight]**   5   **1,250-1,499 grams**
1   **less than 500 grams**   6   **1,500-1,749 grams**
2   **500-749 grams**   7   **1,750-1,999 grams**
3   **750-999 grams**   8   **2,000-2,499 grams**
4   **1,000-1,249 grams**   9   **2,500 grams and over**
5   **1,250-1,499 grams**

√4th **764 Slow fetal growth and fetal malnutrition**
AHA: 3Q, '04, 4; 4Q, '02, 63; 1Q, '94, 8; 2Q, '91, 19; 2Q, '89, 15

√5th **764.0** **"Light-for-dates" without mention of fetal malnutrition** N
Infants underweight for gestational age
"Small-for-dates"

√5th **764.1** **"Light-for-dates" with signs of fetal malnutrition** N
Infants "light-for-dates" classifiable to 764.0, who in addition show signs of fetal malnutrition, such as dry peeling skin and loss of subcutaneous tissue

√5th **764.2** **Fetal malnutrition without mention of "light-for-dates"** N
Infants, not underweight for gestational age, showing signs of fetal malnutrition, such as dry peeling skin and loss of subcutaneous tissue
Intrauterine malnutrition

√5th **764.9** **Fetal growth retardation, unspecified** N
Intrauterine growth retardation
AHA: For code 764.97: 1Q, '97, 6

√4th **765 Disorders relating to short gestation and low birthweight**
INCLUDES   the listed conditions, without further specification, as causes of mortality, morbidity, or additional care, in fetus or newborn
AHA: 1Q, '97, 6; 1Q, '94, 8; 2Q, '91, 19; 2Q, '89, 15

N Newborn Age: 0   P Pediatric Age: 0-17   M Maternity Age: 12-55   A Adult Age: 15-124   Manifestation Code   ◄► Revised Text   ● New Code   ▲ Revised Code Title

224 — Volume 1 • October 2005   *2006 ICD•9•CM*

§ ✓5th **765.0**   **Extreme immaturity**
Note: Usually implies a birthweight of less than 1000 grams.
Use additional code for weeks of gestation (765.20-765.29)
AHA: ▶3Q, '04, 4;◀ 4Q, '02, 63; For code 765.03: 4Q, '01, 51

§ ✓5th **765.1**   **Other preterm infants**
Note: Usually implies a birthweight of 1000-2499.
Prematurity NOS
Prematurity or small size, not classifiable to 765.0 or as "light-for-dates" in 764
Use additional code for weeks of gestation (765.20-765.29)
AHA: ▶3Q, '04, 4;◀ 4Q, '02, 63; For code 765.10: 1Q, '94, 14; For code 765.17: 1Q, '97, 6; For code 765.18: 4Q, '02, 64

✓5th **765.2**   **Weeks of gestation**
AHA: ▶3Q, '04, 4;◀ 4Q, '02, 63

765.20   **Unspecified weeks of gestation**
765.21   **Less than 24 completed weeks of gestation**
765.22   **24 completed weeks of gestation**
765.23   **25-26 completed weeks of gestation**
765.24   **27-28 completed weeks of gestation**
765.25   **29-30 completed weeks of gestation**
765.26   **31-32 completed weeks of gestation**
765.27   **33-34 completed weeks of gestation**
765.28   **35-36 completed weeks of gestation**
AHA: 4Q, '02, 64
765.29   **37 or more completed weeks of gestation**

✓4th **766**   **Disorders relating to long gestation and high birthweight**
INCLUDES   the listed conditions, without further specification, as causes of mortality, morbidity, or additional care, in fetus or newborn

766.0   **Exceptionally large baby**
Note: Usually implies a birthweight of 4500 grams or more.

766.1   **Other "heavy-for-dates" infants**
Other fetus or infant "heavy-" or "large-for-dates" regardless of period of gestation

✓5th **766.2**   **Late infant, not "heavy-for-dates"**
AHA: 4Q, '03, 69

766.21   **Post-term infant**
Infant with gestation period over 40 completed weeks to 42 completed weeks

766.22   **Prolonged gestation of infant**
Infant with gestation period over 42 completed weeks
Postmaturity NOS

✓4th **767**   **Birth trauma**

767.0   **Subdural and cerebral hemorrhage**
Subdural and cerebral hemorrhage, whether described as due to birth trauma or to intrapartum anoxia or hypoxia
Subdural hematoma (localized)
Tentorial tear
Use additional code to identify cause
EXCLUDES   intraventricular hemorrhage (772.10-772.14)
subarachnoid hemorrhage (772.2)

✓5th **767.1**   **Injuries to scalp**
AHA: 4Q, '03, 69

767.11   **Epicranial subaponeurotic hemorrhage (massive)**
Subgaleal hemorrhage
DEF: A hemorrhage that occurs within the space between the galea aponeurotica, or epicranial aponeurosis, which is a thin tendinous structure that is attached to the skull laterally and provides an insertion site for the occipitalis posteriorly and the frontalis muscle anteriorly, and the periosteum of the skull.

767.19   **Other injuries to scalp**
Caput succedaneum
Cephalhematoma
Chignon (from vacuum extraction)

767.2   **Fracture of clavicle**

767.3   **Other injuries to skeleton**
Fracture of: Fracture of:
long bones   skull
EXCLUDES   congenital dislocation of hip (754.30-754.35)
fracture of spine, congenital (767.4)

767.4   **Injury to spine and spinal cord**
Dislocation
Fracture   } of spine or spinal cord
Laceration   due to birth trauma
Rupture

767.5   **Facial nerve injury**
Facial palsy

767.6   **Injury to brachial plexus**
Palsy or paralysis: Palsy or paralysis:
brachial   Klumpke (-Déjérine)
Erb (-Duchenne)

767.7   **Other cranial and peripheral nerve injuries**
Phrenic nerve paralysis

767.8   **Other specified birth trauma**
Eye damage   Rupture of:
Hematoma of: liver
liver (subcapsular)   spleen
testes   Scalpel wound
vulva   Traumatic glaucoma
EXCLUDES   hemorrhage classifiable to 772.0-772.9

767.9   **Birth trauma, unspecified**
Birth injury NOS

✓4th **768**   **Intrauterine hypoxia and birth asphyxia**
Use only when associated with newborn morbidity classifiable elsewhere
AHA: 4Q, '92, 20
DEF: Oxygen intake insufficiency due to interrupted placental circulation or premature separation of placenta.

768.0   **Fetal death from asphyxia or anoxia before onset of labor or at unspecified time**

768.1   **Fetal death from asphyxia or anoxia during labor**

Epicranial Aponeurosis

Skin
Subcutaneous tissues
Areolar space
Frontalis muscle
Epicranial aponeurosis
Pericranium
Frontal sinus
Occipitalis muscle
Inion

§   Requires fifth-digit. See category 764 for codes and definitions.

✓4th
✓5th   Additional Digit Required   RUG III Special Care Dx   RUG III Clinically Complex Dx   Hospice Non-cancer Dx   CD PDx Clinical Dimension PDx   CD SDx Clinical Dimension SDx

Conditions in the Perinatal Period

768.2–770.81

768.2 **Fetal distress before onset of labor, in liveborn** N
infant
Fetal metabolic acidemia before onset of labor, in
liveborn infant

768.3 **Fetal distress first noted during labor, in** N
liveborn infant
Fetal metabolic acidemia first noted during labor, in
liveborn infant

768.4 **Fetal distress, unspecified as to time of onset,** N
in liveborn infant
Fetal metabolic acidemia unspecified as to time of
onset, in liveborn infant
AHA: N-D, '86, 10

768.5 **Severe birth asphyxia** N
Birth asphyxia with neurologic involvement
AHA: N-D, '86, 3

768.6 **Mild or moderate birth asphyxia** N
Birth asphyxia (without mention of neurologic
involvement)
AHA: N-D, '86, 3

768.9 **Unspecified birth asphyxia in liveborn infant** N

Anoxia
Asphyxia } NOS, in liveborn infant
Hypoxia

769 Respiratory distress syndrome N
Cardiorespiratory distress syndrome of newborn
Hyaline membrane disease (pulmonary)
Idiopathic respiratory distress syndrome [IRDS or RDS] of
newborn
Pulmonary hypoperfusion syndrome
EXCLUDES *transient tachypnea of newborn (770.6)*
AHA: 1Q, '89, 10; N-D, '86, 6

DEF: Severe chest contractions upon air intake and expiratory grunting; infant
appears blue due to oxygen deficiency and has rapid respiratory rate;
formerly called hyaline membrane disease.

✓4th **770 Other respiratory conditions of fetus and newborn**

770.0 **Congenital pneumonia** N
Infective pneumonia acquired prenatally
EXCLUDES *pneumonia from infection acquired*
after birth (480.0-486)

AHA: ▶1Q, '05, 10◀

▲ ✓5th **770.1** **Fetal and newborn aspiration**
EXCLUDES ▶*aspiration of postnatal stomach*
contents (770.85, 770.86)
meconium passage during delivery
(763.84)
meconium staining (779.84)◀

DEF: Meconium Aspiration: Aspiration of meconium by the newborn
infant prior to delivery. Presence of meconium in the trachea or
chest x-ray indicating patchy infiltrates in conjunction with chest
hyperextension establishes this diagnosis.

● **770.10** **Fetal and newborn aspiration,** N
unspecified

● **770.11** **Meconium aspiration without** N
respiratory symptoms
Meconium aspiration NOS

● **770.12** **Meconium aspiration with** N
respiratory symptoms
Meconium aspiration pneumonia
Meconium aspiration pneumonitis
Meconium aspiration syndrome NOS
Use additional code to identify any
secondary pulmonary hypertension
(416.8), if applicable

● **770.13** **Aspiration of clear amniotic fluid** N
without respiratory symptoms
Aspiration of clear amniotic fluid NOS

● **770.14** **Aspiration of clear amniotic fluid** N
with respiratory symptoms
Aspiration of clear amniotic fluid with
pneumonia
Aspiration of clear amniotic fluid with
pneumonitis
Use additional code to identify any
secondary pulmonary hypertension
(416.8), if applicable

● **770.15** **Aspiration of blood without** N
respiratory symptoms
Aspiration of blood NOS

● **770.16** **Aspiration of blood with respiratory** N
symptoms
Aspiration of blood with pneumonia
Aspiration of blood with pneumonitis
Use additional code to identify any
secondary pulmonary hypertension
(416.8), if applicable

● **770.17** **Other fetal and newborn aspiration** N
without respiratory symptoms

● **770.18** **Other fetal and newborn aspiration** N
with respiratory symptoms
Other aspiration pneumonia
Other aspiration pneumonitis
Use additional code to identify any
secondary pulmonary hypertension
(416.8), if applicable

770.2 **Interstitial emphysema and related** N
conditions
Pneumomediastinum } originating in the
Pneumopericardium   perinatal period
Pneumothorax

770.3 **Pulmonary hemorrhage** N
Hemorrhage:
alveolar (lung)
intra-alveolar (lung) } originating in the
massive pulmonary   perinatal period

770.4 **Primary atelectasis** N
Pulmonary immaturity NOS
DEF: Alveoli fail to expand causing insufficient air intake by
newborn.

770.5 **Other and unspecified atelectasis** N
Atelectasis:
NOS
partial } originating in the
secondary   perinatal period
Pulmonary collapse

770.6 **Transitory tachypnea of newborn** N
Idiopathic tachypnea of newborn
Wet lung syndrome
EXCLUDES *respiratory distress syndrome (769)*
AHA: 4Q, '95, 4; 1Q, '94, 12; 3Q, '93, 7; 1Q, '89, 10; N-D, '86, 6

DEF: Quick, shallow breathing of newborn; short-term problem.

770.7 **Chronic respiratory disease arising in the** N
perinatal period
Bronchopulmonary dysplasia
Interstitial pulmonary fibrosis of prematurity
Wilson-Mikity syndrome
AHA: 2Q, '91, 19; N-D, '86, 11

✓5th **770.8** **Other respiratory problems after birth** N
AHA: 4Q, '02, 65; 2Q, '98, 10; 2Q, '96, 10

770.81 **Primary apnea of newborn** N
Apneic spells of newborn NOS
Essential apnea of newborn
Sleep apnea of newborn
DEF: Cessation of breathing when a neonate makes no
respiratory effort for 15 seconds, resulting in cyanosis
and bradycardia.

N Newborn Age: 0 ● P Pediatric Age: 0-17 ● M Maternity Age: 12-55 ● A Adult Age: 15-124 ● Manifestation Code ● ▶◀ Revised Text ● ● New Code ● ▲ Revised Code Title

770.82 Other apnea of newborn   N
Obstructive apnea of newborn

770.83 Cyanotic attacks of newborn   N

770.84 Respiratory failure of newborn   N
EXCLUDES   *respiratory distress syndrome (769)*

● **770.85 Aspiration of postnatal stomach contents without respiratory symptoms**   N
Aspiration of postnatal stomach contents NOS

● **770.86 Aspiration of postnatal stomach contents with respiratory symptoms**   N
Aspiration of postnatal stomach contents with pneumonia
Aspiration of postnatal stomach contents with pneumonitis
Use additional code to identify any secondary pulmonary hypertension (416.8), if applicable

770.89 Other respiratory problems after birth   N

770.9 Unspecified respiratory condition of fetus and newborn   N

√4th **771 Infections specific to the perinatal period**
INCLUDES   infections acquired before or during birth or via the umbilicus ▶or during the first 28 days after birth◀
EXCLUDES   *congenital pneumonia (770.0)*
congenital syphilis (090.0-090.9)
maternal infectious disease as a cause of mortality or morbidity in fetus or newborn, but fetus or newborn not manifesting the disease (760.2)
ophthalmia neonatorum due to gonococcus (098.40)
other infections not specifically classified to this category

AHA: N-D, '85, 4

771.0 Congenital rubella   N
Congenital rubella pneumonitis

771.1 Congenital cytomegalovirus infection   N
Congenital cytomegalic inclusion disease

771.2 Other congenital infections   N
Congenital: Congenital:
herpes simplex   toxoplasmosis
listeriosis   tuberculosis
malaria

771.3 Tetanus neonatorum   N
Tetanus omphalitis
EXCLUDES   *hypocalcemic tetany (775.4)*

DEF: Severe infection of central nervous system; due to exotoxin of tetanus bacillus from navel infection prompted by nonsterile technique during umbilical ligation.

771.4 Omphalitis of the newborn   N
Infection:
navel cord
umbilical stump
EXCLUDES   *tetanus omphalitis (771.3)*

DEF: Inflamed umbilicus.

771.5 Neonatal infective mastitis   N
EXCLUDES   *noninfective neonatal mastitis (778.7)*

771.6 Neonatal conjunctivitis and dacryocystitis   N
Ophthalmia neonatorum NOS
EXCLUDES   *ophthalmia neonatorum due to gonococcus (098.40)*

771.7 Neonatal Candida infection   N
Neonatal moniliasis
Thrush in newborn

√5th **771.8 Other infection specific to the perinatal period**   N
Use additional code to identify organism (041.00-041.9)

AHA: 4Q, '02, 66

771.81 Septicemia [sepsis] of newborn   N

771.82 Urinary tract infection of newborn   N

771.83 Bacteremia of newborn   N

771.89 Other infections specific to the perinatal period   N
Intra-amniotic infection of fetus NOS
Infection of newborn NOS

√4th **772 Fetal and neonatal hemorrhage**
EXCLUDES   *hematological disorders of fetus and newborn (776.0-776.9)*

772.0 Fetal blood loss   N
Fetal blood loss from: Fetal exsanguination
cut end of co-twin's cord   Fetal hemorrhage
placenta   into:
ruptured cord   co-twin
vasa previa   mother's circulation

√5th **772.1 Intraventricular hemorrhage**
Intraventricular hemorrhage from any perinatal cause
AHA: 4Q, '01, 49; 3Q, '92, 8; 4Q, '88, 8

772.10 Unspecified grade   N

772.11 Grade I   N
Bleeding into germinal matrix

772.12 Grade II   N
Bleeding into ventricle

772.13 Grade III   N
Bleeding with enlargement of ventricle
AHA: 4Q, '01, 51

772.14 Grade IV   N
Bleeding into cerebral cortex

772.2 Subarachnoid hemorrhage   N
Subarachnoid hemorrhage from any perinatal cause
EXCLUDES   *subdural and cerebral hemorrhage (767.0)*

772.3 Umbilical hemorrhage after birth   N
Slipped umbilical ligature

772.4 Gastrointestinal hemorrhage   N
EXCLUDES   *swallowed maternal blood (777.3)*

772.5 Adrenal hemorrhage   N

772.6 Cutaneous hemorrhage   N
Bruising
Ecchymoses   ⎫
Petechiae   ⎬ in fetus or newborn
Superficial hematoma ⎭

772.8 Other specified hemorrhage of fetus or newborn   N
EXCLUDES   *hemorrhagic disease of newborn (776.0)*
pulmonary hemorrhage (770.3)

772.9 Unspecified hemorrhage of newborn   N

√4th **773 Hemolytic disease of fetus or newborn, due to isoimmunization**
DEF: Hemolytic anemia of fetus or newborn due to maternal antibody formation against fetal erythrocytes; infant blood contains nonmaternal antigen.

773.0 Hemolytic disease due to Rh isoimmunzation   N
Anemia   ⎫ due to RH:
Erythroblastosis (fetalis) ⎪ antibodies
Hemolytic disease ⎬ isoimmunization
(fetus) (newborn) ⎪ maternal/fetal
Jaundice ⎭ incompatibility
Rh hemolytic disease
Rh isoimmunization

√4th √5th Additional Digit Required   RUG III Special Care Dx   RUG III Clinically Complex Dx   Hospice Non-cancer Dx   CD PDx Clinical Dimension PDx   CD SDx Clinical Dimension SDx

2006 ICD•9•CM   October 2005 • Volume 1 — 227

773.1 Hemolytic disease due to ABO isoimmumization [N]

ABO hemolytic disease   ABO isoimmunization

Anemia
Erythroblastosis (fetalis)
Hemolytic disease
 (fetus) (newborn)
Jaundice
} due to ABO:
antibodies
isoimmunization
maternal/fetal
incompatibility

AHA: 3Q, '92, 8

DEF: Incompatible Rh fetal-maternal blood grouping; prematurely destroys red blood cells; detected by Coombs test.

773.2 Hemolytic disease due to other and unspecified isoimmunization [N]

Eythroblastosis (fetalis) (neonatorum) NOS
Hemolytic disease (fetus) (newborn) NOS
Jaundice or anemia due to other and unspecified blood-group incompatibility

AHA: 1Q, '94, 13

773.3 Hydrops fetalis due to isoimmunization [N]

Use additional code to identify type of isoimmunization (773.0-773.2)

DEF: Massive edema of entire body and severe anemia; may result in fetal death or stillbirth.

773.4 Kernicterus due to isoimmunization [N]

Use additional code to identify type of isoimmunization (773.0-773.2)

DEF: Complication of erythroblastosis fetalis associated with severe neural symptoms, high blood bilirubin levels and nerve cell destruction; results in bilirubin-pigmented gray matter of central nervous system.

773.5 Late anemia due to isoimmunization

√4ᵗʰ **774 Other perinatal jaundice**

774.0 *Perinatal jaundice from hereditary hemolyticanemias* [N]

Code first underlying disease (282.0-282.9)

774.1 Perinatal jaundice from other excessive hemolysis [N]

Fetal or neonatal jaundice from:
 bruising
 drugs or toxins transmitted from mother
 infection
 polycythemia
 swallowed maternal blood
Use additional code to identify cause

EXCLUDES jaundice due to isoimmunization (773.0-773.2)

774.2 Neonatal jaundice associated with preterm delivery [N]

Hyperbilirubinemia of prematurity
Jaundice due to delayed conjugation associated with preterm delivery

√5ᵗʰ **774.3 Neonatal jaundice due to delayed conjugation from other causes**

774.30 Neonatal jaundice due to delayed conjugation, cause unspecified [N]

DEF: Jaundice of newborn with abnormal bilirubin metabolism; causes excess accumulated unconjugated bilirubin in blood.

774.31 *Neonatal jaundice due to delayed conjugation in diseases classified elsewhere*

Code first underlying diseases as:
 congenital hypothyroidism (243)
 Crigler-Najjar syndrome (277.4)
 Gilbert's syndrome (277.4)

774.39 Other [N]

Jaundice due to delayed conjugation from causes, such as:
 breast milk inhibitors
 delayed development of conjugating system

774.4 Perinatal jaundice due to hepatocellular damage [N]

Fetal or neonatal hepatitis
Giant cell hepatitis
Inspissated bile syndrome

774.5 *Perinatal jaundice from other causes* [N]

Code first underlying cause as:
 congenital obstruction of bile duct (751.61)
 galactosemia (271.1)
 mucoviscidosis (277.00-277.09)

774.6 Unspecified fetal and neonatal jaundice [N]

Icterus neonatorum
Neonatal hyperbilirubinemia (transient)
Physiologic jaundice NOS in newborn
EXCLUDES that in preterm infants (774.2)

AHA: 1Q, '94, 13; 2Q, '89, 15

774.7 Kernicterus not due to isoimmunization [N]

Bilirubin encephalopathy
Kernicterus of newborn NOS
EXCLUDES kernicterus due to isoimmunization (773.4)

√4ᵗʰ **775 Endocrine and metabolic disturbances specific to the fetus and newborn**

INCLUDES transitory endocrine and metabolic disturbances caused by the infant's response to maternal endocrine and metabolic factors, its removal from them, or its adjustment to extrauterine existence

775.0 Syndrome of "infant of a diabetic mother" [N]

Maternal diabetes mellitus affecting fetus or newborn (with hypoglycemia)

AHA: 1Q, '04, 7-8; 3Q, '91, 5

775.1 Neonatal diabetes mellitus [N]

Diabetes mellitus syndrome in newborn infant

AHA: 3Q, '91, 6

775.2 Neonatal myasthenia gravis [N]

775.3 Neonatal thyrotoxicosis [N]

Neonatal hyperthyroidism (transient)

775.4 Hypocalcemia and hypomagnesemia of newborn [N]

Cow's milk hypocalcemia
Hypocalcemic tetany, neonatal
Neonatal hypoparathyroidism
Phosphate-loading hypocalcemia

775.5 Other transitory neonatal electrolyte disturbances [N]

Dehydration, neonatal

AHA: ▶1Q, '05, 9◄

775.6 Neonatal hypoglycemia [N]

EXCLUDES infant of mother with diabetes mellitus (775.0)

AHA: 1Q, '94, 12

775.7 Late metabolic acidosis of newborn [N]

775.8 Other transitory neonatal endocrine and metabolic disturbances [N]

Amino-acid metabolic disorders described as transitory

775.9 Unspecified endocrine and metabolic disturbances specific to the fetus and newborn [N]

√4ᵗʰ **776 Hematological disorders of fetus and newborn**

INCLUDES disorders specific to the fetus or newborn

776.0 Hemorrhagic disease of newborn [N]

Hemorrhagic diathesis of newborn
Vitamin K deficiency of newborn
EXCLUDES fetal or neonatal hemorrhage (772.0-772.9)

776.1 Transient neonatal thrombocytopenia [N]

Neonatal thrombocytopenia due to:
 exchange transfusion
 idiopathic maternal thrombocytopenia
 isoimmunization

DEF: Temporary decrease in blood platelets of newborn.

[N] Newborn Age: 0 [P] Pediatric Age: 0-17 [M] Maternity Age: 12-55 [A] Adult Age: 15-124 Manifestation Code ▶◀ Revised Text ● New Code ▲ Revised Code Title

776.2 Disseminated intravascular coagulation in newborn [N]

DEF: Disseminated intravascular coagulation of newborn: clotting disorder due to excess thromboplastic agents in blood as a result of disease or trauma; causes blood clotting within vessels and reduces available elements necessary for blood coagulation.

776.3 Other transient neonatal disorders of coagulation [N]

Transient coagulation defect, newborn

776.4 Polycythemia neonatorum [N]

Plethora of newborn   Polycythemia due to:
Polycythemia due to: maternal-fetal transfusion
    donor twin transfusion

DEF: Abnormal increase of total red blood cells of newborn.

776.5 Congenital anemia [N]

Anemia following fetal blood loss

EXCLUDES   *anemia due to isoimmunization (773.0-773.2, 773.5)*

hereditary hemolytic anemias (282.0-282.9)

776.6 Anemia of prematurity [N]

776.7 Transient neonatal neutropenia [N]

Isoimmune neutropenia
Maternal transfer neutropenia

EXCLUDES   *congenital neutropenia (nontransient) (288.0)*

DEF: Decreased neutrophilic leukocytes in blood of newborn.

776.8 Other specified transient hematological disorders [N]

776.9 Unspecified hematological disorder specific to fetus or newborn [N]

✓4ᵗʰ **777 Perinatal disorders of digestive system**

INCLUDES   disorders specific to the fetus and newborn

EXCLUDES   *intestinal obstruction classifiable to 560.0-560.9*

777.1 Meconium obstruction [N]

Congenital fecaliths   Meconium ileus NOS
Delayed passage of meconium   Meconium plug syndrome

EXCLUDES   *meconium ileus in cystic fibrosis (277.01)*

DEF: Meconium blocked digestive tract of newborn.

777.2 Intestinal obstruction due to inspissated milk [N]

777.3 Hematemesis and melena due to swallowed maternal blood [N]

Swallowed blood syndrome in newborn

EXCLUDES   *that not due to swallowed maternal blood (772.4)*

777.4 Transitory ileus of newborn [N]

EXCLUDES   *Hirschsprung's disease (751.3)*

777.5 Necrotizing enterocolitis in fetus or newborn [N]

Pseudomembranous enterocolitis in newborn

DEF: Acute inflammation of small intestine due to pseudomembranous plaque over ulceration; may be due to aggressive antibiotic therapy.

777.6 Perinatal intestinal perforation [N]

Meconium peritonitis

777.8 Other specified perinatal disorders of digestive system [N]

777.9 Unspecified perinatal disorder of digestive system [N]

✓4ᵗʰ **778 Conditions involving the integument and temperature regulation of fetus and newborn**

778.0 Hydrops fetalis not due to isoimmunization [N]

Idiopathic hydrops

EXCLUDES   *hydrops fetalis due to isoimmunization (773.3)*

DEF: Edema of entire body, unrelated to immune response.

778.1 Sclerema neonatorum [N]

Subcutaneous fat necrosis

DEF: Diffuse, rapidly progressing white, waxy, nonpitting hardening of tissue, usually of legs and feet, life-threatening; found in preterm or debilitated infants; unknown etiology.

778.2 Cold injury syndrome of newborn [N]

778.3 Other hypothermia of newborn [N]

778.4 Other disturbances of temperature regulation of newborn [N]

Dehydration fever in newborn
Environmentally-induced pyrexia
Hyperthermia in newborn
Transitory fever of newborn

778.5 Other and unspecified edema of newborn [N]

Edema neonatorum

778.6 Congenital hydrocele [N]

Congenital hydrocele of tunica vaginalis

778.7 Breast engorgement in newborn [N]

Noninfective mastitis of newborn

EXCLUDES   *infective mastitis of newborn (771.5)*

778.8 Other specified conditions involving the integument of fetus and newborn [N]

Urticaria neonatorum

EXCLUDES   *impetigo neonatorum (684)*
pemphigus neonatorum (684)

778.9 Unspecified condition involving the integument and temperature regulation of fetus and newborn [N]

✓4ᵗʰ **779 Other and ill-defined conditions originating in the perinatal period**

779.0 Convulsions in newborn [N]

Fits ⎫
Seizures ⎬ in newborn

AHA: N-D, '94, 11

779.1 Other and unspecified cerebral irritability in newborn [N]

779.2 Cerebral depression, coma, and other abnormal cerebral signs [N]

CNS dysfunction in newborn NOS

779.3 Feeding problems in newborn [N]

Regurgitation of food ⎫
Slow feeding ⎬ in newborn
Vomiting ⎭

AHA: 2Q, '89, 15

779.4 Drug reactions and intoxications specific to newborn [N]

Gray syndrome from chloramphenicol administration in newborn

EXCLUDES   *fetal alcohol syndrome (760.71)*
reactions and intoxications from maternal opiates and tranquilizers (763.5)

779.5 Drug withdrawal syndrome in newborn [N]

Drug withdrawal syndrome in infant of dependent mother

EXCLUDES   *fetal alcohol syndrome (760.71)*

AHA: 3Q, '94, 6

779.6 Termination of pregnancy (fetus) [N]

Fetal death due to: Fetal death due to:
induced abortion   termination of pregnancy

EXCLUDES   *spontaneous abortion (fetus) (761.8)*

779.7 Periventricular leukomalacia [N]

AHA: 4Q, '01, 50, 51

DEF: Necrosis of white matter adjacent to lateral ventricles with the formation of cysts; cause of PVL has not been firmly established, but thought to be related to inadequate blood flow in certain areas of the brain.

✓4ᵗʰ
✓5ᵗʰ Additional Digit Required   RUG III Special Care Dx   RUG III Clinically Complex Dx   Hospice Non-cancer Dx   **CD PDx** Clinical Dimension PDx   **CD SDx** Clinical Dimension SDx

2006 ICD•9•CM   **Volume 1 — 229**

Conditions in the Perinatal Period

779.8–779.9

√5ᵗʰ **779.8 Other specified conditions originating in the perinatal period**
AHA: 4Q, '02, 67; 1Q, '94, 15

779.81 Neonatal bradycardia   N
> EXCLUDES   *abnormality in fetal heart rate or rhythm complicating labor and delivery (763.81-763.83)*
> *bradycardia due to birth asphyxia (768.5-768.9)*

779.82 Neonatal tachycardia   N
> EXCLUDES   *abnormality in fetal heart rate or rhythm complicating labor and delivery (763.81-763.83)*

779.83 Delayed separation of umbilical cord   N
AHA: 4Q, '03, 71

● **779.84 Meconium staining**   N
> EXCLUDES   *meconium aspiration (770.11, 770.12)*
> *meconium passage during delivery (763.84)*

779.89 Other specified conditions originating in the perinatal period   N
▶Use additional code to specify condition◀
AHA: ▶1Q, '05, 9◀

779.9 Unspecified condition originating in the perinatal period   N
Congenital debility NOS
Stillbirth NEC

| N Newborn Age: 0 | P Pediatric Age: 0-17 | M Maternity Age: 12-55 | A Adult Age: 15-124 | Manifestation Code | ▶◀ Revised Text | ● New Code | ▲ Revised Code Title |

230 — Volume 1 • October 2005

2006 ICD•9•CM

16. SYMPTOMS, SIGNS, AND ILL-DEFINED CONDITIONS
(780-799)

This section includes symptoms, signs, abnormal results of laboratory or other investigative procedures, and ill-defined conditions regarding which no diagnosis classifiable elsewhere is recorded.

Signs and symptoms that point rather definitely to a given diagnosis are assigned to some category in the preceding part of the classification. In general, categories 780-796 include the more ill-defined conditions and symptoms that point with perhaps equal suspicion to two or more diseases or to two or more systems of the body, and without the necessary study of the case to make a final diagnosis. Practically all categories in this group could be designated as "not otherwise specified," or as "unknown etiology," or as "transient." The Alphabetic Index should be consulted to determine which symptoms and signs are to be allocated here and which to more specific sections of the classification; the residual subcategories numbered .9 are provided for other relevant symptoms which cannot be allocated elsewhere in the classification.

The conditions and signs or symptoms included in categories 780-796 consist of: (a) cases for which no more specific diagnosis can be made even after all facts bearing on the case have been investigated; (b) signs or symptoms existing at the time of initial encounter that proved to be transient and whose causes could not be determined; (c) provisional diagnoses in a patient who failed to return for further investigation or care; (d) cases referred elsewhere for investigation or treatment before the diagnosis was made; (e) cases in which a more precise diagnosis was not available for any other reason; (f) certain symptoms which represent important problems in medical care and which it might be desired to classify in addition to a known cause.

SYMPTOMS (780-789)
AHA: 1Q, '91, 12; 2Q, '90, 3; 2Q, '90, 5; 2Q, '90, 15; M-A, '85, 3

√4ᵗʰ **780 General symptoms**

√5ᵗʰ **780.0 Alteration of consciousness**

EXCLUDES coma:
  diabetic (250.2-250.3)
  hepatic (572.2)
  originating in the perinatal period (779.2)

AHA: 4Q, '92, 20

780.01 Coma

AHA: 3Q, '96, 16

DEF: State of unconsciousness from which the patient cannot be awakened.

780.02 Transient alteration of awareness

DEF: Temporary, recurring spells of reduced consciousness.

780.03 Persistent vegetative state

DEF: Persistent wakefulness without consciousness due to nonfunctioning cerebral cortex.

780.09 Other
  Drowsiness   Stupor
  Semicoma   Unconsciousness
  Somnolence

780.1 Hallucinations
  Hallucinations: Hallucinations:
  NOS   olfactory
  auditory   tactile
  gustatory
  EXCLUDES those associated with mental disorders, as functional psychoses (295.0-298.9)
    organic brain syndromes (290.0-294.9, 310.0-310.9)
    visual hallucinations (368.16)

DEF: Perception of external stimulus in absence of stimulus; inability to distinguish between real and imagined.

780.2 Syncope and collapse
  Blackout   (Near) (Pre) syncope
  Fainting   Vasovagal attack
  EXCLUDES carotid sinus syncope (337.0)
    heat syncope (992.1)
    neurocirculatory asthenia (306.2)
    orthostatic hypotension (458.0)
    shock NOS (785.50)

AHA: 1Q, '02, 6; 3Q, '95, 14; N-D, '85, 12

DEF: Sudden unconsciousness due to reduced blood flow to brain.

√5ᵗʰ **780.3 Convulsions**
  EXCLUDES convulsions:
    epileptic (345.10-345.91)
    in newborn (779.0)

AHA: 2Q, '97, 8; 1Q, '97, 12; 3Q, '94, 9; 1Q, '93, 24; 4Q, '92, 23; N-D, '87, 12

DEF: Sudden, involuntary contractions of the muscles.

780.31 Febrile convulsions
  Febrile seizure

AHA: 4Q, '98, 39

780.39 Other convulsions
  Convulsive disorder NOS
  Fit NOS
  Seizure NOS

AHA: 4Q, '04, 51; 1Q, '03, 7; 2Q, '99, 17; 4Q, '97, 45

780.4 Dizziness and giddiness
  Light-headedness   Vertigo NOS
  EXCLUDES Ménière's disease and other specified vertiginous syndromes (386.0-386.9)

AHA: 2Q, '03, 11; 2Q, '97, 9; 2Q, '91, 17

DEF: Whirling sensations in head with feeling of falling.

√5ᵗʰ **780.5 Sleep disturbances**
  EXCLUDES ▶ circadian rhythm sleep disorders (327.30-327.39)
    organic hypersomnia (327.10-327.19)
    organic insomnia (327.00-327.09)
    organic sleep apnea (327.20-327.29)
    organic sleep related movement disorders (327.51-327.59)
    parasomnias (327.40-327.49)◄
    that of nonorganic origin (307.40-307.49)

780.50 Sleep disturbance, unspecified

780.51 Insomnia with sleep apnea, unspecified
  DEF: Transient cessation of breathing disturbing sleep.

780.52 Insomnia, unspecified
  DEF: Inability to maintain adequate sleep cycle.

780.53 Hypersomnia with sleep apnea, unspecified

AHA: 1Q, '93, 28; N-D, '85, 4

  DEF: Autonomic response inhibited during sleep; causes insufficient oxygen intake, acidosis and pulmonary hypertension.

780.54 Hypersomnia, unspecified
  DEF: Prolonged sleep cycle.

780.55 Disruptions of 24 hour sleep wake cycle, unspecified

780.56 Dysfunctions associated with sleep stages or arousal from sleep

780.57 Unspecified sleep apnea

AHA: 1Q, '01, 6 ; 1Q, '97, 5; 1Q, '93, 28

780.58 Sleep related movement disorder, unspecified
  EXCLUDES restless leg syndrome (333.99)

AHA: 4Q, '04, 95

780.59 Other

√4ᵗʰ √5ᵗʰ Additional Digit Required   **RUG III Special Care Dx**   **RUG III Clinically Complex Dx**   **Hospice Non-cancer Dx**   **CD PDx** Clinical Dimension PDx   **CD SDx** Clinical Dimension SDx

2006 ICD•9•CM   **October 2005 • Volume 1 — 231**

Symptoms, Signs, and Ill-Defined Conditions

780.6–781.6

780.6 Fever

Chills with fever	Hyperpyrexia NOS
Fever NOS	Pyrexia
Fever of unknown origin (FUO)	Pyrexia of unknown origin

EXCLUDES   pyrexia of unknown origin (during):
in newborn (778.4)
labor (659.2)
the puerperium (672)

AHA: 4Q, '99, 26; 2Q, '91, 8

DEF: Elevated body temperature; no known cause.

√5ᵗʰ 780.7 Malaise and fatigue

EXCLUDES   debility, unspecified (799.3)
fatigue (during):
combat (308.0-308.9)
heat (992.6)
pregnancy (646.8)
neurasthenia (300.5)
senile asthenia (797)

AHA: 4Q, '88, 12; M-A, '87, 8

DEF: Indefinite feeling of debility or lack of good health.

780.71 Chronic fatigue syndrome

AHA: 4Q, '98, 48

DEF: Persistent fatigue, symptoms include weak muscles, sore throat, lymphadenitis, headache, depression and mild fever; no known cause; also called chronic mononucleosis, benign myalgic encephalomyelitis, Iceland disease and neurosthenia.

780.79 Other malaise and fatigue

Asthenia NOS	Postviral (asthenic) syndrome
Lethargy	Tiredness

AHA: 4Q, '04, 78; 1Q, '00, 6; 4Q, '99, 26

DEF: Asthenia: Any weakness, lack of strength or loss of energy, especially neuromuscular.

DEF: Lethargy: Listlessness, drowsiness, stupor and apathy.

DEF: Postviral (asthenic) syndrome: Listlessness, drowsiness, stupor and apathy; follows acute viral infection.

DEF: Tiredness: General exhaustion or fatigue.

780.8 Generalized hyperhidrosis

Diaphoresis
Excessive sweating
Secondary hyperhidrosis

EXCLUDES   focal (localized) (primary) (secondary) hyperhidrosis (705.21-705.22)
Frey's syndrome (705.22)

DEF: Excessive sweating, appears as droplets on skin; general or localized.

√5ᵗʰ 780.9 Other general symptoms

EXCLUDES   hypothermia:
NOS (accidental) (991.6)
due to anesthesia (995.89)
of newborn (778.2-778.3)
memory disturbance as part of a pattern of mental disorder

AHA: 4Q, '02, 67; 4Q, '99, 10; 3Q, '93, 11; N-D, '85, 12

780.91 Fussy infant (baby)   P

780.92 Excessive crying of infant (baby)   P

EXCLUDES ▶◄ excessive crying of child, adolescent or adult (780.95)◄

780.93 Memory loss

Amnesia (retrograde)
Memory loss NOS

EXCLUDES   mild memory disturbance due to organic brain damage (310.1)
transient global amnesia (437.7)

AHA: 4Q, '03, 71

780.94 Early satiety

AHA: 4Q, '03, 72

DEF: The premature feeling of being full; mechanism of satiety is mutlifactorial.

780.95 Other excessive crying

EXCLUDES   excessive crying of infant (baby) (780.92)

780.99 Other general symptoms

Amnesia (retrograde)
Chill(s) NOS
Generalized pain
Hypothermia, not associated with low environmental temperature

AHA: 4Q, '03, 103

√4ᵗʰ 781 Symptoms involving nervous and musculoskeletal systems

EXCLUDES   depression NOS (311)
disorders specifically relating to:
back (724.0-724.9)
hearing (388.0-389.9)
joint (718.0-719.9)
limb (729.0-729.9)
neck (723.0-723.9)
vision (368.0-369.9)
pain in limb (729.5)

781.0 Abnormal involuntary movements   CD PDx

Abnormal head movements	Spasms NOS
Fasciculation	Tremor NOS

EXCLUDES   abnormal reflex (796.1)
chorea NOS (333.5)
infantile spasms (345.60-345.61)
spastic paralysis (342.1, 343.0-344.9)
specified movement disorders classifiable to 333 (333.0-333.9)
that of nonorganic origin (307.2-307.3)

781.1 Disturbances of sensation of smell and taste   CD PDx

Anosmia	Parosmia
Parageusia	

DEF: Anosmia: loss of sense of smell due to organic factors, including loss of olfactory nerve conductivity, cerebral disease, nasal fossae formation and peripheral olfactory nerve diseases; can also be psychological disorder.

DEF: Parageusia: distorted sense of taste, or bad taste in mouth.

DEF: Parosmia: distorted sense of smell.

781.2 Abnormality of gait   CD PDx

Gait:	Gait:
ataxic	spastic
paralytic	staggering

EXCLUDES   ataxia:
NOS (781.3)
locomotor (progressive) (094.0)
difficulty in walking (719.7)

DEF: Abnormal, asymmetric gait.

AHA: 2Q, '04, 15

781.3 Lack of coordination   CD PDx

Ataxia NOS	Muscular incoordination

EXCLUDES   ataxic gait (781.2)
cerebellar ataxia (334.0-334.9)
difficulty in walking (719.7)
vertigo NOS (780.4)

AHA: 4Q, '04, 51; 3Q, '97, 12

781.4 Transient paralysis of limb   CD PDx

Monoplegia, transient NOS

EXCLUDES   paralysis (342.0-344.9)

781.5 Clubbing of fingers   CD PDx

DEF: Enlarged soft tissue of distal fingers.

781.6 Meningismus   CD PDx

Dupré's syndrome	Meningism

AHA: J-F, '87, 7

DEF: Condition with signs and symptoms that resemble meningeal irritation; it is associated with febrile illness and dehydration with no evidence of infection.

N Newborn Age: 0   P Pediatric Age: 0-17   M Maternity Age: 12-55   A Adult Age :15-124   Manifestation Code   ▶◄ Revised Text   ● New Code   ▲ Revised Code Title

781.7 Tetany `CD PDx`
Carpedal spasm
> EXCLUDES   tetanus neonatorum (771.3)
> tetany:
>> hysterical (300.11)
>> newborn (hypocalcemic) (775.4)
>> parathyroid (252.1)
>> psychogenic (306.0)

DEF: Nerve and muscle hyperexcitability; symptoms include muscle spasms, twitching, cramps, laryngospasm with inspiratory stridor, hyperreflexia and choreiform movements.

781.8 Neurologic neglect syndrome `CD PDx`
Asomatognosia   Left-sided neglect
Hemi-akinesia   Sensory extinction
Hemi-inattention   Sensory neglect
Hemispatial neglect   Visuospatial neglect
AHA: 4Q, '94, 37

√5th **781.9 Other symptoms involving nervous and musculoskeletal systems**
AHA: 4Q, '00, 45

781.91 Loss of height `CD PDx`
> EXCLUDES   osteoporosis (733.00-733.09)

781.92 Abnormal posture `CD PDx`
781.93 Ocular torticollis `CD PDx`
AHA: 4Q, '02, 68

DEF: Abnormal head posture as a result of a contracted state of cervical muscles to correct a visual disturbance; either double vision or a visual field defect.

781.94 Facial weakness `CD PDx`
Facial droop
> EXCLUDES   facial weakness due to late effect of cerebrovascular accident (438.83)

AHA: 4Q, '03, 72

781.99 Other symptoms involving nervous `CD PDx` **and musculoskeletal systems**

√4th **782 Symptoms involving skin and other integumentary tissue**
> EXCLUDES   symptoms relating to breast (611.71-611.79)

782.0 Disturbance of skin sensation
Anesthesia of skin   Numbness
Burning or prickling sensation   Paresthesia
Hyperesthesia   Tingling
Hypoesthesia

782.1 Rash and other nonspecific skin eruption
Exanthem
> EXCLUDES   vesicular eruption (709.8)

782.2 Localized superficial swelling, mass, or lump
Subcutaneous nodules
> EXCLUDES   localized adiposity (278.1)

782.3 Edema
Anasarca   Localized edema NOS
Dropsy
> EXCLUDES   ascites (789.5)
> edema of:
>> newborn NOS (778.5)
>> pregnancy (642.0-642.9, 646.1)
> fluid retention (276.6)
> hydrops fetalis (773.3, 778.0)
> hydrothorax (511.8)
> nutritional edema (260, 262)

AHA: 2Q, '00, 18

DEF: Edema: excess fluid in intercellular body tissue.
DEF: Anasarca: massive edema in all body tissues.
DEF: Dropsy: serous fluid accumulated in body cavity or cellular tissue.
DEF: Localized edema: edema in specific body areas.

782.4 Jaundice, unspecified, not of newborn
Cholemia NOS
Icterus NOS
> EXCLUDES   jaundice in newborn (774.0-774.7)
> due to isoimmunization (773.0-773.2, 773.4)

DEF: Bilirubin deposits of skin, causing yellow cast.

782.5 Cyanosis
> EXCLUDES   newborn (770.83)

DEF: Deficient oxygen of blood; causes blue cast to skin.

√5th **782.6 Pallor and flushing**
782.61 Pallor
782.62 Flushing
Excessive blushing

782.7 Spontaneous ecchymoses
Petechiae
> EXCLUDES   ecchymosis in fetus or newborn (772.6)
> purpura (287.0-287.9)

DEF: Hemorrhagic spots of skin; resemble freckles.

782.8 Changes in skin texture
Induration }
Thickening } of skin

782.9 Other symptoms involving skin and integumentary tissues

√4th **783 Symptoms concerning nutrition, metabolism, and development**
783.0 Anorexia
Loss of appetite
> EXCLUDES   anorexia nervosa (307.1)
> loss of appetite of nonorganic origin (307.59)

783.1 Abnormal weight gain
> EXCLUDES   excessive weight gain in pregnancy (646.1)
> obesity (278.00)
> morbid (278.01)

√5th **783.2 Abnormal loss of weight and underweight**
►Use additional code to identify Body Mass Index (BMI), if known (V85.0)◄
AHA: 4Q, '00, 45

783.21 Loss of weight
783.22 Underweight

783.3 Feeding difficulties and mismanagement
Feeding problem (elderly) (infant)
> EXCLUDES   feeding disturbance or problems:
>> in newborn (779.3)
>> of nonorganic origin (307.50-307.59)

AHA: 4Q, '00, 45; 3Q, '97, 12

√5th **783.4 Lack of expected normal physiological development in childhood**
> EXCLUDES   delay in sexual development and puberty (259.0)
> gonadal dysgenesis (758.6)
> pituitary dwarfism (253.3)
> slow fetal growth and fetal malnutrition (764.00-764.99)
> specific delays in mental development (315.0-315.9)

AHA: 4Q, '00, 45; 3Q, '97, 4

783.40 Lack of normal physiological development unspecified
Inadequate development
Lack of development

783.41 Failure to thrive `P`
Failure to gain weight
AHA: 1Q, '03, 12

DEF: Organic failure to thrive: acute or chronic illness that interferes with nutritional intake, absorption, metabolism excretion and energy requirements. Nonorganic FTT is symptom of neglect or abuse.

√4th √5th Additional Digit Required   RUG III Special Care Dx   RUG III Clinically Complex Dx   Hospice Non-cancer Dx   `CD PDx` Clinical Dimension PDx   `CD SDx` Clinical Dimension SDx

Symptoms, Signs, and Ill-Defined Conditions

783.42–785.52

783.42 Delayed milestones [P]
Late talker   Late walker

783.43 Short stature
Growth failure   Lack of growth
Growth retardation   Physical retardation
DEF: Constitutional short stature: stature inconsistent with chronological age. Genetic short stature is when skeletal maturation matches chronological age.

783.5 Polydipsia
Excessive thirst

783.6 Polyphagia
Excessive eating   Hyperalimentation NOS
EXCLUDES   *disorders of eating of nonorganic origin (307.50-307.59)*

783.7 Adult failure to thrive [A]

783.9 Other symptoms concerning nutrition, metabolism, and development
Hypometabolism
EXCLUDES   *abnormal basal metabolic rate (794.7)*
dehydration ▶(276.51)◀
other disorders of fluid, electrolyte, and acid-base balance (276.0-276.9)
AHA: 2Q, '04, 3

✓4ᵗʰ 784 Symptoms involving head and neck
EXCLUDES   *encephalopathy NOS (348.30)*
specific symptoms involving neck classifiable to 723 (723.0-723.9)

784.0 Headache
Facial pain   Pain in head NOS
EXCLUDES   *atypical face pain (350.2)*
migraine (346.0-346.9)
tension headache (307.81)
AHA: 1Q, '90, 4; 3Q, '92, 14

784.1 Throat pain
EXCLUDES   *dysphagia (787.2)*
neck pain (723.1)
sore throat (462)
chronic (472.1)

784.2 Swelling, mass, or lump in head and neck
Space-occupying lesion, intracranial NOS
AHA: 1Q, '03, 8

784.3 Aphasia
EXCLUDES   *developmental aphasia (315.31)*
AHA: 4Q, '04, 78; 4Q. '98, 87; 3Q, '97, 12
DEF: Inability to communicate through speech, written word, or sign language.

✓5ᵗʰ 784.4 Voice disturbance
784.40 Voice disturbance, unspecified
784.41 Aphonia
Loss of voice
784.49 Other
Change in voice   Hypernasality
Dysphonia   Hyponasality
Hoarseness

784.5 Other speech disturbance
Dysarthria   Slurred speech
Dysphasia
EXCLUDES   *stammering and stuttering (307.0)*
that of nonorganic origin (307.0, 307.9)

✓5ᵗʰ 784.6 Other symbolic dysfunction
EXCLUDES   *developmental learning delays (315.0-315.9)*
784.60 Symbolic dysfunction, unspecified
784.61 Alexia and dyslexia
Alexia (with agraphia)
DEF: Alexia: inability to understand written word due to central brain lesion.
DEF: Dyslexia: ability to recognize letters but inability to read, spell, and write words; genetic.

784.69 Other
Acalculia   Agraphia NOS
Agnosia   Apraxia

784.7 Epistaxis
Hemorrhage from nose
Nosebleed
AHA: 3Q, '04, 7

784.8 Hemorrhage from throat
EXCLUDES   *hemoptysis (786.3)*

784.9 Other symptoms involving head and neck
Choking sensation   Mouth breathing
Halitosis   Sneezing

✓4ᵗʰ 785 Symptoms involving cardiovascular system
EXCLUDES   *heart failure NOS (428.9)*

785.0 Tachycardia, unspecified
Rapid heart beat
EXCLUDES   *neonatal tachycardia (779.82)*
paroxysmal tachycardia (427.0-427.2)
AHA: 2Q, '03, 11
DEF: Excessively rapid heart rate.

785.1 Palpitations
Awareness of heart beat
EXCLUDES   *specified dysrhythmias (427.0-427.9)*

785.2 Undiagnosed cardiac murmurs
Heart murmurs NOS
AHA: 4Q, '92, 16

785.3 Other abnormal heart sounds
Cardiac dullness, increased or decreased
Friction fremitus, cardiac
Precordial friction

785.4 Gangrene
Gangrene:
NOS
spreading cutaneous
Gangrenous cellulitis
Phagedena
Code first any associated underlying condition
EXCLUDES   *gangrene of certain sites — see Alphabetic Index*
gangrene with atherosclerosis of the extremities (440.24)
gas gangrene (040.0
AHA: 1Q, '04, 14; 3Q, '90, 15; M-A, '86, 12

DEF: Gangrene: necrosis of skin tissue due to bacterial infection, diabetes, embolus and vascular supply loss.

DEF: Gangrenous cellulitis: group A streptococcal infection; begins with severe cellulitis, spreads to superficial and deep fascia; produces gangrene of underlying tissues.

✓5ᵗʰ 785.5 Shock without mention of trauma
785.50 Shock, unspecified
Failure of peripheral circulation
AHA: 2Q, '96, 10
DEF: Peripheral circulatory failure due to heart insufficiencies.

785.51 Cardiogenic shock
DEF: Shock syndrome: associated with myocardial infarction, cardiac tamponade and massive pulmonary embolism; symptoms include mental torpor, reduced blood pressure, tachycardia, pallor and cold, clammy skin.

785.52 Septic shock
Shock:
Endotoxic
Gram-negative
Code first:
systemic inflammatory response syndrome due to infectious process with organ dysfunction (995.92)
systemic inflammatory response syndrome due to noninfectious process with organ dysfunction (995.94)
AHA: 4Q, '03, 73, 79

[N] Newborn Age: 0   [P] Pediatric Age: 0-17   [M] Maternity Age: 12-55   [A] Adult Age :15-124   Manifestation Code   ▶◀ Revised Text   ● New Code   ▲ Revised Code Title

785.59 Other
Shock:
hypovolemic
> **EXCLUDES** *shock (due to):*
> *anesthetic (995.4)*
> *anaphylactic (995.0)*
> *due to serum (999.4)*
> *electric (994.8)*
> *following abortion (639.5)*
> *lightning (994.0)*
> *obstetrical (669.1)*
> *postoperative (998.0)*
> *traumatic (958.4)*

AHA: 2Q, '00, 3

785.6 Enlargement of lymph nodes
Lymphadenopathy   "Swollen glands"
> **EXCLUDES** *lymphadenitis (chronic) (289.1-289.3)*
> *acute (683)*

785.9 Other symptoms involving cardiovascular system
Bruit (arterial)   Weak pulse

✓4th **786 Symptoms involving respiratory system and other chest symptoms**

✓5th **786.0 Dyspnea and respiratory abnormalities**

786.00 Respiratory abnormality, unspecified

786.01 Hyperventilation
> **EXCLUDES** *hyperventilation, psychogenic (306.1)*

DEF: Rapid breathing causes carbon dioxide loss from blood.

786.02 Orthopnea

DEF: Difficulty breathing except in upright position.

786.03 Apnea
> **EXCLUDES** *apnea of newborn (770.81, 770.82)*
> *sleep apnea (780.51, 780.53, 780.57)*

AHA: 4Q, '98, 50

DEF: Cessation of breathing.

786.04 Cheyne-Stokes respiration
AHA: 4Q, '98, 50

DEF: Rhythmic increase of depth and frequency of breathing with apnea; occurs in frontal lobe and diencephalic dysfunction.

786.05 Shortness of breath
AHA: 4Q, '99, 25; 1Q, '99, 6; 4Q, '98, 50

DEF: Inability to take in sufficient oxygen.

786.06 Tachypnea
> **EXCLUDES** *transitory tachypnea of newborn (770.6)*

AHA: 4Q, '98, 50

DEF: Abnormal rapid respiratory rate; called hyperventilation.

786.07 Wheezing
> **EXCLUDES** *asthma (493.00-493.92)*

AHA: 4Q, '98, 50

DEF: Stenosis of respiratory passageway; causes whistling sound; due to asthma, coryza, croup, emphysema, hay fever, edema, and pleural effusion.

786.09 Other
Respiratory:
distress
insufficiency
> **EXCLUDES** *respiratory distress:*
> *following trauma and surgery (518.5)*
> *newborn (770.89)*
> *syndrome (newborn) (769)*
> *adult (518.5)*
> *respiratory failure (518.81, 518.83-518.84)*
> *newborn (770.84)*

AHA: 2Q, '98, 10; 1Q, '97, 7; 1Q, '90, 9

786.1 Stridor
> **EXCLUDES** *congenital laryngeal stridor (748.3)*

DEF: Obstructed airway causes harsh sound.

786.2 Cough
> **EXCLUDES** *cough:*
> *psychogenic (306.1)*
> *smokers' (491.0)*
> *with hemorrhage (786.3)*

AHA: 4Q. '99, 26

786.3 Hemoptysis
Cough with hemorrhage
Pulmonary hemorrhage NOS
> **EXCLUDES** *pulmonary hemorrhage of newborn (770.3)*

AHA: 4Q, '90, 26

DEF: Coughing up blood or blood-stained sputum.

786.4 Abnormal sputum
Abnormal:
amount
color } (of) sputum
odor
Excessive

✓5th **786.5 Chest pain**

786.50 Chest pain, unspecified
AHA: 1Q, '03, 6; 1Q, '02, 4; 4Q, '99, 25

786.51 Precordial pain
DEF: Chest pain over heart and lower thorax.

786.52 Painful respiration
Pain: Pleurodynia
anterior chest wall
pleuritic
> **EXCLUDES** *epidemic pleurodynia (074.1)*

AHA: N-D, '84, 17

786.59 Other
Discomfort
Pressure   } in chest
Tightness
> **EXCLUDES** *pain in breast (611.71)*

AHA: 1Q, '02, 6

786.6 Swelling, mass, or lump in chest
> **EXCLUDES** *lump in breast (611.72)*

786.7 Abnormal chest sounds
Abnormal percussion, chest   Rales
Friction sounds, chest   Tympany, chest
> **EXCLUDES** *wheezing (786.07)*

786.8 Hiccough
> **EXCLUDES** *psychogenic hiccough (306.1)*

786.9 Other symptoms involving respiratory system and chest
Breath-holding spell

✓4th **787 Symptoms involving digestive system**
> **EXCLUDES** *constipation (564.00-564.09)*
> *pylorospasm (537.81)*
> *congenital (750.5)*

✓5th **787.0 Nausea and vomiting**
Emesis
> **EXCLUDES** *hematemesis NOS (578.0)*
> *vomiting:*
> *bilious, following gastrointestinal surgery (564.3)*
> *cyclical (536.2)*
> *psychogenic (306.4)*
> *excessive, in pregnancy (643.0-643.9)*
> *habit (536.2)*
> *of newborn (779.3)*
> *psychogenic NOS (307.54)*

AHA: M-A, '85, 11

✓4th
✓5th **Additional Digit Required**   RUG III Special Care Dx   RUG III Clinically Complex Dx   Hospice Non-cancer Dx   **CD PDx** Clinical Dimension PDx   **CD SDx** Clinical Dimension SDx

2006 ICD•9•CM   **Volume 1 — 235**

Symptoms, Signs, and Ill-Defined Conditions

787.01–788.5

787.01 Nausea with vomiting

AHA: 1Q, '03, 5

787.02 Nausea alone

AHA: 3Q, '00, 12; 2Q, '97, 9

787.03 Vomiting alone

787.1 Heartburn

Pyrosis   Waterbrash

> EXCLUDES *dyspepsia or indigestion (536.8)*

AHA: 2Q, '01, 6

787.2 Dysphagia

Difficulty in swallowing

AHA: 4Q, '03, 103, 109; 2Q, '01, 4

787.3 Flatulence, eructation, and gas pain

Abdominal distention (gaseous)
Bloating
Tympanites (abdominal) (intestinal)

> EXCLUDES *aerophagy (306.4)*

DEF: Flatulence: excess air or gas in intestine or stomach.

DEF: Eructation: belching, expelling gas through mouth.

DEF: Gas pain: gaseous pressure affecting gastrointestinal system.

787.4 Visible peristalsis

Hyperperistalsis

DEF: Increase in involuntary movements of intestines.

787.5 Abnormal bowel sounds

Absent bowel sounds
Hyperactive bowel sounds

787.6 Incontinence of feces

Encopresis NOS
Incontinence of sphincter ani

> EXCLUDES *that of nonorganic origin (307.7)*

AHA: 1Q, '97, 9

787.7 Abnormal feces

Bulky stools

> EXCLUDES *abnormal stool content (792.1)*
> *melena:*
>   *NOS (578.1)*
>   *newborn (772.4, 777.3)*

√5ᵗʰ **787.9 Other symptoms involving digestive system**

> EXCLUDES *gastrointestinal hemorrhage (578.0-*
> *578.9)*
> *intestinal obstruction (560.0-560.9)*
> *specific functional digestive disorders:*
>   *esophagus (530.0-530.9)*
>   *stomach and duodenum (536.0-*
>   *536.9)*
> *those not elsewhere classified*
>   *(564.00-564.9)*

787.91 Diarrhea

Diarrhea NOS

AHA: 4Q, '95, 54

787.99 Other

Change in bowel habits
Tenesmus (rectal)

DEF: Tenesmus: Painful, ineffective straining at the rectum with limited passage of fecal matter.

√4ᵗʰ **788 Symptoms involving urinary system**

> EXCLUDES *hematuria (599.7)*
> *nonspecific findings on examination of the urine*
>   *(791.0-791.9)*
> *small kidney of unknown cause (589.0-589.9)*
> *uremia NOS (586)*

788.0 Renal colic

Colic (recurrent) of: Colic (recurrent) of:
  kidney   ureter

DEF: Kidney pain.

788.1 Dysuria

Painful urination   Strangury

√5ᵗʰ **788.2 Retention of urine**

> EXCLUDES ▶ *urinary retention due to hyperplasia of*
> *prostate (600.0-600.9 with fifth-*
> *digit 1)*◄

DEF: Inability to void.

788.20 Retention of urine, unspecified

AHA: 2Q, '04, 18; 3Q, '03, 12-13; 1Q, '03, 6; 3Q, '96, 10

788.21 Incomplete bladder emptying

788.29 Other specified retention of urine

√5ᵗʰ **788.3 Urinary incontinence**

Code, if applicable, any causal condition first,
   such as:
   congenital ureterocele (753.23)
   genital prolapse (618.00-618.9)

> EXCLUDES *that of nonorganic origin (307.6)*

AHA: 4Q, '92, 22

788.30 Urinary incontinence, unspecified

Enuresis NOS

788.31 Urge incontinence

AHA: 1Q, '00, 19

DEF: Inability to control urination, upon urge to urinate.

788.32 Stress incontinence, male   ♂

> EXCLUDES *stress incontinence, female*
> *(625.6)*

DEF: Inability to control urination associated with weak sphincter in males.

788.33 Mixed incontinence, (male) (female)

Urge and stress

DEF: Urge, stress incontinence: involuntary discharge of urine due to anatomic displacement.

788.34 Incontinence without sensory awareness

DEF: Involuntary discharge of urine without sensory warning.

788.35 Post-void dribbling

DEF: Involuntary discharge of residual urine after voiding.

788.36 Nocturnal enuresis

DEF: Involuntary discharge of urine during the night.

788.37 Continuous leakage

DEF: Continuous, involuntary urine seepage.

788.38 Overflow incontinence

DEF: Leakage caused by pressure of retained urine in the bladder after the bladder has fully contracted due to weakened bladder muscles or an obstruction of the urethra.

788.39 Other urinary incontinence

√5ᵗʰ **788.4 Frequency of urination and polyuria**

788.41 Urinary frequency

Frequency of micturition

788.42 Polyuria

DEF: Excessive urination.

788.43 Nocturia

DEF: Urination affecting sleep patterns.

788.5 Oliguria and anuria

Deficient secretion of urine
Suppression of urinary secretion

> EXCLUDES *that complicating:*
> *abortion (634-638 with .3, 639.3)*
> *ectopic or molar pregnancy (639.3)*
> *pregnancy, childbirth, or the*
> *puerperium (642.0-642.9,*
> *646.2)*

DEF: Oliguria: diminished urinary secretion related to fluid intake.

DEF: Anuria: lack of urinary secretion due to renal failure or obstructed urinary tract.

Ⓝ Newborn Age: 0   Ⓟ Pediatric Age: 0-17   Ⓜ Maternity Age: 12-55   Ⓐ Adult Age :15-124   Manifestation Code   ▶◄ Revised Text   ● New Code   ▲ Revised Code Title

☑5ᵗʰ 788.6 Other abnormality of urination

788.61 Splitting of urinary stream
Intermittent urinary stream

788.62 Slowing of urinary stream
Weak stream

788.63 Urgency of urination

> **EXCLUDES**   urge incontinence (788.31, 788.33)

AHA: 4Q, '03, 74

DEF: Feeling of intense need to urinate; abrupt sensation of imminent urination.

788.69 Other

788.7 Urethral discharge
Penile discharge   Urethrorrhea

788.8 Extravasation of urine
DEF: Leaking or infiltration of urine into tissues.

788.9 Other symptoms involving urinary system
Extrarenal uremia   Vesical:
Vesical: tenesmus
   pain

AHA: ▶1Q, '05, 12;◀ 4Q, '88, 1

☑4ᵗʰ 789 Other symptoms involving abdomen and pelvis

> **EXCLUDES**   symptoms referable to genital organs:
> female (625.0-625.9)
> male (607.0-608.9)
> psychogenic (302.70-302.79)

The following fifth-digit subclassification is to be used for codes 789.0, 789.3, 789.4, 789.6:

   0 unspecified site
   1 right upper quadrant
   2 left upper quadrant
   3 right lower quadrant
   4 left lower quadrant
   5 periumbilic
   6 epigastric
   7 generalized
   9 other specified site
      Multiple sites

☑5ᵗʰ 789.0 Abdominal pain
Colic: Cramps, abdominal
   NOS
   infantile

> **EXCLUDES**   renal colic (788.0)

AHA: 1Q, '95, 3; **For code 789.06:** 1Q, '02, 5

789.1 Hepatomegaly
Enlargement of liver

789.2 Splenomegaly
Enlargement of spleen

☑5ᵗʰ 789.3 Abdominal or pelvic swelling, mass, or lump
Diffuse or generalized swelling or mass:
   abdominal NOS
   umbilical

> **EXCLUDES**   abdominal distention (gaseous) (787.3)
> ascites (789.5)

☑5ᵗʰ 789.4 Abdominal rigidity

789.5 Ascites
Fluid in peritoneal cavity
AHA: 4Q, '89, 11

DEF: Serous fluid effusion and accumulation in abdominal cavity.

☑5ᵗʰ 789.6 Abdominal tenderness
Rebound tenderness

789.9 Other symptoms involving abdomen and pelvis
Umbilical: Umbilical:
   bleeding   discharge

NONSPECIFIC ABNORMAL FINDINGS (790-796)

AHA: 2Q, '90, 16

☑4ᵗʰ 790 Nonspecific findings on examination of blood

> **EXCLUDES**   abnormality of:
> platelets (287.0-287.9)
> thrombocytes (287.0-287.9)
> white blood cells (288.0-288.9)

☑5ᵗʰ 790.0 Abnormality of red blood cells

> **EXCLUDES**   anemia:
> congenital (776.5)
> newborn, due to isoimmunization (773.0-773.2, 773.5)
> of premature infant (776.6)
> other specified types (280.0-285.9)
> hemoglobin disorders (282.5-282.7)
> polycythemia:
> familial (289.6)
> neonatorum (776.4)
> secondary (289.0)
> vera (238.4)

AHA: 4Q, '00, 46

790.01 Precipitous drop in hematocrit
Drop in hematocrit

790.09 Other abnormality of red blood cells
Abnormal red cell morphology NOS
Abnormal red cell volume NOS
Anisocytosis
Poikilocytosis

790.1 Elevated sedimentation rate

☑5ᵗʰ 790.2 Abnormal glucose

> **EXCLUDES**   diabetes mellitus (250.00-250.93)
> dysmetabolic syndrome X (277.7)
> gestational diabetes (648.8)
> glycosuria (791.5)
> hypoglycemia (251.2)
> that complicating pregnancy, childbirth, or puerperium (648.8)

AHA: 4Q, '03, 74; 3Q, '91, 5

790.21 Impaired fasting glucose
Elevated fasting glucose

790.22 Impaired glucose tolerance test (oral)
Elevated glucose tolerance test

790.29 Other abnormal glucose
Abnormal glucose NOS
Abnormal non-fasting glucose
Pre-diabetes NOS

790.3 Excessive blood level of alcohol
Elevated blood-alcohol

AHA: S-O, '86, 3

790.4 Nonspecific elevation of levels of transaminase or lactic acid dehydrogenase [LDH]

790.5 Other nonspecific abnormal serum enzyme levels
Abnormal serum level of:
   acid phosphatase
   alkaline phosphatase
   amylase
   lipase

> **EXCLUDES**   deficiency of circulating enzymes (277.6)

790.6 Other abnormal blood chemistry
Abnormal blood level of: Abnormal blood level of:
   cobalt   magnesium
   copper   mineral
   iron   zinc
   lithium

> **EXCLUDES**   abnormality of electrolyte or acid-base balance (276.0-276.9)
> hypoglycemia NOS (251.2)
> specific finding indicating abnormality of:
> amino-acid transport and metabolism (270.0-270.9)
> carbohydrate transport and metabolism (271.0-271.9)
> lipid metabolism (272.0-272.9)
> uremia NOS (586)

AHA: 4Q, '88, 1

Symptoms, Signs, and Ill-Defined Conditions

788.6–790.6

☑4ᵗʰ ☑5ᵗʰ Additional Digit Required   RUG III Special Care Dx   RUG III Clinically Complex Dx   Hospice Non-cancer Dx   **CD PDx** Clinical Dimension PDx   **CD SDx** Clinical Dimension SDx

2006 ICD•9•CM   **October 2005 • Volume 1 — 237**

Symptoms, Signs, and Ill-Defined Conditions

790.7–793.89

790.7 Bacteremia

> EXCLUDES   *bacteremia of newborn (771.83)*
> *septicemia (038)*
> Use additional code to identify organism (041)

AHA: 2Q, '03, 7; 4Q, '93, 29; 3Q, '88, 12

DEF: Laboratory finding of bacteria in the blood in the absence of two or more signs of sepsis; transient in nature, progresses to septicemia with severe infectious process.

790.8 Viremia, unspecified

AHA: 4Q, '88, 100

DEF: Presence of a virus in the blood stream.

√5ᵗʰ 790.9 Other nonspecific findings on examination of blood

AHA: 4Q, '93, 29

790.91 Abnormal arterial blood gases

790.92 Abnormal coagulation profile

Abnormal or prolonged:
bleeding time
coagulation time
partial thromboplastin time [PTT]
prothrombintime [PT]

> EXCLUDES   *coagulation (hemorrhagic)*
> *disorders (286.0-286.9)*

790.93 Elevated prostate specific antigen, Ａ♂
(PSA)

790.94 Euthyroid sick syndrome

AHA: 4Q, '97, 45

DEF: Transient alteration of thyroid hormone metabolism due to nonthyroid illness or stress.

790.95 Elevated C-reactive protein (CRP)

DEF: Inflammation in an arterial wall results in elevated C-reactive protein (CRP) in the blood; CRP is a recognized risk factor in cardiovascular disease.

790.99 Other

AHA: 2Q, '03, 14

√4ᵗʰ 791 Nonspecific findings on examination of urine

> EXCLUDES   *hematuria NOS (599.7)*
> *specific findings indicating abnormality of:*
> *amino-acid transport and metabolism (270.0-270.9)*
> *carbohydrate transport and metabolism (271.0-271.9)*

791.0 Proteinuria

Albuminuria
Bence-Jones proteinuria

> EXCLUDES   *postural proteinuria (593.6)*
> *that arising during pregnancy or the puerperium (642.0-642.9, 646.2)*

AHA: 3Q, '91, 8

DEF: Excess protein in urine.

791.1 Chyluria

> EXCLUDES   *filarial (125.0-125.9)*

DEF: Excess chyle in urine.

791.2 Hemoglobinuria

DEF: Free hemoglobin in blood due to rapid hemolysis of red blood cells.

791.3 Myoglobinuria

DEF: Myoglobin (oxygen-transporting pigment) in urine.

791.4 Biliuria

DEF: Bile pigments in urine.

791.5 Glycosuria

> EXCLUDES   *renal glycosuria (271.4)*

DEF: Sugar in urine.

791.6 Acetonuria

Ketonuria

DEF: Excess acetone in urine.

791.7 Other cells and casts in urine

791.9 Other nonspecific findings on examination of urine

Crystalluria
Elevated urine levels of:
17-ketosteroids
catecholamines

Elevated urine levels of:
indolacetic acid
vanillylmandelic acid [VMA]
Melanuria

AHA: ►1Q, '05, 12◄

√4ᵗʰ 792 Nonspecific abnormal findings in other body substances

> EXCLUDES   *that in chromosomal analysis (795.2)*

792.0 Cerebrospinal fluid

792.1 Stool contents

Abnormal stool color
Fat in stool
Mucus in stool

Occult stool
Pus in stool

> EXCLUDES   *blood in stool [melena] (578.1)*
> *newborn (772.4, 777.3)*

AHA: 2Q, '92, 9

792.2 Semen ♂

Abnormal spermatozoa

> EXCLUDES   *azoospermia (606.0)*
> *oligospermia (606.1)*

792.3 Amniotic fluid Ｍ♀

AHA: N-D, '86, 4

DEF: Nonspecific abnormal findings in amniotic fluid.

792.4 Saliva

> EXCLUDES   *that in chromosomal analysis (795.2)*

792.5 Cloudy (hemodialysis) (peritoneal) dialysis effluent

792.9 Other nonspecific abnormal findings in body substances

Peritoneal fluid
Pleural fluid

Synovial fluid
Vaginal fluids

√4ᵗʰ 793 Nonspecific abnormal findings on radiological and other examination of body structure

> INCLUDES   nonspecific abnormal findings of:
> thermography
> ultrasound examination [echogram]
> x-ray examination

> EXCLUDES   *abnormal results of function studies and radioisotope scans (794.0-794.9)*

793.0 Skull and head

> EXCLUDES   *nonspecific abnormal echoencephalogram (794.01)*

793.1 Lung field

Coin lesion
Shadow } (of) lung

DEF: Coin lesion of lung: coin-shaped, solitary pulmonary nodule.

793.2 Other intrathoracic organ

Abnormal:
echocardiogram
heart shadow

Abnormal:
ultrasound cardiogram
Mediastinal shift

793.3 Biliary tract

Nonvisualization of gallbladder

793.4 Gastrointestinal tract

793.5 Genitourinary organs

Filling defect:
bladder
kidney

Filling defect:
ureter

AHA: 4Q, '00, 46

793.6 Abdominal area, including retroperitoneum

793.7 Musculoskeletal system

√5ᵗʰ 793.8 Breast

AHA: 4Q, '01, 51

793.80 Abnormal mammogram, unspecified

793.81 Mammographic microcalcification

DEF: Calcium and cellular debris deposits in the breast that cannot be felt but can be detected on a mammogram; can be a sign of cancer, benign conditions, or changes in the breast tissue as a result of inflammation, injury, or obstructed duct.

793.89 Other abnormal findings on radiological examination of breast

---

Ｎ Newborn Age: 0   Ｐ Pediatric Age: 0-17   Ｍ Maternity Age: 12-55   Ａ Adult Age :15-124   Manifestation Code   ►◄ Revised Text   ● New Code   ▲ Revised Code Title

793.9 **Other**

Abnormal:

  placental finding by x-ray or ultrasound method

  radiological findings in skin and subcutaneous
    tissue

  EXCLUDES   *abnormal finding by radioisotope localization of placenta (794.9)*

√4ᵗʰ **794** **Nonspecific abnormal results of function studies**

  INCLUDES radioisotope:

    scans

    uptake studies

    scintiphotography

√5ᵗʰ **794.0** **Brain and central nervous system**

  794.00 Abnormal function study, unspecified

  794.01 Abnormal echoencephalogram

  794.02 Abnormal electroencephalogram [EEG]

  794.09 Other

    Abnormal brain scan

√5ᵗʰ **794.1** **Peripheral nervous system and special senses**

  794.10 Abnormal response to nerve stimulation, unspecified

  794.11 Abnormal retinal function studies

    Abnormal electroretinogram [ERG]

  794.12 Abnormal electro-oculogram [EOG]

  794.13 Abnormal visually evoked potential

  794.14 Abnormal oculomotor studies

  794.15 Abnormal auditory function studies

    AHA: 1Q, '04, 15-16

  794.16 Abnormal vestibular function studies

  794.17 Abnormal electromyogram [EMG]

    EXCLUDES *that of eye (794.14)*

  794.19 Other

794.2 **Pulmonary**

  Abnormal lung scan   Reduced:

  Reduced: vital capacity

    ventilatory capacity

√5ᵗʰ **794.3** **Cardiovascular**

  794.30 Abnormal function study, unspecified

  794.31 Abnormal electrocardiogram [ECG] [EKG]

    EXCLUDES ▶*long QT syndrome (426.82)*◀

  794.39 Other

    Abnormal: Abnormal:

     ballistocardiogram   vectorcardiogram

     phonocardiogram

794.4 **Kidney**

  Abnormal renal function test

794.5 **Thyroid**

  Abnormal thyroid: Abnormal thyroid:

   scan   uptake

794.6 **Other endocrine function study**

794.7 **Basal metabolism**

  Abnormal basal metabolic rate [BMR]

794.8 **Liver**

  Abnormal liver scan

794.9 **Other**

  Bladder   Placenta

  Pancreas   Spleen

√4ᵗʰ **795** **Other and nonspecific abnormal cytological, histological, immunological and DNA test findings**

  EXCLUDES *nonspecific abnormalities of red blood cells (790.01-790.09)*

√5ᵗʰ **795.0** **Abnormal Papanicolaou smear of cervix and cervical HPV**

  Abnormal thin preparation smear of cervix

  Abnormal cervical cytology

  EXCLUDES *carcinoma in-situ of cervix (233.1)*

    cervical intraepithelial neoplasia I (CIN I) (622.11)

    cervical intraepithelial neoplasia II (CIN II) (622.12)

    cervical intraepithelial neoplasia III (CIN III) (233.1)

    dysplasia (histologically confirmed) of cervix (uteri) NOS (622.10)

    mild dysplasia (histologically confirmed) (622.11)

    moderate dysplasia (histologically confirmed) (622.12)

    severe dysplasia (histologically confirmed) (233.1)

  AHA: 4Q, '02, 69

  795.00 Abnormal glandular Papanicolaou   ♀
    smear of cervix

    Atypical endocervical cells NOS

    Atypical endometrial cells NOS

    Atypical glandular cells NOS

  795.01 Papanicolaou smear of cervix with   ♀
    atypical squamous cells of undetermined significance (ASC-US)

  795.02 Papanicolaou smear of cervix with   ♀
    atypical squamous cells cannot exclude high grade squamous intraepithelial lesion (ASC-H)

  795.03 Papanicolaou smear of cervix with low   ♀
    grade squamous intraepithelial lesion (LGSIL)

  795.04 Papanicolaou smear of cervix with high   ♀
    grade squamous intraepithelial lesion (HGSIL)

    Cytologic evidence of carcinoma

  795.05 Cervical high risk human papillomavirus ♀
    (HPV) DNA test positive

  795.08 Unsatisfactory smear   ♀

    Inadequate sample

  795.09 Other abnormal Papanicolaou smear   ♀
    of cervix and cervical HPV

    ▶Cervical low risk human papillomavirus (HPV) DNA test positive◀

    Use additional code for associated human papillomavirus (079.4)

    EXCLUDES *encounter for Papanicolaou cervical smear to confirm findings of recent normal smear following initial abnormal smear (V72.32)*

795.1 **Nonspecific abnormal Papanicolaou smear of other site**

795.2 **Nonspecific abnormal findings on chromosomal analysis**

  Abnormal karyotype

√5ᵗʰ **795.3** **Nonspecific positive culture findings**

  Positive culture findings in:

   nose   throat

   sputum   wound

  EXCLUDES *that of:*

    blood (790.7-790.8)

    urine (791.9)

  795.31 Nonspecific positive findings for anthrax

    Positive findings by nasal swab

    AHA: 4Q, '02, 70

  795.39 Other nonspecific positive culture findings

795.4 **Other nonspecific abnormal histological findings**

795.5 **Nonspecific reaction to tuberculin skin test without active tuberculosis**

  Abnormal result of   Tuberculin (skin test):

    Mantoux test   positive

  PPD positive   reactor

√4ᵗʰ √5ᵗʰ Additional Digit Required   RUG III Special Care Dx   RUG III Clinically Complex Dx   Hospice Non-cancer Dx   **CD PDx** Clinical Dimension PDx   **CD SDx** Clinical Dimension SDx

2006 ICD•9•CM   October 2005 • Volume 1 — 239

Symptoms, Signs, and Ill-Defined Conditions

795.6–799.9

795.6 False positive serological test for syphilis
False positive Wassermann reaction

√5ᵗʰ **795.7 Other nonspecific immunological findings**

EXCLUDES   *isoimmunization, in pregnancy (656.1-656.2)*
affecting fetus or newborn (773.0-773.2)

AHA: 2Q, '93, 6

795.71 Nonspecific serologic evidence of human immunodeficiency virus [HIV]
Inclusive human immunodeficiency [HIV] test (adult) (infant)

Note: This code is **only** to be used when a test finding is reported as nonspecific. Asymptomatic positive findings are coded to V08. If any HIV infection symptom or condition is present, see code 042. Negative findings are not coded.

EXCLUDES   *acquired immunodeficiency syndrome [AIDS] (042)*
asymptomatic human immunodeficiency virus, [HIV] infection status (V08)
HIV infection, symptomatic (042)
human immunodeficiency virus [HIV] disease (042)
positive (status) NOS (V08)

AHA: 2Q, '04, 11; 1Q, '93, 21; 1Q, '93, 22; 2Q, '92, 11; J-A, '87, 24

795.79 Other and unspecified nonspecific immunological findings
Raised antibody titer
Raised level of immunoglobulins

√4ᵗʰ **796 Other nonspecific abnormal findings**

796.0 Nonspecific abnormal toxicological findings
Abnormal levels of heavy metals or drugs in blood, urine, or other tissue

EXCLUDES   *excessive blood level of alcohol (790.3)*

AHA: 1Q, '97, 16

796.1 Abnormal reflex

796.2 Elevated blood pressure reading without diagnosis of hypertension

Note: This category is to be used to record an episode of elevated blood pressure in a patient in whom no formal diagnosis of hypertension has been made, or as an incidental finding.

AHA: 2Q, '03, 11; 3Q, '90, 4; J-A, '84, 12

796.3 Nonspecific low blood pressure reading

796.4 Other abnormal clinical findings

AHA: 1Q, '97, 16

796.5 Abnormal finding on antenatal screening   Ⓜ ♀

AHA: 4Q, '97, 46

796.6 Abnormal findings on neonatal screening   Ⓝ

EXCLUDES   *nonspecific serologic evidence of human immunodeficiency virus [HIV] (795.71)*

AHA: 4Q, '04, 99

796.9 Other

ILL-DEFINED AND UNKNOWN CAUSES OF MORBIDITY AND MORTALITY (797-799)

797 Senility without mention of psychosis
Old age
Senescence
Senile asthenia
Senile:
debility
exhaustion

EXCLUDES   *senile psychoses (290.0-290.9)*

√4ᵗʰ **798 Sudden death, cause unknown**

798.0 Sudden infant death syndrome   Ⓟ
Cot death
Crib death
Sudden death of nonspecific cause in infancy

DEF: Death of infant under age one due to nonspecific cause.

798.1 Instantaneous death

798.2 Death occurring in less than 24 hours from onset of symptoms, not otherwise explained
Death known not to be violent or instantaneous, for which no cause could be discovered
Died without sign of disease

798.9 Unattended death
Death in circumstances where the body of the deceased was found and no cause could be discovered
Found dead

√4ᵗʰ **799 Other ill-defined and unknown causes of morbidity and mortality**

▲ √5ᵗʰ **799.0 Asphyxia and hypoxemia**

EXCLUDES   ▶*asphyxia and hypoxemia (due to):*◀
carbon monoxide (986)
▶*hypercapnia (786.09)*◀
inhalation of food or foreign body (932-934.9)
newborn (768.0-768.9)
traumatic (994.7)

DEF: Lack of oxygen.

● **799.01 Asphyxia**

● **799.02 Hypoxemia**

799.1 Respiratory arrest
Cardiorespiratory failure

EXCLUDES   *cardiac arrest (427.5)*
failure of peripheral circulation (785.50)
respiratory distress:
NOS (786.09)
acute (518.82)
following trauma and surgery (518.5)
newborn (770.89)
syndrome (newborn) (769)
adult (following trauma and surgery) (518.5)
other (518.82)
respiratory failure (518.81, 518.83-518.84)
newborn (770.84)
respiratory insufficiency (786.09)
acute (518.82)

799.2 Nervousness
"Nerves"

799.3 Debility, unspecified

EXCLUDES   *asthenia (780.79)*
nervous debility (300.5)
neurasthenia (300.5)
senile asthenia (797)

799.4 Cachexia
Wasting disease

EXCLUDES   *nutritional marasmus (261)*

AHA: 3Q, '90, 17

DEF: General ill health and poor nutrition.

√5ᵗʰ **799.8 Other ill-defined conditions**

799.81 Decreased libido   Ⓐ
Decreased sexual desire

EXCLUDES   *psychosexual dysfunction with inhibited sexual desire (302.71)*

AHA: 4Q, '03, 75

799.89 Other ill-defined conditions

799.9 Other unknown and unspecified cause
Undiagnosed disease, not specified as to site or system involved
Unknown cause of morbidity or mortality

AHA: 1Q, '98,.4; 1Q, '90, 20

Ⓝ Newborn Age: 0   Ⓟ Pediatric Age: 0-17   Ⓜ Maternity Age: 12-55   Ⓐ Adult Age :15-124   Manifestation Code   ▶◀ Revised Text   ● New Code   ▲ Revised Code Title

17. INJURY AND POISONING (800-999)

Use E code(s) to identify the cause and intent of the injury or poisoning (E800-E999)

Note:

1. The principle of multiple coding of injuries should be followed wherever possible. Combination categories for multiple injuries are provided for use when there is insufficient detail as to the nature of the individual conditions, or for primary tabulation purposes when it is more convenient to record a single code; otherwise, the component injuries should be coded separately.

Where multiple sites of injury are specified in the titles, the word "with" indicates involvement of both sites, and the word "and" indicates involvement of either or both sites. The word "finger" includes thumb.

2. Categories for "late effect" of injuries are to be found at 905-909.

FRACTURES (800-829)

EXCLUDES   *malunion (733.81)*
nonunion (733.82)
pathological or spontaneous fracture (733.10-733.19)
stress fractures (733.93-733.95)

The terms "condyle," "coronoid process," "ramus," and "symphysis" indicate the portion of the bone fractured, not the name of the bone involved.

The descriptions "closed" and "open" used in the fourth-digit subdivisions include the following terms:

closed (with or without delayed healing):

comminuted	impacted
depressed	linear
elevated	march
fissured	simple
fracture NOS	slipped epiphysis
greenstick	spiral

open (with or without delayed healing):

compound	puncture
infected	with foreign body
missile	

A fracture not indicated as closed or open should be classified as closed.

AHA: 4Q, '90, 26; 3Q, '90, 5; 3Q, '90, 13; 2Q, '90, 7; 2Q, '89, 15, S-O, '85, 3

FRACTURE OF SKULL (800-804)

The following fifth-digit subclassification is for use with the appropriate codes in categories 800, 801, 803, and 804:

  0   unspecified state of consciousness
  1   with no loss of consciousness
  2   with brief [less than one hour] loss of consciousness
  3   with moderate [1-24 hours] loss of consciousness
  4   with prolonged [more than 24 hours] loss of consciousness and return to pre-existing conscious level
  5   with prolonged [more than 24 hours] loss of consciousness, without return to pre-existing conscious level

Use fifth-digit 5 to designate when a patient is unconscious and dies before regaining consciousness, regardless of the duration of the loss of consciousness

  6   with loss of consciousness of unspecified duration
  9   with concussion, unspecified

✓4th **800 Fracture of vault of skull**

  INCLUDES   frontal bone
                      parietal bone

AHA: 4Q, '96, 36

DEF: Fracture of bone that forms skull dome and protects brain.

Fractures

Avulsion · Fracture-dislocation · Impacted · Open (skin broken) · Oblique · Epiphyseal · March · Closed spiral · Comminuted · Linear (fissured) · Greenstick · Depressed

§	✓5th	**800.0**	**Closed without mention of intracranial injury**	CD PDx
§	✓5th	**800.1**	**Closed with cerebral laceration and contusion**	CD PDx
§	✓5th	**800.2**	**Closed with subarachnoid, subdural, and extradural hemorrhage**	CD PDx
§	✓5th	**800.3**	**Closed with other and unspecified intracranial hemorrhage**	CD PDx
§	✓5th	**800.4**	**Closed with intracranial injury of other and unspecified nature**	CD PDx
§	✓5th	**800.5**	**Open without mention of intracranial injury**	CD PDx
§	✓5th	**800.6**	**Open with cerebral laceration and contusion**	CD PDx
§	✓5th	**800.7**	**Open with subarachnoid, subdural, and extradural hemorrhage**	CD PDx
§	✓5th	**800.8**	**Open with other and unspecified intracranial hemorrhage**	CD PDx
§	✓5th	**800.9**	**Open with intracranial injury of other and unspecified nature**	CD PDx

✓4th **801 Fracture of base of skull**

  INCLUDES
fossa:	sinus:
anterior	ethmoid
middle	frontal
posterior	sphenoid bone
occiput bone	temporal bone
orbital roof	

AHA: 4Q, '96, 36

DEF: Fracture of bone that forms skull floor.

§	✓5th	**801.0**	**Closed without mention of intracranial injury**	CD PDx
§	✓5th	**801.1**	**Closed with cerebral laceration and contusion**	CD PDx

            AHA: 4Q, '96, 36

§	✓5th	**801.2**	**Closed with subarachnoid, subdural, and extradural hemorrhage**	CD PDx
§	✓5th	**801.3**	**Closed with other and unspecified intracranial hemorrhage**	CD PDx
§	✓5th	**801.4**	**Closed with intracranial injury of other and unspecified nature**	CD PDx
§	✓5th	**801.5**	**Open without mention of intracranial injury**	CD PDx
§	✓5th	**801.6**	**Open with cerebral laceration and contusion**	CD PDx
§	✓5th	**801.7**	**Open with subarachnoid, subdural, and extradural hemorrhage**	CD PDx
§	✓5th	**801.8**	**Open with other and unspecified intracranial hemorrhage**	CD PDx
§	✓5th	**801.9**	**Open with intracranial injury of other and unspecified nature**	CD PDx

§   Requires fifth-digit. See beginning of section 800-804 for codes and definitions.

✓4th ✓5th Additional Digit Required   **RUG III Special Care Dx**   **RUG III Clinically Complex Dx**   **Hospice Non-cancer Dx**   **CD PDx** Clinical Dimension PDx   **CD SDx** Clinical Dimension SDx

Injury and Poisoning

802–805

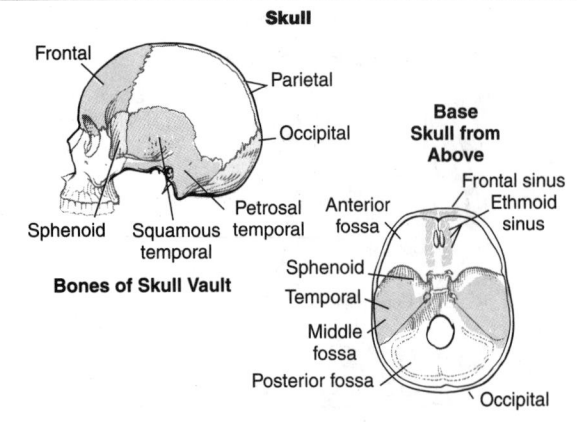

Skull

Frontal

Parietal

Occipital

Petrosal temporal

Sphenoid

Squamous temporal

Bones of Skull Vault

Base Skull from Above

Frontal sinus

Ethmoid sinus

Anterior fossa

Sphenoid

Temporal

Middle fossa

Posterior fossa

Occipital

Facial Fractures

Frontal bone

Nasal bone

Orbital floor

Zygomatic bone (malar) and arch

Type III

Type II

Type I

Maxilla

LeFort Fracture Types

Subcondylar

Body

Angle

Symphysis

Parasymphysis

Common Fracture Sites of Mandible

✓4th **802 Fracture of face bones**
AHA: 4Q, '96, 36

802.0 Nasal bones, closed `CD PDx`
802.1 Nasal bones, open `CD PDx`

✓5th 802.2 **Mandible, closed**
 Inferior maxilla   Lower jaw (bone)

  802.20 Unspecified site `CD PDx`
  802.21 Condylar process `CD PDx`
  802.22 Subcondylar `CD PDx`
  802.23 Coronoid process `CD PDx`
  802.24 Ramus, unspecified `CD PDx`
  802.25 Angle of jaw `CD PDx`
  802.26 Symphysis of body `CD PDx`
  802.27 Alveolar border of body `CD PDx`
  802.28 Body, other and unspecified `CD PDx`
  802.29 Multiple sites `CD PDx`

✓5th 802.3 **Mandible, open**
  802.30 Unspecified site `CD PDx`
  802.31 Condylar process `CD PDx`
  802.32 Subcondylar `CD PDx`
  802.33 Coronoid process `CD PDx`
  802.34 Ramus, unspecified `CD PDx`
  802.35 Angle of jaw `CD PDx`
  802.36 Symphysis of body `CD PDx`
  802.37 Alveolar border of body `CD PDx`
  802.38 Body, other and unspecified `CD PDx`
  802.39 Multiple sites `CD PDx`

 802.4 **Malar and maxillary bones, closed**
  Superior maxilla   Zygoma
  Upper jaw (bone)   Zygomatic arch

 802.5 Malar and maxillary bones, open `CD PDx`
 802.6 Orbital floor (blow-out), closed `CD PDx`
 802.7 Orbital floor (blow-out), open `CD PDx`
 802.8 Other facial bones, closed `CD PDx`
  Alveolus   Palate
  Orbit:
   NOS
   part other than roof or floor
  EXCLUDES orbital:
   floor (802.6)
   roof (801.0-801.9)

 802.9 Other facial bones, open `CD PDx`

✓4th **803 Other and unqualified skull fractures**
  INCLUDES skull NOS   skull multiple NOS
  AHA: 4Q, '96, 36

§ ✓5th 803.0 **Closed without mention of intracranial injury** `CD PDx`

§ ✓5th 803.1 **Closed with cerebral laceration and contusion** `CD PDx`

§ ✓5th 803.2 **Closed with subarachnoid, subdural, and extradural hemorrhage** `CD PDx`

§ ✓5th 803.3 **Closed with other and unspecified intracranial hemorrhage** `CD PDx`

§ ✓5th 803.4 **Closed with intracranial injury of other and unspecified nature** `CD PDx`

§ ✓5th 803.5 **Open without mention of intracranial injury** `CD PDx`

§ ✓5th 803.6 **Open with cerebral laceration and contusion** `CD PDx`

§ ✓5th 803.7 **Open with subarachnoid, subdural, and extradural hemorrhage** `CD PDx`

§ ✓5th 803.8 **Open with other and unspecified intracranial hemorrhage** `CD PDx`

§ ✓5th 803.9 **Open with intracranial injury of other and unspecified nature** `CD PDx`

✓4th **804 Multiple fractures involving skull or face with other bones**
  AHA: 4Q, '96, 36

§ ✓5th 804.0 **Closed without mention of intracranial injury** `CD PDx`

§ ✓5th 804.1 **Closed with cerebral laceration and contusion** `CD PDx`

§ ✓5th 804.2 **Closed with subarachnoid, subdural, and extradural hemorrhage** `CD PDx`

§ ✓5th 804.3 **Closed with other and unspecified intracranial hemorrhage** `CD PDx`

§ ✓5th 804.4 **Closed with intracranial injury of other and unspecified nature** `CD PDx`

§ ✓5th 804.5 **Open without mention of intracranial injury** `CD PDx`

§ ✓5th 804.6 **Open with cerebral laceration and contusion** `CD PDx`

§ ✓5th 804.7 **Open with subarachnoid, subdural, and extradural hemorrage** `CD PDx`

§ ✓5th 804.8 **Open with other and unspecified intracranial hemorrhage** `CD PDx`

§ ✓5th 804.9 **Open with intracranial injury of other and unspecified nature** `CD PDx`

FRACTURE OF NECK AND TRUNK (805-809)

✓4th **805 Fracture of vertebral column without mention of spinal cord injury**
  INCLUDES neural arch   transverse process
         spine   vertebra
         spinous process

  The following fifth-digit subclassification is for use with codes 805.0-805.1:
   0 cervical vertebra, unspecified level
   1 first cervical vertebra
   2 second cervical vertebra
   3 third cervical vertebra
   4 fourth cervical vertebra
   5 fifth cervical vertebra
   6 sixth cervical vertebra
   7 seventh cervical vertebra
   8 multiple cervical vertebrae

§ Requires fifth-digit. See beginning of section 800-804 for codes and definitions.

N Newborn Age: 0   P Pediatric Age: 0-17   M Maternity Age: 12-55   A Adult Age: 15-124   Manifestation Code   ►◄ Revised Text   ● New Code   ▲ Revised Code Title

Vertebral Column

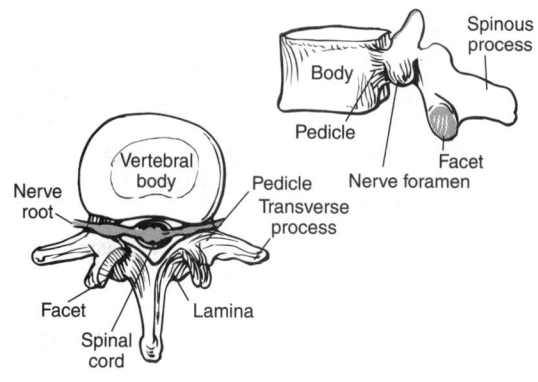

✓5th **805.0 Cervical, closed**   `CD PDx`
Atlas   Axis

✓5th **805.1 Cervical, open**   `CD PDx`

805.2 Dorsal [thoracic], closed   `CD PDx`

805.3 Dorsal [thoracic], open   `CD PDx`

805.4 Lumbar, closed   `CD PDx`
AHA: 4Q, '99, 12

805.5 Lumbar, open   `CD PDx`

805.6 Sacrum and coccyx, closed   `CD PDx`

805.7 Sacrum and coccyx, open   `CD PDx`

805.8 Unspecified, closed   `CD PDx`

805.9 Unspecified, open   `CD PDx`

✓4th **806 Fracture of vertebral column with spinal cord injury**
`INCLUDES` any condition classifiable to 805 with:
complete or incomplete transverse lesion (of cord)
hematomyelia
injury to:
cauda equina
nerve
paralysis
paraplegia
quadriplegia
spinal concussion

✓5th **806.0 Cervical, closed**

806.00 C_1-C_4 level with unspecified spinal cord injury   `CD PDx`
Cervical region NOS with spinal cord injury NOS

806.01 C_1-C_4 level with complete lesion of cord   `CD PDx`

806.02 C_1-C_4 level with anterior cord syndrome   `CD PDx`

806.03 C_1-C_4 level with central cord syndrome   `CD PDx`

806.04 C_1-C_4 level with other specified spinal cord injury   `CD PDx`
C_1-C_4 level with:
incomplete spinal cord lesion NOS
posterior cord syndrome

806.05 C_5-C_7 level with unspecified spinal cord injury   `CD PDx`

806.06 C_5-C_7 level with complete lesion of cord   `CD PDx`

806.07 C_5-C_7 level with anterior cord syndrome   `CD PDx`

806.08 C_5-C_7 level with central cord syndrome   `CD PDx`

806.09 C_5-C_7 level with other specified spinal cord injury   `CD PDx`
C_5-C_7 level with:
incomplete spinal cord lesion NOS
posterior cord syndrome

✓5th **806.1 Cervical, open**

806.10 C_1-C_4 level with unspecified spinal cord injury   `CD PDx`

806.11 C_1-C_4 level with complete lesion of cord   `CD PDx`

806.12 C_1-C_4 level with anterior cord syndrome   `CD PDx`

806.13 C_1-C_4 level with central cord syndrome   `CD PDx`

806.14 C_1-C_4 level with other specified spinal cord injury   `CD PDx`
C_1-C_4 level with:
incomplete spinal cord lesion NOS
posterior cord syndrome

806.15 C_5-C_7 level with unspecified spinal cord injury   `CD PDx`

806.16 C_5-C_7 level with complete lesion of cord   `CD PDx`

806.17 C_5-C_7 level with anterior cord syndrome   `CD PDx`

806.18 C_5-C_7 level with central cord syndrome   `CD PDx`

806.19 C_5-C_7 level with other specified spinal cord injury   `CD PDx`
C_5-C_7 level with:
incomplete spinal cord lesion NOS
posterior cord syndrome

✓5th **806.2 Dorsal [thoracic], closed**

806.20 T_1-T_6 level with unspecified spinal cord injury   `CD PDx`
Thoracic region NOS with spinal cord injury NOS

806.21 T_1-T_6 level with complete lesion of cord   `CD PDx`

806.22 T_1-T_6 level with anterior cord syndrome   `CD PDx`

806.23 T_1-T_6 level with central cord syndrome   `CD PDx`

806.24 T_1-T_6 level with other specified spinal cord injury   `CD PDx`
T_1-T_6 level with:
incomplete spinal cord lesion NOS
posterior cord syndrome

806.25 T_7-T_{12} level with unspecified spinal cord injury   `CD PDx`

806.26 T_7-T_{12} level with complete lesion of cord   `CD PDx`

806.27 T_7-T_{12} level with anterior cord syndrome   `CD PDx`

806.28 T_7-T_{12} level with central cord syndrome   `CD PDx`

✓4th ✓5th **Additional Digit Required**   `RUG III Special Care Dx`   `RUG III Clinically Complex Dx`   `Hospice Non-cancer Dx`   `CD PDx` Clinical Dimension PDx   `CD SDx` Clinical Dimension SDx

2006 ICD•9•CM   **Volume 1 — 243**

Injury and Poisoning

805.0–806.28

Injury and Poisoning

806.29–809.1

806.29 T_7-T_{12} **level with other specified spinal cord injury** `CD PDx`
T_7-T_{12} level with:
incomplete spinal cord lesion NOS
posterior cord syndrome

✓5th **806.3** **Dorsal [thoracic], open**

806.30 T_1-T_6 **level with unspecified spinal cord injury** `CD PDx`

806.31 T_1-T_6 **level with complete lesion of cord** `CD PDx`

806.32 T_1-T_6 **level with anterior cord syndrome** `CD PDx`

806.33 T_1-T_6 **level with central cord syndrome** `CD PDx`

806.34 T_1-T_6 **level with other specified spinal cord injury** `CD PDx`
T_1-T_6 level with:
incomplete spinal cord lesion NOS
posterior cord syndrome

806.35 T_7-T_{12} **level with unspecified spinal cord injury** `CD PDx`

806.36 T_7-T_{12} **level with complete lesion of cord** `CD PDx`

806.37 T_7-T_{12} **level with anterior cord syndrome** `CD PDx`

806.38 T_7-T_{12} **level with central cord syndrome** `CD PDx`

806.39 T_7-T_{12} **level with other specified spinal cord injury** `CD PDx`
T_7-T_{12} level with:
incomplete spinal cord lesion NOS
posterior cord syndrome

806.4 **Lumbar, closed** `CD PDx`
AHA: 4Q, '99, 11, 13

806.5 **Lumbar, open** `CD PDx`

✓5th **806.6** **Sacrum and coccyx, closed**

806.60 **With unspecified spinal cord injury** `CD PDx`

806.61 **With complete cauda equina lesion** `CD PDx`

806.62 **With other cauda equina injury** `CD PDx`

806.69 **With other spinal cord injury** `CD PDx`

✓5th **806.7** **Sacrum and coccyx, open**

806.70 **With unspecified spinal cord injury** `CD PDx`

806.71 **With complete cauda equina lesion** `CD PDx`

806.72 **With other cauda equina injury** `CD PDx`

806.79 **With other spinal cord injury** `CD PDx`

806.8 **Unspecified, closed** `CD PDx`

806.9 **Unspecified, open** `CD PDx`

✓4th **807** **Fracture of rib(s), sternum, larynx, and trachea**

The following fifth-digit subclassification is for use with codes 807.0–807.1:

0 rib(s), unspecified
1 one rib
2 two ribs
3 three ribs
4 four ribs
5 five ribs
6 six ribs
7 seven ribs
8 eight or more ribs
9 multiple ribs, unspecified

✓5th **807.0** **Rib(s), closed** `CD PDx`
✓5th **807.1** **Rib(s), open** `CD PDx`
807.2 **Sternum, closed** `CD PDx`
DEF: Break in flat bone (breast bone) in anterior thorax.

807.3 **Sternum, open** `CD PDx`
DEF: Break, with open wound, in flat bone in mid anterior thorax.

807.4 **Flail chest** `CD PDx`

Ribs, Sternum, Larynx, and Trachea

Pelvis and Pelvic Fractures

807.5 **Larynx and trachea, closed** `CD PDx`
Hyoid bone   Trachea
Thyroid cartilage

807.6 **Larynx and trachea, open** `CD PDx`

✓4th **808** **Fracture of pelvis**

808.0 **Acetabulum, closed** `CD PDx`
808.1 **Acetabulum, open** `CD PDx`
808.2 **Pubis, closed** `CD PDx`
808.3 **Pubis, open** `CD PDx`

✓5th **808.4** **Other specified part, closed**

808.41 **Ilium** `CD PDx`

808.42 **Ischium** `CD PDx`

808.43 **Multiple pelvic fractures with disruption of pelvic circle** `CD PDx`

808.49 **Other** `CD PDx`
Innominate bone
Pelvic rim

✓5th **808.5** **Other specified part, open**

808.51 **Ilium** `CD PDx`

808.52 **Ischium** `CD PDx`

808.53 **Multiple pelvic fractures with disruption of pelvic circle** `CD PDx`

808.59 **Other** `CD PDx`

808.8 **Unspecified, closed** `CD PDx`

808.9 **Unspecified, open** `CD PDx`

✓4th **809** **Ill-defined fractures of bones of trunk**

`INCLUDES`   bones of trunk with other bones except those of skull and face
multiple bones of trunk

`EXCLUDES`   *multiple fractures of:*
pelvic bones alone (808.0–808.9)
ribs alone (807.0–807.1, 807.4)
ribs or sternum with limb bones (819.0–819.1, 828.0–828.1)
skull or face with other bones (804.0–804.9)

809.0 **Fracture of bones of trunk, closed** `CD PDx`

809.1 **Fracture of bones of trunk, open** `CD PDx`

N Newborn Age: 0   **P** Pediatric Age: 0-17   **M** Maternity Age: 12-55   **A** Adult Age: 15-124   `Manifestation Code`   ◄ Revised Text   ● New Code   ▲ Revised Code Title

FRACTURE OF UPPER LIMB (810-819)

✓4th **810 Fracture of clavicle**

INCLUDES   collar bone
              interligamentous part of clavicle

The following fifth-digit subclassification is for use with category 810:

     0 unspecified part
        Clavicle NOS
     1 sternal end of clavicle
     2 shaft of clavicle
     3 acromial end of clavicle

✓5th **810.0 Closed**   `CD PDx`

✓5th **810.1 Open**   `CD PDx`

✓4th **811 Fracture of scapula**

INCLUDES   shoulder blade

The following fifth-digit subclassification is for use with category 811:

     0 unspecified part
     1 acromial process
        Acromion (process)
     2 coracoid process
     3 glenoid cavity and neck of scapula
     9 other

✓5th **811.0 Closed**   `CD PDx`
✓5th **811.1 Open**   `CD PDx`

✓4th **812 Fracture of humerus**

✓5th **812.0 Upper end, closed**

     812.00 Upper end, unspecified part   `CD PDx`
        Proximal end   Shoulder

     812.01 Surgical neck   `CD PDx`
        Neck of humerus NOS

     812.02 Anatomical neck   `CD PDx`

     812.03 Greater tuberosity   `CD PDx`

     812.09 Other   `CD PDx`

Right Clavicle and Scapula, Anterior View

Right Humerus, Anterior View

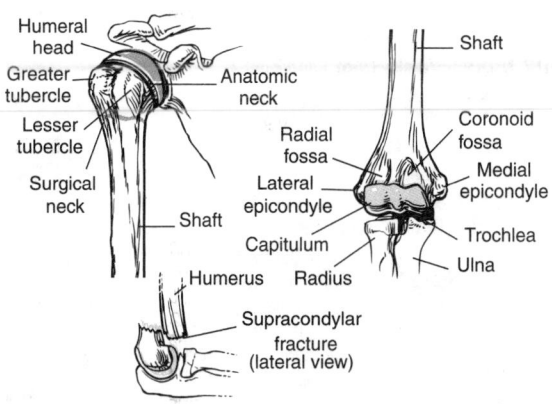

✓5th **812.1 Upper end, open**

     812.10 Upper end, unspecified part   `CD PDx`
     812.11 Surgical neck   `CD PDx`
     812.12 Anatomical neck   `CD PDx`
     812.13 Greater tuberosity   `CD PDx`
     812.19 Other   `CD PDx`
        Head   Upper epiphysis

✓5th **812.2 Shaft or unspecified part, closed**

     812.20 Unspecified part of humerus   `CD PDx`
        Humerus NOS   Upper arm NOS

     812.21 Shaft of humerus   `CD PDx`
        AHA: 3Q, '99, 14

✓5th **812.3 Shaft or unspecified part, open**

     812.30 Unspecified part of humerus   `CD PDx`
     812.31 Shaft of humerus   `CD PDx`

✓5th **812.4 Lower end, closed**
     Distal end of humerus   Elbow

     812.40 Lower end, unspecified part   `CD PDx`
     812.41 Supracondylar fracture of humerus   `CD PDx`
     812.42 Lateral condyle   `CD PDx`
        External condyle

     812.43 Medial condyle   `CD PDx`
        Internal epicondyle

     812.44 Condyle(s), unspecified   `CD PDx`
        Articular process NOS
        Lower epiphysis NOS

     812.49 Other   `CD PDx`
        Multiple fractures of lower end
        Trochlea

✓5th **812.5 Lower end, open**

     812.50 Lower end, unspecified part   `CD PDx`
     812.51 Supracondylar fracture of humerus   `CD PDx`
     812.52 Lateral condyle   `CD PDx`
     812.53 Medial condyle   `CD PDx`
     812.54 Condyle(s), unspecified   `CD PDx`
     812.59 Other   `CD PDx`

✓4th **813 Fracture of radius and ulna**

✓5th **813.0 Upper end, closed**
     Proximal end

     813.00 Upper end of forearm, unspecified   `CD PDx`
     813.01 Olecranon process of ulna   `CD PDx`
     813.02 Coronoid process of ulna   `CD PDx`
     813.03 Monteggia's fracture   `CD PDx`

        DEF: Fracture near the head of the ulnar shaft, causing dislocation of the radial head.

     813.04 Other and unspecified fractures of   `CD PDx`
        proximal end of ulna (alone)
        Multiple fractures of ulna, upper end

     813.05 Head of radius   `CD PDx`
     813.06 Neck of radius   `CD PDx`

Right Radius and Ulna, Anterior View

✓4th ✓5th Additional Digit Required   RUG III Special Care Dx   RUG III Clinically Complex Dx   Hospice Non-cancer Dx   `CD PDx` Clinical Dimension PDx   `CD SDx` Clinical Dimension SDx

2006 ICD•9•CM   **Volume 1 — 245**

Injury and Poisoning

813.07–818.0

813.07 Other and unspecified fractures of `CD PDx`
proximal end of radius (alone)
    Multiple fractures of radius, upper end
813.08 Radius with ulna, upper end `CD PDx`
[any part]

✓5ᵗʰ **813.1 Upper end, open**
813.10 Upper end of forearm, unspecified `CD PDx`
813.11 Olecranon process of ulna `CD PDx`
813.12 Coronoid process of ulna `CD PDx`
813.13 Monteggia's fracture `CD PDx`
813.14 Other and unspecified fractures of `CD PDx`
proximal end of ulna (alone)
813.15 Head of radius `CD PDx`
813.16 Neck of radius `CD PDx`
813.17 Other and unspecified fractures of `CD PDx`
proximal end of radius (alone)
813.18 Radius with ulna, upper end `CD PDx`
[any part]

✓5ᵗʰ **813.2 Shaft, closed**
813.20 Shaft, unspecified `CD PDx`
813.21 Radius (alone) `CD PDx`
813.22 Ulna (alone) `CD PDx`
813.23 Radius with ulna `CD PDx`

✓5ᵗʰ **813.3 Shaft, open**
813.30 Shaft, unspecified `CD PDx`
813.31 Radius (alone) `CD PDx`
813.32 Ulna (alone) `CD PDx`
813.33 Radius with ulna `CD PDx`

✓5ᵗʰ **813.4 Lower end, closed**
    Distal end
813.40 Lower end of forearm, unspecified `CD PDx`
813.41 Colles' fracture `CD PDx`
    Smith's fracture
    DEF: Break of lower end of radius; associated with
    backward movement of the radius lower section.
813.42 Other fractures of distal end of `CD PDx`
radius (alone)
    Dupuytren's fracture, radius
    Radius, lower end
    DEF: Dupuytren's fracture: fracture and dislocation of the
    forearm; the fracture is of the radius above the wrist, and
    the dislocation is of the ulna at the lower end.
813.43 Distal end of ulna (alone) `CD PDx`
    Ulna:
      head   lower epiphysis
      lower end   styloid process
813.44 Radius with ulna, lower end `CD PDx`
813.45 Torus fracture of radius `CD PDx`
    AHA: 4Q, '02, 70

✓5ᵗʰ **813.5 Lower end, open**
813.50 Lower end of forearm, unspecified `CD PDx`
813.51 Colles' fracture `CD PDx`
813.52 Other fractures of distal end of `CD PDx`
radius (alone)

Hand Fractures

Palmar view — Trapezoid, Cuboid, "Fistfighter's" fracture, Trapezium, Scaphoid (fractured), Lunate, Triquetral, Pisiform, Hook of Hamate, Bennett's fracture

Dorsal view — Hamate, Cuboid, Triquetral, Pisiform, Lunate, Ulna, Radius, Colles' fracture, Navicular, Trapezoid, Trapezium

813.53 Distal end of ulna (alone) `CD PDx`
813.54 Radius with ulna, lower end `CD PDx`

✓5ᵗʰ **813.8 Unspecified part, closed**
813.80 Forearm, unspecified `CD PDx`
813.81 Radius (alone) `CD PDx`
    AHA: 2Q, '98, 19
813.82 Ulna (alone) `CD PDx`
813.83 Radius with ulna `CD PDx`

✓5ᵗʰ **813.9 Unspecified part, open**
813.90 Forearm, unspecified `CD PDx`
813.91 Radius (alone) `CD PDx`
813.92 Ulna (alone) `CD PDx`
813.93 Radius with ulna `CD PDx`

✓4ᵗʰ **814 Fracture of carpal bone(s)**

The following fifth-digit subclassification is for use with
category 814:
    0 carpal bone, unspecified
      Wrist NOS
    1 navicular [scaphoid] of wrist
    2 lunate [semilunar] bone of wrist
    3 triquetral [cuneiform] bone of wrist
    4 pisiform
    5 trapezium bone [larger multangular]
    6 trapezoid bone [smaller multangular]
    7 capitate bone [os magnum]
    8 hamate [unciform] bone
    9 other

✓5ᵗʰ **814.0 Closed** `CD PDx`
✓5ᵗʰ **814.1 Open** `CD PDx`

✓4ᵗʰ **815 Fracture of metacarpal bone(s)**
    `INCLUDES` hand [except finger]
                  metacarpus

The following fifth-digit subclassification is for use with
category 815:
    0 metacarpal bone(s), site unspecified
    1 base of thumb [first] metacarpal
      Bennett's fracture
    2 base of other metacarpal bone(s)
    3 shaft of metacarpal bone(s)
    4 neck of metacarpal bone(s)
    9 multiple sites of metacarpus

✓5ᵗʰ **815.0 Closed** `CD PDx`
✓5ᵗʰ **815.1 Open** `CD PDx`

✓4ᵗʰ **816 Fracture of one or more phalanges of hand**
    `INCLUDES` finger(s) thumb

The following fifth-digit subclassification is for use with
category 816:
    0 phalanx or phalanges, unspecified
    1 middle or proximal phalanx or phalanges
    2 distal phalanx or phalanges
    3 multiple sites

✓5ᵗʰ **816.0 Closed** `CD PDx`
✓5ᵗʰ **816.1 Open** `CD PDx`
    AHA: For code 816.12: 4Q, '03, 77

✓4ᵗʰ **817 Multiple fractures of hand bones**
    `INCLUDES` metacarpal bone(s) with phalanx or phalanges
                  of same hand
817.0 Closed `CD PDx`
817.1 Open `CD PDx`

✓4ᵗʰ **818 Ill-defined fractures of upper limb**
    `INCLUDES` arm NOS
                  multiple bones of same upper limb
    `EXCLUDES` *multiple fractures of:*
            metacarpal bone(s) with phalanx or
                phalanges (817.0-817.1)
            phalanges of hand alone (816.0-816.1)
            radius with ulna (813.0-813.9)

818.0 Closed `CD PDx`

N Newborn Age: 0   P Pediatric Age: 0-17   M Maternity Age: 12-55   A Adult Age: 15-124   Manifestation Code   ▶◀ Revised Text   ● New Code   ▲ Revised Code Title

818.1   **Open**   `CD PDx`

✓4ᵗʰ **819 Multiple fractures involving both upper limbs, and upper limb with rib(s) and sternum**
> INCLUDES   arm(s) with rib(s) or sternum
> both arms [any bones]

819.0   **Closed**   `CD PDx`

819.1   **Open**   `CD PDx`

FRACTURE OF LOWER LIMB (820-829)

✓4ᵗʰ **820 Fracture of neck of femur**

✓5ᵗʰ **820.0**   **Transcervical fracture, closed**

820.00   **Intracapsular section, unspecified**   `CD PDx`

820.01   **Epiphysis (separation) (upper)**   `CD PDx`
> Transepiphyseal

820.02   **Midcervical section**   `CD PDx`
> Transcervical NOS
> **AHA:** 3Q, '03, 12

820.03   **Base of neck**   `CD PDx`
> Cervicotrochanteric section

820.09   **Other**   `CD PDx`
> Head of femur   Subcapital

✓5ᵗʰ **820.1**   **Transcervical fracture, open**

820.10   **Intracapsular section, unspecified**   `CD PDx`

820.11   **Epiphysis (separation) (upper)**   `CD PDx`

820.12   **Midcervical section**   `CD PDx`

820.13   **Base of neck**   `CD PDx`

820.19   **Other**   `CD PDx`

✓5ᵗʰ **820.2**   **Pertrochanteric fracture, closed**

820.20   **Trochanteric section, unspecified**   `CD PDx`
> Trochanter: Trochanter:
> NOS   lesser
> greater

820.21   **Intertrochanteric section**   `CD PDx`

820.22   **Subtrochanteric section**   `CD PDx`

✓5ᵗʰ **820.3**   **Pertrochanteric fracture, open**

820.30   **Trochanteric section, unspecified**   `CD PDx`

820.31   **Intertrochanteric section**   `CD PDx`

820.32   **Subtrochanteric section**   `CD PDx`

820.8   **Unspecified part of neck of femur, closed**   `CD PDx`
> Hip NOS   Neck of femur NOS

820.9   **Unspecified part of neck of femur, open**   `CD PDx`

✓4ᵗʰ **821 Fracture of other and unspecified parts of femur**

✓5ᵗʰ **821.0**   **Shaft or unspecified part, closed**

821.00   **Unspecified part of femur**   `CD PDx`
> Thigh   Upper leg
> EXCLUDES   hip NOS (820.8)

821.01   **Shaft**   `CD PDx`
> **AHA:** 1Q, '99, 5

✓5ᵗʰ **821.1**   **Shaft or unspecified part, open**

821.10   **Unspecified part of femur**   `CD PDx`

821.11   **Shaft**   `CD PDx`

✓5ᵗʰ **821.2**   **Lower end, closed**
> Distal end

Right Femur, Anterior View

✓4ᵗʰ Anterior views of
torus compression
fracture

Torus Fracture

821.20   **Lower end, unspecified part**   `CD PDx`

821.21   **Condyle, femoral**   `CD PDx`

821.22   **Epiphysis, lower (separation)**   `CD PDx`

821.23   **Supracondylar fracture of femur**   `CD PDx`

821.29   **Other**   `CD PDx`
> Multiple fractures of lower end

✓5ᵗʰ **821.3**   **Lower end, open**

821.30   **Lower end, unspecified part**   `CD PDx`

821.31   **Condyle, femoral**   `CD PDx`

821.32   **Epiphysis, lower (separation)**   `CD PDx`

821.33   **Supracondylar fracture of femur**   `CD PDx`

821.39   **Other**   `CD PDx`

✓4ᵗʰ **822 Fracture of patella**

822.0   **Closed**   `CD PDx`

822.1   **Open**   `CD PDx`

✓4ᵗʰ **823 Fracture of tibia and fibula**
> EXCLUDES   *Dupuytren's fracture (824.4-824.5)*
> *ankle (824.4-824.5)*
> *radius (813.42, 813.52)*
> *Pott's fracture (824.4-824.5)*
> *that involving ankle (824.0-824.9)*

The following fifth-digit subclassification is for use with category 823:
> **0 tibia alone**
> **1 fibula alone**
> **2 fibula with tibia**

✓5ᵗʰ **823.0**   **Upper end, closed**   `CD PDx`
> Head   Tibia:
> Proximal end   condyles
>   tuberosity

✓5ᵗʰ **823.1**   **Upper end, open**   `CD PDx`

✓5ᵗʰ **823.2**   **Shaft, closed**   `CD PDx`

✓5ᵗʰ **823.3**   **Shaft, open**   `CD PDx`

✓5ᵗʰ **823.4**   **Torus fracture**   `CD PDx`
> **AHA:** 4Q, '02, 70
>
> **DEF:** A bone deformity in children, occurring commonly in the radius or ulna, in which the bone bends and buckles but does not fracture.

✓5ᵗʰ **823.8**   **Unspecified part, closed**   `CD PDx`
> Lower leg NOS
> **AHA:** For code 823.82: 1Q, '97, 8

✓5ᵗʰ **823.9**   **Unspecified part, open**   `CD PDx`

✓4ᵗʰ **824 Fracture of ankle**

824.0   **Medial malleolus, closed**   `CD PDx`
> Tibia involving: Tibia involving:
> ankle   malleolus
> **AHA:** 1Q, '04, 9

824.1   **Medial malleolus, open**   `CD PDx`

824.2   **Lateral malleolus, closed**   `CD PDx`
> Fibula involving:
> ankle
> malleolus

824.3   **Lateral malleolus, open**   `CD PDx`
> **AHA:** 2Q, '02, 3

✓4ᵗʰ / ✓5ᵗʰ **Additional Digit Required**   **RUG III Special Care Dx**   **RUG III Clinically Complex Dx**   **Hospice Non-cancer Dx**   `CD PDx` Clinical Dimension PDx   `CD SDx` Clinical Dimension SDx

2006 ICD•9•CM   **Volume 1 — 247**

824.4 **Bimalleolar, closed** `CD PDx`

Dupuytren's fracture, fibula   Pott's fracture

DEF: Bimalleolar, closed: Breaking of both nodules (malleoli) on either side of ankle joint, without an open wound.

DEF: Dupuytren's fracture (Pott's fracture): The breaking of the farthest end of the lower leg bone (fibula), with injury to the farthest end joint of the other lower leg bone (tibia).

824.5 **Bimalleolar, open** `CD PDx`

824.6 **Trimalleolar, closed** `CD PDx`

Lateral and medial malleolus with anterior or posterior lip of tibia

824.7 **Trimalleolar, open** `CD PDx`

824.8 **Unspecified, closed** `CD PDx`

Ankle NOS

AHA: 3Q, '00, 12

824.9 **Unspecified, open** `CD PDx`

√4ᵗʰ **825 Fracture of one or more tarsal and metatarsal bones**

825.0 **Fracture of calcaneus, closed** `CD PDx`

Heel bone   Os calcis

825.1 **Fracture of calcaneus, open** `CD PDx`

√5ᵗʰ **825.2** **Fracture of other tarsal and metatarsal bones, closed**

825.20 **Unspecified bone(s) of foot [except toes]** `CD PDx`

Instep

825.21 **Astragalus** `CD PDx`

Talus

825.22 **Navicular [scaphoid], foot** `CD PDx`

825.23 **Cuboid** `CD PDx`

825.24 **Cuneiform, foot** `CD PDx`

825.25 **Metatarsal bone(s)** `CD PDx`

825.29 **Other** `CD PDx`

Tarsal with metatarsal bone(s) only

`EXCLUDES` calcaneus (825.0)

√5ᵗʰ **825.3** **Fracture of other tarsal and metatarsal bones, open**

825.30 **Unspecified bone(s) of foot [except toes]** `CD PDx`

825.31 **Astragalus** `CD PDx`

825.32 **Navicular [scaphoid], foot** `CD PDx`

825.33 **Cuboid** `CD PDx`

825.34 **Cuneiform, foot** `CD PDx`

825.35 **Metatarsal bone(s)** `CD PDx`

825.39 **Other** `CD PDx`

√4ᵗʰ **826 Fracture of one or more phalanges of foot**

`INCLUDES` toe(s)

826.0 **Closed**

826.1 **Open**

√4ᵗʰ **827 Other, multiple, and ill-defined fractures of lower limb**

`INCLUDES` leg NOS
multiple bones of same lower limb

`EXCLUDES` *multiple fractures of:*
ankle bones alone (824.4-824.9)
phalanges of foot alone (826.0-826.1)
tarsal with metatarsal bones (825.29, 825.39)
tibia with fibula (823.0-823.9 with fifth-digit 2)

827.0 **Closed** `CD PDx`

827.1 **Open** `CD PDx`

√4ᵗʰ **828 Multiple fractures involving both lower limbs, lower with upper limb, and lower limb(s) with rib(s) and sternum**

`INCLUDES` arm(s) with leg(s) [any bones]
both legs [any bones]
leg(s) with rib(s) or sternum

828.0 **Closed** `CD PDx`

828.1 **Open** `CD PDx`

√4ᵗʰ **829 Fracture of unspecified bones**

829.0 **Unspecified bone, closed**

829.1 **Unspecified bone, open**

Right Tibia and Fibula, Anterior View

Right Foot, Dorsal

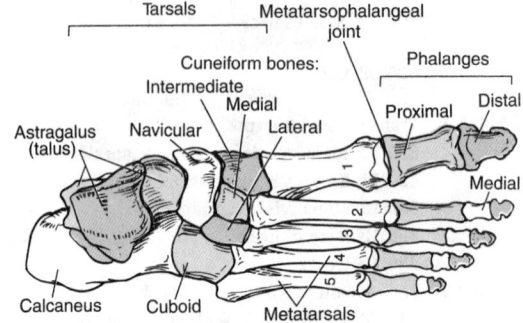

DISLOCATION (830-839)

`INCLUDES` displacement
subluxation

`EXCLUDES` *congenital dislocation (754.0-755.8)*
pathological dislocation (718.2)
recurrent dislocation (718.3)

The descriptions "closed" and "open," used in the fourth-digit subdivisions, include the following terms:

closed: open:
complete   compound
dislocation NOS   infected
partial   with foreign body
simple
uncomplicated

A dislocation not indicated as closed or open should be classified as closed.

AHA: 3Q, '90, 12

√4ᵗʰ **830 Dislocation of jaw**

`INCLUDES` jaw (cartilage) (meniscus)
mandible
maxilla (inferior)
temporomandibular (joint)

830.0 **Closed dislocation**

830.1 **Open dislocation**

√4ᵗʰ **831 Dislocation of shoulder**

`EXCLUDES` *sternoclavicular joint (839.61, 839.71)*
sternum (839.61, 839.71)

The following fifth-digit subclassification is for use with category 831:

0 **shoulder, unspecified**
Humerus NOS

1 **anterior dislocation of humerus**

2 **posterior dislocation of humerus**

3 **inferior dislocation of humerus**

4 **acromioclavicular (joint)**
Clavicle

9 **other**
Scapula

√5ᵗʰ **831.0** **Closed dislocation** `CD PDx`

√5ᵗʰ **831.1** **Open dislocation** `CD PDx`

N Newborn Age: 0   P Pediatric Age: 0-17   M Maternity Age: 12-55   A Adult Age: 15-124   `Manifestation Code`   ▶◀ Revised Text   ● New Code   ▲ Revised Code Title

☑4ᵗʰ **832 Dislocation of elbow**

The following fifth-digit subclassification is for use with category 832:

   0 elbow unspecified
   1 anterior dislocation of elbow
   2 posterior dislocation of elbow
   3 medial dislocation of elbow
   4 lateral dislocation of elbow
   9 other

☑5ᵗʰ **832.0 Closed dislocation** `CD PDx`
☑5ᵗʰ **832.1 Open dislocation** `CD PDx`

☑4ᵗʰ **833 Dislocation of wrist**

The following fifth-digit subclassification is for use with category 833:

   0 wrist, unspecified part
    Carpal (bone)
    Radius, distal end
   1 radioulnar (joint), distal
   2 radiocarpal (joint)
   3 midcarpal (joint)
   4 carpometacarpal (joint)
   5 metacarpal (bone), proximal end
   9 other
    Ulna, distal end

☑5ᵗʰ **833.0 Closed dislocation** `CD PDx`
☑5ᵗʰ **833.1 Open dislocation** `CD PDx`

☑4ᵗʰ **834 Dislocation of finger**

  `INCLUDES` finger(s)   thumb
         phalanx of hand

The following fifth-digit subclassification is for use with category 834:

   0 finger, unspecified part
   1 metacarpophalangeal (joint)
    Metacarpal (bone), distal end
   2 interphalangeal (joint), hand

☑5ᵗʰ **834.0 Closed dislocation**
☑5ᵗʰ **834.1 Open dislocation**

☑4ᵗʰ **835 Dislocation of hip**

The following fifth-digit subclassification is for use with category 835:

   0 dislocation of hip, unspecified
   1 posterior dislocation
   2 obturator dislocation
   3 other anterior dislocation

☑5ᵗʰ **835.0 Closed dislocation** `CD PDx`
☑5ᵗʰ **835.1 Open dislocation** `CD PDx`

☑4ᵗʰ **836 Dislocation of knee**

  `EXCLUDES` *dislocation of knee:*
    old or pathological (718.2)
    recurrent (718.3)
  internal derangement of knee joint (717.0-717.5,
    717.8-717.9)
  old tear of cartilage or meniscus of knee (717.0-
    717.5, 717.8-717.9)

836.0 Tear of medial cartilage or meniscus of knee, current `CD PDx`

  Bucket handle tear:
    NOS   } current injury
    medial meniscus

836.1 Tear of lateral cartilage or meniscus of knee, current `CD PDx`

836.2 Other tear of cartilage or meniscus of knee, current `CD PDx`

  Tear of:
    cartilage
     (semilunar) } current injury, not specified
    meniscus   as medial or lateral

836.3 Dislocation of patella, closed `CD PDx`
836.4 Dislocation of patella, open `CD PDx`

☑5ᵗʰ **836.5 Other dislocation of knee, closed**
  836.50 Dislocation of knee, unspecified `CD PDx`
  836.51 Anterior dislocation of tibia, proximal end `CD PDx`
    Posterior dislocation of femur, distal end
  836.52 Posterior dislocation of tibia, proximal end `CD PDx`
    Anterior dislocation of femur, distal end
  836.53 Medial dislocation of tibia, proximal end `CD PDx`
  836.54 Lateral dislocation of tibia, proximal end `CD PDx`
  836.59 Other `CD PDx`

☑5ᵗʰ **836.6 Other dislocation of knee, open**
  836.60 Dislocation of knee, unspecified `CD PDx`
  836.61 Anterior dislocation of tibia, proximal end `CD PDx`
  836.62 Posterior dislocation of tibia, proximal end `CD PDx`
  836.63 Medial dislocation of tibia, proximal end `CD PDx`
  836.64 Lateral dislocation of tibia, proximal end `CD PDx`
  836.69 Other `CD PDx`

☑4ᵗʰ **837 Dislocation of ankle**

  `INCLUDES` astragalus
        fibula, distal end
        navicular, foot
        scaphoid, foot
        tibia, distal end

837.0 Closed dislocation `CD PDx`
837.1 Open dislocation `CD PDx`

☑4ᵗʰ **838 Dislocation of foot**

The following fifth-digit subclassification is for use with category 838:

   0 foot, unspecified
   1 tarsal (bone), joint unspecified
   2 midtarsal (joint)
   3 tarsometatarsal (joint)
   4 metatarsal (bone), joint unspecified
   5 metatarsophalangeal (joint)
   6 interphalangeal (joint), foot
   9 other
    Phalanx of foot
    Toe(s)

☑5ᵗʰ **838.0 Closed dislocation** `CD PDx`
☑5ᵗʰ **838.1 Open dislocation** `CD PDx`

☑4ᵗʰ **839 Other, multiple, and ill-defined dislocations**

☑5ᵗʰ **839.0 Cervical vertebra, closed**
  Cervical spine   Neck
  839.00 Cervical vertebra, unspecified
  839.01 First cervical vertebra
  839.02 Second cervical vertebra
  839.03 Third cervical vertebra
  839.04 Fourth cervical vertebra
  839.05 Fifth cervical vertebra
  839.06 Sixth cervical vertebra
  839.07 Seventh cervical vertebra
  839.08 Multiple cervical vertebrae

☑5ᵗʰ **839.1 Cervical vertebra, open**
  839.10 Cervical vertebra, unspecified
  839.11 First cervical vertebra
  839.12 Second cervical vertebra
  839.13 Third cervical vertebra
  839.14 Fourth cervical vertebra
  839.15 Fifth cervical vertebra
  839.16 Sixth cervical vertebra
  839.17 Seventh cervical vertebra
  839.18 Multiple cervical vertebrae

☑4ᵗʰ ☑5ᵗʰ Additional Digit Required   RUG III Special Care Dx   RUG III Clinically Complex Dx   Hospice Non-cancer Dx   `CD PDx` Clinical Dimension PDx   `CD SDx` Clinical Dimension SDx

Injury and Poisoning

839.2–847.2

√5ᵗʰ **839.2** **Thoracic and lumbar vertebra, closed**
     839.20 Lumbar vertebra
     839.21 Thoracic vertebra
        Dorsal [thoracic] vertebra

√5ᵗʰ **839.3** **Thoracic and lumbar vertebra, open**
     839.30 Lumbar vertebra
     839.31 Thoracic vertebra

√5ᵗʰ **839.4** **Other vertebra, closed**
     839.40 Vertebra, unspecified site
        Spine NOS
     839.41 Coccyx
     839.42 Sacrum
        Sacroiliac (joint)
     839.49 Other

√5ᵗʰ **839.5** **Other vertebra, open**
     839.50 Vertebra, unspecified site
     839.51 Coccyx
     839.52 Sacrum
     839.59 Other

√5ᵗʰ **839.6** **Other location, closed**
     839.61 Sternum
        Sternoclavicular joint
     839.69 Other
        Pelvis

√5ᵗʰ **839.7** **Other location, open**
     839.71 Sternum
     839.79 Other

     839.8 **Multiple and ill-defined, closed**
        Arm
        Back
        Hand
        Multiple locations, except fingers or toes alone
        Other ill-defined locations
        Unspecified location

     839.9 **Multiple and ill-defined, open**

SPRAINS AND STRAINS OF JOINTS AND ADJACENT MUSCLES
(840-848)

INCLUDES	avulsion		
	hemarthrosis	of:	
	laceration		joint capsule
	rupture		ligament
	sprain		muscle
	strain		tendon
	tear		

EXCLUDES *laceration of tendon in open wounds (880-884 and 890-894 with .2)*

√4ᵗʰ **840** **Sprains and strains of shoulder and upper arm**
     840.0 Acromioclavicular (joint) (ligament)
     840.1 Coracoclavicular (ligament)
     840.2 Coracohumeral (ligament)
     840.3 Infraspinatus (muscle) (tendon)
     840.4 Rotator cuff (capsule)
        EXCLUDES *complete rupture of rotator cuff, nontraumatic (727.61)*
     840.5 Subscapularis (muscle)
     840.6 Supraspinatus (muscle) (tendon)
     840.7 Superior glenoid labrum lesion
        SLAP lesion
        AHA: 4Q, '01, 52
        DEF: Detachment injury of the superior aspect of the glenoid labrum which is the ring of fibrocartilage attached to the rim of the glenoid cavity of the scapula.
     840.8 Other specified sites of shoulder and upper arm
     840.9 Unspecified site of shoulder and upper arm
        Arm NOS   Shoulder NOS

√4ᵗʰ **841** **Sprains and strains of elbow and forearm**
     841.0 Radial collateral ligament
     841.1 Ulnar collateral ligament

     841.2 Radiohumeral (joint)
     841.3 Ulnohumeral (joint)
     841.8 Other specified sites of elbow and forearm
     841.9 Unspecified site of elbow and forearm
        Elbow NOS

√4ᵗʰ **842** **Sprains and strains of wrist and hand**
 √5ᵗʰ **842.0** **Wrist**
     842.00 Unspecified site
     842.01 Carpal (joint)
     842.02 Radiocarpal (joint) (ligament)
     842.09 Other
        Radioulnar joint, distal
 √5ᵗʰ **842.1** **Hand**
     842.10 Unspecified site
     842.11 Carpometacarpal (joint)
     842.12 Metacarpophalangeal (joint)
     842.13 Interphalangeal (joint)
     842.19 Other
        Midcarpal (joint)

√4ᵗʰ **843** **Sprains and strains of hip and thigh**
     843.0 Iliofemoral (ligament)
     843.1 Ischiocapsular (ligament)
     843.8 Other specified sites of hip and thigh
     843.9 Unspecified site of hip and thigh
        Hip NOS   Thigh NOS

√4ᵗʰ **844** **Sprains and strains of knee and leg**
     844.0 Lateral collateral ligament of knee
     844.1 Medial collateral ligament of knee
     844.2 Cruciate ligament of knee
     844.3 Tibiofibular (joint) (ligament), superior
     844.8 Other specified sites of knee and leg
     844.9 Unspecified site of knee and leg
        Knee NOS   Leg NOS

√4ᵗʰ **845** **Sprains and strains of ankle and foot**
 √5ᵗʰ **845.0** **Ankle**
     845.00 Unspecified site
        AHA: 2Q, '02, 3
     845.01 Deltoid (ligament), ankle
        Internal collateral (ligament), ankle
     845.02 Calcaneofibular (ligament)
     845.03 Tibiofibular (ligament), distal
        AHA: 1Q, '04, 9
     845.09 Other
        Achilles tendon
 √5ᵗʰ **845.1** **Foot**
     845.10 Unspecified site
     845.11 Tarsometatarsal (joint) (ligament)
     845.12 Metatarsophalangeal (joint)
     845.13 Interphalangeal (joint), toe
     845.19 Other

√4ᵗʰ **846** **Sprains and strains of sacroiliac region**
     846.0 Lumbosacral (joint) (ligament)   `CD PDx`
     846.1 Sacroiliac ligament   `CD PDx`
     846.2 Sacrospinatus (ligament)   `CD PDx`
     846.3 Sacrotuberous (ligament)   `CD PDx`
     846.8 Other specified sites of sacroiliac region   `CD PDx`
     846.9 Unspecified site of sacroiliac region   `CD PDx`

√4ᵗʰ **847** **Sprains and strains of other and unspecified parts of back**
        EXCLUDES *lumbosacral (846.0)*
     847.0 Neck   `CD PDx`
        Anterior longitudinal (ligament), cervical
        Atlanto-axial (joints)
        Atlanto-occipital (joints)
        Whiplash injury
        EXCLUDES *neck injury NOS (959.0)*
                    thyroid region (848.2)
     847.1 Thoracic   `CD PDx`
     847.2 Lumbar   `CD PDx`

 N Newborn Age: 0   **P** Pediatric Age: 0-17   **M** Maternity Age: 12-55   **A** Adult Age: 15-124   Manifestation Code   ►◄ Revised Text   ● New Code   ▲ Revised Code Title

250 — Volume 1   *2006 ICD•9•CM*

847.3   Sacrum   `CD PDx`
Sacrococcygeal (ligament)

847.4   Coccyx   `CD PDx`

847.9   Unspecified site of back   `CD PDx`
Back NOS

√4ᵗʰ **848   Other and ill-defined sprains and strains**

848.0   Septal cartilage of nose

848.1   Jaw
Temporomandibular (joint) (ligament)

848.2   Thyroid region
Cricoarytenoid (joint) (ligament)
Cricothyroid (joint) (ligament)
Thyroid cartilage

848.3   Ribs

Chondrocostal ⎫
(joint)   ⎬ without mention of
Costal cartilage ⎭ injury to
                     sternum

√5ᵗʰ **848.4   Sternum**

848.40   Unspecified site

848.41   Sternoclavicular (joint) (ligament)

848.42   Chondrosternal (joint)

848.49   Other
Xiphoid cartilage

848.5   Pelvis
Symphysis pubis
EXCLUDES   *that in childbirth (665.6)*

848.8   Other specified sites of sprains and strains

848.9   Unspecified site of sprain and strain

Brain

INTRACRANIAL INJURY, EXCLUDING THOSE WITH SKULL FRACTURE (850-854)

EXCLUDES   *intracranial injury with skull fracture (800-801 and 803-804, except .0 and .5)*
open wound of head without intracranial injury (870.0-873.9)
skull fracture alone (800-801 and 803-804 with .0, .5)

The description "with open intracranial wound," used in the fourth-digit subdivisions, includes those specified as open or with mention of infection or foreign body.

The following fifth-digit subclassification is for use with categories 851-854:

0   unspecified state of consciousness
1   with no loss of consciousness
2   with brief [less than one hour] loss of consciousness
3   with moderate [1-24 hours] loss of consciousness
4   with prolonged [more than 24 hours] loss of consciousness and return to pre-existing conscious level
5   with prolonged [more than 24 hours] loss of consciousness, without return to pre-existing conscious level
Use fifth-digit 5 to designate when a patient is unconscious and dies before regaining consciousness, regardless of the duration of the loss of consciousness
6   with loss of consciousness of unspecified duration
9   with concussion, unspecified

AHA: 1Q, '93, 22

√4ᵗʰ **850   Concussion**
AHA: 4Q, '96, 36; 1Q, '93, 22

INCLUDES   commotio cerebri
EXCLUDES   *concussion with:*
cerebral laceration or contusion (851.0-851.9)
cerebral hemorrhage (852-853)
head injury NOS (959.01)

850.0   With no loss of consciousness
Concussion with mental confusion or disorientation, without loss of consciousness

√5ᵗʰ **850.1   With brief loss of consciousness**
Loss of consciousness for less than one hour
AHA: 4Q, '03, 76; 1Q, '99, 10; 2Q, '92, 5

850.11   With loss of consciousness of 30 minutes or less

850.12   With loss of consciousness from 31 to 59 minutes

850.2   With moderate loss of consciousness
Loss of consciousness for 1-24 hours

850.3   With prolonged loss of consciousness and return to pre-existing conscious level
Loss of consciousness for more than 24 hours with complete recovery

850.4   With prolonged loss of consciousness, without return to pre-existing conscious level

850.5   With loss of consciousness of unspecified duration

850.9   Concussion, unspecified

√4ᵗʰ **851   Cerebral laceration and contusion**
AHA: 4Q, '96, 36; 1Q, '93, 22; 4Q, '90, 24

§ √5ᵗʰ **851.0   Cortex (cerebral) contusion without mention of open intracranial wound**   `CD PDx`

§ √5ᵗʰ **851.1   Cortex (cerebral) contusion with open intracranial wound**   `CD PDx`
AHA: 1Q, '92, 9

§ √5ᵗʰ **851.2   Cortex (cerebral) laceration without mention of open intracranial wound**   `CD PDx`

§ √5ᵗʰ **851.3   Cortex (cerebral) laceration with open intracranial wound**   `CD PDx`

---

§ Requires fifth-digit. See beginning of section 850-854 for codes and definitions.

√4ᵗʰ √5ᵗʰ **Additional Digit Required**   `RUG III Special Care Dx`   `RUG III Clinically Complex Dx`   `Hospice Non-cancer Dx`   `CD PDx` Clinical Dimension PDx   `CD SDx` Clinical Dimension SDx

Injury and Poisoning

851.4–861.22

§ ✓5ᵗʰ **851.4** **Cerebellar or brain stem contusion without mention of open intracranial wound** `CD PDx`

§ ✓5ᵗʰ **851.5** **Cerebellar or brain stem contusion with open intracranial wound** `CD PDx`

§ ✓5ᵗʰ **851.6** **Cerebellar or brain stem laceration without mention of open intracranial wound** `CD PDx`

§ ✓5ᵗʰ **851.7** **Cerebellar or brain stem laceration with open intracranial wound** `CD PDx`

§ ✓5ᵗʰ **851.8** **Other and unspecified cerebral laceration and contusion, without mention of open intracranial wound** `CD PDx`
    Brain (membrane) NOS
    AHA: 4Q, '96, 37

§ ✓5ᵗʰ **851.9** **Other and unspecified cerebral laceration and contusion, with open intracranial wound** `CD PDx`

✓4ᵗʰ **852 Subarachnoid, subdural, and extradural hemorrhage, following injury**
    EXCLUDES *Cerebral contusion or laceration (with hemorrhage) (851.0-851.9)*
    DEF: Bleeding from lining of brain; due to injury.

§ ✓5ᵗʰ **852.0** **Subarachnoid hemorrhage following injury without mention of open intracranial wound** `CD PDx`
    Middle meningeal hemorrhage following injury

§ ✓5ᵗʰ **852.1** **Subarachnoid hemorrhage following injury with open intracranial wound** `CD PDx`

§ ✓5ᵗʰ **852.2** **Subdural hemorrhage following injury without mention of open intracranial wound** `CD PDx`
    AHA: 4Q, '96, 43

§ ✓5ᵗʰ **852.3** **Subdural hemorrhage following injury with open intracranial wound** `CD PDx`

§ ✓5ᵗʰ **852.4** **Extradural hemorrhage following injury without mention of open intracranial wound** `CD PDx`
    Epidural hematoma following injury

§ ✓5ᵗʰ **852.5** **Extradural hemorrhage following injury with open intracranial wound** `CD PDx`

✓4ᵗʰ **853 Other and unspecified intracranial hemorrhage following injury**

§ ✓5ᵗʰ **853.0** **Without mention of open intracranial wound** `CD PDx`
    Cerebral compression due to injury
    Intracranial hematoma following injury
    Traumatic cerebral hemorrhage
    AHA: 3Q, '90, 14

§ ✓5ᵗʰ **853.1** **With open intracranial wound** `CD PDx`

✓4ᵗʰ **854 Intracranial injury of other and unspecified nature**
    INCLUDES brain injury NOS
        cavernous sinus
        intracranial injury
    EXCLUDES *any condition classifiable to 850-853 head injury NOS (959.01)*
    AHA: 4Q, '96, 36; 1Q, '93, 22; 4Q, '90, 24

§ ✓5ᵗʰ **854.0** **Without mention of open intracranial wound** `CD PDx`

§ ✓5ᵗʰ **854.1** **With open intracranial wound** `CD PDx`

INTERNAL INJURY OF THORAX, ABDOMEN, AND PELVIS (860-869)

INCLUDES
blast injuries
blunt trauma
bruise
concussion injuries
    (except cerebral)
crushing   } of internal organs
hematoma
laceration
puncture
tear
traumatic rupture

EXCLUDES *concussion NOS (850.0-850.9)*
flail chest (807.4)
foreign body entering through orifice (930.0-939.9)
injury to blood vessels (901.0-902.9)
The description "with open wound," used in the fourth-digit subdivisions, includes those with mention of infection or foreign body.

✓4ᵗʰ **860 Traumatic pneumothorax and hemothorax**
    AHA: 2Q, '93, 4

    DEF: Traumatic pneumothorax: air or gas leaking into pleural space of lung due to trauma.

    DEF: Traumatic hemothorax: blood buildup in pleural space of lung due to trauma.

860.0 **Pneumothorax without mention of open wound into thorax**

860.1 **Pneumothorax with open wound into thorax**

860.2 **Hemothorax without mention of open wound into thorax**

860.3 **Hemothorax with open wound into thorax**

860.4 **Pneumohemothorax without mention of open wound into thorax**

860.5 **Pneumohemothorax with open wound into thorax**
    CC Excl: see Code 860.0

✓4ᵗʰ **861 Injury to heart and lung**
    EXCLUDES *injury to blood vessels of thorax (901.0-901.9)*

✓5ᵗʰ **861.0** **Heart, without mention of open wound into thorax**
    AHA: 1Q, '92, 9

    861.00 **Unspecified injury**
    861.01 **Contusion**
        Cardiac contusion   Myocardial contusion
        DEF: Bruising within the pericardium with no mention of open wound.

    861.02 **Laceration without penetration of heart chambers**
        DEF: Tearing injury of heart tissue, without penetration of chambers; no open wound.

    861.03 **Laceration with penetration of heart chambers**

✓5ᵗʰ **861.1** **Heart, with open wound into thorax**
    861.10 **Unspecified injury**
    861.11 **Contusion**
    861.12 **Laceration without penetration of heart chambers**
    861.13 **Laceration with penetration of heart chambers**

✓5ᵗʰ **861.2** **Lung, without mention of open wound into thorax**
    861.20 **Unspecified injury**
    861.21 **Contusion**
        DEF: Bruising of lung without mention of open wound.

    861.22 **Laceration**

---

§ Requires fifth-digit. See beginning of section 850-854 for codes and definitions.

N Newborn Age: 0   P Pediatric Age: 0-17   M Maternity Age: 12-55   A Adult Age: 15-124   Manifestation Code   ▶◀ Revised Text   ● New Code   ▲ Revised Code Title

252 — Volume 1   *2006 ICD•9•CM*

✓5ᵗʰ **861.3 Lung, with open wound into thorax**

    861.30 Unspecified injury

    861.31 Contusion

    861.32 Laceration

✓4ᵗʰ **862 Injury to other and unspecified intrathoracic organs**

    EXCLUDES *injury to blood vessels of thorax (901.0-901.9)*

    862.0 Diaphragm, without mention of open wound into cavity

    862.1 Diaphragm, with open wound into cavity

✓5ᵗʰ **862.2 Other specified intrathoracic organs, without mention of open wound into cavity**

    862.21 Bronchus

    862.22 Esophagus

    862.29 Other

        Pleura

        Thymus gland

✓5ᵗʰ **862.3 Other specified intrathoracic organs, with open wound into cavity**

    862.31 Bronchus

    862.32 Esophagus

    862.39 Other

    862.8 Multiple and unspecified intrathoracic organs, without mention of open wound into cavity

        Crushed chest

        Multiple intrathoracic organs

    862.9 Multiple and unspecified intrathoracic organs, with open wound into cavity

✓4ᵗʰ **863 Injury to gastrointestinal tract**

    EXCLUDES *anal sphincter laceration during delivery (664.2)*

        bile duct (868.0-868.1 with fifth-digit 2)

        gallbladder (868.0-868.1 with fifth-digit 2)

    863.0 Stomach, without mention of open wound into cavity

    863.1 Stomach, with open wound into cavity

✓5ᵗʰ **863.2 Small intestine, without mention of open wound into cavity**

    863.20 Small intestine, unspecified site

    863.21 Duodenum

    863.29 Other

✓5ᵗʰ **863.3 Small intestine, with open wound into cavity**

    863.30 Small intestine, unspecified site

    863.31 Duodenum

    863.39 Other

✓5ᵗʰ **863.4 Colon or rectum, without mention of open wound into cavity**

    863.40 Colon, unspecified site

    863.41 Ascending [right] colon

    863.42 Transverse colon

    863.43 Descending [left] colon

    863.44 Sigmoid colon

    863.45 Rectum

    863.46 Multiple sites in colon and rectum

    863.49 Other

✓5ᵗʰ **863.5 Colon or rectum, with open wound into cavity**

    863.50 Colon, unspecified site

    863.51 Ascending [right] colon

    863.52 Transverse colon

    863.53 Descending [left] colon

    863.54 Sigmoid colon

    863.55 Rectum

    863.56 Multiple sites in colon and rectum

    863.59 Other

✓5ᵗʰ **863.8 Other and unspecified gastrointestinal sites, without mention of open wound into cavity**

    863.80 Gastrointestinal tract, unspecified site

    863.81 Pancreas, head

    863.82 Pancreas, body

    863.83 Pancreas, tail

    863.84 Pancreas, multiple and unspecified sites

    863.85 Appendix

    863.89 Other

        Intestine NOS

✓5ᵗʰ **863.9 Other and unspecified gastrointestinal sites, with open wound into cavity**

    863.90 Gastrointestinal tract, unspecified site

    863.91 Pancreas, head

    863.92 Pancreas, body

    863.93 Pancreas, tail

    863.94 Pancreas, multiple and unspecified sites

    863.95 Appendix

    863.99 Other

✓4ᵗʰ **864 Injury to liver**

    The following fifth-digit subclassification is for use with category 864:

    0 unspecified injury

    1 hematoma and contusion

    2 laceration, minor

        Laceration involving capsule only, or without significant involvement of hepatic parenchyma [i.e., less than 1 cm deep]

    3 laceration, moderate

        Laceration involving parenchyma but without major disruption of parenchyma [i.e., less than 10 cm long and less than 3 cm deep]

    4 laceration, major

        Laceration with significant disruption of hepatic parenchyma [i.e., 10 cm long and 3 cm deep]

        Multiple moderate lacerations, with or without hematoma

        Stellate lacerations of liver

    5 laceration, unspecified

    9 other

✓5ᵗʰ **864.0 Without mention of open wound into cavity**

✓5ᵗʰ **864.1 With open wound into cavity**

✓4ᵗʰ **865 Injury to spleen**

    The following fifth-digit subclassification is for use with category 865:

    0 unspecified injury

    1 hematoma without rupture of capsule

    2 capsular tears, without major disruption of parenchyma

    3 laceration extending into parenchyma

    4 massive parenchymal disruption

    9 other

✓5ᵗʰ **865.0 Without mention of open wound into cavity**

✓5ᵗʰ **865.1 With open wound into cavity**

✓4ᵗʰ **866 Injury to kidney**

    The following fifth-digit subclassification is for use with category 866:

    0 unspecified injury

    1 hematoma without rupture of capsule

    2 laceration

    3 complete disruption of kidney parenchyma

✓5ᵗʰ **866.0 Without mention of open wound into cavity**

✓5ᵗʰ **866.1 With open wound into cavity**

✓4ᵗʰ **867 Injury to pelvic organs**

    EXCLUDES *injury during delivery (664.0-665.9)*

    867.0 Bladder and urethra, without mention of open wound into cavity

    AHA: N-D, '85, 15

    867.1 Bladder and urethra, with open wound into cavity

    867.2 Ureter, without mention of open wound into cavity

    867.3 Ureter, with open wound into cavity

✓4ᵗʰ ✓5ᵗʰ Additional Digit Required   RUG III Special Care Dx   RUG III Clinically Complex Dx   Hospice Non-cancer Dx   **CD PDx** Clinical Dimension PDx   **CD SDx** Clinical Dimension SDx

2006 ICD•9•CM   **Volume 1 — 253**

867.4 Uterus, without mention of open wound intocavity ♀

867.5 Uterus, with open wound into cavity ♀

867.6 Other specified pelvic organs, without mention of open wound into cavity
Fallopian tube   Seminal vesicle
Ovary   Vas deferens
Prostate

867.7 Other specified pelvic organs, with open wound into cavity

867.8 Unspecified pelvic organ, without mention of open wound into cavity

867.9 Unspecified pelvic organ, with open wound into cavity

√4ᵗʰ **868 Injury to other intra-abdominal organs**

The following fifth-digit subclassification is for use with category 868:
   0 unspecified intra-abdominal organ
   1 adrenal gland
   2 bile duct and gallbladder
   3 peritoneum
   4 retroperitoneum
   9 other and multiple intra-abdominal organs

√5ᵗʰ **868.0** Without mention of open wound into cavity

√5ᵗʰ **868.1** With open wound into cavity

√4ᵗʰ **869 Internal injury to unspecified or ill-defined organs**
   INCLUDES   internal injury NOS
              multiple internal injury NOS

869.0 Without mention of open wound into cavity

869.1 With open wound into cavity
   AHA: 2Q, '89, 15

OPEN WOUND (870-897)

INCLUDES   animal bite
           avulsion
           cut
           laceration
           puncture wound
           traumatic amputation

EXCLUDES   burn (940.0-949.5)
           crushing (925-929.9)
           puncture of internal organs (860.0-869.1)
           superficial injury (910.0-919.9)
           that incidental to:
              dislocation (830.0-839.9)
              fracture (800.0-829.1)
              internal injury (860.0-869.1)
              intracranial injury (851.0-854.1)

Note: The description "complicated" used in the fourth-digit subdivisions includes those with mention of delayed healing, delayed treatment, foreign body, or infection. Use additional code to identify infection
   AHA: 4Q, '01, 52

OPEN WOUND OF HEAD, NECK, AND TRUNK (870-879)

√4ᵗʰ **870 Open wound of ocular adnexa**

870.0 Laceration of skin of eyelid and periocular area   `CD PDx`

870.1 Laceration of eyelid, full-thickness, not involving lacrimal passages   `CD PDx`

870.2 Laceration of eyelid involving lacrimal passages   `CD PDx`

870.3 Penetrating wound of orbit, without mention of foreign body   `CD PDx`

870.4 Penetrating wound of orbit with foreign body   `CD PDx`
   EXCLUDES   retained (old) foreign body in orbit (376.6)

870.8 Other specified open wounds of ocular adnexa   `CD PDx`

870.9 Unspecified open wound of ocular adnexa   `CD PDx`

√4ᵗʰ **871 Open wound of eyeball**
   EXCLUDES   2nd cranial nerve [optic] injury (950.0-950.9)
              3rd cranial nerve [oculomotor] injury (951.0)

871.0 Ocular laceration without prolapse of intraocular tissue
   AHA: 3Q, '96, 7

   DEF: Tear in ocular tissue without displacing structures.

871.1 Ocular laceration with prolapse or exposure of intraocular tissue

871.2 Rupture of eye with partial loss of intraocular tissue

   DEF: Forcible tearing of eyeball, with tissue loss.

871.3 Avulsion of eye
   Traumatic enucleation

   DEF: Traumatic extraction of eyeball from socket.

871.4 Unspecified laceration of eye

871.5 Penetration of eyeball with magnetic foreign body
   EXCLUDES   retained (old) magnetic foreign body in globe (360.50-360.59)

871.6 Penetration of eyeball with (nonmagnetic) foreign body
   EXCLUDES   retained (old) (nonmagnetic) foreign body in globe (360.60-360.69)

871.7 Unspecified ocular penetration

871.9 Unspecified open wound of eyeball

√4ᵗʰ **872 Open wound of ear**

√5ᵗʰ **872.0** External ear, without mention of complication

872.00 External ear, unspecified site   `CD PDx`

872.01 Auricle, ear   `CD PDx`
   Pinna

   DEF: Open wound of fleshy, outer ear.

872.02 Auditory canal   `CD PDx`

   DEF: Open wound of passage from external ear to eardrum.

√5ᵗʰ **872.1** External ear, complicated

872.10 External ear, unspecified site   `CD PDx`

872.11 Auricle, ear   `CD PDx`

872.12 Auditory canal   `CD PDx`

√5ᵗʰ **872.6** Other specified parts of ear, without mention of complication

872.61 Ear drum   `CD PDx`
   Drumhead   Tympanic membrane

872.62 Ossicles   `CD PDx`

872.63 Eustachian tube   `CD PDx`

   DEF: Open wound of channel between nasopharynx and tympanic cavity.

872.64 Cochlea   `CD PDx`

   DEF: Open wound of snail shell shaped tube of inner ear.

872.69 Other and multiple sites   `CD PDx`

√5ᵗʰ **872.7** Other specified parts of ear, complicated

872.71 Ear drum   `CD PDx`

872.72 Ossicles   `CD PDx`

872.73 Eustachian tube   `CD PDx`

872.74 Cochlea   `CD PDx`

872.79 Other and multiple sites   `CD PDx`

872.8 Ear, part unspecified, without mention of complication   `CD PDx`
   Ear NOS

872.9 Ear, part unspecified, complicated   `CD PDx`

√4ᵗʰ **873 Other open wound of head**

873.0 Scalp, without mention of complication   `CD PDx`

873.1 Scalp, complicated   `CD PDx`

√5ᵗʰ **873.2** Nose, without mention of complication

873.20 Nose, unspecified site   `CD PDx`

N Newborn Age: 0   P Pediatric Age: 0-17   M Maternity Age: 12-55   A Adult Age: 15-124   Manifestation Code   ▶◀ Revised Text   ● New Code   ▲ Revised Code Title

873.21 **Nasal septum** `CD PDx`
DEF: Open wound between nasal passages.

873.22 **Nasal cavity** `CD PDx`
DEF: Open wound of nostrils.

873.23 **Nasal sinus** `CD PDx`
DEF: Open wound of mucous-lined respiratory cavities.

873.29 **Multiple sites** `CD PDx`

√5ᵗʰ 873.3 **Nose, complicated**
873.30 **Nose, unspecified site** `CD PDx`
873.31 **Nasal septum** `CD PDx`
873.32 **Nasal cavity** `CD PDx`
873.33 **Nasal sinus** `CD PDx`
873.39 **Multiple sites** `CD PDx`

√5ᵗʰ 873.4 **Face, without mention of complication**
873.40 **Face, unspecified site** `CD PDx`
873.41 **Cheek** `CD PDx`
873.42 **Forehead** `CD PDx`
Eyebrow
873.43 **Lip** `CD PDx`
873.44 **Jaw** `CD PDx`
873.49 **Other and multiple sites** `CD PDx`

√5ᵗʰ 873.5 **Face, complicated**
873.50 **Face, unspecified site** `CD PDx`
873.51 **Cheek** `CD PDx`
873.52 **Forehead** `CD PDx`
873.53 **Lip** `CD PDx`
873.54 **Jaw** `CD PDx`
873.59 **Other and multiple sites** `CD PDx`

√5ᵗʰ 873.6 **Internal structures of mouth, without mention of complication**
873.60 **Mouth, unspecified site** `CD PDx`
873.61 **Buccal mucosa** `CD PDx`
DEF: Open wound of inside of cheek.
873.62 **Gum (alveolar process)** `CD PDx`
873.63 **Tooth (broken)** `CD PDx`
AHA: 1Q, '04, 17
873.64 **Tongue and floor of mouth** `CD PDx`
873.65 **Palate** `CD PDx`
DEF: Open wound of roof of mouth.
873.69 **Other and multiple sites** `CD PDx`

√5ᵗʰ 873.7 **Internal structures of mouth, complicated**
873.70 **Mouth, unspecified site** `CD PDx`
873.71 **Buccal mucosa** `CD PDx`
873.72 **Gum (alveolar process)** `CD PDx`
873.73 **Tooth (broken)** `CD PDx`
AHA: 1Q, '04, 17
873.74 **Tongue and floor of mouth** `CD PDx`
873.75 **Palate** `CD PDx`
873.79 **Other and multiple sites** `CD PDx`

873.8 **Other and unspecified open wound of head without mention of complication** `CD PDx`
Head NOS

873.9 **Other and unspecified open wound of head, complicated** `CD PDx`

√4ᵗʰ 874 **Open wound of neck**
√5ᵗʰ 874.0 **Larynx and trachea, without mention of complication**
874.00 **Larynx with trachea** `CD PDx`
874.01 **Larynx** `CD PDx`
874.02 **Trachea** `CD PDx`

√5ᵗʰ 874.1 **Larynx and trachea, complicated**
874.10 **Larynx with trachea** `CD PDx`
874.11 **Larynx** `CD PDx`
874.12 **Trachea** `CD PDx`

874.2 **Thyroid gland, without mention of complication** `CD PDx`
874.3 **Thyroid gland, complicated** `CD PDx`
874.4 **Pharynx, without mention of complication** `CD PDx`
Cervical esophagus
874.5 **Pharynx, complicated** `CD PDx`
874.8 **Other and unspecified parts, without mention of complication** `CD PDx`
Nape of neck Throat NOS
Supraclavicular region
874.9 **Other and unspecified parts, complicated** `CD PDx`

√4ᵗʰ 875 **Open wound of chest (wall)**
EXCLUDES open wound into thoracic cavity (860.0-862.9)
traumatic pneumothorax and hemothorax (860.1, 860.3, 860.5)
AHA: 3Q, '93, 17
875.0 **Without mention of complication** `CD PDx`
875.1 **Complicated** `CD PDx`

√4ᵗʰ 876 **Open wound of back**
INCLUDES loin
lumbar region
EXCLUDES open wound into thoracic cavity (860.0-862.9)
traumatic pneumothorax and hemothorax (860.1, 860.3, 860.5)
876.0 **Without mention of complication** `CD PDx`
876.1 **Complicated** `CD PDx`

√4ᵗʰ 877 **Open wound of buttock**
INCLUDES sacroiliac region
877.0 **Without mention of complication** `CD PDx`
877.1 **Complicated** `CD PDx`

√4ᵗʰ 878 **Open wound of genital organs (external), including traumatic amputation**
EXCLUDES injury during delivery (664.0-665.9)
internal genital organs (867.0-867.9)
878.0 **Penis, without mention of complication** `CD PDx` ♂
878.1 **Penis, complicated** `CD PDx` ♂
878.2 **Scrotum and testes, without mention of complication** `CD PDx` ♂
878.3 **Scrotum and testes, complicated** `CD PDx` ♂
878.4 **Vulva, without mention of complication** `CD PDx` ♀
Labium (majus) (minus)
878.5 **Vulva, complicated** `CD PDx` ♀
878.6 **Vagina, without mention of complication** `CD PDx` ♀
878.7 **Vagina, complicated** `CD PDx` ♀
878.8 **Other and unspecified parts, without mention of complication** `CD PDx`
878.9 **Other and unspecified parts, complicated** `CD PDx`

√4ᵗʰ 879 **Open wound of other and unspecified sites, except limbs**
879.0 **Breast, without mention of complication** `CD PDx`
879.1 **Breast, complicated** `CD PDx`
879.2 **Abdominal wall, anterior, without mention of complication** `CD PDx`
Abdominal wall NOS Pubic region
Epigastric region Umbilical region
Hypogastric region
AHA: 2Q, '91, 22
879.3 **Abdominal wall, anterior, complicated** `CD PDx`
879.4 **Abdominal wall, lateral, without mention of complication** `CD PDx`
Flank Iliac (region)
Groin Inguinal region
Hypochondrium
879.5 **Abdominal wall, lateral, complicated** `CD PDx`
879.6 **Other and unspecified parts of trunk, without mention of complication** `CD PDx`
Pelvic region Trunk NOS
Perineum
879.7 **Other and unspecified parts of trunk, complicated** `CD PDx`

√4ᵗʰ √5ᵗʰ Additional Digit Required   RUG III Special Care Dx   RUG III Clinically Complex Dx   Hospice Non-cancer Dx   `CD PDx` Clinical Dimension PDx   `CD SDx` Clinical Dimension SDx

2006 ICD•9•CM   Volume 1 — 255

Injury and Poisoning

879.8–897.7

879.8 Open wound(s) (multiple) of unspecified site(s) without mention of complication `CD PDx`

Multiple open wounds NOS   Open wound NOS

879.9 Open wound(s) (multiple) of unspecified site(s), complicated `CD PDx`

OPEN WOUND OF UPPER LIMB (880-887)

AHA: N-D, '85, 5

✓4ᵗʰ **880** Open wound of shoulder and upper arm

The following fifth-digit subclassification is for use with category 880:

     0 shoulder region
     1 scapular region
     2 axillary region
     3 upper arm
     9 multiple sites

✓5ᵗʰ **880.0** Without mention of complication `CD PDx`
✓5ᵗʰ **880.1** Complicated `CD PDx`
✓5ᵗʰ **880.2** With tendon involvement `CD PDx`

✓4ᵗʰ **881** Open wound of elbow, forearm, and wrist

The following fifth-digit subclassification is for use with category 881:

     0 forearm
     1 elbow
     2 wrist

✓5ᵗʰ **881.0** Without mention of complication `CD PDx`
✓5ᵗʰ **881.1** Complicated `CD PDx`
✓5ᵗʰ **881.2** With tendon involvement `CD PDx`

✓4ᵗʰ **882** Open wound of hand except finger(s) alone
882.0 Without mention of complication `CD PDx`
882.1 Complicated `CD PDx`
882.2 With tendon involvement `CD PDx`

✓4ᵗʰ **883** Open wound of finger(s)
     `INCLUDES` fingernail
                 thumb (nail)
883.0 Without mention of complication `CD PDx`
883.1 Complicated `CD PDx`
883.2 With tendon involvement `CD PDx`

✓4ᵗʰ **884** Multiple and unspecified open wound of upper limb
     `INCLUDES` arm NOS
                  multiple sites of one upper limb
                  upper limb NOS
884.0 Without mention of complication `CD PDx`
884.1 Complicated `CD PDx`
884.2 With tendon involvement `CD PDx`

✓4ᵗʰ **885** Traumatic amputation of thumb (complete) (partial)
     `INCLUDES` thumb(s) (with finger(s) of either hand)
885.0 Without mention of complication `CD PDx`
     AHA: 1Q, '03, 7

885.1 Complicated `CD PDx`

✓4ᵗʰ **886** Traumatic amputation of other finger(s) (complete) (partial)
     `INCLUDES` finger(s) of one or both hands, without mention of thumb(s)
886.0 Without mention of complication `CD PDx`
886.1 Complicated `CD PDx`

✓4ᵗʰ **887** Traumatic amputation of arm and hand (complete) (partial)
887.0 Unilateral, below elbow, without mention of complication `CD PDx`
887.1 Unilateral, below elbow, complicated `CD PDx`
887.2 Unilateral, at or above elbow, without mention of complication `CD PDx`
887.3 Unilateral, at or above elbow, complicated `CD PDx`
887.4 Unilateral, level not specified, without mention of complication `CD PDx`
887.5 Unilateral, level not specified, complicated `CD PDx`

887.6 Bilateral [any level], without mention of complication `CD PDx`
     One hand and other arm

887.7 Bilateral [any level], complicated `CD PDx`

OPEN WOUND OF LOWER LIMB (890-897)

AHA: N-D, '85, 5

✓4ᵗʰ **890** Open wound of hip and thigh
890.0 Without mention of complication `CD PDx`
890.1 Complicated `CD PDx`
890.2 With tendon involvement `CD PDx`

✓4ᵗʰ **891** Open wound of knee, leg [except thigh], and ankle
     `INCLUDES` leg NOS
                  multiple sites of leg, except thigh
     `EXCLUDES` *that of thigh (890.0-890.2)*
                  with multiple sites of lower limb (894.0-894.2)
891.0 Without mention of complication `CD PDx`
891.1 Complicated `CD PDx`
891.2 With tendon involvement `CD PDx`

✓4ᵗʰ **892** Open wound of foot except toe(s) alone
     `INCLUDES` heel
892.0 Without mention of complication `CD PDx`
892.1 Complicated `CD PDx`
892.2 With tendon involvement `CD PDx`

✓4ᵗʰ **893** Open wound of toe(s)
     `INCLUDES` toenail
893.0 Without mention of complication `CD PDx`
893.1 Complicated `CD PDx`
893.2 With tendon involvement `CD PDx`

✓4ᵗʰ **894** Multiple and unspecified open wound of lower limb
     `INCLUDES` lower limb NOS
                  multiple sites of one lower limb, with thigh
894.0 Without mention of complication `CD PDx`
894.1 Complicated `CD PDx`
894.2 With tendon involvement `CD PDx`

✓4ᵗʰ **895** Traumatic amputation of toe(s) (complete) (partial)
     `INCLUDES` toe(s) of one or both feet
895.0 Without mention of complication `CD PDx`
895.1 Complicated `CD PDx`

✓4ᵗʰ **896** Traumatic amputation of foot (complete) (partial)
896.0 Unilateral, without mention of complication `CD PDx`
896.1 Unilateral, complicated `CD PDx`
896.2 Bilateral, without mention of complication `CD PDx`
     `EXCLUDES` *one foot and other leg (897.6-897.7)*
896.3 Bilateral, complicated `CD PDx`

✓4ᵗʰ **897** Traumatic amputation of leg(s) (complete) (partial)
897.0 Unilateral, below knee, without mention of complication `CD PDx`
897.1 Unilateral, below knee, complicated `CD PDx`
897.2 Unilateral, at or above knee, without mention of complication `CD PDx`
897.3 Unilateral, at or above knee, complicated `CD PDx`
897.4 Unilateral, level not specified, without mention of complication `CD PDx`
897.5 Unilateral, level not specified, complicated `CD PDx`
897.6 Bilateral [any level], without mention of complication `CD PDx`
     One foot and other leg
897.7 Bilateral [any level], complicated `CD PDx`
     AHA: 3Q, '90, 5

`N` Newborn Age: 0   `P` Pediatric Age: 0-17   `M` Maternity Age: 12-55   `A` Adult Age: 15-124   `Manifestation Code`   ►◄ Revised Text   ● New Code   ▲ Revised Code Title

INJURY TO BLOOD VESSELS (900-904)

INCLUDES   arterial hematoma
avulsion
cut   of blood vessel,
laceration   secondary to
rupture   other injuries
traumatic aneurysm   e.g., fracture
     or fistula (arteri-   or open
     ovenous)   wound

EXCLUDES   accidental puncture or laceration during medical
procedure (998.2)
intracranial hemorrhage following injury (851.0-
854.1)

AHA: 3Q, '90, 5

√4th 900 Injury to blood vessels of head and neck

    √5th 900.0 Carotid artery
       900.00 Carotid artery, unspecified
       900.01 Common carotid artery
       900.02 External carotid artery
       900.03 Internal carotid artery
    900.1 Internal jugular vein
    √5th 900.8 Other specified blood vessels of head and neck
       900.81 External jugular vein
         Jugular vein NOS
       900.82 Multiple blood vessels of head and neck
       900.89 Other
    900.9 Unspecified blood vessel of head and neck

√4th 901 Injury to blood vessels of thorax
    EXCLUDES   traumatic hemothorax (860.2-860.5)
    901.0 Thoracic aorta
    901.1 Innominate and subclavian arteries
    901.2 Superior vena cava
    901.3 Innominate and subclavian veins
    √5th 901.4 Pulmonary blood vessels
       901.40 Pulmonary vessel(s), unspecified
       901.41 Pulmonary artery
       901.42 Pulmonary vein
    √5th 901.8 Other specified blood vessels of thorax
       901.81 Intercostal artery or vein
       901.82 Internal mammary artery or vein
       901.83 Multiple blood vessels of thorax
       901.89 Other
         Azygos vein   Hemiazygos vein
    901.9 Unspecified blood vessel of thorax

√4th 902 Injury to blood vessels of abdomen and pelvis
    902.0 Abdominal aorta
    √5th 902.1 Inferior vena cava
       902.10 Inferior vena cava, unspecified
       902.11 Hepatic veins
       902.19 Other
    √5th 902.2 Celiac and mesenteric arteries
       902.20 Celiac and mesenteric arteries, unspecified
       902.21 Gastric artery
       902.22 Hepatic artery
       902.23 Splenic artery
       902.24 Other specified branches of celiac axis
       902.25 Superior mesenteric artery (trunk)
       902.26 Primary branches of superior mesenteric artery
         Ileocolic artery
       902.27 Inferior mesenteric artery
       902.29 Other
    √5th 902.3 Portal and splenic veins
       902.31 Superior mesenteric vein and primary subdivisions
         Ileocolic vein

       902.32 Inferior mesenteric vein
       902.33 Portal vein
       902.34 Splenic vein
       902.39 Other
         Cystic vein   Gastric vein
    √5th 902.4 Renal blood vessels
       902.40 Renal vessel(s), unspecified
       902.41 Renal artery
       902.42 Renal vein
       902.49 Other
         Suprarenal arteries
    √5th 902.5 Iliac blood vessels
       902.50 Iliac vessel(s), unspecified
       902.51 Hypogastric artery
       902.52 Hypogastric vein
       902.53 Iliac artery
       902.54 Iliac vein
       902.55 Uterine artery   ♀
       902.56 Uterine vein   ♀
       902.59 Other
    √5th 902.8 Other specified blood vessels of abdomen and pelvis
       902.81 Ovarian artery   ♀
       902.82 Ovarian vein   ♀
       902.87 Multiple blood vessels of abdomen and pelvis
       902.89 Other
    902.9 Unspecified blood vessel of abdomen and pelvis

√4th 903 Injury to blood vessels of upper extremity
    √5th 903.0 Axillary blood vessels
       903.00 Axillary vessel(s), unspecified
       903.01 Axillary artery
       903.02 Axillary vein
    903.1 Brachial blood vessels
    903.2 Radial blood vessels
    903.3 Ulnar blood vessels
    903.4 Palmar artery
    903.5 Digital blood vessels
    903.8 Other specified blood vessels of upper extremity
       Multiple blood vessels of upper extremity
    903.9 Unspecified blood vessel of upper extremity

√4th 904 Injury to blood vessels of lower extremity and unspecified sites
    904.0 Common femoral artery
       Femoral artery above profunda origin
    904.1 Superficial femoral artery
    904.2 Femoral veins
    904.3 Saphenous veins
       Saphenous vein (greater) (lesser)
    √5th 904.4 Popliteal blood vessels
       904.40 Popliteal vessel(s), unspecified
       904.41 Popliteal artery
       904.42 Popliteal vein
    √5th 904.5 Tibial blood vessels
       904.50 Tibial vessel(s), unspecified
       904.51 Anterior tibial artery
       904.52 Anterior tibial vein
       904.53 Posterior tibial artery
       904.54 Posterior tibial vein
    904.6 Deep plantar blood vessels
    904.7 Other specified blood vessels of lower extremity
       Multiple blood vessels of lower extremity
    904.8 Unspecified blood vessel of lower extremity
    904.9 Unspecified site
       Injury to blood vessel NOS

√4th √5th Additional Digit Required   RUG III Special Care Dx   RUG III Clinically Complex Dx   Hospice Non-cancer Dx   **CD PDx** Clinical Dimension PDx   **CD SDx** Clinical Dimension SDx

2006 ICD•9•CM   **Volume 1 — 257**

Injury and Poisoning

905–909.9

LATE EFFECTS OF INJURIES, POISONINGS, TOXIC EFFECTS, AND OTHER EXTERNAL CAUSES (905–909)

Note: These categories are to be used to indicate conditions classifiable to 800-999 as the cause of late effects, which are themselves classified elsewhere. The "late effects" include those specified as such, or as sequelae, which may occur at any time after the acute injury.

✓4ᵗʰ **905 Late effects of musculoskeletal and connective tissue injuries**
AHA: 1Q, '95, 10; 2Q, '94, 3

905.0 Late effect of fracture of skull and face bones
Late effect of injury classifiable to 800-804
AHA: 3Q, '97, 12

905.1 Late effect of fracture of spine and trunk without mention of spinal cord lesion
Late effect of injury classifiable to 805, 807-809

905.2 Late effect of fracture of upper extremities
Late effect of injury classifiable to 810-819

905.3 Late effect of fracture of neck of femur
Late effect of injury classifiable to 820

905.4 Late effect of fracture of lower extremities
Late effect of injury classifiable to 821-827

905.5 Late effect of fracture of multiple and unspecified bones
Late effect of injury classifiable to 828-829

905.6 Late effect of dislocation
Late effect of injury classifiable to 830-839

905.7 Late effect of sprain and strain without mention of tendon injury
Late effect of injury classifiable to 840-848, except tendon injury

905.8 Late effect of tendon injury
Late effect of tendon injury due to:
open wound [injury classifiable to 880-884 with .2, 890-894 with .2]
sprain and strain [injury classifiable to 840-848]
AHA: 2Q, '89, 13; 2Q, '89, 15

905.9 Late effect of traumatic amputation
Late effect of injury classifiable to 885-887, 895-897
EXCLUDES *late amputation stump complication (997.60-997.69)*

✓4ᵗʰ **906 Late effects of injuries to skin and subcutaneous tissues**

906.0 Late effect of open wound of head, neck, and trunk
Late effect of injury classifiable to 870-879

906.1 Late effect of open wound of extremities without mention of tendon injury
Late effect of injury classifiable to 880-884, 890-894 except .2

906.2 Late effect of superficial injury
Late effect of injury classifiable to 910-919

906.3 Late effect of contusion
Late effect of injury classifiable to 920-924

906.4 Late effect of crushing
Late effect of injury classifiable to 925-929

906.5 Late effect of burn of eye, face, head, and neck
Late effect of injury classifiable to 940-941
▶AHA: 4Q, '04, 76◀

906.6 Late effect of burn of wrist and hand
Late effect of injury classifiable to 944
AHA: 4Q, '94, 22

906.7 Late effect of burn of other extremities
Late effect of injury classifiable to 943 or 945
AHA: 4Q, '94, 22

906.8 Late effect of burns of other specified sites
Late effect of injury classifiable to 942, 946-947
AHA: 4Q, '94, 22

906.9 Late effect of burn of unspecified site
Late effect of injury classifiable to 948-949
AHA: 4Q, '94, 22

✓4ᵗʰ **907 Late effects of injuries to the nervous system**

907.0 Late effect of intracranial injury without mention of skull fracture `CD PDx`
Late effect of injury classifiable to 850-854
AHA: 4Q, '03, 103; 3Q, '90, 14

907.1 Late effect of injury to cranial nerve `CD PDx`
Late effect of injury classifiable to 950-951

907.2 Late effect of spinal cord injury `CD PDx`
Late effect of injury classifiable to 806, 952
AHA: 4Q, '03, 103; 4Q, '98, 38

907.3 Late effect of injury to nerve root(s), spinal plexus(es), and other nerves of trunk `CD PDx`
Late effect of injury classifiable to 953-954

907.4 Late effect of injury to peripheral nerve of shoulder girdle and upper limb `CD PDx`
Late effect of injury classifiable to 955

907.5 Late effect of injury to peripheral nerve of pelvic girdle and lower limb `CD PDx`
Late effect of injury classifiable to 956

907.9 Late effect of injury to other and unspecified nerve `CD PDx`
Late effect of injury classifiable to 957

✓4ᵗʰ **908 Late effects of other and unspecified injuries**

908.0 Late effect of internal injury to chest
Late effect of injury classifiable to 860-862

908.1 Late effect of internal injury to intra-abdominal organs
Late effect of injury classifiable to 863-866, 868

908.2 Late effect of internal injury to other internal organs
Late effect of injury classifiable to 867 or 869

908.3 Late effect of injury to blood vessel of head, neck, and extremities
Late effect of injury classifiable to 900, 903-904

908.4 Late effect of injury to blood vessel of thorax, abdomen, and pelvis
Late effect of injury classifiable to 901-902

908.5 Late effect of foreign body in orifice
Late effect of injury classifiable to 930-939

908.6 Late effect of certain complications of trauma
Late effect of complications classifiable to 958

908.9 Late effect of unspecified injury
Late effect of injury classifiable to 959
AHA: 3Q, '00, 4

✓4ᵗʰ **909 Late effects of other and unspecified external causes**

909.0 Late effect of poisoning due to drug, medicinal or biological substance
Late effect of conditions classifiable to 960-979
EXCLUDES *late effect of adverse effect of drug, medicinal or biological substance (909.5)*
AHA: 4Q, '03, 103

909.1 Late effect of toxic effects of nonmedical substances
Late effect of conditions classifiable to 980-989

909.2 Late effect of radiation
Late effect of conditions classifiable to 990

909.3 Late effect of complications of surgical and medical care
Late effect of conditions classifiable to 996-999
AHA: 1Q, '93, 29

909.4 Late effect of certain other external causes
Late effect of conditions classifiable to 991-994

909.5 Late effect of adverse effect of drug, medical or biological substance
EXCLUDES *late effect of poisoning due to drug, medicinal or biological substance (909.0)*
AHA: 4Q, '94, 48

909.9 Late effect of other and unspecified external causes

Ⓝ Newborn Age: 0   Ⓟ Pediatric Age: 0-17   Ⓜ Maternity Age: 12-55   Ⓐ Adult Age: 15-124   Manifestation Code   ▶◀ Revised Text   ● New Code   ▲ Revised Code Title

SUPERFICIAL INJURY (910-919)

EXCLUDES   burn (blisters) (940.0-949.5)
contusion (920-924.9)
foreign body:
granuloma (728.82)
inadvertently left in operative wound (998.4)
residual in soft tissue (729.6)
insect bite, venomous (989.5)
open wound with incidental foreign body
(870.0-897.7)

AHA: 2Q, '89, 15

√4th **910 Superficial injury of face, neck, and scalp except eye**

INCLUDES   cheek   lip
ear   nose
gum   throat

EXCLUDES   eye and adnexa (918.0-918.9)

910.0 **Abrasion or friction burn without mention of infection**

910.1 **Abrasion or friction burn, infected**

910.2 **Blister without mention of infection**

910.3 **Blister, infected**

910.4 **Insect bite, nonvenomous, without mention of infection**

910.5 **Insect bite, nonvenomous, infected**

910.6 **Superficial foreign body (splinter) without major open wound and without mention of infection**

910.7 **Superficial foreign body (splinter) without major open wound, infected**

910.8 **Other and unspecified superficial injury of face, neck, and scalp without mention of infection**

910.9 **Other and unspecified superficial injury of face, neck, and scalp, infected**

√4th **911 Superficial injury of trunk**

INCLUDES   abdominal wall   interscapular region
anus   labium (majus) (minus)
back   penis
breast   perineum
buttock   scrotum
chest wall   testis
flank   vagina
groin   vulva

EXCLUDES   hip (916.0-916.9)
scapular region (912.0-912.9)

911.0 **Abrasion or friction burn without mention of infection**

AHA: 3Q, '01, 10

911.1 **Abrasion or friction burn, infected**

911.2 **Blister without mention of infection**

911.3 **Blister, infected**

911.4 **Insect bite, nonvenomous, without mention of infection**

911.5 **Insect bite, nonvenomous, infected**

911.6 **Superficial foreign body (splinter) without major open wound and without mention of infection**

911.7 **Superficial foreign body (splinter) without major open wound, infected**

911.8 **Other and unspecified superficial injury of trunk without mention of infection**

911.9 **Other and unspecified superficial injury of trunk, infected**

√4th **912 Superficial injury of shoulder and upper arm**

INCLUDES   axilla   scapular region

912.0 **Abrasion or friction burn without mention of infection**

912.1 **Abrasion or friction burn, infected**

912.2 **Blister without mention of infection**

912.3 **Blister, infected**

912.4 **Insect bite, nonvenomous, without mention of infection**

912.5 **Insect bite, nonvenomous, infected**

912.6 **Superficial foreign body (splinter) without major open wound and without mention of infection**

912.7 **Superficial foreign body (splinter) without major open wound, infected**

912.8 **Other and unspecified superficial injury of shoulder and upper arm without mention of infection**

912.9 **Other and unspecified superficial injury of shoulder and upper arm, infected**

√4th **913 Superficial injury of elbow, forearm, and wrist**

913.0 **Abrasion or friction burn without mention of infection**

913.1 **Abrasion or friction burn, infected**

913.2 **Blister without mention of infection**

913.3 **Blister, infected**

913.4 **Insect bite, nonvenomous, without mention of infection**

913.5 **Insect bite, nonvenomous, infected**

913.6 **Superficial foreign body (splinter) without major open wound and without mention of infection**

913.7 **Superficial foreign body (splinter) without major open wound, infected**

913.8 **Other and unspecified superficial injury of elbow, forearm, and wrist without mention of infection**

913.9 **Other and unspecified superficial injury of elbow, forearm, and wrist, infected**

√4th **914 Superficial injury of hand(s) except finger(s) alone**

914.0 **Abrasion or friction burn without mention of infection**

914.1 **Abrasion or friction burn, infected**

914.2 **Blister without mention of infection**

914.3 **Blister, infected**

914.4 **Insect bite, nonvenomous, without mention of infection**

914.5 **Insect bite, nonvenomous, infected**

914.6 **Superficial foreign body (splinter) without major open wound and without mention of infection**

914.7 **Superficial foreign body (splinter) without major open wound, infected**

914.8 **Other and unspecified superficial injury of hand without mention of infection**

914.9 **Other and unspecified superficial injury of hand, infected**

√4th **915 Superficial injury of finger(s)**

INCLUDES   fingernail   thumb (nail)

915.0 **Abrasion or friction burn without mention of infection**

915.1 **Abrasion or friction burn, infected**

915.2 **Blister without mention of infection**

915.3 **Blister, infected**

915.4 **Insect bite, nonvenomous, without mention of infection**

915.5 **Insect bite, nonvenomous, infected**

915.6 **Superficial foreign body (splinter) without major open wound and without mention of infection**

915.7 **Superficial foreign body (splinter) without major open wound, infected**

915.8 **Other and unspecified superficial injury of fingers without mention of infection**

AHA: 4Q, '01, 10

915.9 **Other and unspecified superficial injury of fingers, infected**

√4th **916 Superficial injury of hip, thigh, leg, and ankle**

916.0 **Abrasion or friction burn without mention of infection**

916.1 **Abrasion or friction burn, infected**

916.2 **Blister without mention of infection**

916.3 **Blister, infected**

916.4 **Insect bite, nonvenomous, without mention of infection**

√4th Additional Digit Required   √5th   RUG III Special Care Dx   RUG III Clinically Complex Dx   Hospice Non-cancer Dx   CD PDx Clinical Dimension PDx   CD SDx Clinical Dimension SDx

2006 ICD•9•CM   Volume 1 — 259

Injury and Poisoning

916.5–924.01

916.5   Insect bite, nonvenomous, infected

916.6   Superficial foreign body (splinter) without major open wound and without mention of infection

916.7   Superficial foreign body (splinter) without major open wound, infected

916.8   Other and unspecified superficial injury of hip, thigh, leg, and ankle without mention of infection

916.9   Other and unspecified superficial injury of hip, thigh, leg, and ankle, infected

√4th **917 Superficial injury of foot and toe(s)**

INCLUDES   heel   toenail

917.0   Abrasion or friction burn without mention of infection

917.1   Abrasion or friction burn, infected

917.2   Blister without mention of infection

917.3   Blister, infected

917.4   Insect bite, nonvenomous, without mention of infection

917.5   Insect bite, nonvenomous, infected

917.6   Superficial foreign body (splinter) without major open wound and without mention of infection

917.7   Superficial foreign body (splinter) without major open wound, infected

917.8   Other and unspecified superficial injury of foot and toes without mention of infection

    AHA: 1Q, '03, 13

917.9   Other and unspecified superficial injury of foot and toes, infected

    AHA: 1Q, '03, 13

√4th **918 Superficial injury of eye and adnexa**

EXCLUDES   burn (940.0-940.9)

         foreign body on external eye (930.0-930.9)

918.0   Eyelids and periocular area

    Abrasion   Superficial foreign body

    Insect bite   (splinter)

918.1   Cornea

    Corneal abrasion   Superficial laceration

       EXCLUDES   corneal injury due to contact lens (371.82)

918.2   Conjunctiva

918.9   Other and unspecified superficial injuries of eye

    Eye (ball) NOS

√4th **919 Superficial injury of other, multiple, and unspecified sites**

EXCLUDES   multiple sites classifiable to the same three-digit category (910.0-918.9)

919.0   Abrasion or friction burn without mention of infection

919.1   Abrasion or friction burn, infected

919.2   Blister without mention of infection

919.3   Blister, infected

919.4   Insect bite, nonvenomous, without mention of infection

919.5   Insect bite, nonvenomous, infected

919.6   Superficial foreign body (splinter) without major open wound and without mention of infection

919.7   Superficial foreign body (splinter) without major open wound, infected

919.8   Other and unspecified superficial injury without mention of infection

919.9   Other and unspecified superficial injury, infected

CONTUSION WITH INTACT SKIN SURFACE (920-924)

INCLUDES   bruise   } without fracture or open

        hematoma }   wound

EXCLUDES   concussion (850.0-850.9)

       hemarthrosis (840.0-848.9)

       internal organs (860.0-869.1)

       that incidental to:

          crushing injury (925-929.9)

          dislocation (830.0-839.9)

          fracture (800.0-829.1)

          internal injury (860.0-869.1)

          intracranial injury (850.0-854.1)

          nerve injury (950.0-957.9)

          open wound (870.0-897.7)

920 Contusion of face, scalp, and neck except eye(s)

    Cheek   Mandibular joint area

    Ear (auricle)   Nose

    Gum   Throat

    Lip

√4th **921 Contusion of eye and adnexa**

921.0   Black eye, not otherwise specified

921.1   Contusion of eyelids and periocular area

921.2   Contusion of orbital tissues

921.3   Contusion of eyeball

    AHA: J-A, '85, 16

921.9   Unspecified contusion of eye

    Injury of eye NOS

√4th **922 Contusion of trunk**

922.0   Breast

922.1   Chest wall

922.2   Abdominal wall

    Flank   Groin

√5th 922.3   Back

    AHA: 4Q, '96, 39

    922.31   Back

       EXCLUDES   interscapular region (922.33)

       AHA: 3Q, '99, 14

    922.32   Buttock

    922.33   Interscapular region

922.4   Genital organs

    Labium (majus) (minus)   Vulva

    Penis   Vagina

    Perineum   Testis

    Scrotum

922.8   Multiple sites of trunk

922.9   Unspecified part

    Trunk NOS

√4th **923 Contusion of upper limb**

√5th 923.0   Shoulder and upper arm

    923.00   Shoulder region

    923.01   Scapular region

    923.02   Axillary region

    923.03   Upper arm

    923.09   Multiple sites

√5th 923.1   Elbow and forearm

    923.10   Forearm

    923.11   Elbow

√5th 923.2   Wrist and hand(s), except finger(s) alone

    923.20   Hand(s)

    923.21   Wrist

923.3   Finger

    Fingernail   Thumb (nail)

923.8   Multiple sites of upper limb

923.9   Unspecified part of upper limb

    Arm NOS

√4th **924 Contusion of lower limb and of other and unspecified sites**

√5th 924.0   Hip and thigh

    924.00   Thigh

    924.01   Hip

N Newborn Age: 0   P Pediatric Age: 0-17   M Maternity Age: 12-55   A Adult Age: 15-124   Manifestation Code   ►◄ Revised Text   ● New Code   ▲ Revised Code Title

260 — Volume 1   *2006 ICD•9•CM*

✓5th **924.1 Knee and lower leg**
    924.10 Lower leg
    924.11 Knee

✓5th **924.2 Ankle and foot, excluding toe(s)**
    924.20 Foot
        Heel
    924.21 Ankle

924.3 Toe
    Toenail

924.4 Multiple sites of lower limb

924.5 Unspecified part of lower limb
    Leg NOS

924.8 Multiple sites, not elsewhere classified
    AHA: 1Q, '03, 7

924.9 Unspecified site

CRUSHING INJURY (925-929)

Use additional code to identify any associated injuries,
    such as:
    fractures (800-829)
    internal injuries (860.0-869.1)
    intracranial injuries (850.0-854.1)

EXCLUDES *concussion (850.0-850.9)*
    fractures (800-829)
    internal organs (860.0-869.1)
    that incidental to:
        internal injury (860.0-869.1)
        intracranial injury (850.0-854.1)

AHA: 4Q, '03, 77; 2Q, '93, 7

✓4th **925 Crushing injury of face, scalp, and neck**
    Cheek   Pharynx
    Ear   Throat
    Larynx

925.1 Crushing injury of face and scalp
    Cheek   Ear

925.2 Crushing injury of neck
    Larynx   Throat
    Pharynx

✓4th **926 Crushing injury of trunk**
926.0 External genitalia
    Labium (majus) (minus) Testis
    Penis   Vulva
    Scrotum

✓5th **926.1 Other specified sites**
    926.11 Back
    926.12 Buttock
    926.19 Other
        Breast

926.8 Multiple sites of trunk

926.9 Unspecified site
    Trunk NOS

✓4th **927 Crushing injury of upper limb**
✓5th **927.0 Shoulder and upper arm**
    927.00 Shoulder region `CD PDx`
    927.01 Scapular region `CD PDx`
    927.02 Axillary region `CD PDx`
    927.03 Upper arm `CD PDx`
    927.09 Multiple sites `CD PDx`

✓5th **927.1 Elbow and forearm**
    927.10 Forearm `CD PDx`
    927.11 Elbow `CD PDx`

✓5th **927.2 Wrist and hand(s), except finger(s) alone**
    927.20 Hand(s) `CD PDx`
    927.21 Wrist `CD PDx`

927.3 Finger(s) `CD PDx`
    AHA: 4Q, '03, 77

927.8 Multiple sites of upper limb `CD PDx`

927.9 Unspecified site `CD PDx`
    Arm NOS

✓4th **928 Crushing injury of lower limb**
✓5th **928.0 Hip and thigh**
    928.00 Thigh `CD PDx`
    928.01 Hip `CD PDx`

✓5th **928.1 Knee and lower leg**
    928.10 Lower leg `CD PDx`
    928.11 Knee `CD PDx`

✓5th **928.2 Ankle and foot, excluding toe(s) alone**
    928.20 Foot `CD PDx`
        Heel
    928.21 Ankle `CD PDx`

928.3 Toe(s) `CD PDx`

928.8 Multiple sites of lower limb `CD PDx`

928.9 Unspecified site `CD PDx`
    Leg NOS

✓4th **929 Crushing injury of multiple and unspecified sites**
929.0 Multiple sites, not elsewhere classified

929.9 Unspecified site

EFFECTS OF FOREIGN BODY ENTERING THROUGH ORIFICE (930-939)

EXCLUDES *foreign body:*
    granuloma (728.82)
    inadvertently left in operative wound (998.4,
        998.7)
    in open wound (800-839, 851-897)
    residual in soft tissues (729.6)
    superficial without major open wound (910-
        919 with .6 or .7)

✓4th **930 Foreign body on external eye**
EXCLUDES *foreign body in penetrating wound of:*
    eyeball (871.5-871.6)
        retained (old) (360.5-360.6)
    ocular adnexa (870.4)
        retained (old) (376.6)

930.0 Corneal foreign body

930.1 Foreign body in conjunctival sac

930.2 Foreign body in lacrimal punctum

930.8 Other and combined sites

930.9 Unspecified site
    External eye NOS

931 Foreign body in ear
    Auditory canal   Auricle

932 Foreign body in nose
    Nasal sinus   Nostril

✓4th **933 Foreign body in pharynx and larynx**
933.0 Pharynx
    Nasopharynx   Throat NOS

933.1 Larynx
    Asphyxia due to foreign body
    Choking due to:
        food (regurgitated)
        phlegm

✓4th **934 Foreign body in trachea, bronchus, and lung**
934.0 Trachea

934.1 Main bronchus
    AHA: 3Q, '02, 18

934.8 Other specified parts
    Bronchioles   Lung

934.9 Respiratory tree, unspecified
    Inhalation of liquid or vomitus, lower respiratory
        tract NOS

✓4th **935 Foreign body in mouth, esophagus, and stomach**
935.0 Mouth

935.1 Esophagus
    AHA: 1Q, '88, 13

935.2 Stomach

936 Foreign body in intestine and colon

937 Foreign body in anus and rectum
    Rectosigmoid (junction)

✓4th ✓5th Additional Digit Required   RUG III Special Care Dx   RUG III Clinically Complex Dx   Hospice Non-cancer Dx   `CD PDx` Clinical Dimension PDx   `CD SDx` Clinical Dimension SDx

2006 ICD•9•CM   Volume 1 — 261

Injury and Poisoning

938–944.3

938 Foreign body in digestive system, unspecified
Alimentary tract NOS   Swallowed foreign body

✓4ᵗʰ **939 Foreign body in genitourinary tract**

939.0 Bladder and urethra

939.1 Uterus, any part   ♀

EXCLUDES   *intrauterine contraceptive device:*
complications from (996.32, 996.65)
presence of (V45.51)

939.2 Vulva and vagina   ♀

939.3 Penis   ♂

939.9 Unspecified site

BURNS (940-949)

INCLUDES   burns from:
     electrical heating appliance
     electricity
     flame
     hot object
     lightning
     radiation
     chemical burns (external) (internal)
     scalds

EXCLUDES   *friction burns (910-919 with .0, .1)*
sunburn (692.71, 692.76-692.77)

AHA: 4Q, 94, 22; 2Q, '90, 7; 4Q, '88, 3; M-A, '86, 9

✓4ᵗʰ **940 Burn confined to eye and adnexa**

940.0 Chemical burn of eyelids and periocular area

940.1 Other burns of eyelids and periocular area

940.2 Alkaline chemical burn of cornea and conjunctival sac

940.3 Acid chemical burn of cornea and conjunctival sac

940.4 Other burn of cornea and conjunctival sac

940.5 Burn with resulting rupture and destruction of eyeball

940.9 Unspecified burn of eye and adnexa

✓4ᵗʰ **941 Burn of face, head, and neck**

EXCLUDES   *mouth (947.0)*

The following fifth-digit subclassification is for use with category 941:

   0 face and head, unspecified site
   1 ear [any part]
   2 eye (with other parts of face, head, and neck)
   3 lip(s)
   4 chin
   5 nose (septum)
   6 scalp [any part]
     Temple (region)
   7 forehead and cheek
   8 neck
   9 multiple sites [except with eye] of face, head, and neck

AHA: 4Q, '94, 22; M-A, '86, 9

✓5ᵗʰ **941.0 Unspecified degree**   CD PDx

✓5ᵗʰ **941.1 Erythema [first degree]**   CD PDx

✓5ᵗʰ **941.2 Blisters, epidermal loss [second degree]**   CD PDx

✓5ᵗʰ **941.3 Full-thickness skin loss [third degree NOS]**   CD PDx

✓5ᵗʰ **941.4 Deep necrosis of underlying tissues [deep third degree] without mention of loss of a body part**   CD PDx

✓5ᵗʰ **941.5 Deep necrosis of underlying tissues [deep third degree] with loss of a body part**   CD PDx

✓4ᵗʰ **942 Burn of trunk**

EXCLUDES   *scapular region (943.0-943.5 with fifth-digit 6)*

The following fifth-digit subclassification is for use with category 942:

   0 trunk, unspecified site
   1 breast
   2 chest wall, excluding breast and nipple
   3 abdominal wall
     Flank   Groin
   4 back [any part]
     Buttock
     Interscapular region
   5 genitalia
     Labium (majus) (minus)   Scrotum
     Penis   Testis
     Perineum   Vulva
   9 other and multiple sites of trunk

AHA: 4Q, '94, 22; M-A, '86, 9

✓5ᵗʰ **942.0 Unspecified degree**   CD PDx

✓5ᵗʰ **942.1 Erythema [first degree]**   CD PDx

✓5ᵗʰ **942.2 Blisters, epidermal loss [second degree]**   CD PDx

✓5ᵗʰ **942.3 Full-thickness skin loss [third degree NOS]**   CD PDx

✓5ᵗʰ **942.4 Deep necrosis of underlying tissues [deep third degree] without mention of loss of a body part**   CD PDx

✓5ᵗʰ **942.5 Deep necrosis of underlying tissues [deep third degree] with loss of a body part**   CD PDx

✓4ᵗʰ **943 Burn of upper limb, except wrist and hand**

The following fifth-digit subclassification is for use with category 943:

   0 upper limb, unspecified site
   1 forearm
   2 elbow
   3 upper arm
   4 axilla
   5 shoulder
   6 scapular region
   9 multiple sites of upper limb, except wrist and hand

AHA: 4Q, '94, 22; M-A, '86, 9

✓5ᵗʰ **943.0 Unspecified degree**   CD PDx

✓5ᵗʰ **943.1 Erythema [first degree]**   CD PDx

✓5ᵗʰ **943.2 Blisters, epidermal loss [second degree]**   CD PDx

✓5ᵗʰ **943.3 Full-thickness skin loss [third degree NOS]**   CD PDx

✓5ᵗʰ **943.4 Deep necrosis of underlying tissues [deep third degree] without mention of loss of a body part**   CD PDx

✓5ᵗʰ **943.5 Deep necrosis of underlying tissues [deep third degree] with loss of a body part**   CD PDx

✓4ᵗʰ **944 Burn of wrist(s) and hand(s)**

The following fifth-digit subclassification is for use with category 944:

   0 hand, unspecified site
   1 single digit [finger (nail)] other than thumb
   2 thumb (nail)
   3 two or more digits, not including thumb
   4 two or more digits including thumb
   5 palm
   6 back of hand
   7 wrist
   8 multiple sites of wrist(s) and hand(s)

✓5ᵗʰ **944.0 Unspecified degree**   CD PDx

✓5ᵗʰ **944.1 Erythema [first degree]**   CD PDx

✓5ᵗʰ **944.2 Blisters, epidermal loss [second degree]**   CD PDx

✓5ᵗʰ **944.3 Full-thickness skin loss [third degree NOS]**   CD PDx

---

N Newborn Age: 0   P Pediatric Age: 0-17   M Maternity Age: 12-55   A Adult Age: 15-124   Manifestation Code   ▶◀ Revised Text   ● New Code   ▲ Revised Code Title

262 — Volume 1   *2006 ICD•9•CM*

√5ᵗʰ **944.4** Deep necrosis of underlying tissues [deep third degree] without mention of loss of a body part   `CD PDx`

√5ᵗʰ **944.5** Deep necrosis of underlying tissues [deep third degree] with loss of a body part   `CD PDx`

√4ᵗʰ **945 Burn of lower limb(s)**

The following fifth-digit subclassification is for use with category 945:

- 0 lower limb [leg], unspecified site
- 1 toe(s) (nail)
- 2 foot
- 3 ankle
- 4 lower leg
- 5 knee
- 6 thigh [any part]
- 9 multiple sites of lower limb(s)

AHA: 4Q, '94, 22; M-A, '86, 9

√5ᵗʰ **945.0** Unspecified degree   `CD PDx`

√5ᵗʰ **945.1** Erythema [first degree]   `CD PDx`

√5ᵗʰ **945.2** Blisters, epidermal loss [second degree]   `CD PDx`

√5ᵗʰ **945.3** Full-thickness skin loss [third degree NOS]   `CD PDx`

√5ᵗʰ **945.4** Deep necrosis of underlying tissues [deep third degree] without mention of loss of a body part   `CD PDx`

√5ᵗʰ **945.5** Deep necrosis of underlying tissues [deep third degree] with loss of a body part   `CD PDx`

√4ᵗʰ **946 Burns of multiple specified sites**

INCLUDES burns of sites classifiable to more than one three-digit category in 940-945

EXCLUDES *multiple burns NOS (949.0-949.5)*

AHA: 4Q, '94, 22; M-A, '86, 9

946.0 Unspecified degree   `CD PDx`

946.1 Erythema [first degree]   `CD PDx`

946.2 Blisters, epidermal loss [second degree]   `CD PDx`

946.3 Full-thickness skin loss [third degree NOS]   `CD PDx`

946.4 Deep necrosis of underlying tissues [deep third degree] without mention of loss of a body part   `CD PDx`

946.5 Deep necrosis of underlying tissues [deep third degree] with loss of a body part   `CD PDx`

Burns

Degrees of Burns

First (redness)   Second (blistering)   Third (fill thickness)   Deep Third (deep necrosis)   Eschar

Rule of Nines
Estimation of Total Body Surface Burned

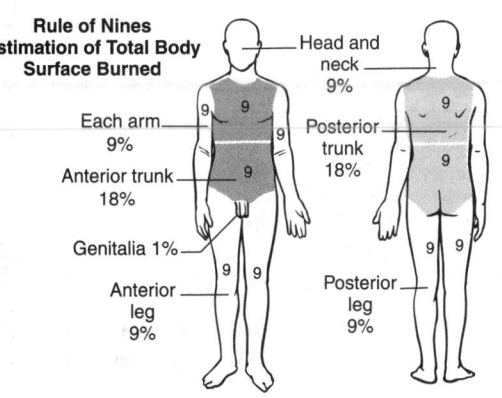

Head and neck 9%
Each arm 9%
Anterior trunk 18%
Genitalia 1%
Anterior leg 9%
Posterior trunk 18%
Posterior leg 9%

√4ᵗʰ **947 Burn of internal organs**

INCLUDES burns from chemical agents (ingested)

AHA: 4Q, '94, 22; M-A, '86, 9

947.0 Mouth and pharynx
   Gum   Tongue

947.1 Larynx, trachea, and lung

947.2 Esophagus

947.3 Gastrointestinal tract
   Colon   Small intestine
   Rectum   Stomach

947.4 Vagina and uterus   ♀

947.8 Other specified sites

947.9 Unspecified site

√4ᵗʰ **948 Burns classified according to extent of body surface involved**

Note: This category is to be used when the site of the burn is unspecified, or with categories 940-947 when the site is specified.

EXCLUDES *sunburn (692.71, 692.76-692.77)*

The following fifth-digit subclassification is for use with category 948 to indicate the percent of body surface with third degree burn; valid digits are in [brackets] under each code:

- 0 less than 10 percent or unspecified
- 1 10-19%
- 2 20-29%
- 3 30-39%
- 4 40-49%
- 5 50-59%
- 6 60-69%
- 7 70-79%
- 8 80-89%
- 9 90% or more of body surface

AHA: 4Q, '94, 22; 4Q, '88, 3; M-A, '86, 9; N-D, '84, 13

√5ᵗʰ **948.0** Burn [any degree] involving less than 10 percent of body surface   `CD PDx`
[0]

√5ᵗʰ **948.1** 10-19 percent of body surface   `CD PDx`
[0-1]

√5ᵗʰ **948.2** 20-29 percent of body surface   `CD PDx`
[0-2]

√5ᵗʰ **948.3** 30-39 percent of body surface   `CD PDx`
[0-3]

√5ᵗʰ **948.4** 40-49 percent of body surface   `CD PDx`
[0-4]

√5ᵗʰ **948.5** 50-59 percent of body surface   `CD PDx`
[0-5]

√5ᵗʰ **948.6** 60-69 percent of body surface   `CD PDx`
[0-6]

√5ᵗʰ **948.7** 70-79 percent of body surface   `CD PDx`
[0-7]

√5ᵗʰ **948.8** 80-89 percent of body surface   `CD PDx`
[0-8]

√5ᵗʰ **948.9** 90 percent or more of body surface   `CD PDx`
[0-9]

√4ᵗʰ **949 Burn, unspecified**

INCLUDES burn NOS multiple burns NOS

EXCLUDES *burn of unspecified site but with statement of the extent of body surface involved (948.0-948.9)*

AHA: 4Q, '94, 22; M-A, '86, 9

949.0 Unspecified degree   `CD PDx`

949.1 Erythema [first degree]   `CD PDx`

949.2 Blisters, epidermal loss [second degree]   `CD PDx`

949.3 Full-thickness skin loss [third degree NOS]   `CD PDx`

949.4 Deep necrosis of underlying tissues [deep third degree] without mention of loss of a body part   `CD PDx`

949.5 Deep necrosis of underlying tissues [deep third degree] with loss of a body part   `CD PDx`

√4ᵗʰ Additional Digit Required   RUG III Special Care Dx   RUG III Clinically Complex Dx   Hospice Non-cancer Dx   `CD PDx` Clinical Dimension PDx   `CD SDx` Clinical Dimension SDx

INJURY TO NERVES AND SPINAL CORD (950-957)

| INCLUDES | division of nerve
lesion in continuity
traumatic neuroma
traumatic transient paralysis | } (with open wound) |

| EXCLUDES | *accidental puncture or laceration during medical procedure (998.2)* |

✓4ᵗʰ **950 Injury to optic nerve and pathways**

   950.0 Optic nerve injury `CD PDx`
      Second cranial nerve

   950.1 Injury to optic chiasm `CD PDx`

   950.2 Injury to optic pathways `CD PDx`

   950.3 Injury to visual cortex `CD PDx`

   950.9 Unspecified `CD PDx`
      Traumatic blindness NOS

✓4ᵗʰ **951 Injury to other cranial nerve(s)**

   951.0 Injury to oculomotor nerve `CD PDx`
      Third cranial nerve

   951.1 Injury to trochlear nerve `CD PDx`
      Fourth cranial nerve

   951.2 Injury to trigeminal nerve `CD PDx`
      Fifth cranial nerve

   951.3 Injury to abducens nerve `CD PDx`
      Sixth cranial nerve

   951.4 Injury to facial nerve `CD PDx`
      Seventh cranial nerve

   951.5 Injury to acoustic nerve `CD PDx`
      Auditory nerve
      Eighth cranial nerve
      Traumatic deafness NOS

   951.6 Injury to accessory nerve `CD PDx`
      Eleventh cranial nerve

   951.7 Injury to hypoglossal nerve `CD PDx`
      Twelfth cranial nerve

   951.8 Injury to other specified cranial nerves `CD PDx`
      Glossopharyngeal [9th cranial] nerve
      Olfactory [1st cranial] nerve
      Pneumogastric [10th cranial] nerve
      Traumatic anosmia NOS
      Vagus [10th cranial] nerve

   951.9 Injury to unspecified cranial nerve `CD PDx`

✓4ᵗʰ **952 Spinal cord injury without evidence of spinal bone injury**

  ✓5ᵗʰ **952.0 Cervical**

   952.00 C_1-C_4 level with unspecified spinal cord injury `CD PDx`
      Spinal cord injury, cervical region NOS

   952.01 C_1-C_4 level with complete lesion of spinal cord `CD PDx`

   952.02 C_1-C_4 level with anterior cord syndrome `CD PDx`

   952.03 C_1-C_4 level with central cord syndrome `CD PDx`

   952.04 C_1-C_4 level with other specified spinal cord injury `CD PDx`
      Incomplete spinal cord lesion at C_1-C_4 level:
        NOS
        with posterior cord syndrome

   952.05 C_5-C_7 level with unspecified spinal cord injury `CD PDx`

   952.06 C_5-C_7 level with complete lesion of spinal cord `CD PDx`

   952.07 C_5-C_7 level with anterior cord syndrome `CD PDx`

   952.08 C_5-C_7 level with central cord syndrome `CD PDx`

   952.09 C_5-C_7 level with other specified spinal cord injury `CD PDx`
      Incomplete spinal cord lesion at C_5-C_7 level:
        NOS
        with posterior cord syndrome

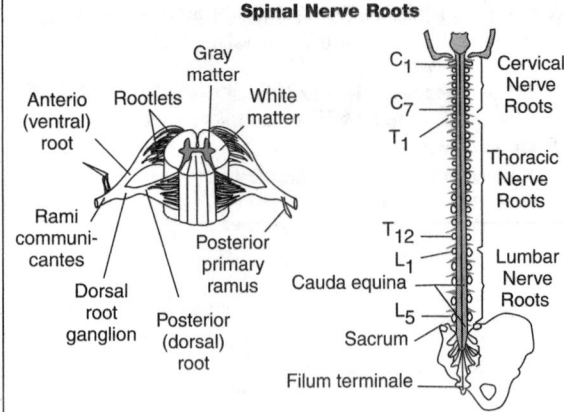

Spinal Nerve Roots

  ✓5ᵗʰ **952.1 Dorsal [thoracic]**

   952.10 T1-T6 level with unspecified spinal cord injury `CD PDx`
      Spinal cord injury, thoracic region NOS

   952.11 T_1-T_6 level with complete lesion of spinal cord `CD PDx`

   952.12 T_1-T_6 level with anterior cord syndrome `CD PDx`

   952.13 T_1-T_6 level with central cord syndrome `CD PDx`

   952.14 T_1-T_6 level with other specified spinal cord injury `CD PDx`
      Incomplete spinal cord lesion at T_1-T_6 level:
        NOS
        with posterior cord syndrome

   952.15 T_7-T_{12} level with unspecified spinal cord injury `CD PDx`

   952.16 T_7-T_{12} level with complete lesion of spinal cord `CD PDx`

   952.17 T_7-T_{12} level with anterior cord syndrome `CD PDx`

   952.18 T_7-T_{12} level with central cord syndrome `CD PDx`

   952.19 T_7-T_{12} level with other specified spinal cord injury `CD PDx`
      Incomplete spinal cord lesion at T_7-T_{12} level:
        NOS
        with posterior cord syndrome

   952.2 Lumbar `CD PDx`

   952.3 Sacral `CD PDx`

   952.4 Cauda equina `CD PDx`

   952.8 Multiple sites of spinal cord `CD PDx`

   952.9 Unspecified site of spinal cord `CD PDx`

✓4ᵗʰ **953 Injury to nerve roots and spinal plexus**

   953.0 Cervical root `CD PDx`

   953.1 Dorsal root `CD PDx`

   953.2 Lumbar root `CD PDx`

   953.3 Sacral root `CD PDx`

   953.4 Brachial plexus `CD PDx`

   953.5 Lumbosacral plexus `CD PDx`

   953.8 Multiple sites `CD PDx`

   953.9 Unspecified site `CD PDx`

✓4ᵗʰ **954 Injury to other nerve(s) of trunk, excluding shoulder and pelvic girdles**

   954.0 Cervical sympathetic `CD PDx`

   954.1 Other sympathetic `CD PDx`
      Celiac ganglion or plexus   Splanchnic nerve(s)
      Inferior mesenteric plexus   Stellate ganglion

   954.8 Other specified nerve(s) of trunk `CD PDx`

   954.9 Unspecified nerve of trunk `CD PDx`

Ⓝ Newborn Age: 0   Ⓟ Pediatric Age: 0-17   Ⓜ Maternity Age: 12-55   Ⓐ Adult Age: 15-124   Manifestation Code   ▶◀ Revised Text   ● New Code   ▲ Revised Code Title

✓4ᵗʰ **955 Injury to peripheral nerve(s) of shoulder girdle and upper limb**

     955.0   **Axillary nerve**   `CD PDx`

     955.1   **Median nerve**   `CD PDx`

     955.2   **Ulnar nerve**   `CD PDx`

     955.3   **Radial nerve**   `CD PDx`

     955.4   **Musculocutaneous nerve**   `CD PDx`

     955.5   **Cutaneous sensory nerve, upper limb**   `CD PDx`

     955.6   **Digital nerve**   `CD PDx`

     955.7   **Other specified nerve(s) of shoulder girdle and upper limb**   `CD PDx`

     955.8   **Multiple nerves of shoulder girdle and upper limb**   `CD PDx`

     955.9   **Unspecified nerve of shoulder girdle and upper limb**   `CD PDx`

✓4ᵗʰ **956 Injury to peripheral nerve(s) of pelvic girdle and lower limb**

     956.0   **Sciatic nerve**   `CD PDx`

     956.1   **Femoral nerve**   `CD PDx`

     956.2   **Posterior tibial nerve**   `CD PDx`

     956.3   **Peroneal nerve**   `CD PDx`

     956.4   **Cutaneous sensory nerve, lower limb**   `CD PDx`

     956.5   **Other specified nerve(s) of pelvic girdle and lower limb**   `CD PDx`

     956.8   **Multiple nerves of pelvic girdle and lower limb**   `CD PDx`

     956.9   **Unspecified nerve of pelvic girdle and lower limb**   `CD PDx`

✓4ᵗʰ **957 Injury to other and unspecified nerves**

     957.0   **Superficial nerves of head and neck**

     957.1   **Other specified nerve(s)**

     957.8   **Multiple nerves in several parts**
         Multiple nerve injury NOS

     957.9   **Unspecified site**
         Nerve injury NOS

CERTAIN TRAUMATIC COMPLICATIONS AND UNSPECIFIED INJURIES (958-959)

✓4ᵗʰ **958 Certain early complications of trauma**

     EXCLUDES   adult respiratory distress syndrome (518.5)
         flail chest (807.4)
         shock lung (518.5)
         that occurring during or following medical procedures (996.0-999.9)

     958.0   **Air embolism**
         Pneumathemia
         EXCLUDES   that complicating:
           abortion (634-638 with .6, 639.6)
           ectopic or molar pregnancy (639.6)
           pregnancy, childbirth, or the puerperium (673.0)

         DEF: Arterial obstruction due to introduction of air bubbles into the veins following surgery or trauma.

     958.1   **Fat embolism**
         EXCLUDES   that complicating:
           abortion (634-638 with .6, 639.6)
           pregnancy, childbirth, or the puerperium (673.8)

         DEF: Arterial blockage due to the entrance of fat in circulatory system, after fracture of large bones or administration of corticosteroids.

     958.2   **Secondary and recurrent hemorrhage**

     958.3   **Posttraumatic wound infection, not elsewhere classified**
         EXCLUDES   infected open wounds–code to complicated open wound of site

         AHA: 4Q, '01, 53; S-O, '85, 10

     958.4   **Traumatic shock**
         Shock (immediate) (delayed) following injury
         EXCLUDES   shock:
           anaphylactic (995.0)
             due to serum (999.4)
           anesthetic (995.4)
           electric (994.8)
           following abortion (639.5)
           lightning (994.0)
           nontraumatic NOS (785.50)
           obstetric (669.1)
           postoperative (998.0)

         DEF: Shock, immediate or delayed following injury.

     958.5   **Traumatic anuria**
         Crush syndrome
         Renal failure following crushing
         EXCLUDES   that due to a medical procedure (997.5)

         DEF: Complete suppression of urinary secretion by kidneys due to trauma.

     958.6   **Volkmann's ischemic contracture**
         Posttraumatic muscle contracture
         DEF: Muscle deterioration due to loss of blood supply from injury or tourniquet; causes muscle contraction and results in inability to extend the muscles fully.

     958.7   **Traumatic subcutaneous emphysema**
         EXCLUDES   subcutaneous emphysema resulting from a procedure (998.81)

     958.8   **Other early complications of trauma**
         AHA: 2Q, '92, 13

         DEF: Compartmental syndrome is abnormal pressure in confined anatomical space, as in swollen muscle restricted by fascia.

✓4ᵗʰ **959 Injury, other and unspecified**

     INCLUDES   injury NOS
     EXCLUDES   injury NOS of:
         blood vessels (900.0-904.9)
         eye (921.0-921.9)
         internal organs (860.0-869.1)
         intracranial sites (854.0-854.1)
         nerves (950.0-951.9, 953.0-957.9)
         spinal cord (952.0-952.9)

✓5ᵗʰ   959.0   **Head, face, and neck**

         959.01   **Head injury, unspecified**
            EXCLUDES   concussion (850.1-850.9)
               with head injury NOS (850.1-850.9)
               head injury NOS with loss of consciousness (850.1-850.5)
               specified intracranial injuries (850.0-854.1)

            AHA: 4Q, '97, 46

         959.09   **Injury of face and neck**

Cheek	Mouth
Ear	Nose
Eyebrow	Throat
Lip	

            AHA: 4Q, '97, 46

✓5ᵗʰ   959.1   **Trunk**
         EXCLUDES   scapular region (959.2)

         AHA: 4Q, '03, 78; 1Q, '99, 10

         959.11   **Other injury of chest wall**

         959.12   **Other injury of abdomen**

         959.13   **Fracture of corpus cavernosum penis**   ♂

         959.14   **Other injury of external genitals**

         959.19   **Other injury of other sites of trunk**
            Injury of trunk NOS

     959.2   **Shoulder and upper arm**

Axilla	Scapular region

     959.3   **Elbow, forearm, and wrist**
         AHA: 1Q, '97, 8

✓4ᵗʰ ✓5ᵗʰ Additional Digit Required   **RUG III** Special Care Dx   **RUG III** Clinically Complex Dx   Hospice Non-cancer Dx   `CD PDx` Clinical Dimension PDx   `CD SDx` Clinical Dimension SDx

959.4 Hand, except finger

959.5 Finger
   Fingernail   Thumb (nail)

959.6 Hip and thigh
   Upper leg

959.7 Knee, leg, ankle, and foot

959.8 Other specified sites, including multiple
   EXCLUDES   multiple sites classifiable to the same
              four-digit category (959.0-959.7)

959.9 Unspecified site

POISONING BY DRUGS, MEDICINAL AND BIOLOGICAL SUBSTANCES (960-979)

INCLUDES   overdose of these substances
           wrong substance given or taken in error

EXCLUDES   adverse effects ["hypersensitivity," "reaction,"
           etc.] of correct substance properly
           administered. Such cases are to be
           classified according to the nature of the
           adverse effect, such as:
           adverse effect NOS (995.2)
           allergic lymphadenitis (289.3)
           aspirin gastritis (535.4)
           blood disorders (280.0-289.9)
           dermatitis:
              contact (692.0-692.9)
              due to ingestion (693.0-693.9)
           nephropathy (583.9)
           [The drug giving rise to the adverse effect may
              be identified by use of categories E930-
              E949.]
           drug dependence (304.0-304.9)
           drug reaction and poisoning affecting the
              newborn (760.0-779.9)
           nondependent abuse of drugs (305.0-305.9)
           pathological drug intoxication (292.2)

Use additional code to specify the effects of the poisoning

AHA: 2Q, '90, 11

✓4ᵗʰ 960 Poisoning by antibiotics

EXCLUDES   antibiotics:
              ear, nose, and throat (976.6)
              eye (976.5)
              local (976.0)

960.0 Penicillins
   Ampicillin   Cloxacillin
   Carbenicillin   Penicillin G

960.1 Antifungal antibiotics
   Amphotericin B   Nystatin
   Griseofulvin   Trichomycin
   EXCLUDES   preparations intended for topical use
              (976.0-976.9)

960.2 Chloramphenicol group
   Chloramphenicol   Thiamphenicol

960.3 Erythromycin and other macrolides
   Oleandomycin   Spiramycin

960.4 Tetracycline group
   Doxycycline   Oxytetracycline
   Minocycline

960.5 Cephalosporin group
   Cephalexin   Cephaloridine
   Cephaloglycin   Cephalothin

960.6 Antimycobacterial antibiotics
   Cycloserine   Rifampin
   Kanamycin   Streptomycin

960.7 Antineoplastic antibiotics
   Actinomycin such as:
      Bleomycin   Daunorubicin
      Cactinomycin   Mitomycin
      Dactinomycin

960.8 Other specified antibiotics

960.9 Unspecified antibiotic

✓4ᵗʰ 961 Poisoning by other anti-infectives

EXCLUDES   anti-infectives:
              ear, nose, and throat (976.6)
              eye (976.5)
              local (976.0)

961.0 Sulfonamides
   Sulfadiazine   Sulfamethoxazole
   Sulfafurazole

961.1 Arsenical anti-infectives

961.2 Heavy metal anti-infectives
   Compounds of: Compounds of:
      antimony   lead
      bismuth   mercury
   EXCLUDES   mercurial diuretics (974.0)

961.3 Quinoline and hydroxyquinoline derivatives
   Chiniofon   Diiodohydroxyquin
   EXCLUDES   antimalarial drugs (961.4)

961.4 Antimalarials and drugs acting on other blood protozoa
   Chloroquine   Proguanil [chloroguanide]
   Cycloguanil   Pyrimethamine
   Primaquine   Quinine

961.5 Other antiprotozoal drugs
   Emetine

961.6 Anthelmintics
   Hexylresorcinol   Thiabendazole
   Piperazine

961.7 Antiviral drugs
   Methisazone
   EXCLUDES   amantadine (966.4)
              cytarabine (963.1)
              idoxuridine (976.5)

961.8 Other antimycobacterial drugs
   Ethambutol   Para-aminosalicylic acid
   Ethionamide   derivatives
   Isoniazid   Sulfones

961.9 Other and unspecified anti-infectives
   Flucytosine
   Nitrofuran derivatives

✓4ᵗʰ 962 Poisoning by hormones and synthetic substitutes

EXCLUDES   oxytocic hormones (975.0)

962.0 Adrenal cortical steroids
   Cortisone derivatives   Fluorinated corticosteroids
   Desoxycorticosterone derivatives

962.1 Androgens and anabolic congeners
   Methandriol   Oxymetholone
   Nandrolone   Testosterone

962.2 Ovarian hormones and synthetic substitutes
   Contraceptives, oral
   Estrogens
   Estrogens and progestogens, combined
   Progestogens

962.3 Insulins and antidiabetic agents
   Acetohexamide   Insulin
   Biguanide derivatives,   Phenformin
      oral   Sulfonylurea derivatives,
   Chlorpropamide   oral
   Glucagon   Tolbutamide
   AHA: M-A, '85, 8

962.4 Anterior pituitary hormones
   Corticotropin
   Gonadotropin
   Somatotropin [growth hormone]

962.5 Posterior pituitary hormones
   Vasopressin
   EXCLUDES   oxytocic hormones (975.0)

962.6 Parathyroid and parathyroid derivatives

962.7 Thyroid and thyroid derivatives
   Dextrothyroxin
   Levothyroxine sodium
   Liothyronine
   Thyroglobulin

962.8 Antithyroid agents
   Iodides   Thiourea
   Thiouracil

 Newborn Age: 0   Pediatric Age: 0-17   Maternity Age: 12-55   Adult Age: 15-124   Manifestation Code   ▶◀ Revised Text   ● New Code   ▲ Revised Code Title

962.9 Other and unspecified hormones and synthetic substitutes

✓4th **963 Poisoning by primarily systemic agents**

963.0 Antiallergic and antiemetic drugs

Antihistamines	Diphenylpyraline
Chlorpheniramine	Thonzylamine
Diphenhydramine	Tripelennamine

EXCLUDES   *phenothiazine-based tranquilizers (969.1)*

963.1 Antineoplastic and immunosuppressive drugs

Azathioprine	Cytarabine
Busulfan	Fluorouracil
Chlorambucil	Mercaptopurine
Cyclophosphamide	thio-TEPA

EXCLUDES   *antineoplastic antibiotics (960.7)*

963.2 Acidifying agents

963.3 Alkalizing agents

963.4 Enzymes, not elsewhere classified
Penicillinase

963.5 Vitamins, not elsewhere classified

Vitamin A	Vitamin D

EXCLUDES   *nicotinic acid (972.2)*
vitamin K (964.3)

963.8 Other specified systemic agents
Heavy metal antagonists

963.9 Unspecified systemic agent

✓4th **964 Poisoning by agents primarily affecting blood constituents**

964.0 Iron and its compounds
Ferric salts
Ferrous sulfate and other ferrous salts

964.1 Liver preparations and other antianemic agents
Folic acid

964.2 Anticoagulants

Coumarin	Phenindione
Heparin	Warfarin sodium

AHA: 1Q, '94, 22

964.3 Vitamin K [phytonadione]

964.4 Fibrinolysis-affecting drugs

Aminocaproic acid	Streptokinase
Streptodornase	Urokinase

964.5 Anticoagulant antagonists and other coagulants

Hexadimethrine	Protamine sulfate

964.6 Gamma globulin

964.7 Natural blood and blood products

Blood plasma	Packed red cells
Human fibrinogen	Whole blood

EXCLUDES   *transfusion reactions (999.4-999.8)*

964.8 Other specified agents affecting blood constituents
Macromolecular blood substitutes
Plasma expanders

964.9 Unspecified agent affecting blood constituents

✓4th **965 Poisoning by analgesics, antipyretics, and antirheumatics**

EXCLUDES   *drug dependence (304.0-304.9)*
nondependent abuse (305.0-305.9)

✓5th **965.0 Opiates and related narcotics**

965.00 Opium (alkaloids), unspecified

965.01 Heroin
Diacetylmorphine

965.02 Methadone

965.09 Other
Codeine [methylmorphine]
Meperidine [pethidine]
Morphine

965.1 Salicylates
Acetylsalicylic acid [aspirin]
Salicylic acid salts
AHA: N-D, '94, 15

965.4 Aromatic analgesics, not elsewhere classified

Acetanilid	Phenacetin [acetophenetidin]
Paracetamol [acetaminophen]	

965.5 Pyrazole derivatives
Aminophenazone [aminopyrine]
Phenylbutazone

✓5th **965.6 Antirheumatics [antiphlogistics]**

EXCLUDES   *salicylates (965.1)*
steroids (962.0-962.9)

AHA: 4Q, '98, 50

965.61 Propionic acid derivatives
Fenoprofen
Flurbiprofen
Ibuprofen
Ketoprofen
Naproxen
Oxaprozin
AHA: 4Q, '98, 50

965.69 Other antirheumatics
Gold salts
Indomethacin

965.7 Other non-narcotic analgesics
Pyrabital

965.8 Other specified analgesics and antipyretics
Pentazocine

965.9 Unspecified analgesic and antipyretic

✓4th **966 Poisoning by anticonvulsants and anti-Parkinsonism drugs**

966.0 Oxazolidine derivatives
Paramethadione
Trimethadione

966.1 Hydantoin derivatives
Phenytoin

966.2 Succinimides
Ethosuximide
Phensuximide

966.3 Other and unspecified anticonvulsants
Primidone

EXCLUDES   *barbiturates (967.0)*
sulfonamides (961.0)

966.4 Anti-Parkinsonism drugs
Amantadine
Ethopropazine [profenamine]
Levodopa [L-dopa]

✓4th **967 Poisoning by sedatives and hypnotics**

EXCLUDES   *drug dependence (304.0-304.9)*
nondependent abuse (305.0-305.9)

967.0 Barbiturates
Amobarbital [amylobarbitone]
Barbital [barbitone]
Butabarbital [butabarbitone]
Pentobarbital [pentobarbitone]
Phenobarbital [phenobarbitone]
Secobarbital [quinalbarbitone]

EXCLUDES   *thiobarbiturate anesthetics (968.3)*

967.1 Chloral hydrate group

967.2 Paraldehyde

967.3 Bromine compounds
Bromide
Carbromal (derivatives)

967.4 Methaqualone compounds

967.5 Glutethimide group

967.6 Mixed sedatives, not elsewhere classified

967.8 Other sedatives and hypnotics

967.9 Unspecified sedative or hypnotic
Sleeping:
drug
pill } NOS
tablet

✓4th **968 Poisoning by other central nervous system depressants and anesthetics**

EXCLUDES   *drug dependence (304.0-304.9)*
nondependent abuse (305.0-305.9)

968.0 Central nervous system muscle-tone depressants

Chlorphenesin (carbamate)	Methocarbamol
Mephenesin	

✓4th ✓5th **Additional Digit Required**   **RUG III Special Care Dx**   **RUG III Clinically Complex Dx**   **Hospice Non-cancer Dx**   **CD PDx** Clinical Dimension PDx   **CD SDx** Clinical Dimension SDx

2006 ICD•9•CM   **Volume 1 — 267**

Injury and Poisoning

968.1–974.4

968.1 **Halothane**

968.2 **Other gaseous anesthetics**
Ether
Halogenated hydrocarbon derivatives, except halothane
Nitrous oxide

968.3 **Intravenous anesthetics**
Ketamine
Methohexital [methohexitone]
Thiobarbiturates, such as thiopental sodium

968.4 **Other and unspecified general anesthetics**

968.5 **Surface [topical] and infiltration anesthetics**
Cocaine   Procaine
Lidocaine [lignocaine]   Tetracaine
AHA: 1Q, '93, 25

968.6 **Peripheral nerve- and plexus-blocking anesthetics**

968.7 **Spinal anesthetics**

968.9 **Other and unspecified local anesthetics**

√4ᵗʰ **969** **Poisoning by psychotropic agents**
  EXCLUDES *drug dependence (304.0-304.9)*
            nondependent abuse (305.0-305.9)

969.0 **Antidepressants**
Amitriptyline
Imipramine
Monoamine oxidase [MAO] inhibitors

969.1 **Phenothiazine-based tranquilizers**
Chlorpromazine   Prochlorperazine
Fluphenazine   Promazine

969.2 **Butyrophenone-based tranquilizers**
Haloperidol   Trifluperidol
Spiperone

969.3 **Other antipsychotics, neuroleptics, and major tranquilizers**

969.4 **Benzodiazepine-based tranquilizers**
Chlordiazepoxide   Lorazepam
Diazepam   Medazepam
Flurazepam   Nitrazepam

969.5 **Other tranquilizers**
Hydroxyzine   Meprobamate

969.6 **Psychodysleptics [hallucinogens]**
Cannabis (derivatives)   Mescaline
Lysergide [LSD]   Psilocin
Marihuana (derivatives) Psilocybin

969.7 **Psychostimulants**
Amphetamine
Caffeine
  EXCLUDES *central appetite depressants (977.0)*
AHA: 2Q, '03, 11

969.8 **Other specified psychotropic agents**

969.9 **Unspecified psychotropic agent**

√4ᵗʰ **970** **Poisoning by central nervous system stimulants**

970.0 **Analeptics**
Lobeline
Nikethamide

970.1 **Opiate antagonists**
Levallorphan
Nalorphine
Naloxone

970.8 **Other specified central nervous system stimulants**
AHA: ▶1Q, '05, 6◀

970.9 **Unspecified central nervous system stimulant**

√4ᵗʰ **971** **Poisoning by drugs primarily affecting the autonomic nervous system**

971.0 **Parasympathomimetics [cholinergics]**
Acetylcholine   Pilocarpine
Anticholinesterase:
  organophosphorus
  reversible

971.1 **Parasympatholytics [anticholinergics and antimuscarinics] and spasmolytics**
Atropine   Quaternary ammonium
Homatropine   derivatives
Hyoscine [scopolamine]
  EXCLUDES *papaverine (972.5)*

971.2 **Sympathomimetics [adrenergics]**
Epinephrine [adrenalin]   Levarterenol [noradrenalin]

971.3 **Sympatholytics [antiadrenergics]**
Phenoxybenzamine   Tolazolinehydrochloride

971.9 **Unspecified drug primarily affecting autonomic nervous system**

√4ᵗʰ **972** **Poisoning by agents primarily affecting the cardiovascular system**

972.0 **Cardiac rhythm regulators**
Practolol   Propranolol
Procainamide   Quinidine
  EXCLUDES *lidocaine (968.5)*

972.1 **Cardiotonic glycosides and drugs of similar action**
Digitalis glycosides   Strophanthins
Digoxin

972.2 **Antilipemic and antiarteriosclerotic drugs**
Clofibrate   Nicotinic acid derivatives

972.3 **Ganglion-blocking agents**
Pentamethonium bromide

972.4 **Coronary vasodilators**
Dipyridamole   Nitrites
Nitrates [nitroglycerin]

972.5 **Other vasodilators**
Cyclandelate   Papaverine
Diazoxide
  EXCLUDES *nicotinic acid (972.2)*

972.6 **Other antihypertensive agents**
Clonidine   Rauwolfia alkaloids
Guanethidine   Reserpine

972.7 **Antivaricose drugs, including sclerosing agents**
Sodium morrhuate   Zinc salts

972.8 **Capillary-active drugs**
Adrenochrome derivatives   Metaraminol

972.9 **Other and unspecified agents primarily affecting the cardiovascular system**

√4ᵗʰ **973** **Poisoning by agents primarily affecting the gastrointestinal system**

973.0 **Antacids and antigastric secretion drugs**
Aluminum hydroxide   Magnesium trisilicate
AHA: 1Q, '03, 19

973.1 **Irritant cathartics**
Bisacodyl   Phenolphthalein
Castor oil

973.2 **Emollient cathartics**
Dioctyl sulfosuccinates

973.3 **Other cathartics, including intestinal atonia drugs**
Magnesium sulfate

973.4 **Digestants**
Pancreatin   Pepsin
Papain

973.5 **Antidiarrheal drugs**
Kaolin   Pectin
  EXCLUDES *anti-infectives (960.0-961.9)*

973.6 **Emetics**

973.8 **Other specified agents primarily affecting the gastrointestinal system**

973.9 **Unspecified agent primarily affecting the gastrointestinal system**

√4ᵗʰ **974** **Poisoning by water, mineral, and uric acid metabolism drugs**

974.0 **Mercurial diuretics**
Chlormerodrin   Mersalyl
Mercaptomerin

974.1 **Purine derivative diuretics**
Theobromine   Theophylline
  EXCLUDES *aminophylline [theophylline ethylenediamine] (975.7)*
            caffeine (969.7)

974.2 **Carbonic acid anhydrase inhibitors**
Acetazolamide

974.3 **Saluretics**
Benzothiadiazides   Chlorothiazide group

974.4 **Other diuretics**
Ethacrynic acid   Furosemide

Ⓝ Newborn Age: 0   Ⓟ Pediatric Age: 0-17   Ⓜ Maternity Age: 12-55   Ⓐ Adult Age: 15-124   Manifestation Code   ▶◀ Revised Text   ● New Code   ▲ Revised Code Title

268 — Volume 1 • October 2005   *2006 ICD•9•CM*

974.5   **Electrolytic, caloric, and water-balance agents**

974.6   **Other mineral salts, not elsewhere classified**

974.7   **Uric acid metabolism drugs**
      Allopurinol   Probenecid
      Colchicine

✓4ᵗʰ **975 Poisoning by agents primarily acting on the smooth and skeletal muscles and respiratory system**

975.0   **Oxytocic agents**
      Ergot alkaloids   Prostaglandins
      Oxytocin

975.1   **Smooth muscle relaxants**
      Adiphenine   Metaproterenol [orciprenaline]
      EXCLUDES   *papaverine (972.5)*

975.2   **Skeletal muscle relaxants**

975.3   **Other and unspecified drugs acting on muscles**

975.4   **Antitussives**
      Dextromethorphan   Pipazethate

975.5   **Expectorants**
      Acetylcysteine   Terpin hydrate
      Guaifenesin

975.6   **Anti-common cold drugs**

975.7   **Antiasthmatics**
      Aminophylline [theophylline ethylenediamine]

975.8   **Other and unspecified respiratory drugs**

✓4ᵗʰ **976 Poisoning by agents primarily affecting skin and mucous membrane, ophthalmological, otorhinolaryngological, and dental drugs**

976.0   **Local anti-infectives and anti-inflammatory drugs**

976.1   **Antipruritics**

976.2   **Local astringents and local detergents**

976.3   **Emollients, demulcents, and protectants**

976.4   **Keratolytics, keratoplastics, other hair treatment drugs and preparations**

976.5   **Eye anti-infectives and other eye drugs**
      Idoxuridine

976.6   **Anti-infectives and other drugs and preparations for ear, nose, and throat**

976.7   **Dental drugs topically applied**
      EXCLUDES   *anti-infectives (976.0)*
                 local anesthetics (968.5)

976.8   **Other agents primarily affecting skin and mucous membrane**
      Spermicides [vaginal contraceptives]

976.9   **Unspecified agent primarily affecting skin and mucous membrane**

✓4ᵗʰ **977 Poisoning by other and unspecified drugs and medicinal substances**

977.0   **Dietetics**
      Central appetite depressants

977.1   **Lipotropic drugs**

977.2   **Antidotes and chelating agents, not elsewhere classified**

977.3   **Alcohol deterrents**

977.4   **Pharmaceutical excipients**
      Pharmaceutical adjuncts

977.8   **Other specified drugs and medicinal substances**
      Contrast media used for diagnostic x-ray procedures
      Diagnostic agents and kits

977.9   **Unspecified drug or medicinal substance**

✓4ᵗʰ **978 Poisoning by bacterial vaccines**

978.0   **BCG**

978.1   **Typhoid and paratyphoid**

978.2   **Cholera**

978.3   **Plague**

978.4   **Tetanus**

978.5   **Diphtheria**

978.6   **Pertussis vaccine, including combinations with a pertussis component**

978.8   **Other and unspecified bacterial vaccines**

978.9   **Mixed bacterial vaccines, except combinations with a pertussis component**

✓4ᵗʰ **979 Poisoning by other vaccines and biological substances**
      EXCLUDES   *gamma globulin (964.6)*

979.0   **Smallpox vaccine**

979.1   **Rabies vaccine**

979.2   **Typhus vaccine**

979.3   **Yellow fever vaccine**

979.4   **Measles vaccine**

979.5   **Poliomyelitis vaccine**

979.6   **Other and unspecified viral and rickettsial vaccines**
      Mumps vaccine

979.7   **Mixed viral-rickettsial and bacterial vaccines, except combinations with a pertussis component**
      EXCLUDES   *combinations with a pertussis component (978.6)*

979.9   **Other and unspecified vaccines and biological substances**

TOXIC EFFECTS OF SUBSTANCES CHIEFLY NONMEDICINAL AS TO SOURCE (980-989)

      EXCLUDES   *burns from chemical agents (ingested) (947.0-947.9)*
                 localized toxic effects indexed elsewhere (001.0-799.9)
                 respiratory conditions due to external agents (506.0-508.9)
      Use additional code to specify the nature of the toxic effect

✓4ᵗʰ **980 Toxic effect of alcohol**

980.0   **Ethyl alcohol**
      Denatured alcohol   Grain alcohol
      Ethanol
      Use additional code to identify any associated:
         acute alcohol intoxication (305.0)
         in alcoholism (303.0)
         drunkenness (simple) (305.0)
         pathological (291.4)

      AHA: 3Q, '96, 16

980.1   **Methyl alcohol**
      Methanol   Wood alcohol

980.2   **Isopropyl alcohol**
      Dimethyl carbinol   Rubbing alcohol
      Isopropanol

980.3   **Fusel oil**
      Alcohol: Alcohol:
         amyl   propyl
         butyl

980.8   **Other specified alcohols**

980.9   **Unspecified alcohol**

981 **Toxic effect of petroleum products**
      Benzine   Petroleum:
      Gasoline   ether
      Kerosene   naphtha
      Paraffin wax   spirit

✓4ᵗʰ **982 Toxic effect of solvents other than petroleum-based**

982.0   **Benzene and homologues**

982.1   **Carbon tetrachloride**

982.2   **Carbon disulfide**
      Carbon bisulfide

982.3   **Other chlorinated hydrocarbon solvents**
      Tetrachloroethylene   Trichloroethylene
      EXCLUDES   *chlorinated hydrocarbon preparations other than solvents (989.2)*

982.4   **Nitroglycol**

982.8   **Other nonpetroleum-based solvents**
      Acetone

✓4ᵗʰ **983 Toxic effect of corrosive aromatics, acids, and caustic alkalis**

983.0   **Corrosive aromatics**
      Carbolic acid or phenol   Cresol

983.1   **Acids**
      Acid: Acid:
         hydrochloric   sulfuric
         nitric

✓4ᵗʰ / ✓5ᵗʰ   Additional Digit Required   RUG III Special Care Dx   RUG III Clinically Complex Dx   Hospice Non-cancer Dx   **CD PDx** Clinical Dimension PDx   **CD SDx** Clinical Dimension SDx

2006 ICD•9•CM   **Volume 1 — 269**

983.2 Caustic alkalis
> Lye   Sodium hydroxide
> Potassium hydroxide

983.9 Caustic, unspecified

√4ᵗʰ **984 Toxic effect of lead and its compounds (including fumes)**
> INCLUDES that from all sources except medicinal substances

984.0 Inorganic lead compounds
> Lead dioxide   Lead salts

984.1 Organic lead compounds
> Lead acetate
> Tetraethyl lead

984.8 Other lead compounds

984.9 Unspecified lead compound

√4ᵗʰ **985 Toxic effect of other metals**
> INCLUDES that from all sources except medicinal substances

985.0 Mercury and its compounds
> Minamata disease

985.1 Arsenic and its compounds

985.2 Manganese and its compounds

985.3 Beryllium and its compounds

985.4 Antimony and its compounds

985.5 Cadmium and its compounds

985.6 Chromium

985.8 Other specified metals
> Brass fumes   Iron compounds
> Copper salts   Nickel compounds
> AHA: 1Q, '88, 5

985.9 Unspecified metal

986 Toxic effect of carbon monoxide
> Carbon monoxide from any source

√4ᵗʰ **987 Toxic effect of other gases, fumes, or vapors**

987.0 Liquefied petroleum gases
> Butane   Propane

987.1 Other hydrocarbon gas

987.2 Nitrogen oxides
> Nitrogen dioxide   Nitrous fumes

987.3 Sulfur dioxide

987.4 Freon
> Dichloromonofluoromethane

987.5 Lacrimogenic gas
> Bromobenzyl cyanide Ethyliodoacetate
> Chloroacetophenone

987.6 Chlorine gas

987.7 Hydrocyanic acid gas

987.8 Other specified gases, fumes, or vapors
> Phosgene   Polyester fumes

987.9 Unspecified gas, fume, or vapor

√4ᵗʰ **988 Toxic effect of noxious substances eaten as food**
> EXCLUDES allergic reaction to food, such as:
> gastroenteritis (558.3)
> rash (692.5, 693.1)
> food poisoning (bacterial) (005.0-005.9)
> toxic effects of food contaminants, such as:
> aflatoxin and other mycotoxin (989.7)
> mercury (985.0)

988.0 Fish and shellfish

988.1 Mushrooms

988.2 Berries and other plants

988.8 Other specified noxious substances eaten as food

988.9 Unspecified noxious substance eaten as food

√4ᵗʰ **989 Toxic effect of other substances, chiefly nonmedicinal as to source**

989.0 Hydrocyanic acid and cyanides
> Potassium cyanide   Sodium cyanide
> EXCLUDES gas and fumes (987.7)

989.1 Strychnine and salts

989.2 Chlorinated hydrocarbons
> Aldrin   DDT
> Chlordane   Dieldrin
> EXCLUDES chlorinated hydrocarbon solvents (982.0-982.3)

989.3 Organophosphate and carbamate
> Carbaryl   Parathion
> Dichlorvos   Phorate
> Malathion   Phosdrin

989.4 Other pesticides, not elsewhere classified
> Mixtures of insecticides

989.5 Venom
> Bites of venomous snakes, lizards, and spiders
> Tick paralysis

989.6 Soaps and detergents

989.7 Aflatoxin and other mycotoxin [food contaminants]

√5ᵗʰ **989.8 Other substances, chiefly nonmedicinal as to source**
> AHA: 4Q, '95, 60

989.81 Asbestos
> EXCLUDES asbestosis (501)
> exposure to asbestos (V15.84)

989.82 Latex

989.83 Silicone
> EXCLUDES silicone used in medical devices, implants and grafts (996.00-996.79)

989.84 Tobacco

989.89 Other

989.9 Unspecified substance, chiefly nonmedicinal as to source

OTHER AND UNSPECIFIED EFFECTS OF EXTERNAL CAUSES
(990-995)

990 Effects of radiation, unspecified
> Complication of: Radiation sickness
> phototherapy
> radiation therapy
> EXCLUDES specified adverse effects of radiation. Such conditions are to be classified according to the nature of the adverse effect, as:
> burns (940.0-949.5)
> dermatitis (692.7-692.8)
> leukemia (204.0-208.9)
> pneumonia (508.0)
> sunburn (692.71, 692.76-692.77)
> [The type of radiation giving rise to the adverse effect may be identified by use of the E codes.]

√4ᵗʰ **991 Effects of reduced temperature**

991.0 Frostbite of face

991.1 Frostbite of hand

991.2 Frostbite of foot

991.3 Frostbite of other and unspecified sites

991.4 Immersion foot
> Trench foot
> DEF: Paresthesia, edema, blotchy cyanosis of foot, the skin is soft (macerated), pale and wrinkled, and the sole is swollen with surface ridging and following sustained immersion in water.

991.5 Chilblains
> Erythema pernio   Perniosis
> DEF: Red, swollen, itchy skin; follows damp cold exposure; also associated with pruritus and a burning feeling, in hands, feet, ears, and face in children, legs and toes in women, and hands and fingers in men.

N Newborn Age: 0   P Pediatric Age: 0-17   M Maternity Age: 12-55   A Adult Age: 15-124   Manifestation Code   ►◄ Revised Text   ● New Code   ▲ Revised Code Title

270 — Volume 1   2006 ICD•9•CM

991.6   Hypothermia
Hypothermia (accidental)
> EXCLUDES   *hypothermia following anesthesia (995.89)*
> *hypothermia not associated with low environmental temperature (780.99)*

DEF: Reduced body temperature due to low environmental temperatures.

991.8   Other specified effects of reduced temperature

991.9   Unspecified effect of reduced temperature
Effects of freezing or excessive cold NOS

√4ᵗʰ 992   Effects of heat and light
> EXCLUDES   *burns (940.0-949.5)*
> *diseases of sweat glands due to heat (705.0-705.9)*
> *malignant hyperpyrexia following anesthesia (995.86)*
> *sunburn (692.71, 692.76-692.77)*

992.0   Heat stroke and sunstroke
Heat apoplexy   Siriasis
Heat pyrexia   Thermoplegia
Ictus solaris

DEF: Headache, vertigo, cramps and elevated body temperature due to high environmental temperatures.

992.1   Heat syncope
Heat collapse

992.2   Heat cramps

992.3   Heat exhaustion, anhydrotic
Heat prostration due to water depletion
> EXCLUDES   *that associated with salt depletion (992.4)*

992.4   Heat exhaustion due to salt depletion
Heat prostration due to salt (and water) depletion

992.5   Heat exhaustion, unspecified
Heat prostration NOS

992.6   Heat fatigue, transient

992.7   Heat edema
DEF: Fluid retention due to high environmental temperatures.

992.8   Other specified heat effects

992.9   Unspecified

√4ᵗʰ 993   Effects of air pressure

993.0   Barotrauma, otitic
Aero-otitis media
Effects of high altitude on ears
DEF: Ringing ears, deafness, pain and vertigo due to air pressure changes.

993.1   Barotrauma, sinus
Aerosinusitis
Effects of high altitude on sinuses

993.2   Other and unspecified effects of high altitude
Alpine sickness   Hypobaropathy
Andes disease   Mountain sickness
Anoxia due to high altitude
AHA: 3Q, '88, 4

993.3   Caisson disease
Bends   Decompression sickness
Compressed-air disease   Divers' palsy or paralysis
DEF: Rapid reduction in air pressure while breathing compressed air; symptoms include skin lesions, joint pains, respiratory and neurological problems.

993.4   Effects of air pressure caused by explosion

993.8   Other specified effects of air pressure

993.9   Unspecified effect of air pressure

√4ᵗʰ 994   Effects of other external causes
> EXCLUDES   *certain adverse effects not elsewhere classified (995.0-995.8)*

994.0   Effects of lightning
Shock from lightning   Struck by lightning NOS
> EXCLUDES   *burns (940.0-949.5)*

994.1   Drowning and nonfatal submersion
Bathing cramp
Immersion
AHA: 3Q, '88, 4

994.2   Effects of hunger
Deprivation of food
Starvation

994.3   Effects of thirst
Deprivation of water

994.4   Exhaustion due to exposure

994.5   Exhaustion due to excessive exertion
Overexertion

994.6   Motion sickness
Air sickness
Seasickness
Travel sickness

994.7   Asphyxiation and strangulation
Suffocation (by):
    bedclothes
    cave-in
    constriction
    mechanical
    plastic bag
    pressure
    strangulation
> EXCLUDES   *asphyxia from:*
> *carbon monoxide (986)*
> *inhalation of food or foreign body (932-934.9)*
> *other gases, fumes, and vapors (987.0-987.9)*

994.8   Electrocution and nonfatal effects of electric current
Shock from electric current
> EXCLUDES   *electric burns (940.0-949.5)*

994.9   Other effects of external causes
Effects of:
    abnormal gravitational [G] forces or states
    weightlessness

√4ᵗʰ 995   Certain adverse effects not elsewhere classified
> EXCLUDES   *complications of surgical and medical care (996.0-999.9)*

995.0   Other anaphylactic shock
Allergic shock ⎫
Anaphylactic   ⎬ NOS or due to adverse effect of
  reaction   ⎪   correct medicinal substance
Anaphylaxis   ⎭   properly administered

Use additional E code to identify external cause, such as:
    adverse effects of correct medicinal substance properly administered [E930-E949]
> EXCLUDES   *anaphylactic reaction to serum (999.4)*
> *anaphylactic shock due to adverse food reaction (995.60-995.69)*

AHA: 4Q, '93, 30

DEF: Immediate sensitivity response after exposure to specific antigen; results in life-threatening respiratory distress; usually followed by vascular collapse, shock, urticaria, angioedema and pruritus.

995.1   Angioneurotic edema
Giant urticaria
> EXCLUDES   *urticaria:*
> *due to serum (999.5)*
> *other specified (698.2, 708.0-708.9, 757.33)*

DEF: Circulatory response of deep dermis, subcutaneous or submucosal tissues; causes localized edema and wheals.

√4ᵗʰ √5ᵗʰ   Additional Digit Required   RUG III Special Care Dx   RUG III Clinically Complex Dx   Hospice Non-cancer Dx   **CD PDx** Clinical Dimension PDx   **CD SDx** Clinical Dimension SDx

2006 ICD•9•CM   Volume 1 — 271

Injury and Poisoning

995.2–995.90

995.2 Unspecified adverse effect of drug, medicinal and biological substance

Adverse effect
Allergic reaction } (due) to correct medicinal
Hypersensitivity } substance properly
Idiosyncrasy } administered

Drug: Drug:
  hypersensitivity NOS   reaction NOS
   EXCLUDES *pathological drug intoxication (292.2)*

AHA: 2Q, '97, 12; 3Q, '95, 13; 3Q, '92, 16

995.3 Allergy, unspecified

Allergic reaction NOS   Idiosyncrasy NOS
Hypersensitivity NOS
   EXCLUDES *allergic reaction NOS to correct*
      medicinal substance properly
      administered (995.2)
      specific types of allergic reaction, such
      as:
        allergic diarrhea (558.3)
        dermatitis (691.0-693.9)
        hayfever (477.0-477.9)

995.4 Shock due to anesthesia

Shock due to anesthesia in which the correct
  substance was properly administered
   EXCLUDES *complications of anesthesia in labor or*
      delivery (668.0-668.9)
      overdose or wrong substance given
      (968.0-969.9)
      postoperative shock NOS (998.0)
      specified adverse effects of anesthesia
      classified elsewhere, such as:
        anoxic brain damage (348.1)
        hepatitis (070.0-070.9), etc.
      unspecified adverse effect of
        anesthesia (995.2)

√5ᵗʰ **995.5 Child maltreatment syndrome**

Use additional code(s), if applicable, to identify any
  associated injuries
Use additional E code to identify:
  nature of abuse (E960-E968)
  perpetrator (E967.0-E967.9)

AHA: 1Q, '98, 11

  995.50 Child abuse, unspecified [P]
  995.51 Child emotional/psychological abuse [P]
  995.52 Child neglect (nutritional) [P]
     AHA: 4Q, '96, 38, 40
  995.53 Child sexual abuse [P]
     AHA: 4Q, '96, 39, 40
  995.54 Child physical abuse [P]
     Battered baby or child syndrome
      EXCLUDES *shaken infant syndrome*
         (995.55)
     AHA: 3Q, '99, 14; 4Q, '96, 39, 40
  995.55 Shaken infant syndrome [P]
     Use additional code(s) to identify any
      associated injuries
     AHA: 4Q, '96, 40, 43
  995.59 Other child abuse and neglect [P]
     Multiple forms of abuse

√5ᵗʰ **995.6 Anaphylactic shock due to adverse food reaction**

Anaphylactic shock due to nonpoisonous foods

AHA: 4Q, '93, 30

  995.60 Due to unspecified food
  995.61 Due to peanuts
  995.62 Due to crustaceans
  995.63 Due to fruits and vegetables
  995.64 Due to tree nuts and seeds
  995.65 Due to fish
  995.66 Due to food additives
  995.67 Due to milk products
  995.68 Due to eggs

  995.69 Due to other specified food

995.7 Other adverse food reactions, not elsewhere classified

Use additional code to identify the type of reaction,
  such as:
  hives (708.0)
  wheezing (786.07)
   EXCLUDES *anaphylactic shock due to adverse food*
      reaction (995.60-995.69)
      asthma (493.0, 493.9)
      dermatitis due to food (693.1)
        in contact with skin (692.5)
      gastroenteritis and colitis due to food
        (558.3)
      rhinitis due to food (477.1)

√5ᵗʰ **995.8 Other specified adverse effects, not elsewhere classified**

  995.80 Adult maltreatment, unspecified [A]
     Abused person NOS
     Use additional code to identify:
      any associated injury
      perpetrator (E967.0-E967.9)
     AHA: 4Q, '96, 41, 43
  995.81 Adult physical abuse [A]
     Battered:
      person syndrome NEC
      man
      spouse
      woman
     Use additional code to identify:
      any association injury
      nature of abuse (E960-E968)
      perpetrator (E967.0-E967.9)
     AHA: 4Q, '96, 42, 43
  995.82 Adult emotional/psychological abuse [A]
     Use additional E code to identify perpetrator
      (E967.0-E967.9)
  995.83 Adult sexual abuse [A]
     Use additional code(s) to identify:
      any associated injury
      perpetrator (E967.0-E967.9)
  995.84 Adult neglect (nutritional) [A]
     Use addition code(s) to identify:
      intent of neglect (E904.0, E968.4)
      perpetrator (E967.0-E967.9)
  995.85 Other adult abuse and neglect [A]
     Multiple forms of abuse and neglect
     Use additional code(s) to identify
      any associated injury
      intent of neglect (E904.0, E968.4)
      nature of abuse (E960-E968)
      perpetrator (E967.0-E967.9)
  995.86 Malignant hyperthermia
     Malignant hyperpyrexia due to anesthesia
     AHA: 4Q, '98, 51
  995.89 Other
     Hypothermia due to anesthesia
     AHA: ▶2Q, '04, 18;◀ 3Q, '03, 12

√5ᵗʰ **995.9 Systemic inflammatory response syndrome (SIRS)**

Code first underlying systemic infection
AHA: ▶2Q, '04, 16;◀ 4Q, '02, 71

DEF: Clinical response to infection or trauma that can trigger an
acute inflammatory reaction and progresses to coagulation,
impaired fibrinolysis, and organ failure; manifested by two or more
of the following symptoms: fever, tachycardia, tachypnea,
leukocytosis or leukopenia.

  **995.90 Systemic inflammatory response
     syndrome, unspecified**
     SIRS NOS

[N] Newborn Age: 0   [P] Pediatric Age: 0-17   [M] Maternity Age: 12-55   [A] Adult Age: 15-124   Manifestation Code   ▶◀ Revised Text   ● New Code   ▲ Revised Code Title

995.91 Systemic inflammatory response syndrome due to infectious process without organ dysfunction
     Sepsis
     AHA: 2Q, '04, 16; 4Q, '03, 79

995.92 Systemic inflammatory response syndrome due to infectious process with organ dysfunction
     Severe sepsis
     Use additional code to specify organ dysfunction, such as:
         acute renal failure (584.5-584.9)
         acute respiratory failure (518.81)
         critical illness myopathy (359.81)
         critical illness polyneuropathy (357.82)
         encephalopathy (348.31)
         hepatic failure (570)
         septic shock (785.52)
     AHA: ▶1Q, '05, 7;◀ 2Q, '04, 16; 4Q, '03, 73, 79

995.93 Systemic inflammatory response syndrome due to noninfectious process without organ dysfunction

995.94 Systemic inflammatory response syndrome due to noninfectious process with organ dysfunction
     Use additional code to specify organ dysfunction, such as:
         acute renal failure (584.5-584.9)
         acute respiratory failure (518.81)
         critical illness myopathy (359.81)
         critical illness polyneuropathy (357.82)
         encephalopathy (348.31)
         hepatic failure (570)
         septic shock (785.52)
     AHA: 4Q, '03, 79

COMPLICATIONS OF SURGICAL AND MEDICAL CARE, NOT ELSEWHERE CLASSIFIED (996-999)

     EXCLUDES   *adverse effects of medicinal agents (001.0-799.9, 995.0-995.8)*
         burns from local applications and irradiation (940.0-949.5)
         complications of:
             conditions for which the procedure was performed
             surgical procedures during abortion, labor, and delivery (630-676.9)
         poisoning and toxic effects of drugs and chemicals (960.0-989.9)
         postoperative conditions in which no complications are present, such as:
             artificial opening status (V44.0-V44.9)
             closure of external stoma (V55.0-V55.9)
             fitting of prosthetic device (V52.0-V52.9)
         specified complications classified elsewhere
             anesthetic shock (995.4)
             electrolyte imbalance (276.0-276.9)
             postlaminectomy syndrome (722.80-722.83)
             postmastectomy lymphedema syndrome (457.0)
             postoperative psychosis (293.0-293.9)
         any other condition classified elsewhere in the Alphabetic Index when described as due to a procedure

Continuum of Illness Due to Infection

Bacteremia ➡ Septicemia ➡ Sepsis

Severe Sepsis with Septic Shock ⬅ Severe Sepsis

⬇

MODS (Multiple Organ Dysfunction Syndrome) ➡ Death

☑4ᵗʰ **996 Complications peculiar to certain specified procedures**
     INCLUDES   complications, not elsewhere classified, in the use of artificial substitutes [e.g., Dacron, metal, Silastic, Teflon] or natural sources [e.g., bone] involving:
         anastomosis (internal)
         graft (bypass) (patch)
         implant
         internal device:
             catheter
             electronic
             fixation
             prosthetic
         reimplant
         transplant
     EXCLUDES   *accidental puncture or laceration during procedure (998.2)*
         complications of internal anastomosis of:
             gastrointestinal tract (997.4)
             urinary tract (997.5)
         ▶*mechanical complication of respirator (V46.14)*◀
         other specified complications classified elsewhere, such as:
             hemolytic anemia (283.1)
             functional cardiac disturbances (429.4)
             serum hepatitis (070.2-070.3)
     AHA: 1Q, '94, 3

☑5ᵗʰ **996.0 Mechanical complication of cardiac device, implant, and graft**
     Breakdown (mechanical)   Obstruction, mechanical
     Displacement   Perforation
     Leakage   Protrusion
     AHA: 2Q, '93, 9

996.00 Unspecified device, implant, and graft

996.01 Due to cardiac pacemaker (electrode)
     AHA: 2Q, '99, 11

996.02 Due to heart valve prosthesis

996.03 Due to coronary bypass graft
     EXCLUDES   *atherosclerosis of graft (414.02, 414.03)*
         embolism [occlusion NOS] [thrombus] of graft (996.72)

996.04 Due to automatic implantable cardiac defibrillator

996.09 Other
     AHA: 2Q, '93, 9

996.1 Mechanical complication of other vascular device, implant, and graft
     Mechanical complications involving:
         aortic (bifurcation) graft (replacement)
         arteriovenous:
             dialysis catheter ⎫
             fistula   ⎬ surgically created
             shunt   ⎭
         balloon (counterpulsation) device, intra-aortic
         carotid artery bypass graft
         femoral-popliteal bypass graft
         umbrella device, vena cava
     EXCLUDES   *atherosclerosis of biological graft (440.30-440.32)*
         embolism [occlusion NOS] [thrombus] of (biological) (synthetic) graft (996.74)
         peritoneal dialysis catheter (996.56)
     AHA: 1Q, '02, 13; 1Q, '95, 3

996.2 Mechanical complication of nervous system device, implant, and graft
     Mechanical complications involving:
         dorsal column stimulator
         electrodes implanted in brain [brain "pacemaker"]
         peripheral nerve graft
         ventricular (communicating) shunt
     AHA: 2Q, '99, 4; S-O, '87, 10

☑4ᵗʰ ☑5ᵗʰ Additional Digit Required   **RUG III Special Care Dx**   **RUG III Clinically Complex Dx**   **Hospice Non-cancer Dx**   **CD PDx** Clinical Dimension PDx   **CD SDx** Clinical Dimension SDx

Injury and Poisoning

996.3–996.62

√5ᵗʰ **996.3 Mechanical complication of genitourinary device, implant, and graft**
AHA: 3Q, '01, 13; S-O, '85, 3

996.30 Unspecified device, implant, and graft

996.31 Due to urethral [indwelling] catheter

996.32 Due to intrauterine contraceptive device ♀

996.39 Other
Cystostomy catheter
Prosthetic reconstruction of vas deferens
Repair (graft) of ureter without mention of resection
EXCLUDES   complications due to:
external stoma of urinary tract (997.5)
internal anastomosis of urinary tract (997.5)

√5ᵗʰ **996.4 Mechanical complication of internal orthopedic device, implant, and graft**
Mechanical complications involving:
external (fixation) device utilizing internal screw(s), pin(s) or other methods of fixation
grafts of bone, cartilage, muscle, or tendon
internal (fixation) device such as nail, plate, rod, etc.
▶Use additional code to identify prosthetic joint with mechanical complication (V43.60-V43.69)◀
EXCLUDES   complications of external orthopedic device, such as:
pressure ulcer due to cast (707.00-707.09)
AHA: 2Q, '99, 10; 2Q, '98, 19; 2Q, '96, 11; 3Q, '95, 16; N-D, '85, 11

● **996.40 Unspecified mechanical complication of internal orthopedic device, implant, and graft**

● **996.41 Mechanical loosening of prosthetic joint**
Aseptic loosening

● **996.42 Dislocation of prosthetic joint**
Instability of prosthetic joint
Subluxation of prosthetic joint

● **996.43 Prosthetic joint implant failure**
Breakage (fracture) of prosthetic joint

● **996.44 Peri-prosthetic fracture around prosthetic joint**

● **996.45 Peri-prosthetic osteolysis**

● **996.46 Articular bearing surface wear of prosthetic joint**

● **996.47 Other mechanical complication of prosthetic joint implant**
Mechanical complication of prosthetic joint NOS

● **996.49 Other mechanical complication of other internal orthopedic device, implant, and graft**
EXCLUDES   mechanical complication of prosthetic joint implant (996.41-996.47)

√5ᵗʰ **996.5 Mechanical complication of other specified prosthetic device, implant, and graft**
Mechanical complications involving:
prosthetic implant in:
bile duct
breast
chin
orbit of eye
nonabsorbable surgical material NOS
other graft, implant, and internal device, not elsewhere classified
AHA: 1Q, '98, 11

996.51 Due to corneal graft

996.52 Due to graft of other tissue, not elsewhere classified
Skin graft failure or rejection
EXCLUDES   failure of artificial skin graft (996.55)
failure of decellularized allodermis (996.55)
sloughing of temporary skin allografts or xenografts (pigskin)—omit code
AHA: 1Q, '96, 10

996.53 Due to ocular lens prosthesis
EXCLUDES   contact lenses—code to condition
AHA: 1Q, '00, 9

996.54 Due to breast prosthesis
Breast capsule (prosthesis)
Mammary implant
AHA: 2Q, '98, 14; 3Q, '92, 4

996.55 Due to artificial skin graft and decellularized allodermis
Dislodgement
Displacement
Failure
Non-adherence
Poor incorporation
Shearing
AHA: 4Q, '98, 52

996.56 Due to peritoneal dialysis catheter
EXCLUDES   mechanical complication of arteriovenous dialysis catheter (996.1)
AHA: 4Q, '98, 54

996.57 Due to insulin pump
AHA: 4Q, '03, 81-82

996.59 Due to other implant and internal device, not elsewhere classified
Nonabsorbable surgical material NOS
Prosthetic implant in:
bile duct
chin
orbit of eye
AHA: 2Q, '99, 13; 3Q, '94, 7

√5ᵗʰ **996.6 Infection and inflammatory reaction due to internal prosthetic device, implant and graft**
Infection (causing obstruction) ⎫ due to (presence of) any device,
Inflammation ⎬ implant, and graft classi-
⎭ fiable to 996.0-996.5
Use additional code to identify specified infections
AHA: 2Q, '89, 16; J-F, '87, 14

996.60 Due to unspecified device, implant and graft

996.61 Due to cardiac device, implant and graft
Cardiac pacemaker or defibrillator:
electrode(s), lead(s)
pulse generator
subcutaneous pocket
Coronary artery bypass graft
Heart valve prosthesis

996.62 Due to other vascular device, implant and graft
Arterial graft
Arteriovenous fistula or shunt
Infusion pump
Vascular catheter (arterial) (dialysis) (venous)
AHA: 2Q, '04, 16; 1Q, '04, 5; 4Q, '03, 107, 111; 2Q, '03, 7; 2Q, '94, 13

N Newborn Age: 0   P Pediatric Age: 0-17   M Maternity Age: 12-55   A Adult Age: 15-124   Manifestation Code   ▶◀ Revised Text   ● New Code   ▲ Revised Code Title

996.63 Due to nervous system device, implant and graft
Electrodes implanted in brain
Peripheral nerve graft
Spinal canal catheter
Ventricular (communicating) shunt (catheter)

996.64 Due to indwelling urinary catheter
Use additional code to identify specified infections, such as:
Cystitis (595.0-595.9)
Sepsis (038.0-038.9)
AHA: 3Q, '93, 6

996.65 Due to other genitourinary device, implant and graft
Intrauterine contraceptive device
AHA: 1Q, '00, 15

996.66 Due to internal joint prosthesis
▶Use additional code to identify infected prosthetic joint (V43.60-V43.69)◀
AHA: 2Q, '91, 18

996.67 Due to other internal orthopedic device, implant and graft
Bone growth stimulator (electrode)
Internal fixation device (pin) (rod) (screw)

996.68 Due to peritoneal dialysis catheter
Exit-site infection or inflammation
AHA: 4Q, '98, 54

996.69 Due to other internal prosthetic device, implant and graft
Breast prosthesis
Ocular lens prosthesis
Prosthetic orbital implant
AHA: 4Q, '03, 108; 4Q, '98, 52

✓5th **996.7 Other complications of internal (biological) (synthetic) prosthetic device, implant and graft**

Complication NOS
occlusion NOS
Embolism
Fibrosis   } due to (presence of) any
Hemorrhage   device, implant, and
Pain   graft classifiable to
Stenosis   996.0-996.5
Thrombus

EXCLUDES   transplant rejection (996.8)
AHA: 1Q, '89, 9; N-D, '86, 5

996.70 Due to unspecified device, implant and graft

996.71 Due to heart valve prosthesis

996.72 Due to other cardiac device, implant and graft
Cardiac pacemaker or defibrillator:
electrode(s), lead(s)
subcutaneous pocket
Coronary artery bypass (graft)
EXCLUDES   occlusion due to
atherosclerosis
(414.02-414.06)
AHA: 3Q, '11, 20

996.73 Due to renal dialysis device, implant and graft
AHA: 2Q, '91, 18

996.74 Due to other vascular device, implant and graft
EXCLUDES   occlusion of biological graft
due to atherosclerosis
(440.30-440.32)
AHA: 1Q, '03, 16, 17

996.75 Due to nervous system device, implant and graft

996.76 Due to genitourinary device, implant and graft
AHA: 1Q, '00, 15

996.77 Due to internal joint prosthesis

996.78 Due to other internal orthopedic device, implant and graft
AHA: 2Q, '03, 14

996.79 Due to other internal prosthetic device, implant and graft
AHA: 2Q, '04, 7; 1Q,'01, 8; 3Q, '95, 14; 3Q, '92, 4

✓5th **996.8 Complications of transplanted organ**
Transplant failure or rejection
Use additional code to identify nature of complication, such as:
Cytomegalovirus (CMV) infection (078.5)
AHA: 3Q, '01, 12; 3Q, '93, 3, 4; 2Q, '93, 11; 1Q, '93, 24

996.80 Transplanted organ, unspecified

996.81 Kidney
AHA: 3Q, '03, 16; 3Q, '98, 6, 7; 3Q, '94, 8; 2Q, '94, 9; 1Q, '93, 24

996.82 Liver
AHA: 3Q, '03, 17; 3Q, '98, 3, 4

996.83 Heart
AHA: 3Q, '03, 16; 4Q, '02, 53; 3Q, '98, 5

996.84 Lung
AHA: 2Q, '03, 12; 3Q, '98, 5

996.85 Bone marrow
Graft-versus-host disease (acute) (chronic)
AHA: 4Q, '90, 4

996.86 Pancreas

996.87 Intestine

996.89 Other specified transplanted organ
AHA: 3Q, '94, 5

✓5th **996.9 Complications of reattached extremity or body part**

996.90 Unspecified extremity

996.91 Forearm

996.92 Hand

996.93 Finger(s)

996.94 Upper extremity, other and unspecified

996.95 Foot and toe(s)

996.96 Lower extremity, other and unspecified

996.99 Other specified body part

✓4th **997 Complications affecting specified body systems, not elsewhere classified**
Use additional code to identify complications
EXCLUDES   the listed conditions when specified as:
causing shock (998.0)
complications of:
anesthesia:
adverse effect (001.0-799.9, 995.0-995.8)
in labor or delivery (668.0-668.9)
poisoning (968.0-969.9)
implanted device or graft (996.0-996.9)
obstetrical procedures (669.0-669.4)
reattached extremity (996.90-996.96)
transplanted organ (996.80-996.89)
AHA: 1Q, '94, 4; 1Q, '93, 26

✓5th **997.0 Nervous system complications**

997.00 Nervous system complication, unspecified

997.01 Central nervous system complication
Anoxic brain damage
Cerebral hypoxia
EXCLUDES   cerebrovascular hemorrhage or
infarction (997.02)

| ✓4th
✓5th Additional Digit Required | RUG III Special Care Dx | RUG III Clinically Complex Dx | Hospice Non-cancer Dx | CD PDx Clinical Dimension PDx | CD SDx Clinical Dimension SDx |

2006 ICD•9•CM

October 2005 • Volume 1 — 275

Injury and Poisoning

997.02–997.79

997.02 Iatrogenic cerebrovascular infarction or hemorrhage
Postoperative stroke
AHA: 2Q, '04, 8; 4Q, '95, 57

997.09 Other nervous system complications

997.1 Cardiac complications
Cardiac:
  arrest
  insufficiency } during or resulting from a procedure
Cardiorespiratory failure
Heart failure

EXCLUDES   *the listed conditions as long-term effects of cardiac surgery or due to the presence of cardiac prosthetic device (429.4)*

AHA: 2Q, '02, 12

997.2 Peripheral vascular complications
Phlebitis or thrombophlebitis during or resulting from a procedure

EXCLUDES   *the listed conditions due to:*
    implant or catheter device (996.62)
    infusion, perfusion, or transfusion (999.2)
    complications affecting blood vessels (997.71-997.79)

AHA: 1Q,'03, 6; 3Q, '02, 24-26

997.3 Respiratory complications
Mendelson's syndrome } resulting from a procedure
Pneumonia (aspiration)

EXCLUDES   *iatrogenic [postoperative] pneumothorax (512.1)*
    iatrogenic pulmonary embolism (415.11)
    Mendelson's syndrome in labor and delivery (668.0)
    specified complications classified elsewhere, such as:
      adult respiratory distress syndrome (518.5)
      pulmonary edema, postoperative (518.4)
      respiratory insufficiency, acute, postoperative (518.5)
      shock lung (518.5)
      tracheostomy complications (519.00-519.09)

AHA: 1Q, '97, 10; 2Q, '93, 3; 2Q, '93, 9; 4Q, '90, 25

DEF: Mendelson's syndrome: acid pneumonitis due to aspiration of gastric acids, may occur after anesthesia or sedation.

997.4 Digestive system complications
Complications of:
  intestinal (internal) anastomosis and bypass, not elsewhere classified, except that involving urinary tract
Hepatic failure
Hepatorenal syndrome } specified as due to a procedure
Intestinal obstruction NOS

EXCLUDES   *gastrostomy complications (536.40-536.49)*
    specified gastrointestinal complications classified elsewhere, such as:
      blind loop syndrome (579.2)
      colostomy and enterostomy complications (569.60-569.69)
      gastrojejunal ulcer (534.0-534.9)
      infection of esophagostomy (530.86)
      infection of external stoma (569.61)
      mechanical complication of esophagostomy (530.87)
      pelvic peritoneal adhesions, female (614.6)
      peritoneal adhesions (568.0)
      peritoneal adhesions with obstruction (560.81)
      postcholecystectomy syndrome (576.0)
      postgastric surgery syndromes (564.2)
      vomiting following gastrointestinal surgery (564.3)

AHA: 2Q, '01, 4-6; 3Q, '99, 4; 2Q, '99, 14; 3Q, '97, 7; 1Q, '97, 11; 2Q, '95, 7; 1Q, '93, 26; 3Q, '92, 15; 2Q, '89, 15; 1Q, '88, 14

997.5 Urinary complications
Complications of:
  external stoma of urinary tract
  internal anastomosis and bypass of urinary tract, including that involving intestinal tract
Oliguria or anuria
Renal:
  failure (acute) } specified as due to procedure
  insufficiency (acute)
Tubular necrosis (acute)

EXCLUDES   *specified complications classified elsewhere, such as:*
    postoperative stricture of:
      ureter (593.3)
      urethra (598.2)

AHA: 3Q, '03, 13; 3Q '96, 10, 15; 4Q, '95, 73; 1Q, '92, 13; 2Q, '89, 16; M-A, '87, 10; S-O, '85, 3

√5ᵗʰ **997.6 Amputation stump complication**
EXCLUDES   *admission for treatment for a current traumatic amputation — code to complicated traumatic amputation*
    phantom limb (syndrome) (353.6)

AHA: 4Q, '95, 82

997.60 Unspecified complication

997.61 Neuroma of amputation stump
DEF: Hyperplasia generated nerve cell mass following amputation.

997.62 Infection (chronic)
Use additional code to identify the organism
AHA: ▶1Q, '05, 14;◀ 4Q, '96, 46

997.69 Other
AHA: ▶1Q, '05, 15◀

√5ᵗʰ **997.7 Vascular complications of other vessels**
EXCLUDES   *peripheral vascular complications (997.2)*

997.71 Vascular complications of mesenteric artery
AHA: 4Q, '01, 53

997.72 Vascular complications of renal artery

997.79 Vascular complications of other vessels

N Newborn Age: 0   P Pediatric Age: 0-17   M Maternity Age: 12-55   A Adult Age: 15-124   Manifestation Code   ▶◀ Revised Text   ● New Code   ▲ Revised Code Title

√5ᵗʰ **997.9 Complications affecting other specified body systems, not elsewhere classified**

> EXCLUDES   *specified complications classified elsewhere, such as:*
> *broad ligament laceration syndrome (620.6)*
> *postartificial menopause syndrome (627.4)*
> *postoperative stricture of vagina (623.2)*

997.91 Hypertension

> EXCLUDES   *essential hypertension (401.0-401.9)*

AHA: 4Q, '95, 57

997.99 Other
Vitreous touch syndrome
AHA: 2Q, '94, 12; 1Q, '94, 17

DEF: Vitreous touch syndrome: vitreous protruding through pupil and attaches to corneal epithelium; causes aqueous fluid in vitreous body; marked by corneal edema, loss of lucidity; complication of cataract surgery.

√4ᵗʰ **998 Other complications of procedures, not elsewhere classified**
AHA: 1Q, '94, 4

998.0 Postoperative shock
Collapse NOS ⎫ during or resulting
Shock (endotoxic) (hypo- ⎬ from a surgical
volemic) (septic) ⎭ procedure

> EXCLUDES   *shock:*
> *anaphylactic due to serum (999.4)*
> *anesthetic (995.4)*
> *electric (994.8)*
> *following abortion (639.5)*
> *obstetric (669.1)*
> *traumatic (958.4)*

√5ᵗʰ **998.1 Hemorrhage or hematoma or seroma complicating a procedure**

> EXCLUDES   *hemorrhage, hematoma, or seroma:*
> *complicating cesarean section or puerperal perineal wound (674.3)*

998.11 Hemorrhage complicating a procedure
AHA: 3Q, '03, 13; 1Q, '03, 4; 4Q, '97, 52; 1Q, '97, 10

998.12 Hematoma complicating a procedure
AHA: 1Q, '03, 6; 3Q, '02, 24, 26

998.13 Seroma complicating a procedure
AHA: 4Q, '96, 46; 1Q, '93, 26; 2Q, '92, 15; S-O, '87, 8

998.2 Accidental puncture or laceration during a procedure
Accidental perforation by catheter or other instrument during a procedure on:
blood vessel
nerve
organ

> EXCLUDES   *iatrogenic [postoperative] pneumothorax (512.1)*
> *puncture or laceration caused by implanted device intentionally left in operation wound (996.0-996.5)*
> *specified complications classified elsewhere, such as:*
> *broad ligament laceration syndrome (620.6)*
> *trauma from instruments during delivery (664.0-665.9)*

AHA: 3Q, '02, 24, 26; 3Q, '94, 6; 3Q, '90, 17; 3Q, '90, 18

√5ᵗʰ **998.3 Disruption of operation wound**
Dehiscence ⎫
Rupture ⎬ of operation wound

> EXCLUDES   *disruption of:*
> *cesarean wound (674.1)*
> *perineal wound, puerperal (674.2)*

AHA: 4Q, '02, 73; 1Q, '93, 19

998.31 Disruption of internal operation wound

998.32 Disruption of external operation wound
Disruption of operation wound NOS
AHA: ▶1Q, '05, 11◀ 4Q, '03, 104, 106

998.4 Foreign body accidentally left during a procedure
Adhesions ⎫ due to foreign body accidentally left
Obstruction ⎬ in operative wound or body
Perforation ⎭ cavity during a procedure

> EXCLUDES   *obstruction or perforation caused by implanted device intentionally left in body (996.0-996.5)*

AHA: 1Q, '89, 9

√5ᵗʰ **998.5 Postoperative infection**

> EXCLUDES   *infection due to:*
> *implanted device (996.60-996.69)*
> *infusion, perfusion, or transfusion (999.3)*
> *postoperative obstetrical wound infection (674.3)*

998.51 Infected postoperative seroma
Use additional code to identify organism
AHA: 4Q, '96, 46

998.59 Other postoperative infection
Abscess:
intra-abdominal ⎫
stitch ⎪
subphrenic ⎬ postoperative
wound ⎪
Septicemia ⎭

Use additional code to identify infection
AHA: 4Q, '04, 76; 4Q, '03, 104, 106-107; 3Q, '98, 3; 3Q, '95, 5; 2Q, '95, 7; 3Q, '94, 6; 1Q, '93, 19; J-F, '87, 14

998.6 Persistent postoperative fistula
AHA: J-F, '87, 14

998.7 Acute reaction to foreign substance accidentally left during a procedure
Peritonitis: Peritonitis:
aseptic   chemical

√5ᵗʰ **998.8 Other specified complications of procedures, not elsewhere classified**
AHA: 4Q, '94, 46; 1Q, '89, 9

998.81 Emphysema (subcutaneous) (surgical) resulting from a procedure

998.82 Cataract fragments in eye following cataract surgery

998.83 Non-healing surgical wound
AHA: 4Q, '96, 47

998.89 Other specified complications
AHA: 3Q, '99, 13; 2Q, '98, 16

998.9 Unspecified complication of procedure, not elsewhere classified
Postoperative complication NOS

> EXCLUDES   *complication NOS of obstetrical, surgery or procedure (669.4)*

AHA: 4Q, '93, 37

√4ᵗʰ √5ᵗʰ Additional Digit Required   RUG III Special Care Dx   RUG III Clinically Complex Dx   Hospice Non-cancer Dx   CD PDx Clinical Dimension PDx   CD SDx Clinical Dimension SDx

2006 ICD•9•CM   **October 2005 • Volume 1 — 277**

Injury and Poisoning

999–999.9

✓4ᵗʰ **999 Complications of medical care, not elsewhere classified**

INCLUDES   complications, not elsewhere classified, of:
     dialysis (hemodialysis) (peritoneal) (renal)
     extracorporeal circulation
     hyperalimentation therapy
     immunization
     infusion
     inhalation therapy
     injection
     inoculation
     perfusion
     transfusion
     vaccination
     ventilation therapy

EXCLUDES   *specified complications classified elsewhere*
     such as:
     complications of implanted device (996.0-
       996.9)
     contact dermatitis due to drugs (692.3)
     dementia dialysis (294.8)
       transient (293.9)
     dialysis disequilibrium syndrome (276.0-
       276.9)
     poisoning and toxic effects of drugs and
       chemicals (960.0-989.9)
     postvaccinal encephalitis (323.5)
     water and electrolyte imbalance (276.0-
       276.9)

999.0 Generalized vaccinia

DEF: Skin eruption, self-limiting; follows vaccination; due to transient viremia with virus localized in skin.

999.1 Air embolism

Air embolism to any site following infusion, perfusion, or transfusion

EXCLUDES   *embolism specified as:*
     complicating:
       abortion (634-638 with .6, 639.6)
       ectopic or molar pregnancy
         (639.6)
       pregnancy, childbirth, or the
         puerperium (673.0)
     due to implanted device (996.7)
     traumatic (958.0)

999.2 Other vascular complications

Phlebitis
Thromboembolism   } *following infusion, perfu-*
Thrombophlebitis   *sion, or transfusion*

EXCLUDES   *the listed conditions when specified as:*
     due to implanted device (996.61-
       996.62. 996.72-996.74)
     postoperative NOS (997.2, 997.71-
       997.79)

AHA: 2Q, '97, 5

999.3 Other infection

Infection
Sepsis   } *following infusion, injection,*
Septicemia   *transfusion, or vaccination*

EXCLUDES   *the listed conditions when specified as:*
     due to implanted device (996.60-
       996.69)
     postoperative NOS (998.51-998.59)

AHA: 2Q, '01, 11, 12; 2Q, '97, 5; J-F, '87, 14

999.4 Anaphylactic shock due to serum

EXCLUDES   *shock:*
     allergic NOS (995.0)
     anaphylactic:
       NOS (995.0)
       due to drugs and chemicals
         (995.0)

DEF: Life-threatening hypersensitivity to foreign serum; causes respiratory distress, vascular collapse, and shock.

999.5 Other serum reaction

Intoxication by serum   Serum sickness
Protein sickness   Urticaria due to serum
Serum rash

EXCLUDES   *serum hepatitis (070.2-070.3)*

DEF: Serum sickness: Hypersensitivity to foreign serum; causes fever, hives, swelling, and lymphadenopathy.

999.6 ABO incompatibility reaction

Incompatible blood transfusion
Reaction to blood group incompatibility in infusion
     or transfusion

999.7 Rh incompatibility reaction

Reactions due to Rh factor in infusion or transfusion

999.8 Other transfusion reaction

Septic shock due to transfusion
Transfusion reaction NOS

EXCLUDES   *postoperative shock (998.0)*

AHA: 3Q, '00, 9

999.9 Other and unspecified complications of medical care, not elsewhere classified

Complications, not elsewhere classified, of:
electroshock   ⎫
inhalation   ⎬ therapy
ultrasound   ⎪
ventilation   ⎭

Unspecified misadventure of medical care

EXCLUDES   *unspecified complication of:*
     phototherapy (990)
     radiation therapy (999)

AHA: 1Q, '03, 19; 2Q, '97, 5

N Newborn Age: 0   P Pediatric Age: 0-17   M Maternity Age: 12-55   A Adult Age: 15-124   Manifestation Code   ▶◀ Revised Text   ● New Code   ▲ Revised Code Title

SUPPLEMENTARY CLASSIFICATION OF FACTORS INFLUENCING HEALTH STATUS AND CONTACT WITH HEALTH SERVICES ▶(V01-V85)◀

This classification is provided to deal with occasions when circumstances other than a disease or injury classifiable to categories 001-999 (the main part of ICD) are recorded as "diagnoses" or "problems." This can arise mainly in three ways:

a) When a person who is not currently sick encounters the health services for some specific purpose, such as to act as a donor of an organ or tissue, to receive prophylactic vaccination, or to discuss a problem which is in itself not a disease or injury. This will be a fairly rare occurrence among hospital inpatients, but will be relatively more common among hospital outpatients and patients of family practitioners, health clinics, etc.

b) When a person with a known disease or injury, whether it is current or resolving, encounters the health care system for a specific treatment of that disease or injury (e.g., dialysis for renal disease; chemotherapy for malignancy; cast change).

c) When some circumstance or problem is present which influences the person's health status but is not in itself a current illness or injury. Such factors may be elicited during population surveys, when the person may or may not be currently sick, or be recorded as an additional factor to be borne in mind when the person is receiving care for some current illness or injury classifiable to categories 001-999.

In the latter circumstances the V code should be used only as a supplementary code and should not be the one selected for use in primary, single cause tabulations. Examples of these circumstances are a personal history of certain diseases, or a person with an artificial heart valve in situ.

AHA: J-F, '87, 8

PERSONS WITH POTENTIAL HEALTH HAZARDS RELATED TO COMMUNICABLE DISEASES (V01-V06)

EXCLUDES   *family history of infectious and parasitic diseases (V18.8)*
personal history of infectious and parasitic diseases (V12.0)

✓4ᵗʰ **V01 Contact with or exposure to communicable diseases**

   V01.0 Cholera
      Conditions classifiable to 001

   V01.1 Tuberculosis
      Conditions classifiable to 010-018

   V01.2 Poliomyelitis
      Conditions classifiable to 045

   V01.3 Smallpox
      Conditions classifiable to 050

   V01.4 Rubella
      Conditions classifiable to 056

   V01.5 Rabies
      Conditions classifiable to 071

   V01.6 Venereal diseases
      Conditions classifiable to 090-099

✓5ᵗʰ **V01.7 Other viral diseases**
      Conditions classifiable to 042-078 and V08, except as above
      AHA: 2Q, '92, 11

      V01.71 Varicella

      V01.79 Other viral diseases

✓5ᵗʰ **V01.8 Other communicable diseases**
      Conditions classifiable to 001-136, except as above
      AHA: J-A, '87, 24

      V01.81 Anthrax
         AHA: 4Q, '02, 70, 78

      V01.82 Exposure to SARS-associated coronavirus
         AHA: 4Q, '03, 46-47

      V01.83 Escherichia coli (E. coli)

      V01.84 Meningococcus

      V01.89 Other communicable diseases

   V01.9 Unspecified communicable disease

✓4ᵗʰ **V02 Carrier or suspected carrier of infectious diseases**
   AHA: 3Q, '95, 18; 3Q, '94, 4

   V02.0 Cholera

   V02.1 Typhoid

   V02.2 Amebiasis

   V02.3 Other gastrointestinal pathogens

   V02.4 Diphtheria

✓5ᵗʰ **V02.5 Other specified bacterial diseases**

      V02.51 Group B streptococcus
         AHA: 1Q, '02, 14; 4Q, '98, 56

      V02.52 Other streptococcus

      V02.59 Other specified bacterial diseases
         Meningococcal   Staphylococcal

✓5ᵗʰ **V02.6 Viral hepatitis**
      Hepatitis Australian-antigen [HAA] [SH] carrier
      Serum hepatitis carrier

      V02.60 Viral hepatitis carrier, unspecified
         AHA: 4Q, '97, 47

      V02.61 Hepatitis B carrier
         AHA: 4Q, '97, 47

      V02.62 Hepatitis C carrier
         AHA: 4Q, '97, 47

      V02.69 Other viral hepatitis carrier
         AHA: 4Q, '97, 47

   V02.7 Gonorrhea

   V02.8 Other venereal diseases

   V02.9 Other specified infectious organism
      AHA: 3Q, '95, 18; 1Q, '93, 22; J-A, '87, 24

✓4ᵗʰ **V03 Need for prophylactic vaccination and inoculation against bacterial diseases**

EXCLUDES ▶ *vaccination not carried out (V64.00-V64.09)*◀
vaccines against combinations of diseases (V06.0-V06.9)

   V03.0 Cholera alone

   V03.1 Typhoid-paratyphoid alone [TAB]

   V03.2 Tuberculosis [BCG]

   V03.3 Plague

   V03.4 Tularemia

   V03.5 Diphtheria alone

   V03.6 Pertussis alone

   V03.7 Tetanus toxoid alone

✓5ᵗʰ **V03.8 Other specified vaccinations against single bacterial diseases**

      V03.81 Hemophilus influenza, type B [Hib]

      V03.82 Streptococcus pneumoniae [pneumococcus]

      V03.89 Other specified vaccination
         AHA: 2Q, '00, 9

   V03.9 Unspecified single bacterial disease

✓4ᵗʰ **V04 Need for prophylactic vaccination and inoculation against certain viral diseases**

EXCLUDES   *vaccines against combinations of diseases (V06.0-V06.9)*

   V04.0 Poliomyelitis

   V04.1 Smallpox

   V04.2 Measles alone

   V04.3 Rubella alone

   V04.4 Yellow fever

   V04.5 Rabies

   V04.6 Mumps alone

   V04.7 Common cold

✓5ᵗʰ **V04.8 Other viral diseases**
      AHA: 4Q, '03, 83

      V04.81 Influenza

      V04.82 Respiratory syncytial virus (RSV)

      V04.89 Other viral diseases

✓4ᵗʰ Additional Digit Required   RUG III Special Care Dx   RUG III Clinically Complex Dx   Hospice Non-cancer Dx   **PDx** Primary Dx use only   **SDx** Secondary Dx use only

V Codes

V05–V09.91

√4ᵗʰ **V05 Need for other prophylactic vaccination and inoculation against single diseases**

> EXCLUDES   *vaccines against combinations of diseases (V06.0-V06.9)*

V05.0 Arthropod-borne viral encephalitis

V05.1 Other arthropod-borne viral diseases

V05.2 Leishmaniasis

V05.3 Viral hepatitis

V05.4 Varicella

> Chickenpox

V05.8 Other specified disease

> AHA: 1Q, '01, 4; 3Q, '91, 20

V05.9 Unspecified single disease

√4ᵗʰ **V06 Need for prophylactic vaccination and inoculation against combinations of diseases**

> Note: Use additional single vaccination codes from categories V03-V05 to identify any vaccinations not included in a combination code.

V06.0 Cholera with typhoid-paratyphoid [cholera+TAB]

V06.1 Diphtheria-tetanus-pertussis, combined [DTP] [DTaP]

> AHA: 4Q, '03, 83; 3Q, '98, 13

V06.2 Diphtheria-tetanus-pertussis with typhoid-paratyphoid [DTP+TAB]

V06.3 Diphtheria-tetanus-pertussis with poliomyelitis [DTP+polio]

V06.4 Measles-mumps-rubella [MMR]

V06.5 Tetanus-diphtheria [Td] [DT]

> AHA: 4Q, '03, 83

V06.6 Streptococcus pneumoniae [pneumococcus] and influenza

V06.8 Other combinations

> EXCLUDES   *multiple single vaccination codes (V03.0-V05.9)*

> AHA: 1Q, '94, 19

V06.9 Unspecified combined vaccine

PERSONS WITH NEED FOR ISOLATION, OTHER POTENTIAL HEALTH HAZARDS AND PROPHYLACTIC MEASURES (V07-V09)

√4ᵗʰ **V07 Need for isolation and other prophylactic measures**

> EXCLUDES   *prophylactic organ removal (V50.41-V50.49)*

V07.0 Isolation

> Admission to protect the individual from his surroundings or for isolation of individual after contact with infectious diseases

V07.1 Desensitization to allergens

V07.2 Prophylactic immunotherapy

> Administration of:
> antivenin
> immune sera [gamma globulin]
> RhoGAM
> tetanus antitoxin

√5ᵗʰ **V07.3 Other prophylactic chemotherapy**

V07.31 Prophylactic fluoride administration

V07.39 Other prophylactic chemotherapy

> EXCLUDES   *maintenance chemotherapy following disease ▶(V58.12)◀*

V07.4 Hormone replacement therapy (postmenopausal) ♀

V07.8 Other specified prophylactic measure

> AHA: 1Q, '92, 11

V07.9 Unspecified prophylactic measure

V08 Asymptomatic human immunodeficiency virus [HIV] infection status

> HIV positive NOS

> Note: This code is *only* to be used when no HIV infection symptoms or conditions are present. If any HIV infection symptoms or conditions are present, see code 042.

> EXCLUDES   *AIDS (042)*
> *human immunodeficiency virus [HIV] disease (042)*
> *exposure to HIV (V01.79)*
> *nonspecific serologic evidence of HIV (795.71)*
> *symptomatic human immunodeficiency virus [HIV] infection (042)*

> AHA: 2Q, '04, 11; 2Q, '99, 8; 3Q, '95, 18

√4ᵗʰ **V09 Infection with drug-resistant microorganisms**

> Note: This category is intended for use as an additional code for infectious conditions classified elsewhere to indicate the presence of drug-resistance of the infectious organism.

> AHA: 3Q, '94, 4; 4Q, '93, 22

V09.0 Infection with microorganisms resistant to penicillins `SDx`

> Methicillin-resistant staphylococcus aureus (MRSA)
> AHA: 4Q, '03, 104, 106

V09.1 Infection with microorganisms resistant to cephalosporins and other B-lactam antibiotics `SDx`

V09.2 Infection with microorganisms resistant to macrolides `SDx`

V09.3 Infection with microorganisms resistant to tetracyclines `SDx`

V09.4 Infection with microorganisms resistant to aminoglycosides `SDx`

√5ᵗʰ **V09.5 Infection with microorganisms resistant to quinolones and fluoroquinolones**

V09.50 Without mention of resistance to multiple quinolones and fluoroquinoles `SDx`

V09.51 With resistance to multiple quinolones and fluoroquinoles `SDx`

V09.6 Infection with microorganisms resistant to sulfonamides `SDx`

√5ᵗʰ **V09.7 Infection with microorganisms resistant to other specified antimycobacterial agents**

> EXCLUDES   *Amikacin (V09.4)*
> *Kanamycin (V09.4)*
> *Streptomycin [SM] (V09.4)*

V09.70 Without mention of resistance to multiple antimycobacterial agents `SDx`

V09.71 With resistance to multiple antimycobacterial agents `SDx`

√5ᵗʰ **V09.8 Infection with microorganisms resistant to other specified drugs**

> Vancomycin (glycopeptide) intermediate staphylococcus aureus (VISA/GISA)
> Vancomycin (glycopeptide) resistant enterococcus (VRE)
> Vancomycin (glycopeptide) resistant staphylococcus aureus (VRSA/GRSA)

V09.80 Without mention of resistance to multiple drugs `SDx`

V09.81 With resistance to multiple drugs `SDx`

√5ᵗʰ **V09.9 Infection with drug-resistant microorganisms, unspecified**

> Drug resistance, NOS

V09.90 Without mention of multiple drug resistance `SDx`

V09.91 With multiple drug resistance `SDx`

> Multiple drug resistance NOS

N Newborn Age: 0   P Pediatric Age: 0-17   M Maternity Age: 12-55   A Adult Age: 15-124   `Manifestation Code`   ▶◀ Revised Text   ● New Code   ▲ Revised Code Title

PERSONS WITH POTENTIAL HEALTH HAZARDS RELATED TO PERSONAL AND FAMILY HISTORY (V10-V19)

> EXCLUDES *obstetric patients where the possibility that the fetus might be affected is the reason for observation or management during pregnancy (655.0-655.9)*

AHA: J-F, '87, 1

√4th **V10 Personal history of malignant neoplasm**
AHA: 4Q, '02, 80; 4Q, '98, 69; 1Q, '95, 4; 3Q, '92, 5; M-J, '85, 10; 2Q, '90, 9

√5th **V10.0 Gastrointestinal tract**
History of conditions classifiable to 140-159

V10.00 Gastrointestinal tract, unspecified

V10.01 Tongue

V10.02 Other and unspecified oral cavity and pharynx

V10.03 Esophagus

V10.04 Stomach

V10.05 Large intestine
AHA: 3Q, '99, 7; 1Q, '95, 4

V10.06 Rectum, rectosigmoid junction, and anus

V10.07 Liver

V10.09 Other
AHA: 4Q, '03, 111

√5th **V10.1 Trachea, bronchus, and lung**
History of conditions classifiable to 162

V10.11 Bronchus and lung

V10.12 Trachea

√5th **V10.2 Other respiratory and intrathoracic organs**
History of conditions classifiable to 160, 161, 163-165

V10.20 Respiratory organ, unspecified

V10.21 Larynx
AHA: 4Q, '03, 108, 110

V10.22 Nasal cavities, middle ear, and accessory sinuses

V10.29 Other

V10.3 Breast
History of conditions classifiable to 174 and 175
AHA: 2Q, '03, 5; 4Q, '01, 66; 4Q, '98, 65; 4Q, '97, 50; 1Q, '91, 16; 1Q, '90, 21

√5th **V10.4 Genital organs**
History of conditions classifiable to 179-187

V10.40 Female genital organ, unspecified ♀

V10.41 Cervix uteri ♀

V10.42 Other parts of uterus ♀

V10.43 Ovary ♀

V10.44 Other female genital organs ♀

V10.45 Male genital organ, unspecified ♂

V10.46 Prostate ♂

V10.47 Testis ♂

V10.48 Epididymis ♂

V10.49 Other male genital organs ♂

√5th **V10.5 Urinary organs**
History of conditions classifiable to 188 and 189

V10.50 Urinary organ, unspecified

V10.51 Bladder

V10.52 Kidney
> EXCLUDES *renal pelvis (V10.53)*

AHA: 2Q, '04, 4

V10.53 Renal pelvis
AHA: 4Q, '01, 55

V10.59 Other

√5th **V10.6 Leukemia**
Conditions classifiable to 204-208
> EXCLUDES *leukemia in remission (204-208)*

AHA: 2Q, '92, 13; 4Q, '91, 26; 4Q, '90, 3

V10.60 Leukemia, unspecified

V10.61 Lymphoid leukemia

V10.62 Myeloid leukemia

V10.63 Monocytic leukemia

V10.69 Other

√5th **V10.7 Other lymphatic and hematopoietic neoplasms**
Conditions classifiable to 200-203
> EXCLUDES *listed conditions in 200-203 in remission*

AHA: 4Q, '90, 3; M-J, '85, 18

V10.71 Lymphosarcoma and reticulosarcoma

V10.72 Hodgkin's disease

V10.79 Other

√5th **V10.8 Personal history of malignant neoplasm of other sites**
History of conditions classifiable to 170-173, 190-195

V10.81 Bone
AHA: 2Q, '03, 13

V10.82 Malignant melanoma of skin

V10.83 Other malignant neoplasm of skin

V10.84 Eye

V10.85 Brain
AHA: 1Q, '01, 6

V10.86 Other parts of nervous system
> EXCLUDES *peripheral sympathetic, and parasympa-thetic nerves (V10.89)*

V10.87 Thyroid

V10.88 Other endocrine glands and related structures

V10.89 Other

V10.9 Unspecified personal history of malignant neoplasm

√4th **V11 Personal history of mental disorder**

V11.0 Schizophrenia
> EXCLUDES *that in remission (295.0-295.9 with fifth-digit 5)*

V11.1 Affective disorders
Personal history of manic-depressive psychosis
> EXCLUDES *that in remission (296.0-296.6 with fifth-digit 5, 6)*

V11.2 Neurosis

V11.3 Alcoholism

V11.8 Other mental disorders

V11.9 Unspecified mental disorder

√4th **V12 Personal history of certain other diseases**
AHA: 3Q, '92, 11

√5th **V12.0 Infectious and parasitic diseases**
> EXCLUDES ▶ *personal history of infectious diseases specific to a body system◄*

V12.00 Unspecified infectious and parasitic disease

V12.01 Tuberculosis

V12.02 Poliomyelitis

V12.03 Malaria

V12.09 Other

V12.1 Nutritional deficiency

V12.2 Endocrine, metabolic, and immunity disorders
> EXCLUDES *history of allergy (V14.0-V14.9, V15.01-V15.09)*

V12.3 Diseases of blood and blood-forming organs

√5th **V12.4 Disorders of nervous system and sense organs**

V12.40 Unspecified disorder of nervous system and sense organs

V12.41 Benign neoplasm of the brain
AHA: 4Q, '97, 48

V12.42 Infections of the central nervous system
Encephalitis   Meningitis

V12.49 Other disorders of nervous system and sense organs
AHA: 4Q, '98, 59

√4th / √5th Additional Digit Required   RUG III Special Care Dx   RUG III Clinically Complex Dx   Hospice Non-cancer Dx   PDx Primary Dx use only   SDx Secondary Dx use only

√5th **V12.5 Diseases of circulatory system**
AHA: 4Q, '95, 61
> EXCLUDES   old myocardial infarction (412)
> postmyocardial infarction syndrome
> (411.0)

V12.50 Unspecified circulatory disease

V12.51 Venous thrombosis and embolism
Pulmonary embolism
AHA: 4Q, '03, 108; 1Q, '02, 15

V12.52 Thrombophlebitis

V12.59 Other
AHA: 4Q, '99, 4; 4Q, '98, 88; 4Q, '97, 37

√5th **V12.6 Diseases of respiratory system**
> EXCLUDES ▶ tuberculosis (V12.01)◀

● **V12.60 Unspecified disease of respiratory system**
● **V12.61 Pneumonia (recurrent)**
● **V12.69 Other diseases of respiratory system**

√5th **V12.7 Diseases of digestive system**
AHA: 1Q, '95, 3; 2Q, '89, 16

V12.70 Unspecified digestive disease

V12.71 Peptic ulcer disease

V12.72 Colonic polyps
AHA: 3Q, '02, 15

V12.79 Other

√4th **V13 Personal history of other diseases**

√5th **V13.0 Disorders of urinary system**

V13.00 Unspecified urinary disorder

V13.01 Urinary calculi

● **V13.02 Urinary (tract) infection**

● **V13.03 Nephrotic syndrome**

V13.09 Other

V13.1 Trophoblastic disease   ♀
> EXCLUDES   supervision during a current pregnancy
> (V23.1)

√5th **V13.2 Other genital system and obstetric disorders**
> EXCLUDES   supervision during a current pregnancy
> of a woman with poor obstetric
> history (V23.0-V23.9)
> habitual aborter (646.3)
> without current pregnancy (629.9)

V13.21 Personal history of pre-term labor   ♀
> EXCLUDES   current pregnancy with history
> of pre-term labor
> (V23.41)
AHA: 4Q, '02, 78

V13.29 Other genital system and obstetric   ♀
disorders

V13.3 Diseases of skin and subcutaneous tissue

V13.4 Arthritis

V13.5 Other musculoskeletal disorders

√5th **V13.6 Congenital malformations**
AHA: 4Q, '98, 63

V13.61 Hypospadias   SDx ♂

V13.69 Other congenital malformations
AHA: 1Q, '04, 16

V13.7 Perinatal problems
> EXCLUDES   low birth weight status (V21.30-
> V21.35)

V13.8 Other specified diseases

V13.9 Unspecified disease

√4th **V14 Personal history of allergy to medicinal agents**

V14.0 Penicillin   SDx

V14.1 Other antibiotic agent   SDx

V14.2 Sulfonamides   SDx

V14.3 Other anti-infective agent   SDx

V14.4 Anesthetic agent   SDx

V14.5 Narcotic agent   SDx

V14.6 Analgesic agent   SDx

V14.7 Serum or vaccine   SDx

V14.8 Other specified medicinal agents   SDx

V14.9 Unspecified medicinal agent   SDx

√4th **V15 Other personal history presenting hazards to health**

√5th **V15.0 Allergy, other than to medicinal agents**
> EXCLUDES   allergy to food substance used as base
> for medicinal agent (V14.0-V14.9)
AHA: 4Q, '00, 42, 49

V15.01 Allergy to peanuts   SDx

V15.02 Allergy to milk products   SDx
> EXCLUDES   lactose intolerance (271.3)
AHA: 1Q, '03, 12

V15.03 Allergy to eggs   SDx

V15.04 Allergy to seafood   SDx
Seafood (octopus) (squid) ink
Shellfish

V15.05 Allergy to other foods   SDx
Food additives
Nuts other than peanuts

V15.06 Allergy to insects   SDx
Bugs
Insect bites and stings
Spiders

V15.07 Allergy to latex   SDx
Latex sensitivity

V15.08 Allergy to radiographic dye   SDx
Contrast media used for diagnostic
x-ray procedures

V15.09 Other allergy, other than to medicinal   SDx
agents

V15.1 Surgery to heart and great vessels   SDx
> EXCLUDES   replacement by transplant or other
> means (V42.1-V42.2, V43.2-V43.4)
AHA: 1Q, '04, 16

V15.2 Surgery to other major organs   SDx
> EXCLUDES   replacement by transplant or other
> means (V42.0-V43.8)

V15.3 Irradiation   SDx
Previous exposure to therapeutic or other ionizing
radiation

√5th **V15.4 Psychological trauma**
> EXCLUDES   history of condition classifiable to 290-
> 316 (V11.0-V11.9)

V15.41 History of physical abuse   SDx
Rape
AHA: 3Q, '99, 15

V15.42 History of emotional abuse   SDx
Neglect
AHA: 3Q, '99, 15

V15.49 Other   SDx
AHA: 3Q, '99, 15

V15.5 Injury   SDx

V15.6 Poisoning   SDx

V15.7 Contraception
> EXCLUDES   current contraceptive management
> (V25.0-V25.4)
> presence of intrauterine contraceptive
> device as incidental finding (V45.5)

√5th **V15.8 Other specified personal history presenting hazards to health**
AHA: 4Q, '95, 62

V15.81 Noncompliance with medical treatment   SDx
AHA: 2Q, '03, 7; 2Q, '01, 11; 12, 13; 2Q '99, 17; 2Q, '97, 11;
1Q, '97, 12; 3Q, '96, 9

V15.82 History of tobacco use   SDx
> EXCLUDES   tobacco dependence (305.1)

V15.84 Exposure to asbestos   SDx

V15.85 Exposure to potentially hazardous   SDx
body fluids

V15.86 Exposure to lead   SDx

N Newborn Age: 0   P Pediatric Age: 0-17   M Maternity Age: 12-55   A Adult Age: 15-124 | Manifestation Code | ▶◀ Revised Text   ● New Code   ▲ Revised Code Title

282 — Volume 1 • October 2005   **2006 ICD•9•CM**

V15.87 History of extracorporeal membrane oxygenation [ECMO] `SDx`
AHA: 4Q, '03, 84

● V15.88 History of fall `SDx`
At risk for falling

V15.89 Other `SDx`
AHA: 1Q, '90, 21; N-D, '84, 12

V15.9 Unspecified personal history presenting hazards to health `SDx`

✓4ᵗʰ **V16 Family history of malignant neoplasm**

V16.0 Gastrointestinal tract
Family history of condition classifiable to 140-159
AHA: 1Q, '99, 4

V16.1 Trachea, bronchus, and lung
Family history of condition classifiable to 162

V16.2 Other respiratory and intrathoracic organs
Family history of condition classifiable to 160-161, 163-165

V16.3 Breast
Family history of condition classifiable to 174
AHA: 4Q, '04, 107; 2Q, '03, 4; 2Q, '00, 8; 1Q, '92, 11

✓5ᵗʰ V16.4 Genital organs
Family history of condition classifiable to 179-187
AHA: 4Q, '97, 48

V16.40 Genital organ, unspecified
V16.41 Ovary
V16.42 Prostate
V16.43 Testis
V16.49 Other

✓5ᵗʰ V16.5 Urinary organs
Family history of condition classifiable to 189
V16.51 Kidney
V16.59 Other

V16.6 Leukemia
Family history of condition classifiable to 204-208

V16.7 Other lymphatic and hematopoietic neoplasms
Family history of condition classifiable to 200-203

V16.8 Other specified malignant neoplasm
Family history of other condition classifiable to 140-199

V16.9 Unspecified malignant neoplasm

✓4ᵗʰ **V17 Family history of certain chronic disabling diseases**

V17.0 Psychiatric condition
EXCLUDES *family history of mental retardation (V18.4)*

V17.1 Stroke (cerebrovascular)

V17.2 Other neurological diseases
Epilepsy   Huntington's chorea

V17.3 Ischemic heart disease

V17.4 Other cardiovascular diseases
AHA: 1Q, '04, 6

V17.5 Asthma

V17.6 Other chronic respiratory conditions

V17.7 Arthritis

✓5ᵗʰ V17.8 Other musculoskeletal diseases
● V17.81 Osteoporosis
● V17.89 Other musculoskeletal diseases

✓4ᵗʰ **V18 Family history of certain other specific conditions**

V18.0 Diabetes mellitus
AHA: 1Q, '04, 8

V18.1 Other endocrine and metabolic diseases

V18.2 Anemia

V18.3 Other blood disorders

V18.4 Mental retardation

V18.5 Digestive disorders

✓5ᵗʰ V18.6 Kidney diseases
V18.61 Polycystic kidney
V18.69 Other kidney diseases

V18.7 Other genitourinary diseases

V18.8 Infectious and parasitic diseases

● V18.9 Genetic disease carrier

✓4ᵗʰ **V19 Family history of other conditions**

V19.0 Blindness or visual loss
V19.1 Other eye disorders
V19.2 Deafness or hearing loss
V19.3 Other ear disorders
V19.4 Skin conditions
V19.5 Congenital anomalies
V19.6 Allergic disorders
V19.7 Consanguinity
V19.8 Other condition

PERSONS ENCOUNTERING HEALTH SERVICES IN CIRCUMSTANCES RELATED TO REPRODUCTION AND DEVELOPMENT (V20-V29)

✓4ᵗʰ **V20 Health supervision of infant or child**

V20.0 Foundling `PDx` `P`

V20.1 Other healthy infant or child receiving care `PDx` `P`
Medical or nursing care supervision of healthy infant in cases of:
maternal illness, physical or psychiatric
socioeconomic adverse condition at home
too many children at home preventing or interfering with normal care
AHA: 1Q, '00, 25; 3Q, '89, 14

V20.2 Routine infant or child health check `PDx` `P`
Developmental testing of infant or child
Immunizations appropriate for age
Routine vision and hearing testing
Use additional code(s) to identify:
special screening examination(s) performed (V73.0-V82.9)
EXCLUDES *special screening for developmental handicaps (V79.3)*
AHA: 1Q, '04, 15

✓4ᵗʰ **V21 Constitutional states in development**

V21.0 Period of rapid growth in childhood `SDx`
V21.1 Puberty `SDx`
V21.2 Other adolescence `SDx`

✓5ᵗʰ V21.3 Low birth weight status
EXCLUDES *history of perinatal problems*
AHA: 4Q, '00, 51

V21.30 Low birth weight status, unspecified `SDx`
V21.31 Low birth weight status, less than 500 grams `SDx`
V21.32 Low birth weight status, 500-999 grams `SDx`
V21.33 Low birth weight status, 1000-1499 grams `SDx`
V21.34 Low birth weight status, 1500-1999 grams `SDx`
V21.35 Low birth weight status, 2000-2500 grams `SDx`

V21.8 Other specified constitutional states in development `SDx`

V21.9 Unspecified constitutional state in development `SDx`

✓4ᵗʰ **V22 Normal pregnancy**
EXCLUDES *pregnancy examination or test, pregnancy unconfirmed (V72.40)*

V22.0 Supervision of normal first pregnancy `PDx` ♀
AHA: 3Q, '99, 16

V22.1 Supervision of other normal pregnancy `PDx` ♀
AHA: 3Q, '99, 16

V22.2 Pregnant state, incidental `SDx` ♀
Pregnant state NOS

✓4ᵗʰ **V23 Supervision of high-risk pregnancy**
AHA: 1Q, 90, 10

V23.0 Pregnancy with history of infertility `M` ♀

✓4ᵗʰ
✓5ᵗʰ Additional Digit Required   RUG III Special Care Dx   RUG III Clinically Complex Dx   Hospice Non-cancer Dx   `PDx` Primary Dx use only   `SDx` Secondary Dx use only

V23.1 **Pregnancy with history of trophoblastic disease**   Ⓜ ♀
Pregnancy with history of:
hydatidiform mole vesicular mole
EXCLUDES   *that without current pregnancy (V13.1)*

V23.2 **Pregnancy with history of abortion**   Ⓜ ♀
Pregnancy with history of conditions classifiable to 634-638
EXCLUDES   *habitual aborter:*
care during pregnancy (646.3)
that without current pregnancy (629.9)

V23.3 **Grand multiparity**   Ⓜ ♀
EXCLUDES   *care in relation to labor and delivery (659.4)*
that without current pregnancy (V61.5)

✓5ᵗʰ V23.4 **Pregnancy with other poor obstetric history**
Pregnancy with history of other conditions classifiable to 630-676

V23.41 **Pregnancy with history of pre-term labor**   Ⓜ ♀
AHA: 4Q, '02, 79

V23.49 **Pregnancy with other poor obstetric history**   Ⓜ ♀

V23.5 **Pregnancy with other poor reproductive history**   Ⓜ ♀
Pregnancy with history of stillbirth or neonatal death

V23.7 **Insufficient prenatal care**   Ⓜ ♀
History of little or no prenatal care

✓5ᵗʰ V23.8 **Other high-risk pregnancy**
AHA: 4Q, '98, 56, 63

V23.81 **Elderly primigravida**   Ⓜ ♀
First pregnancy in a woman who will be 35 years of age or older at expected date of delivery
EXCLUDES   *elderly primigravida complicating pregnancy (659.5)*

V23.82 **Elderly multigravida**   Ⓜ ♀
Second or more pregnancy in a woman who will be 35 years of age or older at expected date of delivery
EXCLUDES   *elderly multigravida complicating pregnancy (659.6)*

V23.83 **Young primigravida**   Ⓜ ♀
First pregnancy in a female less than 16 years old at expected date of delivery
EXCLUDES   *young primigravida complicating pregnancy (659.8)*

V23.84 **Young multigravida**   Ⓜ ♀
Second or more pregnancy in a female less than 16 years old at expected date of delivery
EXCLUDES   *young multigravida complicating pregnancy (659.8)*

V23.89 **Other high-risk pregnancy**   Ⓜ ♀

V23.9 **Unspecified high-risk pregnancy**   Ⓜ ♀

✓4ᵗʰ **V24 Postpartum care and examination**

V24.0 **Immediately after delivery**   PDx Ⓜ ♀
Care and observation in uncomplicated cases

V24.1 **Lactating mother**   PDx ♀
Supervision of lactation

V24.2 **Routine postpartum follow-up**   PDx ♀   ●

✓4ᵗʰ **V25 Encounter for contraceptive management**
AHA: 4Q, '92, 24

✓5ᵗʰ V25.0 **General counseling and advice**

V25.01 **Prescription of oral contraceptives**   ♀

V25.02 **Initiation of other contraceptive measures**
Fitting of diaphragm
Prescription of foams, creams, or other agents
AHA: 3Q, '97, 7

V25.03 **Encounter for emergency contraceptive counseling and prescription**
Encounter for postcoital contraceptive counseling and prescription
AHA: 4Q, '03, 84

V25.09 **Other**
Family planning advice

V25.1 **Insertion of intrauterine contraceptive device**   ♀

V25.2 **Sterilization**
Admission for interruption of fallopian tubes or vas deferens

V25.3 **Menstrual extraction**   ♀
Menstrual regulation

✓5ᵗʰ V25.4 **Surveillance of previously prescribed contraceptive methods**
Checking, reinsertion, or removal of contraceptive device
Repeat prescription for contraceptive method
Routine examination in connection with contraceptive maintenance
EXCLUDES   *presence of intrauterine contraceptive device as incidental finding (V45.5)*

V25.40 **Contraceptive surveillance, unspecified**

V25.41 **Contraceptive pill**   ♀

V25.42 **Intrauterine contraceptive device**   ♀
Checking, reinsertion, or removal of intrauterine device

V25.43 **Implantable subdermal contraceptive**   ♀

V25.49 **Other contraceptive method**
AHA: 3Q, '97, 7

V25.5 **Insertion of implantable subdermal contraceptive**   ♀
AHA: 3Q, '92, 9

V25.8 **Other specified contraceptive management**
Postvasectomy sperm count
EXCLUDES   *sperm count following sterilization reversal (V26.22)*
sperm count for fertility testing (V26.21)
AHA: 3Q, '96, 9

V25.9 **Unspecified contraceptive management**

✓4ᵗʰ **V26 Procreative management**

V26.0 **Tuboplasty or vasoplasty after previous sterilization**
AHA: 2Q, '95, 10

V26.1 **Artificial insemination**   ♀

✓5ᵗʰ V26.2 **Investigation and testing**
EXCLUDES   *postvasectomy sperm count (V25.8)*
AHA: 4Q, '00, 56

V26.21 **Fertility testing**
Fallopian insufflation
Sperm count for fertility testing
EXCLUDES   *genetic counseling and testing ▶(V26.31-V26.33)◀*

V26.22 **Aftercare following sterilization reversal**
Fallopian insufflation following sterilization reversal
Sperm count following sterilization reversal

V26.29 **Other investigation and testing**
AHA: 2Q, '96, 9; N-D, '85, 15

✓5ᵗʰ V26.3 **Genetic counseling and testing**
EXCLUDES   *fertility testing (V26.21)*

V26.31 **Testing for genetic disease carrier status**   ●

V26.32 **Other genetic testing**   ●

V26.33 **Genetic counseling**   ●

V26.4 **General counseling and advice**

✓5ᵗʰ V26.5 **Sterilization status**

V26.51 **Tubal ligation status**   SDx ♀
EXCLUDES   *infertility not due to previous tubal ligation (628.0-628.9)*

V26.52 **Vasectomy status**   SDx ♂

Ⓝ Newborn Age: 0   Ⓟ Pediatric Age: 0-17   Ⓜ Maternity Age: 12-55   Ⓐ Adult Age: 15-124   Manifestation Code   ▶◀ Revised Text   ● New Code   ▲ Revised Code Title

284 — Volume 1 • October 2005   *2006 ICD•9•CM*

V26.8   Other specified procreative management

V26.9   Unspecified procreative management

✓4th **V27 Outcome of delivery**

> Note: This category is intended for the coding of the outcome of delivery on the mother's record.

AHA: 2Q, '91, 16

V27.0   Single liveborn   SDx M♀

> AHA: 2Q, '03, 9; 2Q, '02, 10; 1Q, '01, 10; 3Q, '00, 5; 4Q, '98, 77; 4Q, '95, 59; 1Q, '92, 9

V27.1   Single stillborn   SDx M♀

V27.2   Twins, both liveborn   SDx M♀

V27.3   Twins, one liveborn and one stillborn   SDx M♀

V27.4   Twins, both stillborn   SDx M♀

V27.5   Other multiple birth, all liveborn   SDx M♀

V27.6   Other multiple birth, some liveborn   SDx M♀

V27.7   Other multiple birth, all stillborn   SDx M♀

V27.9   Unspecified outcome of delivery   SDx M♀

> Single birth } outcome to infant
> Multiple birth } unspecified

✓4th **V28 Antenatal screening**

> EXCLUDES   abnormal findings on screening — code to findings
> routine prenatal care (V22.0-V23.9)

AHA: 1Q, '04, 11

V28.0   Screening for chromosomal anomalies by amniocentesis   M♀

V28.1   Screening for raised alpha-fetoprotein levels in amniotic fluid   M♀

V28.2   Other screening based on amniocentesis   M♀

V28.3   Screening for malformation using ultrasonics   ♀

V28.4   Screening for fetal growth retardation using ultrasonics   ♀

V28.5   Screening for isoimmunization   ♀

V28.6   Screening for Streptococcus B   M♀

> AHA: 4Q, '97, 46

V28.8   Other specified antenatal screening   ♀

> AHA: 3Q, '99, 16

V28.9   Unspecified antenatal screening   ♀

✓4th **V29 Observation and evaluation of newborns and infants for suspected condition not found**

> Note: This category is to be used for newborns, within the neonatal period, (the first 28 days of life) who are suspected of having an abnormal condition resulting from exposure from the mother or the birth process, but without signs or symptoms, and, which after examination and observation, is found not to exist.

AHA: 1Q, '00, 25; 4Q, '94, 47; 1Q, '94, 9; 4Q, '92, 21

[1] **V29.0**   Observation for suspected infectious condition   PDx N

> AHA: 1Q, '01, 10

[1] **V29.1**   Observation for suspected neurological condition   PDx N

[1] **V29.2**   Observation for suspected respiratory condition   PDx N

[1] **V29.3**   Observation for suspected genetic or metabolic condition   PDx N

> AHA: 4Q, '98, 59, 68

[1] **V29.8**   Observation for other specified suspected condition   PDx N

> AHA: 2Q, '03, 15

[1] **V29.9**   Observation for unspecified suspected condition   PDx N

> AHA: 1Q, '02, 6

LIVEBORN INFANTS ACCORDING TO TYPE OF BIRTH (V30-V39)

> Note: These categories are intended for the coding of liveborn infants who are consuming health care [e.g., crib or bassinet occupancy].

> The following fourth-digit subdivisions are for use with categories V30-V39:

> ✓5th   **0**   Born in hospital   N
>   **1**   Born before admission to hospital   N
>   **2**   Born outside hospital and not hospitalized

> The following two fifth-digits are for use with the fourth-digit .0, Born in hospital:

>   **0**   delivered without mention of cesarean delivery
>   **1**   delivered by cesarean delivery

AHA: 1Q, '01, 10

✓4th **V30 Single liveborn**   PDx

> AHA: 2Q, '03, 9; 4Q, '98, 46, 59; 1Q, '94, 9; For code V30.00: 1Q, '04, 8, 16; 1Q, '03, 68

✓4th **V31 Twin, mate liveborn**   PDx

> AHA: 3Q, '92, 10

✓4th **V32 Twin, mate stillborn**   PDx

✓4th **V33 Twin, unspecified**   PDx

✓4th **V34 Other multiple, mates all liveborn**   PDx

✓4th **V35 Other multiple, mates all stillborn**   PDx

✓4th **V36 Other multiple, mates live- and stillborn**   PDx

✓4th **V37 Other multiple, unspecified**   PDx

✓4th **V39 Unspecified**   PDx

PERSONS WITH A CONDITION INFLUENCING THEIR HEALTH STATUS (V40-V49)

> Note: These categories are intended for use when these conditions are recorded as "diagnoses" or "problems."

✓4th **V40 Mental and behavioral problems**

   V40.0   Problems with learning

   V40.1   Problems with communication [including speech]

   V40.2   Other mental problems

   V40.3   Other behavioral problems

   V40.9   Unspecified mental or behavioral problem

✓4th **V41 Problems with special senses and other special functions**

   V41.0   Problems with sight

   V41.1   Other eye problems

   V41.2   Problems with hearing

   V41.3   Other ear problems

   V41.4   Problems with voice production

   V41.5   Problems with smell and taste

   V41.6   Problems with swallowing and mastication

   V41.7   Problems with sexual function

> EXCLUDES   marital problems (V61.10)
> psychosexual disorders (302.0-302.9)

   V41.8   Other problems with special functions

   V41.9   Unspecified problem with special functions

✓4th **V42 Organ or tissue replaced by transplant**

> INCLUDES   homologous or heterologous (animal) (human) transplant organ status

AHA: 3Q, '98, 3, 4

   V42.0   Kidney   SDx

> AHA: 1Q, '03, 10; 3Q, '01, 12

   V42.1   Heart   SDx

> AHA: 3Q, '03, 16; 3Q, '01, 13

   V42.2   Heart valve   SDx

   V42.3   Skin   SDx

   V42.4   Bone   SDx

   V42.5   Cornea   SDx

   V42.6   Lung   SDx

   V42.7   Liver   SDx

✓5th   **V42.8**   Other specified organ or tissue

> AHA: 4Q, '98, 64; 4Q, '97, 49

---

[1] A code from the V30–V39 series may be sequenced before the V29 on the newborn record.

✓4th / ✓5th Additional Digit Required   RUG III Special Care Dx   RUG III Clinically Complex Dx   Hospice Non-cancer Dx   PDx Primary Dx use only   SDx Secondary Dx use only

V42.81 **Bone marrow** `SDx`

V42.82 **Peripheral stem cells** `SDx`

V42.83 **Pancreas** `SDx`
  AHA: 1Q, '03, 10; 2Q, '01, 16

V42.84 **Intestines** `SDx`
  AHA: 4Q, '00, 48, 50

V42.89 **Other** `SDx`

V42.9 **Unspecified organ or tissue** `SDx`

√4ᵗʰ V43 **Organ or tissue replaced by other means**
  `INCLUDES` organ or tissue assisted by other means
    replacement of organ by:
      artificial device
      mechanical device
      prosthesis
  `EXCLUDES` *cardiac pacemaker in situ (V45.01)*
    fitting and adjustment of prosthetic device
      (V52.0-V52.9)
    renal dialysis status (V45.1)

V43.0 **Eye globe** `SDx`

V43.1 **Lens** `SDx`
  Pseudophakos
  AHA: 4Q, '98, 65

√5ᵗʰ V43.2 **Heart**
  AHA: 4Q, '03, 85

V43.21 **Heart assist device** `SDx`

V43.22 **Fully implantable artificial heart**

V43.3 **Heart valve** `SDx`
  AHA: 3Q, '02, 13, 14

V43.4 **Blood vessel** `SDx`

V43.5 **Bladder** `SDx`

√5ᵗʰ V43.6 **Joint**

V43.60 **Unspecified joint** `SDx`

V43.61 **Shoulder** `SDx`

V43.62 **Elbow** `SDx`

V43.63 **Wrist** `SDx`

V43.64 **Hip** `SDx`
  AHA: 2Q, '04, 15

V43.65 **Knee** `SDx`

V43.66 **Ankle** `SDx`

V43.69 **Other** `SDx`

V43.7 **Limb** `SDx`

√5ᵗʰ V43.8 **Other organ or tissue**

V43.81 **Larynx** `SDx`

V43.82 **Breast** `SDx`

V43.83 **Artificial skin** `SDx`

V43.89 **Other** `SDx`

√4ᵗʰ V44 **Artificial opening status**
  `EXCLUDES` *artificial openings requiring attention or*
    management (V55.0-V55.9)

V44.0 **Tracheostomy** `SDx`
  AHA: 4Q, '03, 103, 107, 111; 1Q, '01, 6

V44.1 **Gastrostomy** `SDx`
  AHA: 4Q, '03, 103, 107-108, 110; 1Q, '01, 12; 3Q, '97, 12; 1Q, '93, 26

V44.2 **Ileostomy** `SDx`

V44.3 **Colostomy** `SDx`
  AHA: 4Q, '03, 110

V44.4 **Other artificial opening of gastrointestinal** `SDx`
  tract

√5ᵗʰ V44.5 **Cystostomy**

V44.50 **Cystostomy, unspecified** `SDx`

V44.51 **Cutaneous-vesicostomy** `SDx`

V44.52 **Appendico-vesicostomy** `SDx`

V44.59 **Other cystostomy** `SDx`

V44.6 **Other artificial opening of urinary tract** `SDx`
  Nephrostomy   Urethrostomy
  Ureterostomy

V44.7 **Artificial vagina** `SDx`

V44.8 **Other artificial opening status** `SDx`

V44.9 **Unspecified artificial opening status** `SDx`

√4ᵗʰ V45 **Other postprocedural states**
  `EXCLUDES` *aftercare management (V51-V58.9)*
    malfunction or other complication — code to
      condition
  AHA: 4Q, '03, 85

√5ᵗʰ V45.0 **Cardiac device in situ**
  `EXCLUDES` *artificial heart (V43.22)*
    heart assist device (V43.21)

V45.00 **Unspecified cardiac device** `SDx`

V45.01 **Cardiac pacemaker** `SDx`

V45.02 **Automatic implantable cardiac** `SDx`
  defibrillator

V45.09 **Other specified cardiac device** `SDx`
  Carotid sinus pacemaker in situ

V45.1 **Renal dialysis status** `SDx`
  ►Hemodialysis status◄
  Patient requiring intermittent renal dialysis
  ►Peritoneal dialysis status◄
  Presence of arterial-venous shunt (for dialysis)
  `EXCLUDES` *admission for dialysis treatment or*
    session (V56.0)
  AHA: 1Q, '04, 22-23; 2Q, '03, 7; 2Q, '01, 12, 13

V45.2 **Presence of cerebrospinal fluid drainage** `SDx`
  device
  Cerebral ventricle (communicating) shunt, valve, or
    device in situ
  `EXCLUDES` *malfunction (996.2)*
  AHA: 4Q, '03, 106

V45.3 **Intestinal bypass or anastomosis status** `SDx`

V45.4 **Arthrodesis status** `SDx`
  AHA: N-D, '84, 18

√5ᵗʰ V45.5 **Presence of contraceptive device**
  `EXCLUDES` *checking, reinsertion, or removal of*
    device (V25.42)
    complication from device (996.32)
    insertion of device (V25.1)

V45.51 **Intrauterine contraceptive device** `SDx` ♀

V45.52 **Subdermal contraceptive implant** `SDx`

V45.59 **Other** `SDx`

√5ᵗʰ V45.6 **States following surgery of eye and adnexa**
  Cataract extraction
  Filtering bleb   } state following eye
  Surgical eyelid adhesion }   surgery
  `EXCLUDES` *aphakia (379.31)*
    artificial eye globe (V43.0)
  AHA: 4Q, '98, 65; 4Q, '97, 49

V45.61 **Cataract extraction status** `SDx`
  Use additional code for associated
    artificial lens status (V43.1)

V45.69 **Other states following surgery of** `SDx`
  eye and adnexa
  AHA: 2Q, '01, 16; 1Q, '98, 10; 4Q, '97, 19

√5ᵗʰ V45.7 **Acquired absence of organ**
  AHA: 4Q, '01, 66; 4Q, '98, 65; 4Q, '97, 50

V45.71 **Acquired absence of breast**
  AHA: 4Q, '97, 50

V45.72 **Acquired absence of intestine (large) (small)**

V45.73 **Acquired absence of kidney**

V45.74 **Other parts of urinary tract**
  Bladder
  AHA: 4Q, '00, 51

V45.75 **Stomach**
  AHA: 4Q, '00, 51

V45.76 **Lung**
  AHA: 4Q, '00, 51

V45.77 **Genital organs**
  `EXCLUDES` *female genital mutilation*
    status (629.20-629.23)
  AHA: 1Q, '03, 13, 14; 4Q, '00, 51

N Newborn Age: 0 ⬛ P Pediatric Age: 0-17 ⬛ M Maternity Age: 12-55 ⬛ A Adult Age: 15-124 ⬛ Manifestation Code ⬛ ►◄ Revised Text ⬛ ● New Code ⬛ ▲ Revised Code Title

V45.78 Eye
AHA: 4Q, '00, 51

V45.79 Other acquired absence of organ
AHA: 4Q, '00, 51

√5ᵗʰ **V45.8 Other postprocedural status**

V45.81 Aortocoronary bypass status `SDx`
AHA: 4Q, '03, 105; 3Q, '01, 15; 3Q, '97, 16

V45.82 Percutaneous transluminal coronary angioplasty status `SDx`

V45.83 Breast implant removal status `SDx`
AHA: 4Q, '95, 55

V45.84 Dental restoration status `SDx`
Dental crowns status
Dental fillings status
AHA: 4Q, '01, 54

V45.85 Insulin pump status `SDx`

V45.89 Other `SDx`
Presence of neuropacemaker or other electronic device
`EXCLUDES` artificial heart valve in situ (V43.3)
vascular prosthesis in situ (V43.4)

√4ᵗʰ **V46 Other dependence on machines**

V46.0 Aspirator `SDx`

▲ √5ᵗʰ **V46.1 Respirator [Ventilator]**
Iron lung
AHA: 4Q, '03, 103; 1Q, '01, 12; J-F, '87, 7 3

V46.11 Dependence on respirator, status `SDx`
AHA: 4Q, '04, 100

V46.12 Encounter for respirator dependence during power failure `PDx`
AHA: 4Q, '04, 100

● **V46.13 Encounter for weaning from respirator [ventilator]**

● **V46.14 Mechanical complication of respirator [ventilator]**
Mechanical failure of respirator [ventilator]

V46.2 Supplemental oxygen `SDx`
Long-term oxygen therapy
AHA: 4Q, '03, 108; 4Q, '02, 79

V46.8 Other enabling machines `SDx`
Hyperbaric chamber
Possum [Patient-Operated-Selector-Mechanism]
`EXCLUDES` cardiac pacemaker (V45.0)
kidney dialysis machine (V45.1)

V46.9 Unspecified machine dependence `SDx`

√4ᵗʰ **V47 Other problems with internal organs**

V47.0 Deficiencies of internal organs

V47.1 Mechanical and motor problems with internal organs

V47.2 Other cardiorespiratory problems
Cardiovascular exercise intolerance with pain (with):
at rest
less than ordinary activity
ordinary activity

V47.3 Other digestive problems

V47.4 Other urinary problems

V47.5 Other genital problems

V47.9 Unspecified

√4ᵗʰ **V48 Problems with head, neck, and trunk**

V48.0 Deficiencies of head
`EXCLUDES` deficiencies of ears, eyelids, and nose (V48.8)

V48.1 Deficiencies of neck and trunk

V48.2 Mechanical and motor problems with head

V48.3 Mechanical and motor problems with neck and trunk

V48.4 Sensory problem with head

V48.5 Sensory problem with neck and trunk

V48.6 Disfigurements of head

V48.7 Disfigurements of neck and trunk

V48.8 Other problems with head, neck, and trunk

V48.9 Unspecified problem with head, neck, or trunk

√4ᵗʰ **V49 Other conditions influencing health status**

V49.0 Deficiencies of limbs

V49.1 Mechanical problems with limbs

V49.2 Motor problems with limbs

V49.3 Sensory problems with limbs

V49.4 Disfigurements of limbs

V49.5 Other problems of limbs

√5ᵗʰ **V49.6 Upper limb amputation status**
AHA: 4Q, '98, 42; 4Q, '94, 39

V49.60 Unspecified level `SDx`

V49.61 Thumb `SDx`

V49.62 Other finger(s) `SDx`

V49.63 Hand `SDx`

V49.64 Wrist `SDx`
Disarticulation of wrist

V49.65 Below elbow `SDx`

V49.66 Above elbow `SDx`
Disarticulation of elbow

V49.67 Shoulder `SDx`
Disarticulation of shoulder

√5ᵗʰ **V49.7 Lower limb amputation status**
AHA: 4Q, '98, 42; 4Q, '94, 39

V49.70 Unspecified level `SDx`

V49.71 Great toe `SDx`

V49.72 Other toe(s) `SDx`

V49.73 Foot `SDx`

V49.74 Ankle `SDx`
Disarticulation of ankle

V49.75 Below knee `SDx`

V49.76 Above knee `SDx`
Disarticulation of knee

V49.77 Hip `SDx`
Disarticulation of hip

√5ᵗʰ **V49.8 Other specified conditions influencing health status**
AHA: 4Q, '00, 51

V49.81 Asymptomatic postmenopausal status (age-related) (natural) `A` ♀
`EXCLUDES` menopausal and premenopausal disorder (627.0-627.9)
postsurgical menopause (256.2)
premature menopause (256.31)
symptomatic menopause (627.0-627.9)
AHA: 4Q, '02, 79; 4Q, '00, 54

V49.82 Dental sealant status `SDx`
AHA: 4Q, '01, 54

V49.83 Awaiting organ transplant status `SDx`

● **V49.84 Bed confinement status**

V49.89 Other specified conditions influencing health status

V49.9 Unspecified

PERSONS ENCOUNTERING HEALTH SERVICES FOR SPECIFIC PROCEDURES AND AFTERCARE (V50-V59)

Note: Categories V51-V58 are intended for use to indicate a reason for care in patients who may have already been treated for some disease or injury not now present, or who are receiving care to consolidate the treatment, to deal with residual states, or to prevent recurrence.
`EXCLUDES` follow-up examination for medical surveillance following treatment (V67.0-V67.9)

√4ᵗʰ **V50 Elective surgery for purposes other than remedying health states**

V50.0 Hair transplant

√4ᵗʰ / √5ᵗʰ Additional Digit Required   `RUG III Special Care Dx`   `RUG III Clinically Complex Dx`   `Hospice Non-cancer Dx`   `PDx` Primary Dx use only   `SDx` Secondary Dx use only

2006 ICD·9·CM   October 2005 • Volume 1 — 287

V50.1 Other plastic surgery for unacceptable cosmetic appearance
Breast augmentation or reduction
Face-lift
> EXCLUDES   *plastic surgery following healed injury or operation (V51)*

V50.2 Routine or ritual circumcision ♂
Circumcision in the absence of significant medical indication

V50.3 Ear piercing

✓5th **V50.4 Prophylactic organ removal**
> EXCLUDES   *organ donations (V59.0-V59.9)*
> *therapeutic organ removal — code to condition*

AHA: 4Q, '94, 44

V50.41 Breast
AHA: 4Q, '04, 107

V50.42 Ovary ♀

V50.49 Other

V50.8 Other

V50.9 Unspecified

V51 Aftercare involving the use of plastic surgery
Plastic surgery following healed injury or operation
> EXCLUDES   *cosmetic plastic surgery (V50.1)*
> *plastic surgery as treatment for current injury — code to condition*
> *repair of scarred tissue — code to scar*

✓4th **V52 Fitting and adjustment of prosthetic device and implant**
> INCLUDES   removal of device
> EXCLUDES   *malfunction or complication of prosthetic device (996.0-996.7)*
> *status only, without need for care (V43.0-V43.8)*

AHA: 4Q, '95, 55 ; 1Q, '90, 7

V52.0 Artificial arm (complete) (partial)

V52.1 Artificial leg (complete) (partial)

V52.2 Artificial eye

V52.3 Dental prosthetic device

V52.4 Breast prosthesis and implant ♀
> EXCLUDES   *admission for implant insertion (V50.1)*
AHA: 4Q, '95, 80, 81

V52.8 Other specified prosthetic device

V52.9 Unspecified prosthetic device

✓4th **V53 Fitting and adjustment of other device**
> INCLUDES   removal of device
> replacement of device
> EXCLUDES   *status only, without need for care (V45.0-V45.8)*

✓5th **V53.0 Devices related to nervous system and special senses**
AHA: 4Q, '98, 66; 4Q, '97, 51

V53.01 Fitting and adjustment of cerebral ventricular (communicating) shunt
AHA: 4Q, '97, 51

V53.02 Neuropacemaker (brain) (peripheral nerve) (spinal cord)

V53.09 Fitting and adjustment of other devices related to nervous system and special senses
Auditory substitution device
Visual substitution device
AHA: 2Q '99, 4

V53.1 Spectacles and contact lenses

V53.2 Hearing aid

✓5th **V53.3 Cardiac device**
Reprogramming
AHA: 3Q, '92, 3; 1Q, '90, 7; M-J, '87, 8 ; N-D, '84, 18

V53.31 Cardiac pacemaker
> EXCLUDES   *mechanical complication of cardiac pacemaker (996.01)*
AHA: 1Q, '02, 3

V53.32 Automatic implantable cardiac defibrillator

V53.39 Other cardiac device

V53.4 Orthodontic devices

V53.5 Other intestinal appliance
> EXCLUDES   *colostomy (V55.3)*
> *ileostomy (V55.2)*
> *other artificial opening of digestive tract (V55.4)*

V53.6 Urinary devices
Urinary catheter
> EXCLUDES   *cystostomy (V55.5)*
> *nephrostomy (V55.6)*
> *ureterostomy (V55.6)*
> *urethrostomy (V55.6)*

V53.7 Orthopedic devices
Orthopedic: Orthopedic:
  brace   corset
  cast   shoes
> EXCLUDES   *other orthopedic aftercare (V54)*

V53.8 Wheelchair

✓5th **V53.9 Other and unspecified device**
AHA: 2Q, '03, 6

V53.90 Unspecified device

V53.91 Fitting and adjustment of insulin pump
Insulin pump titration

V53.99 Other device

✓4th **V54 Other orthopedic aftercare**
> EXCLUDES   *fitting and adjustment of orthopedic devices (V53.7)*
> *malfunction of internal orthopedic device ▶(996.40-996.49)◄*
> *other complication of nonmechanical nature (996.60-996.79)*

AHA: 3Q, '95, 3

✓5th **V54.0 Aftercare involving internal fixation device**
> EXCLUDES   *malfunction of internal orthopedic device ▶(996.40-996.49)◄*
> *other complication of nonmechanical nature (996.60-996.79)*
> *removal of external fixation device (V54.89)*

AHA: 4Q, '03, 87

V54.01 Encounter for removal of internal fixation device

V54.02 Encounter for lengthening/adjustment of growth rod

V54.09 Other aftercare involving internal fixation device

✓5th **V54.1 Aftercare for healing traumatic fracture**
AHA: 4Q, '02, 80

V54.10 Aftercare for healing traumatic fracture of arm, unspecified

V54.11 Aftercare for healing traumatic fracture of upper arm

V54.12 Aftercare for healing traumatic fracture of lower arm

V54.13 Aftercare for healing traumatic fracture of hip
AHA: 4Q, '03, 103, 105; 2Q, '03, 16

V54.14 Aftercare for healing traumatic fracture of leg, unspecified

V54.15 Aftercare for healing traumatic fracture of upper leg
> EXCLUDES   *aftercare for healing traumatic fracture of hip (V54.13)*

V54.16 Aftercare for healing traumatic fracture of lower leg

V54.17 Aftercare for healing traumatic fracture of vertebrae

V54.19 Aftercare for healing traumatic fracture of other bone
AHA: ▶1Q, '05, 13◄ 4Q, '02, 80

N Newborn Age: 0   P Pediatric Age: 0-17   M Maternity Age: 12-55   A Adult Age: 15-124   Manifestation Code   ▶◄ Revised Text   ● New Code   ▲ Revised Code Title

288 — Volume 1 • October 2005

2006 ICD•9•CM

√5ᵗʰ **V54.2 Aftercare for healing pathologic fracture**
AHA: 4Q, '02, 80

V54.20 Aftercare for healing pathologic fracture of arm, unspecified

V54.21 Aftercare for healing pathologic fracture of upper arm

V54.22 Aftercare for healing pathologic fracture of lower arm

V54.23 Aftercare for healing pathologic fracture of hip

V54.24 Aftercare for healing pathologic fracture of leg, unspecified

V54.25 Aftercare for healing pathologic fracture of upper leg
> EXCLUDES   *aftercare for healing pathologic fracture of hip (V54.23)*

V54.26 Aftercare for healing pathologic fracture of lower leg

V54.27 Aftercare for healing pathologic fracture of vertebrae
AHA: 4Q, '03, 108

V54.29 Aftercare for healing pathologic fracture of other bone
AHA: 4Q, '02, 80

√5ᵗʰ **V54.8 Other orthopedic aftercare**
AHA: 3Q, '01, 19; 4Q, '99, 5

V54.81 Aftercare following joint replacement
Use additional code to identify joint replacement site (V43.60-V43.69)
AHA: 2Q, '04, 15; 4Q, '02, 80

V54.89 Other orthopedic aftercare
Aftercare for healing fracture NOS

V54.9 Unspecified orthopedic aftercare

√4ᵗʰ **V55 Attention to artificial openings**
> INCLUDES   adjustment or repositioning of catheter
> closure
> passage of sounds or bougies
> reforming
> removal or replacement of catheter
> toilet or cleansing
> EXCLUDES   *complications of external stoma (519.00-519.09, 569.60-569.69, 997.4, 997.5)*
> *status only, without need for care (V44.0-V44.9)*

V55.0 Tracheostomy

V55.1 Gastrostomy
AHA: 4Q, '99, 9; 3Q, '97, 7, 8; 1Q, '96, 14; 3Q, '95, 13

V55.2 Ileostomy

V55.3 Colostomy
AHA: 3Q, '97, 9

V55.4 Other artificial opening of digestive tract
AHA: 1Q, '03, 10

V55.5 Cystostomy

V55.6 Other artificial opening of urinary tract
Nephrostomy   Urethrostomy
Ureterostomy

V55.7 Artificial vagina

V55.8 Other specified artificial opening

V55.9 Unspecified artificial opening

√4ᵗʰ **V56 Encounter for dialysis and dialysis catheter care**
Use additional code to identify the associated condition
> EXCLUDES   *dialysis preparation — code to condition*
AHA: 4Q, '98, 66; 1Q, '93, 29

V56.0 Extracorporeal dialysis   PDx
Dialysis (renal) NOS
> EXCLUDES   *dialysis status (V45.1)*
AHA: 1Q, '04, 23; 4Q, '00, 40; 3Q, '98, 6; 2Q, '98, 20

V56.1 Fitting and adjustment of extracorporeal dialysis catheter
Removal or replacement of catheter
Toilet or cleansing
Use additional code for any concurrent extracorporeal dialysis (V56.0)
AHA: 2Q, '98, 20

V56.2 Fitting and adjustment of peritoneal dialysis catheter
Use additional code for any concurrent peritoneal dialysis (V56.8)
AHA: 4Q, '98, 55

√5ᵗʰ **V56.3 Encounter for adequacy testing for dialysis**
AHA: 4Q, '00, 55

V56.31 Encounter for adequacy testing for hemodialysis

V56.32 Encounter for adequacy testing for peritoneal dialysis
Peritoneal equilibration test

V56.8 Other dialysis
Peritoneal dialysis
AHA: 4Q, '98, 55

√4ᵗʰ **V57 Care involving use of rehabilitation procedures**
Use additional code to identify underlying condition
AHA: 1Q, '02, 19; 3Q, '97, 12; 1Q, '90, 6; S-O, '86, 3

V57.0 Breathing exercises

V57.1 Other physical therapy
Therapeutic and remedial exercises, except breathing
AHA: 2Q, '04, 15; 4Q, '02, 56; 4Q, '99, 5

√5ᵗʰ **V57.2 Occupational therapy and vocational rehabilitation**

V57.21 Encounter for occupational therapy
AHA: 4Q, '99,

V57.22 Encounter for vocational therapy

V57.3 Speech therapy
AHA: 4Q, '97, 36

V57.4 Orthoptic training

√5ᵗʰ **V57.8 Other specified rehabilitation procedure**

V57.81 Orthotic training
Gait training in the use of artificial limbs

V57.89 Other
Multiple training or therapy
AHA: 4Q, '03, 105-106, 108; 2Q, '03, 16; 3Q, '01, 21; 3Q, '97, 11, 12; S-O, '86, 4

V57.9 Unspecified rehabilitation procedure

√4ᵗʰ **V58 Encounter for other and unspecified procedures and aftercare**
> EXCLUDES   *convalescence and palliative care (V66)*

V58.0 Radiotherapy   PDx
Encounter or admission for radiotherapy
> EXCLUDES   *encounter for radioactive implant — code to condition*
> *radioactive iodine therapy — code to condition*
AHA: 3Q, '92, 5; 2Q, '90, 7; J-F, '87, 13

▲ √5ᵗʰ **V58.1 Encounter for antineoplastic chemotherapy and immunotherapy**
Encounter or admission for chemotherapy
> EXCLUDES   ▶*chemotherapy and immunotherapy for nonneoplastic conditions — code to condition*◀
> *prophylactic chemotherapy against disease which has never been present (V03.0-V07.9)*
AHA: 1Q, '04, 13; 2Q, '03, 16; 3Q, '93, 4; 2Q, '92, 6; 2Q, '91, 17; 2Q, '90, 7; S-O, '84, 5

● **V58.11 Encounter for antineoplastic chemotherapy**   PDx

● **V58.12 Encounter for antineoplastic immunotherapy**   PDx

V58.2 Blood transfusion, without reported diagnosis

V58.3 Attention to surgical dressings and sutures
Change of dressings
Removal of sutures

√4ᵗʰ Additional Digit Required   RUG III Special Care Dx   RUG III Clinically Complex Dx   Hospice Non-cancer Dx   PDx Primary Dx use only   SDx Secondary Dx use only

2006 ICD•9•CM   October 2005 • Volume 1 — 289

√5ᵗʰ **V58.4 Other aftercare following surgery**

Note: Codes from this subcategory should be used in conjunction with other aftercare codes to fully identify the reason for the aftercare encounter

> **EXCLUDES** *aftercare following sterilization reversal surgery (V26.22)*
> *attention to artificial openings (V55.0-V55.9)*
> *orthopedic aftercare (V54.0-V54.9)*

AHA: 4Q, '99, 9; N-D, '87, 9

V58.41 Encounter for planned postoperative wound closure

> **EXCLUDES** *disruption of operative wound (998.3)*

AHA: 4Q, '99, 15

V58.42 Aftercare following surgery for neoplasm
Conditions classifiable to 140-239

AHA: 4Q, '02, 80

V58.43 Aftercare following surgery for injury and trauma
Conditions classifiable to 800-999

> **EXCLUDES** *aftercare for healing traumatic fracture (V54.10-V54.19)*

AHA: 4Q, '02, 80

V58.44 Aftercare following organ transplant
Use additional code to identify the organ transplanted (V42.0-V42.9)

AHA: 4Q, '04, 101

V58.49 Other specified aftercare following surgery
AHA: 1Q, '96, 8, 9

V58.5 Orthodontics

> **EXCLUDES** *fitting and adjustment of orthodontic device (V53.4)*

√5ᵗʰ **V58.6 Long-term (current) drug use**

> **EXCLUDES** *drug abuse (305.00-305.93)*
> *drug dependence (304.00-304.93)*
> *hormone replacement therapy (postmenopausal) (V07.4)*

AHA: 4Q, '03, 85; 4Q, '02, 84; 3Q, '02, 15; 4Q, '95, 61

V58.61 Long-term (current) use of anticoagulants

> **EXCLUDES** *long-term (current) use of aspirin (V58.66)*

AHA: 3Q, '04, 7; 4Q, '03, 108; 3Q, '02, 13-16; 1Q, '02, 15, 16

V58.62 Long-term (current) use of antibiotics
AHA: 4Q, '98, 59

V58.63 Long-term (current) use of antiplatelets/antithrombotics

> **EXCLUDES** *long-term (current) use of aspirin (V58.66)*

V58.64 Long-term (current) use of non-steroidal anti-inflammatories (NSAID)

> **EXCLUDES** *long-term (current) use of aspirin (V58.66)*

V58.65 Long-term (current) use of steroids

V58.66 Long-term (current) use of aspirin
AHA: 4Q, '04, 102

V58.67 Long-term (current) use of insulin
AHA: 4Q, '04, 55-56, 103

V58.69 Long-term (current) use of other medications
High-risk medications

AHA: 2Q, '04, 10; 1Q, '04, 13; 1Q, '03, 11; 2Q, '00, 8; 3Q, '99, 13; 2Q, '99, 17; 1Q, '97, 12; 2Q, '96, 7

√5ᵗʰ **V58.7 Aftercare following surgery to specified body systems, not elsewhere classified**

Note: Codes from this subcategory should be used in conjunction with other aftercare codes to fully identify the reason for the aftercare encounter

> **EXCLUDES** *aftercare following organ transplant (V58.44)*
> *aftercare following surgery for neoplasm (V58.42)*

AHA: 4Q, '03, 104; 4Q, '02, 80

V58.71 Aftercare following surgery of the sense organs, NEC
Conditions classifiable to 360-379, 380-389

V58.72 Aftercare following surgery of the nervous system, NEC
Conditions classifiable to 320-359

> **EXCLUDES** *aftercare following surgery of the sense organs, NEC (V58.71)*

V58.73 Aftercare following surgery of the circulatory system, NEC
Conditions classifiable to 390-459

AHA: 4Q, '03, 105

V58.74 Aftercare following surgery of the respiratory system, NEC
Conditions classifiable to 460-519

V58.75 Aftercare following surgery of the teeth, oral cavity and digestive system, NEC
Conditions classifiable to 520-579

V58.76 Aftercare following surgery of the genitourinary system, NEC
Conditions classifiable to 580-629

> **EXCLUDES** *aftercare following sterilization reversal (V26.22)*

AHA: ▶1Q, '05, 11-12◀

V58.77 Aftercare following surgery of the skin and subcutaneous tissue, NEC
Conditions classifiable to 680-709

V58.78 Aftercare following surgery of the musculoskeletal system, NEC
Conditions classifiable to 710-739

√5ᵗʰ **V58.8 Other specified procedures and aftercare**
AHA: 4Q, '94, 45; 2Q, '94, 8

V58.81 Fitting and adjustment of vascular catheter
Removal or replacement of catheter
Toilet or cleansing

> **EXCLUDES** *complication of renal dialysis (996.73)*
> *complication of vascular catheter (996.74)*
> *dialysis preparation — code to condition*
> *encounter for dialysis (V56.0-V56.8)*
> *fitting and adjustment of dialysis catheter (V56.1)*

V58.82 Fitting and adjustment of nonvascular catheter, NEC
Removal or replacement of catheter
Toilet or cleansing

> **EXCLUDES** *fitting and adjustment of peritoneal dialysis catheter (V56.2)*
> *fitting and adjustment of urinary catheter (V53.6)*

Ⓝ Newborn Age: 0   Ⓟ Pediatric Age: 0-17   Ⓜ Maternity Age: 12-55   Ⓐ Adult Age: 15-124   ▮Manifestation Code   ▶◀ Revised Text   ● New Code   ▲ Revised Code Title

290 — Volume 1 • October 2005   **2006 ICD•9•CM**

V58.83 Encounter for therapeutic drug monitoring
Use additional code for any associated long-term (current) drug use (V58.61-V58.69)

> EXCLUDES   *blood-drug testing for medicolegal reasons (V70.4)*

AHA: 2Q, '04, 10; 1Q, '04, 13; 4Q, '03, 85; 4Q, '02, 84; 3Q, '02, 13-16

DEF: Drug monitoring: Measurement of the level of a specific drug in the body or measurement of a specific function to assess effectiveness of a drug.

V58.89 Other specified aftercare
AHA: 4Q, '98, 59

V58.9 Unspecified aftercare

✓4ᵗʰ **V59 Donors**

> EXCLUDES   *examination of potential donor (V70.8)*
> *self-donation of organ or tissue — code to condition*

AHA: 4Q, '95, 62; 1Q, '90, 10; N-D, '84, 8

✓5ᵗʰ **V59.0 Blood**
    V59.01 Whole blood   `PDx`
    V59.02 Stem cells   `PDx`
    V59.09 Other   `PDx`
  V59.1 Skin   `PDx`
  V59.2 Bone   `PDx`
  V59.3 Bone marrow   `PDx`
  V59.4 Kidney   `PDx`
  V59.5 Cornea   `PDx`
  V59.6 Liver   `PDx`

● ✓5ᵗʰ **V59.7 Egg (oocyte) (ovum)**
    V59.70 Egg (oocyte) (ovum) donor, unspecified   `PDx`

●   **V59.71 Egg (oocyte) (ovum) donor, under age 35, anonymous recipient**   `PDx`
      Egg donor, under age 35 NOS

●   **V59.72 Egg (oocyte) (ovum) donor, under age 35, designated recipient**   `PDx`

●   **V59.73 Egg (oocyte) (ovum) donor, age 35 and over, anonymous recipient**   `PDx`
      Egg donor, age 35 and over NOS

●   **V59.74 Egg (oocyte) (ovum) donor, age 35 and over, designated recipient**   `PDx`

  V59.8 Other specified organ or tissue   `PDx`
    AHA: 3Q, '02, 20

  V59.9 Unspecified organ or tissue   `PDx`

PERSONS ENCOUNTERING HEALTH SERVICES IN OTHER CIRCUMSTANCES (V60-V69)

✓4ᵗʰ **V60 Housing, household, and economic circumstances**

  V60.0 Lack of housing   `SDx`
    Hobos   Transients
    Social migrants   Vagabonds
    Tramps

  V60.1 Inadequate housing   `SDx`
    Lack of heating   Technical defects in
    Restriction of space   home preventing
                     adequate care

  V60.2 Inadequate material resources   `SDx`
    Economic problem
    Poverty NOS

  V60.3 Person living alone   `SDx`

  V60.4 No other household member able to render care   `SDx`
    Person requiring care (has) (is):
      family member too handicapped, ill, or otherwise unsuited to render care
      partner temporarily away from home
      temporarily away from usual place of abode

> EXCLUDES   *holiday relief care (V60.5)*

  V60.5 Holiday relief care   `SDx`
    Provision of health care facilities to a person normally cared for at home, to enable relatives to take a vacation

  V60.6 Person living in residential institution   `SDx`
    Boarding school resident

  V60.8 Other specified housing or economic circumstances   `SDx`

  V60.9 Unspecified housing or economic circumstance   `SDx`

✓4ᵗʰ **V61 Other family circumstances**

> INCLUDES   when these circumstances or fear of them, affecting the person directly involved or others, are mentioned as the reason, justified or not, for seeking or receiving medical advice or care

AHA: 1Q, '90, 9

  V61.0 Family disruption
    Divorce   Estrangement

✓5ᵗʰ **V61.1 Counseling for marital and partner problems**

> EXCLUDES   *problems related to:*
> *psychosexual disorders (302.0-302.9)*
> *sexual function (V41.7)*

    V61.10 Counseling for marital and partner problems, unspecified
      Marital conflict
      ▶Marital relationship problem◀
      Partner conflict
      ▶Partner relationship problem◀

    V61.11 Counseling for victim of spousal and partner abuse

> EXCLUDES   *encounter for treatment of current injuries due to abuse (995.80-995.85)*

    V61.12 Counseling for perpetrator of spousal and partner abuse

✓5ᵗʰ **V61.2 Parent-child problems**

    V61.20 Counseling for parent-child problem, unspecified
      Concern about behavior of child
      Parent-child conflict
      ▶Parent-child relationship problem◀

    V61.21 Counseling for victim of child abuse
      Child battering   Child neglect

> EXCLUDES   *current injuries due to abuse (995.50-995.59)*

    V61.22 Counseling for perpetrator of parental child abuse

> EXCLUDES   *counseling for non-parental abuser (V62.83)*

    V61.29 Other
      Problem concerning adopted or foster child
      AHA: 3Q, '99, 16

  V61.3 Problems with aged parents or in-laws

✓5ᵗʰ **V61.4 Health problems within family**

    V61.41 Alcoholism in family

    V61.49 Other
      Care of   ⎱ sick or handicapped person
      Presence of ⎰ in family or household

  V61.5 Multiparity

  V61.6 Illegitimacy or illegitimate pregnancy   `M` ♀

  V61.7 Other unwanted pregnancy   `M` ♀

  V61.8 Other specified family circumstances
    Problems with family members NEC
    ▶Sibling relationship problem◀

  V61.9 Unspecified family circumstance

✓4ᵗʰ ✓5ᵗʰ Additional Digit Required   `RUG III Special Care Dx`   `RUG III Clinically Complex Dx`   `Hospice Non-cancer Dx`   `PDx` Primary Dx use only   `SDx` Secondary Dx use only

2006 ICD•9•CM   October 2005 • Volume 1 — 291

V Codes

V62–V65.41

☑4ᵗʰ **V62 Other psychosocial circumstances**

  INCLUDES those circumstances or fear of them, affecting the person directly involved or others, mentioned as the reason, justified or not, for seeking or receiving medical advice or care

  EXCLUDES previous psychological trauma (V15.41-V15.49)

V62.0 Unemployment SDx
  EXCLUDES circumstances when main problem is economic inadequacy or poverty (V60.2)

V62.1 Adverse effects of work environment SDx

V62.2 Other occupational circumstances or maladjustment SDx
  Career choice problem
  Dissatisfaction with employment
  ▶Occupational problem◀

V62.3 Educational circumstances SDx
  ▶Academic problem◀
  Dissatisfaction with school environment
  Educational handicap

V62.4 Social maladjustment SDx
  ▶Acculturation problem◀
  Cultural deprivation
  Political, religious, or sex discrimination
  Social:
    isolation
    persecution

V62.5 Legal circumstances SDx
  Imprisonment   Litigation
  Legal investigation   Prosecution

V62.6 Refusal of treatment for reasons of religion or conscience SDx

☑5ᵗʰ **V62.8 Other psychological or physical stress, not elsewhere classified**

  V62.81 Interpersonal problems, not elsewhere classified SDx
    ▶Relational problem NOS◀

  V62.82 Bereavement, uncomplicated SDx
    EXCLUDES bereavement as adjustment reaction (309.0)

  V62.83 Counseling for perpetrator of physical/sexual abuse SDx
    EXCLUDES counseling for perpetrator of parental child abuse (V61.22)
      counseling for perpetrator of spousal and partner abuse (V61.12)

  V62.84 Suicidal ideation SDx
    EXCLUDES suicidal tendencies (300.9)

  V62.89 Other SDx
    ▶Borderline intellectual functioning◀
    Life circumstance problems
    Phase of life problems
    ▶Religious or spiritual problem◀

V62.9 Unspecified psychosocial circumstance SDx

☑5ᵗʰ **V63 Unavailability of other medical facilities for care**
  AHA: 1Q, '91, 21

V63.0 Residence remote from hospital or other health care facility

V63.1 Medical services in home not available
  EXCLUDES no other household member able to render care (V60.4)
  AHA: 4Q, '01, 67; 1Q, '01, 12

V63.2 Person awaiting admission to adequate facility elsewhere

V63.8 Other specified reasons for unavailability of medical facilities
  Person on waiting list undergoing social agency investigation

V63.9 Unspecified reason for unavailability of medical facilities

☑4ᵗʰ **V64 Persons encountering health services for specific procedures, not carried out**

▲ ☑5ᵗʰ **V64.0 Vaccination not carried out**
● **V64.00 Vaccination not carried out, unspecified reason** SDx
● **V64.01 Vaccination not carried out because of acute illness** SDx
● **V64.02 Vaccination not carried out because of chronic illness or condition** SDx
● **V64.03 Vaccination not carried out because of immune compromised state** SDx
● **V64.04 Vaccination not carried out because of allergy to vaccine or component** SDx
● **V64.05 Vaccination not carried out because of aregiver refusal** SDx
● **V64.06 Vaccination not carried out because of patient refusal** SDx
● **V64.07 Vaccination not carried out for religious reasons** SDx
● **V64.08 Vaccination not carried out because patient had disease being vaccinated against** SDx
● **V64.09 Vaccination not carried out for other reason** SDx

V64.1 Surgical or other procedure not carried out because of contraindication SDx

V64.2 Surgical or other procedure not carried out because of patient's decision SDx
  AHA: 2Q, '01, 8

V64.3 Procedure not carried out for other reasons SDx

☑5ᵗʰ **V64.4 Closed surgical procedure converted to open procedure**
  AHA: 4Q, '03, 87; 4Q, '98, 68; 4Q, '97, 52

  V64.41 Laparoscopic surgical procedure converted to open procedure SDx

  V64.42 Thoracoscopic surgical procedure converted to open procedure SDx

  V64.43 Arthroscopic surgical procedure converted to open procedure SDx

☑4ᵗʰ **V65 Other persons seeking consultation**

V65.0 Healthy person accompanying sick person
  Boarder

☑5ᵗʰ **V65.1 Person consulting on behalf of another person**
  Advice or treatment for nonattending third party
  EXCLUDES concern (normal) about sick person in family (V61.41-V61.49)
  AHA: 4Q, '03, 84

  V65.11 Pediatric pre-birth visit for expectant mother M ♀

  V65.19 Other person consulting on behalf of another person

V65.2 Person feigning illness
  Malingerer   Peregrinating patient
  AHA: 3Q, '99, 20

V65.3 Dietary surveillance and counseling
  Dietary surveillance and counseling (in):
    NOS   gastritis
    colitis   hypercholesterolemia
    diabetes mellitus hypoglycemia
    food allergies or obesity
      intolerance

☑5ᵗʰ **V65.4 Other counseling, not elsewhere classified**
  Health: Health:
    advice   instruction
    education
  EXCLUDES counseling (for):
    contraception (V25.40-V25.49)
    genetic ▶(V26.31-V26.33)◀
    on behalf of third party (V65.11-V65.19)
    procreative management (V26.4)

V65.40 Counseling NOS
V65.41 Exercise counseling

N Newborn Age: 0   P Pediatric Age: 0-17   M Maternity Age: 12-55   A Adult Age: 15-124 | Manifestation Code | ▶◀ Revised Text   ● New Code   ▲ Revised Code Title

V65.42 Counseling on substance use and abuse

V65.43 Counseling on injury prevention

V65.44 Human immunodeficiency virus [HIV] counseling

V65.45 Counseling on other sexually transmitted diseases

V65.46 Encounter for insulin pump training

V65.49 Other specified counseling
AHA: 2Q, '00, 8

V65.5 Person with feared complaint in whom no diagnosis was made
Feared condition not demonstrated
Problem was normal state
"Worried well"

V65.8 Other reasons for seeking consultation
EXCLUDES specified symptoms
AHA: 3Q, '92, 4

V65.9 Unspecified reason for consultation

✓4th V66 Convalescence and palliative care

V66.0 Following surgery PDx

V66.1 Following radiotherapy PDx

V66.2 Following chemotherapy PDx

V66.3 Following psychotherapy and other treatment for mental disorder PDx

V66.4 Following treatment of fracture PDx

V66.5 Following other treatment PDx

V66.6 Following combined treatment PDx

V66.7 Encounter for palliative care SDx
End of life care   Terminal care
Hospice care
Code first underlying disease
AHA: 4Q, '03, 107; 1Q, '98, 11; 4Q, '96, 47, 48

V66.9 Unspecified convalescence PDx
AHA: 4Q, '99, 8

✓4th V67 Follow-up examination
INCLUDES surveillance only following completed treatment
EXCLUDES surveillance of contraception (V25.40-V25.49)
AHA: 2Q, '03, 5

✓5th V67.0 Following surgery
AHA: 4Q, '00, 56; 4Q, '98, 69; 4Q, '97, 50; 2Q, '95, 8;1Q, '95, 4; 3Q, '92, 11

V67.00 Following surgery, unspecified

V67.01 Follow-up vaginal pap smear ♀
Vaginal pap-smear, status-post hysterectomy for malignant condition
Use additional code to identify:
acquired absence of uterus (V45.77)
personal history of malignant neoplasm (V10.40-V10.44)
EXCLUDES vaginal pap smear status-post hysterectomy for non-malignant condition (V76.47)

V67.09 Following other surgery
EXCLUDES sperm count following steriliz-ation reversal (V26.22)
sperm count for fertility testing (V26.21)
AHA: 3Q, '02, 16; 3Q, '02, 15

V67.1 Following radiotherapy

V67.2 Following chemotherapy
Cancer chemotherapy follow-up

V67.3 Following psychotherapy and other treatment for mental disorder

V67.4 Following treatment of healed fracture
EXCLUDES current (healing) fracture aftercare (V54.0-V54.9)
AHA: 1Q, '90, 7

✓5th V67.5 Following other treatment

V67.51 Following completed treatment with high-risk medications, not elsewhere classified
EXCLUDES long-term (current) drug use (V58.61-V58.69)
AHA: 1Q, '99, 5, 6;4Q, '95, 61 ; 1Q, '90, 18

V67.59 Other

V67.6 Following combined treatment

V67.9 Unspecified follow-up examination

✓4th V68 Encounters for administrative purposes

V68.0 Issue of medical certificates PDx
Issue of medical certificate of:
cause of death
fitness
incapacity
EXCLUDES encounter for general medical examination (V70.0-V70.9)

V68.1 Issue of repeat prescriptions PDx
Issue of repeat prescription for:
appliance
glasses
medications
EXCLUDES repeat prescription for contraceptives (V25.41-V25.49)

V68.2 Request for expert evidence PDx

✓5th V68.8 Other specified administrative purpose

V68.81 Referral of patient without examination or treatment PDx

V68.89 Other PDx

V68.9 Unspecified administrative purpose PDx

✓4th V69 Problems related to lifestyle
AHA: 4Q, '94, 48

V69.0 Lack of physical exercise

V69.1 Inappropriate diet and eating habits
EXCLUDES anorexia nervosa (307.1)
bulimia (783.6)
malnutrition and other nutritional deficiencies (260-269.9)
other and unspecified eating disorders (307.50-307.59)

V69.2 High-risk sexual behavior

V69.3 Gambling and betting
EXCLUDES pathological gambling (312.31)

V69.4 Lack of adequate sleep
Sleep deprivation
EXCLUDES insomnia (780.52)

V69.5 Behavioral insomnia of childhood

V69.8 Other problems related to lifestyle
Self-damaging behavior

V69.9 Problem related to lifestyle, unspecified

PERSONS WITHOUT REPORTED DIAGNOSIS ENCOUNTERED DURING EXAMINATION AND INVESTIGATION OF INDIVIDUALS AND POPULATIONS ▶(V70-V85)◀

Note: Nonspecific abnormal findings disclosed at the time of these examinations are classifiable to categories 790-796.

✓4th V70 General medical examination
Use additional code(s) to identify any special screening examination(s) performed (V73.0-V82.9)

V70.0 Routine general medical examination at a health care facility PDx
Health checkup
EXCLUDES health checkup of infant or child (V20.2)
▶pre-procedural general physical examination (V72.83)◀

V70.1 General psychiatric examination, requested by the authority PDx

V70.2 General psychiatric examination, other and unspecified PDx

✓4th ✓5th Additional Digit Required   RUG III Special Care Dx   RUG III Clinically Complex Dx   Hospice Non-cancer Dx   PDx Primary Dx use only   SDx Secondary Dx use only

2006 ICD•9•CM   October 2005 • Volume 1 — 293

V70.3 **Other medical examination for administrative purposes** `PDx`

General medical examination for:
- admission to old age home
- adoption
- camp
- driving license
- immigration and naturalization
- insurance certification
- marriage
- prison
- school admission
- sports competition

`EXCLUDES`   attendance for issue of medical certificates (V68.0)
pre-employment screening (V70.5)

AHA: 1Q, '90, 6

V70.4 **Examination for medicolegal reasons** `PDx`

Blood-alcohol tests
Blood-drug tests
Paternity testing

`EXCLUDES`   examination and observation following:
accidents (V71.3, V71.4)
assault (V71.6)
rape (V71.5)

V70.5 **Health examination of defined subpopulations** `PDx`

Armed forces personnel	Prisoners
Inhabitants of institutions	Prostitutes
Occupational health examinations	Refugees
	School children
Pre-employment screening	Students
Preschool children	

V70.6 **Health examination in population surveys** `PDx`

`EXCLUDES`   special screening (V73.0-V82.9)

V70.7 **Examination of participant in clinical trial**

Examination of participant or control in clinical research

AHA: 4Q, '01, 55

V70.8 **Other specified general medical examinations** `PDx`

Examination of potential donor of organ or tissue

V70.9 **Unspecified general medical examination** `PDx`

✓4ᵗʰ **V71** **Observation and evaluation for suspected conditions not found**

`INCLUDES`   This category is to be used when persons without a diagnosis are suspected of having an abnormal condition, without signs or symptoms, which requires study, but after examination and observation, is found not to exist. This category is also for use for administrative and legal observation status.

AHA: 4Q, '94, 47; 2Q, '90, 5; M-A, '87, 1

✓5ᵗʰ **V71.0** **Observation for suspected mental condition**

V71.01 **Adult antisocial behavior** `PDx` `A`

Dyssocial behavior or gang activity in adult without manifest psychiatric disorder

V71.02 **Childhood or adolescent antisocial behavior** `PDx`

Dyssocial behavior or gang activity in child or adolescent without manifest psychiatric disorder

V71.09 **Other suspected mental condition** `PDx`

V71.1 **Observation for suspected malignant neoplasm** `PDx`

V71.2 **Observation for suspected tuberculosis** `PDx`

V71.3 **Observation following accident at work** `PDx`

V71.4 **Observation following other accident** `PDx`

Examination of individual involved in motor vehicle traffic accident

V71.5 **Observation following alleged rape or seduction** `PDx`

Examination of victim or culprit

V71.6 **Observation following other inflicted injury** `PDx`

Examination of victim or culprit

V71.7 **Observation for suspected cardiovascular disease** `PDx`

AHA: 1Q, '04, 6; 3Q, '90, 10; S-O, '87, 10

✓5ᵗʰ **V71.8** **Observation and evaluation for other specified suspected conditions** `PDx`

AHA: 4Q, '00, 54 ; 1Q, '90, 19

V71.81 **Abuse and neglect** `PDx`

`EXCLUDES`   adult abuse and neglect (995.80-995.85)
child abuse and neglect (995.50-995.59)

AHA: 4Q, '00, 55

V71.82 **Observation and evaluation for suspected exposure to anthrax** `PDx`

AHA: 4Q, '02, 70, 85

V71.83 **Observation and evaluation for suspected exposure to other biological agent** `PDx`

AHA: 4Q, '03, 47

V71.89 **Other specified suspected conditions** `PDx`

AHA: 2Q, '03, 15

V71.9 **Observation for unspecified suspected condition** `PDx`

AHA: 1Q, '02, 6

✓4ᵗʰ **V72** **Special investigations and examinations**

`INCLUDES`   routine examination of specific system
`EXCLUDES`   general medical examination (V70.0-V70.4)
general screening examination of defined population groups (V70.5, V70.6, V70.7)
routine examination of infant or child (V20.2)

Use additional code(s) to identify any special screening examination(s) performed (V73.0-V82.9)

V72.0 **Examination of eyes and vision** `PDx`

AHA: 1Q, '04, 15

V72.1 **Examination of ears and hearing** `PDx`

AHA: 1Q, '04, 15

V72.2 **Dental examination** `PDx`

✓5ᵗʰ **V72.3** **Gynecological examination**

`EXCLUDES`   cervical Papanicolaou smear without general gynecological examination (V76.2)
routine examination in contraceptive management (V25.40-V25.49)

V72.31 **Routine gynecological examination** `PDx` ♀

General gynecological examination with or without Papanicolaou cervical smear
Pelvic examination (annual) (periodic)
Use additional code to identify routine vaginal Papanicolaou smear (V76.47)

V72.32 **Encounter for Papanicolaou cervical smear to confirm findings of recent normal smear following initial abnormal smear** `PDx` ♀

✓5ᵗʰ **V72.4** **Pregnancy examination or test**

V72.40 **Pregnancy examination or test, pregnancy unconfirmed** `PDx` ♀

Possible pregnancy, not (yet) confirmed

V72.41 **Pregnancy examination or test, negative result** `PDx` ♀

V72.42 **Pregnancy examination or test, positive result** `PDx` ♀

V72.5 **Radiological examination, not elsewhere classified**

Routine chest x-ray

`EXCLUDES`   examination for suspected tuberculosis (V71.2)

AHA: 1Q, '90, 19

| `N` Newborn Age: 0 | `P` Pediatric Age: 0-17 | `M` Maternity Age: 12-55 | `A` Adult Age: 15-124 | `Manifestation Code` | ▶◀ Revised Text | ● New Code | ▲ Revised Code Title |

V72.6 Laboratory examination
> EXCLUDES   *that for suspected disorder (V71.0-V71.9)*

AHA: 1Q, '90, 22

V72.7 Diagnostic skin and sensitization tests PDx
Allergy tests   Skin tests for hypersensitivity
> EXCLUDES   *diagnostic skin tests for bacterial diseases (V74.0-V74.9)*

√5ᵗʰ **V72.8 Other specified examinations**

V72.81 Pre-operative cardiovascular examination PDx
▶Pre-procedural cardiovascular examination◀

V72.82 Pre-operative respiratory examination PDx
▶Pre-procedural respiratory examination◀
AHA: 3Q, '96, 14

V72.83 Other specified pre-operative examination PDx
▶Other pre-procedural examination
Pre-procedural general physical examination◀
> EXCLUDES ▶ *routine general medical examination (V70.0)*◀

AHA: 3Q, '96, 14

V72.84 Pre-operative examination, unspecified PDx
▶Pre-procedural examination, unspecified◀

V72.85 Other specified examination PDx
AHA: 1Q, '04, 12

V72.86 Encounter for blood typing

V72.9 Unspecified examination PDx

√4ᵗʰ **V73 Special screening examination for viral and chlamydial diseases**
AHA: 1Q, '04, 11

V73.0 Poliomyelitis
V73.1 Smallpox
V73.2 Measles
V73.3 Rubella
V73.4 Yellow fever
V73.5 Other arthropod-borne viral diseases
Dengue fever   Viral encephalitis:
Hemorrhagic fever   mosquito-borne
                          tick-borne
V73.6 Trachoma
√5ᵗʰ **V73.8 Other specified viral and chlamydial diseases**
V73.88 Other specified chlamydial diseases
V73.89 Other specified viral diseases
√5ᵗʰ **V73.9 Unspecified viral and chlamydial disease**
V73.98 Unspecified chlamydial disease
V73.99 Unspecified viral disease

√4ᵗʰ **V74 Special screening examination for bacterial and spirochetal diseases**
> INCLUDES   diagnostic skin tests for these diseases

AHA: 1Q, '04, 11

V74.0 Cholera
V74.1 Pulmonary tuberculosis
V74.2 Leprosy [Hansen's disease]
V74.3 Diphtheria
V74.4 Bacterial conjunctivitis
V74.5 Venereal disease
V74.6 Yaws
V74.8 Other specified bacterial and spirochetal diseases
Brucellosis   Tetanus
Leptospirosis   Whooping cough
Plague
V74.9 Unspecified bacterial and spirochetal disease

√4ᵗʰ **V75 Special screening examination for other infectious diseases**
AHA: 1Q, '04, 11

V75.0 Rickettsial diseases

V75.1 Malaria
V75.2 Leishmaniasis
V75.3 Trypanosomiasis
Chagas' disease   Sleeping sickness
V75.4 Mycotic infections
V75.5 Schistosomiasis
V75.6 Filariasis
V75.7 Intestinal helminthiasis
V75.8 Other specified parasitic infections
V75.9 Unspecified infectious disease

√4ᵗʰ **V76 Special screening for malignant neoplasms**
AHA: 1Q, '04, 11

V76.0 Respiratory organs
√5ᵗʰ **V76.1 Breast**
AHA: 4Q, '98, 67

V76.10 Breast screening, unspecified
V76.11 Screening mammogram for high-risk patient ♀
AHA: 2Q, '03, 4

V76.12 Other screening mammogram
AHA: 2Q, '03, 3-4

V76.19 Other screening breast examination

V76.2 Cervix ♀
Routine cervical Papanicolaou smear
> EXCLUDES   *that as part of a general gynecological examination (V72.31)*

V76.3 Bladder
√5ᵗʰ **V76.4 Other sites**
V76.41 Rectum
V76.42 Oral cavity
V76.43 Skin
V76.44 Prostate ♂
V76.45 Testis ♂
V76.46 Ovary ♀
AHA: 4Q, '00, 52

V76.47 Vagina ♀
Vaginal pap smear status-post hysterectomy for non-malignant condition
Use additional code to identify acquired absence of uterus (V45.77)
> EXCLUDES   *vaginal pap smear status-post hysterectomy for malignant condition (V67.01)*

AHA: 4Q, '00, 52

V76.49 Other sites
AHA: 1Q, '99, 4

√5ᵗʰ **V76.5 Intestine**
AHA: 4Q, '00, 52

V76.50 Intestine, unspecified
V76.51 Colon
> EXCLUDES   *rectum (V76.41)*

AHA: 4Q, '01, 56

V76.52 Small intestine
√5ᵗʰ **V76.8 Other neoplasm**
AHA: 4Q, '00, 52

V76.81 Nervous system
V76.89 Other neoplasm
V76.9 Unspecified

√4ᵗʰ **V77 Special screening for endocrine, nutritional, metabolic, and immunity disorders**
AHA: 1Q, '04, 11

V77.0 Thyroid disorders
V77.1 Diabetes mellitus
V77.2 Malnutrition
V77.3 Phenylketonuria [PKU]
V77.4 Galactosemia
V77.5 Gout

√4ᵗʰ Additional Digit Required   RUG III Special Care Dx   RUG III Clinically Complex Dx   Hospice Non-cancer Dx   **PDx** Primary Dx use only   **SDx** Secondary Dx use only
√5ᵗʰ

V Codes

V77.6–V85.4

V77.6   **Cystic fibrosis**
Screening for mucoviscidosis

V77.7   **Other inborn errors of metabolism**

V77.8   **Obesity**

✓5th **V77.9**   **Other and unspecified endocrine, nutritional, metabolic, and immunity disorders**
AHA: 4Q, '00, 53

     V77.91 Screening for lipoid disorders
Screening for cholesterol level
Screening for hypercholesterolemia
Screening for hyperlipidemia

     V77.99 Other and unspecified endocrine, nutritional, metabolic, and immunity disorders

✓4th **V78 Special screening for disorders of blood and blood-forming organs**
AHA: 1Q, '04, 11

V78.0   **Iron deficiency anemia**

V78.1   **Other and unspecified deficiency anemia**

V78.2   **Sickle cell disease or trait**

V78.3   **Other hemoglobinopathies**

V78.8   **Other disorders of blood and blood-forming organs**

V78.9   **Unspecified disorder of blood and blood-forming organs**

✓4th **V79 Special screening for mental disorders and developmental handicaps**
AHA: 1Q, '04, 11

V79.0   **Depression**

V79.1   **Alcoholism**

V79.2   **Mental retardation**

V79.3   **Developmental handicaps in early childhood**

V79.8   **Other specified mental disorders and developmental handicaps**

V79.9   **Unspecified mental disorder and developmental handicap**

✓4th **V80 Special screening for neurological, eye, and ear diseases**
AHA: 1Q, '04, 11

V80.0   **Neurological conditions**

V80.1   **Glaucoma**

V80.2   **Other eye conditions**
Screening for: Screening for:
  cataract   senile macular lesions
  congenital anomaly of eye
     EXCLUDES   *general vision examination (V72.0)*

V80.3   **Ear diseases**
     EXCLUDES   *general hearing examination (V72.1)*

✓4th **V81 Special screening for cardiovascular, respiratory, and genitourinary diseases**
AHA: 1Q, '04, 11

V81.0   **Ischemic heart disease**

V81.1   **Hypertension**

V81.2   **Other and unspecified cardiovascular conditions**

V81.3   **Chronic bronchitis and emphysema**

V81.4   **Other and unspecified respiratory conditions**
     EXCLUDES   *screening for:*
         lung neoplasm (V76.0)
         pulmonary tuberculosis (V74.1)

V81.5   **Nephropathy**
Screening for asymptomatic bacteriuria

V81.6   **Other and unspecified genitourinary conditions**

✓4th **V82 Special screening for other conditions**
AHA: 1Q, '04, 11

V82.0   **Skin conditions**

V82.1   **Rheumatoid arthritis**

V82.2   **Other rheumatic disorders**

V82.3   **Congenital dislocation of hip**

V82.4   **Maternal postnatal screening for chromosomal anomalies**   ♀
     EXCLUDES   *antenatal screening by amniocentesis (V28.0)*

V82.5   **Chemical poisoning and other contamination**
Screening for:
  heavy metal poisoning
  ingestion of radioactive substance
  poisoning from contaminated water supply
  radiation exposure

V82.6   **Multiphasic screening**

✓5th **V82.8**   **Other specified conditions**
AHA: 4Q, '00, 53

     V82.81 Osteoporosis
Use additional code to identify:
  hormone replacement therapy (postmenopausal) status (V07.4)
  postmenopausal (age-related) (natural) status (V49.81)
AHA: 4Q, '00, 54

     V82.89 Other specified conditions

V82.9   **Unspecified condition**

✓4th **V83 Genetic carrier status**
AHA: 4Q, '02, 79; 4Q, '01, 54

✓5th **V83.0**   **Hemophilia A carrier**
     V83.01 Asymptomatic hemophilia A carrier
     V83.02 Symptomatic hemophilia A carrier

✓5th **V83.8**   **Other genetic carrier status**
     V83.81 Cystic fibrosis gene carrier
     V83.89 Other genetic carrier status

✓4th **V84 Genetic susceptibility to disease**
     INCLUDES   confirmed abnormal gene
Use additional code, if applicable, for any associated family history of the disease (V16-V19)
AHA: 4Q, '04, 106

✓5th **V84.0**   **Genetic susceptibility to malignant neoplasm**
Code first, if applicable, any current malignant neoplasms (140.0-195.8, 200.0-208.9, 230.0-234.9)
Use additional code, if applicable, for any personal history of malignant neoplasm (V10.0-V10.9)

     V84.01 Genetic susceptibility to malignant neoplasm of breast   SDx
AHA: 4Q, '04, 107

     V84.02 Genetic susceptibility to malignant neoplasm of ovary   ♀ SDx

     V84.03 Genetic susceptibility to malignant neoplasm of prostate   ♂ SDx

     V84.04 Genetic susceptibility to malignant neoplasm of endometrium   ♀ SDx

     V84.09 Genetic susceptibility to other malignant neoplasm

V84.8   **Genetic susceptibility to other disease**   SDx

● ✓4th **V85 Body Mass Index**
Kilograms per meters squared
Note: BMI adult codes are for use for persons over 20 years old

●   **V85.0**   **Body Mass Index less than 19, adult**   SDx

●   **V85.1**   **Body Mass Index between 19-24, adult**   SDx

● ✓5th **V85.2**   **Body Mass Index between 25-29, adult**
●   **V85.21 Body Mass Index 25.0-25.9, adult**   SDx
●   **V85.22 Body Mass Index 26.0-26.9, adult**   SDx
●   **V85.23 Body Mass Index 27.0-27.9, adult**   SDx
●   **V85.24 Body Mass Index 28.0-28.9, adult**   SDx
●   **V85.25 Body Mass Index 29.0-29.9, adult**   SDx

● ✓5th **V85.3**   **Body Mass Index between 30-39, adult**
●   **V85.30 Body Mass Index 30.0-30.9, adult**   SDx
●   **V85.31 Body Mass Index 31.0-31.9, adult**   SDx
●   **V85.32 Body Mass Index 32.0-32.9, adult**   SDx
●   **V85.33 Body Mass Index 33.0-33.9, adult**   SDx
●   **V85.34 Body Mass Index 34.0-34.9, adult**   SDx
●   **V85.35 Body Mass Index 35.0-35.9, adult**   SDx
●   **V85.36 Body Mass Index 36.0-36.9, adult**   SDx
●   **V85.37 Body Mass Index 37.0-37.9, adult**   SDx
●   **V85.38 Body Mass Index 38.0-38.9, adult**   SDx
●   **V85.39 Body Mass Index 39.0-39.9, adult**   SDx

●   **V85.4**   **Body Mass Index 40 and over, adult**   SDx

N Newborn Age: 0   P Pediatric Age: 0-17   M Maternity Age: 12-55   A Adult Age: 15-124   Manifestation Code   ►◄ Revised Text   ● New Code   ▲ Revised Code Title

SUPPLEMENTARY CLASSIFICATION OF EXTERNAL CAUSES OF INJURY AND POISONING (E800-E999)

This section is provided to permit the classification of environmental events, circumstances, and conditions as the cause of injury, poisoning, and other adverse effects. Where a code from this section is applicable, it is intended that it shall be used in addition to a code from one of the main chapters of ICD-9-CM, indicating the nature of the condition. Certain other conditions which may be stated to be due to external causes are classified in Chapters 1 to 16 of ICD-9-CM. For these, the "E" code classification should be used as an additional code for more detailed analysis.

Machinery accidents [other than those connected with transport] are classifiable to category E919, in which the fourth-digit allows a broad classification of the type of machinery involved. If a more detailed classification of type of machinery is required, it is suggested that the "Classification of Industrial Accidents according to Agency," prepared by the International Labor Office, be used in addition. This is reproduced in Appendix D for optional use.

Categories for "late effects" of accidents and other external causes are to be found at E929, E959, E969, E977, E989, and E999.

DEFINITIONS AND EXAMPLES RELATED TO TRANSPORT ACCIDENTS

(a) A **transport accident** (E800-E848) is any accident involving a device designed primarily for, or being used at the time primarily for, conveying persons or goods from one place to another.

INCLUDES   accidents involving:
     aircraft and spacecraft (E840-E845)
     watercraft (E830-E838)
     motor vehicle (E810-E825)
     railway (E800-E807)
     other road vehicles (E826-E829)

In classifying accidents which involve more than one kind of transport, the above order of precedence of transport accidents should be used.

Accidents involving agricultural and construction machines, such as tractors, cranes, and bulldozers, are regarded as transport accidents only when these vehicles are under their own power on a highway [otherwise the vehicles are regarded as machinery]. Vehicles which can travel on land or water, such as hovercraft and other amphibious vehicles, are regarded as watercraft when on the water, as motor vehicles when on the highway, and as off-road motor vehicles when on land, but off the highway.

EXCLUDES   *accidents:*
     in sports which involve the use of transport but where the transport vehicle itself was not involved in the accident
     involving vehicles which are part of industrial equipment used entirely on industrial premises
     occurring during transportation but unrelated to the hazards associated with the means of transportation [e.g., injuries received in a fight on board ship; transport vehicle involved in a cataclysm such as an earthquake]
     to persons engaged in the maintenance or repair of transport equipment or vehicle not in motion, unlesss injured by another vehicle in motion

(b) A **railway accident** is a transport accident involving a railway train or other railway vehicle operated on rails, whether in motion or not.

EXCLUDES   *accidents:*
     in repair shops
     in roundhouse or on turntable
     on railway premises but not involving a train or other railway vehicle

(c) A **railway train** or **railway vehicle** is any device with or without cars coupled to it, desiged for traffic on a railway.

INCLUDES   interurban:
     electric car   (operated chiefly on its
     streetcar   own right-of-way, not open to other traffic)

     railway train, any power [diesel] [electric] [steam]
     funicular
     monorail or two-rail
     subterranean or elevated
     other vehicle designed to run on a railway track

EXCLUDES   *interurban electric cars [streetcars] specified to be operating on a right-of-way that forms part of the public street or highway [definition (n)]*

(d) A **railway** or **railroad** is a right-of-way designed for traffic on rails, which is used by carriages or wagons transporting passengers or freight, and by other rolling stock, and which is not open to other public vehicular traffic.

(e) A **motor vehicle accident** is a transport accident involving a motor vehicle. It is defined as a motor vehicle traffic accident or as a motor vehicle nontraffic accident according to whether the accident occurs on a public highway or elsewhere.

EXCLUDES   *injury or damage due to cataclysm*
     injury or damage while a motor vehicle, not under its own power, is being loaded on, or unloaded from, another conveyance

(f) A **motor vehicle traffic accident** is any motor vehicle accident occurring on a public highway [i.e., originating, terminating, or involving a vehicle partially on the highway]. A motor vehicle accident is assumed to have occurred on the highway unless another place is specified, except in the case of accidents involving only off-road motor vehicles which are classified as nontraffic accidents unless the contrary is stated.

(g) A **motor vehicle nontraffic accident** is any motor vehicle accident which occurs entirely in any place other than a public highway.

(h) A **public highway [trafficway]** or **street** is the entire width between property lines [or other boundary lines] of every way or place, of which any part is open to the use of the public for purposes of vehicular traffic as a matter of right or custom. A **roadway** is that part of the public highway designed, improved, and ordinarily used, for vehicular travel.

INCLUDES   approaches (public) to:
     docks
     public building
     station

EXCLUDES   *driveway (private)*
     parking lot
     ramp
     roads in:
       airfield
       farm
       industrial premises
       mine
       private grounds
       quarry

     ▨4ᵗʰ Fourth-digit Required   ▶◀ Revised Text   ● New Code   ▲ Revised Code Title

(i) A **motor vehicle** is any mechanically or electrically powered device, not operated on rails, upon which any person or property may be transported or drawn upon a highway. Any object such as a trailer, coaster, sled, or wagon being towed by a motor vehicle is considerd a part of the motor vehicle.

INCLUDES	automobile [any type]
	bus
	construction machinery, farm and industrial machinery, steam roller, tractor, army tank, highway grader, or similar vehicle on wheels or treads, while in transport under own power
	fire engine (motorized)
	motorcycle
	motorized bicycle [moped] or scooter
	trolley bus not operating on rails
	truck
	van

EXCLUDES *devices used solely to move persons or materials within the confines of a building and its premises, such as:*
building elevator
coal car in mine
electric baggage or mail truck used solely within a railroad station
electric truck used solely within an industrial plant
moving overhead crane

(j) A **motorcycle** is a two-wheeled motor vehicle having one or two riding saddles and sometimes having a third wheel for the support of a sidecar. The sidecar is considered part of the motorcycle.

INCLUDES	motorized:
	bicycle [moped]
	scooter
	tricycle

(k) An **off-road motor vehicle** is a motor vehicle of special design, to enable it to negotiate rough or soft terrain or snow. Examples of special design are high construction, special wheels and tires, driven by treads, or support on a cushion of air.

INCLUDES	all terrain vehicle [ATV]
	army tank
	hovercraft, on land or swamp
	snowmobile

(l) A **driver** of a motor vehicle is the occupant of the motor vehicle operating it or intending to operate it. A **motorcyclist** is the driver of a motorcycle. Other authorized occupants of a motor vehicle are **passengers**.

(m) An **other road vehicle** is any device, except a motor vehicle, in, on, or by which any person or property may be transported on a highway.

INCLUDES	animal carrying a person or goods
	animal-drawn vehicles
	animal harnessed to conveyance
	bicycle [pedal cycle]
	streetcar
	tricycle (pedal)

EXCLUDES *pedestrian conveyance [definition (q)]*

(n) A **streetcar** is a device designed and used primarily for transporting persons within a municipality, running on rails, usually subject to normal traffic control signals, and operated principally on a right-of-way that forms part of the traffic way. A trailer being towed by a streetcar is considered a part of the streetcar.

INCLUDES	interurban or intraurban electric or streetcar, when specified to be operating on a street or public highway
	tram (car)
	trolley (car)

(o) A **pedal cycle** is any road transport vehicle operated solely by pedals.

INCLUDES	bicycle
	pedal cycle
	tricycle

EXCLUDES *motorized bicycle [definition (i)]*

(p) A **pedal cyclist** is any person riding on a pedal cycle or in a sidecar attached to such a vehicle.

(q) A **pedestrian conveyance** is any human powered device by which a pedestrian may move other than by walking or by which a walking person may move another pedestrian.

INCLUDES	baby carriage
	coaster wagon
	ice skates
	perambulator
	pushcart
	pushchair
	roller skates
	scooter
	skateboard
	skis
	sled
	wheelchair

(r) A **pedestrian** is any person involved in an accident who was not at the time of the accident riding in or on a motor vehicle, railroad train, streetcar, animal-drawn or other vehicle, or on a bicycle or animal.

INCLUDES	person:
	changing tire of vehicle
	in or operating a pedestrian conveyance
	making adjustment to motor of vehicle
	on foot

(s) A **watercraft** is any device for transporting passengers or goods on the water.

(t) A **small boat** is any watercraft propelled by paddle, oars, or small motor, with a passenger capacity of less than ten.

INCLUDES	boat NOS
	canoe
	coble
	dinghy
	punt
	raft
	rowboat
	rowing shell
	scull
	skiff
	small motorboat

EXCLUDES *barge*
lifeboat (used after abandoning ship)
raft (anchored) being used as a diving platform
yacht

(u) An **aircraft** is any device for transporting passengers or goods in the air.

INCLUDES	airplane [any type]
	balloon
	bomber
	dirigible
	glider (hang)
	military aircraft
	parachute

(v) A **commercial transport aircraft** is any device for collective passenger or freight transportation by air, whether run on commercial lines for profit or by government authorities, with the exception of military craft.

▨4ᵗʰ Fourth-digit Required   ▶◀ Revised Text   ● New Code   ▲ Revised Code Title

RAILWAY ACCIDENTS (E800-E807)

Note: For definitions of railway accident and related terms see definitions (a) to (d).

EXCLUDES *accidents involving railway train and:*
aircraft (E840.0-E845.9)
motor vehicle (E810.0-E825.9)
watercraft (E830.0-E838.9)

The following fourth-digit subdivisions are for use with categories E800-E807 to identify the injured person:

.0 Railway employee

Any person who by virtue of his employment in connection with a railway, whether by the railway company or not, is at increased risk of involvement in a railway accident, such as:
catering staff of train
driver
guard
porter
postal staff on train
railway fireman
shunter
sleeping car attendant

.1 Passenger on railway

Any authorized person traveling on a train, except a railway employee.

EXCLUDES *intending passenger waiting at station (.8)*
unauthorized rider on railway vehicle (.8)

.2 Pedestrian

See definition (r)

.3 Pedal cyclist

See definition (p)

.8 Other specified person

Intending passenger or bystander waiting at station
Unauthorized rider on railway vehicle

.9 Unspecified person

✓4ᵗʰ **E800 Railway accident involving collision with rolling stock**

INCLUDES collision between railway trains or railway vehicles, any kind
collision NOS on railway
derailment with antecedent collision with rolling stock or NOS

✓4ᵗʰ **E801 Railway accident involving collision with other object**

INCLUDES collision of railway train with:
buffers
fallen tree on railway
gates
platform
rock on railway
streetcar
other nonmotor vehicle
other object

EXCLUDES *collision with:*
aircraft (E840.0-E842.9)
motor vehicle (E810.0-E810.9, E820.0-E822.9)

✓4ᵗʰ **E802 Railway accident involving derailment without antecedent collision**

✓4ᵗʰ **E803 Railway accident involving explosion, fire, or burning**

EXCLUDES *explosion or fire, with antecedent derailment (E802.0-E802.9)*
explosion or fire, with mention of antecedent collision (E800.0-E801.9)

✓4ᵗʰ **E804 Fall in, on, or from railway train**

INCLUDES fall while alighting from or boarding railway train

EXCLUDES *fall related to collision, derailment, or explosion of railway train (E800.0-E803.9)*

✓4ᵗʰ **E805 Hit by rolling stock**

INCLUDES crushed
injured   } by railway train or
killed   part
knocked down
run over

EXCLUDES *pedestrian hit by object set in motion by railway train (E806.0-E806.9)*

✓4ᵗʰ **E806 Other specified railway accident**

INCLUDES hit by object falling in railway train
injured by door or window on railway train
nonmotor road vehicle or pedestrian hit by object set in motion by railway train
railway train hit by falling:
earth NOS
rock
tree
other object

EXCLUDES *railway accident due to cataclysm (E908-E909)*

✓4ᵗʰ **E807 Railway accident of unspecified nature**

INCLUDES found dead   } on railway right-of-way
injured   NOS

railway accident NOS

MOTOR VEHICLE TRAFFIC ACCIDENTS (E810-E819)

Note: For definitions of motor vehicle traffic accident, and related terms, see definitions (e) to (k).

EXCLUDES *accidents involving motor vehicle and aircraft (E840.0-E845.9)*

The following fourth-digit subdivisions are for use with categories E810-E819 to identify the injured person:

.0 Driver of motor vehicle other than motorcycle

See definition (1)

.1 Passenger in motor vehicle other than motorcycle

See definition (1)

.2 Motorcyclist

See definition (1)

.3 Passenger on motorcycle

See definition (1)

.4 Occupant of streetcar

.5 Rider of animal; occupant of animal-drawn vehicle

.6 Pedal cyclist

See definition (p)

.7 Pedestrian

See definition (r)

.8 Other specified person

Occupant of vehicle other than above
Person in railway train involved in accident
Unauthorized rider of motor vehicle

.9 Unspecified person

✓4ᵗʰ **E810 Motor vehicle traffic accident involving collision with train**

EXCLUDES *motor vehicle collision with object set in motion by railway train (E815.0-E815.9)*
railway train hit by object set in motion by motor vehicle (E818.0-E818.9)

✓4ᵗʰ **E811 Motor vehicle traffic accident involving re-entrant collision with another motor vehicle**

INCLUDES collision between motor vehicle which accidentally leaves the roadway then re-enters the same roadway, or the opposite roadway on a divided highway, and another motor vehicle

EXCLUDES *collision on the same roadway when none of the motor vehicles involved have left and re-entered the highway (E812.0-E812.9)*

✓4ᵗʰ Fourth-digit Required   ▶◀ Revised Text   ● New Code   ▲ Revised Code Title

E Codes

E812–E819

§ ✓4th **E812 Other motor vehicle traffic accident involving collision with motor vehicle**

INCLUDES   collision with another motor vehicle parked, stopped, stalled, disabled, or abandoned on the highway

motor vehicle collision NOS

EXCLUDES   *collision with object set in motion by another motor vehicle (E815.0-E815.9)*

re-entrant collision with another motor vehicle (E811.0-E811.9)

§ ✓4th **E813 Motor vehicle traffic accident involving collision with other vehicle**

INCLUDES   collision between motor vehicle, any kind, and:

other road (nonmotor transport) vehicle, such as:

     animal carrying a person

     animal-drawn vehicle

     pedal cycle

     streetcar

EXCLUDES   *collision with:*

     object set in motion by nonmotor road vehicle (E815.0-E815.9)

     pedestrian (E814.0-E814.9)

nonmotor road vehicle hit by object set in motion by motor vehicle (E818.0-E818.9)

§ ✓4th **E814 Motor vehicle traffic accident involving collision with pedestrian**

INCLUDES   collision between motor vehicle, any kind, and pedestrian

pedestrian dragged, hit, or run over by motor vehicle, any kind

EXCLUDES   *pedestrian hit by object set in motion by motor vehicle (E818.0-E818.9)*

§ ✓4th **E815 Other motor vehicle traffic accident involving collision on the highway**

INCLUDES   collision (due to loss of control) (on highway) between motor vehicle, any kind, and:

     abutment (bridge) (overpass)

     animal (herded) (unattended)

     fallen stone, traffic sign, tree, utility pole

     guard rail or boundary fence

     interhighway divider

     landslide (not moving)

     object set in motion by railway train or road vehicle (motor) (nonmotor)

     object thrown in front of motor vehicle

     other object, fixed, movable, or moving

     safety island

     temporary traffic sign or marker

     wall of cut made for road

EXCLUDES   *collision with:*

     any object off the highway (resulting from loss of control) (E816.0-E816.9)

     any object which normally would have been off the highway and is not stated to have been on it (E816.0-E816.9)

motor vehicle parked, stopped, stalled, disabled, or abandoned on highway (E812.0-E812.9)

moving landslide (E909)

motor vehicle hit by object:

     set in motion by railway train or road vehicle (motor) (nonmotor) (E818.0-E818.9)

     thrown into or on vehicle (E818.0-E818.9)

§ ✓4th **E816 Motor vehicle traffic accident due to loss of control, without collision on the highway**

INCLUDES   motor vehicle:

     failing to make curve ⎤   and:

     going out of control   coliding with

       (due to):   object off

     blowout   the high-

     burst tire   way

     driver falling   overturning

       asleep   stopping

     driver inattention   abruptly

     excessive speed   off the

     failure of mech-   highway

       anical part ⎦

EXCLUDES   *collision on highway following loss of control (E810.0-E815.9)*

loss of control of motor vehicle following collision on the highway (E810.0-E815.9)

§ ✓4th **E817 Noncollision motor vehicle traffic accident while boarding or alighting**

INCLUDES   fall down stairs of motor ⎤

     bus

   fall from car in street   while boarding

   injured by moving part of ⎬ or alighting

     the vehicle

   trapped by door of motor ⎦

     bus

§ ✓4th **E818 Other noncollision motor vehicle traffic accident**

INCLUDES   accidental poisoning from exhaust gas generated by

breakage of any part of

explosion of any part of

fall, jump, or being accidentally pushed from   motor vehicle

fire starting in   while

hit by object thrown into or on   in

injured by being thrown against some part of, or object in   motion

injury from moving part of

object falling in or on

object thrown on

collision of railway train or road vehicle except motor vehicle, with object set in motion by motor vehicle

motor vehicle hit by object set in motion by railway train or road vehicle (motor) (nonmotor)

pedestrian, railway train, or road vehicle (motor) (nonmotor) hit by object set in motion by motor vehicle

EXCLUDES   *collision between motor vehicle and:*

     object set in motion by railway train or road vehicle (motor) (nonmotor) (E815.0-E815.9)

     object thrown towards the motor vehicle (E815.0-E815.9)

person overcome by carbon monoxide generated by stationary motor vehicle off the roadway with motor running (E868.2)

§ ✓4th **E819 Motor vehicle traffic accident of unspecified nature**

INCLUDES   motor vehicle traffic accident NOS

traffic accident NOS

§   Requires fourth-digit. See beginning of section E810-E819 for codes and definitions.

✓4th Fourth-digit Required   ▶◀ Revised Text   ● New Code   ▲ Revised Code Title

MOTOR VEHICLE NONTRAFFIC ACCIDENTS (E820-E825)

Note: For definitions of motor vehicle nontraffic accident and related terms see definition (a) to (k).

INCLUDES accidents involving motor vehicles being used in recreational or sporting activities off the highway

collision and noncollision motor vehicle accidents occurring entirely off the highway

EXCLUDES *accidents involving motor vehicle and:*
aircraft (E840.0-E845.9)
watercraft (E830.0-E838.9)
accidents, not on the public highway, involving agricultural and construction machinery but not involving another motor vehicle (E919.0, E919.2, E919.7)

The following fourth-digit subdivisions are for use with categories E820-E825 to identify the injured person:

.0 Driver of motor vehicle other than motorcycle
See definition (l)

.1 Passenger in motor vehicle other than motorcycle
See definition (l)

.2 Motorcyclist
See definition (l)

.3 Passenger on motorcycle
See definition (l)

.4 Occupant of streetcar

.5 Rider of animal; occupant of animal-drawn vehicle

.6 Pedal cyclist
See definition (p)

.7 Pedestrian
See definition (r)

.8 Other specified person
Occupant of vehicle other than above
Person on railway train involved in accident
Unauthorized rider of motor vehicle

.9 Unspecified person

✓4ᵗʰ **E820 Nontraffic accident involving motor-driven snow vehicle**

INCLUDES breakage of part of
fall from
hit by | motor-driven snow vehicle (not on public highway)
overturning of
run over or dragged by

collision of motor-driven snow vehicle with:
animal (being ridden) (-drawn vehicle)
another off-road motor vehicle
other motor vehicle, not on public highway
railway train
other object, fixed or movable
injury caused by rough landing of motor-driven snow vehicle (after leaving ground on rough terrain)

EXCLUDES *accident on the public highway involving motor driven snow vehicle (E810.0-E819.9)*

✓4ᵗʰ **E821 Nontraffic accident involving other off-road motor vehicle**

INCLUDES breakage of part of
fall from
hit by | off-road motor vehicle, except snow vehicle (not on public highway)
overturning of
run over or dragged by
thrown against some part of or object in

collision with:
animal (being ridden) (-drawn vehicle)
another off-road motor vehicle, except snow vehicle
other motor vehicle, not on public highway
other object, fixed or movable

EXCLUDES *accident on public highway involving off-road motor vehicle (E810.0-E819.9)*
collision between motor driven snow vehicle and other off-road motor vehicle (E820.0-E820.9)
hovercraft accident on water (E830.0-E838.9)

✓4ᵗʰ **E822 Other motor vehicle nontraffic accident involving collision with moving object**

INCLUDES collision, not on public highway, between motor vehicle, except off-road motor vehicle and:
animal
nonmotor vehicle
other motor vehicle, except off-road motor vehicle
pedestrian
railway train
other moving object

EXCLUDES *collision with:*
motor-driven snow vehicle (E820.0-E820.9)
other off-road motor vehicle (E821.0-E821.9)

✓4ᵗʰ **E823 Other motor vehicle nontraffic accident involving collision with stationary object**

INCLUDES collision, not on public highway, between motor vehicle, except off-road motor vehicle, and any object, fixed or movable, but not in motion

✓4ᵗʰ **E824 Other motor vehicle nontraffic accident while boarding and alighting**

INCLUDES fall
injury from moving part of motor vehicle | while boarding or alighting from motor vehicle, except off-road motor vehicle, not on public highway
trapped by door of motor vehicle

---

§ ✓4ᵗʰ **E825 Other motor vehicle nontraffic accident of other and unspecified nature**

INCLUDES

accidental poisoning from carbon monoxide generated by	
breakage of any part of	
explosion of any part of	motor vehicle while in motion, not on public highway
fall, jump, or being accidentally pushed from	
fire starting in	
hit by object thrown into, towards, or on	
injured by being thrown against some part of, or object in	
injury from moving part of	
object falling in or on	

motor vehicle nontraffic accident NOS

EXCLUDES *fall from or in stationary motor vehicle (E884.9, E885.9)*
overcome by carbon monoxide or exhaust gas generated by stationary motor vehicle off the roadway with motor running (E868.2)
struck by falling object from or in stationary motor vehicle (E916)

OTHER ROAD VEHICLE ACCIDENTS (E826-E829)

Note: Other road vehicle accidents are transport accidents involving road vehicles other than motor vehicles. For definitions of other road vehicle and related terms see definitions (m) to (o).

INCLUDES accidents involving other road vehicles being used in recreational or sporting activities

EXCLUDES *collision of other road vehicle [any] with:*
aircraft (E840.0-E845.9)
motor vehicle (E813.0-E813.9, E820.0-E822.9)
railway train (E801.0-E801.9)

The following fourth-digit subdivisions are for use with categories E826-E829 to identify the injured person.

.0 **Pedestrian**
    See definition (r)
.1 **Pedal cyclist**
    See definition (p)
.2 **Rider of animal**
.3 **Occupant of animal-drawn vehicle**
.4 **Occupant of streetcar**
.8 **Other specified person**
.9 **Unspecified person**

✓4ᵗʰ **E826 Pedal cycle accident**

[0-9] INCLUDES breakage of any part of pedal cycle
collision between pedal cycle and:
    animal (being ridden) (herded) (unattended)
    another pedal cycle
    any pedestrian
    nonmotor road vehicle
    other object, fixed, movable, or moving, not set in motion by motor vehicle, railway train, or aircraft
entanglement in wheel of pedal cycle
fall from pedal cycle
hit by object falling or thrown on the pedal cycle
pedal cycle accident NOS
pedal cycle overturned

✓4ᵗʰ **E827 Animal-drawn vehicle accident**

[0,2-4,8,9] INCLUDES breakage of any part of vehicle
collision between animal-drawn vehicle and:
    animal (being ridden) (herded) (unattended)
    nonmotor road vehicle, except pedal cycle
    pedestrian, pedestrian conveyance, or pedestrian vehicle
    other object, fixed, movable, or moving, not set in motion by motor vehicle, railway train, or aircraft

fall from	
knocked down by	animal-drawn vehicle
overturning of	
run over by	
thrown from	

EXCLUDES *collision of animal-drawn vehicle with pedal cycle (E826.0-E826.9)*

✓4ᵗʰ **E828 Accident involving animal being ridden**

[0,2,4,8,9] INCLUDES collision between animal being ridden and:
    another animal
    nonmotor road vehicle, except pedal cycle, and animal-drawn vehicle
    pedestrian, pedestrian conveyance, or pedestrian vehicle
    other object, fixed, movable, or moving, not set in motion by motor vehicle, railway train, or aircraft

fall from	
knocked down by	animal being ridden
thrown from	
trampled by	

ridden animal stumbled and fell

EXCLUDES *collision of animal being ridden with:*
animal-drawn vehicle (E827.0-E827.9)
pedal cycle (E826.0-E826.9)

✓4ᵗʰ **E829 Other road vehicle accidents**

[0,4,8,9] INCLUDES

accident while boarding or alighting from	
blow from object in	streetcar nonmotor road vehicle not classifiable to E826-E828
breakage of any part of	
caught in door of	
derailment of	
fall in, on, or from	
fire in	

collision between streetcar or nonmotor road vehicle, except as in E826-E828, and:
    animal (not being ridden)
    another nonmotor road vehicle not classifiable to E826-E828
    pedestrian
    other object, fixed, movable, or moving, not set in motion by motor vehicle, railway train, or aircraft
nonmotor road vehicle accident NOS
streetcar accident NOS

EXCLUDES *collision with:*
animal being ridden (E828.0-E828.9)
animal-drawn vehicle (E827.0-E827.9)
pedal cycle (E826.0-E826.9)

---

§ Requires fourth-digit. Valid digits are in [brackets] under each code. See beginning of section E820-E825 for codes and definitions.

✓4ᵗʰ Fourth-digit Required   ►◄ Revised Text   ● New Code   ▲ Revised Code Title

WATER TRANSPORT ACCIDENTS (E830-E838)

Note: For definitions of water transport accident and related terms see definitions (a), (s), and (t).

INCLUDES   watercraft accidents in the course of recreational activities

EXCLUDES   *accidents involving both aircraft, including objects set in motion by aircraft, and watercraft (E840.0-E845.9)*

The following fourth-digit subdivisions are for use with categories E830-E838 to identify the injured person:

.0 Occupant of small boat, unpowered

.1 Occupant of small boat, powered

See definition (t)

EXCLUDES *water skier (.4)*

.2 Occupant of other watercraft — crew

Persons:

engaged in operation of watercraft

providing passenger services [cabin attendants, ship's physician, catering personnel]

working on ship during voyage in other capacity [musician in band, operators of shops and beauty parlors]

.3 Occupant of other watercraft — other than crew

Passenger

Occupant of lifeboat, other than crew, after abandoning ship

.4 Water skier

.5 Swimmer

.6 Dockers, stevedores

Longshoreman employed on the dock in loading and unloading ships

.8 Other specified person

Immigration and custom officials on board ship

Person:

accompanying passenger or member of crew visiting boat

Pilot (guiding ship into port)

.9 Unspecified person

✓4th **E830 Accident to watercraft causing submersion**

INCLUDES   submersion and drowning due to:

boat overturning

boat submerging

falling or jumping from burning ship

falling or jumping from crushed watercraft

ship sinking

other accident to watercraft

✓4th **E831 Accident to watercraft causing other injury**

INCLUDES   any injury, except submersion and drowning, as a result of an accident to watercraft

burned while ship on fire

crushed between ships in collision

crushed by lifeboat after abandoning ship

fall due to collision or other accident to watercraft

hit by falling object due to accident to watercraft

injured in watercraft accident involving collision

struck by boat or part thereof after fall or jump from damaged boat

EXCLUDES *burns from localized fire or explosion on board ship (E837.0-E837.9)*

✓4th **E832 Other accidental submersion or drowning in water transport accident**

INCLUDES   submersion or drowning as a result of an accident other than accident to the watercraft, such as:

fall:

from gangplank

from ship

overboard

thrown overboard by motion of ship

washed overboard

EXCLUDES *submersion or drowning of swimmer or diver who voluntarily jumps from boat not involved in an accident (E910.0-E910.9)*

✓4th **E833 Fall on stairs or ladders in water transport**

EXCLUDES *fall due to accident to watercraft (E831.0-E831.9)*

✓4th **E834 Other fall from one level to another in water transport**

EXCLUDES *fall due to accident to watercraft (E831.0-E831.9)*

✓4th **E835 Other and unspecified fall in water transport**

EXCLUDES *fall due to accident to watercraft (E831.0-E831.9)*

✓4th **E836 Machinery accident in water transport**

INCLUDES   injuries in water transport caused by:

deck

engine room

galley   } machinery

laundry

loading

✓4th **E837 Explosion, fire, or burning in watercraft**

INCLUDES   explosion of boiler on steamship

localized fire on ship

EXCLUDES *burning ship (due to collision or explosion) resulting in:*

submersion or drowning (E830.0-E830.9)

other injury (E831.0-E831.9)

✓4th **E838 Other and unspecified water transport accident**

INCLUDES   accidental poisoning by gases or fumes on ship

atomic power plant malfunction in watercraft

crushed between ship and stationary object [wharf]

crushed between ships without accident to watercraft

crushed by falling object on ship or while loading or unloading

hit by boat while water skiing

struck by boat or part thereof (after fall from boat)

watercraft accident NOS

AIR AND SPACE TRANSPORT ACCIDENTS (E840-E845)

Note: For definition of aircraft and related terms see definitions (u) and (v).

The following fourth-digit subdivisions are for use with categories E840-E845 to identify the injured person. Valid fourth digits are in [brackets] under codes E842-E845.

.0 Occupant of spacecraft

.1 Occupant of military aircraft, any
Crew in military aircraft [air force] [army] [national guard] [navy]
Passenger (civilian) (military) in military aircraft [air force] [army] [national guard] [navy]
Troops in military aircraft [air force] [army] [national guard] [navy]

> EXCLUDES *occupants of aircraft operated under jurisdiction of police departments (.5)*
> *parachutist (.7)*

.2 Crew of commercial aircraft (powered) in surface to surface transport

.3 Other occupant of commercial aircraft (powered) in surface to surface transport
Flight personnel:
not part of crew
on familiarization flight
Passenger on aircraft (powered) NOS

.4 Occupant of commercial aircraft (powered) in surface to air transport
Occupant [crew] [passenger] of aircraft (powered) engaged in activities, such as:
aerial spraying (crops) (fire retardants)
air drops of emergency supplies
air drops of parachutists, except from military craft
crop dusting
lowering of construction material [bridge or telephone pole]
sky writing

.5 Occupant of other powered aircraft
Occupant [crew][passenger] of aircraft [powered] engaged in activities, such as:
aerobatic flying
aircraft racing
rescue operation
storm surveillance
traffic surveillance
Occupant of private plane NOS

.6 Occupant of unpowered aircraft, except parachutist
Occupant of aircraft classifiable to E842

.7 Parachutist (military) (other)
Person making voluntary descent

> EXCLUDES *person making descent after accident to aircraft (.1-.6)*

.8 Ground crew, airline employee
Persons employed at airfields (civil) (military) or launching pads, not occupants of aircraft

.9 Other person

✓4ᵗʰ E840 Accident to powered aircraft at takeoff or landing

| INCLUDES | collision of aircraft with any object, fixed, movable, or moving
crash
explosion on aircraft
fire on aircraft
forced landing | } while taking off or landing |

✓4ᵗʰ E841 Accident to powered aircraft, other and unspecified

INCLUDES   aircraft accident NOS
aircraft crash or wreck NOS
any accident to powered aircraft while in transit or when not specified whether in transit, taking off, or landing
collision of aircraft with another aircraft, bird, or any object, while in transit
explosion on aircraft while in transit
fire on aircraft while in transit

✓4ᵗʰ E842 Accident to unpowered aircraft

[6-9]   INCLUDES   any accident, except collision with powered aircraft, to:
balloon
glider
hang glider
kite carrying a person
hit by object falling from unpowered aircraft

✓4ᵗʰ E843 Fall in, on, or from aircraft

[0-9]   INCLUDES   accident in boarding or alighting from aircraft, any kind
fall in, on, or from aircraft [any kind], while in transit, taking off, or landing, except when as a result of an accident to aircraft

✓4ᵗʰ E844 Other specified air transport accidents

[0-9]   INCLUDES   hit by:
aircraft
object falling from aircraft
injury by or from:
machinery on aircraft
rotating propeller
voluntary parachute descent
poisoning by carbon monoxide from aircraft while in transit
} without accident to aircraft
sucked into jet
any accident involving other transport vehicle (motor) (nonmotor) due to being hit by object set in motion by aircraft (powered)

> EXCLUDES *air sickness (E903)*
> *effects of:*
> *high altitude (E902.0-E902.1)*
> *pressure change (E902.0-E902.1)*
> *injury in parachute descent due to accident to aircraft (E840.0-E842-9)*

✓4ᵗʰ E845 Accident involving spacecraft

[0,8,9]   INCLUDES   launching pad accident
EXCLUDES   *effects of weightlessness in spacecraft (E928.0)*

✓4ᵗʰ Fourth-digit Required   ◄► Revised Text   ● New Code   ▲ Revised Code Title

VEHICLE ACCIDENTS NOT ELSEWHERE CLASSIFIABLE (E846-E848)

E846 Accidents involving powered vehicles used solely within the buildings and premises of industrial or commercial establishment

Accident to, on, or involving:
    battery powered airport passenger vehicle
    battery powered trucks (baggage) (mail)
    coal car in mine
    logging car
    self propelled truck, industrial
    station baggage truck (powered)
    tram, truck, or tub (powered) in mine or quarry

Collision with:
    pedestrian
    other vehicle or object within premises

Explosion of ⎫
Fall from   ⎬ powered vehicle, industrial
Overturning of ⎪   or commercial
Struck by ⎭

EXCLUDES   accidental poisoning by exhaust gas from vehicle not elsewhere classifiable (E868.2)
                 injury by crane, lift (fork), or elevator (E919.2)

E847 Accidents involving cable cars not running on rails

Accident to, on, or involving:
    cable car, not on rails
    ski chair-lift
    ski-lift with gondola
    téléférique

Breakage of cable
Caught or dragged by ⎫
Fall or jump from   ⎬ cable car, not on rails
Object thrown from or in ⎭

E848 Accidents involving other vehicles, not elsewhere classifiable

Accident to, on, or involving:
    ice yacht
    land yacht
    nonmotor, nonroad vehicle NOS

✓4ᵗʰ **E849 Place of occurrence**

The following category is for use to denote the place where the injury or poisoning occurred.

E849.0 Home

Apartment	Private:
Boarding house	garage
Farm house	garden
Home premises	home
House (residential)	walk
Noninstitutional	Swimming pool in private
place of residence	house or garden
Private:	Yard of home
driveway	

EXCLUDES   home under construction but not yet occupied (E849.3)
                 institutional place of residence (E849.7)

E849.1 Farm

Farm:
    buildings
    land under cultivation

EXCLUDES   farm house and home premises of farm (E849.0)

E849.2 Mine and quarry

Gravel pit	Tunnel under
Sand pit	construction

E849.3 Industrial place and premises

Building under	Industrial yard
construction	Loading platform (factory)
Dockyard	(store)
Dry dock	Plant, industrial
Factory	Railway yard
building	Shop (place of work)
premises	Warehouse
Garage (place of work)	Workhouse

E849.4 Place for recreation and sport

Amusement park	Public park
Baseball field	Racecourse
Basketball court	Resort NOS
Beach resort	Riding school
Cricket ground	Rifle range
Fives court	Seashore resort
Football field	Skating rink
Golf course	Sports palace
Gymnasium	Stadium
Hockey field	Swimming pool, public
Holiday camp	Tennis court
Ice palace	Vacation resort
Lake resort	
Mountain resort	
Playground, including school playground	

EXCLUDES   that in private house or garden (E849.0)

E849.5 Street and highway

E849.6 Public building

Building (including adjacent grounds) used by the general public or by a particular group of the public, such as:

airport	music hall
bank	nightclub
café	office
casino	office building
church	opera house
cinema	post office
clubhouse	public hall
courthouse	radio broadcasting station
dance hall	restaurant
garage building (for	school (state) (public)
car storage)	(private)
hotel	shop, commercial
market (grocery or	station (bus) (railway)
other	store
commodity)	theater
movie house	

EXCLUDES   home garage (E849.0)
                 industrial building or workplace (E849.3)

E849.7 Residential institution

Children's home	Old people's home
Dormitory	Orphanage
Hospital	Prison
Jail	Reform school

E849.8 Other specified places

Beach NOS	Pond or pool (natural)
Canal	Prairie
Caravan site NOS	Public place NOS
Derelict house	Railway line
Desert	Reservoir
Dock	River
Forest	Sea
Harbor	Seashore NOS
Hill	Stream
Lake NOS	Swamp
Mountain	Trailer court
Parking lot	Woods
Parking place	

E849.9 Unspecified place

✓4ᵗʰ Fourth-digit Required   ▶◀ Revised Text   ● New Code   ▲ Revised Code Title

ACCIDENTAL POISONING BY DRUGS, MEDICINAL SUBSTANCES, AND BIOLOGICALS (E850-E858)

INCLUDES   accidental overdose of drug, wrong drug given or taken in error, and drug taken inadvertently

accidents in the use of drugs and biologicals in medical and surgical procedures

EXCLUDES   *administration with suicidal or homicidal intent or intent to harm, or in circumstances classifiable to E980-E989 (E950.0-E950.5, E962.0, E980.0-E980.5)*

correct drug properly administered in therapeutic or prophylactic dosage, as the cause of adverse effect (E930.0-E949.9)

See Alphabetic Index for more complete list of specific drugs to be classified under the fourth-digit subdivisions. The American Hospital Formulary numbers can be used to classify new drugs listed by the American Hospital Formulary Service (AHFS). See Appendix C.

√4ᵗʰ **E850 Accidental poisoning by analgesics, antipyretics, and antirheumatics**

E850.0 Heroin
     Diacetylmorphine

E850.1 Methadone

E850.2 Other opiates and related narcotics
     Codeine [methylmorphine]   Morphine
     Meperidine [pethidine]   Opium (alkaloids)

E850.3 Salicylates
     Acetylsalicylic acid [aspirin]
     Amino derivatives of salicylic acid
     Salicylic acid salts

E850.4 Aromatic analgesics, not elsewhere classified
     Acetanilid
     Paracetamol [acetaminophen]
     Phenacetin [acetophenetidin]

E850.5 Pyrazole derivatives
     Aminophenazone [amidopyrine]
     Phenylbutazone

E850.6 Antirheumatics [antiphlogistics]
     Gold salts   Indomethacin
     EXCLUDES   *salicylates (E850.3)*
         steroids (E858.0)

E850.7 Other non-narcotic analgesics
     Pyrabital

E850.8 Other specified analgesics and antipyretics
     Pentazocine

E850.9 Unspecified analgesic or antipyretic

E851 Accidental poisoning by barbiturates
     Amobarbital [amylobarbitone]   Pentobarbital [pentobarbitone]
     Barbital [barbitone]   Phenobarbital [phenobarbitone]
     Butabarbital [butabarbitone]   Secobarbital [quinalbarbitone]
     EXCLUDES   *thiobarbiturates (E855.1)*

√4ᵗʰ **E852 Accidental poisoning by other sedatives and hypnotics**

E852.0 Chloral hydrate group

E852.1 Paraldehyde

E852.2 Bromine compounds
     Bromides   Carbromal (derivatives)

E852.3 Methaqualone compounds

E852.4 Glutethimide group

E852.5 Mixed sedatives, not elsewhere classified

E852.8 Other specified sedatives and hypnotics

E852.9 Unspecified sedative or hypnotic
     Sleeping:
         drug
         pill   } NOS
         tablet

√4ᵗʰ **E853 Accidental poisoning by tranquilizers**

E853.0 Phenothiazine-based tranquilizers
     Chlorpromazine   Prochlorperazine
     Fluphenazine   Promazine

E853.1 Butyrophenone-based tranquilizers
     Haloperidol   Trifluperidol
     Spiperone

E853.2 Benzodiazepine-based tranquilizers
     Chlordiazepoxide   Lorazepam
     Diazepam   Medazepam
     Flurazepam   Nitrazepam

E853.8 Other specified tranquilizers
     Hydroxyzine   Meprobamate

E853.9 Unspecified tranquilizer

√4ᵗʰ **E854 Accidental poisoning by other psychotropic agents**

E854.0 Antidepressants
     Amitriptyline
     Imipramine
     Monoamine oxidase [MAO] inhibitors

E854.1 Psychodysleptics [hallucinogens]
     Cannabis derivatives   Mescaline
     Lysergide [LSD]   Psilocin
     Marihuana (derivatives)   Psilocybin

E854.2 Psychostimulants
     Amphetamine   Caffeine
     EXCLUDES   *central appetite depressants (E858.8)*

E854.3 Central nervous system stimulants
     Analeptics   Opiate antagonists

E854.8 Other psychotropic agents

√4ᵗʰ **E855 Accidental poisoning by other drugs acting on central and autonomic nervous system**

E855.0 Anticonvulsant and anti-Parkinsonism drugs
     Amantadine
     Hydantoin derivatives
     Levodopa [L-dopa]
     Oxazolidine derivatives [paramethadione]
         [trimethadione]
     Succinimides

E855.1 Other central nervous system depressants
     Ether
     Gaseous anesthetics
     Halogenated hydrocarbon derivatives
     Intravenous anesthetics
     Thiobarbiturates, such as thiopental sodium

E855.2 Local anesthetics
     Cocaine   Procaine
     Lidocaine [lignocaine]   Tetracaine

E855.3 Parasympathomimetics [cholinergics]
     Acetylcholine   Pilocarpine
     Anticholinesterase:
         organophosphorus
         reversible

E855.4 Parasympatholytics [anticholinergics and antimuscarinics] and spasmolytics
     Atropine
     Homatropine
     Hyoscine [scopolamine]
     Quaternary ammonium derivatives

E855.5 Sympathomimetics [adrenergics]
     Epinephrine [adrenalin]
     Levarterenol [noradrenalin]

E855.6 Sympatholytics [antiadrenergics]
     Phenoxybenzamine
     Tolazoline hydrochloride

E855.8 Other specified drugs acting on central and autonomic nervous systems

E855.9 Unspecified drug acting on central and autonomic nervous systems

E856 Accidental poisoning by antibiotics

E857 Accidental poisoning by other anti-infectives

√4ᵗʰ **E858 Accidental poisoning by other drugs**

E858.0 Hormones and synthetic substitutes

E858.1 Primarily systemic agents

E858.2 Agents primarily affecting blood constituents

E858.3 Agents primarily affecting cardiovascular system

E858.4 Agents primarily affecting gastrointestinal system

√4ᵗʰ Fourth-digit Required   ►◄ Revised Text   ● New Code   ▲ Revised Code Title

E858.5   Water, mineral, and uric acid metabolism drugs

E858.6   Agents primarily acting on the smooth and skeletal muscles and respiratory system

E858.7   Agents primarily affecting skin and mucous membrane, ophthalmological, otorhinolaryngological, and dental drugs

E858.8   Other specified drugs

Central appetite depressants

E858.9   Unspecified drug

ACCIDENTAL POISONING BY OTHER SOLID AND LIQUID SUBSTANCES, GASES, AND VAPORS (E860-E869)

Note: Categories in this section are intended primarily to indicate the external cause of poisoning states classifiable to 980-989. They may also be used to indicate external causes of localized effects classifiable to 001-799.

✓4ᵗʰ E860 Accidental poisoning by alcohol, not elsewhere classified

E860.0   Alcoholic beverages

Alcohol in preparations intended for consumption

E860.1   Other and unspecified ethyl alcohol and its products

| Denatured alcohol | Grain alcohol NOS |
| Ethanol NOS | Methylated spirit |

E860.2   Methyl alcohol

| Methanol | Wood alcohol |

E860.3   Isopropyl alcohol

| Dimethyl carbinol | Rubbing alcohol subsitute |
| Isopropanol | Secondary propyl alcohol |

E860.4   Fusel oil

Alcohol:	Alcohol:
amyl	propyl
butyl	

E860.8   Other specified alcohols

E860.9   Unspecified alcohol

✓4ᵗʰ E861 Accidental poisoning by cleansing and polishing agents, disinfectants, paints, and varnishes

E861.0   Synthetic detergents and shampoos

E861.1   Soap products

E861.2   Polishes

E861.3   Other cleansing and polishing agents

Scouring powders

E861.4   Disinfectants

Household and other disinfectants not ordinarily used on the person

EXCLUDES   *carbolic acid or phenol (E864.0)*

E861.5   Lead paints

E861.6   Other paints and varnishes

| Lacquers | Paints, other than lead |
| Oil colors | White washes |

E861.9   Unspecified

✓4ᵗʰ E862 Accidental poisoning by petroleum products, other solvents and their vapors, not elsewhere classified

E862.0   Petroleum solvents

Petroleum:	Petroleum:
ether	naphtha
benzine	

E862.1   Petroleum fuels and cleaners

Antiknock additives to petroleum fuels

Gas oils

Gasoline or petrol

Kerosene

EXCLUDES   *kerosene insecticides (E863.4)*

E862.2   Lubricating oils

E862.3   Petroleum solids

Paraffin wax

E862.4   Other specified solvents

Benzene

E862.9   Unspecified solvent

✓4ᵗʰ E863 Accidental poisoning by agricultural and horticultural chemical and pharmaceutical preparations other than plant foods and fertilizers

EXCLUDES   *plant foods and fertilizers (E866.5)*

E863.0   Insecticides of organochlorine compounds

Benzene hexachloride	Dieldrin
Chlordane	Endrine
DDT	Toxaphene

E863.1   Insecticides of organophosphorus compounds

Demeton	Parathion
Diazinon	Phenylsulphthion
Dichlorvos	Phorate
Malathion	Phosdrin
Methyl parathion	

E863.2   Carbamates

| Aldicarb | Propoxur |
| Carbaryl | |

E863.3   Mixtures of insecticides

E863.4   Other and unspecified insecticides

Kerosene insecticides

E863.5   Herbicides

2, 4-Dichlorophenoxyacetic acid [2, 4-D]

2, 4, 5-Trichlorophenoxyacetic acid [2, 4, 5-T]

Chlorates

Diquat

Mixtures of plant foods and fertilizers with herbicides

Paraquat

E863.6   Fungicides

Organic mercurials (used in seed dressing)

Pentachlorophenols

E863.7   Rodenticides

Fluoroacetates	Warfarin
Squill and derivatives	Zinc phosphide
Thallium	

E863.8   Fumigants

| Cyanides | Phosphine |
| Methyl bromide | |

E863.9   Other and unspecified

✓4ᵗʰ E864 Accidental poisoning by corrosives and caustics, not elsewhere classified

EXCLUDES   *those as components of disinfectants (E861.4)*

E864.0   Corrosive aromatics

Carbolic acid or phenol

E864.1   Acids

Acid:	Acid:
hydrochloric	sulfuric
nitric	

E864.2   Caustic alkalis

Lye

E864.3   Other specified corrosives and caustics

E864.4   Unspecified corrosives and caustics

✓4ᵗʰ E865 Accidental poisoning from poisonous foodstuffs and poisonous plants

INCLUDES   any meat, fish, or shellfish

plants, berries, and fungi eaten as, or in mistake for, food, or by a child

EXCLUDES   *anaphylactic shock due to adverse food reaction (995.60-995.69)*

food poisoning (bacterial) (005.0-005.9)

poisoning and toxic reactions to venomous plants (E905.6-E905.7)

E865.0   Meat

E865.1   Shellfish

E865.2   Other fish

E865.3   Berries and seeds

E865.4   Other specified plants

E865.5   Mushrooms and other fungi

E865.8   Other specified foods

E865.9   Unspecified foodstuff or poisonous plant

E Codes

E866–E872.5

☑4ᵗʰ **E866 Accidental poisoning by other and unspecified solid and liquid substances**

> EXCLUDES   these substances as a component of:
> medicines (E850.0-E858.9)
> paints (E861.5-E861.6)
> pesticides (E863.0-E863.9)
> petroleum fuels (E862.1)

E866.0 Lead and its compounds and fumes

E866.1 Mercury and its compounds and fumes

E866.2 Antimony and its compounds and fumes

E866.3 Arsenic and its compounds and fumes

E866.4 Other metals and their compounds and fumes

> Beryllium (compounds)   Iron (compounds)
> Brass fumes   Manganese (compounds)
> Cadmium (compounds)   Nickel (compounds)
> Copper salts   Thallium (compounds)

E866.5 Plant foods and fertilizers

> EXCLUDES   mixtures with herbicides (E863.5)

E866.6 Glues and adhesives

E866.7 Cosmetics

E866.8 Other specified solid or liquid substances

E866.9 Unspecified solid or liquid substance

E867 Accidental poisoning by gas distributed by pipeline

> Carbon monoxide from incomplete combustion of piped gas
> Coal gas NOS
> Liquefied petroleum gas distributed through pipes (pure or mixed with air)
> Piped gas (natural) (manufactured)

☑4ᵗʰ **E868 Accidental poisoning by other utility gas and other carbon monoxide**

E868.0 Liquefied petroleum gas distributed in mobile containers

> Butane
> Liquefied hydrocarbon gas NOS
> Propane
> } or carbon monoxide from incomplete conbustion of these gases

E868.1 Other and unspecified utility gas

> Acetylene
> Gas NOS used for lighting, heating, or cooking
> Water gas
> } or carbon monoxide from incomplete conbustion of these gases

E868.2 Motor vehicle exhaust gas

> Exhaust gas from:
> farm tractor, not in transit
> gas engine
> motor pump
> motor vehicle, not in transit
> any type of combustion engine not in watercraft

> EXCLUDES   poisoning by carbon monoxide from:
> aircraft while in transit (E844.0-E844.9)
> motor vehicle while in transit (E818.0-E818.9)
> watercraft whether or not in transit (E838.0-E838.9)

E868.3 Carbon monoxide from incomplete combustion of other domestic fuels

> Carbon monoxide from incomplete combustion of:
> coal
> coke
> kerosene
> wood
> } in domestic stove or fireplace

> EXCLUDES   carbon monoxide from smoke and fumes due to conflagration (E890.0-E893.9)

E868.8 Carbon monoxide from other sources

> Carbon monoxide from:
> blast furnace gas
> incomplete combustion of fuels in industrial use
> kiln vapor

E868.9 Unspecified carbon monoxide

☑4ᵗʰ **E869 Accidental poisoning by other gases and vapors**

> EXCLUDES   effects of gases used as anesthetics (E855.1, E938.2)
> fumes from heavy metals (E866.0-E866.4)
> smoke and fumes due to conflagration or explosion (E890.0-E899)

E869.0 Nitrogen oxides

E869.1 Sulfur dioxide

E869.2 Freon

E869.3 Lacrimogenic gas [tear gas]

> Bromobenzyl cyanide   Ethyliodoacetate
> Chloroacetophenone

E869.4 Second-hand tobacco smoke

E869.8 Other specified gases and vapors

> Chlorine   Hydrocyanic acid gas

E869.9 Unspecified gases and vapors

MISADVENTURES TO PATIENTS DURING SURGICAL AND MEDICAL CARE (E870-E876)

> EXCLUDES   accidental overdose of drug and wrong drug given in error (E850.0-E858.9)
> surgical and medical procedures as the cause of abnormal reaction by the patient, without mention of misadventure at the time of procedure (E878.0-E879.9)

☑4ᵗʰ **E870 Accidental cut, puncture, perforation, or hemorrhage during medical care**

E870.0 Surgical operation

E870.1 Infusion or transfusion

E870.2 Kidney dialysis or other perfusion

E870.3 Injection or vaccination

E870.4 Endoscopic examination

E870.5 Aspiration of fluid or tissue, puncture, and catheterization

> Abdominal paracentesis   Lumbar puncture
> Aspirating needle biopsy   Thoracentesis
> Blood sampling

> EXCLUDES   heart catheterization (E870.6)

E870.6 Heart catheterization

E870.7 Administration of enema

E870.8 Other specified medical care

E870.9 Unspecified medical care

☑4ᵗʰ **E871 Foreign object left in body during procedure**

E871.0 Surgical operation

E871.1 Infusion or transfusion

E871.2 Kidney dialysis or other perfusion

E871.3 Injection or vaccination

E871.4 Endoscopic examination

E871.5 Aspiration of fluid or tissue, puncture, and catheterization

> Abdominal paracentesis   Lumbar puncture
> Aspiration needle biopsy   Thoracentesis
> Blood sampling

> EXCLUDES   heart catheterization (E871.6)

E871.6 Heart catheterization

E871.7 Removal of catheter or packing

E871.8 Other specified procedures

E871.9 Unspecified procedure

☑4ᵗʰ **E872 Failure of sterile precautions during procedure**

E872.0 Surgical operation

E872.1 Infusion or transfusion

E872.2 Kidney dialysis and other perfusion

E872.3 Injection or vaccination

E872.4 Endoscopic examination

E872.5 Aspiration of fluid or tissue, puncture, and catheterization

> Abdominal paracentesis   Lumbar puncture
> Aspiration needle biopsy   Thoracentesis
> Blood sampling

> EXCLUDES   heart catheterization (E872.6)

E872.6   Heart catheterization

E872.8   Other specified procedures

E872.9   Unspecified procedure

√4th **E873 Failure in dosage**

> EXCLUDES   *accidental overdose of drug, medicinal or biological substance (E850.0-E858.9)*

E873.0   **Excessive amount of blood or other fluid during transfusion or infusion**

E873.1   **Incorrect dilution of fluid during infusion**

E873.2   **Overdose of radiation in therapy**

E873.3   **Inadvertent exposure of patient to radiation during medical care**

E873.4   **Failure in dosage in electroshock or insulin-shock therapy**

E873.5   **Inappropriate [too hot or too cold] temperature in local application and packing**

E873.6   **Nonadministration of necessary drug or medicinal substance**

E873.8   **Other specified failure in dosage**

E873.9   **Unspecified failure in dosage**

√4th **E874 Mechanical failure of instrument or apparatus during procedure**

E874.0   **Surgical operation**

E874.1   **Infusion and transfusion**
> Air in system

E874.2   **Kidney dialysis and other perfusion**

E874.3   **Endoscopic examination**

E874.4   **Aspiration of fluid or tissue, puncture, and catheterization**
> Abdominal paracentesis   Lumbar puncture
> Aspiration needle biopsy   Thoracentesis
> Blood sampling
>> EXCLUDES   *heart catheterization (E874.5)*

E874.5   **Heart catheterization**

E874.8   **Other specified procedures**

E874.9   **Unspecified procedure**

√4th **E875 Contaminated or infected blood, other fluid, drug, or biological substance**

> INCLUDES   presence of:
> bacterial pyrogens
> endotoxin-producing bacteria
> serum hepatitis-producing agent

E875.0   **Contaminated substance transfused or infused**

E875.1   **Contaminated substance injected or used for vaccination**

E875.2   **Contaminated drug or biological substance administered by other means**

E875.8   **Other**

E875.9   **Unspecified**

√4th **E876 Other and unspecified misadventures during medical care**

E876.0   **Mismatched blood in transfusion**

E876.1   **Wrong fluid in infusion**

E876.2   **Failure in suture and ligature during surgical operation**

E876.3   **Endotracheal tube wrongly placed during anesthetic procedure**

E876.4   **Failure to introduce or to remove other tube or instrument**
> EXCLUDES   *foreign object left in body during procedure (E871.0-E871.9)*

E876.5   **Performance of inappropriate operation**

E876.8   **Other specified misadventures during medical care**
> Performance of inappropriate treatment NEC

E876.9   **Unspecified misadventure during medical care**

SURGICAL AND MEDICAL PROCEDURES AS THE CAUSE OF ABNORMAL REACTION OF PATIENT OR LATER COMPLICATION, WITHOUT MENTION OF MISADVENTURE AT THE TIME OF PROCEDURE (E878-E879)

> INCLUDES   procedures as the cause of abnormal reaction, such as:
> displacement or malfunction of prosthetic device
> hepatorenal failure, postoperative
> malfunction of external stoma
> postoperative intestinal obstruction
> rejection of transplanted organ

> EXCLUDES   *anesthetic management properly carried out as the cause of adverse effect (E937.0-E938.9)*
> *infusion and transfusion, without mention of misadventure in the technique of procedure (E930.0-E949.9)*

√4th **E878 Surgical operation and other surgical procedures as the cause of abnormal reaction of patient, or of later complication, without mention of misadventure at the time of operation**

E878.0   **Surgical operation with transplant of whole organ**
> Transplantation of: Transplantation of:
> heart   liver
> kidney

E878.1   **Surgical operation with implant of artificial internal device**
> Cardiac pacemaker   Heart valve prosthesis
> Electrodes implanted in   Internal orthopedic
> brain   device

E878.2   **Surgical operation with anastomosis, bypass, or graft, with natural or artificial tissues used as implant**
> Anastomosis: Graft of blood vessel,
> arteriovenous   tendon, or skin
> gastrojejunal
>> EXCLUDES   *external stoma (E878.3)*

E878.3   **Surgical operation with formation of external stoma**
> Colostomy   Gastrostomy
> Cystostomy   Ureterostomy
> Duodenostomy

E878.4   **Other restorative surgery**

E878.5   **Amputation of limb(s)**

E878.6   **Removal of other organ (partial) (total)**

E878.8   **Other specified surgical operations and procedures**

E878.9   **Unspecified surgical operations and procedures**

√4th **E879 Other procedures, without mention of misadventure at the time of procedure, as the cause of abnormal reaction of patient, or of later complication**

E879.0   **Cardiac catheterization**

E879.1   **Kidney dialysis**

E879.2   **Radiological procedure and radiotherapy**
> EXCLUDES   *radio-opaque dyes for diagnostic x-ray procedures (E947.8)*

E879.3   **Shock therapy**
> Electroshock therapy
> Insulin-shock therapy

E879.4   **Aspiration of fluid**
> Lumbar puncture
> Thoracentesis

E879.5   **Insertion of gastric or duodenal sound**

E879.6   **Urinary catheterization**

E879.7   **Blood sampling**

E879.8   **Other specified procedures**
> Blood transfusion

E879.9   **Unspecified procedure**

√4th Fourth-digit Required   ▶◀ Revised Text   ● New Code   ▲ Revised Code Title

ACCIDENTAL FALLS (E880-E888)

EXCLUDES   *falls (in or from):*
  burning building (E890.8, E891.8)
  into fire (E890.0-E899)
  into water (with submersion or drowning)
    (E910.0-E910.9)
  machinery (in operation) (E919.0-E919.9)
  on edged, pointed, or sharp object (E920.0-
    E920.9)
  transport vehicle (E800.0-E845.9)
  vehicle not elsewhere classifiable (E846-E848)

✓4ᵗʰ **E880 Fall on or from stairs or steps**

E880.0 Escalator

E880.1 Fall on or from sidewalk curb

EXCLUDES   *fall from moving sidewalk (E885.9)*

E880.9 Other stairs or steps

✓4ᵗʰ **E881 Fall on or from ladders or scaffolding**

E881.0 Fall from ladder

E881.1 Fall from scaffolding

E882 Fall from or out of building or other structure

Fall from:	Fall from:
balcony	turret
bridge	viaduct
building	wall
flagpole	window
tower	Fall through roof

EXCLUDES   *collapse of a building or structure (E916)*
  fall or jump from burning building (E890.8,
    E891.8)

✓4ᵗʰ **E883 Fall into hole or other opening in surface**

INCLUDES   fall into: fall into:

cavity	shaft
dock	swimming pool
hole	tank
pit	well
quarry	

EXCLUDES   *fall into water NOS (E910.9)*
  that resulting in drowning or submersion
    without mention of injury (E910.0-E910.9)

**E883.0 Accident from diving or jumping into water
[swimming pool]**
  Strike or hit:
    against bottom when jumping or diving into water
    wall or board of swimming pool
    water surface

EXCLUDES   *diving with insufficient air supply*
    (E913.2)
  effects of air pressure from diving
    (E902.2)

E883.1 Accidental fall into well

E883.2 Accidental fall into storm drain or manhole

E883.9 Fall into other hole or other opening in surface

✓4ᵗʰ **E884 Other fall from one level to another**

E884.0 Fall from playground equipment

EXCLUDES   *recreational machinery (E919.8)*

E884.1 Fall from cliff

E884.2 Fall from chair

E884.3 Fall from wheelchair

E884.4 Fall from bed

E884.5 Fall from other furniture

E884.6 Fall from commode
  Toilet

E884.9 Other fall from one level to another

Fall from:	Fall from:
embankment	stationary vehicle
haystack	tree

✓4ᵗʰ **E885 Fall on same level from slipping, tripping, or stumbling**

E885.0 Fall from (nonmotorized) scooter

E885.1 Fall from roller skates
  In-line skates

E885.2 Fall from skateboard

E885.3 Fall from skis

E885.4 Fall from snowboard

E885.9 Fall from other slipping, tripping, or stumbling
  Fall on moving sidewalk

✓4ᵗʰ **E886 Fall on same level from collision, pushing, or shoving, by or
with other person**

EXCLUDES   *crushed or pushed by a crowd or human*
    stampede (E917.1, E917.6)

E886.0 In sports
  Tackles in sports

EXCLUDES   *kicked, stepped on, struck by object, in*
    sports (E917.0, E917.5)

E886.9 Other and unspecified
  Fall from collision of pedestrian (conveyance) with
    another pedestrian (conveyance)

E887 Fracture, cause unspecified

✓4ᵗʰ **E888 Other and unspecified fall**
  Accidental fall NOS   Fall on same level NOS

E888.0 Fall resulting in striking against sharp object
  Use additional external cause code to identify object
    (E920)

E888.1 Fall resulting in striking against other object

E888.8 Other fall

E888.9 Unspecified fall
  Fall NOS

ACCIDENTS CAUSED BY FIRE AND FLAMES (E890-E899)

INCLUDES   asphyxia or poisoning due to conflagration or
    ignition
  burning by fire
  secondary fires resulting from explosion

EXCLUDES   *arson (E968.0)*
  fire in or on:
    machinery (in operation) (E919.0-E919.9)
    transport vehicle other than stationary
      vehicle (E800.0-E845.9)
    vehicle not elsewhere classifiable (E846-
      E848)

✓4ᵗʰ **E890 Conflagration in private dwelling**

INCLUDES   conflagration in: conflagration in:

apartment	lodging house
boarding house	mobile home
camping place	private garage
caravan	rooming house
farmhouse	tenement
house	

  conflagration originating from sources
    classifiable to E893-E898 in the above
    buildings

E890.0 Explosion caused by conflagration

**E890.1 Fumes from combustion of polyvinylchloride [PVC]
and similar material in conflagration**

E890.2 Other smoke and fumes from conflagration

Carbon monoxide	
Fumes NOS	from conflagration in
Smoke NOS	private building

E890.3 Burning caused by conflagration

E890.8 Other accident resulting from conflagration

Collapse of	
Fall from	burning private
Hit by object falling from	building
Jump from	

**E890.9 Unspecified accident resulting from conflagration in
private dwelling**

✓4ᵗʰ Fourth-digit Required   ▶◀ Revised Text   ● New Code   ▲ Revised Code Title

☑4ᵗʰ **E891 Conflagration in other and unspecified building or structure**

Conflagration in: Conflagration in:
  barn   farm outbuildings
  church   hospital
  convalescent and other   hotel
    residential home   school
  dormitory of educational   store
    institution   theater
  factory
Conflagration originating from sources classifiable to E893-E898, in the above buildings

E891.0 Explosion caused by conflagration

E891.1 Fumes from combustion of polyvinylchloride [PVC] and similar material in conflagration

E891.2 Other smoke and fumes from conflagration

Carbon monoxide ⎤ from conflagration in
Fumes NOS   ⎬ building or
Smoke NOS   ⎦ structure

E891.3 Burning caused by conflagration

E891.8 Other accident resulting from conflagration

Collapse of   ⎤
Fall from   ⎬ burning building or
Hit by object falling from ⎭ structure
Jump from

E891.9 Unspecified accident resulting from conflagration of other and unspecified building or structure

E892 Conflagration not in building or structure

Fire (uncontrolled) (in) (of):   Fire (uncontrolled) (in) (of):
  forest   prairie
  grass   transport vehicle [any],
  hay   except while in
  lumber   transit
  mine   tunnel

☑4ᵗʰ **E893 Accident caused by ignition of clothing**

EXCLUDES   *ignition of clothing:*
             from highly inflammable material (E894)
             with conflagration (E890.0-E892)

E893.0 From controlled fire in private dwelling

Ignition of clothing from:
  normal fire (charcoal) (coal)
    (electric) (gas) (wood) in: ⎤ in private
  brazier   ⎬ dwelling
  fireplace   ⎥ (as listed
  furnace   ⎥ in E890)
  stove   ⎦

E893.1 From controlled fire in other building or structure

Ignition of clothing from:
  normal fire (charcoal) ⎤
    (coal) (electric)   ⎥
    (gas) (wood) in: ⎬ in other building or
  brazier   ⎥ structure (as
  fireplace   ⎥ listed in E81)
  furnace   ⎥
  stove   ⎦

E893.2 From controlled fire not in building or structure

Ignition of clothing from:
  bonfire (controlled)
  brazier fire (controlled), not in building or
    structure
  trash fire (controlled)

  EXCLUDES   *conflagration not in building (E892)*
               trash fire out of control (E892)

E893.8 From other specified sources

Ignition of clothing from: Ignition of clothing from:
  blowlamp   cigarette
  blowtorch   lighter
  burning bedspread   matches
  candle   pipe
  cigar   welding torch

E893.9 Unspecified source

Ignition of clothing (from controlled fire NOS) (in building NOS) NOS

E894 Ignition of highly inflammable material

Ignition of:
  benzine   ⎤
  gasoline ⎥
  fat   ⎬ (with ignition of clothing)
  kerosene ⎥
  paraffin ⎥
  petrol   ⎦

EXCLUDES   *ignition of highly inflammable material with:*
             conflagration (E890.0-E892)
             explosion (E923.0-E923.9)

E895 Accident caused by controlled fire in private dwelling

Burning by (flame of) normal fire ⎤
  (charcoal) (coal) (electric)   ⎥
  (gas) (wood) in: ⎥ in private dwelling (as
  brazier   ⎬ listed in E890)
  fireplace   ⎥
  furnace   ⎥
  stove   ⎦

EXCLUDES   *burning by hot objects not producing fire or*
             flames (E924.0-E924.9)
           ignition of clothing from these sources (E893.0)
           poisoning by carbon monoxide from incomplete
             combustion of fuel (E867-E868.9)
           that with conflagration (E890.0-E890.9)

E896 Accident caused by controlled fire in other and unspecified building or structure

Burning by (flame of) normal fire (charcoal) (coal) (electric)
  (gas) (wood) in:
  brazier   ⎤
  fireplace ⎬ in other building or structure (as
  furnace   ⎥ listed in E891)
  stove   ⎦

EXCLUDES   *burning by hot objects not producing fire or*
             flames (E924.0-E924.9)
           ignition of clothing from these sources (E893.1)
           poisoning by carbon monoxide from incomplete
             combustion of fuel (E867-E868.9)
           that with conflagration (E891.0-E891.9)

E897 Accident caused by controlled fire not in building or structure

Burns from flame of: ⎤
  bonfire   ⎥
  brazier fire, not in building or structure ⎬ controlled
  trash fire   ⎦

EXCLUDES   *ignition of clothing from these sources (E893.2)*
           trash fire out of control (E892)
           that with conflagration (E892)

☑4ᵗʰ **E898 Accident caused by other specified fire and flames**

EXCLUDES   *conflagration (E890.0-E892)*
           that with ignition of:
             clothing (E893.0-E893.9)
             highly inflammable material (E894)

E898.0 Burning bedclothes

Bed set on fire NOS

E898.1 Other

Burning by: Burning by:
  blowlamp   lamp
  blowtorch   lighter
  candle   matches
  cigar   pipe
  cigarette   welding torch
  fire in room NOS

E899 Accident caused by unspecified fire

Burning NOS

ACCIDENTS DUE TO NATURAL AND ENVIRONMENTAL FACTORS (E900-E909)

☑4ᵗʰ **E900 Excessive heat**

E900.0 Due to weather conditions

Excessive heat as the external cause of:
  ictus solaris   sunstroke
  siriasis

E900.1 Of man-made origin

Heat (in):
- boiler room
- drying room
- factory
- furnace room

Heat (in):
- generated in transport vehicle
- kitchen

E900.9 Of unspecified origin

✓4ᵗʰ **E901 Excessive cold**

E901.0 Due to weather conditions

Excessive cold as the cause of:
- chilblains NOS
- immersion foot

E901.1 Of man-made origin

Contact with or inhalation of:
- dry ice
- liquid air
- liquid hydrogen
- liquid nitrogen

Prolonged exposure in:
- deep freeze unit
- refrigerator

E901.8 Other specified origin

E901.9 Of unspecified origin

✓4ᵗʰ **E902 High and low air pressure and changes in air pressure**

E902.0 Residence or prolonged visit at high altitude

Residence or prolonged visit at high altitude as the cause of:
- Acosta syndrome
- Alpine sickness
- altitude sickness
- Andes disease
- anoxia, hypoxia
- barotitis, barodontalgia, barosinusitis, otitic barotrauma
- hypobarism, hypobaropathy
- mountain sickness
- range disease

E902.1 In aircraft

Sudden change in air pressure in aircraft during ascent or descent as the cause of:
- aeroneurosis
- aviators' disease

E902.2 Due to diving

High air pressure from rapid descent in water

Reduction in atmospheric pressure while surfacing from deep water diving

} as the cause of:
- caisson disease
- divers' disease
- divers' palsy or paralysis

E902.8 Due to other specified causes

Reduction in atmospheric pressure whilesurfacing from underground

E902.9 Unspecified cause

E903 Travel and motion

✓4ᵗʰ **E904 Hunger, thirst, exposure, and neglect**

> EXCLUDES   *any condition resulting from homicidal intent (E968.0-E968.9)*
>
> *hunger, thirst, and exposure resulting from accidents connected with transport (E800.0-E848)*

E904.0 Abandonment or neglect of infants and helpless persons

Exposure to weather conditions

Hunger or thirst

} resulting from abandonment or neglect

Desertion of newborn
Inattention at or after birth
Lack of care (helpless person) (infant)

> EXCLUDES   *criminal [purposeful] neglect (E968.4)*

E904.1 Lack of food

Lack of food as the cause of:
- inanition
- insufficient nourishment
- starvation

> EXCLUDES   *hunger resulting from abandonment or neglect (E904.0)*

E904.2 Lack of water

Lack of water as the cause of:
- dehydration
- inanition

> EXCLUDES   *dehydration due to acute fluid loss* ▶*(276.51)*◀

E904.3 Exposure (to weather conditions), not elsewhere classifiable

Exposure NOS   Struck by hailstones
Humidity

> EXCLUDES   *struck by lightning (E907)*

E904.9 Privation, unqualified

Destitution

✓4ᵗʰ **E905 Venomous animals and plants as the cause of poisoning and toxic reactions**

> INCLUDES   chemical released by animal
>
> insects
>
> release of venom through fangs, hairs, spines, tentacles, and other venom apparatus

> EXCLUDES   *eating of poisonous animals or plants (E865.0-E865.9)*

E905.0 Venomous snakes and lizards

Cobra   Mamba
Copperhead snake   Rattlesnake
Coral snake   Sea snake
Fer de lance   Snake (venomous)
Gila monster   Viper
Krait   Water moccasin

> EXCLUDES   *bites of snakes and lizards known to be nonvenomous (E906.2)*

E905.1 Venomous spiders

Black widow spider   Tarantula (venomous)
Brown spider

E905.2 Scorpion

E905.3 Hornets, wasps, and bees

Yellow jacket

E905.4 Centipede and venomous millipede (tropical)

E905.5 Other venomous arthropods

Sting of: Sting of:
- ant   caterpillar

E905.6 Venomous marine animals and plants

Puncture by sea urchin spine

Sting of:
- coral
- jelly fish
- nematocysts

Sting of:
- sea anemone
- sea cucumber
- other marine animal or plant

> EXCLUDES   *bites and other injuries caused by nonvenomous marine animal (E906.2-E906.8)*
>
> *bite of sea snake (venomous) (E905.0)*

E905.7 Poisoning and toxic reactions caused by other plants

Injection of poisons or toxins into or through skin by plant thorns, spines, or other mechanisms

> EXCLUDES   *puncture wound NOS by plant thorns or spines (E920.8)*

E905.8 Other specified

E905.9 Unspecified

Sting NOS   Venomous bite NOS

✓4ᵗʰ **E906 Other injury caused by animals**

> EXCLUDES   *poisoning and toxic reactions caused by venomous animals and insects (E905.0-E905.9)*
>
> *road vehicle accident involving animals (E827.0-E828.9)*
>
> *tripping or falling over an animal (E885.9)*

✓4ᵗʰ Fourth-digit Required   ◄► Revised Text   ● New Code   ▲ Revised Code Title

E906.0 **Dog bite**

E906.1 **Rat bite**

E906.2 **Bite of nonvenomous snakes and lizards**

E906.3 **Bite of other animal except arthropod**

    Cats   Rodents, except rats

    Moray eel   Shark

E906.4 **Bite of nonvenomous arthropod**

    Insect bite NOS

E906.5 **Bite by unspecified animal**

    Animal bite NOS

E906.8 **Other specified injury caused by animal**

    Butted by animal

    Fallen on by horse or other animal, not being ridden

    Gored by animal

    Implantation of quills of porcupine

    Pecked by bird

    Run over by animal, not being ridden

    Stepped on by animal, not being ridden

       EXCLUDES *injury by animal being ridden (E828.0-E828.9)*

E906.9 **Unspecified injury caused by animal**

E907 **Lightning**

    EXCLUDES *injury from:*

        fall of tree or other object caused by lightning (E916)

        fire caused by lightning (E890.0-E892)

✓4ᵗʰ E908 **Cataclysmic storms, and floods resulting from storms**

    EXCLUDES *collapse of dam or man-made structure causing flood (E909.3)*

E908.0 **Hurricane**

    Storm surge

    "Tidal wave" caused by storm action

    Typhoon

E908.1 **Tornado**

    Cyclone

    Twisters

E908.2 **Floods**

    Torrential rainfall

    Flash flood

       EXCLUDES *collapse of dam or man-made structure causing flood (E909.3)*

E908.3 **Blizzard (snow) (ice)**

E908.4 **Dust storm**

E908.8 **Other cataclysmic storms**

E908.9 **Unspecified cataclysmic storms, and floods resulting from storms**

    Storm NOS

✓4ᵗʰ E909 **Cataclysmic earth surface movements and eruptions**

E909.0 **Earthquakes**

E909.1 **Volcanic eruptions**

    Burns from lava

    Ash inhalation

E909.2 **Avalanche, landslide, or mudslide**

E909.3 **Collapse of dam or man-made structure**

E909.4 **Tidalwave caused by earthquake**

    Tidalwave NOS

    Tsunami

       EXCLUDES *tidalwave caused by tropical storm (E908.0)*

E909.8 **Other cataclysmic earth surface movements and eruptions**

E909.9 **Unspecified cataclysmic earth surface movements and eruptions**

ACCIDENTS CAUSED BY SUBMERSION, SUFFOCATION, AND FOREIGN BODIES (E910-E915)

✓4ᵗʰ E910 **Accidental drowning and submersion**

    INCLUDES immersion

        swimmers' cramp

    EXCLUDES *diving accident (NOS) (resulting in injury except drowning) (E883.0)*

        diving with insufficient air supply (E913.2)

        drowning and submersion due to:

          cataclysm (E908-E909)

          machinery accident (E919.0-E919.9)

          transport accident (E800.0-E845.9)

        effect of high and low air pressure (E902.2)

        injury from striking against objects while in running water (E917.2)

E910.0 **While water-skiing**

    Fall from water skis with submersion or drowning

       EXCLUDES *accident to water-skier involving a watercraft and resulting in submersion or other injury (E830.4, E831.4)*

E910.1 **While engaged in other sport or recreational activity with diving equipment**

    Scuba diving NOS   Underwater spear

    Skin diving NOS   fishing NOS

E910.2 **While engaged in other sport or recreational activity without diving equipment**

    Fishing or hunting, except from boat or with diving equipment

    Ice skating

    Playing in water

    Surfboarding

    Swimming NOS

    Voluntarily jumping from boat, not involved in accident, for swim NOS

    Wading in water

       EXCLUDES *jumping into water to rescue another person (E910.3)*

E910.3 **While swimming or diving for purposes other than recreation or sport**

    Marine salvage

    Pearl diving

    Placement of fishing nets   (with diving

    Rescue (attempt) of   equipment)

       another person

    Underwater construction

      or repairs

E910.4 **In bathtub**

E910.8 **Other accidental drowning or submersion**

    Drowning in: Drowning in:

      quenching tank   swimming pool

E910.9 **Unspecified accidental drowning or submersion**

    Accidental fall into water NOS

    Drowning NOS

E911 **Inhalation and ingestion of food causing obstruction of respiratory tract or suffocation**

    Aspiration and inhalation of food [any] (into respiratory tract) NOS

    Asphyxia by

    Choked on   food [including bone, seed in

    Suffocation by   food, regurgitated food]

    Compression of trachea

    Interruption of respiration   by food lodged in

    Obstruction of respiration   esophagus

    Obstruction of pharynx by food (bolus)

       EXCLUDES *injury, except asphyxia and obstruction of respiratory passage, caused by food (E915)*

        obstruction of esophagus by food without mention of asphyxia or obstruction of respiratory passage (E915)

E912 Inhalation and ingestion of other object causing obstruction of respiratory tract or suffocation

Aspiration and inhalation of foreign body except food (into respiratory tract) NOS

Foreign object [bean] [marble] in nose

Obstruction of pharynx by foreign body

Compression

Interruption of respiration } by foreign body in

Obstruction of respiration } esophagus

> **EXCLUDES**   injury, except asphyxia and obstruction of respiratory passage, caused by foreign body (E915)
>
> obstruction of esophagus by foreign body without mention of asphyxia or obstruction in respiratory passage (E915)

✓4ᵗʰ E913 Accidental mechanical suffocation

> **EXCLUDES**   mechanical suffocation from or by:
> accidental inhalation or ingestion of:
> food (E911)
> foreign object (E912)
> cataclysm (E908-E909)
> explosion (E921.0-E921.9, E923.0-E923.9)
> machinery accident (E919.0-E919.9)

E913.0 In bed or cradle

> **EXCLUDES**   suffocation by plastic bag (E913.1)

E913.1 By plastic bag

E913.2 Due to lack of air (in closed place)

Accidentally closed up in refrigerator or other airtight enclosed space

Diving with insufficient air supply

> **EXCLUDES**   suffocation by plastic bag (E913.1)

E913.3 By falling earth or other substance

Cave-in NOS

> **EXCLUDES**   cave-in caused by cataclysmic earth surface movements and eruptions (E909)
>
> struck by cave-in without asphyxiation or suffocation (E916)

E913.8 Other specified means

Accidental hanging, except in bed or cradle

E913.9 Unspecified means

Asphyxia, mechanical NOS   Suffocation NOS

Strangulation NOS

E914 Foreign body accidentally entering eye and adnexa

> **EXCLUDES**   corrosive liquid (E924.1)

E915 Foreign body accidentally entering other orifice

> **EXCLUDES**   aspiration and inhalation of foreign body, any, (into respiratory tract) NOS (E911-E912)

OTHER ACCIDENTS (E916-E928)

E916 Struck accidentally by falling object

Collapse of building, except on fire

Falling:
rock
snowslide NOS
stone
tree

Object falling from:
machine, not in operation
stationary vehicle

Code first:
collapse of building on fire (E890.0-E891.9)
falling object in:
cataclysm (E908-E909)
machinery accidents (E919.0-E919.9)
transport accidents (E800.0-E845.9)
vehicle accidents not elsewhere classifiable (E846-E848)
object set in motion by:
explosion (E921.0-E921.9, E923.0-E923.9)
firearm (E922.0-E922.9)
projected object (E917.0-E917.9)

✓4ᵗʰ E917 Striking against or struck accidentally by objects or persons

> **INCLUDES**   bumping into or against   object (moving) (projected) (stationary)   colliding with   kicking against   stepping on   pedestrian conveyance   struck by   person

> **EXCLUDES**   fall from:
> collision with another person, except when caused by a crowd (E886.0-E886.9)
> stumbling over object (E885.9)
> fall resulting in striking against object (E888.0, E888.1)
> injury caused by:
> assault (E960.0-E960.1, E967.0-E967.9)
> cutting or piercing instrument (E920.0-E920.9)
> explosion (E921.0-E921.9, E923.0-E923.9)
> firearm (E922.0-E922.9)
> machinery (E919.0-E919.9)
> transport vehicle (E800.0-E845.9)
> vehicle not elsewhere classifiable (E846-E848)

E917.0 In sports without subsequent fall

Kicked or stepped on during game (football) (rugby)

Struck by hit or thrown ball

Struck by hockey stick or puck

E917.1 Caused by a crowd, by collective fear or panic without subsequent fall

Crushed

Pushed } by crowd or human stampede

Stepped on

E917.2 In running water without subsequent fall

> **EXCLUDES**   drowning or submersion (E910.0-E910.9)
>
> that in sports (E917.0, E917.5)

E917.3 Furniture without subsequent fall

> **EXCLUDES**   fall from furniture (E884.2, E884.4-E884.5)

E917.4 Other stationary object without subsequent fall

Bath tub

Fence

Lamp-post

E917.5 Object in sports with subsequent fall

Knocked down while boxing

E917.6 Caused by a crowd, by collective fear or panic with subsequent fall

E917.7 Furniture with subsequent fall

> **EXCLUDES**   fall from furniture (E884.2, E884.4-E884.5)

E917.8 Other stationary object with subsequent fall

Bath tub

Fence

Lamp-post

E917.9 Other striking against with or without subsequent fall

E918 Caught accidentally in or between objects

Caught, crushed, jammed, or pinched in or between moving or stationary objects, such as:

escalator

folding object

hand tools, appliances, or implements

sliding door and door frame

under packing crate

washing machine wringer

> **EXCLUDES**   injury caused by:
> cutting or piercing instrument (E920.0-E920.9)
> machinery (E919.0-E919.9)
> transport vehicle (E800.0-E845.9)
> vehicle not elsewhere classifiable (E846-E848)
> struck accidentally by:
> falling object (E916)
> object (moving) (projected) (E917.0-E917.9)

☑4ᵗʰ E919 Accidents caused by machinery

INCLUDES
burned by
caught in (moving parts of)
collapse of
crushed by
cut or pierced by
drowning or submersion
    caused by
explosion of, on, in
fall from or into moving
    part of   machinery
fire starting in or on   (accident)
mechanical suffocation
    caused by
object falling from, on, in
    motion by
overturning of
pinned under
run over by
struck by
thrown from

caught between machinery and other object
machinery accident NOS

EXCLUDES
accidents involving machinery, not in operation (E884.9, E916-E918)
injury caused by:
    electric current in connection with machinery (E925.0-E925.9)
    escalator (E880.0, E918)
    explosion of pressure vessel in connection with machinery (E921.0-E921.9)
    moving sidewalk (E885.9)
    powered hand tools, appliances, and implements (E916-E918, E920.0-E921.9, E923.0-E926.9)
    transport vehicle accidents involving machinery (E800.0-E848)
poisoning by carbon monoxide generated by machine (E868.8)

E919.0 Agricultural machines

Animal-powered	Farm tractor
agricultural machine	Harvester
Combine	Hay mower or rake
Derrick, hay	Reaper
Farm machinery NOS	Thresher

EXCLUDES
that in transport under own power on the highway (E810.0-E819.9)
that being towed by another vehicle on the highway (E810.0-E819.9, E827.0-E827.9, E829.0-E829.9)
that involved in accident classifiable to E820-E829 (E820.0-E829.9)

E919.1 Mining and earth-drilling machinery

Bore or drill (land) (seabed)	Shaft lift
Shaft hoist	Under-cutter

EXCLUDES
coal car, tram, truck, and tub in mine (E846)

E919.2 Lifting machines and appliances

Chain hoist	
Crane	
Derrick	except in
Elevator (building) (grain)	agricultural
Forklift truck	or mining
Lift	operations
Pulley block	
Winch	

EXCLUDES
that being towed by another vehicle on the highway (E810.0-E819.9, E827.0-E827.9, E829.0-829.9)
that in transport under own power on the highway (E810.0-E819.9)
that involved in accident classifiable to E820-E829 (E820.0-E829.9)

E919.3 Metalworking machines

	Metal:
Abrasive wheel	
Forging machine	drilling machine
Lathe	milling machine
Mechanical shears	power press
	rolling-mill
	sawing machine

E919.4 Woodworking and forming machines

Band saw	Overhead plane
Bench saw	Powered saw
Circular saw	Radial saw
Molding machine	Sander

EXCLUDES *hand saw (E920.1)*

E919.5 Prime movers, except electrical motors

Gas turbine
Internal combustion engine
Steam engine
Water driven turbine

EXCLUDES
that being towed by other vehicle on the highway (E810.0-E819.9, E827.0-E827.9, E829.0-E829.9)
that in transport under own power on the highway (E810.0-E819.9)

E919.6 Transmission machinery

Transmission:	Transmission:
belt	pinion
cable	pulley
chain	shaft
gear	

E919.7 Earth moving, scraping, and other excavating machines

Bulldozer	Steam shovel
Road scraper	

EXCLUDES
that being towed by other vehicle on the highway (E810.0-E819.9, E827.0-E827.9, E829.0-E829.9)
that in transport under own power on the highway (E810.0-E819.9)

E919.8 Other specified machinery

Machines for manufacture of:
  clothing
  foodstuffs and beverages
  paper
Printing machine
Recreational machinery
Spinning, weaving, and textile machines

E919.9 Unspecified machinery

☑4ᵗʰ E920 Accidents caused by cutting and piercing instruments or objects

INCLUDES

	object:
accidental injury (by)	edged
	pointed
	sharp

E920.0 Powered lawn mower

E920.1 Other powered hand tools

Any powered hand tool [compressed air] [electric] [explosive cartridge] [hydraulic power], such as:
  drill
  hand saw
  hedge clipper
  rivet gun
  snow blower
  staple gun

EXCLUDES *band saw (E919.4)*
bench saw (E919.4)

E920.2 Powered household appliances and implements

	Electric:
Blender	fan
Electric:	knife
beater or mixer	sewing machine
can opener	Garbage disposal appliance

E920.3 Knives, swords, and daggers

E920.4 Other hand tools and implements
Axe
Can opener NOS
Chisel
Fork
Hand saw
Hoe
Ice pick
Needle (sewing)
Paper cutter
Pitchfork
Rake
Scissors
Screwdriver
Sewing machine, not powered
Shovel

E920.5 Hypodermic needle
Contaminated needle
Needle stick

E920.8 Other specified cutting and piercing instruments or objects
Arrow
Broken glass
Dart
Edge of stiff paper
Lathe turnings
Nail
Plant thorn
Splinter
Tin can lid

> EXCLUDES *animal spines or quills (E906.8)*
> *flying glass due to explosion (E921.0-E923.9)*

E920.9 Unspecified cutting and piercing instrument or object

✓4ᵗʰ **E921 Accident caused by explosion of pressure vessel**

> INCLUDES *accidental explosion of pressure vessels, whether or not part of machinery*

> EXCLUDES *explosion of pressure vessel on transport vehicle (E800.0-E845.9)*

E921.0 Boilers

E921.1 Gas cylinders
Air tank
Pressure gas tank

E921.8 Other specified pressure vessels
Aerosol can
Automobile tire
Pressure cooker

E921.9 Unspecified pressure vessel

✓4ᵗʰ **E922 Accident caused by firearm, and air gun missile**

E922.0 Handgun
Pistol
Revolver

> EXCLUDES *Verey pistol (E922.8)*

E922.1 Shotgun (automatic)

E922.2 Hunting rifle

E922.3 Military firearms
Army rifle
Machine gun

E922.4 Air gun
BB gun
Pellet gun

E922.5 Paintball gun

E922.8 Other specified firearm missile
Verey pistol [flare]

E922.9 Unspecified firearm missile
Gunshot wound NOS
Shot NOS

✓4ᵗʰ **E923 Accident caused by explosive material**

> INCLUDES *flash burns and other injuries resulting from explosion of explosive material*
> *ignition of highly explosive material with explosion*

> EXCLUDES *explosion:*
> *in or on machinery (E919.0-E919.9)*
> *on any transport vehicle, except stationary motor vehicle (E800.0-E848)*
> *with conflagration (E890.0, E891.0,E892)*
> *secondary fires resulting from explosion (E890.0-E899)*

E923.0 Fireworks

E923.1 Blasting materials
Blasting cap
Detonator
Dynamite
Explosive [any] used in blasting operations

E923.2 Explosive gases
Acetylene
Butane
Coal gas
Explosion in mine NOS
Fire damp
Gasoline fumes
Methane
Propane

E923.8 Other explosive materials
Bomb
Explosive missile
Grenade
Mine
Shell
Torpedo
Explosion in munitions:
dump
factory

E923.9 Unspecified explosive material
Explosion NOS

✓4ᵗʰ **E924 Accident caused by hot substance or object, caustic or corrosive material, and steam**

> EXCLUDES *burning NOS (E899)*
> *chemical burn resulting from swallowing a corrosive substance (E860.0-E864.4)*
> *fire caused by these substances and objects (E890.0-E894)*
> *radiation burns (E926.0-E926.9)*
> *therapeutic misadventures (E870.0-E876.9)*

E924.0 Hot liquids and vapors, including steam
Burning or scalding by:
boiling water
hot or boiling liquids not primarily caustic or corrosive
liquid metal
steam
other hot vapor

> EXCLUDES *hot (boiling) tap water (E924.2)*

E924.1 Caustic and corrosive substances
Burning by:
acid [any kind]
ammonia
caustic oven cleaner
or other substance
Burning by:
corrosive substance
lye
vitriol

E924.2 Hot (boiling) tap water

E924.8 Other
Burning by:
heat from electric heating appliance
hot object NOS
light bulb
steam pipe

E924.9 Unspecified

✓4ᵗʰ **E925 Accident caused by electric current**

> INCLUDES *electric current from exposed wire, faulty appliance, high voltage cable, live rail, or open electric socket as the cause of:*
> burn
> cardiac fibrillation
> convulsion
> electric shock
> electrocution
> puncture wound
> respiratory paralysis

> EXCLUDES *burn by heat from electrical appliance (E924.8)*
> *lightning (E907)*

E925.0 Domestic wiring and appliances

E925.1 Electric power generating plants, distribution stations, transmission lines
Broken power line

E925.2 Industrial wiring, appliances, and electrical machinery
Conductors
Control apparatus
Electrical equipment and machinery
Transformers

E925.8 Other electric current
Wiring and appliances in or on:
farm [not farmhouse]
outdoors
public building
residential institutions
schools

✓4ᵗʰ Fourth-digit Required   ▶◀ Revised Text   ● New Code   ▲ Revised Code Title

E925.9　Unspecified electric current
　　　Burns or other injury from electric current NOS
　　　Electric shock NOS
　　　Electrocution NOS

✓4ᵗʰ **E926　Exposure to radiation**
　　EXCLUDES　*abnormal reaction to or complication of treatment without mention of misadventure (E879.2)*
　　　　　atomic power plant malfunction in water transport (E838.0-E838.9)
　　　　　misadventure to patient in surgical and medical procedures (E873.2-E873.3)
　　　　　use of radiation in war operations (E996-E997.9)

E926.0　Radiofrequency radiation

Overexposure to:	from:
microwave radiation radar radiation radiofrequency radiofrequency radiation [any]	high-powered radio and television transmitters industrial radiofrequency induction heaters radar installations

E926.1　Infrared heaters and lamps
　　　Exposure to infrared radiation from heaters and lamps as the cause of:
　　　　blistering
　　　　burning
　　　　charring
　　　　inflammatory change
　　EXCLUDES　*physical contact with heater or lamp (E924.8)*

E926.2　Visible and ultraviolet light sources

Arc lamps	Oxygas welding torch
Black light sources	Sun rays
Electrical welding arc	Tanning bed

　　EXCLUDES　*excessive heat from these sources (E900.1-E900.9)*

E926.3　X-rays and other electromagnetic ionizing radiation
　　　Gamma rays　　　X-rays (hard) (soft)

E926.4　Lasers

E926.5　Radioactive isotopes
　　　Radiobiologicals　　　Radiopharmaceuticals

E926.8　Other specified radiation
　　　Artificially accelerated beams of ionized particles generated by:
　　　　betatrons
　　　　synchrotrons

E926.9　Unspecified radiation
　　　Radiation NOS

E927　Overexertion and strenuous movements

Excessive physical exercise	Strenuous movements in:
Overexertion (from): lifting pulling pushing	recreational activities other activities

✓4ᵗʰ **E928　Other and unspecified environmental and accidental causes**

E928.0　Prolonged stay in weightless environment
　　　Weightlessness in spacecraft (simulator)

E928.1　Exposure to noise
　　　Noise (pollution)　　　Supersonic waves
　　　Sound waves

E928.2　Vibration

E928.3　Human bite

E928.4　External constriction caused by hair

E928.5　External constriction caused by other object

E928.8　Other

E928.9　Unspecified accident

Accident NOS Blow NOS Casualty (not due to war) Decapitation	}	stated as accidentally inflicted
Knocked down Killed Injury [any part of body, or unspecified] Mangled Wound	}	stated as accidentally inflicted, but not otherwise specified

　　EXCLUDES　*fracture, cause unspecified (E887)*
　　　　　injuries undetermined whether accidentally or purposely inflicted (E980.0-E989)

LATE EFFECTS OF ACCIDENTAL INJURY (E929)

Note: This category is to be used to indicate accidental injury as the cause of death or disability from late effects, which are themselves classifiable elsewhere. The "late effects" include conditions reported as such, or as sequelae which may occur at any time after the attempted suicide or self-inflicted injury.

✓4ᵗʰ **E929　Late effects of accidental injury**
　　EXCLUDES　*late effects of:*
　　　　　surgical and medical procedures (E870.0-E879.9)
　　　　　therapeutic use of drugs and medicines (E930.0-E949.9)

E929.0　Late effects of motor vehicle accident
　　　Late effects of accidents classifiable to E810-E825

E929.1　Late effects of other transport accident
　　　Late effects of accidents classifiable to E800-E807, E826-E838, E840-E848

E929.2　Late effects of accidental poisoning
　　　Late effects of accidents classifiable to E850-E858, E860-E869

E929.3　Late effects of accidental fall
　　　Late effects of accidents classifiable to E880-E888

E929.4　Late effects of accident caused by fire
　　　Late effects of accidents classifiable to E890-E899

E929.5　Late effects of accident due to natural and environmental factors
　　　Late effects of accidents classifiable to E900-E909

E929.8　Late effects of other accidents
　　　Late effects of accidents classifiable to E910-E928.8

E929.9　Late effects of unspecified accident
　　　Late effects of accidents classifiable to E928.9

DRUGS, MEDICINAL AND BIOLOGICAL SUBSTANCES CAUSING ADVERSE EFFECTS IN THERAPEUTIC USE (E930-E949)

　　INCLUDES　correct drug properly administered in therapeutic or prophylactic dosage, as the cause of any adverse effect including allergic or hypersensitivity reactions
　　EXCLUDES　*accidental overdose of drug and wrong drug given or taken in error (E850.0-E858.9)*
　　　　　accidents in the technique of administration of drug or biological substance, such as accidental puncture during injection, or contamination of drug (E870.0-E876.9)
　　　　　administration with suicidal or homicidal intent or intent to harm, or in circumstances classifiable to E980-E989 (E950.0-E950.5, E962.0, E980.0-E980.5)

See Alphabetic Index for more complete list of specific drugs to be classified under the fourth-digit subdivisions. The American Hospital Formulary numbers can be used to classify new drugs listed by the American Hospital Formulary Service (AHFS). See Appendix C.

✓4ᵗʰ **E930　Antibiotics**
　　EXCLUDES　*that used as eye, ear, nose, and throat [ENT] and local anti-infectives (E946.0-E946.9)*

E930.0 Penicillins

Natural	Semisynthetic, such as:
Synthetic	cloxacillin
Semisynthetic, such as:	nafcillin
ampicillin	oxacillin

E930.1 Antifungal antibiotics

Amphotericin B	Hachimycin [trichomycin]
Griseofulvin	Nystatin

E930.2 Chloramphenicol group

Chloramphenicol	Thiamphenicol

E930.3 Erythromycin and other macrolides

Oleandomycin	Spiramycin

E930.4 Tetracycline group

Doxycycline	Oxytetracycline
Minocycline	

E930.5 Cephalosporin group

Cephalexin	Cephaloridine
Cephaloglycin	Cephalothin

E930.6 Antimycobacterial antibiotics

Cycloserine	Rifampin
Kanamycin	Streptomycin

E930.7 Antineoplastic antibiotics

Actinomycins, such as:	Actinomycins, such as:
Bleomycin	Daunorubicin
Cactinomycin	Mitomycin
Dactinomycin	

> **EXCLUDES** other antineoplastic drugs (E933.1)

E930.8 Other specified antibiotics

E930.9 Unspecified antibiotic

☑4ᵗʰ **E931 Other anti-infectives**

> **EXCLUDES** ENT, and local anti-infectives (E946.0-E946.9)

E931.0 Sulfonamides

Sulfadiazine	Sulfamethoxazole
Sulfafurazole	

E931.1 Arsenical anti-infectives

E931.2 Heavy metal anti-infectives

Compounds of:	Compounds of:
antimony	lead
bismuth	mercury

> **EXCLUDES** mercurial diuretics (E944.0)

E931.3 Quinoline and hydroxyquinoline derivatives

Chiniofon	Diiodohydroxyquin

> **EXCLUDES** antimalarial drugs (E931.4)

E931.4 Antimalarials and drugs acting on other blood protozoa

Chloroquine phosphate	Proguanil [chloroguanide]
Cycloguanil	Pyrimethamine
Primaquine	Quinine (sulphate)

E931.5 Other antiprotozoal drugs

Emetine

E931.6 Anthelmintics

Hexylresorcinol	Piperazine
Male fern oleoresin	Thiabendazole

E931.7 Antiviral drugs

Methisazone

> **EXCLUDES** amantadine (E936.4)
> cytarabine (E933.1)
> idoxuridine (E946.5)

E931.8 Other antimycobacterial drugs

Ethambutol	Para-aminosalicylic
Ethionamide	acid derivatives
Isoniazid	Sulfones

E931.9 Other and unspecified anti-infectives

Flucytosine	Nitrofuranderivatives

☑4ᵗʰ **E932 Hormones and synthetic substitutes**

E932.0 Adrenal cortical steroids

Cortisone derivatives	Fluorinated corticosteroid
Desoxycorticosterone derivatives	

E932.1 Androgens and anabolic congeners

Nandrolone phenpropionate
Oxymetholone
Testosterone and preparations

E932.2 Ovarian hormones and synthetic substitutes

Contraceptives, oral
Estrogens
Estrogens and progestogens combined
Progestogens

E932.3 Insulins and antidiabetic agents

Acetohexamide	Phenformin
Biguanide derivatives, oral	Sulfonylurea
Chlorpropamide	derivatives,
Glucagon	oral
Insulin	Tolbutamide

> **EXCLUDES** adverse effect of insulin administered for shock therapy (E879.3)

E932.4 Anterior pituitary hormones

Corticotropin
Gonadotropin
Somatotropin [growth hormone]

E932.5 Posterior pituitary hormones

Vasopressin

> **EXCLUDES** oxytocic agents (E945.0)

E932.6 Parathyroid and parathyroid derivatives

E932.7 Thyroid and thyroid derivatives

Dextrothyroxine	Liothyronine
Levothyroxine sodium	Thyroglobulin

E932.8 Antithyroid agents

Iodides	Thiourea
Thiouracil	

E932.9 Other and unspecified hormones and synthetic substitutes

☑4ᵗʰ **E933 Primarily systemic agents**

E933.0 Antiallergic and antiemetic drugs

Antihistamines	Diphenylpyraline
Chlorpheniramine	Thonzylamine
Diphenhydramine	Tripelennamine

> **EXCLUDES** phenothiazine-based tranquilizers (E939.1)

E933.1 Antineoplastic and immunosuppressive drugs

Azathioprine
Busulfan
Chlorambucil
Cyclophosphamide
Cytarabine
Fluorouracil
Mechlorethamine hydrochloride
Mercaptopurine
Triethylenethiophosphoramide [thio-TEPA]

> **EXCLUDES** antineoplastic antibiotics (E930.7)

E933.2 Acidifying agents

E933.3 Alkalizing agents

E933.4 Enzymes, not elsewhere classified

Penicillinase

E933.5 Vitamins, not elsewhere classified

Vitamin A	Vitamin D

> **EXCLUDES** nicotinic acid (E942.2)
> vitamin K (E934.3)

E933.8 Other systemic agents, not elsewhere classified

Heavy metal antagonists

E933.9 Unspecified systemic agent

☑4ᵗʰ **E934 Agents primarily affecting blood constituents**

E934.0 Iron and its compounds

Ferric salts
Ferrous sulphate and other ferrous salts

E934.1 Liver preparations and other antianemic agents

Folic acid

E934.2 Anticoagulants

Coumarin	Prothrombin synthesis
Heparin	inhibitor
Phenindione	Warfarin sodium

E934.3 Vitamin K [phytonadione]

E934.4 Fibrinolysis-affecting drugs

Aminocaproic acid	Streptokinase
Streptodornase	Urokinase

☑4ᵗʰ Fourth-digit Required   ►◄ Revised Text   ● New Code   ▲ Revised Code Title

E934.5 Anticoagulant antagonists and other coagulants
Hexadimethrine bromide
Protamine sulfate

E934.6 Gamma globulin

E934.7 Natural blood and blood products
Blood plasma   Packed red cells
Human fibrinogen   Whole blood

E934.8 Other agents affecting blood constituents
Macromolecular blood substitutes

E934.9 Unspecified agent affecting blood constituents

✓4th **E935 Analgesics, antipyretics, and antirheumatics**

E935.0 Heroin
Diacetylmorphine

E935.1 Methadone

E935.2 Other opiates and related narcotics
Codeine [methylmorphine]   Morphine
Meperidine [pethidine]   Opium (alkaloids)

E935.3 Salicylates
Acetylsalicylic acid [aspirin]
Amino derivatives of salicylic acid
Salicylic acid salts

E935.4 Aromatic analgesics, not elsewhere classified
Acetanilid
Paracetamol [acetaminophen]
Phenacetin [acetophenetidin]

E935.5 Pyrazole derivatives
Aminophenazone [aminopyrine]
Phenylbutazone

E935.6 Antirheumatics [antiphlogistics]
Gold salts   Indomethacin
> **EXCLUDES**   salicylates (E935.3)
>   steroids (E932.0)

E935.7 Other non-narcotic analgesics
Pyrabital

E935.8 Other specified analgesics and antipyretics
Pentazocine

E935.9 Unspecified analgesic and antipyretic

✓4th **E936 Anticonvulsants and anti-Parkinsonism drugs**

E936.0 Oxazolidine derivatives
Paramethadione
Trimethadione

E936.1 Hydantoin derivatives
Phenytoin

E936.2 Succinimides
Ethosuximide
Phensuximide

E936.3 Other and unspecified anticonvulsants
Beclamide
Primidone

E936.4 Anti-Parkinsonism drugs
Amantadine
Ethopropazine [profenamine]
Levodopa [L-dopa]

✓4th **E937 Sedatives and hypnotics**

E937.0 Barbiturates
Amobarbital [amylobarbitone]
Barbital [barbitone]
Butabarbital [butabarbitone]
Pentobarbital [pentobarbitone]
Phenobarbital [phenobarbitone]
Secobarbital [quinalbarbitone]
> **EXCLUDES**   thiobarbiturates (E938.3)

E937.1 Chloral hydrate group

E937.2 Paraldehyde

E937.3 Bromine compounds
Bromide
Carbromal (derivatives)

E937.4 Methaqualone compounds

E937.5 Glutethimide group

E937.6 Mixed sedatives, not elsewhere classified

E937.8 Other sedatives and hypnotics

E937.9 Unspecified
Sleeping:
  drug ⎫
  pill   ⎬ NOS
  tablet ⎭

✓4th **E938 Other central nervous system depressants and anesthetics**

E938.0 Central nervous system muscle-tone depressants
Chlorphenesin (carbamate)
Mephenesin
Methocarbamol

E938.1 Halothane

E938.2 Other gaseous anesthetics
Ether
Halogenated hydrocarbon derivatives, except halothane
Nitrous oxide

E938.3 Intravenous anesthetics
Ketamine
Methohexital [methohexitone]
Thiobarbiturates, such as thiopental sodium

E938.4 Other and unspecified general anesthetics

E938.5 Surface and infiltration anesthetics
Cocaine   Procaine
Lidocaine [lignocaine]   Tetracaine

E938.6 Peripheral nerve- and plexus-blocking anesthetics

E938.7 Spinal anesthetics

E938.9 Other and unspecified local anesthetics

✓4th **E939 Psychotropic agents**

E939.0 Antidepressants
Amitriptyline
Imipramine
Monoamine oxidase [MAO] inhibitors

E939.1 Phenothiazine-based tranquilizers
Chlorpromazine   Prochlorperazine
Fluphenazine   Promazine
Phenothiazine

E939.2 Butyrophenone-based tranquilizers
Haloperidol   Trifluperidol
Spiperone

E939.3 Other antipsychotics, neuroleptics, and major tranquilizers

E939.4 Benzodiazepine-based tranquilizers
Chlordiazepoxide   Lorazepam
Diazepam   Medazepam
Flurazepam   Nitrazepam

E939.5 Other tranquilizers
Hydroxyzine   Meprobamate

E939.6 Psychodysleptics [hallucinogens]
Cannabis (derivatives)   Mescaline
Lysergide [LSD]   Psilocin
Marihuana (derivatives)   Psilocybin

E939.7 Psychostimulants
Amphetamine   Caffeine
> **EXCLUDES**   central appetite depressants (E947.0)

E939.8 Other psychotropic agents

E939.9 Unspecified psychotropic agent

✓4th **E940 Central nervous system stimulants**

E940.0 Analeptics
Lobeline   Nikethamide

E940.1 Opiate antagonists
Levallorphan   Naloxone
Nalorphine

E940.8 Other specified central nervous system stimulants

E940.9 Unspecified central nervous system stimulant

✓4th **E941 Drugs primarily affecting the autonomic nervous system**

E941.0 Parasympathomimetics [cholinergics]
Acetylcholine
Anticholinesterase:
  organophosphorus
  reversible
Pilocarpine

     ✓4th Fourth-digit Required   ▶◀ Revised Text   ● New Code   ▲ Revised Code Title

E Codes

E941.1–E948.0

E941.1 Parasympatholytics [anticholinergics and antimuscarinics] and spasmolytics

Atropine　　　　　　　　Hyoscine [scopolamine]
Homatropine　　　　　　Quaternary ammonium
　　　　　　　　　　　　　　derivatives

EXCLUDES *papaverine (E942.5)*

E941.2 Sympathomimetics [adrenergics]

Epinephrine [adrenalin]　Levarterenol [noradrenalin]

E941.3 Sympatholytics [antiadrenergics]

Phenoxybenzamine
Tolazolinehydrochloride

E941.9 Unspecified drug primarily affecting the autonomic nervous system

✓4th **E942 Agents primarily affecting the cardiovascular system**

E942.0 Cardiac rhythm regulators

Practolol　　　　　　　Propranolol
Procainamide　　　　　Quinidine

E942.1 Cardiotonic glycosides and drugs of similar action

Digitalis glycosides　　Strophanthins
Digoxin

E942.2 Antilipemic and antiarteriosclerotic drugs

Cholestyramine　　　　Nicotinic acid derivatives
Clofibrate　　　　　　　Sitosterols

EXCLUDES *dextrothyroxine (E932.7)*

E942.3 Ganglion-blocking agents

Pentamethonium bromide

E942.4 Coronary vasodilators

Dipyridamole　　　　　Nitrites
Nitrates [nitroglycerin]　Prenylamine

E942.5 Other vasodilators

Cyclandelate　　　　　Hydralazine
Diazoxide　　　　　　　Papaverine

E942.6 Other antihypertensive agents

Clonidine　　　　　　　Rauwolfia alkaloids
Guanethidine　　　　　Reserpine

E942.7 Antivaricose drugs, including sclerosing agents

Monoethanolamine　　Zinc salts

E942.8 Capillary-active drugs

Adrenochrome derivatives
Bioflavonoids
Metaraminol

E942.9 Other and unspecified agents primarily affecting the cardiovascular system

✓4th **E943 Agents primarily affecting gastrointestinal system**

E943.0 Antacids and antigastric secretion drugs

Aluminum hydroxide
Magnesium trisilicate

E943.1 Irritant cathartics

Bisacodyl　　　　　　　Phenolphthalein
Castor oil

E943.2 Emollient cathartics

Sodium dioctyl sulfosuccinate

E943.3 Other cathartics, including intestinal atonia drugs

Magnesium sulfate

E943.4 Digestants

Pancreatin　　　　　　Pepsin
Papain

E943.5 Antidiarrheal drugs

Bismuth subcarbonatePectin
Kaolin

EXCLUDES *anti-infectives (E930.0-E931.9)*

E943.6 Emetics

E943.8 Other specified agents primarily affecting the gastrointestinal system

E943.9 Unspecified agent primarily affecting the gastrointestinal system

✓4th **E944 Water, mineral, and uric acid metabolism drugs**

E944.0 Mercurial diuretics

Chlormerodrin　　　　Mercurophylline
Mercaptomerin　　　　Mersalyl

E944.1 Purine derivative diuretics

Theobromine　　　　　Theophylline

EXCLUDES *aminophylline [theophylline ethylenediamine] (E945.7)*

E944.2 Carbonic acid anhydrase inhibitors

Acetazolamide

E944.3 Saluretics

Benzothiadiazides　　Chlorothiazide group

E944.4 Other diuretics

Ethacrynic acid　　　Furosemide

E944.5 Electrolytic, caloric, and water-balance agents

E944.6 Other mineral salts, not elsewhere classified

E944.7 Uric acid metabolism drugs

Cinchophen and congeners　Phenoquin
Colchicine　　　　　　　　　Probenecid

✓4th **E945 Agents primarily acting on the smooth and skeletal muscles and respiratory system**

E945.0 Oxytocic agents

Ergot alkaloids
Prostaglandins

E945.1 Smooth muscle relaxants

Adiphenine
Metaproterenol [orciprenaline]

EXCLUDES *papaverine (E942.5)*

E945.2 Skeletal muscle relaxants

Alcuronium chloride
Suxamethonium chloride

E945.3 Other and unspecified drugs acting on muscles

E945.4 Antitussives

Dextromethorphan　　Pipazethate hydrochloride

E945.5 Expectorants

Acetylcysteine　　　　Ipecacuanha
Cocillana　　　　　　　Terpin hydrate
Guaifenesin [glyceryl
　guaiacolate]

E945.6 Anti-common cold drugs

E945.7 Antiasthmatics

Aminophylline [theophylline ethylenediamine]

E945.8 Other and unspecified respiratory drugs

✓4th **E946 Agents primarily affecting skin and mucous membrane, ophthalmological, otorhinolaryngological, and dental drugs**

E946.0 Local anti-infectives and anti-inflammatory drugs

E946.1 Antipruritics

E946.2 Local astringents and local detergents

E946.3 Emollients, demulcents, and protectants

E946.4 Keratolytics, kerstoplastics, other hair treatment drugs and preparations

E946.5 Eye anti-infectives and other eye drugs

Idoxuridine

E946.6 Anti-infectives and other drugs and preparations for ear, nose, and throat

E946.7 Dental drugs topically applied

E946.8 Other agents primarily affecting skin and mucous membrane

Spermicides

E946.9 Unspecified agent primarily affecting skin and mucous membrane

✓4th **E947 Other and unspecified drugs and medicinal substances**

E947.0 Dietetics

E947.1 Lipotropic drugs

E947.2 Antidotes and chelating agents, not elsewhere classified

E947.3 Alcohol deterrents

E947.4 Pharmaceutical excipients

E947.8 Other drugs and medicinal substances

Contrast media used for diagnostic x-ray procedures
Diagnostic agents and kits

E947.9 Unspecified drug or medicinal substance

✓4th **E948 Bacterial vaccines**

E948.0 BCG vaccine

✓4th Fourth-digit Required　▶◀ Revised Text　● New Code　▲ Revised Code Title

E948.1 Typhoid and paratyphoid

E948.2 Cholera

E948.3 Plague

E948.4 Tetanus

E948.5 Diphtheria

E948.6 Pertussis vaccine, including combinations with a pertussis component

E948.8 Other and unspecified bacterial vaccines

E948.9 Mixed bacterial vaccines, except combinations with a pertussis component

✓4ᵗʰ E949 Other vaccines and biological substances

> **EXCLUDES** *gamma globulin (E934.6)*

E949.0 Smallpox vaccine

E949.1 Rabies vaccine

E949.2 Typhus vaccine

E949.3 Yellow fever vaccine

E949.4 Measles vaccine

E949.5 Poliomyelitis vaccine

E949.6 Other and unspecified viral and rickettsial vaccines
Mumps vaccine

E949.7 Mixed viral-rickettsial and bacterial vaccines, except combinations with a pertussis component

> **EXCLUDES** *combinations with a pertussis component (E948.6)*

E949.9 Other and unspecified vaccines and biological substances

SUICIDE AND SELF-INFLICTED INJURY (E950-E959)

> **INCLUDES** injuries in suicide and attempted suicide
> self-inflicted injuries specified as intentional

✓4ᵗʰ E950 Suicide and self-inflicted poisoning by solid or liquid substances

E950.0 Analgesics, antipyretics, and antirheumatics

E950.1 Barbiturates

E950.2 Other sedatives and hypnotics

E950.3 Tranquilizers and other psychotropic agents

E950.4 Other specified drugs and medicinal substances

E950.5 Unspecified drug or medicinal substance

E950.6 Agricultural and horticultural chemical and pharmaceutical preparations other than plant foods and fertilizers

E950.7 Corrosive and caustic substances
Suicide and self-inflicted poisoning by substances classifiable to E864

E950.8 Arsenic and its compounds

E950.9 Other and unspecified solid and liquid substances

✓4ᵗʰ E951 Suicide and self-inflicted poisoning by gases in domestic use

E951.0 Gas distributed by pipeline

E951.1 Liquefied petroleum gas distributed in mobile containers

E951.8 Other utility gas

✓4ᵗʰ E952 Suicide and self-inflicted poisoning by other gases and vapors

E952.0 Motor vehicle exhaust gas

E952.1 Other carbon monoxide

E952.8 Other specified gases and vapors

E952.9 Unspecified gases and vapors

✓4ᵗʰ E953 Suicide and self-inflicted injury by hanging, strangulation, and suffocation

E953.0 Hanging

E953.1 Suffocation by plastic bag

E953.8 Other specified means

E953.9 Unspecified means

E954 Suicide and self-inflicted injury by submersion [drowning]

✓4ᵗʰ E955 Suicide and self-inflicted injury by firearms, air guns and explosives

E955.0 Handgun

E955.1 Shotgun

E955.2 Hunting rifle

E955.3 Military firearms

E955.4 Other and unspecified firearm
Gunshot NOS   Shot NOS

E955.5 Explosives

E955.6 Air gun
BB gun   Pellet gun

E955.7 Paintball gun

E955.9 Unspecified

E956 Suicide and self-inflicted injury by cutting and piercing instrument

✓4ᵗʰ E957 Suicide and self-inflicted injuries by jumping from high place

E957.0 Residential premises

E957.1 Other man-made structures

E957.2 Natural sites

E957.9 Unspecified

✓4ᵗʰ E958 Suicide and self-inflicted injury by other and unspecified means

E958.0 Jumping or lying before moving object

E958.1 Burns, fire

E958.2 Scald

E958.3 Extremes of cold

E958.4 Electrocution

E958.5 Crashing of motor vehicle

E958.6 Crashing of aircraft

E958.7 Caustic substances, except poisoning

> **EXCLUDES** *poisoning by caustic substance (E950.7)*

E958.8 Other specified means

E958.9 Unspecified means

E959 Late effects of self-inflicted injury

> Note: This category is to be used to indicate circumstances classifiable to E950-E958 as the cause of death or disability from late effects, which are themselves classifiable elsewhere. The "late effects" include conditions reported as such, or as sequelae which may occur at any time after the attempted suicide or self-inflicted injury.

HOMICIDE AND INJURY PURPOSELY INFLICTED BY OTHER PERSONS (E960-E969)

> **INCLUDES** injuries inflicted by another person with intent to injure or kill, by any means

> **EXCLUDES** *injuries due to:*
> *legal intervention (E970-E978)*
> *operations of war (E990-E999)*
> *terrorism (E979)*

✓4ᵗʰ E960 Fight, brawl, rape

E960.0 Unarmed fight or brawl
Beatings NOS
Brawl or fight with hands, fists, feet
Injured or killed in fight NOS

> **EXCLUDES** *homicidal:*
> *injury by weapons (E965.0-E966, E969)*
> *strangulation (E963)*
> *submersion (E964)*

E960.1 Rape

E961 Assault by corrosive or caustic substance, except poisoning
Injury or death purposely caused by corrosive or caustic substance, such as:
acid [any]
corrosive substance
vitriol

> **EXCLUDES** *burns from hot liquid (E968.3)*
> *chemical burns from swallowing a corrosive substance (E962.0-E962.9)*

✓4ᵗʰ Fourth-digit Required   ▶◀ Revised Text   ● New Code   ▲ Revised Code Title

E Codes

E962–E978

✓4ᵗʰ **E962 Assault by poisoning**

E962.0 Drugs and medicinal substances
>Homicidal poisoning by any drug or medicinal substance

E962.1 Other solid and liquid substances

E962.2 Other gases and vapors

E962.9 Unspecified poisoning

E963 Assault by hanging and strangulation
>Homicidal (attempt):   Homicidal (attempt):
>garrotting or ligature   strangulation
>hanging   suffocation

E964 Assault by submersion [drowning]

✓4ᵗʰ **E965 Assault by firearms and explosives**

E965.0 Handgun
>Pistol   Revolver

E965.1 Shotgun

E965.2 Hunting rifle

E965.3 Military firearms

E965.4 Other and unspecified firearm

E965.5 Antipersonnel bomb

E965.6 Gasoline bomb

E965.7 Letter bomb

E965.8 Other specified explosive
>Bomb NOS (placed in):   Dynamite
>car
>house

E965.9 Unspecified explosive

E966 Assault by cutting and piercing instrument
>Assassination (attempt), homicide (attempt) by any instrument classifiable under E920
>Homicidal:
>cut
>puncture   } any part of body
>stab
>Stabbed

✓4ᵗʰ **E967 Perpetrator of child and adult abuse**
>Note: Selection of the correct perpetrator code is based on the relationship between the perpetrator and the victim

E967.0 By father, stepfather, or boyfriend
>Male partner of child's parent or guardian

E967.1 By other specified person

E967.2 By mother, stepmother, or girlfriend
>Female partner of child's parent or guardian

E967.3 By spouse or partner
>Abuse of spouse or partner by ex-spouse or ex-partner

E967.4 By child

E967.5 By sibling

E967.6 By grandparent

E967.7 By other relative

E967.8 By non-related caregiver

E967.9 By unspecified person

✓4ᵗʰ **E968 Assault by other and unspecified means**

E968.0 Fire
>Arson
>Homicidal burns NOS
>>**EXCLUDES** *burns from hot liquid (E968.3)*

E968.1 Pushing from a high place

E968.2 Striking by blunt or thrown object

E968.3 Hot liquid
>Homicidal burns by scalding

E968.4 Criminal neglect
>Abandonment of child, infant, or other helpless person with intent to injure or kill

E968.5 Transport vehicle
>Being struck by other vehicle or run down with intent to injure
>Pushed in front of, thrown from, or dragged by moving vehicle with intent to injure

E968.6 Air gun
>BB gun
>Pellet gun

E968.7 Human bite

E968.8 Other specified means

E968.9 Unspecified means
>Assassination (attempt) NOS
>Homicidal (attempt):
>injury NOS
>wound NOS
>Manslaughter (nonaccidental)
>Murder (attempt) NOS
>Violence, non-accidental

E969 Late effects of injury purposely inflicted by other person
>Note: This category is to be used to indicate circumstances classifiable to E960-E968 as the cause of death or disability from late effects, which are themselves classifiable elsewhere. The "late effects" include conditions reported as such, or as sequelae which may occur at any time after injury purposely inflicted by another person.

LEGAL INTERVENTION (E970-E978)

>**INCLUDES** injuries inflicted by the police or other law-enforcing agents, including military on duty, in the course of arresting or attempting to arrest lawbreakers, suppressing disturbances, maintaining order, and other legal action
>legal execution
>**EXCLUDES** *injuries caused by civil insurrections (E990.0-E999)*

E970 Injury due to legal intervention by firearms
>Gunshot wound   Injury by:
>Injury by: rifle pellet or
>machine gun   rubber bullet
>revolver   shot NOS

E971 Injury due to legal intervention by explosives
>Injury by: Injury by:
>dynamite   grenade
>explosive shell   mortar bomb

E972 Injury due to legal intervention by gas
>Asphyxiation by gas   Poisoning by gas
>Injury by tear gas

E973 Injury due to legal intervention by blunt object
>Hit, struck by: Hit, struck by:
>baton (nightstick)   stave
>blunt object

E974 Injury due to legal intervention by cutting and piercing instrument
>Cut   Injured by bayonet
>Incised wound   Stab wound

E975 Injury due to legal intervention by other specified means
>Blow   Manhandling

E976 Injury due to legal intervention by unspecified means

E977 Late effects of injuries due to legal intervention
>Note: This category is to be used to indicate circumstances classifiable to E970-E976 as the cause of death or disability from late effects, which are themselves classifiable elsewhere. The "late effects" include conditions reported as such, or as sequelae, which may occur at any time after the injury due to legal intervention.

E978 Legal execution
>All executions performed at the behest of the judiciary or ruling authority [whether permanent or temporary] as:
>asphyxiation by gas
>beheading, decapitation (by guillotine)
>capital punishment
>electrocution
>hanging
>poisoning
>shooting
>other specified means

✓4ᵗʰ Fourth-digit Required   ▶◀ Revised Text   ● New Code   ▲ Revised Code Title

TERRORISM (E979)

✓4th **E979 Terrorism**

Injuries resulting from the unlawful use of force or violence against persons or property to intimidate or coerce a Government, the civilian population, or any segment thereof, in furtherance of political or social objective

E979.0 Terrorism involving explosion of marine weapons

Depth-charge
Marine mine
Mine NOS, at sea or in harbour
Sea-based artillery shell
Torpedo
Underwater blast

E979.1 Terrorism involving destruction of aircraft

Aircraft used as a weapon
Aircraft:
    burned
    exploded
    shot down
Crushed by falling aircraft

E979.2 Terrorism involving other explosions and fragments

Antipersonnel bomb (fragments)
Blast NOS
Explosion (of):
    artillery shell
    breech-block
    cannon block
    mortar bomb
    munitions being used in terrorism
    NOS
Fragments from:
    artillery shell
    bomb
    grenade
    guided missile
    land-mine
    rocket
    shell
    shrapnel
Mine NOS

E979.3 Terrorism involving fires, conflagration and hot substances

Burning building or structure:
    collapse of
    fall from
    hit by falling object in
    jump from
Conflagration NOS
Fire (causing):
    Asphyxia
    Burns
    NOS
    Other injury
Melting of fittings and furniture in burning
Petrol bomb
Smouldering building or structure

E979.4 Terrorism involving firearms

Bullet:
    carbine
    machine gun
    pistol
    rifle
    rubber (rifle)
Pellets (shotgun)

E979.5 Terrorism involving nuclear weapons

Blast effects
Exposure to ionizing radiation from nuclear weapon
Fireball effects
Heat from nuclear weapon
Other direct and secondary effects of nuclear weapons

E979.6 Terrorism involving biological weapons

Anthrax
Cholera
Smallpox

E979.7 Terrorism involving chemical weapons

Gases, fumes, chemicals
Hydrogen cyanide
Phosgene
Sarin

E979.8 Terrorism involving other means

Drowning and submersion
Lasers
Piercing or stabbing instruments
Terrorism NOS

E979.9 Terrorism, secondary effects

Note: This code is for use to identify conditions occurring subsequent to a terrorist attack not those that are due to the initial terrorist act

EXCLUDES *late effect of terrorist attack (E999.1)*

INJURY UNDETERMINED WHETHER ACCIDENTALLY OR PURPOSELY INFLICTED (E980-E989)

Note: Categories E980-E989 are for use when it is unspecified or it cannot be determined whether the injuries are accidental (unintentional), suicide (attempted), or assault.

✓4th **E980 Poisoning by solid or liquid substances, undetermined whether accidentally or purposely inflicted**

E980.0 Analgesics, antipyretics, and antirheumatics

E980.1 Barbiturates

E980.2 Other sedatives and hypnotics

E980.3 Tranquilizers and other psychotropic agents

E980.4 Other specified drugs and medicinal substances

E980.5 Unspecified drug or medicinal substance

E980.6 Corrosive and caustic substances

Poisoning, undetermined whether accidental or purposeful, by substances classifiable to E864

E980.7 Agricultural and horticultural chemical and pharmaceutical preparations other than plant foods and fertilizers

E980.8 Arsenic and its compounds

E980.9 Other and unspecified solid and liquid substances

✓4th **E981 Poisoning by gases in domestic use, undetermined whether accidentally or purposely inflicted**

E981.0 Gas distributed by pipeline

E981.1 Liquefied petroleum gas distributed in mobile containers

E981.8 Other utility gas

✓4th **E982 Poisoning by other gases, undetermined whether accidentally or purposely inflicted**

E982.0 Motor vehicle exhaust gas

E982.1 Other carbon monoxide

E982.8 Other specified gases and vapors

E982.9 Unspecified gases and vapors

✓4th **E983 Hanging, strangulation, or suffocation, undetermined whether accidentally or purposely inflicted**

E983.0 Hanging

E983.1 Suffocation by plastic bag

E983.8 Other specified means

E983.9 Unspecified means

E984 Submersion [drowning], undetermined whether accidentally or purposely inflicted

✓4th **E985 Injury by firearms, air guns and explosives, undetermined whether accidentally or purposely inflicted**

E985.0 Handgun

E985.1 Shotgun

E985.2 Hunting rifle

E985.3 Military firearms

E985.4 Other and unspecified firearm

E985.5 Explosives

E985.6 Air gun

BB gun   Pellet gun

E985.7 Paintball gun

✓4th Fourth-digit Required   ►◄ Revised Text   ● New Code   ▲ Revised Code Title

E986 Injury by cutting and piercing instruments, undetermined whether accidentally or purposely inflicted

☑4ᵗʰ E987 Falling from high place, undetermined whether accidentally or purposely inflicted

E987.0 Residential premises

E987.1 Other man-made structures

E987.2 Natural sites

E987.9 Unspecified site

☑4ᵗʰ E988 Injury by other and unspecified means, undetermined whether accidentally or purposely inflicted

E988.0 Jumping or lying before moving object

E988.1 Burns, fire

E988.2 Scald

E988.3 Extremes of cold

E988.4 Electrocution

E988.5 Crashing of motor vehicle

E988.6 Crashing of aircraft

E988.7 Caustic substances, except poisoning

E988.8 Other specified means

E988.9 Unspecified means

E989 Late effects of injury, undetermined whether accidentally or purposely inflicted

Note: This category is to be used to indicate circumstances classifiable to E980-E988 as the cause of death or disability from late effects, which are themselves classifiable elsewhere. The "late effects" include conditions reported as such, or as sequelae, which may occur at any time after injury, undetermined whether accidentally or purposely inflicted.

INJURY RESULTING FROM OPERATIONS OF WAR (E990-E999)

| INCLUDES | injuries to military personnel and civilians caused by war and civil insurrections and occurring during the time of war and insurrection |

| EXCLUDES | accidents during training of military personnel manufacture of war material and transport, unless attributable to enemy action |

☑4ᵗʰ E990 Injury due to war operations by fires and conflagrations

| INCLUDES | asphyxia, burns, or other injury originating from fire caused by a fire-producing device or indirectly by any conventional weapon |

E990.0 From gasoline bomb

E990.9 From other and unspecified source

☑4ᵗʰ E991 Injury due to war operations by bullets and fragments

E991.0 Rubber bullets (rifle)

E991.1 Pellets (rifle)

E991.2 Other bullets

Bullet [any, except rubber bullets and pellets]
carbine
machine gun
pistol
rifle
shotgun

E991.3 Antipersonnel bomb (fragments)

E991.9 Other and unspecified fragments

Fragments from: Fragments from:
artillery shell   land mine
bombs, except   rockets
  anti-personnel   shell
grenade   Shrapnel
guided missile

E992 Injury due to war operations by explosion of marine weapons

Depth charge   Sea-based artillery shell
Marine mines   Torpedo
Mine NOS, at sea or in harbor   Underwater blast

E993 Injury due to war operations by other explosion

Accidental explosion of   Explosion of:
  munitions being used   artillery shell
  in war   breech block
Accidental explosion of own   cannon block
  weapons   mortar bomb
Air blast NOS   Injury by weapon burst
Blast NOS
Explosion NOS

E994 Injury due to war operations by destruction of aircraft

Airplane: Airplane:
  burned   shot down
  exploded   Crushed by falling
                                airplane

E995 Injury due to war operations by other and unspecified forms of conventional warfare

Battle wounds
Bayonet injury
Drowned in war operations

E996 Injury due to war operations by nuclear weapons

Blast effects
Exposure to ionizing radiation from nuclear weapons
Fireball effects
Heat
Other direct and secondary effects of nuclear weapons

☑4ᵗʰ E997 Injury due to war operations by other forms of unconventional warfare

E997.0 Lasers

E997.1 Biological warfare

E997.2 Gases, fumes, and chemicals

E997.8 Other specified forms of unconventional warfare

E997.9 Unspecified form of unconventional warfare

E998 Injury due to war operations but occurring after cessation of hostilities

Injuries due to operations of war but occurring after cessation of hostilities by any means classifiable under E990-E997

Injuries by explosion of bombs or mines placed in the course of operations of war, if the explosion occurred after cessation of hostilities

☑4ᵗʰ E999 Late effect of injury due to war operations and terrorism

Note: This category is to be used to indicate circumstances classifiable to E979, E990-E998 as the cause of death or disability from late effects, which are themselves classifiable elsewhere. The "late effects" include conditions reported as such, or as sequelae, which may occur at any time after the injury, resulting from operations of war or terrorism

E999.0 Late effect of injury due to war operations

E999.1 Late effect of injury due to terrorism

☑4ᵗʰ Fourth-digit Required   ▶◀ Revised Text   ● New Code   ▲ Revised Code Title

Official ICD-9-CM Government Appendixes

MORPHOLOGY OF NEOPLASMS

The World Health Organization has published an adaptation of the International Classification of Diseases for oncology (ICD-O). It contains a coded nomenclature for the morphology of neoplasms, which is reproduced here for those who wish to use it in conjunction with Chapter 2 of the International Classification of Diseases, 9th Revision, Clinical Modification.

The morphology code numbers consist of five digits; the first four identify the histological type of the neoplasm and the fifth indicates its behavior. The one-digit behavior code is as follows:

/0   Benign
/1   Uncertain whether benign or malignant
      Borderline malignancy
/2   Carcinoma in situ
      Intraepithelial
      Noninfiltrating
      Noninvasive
/3   Malignant, primary site
/6   Malignant, metastatic site
      Secondary site
/9   Malignant, uncertain whether primary or
      metastatic site

In the nomenclature below, the morphology code numbers include the behavior code appropriate to the histological type of neoplasm, but this behavior code should be changed if other reported information makes this necessary. For example, "chordoma (M9370/3)" is assumed to be malignant; the term "benign chordoma" should be coded M9370/0. Similarly, "superficial spreading adenocarcinoma (M8143/3)" described as "noninvasive" should be coded M8143/2 and "melanoma (M8720/3)" described as "secondary" should be coded M8720/6.

The following table shows the correspondence between the morphology code and the different sections of Chapter 2:

Morphology Code Histology/Behavior		ICD-9-CM Chapter 2
Any	0 210-229	Benign neoplasms
M8000-M8004	1 239	Neoplasms of unspecified nature
M8010+	1 235-238	Neoplasms of uncertain behavior
Any	2 230-234	Carcinoma in situ
Any	3 140-195 200-208	Malignant neoplasms, stated or presumed to be primary
Any	6 196-198	Malignant neoplasms, stated or presumed to be secondary

The ICD-O behavior digit /9 is inapplicable in an ICD context, since all malignant neoplasms are presumed to be primary (/3) or secondary (/6) according to other information on the medical record.

Only the first-listed term of the full ICD-O morphology nomenclature appears against each code number in the list below. The ICD-9-CM Alphabetical Index (Volume 2), however, includes all the ICD-O synonyms as well as a number of other morphological names still likely to be encountered on medical records but omitted from ICD-O as outdated or otherwise undesirable.

A coding difficulty sometimes arises where a morphological diagnosis contains two qualifying adjectives that have different code numbers. An example is "transitional cell epidermoid carcinoma." "Transitional cell carcinoma NOS" is M8120/3 and "epidermoid carcinoma NOS" is M8070/3. In such circumstances, the higher number (M8120/3 in this example) should be used, as it is usually more specific.

CODED NOMENCLATURE FOR MORPHOLOGY OF NEOPLASMS

M800   Neoplasms NOS
M8000/0   Neoplasm, benign
M8000/1   Neoplasm, uncertain whether benign or malignant
M8000/3   Neoplasm, malignant
M8000/6   Neoplasm, metastatic
M8000/9   Neoplasm, malignant, uncertain whether primary or metastatic
M8001/0   Tumor cells, benign
M8001/1   Tumor cells, uncertain whether benign or malignant
M8001/3   Tumor cells, malignant
M8002/3   Malignant tumor, small cell type
M8003/3   Malignant tumor, giant cell type
M8004/3   Malignant tumor, fusiform cell type

M801-M804   Epithelial neoplasms NOS
M8010/0   Epithelial tumor, benign
M8010/2   Carcinoma in situ NOS
M8010/3   Carcinoma NOS
M8010/6   Carcinoma, metastatic NOS
M8010/9   Carcinomatosis
M8011/0   Epithelioma, benign
M8011/3   Epithelioma, malignant
M8012/3   Large cell carcinoma NOS
M8020/3   Carcinoma, undifferentiated type NOS
M8021/3   Carcinoma, anaplastic type NOS
M8022/3   Pleomorphic carcinoma
M8030/3   Giant cell and spindle cell carcinoma
M8031/3   Giant cell carcinoma
M8032/3   Spindle cell carcinoma
M8033/3   Pseudosarcomatous carcinoma
M8034/3   Polygonal cell carcinoma
M8035/3   Spheroidal cell carcinoma
M8040/1   Tumorlet
M8041/3   Small cell carcinoma NOS
M8042/3   Oat cell carcinoma
M8043/3   Small cell carcinoma, fusiform cell type

M805-M808   Papillary and squamous cell neoplasms
M8050/0   Papilloma NOS (except Papilloma of urinary bladder M8120/1)
M8050/2   Papillary carcinoma in situ
M8050/3   Papillary carcinoma NOS
M8051/0   Verrucous papilloma
M8051/3   Verrucous carcinoma NOS
M8052/0   Squamous cell papilloma
M8052/3   Papillary squamous cell carcinoma
M8053/0   Inverted papilloma
M8060/0   Papillomatosis NOS

M8070/2   Squamous cell carcinoma in situ NOS
M8070/3   Squamous cell carcinoma NOS
M8070/6   Squamous cell carcinoma, metastatic NOS
M8071/3   Squamous cell carcinoma, keratinizing type NOS
M8072/3   Squamous cell carcinoma, large cell, nonkeratinizing type
M8073/3   Squamous cell carcinoma, small cell, nonkeratinizing type
M8074/3   Squamous cell carcinoma, spindle cell type
M8075/3   Adenoid squamous cell carcinoma
M8076/2   Squamous cell carcinoma in situ with questionable stromal invasion
M8076/3   Squamous cell carcinoma, microinvasive
M8080/2   Queyrat's erythroplasia
M8081/2   Bowen's disease
M8082/3   Lymphoepithelial carcinoma

M809-M811   Basal cell neoplasms
M8090/1   Basal cell tumor
M8090/3   Basal cell carcinoma NOS
M8091/3   Multicentric basal cell carcinoma
M8092/3   Basal cell carcinoma, morphea type
M8093/3   Basal cell carcinoma, fibroepithelial type
M8094/3   Basosquamous carcinoma
M8095/3   Metatypical carcinoma
M8096/0   Intraepidermal epithelioma of Jadassohn
M8100/0   Trichoepithelioma
M8101/0   Trichofolliculoma
M8102/0   Tricholemmoma
M8110/0   Pilomatrixoma

M812-M813   Transitional cell papillomas and carcinomas
M8120/0   Transitional cell papilloma NOS
M8120/1   Urothelial papilloma
M8120/2   Transitional cell carcinoma in situ
M8120/3   Transitional cell carcinoma NOS
M8121/0   Schneiderian papilloma
M8121/1   Transitional cell papilloma, inverted type
M8121/3   Schneiderian carcinoma
M8122/3   Transitional cell carcinoma, spindle cell type
M8123/3   Basaloid carcinoma
M8124/3   Cloacogenic carcinoma
M8130/3   Papillary transitional cell carcinoma

M814-M838   Adenomas and adenocarcinomas
M8140/0   Adenoma NOS
M8140/1   Bronchial adenoma NOS
M8140/2   Adenocarcinoma in situ
M8140/3   Adenocarcinoma NOS
M8140/6   Adenocarcinoma, metastatic NOS
M8141/3   Scirrhous adenocarcinoma
M8142/3   Linitis plastica
M8143/3   Superficial spreading adenocarcinoma
M8144/3   Adenocarcinoma, intestinal type
M8145/3   Carcinoma, diffuse type
M8146/0   Monomorphic adenoma
M8147/0   Basal cell adenoma
M8150/0   Islet cell adenoma
M8150/3   Islet cell carcinoma
M8151/0   Insulinoma NOS
M8151/3   Insulinoma, malignant
M8152/0   Glucagonoma NOS
M8152/3   Glucagonoma, malignant
M8153/1   Gastrinoma NOS

Appendix A: Morphology of Neoplasms

M8153/3	Gastrinoma, malignant
M8154/3	Mixed islet cell and exocrine adenocarcinoma
M8160/0	Bile duct adenoma
M8160/3	Cholangiocarcinoma
M8161/0	Bile duct cystadenoma
M8161/3	Bile duct cystadenocarcinoma
M8170/0	Liver cell adenoma
M8170/3	Hepatocellular carcinoma NOS
M8180/0	Hepatocholangioma, benign
M8180/3	Combined hepatocellular carcinoma and cholangiocarcinoma
M8190/0	Trabecular adenoma
M8190/3	Trabecular adenocarcinoma
M8191/0	Embryonal adenoma
M8200/0	Eccrine dermal cylindroma
M8200/3	Adenoid cystic carcinoma
M8201/3	Cribriform carcinoma
M8210/0	Adenomatous polyp NOS
M8210/3	Adenocarcinoma in adenomatous polyp
M8211/0	Tubular adenoma NOS
M8211/3	Tubular adenocarcinoma
M8220/0	Adenomatous polyposis coli
M8220/3	Adenocarcinoma in adenomatous polyposis coli
M8221/0	Multiple adenomatous polyps
M8230/3	Solid carcinoma NOS
M8231/3	Carcinoma simplex
M8240/1	Carcinoid tumor NOS
M8240/3	Carcinoid tumor, malignant
M8241/1	Carcinoid tumor, argentaffin NOS
M8241/3	Carcinoid tumor, argentaffin, malignant
M8242/1	Carcinoid tumor, nonargentaffin NOS
M8242/3	Carcinoid tumor, nonargentaffin, malignant
M8243/3	Mucocarcinoid tumor, malignant
M8244/3	Composite carcinoid
M8250/1	Pulmonary adenomatosis
M8250/3	Bronchiolo-alveolar adenocarcinoma
M8251/0	Alveolar adenoma
M8251/3	Alveolar adenocarcinoma
M8260/0	Papillary adenoma NOS
M8260/3	Papillary adenocarcinoma NOS
M8261/1	Villous adenoma NOS
M8261/3	Adenocarcinoma in villous adenoma
M8262/3	Villous adenocarcinoma
M8263/3	Tubulovillous adenoma
M8270/0	Chromophobe adenoma
M8270/3	Chromophobe carcinoma
M8280/0	Acidophil adenoma
M8280/3	Acidophil carcinoma
M8281/0	Mixed acidophil-basophil adenoma
M8281/3	Mixed acidophil-basophil carcinoma
M8290/0	Oxyphilic adenoma
M8290/3	Oxyphilic adenocarcinoma
M8300/0	Basophil adenoma
M8300/3	Basophil carcinoma
M8310/0	Clear cell adenoma
M8310/3	Clear cell adenocarcinoma NOS
M8311/1	Hypernephroid tumor
M8312/3	Renal cell carcinoma
M8313/0	Clear cell adenofibroma
M8320/3	Granular cell carcinoma
M8321/0	Chief cell adenoma
M8322/0	Water-clear cell adenoma
M8322/3	Water-clear cell adenocarcinoma
M8323/0	Mixed cell adenoma
M8323/3	Mixed cell adenocarcinoma
M8324/0	Lipoadenoma
M8330/0	Follicular adenoma
M8330/3	Follicular adenocarcinoma NOS
M8331/3	Follicular adenocarcinoma, well differentiated type

M8332/3	Follicular adenocarcinoma, trabecular type
M8333/0	Microfollicular adenoma
M8334/0	Macrofollicular adenoma
M8340/3	Papillary and follicular adenocarcinoma
M8350/3	Nonencapsulated sclerosing carcinoma
M8360/1	Multiple endocrine adenomas
M8361/1	Juxtaglomerular tumor
M8370/0	Adrenal cortical adenoma NOS
M8370/3	Adrenal cortical carcinoma
M8371/0	Adrenal cortical adenoma, compact cell type
M8372/0	Adrenal cortical adenoma, heavily pigmented variant
M8373/0	Adrenal cortical adenoma, clear cell type
M8374/0	Adrenal cortical adenoma, glomerulosa cell type
M8375/0	Adrenal cortical adenoma, mixed cell type
M8380/0	Endometrioid adenoma NOS
M8380/1	Endometrioid adenoma, borderline malignancy
M8380/3	Endometrioid carcinoma
M8381/0	Endometrioid adenofibroma NOS
M8381/1	Endometrioid adenofibroma, borderline malignancy
M8381/3	Endometrioid adenofibroma, malignant

M839-M842 Adnexal and skin appendage neoplasms

M8390/0	Skin appendage adenoma
M8390/3	Skin appendage carcinoma
M8400/0	Sweat gland adenoma
M8400/1	Sweat gland tumor NOS
M8400/3	Sweat gland adenocarcinoma
M8401/0	Apocrine adenoma
M8401/3	Apocrine adenocarcinoma
M8402/0	Eccrine acrospiroma
M8403/0	Eccrine spiradenoma
M8404/0	Hidrocystoma
M8405/0	Papillary hydradenoma
M8406/0	Papillary syringadenoma
M8407/0	Syringoma NOS
M8410/0	Sebaceous adenoma
M8410/3	Sebaceous adenocarcinoma
M8420/0	Ceruminous adenoma
M8420/3	Ceruminous adenocarcinoma

M843 Mucoepidermoid neoplasms

M8430/1	Mucoepidermoid tumor
M8430/3	Mucoepidermoid carcinoma

M844-M849 Cystic, mucinous, and serous neoplasms

M8440/0	Cystadenoma NOS
M8440/3	Cystadenocarcinoma NOS
M8441/0	Serous cystadenoma NOS
M8441/1	Serous cystadenoma, borderline malignancy
M8441/3	Serous cystadenocarcinoma NOS
M8450/0	Papillary cystadenoma NOS
M8450/1	Papillary cystadenoma, borderline malignancy
M8450/3	Papillary cystadenocarcinoma NOS
M8460/0	Papillary serous cystadenoma NOS
M8460/1	Papillary serous cystadenoma, borderline malignancy
M8460/3	Papillary serous cystadenocarcinoma
M8461/0	Serous surface papilloma NOS
M8461/1	Serous surface papilloma, borderline malignancy
M8461/3	Serous surface papillary carcinoma
M8470/0	Mucinous cystadenoma NOS
M8470/1	Mucinous cystadenoma, borderline malignancy

M8470/3	Mucinous cystadenocarcinoma NOS
M8471/0	Papillary mucinous cystadenoma NOS
M8471/1	Papillary mucinous cystadenoma, borderline malignancy
M8471/3	Papillary mucinous cystadenocarcinoma
M8480/0	Mucinous adenoma
M8480/3	Mucinous adenocarcinoma
M8480/6	Pseudomyxoma peritonei
M8481/3	Mucin-producing adenocarcinoma
M8490/3	Signet ring cell carcinoma
M8490/6	Metastatic signet ring cell carcinoma

M850-M854 Ductal, lobular, and medullary neoplasms

M8500/2	Intraductal carcinoma, noninfiltrating NOS
M8500/3	Infiltrating duct carcinoma
M8501/2	Comedocarcinoma, noninfiltrating
M8501/3	Comedocarcinoma NOS
M8502/3	Juvenile carcinoma of the breast
M8503/0	Intraductal papilloma
M8503/2	Noninfiltrating intraductal papillary adenocarcinoma
M8504/0	Intracystic papillary adenoma
M8504/2	Noninfiltrating intracystic carcinoma
M8505/0	Intraductal papillomatosis NOS
M8506/0	Subareolar duct papillomatosis
M8510/3	Medullary carcinoma NOS
M8511/3	Medullary carcinoma with amyloid stroma
M8512/3	Medullary carcinoma with lymphoid stroma
M8520/2	Lobular carcinoma in situ
M8520/3	Lobular carcinoma NOS
M8521/3	Infiltrating ductular carcinoma
M8530/3	Inflammatory carcinoma
M8540/3	Paget's disease, mammary
M8541/3	Paget's disease and infiltrating duct carcinoma of breast
M8542/3	Paget's disease, extramammary (except Paget's disease of bone)

M855 Acinar cell neoplasms

M8550/0	Acinar cell adenoma
M8550/1	Acinar cell tumor
M8550/3	Acinar cell carcinoma

M856-M858 Complex epithelial neoplasms

M8560/3	Adenosquamous carcinoma
M8561/0	Adenolymphoma
M8570/3	Adenocarcinoma with squamous metaplasia
M8571/3	Adenocarcinoma with cartilaginous and osseous metaplasia
M8572/3	Adenocarcinoma with spindle cell metaplasia
M8573/3	Adenocarcinoma with apocrine metaplasia
M8580/0	Thymoma, benign
M8580/3	Thymoma, malignant

M859-M867 Specialized gonadal neoplasms

M8590/1	Sex cord-stromal tumor
M8600/0	Thecoma NOS
M8600/3	Theca cell carcinoma
M8610/0	Luteoma NOS
M8620/0	Granulosa cell tumor NOS
M8620/3	Granulosa cell tumor, malignant
M8621/1	Granulosa cell-theca cell tumor
M8630/0	Androblastoma, benign
M8630/1	Androblastoma NOS
M8630/3	Androblastoma, malignant
M8631/0	Sertoli-Leydig cell tumor
M8632/0	Gynandroblastoma
M8640/0	Tubular androblastoma NOS
M8640/3	Sertoli cell carcinoma
M8641/0	Tubular androblastoma with lipid storage

M8650/0	Leydig cell tumor, benign
M8650/1	Leydig cell tumor NOS
M8650/3	Leydig cell tumor, malignant
M8660/0	Hilar cell tumor
M8670/0	Lipid cell tumor of ovary
M8671/0	Adrenal rest tumor

M868-M871 Paragangliomas and glomus tumors

M8680/1	Paraganglioma NOS
M8680/3	Paraganglioma, malignant
M8681/1	Sympathetic paraganglioma
M8682/1	Parasympathetic paraganglioma
M8690/1	Glomus jugulare tumor
M8691/1	Aortic body tumor
M8692/1	Carotid body tumor
M8693/1	Extra-adrenal paraganglioma NOS
M8693/3	Extra-adrenal paraganglioma, malignant
M8700/0	Pheochromocytoma NOS
M8700/3	Pheochromocytoma, malignant
M8710/3	Glomangiosarcoma
M8711/0	Glomus tumor
M8712/0	Glomangioma

M872-M879 Nevi and melanomas

M8720/0	Pigmented nevus NOS
M8720/3	Malignant melanoma NOS
M8721/3	Nodular melanoma
M8722/0	Balloon cell nevus
M8722/3	Balloon cell melanoma
M8723/0	Halo nevus
M8724/0	Fibrous papule of the nose
M8725/0	Neuronevus
M8726/0	Magnocellular nevus
M8730/0	Nonpigmented nevus
M8730/3	Amelanotic melanoma
M8740/0	Junctional nevus
M8740/3	Malignant melanoma in junctional nevus
M8741/2	Precancerous melanosis NOS
M8741/3	Malignant melanoma in precancerous melanosis
M8742/2	Hutchinson's melanotic freckle
M8742/3	Malignant melanoma in Hutchinson's melanotic freckle
M8743/3	Superficial spreading melanoma
M8750/0	Intradermal nevus
M8760/0	Compound nevus
M8761/1	Giant pigmented nevus
M8761/3	Malignant melanoma in giant pigmented nevus
M8770/0	Epithelioid and spindle cell nevus
M8771/3	Epithelioid cell melanoma
M8772/3	Spindle cell melanoma NOS
M8773/3	Spindle cell melanoma, type A
M8774/3	Spindle cell melanoma, type B
M8775/3	Mixed epithelioid and spindle cell melanoma
M8780/0	Blue nevus NOS
M8780/3	Blue nevus, malignant
M8790/0	Cellular blue nevus

M880 Soft tissue tumors and sarcomas NOS

M8800/0	Soft tissue tumor, benign
M8800/3	Sarcoma NOS
M8800/9	Sarcomatosis NOS
M8801/3	Spindle cell sarcoma
M8802/3	Giant cell sarcoma (except of bone M9250/3)
M8803/3	Small cell sarcoma
M8804/3	Epithelioid cell sarcoma

M881-M883 Fibromatous neoplasms

M8810/0	Fibroma NOS
M8810/3	Fibrosarcoma NOS
M8811/0	Fibromyxoma
M8811/3	Fibromyxosarcoma
M8812/0	Periosteal fibroma
M8812/3	Periosteal fibrosarcoma
M8813/0	Fascial fibroma
M8813/3	Fascial fibrosarcoma
M8814/3	Infantile fibrosarcoma
M8820/0	Elastofibroma
M8821/1	Aggressive fibromatosis
M8822/1	Abdominal fibromatosis
M8823/1	Desmoplastic fibroma
M8830/0	Fibrous histiocytoma NOS
M8830/1	Atypical fibrous histiocytoma
M8830/3	Fibrous histiocytoma, malignant
M8831/0	Fibroxanthoma NOS
M8831/1	Atypical fibroxanthoma
M8831/3	Fibroxanthoma, malignant
M8832/0	Dermatofibroma NOS
M8832/1	Dermatofibroma protuberans
M8832/3	Dermatofibrosarcoma NOS

M884 Myxomatous neoplasms

M8840/0	Myxoma NOS
M8840/3	Myxosarcoma

M885-M888 Lipomatous neoplasms

M8850/0	Lipoma NOS
M8850/3	Liposarcoma NOS
M8851/0	Fibrolipoma
M8851/3	Liposarcoma, well differentiated type
M8852/0	Fibromyxolipoma
M8852/3	Myxoid liposarcoma
M8853/3	Round cell liposarcoma
M8854/3	Pleomorphic liposarcoma
M8855/3	Mixed type liposarcoma
M8856/0	Intramuscular lipoma
M8857/0	Spindle cell lipoma
M8860/0	Angiomyolipoma
M8860/3	Angiomyoliposarcoma
M8861/0	Angiolipoma NOS
M8861/1	Angiolipoma, infiltrating
M8870/0	Myelolipoma
M8880/0	Hibernoma
M8881/0	Lipoblastomatosis

M889-M892 Myomatous neoplasms

M8890/0	Leiomyoma NOS
M8890/1	Intravascular leiomyomatosis
M8890/3	Leiomyosarcoma NOS
M8891/1	Epithelioid leiomyoma
M8891/3	Epithelioid leiomyosarcoma
M8892/1	Cellular leiomyoma
M8893/0	Bizarre leiomyoma
M8894/0	Angiomyoma
M8894/3	Angiomyosarcoma
M8895/0	Myoma
M8895/3	Myosarcoma
M8900/0	Rhabdomyoma NOS
M8900/3	Rhabdomyosarcoma NOS
M8901/3	Pleomorphic rhabdomyosarcoma
M8902/3	Mixed type rhabdomyosarcoma
M8903/0	Fetal rhabdomyoma
M8904/0	Adult rhabdomyoma
M8910/3	Embryonal rhabdomyosarcoma
M8920/3	Alveolar rhabdomyosarcoma

M893-M899 Complex mixed and stromal neoplasms

M8930/3	Endometrial stromal sarcoma
M8931/1	Endolymphatic stromal myosis
M8932/0	Adenomyoma
M8940/0	Pleomorphic adenoma
M8940/3	Mixed tumor, malignant NOS
M8950/3	Mullerian mixed tumor
M8951/3	Mesodermal mixed tumor
M8960/1	Mesoblastic nephroma
M8960/3	Nephroblastoma NOS
M8961/3	Epithelial nephroblastoma
M8962/3	Mesenchymal nephroblastoma
M8970/3	Hepatoblastoma
M8980/3	Carcinosarcoma NOS
M8981/3	Carcinosarcoma, embryonal type
M8982/0	Myoepithelioma
M8990/0	Mesenchymoma, benign
M8990/1	Mesenchymoma NOS
M8990/3	Mesenchymoma, malignant
M8991/3	Embryonal sarcoma

M900-M903 Fibroepithelial neoplasms

M9000/0	Brenner tumor NOS
M9000/1	Brenner tumor, borderline malignancy
M9000/3	Brenner tumor, malignant
M9010/0	Fibroadenoma NOS
M9011/0	Intracanalicular fibroadenoma NOS
M9012/0	Pericanalicular fibroadenoma
M9013/0	Adenofibroma NOS
M9014/0	Serous adenofibroma
M9015/0	Mucinous adenofibroma
M9020/0	Cellular intracanalicular fibroadenoma
M9020/1	Cystosarcoma phyllodes NOS
M9020/3	Cystosarcoma phyllodes, malignant
M9030/0	Juvenile fibroadenoma

M904 Synovial neoplasms

M9040/0	Synovioma, benign
M9040/3	Synovial sarcoma NOS
M9041/3	Synovial sarcoma, spindle cell type
M9042/3	Synovial sarcoma, epithelioid cell type
M9043/3	Synovial sarcoma, biphasic type
M9044/3	Clear cell sarcoma of tendons and aponeuroses

M905 Mesothelial neoplasms

M9050/0	Mesothelioma, benign
M9050/3	Mesothelioma, malignant
M9051/0	Fibrous mesothelioma, benign
M9051/3	Fibrous mesothelioma, malignant
M9052/0	Epithelioid mesothelioma, benign
M9052/3	Epithelioid mesothelioma, malignant
M9053/0	Mesothelioma, biphasic type, benign
M9053/3	Mesothelioma, biphasic type, malignant
M9054/0	Adenomatoid tumor NOS

M906-M909 Germ cell neoplasms

M9060/3	Dysgerminoma
M9061/3	Seminoma NOS
M9062/3	Seminoma, anaplastic type
M9063/3	Spermatocytic seminoma
M9064/3	Germinoma
M9070/3	Embryonal carcinoma NOS
M9071/3	Endodermal sinus tumor
M9072/3	Polyembryoma
M9073/1	Gonadoblastoma
M9080/0	Teratoma, benign
M9080/1	Teratoma NOS
M9080/3	Teratoma, malignant NOS
M9081/3	Teratocarcinoma
M9082/3	Malignant teratoma, undifferentiated type
M9083/3	Malignant teratoma, intermediate type
M9084/0	Dermoid cyst
M9084/3	Dermoid cyst with malignant transformation
M9090/0	Struma ovarii NOS
M9090/3	Struma ovarii, malignant
M9091/1	Strumal carcinoid

M910 Trophoblastic neoplasms

M9100/0	Hydatidiform mole NOS
M9100/1	Invasive hydatidiform mole
M9100/3	Choriocarcinoma
M9101/3	Choriocarcinoma combined with teratoma
M9102/3	Malignant teratoma, trophoblastic

M911 Mesonephromas

M9110/0	Mesonephroma, benign
M9110/1	Mesonephric tumor
M9110/3	Mesonephroma, malignant
M9111/1	Endosalpingioma

M912-M916 Blood vessel tumors

M9120/0	Hemangioma NOS
M9120/3	Hemangiosarcoma
M9121/0	Cavernous hemangioma
M9122/0	Venous hemangioma
M9123/0	Racemose hemangioma
M9124/3	Kupffer cell sarcoma
M9130/0	Hemangioendothelioma, benign
M9130/1	Hemangioendothelioma NOS
M9130/3	Hemangioendothelioma, malignant
M9131/0	Capillary hemangioma
M9132/0	Intramuscular hemangioma
M9140/3	Kaposi's sarcoma
M9141/0	Angiokeratoma
M9142/0	Verrucous keratotic hemangioma
M9150/0	Hemangiopericytoma, benign
M9150/1	Hemangiopericytoma NOS
M9150/3	Hemangiopericytoma, malignant
M9160/0	Angiofibroma NOS
M9161/1	Hemangioblastoma

M917 Lymphatic vessel tumors

M9170/0	Lymphangioma NOS
M9170/3	Lymphangiosarcoma
M9171/0	Capillary lymphangioma
M9172/0	Cavernous lymphangioma
M9173/0	Cystic lymphangioma
M9174/0	Lymphangiomyoma
M9174/1	Lymphangiomyomatosis
M9175/0	Hemolymphangioma

M918-M920 Osteomas and osteosarcomas

M9180/0	Osteoma NOS
M9180/3	Osteosarcoma NOS
M9181/3	Chondroblastic osteosarcoma
M9182/3	Fibroblastic osteosarcoma
M9183/3	Telangiectatic osteosarcoma
M9184/3	Osteosarcoma in Paget's disease of bone
M9190/3	Juxtacortical osteosarcoma
M9191/0	Osteoid osteoma NOS
M9200/0	Osteoblastoma

M921-M924 Chondromatous neoplasms

M9210/0	Osteochondroma
M9210/1	Osteochondromatosis NOS
M9220/0	Chondroma NOS
M9220/1	Chondromatosis NOS
M9220/3	Chondrosarcoma NOS
M9221/0	Juxtacortical chondroma
M9221/3	Juxtacortical chondrosarcoma
M9230/0	Chondroblastoma NOS
M9230/3	Chondroblastoma, malignant
M9240/3	Mesenchymal chondrosarcoma
M9241/0	Chondromyxoid fibroma

M925 Giant cell tumors

M9250/1	Giant cell tumor of bone NOS
M9250/3	Giant cell tumor of bone, malignant
M9251/1	Giant cell tumor of soft parts NOS
M9251/3	Malignant giant cell tumor of soft parts

M926 Miscellaneous bone tumors

M9260/3	Ewing's sarcoma
M9261/3	Adamantinoma of long bones
M9262/0	Ossifying fibroma

M927-M934 Odontogenic tumors

M9270/0	Odontogenic tumor, benign
M9270/1	Odontogenic tumor NOS
M9270/3	Odontogenic tumor, malignant
M9271/0	Dentinoma
M9272/0	Cementoma NOS
M9273/0	Cementoblastoma, benign
M9274/0	Cementifying fibroma
M9275/0	Gigantiform cementoma
M9280/0	Odontoma NOS
M9281/0	Compound odontoma
M9282/0	Complex odontoma
M9290/0	Ameloblastic fibro-odontoma
M9290/3	Ameloblastic odontosarcoma
M9300/0	Adenomatoid odontogenic tumor

M9301/0	Calcifying odontogenic cyst
M9310/0	Ameloblastoma NOS
M9310/3	Ameloblastoma, malignant
M9311/0	Odontoameloblastoma
M9312/0	Squamous odontogenic tumor
M9320/0	Odontogenic myxoma
M9321/0	Odontogenic fibroma NOS
M9330/0	Ameloblastic fibroma
M9330/3	Ameloblastic fibrosarcoma
M9340/0	Calcifying epithelial odontogenic tumor

M935-M937 Miscellaneous tumors

M9350/1	Craniopharyngioma
M9360/1	Pinealoma
M9361/1	Pineocytoma
M9362/3	Pineoblastoma
M9363/0	Melanotic neuroectodermal tumor
M9370/3	Chordoma

M938-M948 Gliomas

M9380/3	Glioma, malignant
M9381/3	Gliomatosis cerebri
M9382/3	Mixed glioma
M9383/1	Subependymal glioma
M9384/1	Subependymal giant cell astrocytoma
M9390/0	Choroid plexus papilloma NOS
M9390/3	Choroid plexus papilloma, malignant
M9391/0	Ependymoma NOS
M9392/3	Ependymoma, anaplastic type
M9393/1	Papillary ependymoma
M9394/1	Myxopapillary ependymoma
M9400/3	Astrocytoma NOS
M9401/3	Astrocytoma, anaplastic type
M9410/3	Protoplasmic astrocytoma
M9411/3	Gemistocytic astrocytoma
M9420/3	Fibrillary astrocytoma
M9421/3	Pilocytic astrocytoma
M9422/3	Spongioblastoma NOS
M9423/3	Spongioblastoma polare
M9430/3	Astroblastoma
M9440/3	Glioblastoma NOS
M9441/3	Giant cell glioblastoma
M9442/3	Glioblastoma with sarcomatous component
M9443/3	Primitive polar spongioblastoma
M9450/3	Oligodendroglioma NOS
M9451/3	Oligodendroglioma, anaplastic type
M9460/3	Oligodendroblastoma
M9470/3	Medulloblastoma NOS
M9471/3	Desmoplastic medulloblastoma
M9472/3	Medullomyoblastoma
M9480/3	Cerebellar sarcoma NOS
M9481/3	Monstrocellular sarcoma

M949-M952 Neuroepitheliomatous neoplasms

M9490/0	Ganglioneuroma
M9490/3	Ganglioneuroblastoma
M9491/0	Ganglioneuromatosis
M9500/0	Neuroblastoma NOS
M9501/0	Medulloepithelioma NOS
M9502/3	Teratoid medulloepithelioma
M9503/3	Neuroepithelioma NOS
M9504/3	Spongioneuroblastoma
M9505/1	Ganglioglioma
M9506/0	Neurocytoma
M9507/0	Pacinian tumor
M9510/3	Retinoblastoma NOS
M9511/3	Retinoblastoma, differentiated type
M9512/3	Retinoblastoma, undifferentiated type
M9520/3	Olfactory neurogenic tumor
M9521/3	Esthesioneurocytoma
M9522/3	Esthesioneuroblastoma
M9523/3	Esthesioneuroepithelioma

M953 Meningiomas

M9530/0	Meningioma NOS
M9530/1	Meningiomatosis NOS

M9530/3	Meningioma, malignant
M9531/0	Meningotheliomatous meningioma
M9532/0	Fibrous meningioma
M9533/0	Psammomatous meningioma
M9534/0	Angiomatous meningioma
M9535/0	Hemangioblastic meningioma
M9536/0	Hemangiopericytic meningioma
M9537/0	Transitional meningioma
M9538/1	Papillary meningioma
M9539/3	Meningeal sarcomatosis

M954-M957 Nerve sheath tumor

M9540/0	Neurofibroma NOS
M9540/1	Neurofibromatosis NOS
M9540/3	Neurofibrosarcoma
M9541/0	Melanotic neurofibroma
M9550/0	Plexiform neurofibroma
M9560/0	Neurilemmoma NOS
M9560/1	Neurinomatosis
M9560/3	Neurilemmoma, malignant
M9570/0	Neuroma NOS

M958 Granular cell tumors and alveolar soft part sarcoma

M9580/0	Granular cell tumor NOS
M9580/3	Granular cell tumor, malignant
M9581/3	Alveolar soft part sarcoma

M959-M963 Lymphomas, NOS or diffuse

M9590/0	Lymphomatous tumor, benign
M9590/3	Malignant lymphoma NOS
M9591/3	Malignant lymphoma, non Hodgkin's type
M9600/3	Malignant lymphoma, undifferentiated cell type NOS
M9601/3	Malignant lymphoma, stem cell type
M9602/3	Malignant lymphoma, convoluted cell type NOS
M9610/3	Lymphosarcoma NOS
M9611/3	Malignant lymphoma, lymphoplasmacytoid type
M9612/3	Malignant lymphoma, immunoblastic type
M9613/3	Malignant lymphoma, mixed lymphocytic-histiocytic NOS
M9614/3	Malignant lymphoma, centroblastic-centrocytic, diffuse
M9615/3	Malignant lymphoma, follicular center cell NOS
M9620/3	Malignant lymphoma, lymphocytic, well differentiated NOS
M9621/3	Malignant lymphoma, lymphocytic, intermediate differentiation NOS
M9622/3	Malignant lymphoma, centrocytic
M9623/3	Malignant lymphoma, follicular center cell, cleaved NOS
M9630/3	Malignant lymphoma, lymphocytic, poorly differentiated NOS
M9631/3	Prolymphocytic lymphosarcoma
M9632/3	Malignant lymphoma, centroblastic type NOS
M9633/3	Malignant lymphoma, follicular center cell, noncleaved NOS

M964 Reticulosarcomas

M9640/3	Reticulosarcoma NOS
M9641/3	Reticulosarcoma, pleomorphic cell type
M9642/3	Reticulosarcoma, nodular

M965-M966 Hodgkin's disease

M9650/3	Hodgkin's disease NOS
M9651/3	Hodgkin's disease, lymphocytic predominance
M9652/3	Hodgkin's disease, mixed cellularity
M9653/3	Hodgkin's disease, lymphocytic depletion NOS
M9654/3	Hodgkin's disease, lymphocytic depletion, diffuse fibrosis
M9655/3	Hodgkin's disease, lymphocytic depletion, reticular type

M9656/3	*Hodgkin's disease, nodular sclerosis NOS*
M9657/3	*Hodgkin's disease, nodular sclerosis, cellular phase*
M9660/3	*Hodgkin's paragranuloma*
M9661/3	*Hodgkin's granuloma*
M9662/3	*Hodgkin's sarcoma*
M969	**Lymphomas, nodular or follicular**
M9690/3	*Malignant lymphoma, nodular NOS*
M9691/3	*Malignant lymphoma, mixed lymphocytic-histiocytic, nodular*
M9692/3	*Malignant lymphoma, centroblastic-centrocytic, follicular*
M9693/3	*Malignant lymphoma, lymphocytic, well differentiated, nodular*
M9694/3	*Malignant lymphoma, lymphocytic, intermediate differentiation, nodular*
M9695/3	*Malignant lymphoma, follicular center cell, cleaved, follicular*
M9696/3	*Malignant lymphoma, lymphocytic, poorly differentiated, nodular*
M9697/3	*Malignant lymphoma, centroblastic type, follicular*
M9698/3	*Malignant lymphoma, follicular center cell, noncleaved, follicular*
M970	**Mycosis fungoides**
M9700/3	*Mycosis fungoides*
M9701/3	*Sezary's disease*
M971-M972	**Miscellaneous reticuloendothelial neoplasms**
M9710/3	*Microglioma*
M9720/3	*Malignant histiocytosis*
M9721/3	*Histiocytic medullary reticulosis*
M9722/3	*Letterer-Siwe's disease*

M973	**Plasma cell tumors**
M9730/3	*Plasma cell myeloma*
M9731/0	*Plasma cell tumor, benign*
M9731/1	*Plasmacytoma NOS*
M9731/3	*Plasma cell tumor, malignant*
M974	**Mast cell tumors**
M9740/1	*Mastocytoma NOS*
M9740/3	*Mast cell sarcoma*
M9741/3	*Malignant mastocytosis*
M975	**Burkitt's tumor**
M9750/3	*Burkitt's tumor*
M980-M994	**Leukemias**
M980	**Leukemias NOS**
M9800/3	*Leukemia NOS*
M9801/3	*Acute leukemia NOS*
M9802/3	*Subacute leukemia NOS*
M9803/3	*Chronic leukemia NOS*
M9804/3	*Aleukemic leukemia NOS*
M981	**Compound leukemias**
M9810/3	*Compound leukemia*
M982	**Lymphoid leukemias**
M9820/3	*Lymphoid leukemia NOS*
M9821/3	*Acute lymphoid leukemia*
M9822/3	*Subacute lymphoid leukemia*
M9823/3	*Chronic lymphoid leukemia*
M9824/3	*Aleukemic lymphoid leukemia*
M9825/3	*Prolymphocytic leukemia*
M983	**Plasma cell leukemias**
M9830/3	*Plasma cell leukemia*
M984	**Erythroleukemias**
M9840/3	*Erythroleukemia*
M9841/3	*Acute erythremia*
M9842/3	*Chronic erythremia*
M985	**Lymphosarcoma cell leukemias**
M9850/3	*Lymphosarcoma cell leukemia*

M986	**Myeloid leukemias**
M9860/3	*Myeloid leukemia NOS*
M9861/3	*Acute myeloid leukemia*
M9862/3	*Subacute myeloid leukemia*
M9863/3	*Chronic myeloid leukemia*
M9864/3	*Aleukemic myeloid leukemia*
M9865/3	*Neutrophilic leukemia*
M9866/3	*Acute promyelocytic leukemia*
M987	**Basophilic leukemias**
M9870/3	*Basophilic leukemia*
M988	**Eosinophilic leukemias**
M9880/3	*Eosinophilic leukemia*
M989	**Monocytic leukemias**
M9890/3	*Monocytic leukemia NOS*
M9891/3	*Acute monocytic leukemia*
M9892/3	*Subacute monocytic leukemia*
M9893/3	*Chronic monocytic leukemia*
M9894/3	*Aleukemic monocytic leukemia*
M990-M994	**Miscellaneous leukemias**
M9900/3	*Mast cell leukemia*
M9910/3	*Megakaryocytic leukemia*
M9920/3	*Megakaryocytic myelosis*
M9930/3	*Myeloid sarcoma*
M9940/3	*Hairy cell leukemia*
M995-M997	**Miscellaneous myeloproliferative and lymphoproliferative disorders**
M9950/1	*Polycythemia vera*
M9951/1	*Acute panmyelosis*
M9960/1	*Chronic myeloproliferative disease*
M9961/1	*Myelosclerosis with myeloid metaplasia*
M9962/1	*Idiopathic thrombocythemia*
M9970/1	*Chronic lymphoproliferative disease*

Appendix B
was officially deleted
October 1, 2004

CLASSIFICATION OF DRUGS BY AMERICAN HOSPITAL FORMULARY SERVICE LIST NUMBER AND THEIR ICD-9-CM EQUIVALENTS

The coding of adverse effects of drugs is keyed to the continually revised Hospital Formulary of the American Hospital Formulary Service (AHFS) published under the direction of the American Society of Hospital Pharmacists.

The following section gives the ICD-9-CM diagnosis code for each AHFS list.

AHFS* List		ICD-9-CM Diagnosis Code
4:00	ANTIHISTAMINE DRUGS	963.0
8:00	ANTI-INFECTIVE AGENTS	
8:04	Amebacides	961.5
	hydroxyquinoline derivatives	961.3
	arsenical anti-infectives	961.1
8:08	Anthelmintics	961.6
	quinoline derivatives	961.3
8:12.04	Antifungal Antibiotics	960.1
	nonantibiotics	961.9
8:12.06	Cephalosporins	960.5
8:12.08	Chloramphenicol	960.2
8:12.12	The Erythromycins	960.3
8:12.16	The Penicillins	960.0
8:12.20	The Streptomycins	960.6
8:12.24	The Tetracyclines	960.4
8:12.28	Other Antibiotics	960.8
	antimycobacterial antibiotics	960.6
	macrolides	960.3
8:16	Antituberculars	961.8
	antibiotics	960.6
8:18	Antivirals	961.7
8:20	Plasmodicides (antimalarials)	961.4
8:24	Sulfonamides	961.0
8:26	The Sulfones	961.8
8:28	Treponemicides	961.2
8:32	Trichomonacides	961.5
	hydroxyquinoline derivatives	961.3
	nitrofuran derivatives	961.9
8:36	Urinary Germicides	961.9
	quinoline derivatives	961.3
8:40	Other Anti-Infectives	961.9
10:00	ANTINEOPLASTIC AGENTS	963.1
	antibiotics	960.7
	progestogens	962.2
12:00	AUTONOMIC DRUGS	
12:04	Parasympathomimetic (Cholinergic) Agents	971.0
12:08	Parasympatholytic (Cholinergic Blocking) Agents	971.1
12:12	Sympathomimetic (Adrenergic) Agents	971.2
12:16	Sympatholytic (Adrenergic Blocking) Agents	971.3
12:20	Skeletal Muscle Relaxants	975.2
	central nervous system muscle-tone depressants	968.0
16:00	BLOOD DERIVATIVES	964.7
20:00	BLOOD FORMATION AND COAGULATION	
20:04	Antianemia Drugs	964.1
20:04.04	Iron Preparations	964.0
20:04.08	Liver and Stomach Preparations	964.1
20:12.04	Anticoagulants	964.2
20:12.08	Antiheparin Agents	964.5
20:12.12	Coagulants	964.5
20:12.16	Hemostatics	964.5
	capillary-active drugs	972.8
	fibrinolysis-affecting agents	964.4
	natural products	964.7
24:00	CARDIOVASCULAR DRUGS	
24:04	Cardiac Drugs	972.9
	cardiotonic agents	972.1
	rhythm regulators	972.0
24:06	Antilipemic Agents	972.2
	thyroid derivatives	962.7
24:08	Hypotensive Agents	972.6
	adrenergic blocking agents	971.3
	ganglion-blocking agents	972.3
	vasodilators	972.5
24:12	Vasodilating Agents	972.5
	coronary	972.4
	nicotinic acid derivatives	972.2

AHFS* List		ICD-9-CM Diagnosis Code
24:16	Sclerosing Agents	972.7
28:00	CENTRAL NERVOUS SYSTEM DRUGS	
28:04	General Anesthetics	968.4
	gaseous anesthetics	968.2
	halothane	968.1
	intravenous anesthetics	968.3
28:08	Analgesics and Antipyretics	965.9
	antirheumatics	965.61-965.69
	aromatic analgesics	965.4
	non-narcotics NEC	965.7
	opium alkaloids	965.00
	heroin	965.01
	methadone	965.02
	specified type NEC	965.09
	pyrazole derivatives	965.5
	salicylates	965.1
	specified type NEC	965.8
28:10	Narcotic Antagonists	970.1
28:12	Anticonvulsants	966.3
	barbiturates	967.0
	benzodiazepine-based tranquilizers	969.4
	bromides	967.3
	hydantoin derivatives	966.1
	oxazolidine derivative	966.0
	succinimides	966.2
28:16.04	Antidepressants	969.0
28:16.08	Tranquilizers	969.5
	benzodiazepine-based	969.4
	butyrophenone-based	969.2
	major NEC	969.3
	phenothiazine-based	969.1
28:16.12	Other Psychotherapeutic Agents	969.8
28:20	Respiratory and Cerebral Stimulants	970.9
	analeptics	970.0
	anorexigenic agents	977.0
	psychostimulants	969.7
	specified type NEC	970.8
28:24	Sedatives and Hypnotics	967.9
	barbiturates	967.0
	benzodiazepine-based tranquilizers	969.4
	chloral hydrate group	967.1
	glutethamide group	967.5
	intravenous anesthetics	968.3
	methaqualone	967.4
	paraldehyde	967.2
	phenothiazine-based tranquilizers	969.1
	specified type NEC	967.8
	thiobarbiturates	968.3
	tranquilizer NEC	969.5
36:00	DIAGNOSTIC AGENTS	977.8
40:00	ELECTROLYTE, CALORIC, AND WATER BALANCE AGENTS NEC	974.5
40:04	Acidifying Agents	963.2
40:08	Alkalinizing Agents	963.3
40:10	Ammonia Detoxicants	974.5
40:12	Replacement Solutions NEC	974.5
	plasma volume expanders	964.8
40:16	Sodium-Removing Resins	974.5
40:18	Potassium-Removing Resins	974.5
40:20	Caloric Agents	974.5
40:24	Salt and Sugar Substitutes	974.5
40:28	Diuretics NEC	974.4
	carbonic acid anhydrase inhibitors	974.2
	mercurials	974.0
	purine derivatives	974.1
	saluretics	974.3
40:36	Irrigating Solutions	974.5
40:40	Uricosuric Agents	974.7
44:00	ENZYMES NEC	963.4
	fibrinolysis-affecting agents	964.4
	gastric agents	973.4

Appendix C: Classification of Drugs by AHFS List

AHFS* List		ICD-9-CM Diagnosis Code
48:00	EXPECTORANTS AND COUGH PREPARATIONS	
	antihistamine agents	963.0
	antitussives	975.4
	codeine derivatives	965.09
	expectorants	975.5
	narcotic agents NEC	965.09
52:00	EYE, EAR, NOSE, AND THROAT PREPARATIONS	
52:04	Anti-Infectives	
	ENT	976.6
	ophthalmic	976.5
52:04.04	Antibiotics	
	ENT	976.6
	ophthalmic	976.5
52:04.06	Antivirals	
	ENT	976.6
	ophthalmic	976.5
52:04.08	Sulfonamides	
	ENT	976.6
	ophthalmic	976.5
52:04.12	Miscellaneous Anti-Infectives	
	ENT	976.6
	ophthalmic	976.5
52:08	Anti-Inflammatory Agents	
	ENT	976.6
	ophthalmic	976.5
52:10	Carbonic Anhydrase Inhibitors	974.2
52:12	Contact Lens Solutions	976.5
52:16	Local Anesthetics	968.5
52:20	Miotics	971.0
52:24	Mydriatics	
	adrenergics	971.2
	anticholinergics	971.1
	antimuscarinics	971.1
	parasympatholytics	971.1
	spasmolytics	971.1
	sympathomimetics	971.2
52:28	Mouth Washes and Gargles	976.6
52:32	Vasoconstrictors	971.2
52:36	Unclassified Agents	
	ENT	976.6
	ophthalmic	976.5
56:00	GASTROINTESTINAL DRUGS	
56:04	Antacids and Absorbents	973.0
56:08	Anti-Diarrhea Agents	973.5
56:10	Antiflatulents	973.8
56:12	Cathartics NEC	973.3
	emollients	973.2
	irritants	973.1
56:16	Digestants	973.4
56:20	Emetics and Antiemetics	
	antiemetics	963.0
	emetics	973.6
56:24	Lipotropic Agents	977.1
60:00	GOLD COMPOUNDS	965.69
64:00	HEAVY METAL ANTAGONISTS	963.8
68:00	HORMONES AND SYNTHETIC SUBSTITUTES	
68:04	Adrenals	962.0
68:08	Androgens	962.1
68:12	Contraceptives	962.2
68:16	Estrogens	962.2
68:18	Gonadotropins	962.4
68:20	Insulins and Antidiabetic Agents	962.3
68:20.08	Insulins	962.3
68:24	Parathyroid	962.6
68:28	Pituitary	
	anterior	962.4
	posterior	962.5
68:32	Progestogens	962.2
68:34	Other Corpus Luteum Hormones	962.2
68:36	Thyroid and Antithyroid	
	antithyroid	962.8
	thyroid	962.7

AHFS* List		ICD-9-CM Diagnosis Code
72:00	LOCAL ANESTHETICS NEC	968.9
	topical (surface) agents	968.5
	infiltrating agents (intradermal) (subcutaneous) (submucosal)	968.5
	nerve blocking agents (peripheral) (plexus) (regional)	968.6
	spinal	968.7
76:00	OXYTOCICS	975.0
78:00	RADIOACTIVE AGENTS	990
80:00	SERUMS, TOXOIDS, AND VACCINES	
80:04	Serums	979.9
	immune globulin (gamma) (human)	964.6
80:08	Toxoids NEC	978.8
	diphtheria	978.5
	and tetanus	978.9
	with pertussis component	978.6
	tetanus	978.4
	and diphtheria	978.9
	with pertussis component	978.6
80:12	Vaccines NEC	979.9
	bacterial NEC	978.8
	with	
	other bacterial component	978.9
	pertussis component	978.6
	viral and rickettsial component	979.7
	rickettsial NEC	979.6
	with	
	bacterial component	979.7
	pertussis component	978.6
	viral component	979.7
	viral NEC	979.6
	with	
	bacterial component	979.7
	pertussis component	978.6
	rickettsial component	979.7
84:00	SKIN AND MUCOUS MEMBRANE PREPARATIONS	
84:04	Anti-Infectives	976.0
84:04.04	Antibiotics	976.0
84:04.08	Fungicides	976.0
84:04.12	Scabicides and Pediculicides	976.0
84:04.16	Miscellaneous Local Anti-Infectives	976.0
84:06	Anti-Inflammatory Agents	976.0
84:08	Antipruritics and Local Anesthetics	
	antipruritics	976.1
	local anesthetics	968.5
84:12	Astringents	976.2
84:16	Cell Stimulants and Proliferants	976.8
84:20	Detergents	976.2
84:24	Emollients, Demulcents, and Protectants	976.3
84:28	Keratolytic Agents	976.4
84:32	Keratoplastic Agents	976.4
84:36	Miscellaneous Agents	976.8
86:00	SPASMOLYTIC AGENTS	975.1
	antiasthmatics	975.7
	papaverine	972.5
	theophyllin	974.1
88:00	VITAMINS	
88:04	Vitamin A	963.5
88:08	Vitamin B Complex	963.5
	hematopoietic vitamin	964.1
	nicotinic acid derivatives	972.2
88:12	Vitamin C	963.5
88:16	Vitamin D	963.5
88:20	Vitamin E	963.5
88:24	Vitamin K Activity	964.3
88:28	Multivitamin Preparations	963.5
92:00	UNCLASSIFIED THERAPEUTIC AGENTS	977.8

* American Hospital Formulary Service

CLASSIFICATION OF INDUSTRIAL ACCIDENTS ACCORDING TO AGENCY

Annex B to the Resolution concerning Statistics of Employment Injuries adopted by the Tenth International Conference of Labor Statisticians on 12 October 1962

1 MACHINES

11 Prime-Movers, except Electrical Motors
111 *Steam engines*
112 *Internal combustion engines*
119 *Others*
12 Transmission Machinery
121 *Transmission shafts*
122 *Transmission belts, cables, pulleys, pinions, chains, gears*
129 *Others*
13 Metalworking Machines
131 *Power presses*
132 *Lathes*
133 *Milling machines*
134 *Abrasive wheels*
135 *Mechanical shears*
136 *Forging machines*
137 *Rolling-mills*
139 *Others*
14 Wood and Assimilated Machines
141 *Circular saws*
142 *Other saws*
143 *Molding machines*
144 *Overhand planes*
149 *Others*
15 Agricultural Machines
151 *Reapers (including combine reapers)*
152 *Threshers*
159 *Others*
16 Mining Machinery
161 *Under-cutters*
169 *Others*
19 Other Machines Not Elsewhere Classified
191 *Earth-moving machines, excavating and scraping machines, except means of transport*
192 *Spinning, weaving and other textile machines*
193 *Machines for the manufacture of foodstuffs and beverages*
194 *Machines for the manufacture of paper*
195 *Printing machines*
199 *Others*

2 MEANS OF TRANSPORT AND LIFTING EQUIPMENT

21 Lifting Machines and Appliances
211 *Cranes*
212 *Lifts and elevators*
213 *Winches*
214 *Pulley blocks*
219 *Others*
22 Means of Rail Transport
221 *Inter-urban railways*
222 *Rail transport in mines, tunnels, quarries, industrial establishments, docks, etc.*
229 *Others*
23 Other Wheeled Means of Transport, Excluding Rail Transport
231 *Tractors*
232 *Lorries*
233 *Trucks*
234 *Motor vehicles, not elsewhere classified*
235 *Animal-drawn vehicles*
236 *Hand-drawn vehicles*
239 *Others*
24 Means of Air Transport
25 Means of Water Transport
251 *Motorized means of water transport*
252 *Non-motorized means of water transport*
26 Other Means of Transport
261 *Cable-cars*
262 *Mechanical conveyors, except cable-cars*
269 *Others*

3 OTHER EQUIPMENT

31 Pressure Vessels
311 *Boilers*
312 *Pressurized containers*
313 *Pressurized piping and accessories*
314 *Gas cylinders*
315 *Caissons, diving equipment*
319 *Others*
32 Furnaces, Ovens, Kilns
321 *Blast furnaces*
322 *Refining furnaces*
323 *Other furnaces*
324 *Kilns*
325 *Ovens*
33 Refrigerating Plants
34 Electrical Installations, Including Electric Motors, but Excluding Electric Hand Tools
341 *Rotating machines*
342 *Conductors*
343 *Transformers*
344 *Control apparatus*
349 *Others*
35 Electric Hand Tools
36 Tools, Implements, and Appliances, Except Electric Hand Tools
361 *Power-driven hand tools, except electric hand tools*
362 *Hand tools, not power-driven*
369 *Others*
37 Ladders, Mobile Ramps
38 Scaffolding
39 Other Equipment, Not Elsewhere Classified

4 MATERIALS, SUBSTANCES AND RADIATIONS

41 Explosives
42 Dusts, Gases, Liquids and Chemicals, Excluding Explosives
421 *Dusts*
422 *Gases, vapors, fumes*
423 *Liquids, not elsewhere classified*
424 *Chemicals, not elsewhere classified*
43 Flying Fragments
44 Radiations
441 *Ionizing radiations*
449 *Others*
49 Other Materials and Substances Not Elsewhere Classified

5 WORKING ENVIRONMENT

51 Outdoor
511 *Weather*
512 *Traffic and working surfaces*
513 *Water*
519 *Others*
52 Indoor
521 *Floors*
522 *Confined quarters*
523 *Stairs*
524 *Other traffic and working surfaces*
525 *Floor openings and wall openings*
526 *Environmental factors (lighting, ventilation, temperature, noise, etc.)*
529 *Others*
53 Underground
531 *Roofs and faces of mine roads and tunnels, etc.*
532 *Floors of mine roads and tunnels, etc.*
533 *Working-faces of mines, tunnels, etc.*
534 *Mine shafts*
535 *Fire*
536 *Water*
539 *Others*

6 OTHER AGENCIES, NOT ELSEWHERE CLASSIFIED

61 Animals
611 *Live animals*
612 *Animal products*
69 Other Agencies, Not Elsewhere Classified

7 AGENCIES NOT CLASSIFIED FOR LACK OF SUFFICIENT DATA

LIST OF THREE-DIGIT CATEGORIES

1. INFECTIOUS AND PARASITIC DISEASES

Intestinal infectious diseases (001-009)
001 Cholera
002 Typhoid and paratyphoid fevers
003 Other salmonella infections
004 Shigellosis
005 Other food poisoning (bacterial)
006 Amebiasis
007 Other protozoal intestinal diseases
008 Intestinal infections due to other organisms
009 Ill-defined intestinal infections

Tuberculosis (010-018)
010 Primary tuberculous infection
011 Pulmonary tuberculosis
012 Other respiratory tuberculosis
013 Tuberculosis of meninges and central nervous system
014 Tuberculosis of intestines, peritoneum, and mesenteric glands
015 Tuberculosis of bones and joints
016 Tuberculosis of genitourinary system
017 Tuberculosis of other organs
018 Miliary tuberculosis

Zoonotic bacterial diseases (020-027)
020 Plague
021 Tularemia
022 Anthrax
023 Brucellosis
024 Glanders
025 Melioidosis
026 Rat-bite fever
027 Other zoonotic bacterial diseases

Other bacterial diseases (030-042)
030 Leprosy
031 Diseases due to other mycobacteria
032 Diphtheria
033 Whooping cough
034 Streptococcal sore throat and scarlatina
035 Erysipelas
036 Meningococcal infection
037 Tetanus
038 Septicemia
039 Actinomycotic infections
040 Other bacterial diseases
041 Bacterial infection in conditions classified elsewhere and of unspecified site

Human immunodeficiency virus (042)
042 Human immunodeficiency virus [HIV] disease

Poliomyelitis and other non-arthropod-borne viral diseases of central nervous system (045-049)
045 Acute poliomyelitis
046 Slow virus infection of central nervous system
047 Meningitis due to enterovirus
048 Other enterovirus diseases of central nervous system
049 Other non-arthropod-borne viral diseases of central nervous system

Viral diseases accompanied by exanthem (050-057)
050 Smallpox
051 Cowpox and paravaccinia
052 Chickenpox
053 Herpes zoster
054 Herpes simplex
055 Measles
056 Rubella
057 Other viral exanthemata

Arthropod-borne viral diseases (060-066)
060 Yellow fever
061 Dengue
062 Mosquito-borne viral encephalitis
063 Tick-borne viral encephalitis
064 Viral encephalitis transmitted by other and unspecified arthropods
065 Arthropod-borne hemorrhagic fever
066 Other arthropod-borne viral diseases

Other diseases due to viruses and Chlamydiae (070-079)
070 Viral hepatitis
071 Rabies
072 Mumps
073 Ornithosis
074 Specific diseases due to Coxsackievirus
075 Infectious mononucleosis
076 Trachoma
077 Other diseases of conjunctiva due to viruses and Chlamydiae
078 Other diseases due to viruses and Chlamydiae
079 Viral infection in conditions classified elsewhere and of unspecified site

Rickettsioses and other arthropod-borne diseases (080-088)
080 Louse-borne [epidemic] typhus
081 Other typhus
082 Tick-borne rickettsioses
083 Other rickettsioses
084 Malaria
085 Leishmaniasis
086 Trypanosomiasis
087 Relapsing fever
088 Other arthropod-borne diseases

Syphilis and other venereal diseases (090-099)
090 Congenital syphilis
091 Early syphilis, symptomatic
092 Early syphilis, latent
093 Cardiovascular syphilis
094 Neurosyphilis
095 Other forms of late syphilis, with symptoms
096 Late syphilis, latent
097 Other and unspecified syphilis
098 Gonococcal infections
099 Other venereal diseases

Other spirochetal diseases (100-104)
100 Leptospirosis
101 Vincent's angina
102 Yaws
103 Pinta
104 Other spirochetal infection

Mycoses (110-118)
110 Dermatophytosis
111 Dermatomycosis, other and unspecified
112 Candidiasis
114 Coccidioidomycosis
115 Histoplasmosis
116 Blastomycotic infection
117 Other mycoses
118 Opportunistic mycoses

Helminthiases (120-129)
120 Schistosomiasis [bilharziasis]
121 Other trematode infections
122 Echinococcosis
123 Other cestode infection
124 Trichinosis
125 Filarial infection and dracontiasis
126 Ancylostomiasis and necatoriasis
127 Other intestinal helminthiases
128 Other and unspecified helminthiases
129 Intestinal parasitism, unspecified

Other infectious and parasitic diseases (130-136)
130 Toxoplasmosis
131 Trichomoniasis
132 Pediculosis and phthirus infestation
133 Acariasis
134 Other infestation
135 Sarcoidosis
136 Other and unspecified infectious and parasitic diseases

Late effects of infectious and parasitic diseases (137-139)
137 Late effects of tuberculosis
138 Late effects of acute poliomyelitis
139 Late effects of other infectious and parasitic diseases

2. NEOPLASMS

Malignant neoplasm of lip, oral cavity, and pharynx (140-149)
140 Malignant neoplasm of lip
141 Malignant neoplasm of tongue
142 Malignant neoplasm of major salivary glands
143 Malignant neoplasm of gum
144 Malignant neoplasm of floor of mouth
145 Malignant neoplasm of other and unspecified parts of mouth
146 Malignant neoplasm of oropharynx
147 Malignant neoplasm of nasopharynx
148 Malignant neoplasm of hypopharynx
149 Malignant neoplasm of other and ill-defined sites within the lip, oral cavity, and pharynx

Malignant neoplasm of digestive organs and peritoneum (150-159)
150 Malignant neoplasm of esophagus
151 Malignant neoplasm of stomach
152 Malignant neoplasm of small intestine, including duodenum
153 Malignant neoplasm of colon
154 Malignant neoplasm of rectum, rectosigmoid junction, and anus
155 Malignant neoplasm of liver and intrahepatic bile ducts
156 Malignant neoplasm of gallbladder and extrahepatic bile ducts
157 Malignant neoplasm of pancreas
158 Malignant neoplasm of retroperitoneum and peritoneum
159 Malignant neoplasm of other and ill-defined sites within the digestive organs and peritoneum

Malignant neoplasm of respiratory and intrathoracic organs (160-165)
160 Malignant neoplasm of nasal cavities, middle ear, and accessory sinuses
161 Malignant neoplasm of larynx
162 Malignant neoplasm of trachea, bronchus, and lung
163 Malignant neoplasm of pleura
164 Malignant neoplasm of thymus, heart, and mediastinum
165 Malignant neoplasm of other and ill-defined sites within the respiratory system and intrathoracic organs

Malignant neoplasm of bone, connective tissue, skin, and breast (170-176)
170 Malignant neoplasm of bone and articular cartilage
171 Malignant neoplasm of connective and other soft tissue
172 Malignant melanoma of skin
173 Other malignant neoplasm of skin
174 Malignant neoplasm of female breast
175 Malignant neoplasm of male breast
176 Kaposi's sarcoma

Malignant neoplasm of genitourinary organs (179-189)
179 Malignant neoplasm of uterus, part unspecified
180 Malignant neoplasm of cervix uteri
181 Malignant neoplasm of placenta
182 Malignant neoplasm of body of uterus
183 Malignant neoplasm of ovary and other uterine adnexa
184 Malignant neoplasm of other and unspecified female genital organs
185 Malignant neoplasm of prostate

186 Malignant neoplasm of testis
187 Malignant neoplasm of penis and other male genital organs
188 Malignant neoplasm of bladder
189 Malignant neoplasm of kidney and other unspecified urinary organs

Malignant neoplasm of other and unspecified sites (190-199)
190 Malignant neoplasm of eye
191 Malignant neoplasm of brain
192 Malignant neoplasm of other and unspecified parts of nervous system
193 Malignant neoplasm of thyroid gland
194 Malignant neoplasm of other endocrine glands and related structures
195 Malignant neoplasm of other and ill-defined sites
196 Secondary and unspecified malignant neoplasm of lymph nodes
197 Secondary malignant neoplasm of respiratory and digestive systems
198 Secondary malignant neoplasm of other specified sites
199 Malignant neoplasm without specification of site

Malignant neoplasm of lymphatic and hematopoietic tissue (200-208)
200 Lymphosarcoma and reticulosarcoma
201 Hodgkin's disease
202 Other malignant neoplasm of lymphoid and histiocytic tissue
203 Multiple myeloma and immunoproliferative neoplasms
204 Lymphoid leukemia
205 Myeloid leukemia
206 Monocytic leukemia
207 Other specified leukemia
208 Leukemia of unspecified cell type

Benign neoplasms (210-229)
210 Benign neoplasm of lip, oral cavity, and pharynx
211 Benign neoplasm of other parts of digestive system
212 Benign neoplasm of respiratory and intrathoracic organs
213 Benign neoplasm of bone and articular cartilage
214 Lipoma
215 Other benign neoplasm of connective and other soft tissue
216 Benign neoplasm of skin
217 Benign neoplasm of breast
218 Uterine leiomyoma
219 Other benign neoplasm of uterus
220 Benign neoplasm of ovary
221 Benign neoplasm of other female genital organs
222 Benign neoplasm of male genital organs
223 Benign neoplasm of kidney and other urinary organs
224 Benign neoplasm of eye
225 Benign neoplasm of brain and other parts of nervous system
226 Benign neoplasm of thyroid gland
227 Benign neoplasm of other endocrine glands and related structures
228 Hemangioma and lymphangioma, any site
229 Benign neoplasm of other and unspecified sites

Carcinoma in situ (230-234)
230 Carcinoma in situ of digestive organs
231 Carcinoma in situ of respiratory system
232 Carcinoma in situ of skin
233 Carcinoma in situ of breast and genitourinary system
234 Carcinoma in situ of other and unspecified sites

Neoplasms of uncertain behavior (235-238)
235 Neoplasm of uncertain behavior of digestive and respiratory systems
236 Neoplasm of uncertain behavior of genitourinary organs
237 Neoplasm of uncertain behavior of endocrine glands and nervous system
238 Neoplasm of uncertain behavior of other and unspecified sites and tissues

Neoplasms of unspecified nature (239)
239 Neoplasm of unspecified nature

3. ENDOCRINE, NUTRITIONAL AND METABOLIC DISEASES, AND IMMUNITY DISORDERS

Disorders of thyroid gland (240-246)
240 Simple and unspecified goiter
241 Nontoxic nodular goiter
242 Thyrotoxicosis with or without goiter
243 Congenital hypothyroidism
244 Acquired hypothyroidism
245 Thyroiditis
246 Other disorders of thyroid

Diseases of other endocrine glands (250-259)
250 Diabetes mellitus
251 Other disorders of pancreatic internal secretion
252 Disorders of parathyroid gland
253 Disorders of the pituitary gland and its hypothalamic control
254 Diseases of thymus gland
255 Disorders of adrenal glands
256 Ovarian dysfunction
257 Testicular dysfunction
258 Polyglandular dysfunction and related disorders
259 Other endocrine disorders

Nutritional deficiencies (260-269)
260 Kwashiorkor
261 Nutritional marasmus
262 Other severe protein-calorie malnutrition
263 Other and unspecified protein-calorie malnutrition
264 Vitamin A deficiency
265 Thiamine and niacin deficiency states
266 Deficiency of B-complex components
267 Ascorbic acid deficiency
268 Vitamin D deficiency
269 Other nutritional deficiencies

Other metabolic disorders and immunity disorders (270-279)
270 Disorders of amino-acid transport and metabolism
271 Disorders of carbohydrate transport and metabolism
272 Disorders of lipoid metabolism
273 Disorders of plasma protein metabolism
274 Gout
275 Disorders of mineral metabolism
276 Disorders of fluid, electrolyte, and acid-base balance
277 Other and unspecified disorders of metabolism
278 Overweight, obesity and other hyperalimentation
279 Disorders involving the immune mechanism

4. DISEASES OF BLOOD AND BLOOD-FORMING ORGANS (280-289)
280 Iron deficiency anemias
281 Other deficiency anemias
282 Hereditary hemolytic anemias
283 Acquired hemolytic anemias
284 Aplastic anemia
285 Other and unspecified anemias
286 Coagulation defects
287 Purpura and other hemorrhagic conditions
288 Diseases of white blood cells
289 Other diseases of blood and blood-forming organs

5. MENTAL DISORDERS

Organic psychotic conditions (290-294)
290 Senile and presenile organic psychotic conditions
291 Alcoholic psychoses
292 Drug psychoses
293 Transient organic psychotic conditions
294 Other organic psychotic conditions (chronic)

Other psychoses (295-299)
295 Schizophrenic psychoses
296 Affective psychoses
297 Paranoid states
298 Other nonorganic psychoses
299 Psychoses with origin specific to childhood

Neurotic disorders, personality disorders, and other nonpsychotic mental disorders (300-316)
300 Neurotic disorders
301 Personality disorders
302 Sexual deviations and disorders
303 Alcohol dependence syndrome
304 Drug dependence
305 Nondependent abuse of drugs
306 Physiological malfunction arising from mental factors
307 Special symptoms or syndromes, not elsewhere classified
308 Acute reaction to stress
309 Adjustment reaction
310 Specific nonpsychotic mental disorders following organic brain damage
311 Depressive disorder, not elsewhere classified
312 Disturbance of conduct, not elsewhere classified
313 Disturbance of emotions specific to childhood and adolescence
314 Hyperkinetic syndrome of childhood
315 Specific delays in development
316 Psychic factors associated with diseases classified elsewhere

Mental retardation (317-319)
317 Mild mental retardation
318 Other specified mental retardation
319 Unspecified mental retardation

6. DISEASES OF THE NERVOUS SYSTEM AND SENSE ORGANS

Inflammatory diseases of the central nervous system (320-326)
320 Bacterial meningitis
321 Meningitis due to other organisms
322 Meningitis of unspecified cause
323 Encephalitis, myelitis, and encephalomyelitis
324 Intracranial and intraspinal abscess
325 Phlebitis and thrombophlebitis of intracranial venous sinuses
326 Late effects of intracranial abscess or pyogenic infection

Organic Sleep Disorders (327)
327 Organic sleep disorders

Hereditary and degenerative diseases of the central nervous system (330-337)
330 Cerebral degenerations usually manifest in childhood
331 Other cerebral degenerations
332 Parkinson's disease
333 Other extrapyramidal diseases and abnormal movement disorders
334 Spinocerebellar disease
335 Anterior horn cell disease
336 Other diseases of spinal cord
337 Disorders of the autonomic nervous system

Other disorders of the central nervous system (340-349)

340 Multiple sclerosis
341 Other demyelinating diseases of central nervous system
342 Hemiplegia and hemiparesis
343 Infantile cerebral palsy
344 Other paralytic syndromes
345 Epilepsy
346 Migraine
347 Cataplexy and narcolepsy
348 Other conditions of brain
349 Other and unspecified disorders of the nervous system

Disorders of the peripheral nervous system (350-359)

350 Trigeminal nerve disorders
351 Facial nerve disorders
352 Disorders of other cranial nerves
353 Nerve root and plexus disorders
354 Mononeuritis of upper limb and mononeuritis multiplex
355 Mononeuritis of lower limb
356 Hereditary and idiopathic peripheral neuropathy
357 Inflammatory and toxic neuropathy
358 Myoneural disorders
359 Muscular dystrophies and other myopathies

Disorders of the eye and adnexa (360-379)

360 Disorders of the globe
361 Retinal detachments and defects
362 Other retinal disorders
363 Chorioretinal inflammations and scars and other disorders of choroid
364 Disorders of iris and ciliary body
365 Glaucoma
366 Cataract
367 Disorders of refraction and accommodation
368 Visual disturbances
369 Blindness and low vision
370 Keratitis
371 Corneal opacity and other disorders of cornea
372 Disorders of conjunctiva
373 Inflammation of eyelids
374 Other disorders of eyelids
375 Disorders of lacrimal system
376 Disorders of the orbit
377 Disorders of optic nerve and visual pathways
378 Strabismus and other disorders of binocular eye movements
379 Other disorders of eye

Diseases of the ear and mastoid process (380-389)

380 Disorders of external ear
381 Nonsuppurative otitis media and Eustachian tube disorders
382 Suppurative and unspecified otitis media
383 Mastoiditis and related conditions
384 Other disorders of tympanic membrane
385 Other disorders of middle ear and mastoid
386 Vertiginous syndromes and other disorders of vestibular system
387 Otosclerosis
388 Other disorders of ear
389 Hearing loss

7. DISEASES OF THE CIRCULATORY SYSTEM

Acute rheumatic fever (390-392)

390 Rheumatic fever without mention of heart involvement
391 Rheumatic fever with heart involvement
392 Rheumatic chorea

Chronic rheumatic heart disease (393-398)

393 Chronic rheumatic pericarditis
394 Diseases of mitral valve
395 Diseases of aortic valve
396 Diseases of mitral and aortic valves
397 Diseases of other endocardial structures
398 Other rheumatic heart disease

Hypertensive disease (401-405)

401 Essential hypertension
402 Hypertensive heart disease
403 Hypertensive kidney disease
404 Hypertensive heart and kidney disease
405 Secondary hypertension

Ischemic heart disease (410-414)

410 Acute myocardial infarction
411 Other acute and subacute form of ischemic heart disease
412 Old myocardial infarction
413 Angina pectoris
414 Other forms of chronic ischemic heart disease

Diseases of pulmonary circulation (415-417)

415 Acute pulmonary heart disease
416 Chronic pulmonary heart disease
417 Other diseases of pulmonary circulation

Other forms of heart disease (420-429)

420 Acute pericarditis
421 Acute and subacute endocarditis
422 Acute myocarditis
423 Other diseases of pericardium
424 Other diseases of endocardium
425 Cardiomyopathy
426 Conduction disorders
427 Cardiac dysrhythmias
428 Heart failure
429 Ill-defined descriptions and complications of heart disease

Cerebrovascular disease (430-438)

430 Subarachnoid hemorrhage
431 Intracerebral hemorrhage
432 Other and unspecified intracranial hemorrhage
433 Occlusion and stenosis of precerebral arteries
434 Occlusion of cerebral arteries
435 Transient cerebral ischemia
436 Acute but ill-defined cerebrovascular disease
437 Other and ill-defined cerebrovascular disease
438 Late effects of cerebrovascular disease

Diseases of arteries, arterioles, and capillaries (440-448)

440 Atherosclerosis
441 Aortic aneurysm and dissection
442 Other aneurysm
443 Other peripheral vascular disease
444 Arterial embolism and thrombosis
445 Atheroembolism
446 Polyarteritis nodosa and allied conditions
447 Other disorders of arteries and arterioles
448 Diseases of capillaries

Diseases of veins and lymphatics, and other diseases of circulatory system (451-459)

451 Phlebitis and thrombophlebitis
452 Portal vein thrombosis
453 Other venous embolism and thrombosis
454 Varicose veins of lower extremities
455 Hemorrhoids
456 Varicose veins of other sites
457 Noninfective disorders of lymphatic channels
458 Hypotension
459 Other disorders of circulatory system

8. DISEASES OF THE RESPIRATORY SYSTEM

Acute respiratory infections (460-466)

460 Acute nasopharyngitis [common cold]
461 Acute sinusitis
462 Acute pharyngitis
463 Acute tonsillitis
464 Acute laryngitis and tracheitis
465 Acute upper respiratory infections of multiple or unspecified sites
466 Acute bronchitis and bronchiolitis

Other diseases of upper respiratory tract (470-478)

470 Deviated nasal septum
471 Nasal polyps
472 Chronic pharyngitis and nasopharyngitis
473 Chronic sinusitis
474 Chronic disease of tonsils and adenoids
475 Peritonsillar abscess
476 Chronic laryngitis and laryngotracheitis
477 Allergic rhinitis
478 Other diseases of upper respiratory tract

Pneumonia and influenza (480-487)

480 Viral pneumonia
481 Pneumococcal pneumonia [Streptococcus pneumoniae pneumonia]
482 Other bacterial pneumonia
483 Pneumonia due to other specified organism
484 Pneumonia in infectious diseases classified elsewhere
485 Bronchopneumonia, organism unspecified
486 Pneumonia, organism unspecified
487 Influenza

Chronic obstructive pulmonary disease and allied conditions (490-496)

490 Bronchitis, not specified as acute or chronic
491 Chronic bronchitis
492 Emphysema
493 Asthma
494 Bronchiectasis
495 Extrinsic allergic alveolitis
496 Chronic airways obstruction, not elsewhere classified

Pneumoconioses and other lung diseases due to external agents (500-508)

500 Coal workers' pneumoconiosis
501 Asbestosis
502 Pneumoconiosis due to other silica or silicates
503 Pneumoconiosis due to other inorganic dust
504 Pneumopathy due to inhalation of other dust
505 Pneumoconiosis, unspecified
506 Respiratory conditions due to chemical fumes and vapors
507 Pneumonitis due to solids and liquids
508 Respiratory conditions due to other and unspecified external agents

Other diseases of respiratory system (510-519)

510 Empyema
511 Pleurisy
512 Pneumothorax
513 Abscess of lung and mediastinum
514 Pulmonary congestion and hypostasis
515 Postinflammatory pulmonary fibrosis
516 Other alveolar and parietoalveolar pneumopathy
517 Lung involvement in conditions classified elsewhere
518 Other diseases of lung
519 Other diseases of respiratory system

9. DISEASES OF THE DIGESTIVE SYSTEM

Diseases of oral cavity, salivary glands, and jaws (520-529)

520 Disorders of tooth development and eruption
521 Diseases of hard tissues of teeth
522 Diseases of pulp and periapical tissues
523 Gingival and periodontal diseases
524 Dentofacial anomalies, including malocclusion
525 Other diseases and conditions of the teeth and supporting structures
526 Diseases of the jaws
527 Diseases of the salivary glands

528 Diseases of the oral soft tissues, excluding lesions specific for gingiva and tongue
529 Diseases and other conditions of the tongue

Diseases of esophagus, stomach, and duodenum (530-537)
530 Diseases of esophagus
531 Gastric ulcer
532 Duodenal ulcer
533 Peptic ulcer, site unspecified
534 Gastrojejunal ulcer
535 Gastritis and duodenitis
536 Disorders of function of stomach
537 Other disorders of stomach and duodenum

Appendicitis (540-543)
540 Acute appendicitis
541 Appendicitis, unqualified
542 Other appendicitis
543 Other diseases of appendix

Hernia of abdominal cavity (550-553)
550 Inguinal hernia
551 Other hernia of abdominal cavity, with gangrene
552 Other hernia of abdominal cavity, with obstruction, but without mention of gangrene
553 Other hernia of abdominal cavity without mention of obstruction or gangrene

Noninfective enteritis and colitis (555-558)
555 Regional enteritis
556 Ulcerative colitis
557 Vascular insufficiency of intestine
558 Other noninfective gastroenteritis and colitis

Other diseases of intestines and peritoneum (560-569)
560 Intestinal obstruction without mention of hernia
562 Diverticula of intestine
564 Functional digestive disorders, not elsewhere classified
565 Anal fissure and fistula
566 Abscess of anal and rectal regions
567 Peritonitis and retroperitoneal infections
568 Other disorders of peritoneum
569 Other disorders of intestine

Other diseases of digestive system (570-579)
570 Acute and subacute necrosis of liver
571 Chronic liver disease and cirrhosis
572 Liver abscess and sequelae of chronic liver disease
573 Other disorders of liver
574 Cholelithiasis
575 Other disorders of gallbladder
576 Other disorders of biliary tract
577 Diseases of pancreas
578 Gastrointestinal hemorrhage
579 Intestinal malabsorption

10. DISEASES OF THE GENITOURINARY SYSTEM

Nephritis, nephrotic syndrome, and nephrosis (580-589)
580 Acute glomerulonephritis
581 Nephrotic syndrome
582 Chronic glomerulonephritis
583 Nephritis and nephropathy, not specified as acute or chronic
584 Acute renal failure
585 Chronic kidney disease (CKD)
586 Renal failure, unspecified
587 Renal sclerosis, unspecified
588 Disorders resulting from impaired renal function
589 Small kidney of unknown cause

Other diseases of urinary system (590-599)
590 Infections of kidney
591 Hydronephrosis
592 Calculus of kidney and ureter
593 Other disorders of kidney and ureter

594 Calculus of lower urinary tract
595 Cystitis
596 Other disorders of bladder
597 Urethritis, not sexually transmitted, and urethral syndrome
598 Urethral stricture
599 Other disorders of urethra and urinary tract

Diseases of male genital organs (600-608)
600 Hyperplasia of prostate
601 Inflammatory diseases of prostate
602 Other disorders of prostate
603 Hydrocele
604 Orchitis and epididymitis
605 Redundant prepuce and phimosis
606 Infertility, male
607 Disorders of penis
608 Other disorders of male genital organs

Disorders of breast (610-611)
610 Benign mammary dysplasias
611 Other disorders of breast

Inflammatory disease of female pelvic organs (614-616)
614 Inflammatory disease of ovary, fallopian tube, pelvic cellular tissue, and peritoneum
615 Inflammatory diseases of uterus, except cervix
616 Inflammatory disease of cervix, vagina, and vulva

Other disorders of female genital tract (617-629)
617 Endometriosis
618 Genital prolapse
619 Fistula involving female genital tract
620 Noninflammatory disorders of ovary, fallopian tube, and broad ligament
621 Disorders of uterus, not elsewhere classified
622 Noninflammatory disorders of cervix
623 Noninflammatory disorders of vagina
624 Noninflammatory disorders of vulva and perineum
625 Pain and other symptoms associated with female genital organs
626 Disorders of menstruation and other abnormal bleeding from female genital tract
627 Menopausal and postmenopausal disorders
628 Infertility, female
629 Other disorders of female genital organs

11. COMPLICATIONS OF PREGNANCY, CHILDBIRTH AND THE PUERPERIUM

Ectopic and molar pregnancy and other pregnancy with abortive outcome (630-639)
630 Hydatidiform mole
631 Other abnormal product of conception
632 Missed abortion
633 Ectopic pregnancy
634 Spontaneous abortion
635 Legally induced abortion
636 Illegally induced abortion
637 Unspecified abortion
638 Failed attempted abortion
639 Complications following abortion and ectopic and molar pregnancies

Complications mainly related to pregnancy (640-648)
640 Hemorrhage in early pregnancy
641 Antepartum hemorrhage, abruptio placentae, and placenta previa
642 Hypertension complicating pregnancy, childbirth, and the puerperium
643 Excessive vomiting in pregnancy
644 Early or threatened labor
645 Prolonged pregnancy
646 Other complications of pregnancy, not elsewhere classified
647 Infective and parasitic conditions in the mother classifiable elsewhere but complicating pregnancy, childbirth, and the puerperium

648 Other current conditions in the mother classifiable elsewhere but complicating pregnancy, childbirth, and the puerperium

Normal delivery, and other indications for care in pregnancy, labor, and delivery (650-659)
650 Normal delivery
651 Multiple gestation
652 Malposition and malpresentation of fetus
653 Disproportion
654 Abnormality of organs and soft tissues of pelvis
655 Known or suspected fetal abnormality affecting management of mother
656 Other fetal and placental problems affecting management of mother
657 Polyhydramnios
658 Other problems associated with amniotic cavity and membranes
659 Other indications for care or intervention related to labor and delivery and not elsewhere classified

Complications occurring mainly in the course of labor and delivery (660-669)
660 Obstructed labor
661 Abnormality of forces of labor
662 Long labor
663 Umbilical cord complications
664 Trauma to perineum and vulva during delivery
665 Other obstetrical trauma
666 Postpartum hemorrhage
667 Retained placenta or membranes, without hemorrhage
668 Complications of the administration of anesthetic or other sedation in labor and delivery
669 Other complications of labor and delivery, not elsewhere classified

Complications of the puerperium (670-677)
670 Major puerperal infection
671 Venous complications in pregnancy and the puerperium
672 Pyrexia of unknown origin during the puerperium
673 Obstetrical pulmonary embolism
674 Other and unspecified complications of the puerperium, not elsewhere classified
675 Infections of the breast and nipple associated with childbirth
676 Other disorders of the breast associated with childbirth, and disorders of lactation
677 Late effect of complication of pregnancy, childbirth, and the puerperium

12. DISEASES OF THE SKIN AND SUBCUTANEOUS TISSUE

Infections of skin and subcutaneous tissue (680-686)
680 Carbuncle and furuncle
681 Cellulitis and abscess of finger and toe
682 Other cellulitis and abscess
683 Acute lymphadenitis
684 Impetigo
685 Pilonidal cyst
686 Other local infections of skin and subcutaneous tissue

Other inflammatory conditions of skin and subcutaneous tissue (690-698)
690 Erythematosquamous dermatosis
691 Atopic dermatitis and related conditions
692 Contact dermatitis and other eczema
693 Dermatitis due to substances taken internally
694 Bullous dermatoses
695 Erythematous conditions
696 Psoriasis and similar disorders
697 Lichen
698 Pruritus and related conditions

Other diseases of skin and subcutaneous tissue (700-709)
700   Corns and callosities
701   Other hypertrophic and atrophic conditions of skin
702   Other dermatoses
703   Diseases of nail
704   Diseases of hair and hair follicles
705   Disorders of sweat glands
706   Diseases of sebaceous glands
707   Chronic ulcer of skin
708   Urticaria
709   Other disorders of skin and subcutaneous tissue

13.   DISEASES OF THE MUSCULOSKELETAL SYSTEM AND CONNECTIVE TISSUE

Arthropathies and related disorders (710-719)
710   Diffuse diseases of connective tissue
711   Arthropathy associated with infections
712   Crystal arthropathies
713   Arthropathy associated with other disorders classified elsewhere
714   Rheumatoid arthritis and other inflammatory polyarthropathies
715   Osteoarthrosis and allied disorders
716   Other and unspecified arthropathies
717   Internal derangement of knee
718   Other derangement of joint
719   Other and unspecified disorder of joint
Dorsopathies (720-724)
720   Ankylosing spondylitis and other inflammatory spondylopathies
721   Spondylosis and allied disorders
722   Intervertebral disc disorders
723   Other disorders of cervical region
724   Other and unspecified disorders of back

Rheumatism, excluding the back (725-729)
725   Polymyalgia rheumatica
726   Peripheral enthesopathies and allied syndromes
727   Other disorders of synovium, tendon, and bursa
728   Disorders of muscle, ligament, and fascia
729   Other disorders of soft tissues

Osteopathies, chondropathies, and acquired musculoskeletal deformities (730-739)
730   Osteomyelitis, periostitis, and other infections involving bone
731   Osteitis deformans and osteopathies associated with other disorders classified elsewhere
732   Osteochondropathies
733   Other disorders of bone and cartilage
734   Flat foot
735   Acquired deformities of toe
736   Other acquired deformities of limbs
737   Curvature of spine
738   Other acquired deformity
739   Nonallopathic lesions, not elsewhere classified

14.   CONGENITAL ANOMALIES
740   Anencephalus and similar anomalies
741   Spina bifida
742   Other congenital anomalies of nervous system
743   Congenital anomalies of eye
744   Congenital anomalies of ear, face, and neck
745   Bulbus cordis anomalies and anomalies of cardiac septal closure
746   Other congenital anomalies of heart
747   Other congenital anomalies of circulatory system
748   Congenital anomalies of respiratory system
749   Cleft palate and cleft lip
750   Other congenital anomalies of upper alimentary tract
751   Other congenital anomalies of digestive system
752   Congenital anomalies of genital organs

753   Congenital anomalies of urinary system
754   Certain congenital musculoskeletal deformities
755   Other congenital anomalies of limbs
756   Other congenital musculoskeletal anomalies
757   Congenital anomalies of the integument
758   Chromosomal anomalies
759   Other and unspecified congenital anomalies

15.   CERTAIN CONDITIONS ORIGINATING IN THE PERINATAL PERIOD

Maternal causes of perinatal morbidity and mortality (760-763)
760   Fetus or newborn affected by maternal conditions which may be unrelated to present pregnancy
761   Fetus or newborn affected by maternal complications of pregnancy
762   Fetus or newborn affected by complications of placenta, cord, and membranes
763   Fetus or newborn affected by other complications of labor and delivery

Other conditions originating in the perinatal period (764-779)
764   Slow fetal growth and fetal malnutrition
765   Disorders relating to short gestation and unspecified low birthweight
766   Disorders relating to long gestation and high birthweight
767   Birth trauma
768   Intrauterine hypoxia and birth asphyxia
769   Respiratory distress syndrome
770   Other respiratory conditions of fetus and newborn
771   Infections specific to the perinatal period
772   Fetal and neonatal hemorrhage
773   Hemolytic disease of fetus or newborn, due to isoimmunization
774   Other perinatal jaundice
775   Endocrine and metabolic disturbances specific to the fetus and newborn
776   Hematological disorders of fetus and newborn
777   Perinatal disorders of digestive system
778   Conditions involving the integument and temperature regulation of fetus and newborn
779   Other and ill-defined conditions originating in the perinatal period

16.   SYMPTOMS, SIGNS, AND ILL-DEFINED CONDITIONS

Symptoms (780-789)
780   General symptoms
781   Symptoms involving nervous and musculoskeletal systems
782   Symptoms involving skin and other integumentary tissue
783   Symptoms concerning nutrition, metabolism, and development
784   Symptoms involving head and neck
785   Symptoms involving cardiovascular system
786   Symptoms involving respiratory system and other chest symptoms
787   Symptoms involving digestive system
788   Symptoms involving urinary system
789   Other symptoms involving abdomen and pelvis

Nonspecific abnormal findings (790-796)
790   Nonspecific findings on examination of blood
791   Nonspecific findings on examination of urine
792   Nonspecific abnormal findings in other body substances
793   Nonspecific abnormal findings on radiological and other examination of body structure
794   Nonspecific abnormal results of function studies

795   Nonspecific abnormal histological and immunological findings
796   Other nonspecific abnormal findings

Ill-defined and unknown causes of morbidity and mortality (797-799)
797   Senility without mention of psychosis
798   Sudden death, cause unknown
799   Other ill-defined and unknown causes of morbidity and mortality

17.   INJURY AND POISONING

Fracture of skull (800-804)
800   Fracture of vault of skull
801   Fracture of base of skull
802   Fracture of face bones
803   Other and unqualified skull fractures
804   Multiple fractures involving skull or face with other bones

Fracture of spine and trunk (805-809)
805   Fracture of vertebral column without mention of spinal cord lesion
806   Fracture of vertebral column with spinal cord lesion
807   Fracture of rib(s), sternum, larynx, and trachea
808   Fracture of pelvis
809   Ill-defined fractures of bones of trunk

Fracture of upper limb (810-819)
810   Fracture of clavicle
811   Fracture of scapula
812   Fracture of humerus
813   Fracture of radius and ulna
814   Fracture of carpal bone(s)
815   Fracture of metacarpal bone(s)
816   Fracture of one or more phalanges of hand
817   Multiple fractures of hand bones
818   Ill-defined fractures of upper limb
819   Multiple fractures involving both upper limbs, and upper limb with rib(s) and sternum

Fracture of lower limb (820-829)
820   Fracture of neck of femur
821   Fracture of other and unspecified parts of femur
822   Fracture of patella
823   Fracture of tibia and fibula
824   Fracture of ankle
825   Fracture of one or more tarsal and metatarsal bones
826   Fracture of one or more phalanges of foot
827   Other, multiple, and ill-defined fractures of lower limb
828   Multiple fractures involving both lower limbs, lower with upper limb, and lower limb(s) with rib(s) and sternum
829   Fracture of unspecified bones

Dislocation (830-839)
830   Dislocation of jaw
831   Dislocation of shoulder
832   Dislocation of elbow
833   Dislocation of wrist
834   Dislocation of finger
835   Dislocation of hip
836   Dislocation of knee
837   Dislocation of ankle
838   Dislocation of foot
839   Other, multiple, and ill-defined dislocations

Sprains and strains of joints and adjacent muscles (840-848)
840   Sprains and strains of shoulder and upper arm
841   Sprains and strains of elbow and forearm
842   Sprains and strains of wrist and hand
843   Sprains and strains of hip and thigh
844   Sprains and strains of knee and leg
845   Sprains and strains of ankle and foot
846   Sprains and strains of sacroiliac region
847   Sprains and strains of other and unspecified parts of back

Appendix E: List of Three-Digit Categories

848 Other and ill-defined sprains and strains

Intracranial injury, excluding those with skull fracture (850-854)

850 Concussion
851 Cerebral laceration and contusion
852 Subarachnoid, subdural, and extradural hemorrhage, following injury
853 Other and unspecified intracranial hemorrhage following injury
854 Intracranial injury of other and unspecified nature

Internal injury of chest, abdomen, and pelvis (860-869)

860 Traumatic pneumothorax and hemothorax
861 Injury to heart and lung
862 Injury to other and unspecified intrathoracic organs
863 Injury to gastrointestinal tract
864 Injury to liver
865 Injury to spleen
866 Injury to kidney
867 Injury to pelvic organs
868 Injury to other intra-abdominal organs
869 Internal injury to unspecified or ill-defined organs

Open wound of head, neck, and trunk (870-879)

870 Open wound of ocular adnexa
871 Open wound of eyeball
872 Open wound of ear
873 Other open wound of head
874 Open wound of neck
875 Open wound of chest (wall)
876 Open wound of back
877 Open wound of buttock
878 Open wound of genital organs (external), including traumatic amputation
879 Open wound of other and unspecified sites, except limbs

Open wound of upper limb (880-887)

880 Open wound of shoulder and upper arm
881 Open wound of elbow, forearm, and wrist
882 Open wound of hand except finger(s) alone
883 Open wound of finger(s)
884 Multiple and unspecified open wound of upper limb
885 Traumatic amputation of thumb (complete) (partial)
886 Traumatic amputation of other finger(s) (complete) (partial)
887 Traumatic amputation of arm and hand (complete) (partial)

Open wound of lower limb (890-897)

890 Open wound of hip and thigh
891 Open wound of knee, leg [except thigh], and ankle
892 Open wound of foot except toe(s) alone
893 Open wound of toe(s)
894 Multiple and unspecified open wound of lower limb
895 Traumatic amputation of toe(s) (complete) (partial)
896 Traumatic amputation of foot (complete) (partial)
897 Traumatic amputation of leg(s) (complete) (partial)

Injury to blood vessels (900-904)

900 Injury to blood vessels of head and neck
901 Injury to blood vessels of thorax
902 Injury to blood vessels of abdomen and pelvis
903 Injury to blood vessels of upper extremity
904 Injury to blood vessels of lower extremity and unspecified sites

Late effects of injuries, poisonings, toxic effects, and other external causes (905-909)

905 Late effects of musculoskeletal and connective tissue injuries
906 Late effects of injuries to skin and subcutaneous tissues
907 Late effects of injuries to the nervous system
908 Late effects of other and unspecified injuries
909 Late effects of other and unspecified external causes

Superficial injury (910-919)

910 Superficial injury of face, neck, and scalp except eye
911 Superficial injury of trunk
912 Superficial injury of shoulder and upper arm
913 Superficial injury of elbow, forearm, and wrist
914 Superficial injury of hand(s) except finger(s) alone
915 Superficial injury of finger(s)
916 Superficial injury of hip, thigh, leg, and ankle
917 Superficial injury of foot and toe(s)
918 Superficial injury of eye and adnexa
919 Superficial injury of other, multiple, and unspecified sites

Contusion with intact skin surface (920-924)

920 Contusion of face, scalp, and neck except eye(s)
921 Contusion of eye and adnexa
922 Contusion of trunk
923 Contusion of upper limb
924 Contusion of lower limb and of other and unspecified sites

Crushing injury (925-929)

925 Crushing injury of face, scalp, and neck
926 Crushing injury of trunk
927 Crushing injury of upper limb
928 Crushing injury of lower limb
929 Crushing injury of multiple and unspecified sites

Effects of foreign body entering through orifice (930-939)

930 Foreign body on external eye
931 Foreign body in ear
932 Foreign body in nose
933 Foreign body in pharynx and larynx
934 Foreign body in trachea, bronchus, and lung
935 Foreign body in mouth, esophagus, and stomach
936 Foreign body in intestine and colon
937 Foreign body in anus and rectum
938 Foreign body in digestive system, unspecified
939 Foreign body in genitourinary tract

Burns (940-949)

940 Burn confined to eye and adnexa
941 Burn of face, head, and neck
942 Burn of trunk
943 Burn of upper limb, except wrist and hand
944 Burn of wrist(s) and hand(s)
945 Burn of lower limb(s)
946 Burns of multiple specified sites
947 Burn of internal organs
948 Burns classified according to extent of body surface involved
949 Burn, unspecified

Injury to nerves and spinal cord (950-957)

950 Injury to optic nerve and pathways
951 Injury to other cranial nerve(s)
952 Spinal cord injury without evidence of spinal bone injury
953 Injury to nerve roots and spinal plexus
954 Injury to other nerve(s) of trunk excluding shoulder and pelvic girdles
955 Injury to peripheral nerve(s) of shoulder girdle and upper limb
956 Injury to peripheral nerve(s) of pelvic girdle and lower limb
957 Injury to other and unspecified nerves

Certain traumatic complications and unspecified injuries (958-959)

958 Certain early complications of trauma
959 Injury, other and unspecified

Poisoning by drugs, medicinals and biological substances (960-979)

960 Poisoning by antibiotics
961 Poisoning by other anti-infectives
962 Poisoning by hormones and synthetic substitutes
963 Poisoning by primarily systemic agents
964 Poisoning by agents primarily affecting blood constituents
965 Poisoning by analgesics, antipyretics, and antirheumatics
966 Poisoning by anticonvulsants and anti-Parkinsonism drugs
967 Poisoning by sedatives and hypnotics
968 Poisoning by other central nervous system depressants and anesthetics
969 Poisoning by psychotropic agents
970 Poisoning by central nervous system stimulants
971 Poisoning by drugs primarily affecting the autonomic nervous system
972 Poisoning by agents primarily affecting the cardiovascular system
973 Poisoning by agents primarily affecting the gastrointestinal system
974 Poisoning by water, mineral, and uric acid metabolism drugs
975 Poisoning by agents primarily acting on the smooth and skeletal muscles and respiratory system
976 Poisoning by agents primarily affecting skin and mucous membrane, ophthalmological, otorhinolaryngological, and dental drugs
977 Poisoning by other and unspecified drugs and medicinals
978 Poisoning by bacterial vaccines
979 Poisoning by other vaccines and biological substances

Toxic effects of substances chiefly nonmedicinal as to source (980-989)

980 Toxic effect of alcohol
981 Toxic effect of petroleum products
982 Toxic effect of solvents other than petroleum-based
983 Toxic effect of corrosive aromatics, acids, and caustic alkalis
984 Toxic effect of lead and its compounds (including fumes)
985 Toxic effect of other metals
986 Toxic effect of carbon monoxide
987 Toxic effect of other gases, fumes, or vapors
988 Toxic effect of noxious substances eaten as food
989 Toxic effect of other substances, chiefly nonmedicinal as to source

Other and unspecified effects of external causes (990-995)

990 Effects of radiation, unspecified
991 Effects of reduced temperature
992 Effects of heat and light
993 Effects of air pressure
994 Effects of other external causes
995 Certain adverse effects, not elsewhere classified

Complications of surgical and medical care, not elsewhere classified (996-999)

996 Complications peculiar to certain specified procedures
997 Complications affecting specified body systems, not elsewhere classified
998 Other complications of procedures, not elsewhere classified
999 Complications of medical care, not elsewhere classified

SUPPLEMENTARY CLASSIFICATION OF FACTORS INFLUENCING HEALTH STATUS AND CONTACT WITH HEALTH SERVICES

Persons with potential health hazards related to communicable diseases (V01-V09)
V01 Contact with or exposure to communicable diseases
V02 Carrier or suspected carrier of infectious diseases
V03 Need for prophylactic vaccination and inoculation against bacterial diseases
V04 Need for prophylactic vaccination and inoculation against certain viral diseases
V05 Need for other prophylactic vaccination and inoculation against single diseases
V06 Need for prophylactic vaccination and inoculation against combinations of diseases
V07 Need for isolation and other prophylactic measures
V08 Asymptomatic human immunodeficiency virus [HIV] infection status
V09 Infection with drug-resistant microorganisms

Persons with potential health hazards related to personal and family history (V10-V19)
V10 Personal history of malignant neoplasm
V11 Personal history of mental disorder
V12 Personal history of certain other diseases
V13 Personal history of other diseases
V14 Personal history of allergy to medicinal agents
V15 Other personal history presenting hazards to health
V16 Family history of malignant neoplasm
V17 Family history of certain chronic disabling diseases
V18 Family history of certain other specific conditions
V19 Family history of other conditions

Persons encountering health services in circumstances related to reproduction and development (V20-V29)
V20 Health supervision of infant or child
V21 Constitutional states in development
V22 Normal pregnancy
V23 Supervision of high-risk pregnancy
V24 Postpartum care and examination
V25 Encounter for contraceptive management
V26 Procreative management
V27 Outcome of delivery
V28 Antenatal screening
V29 Observation and evaluation of newborns and infants for suspected condition not found

Liveborn infants according to type of birth (V30-V39)
V30 Single liveborn
V31 Twin, mate liveborn
V32 Twin, mate stillborn
V33 Twin, unspecified
V34 Other multiple, mates all liveborn
V35 Other multiple, mates all stillborn
V36 Other multiple, mates live- and stillborn
V37 Other multiple, unspecified
V39 Unspecified

Persons with a condition influencing their health status (V40-V49)
V40 Mental and behavioral problems
V41 Problems with special senses and other special functions
V42 Organ or tissue replaced by transplant
V43 Organ or tissue replaced by other means
V44 Artificial opening status
V45 Other postprocedural states
V46 Other dependence on machines
V47 Other problems with internal organs
V48 Problems with head, neck, and trunk
V49 Problems with limbs and other problems

Persons encountering health services for specific procedures and aftercare (V50-V59)
V50 Elective surgery for purposes other than remedying health states
V51 Aftercare involving the use of plastic surgery
V52 Fitting and adjustment of prosthetic device
V53 Fitting and adjustment of other device
V54 Other orthopedic aftercare
V55 Attention to artificial openings
V56 Encounter for dialysis and dialysis catheter care
V57 Care involving use of rehabilitation procedures
V58 Encounter for other and unspecified procedures and aftercare
V59 Donors

Persons encountering health services in other circumstances (V60-V69)
V60 Housing, household, and economic circumstances
V61 Other family circumstances
V62 Other psychosocial circumstances
V63 Unavailability of other medical facilities for care
V64 Persons encountering health services for specific procedures, not carried out
V65 Other persons seeking consultation
V66 Convalescence and palliative care
V67 Follow-up examination
V68 Encounters for administrative purposes
V69 Problems related to lifestyle

Persons without reported diagnosis encountered during examination and investigation of individuals and populations (V70-V85)
V70 General medical examination
V71 Observation and evaluation for suspected conditions not found
V72 Special investigations and examinations
V73 Special screening examination for viral and chlamydial diseases
V74 Special screening examination for bacterial and spirochetal diseases
V75 Special screening examination for other infectious diseases
V76 Special screening for malignant neoplasms
V77 Special screening for endocrine, nutritional, metabolic, and immunity disorders
V78 Special screening for disorders of blood and blood-forming organs
V79 Special screening for mental disorders and developmental handicaps
V80 Special screening for neurological, eye, and ear diseases
V81 Special screening for cardiovascular, respiratory, and genitourinary diseases
V82 Special screening for other conditions
V83 Genetic carrier status
V84 Genetic susceptibility to disease
V85 Body Mass Index

SUPPLEMENTARY CLASSIFICATION OF EXTERNAL CAUSES OF INJURY AND POISONING

Railway accidents (E800-E807)
E800 Railway accident involving collision with rolling stock
E801 Railway accident involving collision with other object
E802 Railway accident involving derailment without antecedent collision
E803 Railway accident involving explosion, fire, or burning
E804 Fall in, on, or from railway train
E805 Hit by rolling stock
E806 Other specified railway accident
E807 Railway accident of unspecified nature

Motor vehicle traffic accidents (E810-E819)
E810 Motor vehicle traffic accident involving collision with train
E811 Motor vehicle traffic accident involving re-entrant collision with another motor vehicle
E812 Other motor vehicle traffic accident involving collision with another motor vehicle
E813 Motor vehicle traffic accident involving collision with other vehicle
E814 Motor vehicle traffic accident involving collision with pedestrian
E815 Other motor vehicle traffic accident involving collision on the highway
E816 Motor vehicle traffic accident due to loss of control, without collision on the highway
E817 Noncollision motor vehicle traffic accident while boarding or alighting
E818 Other noncollision motor vehicle traffic accident
E819 Motor vehicle traffic accident of unspecified nature

Motor vehicle nontraffic accidents (E820-E825)
E820 Nontraffic accident involving motor-driven snow vehicle
E821 Nontraffic accident involving other off-road motor vehicle
E822 Other motor vehicle nontraffic accident involving collision with moving object
E823 Other motor vehicle nontraffic accident involving collision with stationary object
E824 Other motor vehicle nontraffic accident while boarding and alighting
E825 Other motor vehicle nontraffic accident of other and unspecified nature

Other road vehicle accidents (E826-E829)
E826 Pedal cycle accident
E827 Animal-drawn vehicle accident
E828 Accident involving animal being ridden
E829 Other road vehicle accidents

Water transport accidents (E830-E838)
E830 Accident to watercraft causing submersion
E831 Accident to watercraft causing other injury
E832 Other accidental submersion or drowning in water transport accident
E833 Fall on stairs or ladders in water transport
E834 Other fall from one level to another in water transport
E835 Other and unspecified fall in water transport
E836 Machinery accident in water transport
E837 Explosion, fire, or burning in watercraft
E838 Other and unspecified water transport accident

Air and space transport accidents (E840-E845)
E840 Accident to powered aircraft at takeoff or landing
E841 Accident to powered aircraft, other and unspecified
E842 Accident to unpowered aircraft
E843 Fall in, on, or from aircraft
E844 Other specified air transport accidents
E845 Accident involving spacecraft

Vehicle accidents, not elsewhere classifiable (E846-E849)
E846 Accidents involving powered vehicles used solely within the buildings and premises of an industrial or commercial establishment
E847 Accidents involving cable cars not running on rails
E848 Accidents involving other vehicles, not elsewhere classifiable
E849 Place of occurrence

Accidental poisoning by drugs, medicinal substances, and biologicals (E850-E858)
E850 Accidental poisoning by analgesics, antipyretics, and antirheumatics
E851 Accidental poisoning by barbiturates
E852 Accidental poisoning by other sedatives and hypnotics
E853 Accidental poisoning by tranquilizers

E854 Accidental poisoning by other psychotropic agents
E855 Accidental poisoning by other drugs acting on central and autonomic nervous systems
E856 Accidental poisoning by antibiotics
E857 Accidental poisoning by anti-infectives
E858 Accidental poisoning by other drugs

Accidental poisoning by other solid and liquid substances, gases, and vapors (E860-E869)
E860 Accidental poisoning by alcohol, not elsewhere classified
E861 Accidental poisoning by cleansing and polishing agents, disinfectants, paints, and varnishes
E862 Accidental poisoning by petroleum products, other solvents and their vapors, not elsewhere classified
E863 Accidental poisoning by agricultural and horticultural chemical and pharmaceutical preparations other than plant foods and fertilizers
E864 Accidental poisoning by corrosives and caustics, not elsewhere classified
E865 Accidental poisoning from poisonous foodstuffs and poisonous plants
E866 Accidental poisoning by other and unspecified solid and liquid substances
E867 Accidental poisoning by gas distributed by pipeline
E868 Accidental poisoning by other utility gas and other carbon monoxide
E869 Accidental poisoning by other gases and vapors

Misadventures to patients during surgical and medical care (E870-E876)
E870 Accidental cut, puncture, perforation, or hemorrhage during medical care
E871 Foreign object left in body during procedure
E872 Failure of sterile precautions during procedure
E873 Failure in dosage
E874 Mechanical failure of instrument or apparatus during procedure
E875 Contaminated or infected blood, other fluid, drug, or biological substance
E876 Other and unspecified misadventures during medical care

Surgical and medical procedures as the cause of abnormal reaction of patient or later complication, without mention of misadventure at the time of procedure (E878-E879)
E878 Surgical operation and other surgical procedures as the cause of abnormal reaction of patient, or of later complication, without mention of misadventure at the time of operation
E879 Other procedures, without mention of misadventure at the time of procedure, as the cause of abnormal reaction of patient, or of later complication

Accidental falls (E880-E888)
E880 Fall on or from stairs or steps
E881 Fall on or from ladders or scaffolding
E882 Fall from or out of building or other structure
E883 Fall into hole or other opening in surface
E884 Other fall from one level to another
E885 Fall on same level from slipping, tripping, or stumbling
E886 Fall on same level from collision, pushing or shoving, by or with other person
E887 Fracture, cause unspecified
E888 Other and unspecified fall

Accidents caused by fire and flames (E890-E899)
E890 Conflagration in private dwelling
E891 Conflagration in other and unspecified building or structure

E892 Conflagration not in building or structure
E893 Accident caused by ignition of clothing
E894 Ignition of highly inflammable material
E895 Accident caused by controlled fire in private dwelling
E896 Accident caused by controlled fire in other and unspecified building or structure
E897 Accident caused by controlled fire not in building or structure
E898 Accident caused by other specified fire and flames
E899 Accident caused by unspecified fire

Accidents due to natural and environmental factors (E900-E909)
E900 Excessive heat
E901 Excessive cold
E902 High and low air pressure and changes in air pressure
E903 Travel and motion
E904 Hunger, thirst, exposure, and neglect
E905 Venomous animals and plants as the cause of poisoning and toxic reactions
E906 Other injury caused by animals
E907 Lightning
E908 Cataclysmic storms, and floods resulting from storms
E909 Cataclysmic earth surface movements and eruptions

Accidents caused by submersion, suffocation, and foreign bodies (E910-E915)
E910 Accidental drowning and submersion
E911 Inhalation and ingestion of food causing obstruction of respiratory tract or suffocation
E912 Inhalation and ingestion of other object causing obstruction of respiratory tract or suffocation
E913 Accidental mechanical suffocation
E914 Foreign body accidentally entering eye and adnexa
E915 Foreign body accidentally entering other orifice

Other accidents (E916-E928)
E916 Struck accidentally by falling object
E917 Striking against or struck accidentally by objects or persons
E918 Caught accidentally in or between objects
E919 Accidents caused by machinery
E920 Accidents caused by cutting and piercing instruments or objects
E921 Accident caused by explosion of pressure vessel
E922 Accident caused by firearm missile
E923 Accident caused by explosive material
E924 Accident caused by hot substance or object, caustic or corrosive material, and steam
E925 Accident caused by electric current
E926 Exposure to radiation
E927 Overexertion and strenuous movements
E928 Other and unspecified environmental and accidental causes

Late effects of accidental injury (E929)
E929 Late effects of accidental injury

Drugs, medicinal and biological substances causing adverse effects in therapeutic use (E930-E949)
E930 Antibiotics
E931 Other anti-infectives
E932 Hormones and synthetic substitutes
E933 Primarily systemic agents
E934 Agents primarily affecting blood constituents
E935 Analgesics, antipyretics, and antirheumatics
E936 Anticonvulsants and anti-Parkinsonism drugs
E937 Sedatives and hypnotics

E938 Other central nervous system depressants and anesthetics
E939 Psychotropic agents
E940 Central nervous system stimulants
E941 Drugs primarily affecting the autonomic nervous system
E942 Agents primarily affecting the cardiovascular system
E943 Agents primarily affecting gastrointestinal system
E944 Water, mineral, and uric acid metabolism drugs
E945 Agents primarily acting on the smooth and skeletal muscles and respiratory system
E946 Agents primarily affecting skin and mucous membrane, ophthalmological, otorhinolaryngological, and dental drugs
E947 Other and unspecified drugs and medicinal substances
E948 Bacterial vaccines
E949 Other vaccines and biological substances

Suicide and self-inflicted injury (E950-E959)
E950 Suicide and self-inflicted poisoning by solid or liquid substances
E951 Suicide and self-inflicted poisoning by gases in domestic use
E952 Suicide and self-inflicted poisoning by other gases and vapors
E953 Suicide and self-inflicted injury by hanging, strangulation, and suffocation
E954 Suicide and self-inflicted injury by submersion [drowning]
E955 Suicide and self-inflicted injury by firearms and explosives
E956 Suicide and self-inflicted injury by cutting and piercing instruments
E957 Suicide and self-inflicted injuries by jumping from high place
E958 Suicide and self-inflicted injury by other and unspecified means
E959 Late effects of self-inflicted injury

Homicide and injury purposely inflicted by other persons (E960-E969)
E960 Fight, brawl, and rape
E961 Assault by corrosive or caustic substance, except poisoning
E962 Assault by poisoning
E963 Assault by hanging and strangulation
E964 Assault by submersion [drowning]
E965 Assault by firearms and explosives
E966 Assault by cutting and piercing instrument
E967 Child and adult battering and other maltreatment
E968 Assault by other and unspecified means
E969 Late effects of injury purposely inflicted by other person

Legal intervention (E970-E978)
E970 Injury due to legal intervention by firearms
E971 Injury due to legal intervention by explosives
E972 Injury due to legal intervention by gas
E973 Injury due to legal intervention by blunt object
E974 Injury due to legal intervention by cutting and piercing instruments
E975 Injury due to legal intervention by other specified means
E976 Injury due to legal intervention by unspecified means
E977 Late effects of injuries due to legal intervention
E978 Legal execution

Terrorism (E979)
E979 Terrorism

Injury undetermined whether accidentally or purposely inflicted (E980-E989)
E980 Poisoning by solid or liquid substances, undetermined whether accidentally or purposely inflicted

E981 Poisoning by gases in domestic use, undetermined whether accidentally or purposely inflicted

E982 Poisoning by other gases, undetermined whether accidentally or purposely inflicted

E983 Hanging, strangulation, or suffocation, undetermined whether accidentally or purposely inflicted

E984 Submersion [drowning], undetermined whether accidentally or purposely inflicted

E985 Injury by firearms and explosives, undetermined whether accidentally or purposely inflicted

E986 Injury by cutting and piercing instruments, undetermined whether accidentally or purposely inflicted

E987 Falling from high place, undetermined whether accidentally or purposely inflicted

E988 Injury by other and unspecified means, undetermined whether accidentally or purposely inflicted

E989 Late effects of injury, undetermined whether accidentally or purposely inflicted

Injury resulting from operations of war (E990-E999)

E990 Injury due to war operations by fires and conflagrations

E991 Injury due to war operations by bullets and fragments

E992 Injury due to war operations by explosion of marine weapons

E993 Injury due to war operations by other explosion

E994 Injury due to war operations by destruction of aircraft

E995 Injury due to war operations by other and unspecified forms of conventional warfare

E996 Injury due to war operations by nuclear weapons

E997 Injury due to war operations by other forms of unconventional warfare

E998 Injury due to war operations but occurring after cessation of hostilities

E999 Late effects of injury due to war operations

A

Abbe operation
construction of vagina 70.61
intestinal anastomosis — *see* Anastomosis,
    intestine

Abciximab, infusion 99.20

Abdominocentesis 54.91

Abdominohysterectomy 68.4

Abdominoplasty 86.83

Abdominoscopy 54.21

Abdominouterotomy 68.0
obstetrical 74.99

Abduction, arytenoid 31.69

Ablation
biliary tract (lesion) by ERCP 51.64
endometrial (hysteroscopic) 68.23
inner ear (cryosurgery) (ultrasound) 20.79
    by injection 20.72
lesion
    esophagus 42.39
        endoscopic 42.33
    heart
        by peripherally inserted catheter 37.34
        endovascular approach 37.34
        maze procedure (Cox-maze)
            endovascular approach 37.34
            open (trans-thoracic) approach 37.33
            trans-thoracic approach 37.33
    intestine
        large 45.49
            endoscopic 45.43
    large intestine 45.49
        endoscopic 45.43
    pituitary 07.69
        by
            cobalt 60 92.32
            implantation (strontium-yttrium) (Y) NEC
                07.68
                transfrontal approach 07.64
                transsphenoidal approach 07.65
            proton beam (Bragg peak) 92.33
    prostate
        by
            cryoablation 60.62
            laser, transurethral 60.21
            radical cryosurgical ablation (RCSA) 60.62
            radiofrequency thermotherapy 60.97
            transurethral needle ablation (TUNA)
                60.97
    tissue
        heart — *see* Ablation, lesion, heart

Abortion, therapeutic 69.51
by
    aspiration curettage 69.51
    dilation and curettage 69.01
    hysterectomy — *see* Hysterectomy
    hysterotomy 74.91
    insertion
        laminaria 69.93
        prostaglandin suppository 96.49
    intra-amniotic injection (saline) 75.0

Abrasion
corneal epithelium 11.41
    for smear or culture 11.21
epicardial surface 36.39
pleural 34.6
skin 86.25

Abscission, cornea 11.49

Absorptiometry
photon (dual) (single) 88.98

Aburel operation (intra-amniotic injection for
    abortion) 75.0

Accouchement forcé 73.99

Acetabulectomy 77.85

Acetabuloplasty NEC 81.40
with prosthetic implant 81.52

Achillorrhaphy 83.64
delayed 83.62

Achillotenotomy 83.11
plastic 83.85

Achillotomy 83.11
plastic 83.85

Acid peel, skin 86.24

Acromionectomy 77.81

Acromioplasty 81.83
for recurrent dislocation of shoulder 81.82
partial replacement 81.81
total replacement 81.80

Actinotherapy 99.82

Activities of daily living (ADL)
therapy 93.83
training for the blind 93.78

Acupuncture 99.92
with smouldering moxa 93.35
for anesthesia 99.91

Adams operation
advancement of round ligament 69.22
crushing of nasal septum 21.88
excision of palmar fascia 82.35

Adenectomy — *see also* Excision, by site
prostate NEC 60.69
    retropubic 60.4

Adenoidectomy (without tonsillectomy) 28.6
with tonsillectomy 28.3

Adhesiolysis — *see also* Lysis, adhesions
for collapse of lung 33.39
middle ear 20.23

Adipectomy 86.83

Adjustment
cardiac pacemaker program (reprogramming) —
    omit code
cochlear prosthetic device (external
    components) 95.49
dental 99.97
gastric restrictive device (laparoscopic) 44.98
occlusal 24.8
spectacles 95.31

Administration (of) — *see also* Injection
adhesion barrier substance 99.77
antitoxins NEC 99.58
    botulism 99.57
    diphtheria 99.58
    gas gangrene 99.58
    scarlet fever 99.58
    tetanus 99.56
Bender Visual-Motor Gestalt test 94.02
Benton Visual Retention test 94.02
inhaled nitric oxide 00.12
intelligence test or scale (Stanford-Binet)
    (Wechsler) (adult) (children) 94.01
Minnesota Multiphasic Personality Inventory
    (MMPI) 94.02
MMPI (Minnesota Multiphasic Personality
    Inventory) 94.02
neuroprotective agent 99.75
psychologic test 94.02
Stanford-Binet test 94.01
toxoid
    diphtheria 99.36
        with tetanus and pertussis, combined
            (DTP) 99.39
    tetanus 99.38
        with diphtheria and pertussis, combined
            (DTP) 99.39
vaccine — *see also* Vaccination
    BCG 99.33
    measles-mumps-rubella (MMR) 99.48
    poliomyelitis 99.41
    TAB 99.32
Wechsler
    Intelligence Scale (adult) (children) 94.01
    Memory Scale 94.02

Adrenalectomy (unilateral) 07.22
with partial removal of remaining gland 07.29
bilateral 07.3
    partial 07.29
    subtotal 07.29
complete 07.3
partial NEC 07.29
remaining gland 07.3
subtotal NEC 07.29
total 07.3

Adrenalorrhaphy 07.44

Adrenalotomy (with drainage) 07.41

Advancement
extraocular muscle 15.12
    multiple (with resection or recession) 15.3
eyelid muscle 08.59
eye muscle 15.12
    multiple (with resection or recession) 15.3
graft — *see* Graft
leaflet (heart) 35.10
pedicle (flap) 86.72
profundus tendon (Wagner) 82.51
round ligament 69.22
tendon 83.71
    hand 82.51
        profundus (Wagner) 82.51
Wagner (profundus tendon) 82.51

Albee operation
bone peg, femoral neck 78.05
graft for slipping patella 78.06
sliding inlay graft, tibia 78.07

Albert operation (arthrodesis of knee) 81.22

Aldridge (-Studdiford) operation (urethral sling)
    59.5

Alexander operation
prostatectomy
    perineal 60.62
    suprapubic 60.3
shortening of round ligaments 69.22

Alexander-Adams operation (shortening of round
    ligaments) 69.22

Alimentation, parenteral 99.29

Allograft — *see* Graft

Almoor operation (extrapetrosal drainage) 20.22

Altemeier operation (perineal rectal pull-
    through) 48.49

Alveolectomy (interradicular) (intraseptal)
    (radical) (simple) (with graft) (with implant)
    24.5

Alveoloplasty (with graft or implant) 24.5

Alveolotomy (apical) 24.0

Ambulatory cardiac monitoring (ACM) 89.50

Ammon operation (dacryocystotomy) 09.53

Amniocentesis (transuterine) (diagnostic) 75.1
with intra-amniotic injection of saline 75.0

Amniography 87.81

Amnioinfusion 75.37

Amnioscopy, internal 75.31

Amniotomy 73.09
to induce labor 73.01

Amputation (cineplastic) (closed flap) (guillotine)
    (kineplastic) (open) 84.91
abdominopelvic 84.19
above-elbow 84.07
above-knee (AK) 84.17
ankle (disarticulation) 84.13
    through malleoli of tibia and fibula 84.14
arm NEC 84.00
    through
        carpals 84.03
        elbow (disarticulation) 84.06
        forearm 84.05
        humerus 84.07
        shoulder (disarticulation) 84.08
        wrist (disarticulation) 84.04
        upper 84.07
Batch-Spittler-McFaddin (knee disarticulation)
    84.16
below-knee (BK) NEC 84.15
    conversion into above-knee amputation
        84.17
Boyd (hip disarticulation) 84.18
Callander's (knee disarticulation) 84.16
carpals 84.03
cervix 67.4
Chopart's (midtarsal) 84.12
clitoris 71.4
Dieffenbach (hip disarticulation) 84.18
Dupuytren's (shoulder disarticulation) 84.08
ear, external 18.39
elbow (disarticulation) 84.06
finger, except thumb 84.01
    thumb 84.02
foot (middle) 84.12
forearm 84.05

2006 ICD-9-CM

✓ Additional Digit Required — Refer to the Tabular List (Numeric Code Section) for Additional Digit Selection
▶◀ Revised Text   ● New Line   ▲ Revised Code

Volume 3 — 1

Amputation — *continued*
forefoot 84.12
forequarter 84.09
Gordon-Taylor (hindquarter) 84.19
Gritti-Stokes (knee disarticulation) 84.16
Guyon (ankle) 84.13
hallux 84.11
hand 84.03
Hey's (foot) 84.12
hindquarter 84.19
hip (disarticulation) 84.18
humerus 84.07
interscapulothoracic 84.09
interthoracoscapular 84.09
King-Steelquist (hindquarter) 84.19
Kirk (thigh) 84.17
knee (disarticulation) 84.16
Kutler (revision of current traumatic
    amputation of finger) 84.01
Larry (shoulder disarticulation) 84.08
leg NEC 84.10
    above knee (AK) 84.17
    below knee (BK) 84.15
    through
        ankle (disarticulation) 84.13
        femur (AK) 84.17
        foot 84.12
        hip (disarticulation) 84.18
        tibia and fibula (BK) 84.15
Lisfranc
    foot 84.12
    shoulder (disarticulation) 84.08
Littlewood (forequarter) 84.09
lower limb NEC (*see also* Amputation, leg)
    84.10
Mazet (knee disarticulation) 84.16
metacarpal 84.03
metatarsal 84.11
    head (bunionectomy) 77.59
metatarsophalangeal (joint) 84.11
midtarsal 84.12
nose 21.4
penis (circle) (complete) (flap) (partial) (radical)
    64.3
Pirogoff's (ankle amputation through malleoli of
    tibia and fibula) 84.14
ray
    finger 84.01
    foot 84.11
    toe (metatarsal head) 84.11
root (tooth) (apex) 23.73
    with root canal therapy 23.72
shoulder (disarticulation) 84.08
Sorondo-Ferré (hindquarter) 84.19
S.P. Rogers (knee disarticulation) 84.16
supracondylar, above-knee 84.17
supramalleolar, foot 84.14
Syme's (ankle amputation through malleoli of
    tibia and fibula) 84.14
thigh 84.17
thumb 84.02
toe (through metatarsophalangeal joint) 84.11
transcarpal 84.03
transmetatarsal 84.12
upper limb NEC (*see also* Amputation, arm)
    84.00
wrist (disarticulation) 84.04
Amygdalohippocampotomy 01.39
Amygdalotomy 01.39
Analysis
cardiac rhythm device (CRT-D) (CRT-P)
    (AICD) (pacemaker) — *see* Interrogation
character 94.03
gastric 89.39
psychologic 94.31
transactional
    group 94.44
    individual 94.39
Anastomosis
abdominal artery to coronary artery 36.17
accessory-facial nerve 04.72
accessory-hypoglossal nerve 04.73
anus (with formation of endorectal ileal pouch)
    45.95
aorta (descending)-pulmonary (artery) 39.0

Anastomosis — *continued*
aorta-renal artery 39.24
aorta-subclavian artery 39.22
aortoceliac 39.26
aorto(ilio)femoral 39.25
aortomesenteric 39.26
appendix 47.99
arteriovenous NEC 39.29
    for renal dialysis 39.27
artery (suture of distal to proximal end) 39.31
    with
        bypass graft 39.29
            extracranial-intracranial [EC-IC] 39.28
        excision or resection of vessel — *see*
            Arteriectomy, with anastomosis, by
            site
    revision 39.49
bile ducts 51.39
bladder NEC 57.88
    with
        isolated segment of intestine 57.87
            [45.50]
            colon (sigmoid) 57.87 [45.52]
            ileum 57.87 [45.51]
        open loop of ileum 57.87 [45.51]
    to intestine 57.88
        ileum 57.87 [45.51]
bowel (*see also* Anastomosis, intestine) 45.90
bronchotracheal 33.48
bronchus 33.48
carotid-subclavian artery 39.22
caval-mesenteric vein 39.1
caval-pulmonary artery 39.21
cervicoesophageal 42.59
colohypopharyngeal (intrathoracic) 42.55
    antesternal or antethoracic 42.65
common bile duct 51.39
common pulmonary trunk and left atrium
    (posterior wall) 35.82
cystic bile duct 51.39
cystocolic 57.88
epididymis to vas deferens 63.83
esophagocolic (intrathoracic) NEC 42.56
    with interposition 42.55
    antesternal or antethoracic NEC 42.66
        with interposition 42.65
esophagocologastric (intrathoracic) 42.55
    antesternal or antethoracic 42.65
esophagoduodenal (intrathoracic) NEC 42.54
    with interposition 42.53
esophagoenteric (intrathoracic) NEC (*see also*
    Anastomosis, esophagus, to intestinal
    segment) 42.54
    antesternal or antethoracic NEC (*see also*
        Anastomosis, esophagus, antesternal,
        to intestinal segment) 42.64
esophagoesophageal (intrathoracic) 42.51
    antesternal or antethoracic 42.61
esophagogastric (intrathoracic) 42.52
    antesternal or antethoracic 42.62
esophagus (intrapleural) (intrathoracic)
    (retrosternal) NEC 42.59
    with
        gastrectomy (partial) 43.5
            complete or total 43.99
        interposition (of) NEC 42.58
            colon 42.55
            jejunum 42.53
            small bowel 42.53
    antesternal or antethoracic NEC 42.69
        with
            interposition (of) NEC 42.68
                colon 42.65
                jejunal loop 42.63
                small bowel 42.63
                rubber tube 42.68
        to intestinal segment NEC 42.64
            with interposition 42.68
            colon NEC 42.66
                with interposition 42.65
            small bowel NEC 42.64
                with interposition 42.63
    to intestinal segment (intrathoracic) NEC
        42.54
        with interposition 42.58

Anastomosis — *continued*
esophagus NEC — *continued*
    to intestinal segment NEC — *continued*
        antesternal or antethoracic NEC 42.64
            with interposition 42.68
        colon (intrathoracic) NEC 42.56
            with interposition 42.55
            antesternal or antethoracic 42.66
                with interposition 42.65
        small bowel NEC 42.54
            with interposition 42.53
            antesternal or antethoracic 42.64
                with interposition 42.63
facial-accessory nerve 04.72
facial-hypoglossal nerve 04.71
fallopian tube 66.73
    by reanastomosis 66.79
gallbladder 51.35
    to
        hepatic ducts 51.31
        intestine 51.32
        pancreas 51.33
        stomach 51.34
gastroepiploic artery to coronary artery 36.17
hepatic duct 51.39
hypoglossal-accessory nerve 04.73
hypoglossal-facial nerve 04.71
ileal loop to bladder 57.87 [45.51]
ileoanal 45.95
ileorectal 45.93
inferior vena cava and portal vein 39.1
internal mammary artery (to)
    coronary artery (single vessel) 36.15
        double vessel 36.16
    myocardium 36.2
intestine 45.90
    large-to-anus 45.95
    large-to-large 45.94
    large-to-rectum 45.94
    large-to-small 45.93
    small-to-anus 45.95
    small-to-large 45.93
    small-to-rectal stump 45.92
    small-to-small 45.91
intrahepatic 51.79
intrathoracic vessel NEC 39.23
kidney (pelvis) 55.86
lacrimal sac to conjunctiva 09.82
left-to-right (systemic-pulmonary artery) 39.0
lymphatic (channel) (peripheral) 40.9
mesenteric-caval 39.1
mesocaval 39.1
nasolacrimal 09.81
nerve (cranial) (peripheral) NEC 04.74
    accessory-facial 04.72
    accessory-hypoglossal 04.73
    hypoglossal-facial 04.71
pancreas (duct) (to) 52.96
    bile duct 51.39
    gall bladder 51.33
    intestine 52.96
    jejunum 52.96
    stomach 52.96
pleurothecal (with valve) 03.79
portacaval 39.1
portal vein to inferior vena cava 39.1
pulmonary-aortic (Pott's) 39.0
pulmonary artery and superior vena cava 39.21
pulmonary-innominate artery (Blalock) 39.0
pulmonary-subclavian artery (Blalock-Taussig)
    39.0
pulmonary vein and azygos vein 39.23
pyeloileocutaneous 56.51
pyeloureterovesical 55.86
radial artery 36.19
rectum, rectal NEC 48.74
    stump to small intestine 45.92
renal (pelvis) 55.86
    vein and splenic vein 39.1
renoportal 39.1
salpingothecal (with valve) 03.79
splenic to renal veins 39.1
splenorenal (venous) 39.1
    arterial 39.26
subarachnoid-peritoneal (with valve) 03.71
subarachnoid-ureteral (with valve) 03.72

☑ Additional Digit Required — Refer to the Tabular List (Numeric Code Section) for Additional Digit Selection

Anastomosis — *continued*
  subclavian-aortic 39.22
  superior vena cava to pulmonary artery 39.21
  systemic-pulmonary artery 39.0
  thoracic artery (to)
    coronary artery (single) 36.15
      double 36.16
    myocardium 36.2
  ureter (to) NEC 56.79
    bladder 56.74
    colon 56.71
    ileal pouch (bladder) 56.51
    ileum 56.71
    intestine 56.71
    skin 56.61
  ureterocalyceal 55.86
  ureterocolic 56.71
  ureterovesical 56.74
  urethra (end-to-end) 58.44
  vas deferens 63.82
  veins (suture of proximal to distal end) (with
      bypass graft) 39.29
    with excision or resection of vessel — *see*
        Phlebectomy, with anastomosis, by
        site
    mesenteric to vena cava 39.1
    portal to inferior vena cava 39.1
    revision 39.49
    splenic and renal 39.1
  ventricle, ventricular (intracerebral) (with valve)
      (*see also* Shunt, ventricular) 02.2
  ventriculoatrial (with valve) 02.32
  ventriculocaval (with valve) 02.32
  ventriculomastoid (with valve) 02.31
  ventriculopleural (with valve) 02.33
  vesicle — *see* Anastomosis, bladder
Anderson operation (tibial lengthening) 78.37
Anel operation (dilation of lacrimal duct) 09.42
Anesthesia
  acupuncture for 99.91
  cryoanalgesia, nerve (cranial) (peripheral) 04.2
  spinal — *omit code*
Aneurysmectomy 38.60
  with
    anastomosis 38.30
      abdominal
        artery 38.36
        vein 38.37
      aorta (arch) (ascending) (descending) 38.34
      head and neck NEC 38.32
      intracranial NEC 38.31
      lower limb
        artery 38.38
        vein 38.39
      thoracic NEC 38.35
      upper limb (artery) (vein) 38.33
    graft replacement (interposition) 38.40
      abdominal
        aorta 38.44
        artery 38.46
        vein 38.47
      aorta (arch) (ascending) (descending
          thoracic)
        abdominal 38.44
        thoracic 38.45
        thoracoabdominal 38.45 *[38.44]*
      head and neck NEC 38.42
      intracranial NEC 38.41
      lower limb
        artery 38.48
        vein 38.49
      thoracic NEC 38.45
      upper limb (artery) (vein) 38.43
  abdominal
    artery 38.66
    vein 38.67
  aorta (arch) (ascending) (descending) 38.64
  atrial, auricular 37.32
  head and neck NEC 38.62
  heart 37.32
  intracranial NEC 38.61
  lower limb
    artery 38.68
    vein 38.69
  sinus of Valsalva 35.39

Aneurysmectomy — *continued*
  thoracic NEC 38.65
  upper limb (artery) (vein) 38.63
  ventricle (myocardium) 37.32
Aneurysmoplasty — *see* Aneurysmorrhaphy
Aneurysmorrhaphy NEC 39.52
  by or with
    anastomosis — *see* Aneurysmectomy, with
        anastomosis, by site
    clipping 39.51
    coagulation 39.52
    electrocoagulation 39.52
    endovascular graft
      abdominal aorta 39.71
      lower extremity artery(s) 39.79
      thoracic aorta 39.73   ▲
      upper extremity artery(s) 39.79
    excision or resection — *see also*
        Aneurysmectomy, by site
      with
        anastomosis — *see* Aneurysmectomy,
            with anastomosis, by site
        graft replacement — *see*
            Aneurysmectomy, with graft
            replacement, by site
    filipuncture 39.52
    graft replacement — *see* Aneurysmectomy,
        with graft replacement, by site
    methyl methacrylate 39.52
    suture 39.52
    wiring 39.52
    wrapping 39.52
  Matas' 39.52
Aneurysmotomy — *see* Aneurysmectomy
Angiectomy
  with
    anastomosis 38.30
      abdominal
        artery 38.36
        vein 38.37
      aorta (arch) (ascending) (descending)
          38.34
      head and neck NEC 38.32
      intracranial NEC 38.31
      lower limb
        artery 38.38
        vein 38.39
      thoracic vessel NEC 38.35
      upper limb (artery) (vein) 38.33
    graft replacement (interposition) 38.40
      abdominal
        aorta 38.44
        artery 38.46
        vein 38.47
      aorta (arch) (ascending) (descending
          thoracic)
        abdominal 38.44
        thoracic 38.45
        thoracoabdominal 38.45 *[38.44]*
      head and neck NEC 38.42
      intracranial NEC 38.41
      lower limb
        artery 38.48
        vein 38.49
      thoracic vessel NEC 38.45
      upper limb (artery) (vein) 38.43
Angiocardiography (selective) 88.50
  carbon dioxide (negative contrast) 88.58
  combined right and left heart 88.54
  left heart (aortic valve) (atrium) (ventricle)
      (ventricular outflow tract) 88.53
    combined with right heart 88.54
  right heart (atrium) (pulmonary valve)
      (ventricle) (ventricular outflow tract)
      88.52
    combined with left heart 88.54
  vena cava (inferior) (superior) 88.51
Angiography (arterial) (*see also* Arteriography)
      88.40
  by radioisotope — *see* Scan, radioisotope, by
      site
  by ultrasound — *see* Ultrasonography, by site
  basilar 88.41
  brachial 88.49
  carotid (internal) 88.41

Angiography (*see also* Arteriography) — *continued*
  celiac 88.47
  cerebral (posterior circulation) 88.41
  coronary NEC 88.57
  eye (fluorescein) 95.12
  femoral 88.48
  heart 88.50
  intra-abdominal NEC 88.47
  intracranial 88.41
  intrathoracic vessels NEC 88.44
  lower extremity NEC 88.48
  neck 88.41
  placenta 88.46
  pulmonary 88.43
  renal 88.45
  specified artery NEC 88.49
  transfemoral 88.48
  upper extremity NEC 88.49
  veins — *see* Phlebography
  vertebral 88.41
Angioplasty (laser) — *see also* Repair, blood
      vessel

> *Note* — Also use 00.40, 00.41, 00.42, or   ●
> 00.43 to show the total number of vessels   ●
> treated. In addition, use 00.45, 00.46,   ●
> 00.47, or 00.48 to show the number of   ●
> vascular stents inserted.   ●

  balloon (percutaneous transluminal) NEC
      39.50
    coronary artery 00.66   ▲
  coronary 36.09
    open chest approach 36.03
    percutaneous transluminal (balloon)
        00.66   ▲
  percutaneous transluminal (balloon)
    basilar 00.61
    carotid 00.61
    cerebral (intracranial) 00.62
    cerebrovascular
      cerebral (intracranial) 00.62
      precerebral (extracranial) 00.61
        carotid 00.61
    coronary (balloon) 00.66   ▲
    femoropopliteal 39.50
    iliac 39.50
    lower extremity NOS 39.50
    mesenteric 39.50
    peripheral NEC 39.50
    precerebral (extracranial) 00.61
        carotid 00.61
    renal 39.50
    subclavian 39.50
    upper extremity NOS 39.50
    vertebral 00.61
  specified site NEC 39.50
    cerebrovascular
      cerebral (intracranial) 00.62
      precerebral (extracranial) 00.61
    peripheral 39.50
Angiorrhaphy 39.30
  artery 39.31
  vein 39.32
Angioscopy, percutaneous 38.22
  eye (fluorescein) 95.12
Angiotomy 38.00
  abdominal
    artery 38.06
    vein 38.07
  aorta (arch) (ascending) (descending) 38.04
  head and neck NEC 38.02
  intracranial NEC 38.01
  lower limb
    artery 38.08
    vein 38.09
  thoracic NEC 38.05
  upper limb (artery) (vein) 38.03
Angiotripsy 39.98
Ankylosis, production of — *see* Arthrodesis
Annuloplasty (heart) (posteromedial) 35.33
Anoplasty 49.79
  with hemorrhoidectomy 49.46

☑ Additional Digit Required — Refer to the Tabular List (Numeric Code Section) for Additional Digit Selection

Anoscopy 49.21
Antibiogram — *see* Examination, microscopic
Antiembolic filter, vena cava 38.7
Antiphobic treatment 94.39
Antrectomy
  mastoid 20.49
  maxillary 22.39
    radical 22.31
  pyloric 43.6
Antrostomy — *see* Antrotomy
Antrotomy (exploratory) (nasal sinus) 22.2
  Caldwell-Luc (maxillary sinus) 22.39
    with removal of membrane lining 22.31
  intranasal 22.2
    with external approach (Caldwell-Luc) 22.39
      radical 22.31
  maxillary (simple) 22.2
    with Caldwell-Luc approach 22.39
      with removal of membrane lining 22.31
    external (Caldwell-Luc approach) 22.39
      with removal of membrane lining 22.31
    radical (with removal of membrane lining)
      22.31
Antrum window operation — *see* Antrotomy,
  maxillary
Aorticopulmonary window operation 39.59
Aortogram, aortography (abdominal) (retrograde)
  (selective) (translumbar) 88.42
Aortoplasty (aortic valve) (gusset type) 35.11
Aortotomy 38.04
Apexcardiogram (with ECG lead) 89.57
Apheresis, therapeutic — *see* category 99.7 ☑
Apicectomy
  lung 32.3
  petrous pyramid 20.59
  tooth (root) 23.73
    with root canal therapy 23.72
Apicoectomy 23.73
  with root canal therapy 23.72
Apicolysis (lung) 33.39
Apicostomy, alveolar 24.0
Aponeurectomy 83.42
  hand 82.33
Aponeurorrhaphy (*see also* Suture, tendon) 83.64
  hand (*see also* Suture, tendon, hand) 82.45
Aponeurotomy 83.13
  hand 82.11
Appendectomy (with drainage) 47.09
  incidental 47.19
    laparoscopic 47.11
  laparoscopic 47.01
Appendicectomy (with drainage) 47.09
  incidental 47.19
    laparoscopic 47.11
  laparoscopic 47.01
Appendicocecostomy 47.91
Appendicoenterostomy 47.91
Appendicolysis 54.59
  with appendectomy 47.09
    laparoscopic 47.01
    other 47.09
  laparoscopic 54.51
Appendicostomy 47.91
  closure 47.92
Appendicotomy 47.2
Application
  adhesion barrier substance 99.77
  anti-shock trousers 93.58
  arch bars (orthodontic) 24.7
    for immobilization (fracture) 93.55
  barrier substance, adhesion 99.77
  Barton's tongs (skull) (with synchronous
    skeletal traction) 02.94
  bone growth stimulator (surface)
    (transcutaneous) 99.86
  bone morphogenetic protein ▶(Infuse™)
    (OP-1™)◀ (recombinant) (rhBMP) 84.52
  Bryant's traction 93.44
    with reduction of fracture or dislocation —
      see Reduction, fracture *and*
      Reduction, dislocation
  Buck's traction 93.46

Application — *continued*
  caliper tongs (skull) (with synchronous skeletal
    traction) 02.94
  cast (fiberglass) (plaster) (plastic) NEC 93.53
    with reduction of fracture or dislocation —
      see Reduction, fracture *and*
      Reduction, dislocation
    spica 93.51
  cervical collar 93.52
    with reduction of fracture or dislocation —
      see Reduction, fracture *and*
      Reduction, dislocation
  clamp, cerebral aneurysm (Crutchfield)
    (Silverstone) 39.51
  croupette, croup tent 93.94
  crown (artificial) 23.41
  Crutchfield tongs (skull) (with synchronous
    skeletal traction) 02.94
  Dunlop's traction 93.44
    with reduction of fracture or dislocation —
      see Reduction, fracture *and*
      Reduction, dislocation
  elastic stockings 93.59
  electronic gaiter 93.59
  external ▶fixator◀ device (bone) 78.10
    carpal, metacarpal 78.14
    clavicle 78.11
    femur 78.15
    fibula 78.17
    humerus 78.12
    hybrid device or system 84.73 ●
    Ilizarov type 84.72 ●
    monoplanar system or device 84.71 ●
    patella 78.16
    pelvic 78.19
    phalanges (foot) (hand) 78.19
    radius 78.13
    ring device or system 84.72 ●
    scapula 78.11
    Sheffield type 84.72 ●
    specified site NEC 78.19
    tarsal, metatarsal 78.18
    thorax (ribs) (sternum) 78.11
    tibia 78.17
    ulna 78.13
    vertebrae 78.19
  forceps, with delivery — *see* Delivery, forceps
  graft — *see* Graft
  gravity (G-) suit 93.59
  intermittent pressure device 93.59
  Jewett extension brace 93.59
  Jobst pumping unit (reduction of edema) 93.59
  Lyman Smith traction 93.44
    with reduction of fracture or dislocation —
      see Reduction, fracture *and*
      Reduction, dislocation
  MAST (military anti-shock trousers) 93.58
  Minerva jacket 93.52
  minifixator device (bone) — *see* category 78.1 ☑
  neck support (molded) 93.52
  obturator (orthodontic) 24.7
  orthodontic appliance (obturator) (wiring) 24.7
  pelvic sling 93.44
    with reduction of fracture or dislocation —
      see Reduction, fracture *and*
      Reduction, dislocation
  peridontal splint (orthodontic) 24.7
  plaster jacket 93.51
    Minerva 93.52
  pressure
    dressing (bandage) (Gibney) (Robert Jones')
      (Shanz) 93.56
    trousers (anti-shock) (MAST) 93.58
  prosthesis for missing ear 18.71
  Russell's traction 93.44
    with reduction of fracture or dislocation —
      see Reduction, fracture *and*
      Reduction, dislocation
  splint, for immobilization (plaster) (pneumatic)
    (tray) 93.54
    with fracture reduction — *see* Reduction,
      fracture
  stereotactic head frame 93.59
  substance, adhesion barrier 99.77

Application — *continued*
  Thomas collar 93.52
    with reduction of fracture or dislocation —
      see Reduction, fracture *and*
      Reduction, dislocation
  traction
    with reduction of fracture or dislocation —
      see Reduction, fracture *and*
      Reduction, dislocation
    adhesive tape (skin) 93.46
    boot 93.46
    Bryant's 93.44
    Buck's 93.46
    Cotrel's 93.42
    Dunlop's 93.44
    gallows 93.46
    Lyman Smith 93.44
    Russell's 93.44
    skeletal NEC 93.44
      intermittent 93.43
    skin, limbs NEC 93.46
    spinal NEC 93.42
      with skull device (halo) (caliper)
        (Crutchfield) (Gardner-Wells) (Vinke)
        (tongs) 93.41
        with synchronous insertion 02.94
    Thomas' splint 93.45
  Unna's paste boot 93.53
  vasopneumatic device 93.58
  Velpeau dressing 93.59
  Vinke tongs (skull) (with synchronous skeletal
    traction) 02.94
  wound dressing NEC 93.57
Aquapheresis 99.78
Arc lamp — *see* Photocoagulation
Arrest
  bone growth (epiphyseal) 78.20
    by stapling — *see* Stapling, epiphyseal plate
    femur 78.25
    fibula 78.27
    humerus 78.22
    radius 78.23
    tibia 78.27
    ulna 78.23
  cardiac, induced (anoxic) (circulatory) 39.63
  circulatory, induced (anoxic) 39.63
  hemorrhage — *see* Control, hemorrhage
Arslan operation (fenestration of inner ear) 20.61
Arteriectomy 38.60
  with
    anastomosis 38.30
      abdominal 38.36
      aorta (arch) (ascending) (descending)
        38.34
      head and neck NEC 38.32
      intracranial NEC 38.31
      lower limb 38.38
      thoracic NEC 38.35
      upper limb 38.33
    graft replacement (interposition) 38.40
      abdominal
        aorta 38.44
      aorta (arch) (ascending) (descending
        thoracic) (thoracic)
        abdominal 38.44
        thoracic 38.45
        thoracoabdominal 38.45 *[38.44]*
      head and neck NEC 38.42
      intracranial NEC 38.41
      lower limb 38.48
      thoracic NEC 38.45
      upper limb 38.43
  abdominal 38.66
  aorta (arch) (ascending) (descending) 38.64
  head and neck NEC 38.62
  intracranial NEC 38.61
  lower limb 38.68
  thoracic NEC 38.65
  upper limb 38.63
Arteriography (contrast) (fluoroscopic)
  (retrograde) 88.40
  by
    radioisotope — *see* Scan, radioisotope
    ultrasound (Doppler) — *see*
      Ultrasonography, by site

Arteriography — Aspiration

Aspiration — *continued*
joint 81.91
for arthrography — *see* Arthrogram
kidney (cyst) (pelvis) (percutaneous)
(therapeutic) 55.92
diagnostic 55.23
liver (percutaneous) 50.91
lung (percutaneous) (puncture) (needle) (trocar)
33.93
middle ear 20.09
with intubation 20.01
muscle 83.95
hand 82.93
nail 86.01
nasal sinus 22.00
by puncture 22.01
through natural ostium 22.02
nasotracheal 96.04
with lavage 96.56
orbit, diagnostic 16.22
ovary 65.91
percutaneous — *see* Aspiration, by site
pericardium (wound) 37.0
pituitary gland 07.72
pleural cavity 34.91
prostate (percutaneous) 60.91
Rathke's pouch 07.72
seminal vesicles 60.71
seroma — *see* Aspiration, by site
skin 86.01
soft tissue NEC 83.95
hand 82.93
spermatocele 63.91
spinal (puncture) 03.31
spleen (cyst) 41.1
stem cell 99.79
subarachnoid space (cerebral) 01.09
subcutaneous tissue 86.01
subdural space (cerebral) 01.09
tendon 83.95
hand 82.93
testis 62.91
thymus 07.92
thyroid (field) (gland) 06.01
postoperative 06.02
trachea 96.04
with lavage 96.56
percutaneous 31.99
tunica vaginalis (hydrocele) (percutaneous)
61.91
vitreous (and replacement) 14.72
diagnostic 14.11
Assessment
fitness to testify 94.11
mental status 94.11
nutritional status 89.39
personality 94.03
temperament 94.02
vocational 93.85
Assistance
cardiac (*see also* Resuscitation, cardiac)
extracorporeal circulation 39.61
endotracheal respiratory — *see* category
96.7 ☑
hepatic, extracorporeal 50.92
respiratory (endotracheal) (mechanical) — *see*
Ventilation, mechanical
Astragalectomy 77.98
Asymmetrogammagram — *see* Scan,
radioisotope
Atherectomy
cerebrovascular — *see* Angioplasty
coronary — *see* Angioplasty
peripheral 39.50
Atriocommissuropexy (mitral valve) 35.12
Atrioplasty NEC 37.99
combined with repair of valvular and
ventricular septal defects — *see* Repair,
endocardial cushion defect
septum (heart) NEC 35.71
Atrioseptopexy (*see also* Repair, atrial septal
defect) 35.71
Atrioseptoplasty (*see also* Repair, atrial septal
defect) 35.71

Atrioseptostomy (balloon) 35.41
Atriotomy 37.11
Atrioventriculostomy (cerebral-heart) 02.32
Attachment
eye muscle
orbicularis oculi to eyebrow 08.36
rectus to frontalis 15.9
pedicle (flap) graft 86.74
hand 86.73
lip 27.57
mouth 27.57
pharyngeal flap (for cleft palate repair) 27.62
secondary or subsequent 27.63
retina — *see* Reattachment, retina
Atticoantrostomy (ear) 20.49
Atticoantrotomy (ear) 20.49
Atticotomy (ear) 20.23
Audiometry (Békésy 5-tone) (impedance)
(stapedial reflex response) (subjective) 95.41
Augmentation
bladder 57.87
breast — *see* Mammoplasty, augmentation
buttock ("fanny-lift") 86.89
chin 76.68
genioplasty 76.68
mammoplasty — *see* Mammoplasty,
augmentation
outflow tract (pulmonary valve) (gusset type)
35.26
in total repair of tetralogy of Fallot 35.81
vocal cord(s) 31.0
Auriculectomy 18.39
Autograft — *see* Graft
Autologous — *see* Blood, transfusion
Autopsy 89.8
Autotransfusion (whole blood) — *see* Blood,
transfusion
Autotransplant, autotransplantation — *see also*
Reimplantation
adrenal tissue (heterotopic) (orthotopic) 07.45
kidney 55.61
lung — *see* Transplant, transplantation, lung
33.5 ☑
ovary 65.72
laparoscopic 65.75
pancreatic tissue 52.81
parathyroid tissue (heterotopic) (orthotopic)
06.95
thyroid tissue (heterotopic) (orthotopic) 06.94
tooth 23.5
Avulsion, nerve (cranial) (peripheral) NEC 04.07
acoustic 04.01
phrenic 33.31
sympathetic 05.29
Azygography 88.63

B

Bacterial smear — *see* Examination, microscopic
Baffes operation (interatrial transposition of
venous return) 35.91
Baffle, atrial or interatrial 35.91
Balanoplasty 64.49
Baldy-Webster operation (uterine suspension)
69.22
Ballistocardiography 89.59
Balloon
angioplasty — *see* Angioplasty, balloon
pump, intra-aortic 37.61
systostomy (atrial) 35.41
Ball operation
herniorrhaphy — *see* Repair, hernia, inguinal
undercutting 49.02
Bandage 93.57
elastic 93.56
Banding
gastric 44.68
vertical 44.68
pulmonary artery 38.85

Bankhart operation (capsular repair into glenoid,
for shoulder dislocation) 81.82
Bardenheurer operation (ligation of innominate
artery) 38.85
Barium swallow 87.61
Barkan operation (goniotomy) 12.52
with goniopuncture 12.53
Barr operation (transfer of tibialis posterior
tendon) 83.75
Barsky operation (closure of cleft hand) 82.82
Basal metabolic rate 89.39
Bassett operation (vulvectomy with inguinal
lymph node dissection) 71.5 *[40.3]*
Bassini operation — *see* Repair, hernia, inguinal
Batch-Spittler-McFaddin operation (knee
disarticulation) 84.16
Batista operation (partial ventriculectomy)
(ventricular reduction) (ventricular
remodeling) 37.35
Bearing surface, hip replacement   •
ceramic-on-ceramic 00.76   •
metal-on-metal 00.75   •
metal on polyethylene 00.74   •
Beck operation
aorta-coronary sinus shunt 36.39
epicardial poudrage 36.39
Beck-Jianu operation (permanent gastrostomy)
43.19
Behavior modification 94.33
Bell-Beuttner operation (subtotal abdominal
hysterectomy) 68.39
laparoscopic 68.31
Belsey operation (esophagogastric sphincter)
44.65
Benenenti operation (rotation of bulbous
urethra) 58.49
Berke operation (levator resection of eyelid) 08.33
Bicuspidization of heart valve 35.10
aortic 35.11
mitral 35.12
Bicycle dynamometer 93.01
Biesenberger operation (size reduction of breast,
bilateral) 85.32
unilateral 85.31
Bifurcation, bone (*see also* Osteotomy) 77.30
Bigelow operation (litholapaxy) 57.0
Bililite therapy (ultraviolet) 99.82
Billroth I operation (partial gastrectomy with
gastroduodenostomy) 43.6
Billroth II operation (partial gastrectomy with
gastrojejunostomy) 43.7
Binnie operation (hepatopexy) 50.69
Biofeedback, psychotherapy 94.39
Biopsy
abdominal wall 54.22
adenoid 28.11
adrenal gland NEC 07.11
closed 07.11
open 07.12
percutaneous (aspiration) (needle) 07.11
alveolus 24.12
anus 49.23
appendix 45.26
artery (any site) 38.21
aspiration — *see* Biopsy, by site
bile ducts 51.14
closed (endoscopic) 51.14
open 51.13
percutaneous (needle) 51.12
bladder 57.33
closed 57.33
open 57.34
transurethral 57.33
blood vessel (any site) 38.21
bone 77.40
carpal, metacarpal 77.44
clavicle 77.41
facial 76.11
femur 77.45
fibula 77.47

☑ Additional Digit Required — Refer to the Tabular List (Numeric Code Section) for Additional Digit Selection

▶◀ Revised Text   ● New Line   ▲ Revised Code

Biopsy — *continued*
  bone — *continued*
    humerus 77.42
    marrow 41.31
    patella 77.46
    pelvic 77.49
    phalanges (foot) (hand) 77.49
    radius 77.43
    scapula 77.41
    specified site NEC 77.49
    tarsal, metatarsal 77.48
    thorax (ribs) (sternum) 77.41
    tibia 77.47
    ulna 77.43
    vertebrae 77.49
  bowel — *see* Biopsy, intestine
  brain NEC 01.13
    closed 01.13
    open 01.14
    percutaneous (needle) 01.13
  breast 85.11
    blind 85.11
    closed 85.11
    open 85.12
    percutaneous (needle) (Vimm-Silverman)
      85.11
  bronchus NEC 33.24
    brush 33.24
    closed (endoscopic) 33.24
    open 33.25
    washings 33.24
  bursa 83.21
  cardioesophageal (junction) 44.14
    closed (endoscopic) 44.14
    open 44.15
  cecum 45.25
    brush 45.25
    closed (endoscopic) 45.25
    open 45.26
  cerebral meninges NEC 01.11
    closed 01.11
    open 01.12
    percutaneous (needle) 01.11
  cervix (punch) 67.12
    conization (sharp) 67.2
  chest wall 34.23
  clitoris 71.11
  colon 45.25
    brush 45.25
    closed (endoscopic) 45.25
    open 45.26
  conjunctiva 10.21
  cornea 11.22
  cul-de-sac 70.23
  diaphragm 34.27
  duodenum 45.14
    brush 45.14
    closed (endoscopic) 45.14
    open 45.15
  ear (external) 18.12
    middle or inner 20.32
  endocervix 67.11
  endometrium NEC 68.16
    by
      aspiration curettage 69.59
      dilation and curettage 69.09
    closed (endoscopic) 68.16
    open 68.13
  epididymis 63.01
  esophagus 42.24
    closed (endoscopic) 42.24
    open 42.25
  extraocular muscle or tendon 15.01
  eye 16.23
    muscle (oblique) (rectus) 15.01
  eyelid 08.11
  fallopian tube 66.11
  fascia 83.21
  fetus 75.33
  gallbladder 51.12
    closed (endoscopic) 51.14
    open 51.13
    percutaneous (needle) 51.12
  ganglion (cranial) (peripheral) NEC 04.11
    closed 04.11
    open 04.12

Biopsy — *continued*
  ganglion NEC — *continued*
    percutaneous (needle) 04.11
    sympathetic nerve 05.11
  gum 24.11
  heart 37.25
  hypophysis (*see also* Biopsy, pituitary gland)
    07.15
  ileum 45.14
    brush 45.14
    closed (endoscopic) 45.14
    open 45.15
  intestine NEC 45.27
    large 45.25
      brush 45.25
      closed (endoscopic) 45.25
      open 45.26
    small 45.14
      brush 45.14
      closed (endoscopic) 45.14
      open 45.15
  intra-abdominal mass 54.24
    closed 54.24
    percutaneous (needle) 54.24
  iris 12.22
  jejunum 45.14
    brush 45.14
    closed (endoscopic) 45.14
    open 45.15
  joint structure (aspiration) 80.30
    ankle 80.37
    elbow 80.32
    foot and toe 80.38
    hand and finger 80.34
    hip 80.35
    knee 80.36
    shoulder 80.31
    specified site NEC 80.39
    spine 80.39
    wrist 80.33
  kidney 55.23
    closed 55.23
    open 55.24
    percutaneous (aspiration) (needle) 55.23
  labia 71.11
  lacrimal
    gland 09.11
    sac 09.12
  larynx 31.43
    brush 31.43
    closed (endoscopic) 31.43
    open 31.45
  lip 27.23
  liver 50.11
    closed 50.11
    laparoscopic 50.19
    open 50.12
    percutaneous (aspiration) (needle) 50.11
  lung NEC 33.27
    brush 33.24
    closed (percutaneous) (needle) 33.26
      brush 33.24
      endoscopic 33.27
        brush 33.24
    endoscopic 33.27
      brush 33.24
    open 33.28
    transbronchial 33.27
  lymphatic structure (channel) (node) (vessel)
    40.11
  mediastinum NEC 34.25
    closed 34.25
    open 34.26
    percutaneous (needle) 34.25
  meninges (cerebral) NEC 01.11
    closed 01.11
    open 01.12
    percutaneous (needle) 01.11
    spinal 03.32
  mesentery 54.23
  mouth NEC 27.24
  muscle 83.21
    extraocular 15.01
    ocular 15.01
  nasopharynx 29.12

Biopsy — *continued*
  nerve (cranial) (peripheral) NEC 04.11
    closed 04.11
    open 04.12
    percutaneous (needle) 04.11
    sympathetic 05.11
  nose, nasal 21.22
    sinus 22.11
      closed (endoscopic) (needle) 22.11
      open 22.12
  ocular muscle or tendon 15.01
  omentum
    closed 54.24
    open 54.23
    percutaneous (needle) 54.24
  orbit 16.23
    by aspiration 16.22
  ovary 65.12
    by aspiration 65.11
    laparoscopic 65.13
  palate (bony) 27.21
    soft 27.22
  pancreas 52.11
    closed (endoscopic) 52.11
    open 52.12
    percutaneous (aspiration) (needle) 52.11
  pancreatic duct 52.14
    closed (endoscopic) 52.14
  parathyroid gland 06.13
  penis 64.11
  perianal tissue 49.22
  pericardium 37.24
  periprostatic 60.15
  perirectal tissue 48.26
  perirenal tissue 59.21
  peritoneal implant
    closed 54.24
    open 54.23
    percutaneous (needle) 54.24
  peritoneum
    closed 54.24
    open 54.23
    percutaneous (needle) 54.24
  periurethral tissue 58.24
  perivesical tissue 59.21
  pharynx, pharyngeal 29.12
  pineal gland 07.17
  pituitary gland 07.15
    transfrontal approach 07.13
    transsphenoidal approach 07.14
  pleura, pleural 34.24
  prostate NEC 60.11
    closed (transurethral) 60.11
    open 60.12
    percutaneous (needle) 60.11
    transrectal 60.11
  rectum 48.24
    brush 48.24
    closed (endoscopic) 48.24
    open 48.25
  retroperitoneal tissue 54.24
  salivary gland or duct 26.11
    closed (needle) 26.11
    open 26.12
  scrotum 61.11
  seminal vesicle NEC 60.13
    closed 60.13
    open 60.14
    percutaneous (needle) 60.13
  sigmoid colon 45.25
    brush 45.25
    closed (endoscopic) 45.25
    open 45.26
  sinus, nasal 22.11
    closed (endoscopic) (needle) 22.11
    open 22.12
  skin (punch) 86.11
  skull 01.15
  soft palate 27.22
  soft tissue NEC 83.21
  spermatic cord 63.01
  sphincter of Oddi 51.14
    closed (endoscopic) 51.14
    open 51.13
  spinal cord (meninges) 03.32

☑ Additional Digit Required — Refer to the Tabular List (Numeric Code Section) for Additional Digit Selection

►◄ Revised Text   ● New Line   ▲ Revised Code

Bypass — *continued*
  gastroenterostomy 44.39
    laparoscopic 44.38
  gastroepiploic-coronary artery 36.17
  gastrogastrostomy 44.39
    laparoscopic 44.38
  graft, pressurized treatment 00.16
  heart-lung (complete) (partial) 39.61
    open 39.61
    percutaneous (closed) 39.66
  high gastric 44.31
  ileo-jejunal 45.91
  internal mammary-coronary artery (single)
    36.15
    double vessel 36.16
  jejunal-ileum 45.91
  pulmonary 39.61
    open 39.61
    percutaneous (closed) 39.66
  shunt
    intestine
      large-to-large 45.94
      small-to-large 45.93
      small-to-small 45.91
    stomach 44.39
      high gastric 44.31
      laparoscopic 44.38
  terminal ileum 45.93
  vascular (arterial) (graft) (mandril grown graft)
    (vein graft) NEC 39.29
    aorta-carotid-brachial 39.22
    aorta-iliac-femoral 39.25
    aorta-renal 39.24
    aorta-subclavian-carotid 39.22
    aortic-superior mesenteric 39.26
    aortocarotid 39.22
    aortoceliac 39.26
    aortocoronary (*see also* Bypass,
      aortocoronary) 36.10
    aortofemoral 39.25
    aortofemoral-popliteal 39.25
    aortoiliac 39.25
      to popliteal 39.25
    aortoiliofemoral 39.25
    aortomesenteric 39.26
    aortopopliteal 39.25
    aortorenal 39.24
    aortosubclavian 39.22
    axillary-brachial 39.29
    axillary-femoral (superficial) 39.29
    axillofemoral (superficial) 39.29
    carotid-cerebral 39.28
    carotid-vertebral 39.28
    carotid to subclavian artery 39.22
    common hepatic-common iliac-renal 39.26
    coronary (*see also* Bypass, aortocoronary)
      36.10
    extracranial-intracranial [EC-IC] 39.28
    femoral-femoral 39.29
    femoroperoneal 39.29
    femoropopliteal (reversed saphenous vein)
      (saphenous) 39.29
    femorotibial (anterior) (posterior) 39.29
    iliofemoral 39.25
    ilioiliac 39.26
    internal mammary-coronary artery (single)
      36.15
      double vessel 36.16
    intra-abdominal (arterial) NEC 39.26
      venous NEC 39.1
    intrathoracic NEC 39.23
    peripheral artery NEC 39.29
    popliteal-tibial 39.29
    renal artery 39.24
    splenorenal (venous) 39.1
      arterial 39.26
    subclavian-axillary 39.29
    subclavian-carotid 39.22
    subclavian-subclavian 39.22
    Y graft to renal arteries 39.24

C

Caldwell operation (sulcus extension) 24.91
Caldwell-Luc operation (maxillary sinusotomy)
  22.39
  with removal of membrane lining 22.31
Calibration, urethra 89.29
Calicectomy (renal) 55.4
Callander operation (knee disarticulation) 84.16
Caloric test, vestibular function 95.44
Calycectomy (renal) 55.4
Calyco-ileoneocystostomy 55.86
Calycotomy (renal) 55.11
Campbell operation
  bone block, ankle 81.11
  fasciotomy (iliac crest) 83.14
  reconstruction of anterior cruciate ligament
    81.45
Campimetry 95.05
Canaliculodacryocystorhinostomy 09.81
Canaliculoplasty 09.73
Canaliculorhinostomy 09.81
Canaloplasty, external auditory meatus 18.6
Cannulation — *see also* Insertion, catheter
  ampulla of Vater 51.99
  antrum 22.01
  arteriovenous 39.93
  artery 38.91
  caval-mesenteric vein 39.1
  cisterna chyli 40.61
  Eustachian tube 20.8
  lacrimal apparatus 09.42
  lymphatic duct, left (thoracic) 40.61
  nasal sinus (by puncture) 22.01
    through natural ostium 22.02
  pancreatic duct 52.92
    by retrograde endoscopy (ERP) 52.93
  renoportal 39.1
  sinus (nasal) (by puncture) 22.01
    through natural ostium 22.02
  splenorenal (venous) 39.1
    arterial 39.26
  thoracic duct (cervical approach) (thoracic
    approach) 40.61
Cannulization — *see* Cannulation
Canthocystostomy 09.82
Canthoplasty 08.59
Canthorrhaphy 08.52
  division or severing 08.02
Canthotomy 08.51
Capsulectomy
  joint (*see also* Arthrectomy) 80.90
  kidney 55.91
  lens 13.65
    with extraction of lens 13.51
  ovary 65.29
    laparoscopic 65.25
Capsulo-iridectomy 13.65
Capsuloplasty — *see* Arthroplasty
Capsulorrhaphy 81.96
  with arthroplasty — *see* Arthroplasty
  ankle 81.94
  foot 81.94
  lower extremity NEC 81.95
  upper extremity 81.93
Capsulotomy
  joint (*see also* Division, joint capsule) 80.40
    for claw toe repair 77.57
  lens 13.64
    with
      discission of lens 13.2
      removal of foreign body 13.02
        by magnet extraction 13.01
Cardiac
  mapping 37.27
  massage (external) (closed chest) 99.63
    open chest 37.91
  retraining 93.36
Cardiac support device (CSD) 37.41   ●
Cardiectomy (stomach) 43.5
Cardiocentesis 37.0
Cardiography (*see also* Angiocardiography) 88.50

Cardiolysis 37.10
Cardiomyopexy 36.39
Cardiomyotomy 42.7
Cardio-omentopexy 36.39
Cardiopericardiopexy 36.39
Cardioplasty (stomach and esophagus) 44.65
  stomach alone 44.66
    laparoscopic 44.67
Cardioplegia 39.63
Cardiopneumopexy 36.39
Cardiorrhaphy 37.49   ▲
Cardioschisis 37.12
Cardiosplenopexy 36.39
Cardiotomy (exploratory) 37.11
Cardiovalvulotomy — *see* Valvulotomy, heart
Cardioversion (external) 99.62
  atrial 99.61
Carotid pulse tracing with ECG lead 89.56
Carpectomy (partial) 77.84
  total 77.94
Carroll and Taber arthroplasty (proximal
  interphalangeal joint) 81.72
Casting (for immobilization) NEC 93.53
  with fracture-reduction — *see* Reduction,
    fracture
Castration
  female (oophorectomy, bilateral) 65.51
    laparoscopic 65.53
  male 62.41
C.A.T. (computerized axial tomography) (*see also*
  Scan, C.A.T.) 88.38
Catheterization — *see also* Insertion, catheter
  arteriovenous 39.93
  artery 38.91
  bladder, indwelling 57.94
    percutaneous (cystostomy) 57.17
    suprapubic NEC 57.18
  bronchus 96.05
    with lavage 96.56
  cardiac (right) 37.21
    combined left and right 37.23
    left 37.22
      combined with right heart 37.23
    right 37.21
      combined with left heart 37.23
  central venous NEC 38.93
    peripherally inserted central catheter (PICC)
      38.93
  chest 34.04
    revision (with lysis of adhesions) 34.04
  Eustachian tube 20.8
  heart (right) 37.21
    combined left and right 37.23
    left 37.22
      combined with right heart 37.23
    right 37.21
      combined with left heart 37.23
  hepatic vein 38.93
  inferior vena cava 38.93
  intercostal space (with water seal), for drainage
    34.04
    revision (with lysis of adhesions) 34.04
  lacrimonasal duct 09.44
  laryngeal 96.05
  nasolacrimal duct 09.44
  pancreatic cyst 52.01
  renal vein 38.93
  Swan-Ganz (pulmonary) 89.64
  transtracheal for oxygenation 31.99
  umbilical vein 38.92
  ureter (to kidney) 59.8
    for retrograde pyelogram 87.74
  urethra, indwelling 57.94
  vein NEC 38.93
    for renal dialysis 38.95
Cattell operation (herniorrhaphy) 53.51
Cauterization — *see also* Destruction, lesion, by
  site
  anus NEC 49.39
    endoscopic 49.31
  Bartholin's gland 71.24
  broad ligament 69.19

☑ Additional Digit Required — Refer to the Tabular List (Numeric Code Section) for Additional Digit Selection

Cauterization — *see also* Destruction, lesion, by site — *continued*
 bronchus 32.09
  endoscopic 32.01
 canaliculi 09.73
 cervix 67.32
 chalazion 08.25
 choroid plexus 02.14
 conjunctiva 10.33
  lesion 10.32
 cornea (fistula) (ulcer) 11.42
 ear, external 18.29
 endometrial implant — *see* Excision, lesion, by site
 entropion 08.41
 esophagus 42.39
  endoscopic 42.33
 eyelid 08.25
  for entropion or ectropion 08.41
 fallopian tube 66.61
  by endoscopy (hysteroscopy) (laparoscopy) 66.29
 hemorrhoids 49.43
 iris 12.41
 lacrimal
  gland 09.21
  punctum 09.72
   for eversion 09.71
  sac 09.6
 larynx 30.09
 liver 50.29
 lung 32.29
  endoscopic 32.28
 meibomian gland 08.25
 nose, for epistaxis (with packing) 21.03
 ovary 65.29
  laparoscopic 65.25
 palate (bony) 27.31
 pannus (superficial) 11.42
 pharynx 29.39
 punctum, lacrimal 09.72
  for eversion 09.71
 rectum 48.32
  radical 48.31
 round ligament 69.19
 sclera 12.84
  with iridectomy 12.62
 skin 86.3
 subcutaneous tissue 86.3
 tonsillar fossa 28.7
 urethra 58.39
  endoscopic 58.31
 uterosacral ligament 69.19
 uterotubal ostia 66.61
 uterus 68.29
 vagina 70.33
 vocal cords 30.09
 vulva 71.3
Cavernoscopy 34.21
Cavernostomy 33.1
Cavernotomy, kidney 55.39
Cavography (inferior vena cava) 88.51
Cecectomy (with resection of terminal ileum) 45.72
Cecil operation (urethral reconstruction) 58.46
Cecocoloplicopexy 46.63
Cecocolostomy 45.94
Cecofixation 46.64
Ceco-ileostomy 45.93
Cecopexy 46.64
Cecoplication 46.62
Cecorrhaphy 46.75
Cecosigmoidostomy 45.94
Cecostomy (tube) (*see also* Colostomy) 46.10
Cecotomy 45.03
Celiocentesis 54.91
Celioscopy 54.21
Celiotomy, exploratory 54.11
Cell block and Papanicolaou smear — *see* Examination, microscopic
Cephalogram 87.17
 dental 87.12
 orthodontic 87.12

Cephalometry, cephalometrics 87.17
 echo 88.78
 orthodontic 87.12
 ultrasound (sonar) 88.78
 x-ray 87.81
Cephalotomy, fetus 73.8
Cerclage
 anus 49.72
 cervix 67.59
  transabdominal 67.51
  transvaginal 67.59
 isthmus uteri (cervix) 67.59
 retinal reattachment (*see also* Buckling, scleral) 14.49
 sclera (*see also* Buckling, scleral) 14.49
Cervicectomy (with synchronous colporrhaphy) 67.4
Cervicoplasty 67.69
Cesarean section 74.99
 classical 74.0
 corporeal 74.0
 extraperitoneal 74.2
 fundal 74.0
 laparotrachelotomy 74.1
 Latzko 74.2
 low cervical 74.1
 lower uterine segment 74.1
 peritoneal exclusion 74.4
 specified type NEC 74.4
 supravesical 74.2
 transperitoneal 74.4
  classical 74.0
  low cervical 74.1
 upper uterine segment 74.0
 vaginal 74.4
 Waters 74.2
Chandler operation (hip fusion) 81.21
Change — *see also* Replacement
 cast NEC 97.13
  lower limb 97.12
  upper limb 97.11
 cystostomy catheter or tube 59.94
 gastrostomy tube 97.02
 length
  bone — *see either* category 78.2 ☑
    Shortening, bone or category 78.3 ☑
    Lengthening, bone
   muscle 83.85
    hand 82.55
   tendon 83.85
    hand 82.55
 nephrostomy catheter or tube 55.93
 pyelostomy catheter or tube 55.94
 tracheostomy tube 97.23
 ureterostomy catheter or tube 59.93
 urethral catheter, indwelling 57.95
Character analysis, psychologic 94.03
Charles operation (correction of lymphedema) 40.9
Charnley operation (compression arthrodesis)
 ankle 81.11
 hip 81.21
 knee 81.22
Cheatle-Henry operation — *see* Repair, hernia, femoral
Check
 automatic implantable cardioverter/defibrillatory (AICD) (interrogation only) 89.49
 CRT-D (cardiac resynchronization defibrillator) (interrogation only) 89.49
 CRT-P (cardiac resynchronization pacemaker) (interrogation only) 89.45
 pacemaker, artificial (cardiac) (function) (interrogation only) (rate) 89.45
  amperage threshold 89.48
  artifact wave form 89.46
  electrode impedance 89.47
  voltage threshold 89.48
 vision NEC 95.09
Cheiloplasty 27.59
Cheilorrhaphy 27.51
Cheilostomatoplasty 27.59

Cheilotomy 27.0
Chemical peel, skin 86.24
Chemocauterization — *see also* Destruction, lesion, by site
 corneal epithelium 11.41
 palate 27.31
Chemodectomy 39.8
Chemoembolization 99.25
Chemolysis
 nerve (peripheral) 04.2
 spinal canal structure 03.8
Chemoneurolysis 04.2
Chemonucleolysis (nucleus pulposus) 80.52
Chemopallidectomy 01.42
Chemopeel (skin) 86.24
Chemosurgery
 esophagus 42.39
  endoscopic 42.33
 Mohs' 86.24
 skin (superficial) 86.24
 stomach 43.49
  endoscopic 43.41
Chemothalamectomy 01.41
Chemotherapy — *see also* Immunotherapy
 Antabuse 94.25
 for cancer NEC 99.25
  brain wafer implantation 00.10
  implantation of chemotherapeutic agent 00.10
   interstitial implantation 00.10
   intracavitary implantation 00.10
   wafer chemotherapy 00.10
 lithium 94.22
 methadone 94.25
 palate (bony) 27.31
Chevalier-Jackson operation (partial laryngectomy) 30.29
Child operation (radical subtotal pancreatectomy) 52.53
Cholangiocholangiostomy 51.39
Cholangiocholecystocholedochectomy 51.22
Cholangio-enterostomy 51.39
Cholangiogastrostomy 51.39
Cholangiogram 87.54
 endoscopic retrograde (ERC) 51.11
 intraoperative 87.53
 intravenous 87.52
 percutaneous hepatic 87.51
 transhepatic 87.53
Cholangiography (*see also* Cholangiogram) 87.54
Cholangiojejunostomy (intrahepatic) 51.39
Cholangiopancreatography, endoscopic retrograde (ERCP) 51.10
Cholangiostomy 51.59
Cholangiotomy 51.59
Cholecystectomy (total) 51.22
 laparoscopic 51.23
 partial 51.21
  laparoscopic 51.24
Cholecystenterorrhaphy 51.91
Cholecystocecostomy 51.32
Cholecystocholangiogram 87.59
Cholecystocolostomy 51.32
Cholecystoduodenostomy 51.32
Cholecystoenterostomy (Winiwater) 51.32
Cholecystogastrostomy 51.34
Cholecystogram 87.59
Cholecystoileostomy 51.32
Cholecystojejunostomy (Roux-en-Y) (with jejunojejunostomy) 51.32
Cholecystopancreatostomy 51.33
Cholecystopexy 51.99
Cholecystorrhaphy 51.91
Cholecystostomy NEC 51.03
 by trocar 51.02
Cholecystotomy 51.04
 percutaneous 51.01
Choledochectomy 51.63
Choledochoduodenostomy 51.36
Choledochoenterostomy 51.36

☑ Additional Digit Required — Refer to the Tabular List (Numeric Code Section) for Additional Digit Selection

Choledochojejunostomy 51.36
Choledocholithotomy 51.41
  endoscopic 51.88
Choledocholithotripsy 51.41
  endoscopic 51.88
Choledochopancreatostomy 51.39
Choledochoplasty 51.72
Choledochorrhaphy 51.71
Choledochoscopy 51.11
Choledochostomy 51.51
Choledochotomy 51.51
Cholelithotomy 51.04
Chondrectomy 80.90
  ankle 80.97
  elbow 80.92
  foot and toe 80.98
  hand and finger 80.94
  hip 80.95
  intervertebral cartilage — *see* category 80.5 ☑
  knee (semilunar cartilage) 80.6
  nasal (submucous) 21.5
  semilunar cartilage (knee) 80.6
  shoulder 80.91
  specified site NEC 80.99
  spine — *see* category 80.5 ☑
  wrist 80.93
Chondroplasty — *see* Arthroplasty
Chondrosternoplasty (for pectus excavatum repair) 34.74
Chondrotomy (*see also* Division, cartilage) 80.40
  nasal 21.1
Chopart operation (midtarsal amputation) 84.12
Chordectomy, vocal 30.22
Chordotomy (spinothalmic) (anterior) (posterior) NEC 03.29
  percutaneous 03.21
  stereotactic 03.21
Ciliarotomy 12.55
Ciliectomy (ciliary body) 12.44
  eyelid margin 08.20
Cinch, cinching
  for scleral buckling (*see also* Buckling, scleral) 14.49
  ocular muscle (oblique) (rectus) 15.22
    multiple (two or more muscles) 15.4
Cineangiocardiography (*see also* Angiocardiography) 88.50
Cineplasty, cineplastic prosthesis
  amputation — *see* Amputation
  arm 84.44
  biceps 84.44
  extremity 84.40
    lower 84.48
    upper 84.44
  leg 84.48
Cineradiograph — *see* Radiography
Cingulumotomy (brain) (percutaneous radiofrequency) 01.32
Circumcision (male) 64.0
  female 71.4
CISH (classic infrafascial SEMM hysterectomy) 68.31
Clagett operation (closure of chest wall following open flap drainage) 34.72
Clamp and cautery, hemorrhoids 49.43
Clamping
  aneurysm (cerebral) 39.51
  blood vessel — *see* Ligation, blood vessel
  ventricular shunt 02.43
Clavicotomy 77.31
  fetal 73.8
Claviculectomy (partial) 77.81
  total 77.91
Clayton operation (resection of metatarsal heads and bases of phalanges) 77.88
Cleaning, wound 96.59
Clearance
  bladder (transurethral) 57.0
  pelvic
    female 68.8
    male 57.71

Clearance — *continued*
  prescalene fat pad 40.21
  renal pelvis (transurethral) 56.0
  ureter (transurethral) 56.0
Cleidotomy 77.31
  fetal 73.8
Clipping
  aneurysm (basilar) (carotid) (cerebellar) (cerebellopontine) (communicating artery) (vertebral) 39.51
  arteriovenous fistula 39.53
  frenulum, frenum
    labia (lips) 27.91
    lingual (tongue) 25.91
  tip of uvula 27.72
Clitoridectomy 71.4
Clitoridotomy 71.4
Clivogram 87.02
Closure — *see also* Repair
  abdominal wall 54.63
    delayed (granulating wound) 54.62
    secondary 54.61
    tertiary 54.62
  amputation stump, secondary 84.3
  aorticopulmonary fenestration (fistula) 39.59
  appendicostomy 47.92
  artificial opening
    bile duct 51.79
    bladder 57.82
    bronchus 33.42
    common duct 51.72
    esophagus 42.83
    gallbladder 51.92
    hepatic duct 51.79
    intestine 46.50
      large 46.52
      small 46.51
    kidney 55.82
    larynx 31.62
    rectum 48.72
    stomach 44.62
    thorax 34.72
    trachea 31.72
    ureter 56.83
    urethra 58.42
  atrial septal defect (*see also* Repair, atrial septal defect) 35.71
    with umbrella device (King-Mills type) 35.52
    combined with repair of valvular and ventricular septal defects — *see* Repair, endocardial cushion defect
  bronchostomy 33.42
  cecostomy 46.52
  cholecystostomy 51.92
  cleft hand 82.82
  colostomy 46.52
  cystostomy 57.82
  diastema (alveolar) (dental) 24.8
  disrupted abdominal wall (postoperative) 54.61
  duodenostomy 46.51
  encephalocele 02.12
  endocardial cushion defect (*see also* Repair, endocardial cushion defect) 35.73
  enterostomy 46.50
  esophagostomy 42.83
  fenestration
    aorticopulmonary 39.59
    septal, heart (*see also* Repair, heart, septum) 35.70
  filtering bleb, corneoscleral (postglaucoma) 12.66
  fistula
    abdominothoracic 34.83
    anorectal 48.73
    anovaginal 70.73
    antrobuccal 22.71
    anus 49.73
    aorticopulmonary (fenestration) 39.59
    aortoduodenal 39.59
    appendix 47.92
    biliary tract 51.79
    bladder NEC 57.84
    branchial cleft 29.52
    bronchocutaneous 33.42
    bronchoesophageal 33.42

Closure — *see also* Repair — *continued*
  fistula — *continued*
    bronchomediastinal 34.73
    bronchopleural 34.73
    bronchopleurocutaneous 34.73
    bronchopleuromediastinal 34.73
    bronchovisceral 33.42
    bronchus 33.42
    cecosigmoidal 46.76
    cerebrospinal fluid 02.12
    cervicoaural 18.79
    cervicosigmoidal 67.62
    cervicovesical 57.84
    cervix 67.62
    cholecystocolic 51.93
    cholecystoduodenal 51.93
    cholecystoenteric 51.93
    cholecystogastric 51.93
    cholecystojejunal 51.93
    cisterna chyli 40.63
    colon 46.76
    colovaginal 70.72
    common duct 51.72
    cornea 11.49
      with lamellar graft (homograft) 11.62
        autograft 11.61
    diaphragm 34.83
    duodenum 46.72
    ear, middle 19.9
    ear drum 19.4
    enterocolic 46.74
    enterocutaneous 46.74
    enterouterine 69.42
    enterovaginal 70.74
    enterovesical 57.83
    esophagobronchial 33.42
    esophagocutaneous 42.84
    esophagopleurocutaneous 34.73
    esophagotracheal 31.73
    esophagus NEC 42.84
    fecal 46.79
    gallbladder 51.93
    gastric NEC 44.63
    gastrocolic 44.63
    gastroenterocolic 44.63
    gastroesophageal 42.84
    gastrojejunal 44.63
    gastrojejunocolic 44.63
    heart valve — *see* Repair, heart, valve
    hepatic duct 51.79
    hepatopleural 34.73
    hepatopulmonary 34.73
    ileorectal 46.74
    ileosigmoidal 46.74
    ileovesical 57.83
    ileum 46.74
    in ano 49.73
    intestine 46.79
      large 46.76
      small NEC 46.74
    intestinocolonic 46.74
    intestinoureteral 56.84
    intestinouterine 69.42
    intestinovaginal 70.74
    intestinovesical 57.83
    jejunum 46.74
    kidney 55.83
    lacrimal 09.99
    laryngotracheal 31.62
    larynx 31.62
    lymphatic duct, left (thoracic) 40.63
    mastoid (antrum) 19.9
    mediastinobronchial 34.73
    mediastinocutaneous 34.73
    mouth (external) 27.53
    nasal 21.82
      sinus 22.71
    nasolabial 21.82
    nasopharyngeal 21.82
    oroantral 22.71
    oronasal 21.82
    oval window (ear) 20.93
    pancreaticoduodenal 52.95
    perilymph 20.93
    perineorectal 48.73
    perineosigmoidal 46.76

Closure — *see also* Repair — *continued*
fistula — *continued*
perineourethroscrotal 58.43
perineum 71.72
perirectal 48.93
pharyngoesophageal 29.53
pharynx NEC 29.53
pleura, pleural NEC 34.93
pleurocutaneous 34.73
pleuropericardial 37.49 ▲
pleuroperitoneal 34.83
pulmonoperitoneal 34.83
rectolabial 48.73
rectoureteral 56.84
rectourethral 58.43
rectovaginal 70.73
rectovesical 57.83
rectovesicovaginal 57.83
rectovulvar 48.73
rectum NEC 48.73
renal 55.83
reno-intestinal 55.83
round window 20.93
salivary (gland) (duct) 26.42
scrotum 61.42
sigmoidovaginal 70.74
sigmoidovesical 57.83
splenocolic 41.95
stomach NEC 44.63
thoracic duct 40.63
thoracoabdominal 34.83
thoracogastric 34.83
thoracointestinal 34.83
thorax NEC 34.73
trachea NEC 31.73
tracheoesophageal 31.73
tympanic membrane (*see also*
Tympanoplasty) 19.4
umbilicourinary 57.51
ureter 56.84
ureterocervical 56.84
ureterorectal 56.84
ureterosigmoidal 56.84
ureterovaginal 56.84
ureterovesical 56.84
urethra 58.43
urethroperineal 58.43
urethroperineovesical 57.84
urethrorectal 58.43
urethroscrotal 58.43
urethrovaginal 58.43
uteroenteric 69.42
uterointestinal 69.42
uterorectal 69.42
uteroureteric 56.84
uterovaginal 69.42
uterovesical 57.84
vagina 70.75
vaginocutaneous 70.75
vaginoenteric 70.74
vaginoperineal 70.75
vaginovesical 57.84
vesicocervicovaginal 57.84
vesicocolic 57.83
vesicocutaneous 57.84
vesicoenteric 57.83
vesicometrorectal 57.83
vesicoperineal 57.84
vesicorectal 57.83
vesicosigmoidal 57.83
vesicosigmoidovaginal 57.83
vesicoureteral 56.84
vesicoureterovaginal 56.84
vesicourethral 57.84
vesicourethrorectal 57.83
vesicouterine 57.84
vesicovaginal 57.84
vulva 71.72
vulvorectal 48.73
foramen ovale (patent) 35.71
with
prosthesis (open heart technique) 35.51
closed heart technique 35.52
tissue graft 35.61
gastroduodenostomy 44.5
gastrojejunostomy 44.5

Closure — *see also* Repair — *continued*
gastrostomy 44.62
ileostomy 46.51
jejunostomy 46.51
laceration — *see also* Suture, by site
liver 50.61
laparotomy, delayed 54.62
meningocele (spinal) 03.51
cerebral 02.12
myelomeningocele 03.52
nephrostomy 55.82
palmar cleft 82.82
patent ductus arteriosus 38.85
pelviostomy 55.82
peptic ulcer (bleeding) (perforated) 44.40
perforation
ear drum (*see also* Tympanoplasty) 19.4
esophagus 42.82
nasal septum 21.88
tympanic membrane (*see also*
Tympanoplasty) 19.4
proctostomy 48.72
punctum, lacrimal (papilla) 09.91
pyelostomy 55.82
rectostomy 48.72
septum defect (heart) (*see also* Repair, heart,
septum) 35.70
sigmoidostomy 46.52
skin (V-Y type) 86.59
stoma
bile duct 51.79
bladder 57.82
bronchus 33.42
common duct 51.72
esophagus 42.83
gallbladder 51.92
hepatic duct 51.79
intestine 46.50
large 46.52
small 46.51
kidney 55.82
larynx 31.62
rectum 48.72
stomach 44.62
thorax 34.72
trachea 31.72
ureter 56.83
urethra 58.42
thoracostomy 34.72
tracheostomy 31.72
ulcer (bleeding) (peptic) (perforated) 44.40
duodenum 44.42
gastric 44.41
intestine (perforated) 46.79
skin 86.59
stomach 44.41
ureterostomy 56.83
urethrostomy 58.42
vagina 70.8
vascular
percutaneous puncture — *omit code*
vesicostomy 57.22
wound — *see also* Suture, by site
with graft — *see* Graft
with tissue adhesive 86.59

Coagulation, electrocoagulation — *see also*
Destruction, lesion, by site
aneurysm (cerebral) (peripheral vessel) 39.52
arteriovenous fistula 39.53
brain tissue (incremental) (radio-frequency)
01.59
broad ligament 69.19
cervix 67.32
ear
external 18.29
inner 20.79
middle 20.51
fallopian tube 66.61
gasserian ganglion 04.05
nose for epistaxis (with packing) 21.03
ovary 65.29
laparoscopic 65.25
pharynx (by diathermy) 29.39
prostatic bed 60.94

Coagulation, electrocoagulation — *see also*
Destruction, lesion, by site — *continued*
rectum (polyp) 48.32
radical 48.31
retina (for)
destruction of lesion 14.21
reattachment 14.51
repair of tear 14.31
round ligament 69.19
semicircular canals 20.79
spinal cord (lesion) 03.4
urethrovesical junction, transurethral 57.49
uterosacral ligament 69.19
uterus 68.29
vagina 70.33
vulva 71.3
Coating, aneurysm of brain 39.52
Cobalt-60 therapy (treatment) 92.23
Coccygectomy (partial) 77.89
total 77.99
Coccygotomy 77.39
"Cocked hat" procedure (metacarpal lengthening
and transfer of local flap) 82.69
Cockett operation (varicose vein)
lower limb 38.59
upper limb 38.53
Cody tack (perforation of footplate) 19.0
Coffey operation (uterine suspension) (Meig's
modification) 69.22
Cole operation (anterior tarsal wedge osteotomy)
77.28
Colectomy (partial) (segmental) (subtotal) 45.79
cecum (with terminal ileum) 45.72
left (Hartmann) (lower) (radical) 45.75
multiple segmental 45.71
right (radical) 45.73
sigmoid 45.76
terminal ileum with cecum 45.72
total 45.8
transverse 45.74
Collapse, lung, surgical 33.39
by
destruction of phrenic nerve 33.31
pneumoperitoneum 33.33
pneumothorax, artificially-induced 33.32
thoracoplasty 33.34
Collection, sperm for artificial insemination
99.96
Collis-Nissen operation (hiatal hernia repair with
esophagogastroplasty) 53.80
Colocentesis 45.03
Colocolostomy 45.94
proximal to distal segment 45.79
Colocystoplasty 57.87 *[45.52]*
Colofixation 46.64
Coloileotomy 45.00
Colonna operation
adductor tenotomy (first stage) 83.12
hip arthroplasty (second stage) 81.40
reconstruction of hip (second stage) 81.40
Colonoscopy 45.23
with biopsy 45.25
rectum 48.24
fiberoptic (flexible) 45.23
intraoperative 45.21
through stoma (artificial) 45.22
transabdominal 45.21
Colopexy 46.63
Coloplication 46.64
Coloproctostomy 45.94
Colorectosigmoidostomy 45.94
Colorectostomy 45.94
Colorrhaphy 46.75
Coloscopy — *see* Colonoscopy
Colosigmoidostomy 45.94
Colostomy (ileo-ascending) (ileotransverse)
(perineal) (transverse) 46.10
with anterior rectal resection 48.62
delayed opening 46.14
loop 46.03
permanent (magnetic) 46.13
temporary 46.11

Costectomy — *continued*
  associated with thoracic operation — *omit code*
Costochondrectomy 77.91
  associated with thoracic operation — *omit code*
Costosternoplasty (pectus excavatum repair)
  34.74
Costotomy 77.31
Costotransversectomy 77.91
  associated with thoracic operation — *omit code*
Counseling (for) NEC 94.49
  alcoholism 94.46
  drug addiction 94.45
  employers 94.49
  family (medical) (social) 94.49
  marriage 94.49
  ophthalmologic (with instruction) 95.36
  pastoral 94.49
Countershock, cardiac NEC 99.62
Coventry operation (tibial wedge osteotomy)
  77.27
CPAP (continuous positive airway pressure) 93.90
Craniectomy 01.25
  linear (opening of cranial suture) 02.01
  reopening of site 01.23
  strip (opening of cranial suture) 02.01
Cranioclasis, fetal 73.8
Cranioplasty 02.06
  with synchronous repair of encephalocele 02.12
Craniotomy 01.24
  as operative approach — *omit code*
  fetal 73.8
  for decompression of fracture 02.02
  reopening of site 01.23
Craterization, bone (see also Excision, lesion,
  bone) 77.60
Crawford operation (tarso-frontalis sling of eyelid)
  08.32
Creation — *see also* Formation
  cardiac ▶device (defibrillator) (pacemaker)◀
      pocket
    with initial insertion of ▶cardiac device◀
        — *omit code*
    new site (skin) (subcutaneous) 37.79
  conduit
    ileal (urinary) 56.51
    left ventricle and aorta 35.93
    right atrium and pulmonary artery 35.94
    right ventricle and pulmonary (distal) artery
        35.92
      in repair of
        pulmonary artery atresia 35.92
        transposition of great vessels 35.92
        truncus arteriosus 35.83
  endorectal ileal pouch (J-pouch) (H-pouch) (S-
      pouch) (with anastomosis to anus) 45.95
  esophagogastric sphincteric competence NEC
      44.66
    laparoscopic 44.67
  Hartmann pouch — *see* Colectomy, by site
  interatrial fistula 35.42
  pericardial window 37.12
  pleural window, for drainage 34.09
  pocket
    cardiac ▶device (defibrillator) (pacemaker)◀
      with initial insertion of ▶cardiac device◀
          — *omit code*
      new site (skin) (subcutaneous) 37.79
    loop recorder 37.79   ▲
    thalamic stimulator pulse generator
      with initial insertion of battery package —
          omit code
      new site (skin) (subcutaneous) 86.09
  shunt — *see also* Shunt
    arteriovenous fistula, for dialysis 39.93
    left-to-right (systemic to pulmonary
        circulation) 39.0
  subcutaneous tunnel for esophageal
      anastomosis 42.86
    with anastomosis — *see* Anastomosis,
        esophagus, antesternal
  syndactyly (finger) (toe) 86.89
  thalamic stimulator pulse generator pocket
    with initial insertion of battery package —
        omit code

Creation — *see also* Formation — *continued*
  thalamic stimulator pulse generator pocket —
      continued
      new site (skin) (subcutaneous) 86.09
  tracheoesophageal fistula 31.95
  window
    pericardial 37.12
    pleura, for drainage 34.09
Credé maneuver 73.59
Cricoidectomy 30.29
Cricothyreotomy (for assistance in breathing)
  31.1
Cricothyroidectomy 30.29
Cricothyrostomy 31.1
Cricothyrotomy (for assistance in breathing) 31.1
Cricotomy (for assistance in breathing) 31.1
Cricotracheotomy (for assistance in breathing)
  31.1
Crisis intervention 94.35
Croupette, croup tent 93.94
Crown, dental (ceramic) (gold) 23.41
Crushing
  bone — *see* category 78.4 ☑
  calculus
    bile (hepatic) passage 51.49
      endoscopic 51.88
    bladder (urinary) 57.0
    pancreatic duct 52.09
      endoscopic 52.94
  fallopian tube (see also Ligation, fallopian tube)
      66.39
  ganglion — *see* Crushing, nerve
  hemorrhoids 49.45
  nasal septum 21.88
  nerve (cranial) (peripheral) NEC 04.03
    acoustic 04.01
    auditory 04.01
    phrenic 04.03
      for collapse of lung 33.31
    sympathetic 05.0
    trigeminal 04.02
    vestibular 04.01
  vas deferens 63.71
Cryoablation — *see* Ablation
Cryoanalgesia
  nerve (cranial) (peripheral) 04.2
Cryoconization, cervix 67.33
Cryodestruction — *see* Destruction, lesion, by
  site
Cryoextraction, lens (see also Extraction,
  cataract, intracapsular) 13.19
Cryohypophysectomy (complete) (total) (*see also*
  Hypophysectomy) 07.69
Cryoleucotomy 01.32
Cryopexy, retinal — *see* Cryotherapy, retina
Cryoprostatectomy 60.62
Cryoretinopexy (for)
  reattachment 14.52
  repair of tear or defect 14.32
Cryosurgery — *see* Cryotherapy
Cryothalamectomy 01.41
Cryotherapy — *see also* Destruction, lesion, by
  site
  bladder 57.59
  brain 01.59
  cataract 13.19
  cervix 67.33
  choroid — *see* Cryotherapy, retina
  ciliary body 12.72
  corneal lesion (ulcer) 11.43
    to reshape cornea 11.79
  ear
    external 18.29
    inner 20.79
  esophagus 42.39
    endoscopic 42.33
  eyelid 08.25
  hemorrhoids 49.44
  iris 12.41
  nasal turbinates 21.61
  palate (bony) 27.31
  prostate 60.62

Cryotherapy — *see also* Destruction, lesion, by
  site — *continued*
  retina (for)
    destruction of lesion 14.22
    reattachment 14.52
    repair of tear 14.32
  skin 86.3
  stomach 43.49
    endoscopic 43.41
  subcutaneous tissue 86.3
  turbinates (nasal) 21.61
  warts 86.3
    genital 71.3
Cryptectomy (anus) 49.39
  endoscopic 49.31
Cryptorchidectomy (unilateral) 62.3
  bilateral 62.41
Cryptotomy (anus) 49.39
  endoscopic 49.31
Cuirass 93.99
Culdocentesis 70.0
Culdoplasty 70.92
Culdoscopy (exploration) (removal of foreign body
  or lesion) 70.22
Culdotomy 70.12
Culp-Deweerd operation (spiral flap pyeloplasty)
  55.87
Culp-Scardino operation (ureteral flap
  pyeloplasty) 55.87
Culture (and sensitivity) — *see* Examination,
  microscopic
Curettage (with packing) (with secondary closure)
  — *see also* Dilation and curettage
  adenoids 28.6
  anus 49.39
    endoscopic 49.31
  bladder 57.59
    transurethral 57.49
  bone (see also Excision, lesion, bone) 77.60
  brain 01.59
  bursa 83.39
    hand 82.29
  cartilage (see also Excision, lesion, joint) 80.80
  cerebral meninges 01.51
  chalazion 08.25
  conjunctiva (trachoma follicles) 10.33
  corneal epithelium 11.41
    for smear or culture 11.21
  ear, external 18.29
  eyelid 08.25
  joint (see also Excision, lesion, joint) 80.80
  meninges (cerebral) 01.51
    spinal 03.4
  muscle 83.32
    hand 82.22
  nerve (peripheral) 04.07
    sympathetic 05.29
  sclera 12.84
  skin 86.3
  spinal cord (meninges) 03.4
  subgingival 24.31
  tendon 83.39
    sheath 83.31
      hand 82.21
  uterus (with dilation) 69.09
    aspiration (diagnostic) NEC 69.59
      after abortion or delivery 69.52
      to terminate pregnancy 69.51
    following delivery or abortion 69.02
Curette evacuation, lens 13.2
Curtis operation (interphalangeal joint
  arthroplasty) 81.72
Cutaneolipectomy 86.83
Cutdown, venous 38.94
Cutting
  nerve (cranial) (peripheral) NEC 04.03
    acoustic 04.01
    auditory 04.01
    root, spinal 03.1
    sympathetic 05.0
    trigeminal 04.02
    vestibular 04.01
  pedicle (flap) graft 86.71

Cutting — *continued*
pylorus (with wedge resection) 43.3
spinal nerve root 03.1
ureterovesical orifice 56.1
urethral sphincter 58.5
CVP (central venous pressure monitoring) 89.62
Cyclectomy (ciliary body) 12.44
eyelid margin 08.20
Cyclicotomy 12.55
Cycloanemization 12.74
Cyclocryotherapy 12.72
Cyclodialysis (initial) (subsequent) 12.55
Cyclodiathermy (penetrating) (surface) 12.71
Cycloelectrolysis 12.71
Cyclophotocoagulation 12.73
Cyclotomy 12.55
Cystectomy — *see also* Excision, lesion, by site
gallbladder — *see* Cholecystectomy
urinary (partial) (subtotal) 57.6
complete (with urethrectomy) 57.79
radical 57.71
with pelvic exenteration (female) 68.8
total (with urethrectomy) 57.79
Cystocolostomy 57.88
Cystogram, cystography NEC 87.77
Cystolitholapaxy 57.0
Cystolithotomy 57.19
Cystometrogram 89.22
Cystopexy NEC 57.89
Cystoplasty NEC 57.89
Cystoproctostomy 57.88
Cystoprostatectomy, radical 57.71
Cystopyelography 87.74
Cystorrhaphy 57.81
Cystoscopy (transurethral) 57.32
with biopsy 57.33
for
control of hemorrhage
bladder 57.93
prostate 60.94
retrograde pyelography 87.74
ileal conduit 56.35
through stoma (artificial) 57.31
Cystostomy
closed (suprapubic) (percutaneous) 57.17
open (suprapubic) 57.18
percutaneous (closed) (suprapubic) 57.17
suprapubic
closed 57.17
open 57.18
Cystotomy (open) (for removal of calculi) 57.19
Cystourethrogram (retrograde) (voiding) 87.76
Cystourethropexy (by) 59.79
levator muscle sling 59.71
retropubic suspension 59.5
suprapubic suspension 59.4
Cystourethroplasty 57.85
Cystourethroscopy 57.32
with biopsy
bladder 57.33
ureter 56.33
Cytology — *see* Examination, microscopic

D

Dacryoadenectomy 09.20
partial 09.22
total 09.23
Dacryoadenotomy 09.0
Dacryocystectomy (complete) (partial) 09.6
Dacryocystogram 87.05
Dacryocystorhinostomy (DCR) (by intubation)
(external) (intranasal) 09.81
Dacryocystostomy 09.53
Dacryocystosyringotomy 09.53
Dacryocystotomy 09.53
Dahlman operation (excision of esophageal
diverticulum) 42.31
Dana operation (posterior rhizotomy) 03.1

Danforth operation (fetal) 73.8
Darrach operation (ulnar resection) 77.83
Davis operation (intubated ureterotomy) 56.2
Deaf training 95.49
Debridement
abdominal wall 54.3
bone (*see also* Excision, lesion, bone) 77.60
fracture — *see* Debridement, open fracture
brain 01.59
burn (skin) 86.28
excisional 86.22
nonexcisional 86.28
bursa 83.5 •
cerebral meninges 01.51
dental 96.54
fascia 83.39 •
flap graft 86.75
graft (flap) (pedicle) 86.75
heart valve (calcified) — *see* Valvuloplasty,
heart
infection (skin) 86.28
excisional 86.22
nail (bed) (fold) 86.27
nonexcisional 86.28
joint — *see* Excision, lesion, joint
meninges (cerebral) 01.51
spinal 03.4
muscle 83.45
hand 82.36
nail (bed) (fold) 86.27
nerve (peripheral) 04.07
open fracture (compound) 79.60
arm NEC 79.62
carpal, metacarpal 79.63
facial bone 76.2
femur 79.65
fibula 79.66
foot NEC 79.67
hand NEC 79.63
humerus 79.61
leg NEC 79.66
phalanges
foot 79.68
hand 79.64
radius 79.62
specified site NEC 79.69
tarsal, metatarsal 79.67
tibia 79.66
ulna 79.62
patella 77.66
pedicle graft 86.75
skin or subcutaneous tissue (burn) (infection)
(wound) 86.28
cardioverter/defibrillator (automatic) pocket
37.99
excisional 86.22
graft 86.75
nail, nail bed, or nail fold 86.27
nonexcisional 86.28
pacemaker pocket 37.79
pocket
cardiac pacemaker 37.79
cardioverter/defibrillator (automatic)
37.99
skull 01.25
compound fracture 02.02
spinal cord (meninges) 03.4
wound (skin) 86.28
excisional 86.22
nonexcisional 86.28
Decapitation, fetal 73.8
Decapsulation, kidney 55.91
Declotting — *see also* Removal, thrombus
arteriovenous cannula or shunt 39.49
Decompression
anus (imperforate) 48.0
biliary tract 51.49
by intubation 51.43
endoscopic 51.87
percutaneous 51.98
brain 01.24
carpal tunnel 04.43
cauda equina 03.09
chamber 93.97

Decompression — *continued*
colon 96.08
by incision 45.03
endoscopic (balloon) 46.85
common bile duct 51.42
by intubation 51.43
endoscopic 51.87
percutaneous 51.98
cranial 01.24
for skull fracture 02.02
endolymphatic sac 20.79
ganglion (peripheral) NEC 04.49
cranial NEC 04.42
gastric 96.07
heart 37.0
intestine 96.08
by incision 45.00
endoscopic (balloon) 46.85
intracranial 01.24
labyrinth 20.79
laminectomy 03.09
laminotomy 03.09
median nerve 04.43
muscle 83.02
hand 82.02
nerve (peripheral) NEC 04.49
auditory 04.42
cranial NEC 04.42
median 04.43
trigeminal (root) 04.41
orbit (*see also* Orbitotomy) 16.09
pancreatic duct 52.92
endoscopic 52.93
pericardium 37.0
rectum 48.0
skull fracture 02.02
spinal cord (canal) 03.09
tarsal tunnel 04.44
tendon (sheath) 83.01
hand 82.01
thoracic outlet
by
myotomy (division of scalenus anticus
muscle) 83.19
tenotomy 83.13
trigeminal (nerve root) 04.41
Decortication
arterial 05.25
brain 01.51
cerebral meninges 01.51
heart 37.31
kidney 55.91
lung (partial) (total) 34.51
nasal turbinates — *see* Turbinectomy
nose 21.89
ovary 65.29
laparoscopic 65.25
periarterial 05.25
pericardium 37.31
ventricle, heart (complete) 37.31
Decoy, E2F 00.16
Deepening
alveolar ridge 24.5
buccolabial sulcus 24.91
lingual sulcus 24.91
Defatting, flap or pedicle graft 86.75
Defibrillation, electric (external) (internal) 99.62
automatic cardioverter/defibrillator — *see*
category 37.9 ☑
de Grandmont operation (tarsectomy) 08.35
Delaying of pedicle graft 86.71
Delivery (with)
assisted spontaneous 73.59
breech extraction (assisted) 72.52
partial 72.52
with forceps to aftercoming head 72.51
total 72.54
with forceps to aftercoming head 72.53
unassisted (spontaneous delivery) — *omit
code*
cesarean section — *see* Cesarean section
Credé maneuver 73.59
De Lee maneuver 72.4

Delivery — *continued*
forceps 72.9
application to aftercoming head (Piper) 72.6
with breech extraction
partial 72.51
total 72.53
Barton's 72.4
failed 73.3
high 72.39
with episiotomy 72.31
low (outlet) 72.0
with episiotomy 72.1
mid 72.29
with episiotomy 72.21
outlet (low) 72.0
with episiotomy 72.1
rotation of fetal head 72.4
trial 73.3
instrumental NEC 72.9
specified NEC 72.8
key-in-lock rotation 72.4
Kielland rotation 72.4
Malström's extraction 72.79
with episiotomy 72.71
manually assisted (spontaneous) 73.59
spontaneous (unassisted) 73.59
assisted 73.59
vacuum extraction 72.79
with episiotomy 72.71

Delorme operation
pericardiectomy 37.31
proctopexy 48.76
repair of prolapsed rectum 48.76
thoracoplasty 33.34

Denervation
aortic body 39.8
carotid body 39.8
facet, percutaneous (radiofrequency) 03.96
ovarian 65.94
paracervical uterine 69.3
uterosacral 69.3

Denker operation (radical maxillary antrotomy) 22.31

Dennis-Barco operation — *see* Repair, hernia, femoral

Denonvillier operation (limited rhinoplasty) 21.86

Densitometry, bone (serial) (radiographic) 88.98

Depilation, skin 86.92

Derlacki operation (tympanoplasty) 19.4

Dermabond 86.59

Dermabrasion (laser) 86.25
for wound debridement 86.28

Derotation — *see* Reduction, torsion

Desensitization
allergy 99.12
psychologic 94.33

Desmotomy (*see also* Division, ligament) 80.40

Destruction
breast 85.20
chorioretinopathy (*see also* Destruction, lesion, choroid) 14.29
ciliary body 12.74
epithelial downgrowth, anterior chamber 12.93
fallopian tube 66.39
with
crushing (and ligation) 66.31
by endoscopy (laparoscopy) 66.21
division (and ligation) 66.32
by endoscopy (culdoscopy)
(hysteroscopy) (laparoscopy)
(peritoneoscopy) 66.22
ligation 66.39
with
crushing 66.31
by endoscopy (laparoscopy) 66.21
division 66.32
by endoscopy (culdoscopy)
(hysteroscopy)
(laparoscopy)
(peritoneoscopy) 66.22
fetus 73.8

Destruction — *continued*
hemorrhoids 49.49
by
cryotherapy 49.44
sclerotherapy 49.42
inner ear NEC 20.79
by injection 20.72
intervertebral disc (NOS) 80.50
by injection 80.52
by other specified method 80.59
herniated (nucleus pulposus) 80.51
lacrimal sac 09.6
lesion (local)
anus 49.39
endoscopic 49.31
Bartholin's gland 71.24
by
aspiration 71.21
excision 71.24
incision 71.22
marsupialization 71.23
biliary ducts 51.69
endoscopic 51.64
bladder 57.59
transurethral 57.49
bone — *see* Excision, lesion, bone
bowel — *see* Destruction, lesion, intestine
brain (transtemporal approach) NEC 01.59
by stereotactic radiosurgery 92.30
cobalt 60 92.32
linear accelerator (LINAC) 92.31
multi-source 92.32
particle beam 92.33
particulate 92.33
radiosurgery NEC 92.39
single source photon 92.31
breast NEC 85.20
bronchus NEC 32.09
endoscopic 32.01
cerebral NEC 01.59
meninges 01.51
cervix 67.39
by
cauterization 67.32
cryosurgery, cryoconization 67.33
electroconization 67.32
choroid 14.29
by
cryotherapy 14.22
diathermy 14.21
implantation of radiation source 14.27
photocoagulation 14.25
laser 14.24
xenon arc 14.23
radiation therapy 14.26
ciliary body (nonexcisional) 12.43
by excision 12.44
conjunctiva 10.32
by excision 10.31
cornea NEC 11.49
by
cryotherapy 11.43
electrocauterization 11.42
thermocauterization 11.42
cul-de-sac 70.32
duodenum NEC 45.32
by excision 45.31
endoscopic 45.30
endoscopic 45.30
esophagus (chemosurgery) (cryosurgery)
(electroresection) (fulguration) NEC
42.39
by excision 42.32
endoscopic 42.33
endoscopic 42.33
eye NEC 16.93
eyebrow 08.25
eyelid 08.25
excisional — *see* Excision, lesion, eyelid
heart 37.33
by catheter ablation 37.34
intestine (large) 45.49
by excision 45.41
endoscopic 45.43
polypectomy 45.42

Destruction — *continued*
lesion — *continued*
intestine — *continued*
endoscopic 45.43
polypectomy 45.42
small 45.34
by excision 45.33
intranasal 21.31
iris (nonexcisional) NEC 12.41
by excision 12.42
kidney 55.39
by marsupialization 55.31
lacrimal sac 09.6
larynx 30.09
liver 50.29
lung 32.29
endoscopic 32.28
meninges (cerebral) 01.51
spinal 03.4
nerve (peripheral) 04.07
sympathetic 05.29
nose 21.30
intranasal 21.31
specified NEC 21.32
ovary
by
aspiration 65.91
excision 65.29
laparoscopic 65.25
cyst by rupture (manual) 65.93
palate (bony) (local) 27.31
wide 27.32
pancreas 52.22
by marsupialization 52.3
endoscopic 52.21
pancreatic duct 52.22
endoscopic 52.21
penis 64.2
pharynx (excisional) 29.39
pituitary gland
by stereotactic radiosurgery 92.30
cobalt 60 92.32
linear accelerator (LINAC) 92.31
multi-source 92.32
particle beam 92.33
particulate 92.33
radiosurgery NEC 92.39
single source photon 92.31
rectum (local) 48.32
by
cryosurgery 48.34
electrocoagulation 48.32
excision 48.35
fulguration 48.32
laser (Argon) 48.33
polyp 48.36
radical 48.31
retina 14.29
by
cryotherapy 14.22
diathermy 14.21
implantation of radiation source 14.27
photocoagulation 14.25
laser 14.24
xenon arc 14.23
radiation therapy 14.26
salivary gland NEC 26.29
by marsupialization 26.21
sclera 12.84
scrotum 61.3
skin NEC 86.3
sphincter of Oddi 51.69
endoscopic 51.64
spinal cord (meninges) 03.4
spleen 41.42
by marsupialization 41.41
stomach NEC 43.49
by excision 43.42
endoscopic 43.41
endoscopic 43.41
subcutaneous tissue NEC 86.3
testis 62.2
tongue 25.1
urethra (excisional) 58.39
endoscopic 58.31
uterus 68.29

Destruction — *continued*
nerve (cranial) (peripheral) (by cryoanalgesia)
(by radiofrequency) 04.2
sympathetic, by injection of neurolytic agent
05.32
neuroma
acoustic 04.01
by craniotomy 04.01
by stereotactic radiosurgery 92.30
cobalt 60 92.32
linear accelerator (LINAC) 92.31
multi-source 92.32
particle beam 92.33
particulate 92.33
radiosurgery NEC 92.39
single source photon 92.31
cranial 04.07
Morton's 04.07
peripheral
Morton's 04.07
prostate (prostatic tissue)
by
cryotherapy 60.62
microwave 60.96
radiofrequency 60.97
transurethral microwave thermotherapy
(TUMT) 60.96
transurethral needle ablation (TUNA) 60.97
TULIP (transurethral (ultrasound) guided
laser induced prostatectomy) 60.21
TUMT (transurethral microwave
thermotherapy) 60.96
TUNA (transurethral needle ablation) 60.97
semicircular canals, by injection 20.72
vestibule, by injection 20.72
Detachment, uterosacral ligaments 69.3
Determination
mental status (clinical) (medicolegal)
(psychiatric) NEC 94.11
psychologic NEC 94.09
vital capacity (pulmonary) 89.37
Detorsion
intestine (twisted) (volvulus) 46.80
large 46.82
endoscopic (balloon) 46.85
small 46.81
kidney 55.84
ovary 65.95
spermatic cord 63.52
with orchiopexy 62.5
testis 63.52
with orchiopexy 62.5
volvulus 46.80
endoscopic (balloon) 46.85
Detoxification therapy 94.25
alcohol 94.62
with rehabilitation 94.63
combined alcohol and drug 94.68
with rehabilitation 94.69
drug 94.65
with rehabilitation 94.66
combined alcohol and drug 94.68
with rehabilitation 94.69
Devascularization, stomach 44.99
Device
CorCap™ 37.41 •
external fixator — *see* Fixator, external •
Dewebbing
esophagus 42.01
syndactyly (fingers) (toes) 86.85
Dextrorotation — *see* Reduction, torsion
Dialysis
hemodiafiltration, hemofiltration
(extracorporeal) 39.95
kidney (extracorporeal) 39.95
liver 50.92
peritoneal 54.98
renal (extracorporeal) 39.95
Diaphanoscopy
nasal sinuses 89.35
skull (newborn) 89.16
Diaphysectomy — *see* category 77.8 ☑
Diathermy 93.34
choroid — *see* Diathermy, retina

Diathermy — *continued*
nasal turbinates 21.61
retina
for
destruction of lesion 14.21
reattachment 14.51
repair of tear 14.31
surgical — *see* Destruction, lesion, by site
turbinates (nasal) 21.61
Dickson operation (fascial transplant) 83.82
Dickson-Diveley operation (tendon transfer and
arthrodesis to correct claw toe) 77.57
Dieffenbach operation (hip disarticulation) 84.18
Dilation
achalasia 42.92
ampulla of Vater 51.81
endoscopic 51.84
anus, anal (sphincter) 96.23
biliary duct
endoscopic 51.84
pancreatic duct 52.99
endoscopic 52.98
percutaneous (endoscopy) 51.98
sphincter
of Oddi 51.81
endoscopic 51.84
pancreatic 51.82
endoscopic 51.85
bladder 96.25
neck 57.92
bronchus 33.91
cervix (canal) 67.0
obstetrical 73.1
to assist delivery 73.1
choanae (nasopharynx) 29.91
colon (endoscopic) (balloon) 46.85
colostomy stoma 96.24
duodenum (endoscopic) (balloon) 46.85
endoscopic — *see* Dilation, by site
enterostomy stoma 96.24
esophagus (by bougie) (by sound) 42.92
fallopian tube 66.96
foreskin (newborn) 99.95
frontonasal duct 96.21
gastrojejunostomy site, endoscopic 44.22
heart valve — *see* Valvulotomy, heart
ileostomy stoma 96.24
ileum (endoscopic) (balloon) 46.85
intestinal stoma (artificial) 96.24
intestine (endoscopic) (balloon) 46.85
jejunum (endoscopic) (balloon) 46.85
lacrimal
duct 09.42
punctum 09.41
larynx 31.98
lymphatic structure(s) (peripheral) 40.9
nares 21.99
nasolacrimal duct (retrograde) 09.43
with insertion of tube or stent 09.44
nasopharynx 29.91
pancreatic duct 52.99
endoscopic 52.98
pharynx 29.91
prostatic urethra (transurethral) (balloon) 60.95
punctum, lacrimal papilla 09.41
pylorus
by incision 44.21
endoscopic 44.22
rectum 96.22
salivary duct 26.91
sphenoid ostia 22.52
sphincter
anal 96.23
cardiac 42.92
of Oddi 51.81
endoscopic 51.84
pancreatic 51.82
endoscopic 51.85
pylorus, endoscopic 44.22
by incision 44.21
Stenson's duct 26.91
trachea 31.99
ureter 59.8
meatus 56.91
ureterovesical orifice 59.8

Dilation — *continued*
urethra 58.6
prostatic (transurethral) (balloon) 60.95
urethrovesical junction 58.6
vagina (instrumental) (manual) NEC 96.16
vesical neck 57.92
Wharton's duct 26.91
Wirsung's duct 52.99
endoscopic 52.98
Dilation and curettage, uterus (diagnostic) 69.09
after
abortion 69.02
delivery 69.02
to terminate pregnancy 69.01
Diminution, ciliary body 12.74
Disarticulation 84.91
ankle 84.13
elbow 84.06
finger, except thumb 84.01
thumb 84.02
hip 84.18
knee 84.16
shoulder 84.08
thumb 84.02
toe 84.11
wrist 84.04
Discectomy — *see* Diskectomy
Discission
capsular membrane 13.64
cataract (Wheeler knife) (Ziegler knife) 13.2
congenital 13.69
secondary membrane 13.64
iris 12.12
lens (capsule) (Wheeler knife) (Ziegler knife)
(with capsulotomy) 13.2
orbitomaxillary, radical 16.51
pupillary 13.2
secondary membrane (after cataract) 13.64
vitreous strands (posterior approach) 14.74
anterior approach 14.73
Discogram, diskogram 87.21
Discolysis (by injection) 80.52
Diskectomy (discectomy), intervertebral 80.51
herniated (nucleus pulposus) 80.51
percutaneous 80.59
Dispensing (with fitting)
contact lens 95.32
low vision aids NEC 95.33
spectacles 95.31
Dissection — *see also* Excision
aneurysm 38.60
artery-vein-nerve bundle 39.91
branchial cleft fistula or sinus 29.52
bronchus 32.1
femoral hernia 53.29
groin, radical 40.54
larynx block (en bloc) 30.3
mediastinum with pneumonectomy 32.5
neck, radical 40.40
with laryngectomy 30.4
bilateral 40.42
unilateral 40.41
orbital fibrous bands 16.92
pterygium (with reposition) 11.31
radical neck — *see* Dissection, neck, radical
retroperitoneal NEC 59.00
thoracic structures (block) (en bloc) (radical)
(brachial plexus, bronchus, lobe of lung,
ribs, and sympathetic nerves) 32.6
vascular bundle 39.91
Distention, bladder (therapeutic) (intermittent)
96.25
Diversion
biliopancreatic (BPD) 43.7 *[45.51] [45.91]*
with duodenal switch 43.89 *[45.51] [45.91]*
urinary
cutaneous 56.61
ileal conduit 56.51
internal NEC 56.71
ureter to
intestine 56.71
skin 56.61
uretero-ileostomy 56.51
Diversional therapy 93.81

Diverticulectomy

bladder (suprapubic) 57.59
  transurethral approach 57.49
duodenum 45.31
  endoscopic 45.30
esophagus 42.31
  endoscopic 42.33
esophagomyotomy 42.7
hypopharyngeal (by cricopharyngeal myotomy)
  29.32
intestine
  large 45.41
    endoscopic 45.43
  small 45.33
kidney 55.39
Meckel's 45.33
pharyngeal (by cricopharyngeal myotomy)
  29.32
pharyngoesophageal (by cricopharyngeal
  myotomy) 29.32
stomach 43.42
  endoscopic 43.41
urethra 58.39
  endoscopic 58.31

Division

Achilles tendon 83.11
adductor tendon (hip) 83.12
adhesions — see Lysis, adhesions
angle of mandible (open) 76.62
  closed 76.61
anterior synechiae 12.32
aponeurosis 83.13
arcuate ligament (spine) — omit code
arteriovenous fistula (with ligation) 39.53
artery (with ligation) 38.80
  abdominal 38.86
  aorta (arch) (ascending) (descending) 38.84
  head and neck NEC 38.82
  intracranial NEC 38.81
  lower limb 38.88
  thoracic NEC 38.85
  upper limb 38.83
bladder neck 57.91
blepharorrhaphy 08.02
blood vessels, cornea 10.1
bone (see also Osteotomy) 77.30
brain tissue 01.32
  cortical adhesions 02.91
canaliculus 09.52
canthorrhaphy 08.02
cartilage 80.40
  ankle 80.47
  elbow 80.42
  foot and toe 80.48
  hand and finger 80.44
  hip 80.45
  knee 80.46
  shoulder 80.41
  specified site NEC 80.49
  spine 80.49
  wrist 80.43
cerebral tracts 01.32
chordae tendineae 35.32
common wall between posterior left atrium and
  coronary sinus (with roofing of resultant
  defect with patch graft) 35.82
congenital web
  larynx 31.98
  pharynx 29.54
endometrial synechiae 68.21
fallopian tube — see Ligation, fallopian tube
fascia 83.14
  hand 82.12
frenulum, frenum
  labial 27.91
  lingual 25.91
  tongue 25.91
ganglion, sympathetic 05.0
glossopharyngeal nerve 29.92
goniosynechiae 12.31
hypophyseal stalk (see also Hypophysectomy,
  partial) 07.63
iliotibial band 83.14
isthmus
  horseshoe kidney 55.85

Division — continued
isthmus — continued
  thyroid 06.91
joint capsule 80.40
  ankle 80.47
  elbow 80.42
  foot and toe 80.48
  hand and finger 80.44
  hip 80.45
  knee 80.46
  shoulder 80.41
  specified site NEC 80.49
  wrist 80.43
labial frenum 27.91
lacrimal ductules 09.0
laryngeal nerve (external) (recurrent) (superior)
  31.91
ligament 80.40
  ankle 80.47
  arcuate (spine) — omit code
  canthal 08.36
  elbow 80.42
  foot and toe 80.48
  hand and finger 80.44
  hip 80.45
  knee 80.46
  palpebrae 08.36
  shoulder 80.41
  specified site NEC 80.49
  spine 80.49
    arcuate — omit code
    flavum — omit code
  uterosacral 69.3
  wrist 80.43
ligamentum flavum (spine) — omit code
meninges (cerebral) 01.31
muscle 83.19
  hand 82.19
nasolacrimal duct stricture (with drainage)
  09.59
nerve (cranial) (peripheral) NEC 04.03
  acoustic 04.01
  adrenal gland 07.42
  auditory 04.01
  glossopharyngeal 29.92
  lacrimal branch 05.0
  laryngeal (external) (recurrent) (superior)
    31.91
  phrenic 04.03
    for collapse of lung 33.31
  root, spinal or intraspinal 03.1
  sympathetic 05.0
  tracts
    cerebral 01.32
    spinal cord 03.29
      percutaneous 03.21
  trigeminal 04.02
  vagus (see also Vagotomy) 44.00
  vestibular 04.01
otosclerotic process or material, middle ear
  19.0
papillary muscle (heart) 35.31
patent ductus arteriosus 38.85
penile adhesions 64.93
posterior synechiae 12.33
pylorus (with wedge resection) 43.3
rectum (stricture) 48.91
scalenus anticus muscle 83.19
Skene's gland 71.3
soft tissue NEC 83.19
  hand 82.19
sphincter
  anal (external) (internal) 49.59
    left lateral 49.51
    posterior 49.52
  cardiac 42.7
  of Oddi 51.82
    endoscopic 51.85
  pancreatic 51.82
    endoscopic 51.85
spinal
  cord tracts 03.29
    percutaneous 03.21
  nerve root 03.1
symblepharon (with insertion of conformer)
  10.5

Division — continued
synechiae
  endometrial 68.21
  iris (posterior) 12.33
    anterior 12.32
tarsorrhaphy 08.02
tendon 83.13
  Achilles 83.11
  adductor (hip) 83.12
  hand 82.11
trabeculae carneae cordis (heart) 35.35
tympanum 20.23
uterosacral ligaments 69.3
vaginal septum 70.14
vas deferens 63.71
vein (with ligation) 38.80
  abdominal 38.87
  head and neck NEC 38.82
  intracranial NEC 38.81
  lower limb 38.89
    varicose 38.59
  thoracic NEC 38.85
  upper limb 38.83
  varicose 38.50
    abdominal 38.57
    head and neck NEC 38.52
    intracranial NEC 38.51
    lower limb 38.59
    thoracic NEC 38.55
    upper limb 38.53
vitreous, cicatricial bands (posterior approach)
  14.74
  anterior approach 14.73

Doleris operation (shortening of round ligaments)
  69.22
D'Ombrain operation (excision of pterygium with
  corneal graft) 11.32
Domestic tasks therapy 93.83
Dopplergram, Doppler flow mapping — see also
  Ultrasonography
  aortic arch 88.73
  head and neck 88.71
  heart 88.72
  thorax NEC 88.73
Dorrance operation (push-back operation for cleft
  palate) 27.62
Dotter operation (transluminal angioplasty)
  39.59
Douche, vagina 96.44
Douglas' operation (suture of tongue to lip for
  micrognathia) 25.59
Doyle operation (paracervical uterine
  denervation) 69.3
Drainage
  by
    anastomosis — see Anastomosis
    aspiration — see Aspiration
    incision — see Incision
  abdomen 54.19
    percutaneous 54.91
  abscess — see also Drainage, by site and
      Incision, by site
    appendix 47.2
      with appendectomy 47.09
        laparoscopic 47.01
    parapharyngeal (oral) (transcervical) 28.0
    peritonsillar (oral) (transcervical) 28.0
    retropharyngeal (oral) (transcervical) 28.0
    thyroid (field) (gland) 06.09
      percutaneous (needle) 06.01
      postoperative 06.02
    tonsil, tonsillar (oral) (transcervical) 28.0
  antecubital fossa 86.04
  appendix 47.91
    with appendectomy 47.09
      laparoscopic 47.01
    abscess 47.2
      with appendectomy 47.09
        laparoscopic 47.01
  axilla 86.04
  bladder (without incision) 57.0
    by indwelling catheter 57.94
      percutaneous suprapubic (closed) 57.17
      suprapubic NEC 57.18

Diverticulectomy — Drainage

Index

Drainage — *continued*
buccal space 27.0
bursa 83.03
by aspiration 83.94
hand 82.92
hand 82.03
by aspiration 82.92
radial 82.03
ulnar 82.03
cerebrum, cerebral (meninges) (ventricle) (incision) (trephination) 01.39
by
anastomosis — *see* Shunt, ventricular
aspiration 01.09
through previously implanted catheter 01.02
chest (closed) 34.04
open (by incision) 34.09
cranial sinus (incision) (trephination) 01.21
by aspiration 01.09
cul-de-sac 70.12
by aspiration 70.0
cyst — *see also* Drainage, by site *and* Incision, by site
pancreas (by catheter) 52.01
by marsupialization 52.3
internal (anastomosis) 52.4
pilonidal 86.03
spleen, splenic (by marsupialization) 41.41
duodenum (tube) 46.39
by incision 45.01
ear
external 18.09
inner 20.79
middle (by myringotomy) 20.09
with intubation 20.01
epidural space, cerebral (incision) (trephination) 01.24
by aspiration 01.09
extradural space, cerebral (incision) (trephination) 01.24
by aspiration 01.09
extraperitoneal 54.0
facial region 27.0
fascial compartments, head and neck 27.0
fetal hydrocephalic head (needling) (trocar) 73.8
gallbladder 51.04
by
anastomosis 51.35
aspiration 51.01
incision 51.04
groin region (abdominal wall) (inguinal) 54.0
skin 86.04
subcutaneous tissue 86.04
hematoma — *see* Drainage, by site *and* Incision, by site
hydrocephalic head (needling) (trocar) 73.8
hypochondrium 54.0
intra-abdominal 54.19
iliac fossa 54.0
infratemporal fossa 27.0
intracranial space (epidural) (extradural) (incision) (trephination) 01.24
by aspiration 01.09
subarachnoid or subdural (incision) (trephination) 01.31
by aspiration 01.09
intraperitoneal 54.19
percutaneous 54.91
kidney (by incision) 55.01
by
anastomosis 55.86
catheter 59.8
pelvis (by incision) 55.11
liver 50.0
by aspiration 50.91
Ludwig's angina 27.0
lung (by incision) 33.1
by punch (needle) (trocar) 33.93
midpalmar space 82.04
mouth floor 27.0
mucocele, nasal sinus 22.00
by puncture 22.01
through natural ostium 22.02
omentum 54.19
percutaneous 54.91

Drainage — *continued*
ovary (aspiration) 65.91
by incision 65.09
laparoscopic 65.01
palmar space (middle) 82.04
pancreas (by catheter) 52.01
by anastomosis 52.96
parapharyngeal 28.0
paronychia 86.04
parotid space 27.0
pelvic peritoneum (female) 70.12
male 54.19
pericardium 37.0
perigastric 54.19
percutaneous 54.91
perineum
female 71.09
male 86.04
perisplenic tissue 54.19
percutaneous 54.91
peritoneum 54.19
pelvic (female) 70.12
percutaneous 54.91
peritonsillar 28.0
pharyngeal space, lateral 27.0
pilonidal cyst or sinus 86.03
pleura (closed) 34.04
open (by incision) 34.09
popliteal space 86.04
postural 93.99
postzygomatic space 27.0
pseudocyst, pancreas 52.3
by anastomosis 52.4
pterygopalatine fossa 27.0
retropharyngeal 28.0
scrotum 61.0
skin 86.04
spinal (canal) (cord) 03.09
by anastomosis — *see* Shunt, spinal
diagnostic 03.31
spleen 41.2
cyst (by marsupialization) 41.41
subarachnoid space, cerebral (incision) (trephination) 01.31
by aspiration 01.09
subcutaneous tissue 86.04
subdiaphragmatic 54.19
percutaneous 54.91
subdural space, cerebral (incision) (trephination) 01.31
by aspiration 01.09
subhepatic space 54.19
percutaneous 54.91
sublingual space 27.0
submental space 27.0
subphrenic space 54.19
percutaneous 54.91
supraclavicular fossa 86.04
temporal pouches 27.0
tendon (sheath) 83.01
hand 82.01
thenar space 82.04
thorax (closed) 34.04
open (by incision) 34.09
thyroglossal tract (by incision) 06.09
by aspiration 06.01
thyroid (field) (gland) (by incision) 06.09
by aspiration 06.01
postoperative 06.02
tonsil 28.0
tunica vaginalis 61.0
ureter (by catheter) 59.8
by
anastomosis NEC (*see also* Anastomosis, ureter) 56.79
incision 56.2
ventricle (cerebral) (incision) NEC 02.39
by
anastomosis — *see* Shunt, ventricular
aspiration 01.09
through previously implanted catheter 01.02
vertebral column 03.09
Drawing test 94.08
Dressing
burn 93.57

Dressing — *continued*
ulcer 93.56
wound 93.57
Drilling
bone — *see also* Incision, bone 77.10
ovary 65.99
Drotrecogin alfa (activated), infusion 00.11
Ductogram, mammary 87.35
Duhamel operation (abdominoperineal pull-through) 48.65
Dührssen's
incisions (cervix, to assist delivery) 73.93
operation (vaginofixation of uterus) 69.22
Dunn operation (triple arthrodesis) 81.12
Duodenectomy 45.62
with
gastrectomy — *see* Gastrectomy
pancreatectomy — *see* Pancreatectomy
Duodenocholedochotomy 51.51
Duodenoduodenostomy 45.91
proximal to distal segment 45.62
Duodenoileostomy 45.91
Duodenojejunostomy 45.91
Duodenoplasty 46.79
Duodenorrhaphy 46.71
Duodenoscopy 45.13
through stoma (artificial) 45.12
transabdominal (operative) 45.11
Duodenostomy 46.39
Duodenotomy 45.01
Dupuytren operation
fasciectomy 82.35
fasciotomy 82.12
with excision 82.35
shoulder disarticulation 84.08
Durabond 86.59
Duraplasty 02.12
Durham (-Caldwell) operation (transfer of biceps femoris tendon) 83.75
DuToit and Roux operation (staple capsulorrhaphy of shoulder) 81.82
DuVries operation (tenoplasty) 83.88
Dwyer operation
fasciotomy 83.14
soft tissue release NEC 83.84
wedge osteotomy, calcaneus 77.28

E

E2F decoy 00.16
Eagleton operation (extrapetrosal drainage) 20.22
ECG — *see* Electrocardiogram
Echocardiography 88.72
intracardiac (heart chambers) (ICE) 37.28
intravascular (coronary vessels) 00.24
transesophageal 88.72
monitoring (Doppler) (ultrasound) 89.68
Echoencephalography 88.71
Echography — *see* Ultrasonography
Echogynography 88.79
Echoplacentogram 88.78
ECMO (extracorporeal membrane oxygenation) 39.65
Eden-Hybinette operation (glenoid bone block) 78.01
Educational therapy (bed-bound children) (handicapped) 93.82
EEG (electroencephalogram) 89.14
monitoring (radiographic) (video) 89.19
Effler operation (heart) 36.2
Effleurage 93.39
EGD (esophagogastroduodenoscopy) 45.13
with closed biopsy 45.16
Eggers operation
tendon release (patellar retinacula) 83.13
tendon transfer (biceps femoris tendon) (hamstring tendon) 83.75
EKG (*see also* Electrocardiogram) 89.52

Index

Endoscopy — ESWL

Ethmoidectomy 22.63
Ethmoidotomy 22.51
Evacuation
  abscess — see Drainage, by site
  anterior chamber (eye) (aqueous) (hyphema)
    12.91
  cyst — see also Excision, lesion, by site
    breast 85.91
    kidney 55.01
    liver 50.29
  hematoma — see also Incision, hematoma
    obstetrical 75.92
      incisional 75.91
  hemorrhoids (thrombosed) 49.47
  pelvic blood clot (by incision) 54.19
    by
      culdocentesis 70.0
      culdoscopy 70.22
  retained placenta
    with curettage 69.02
    manual 75.4
  streptothrix from lacrimal duct 09.42
Evaluation (of)
  audiological 95.43
  cardiac rhythm device (CRT-D) (CRT-P) (AICD)
    (pacemaker) — see Interrogation
  criminal responsibility, psychiatric 94.11
  functional (physical therapy) 93.01
  hearing NEC 95.49
  orthotic (for brace fitting) 93.02
  prosthetic (for artificial limb fitting) 93.03
  psychiatric NEC 94.19
    commitment 94.13
  psychologic NEC 94.08
  testimentary capacity, psychiatric 94.11
Evans operation (release of clubfoot) 83.84
Evisceration
  eyeball 16.39
    with implant (into scleral shell) 16.31
  ocular contents 16.39
    with implant (into scleral shell) 16.31
  orbit (see also Exenteration, orbit) 16.59
  pelvic (anterior) (posterior) (partial) (total)
    (female) 68.8
    male 57.71
Evulsion
  nail (bed) (fold) 86.23
  skin 86.3
  subcutaneous tissue 86.3
Examination (for)
  breast
    manual 89.36
    radiographic NEC 87.37
    thermographic 88.85
    ultrasonic 88.73
  cervical rib (by x-ray) 87.43
  colostomy stoma (digital) 89.33
  dental (oral mucosa) (peridontal) 89.31
    radiographic NEC 87.12
  enterostomy stoma (digital) 89.33
  eye 95.09
    color vision 95.06
    comprehensive 95.02
    dark adaptation 95.07
    limited (with prescription of spectacles)
      95.01
    under anesthesia 95.04
  fetus, intrauterine 75.35
  general physical 89.7
  glaucoma 95.03
  gynecological 89.26
  hearing 95.47

Examination — continued
  microscopic (specimen) (of) 91.9 ☑

> Note — Use the following fourth-digit
> subclassification with categories 90-91 to
> identify type of examination:
>   1 bacterial smear
>   2 culture
>   3 culture and sensitivity
>   4 parasitology
>   5 toxicology
>   6 cell block and Papanicolaou smear
>   9 other microscopic examination

    adenoid 90.3 ☑
    adrenal gland 90.1 ☑
    amnion 91.4 ☑
    anus 90.9 ☑
    appendix 90.9 ☑
    bile ducts 91.0 ☑
    bladder 91.3 ☑
    blood 90.5 ☑
    bone 91.5 ☑
      marrow 90.6 ☑
    brain 90.0 ☑
    breast 91.6 ☑
    bronchus 90.4 ☑
    bursa 91.5 ☑
    cartilage 91.5 ☑
    cervix 91.4 ☑
    chest wall 90.4 ☑
    chorion 91.4 ☑
    colon 90.9 ☑
    cul-de-sac 91.1 ☑
    dental 90.8 ☑
    diaphragm 90.4 ☑
    duodenum 90.8 ☑
    ear 90.3 ☑
    endocrine gland NEC 90.1 ☑
    esophagus 90.8 ☑
    eye 90.2 ☑
    fallopian tube 91.4 ☑
    fascia 91.5 ☑
    female genital tract 91.4 ☑
    fetus 91.4 ☑
    gallbladder 91.0 ☑
    hair 91.6 ☑
    ileum 90.9 ☑
    jejunum 90.9 ☑
    joint fluid 91.5 ☑
    kidney 91.2 ☑
    large intestine 90.9 ☑
    larynx 90.3 ☑
    ligament 91.5 ☑
    liver 91.0 ☑
    lung 90.4 ☑
    lymph (node) 90.7 ☑
    meninges 90.0 ☑
    mesentery 91.1 ☑
    mouth 90.8 ☑
    muscle 91.5 ☑
    musculoskeletal system 91.5 ☑
    nails 91.6 ☑
    nerve 90.0 ☑
    nervous system 90.0 ☑
    nose 90.3 ☑
    omentum 91.1 ☑
    operative wound 91.7 ☑
    ovary 91.4 ☑
    pancreas 91.0 ☑
    parathyroid gland 90.1 ☑
    penis 91.3 ☑
    perirenal tissue 91.2 ☑
    peritoneum (fluid) 91.1 ☑
    periureteral tissue 91.2 ☑
    perivesical (tissue) 91.3 ☑
    pharynx 90.3 ☑
    pineal gland 90.1 ☑
    pituitary gland 90.1 ☑
    placenta 91.4 ☑
    pleura (fluid) 90.4 ☑
    prostate 91.3 ☑
    rectum 90.9 ☑
    retroperitoneum 91.1 ☑
    semen 91.3 ☑
    seminal vesicle 91.3 ☑

Examination — continued
  microscopic — continued
    sigmoid 90.9 ☑
    skin 91.6 ☑
    small intestine 90.9 ☑
    specified site NEC 91.8 ☑
    spinal fluid 90.0 ☑
    spleen 90.6 ☑
    sputum 90.4 ☑
    stomach 90.8 ☑
    stool 90.9 ☑
    synovial membrane 91.5 ☑
    tendon 91.5 ☑
    thorax NEC 90.4 ☑
    throat 90.3 ☑
    thymus 90.1 ☑
    thyroid gland 90.1 ☑
    tonsil 90.3 ☑
    trachea 90.4 ☑
    ureter 91.2 ☑
    urethra 91.3 ☑
    urine 91.3 ☑
    uterus 91.4 ☑
    vagina 91.4 ☑
    vas deferens 91.3 ☑
    vomitus 90.8 ☑
    vulva 91.4 ☑
  neurologic 89.13
  neuro-ophthalmology 95.03
  opthalmoscopic 16.21
  panorex, mandible 87.12
  pelvic (manual) 89.26
    instrumental (by pelvimeter) 88.25
    pelvimetric 88.25
  physical, general 89.7
  postmortem 89.8
  rectum (digital) 89.34
    endoscopic 48.23
      through stoma (artificial) 48.22
      transabdominal 48.21
  retinal disease 95.03
  specified type (manual) NEC 89.39
  thyroid field, postoperative 06.02
  uterus (digital) 68.11
    endoscopic 68.12
  vagina 89.26
    endoscopic 70.21
  visual field 95.05
Exchange transfusion 99.01
  intrauterine 75.2
Excision
  aberrant tissue — see Excision, lesion, by site
    of tissue origin
  abscess — see Excision, lesion, by site
  accessory tissue — see also Excision, lesion, by
    site of tissue origin
    lung 32.29
      endoscopic 32.28
    spleen 41.93
  adenoids (tag) 28.6
    with tonsillectomy 28.3
  adenoma — see Excision, lesion, by site
  adrenal gland (see also Adrenalectomy) 07.22
  ampulla of Vater (with reimplantation of
    common duct) 51.62
  anal papilla 49.39
    endoscopic 49.31
  aneurysm (arteriovenous) (see also
    Aneurysmectomy) 38.60
    coronary artery 36.91
    heart 37.32
    myocardium 37.32
    sinus of Valsalva 35.39
    ventricle (heart) 37.32
  anus (complete) (partial) 49.6
  aortic subvalvular ring 35.35
  apocrine gland 86.3
  aponeurosis 83.42
    hand 82.33
  appendiceal stump 47.09
    laparoscopic 47.01
  appendices epiploicae 54.4
  appendix (see also Appendectomy) 47.01, 47.09
    epididymis 63.3
    testis 62.2
  arcuate ligament (spine) — omit code

Excision — *continued*
  arteriovenous fistula (*see also*
    Aneurysmectomy) 38.60
  artery (*see also* Arteriectomy) 38.60
  Baker's cyst, knee 83.39
  Bartholin's gland 71.24
  basal ganglion 01.59
  bile duct 51.69
    endoscopic 51.64
  bladder — *see also* Cystectomy
  bleb (emphysematous), lung 32.29
    endoscopic 32.28
  blood vessel (*see also* Angiectomy) 38.60
  bone (ends) (partial), except facial — *see*
    category 77.8 ☑
    facial NEC 76.39
      total 76.45
        with reconstruction 76.44
    for graft (autograft) (homograft) — *see*
      category 77.7 ☑
    fragments (chips) (*see also* Incision, bone)
      77.10
    joint (*see also* Arthrotomy) 80.10
    necrotic (*see also* Sequestrectomy, bone)
      77.00
    heterotopic, from
      muscle 83.32
        hand 82.22
      skin 86.3
      tendon 83.31
        hand 82.21
    mandible 76.31
      with arthrodesis — *see* Arthrodesis
      total 76.42
        with reconstruction 76.41
    spur — *see* Excision, lesion, bone
    total, except facial — *see* category 77.9 ☑
      facial NEC 76.45
        with reconstruction 76.44
      mandible 76.42
        with reconstruction 76.41
  brain 01.59
    hemisphere 01.52
    lobe 01.53
  branchial cleft cyst or vestige 29.2
  breast (*see also* Mastectomy) 85.41
    aberrant tissue 85.24
    accessory 85.24
    ectopic 85.24
    nipple 85.25
      accessory 85.24
    segmental 85.23
    supernumerary 85.24
    wedge 85.21
  broad ligament 69.19
  bronchogenic cyst 32.09
    endoscopic 32.01
  bronchus (wide sleeve) NEC 32.1
  buccal mucosa 27.49
  bulbourethral gland 58.92
  bulbous tuberosities (mandible) (maxilla)
    (fibrous) (osseous) 24.31
  bunion (*see also* Bunionectomy) 77.59
  bunionette (with osteotomy) 77.54
  bursa 83.5
    hand 82.31
  canal of Nuck 69.19
  cardioma 37.33
  carotid body (lesion) (partial) (total) 39.8
  cartilage (*see also* Chondrectomy) 80.90
    intervertebral — *see* category 80.5 ☑
    knee (semilunar) 80.6
    larynx 30.29
    nasal (submucous) 21.5
  caruncle, urethra 58.39
    endoscopic 58.31
  cataract (*see also* Extraction, cataract) 13.19
    secondary membrane (after cataract) 13.65
  cervical
    rib 77.91
    stump 67.4
  cervix (stump) NEC 67.4
    cold (knife) 67.2
    conization 67.2
    cryoconization 67.33
    electroconization 67.32

Excision — *continued*
  chalazion (multiple) (single) 08.21
  cholesteatoma — *see* Excision, lesion, by site
  choroid plexus 02.14
  cicatrix (skin) 86.3
  cilia base 08.20
  ciliary body, prolapsed 12.98
  clavicle (head) (partial) 77.81
    total (complete) 77.91
  clitoris 71.4
  coarctation of aorta (end-to-end anastomosis)
    38.64
    with
      graft replacement (interposition)
        abdominal 38.44
        thoracic 38.45
        thoracoabdominal 38.45 [38.44]
  common
    duct 51.63
    wall between posterior and coronary sinus
      (with roofing of resultant defect with
      patch graft) 35.82
  condyle — *see* category 77.8 ☑
    mandible 76.5
  conjunctival ring 10.31
  cornea 11.49
    epithelium (with chemocauterization) 11.41
    for smear or culture 11.21
  costal cartilage 80.99
  cul-de-sac (Douglas') 70.92
  cusp, heart valve 35.10
    aortic 35.11
    mitral 35.12
    tricuspid 35.14
  cyst — *see also* Excision, lesion, by site
    apical (tooth) 23.73
      with root canal therapy 23.72
    Baker's (popliteal) 83.39
    breast 85.21
    broad ligament 69.19
    bronchogenic 32.09
      endoscopic 32.01
    cervix 67.39
    dental 24.4
    dentigerous 24.4
    epididymis 63.2
    fallopian tube 66.61
    Gartner's duct 70.33
    hand 82.22
    labia 71.3
    lung 32.29
      endoscopic 32.28
    mesonephric duct 69.19
    Morgagni
      female 66.61
      male 62.2
    müllerian duct 60.73
    nasolabial 27.49
    nasopalatine 27.31
      by wide excision 27.32
    ovary 65.29
      laparoscopic 65.25
    parovarian 69.19
    pericardium 37.31
    periodontal (apical) (lateral) 24.4
    popliteal (Baker's), knee 83.39
    radicular 24.4
    spleen 41.42
    synovial (membrane) 83.39
    thyroglossal (with resection of hyoid bone)
      06.7
    urachal (bladder) 57.51
      abdominal wall 54.3
    vagina (Gartner's duct) 70.33
  cystic
    duct remnant 51.61
    hygroma 40.29
  dentinoma 24.4
  diaphragm 34.81
  disc, intervertebral NOS 80.50
    herniated (nucleus pulposus) 80.51
    other specified (diskectomy) 80.51
  diverticulum
    ampulla of Vater 51.62
    anus 49.39
      endoscopic 49.31

Excision — *continued*
  diverticulum — *continued*
    bladder 57.59
      transurethral 57.49
    duodenum 45.31
      endoscopic 45.30
    esophagus (local) 42.31
      endoscopic 42.33
    hypopharyngeal (by cricopharyngeal
      myotomy) 29.32
    intestine
      large 45.41
        endoscopic 45.43
      small NEC 45.33
    Meckel's 45.33
    pharyngeal (by cricopharyngeal myotomy)
      29.32
    pharyngoesophageal (by cricopharyngeal
      myotomy) 29.32
    stomach 43.42
      endoscopic 43.41
    urethra 58.39
      endoscopic 58.31
    ventricle, heart 37.33
  duct
    müllerian 69.19
    paramesonephric 69.19
    thyroglossal (with resection of hyoid bone)
      06.7
  ear, external (complete) NEC 18.39
    partial 18.29
    radical 18.31
  ectopic
    abdominal fetus 74.3
    tissue — *see also* Excision, lesion, by site of
      tissue origin
      bone, from muscle 83.32
      breast 85.24
      lung 32.29
        endoscopic 32.28
      spleen 41.93
  empyema pocket, lung 34.09
  epididymis 63.4
  epiglottis 30.21
  epithelial downgrowth, anterior chamber (eye)
    12.93
  epulis (gingiva) 24.31
  esophagus (*see also* Esophagectomy) 42.40
  exostosis (*see also* Excision, lesion, bone) 77.60
    auditory canal, external 18.29
    facial bone 76.2
    first metatarsal (hallux valgus repair) — *see*
      Bunionectomy
  eye 16.49
    with implant (into Tenon's capsule) 16.42
      with attachment of muscles 16.41
  eyelid 08.20
    redundant skin 08.86
  falciform ligament 54.4
  fallopian tube — *see* Salpingectomy
  fascia 83.44
    for graft 83.43
      hand 82.34
    hand 82.35
      for graft 82.34
  fat pad NEC 86.3
    knee (infrapatellar) (prepatellar) 86.3
    scalene 40.21
  fibroadenoma, breast 85.21
  fissure, anus 49.39
    endoscopic 49.31
  fistula — *see also* Fistulectomy
    anal 49.12
    arteriovenous (*see also* Aneurysmectomy)
      38.60
    ileorectal 46.74
    lacrimal
      gland 09.21
      sac 09.6
    rectal 48.73
    vesicovaginal 57.84
  frenulum, frenum
    labial (lip) 27.41
    lingual (tongue) 25.92
  ganglion (hand) (tendon sheath) (wrist) 82.21
    gasserian 04.05

☑ Additional Digit Required — Refer to the Tabular List (Numeric Code Section) for Additional Digit Selection

Excision — Excision

Excision — *continued*
  lesion — *continued*
    muscle 83.32
      hand 82.22
      ocular 15.13
    myocardium 37.33
    nail 86.23
    nasal sinus 22.60
      antrum 22.62
        with Caldwell-Luc approach 22.61
        specified approach NEC 22.62
      ethmoid 22.63
      frontal 22.42
      maxillary 22.62
        with Caldwell-Luc approach 22.61
        specified approach NEC 22.62
      sphenoid 22.64
    nasopharynx 29.3 ☑
    nerve (cranial) (peripheral) 04.07
      sympathetic 05.29
    nonodontogenic 24.31
    nose 21.30
      intranasal 21.31
        polyp 21.31
      skin 21.32
      specified site NEC 21.32
    odontogenic 24.4
    omentum 54.4
    orbit 16.92
    ovary 65.29
      by wedge resection 65.22
        laparoscopic 65.24
      that by laparoscope 65.25
    palate (bony) 27.31
      by wide excision 27.32
      soft 27.49
    pancreas (local) 52.22
      endoscopic 52.21
    parathyroid 06.89
    parotid gland or duct NEC 26.29
    pelvic wall 54.3
    pelvirectal tissue 48.82
    penis 64.2
    pericardium 37.31
    perineum (female) 71.3
      male 86.3
    periprostatic tissue 60.82
    perirectal tissue 48.82
    perirenal tissue 59.91
    peritoneum 54.4
    perivesical tissue 59.91
    pharynx 29.39
      diverticulum 29.32
    pineal gland 07.53
    pinna 18.29
      radical 18.31
    pituitary (gland) (*see also* Hypophysectomy,
        partial) 07.63
      by stereotactic radiosurgery 92.30
        cobalt 60 92.32
        linear accelerator (LINAC) 92.31
        multi-source 92.32
        particle beam 92.33
        particulate 92.33
        radiosurgery NEC 92.39
        single source photon 92.31
    pleura 34.59
    pouch of Douglas 70.32
    preauricular (ear) 18.21
    presacral 54.4
    prostate (transurethral) 60.61
    pulmonary (fibrosis) 32.29
      endoscopic 32.28
    rectovaginal septum 48.82
    rectum 48.35
      polyp (endoscopic) 48.36
    retroperitoneum 54.4
    salivary gland or duct NEC 26.29
      en bloc 26.32
    sclera 12.84
    scrotum 61.3
    sinus (nasal) — *see* Excision, lesion, nasal
        sinus
    Skene's gland 71.3

Excision — *continued*
  lesion — *continued*
    skin 86.3
      breast 85.21
      nose 21.32
      radical (wide) (involving underlying or
          adjacent structure) (with flap
          closure) 86.4
      scrotum 61.3
    skull 01.6
    soft tissue NEC 83.39
      hand 82.29
    spermatic cord 63.3
    sphincter of Oddi 51.62
      endoscopic 51.64
    spinal cord (meninges) 03.4
    spleen (cyst) 41.42
    stomach NEC 43.42
      endoscopic 43.41
        polyp 43.41
      polyp (endoscopic) 43.41
    subcutaneous tissue 86.3
      breast 85.21
    subgingival 24.31
    sweat gland 86.3
    tendon 83.39
      hand 82.29
      ocular 15.13
      sheath 83.31
        hand 82.21
    testis 62.2
    thorax 34.4
    thymus 07.81
    thyroid 06.31
      substernal or transsternal route 06.51
    tongue 25.1
    tonsil 28.92
    trachea 31.5
    tunica vaginalis 61.92
    ureter 56.41
    urethra 58.39
      endoscopic 58.31
    uterine ligament 69.19
    uterosacral ligament 69.19
    uterus 68.29
    vagina 70.33
    vein 38.60
      abdominal 38.67
      head and neck NEC 38.62
      intracranial NEC 38.61
      lower limb 38.69
      thoracic NEC 38.65
      upper limb 38.63
    ventricle (heart) 37.33
    vocal cords 30.09
    vulva 71.3
  ligament (*see also* Arthrectomy) 80.90
    broad 69.19
    round 69.19
    uterine 69.19
    uterosacral 69.19
  ligamentum flavum (spine) — *omit code*
  lingual tonsil 28.5
  lip 27.43
  liver (partial) 50.22
  loose body
    bone — *see* Sequestrectomy, bone
    joint 80.10
  lung (complete) (with mediastinal dissection)
      32.5
    accessory or ectopic tissue 32.29
      endoscopic 32.28
    segmental 32.3
    specified type NEC 32.29
      endoscopic 32.28
    volume reduction surgery 32.22
    wedge 32.29
  lymph, lymphatic
    drainage area 40.29
      radical — *see* Excision, lymph, node,
          radical
      regional (with lymph node, skin,
          subcutaneous tissue, and fat) 40.3

Excision — *continued*
  lymph, lymphatic — *continued*
    node (simple) NEC 40.29
      with
        lymphatic drainage area (including
            skin, subcutaneous tissue, and
            fat) 40.3
        mastectomy — *see* Mastectomy,
            radical
        muscle and deep fascia — *see*
            Excision, lymph, node, radical
      axillary 40.23
        radical 40.51
        regional (extended) 40.3
      cervical (deep) (with excision of scalene
          fat pad) 40.21
        with laryngectomy 30.4
        radical (including muscle and deep
            fascia) 40.40
          bilateral 40.42
          unilateral 40.41
        regional (extended) 40.3
        superficial 40.29
      groin 40.24
        radical 40.54
        regional (extended) 40.3
      iliac 40.29
        radical 40.53
        regional (extended) 40.3
      inguinal (deep) (superficial) 40.24
        radical 40.54
        regional (extended) 40.3
      jugular — *see* Excision, lymph, node,
          cervical
      mammary (internal) 40.22
        external 40.29
          radical 40.59
          regional (extended) 40.3
        radical 40.59
          regional (extended) 40.3
      paratracheal — *see* Excision, lymph,
          node, cervical
      periaortic 40.29
        radical 40.52
        regional (extended) 40.3
      radical 40.50
        with mastectomy — *see* Mastectomy,
            radical
        specified site NEC 40.59
      regional (extended) 40.3
      sternal — *see* Excision, lymph, node,
          mammary
    structure(s) (simple) NEC 40.29
      radical 40.59
      regional (extended) 40.3
    lymphangioma (simple) — *see also* Excision,
        lymph, lymphatic, node 40.29
    lymphocele 40.29
    mastoid (*see also* Mastoidectomy) 20.49
    median bar, transurethral approach 60.29
    meibomian gland 08.20
    meniscus (knee) 80.6
      acromioclavicular 80.91
      jaw 76.5
      sternoclavicular 80.91
      temporomandibular (joint) 76.5
      wrist 80.93
    müllerian duct cyst 60.73
    muscle 83.45
      for graft 83.43
      hand 82.34
      hand 82.36
        for graft 82.34
    myositis ossificans 83.32
      hand 82.22
    nail (bed) (fold) 86.23
    nasolabial cyst 27.49
    nasopalatine cyst 27.31
      by wide excision 27.32
    neoplasm — *see* Excision, lesion, by site
    nerve (cranial) (peripheral) NEC 04.07
      sympathetic 05.29
    neuroma (Morton's) (peripheral nerve) 04.07
      acoustic
        by craniotomy 04.01

Exercise NEC — *continued*
 breathing 93.18
 musculoskeletal
  active NEC 93.12
  passive NEC 93.17
 neurologic 89.13
 passive musculoskeletal NEC 93.17
 resistive 93.13
Exfoliation, skin, by chemical 86.24
Exostectomy (*see also* Excision, lesion, bone)
  77.60
 first metatarsal (hallux valgus repair) — *see*
  Bunionectomy
 hallux valgus repair (with wedge osteotomy) —
  see Bunionectomy
Expiratory flow rate 89.38
Explant, explantation — *see* Removal
Exploration — *see also* Incision
 abdomen 54.11
 abdominal wall 54.0
 adrenal (gland) 07.41
  field 07.00
   bilateral 07.02
   unilateral 07.01
 artery 38.00
  abdominal 38.06
  aorta (arch) (ascending) (descending) 38.04
  head and neck NEC 38.02
  intracranial NEC 38.01
  lower limb 38.08
  thoracic NEC 38.05
  upper limb 38.03
 auditory canal, external 18.02
 axilla 86.09
 bile duct(s) 51.59
  common duct 51.51
   endoscopic 51.11
    for
     relief of obstruction 51.42
      endoscopic 51.84
     removal of calculus 51.41
      endoscopic 51.88
    laparoscopic 51.11
   for relief of obstruction 51.49
    endoscopic 51.84
 bladder (by incision) 57.19
  endoscopic 57.32
   through stoma (artificial) 57.31
 bone (*see also* Incision, bone) 77.10
 brain (tissue) 01.39
 breast 85.0
 bronchus 33.0
  endoscopic — *see* Bronchoscopy
 bursa 83.03
  hand 82.03
 carotid body 39.8
 carpal tunnel 04.43
 choroid 14.9
 ciliary body 12.44
 colon 45.03
 common bile duct 51.51
  endoscopic 51.11
   for
    relief of obstruction 51.42
     endoscopic 51.84
    removal of calculus 51.41
     endoscopic 51.88
 coronary artery 36.99
 cranium 01.24
 cul-de-sac 70.12
  endoscopic 70.22
 disc space 03.09
 duodenum 45.01
 endoscopic — *see* Endoscopy, by site
 epididymis 63.92
 esophagus (by incision) NEC 42.09
  endoscopic — *see* Esophagoscopy
 ethmoid sinus 22.51
 eyelid 08.09
 fallopian tube 66.01
 fascia 83.09
  hand 82.09
 flank 54.0
 fossa (superficial) NEC 86.09
  pituitary 07.71

Exploration — *see also* Incision — *continued*
 frontal sinus 22.41
 frontonasal duct 96.21
 gallbladder 51.04
 groin (region) (abdominal wall) (inguinal) 54.0
  skin and subcutaneous tissue 86.09
 heart 37.11
 hepatic duct 51.59
 hypophysis 07.72
 ileum 45.02
 inguinal canal (groin) 54.0
 intestine (by incision) NEC 45.00
  large 45.03
  small 45.02
 intrathoracic 34.02
 jejunum 45.02
 joint structures (*see also* Arthrotomy) 80.10
 kidney 55.01
  pelvis 55.11
 labia 71.09
 lacrimal
  gland 09.0
  sac 09.53
 laparotomy site 54.12
 larynx (by incision) 31.3
  endoscopic 31.42
 liver 50.0
 lung (by incision) 33.1
 lymphatic structure(s) (channel) (node) (vessel)
  40.0
 mastoid 20.21
 maxillary antrum or sinus (Caldwell-Luc
  approach) 22.39
 mediastinum 34.1
  endoscopic 34.22
 middle ear (transtympanic) 20.23
 muscle 83.02
  hand 82.02
 neck (*see also* Exploration, thyroid) 06.09
 nerve (cranial) (peripheral) NEC 04.04
  auditory 04.01
  root (spinal) 03.09
 nose 21.1
 orbit (*see also* Orbitotomy) 16.09
 pancreas 52.09
  endoscopic 52.13
 pancreatic duct 52.09
  endoscopic 52.13
 pelvis (by laparotomy) 54.11
  by colpotomy 70.12
 penis 64.92
 perinephric area 59.09
 perineum (female) 71.09
  male 86.09
 peripheral vessels
  lower limb
   artery 38.08
   vein 38.09
  upper limb (artery) (vein) 38.03
 periprostatic tissue 60.81
 perirenal tissue 59.09
 perivesical tissue 59.19
 petrous pyramid air cells 20.22
 pilonidal sinus 86.03
 pineal (gland) 07.52
  field 07.51
 pituitary (gland) 07.72
  fossa 07.71
 pleura 34.09
 popliteal space 86.09
 prostate 60.0
 rectum (*see also* Proctoscopy) 48.23
  by incision 48.0
 retroperitoneum 54.0
 retropubic 59.19
 salivary gland 26.0
 sclera (by incision) 12.89
 scrotum 61.0
 shunt
  ventriculoperitoneal at
   peritoneal site 54.95
   ventricular site 02.41
 sinus
  ethmoid 22.51
  frontal 22.41
  maxillary (Caldwell-Luc approach) 22.39

Exploration — *see also* Incision — *continued*
 sinus — *continued*
  sphenoid 22.52
  tract, skin and subcutaneous tissue 86.09
 skin 86.09
 soft tissue NEC 83.09
  hand 82.09
 spermatic cord 63.93
 sphenoidal sinus 22.52
 spinal (canal) (nerve root) 03.09
 spleen 41.2
 stomach (by incision) 43.0
  endoscopic — *see* Gastroscopy
 subcutaneous tissue 86.09
 subdiaphragmatic space 54.11
 superficial fossa 86.09
 tarsal tunnel 04.44
 tendon (sheath) 83.01
  hand 82.01
 testes 62.0
 thymus (gland) 07.92
  field 07.91
 thyroid (field) (gland) (by incision) 06.09
  postoperative 06.02
 trachea (by incision) 31.3
  endoscopic — *see* Tracheoscopy
 tunica vaginalis 61.0
 tympanum 20.09
  transtympanic route 20.23
 ureter (by incision) 56.2
  endoscopic 56.31
 urethra (by incision) 58.0
  endoscopic 58.22
 uterus (corpus) 68.0
  cervix 69.95
  digital 68.11
  postpartal, manual 75.7
 vagina (by incision) 70.14
  endoscopic 70.21
 vas deferens 63.6
 vein 38.00
  abdominal 38.07
  head and neck NEC 38.02
  intracranial NEC 38.01
  lower limb 38.09
  thoracic NEC 38.05
  upper limb 38.03
 vulva (by incision) 71.09
Exposure — *see also* Incision, by site
 tooth (for orthodontic treatment) 24.6
Expression, trachoma follicles 10.33
Exsanguination transfusion 99.01
Extension
 buccolabial sulcus 24.91
 limb, forced 93.25
 lingual sulcus 24.91
 mandibular ridge 76.43
Exteriorization
 esophageal pouch 42.12
 intestine 46.03
  large 46.03
  small 46.01
 maxillary sinus 22.9
 pilonidal cyst or sinus (open excision) (with
  partial closure) 86.21
Extirpation — *see also* Excision, by site
 aneurysm — *see* Aneurysmectomy
 arteriovenous fistula — *see* Aneurysmectomy
 lacrimal sac 09.6
 larynx 30.3
  with radical neck dissection (with
   synchronous thyroidectomy)(with
   synchronous tracheostomy) 30.4
 nerve, tooth (*see also* Therapy, root canal)
  23.70
 varicose vein (peripheral) (lower limb) 38.59
  upper limb 38.53
Extracorporeal
 circulation (regional), except hepatic 39.61
  hepatic 50.92
  percutaneous 39.66
 hemodialysis 39.95
 membrane oxygenation (ECMO) 39.65
 photopheresis, therapeutic 99.88

Extracorporeal — *continued*
  shockwave lithotripsy (ESWL) NEC 98.59
    bile duct 98.52
    bladder 98.51
    gallbladder 98.52
    kidney 98.51
    renal pelvis 98.51
    specified site NEC 98.59
    ureter 98.51
Extracranial-intracranial bypass [EC-IC] 39.28
Extraction
  breech (partial) 72.52
    with forceps to aftercoming head 72.51
    total 72.54
      with forceps to aftercoming head 72.53
  cataract 13.19
    after cataract (by)
      capsulectomy 13.65
      capsulotomy 13.64
      discission 13.64
      excision 13.65
      iridocapsulectomy 13.65
      mechanical fragmentation 13.66
      needling 13.64
      phacofragmentation (mechanical) 13.66
    aspiration (simple) (with irrigation) 13.3
    cryoextraction (intracapsular approach) 13.19
      temporal inferior route (in presence of fistulization bleb) 13.11
    curette evacuation (extracapsular approach) 13.2
    emulsification (and aspiration) 13.41
    erysiphake (intracapsular approach) 13.19
      temporal inferior route (in presence of fistulization bleb) 13.11
    extracapsular approach (with iridectomy) NEC 13.59
      by temporal inferior route (in presence of fistulization bleb) 13.51
      aspiration (simple) (with irrigation) 13.3
      curette evacuation 13.2
      emulsification (and aspiration) 13.41
      linear extraction 13.2
      mechanical fragmentation with aspiration by
        posterior route 13.42
        specified route NEC 13.43
      phacoemulsification (ultrasonic) (with aspiration) 13.41
      phacofragmentation (mechanical)
        with aspiration by
          posterior route 13.42
          specified route NEC 13.43
        ultrasonic (with aspiration) 13.41
      rotoextraction (mechanical) with aspiration by
        posterior route 13.42
        specified route NEC 13.43
    intracapsular (combined) (simple) (with iridectomy) (with suction) (with zonulolysis) 13.19
      by temporal inferior route (in presence of fistulization bleb) 13.11
    linear extraction (extracapsular approach) 13.2
    phacoemulsification (and aspiration) 13.41
    phacofragmentation (mechanical)
      with aspiration by
        posterior route 13.42
        specified route NEC 13.43
      ultrasonic 13.41
    rotoextraction (mechanical)
      with aspiration by
        posterior route 13.42
        specified route NEC 13.43
    secondary membranous (after cataract) (by)
      capsulectomy 13.65
      capsulotomy 13.64
      discission 13.64
      excision 13.65
      iridocapsulectomy 13.65
      mechanical fragmentation 13.66
      needling 13.64
      phacofragmentation (mechanical) 13.66

Extraction — *continued*
  common duct stones (percutaneous) (through sinus tract) (with basket) 51.96
  foreign body — *see* Removal, foreign body
  kidney stone(s), percutaneous 55.03
    with fragmentation procedure 55.04
  lens (eye) (*see also* Extraction, cataract) 13.19
  Malström's 72.79
    with episiotomy 72.71
  menstrual, menses 69.6
  milk from lactating breast (manual) (pump) 99.98
  tooth (by forceps) (multiple) (single) NEC 23.09
    with mucoperiosteal flap elevation 23.19
    deciduous 23.01
    surgical NEC (*see also* Removal, tooth, surgical) 23.19
  vacuum, fetus 72.79
    with episiotomy 72.71
  vitreous (*see also* Removal, vitreous) 14.72

F

Face lift 86.82
Facetectomy 77.89
Facilitation, intraocular circulation NEC 12.59
Failed (trial) forceps 73.3
Family
  counselling (medical) (social) 94.49
  therapy 94.42
Farabeuf operation (ischiopubiotomy) 77.39
Fasanella-Servatt operation (blepharoptosis repair) 08.35
Fasciaplasty — *see* Fascioplasty
Fascia sling operation — *see* Operation, sling
Fasciectomy 83.44
  for graft 83.43
    hand 82.34
  hand 82.35
    for graft 82.34
  palmar (release of Dupuytren's contracture) 82.35
Fasciodesis 83.89
  hand 82.89
Fascioplasty (*see also* Repair, fascia) 83.89
  hand (*see also* Repair, fascia, hand) 82.89
Fasciorrhaphy — *see* Suture, fascia
Fasciotomy 83.14
  Dupuytren's 82.12
    with excision 82.35
  Dwyer 83.14
  hand 82.12
  Ober-Yount 83.14
  orbital (*see also* Orbitotomy) 16.09
  palmar (release of Dupuytren's contracture) 82.12
    with excision 82.35
Fenestration
  aneurysm (dissecting), thoracic aorta 39.54
  aortic aneurysm 39.54
  cardiac valve 35.10
  chest wall 34.01
  ear
    inner (with graft) 20.61
      revision 20.62
    tympanic 19.55
  labyrinth (with graft) 20.61
  Lempert's (endaural) 19.9
  operation (aorta) 39.54
  oval window, ear canal 19.55
  palate 27.1
  pericardium 37.12
  semicircular canals (with graft) 20.61
  stapes foot plate (with vein graft) 19.19
    with incus replacement 19.11
  tympanic membrane 19.55
  vestibule (with graft) 20.61
Ferguson operation (hernia repair) 53.00
Fetography 87.81
Fetoscopy 75.31
Fiberoscopy — *see* Endoscopy, by site

Fibroidectomy, uterine 68.29
Fick operation (perforation of foot plate) 19.0
Filipuncture (aneurysm) (cerebral) 39.52
Filleting
  hammer toe 77.56
  pancreas 52.3
Filling, tooth (amalgam) (plastic) (silicate) 23.2
  root canal (*see also* Therapy, root canal) 23.70
Fimbriectomy (*see also* Salpingectomy, partial) 66.69
  Uchida (with tubal ligation) 66.32
Finney operation (pyloroplasty) 44.29
Fissurectomy, anal 49.39
  endoscopic 49.31
  skin (subcutaneous tissue) 49.04
Fistulectomy — *see also* Closure, fistula, by site
  abdominothoracic 34.83
  abdominouterine 69.42
  anus 49.12
  appendix 47.92
  bile duct 51.79
  biliary tract NEC 51.79
  bladder (transurethral approach) 57.84
  bone (*see also* Excision, lesion, bone) 77.60
  branchial cleft 29.52
  bronchocutaneous 33.42
  bronchoesophageal 33.42
  bronchomediastinal 34.73
  bronchopleural 34.73
  bronchopleurocutaneous 34.73
  bronchopleuromediastinal 34.73
  bronchovisceral 33.42
  cervicosigmoidal 67.62
  cholecystogastroenteric 51.93
  cornea 11.49
  diaphragm 34.83
  enterouterine 69.42
  esophagopleurocutaneous 34.73
  esophagus NEC 42.84
  fallopian tube 66.73
  gallbladder 51.93
  gastric NEC 44.63
  hepatic duct 51.79
  hepatopleural 34.73
  hepatopulmonary 34.73
  intestine
    large 46.76
    small 46.74
  intestinouterine 69.42
  joint (*see also* Excision, lesion, joint) 80.80
  lacrimal
    gland 09.21
    sac 09.6
  laryngotracheal 31.62
  larynx 31.62
  mediastinocutaneous 34.73
  mouth NEC 27.53
  nasal 21.82
    sinus 22.71
  nasolabial 21.82
  nasopharyngeal 21.82
  oroantral 22.71
  oronasal 21.82
  pancreas 52.95
  perineorectal 71.72
  perineosigmoidal 71.72
  perirectal, not opening into rectum 48.93
  pharyngoesophageal 29.53
  pharynx NEC 29.53
  pleura 34.73
  rectolabial 71.72
  rectourethral 58.43
  rectouterine 69.42
  rectovaginal 70.73
  rectovesical 57.83
  rectovulvar 71.72
  rectum 48.73
  salivary (duct) (gland) 26.42
  scrotum 61.42
  skin 86.3
  stomach NEC 44.63
  subcutaneous tissue 86.3
  thoracoabdominal 34.83
  thoracogastric 34.83
  thoracointestinal 34.83

☑ Additional Digit Required — Refer to the Tabular List (Numeric Code Section) for Additional Digit Selection

☑ Additional Digit Required — Refer to the Tabular List (Numeric Code Section) for Additional Digit Selection
▶◀ Revised Text   ● New Line   ▲ Revised Code

2006 ICD-9-CM   October 2005 • Volume 3 — 29

Formation — *continued*
  pocket
    cardiac ▶device (defibrillator) (pacemaker)◀
      with initial insertion of ▶cardiac device◀
        — *omit code*
      new site (skin) (subcutaneous) 37.79
      loop recorder 37.79   ●
    thalamic stimulator pulse generator
      with initial insertion of battery package —
        omit code
      new site (skin) (subcutaneous) 86.09
  pupil 12.39
    by iridectomy 12.14
  rectovaginal fistula 48.99
  reversed gastric tube (intrathoracic)
    (retrosternal) 42.58
    antesternal or antethoracic 42.68
  septal defect, interatrial 35.42
  shunt
    abdominovenous 54.94
    arteriovenous 39.93
    peritoneojugular 54.94
    peritoneo-vascular 54.94
    pleuroperitoneal 34.05
    transjugular intrahepatic portosystemic
      [TIPS] 39.1
  subcutaneous tunnel
    esophageal 42.86
      with anastomosis — *see* Anastomosis,
        esophagus, antesternal
    pulse generator lead wire 86.99
      with initial procedure — *omit code*
    thalamic stimulator pulse generator pocket
      with initial insertion of battery package —
        omit code
      new site (skin) (subcutaneous) 86.09
  syndactyly (finger) (toe) 86.89
  tracheoesophageal 31.95
  tubulovalvular fistula (Beck-Jianu) (Frank's)
    (Janeway) (Spivack's) (Ssabanejew-Frank)
    43.19
  uretero-ileostomy, cutaneous 56.51
  ureterostomy, cutaneous 56.61
    ileal 56.51
  urethrovaginal fistula 58.0
  window
    pericardial 37.12
    pleural (for drainage) 34.09
Fothergill (-Donald) operation (uterine
  suspension) 69.22
Fowler operation
  arthroplasty of metacarpophalangeal joint
    81.72
  release (mallet finger repair) 82.84
  tenodesis (hand) 82.85
  thoracoplasty 33.34
Fox operation (entropion repair with wedge
  resection) 08.43
Fracture, surgical (*see also* Osteoclasis) 78.70
  turbinates (nasal) 21.62
Fragmentation
  lithotriptor — *see* Lithotripsy
  mechanical
    cataract (with aspiration) 13.43
      posterior route 13.42
      secondary membrane 13.66
    secondary membrane (after cataract) 13.66
  ultrasonic
    cataract (with aspiration) 13.41
    stones, urinary (Kock pouch) 59.95
    urinary stones 59.95
      percutaneous nephrostomy 55.04
Franco operation (suprapubic cystotomy) 57.18
Frank operation (permanent gastrostomy) 43.19
Frazier (-Spiller) operation (subtemporal
  trigeminal rhizotomy) 04.02
Fredet-Ramstedt operation (pyloromyotomy)
  (with wedge resection) 43.3
Freeing
  adhesions — *see* Lysis, adhesions
  anterior synechiae (with injection of air or
    liquid) 12.32
  artery-vein-nerve bundle 39.91
  extraocular muscle, entrapped 15.7

Freeing — *continued*
  goniosynechiae (with injection of air or liquid)
    12.31
  intestinal segment for interposition 45.50
    large 45.52
    small 45.51
  posterior synechiae 12.33
  synechiae (posterior) 12.33
    anterior (with injection of air or liquid) 12.32
  vascular bundle 39.91
  vessel 39.91
Freezing
  gastric 96.32
  prostate 60.62
Frenckner operation (intrapetrosal drainage)
  20.22
Frenectomy
  labial 27.41
  lingual 25.92
  lip 27.41
  maxillary 27.41
  tongue 25.92
Frenotomy
  labial 27.91
  lingual 25.91
Frenulumectomy — *see* Frenectomy
Frickman operation (abdominal proctopexy)
  48.75
Frommel operation (shortening of uterosacral
  ligaments) 69.22
Fulguration — *see also* Electrocoagulation and
    Destruction, lesion, by site
  adenoid fossa 28.7
  anus 49.39
    endoscopic 49.31
  bladder (transurethral) 57.49
    suprapubic 57.59
  choroid 14.21
  duodenum 45.32
    endoscopic 45.30
  esophagus 42.39
    endoscopic 42.33
  large intestine 45.49
    endoscopic 45.43
      polypectomy 45.42
  penis 64.2
  perineum, female 71.3
  prostate, transurethral 60.29
  rectum 48.32
    radical 48.31
  retina 14.21
  scrotum 61.3
  Skene's gland 71.3
  skin 86.3
  small intestine NEC 45.34
    duodenum 45.32
      endoscopic 45.30
  stomach 43.49
    endoscopic 43.41
  subcutaneous tissue 86.3
  tonsillar fossa 28.7
  urethra 58.39
    endoscopic 58.31
  vulva 71.3
Function
  study — *see also* Scan, radioisotope
    gastric 89.39
    muscle 93.08
      ocular 95.25
    nasal 89.12
    pulmonary — *see* categories 89.37-89.38
    renal 92.03
    thyroid 92.01
    urethral sphincter 89.23
Fundectomy, uterine 68.39
Fundoplication (esophageal) (Nissen's) 44.66
  laparoscopic 44.67
Fundusectomy, gastric 43.89
Fusion
  atlas-axis (spine) — *see* Fusion, spinal, atlas-
    axis
  bone (*see also* Osteoplasty) 78.40
  cervical (spine) (C$_2$ level or below) — *see*
    Fusion, spinal, cervical

Fusion — *continued*
  claw toe 77.57
  craniocervical — *see* Fusion, spinal,
    craniocervical
  dorsal, dorsolumbar — *see* Fusion, spinal,
    dorsal, dorsolumbar
  epiphyseal-diaphyseal (*see also* Arrest, bone
    growth) 78.20
  epiphysiodesis (*see also* Arrest, bone growth)
    78.20
  hammer toe 77.56
  joint (with bone graft) (*see also* Arthrodesis)
    81.20
    ankle 81.11
    claw toe 77.57
    foot NEC 81.17
    hammer toe 77.56
    hip 81.21
    interphalangeal, finger 81.28
    ischiofemoral 81.21
    metatarsophalangeal 81.16
    midtarsal 81.14
    overlapping toe(s) 77.58
    pantalar 81.11
    spinal (*see also* Fusion, spinal) 81.00
    subtalar 81.13
    tarsal joints NEC 81.17
    tarsometatarsal 81.15
    tibiotalar 81.11
    toe NEC 77.58
      claw toe 77.57
      hammer toe 77.56
      overlapping toe(s) 77.58
  lip to tongue 25.59
  lumbar, lumbosacral — *see* Fusion, spinal,
    lumbar, lumbosacral
  occiput — C$_2$ (spinal) — *see* Fusion, spinal,
    occiput
  spinal (with graft) (with internal fixation) (with
    instrumentation) 81.00

  ┌───┐
  │ Note: Also use either 81.62, 81.63, or 81.64 │
  │ as an additional code to show the total   │
  │ number of vertebrae fused   │
  └───┘

    anterior lumbar interbody fusion (ALIF)   ●
      81.06   ●
    atlas-axis (anterior transoral) (posterior)
      81.01
      for pseudarthrosis 81.31
    cervical (C$_2$ level or below) NEC 81.02
      anterior (interbody), anterolateral
        technique 81.02
        for pseudarthrosis 81.32
      C$_1$-C$_2$ level (anterior) (posterior) 81.01
        for pseudarthrosis 81.31
      for pseudarthrosis 81.32
      posterior (interbody), posterolateral
        technique 81.03
        for pseudarthrosis 81.33
    craniocervical (anterior transoral)
      (posterior) 81.01
      for pseudarthrosis 81.31
    dorsal, dorsolumbar NEC 81.05
      anterior (interbody), anterolateral
        technique 81.04
        for pseudarthrosis 81.34
      for pseudarthrosis 81.35
      posterior (interbody), posterolateral
        technique 81.05
        for pseudarthrosis 81.35
    lumbar, lumbosacral NEC 81.08
      anterior (interbody), anterolateral
        technique 81.06
        for pseudarthrosis 81.36
      for pseudarthrosis 81.38
      lateral transverse process technique
        81.07
        for pseudarthrosis 81.37
      posterior (interbody), posterolateral
        technique 81.08
        for pseudarthrosis 81.38
    number of vertebrae — *see* codes 81.62-
      81.64
    occiput — C$_2$ (anterior transoral) (posterior)
      81.01
      for pseudarthrosis 81.31

Graft, grafting — *continued*
breast (*see also* Mammoplasty) 85.89
buccal sulcus 27.99
cartilage (joint) — *see also* Arthroplasty
    nose — *see* Graft, nose
chest wall (mesh) (silastic) 34.79
conjunctiva (free) (mucosa) 10.44
    for symblepharon repair 10.41
cornea (*see also* Keratoplasty) 11.60
dermal-fat 86.69
dermal regenerative 86.67
dura 02.12
ear
    auricle 18.79
external auditory meatus 18.6
    inner 20.61
    pedicle preparation 86.71
esophagus NEC 42.87
    with interposition (intrathoracic) NEC 42.58
        antesternal or antethoracic NEC 42.68
        colon (intrathoracic) 42.55
            antesternal or antethoracic 42.65
        small bowel (intrathoracic) 42.53
            antesternal or antethoracic 42.63
eyebrow (*see also* Reconstruction, eyelid, with
    graft) 08.69
eyelid (*see also* Reconstruction, eyelid, with
    graft) 08.69
    free mucous membrane 08.62
eye socket (skin) (cartilage) (bone) 16.63
fallopian tube 66.79
fascia 83.82
    with hernia repair — *see* Repair, hernia
    eyelid 08.32
    hand 82.72
    tarsal cartilage 08.69
fat pad NEC 86.89
    with skin graft — *see* Graft, skin, full-
        thickness
flap (advanced) (rotating) (sliding) — *see also*
    Graft, skin, pedicle
    tarsoconjunctival 08.64
hair-bearing skin 86.64
hand
    fascia 82.72
    free skin 86.62
    muscle 82.72
    pedicle (flap) 86.73
    tendon 82.79
heart, for revascularization — *see* category
    36.3 ☑
joint — *see* Arthroplasty
larynx 31.69
lip 27.56
    full-thickness 27.55
lymphatic structure(s) (channel) (node) (vessel)
    40.9
mediastinal fat to myocardium 36.39
meninges (cerebral) 02.12
mouth, except palate 27.56
    full-thickness 27.55
muscle 83.82
    hand 82.72
myocardium, for revascularization 36.39
nasolabial flaps 21.86
nerve (cranial) (peripheral) 04.5
nipple 85.86
nose 21.89
    with
        augmentation 21.85
        rhinoplasty — *see* Rhinoplasty
        total reconstruction 21.83
    septum 21.88
    tip 21.86
omentum 54.74
    to myocardium 36.39
orbit (bone) (cartilage) (skin) 16.63
outflow tract (patch) (pulmonary valve) 35.26
    in total repair of tetralogy of Fallot 35.81
ovary 65.92
palate 27.69
    for cleft palate repair 27.62
pedicle — *see* Graft, skin, pedicle
penis (rib) (skin) 64.49
pigskin 86.65
pinch — *see* Graft, skin, free

Graft, grafting — *continued*
pocket — *see* Graft, skin, pedicle
porcine 86.65
postauricular (Wolff) 18.79
razor — *see* Graft, skin, free
rope — *see* Graft, skin, pedicle
saphenous vein in aortocoronary bypass — *see*
    Bypass, aortocoronary
scrotum 61.49
skin (partial-thickness) (split-thickness) 86.69
    amnionic membrane 86.66
    auditory meatus (ear) 18.6
    dermal-fat 86.69
        for breast augmentation 85.50
    dermal regenerative 86.67
    ear
        auditory meatus 18.6
        postauricular 18.79
    eyelid 08.61
    flap — *see* Graft, skin, pedicle
    free (autogenous) NEC 86.60
        lip 27.56
        thumb 86.62
            for
                pollicization 82.61
                reconstruction 82.69
    full-thickness 86.63
        breast 85.83
        hand 86.61
    hair-bearing 86.64
        eyelid or eyebrow 08.63
    hand 86.62
        full-thickness 86.61
    heterograft 86.65
    homograft 86.66
    island flap 86.70
    mucous membrane 86.69
        eyelid 08.62
    nose — *see* Graft, nose
    pedicle (flap) (tube) 86.70
        advancement 86.72
        attachment to site (advanced) (double)
            (rotating) (sliding) 86.74
            hand (cross finger) (pocket) 86.73
            lip 27.57
            mouth 27.57
            thumb 86.73
               for
                  pollicization 82.61
                  reconstruction NEC 82.69
        breast 85.84
            transverse rectus abdominis
               musculocutaneous (TRAM) 85.7
        defatting 86.75
        delayed 86.71
        design and raising 86.71
        elevation 86.71
        preparation of (cutting) 86.71
        revision 86.75
        sculpturing 86.71
        transection 86.71
        transfer 86.74
        trimming 86.71
    postauricular 18.79
    rotation flap 86.70
    specified site NEC 86.69
        full-thickness 86.63
    tarsal cartilage 08.69
temporalis muscle to orbit 16.63
    with exenteration of orbit 16.59
tendon 83.81
    for joint repair — *see* Arthroplasty
    hand 82.79
testicle 62.69
thumb (for reconstruction) NEC 82.69
tongue (mucosal) (skin) 25.59
trachea 31.79
tubular (tube) — *see* Graft, skin, pedicle
tunnel — *see* Graft, skin, pedicle
tympanum (*see also* Tympanoplasty) 19.4
ureter 56.79
vein (patch) 39.58
    with
        excision or resection of vessel — *see*
            Phlebectomy, with graft
            replacement

Graft, grafting — *continued*
vein — *continued*
    with — *continued*
        synthetic patch (Dacron) (Teflon) 39.57
        tissue patch (vein) (autogenous)
            (homograft) 39.56
    vermilion border (lip) 27.56
Grattage, conjunctiva 10.31
Green operation (scapulopexy) 78.41
Grice operation (subtalar arthrodesis) 81.13
Grip, strength 93.04
Gritti-Stokes operation (knee disarticulation)
    84.16
Gross operation (herniorrhaphy) 53.49
Group therapy 94.44
Guttering, bone (*see also* Excision, lesion, bone)
    77.60
Guyon operation (amputation of ankle) 84.13

H

Hagner operation (epididymotomy) 63.92
Halsted operation — *see* Repair, hernia, inguinal
Hampton operation (anastomosis small intestine
    to rectal stump) 45.92
Hanging hip operation (muscle release) 83.19
Harelip operation 27.54
Harrison-Richardson operation (vaginal
    suspension) 70.77
Hartmann resection (of intestine) (with pouch) —
    see Colectomy, by site
Harvesting
    bone marrow 41.91
    stem cells 99.79
Hauser operation
    achillotenotomy 83.11
    bunionectomy with adductor tendon transfer
        77.53
    stabilization of patella 81.44
Heaney operation (vaginal hysterectomy) 68.59
    laparoscopically assisted (LAVH) 68.51
Hearing aid (with battery replacement) 95.49
Hearing test 95.47
Hegar operation (perineorrhaphy) 71.79
Heine operation (cyclodialysis) 12.55
Heineke-Mikulicz operation (pyloroplasty) 44.29
Heller operation (esophagomyotomy) 42.7
Hellström operation (transplantation of aberrant
    renal vessel) 39.55
Hemicolectomy
    left 45.75
    right (extended) 45.73
Hemicystectomy 57.6
Hemigastrectomy — *see* Gastrectomy
Hemiglossectomy 25.2
Hemilaminectomy (decompression) (exploration)
    03.09
Hemilaryngectomy (anterior) (lateral) (vertical)
    30.1
Hemimandibulectomy 76.31
Hemimastectomy (radical) 85.23
Hemimaxillectomy (with bone graft) (with
    prosthesis) 76.39
Heminephrectomy 55.4
Hemipelvectomy 84.19
Hemispherectomy (cerebral) 01.52
Hemithyroidectomy (with removal of isthmus)
    (with removal of portion of remaining lobe)
    06.2
Hemodiafiltration (extracorporeal) 39.95
Hemodialysis (extracorporeal) 39.95
Hemodilution 99.03
Hemofiltration (extracorporeal) 39.95
Hemorrhage control — *see* Control, hemorrhage
Hemorrhoidectomy 49.46
    by
        cautery, cauterization 49.43
        crushing 49.45

Hemorrhoidectomy — *continued*
  by — *continued*
    cryotherapy, cryosurgery 49.44
    excision 49.46
    injection 49.42
    ligation 49.45
Hemostasis — *see* Control, hemorrhage
Henley operation (jejunal transposition) 43.81
Hepatectomy (complete) (total) 50.4
  partial or subtotal 50.22
Hepatic assistance, extracorporeal 50.92
Hepaticocholangiojejunostomy 51.37
Hepaticocystoduodenostomy 51.37
Hepaticodochotomy 51.59
Hepaticoduodenostomy 51.37
Hepaticojejunostomy 51.37
Hepaticolithectomy 51.49
  endoscopic 51.88
Hepaticolithotomy 51.49
  endoscopic 51.88
Hepaticostomy 51.59
Hepaticotomy 51.59
Hepatocholangiocystoduodenostomy 51.37
Hepatocholedochostomy 51.43
  endoscopic 51.87
Hepatoduodenostomy 50.69
Hepatogastrostomy 50.69
Hepatojejunostomy 50.69
Hepatolithotomy
  hepatic duct 51.49
  liver 50.0
Hepatopexy 50.69
Hepatorrhaphy 50.61
Hepatostomy (external) (internal) 50.69
Hepatotomy (with packing) 50.0
Hernioplasty — *see* Repair, hernia
Herniorrhaphy — *see* Repair, hernia
Herniotomy — *see* Repair, hernia
Heterograft — *see* Graft
Heterotransplant, heterotransplantation — *see* Transplant
Hey operation (amputation of foot) 84.12
Hey-Groves operation (reconstruction of anterior cruciate ligament) 81.45
Heyman operation (soft tissue release for clubfoot) 83.84
Heyman-Herndon (-Strong) operation (correction of metatarsus varus) 80.48
Hibbs operation (lumbar spinal fusion) — *see* Fusion, lumbar
Higgins operation — *see* Repair, hernia, femoral
High forceps delivery 72.39
  with episiotomy 72.31
Hill-Allison operation (hiatal hernia repair, transpleural approach) 53.80
Hinging, mitral valve 35.12
His bundle recording 37.29
Hitchcock operation (anchoring tendon of biceps) 83.88
Hofmeister operation (gastrectomy) 43.7
Hoke operation
  midtarsal fusion 81.14
  triple arthrodesis 81.12
Holth operation
  iridencleisis 12.63
  sclerectomy 12.65
Homan operation (correction of lymphedema) 40.9
Homograft — *see* Graft
Homotransplant, homotransplantation — *see* Transplant
Hosiery, elastic 93.59
Hutch operation (ureteroneocystostomy) 56.74
Hybinette-Eden operation (glenoid bone block) 78.01
Hydrocelectomy
  canal of Nuck (female) 69.19
    male 63.1
  round ligament 69.19

Hydrocelectomy — *continued*
  spermatic cord 63.1
  tunica vaginalis 61.2
Hydrotherapy 93.33
  assisted exercise in pool 93.31
  whirlpool 93.32
Hymenectomy 70.31
Hymenoplasty 70.76
Hymenorrhaphy 70.76
Hymenotomy 70.11
Hyperalimentation (parenteral) 99.15
Hyperbaric oxygenation 93.95
  wound 93.59
Hyperextension, joint 93.25
Hyperthermia NEC 93.35
  for cancer treatment (interstitial) (local) (radiofrequency) (regional) (ultrasound) (whole-body) 99.85
Hypnodrama, psychiatric 94.32
Hypnosis (psychotherapeutic) 94.32
  for anesthesia — *omit code*
Hypnotherapy 94.32
Hypophysectomy (complete) (total) 07.69
  partial or subtotal 07.63
    transfrontal approach 07.61
    transsphenoidal approach 07.62
  specified approach NEC 07.68
  transfrontal approach (complete) (total) 07.64
    partial 07.61
  transsphenoidal approach (complete) (total) 07.65
    partial 07.62
Hypothermia (central) (local) 99.81
  gastric (cooling) 96.31
    freezing 96.32
  systemic (in open heart surgery) 39.62
Hypotympanotomy 20.23
Hysterectomy 68.9
  abdominal 68.4
    partial or subtotal (supracervical) (supravaginal) 68.39
    radical (modified) (Wertheim's) 68.6
  supracervical 68.39
    classic infrafascial SEMM hysterectomy (CISH) 68.31
    laparoscopically assisted (LASH) 68.31
  vaginal (complete) (partial) (subtotal) (total) 68.59
    laparoscopically assisted (LAVH) 68.51
    radical (Schauta) 68.7
Hysterocolpectomy (radical) (vaginal) 68.7
  abdominal 68.6
Hysterogram NEC 87.85
  percutaneous 87.84
Hysterolysis 54.59
  laparoscopic 54.51
Hysteromyomectomy 68.29
Hysteropexy 69.22
Hysteroplasty 69.49
Hysterorrhaphy 69.41
Hysterosalpingography gas (contrast) 87.82
  opaque dye (contrast) 87.83
Hysterosalpingostomy 66.74
Hysteroscopy 68.12
  with
    ablation
      endometrial 68.23
    biopsy 68.16
Hysterotomy (with removal of foreign body) (with removal of hydatidiform mole) 68.0
  for intrauterine transfusion 75.2
  obstetrical 74.99
    for termination of pregnancy 74.91
Hysterotrachelectomy 67.4
Hysterotracheloplasty 69.49
Hysterotrachelorrhaphy 69.41
Hysterotrachelotomy 69.95

I

ICCE (intracapsular cataract extraction) 13.19
Ileal
  bladder
    closed 57.87 *[45.51]*
      open (ileoureterostomy) 56.51
    conduit (ileoureterostomy) 56.51
Ileocecostomy 45.93
Ileocolectomy 45.73
Ileocolostomy 45.93
Ileocolotomy 45.00
Ileocystoplasty (isolated segment anastomosis) (open loop) 57.87 *[45.51]*
Ileoduodenotomy 45.01
Ileoectomy (partial) 45.62
  with cecectomy 45.72
Ileoentectropy 46.99
Ileoesophagostomy 42.54
Ileoileostomy 45.91
  proximal to distal segment 45.62
Ileoloopogram 87.78
Ileopancreatostomy 52.96
Ileopexy 46.61
Ileoproctostomy 45.93
Ileorectostomy 45.93
Ileorrhaphy 46.73
Ileoscopy 45.13
  through stoma (artificial) 45.12
  transabdominal (operative) 45.11
Ileosigmoidostomy 45.93
Ileostomy 46.20
  continent (permanent) 46.22
  for urinary diversion 56.51
  delayed opening 46.24
  Hendon (temporary) 46.21
  loop 46.01
  Paul (temporary) 46.21
  permanent 46.23
    continent 46.22
  repair 46.41
  revision 46.41
  tangential (temporary) 46.21
  temporary 46.21
  transplantation to new site 46.23
  tube (temporary) 46.21
  ureteral
    external 56.51
    internal 56.71
Ileotomy 45.02
Ileotransversostomy 45.93
Ileoureterostomy (Bricker's) (ileal bladder) 56.51
Imaging (diagnostic)
  diagnostic, not elsewhere classified 88.90
  endovascular ultrasound — *see* Imaging, intravascular ultrasound
  intraoperative
    iMRI — *see* Imaging, magnetic resonance
    intravascular — *see* Imaging, intravascular ultrasound
  intravascular ultrasound (IVUS) 00.29
    aorta 00.22
    aortic arch 00.22
    carotid vessel 00.21
    cerebral vessel, extracranial 00.21
    coronary vessel 00.24
    intrathoracic vessel 00.22
    other specified vessel 00.28
    peripheral vessel 00.23
    renal vessel 00.25
    vena cava (inferior) (superior) 00.22
  magnetic resonance (nuclear) (proton) NEC 88.97
    abdomen 88.97
    bladder (urinary) 88.95
    bone marrow blood supply 88.94
    brain (brain stem) 88.91
      intraoperative (iMRI) 88.96
      real-time 88.96
    chest (hilar) (mediastinal) 88.92
    computer assisted surgery (CAS) with MR/MRA 00.32
    extremity (upper) (lower) 88.94

Imaging — Implant, implantation

Imaging — *continued*
  magnetic resonance NEC — *continued*
    eye orbit 88.97
    face 88.97
    head NEC 88.97
    musculoskeletal 88.94
    myocardium 88.92
    neck 88.97
    orbit of eye 88.97
    prostate 88.95
    specified site NEC 88.97
    spinal canal (cord) (spine) 88.93
Immobilization (by)
  with fracture-reduction — *see* Reduction,
      fracture
  bandage 93.59
  bone 93.53
  cast NEC 93.53
    with reduction of fracture or dislocation —
        see Reduction, fracture, *and*
        Reduction, dislocation
  device NEC 93.59
  pressure dressing 93.56
  splint (plaster) (tray) 93.54
    with reduction of fracture or dislocation —
        see Reduction, fracture, *and*
        Reduction, dislocation
  stereotactic head frame 93.59
Immunization — *see also* Vaccination
  allergy 99.12
  autoimmune disease 99.13
  BCG 99.33
  brucellosis 99.55
  cholera 99.31
  diphtheria 99.36
  DPT 99.39
  epidemic parotitis 99.46
  German measles 99.47
  Hemophilus influenzae 99.52
  influenza 99.52
  measles 99.45
  meningococcus 99.55
  mumps 99.46
  pertussis 99.37
  plague 99.34
  poliomyelitis 99.41
  rabies 99.44
  rubella 99.47
  salmonella 99.55
  smallpox 99.42
  staphylococcus 99.55
  TAB 99.32
  tetanus 99.38
  triple vaccine 99.48
  tuberculosis 99.33
  tularemia 99.35
  typhoid-paratyphoid 99.32
  typhus 99.55
  viral NEC 99.55
  whooping cough 99.37
  yellow fever 99.43
Immunoadsorption
  extracorporeal (ECI) 99.76
Immunotherapy, antineoplastic 99.28
  C-Parvum 99.28
  Interferon 99.28
  interleukin-2 (low-dose) 99.28
    high-dose 00.15
  Levamisole 99.28
  Proleukin (low-dose) 99.28
    high-dose 00.15
  Thymosin 99.28
Implant, implantation
  abdominal artery to coronary artery 36.17
  artery
    aortic branches to heart muscle 36.2
    mammary to ventricular wall (Vineberg) 36.2
  baffle, atrial or interatrial 35.91
  biliary fistulous tract into stomach or intestine
      51.39
  bipolar endoprosthesis (femoral head) 81.52
  bladder sphincter, artificial (inflatable) 58.93
  blood vessels to myocardium 36.2

Implant, implantation — *continued*
  bone growth stimulator (invasive)
      (percutaneous) (semi-invasive) — *see*
      category 78.9 ☑
  bone morphogenetic protein ▶(Infuse™)
      (OP-1™)◀ (recombinant) (rhBMP) 84.52
  bone void filler 84.55
    that with kyphoplasty 81.66
    that with vertebroplasty 81.65
  breast (for augmentation) (bilateral) 85.54
    unilateral 85.53
  cardiac resynchronization device
    defibrillator (CRT-D) ▶(device and one or
        more leads)◀ (total system) 00.51
      left ventricular coronary venous lead only
          00.52
      pulse generator only 00.54
    pacemaker (CRT-P) ▶(device and one or
        more leads)◀ (total system) 00.50
      left ventricular coronary venous lead only
          00.52
      pulse generator only 00.53
  cardiac support device (CSD) 37.41   ●
  cardiomyostimulation system 37.67
  cardioverter/defibrillator (automatic) 37.94
    leads only (patch electrodes) (sensing)
        (pacing) 37.95
    pulse generator only 37.96
    total system 37.94
  chest wall (mesh) (silastic) 34.79
  chin (polyethylene) (silastic) 76.68
  cochlear (electrode) 20.96
    prosthetic device (electrode and receiver)
        20.96
      channel (single) 20.97
        multiple 20.98
      electrode only 20.99
      internal coil only 20.99
  CorCap™ 37.41   ●
  cornea 11.73
  CRT-D (cardiac resynchronization defibrillator)
      ▶(device and one or more leads)◀ 00.51
    left ventricular coronary venous lead only
        00.52
    pulse generator only 00.54
  CRT-P (cardiac resynchronization pacemaker)
      ▶(device and one or more leads)◀ 00.50
    left ventricular coronary venous lead only
        00.52
    pulse generator only 00.53
  custodis eye 14.41
  dental (endosseous) (prosthetic) 23.6
  device
    adjustable gastric band and port 44.95
    cardiac support device (CSD) 37.41   ●
    CorCap™ 37.41   ●
    epicardial support device 37.41   ●
    Lap-Band™ 44.95
    left atrial appendage 37.90
    left atrial filter 37.90
    left atrial occluder 37.90
    prosthetic cardiac support device 37.41   ●
    vascular access 86.07
    ventricular support device 37.41   ●
  diaphragmatic pacemaker 34.85
  electrode(s)
    brain 02.93
      depth 02.93
      foramen ovale 02.93
      sphenoidal 02.96
    cardiac (initial) (transvenous) 37.70
      atrium (initial) 37.73
        replacement 37.76
      atrium and ventricle (initial) 37.72
        replacement 37.76
      epicardium (sternotomy or thoracotomy
          approach) 37.74
      left ventricular coronary venous system
          00.52
      temporary transvenous pacemaker
          system 37.78
        during and immediately following
            cardiac surgery 39.64
      ventricle (initial) 37.71
        replacement 37.76

Implant, implantation — *continued*
  electrode(s) — *continued*
    depth 02.93
    foramen ovale 02.93
    heart (*see also* Implant, electrode(s), cardiac)
        37.70
    intracranial 02.93
    osteogenic (invasive) for bone growth
        stimulation — *see* category 78.9 ☑
    peripheral nerve 04.92
    sacral nerve 04.92
    sphenoidal 02.96
    spine 03.93
  electroencephalographic receiver
    brain 02.93
    intracranial 02.93
  electronic stimulator
    anus (subcutaneous) 49.92
    bladder 57.96
    bone growth (invasive) (percutaneous) (semi-
        invasive) 78.9 ☑
    brain — *see* Implant, neurostimulator, brain
    carotid sinus 39.8
    cochlear 20.96
      channel (single) 20.97
        multiple 20.98
    intracranial — *see* Implant, neurostimulator,
        intracranial
    peripheral nerve — *see* Implant,
        neurostimulator, peripheral nerve
    phrenic nerve 34.85
    skeletal muscle 83.92
    spine — *see* Implant, neurostimulator, spine
    ureter 56.92
  electrostimulator — *see* Implant, electronic
      stimulator, by site
  endoprosthesis
    bile duct 51.87
    femoral head (bipolar) 81.52
    pancreatic duct 52.93
  endosseous (dental) 23.6
  epidural pegs 02.93
  epikeratoprosthesis 11.73
  estradiol (pellet) 99.23
  eye (Iowa type) 16.61
    integrated 16.41
  facial bone, synthetic (alloplastic) 76.92
  fallopian tube (Mulligan hood) (silastic tube)
      (stent) 66.93
    into uterus 66.74
  gastroepiploic artery to coronary artery 36.17
  half-heart 37.62
  hearing device, electromagnetic 20.95
  heart
    artificial 37.52
      total replacement system 37.52
    assist system NEC 37.62
      external 37.65
      extrinsic 37.68
      implantable 37.66
      non-implantable 37.62
      percutaneous external 37.68
      pVAD 37.68
    auxiliary ventricle 37.62
    cardiac support device (CSD) 37.41   ●
    circulatory assist system — *see* Implant,
        heart, assist system
    CorCap™ 37.41   ●
    epicardial support device 37.41   ●
    pacemaker (*see also* Implant, pacemaker,
        cardiac) 37.80
    prosthetic cardiac support device 37.41   ●
    total replacement system 37.52
    valve(s)
      prosthesis or synthetic device (partial)
          (synthetic) (total) 35.20
        aortic 35.22
        mitral 35.24
        pulmonary 35.26
        tricuspid 35.28
      tissue graft 35.20
        aortic 35.21
        mitral 35.23
        pulmonary 35.25
        tricuspid 35.27
    ventricular support device 37.41   ●

Implant, implantation — *continued*
　inert material
　　breast (for augmentation) (bilateral) 85.54
　　　unilateral 85.53
　　larynx 31.0
　　nose 21.85
　　orbit (eye socket) 16.69
　　　reinsertion 16.62
　　scleral shell (cup) (with evisceration of
　　　eyeball) 16.31
　　　reinsertion 16.62
　　Tenon's capsule (with enucleation of eyeball)
　　　16.42
　　　with attachment of muscles 16.41
　　　reinsertion 16.62
　　urethra 59.79
　　vocal cord(s) 31.0
　infusion pump 86.06
　interbody spinal fusion device 84.51
　joint (prosthesis) (silastic) (Swanson type) NEC
　　81.96
　　ankle (total) 81.56
　　　revision 81.59
　　carpocarpal, carpometacarpal 81.74
　　elbow (total) 81.84
　　　revision 81.97
　　extremity (bioelectric) (cineplastic)
　　　(kineplastic) 84.40
　　　lower 84.48
　　　　revision 81.59
　　　upper 84.44
　　　　revision 81.97
　　femoral (bipolar endoprosthesis) 81.52
　　　revision NOS 81.53　●
　　　　acetabular and femoral
　　　　　components (total) 00.70　●
　　　　acetabular component only 00.71　●
　　　　acetabular liner and/or femoral
　　　　　head only 00.73　●
　　　　femoral component only 00.72　●
　　　　femoral head only and/or
　　　　　acetabular liner 00.73　●
　　　　total (acetabular and femoral
　　　　　components) 00.70　●
　　finger 81.71
　　hand (metacarpophalangeal)
　　　(interphalangeal) 81.71
　　　revision 81.97
　　hip (partial) 81.52
　　　revision ▶NOS◀ 81.53
　　　　acetabular and femoral
　　　　　components (total) 00.70　●
　　　　acetabular component only 00.71　●
　　　　acetabular liner and/or femoral
　　　　　head only 00.73　●
　　　　femoral component only 00.72　●
　　　　femoral head only and/or
　　　　　acetabular liner 00.73　●
　　　　partial
　　　　　acetabular component only 00.71　●
　　　　　acetabular liner and/or femoral
　　　　　　head only 00.73　●
　　　　　femoral component only 00.72　●
　　　　　femoral head only and/or
　　　　　　acetabular liner 00.73　●
　　　　total (acetabular and femoral
　　　　　components) 00.70　●
　　　total 81.51
　　　　revision ▶(acetabular and femoral
　　　　　components)◀ 00.70　▲
　　interphalangeal 81.71
　　　revision 81.97
　　knee (partial) (total) 81.54
　　　revision ▶NOS◀ 81.55
　　　　femoral component 00.82　●
　　　　partial　●
　　　　　femoral component 00.82　●
　　　　　patellar component 00.83　●
　　　　　tibial component 00.81　●
　　　　　tibial insert 00.84　●
　　　　patellar component 00.83　●
　　　　tibial component 00.81　●
　　　　tibial insert 00.84　●
　　　　total (all components) 00.80　●
　　metacarpophalangeal 81.71
　　　revision 81.97

Implant, implantation — *continued*
　joint NEC — *continued*
　　shoulder (partial) 81.81
　　　revision 81.97
　　　total replacement 81.80
　　toe 81.57
　　　for hallux valgus repair 77.59
　　　revision 81.59
　　wrist (partial) 81.74
　　　revision 81.97
　　　total replacement 81.73
　kidney, mechanical 55.97
　Lap-Band™ 44.95
　larynx 31.0
　leads (cardiac) — *see* Implant, electrode(s),
　　cardiac
　limb lengthening device, internal (NOS)
　　84.54
　　with kinetic distraction 84.53
　mammary artery
　　in ventricle (Vineberg) 36.2
　　to coronary artery (single vessel) 36.15
　　　double vessel 36.16
　Mulligan hood, fallopian tube 66.93
　nerve (peripheral) 04.79
　neuropacemaker— *see* Implant,
　　neurostimulator, by site
　neurostimulator
　　brain 02.93
　　electrodes
　　　brain 02.93
　　　intracranial 02.93
　　　peripheral nerve 04.92
　　　sacral nerve 04.92
　　　spine 03.93
　　intracranial 02.93
　　peripheral nerve 04.92
　　pulse generator 86.96
　　　dual array 86.95
　　　　rechargeable 86.98　●
　　　single array 86.94
　　　　rechargeable 86.97　●
　　spine 03.93
　nose 21.85
　Ommaya reservoir 02.2
　orbit 16.69
　　reinsertion 16.62
　outflow tract prosthesis (heart) (gusset type)
　　in
　　　pulmonary valvuloplasty 35.26
　　　total repair of tetralogy of Fallot 35.81
　ovary into uterine cavity 65.72
　　laparoscopic 65.75
　pacemaker
　　brain — *see* Implant, neurostimulator, brain
　　cardiac (device) (initial) (permanent)
　　　(replacement) 37.80
　　　dual-chamber device (initial) 37.83
　　　　replacement 37.87
　　　resynchronization device (CRT-P)
　　　　device only (initial) (replacement) 00.53
　　　　total system ▶(device and one or more
　　　　　leads)◀ 00.50
　　　　transvenous lead into left ventricular
　　　　　coronary venous system 00.52
　　　single-chamber device (initial) 37.81
　　　　rate responsive 37.82
　　　　replacement 37.85
　　　　　rate responsive 37.86
　　　temporary transvenous pacemaker
　　　　system 37.78
　　　　during and immediately following
　　　　　cardiac surgery 39.64
　　carotid sinus 39.8
　　diaphragm 34.85
　　intracranial — *see* Implant, neurostimulator,
　　　intracranial
　　neural — *see* Implant, neurostimulator, by
　　　site
　　peripheral nerve — *see* Implant,
　　　neurostimulator, peripheral nerve
　　spine — *see* Implant, neurostimulator, spine
　pancreas (duct) 52.96
　penis, prosthesis (internal)
　　inflatable 64.97
　　non-inflatable 64.95

Implant, implantation — *continued*
　port, vascular access device 86.07
　premaxilla 76.68
　progesterone (subdermal) 99.23
　prosthesis, prosthetic device
　　acetabulum (Aufranc-Turner) 81.52
　　ankle (total) 81.56
　　arm (bioelectric) (cineplastic) (kineplastic)
　　　84.44
　　breast (Cronin) (Dow-Corning) (Perras-
　　　Pappillon) (bilateral) 85.54
　　　unilateral 85.53
　　cardiac support device (CSD) (CorCap™)　●
　　　37.41　●
　　cochlear 20.96
　　　channel (single) 20.97
　　　multiple 20.98
　　extremity (bioelectric) (cineplastic)
　　　(kineplastic) 84.40
　　　lower 84.48
　　　upper 84.44
　　fallopian tube (Mulligan hood) (stent) 66.93
　　femoral head (Austin-Moore) (bipolar)
　　　(Eicher) (Thompson) 81.52
　　　revision NOS 81.53　●
　　　　acetabular and femoral
　　　　　components (total) 00.70　●
　　　　acetabular component only 00.71　●
　　　　acetabular liner and/or femoral
　　　　　head only 00.73　●
　　　　femoral component only 00.72　●
　　　　femoral head only and/or
　　　　　acetabular liner 00.73　●
　　　　partial
　　　　　acetabular component only 00.71　●
　　　　　acetabular liner and/or femoral
　　　　　　head only 00.73　●
　　　　　femoral component only 00.72　●
　　　　　femoral head only and/or
　　　　　　acetabular liner 00.73　●
　　　　total (acetabular and femoral
　　　　　components) 00.70　●
　　joint (Swanson type) NEC 81.96
　　　ankle (total) 81.56
　　　carpocarpal, carpometacarpal 81.74
　　　elbow (total) 81.84
　　　finger 81.71
　　　hand (metacarpophalangeal)
　　　　(interphalangeal) 81.71
　　　hip (partial) 81.52
　　　　revision NOS 81.53　●
　　　　　acetabular and femoral
　　　　　　components (total) 00.70　●
　　　　　acetabular component only 00.71　●
　　　　　acetabular liner and/or femoral
　　　　　　head only 00.73　●
　　　　　femoral component only 00.72　●
　　　　　femoral head only and/or
　　　　　　acetabular liner 00.73　●
　　　　　partial
　　　　　　acetabular component only
　　　　　　　00.71　●
　　　　　　acetabular liner and/or
　　　　　　　femoral head only 00.73　●
　　　　　　femoral component only 00.72　●
　　　　　　femoral head only and/or
　　　　　　　acetabular liner 00.73　●
　　　　　total (acetabular and femoral
　　　　　　components) 00.70　●
　　　　total 81.51
　　　　　revision (acetabular and
　　　　　　femoral components 00.70　●
　　　interphalangeal 81.71
　　　knee (partial) (total) 81.54
　　　　revision ▶NOS◀ 81.55
　　　　　femoral component 00.82　●
　　　　　partial　●
　　　　　　femoral component 00.82　●
　　　　　　patellar component 00.83　●
　　　　　　tibial component 00.81　●
　　　　　　tibial insert 00.84　●
　　　　　patellar component 00.83　●
　　　　　tibial component 00.81　●
　　　　　tibial insert 00.84　●
　　　　　total (all components) 00.80　●
　　　metacarpophalangeal 81.71

☑ Additional Digit Required — Refer to the Tabular List (Numeric Code Section) for Additional Digit Selection

Implant, implantation — *continued*
 prosthesis, prosthetic device — *continued*
  joint NEC — *continued*
   shoulder (partial) 81.81
    total 81.80
   spine NEC 84.59 ●
    interspinous process decompression ●
     device 84.58 ●
   toe 81.57
    for hallux valgus repair 77.59
   wrist (partial) 81.74
    total 81.73
  leg (bioelectric) (cineplastic) (kineplastic)
    84.48
  outflow tract (heart) (gusset type)
   in
    pulmonary valvuloplasty 35.26
    total repair of tetralogy of Fallot 35.81
  penis (internal) (non-inflatable) 64.95
   inflatable (internal) 64.97
  skin (dermal regenerative) (matrix) 86.67
  testicular (bilateral) (unilateral) 62.7
 pulsation balloon (phase-shift) 37.61
 pump, infusion 86.06
 radial artery 36.19
 radioactive isotope 92.27
 radium (radon) 92.27
 retinal attachment 14.41
  with buckling 14.41
 Rickham reservoir 02.2
 silicone
  breast (bilateral) 85.54
   unilateral 85.53
  skin (for filling of defect) 86.02
   for augmentation NEC 86.89
 stimoceiver — *see* Implant, neurostimulator, by
   site
 subdural
  grids 02.93
  strips 02.93
 Swanson prosthesis (joint) (silastic) NEC 81.96
  carpocarpal, carpometacarpal 81.74
  finger 81.71
  hand (metacarpophalangeal)
    (interphalangeal) 81.71
  interphalangeal 81.71
  knee (partial) (total) 81.54
   revision 81.55
  metacarpophalangeal 81.71
  toe 81.57
   for hallux valgus repair 77.59
  wrist (partial) 81.74
   total 81.73
 systemic arteries into myocardium (Vineberg
   type operation) 36.2
 Tandem™ heart 37.68
 testicular prosthesis (bilateral) (unilateral) 62.7
 tissue expander (skin) NEC 86.93
  breast 85.95
 tissue mandril (for vascular graft) 39.99
  with
   blood vessel repair 39.56
   vascular bypass or shunt — *see* Bypass,
     vascular
 tooth (bud) (germ) 23.5
  prosthetic 23.6
 umbrella, vena cava 38.7
 ureters into
  bladder 56.74
  intestine 56.71
   external diversion 56.51
  skin 56.61
 urethra
  for repair of urinary stress incontinence
   collagen 59.72
   fat 59.72
   polytef 59.72
 urethral sphincter, artificial (inflatable) 58.93
 urinary sphincter, artificial (inflatable) 58.93
 vascular access device 86.07
 vitreous (silicone) 14.75
  for retinal reattachment 14.41
   with buckling 14.41
 vocal cord(s) (paraglottic) 31.98
Implosion (psychologic desensitization) 94.33

Incision (and drainage)
 with
  exploration — *see* Exploration
  removal of foreign body — *see* Removal,
    foreign body
 abdominal wall 54.0
  as operative approach — *omit code*
 abscess — *see also* Incision, by site
  appendix 47.2
   with appendectomy 47.09
    laparoscopic 47.01
  extraperitoneal 54.0
  ischiorectal 49.01
  lip 27.0
  omental 54.19
  perianal 49.01
  perigastric 54.19
  perisplenic 54.19
  peritoneal NEC 54.19
   pelvic (female) 70.12
  retroperitoneal 54.0
  sclera 12.89
  skin 86.04
  subcutaneous tissue 86.04
  subdiaphragmatic 54.19
  subhepatic 54.19
  subphrenic 54.19
  vas deferens 63.6
 adrenal gland 07.41
 alveolus, alveolar bone 24.0
 antecubital fossa 86.09
 anus NEC 49.93
  fistula 49.11
  septum 49.91
 appendix 47.2
 artery 38.00
  abdominal 38.06
   aorta (arch) (ascending) (descending)
     38.04
  head and neck NEC 38.02
  intracranial NEC 38.01
  lower limb 38.08
  thoracic NEC 38.05
  upper limb 38.03
 atrium (heart) 37.11
 auditory canal or meatus, external 18.02
 auricle 18.09
 axilla 86.09
 Bartholin's gland or cyst 71.22
 bile duct (with T or Y tube insertion) NEC
   51.59
  common (exploratory) 51.51
   for
    relief of obstruction NEC 51.42
    removal of calculus 51.41
  for
   exploration 51.59
   relief of obstruction 51.49
 bladder 57.19
  neck (transurethral) 57.91
  percutaneous suprapubic (closed) 57.17
  suprapubic NEC 57.18
 blood vessel (*see also* Angiotomy) 38.00
 bone 77.10
  alveolus, alveolar 24.0
  carpals, metacarpals 77.14
  clavicle 77.11
  facial 76.09
  femur 77.15
  fibula 77.17
  humerus 77.12
  patella 77.16
  pelvic 77.19
  phalanges (foot) (hand) 77.19
  radius 77.13
  scapula 77.11
  skull 01.24
  specified site NEC 77.19
  tarsals, metatarsals 77.18
  thorax (ribs) (sternum) 77.11
  tibia 77.17
  ulna 77.13
  vertebrae 77.19
 brain 01.39
  cortical adhesions 02.91

Incision — *continued*
 breast (skin) 85.0
  with removal of tissue expander 85.96
 bronchus 33.0
 buccal space 27.0
 bulbourethral gland 58.91
 bursa 83.03
  hand 82.03
  pharynx 29.0
 carotid body 39.8
 cerebral (meninges) 01.39
  epidural or extradural space 01.24
  subarachnoid or subdural space 01.31
 cerebrum 01.39
 cervix 69.95
  to
   assist delivery 73.93
   replace inverted uterus 75.93
 chalazion 08.09
  with removal of capsule 08.21
 cheek 86.09
 chest wall (for extrapleural drainage) (for
   removal of foreign body) 34.01
  as operative approach — *omit code*
 common bile duct (for exploration) 51.51
  for
   relief of obstruction 51.42
   removal of calculus 51.41
 common wall between posterior left atrium and
   coronary sinus (with roofing of resultant
   defect with patch graft) 35.82
 conjunctiva 10.1
 cornea 11.1
  radial (refractive) 11.75
 cranial sinus 01.21
 craniobuccal pouch 07.72
 cul-de-sac 70.12
 cyst
  dentigerous 24.0
  radicular (apical) (periapical) 24.0
 Dührssen's (cervix, to assist delivery) 73.93
 duodenum 45.01
 ear
  external 18.09
  inner 20.79
  middle 20.23
 endocardium 37.11
 endolymphatic sac 20.79
 epididymis 63.92
 epidural space, cerebral 01.24
 epigastric region 54.0
  intra-abdominal 54.19
 esophagus, esophageal NEC 42.09
  web 42.01
 exploratory — *see* Exploration
 extradural space (cerebral) 01.24
 extrapleural 34.01
 eyebrow 08.09
 eyelid 08.09
  margin (trichiasis) 08.01
 face 86.09
 fallopian tube 66.01
 fascia 83.09
  with division 83.14
   hand 82.12
  hand 82.09
   with division 82.12
 fascial compartments, head and neck 27.0
 fistula, anal 49.11
 flank 54.0
 furuncle — *see* Incision, by site
 gallbladder 51.04
 gingiva 24.0
 gluteal 86.09
 groin region (abdominal wall) (inguinal) 54.0
  skin 86.09
  subcutaneous tissue 86.09
 gum 24.0
 hair follicles 86.09
 heart 37.10
  valve — *see* Valvulotomy
 hematoma — *see also* Incision, by site
  axilla 86.04
  broad ligament 69.98
  ear 18.09
  episiotomy site 75.91

Incision — *continued*
  hematoma — *see also* Incision, by site — *continued*
    fossa (superficial) NEC 86.04
    groin region (abdominal wall) (inguinal) 54.0
      skin 86.04
      subcutaneous tissue 86.04
    laparotomy site 54.12
    mediastinum 34.1
    perineum (female) 71.09
      male 86.04
    popliteal space 86.04
    scrotum 61.0
    skin 86.04
    space of Retzius 59.19
    subcutaneous tissue 86.04
    vagina (cuff) 70.14
      episiotomy site 75.91
      obstetrical NEC 75.92
  hepatic ducts 51.59
  hordeolum 08.09
  hygroma — *see also* Incision, by site
    cystic 40.0
  hymen 70.11
  hypochondrium 54.0
    intra-abdominal 54.19
  hypophysis 07.72
  iliac fossa 54.0
  ingrown nail 86.09
  intestine 45.00
    large 45.03
    small 45.02
  intracerebral 01.39
  intracranial (epidural space) (extradural space) 01.24
    subarachnoid or subdural space 01.31
  intraperitoneal 54.19
  ischiorectal tissue 49.02
    abscess 49.01
  joint structures (*see also* Arthrotomy) 80.10
  kidney 55.01
    pelvis 55.11
  labia 71.09
  lacrimal
    canaliculus 09.52
    gland 09.0
    passage NEC 09.59
    punctum 09.51
    sac 09.53
  larynx NEC 31.3
  ligamentum flavum (spine) — *omit code*
  liver 50.0
  lung 33.1
  lymphangioma 40.0
  lymphatic structure (channel) (node) (vessel) 40.0
  mastoid 20.21
  mediastinum 34.1
  meibomian gland 08.09
  meninges (cerebral) 01.31
    spinal 03.09
  midpalmar space 82.04
  mouth NEC 27.92
    floor 27.0
  muscle 83.02
    with division 83.19
      hand 82.19
    hand 82.02
      with division 82.19
  myocardium 37.11
  nailbed or nailfold 86.09
  nasolacrimal duct (stricture) 09.59
  neck 86.09
  nerve (cranial) (peripheral) NEC 04.04
    root (spinal) 03.1
  nose 21.1
  omentum 54.19
  orbit (*see also* Orbitotomy) 16.09
  ovary 65.09
    laparoscopic 65.01
  palate 27.1
  palmar space (middle) 82.04
  pancreas 52.09
  pancreatic sphincter 51.82
    endoscopic 51.85

Incision — *continued*
  parapharyngeal (oral) (transcervical) 28.0
  paronychia 86.09
  parotid
    gland or duct 26.0
    space 27.0
  pelvirectal tissue 48.81
  penis 64.92
  perianal (skin) (tissue) 49.02
    abscess 49.01
  perigastric 54.19
  perineum (female) 71.09
    male 86.09
  peripheral vessels
    lower limb
      artery 38.08
      vein 38.09
    upper limb (artery) (vein) 38.03
  periprostatic tissue 60.81
  perirectal tissue 48.81
  perirenal tissue 59.09
  perisplenic 54.19
  peritoneum 54.95
    by laparotomy 54.19
    pelvic (female) 70.12
      male 54.19
  periureteral tissue 59.09
  periurethral tissue 58.91
  perivesical tissue 59.19
  petrous pyramid (air cells) (apex) (mastoid) 20.22
  pharynx, pharyngeal (bursa) 29.0
    space, lateral 27.0
  pilonidal sinus (cyst) 86.03
  pineal gland 07.52
  pituitary (gland) 07.72
  pleura NEC 34.09
  popliteal space 86.09
  postzygomatic space 27.0
  pouch of Douglas 70.12
  prostate (perineal approach) (transurethral approach) 60.0
  pterygopalatine fossa 27.0
  pulp canal (tooth) 24.0
  Rathke's pouch 07.72
  rectovaginal septum 48.81
  rectum 48.0
    stricture 48.91
  renal pelvis 55.11
  retroperitoneum 54.0
  retropharyngeal (oral) (transcervical) 28.0
  salivary gland or duct 26.0
  sclera 12.89
  scrotum 61.0
  sebaceous cyst 86.04
  seminal vesicle 60.72
  sinus — *see* Sinusotomy
  Skene's duct or gland 71.09
  skin 86.09
    with drainage 86.04
    breast 85.0
    cardiac pacemaker pocket, new site 37.79
    ear 18.09
    nose 21.1
    subcutaneous tunnel for pulse generator lead wire 86.99
      with initial procedure — *omit code*
    thalamic stimulator pulse generator pocket, new site 86.09
      with initial insertion of battery package — *omit code*
    tunnel, subcutaneous for pulse generator lead wire 86.99
      with initial procedure — *omit code*
  skull (bone) 01.24
  soft tissue NEC 83.09
    with division 83.19
      hand 82.19
    hand 82.09
      with division 82.19
  space of Retzius 59.19
  spermatic cord 63.93
  sphincter of Oddi 51.82
    endoscopic 51.85
  spinal
    cord 03.09
    nerve root 03.1

Incision — *continued*
  spleen 41.2
  stomach 43.0
  stye 08.09
  subarachnoid space, cerebral 01.31
  subcutaneous tissue 86.09
    with drainage 86.04
    tunnel
      esophageal 42.86
        with anastomosis — *see* Anastomosis, esophagus, antesternal
      pulse generator lead wire 86.99
        with initial procedure — *omit code*
  subdiaphragmatic space 54.19
  subdural space, cerebral 01.31
  sublingual space 27.0
  submandibular space 27.0
  submaxillary 86.09
    with drainage 86.04
  submental space 27.0
  subphrenic space 54.19
  supraclavicular fossa 86.09
    with drainage 86.04
  sweat glands, skin 86.04
  temporal pouches 27.0
  tendon (sheath) 83.01
    with division 83.13
      hand 82.11
    hand 82.01
      with division 82.11
  testis 62.0
  thenar space 82.04
  thymus 07.92
  thyroid (field) (gland) NEC 06.09
    postoperative 06.02
  tongue NEC 25.94
    for tongue tie 25.91
  tonsil 28.0
  trachea NEC 31.3
  tunica vaginalis 61.0
  umbilicus 54.0
  urachal cyst 54.0
  ureter 56.2
  urethra 58.0
  uterus (corpus) 68.0
    cervix 69.95
    for termination of pregnancy 74.91
    septum (congenital) 68.22
  uvula 27.71
  vagina (cuff) (septum) (stenosis) 70.14
    for
      incisional hematoma (episiotomy) 75.91
      obstetrical hematoma NEC 75.92
      pelvic abscess 70.12
  vas deferens 63.6
  vein 38.00
    abdominal 38.07
    head and neck NEC 38.02
    intracranial NEC 38.01
    lower limb 38.09
    thoracic NEC 38.05
    upper limb 38.03
  vertebral column 03.09
  vulva 71.09
    obstetrical 75.92
  web, esophageal 42.01
Incudectomy NEC 19.3
  with
    stapedectomy (*see also* Stapedectomy) 19.19
    tympanoplasty — *see* Tympanoplasty
Incudopexy 19.19
Incudostapediopexy 19.19
  with incus replacement 19.11
Indentation, sclera, for buckling (*see also* Buckling, scleral) 14.49
Indicator dilution flow measurement 89.68
Induction
  abortion
    by
      D and C 69.01
      insertion of prostaglandin suppository 96.49
      intra-amniotic injection (prostaglandin) (saline) 75.0

Incision — Induction

Induction — *continued*
  labor
    medical 73.4
    surgical 73.01
      intra- and extra-amniotic injection 73.1
      stripping of membranes 73.1
Inflation
  belt wrap 93.99
  Eustachian tube 20.8
  fallopian tube 66.8
    with injection of therapeutic agent 66.95
Infolding, sclera, for buckling (*see also*
    Buckling, scleral) 14.49
Infraction, turbinates (nasal) 21.62
Infundibulectomy
  hypophyseal (*see also* Hypophysectomy, partial)
    07.63
  ventricle (heart) (right) 35.34
    in total repair of tetralogy of Fallot 35.81
Infusion (intra-arterial) (intravenous)
  Abciximab 99.20
  antibiotic
    oxazolidinone class 00.14
  antineoplastic agent (chemotherapeutic) 99.25
    biological response modifier [BRM] 99.28
    high-dose interleukin-2 00.15
    low-dose interleukin-2 99.28
  biological response modifier [BRM],
    antineoplastic agent 99.28
    high-dose interleukin-2 00.15
    low-dose interleukin-2 99.28
  cancer chemotherapy agent NEC 99.25
  drotrecogin alfa (activated) 00.11
  electrolytes 99.18
  enzymes, thrombolytic (streptokinase) (tissue
    plasminogen activator) (TPA) (urokinase)
    direct coronary artery 36.04
    intravenous 99.10
  Eptifibatide 99.20
  GP IIb/IIIa inhibitor 99.20
  hormone substance NEC 99.24
  human B-type natriuretic peptide (hBNP) 00.13
  immunosuppressive antibody therapy 00.18 ●
  nesiritide 00.13
  neuroprotective agent 99.75
  nimodipine 99.75
  nutritional substance — *see* Nutrition
  platelet inhibitor
    direct coronary artery 36.04
    intravenous 99.20
  Proleukin (low-dose) 99.28
    high-dose 00.15
  prophylactic substance NEC 99.29
  radioimmunoconjugate 92.28
  radioimmunotherapy 92.28
  radioisotope (liquid brachytherapy   ●
    (liquid I-125) 92.20   ●
  recombinant protein 00.11
  reteplase 99.10
  therapeutic substance NEC 99.29
  thrombolytic agent (enzyme) (streptokinase)
    99.10
    with percutaneous transluminal angioplasty

Note — Also use 00.40, 00.41, 00.42, or ●   *00.43 to show the total number of vessels* ●   *treated.* ●

      coronary 00.66   ▲
      non-coronary vessel(s) 39.50
      specified site NEC 39.50
    direct intracoronary artery 36.04
  tirofiban (HCl) 99.20
  vaccine
    tumor 99.28
  vasopressor 00.17
Injection (into) (hypodermically) (intramuscularly)
    (intravenously) (acting locally or
    systemically)
  Actinomycin D, for cancer chemotherapy 99.25
  adhesion barrier substance 99.77
  alcohol
    nerve — *see* Injection, nerve
    spinal 03.8

Injection — *continued*
  anterior chamber, eye (air) (liquid) (medication)
    12.92
  antibiotic 99.21
    oxazolidinone class 00.14
  anticoagulant 99.19
  anti-D (Rhesus) globulin 99.11
  antidote NEC 99.16
  anti-infective NEC 99.22
  antineoplastic agent (chemotherapeutic) NEC
    99.25
    biological response modifier [BRM] 99.28
    high-dose interleukin-2 00.15
    low-dose interleukin-2 99.28
  antivenin 99.16
  barrier substance, adhesion 99.77
  BCG
    for chemotherapy 99.25
    vaccine 99.33
  biological response modifier [BRM], antineo-
    plastic agent 99.28
    high-dose interleukin-2 00.15
    low-dose interleukin-2 99.28
  bone marrow 41.92
    transplant — *see* Transplant, bone, marrow
  breast (therapeutic agent) 85.92
    inert material (silicone) (bilateral) 85.52
      unilateral 85.51
  bursa (therapeutic agent) 83.96
    hand 82.94
  cancer chemotherapeutic agent 99.25
  caudal — *see* Injection, spinal
  cortisone 99.23
  costochondral junction 81.92
  dinoprost-tromethine, intraamniotic 75.0
  ear, with alcohol 20.72
  electrolytes 99.18
  enzymes, thrombolytic (streptokinase) (tissue
    plasminogen activator) (TPA) (urokinase)
    direct coronary artery 36.04
    intravenous 99.10
  epidural, spinal — *see* Injection, spinal
  esophageal varices or blood vessel (endoscopic)
    (sclerosing agent) 42.33
  Eustachian tube (inert material) 20.8
  eye (orbit) (retrobulbar) 16.91
    anterior chamber 12.92
    subconjunctival 10.91
  fascia 83.98
    hand 82.96
  gamma globulin 99.14
  ganglion, sympathetic 05.39
    ciliary 12.79
    paravertebral stellate 05.39
  gel, adhesion barrier — *see* Injection, adhesion
    barrier substance
  globulin
    anti-D (Rhesus) 99.11
    gamma 99.14
    Rh immune 99.11
  heart 37.92
  heavy metal antagonist 99.16
  hemorrhoids (sclerosing agent) 49.42
  hormone NEC 99.24
  human B-type natriuretic peptide (hBNP) 00.13
  immune sera 99.14
  inert material — *see* Implant, inert material
  inner ear, for destruction 20.72
  insulin 99.17
  intervertebral space for herniated disc 80.52
  intra-amniotic
    for induction of
      abortion 75.0
      labor 73.1
  intrathecal — *see* Injection, spinal
  joint (therapeutic agent) 81.92
    temporomandibular 76.96
  kidney (cyst) (therapeutic substance) NEC
    55.96
  larynx 31.0
  ligament (joint) (therapeutic substance) 81.92
  liver 50.94
  lung, for surgical collapse 33.32
  Methotrexate, for cancer chemotherapy 99.25

Injection — *continued*
  nerve (cranial) (peripheral) 04.80
    agent NEC 04.89
      alcohol 04.2
      anesthetic for analgesia 04.81
        for operative anesthesia — *omit code*
      neurolytic 04.2
      phenol 04.2
    laryngeal (external) (recurrent) (superior)
      31.91
    optic 16.91
    sympathetic 05.39
      alcohol 05.32
      anesthetic for analgesia 05.31
      neurolytic agent 05.32
      phenol 05.32
  nesiritide 00.13
  neuroprotective agent 99.75
  nimodipine 99.75
  orbit 16.91
  pericardium 37.93
  peritoneal cavity
    air 54.96
    locally-acting therapeutic substance 54.97
  platelet inhibitor
    direct coronary artery 36.04
    intravenous 99.20
  prophylactic substance NEC 99.29
  prostate 60.92
  radioimmunoconjugate 92.28
  radioimmunotherapy 92.28
  radioisotopes (intracavitary) (intravenous) 92.28
  renal pelvis (cyst) 55.96
  retrobulbar (therapeutic substance) 16.91
    for anesthesia — *omit code*
  Rh immune globulin 99.11
  RhoGAM 99.11
  sclerosing agent NEC 99.29
    esophageal varices (endoscopic) 42.33
    hemorrhoids 49.42
    pleura 34.92
      treatment of malignancy (cytotoxic agent)
        34.92 *[99.25]*
        with tetracycline 34.92 *[99.21]*
    varicose vein 39.92
    vein NEC 39.92
  semicircular canals, for destruction 20.72
  silicone — *see* Implant, inert material
  skin (sclerosing agent) (filling material) 86.02
  soft tissue 83.98
    hand 82.96
  spinal (canal) NEC 03.92
    alcohol 03.8
    anesthetic agent for analgesia 03.91
      for operative anesthesia — *omit code*
    contrast material (for myelogram) 87.21
    destructive agent NEC 03.8
    neurolytic agent NEC 03.8
    phenol 03.8
    proteolytic enzyme (chymopapain)
      (chymodiactin) 80.52
    saline (hypothermic) 03.92
    steroid NEC 03.92
  spinal nerve root (intrathecal) — *see* Injection,
    spinal
  steroid NEC 99.23
  subarachnoid, spinal — *see* Injection, spinal
  subconjunctival 10.91
  tendon 83.97
    hand 82.95
  testis 62.92
  therapeutic agent NEC 99.29
  thoracic cavity 34.92
  thrombolytic agent (enzyme) (streptokinase)
    99.10
    with percutaneous transluminal angioplasty

Note — Also use 00.40, 00.41, 00.42, or ●   *00.43 to show the total number of vessels* ●   *treated.* ●

      coronary 00.66   ▲
      non-coronary vessel(s) 39.50
      specified site NEC 39.50
    direct intracoronary artery 36.04
  trachea 31.94
  tranquilizer 99.26

Injection — *continued*
  tunica vaginalis (with aspiration) 61.91
  tympanum 20.94
  urethra (inert material)
    for repair of urinary stress incontinence
      collagen implant 59.72
      endoscopic injection of implant 59.72
      fat implant 59.72
      polytef implant 59.72
  vaccine
    tumor 99.28
  varices, esophagus (endoscopic) (sclerosing agent) 42.33
  varicose vein (sclerosing agent) 39.92
    esophagus (endoscopic) 42.33
  vestibule, for destruction 20.72
  vitreous substitute (silicone) 14.75
    for reattachment of retina 14.59
  vocal cords 31.0
Inlay, tooth 23.3
Inoculation
  antitoxins — *see* Administration, antitoxins
  toxoids — *see* Administration, toxoids
  vaccine — *see* Administration, vaccine
Insemination, artificial 69.92
Insertion
  airway
    esophageal obturator 96.03
    nasopharynx 96.01
    oropharynx 96.02
  Allen-Brown cannula 39.93
  arch bars (orthodontic) 24.7
    for immobilization (fracture) 93.55
  atrial septal umbrella 35.52
  Austin-Moore prosthesis 81.52
  baffle, heart (atrial) (interatrial) (intra-atrial) 35.91
  bag, cervix (nonobstetrical) 67.0
    after delivery or abortion 75.8
    to assist delivery or induce labor 73.1
  Baker's (tube) (for stenting) 46.85
  balloon
    gastric 44.93
    heart (pulsation-type) (Kantrowitz) 37.61
    intestine (for decompression) (for dilation) 46.85
  band (adjustable)
    gastric, laparoscopic 44.95
    Lap-Band™ 44.95
  Barton's tongs (skull) (with synchronous skeletal traction) 02.94
  bipolar endoprosthesis (femoral head) 81.52
  Blakemore-Sengstaken tube 96.06
  bone growth stimulator (invasive) (percutaneous) (semi-invasive) — *see* category 78.9 ☑
  bone morphogenetic protein ▶(Infuse™) (OP-1™)◀ (recombinant) (rhBMP) 84.52
  bone void filler 84.55
    that with kyphoplasty 81.66
    that with vertebroplasty 81.65
  bougie, cervix, nonobstetrical 67.0
    to assist delivery or induce labor 73.1
  breast implant (for augmentation) (bilateral) 85.54
    unilateral 85.53
  bridge (dental) (fixed) 23.42
    removable 23.43
  bubble (balloon), stomach 44.93
  caliper tongs (skull) (with synchronous skeletal traction) 02.94
  cannula
    Allen-Brown 39.93
    for extracorporeal membrane oxygenation (ECMO) — *omit code*
    nasal sinus (by puncture) 22.01
      through natural ostium 22.02
    pancreatic duct 52.92
      endoscopic 52.93
    vessel to vessel 39.93
  cardiac resynchronization device
    defibrillator (CRT-D) (total system) ▶(device and one or more leads)◀ 00.51
      left ventricular coronary venous lead only 00.52

Insertion — *continued*
  cardiac resynchronization device — *continued*
    defibrillator — *continued*
      pulse generator only 00.54
    pacemaker (CRT-P) (total system) ▶(device and one or more leads)◀ 00.50
      left ventricular coronary venous lead only 00.52
      pulse generator only 00.53
  cardiac support device (CSD) (CorCap™) ● 37.41 ●
  carotid artery stent(s) (stent graft) 00.63

> *Note* — Also use 00.40, 00.41, 00.42, or ●
> 00.43 to show the total number of vessels ●
> treated. In addition, use 00.45, 00.46, ●
> 00.47, or 00.48 to show the number of ●
> vascular stents inserted. ●

  catheter
    abdomen of fetus, for intrauterine transfusion 75.2
    anterior chamber (eye), for permanent drainage (glaucoma) 12.79
    artery 38.91
    bile duct(s) 51.59
      common 51.51
        endoscopic 51.87
      endoscopic 51.87
    bladder, indwelling 57.94
      suprapubic 57.18
        percutaneous (closed) 57.17
    bronchus 96.05
      with lavage 96.56
    central venous NEC 38.93
      for
        hemodialysis 38.95
        pressure monitoring 89.62
        peripherally inserted central catheter (PICC) 38.93
    chest 34.04
      revision (with lysis of adhesions) 34.04
    cranial cavity 01.26 ●
    esophagus (nonoperative) 96.06
      permanent tube 42.81
    intercostal (with water seal), for drainage 34.04
      revision (with lysis of adhesions) 34.04
    spinal canal space (epidural) (subarachnoid) (subdural) for infusion of therapeutic or palliative substances 03.90
    Swan-Ganz (pulmonary) 89.64
    transtracheal for oxygenation 31.99
    vein NEC 38.93
      for renal dialysis 38.95
  chest tube 34.04
  choledochohepatic tube (for decompression) 51.43
    endoscopic 51.87
  cochlear prosthetic device — *see* Implant, cochlear prosthetic device
  contraceptive device (intrauterine) 69.7
  CorCap™ 37.41 ●
  cordis cannula 54.98
  coronary (artery)

> *Note* — Also use 00.40, 00.41, 00.42, or ●
> 00.43 to show the total number of vessels ●
> treated. In addition, use 00.45, 00.46, ●
> 00.47, or 00.48 to show the number of ●
> vascular stents inserted. ●

    stent, drug-eluting 36.07
    stent, non-drug-eluting 36.06
  Crosby-Cooney button 54.98
  CRT-D (cardiac resynchronization defibrillator) ▶(device and one or more leads)◀ 00.51
    left ventricular coronary venous lead only 00.52
    pulse generator only 00.54
  CRT-P (cardiac resynchronization pacemaker) ▶(device and one or more leads)◀ 00.50
    left ventricular coronary venous lead only 00.52
    pulse generator only 00.53
  Crutchfield tongs (skull) (with synchronous skeletal traction) 02.94
  Davidson button 54.98

Insertion — *continued*
  denture (total) 99.97
  device
    adjustable gastric band and port 44.95
    cardiac support device (CSD) 37.41 ●
    CorCap™ 37.41 ●
    epicardial support device 37.41 ●
    Lap-Band™ 44.95
    left atrial appendage 37.90
    left atrial filter 37.90
    left atrial occluder 37.90
    prosthetic cardiac support device 37.41 ●
    vascular access 86.07
    ventricular support device 37.41 ●
  diaphragm, vagina 96.17
  drainage tube
    kidney 55.02
    pelvis 55.12
    renal pelvis 55.12
  elbow prosthesis (total) 81.84
    revision 81.97
  electrode(s)
    bone growth stimulator (invasive) (percutaneous) (semi-invasive) — *see* category 78.9 ☑
    brain 02.93
      depth 02.93
      foramen ovale 02.93
      sphenoidal 02.96
    depth 02.93
    foramen ovale 02.93
    heart (initial) (transvenous) 37.70
      atrium (initial) 37.73
        replacement 37.76
      atrium and ventricle (initial) 37.72
        replacement 37.76
      epicardium (sternotomy or thoracotomy approach) 37.74
      left ventricular coronary venous system 00.52
      temporary transvenous pacemaker system 37.78
        during and immediately following cardiac surgery 39.64
      ventricle (initial) 37.71
        replacement 37.76
    intracranial 02.93
    osteogenic (for bone growth stimulation) — *see* category 78.9 ☑
    peripheral nerve 04.92
    sacral nerve 04.92
    sphenoidal 02.96
    spine 03.93
  electroencephalographic receiver — *see* Implant, electroencephalographic receiver, by site
  electronic stimulator — *see* Implant, electronic stimulator, by site
  electrostimulator — *see* Implant, electronic stimulator, by site
  endograft(s), endovascular graft(s)
    endovascular, abdominal aorta 39.71 ●
    endovascular, head and neck vessels 39.72 ●
    endovascular, other vessels (for aneurysm) 39.79
    endovascular, thoracic aorta 39.73 ●
  endoprosthesis
    bile duct 51.87
    femoral head (bipolar) 81.52
    pancreatic duct 52.93
  epidural pegs 02.93
  external fixation device (bone) — *see* category 78.1 ☑
  facial bone implant (alloplastic) (synthetic) 76.92
  filling material, skin (filling of defect) 86.02
  filter
    vena cava (inferior) (superior) (transvenous) 38.7
  fixator, mini device (bone) — *see* category 78.1 ☑
  frame (stereotactic)
    for radiosurgery 93.59
  Gardner Wells tongs (skull) (with synchronous skeletal traction) 02.94
  gastric bubble (balloon) 44.93
  globe, into eye socket 16.69
  Greenfield filter 38.7

☑ Additional Digit Required — Refer to the Tabular List (Numeric Code Section) for Additional Digit Selection
▶◀ Revised Text   ● New Line   ▲ Revised Code

2006 ICD-9-CM   **October 2005 • Volume 3 — 39**

Insertion — *continued*
  prosthesis, prosthetic device — *continued*
    hip (partial) 81.52
      revision ▶NOS◀ 81.53
        acetabular and femoral
          components (total) 00.70 ●
        acetabular component only 00.71 ●
        acetabular liner and/or femoral
          head only 00.73 ●
        femoral component only 00.72 ●
        femoral head only and/or
          acetabular liner 00.73 ●
        partial ●
          acetabular component only 00.71 ●
          acetabular liner and/or femoral ●
            head only 00.73 ●
          femoral component only 00.72 ●
          femoral head only and/or
            acetabular liner 00.73 ●
        total (acetabular and femoral
          components) 00.70 ●
      total 81.51
        revision
          acetabular and femoral
            components (total) 00.70 ●
          total (acetabular and femoral
            components) 00.70 ●
    joint — *see* Arthroplasty
    knee (partial) (total) 81.54
      revision ▶NOS◀ 81.55
        femoral component 00.82 ●
        partial ●
          femoral component 00.82 ●
          patellar component 00.83 ●
          tibial component 00.81 ●
          tibial insert 00.84 ●
        patellar component 00.83 ●
        tibial component 00.81 ●
        tibial insert 00.84 ●
        total (all components) 00.80 ●
    leg (bioelectric) (cineplastic) (kineplastic)
      84.48
    ocular (secondary) 16.61
      with orbital exenteration 16.42
    outflow tract (gusset type) (heart)
      in
        pulmonary valvuloplasty 35.26
        total repair of tetralogy of Fallot 35.81
    penis (internal) (noninflatable) 64.95
      with
        construction 64.43
        reconstruction 64.44
      inflatable (internal) 64.97
    Rosen (for urinary incontinence) 59.79
    shoulder
      partial 81.81
      revision 81.97
      total 81.80
    spine
      artificial disc, NOS 84.60
        cervical 84.62
          nucleus 84.61
          partial 84.61
          total 84.62
        lumbar, lumbosacral 84.65
          nucleus 84.64
          partial 84.64
          total 84.65
        thoracic (partial) (total) 84.63
      other device 84.59
    testicular (bilateral) (unilateral) 62.7
    toe 81.57
      hallux valgus repair 77.59
    pseudophakos (*see also* Insertion, lens) 13.70
    pump, infusion 86.06
    radioactive isotope 92.27
    radium 92.27
    radon seeds 92.27
    Reuter bobbin (with intubation) 20.01
    Rickham reservoir 02.2
    Rosen prosthesis (for urinary incontinence)
      59.79
    Scribner shunt 39.93
    Sengstaken-Blakemore tube 96.06

Insertion — *continued*
  sensor
    intra-arterial, for continuous blood gas
      monitoring 89.60
  sieve, vena cava 38.7
  skeletal muscle stimulator 83.92
  skull
    plate 02.05
    stereotactic frame 93.59
    tongs (Barton) (caliper) (Garder Wells) (Vinke)
      (with synchronous skeletal traction)
      02.94
  spacer (cement) ▶(joint)◀ 84.56   ▲
    spine 84.51
  sphenoidal electrodes 02.96
  spine
    bone void filler
      that with kyphoplasty 81.66
      that with vertebroplasty 81.65
    cage (BAK) 84.51
    interbody spinal fusion device 84.51
    interspinous process decompression ●
      device 84.58 ●
    spacer 84.51
  Spitz-Holter valve 02.2
  Steinmann pin 93.44
    with reduction of fracture or dislocation
      — *see* Reduction, fracture *and*
      Reduction, dislocation
  stent(s) (stent graft)
    artery (bare) (bonded) (drug-coated) (non-
      drug-eluting)

    ┌─────────────────────────────────────┐
    │ *Note — Also use 00.40, 00.41, 00.42, or* ● │
    │ *00.43 to show the total number of vessels* ● │
    │ *treated. In addition, use 00.45, 00.46,* ● │
    │ *00.47, or 00.48 to show the number of* ● │
    │ *vascular stents inserted.* ● │
    └─────────────────────────────────────┘

      basilar 00.64
      carotid 00.63
      cerebrovascular
        cerebral (intracranial) 00.65
        precerebral (extracranial) 00.64
          carotid 00.63
      coronary (bare) (bonded) (drug-coated)
        (non-drug-eluting) 36.06
          drug-eluting 36.07
      extracranial 00.64
        carotid 00.63
      intracranial 00.65
      non-coronary vessel
        basilar 00.64
        carotid 00.63
        extracranial 00.64
        intracranial 00.65
        peripheral 39.90
          bare, drug-coated 39.90
          drug-eluting 00.55
        vertebral 00.64
    bile duct 51.43
      endoscopic 51.87
      percutaneous transhepatic 51.98
    coronary (artery) (bare) (bonded) (drug-
      coated) (non-drug-eluting) 36.06

    ┌─────────────────────────────────────┐
    │ *Note — Also use 00.40, 00.41, 00.42, or* ● │
    │ *00.43 to show the total number of vessels* ● │
    │ *treated. In addition, use 00.45, 00.46,* ● │
    │ *00.47, or 00.48 to show the number of* ● │
    │ *vascular stents inserted.* ● │
    └─────────────────────────────────────┘

      drug-eluting 36.07
    esophagus (endoscopic) (fluoroscopic) 42.81
    non-coronary vessel

    ┌─────────────────────────────────────┐
    │ *Note — Also use 00.40, 00.41, 00.42, or* ● │
    │ *00.43 to show the total number of vessels* ● │
    │ *treated. In addition, use 00.45, 00.46,* ● │
    │ *00.47, or 00.48 to show the number of* ● │
    │ *vascular stents inserted.* ● │
    └─────────────────────────────────────┘

      with angioplasty or atherectomy 39.50
      with bypass — *omit code*
        basilar 00.64
        carotid 00.63
        extracranial 00.64
        intracranial 00.65

Insertion — *continued*
  stent(s) — *continued*
    non-coronary vessel — *continued*
      peripheral 39.90
        bare, drug-coated 39.90
        drug-eluting 00.55
      vertebral 00.64
    pancreatic duct 52.92
      endoscopic 52.93
    peripheral vessel 39.90

    ┌─────────────────────────────────────┐
    │ *Note — Also use 00.40, 00.41, 00.42, or* ● │
    │ *00.43 to show the total number of vessels* ● │
    │ *treated. In addition, use 00.45, 00.46,* ● │
    │ *00.47, or 00.48 to show the number of* ● │
    │ *vascular stents inserted.* ● │
    └─────────────────────────────────────┘

      bare, drug-coated 39.90
      drug-eluting 00.55
    precerebral 00.64

    ┌─────────────────────────────────────┐
    │ *Note — Also use 00.40, 00.41, 00.42, or* ● │
    │ *00.43 to show the total number of vessels* ● │
    │ *treated. In addition, use 00.45, 00.46,* ● │
    │ *00.47, or 00.48 to show the number of* ● │
    │ *vascular stents inserted.* ● │
    └─────────────────────────────────────┘

      subclavian 39.90

    ┌─────────────────────────────────────┐
    │ *Note — Also use 00.40, 00.41, 00.42, or* ● │
    │ *00.43 to show the total number of vessels* ● │
    │ *treated. In addition, use 00.45, 00.46,* ● │
    │ *00.47, or 00.48 to show the number of* ● │
    │ *vascular stents inserted.* ● │
    └─────────────────────────────────────┘

      bare, drug-coated 39.90
      drug-eluting 00.55
    tracheobronchial 96.05
    vertebral 00.64

    ┌─────────────────────────────────────┐
    │ *Note — Also use 00.40, 00.41, 00.42, or* ● │
    │ *00.43 to show the total number of vessels* ● │
    │ *treated. In addition, use 00.45, 00.46,* ● │
    │ *00.47, or 00.48 to show the number of* ● │
    │ *vascular stents inserted.* ● │
    └─────────────────────────────────────┘

  stimoceiver — *see* Implant, neurostimulator, by
    site
  stimulator for bone growth — *see* category
    78.9 ☑
  subdural
    grids 02.93
    strips 02.93
  suppository
    prostaglandin (for abortion) 96.49
    vagina 96.49
  Swan-Ganz catheter (pulmonary) 89.64
  tampon
    esophagus 96.06
    uterus 69.91
    vagina 96.14
      after delivery or abortion 75.8
  Tandem™ heart 37.68
  testicular prosthesis (bilateral) (unilateral) 62.7
  tissue expander (skin) NEC 86.93
    breast 85.95
  tissue mandril (peripheral vessel) (Dacron)
    (Spark's type) 39.99
    with
      blood vessel repair 39.56
      vascular bypass or shunt — *see* Bypass,
        vascular
  tongs, skull (with synchronous skeletal
    traction) 02.94
  totally implanted device for bone growth
    (invasive) — *see* category 78.9 ☑
  tube — *see also* Catheterization *and* Intubation
    bile duct 51.43
      endoscopic 51.87
    chest 34.04
      revision (with lysis of adhesions) 34.04
    endotracheal 96.04
    esophagus (nonoperative) (Sengstaken)
      96.06
      permanent (silicone) (Souttar) 42.81
    feeding
      esophageal 42.81
      gastric 96.6

Insertion — *continued*
tube — *see also* Catheterization *and* Intubation — *continued*
  feeding — *continued*
    nasogastric 96.6
    gastric
      by gastrostomy — *see* category 43.1 ☑
      for
        decompression, intestinal 96.07
        feeding 96.6
    intercostal (with water seal), for drainage 34.04
      revision (with lysis of adhesions) 34.04
    Miller-Abbott (for intestinal decompression) 96.08
    nasobiliary (drainage) 51.86
    nasogastric (for intestinal decompression) NEC 96.07
    naso-intestinal 96.08
    nasopancreatic drainage (endoscopic) 52.97
    pancreatic duct 52.92
      endoscopic 52.93
    rectum 96.09
    stomach (nasogastric) (for intestinal decompression) NEC 96.07
      for feeding 96.6
    tracheobronchial 96.05
  umbrella device
    atrial septum (King-Mills) 35.52
    vena cava (Mobitz-Uddin) 38.7
  ureteral stent (transurethral) 59.8
    with ureterotomy 59.8 [56.2]
  urinary sphincter, artificial (AUS) (inflatable) 58.93
  vaginal mold 96.15
  valve
    Holter 02.2
    Hufnagel — *see* Replacement, heart valve
    pharyngeal (artificial) 31.75
    Spitz-Holter 02.2
    vas deferens 63.95
  vascular access device, totally implantable 86.07
  vena cava sieve or umbrella 38.7
  Vinke tongs (skull) (with synchronous skeletal traction) 02.94
Instillation
  bladder 96.49
  digestive tract, except gastric gavage 96.43
  genitourinary NEC 96.49
  radioisotope (intracavitary) (intravenous) 92.28
Insufflation
  Eustachian tube 20.8
  fallopian tube (air) (dye) (gas) (saline) 66.8
    for radiography — *see* Hysterosalpingography
    therapeutic substance 66.95
  lumbar retroperitoneal, bilateral 88.15
Intercricothyroidotomy (for assistance in breathing) 31.1
Intermittent positive pressure breathing (IPPB) 93.91
Interposition operation
  esophageal reconstruction (intrathoracic) (retrosternal) NEC (*see also* Anastomosis, esophagus, with, interposition) 42.58
  antesternal or antethoracic NEC (*see also* Anastomosis, esophagus, antesternal, with, interposition) 42.68
  uterine suspension 69.21
Interruption
  vena cava (inferior) (superior) 38.7
Interrogation
  cardioverter-defibrillator, automatic (AICD)
    with NIPS (arrhythmia induction) 37.26
    interrogation only (bedside device check) 89.49
  CRT-D (cardiac resynchronization defibrillator)
    with NIPS (arrhythmia induction) 37.26
    interrogation only (bedside device check) 89.49
  CRT-P (cardiac resynchronization pacemaker)
    with NIPS (arrhythmia induction) 37.26

Interrogation — *continued*
  CRT-P — *continued*
    interrogation only (bedside device check) 89.45
  pacemaker
    with NIPS (arrhythmia induction) 37.26
    interrogation only (bedside device check) 89.45
Interview (evaluation) (diagnostic)
  medical, except psychiatric 89.05
    brief (abbreviated history) 89.01
    comprehensive (history and evaluation of new problem) 89.03
    limited (interval history) 89.02
    specified type NEC 89.04
  psychiatric NEC 94.19
    follow-up 94.19
    initial 94.19
    pre-commitment 94.13
Intimectomy 38.10
  abdominal 38.16
  aorta (arch) (ascending) (descending) 38.14
  head and neck NEC 38.12
  intracranial NEC 38.11
  lower limb 38.18
  thoracic NEC 38.15
  upper limb 38.13
Introduction
  orthodontic appliance 24.7
  therapeutic substance (acting locally or systemically) NEC 99.29
    bursa 83.96
      hand 82.94
    fascia 83.98
      hand 82.96
    heart 37.92
    joint 81.92
      temporomandibular 76.96
    ligament (joint) 81.92
    pericardium 37.93
    soft tissue NEC 83.98
      hand 82.96
    tendon 83.97
      hand 82.95
    vein 39.92
Intubation — *see also* Catheterization and Insertion
  bile duct(s) 51.59
    common 51.51
      endoscopic 51.87
    endoscopic 51.87
  esophagus (nonoperative) (Sengstaken) 96.06
    permanent tube (silicone) (Souttar) 42.81
  Eustachian tube 20.8
  intestine (for decompression) 96.08
  lacrimal for
    dilation 09.42
    tear drainage, intranasal 09.81
  larynx 96.05
  nasobiliary (drainage) 51.86
  nasogastric
    for
      decompression, intestinal 96.07
      feeding 96.6
  nasolacrimal (duct) (with irrigation) 09.44
  nasopancreatic drainage (endoscopic) 52.97
  naso-intestinal 96.08
  respiratory tract NEC 96.05
  small intestine (Miller-Abbott) 96.08
  stomach (nasogastric) (for intestinal decompression) NEC 96.07
    for feeding 96.6
  trachea 96.04
  ventriculocisternal 02.2
Invagination, diverticulum
  gastric 44.69
    laparoscopic 44.68
  pharynx 29.59
  stomach 44.69
    laparoscopic 44.68
Inversion
  appendix 47.99
  diverticulum
    gastric 44.69
      laparoscopic 44.68

Inversion — *continued*
  diverticulum — *continued*
    intestine
      large 45.49
        endoscopic 45.43
      small 45.34
    stomach 44.69
      laparoscopic 44.68
  tunica vaginalis 61.49
Ionization, medical 99.27
Iontherapy 99.27
Iontophoresis 99.27
Iridectomy (basal) (buttonhole) (optical) (peripheral) (total) 12.14
  with
    capsulectomy 13.65
    cataract extraction — *see* Extraction, cataract
    filtering operation (for glaucoma) NEC 12.65
    scleral
      fistulization 12.65
      thermocauterization 12.62
      trephination 12.61
Iridencleisis 12.63
Iridesis 12.63
Irido-capsulectomy 13.65
Iridocyclectomy 12.44
Iridocystectomy 12.42
Iridodesis 12.63
Iridoplasty NEC 12.39
Iridosclerectomy 12.65
Iridosclerotomy 12.69
Iridotasis 12.63
Iridotomy 12.12
  by photocoagulation 12.12
  with transfixion 12.11
  for iris bombé 12.11
  specified type NEC 12.12
Iron lung 93.99
Irradiation
  gamma, stereotactic 92.32
Irrigation
  anterior chamber (eye) 12.91
  bronchus NEC 96.56
  canaliculus 09.42
  catheter
    ureter 96.46
    urinary, indwelling NEC 96.48
    vascular 96.57
    ventricular 02.41
    wound 96.58
  cholecystostomy 96.41
  cornea 96.51
    with removal of foreign body 98.21
  corpus cavernosum 64.98
  cystostomy 96.47
  ear (removal of cerumen) 96.52
  enterostomy 96.36
  eye 96.51
    with removal of foreign body 98.21
  gastrostomy 96.36
  lacrimal
    canaliculi 09.42
    punctum 09.41
  muscle 83.02
    hand 82.02
  nasal
    passages 96.53
    sinus 22.00
  nasolacrimal duct 09.43
    with insertion of tube or stent 09.44
  nephrostomy 96.45
  peritoneal 54.25
  pyelostomy 96.45
  rectal 96.39
  stomach 96.33
  tendon (sheath) 83.01
    hand 82.01
  trachea NEC 96.56
  traumatic cataract 13.3
  tube
    biliary NEC 96.41
    nasogastric NEC 96.34

Irrigation — *continued*
   tube — *continued*
      pancreatic 96.42
      ureterostomy 96.46
      ventricular shunt 02.41
      wound (cleaning) NEC 96.59
Irving operation (tubal ligation) 66.32
Irwin operation (*see also* Osteotomy) 77.30
Ischiectomy (partial) 77.89
   total 77.99
Ischiopubiotomy 77.39
Isolation
   after contact with infectious disease 99.84
   ileal loop 45.51
   intestinal segment or pedicle flap
      large 45.52
      small 45.51
Isthmectomy, thyroid (*see also* Thyroidectomy,
   partial) 06.39

J

Jaboulay operation (gastroduodenostomy) 44.39
   laparoscopic 44.38
Janeway operation (permanent gastrostomy)
   43.19
Jatene operation (arterial switch) 35.84
Jejunectomy 45.62
Jejunocecostomy 45.93
Jejunocholecystostomy 51.32
Jejunocolostomy 45.93
Jejunoileostomy 45.91
Jejunojejunostomy 45.91
Jejunopexy 46.61
Jejunorrhaphy 46.73
Jejunostomy (feeding) 46.39
   delayed opening 46.31
   loop 46.01
   percutaneous (endoscopic) (PEJ) 46.32
   revision 46.41
Jejunotomy 45.02
Johanson operation (urethral reconstruction)
   58.46
Jones operation
   claw toe (transfer of extensor hallucis longus
      tendon) 77.57
      modified (with arthrodesis) 77.57
   dacryocystorhinostomy 09.81
   hammer toe (interphalangeal fusion) 77.56
      modified (tendon transfer with arthrodesis)
         77.57
   repair of peroneal tendon 83.88
Joplin operation (exostectomy with tendon
   transfer) 77.53

K

Kader operation (temporary gastrostomy) 43.19
Kasai portoenterostomy 51.37
Kaufman operation (for urinary stress
   incontinence) 59.79
Kazanjian operation (buccal vestibular sulcus
   extension) 24.91
Kehr operation (hepatopexy) 50.69
Keller operation (bunionectomy) 77.59
Kelly (-Kennedy) operation (urethrovesical
   plication) 59.3
Kelly-Stoeckel operation (urethrovesical
   plication) 59.3
Kelotomy 53.9
Keratectomy (complete) (partial) (superficial)
   11.49
   for pterygium 11.39
      with corneal graft 11.32
Keratocentesis (for hyphema) 12.91
Keratomileusis 11.71
Keratophakia 11.72

Keratoplasty (tectonic) (with autograft) (with
   homograft) 11.60
   lamellar (nonpenetrating) (with homograft)
      11.62
      with autograft 11.61
   penetrating (full-thickness) (with homograft)
      11.64
      with autograft 11.63
   perforating — *see* Keratoplasty, penetrating
   refractive 11.71
   specified type NEC 11.69
Keratoprosthesis 11.73
Keratotomy (delimiting) (posterior) 11.1
   radial (refractive) 11.75
Kerr operation (low cervical cesarean section)
   74.1
Kessler operation (arthroplasty, carpometacarpal
   joint) 81.74
Kidner operation (excision of accessory navicular
   bone) (with tendon transfer) 77.98
Killian operation (frontal sinusotomy) 22.41
Kineplasty — *see* Cineplasty
King-Steelquist operation (hind-quarter
   amputation) 84.19
Kirk operation (amputation through thigh) 84.17
Kock pouch
   bowel anastomosis — *omit code*
   continent ileostomy 46.22
   cutaneous uretero-ileostomy 56.51
   ESWL (extracorporeal shockwave lithotripsy)
      98.51
   removal, calculus 57.19
   revision, cutaneous uretero-ileostomy 56.52
   urinary diversion procedure 56.51
Kockogram (ileal conduitogram) 87.78
Kockoscopy 45.12
Kondoleon operation (correction of lymphedema)
   40.9
Krause operation (sympathetic denervation)
   05.29
Kroener operation (partial salpingectomy) 66.69
Kroenlein operation (lateral orbitotomy) 16.01
Krönig operation (low cervical cesarean section)
   74.1
Krukenberg operation (reconstruction of below-
   elbow amputation) 82.89
Kuhnt-Szymanowski operation (ectropion repair
   with lid reconstruction) 08.44
Kyphoplasty 81.66

L

Labbe operation (gastrotomy) 43.0
Labiectomy (bilateral) 71.62
   unilateral 71.61
Labyrinthectomy (transtympanic) 20.79
Labyrinthotomy (transtympanic) 20.79
Ladd operation (mobilization of intestine) 54.95
Lagrange operation (iridosclerectomy) 12.65
Lambrinudi operation (triple arthrodesis) 81.12
Laminectomy (decompression) (for exploration)
   03.09
   as operative approach — *omit code*
   with
      excision of herniated intervertebral disc
         (nucleus pulposus) 80.51
      excision of other intraspinal lesion (tumor)
         03.4
   reopening of site 03.02
Laminography — *see* Radiography
Laminoplasty, expansile 03.09
Laminotomy (decompression) (for exploration)
   03.09
   as operative approach — *omit code*
   reopening of site 03.02
Langenbeck operation (cleft palate repair) 27.62
Laparoamnioscopy 75.31
Laparorrhaphy 54.63

Laparoscopy 54.21
   with
      biopsy (intra-abdominal) 54.24
         uterine ligaments 68.15
         uterus 68.16
      destruction of fallopian tubes — *see*
         Destruction, fallopian tube
Laparotomy NEC 54.19
   as operative approach — *omit code*
   exploratory (pelvic) 54.11
   reopening of recent operative site (for control of
      hemorrhage) (for exploration) (for incision
      of hematoma) 54.12
Laparotrachelotomy 74.1
Lapidus operation (bunionectomy with
   metatarsal osteotomy) 77.51
Larry operation (shoulder disarticulation) 84.08
Laryngectomy
   with radical neck dissection (with synchronous
      thyroidectomy) (with synchronous
      tracheostomy) 30.4
   complete (with partial laryngectomy) (with
      synchronous tracheostomy) 30.3
      with radical neck dissection (with
         synchronous thyroidectomy) (with
         synchronous tracheostomy) 30.4
   frontolateral partial (extended) 30.29
   glottosupraglottic partial 30.29
   lateral partial 30.29
   partial (frontolateral) (glottosupraglottic)
      (lateral) (submucous) (supraglottic)
      (vertical) 30.29
   radical (with synchronous thyroidectomy) (with
      synchronous tracheostomy) 30.4
   submucous (partial) 30.29
   supraglottic partial 30.29
   total (with partial pharyngectomy) (with
      synchronous tracheostomy) 30.3
      with radical neck dissection (with
         synchronous thyroidectomy) (with
         synchronous tracheostomy) 30.4
   vertical partial 30.29
   wide field 30.3
Laryngocentesis 31.3
Laryngoesophagectomy 30.4
Laryngofissure 30.29
Laryngogram 87.09
   contrast 87.07
Laryngopharyngectomy (with synchronous
   tracheostomy) 30.3
   radical (with synchronous thyroidectomy) 30.4
Laryngopharyngoesophagectomy (with
   synchronous tracheostomy) 30.3
   with radical neck dissection (with synchronous
      thyroidectomy) 30.4
Laryngoplasty 31.69
Laryngorrhaphy 31.61
Laryngoscopy (suspension) (through artificial
   stoma) 31.42
Laryngostomy (permanent) 31.29
   revision 31.63
   temporary (emergency) 31.1
Laryngotomy 31.3
Laryngotracheobronchoscopy 33.23
   with biopsy 33.24
Laryngotracheoscopy 31.42
Laryngotracheostomy (permanent) 31.29
   temporary (emergency) 31.1
Laryngotracheotomy (temporary) 31.1
   permanent 31.29
Laser — *see also* Coagulation, Destruction, and
   Photocoagulation by site
   angioplasty, percutaneous transluminal 39.59
   coronary — *see* Angioplasty, coronary
Lash operation
   internal cervical os repair 67.59
   laparoscopic supracervical hysterectomy 68.31
LASIK (laser-assisted in situ keratomileusis)
   11.71
Latzko operation
   cesarean section 74.2
   colpocleisis 70.8   ▲

☑ Additional Digit Required — Refer to the Tabular List (Numeric Code Section) for Additional Digit Selection

Lavage
antral 22.00
bronchus NEC 96.56
diagnostic (endoscopic) bronchoalveolar
lavage (BAL) 33.24
endotracheal 96.56
gastric 96.33
lung (total) (whole) 33.99
diagnostic (endoscopic) bronchoalveolar
lavage (BAL) 33.24
nasal sinus(es) 22.00
by puncture 22.01
through natural ostium 22.02
peritoneal (diagnostic) 54.25
trachea NEC 96.56
Leadbetter operation (urethral reconstruction)
58.46
Leadbetter-Politano operation
(ureteroneocystostomy) 56.74
Le Fort operation (colpocleisis) 70.8
LEEP (loop electrosurgical excision procedure) of
cervix 67.32
LeMesurier operation (cleft lip repair) 27.54
Lengthening
bone (with bone graft) 78.30
femur 78.35
for reconstruction of thumb 82.69
specified site NEC (see also category 78.3 ☑)
78.39
tibia 78.37
ulna 78.33
extraocular muscle NEC 15.21
multiple (two or more muscles) 15.4
fascia 83.89
hand 82.89
hamstring NEC 83.85
heel cord 83.85
leg
femur 78.35
tibia 78.37
levator palpebrae muscle 08.38
muscle 83.85
extraocular 15.21
multiple (two or more muscles) 15.4
hand 82.55
palate 27.62
secondary or subsequent 27.63
tendon 83.85
for claw toe repair 77.57
hand 82.55
Leriche operation (periarterial sympathectomy)
05.25
Leucotomy, leukotomy 01.32
Leukopheresis, therapeutic 99.72
Lid suture operation (blepharoptosis) 08.31
Ligation
adrenal vessel (artery) (vein) 07.43
aneurysm 39.52
appendages, dermal 86.26
arteriovenous fistula 39.53
coronary artery 36.99
artery 38.80
abdominal 38.86
adrenal 07.43
aorta (arch) (ascending) (descending) 38.84
coronary (anomalous) 36.99
ethmoidal 21.04
external carotid 21.06
for control of epistaxis — see Control,
epistaxis
head and neck NEC 38.82
intracranial NEC 38.81
lower limb 38.88
maxillary (transantral) 21.05
middle meningeal 02.13
thoracic NEC 38.85
thyroid 06.92
upper limb 38.83
atrium, heart 37.99
auricle, heart 37.99
bleeding vessel — see Control, hemorrhage
blood vessel 38.80
abdominal
artery 38.86

Ligation — continued
blood vessel — continued
abdominal — continued
vein 38.87
adrenal 07.43
aorta (arch) (ascending) (descending) 38.84
esophagus 42.91
endoscopic 42.33
head and neck 38.82
intracranial NEC 38.81
lower limb
artery 38.88
vein 38.89
meningeal (artery) (longitudinal sinus) 02.13
thoracic NEC 38.85
thyroid 06.92
upper limb (artery) (vein) 38.83
bronchus 33.92
cisterna chyli 40.64
coronary
artery (anomalous) 36.99
sinus 36.39
dermal appendage 86.26
ductus arteriosus, patent 38.85
esophageal vessel 42.91
endoscopic 42.33
ethmoidal artery 21.04
external carotid artery 21.06
fallopian tube (bilateral) (remaining) (solitary)
66.39
by endoscopy (culdoscopy) (hysteroscopy)
(laparoscopy) (peritoneoscopy) 66.29
with
crushing 66.31
by endoscopy (laparoscopy) 66.21
division 66.32
by endoscopy (culdoscopy)
(laparoscopy) (peritoneoscopy)
66.22
Falope ring 66.39
by endoscopy (laparoscopy) 66.29
unilateral 66.92
fistula, arteriovenous 39.53
coronary artery 36.99
gastric
artery 38.86
varices 44.91
endoscopic 43.41
hemorrhoids 49.45
longitudinal sinus (superior) 02.13
lymphatic (channel) (peripheral) 40.9
thoracic duct 40.64
maxillary artery 21.05
meningeal vessel 02.13
spermatic
cord 63.72
varicocele 63.1
vein (high) 63.1
splenic vessels 38.86
subclavian artery 38.85
superior longitudinal sinus 02.13
supernumerary digit 86.26
thoracic duct 40.64
thyroid vessel (artery) (vein) 06.92
toes (supernumerary) 86.26
tooth 93.55
impacted 24.6
ulcer (peptic) (base) (bed) (bleeding vessel)
44.40
duodenal 44.42
gastric 44.41
ureter 56.95
varices
esophageal 42.91
endoscopic 42.33
gastric 44.91
endoscopic 43.41
peripheral vein (lower limb) 38.59
upper limb 38.53
varicocele 63.1
vas deferens 63.71
vein 38.80
abdominal 38.87
adrenal 07.43
head and neck NEC 38.82
intracranial NEC 38.81

Ligation — continued
vein — continued
lower limb 38.89
spermatic, high 63.1
thoracic NEC 38.85
thyroid 06.92
upper limb 38.83
varicose 38.50
abdominal 38.57
esophagus 42.91
endoscopic 42.33
gastric 44.91
endoscopic 43.41
head and neck NEC 38.52
intracranial NEC 38.51
lower limb 38.59
stomach 44.91
thoracic NEC 38.55
upper limb 38.53
vena cava, inferior 38.7
venous connection between anomalous vein to
left innominate vein 35.82
superior vena cava 35.82
wart 86.26
Light coagulation — see Photocoagulation
Lindholm operation (repair of ruptured tendon)
83.88
Lingulectomy, lung 32.3
Linton operation (varicose vein) 38.59
Lipectomy (subcutaneous tissue) (abdominal)
(submental) 86.83
Liposuction 86.83
Lip reading training 95.49
Lip shave 27.43
Lisfranc operation
foot amputation 84.12
shoulder disarticulation 84.08
Litholapaxy, bladder 57.0
by incision 57.19
Lithotomy
bile passage 51.49
bladder (urinary) 57.19
common duct 51.41
percutaneous 51.96
gallbladder 51.04
hepatic duct 51.49
kidney 55.01
percutaneous 55.03
ureter 56.2
Lithotripsy
bile duct NEC 51.49
extracorporeal shockwave (ESWL) 98.52
bladder 57.0
with ultrasonic fragmentation 57.0 [59.95]
extracorporeal shockwave (ESWL) 98.51
extracorporeal shockwave (ESWL) NEC 98.59
bile duct 98.52
bladder (urinary) 98.51
gallbladder 98.52
kidney 98.51
Kock pouch 98.51
renal pelvis 98.51
specified site NEC 98.59
ureter 98.51
gallbladder NEC 51.04
endoscopic 51.88
extracorporeal shockwave (ESWL) 98.52
kidney 56.0
extracorporeal shockwave (ESWL) 98.51
percutaneous nephrostomy with
fragmentation (laser) (ultrasound)
55.04
renal pelvis 56.0
extracorporeal shockwave (ESWL) 98.51
percutaneous nephrostomy with
fragmentation (laser) (ultrasound)
55.04
ureter 56.0
extracorporeal shockwave (ESWL) 98.51
Littlewood operation (forequarter amputation)
84.09
LLETZ (large loop excision of the transformation
zone) of cervix 67.32

Lloyd-Davies operation (abdominoperineal resection) 48.5

Lobectomy
brain 01.53
  partial 01.59
liver (with partial excision of adjacent lobes) 50.3
lung (complete) 32.4
  partial 32.3
  segmental (with resection of adjacent lobes) 32.4
thyroid (total) (unilateral) (with removal of isthmus) (with removal of portion of remaining lobe) 06.2
  partial (see also Thyroidectomy, partial) 06.39
  substernal 06.51
  subtotal (see also Thyroidectomy, partial) 06.39

Lobotomy, brain 01.32

Localization, placenta 88.78
by RISA injection 92.17

Longmire operation (bile duct anastomosis) 51.39

Loop ileal stoma (see also Ileostomy) 46.01

Loopogram 87.78

Looposcopy (ileal conduit) 56.35

Lord operation
dilation of anal canal for hemorrhoids 49.49
hemorrhoidectomy 49.49
orchidopexy 62.5

Lower GI series (x-ray) 87.64

Lucas and Murray operation (knee arthrodesis with plate) 81.22

Lumpectomy
breast 85.21
specified site — see Excision, lesion, by site

Lymphadenectomy (simple) (see also Excision, lymph, node) 40.29

Lymphadenotomy 40.0

Lymphangiectomy (radical) (see also Excision, lymph, node, by site, radical) 40.50

Lymphangiogram
abdominal 88.04
cervical 87.08
intrathoracic 87.34
lower limb 88.36
pelvic 88.04
upper limb 88.34

Lymphangioplasty 40.9

Lymphangiorrhaphy 40.9

Lymphangiotomy 40.0

Lymphaticostomy 40.9
thoracic duct 40.62

Lysis
adhesions

> *Note:*
> *blunt — omit code*
> *digital — omit code*
> *manual — omit code*
> *mechanical — omit code*
> *without instrumentation — omit code*

  abdominal 54.59
    laparoscopic 54.51
  appendiceal 54.59
    laparoscopic 54.51
  artery-vein-nerve bundle 39.91
  biliary tract 54.59
    laparoscopic 54.51
  bladder (neck) (intraluminal) 57.12
    external 59.11
      laparoscopic 59.12
    transurethral 57.41
  blood vessels 39.91
  bone — see category 78.4 ☑
  bursa 83.91
    by stretching or manipulation 93.28
    hand 82.91
  cartilage of joint 93.26
  chest wall 33.99
  choanae (nasopharynx) 29.54

Lysis — continued
adhesions — continued
  conjunctiva 10.5
  corneovitreal 12.34
  cortical (brain) 02.91
  ear, middle 20.23
  Eustachian tube 20.8
  extraocular muscle 15.7
  extrauterine 54.59
    laparoscopic 54.51
  eyelid 08.09
    and conjunctiva 10.5
  eye muscle 15.7
  fallopian tube 65.89
    laparoscopic 65.81
  fascia 83.91
    hand 82.91
      by stretching or manipulation 93.26
  gallbladder 54.59
    laparoscopic 54.51
  ganglion (peripheral) NEC 04.49
    cranial NEC 04.42
  hand 82.91
    by stretching or manipulation 93.26
  heart 37.10
  intestines 54.59
    laparoscopic 54.51
  iris (posterior) 12.33
    anterior 12.32
  joint (capsule) (structure) (see also Division, joint capsule) 80.40
  kidney 59.02
    laparoscopic 59.03
  labia (vulva) 71.01
  larynx 31.92
  liver 54.59
    laparoscopic 54.51
  lung (for collapse of lung) 33.39
  mediastinum 34.99
  meninges (spinal) 03.6
    cortical 02.91
  middle ear 20.23
  muscle 83.91
    by stretching or manipulation 93.27
    extraocular 15.7
    hand 82.91
      by stretching or manipulation 93.26
  nasopharynx 29.54
  nerve (peripheral) NEC 04.49
    cranial NEC 04.42
    roots, spinal 03.6
    trigeminal 04.41
  nose, nasal 21.91
  ocular muscle 15.7
  ovary 65.89
    laparoscopic 65.81
  pelvic 54.59
    laparoscopic 54.51
  penile 64.93
  pericardium 37.12
  perineal (female) 71.01
  peripheral vessels 39.91
  perirectal 48.81
  perirenal 59.02
    laparoscopic 59.03
  peritoneum (pelvic) 54.59
    laparoscopic 54.51
  periureteral 59.02
    laparoscopic 59.03
  perivesical 59.11
    laparoscopic 59.12
  pharynx 29.54
  pleura (for collapse of lung) 33.39
  spermatic cord 63.94
  spinal (cord) (meninges) (nerve roots) 03.6
  spleen 54.59
    laparoscopic 54.51
  tendon 83.91
    by stretching or manipulation 93.27
    hand 82.91
      by stretching or manipulation 93.26
  thorax 34.99
  tongue 25.93
  trachea 31.92
  tubo-ovarian 65.89
    laparoscopic 65.81

Lysis — continued
adhesions — continued
  ureter 59.02
    with freeing or repositioning of ureter 59.02
    intraluminal 56.81
    laparoscopic 59.03
  urethra (intraluminal) 58.5
  uterus 54.59
    intraluminal 68.21
    laparoscopic 54.51
    peritoneal 54.59
      laparoscopic 54.51
  vagina (intraluminal) 70.13
  vitreous (posterior approach) 14.74
    anterior approach 14.73
  vulva 71.01
  goniosynechiae (with injection of air or liquid) 12.31
  synechiae (posterior) 12.33
    anterior (with injection of air or liquid) 12.32

M

Madlener operation (tubal ligation) 66.31

Magnet extraction
foreign body
  anterior chamber, eye 12.01
  choroid 14.01
  ciliary body 12.01
  conjunctiva 98.22
  cornea 11.0
  eye, eyeball NEC 98.21
    anterior segment 12.01
    posterior segment 14.01
  intraocular (anterior segment) 12.01
  iris 12.01
  lens 13.01
  orbit 98.21
  retina 14.01
  sclera 12.01
  vitreous 14.01

Magnetic resonance imaging (nuclear) — see Imaging, magnetic resonance

Magnuson (-Stack) operation (arthroplasty for recurrent shoulder dislocation) 81.82

Malleostapediopexy 19.19
with incus replacement 19.11

Malström's vacuum extraction 72.79
with episiotomy 72.71

Mammaplasty — see Mammoplasty

Mammectomy — see also Mastectomy
subcutaneous (unilateral) 85.34
  with synchronous implant 85.33
  bilateral 85.36
    with synchronous implant 85.35

Mammilliplasty 85.87

Mammography NEC 87.37

Mammoplasty 85.89
with
  full-thickness graft 85.83
  muscle flap 85.85
  pedicle graft 85.84
  split-thickness graft 85.82
amputative (reduction) (bilateral) 85.32
  unilateral 85.31
augmentation 85.50
with
  breast implant (bilateral) 85.54
    unilateral 85.53
  injection into breast (bilateral) 85.52
    unilateral 85.51
reduction (bilateral) 85.32
  unilateral 85.31
revision 85.89
size reduction (gynecomastia) (bilateral) 85.32
  unilateral 85.31

Mammotomy 85.0

Manchester (-Donald) (-Fothergill) operation (uterine suspension) 69.22

Mandibulectomy (partial) 76.31
total 76.42
  with reconstruction 76.41

Maneuver (method)
Bracht 72.52
Credé 73.59
De Lee (key-in-lock) 72.4
Kristeller 72.54
Lovset's (extraction of arms in breech birth) 72.52
Mauriceau (-Smellie-Veit) 72.52
Pinard (total breech extraction) 72.54
Prague 72.52
Ritgen 73.59
Scanzoni (rotation) 72.4
Van Hoorn 72.52
Wigand-Martin 72.52

Manipulation
with reduction of fracture or dislocation — *see* Reduction, fracture *and* Reduction, dislocation
enterostomy stoma (with dilation) 96.24
intestine (intra-abdominal) 46.80
large 46.82
small 46.81
joint
adhesions 93.26
temporomandibular 76.95
dislocation — *see* Reduction, dislocation
lacrimal passage (tract) NEC 09.49
muscle structures 93.27
musculoskeletal (physical therapy) NEC 93.29
nasal septum, displaced 21.88
osteopathic NEC 93.67
for general mobilization (general articulation) 93.61
high-velocity, low-amplitude forces (thrusting) 93.62
indirect forces 93.65
isotonic, isometric forces 93.64
low-velocity, high-amplitude forces (springing) 93.63
to move tissue fluids 93.66
rectum 96.22
salivary duct 26.91
stomach, intraoperative 44.92
temporomandibular joint NEC 76.95
ureteral calculus by catheter
with removal 56.0
without removal 59.8
uterus NEC 69.98
gravid 75.99
inverted
manual replacement (following delivery) 75.94
surgical — *see* Repair, inverted uterus

Manometry
esophageal 89.32
spinal fluid 89.15
urinary 89.21

Manual arts therapy 93.81

Mapping
cardiac (electrophysiologic) 37.27
doppler (flow) 88.72
electrocardiogram only 89.52

Marckwald operation (cervical os repair) 67.59

Marshall-Marchetti (-Krantz) operation (retropubic urethral suspension) 59.5

Marsupialization — *see also* Destruction, lesion, by site
cyst
Bartholin's 71.23
brain 01.59
cervical (nabothian) 67.31
dental 24.4
dentigerous 24.4
kidney 55.31
larynx 30.01
liver 50.21
ovary 65.21
laparoscopic 65.23
pancreas 52.3
pilonidal (open excision) (with partial closure) 86.21
salivary gland 26.21
spinal (intraspinal) (meninges) 03.4
spleen, splenic 41.41

Marsupialization — *see also* Destruction, lesion, by site — *continued*
lesion
brain 01.59
cerebral 01.59
liver 50.21
pilonidal cyst or sinus (open excision) (with partial closure) 86.21
pseudocyst, pancreas 52.3
ranula, salivary gland 26.21

Massage
cardiac (external) (manual) (closed) 99.63
open 37.91
prostatic 99.94
rectal (for levator spasm) 99.93

MAST (military anti-shock trousers) 93.58

Mastectomy (complete) (prophylactic) (simple) (unilateral) 85.41
with
excision of regional lymph nodes 85.43
bilateral 85.44
preservation of skin and nipple 85.34
with synchronous implant 85.33
bilateral 85.36
with synchronous implant 85.35
bilateral 85.42
extended
radical (Urban) (unilateral) 85.47
bilateral 85.48
simple (with regional lymphadenectomy) (unilateral) 85.43
bilateral 85.44
modified radical (unilateral) 85.43
bilateral 85.44
partial 85.23
radical (Halsted) (Meyer) (unilateral) 85.45
bilateral 85.46
extended (Urban) (unilateral) 85.47
bilateral 85.48
modified (unilateral) 85.43
bilateral 85.44
subcutaneous 85.34
with synchronous implant 85.33
bilateral 85.36
with synchronous implant 85.35
subtotal 85.23

Masters' stress test (two-step) 89.42

Mastoidectomy (cortical) (conservative) 20.49
complete (simple) 20.41
modified radical 20.49
radical 20.42
modified 20.49
simple (complete) 20.41

Mastoidotomy 20.21

Mastoidotympanectomy 20.42

Mastopexy 85.6

Mastoplasty — *see* Mammoplasty

Mastorrhaphy 85.81

Mastotomy 85.0

Matas operation (aneurysmorrhaphy) 39.52

Mayo operation
bunionectomy 77.59
herniorrhaphy 53.49
vaginal hysterectomy 68.59
laparoscopically assisted (LAVH) 68.51

Mazet operation (knee disarticulation) 84.16

McBride operation (bunionectomy with soft tissue correction) 77.53

McBurney operation — *see* Repair, hernia, inguinal

McCall operation (enterocele repair) 70.92

McCauley operation (release of clubfoot) 83.84

McDonald operation (encirclement suture, cervix) 67.59

McIndoe operation (vaginal construction) 70.61

McKeever operation (fusion of first metatarsophalangeal joint for hallux valgus repair) 77.52

McKissock operation (breast reduction) 85.33

McReynolds operation (transposition of pterygium) 11.31

McVay operation
femoral hernia — *see* Repair, hernia, femoral
inguinal hernia — *see* Repair, hernia, inguinal

Measurement
airway resistance 89.38
anatomic NEC 89.39
arterial blood gases 89.65
basal metabolic rate (BMR) 89.39
blood gases
arterial 89.65
continuous intra-arterial 89.60
venous 89.66
body 93.07
cardiac output (by)
Fick method 89.67
indicator dilution technique 89.68
oxygen consumption technique 89.67
thermodilution indicator 89.68
cardiovascular NEC 89.59
central venous pressure 89.62
coronary blood flow 89.69
gastric function NEC 89.39
girth 93.07
intelligence 94.01
intracranial pressure 01.18
intraocular tension or pressure 89.11
as part of extended ophthalmologic work-up 95.03
intrauterine pressure 89.62
limb length 93.06
lung volume 89.37
mixed venous blood gases 89.66
physiologic NEC 89.39
portovenous pressure 89.62
range of motion 93.05
renal clearance 89.29
respiratory NEC 89.38
skin fold thickness 93.07
skull circumference 93.07
sphincter of Oddi pressure 51.15
systemic arterial
blood gases 89.65
continuous intra-arterial 89.60
pressure 89.61
urine (bioassay) (chemistry) 89.29
vascular 89.59
venous blood gases 89.66
vital capacity (pulmonary) 89.37

Meatoplasty
ear 18.6
urethra 58.47

Meatotomy
ureter 56.1
urethra 58.1
internal 58.5

Mechanical ventilation — *see* Ventilation

Mediastinectomy 34.3

Mediastinoscopy (transpleural) 34.22

Mediastinotomy 34.1
with pneumonectomy 32.5

Meloplasty, facial 86.82

Meningeorrhaphy (cerebral) 02.12
spinal NEC 03.59
for
meningocele 03.51
myelomeningocele 03.52

Meniscectomy (knee) NEC 80.6
acromioclavicular 80.91
sternoclavicular 80.91
temporomandibular (joint) 76.5
wrist 80.93

Menstrual extraction or regulation 69.6

Mentoplasty (augmentation) (with graft) (with implant) 76.68
reduction 76.67

Mesenterectomy 54.4

Mesenteriopexy 54.75

Mesenteriplication 54.75

Mesocoloplication 54.75

Mesopexy 54.75

Metatarsectomy 77.98

Metroplasty 69.49

Mid forceps delivery 72.29

Mikulicz operation (exteriorization of intestine) (first stage) 46.03
  second stage 46.04
Miles operation (proctectomy) 48.5
Military anti-shock trousers (MAST) 93.58
Millard operation (cheiloplasty) 27.54
Miller operation
  midtarsal arthrodesis 81.14
  urethrovesical suspension 59.4
Millin-Read operation (urethrovesical suspension) 59.4
Mist therapy 93.94
Mitchell operation (hallux valgus repair) 77.51
Mobilization
  joint NEC 93.16
  mandible 76.95
  neostrophingic (mitral valve) 35.12
  spine 93.15
  stapes (transcrural) 19.0
  testis in scrotum 62.5
Mohs operation (chemosurgical excision of skin) 86.24
Molegraphy 87.81
Monitoring
  cardiac output (by)
    ambulatory (ACM) 89.50
    electrographic 89.54
      during surgery — *omit code*
    Fick method 89.67
    Holter-type device 89.50
    indicator dilution technique 89.68
    oxygen consumption technique 89.67
    specified technique NEC 89.68
    telemetry (cardiac) 89.54
    thermodilution indicator 89.68
    transesophageal (Doppler) (ultrasound) 89.68
  central venous pressure 89.62
  circulatory NEC 89.69
  continuous intra-arterial blood gas 89.60
  coronary blood flow (coincidence counting technique) 89.69
  electroencephalographic 89.19
    radio-telemetered 89.19
    video 89.19
  fetus (fetal heart)
    antepartum
      nonstress (fetal activity acceleration determinations) 75.34
      oxytocin challenge (contraction stress test) 75.35
      ultrasonography (early pregnancy) (Doppler) 88.78
    intrapartum (during labor) (extrauterine) (external) 75.34
      ausculatory (stethoscopy) — *omit code*
      internal (with contraction measurements) (ECG) 75.32
      intrauterine (direct) (ECG) 75.32
      phonocardiographic (extrauterine) 75.34
      pulsed ultrasound (Doppler) 88.78
      transcervical fetal oxygen saturation monitoring 75.38
      transcervical fetal SpO$_2$ monitoring 75.38
  Holter-type device (cardiac) 89.50
  intracranial pressure 01.18
  pulmonary artery
    pressure 89.63
    wedge 89.64
  sleep (recording) — *see* categories 89.17-89.18
  systemic arterial pressure 89.61
  telemetry (cardiac) 89.54
  transesophageal cardiac output (Doppler) 89.68
  ventricular pressure (cardiac) 89.62
Moore operation (arthroplasty) 81.52
Moschowitz
  enterocele repair 70.92
  herniorrhaphy — *see* Repair, hernia, femoral
  sigmoidopexy 46.63
Mountain resort sanitarium 93.98
Mouth-to-mouth resuscitation 93.93
Moxibustion 93.35
MRI — *see* Imaging, magnetic resonance

Muller operation (banding of pulmonary artery) 38.85
Multiple sleep latency test (MSLT) 89.18
Mumford operation (partial claviculectomy) 77.81
Musculoplasty (*see also* Repair, muscle) 83.87
  hand (*see also* Repair, muscle, hand) 82.89
Music therapy 93.84
Mustard operation (interatrial transposition of venous return) 35.91
Myectomy 83.45
  anorectal 48.92
  eye muscle 15.13
    multiple 15.3
  for graft 83.43
    hand 82.34
  hand 82.36
    for graft 82.34
  levator palpebrae 08.33
  rectal 48.92
Myelogram, myelography (air) (gas) 87.21
  posterior fossa 87.02
Myelotomy
  spine, spinal (cord) (tract) (one-stage) (two-stage) 03.29
    percutaneous 03.21
Myocardiectomy (infarcted area) 37.33
Myocardiotomy 37.11
Myoclasis 83.99
  hand 82.99
Myomectomy (uterine) 68.29
  broad ligament 69.19
Myoplasty (*see also* Repair, muscle) 83.87
  hand (*see also* Repair, muscle, hand) 82.89
  mastoid 19.9
Myorrhaphy 83.65
  hand 82.46
Myosuture 83.65
  hand 82.46
Myotasis 93.27
Myotenontoplasty (*see also* Repair, tendon) 83.88
  hand 82.86
Myotenoplasty (*see also* Repair, tendon) 83.88
  hand 82.86
Myotenotomy 83.13
  hand 82.11
Myotomy 83.02
  with division 83.19
    hand 82.19
  colon NEC 46.92
    sigmoid 46.91
  cricopharyngeal 29.31
    that for pharyngeal (pharyngoesophageal) diverticulectomy 29.32
  esophagus 42.7
  eye (oblique) (rectus) 15.21
    multiple (two or more muscles) 15.4
  hand 82.02
    with division 82.19
  levator palpebrae 08.38
  sigmoid (colon) 46.91
Myringectomy 20.59
Myringodectomy 20.59
Myringomalleolabyrinthopexy 19.52
Myringoplasty (epitympanic, type I) (by cauterization) (by graft) 19.4
  revision 19.6
Myringostapediopexy 19.53
Myringostomy 20.01
Myringotomy (with aspiration) (with drainage) 20.09
  with insertion of tube or drainage device (button) (grommet) 20.01

N

Nailing, intramedullary — *see* Reduction, fracture with internal fixation
Narcoanalysis 94.21
Narcosynthesis 94.21
Narrowing, palpebral fissure 08.51

Nasopharyngogram 87.09
  contrast 87.06
Necropsy 89.8
Needleoscopy (fetus) 75.31
Needling
  Bartholin's gland (cyst) 71.21
  cataract (secondary) 13.64
  fallopian tube 66.91
  hydrocephalic head 73.8
  lens (capsule) 13.2
  pupillary membrane (iris) 12.35
Nephrectomy (complete) (total) (unilateral) 55.51
  bilateral 55.54
  partial (wedge) 55.4
  remaining or solitary kidney 55.52
  removal transplanted kidney 55.53
Nephrocolopexy 55.7
Nephrocystanastomosis NEC 56.73
Nephrolithotomy 55.01
Nephrolysis 59.02
  laparoscopic 59.03
Nephropexy 55.7
Nephroplasty 55.89
Nephropyeloplasty 55.87
Nephropyeloureterostomy 55.86
Nephrorrhaphy 55.81
Nephroscopy 55.21
Nephrostolithotomy, percutaneous 55.03
Nephrostomy (with drainage tube) 55.02
  closure 55.82
  percutaneous 55.03
    with fragmentation (ultrasound) 55.04
Nephrotomogram, nephrotomography NEC 87.72
Nephrotomy 55.01
Nephroureterectomy (with bladder cuff) 55.51
Nephroureterocystectomy 55.51 *[57.79]*
Nerve block (cranial) (peripheral) NEC (*see also* Block, by site) 04.81
Neurectasis (cranial) (peripheral) 04.91
Neurectomy (cranial) (infraorbital) (occipital) (peripheral) (spinal) NEC 04.07
  gastric (vagus) (*see also* Vagotomy) 44.00
  opticociliary 12.79
  paracervical 05.22
  presacral 05.24
  retrogasserian 04.07
  sympathetic — *see* Sympathectomy
  trigeminal 04.07
  tympanic 20.91
Neurexeresis NEC 04.07
Neuroablation
  radiofrequency 04.2
Neuroanastomosis (cranial) (peripheral) NEC 04.74
  accessory-facial 04.72
  accessory-hypoglossal 04.73
  hypoglossal-facial 04.71
Neurolysis (peripheral nerve) NEC 04.49
  carpal tunnel 04.43
  cranial nerve NEC 04.42
  spinal (cord) (nerve roots) 03.6
  tarsal tunnel 04.44
  trigeminal nerve 04.41
Neuroplasty (cranial) (peripheral) NEC 04.79
  of old injury (delayed repair) 04.76
  revision 04.75
Neurorrhaphy (cranial) (peripheral) 04.3
Neurotomy (cranial) (peripheral) (spinal) NEC 04.04
  acoustic 04.01
  glossopharyngeal 29.92
  lacrimal branch 05.0
  retrogasserian 04.02
  sympathetic 05.0
  vestibular 04.01
Neurotripsy (peripheral) NEC 04.03
  trigeminal 04.02
Nicola operation (tenodesis for recurrent dislocation of shoulder) 81.82
Nimodipine, infusion 99.75

NIPS (non-invasive programmed electrical stimulation) 37.26
Nissen operation (fundoplication of stomach) 44.66
  laparoscopic 44.67
Noble operation (plication of small intestine) 46.62
Norman Miller operation (vaginopexy) 70.77
Norton operation (extraperitoneal cesarean section) 74.2
Nuclear magnetic resonance imaging — see Imaging, magnetic resonance
Nutrition, concentrated substances
  enteral infusion (of) 96.6
  parenteral, total 99.15
  peripheral parenteral 99.15

O

Ober (-Yount) operation (gluteal-iliotibial fasciotomy) 83.14
Obliteration
  bone cavity (see also Osteoplasty) 78.40
  calyceal diverticulum 55.39
  canaliculi 09.6
  cerebrospinal fistula 02.12
  cul-de-sac 70.92
  frontal sinus (with fat) 22.42
  lacrimal punctum 09.91
  lumbar pseudomeningocele 03.51
  lymphatic structure(s) (peripheral) 40.9
  maxillary sinus 22.31
  meningocele (sacral) 03.51
  pelvic 68.8
  pleural cavity 34.6
  sacral meningocele 03.51
  Skene's gland 71.3
  tympanomastoid cavity 19.9
  vagina, vaginal (partial) (total) 70.4
    vault 70.8
Occlusal molds (dental) 89.31
Occlusion
  artery
    by embolization — see Embolization, artery
    by endovascular approach — see Embolization, artery
    by ligation — see Ligation, artery
  fallopian tube — see Ligation, fallopian tube
  patent ductus arteriosus (PDA) 38.85
  vein
    by embolization — see Embolization, vein
    by endovascular approach — see Embolization, vein
    by ligation — see Ligation, vein
  vena cava (surgical) 38.7
Occupational therapy 93.83
O'Donoghue operation (triad knee repair) 81.43
Odontectomy NEC (see also Removal, tooth, surgical) 23.19
Oleothorax 33.39
Olshausen operation (uterine suspension) 69.22
Omentectomy 54.4
Omentofixation 54.74
Omentopexy 54.74
Omentoplasty 54.74
Omentorrhaphy 54.74
Omentotomy 54.19
Omphalectomy 54.3
Onychectomy 86.23
Onychoplasty 86.86
Onychotomy 86.09
  with drainage 86.04
Oophorectomy (unilateral) 65.39
  with salpingectomy 65.49
    laparoscopic 65.41
  bilateral (same operative episode) 65.51
    laparoscopic 65.53
    with salpingectomy 65.61
      laparoscopic 65.63
  laparoscopic 65.31

Oophorectomy — continued
  partial 65.29
    laparoscopic 65.25
    wedge 65.22
      that by laparoscope 65.24
  remaining ovary 65.52
    laparoscopic 65.54
    with tube 65.62
      laparoscopic 65.64
Oophorocystectomy 65.29
  laparoscopic 65.25
Oophoropexy 65.79
Oophoroplasty 65.79
Oophororrhaphy 65.71
  laparoscopic 65.74
Oophorostomy 65.09
  laparoscopic 65.01
Oophorotomy 65.09
  laparoscopic 65.01
Opening
  bony labyrinth (ear) 20.79
  cranial suture 02.01
  heart valve
    closed heart technique — see Valvulotomy, by site
    open heart technique — see Valvuloplasty, by site
  spinal dura 03.09
Operation
  Abbe
    construction of vagina 70.61
    intestinal anastomosis — see Anastomosis, intestine
  abdominal (region) NEC 54.99
  abdominoperineal NEC 48.5
  Aburel (intra-amniotic injection for abortion) 75.0
  Adams
    advancement of round ligament 69.22
    crushing of nasal septum 21.88
    excision of palmar fascia 82.35
  adenoids NEC 28.99
  adrenal (gland) (nerve) (vessel) NEC 07.49
  Albee
    bone peg, femoral neck 78.05
    graft for slipping patella 78.06
    sliding inlay graft, tibia 78.07
  Albert (arthrodesis, knee) 81.22
  Aldridge (-Studdiford) (urethral sling) 59.5
  Alexander
    prostatectomy
      perineal 60.62
      suprapubic 60.3
    shortening of round ligaments of uterus 69.22
  Alexander-Adams (shortening of round ligaments of uterus) 69.22
  Almoor (extrapetrosal drainage) 20.22
  Altemeier (perineal rectal pull-through) 48.49
  Ammon (dacryocystotomy) 09.53
  Anderson (tibial lengthening) 78.37
  Anel (dilation of lacrimal duct) 09.42
  anterior chamber (eye) NEC 12.99
  anti-incontinence NEC 59.79
  antrum window (nasal sinus) 22.2
    with Caldwell-Luc approach 22.39
  anus NEC 49.99
  aortic body NEC 39.8
  aorticopulmonary window 39.59
  appendix NEC 47.99
  Arslan (fenestration of inner ear) 20.61
  artery NEC 39.99
  Asai (larynx) 31.75
  Baffes (interatrial transposition of venous return) 35.91
  Baldy-Webster (uterine suspension) 69.22
  Ball
    herniorrhaphy — see Repair, hernia, inguinal
    undercutting 49.02
  Bankhart (capsular repair into glenoid, for shoulder dislocation) 81.82
  Bardenheurer (ligation of innominate artery) 38.85

Operation — continued
  Barkan (goniotomy) 12.52
    with goniopuncture 12.53
  Barr (transfer of tibialis posterior tendon) 83.75
  Barsky (closure of cleft hand) 82.82
  Bassett (vulvectomy with inguinal lymph node dissection) 71.5 [40.3]
  Bassini (herniorrhaphy) — see Repair, hernia, inguinal
  Batch-Spittler-McFaddin (knee disarticulation) 84.16
  Batista (partial ventriculectomy) (ventricular reduction) (ventricular remodeling) 37.35
  Beck I (epicardial poudrage) 36.39
  Beck II (aorta-coronary sinus shunt) 36.39
  Beck-Jianu (permanent gastrostomy) 43.19
  Bell-Beuttner (subtotal abdominal hysterectomy) 68.39
  Belsey (esophagogastric sphincter) 44.65
  Benenenti (rotation of bulbous urethra) 58.49
  Berke (levator resection eyelid) 08.33
  Biesenberger (size reduction of breast, bilateral) 85.32
    unilateral 85.31
  Bigelow (litholapaxy) 57.0
  biliary (duct) (tract) NEC 51.99
  Billroth I (partial gastrectomy with gastroduodenostomy) 43.6
  Billroth II (partial gastrectomy with gastrojejunostomy) 43.7
  Binnie (hepatopexy) 50.69
  Bischoff (ureteroneocystostomy) 56.74
  bisection hysterectomy 68.39
    laparoscopic 68.31
  Bishoff (spinal myelotomy) 03.29
  bladder NEC 57.99
    flap 56.74
  Blalock (systemic-pulmonary anastomosis) 39.0
  Blalock-Hanlon (creation of atrial septal defect) 35.42
  Blalock-Taussig (subclavian-pulmonary anastomosis) 39.0
  Blascovic (resection and advancement of levator palpebrae superioris) 08.33
  blood vessel NEC 39.99
  Blount
    femoral shortening (with blade plate) 78.25
    by epiphyseal stapling 78.25
  Boari (bladder flap) 56.74
  Bobb (cholelithotomy) 51.04
  bone NEC — see category 78.4 ☑
    facial 76.99
    injury NEC — see category 79.9 ☑
    marrow NEC 41.98
    skull NEC 02.99
  Bonney (abdominal hysterectomy) 68.4
  Borthen (iridotasis) 12.63
  Bost
    plantar dissection 80.48
    radiocarpal fusion 81.26
  Bosworth
    arthroplasty for acromioclavicular separation 81.83
    fusion of posterior lumbar spine 81.08
      for pseudarthrosis 81.38
    resection of radial head ligaments (for tennis elbow) 80.92
    shelf procedure, hip 81.40
  Bottle (repair of hydrocele of tunica vaginalis) 61.2
  Boyd (hip disarticulation) 84.18
  brain NEC 02.99
  Brauer (cardiolysis) 37.10
  breast NEC 85.99
  Bricker (ileoureterostomy) 56.51
  Bristow (repair of shoulder dislocation) 81.82
  Brock (pulmonary valvulotomy) 35.03
  Brockman (soft tissue release for clubfoot) 83.84
  bronchus NEC 33.98
  Browne (-Denis) (hypospadias repair) 58.45
  Brunschwig (temporary gastrostomy) 43.19
  buccal cavity NEC 27.99
  Bunnell (tendon transfer) 82.56

☑ Additional Digit Required — Refer to the Tabular List (Numeric Code Section) for Additional Digit Selection

Operation — *continued*

Burch procedure (retropubic urethral
    suspension for urinary stress
    incontinence) 59.5
Burgess (amputation of ankle) 84.14
bursa NEC 83.99
    hand 82.99
bypass — *see* Bypass
Caldwell (sulcus extension) 24.91
Caldwell-Luc (maxillary sinusotomy) 22.39
    with removal of membrane lining 22.31
Callander (knee disarticulation) 84.16
Campbell
    bone block, ankle 81.11
    fasciotomy (iliac crest) 83.14
    reconstruction of anterior cruciate ligaments
        81.45
canthus NEC 08.99
cardiac NEC 37.99
    septum NEC 35.98
    valve NEC 35.99
carotid body or gland NEC 39.8
Carroll and Taber (arthroplasty proximal
    interphalangeal joint) 81.72
Cattell (herniorrhaphy) 53.51
Cecil (urethral reconstruction) 58.46
cecum NEC 46.99
cerebral (meninges) NEC 02.99
cervix NEC 69.99
Chandler (hip fusion) 81.21
Charles (correction of lymphedema) 40.9
Charnley (compression arthrodesis)
    ankle 81.11
    hip 81.21
    knee 81.22
Cheatle-Henry — *see* Repair, hernia, femoral
chest cavity NEC 34.99
Chevalier-Jackson (partial laryngectomy) 30.29
Child (radical subtotal pancreatectomy) 52.53
Chopart (midtarsal amputation) 84.12
chordae tendineae NEC 35.32
choroid NEC 14.9
ciliary body NEC 12.98
cisterna chyli NEC 40.69
Clagett (closure of chest wall following open
    flap drainage) 34.72
Clayton (resection of metatarsal heads and
    bases of phalanges) 77.88
clitoris NEC 71.4
cocked hat (metacarpal lengthening and
    transfer of local flap) 82.69
Cockett (varicose vein)
    lower limb 38.59
    upper limb 38.53
Cody tack (perforation of footplate) 19.0
Coffey (uterine suspension) (Meigs'
    modification) 69.22
Cole (anterior tarsal wedge osteotomy) 77.28
Collis-Nissen (hiatal hernia repair) 53.80
colon NEC 46.99
Colonna
    adductor tenotomy (first stage) 83.12
    hip arthroplasty (second stage) 81.40
    reconstruction of hip (second stage) 81.40
commando (radical glossectomy) 25.4
conjunctiva NEC 10.99
    destructive NEC 10.33
cornea NEC 11.99
Coventry (tibial wedge osteotomy) 77.27
Cox-maze procedure (ablation or destruction of
    heart tissue) — *see* Operation, maze
    procedure
Crawford (tarso-frontalis sling of eyelid) 08.32
cul-de-sac NEC 70.92
Culp-Deweerd (spiral flap pyeloplasty) 55.87
Culp-Scardino (ureteral flap pyeloplasty) 55.87
Curtis (interphalangeal joint arthroplasty)
    81.72
cystocele NEC 70.51
Dahlman (excision of esophageal diverticulum)
    42.31
Dana (posterior rhizotomy) 03.1
Danforth (fetal) 73.8
Darrach (ulnar resection) 77.83

Operation — *continued*

Davis (intubated ureterotomy) 56.2
de Grandmont (tarsectomy) 08.35
Delorme
    pericardiectomy 37.31
    proctopexy 48.76
    repair of prolapsed rectum 48.76
    thoracoplasty 33.34
Denker (radical maxillary antrotomy) 22.31
Dennis-Varco (herniorrhaphy) — *see* Repair,
    hernia, femoral
Denonvillier (limited rhinoplasty) 21.86
dental NEC 24.99
    orthodontic NEC 24.8
Derlacki (tympanoplasty) 19.4
diaphragm NEC 34.89
Dickson (fascial transplant) 83.82
Dickson-Diveley (tendon transfer and
    arthrodesis to correct claw toe) 77.57
Dieffenbach (hip disarticulation) 84.18
digestive tract NEC 46.99
Doléris (shortening of round ligaments) 69.22
D'Ombrain (excision of pterygium with corneal
    graft) 11.32
Dorrance (push-back operation for cleft palate)
    27.62
Dotter (transluminal angioplasty) 39.59
Douglas (suture of tongue to lip for
    micrognathia) 25.59
Doyle (paracervical uterine denervation) 69.3
Dühamel (abdominoperineal pull-through)
    48.65
Dührssen (vaginofixation of uterus) 69.22
Dunn (triple arthrodesis) 81.12
duodenum NEC 46.99
Dupuytren
    fasciectomy 82.35
    fasciotomy 82.12
        with excision 82.35
    shoulder disarticulation 84.08
Durham (-Caldwell) (transfer of biceps femoris
    tendon) 83.75
DuToit and Roux (staple capsulorrhaphy of
    shoulder) 81.82
DuVries (tenoplasty) 83.88
Dwyer
    fasciotomy 83.14
    soft tissue release NEC 83.84
    wedge osteotomy, calcaneus 77.28
Eagleton (extrapetrosal drainage) 20.22
ear (external) NEC 18.9
    middle or inner NEC 20.99
Eden-Hybinette (glenoid bone block) 78.01
Effler (heart) 36.2
Eggers
    tendon release (patellar retinacula) 83.13
    tendon transfer (biceps femoris tendon)
        (hamstring tendon) 83.75
Elliot (scleral trephination with iridectomy)
    12.61
Ellis Jones (repair of peroneal tendon) 83.88
Ellison (reinforcement of collateral ligament)
    81.44
Elmslie-Cholmeley (tarsal wedge osteotomy)
    77.28
Eloesser
    thoracoplasty 33.34
    thoracostomy 34.09
Emmet (cervix) 67.61
endorectal pull-through 48.41
epididymis NEC 63.99
esophagus NEC 42.99
Estes (ovary) 65.72
    laparoscopic 65.75
Estlander (thoracoplasty) 33.34
Evans (release of clubfoot) 83.84
extraocular muscle NEC 15.9
    multiple (two or more muscles) 15.4
        with temporary detachment from globe
            15.3
    revision 15.6
    single 15.29
        with temporary detachment from globe
            15.19
eyeball NEC 16.99
eyelid(s) NEC 08.99

Operation — *continued*

face NEC 27.99
facial bone or joint NEC 76.99
fallopian tube NEC 66.99
Farabeuf (ischiopubiotomy) 77.39
Fasanella-Servatt (blepharoptosis repair) 08.35
fascia NEC 83.99
    hand 82.99
female (genital organs) NEC 71.9
    hysterectomy NEC 68.9
fenestration (aorta) 39.54
Ferguson (hernia repair) 53.00
Fick (perforation of footplate) 19.0
filtering (for glaucoma) 12.79
    with iridectomy 12.65
Finney (pyloroplasty) 44.29
fistulizing, sclera NEC 12.69
Foley (pyeloplasty) 55.87
Fontan (creation of conduit between right
    atrium and pulmonary artery) 35.94
Fothergill (-Donald) (uterine suspension) 69.22
Fowler
    arthroplasty of metacarpophalangeal joint
        81.72
    release (mallet finger repair) 82.84
    tenodesis (hand) 82.85
    thoracoplasty 33.34
Fox (entropion repair with wedge resection)
    08.43
Franco (suprapubic cystotomy) 57.19
Frank (permanent gastrostomy) 43.19
Frazier (-Spiller) (subtemporal trigeminal
    rhizotomy) 04.02
Fredet-Ramstedt (pyloromyotomy) (with wedge
    resection) 43.3
Frenckner (intrapetrosal drainage) 20.22
Frickman (abdominal proctopexy) 48.75
Frommel (shortening of uterosacral ligaments)
    69.22
Gabriel (abdominoperineal resection of rectum)
    48.5
gallbladder NEC 51.99
ganglia NEC 04.99
    sympathetic 05.89
Gant (wedge osteotomy of trochanter) 77.25
Garceau (tibial tendon transfer) 83.75
Gardner (spinal meningocele repair) 03.51
gastric NEC 44.99
Gelman (release of clubfoot) 83.84
genital organ NEC
    female 71.9
    male 64.99
Ghormley (hip fusion) 81.21
Gifford
    destruction of lacrimal sac 09.6
    keratotomy (delimiting) 11.1
Gill
    arthrodesis of shoulder 81.23
    laminectomy 03.09
Gill-Stein (carporadial arthrodesis) 81.25
Gilliam (uterine suspension) 69.22
Girdlestone
    laminectomy with spinal fusion 81.00
    muscle transfer for claw toe 77.57
    resection of femoral head and neck
        ▶(without insertion of joint
            prosthesis)◀ 77.85   ●
        with replacement prosthesis — *see*   ●
            Implant, joint, hip   ●
    resection of hip prosthesis 80.05   ●
        with replacement prosthesis — *see*   ●
            Implant, joint, hip   ●
Girdlestone-Taylor (muscle transfer for claw toe
    repair) 77.57
glaucoma NEC 12.79
Glenn (anastomosis of superior vena cava to
    right pulmonary artery) 39.21
globus pallidus NEC 01.42
Goebel-Frangenheim-Stoeckel (urethrovesical
    suspension) 59.4
Goldner (clubfoot release) 80.48
Goldthwait
    ankle stabilization 81.11
    patella stabilization 81.44
    tendon transfer for patella dislocation 81.44
Goodall-Power (vagina) 70.4

Operation — *continued*
　Gordon-Taylor (hindquarter amputation) 84.19
　Graber-Duvernay (drilling femoral head) 77.15
　Green (scapulopexy) 78.41
　Grice (subtalar arthrodesis) 81.13
　Gritti-Stokes (knee disarticulation) 84.16
　Gross (herniorrhaphy) 53.49
　gum NEC 24.39
　Guyon (amputation of ankle) 84.13
　Hagner (epididymotomy) 63.92
　Halsted — *see* Repair, hernia, inguinal
　Hampton (anastomosis small intestine to rectal
　　stump) 45.92
　hanging hip (muscle release) 83.19
　harelip 27.54
　Harrison-Richardson (vaginal suspension)
　　70.77
　Hartmann — *see* Colectomy, by site
　Hauser
　　achillotenotomy 83.11
　　bunionectomy with adductor tendon transfer
　　　77.53
　　stabilization of patella 81.44
　Heaney (vaginal hysterectomy) 68.59
　　laparoscopically assisted (LAVH) 68.51
　heart NEC 37.99
　　valve NEC 35.99
　　　adjacent structure NEC 35.39
　Hegar (perineorrhaphy) 71.79
　Heine (cyclodialysis) 12.55
　Heineke-Mikulicz (pyloroplasty) — *see* category
　　44.2 ☑
　Heller (esophagomyotomy) 42.7
　Hellström (transplantation of aberrant renal
　　vessel) 39.55
　hemorrhoids NEC 49.49
　Henley (jejunal transposition) 43.81
　hepatic NEC 50.99
　hernia — *see* Repair, hernia
　Hey (amputation of foot) 84.12
　Hey-Groves (reconstruction of anterior cruciate
　　ligament) 81.45
　Heyman (soft tissue release for clubfoot) 83.84
　Heyman-Herndon (-Strong) (correction of
　　metatarsus varus) 80.48
　Hibbs (lumbar spinal fusion) — *see* Fusion,
　　lumbar
　Higgins — *see* Repair, hernia, femoral
　Hill-Allison (hiatal hernia repair, transpleural
　　approach) 53.80
　Hitchcock (anchoring tendon of biceps) 83.88
　Hofmeister (gastrectomy) 43.7
　Hoke
　　midtarsal fusion 81.14
　　triple arthrodesis 81.12
　Holth
　　iridencleisis 12.63
　　sclerectomy 12.65
　Homan (correction of lymphedema) 40.9
　Hutch (ureteroneocystostomy) 56.74
　Hybinette-eden (glenoid bone block) 78.01
　hymen NEC 70.91
　hypopharynx NEC 29.99
　hypophysis NEC 07.79
　ileal loop 56.51
　ileum NEC 46.99
　intestine NEC 46.99
　iris NEC 12.97
　　inclusion 12.63
　Irving (tubal ligation) 66.32
　Irwin (*see also* Osteotomy) 77.30
　Jaboulay (gastroduodenostomy) 44.39
　　laparoscopic 44.38
　Janeway (permanent gastrostomy) 43.19
　Jatene (arterial switch) 35.84
　jejunum NEC 46.99
　Johanson (urethral reconstruction) 58.46
　joint (capsule) (ligament) (structure) NEC 81.99
　　facial NEC 76.99
　Jones
　　claw toe (transfer of extensor hallucis longus
　　　tendon) 77.57
　　　modified (with arthrodesis) 77.57
　　dacryocystorhinostomy 09.81
　　hammer toe (interphalangeal fusion) 77.56
　　modified (tendon transfer with arthrodesis)
　　　77.57

Operation — *continued*
　Jones — *continued*
　　repair of peroneal tendon 83.88
　Joplin (exostectomy with tendon transfer) 77.53
　Kader (temporary gastrostomy) 43.19
　Kaufman (for urinary stress incontinence)
　　59.79
　Kazanjian (buccal vestibular sulcus extension)
　　24.91
　Kehr (hepatopexy) 50.69
　Keller (bunionectomy) 77.59
　Kelly (-Kennedy) (urethrovesical plication) 59.3
　Kelly-Stoeckel (urethrovesical plication) 59.3
　Kerr (cesarean section) 74.1
　Kessler (arthroplasty, carpometacarpal joint)
　　81.74
　Kidner (excision of accessory navicular bone)
　　(with tendon transfer) 77.98
　kidney NEC 55.99
　Killian (frontal sinusotomy) 22.41
　King-Steelquist (hindquarter amputation) 84.19
　Kirk (amputation through thigh) 84.17
　Kock pouch
　　bowel anastomosis — *omit code*
　　continent ileostomy 46.22
　　cutaneous uretero-ileostomy 56.51
　　ESWL (electrocorporeal shockwave
　　　lithotripsy) 98.51
　　removal, calculus 57.19
　　revision, cutaneous uretero-ileostomy 56.52
　　urinary diversion procedure 56.51
　Kondoleon (correction of lymphedema) 40.9
　Krause (sympathetic denervation) 05.29
　Kroener (partial salpingectomy) 66.69
　Kroenlein (lateral orbitotomy) 16.01
　Krönig (low cervical cesarean section) 74.1
　Krukenberg (reconstruction of below-elbow
　　amputation) 82.89
　Kuhnt-Szymanowski (ectropion repair with lid
　　reconstruction) 08.44
　Labbe (gastrotomy) 43.0
　labia NEC 71.8
　lacrimal
　　gland 09.3
　　system NEC 09.99
　Ladd (mobilization of intestine) 54.95
　Lagrange (iridosclerectomy) 12.65
　Lambrinudi (triple arthrodesis) 81.12
　Langenbeck (cleft palate repair) 27.62
　Lapidus (bunionectomy with metatarsal
　　osteotomy) 77.51
　Larry (shoulder disarticulation) 84.08
　larynx NEC 31.98
　Lash
　　internal cervical os repair 67.59
　　laparoscopic supracervical hysterectomy
　　　68.31
　Latzko
　　cesarean section, extraperitoneal 74.2
　　colpocleisis 70.8
　Leadbetter (urethral reconstruction) 58.46
　Leadbetter-Politano (ureteroneocystostomy)
　　56.74
　Le Fort (colpocleisis) 70.8
　LeMesurier (cleft lip repair) 27.54
　lens NEC 13.9
　Leriche (periarterial sympathectomy) 05.25
　levator muscle sling
　　eyelid ptosis repair 08.33
　　urethrovesical suspension 59.71
　　urinary stress incontinence 59.71
　lid suture (blepharoptosis) 08.31
　ligament NEC 81.99
　　broad NEC 69.98
　　round NEC 69.98
　　uterine NEC 69.98
　Lindholm (repair of ruptured tendon) 83.88
　Linton (varicose vein) 38.59
　lip NEC 27.99
　Lisfranc
　　foot amputation 84.12
　　shoulder disarticulation 84.08
　Littlewood (forequarter amputation) 84.09
　　liver NEC 50.99
　Lloyd-Davies (abdominoperineal resection)
　　48.5

Operation — *continued*
　Longmire (bile duct anastomosis) 51.39
　Lord
　　dilation of anal canal for hemorrhoids 49.49
　　hemorrhoidectomy 49.49
　　orchidopexy 62.5
　Lucas and Murray (knee arthrodesis with plate)
　　81.22
　lung NEC 33.99
　lung volume reduction 32.22
　lymphatic structure(s) NEC 40.9
　　duct, left (thoracic) NEC 40.69
　Madlener (tubal ligation) 66.31
　Magnuson (-Stack) (arthroplasty for recurrent
　　shoulder dislocation) 81.82
　male genital organs NEC 64.99
　Manchester (-Donald) (-Fothergill) (uterine
　　suspension) 69.22
　mandible NEC 76.99
　　orthognathic 76.64
　Marckwald (cervical os repair) 67.59
　Marshall-Marchetti (-Krantz) (retropubic
　　urethral suspension) 59.5
　Matas (aneurysmorrhaphy) 39.52
　Mayo
　　bunionectomy 77.59
　　herniorrhaphy 53.49
　　vaginal hysterectomy 68.59
　　　laparoscopically assisted (LAVH) 68.51
　maze procedure (ablation or destruction of
　　heart tissue)
　　by incision (open) 37.33
　　by peripherally inserted catheter 37.34
　　endovascular approach 37.34
　　trans-thoracic approach 37.33
　Mazet (knee disarticulation) 84.16
　McBride (bunionectomy with soft tissue
　　correction) 77.53
　McBurney — *see* Repair, hernia, inguinal
　McCall (enterocele repair) 70.92
　McCauley (release of clubfoot) 83.84
　McDonald (encirclement suture, cervix) 67.59
　McIndoe (vaginal construction) 70.61
　McKeever (fusion of first metatarsophalangeal
　　joint for hallux valgus repair) 77.52
　McKissock (breast reduction) 85.33
　McReynolds (transposition of pterygium) 11.31
　McVay
　　femoral hernia — *see* Repair, hernia, femoral
　　inguinal hernia — *see* Repair, hernia,
　　　inguinal
　meninges (spinal) NEC 03.99
　　cerebral NEC 02.99
　mesentery NEC 54.99
　Mikulicz (exteriorization of intestine) (first
　　stage) 46.03
　　second stage 46.04
　Miles (complete proctectomy) 48.5
　Millard (cheiloplasty) 27.54
　Miller
　　midtarsal arthrodesis 81.14
　　urethrovesical suspension 59.4
　Millin-Read (urethrovesical suspension) 59.4
　Mitchell (hallux valgus repair) 77.51
　Mohs (chemosurgical excision of skin) 86.24
　Moore (arthroplasty) 81.52
　Moschowitz
　　enterocele repair 70.92
　　herniorrhaphy — *see* Repair, hernia, femoral
　　sigmoidopexy 46.63
　mouth NEC 27.99
　Muller (banding of pulmonary artery) 38.85
　Mumford (partial claviculectomy) 77.81
　muscle NEC 83.99
　　extraocular — *see* Operation, extraocular
　　hand NEC 82.99
　　papillary heart NEC 35.31
　musculoskeletal system NEC 84.99
　Mustard (interatrial transposition of venous
　　return) 35.91
　nail (finger) (toe) NEC 86.99
　nasal sinus NEC 22.9
　nasopharynx NEC 29.99
　nerve (cranial) (peripheral) NEC 04.99
　　adrenal NEC 07.49
　　sympathetic NEC 05.89

☑ Additional Digit Required — Refer to the Tabular List (Numeric Code Section) for Additional Digit Selection

Operation — *continued*
nervous system NEC 05.9
Nicola (tenodesis for recurrent dislocation of shoulder) 81.82
nipple NEC 85.99
Nissen (fundoplication of stomach) 44.66
  laparoscopic 44.67
Noble (plication of small intestine) 46.62
node (lymph) NEC 40.9
Norman Miller (vaginopexy) 70.77
Norton (extraperitoneal cesarean operation) 74.2
nose, nasal NEC 21.99
  sinus NEC 22.9
Ober (-Yount) (gluteal-iliotibial fasciotomy) 83.14
obstetric NEC 75.99
ocular NEC 16.99
  muscle — *see* Operation, extraocular muscle
O'Donoghue (triad knee repair) 81.43
Olshausen (uterine suspension) 69.22
omentum NEC 54.99
ophthalmologic NEC 16.99
oral cavity NEC 27.99
orbicularis muscle sling 08.36
orbit NEC 16.98
oropharynx NEC 29.99
orthodontic NEC 24.8
orthognathic NEC 76.69
Oscar Miller (midtarsal arthrodesis) 81.14
Osmond-Clark (soft tissue release with peroneus brevis tendon transfer) 83.75
ovary NEC 65.99
Oxford (for urinary incontinence) 59.4
palate NEC 27.99
palpebral ligament sling 08.36
Panas (linear proctotomy) 48.0
Pancoast (division of trigeminal nerve at foramen ovale) 04.02
pancreas NEC 52.99
pantaloon (revision of gastric anastomosis) 44.5
papillary muscle (heart) NEC 35.31
Paquin (ureteroneocystostomy) 56.74
parathyroid gland(s) NEC 06.99
parotid gland or duct NEC 26.99
Partsch (marsupialization of dental cyst) 24.4
Pattee (auditory canal) 18.6
Peet (splanchnic resection) 05.29
Pemberton
  osteotomy of ilium 77.39
  rectum (mobilization and fixation for prolapse repair) 48.76
penis NEC 64.98
Pereyra (paraurethral suspension) 59.6
pericardium NEC 37.99
perineum (female) NEC 71.8
  male NEC 86.99
perirectal tissue NEC 48.99
perirenal tissue NEC 59.92
peritoneum NEC 54.99
periurethral tissue NEC 58.99
perivesical tissue NEC 59.92
pharyngeal flap (cleft palate repair) 27.62
  secondary or subsequent 27.63
pharynx, pharyngeal (pouch) NEC 29.99
pineal gland NEC 07.59
Pinsker (obliteration of nasoseptal telangiectasia) 21.07
Piper (forceps) 72.6
Pirogoff (ankle amputation through malleoli of tibia and fibula) 84.14
pituitary gland NEC 07.79
plastic — *see* Repair, by site
pleural cavity NEC 34.99
Politano-Leadbetter (ureteroneocystostomy) 56.74
pollicization (with nerves and blood supply) 82.61
Polya (gastrectomy) 43.7
Pomeroy (ligation and division of fallopian tubes) 66.32
Poncet
  lengthening of Achilles tendon 83.85
  urethrostomy, perineal 58.0
Porro (cesarean section) 74.99
posterior chamber (eye) NEC 14.9

Operation — *continued*
Potts-Smith (descending aorta-left pulmonary artery anastomosis) 39.0
Printen and Mason (high gastric bypass) 44.31
prostate NEC (*see also* Prostatectomy) 60.69
  specified type 60.99
pterygium 11.39
  with corneal graft 11.32
Puestow (pancreaticojejunostomy) 52.96
pull-through NEC 48.49
pulmonary NEC 33.99
push-back (cleft palate repair) 27.62
Putti-Platt (capsulorrhaphy of shoulder for recurrent dislocation) 81.82
pyloric exclusion 44.39
  laparoscopic 44.38
pyriform sinus NEC 29.99
"rabbit ear" (anterior urethropexy) (Tudor) 59.79
Ramadier (intrapetrosal drainage) 20.22
Ramstedt (pyloromyotomy) (with wedge resection) 43.3
Rankin
  exteriorization of intestine 46.03
  proctectomy (complete) 48.5
Rashkind (balloon septostomy) 35.41
Rastelli (creation of conduit between right ventricle and pulmonary artery) 35.92
  in repair of
    pulmonary artery atresia 35.92
    transposition of great vessels 35.92
    truncus arteriosus 35.83
Raz-Pereyra procedure (bladder neck suspension) 59.79
rectal NEC 48.99
rectocele NEC 70.52
re-entry (aorta) 39.54
renal NEC 55.99
respiratory (tract) NEC 33.99
retina NEC 14.9
Ripstein (repair of rectal prolapse) 48.75
Rodney Smith (radical subtotal pancreatectomy) 52.53
Roux-en-Y
  bile duct 51.36
  cholecystojejunostomy 51.32
  esophagus (intrathoracic) 42.54
  gastroenterostomy 44.39
    laparoscopic 44.38
  gastrojejunostomy 44.39
    laparoscopic 44.38
  pancreaticojejunostomy 52.96
Roux-Goldthwait (repair of patellar dislocation) 81.44
Roux-Herzen-Judine (jejunal loop interposition) 42.63
Ruiz-Mora (proximal phalangectomy for hammer toe) 77.99
Russe (bone graft of scaphoid) 78.04
Saemisch (corneal section) 11.1
salivary gland or duct NEC 26.99
Salter (innominate osteotomy) 77.39
Sauer-Bacon (abdominoperineal resection) 48.5
Schanz (femoral osteotomy) 77.35
Schauta (-Amreich) (radical vaginal hysterectomy) 68.7
Schede (thoracoplasty) 33.34
Scheie
  cautery of sclera 12.62
  sclerostomy 12.62
Schlatter (total gastrectomy) 43.99
Schroeder (endocervical excision) 67.39
Schuchardt (nonobstetrical episiotomy) 71.09
Schwartze (simple mastoidectomy) 20.41
sclera NEC 12.89
Scott
  intestinal bypass for obesity 45.93
  jejunocolostomy (bypass) 45.93
scrotum NEC 61.99
Seddon-Brooks (transfer of pectoralis major tendon) 83.75
Semb (apicolysis of lung) 33.39
seminal vesicle NEC 60.79
Senning (correction of transposition of great vessels) 35.91
Sever (division of soft tissue of arm) 83.19

Operation — *continued*
Sewell (heart) 36.2
sex transformation NEC 64.5
Sharrard (iliopsoas muscle transfer) 83.77
shelf (hip arthroplasty) 81.40
Shirodkar (encirclement suture, cervix) 67.59
sigmoid NEC 46.99
Silver (bunionectomy) 77.59
Sistrunk (excision of thyroglossal cyst) 06.7
Skene's gland NEC 71.8
skin NEC 86.99
skull NEC 02.99
sling
  eyelid
    fascia lata, palpebral 08.36
    frontalis fascial 08.32
    levator muscle 08.33
    orbicularis muscle 08.36
    palpebrae ligament, fascia lata 08.36
    tarsus muscle 08.35
  fascial (fascia lata)
    eye 08.32
    for facial weakness (trigeminal nerve paralysis) 86.81
    palpebral ligament 08.36
    tongue 25.59
  tongue (fascial) 25.59
  urethra (suprapubic) 59.4
    retropubic 59.5
  urethrovesical 59.5
Slocum (pes anserinus transfer) 81.47
Sluder (tonsillectomy) 28.2
Smith (open osteotomy of mandible) 76.62
Smith-Peterson (radiocarpal arthrodesis) 81.25
Smithwick (sympathectomy) 05.29
Soave (endorectal pull-through) 48.41
soft tissue NEC 83.99
  hand 82.99
Sonneberg (inferior maxillary neurectomy) 04.07
Sorondo-Ferré (hindquarter amputation) 84.19
Soutter (iliac crest fasciotomy) 83.14
Spalding-Richardson (uterine suspension) 69.22
spermatic cord NEC 63.99
sphincter of Oddi NEC 51.89
spinal (canal) (cord) (structures) NEC 03.99
Spinelli (correction of inverted uterus) 75.93
Spivack (permanent gastrostomy) 43.19
spleen NEC 41.99
S.P. Rogers (knee disarticulation) 84.16
Ssabanejew-Frank (permanent gastrostomy) 43.19
Stacke (simple mastoidectomy) 20.41
Stallard (conjunctivocystorhinostomy) 09.82
  with insertion of tube or stent 09.83
Stamm (-Kader) (temporary gastrostomy) 43.19
Steinberg 44.5
Steindler
  fascia stripping (for cavus deformity) 83.14
  flexorplasty (elbow) 83.77
  muscle transfer 83.77
sterilization NEC
  female (*see also* specific operation) 66.39
  male (*see also* Ligation, vas deferens) 63.70
Stewart (renal plication with pyeloplasty) 55.87
stomach NEC 44.99
Stone (anoplasty) 49.79
Strassman (metroplasty) 69.49
  metroplasty (Jones modification) 69.49
  uterus 68.22
Strayer (gastrocnemius recession) 83.72
stress incontinence — *see* Repair, stress incontinence
Stromeyer-Little (hepatotomy) 50.0
Strong (unbridling of celiac artery axis) 39.91
Sturmdorf (conization of cervix) 67.2
subcutaneous tissue NEC 86.99
sublingual gland or duct NEC 26.99
submaxillary gland or duct NEC 26.99
Summerskill (dacryocystorhinostomy by intubation) 09.81
Surmay (jejunostomy) 46.39
Swenson
  bladder reconstruction 57.87
  proctectomy 48.49

Operation — *continued*
Swinney (urethral reconstruction) 58.46
Syme
  ankle amputation through malleoli of tibia
    and fibula 84.14
  urethrotomy, external 58.0
sympathetic nerve NEC 05.89
Taarnhoj (trigeminal nerve root decompression)
  04.41
Tack (sacculotomy) 20.79
Talma-Morison (omentopexy) 54.74
Tanner (devascularization of stomach) 44.99
TAPVC NEC 35.82
tarsus NEC 08.99
  muscle sling 08.35
tendon NEC 83.99
  extraocular NEC 15.9
  hand NEC 82.99
testis NEC 62.99
tetralogy of Fallot
  partial repair — *see* specific procedure
  total (one-stage) 35.81
Thal (repair of esophageal stricture) 42.85
thalamus 01.41
  by stereotactic radiosurgery 92.32
    cobalt 60 92.32
    linear accelerator (LINAC) 92.31
    multi-source 92.32
    particle beam 92.33
    particulate 92.33
    radiosurgery NEC 92.39
    single source photon 92.31
Thiersch
  anus 49.79
  skin graft 86.69
    hand 86.62
Thompson
  cleft lip repair 27.54
  correction of lymphedema 40.9
  quadricepsplasty 83.86
  thumb apposition with bone graft 82.69
thoracic duct NEC 40.69
thorax NEC 34.99
Thorek (partial cholecystectomy) 51.21
three-snip, punctum 09.51
thymus NEC 07.99
thyroid gland NEC 06.98
TKP (thermokeratoplasty) 11.74
Tomkins (metroplasty) 69.49
tongue NEC 25.99
  flap, palate 27.62
  tie 25.91
tonsil NEC 28.99
Torek (-Bevan) (orchidopexy) (first stage)
  (second stage) 62.5
Torkildsen (ventriculocisternal shunt) 02.2
Torpin (cul-de-sac resection) 70.92
Toti (dacryocystorhinostomy) 09.81
Touchas 86.83
Touroff (ligation of subclavian artery) 38.85
trabeculae corneae cordis (heart) NEC 35.35
trachea NEC 31.99
Trauner (lingual sulcus extension) 24.91
truncus arteriosus NEC 35.83
Tsuge (macrodactyly repair) 82.83
Tudor "rabbit ear" (anterior urethropexy) 59.79
Tuffier
  apicolysis of lung 33.39
  vaginal hysterectomy 68.59
    laparoscopically assisted (LAVH) 68.51
tunica vaginalis NEC 61.99
Turco (release of joint capsules in clubfoot)
  80.48
Uchida (tubal ligation with or without
  fimbriectomy) 66.32
umbilicus NEC 54.99
urachus NEC 57.51
Urban (mastectomy) (unilateral) 85.47
  bilateral 85.48
ureter NEC 56.99
urethra NEC 58.99
urinary system NEC 59.99
uterus NEC 69.99
  supporting structures NEC 69.98
uvula NEC 27.79
vagina NEC 70.91

Operation — *continued*
vascular NEC 39.99
vas deferens NEC 63.99
  ligation NEC 63.71
vein NEC 39.99
vena cava sieve 38.7
vertebra NEC 78.49
vesical (bladder) NEC 57.99
vessel NEC 39.99
  cardiac NEC 36.99
Vicq d'Azyr (larynx) 31.1
Vidal (varicocele ligation) 63.1
Vineberg (implantation of mammary artery into
  ventricle) 36.2
vitreous NEC 14.79
vocal cord NEC 31.98
von Kraske (proctectomy) 48.64
Voss (hanging hip operation) 83.19
Vulpius (-Compere) (lengthening of
  gastrocnemius muscle) 83.85
vulva NEC 71.8
Ward-Mayo (vaginal hysterectomy) 68.59
  laparoscopically assisted (LAVH) 68.51
Wardill (cleft palate) 27.62
Waters (extraperitoneal cesarean section) 74.2
Waterston (aorta-right pulmonary artery
  anastomosis) 39.0
Watkins (-Wertheim) (uterus interposition)
  69.21
Watson-Jones
  hip arthrodesis 81.21
  reconstruction of lateral ligaments, ankle
    81.49
  shoulder arthrodesis (extra-articular) 81.23
  tenoplasty 83.88
Weir
  appendicostomy 47.91
  correction of nostrils 21.86
Wertheim (radical hysterectomy) 68.6
West (dacryocystorhinostomy) 09.81
Wheeler
  entropion repair 08.44
  halving procedure (eyelid) 08.24
Whipple (radical pancreaticoduodenectomy)
  52.7
  Child modification (radical subtotal
    pancreatectomy) 52.53
  Rodney Smith modification (radical subtotal
    pancreatectomy) 52.53
White (lengthening of tendo calcaneus by
  incomplete tenotomy) 83.11
Whitehead
  glossectomy, radical 25.4
  hemorrhoidectomy 49.46
Whitman
  foot stabilization (talectomy) 77.98
  hip reconstruction 81.40
  repair of serratus anterior muscle 83.87
  talectomy 77.98
  trochanter wedge osteotomy 77.25
Wier (entropion repair) 08.44
Williams-Richardson (vaginal construction)
  70.61
Wilms (thoracoplasty) 33.34
Wilson (angulation osteotomy for hallux valgus)
  77.51
window
  antrum (nasal sinus) — *see* Antrotomy,
    maxillary
  aorticopulmonary 39.59
  bone cortex (*see also* Incision, bone) 77.10
    facial 76.09
  nasoantral — *see* Antrotomy, maxillary
  pericardium 37.12
  pleural 34.09
Winiwarter (cholecystoenterostomy) 51.32
Witzel (temporary gastrostomy) 43.19
Woodward (release of high riding scapula)
  81.83
Young
  epispadias repair 58.45
  tendon transfer (anterior tibialis) (repair of
    flat foot) 83.75
Yount (division of iliotibial band) 83.14
Zancolli
  capsuloplasty 81.72

Operation — *continued*
  Zancolli — *continued*
    tendon transfer (biceps) 82.56
  Ziegler (iridectomy) 12.14
Operculectomy 24.6
Ophthalmectomy 16.49
  with implant (into Tenon's capsule) 16.42
    with attachment of muscles 16.41
Ophthalmoscopy 16.21
Opponensplasty (hand) 82.56
Orbitomaxillectomy, radical 16.51
Orbitotomy (anterior) (frontal) (temporofrontal)
  (transfrontal) NEC 16.09
  with
    bone flap 16.01
    insertion of implant 16.02
  Kroenlein (lateral) 16.01
  lateral 16.01
Orchidectomy (with epididymectomy) (unilateral)
  62.3
  bilateral (radical) 62.41
  remaining or solitary testis 62.42
Orchidopexy 62.5
Orchidoplasty 62.69
Orchidorrhaphy 62.61
Orchidotomy 62.0
Orchiectomy (with epididymectomy) (unilateral)
  62.3
  bilateral (radical) 62.41
  remaining or solitary testis 62.42
Orchiopexy 62.5
Orchioplasty 62.69
Orthoroentgenography — *see* Radiography
Oscar Miller operation (midtarsal arthrodesis)
  81.14
Osmond-Clark operation (soft tissue release with
  peroneus brevis tendon transfer) 83.75
Ossiculectomy NEC 19.3
  with
    stapedectomy (*see also* Stapedectomy) 19.19
    stapes mobilization 19.0
    tympanoplasty 19.53
      revision 19.6
Ossiculotomy NEC 19.3
Ostectomy (partial), except facial — *see also*
  category 77.8 ☑
  facial NEC 76.39
    total 76.45
      with reconstruction 76.44
  first metatarsal head — *see* Bunionectomy
  for graft (autograft) (homograft) — *see also*
    category 77.7 ☑
    mandible 76.31
      total 76.42
        with reconstruction 76.41
  total, except facial — *see also* category 77.9 ☑
    facial NEC 76.45
      with reconstruction 76.44
    mandible 76.42
      with reconstruction 76.41
Osteoarthrotomy (*see also* Osteotomy) 77.30
Osteoclasis 78.70
  carpal, metacarpal 78.74
  clavicle 78.71
  ear 20.79
  femur 78.75
  fibula 78.77
  humerus 78.72
  patella 78.76
  pelvic 78.79
  phalanges (foot) (hand) 78.79
  radius 78.73
  scapula 78.71
  specified site NEC 78.79
  tarsal, metatarsal 78.78
  thorax (ribs) (sternum) 78.71
  tibia 78.77
  ulna 78.73
  vertebrae 78.79
Osteolysis — *see* category 78.4 ☑
Osteopathic manipulation (*see also*
  Manipulation, osteopathic) 93.67

Osteoplasty NEC — *see* category 78.4 ☑
 with bone graft — *see* Graft, bone
 for
  bone lengthening — *see* Lengthening, bone
  bone shortening — *see* Shortening, bone
  repair of malunion or nonunion of fracture
   — *see* Repair, fracture, malunion or
   nonunion
 carpal, metacarpal 78.44
 clavicle 78.41
 cranium NEC 02.06
  with
   flap (bone) 02.03
   graft (bone) 02.04
 facial bone NEC 76.69
 femur 78.45
 fibula 78.47
 humerus 78.42
 mandible, mandibular NEC 76.64
  body 76.63
  ramus (open) 76.62
   closed 76.61
 maxilla (segmental) 76.65
  total 76.66
 nasal bones 21.89
 patella 78.46
 pelvic 78.49
 phalanges (foot) (hand) 78.49
 radius 78.43
 scapula 78.41
 skull NEC 02.06
  with
   flap (bone) 02.03
   graft (bone) 02.04
 specified site NEC 78.49
 tarsal, metatarsal 78.48
 thorax (ribs) (sternum) 78.41
 tibia 78.47
 ulna 78.43
 vertebrae 78.49
Osteorrhaphy (*see also* Osteoplasty) 78.40
Osteosynthesis (fracture) — *see* Reduction,
 fracture
Osteotomy (adduction) (angulation) (block)
 (derotational) (displacement) (partial)
 (rotational) 77.30
 carpals, metacarpals 77.34
  wedge 77.24
 clavicle 77.31
  wedge 77.21
 facial bone NEC 76.69
 femur 77.35
  wedge 77.25
 fibula 77.37
  wedge 77.27
 humerus 77.32
  wedge 77.22
 mandible (segmental) (subapical) 76.64
  angle (open) 76.62
   closed 76.61
  body 76.63
  Gigli saw 76.61
  ramus (open) 76.62
   closed 76.61
 maxilla (segmental) 76.65
  total 76.66
 metatarsal 77.38
  wedge 77.28
   for hallux valgus repair 77.51
 patella 77.36
  wedge 77.26
 pelvic 77.39
  wedge 77.29
 phalanges (foot) (hand) 77.39
  for repair of
   bunion — *see* Bunionectomy
   bunionette 77.54
   hallux valgus — *see* Bunionectomy
  wedge 77.29
   for repair of
    bunion — *see* Bunionectomy
    bunionette 77.54
    hallux valgus — *see* Bunionectomy
 radius 77.33
  wedge 77.23

Osteotomy — *continued*
 scapula 77.31
  wedge 77.21
 specified site NEC 77.39
  wedge 77.29
 tarsal 77.38
  wedge 77.28
 thorax (ribs) (sternum) 77.31
  wedge 77.21
 tibia 77.37
  wedge 77.27
 toe 77.39
  for repair of
   bunion — *see* Bunionectomy
   bunionette 77.54
   hallux valgus — *see* Bunionectomy
  wedge 77.29
   for repair of
    bunion — *see* Bunionectomy
    bunionette 77.54
    hallux valgus — *see* Bunionectomy
 ulna 77.33
  wedge 77.23
 vertebrae 77.39
  wedge 77.29
Otonecrectomy (inner ear) 20.79
Otoplasty (external) 18.79
 auditory canal or meatus 18.6
 auricle 18.79
 cartilage 18.79
  reconstruction 18.71
 prominent or protruding 18.5
Otoscopy 18.11
Outfolding, sclera, for buckling (*see also*
 Buckling, scleral) 14.49
Outfracture, turbinates (nasal) 21.62
Output and clearance, circulatory 92.05
Overdistension, bladder (therapeutic) 96.25
Overlapping, sclera, for buckling (*see also*
 Buckling, scleral) 14.49
Oversewing
 pleural bleb 32.21
 ulcer crater (peptic) 44.40
  duodenum 44.42
  stomach 44.41
Oxford operation (for urinary incontinence) 59.4
Oximetry
 fetal pulse 75.38
Oxygenation 93.96
 extracorporeal membrane (ECMO) 39.65
 hyperbaric 93.95
  wound 93.59
Oxygen therapy (catalytic) (pump) 93.96
 hyperbaric 93.95

P

Pacemaker
 cardiac — *see also* Insertion, pacemaker,
  cardiac
  intraoperative (temporary) 39.64
  temporary (during and immediately following
   cardiac surgery) 39.64
Packing — *see also* Insertion, pack
 auditory canal 96.11
 nose, for epistaxis (anterior) 21.01
  posterior (and anterior) 21.02
 rectal 96.19
 sella turcica 07.79
 vaginal 96.14
Palatoplasty 27.69
 for cleft palate 27.62
  secondary or subsequent 27.63
Palatorrhaphy 27.61
 for cleft palate 27.62
Pallidectomy 01.42
Pallidoansotomy 01.42
Pallidotomy 01.42
 by stereotactic radiosurgery 92.32
  cobalt 60 92.32
  linear accelerator (LINAC) 92.31
  multi-source 92.32

Pallidotomy — *continued*
 by stereotactic radiosurgery — *continued*
  particle beam 92.33
  particulate 92.33
  radiosurgery NEC 92.39
  single source photon 92.31
Panas operation (linear proctotomy) 48.0
Pancoast operation (division of trigeminal nerve
 at foramen ovale) 04.02
Pancreatectomy (total) (with synchronous
 duodenectomy) 52.6
 partial NEC 52.59
  distal (tail) (with part of body) 52.52
  proximal (head) (with part of body) (with
   synchronous duodenectomy) 52.51
  radical 52.53
   subtotal 52.53
 radical 52.7
  subtotal 52.53
Pancreaticocystoduodenostomy 52.4
Pancreaticocystoenterostomy 52.4
Pancreaticocystogastrostomy 52.4
Pancreaticocystojejunostomy 52.4
Pancreaticoduodenectomy (total) 52.6
 partial NEC 52.59
  proximal 52.51
  radical subtotal 52.53
 radical (one-stage) (two-stage) 52.7
  subtotal 52.53
Pancreaticoduodenostomy 52.96
Pancreaticoenterostomy 52.96
Pancreaticogastrostomy 52.96
Pancreaticoileostomy 52.96
Pancreaticojejunostomy 52.96
Pancreatoduodenectomy (total) 52.6
 partial NEC 52.59
 radical (one-stage) (two-stage) 52.7
  subtotal 52.53
Pancreatogram 87.66
 endoscopic retrograde (ERP) 52.13
Pancreatolithotomy 52.09
 endoscopic 52.94
Pancreatotomy 52.09
Pancreolithotomy 52.09
 endoscopic 52.94
Panendoscopy 57.32
 specified site, other than bladder — *see*
  Endoscopy, by site
 through artificial stoma 57.31
Panhysterectomy (abdominal) 68.4
 vaginal 68.59
  laparoscopically assisted (LAVH) 68.51
Panniculectomy 86.83
Panniculotomy 86.83
Pantaloon operation (revision of gastric
 anastomosis) 44.5
Papillectomy, anal 49.39
 endoscopic 49.31
Papillotomy (pancreas) 51.82
 endoscopic 51.85
Paquin operation (ureteroneocystostomy) 56.74
Paracentesis
 abdominal (percutaneous) 54.91
 anterior chamber, eye 12.91
 bladder 57.11
 cornea 12.91
 eye (anterior chamber) 12.91
 thoracic, thoracis 34.91
 tympanum 20.09
  with intubation 20.01
Parasitology — *see* Examination, microscopic
Parathyroidectomy (partial) (subtotal) NEC 06.89
 complete 06.81
 ectopic 06.89
 global removal 06.81
 mediastinal 06.89
 total 06.81
Parenteral nutrition, total 99.15
 peripheral 99.15
Parotidectomy 26.30
 complete 26.32

Parotidectomy — *continued*
partial 26.31
radical 26.32
Partsch operation (marsupialization of dental cyst) 24.4
Passage — *see* Insertion and Intubation
Passage of sounds, urethra 58.6
Patch
blood, spinal (epidural) 03.95
graft — *see* Graft
spinal, blood (epidural) 03.95
subdural, brain 02.12
Patellapexy 78.46
Patellaplasty NEC 78.46
Patellectomy 77.96
partial 77.86
Pattee operation (auditory canal) 18.6
Pectenotomy (*see also* Sphincterotomy, anal) 49.59
Pedicle flap — *see* Graft, skin, pedicle
Peet operation (splanchnic resection) 05.29
PEG (percutaneous endoscopic gastrostomy) 43.11
PEJ (percutaneous endoscopic jejunostomy) 46.32
Pelvectomy, kidney (partial) 55.4
Pelvimetry 88.25
gynecological 89.26
Pelviolithotomy 55.11
Pelvioplasty, kidney 55.87
Pelviostomy 55.12
closure 55.82
Pelviotomy 77.39
to assist delivery 73.94
Pelvi-ureteroplasty 55.87
Pemberton operation
osteotomy of ilium 77.39
rectum (mobilization and fixation for prolapse repair) 48.76
Penectomy 64.3
Pereyra operation (paraurethral suspension) 59.6
Perforation
stapes footplate 19.0
Perfusion NEC 39.97
carotid artery 39.97
coronary artery 39.97
for
chemotherapy NEC 99.25
hormone therapy NEC 99.24
head 39.97
hyperthermic (lymphatic), localized region or site 93.35
intestine (large) (local) 46.96
small 46.95
kidney, local 55.95
limb (lower) (upper) 39.97
liver, localized 50.93
neck 39.97
subarachnoid (spinal cord) (refrigerated saline) 03.92
total body 39.96
Pericardiectomy 37.31
Pericardiocentesis 37.0
Pericardiolysis 37.12
Pericardioplasty 37.49   ▲
Pericardiorrhaphy 37.49   ▲
Pericardiostomy (tube) 37.12
Pericardiotomy 37.12
Peridectomy 10.31
Perilimbal suction 89.11
Perimetry 95.05
Perineoplasty 71.79
Perineorrhaphy 71.71
obstetrical laceration (current) 75.69
Perineotomy (nonobstetrical) 71.09
to assist delivery — *see* Episiotomy
Periosteotomy (*see also* Incision, bone) 77.10
facial bone 76.09
Perirectofistulectomy 48.93
Peritectomy 10.31
Peritomy 10.1
Peritoneocentesis 54.91

Peritoneoscopy 54.21
Peritoneotomy 54.19
Peritoneumectomy 54.4
Phacoemulsification (ultrasonic) (with aspiration) 13.41
Phacofragmentation (mechanical) (with aspiration) 13.43
posterior route 13.42
ultrasonic 13.41
Phalangectomy (partial) 77.89
claw toe 77.57
cockup toe 77.58
hammer toe 77.56
overlapping toe 77.58
total 77.99
Phalangization (fifth metacarpal) 82.81
Pharyngeal flap operation (cleft palate repair) 27.62
secondary or subsequent 27.63
Pharyngectomy (partial) 29.33
with laryngectomy 30.3
Pharyngogram 87.09
contrast 87.06
Pharyngolaryngectomy 30.3
Pharyngoplasty (with silastic implant) 29.4
for cleft palate 27.62
secondary or subsequent 27.63
Pharyngorrhaphy 29.51
for cleft palate 27.62
Pharyngoscopy 29.11
Pharyngotomy 29.0
Phenopeel (skin) 86.24
Phlebectomy 38.60
with
anastomosis 38.30
abdominal 38.37
head and neck NEC 38.32
intracranial NEC 38.31
lower limb 38.39
thoracic NEC 38.35
upper limb 38.33
graft replacement 38.40
abdominal 38.47
head and neck NEC 38.42
intracranial NEC 38.41
lower limb 38.49
thoracic NEC 38.45
upper limb 38.43
abdominal 38.67
head and neck NEC 38.62
intracranial NEC 38.61
lower limb 38.69
thoracic NEC 38.65
upper limb 38.63
varicose 38.50
abdominal 38.57
head and neck NEC 38.52
intracranial NEC 38.51
lower limb 38.59
thoracic NEC 38.55
upper limb 38.53
Phlebogoniostomy 12.52
Phlebography (contrast) (retrograde) 88.60
by radioisotope — *see* Scan, radioisotope, by site
adrenal 88.65
femoral 88.66
head 88.61
hepatic 88.64
impedance 88.68
intra-abdominal NEC 88.65
intrathoracic NEC 88.63
lower extremity NEC 88.66
neck 88.61
portal system 88.64
pulmonary 88.62
specified site NEC 88.67
vena cava (inferior) (superior) 88.51
Phleborrhaphy 39.32
Phlebotomy 38.99
Phonocardiogram, with ECG lead 89.55
Photochemotherapy NEC 99.83
extracorporeal 99.88

Photocoagulation
ciliary body 12.73
eye, eyeball 16.99
iris 12.41
macular hole — *see* Photocoagulation, retina
orbital lesion 16.92
retina
for
destruction of lesion 14.25
reattachment 14.55
repair of tear or defect 14.35
laser (beam)
for
destruction of lesion 14.24
reattachment 14.54
repair of tear or defect 14.34
xenon arc
for
destruction of lesion 14.23
reattachment 14.53
repair of tear or defect 14.33
Photography 89.39
fundus 95.11
Photopheresis, therapeutic 99.88
Phototherapy NEC 99.83
newborn 99.83
ultraviolet 99.82
Phrenemphraxis 04.03
for collapse of lung 33.31
Phrenicectomy 04.03
for collapse of lung 33.31
Phrenicoexeresis 04.03
for collapse of lung 33.31
Phrenicotomy 04.03
for collapse of lung 33.31
Phrenicotripsy 04.03
for collapse of lung 33.31
Phrenoplasty 34.84
Physical medicine — *see* Therapy, physical
Physical therapy — *see* Therapy, physical
Physiotherapy, chest 93.99
PICC (peripherally inserted central catheter) 38.93
Piercing ear, external (pinna) 18.01
Pigmenting, skin 86.02
Pilojection (aneurysm) (Gallagher) 39.52
Pinealectomy (complete) (total) 07.54
partial 07.53
Pinealotomy (with drainage) 07.52
Pinning
bone — *see* Fixation, bone, internal
ear 18.5
Pinsker operation (obliteration of nasoseptal telangiectasia) 21.07
Piper operation (forceps) 72.6
Pirogoff operation (ankle amputation through malleoli of tibia and fibula) 84.14
Pituitectomy (complete) (total) (*see also* Hypophysectomy) 07.69
Placentogram, placentography 88.46
with radioisotope (RISA) 92.17
Planing, skin 86.25
Plantation, tooth (bud) (germ) 23.5
prosthetic 23.6
Plasma exchange 99.07
Plasmapheresis, therapeutic 99.71
Plastic repair — *see* Repair, by site
Plasty — *see also* Repair, by site
bladder neck (V-Y) 57.85
skin (without graft) 86.89
subcutaneous tissue 86.89
Platelet inhibitor (GP IIb/IIIa inhibitor only), infusion 99.20
Plateletpheresis, therapeutic 99.74
Play
psychotherapy 94.36
therapy 93.81
Pleating
eye muscle 15.22
multiple (two or more muscles) 15.4
sclera, for buckling (*see also* Buckling, scleral) 14.49

Plethysmogram (carotid) 89.58
　air-filled (pneumatic) 89.58
　capacitance 89.58
　cerebral 89.58
　differential 89.58
　oculoplethysmogram 89.58
　penile 89.58
　photoelectric 89.58
　regional 89.58
　respiratory function measurement (body) 89.38
　segmental 89.58
　strain-gauge 89.58
　thoracic impedance 89.38
　venous occlusion 89.58
　water-filled 89.58
Plethysmography
　penile 89.58
Pleurectomy NEC 34.59
Pleurocentesis 34.91
Pleurodesis 34.6
　chemical 34.92
　　with cancer chemotherapy substance 34.92
　　　[99.25]
　　tetracycline 34.92 *[99.21]*
Pleurolysis (for collapse of lung) 33.39
Pleuropexy 34.99
Pleurosclerosis 34.6
　chemical 34.92
　　with cancer chemotherapy substance 34.92
　　　[99.25]
　　tetracycline 34.92 *[99.21]*
Pleurotomy 34.09
Plexectomy
　choroid 02.14
　hypogastric 05.24
Plication
　aneurysm
　　heart 37.32
　annulus, heart valve 35.33
　bleb (emphysematous), lung 32.21
　broad ligament 69.22
　diaphragm (for hernia repair) (thoracic
　　approach) (thoracoabdominal approach)
　　53.81
　eye muscle (oblique) (rectus) 15.22
　　multiple (two or more muscles) 15.4
　fascia 83.89
　　hand 82.89
　inferior vena cava 38.7
　intestine (jejunum) (Noble) 46.62
　Kelly (-Stoeckel) (urethrovesical junction) 59.3
　levator, for blepharoptosis 08.34
　ligament (*see also* Arthroplasty) 81.96
　　broad 69.22
　　round 69.22
　　uterosacral 69.22
　mesentery 54.75
　round ligament 69.22
　sphincter, urinary bladder 57.85
　stomach 44.69
　　laparoscopic 44.68
　superior vena cava 38.7
　tendon 83.85
　　hand 82.55
　tricuspid valve (with repositioning) 35.14
　ureter 56.89
　urethra 58.49
　urethrovesical junction 59.3
　vein (peripheral) 39.59
　vena cava (inferior) (superior) 38.7
　ventricle (heart)
　　aneurysm 37.32
Plicotomy, tympanum 20.23
Plombage, lung 33.39
Pneumocentesis 33.93
Pneumocisternogram 87.02
Pneumoencephalogram 87.01
Pneumogram, pneumography
　extraperitoneal 88.15
　mediastinal 87.33
　orbit 87.14
　pelvic 88.13
　peritoneum NEC 88.13

Pneumogram, pneumography — *continued*
　presacral 88.15
　retroperitoneum 88.15
Pneumogynecography 87.82
Pneumomediastinography 87.33
Pneumonectomy (complete) (extended) (radical)
　(standard) (total) (with mediastinal
　dissection) 32.5
　partial
　　complete excision, one lobe 32.4
　　resection (wedge), one lobe 32.3
Pneumonolysis (for collapse of lung) 33.39
Pneumonotomy (with exploration) 33.1
Pneumoperitoneum (surgically-induced) 54.96
　for collapse of lung 33.33
　pelvic 88.12
Pneumothorax (artificial) (surgical) 33.32
　intrapleural 33.32
Pneumoventriculogram 87.02
Politano-Leadbetter operation
　(ureteroneocystostomy) 56.74
Politzerization, Eustachian tube 20.8
Pollicization (with carry over of nerves and blood
　supply) 82.61
Polya operation (gastrectomy) 43.7
Polypectomy — *see also* Excision, lesion, by site
　esophageal 42.32
　　endoscopic 42.33
　gastric (endoscopic) 43.41
　large intestine (colon) 45.42
　nasal 21.31
　rectum (endoscopic) 48.36
Polysomnogram 89.17
Pomeroy operation (ligation and division of
　fallopian tubes) 66.32
Poncet operation
　lengthening of Achilles tendon 83.85
　urethrostomy, perineal 58.0
Porro operation (cesarean section) 74.99
Portoenterostomy (Kasai) 51.37
Positrocephalogram 92.11
Positron emission tomography (PET) — *see*
　Scan, radioisotope
Postmortem examination 89.8
Potts-Smith operation (descending aorta-left
　pulmonary artery anastomosis) 39.0
Poudrage
　intrapericardial 36.39
　pleural 34.6
PPN (peripheral parenteral nutrition) 99.15
Preparation (cutting), pedicle (flap) graft 86.71
Preputiotomy 64.91
Prescription for glasses 95.31
Pressure support
　ventilation [PSV] — *see* category 96.7 ☑
Pressurized
　graft treatment 00.16
Printen and Mason operation (high gastric
　bypass) 44.31
Probing
　canaliculus, lacrimal (with irrigation) 09.42
　lacrimal
　　canaliculi 09.42
　　punctum (with irrigation) 09.41
　nasolacrimal duct (with irrigation) 09.43
　　with insertion of tube or stent 09.44
　salivary duct (for dilation of duct) (for removal
　　of calculus) 26.91
　　with incision 26.0
Procedure — *see also* specific procedure
　diagnostic NEC
　　abdomen (region) 54.29
　　adenoid 28.19
　　adrenal gland 07.19
　　alveolus 24.19
　　amnion 75.35
　　anterior chamber, eye 12.29
　　anus 49.29
　　appendix 45.28
　　biliary tract 51.19
　　bladder 57.39

Procedure — *see also* specific procedure —
　continued
　diagnostic NEC — *continued*
　　blood vessel (any site) 38.29
　　bone 78.80
　　　carpal, metacarpal 78.84
　　　clavicle 78.81
　　　facial 76.19
　　　femur 78.85
　　　fibula 78.87
　　　humerus 78.82
　　　marrow 41.38
　　　patella 78.86
　　　pelvic 78.89
　　　phalanges (foot) (hand) 78.89
　　　radius 78.83
　　　scapula 78.81
　　　specified site NEC 78.89
　　　tarsal, metatarsal 78.88
　　　thorax (ribs) (sternum) 78.81
　　　tibia 78.87
　　　ulna 78.83
　　　vertebrae 78.89
　　brain 01.18
　　breast 85.19
　　bronchus 33.29
　　buccal 27.24
　　bursa 83.29
　　canthus 08.19
　　cecum 45.28
　　cerebral meninges 01.18
　　cervix 67.19
　　chest wall 34.28
　　choroid 14.19
　　ciliary body 12.29
　　clitoris 71.19
　　colon 45.28
　　conjunctiva 10.29
　　cornea 11.29
　　cul-de-sac 70.29
　　dental 24.19
　　diaphragm 34.28
　　duodenum 45.19
　　ear
　　　external 18.19
　　　inner and middle 20.39
　　epididymis 63.09
　　esophagus 42.29
　　Eustachian tube 20.39
　　extraocular muscle or tendon 15.09
　　eye 16.29
　　　anterior chamber 12.29
　　　posterior chamber 14.19
　　eyeball 16.29
　　eyelid 08.19
　　fallopian tube 66.19
　　fascia (any site) 83.29
　　fetus 75.35
　　gallbladder 51.19
　　ganglion (cranial) (peripheral) 04.19
　　　sympathetic 05.19
　　gastric 44.19
　　globus pallidus 01.18
　　gum 24.19
　　heart 37.29
　　hepatic 50.19
　　hypophysis 07.19
　　ileum 45.19
　　intestine 45.29
　　　large 45.28
　　　small 45.19
　　iris 12.29
　　jejunum 45.19
　　joint (capsule) (ligament) (structure) NEC
　　　81.98
　　　facial 76.19
　　kidney 55.29
　　labia 71.19
　　lacrimal (system) 09.19
　　large intestine 45.28
　　larynx 31.48
　　ligament 81.98
　　　uterine 68.19
　　liver 50.19
　　lung 33.29

Procedure — *see also* specific procedure — continued
  diagnostic NEC — *continued*
    lymphatic structure (channel) (gland) (node) (vessel) 40.19
    mediastinum 34.29
    meninges (cerebral) 01.18
      spinal 03.39
    mouth 27.29
    muscle 83.29
      extraocular (oblique) (rectus) 15.09
      papillary (heart) 37.29
    nail 86.19
    nasopharynx 29.19
    nerve (cranial) (peripheral) NEC 04.19
      sympathetic 05.19
    nipple 85.19
    nose, nasal 21.29
      sinus 22.19
    ocular 16.29
      muscle 15.09
    omentum 54.29
    ophthalmologic 16.29
    oral (cavity) 27.29
    orbit 16.29
    orthodontic 24.19
    ovary 65.19
      laparoscopic 65.14
    palate 27.29
    pancreas 52.19
    papillary muscle (heart) 37.29
    parathyroid gland 06.19
    penis 64.19
    perianal tissue 49.29
    pericardium 37.29
    periprostatic tissue 60.18
    perirectal tissue 48.29
    perirenal tissue 59.29
    peritoneum 54.29
    periurethral tissue 58.29
    perivesical tissue 59.29
    pharynx 29.19
    pineal gland 07.19
    pituitary gland 07.19
    pleura 34.28
    posterior chamber, eye 14.19
    prostate 60.18
    pulmonary 33.29
    rectosigmoid 48.29
    rectum 48.29
    renal 55.29
    respiratory 33.29
    retina 14.19
    retroperitoneum 59.29
    salivary gland or duct 26.19
    sclera 12.29
    scrotum 61.19
    seminal vesicle 60.19
    sigmoid 45.28
    sinus, nasal 22.19
    skin 86.19
    skull 01.19
    soft tissue 83.29
    spermatic cord 63.09
    sphincter of Oddi 51.19
    spine, spinal (canal) (cord) (meninges) (structure) 03.39
    spleen 41.39
    stomach 44.19
    subcutaneous tissue 86.19
    sympathetic nerve 05.19
    tarsus 09.19
    tendon NEC 83.29
      extraocular 15.09
    testicle 62.19
    thalamus 01.18
    thoracic duct 40.19
    thorax 34.28
    thymus 07.19
    thyroid gland 06.19
    tongue 25.09
    tonsils 28.19
    tooth 24.19
    trachea 31.49
    tunica vaginalis 61.19
    ureter 56.39

Procedure — *see also* specific procedure — continued
  diagnostic NEC — *continued*
    urethra 58.29
    uterus and supporting structures 68.19
    uvula 27.29
    vagina 70.29
    vas deferens 63.09
    vesical 57.39
    vessel (blood) (any site) 38.29
    vitreous 14.19
    vulva 71.19
  fistulizing, sclera NEC 12.69
  miscellaneous (nonoperative) NEC 99.99
  respiratory (nonoperative) NEC 93.99
  surgical — *see* Operation

Proctectasis 96.22
Proctectomy (partial) (*see also* Resection, rectum) 48.69
  abdominoperineal 48.5
  complete (Miles) (Rankin) 48.5
  pull-through 48.49
Proctoclysis 96.37
Proctolysis 48.99
Proctopexy (Delorme) 48.76
  abdominal (Ripstein) 48.75
Proctoplasty 48.79
Proctorrhaphy 48.71
Proctoscopy 48.23
  with biopsy 48.24
  through stoma (artificial) 48.22
  transabdominal approach 48.21
Proctosigmoidectomy (*see also* Resection, rectum) 48.69
Proctosigmoidopexy 48.76
Proctosigmoidoscopy (rigid) 48.23
  with biopsy 48.24
  flexible 45.24
  through stoma (artificial) 48.22
  transabdominal approach 48.21
Proctostomy 48.1
Proctotomy (decompression) (linear) 48.0
Production — *see also* Formation and Creation
  atrial septal defect 35.42
  subcutaneous tunnel for esophageal anastomosis 42.86
    with anastomosis — *see* Anastomosis, esophagus, antesternal
Prognathic recession 76.64
Prophylaxis, dental (scaling) (polishing) 96.54
Prostatectomy (complete) (partial) NEC 60.69
  loop 60.29
  perineal 60.62
  radical (any approach) 60.5
  retropubic (punch) (transcapsular) 60.4
  suprapubic (punch) (transvesical) 60.3
  transcapsular NEC 60.69
    retropubic 60.4
  transperineal 60.62
  transurethral 60.29
    ablation (contact) (noncontact) by laser 60.21
    electrovaporization 60.29
    enucleative 60.29
    resection of prostate (TURP) 60.29
    ultrasound guided laser induced (TULIP) 60.21
  transvesical punch (suprapubic) 60.3
Prostatocystotomy 60.0
Prostatolithotomy 60.0
Prostatotomy (perineal) 60.0
Prostatovesiculectomy 60.5
Protection (of)
  individual from his surroundings 99.84
  surroundings from individual 99.84
Psychoanalysis 94.31
Psychodrama 94.43
Psychotherapy NEC 94.39
  biofeedback 94.39
  exploratory verbal 94.37
  group 94.44
    for psychosexual dysfunctions 94.41

Psychotherapy NEC — *continued*
  play 94.36
  psychosexual dysfunctions 94.34
  supportive verbal 94.38
PTCA (percutaneous transluminal coronary angioplasty) — *see* Angioplasty, balloon, coronary
Ptyalectasis 26.91
Ptyalithotomy 26.0
Ptyalolithotomy 26.0
Pubiotomy 77.39
  assisting delivery 73.94
Pubococcygeoplasty 59.71
Puestow operation (pancreaticojejunostomy) 52.96
Pull-through
  abdomino-anal 48.49
  abdominoperineal 48.49
    Duhamel type 48.65
  endorectal 48.41
Pulmowrap 93.99
Pulpectomy (*see also* Therapy, root canal) 23.70
Pulpotomy (*see also* Therapy, root canal) 23.70
Pump-oxygenator, for extracorporeal circulation 39.61
  percutaneous 39.66
Punch
  operation
    bladder neck, transurethral 57.49
    prostate — *see* Prostatectomy
  resection, vocal cords 30.22
Puncture
  antrum (nasal) (bilateral) (unilateral) 22.01
  artery NEC 38.98
    for
      arteriography (*see also* Arteriography) 88.40
      coronary arteriography (*see also* Arteriography, coronary) 88.57
      percutaneous vascular closure — *omit code*
  bladder, suprapubic (for drainage) NEC 57.18
    needle 57.11
    percutaneous (suprapubic) 57.17
  bursa 83.94
    hand 82.92
  cisternal 01.01
    with contrast media 87.02
  cranial 01.09
    with contrast media 87.02
  craniobuccal pouch 07.72
  craniopharyngioma 07.72
  fallopian tube 66.91
  fontanel, anterior 01.09
  heart 37.0
    for intracardiac injection 37.92
  hypophysis 07.72
  iris 12.12
  joint 81.91
  kidney (percutaneous) 55.92
  larynx 31.98
  lumbar (diagnostic) (removal of dye) 03.31
  lung (for aspiration) 33.93
  nasal sinus 22.01
  pericardium 37.0
  pituitary gland 07.72
  pleural cavity 34.91
  Rathke's pouch 07.72
  spinal 03.31
  spleen 41.1
    for biopsy 41.32
  sternal (for bone marrow biopsy) 41.31
    donor for bone marrow transplant 41.91
  vein NEC 38.99
    for
      phlebography (*see also* Phlebography) 88.60
      transfusion — *see* Transfusion
  ventricular shunt tubing 01.02
Pupillotomy 12.35
Push-back operation (cleft palate repair) 27.62
Putti-Platt operation (capsulorrhaphy of shoulder for recurrent dislocation) 81.82

pVAD (percutaneous ventricular assist device) 37.68
Pyelogram (intravenous) 87.73
   infusion (continuous) (diuretic) 87.73
   percutaneous 87.75
   retrograde 87.74
Pyeloileostomy 56.71
Pyelolithotomy 55.11
Pyeloplasty 55.87
Pyelorrhaphy 55.81
Pyeloscopy 55.22
Pyelostolithotomy, percutaneous 55.03
Pyelostomy 55.12
   closure 55.82
Pyelotomy 55.11
Pyeloureteroplasty 55.87
Pylorectomy 43.6
Pyloroduodenotomy — *see category* 44.2 ☑
Pyloromyotomy (Ramstedt) (with wedge resection) 43.3
Pyloroplasty (Finney) (Heineke-Mikulicz) 44.29
   dilation, endoscopic 44.22
      by incision 44.21
   not elsewhere classified 44.29
   revision 44.29
Pylorostomy — *see* Gastrostomy

Q

Quadrant resection of breast 85.22
Quadricepsplasty (Thompson) 83.86
Quarantine 99.84
Quenuthoracoplasty 77.31
Quotient, respiratory 89.38

R

Rachicentesis 03.31
Rachitomy 03.09
Radiation therapy — *see also* Therapy, radiation
   teleradiotherapy — *see* Teleradiotherapy
Radical neck dissection — *see* Dissection, neck
Radicotomy 03.1
Radiculectomy 03.1
Radiculotomy 03.1
Radiography (diagnostic) NEC 88.39
   abdomen, abdominal (flat plate) NEC 88.19
      wall (soft tissue) NEC 88.09
   adenoid 87.09
   ankle (skeletal) 88.28
      soft tissue 88.37
   bone survey 88.31
   bronchus 87.49
   chest (routine) 87.44
      wall NEC 87.39
   clavicle 87.43
   computer assisted surgery (CAS) with fluoroscopy 00.33
   contrast (air) (gas) (radio-opaque substance) NEC
      abdominal wall 88.03
      arteries (by fluoroscopy) — *see* Arteriography
      bile ducts NEC 87.54
      bladder NEC 87.77
      brain 87.02
      breast 87.35
      bronchus NEC (transcricoid) 87.32
         endotracheal 87.31
      epididymis 87.93
      esophagus 87.61
      fallopian tubes
         gas 87.82
         opaque dye 87.83
      fistula (sinus tract) — *see also* Radiography, contrast, by site
         abdominal wall 88.03
         chest wall 87.38
      gallbladder NEC 87.59
      intervertebral disc(s) 87.21

Radiography NEC — *continued*
   contrast NEC — *continued*
      joints 88.32
      larynx 87.07
      lymph — *see* Lymphangiogram
      mammary ducts 87.35
      mediastinum 87.33
      nasal sinuses 87.15
      nasolacrimal ducts 87.05
      nasopharynx 87.06
      orbit 87.14
      pancreas 87.66
      pelvis
         gas 88.12
         opaque dye 88.11
      peritoneum NEC 88.13
      retroperitoneum NEC 88.15
      seminal vesicles 87.91
      sinus tract — *see also* Radiography, contrast, by site
         abdominal wall 88.03
         chest wall 87.38
         nose 87.15
      skull 87.02
      spinal disc(s) 87.21
      trachea 87.32
      uterus
         gas 87.82
         opaque dye 87.83
      vas deferens 87.94
      veins (by fluoroscopy) — *see* Phlebography
      vena cava (inferior) (superior) 88.51
   dental NEC 87.12
   diaphragm 87.49
   digestive tract NEC 87.69
      barium swallow 87.61
      lower GI series 87.64
      small bowel series 87.63
      upper GI series 87.62
   elbow (skeletal) 88.22
      soft tissue 88.35
   epididymis NEC 87.95
   esophagus 87.69
      barium-swallow 87.61
   eye 95.14
   face, head, and neck 87.09
   facial bones 87.16
   fallopian tubes 87.85
   foot 88.28
   forearm (skeletal) 88.22
      soft tissue 88.35
   frontal area, facial 87.16
   genital organs
      female NEC 87.89
      male NEC 87.99
   hand (skeletal) 88.23
      soft tissue 88.35
   head NEC 87.09
   heart 87.49
   hip (skeletal) 88.26
      soft tissue 88.37
   intestine NEC 87.65
   kidney-ureter-bladder (KUB) 87.79
   knee (skeletal) 88.27
      soft tissue 88.37
   KUB (kidney-ureter-bladder) 87.79
   larynx 87.09
   lower leg (skeletal) 88.27
      soft tissue 88.37
   lower limb (skeletal) NEC 88.29
      soft tissue NEC 88.37
   lung 87.49
   mandible 87.16
   maxilla 87.16
   mediastinum 87.49
   nasal sinuses 87.16
   nasolacrimal duct 87.09
   nasopharynx 87.09
   neck NEC 87.09
   nose 87.16
   orbit 87.16
   pelvis (skeletal) 88.26
      pelvimetry 88.25
      soft tissue 88.19
   prostate NEC 87.92
   retroperitoneum NEC 88.16

Radiography NEC — *continued*
   ribs 87.43
   root canal 87.12
   salivary gland 87.09
   seminal vesicles NEC 87.92
   shoulder (skeletal) 88.21
      soft tissue 88.35
   skeletal NEC 88.33
      series (whole or complete) 88.31
   skull (lateral, sagittal or tangential projection) NEC 87.17
   spine NEC 87.29
      cervical 87.22
      lumbosacral 87.24
      sacrococcygeal 87.24
      thoracic 87.23
   sternum 87.43
   supraorbital area 87.16
   symphysis menti 87.16
   teeth NEC 87.12
      full-mouth 87.11
   thigh (skeletal) 88.27
      soft tissue 88.37
   thyroid region 87.09
   tonsils and adenoids 87.09
   trachea 87.49
   ultrasonic — *see* Ultrasonography
   upper arm (skeletal) 88.21
      soft tissue 88.35
   upper limb (skeletal) NEC 88.24
      soft tissue NEC 88.35
   urinary system NEC 87.79
   uterus NEC 87.85
      gravid 87.81
   uvula 87.09
   vas deferens NEC 87.95
   wrist 88.23
   zygomaticomaxillary complex 87.16
Radioimmunotherapy 92.28
Radioisotope
   scanning — *see* Scan, radioisotope
   therapy — *see* Therapy, radioisotope
Radiology
   diagnostic — *see* Radiography
   therapeutic — *see* Therapy, radiation
Radiosurgery, stereotactic 92.30
   cobalt 60 92.32
   linear accelerator (LINAC) 92.31
   multi-source 92.32
   particle beam 92.33
   particulate 92.33
   radiosurgery NEC 92.39
   single source photon 92.31
Raising, pedicle graft 86.71
Ramadier operation (intrapetrosal drainage) 20.22
Ramisection (sympathetic) 05.0
Ramstedt operation (pyloromyotomy) (with wedge resection) 43.3
Range of motion testing 93.05
Rankin operation
   exteriorization of intestine 46.03
   proctectomy (complete) 48.5
Rashkind operation (balloon septostomy) 35.41
Rastelli operation (creation of conduit between right ventricle and pulmonary artery) 35.92
   in repair of
      pulmonary artery atresia 35.92
      transposition of great vessels 35.92
      truncus arteriosus 35.83
Raz-Pereyra procedure (bladder neck suspension) 59.79
RCSA (radical cryosurgical ablation) of prostate 60.62
Readjustment — *see* Adjustment
Reamputation, stump 84.3
Reanastomosis — *see* Anastomosis
Reattachment
   amputated ear 18.72
   ankle 84.27
   arm (upper) NEC 84.24

Index

Reattachment — Reduction

Reattachment — continued
choroid and retina NEC 14.59
by
cryotherapy 14.52
diathermy 14.51
electrocoagulation 14.51
photocoagulation 14.55
laser 14.54
xenon arc 14.53
ear (amputated) 18.72
extremity 84.29
ankle 84.27
arm (upper) NEC 84.24
fingers, except thumb 84.22
thumb 84.21
foot 84.26
forearm 84.23
hand 84.23
leg (lower) NEC 84.27
thigh 84.28
thumb 84.21
toe 84.25
wrist 84.23
finger 84.22
thumb 84.21
foot 84.26
forearm 84.23
hand 84.23
joint capsule (see also Arthroplasty) 81.96
leg (lower) NEC 84.27
ligament — see also Arthroplasty
uterosacral 69.22
muscle 83.74
hand 82.54
papillary (heart) 35.31
nerve (peripheral) 04.79
nose (amputated) 21.89
papillary muscle (heart) 35.31
penis (amputated) 64.45
retina (and choroid) NEC 14.59
by
cryotherapy 14.52
diathermy 14.51
electrocoagulation 14.51
photocoagulation 14.55
laser 14.54
xenon arc 14.53
tendon (to tendon) 83.73
hand 82.53
to skeletal attachment 83.88
hand 82.85
thigh 84.28
thumb 84.21
toe 84.25
tooth 23.5
uterosacral ligament(s) 69.22
vessels (peripheral) 39.59
renal, aberrant 39.55
wrist 84.23
Recession
extraocular muscle 15.11
multiple (two or more muscles) (with
advancement or resection) 15.3
gastrocnemius tendon (Strayer operation) 83.72
levator palpebrae (superioris) muscle 08.38
prognathic jaw 76.64
tendon 83.72
hand 82.52
Reclosure — see also Closure
disrupted abdominal wall (postoperative) 54.61
Reconstruction (plastic) — see also Construction
and Repair, by site
alveolus, alveolar (process) (ridge) (with graft or
implant) 24.5
artery (graft) — see Graft, artery
artificial stoma, intestine 46.40
auditory canal (external) 18.6
auricle (ear) 18.71
bladder 57.87
with
ileum 57.87 [45.51]
sigmoid 57.87 [45.52]
bone, except facial (see also Osteoplasty) 78.40
facial NEC 76.46
with total ostectomy 76.44
mandible 76.43
with total mandibulectomy 76.41

Reconstruction — see also Construction and
Repair, by site — continued
breast, total 85.7
bronchus 33.48
canthus (lateral) 08.59
cardiac annulus 35.33
chest wall (mesh) (silastic) 34.79
cleft lip 27.54
conjunctival cul-de-sac 10.43
with graft (buccal mucous membrane) (free)
10.42
cornea NEC 11.79
diaphragm 34.84
ear (external) (auricle) 18.71
external auditory canal 18.6
meatus (new) (osseous skin-lined) 18.6
ossicles 19.3
prominent or protruding 18.5
eyebrow 08.70
eyelid 08.70
with graft or flap 08.69
hair follicle 08.63
mucous membrane 08.62
skin 08.61
tarsoconjunctival (one-stage) (two-stage)
08.64
full-thickness 08.74
involving lid margin 08.73
partial-thickness 08.72
involving lid margin 08.71
eye socket 16.64
with graft 16.63
fallopian tube 66.79
foot and toes (with fixation device) 81.57
with prosthetic implant 81.57
frontonasal duct 22.79
hip (total) (with prosthesis) 81.51
intraoral 27.59
joint — see Arthroplasty
lymphatic (by transplantation) 40.9
mandible 76.43
with total mandibulectomy 76.41
mastoid cavity 19.9
mouth 27.59
nipple NEC 85.87
nose (total) (with arm flap) (with forehead flap)
21.83
ossicles (graft) (prosthesis) NEC 19.3
with
stapedectomy 19.19
tympanoplasty 19.53
pelvic floor 71.79
penis (rib graft) (skin graft) (myocutaneous flap)
64.44
pharynx 29.4
scrotum (with pedicle flap) (with rotational flap)
61.49
skin (plastic) (without graft) NEC 86.89
with graft — see Graft, skin
subcutaneous tissue (plastic) (without skin
graft) NEC 86.89
with graft — see Graft, skin
tendon pulley (with graft) (with local tissue)
83.83
for opponensplasty 82.71
hand 82.71
thumb (osteoplastic) (with bone graft) (with skin
graft) 82.69
trachea (with graft) 31.75
umbilicus 53.49
ureteropelvic junction 55.87
urethra 58.46
vagina 70.62
vas deferens, surgically divided 63.82
Recontour, gingiva 24.2
Recreational therapy 93.81
Rectectomy (see also Resection, rectum) 48.69
Rectopexy (Delorme) 48.76
abdominal (Ripstein) 48.75
Rectoplasty 48.79
Rectorectostomy 48.74
Rectorrhaphy 48.71
Rectosigmoidectomy (see also Resection,
rectum) 48.69
transsacral 48.61

Rectosigmoidostomy 45.94
Rectostomy 48.1
closure 48.72
Red cell survival studies 92.05
Reduction
adipose tissue 86.83
batwing arms 86.83
breast (bilateral) 85.32
unilateral 85.31
bulbous tuberosities (mandible) (maxilla)
(fibrous) (osseous) 24.31
buttocks 86.83
diastasis, ankle mortise (closed) 79.77
open 79.87
dislocation (of joint) (manipulation) (with cast)
(with splint) (with traction device) (closed)
79.70
with fracture — see Reduction, fracture, by
site
ankle (closed) 79.77
open 79.87
elbow (closed) 79.72
open 79.82
finger (closed) 79.74
open 79.84
foot (closed) 79.78
open 79.88
hand (closed) 79.74
open 79.84
hip (closed) 79.75
open 79.85
knee (closed) 79.76
open 79.86
open (with external fixation) (with internal
fixation) 79.80
specified site NEC 79.89
shoulder (closed) 79.71
open 79.81
specified site (closed) NEC 79.79
open 79.89
temporomandibular (closed) 76.93
open 76.94
toe (closed) 79.78
open 79.88
wrist (closed) 79.73
open 79.83
elephantiasis, scrotum 61.3
epistaxis (see also Control, epistaxis) 21.00
fracture (bone) (with cast) (with splint) (with
traction device) (closed) 79.00
with internal fixation 79.10
alveolar process (with stabilization of teeth)
mandible (closed) 76.75
open 76.77
maxilla (closed) 76.73
open 76.77
open 76.77
ankle — see Reduction, fracture, leg
arm (closed) NEC 79.02
with internal fixation 79.12
open 79.22
with internal fixation 79.32
blow-out — see Reduction, fracture, orbit
carpal, metacarpal (closed) 79.03
with internal fixation 79.13
open 79.23
with internal fixation 79.33
epiphysis — see Reduction, separation
facial (bone) NEC 76.70
closed 76.78
open 76.79
femur (closed) 79.05
with internal fixation 79.15
open 79.25
with internal fixation 79.35
fibula (closed) 79.06
with internal fixation 79.16
open 79.26
with internal fixation 79.36
foot (closed) NEC 79.07
with internal fixation 79.17
open 79.27
with internal fixation 79.37
hand (closed) NEC 79.03
with internal fixation 79.13

Reduction — Reinsertion

Reduction — *continued*
  fracture — *continued*
    hand NEC — *continued*
      open 79.23
        with internal fixation 79.33
      humerus (closed) 79.01
        with internal fixation 79.11
          open 79.21
            with internal fixation 79.31
      jaw (lower) — *see also* Reduction, fracture, mandible
        upper — *see* Reduction, fracture, maxilla
      larynx 31.64
      leg (closed) NEC 79.06
        with internal fixation 79.16
          open 79.26
            with internal fixation 79.36
      malar (closed) 76.71
        open 76.72
      mandible (with dental wiring) (closed) 76.75
        open 76.76
      maxilla (with dental wiring) (closed) 76.73
        open 76.74
      nasal (closed) 21.71
        open 21.72
      open 79.20
        with internal fixation 79.30
        specified site NEC 79.29
          with internal fixation 79.39
      orbit (rim) (wall) (closed) 76.78
        open 76.79
      patella (open) (with internal fixation) 79.36
      phalanges
        foot (closed) 79.08
          with internal fixation 79.18
            open 79.28
              with internal fixation 79.38
        hand (closed) 79.04
          with internal fixation 79.14
            open 79.24
              with internal fixation 79.34
      radius (closed) 79.02
        with internal fixation 79.12
          open 79.22
            with internal fixation 79.32
      skull 02.02
      specified site (closed) NEC 79.09
        with internal fixation 79.19
          open 79.29
            with internal fixation 79.39
      spine 03.53
      tarsal, metatarsal (closed) 79.07
        with internal fixation 79.17
          open 79.27
            with internal fixation 79.37
      tibia (closed) 79.06
        with internal fixation 79.16
          open 79.26
            with internal fixation 79.36
      ulna (closed) 79.02
        with internal fixation 79.12
          open 79.22
            with internal fixation 79.32
      vertebra 03.53
      zygoma, zygomatic arch (closed) 76.71
        open 76.72
    fracture dislocation — *see* Reduction, fracture
    heart volume 37.35
    hemorrhoids (manual) 49.41
    hernia — *see also* Repair, hernia
      manual 96.27
    intussusception (open) 46.80
      with
        fluoroscopy 96.29
        ionizing radiation enema 96.29
        ultrasonography guidance 96.29
      hydrostatic 96.29
      large intestine 46.82
        endoscopic (balloon) 46.85
      pneumatic 96.29
      small intestine 46.81
    lung volume 32.22
    malrotation, intestine (manual) (surgical) 46.80
      large 46.82
        endoscopic (balloon) 46.85
      small 46.81

Reduction — *continued*
  mammoplasty (bilateral) 85.32
    unilateral 85.31
  prolapse
    anus (operative) 49.94
    colostomy (manual) 96.28
    enterostomy (manual) 96.28
    ileostomy (manual) 96.28
    rectum (manual) 96.26
    uterus
      by pessary 96.18
      surgical 69.22
  ptosis overcorrection 08.37
  retroversion, uterus by pessary 96.18
  separation, epiphysis (with internal fixation) (closed) 79.40
    femur (closed) 79.45
      open 79.55
    fibula (closed) 79.46
      open 79.56
    humerus (closed) 79.41
      open 79.51
    open 79.50
    specified site (closed) NEC — *see also* category 79.4 ☑
      open — *see* category 79.5 ☑
    tibia (closed) 79.46
      open 79.56
  size
    abdominal wall (adipose) (pendulous) 86.83
    arms (adipose) (batwing) 86.83
    breast (bilateral) 85.32
      unilateral 85.31
    buttocks (adipose) 86.83
    finger (macrodactyly repair) 82.83
    skin 86.83
    subcutaneous tissue 86.83
    thighs (adipose) 86.83
  torsion
    intestine (manual) (surgical) 46.80
      large 46.82
        endoscopic (balloon) 46.85
      small 46.81
    kidney pedicle 55.84
    omentum 54.74
    spermatic cord 63.52
      with orchiopexy 62.5
    testis 63.52
      with orchiopexy 62.5
    uterus NEC 69.98
      gravid 75.99
  ventricular 37.35
  volvulus
    intestine 46.80
      large 46.82
        endoscopic (balloon) 46.85
      small 46.81
    stomach 44.92
Reefing, joint capsule (*see also* Arthroplasty) 81.96
Re-entry operation (aorta) 39.54
Re-establishment, continuity — *see also* Anastomosis
  bowel 46.50
  fallopian tube 66.79
  vas deferens 63.82
Referral (for)
  psychiatric aftercare (halfway house) (outpatient clinic) 94.52
  psychotherapy 94.51
  rehabilitation
    alcoholism 94.53
    drug addiction 94.54
    psychologic NEC 94.59
    vocational 94.55
Reformation
  cardiac pacemaker pocket, new site (skin) (subcutaneous) 37.79
  cardioverter/defibrillator (automatic) pocket, new site (skin) (subcutaneous) 37.99
  chamber of eye 12.99
Refracture
  bone (for faulty union) (*see also* Osteoclasis) 78.70
  nasal bones 21.88

Refusion
  spinal NOS 81.30

> *Note: Also use either 81.62, 81.63, or 81.64 as an additional code to show the total number of vertebrae fused*

    atlas-axis (anterior) (transoral) (posterior) 81.31
    cervical (C_2 level or below) NEC 81.32
      anterior (interbody), anterolateral technique 81.32
      C_1-C_2 level (anterior) (posterior) 81.31
      posterior (interbody), posterolateral technique 81.33
    craniocervical (anterior) (transoral) (posterior) 81.31
    dorsal, dorsolumbar NEC 81.35
      anterior (interbody), anterolateral technique 81.34
      posterior (interbody), posterolateral technique 81.35
    lumbar, lumbosacral NEC 81.38
      anterior (interbody), anterolateral technique 81.36
      anterior lumbar interbody fusion (ALIF) 81.36 ●●
      lateral transverse process technique 81.37
      posterior (interbody), posterolateral technique 81.38
      posterior lumbar interbody fusion (PLIF) 81.38 ●
      transforaminal lumbar interbody fusion (TLIF) 81.38 ●●●
    number of vertebrae — *see* codes 81.62-81.64
    occiput — C_2 (anterior) (transoral) (posterior) 81.31
    refusion NEC 81.39
Regional blood flow study 92.05
Regulation, menstrual 69.6
Rehabilitation programs NEC 93.89
  alcohol 94.61
    with detoxification 94.63
    combined alcohol and drug 94.67
      with detoxification 94.69
  drug 94.64
    with detoxification 94.66
    combined drug and alcohol 94.67
      with detoxification 94.69
  sheltered employment 93.85
  vocational 93.85
Reimplantation
  adrenal tissue (heterotopic) (orthotopic) 07.45
  artery 39.59
    renal, aberrant 39.55
  bile ducts following excision of ampulla of Vater 51.62
  extremity — *see* Reattachment, extremity
  fallopian tube into uterus 66.74
  kidney 55.61
  lung 33.5 ☑
  ovary 65.72
    laparoscopic 65.75
  pancreatic tissue 52.81
  parathyroid tissue (heterotopic) (orthotopic) 06.95
  pulmonary artery for hemitruncus repair 35.83
  renal vessel, aberrant 39.55
  testis in scrotum 62.5
  thyroid tissue (heterotopic) (orthotopic) 06.94
  tooth 23.5
  ureter into bladder 56.74
Reinforcement — *see also* Repair, by site
  sclera NEC 12.88
    with graft 12.87
Reinsertion — *see also* Insertion or Revision
  cystostomy tube 59.94
  fixation device (internal) (*see also* Fixation, bone, internal) 78.50
  heart valve (prosthetic) 35.95
  Holter (-Spitz) valve 02.42
  implant (expelled) (extruded)
    eyeball (with conjunctival graft) 16.62

Reinsertion — *see also* Insertion or Revision — *continued*
  implant — *continued*
    orbital 16.62
  nephrostomy tube 55.93
  pyelostomy tube 55.94
  ureteral stent (transurethral) 59.8
    with ureterotomy 59.8 [56.2]
  ureterostomy tube 59.93
  valve
    heart (prosthetic) 35.95
    ventricular (cerebral) 02.42

Relaxation (*see also* Release training) 94.33

Release
  carpal tunnel (for nerve decompression) 04.43
  celiac artery axis 39.91
  central slip, extensor tendon hand (mallet finger repair) 82.84
  chordee 64.42
  clubfoot NEC 83.84
  de Quervain's tenosynovitis 82.01
  Dupuytren's contracture (by palmar fasciectomy) 82.35
    by fasciotomy (subcutaneous) 82.12
      with excision 82.35
  Fowler (mallet finger repair) 82.84
  joint (capsule) (adherent) (constrictive) (*see also* Division, joint capsule) 80.40
  laryngeal 31.92
  ligament (*see also* Division, ligament) 80.40
    median arcuate 39.91
  median arcuate ligament 39.91
  muscle (division) 83.19
    hand 82.19
  nerve (peripheral) NEC 04.49
    cranial NEC 04.42
    trigeminal 04.41
  pressure, intraocular 12.79
  scar tissue
    skin 86.84
    stoma — *see* Revision, stoma
  tarsal tunnel 04.44
  tendon 83.13
    hand 82.11
      extensor, central slip (repair mallet finger) 82.84
    sheath 83.01
      hand 82.01
  tenosynovitis 83.01
    abductor pollicis longus 82.01
    de Quervain's 82.01
    external pollicis brevis 82.01
    hand 82.01
  torsion
    intestine 46.80
      large 46.82
        endoscopic (balloon) 46.85
      small 46.81
    kidney pedicle 55.84
    ovary 65.95
    testes 63.52
  transverse carpal ligament (for nerve decompression) 04.43
  trigger finger or thumb 82.01
  urethral stricture 58.5
  Volkmann's contracture
    excision of scar, muscle 83.32
    fasciotomy 83.14
    muscle transplantation 83.77
  web contracture (skin) 86.84

Relief — *see* Release

Relocation — *see also* Revision
  cardiac ►device (CRT-D) (CRT-P) (defibrillator) (pacemaker)◄ pocket, new site (skin) (subcutaneous) 37.79
  CRT-D pocket 37.79 ▲
  CRT-P pocket 37.79
  subcutaneous device pocket NEC 86.09

Remobilization
  joint 93.16
  stapes 19.0

Remodel
  ventricle 37.35

Removal — *see also* Excision
  Abrams bar (chest wall) 34.01

Removal — *see also* Excision — *continued*
  abscess — *see* Incision, by site
  adenoid tag(s) 28.6
  anal sphincter
    with revision 49.75
    without revision 49.76
  arch bars (orthodontic) 24.8
    immobilization device 97.33
  arterial graft or prosthesis 39.49
  arteriovenous shunt (device) 39.43
    with creation of new shunt 39.42
  Barton's tongs (skull) 02.95
    with synchronous replacement 02.94
  bladder sphincter, artificial 58.99
    with replacement 58.93
  blood clot — *see also* Incision, by site
    bladder (by incision) 57.19
      without incision 57.0
    kidney (without incision) 56.0
      by incision 55.01
    ureter
      by incision 56.2
  bone fragment (chip) (*see also* Incision, bone) 77.10
    joint (*see also* Arthrotomy) 80.10
    necrotic (*see also* Sequestrectomy, bone) 77.00
      joint (*see also* Arthrotomy) 80.10
    skull 01.25
      with debridement compound fracture 02.02
  bone growth stimulator — *see* category 78.6 ☑
  bony spicules, spinal canal 03.53
  brace 97.88
  breast implant 85.94
    tissue expander 85.96
  calcareous deposit
    bursa 83.03
      hand 82.03
    tendon, intratendinous 83.39
      hand 82.29
  calcification, heart valve leaflets —*see* Valvuloplasty, heart
  calculus
    bile duct (by incision) 51.49
      endoscopic 51.88
      laparoscopic 51.88
      percutaneous 51.98
    bladder (by incision) 57.19
      without incision 57.0
    common duct (by incision) 51.41
      endoscopic 51.88
      laparoscopic 51.88
      percutaneous 51.96
    gallbladder 51.04
      endoscopic 51.88
      laparoscopic 51.88
    kidney (by incision) 55.01
      without incision (transurethral) 56.0
      percutaneous 55.03
        with fragmentation (ultrasound) 55.04
      renal pelvis (by incision) 55.11
        percutaneous nephrostomy 55.03
          with fragmentation 55.04
        transurethral 56.0
    lacrimal
      canaliculi 09.42
        by incision 09.52
      gland 09.3
        by incision 09.0
      passage(s) 09.49
        by incision 09.59
      punctum 09.41
        by incision 09.51
      sac 09.49
        by incision 09.53
    pancreatic duct (by incision) 52.09
      endoscopic 52.94
    perirenal tissue 59.09
    pharynx 29.39
    prostate 60.0
    salivary gland (by incision) 26.0
      by probe 26.91
    ureter (by incision) 56.2
      without incision 56.0

Removal — *see also* Excision — *continued*
  calculus — *continued*
    urethra (by incision) 58.0
      without incision 58.6
  caliper tongs (skull) 02.95
  cannula
    for extracorporeal membrane oxygenation (ECMO) — *omit code*
  cardiac pacemaker (device) (initial) (permanent) (cardiac resynchronization device, CRT-P) 37.89
    with replacement (by)
      cardiac resynchronization pacemaker (CRT-P)
        device only 00.53
        total system 00.50
      dual-chamber 37.87
      single-chamber device 37.85
        rate responsive 37.86
  cardioverter/defibrillator pulse generator
    without replacement (cardiac resynchronization defibrillator device (CRT-D)) 37.99
  cast 97.88
    with reapplication 97.13
      lower limb 97.12
      upper limb 97.11
  catheter (indwelling) — *see also* Removal, tube
    bladder 97.64
    cranial cavity 01.27 ●
    middle ear (tympanum) 20.1
    ureter 97.62
    urinary 97.64
    ventricular (cerebral) 02.43
      with synchronous replacement 02.42
  cerclage material, cervix 69.96
  cerumen, ear 96.52
  corneal epithelium 11.41
    for smear or culture 11.21
  coronary artery obstruction (thrombus) 36.09
    direct intracoronary artery infusion 36.04
    open chest approach 36.03
    percutaneous transluminal (balloon) 00.66 ▲

> *Note — Also use 00.40, 00.41, 00.42, or 00.43 to show the total number of vessels treated. In addition, use 00.45, 00.46, 00.47, or 00.48 to show the number of vascular stents inserted.* ● ● ● ● ●

  Crutchfield tongs (skull) 02.95
    with synchronous replacement 02.94
  cyst — *see also* Excision, lesion, by site
    dental 24.4
    lung 32.29
      endoscopic 32.28
  cystic duct remnant 51.61
  decidua (by)
    aspiration curettage 69.52
    curettage (D and C) 69.02
    manual 75.4
  dental wiring (immobilization device) 97.33
    orthodontic 24.8
  device (therapeutic) NEC 97.89
    abdomen NEC 97.86
    digestive system NEC 97.59
    drainage — *see* Removal, tube
    external fixation device 97.88
      mandibular NEC 97.36
      minifixator (bone) — *see* category 78.6 ☑
    for musculoskeletal immobilization NEC 97.88
    genital tract NEC 97.79
    head and neck NEC 97.39
    intrauterine contraceptive 97.71
    spine 80.09 ●
    thorax NEC 97.49
    trunk NEC 97.87
    urinary system NEC 97.69
  diaphragm, vagina 97.73
  drainage device — *see* Removal, tube
  dye, spinal canal 03.31
  ectopic fetus (from) 66.02
    abdominal cavity 74.3
    extraperitoneal (intraligamentous) 74.3

Removal — *see also* Excision — *continued*
ectopic fetus — *continued*
  fallopian tube (by salpingostomy) 66.02
    by salpingotomy 66.01
    with salpingectomy 66.62
  intraligamentous 74.3
  ovarian 74.3
  peritoneal (following uterine or tubal
    rupture) 74.3
  site NEC 74.3
  tubal (by salpingostomy) 66.02
    by salpingotomy 66.01
    with salpingectomy 66.62
electrodes
  bone growth stimulator — *see* category
    78.6 ☑
  brain 01.22
    depth 01.22
      with synchronous replacement 02.93
    foramen ovale 01.22
      with synchronous replacement 02.93
    sphenoidal — *omit code*
      with synchronous replacement 02.96
  cardiac pacemaker (atrial) (transvenous)
    (ventricular) 37.77
    with replacement 37.76
  depth 01.22
    with synchronous replacement 02.93
  epicardial (myocardial) 37.77
    with replacement (by)
      atrial and/or ventricular lead(s)
        (electrode) 37.76
      epicardial lead 37.74
  epidural pegs 01.22
    with synchronous replacement 02.93
  foramen ovale 01.22
    with synchronous replacement 02.93
  intracranial 01.22
    with synchronous replacement 02.93
  peripheral nerve 04.93
    with synchronous replacement 04.92
  sacral nerve 04.93
  sphenoidal — *omit code*
    with synchronous replacement 02.96
  spinal 03.94
    with synchronous replacement 03.93
  temporary transvenous pacemaker system
    — *omit code*
electroencephalographic receiver (brain)
  (intracranial) 01.22
  with synchronous replacement 02.93
electronic
  stimulator — *see* Removal, neurostimulator,
    by site
    bladder 57.98
    bone 78.6 ☑
    skeletal muscle 83.93
      with synchronous replacement 83.92
    ureter 56.94
electrostimulator — *see* Removal, electronic,
  stimulator, by site
embolus 38.00
  with endarterectomy — *see* Endarterectomy
  abdominal
    artery 38.06
    vein 38.07
  aorta (arch) (ascending) (descending) 38.04
  arteriovenous shunt or cannula 39.49
  bovine graft 39.49
  head and neck vessel NEC 38.02
  intracranial vessel NEC 38.01
  lower limb
    artery 38.08
    vein 38.09
  pulmonary (artery) (vein) 38.05
  thoracic vessel NEC 38.05
  upper limb (artery) (vein) 38.03
embryo — *see* Removal, ectopic fetus
encircling tube, eye (episcleral) 14.6
epithelial downgrowth, anterior chamber 12.93
external fixation device 97.88
  mandibular NEC 97.36
  minifixator (bone) — *see* category 78.6 ☑
extrauterine embryo — *see* Removal, ectopic
  fetus

Removal — *see also* Excision — *continued*
eyeball 16.49
  with implant 16.42
    with attachment of muscles 16.41
fallopian tube — *see* Salpingectomy
feces (impacted) (by flushing) (manual) 96.38
fetus, ectopic — *see* Removal, ectopic fetus
fingers, supernumerary 86.26
fixation device
  external 97.88
    mandibular NEC 97.36
    minifixator (bone) — *see* category 78.6 ☑
  internal 78.60
    carpal, metacarpal 78.64
    clavicle 78.61
    facial (bone) 76.97
    femur 78.65
    fibula 78.67
    humerus 78.62
    patella 78.66
    pelvic 78.69
    phalanges (foot) (hand) 78.69
    radius 78.63
    scapula 78.61
    specified site NEC 78.69
    tarsal, metatarsal 78.68
    thorax (ribs) (sternum) 78.61
    tibia 78.67
    ulna 78.63
    vertebrae 78.69
foreign body NEC (*see also* Incision, by site)
    98.20
  abdominal (cavity) 54.92
    wall 54.0
  adenoid 98.13
    by incision 28.91
  alveolus, alveolar bone 98.22
    by incision 24.0
  antecubital fossa 98.27
    by incision 86.05
  anterior chamber 12.00
    by incision 12.02
      with use of magnet 12.01
  anus (intraluminal) 98.05
    by incision 49.93
  artificial stoma (intraluminal) 98.18
  auditory canal, external 18.02
  axilla 98.27
    by incision 86.05
  bladder (without incision) 57.0
    by incision 57.19
  bone, except fixation device (*see also*
    Incision, bone) 77.10
    alveolus, alveolar 98.22
      by incision 24.0
  brain 01.39
    without incision into brain 01.24
  breast 85.0
  bronchus (intraluminal) 98.15
    by incision 33.0
  bursa 83.03
    hand 82.03
  canthus 98.22
    by incision 08.51
  cerebral meninges 01.31
  cervix (intraluminal) NEC 98.16
    penetrating 69.97
  choroid (by incision) 14.00
    with use of magnet 14.01
    without use of magnet 14.02
  ciliary body (by incision) 12.00
    with use of magnet 12.01
    without use of magnet 12.02
  conjunctiva (by magnet) 98.22
    by incision 10.0
  cornea 98.21
    by
      incision 11.1
      magnet 11.0
  duodenum 98.03
    by incision 45.01
  ear (intraluminal) 98.11
    with incision 18.09
  epididymis 63.92
  esophagus (intraluminal) 98.02
    by incision 42.09

Removal — *see also* Excision — *continued*
foreign body NEC (*see also* Incision, by site) —
    continued
  extrapleural (by incision) 34.01
  eye, eyeball (by magnet) 98.21
    anterior segment (by incision) 12.00
      with use of magnet 12.01
      without use of magnet 12.02
    posterior segment (by incision) 14.00
      with use of magnet 14.01
      without use of magnet 14.02
    superficial 98.21
  eyelid 98.22
    by incision 08.09
  fallopian tube
    by salpingostomy 66.02
    by salpingotomy 66.01
  fascia 83.09
    hand 82.09
  foot 98.28
  gall bladder 51.04
  groin region (abdominal wall) (inguinal) 54.0
  gum 98.22
    by incision 24.0
  hand 98.26
  head and neck NEC 98.22
  heart 37.11
  internal fixation device — *see* Removal,
    fixation device, internal
  intestine
    by incision 45.00
    large (intraluminal) 98.04
      by incision 45.03
    small (intraluminal) 98.03
      by incision 45.02
  intraocular (by incision) 12.00
    with use of magnet 12.01
    without use of magnet 12.02
  iris (by incision) 12.00
    with use of magnet 12.01
    without use of magnet 12.02
  joint structures (*see also* Arthrotomy) 80.10
  kidney (transurethral) (by endoscopy) 56.0
    by incision 55.01
    pelvis (transurethral) 56.0
      by incision 55.11
  labia 98.23
    by incision 71.09
  lacrimal
    canaliculi 09.42
      by incision 09.52
    gland 09.3
      by incision 09.0
    passage(s) 09.49
      by incision 09.59
    punctum 09.41
      by incision 09.51
    sac 09.49
      by incision 09.53
  large intestine (intraluminal) 98.04
    by incision 45.03
  larynx (intraluminal) 98.14
    by incision 31.3
  lens 13.00
    by incision 13.02
      with use of magnet 13.01
  liver 50.0
  lower limb, except foot 98.29
    foot 98.28
  lung 33.1
  mediastinum 34.1
  meninges (cerebral) 01.31
    spinal 03.01
  mouth (intraluminal) 98.01
    by incision 27.92
  muscle 83.02
    hand 82.02
  nasal sinus 22.50
    antrum 22.2
      with Caldwell-Luc approach 22.39
    ethmoid 22.51
    frontal 22.41
    maxillary 22.2
      with Caldwell-Luc approach 22.39
    sphenoid 22.52

Removal — *see also* Excision — *continued*
foreign body NEC (*see also* Incision, by site) —
continued
nerve (cranial) (peripheral) NEC 04.04
root 03.01
nose (intraluminal) 98.12
by incision 21.1
oral cavity (intraluminal) 98.01
by incision 27.92
orbit (by magnet) 98.21
by incision 16.1
palate (penetrating) 98.22
by incision 27.1
pancreas 52.09
penis 98.24
by incision 64.92
pericardium 37.12
perineum (female) 98.23
by incision 71.09
male 98.25
by incision 86.05
perirenal tissue 59.09
peritoneal cavity 54.92
perivesical tissue 59.19
pharynx (intraluminal) 98.13
by pharyngotomy 29.0
pleura (by incision) 34.09
popliteal space 98.29
by incision 86.05
rectum (intraluminal) 98.05
by incision 48.0
renal pelvis (transurethral) 56.0
by incision 56.1
retina (by incision) 14.00
with use of magnet 14.01
without use of magnet 14.02
retroperitoneum 54.92
sclera (by incision) 12.00
with use of magnet 12.01
without use of magnet 12.02
scrotum 98.24
by incision 61.0
sinus (nasal) 22.50
antrum 22.2
with Caldwell-Luc approach 22.39
ethmoid 22.51
frontal 22.41
maxillary 22.2
with Caldwell-Luc approach 22.39
sphenoid 22.52
skin NEC 98.20
by incision 86.05
skull 01.24
with incision into brain 01.39
small intestine (intraluminal) 98.03
by incision 45.02
soft tissue NEC 83.09
hand 82.09
spermatic cord 63.93
spinal (canal) (cord) (meninges) 03.01
stomach (intraluminal) 98.03
bubble (balloon) 44.94
by incision 43.0
subconjunctival (by magnet) 98.22
by incision 10.0
subcutaneous tissue NEC 98.20
by incision 86.05
supraclavicular fossa 98.27
by incision 86.05
tendon (sheath) 83.01
hand 82.01
testis 62.0
thorax (by incision) 34.09
thyroid (field) (gland) (by incision) 06.09
tonsil 98.13
by incision 28.91
trachea (intraluminal) 98.15
by incision 31.3
trunk NEC 98.25
tunica vaginalis 98.24
upper limb, except hand 98.27
hand 98.26
ureter (transurethral) 56.0
by incision 56.2
urethra (intraluminal) 98.19
by incision 58.0

Removal — *see also* Excision — *continued*
foreign body NEC (*see also* Incision, by site) —
continued
uterus (intraluminal) 98.16
vagina (intraluminal) 98.17
by incision 70.14
vas deferens 63.6
vitreous (by incision) 14.00
with use of magnet 14.01
without use of magnet 14.02
vulva 98.23
by incision 71.09
gallstones
bile duct (by incision) NEC 51.49
endoscopic 51.88
common duct (by incision) 51.41
endoscopic 51.88
percutaneous 51.96
duodenum 45.01
gallbladder 51.04
endoscopic 51.88
laparoscopic 51.88
hepatic ducts 51.49
endoscopic 51.88
intestine 45.00
large 45.03
small NEC 45.02
liver 50.0
Gardner Wells tongs (skull) 02.95
with synchronous replacement 02.94
gastric band (adjustable), laparoscopic
44.97
gastric bubble (balloon) 44.94
granulation tissue — *see also* Excision, lesion,
by site
with repair — *see* Repair, by site
cranial 01.6
skull 01.6
halo traction device (skull) 02.95
with synchronous replacement 02.94
heart assist system
with replacement 37.63
intra-aortic balloon pump (IABP) 97.44
nonoperative 97.44
open removal 37.64
percutaneous external device 97.44
hematoma — *see* Drainage, by site
Hoffman minifixator device (bone) — *see*
category 78.6 ☑
hydatidiform mole 68.0
impacted
feces (rectum) (by flushing) (manual) 96.38
tooth 23.19
from nasal sinus (maxillary) 22.61
implant
breast 85.94
cochlear prosthetic device 20.99
cornea 11.92
lens (prosthetic) 13.8
middle ear NEC 20.99
ocular 16.71
posterior segment 14.6
orbit 16.72
retina 14.6
tympanum 20.1
internal fixation device — *see* Removal, fixation
device, internal
intra-aortic balloon pump (IABP) 97.44
intrauterine contraceptive device (IUD) 97.71
joint (structure) NOS 80.90
ankle 80.97
elbow 80.92
foot and toe 80.98
hand and finger 80.94
hip 80.95
knee 80.96
other specified sites 80.99
shoulder 80.91
spine 80.99
toe 80.98
wrist 80.93
Kantrowitz heart pump 37.64
nonoperative 97.44
keel (tantalum plate), larynx 31.98
kidney — *see also* Nephrectomy
mechanical 55.98

Removal — *see also* Excision — *continued*
kidney — *see also* Nephrectomy — *continued*
transplanted or rejected 55.53
laminaria (tent), uterus 97.79
leads (cardiac) — *see* Removal, electrodes,
cardiac pacemaker
lesion — *see* Excision, lesion, by site
ligamentum flavum (spine) — *omit code*
ligature
fallopian tube 66.79
ureter 56.86
vas deferens 63.84
limb lengthening device, internal — *see*
category 78.6 ☑
loop recorder 86.05
loose body
bone — *see* Sequestrectomy, bone
joint 80.10
mesh (surgical) — *see* Removal, foreign
body, by site
lymph node — *see* Excision, lymph, node
minifixator device (bone) — *see* category
78.6 ☑
external fixation device 97.88
Mulligan hood, fallopian tube 66.94
with synchronous replacement 66.93
muscle stimulator (skeletal) 83.93
with replacement 83.92
myringotomy device or tube 20.1
nail (bed) (fold) 86.23
internal fixation device — *see* Removal,
fixation device, internal
necrosis
skin 86.28
excisional 86.22
neuropacemaker — *see* Removal,
neurostimulator, by site
neurostimulator
brain 01.22
with synchronous replacement 02.93
electrodes
brain 01.22
with synchronous replacement
02.93
intracranial 01.22
with synchronous replacement
02.93
peripheral nerve 04.93
with synchronous replacement
04.92
sacral nerve 04.93
with synchronous replacement
04.92
spinal 03.94
with synchronous replacement
03.93
intracranial 01.22
with synchronous replacement 02.93
peripheral nerve 04.93
with synchronous replacement 04.92
pulse generator (single array, dual array)
86.05
with synchronous replacement 86.96
dual array 86.95
rechargeable 86.98   ●
single array 86.94
rechargeable 86.97   ●
spinal 03.94
with synchronous replacement 03.93
nonabsorbable surgical material NEC — *see*
Removal, foreign body, by site
odontoma (tooth) 24.4
orbital implant 16.72
osteocartilagenous loose body, joint structures
(*see also* Arthrotomy) 80.10
outer attic wall (middle ear) 20.59
ovo-testis (unilateral) 62.3
bilateral 62.41
pacemaker
brain (intracranial) — *see* Removal,
neurostimulator
cardiac (device) (initial) (permanent) 37.89
with replacement
dual-chamber device 37.87
single-chamber device 37.85
rate responsive 37.86

Removal — *see also* Excision — *continued*
　pacemaker — *continued*
　　cardiac — *continued*
　　　electrodes (atrial) (transvenous)
　　　　　(ventricular) 37.77
　　　　with replacement 37.76
　　　epicardium (myocardium) 37.77
　　　　with replacement (by)
　　　　　atrial and/or ventricular lead(s)
　　　　　　(electrode) 37.76
　　　　　epicardial lead 37.74
　　　temporary transvenous pacemaker
　　　　system — *omit code*
　　intracranial — *see* Removal, neurostimulator
　　neural — *see* Removal, neurostimulator
　　peripheral nerve — *see* Removal,
　　　neurostimulator
　　spine — *see* Removal, neurostimulator
　pack, packing
　　dental 97.34
　　intrauterine 97.72
　　nasal 97.32
　　rectum 97.59
　　trunk NEC 97.85
　　vagina 97.75
　　vulva 97.75
　pantopaque dye, spinal canal 03.31
　patella (complete) 77.96
　　partial 77.86
　pectus deformity implant device 34.01
　pelvic viscera, en masse (female) 68.8
　　male 57.71
　pessary, vagina NEC 97.74
　pharynx (partial) 29.33
　phlebolith — *see* Removal, embolus
　placenta (by)
　　aspiration curettage 69.52
　　D and C 69.02
　　manual 75.4
　plaque, dental 96.54
　plate, skull 02.07
　　with synchronous replacement 02.05
　polyp — *see also* Excision, lesion, by site
　　esophageal 42.32
　　　endoscopic 42.33
　　gastric (endoscopic) 43.41
　　intestine 45.41
　　　endoscopic 45.42
　　nasal 21.31
　prosthesis
　　bile duct 51.95
　　　nonoperative 97.55
　　cochlear prosthetic device 20.99
　　dental 97.35
　　eye 97.31
　　facial bone 76.99
　　fallopian tube 66.94
　　　with synchronous replacement 66.93
　　joint structures 80.00
　　　ankle 80.07
　　　elbow 80.02
　　　foot and toe 80.08
　　　hand and finger 80.04
　　　hip 80.05
　　　knee 80.06
　　　shoulder 80.01
　　　specified site NEC 80.09
　　　spine 80.09
　　　wrist 80.03
　　lens 13.8
　　penis (internal) without replacement 64.96
　　Rosen (urethra) 59.99
　　testicular, by incision 62.0
　　urinary sphincter, artificial 58.99
　　　with replacement 58.93
　pseudophakos 13.8
　pterygium 11.39
　　with corneal graft 11.32
　pulse generator
　　cardiac pacemaker 37.86
　　cardioverter/defibrillator 37.99
　　neurostimulator — *see* Removal,
　　　neurostimulator, pulse generator
　pump assist device, heart 37.64
　　with replacement 37.63
　　nonoperative 97.44

Removal — *see also* Excision — *continued*
　radioactive material — *see* Removal, foreign
　　body, by site
　redundant skin, eyelid 08.86
　rejected organ
　　kidney 55.53
　　testis 62.42
　reservoir, ventricular (Ommaya) (Rickham)
　　02.43
　　with synchronous replacement 02.42
　retained placenta (by)
　　aspiration curettage 69.52
　　D and C 69.02
　　manual 75.4
　retinal implant 14.6
　rhinolith 21.31
　rice bodies, tendon sheaths 83.01
　　hand 82.01
　Roger-Anderson minifixator device (bone) — *see*
　　category 78.6 ☑
　root, residual (tooth) (buried) (retained) 23.11
　Rosen prosthesis (urethra) 59.99
　Scribner shunt 39.43
　scleral buckle or implant 14.6
　secondary membranous cataract (with
　　iridectomy) 13.65
　secundines (by)
　　aspiration curettage 69.52
　　D and C 69.02
　　manual 75.4
　sequestrum — *see* Sequestrectomy
　seton, anus 49.93
　Shepard's tube (ear) 20.1
　Shirodkar suture, cervix 69.96
　shunt
　　arteriovenous 39.43
　　　with creation of new shunt 39.42
　　lumbar-subarachnoid NEC 03.98
　　pleurothecal 03.98
　　salpingothecal 03.98
　　spinal (thecal) NEC 03.98
　　subarachnoid-peritoneal 03.98
　　subarachnoid-ureteral 03.98
　silastic tubes
　　ear 20.1
　　fallopian tubes 66.94
　　　with synchronous replacement 66.93
　skin
　　necrosis or slough 86.28
　　　excisional 86.22
　　　superficial layer (by dermabrasion) 86.25
　skull tongs 02.95
　　with synchronous replacement 02.94
　spacer (cement) (joint) 84.57　　　　　　●
　splint 97.88
　stent
　　bile duct 97.55
　　larynx 31.98
　　ureteral 97.62
　　urethral 97.65
　stimoceiver — *see* Removal, neurostimulator
　subdural
　　grids 01.22
　　strips 01.22
　supernumerary digit(s) 86.26
　suture(s) NEC 97.89
　　abdominal wall 97.83
　　by incision — *see* Incision, by site
　　genital tract 97.79
　　head and neck 97.38
　　thorax 97.43
　　trunk NEC 97.84
　symblepharon — *see* Repair, symblepharon
　temporary transvenous pacemaker system —
　　omit code
　testis (unilateral) 62.3
　　bilateral 62.41
　　remaining or solitary 62.42
　thrombus 38.00
　　with endarterectomy — *see* Endarterectomy
　　abdominal
　　　artery 38.06
　　　vein 38.07
　　aorta (arch) (ascending) (descending) 38.04
　　arteriovenous shunt or cannula 39.49
　　bovine graft 39.49

Removal — *see also* Excision — *continued*
　thrombus — *continued*
　　coronary artery 36.09
　　head and neck vessel NEC 38.02
　　intracranial vessel NEC 38.01
　　lower limb
　　　artery 38.08
　　　vein 38.09
　　pulmonary (artery) (vein) 38.05
　　thoracic vessel NEC 38.05
　　upper limb (artery) (vein) 38.03
　tissue expander (skin) NEC 86.05
　　breast 85.96
　toes, supernumerary 86.26
　tongs, skull 02.95
　　with synchronous replacement 02.94
　tonsil tag 28.4
　tooth (by forceps) (multiple) (single) NEC 23.09
　　deciduous 23.01
　　surgical NEC 23.19
　　　impacted 23.19
　　　residual root 23.11
　　　root apex 23.73
　　　　with root canal therapy 23.72
　trachoma follicles 10.33
　T-tube (bile duct) 97.55
　tube
　　appendix 97.53
　　bile duct (T-tube) NEC 97.55
　　cholecystostomy 97.54
　　cranial cavity 01.27　　　　　　　　　●
　　cystostomy 97.63
　　ear (button) 20.1
　　gastrostomy 97.51
　　large intestine 97.53
　　liver 97.55
　　mediastinum 97.42
　　nephrostomy 97.61
　　pancreas 97.56
　　peritoneum 97.82
　　pleural cavity 97.41
　　pyelostomy 97.61
　　retroperitoneum 97.81
　　small intestine 97.52
　　thoracotomy 97.41
　　tracheostomy 97.37
　　tympanostomy 20.1
　　tympanum 20.1
　　ureterostomy 97.62
　ureteral splint (stent) 97.62
　urethral sphincter, artificial 58.99
　　with replacement 58.93
　urinary sphincter, artificial 58.99
　　with replacement 58.93
　utricle 20.79
　valve
　　vas deferens 63.85
　　ventricular (cerebral) 02.43
　vascular graft or prosthesis 39.49
　ventricular shunt or reservoir 02.43
　　with synchronous replacement 02.42
　Vinke tongs (skull) 02.95
　　with synchronous replacement 02.94
　vitreous (with replacement) 14.72
　　anterior approach (partial) 14.71
　　open sky technique 14.71
　Wagner-Brooker minifixator device (bone) —
　　see category 78.6 ☑
　wiring, dental (immobilization device) 97.33
　　orthodontic 24.8

Renipuncture (percutaneous) 55.92

Renogram 92.03

Renotransplantation NEC 55.69

> *Note — To report donor source:*
> 　*cadaver 00.93*
> 　*live non-related donor 00.92*
> 　*live related donor 00.91*
> 　*live unrelated donor 00.92*

Reopening — *see also* Incision, by site
　blepharorrhaphy 08.02
　canthorrhaphy 08.02
　cilia base 08.71
　craniotomy or craniectomy site 01.23

Reopening — *see also* Incision, by site —
    continued
  fallopian tube (divided) 66.79
  iris in anterior chambers 12.97
  laminectomy or laminotomy site 03.02
  laparotomy site 54.12
  osteotomy site (*see also* Incision, bone) 77.10
    facial bone 76.09
  tarsorrhaphy 08.02
  thoracotomy site (for control of hemorrhage)
    (for examination) (for exploration) 34.03
  thyroid field wound (for control of hemorrhage)
    (for examination) (for exploration) (for
    removal of hematoma) 06.02
Repacking — *see* Replacement, pack, by site
Repair
  abdominal wall 54.72
  adrenal gland 07.44
  alveolus, alveolar (process) (ridge) (with graft)
    (with implant) 24.5
  anal sphincter 49.79
    artificial sphincter
      implantation 49.75
      revision 49.75
    laceration (by suture) 49.71
      obstetric (current) 75.62
      old 49.79
  aneurysm (false) (true) 39.52
    by or with
      clipping 39.51
      coagulation 39.52
      coil (endovascular approach) 39.79
        head and neck 39.72
      electrocoagulation 39.52
        excision or resection of vessel — *see*
          also Aneurysmectomy, by site
        with
          anastomosis — *see* Aneurysmectomy,
            with anastomosis, by site
          graft replacement — *see*
            Aneurysmectomy, with graft
            replacement, by site
    endovascular graft 39.79
      abdominal aorta 39.71
      head and neck 39.72
      lower extremity artery(s) 39.79
      thoracic aorta 39.73   ▲
      upper extremity artery(s) 39.79
    filipuncture 39.52
    graft replacement — *see*
      Aneurysmectomy, with graft
      replacement, by site
    ligation 39.52
    liquid tissue adhesive (glue) 39.79
      endovascular approach 39.79
        head and neck 39.72
    methyl methacrylate 39.52
      endovascular approach 39.79
        head and neck 39.72
    occlusion 39.52
      endovascular approach 39.79
        head and neck 39.72
    suture 39.52
    trapping 39.52
    wiring 39.52
    wrapping (gauze) (methyl methacrylate)
      (plastic) 39.52
    coronary artery 36.91
    heart 37.32
    sinus of Valsalva 35.39
    thoracic aorta (dissecting), by fenestration
      39.54
  anomalous pulmonary venous connection
    (total)
    one-stage 35.82
    partial — *see* specific procedure
    total 35.82
  anus 49.79
    laceration (by suture) 49.71
      obstetric (current) 75.62
      old 49.79
  aorta 39.31
  aorticopulmonary window 39.59

Repair — *continued*
  arteriovenous fistula 39.53
    by or with
      clipping 39.53
      coagulation 39.53
      coil (endovascular approach) 39.79
        head and neck vessels 39.72
      division 39.53
      excision or resection — *see also*
        Aneurysmectomy, by site
        with
          anastomosis — *see* Aneurysmectomy,
            with anastomosis, by site
          graft replacement — *see*
            Aneurysmectomy, with graft
            replacement, by site
      ligation 39.53
        coronary artery 36.99
      occlusion 39.53
        endovascular approach 39.79
          head and neck 39.72
      suture 39.53
  artery NEC 39.59
    by
      endovascular approach
        abdominal aorta 39.71   ●
        head and neck (embolization or
          occlusion) 39.72
        other repair (of aneurysm) 39.79
        percutaneous repair of intracranial
          vessel(s) (for stent insertion)
          00.62

> *Note* — *Also use 00.40, 00.41, 00.42, or* ●
> *00.43 to show the total number of vessels* ●
> *treated. In addition, use 00.45, 00.46,* ●
> *00.47, or 00.48 to show the number of* ●
> *vascular stents inserted.* ●

        percutaneous repair of precerebral
          (extracranial) vessel(s) (for
          stent insertion) 00.61

> *Note* — *Also use 00.40, 00.41, 00.42, or* ●
> *00.43 to show the total number of vessels* ●
> *treated. In addition, use 00.45, 00.46,* ●
> *00.47, or 00.48 to show the number of* ●
> *vascular stents inserted.* ●

        thoracic aorta 39.73   ●
        non-coronary percutaneous transluminal
          angioplasty or atherectomy

> *Note* — *Also use 00.40, 00.41, 00.42, or* ●
> *00.43 to show the total number of vessels* ●
> *treated. In addition, use 00.45, 00.46,* ●
> *00.47, or 00.48 to show the number of* ●
> *vascular stents inserted.* ●

        basilar 00.61
        carotid 00.61
        femoropopliteal 39.50
        iliac 39.50
        lower extremity NOS 39.50
        mesenteric 39.50
        renal 39.50
        upper extremity NOS 39.50
        vertebral 00.61
    with
      patch graft 39.58
        with excision or resection of vessel —
          see Arteriectomy, with graft
          replacement, by site
        synthetic (Dacron) (Teflon) 39.57
        tissue (vein) (autogenous) (homograft)
          39.56
      suture 39.31
    coronary NEC 36.99
      by angioplasty — *see* Angioplasty,
        coronary
      by atherectomy — *see* Angioplasty,
        coronary
  artificial opening — *see* Repair, stoma
  atrial septal defect 35.71
    with
      prosthesis (open heart technique) 35.51
        closed heart technique 35.52
      tissue graft 35.61

Repair — *continued*
  atrial septal defect — *continued*
    combined with repair of valvular and
      ventricular septal defects — *see*
      Repair, endocardial cushion defect
    in total repair of total anomalous pulmonary
      venous connection 35.82
  atrioventricular canal defect (any type) 35.73
    with
      prosthesis 35.54
      tissue graft 35.63
  bifid digit (finger) 82.89
  bile duct NEC 51.79
    laceration (by suture) NEC 51.79
      common bile duct 51.71
  bladder NEC 57.89
    exstrophy 57.86
    for stress incontinence — *see* Repair, stress
      incontinence
    laceration (by suture) 57.81
      obstetric (current) 75.61
      old 57.89
    neck 57.85
  blepharophimosis 08.59
  blepharoptosis 08.36
    by
      frontalis muscle technique (with)
        fascial sling 08.32
        suture 08.31
      levator muscle technique 08.34
        with resection or advancement 08.33
      orbicularis oculi muscle sling 08.36
      tarsal technique 08.35
  blood vessel NEC 39.59
    with
      patch graft 39.58
        with excision or resection — *see*
          Angiectomy, with graft
          replacement
        synthetic (Dacron) (Teflon) 39.57
        tissue (vein) (autogenous) (homograft)
          39.56
      resection — *see* Angiectomy
      suture 39.30
    coronary artery NEC 36.99
      by angioplasty — *see* Angioplasty,
        coronary
      by atherectomy — *see* Angioplasty,
        coronary
    peripheral vessel NEC 39.59
      by angioplasty 39.50

> *Note* — *Also use 00.40, 00.41, 00.42, or* ●
> *00.43 to show the total number of vessels* ●
> *treated. In addition, use 00.45, 00.46,* ●
> *00.47, or 00.48 to show the number of* ●
> *vascular stents inserted.* ●

      by atherectomy 39.50

> *Note* — *Also use 00.40, 00.41, 00.42, or* ●
> *00.43 to show the total number of vessels* ●
> *treated. In addition, use 00.45, 00.46,* ●
> *00.47, or 00.48 to show the number of* ●
> *vascular stents inserted.* ●

      by endovascular approach 39.79
  bone NEC (*see also* Osteoplasty) — *see*
    category 78.4 ☑
    by synostosis technique — *see* Arthrodesis
    accessory sinus 22.79
    cranium NEC 02.06
      with
        flap (bone) 02.03
        graft (bone) 02.04
    for malunion, nonunion, or delayed union of
      fracture — *see* Repair, fracture,
      malunion or nonunion
    nasal 21.89
    skull NEC 02.06
      with
        flap (bone) 02.03
        graft (bone) 02.04
  bottle, hydrocele of tunica vaginalis 61.2
  brain (trauma) NEC 02.92
  breast (plastic) (*see also* Mammoplasty) 85.89
  broad ligament 69.29

☑ Additional Digit Required — Refer to the Tabular List (Numeric Code Section) for Additional Digit Selection

Repair — continued

bronchus NEC 33.48
  laceration (by suture) 33.41
bunionette (with osteotomy) 77.54
canaliculus, lacrimal 09.73
canthus (lateral) 08.59
cardiac pacemaker NEC 37.89
  electrode(s) (lead) NEC 37.75
cardioverter/defibrillator (automatic) pocket
  (skin) (subcutaneous) 37.99
cerebral meninges 02.12
cervix 67.69
  internal os 67.59
    transabdominal 67.51
    transvaginal 67.59
  laceration (by suture) 67.61
    obstetric (current) 75.51
    old 67.69
chest wall (mesh) (silastic) NEC 34.79
chordae tendineae 35.32
choroid NEC 14.9
  with retinal repair — see Repair, retina
cisterna chyli 40.69
claw toe 77.57
cleft
  hand 82.82
  laryngotracheal 31.69
  lip 27.54
  palate 27.62
    secondary or subsequent 27.63
coarctation of aorta — see Excision, coarctation
  of aorta
cochlear prosthetic device 20.99
  external components only 95.49
cockup toe 77.58
colostomy 46.43
conjunctiva NEC 10.49
  with scleral repair 12.81
  laceration 10.6
    with repair of sclera 12.81
  late effect of trachoma 10.49
cornea NEC 11.59
  with
    conjunctival flap 11.53
    transplant — see Keratoplasty
  postoperative dehiscence 11.52
coronary artery NEC 36.99
  by angioplasty — see Angioplasty, coronary
  by atherectomy — see Angioplasty, coronary
cranium NEC 02.06
  with
    flap (bone) 02.03
    graft (bone) 02.04
cusp, valve — see Repair, heart, valve
cystocele 70.51
  and rectocele 70.50
dental arch 24.8
diaphragm NEC 34.84
diastasis recti 83.65
diastematomyelia 03.59
ear (external) 18.79
  auditory canal or meatus 18.6
  auricle NEC 18.79
  cartilage NEC 18.79
  laceration (by suture) 18.4
  lop ear 18.79
  middle NEC 19.9
  prominent or protruding 18.5
ectropion 08.49
  by or with
    lid reconstruction 08.44
    suture (technique) 08.42
    thermocauterization 08.41
    wedge resection 08.43
encephalocele (cerebral) 02.12
endocardial cushion defect 35.73
  with
    prosthesis (grafted to septa) 35.54
    tissue graft 35.63
enterocele (female) 70.92
  male 53.9
enterostomy 46.40
entropion 08.49
  by or with
    lid reconstruction 08.44
    suture (technique) 08.42

Repair — continued

entropion — continued
  by or with — continued
    thermocauterization 08.41
    wedge resection 08.43
epicanthus (fold) 08.59
epididymis (and spermatic cord) NEC 63.59
  with vas deferens 63.89
epiglottis 31.69
episiotomy
  routine following delivery — see Episiotomy
  secondary 75.69
epispadias 58.45
esophagus, esophageal NEC 42.89
  fistula NEC 42.84
  stricture 42.85
exstrophy of bladder 57.86
eye, eyeball 16.89
  multiple structures 16.82
  rupture 16.82
  socket 16.64
    with graft 16.63
eyebrow 08.89
  linear 08.81
eyelid 08.89
  full-thickness 08.85
    involving lid margin 08.84
  laceration 08.81
    full-thickness 08.85
      involving lid margin 08.84
    partial-thickness 08.83
      involving lid margin 08.82
  linear 08.81
  partial-thickness 08.83
    involving lid margin 08.82
  retraction 08.38
fallopian tube (with prosthesis) 66.79
  by
    anastomosis 66.73
    reanastomosis 66.79
    reimplantation into
      ovary 66.72
      uterus 66.74
    suture 66.71
false aneurysm — see Repair, aneurysm
fascia 83.89
  by or with
    arthroplasty — see Arthroplasty
    graft (fascial) (muscle) 83.82
      hand 82.72
      tendon 83.81
        hand 82.79
    suture (direct) 83.65
      hand 82.46
  hand 82.89
    by
      graft NEC 82.79
        fascial 82.72
        muscle 82.72
      suture (direct) 82.46
  joint — see Arthroplasty
filtering bleb (corneal) (scleral) (by excision)
  12.82
  by
    corneal graft (see also Keratoplasty) 11.60
    scleroplasty 12.82
    suture 11.51
      with conjunctival flap 11.53
fistula — see also Closure, fistula
  anovaginal 70.73
  arteriovenous 39.53
    clipping 39.53
    coagulation 39.53
      endovascular approach 39.79
      head and neck 39.72
    division 39.53
    excision or resection — see also
      Aneurysmectomy, by site
      with
        anastomosis — see Aneurysmectomy,
          with anastomosis, by site
        graft replacement — see
          Aneurysmectomy, with graft
          replacement, by site
    ligation 39.53
      coronary artery 36.99

Repair — continued

fistula — see also Closure, fistula — continued
  arteriovenous — continued
    occlusion 39.53
      endovascular approach 39.79
      head and neck 39.72
    suture 39.53
  cervicovesical 57.84
  cervix 67.62
  choledochoduodenal 51.72
  colovaginal 70.72
  enterovaginal 70.74
  enterovesical 57.83
  esophagocutaneous 42.84
  ileovesical 57.83
  intestinovaginal 70.74
  intestinovesical 57.83
  oroantral 22.71
  perirectal 48.93
  pleuropericardial 37.49   ▲
  rectovaginal 70.73
  rectovesical 57.83
  rectovesicovaginal 57.83
  scrotum 61.42
  sigmoidovaginal 70.74
  sinus
    nasal 22.71
    of Valsalva 35.39
  splenocolic 41.95
  urethroperineovesical 57.84
  urethrovesical 57.84
  urethrovesicovaginal 57.84
  uterovesical 57.84
  vagina NEC 70.75
  vaginocutaneous 70.75
  vaginoenteric NEC 70.74
  vaginoileal 70.74
  vaginoperineal 70.75
  vaginovesical 57.84
  vesicocervicovaginal 57.84
  vesicocolic 57.83
  vesicocutaneous 57.84
  vesicoenteric 57.83
  vesicointestinal 57.83
  vesicometrorectal 57.83
  vesicoperineal 57.84
  vesicorectal 57.83
  vesicosigmoidal 57.83
  vesicosigmoidovaginal 57.83
  vesicourethral 57.84
  vesicourethrorectal 57.83
  vesicouterine 57.84
  vesicovaginal 57.84
  vulva 71.72
  vulvorectal 48.73
foramen ovale (patent) 35.71
  with
    prosthesis (open heart technique) 35.51
      closed heart technique 35.52
    tissue graft 35.61
fracture — see also Reduction, fracture
  larynx 31.64
  malunion or nonunion (delayed) NEC — see
    category 78.4 ☑
    with
      graft — see Graft, bone
      insertion (of)
        bone growth stimulator (invasive) —
          see category 78.9 ☑
        internal fixation device 78.5 ☑
      manipulation for realignment — see
        Reduction, fracture, by site,
        closed
    osteotomy
      with
        correction of alignment — see
          category 77.3 ☑
        with internal fixation device
          — see categories
          77.3 ☑ [78.5 ☑]
        with intramedullary rod —
          see categories
          77.3 ☑ [78.5 ☑]
    replacement arthroplasty — see
      Arthroplasty

☑ Additional Digit Required — Refer to the Tabular List (Numeric Code Section) for Additional Digit Selection

Repair — *continued*
  fracture — *see also* Reduction, fracture —
      continued
    malunion or nonunion NEC — *see* category
        78.4 ☑ — *continued*
      with — *continued*
        sequestrectomy — *see* category 77.0 ☑
          Sofield type procedure — *see*
              categories 77.3 ☑ [78.5 ☑]
          synostosis technique — *see*
              Arthrodesis
      vertebra 03.53
  funnel chest (with implant) 34.74
  gallbladder 51.91
  gastroschisis 54.71
  great vessels NEC 39.59
    laceration (by suture) 39.30
      artery 39.31
      vein 39.32
  hallux valgus NEC 77.59
    resection of joint with prosthetic implant
        77.59
  hammer toe 77.56
  hand 82.89
    with graft or implant 82.79
      fascia 82.72
      muscle 82.72
      tendon 82.79
  heart 37.49   ▲
    assist system 37.63
    septum 35.70
      with
        prosthesis 35.50
        tissue graft 35.60
      atrial 35.71
        with
          prosthesis (open heart technique)
              35.51
            closed heart technique 35.52
          tissue graft 35.61
        combined with repair of valvular and
            ventricular septal defects — *see*
            Repair, endocardial cushion
            defect
        in total repair of
          tetralogy of Fallot 35.81
          total anomalous pulmonary venous
              connection 35.82
          truncus arteriosus 35.83
        combined with repair of valvular defect —
            see Repair, endocardial cushion
            defect
      ventricular 35.72
        with
          prosthesis 35.53
          tissue graft 35.62
        combined with repair of valvular and
            atrial septal defects — *see*
            Repair, endocardial cushion
            defect
        in total repair of
          tetralogy of Fallot 35.81
          total anomalous pulmonary venous
              connection 35.82
          truncus arteriosus 35.83
    total replacement system 37.52
      implantable battery 37.54
      implantable controller 37.54
      thoracic unit 37.53
      transcutaneous energy transfer (TET)
          device 37.54
    valve (cusps) (open heart technique) 35.10
      with prosthesis or tissue graft 35.20
      aortic (without replacement) 35.11
        with
          prosthesis 35.22
          tissue graft 35.21
        combined with repair of atrial and
            ventricular septal defects — *see*
            Repair, endocardial cushion defect
      mitral (without replacement) 35.12
        with
          prosthesis 35.24
          tissue graft 35.23

Repair — *continued*
  heart — *continued*
    valve — *continued*
      pulmonary (without replacement) 35.13
        with
          prosthesis 35.26
          in total repair of tetralogy of
              Fallot 35.81
          tissue graft 35.25
      tricuspid (without replacement) 35.14
        with
          prosthesis 35.28
          tissue graft 35.27
  hepatic duct 51.79
  hernia NEC 53.9
    anterior abdominal wall NEC 53.59
      with prosthesis or graft 53.69
    colostomy 46.42
    crural 53.29
    cul-de-sac (Douglas') 70.92
    diaphragmatic
      abdominal approach 53.7
      thoracic, thoracoabdominal approach
          53.80
    epigastric 53.59
      with prosthesis or graft 53.69
    esophageal hiatus
      abdominal approach 53.7
      thoracic, thoracoabdominal approach
          53.80
    fascia 83.89
      hand 82.89
    femoral (unilateral) 53.29
      with prosthesis or graft 53.21
      bilateral 53.39
        with prosthesis or graft 53.31
    Ferguson 53.00
    Halsted 53.00
    Hill-Allison (hiatal hernia repair,
        transpleural approach) 53.80
    hypogastric 53.59
      with prosthesis or graft 53.69
    incisional 53.51
      with prosthesis or graft 53.61
    inguinal (unilateral) 53.00
      with prosthesis or graft 53.05
      bilateral 53.10
        with prosthesis or graft 53.17
        direct 53.11
          with prosthesis or graft 53.14
        direct and indirect 53.13
          with prosthesis or graft 53.16
        indirect 53.12
          with prosthesis or graft 53.15
      direct (unilateral) 53.01
        with prosthesis or graft 53.03
        and indirect (unilateral) 53.01
          with prosthesis or graft 53.03
          bilateral 53.13
            with prosthesis or graft 53.16
        bilateral 53.11
          with prosthesis or graft 53.14
      indirect (unilateral) 53.02
        with prosthesis or graft 53.04
        and direct (unilateral) 53.01
          with prosthesis or graft 53.03
          bilateral 53.13
            with prosthesis or graft 53.16
        bilateral 53.12
          with prosthesis or graft 53.15
    internal 53.9
    ischiatic 53.9
    ischiorectal 53.9
    lumbar 53.9
    manual 96.27
    obturator 53.9
    omental 53.9
    paraesophageal 53.7
    parahiatal 53.7
    paraileostomy 46.41
    parasternal 53.82
    paraumbilical 53.49
      with prosthesis 53.41
    pericolostomy 46.42
    perineal (enterocele) 53.9
    preperitoneal 53.29

Repair — *continued*
  hernia NEC — *continued*
    pudendal 53.9
    retroperitoneal 53.9
    sciatic 53.9
    scrotal — *see* Repair, hernia, inguinal
    spigelian 53.59
      with prosthesis or graft 53.69
    umbilical 53.49
      with prosthesis 53.41
    uveal 12.39
    ventral 53.59
      incisional 53.51
        with prosthesis or graft 53.61
  hydrocele
    round ligament 69.19
    spermatic cord 63.1
    tunica vaginalis 61.2
  hymen 70.76
  hypospadias 58.45
  ileostomy 46.41
  ingrown toenail 86.23
  intestine, intestinal NEC 46.79
    fistula — *see* Closure, fistula, intestine
    laceration
      large intestine 46.75
      small intestine NEC 46.73
    stoma — *see* Repair, stoma
  inverted uterus NEC 69.29
    manual
      nonobstetric 69.94
      obstetric 75.94
    obstetrical
      manual 75.94
      surgical 75.93
    vaginal approach 69.23
  iris (rupture) NEC 12.39
  jejunostomy 46.41
  joint (capsule) (cartilage) NEC (*see also*
      Arthroplasty) 81.96
  kidney NEC 55.89
  knee (joint) NEC 81.47
    collateral ligaments 81.46
    cruciate ligaments 81.45
    five-in-one 81.42
    triad 81.43
  labia — *see* Repair, vulva
  laceration — *see* Suture, by site
  lacrimal system NEC 09.99
    canaliculus 09.73
    punctum 09.72
      for eversion 09.71
  laryngostomy 31.62
  laryngotracheal cleft 31.69
  larynx 31.69
    fracture 31.64
    laceration 31.61
  leads (cardiac) NEC 37.75
  ligament (*see also* Arthroplasty) 81.96
    broad 69.29
    collateral, knee NEC 81.46
    cruciate, knee NEC 81.45
    round 69.29
    uterine 69.29
  lip NEC 27.59
    cleft 27.54
    laceration (by suture) 27.51
  liver NEC 50.69
    laceration 50.61
  lop ear 18.79
  lung NEC 33.49
  lymphatic (channel) (peripheral) NEC 40.9
    duct, left (thoracic) NEC 40.69
  macrodactyly 82.83
  mallet finger 82.84
  mandibular ridge 76.64
  mastoid (antrum) (cavity) 19.9
  meninges (cerebral) NEC 02.12
    spinal NEC 03.59
      meningocele 03.51
      myelomeningocele 03.52
  meningocele (spinal) 03.51
    cranial 02.12
  mesentery 54.75
  mouth NEC 27.59
    laceration NEC 27.52

Repair — continued
　muscle NEC 83.87
　　by
　　　graft or implant (fascia) (muscle) 83.82
　　　　hand 82.72
　　　　tendon 83.81
　　　　　hand 82.79
　　　suture (direct) 83.65
　　　　hand 82.46
　　　transfer or transplantation (muscle) 83.77
　　　　hand 82.58
　　hand 82.89
　　　by
　　　　graft or implant NEC 82.79
　　　　　fascia 82.72
　　　　suture (direct) 82.46
　　　　transfer or transplantation (muscle)
　　　　　82.58
　musculotendinous cuff, shoulder 83.63
　myelomeningocele 03.52
　nasal
　　septum (perforation) NEC 21.88
　　sinus NEC 22.79
　　　fistula 22.71
　nasolabial flaps (plastic) 21.86
　nasopharyngeal atresia 29.4
　nerve (cranial) (peripheral) NEC 04.79
　　old injury 04.76
　　revision 04.75
　　sympathetic 05.81
　nipple NEC 85.87
　nose (external) (internal) (plastic) NEC (see also
　　　Rhinoplasty) 21.89
　　laceration (by suture) 21.81
　notched lip 27.59
　omentum 54.74
　omphalocele 53.49
　　with prosthesis 53.41
　orbit 16.89
　　wound 16.81
　ostium
　　primum defect 35.73
　　　with
　　　　prosthesis 35.54
　　　　tissue graft 35.63
　　secundum defect 35.71
　　　with
　　　　prosthesis (open heart technique)
　　　　　35.51
　　　　　closed heart technique 35.52
　　　　tissue graft 35.61
　ovary 65.79
　　with tube 65.73
　　　laparoscopic 65.76
　overlapping toe 77.58
　pacemaker
　　cardiac
　　　device (permanent) 37.89
　　　electrodes (leads) NEC 37.75
　　　pocket (skin) (subcutaneous) 37.79
　palate NEC 27.69
　　cleft 27.62
　　　secondary or subsequent 27.63
　　laceration (by suture) 27.61
　pancreas NEC 52.95
　　Wirsung's duct 52.99
　papillary muscle (heart) 35.31
　patent ductus arteriosus 38.85
　pectus deformity (chest) (carinatum)
　　　(excavatum) 34.74
　pelvic floor NEC 70.79
　　obstetric laceration (current) 75.69
　　　old 70.79
　penis NEC 64.49
　　for epispadias or hypospadias 58.45
　　inflatable prosthesis 64.99
　　laceration 64.41
　pericardium 37.49　　　　　　　　　　　▲
　perineum (female) 71.79
　　laceration (by suture) 71.71
　　　obstetric (current) 75.69
　　　old 71.79
　　male NEC 86.89
　　　laceration (by suture) 86.59
　peritoneum NEC 54.73
　　by suture 54.64

Repair — continued
　pharynx NEC 29.59
　　laceration (by suture) 29.51
　　plastic 29.4
　pleura NEC 34.93
　postcataract wound dehiscence 11.52
　　with conjunctival flap 11.53
　pouch of Douglas 70.52
　primum ostium defect 35.73
　　with
　　　prosthesis 35.54
　　　tissue graft 35.63
　prostate 60.93
　ptosis, eyelid — see Repair, blepharoptosis
　punctum, lacrimal NEC 09.72
　　for correction of eversion 09.71
　quadriceps (mechanism) 83.86
　rectocele (posterior colporrhaphy) 70.52
　　and cystocele 70.50
　rectum NEC 48.79
　　laceration (by suture) 48.71
　　prolapse NEC 48.76
　　　abdominal approach 48.75
　retina, retinal
　　detachment 14.59
　　　by
　　　　cryotherapy 14.52
　　　　diathermy 14.51
　　　　photocoagulation 14.55
　　　　　laser 14.54
　　　　　xenon arc 14.53
　　　　scleral buckling (see also Buckling,
　　　　　scleral) 14.49
　　tear or defect 14.39
　　　by
　　　　cryotherapy 14.32
　　　　diathermy 14.31
　　　　photocoagulation 14.35
　　　　　laser 14.34
　　　　　xenon arc 14.33
　retroperitoneal tissue 54.73
　rotator cuff (suture) 83.63
　round ligament 69.29
　ruptured tendon NEC 83.88
　　hand 82.86
　salivary gland or duct NEC 26.49
　sclera, scleral 12.89
　　fistula 12.82
　　staphyloma NEC 12.86
　　　with graft 12.85
　scrotum 61.49
　sinus
　　nasal NEC 22.79
　　of Valsalva (aneurysm) 35.39
　skin (plastic) (without graft) 86.89
　　laceration (by suture) 86.59
　skull NEC 02.06
　　with
　　　flap (bone) 02.03
　　　graft (bone) 02.04
　spermatic cord NEC 63.59
　　laceration (by suture) 63.51
　sphincter ani 49.79
　　laceration (by suture) 49.71
　　　obstetric (current) 75.62
　　　old 49.79
　spina bifida NEC 03.59
　　meningocele 03.51
　　myelomeningocele 03.52
　spinal (cord) (meninges) (structures) NEC 03.59
　　meningocele 03.51
　　myelomeningocele 03.52
　spleen 41.95
　sternal defect 78.41
　stoma
　　bile duct 51.79
　　bladder 57.22
　　bronchus 33.42
　　common duct 51.72
　　esophagus 42.89
　　gallbladder 51.99
　　hepatic duct 51.79
　　intestine 46.40
　　　large 46.43
　　　small 46.41
　　kidney 55.89

Repair — continued
　stoma — continued
　　larynx 31.63
　　rectum 48.79
　　stomach 44.69
　　　laparoscopic 44.68
　　thorax 34.79
　　trachea 31.74
　　ureter 56.62
　　urethra 58.49
　stomach NEC 44.69
　　laceration (by suture) 44.61
　　laparoscopic 44.68
　stress incontinence (urinary) NEC 59.79
　　by
　　　anterior urethropexy 59.79
　　　Burch 59.5
　　　cystourethropexy (with levator muscle
　　　　sling) 59.71
　　　injection of implant (collagen) (fat)
　　　　(polytef) 59.72
　　　paraurethral suspension (Pereyra) 59.6
　　　periurethral suspension 59.6
　　　plication of urethrovesical junction 59.3
　　　pubococcygeal sling 59.71
　　　retropubic urethral suspension 59.5
　　　suprapubic sling 59.4
　　　tension free vaginal tape 59.79
　　　urethrovesical suspension 59.4
　　　　gracilis muscle transplant 59.71
　　　　levator muscle sling 59.71
　subcutaneous tissue (plastic) (without skin
　　　graft) 86.89
　　laceration (by suture) 86.59
　supracristal defect (heart) 35.72
　　with
　　　prosthesis 35.53
　　　tissue graft 35.62
　symblepharon NEC 10.49
　　by division (with insertion of conformer) 10.5
　　with free graft 10.41
　syndactyly 86.85
　synovial membrane, joint — see Arthroplasty
　telecanthus 08.59
　tendon 83.88
　　by or with
　　　arthroplasty — see Arthroplasty
　　　graft or implant (tendon) 83.81
　　　　fascia 83.82
　　　　　hand 82.72
　　　　hand 82.79
　　　　muscle 83.82
　　　　　hand 82.72
　　　suture (direct) (immediate) (primary) (see
　　　　also Suture, tendon) 83.64
　　　　hand 82.45
　　　transfer or transplantation (tendon) 83.75
　　　　hand 82.56
　　hand 82.86
　　　by
　　　　graft or implant (tendon) 82.79
　　　　suture (direct) (immediate) (primary)
　　　　　(see also Suture, tendon, hand)
　　　　　82.45
　　　　transfer or transplantation (tendon)
　　　　　82.56
　　rotator cuff (direct suture) 83.63
　　ruptured NEC 83.88
　　　hand 82.86
　　sheath (direct suture) 83.61
　　　hand 82.41
　testis NEC 62.69
　tetralogy of Fallot
　　partial — see specific procedure
　　total (one-stage) 35.81
　thoracic duct NEC 40.69
　thoracostomy 34.72
　thymus (gland) 07.93
　tongue NEC 25.59
　tooth NEC 23.2
　　by
　　　crown (artificial) 23.41
　　　filling (amalgam) (plastic) (silicate) 23.2
　　　inlay 23.3
　total anomalous pulmonary venous connection
　　partial — see specific procedure

Index

Repair — Replacement

Repair — *continued*
total anomalous pulmonary venous connection
— *continued*
total (one-stage) 35.82
trachea NEC 31.79
laceration (by suture) 31.71
tricuspid atresia 35.94
truncus arteriosus
partial — *see* specific procedure
total (one-stage) 35.83
tunica vaginalis 61.49
laceration (by suture) 61.41
tympanum — *see* Tympanoplasty
ureter NEC 56.89
laceration (by suture) 56.82
ureterocele 56.89
urethra NEC 58.49
laceration (by suture) 58.41
obstetric (current) 75.61
old 58.49
meatus 58.47
urethrocele (anterior colporrhaphy) (female)
70.51
and rectocele 70.50
urinary sphincter, artificial (component) 58.99
urinary stress incontinence — *see* Repair,
stress incontinence
uterus, uterine 69.49
inversion — *see* Repair, inverted uterus
laceration (by suture) 69.41
obstetric (current) 75.50
old 69.49
ligaments 69.29
by
interposition 69.21
plication 69.22
uvula 27.73
with synchronous cleft palate repair 27.62
vagina, vaginal (cuff) (wall) NEC 70.79
anterior 70.51
with posterior repair 70.50
cystocele 70.51
and rectocele 70.50
enterocele 70.92
laceration (by suture) 70.71
obstetric (current) 75.69
old 70.79
posterior 70.52
with anterior repair 70.50
rectocele 70.52
and cystocele 70.50
urethrocele 70.51
and rectocele 70.50
varicocele 63.1
vas deferens 63.89
by
anastomosis 63.82
to epididymis 63.83
reconstruction 63.82
laceration (by suture) 63.81
vein NEC 39.59
with
patch graft 39.58
with excision or resection of vessel —
see Phlebectomy, with graft
replacement, by site
synthetic (Dacron) (Teflon) 39.57
tissue (vein) (autogenous)
(homograft) 39.56
suture 39.32
by
endovascular approach
head and neck (embolization or
occlusion) 39.72
ventricular septal defect 35.72
with
prosthesis 35.53
in total repair of tetralogy of Fallot
35.81
tissue graft 35.62
combined with repair of valvular and atrial
septal defects — *see* Repair,
endocardial cushion defect
in total repair of
tetralogy of Fallot 35.81
truncus arteriosus 35.83

Repair — *continued*
vertebral arch defect (spina bifida) 03.59
vulva NEC 71.79
laceration (by suture) 71.71
obstetric (current) 75.69
old 71.79
Wirsung's duct 52.99
wound (skin) (without graft) 86.59
abdominal wall 54.63
dehiscence 54.61
postcataract dehiscence (corneal) 11.52
Replacement
acetabulum (with prosthesis) 81.52
ankle, total 81.56
revision 81.59
aortic valve (with prosthesis) 35.22
with tissue graft 35.21
artery — *see* Graft, artery
bag — *see* Replacement, pack or bag
Barton's tongs (skull) 02.94
bladder
with
ileal loop 57.87 *[45.51]*
sigmoid 57.87 *[45.52]*
sphincter, artificial 58.93
caliper tongs (skull) 02.94
cannula
arteriovenous shunt 39.94
pancreatic duct 97.05
vessel-to-vessel (arteriovenous) 39.94
cardiac resynchronization device
defibrillator (CRT-D) ▶(device and one or
more leads)◀ (total system) 00.51
left ventricular coronary venous lead only
00.52
pulse generator only 00.54
pacemaker (CRT-P) ▶(device and one or
more leads)◀ (total system) 00.50
left ventricular coronary venous lead only
00.52
pulse generator only 00.53
cardioverter/defibrillator (total system) 37.94
leads only (electrodes) (sensing) (pacing)
37.97
pulse generator only 37.98
cast NEC 97.13
lower limb 97.12
upper limb 97.11
catheter
bladder (indwelling) 57.95
cystostomy 59.94
ventricular shunt (cerebral) 02.42
wound 97.15
CRT-D (cardiac resynchronization defibrillator)
▶(device and one or more leads)◀ 00.51
left ventricular coronary venous lead only
00.52
pulse generator only 00.54
CRT-P (cardiac resynchronization pacemaker)
▶(device and one or more leads)◀ 00.50
left ventricular coronary venous lead only
00.52
pulse generator only 00.53
Crutchfield tongs (skull) 02.94
cystostomy tube (catheter) 59.94
diaphragm, vagina 97.24
disc — *see* Replacement, intervertebral disc
drain — *see also* Replacement, tube
vagina 97.26
vulva 97.26
wound, musculoskeletal or skin 97.16
ear (prosthetic) 18.71
elbow (joint), total 81.84
electrode(s) — *see* Implant, electrode or lead by
site or name of device
brain
depth 02.93
foramen ovale 02.93
sphenoidal 02.96
depth 02.93
foramen ovale 02.93
intracranial 02.93
pacemaker — *see* Replacement,
pacemaker, electrode(s)
peripheral nerve 04.92
sacral nerve 04.92

Replacement — *continued*
electrode(s) — *see* Implant, electrode or lead by
site or name of device — *continued*
sphenoidal 02.96
spine 03.93
electroencephalographic receiver (brain)
(intracranial) 02.93
electronic
cardioverter/defibrillator — *see*
Replacement, cardioverter/defibrillator
leads (electrode)(s) — *see* Replacement,
electrode(s)
stimulator — *see also* Implant, electronic
stimulator, by site
bladder 57.97
muscle (skeletal) 83.92
ureter 56.93
electrostimulator — *see* Implant, electronic
stimulator, by site
enterostomy device (tube)
large intestine 97.04
small intestine 97.03
epidural pegs 02.93
femoral head, by prosthesis 81.52
revision 81.53
Gardner Wells tongs (skull) 02.94
gastric band, laparoscopic 44.96
gastric port device (subcutaneous) 44.96
graft — *see* Graft
halo traction device (skull) 02.94
Harrington rod (with refusion of spine) — *see*
Refusion, spinal
heart
artificial
total replacement system 37.52
implantable battery 37.54
implantable controller 37.54
thoracic unit 37.53
transcutaneous energy transfer (TET)
device 37.54
total replacement system 37.52
implantable battery 37.54
implantable controller 37.54
thoracic unit 37.53
transcutaneous energy transfer (TET)
device 37.54
valve (with prosthesis) (with tissue graft)
35.20
aortic (with prosthesis) 35.22
with tissue graft 35.21
mitral (with prosthesis) 35.24
with tissue graft 35.23
poppet (prosthetic) 35.95
pulmonary (with prosthesis) 35.26
with tissue graft 35.25
in total repair of tetralogy of Fallot
35.81
tricuspid (with prosthesis) 35.28
with tissue graft 35.27
hip (partial) (with fixation device) (with
prosthesis) (with traction) 81.52
acetabulum 81.52
revision 81.53
femoral head 81.52
revision 81.53
total 81.51
revision 81.53
intervertebral disc
artificial, NOS 84.60
cervical 84.62
nucleus 84.61
partial 84.61
total 84.62
lumbar, lumbosacral 84.65
nucleus 84.64
partial 84.64
total 84.65
thoracic (partial) (total) 84.63
inverted uterus — *see* Repair, inverted uterus
iris NEC 12.39
kidney, mechanical 55.97
knee (bicompartmental) (hemijoint) (partial)
(total) (tricompartmental)
(unicompartmental) 81.54
revision 81.55
laryngeal stent 31.93

Replacement — *continued*
leads (electrode)(s) — *see* Replacement,
    electrode(s)
mechanical kidney 55.97
mitral valve (with prosthesis) 35.24
    with tissue graft 35.23
Mulligan hood, fallopian tube 66.93
muscle stimulator (skeletal) 83.92
nephrostomy tube 55.93
neuropacemaker — *see* Implant,
    neurostimulator, by site
neurostimulator (*see also* Implant,
    neurostimulator, by site)
    skeletal muscle 83.92
pacemaker
    brain — *see* Implant, neurostimulator, brain
    cardiac device (initial) (permanent)
        dual-chamber device 37.87
        resynchronization — *see* Replacement,
            CRT-P
        single-chamber device 37.85
            rate responsive 37.86
        electrode(s), cardiac (atrial) (transvenous)
            (ventricular) 37.76
            epicardium (myocardium) 37.74
            left ventricular coronary venous system
                00.52
        intracranial — *see* Implant, neurostimulator,
            intracranial
        neural — *see* Implant, neurostimulator, by
            site
        peripheral nerve — *see* Implant,
            neurostimulator, peripheral nerve
        sacral nerve — *see* Implant,
            neurostimulator, sacral nerve
        spine — *see* Implant, neurostimulator, spine
        temporary transvenous pacemaker system
            37.78
    pack or bag
        nose 97.21
        teeth, tooth 97.22
        vagina 97.26
        vulva 97.26
        wound 97.16
    pessary, vagina NEC 97.25
    prosthesis
        acetabulum 81.53
        arm (bioelectric) (cineplastic) (kineplastic)
            84.44
        biliary tract 51.99
        cochlear 20.96
        channel (single) 20.97
            multiple 20.98
        elbow 81.97
        extremity (bioelectric) (cineplastic)
            (kineplastic) 84.40
            lower 84.48
            upper 84.44
        fallopian tube (Mulligan hood) (stent) 66.93
        femur 81.53
        knee 81.55
        leg (bioelectric) (cineplastic) (kineplastic)
            84.48
        penis (internal) (non-inflatable) 64.95
            inflatable (internal) 64.97
    pulmonary valve (with prosthesis) 35.26
        with tissue graft 35.25
        in total repair of tetralogy of Fallot 35.81
    pyelostomy tube 55.94
    rectal tube 96.09
    shoulder NEC 81.83
        partial 81.81
        total 81.80
    skull
        plate 02.05
        tongs 02.94
    specified appliance or device NEC 97.29
    stent
        bile duct 97.05
        fallopian tube 66.93
        larynx 31.93
        pancreatic duct 97.05
        trachea 31.93
    stimoceiver — *see* Implant, stimoceiver, by site
    subdural
        grids 02.93

Replacement — *continued*
subdural — *continued*
    strips 02.93
testis in scrotum 62.5
tongs, skull 02.94
tracheal stent 31.93
tricuspid valve (with prosthesis) 35.28
    with tissue graft 35.27
tube
    bile duct 97.05
    bladder 57.95
    cystostomy 59.94
    esophagostomy 97.01
    gastrostomy 97.02
    large intestine 97.04
    nasogastric 97.01
    nephrostomy 55.93
    pancreatic duct 97.05
    pyelostomy 55.94
    rectal 96.09
    small intestine 97.03
    tracheostomy 97.23
    ureterostomy 59.93
    ventricular (cerebral) 02.42
umbilical cord, prolapsed 73.92
ureter (with)
    bladder flap 56.74
    ileal segment implanted into bladder 56.89
        [45.51]
ureterostomy tube 59.93
urethral sphincter, artificial 58.93
urinary sphincter, artificial 58.93
valve
    heart — *see also* Replacement, heart valve
        poppet (prosthetic) 35.95
    ventricular (cerebral) 02.42
ventricular shunt (catheter) (valve) 02.42
Vinke tongs (skull) 02.94
vitreous (silicone) 14.75
    for retinal reattachment 14.59

Replant, replantation — *see also* Reattachment
extremity — *see* Reattachment, extremity
penis 64.45
scalp 86.51
tooth 23.5

Reposition
cardiac pacemaker
    electrode(s) (atrial) (transvenous)
        (ventricular) 37.75
    pocket 37.79
cardioverter/defibrillator (automatic)
    lead(s) (sensing) (pacing) (epicardial patch)
        37.99
    pocket 37.99
    pulse generator 37.99
cilia base 08.71
iris 12.39
neurostimulator
    leads
        subcutaneous, without device
            replacement 86.09
        within brain 02.93
        within or over peripheral nerve 04.92
        within or over sacral nerve 04.92
        within spine 03.93
    pulse generator
        subcutaneous, without device
            replacement 86.09
renal vessel, aberrant 39.55
subcutaneous device pocket NEC 86.09
thyroid tissue 06.94
tricuspid valve (with plication) 35.14

Resection — *see also* Excision, by site
abdominoendorectal (combined) 48.5
abdominoperineal (rectum) 48.5
    pull-through (Altemeier) (Swenson) NEC
        48.49
        Duhamel type 48.65
alveolar process and palate (en bloc) 27.32
aneurysm — *see* Aneurysmectomy
aortic valve (for subvalvular stenosis) 35.11
artery — *see* Arteriectomy
bile duct NEC 51.69
    common duct NEC 51.63

Resection — *see also* Excision, by site —
    continued
bladder (partial) (segmental) (transvesical)
    (wedge) 57.6
    complete or total 57.79
    lesion NEC 57.59
        transurethral approach 57.49
    neck 57.59
        transurethral approach 57.49
blood vessel — *see* Angiectomy
brain 01.59
    by
        stereotactic radiosurgery 92.30
            cobalt 60 92.32
            linear accelerator (LINAC) 92.31
            multi-source 92.32
            particle beam 92.33
            particulate 92.33
            radiosurgery NEC 92.39
            single source photon 92.31
    hemisphere 01.52
    lobe 01.53
breast — *see also* Mastectomy
    quadrant 85.22
    segmental 85.23
broad ligament 69.19
bronchus (sleeve) (wide sleeve) 32.1
    block (en bloc) (with radical dissection of
        brachial plexus, bronchus, lobe of
        lung, ribs, and sympathetic nerves)
        32.6
bursa 83.5
    hand 82.31
cecum (and terminal ileum) 45.72
cerebral meninges 01.51
chest wall 34.4
clavicle 77.81
clitoris 71.4
colon (partial) (segmental) 45.79
    ascending (cecum and terminal ileum) 45.72
    cecum (and terminal ileum) 45.72
    complete 45.8
    descending (sigmoid) 45.76
    for interposition 45.52
    Hartmann 45.75
    hepatic flexure 45.73
    left radical (hemicolon) 45.75
    multiple segmental 45.71
    right radical (hemicolon) (ileocolectomy)
        45.73
    segmental NEC 45.79
        multiple 45.71
    sigmoid 45.76
    splenic flexure 45.75
    total 45.8
    transverse 45.74
conjunctiva, for pterygium 11.39
    corneal graft 11.32
cornual (fallopian tube) (unilateral) 66.69
    bilateral 66.63
diaphragm 34.81
endaural 20.79
endorectal (pull-through) (Soave) 48.41
    combined abdominal 48.5
esophagus (partial) (subtotal) (*see also*
    Esophagectomy) 42.41
    total 42.42
exteriorized intestine — *see* Resection,
    intestine, exteriorized
fascia 83.44
    for graft 83.43
    hand 82.34
    hand 82.35
        for graft 82.34
gallbladder (total) 51.22
gastric (partial) (sleeve) (subtotal) NEC (*see also*
    Gastrectomy) 43.89
    with anastomosis NEC 43.89
        esophagogastric 43.5
        gastroduodenal 43.6
        gastrogastric 43.89
        gastrojejunal 43.7
    complete or total NEC 43.99
        with intestinal interposition 43.91
    radical NEC 43.99
        with intestinal interposition 43.91

Resection — *see also* Excision, by site — *continued*
  gastric NEC (*see also* Gastrectomy) — *continued*
    wedge 43.42
      endoscopic 43.41
  hallux valgus (joint) — *see also* Bunionectomy
    with prosthetic implant 77.59
  hepatic
    duct 51.69
    flexure (colon) 45.73
  infundibula, heart (right) 35.34
  intestine (partial) NEC 45.79
    cecum (with terminal ileum) 45.72
    exteriorized (large intestine) 46.04
      small intestine 46.02
    for interposition 45.50
      large intestine 45.52
      small intestine 45.51
    hepatic flexure 45.73
    ileum 45.62
      with cecum 45.72
    large (partial) (segmental) NEC 45.79
      for interposition 45.52
      multiple segmental 45.71
      total 45.8
    left hemicolon 45.75
    multiple segmental (large intestine) 45.71
      small intestine 45.61
    right hemicolon 45.73
    segmental (large intestine) 45.79
      multiple 45.71
      small intestine 45.62
        multiple 45.61
    sigmoid 45.76
    small (partial) (segmental) NEC 45.62
      for interposition 45.51
      multiple segmental 45.61
      total 45.63
    total
      large intestine 45.8
      small intestine 45.63
  joint structure NEC (*see also* Arthrectomy) 80.90
  kidney (segmental) (wedge) 55.4
  larynx — *see also* Laryngectomy
    submucous 30.29
  lesion — *see* Excision, lesion, by site
  levator palpebrae muscle 08.33
  ligament (*see also* Arthrectomy) 80.90
    broad 69.19
    round 69.19
    uterine 69.19
  lip (wedge) 27.43
  liver (partial) (wedge) 50.22
    lobe (total) 50.3
    total 50.4
  lung (wedge) NEC 32.29
    endoscopic 32.28
    segmental (any part) 32.3
    volume reduction 32.22
  meninges (cerebral) 01.51
    spinal 03.4
  mesentery 54.4
  muscle 83.45
    extraocular 15.13
      with
        advancement or recession of other eye muscle 15.3
        suture of original insertion 15.13
      levator palpebrae 08.33
      Müller's, for blepharoptosis 08.35
      orbicularis oculi 08.20
      tarsal, for blepharoptosis 08.35
    for graft 83.43
      hand 82.34
    hand 82.36
      for graft 82.34
    ocular — *see* Resection, muscle, extraocular
  myocardium 37.33
  nasal septum (submucous) 21.5
  nerve (cranial) (peripheral) NEC 04.07
    phrenic 04.03
      for collapse of lung 33.31
    sympathetic 05.29
    vagus — *see* Vagotomy

Resection — *see also* Excision, by site — *continued*
  nose (complete) (extended) (partial) (radical) 21.4
  omentum 54.4
  orbitomaxillary, radical 16.51
  ovary (*see also* Oophorectomy)
    wedge 65.22
      laparoscopic 65.24
  palate (bony) (local) 27.31
    by wide excision 27.32
    soft 27.49
  pancreas (total) (with synchronous duodenectomy) 52.6
    partial NEC 52.59
      distal (tail) (with part of body) 52.52
      proximal (head) (with part of body) (with synchronous duodenectomy) 52.51
      radical subtotal 52.53
    radical (one-stage) (two-stage) 52.7
    subtotal 52.53
  pancreaticoduodenal (*see also* Pancreatectomy) 52.6
  pelvic viscera (en masse) (female) 68.8
    male 57.71
  penis 64.3
  pericardium (partial) (for)
    chronic constrictive pericarditis 37.31
    drainage 37.12
    removal of adhesions 37.31
  peritoneum 54.4
  pharynx (partial) 29.33
  phrenic nerve 04.03
    for collapse of lung 33.31
  prostate — *see also* Prostatectomy
    transurethral (punch) 60.29
  pterygium 11.39
  radial head 77.83
  rectosigmoid (*see also* Resection, rectum) 48.69
  rectum (partial) NEC 48.69
    with
      pelvic exenteration 68.8
      transsacral sigmoidectomy 48.61
    abdominoendorectal (combined) 48.5
    abdominoperineal 48.5
      pull-through NEC 48.49
        Duhamel type 48.65
    anterior 48.63
      with colostomy (synchronous) 48.62
    Duhamel 48.65
    endorectal 48.41
      combined abdominal 48.5
    posterior 48.64
    pull-through NEC 48.49
      endorectal 48.41
    submucosal (Soave) 48.41
      combined abdominal 48.5
  rib (transaxillary) 77.91
    as operative approach — *omit code*
    incidental to thoracic operation — *omit code*
  right ventricle (heart), for infundibular stenosis 35.34
  root (tooth) (apex) 23.73
    with root canal therapy 23.72
    residual or retained 23.11
  round ligament 69.19
  sclera 12.65
    with scleral buckling (*see also* Buckling, scleral) 14.49
    lamellar (for retinal reattachment) 14.49
      with implant 14.41
  scrotum 61.3
  soft tissue NEC 83.49
    hand 82.39
  sphincter of Oddi 51.89
  spinal cord (meninges) 03.4
  splanchnic 05.29
  splenic flexure (colon) 45.75
  sternum 77.81
  stomach (partial) (sleeve) (subtotal) NEC (*see also* Gastrectomy) 43.89
    with anastomosis NEC 43.89
      esophagogastric 43.5
      gastroduodenal 43.6
      gastrogastric 43.89
      gastrojejunal 43.7

Resection — *see also* Excision, by site — *continued*
  stomach NEC (*see also* Gastrectomy) — *continued*
    complete or total NEC 43.99
      with intestinal interposition 43.91
    fundus 43.89
    radical NEC 43.99
      with intestinal interposition 43.91
    wedge 43.42
      endoscopic 43.41
  submucous
    larynx 30.29
    nasal septum 21.5
    vocal cords 30.22
  synovial membrane (complete) (partial) (*see also* Synovectomy) 80.70
  tarsolevator 08.33
  tendon 83.42
    hand 82.33
  thoracic structures (block) (en bloc) (radical) (brachial plexus, bronchus, lobes of lung, ribs, and sympathetic nerves) 32.6
  thorax 34.4
  tongue 25.2
    wedge 25.1
  tooth root 23.73
    with root canal therapy 23.72
    apex (abscess) 23.73
      with root canal therapy 23.72
    residual or retained 23.11
  trachea 31.5
  transurethral
    bladder NEC 57.49
    prostate 60.29
  transverse colon 45.74
  turbinates — *see* Turbinectomy
  ureter (partial) 56.41
    total 56.42
  uterus — *see* Hysterectomy
  vein — *see* Phlebectomy
  ventricle (heart) 37.35
    infundibula 35.34
  vesical neck 57.59
    transurethral 57.49
  vocal cords (punch) 30.22

Respirator, volume-controlled (Bennett) (Byrd) — *see* Ventilation

Restoration
  cardioesophageal angle 44.66
    laparoscopic 44.67
  dental NEC 23.49
    by
      application of crown (artificial) 23.41
      insertion of bridge (fixed) 23.42
        removable 23.43
  extremity — *see* Reattachment, extremity
  eyebrow 08.70
    with graft 08.63
  eye socket 16.64
    with graft 16.63
  tooth NEC 23.2
    by
      crown (artificial) 23.41
      filling (amalgam) (plastic) (silicate) 23.2
      inlay 23.3

Restrictive
  gastric band, laparoscopic 44.95

Resuscitation
  artificial respiration 93.93
  cardiac 99.60
    cardioversion 99.62
      atrial 99.61
    defibrillation 99.62
    external massage 99.63
      open chest 37.91
    intracardiac injection 37.92
  cardiopulmonary 99.60
  endotracheal intubation 96.04
  manual 93.93
  mouth-to-mouth 93.93
  pulmonary 93.93

Resuture
  abdominal wall 54.61
  cardiac septum prosthesis 35.95

☑ Additional Digit Required — Refer to the Tabular List (Numeric Code Section) for Additional Digit Selection

Resuture — Revision

Revision — *continued*
pocket — *continued*
thalamic stimulator pulse generator
with initial insertion of battery package —
omit code
new site (skin) (subcutaneous) 86.09
previous mastectomy site — *see* categories
85.0-85.99
proctostomy 48.79
prosthesis
acetabular and femoral components
(total) 00.70 ●
acetabular component only 00.71 ●
acetabular liner and/or femoral head
only 00.73 ●
ankle 81.59
breast 85.93
elbow 81.97
femoral component only 00.72 ●
femoral head ▶only and/or acetabular
liner◀ 00.73 ▲
foot 81.59
hand 81.97
heart valve (poppet) 35.95
hip 81.53
acetabular and femoral components
(total) 00.70 ●
acetabular component only 00.71 ●
acetabular liner and/or femoral head
only 00.73 ●
femoral component only 00.72 ●
femoral head only and/or acetabular ●
liner 00.73 ●
partial ●
acetabular component only 00.71 ●
acetabular liner and/or femoral ●
head only 00.73 ●
femoral component only 00.72 ●
femoral head only and/or ●
acetabular liner 00.73 ●
total (acetabular and femoral ●
components) 00.70 ●
knee ▶NOS◀ 81.55
femoral component 00.82 ●
partial ●
femoral component 00.82 ●
patellar component 00.83 ●
tibial component 00.81 ●
tibial insert 00.84 ●
patellar component 00.83 ●
tibial component 00.81 ●
tibial insert 00.84 ●
total (all components) 00.80 ●
lower extremity NEC 81.59
shoulder 81.97
toe 81.59
upper extremity 81.97
wrist 81.97
ptosis overcorrection 08.37
pyelostomy 55.12
pyloroplasty 44.29
rhinoplasty 21.84
scar
skin 86.84
with excision 86.3
scleral fistulization 12.66
shoulder replacement (prosthesis) 81.97
shunt
arteriovenous (cannula) (for dialysis) 39.42
lumbar-subarachnoid NEC 03.97
peritoneojugular 54.99
peritoneovascular 54.99
pleurothecal 03.97
salpingothecal 03.97
spinal (thecal) NEC 03.97
subarachnoid-peritoneal 03.97
subarachnoid-ureteral 03.97
ventricular (cerebral) 02.42
ventriculoperitoneal
at peritoneal site 54.95
at ventricular site 02.42
stapedectomy NEC 19.29
with incus replacement (homograft)
(prosthesis) 19.21
stoma
bile duct 51.79

Revision — *continued*
stoma — *continued*
bladder (vesicostomy) 57.22
bronchus 33.42
common duct 51.72
esophagus 42.89
gallbladder 51.99
hepatic duct 51.79
intestine 46.40
large 46.43
small 46.41
kidney 55.89
larynx 31.63
rectum 48.79
stomach 44.69
laparoscopic 44.68
thorax 34.79
trachea 31.74
ureter 56.62
urethra 58.49
tack operation 20.79
toe replacement (prosthesis) 81.59
tracheostomy 31.74
tunnel
pulse generator lead wire 86.99
with initial procedure — *omit code*
tympanoplasty 19.6
uretero-ileostomy, cutaneous 56.52
ureterostomy (cutaneous) (stoma) NEC 56.62
ileal 56.52
urethrostomy 58.49
urinary conduit 56.52
vascular procedure (previous) NEC 39.49
ventricular shunt (cerebral) 02.42
vesicostomy stoma 57.22
wrist replacement (prosthesis) 81.97
Rhinectomy 21.4
Rhinocheiloplasty 27.59
cleft lip 27.54
Rhinomanometry 89.12
Rhinoplasty (external) (internal) NEC 21.87
augmentation (with graft) (with synthetic
implant) 21.85
limited 21.86
revision 21.84
tip 21.86
twisted nose 21.84
Rhinorrhaphy (external) (internal) 21.81
for epistaxis 21.09
Rhinoscopy 21.21
Rhinoseptoplasty 21.84
Rhinotomy 21.1
Rhizotomy (radiofrequency) (spinal) 03.1
acoustic 04.01
trigeminal 04.02
Rhytidectomy (facial) 86.82
eyelid
lower 08.86
upper 08.87
Rhytidoplasty (facial) 86.82
Ripstein operation (repair of prolapsed rectum)
48.75
Rodney Smith operation (radical subtotal
pancreatectomy) 52.53
Roentgenography — *see also* Radiography
cardiac, negative contrast 88.58
Rolling of conjunctiva 10.33
Root
canal (tooth) (therapy) 23.70
with
apicoectomy 23.72
irrigation 23.71
resection (tooth) (apex) 23.73
with root canal therapy 23.72
residual or retained 23.11
Rotation of fetal head
forceps (instrumental) (Kielland) (Scanzoni)
(key-in-lock) 72.4
manual 73.51
Routine
chest x-ray 87.44
psychiatric visit 94.12

Roux-en-Y operation
bile duct 51.36
cholecystojejunostomy 51.32
esophagus (intrathoracic) 42.54
gastroenterostomy 44.39
laparoscopic 44.38
gastrojejunostomy 44.39
laparoscopic 44.38
pancreaticojejunostomy 52.96
Roux-Goldthwait operation (repair of recurrent
patellar dislocation) 81.44
Roux-Herzen-Judine operation (jejunal loop
interposition) 42.63
Rubin test (insufflation of fallopian tube) 66.8
Ruiz-Mora operation (proximal phalangectomy
for hammer toe) 77.99
Rupture
esophageal web 42.01
joint adhesions, manual 93.26
membranes, artificial 73.09
for surgical induction of labor 73.01
ovarian cyst, manual 65.93
Russe operation (bone graft of scaphoid) 78.04

S

Sacculotomy (tack) 20.79
Sacrectomy (partial) 77.89
total 77.99
Saemisch operation (corneal section) 11.1
Salpingectomy (bilateral) (total) (transvaginal)
66.51
with oophorectomy 65.61
laparoscopic 65.63
partial (unilateral) 66.69
with removal of tubal pregnancy 66.62
bilateral 66.63
for sterilization 66.39
by endoscopy 66.29
remaining or solitary tube 66.52
with ovary 65.62
laparoscopic 65.64
unilateral (total) 66.4
with
oophorectomy 65.49
laparoscopic 65.41
removal of tubal pregnancy 66.62
partial 66.69
Salpingography 87.85
Salpingohysterostomy 66.74
Salpingo-oophorectomy (unilateral) 65.49
that by laparoscope 65.41
bilateral (same operative episode) 65.61
laparoscopic 65.63
remaining or solitary tube and ovary 65.62
laparoscopic 65.64
Salpingo-oophoroplasty 65.73
laparoscopic 65.76
Salpingo-oophororrhaphy 65.79
Salpingo-oophorostomy 66.72
Salpingo-oophorotomy 65.09
laparoscopic 65.01
Salpingoplasty 66.79
Salpingorrhaphy 66.71
Salpingosalpingostomy 66.73
Salpingostomy (for removal of non-ruptured
ectopic pregnancy) 66.02
Salpingotomy 66.01
Salpingo-uterostomy 66.74
Salter operation (innominate osteotomy) 77.39
Salvage (autologous blood) (intraoperative)
(perioperative) (postoperative) 99.00
**Sampling, blood for genetic determination of
fetus** 75.33
Sandpapering (skin) 86.25
Saucerization
bone (*see also* Excision, lesion, bone) 77.60
rectum 48.99
Sauer-Bacon operation (abdominoperineal
resection) 48.5

Scalenectomy 83.45
Scalenotomy 83.19
Scaling and polishing, dental 96.54
Scan, scanning
  C.A.T. (computerized axial tomography) 88.38
    with computer assisted surgery (CAS)
      00.31
    abdomen 88.01
    bone 88.38
      mineral density 88.98
    brain 87.03
    head 87.03
    kidney 87.71
    skeletal 88.38
      mineral density 88.98
    thorax 87.41
  computerized axial tomography (C.A.T.) (see
    also Scan, C.A.T.) 88.38
  C.T. — see Scan, C.A.T.
  gallium — see Scan, radioisotope
  liver 92.02
  MUGA (multiple gated acquisition) — see Scan,
    radioisotope
  positron emission tomography (PET) — see
    Scan, radioisotope
  radioisotope
    adrenal 92.09
    bone 92.14
      marrow 92.05
    bowel 92.04
    cardiac output 92.05
    cardiovascular 92.05
    cerebral 92.11
    circulation time 92.05
    eye 95.16
    gastrointestinal 92.04
    head NEC 92.12
    hematopoietic 92.05
    intestine 92.04
    iodine-131 92.01
    kidney 92.03
    liver 92.02
    lung 92.15
    lymphatic system 92.16
    myocardial infarction 92.05
    pancreatic 92.04
    parathyroid 92.13
    pituitary 92.11
    placenta 92.17
    protein-bound iodine 92.01
    pulmonary 92.15
    radio-iodine uptake 92.01
    renal 92.03
    specified site NEC 92.19
    spleen 92.05
    thyroid 92.01
    total body 92.18
    uterus 92.19
  renal 92.03
  thermal — see Thermography
Scapulectomy (partial) 77.81
  total 77.91
Scapulopexy 78.41
Scarification
  conjunctiva 10.33
  nasal veins (with packing) 21.03
  pericardium 36.39
  pleura 34.6
    chemical 34.92
      with cancer chemotherapy substance
        34.92 [99.25]
        tetracycline 34.92 [99.21]
Schanz operation (femoral osteotomy) 77.35
Schauta (-Amreich) operation (radical vaginal
  hysterectomy) 68.7
Schede operation (thoracoplasty) 33.34
Scheie operation
  cautery of sclera 12.62
  sclerostomy 12.62
Schlatter operation (total gastrectomy) 43.99
Schroeder operation (endocervical excision)
  67.39
Schuchardt operation (nonobstetrical episiotomy)
  71.09

Schwartze operation (simple mastoidectomy)
  20.41
Scintiphotography — see Scan, radioisotope
Scintiscan — see Scan, radioisotope
Sclerectomy (punch) (scissors) 12.65
  for retinal reattachment 14.49
  Holth's 12.65
  trephine 12.61
    with implant 14.41
Scleroplasty 12.89
Sclerosis — see Sclerotherapy
Sclerostomy (Scheie's) 12.62
Sclerotherapy
  esophageal varices (endoscopic) 42.33
  hemorrhoids 49.42
  pleura 34.92
    treatment of malignancy (cytotoxic agent)
      34.92 [99.25]
      with tetracycline 34.92 [99.21]
  varicose vein 39.92
  vein NEC 39.92
Sclerotomy (exploratory) 12.89
  anterior 12.89
    with
      iridectomy 12.65
      removal of vitreous 14.71
  posterior 12.89
    with
      iridectomy 12.65
      removal of vitreous 14.72
Scott operation
  intestinal bypass for obesity 45.93
  jejunocolostomy (bypass) 45.93
Scraping
  corneal epithelium 11.41
    for smear or culture 11.21
  trachoma follicles 10.33
Scrotectomy (partial) 61.3
Scrotoplasty 61.49
Scrotorrhaphy 61.41
Scrotomy 61.0
Scrub, posterior nasal (adhesions) 21.91
Sculpturing, heart valve — see Valvuloplasty,
  heart
Section — see also Division and Incision
  cesarean — see Cesarean section
  ganglion, sympathetic 05.0
  hypophyseal stalk (see also Hypophysectomy,
    partial) 07.63
  ligamentum flavum (spine) — omit code
  nerve (cranial) (peripheral) NEC 04.03
    acoustic 04.01
    spinal root (posterior) 03.1
    sympathetic 05.0
    trigeminal tract 04.02
  Saemisch (corneal) 11.1
  spinal ligament 80.49
    arcuate — omit code
    flavum — omit code
  tooth (impacted) 23.19
Seddon-Brooks operation (transfer of pectoralis
  major tendon) 83.75
Semb operation (apicolysis of lung) 33.39
Senning operation (correction of transposition of
  great vessels) 35.91
Separation
  twins (attached) (conjoined) (Siamese) 84.93
    asymmetrical (unequal) 84.93
    symmetrical (equal) 84.92
Septectomy
  atrial (closed) 35.41
    open 35.42
    transvenous method (balloon) 35.41
  submucous (nasal) 21.5
Septoplasty NEC 21.88
  with submucous resection of septum 21.5
Septorhinoplasty 21.84
Septostomy (atrial) (balloon) 35.41
Septotomy, nasal 21.1
Sequestrectomy
  bone 77.00
    carpals, metacarpals 77.04

Sequestrectomy — continued
  bone — continued
    clavicle 77.01
    facial 76.01
    femur 77.05
    fibula 77.07
    humerus 77.02
    nose 21.32
    patella 77.06
    pelvic 77.09
    phalanges (foot) (hand) 77.09
    radius 77.03
    scapula 77.01
    skull 01.25
    specified site NEC 77.09
    tarsals, metatarsals 77.08
    thorax (ribs) (sternum) 77.01
    tibia 77.07
    ulna 77.03
    vertebrae 77.09
  nose 21.32
  skull 01.25
Sesamoidectomy 77.98
Setback, ear 18.5
Sever operation (division of soft tissue of arm)
  83.19
Severing of blepharorrhaphy 08.02
Sewell operation (heart) 36.2
Sharrard operation (iliopsoas muscle transfer)
  83.77
Shaving
  bone (see also Excision, lesion, bone) 77.60
  cornea (epithelium) 11.41
    for smear or culture 11.21
  patella 77.66
Shelf operation (hip arthroplasty) 81.40
Shirodkar operation (encirclement suture, cervix)
  67.59
Shock therapy
  chemical 94.24
  electroconvulsive 94.27
  electrotonic 94.27
  insulin 94.24
  subconvulsive 94.26
Shortening
  bone (fusion) 78.20
    femur 78.25
    specified site NEC (see category 78.2 ☑)
    tibia 78.27
    ulna 78.23
  endopelvic fascia 69.22
  extraocular muscle NEC 15.22
    multiple (two or more muscles) 15.4
  eyelid margin 08.71
  eye muscle NEC 15.22
    multiple (two or more muscles) (with
      lengthening) 15.4
  finger (macrodactyly repair) 82.83
  heel cord 83.85
  levator palpebrae muscle 08.33
  ligament — see also Arthroplasty
    round 69.22
    uterosacral 69.22
  muscle 83.85
    extraocular 15.22
      multiple (two or more muscles) 15.4
    hand 82.55
  sclera (for repair of retinal detachment) 14.59
    by scleral buckling (see also Buckling,
      scleral) 14.49
  tendon 83.85
    hand 82.55
  ureter (with reimplantation) 56.41
Shunt — see also Anastomosis and Bypass,
  vascular
  abdominovenous 54.94
  aorta-coronary sinus 36.39
  aorta (descending)-pulmonary (artery) 39.0
  aortocarotid 39.22
  aortoceliac 39.26
  aortofemoral 39.25
  aortoiliac 39.25
  aortoiliofemoral 39.25
  aortomesenteric 39.26

2006 ICD-9-CM

☑ Additional Digit Required — Refer to the Tabular List (Numeric Code Section) for Additional Digit Selection
▶◀ Revised Text   ● New Line   ▲ Revised Code

Volume 3 — 73

Shunt — *see also* Anastomosis and Bypass, vascular — *continued*
  aorto-myocardial (graft) 36.2
  aortorenal 39.24
  aortosubclavian 39.22
  apicoaortic 35.93
  arteriovenous NEC 39.29
    for renal dialysis (by)
      anastomosis 39.27
      external cannula 39.93
  ascending aorta to pulmonary artery (Waterston) 39.0
  axillary-femoral 39.29
  carotid-carotid 39.22
  carotid-subclavian 39.22
  caval-mesenteric 39.1
  corpora cavernosa-corpus spongiosum 64.98
  corpora-saphenous 64.98
  descending aorta to pulmonary artery (Potts-Smith) 39.0
  endolymphatic (-subarachnoid) 20.71
  endolymph-perilymph 20.71
  extracranial-intracranial (EC-IC) 39.28
  femoroperoneal 39.29
  femoropopliteal 39.29
  iliofemoral 39.25
  ilioiliac 39.25
  intestinal
    large-to-large 45.94
    small-to-large 45.93
    small-to-small 45.91
  left subclavian to descending aorta (Blalock-Park) 39.0
  left-to-right (systemic-pulmonary artery) 39.0
  left ventricle (heart) (apex) and aorta 35.93
  lienorenal 39.1
  lumbar-subarachnoid (with valve) NEC 03.79
  mesocaval 39.1
  peritoneal-jugular 54.94
  peritoneo-vascular 54.94
  peritoneovenous 54.94
  pleuroperitoneal 34.05
  pleurothecal (with valve) 03.79
  portacaval (double) 39.1
  portal-systemic 39.1
  portal vein to vena cava 39.1
  pulmonary-innominate 39.0
  pulmonary vein to atrium 35.82
  renoportal 39.1
  right atrium and pulmonary artery 35.94
  right ventricle and pulmonary artery (distal) 35.92
    in repair of
      pulmonary artery atresia 35.92
      transposition of great vessels 35.92
      truncus arteriosus 35.83
  salpingothecal (with valve) 03.79
  semicircular-subarachnoid 20.71
  spinal (thecal) (with valve) NEC 03.79
    subarachnoid-peritoneal 03.71
    subarachnoid-ureteral 03.72
  splenorenal (venous) 39.1
    arterial 39.26
  subarachnoid-peritoneal (with valve) 03.71
  subarachnoid-ureteral (with valve) 03.72
  subclavian-pulmonary 39.0
  subdural-peritoneal (with valve) 02.34
  superior mesenteric-caval 39.1
  systemic-pulmonary artery 39.0
  transjugular intrahepatic portosystemic [TIPS] 39.1
  vena cava to pulmonary artery (Green) 39.21
  ventricular (cerebral) (with valve) 02.2
    to
      abdominal cavity or organ 02.34
      bone marrow 02.39
      cervical subarachnoid space 02.2
      circulatory system 02.32
      cisterna magna 02.2
      extracranial site NEC 02.39
      gallbladder 02.34
      head or neck structure 02.31
      intracerebral site NEC 02.2
      lumbar site 02.39

Shunt — *see also* Anastomosis and Bypass, vascular — *continued*
  ventricular — *continued*
    to — *continued*
      mastoid 02.31
      nasopharynx 02.31
      thoracic cavity 02.33
      ureter 02.35
      urinary system 02.35
      venous system 02.32
  ventriculoatrial (with valve) 02.32
  ventriculocaval (with valve) 02.32
  ventriculocisternal (with valve) 02.2
  ventriculolumbar (with valve) 02.39
  ventriculomastoid (with valve) 02.31
  ventriculonasopharyngeal 02.31
  ventriculopleural (with valve) 02.33
Sialoadenectomy (parotid) (sublingual) (submaxillary) 26.30
  complete 26.32
  partial 26.31
  radical 26.32
Sialoadenolithotomy 26.0
Sialoadenotomy 26.0
Sialodochoplasty NEC 26.49
Sialogram 87.09
Sialolithotomy 26.0
Sieve, vena cava 38.7
Sigmoid bladder 57.87 [45.52]
Sigmoidectomy 45.76
Sigmoidomyotomy 46.91
Sigmoidopexy (Moschowitz) 46.63
Sigmoidoproctectomy (*see also* Resection, rectum) 48.69
Sigmoidoproctostomy 45.94
Sigmoidorectostomy 45.94
Sigmoidorrhaphy 46.75
Sigmoidoscopy (rigid) 48.23
  with biopsy 45.25
  flexible 45.24
  through stoma (artificial) 45.22
  transabdominal 45.21
Sigmoidosigmoidostomy 45.94
  proximal to distal segment 45.76
Sigmoidostomy (*see also* Colostomy) 46.10
Sigmoidotomy 45.03
Sign language 93.75
Silver operation (bunionectomy) 77.59
Sinogram
  abdominal wall 88.03
  chest wall 87.38
  retroperitoneum 88.14
Sinusectomy (nasal) (complete) (partial) (with turbinectomy) 22.60
  antrum 22.62
    with Caldwell-Luc approach 22.61
  ethmoid 22.63
  frontal 22.42
  maxillary 22.62
    with Caldwell-Luc approach 22.61
  sphenoid 22.64
Sinusotomy (nasal) 22.50
  antrum (intranasal) 22.2
    with external approach (Caldwell-Luc) 22.39
      radical (with removal of membrane lining) 22.31
  ethmoid 22.51
  frontal 22.41
  maxillary (intranasal) 22.2
    external approach (Caldwell-Luc) 22.39
      radical (with removal of membrane lining) 22.31
  multiple 22.53
  perinasal 22.50
  sphenoid 22.52
Sistrunk operation (excision of thyroglossal cyst) 06.7
Size reduction
  abdominal wall (adipose) (pendulous) 86.83
  arms (adipose) (batwing) 86.83
  breast (bilateral) 85.32
    unilateral 85.31

Size reduction — *continued*
  buttocks (adipose) 86.83
  skin 86.83
  subcutaneous tissue 86.83
  thighs (adipose) 86.83
Skeletal series (x-ray) 88.31
Sling — *see also* Operation, sling
  fascial (fascia lata)
    for facial weakness (trigeminal nerve paralysis) 86.81
    mouth 86.81
    orbicularis (mouth) 86.81
    tongue 25.59
  levator muscle (urethrocystopexy) 59.71
  pubococcygeal 59.71
  rectum (puborectalis) 48.76
  tongue (fascial) 25.59
Slitting
  canaliculus for
    passage of tube 09.42
    removal of streptothrix 09.42
  lens 13.2
  prepuce (dorsal) (lateral) 64.91
Slocum operation (pes anserinus transfer) 81.47
Sluder operation (tonsillectomy) 28.2
Small bowel series (x-ray) 87.63
Smith operation (open osteotomy of mandible) 76.62
Smith-Peterson operation (radiocarpal arthrodesis) 81.25
Smithwick operation (sympathectomy) 05.29
Snaring, polyp, colon (endoscopic) 45.42
Snip, punctum (with dilation) 09.51
Soave operation (endorectal pull-through) 48.41
Somatotherapy, psychiatric NEC 94.29
Sonneberg operation (inferior maxillary neurectomy) 04.07
Sorondo-Ferré operation (hindquarter amputation) 84.19
Soutter operation (iliac crest fasciotomy) 83.14
Spaulding-Richardson operation (uterine suspension) 69.22
Spectrophotometry NEC 89.39
  blood 89.39
  placenta 89.29
  urine 89.29
Speech therapy NEC 93.75
Spermatocelectomy 63.2
Spermatocystectomy 60.73
Spermatocystotomy 60.72
Sphenoidectomy 22.64
Sphenoidotomy 22.52
Sphincterectomy, anal 49.6
Sphincteroplasty
  anal 49.79
    obstetrical laceration (current) 75.62
      old 49.79
  bladder neck 57.85
  pancreas 51.83
  sphincter of Oddi 51.83
Sphincterorrhaphy, anal 49.71
  obstetrical laceration (current) 75.62
    old 49.79
Sphincterotomy
  anal (external) (internal) 49.59
    left lateral 49.51
    posterior 49.52
  bladder (neck) (transurethral) 57.91
  choledochal 51.82
    endoscopic 51.85
  iris 12.12
  pancreatic 51.82
    endoscopic 51.85
  sphincter of Oddi 51.82
    endoscopic 51.85
  transduodenal ampullary 51.82
    endoscopic 51.85
Spinal anesthesia — *omit code*
Spinelli operation (correction of inverted uterus) 75.93
Spirometry (incentive) (respiratory) 89.37

Spivack operation (permanent gastrostomy) 43.19
Splanchnicectomy 05.29
Splanchnicotomy 05.0
Splenectomy (complete) (total) 41.5
    partial 41.43
Splenogram 88.64
    radioisotope 92.05
Splenolysis 54.59
    laparoscopic 54.51
Splenopexy 41.95
Splenoplasty 41.95
Splenoportogram (by splenic arteriography) 88.64
Splenorrhaphy 41.95
Splenotomy 41.2
Splinting
    dental (for immobilization) 93.55
        orthodontic 24.7
    musculoskeletal 93.54
    ureteral 56.2
Splitting — *see also* Division
    canaliculus 09.52
    lacrimal papilla 09.51
    spinal cord tracts 03.29
        percutaneous 03.21
    tendon sheath 83.01
        hand 82.01
Spondylosyndesis (*see also* Fusion, spinal) 81.00
S.P. Rogers operation (knee disarticulation) 84.16
Ssabanejew-Frank operation (permanent gastrostomy) 43.19
Stab, intercostal 34.09
Stabilization, joint — *see also* Arthrodesis
    patella (for recurrent dislocation) 81.44
Stacke operation (simple mastoidectomy) 20.41
Stallard operation (conjunctivocystorhinostomy) 09.82
    with insertion of tube or stent 09.83
Stamm (-Kader) operation (temporary gastrostomy) 43.19
Stapedectomy 19.19
    with incus replacement (homograft) (prosthesis) 19.11
    revision 19.29
        with incus replacement 19.21
Stapediolysis 19.0
Stapling
    artery 39.31
    blebs, lung (emphysematous) 32.21
    diaphysis (*see also* Stapling, epiphyseal plate) 78.20
    epiphyseal plate 78.20
        femur 78.25
        fibula 78.27
        humerus 78.22
        radius 78.23
        specified site NEC 78.29
        tibia 78.27
        ulna 78.23
    gastric varices 44.91
    graft — *see* Graft
    vein 39.32
STARR (stapled transanal rectal resection) 70.52 ●
                                                     ●
Steinberg operation 44.5
Steindler operation
    fascia stripping (for cavus deformity) 83.14
    flexorplasty (elbow) 83.77
    muscle transfer 83.77
Stereotactic head frame application 93.59
Stereotactic radiosurgery 92.30
    cobalt 60 92.32
    linear accelerator (LINAC) 92.31
    multi-source 92.32
    particle beam 92.33
    particulate 92.33
    radiosurgery NEC 92.39
    single source photon 92.31
Sterilization
    female (*see also* specific operation) 66.39

Sterilization — *continued*
    male NEC (*see also* Ligation, vas deferens) 63.70
Sternotomy 77.31
    as operative approach — *omit code*
    for bone marrow biopsy 41.31
Stewart operation (renal plication with pyeloplasty) 55.87
Stimulation (electronic) — *see also* Implant, electronic stimulator
    bone growth (percutaneous) — *see* category 78.9 ☑
        transcutaneous (surface) 99.86
    cardiac (external) 99.62
        internal 37.91
    carotid sinus 99.64
    defibrillator
        non-invasive programmed electrical stimulation (NIPS) 37.26
    electrophysiologic, cardiac 37.26
    nerve, peripheral or spinal cord, transcutaneous 93.39
Stitch, Kelly-Stoeckel (urethra) 59.3
Stomatoplasty 27.59
Stomatorrhaphy 27.52
Stone operation (anoplasty) 49.79
Strassman operation (metroplasty) 69.49
Strayer operation (gastrocnemius recession) 83.72
Stretching
    eyelid (with elongation) 08.71
    fascia 93.28
    foreskin 99.95
    iris 12.63
    muscle 93.27
    nerve (cranial) (peripheral) 04.91
    tendon 93.27
Stripping
    bone (*see also* Incision, bone) 77.10
    carotid sinus 39.8
    cranial suture 02.01
    fascia 83.14
        hand 82.12
    membranes for surgical induction of labor 73.1
    meninges (cerebral) 01.51
        spinal 03.4
    saphenous vein, varicose 38.59
    subdural membrane (cerebral) 01.51
        spinal 03.4
    varicose veins (lower limb) 38.59
        upper limb 38.53
    vocal cords 30.09
Stromeyer-Little operation (hepatotomy) 50.0
Strong operation (unbridling of celiac artery axis) 39.91
Stryker frame 93.59
Study
    bone mineral density 88.98
    bundle of His 37.29
    color vision 95.06
    conduction, nerve (median) 89.15
    dark adaptation, eye 95.07
    electrophysiologic stimulation and recording, cardiac 37.26
    function — *see also* Function, study
        radioisotope — *see* Scan, radioisotope
    lacrimal flow (radiographic) 87.05
    ocular motility 95.15
    pulmonary function — *see* categories 89.37-89.38
    radiographic — *see* Radiography
    radio-iodinated triolein 92.04
    renal clearance 92.03
    spirometer 89.37
    tracer — *see also* Scan, radioisotope eye (P^{32}) 95.16
    ultrasonic — *see* Ultrasonography
    visual field 95.05
    xenon flow NEC 92.19
        cardiovascular 92.05
        pulmonary 92.15
Sturmdorf operation (conization of cervix) 67.2
Submucous resection
    larynx 30.29

Submucous resection — *continued*
    nasal septum 21.5
Summerskill operation (dacryocystorhinostomy by intubation) 09.81
Surgery
    computer assisted (CAS) 00.39
        CAS with CT/CTA 00.31
        CAS with fluoroscopy 00.33
        CAS with MR/MRA 00.32
        CAS with multiple datasets 00.35
            imageless 00.34
        other CAS 00.39
    IGS — *see* Surgery, computer assisted
    image guided — *see* Surgery, computer assisted
    navigation (CT-free, IGN image guided, imageless) — *see* Surgery, computer assisted
Surmay operation (jejunostomy) 46.39
Suspension
    balanced, for traction 93.45
    bladder NEC 57.89
    diverticulum, pharynx 29.59
    kidney 55.7
    Olshausen (uterus) 69.22
    ovary 65.79
    paraurethral (Pereyra) 59.6
    periurethral 59.6
    urethra (retropubic) (sling) 59.5
    urethrovesical
        Goebel-Frangenheim-Stoeckel 59.4
        gracilis muscle transplant 59.71
        levator muscle sling 59.71
        Marshall-Marchetti (-Krantz) 59.5
        Millin-Read 59.4
        suprapubic 59.4
    uterus (abdominal or vaginal approach) 69.22
    vagina 70.77
Suture (laceration)
    abdominal wall 54.63
        secondary 54.61
    adenoid fossa 28.7
    adrenal (gland) 07.44
    aneurysm (cerebral) (peripheral) 39.52
    anus 49.71
        obstetric laceration (current) 75.62
        old 49.79
    aorta 39.31
    aponeurosis (*see also* Suture, tendon) 83.64
    arteriovenous fistula 39.53
    artery 39.31
        percutaneous puncture closure — *omit code*
    bile duct 51.79
    bladder 57.81
        obstetric laceration (current) 75.61
    blood vessel NEC 39.30
        artery 39.31
        percutaneous puncture closure — *omit code*
        vein 39.32
    breast (skin) 85.81
    bronchus 33.41
    bursa 83.99
        hand 82.99
    canaliculus 09.73
    cecum 46.75
    cerebral meninges 02.11
    cervix (traumatic laceration) 67.61
        internal os, encirclement 67.59
        obstetric laceration (current) 75.51
        old 67.69
    chest wall 34.71
    cleft palate 27.62
    clitoris 71.4
    colon 46.75
    common duct 51.71
    conjunctiva 10.6
    cornea 11.51
        with conjunctival flap 11.53
    corneoscleral 11.51
        with conjunctival flap 11.53
    diaphragm 34.82
    duodenum 46.71
        ulcer (bleeding) (perforated) 44.42
        endoscopic 44.43

2006 ICD-9-CM

☑ Additional Digit Required — Refer to the Tabular List (Numeric Code Section) for Additional Digit Selection
▶◀ Revised Text   ● New Line   ▲ Revised Code

October 2005 • Volume 3 — 75

Suture — *continued*
  dura mater (cerebral) 02.11
    spinal 03.59
  ear, external 18.4
  enterocele 70.92
  entropion 08.42
  epididymis (and)
    spermatic cord 63.51
    vas deferens 63.81
  episiotomy — *see* Episiotomy
  esophagus 42.82
  eyeball 16.89
  eyebrow 08.81
  eyelid 08.81
    with entropion or ectropion repair 08.42
  fallopian tube 66.71
  fascia 83.65
    hand 82.46
    to skeletal attachment 83.89
      hand 82.89
  gallbladder 51.91
  ganglion, sympathetic 05.81
  gingiva 24.32
  great vessel 39.30
    artery 39.31
    vein 39.32
  gum 24.32
  heart 37.49 ▲
  hepatic duct 51.79
  hymen 70.76
  ileum 46.73
  intestine 46.79
    large 46.75
    small 46.73
  jejunum 46.73
  joint capsule 81.96
    with arthroplasty — *see* Arthroplasty
      ankle 81.94
      foot 81.94
      lower extremity NEC 81.95
      upper extremity 81.93
  kidney 55.81
  labia 71.71
  laceration — *see* Suture, by site
  larynx 31.61
  ligament 81.96
    with arthroplasty — *see* Arthroplasty
      ankle 81.94
    broad 69.29
    Cooper's 54.64
    foot and toes 81.94
    gastrocolic 54.73
    knee 81.95
    lower extremity NEC 81.95
    sacrouterine 69.29
    upper extremity 81.93
    uterine 69.29
  ligation — *see* Ligation
  lip 27.51
  liver 50.61
  lung 33.43
  meninges (cerebral) 02.11
    spinal 03.59
  mesentery 54.75
  mouth 27.52
  muscle 83.65
    hand 82.46
    ocular (oblique) (rectus) 15.7
  nerve (cranial) (peripheral) 04.3
    sympathetic 05.81
  nose (external) (internal) 21.81
    for epistaxis 21.09
  obstetric laceration NEC 75.69
    bladder 75.61
    cervix 75.51
    corpus uteri 75.52
    pelvic floor 75.69
    perineum 75.69
    rectum 75.62
    sphincter ani 75.62
    urethra 75.61
    uterus 75.50
    vagina 75.69
    vulva 75.69
  omentum 54.64

Suture — *continued*
  ovary 65.71
    laparoscopic 65.74
  palate 27.61
    cleft 27.62
  palpebral fissure 08.59
  pancreas 52.95
  pelvic floor 71.71
    obstetric laceration (current) 75.69
  penis 64.41
  peptic ulcer (bleeding) (perforated) 44.40
  pericardium 37.49   ▲
  perineum (female) 71.71
    after delivery 75.69
      episiotomy repair — *see* Episiotomy
    male 86.59
  periosteum 78.20
    carpal, metacarpal 78.24
    femur 78.25
    fibula 78.27
    humerus 78.22
    pelvic 78.29
    phalanges (foot) (hand) 78.29
    radius 78.23
    specified site NEC 78.29
    tarsal, metatarsal 78.28
    tibia 78.27
    ulna 78.23
    vertebrae 78.29
  peritoneum 54.64
  periurethral tissue to symphysis pubis 59.5
  pharynx 29.51
  pleura 34.93
  rectum 48.71
    obstetric laceration (current) 75.62
  retina (for reattachment) 14.59
  sacrouterine ligament 69.29
  salivary gland 26.41
  scalp 86.59
    replantation 86.51
  sclera (with repair of conjunctiva) 12.81
  scrotum (skin) 61.41
  secondary
    abdominal wall 54.61
    episiotomy 75.69
    peritoneum 54.64
  sigmoid 46.75
  skin (mucous membrane) (without graft) 86.59
    with graft — *see* Graft, skin
    breast 85.81
    ear 18.4
    eyebrow 08.81
    eyelid 08.81
    nose 21.81
    penis 64.41
    scalp 86.59
      replantation 86.51
    scrotum 61.41
    vulva 71.71
  specified site NEC — *see* Repair, by site
  spermatic cord 63.51
  sphincter ani 49.71
    obstetric laceration (current) 75.62
    old 49.79
  spinal meninges 03.59
  spleen 41.95
  stomach 44.61
    ulcer (bleeding) (perforated) 44.41
      endoscopic 44.43
  subcutaneous tissue (without skin graft) 86.59
    with graft — *see* Graft, skin
  tendon (direct) (immediate) (primary) 83.64
    delayed (secondary) 83.62
      hand NEC 82.43
        flexors 82.42
    hand NEC 82.45
      delayed (secondary) 82.43
      flexors 82.44
        delayed (secondary) 82.42
    ocular 15.7
    rotator cuff 83.63
    sheath 83.61
      hand 82.41
    supraspinatus (rotator cuff repair) 83.63
    to skeletal attachment 83.88
      hand 82.85

Suture — *continued*
  Tenon's capsule 15.7
  testis 62.61
  thymus 07.93
  thyroid gland 06.93
  tongue 25.51
  tonsillar fossa 28.7
  trachea 31.71
  tunica vaginalis 61.41
  ulcer (bleeding) (perforated) (peptic) 44.40
    duodenum 44.42
      endoscopic 44.43
    gastric 44.41
      endoscopic 44.43
    intestine 46.79
    skin 86.59
    stomach 44.41
      endoscopic 44.43
  ureter 56.82
  urethra 58.41
    obstetric laceration (current) 75.61
  uterosacral ligament 69.29
  uterus 69.41
    obstetric laceration (current) 75.50
      old 69.49
  uvula 27.73
  vagina 70.71
    obstetric laceration (current) 75.69
      old 70.79
  vas deferens 63.81
  vein 39.32
  vulva 71.71
    obstetric laceration (current) 75.69
      old 71.79

Suture-ligation — *see also* Ligation
  blood vessel — *see* Ligation, blood vessel
Sweep, anterior iris 12.97
Swenson operation
  bladder reconstruction 57.87
  proctectomy 48.49
Swinney operation (urethral reconstruction) 58.46
Switch, switching
  coronary arteries 35.84
  great arteries, total 35.84
Syme operation
  ankle amputation through malleoli of tibia and
    fibula 84.14
  urethrotomy, external 58.0
Sympathectomy NEC 05.29
  cervical 05.22
  cervicothoracic 05.22
  lumbar 05.23
  periarterial 05.25
  presacral 05.24
  renal 05.29
  thoracolumbar 05.23
  tympanum 20.91
Sympatheticotripsy 05.0
Symphysiotomy 77.39
  assisting delivery (obstetrical) 73.94
  kidney (horseshoe) 55.85
Symphysis, pleural 34.6
Synchondrotomy (*see also* Division, cartilage)
  80.40
Syndactylization 86.89
Syndesmotomy (*see also* Division, ligament)
  80.40
Synechiotomy
  endometrium 68.21
  iris (posterior) 12.33
    anterior 12.32
Synovectomy (joint) (complete) (partial) 80.70
  ankle 80.77
  elbow 80.72
  foot and toe 80.78
  hand and finger 80.74
  hip 80.75
  knee 80.76
  shoulder 80.71
  specified site NEC 80.79
  spine 80.79
  tendon sheath 83.42
    hand 82.33
  wrist 80.73

☑ Additional Digit Required — Refer to the Tabular List (Numeric Code Section) for Additional Digit Selection

Syringing
  lacrimal duct or sac 09.43
  nasolacrimal duct 09.43
    with
      dilation 09.43
      insertion of tube or stent 09.44

T

Taarnhoj operation (trigeminal nerve root decompression) 04.41
Tack operation (sacculotomy) 20.79
Take-down
  anastomosis
    arterial 39.49
    blood vessel 39.49
    gastric, gastrointestinal 44.5
    intestine 46.93
    stomach 44.5
    vascular 39.49
    ventricular 02.43
  arterial bypass 39.49
  arteriovenous shunt 39.43
    with creation of new shunt 39.42
  cecostomy 46.52
  colostomy 46.52
  duodenostomy 46.51
  enterostomy 46.50
  esophagostomy 42.83
  gastroduodenostomy 44.5
  gastrojejunostomy 44.5
  ileostomy 46.51
  intestinal stoma 46.50
    large 46.52
    small 46.51
  jejunoileal bypass 46.93
  jejunostomy 46.51
  laryngostomy 31.62
  sigmoidostomy 46.52
  stoma
    bile duct 51.79
    bladder 57.82
    bronchus 33.42
    common duct 51.72
    esophagus 42.83
    gall bladder 51.92
    hepatic duct 51.79
    intestine 46.50
      large 46.52
      small 46.51
    kidney 55.82
    larynx 31.62
    rectum 48.72
    stomach 44.62
    thorax 34.72
    trachea 31.72
    ureter 56.83
    urethra 58.42
  systemic-pulmonary artery anastomosis 39.49
    in total repair of tetralogy of Fallot 35.81
  tracheostomy 31.72
  vascular anastomosis or bypass 39.49
  ventricular shunt (cerebral) 02.43
Talectomy 77.98
Talma-Morison operation (omentopexy) 54.74
Tamponade
  esophageal 96.06
  intrauterine (nonobstetric) 69.91
    after delivery or abortion 75.8
    antepartum 73.1
  vagina 96.14
    after delivery or abortion 75.8
    antepartum 73.1
Tanner operation (devascularization of stomach) 44.99
Tap
  abdomen 54.91
  chest 34.91
  cisternal 01.01
  cranial 01.09
  joint 81.91
  lumbar (diagnostic) (removal of dye) 03.31
  perilymphatic 20.79
  spinal (diagnostic) 03.31

Tap — *continued*
  subdural (through fontanel) 01.09
  thorax 34.91
Tarsectomy 08.20
  de Grandmont 08.35
Tarsoplasty (*see also* Reconstruction, eyelid) 08.70
Tarsorrhaphy (lateral) 08.52
  division or severing 08.02
Tattooing
  cornea 11.91
  skin 86.02
Tautening, eyelid for entropion 08.42
Telemetry (cardiac) 89.54
Teleradiotherapy
  beta particles 92.25
  Betatron 92.24
  cobalt-60 92.23
  electrons 92.25
  iodine-125 92.23
  linear accelerator 92.24
  neutrons 92.26
  particulate radiation NEC 92.26
  photons 92.24
  protons 92.26
  radioactive cesium 92.23
  radioisotopes NEC 92.23
Temperature gradient study (*see also* Thermography) 88.89
Temperament assessment 94.02
Tendinoplasty — *see* Repair, tendon
Tendinosuture (immediate) (primary) (*see also* Suture, tendon) 83.64
  hand (*see also* Suture, tendon, hand) 82.45
Tendolysis 83.91
  hand 82.91
Tendoplasty — *see* Repair, tendon
Tenectomy 83.39
  eye 15.13
    levator palpebrae 08.33
    multiple (two or more tendons) 15.3
  hand 82.29
  levator palpebrae 08.33
  tendon sheath 83.31
    hand 82.21
Tenodesis (tendon fixation to skeletal attachment) 83.88
  Fowler 82.85
  hand 82.85
Tenolysis 83.91
  hand 82.91
Tenomyoplasty (*see also* Repair, tendon) 83.88
  hand (*see also* Repair, tendon, hand) 82.86
Tenomyotomy — *see* Tenonectomy
Tenonectomy 83.42
  for graft 83.41
    hand 82.32
  hand 82.33
    for graft 82.32
Tenontomyoplasty — *see* Repair, tendon
Tenontoplasty — *see* Repair, tendon
Tenoplasty (*see also* Repair, tendon) 83.88
  hand (*see also* Repair, tendon, hand) 82.86
Tenorrhaphy (*see also* Suture, tendon) 83.64
  hand (*see also* Suture, tendon, hand) 82.45
  to skeletal attachment 83.88
    hand 82.85
Tenosuspension 83.88
  hand 82.86
Tenosuture (*see also* Suture, tendon) 83.64
  hand (*see also* Suture, tendon, hand) 82.45
  to skeletal attachment 83.88
    hand 82.85
Tenosynovectomy 83.42
  hand 82.33
Tenotomy 83.13
  Achilles tendon 83.11
  adductor (hip) (subcutaneous) 83.12
  eye 15.12
    levator palpebrae 08.38
    multiple (two or more tendons) 15.4
  hand 82.11
  levator palpebrae 08.38

Tenotomy — *continued*
  pectoralis minor tendon (decompression thoracic outlet) 83.13
  stapedius 19.0
  tensor tympani 19.0
Tenovaginotomy — *see* Tenotomy
Tensing, orbicularis oculi 08.59
Termination of pregnancy
  by
    aspiration curettage 69.51
    dilation and curettage 69.01
    hysterectomy — *see* Hysterectomy
    hysterotomy 74.91
    intra-amniotic injection (saline) 75.0
Test, testing (for)
  14 C-Urea breath 89.39
  auditory function
    NEC 95.46
  Bender Visual-Motor Gestalt 94.02
  Benton Visual Retention 94.02
  cardiac (vascular)
    function NEC 89.59
    stress 89.44
      bicycle ergometer 89.43
      Masters' two-step 89.42
      treadmill 89.41
  Denver developmental (screening) 94.02
  fetus, fetal
    nonstress (fetal activity acceleration determinations) 75.34
    oxytocin challenge (contraction stress) 75.35
    sensitivity (to oxytocin) — *omit code*
  function
    cardiac NEC 89.59
    hearing NEC 95.46
    muscle (by)
      electromyography 93.08
      manual 93.04
    neurologic NEC 89.15
    vestibular 95.46
      clinical 95.44
  glaucoma NEC 95.26
  hearing 95.47
    clinical NEC 95.42
  intelligence 94.01
  internal jugular-subclavian venous reflux 89.62
  intracarotid amobarbital (Wada) 89.10
  Masters' two-step stress (cardiac) 89.42
  muscle function (by)
    electromyography 93.08
    manual 93.04
  neurologic function NEC 89.15
  nocturnal penile tumescence 89.29
  provocative, for glaucoma 95.26
  psychologic NEC 94.08
  psychometric 94.01
  radio-cobalt B$_{12}$ Schilling 92.04
  range of motion 93.05
  rotation (Bárány chair) (hearing) 95.45
  sleep disorder function — *see* categories 89.17-89.18
  Stanford-Binet 94.01
  tuning fork (hearing) 95.42
  Thallium stress (transesophageal pacing) 89.44
  Urea breath, (14 C) 89.39
  vestibular function NEC 95.46
    thermal 95.44
  Wada (hemispheric function) 89.10
  whispered speech (hearing) 95.42
TEVAP (transurethral electrovaporization of prostate) 60.29
Thalamectomy 01.41
Thalamotomy 01.41
  by stereotactic radiosurgery 92.32
    cobalt 60 92.32
    linear accelerator (LINAC) 92.31
    multi-source 92.32
    particle beam 92.33
    particulate 92.33
    radiosurgery NEC 92.39
    single source photon 92.31
Thal operation (repair of esophageal stricture) 42.85

Thyroidectomy NEC — *continued*
  substernal — *continued*
    partial or subtotal 06.51
  transoral route (lingual) 06.6
  transsternal route (*see also* Thyroidectomy, substernal) 06.50
  unilateral (with removal of isthmus) (with removal of portion of other lobe) 06.2
Thyroidorrhaphy 06.93
Thyroidotomy (field) (gland) NEC 06.09
  postoperative 06.02
Thyrotomy 31.3
  with tantalum plate 31.69
Tirofiban (HCl), infusion 99.20
Toilette
  skin — *see* Debridement, skin or subcutaneous tissue
  tracheostomy 96.55
Token economy (behavior therapy) 94.33
Tomkins operation (metroplasty) 69.49
Tomography — *see also* Radiography
  abdomen NEC 88.02
  cardiac 87.42
  computerized axial NEC 88.38
    abdomen 88.01
    bone 88.38
      quantitative 88.98
    brain 87.03
    head 87.03
    kidney 87.71
    skeletal 88.38
      quantitative 88.98
    thorax 87.41
  head NEC 87.04
  kidney NEC 87.72
  lung 87.42
  thorax NEC 87.42
Tongue tie operation 25.91
Tonography 95.26
Tonometry 89.11
Tonsillectomy 28.2
  with adenoidectomy 28.3
Tonsillotomy 28.0
Topectomy 01.32
Torek (-Bevan) operation (orchidopexy) (first stage) (second stage) 62.5
Torkildsen operation (ventriculocisternal shunt) 02.2
Torpin operation (cul-de-sac resection) 70.92
Toti operation (dacryocystorhinostomy) 09.81
Touchas operation 86.83
Touroff operation (ligation of subclavian artery) 38.85
Toxicology — *see* Examination, microscopic
TPN (total parenteral nutrition) 99.15
Trabeculectomy ab externo 12.64
Trabeculodialysis 12.59
Trabeculotomy ab externo 12.54
Trachelectomy 67.4
Trachelopexy 69.22
Tracheloplasty 67.69
Trachelorrhaphy (Emmet) (suture) 67.61
  obstetrical 75.51
Trachelotomy 69.95
  obstetrical 73.93
Tracheocricotomy (for assistance in breathing) 31.1
Tracheofissure 31.1
Tracheography 87.32
Tracheolaryngotomy (emergency) 31.1
  permanent opening 31.29
Tracheoplasty 31.79
  with artificial larynx 31.75
Tracheorrhaphy 31.71
Tracheoscopy NEC 31.42
  through tracheotomy (stoma) 31.41
Tracheostomy (emergency) (temporary) (for assistance in breathing) 31.1
  mediastinal 31.21
  permanent NEC 31.29
  revision 31.74

Tracheotomy (emergency) (temporary) (for assistance in breathing) 31.1
  permanent 31.29
Tracing, carotid pulse with ECG lead 89.56
Traction
  with reduction of fracture or dislocation — *see* Reduction, fracture *and* Reduction, dislocation
  adhesive tape (skin) 93.46
  boot 93.46
  Bryant's (skeletal) 93.44
  Buck's 93.46
  caliper tongs 93.41
    with synchronous insertion of device 02.94
  Cortel's (spinal) 93.42
  Crutchfield tongs 93.41
    with synchronous insertion of device 02.94
  Dunlop's (skeletal) 93.44
  gallows 93.46
  Gardner Wells 93.41
    with synchronous insertion of device 02.94
  halo device, skull 93.41
    with synchronous insertion of device 02.94
  Lyman Smith (skeletal) 93.44
  manual, intermittent 93.21
  mechanical, intermittent 93.21
  Russell's (skeletal) 93.44
  skeletal NEC 93.44
    intermittent 93.43
  skin, limbs NEC 93.46
  spinal NEC 93.42
    with skull device (halo) (caliper) (Crutchfield) (Gardner Wells) (Vinke) (tongs) 93.41
    with synchronous insertion of device 02.94
  Thomas' splint 93.45
  Vinke tongs 93.41
    with synchronous insertion of device 02.94
Tractotomy
  brain 01.32
  medulla oblongata 01.32
  mesencephalon 01.32
  percutaneous 03.21
  spinal cord (one-stage) (two-stage) 03.29
  trigeminal (percutaneous) (radiofrequency) 04.02
Training (for) (in)
  ADL (activities of daily living) 93.83
    for the blind 93.78
  ambulation 93.22
  braille 93.77
  crutch walking 93.24
  dyslexia 93.71
  dysphasia 93.72
  esophageal speech (postlaryngectomy) 93.73
  gait 93.22
  joint movements 93.14
  lip reading 93.75
  Moon (blind reading) 93.77
  orthoptic 95.35
  prenatal (natural childbirth) 93.37
  prosthetic or orthotic device usage 93.24
  relaxation 94.33
  speech NEC 93.75
    esophageal 93.73
    for correction of defect 93.74
  use of lead dog for the blind 93.76
  vocational 93.85
TRAM (transverse rectus abdominis musculocutaneous) flap of breast 85.7
Transactional analysis
  group 94.44
  individual 94.39
Transection — *see also* Division
  artery (with ligation) (*see also* Division, artery) 38.80
    renal, aberrant (with reimplantation) 39.55
  bone (*see also* Osteotomy) 77.30
  fallopian tube (bilateral) (remaining) (solitary) 66.39
    by endoscopy 66.22
    unilateral 66.92
  isthmus, thyroid 06.91
Transection — *see also* Division
  muscle 83.19
    eye 15.13
      multiple (two or more muscles) 15.3
    hand 82.19

Transection — *see also* Division — *continued*
  nerve (cranial) (peripheral) NEC 04.03
    acoustic 04.01
    root (spinal) 03.1
    sympathetic 05.0
    tracts in spinal cord 03.29
    trigeminal 04.02
    vagus (transabdominal) (*see also* Vagotomy) 44.00
  pylorus (with wedge resection) 43.3
  renal vessel, aberrant (with reimplantation) 39.55
  spinal
    cord tracts 03.29
    nerve root 03.1
  tendon 83.13
    hand 82.11
  uvula 27.71
  vas deferens 63.71
  vein (with ligation) (*see also* Division, vein) 38.80
    renal, aberrant (with reimplantation) 39.55
    varicose (lower limb) 38.59
Transfer, transference
  bone shaft, fibula into tibia 78.47
  digital (to replace absent thumb) 82.69
    finger (to thumb) (same hand) 82.61
      to
        finger, except thumb 82.81
        opposite hand (with amputation) 82.69 [84.01]
      toe (to thumb) (with amputation) 82.69 [84.11]
      to finger, except thumb 82.81 [84.11]
  fat pad NEC 86.89
    with skin graft — *see* Graft, skin, full-thickness
  finger (to replace absent thumb) (same hand) 82.61
    to
      finger, except thumb 82.81
      opposite hand (with amputation) 82.69 [84.01]
  muscle origin 83.77
    hand 82.58
  nerve (cranial) (peripheral) (radial anterior) (ulnar) 04.6
  pedicle graft 86.74
  pes anserinus (tendon) (repair of knee) 81.47
  tarsoconjunctival flap, from opposing lid 08.64
  tendon 83.75
    hand 82.56
    pes anserinus (repair of knee) 81.47
  toe-to-thumb (free) (pedicle) (with amputation) 82.69 [84.11]
Transfixion — *see also* Fixation
  iris (bombé) 12.11
Transfusion (of) 99.03
  antihemophilic factor 99.06
  antivenin 99.16
  autologous blood
    collected prior to surgery 99.02
    intraoperative 99.00
    perioperative 99.00
    postoperative 99.00
    previously collected 99.02
    salvage 99.00
  blood (whole) NOS 99.03
    expander 99.08
    surrogate 99.09
  bone marrow 41.00
    allogeneic 41.03
      with purging 41.02
    allograft 41.03
      with purging 41.02
    autograft 41.01
      with purging 41.09
    autologous 41.01
      with purging 41.09
  coagulation factors 99.06
  Dextran 99.08
  exchange 99.01
    intraperitoneal 75.2
    in utero (with hysterotomy) 75.2
  exsanguination 99.01

2006 ICD-9-CM

☑ Additional Digit Required — Refer to the Tabular List (Numeric Code Section) for Additional Digit Selection
▶◀ Revised Text   ● New Line   ▲ Revised Code

Volume 3 — 79

Ultrasonography
abdomen 88.76
aortic arch 88.73
biliary tract 88.74
breast 88.73
deep vein thrombosis 88.77
digestive system 88.74
eye 95.13
head and neck 88.71
heart 88.72
intestine 88.74
intravascular — see Ultrasound, intravascular (IVUS)
lung 88.73
midline shift, brain 88.71
multiple sites 88.79
peripheral vascular system 88.77
retroperitoneum 88.76
therapeutic — see Ultrasound
thorax NEC 88.73
total body 88.79
urinary system 88.75
uterus 88.79
gravid 88.78

Ultrasound
diagnostic — see Ultrasonography
fragmentation (of)
cataract (with aspiration) 13.41
urinary calculus, stones (Kock pouch) 59.95
heart 88.72
intracardiac (heart chambers) (ICE) 37.28
intravascular (coronary vessels) (IVUS) 00.24
non-invasive 88.72
inner ear 20.79
intravascular (IVUS) 00.29
aorta 00.22
aortic arch 00.22
cerebral vessel, extracranial 00.21
coronary vessel 00.24
intrathoracic vessel 00.22
other specified vessel 00.28
peripheral vessel 00.23
renal vessel 00.25
vena cava (inferior) (superior) 00.22
therapeutic
head 00.01
heart 00.02
neck 00.01
other therapeutic ultrasound 00.09
peripheral vascular vessels 00.03
vessels of head and neck 00.01
therapy 93.35

Umbilectomy 54.3

Unbridling
blood vessel, peripheral 39.91
celiac artery axis 39.91

Uncovering — see Incision, by site

Undercutting
hair follicle 86.09
perianal tissue 49.02

Unroofing — see also Incision, by site
external
auditory canal 18.02
ear NEC 18.09
kidney cyst 55.39

UPP (urethral pressure profile) 89.25

Upper GI series (x-ray) 87.62

UPPP (uvulopalatopharyngoplasty) 27.69 *[29.4]*

Uranoplasty (for cleft palate repair) 27.62

Uranorrhaphy (for cleft palate repair) 27.62

Uranostaphylorrhaphy 27.62

Urban operation (mastectomy) (unilateral) 85.47
bilateral 85.48

Ureterectomy 56.40
with nephrectomy 55.51
partial 56.41
total 56.42

Ureterocecostomy 56.71

Ureterocelectomy 56.41

Ureterocolostomy 56.71

Ureterocystostomy 56.74

Ureteroenterostomy 56.71

Ureteroileostomy (internal diversion) 56.71
external diversion 56.51

Ureterolithotomy 56.2

Ureterolysis 59.02
with freeing or repositioning of ureter 59.02
laparoscopic 59.03

Ureteroneocystostomy 56.74

Ureteropexy 56.85

Ureteroplasty 56.89

Ureteroplication 56.89

Ureteroproctostomy 56.71

Ureteropyelography (intravenous) (diuretic infusion) 87.73
percutaneous 87.75
retrograde 87.74

Ureteropyeloplasty 55.87

Ureteropyelostomy 55.86

Ureterorrhaphy 56.82

Ureteroscopy 56.31
with biopsy 56.33

Ureterosigmoidostomy 56.71

Ureterostomy (cutaneous) (external) (tube) 56.61
closure 56.83
ileal 56.51

Ureterotomy 56.2

Ureteroureterostomy (crossed) 56.75
lumbar 56.41
resection with end-to-end anastomosis 56.41
spatulated 56.41

Urethral catheterization, indwelling 57.94

Urethral pressure profile (UPP) 89.25

Urethrectomy (complete) (partial) (radical) 58.39
with
complete cystectomy 57.79
pelvic exenteration 68.8
radical cystectomy 57.71

Urethrocystography (retrograde) (voiding) 87.76

Urethrocystopexy (by) 59.79
levator muscle sling 59.71
retropubic suspension 59.5
suprapubic suspension 59.4

Urethrolithotomy 58.0

Urethrolysis 58.5

Urethropexy 58.49
anterior 59.79

Urethroplasty 58.49
augmentation 59.79
collagen implant 59.72
fat implant 59.72
injection (endoscopic) of implant into urethra 59.72
polytef implant 59.72

Urethrorrhaphy 58.41

Urethroscopy 58.22
for control of hemorrhage of prostate 60.94
perineal 58.21

Urethrostomy (perineal) 58.0

Urethrotomy (external) 58.0
internal (endoscopic) 58.5

Uroflowmetry (UFR) 89.24

Urography (antegrade) (excretory) (intravenous) 87.73
retrograde 87.74

Uteropexy (abdominal approach) (vaginal approach) 69.22

UVP (uvulopalatopharyngoplasty) 27.69 *[29.4]*

Uvulectomy 27.72

Uvulopalatopharyngoplasty (UPPP) 27.69 *[29.4]*

Uvulotomy 27.71

V

Vaccination (prophylactic) (against) 99.59
anthrax 99.55
brucellosis 99.55
cholera 99.31
common cold 99.51
disease NEC 99.55
arthropod-borne viral NEC 99.54
encephalitis, arthropod-borne viral 99.53
German measles 99.47

Vaccination — continued
hydrophobia 99.44
infectious parotitis 99.46
influenza 99.52
measles 99.45
mumps 99.46
paratyphoid fever 99.32
pertussis 99.37
plague 99.34
poliomyelitis 99.41
rabies 99.44
Rocky Mountain spotted fever 99.55
rubella 99.47
rubeola 99.45
smallpox 99.42
Staphylococcus 99.55
Streptococcus 99.55
tuberculosis 99.33
tularemia 99.35
tumor 99.28
typhoid 99.32
typhus 99.55
undulant fever 99.55
yellow fever 99.43

Vacuum extraction, fetal head 72.79
with episiotomy 72.71

VAD (vascular access device) — see Implant, heart assist system

Vagectomy (subdiaphragmatic) (see also Vagotomy) 44.00

Vaginal douche 96.44

Vaginectomy 70.4

Vaginofixation 70.77

Vaginoperineotomy 70.14

Vaginoplasty 70.79

Vaginorrhaphy 70.71
obstetrical 75.69

Vaginoscopy 70.21

Vaginotomy 70.14
for
culdocentesis 70.0
pelvic abscess 70.12

Vagotomy (gastric) 44.00
parietal cell 44.02
selective NEC 44.03
highly 44.02
Holle's 44.02
proximal 44.02
truncal 44.01

Valvotomy — see Valvulotomy

Valvulectomy, heart — see Valvuloplasty, heart

Valvuloplasty
heart (open heart technique) (without valve replacement) 35.10
with prosthesis or tissue graft — see Replacement, heart, valve, by site
aortic valve 35.11
percutaneous (balloon) 35.96
combined with repair of atrial and ventricular septal defects — see Repair, endocardial cushion defect
mitral valve 35.12
percutaneous (balloon) 35.96
pulmonary valve 35.13
in total repair of tetralogy of Fallot 35.81
percutaneous (balloon) 35.96
tricuspid valve 35.14

Valvulotomy
heart (closed heart technique) (transatrial) (transventricular) 35.00
aortic valve 35.01
mitral valve 35.02
open heart technique — see Valvuloplasty, heart
pulmonary valve 35.03
in total repair of tetralogy of Fallot 35.81
tricuspid valve 35.04

Varicocelectomy, spermatic cord 63.1

Varicotomy, peripheral vessels (lower limb) 38.59
upper limb 38.53

Vascular closure, percutaneous puncture — *omit code*

Vascularization — see Revascularization

Vasectomy (complete) (partial) 63.73

2006 ICD-9-CM

☑ Additional Digit Required — Refer to the Tabular List (Numeric Code Section) for Additional Digit Selection
►◄ Revised Text   ● New Line   ▲ Revised Code

Volume 3 — 81

Vasogram 87.94
Vasoligation 63.71
   gastric 38.86
Vasorrhaphy 63.81
Vasostomy 63.6
Vasotomy 63.6
Vasotripsy 63.71
Vasovasostomy 63.82
Vectorcardiogram (VCG) (with ECG) 89.53
Venectomy — see Phlebectomy
Venipuncture NEC 38.99
   for injection of contrast material — see
     Phlebography
Venography — see Phlebography
Venorrhaphy 39.32
Venotomy 38.00
   abdominal 38.07
   head and neck NEC 38.02
   intracranial NEC 38.01
   lower limb 38.09
   thoracic NEC 38.05
   upper limb 38.03
Venotripsy 39.98
Venovenostomy 39.29
Ventilation
   bi-level airway pressure 93.90
   continuous positive airway pressure [CPAP]
     93.90
   endotracheal respiratory assistance — see
     category 96.7 ☑
   intermittent mandatory ventilation [IMV] — see
     category 96.7 ☑
   intermittent positive pressure breathing [IPPB]
     93.91
   mechanical
     endotracheal respiratory assistance — see
       category 96.7 ☑
     intermittent mandatory ventilation [IMV] —
       see category 96.7 ☑
     other continuous (unspecified duration)
       96.70
       for less than 96 consecutive hours 96.71
       for 96 consecutive hours or more 96.72
     positive and expiratory pressure [PEEP] —
       see category 96.7 ☑
     pressure support ventilation [PSV] —see
       category 96.7 ☑
   negative pressure (continuous) [CNP] 93.99
   non-invasive positive pressure (NIPPV) 93.90
Ventriculectomy, heart
   partial 37.35
Ventriculocholecystostomy 02.34
Ventriculocisternostomy 02.2
Ventriculocordectomy 30.29
Ventriculogram, ventriculography (cerebral) 87.02
   cardiac
     left ventricle (outflow tract) 88.53
       combined with right heart 88.54
     right ventricle (outflow tract) 88.52
       combined with left heart 88.54
     radionuclide cardiac 92.05
Ventriculomyocardiotomy 37.11
Ventriculoperitoneostomy 02.34
Ventriculopuncture 01.09
   through previously implanted catheter or
     reservoir (Ommaya) (Rickham) 01.02
Ventriculoseptopexy (see also Repair, ventricular
   septal defect) 35.72
Ventriculoseptoplasty (see also Repair,
   ventricular septal defect) 35.72
Ventriculostomy 02.2
Ventriculotomy
   cerebral 02.2
   heart 37.11
Ventriculoureterostomy 02.35
Ventriculovenostomy 02.32
Ventrofixation, uterus 69.22
Ventrohysteropexy 69.22
Ventrosuspension, uterus 69.22
VEP (visual evoked potential) 95.23

Version, obstetrical (bimanual) (cephalic)
   (combined) (internal) (podalic) 73.21
   with extraction 73.22
   Braxton Hicks 73.21
     with extraction 73.22
   external (bipolar) 73.91
   Potter's (podalic) 73.21
     with extraction 73.22
   Wigand's (external) 73.91
   Wright's (cephalic) 73.21
     with extraction 73.22
Vertebroplasty (percutaneous) 81.65
Vesicolithotomy (suprapubic) 57.19
Vesicostomy 57.21
Vesicourethroplasty 57.85
Vesiculectomy 60.73
   with radical prostatectomy 60.5
Vesiculogram, seminal 87.92
   contrast 87.91
Vesiculotomy 60.72
Vestibuloplasty (buccolabial) (lingual) 24.91
Vestibulotomy 20.79
Vicq D'azyr operation (larynx) 31.1
Vidal operation (varicocele ligation) 63.1
Vidianectomy 05.21
Villusectomy (see also Synovectomy) 80.70
Vision check 95.09
Visual evoked potential (VEP) 95.23
Vitrectomy (mechanical) (posterior approach) 14.74
   with scleral buckling 14.49
   anterior approach 14.73
Vocational
   assessment 93.85
   retraining 93.85
   schooling 93.82
Voice training (postlaryngectomy) 93.73
von Kraske operation (proctectomy) 48.64
Voss operation (hanging hip operation) 83.19
Vulpius (-Compere) operation (lengthening of
   gastrocnemius muscle) 83.85
Vulvectomy (bilateral) (simple) 71.62
   partial (unilateral) 71.61
   radical (complete) 71.5
   unilateral 71.61
V-Y operation (repair)
   bladder 57.89
     neck 57.85
   ectropion 08.44
   lip 27.59
   skin (without graft) 86.89
   subcutaneous tissue (without skin graft) 86.89
   tongue 25.59

W

Wada test (hemispheric function) 89.10
Ward-Mayo operation (vaginal hysterectomy)
   68.59
   laparoscopically assisted (LAVH) 68.51
Washing — see Lavage and Irrigation
Waterston operation (aorta-right pulmonary
   artery anastomosis) 39.0
Watkins (-Wertheim) operation (uterus
   interposition) 69.21
Watson-Jones operation
   hip arthrodesis 81.21
   reconstruction of lateral ligaments, ankle 81.49
   shoulder arthrodesis (extra-articular) 81.23
   tenoplasty 83.88
Webbing (syndactylization) 86.89
Weir operation
   appendicostomy 47.91
   correction of nostrils 21.86
Wertheim operation (radical hysterectomy) 68.6
West operation (dacryocystorhinostomy) 09.81
Wheeler operation
   entropion repair 08.44
   halving procedure (eyelid) 08.24
Whipple operation (radical
   pancreaticoduodenectomy) 52.7

Whipple operation — continued
   Child modification (radical subtotal
     pancreatectomy) 52.53
   Rodney Smith modification (radical subtotal
     pancreatectomy) 52.53
White operation (lengthening of tendo calcaneus
   by incomplete tenotomy) 83.11
Whitehead operation
   glossectomy, radical 25.4
   hemorrhoidectomy 49.46
Whitman operation
   foot stabilization (talectomy) 77.98
   hip reconstruction 81.40
   repair of serratus anterior muscle 83.87
   talectomy 77.98
   trochanter wedge osteotomy 77.25
Wier operation (entropion repair) 08.44
Williams-Richardson operation (vaginal
   construction) 70.61
Wilms operation (thoracoplasty) 33.34
Wilson operation (angulation osteotomy for
   hallux valgus) 77.51
Window operation
   antrum (nasal sinus) — see Antrotomy,
     maxillary
   aorticopulmonary 39.59
   bone cortex (see also Incision, bone) 77.10
     facial 76.09
   nasoantral — see Antrotomy, maxillary
   pericardium 37.12
   pleura 34.09
Winiwarter operation (cholecystoenterostomy)
   51.32
Wiring
   aneurysm 39.52
   dental (for immobilization) 93.55
     with fracture-reduction — see Reduction,
       fracture
     orthodontic 24.7
Wirsungojejunostomy 52.96
Witzel operation (temporary gastrostomy) 43.19
Woodward operation (release of high riding
   scapula) 81.83
Wrapping, aneurysm (gauze) (methyl
   methacrylate) (plastic) 39.52

X

Xenograft 86.65
Xerography, breast 87.36
Xeromammography 87.36
Xiphoidectomy 77.81
X-ray
   chest (routine) 87.44
     wall NEC 87.39
   contrast — see Radiography, contrast
   diagnostic — see Radiography
   injection of radio-opaque substance — see
     Radiography, contrast
   skeletal series, whole or complete 88.31
   therapeutic — see Therapy, radiation

Y

Young operation
   epispadias repair 58.45
   tendon transfer (anterior tibialis) (repair of flat
     foot) 83.75
Yount operation (division of iliotibial band) 83.14

Z

Zancolli operation
   capsuloplasty 81.72
   tendon transfer (biceps) 82.56
Ziegler operation (iridectomy) 12.14
Zonulolysis (with lens extraction) (see also
   Extraction, cataract, intracapsular) 13.19
Z-plasty
   epicanthus 08.59
   eyelid (see also Reconstruction, eyelid) 08.70
   hypopharynx 29.4
   skin (scar) (web contracture) 86.84
     with excision of lesion 86.3

☑ Additional Digit Required — Refer to the Tabular List (Numeric Code Section) for Additional Digit Selection

00. PROCEDURES AND INTERVENTIONS, NOT ELSEWHERE CLASSIFIED (00)

√3rd **00   Procedures and interventions, not elsewhere classified**

√4th **00.0   Therapeutic ultrasound**

> EXCLUDES   *diagnostic ultrasound (non-invasive) (88.71-88.79)*
> *intracardiac echocardiography [ICE] (heart chamber(s)) (37.28)*
> *intravascular imaging (adjunctive) (00.21-00.29)*

AHA: 4Q, '02, 90

DEF: Interventional treatment modality using lower frequency and higher intensity levels of ultrasound energy than used in diagnostic ultrasound modality for the purpose of limiting intimal hyperpalsia, or restenosis, associated with atherosclerotic vascular disease.

00.01   Therapeutic ultrasound of vessels of head and neck

Anti-restenotic ultrasound
Intravascular non-ablative ultrasound

> EXCLUDES   *diagnostic ultrasound of:*
> *eye (95.13)*
> *head and neck (88.71)*
> *that of inner ear (20.79)*
> *ultrasonic:*
> *angioplasty of non-coronary vessel (39.50)*
> *embolectomy (38.01, 38.02)*
> *endarterectomy (38.11, 38.12)*
> *thrombectomy (38.01, 38.02)*

00.02   Therapeutic ultrasound of heart

Anti-restenotic ultrasound
Intravascular non-ablative ultrasound

> EXCLUDES   *diagnostic ultrasound of heart (88.72)*
> *ultrasonic ablation of heart lesion (37.34)*
> *ultrasonic angioplasty of coronary vessels ▶(00.66, 36.09)◀*

00.03   Therapeutic ultrasound of peripheral vascular vessels

Anti-restenotic ultrasound
Intravascular non-ablative ultrasound

> EXCLUDES   *diagnostic ultrasound of peripheral vascular system (88.77)*
> *ultrasonic angioplasty of: non-coronary vessel (39.50)*

00.09   Other therapeutic ultrasound

> EXCLUDES   *ultrasonic:*
> *fragmentation of urinary stones (59.95)*
> *percutaneous nephrostomy with fragmentation (55.04)*
> *physical therapy (93.35)*
> *transurethral guided laser induced prostatectomy (TULIP) (60.21)*

√4th **00.1   Pharmaceuticals**

00.10   Implantation of chemotherapeutic agent

Brain wafer chemotherapy
Interstitial/intracavitary

> EXCLUDES   *injection or infusion of cancer chemotherapeutic substance (99.25)*

AHA: 4Q, '02, 93

DEF: Brain wafer chemotherapy: Placement of wafers containing antineoplastic agent against the wall of the resection cavity subsequent to the surgeon completing a tumor excision to deliver chemotherapy directly to the tumor site; used to treat glioblastoma multiforme (GBM).

00.11   Infusion of drotrecogin alfa (activated)

Infusion of recombinant protein

AHA: 4Q, '02, 93

00.12   Administration of inhaled nitric oxide

Nitric oxide therapy

AHA: 4Q, '02, 94

00.13   Injection or infusion of nesiritide

Human B-type natriuretic peptide (hBNP)

AHA: 4Q, '02, 94

00.14   Injection or infusion of oxazolidinone class of antibiotics

Linezolid injection

AHA: 4Q, '02, 95

00.15   High-dose infusion interleukin-2 [IL-2]

Infusion (IV bolus, CIV) interleukin
Injection of aldesleukin

> EXCLUDES   *low-dose infusion interleukin-2 (99.28)*

AHA: 4Q, '03, 92

DEF: A high-dose anti-neoplastic therapy using a biological response modifier (BRM); the body naturally produces substances called interleukins, which are multifunction cytokines in the generation of an immune response.

00.16   Pressurized treatment of venous bypass Adj **graft [conduit] with pharmaceutical substance**

Ex-vivo treatment of vessel
Hyperbaric pressurized graft [conduit]

DEF: Ex-vivo process of delivering small nucleic acid molecules that block protein transcription factors essential for the expression of genes controlling cell proliferation into graft tissue under nondistending pressure; reduces intimal hyperplasia and vein graft failure.

00.17   Infusion of vasopressor agent

00.18   Infusion of immunosuppressive antibody therapy during induction phase of solid organ transplantation

Monoclonal antibody therapy
Polyclonal antibody therapy

√3rd
√4th Additional Digit Required   RUG III Special Care Procedure   RUG III Clinically Complex Procedure   RUG III Extensive Services Procedure   RUG III Rehab Procedure

2006 ICD•9•CM   October 2005 • Volume 3 — 83

√4ᵗʰ **00.2** **Intravascular imaging of blood vessels**
▶Note: Real-time imaging of lumen of blood vessel(s)
  using sound waves◀
Endovascular ultrasonography
▶Intravascular [ultrasound] imaging of blood vessels◀
Intravascular ultrasound (IVUS)
Code also any synchronous diagnostic or therapeutic
  procedures
  EXCLUDES ▶ *adjunct vascular system procedures,*
    number of vessels treated (00.40-
    00.43)
    diagnostic procedures on blood vessels
    (38.21-38.29)
    diagnostic ultrasound of peripheral
    vascular system (88.77)
    magnetic resonance imaging (MRI)
    (88.91-88.97)◀
    therapeutic ultrasound (00.01-00.09)

00.21 **Intravascular imaging of extracranial**
  cerebral vessels
  Common carotid vessels and branches
  Intravascular ultrasound (IVUS),
    extracranial cerebral vessels
    EXCLUDES *diagnostic ultrasound (non-*
      invasive) of head and
      neck (88.71)

00.22 **Intravascular imaging of intrathoracic**
  vessels
  Aorta and aortic arch
  Intravascular ultrasound (IVUS),
    intrathoracic vessels
  Vena cava (superior) (inferior)
    EXCLUDES *diagnostic ultrasound (non-*
      invasive) of other sites of
      thorax (88.73)

00.23 **Intravascular imaging of peripheral vessels**
  Imaging of:
    vessels of arm(s)
    vessels of leg(s)
  Intravascular ultrasound (IVUS), peripheral
    vessels
    EXCLUDES *diagnostic ultrasound (non-*
      invasive) of peripheral
      vascular system (88.77)

00.24 **Intravascular imaging of coronary vessels**
  Intravascular ultrasound (IVUS), coronary
    vessels
    EXCLUDES *diagnostic ultrasound (non-*
      invasive) of heart (88.72)
      intracardiac echocardiography
      [ICE] (ultrasound of heart
      chamber(s)) (37.28)

00.25 **Intravascular imaging of renal vessels**
  Intravascular ultrasound (IVUS), renal
    vessels
  Renal artery
    EXCLUDES *diagnostic ultrasound (non-*
      invasive) of urinary
      system (88.75)

00.28 **Intravascular imaging, other specified**
  vessel(s)

00.29 **Intravascular imaging, unspecified vessel(s)**

√4ᵗʰ **00.3** **Computer assisted surgery [CAS]**
  CT-free navigation
  Image guided navigation (IGN)
  Image guided surgery (IGS)
  Imageless navigation
  Code also diagnostic or therapeutic procedure
    EXCLUDES *stereotactic frame application only*
      (93.59)

00.31 **Computer assisted surgery with** `Adj`
  CT/CTA
  AHA: 4Q, '04, 113

00.32 **Computer assisted surgery with** `Adj`
  MR/MRA
  AHA: 4Q, '04, 113

00.33 **Computer assisted surgery with** `Adj`
  fluoroscopy

00.34 **Imageless computer assisted surgery** `Adj`

00.35 **Computer assisted surgery with** `Adj`
  multiple datasets

00.39 **Other computer assisted surgery** `Adj`
  Computer assisted surgery NOS

● √4ᵗʰ **00.4** **Adjunct vascular system procedures**
  Note: These codes can apply to both coronary and
    peripheral vessels. These codes are to be used
    in conjunction with other therapeutic
    procedure codes to provide additional
    information on the number of vessels upon
    which a procedure was performed and/or the
    number of stents inserted. As appropriate,
    code both the number of vessels operated on
    (00.40-00.43), and the number of stents
    inserted (00.45-00.48).
  Code also any:
    angioplasty or atherectomy (00.61-00.62, 00.66,
      39.50)
    endarterectomy (38.10-38.18)
    insertion of vascular stent(s) (00.55, 00.63-00.65,
      36.06-36.07, 39.90)
    other removal of coronary artery obstruction
      (36.09)

● **00.40** **Procedure on single vessel** `Adj`
  Number of vessels, unspecified
    EXCLUDES *(aorto)coronary bypass (36.10-*
      36.19)
      intravascular imaging of blood
      vessels (00.21-00.29)

● **00.41** **Procedure on two vessels** `Adj`
    EXCLUDES *(aorto)coronary bypass (36.10-*
      36.19)
      intravascular imaging of blood
      vessels (00.21-00.29)

● **00.42** **Procedure on three vessels** `Adj`
    EXCLUDES *(aorto)coronary bypass (36.10-*
      36.19)
      intravascular imaging of blood
      vessels (00.21-00.29)

● **00.43** **Procedure on four or more vessels** `Adj`
    EXCLUDES *(aorto)coronary bypass (36.10-*
      36.19)
      intravascular imaging of blood
      vessels (00.21-00.29)

● **00.45** **Insertion of one vascular stent** `Adj`
  Number of stents, unspecified

● **00.46** **Insertion of two vascular stents** `Adj`

● **00.47** **Insertion of three vascular stents** `Adj`

● **00.48** **Insertion of four or more vascular** `Adj`
  stents

N Newborn Age: 0 P Pediatric Age: 0-17 M Maternity Age: 12-55 A Adult Age: 15-124 `Adj` Adjunct Code ▶◀ Revised Text ● New Code ▲ Revised Code Title

84 — Volume 3 • October 2005 *2006 ICD•9•CM*

✓4ᵗʰ **00.5**   **Other cardiovascular procedures**
AHA: 4Q, '02, 95

00.50   **Implantation of cardiac resynchronization pacemaker without mention of defibrillation, total system [CRT-P]**
Biventricular pacing without internal cardiac defibrillator
Implantation of cardiac resynchronization (biventricular) pulse generator pacing device, formation of pocket, transvenous leads including placement of lead into left ventricular coronary venous system, and intraoperative procedures for evaluation of lead signals
▶That with CRT-P generator and one or more leads◀

EXCLUDES   *implantation of cardiac resynchronization defibrillator, total system [CRT-D] (00.51)*
insertion or replacement of any type pacemaker device (37.80-37.87)
replacement of cardiac resynchronization: defibrillator, pulse generator only [CRT-D] (00.54) pacemaker, pulse generator only [CRT-P] (00.53)

AHA: 4Q, '02, 100

DEF: Cardiac resynchronization pacemaker: CRT-P, or bi-ventricular pacing, adds a third lead to traditional pacemaker designs that connects to the left ventricle. The device provides electrical stimulation to the right atrium, right ventricle, and left ventricle, and coordinates ventricular contractions to improve cardiac output.

00.51   **Implantation of cardiac resynchronization defibrillator, total system [CRT-D]**
Biventricular pacing with internal cardiac defibrillator
Implantation of cardiac resynchronization (biventricular) pulse generator with defibrillator [AICD], formation of pocket, transvenous leads, including placement of lead into left ventricular coronary venous system, intraoperative procedures for evaluation of lead signals, and obtaining defibrillator threshold measurements
▶That with CRT-D generator and one or more leads◀

EXCLUDES   *implantation of cardiac resynchronization pacemaker, total system [CRT-P] (00.50)*
implantation or replacement of automatic cardioverter/ defibrillator, total system [AICD] (37.94)
replacement of cardiac resynchronization defibrillator, pulse generator only [CRT-D] (00.54)

AHA: 4Q, '02, 99, 100

00.52   **Implantation or replacement of transvenous lead [electrode] into left ventricular coronary venous system**

EXCLUDES   *implantation of cardiac resynchronization: defibrillator, total system [CRT-D] (00.51) pacemaker, total system [CRT-P] (00.50)*
initial insertion of transvenous lead [electrode] (37.70-37.72)
replacement of transvenous atrial and/or ventricular lead(s) [electrodes] (37.76)

00.53   **Implantation or replacement of cardiac resynchronization pacemaker, pulse generator only [CRT-P]**
Implantation of CRT-P device with removal of any existing CRT-P or other pacemaker device

EXCLUDES   *implantation of cardiac resynchronization pacemaker, total system [CRT-P] (00.50)*
implantation or replacement of cardiac resynchron-ization defibrillator, pulse generator only [CRT-D] (00.54)
insertion or replacement of any type pacemaker device (37.80-37.87)

00.54   **Implantation or replacement of cardiac resynchronization defibrillator, pulse generator device only [CRT-D]**
Implantation of CRT-D device with removal of any existing CRT-D, CRT-P, pacemaker, or defibrillator device

EXCLUDES   *implantation of automatic cardioverter/defibrillator pulse generator only (37.96)*
implantation of cardiac resynchronization defibrillator, total system [CRT-D] (00.51)
implantation or replacement of cardiac resynchronization pacemaker, pulse gener-ator only [CRT-P] (00.53)

AHA: 4Q, '02, 100

✓3ʳᵈ
✓4ᵗʰ   Additional Digit Required   RUG III Special Care Procedure   RUG III Clinically Complex Procedure   RUG III Extensive Services Procedure   RUG III Rehab Procedure

2006 ICD•9•CM   October 2005 • Volume 3 — 85

00.55 **Insertion of drug-eluting peripheral vessel stent(s)**
Endograft(s)
Endovascular graft(s)
Stent graft(s)
▶Code also any:
angioplasty or atherectomy of other non-coronary vessel(s) (39.50)
number of vascular stents inserted (00.45-00.48)
number of vessels treated (00.40-00.43)◀

> EXCLUDES   *drug-coated peripheral stents, e.g., heparin coated (39.90)*
> *insertion of cerebrovascular stent(s) (00.63-00.65)*
> *insertion of drug-eluting coronary artery stent (36.07)*
> *insertion of non-drug-eluting stent(s):*
> *coronary artery (36.06)*
> *peripheral vessel (39.90)*
> *that for aneurysm repair (39.71-39.79)*

AHA: 4Q, '02, 101

✓4ᵗʰ **00.6** **Procedures on blood vessels**

00.61 **Percutaneous angioplasty or atherectomy of precerebral (extracranial) vessel(s)**
Basilar
Carotid
Vertebral
Code also any:
injection or infusion of thrombolytic agent (99.10)
▶number of vascular stents inserted (00.45-00.48)
number of vessels treated (00.40-00.43)◀
percutaneous insertion of carotid artery stent(s) (00.63)
percutaneous insertion of other precerebral artery stent(s) (00.64)

> EXCLUDES   *angioplasty or atherectomy of other non-coronary vessel(s) (39.50)*
> *removal of cerebrovascular obstruction of vessel(s) by open approach (38.01-38.02, 38.11-38.12, 38.31-38.32, 38.41-38.42)*

00.62 **Percutaneous angioplasty or atherectomy of intracranial vessel(s)**
Code also any:
injection or infusion of thrombolytic agent (99.10)
▶number of vascular stents inserted (00.45-00.48)
number of vessels treated (00.40-00.43)◀
percutaneous insertion of intracranial stent(s) (00.65)

> EXCLUDES   *angioplasty or atherectomy of other non-coronary vessel(s) (39.50)*
> *removal of cerebrovascular obstruction of vessel(s) by open approach (38.01-38.02, 38.11-38.12, 38.31-38.32, 38.41-38.42)*

00.63 **Percutaneous insertion of carotid artery stent(s)**
Includes the use of any embolic protection device, distal protection device, filter device, or stent delivery system
Non-drug-eluting stent
▶Code also any:
number of vascular stents inserted (00.45-00.48)
number of vessels treated (00.40-00.43)
percutaneous angioplasty or atherectomy of precerebral vessel(s) (00.61)◀

> EXCLUDES ▶ *angioplasty or atherectomy of other non-coronary vessel(s) (39.50)*
> *insertion of drug-eluting peripheral vessel stent(s) (00.55)*◀

00.64 **Percutaneous insertion of other precerebral (extracranial) artery stent(s)**
Includes the use of any embolic protection device, distal protection device, filter device, or stent delivery system
Basilar stent
Vertebral stent
▶Code also any:
number of vascular stents inserted (00.45-00.48)
number of vessels treated (00.40-00.43)
percutaneous angioplasty or atherectomy of precerebral vessel(s) (00.61)◀

> EXCLUDES ▶ *angioplasty or atherectomy of other non-coronary vessel(s) (39.50)*
> *insertion of drug-eluting peripheral vessel stent(s) (00.55)*◀

00.65 **Percutaneous insertion of intracranial vascular stent(s)**
Includes the use of any embolic protection device, distal protection device, filter device, or stent delivery system
▶Code also any:
number of vascular stents inserted (00.45-00.48)
number of vessels treated (00.40-00.43)
percutaneous angioplasty or atherectomy of intracranial vessel(s) (00.62)◀

> EXCLUDES ▶ *angioplasty or atherectomy of other non-coronary vessel(s) (39.50)*
> *insertion of drug-eluting peripheral vessel stent(s) (00.55)*◀

● **00.66** **Percutaneous transluminal coronary angioplasty [PTCA] or coronary atherectomy**
Balloon angioplasty of coronary artery
Coronary atherectomy
Percutaneous coronary angioplasty NOS
PTCA NOS
Code also any:
injection or infusion of thrombolytic agent (99.10)
insertion of coronary artery stent(s) (36.06-36.07)
intracoronary artery thrombolytic infusion (36.04)
number of vascular stents inserted (00.45-00.48)
number of vessels treated (00.40-00.43)

AHA: **These references pertain to deleted PTCA codes (36.01, 36.02, 36.05):** 1Q, '04, 10; 3Q, '03, 9; 4Q, '02, 114; 3Q, '02, 19; 1Q, '01, 9; 2Q, '01, 24; 1Q, '00, 11; 1Q, '99, 17; 4Q, '98, 74, 85; 1Q, '97, 3; 1Q, '94, 3; 3Q, '91, 24

DEF: Balloon angioplasty: Insertion of catheter with inflation of balloon to flatten plaque and widen vessels.

N Newborn Age: 0   P Pediatric Age: 0-17   M Maternity Age: 12-55   A Adult Age: 15-124   Adj Adjunct Code   ▶◀ Revised Text   ● New Code   ▲ Revised Code Title

● ✓4ᵗʰ **00.7**   **Other hip procedures**

● **00.70**   **Revision of hip replacement, both acetabular and femoral components**
Total hip revision
Code also any:
removal of (cement) (joint) spacer (84.57)
type of bearing surface, if known (00.74-00.76)
EXCLUDES   *revision of hip replacement, acetabular component only (00.71)*
revision of hip replacement, femoral component only (00.72)
revision of hip replacement, not otherwise specified (81.53)
revision with replacement of acetabular liner and/or femoral head only (00.73)

● **00.71**   **Revision of hip replacement, acetabular component**
Partial, acetabular component only
That with:
exchange of acetabular cup and liner
exchange of femoral head
Code also any type of bearing surface, if known (00.74-00.76)
EXCLUDES   *revision of hip replacement, both acetabular and femoral components (00.70)*
revision of hip replacement, femoral component (00.72)
revision of hip replacement, not otherwise specified (81.53)
revision with replacement of acetabular liner and/or femoral head only (00.73)

● **00.72**   **Revision of hip replacement, femoral component**
Partial, femoral component only
That with:
exchange of acetabular liner
exchange of femoral stem and head
Code also any type of bearing surface, if known (00.74-00.76)
EXCLUDES   *revision of hip replacement, acetabular component (00.71)*
revision of hip replacement, both acetabular and femoral components (00.70)
revision of hip replacement, not otherwise specified (81.53)
revision with replacement of acetabular liner and/or femoral head only (00.73)

● **00.73**   **Revision of hip replacement, acetabular liner and/or femoral head only**
Code also any type of bearing surface, if known (00.74-00.76)

● **00.74**   **Hip replacement bearing surface, metal on polyethylene**   `Adj`

● **00.75**   **Hip replacement bearing surface, metal-on-metal**   `Adj`

● **00.76**   **Hip replacement bearing surface, ceramic-on-ceramic**   `Adj`

● ✓4ᵗʰ **00.8**   **Other knee procedures**
Note: Report up to two components using 00.81-00.83 to describe revision of knee replacements. If all three components are revised, report 00.80.

● **00.80**   **Revision of knee replacement, total (all components)**
Replacement of femoral, tibial, and patellar components (all components)
Code also any removal of (cement) (joint) spacer (84.57)
EXCLUDES   *revision of only one or two components (tibial, femoral or patellar component) (00.81-00.84)*

● **00.81**   **Revision of knee replacement, tibial component**
Replacement of tibial baseplate and tibial insert (liner)
EXCLUDES   *revision of knee replacement, total (all components) (00.80)*

● **00.82**   **Revision of knee replacement, femoral component**
That with replacement of tibial insert (liner)
EXCLUDES   *revision of knee replacement, total (all components) (00.80)*

● **00.83**   **Revision of knee replacement, patellar component**
EXCLUDES   *revision of knee replacement, total (all components) (00.80)*

● **00.84**   **Revision of total knee replacement, tibial insert (liner)**
Replacement of tibial insert (liner)
EXCLUDES   *that with replacement of tibial component (tibial baseplate and liner) (00.81)*

✓4ᵗʰ **00.9**   **Other procedures and interventions**

00.91   **Transplant from live related donor**   `Adj`
Code also organ transplant procedure

00.92   **Transplant from live non-related donor**   `Adj`
Code also organ transplant procedure
AHA: 4Q, '04, 117

00.93   **Transplant from cadaver**   `Adj`
Code also organ transplant procedure

✓3ʳᵈ **Additional Digit Required**   RUG III Special Care Procedure   RUG III Clinically Complex Procedure   RUG III Extensive Services Procedure   RUG III Rehab Procedure
✓4ᵗʰ

2006 ICD•9•CM   October 2005 • Volume 3 — 87

Operations on the Nervous System

01–01.42

1. OPERATIONS ON THE NERVOUS SYSTEM (01-05)

√3ʳᵈ **01   Incision and excision of skull, brain, and cerebral meninges**

√4ᵗʰ **01.0   Cranial puncture**

01.01   Cisternal puncture
Cisternal tap

EXCLUDES   pneumocisternogram (87.02)

DEF: Needle insertion through subarachnoid space to withdraw cerebrospinal fluid.

01.02   Ventriculopuncture through previously implanted catheter
Puncture of ventricular shunt tubing

DEF: Piercing of artificial, fluid-diverting tubing in the brain for withdrawal of cerebrospinal fluid.

01.09   Other cranial puncture
Aspiration of:
     subarac hnoid space
     subdural space
Cranial aspiration NOS
Puncture of anterior fontanel
Subdural tap (through fontanel)

√4ᵗʰ **01.1   Diagnostic procedures on skull, brain, and cerebral meninges**

01.11   Closed [percutaneous] [needle] biopsy of cerebral meninges
Burr hole approach

DEF: Needle excision of tissue sample through skin into cerebral membranes; no other procedure performed.

01.12   Open biopsy of cerebral meninges

DEF: Open surgical excision of tissue sample from cerebral membrane.

01.13   Closed [percutaneous] [needle] biopsy of brain
Burr hole approach
Stereotactic method

AHA: M-A, '87, 9

DEF: Removal by needle of brain tissue sample through skin.

01.14   Open biopsy of brain

DEF: Open surgical excision of brain tissue sample.

01.15   Biopsy of skull

01.18   Other diagnostic procedures on brain and cerebral meninges

EXCLUDES   cerebral:
     arteriography (88.41)
     thermography (88.81)
     contrast radiogram of brain
       (87.01-87.02)
     echoencephalogram (88.71)
     electroencephalogram (89.14)
     microscopic examination of
       specimen from nervous
       system and of spinal
       fluid (90.01-90.09)
     neurologic examination (89.13)
     phlebography of head and
       neck (88.61)
     pneumoencephalogram (87.01)
     radioisotope scan:
       cerebral (92.11)
       head NEC (92.12)
     tomography of head:
       C.A.T. scan (87.03)
       other (87.04)

AHA: 3Q, '98, 12

01.19   Other diagnostic procedures on skull

EXCLUDES   transillumination of skull
     (89.16)
     x-ray of skull (87.17)

√4ᵗʰ **01.2   Craniotomy and craniectomy**

EXCLUDES   decompression of skull fracture (02.02)
     exploration of orbit (16.01-16.09)
     that as operative approach — omit code

AHA: 1Q, '91, 1

DEF: Craniotomy: Incision into skull.

DEF: Craniectomy: Excision of part of skull.

01.21   Incision and drainage of cranial sinus

DEF: Incision for drainage, including drainage of air cavities in skull bones.

01.22   Removal of intracranial neurostimulator lead(s)
Code also any removal of neurostimulator pulse generator (86.05)

EXCLUDES   removal with synchronous replacement (02.93)

01.23   Reopening of craniotomy site

DEF: Reopening of skull incision.

01.24   Other craniotomy
Cranial: Craniotomy with
   decompression   removal of:
   exploration   epidural abscess
   trephination   extradural hematoma
Craniotomy NOS   foreign body of skull

EXCLUDES   removal of foreign body with incision into brain (01.39)

AHA: 2Q, '91, 14

01.25   Other craniectomy
Debridement of skull NOS
Sequestrectomy of skull

EXCLUDES   debridement of compound fracture of skull (02.02)
     strip craniectomy (02.01)

● **01.26   Insertion of catheter into cranial cavity**
Code also any concomitant procedure (e.g. resection (01.59))

● **01.27   Removal of catheter from cranial cavity**

√4ᵗʰ **01.3   Incision of brain and meninges**

01.31   Incision of cerebral meninges
Drainage of:
     intracranial hygroma
     subarachnoid abscess (cerebral)
     subdural empyema

01.32   Lobotomy and tractotomy
Division of: Percutaneous
   brain tissue   (radiofrequency)
   cerebral tracts   cingulotomy

DEF: Lobotomy: Incision of nerve fibers of brain lobe, usually frontal.

DEF: Tractotomy: Severing of a nerve fiber group to relieve pain.

01.39   Other incision of brain
Amygdalohippocampotomy
Drainage of intracerebral hematoma
Incision of brain NOS

EXCLUDES   division of cortical adhesions (02.91)

√4ᵗʰ **01.4   Operations on thalamus and globus pallidus**

01.41   Operations on thalamus
Chemothalamectomy   Thalamotomy

EXCLUDES   that by stereotactic radiosurgery (92.30-92.39)

01.42   Operations on globus pallidus
Pallidoansectomy   Pallidotomy

EXCLUDES   that by stereotactic radiosurgery (92.30-92.39)

Ⓝ Newborn Age: 0   Ⓟ Pediatric Age: 0-17   Ⓜ Maternity Age: 12-55   Ⓐ Adult Age: 15-124   **Adj** Adjunct Code   ▶◀ Revised Text   ● New Code   ▲ Revised Code Title

√4ᵗʰ **01.5 Other excision or destruction of brain and meninges**
AHA: 4Q, '93, 33

01.51 Excision of lesion or tissue of cerebral meninges
Decortication ⎫
Resection ⎬ of (cerebral)
Stripping of subdural ⎭ meninges
    membrane

EXCLUDES *biopsy of cerebral meninges (01.11-01.12)*

01.52 Hemispherectomy
DEF: Removal of one half of the brain. Most often performed for malignant brain tumors or intractable epilepsy.

01.53 Lobectomy of brain
DEF: Excision of a brain lobe.

01.59 Other excision or destruction of lesion or tissue of brain
Curettage of brain
Debridement of brain
Marsupialization of brain cyst
Transtemporal (mastoid) excision of brain tumor

EXCLUDES *biopsy of brain (01.13-01.14)*
that by stereotactic radiosurgery (92.30-92.39)

AHA: 3Q, '99, 7; 1Q, '99, 9; 3Q, '98, 12; 1Q, '98, 6

01.6 Excision of lesion of skull
Removal of granulation tissue of cranium
EXCLUDES *biopsy of skull (01.15)*
sequestrectomy (01.25)

√3ʳᵈ **02 Other operations on skull, brain, and cerebral meninges**

√4ᵗʰ **02.0 Cranioplasty**
EXCLUDES *that with synchronous repair of encephalocele (02.12)*

02.01 Opening of cranial suture
Linear craniectomy
Strip craniectomy
DEF: Opening of the lines of junction between the bones of the skull for removal of strips of skull bone.

02.02 Elevation of skull fracture fragments
Debridement of compound fracture of skull
Decompression of skull fracture
Reduction of skull fracture
Code also any synchronous debridement of brain (01.59)
EXCLUDES *debridement of skull NOS (01.25)*
removal of granulation tissue of cranium (01.6)

02.03 Formation of cranial bone flap
Repair of skull with flap

02.04 Bone graft to skull
Pericranial graft (autogenous) (heterogenous)

02.05 Insertion of skull plate
Replacement of skull plate

02.06 Other cranial osteoplasty
Repair of skull NOS
Revision of bone flap of skull
AHA: ▶1Q, '05, 11;◀ 3Q, '98, 9

DEF: Plastic surgery repair of skull bones.

02.07 Removal of skull plate
EXCLUDES *removal with synchronous replacement (02.05)*

√4ᵗʰ **02.1 Repair of cerebral meninges**
EXCLUDES *marsupialization of cerebral lesion (01.59)*

02.11 Simple suture of dura mater of brain

02.12 Other repair of cerebral meninges
Closure of fistula of cerebrospinal fluid
Dural graft
Repair of encephalocele including synchronous cranioplasty
Repair of meninges NOS
Subdural patch

02.13 Ligation of meningeal vessel
Ligation of:
longitudinal sinus
middle meningeal artery

02.14 Choroid plexectomy
Cauterization of choroid plexus
DEF: Excision or destruction of the ependymal cells that form the membrane lining in the third, fourth, and lateral ventricles of the brain and secrete cerebrospinal fluid.

02.2 Ventriculostomy
Anastomosis of ventricle to:
cervical subarachnoid space
cisterna magna
Insertion of Holter valve
Ventriculocisternal intubation
DEF: Surgical creation of an opening of ventricle; often performed to drain cerebrospinal fluid in treating hydrocephalus.

√4ᵗʰ **02.3 Extracranial ventricular shunt**
INCLUDES that with insertion of valve
DEF: Placement of shunt or creation of artificial passage leading from skull cavities to site outside skull to relieve excess cerebrospinal fluid created in the chorioid plexuses of the third and fourth ventricles of the brain.

02.31 Ventricular shunt to structure in head and neck
Ventricle to nasopharynx shunt
Ventriculomastoid anastomosis

02.32 Ventricular shunt to circulatory system
Ventriculoatrial anastomosis
Ventriculocaval shunt

02.33 Ventricular shunt to thoracic cavity
Ventriculopleural anastomosis

02.34 Ventricular shunt to abdominal cavity and organs
Ventriculocholecystostomy
Ventriculoperitoneostomy

02.35 Ventricular shunt to urinary system
Ventricle to ureter shunt

02.39 Other operations to establish drainage of ventricle
Ventricle to bone marrow shunt
Ventricular shunt to extracranial site NEC

√4ᵗʰ **02.4 Revision, removal, and irrigation of ventricular shunt**
EXCLUDES *revision of distal catheter of ventricular shunt (54.95)*

02.41 Irrigation and exploration of ventricular shunt
Exploration of ventriculoperitoneal shunt at ventricular site
Re-programming of ventriculoperitoneal shuntx

02.42 Replacement of ventricular shunt
Reinsertion of Holter valve
Replacement of ventricular catheter
Revision of ventriculoperitoneal shunt at ventricular site
AHA: N-D, '86, 8

02.43 Removal of ventricular shunt
AHA: N-D, '86, 8

√3ʳᵈ / √4ᵗʰ Additional Digit Required   RUG III Special Care Procedure   RUG III Clinically Complex Procedure   RUG III Extensive Services Procedure   RUG III Rehab Procedure

2006 ICD•9•CM   **October 2005 • Volume 3 — 89**

Operations on the Nervous System

02.9–03.29

√4th **02.9**   **Other operations on skull, brain, and cerebral meninges**

EXCLUDES   *operations on:*
pineal gland (07.17, 07.51-07.59)
pituitary gland [hypophysis] (07.13-07.15, 07.61-07.79)

02.91   **Lysis of cortical adhesions**

DEF: Breaking up of fibrous structures in brain outer layer.

02.92   **Repair of brain**

02.93   **Implantation or replacement of intracranial neurostimulator lead(s)**

Implantation, insertion, placement, or replacement of intracranial:
brain pacemaker [neuropacemaker]
depth electrodes
epidural pegs
electroencephalographic receiver
foramen ovale electrodes
intracranial electrostimulator
subdural grids
subdural strips
Code also any insertion of neurostimulator pulse generator (86.94-86.96)

AHA: 4Q, '97, 57; 4Q, '92, 28

02.94   **Insertion or replacement of skull tongs or halo traction device**

AHA: 3Q, '01, 8; 3Q, '96, 14

DEF: Halo traction device: Metal or plastic band encircles the head or neck secured to the skull with four pins and attached to a metal chest plate by rods; provides support and stability for the head and neck.

DEF: Skull tongs: Device inserted into each side of the skull used to apply parallel traction to the long axis of the cervical spine.

02.95   **Removal of skull tongs or halo traction device**

02.96   **Insertion of sphenoidal electrodes**

AHA: 4Q, '92, 28

02.99   **Other**

EXCLUDES   *chemical shock therapy (94.24)*
electroshock therapy:
subconvulsive (94.26)
other (94.27)

√3rd **03**   **Operations on spinal cord and spinal canal structures**

Code also any application or administration of an adhesion barrier substance (99.77)

√4th **03.0**   **Exploration and decompression of spinal canal structures**

03.01   **Removal of foreign body from spinal canal**

03.02   **Reopening of laminectomy site**

Laminotomy with Decompression

Spinal nerve — Herniated disk — Spinal cord — Lamina

Laminotomy decompresses spinal nerve

03.09   **Other exploration and decompression of spinal canal**

Decompression:
laminectomy
laminotomy
Expansile laminoplasty
Exploration of spinal nerve root
Foraminotomy

EXCLUDES   *drainage of spinal fluid by anastomosis (03.71-03.79)*
laminectomy with excision of intervertebral disc (80.51)
spinal tap (03.31)
that as operative approach — omit code

AHA: ▶3Q, '04, 6;◀ 4Q, '02, 109; 2Q, '02, 15; 4Q, '99, 14; 2Q, '97, 6; 2Q, '95, 9; 2Q, '95, 10; 2Q, '90, 22; S-Q, '86, 12

DEF: Decompression of spinal canal: Excision of bone pieces, hematoma or other lesion to relieve spinal cord pressure.
DEF: Expansile laminoplasty: Lamina is incised at the level of the pedicle to relieve pressure; no tissue is excised.
DEF: Foraminotomy: Removal of root opening between vertebrae to relieve nerve root pressure.

03.1   **Division of intraspinal nerve root**

Rhizotomy

DEF: Rhizotomy: Surgical severing of spinal nerve roots within spinal canal for pain relief.

√4th **03.2**   **Chordotomy**

DEF: Chordotomy: Surgical cutting of lateral spinothalamic tract of spinal cord to relieve pain.

03.21   **Percutaneous chordotomy**

Stereotactic chordotomy

DEF: Percutaneous chordotomy: Insertion of hollow needle through skin to interrupt spinal nerve root.

DEF: Stereotactic chordotomy: Use of three-dimensional imaging to locate spinal nerve root for surgical interruption.

03.29   **Other chordotomy**

Chordotomy NOS
Tractotomy (one-stage) (two-stage) of spinal cord
Transection of spinal cord tracts

DEF: Tractotomy (one stage) (two stages) of the spinal cord: Surgical incision or severing of a nerve tract of spinal cord.
DEF: Transection of spinal cord tracts: Use of transverse incision to divide spinal nerve root.

N Newborn Age: 0   P Pediatric Age: 0-17   M Maternity Age: 12-55   A Adult Age: 15-124   Adj Adjunct Code   ►◄ Revised Text   ● New Code   ▲ Revised Code Title

Operations on the Nervous System

03.3–04.02

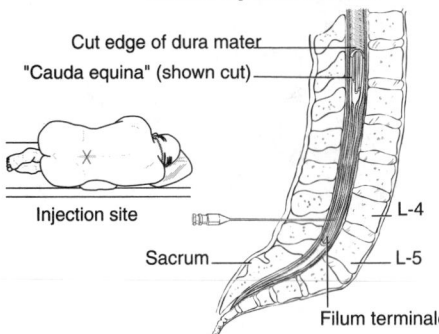

Lumbar Spinal Puncture

Cut edge of dura mater

"Cauda equina" (shown cut)

Injection site

Sacrum

L-4

L-5

Filum terminale

☑4th **03.3**   **Diagnostic procedures on spinal cord and spinal canal structures**

03.31   **Spinal tap**

Lumbar puncture for removal of dye

`EXCLUDES`   *lumbar puncture for injection of dye [myelogram] (87.21)*

AHA: 2Q, '90, 22

DEF: Puncture into lumbar subarachnoid space to tap cerebrospinal fluid.

03.32   **Biopsy of spinal cord or spinal meninges**

03.39   **Other diagnostic procedures on spinal cord and spinal canal structures**

`EXCLUDES`   *microscopic examination of specimen from nervous system or of spinal fluid (90.01-90.09)*
x-ray of spine (87.21-87.29)

03.4   **Excision or destruction of lesion of spinal cord or spinal meninges**

Curettage
Debridement
Marsupialization of cyst } of spinal cord or spinal meninges
Resection

`EXCLUDES`   *biopsy of spinal cord or meninges (03.32)*

AHA: 3Q, '95, 5

☑4th **03.5**   **Plastic operations on spinal cord structures**

03.51   **Repair of spinal meningocele**

Repair of meningocele NOS

DEF: Restoration of hernial protrusion of spinal meninges through defect in vertebral column.

03.52   **Repair of spinal myelomeningocele**

DEF: Restoration of hernial protrusion of spinal cord and meninges through defect in vertebral column.

03.53   **Repair of vertebral fracture**

Elevation of spinal bone fragments
Reduction of fracture of vertebrae
Removal of bony spicules from spinal canal

`EXCLUDES`   *kyphoplasty ▶(81.66)◀*
vertebroplasty ▶(81.65)◀

AHA: 4Q, '04, 126; 4Q, '99, 11, 12, 13;3Q, '96, 14

03.59   **Other repair and plastic operations on spinal cord structures**

Repair of:
diastematomyelia
spina bifida NOS
spinal cord NOS
spinal meninges NOS
vertebral arch defect

03.6   **Lysis of adhesions of spinal cord and nerve roots**

AHA: 2Q, '98, 18

☑4th **03.7**   **Shunt of spinal theca**

`INCLUDES`   that with valve

DEF: Surgical passage created from spinal cord dura mater to another channel.

03.71   **Spinal subarachnoid-peritoneal shunt**

03.72   **Spinal subarachnoid-ureteral shunt**

03.79   **Other shunt of spinal theca**

Lumbar-subarachnoid shunt NOS
Pleurothecal anastomosis
Salpingothecal anastomosis

AHA: 1Q, '97, 7

03.8   **Injection of destructive agent into spinal canal**

☑4th **03.9**   **Other operations on spinal cord and spinal canal structures**

03.90   **Insertion of catheter into spinal canal for infusion of therapeutic or palliative substances**

Insertion of catheter into epidural, subarachnoid, or subdural space of spine with intermittent or continuous infusion of drug (with creation of any reservoir)
Code also any implantation of infusion pump (86.06)

03.91   **Injection of anesthetic into spinal canal for analgesia**

`EXCLUDES`   *that for operative anesthesia — omit code*

AHA: 3Q, '00, 15; 1Q, '99, 8; 2Q, '98, 18

03.92   **Injection of other agent into spinal canal**

Intrathecal injection of steroid
Subarachnoid perfusion of refrigerated saline

`EXCLUDES`   *injection of:*
contrast material for myelogram (87.21)
destructive agent into spinal canal (03.8)

AHA: 2Q, '03, 6; 3Q, '00, 15; 2Q, '98, 18

03.93   **Implantation or replacement of spinal neurostimulator lead(s)**

Code also any insertion of neurostimulator pulse generator (86.94-86.96)

AHA: 1Q, '00, 19

03.94   **Removal of spinal neurostimulator lead(s)**

Code also any removal of neurostimulator pulse generator (86.05)

03.95   **Spinal blood patch**

DEF: Injection of blood into epidural space to patch hole in outer spinal membrane when blood clots.

03.96   **Percutaneous denervation of facet**

03.97   **Revision of spinal thecal shunt**

AHA: 2Q, '99, 4

03.98   **Removal of spinal thecal shunt**

03.99   **Other**

☑3rd **04**   **Operations on cranial and peripheral nerves**

☑4th **04.0**   **Incision, division, and excision of cranial and peripheral nerves**

`EXCLUDES`   *opticociliary neurectomy (12.79)*
sympathetic ganglionectomy (05.21-05.29)

04.01   **Excision of acoustic neuroma**

That by craniotomy

`EXCLUDES`   *that by stereotactic radiosurgery (92.3)*

AHA: 2Q, '98, 20; 2Q, '95, 8; 4Q, '92, 26

04.02   **Division of trigeminal nerve**

Retrogasserian neurotomy

DEF: Transection of sensory root fibers of trigeminal nerve for relief of trigeminal neuralgia.

☑3rd **Additional Digit Required**   **RUG III Special Care Procedure**   **RUG III Clinically Complex Procedure**   **RUG III Extensive Services Procedure**   **RUG III Rehab Procedure**
☑4th

2006 ICD•9•CM   **October 2005 • Volume 3 — 91**

Operations on the Nervous System

04.03–05.19

04.03　Division or crushing of other cranial and peripheral nerves

> EXCLUDES　*that of:*
> *glossopharyngeal nerve (29.92)*
> *laryngeal nerve (31.91)*
> *nerves to adrenal glands (07.42)*
> *phrenic nerve for collapse of lung (33.31)*
> *vagus nerve (44.00-44.03)*

AHA: 2Q, '98, 20

04.04　Other incision of cranial and peripheral nerves

04.05　Gasserian ganglionectomy

04.06　Other cranial or peripheral ganglionectomy

> EXCLUDES　*sympathetic ganglionectomy (05.21-05.29)*

04.07　Other excision or avulsion of cranial and peripheral nerves

Curettage ⎫
Debridement ⎬ of peripheral nerve
Resection ⎭

Excision of peripheral neuroma [Morton's]

> EXCLUDES　*biopsy of cranial or peripheral nerve (04.11-04.12)*

AHA: 2Q, '95, 8; 4Q, '92, 26

✓4th　04.1　Diagnostic procedures on peripheral nervous system

04.11　Closed [percutaneous] [needle] biopsy of cranial or peripheral nerve or ganglion

04.12　Open biopsy of cranial or peripheral nerve or ganglion

04.19　Other diagnostic procedures on cranial and peripheral nerves and ganglia

> EXCLUDES　*microscopic examination of specimen from nervous system (90.01-90.09)*
> *neurologic examination (89.13)*

04.2　Destruction of cranial and peripheral nerves

Destruction of cranial or peripheral nerves by:
cryoanalgesia
injection of neurolytic agent
radiofrequency
Radiofrequency ablation

AHA: 3Q, '02, 10, 11; 4Q, '95, 74

DEF: Radiofrequency ablation: High frequency radio waves are applied to injure the nerve resulting in interruption of the pain signal.

04.3　Suture of cranial and peripheral nerves

✓4th　04.4　Lysis of adhesions and decompression of cranial and peripheral nerves

04.41　Decompression of trigeminal nerve root

04.42　Other cranial nerve decompression

AHA: 3Q, '02, 13

04.43　Release of carpal tunnel

04.44　Release of tarsal tunnel

04.49　Other peripheral nerve or ganglion decompression or lysis of adhesions

Peripheral nerve neurolysis NOS

AHA: 2Q, '95, 8;

04.5　Cranial or peripheral nerve graft

04.6　Transposition of cranial and peripheral nerves

Nerve transplantation

DEF: Relocation of cranial or peripheral nerves without detaching or severing them.

✓4th　04.7　Other cranial or peripheral neuroplasty

04.71　Hypoglossal-facial anastomosis

DEF: Surgical connection of hypoglossal nerve to facial nerve.

Release of Carpal Tunnel

Median nerve

(Deep) transverse carpal ligament being cut

04.72　Accessory-facial anastomosis

DEF: Surgical connection of accessory nerve to facial nerve.

04.73　Accessory-hypoglossal anastomosis

DEF: Surgical connection of accessory nerve to hypoglossal nerve.

04.74　Other anastomosis of cranial or peripheral nerve

04.75　Revision of previous repair of cranial and peripheral nerves

04.76　Repair of old traumatic injury of cranial and peripheral nerves

04.79　Other neuroplasty

✓4th　04.8　Injection into peripheral nerve

> EXCLUDES　*destruction of nerve (by injection of neurolytic agent) (04.2)*

04.80　Peripheral nerve injection, not otherwise specified

04.81　Injection of anesthetic into peripheral nerve for analgesia

> EXCLUDES　*that for operative anesthesia — omit code*

AHA: 1Q, '00, 7

04.89　Injection of other agent, except neurolytic

> EXCLUDES　*injection of neurolytic agent (04.2)*

✓4th　04.9　Other operations on cranial and peripheral nerves

04.91　Neurectasis

DEF: Surgical stretching of peripheral or cranial nerve.

04.92　Implantation or replacement of peripheral neurostimulator lead(s)

Code also any insertion of neurostimulator pulse generator (86.94-86.96)

AHA: ▶2Q, '04, 7;◀ 3Q, '01, 16; 2Q, '00, 22; 3Q, '96, 12

DEF: Placement of or removal and replacement of neurostimulator lead(s) during the same episode.

04.93　Removal of peripheral neurostimulator lead(s)

Code also any removal of neurostimulator pulse generator (86.05)

AHA: 3Q, '01, 16

DEF: Removal of test neurostimulator or permanent neurostimulator when a permanent device is not placed during the same episode.

04.99　Other

✓3rd　05　Operations on sympathetic nerves or ganglia

> EXCLUDES　*paracervical uterine denervation (69.3)*

05.0　Division of sympathetic nerve or ganglion

> EXCLUDES　*that of nerves to adrenal glands (07.42)*

✓4th　05.1　Diagnostic procedures on sympathetic nerves or ganglia

05.11　Biopsy of sympathetic nerve or ganglion

05.19　Other diagnostic procedures on sympathetic nerves or ganglia

---

N Newborn Age: 0　　P Pediatric Age: 0-17　　M Maternity Age: 12-55　　A Adult Age: 15-124　　Adj Adjunct Code　　◀▶ Revised Text　　● New Code　　▲ Revised Code Title

✓4ᵗʰ **05.2**   **Sympathectomy**

DEF: Sympathectomy: Division of nerve pathway at a specific site of a sympathetic nerve.

05.21   **Sphenopalatine ganglionectomy**

05.22   **Cervical sympathectomy**

05.23   **Lumbar sympathectomy**

DEF: Excision, resection of lumber chain nerve group to relieve causalgia, Raynaud's disease, or lower extremity thromboangiitis.

05.24   **Presacral sympathectomy**

DEF: Excision or resection of hypogastric nerve network.

05.25   **Periarterial sympathectomy**

DEF: Removal of arterial sheath containing sympathetic nerve fibers.

05.29   **Other sympathectomy and ganglionectomy**

Excision or avulsion of sympathetic nerve NOS
Sympathetic ganglionectomy NOS

EXCLUDES   *biopsy of sympathetic nerve or ganglion (05.11)*
opticociliary neurectomy (12.79)
periarterial sympathectomy (05.25)
tympanosympathectomy (20.91)

✓4ᵗʰ **05.3**   **Injection into sympathetic nerve or ganglion**

EXCLUDES   *injection of ciliary sympathetic ganglion (12.79)*

05.31   **Injection of anesthetic into sympathetic nerve for analgesia**

05.32   **Injection of neurolytic agent into sympathetic nerve**

05.39   **Other injection into sympathetic nerve or ganglion**

✓4ᵗʰ **05.8**   **Other operations on sympathetic nerves or ganglia**

05.81   **Repair of sympathetic nerve or ganglion**

05.89   **Other**

05.9   **Other operations on nervous system**

Operations on the Nervous System

05.2–05.9

✓3ʳᵈ
✓4ᵗʰ Additional Digit Required   RUG III Special Care Procedure   RUG III Clinically Complex Procedure   RUG III Extensive Services Procedure   RUG III Rehab Procedure

2006 ICD•9•CM   **Volume 3 — 93**

Operations on the Endocrine System

06–06.99

2. OPERATIONS ON THE ENDOCRINE SYSTEM (06-07)

√3rd **06**   **Operations on thyroid and parathyroid glands**
  INCLUDES   incidental resection of hyoid bone

√4th **06.0**   **Incision of thyroid field**
    EXCLUDES   division of isthmus (06.91)

06.01   **Aspiration of thyroid field**
    Percutaneous or needle drainage of thyroid field
      EXCLUDES   aspiration biopsy of thyroid (06.11)
        drainage by incision (06.09)
        postoperative aspiration of field (06.02)

06.02   **Reopening of wound of thyroid field**
    Reopening of wound of thyroid field for:
      control of (postoperative) hemorrhage
      examination
      exploration
      removal of hematoma

06.09   **Other incision of thyroid field**
    Drainage of hematoma
    Drainage of thyroglossal tract
    Exploration:
      neck
      thyroid (field)   } by incision
    Removal of foreign body
    Thyroidotomy NOS
      EXCLUDES   postoperative exploration (06.02)
        removal of hematoma by aspiration (06.01)

√4th **06.1**   **Diagnostic procedures on thyroid and parathyroid glands**

06.11   **Closed [percutaneous] [needle] biopsy of thyroid gland**
    Aspiration biopsy of thyroid
    DEF: Insertion of needle-type device for removal of thyroid tissue sample.

06.12   **Open biopsy of thyroid gland**

06.13   **Biopsy of parathyroid gland**

06.19   **Other diagnostic procedures on thyroid and parathyroid glands**
      EXCLUDES   radioisotope scan of:
        parathyroid (92.13)
        thyroid (92.01)
        soft tissue x-ray of thyroid field (87.09)

Thyroidectomy

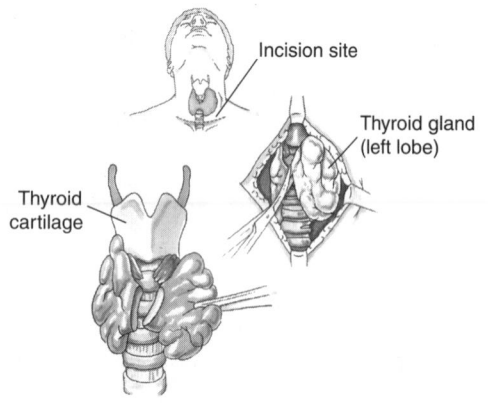

Incision site

Thyroid gland (left lobe)

Thyroid cartilage

06.2   **Unilateral thyroid lobectomy**
    Complete removal of one lobe of thyroid (with removal of isthmus or portion of other lobe)
    Hemithyroidectomy
      EXCLUDES   partial substernal thyroidectomy (06.51)
    DEF: Excision of thyroid lobe.

√4th **06.3**   **Other partial thyroidectomy**

06.31   **Excision of lesion of thyroid**
      EXCLUDES   biopsy of thyroid (06.11-06.12)
    DEF: Removal of growth on thyroid.

06.39   **Other**
    Isthmectomy   Partial thyroidectomy NOS
      EXCLUDES   partial substernal thyroidectomy (06.51)

06.4   **Complete thyroidectomy**
      EXCLUDES   complete substernal thyroidectomy (06.52)
        that with laryngectomy (30.3-30.4)

√4th **06.5**   **Substernal thyroidectomy**
    DEF: Removal of thyroid tissue below breastbone.

06.50   **Substernal thyroidectomy, not otherwise specified**

06.51   **Partial substernal thyroidectomy**

06.52   **Complete substernal thyroidectomy**

06.6   **Excision of lingual thyroid**
    Excision of thyroid by:
      submental route
      transoral route
    DEF: Excision of thyroid tissue at base of tongue.

06.7   **Excision of thyroglossal duct or tract**

√4th **06.8**   **Parathyroidectomy**
    DEF: Removal of parathyroid glands.

06.81   **Complete parathyroidectomy**

06.89   **Other parathyroidectomy**
    Parathyroidectomy NOS
    Partial parathyroidectomy
      EXCLUDES   biopsy of parathyroid (06.13)

√4th **06.9**   **Other operations on thyroid (region) and parathyroid**

06.91   **Division of thyroid isthmus**
    Transection of thyroid isthmus
    DEF: Cutting or division of tissue at narrowest point of thyroid.

06.92   **Ligation of thyroid vessels**

06.93   **Suture of thyroid gland**

06.94   **Thyroid tissue reimplantation**
    Autotransplantation of thyroid tissue
    DEF: Placement of thyroid tissue graft into functional site.

    DEF: Autotransplantation of thyroid tissue: Tissue graft from patient thyroid tissue to another site on thyroid.

06.95   **Parathyroid tissue reimplantation**
    Autotransplantation of parathyroid tissue
    DEF: Placement of parathyroid tissue graft into functional site.

    DEF: Autotransplantation of parathyroid tissue: Use of patient parathyroid tissue for graft.

06.98   **Other operations on thyroid glands**

06.99   **Other operations on parathyroid glands**

N Newborn Age: 0   P Pediatric Age: 0-17   M Maternity Age: 12-55   A Adult Age: 15-124   Adj Adjunct Code   ◄► Revised Text   ● New Code   ▲ Revised Code Title

94 — Volume 3   2006 ICD•9•CM

√3rd **07**   **Operations on other endocrine glands**

INCLUDES   operations on:
     adrenal glands   pituitary gland
     pineal gland   thymus

EXCLUDES   operations on:
     aortic and carotid bodies (39.8)
     ovaries (65.0-65.99)
     pancreas (52.01-52.99)
     testes (62.0-62.99)

√4th **07.0**   **Exploration of adrenal field**
       EXCLUDES   incision of adrenal (gland) (07.41)

07.00   **Exploration of adrenal field, not otherwise specified**

07.01   **Unilateral exploration of adrenal field**
DEF: Investigation of one adrenal gland for diagnostic reasons.

07.02   **Bilateral exploration of adrenal field**
DEF: Investigation of both adrenal glands for diagnostic reasons.

√4th **07.1**   **Diagnostic procedures on adrenal glands, pituitary gland, pineal gland, and thymus**

07.11   **Closed [percutaneous] [needle] biopsy of adrenal gland**

07.12   **Open biopsy of adrenal gland**

07.13   **Biopsy of pituitary gland, transfrontal approach**
DEF: Excision of pituitary gland tissue for exam through frontal bone.

07.14   **Biopsy of pituitary gland, transsphenoidal approach**
DEF: Excision of pituitary gland tissue for exam through sphenoid bone.

07.15   **Biopsy of pituitary gland, unspecified approach**

07.16   **Biopsy of thymus**

07.17   **Biopsy of pineal gland**

07.19   **Other diagnostic procedures on adrenal glands, pituitary gland, pineal gland, and thymus**
       EXCLUDES   microscopic examination of specimen from endocrine gland (90.11-90.19)
             radioisotope scan of pituitary gland (92.11)

√4th **07.2**   **Partial adrenalectomy**

07.21   **Excision of lesion of adrenal gland**
       EXCLUDES   biopsy of adrenal gland (07.11-07.12)

07.22   **Unilateral adrenalectomy**
Adrenalectomy NOS
       EXCLUDES   excision of remaining adrenal gland (07.3)
DEF: Excision of one adrenal gland.

07.29   **Other partial adrenalectomy**
Partial adrenalectomy NOS

07.3   **Bilateral adrenalectomy**
Excision of remaining adrenal gland
       EXCLUDES   bilateral partial adrenalectomy (07.29)

√4th **07.4**   **Other operations on adrenal glands, nerves, and vessels**

07.41   **Incision of adrenal gland**
Adrenalotomy (with drainage)

07.42   **Division of nerves to adrenal glands**

07.43   **Ligation of adrenal vessels**

07.44   **Repair of adrenal gland**

07.45   **Reimplantation of adrenal tissue**
Autotransplantation of adrenal tissue
DEF: Placement of adrenal tissue graft into functional site.

DEF: Autotransplantation of adrenal tissue: Use of tissue graft from the patient's own body.

07.49   **Other**

√4th **07.5**   **Operations on pineal gland**

07.51   **Exploration of pineal field**
       EXCLUDES   that with incision of pineal gland (07.52)

07.52   **Incision of pineal gland**

07.53   **Partial excision of pineal gland**
       EXCLUDES   biopsy of pineal gland (07.17)

07.54   **Total excision of pineal gland**
Pinealectomy (complete) (total)

07.59   **Other operations on pineal gland**

√4th **07.6**   **Hypophysectomy**
DEF: Excision, destruction of pituitary gland.

07.61   **Partial excision of pituitary gland, transfrontal approach**

Cryohypophysectomy, partial
Division of hypophyseal stalk
Excision of lesion of pituitary [hypophysis]   }   transfrontal approach
Hypophysectomy, subtotal
Infundibulectomy, hypophyseal

       EXCLUDES   biopsy of pituitary gland, transfrontal approach (07.13)
DEF: Removal of pituitary gland, partial, through frontal bone.

07.62   **Partial excision of pituitary gland, transsphenoidal approach**
       EXCLUDES   biopsy of pituitary gland, transsphenoidal approach (07.14)
DEF: Removal of pituitary gland, partial, through sphenoid bone.

07.63   **Partial excision of pituitary gland, unspecified approach**
       EXCLUDES   biopsy of pituitary gland NOS (07.15)

07.64   **Total excision of pituitary gland, transfrontal approach**

Ablation of pituitary by implantation (strontiumyttrium)   }   transfrontal approach
Cryohypophysectomy, complete

DEF: Removal of pituitary gland, total, through frontal bone.

07.65   **Total excision of pituitary gland, transsphenoidal approach**
DEF: Removal of pituitary gland, total, through sphenoid bone.

07.68   **Total excision of pituitary gland, other specified approach**
DEF: Destroy or remove pituitary gland by a specified approach, other than those listed.

√3rd √4th   Additional Digit Required   RUG III Special Care Procedure   RUG III Clinically Complex Procedure   RUG III Extensive Services Procedure   RUG III Rehab Procedure

2006 ICD•9•CM   **Volume 3 — 95**

Operations on the Endocrine System

07.69–07.99

07.69 **Total excision of pituitary gland, unspecified approach**
Hypophysectomy NOS
Pituitectomy NOS

✓4th 07.7 **Other operations on hypophysis**

07.71 **Exploration of pituitary fossa**
EXCLUDES exploration with incision of pituitary gland (07.72)
DEF: Exploration of region of pituitary gland.

07.72 **Incision of pituitary gland**
Aspiration of: Aspiration of:
craniobuccal pouch   pituitary gland
craniopharyngioma   Rathke's pouch
hypophysis

07.79 **Other**
Insertion of pack into sella turcica

✓4th 07.8 **Thymectomy**

07.80 **Thymectomy, not otherwise specified**

07.81 **Partial excision of thymus**
EXCLUDES biopsy of thymus (07.16)

07.82 **Total excision of thymus**

✓4th 07.9 **Other operations on thymus**

07.91 **Exploration of thymus field**
EXCLUDES exploration with incision of thymus (07.92)

07.92 **Incision of thymus**

07.93 **Repair of thymus**

07.94 **Transplantation of thymus**
DEF: Placement of thymus tissue grafts into functional area of gland.

07.99 **Other**
Thymopexy

N Newborn Age: 0   P Pediatric Age: 0-17   M Maternity Age: 12-55   A Adult Age: 15-124   Adj Adjunct Code   ▶◀ Revised Text   ● New Code   ▲ Revised Code Title

96 — Volume 3   2006 ICD•9•CM

3. OPERATIONS ON THE EYE (08-16)

√3rd **08**   **Operations on eyelids**
> INCLUDES   operations on the eyebrow

√4th **08.0**   **Incision of eyelid**

08.01   **Incision of lid margin**
> DEF: Cutting into eyelid edge.

08.02   **Severing of blepharorrhaphy**
> DEF: Freeing of eyelids previously sutured shut.

08.09   **Other incision of eyelid**

√4th **08.1**   **Diagnostic procedures on eyelid**

08.11   **Biopsy of eyelid**

08.19   **Other diagnostic procedures on eyelid**

√4th **08.2**   **Excision or destruction of lesion or tissue of eyelid**
> Code also any synchronous reconstruction (08.61-08.74)
> EXCLUDES   *biopsy of eyelid (08.11)*

08.20   **Removal of lesion of eyelid, not otherwise specified**
> Removal of meibomian gland NOS

08.21   **Excision of chalazion**

08.22   **Excision of other minor lesion of eyelid**
> Excision of: Excision of:
> verruca   wart

08.23   **Excision of major lesion of eyelid, partial-thickness**
> Excision involving one-fourth or more of lid margin, partial-thickness
> DEF: Excision of lesion not in all eyelid layers.

08.24   **Excision of major lesion of eyelid, full-thickness**
> Excision involving one-fourth or more of lid margin, full-thickness
> Wedge resection of eyelid
> DEF: Excision of growth in all eyelid layers, full thickness.

08.25   **Destruction of lesion of eyelid**

√4th **08.3**   **Repair of blepharoptosis and lid retraction**

08.31   **Repair of blepharoptosis by frontalis muscle technique with suture**
> DEF: Correction of drooping upper eyelid with suture of frontalis muscle.

08.32   **Repair of blepharoptosis by frontalis muscle technique with fascial sling**
> DEF: Correction of drooping upper eyelid with fascial tissue sling of frontalis muscle.

08.33   **Repair of blepharoptosis by resection or advancement of levator muscle or aponeurosis**
> DEF: Correction of drooping upper eyelid with levator muscle, extended, cut, or by expanded tendon.

08.34   **Repair of blepharoptosis by other levator muscle techniques**

08.35   **Repair of blepharoptosis by tarsal technique**
> DEF: Correction of drooping upper eyelid with tarsal muscle.

08.36   **Repair of blepharoptosis by other techniques**
> Correction of eyelid ptosis NOS
> Orbicularis oculi muscle sling for correction of blepharoptosis

08.37   **Reduction of overcorrection of ptosis**
> DEF: Correction, release of previous plastic repair of drooping eyelid.

08.38   **Correction of lid retraction**
> DEF: Fixing of withdrawn eyelid into normal position.

√4th **08.4**   **Repair of entropion or ectropion**

08.41   **Repair of entropion or ectropion by thermocauterization**
> DEF: Restoration of eyelid margin to normal position with heat cautery.

08.42   **Repair of entropion or ectropion by suture technique**
> DEF: Restoration of eyelid margin to normal position by suture.

08.43   **Repair of entropion or ectropion with wedge resection**
> DEF: Restoration of eyelid margin to normal position by removing tissue.

08.44   **Repair of entropion or ectropion with lid reconstruction**
> DEF: Reconstruction of eyelid margin.

08.49   **Other repair of entropion or ectropion**

√4th **08.5**   **Other adjustment of lid position**

08.51   **Canthotomy**
> DEF: Incision into outer canthus of eye.

08.52   **Blepharorrhaphy**
> Canthorrhaphy   Tarsorrhaphy
> DEF: Suture together of eyelids, partial or repair; done to shorten palpebral fissure or protect cornea.

08.59   **Other**
> Canthoplasty NOS
> Repair of epicanthal fold

√4th **08.6**   **Reconstruction of eyelid with flaps or grafts**
> EXCLUDES   *that associated with repair of entropion and ectropion (08.44)*

08.61   **Reconstruction of eyelid with skin flap or graft**
> DEF: Rebuild of eyelid by graft or flap method.

08.62   **Reconstruction of eyelid with mucous membrane flap or graft**
> DEF: Rebuild of eyelid with mucous membrane by graft or flap method.

08.63   **Reconstruction of eyelid with hair follicle graft**
> DEF: Rebuild of eyelid with hair follicle graft.

08.64   **Reconstruction of eyelid with tarsoconjunctival flap**
> Transfer of tarsoconjunctival flap from opposing lid
> DEF: Recreation of eyelid with tarsoconjunctival tissue.

08.69   **Other reconstruction of eyelid with flaps or grafts**

√4th **08.7**   **Other reconstruction of eyelid**
> EXCLUDES   *that associated with repair of entropion and ectropion (08.44)*

08.70   **Reconstruction of eyelid, not otherwise specified**
> AHA: 2Q, '96, 11

08.71   **Reconstruction of eyelid involving lid margin, partial-thickness**
> DEF: Repair of eyelid margin not using all lid layers.

08.72   **Other reconstruction of eyelid, partial-thickness**
> DEF: Reshape of eyelid not using all lid layers.

√3rd
√4th   Additional Digit Required   RUG III Special Care Procedure   RUG III Clinically Complex Procedure   RUG III Extensive Services Procedure   RUG III Rehab Procedure

Operations on the Eye

08.73–10.1

08.73　Reconstruction of eyelid involving lid margin, full-thickness

DEF: Repair of eyelid and margin using all tissue layers.

08.74　Other reconstruction of eyelid, full-thickness

DEF: Other repair of eyelid using all tissue layers.

✓4ᵗʰ **08.8　Other repair of eyelid**

08.81　Linear repair of laceration of eyelid or eyebrow

08.82　Repair of laceration involving lid margin, partial-thickness

DEF: Repair of laceration not involving all layers of eyelid margin.

08.83　Other repair of laceration of eyelid, partial thickness

DEF: Repair of eyelid tear not involving all eyelid layers.

08.84　Repair of laceration involving lid margin, full-thickness

DEF: Repair of eyelid margin tear involving all margin layers.

08.85　Other repair of laceration of eyelid, full-thickness

DEF: Repair of eyelid tear involving all layers.

08.86　Lower eyelid rhytidectomy

DEF: Removal of wrinkles from lower eyelid.

08.87　Upper eyelid rhytidectomy

AHA: 2Q, '96, 11

DEF: Removal of wrinkles from upper eyelid.

08.89　Other eyelid repair

AHA: 1Q, '00, 22

✓4ᵗʰ **08.9　Other operations on eyelids**

08.91　Electrosurgical epilation of eyelid

DEF: Electrical removal of eyelid hair roots.

08.92　Cryosurgical epilation of eyelid

DEF: Removal of eyelid hair roots by freezing.

08.93　Other epilation of eyelid

08.99　Other

✓3ʳᵈ **09　Operations on lacrimal system**

09.0　Incision of lacrimal gland

Incision of lacrimal cyst (with drainage)

✓4ᵗʰ **09.1　Diagnostic procedures on lacrimal system**

09.11　Biopsy of lacrimal gland

09.12　Biopsy of lacrimal sac

09.19　Other diagnostic procedures on lacrimal system

EXCLUDES　contrast dacryocystogram (87.05)
soft tissue x-ray of nasolacrimal duct (87.09)

✓4ᵗʰ **09.2　Excision of lesion or tissue of lacrimal gland**

09.20　Excision of lacrimal gland, not otherwise specified

09.21　Excision of lesion of lacrimal gland

EXCLUDES　biopsy of lacrimal gland (09.11)

09.22　Other partial dacryoadenectomy

EXCLUDES　biopsy of lacrimal gland (09.11)

DEF: Excision, partial, of tear gland.

09.23　Total dacryoadenectomy

DEF: Excision, total, of tear gland.

09.3　Other operations on lacrimal gland

✓4ᵗʰ **09.4　Manipulation of lacrimal passage**

INCLUDES　removal of calculus
that with dilation

EXCLUDES　contrast dacryocystogram (87.05)

09.41　Probing of lacrimal punctum

DEF: Exploration of tear duct entrance with flexible rod.

09.42　Probing of lacrimal canaliculi

DEF: Exploration of tear duct with flexible rod.

09.43　Probing of nasolacrimal duct

EXCLUDES　that with insertion of tube or stent (09.44)

DEF: Exploration of passage between tear sac and nose with flexible rod.

09.44　Intubation of nasolacrimal duct

Insertion of stent into nasolacrimal duct

AHA: 2Q, '94, 11

09.49　Other manipulation of lacrimal passage

✓4ᵗʰ **09.5　Incision of lacrimal sac and passages**

09.51　Incision of lacrimal punctum

09.52　Incision of lacrimal canaliculi

09.53　Incision of lacrimal sac

DEF: Cutting into lacrimal pouch of tear gland.

09.59　Other incision of lacrimal passages

Incision (and drainage) of nasolacrimal duct NOS

09.6　Excision of lacrimal sac and passage

EXCLUDES　biopsy of lacrimal sac (09.12)

DEF: Removal of pouch and passage of tear gland.

✓4ᵗʰ **09.7　Repair of canaliculus and punctum**

EXCLUDES　repair of eyelid (08.81-08.89)

09.71　Correction of everted punctum

DEF: Repair of an outwardly turned tear duct entrance.

09.72　Other repair of punctum

09.73　Repair of canaliculus

✓4ᵗʰ **09.8　Fistulization of lacrimal tract to nasal cavity**

09.81　Dacryocystorhinostomy [DCR]

DEF: Creation of entrance between tear gland and nasal passage for tear flow.

09.82　Conjunctivocystorhinostomy

Conjunctivodacryocystorhinostomy [CDCR]

EXCLUDES　that with insertion of tube or stent (09.83)

DEF: Creation of tear drainage path from lacrimal sac to nasal cavity through conjunctiva.

09.83　Conjunctivorhinostomy with insertion of tube or stent

DEF: Creation of passage between eye sac membrane and nasal cavity with tube or stent.

✓4ᵗʰ **09.9　Other operations on lacrimal system**

09.91　Obliteration of lacrimal punctum

DEF: Destruction, total of tear gland opening in eyelid.

09.99　Other

AHA: 2Q, '94, 11

✓3ʳᵈ **10　Operations on conjunctiva**

10.0　Removal of embedded foreign body from conjunctiva by incision

EXCLUDES　removal of:
embedded foreign body without incision (98.22)
superficial foreign body (98.21)

10.1　Other incision of conjunctiva

 Newborn Age: 0　　 Pediatric Age: 0-17　　 Maternity Age: 12-55　　 Adult Age: 15-124　　**Adj** Adjunct Code　　▶◀ Revised Text　　● New Code　　▲ Revised Code Title

✓4th **10.2 Diagnostic procedures on conjunctiva**
     10.21 Biopsy of conjunctiva
     10.29 Other diagnostic procedures on conjunctiva

✓4th **10.3 Excision or destruction of lesion or tissue of conjunctiva**
     10.31 Excision of lesion or tissue of conjunctiva
         Excision of ring of conjunctiva around cornea
         EXCLUDES *biopsy of conjunctiva (10.21)*
         AHA: 4Q, '00, 41; 3Q, '96, 7

         DEF: Removal of growth or tissue from eye membrane.

     10.32 Destruction of lesion of conjunctiva
         EXCLUDES *excision of lesion (10.31)*
         thermocauterization for entropion (08.41)

         DEF: Destruction of eye membrane growth; not done by excision.

     10.33 Other destructive procedures on conjunctiva
         Removal of trachoma follicles

✓4th **10.4 Conjunctivoplasty**

     DEF: Correction of conjunctiva by plastic surgery.

     10.41 Repair of symblepharon with free graft
         AHA: 3Q, '96, 7

     10.42 Reconstruction of conjunctival cul-de-sac with free graft
         EXCLUDES *revision of enucleation socket with graft (16.63)*

         DEF: Rebuilding of eye membrane fold with graft of unattached tissue.

     10.43 Other reconstruction of conjunctival cul-de-sac
         EXCLUDES *revision of enucleation socket (16.64)*

     10.44 Other free graft to conjunctiva
     10.49 Other conjunctivoplasty
         EXCLUDES *repair of cornea with conjunctival flap (11.53)*

10.5 Lysis of adhesions of conjunctiva and eyelid
     Division of symblepharon (with insertion of conformer)

10.6 Repair of laceration of conjunctiva
     EXCLUDES *that with repair of sclera (12.81)*

✓4th **10.9 Other operations on conjunctiva**
     10.91 Subconjunctival injection
         AHA: 3Q, '96, 7

     10.99 Other

✓3rd **11 Operations on cornea**
     11.0 Magnetic removal of embedded foreign body from cornea
         EXCLUDES *that with incision (11.1)*

     11.1 Incision of cornea
         Incision of cornea for removal of foreign body

✓4th **11.2 Diagnostic procedures on cornea**
     11.21 Scraping of cornea for smear or culture
     11.22 Biopsy of cornea
     11.29 Other diagnostic procedures on cornea

✓4th **11.3 Excision of pterygium**
     11.31 Transposition of pterygium
         DEF: Cutting into membranous structure extending from eye membrane to cornea and suturing it in a downward position.

     11.32 Excision of pterygium with corneal graft
         DEF: Surgical removal and repair of membranous structure extending from eye membrane to cornea using corneal tissue transplant.

     11.39 Other excision of pterygium

✓4th **11.4 Excision or destruction of tissue or other lesion of cornea**
     11.41 Mechanical removal of corneal epithelium
         That by chemocauterization
         EXCLUDES *that for smear or culture (11.21)*

         AHA: 3Q, '02, 20

         DEF: Removal of outer layer of cornea by mechanical means.

     11.42 Thermocauterization of corneal lesion
         DEF: Destruction of corneal lesion by electrical cautery.

     11.43 Cryotherapy of corneal lesion
         DEF: Destruction of corneal lesion by cold therapy.

     11.49 Other removal or destruction of corneal lesion
         Excision of cornea NOS
         EXCLUDES *biopsy of cornea (11.22)*

✓4th **11.5 Repair of cornea**
     11.51 Suture of corneal laceration
         AHA: 3Q, '96, 7

     11.52 Repair of postoperative wound dehiscence of cornea
         DEF: Repair of ruptured postoperative corneal wound.

     11.53 Repair of corneal laceration or wound with conjunctival flap
         DEF: Correction corneal wound or tear with conjunctival tissue.

     11.59 Other repair of cornea

✓4th **11.6 Corneal transplant**
     EXCLUDES *excision of pterygium with corneal graft (11.32)*

     11.60 Corneal transplant, not otherwise specified
         Note: To report donor source — see codes 00.91-00.93
         Keratoplasty NOS

     11.61 Lamellar keratoplasty with autograft
         DEF: Restoration of sight using patient's own corneal tissue, partial thickness.

     11.62 Other lamellar keratoplasty
         AHA: S-O, '85, 6

         DEF: Restoration of sight using donor corneal tissue, partial thickness.

     11.63 Penetrating keratoplasty with autograft
         Perforating keratoplasty with autograft

     11.64 Other penetrating keratoplasty
         Perforating keratoplasty (with homograft)

     11.69 Other corneal transplant

✓4th **11.7 Other reconstructive and refractive surgery on cornea**
     11.71 Keratomileusis
         DEF: Restoration of corneal shape by removing portion of cornea, freezing, reshaping curve and reattaching it.

     11.72 Keratophakia
         DEF: Correction of eye lens loss by dissecting the central zone of the cornea and replacing it with a thickened graft of the cornea.

     11.73 Keratoprosthesis
         DEF: Placement of corneal artificial implant.

     11.74 Thermokeratoplasty
         DEF: Reshaping and reforming cornea by heat application.

Operations on the Eye

10.2–11.74

✓3rd ✓4th Additional Digit Required   RUG III Special Care Procedure   RUG III Clinically Complex Procedure   RUG III Extensive Services Procedure   RUG III Rehab Procedure

2006 ICD•9•CM   **Volume 3 — 99**

11.75   Radial keratotomy

DEF: Incisions around cornea radius to correct nearsightedness.

11.76   Epikeratophakia

DEF: Repair lens loss by cornea graft sutured to central corneal zone.

11.79   Other

AHA: 3Q, '02, 20

✓4th **11.9   Other operations on cornea**

11.91   Tattooing of cornea

11.92   Removal of artificial implant from cornea

11.99   Other

✓3rd **12   Operations on iris, ciliary body, sclera, and anterior chamber**

EXCLUDES   *operations on cornea (11.0-11.99)*

✓4th **12.0   Removal of intraocular foreign body from anterior segment of eye**

12.00   Removal of intraocular foreign body from anterior segment of eye, not otherwise specified

12.01   Removal of intraocular foreign body from anterior segment of eye with use of magnet

12.02   Removal of intraocular foreign body from anterior segment of eye without use of magnet

✓4th **12.1   Iridotomy and simple iridectomy**

EXCLUDES   *iridectomy associated with:*
cataract extraction (13.11-13.69)
removal of lesion (12.41-12.42)
scleral fistulization (12.61-12.69)

12.11   Iridotomy with transfixion

12.12   Other iridotomy

Corectomy
Discission of iris
Iridotomy NOS

DEF: Corectomy: Incision into iris (also called iridectomy).

12.13   Excision of prolapsed iris

DEF: Removal of downwardly placed portion of iris.

12.14   Other iridectomy

Iridectomy (basal) (peripheral) (total)

DEF: Removal, partial or total of iris.

✓4th **12.2   Diagnostic procedures on iris, ciliary body, sclera, and anterior chamber**

12.21   Diagnostic aspiration of anterior chamber of eye

DEF: Suction withdrawal of fluid from anterior eye chamber for diagnostic reasons.

12.22   Biopsy of iris

12.29   Other diagnostic procedures on iris, ciliary body, sclera, and anterior chamber

✓4th **12.3   Iridoplasty and coreoplasty**

DEF: Correction of abnormal iris or pupil by plastic surgery.

12.31   Lysis of goniosynechiae

Lysis of goniosynechiae by injection of air or liquid

DEF: Freeing of fibrous structures between cornea and iris by injecting air or liquid.

12.32   Lysis of other anterior synechiae

Lysis of anterior synechiae:
NOS
by injection of air or liquid

12.33   Lysis of posterior synechiae

Lysis of iris adhesions NOS

12.34   Lysis of corneovitreal adhesions

DEF: Release of adhesions of cornea and vitreous body.

12.35   Coreoplasty

Needling of pupillary membrane

DEF: Correction of an iris defect.

12.39   Other iridoplasty

✓4th **12.4   Excision or destruction of lesion of iris and ciliary body**

12.40   Removal of lesion of anterior segment of eye, not otherwise specified

12.41   Destruction of lesion of iris, nonexcisional

Destruction of lesion of iris by:
cauterization
cryotherapy
photocoagulation

12.42   Excision of lesion of iris

EXCLUDES   *biopsy of iris (12.22)*

12.43   Destruction of lesion of ciliary body, nonexcisional

12.44   Excision of lesion of ciliary body

✓4th **12.5   Facilitation of intraocular circulation**

12.51   Goniopuncture without goniotomy

DEF: Stab incision into anterior chamber of eye to relieve optic pressure.

12.52   Goniotomy without goniopuncture

DEF: Incision into Schlemm's canal to drain aqueous and relieve pressure.

12.53   Goniotomy with goniopuncture

12.54   Trabeculotomy ab externo

DEF: Incision into supporting connective tissue strands of eye capsule, via exterior approach.

12.55   Cyclodialysis

DEF: Creation of passage between anterior chamber and suprachoroidal space.

12.59   Other facilitation of intraocular circulation

✓4th **12.6   Scleral fistulization**

EXCLUDES   *exploratory sclerotomy (12.89)*

12.61   Trephination of sclera with iridectomy

DEF: Cut around sclerocornea to remove part of the iris.

12.62   Thermocauterization of sclera with iridectomy

DEF: Destruction of outer eyeball layer with partial excision of iris using heat.

12.63   Iridencleisis and iridotasis

DEF: Creation of permanent drain in iris by transposing or stretching iris tissue.

12.64   Trabeculectomy ab externo

DEF: Excision of supporting connective tissue strands of eye capsule, via exterior approach.

Trabeculectomy Ab Externo

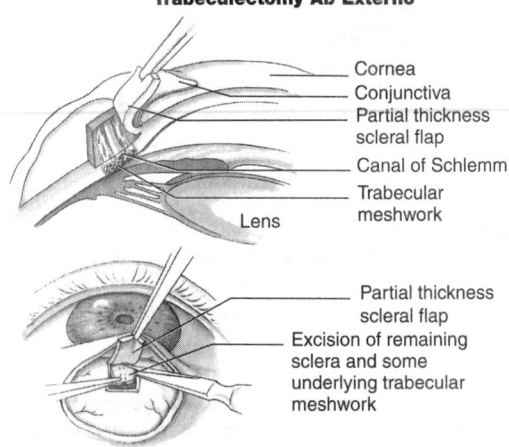

Cornea
Conjunctiva
Partial thickness scleral flap
Canal of Schlemm
Trabecular meshwork
Lens

Partial thickness scleral flap
Excision of remaining sclera and some underlying trabecular meshwork

---

N Newborn Age: 0   P Pediatric Age: 0-17   M Maternity Age: 12-55   A Adult Age: 15-124   Adj Adjunct Code   ◄ Revised Text   ● New Code   ▲ Revised Code Title

12.65   **Other scleral fistulization with iridectomy**

DEF: Creation of outer eyeball layer passage with partial excision of iris.

12.66   **Postoperative revision of scleral fistulization procedure**

Revision of filtering bleb

EXCLUDES   *repair of fistula (12.82)*

AHA: 2Q, '01, 16

12.69   **Other fistulizing procedure**

AHA: S-O, '85, 6

√4th **12.7**   **Other procedures for relief of elevated intraocular pressure**

12.71   **Cyclodiathermy**

DEF: Destruction of ciliary body tissue with heat.

12.72   **Cyclocryotherapy**

DEF: Destruction of ciliary body tissue by freezing.

12.73   **Cyclophotocoagulation**

DEF: Destruction of ciliary body tissue by high energy light source.

12.74   **Diminution of ciliary body, not otherwise specified**

12.79   **Other glaucoma procedures**

AHA: 2Q, '98, 16

√4th **12.8**   **Operations on sclera**

EXCLUDES   *those associated with:*
retinal reattachment (14.41-14.59)
scleral fistulization (12.61-12.69)

12.81   **Suture of laceration of sclera**

Suture of sclera with synchronous repair of conjunctiva

12.82   **Repair of scleral fistula**

EXCLUDES   *postoperative revision of scleral fistulization procedure (12.66)*

12.83   **Revision of operative wound of anterior segment, not elsewhere classified**

EXCLUDES   *postoperative revision of scleral fistulization procedure (12.66)*

12.84   **Excision or destruction of lesion of sclera**

12.85   **Repair of scleral staphyloma with graft**

DEF: Repair of protruding outer eyeball layer with a graft.

12.86   **Other repair of scleral staphyloma**

12.87   **Scleral reinforcement with graft**

DEF: Restoration of outer eyeball shape with tissue graft.

12.88   **Other scleral reinforcement**

12.89   **Other operations on sclera**

Exploratory sclerotomy

√4th **12.9**   **Other operations on iris, ciliary body, and anterior chamber**

12.91   **Therapeutic evacuation of anterior chamber**

Paracentesis of anterior chamber

EXCLUDES   *diagnostic aspiration (12.21)*

12.92   **Injection into anterior chamber**

Injection of:
air   into anterior
liquid   chamber
medication

AHA: J-A, '84, 1

12.93   **Removal or destruction of epithelial downgrowth from anterior chamber**

EXCLUDES   *that with iridectomy (12.41-12.42)*

DEF: Excision or destruction of epithelial overgrowth in anterior eye chamber.

12.97   **Other operations on iris**

12.98   **Other operations on ciliary body**

12.99   **Other operations on anterior chamber**

√3rd **13**   **Operations on lens**

√4th **13.0**   **Removal of foreign body from lens**

EXCLUDES   *removal of pseudophakos (13.8)*

13.00   **Removal of foreign body from lens, not otherwise specified**

13.01   **Removal of foreign body from lens with use of magnet**

13.02   **Removal of foreign body from lens without use of magnet**

√4th **13.1**   **Intracapsular extraction of lens**

Code also any synchronous insertion of pseudophakos (13.71)

AHA: S-O, '85, 6

13.11   **Intracapsular extraction of lens by temporal inferior route**

DEF: Extraction of lens and capsule via anterior approach through outer side of eyeball.

13.19   **Other intracapsular extraction of lens**

Cataract extraction NOS
Cryoextraction of lens
Erysiphake extraction of cataract
Extraction of lens NOS

13.2   **Extracapsular extraction of lens by linear extraction technique**

AHA: S-O, '85, 6

DEF: Excision of lens without the posterior capsule at junction between the cornea and outer eyeball layer by means of a linear incision.

13.3   **Extracapsular extraction of lens by simple aspiration (and irrigation) technique**

Irrigation of traumatic cataract

AHA: S-O, '85, 6

DEF: Removal of lens without the posterior capsule by suctioning and flushing out the area.

√4th **13.4**   **Extracapsular extraction of lens by fragmentation and aspiration technique**

AHA: S-O, '85, 6

DEF: Removal of lens after division into smaller pieces with posterior capsule left intact.

13.41   **Phacoemulsification and aspiration of cataract**

AHA: 3Q, '96, 4; 1Q, '94, 16

13.42   **Mechanical phacofragmentation and aspiration of cataract by posterior route**

Code also any synchronous vitrectomy (14.74)

**Extraction of Lens
(with insertion of intraocular lens prosthesis)**

Iris
Lens cataract removed
Iris
Lens
Intraocular lens insertion

√3rd
√4th Additional Digit Required   RUG III Special Care Procedure   RUG III Clinically Complex Procedure   RUG III Extensive Services Procedure   RUG III Rehab Procedure

2006 ICD•9•CM   **Volume 3 — 101**

Operations on the Eye

13.43–14.49

Laser Surgery (YAG)

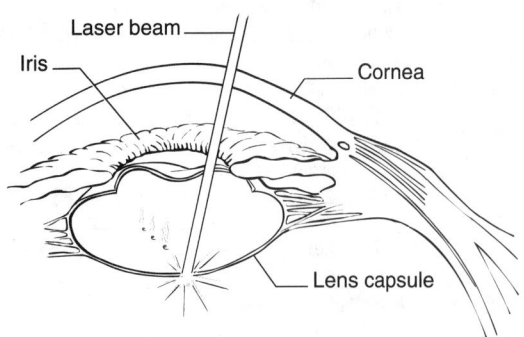

- Laser beam
- Iris
- Cornea
- Lens capsule

13.43   **Mechanical phacofragmentation and other aspiration of cataract**

✓4th **13.5**   **Other extracapsular extraction of lens**
Code also any synchronous insertion of pseudophakos (13.71)
AHA: S-O, '85, 6

    13.51   **Extracapsular extraction of lens by temporal inferior route**
DEF: Removal of lens through outer eyeball with posterior capsule left intact.

    13.59   **Other extracapsular extraction of lens**

✓4th **13.6**   **Other cataract extraction**
Code also any synchronous insertion of pseudophakos (13.71)
AHA: S-O, '85, 6

    13.64   **Discission of secondary membrane [after cataract]**
DEF: Breaking up of fibrotic lens capsule developed after previous lens extraction.

    13.65   **Excision of secondary membrane [after cataract]**
Capsulectomy
DEF: Capsulectomy: Excision of lens capsule membrane after previous lens extraction.

    13.66   **Mechanical fragmentation of secondary membrane [after cataract]**
DEF: Breaking up and removal of fibrotic lens capsule developed after previous lens extraction.

    13.69   **Other cataract extraction**

✓4th **13.7**   **Insertion of prosthetic lens [pseudophakos]**
AHA: J-A, '84, 1

DEF: Insertion of ocular implant, following lens extraction.

    13.70   **Insertion of pseudophakos, not otherwise specified**

    13.71   **Insertion of intraocular lens prosthesis at time of cataract extraction, one-stage**
Code also synchronous extraction of cataract (13.11-13.69)
AHA: 3Q, '96, 4

    13.72   **Secondary insertion of intraocular lens prosthesis**

13.8   **Removal of implanted lens**
Removal of pseudophakos

13.9   **Other operations on lens**
AHA: 1Q, '00, 9

✓3rd **14**   **Operations on retina, choroid, vitreous, and posterior chamber**

✓4th **14.0**   **Removal of foreign body from posterior segment of eye**
EXCLUDES   removal of surgically implanted material (14.6)

    14.00   **Removal of foreign body from posterior segment of eye, not otherwise specified**

    14.01   **Removal of foreign body from posterior segment of eye with use of magnet**

    14.02   **Removal of foreign body from posterior segment of eye without use of magnet**

✓4th **14.1**   **Diagnostic procedures on retina, choroid, vitreous, and posterior chamber**

    14.11   **Diagnostic aspiration of vitreous**

    14.19   **Other diagnostic procedures on retina, choroid, vitreous, and posterior chamber**

✓4th **14.2**   **Destruction of lesion of retina and choroid**
INCLUDES   destruction of chorioretinopathy or isolated chorioretinal lesion
EXCLUDES   that for repair of retina (14.31-14.59)
DEF: Destruction of damaged retina and choroid tissue.

    14.21   **Destruction of chorioretinal lesion by diathermy**

    14.22   **Destruction of chorioretinal lesion by cryotherapy**

    14.23   **Destruction of chorioretinal lesion by xenon arc photocoagulation**

    14.24   **Destruction of chorioretinal lesion by laser photocoagulation**

    14.25   **Destruction of chorioretinal lesion by photocoagulation of unspecified type**

    14.26   **Destruction of chorioretinal lesion by radiation therapy**

    14.27   **Destruction of chorioretinal lesion by implantation of radiation source**

    14.29   **Other destruction of chorioretinal lesion**
Destruction of lesion of retina and choroid NOS

✓4th **14.3**   **Repair of retinal tear**
INCLUDES   repair of retinal defect
EXCLUDES   repair of retinal detachment (14.41-14.59)

    14.31   **Repair of retinal tear by diathermy**

    14.32   **Repair of retinal tear by cryotherapy**

    14.33   **Repair of retinal tear by xenon arc photocoagulation**

    14.34   **Repair of retinal tear by laser photocoagulation**
AHA: 1Q, '94, 17

    14.35   **Repair of retinal tear by photocoagulation of unspecified type**

    14.39   **Other repair of retinal tear**

✓4th **14.4**   **Repair of retinal detachment with scleral buckling and implant**
DEF: Placement of material around eye to indent sclera and close a hole or tear or to reduce vitreous traction.

    14.41   **Scleral buckling with implant**
AHA: 3Q, '96, 6

    14.49   **Other scleral buckling**
Scleral buckling with:
air tamponade
resection of sclera
vitrectomy
AHA: 1Q, '94, 16

N Newborn Age: 0   P Pediatric Age: 0-17   M Maternity Age: 12-55   A Adult Age: 15-124   Adj Adjunct Code   ◄ Revised Text   ● New Code   ▲ Revised Code Title

102 — Volume 3   *2006 ICD•9•CM*

✓4th **14.5** **Other repair of retinal detachment**
> INCLUDES   that with drainage

14.51 **Repair of retinal detachment with diathermy**

14.52 **Repair of retinal detachment with cryotherapy**

14.53 **Repair of retinal detachment with xenon arc photocoagulation**

14.54 **Repair of retinal detachment with laser photocoagulation**
> AHA: N-D, '87, 10

14.55 **Repair of retinal detachment with photocoagulation of unspecified type**

14.59 **Other**

14.6 **Removal of surgically implanted material from posterior segment of eye**

✓4th **14.7** **Operations on vitreous**

14.71 **Removal of vitreous, anterior approach**
Open sky technique
Removal of vitreous, anterior approach (with replacement)
DEF: Removal of all or part of the eyeball fluid via the anterior segment of the eyeball.

14.72 **Other removal of vitreous**
Aspiration of vitreous by posterior sclerotomy

14.73 **Mechanical vitrectomy by anterior approach**
> AHA: 3Q, '96, 4, 5

DEF: Removal of abnormal tissue in eyeball fluid to control fibrotic overgrowth in severe intraocular injury.

14.74 **Other mechanical vitrectomy**
> AHA: 3Q, '96, 4, 5

14.75 **Injection of vitreous substitute**
> EXCLUDES   that associated with removal (14.71-14.72)

> AHA: 1Q, '98, 6; 3Q, '96, 4, 5; 1Q, '94, 17

14.79 **Other operations on vitreous**
> AHA: 3Q, '99, 12; 1Q, '99, 11; 1Q, '98, 6

14.9 **Other operations on retina, choroid, and posterior chamber**
> AHA: 3Q, '96, 5

✓3rd **15** **Operations on extraocular muscles**

✓4th **15.0** **Diagnostic procedures on extraocular muscles or tendons**

15.01 **Biopsy of extraocular muscle or tendon**

15.09 **Other diagnostic procedures on extraocular muscles and tendons**

✓4th **15.1** **Operations on one extraocular muscle involving temporary detachment from globe**

15.11 **Recession of one extraocular muscle**
> AHA: 3Q, '96, 3

DEF: Detachment of exterior eye muscle with posterior reattachment to correct strabismus.

15.12 **Advancement of one extraocular muscle**
DEF: Detachment of exterior eye muscle with forward reattachment to correct strabismus.

15.13 **Resection of one extraocular muscle**

15.19 **Other operations on one extraocular muscle involving temporary detachment from globe**
> EXCLUDES   transposition of muscle (15.5)

✓4th **15.2** **Other operations on one extraocular muscle**

15.21 **Lengthening procedure on one extraocular muscle**
DEF: Extension of exterior eye muscle length.

Lengthening Procedure on One Extraocular Muscle

Proposed second cut
Lengthened muscle
Extraocular muscle

Shortening Procedure on One Extraocular Muscle

To be resected
Muscle advanced and reattached
Iris

15.22 **Shortening procedure on one extraocular muscle**
DEF: Shortening of exterior eye muscle.

15.29 **Other**

15.3 **Operations on two or more extraocular muscles involving temporary detachment from globe, one or both eyes**
> AHA: 3Q, '96, 3

15.4 **Other operations on two or more extraocular muscles, one or both eyes**

15.5 **Transposition of extraocular muscles**
> EXCLUDES   that for correction of ptosis (08.31-08.36)

DEF: Relocation of exterior eye muscle to a more functional site.

15.6 **Revision of extraocular muscle surgery**
DEF: Repair of previous exterior eye muscle surgery.

15.7 **Repair of injury of extraocular muscle**
Freeing of entrapped extraocular muscle
Lysis of adhesions of extraocular muscle
Repair of laceration of extraocular muscle, tendon, or Tenon's capsule

15.9 **Other operations on extraocular muscles and tendons**

✓3rd **16** **Operations on orbit and eyeball**
> EXCLUDES   reduction of fracture of orbit (76.78-76.79)

✓4th **16.0** **Orbitotomy**

16.01 **Orbitotomy with bone flap**
Orbitotomy with lateral approach
DEF: Incision into orbital bone with insertion of small bone piece.

✓3rd
✓4th **Additional Digit Required**   RUG III Special Care Procedure   RUG III Clinically Complex Procedure   RUG III Extensive Services Procedure   RUG III Rehab Procedure

2006 ICD•9•CM   Volume 3 — 103

Operations on the Eye

16.02–16.99

16.02   **Orbitotomy with insertion of orbital implant**

> EXCLUDES   *that with bone flap (16.01)*

16.09   **Other orbitotomy**

16.1   **Removal of penetrating foreign body from eye, not otherwise specified**

> EXCLUDES   *removal of nonpenetrating foreign body (98.21)*

DEF: Removal of foreign body from an unspecified site in eye.

✓4ᵗʰ **16.2**   **Diagnostic procedures on orbit and eyeball**

16.21   **Ophthalmoscopy**

16.22   **Diagnostic aspiration of orbit**

16.23   **Biopsy of eyeball and orbit**

16.29   **Other diagnostic procedures on orbit and eyeball**

> EXCLUDES   *examination of form and structure of eye (95.11-95.16)*
> *general and subjective eye examination (95.01-95.09)*
> *microscopic examination of specimen from eye (90.21-90.29)*
> *objective functional tests of eye (95.21-95.26)*
> *ocular thermography (88.82)*
> *tonometry (89.11)*
> *x-ray of orbit (87.14, 87.16)*

✓4ᵗʰ **16.3**   **Evisceration of eyeball**

DEF: Removal of eyeball, leaving sclera and occasionally cornea.

16.31   **Removal of ocular contents with synchronous implant into scleral shell**

DEF: Removal of eyeball leaving outer eyeball layer with ocular implant into shell.

16.39   **Other evisceration of eyeball**

✓4ᵗʰ **16.4**   **Enucleation of eyeball**

DEF: Removal of entire eyeball after severing eye muscles and optic nerves.

16.41   **Enucleation of eyeball with synchronous implant into Tenon's capsule with attachment of muscles**

Integrated implant of eyeball

DEF: Removal of eyeball with insertion of ocular implant and muscle attachment.

16.42   **Enucleation of eyeball with other synchronous implant**

16.49   **Other enucleation of eyeball**

Removal of eyeball NOS

✓4ᵗʰ **16.5**   **Exenteration of orbital contents**

16.51   **Exenteration of orbit with removal of adjacent structures**

Radical orbitomaxillectomy

DEF: Removal of contents of bony cavity of eye as well as related tissues and structures.

DEF: Radical orbitomaxillectomy: Removal of contents of bony cavity of eye, related tissues and structures, and a portion of maxillary bone.

16.52   **Exenteration of orbit with therapeutic removal of orbital bone**

16.59   **Other exenteration of orbit**

Evisceration of orbit NOS

Exenteration of orbit with temporalis muscle transplant

✓4ᵗʰ **16.6**   **Secondary procedures after removal of eyeball**

> EXCLUDES   *that with synchronous:*
> *enucleation of eyeball (16.41-16.42)*
> *evisceration of eyeball (16.31)*

16.61   **Secondary insertion of ocular implant**

DEF: Insertion of ocular implant after previous eye removal.

16.62   **Revision and reinsertion of ocular implant**

DEF: Reimplant or correction of ocular implant.

16.63   **Revision of enucleation socket with graft**

DEF: Implant of tissue to correct socket after eye removal.

16.64   **Other revision of enucleation socket**

16.65   **Secondary graft to exenteration cavity**

DEF: Implant of tissue in place of eye after removal.

16.66   **Other revision of exenteration cavity**

16.69   **Other secondary procedures after removal of eyeball**

✓4ᵗʰ **16.7**   **Removal of ocular or orbital implant**

16.71   **Removal of ocular implant**

16.72   **Removal of orbital implant**

✓4ᵗʰ **16.8**   **Repair of injury of eyeball and orbit**

16.81   **Repair of wound of orbit**

> EXCLUDES   *reduction of orbital fracture (76.78-76.79)*
> *repair of extraocular muscles (15.7)*

16.82   **Repair of rupture of eyeball**

Repair of multiple structures of eye

> EXCLUDES   *repair of laceration of:*
> *cornea (11.51-11.59)*
> *sclera (12.81)*

16.89   **Other repair of injury of eyeball or orbit**

✓4ᵗʰ **16.9**   **Other operations on orbit and eyeball**

> EXCLUDES   *irrigation of eye (96.51)*
> *prescription and fitting of low vision aids (95.31-95.33)*
> *removal of:*
> *eye prosthesis NEC (97.31)*
> *nonpenetrating foreign body from eye without incision (98.21)*

16.91   **Retrobulbar injection of therapeutic agent**

> EXCLUDES   *injection of radiographic contrast material (87.14)*
> *opticociliary injection (12.79)*

16.92   **Excision of lesion of orbit**

> EXCLUDES   *biopsy of orbit (16.23)*

16.93   **Excision of lesion of eye, unspecified structure**

> EXCLUDES   *biopsy of eye NOS (16.23)*

16.98   **Other operations on orbit**

16.99   **Other operations on eyeball**

Ⓝ Newborn Age: 0   Ⓟ Pediatric Age: 0-17   Ⓜ Maternity Age: 12-55   Ⓐ Adult Age: 15-124   ▶◀ Revised Text   ● New Code   ▲ Revised Code Title

104 — Volume 3   *2006 ICD•9•CM*

4. OPERATIONS ON THE EAR (18-20)

√3rd **18   Operations on external ear**

INCLUDES   operations on:
    external auditory canal
    skin and cartilage of:
        auricle
        meatus

√4th **18.0   Incision of external ear**

EXCLUDES   *removal of intraluminal foreign body (98.11)*

18.01   Piercing of ear lobe
    Piercing of pinna

18.02   Incision of external auditory canal

18.09   Other incision of external ear

√4th **18.1   Diagnostic procedures on external ear**

18.11   Otoscopy

DEF: Exam of the ear with instrument designed for visualization.

18.12   Biopsy of external ear

18.19   Other diagnostic procedures on external ear

EXCLUDES   *microscopic examination of specimen from ear (90.31-90.39)*

√4th **18.2   Excision or destruction of lesion of external ear**

18.21   Excision of preauricular sinus
    Radical excision of preauricular sinus or cyst

EXCLUDES   *excision of preauricular remnant [appendage] (18.29)*

DEF: Excision of preauricular sinus or cyst with adjacent tissues.

18.29   Excision or destruction of other lesion of external ear
    Cauterization
    Coagulation
    Cryosurgery   } of external ear
    Curettage
    Electrocoagulation
    Enucleation

    Excision of:
        exostosis of external auditory canal
        preauricular remnant [appendage]
    Partial excision of ear

EXCLUDES   *biopsy of external ear (18.12)*
    radical excision of lesion (18.31)
    removal of cerumen (96.52)

√4th **18.3   Other excision of external ear**

EXCLUDES   *biopsy of external ear (18.12)*

18.31   Radical excision of lesion of external ear

EXCLUDES   *radical excision of preauricular sinus (18.21)*

DEF: Removal of damaged, diseased ear and adjacent tissue.

18.39   Other
    Amputation of external ear

EXCLUDES   *excision of lesion (18.21-18.29, 18.31)*

18.4   Suture of laceration of external ear

18.5   Surgical correction of prominent ear
    Ear:
        pinning
        setback

DEF: Reformation of protruding outer ear.

18.6   Reconstruction of external auditory canal
    Canaloplasty of external auditory meatus
    Construction [reconstruction] of external meatus of ear:
        osseous portion
        skin-lined portion (with skin graft)

DEF: Repair of outer ear canal.

√4th **18.7   Other plastic repair of external ear**

18.71   Construction of auricle of ear
    Prosthetic appliance for absent ear
    Reconstruction:
        auricle
        ear

DEF: Reformation or repair of external ear flap.

18.72   Reattachment of amputated ear

18.79   Other plastic repair of external ear
    Otoplasty NOS   Repair of lop ear
    Postauricular skin graft

AHA: 3Q, '03, 12

DEF: Postauricular skin graft: Graft repair behind ear.

DEF: Repair of lop ear: Reconstruction of ear that is at right angle to head.

18.9   Other operations on external ear

EXCLUDES   *irrigation of ear (96.52)*
    packing of external auditory canal (96.11)
    removal of:
        cerumen (96.52)
        foreign body (without incision) (98.11)

√3rd **19   Reconstructive operations on middle ear**

19.0   Stapes mobilization
    Division, otosclerotic:
        material
        process
    Remobilization of stapes
    Stapediolysis
    Transcrural stapes mobilization

EXCLUDES   *that with synchronous stapedectomy (19.11-19.19)*

DEF: Repair of innermost bone of middle ear to enable movement and response to sound.

√4th **19.1   Stapedectomy**

EXCLUDES   *revision of previous stapedectomy (19.21-19.29)*
    stapes mobilization only (19.0)

DEF: Removal of innermost bone of middle ear.

19.11   Stapedectomy with incus replacement
    Stapedectomy with incus:
        homograft
        prosthesis

DEF: Removal of innermost bone of middle ear with autograft or prosthesis replacement.

19.19   Other stapedectomy

√4th **19.2   Revision of stapedectomy**

19.21   Revision of stapedectomy with incus replacement

19.29   Other revision of stapedectomy

19.3   Other operations on ossicular chain
    Incudectomy NOS
    Ossiculectomy NOS
    Reconstruction of ossicles, second stage

DEF: Incudectomy: Excision of middle bone of middle ear, not otherwise specified.

DEF: Ossiculectomy: Excision of middle ear bones, not otherwise specified.

DEF: Reconstruction of ossicles, second stage: Repair of middle ear bones following previous surgery.

√3rd
√4th Additional Digit Required   RUG III Special Care Procedure   RUG III Clinically Complex Procedure   RUG III Extensive Services Procedure   RUG III Rehab Procedure

2006 ICD•9•CM   Volume 3 — 105

Operations on the Ear

19.4–20.72

Stapedectomy with Incus Replacement

19.4 Myringoplasty
Epitympanic, type I   Myringoplasty by:
Myringoplasty by: graft
    cauterization   Tympanoplasty (type I)
DEF: Epitympanic, type I: Repair over or upon eardrum.

DEF: Myringoplasty by cauterization: Plastic repair of tympanic membrane of eardrum by heat.

DEF: Graft: Plastic repair using implanted tissue.

DEF: Tympanoplasty (type I): Reconstruction of eardrum to restore hearing.

✓4th 19.5 Other tympanoplasty

19.52 Type II tympanoplasty
Closure of perforation with graft against incus or malleus

19.53 Type III tympanoplasty
Graft placed in contact with mobile and intact stapes
AHA: M-A, '85, 15

19.54 Type IV tympanoplasty
Mobile footplate left exposed with air pocket between round window and graft

19.55 Type V tympanoplasty
Fenestra in horizontal semicircular canal covered by graft

19.6 Revision of tympanoplasty
DEF: Repair or correction of previous plastic surgery on eardrum.

19.9 Other repair of middle ear
Closure of mastoid fistula
Mastoid myoplasty
Obliteration of tympanomastoid cavity
DEF: Closure of mastoid fistula: Closing of abnormal channel in mastoid.

DEF: Mastoid myoplasty: Restoration or repair of mastoid muscle.

DEF: Obliteration of tympanomastoid cavity: Removal, total, of functional elements of middle ear.

✓3rd 20 Other operations on middle and inner ear

✓4th 20.0 Myringotomy
DEF: Myringotomy: Puncture of tympanic membrane or eardrum, also called tympanocentesis

20.01 Myringotomy with insertion of tube
Myringostomy

20.09 Other myringotomy
Aspiration of middle ear NOS

20.1 Removal of tympanostomy tube

✓4th 20.2 Incision of mastoid and middle ear

20.21 Incision of mastoid

20.22 Incision of petrous pyramid air cells

20.23 Incision of middle ear
Atticotomy
Division of tympanum
Lysis of adhesions of middle ear
EXCLUDES   division of otosclerotic process (19.0)
    stapediolysis (19.0)
    that with stapedectomy (19.11-19.19)

✓4th 20.3 Diagnostic procedures on middle and inner ear

20.31 Electrocochleography
DEF: Measure of electric potential of eighth cranial nerve by electrode applied sound.

20.32 Biopsy of middle and inner ear

20.39 Other diagnostic procedures on middle and inner ear
EXCLUDES   auditory and vestibular function tests (89.13, 95.41-95.49)
    microscopic examination of specimen from ear (90.31-90.39)

✓4th 20.4 Mastoidectomy
Code also any:
    skin graft (18.79)
    tympanoplasty (19.4-19.55)
EXCLUDES   that with implantation of cochlear prosthetic device (20.96-20.98)
DEF: Mastoidectomy: Excision of bony protrusion behind ear.

20.41 Simple mastoidectomy

20.42 Radical mastoidectomy

20.49 Other mastoidectomy
Atticoantrostomy
Mastoidectomy:
    NOS
    modified radical
DEF: Atticoantrotomy: Opening of cavity of mastoid bone and middle ear.

✓4th 20.5 Other excision of middle ear
EXCLUDES   that with synchronous mastoidectomy (20.41-20.49)

20.51 Excision of lesion of middle ear
EXCLUDES   biopsy of middle ear (20.32)

20.59 Other
Apicectomy of petrous pyramid
Tympanectomy

✓4th 20.6 Fenestration of inner ear

20.61 Fenestration of inner ear (initial)
Fenestration of:
    labyrinth   } with graft (skin)
    semicircular canals   (vein)
    vestibule
EXCLUDES   that with tympanoplasty, type V (19.55)
DEF: Creation of inner ear opening.

20.62 Revision of fenestration of inner ear

✓4th 20.7 Incision, excision, and destruction of inner ear

20.71 Endolymphatic shunt
DEF: Insertion of tube to drain fluid in inner ear cavities.

20.72 Injection into inner ear
Destruction by injection (alcohol):
    inner ear
    semicircular canals
    vestibule

N Newborn Age: 0   P Pediatric Age: 0-17   M Maternity Age: 12-55   A Adult Age: 15-124   Adj Adjunct Code   ◄► Revised Text   ● New Code   ▲ Revised Code Title

106 — Volume 3   2006 ICD•9•CM

20.79   **Other incision, excision, and destruction of inner ear**
Decompression of labyrinth
Drainage of inner ear
Fistulization:
    endolymphatic sac
    labyrinth
Incision of endolymphatic sac
Labyrinthectomy (transtympanic)
Opening of bony labyrinth
Perilymphatic tap

> **EXCLUDES**   *biopsy of inner ear (20.32)*

DEF: Decompression of labyrinth: Controlled relief of pressure in cavities of inner ear.

DEF: Drainage of inner ear: Removal of fluid from inner ear.

DEF: Fistulization of endolymphatic sac: Creation of passage to fluid sac in inner ear cavities.

DEF: Fistulization of labyrinth: Creation of passage to inner ear cavities.

DEF: Incision of endolymphatic sac: Cutting into fluid sac in inner ear cavities.

DEF: Labyrinthectomy (transtympanic): Excision of cavities across eardrum.

DEF: Opening of bony labyrinth: Cutting into inner ear bony cavities.

DEF: Perilymphatic tap: Puncture or incision into fluid sac of inner ear cavities.

20.8   **Operations on Eustachian tube**
Catheterization
Inflation
Injection (Teflon paste)
Insufflation (boric acid-   }   of Eustachian
    salicylic acid)   tube
Intubation
Politzerization

DEF: Catheterization: Passing catheter into passage between pharynx and middle ear.

DEF: Inflation: Blowing air, gas or liquid into passage between pharynx and middle ear to inflate.

DEF: Injection (Teflon paste): Forcing fluid (Teflon paste) into passage between pharynx and middle ear.

DEF: Insufflation (boric acid-salicylic acid): Blowing gas or liquid into passage between pharynx and middle ear.

DEF: Intubation: Placing tube into passage between pharynx and middle ear.

DEF: Politzerization: Inflating passage between pharynx and middle ear with Politzer bag.

√4th **20.9**   **Other operations on inner and middle ear**

20.91   **Tympanosympathectomy**
DEF: Excision or chemical suppression of impulses of middle ear nerves.

20.92   **Revision of mastoidectomy**
AHA: 2Q, '98, 20

DEF: Correction of previous removal of mastoid cells from temporal or mastoid bone.

20.93   **Repair of oval and round windows**
Closure of fistula: Closure of fistula:
    oval window   round window
    perilymph
DEF: Restoration of middle ear openings.

20.94   **Injection of tympanum**

20.95   **Implantation of electromagnetic hearing device**
Bone conduction hearing device

> **EXCLUDES**   *cochlear prosthetic device (20.96-20.98)*

AHA: 4Q, '89, 5

20.96   **Implantation or replacement of cochlear prosthetic device, not otherwise specified**
Implantation of receiver (within skull) and insertion of electrode(s) in the cochlea

> **INCLUDES**   mastoidectomy

> **EXCLUDES**   *electromagnetic hearing device (20.95)*

AHA: 4Q, '89, 5

20.97   **Implantation or replacement of cochlear prosthetic device, single channel**
Implantation of receiver (within skull) and insertion of electrode in the cochlea

> **INCLUDES**   mastoidectomy

> **EXCLUDES**   *electromagnetic hearing device (20.95)*

AHA: 4Q, '89, 5

20.98   **Implantation or replacement of cochlear prosthetic device, multiple channel**
Implantation of receiver (within skull) and insertion of electrodes in the cochlea

> **INCLUDES**   mastoidectomy

> **EXCLUDES**   *electromagnetic hearing device (20.95)*

AHA: 4Q, '89, 5

20.99   **Other operations on middle and inner ear**
Repair or removal of cochlear prosthetic device (receiver) (electrode)

> **EXCLUDES**   *adjustment (external components) of cochlear prosthetic device (95.49)*
> *fitting of hearing aid (95.48)*

AHA: 4Q, '89, 7

√3rd
√4th   Additional Digit Required   RUG III Special Care Procedure   RUG III Clinically Complex Procedure   RUG III Extensive Services Procedure   RUG III Rehab Procedure

2006 ICD•9•CM   **Volume 3 — 107**

Operations on the Nose, Mouth, and Pharynx

21–21.87

5. OPERATIONS ON THE NOSE, MOUTH, AND PHARYNX (21-29)

√3ʳᵈ **21 Operations on nose**

INCLUDES   operations on:
bone ⎫
skin ⎬ of nose

AHA: 1Q, '94, 5

√4ᵗʰ **21.0 Control of epistaxis**

21.00 Control of epistaxis, not otherwise specified

21.01 Control of epistaxis by anterior nasal packing

21.02 Control of epistaxis by posterior (and anterior) packing

21.03 Control of epistaxis by cauterization (and packing)

21.04 Control of epistaxis by ligation of ethmoidal arteries

21.05 Control of epistaxis by (transantral) ligation of the maxillary artery

21.06 Control of epistaxis by ligation of the external carotid artery

21.07 Control of epistaxis by excision of nasal mucosa and skin grafting of septum and lateral nasal wall

21.09 Control of epistaxis by other means

21.1 Incision of nose
Chondrotomy   Nasal septotomy
Incision of skin of nose

DEF: Chondrotomy: Incision or division of nasal cartilage.

DEF: Nasal septotomy: Incision into bone dividing nose into two chambers.

√4ᵗʰ **21.2 Diagnostic procedures on nose**

21.21 Rhinoscopy

DEF: Visualization of nasal passage with nasal speculum.

21.22 Biopsy of nose

21.29 Other diagnostic procedures on nose
EXCLUDES   microscopic examination of specimen from nose (90.31-90.39)
nasal:
function study (89.12)
x-ray (87.16)
rhinomanometry (89.12)

√4ᵗʰ **21.3 Local excision or destruction of lesion of nose**
EXCLUDES   biopsy of nose (21.22)
nasal fistulectomy (21.82)

21.30 Excision or destruction of lesion of nose, not otherwise specified

21.31 Local excision or destruction of intranasal lesion
Nasal polypectomy

21.32 Local excision or destruction of other lesion of nose
AHA: 2Q, '89, 16

21.4 Resection of nose
Amputation of nose

21.5 Submucous resection of nasal septum

DEF: Resection, partial, of nasal septum with mucosa reimplanted after excision.

√4ᵗʰ **21.6 Turbinectomy**

DEF: Removal, partial, or total of turbinate bones; inferior turbinate is most often excised.

21.61 Turbinectomy by diathermy or cryosurgery
DEF: Destruction of turbinate bone by heat or freezing.

Excision of Turbinate

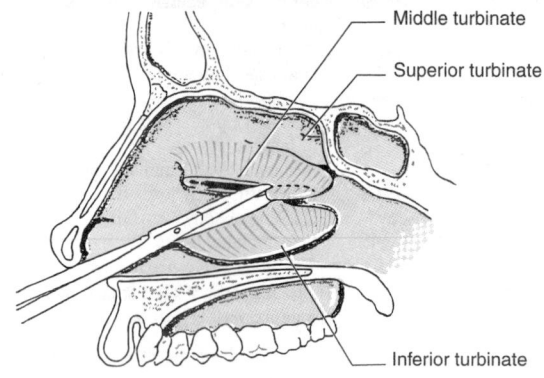

Middle turbinate
Superior turbinate
Inferior turbinate

21.62 Fracture of the turbinates
DEF: Surgical breaking of turbinate bones.

21.69 Other turbinectomy
EXCLUDES   turbinectomy associated with sinusectomy (22.31-22.39, 22.42, 22.60-22.64)

√4ᵗʰ **21.7 Reduction of nasal fracture**

21.71 Closed reduction of nasal fracture

21.72 Open reduction of nasal fracture

√4ᵗʰ **21.8 Repair and plastic operations on the nose**

21.81 Suture of laceration of nose

21.82 Closure of nasal fistula
Nasolabial ⎫
Nasopharyngeal ⎬ fistulectomy
Oronasal ⎭

DEF: Sealing off crack or hole between nose and lip, nose and pharynx, or nose and mouth.

21.83 Total nasal reconstruction
Reconstruction of nose with:
arm flap
forehead flap

DEF: Reformation, plastic, of nasal structure with tissue flap from arm or forehead.

21.84 Revision rhinoplasty
Rhinoseptoplasty
Twisted nose rhinoplasty

DEF: Rhinoseptoplasty: Repair of nose and the bone dividing the nose into two chambers.

DEF: Twisted nose rhinoplasty: Repair of nose alignment following reconstructive surgery.

21.85 Augmentation rhinoplasty
Augmentation rhinoplasty with:
graft
synthetic implant

DEF: Implant of tissue or synthetic graft to enlarge nose.

21.86 Limited rhinoplasty
Plastic repair of nasolabial flaps
Tip rhinoplasty

DEF: Plastic repair of nasolabial flaps: Reconstruction of nasal area above lips.

DEF: Tip rhinoplasty: Reconstruction or restoration of nasal tip.

21.87 Other rhinoplasty
Rhinoplasty NOS

Ⓝ Newborn Age: 0   Ⓟ Pediatric Age: 0-17   Ⓜ Maternity Age: 12-55   Ⓐ Adult Age: 15-124   Adj Adjunct Code   ▶◀ Revised Text   ● New Code   ▲ Revised Code Title

21.88 Other septoplasty
Crushing of nasal septum
Repair of septal perforation
> EXCLUDES septoplasty associated with submucous resection of septum (21.5)

DEF: Crushing of nasal septum: Division and reconstruction of defects in bone dividing nasal chambers.

DEF: Repair of septal perforation: Repair of hole in bone dividing nasal chambers with adjacent tissue.

21.89 Other repair and plastic operations on nose
Reattachment of amputated nose

✓4th **21.9 Other operations on nose**

21.91 Lysis of adhesions of nose
Posterior nasal scrub

DEF: Posterior nasal scrub: Clearing out of abnormal adhesions in posterior nasal area.

21.99 Other
> EXCLUDES dilation of frontonasal duct (96.21)
> irrigation of nasal passages (96.53)
> removal of:
> intraluminal foreign body without incision (98.12)
> nasal packing (97.32)
> replacement of nasal packing (97.21)

✓3rd **22 Operations on nasal sinuses**

✓4th **22.0 Aspiration and lavage of nasal sinus**

22.00 Aspiration and lavage of nasal sinus, not otherwise specified

22.01 Puncture of nasal sinus for aspiration or lavage

22.02 Aspiration or lavage of nasal sinus through natural ostium
DEF: Withdrawal of fluid and washing of nasal cavity through natural opening.

✓4th **22.1 Diagnostic procedures on nasal sinus**

22.11 Closed [endoscopic] [needle] biopsy of nasal sinus

22.12 Open biopsy of nasal sinus

22.19 Other diagnostic procedures on nasal sinuses
Endoscopy without biopsy
> EXCLUDES transillumination of sinus (89.35)
> x-ray of sinus (87.15-87.16)

22.2 Intranasal antrotomy
> EXCLUDES antrotomy with external approach (22.31-22.39)

DEF: Incision of intranasal sinus.

✓4th **22.3 External maxillary antrotomy**

22.31 Radical maxillary antrotomy
Removal of lining membrane of maxillary sinus using Caldwell-Luc approach

DEF: Caldwell-Luc approach: Removal of membrane lining the maxillary cavity through incision above canine teeth.

22.39 Other external maxillary antrotomy
Exploration of maxillary antrum with Caldwell-Luc approach

✓4th **22.4 Frontal sinusotomy and sinusectomy**

22.41 Frontal sinusotomy

22.42 Frontal sinusectomy
Excision of lesion of frontal sinus
Obliteration of frontal sinus (with fat)
> EXCLUDES biopsy of nasal sinus (22.11-22.12)

✓4th **22.5 Other nasal sinusotomy**

22.50 Sinusotomy, not otherwise specified

22.51 Ethmoidotomy

22.52 Sphenoidotomy

22.53 Incision of multiple nasal sinuses

✓4th **22.6 Other nasal sinusectomy**
> INCLUDES that with incidental turbinectomy
> EXCLUDES biopsy of nasal sinus (22.11-22.12)

22.60 Sinusectomy, not otherwise specified

22.61 Excision of lesion of maxillary sinus with Caldwell-Luc approach

22.62 Excision of lesion of maxillary sinus with other approach

22.63 Ethmoidectomy
DEF: Removal of ethmoid cells and bone, partial or total includes excising mucosal lining, partial or total.

22.64 Sphenoidectomy
DEF: Removal of wedge shaped sphenoid bone at base of brain.

✓4th **22.7 Repair of nasal sinus**

22.71 Closure of nasal sinus fistula
Repair of oro-antral fistula

22.79 Other repair of nasal sinus
Reconstruction of frontonasal duct
Repair of bone of accessory sinus

22.9 Other operations on nasal sinuses
Exteriorization of maxillary sinus
Fistulization of sinus
> EXCLUDES dilation of frontonasal duct (96.21)

DEF: Exteriorization of maxillary sinus: Creation of external maxillary cavity opening.

DEF: Fistulization of sinus: Creation of fistula canal in nasal cavity.

✓3rd **23 Removal and restoration of teeth**

✓4th **23.0 Forceps extraction of tooth**

23.01 Extraction of deciduous tooth

23.09 Extraction of other tooth
Extraction of tooth NOS

✓4th **23.1 Surgical removal of tooth**

23.11 Removal of residual root

23.19 Other surgical extraction of tooth
Odontectomy NOS
Removal of impacted tooth
Tooth extraction with elevation of mucoperiosteal flap

23.2 Restoration of tooth by filling

23.3 Restoration of tooth by inlay
DEF: Restoration of tooth by cementing in a molded filling.

✓4th **23.4 Other dental restoration**

23.41 Application of crown

23.42 Insertion of fixed bridge

23.43 Insertion of removable bridge

23.49 Other

23.5 Implantation of tooth
DEF: Insertion of a sound tooth to replace extracted tooth.

23.6 Prosthetic dental implant
Endosseous dental implant
DEF: Implant of artificial denture within bone covering tooth socket.

✓4th **23.7 Apicoectomy and root canal therapy**

23.70 Root canal, not otherwise specified

23.71 Root canal therapy with irrigation

✓3rd ✓4th Additional Digit Required   RUG III Special Care Procedure   RUG III Clinically Complex Procedure   RUG III Extensive Services Procedure   RUG III Rehab Procedure

2006 ICD•9•CM   Volume 3 — 109

Operations on the Nose, Mouth, and Pharynx

23.72–26.0

23.72 Root canal therapy with apicoectomy

DEF: Removal of tooth root to treat damaged root canal tissue.

23.73 Apicoectomy

√3rd **24 Other operations on teeth, gums, and alveoli**

24.0 Incision of gum or alveolar bone
Apical alveolotomy

√4th **24.1 Diagnostic procedures on teeth, gums, and alveoli**

24.11 Biopsy of gum

24.12 Biopsy of alveolus

24.19 Other diagnostic procedures on teeth, gums, and alveoli

EXCLUDES *dental:*
examination (89.31)
x-ray:
full-mouth (87.11)
other (87.12)
microscopic examination of dental specimen (90.81-90.89)

24.2 Gingivoplasty
Gingivoplasty with bone or soft tissue graft

DEF: Repair of gum tissue.

√4th **24.3 Other operations on gum**

24.31 Excision of lesion or tissue of gum

EXCLUDES *biopsy of gum (24.11)*
excision of odontogenic lesion (24.4)

24.32 Suture of laceration of gum

24.39 Other

24.4 Excision of dental lesion of jaw
Excision of odontogenic lesion

24.5 Alveoloplasty
Alveolectomy (interradicular) (intraseptal) (radical) (simple) (with graft or implant)

EXCLUDES *biopsy of alveolus (24.12)*
en bloc resection of alveolar process and palate (27.32)

DEF: Repair or correction of bony tooth socket.

24.6 Exposure of tooth

24.7 Application of orthodontic appliance
Application, insertion, or fitting of:
arch bars   orthodontic wiring
orthodontic obturator   periodontal splint

EXCLUDES *nonorthodontic dental wiring (93.55)*

24.8 Other orthodontic operation
Closure of diastema   Removal of arch bars
(alveolar) (dental)   Repair of dental arch
Occlusal adjustment

EXCLUDES *removal of nonorthodontic wiring (97.33)*

√4th **24.9 Other dental operations**

24.91 Extension or deepening of buccolabial or lingual sulcus

24.99 Other

EXCLUDES *dental:*
debridement (96.54)
examination (89.31)
prophylaxis (96.54)
scaling and polishing (96.54)
wiring (93.55)
fitting of dental appliance [denture] (99.97)
microscopic examination of dental specimen (90.81-90.89)
removal of dental:
packing (97.34)
prosthesis (97.35)
wiring (97.33)
replacement of dental packing (97.22)

√3rd **25 Operations on tongue**

√4th **25.0 Diagnostic procedures on tongue**

25.01 Closed [needle] biopsy of tongue

25.02 Open biopsy of tongue
Wedge biopsy

25.09 Other diagnostic procedures on tongue

25.1 Excision or destruction of lesion or tissue of tongue

EXCLUDES *biopsy of tongue (25.01-25.02)*
frenumectomy:
labial (27.41)
lingual (25.92)

AHA: 2Q, '02, 5

25.2 Partial glossectomy

25.3 Complete glossectomy
Glossectomy NOS
Code also any neck dissection (40.40-40.42)

25.4 Radical glossectomy
Code also any:
neck dissection (40.40-40.42)
tracheostomy (31.1-31.29)

√4th **25.5 Repair of tongue and glossoplasty**

25.51 Suture of laceration of tongue

25.59 Other repair and plastic operations on tongue
Fascial sling of tongue
Fusion of tongue (to lip)
Graft of mucosa or skin to tongue

EXCLUDES *lysis of adhesions of tongue (25.93)*

AHA: 1Q, '97, 5

√4th **25.9 Other operations on tongue**

25.91 Lingual frenotomy

EXCLUDES *labial frenotomy (27.91)*

DEF: Extension of groove between cheek and lips or cheek and tongue.

25.92 Lingual frenectomy

EXCLUDES *labial frenectomy (27.41)*

DEF: Frenectomy: Removal of vertical membrane attaching tongue to floor of mouth.

25.93 Lysis of adhesions of tongue

25.94 Other glossotomy

25.99 Other

√3rd **26 Operations on salivary glands and ducts**

INCLUDES operations on:
lesser salivary ⎤
parotid   ⎥ gland and duct
sublingual   ⎥
submaxillary   ⎦

Code also any neck dissection (40.40-40.42)

26.0 Incision of salivary gland or duct

N Newborn Age: 0   P Pediatric Age: 0-17   M Maternity Age: 12-55   A Adult Age: 15-124   Adj Adjunct Code   ▶◀ Revised Text   ● New Code   ▲ Revised Code Title

√4th **26.1**   **Diagnostic procedures on salivary glands and ducts**

26.11   **Closed [needle] biopsy of salivary gland or duct**

26.12   **Open biopsy of salivary gland or duct**

26.19   **Other diagnostic procedures on salivary glands and ducts**

EXCLUDES   *x-ray of salivary gland (87.09)*

√4th **26.2**   **Excision of lesion of salivary gland**

26.21   **Marsupialization of salivary gland cyst**

DEF: Creation of pouch of salivary gland cyst to drain and promote healing.

26.29   **Other excision of salivary gland lesion**

EXCLUDES   *biopsy of salivary gland (26.11-26.12)*
salivary fistulectomy (26.42)

√4th **26.3**   **Sialoadenectomy**

DEF: Removal of salivary gland.

26.30   **Sialoadenectomy, not otherwise specified**

26.31   **Partial sialoadenectomy**

26.32   **Complete sialoadenectomy**
En bloc excision of salivary gland lesion
Radical sialoadenectomy

√4th **26.4**   **Repair of salivary gland or duct**

26.41   **Suture of laceration of salivary gland**

26.42   **Closure of salivary fistula**

DEF: Closing of abnormal opening in salivary gland.

26.49   **Other repair and plastic operations on salivary gland or duct**
Fistulization of salivary gland
Plastic repair of salivary gland or duct NOS
Transplantation of salivary duct opening

√4th **26.9**   **Other operations on salivary gland or duct**

26.91   **Probing of salivary duct**

26.99   **Other**

√3rd **27**   **Other operations on mouth and face**

INCLUDES   operations on:
lips
palate
soft tissue of face and mouth, except tongue and gingiva

EXCLUDES   operations on:
gingiva (24.0-24.99)
tongue (25.01-25.99)

27.0   **Drainage of face and floor of mouth**
Drainage of: Drainage of:
facial region (abscess)   Ludwig's angina
fascial compartment of face

EXCLUDES   *drainage of thyroglossal tract (06.09)*

27.1   **Incision of palate**

√4th **27.2**   **Diagnostic procedures on oral cavity**

27.21   **Biopsy of bony palate**

27.22   **Biopsy of uvula and soft palate**

27.23   **Biopsy of lip**

27.24   **Biopsy of mouth, unspecified structure**

27.29   **Other diagnostic procedures on oral cavity**

EXCLUDES   *soft tissue x-ray (87.09)*

√4th **27.3**   **Excision of lesion or tissue of bony palate**

27.31   **Local excision or destruction of lesion or tissue of bony palate**
Local excision or destruction of palate by:
cautery   cryotherapy
chemotherapy

EXCLUDES   *biopsy of bony palate (27.21)*

27.32   **Wide excision or destruction of lesion or tissue of bony palate**
En bloc resection of alveolar process and palate

√4th **27.4**   **Excision of other parts of mouth**

27.41   **Labial frenectomy**

EXCLUDES   *division of labial frenum (27.91)*

DEF: Removal of mucous membrane fold of lip.

27.42   **Wide excision of lesion of lip**

27.43   **Other excision of lesion or tissue of lip**

27.49   **Other excision of mouth**

EXCLUDES   *biopsy of mouth NOS (27.24)*
excision of lesion of:
palate (27.31-27.32)
tongue (25.1)
uvula (27.72)
fistulectomy of mouth (27.53)
frenectomy of:
lip (27.41)
tongue (25.92)

√4th **27.5**   **Plastic repair of mouth**

EXCLUDES   *palatoplasty (27.61-27.69)*

27.51   **Suture of laceration of lip**

27.52   **Suture of laceration of other part of mouth**

27.53   **Closure of fistula of mouth**

EXCLUDES   *fistulectomy:*
nasolabial (21.82)
oro-antral (22.71)
oronasal (21.82)

27.54   **Repair of cleft lip**

27.55   **Full-thickness skin graft to lip and mouth**

27.56   **Other skin graft to lip and mouth**

27.57   **Attachment of pedicle or flap graft to lip and mouth**
AHA: 1Q, '96, 14

DEF: Repair of lip or mouth with tissue pedicle or flap still connected to original vascular base.

27.59   **Other plastic repair of mouth**

√4th **27.6**   **Palatoplasty**

27.61   **Suture of laceration of palate**

27.62   **Correction of cleft palate**
Correction of cleft palate by push-back operation

EXCLUDES   *revision of cleft palate repair (27.63)*

27.63   **Revision of cleft palate repair**
Secondary:
attachment of pharyngeal flap
lengthening of palate
AHA: 1Q, '96, 14

27.64   **Insertion of palatal implant**

DEF: ▶Nonabsorbable polyester implants into the soft palate at the back of the roof of the mouth; one implant placed at the soft palate midline and two are positioned on either side; to support and stiffen the palate reducing vibration (snoring).◀

27.69   **Other plastic repair of palate**
Code also any insertion of palatal implant (27.64)

EXCLUDES   *fistulectomy of mouth (27.53)*

AHA: 3Q, '99, 22; 1Q, '97, 14; 3Q, '92, 18

√4th **27.7**   **Operations on uvula**

27.71   **Incision of uvula**

27.72   **Excision of uvula**

EXCLUDES   *biopsy of uvula (27.22)*

27.73   **Repair of uvula**

EXCLUDES   *that with synchronous cleft palate repair (27.62)*
uranostaphylorrhaphy (27.62)

27.79   **Other operations on uvula**
AHA: 3Q, '92, 18

√3rd √4th   Additional Digit Required   RUG III Special Care Procedure   RUG III Clinically Complex Procedure   RUG III Extensive Services Procedure   RUG III Rehab Procedure

2006 ICD•9•CM   February 2005 • Volume 3 — 111

Operations on the Nose, Mouth, and Pharynx

27.9–29.99

√4th **27.9** **Other operations on mouth and face**

27.91 **Labial frenotomy**

Division of labial frenum

EXCLUDES   lingual frenotomy (25.91)

DEF: Division of labial frenum: Cutting and separating mucous membrane fold of lip.

27.92 **Incision of mouth, unspecified structure**

EXCLUDES   incision of:
gum (24.0)
palate (27.1)
salivary gland or duct (26.0)
tongue (25.94)
uvula (27.71)

27.99 **Other operations on oral cavity**

Graft of buccal sulcus

EXCLUDES   removal of:
intraluminal foreign body (98.01)
penetrating foreign body from mouth without incision (98.22)

DEF: Graft of buccal sulcus: Implant of tissue into groove of interior cheek lining.

√3rd **28** **Operations on tonsils and adenoids**

28.0 **Incision and drainage of tonsil and peritonsillar structures**

Drainage (oral) (transcervical) of:
parapharyngeal
peritonsillar   } abscess
retropharyngeal
tonsillar

√4th **28.1** **Diagnostic procedures on tonsils and adenoids**

28.11 **Biopsy of tonsils and adenoids**

28.19 **Other diagnostic procedures on tonsils and adenoids**

EXCLUDES   soft tissue x-ray (87.09)

28.2 **Tonsillectomy without adenoidectomy**

AHA: 1Q, '97, 5; 2Q, '90, 23

28.3 **Tonsillectomy with adenoidectomy**

28.4 **Excision of tonsil tag**

28.5 **Excision of lingual tonsil**

28.6 **Adenoidectomy without tonsillectomy**

Excision of adenoid tag

28.7 **Control of hemorrhage after tonsillectomy and adenoidectomy**

√4th **28.9** **Other operations on tonsils and adenoids**

28.91 **Removal of foreign body from tonsil and adenoid by incision**

EXCLUDES   that without incision (98.13)

28.92 **Excision of lesion of tonsil and adenoid**

EXCLUDES   biopsy of tonsil and adenoid (28.11)

28.99 **Other**

√3rd **29** **Operations on pharynx**

INCLUDES   operations on: operations on:
hypopharynx   pharyngeal pouch
nasopharynx   pyriform sinus
oropharynx

29.0 **Pharyngotomy**

Drainage of pharyngeal bursa

EXCLUDES   incision and drainage of retropharyngeal abscess (28.0)
removal of foreign body (without incision) (98.13)

√4th **29.1** **Diagnostic procedures on pharynx**

29.11 **Pharyngoscopy**

29.12 **Pharyngeal biopsy**

Biopsy of supraglottic mass

29.19 **Other diagnostic procedures on pharynx**

EXCLUDES   x-ray of nasopharynx:
contrast (87.06)
other (87.09)

29.2 **Excision of branchial cleft cyst or vestige**

EXCLUDES   branchial cleft fistulectomy (29.52)

√4th **29.3** **Excision or destruction of lesion or tissue of pharynx**

AHA: 2Q, '89, 18

29.31 **Cricopharyngeal myotomy**

EXCLUDES   that with pharyngeal diverticulectomy (29.32)

DEF: Removal of outward pouching of throat.

29.32 **Pharyngeal diverticulectomy**

29.33 **Pharyngectomy (partial)**

EXCLUDES   laryngopharyngectomy (30.3)

29.39 **Other excision or destruction of lesion or tissue of pharynx**

29.4 **Plastic operation on pharynx**

Correction of nasopharyngeal atresia

EXCLUDES   pharyngoplasty associated with cleft palate repair (27.62-27.63)

AHA: 3Q, '99, 22; 1Q, '97, 5; 3Q, '92, 18

DEF: Correction of nasopharyngeal atresia: Construction of normal opening for throat stricture behind nose.

√4th **29.5** **Other repair of pharynx**

29.51 **Suture of laceration of pharynx**

29.52 **Closure of branchial cleft fistula**

DEF: Sealing off an abnormal opening of the branchial fissure in throat.

29.53 **Closure of other fistula of pharynx**

Pharyngoesophageal fistulectomy

29.54 **Lysis of pharyngeal adhesions**

29.59 **Other**

AHA: 2Q, '89, 18

√4th **29.9** **Other operations on pharynx**

29.91 **Dilation of pharynx**

Dilation of nasopharynx

29.92 **Division of glossopharyngeal nerve**

29.99 **Other**

EXCLUDES   insertion of radium into pharynx and nasopharynx (92.27)
removal of intraluminal foreign body (98.13)

N Newborn Age: 0   P Pediatric Age: 0-17   M Maternity Age: 12-55   A Adult Age: 15-124   Adj Adjunct Code   ◄ Revised Text   ● New Code   ▲ Revised Code Title

6. OPERATIONS ON THE RESPIRATORY SYSTEM (30-34)

✓3rd **30**   **Excision of larynx**

✓4th   **30.0**   **Excision or destruction of lesion or tissue of larynx**

     30.01   **Marsupialization of laryngeal cyst**

       DEF: Incision of cyst of larynx with the edges sutured open to create pouch.

     30.09   **Other excision or destruction of lesion or tissue of larynx**

       Stripping of vocal cords

       EXCLUDES   *biopsy of larynx (31.43)*
                laryngeal fistulectomy (31.62)
                laryngotracheal fistulectomy (31.62)

   30.1   **Hemilaryngectomy**

     DEF: Excision of one side (half) of larynx.

✓4th   **30.2**   **Other partial laryngectomy**

     30.21   **Epiglottidectomy**

     30.22   **Vocal cordectomy**

       Excision of vocal cords

     30.29   **Other partial laryngectomy**

       Excision of laryngeal cartilage

   30.3   **Complete laryngectomy**

     Block dissection of larynx (with thyroidectomy) (with synchronous tracheostomy)

     Laryngopharyngectomy

     EXCLUDES   *that with radical neck dissection (30.4)*

   30.4   **Radical laryngectomy**

     Complete [total] laryngectomy with radical neck dissection (with thyroidectomy) (with synchronous tracheostomy)

✓3rd **31**   **Other operations on larynx and trachea**

   31.0   **Injection of larynx**

     Injection of inert material into larynx or vocal cords

   31.1   **Temporary tracheostomy**

     Tracheotomy for assistance in breathing

     AHA: 1Q, '97, 6; 3Q, '91, 20

✓4th   **31.2**   **Permanent tracheostomy**

     31.21   **Mediastinal tracheostomy**

       DEF: Placement of artificial breathing tube in windpipe through mediastinum, for long-term use.

     31.29   **Other permanent tracheostomy**

       EXCLUDES   *that with laryngectomy (30.3-30.4)*

       AHA: 2Q, '02, 6

   31.3   **Other incision of larynx or trachea**

     EXCLUDES   *that for assistance in breathing (31.1-31.29)*

✓4th   **31.4**   **Diagnostic procedures on larynx and trachea**

     31.41   **Tracheoscopy through artificial stoma**

       EXCLUDES   *that with biopsy (31.43-31.44)*

       DEF: Exam by scope of trachea through an artificial opening.

Temporary Tracheostomy

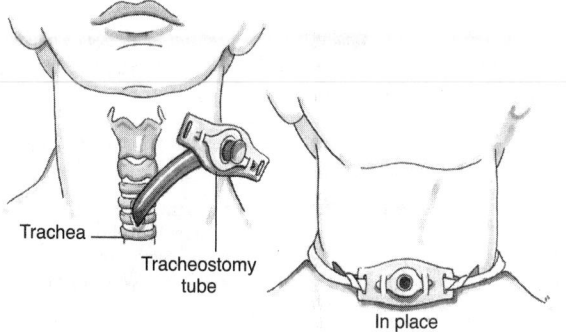

Trachea — Tracheostomy tube — In place

Closed Endoscopic Biopsy of Larynx

Laryngoscope — Palate — Trachea

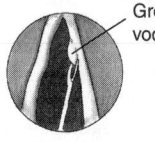

Growth on vocal cord

     31.42   **Laryngoscopy and other tracheoscopy**

       EXCLUDES   *that with biopsy (31.43-31.44)*

     31.43   **Closed [endoscopic] biopsy of larynx**

     31.44   **Closed [endoscopic] biopsy of trachea**

     31.45   **Open biopsy of larynx or trachea**

     31.48   **Other diagnostic procedures on larynx**

       EXCLUDES   *contrast laryngogram (87.07)*
               microscopic examination of specimen from larynx (90.31-90.39)
               soft tissue x-ray of larynx NEC (87.09)

     31.49   **Other diagnostic procedures on trachea**

       EXCLUDES   *microscopic examination of specimen from trachea (90.41-90.49)*
               x-ray of trachea (87.49)

   31.5   **Local excision or destruction of lesion or tissue of trachea**

     EXCLUDES   *biopsy of trachea (31.44-31.45)*
               laryngotracheal fistulectomy (31.62)
               tracheoesophageal fistulectomy (31.73)

✓4th   **31.6**   **Repair of larynx**

     31.61   **Suture of laceration of larynx**

     31.62   **Closure of fistula of larynx**

       Laryngotracheal fistulectomy

       Take-down of laryngostomy

       DEF: Laryngotracheal fistulectomy: Excision and closing of passage between voice box and trachea.

       DEF: Take-down of laryngostomy: Removal of laryngostomy tube and restoration of voice box.

     31.63   **Revision of laryngostomy**

     31.64   **Repair of laryngeal fracture**

       DEF: Alignment and positioning of harder structures of larynx such as hyoid bone; following fracture.

     31.69   **Other repair of larynx**

       Arytenoidopexy

       Graft of larynx

       Transposition of vocal cords

       EXCLUDES   *construction of artificial larynx (31.75)*

       DEF: Arytenoidopexy: Fixation of pitcher-shaped cartilage in voice box.

       DEF: Graft of larynx: Implant of graft tissue into voice box.

       DEF: Transposition of the vocal cords: Placement of vocal cords into more functional positions.

✓4th   **31.7**   **Repair and plastic operations on trachea**

     31.71   **Suture of laceration of trachea**

✓3rd ✓4th **Additional Digit Required**   RUG III Special Care Procedure   RUG III Clinically Complex Procedure   RUG III Extensive Services Procedure   RUG III Rehab Procedure

2006 ICD•9•CM   **Volume 3 — 113**

31.72 Closure of external fistula of trachea
Closure of tracheotomy

31.73 Closure of other fistula of trachea
Tracheoesophageal fistulectomy

> EXCLUDES   *laryngotracheal fistulectomy (31.62)*

DEF: Tracheoesophageal fistulectomy: Excision and closure of abnormal opening between windpipe and esophagus.

31.74 Revision of tracheostomy

31.75 Reconstruction of trachea and construction of artificial larynx
Tracheoplasty with artificial larynx

31.79 Other repair and plastic operations on trachea

√4th **31.9 Other operations on larynx and trachea**

31.91 Division of laryngeal nerve

31.92 Lysis of adhesions of trachea or larynx

31.93 Replacement of laryngeal or tracheal stent

DEF: Removal and substitution of tubed molding into larynx or trachea.

31.94 Injection of locally-acting therapeutic substance into trachea

31.95 Tracheoesophageal fistulization

DEF: Creation of passage between trachea and esophagus.

31.98 Other operations on larynx

Dilation
Division of congenital web } of larynx
Removal of keel or stent

> EXCLUDES   *removal of intraluminal foreign body from larynx without incision (98.14)*

DEF: Dilation: Increasing larynx size by stretching.

DEF: Division of congenital web: Cutting and separating congenital membranes around larynx.

DEF: Removal of keel or stent: Removal of prosthetic device from larynx.

31.99 Other operations on trachea

> EXCLUDES   *removal of:*
> *intraluminal foreign body from trachea without incision (98.15)*
> *tracheostomy tube (97.37)*
> *replacement of tracheostomy tube (97.23)*
> *tracheostomy toilette (96.55)*

AHA: 1Q, '97, 14

√3rd **32 Excision of lung and bronchus**

> INCLUDES   rib resection
> sternotomy
> sternum-splitting } as operative
> incision   approach
> thoracotomy

Code also any synchronous bronchoplasty (33.48)

DEF: Rib resection: Cutting of ribs to access operative field.

DEF: Sternotomy: Cut through breastbone as an operative approach.

DEF: Sternum-splitting incision: Breaking through breastbone to access operative field.

√4th **32.0 Local excision or destruction of lesion or tissue of bronchus**

> EXCLUDES   *biopsy of bronchus (33.24-33.25)*
> *bronchial fistulectomy (33.42)*

AHA: 4Q, '88, 11

Lung Volume Reduction

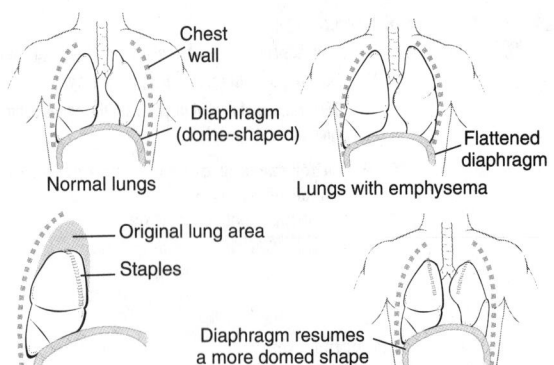

32.01 Endoscopic excision or destruction of lesion or tissue of bronchus

32.09 Other local excision or destruction of lesion or tissue of bronchus

> EXCLUDES   *that by endoscopic approach (32.01)*

32.1 Other excision of bronchus
Resection (wide sleeve) of bronchus

> EXCLUDES   *radical dissection [excision] of bronchus (32.6)*

DEF: Resection (wide sleeve) of bronchus: Excision and partial, lengthwise removal of a lung branch.

√4th **32.2 Local excision or destruction of lesion or tissue of lung**

32.21 Plication of emphysematous bleb

DEF: Stitching of a swollen vesicle into folds or tuck.

32.22 Lung volume reduction surgery

AHA: 1Q, '97, 6; 3Q, '96, 20; 4Q, '95, 64

DEF: Excision of portion of lung(s) to reduce respiratory effort in moderate to severe emphysema.

32.28 Endoscopic excision or destruction of lesion or tissue of lung

> EXCLUDES   *biopsy of lung (33.26-33.27)*

32.29 Other local excision or destruction of lesion or tissue of lung
Resection of lung:
NOS
wedge

> EXCLUDES   *biopsy of lung (33.26-33.27)*
> *that by endoscopic approach (32.28)*
> *wide excision of lesion of lung (32.3)*

AHA: 3Q, '99, 3

32.3 Segmental resection of lung
Partial lobectomy

32.4 Lobectomy of lung
Lobectomy with segmental resection of adjacent lobes of lung

> EXCLUDES   *that with radical dissection [excision] of thoracic structures (32.6)*

32.5 Complete pneumonectomy
Excision of lung NOS
Pneumonectomy (with mediastinal dissection)
AHA: 1Q, '99, 6

32.6 Radical dissection of thoracic structures
Block [en bloc] dissection of bronchus, lobe of lung, brachial plexus, intercostal structure, ribs (transverse process), and sympathetic nerves

---

Ⓝ Newborn Age: 0   Ⓟ Pediatric Age: 0-17   Ⓜ Maternity Age: 12-55   Ⓐ Adult Age: 15-124   **Adj** Adjunct Code   ◄ Revised Text   ● New Code   ▲ Revised Code Title

114 — Volume 3   *2006 ICD•9•CM*

32.9   Other excision of lung

> **EXCLUDES**   *biopsy of lung and bronchus (33.24-33.27)*
>
> *pulmonary decortication (34.51)*

√3rd 33   Other operations on lung and bronchus

> **INCLUDES**   rib resection
> sternotomy   as operative
> sternum-splitting incision   approach
> thoracotomy

33.0   Incision of bronchus

33.1   Incision of lung

> **EXCLUDES** *puncture of lung (33.93)*

√4th 33.2   Diagnostic procedures on lung and bronchus

33.21   Bronchoscopy through artificial stoma

> **EXCLUDES**   *that with biopsy (33.24, 33.27)*

DEF: Visual exam of lung and its branches via tube through artificial opening.

33.22   Fiber-optic bronchoscopy

> **EXCLUDES**   *that with biopsy (33.24, 33.27)*

AHA: 1Q, '04, 4

DEF: Exam of lung and bronchus via flexible optical instrument for visualization.

33.23   Other bronchoscopy

> **EXCLUDES**   *that for:*
> *aspiration (96.05)*
> *biopsy (33.24, 33.27)*

AHA: 3Q, '02, 18; 1Q, '99, 6

33.24   Closed [endoscopic] biopsy of bronchus

Bronchoscopy (fiberoptic) (rigid) with:
brush biopsy of "lung"
brushing or washing for specimen collection
excision (bite) biopsy
Diagnostic bronchoalveolar lavage (BAL)

> **EXCLUDES**   *closed biopsy of lung, other than brush biopsy of "lung" (33.26, 33.27)*
> *whole lung lavage (33.99)*

AHA: ▶3Q, '04, 9;◀ 3Q, '02, 16; 4Q, '92, 27; 3Q, '91, 15

DEF: Bronchoalveolar lavage (BAL): Saline is introduced into the subsegment of a lobe and retrieved using gentle suction; also called 'liquid biopsy'.

DEF: Brush biopsy: Obtaining cell or tissue samples via bristled instrument without incision.

33.25   Open biopsy of bronchus

> **EXCLUDES**   *open biopsy of lung (33.28)*

33.26   Closed [percutaneous] [needle] biopsy of lung

> **EXCLUDES**   *endoscopic biopsy of lung (33.27)*

AHA: 3Q, '92, 12

33.27   Closed endoscopic biopsy of lung

Fiber-optic (flexible) bronchoscopy with fluoroscopic guidance with biopsy
Transbronchial lung biopsy

> **EXCLUDES**   *brush biopsy of "lung" (33.24)*
> *percutaneous biopsy of lung (33.26)*

AHA: ▶3Q, '04, 9;◀ 3Q, '02, 16; 4Q, '92, 27; 3Q, '91, 15; S-O, '86, 11

33.28   Open biopsy of lung

AHA: 3Q, '99, 3; 3Q, '92, 12

Bronchoscopy with Bite Biopsy

33.29   Other diagnostic procedures on lung and bronchus

> **EXCLUDES**   *contrast bronchogram:*
> *endotracheal (87.31)*
> *other (87.32)*
> *lung scan (92.15)*
> *magnetic resonance imaging (88.92)*
> *microscopic examination of specimen from bronchus or lung (90.41-90.49)*
> *routine chest x-ray (87.44)*
> *ultrasonography of lung (88.73)*
> *vital capacity determination (89.37)*
> *x-ray of bronchus or lung NOS (87.49)*

√4th 33.3   Surgical collapse of lung

33.31   Destruction of phrenic nerve for collapse of lung

DEF: Therapeutic deadening or destruction of diaphragmatic nerve to collapse the lung.

33.32   Artificial pneumothorax for collapse of lung

Thoracotomy for collapse of lung

DEF: Forcing air or gas into diaphragmatic space to achieve therapeutic collapse of lung.

DEF: Thoracotomy for collapse of lung: Incision into chest for therapeutic collapse of lung.

33.33   Pneumoperitoneum for collapse of lung

DEF: Forcing air or gas into abdominal serous membrane to achieve therapeutic collapse of lung.

33.34   Thoracoplasty

DEF: Removal of ribs for therapeutic collapse of lungs.

33.39   Other surgical collapse of lung

Collapse of lung NOS

√4th 33.4   Repair and plastic operation on lung and bronchus

33.41   Suture of laceration of bronchus

33.42   Closure of bronchial fistula

Closure of bronchostomy
Fistulectomy:
bronchocutaneous
bronchoesophageal
bronchovisceral

> **EXCLUDES**   *closure of fistula:*
> *bronchomediastinal (34.73)*
> *bronchopleural (34.73)*
> *bronchopleuromediastinal (34.73)*

DEF: Closure of bronchostomy: Removal of bronchostomy tube and repair of surgical wound.

DEF: Fistulectomy: Closure of abnormal passage.
Bronchocutaneous: Between skin and lung branch.
Bronchoesophagus: Between esophagus and lung branch.
Bronchovisceral: Between an internal organ and lung branch.

√3rd
√4th Additional Digit Required   RUG III Special Care Procedure   RUG III Clinically Complex Procedure   RUG III Extensive Services Procedure   RUG III Rehab Procedure

2006 ICD•9•CM

February 2005 • Volume 3 — 115

Operations on the Respiratory System

33.43–34.28

33.43   **Closure of laceration of lung**

33.48   **Other repair and plastic operations on bronchus**

33.49   **Other repair and plastic operations on lung**
> EXCLUDES   *closure of pleural fistula (34.73)*

√4ᵗʰ **33.5**   **Lung transplant**
> Note: To report donor source — see codes 00.91-00.93
> Code also cardiopulmonary bypass [extracorporeal circulation] [heart-lung machine] (39.61)
> EXCLUDES   *combined heart-lung transplantation (33.6)*

AHA: 4Q, '95, 75

33.50   **Lung transplantation, not otherwise specified**

33.51   **Unilateral lung transplantation**

33.52   **Bilateral lung transplantation**
> Double-lung transplantation
> En bloc transplantation
> DEF: Sequential excision and implant of both lungs.

33.6   **Combined heart-lung transplantation**
> Note: To report donor source — see codes 00.91-00.93
> Code also cardiopulmonary bypass [extracorporeal circulation] [heart-lung machine] (39.61)

√4ᵗʰ **33.9**   **Other operations on lung and bronchus**

33.91   **Bronchial dilation**
> AHA: 1Q, '97, 14

33.92   **Ligation of bronchus**
> DEF: Tying off of a lung branch.

33.93   **Puncture of lung**
> EXCLUDES   *needle biopsy (33.26)*
> DEF: Piercing of lung with surgical instrument.

33.98   **Other operations on bronchus**
> EXCLUDES   *bronchial lavage (96.56)*
> *removal of intraluminal foreign body from bronchus without incision (98.15)*

33.99   **Other operations on lung**
> Whole lung lavage
> EXCLUDES   *other continuous mechanical ventilation (96.70-96.72)*
> *respiratory therapy (93.90-93.99)*

AHA: 3Q, '02, 17

√3ʳᵈ **34**   **Operations on chest wall, pleura, mediastinum, and diaphragm**
> EXCLUDES   *operations on breast (85.0-85.99)*

√4ᵗʰ **34.0**   **Incision of chest wall and pleura**
> EXCLUDES   *that as operative approach — omit code*

34.01   **Incision of chest wall**
> Extrapleural drainage
> EXCLUDES   *incision of pleura (34.09)*

AHA: 3Q, '00, 12; 1Q, '92, 13

DEF: Extrapleural drainage: Incision to drain fluid from external pleura.

34.02   **Exploratory thoracotomy**

34.03   **Reopening of recent thoracotomy site**

34.04   **Insertion of intercostal catheter for drainage**
> Chest tube
> Closed chest drainage
> Revision of intercostal catheter (chest tube) (with lysis of adhesions)

AHA: 2Q, '03, 7; 1Q, '99, 10; 2Q, '99, 12;1Q, '95, 5; 1Q, '92, 12

DEF: Insertion of catheter between ribs for drainage.

34.05   **Creation of pleuroperitoneal shunt**
> AHA: 4Q, '94, 50

34.09   **Other incision of pleura**
> Creation of pleural window for drainage
> Intercostal stab
> Open chest drainage
> EXCLUDES   *thoracoscopy (34.21)*
> *thoracotomy for collapse of lung (33.32)*

AHA: 3Q, '02, 22; 1Q, '94, 7; 4Q, '94, 50

DEF: Creation of pleural window: Creation of circumscribed drainage hole in serous membrane of chest.

DEF: Intercostal stab: Creation of penetrating stab wound between ribs.

DEF: Open chest drainage: Insertion of tube through ribs and serous membrane of chest for drainage.

34.1   **Incision of mediastinum**
> EXCLUDES   *mediastinoscopy (34.22)*
> *mediastinotomy associated with pneumonectomy (32.5)*

AHA: 3Q, '92, 12

√4ᵗʰ **34.2**   **Diagnostic procedures on chest wall, pleura, mediastinum, and diaphragm**

34.21   **Transpleural thoracoscopy**
> AHA: 3Q, '02, 27
> DEF: Exam of chest through serous membrane using scope.

34.22   **Mediastinoscopy**
> Code also any lymph node biopsy (40.11)
> DEF: Exam of lung cavity and heart using scope.

34.23   **Biopsy of chest wall**

34.24   **Pleural biopsy**
> AHA: 3Q, '02, 22, 27; 1Q, '92, 14

34.25   **Closed [percutaneous] [needle] biopsy of mediastinum**

34.26   **Open biopsy of mediastinum**

34.27   **Biopsy of diaphragm**

34.28   **Other diagnostic procedures on chest wall, pleura, and diaphragm**
> EXCLUDES   *angiocardiography (88.50-88.58)*
> *aortography (88.42)*
> *arteriography of:*
> *intrathoracic vessels NEC (88.44)*
> *pulmonary arteries (88.43)*
> *microscopic examination of specimen from chest wall, pleura, and diaphragm (90.41-90.49)*
> *phlebography of:*
> *intrathoracic vessels NEC (88.63)*
> *pulmonary veins (88.62)*
> *radiological examinations of thorax:*
> *C.A.T. scan (87.41)*
> *diaphragmatic x-ray (87.49)*
> *intrathoracic lymphangiogram (87.34)*
> *routine chest x-ray (87.44)*
> *sinogram of chest wall (87.38)*
> *soft tissue x-ray of chest wall NEC (87.39)*
> *tomogram of thorax NEC (87.42)*
> *ultrasonography of thorax (88.73)*

| Ⓝ Newborn Age: 0 | Ⓟ Pediatric Age: 0-17 | Ⓜ Maternity Age: 12-55 | Ⓐ Adult Age: 15-124 | **Adj** Adjunct Code | ◄► Revised Text | ● New Code | ▲ Revised Code Title |

34.29   Other diagnostic procedures on mediastinum

> EXCLUDES   mediastinal:
> pneumogram (87.33)
> x-ray NEC (87.49)

34.3   Excision or destruction of lesion or tissue of mediastinum

> EXCLUDES   biopsy of mediastinum (34.25-34.26)
> mediastinal fistulectomy (34.73)

34.4   Excision or destruction of lesion of chest wall

Excision of lesion of chest wall NOS (with excision of ribs)

> EXCLUDES   biopsy of chest wall (34.23)
> costectomy not incidental to thoracic procedure (77.91)
> excision of lesion of:
> breast (85.20-85.25)
> cartilage (80.89)
> skin (86.2-86.3)
> fistulectomy (34.73)

✓4ᵗʰ 34.5   Pleurectomy

34.51   Decortication of lung

DEF: Removal of thickened serous membrane for lung expansion.

34.59   Other excision of pleura

Excision of pleural lesion

> EXCLUDES   biopsy of pleura (34.24)
> pleural fistulectomy (34.73)

34.6   Scarification of pleura

Pleurosclerosis

> EXCLUDES   injection of sclerosing agent (34.92)

AHA: 1Q, '92, 12

DEF: Destruction of fluid-secreting serous membrane cells of chest.

✓4ᵗʰ 34.7   Repair of chest wall

34.71   Suture of laceration of chest wall

> EXCLUDES   suture of skin and subcutaneous tissue alone (86.59)

34.72   Closure of thoracostomy

34.73   Closure of other fistula of thorax

Closure of:
bronchopleural
bronchopleurocutaneous   } fistula
bronchopleuromediastinal

34.74   Repair of pectus deformity

Repair of:
pectus carinatum   } (with implant)
pectus excavatum

AHA: ▶2Q, '04, 6◀

DEF: Pectus carinatum repair: Restoration of prominent chest bone defect with implant.

DEF: Pectus excavatum: Restoration of depressed chest bone defect with implant.

34.79   Other repair of chest wall

Repair of chest wall NOS

AHA: ▶2Q, '04, 6;◀ J-F, '87, 13

✓4ᵗʰ 34.8   Operations on diaphragm

34.81   Excision of lesion or tissue of diaphragm

> EXCLUDES   biopsy of diaphragm (34.27)

34.82   Suture of laceration of diaphragm

34.83   Closure of fistula of diaphragm

Thoracicoabdominal
Thoracicogastric   } fistulectomy
Thoracicointestinal

DEF: Fistulectomy: Closure of abnormal passage.

34.84   Other repair of diaphragm

> EXCLUDES   repair of diaphragmatic hernia (53.7-53.82)

34.85   Implantation of diaphragmatic pacemaker

34.89   Other operations on diaphragm

✓4ᵗʰ 34.9   Other operations on thorax

34.91   Thoracentesis

AHA: S-O, '85, 6

DEF: Puncture of pleural cavity for fluid aspiration, also called pleurocentesis.

34.92   Injection into thoracic cavity

Chemical pleurodesis
Injection of cytotoxic agent or tetracycline
Requires additional code for any cancer chemotherapeutic substance (99.25)

> EXCLUDES   that for collapse of lung (33.32)

AHA: 1Q, '92, 12; 2Q, '89, 17

DEF: Chemical pleurodesis: Tetracycline hydrochloride injections to create adhesions between parietal and visceral pleura for treatment of pleural effusion.

34.93   Repair of pleura

34.99   Other

> EXCLUDES   removal of:
> mediastinal drain (97.42)
> sutures (97.43)
> thoracotomy tube (97.41)

AHA: 1Q, '00, 17; 1Q, '88, 9

DEF: Pleural tent: Extrapleural mobilization of parietal pleura that allows draping of membrane over visceral pleura to eliminate intrapleural dead space and seal visceral pleura.

Operations on the Respiratory System

34.29–34.99

✓3ʳᵈ
✓4ᵗʰ Additional Digit Required   RUG III Special Care Procedure   RUG III Clinically Complex Procedure   RUG III Extensive Services Procedure   RUG III Rehab Procedure

2006 ICD•9•CM   **February 2005 • Volume 3 — 117**

Operations on the Cardiovascular System

35–35.41

7. OPERATIONS ON THE CARDIOVASCULAR SYSTEM (35-39)

√3rd **35** **Operations on valves and septa of heart**

INCLUDES sternotomy (median) (transverse) thoractotomy } as operative approach

Code also cardiopulmonary bypass [extracorporeal circulation] [heart-lung machine] (39.61)

√4th **35.0** **Closed heart valvotomy**

EXCLUDES percutaneous (balloon) valvuloplasty (35.96)

DEF: Incision into valve to restore function.

35.00 **Closed heart valvotomy, unspecified valve**
35.01 **Closed heart valvotomy, aortic valve**
35.02 **Closed heart valvotomy, mitral valve**
35.03 **Closed heart valvotomy, pulmonary valve**
35.04 **Closed heart valvotomy, tricuspid valve**

√4th **35.1** **Open heart valvuloplasty without replacement**

INCLUDES open heart valvotomy

Code also cardiopulmonary bypass, if performed [extracorporeal circulation] [heart-lung machine] (39.61)

EXCLUDES that associated with repair of:
endocardial cushion defect (35.54,35.63,35.73)
percutaneous (balloon) valvuloplasty 112(35.96)
valvular defect associated with atrial and ventricular septal defects (35.54, 35.63, 35.73)

DEF: Incision into heart for plastic repair of valve without replacing valve.

35.10 **Open heart valvuloplasty without replacement, unspecified valve**

35.11 **Open heart valvuloplasty of aortic valve without replacement**

35.12 **Open heart valvuloplasty of mitral valve without replacement**

AHA: 1Q, '97, 13

35.13 **Open heart valvuloplasty of pulmonary valve without replacement**

35.14 **Open heart valvuloplasty of tricuspid valve without replacement**

√4th **35.2** **Replacement of heart valve**

INCLUDES excision of heart valve with replacement

Code also cardiopulmonary bypass [extracorporeal circulation] [heart-lung machine] (39.61)

EXCLUDES that associated with repair of:
endocardial cushion defect (35.54,35.63, 35.73)
valvular defect associated with atrial and ventricular septal defects (35.54, 35.63, 35.73)

DEF: Removal and replacement of valve with tissue from patient, animal, other human, or prosthetic (synthetic) valve.

35.20 **Replacement of unspecified heart valve**
Repair of unspecified heart valve with tissue graft or prosthetic implant

35.21 **Replacement of aortic valve with tissue graft**
Repair of aortic valve with tissue graft (autograft) (heterograft) (homograft)

AHA: 2Q, '97, 8

35.22 **Other replacement of aortic valve**
Repair of aortic valve with replacement:
NOS
prosthetic (partial) (synthetic) (total)

AHA: 1Q, '96, 11

35.23 **Replacement of mitral valve with tissue graft**
Repair of mitral valve with tissue graft (autograft) (heterograft) (homograft)

35.24 **Other replacement of mitral valve**
Repair of mitral valve with replacement:
NOS
prosthetic (partial) (synthetic) (total)

AHA: 4Q, '97, 55

35.25 **Replacement of pulmonary valve with tissue graft**
Repair of pulmonary valve with tissue graft (autograft) (heterograft) (homograft)

AHA: 1Q, '04, 16; 2Q, '97, 8

35.26 **Other replacement of pulmonary valve**
Repair of pulmonary valve with replacement:
NOS
prosthetic (partial) (synthetic) (total)

35.27 **Replacement of tricuspid valve with tissue graft**
Repair of tricuspid valve with tissue graft (autograft) (heterograft) (homograft)

35.28 **Other replacement of tricuspid valve**
Repair of tricuspid valve with replacement:
NOS
prosthetic (partial) (synthetic) (total)

√4th **35.3** **Operations on structures adjacent to heart valves**
Code also cardiopulmonary bypass [extracorporeal circulation] [heart-lung machine] (39.61)

35.31 **Operations on papillary muscle**
Division
Reattachment } of papillary
Repair muscle

35.32 **Operations on chordae tendineae**
Division } chordae
Repair tendineae

35.33 **Annuloplasty**
Plication of annulus

AHA: 1Q, '97, 13; 1Q, '88, 10

DEF: Plication of annulus: Tuck stitched in valvular ring for tightening.

35.34 **Infundibulectomy**
Right ventricular infundibulectomy

DEF: Infundibulectomy: Excision of funnel-shaped heart passage.

DEF: Right ventricular infundibulectomy: Excision of funnel-shaped passage in right upper heart chamber.

35.35 **Operations on trabeculae carneae cordis**
Division } of trabeculae carneae
Excision cordis

Excision of aortic subvalvular ring

35.39 **Operations on other structures adjacent to valves of heart**
Repair of sinus of Valsalva (aneurysm)

√4th **35.4** **Production of septal defect in heart**

35.41 **Enlargement of existing atrial septal defect**
Rashkind procedure
Septostomy (atrial) (balloon)

DEF: Enlargement of partition wall defect in lower heart chamber to improve function.

DEF: Rashkind procedure: Enlargement of partition wall defect between the two lower heart chambers by balloon catheter.

N Newborn Age: 0　　P Pediatric Age: 0-17　　M Maternity Age: 12-55　　A Adult Age: 15-124　　Adj Adjunct Code　　◄ Revised Text　　● New Code　　▲ Revised Code Title

35.42　Creation of septal defect in heart
　　Blalock-Hanlon operation
　　DEF: Blalock-Hanlon operation: Removal of partition wall defect in lower heart chamber.

✓4th **35.5　Repair of atrial and ventricular septa with prosthesis**
　　INCLUDES　repair of septa with synthetic implant or patch
　　Code also cardiopulmonary bypass [extracorporeal circulation] [heart-lung machine] (39.61)

35.50　Repair of unspecified septal defect of heart with prosthesis
　　EXCLUDES　*that associated with repair of:*
　　　　endocardial cushion defect (35.54)
　　　　septal defect associated with valvular defect (35.54)

35.51　Repair of atrial septal defect with prosthesis, open technique
　　Atrioseptoplasty
　　Correction of atrial septal defect
　　Repair:
　　　foramen ovale (patent)
　　　ostium secundum defect ⎫ with prosthesis

　　EXCLUDES　*that associated with repair of:*
　　　　atrial septal defect associated with valvular and ventricular septal defects (35.54)
　　　　endocardial cushion defect (35.54)

　　DEF: Repair of opening or weakening in septum separating the atria; prosthesis implanted through heart incision.

35.52　Repair of atrial septal defect with prosthesis, closed technique
　　Insertion of atrial septal umbrella [King-Mills]

　　AHA: 3Q, '98, 11

　　DEF: Correction of partition wall defect in lower heart chamber with artificial material; without incision into heart.

　　DEF: Insertion of atrial septal umbrella (King-Mills): Correction of partition wall defect in lower heart chamber with atrial septal umbrella.

35.53　Repair of ventricular septal defect with prosthesis
　　Correction of ventricular septal defect
　　Repair of supracristal defect ⎫ with prosthesis

　　EXCLUDES　*that associated with repair of:*
　　　　endocardial cushion defect (35.54)
　　　　ventricular defect associated with valvular and atrial septal defects (35.54)

35.54　Repair of endocardial cushion defect with prosthesis
　　Repair:
　　　atrioventricular canal
　　　ostium primum defect
　　　valvular defect associated with atrial and ventricular septal defects ⎫ with prosthesis (grafted to septa)

　　EXCLUDES　*repair of isolated:*
　　　　atrial septal defect (35.51-35.52)
　　　　valvular defect (35.20, 35.22, 35.24, 35.26, 35.28)
　　　　ventricular septal defect (35.53)

✓4th **35.6　Repair of atrial and ventricular septa with tissue graft**
　　Code also cardiopulmonary bypass [extracorporeal circulation] [heart-lung machine] (39.61)

35.60　Repair of unspecified septal defect of heart with tissue graft
　　EXCLUDES　*that associated with repair of:*
　　　　endocardial cushion defect (35.63)
　　　　septal defect associated with valvular defect (35.63)

35.61　Repair of atrial septal defect with tissue graft
　　Atrioseptoplasty
　　Correction of atrial septal defect
　　Repair:
　　　foramen ovale (patent)
　　　ostium secundum defect ⎫ with tissue graft

　　EXCLUDES　*that associated with repair of:*
　　　　atrial septal defect associated with valvular and ventricular septal defects (35.63)
　　　　endocardial cushion defect (35.63)

35.62　Repair of ventricular septal defect with tissue graft
　　Correction of ventricular septal defect
　　Repair of supracristal defect ⎫ with tissue graft

　　EXCLUDES　*that associated with repair of:*
　　　　endocardial cushion defect (35.63)
　　　　ventricular defect associated with valvular and atrial septal defects (35.63)

✓3rd ✓4th　Additional Digit Required　　RUG III Special Care Procedure　　RUG III Clinically Complex Procedure　　RUG III Extensive Services Procedure　　RUG III Rehab Procedure

2006 ICD•9•CM　　　　Volume 3 — 119

35.63   **Repair of endocardial cushion defect with tissue graft**

Repair of:

atrioventricular canal
ostium primum defect
valvular defect
    associated with
    atrial and
    ventricular septal
    defects   } with tissue graft

> **EXCLUDES**   *repair of isolated:*
> *atrial septal defect (35.61)*
> *valvular defect (35.20-*
> *35.21, 35.23, 35.25,*
> *35.27)*
> *ventricular septal defect*
> *(35.62)*

✓4ᵗʰ 35.7   **Other and unspecified repair of atrial and ventricular septa**

Code also cardiopulmonary bypass [extracorporeal circulation] [heart-lung machine] (39.61)

35.70   **Other and unspecified repair of unspecified septal defect of heart**

Repair of septal defect NOS

> **EXCLUDES**   *that associated with repair of:*
> *endocardial cushion defect*
> *(35.73)*
> *septal defect associated*
> *with valvular defect*
> *(35.73)*

35.71   **Other and unspecified repair of atrial septal defect**

Repair NOS:

atrial septum
foramen ovale (patent)
ostium secundum defect

> **EXCLUDES**   *that associated with repair of:*
> *atrial septal defect*
> *associated with*
> *valvular and*
> *ventricular septal*
> *defects (35.73)*
> *endocardial cushion defect*
> *(35.73)*

35.72   **Other and unspecified repair of ventricular septal defect**

Repair NOS:

supracristal defect
ventricular septum

> **EXCLUDES**   *that associated with repair of:*
> *endocardial cushion defect*
> *(35.73)*
> *ventricular septal defect*
> *associated with*
> *valvular and atrial*
> *septal defects (35.73)*

35.73   **Other and unspecified repair of endocardial cushion defect**

Repair NOS:

atrioventricular canal
ostium primum defect
valvular defect associated with atrial and
    ventricular septal defects

> **EXCLUDES**   *repair of isolated:*
> *atrial septal defect (35.71)*
> *valvular defect (35.20,*
> *35.22, 35.24, 35.26,*
> *35.28)*
> *ventricular septal defect*
> *(35.72)*

✓4ᵗʰ 35.8   **Total repair of certain congenital cardiac anomalies**

Note: For partial repair of defect [e.g. repair of atrial septal defect in tetralogy of Fallot] — code to specific procedure

35.81   **Total repair of tetralogy of Fallot**

One-stage total correction of tetralogy of Fallot with or without:

commissurotomy of pulmonary valve
infundibulectomy
outflow tract prosthesis
patch graft of outflow tract
prosthetic tube for pulmonary artery
repair of ventricular septal defect (with
    prosthesis)
take-down of previous systemic-
    pulmonary artery anastomosis

35.82   **Total repair of total anomalous pulmonary venous connection**

One-stage total correction of total
    anomalous pulmonary venous
    connection with or without:

anastomosis between (horizontal)
    common pulmonary trunk and
    posterior wall of left atrium (side-
    to-side)
enlargement of foramen ovale
incision [excision] of common wall
    between posterior left atrium and
    coronary sinus and roofing of
    resultant defect with patch graft
    (synthetic)
ligation of venous connection (descending
    anomalous vein) (to left innominate
    vein) (to superior vena cava)
repair of atrial septal defect (with
    prosthesis)

35.83   **Total repair of truncus arteriosus**

One-stage total correction of truncus
    arteriosus with or without:

construction (with aortic homograft) (with
    prosthesis) of a pulmonary artery
    placed from right ventricle to
    arteries supplying the lung
ligation of connections between aorta and
    pulmonary artery
repair of ventricular septal defect (with
    prosthesis)

35.84   **Total correction of transposition of great vessels, not elsewhere classified**

Arterial switch operation [Jatene]
Total correction of transposition of great
    arteries at the arterial level by
    switching the great arteries, including
    the left or both coronary arteries,
    implanted in the wall of the
    pulmonary artery

> **EXCLUDES**   *baffle operation [Mustard]*
> *[Senning] (35.91)*
> *creation of shunt between*
> *right ventricle and*
> *pulmonary artery*
> *[Rastelli] (35.92)*

✓4ᵗʰ 35.9   **Other operations on valves and septa of heart**

Code also cardiopulmonary bypass, if performed
[extracorporeal circulation] [heart-lung
machine] (39.61)

N Newborn Age: 0   **P** Pediatric Age: 0-17   **M** Maternity Age: 12-55   **A** Adult Age: 15-124   **Adj** Adjunct Code   ▶◀ Revised Text   ● New Code   ▲ Revised Code Title

35.91 Interatrial transposition of venous return

Baffle:
  atrial
  interatrial
Mustard's operation
Resection of atrial septum and insertion of patch to direct systemic venous return to tricuspid valve and pulmonary venous return to mitral valve

DEF: Atrial baffle: Correction of venous flow of abnormal or deviated lower heart chamber.

DEF: Interatrial baffle: Correction of venous flow between abnormal lower heart chambers.

DEF: Mustard's operation: Creates intra-atrial baffle using pericardial tissue to correct transposition of the great vessels.

35.92 Creation of conduit between right ventricle and pulmonary artery

Creation of shunt between right ventricle and (distal) pulmonary artery

EXCLUDES   *that associated with total repair of truncus arteriosus (35.83)*

35.93 Creation of conduit between left ventricle and aorta

Creation of apicoaortic shunt
Shunt between apex of left ventricle and aorta

35.94 Creation of conduit between atrium and pulmonary artery

Fontan procedure

35.95 Revision of corrective procedure on heart

Replacement of prosthetic heart valve poppet
Resuture of prosthesis of:
  septum
  valve

EXCLUDES   *complete revision — code to specific procedure replacement of prosthesis or graft of:*
      septum (35.50-35.63)
      valve (35.20-35.28)

DEF: Replacement of prosthetic heart valve poppet: Removal and replacement of valve-supporting prosthesis.

DEF: Resuture of prosthesis of septum: Restitching of prosthesis in partition wall.

DEF: Resuture of prosthesis of valve: Restitching of prosthetic valve.

35.96 Percutaneous valvuloplasty

Percutaneous balloon valvuloplasty

AHA: 3Q, '04, 10; M-J, '86, 6; N-D, '85, 10

DEF: Repair of valve with catheter.

DEF: Percutaneous balloon valvuloplasty: Repair of valve with inflatable catheter.

35.98 Other operations on septa of heart

35.99 Other operations on valves of heart

√3rd **36 Operations on vessels of heart**

INCLUDES sternotomy (median)   } as operative
         (transverse)   } approach
      thoracotomy

Code also any:
  injection or infusion of platelet inhibitor (99.20)
  ▶injection or infusion of thrombolytic agent (99.10)◄
Code also cardiopulmonary bypass, if performed [extracorporeal circulation] [heart-lung machine] (39.61)

√4th **36.0 Removal of coronary artery obstruction and insertion of stent(s)**

AHA: 4Q, '95, 66; 2Q, '94, 13; 1Q, '94, 3; 2Q, '90, 23; N-D, '86, 8;

36.03 Open chest coronary artery angioplasty

Coronary (artery):
  endarterectomy (with patch graft)
  thromboendarterectomy (with patch graft)
Open surgery for direct relief of coronary artery obstruction
▶Code also any:
  insertion of drug-eluting coronary stent(s) (36.07)
  insertion of non-drug-eluting coronary stent(s) (36.06)
  number of vascular stents inserted (00.45-00.48)
  number of vessels treated (00.40-00.43)◄

EXCLUDES   *that with coronary artery bypass graft (36.10-36.19)*

AHA: 2Q, '01, 24; 3Q, '93, 7

DEF: Endarterectomy (with patch graft): Excision of thickened material within coronary artery; repair with patch graft.

DEF: Thromboendarterectomy (with patch graft): Excision of blood clot and thickened material within coronary artery; repair with patch graft.

DEF: Open surgery for direct relief of coronary artery obstruction: Removal of coronary artery obstruction through opening in chest.

36.04 Intracoronary artery thrombolytic infusion

That by direct coronary artery injection, infusion, or catheterization
  enzyme infusion
  platelet inhibitor

EXCLUDES   *infusion of platelet inhibitor (99.20)*
      infusion of thrombolytic agent (99.10)
      ▶*that associated with any procedure in 36.03*◄

AHA: 4Q, '02, 114; 3Q, '02, 20; 2Q, '01, 24; 4Q, '98, 85; 1Q, '97, 3; 4Q, '95, 67

DEF: Infusion of clot breaking solution into intracoronary artery.

PTCA (Balloon Angioplasty)

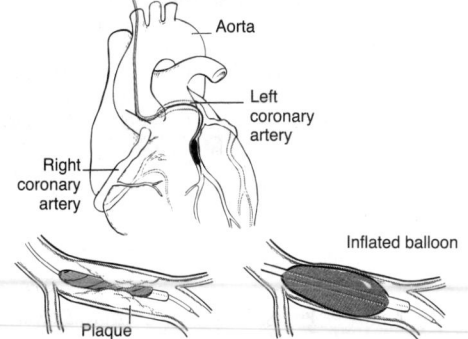

√3rd √4th Additional Digit Required   RUG III Special Care Procedure   RUG III Clinically Complex Procedure   RUG III Extensive Services Procedure   RUG III Rehab Procedure

2006 ICD•9•CM   October 2005 • Volume 3 — 121

Operations on the Cardiovascular System

36.06–36.2

36.06 Insertion of non-drug-eluting coronary artery stent(s)

Bare stent(s)
Bonded stent(s)
Drug-coated stent(s), e.g., heparin coated
Endograft(s)
Endovascular graft(s)
Stent graft(s)
Code also any:
▶number of vascular stents inserted
(00.45-00.48)
number of vessels treated (00.40-00.43)◀
open chest coronary artery angioplasty
(36.03)
percutaneous transluminal coronary
angioplasty [PTCA] or coronary
atherectomy ▶(00.66)◀

> **EXCLUDES** *insertion of drug-eluting coronary artery stent(s) (36.07)*

AHA: 2Q, '04, 3; 4Q, '02, 101; 1Q,'01, 9; 2Q, '01, 24;
1Q, '00, 11; 1Q, '99, 17

DEF: Percutaneous implant via catheter of metal stent, to enlarge, maintain lumen size of coronary artery.

36.07 Insertion of drug-eluting coronary artery stent(s)

Endograft(s)
Endovascular graft(s)
Stent graft(s)
Code also any:
▶number of vascular stents inserted
(00.45-00.48)
number of vessels treated (00.40-00.43)◀
open chest coronary artery angioplasty
(36.03)
percutaneous transluminal coronary
angioplasty [PTCA] or coronary
atherectomy ▶(00.66)◀

> **EXCLUDES** *drug-coated stents, e.g., heparin coated (36.06)*
> *insertion of non-drug-eluting coronary artery stent(s) (36.06)*

AHA: 4Q, '02, 101

DEF: Drug-eluting stent technology developed to prevent the accumulation of scar tissue that can narrow reopened coronary arteries. A special polymer is used to coat the drug onto the stent, which slowly releases into the coronary artery wall tissue.

36.09 Other removal of coronary artery obstruction

Coronary angioplasty NOS
▶Code also any:
number of vascular stents inserted
(00.45-00.48)
number of vessels treated (00.40-00.43)◀

> **EXCLUDES** *that by open angioplasty (36.03)*
> *that by percutaneous transluminal coronary angioplasty [PTCA] or coronary atherectomy ▶(00.66)◀*

✓4ᵗʰ 36.1 Bypass anastomosis for heart revascularization

▶Note: Do not assign codes from series 00.40-00.43
with codes from series 36.10-36.19◀
Code also:
cardiopulmonary bypass [extracorporeal
circulation] [heart-lung machine] (39.61)
pressurized treatment of venous bypass graft
[conduit] with pharmaceutical substance, if
performed (00.16)

AHA: 2Q, '96, 7; 3Q, '95, 7; 3Q, '93, 8; 1Q, '91, 7; 2Q, '90, 24; 4Q, '89, 3

DEF: Insertion of tube to bypass blocked coronary artery, correct coronary blood flow.

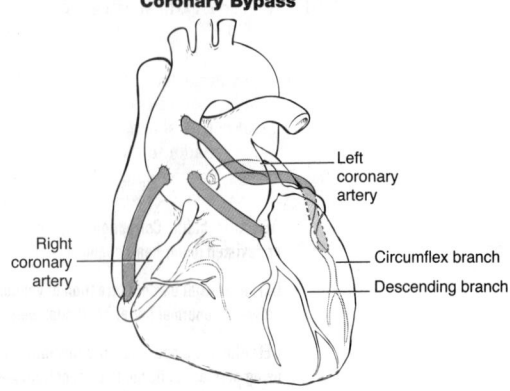

Coronary Bypass

Left coronary artery
Right coronary artery
Circumflex branch
Descending branch

36.10 Aortocoronary bypass for heart revascularization, not otherwise specified

Direct revascularization:
cardiac ⎫
coronary ⎬ with catheter stent,
heart muscle ⎪ prosthesis, or
myocardial ⎭ vein graft

Heart revascularization NOS

AHA: 2Q, '96, 7

36.11 (Aorto)coronary bypass of one coronary artery

AHA: 3Q, '02, 4, 9; 4Q, '89, 3

36.12 (Aorto)coronary bypass of two coronary arteries

AHA: 3Q, '02, 8; 4Q, '99, 15; 2Q, '96, 7; 3Q, '97, 14; 4Q, '89, 3

36.13 (Aorto)coronary bypass of three coronary arteries

AHA: 3Q, '02, 6, 7, 9; 2Q, '96, 7; 4Q, '89, 3

36.14 (Aorto)coronary bypass of four or more coronary arteries

AHA: 3Q, '02, 5; 2Q, '96, 7; 4Q, '89, 3

36.15 Single internal mammary-coronary artery bypass

Anastomosis (single):
mammary artery to coronary artery
thoracic artery to coronary artery

AHA: 3Q, '02, 4-9; 4Q, '99, 15; 3Q, '97, 14; 2Q, '96, 7

36.16 Double internal mammary-coronary artery bypass

Anastomosis, double:
mammary artery to coronary artery
thoracic artery to coronary artery

AHA: 3Q, '02, 6, 8, 9; 2Q, '96, 7

36.17 Abdominal-coronary artery bypass

Anastomosis:
gastroepiploic artery to coronary artery

AHA: 3Q, '97, 14; 4Q, '96, 64

36.19 Other bypass anastomosis for heart revascularization

AHA: 2Q, '96, 7

36.2 Heart revascularization by arterial implant

Implantation of:
aortic branches [ascending aortic branches] into
heart muscle
blood vessels into myocardium
internal mammary artery [internal thoracic
artery] into:
heart muscle
myocardium
ventricle
ventricular wall
Indirect heart revascularization NOS

N Newborn Age: 0   P Pediatric Age: 0-17   M Maternity Age: 12-55   A Adult Age: 15-124   Adj Adjunct Code   ◀▶ Revised Text   ● New Code   ▲ Revised Code Title

Transmyocardial Revascularization

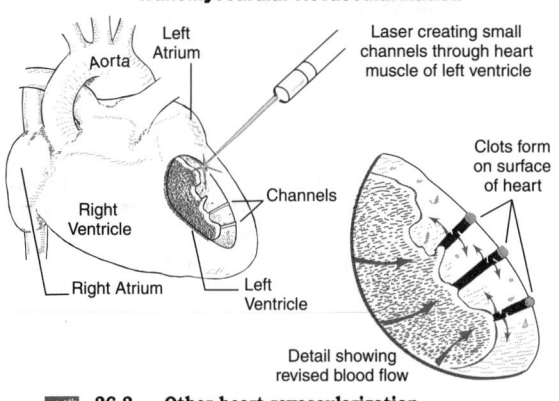

✓4th **36.3**   **Other heart revascularization**

36.31   **Open chest transmyocardial revascularization**

DEF: Transmyocardial revascularization (TMR): Laser creation of channels through myocardium allows oxygenated blood flow from sinusoids to myocardial tissue.

36.32   **Other transmyocardial revascularization**

Percutaneous transmyocardial revascularization

Thoracoscopic transmyocardial revascularization

AHA: 4Q, '98, 74

36.39   **Other heart revascularization**

Abrasion of epicardium

Cardio-omentopexy

Intrapericardial poudrage

Myocardial graft:

    mediastinal fat

    omentum

    pectoral muscles

DEF: Cardio-omentopexy: Suture of omentum segment to heart after drawing segment through incision in diaphragm.

DEF: Intrapericardial poudrage: Application of powder to heart lining to promote fusion.

DEF: Myocardial graft:

    Mediastinal fat: Implantation in heart muscle of fat from cavity containing heart and structures.

    Omentopexy: Suture of omentum to heart.

✓4th **36.9**   **Other operations on vessels of heart**

Code also cardiopulmonary bypass [extracorporeal circulation] [heart-lung machine] (39.61)

36.91   **Repair of aneurysm of coronary vessel**

36.99   **Other operations on vessels of heart**

Exploration ⎫
Incision   ⎬ of coronary artery
Ligation   ⎭

Repair of arteriovenous fistula

AHA: 3Q, '03, 18; 1Q, '94, 3

✓3rd **37**   **Other operations on heart and pericardium**

Code also any injection or infusion of platelet inhibitor (99.20)

37.0   **Pericardiocentesis**

DEF: Puncture of the heart lining to withdraw fluid.

✓4th **37.1**   **Cardiotomy and pericardiotomy**

Code also cardiopulmonary bypass [extracorporeal circulation] [heart-lung machine] (39.61)

37.10   **Incision of heart, not otherwise specified**

Cardiolysis NOS

37.11   **Cardiotomy**

Incision of: Incision of:

   atrium   myocardium

   endocardium   ventricle

37.12   **Pericardiotomy**

Pericardial window   Pericardiolysis

operation   Pericardiotomy

DEF: Pericardial window operation: Incision into heart lining for drainage.

DEF: Pericardiolysis: Destruction of heart tissue lining.

✓4th **37.2**   **Diagnostic procedures on heart and pericardium**

37.21   **Right heart cardiac catheterization**

Cardiac catheterization NOS

EXCLUDES   *that with catheterization of left heart (37.23)*

AHA: ▶3Q, '04, 10;◄ 3Q, '03, 9; 2Q, '90, 23; M-J, '87, 11

37.22   **Left heart cardiac catheterization**

EXCLUDES   *that with catheterization of right heart (37.23)*

AHA: ▶3Q, '04, 10; 2Q, '04, 3;◄ 1Q, '00, 21; 2Q, '90, 23; 4Q, '88, 4; M-J, '87, 11

37.23   **Combined right and left heart cardiac catheterization**

AHA: ▶3Q, '04, 10;◄ 2Q, '01, 8; 1Q, '00, 20; 3Q, '98, 11; 2Q, '90, 23; M-J, '87, 11

37.24   **Biopsy of pericardium**

37.25   **Biopsy of heart**

AHA: 3Q, '03, 16; 3Q, '94, 8

37.26   **Cardiac electrophysiologic stimulation and recording studies**

Electrophysiologic studies [EPS]

Non-invasive programmed electrical stimulation (NIPS)

Programmed electrical stimulation

Code also any concomitant procedure

EXCLUDES   *device interrogation only without arrhythmia induction (bedside check) (89.45-89.49)*

His bundle recording (37.29)

AHA: 3Q, '03, 23; 2Q, '03, 19; 1Q, '99, 3; 2Q, '97, 10; 3Q, '90, 11

DEF: Diagnostic mapping and measurement of intracardiac electrical activity; requires inserting three to six catheters into heart blood vessels and positioning catheters under fluoroscopic guidance to determine site of the tachycardia or abnormal impulse pathway; may also be used to terminate arrhythmias.

37.27   **Cardiac mapping**

Code also any concomitant procedure

EXCLUDES   *electrocardiogram (89.52)*

His bundle recording (37.29)

Intracardiac Echocardiography

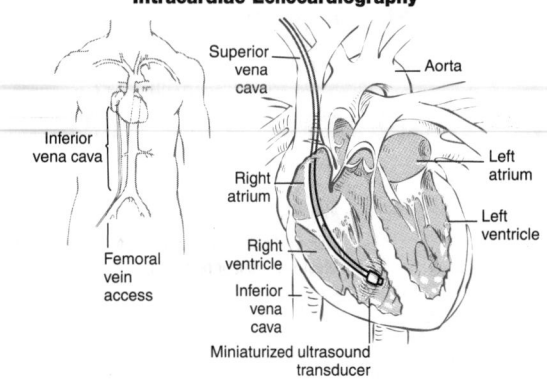

✓3rd ✓4th   Additional Digit Required   RUG III Special Care Procedure   RUG III Clinically Complex Procedure   RUG III Extensive Services Procedure   RUG III Rehab Procedure

2006 ICD•9•CM   **February 2005 • Volume 3 — 123**

Operations on the Cardiovascular System

37.28–37.53

37.28   Intracardiac echocardiography

Echocardiography of heart chambers
ICE
Code also any synchronous Doppler flow
     mapping (88.72)

> **EXCLUDES**   *intravascular imaging of coronary vessels (intravascular ultrasound) (IVUS) (00.24)*

AHA: 4Q, '01, 62

DEF: Creation of a two-dimensional graphic of heart using endoscopic echocardiographic equipment.

37.29   Other diagnostic procedures on heart and pericardium

> **EXCLUDES**   *angiocardiography (88.50-88.58)*
> *cardiac function tests (89.41-89.69)*
> *cardiovascular radioisotopic scan and function study (92.05)*
> *coronary arteriography (88.55-88.57)*
> *diagnostic pericardiocentesis (37.0)*
> *diagnostic ultrasound of heart (88.72)*
> *x-ray of heart (87.49)*

AHA: S-O, '87, 3

√4ᵗʰ 37.3   Pericardiectomy and excision of lesion of heart

Code also cardiopulmonary bypass [extracorporeal circulation] [heart-lung machine] (39.61)

37.31   Pericardiectomy

Excision of:
     adhesions of pericardium
     constricting scar of:
         epicardium
         pericardium

DEF: Excision of a portion of heart lining.

37.32   Excision of aneurysm of heart

Repair of aneurysm of heart

37.33   Excision or destruction of other lesion or tissue of heart, open approach

Ablation of heart tissue (cryoablation) (electrocurrent) (laser) (microwave) (radiofrequency) (resection), open chest approach
Cox-maze procedure
Maze procedure
Modified maze procedure, trans-thoracic approach

> **EXCLUDES**   *ablation, excision or destruction of lesion or tissue of heart, endovascular approach (37.34)*

AHA: 4Q, '03, 93-94; 2Q, '94, 12

37.34   Excision or destruction of other lesion or tissue of heart, other approach

Ablation of heart tissue (cryoablation) (electrocurrent) (laser) (microwave) (radiofrequency) (resection), via peripherally inserted catheter
Modified maze procedure, endovascular approach

AHA: 4Q, '03, 93-95; 1Q, '00, 20

DEF: Destruction of heart tissue or lesion by freezing, electric current or resection.

37.35   Partial ventriculectomy

Ventricular reduction surgery
Ventricular remodeling
Code also any synchronous:
     mitral valve repair (35.02, 35.12)
     mitral valve replacement (35.23-35.24)

AHA: 4Q, '97, 54, 55

DEF: Removal of elliptical slice of ventricle between anterior and posterior papillary muscle; also called Batiste operation.

√4ᵗʰ 37.4   Repair of heart and pericardium

AHA: 2Q, '90, 24

●   **37.41   Implantation of prosthetic cardiac support device around the heart**

Cardiac support device (CSD)
Epicardial support device
Fabric (textile) (mesh) device
Ventricular support device on surface of heart
Code also any:
     cardiopulmonary bypass [extracorporeal circulation] [heart-lung machine] if performed (39.61)
     mitral valve repair (35.02, 35.12)
     mitral valve replacement (35.23-35.24)
     transesophageal echocardiography (88.72)

> **EXCLUDES**   *circulatory assist systems (37.61-37.68)*

●   **37.49   Other repair of heart and pericardium**

√4ᵗʰ 37.5   Heart replacement procedures

AHA: 4Q, '03, 96

37.51   Heart transplantation

> **EXCLUDES**   *combined heart-lung transplantation (33.6)*

37.52   Implantation of total replacement heart system

Artificial heart
Implantation of fully implantable total replacement heart system, including ventriculectomy

> **EXCLUDES**   *implantation of heart assist system [VAD] (37.62, 37.65, 37.66)*

37.53   Replacement or repair of thoracic unit of total replacement heart system

> **EXCLUDES**   *replacement and repair of heart assist system [VAD] (37.63)*

Ventricular Reduction Surgery

N Newborn Age: 0   **P** Pediatric Age: 0-17   **M** Maternity Age: 12-55   **A** Adult Age: 15-124   **Adj** Adjunct Code   ►◄ Revised Text   ● New Code   ▲ Revised Code Title

124 — Volume 3 • October 2005   *2006 ICD•9•CM*

37.54 Replacement or repair of other implantable component of total replacement heart system
Implantable battery
Implantable controller
Transcutaneous energy transfer [TET] device

> EXCLUDES *replacement and repair of heart assist system [VAD] (37.63)*
> *replacement or repair of thoracic unit of total replacement heart system (37.53)*

✓4th **37.6 Implantation of heart and circulatory assist system**
> EXCLUDES ▶ *implantation of prosthetic cardiac support system (37.41)*◄

AHA: 4Q, '95, 68

DEF: Implant of device for assisting heart in circulating blood.

37.61 Implant of pulsation balloon

37.62 Insertion of non-implantable heart assist system
Insertion of heart assist system, NOS
Insertion of heart pump

> EXCLUDES *implantation of total replacement heart system (37.52)*
> *insertion of percutaneous external heart assist device (37.68)*

AHA: 4Q, '03, 116; 2Q, '90, 25

37.63 Repair of heart assist system
Replacement of parts of an existing ventricular assist device (VAD)

> EXCLUDES *replacement or repair of other implantable component of total replacement heart system [artificial heart] (37.54)*
> *replacement or repair of thoracic unit of total replacement heart system [artificial heart] (37.53)*

37.64 Removal of heart assist system

> EXCLUDES *explantation [removal] of percutaneous external heart assist device (97.44)*
> *that with replacement of implant (37.63)*
> *nonoperative removal of heart assist system (97.44)*

37.65 Implant of external heart assist system
Note: Device (outside the body but connected to heart) with external circulation and pump

> INCLUDES *open chest (sternotomy) procedure for cannulae attachments*

> EXCLUDES *implantation of total replacement heart system (37.52)*
> *implant of pulsation balloon (37.61)*
> *insertion of percutaneous external heart assist device (37.68)*

DEF: Insertion of short-term circulatory support device with pump outside body.

37.66 Insertion of implantable heart assist system
Note: Device directly connected to the heart and implanted in the upper left quadrant of peritoneal cavity
Axial flow heart assist system
Diagonal pump heart assist system
Left ventricular assist device (LVAD)
Pulsatile heart assist system
Right ventricular assist device (RVAD)
Rotary pump heart assist system
Transportable, implantable heart assist system
Ventricular assist device (VAD) not otherwise specified

> EXCLUDES *implantation of total replacement heart system [artificial heart] (37.52)*
> *implant of pulsation balloon (37.61)*
> *insertion of percutaneous external heart assist device (37.68)*

AHA: 4Q, '03, 116; 1Q, '98, 8

DEF: Insertion of long-term circulatory support device with pump in body.

37.67 Implantation of cardiomyostimulation system
Note: Two-step open procedure consisting of tranfer of one end of the latissimus dorsi muscle; wrapping it around the heart; rib resection; implantation of epicardial cardiac pacing leads into the right ventricle; tunneling and pocket creation for the cardiomyostimulator.

AHA: 4Q, '98, 75; 1Q, '98, 8

37.68 Insertion of percutaneous external heart assist device
Circulatory assist device
Extrinsic heart assist device
pVAD
Percutaneous heart assist device

> INCLUDES *percutaneous [femoral] insertion of cannulae attachments*

▲ ✓4th **37.7 Insertion, revision, replacement, and removal of pacemaker leads; insertion of temporary pacemaker system; or revision of cardiac device pocket**
Code also any insertion and replacement of pacemaker device (37.80-37.87)

> EXCLUDES *implantation or replacement of transvenous lead [electrode] into left ventricular cardiac venous system (00.52)*

AHA: 1Q, '94, 16; 3Q, '92, 3; M-J, '87, 1

37.70 Initial insertion of lead [electrode], not otherwise specified

> EXCLUDES *insertion of temporary transvenous pacemaker system (37.78)*
> *replacement of atrial and/or ventricular lead(s) (37.76)*

37.71 Initial insertion of transvenous lead [electrode] into ventricle

> EXCLUDES *insertion of temporary transvenous pacemaker system (37.78)*
> *replacement of atrial and/or ventricular lead(s) (37.76)*

✓3rd ✓4th Additional Digit Required   RUG III Special Care Procedure   RUG III Clinically Complex Procedure   RUG III Extensive Services Procedure   RUG III Rehab Procedure

2006 ICD•9•CM   **October 2005 • Volume 3 — 125**

Operations on the Cardiovascular System

37.72–37.89

37.72   Initial insertion of transvenous leads [electrodes] into atrium and ventricle

> EXCLUDES   insertion of temporary transvenous pacemaker system (37.78)
> replacement of atrial and/or ventricular lead(s) (37.76)

AHA: 2Q, '97, 4

37.73   Initial insertion of transvenous lead [electrode] into atrium

> EXCLUDES   insertion of temporary transvenous pacemaker system (37.78)
> replacement of atrial and/or ventricular lead(s) (37.76)

37.74   Insertion or replacement of epicardial lead [electrode] into epicardium

Insertion or replacement of epicardial lead by:
     sternotomy
     thoracotomy

> EXCLUDES   replacement of atrial and/or ventricular lead(s) (37.76)

37.75   Revision of lead [electrode]

Repair of electrode [removal with re-insertion]
Repositioning of lead [electrode]
Revision of lead NOS

> EXCLUDES   repositioning of temporary transvenous pacemaker system — omit code

AHA: 2Q, '99, 11

37.76   Replacement of transvenous atrial and/or ventricular lead(s) [electrode]

Removal or abandonment of existing transvenous or epicardial lead(s) with transvenous lead(s) replacement

> EXCLUDES   replacement of epicardial lead [electrode] (37.74)

37.77   Removal of lead(s) [electrode] without replacement

Removal:
     epicardial lead (transthoracic approach)
     transvenous lead(s)

> EXCLUDES   removal of temporary transvenous pacemaker system — omit code
> that with replacement of:
>   atrial and/or ventricular lead(s) [electrode] (37.76)
>   epicardial lead [electrode] (37.74)

Insertion of Pacemaker

Lead

Subclavian vein

Pulse generator

Electrode

37.78   Insertion of temporary transvenous pacemaker system

> EXCLUDES   intraoperative cardiac pacemaker (39.64)

AHA: 3Q, '93, 12; 1Q, '89, 2

37.79   Revision or relocation of cardiac device pocket

Debridement and reforming pocket (skin and subcutaneous tissue)
Relocation of pocket [creation of new pocket] pacemaker or CRT-P
▶Revision or relocation of pacemaker, defibrillator, or other implanted cardiac device pocket◀

✓4ᵗʰ **37.8   Insertion, replacement, removal, and revision of pacemaker device**

Code also any lead insertion, lead replacement, lead removal and/or lead revision (37.70-37.77)

> EXCLUDES   implantation of cardiac resynchronization pacemaker, total system [CRT-P] (00.50)
> implantation or replacement of cardiac resynchronization pacemaker, pulse generator only [CRT-P] (00.53)

AHA: M-J, '87, 1

37.80   Insertion of permanent pacemaker, initial or replacement, type of device not specified

37.81   Initial insertion of single-chamber device, not specified as rate responsive

> EXCLUDES   replacement of existing pacemaker device (37.85-37.87)

37.82   Initial insertion of single-chamber device, rate responsive

Rate responsive to physiologic stimuli other than atrial rate

> EXCLUDES   replacement of existing pacemaker device (37.85-37.87)

37.83   Initial insertion of dual-chamber device

Atrial ventricular sequential device

> EXCLUDES   replacement of existing pacemaker device (37.85-37.87)

AHA: 2Q, '97, 4

37.85   Replacement of any type pacemaker device with single-chamber device, not specified as rate responsive

37.86   Replacement of any type pacemaker device with single-chamber device, rate responsive

Rate responsive to physiologic stimuli other than atrial rate

37.87   Replacement of any type pacemaker device with dual-chamber device

Atrial ventricular sequential device

37.89   Revision or removal of pacemaker device

Removal without replacement of cardiac resynchronization pacemaker device [CRT-P]
Repair of pacemaker device

> EXCLUDES   removal of temporary transvenous pacemaker system — omit code
> replacement of existing pacemaker device (37.85-37.87)
> replacement of existing pacemaker device with CRT-P pacemaker device (00.53)

AHA: N-D, '86, 1

N Newborn Age: 0   P Pediatric Age: 0-17   M Maternity Age: 12-55   A Adult Age: 15-124   Adj Adjunct Code   ▶◀ Revised Text   ● New Code   ▲ Revised Code Title

Left Atrial Appendage Device Insertion

Automatic Implantable Cardioverter/Defibrillator

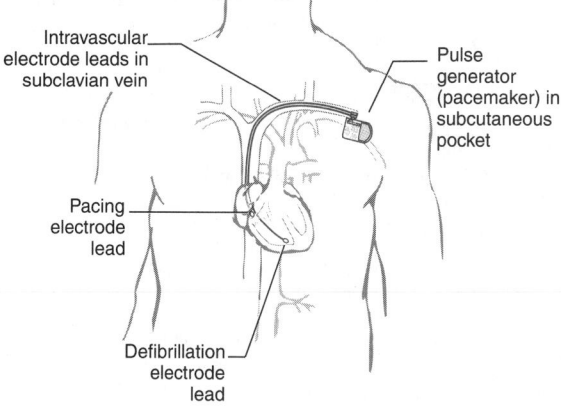

√4th **37.9　Other operations on heart and pericardium**
AHA: 3Q, '90, 11

37.90　Insertion of left atrial appendage device
Left atrial filter
Left atrial occluder
Transseptal catheter technique
AHA: 4Q, '04, 121

DEF: Implantation of a filtering device within the left
atrial appendage (LAA) to block emboli from exiting the
LAA causing stroke or systemic thromboembolism.

37.91　Open chest cardiac massage
EXCLUDES　*closed chest cardiac massage
(99.63)*
AHA: 4Q, '88, 12

DEF: Massage of heart through opening in chest wall to
reinstate or maintain circulation.

37.92　Injection of therapeutic substance into heart
**37.93　Injection of therapeutic substance into
pericardium**
**37.94　Implantation or replacement of automatic
cardioverter/defibrillator, total system [AICD]**
Implantation of defibrillator with leads
(epicardial patches), formation of pocket
(abdominal fascia) (subcutaneous), any
transvenous leads, intraoperative
procedures for evaluation of lead
signals, and obtaining defibrillator
threshold measurements
(electrophysiologic studies [EPS])
Techniques:
lateral thoracotomy
medial sternotomy
subxiphoid procedure
Code also extracorporeal circulation, if
performed (39.61)
Code also any concomitant procedure [e.g.,
coronary bypass] (36.01-36.19)
EXCLUDES　*implantation of cardiac
resynchronization
defibrillator, total system
[CRT-D] (00.51)*
AHA: 2Q, '03, 19; 3Q, '99, 12; 1Q, '99, 3; 3Q, '90, 11;
S-O, '87, 5

DEF: Direct insertion of defibrillator/cardioverter system
to deliver shock and restore heart rhythm; code also
used for replacing system.

**37.95　Implantation of automatic
cardioverter/defibrillator lead(s) only**
AHA: 3Q, '90, 11

**37.96　Implantation of automatic cardioverter/
defibrillator pulse generator only**
*implantation or replacement of
cardiac resynchroniz-
ation defibrillator, pulse
generator device only
[CRT-D] (00.54)*
EXCLUDES
AHA: 3Q, '90, 11

**37.97　Replacement of automatic
cardioverter/defibrillator lead(s) only**
AHA: 3Q, '90, 11

**37.98　Replacement of automatic cardioverter/
defibrillator pulse generator only**
EXCLUDES　*replacement of cardiac
resynchronization
defibrillator, pulse
generator device only
[CRT-D] (00.54)*
AHA: 1Q, '99, 3; 3Q, '90, 11

37.99　Other
Removal of cardioverter/defibrillator pulse
generator only without replacement
Removal without replacement of cardiac
resynchronization defibrillator device
[CRT-D]
Repositioning of lead(s) (sensing) (pacing)
[electrode]
Repositioning of pulse generator
Revision of cardioverter/defibrillator
(automatic) pocket
Revision or relocation of CRT-D pocket
EXCLUDES　*cardiac retraining (93.36)
conversion of cardiac rhythm
(99.60-99.69)
▶implantation of prosthetic
cardiac support device
(37.41)◀
insertion of left atrial
appendage device
(37.90)
maze procedure (Cox-maze),
open (37.33)
maze procedure, endovascular
approach (37.34)*
AHA: 1Q, '97, 12; 1Q, '94, 19; 3Q, '90, 11; 1Q, '89, 11

√3rd √4th Additional Digit Required　　RUG III Special Care Procedure　　RUG III Clinically Complex Procedure　　RUG III Extensive Services Procedure　　RUG III Rehab Procedure

2006 ICD•9•CM　　　　　　　　　　　　　　　　　　October 2005 • Volume 3 — 127

Operations on the Cardiovascular System

37.9–37.99

√3ʳᵈ **38   Incision, excision, and occlusion of vessels**

Code also any application or administration of an adhesion barrier substance (99.77)

Code also cardiopulmonary bypass [extracorporeal circulation] [heart-lung machine] (39.61)

> **EXCLUDES**   *that of coronary vessels (36.01-36.99)*

The following fourth-digit subclassification is for use with appropriate categories in section 38.0, 38.1, 38.3, 38.5, 38.6, and 38.8 according to site. Valid fourth-digits are in [brackets] under each code.

0   unspecified

1   intracranial vessels
    Cerebral (anterior) (middle)
    Circle of Willis
    Posterior communicating artery

2   other vessels of head and neck
    Carotid artery (common) (external) (internal)
    Jugular vein (external) (internal)

3   upper limb vessels
    Axillary   Radial
    Brachial   Ulnar

4   aorta

5   other thoracic vessels
    Innominate   Vena cava, superior
    Pulmonary (artery) (vein)
    Subclavian

6   abdominal arteries
    Celiac   Mesenteric
    Gastric   Renal
    Hepatic   Splenic
    Iliac   Umbilical
    EXCLUDES *abdominal aorta (4)*

7   abdominal veins
    Iliac   Splenic
    Portal   Vena cava (inferior)
    Renal

8   lower limb arteries
    Femoral (common)   Popliteal
    (superficial)   Tibial

9   lower limb veins
    Femoral   Saphenous
    Popliteal   Tibial

§ √4ᵗʰ **38.0   Incision of vessel**
[0-9]
    Embolectomy   Thrombectomy
    EXCLUDES *puncture or catheterization of any:*
       artery (38.91, 38.98)
       vein (38.92-38.95, 38.99)
    AHA: 2Q, '98, 23; **For code 38.08:** 1Q, '03, 17; **For code 38.09:** 1Q, '03, 17

    DEF: Incision into vessel to remove mobile or stationary blood clot.

§ √4ᵗʰ **38.1   Endarterectomy**
[0-6,8]
    Endarterectomy with:
      embolectomy
      patch graft
      temporary bypass during procedure
      thrombectomy
    ►Code also any:
      number of vascular stents inserted (00.45-00.48)
      number of vessels treated (00.40-00.43)◄
    AHA: 1Q, '00, 16; 2Q, '99, 5; 2Q, '95, 16; **For code 38.12:** 1Q, '02, 10

    DEF: Excision of tunica intima of artery to relieve arterial walls thickened by plaque or chronic inflammation.

√4ᵗʰ **38.2   Diagnostic procedures on blood vessels**
    EXCLUDES ►*adjunct vascular system procedures (00.40-00.43)*◄

38.21   Biopsy of blood vessel

38.22   Percutaneous angioscopy
    EXCLUDES *angioscopy of eye (95.12)*

    DEF: Exam, with fiberoptic catheter inserted through peripheral artery to visualize inner lining of blood vessels.

Endarterectomy of Aortic Bifurcation

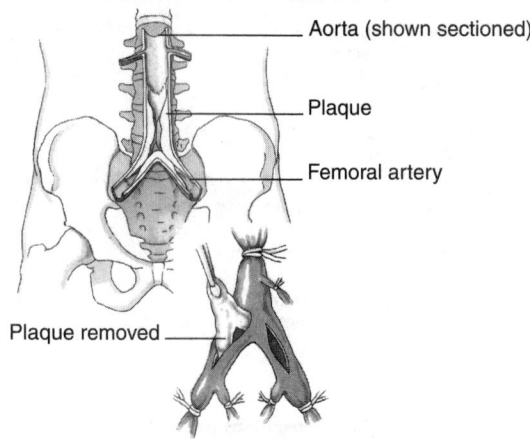

- Aorta (shown sectioned)
- Plaque
- Femoral artery
- Plaque removed

38.29   Other diagnostic procedures on blood vessels
    EXCLUDES *blood vessel thermography (88.86)*
      circulatory monitoring (89.61-89.69)
      contrast:
        angiocardiography (88.50-88.58)
        arteriography (88.40-88.49)
        phlebography (88.60-88.67)
      impedance phlebography (88.68)
      peripheral vascular ultrasonography (88.77)
      plethysmogram (89.58)
    AHA: 3Q, '00, 16; 1Q, '99, 7

§ √4ᵗʰ **38.3   Resection of vessel with anastomosis**
[0-9]
    Angiectomy
    Excision of:
      aneurysm (arteriovenous) ⎫
                       ⎬ with anastomosis
      blood vessel (lesion)   ⎭

    DEF: Reconstruction and reconnection of vessel after partial excision.

Methods of Vessel Anastomoses

End-to-end   Side-to-side

Oblique cut   Fish mouth

Funnelization   End-to-side

---

§   Requires fourth-digit. Valid digits are in [brackets] under each code. See category 38 for definitions.

[N] Newborn Age: 0   [P] Pediatric Age: 0-17   [M] Maternity Age: 12-55   [A] Adult Age: 15-124   **Adj** Adjunct Code   ►◄ Revised Text   ● New Code   ▲ Revised Code Title

§§ ✓4ᵗʰ **38.4**   **Resection of vessel with replacement**
[0-9]   Angiectomy
            Excision of:
                aneurysm (arteriovenous) or ⎫
                blood vessel (lesion)   ⎬ with replacement
                                             ⎭

> EXCLUDES   *endovascular repair of aneurysm*
>   *(39.71-39.79)*

Requires the use of one of the following fourth-digit
subclassifications to identify site:

0 unspecified site
1 intracranial vessels
        Cerebral (anterior) (middle)
        Circle of Willis
        Posterior communicating artery
2 other vessels of head and neck
        Carotid artery (common) (external) (internal)
        Jugular vein (external) (internal)
3 upper limb vessels
        Axillary   Radial
        Brachial   Ulnar
4 aorta, abdominal
        Code also any thoracic vessel involvement
            (thoracoabdominal procedure) (38.45)
5 thoracic vessel
        Aorta (thoracic)
        Innominate   Subclavian
        Pulmonary (artery) (vein)   Vena cava, superior
        Code also any abdominal aorta involvement
            (thoracoabdominal procedure) (38.44)
6 abdominal arteries
        Celiac   Mesenteric
        Gastric   Renal
        Hepatic   Splenic
        Iliac   Umbilical

> EXCLUDES   *abdominal aorta (4)*

7 abdominal veins
        Iliac   Splenic
        Portal   Vena cava (inferior)
        Renal
8 lower limb arteries
        Femoral (common) (superficial)
        Tibial
9 lower limb veins
        Femoral   Saphenous
        Popliteal   Tibial

AHA: 2Q, '99, 5, 6
DEF: Excision of aneurysm (arteriovenous): Excision and
replacement of segment of stretched or bulging blood vessel.
DEF: Excision of blood vessel (lesion): Excision and replacement of
segment of vessel containing lesion.

§ ✓4ᵗʰ **38.5**   **Ligation and stripping of varicose veins**
[0-3,5,7,9]   EXCLUDES   *ligation of varices:*
                            esophageal (42.91)
                            gastric (44.91)

AHA: For code 38.59: 2Q, '97, 7

DEF: Ligation of varicose veins: Typing off vein with thread or wire
to eliminate blood flow; stripping involves excising length of vein.

§ ✓4ᵗʰ **38.6**   **Other excision of vessels**
[0-9]   Excision of blood vessel (lesion) NOS
            EXCLUDES   *excision of vessel for aortocoronary*
                        bypass (36.10-36.14)
                       excision with:
                        anastomosis (38.30-38.39)
                        graft replacement (38.40-38.49)
                        implant (38.40-38.49)

AHA: 3Q, '90, 17

38.7   **Interruption of the vena cava**
        Insertion of implant or sieve in vena cava
        Ligation of vena cava (inferior) (superior)
        Plication of vena cava

AHA: 2Q, '94, 9; S-0, '85, 5

DEF: Interruption of the blood flow through the venous heart vessels
to prevent clots from reaching the chambers of the heart by means
of implanting a sieve or implant, separating off a portion or by
narrowing the venous blood vessels.

§ ✓4ᵗʰ **38.8**   **Other surgical occlusion of vessels**
[0-9]   Clamping ⎫
            Division ⎬ of blood vessel
            Ligation ⎭
            Occlusion

> EXCLUDES   *adrenal vessels (07.43)*
>   *esophageal varices (42.91)*
>   *gastric or duodenal vessel for ulcer*
>   *(44.40-44.49)*
>   *gastric varices (44.91)*
>   *meningeal vessel (02.13)*
>   *percutaneous transcatheter infusion*
>   *embolization (99.29)*
>   *spermatic vein for varicocele (63.1)*
>   *surgical occlusion of vena cava (38.7)*
>   *that for chemoembolization (99.25)*
>   *that for control of (postoperative)*
>   *hemorrhage:*
>   *anus (49.95)*
>   *bladder (57.93)*
>   *following vascular procedure (39.41)*
>   *nose (21.00-21.09)*
>   *prostate (60.94)*
>   *tonsil (28.7)*
>   *thyroid vessel (06.92)*

AHA: 2Q, '90, 23; M-A, '87, 9; **For code 38.85:** 1Q, '03, 15;
For code 38.86: ▶1Q, '05, 14;◄ N-D, '87, 4

✓4ᵗʰ **38.9**   **Puncture of vessel**
            EXCLUDES   *that for circulatory monitoring (89.60-*
                        89.69)

38.91   **Arterial catheterization**
AHA: ▶1Q, '05, 14;◄ 1Q, '97, 3; 1Q, '95, 3; 2Q, '91, 15;
     2Q, '90, 23

38.92   **Umbilical vein catheterization**

38.93   **Venous catheterization, not elsewhere**
            classified
            EXCLUDES   *that for cardiac catheterization*
                        (37.21-37.23)
                       that for renal dialysis (38.95)

AHA: 3Q, '00, 9 ;2Q, '98, 24; 1Q, '96, 3; 2Q, '96, 15;
     3Q, '91, 13; 4Q, '90, 14; 2Q, '90, 24; 3Q, '88, 13

38.94   **Venous cutdown**
            DEF: Incision of vein to place needle or catheter.

38.95   **Venous catheterization for renal dialysis**
            EXCLUDES   *insertion of totally implantable*
                        vascular access device
                        [VAD] (86.07)

AHA: 3Q, '98, 13; 2Q, '94, 11

38.98   **Other puncture of artery**
            EXCLUDES   *that for:*
                        arteriography (88.40-88.49)
                        coronary arteriography
                        (88.55-88.57)

---

§ Tequires fourth-digit. Valid digits are in [brackets] under each code. See category 38 for definitions.
§§ Requires fourth-digit. Valid digits are in [brackets]. See code 38.4 for definitions.

✓3ʳᵈ
✓4ᵗʰ Additional Digit Required   RUG III Special Care Procedure   RUG III Clinically Complex Procedure   RUG III Extensive Services Procedure   RUG III Rehab Procedure

38.99   **Other puncture of vein**

Phlebotomy

EXCLUDES   *that for:*
angiography (88.60-88.68)
extracorporeal circulation (39.61, 50.92)
injection or infusion of:
sclerosing solution (39.92)
therapeutic or prophylactic substance (99.11-99.29)
perfusion (39.96, 39.97)
phlebography (88.60-88.68)
transfusion (99.01-99.09)

AHA: 4Q, '94, 50; 1Q, '88, 11

√3rd   **39**   **Other operations on vessels**

EXCLUDES   *those on coronary vessels (36.0-36.99)*

39.0   **Systemic to pulmonary artery shunt**

Descending aorta-pulmonary artery
Left to right   } anastomosis (graft)
Subclavian-pulmonary

Code also cardiopulmonary bypass [extracorporeal circulation] [heart-lung machine] (39.61)

DEF: Descending aorta-pulmonary artery anastomosis (graft): Connection of descending main heart artery to pulmonary artery.
DEF: Left to right anastomosis (graft): Connection of systemic arterial blood vessel to venous pulmonary system.
DEF: Subclavian-pulmonary anastomosis (graft): Connection of subclavian artery to pulmonary artery.

39.1   **Intra-abdominal venous shunt**

Anastomosis:
mesocaval
portacaval
portal vein to inferior vena cava
splenic and renal veins
transjugular intrahepatic portosystemic shunt [TIPS]

EXCLUDES   *peritoneovenous shunt (54.94)*

AHA: 2Q, '02, 4; 4Q, '94, 50; 4Q, '93, 31; 2Q, '93, 8

DEF: Connection of two venous blood vessels within abdominal cavity.

√4th   **39.2**   **Other shunt or vascular bypass**

Code also pressurized treatment of venous bypass graft [conduit] with pharmaceutical substance, if performed (00.16)

DEF: Creation of supplemental blood flow to area with inadequate blood supply due to disease or injury of vessels.

39.21   **Caval-pulmonary artery anastomosis**

Code also cardiopulmonary bypass (39.61)

39.22   **Aorta-subclavian-carotid bypass**

Bypass (arterial):
aorta to carotid and brachial
aorta to subclavian and carotid
carotid to subclavian

39.23   **Other intrathoracic vascular shunt or bypass**

Intrathoracic (arterial) bypass graft NOS

EXCLUDES   *coronary artery bypass (36.10-36.19)*

39.24   **Aorta-renal bypass**

39.25   **Aorta-iliac-femoral bypass**

Bypass:
aortofemoral   aortopopliteal
aortoiliac   iliofemoral [iliac-
aortoiliac to popliteal   femoral]

AHA: 1Q, '03, 16; 4Q, '90, 27; 1Q, '88, 10

39.26   **Other intra-abdominal vascular shunt or bypass**

Bypass:
aortoceliac
aortic-superior mesenteric
common hepatic-common iliac-renal
Intra-abdominal arterial bypass graft NOS

EXCLUDES   *peritoneovenous shunt (54.94)*

Typical Venous Cutdown

Vein mobilized, opened by oblique cut, catheter inserted

Distal vein tied

Saphenous vein (typical site) accessed by transverse incision

---

39.27   **Arteriovenostomy for renal dialysis**

Anastomosis for renal dialysis
Formation of (peripheral) arteriovenous fistula for renal [kidney] dialysis
Code also any renal dialysis (39.95)

39.28   **Extracranial-intracranial (EC-IC) vascular bypass**

AHA: 2Q, '92, 7; 4Q, '91, 22

39.29   **Other (peripheral) vascular shunt or bypass**

Bypass (graft):
axillary-brachial
axillary-femoral [axillofemoral] (superficial)
brachial
femoral-femoral
femoroperoneal
femoropopliteal (arteries)
femorotibial (anterior) (posterior)
popliteal
vascular NOS

EXCLUDES   *peritoneovenous shunt (54.94)*

AHA: 1Q, '03, 17; 1Q, '02, 13; S-O, '85, 13

√4th   **39.3**   **Suture of vessel**

Repair of laceration of blood vessel

EXCLUDES   *any other vascular puncture closure device — omit code*
suture of aneurysm (39.52)
that for control of hemorrhage (postoperative):
anus (49.95)
bladder (57.93)
following vascular procedure (39.41)
nose (21.00-21.09)
prostate (60.94)
tonsil (28.7)

39.30   **Suture of unspecified blood vessel**

39.31   **Suture of artery**

39.32   **Suture of vein**

√4th   **39.4**   **Revision of vascular procedure**

39.41   **Control of hemorrhage following vascular surgery**

EXCLUDES   *that for control of hemorrhage (postoperative):*
anus (49.95)
bladder (57.93)
nose (21.00-21.09)
prostate (60.94)
tonsil (28.7)

39.42   **Revision of arteriovenous shunt for renal dialysis**

Conversion of renal dialysis:
end-to-end anastomosis to end-to-side
end-to-side anastomosis to end-to-end
vessel-to-vessel cannula to arteriovenous shunt
Removal of old arteriovenous shunt and creation of new shunt

EXCLUDES   *replacement of vessel-to-vessel cannula (39.94)*

AHA: 2Q, '94, 15; 4Q, '93, 33

N Newborn Age: 0   P Pediatric Age: 0-17   M Maternity Age: 12-55   A Adult Age: 15-124   Adj Adjunct Code   ◄► Revised Text   ● New Code   ▲ Revised Code Title

130 — Volume 3   **2006 ICD•9•CM**

39.43   Removal of arteriovenous shunt for renal dialysis
> **EXCLUDES**   *that with replacement [revision] of shunt (39.42)*

39.49   Other revision of vascular procedure
Declotting (graft)
Revision of:
  anastomosis of blood vessel
  vascular procedure (previous)
AHA: 2Q, '98, 17; 1Q, '97, 3; 2Q, '94, 15

DEF: Declotting (graft): Removal of clot from graft.

√4ᵗʰ **39.5   Other repair of vessels**

39.50   Angioplasty or atherectomy of other non-coronary vessel(s)
Percutaneous transluminal angioplasty (PTA) of non-coronary vessels:
  lower extremity vessels
  mesenteric artery
  renal artery
  upper extremity vessels
Code also any:
  injection or infusion of thrombolytic agent (99.10)
  insertion of non-coronary stent(s) or stent grafts(s) (39.90)
  ▶number of vascular stents inserted (00.45-00.48)
  number of vessels treated (00.40-00.43)◀
> **EXCLUDES**   *percutaneous angioplasty or atherectomy of precerebral or cerebral vessel(s) (00.61-00.62)*
AHA: 3Q, '03, 10; 1Q, '02, 13; 2Q, '01, 23; 2Q, '00, 10; 1Q, '00, 12; 2Q, '98, 17; 1Q, '97, 3; 4Q, '96, 63; 4Q, '95, 66

39.51   Clipping of aneurysm
> **EXCLUDES**   *clipping of arteriovenous fistula (39.53)*

39.52   Other repair of aneurysm
Repair of aneurysm by:
  coagulation
  electrocoagulation
  filipuncture
  methyl methacrylate
  suture
  wiring
  wrapping
> **EXCLUDES**   *endovascular repair of aneurysm (39.71-39.79)*
> *re-entry operation (aorta) (39.54)*
> *that with:*
> *graft replacement (38.40-38.49)*
> *resection (38.30-38.49, 38.60-38.69)*
AHA: 3Q, '02, 25, 26; 1Q, '99, 15, 16, 17; 1Q, '88, 10

DEF: Application of device in abnormally stretched blood vessel to prevent movement of material collected in vessel.
DEF: Repair of aneurysm by: Coagulation: Clotting or solidifying. Electrocoagulation: Electrically produced clotting. Filipuncture: Insertion of wire or thread. Methyl methacrylate: Injection or insertion of plastic material. Suture: Stitching. Wiring: Insertion of wire. Wrapping: Compression.

39.53   Repair of arteriovenous fistula
Embolization of carotid cavernous fistula
Repair of arteriovenous fistula by:
  clipping
  coagulation
  ligation and division
> **EXCLUDES**   *repair of:*
> *arteriovenous shunt for renal dialysis (39.42)*
> *head and neck vessels, endovascular approach (39.72)*
> *that with:*
> *graft replacement (38.40-38.49)*
> *resection (38.30-38.49, 38.60-38.69)*
AHA: 1Q, '00, 8

DEF: Correction of arteriovenous fistula by application of clamps, causing coagulation or by tying off and dividing the connection.

39.54   Re-entry operation (aorta)
Fenestration of dissecting aneurysm of thoracic aorta
Code also cardiopulmonary bypass [extracorporeal circulation] [heart-lung machine] (39.61)
DEF: Re-entry operation: Creation of passage between stretched wall of the vessel and major arterial channel to heart.
DEF: Fenestration of dissecting aneurysm of thoracic aorta: Creation of passage between stretched arterial heart vessel and functional part of vessel.

39.55   Reimplantation of aberrant renal vessel
DEF: Reimplant of renal vessel into normal position.

39.56   Repair of blood vessel with tissue patch graft
> **EXCLUDES**   *that with resection (38.40-38.49)*
AHA: 1Q, '04, 16

39.57   Repair of blood vessel with synthetic patch graft
> **EXCLUDES**   *that with resection (38.40-38.49)*

39.58   Repair of blood vessel with unspecified type of patch graft
> **EXCLUDES**   *that with resection (38.40-38.49)*

39.59   Other repair of vessel
Aorticopulmonary window operation
Arterioplasty NOS
Construction of venous valves (peripheral)
Plication of vein (peripheral)
Reimplantation of artery
Code also cardiopulmonary bypass [extracorporeal circulation] [heart-lung machine] (39.61)
> **EXCLUDES**   *interruption of the vena cava (38.7)*
> *reimplantation of renal artery (39.55)*
> *that with:*
> *graft (39.56-39.58)*
> *resection (38.30-38.49, 38.60-38.69)*
AHA: 4Q, '93, 31; 2Q, '89, 17; N-D, '86, 8; S-O, '85, 5; M-A, '85, 15

DEF: Aorticopulmonary window operation: Repair of abnormal opening between major heart arterial vessel above valves and pulmonary artery.

DEF: Construction of venous valves (peripheral): Reconstruction of valves within peripheral veins.

DEF: Plication of vein (peripheral): Shortening of peripheral vein.

DEF: Reimplantation of artery: Reinsertion of artery into its normal position.

√3ʳᵈ
√4ᵗʰ Additional Digit Required   RUG III Special Care Procedure   RUG III Clinically Complex Procedure   RUG III Extensive Services Procedure   RUG III Rehab Procedure

2006 ICD•9•CM   October 2005 • Volume 3 — 131

Operations on the Cardiovascular System

39.43–39.59

Operations on the Cardiovascular System

39.6–39.73

Endovascular Repair of Abdominal Aortic Aneurysm

Renal arteries

Abdominal aortic aneurysm

Stent

Common iliac arteries

√4ᵗʰ **39.6 Extracorporeal circulation and procedures auxiliary to heart surgery**
AHA: 1Q, '95, 5

39.61 Extracorporeal circulation auxiliary to open heart surgery
Artificial heart and lung
Cardiopulmonary bypass
Pump oxygenator
EXCLUDES extracorporeal hepatic assistance (50.92)
extracorporeal membrane oxygenation [ECMO] (39.65)
hemodialysis (39.95)
percutaneous cardiopulmonary bypass (39.66)
AHA: 1Q, '04, 16; 3Q, '02, 5; 4Q, '97, 55; 3Q, '97, 14; 2Q, '97, 8; 2Q, '90, 24

39.62 Hypothermia (systemic) incidental to open heart surgery

39.63 Cardioplegia
Arrest:
anoxic
circulatory
DEF: Purposely inducing electromechanical cardiac arrest.

39.64 Intraoperative cardiac pacemaker
Temporary pacemaker used during and immediately following cardiac surgery
AHA: 1Q, '89, 2; M-J, '87, 3

39.65 Extracorporeal membrane oxygenation [ECMO]
EXCLUDES extracorporeal circulation auxiliary to open heart surgery (39.61)
percutaneous cardiopulmonary bypass (39.66)
AHA: 2Q, '90, 23; 2Q, '89, 17; 4Q, '88, 5
DEF: Creation of closed-chest, heart-lung bypass or Bard cardiopulmonary assist system with tube insertion.

39.66 Percutaneous cardiopulmonary bypass
Closed chest
EXCLUDES extracorporeal circulation auxiliary to open heart surgery (39.61)
extracorporeal hepatic assistance (50.92)
extracorporeal membrane oxy-genation [ECMO] (39.65)
hemodialysis (39.95)
AHA: 3Q, '96, 11
DEF: Use of mechanical pump system to oxygenate and pump blood throughout the body via catheter in the femoral artery and vein.

√4ᵗʰ **39.7 Endovascular repair of vessel**
Endoluminal repair
EXCLUDES angioplasty or atherectomy of other non-coronary vessel(s) (39.50)
insertion of non-drug-eluting peripheral vessel stent(s) (39.90)
other repair of aneurysm (39.52)
percutaneous insertion of carotid artery stent(s) (00.63)
percutaneous insertion of intracranial stent(s) (00.65)
percutaneous insertion of other precerebral artery stent(s) (00.64)
resection of abdominal aorta with replacement (38.44)
resection of lower limb arteries with replacement (38.48)
resection of thoracic aorta with replacement (38.45)
resection of upper limb vessels with replacement (38.43)

39.71 Endovascular implantation of graft in abdominal aorta
Endovascular repair of abdominal aortic aneurysm with graft
Stent graft(s)
AHA: 1Q, '02, 13; 4Q, '00, 63, 64
DEF: Replacement of a section of abdominal aorta with mesh graft; via catheters inserted through femoral arteries.

39.72 Endovascular repair or occlusion of head and neck vessels
Coil embolization or occlusion
Endograft(s)
Endovascular graft(s)
Liquid tissue adhesive (glue) embolization or occlusion
Other implant or substance for repair, embolization or occlusion
That for repair of aneurysm, arteriovenous malformation [AVM] or fistula
AHA: 4Q, '02, 103
DEF: Coil embolization or occlusion: Utilizing x-ray guidance a neuro-microcatheter is guided from entry in the femoral artery in the groin to the site of the aneurysm of the head and neck vessels for delivery of micro-coils that act to stop blood flow to the arteriovenous malfomation (AVM).

39.73 Endovascular implantation of graft in thoracic aorta
Endograft(s)
Endovascular graft(s)
Endovascular repair of defect of thoracic aorta with graft(s) or device(s)
Stent graft(s) or device(s)
That for repair of aneurysm, dissection, or injury
EXCLUDES fenestration of dissecting aneurysm of thoracic aorta (39.54)

External Arteriovenous Shunt

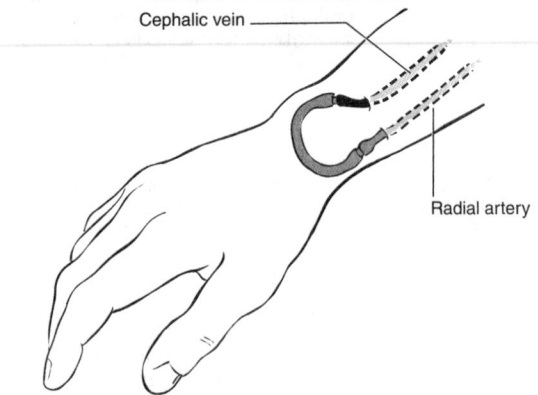

Cephalic vein

Radial artery

N Newborn Age: 0   P Pediatric Age: 0-17   M Maternity Age: 12-55   A Adult Age: 15-124   **Adj** Adjunct Code   ◄► Revised Text   ● New Code   ▲ Revised Code Title

132 — Volume 3 • October 2005   *2006 ICD•9•CM*

39.79 **Other endovascular repair (of aneurysm) of other vessels**
Coil embolization or occlusion
Endograft(s)
Endovascular graft(s)
Liquid tissue adhesive (glue) embolization or occlusion
Other implant or substance for repair, embolization or occlusion
EXCLUDES ▶endovascular implantation of graft in thoracic aorta (39.73)◀
endovascular repair or occlusion of head and neck vessels (39.72)
insertion of drug-eluting peripheral vessel stent(s) (00.55)
insertion of non-drug-eluting peripheral vessel stent(s) (for other than aneurysm repair) (39.90)
non-endovascular repair of arteriovenous fistula (39.53)
other surgical occlusion of vessels–see category 38.8
percutaneous transcatheter infusion (99.29)
transcatheter embolization for gastric or duodenal bleeding (44.44)
AHA: 4Q, '02, 103; 3Q, '01, 17,18; 4Q, '00, 64

39.8 **Operations on carotid body and other vascular bodies**
Chemodectomy
Denervation of:
aortic body
carotid body
Glomectomy, carotid
Implantation into carotid body:
electronic stimulator
pacemaker
EXCLUDES excision of glomus jugulare (20.51)
DEF: Chemodectomy: Removal of a chemoreceptor vascular body.
DEF: Denervation of aortic body: Destruction of nerves attending the major heart blood vessels.
DEF: Destruction of carotid body: Destruction of nerves of carotid artery.
DEF: Glomectomy, carotid: Removal of the carotid artery framework.

√4ᵗʰ 39.9 **Other operations on vessels**

39.90 **Insertion of non-drug-eluting peripheral vessel stent(s)**
Bare stent(s)
Bonded stent(s)
Drug-coated stent(s), e.g., heparin coated
Endograft(s)
Endovascular graft(s)
Endovascular recanalization techniques
Stent graft(s)
Code also any:
non-coronary angioplasty or atherectomy (39.50)
▶number of vascular stents inserted (00.45-00.48)
number of vessels treated (00.40-00.43)◀
EXCLUDES insertion of drug-eluting, peripheral vessel stent(s) (00.55)
percutaneous insertion of carotid artery stent(s) (00.63)
percutaneous insertion of intracranial stent(s) (00.65)
percutaneous insertion of other precerebral artery stent(s) (00.64)
that for aneurysm repair (39.71-39.79)
AHA: 4Q, '02, 101; 1Q, '00, 12; 4Q, '96, 63

39.91 **Freeing of vessel**
Dissection and freeing of adherent tissue:
artery-vein-nerve bundle
vascular bundle
AHA: 3Q, '02, 12

39.92 **Injection of sclerosing agent into vein**
EXCLUDES injection:
esophageal varices (42.33)
hemorrhoids (49.42)
AHA: 2Q, '92, 17

39.93 **Insertion of vessel-to-vessel cannula**
Formation of:
arteriovenous:
fistula ⎫ by external
shunt ⎭ cannula
Code also any renal dialysis (39.95)
AHA: 3Q, '88, 13; S-O, '85, 5 & 12

39.94 **Replacement of vessel-to-vessel cannula**
Revision of vessel-to-vessel cannula

39.95 **Hemodialysis**
Artificial kidney
Hemofiltration
Hemodiafiltration
Renal dialysis
EXCLUDES peritoneal dialysis (54.98)
AHA: 1Q, '04, 22; 4Q, '03, 111; 2Q, '01, 2-14; 4Q, '00, 40; 2Q, '98, 20; S-O, '86, 11
DEF: Filtration process to treat acute and chronic renal failure by eliminating toxic end products of nitrogen metabolism from blood.

39.96 **Total body perfusion**
Code also substance perfused (99.21-99.29)

39.97 **Other perfusion**
Perfusion NOS
Perfusion, local [regional] of:
carotid artery
coronary artery
head
Perfusion, local [regional] of:
lower limb
neck
upper limb
Code also substance perfused (99.21-99.29)
EXCLUDES perfusion of:
kidney (55.95)
large intestine (46.96)
liver (50.93)
small intestine (46.95)
AHA: 3Q, '96, 11

39.98 **Control of hemorrhage, not otherwise specified**
Angiotripsy
Control of postoperative hemorrhage NOS
Venotripsy
EXCLUDES control of hemorrhage (postoperative):
anus (49.95)
bladder (57.93)
following vascular procedure (39.41)
nose (21.00-21.09)
prostate (60.94)
tonsil (28.7)
that by:
ligation (38.80-38.89)
suture (39.30-39.32)
DEF: Angiotripsy: Clamping of tissue to stop arterial blood flow.
DEF: Venotripsy: Clamping of tissue to stop venous blood flow.

39.99 **Other operations on vessels**
EXCLUDES injection or infusion of therapeutic or prophylactic substance (99.11-99.29)
transfusion of blood and blood components (99.01-99.09)
AHA: 1Q, '89, 11

√3ʳᵈ
√4ᵗʰ Additional Digit Required   RUG III Special Care Procedure   RUG III Clinically Complex Procedure   RUG III Extensive Services Procedure   RUG III Rehab Procedure

2006 ICD•9•CM   **October 2005 • Volume 3 — 133**

Operations on the Hemic and Lymphatic Systems

40–41.05

8. OPERATIONS ON THE HEMIC AND LYMPHATIC SYSTEMS (40–41)

√3rd **40 Operations on lymphatic system**

40.0 Incision of lymphatic structures

√4th **40.1 Diagnostic procedures on lymphatic structures**

40.11 Biopsy of lymphatic structure

40.19 Other diagnostic procedures on lymphatic structures

> EXCLUDES   lymphangiogram:
>   abdominal (88.04)
>   cervical (87.08)
>   intrathoracic (87.34)
>   lower limb (88.36)
>   upper limb (88.34)
>   microscopic examination of
>   specimen (90.71-90.79)
>   radioisotope scan (92.16)
>   thermography (88.89)

√4th **40.2 Simple excision of lymphatic structure**

> EXCLUDES   biopsy of lymphatic structure (40.11)

DEF: Removal of lymphatic structure only.

40.21 Excision of deep cervical lymph node

AHA: 4Q, '99, 16

40.22 Excision of internal mammary lymph node

40.23 Excision of axillary lymph node

AHA: 2Q, '02, 7

40.24 Excision of inguinal lymph node

40.29 Simple excision of other lymphatic structure

> Excision of:
>   cystic hygroma
>   lymphangioma
> Simple lymphadenectomy

AHA: 1Q, '99, 6

DEF: Lymphangioma: Removal of benign congenital lymphatic malformation.

DEF: Simple lymphadenectomy: Removal of lymph node.

40.3 Regional lymph node excision

> Extended regional lymph node excision
> Regional lymph node excision with excision of lymphatic drainage area including skin, subcutaneous tissue, and fat

AHA: 2Q, '92, 7

DEF: Extended regional lymph node excision: Removal of lymph node group, including area around nodes.

√4th **40.4 Radical excision of cervical lymph nodes**

> Resection of cervical lymph nodes down to muscle and deep fascia

> EXCLUDES   that associated with radical laryngectomy (30.4)

40.40 Radical neck dissection, not otherwise specified

40.41 Radical neck dissection, unilateral

AHA: 2Q, '99, 6

DEF: Dissection, total, of cervical lymph nodes on one side of neck.

40.42 Radical neck dissection, bilateral

DEF: Dissection, total, of cervical lymph nodes on both sides of neck.

√4th **40.5 Radical excision of other lymph nodes**

> EXCLUDES   that associated with radical mastectomy (85.45-85.48)

40.50 Radical excision of lymph nodes, not otherwise specified

> Radical (lymph) node dissection NOS

40.51 Radical excision of axillary lymph nodes

40.52 Radical excision of periaortic lymph nodes

40.53 Radical excision of iliac lymph nodes

40.54 Radical groin dissection

40.59 Radical excision of other lymph nodes

> EXCLUDES   radical neck dissection (40.40-40.42)

√4th **40.6 Operations on thoracic duct**

40.61 Cannulation of thoracic duct

DEF: Placement of cannula in main lymphatic duct of chest.

40.62 Fistulization of thoracic duct

DEF: Creation of passage in main lymphatic duct of chest.

40.63 Closure of fistula of thoracic duct

DEF: Closure of fistula in main lymphatic duct of chest.

40.64 Ligation of thoracic duct

DEF: Tying off main lymphatic duct of chest.

40.69 Other operations on thoracic duct

40.9 Other operations on lymphatic structures

> Anastomosis
> Dilation
> Ligation
> Obliteration   } of peripheral lymphatics
> Reconstruction
> Repair
> Transplantation

> Correction of lymphedema of limb, NOS

> EXCLUDES   reduction of elephantiasis of scrotum (61.3)

√3rd **41 Operations on bone marrow and spleen**

√4th **41.0 Bone marrow or hematopoietic stem cell transplant**

> Note: To report donor source — see codes 00.91-00.93

> EXCLUDES   aspiration of bone marrow from donor (41.91)

AHA: 4Q, '00, 64; 1Q, '91, 3; 4Q, '91, 26

41.00 Bone marrow transplant, not otherwise specified

41.01 Autologous bone marrow transplant without purging

> EXCLUDES   that with purging (41.09)

DEF: Transplant of patient's own bone marrow.

41.02 Allogeneic bone marrow transplant with purging

> Allograft of bone marrow with in vitro removal (purging) of T-cells

DEF: Transplant of bone marrow from donor to patient after donor marrow purged of undesirable cells.

41.03 Allogeneic bone marrow transplant without purging

> Allograft of bone marrow NOS

41.04 Autologous hematopoietic stem cell transplant without purging

> EXCLUDES   that with purging (41.07)

AHA: 4Q, '94, 52

41.05 Allogeneic hematopoietic stem cell transplant without purging

> EXCLUDES   that with purging (41.08)

AHA: 4Q, '97, 55

N Newborn Age: 0   P Pediatric Age: 0-17   M Maternity Age: 12-55   A Adult Age: 15-124   Adj Adjunct Code   ◄ Revised Text   ● New Code   ▲ Revised Code Title

Partial Splenectomy

Total Splenectomy

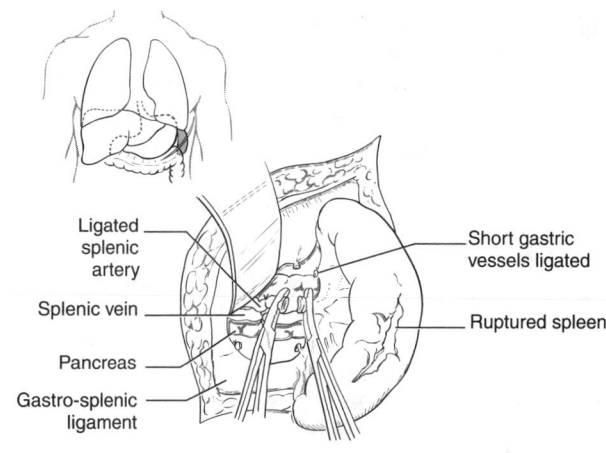

41.06   **Cord blood stem cell transplant**
     AHA: 4Q, '97, 56

41.07   **Autologous hematopoietic stem cell transplant with purging**
     Cell depletion

41.08   **Allogeneic hematopoietic stem cell transplant with purging**
     Cell depletion

41.09   **Autologous bone marrow transplant with purging**
     With extracorporeal purging of malignant cells from marrow
     Cell depletion

41.1   **Puncture of spleen**
     EXCLUDES   *aspiration biopsy of spleen (41.32)*

41.2   **Splenotomy**

✓4ᵗʰ **41.3**   **Diagnostic procedures on bone marrow and spleen**

41.31   **Biopsy of bone marrow**

41.32   **Closed [aspiration] [percutaneous] biopsy of spleen**
     Needle biopsy of spleen

41.33   **Open biopsy of spleen**

41.38   **Other diagnostic procedures on bone marrow**
     EXCLUDES   *microscopic examination of specimen from bone marrow (90.61-90.69)*
     radioisotope scan (92.05)

41.39   **Other diagnostic procedures on spleen**
     EXCLUDES   *microscopic examination of specimen from spleen (90.61-90.69)*
     radioisotope scan (92.05)

✓4ᵗʰ **41.4**   **Excision or destruction of lesion or tissue of spleen**
     Code also any application or administration of an adhesion barrier substance (99.77)
     EXCLUDES   *excision of accessory spleen (41.93)*

41.41   **Marsupialization of splenic cyst**
     DEF: Incision of cyst of spleen with edges sutured open to create pouch.

41.42   **Excision of lesion or tissue of spleen**
     EXCLUDES   *biopsy of spleen (41.32-41.33)*

41.43   **Partial splenectomy**
     DEF: Removal of spleen, partial.

41.5   **Total splenectomy**
     Splenectomy NOS
     Code also any application or administration of an adhesion barrier substance (99.77)

✓4ᵗʰ **41.9**   **Other operations on spleen and bone marrow**
     Code also any application or administration of an adhesion barrier substance (99.77)

41.91   **Aspiration of bone marrow from donor for transplant**
     EXCLUDES   *biopsy of bone marrow (41.31)*
     AHA: 1Q, '91, 3

41.92   **Injection into bone marrow**
     EXCLUDES   *bone marrow transplant (41.00-41.03)*
     AHA: 3Q, '96, 17

41.93   **Excision of accessory spleen**

41.94   **Transplantation of spleen**

41.95   **Repair and plastic operations on spleen**

41.98   **Other operations on bone marrow**

41.99   **Other operations on spleen**

✓3ʳᵈ ✓4ᵗʰ   Additional Digit Required   RUG III Special Care Procedure   RUG III Clinically Complex Procedure   RUG III Extensive Services Procedure   RUG III Rehab Procedure

Operations on the Digestive System

42–42.58

9. OPERATIONS ON THE DIGESTIVE SYSTEM (42-54)

√3rd **42 Operations on esophagus**

√4th **42.0 Esophagotomy**

42.01 Incision of esophageal web
DEF: Cutting into congenital esophageal membrane.

42.09 Other incision of esophagus
Esophagotomy NOS
EXCLUDES esophagomyotomy (42.7)
esophagostomy (42.10-42.19)

√4th **42.1 Esophagostomy**

42.10 Esophagostomy, not otherwise specified

42.11 Cervical esophagostomy
DEF: Creation of opening into upper region of esophagus.

42.12 Exteriorization of esophageal pouch
DEF: Transfer of section of esophageal pouch to exterior of the body.

42.19 Other external fistulization of esophagus
Thoracic esophagostomy
Code also any resection (42.40-42.42)

√4th **42.2 Diagnostic procedures on esophagus**

42.21 Operative esophagoscopy by incision
DEF: Esophageal examination with an endoscope through incision.

42.22 Esophagoscopy through artificial stoma
EXCLUDES that with biopsy (42.24)

42.23 Other esophagoscopy
EXCLUDES that with biopsy (42.24)
AHA: 1Q, '00, 20; 3Q, '98, 11

42.24 Closed [endoscopic] biopsy of esophagus
Brushing or washing for specimen collection
Esophagoscopy with biopsy
Suction biopsy of the esophagus
EXCLUDES esophagogastroduodenoscopy [EGD] with closed biopsy (45.16)

DEF: Scope passed through mouth and throat to obtain biopsy specimen, usually by brushing and swabbing.

42.25 Open biopsy of esophagus

42.29 Other diagnostic procedures on esophagus
EXCLUDES barium swallow (87.61)
esophageal manometry (89.32)
microscopic examination of specimen from esophagus (90.81-90.89)

AHA: 3Q, '96, 12

√4th **42.3 Local excision or destruction of lesion or tissue of esophagus**

42.31 Local excision of esophageal diverticulum

42.32 Local excision of other lesion or tissue of esophagus
EXCLUDES biopsy of esophagus (42.24-42.25)
esophageal fistulectomy (42.84)

42.33 Endoscopic excision or destruction of lesion or tissue of esophagus
Ablation of esophageal neoplasm
Control of esophageal bleeding
Esophageal polypectomy
Esophageal varices
Injection of esophageal varices
} by endoscopic approach

EXCLUDES biopsy of esophagus (42.24-42.25)
fistulectomy (42.84)
open ligation of esophageal varices (42.91)

42.39 Other destruction of lesion or tissue of esophagus
EXCLUDES that by endoscopic approach (42.33)

√4th **42.4 Excision of esophagus**
EXCLUDES esophagogastrectomy NOS (43.99)

42.40 Esophagectomy, not otherwise specified

42.41 Partial esophagectomy
Code also any synchronous:
anastomosis other than end-to-end (42.51-42.69)
esophagostomy (42.10-42.19)
gastrostomy (43.11-43.19)

DEF: Surgical removal of any part of esophagus.

42.42 Total esophagectomy
Code also any synchronous:
gastrostomy (43.11-43.19)
interposition or anastomosis other than end-to-end (42.51-42.69)
EXCLUDES esophagogastrectomy (43.99)

AHA: 4Q, '88, 11

DEF: Surgical removal of entire esophagus.

√4th **42.5 Intrathoracic anastomosis of esophagus**
Code also any synchronous:
esophagectomy (42.40-42.42)
gastrostomy (43.1)

DEF: Connection of esophagus to conduit within chest.

42.51 Intrathoracic esophagoesophagostomy
DEF: Connection of both ends of esophagus within chest cavity.

42.52 Intrathoracic esophagogastrostomy
DEF: Connection of esophagus to stomach within chest; follows esophagogastrectomy.

42.53 Intrathoracic esophageal anastomosis with interposition of small bowel

42.54 Other intrathoracic esophagoenterostomy
Anastomosis of esophagus to intestinal segment NOS

42.55 Intrathoracic esophageal anastomosis with interposition of colon

42.56 Other intrathoracic esophagocolostomy
Esophagocolostomy NOS

42.58 Intrathoracic esophageal anastomosis with other interposition
Construction of artificial esophagus
Retrosternal formation of reversed gastric tube

DEF: Construction of artificial esophagus: Creation of artificial esophagus.

DEF: Retrosternal anastomosis of reversed gastric tube: Formation of gastric tube behind breastbone.

N Newborn Age: 0 P Pediatric Age: 0-17 M Maternity Age: 12-55 A Adult Age: 15-124 Adj Adjunct Code ◄ Revised Text ● New Code ▲ Revised Code Title

136 — Volume 3

2006 ICD•9•CM

42.59   **Other intrathoracic anastomosis of esophagus**
     AHA: 4Q, '88, 11

√4ᵗʰ   **42.6**   **Antesternal anastomosis of esophagus**
     Code also any synchronous:
       esophagectomy (42.40-42.42)
       gastrostomy (43.1)

     42.61   **Antesternal esophagoesophagostomy**

     42.62   **Antesternal esophagogastrostomy**

     42.63   **Antesternal esophageal anastomosis with interposition of small bowel**

     42.64   **Other antesternal esophagoenterostomy**
         Antethoracic:
           esophagoenterostomy
           esophagoileostomy
           esophagojejunostomy

     42.65   **Antesternal esophageal anastomosis with interposition of colon**
         DEF: Connection of esophagus with colon segment.

     42.66   **Other antesternal esophagocolostomy**
         Antethoracic esophagocolostomy

     42.68   **Other antesternal esophageal anastomosis with interposition**

     42.69   **Other antesternal anastomosis of esophagus**

42.7   **Esophagomyotomy**
     DEF: Division of esophageal muscle, usually distal.

√4ᵗʰ   **42.8**   **Other repair of esophagus**

     42.81   **Insertion of permanent tube into esophagus**
         AHA: 1Q, '97, 15

     42.82   **Suture of laceration of esophagus**

     42.83   **Closure of esophagostomy**

     42.84   **Repair of esophageal fistula, not elsewhere classified**
         `EXCLUDES`   *repair of fistula:*
           bronchoesophageal (33.42)
           esophagopleurocutaneous (34.73)
           pharyngoesophageal (29.53)
           tracheoesophageal (31.73)

     42.85   **Repair of esophageal stricture**

     42.86   **Production of subcutaneous tunnel without esophageal anastomosis**
         DEF: Surgical formation of esophageal passage, without cutting, and reconnection.

     42.87   **Other graft of esophagus**
         `EXCLUDES`   *antesternal esophageal anastomosis with interposition of:*
           colon (42.65)
           small bowel (42.63)
          antesternal esophageal anastomosis with other interposition (42.68)
         intrathoracic esophageal anastomosis with interposition of:
           colon (42.55)
           small bowel (42.53)
          intrathoracic esophageal anastomosis with other interposition (42.58)

     42.89   **Other repair of esophagus**

√4ᵗʰ   **42.9**   **Other operations on esophagus**

     42.91   **Ligation of esophageal varices**
         `EXCLUDES`   *that by endoscopic approach (42.33)*
         DEF: Destruction of dilated veins by suture strangulation.

     42.92   **Dilation of esophagus**
         Dilation of cardiac sphincter
         `EXCLUDES`   *intubation of esophagus (96.03, 96.06-96.08)*
         DEF: Passing of balloon or hydrostatic dilators through esophagus to enlarge esophagus and relieve obstruction.

42.99   **Other**
     `EXCLUDES`   *insertion of Sengstaken tube (96.06)*
          intubation of esophagus (96.03, 96.06-96.08)
          removal of intraluminal foreign body from esophagus without incision (98.02)
          tamponade of esophagus (96.06)

√3ʳᵈ   **43**   **Incision and excision of stomach**
     Code also any application or administration of an adhesion barrier substance (99.77)

     43.0   **Gastrotomy**
         `EXCLUDES`   *gastrostomy (43.11-43.19)*
          that for control of hemorrhage (44.49)
         AHA: 3Q, '89, 14

√4ᵗʰ   **43.1**   **Gastrostomy**
     AHA: S-O, '85, 5

     43.11   **Percutaneous [endoscopic] gastrostomy [PEG]**
         Percutaneous transabdominal gastrostomy
         DEF: Endoscopic positioning of tube through abdominal wall into stomach.

     43.19   **Other gastrostomy**
         `EXCLUDES`   *percutaneous [endoscopic] gastrostomy [PEG] (43.11)*
         AHA: 1Q, '92, 14; 3Q, '89, 14

     43.3   **Pyloromyotomy**
         DEF: Cutting into longitudinal and circular muscular membrane between stomach and small intestine.

√4ᵗʰ   **43.4**   **Local excision or destruction of lesion or tissue of stomach**

     43.41   **Endoscopic excision or destruction of lesion or tissue of stomach**
         Gastric polypectomy by endoscopic approach
         Gastric varices by endoscopic approach
         `EXCLUDES`   *biopsy of stomach (44.14-44.15)*
          control of hemorrhage (44.43)
          open ligation of gastric varices (44.91)
         AHA: 3Q, '96, 10

     43.42   **Local excision of other lesion or tissue of stomach**
         `EXCLUDES`   *biopsy of stomach (44.14-44.15)*
          gastric fistulectomy (44.62-44.63)
          partial gastrectomy (43.5-43.89)

     43.49   **Other destruction of lesion or tissue of stomach**
         `EXCLUDES`   *that by endoscopic approach (43.41)*
         AHA: N-D, '87, 5; S-O, '85, 6

     43.5   **Partial gastrectomy with anastomosis to esophagus**
         Proximal gastrectomy

√3ᵗʰ / √4ᵗʰ   Additional Digit Required   RUG III Special Care Procedure   RUG III Clinically Complex Procedure   RUG III Extensive Services Procedure   RUG III Rehab Procedure

2006 ICD•9•CM   Volume 3 — 137

Operations on the Digestive System

43.6–44.19

Biliopancreatic Diversion without Duodenal Switch

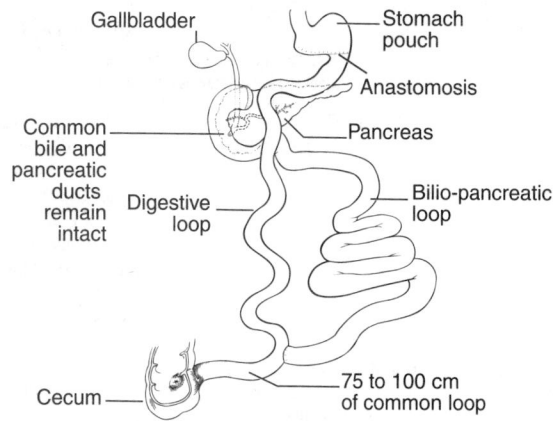

43.6   **Partial gastrectomy with anastomosis to duodenum**
Billroth I operation   Gastropylorectomy
Distal gastrectomy

43.7   **Partial gastrectomy with anastomosis to jejunum**
Billroth II operation
AHA: 3Q, '03, 7

✓4th **43.8**   **Other partial gastrectomy**

    43.81   **Partial gastrectomy with jejunal transposition**
Henley jejunal transposition operation
Code also any synchronous intestinal resection (45.51)

    43.89   **Other**
Partial gastrectomy with bypass
gastrogastrostomy
Sleeve resection of stomach
AHA: 3Q, '03, 6-8

✓4th **43.9**   **Total gastrectomy**

    43.91   **Total gastrectomy with intestinal interposition**

    43.99   **Other total gastrectomy**
Complete gastroduodenectomy
Esophagoduodenostomy with complete gastrectomy
Esophagogastrectomy NOS
Esophagojejunostomy with complete gastrectomy
Radical gastrectomy

✓3rd **44**   **Other operations on stomach**
Code also any application or administration of an adhesion barrier substance (99.77)

✓4th **44.0**   **Vagotomy**

    44.00   **Vagotomy, not otherwise specified**
Division of vagus nerve NOS
DEF: Cutting of vagus nerve to reduce acid production.

Partial Gastrectomy with Anastomosis to Duodenum

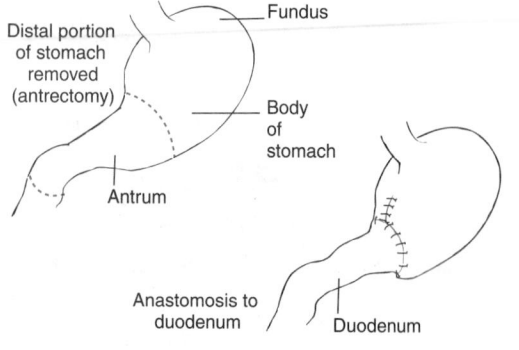

Types of Vagotomy Procedures

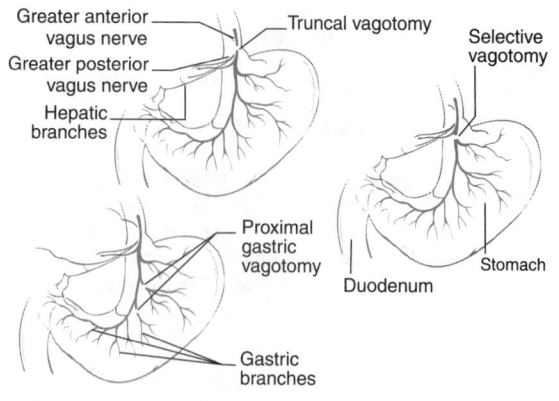

44.01   **Truncal vagotomy**
DEF: Surgical removal of vagus nerve segment near stomach branches.

44.02   **Highly selective vagotomy**
Parietal cell vagotomy
Selective proximal vagotomy
DEF: Cutting select gastric branches of vagus nerve to reduce acid production and preserve other nerve functions.

44.03   **Other selective vagotomy**

✓4th **44.1**   **Diagnostic procedures on stomach**

    44.11   **Transabdominal gastroscopy**
Intraoperative gastroscopy
EXCLUDES   *that with biopsy (44.14)*

    44.12   **Gastroscopy through artificial stoma**
EXCLUDES   *that with biopsy (44.14)*

    44.13   **Other gastroscopy**
EXCLUDES   *that with biopsy (44.14)*
AHA: 1Q, '88, 15; N-D, '87, 5

    44.14   **Closed [endoscopic] biopsy of stomach**
Brushing or washing for specimen collection
EXCLUDES   *esophagogastroduodenoscopy [EGD] with closed biopsy (45.16)*
AHA: 1Q, '88, 15; N-D, '87, 5

    44.15   **Open biopsy of stomach**

    44.19   **Other diagnostic procedures on stomach**
EXCLUDES   *gastric lavage (96.33)*
microscopic examination of specimen from stomach (90.81-90.89)
upper GI series (87.62)

Biliopancreatic Diversion with Duodenal Switch

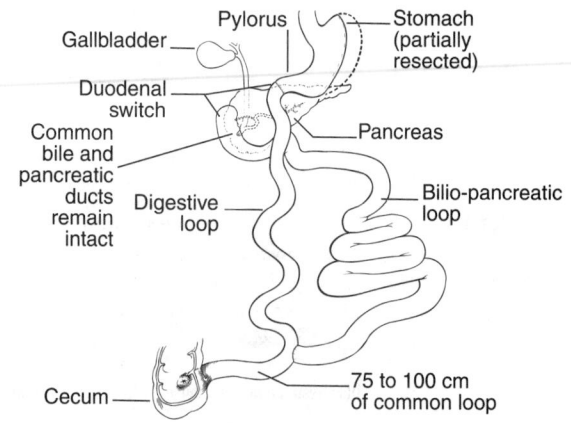

N Newborn Age: 0   P Pediatric Age: 0-17   M Maternity Age: 12-55   A Adult Age: 15-124   **Adj** Adjunct Code   ◄► Revised Text   ● New Code   ▲ Revised Code Title

138 — Volume 3   *2006 ICD•9•CM*

Roux-en-Y Operation (Gastrojejunostomy without gastrectomy)

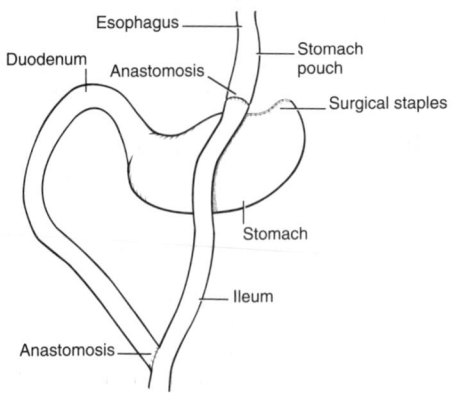

✓4ᵗʰ **44.2   Pyloroplasty**

44.21   Dilation of pylorus by incision
DEF: Cutting and suturing pylorus to relieve obstruction.

44.22   Endoscopic dilation of pylorus
Dilation with balloon endoscope
Endoscopic dilation of gastrojejunostomy site
AHA: 2Q, '01, 17

44.29   Other pyloroplasty
Pyloroplasty NOS
Revision of pylorus
AHA: 3Q, '99, 3

✓4ᵗʰ **44.3   Gastroenterostomy without gastrectomy**

44.31   High gastric bypass
Printen and Mason gastric bypass
AHA: M-J, '85, 17

DEF: Connection of middle part of small intestine to upper stomach to divert food passage from upper intestine.

44.32   Percutaneous [endoscopic] gastrojejunostomy
Endoscopic conversion of gastrostomy to jejunostomy
DEF: Percutaneous placement of a thin feeding tube through a gastrostomy tube and then pulling the tube into the proximal end of the jejunum.

44.38   Laparoscopic gastroenterostomy
Bypass:
gastroduodenostomy
gastroenterostomy
gastrogastrostomy
Laparoscopic gastrojejunostomy without gastrectomy NEC
EXCLUDES   gastroenterostomy, open approach (44.39)

44.39   Other gastroenterostomy
Bypass:
gastroduodenostomy
gastroenterostomy
gastrogastrostomy
Gastrojejunostomy without gastrectomy NOS
AHA: 3Q, '03, 6; 1Q, '01, 16, 17

✓4ᵗʰ **44.4   Control of hemorrhage and suture of ulcer of stomach or duodenum**

44.40   Suture of peptic ulcer, not otherwise specified

44.41   Suture of gastric ulcer site
EXCLUDES   ligation of gastric varices (44.91)

44.42   Suture of duodenal ulcer site
AHA: J-F, '87, 11

44.43   Endoscopic control of gastric or duodenal bleeding
AHA: ▶2Q, '04, 12;◀ 2Q, '92, 17; N-D, '87, 4

44.44   Transcatheter embolization for gastric or duodenal bleeding
EXCLUDES   surgical occlusion of abdominal vessels (38.86-38.87)
AHA: 1Q, '88, 15; N-D, '87, 4
DEF: Therapeutic blocking of stomach or upper small intestine blood vessel to stop hemorrhaging; accomplished by introducing various substances using a catheter.

44.49   Other control of hemorrhage of stomach or duodenum
That with gastrotomy

44.5   Revision of gastric anastomosis
Closure of: Closure of:
gastric anastomosis   gastrojejunostomy
gastroduodenostomy   Pantaloon operation

✓4ᵗʰ **44.6   Other repair of stomach**

44.61   Suture of laceration of stomach
EXCLUDES   that of ulcer site (44.41)

44.62   Closure of gastrostomy

44.63   Closure of other gastric fistula
Closure of:
gastrocolic fistula
gastrojejunocolic fistula

44.64   Gastropexy
AHA: M-J, '85, 17
DEF: Suturing of stomach into position.

44.65   Esophagogastroplasty
Belsey operation
Esophagus and stomach cardioplasty
AHA: M-J, '85, 17

44.66   Other procedures for creation of esophagogastric sphincteric competence
Fundoplication
Gastric cardioplasty
Nissen's fundoplication
Restoration of cardio-esophageal angle
EXCLUDES   that by laparoscopy (44.67)
AHA: 2Q, '03, 12; 2Q, '01, 3, 5, 6; 3Q, '98, 10; M-J, '85, 17

44.67   Laparoscopic procedures for creation of esophagogastric sphincteric competence
Fundoplication
Gastric cardioplasty
Nissen's fundoplication
Restoration of cardio-esophageal angle

44.68   Laparoscopic gastroplasty
Banding
Silastic vertical banding
Vertical banded gastroplasty (VBG)
Code also any synchronous laparoscopic gastroenterostomy (44.38)
EXCLUDES   insertion, laparoscopic adjustable gastric band (restrictive procedure) (44.95)
other repair of stomach, open approach (44.61-44.65, 44.69)

44.69   Other
Inversion of gastric diverticulum
Repair of stomach NOS
AHA: 3Q, '03, 8; 2Q, '01, 3; 3Q, '99, 3; M-J, '85, 17; N-D, '84, 13
DEF: Inversion of gastric diverticulum: Turning stomach inward to repair outpouch of wall.

✓3ʳᵈ
✓4ᵗʰ   Additional Digit Required   RUG III Special Care Procedure   RUG III Clinically Complex Procedure   RUG III Extensive Services Procedure   RUG III Rehab Procedure

√4th **44.9** **Other operations on stomach**

44.91 **Ligation of gastric varices**

EXCLUDES *that by endoscopic approach (43.41)*

DEF: Destruction of dilated veins by suture or strangulation.

44.92 **Intraoperative manipulation of stomach**
Reduction of gastric volvulus

44.93 **Insertion of gastric bubble (balloon)**

44.94 **Removal of gastric bubble (balloon)**

44.95 **Laparoscopic gastric restrictive procedure**
Adjustable gastric band and port insertion

EXCLUDES *laparoscopic gastroplasty (44.68)*
other repair of stomach (44.69)

44.96 **Laparoscopic revision of gastric restrictive procedure**
Revision or replacement of:
adjustable gastric band
subcutaneous gastric port device

44.97 **Laparoscopic removal of gastric restrictive device(s)**
Removal of either or both:
adjustable gastric band
subcutaneous port device

EXCLUDES *nonoperative removal of gastric restrictive device(s) (97.86)*
open removal of gastric restrictive device(s) (44.99)

44.98 **(Laparoscopic) adjustment of size of adjustable gastric restrictive device**
Infusion of saline for device tightening
Withdrawal of saline for device loosening
Code also any:
abdominal ultrasound (88.76)
abdominal wall fluoroscopy (88.09)
barium swallow (87.61)

44.99 **Other**

EXCLUDES *change of gastrostomy tube (97.02)*
dilation of cardiac sphincter (42.92)
gastric:
cooling (96.31)
freezing (96.32)
gavage (96.35)
hypothermia (96.31)
lavage (96.33)
insertion of nasogastric tube (96.07)
irrigation of gastrostomy (96.36)
irrigation of nasogastric tube (96.34)
removal of:
gastrostomy tube (97.51)
intraluminal foreign body from stomach without incision (98.03)
replacement of:
gastrostomy tube (97.02)
(naso-)gastric tube (97.01)

AHA: ▶3Q, '04, 5◀

√3rd **45** **Incision, excision, and anastomosis of intestine**
Code also any application or administration of an adhesion barrier substance (99.77)

√4th **45.0** **Enterotomy**

EXCLUDES *duodenocholedochotomy (51.41-51.42, 51.51)*
that for destruction of lesion (45.30-45.34)
that of exteriorized intestine (46.14, 46.24, 46.31)

45.00 **Incision of intestine, not otherwise specified**

45.01 **Incision of duodenum**

45.02 **Other incision of small intestine**

45.03 **Incision of large intestine**

EXCLUDES *proctotomy (48.0)*

√4th **45.1** **Diagnostic procedures on small intestine**
Code also any laparotomy (54.11-54.19)

45.11 **Transabdominal endoscopy of small intestine**
Intraoperative endoscopy of small intestine

EXCLUDES *that with biopsy (45.14)*

DEF: Endoscopic exam of small intestine through abdominal wall.

DEF: Intraoperative endoscope of small intestine: Endoscopic exam of small intestine during surgery.

45.12 **Endoscopy of small intestine through artificial stoma**

EXCLUDES *that with biopsy (45.14)*

AHA: M-J, '85, 17

45.13 **Other endoscopy of small intestine**
Esophagogastroduodenoscopy [EGD]

EXCLUDES *that with biopsy (45.14, 45.16)*

AHA: ▶3Q, '04, 5◀ N-D, '87, 5

45.14 **Closed [endoscopic] biopsy of small intestine**
Brushing or washing for specimen collection

EXCLUDES *esophagogastroduodenoscopy [EGD] with closed biopsy π(45.16)*

45.15 **Open biopsy of small intestine**

45.16 **Esophagogastroduodenoscopy [EGD] with closed biopsy**
Biopsy of one or more sites involving esophagus, stomach, and/or duodenum

AHA: 2Q, '01, 9

45.19 **Other diagnostic procedures on small intestine**

EXCLUDES *microscopic examination of specimen from small intestine (90.91-90.99)*
radioisotope scan (92.04)
ultrasonography (88.74)
x-ray (87.61-87.69)

√4th **45.2** **Diagnostic procedures on large intestine**
Code also any laparotomy (54.11-54.19)

45.21 **Transabdominal endoscopy of large intestine**
Intraoperative endoscopy of large intestine

EXCLUDES *that with biopsy (45.25)*

DEF: Endoscopic exam of large intestine through abdominal wall.

DEF: Intraoperative endoscopy of large intestine: Endoscopic exam of large intestine during surgery.

Esophagogastroduodenoscopy

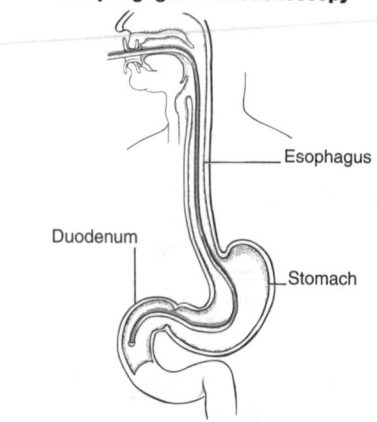

Esophagus

Duodenum

Stomach

N Newborn Age: 0   P Pediatric Age: 0-17   M Maternity Age: 12-55   A Adult Age: 15-124   Adj Adjunct Code   ▶◀ Revised Text   ● New Code   ▲ Revised Code Title

45.22 Endoscopy of large intestine through artificial stoma

> **EXCLUDES** *that with biopsy (45.25)*

DEF: Endoscopic exam of large intestine lining from rectum to cecum via colostomy stoma.

45.23 Colonoscopy
Flexible fiberoptic colonoscopy

> **EXCLUDES** *endoscopy of large intestine through artificial stoma (45.22)*
> *flexible sigmoidoscopy (45.24)*
> *rigid proctosigmoidoscopy (48.23)*
> *transabdominal endoscopy of large intestine (45.21)*

AHA: S-O, '85, 5

DEF: Endoscopic exam of descending colon, splenic flexure, transverse colon, hepatic flexure and cecum.

45.24 Flexible sigmoidoscopy
Endoscopy of descending colon

> **EXCLUDES** *rigid proctosigmoidoscopy (48.23)*

DEF: Endoscopic exam of anus, rectum and sigmoid colon.

45.25 Closed [endoscopic] biopsy of large intestine
Biopsy, closed, of unspecified intestinal site
Brushing or washing for specimen collection
Colonoscopy with biopsy

> **EXCLUDES** *proctosigmoidoscopy with biopsy (48.24)*

AHA: 1Q, '03, 10

45.26 Open biopsy of large intestine
45.27 Intestinal biopsy, site unspecified
45.28 Other diagnostic procedures on large intestine
45.29 Other diagnostic procedures on intestine, site unspecified

> **EXCLUDES** *microscopic examination of specimen (90.91-90.99)*
> *scan and radioisotope function study (92.04)*
> *ultrasonography (88.74)*
> *x-ray (87.61-87.69)*

√4ᵗʰ 45.3 Local excision or destruction of lesion or tissue of small intestine

45.30 Endoscopic excision or destruction of lesion of duodenum

> **EXCLUDES** *biopsy of duodenum (45.14-45.15)*
> *control of hemorrhage (44.43)*
> *fistulectomy (46.72)*

45.31 Other local excision of lesion of duodenum

> **EXCLUDES** *biopsy of duodenum (45.14-45.15)*
> *fistulectomy (46.72)*
> *multiple segmental resection (45.61)*
> *that by endoscopic approach (45.30)*

45.32 Other destruction of lesion of duodenum

> **EXCLUDES** *that by endoscopic approach (45.30)*

AHA: N-D, '87, 5; S-O, '85, 6

45.33 Local excision of lesion or tissue of small intestine, except duodenum
Excision of redundant mucosa of ileostomy

> **EXCLUDES** *biopsy of small intestine (45.14-45.15)*
> *fistulectomy (46.74)*
> *multiple segmental resection (45.61)*

45.34 Other destruction of lesion of small intestine, except duodenum

√4ᵗʰ 45.4 Local excision or destruction of lesion or tissue of large intestine

AHA: N-D, '87, 11

45.41 Excision of lesion or tissue of large intestine
Excision of redundant mucosa of colostomy

> **EXCLUDES** *biopsy of large intestine (45.25-45.27)*
> *endoscopic polypectomy of large intestine (45.42)*
> *fistulectomy (46.76)*
> *multiple segmental resection (45.71)*
> *that by endoscopic approach (45.42-45.43)*

45.42 Endoscopic polypectomy of large intestine

> **EXCLUDES** *that by open approach (45.41)*

AHA: 2Q, '90, 25

DEF: Endoscopic removal of polyp from large intestine.

45.43 Endoscopic destruction of other lesion or tissue of large intestine
Endoscopic ablation of tumor of large intestine
Endoscopic control of colonic bleeding

> **EXCLUDES** *endoscopic polypectomy of large intestine (45.42)*

AHA: 4Q, '02, 61

45.49 Other destruction of lesion of large intestine

> **EXCLUDES** *that by endoscopic approach (45.43)*

√4ᵗʰ 45.5 Isolation of intestinal segment
Code also any synchronous:
anastomosis other than end-to-end (45.90-45.94)
enterostomy (46.10-46.39)

45.50 Isolation of intestinal segment, not otherwise specified
Isolation of intestinal pedicle flap
Reversal of intestinal segment

DEF: Isolation of small intestinal pedicle flap: Separation of intestinal pedicle flap.
DEF: Reversal of intestinal segment: Separation of intestinal segment.

45.51 Isolation of segment of small intestine
Isolation of ileal loop
Resection of small intestine for interposition

AHA: 3Q, '03, 6-8; 2Q, '03, 11; 3Q, '00, 7

45.52 Isolation of segment of large intestine
Resection of colon for interposition

√4ᵗʰ 45.6 Other excision of small intestine
Code also any synchronous:
anastomosis other than end-to-end (45.90-45.93, 45.95)
colostomy (46.10-46.13)
enterostomy (46.10-46.39)

> **EXCLUDES** *cecectomy (45.72)*
> *enterocolectomy (45.79)*
> *gastroduodenectomy (43.6-43.99)*
> *ileocolectomy (45.73)*
> *pancreatoduodenectomy (52.51-52.7)*

45.61 Multiple segmental resection of small intestine
Segmental resection for multiple traumatic lesions of small intestine

45.62 Other partial resection of small intestine
Duodenectomy   Jejunectomy
Ileectomy

> **EXCLUDES** *duodenectomy with synchronous pancreatectomy (52.51-52.7)*
> *resection of cecum and terminal ileum (45.72)*

AHA: 1Q, '04, 10; 1Q, '03, 18

√3ʳᵈ √4ᵗʰ Additional Digit Required   RUG III Special Care Procedure   RUG III Clinically Complex Procedure   RUG III Extensive Services Procedure   RUG III Rehab Procedure

2006 ICD•9•CM

Volume 3 — 141

Operations on the Digestive System

45.63–46.32

Colectomy

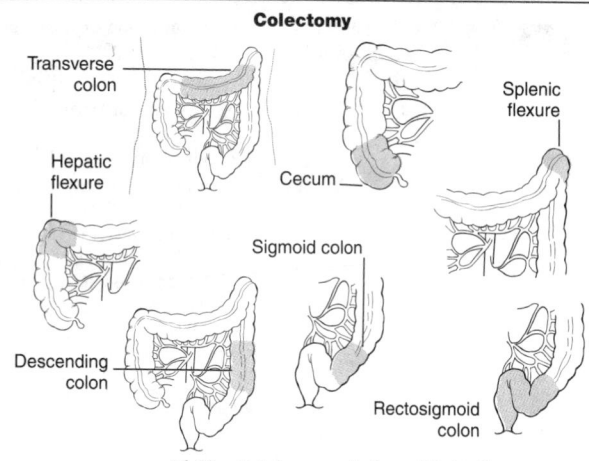

Transverse colon
Splenic flexure
Hepatic flexure
Cecum
Sigmoid colon
Descending colon
Rectosigmoid colon

45.63   Total removal of small intestine

√4th **45.7   Partial excision of large intestine**
Code also any synchronous:
anastomosis other than end-to-end (45.92-45.94)
enterostomy (46.10-46.39)
AHA: 4Q, '92, 27

45.71   Multiple segmental resection of large intestine
Segmental resection for multiple traumatic lesions of large intestine

45.72   Cecectomy
Resection of cecum and terminal ileum

45.73   Right hemicolectomy
Ileocolectomy
Right radical colectomy
AHA: 3Q, '99, 10

45.74   Resection of transverse colon

45.75   Left hemicolectomy
EXCLUDES   proctosigmoidectomy (48.41-48.69)
second stage Mikulicz operation (46.04)
DEF: Excision of left descending large intestine.

45.76   Sigmoidectomy
AHA: 1Q, '96, 9; 3Q, '89, 15

45.79   Other partial excision of large intestine
Enterocolectomy NEC
AHA: 1Q, '03, 18; 3Q, '97, 9; 2Q, '91, 16

45.8   Total intra-abdominal colectomy
Excision of cecum, colon, and sigmoid
EXCLUDES   coloproctectomy (48.41-48.69)

√4th **45.9   Intestinal anastomosis**
Code also any synchronous resection (45.31-45.8, 48.41-48.69)
EXCLUDES   end-to-end anastomosis — omit code

45.90   Intestinal anastomosis, not otherwise specified

45.91   Small-to-small intestinal anastomosis
AHA: 3Q, '03, 6-8; M-J, '85, 17

45.92   Anastomosis of small intestine to rectal stump
Hampton procedure

45.93   Other small-to-large intestinal anastomosis
AHA: 1Q, '03, 18; N-D, '86, 11

45.94   Large-to-large intestinal anastomosis
EXCLUDES   rectorectostomy (48.74)
AHA: 3Q, '89, 15

45.95   Anastomosis to anus
Formation of endorectal ileal pouch (J-pouch) (H-pouch) (S-pouch) with anastomosis of small intestine to anus

Intestinal Anastomosis

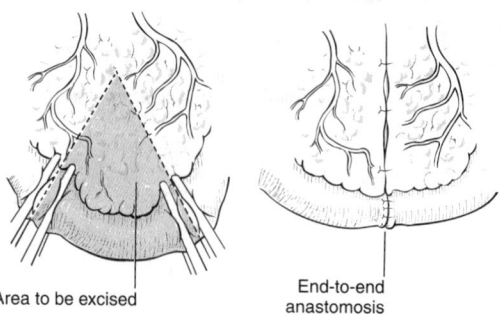

Area to be excised
End-to-end anastomosis

√3rd **46   Other operations on intestine**
Code also any application or administration of an adhesion barrier substance (99.77)

√4th **46.0   Exteriorization of intestine**
INCLUDES   loop enterostomy
multiple stage resection of intestine
DEF: Bringing intestinal segment to body surface.

46.01   Exteriorization of small intestine
Loop ileostomy

46.02   Resection of exteriorized segment of small intestine

46.03   Exteriorization of large intestine
Exteriorization of intestine NOS
First stage Mikulicz exteriorization of intestine
Loop colostomy

46.04   Resection of exteriorized segment of large intestine
Resection of exteriorized segment of intestine NOS
Second stage Mikulicz operation

√4th **46.1   Colostomy**
Code also any synchronous resection (45.49, 45.71-45.79, 45.8)
EXCLUDES   loop colostomy (46.03)
that with abdominoperineal resection of rectum (48.5)
that with synchronous anterior rectal resection (48.62)
DEF: Creation of opening from large intestine through abdominal wall to body surface.

46.10   Colostomy, not otherwise specified

46.11   Temporary colostomy

46.13   Permanent colostomy

46.14   Delayed opening of colostomy

√4th **46.2   Ileostomy**
Code also any synchronous resection (45.34, 45.61-45.63)
EXCLUDES   loop ileostomy (46.01)
DEF: Creation of artificial anus by bringing ileum through abdominal wall to body surface.

46.20   Ileostomy, not otherwise specified

46.21   Temporary ileostomy

46.22   Continent ileostomy
AHA: M-J, '85, 17
DEF: Creation of opening from third part of small intestine through abdominal wall, with pouch outside abdomen.

46.23   Other permanent ileostomy

46.24   Delayed opening of ileostomy

√4th **46.3   Other enterostomy**
Code also any synchronous resection (45.61-45.8)

46.31   Delayed opening of other enterostomy

46.32   Percutaneous (endoscopic) jejunostomy [PEJ]
DEF: Endoscopic placement of tube in midsection of small intestine through abdominal wall.

N Newborn Age: 0   P Pediatric Age: 0-17   M Maternity Age: 12-55   A Adult Age: 15-124   Adj Adjunct Code   ▶◀ Revised Text   ● New Code   ▲ Revised Code Title

46.39   **Other**
Duodenostomy   Feeding enterostomy
AHA: 3Q, '89, 15

✓4th   **46.4**   **Revision of intestinal stoma**
DEF: Revision of opening surgically created from intestine through abdominal wall, to skin surface.

46.40   **Revision of intestinal stoma, not otherwise specified**
Plastic enlargement of intestinal stoma
Reconstruction of stoma of intestine
Release of scar tissue of intestinal stoma
    EXCLUDES   *excision of redundant mucosa (45.41)*

46.41   **Revision of stoma of small intestine**
    EXCLUDES   *excision of redundant mucosa (45.33)*

46.42   **Repair of pericolostomy hernia**

46.43   **Other revision of stoma of large intestine**
    EXCLUDES   *excision of redundant mucosa (45.41)*

    AHA: 2Q, '02, 9

✓4th   **46.5**   **Closure of intestinal stoma**
Code also any synchronous resection (45.34, 45.49, 45.61-45.8)

46.50   **Closure of intestinal stoma, not otherwise specified**

46.51   **Closure of stoma of small intestine**

46.52   **Closure of stoma of large intestine**
Closure or take-down of cecostomy
Closure or take-down of colostomy
Closure or take-down of sigmoidostomy
    AHA: 3Q, '97, 9; 2Q, '91, 16; N-D, '87, 8

✓4th   **46.6**   **Fixation of intestine**
46.60   **Fixation of intestine not otherwise specified**
Fixation of intestine to abdominal wall

46.61   **Fixation of small intestine to abdominal wall**
Ileopexy

46.62   **Other fixation of small intestine**
Noble plication of small intestine
Plication of jejunum
DEF: Noble plication of small intestine: Fixing small intestine into place with tuck in small intestine.

DEF: Plication of jejunum: Fixing small intestine into place with tuck in midsection.

46.63   **Fixation of large intestine to abdominal wall**
Cecocoloplicopexy
Sigmoidopexy   (Moschowitz)

46.64   **Other fixation of large intestine**
Cecofixation   Colofixation

✓4th   **46.7**   **Other repair of intestine**
    EXCLUDES   *closure of:*
       ulcer of duodenum (44.42)
       vesicoenteric fistula (57.83)

46.71   **Suture of laceration of duodenum**

46.72   **Closure of fistula of duodenum**

46.73   **Suture of laceration of small intestine, except duodenum**

46.74   **Closure of fistula of small intestine, except duodenum**
    EXCLUDES   *closure of:*
       artificial stoma (46.51)
       vaginal fistula (70.74)
       repair of gastrojejunocolic fistula (44.63)

46.75   **Suture of laceration of large intestine**

46.76   **Closure of fistula of large intestine**
    EXCLUDES   *closure of:*
       gastrocolic fistula (44.63)
       rectal fistula (48.73)
       sigmoidovesical fistula (57.83)
       stoma (46.52)
       vaginal fistula (70.72-70.73)
       vesicocolic fistula (57.83)
       vesicosigmoidovaginal fistula (57.83)
    AHA: 3Q, '99, 8

46.79   **Other repair of intestine**
Duodenoplasty
AHA: 3Q, '02, 11

✓4th   **46.8**   **Dilation and manipulation of intestine**
AHA: 1Q, '03, 14

46.80   **Intra-abdominal manipulation of intestine, not otherwise specifie**
Correction of intestinal malrotation
Reduction of:
    intestinal torsion
    intestinal volvulus
    intussusception
    EXCLUDES   *reduction of intussusception with:*
       fluoroscopy (96.29)
       ionizing radiation enema (96.29)
       ultrasonography guidance (96.29)
    AHA: 4Q, '98, 82
DEF: Correction of intestinal malrotation: Repair of abnormal rotation.
DEF: Reduction of:
    Intestinal torsion: Repair of twisted segment.
    Intestinal volvulus: Repair of a knotted segment.
    Intussusception: Repair of prolapsed segment.

46.81   **Intra-abdominal manipulation of small intestine**

46.82   **Intra-abdominal manipulation of large intestine**

46.85   **Dilation of intestine**
Dilation (balloon) of duodenum
Dilation (balloon) of jejunum
Endoscopic dilation (balloon) of large intestine
That through rectum or colostomy
AHA: 3Q, '89, 15

✓4th   **46.9**   **Other operations on intestines**
46.91   **Myotomy of sigmoid colon**
46.92   **Myotomy of other parts of colon**
46.93   **Revision of anastomosis of small intestine**
46.94   **Revision of anastomosis of large intestine**
46.95   **Local perfusion of small intestine**
Code also substance perfused (99.21-99.29)
46.96   **Local perfusion of large intestine**
Code also substance perfused (99.21-99.29)
46.97   **Transplant of intestine**
Note: To report donor source — see codes 00.91-00.93
AHA: 4Q, '00, 66

✓3rd
✓4th   Additional Digit Required   RUG III Special Care Procedure   RUG III Clinically Complex Procedure   RUG III Extensive Services Procedure   RUG III Rehab Procedure

2006 ICD•9•CM   **Volume 3 — 143**

Operations on the Digestive System

46.99–48.49

46.99   **Other**
     Ileoentectomy
     EXCLUDES   diagnostic procedures on
         intestine (45.11-45.29)
         dilation of enterostomy stoma
         (96.24)
         intestinal intubation (96.08)
         removal of:
           intraluminal foreign body
             from large intestine
             without incision
             (98.04)
           intraluminal foreign body
             from small intestine
             without incision
             (98.03)
           tube from large intestine
             (97.53)
           tube from small intestine
             (97.52)
         replacement of:
           large intestine tube or
             enterostomy device
             (97.04)
           small intestine tube or
             enterostomy device
             (97.03)

     AHA: 3Q, '99, 11; 1Q, '89, 11

✓3rd 47   **Operations on appendix**
     Code also any application or administration of an adhesion
     barrier substance (99.77)
     INCLUDES   appendiceal stump

✓4th 47.0   **Appendectomy**
     EXCLUDES   incidental appendectomy, so described
         (47.11, 47.19)
     AHA: 4Q, '96, 64; 3Q, '92, 12

     47.01   **Laparoscopic appendectomy**
         AHA: 1Q, '01, 15; 4Q, '96, 64

     47.09   **Other appendectomy**
         AHA: 4Q, '97, 52

✓4th 47.1   **Incidental appendectomy**
     DEF: Removal of appendix during abdominal surgery as
     prophylactic measure, without significant appendiceal pathology.

     47.11   **Laparoscopic incidental appendectomy**
     47.19   **Other incidental appendectomy**
         AHA: 4Q, '96, 65

     47.2   **Drainage of appendiceal abscess**
         EXCLUDES   that with appendectomy (47.0)

✓4th 47.9   **Other operations on appendix**
     47.91   **Appendicostomy**
     47.92   **Closure of appendiceal fistula**
     47.99   **Other**
         Anastomosis of appendix
         EXCLUDES   diagnostic procedures on
             appendix (45.21-45.29)
         AHA: 3Q, '01, 16

✓3rd 48   **Operations on rectum, rectosigmoid, and perirectal tissue**
     Code also any application or administration of an adhesion
     barrier substance (99.77)

     48.0   **Proctotomy**
         Decompression of imperforate anus
         Panas' operation [linear proctotomy]
         EXCLUDES   incision of perirectal tissue (48.81)
         AHA: 3Q, '99, 8

         DEF: Incision into rectal portion of large intestine.

         DEF: Decompression of imperforate anus: opening a closed anus by
         means of an incision.

         DEF: Panas' operation (linear proctotomy): Linear incision into
         rectal portion of large intestine

     48.1   **Proctostomy**

✓4th 48.2   **Diagnostic procedures on rectum, rectosigmoid, and perirectal tissue**

     48.21   **Transabdominal proctosigmoidoscopy**
         Intraoperative proctosigmoidoscopy
         EXCLUDES   that with biopsy (48.24)

     48.22   **Proctosigmoidoscopy through artificial stoma**
         EXCLUDES   that with biopsy (48.24)

     48.23   **Rigid proctosigmoidoscopy**
         EXCLUDES   flexible sigmoidoscopy (45.24)
         AHA: 1Q, '01, 8
         DEF: Endoscopic exam of anus, rectum and lower
         sigmoid colon.

     48.24   **Closed [endoscopic] biopsy of rectum**
         Brushing or washing for specimen collection
         Proctosigmoidoscopy with biopsy
         AHA: 1Q, '03, 12

     48.25   **Open biopsy of rectum**
     48.26   **Biopsy of perirectal tissue**
     48.29   **Other diagnostic procedures on rectum, rectosigmoid, and perirectal tissue**
         EXCLUDES   digital examination of rectum
             (89.34)
           lower GI series (87.64)
           microscopic examination of
             specimen from rectum
             (90.91-90.99)

✓4th 48.3   **Local excision or destruction of lesion or tissue of rectum**

     48.31   **Radical electrocoagulation of rectal lesion or tissue**
         DEF: Destruction of lesion or tissue of large intestine,
         rectal part.

     48.32   **Other electrocoagulation of rectal lesion or tissue**
         AHA: 2Q, '98, 18

     48.33   **Destruction of rectal lesion or tissue by laser**

     48.34   **Destruction of rectal lesion or tissue by cryosurgery**

     48.35   **Local excision of rectal lesion or tissue**
         EXCLUDES   biopsy of rectum (48.24-48.25)
           [endoscopic] polypectomy of
             rectum (48.36)
           excision of perirectal tissue
             (48.82)
           hemorrhoidectomy (49.46)
           rectal fistulectomy (48.73)

     48.36   **[Endoscopic] polypectomy of rectum**
         AHA: 4Q, '95, 65

✓4th 48.4   **Pull-through resection of rectum**
     Code also any synchronous anastomosis other than
     end-to-end (45.90, 45.92-45.95)

     48.41   **Soave submucosal resection of rectum**
         Endorectal pull-through operation
         DEF: Soave submucosal resection: Resection of submuco-
         sal rectal part of large intestine by pull-through technique.
         DEF: Endorectal pull-through operation: Resection of
         interior large intestine by pull-through technique.

     48.49   **Other pull-through resection of rectum**
         Abdominoperineal pull-through
         Altemeier operation
         Swenson proctectomy
         EXCLUDES   Duhamel abdominoperineal
             pull-through (48.65)
         AHA: 3Q, '01, 8; 2Q, '99, 13
         DEF: Abdominoperineal pull-through: Resection of large
         intestine, latter part, by pull-through of abdomen,
         scrotum or vulva and anus.
         DEF: Swenson proctatectomy: Excision of large intestine,
         rectal by pull-through and preserving muscles that close
         the anus.

N Newborn Age: 0   **P** Pediatric Age: 0-17   **M** Maternity Age: 12-55   **A** Adult Age: 15-124   **Adj** Adjunct Code   ▶◀ Revised Text   ● New Code   ▲ Revised Code Title

48.5 **Abdominoperineal resection of rectum**
Combined abdominoendorectal resection
Complete proctectomy
Code also any synchronous anastomosis other than end-to-end (45.90, 45.92-45.95)

INCLUDES   with synchronous colostomy

EXCLUDES   *Duhamel abdominoperineal pull-through (48.65)*
that as part of pelvic exenteration (68.8)

AHA: 2Q, '97, 5

DEF: Rectal excision through cavities formed by abdomen, anus, vulva or scrotum.

✓4ᵗʰ **48.6** **Other resection of rectum**
Code also any synchronous anastomosis other than end-to-end (45.90, 45.92-45.95)

48.61 **Transsacral rectosigmoidectomy**
DEF: Excision through sacral bone area of sigmoid and last parts of large intestine.

48.62 **Anterior resection of rectum with synchronous colostomy**
DEF: Resection of front terminal end of large intestine and creation of colostomy.

48.63 **Other anterior resection of rectum**
EXCLUDES   *that with synchronous colostomy (48.62)*

AHA: 1Q, '96, 9

48.64 **Posterior resection of rectum**

48.65 **Duhamel resection of rectum**
Duhamel abdominoperineal pull-through

48.69 **Other**
Partial proctectomy
Rectal resection NOS
AHA: J-F, '87, 11; N-D, '86, 11

✓4ᵗʰ **48.7** **Repair of rectum**
EXCLUDES   *repair of:*
current obstetric laceration (75.62)
vaginal rectocele (70.50, 70.52)

48.71 **Suture of laceration of rectum**

48.72 **Closure of proctostomy**

48.73 **Closure of other rectal fistula**
EXCLUDES   *fistulectomy:*
perirectal (48.93)
rectourethral (58.43)
rectovaginal (70.73)
rectovesical (57.83)
rectovesicovaginal (57.83)

48.74 **Rectorectostomy**
Rectal anastomosis NOS
DEF: Connection of two cut portions of large intestine, rectal end.

48.75 **Abdominal proctopexy**
Frickman procedure
Ripstein repair of rectal prolapse
DEF: Fixation of rectum to adjacent abdominal structures.

48.76 **Other proctopexy**
Delorme repair of prolapsed rectum
Proctosigmoidopexy
Puborectalis sling operation
EXCLUDES   *manual reduction of rectal prolapse (96.26)*

DEF: Delorme repair of prolapsed rectum: Fixation of collapsed large intestine, rectal part.

DEF: Proctosigmoidopexy: Suturing of twisted large intestine, rectal part.

DEF: Puborectalis sling operation: Fixation of large intestine, rectal part by forming puborectalis muscle into sling.

48.79 **Other repair of rectum**
Repair of old obstetric laceration of rectum
EXCLUDES   *anastomosis to:*
large intestine (45.94)
small intestine (45.92-45.93)
repair of:
current obstetrical laceration (75.62)
vaginal rectocele (70.50, 70.52)

✓4ᵗʰ **48.8** **Incision or excision of perirectal tissue or lesion**
INCLUDES   pelvirectal tissue
rectovaginal septum

48.81 **Incision of perirectal tissue**
Incision of rectovaginal septum

48.82 **Excision of perirectal tissue**
EXCLUDES   *perirectal biopsy (48.26)*
perirectofistulectomy (48.93)
rectal fistulectomy (48.73)

✓4ᵗʰ **48.9** **Other operations on rectum and perirectal tissue**

48.91 **Incision of rectal stricture**

48.92 **Anorectal myectomy**
DEF: Excision of anorectal muscle.

48.93 **Repair of perirectal fistula**
EXCLUDES   *that opening into rectum (48.73)*

DEF: Closure of abdominal passage in tissue around large intestine, rectal part.

48.99 **Other**
EXCLUDES   *digital examination of rectum (89.34)*
dilation of rectum (96.22)
insertion of rectal tube (96.09)
irrigation of rectum (96.38-96.39)
manual reduction of rectal prolapse (96.26)
proctoclysis (96.37)
rectal massage (99.93)
rectal packing (96.19)
removal of:
impacted feces (96.38)
intraluminal foreign body from rectum without incision (98.05)
rectal packing (97.59)
transanal enema (96.39)

✓3ʳᵈ **49** **Operations on anus**
Code also any application or administration of an adhesion barrier substance (99.77)

✓4ᵗʰ **49.0** **Incision or excision of perianal tissue**

49.01 **Incision of perianal abscess**

49.02 **Other incision of perianal tissue**
Undercutting of perianal tissue
EXCLUDES   *anal fistulotomy (49.11)*

49.03 **Excision of perianal skin tags**

49.04 **Other excision of perianal tissue**
EXCLUDES   *anal fistulectomy (49.12)*
biopsy of perianal tissue (49.22)

AHA: 1Q, '01, 8

✓4ᵗʰ **49.1** **Incision or excision of anal fistula**
EXCLUDES   *closure of anal fistula (49.73)*

49.11 **Anal fistulotomy**

49.12 **Anal fistulectomy**

✓4ᵗʰ **49.2** **Diagnostic procedures on anus and perianal tissue**

49.21 **Anoscopy**

49.22 **Biopsy of perianal tissue**

49.23 **Biopsy of anus**

✓3ʳᵈ ✓4ᵗʰ Additional Digit Required   RUG III Special Care Procedure   RUG III Clinically Complex Procedure   RUG III Extensive Services Procedure   RUG III Rehab Procedure

Operations on the Digestive System

49.29–50.12

49.29   **Other diagnostic procedures on anus and perianal tissue**

> **EXCLUDES**   *microscopic examination of specimen from anus (90.91-90.99)*

√4ᵗʰ **49.3**   **Local excision or destruction of other lesion or tissue of anus**

Anal cryptotomy
Cauterization of lesion of anus

> **EXCLUDES**   *biopsy of anus (49.23)*
> *control of (postoperative) hemorrhage of anus (49.95)*
> *hemorrhoidectomy (49.46)*

49.31   **Endoscopic excision or destruction of lesion or tissue of anus**

49.39   **Other local excision or destruction of lesion or tissue of anus**

> **EXCLUDES**   *that by endoscopic approach (49.31)*

AHA: 1Q, '01, 8

√4ᵗʰ **49.4**   **Procedures on hemorrhoids**

49.41   **Reduction of hemorrhoids**

DEF: Manual manipulation to reduce hemorrhoids.

49.42   **Injection of hemorrhoids**

49.43   **Cauterization of hemorrhoids**

Clamp and cautery of hemorrhoids

49.44   **Destruction of hemorrhoids by cryotherapy**

49.45   **Ligation of hemorrhoids**

49.46   **Excision of hemorrhoids**

Hemorrhoidectomy NOS

49.47   **Evacuation of thrombosed hemorrhoids**

DEF: Removal of clotted material from hemorrhoid.

49.49   **Other procedures on hemorrhoids**

Lord procedure

√4ᵗʰ **49.5**   **Division of anal sphincter**

49.51   **Left lateral anal sphincterotomy**

49.52   **Posterior anal sphincterotomy**

49.59   **Other anal sphincterotomy**

Division of sphincter NOS

49.6   **Excision of anus**

√4ᵗʰ **49.7**   **Repair of anus**

> **EXCLUDES**   *repair of current obstetric laceration (75.62)*

49.71   **Suture of laceration of anus**

49.72   **Anal cerclage**

DEF: Encircling anus with ring or sutures.

49.73   **Closure of anal fistula**

> **EXCLUDES**   *excision of anal fistula (49.12)*

49.74   **Gracilis muscle transplant for anal incontinence**

DEF: Moving pubic attachment of gracilis muscle to restore anal control.

49.75   **Implantation or revision of artificial anal sphincter**

Removal with subsequent replacement
Replacement during same or subsequent operative episode

AHA: 4Q, '02, 105

49.76   **Removal of artificial anal sphincter**

Explantation or removal without replacement

> **EXCLUDES**   *revision with implantation during same operative episode (49.75)*

AHA: 4Q, '02, 105

49.79   **Other repair of anal sphincter**

Repair of old obstetric laceration of anus

> **EXCLUDES**   *anoplasty with synchronous hemorrhoidectomy (49.46)*
> *repair of current obstetric laceration (75.62)*

AHA: 2Q, '98, 16; 1Q, '97, 9

√4ᵗʰ **49.9**   **Other operations on anus**

> **EXCLUDES**   *dilation of anus (sphincter) (96.23)*

49.91   **Incision of anal septum**

49.92   **Insertion of subcutaneous electrical anal stimulator**

49.93   **Other incision of anus**

Removal of:
    foreign body from anus with incision
    seton from anus

> **EXCLUDES**   *anal fistulotomy (49.11)*
> *removal of intraluminal foreign body without incision (98.05)*

49.94   **Reduction of anal prolapse**

> **EXCLUDES**   *manual reduction of rectal prolapse (96.26)*

DEF: Manipulation of displaced anal tissue to normal position.

49.95   **Control of (postoperative) hemorrhage of anus**

49.99   **Other**

√3ʳᵈ **50**   **Operations on liver**

Code also any application or administration of an adhesion barrier substance (99.77)

50.0   **Hepatotomy**

Incision of abscess of liver
Removal of gallstones from liver
Stromeyer-Little operation

√4ᵗʰ **50.1**   **Diagnostic procedures on liver**

50.11   **Closed (percutaneous) [needle] biopsy of liver**

Diagnostic aspiration of liver

AHA: 4Q, '88, 12

50.12   **Open biopsy of liver**

Wedge biopsy

Dynamic Graciloplasty

Rectum
Generator
Electrodes
Gracilis muscle (transpositional)
Neosphincter
Anal opening

Closed Liver Biopsy

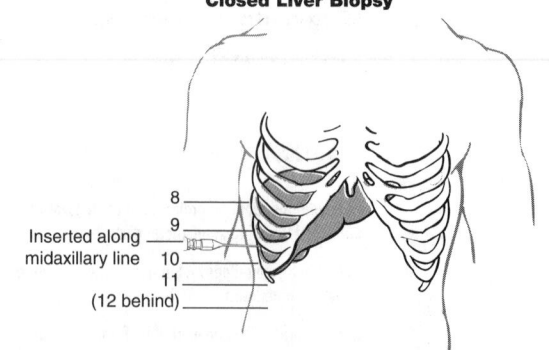

Inserted along midaxillary line
8
9
10
11
(12 behind)

N Newborn Age: 0   **P** Pediatric Age: 0-17   **M** Maternity Age: 12-55   **A** Adult Age: 15-124   **Adj** Adjunct Code   ◄ Revised Text   ● New Code   ▲ Revised Code Title

Liver Biopsy (Open, Wedge)

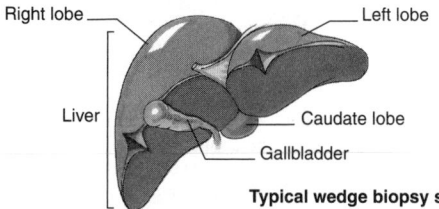

Right lobe — Liver — Left lobe — Caudate lobe — Gallbladder

Typical wedge biopsy sites

50.19　Other diagnostic procedures on liver
Laparoscopic liver biopsy
EXCLUDES　*liver scan and radioisotope function study (92.02)*
microscopic examination of specimen from liver (91.01-91.09)

✓4ᵗʰ **50.2　Local excision or destruction of liver tissue or lesion**

50.21　Marsupialization of lesion of liver
DEF: Exteriorizing lesion by incision and suturing cut edges to skin to create opening.

50.22　Partial hepatectomy
Wedge resection of liver
EXCLUDES　*biopsy of liver (50.11-50.12)*
hepatic lobectomy (50.3)

50.29　Other destruction of lesion of liver
Cauterization
Enucleation　} of hepatic lesion
Evacuation
EXCLUDES　*percutaneous aspiration of lesion (50.91)*
AHA: 2Q, '03, 9

50.3　Lobectomy of liver
Total hepatic lobectomy with partial excision of other lobe

50.4　Total hepatectomy

✓4ᵗʰ **50.5　Liver transplant**
Note: To report donor source — see codes 00.91-00.93

50.51　Auxiliary liver transplant
Auxiliary hepatic transplantation leaving patient's own liver in situ

50.59　Other transplant of liver

✓4ᵗʰ **50.6　Repair of liver**

50.61　Closure of laceration of liver

50.69　Other repair of liver
Hepatopexy

✓4ᵗʰ **50.9　Other operations on liver**
EXCLUDES　*lysis of adhesions (54.5)*

50.91　Percutaneous aspiration of liver
EXCLUDES　*percutaneous biopsy (50.11)*
DEF: Incision into liver through body wall to withdraw fluid.

50.92　Extracorporeal hepatic assistance
Liver dialysis
AHA: 2Q, '01, 21
DEF: Devices used outside body to assist liver function.

50.93　Localized perfusion of liver

50.94　Other injection of therapeutic substance into liver

50.99　Other

✓3ʳᵈ **51　Operations on gallbladder and biliary tract**
Code also any application or administration of an adhesion barrier substance (99.77)
INCLUDES　operations on:
ampulla of Vater
common bile duct
cystic duct
hepatic duct
intrahepatic bile duct
sphincter of Oddi

✓4ᵗʰ **51.0　Cholecystotomy and cholecystostomy**

51.01　Percutaneous aspiration of gallbladder
Percutaneous cholecystotomy for drainage
That by: needle or catheter
EXCLUDES　*needle biopsy (51.12)*

51.02　Trocar cholecystostomy
AHA: 3Q, '89, 18
DEF: Creating opening in gallbladder with catheter.

51.03　Other cholecystostomy

51.04　Other cholecystotomy
Cholelithotomy NOS

✓4ᵗʰ **51.1　Diagnostic procedures on biliary tract**
EXCLUDES　*that for endoscopic procedures classifiable to 51.64, 51.84-51.88, 52.14, 52.21, 52.93 -52.94, 52.97-52.98*
AHA: 2Q, '97, 7

51.10　Endoscopic retrograde cholangiopancreatography [ERCP]
EXCLUDES　*endoscopic retrograde:*
cholangiography [ERC] (51.11)
pancreatography [ERP] (52.13)
AHA: 4Q, '03, 118; 3Q, '03, 17; 1Q, '01, 8; 2Q, '99, 13
DEF: Endoscopic and radioscopic exam of pancreatic and common bile ducts with contrast material injected in opposite direction of normal flow through catheter.

51.11　Endoscopic retrograde cholangiography [ERC]
Laparoscopic exploration of common bile duct
EXCLUDES　*endoscopic retrograde:*
cholangiopancreatography [ERCP] (51.10)
pancreatography [ERP] (52.13)
AHA: 1Q, '96, 12; 3Q, '89, 18; 4Q, '88, 7
DEF: Endoscopic and radioscopic exam of common bile ducts with contrast material injected in opposite direction of normal flow through catheter.

51.12　Percutaneous biopsy of gallbladder or bile ducts
Needle biopsy of gallbladder

51.13　Open biopsy of gallbladder or bile ducts

51.14　Other closed [endoscopic] biopsy of biliary duct or sphincter of Oddi
Brushing or washing for specimen collection
Closed biopsy of biliary duct or sphincter of Oddi by procedures classifiable to 51.10-51.11, 52.13
DEF: Endoscopic biopsy of muscle tissue around pancreatic and common bile ducts.

51.15　Pressure measurement of sphincter of Oddi
Pressure measurement of sphincter by procedures classifiable to 51.10-51.11, 52.13
DEF: Pressure measurement tests of muscle tissue surrounding pancreatic and common bile ducts.

51.19　Other diagnostic procedures on biliary tract
EXCLUDES　*biliary tract x-ray (87.51-87.59)*
microscopic examination of specimen from biliary tract (91.01-91.09)

✓3ʳᵈ
✓4ᵗʰ　Additional Digit Required　　RUG III Special Care Procedure　　RUG III Clinically Complex Procedure　　RUG III Extensive Services Procedure　　RUG III Rehab Procedure

2006 ICD•9•CM　　　　　　　　　　　　　　　　　　　　　　　　　　　　　　　**Volume 3 — 147**

Operations on the Digestive System

51.2–51.85

Laparoscopic Cholecystectomy by Laser

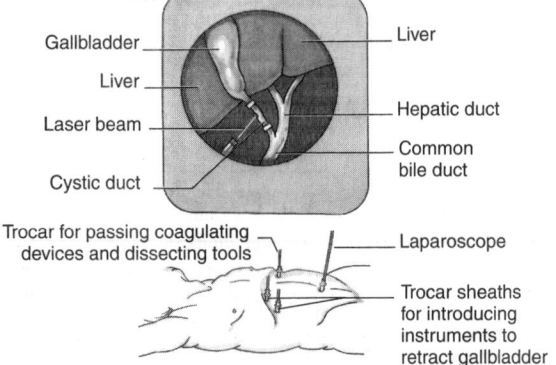

Gallbladder — Liver

Liver

Laser beam

Cystic duct

Trocar for passing coagulating devices and dissecting tools

Liver

Hepatic duct

Common bile duct

Laparoscope

Trocar sheaths for introducing instruments to retract gallbladder

✓4ᵗʰ **51.2 Cholecystectomy**
AHA: 1Q, '93, 17; 4Q, '91, 26; 3Q, '89, 18

51.21 Other partial cholecystectomy
Revision of prior cholecystectomy
EXCLUDES *that by laparoscope (51.24)*
AHA: 4Q, '96, 69

51.22 Cholecystectomy
EXCLUDES *laparoscopic cholecystectomy (51.23)*
AHA: 4Q, '97, 52; 2Q, '91, 16

51.23 Laparoscopic cholecystectomy
That by laser
AHA: 3Q, '98, 10; 4Q, '97, 52; 1Q, '96, 12; 2Q, '95, 11; 4Q, '91, 26
DEF: Endoscopic removal of gallbladder.

51.24 Laparoscopic partial cholecystectomy
AHA: 4Q, '96, 69

✓4ᵗʰ **51.3 Anastomosis of gallbladder or bile duct**
EXCLUDES *resection with end-to-end anastomosis (51.61-51.69)*

51.31 Anastomosis of gallbladder to hepatic ducts
51.32 Anastomosis of gallbladder to intestine
51.33 Anastomosis of gallbladder to pancreas
51.34 Anastomosis of gallbladder to stomach
51.35 Other gallbladder anastomosis
Gallbladder anastomosis NOS

51.36 Choledochoenterostomy
DEF: Connection of common bile duct to intestine.

51.37 Anastomosis of hepatic duct to gastrointestinal tract
Kasai portoenterostomy
AHA: 2Q, '02, 12
DEF: Kaisi portoenterostomy: A duct to drain bile from the liver is formed by anastomosing the porta hepatis to a loop of bowel.

51.39 Other bile duct anastomosis
Anastomosis of bile duct NOS
Anastomosis of unspecified bile duct to:
intestine   pancreas
liver   stomach

✓4ᵗʰ **51.4 Incision of bile duct for relief of obstruction**

51.41 Common duct exploration for removal of calculus
EXCLUDES *percutaneous extraction (51.96)*
AHA: 1Q, '96, 12; 3Q, '89, 18; 4Q, '88, 7

51.42 Common duct exploration for relief of other obstruction
AHA: 3Q, '89, 18

51.43 Insertion of choledochohepatic tube for decompression
Hepatocholedochostomy
AHA: 3Q, '89, 18; 4Q, '88, 7

51.49 Incision of other bile ducts for relief of obstruction
AHA: 3Q, '89, 18

✓4ᵗʰ **51.5 Other incision of bile duct**
EXCLUDES *that for relief of obstruction (51.41-51.49)*

51.51 Exploration of common duct
Incision of common bile duct
AHA: 2Q, '97, 16; 1Q, '96, 12

51.59 Incision of other bile duct
AHA: 2Q, '97, 16; 3Q, '89, 18

✓4ᵗʰ **51.6 Local excision or destruction of lesion or tissue of biliary ducts and sphincter of Oddi**
Code also anastomosis other than end-to-end (51.31, 51.36-51.39)
EXCLUDES *biopsy of bile duct (51.12-51.13)*

51.61 Excision of cystic duct remnant
AHA: 3Q, '89, 18

51.62 Excision of ampulla of Vater (with reimplantation of common duct)

51.63 Other excision of common duct
Choledochectomy
EXCLUDES *fistulectomy (51.72)*

51.64 Endoscopic excision or destruction of lesion of biliary ducts or sphincter of Oddi
Excision or destruction of lesion of biliary duct by procedures classifiable to 51.10-51.11, 52.13

51.69 Excision of other bile duct
Excision of lesion of bile duct NOS
EXCLUDES *fistulectomy (51.79)*

✓4ᵗʰ **51.7 Repair of bile ducts**
51.71 Simple suture of common bile duct
51.72 Choledochoplasty
Repair of fistula of common bile duct

51.79 Repair of other bile ducts
Closure of artificial opening of bile duct NOS
Suture of bile duct NOS
EXCLUDES *operative removal of prosthetic device (51.95)*

✓4ᵗʰ **51.8 Other operations on biliary ducts and sphincter of Oddi**

51.81 Dilation of sphincter of Oddi
Dilation of ampulla of Vater
EXCLUDES *that by endoscopic approach (51.84)*
DEF: Dilation of muscle around common bile and pancreatic ducts; to mitigate constriction obstructing bile flow.

51.82 Pancreatic sphincterotomy
Incision of pancreatic sphincter
Transduodenal ampullary sphincterotomy
EXCLUDES *that by endoscopic approach (51.85)*
DEF: Pancreatic sphincterotomy: Division of muscle around common bile and pancreatic ducts.
DEF: Transduodenal ampullary sphincterotomy: Incision into muscle around common bile and pancreatic ducts; closing approach through first section of small intestine.

51.83 Pancreatic sphincteroplasty
51.84 Endoscopic dilation of ampulla and biliary duct
Dilation of ampulla and biliary duct by procedures classifiable to 51.10-51.11, 52.13

51.85 Endoscopic sphincterotomy and papillotomy
Sphincterotomy and papillotomy by procedures classifiable to 51.10-51.11, 52.13
AHA: 4Q, '03, 118; 3Q, '03, 17; 2Q, '97, 7
DEF: Incision of muscle around common bile and pancreatic ducts and closing the duodenal papilla.

Ⓝ Newborn Age: 0   Ⓟ Pediatric Age: 0-17   Ⓜ Maternity Age: 12-55   Ⓐ Adult Age: 15-124   **Adj** Adjunct Code   ►◄ Revised Text   ● New Code   ▲ Revised Code Title

51.86 Endoscopic insertion of nasobiliary drainage tube

Insertion of nasobiliary tube by procedures classifiable to 51.10-51.11, 52.13

51.87 Endoscopic insertion of stent (tube) into bile duct

Endoprosthesis of bile duct

Insertion of stent into bile duct by procedures classifiable to 51.10-51.11, 52.13

> **EXCLUDES** *nasobiliary drainage tube (51.86)*
> *replacement of stent (tube) (97.05)*

AHA: 3Q, '03, 17

51.88 Endoscopic removal of stone(s) from biliary tract

Laparoscopic removal of stone(s) from biliary tract

Removal of biliary tract stone(s) by procedures classifiable to 51.10-51.11, 52.13

> **EXCLUDES** *percutaneous extraction of common duct stones (51.96)*

AHA: 2Q, '00, 11; 2Q, '97, 7

51.89 Other operations on sphincter of Oddi

51.9 Other operations on biliary tract

51.91 Repair of laceration of gallbladder

51.92 Closure of cholecystostomy

51.93 Closure of other biliary fistula

Cholecystogastroenteric fistulectomy

51.94 Revision of anastomosis of biliary tract

51.95 Removal of prosthetic device from bile duct

> **EXCLUDES** *nonoperative removal (97.55)*

51.96 Percutaneous extraction of common duct stones

AHA: 4Q, '88, 7

51.98 Other percutaneous procedures on biliary tract

Percutaneous biliary endoscopy via existing T-tube or other tract for:
dilation of biliary duct stricture
removal of stone(s) except common duct stone
exploration (postoperative)

Percutaneous transhepatic biliary drainage

> **EXCLUDES** *percutaneous aspiration of gallbladder (51.01)*
> *percutaneous biopsy and/or collection of specimen by brushing or washing (51.12)*
> *percutaneous removal of common duct stone(s) (51.96)*

AHA: 1Q, '97, 14; 3Q, '89, 18; N-D, '87, 1

51.99 Other

Insertion or replacement of biliary tract prosthesis

> **EXCLUDES** *biopsy of gallbladder (51.12-51.13)*
> *irrigation of cholecystostomy and other biliary tube (96.41)*
> *lysis of peritoneal adhesions (54.5)*
> *nonoperative removal of:*
> *cholecystostomy tube (97.54)*
> *tube from biliary tract or liver (97.55)*

52 Operations on pancreas

Code also any application or administration of an adhesion barrier substance (99.77)

> **INCLUDES** operations on pancreatic duct

52.0 Pancreatotomy

52.01 Drainage of pancreatic cyst by catheter

52.09 Other pancreatotomy

Pancreatolithotomy

> **EXCLUDES** *drainage by anastomosis (52.4, 52.96)*
> *incision of pancreatic sphincter (51.82)*
> *marsupialization of cyst (52.3)*

DEF: Pancreatolithotomy: Incision into pancreas to remove stones.

52.1 Diagnostic procedures on pancreas

52.11 Closed [aspiration] [needle] [percutaneous] biopsy of pancreas

52.12 Open biopsy of pancreas

52.13 Endoscopic retrograde pancreatography [ERP]

> **EXCLUDES** *endoscopic retrograde:*
> *cholangiography [ERC] (51.11)*
> *cholangiopancreatography [ERCP] (51.10)*
> *that for procedures classifiable to 51.14-51.15, 51.64, 51.84-51.88, 52.14, 52.21, 52.92-52.94, 52.97-52.98*

52.14 Closed [endoscopic] biopsy of pancreatic duct

Closed biopsy of pancreatic duct by procedures classifiable to 51.10-51.11, 52.13

52.19 Other diagnostic procedures on pancreas

> **EXCLUDES** *contrast pancreatogram (87.66)*
> *endoscopic retrograde pancreatography [ERP] (52.13)*
> *microscopic examination of specimen from pancreas (91.01-91.09)*

52.2 Local excision or destruction of pancreas and pancreatic duct

> **EXCLUDES** *biopsy of pancreas (52.11-52.12, 52.14)*
> *pancreatic fistulectomy (52.95)*

52.21 Endoscopic excision or destruction of lesion or tissue of pancreatic duct

Excision or destruction of lesion or tissue of pancreatic duct by procedures classifiable to 51.10-51.11, 52.13

52.22 Other excision or destruction of lesion or tissue of pancreas or pancreatic duct

52.3 Marsupialization of pancreatic cyst

> **EXCLUDES** *drainage of cyst by catheter (52.01)*

DEF: Incision into pancreas and suturing edges to form pocket; promotes drainage and healing.

52.4 Internal drainage of pancreatic cyst

Pancreaticocystoduodenostomy
Pancreaticocystogastrostomy
Pancreaticocystojejunostomy

DEF: Withdrawing fluid from pancreatic cyst by draining it through a created passage to another organ.

DEF: Pancreaticocystoduodenostomy: Creation of passage from pancreatic cyst to first portion of small intestine.

DEF: Pancreaticocystogastrostomy: Creation of passage from pancreatic cyst to stomach.

DEF: Pancreaticocystojejunostomy: Creation of passage from pancreatic cyst to midsection of small intestine.

Operations on the Digestive System

51.86–52.4

■ Additional Digit Required   RUG III Special Care Procedure   RUG III Clinically Complex Procedure   RUG III Extensive Services Procedure   RUG III Rehab Procedure

2006 ICD•9•CM   Volume 3 — 149

Operations on the Digestive System

52.5–53.02

✓4th **52.5** **Partial pancreatectomy**
> EXCLUDES   *pancreatic fistulectomy (52.95)*

52.51 **Proximal pancreatectomy**
Excision of head of pancreas (with part of body)
Proximal pancreatectomy with synchronous duodenectomy

52.52 **Distal pancreatectomy**
Excision of tail of pancreas (with part of body)

52.53 **Radical subtotal pancreatectomy**

52.59 **Other partial pancreatectomy**

52.6 **Total pancreatectomy**
Pancreatectomy with synchronous duodenectomy
AHA: 4Q, '96, 71

52.7 **Radical pancreaticoduodenectomy**
One-stage pancreaticoduodenal resection with choledochojejunal anastomosis, pancreaticojejunal anastomosis, and gastrojejunostomy
Two-stage pancreaticoduodenal resection (first stage) (second stage)
Radical resection of the pancreas
Whipple procedure
> EXCLUDES   *radical subtotal pancreatectomy (52.53)*

AHA: 1Q, '01, 13

DEF: Whipple procedure: pancreaticoduodenectomy involving the removal of the head of the pancreas and part of the small intestines; pancreaticojejunostomy, choledochojejunal anastomosis, and gastrojejunostomy included in the procedure.

✓4th **52.8** **Transplant of pancreas**
Note: To report donor source — see codes 00.91-00.93

52.80 **Pancreatic transplant, not otherwise specified**

52.81 **Reimplantation of pancreatic tissue**

52.82 **Homotransplant of pancreas**

52.83 **Heterotransplant of pancreas**

52.84 **Autotransplantation of cells of islets of Langerhans**
Homotransplantation of islet cells of pancreas
AHA: 4Q, '96, 70, 71

DEF: Transplantation of Islet cells from pancreas to another location of same patient.

52.85 **Allotransplantation of cells of islets of Langerhans**
Heterotransplantation of islet cells of pancreas
AHA: 4Q, '96, 70, 71

DEF: Transplantation of Islet cells from one individual to another.

52.86 **Transplantation of cells of islets of Langerhans, not otherwise specified**
AHA: 4Q, '96, 70

✓4th **52.9** **Other operations on pancreas**
DEF: Placement of tube into pancreatic duct, without an endoscope.

52.92 **Cannulation of pancreatic duct**
> EXCLUDES   *that by endoscopic approach (52.93)*

52.93 **Endoscopic insertion of stent (tube) into pancreatic duct**
Insertion of cannula or stent into pancreatic duct by procedures classifiable to 51.10-51.11, 52.13
> EXCLUDES   *endoscopic insertion of nasopancreatic drainage tube (52.97)*
> *replacement of stent (tube) (97.05)*

AHA: 2Q, '97, 7

52.94 **Endoscopic removal of stone(s) from pancreatic duct**
Removal of stone(s) from pancreatic duct by procedures classifiable to 51.10-51.11, 52.13

52.95 **Other repair of pancreas**
Fistulectomy } of pancreas
Simple suture }

52.96 **Anastomosis of pancreas**
Anastomosis of pancreas (duct) to:
intestine   stomach
jejunum
> EXCLUDES   *anastomosis to:*
> *bile duct (51.39)*
> *gallbladder (51.33)*

52.97 **Endoscopic insertion of nasopancreatic drainage tube**
Insertion of nasopancreatic drainage tube by procedures classifiable to 51.10-51.11, 52.13
> EXCLUDES   *drainage of pancreatic cyst by catheter (52.01)*
> *replacement of stent (tube) (97.05)*

52.98 **Endoscopic dilation of pancreatic duct**
Dilation of Wirsung's duct by procedures classifiable to 51.10-51.11, 52.13

52.99 **Other**
Dilation of pancreatic [Wirsung's] duct } by open
Repair of pancreatic [Wirsung's] duct } approach
> EXCLUDES   *irrigation of pancreatic tube (96.42)*
> *removal of pancreatic tube (97.56)*

✓3rd **53** **Repair of hernia**
Code also any application or administration of an adhesion barrier substance (99.77)
> INCLUDES   hernioplasty   herniotomy
> herniorrhaphy
> EXCLUDES   *manual reduction of hernia (96.27)*

AHA: 3Q, '94, 8

DEF: Repair of hernia: Restoration of abnormally protruding organ or tissue.

DEF: Herniorrhaphy: Repair of hernia.

DEF: Herniotomy: Division of constricted, strangulated, irreducible hernia.

✓4th **53.0** **Unilateral repair of inguinal hernia**

53.00 **Unilateral repair of inguinal hernia, not otherwise specified**
Inguinal herniorrhaphy NOS
AHA: 3Q, '03, 10

53.01 **Repair of direct inguinal hernia**
AHA: 4Q, '96, 66

53.02 **Repair of indirect inguinal hernia**

Indirect Repair of Hernia

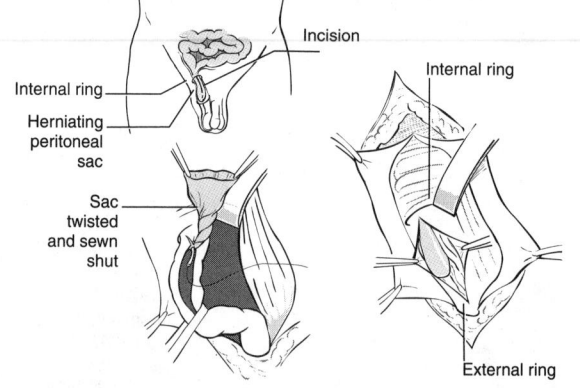

N Newborn Age: 0   P Pediatric Age: 0-17   M Maternity Age: 12-55   A Adult Age: 15-124   Adj Adjunct Code   ►◄ Revised Text   ● New Code   ▲ Revised Code Title

150 — Volume 3

2006 ICD•9•CM

53.03   **Repair of direct inguinal hernia with graft or prosthesis**

53.04   **Repair of indirect inguinal hernia with graft or prosthesis**

53.05   **Repair of inguinal hernia with graft or prosthesis, not otherwise specified**

✓4ᵗʰ **53.1**   **Bilateral repair of inguinal hernia**

53.10   **Bilateral repair of inguinal hernia, not otherwise specified**

53.11   **Bilateral repair of direct inguinal hernia**

53.12   **Bilateral repair of indirect inguinal hernia**

53.13   **Bilateral repair of inguinal hernia, one direct and one indirect**

53.14   **Bilateral repair of direct inguinal hernia with graft or prosthesis**

53.15   **Bilateral repair of indirect inguinal hernia with graft or prosthesis**

53.16   **Bilateral repair of inguinal hernia, one direct and one indirect, with graft or prosthesis**

53.17   **Bilateral inguinal hernia repair with graft or prosthesis, not otherwise specified**

✓4ᵗʰ **53.2**   **Unilateral repair of femoral hernia**

53.21   **Unilateral repair of femoral hernia with graft or prosthesis**

53.29   **Other unilateral femoral herniorrhaphy**

✓4ᵗʰ **53.3**   **Bilateral repair of femoral hernia**

53.31   **Bilateral repair of femoral hernia with graft or prosthesis**

53.39   **Other bilateral femoral herniorrhaphy**

✓4ᵗʰ **53.4**   **Repair of umbilical hernia**

     EXCLUDES   *repair of gastroschisis (54.71)*

53.41   **Repair of umbilical hernia with prosthesis**

53.49   **Other umbilical herniorrhaphy**

✓4ᵗʰ **53.5**   **Repair of other hernia of anterior abdominal wall (without graft or prosthesis)**

53.51   **Incisional hernia repair**

     AHA: 3Q, '03, 6

53.59   **Repair of other hernia of anterior abdominal wall**

     Repair of hernia: Repair of hernia:
       epigastric   spigelian
       hypogastric   ventral

     AHA: 3Q, '03, 6; 3Q, '96, 15

✓4ᵗʰ **53.6**   **Repair of other hernia of anterior abdominal wall with graft or prosthesis**

53.61   **Incisional hernia repair with prosthesis**

     AHA: 3Q, '03, 11

53.69   **Repair of other hernia of anterior abdominal wall with prosthesis**

53.7   **Repair of diaphragmatic hernia, abdominal approach**

✓4ᵗʰ **53.8**   **Repair of diaphragmatic hernia, thoracic approach**

     DEF: Repair of diaphragmatic hernia though abdomen and thorax.

53.80   **Repair of diaphragmatic hernia with thoracic approach, not otherwise specified**

     Thoracoabdominal repair of diaphragmatic hernia

53.81   **Plication of the diaphragm**

     DEF: Tuck repair of diaphragmatic hernia.

53.82   **Repair of parasternal hernia**

     DEF: Repair of hernia protruding into breastbone area.

53.9   **Other hernia repair**

     Repair of hernia: Repair of hernia:
       ischiatic   omental
       ischiorectal   retroperitoneal
       lumbar   sciatic
       obturator

     EXCLUDES   *relief of strangulated hernia with exteriorization of intestine (46.01, 46.03)*
                 repair of pericolostomy hernia (46.42)
                 repair of vaginal enterocele (70.92)

✓3ʳᵈ **54**   **Other operations on abdominal region**

     Code also any application or administration of an adhesion barrier substance (99.77)

     INCLUDES   operations on: operations on:
                   epigastric region   male pelvic cavity
                   flank   mesentery
                   groin region   omentum
                   hypochondrium   peritoneum
                   inguinal region   retroperitoneal
                   loin region   tissue space

     EXCLUDES   *female pelvic cavity (69.01-70.92)*
                 hernia repair (53.00-53.9)
                 obliteration of cul-de-sac (70.92)
                 retroperitoneal tissue dissection (59.00-59.09)
                 skin and subcutaneous tissue of abdominal wall (86.01-86.99)

54.0   **Incision of abdominal wall**

     Drainage of: Drainage of:
       abdominal wall   retroperitoneal abscess
       extraperitoneal abscess

     EXCLUDES   *incision of peritoneum (54.95)*
                 laparotomy (54.11-54.19)

     AHA: 1Q, '97, 11; N-D, '87, 12

✓4ᵗʰ **54.1**   **Laparotomy**

     AHA: 1Q, '92, 13

     DEF: Incision into abdomen.

54.11   **Exploratory laparotomy**

     EXCLUDES   *exploration incidental to intra-abdominal surgery — omit code*

     AHA: 3Q, '89, 14; 4Q, '88, 12

     DEF: Exam of peritoneal cavity through incision into abdomen.

54.12   **Reopening of recent laparotomy site**

     Reopening of recent laparotomy site for:
       control of hemorrhage
       exploration
       incision of hematoma

54.19   **Other laparotomy**

     Drainage of intraperitoneal abscess or hematoma

     EXCLUDES   *culdocentesis (70.0)*
                 drainage of appendiceal abscess (47.2)
                 exploration incidental to intra-abdominal surgery — omit code
                 Ladd operation (54.95)
                 percutaneous drainage of abdomen (54.91)
                 removal of foreign body (54.92)

     AHA: 3Q, '03, 17

✓4ᵗʰ **54.2**   **Diagnostic procedures of abdominal region**

54.21   **Laparoscopy**

     Peritoneoscopy

     EXCLUDES   *laparoscopic cholecystectomy (51.23)*
                 that incidental to destruction of fallopian tubes (66.21-66.29)

     DEF: Endoscopic exam of peritoneal cavity through abdominal incision.

✓3ʳᵈ ✓4ᵗʰ **Additional Digit Required**   RUG III Special Care Procedure   RUG III Clinically Complex Procedure   RUG III Extensive Services Procedure   RUG III Rehab Procedure

2006 ICD•9•CM   **Volume 3 — 151**

Operations on the Digestive System

54.22–54.74

54.22   **Biopsy of abdominal wall or umbilicus**

54.23   **Biopsy of peritoneum**
Biopsy of:
  mesentery
  omentum
  peritoneal implant
> EXCLUDES   closed biopsy of:
>   omentum (54.24)
>   peritoneum (54.24)

54.24   **Closed [percutaneous] [needle] biopsy of intra-abdominal mass**
Closed biopsy of:
  omentum
  peritoneal implant
  peritoneum
> EXCLUDES   that of:
>   fallopian tube (66.11)
>   ovary (65.11)
>   uterine ligaments (68.15)
>   uterus (68.16)

AHA: 4Q, '97, 57

54.25   **Peritoneal lavage**
Diagnostic peritoneal lavage
> EXCLUDES   peritoneal dialysis (54.98)

AHA: 2Q, '98, 19; 4Q, '93, 28

DEF: Irrigation of peritoneal cavity with siphoning of liquid contents for analysis.

54.29   **Other diagnostic procedures on abdominal region**
> EXCLUDES
>   abdominal lymphangiogram (88.04)
>   abdominal x-ray NEC (88.19)
>   angiocardiography of venae cavae (88.51)
>   C.A.T. scan of abdomen (88.01)
>   contrast x-ray of abdominal cavity (88.11-88.15)
>   intra-abdominal arteriography NEC (88.47)
>   microscopic examination of peritoneal and retroperitoneal specimen (91.11-91.19)
>   phlebography of:
>   intra-abdominal vessels NEC (88.65)
>   portal venous system (88.64)
>   sinogram of abdominal wall (88.03)
>   soft tissue x-ray of abdominal wall NEC (88.09)
>   tomography of abdomen NEC (88.02)
>   ultrasonography of abdomen and retroperitoneum (88.76)

54.3   **Excision or destruction of lesion or tissue of abdominal wall or umbilicus**
Debridement of abdominal wall
Omphalectomy
> EXCLUDES   biopsy of abdominal wall or umbilicus (54.22)
>   size reduction operation (86.83)
>   that of skin of abdominal wall (86.22, 86.26, 86.3)

AHA: 1Q, '89, 11

54.4   **Excision or destruction of peritoneal tissue**
Excision of:
  appendices epiploicae
  falciform ligament
  gastrocolic ligament
  lesion of:
    mesentery
    omentum
    peritoneum
  presacral lesion NOS
  retroperitoneal lesion NOS
> EXCLUDES   biopsy of peritoneum (54.23)
>   endometrectomy of cul-de-sac (70.32)

√4ᵗʰ **54.5**   **Lysis of peritoneal adhesions**
Freeing of adhesions of:
  biliary tract
  intestines
  liver
  pelvic peritoneum
  peritoneum
  spleen
  uterus
> EXCLUDES   lysis of adhesions of:
>   bladder (59.11)
>   fallopian tube and ovary (65.81, 65.89)
>   kidney (59.02)
>   ureter (59.02-59.03)

AHA: 3Q, '94, 8; 4Q, '90, 18

54.51   **Laparoscopic lysis of peritoneal adhesions**
AHA: 3Q, '03, 6-7; 4Q, '96, 65

54.59   **Other lysis of peritoneal adhesions**
AHA: 3Q, '03, 11; 1Q, '03, 14; 4Q, '96, 66

√4ᵗʰ **54.6**   **Suture of abdominal wall and peritoneum**

54.61   **Reclosure of postoperative disruption of abdominal wall**

54.62   **Delayed closure of granulating abdominal wound**
Tertiary subcutaneous wound closure
DEF: Closure of outer layers of abdominal wound; follows procedure to close initial layers of wound.

54.63   **Other suture of abdominal wall**
Suture of laceration of abdominal wall
> EXCLUDES   closure of operative wound — omit code

54.64   **Suture of peritoneum**
Secondary suture of peritoneum
> EXCLUDES   closure of operative wound — omit code

√4ᵗʰ **54.7**   **Other repair of abdominal wall and peritoneum**

54.71   **Repair of gastroschisis**
AHA: 2Q, '02, 9

DEF: Repair of congenital fistula of abdominal wall.

54.72   **Other repair of abdominal wall**

54.73   **Other repair of peritoneum**
Suture of gastrocolic ligament

54.74   **Other repair of omentum**
Epiplorrhaphy
Graft of omentum
Omentopexy
Reduction of torsion of omentum
> EXCLUDES   cardio-omentopexy (36.39)

AHA: J-F, '87, 11

DEF: Epiplorrhaphy: Suture of abdominal serous membrane.

DEF: Graft of omentum: Implantation of tissue into abdominal serous membrane.

DEF: Omentopexy: Anchoring of abdominal serous membrane.

DEF: Reduction of torsion of omentum: Reduction of twisted abdominal serous membrane.

N Newborn Age: 0   P Pediatric Age: 0-17   M Maternity Age: 12-55   A Adult Age: 15-124   Adj Adjunct Code   ◄► Revised Text   ● New Code   ▲ Revised Code Title

54.75 Other repair of mesentery
Mesenteric plication
Mesenteropexy
DEF: Creation of folds in mesentery for shortening.

DEF: Mesenteriopexy: Fixation of torn, incised mesentery.

√4ᵗʰ **54.9 Other operations of abdominal region**
> EXCLUDES   removal of ectopic pregnancy (74.3)

54.91 Percutaneous abdominal drainage
Paracentesis
> EXCLUDES   creation of cutaneoperitoneal
> fistula (54.93)

AHA: 3Q, '99, 9; 2Q, '99, 14; 3Q, '98, 12; 1Q, '92, 14; 2Q, '90, 25

DEF: Puncture for removal of fluid.

54.92 Removal of foreign body from peritoneal cavity

AHA: 1Q, '89, 11

54.93 Creation of cutaneoperitoneal fistula

AHA: 2Q, '95, 10; N-D, '84, 6

DEF: Creation of opening between skin and peritoneal cavity.

54.94 Creation of peritoneovascular shunt
Peritoneovenous shunt

AHA: 1Q, '94, 7; 1Q, '88, 9; S-O, '85, 6

DEF: Peritoneovascular shunt: Construction of shunt to connect peritoneal cavity with vascular system.

DEF: Peritoneovenous shunt: Construction of shunt to connect peritoneal cavity with vein.

54.95 Incision of peritoneum
Exploration of ventriculoperitoneal shunt at peritoneal site
Ladd operation
Revision of distal catheter of ventricular shunt
Revision of ventriculoperitoneal shunt at peritoneal site
> EXCLUDES   that incidental to laparotomy
> (54.11-54.19)

AHA: 4Q, '95, 65

DEF: Ladd operation: Peritoneal attachment of incompletely rotated cecum, obstructing duodenum.

54.96 Injection of air into peritoneal cavity
Pneumoperitoneum
> EXCLUDES   that for:
> collapse of lung (33.33)
> radiography (88.12-88.13,
> 88.15)

54.97 Injection of locally-acting therapeutic substance into peritoneal cavity
> EXCLUDES   peritoneal dialysis (54.98)

54.98 Peritoneal dialysis
> EXCLUDES   peritoneal lavage (diagnostic)
> (54.25)

AHA: 4Q, '93, 28; N-D, '84, 6

DEF: Separation of blood elements by diffusion through membrane.

54.99 Other
> EXCLUDES   removal of:
> abdominal wall sutures
> (97.83)
> peritoneal drainage device
> (97.82)
> retroperitoneal drainage
> device (97.81)

AHA: 1Q, '99, 4

√3ᵗʰ
√4ᵗʰ Additional Digit Required   RUG III Special Care Procedure   RUG III Clinically Complex Procedure   RUG III Extensive Services Procedure   RUG III Rehab Procedure

Operations on the Urinary System

55–55.53

10. OPERATIONS ON THE URINARY SYSTEM (55-59)

√3rd **55**   **Operations on kidney**

Code also any application or administration of an adhesion barrier substance (99.77)

INCLUDES   operations on renal pelvis

EXCLUDES   *perirenal tissue (59.00-59.09, 59.21-59.29, 59.91-59.92)*

√4th **55.0**   **Nephrotomy and nephrostomy**

EXCLUDES   *drainage by:*
     anastomosis (55.86)
     aspiration (55.92)

55.01   **Nephrotomy**

Evacuation of renal cyst
Exploration of kidney
Nephrolithotomy

DEF: Nephrotomy: Incision into kidney.

DEF: Evacuation of renal cyst: Draining contents of cyst.

DEF: Exploration of kidney: Exploration through incision.

DEF: Nephrolithotomy: Removal of kidney stone through incision.

55.02   **Nephrostomy**

AHA: 2Q, '97, 4

55.03   **Percutaneous nephrostomy without fragmentation**

Nephrostolithotomy, percutaneous (nephroscopic)
Percutaneous removal of kidney stone(s) by:
   forceps extraction (nephroscopic)
   basket extraction
Pyelostolithotomy, percutaneous (nephroscopic)
With placement of catheter down ureter

EXCLUDES   *percutaneous removal by fragmentation (55.04)*
     repeat nephroscopic removal during current episode (55.92)

AHA: 2Q, '96, 5

DEF: Insertion of tube through abdominal wall without breaking up stones.

DEF: Nephrostolithotomy: Insertion of tube through the abdominal wall to remove stones.

DEF: Basket extraction: Removal, percutaneous of stone with grasping forceps.

DEF: Pyelostolithotomy: Removal, percutaneous of stones from funnel-shaped portion of kidney.

55.04   **Percutaneous nephrostomy with fragmentation**

Percutaneous nephrostomy with disruption of kidney stone by ultrasonic energy and extraction (suction) through endoscope
With placement of catheter down ureter
With fluoroscopic guidance

EXCLUDES   *repeat fragmentation during current episode (59.95)*

AHA: 1Q, '89, 1; S-O, '86, 11

DEF: Insertion of tube through abdominal wall into kidney to break up stones.

√4th **55.1**   **Pyelotomy and pyelostomy**

EXCLUDES   *drainage by anastomosis (55.86)*
     percutaneous pyelostolithotomy (55.03)
     removal of calculus without incision (56.0)

55.11   **Pyelotomy**

Exploration of renal pelvis
Pyelolithotomy

55.12   **Pyelostomy**

Insertion of drainage tube into renal pelvis

√4th **55.2**   **Diagnostic procedures on kidney**

55.21   **Nephroscopy**

DEF: Endoscopic exam of renal pelvis; retrograde through ureter, percutaneous or open exposure.

55.22   **Pyeloscopy**

DEF: Fluoroscopic exam of kidney pelvis, calyces and ureters; follows IV or retrograde injection of contrast.

55.23   **Closed [percutaneous] [needle] biopsy of kidney**

Endoscopic biopsy via existing nephrostomy, nephrotomy, pyelostomy, or pyelotomy

55.24   **Open biopsy of kidney**

55.29   **Other diagnostic procedures on kidney**

EXCLUDES   *microscopic examination of specimen from kidney (91.21-91.29)*
     pyelogram:
       intravenous (87.73)
       percutaneous (87.75)
       retrograde (87.74)
     radioisotope scan (92.03)
     renal arteriography (88.45)
     tomography:
       C.A.T scan (87.71)
       other (87.72)

√4th **55.3**   **Local excision or destruction of lesion or tissue of kidney**

55.31   **Marsupialization of kidney lesion**

DEF: Exteriorization of lesion by incising anterior wall and suturing cut edges to create open pouch.

55.39   **Other local destruction or excision of renal lesion or tissue**

Obliteration of calyceal diverticulum

EXCLUDES   *biopsy of kidney (55.23-55.24)*
     partial nephrectomy (55.4)
     percutaneous aspiration of kidney (55.92)
     wedge resection of kidney (55.4)

55.4   **Partial nephrectomy**

Calycectomy
Wedge resection of kidney
Code also any synchronous resection of ureter (56.40-56.42)

DEF: Surgical removal of a part of the kidney.

DEF: Calycectomy: Removal of indentations in kidney.

√4th **55.5**   **Complete nephrectomy**

Code also any synchronous excision of:
   adrenal gland (07.21-07.3)
   bladder segment (57.6)
   lymph nodes (40.3, 40.52-40.59)

55.51   **Nephroureterectomy**

Nephroureterectomy with bladder cuff
Total nephrectomy (unilateral)

EXCLUDES   *removal of transplanted kidney (55.53)*

DEF: Complete removal of the kidney and all or portion of the ureter.

DEF: Nephroureterectomy with bladder cuff: Removal of kidney, ureter, and portion of bladder attached to ureter.

DEF: Total nephrectomy (unilateral): Complete excision of one kidney.

55.52   **Nephrectomy of remaining kidney**

Removal of solitary kidney

EXCLUDES   *removal of transplanted kidney (55.53)*

55.53   **Removal of transplanted or rejected kidney**

N Newborn Age: 0   P Pediatric Age: 0-17   M Maternity Age: 12-55   A Adult Age: 15-124   Adj Adjunct Code   ►◄ Revised Text   ● New Code   ▲ Revised Code Title

Operations on the Urinary System

55.54 Bilateral nephrectomy

     EXCLUDES *complete nephrectomy NOS (55.51)*

     DEF: Removal of both kidneys same operative session.

✓4ᵗʰ **55.6 Transplant of kidney**

     Note: To report donor source — see codes 00.91-00.93

     55.61 Renal autotransplantation

     55.69 Other kidney transplantation

         AHA: ▶4Q, '04, 117;◀ 4Q, '96, 71

55.7 Nephropexy

     Fixation or suspension of movable [floating] kidney

✓4ᵗʰ **55.8 Other repair of kidney**

     55.81 Suture of laceration of kidney

     55.82 Closure of nephrostomy and pyelostomy

         DEF: Removal of tube from kidney and closure of site of tube insertion.

     55.83 Closure of other fistula of kidney

     55.84 Reduction of torsion of renal pedicle

         DEF: Restoration of twisted renal pedicle into normal position.

     55.85 Symphysiotomy for horseshoe kidney

         DEF: Division of congenitally malformed kidney into two parts.

     55.86 Anastomosis of kidney

         Nephropyeloureterostomy
         Pyeloureterovesical anastomosis
         Ureterocalyceal anastomosis

         EXCLUDES *nephrocystanastomosis NOS (56.73)*

         DEF: Nephropyeloureterostomy: Creation of passage between kidney and ureter.

         DEF: Pyeloureterovesical anastomosis: Creation of passage between kidney and bladder.

         DEF: Ureterocalyceal anastomosis: Creation of passage between ureter and kidney indentations.

     55.87 Correction of ureteropelvic junction

     55.89 Other

✓4ᵗʰ **55.9 Other operations on kidney**

     EXCLUDES *lysis of perirenal adhesions (59.02)*

     55.91 Decapsulation of kidney

         Capsulectomy ⎫ of kidney
         Decortication ⎭

Symphysiotomy for Horseshoe Kidney

- Proposed second cut
- Lengthened muscle
- Extraocular muscle

55.92 Percutaneous aspiration of kidney (pelvis)

     Aspiration of renal cyst   Renipuncture

     EXCLUDES *percutaneous biopsy of kidney (55.23)*

     AHA: N-D, '84, 20

     DEF: Insertion of needle into kidney to withdraw fluid.

55.93 Replacement of nephrostomy tube

55.94 Replacement of pyelostomy tube

55.95 Local perfusion of kidney

     DEF: Fluid passage through kidney.

55.96 Other injection of therapeutic substance into kidney

     Injection into renal cyst

55.97 Implantation or replacement of mechanical kidney

55.98 Removal of mechanical kidney

55.99 Other

     EXCLUDES *removal of pyelostomy or nephrostomy tube (97.61)*

✓3ʳᵈ **56 Operations on ureter**

     Code also any application or administration of an adhesion barrier substance (99.77)

     56.0 Transurethral removal of obstruction from ureter and renal pelvis

         Removal of:
         blood clot ⎫ from ureter or renal pelvis
         calculus ⎬ without incision
         foreign body ⎭

         EXCLUDES *manipulation without removal of obstruction (59.8)*
         that by incision (55.11,56.2)
         transurethral insertion of ureteral stent for passage of calculus (59.8)

         AHA: 1Q, '89, 1; S-O, '86, 12

         DEF: Removal of obstruction by tube inserted through urethra to ureter.

     56.1 Ureteral meatotomy

         DEF: Incision into ureteral meatus to enlarge passage.

     56.2 Ureterotomy

         Incision of ureter for: Incision of ureter for:
         drainage   removal of calculus
         exploration

         EXCLUDES *cutting of ureterovesical orifice (56.1)*
         removal of calculus without incision (56.0)
         transurethral insertion of ureteral stent for passage of calculus (59.8)
         urinary diversion (56.51-56.79)

         AHA: S-O, '86, 10

✓4ᵗʰ **56.3 Diagnostic procedures on ureter**

     56.31 Ureteroscopy

     56.32 Closed percutaneous biopsy of ureter

         EXCLUDES *endoscopic biopsy of ureter (56.33)*

     56.33 Closed endoscopic biopsy of ureter

         Cystourethroscopy with ureteral biopsy
         Transurethral biopsy of ureter
         Ureteral endoscopy with biopsy through ureterotomy
         Ureteroscopy with biopsy

         EXCLUDES *percutaneous biopsy of ureter (56.32)*

     56.34 Open biopsy of ureter

     56.35 Endoscopy (cystoscopy) (looposcopy) of ileal conduit

         DEF: Endoscopic exam of created opening between ureters and one end of small intestine; other end used to form artificial opening.

✓3ʳᵈ
✓4ᵗʰ
  Additional Digit Required   RUG III Special Care Procedure   RUG III Clinically Complex Procedure   RUG III Extensive Services Procedure   RUG III Rehab Procedure

2006 ICD•9•CM   **February 2005 • Volume 3 — 155**

Operations on the Urinary System

56.39–57.11

56.39 **Other diagnostic procedures on ureter**
EXCLUDES *microscopic examination of specimen from ureter (91.21-91.29)*

✓4th **56.4** **Ureterectomy**
Code also anastomosis other than end-to-end (56.51-56.79)
EXCLUDES *fistulectomy (56.84)*
nephroureterectomy (55.51-55.54)

56.40 **Ureterectomy, not otherwise specified**

56.41 **Partial ureterotomy**
Excision of lesion of ureter
Shortening of ureter with reimplantation
EXCLUDES *biopsy of ureter (56.32-56.34)*

56.42 **Total ureterectomy**

✓4th **56.5** **Cutaneous uretero-ileostomy**

56.51 **Formation of cutaneous uretero-ileostomy**
Construction of ileal conduit
External ureteral ileostomy
Formation of open ileal bladder
Ileal loop operation
Ileoureterostomy (Bricker's) (ileal bladder)
Transplantation of ureter into ileum with external diversion
EXCLUDES *closed ileal bladder (57.87)*
replacement of ureteral defect by ileal segment (56.89)

DEF: Creation of urinary passage by connecting the terminal end of small intestine to ureter then connected to opening through abdominal wall.

DEF: Construction of ileal conduit: Formation of conduit from terminal end of small intestine.

56.52 **Revision of cutaneous uretero-ileostomy**
AHA: 3Q, '96, 15; 4Q, '88, 7

✓4th **56.6** **Other external urinary diversion**

56.61 **Formation of other cutaneous ureterostomy**
Anastomosis of ureter to skin
Ureterostomy NOS

56.62 **Revision of other cutaneous ureterostomy**
Revision of ureterostomy stoma
EXCLUDES *nonoperative removal of ureterostomy tube (97.62)*

✓4th **56.7** **Other anastomosis or bypass of ureter**
EXCLUDES *ureteropyelostomy (55.86)*

56.71 **Urinary diversion to intestine**
Anastomosis of ureter to intestine
Internal urinary diversion NOS
Code also any synchronous colostomy (46.10-46.13)
EXCLUDES *external ureteral ileostomy (56.51)*

56.72 **Revision of ureterointestinal anastomosis**
EXCLUDES *revision of external ureteral ileostomy (56.52)*

56.73 **Nephrocystanastomosis, not otherwise specified**
DEF: Connection of kidney to bladder.

56.74 **Ureteroneocystostomy**
Replacement of ureter with bladder flap
Ureterovesical anastomosis
DEF: Transfer of ureter to another site in bladder.

DEF: Ureterovesical anastomosis: Implantation of ureter into bladder.

56.75 **Transureteroureterostomy**
EXCLUDES *ureteroureterostomy associated with partial resection (56.41)*

DEF: Separating one ureter and joining the ends to the opposite ureter.

56.79 **Other**

✓4th **56.8** **Repair of ureter**

56.81 **Lysis of intraluminal adhesions of ureter**
EXCLUDES *lysis of periureteral adhesions (59.01-59.02)*
ureterolysis (59.02-59.03)

DEF: Destruction of adhesions within urethral cavity.

56.82 **Suture of laceration of ureter**

56.83 **Closure of ureterostomy**

56.84 **Closure of other fistula of ureter**

56.85 **Ureteropexy**

56.86 **Removal of ligature from ureter**

56.89 **Other repair of ureter**
Graft of ureter
Replacement of ureter with ileal segment implanted into bladder
Ureteroplication

DEF: Graft of ureter: Tissue from another site for graft replacement or repair of ureter.

DEF: Replacement of ureter with ileal segment implanted into bladder and ureter replacement with terminal end of small intestine.

DEF: Ureteroplication: Creation of tucks in ureter.

✓4th **56.9** **Other operations on ureter**

56.91 **Dilation of ureteral meatus**

56.92 **Implantation of electronic ureteral stimulator**

56.93 **Replacement of electronic ureteral stimulator**

56.94 **Removal of electronic ureteral stimulator**
EXCLUDES *that with synchronous replacement (56.93)*

56.95 **Ligation of ureter**

56.99 **Other**
EXCLUDES *removal of ureterostomy tube and ureteral catheter (97.62)*
ureteral catheterization (59.8)

✓3rd **57** **Operations on urinary bladder**
Code also any application or administration of an adhesion barrier substance (99.77)
EXCLUDES *perivesical tissue (59.11-59.29, 59.91-59.92)*
ureterovesical orifice (56.0-56.99)

57.0 **Transurethral clearance of bladder**
Drainage of bladder without incision
Removal of:
blood clot ⎫ from bladder
calculus ⎬ without
foreign body ⎭ incision
EXCLUDES *that by incision (57.19)*
AHA: S-O, '86, 11

DEF: Insertion of device through urethra to cleanse bladder.

✓4th **57.1** **Cystotomy and cystostomy**
EXCLUDES *cystotomy and cystostomy as operative approach — omit code*
DEF: Cystotomy: Incision of bladder.

DEF: Cystostomy: Creation of opening into bladder.

57.11 **Percutaneous aspiration of bladder**

N Newborn Age: 0   P Pediatric Age: 0-17   M Maternity Age: 12-55   A Adult Age: 15-124   Adj Adjunct Code   ▶◀ Revised Text   ● New Code   ▲ Revised Code Title

156 — Volume 3   *2006 ICD•9•CM*

57.12   **Lysis of intraluminal adhesions with incision into bladder**

     EXCLUDES   *transurethral lysis of intraluminal adhesions (57.41)*

     DEF: Incision into bladder to destroy lesions.

57.17   **Percutaneous cystostomy**
     Closed cystostomy
     Percutaneous suprapubic cystostomy

     EXCLUDES   *removal of cystostomy tube (97.63)*
         replacement of cystostomy tube (59.94)

     DEF: Incision through body wall into bladder to insert tube.

     DEF: Percutaneous (closed) suprapubic cystostomy: Incision above pubic arch, through body wall, into the bladder to insert tube.

57.18   **Other suprapubic cystostomy**

     EXCLUDES   *percutaneous cystostomy (57.17)*
         removal of cystostomy tube (97.63)
         replacement of cystostomy tube (59.94)

57.19   **Other cystotomy**
     Cystolithotomy

     EXCLUDES   *percutaneous cystostomy (57.17)*
         suprapubic cystostomy (57.18)

     AHA: 4Q, '95, 73; S-O, '86, 11

✓4th 57.2   **Vesicostomy**

     EXCLUDES   *percutaneous cystostomy (57.17)*
         suprapubic cystostomy (57.18)

57.21   **Vesicostomy**
     Creation of permanent opening from bladder to skin using a bladder flap

     DEF: Creation of permanent opening from the bladder to the skin using bladder tissue.

57.22   **Revision or closure of vesicostomy**

     EXCLUDES   *closure of cystostomy (57.82)*

✓4th 57.3   **Diagnostic procedures on bladder**

57.31   **Cystoscopy through artificial stoma**

57.32   **Other cystoscopy**
     Transurethral cystoscopy

     EXCLUDES   *cystourethroscopy with ureteral biopsy (56.33)*
         retrograde pyelogram (87.74)
         that for control of hemorrhage (postoperative):
             bladder (57.93)
             prostate (60.94)

     AHA: 1Q, '01, 14

57.33   **Closed [transurethral] biopsy of bladder**

57.34   **Open biopsy of bladder**

Transurethral Cystourethroscopy

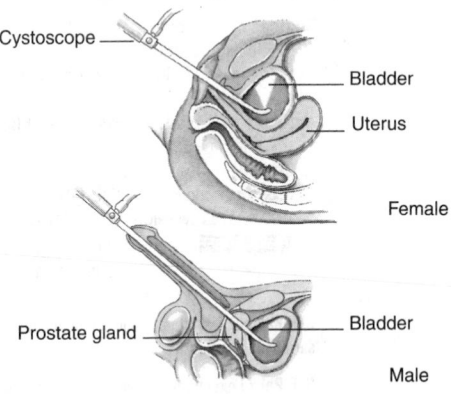

Cystoscope — Bladder — Uterus — Female

Prostate gland — Bladder — Male

57.39   **Other diagnostic procedures on bladder**

     EXCLUDES   *cystogram NEC (87.77)*
         microscopic examination of specimen from bladder (91.31-91.39)
         retrograde cystourethrogram (87.76)
         therapeutic distention of bladder (96.25)

✓4th 57.4   **Transurethral excision or destruction of bladder tissue**

     DEF: Destruction of bladder tissue with instrument inserted into urethra.

57.41   **Transurethral lysis of intraluminal adhesions**

57.49   **Other transurethral excision or destruction of lesion or tissue of bladder**
     Endoscopic resection of bladder lesion

     EXCLUDES   *transurethral biopsy of bladder (57.33)*
         transurethral fistulectomy (57.83-57.84)

✓4th 57.5   **Other excision or destruction of bladder tissue**

     EXCLUDES   *that with transurethral approach (57.41-57.49)*

57.51   **Excision of urachus**
     Excision of urachal sinus of bladder

     EXCLUDES   *excision of urachal cyst of abdominal wall (54.3)*

57.59   **Open excision or destruction of other lesion or tissue of bladder**
     Endometrectomy of bladder
     Suprapubic excision of bladder lesion

     EXCLUDES   *biopsy of bladder (57.33-57.34)*
         fistulectomy of bladder (57.83-57.84)

     DEF: Endometrectomy of bladder: Removal of inner lining.

     DEF: Suprapubic excision of bladder lesion: Removal of lesion by excision above suprapubic bone arch.

57.6   **Partial cystectomy**
     Excision of bladder dome
     Trigonectomy
     Wedge resection of bladder

✓3rd ✓4th Additional Digit Required   RUG III Special Care Procedure   RUG III Clinically Complex Procedure   RUG III Extensive Services Procedure   RUG III Rehab Procedure

2006 ICD•9•CM   Volume 3 — 157

Operations on the Urinary System

57.7–58.29

√4ᵗʰ **57.7**   **Total cystectomy**

> INCLUDES   total cystectomy with urethrectomy

57.71   **Radical cystectomy**

Pelvic exenteration in male
Removal of bladder, prostate, seminal vesicles and fat
Removal of bladder, urethra, and fat in a female
Code also any:
    lymph node dissection (40.3, 40.5)
    urinary diversion (56.51-56.79)

> EXCLUDES   that as part of pelvic exenteration in female (68.8)

DEF: Radical cystectomy: Removal of bladder and surrounding tissue.

DEF: Pelvic exenteration in male: Excision of bladder, prostate, seminal vessels and fat.

57.79   **Other total cystectomy**

√4ᵗʰ **57.8**   **Other repair of urinary bladder**

> EXCLUDES   repair of:
>   current obstetric laceration (75.61)
>   cystocele (70.50-70.51)
>   that for stress incontinence (59.3-59.79)

57.81   **Suture of laceration of bladder**

57.82   **Closure of cystostomy**

57.83   **Repair of fistula involving bladder and intestine**

Rectovesicovaginal   ⎫
Vesicosigmoidovaginal ⎬ fistulectomy
               ⎭

57.84   **Repair of other fistula of bladder**

Cervicovesical   ⎫
Urethroperineovesical ⎬
Uterovesical   ⎬ fistulectomy
Vaginovesical   ⎭

> EXCLUDES   vesicoureterovaginal fistulectomy (56.84)

57.85   **Cystourethroplasty and plastic repair of bladder neck**

Plication of sphincter of urinary bladder
V-Y plasty of bladder neck

DEF: Cystourethroplasty: Reconstruction of narrowed portion of bladder.

DEF: Plication of sphincter or urinary bladder: Creation of tuck in bladder sphincter.

DEF: V-Y plasty of bladder neck: Surgical reconstruction of the narrowed portion of bladder by V-Y technique.

57.86   **Repair of bladder exstrophy**

DEF: Surgical correction of a congenital bladder wall defect.

57.87   **Reconstruction of urinary bladder**

Anastomosis of bladder with isolated segment of ileum
Augmentation of bladder
Replacement of bladder with ileum or sigmoid [closed ileal bladder]
Code also resection of intestine (45.50-45.52)

AHA: 2Q, '03, 11; 3Q, '00, 7

DEF: Anastomosis of bladder with isolated segment of ileum: Creation of connection between bladder and separated terminal end of small intestine.

57.88   **Other anastomosis of bladder**

Anastomosis of bladder to intestine NOS
Cystocolic anastomosis

> EXCLUDES   formation of closed ileal bladder (57.87)

57.89   **Other repair of bladder**

Bladder suspension, not elsewhere classified
Cystopexy NOS
Repair of old obstetric laceration of bladder

> EXCLUDES   repair of current obstetric laceration (75.61)

√4ᵗʰ **57.9**   **Other operations on bladder**

57.91   **Sphincterotomy of bladder**

Division of bladder neck

AHA: 2Q, '90, 26

57.92   **Dilation of bladder neck**

57.93   **Control of (postoperative) hemorrhage of bladder**

57.94   **Insertion of indwelling urinary catheter**

57.95   **Replacement of indwelling urinary catheter**

57.96   **Implantation of electronic bladder stimulator**

57.97   **Replacement of electronic bladder stimulator**

57.98   **Removal of electronic bladder stimulator**

> EXCLUDES   that with synchronous replacement (57.97)

57.99   **Other**

> EXCLUDES   irrigation of:
>   cystostomy (96.47)
>   other indwelling urinary catheter (96.48)
> lysis of external adhesions (59.11)
> removal of:
>   cystostomy tube (97.63)
>   other urinary drainage device (97.64)
> therapeutic distention of bladder (96.25)

√3ʳᵈ **58**   **Operations on urethra**

Code also any application or administration of an adhesion barrier substance (99.77)

> INCLUDES   operations on:
>   bulbourethral gland [Cowper's gland]
>   periurethral tissue

58.0   **Urethrotomy**

Excision of urethral septum
Formation of urethrovaginal fistula
Perineal urethrostomy
Removal of calculus from urethra by incision

> EXCLUDES   drainage of bulbourethral gland or periurethral tissue (58.91)
> internal urethral meatotomy (58.5)
> removal of urethral calculus without incision (58.6)

58.1   **Urethral meatotomy**

> EXCLUDES   internal urethral meatotomy (58.5)

DEF: Incision of urethra to enlarge passage.

√4ᵗʰ **58.2**   **Diagnostic procedures on urethra**

58.21   **Perineal urethroscopy**

58.22   **Other urethroscopy**

58.23   **Biopsy of urethra**

58.24   **Biopsy of periurethral tissue**

DEF: Removal for biopsy of tissue around urethra.

58.29   **Other diagnostic procedures on urethra and periurethral tissue**

> EXCLUDES   microscopic examination of specimen from urethra (91.31-91.39)
> retrograde cystourethrogram (87.76)
> urethral pressure profile (89.25)
> urethral sphincter electromyogram (89.23)

Ⓝ Newborn Age: 0   Ⓟ Pediatric Age: 0-17   Ⓜ Maternity Age: 12-55   Ⓐ Adult Age: 15-124   **Adj** Adjunct Code   ▶◀ Revised Text   ● New Code   ▲ Revised Code Title

Operations on the Urinary System

✓4ᵗʰ **58.3 Excision or destruction of lesion or tissue of urethra**

> EXCLUDES   *biopsy of urethra (58.23)*
> *excision of bulbourethral gland (58.92)*
> *fistulectomy (58.43)*
> *urethrectomy as part of:*
>   *complete cystectomy (57.79)*
>   *pelvic evisceration (68.8)*
>   *radical cystectomy (57.71)*

58.31 Endoscopic excision or destruction of lesion or tissue of urethra
Fulguration of urethral lesion

58.39 Other local excision or destruction of lesion or tissue of urethra
Excision of:
   congenital valve ⎫
   lesion   ⎬ of urethra
   stricture   ⎭

Urethrectomy
> EXCLUDES   *that by endoscopic appoach (58.31)*

✓4ᵗʰ **58.4 Repair of urethra**
> EXCLUDES   *repair of current obstetric laceration (75.61)*

58.41 Suture of laceration of urethra

58.42 Closure of urethrostomy

58.43 Closure of other fistula of urethra
> EXCLUDES   *repair of urethroperineovesical fistula (57.84)*

58.44 Reanastomosis of urethra
Anastomosis of urethra
DEF: Repair of severed urethra.

58.45 Repair of hypospadias or epispadias
AHA: 3Q, '97, 6; 4Q, '96, 35

DEF: Repair of abnormal urethral opening.

58.46 Other reconstruction of urethra
Urethral construction

58.47 Urethral meatoplasty
DEF: Reconstruction of urethral opening.

58.49 Other repair of urethra
Benenenti rotation of bulbous urethra
Repair of old obstetric laceration of urethra
Urethral plication
> EXCLUDES   *repair of:*
>   *current obstetric laceration (75.61)*
>   *urethrocele (70.50-70.51)*

58.5 Release of urethral stricture
Cutting of urethral sphincter
Internal urethral meatotomy
Urethrolysis
AHA: 1Q, '97, 13

58.6 Dilation of urethra
Dilation of urethrovesical junction
Passage of sounds through urethra
Removal of calculus from urethra without incision
> EXCLUDES   *urethral calibration (89.29)*
AHA: 1Q, '01, 14; 1Q, '97, 13

✓4ᵗʰ **58.9 Other operations on urethra and periurethral tissue**
58.91 Incision of periurethral tissue
Drainage of bulbourethral gland
DEF: Incision of tissue around urethra.

58.92 Excision of periurethral tissue
> EXCLUDES   *biopsy of periurethral tissue (58.24)*
> *lysis of periurethral adhesions (59.11-59.12)*

58.93 Implantation of artificial urinary sphincter [AUS]
Placement of inflatable:
   urethral sphincter
   bladder sphincter
Removal with replacement of sphincter device [AUS]
With pump and/or reservoir

58.99 Other
Repair of inflatable sphincter pump and/or reservoir
Surgical correction of hydraulic pressure of inflatable sphincter device
Removal of inflatable urinary sphincter without replacement
> EXCLUDES   *removal of:*
>   *intraluminal foreign body from urethra without incision (98.19)*
>   *urethral stent (97.65)*

✓3ʳᵈ **59 Other operations on urinary tract**
Code also any application or administration of an adhesion barrier substance (99.77)

✓4ᵗʰ **59.0 Dissection of retroperitoneal tissue**
59.00 Retroperitoneal dissection, not otherwise specified

59.02 Other lysis of perirenal or periureteral adhesions
> EXCLUDES   *that by laparoscope (59.03)*

59.03 Laparoscopic lysis of perirenal or periureteral adhesions

59.09 Other incision of perirenal or periureteral tissue
Exploration of perinephric area
Incision of perirenal abscess
DEF: Exploration of the perinephric area: Exam of tissue around the kidney by incision.

DEF: Incision of perirenal abscess: Incising abscess in tissue around kidney.

✓4ᵗʰ **59.1 Incision of perivesical tissue**
DEF: Incising tissue around bladder.

59.11 Other lysis of perivesical adhesions
59.12 Laparoscopic lysis of perivesical adhesions
59.19 Other incision of perivesical tissue
Exploration of perivesical tissue
Incision of hematoma of space of Retzius
Retropubic exploration

✓4ᵗʰ **59.2 Diagnostic procedures on perirenal and perivesical tissue**
59.21 Biopsy of perirenal or perivesical tissue
59.29 Other diagnostic procedures on perirenal tissue, perivesical tissue, and retroperitoneum
> EXCLUDES   *microscopic examination of specimen from:*
>   *perirenal tissue (91.21-91.29)*
>   *perivesical tissue (91.31-91.39)*
>   *retroperitoneum NEC (91.11-91.19)*
>   *retroperitoneal x-ray (88.14-88.16)*

✓3ʳᵈ ✓4ᵗʰ Additional Digit Required   RUG III Special Care Procedure   RUG III Clinically Complex Procedure   RUG III Extensive Services Procedure   RUG III Rehab Procedure

2006 ICD•9•CM   **Volume 3 — 159**

Operations on the Urinary System

59.3–59.99

59.3   **Plication of urethrovesical junction**
Kelly-Kennedy operation on urethra
Kelly-Stoeckel urethral plication

DEF: Suturing a tuck in tissues around urethra at junction with bladder; changes angle of junction and provides support.

59.4   **Suprapubic sling operation**
Goebel-Frangenheim-Stoeckel urethrovesical suspension
Millin-Read urethrovesical suspension
Oxford operation for urinary incontinence
Urethrocystopexy by suprapubic suspension

DEF: Suspension of urethra from suprapubic periosteum to restore support to bladder and urethra.

59.5   **Retropubic urethral suspension**
Burch procedure
Marshall-Marchetti-Krantz operation
Suture of periurethral tissue to symphysis pubis
Urethral suspension NOS

AHA: 1Q, '97, 11

DEF: Suspension of urethra from pubic bone with suture placed from symphysis pubis to paraurethral tissues; elevates urethrovesical angle, restores urinary continence.

59.6   **Paraurethral suspension**
Pereyra paraurethral suspension
Periurethral suspension

DEF: Suspension of bladder neck from fibrous membranes of anterior abdominal wall; upward traction applied; changes angle of urethra, improves urinary control.

√4ᵗʰ **59.7**   **Other repair of urinary stress incontinence**

59.71   **Levator muscle operation for urethrovesical suspension**
Cystourethropexy with levator muscle sling
Gracilis muscle transplant for urethrovesical suspension
Pubococcygeal sling

59.72   **Injection of implant into urethra and/or bladder neck**
Collagen implant
Endoscopic injection of implant
Fat implant
Polytef implant

AHA: 4Q, '95, 72, 73

DEF: Injection of collagen into submucosal tissues to increase tissue bulk and improve urinary control.

59.79   **Other**
Anterior urethropexy
Repair of stress incontinence NOS
Tudor "rabbit ear" urethropexy

AHA: 2Q, '01, 20; 1Q, '00, 14, 15

DEF: Pubovaginal sling for treatment of stress incontinence: A strip of fascia is harvested and the vaginal epithelium is mobilized and then sutured to the midline at the urethral level to the rectus muscle to create a sling supporting the bladder.

DEF: Vaginal wall sling with bone anchors for treatment of stress incontinence: A sling for the bladder is formed by a suture attachment of vaginal wall to the abdominal wall. In addition, a suture is run from the vagina to a bone anchor placed in the pubic bone.

DEF: Transvaginal endoscopic bladder neck suspension for treatment of stress incontinence: Endoscopic surgical suturing of the vaginal epithelium and the pubocervical fascia at the bladder neck level on both sides of the urethra. Two supporting sutures are run from the vagina to an anchor placed in the pubic bone on each side.

59.8   **Ureteral catheterization**
Drainage of kidney by catheter
Insertion of ureteral stent
Ureterovesical orifice dilation
Code also any ureterotomy (56.2)

EXCLUDES   that for:
transurethral removal of calculus or clot from ureter and renal pelvis (56.0)
retrograde pyelogram (87.74)

AHA: 2Q, '03, 11; 3Q, '00, 7; 1Q, '89, 1; S-O, '86, 10

√4ᵗʰ **59.9**   **Other operations on urinary system**
EXCLUDES   nonoperative removal of therapeutic device (97.61-97.69)

59.91   **Excision of perirenal or perivesical tissue**
EXCLUDES   biopsy of perirenal or perivesical tissue (59.21)

59.92   **Other operations on perirenal or perivesical tissue**

59.93   **Replacement of ureterostomy tube**
Change of ureterostomy tube
Reinsertion of ureterostomy tube
EXCLUDES   nonoperative removal of ureterostomy tube (97.62)

59.94   **Replacement of cystostomy tube**
EXCLUDES   nonoperative removal of cystostomy tube (97.63)

59.95   **Ultrasonic fragmentation of urinary stones**
Shattered urinary stones
EXCLUDES   percutaneous nephrostomy with fragmentation (55.04)
shockwave disintegration (98.51)

AHA: 1Q, '89, 1; S-O, '86, 11

59.99   **Other**
EXCLUDES   instillation of medication into urinary tract (96.49)
irrigation of urinary tract (96.45-96.48)

N Newborn Age: 0   P Pediatric Age: 0-17   M Maternity Age: 12-55   A Adult Age: 15-124   Adj Adjunct Code   ►◄ Revised Text   ● New Code   ▲ Revised Code Title

11. OPERATIONS ON THE MALE GENITAL ORGANS (60-64)

☑3ʳᵈ 60 Operations on prostate and seminal vesicles

Code also any application or administration of an adhesion barrier substance (99.77)

INCLUDES operations on periprostatic tissue

EXCLUDES *that associated with radical cystectomy (57.71)*

60.0 Incision of prostate ♂
Drainage of prostatic abscess
Prostatolithotomy
EXCLUDES *drainage of periprostatic tissue only (60.81)*

☑4ᵗʰ 60.1 Diagnostic procedures on prostate and seminal vesicles

60.11 Closed [percutaneous] [needle] biopsy of prostate ♂
Approach:
transrectal
transurethral
Punch biopsy
DEF: Excision of prostate tissue by closed technique for biopsy.

60.12 Open biopsy of prostate ♂

60.13 Closed [percutaneous] biopsy of seminal vesicles ♂
Needle biopsy of seminal vesicles

60.14 Open biopsy of seminal vesicles ♂

60.15 Biopsy of periprostatic tissue ♂

60.18 Other diagnostic procedures on prostate and periprostatic tissue ♂
EXCLUDES *microscopic examination of specimen from prostate (91.31-91.39)*
x-ray of prostate (87.92)

60.19 Other diagnostic procedures on seminal vesicles ♂
EXCLUDES *microscopic examination of specimen from seminal vesicles (91.31-91.39)*
x-ray:
contrast seminal vesiculogram (87.91)
other (87.92)

☑4ᵗʰ 60.2 Transurethral prostatectomy
EXCLUDES *local excision of lesion of prostate (60.61)*
AHA: 2Q, '94, 9; 3Q, '92, 13

60.21 Transurethral (ultrasound) guided laser induced prostatectomy (TULIP) ♂
Ablation (contact) (noncontact) by laser
AHA: 4Q, '95, 7

60.29 Other transurethral prostatectomy ♂
Excision of median bar by transurethral approach
Transurethral electrovaporization of prostate (TEVAP)
Transurethral enucleative procedure
Transurethral prostatectomy NOS
Transurethral resection of prostate (TURP)
DEF: Excision of median bar by transurethral approach: Removal of fibrous structure of prostate.

AHA: 3Q, '97, 3

Transurethral Prostatectomy

Resectoscope

Adenomatous prostate

60.3 Suprapubic prostatectomy ♂
Transvesical prostatectomy
EXCLUDES *local excision of lesion of prostate (60.61)*
radical prostatectomy (60.5)
DEF: Resection of prostate through incision in abdomen above pubic arch.

60.4 Retropubic prostatectomy ♂
EXCLUDES *local excision of lesion of prostate (60.61)*
radical prostatectomy (60.5)
DEF: Removal of the prostate using an abdominal approach with direct cutting into prostatic capsule.

60.5 Radical prostatectomy ♂
Prostatovesiculectomy
Radical prostatectomy by any approach
EXCLUDES *cystoprostatectomy (57.71)*
AHA: 3Q, '93, 12

DEF: Radical prostatectomy: Removal of prostate, epididymis and vas ampullae.

DEF: Prostatovesiculectomy: Removal of prostate and epididymis.

☑4ᵗʰ 60.6 Other prostatectomy

60.61 Local excision of lesion of prostate ♂
Excision of prostatic lesion by any approach
EXCLUDES *biopsy of prostate (60.11-60.12)*

60.62 Perineal prostatectomy ♂
Cryoablation of prostate
Cryoprostatectomy
Cryosurgery of prostate
Radical cryosurcial ablation of prostate (RCSA)
EXCLUDES *local excision of lesion of prostate (60.61)*

AHA: 4Q, '95, 71

DEF: Excision of prostate tissue through incision between scrotum and anus.

60.69 Other ♂

☑4ᵗʰ 60.7 Operations on seminal vesicles

60.71 Percutaneous aspiration of seminal vesicle ♂
EXCLUDES *needle biopsy of seminal vesicle (60.13)*

60.72 Incision of seminal vesicle ♂

60.73 Excision of seminal vesicle ♂
Excision of Müllerian duct cyst
Spermatocystectomy
EXCLUDES *biopsy of seminal vesicle (60.13-60.14)*
prostatovesiculectomy (60.5)

☑3ʳᵈ
☑4ᵗʰ Additional Digit Required   RUG III Special Care Procedure   RUG III Clinically Complex Procedure   RUG III Extensive Services Procedure   RUG III Rehab Procedure

2006 ICD•9•CM

Volume 3 — 161

Operations on the Male Genital Organs

60–60.73

Operations on the Male Genital Organs

60.79–62.41

60.79   Other operations on seminal vesicles   ♂

✓4ᵗʰ **60.8**   Incision or excision of periprostatic tissue

60.81   Incision of periprostatic tissue   ♂
> Drainage of periprostatic abscess

60.82   Excision of periprostatic tissue   ♂
> Excision of lesion of periprostatic tissue
> EXCLUDES   biopsy of periprostatic tissue (60.15)

✓4ᵗʰ **60.9**   Other operations on prostate

60.91   Percutaneous aspiration of prostate   ♂
> EXCLUDES   needle biopsy of prostate (60.11)

60.92   Injection into prostate   ♂

60.93   Repair of prostate   ♂

60.94   Control of (postoperative) hemorrhage of prostate   ♂
> Coagulation of prostatic bed
> Cystoscopy for control of prostatic hemorrhage

60.95   Transurethral balloon dilation of the prostatic urethra   ♂
> AHA: 4Q, '91, 23
>
> DEF: Insertion and inflation of balloon to stretch prostate passage.

60.96   Transurethral destruction of prostate tissue by microwave thermotherapy   ♂
> Transurethral microwave thermotherapy (TUMT) of prostate
> EXCLUDES   Prostatectomy:
>   other (60.61-60.69)
>   radical (60.5)
>   retropubic (60.4)
>   suprapubic (60.3)
>   transurethral (60.21-60.29)
>
> AHA: 4Q, '00, 67

60.97   Other transurethral destruction of prostate tissue by other thermotherapy   ♂
> Radiofrequency thermotherapy
> Transurethral needle ablation (TUNA) of prostate
> EXCLUDES   Prostatectomy:
>   other (60.61-60.69)
>   radical (60.5)
>   retropubic (60.4)
>   suprapubic (60.3)
>   transurethral (60.21-60.29)
>
> AHA: 4Q, '00, 67

60.99   Other   ♂
> EXCLUDES   prostatic massage (99.94)
>
> AHA: 3Q, '90, 12

✓3ʳᵈ **61**   Operations on scrotum and tunica vaginalis

61.0   Incision and drainage of scrotum and tunica vaginalis   ♂
> EXCLUDES   percutaneous aspiration of hydrocele (61.91)

✓4ᵗʰ **61.1**   Diagnostic procedures on scrotum and tunica vaginalis

61.11   Biopsy of scrotum or tunica vaginalis   ♂

61.19   Other diagnostic procedures on scrotum and tunica vaginalis   ♂

61.2   Excision of hydrocele (of tunica vaginalis)   ♂
> Bottle repair of hydrocele of tunica vaginalis
> EXCLUDES   percutaneous aspiration of hydrocele (61.91)
>
> DEF: Removal of fluid collected in serous membrane of testes.

Hydrocelectomy

Scrotal skin incised

Sac opened

Fluid-filled sac mobilized

Excess tissue trimmed

Testis

Remaining sacular tissue folded back and sewn to itself to preclude recurrence ("bottle" procedure)

61.3   Excision or destruction of lesion or tissue of scrotum   ♂
> Fulguration of lesion ⎱
> Reduction of elephantiasis ⎰ of scrotum
> Partial scrotectomy
> EXCLUDES   biopsy of scrotum (61.11)
>   scrotal fistulectomy (61.42)

✓4ᵗʰ **61.4**   Repair of scrotum and tunica vaginalis

61.41   Suture of laceration of scrotum and tunica vaginalis   ♂

61.42   Repair of scrotal fistula   ♂

61.49   Other repair of scrotum and tunica vaginalis   ♂
> Reconstruction with rotational or pedicle flaps

✓4ᵗʰ **61.9**   Other operations on scrotum and tunica vaginalis

61.91   Percutaneous aspiration of tunica vaginalis   ♂
> Aspiration of hydrocele of tunica vaginalis

61.92   Excision of lesion of tunica vaginalis other than hydrocele   ♂
> Excision of hematocele of tunica vaginalis
> DEF: Removal of blood collected in tunica vaginalis.

61.99   Other   ♂
> EXCLUDES   removal of foreign body from scrotum without incision (98.24)

✓3ʳᵈ **62**   Operations on testes

62.0   Incision of testis   ♂

✓4ᵗʰ **62.1**   Diagnostic procedures on testes

62.11   Closed [percutaneous] [needle] biopsy of testis   ♂

62.12   Open biopsy of testis   ♂

62.19   Other diagnostic procedures on testes   ♂

62.2   Excision or destruction of testicular lesion   ♂
> Excision of appendix testis
> Excision of cyst of Morgagni in the male
> EXCLUDES   biopsy of testis (62.11-62.12)

62.3   Unilateral orchiectomy   ♂
> Orchidectomy (with epididymectomy) NOS

✓4ᵗʰ **62.4**   Bilateral orchiectomy
> Male castration
> Radical bilateral orchiectomy (with epididymectomy)
> Code also any synchronous lymph node dissection (40.3, 40.5)
>
> DEF: Removal of both testes.
>
> DEF: Radical bilateral orchiectomy (with epididymectomy): Excision of both testes and structures that store sperm.

62.41   Removal of both testes at same operative episode   ♂
> Bilateral orchiectomy NOS

N Newborn Age: 0   P Pediatric Age: 0-17   M Maternity Age: 12-55   A Adult Age: 15-124   Adj Adjunct Code   ◄► Revised Text   ● New Code   ▲ Revised Code Title

162 — Volume 3   *2006 ICD•9•CM*

62.42   **Removal of remaining testis** ♂
Removal of solitary testis

62.5   **Orchiopexy** ♂
Mobilization and replacement of testis in scrotum
Orchiopexy with detorsion of testis
Torek (-Bevan) operation (orchidopexy) (first stage) (second stage)
Transplantation to and fixation of testis in scrotum

DEF: Fixation of testis in scrotum.

DEF: Orchiopexy with detorsion of testis: Fixation and placement of testis in scrotum after correcting angle.

DEF: Torek operation (first stage) (second stage): Transfer of congenitally undescended testis from inguinal canal to scrotum.

DEF: Transplantation to and fixation of testis in scrotum: Transfer of displaced testis to scrotum.

✓4th **62.6**   **Repair of testes**
EXCLUDES   reduction of torsion (63.52)

62.61   **Suture of laceration of testis** ♂

62.69   **Other repair of testis** ♂
Testicular graft

62.7   **Insertion of testicular prosthesis** ♂

✓4th **62.9**   **Other operations on testes**

62.91   **Aspiration of testis** ♂
EXCLUDES   percutaneous biopsy of testis (62.11)

62.92   **Injection of therapeutic substance into testis** ♂

62.99   **Other** ♂

✓3rd **63**   **Operations on spermatic cord, epididymis, and vas deferens**

✓4th **63.0**   **Diagnostic procedures on spermatic cord, epididymis, and vas deferens**

63.01   **Biopsy of spermatic cord, epididymis, or vas deferens** ♂

63.09   **Other diagnostic procedures on spermatic cord, epididymis, and vas deferens** ♂
EXCLUDES   contrast epididymogram (87.93)
contrast vasogram (87.94)
other x-ray of epididymis and vas deferens (87.95)

63.1   **Excision of varicocele and hydrocele of spermatic cord** ♂
High ligation of spermatic vein
Hydrocelectomy of canal of Nuck

DEF: Removal of a swollen vein and collected fluid from spermatic cord.

DEF: High ligation of spermatic vein: Tying off of spermatic vein.

DEF: Hydrocelectomy of canal of Nuck: Removal of fluid collected from serous membrane of inguinal canal.

Varicocelectomy

Ligated veins
Pampiniform plexus
Vas deferens
Artery
Ligated veins

63.2   **Excision of cyst of epididymis** ♂
Spermatocelectomy

63.3   **Excision of other lesion or tissue of spermatic cord and epididymis** ♂
Excision of appendix epididymis
EXCLUDES   biopsy of spermatic cord or epididymis (63.01)

63.4   **Epididymectomy** ♂
EXCLUDES   that synchronous with orchiectomy (62.3-62.42)

✓4th **63.5**   **Repair of spermatic cord and epididymis**

63.51   **Suture of laceration of spermatic cord and epididymis** ♂

63.52   **Reduction of torsion of testis or spermatic cord** ♂
EXCLUDES   that associated with orchiopexy (62.5)

DEF: Correction of twisted testicle or spermatic cord.

63.53   **Transplantation of spermatic cord** ♂

63.59   **Other repair of spermatic cord and epididymis** ♂

63.6   **Vasotomy** ♂
Vasostomy

DEF: Vasotomy: Incision of ducts carrying sperm from testicles.

DEF: Vasostomy: Creation of an opening into duct.

✓4th **63.7**   **Vasectomy and ligation of vas deferens**

63.70   **Male sterilization procedure, not otherwise specified** ♂

63.71   **Ligation of vas deferens** ♂
Crushing of vas deferens
Division of vas deferens

63.72   **Ligation of spermatic cord** ♂

63.73   **Vasectomy** ♂
AHA: 2Q, '98, 13

✓4th **63.8**   **Repair of vas deferens and epididymis**

63.81   **Suture of laceration of vas deferens and epididymis** ♂

63.82   **Reconstruction of surgically divided vas deferens** ♂

63.83   **Epididymovasostomy** ♂
DEF: Creation of new connection between vas deferens and epididymis.

63.84   **Removal of ligature from vas deferens** ♂

63.85   **Removal of valve from vas deferens** ♂

63.89   **Other repair of vas deferens and epididymis** ♂

✓4th **63.9**   **Other operations on spermatic cord, epididymis, and vas deferens**

63.91   **Aspiration of spermatocele** ♂
DEF: Puncture of cystic distention of epididymis.

63.92   **Epididymotomy** ♂
DEF: Incision of epididymis.

63.93   **Incision of spermatic cord** ♂
DEF: Incision into sperm storage structure.

63.94   **Lysis of adhesions of spermatic cord** ♂

63.95   **Insertion of valve in vas deferens** ♂

63.99   **Other** ♂

✓3rd **64**   **Operations on penis**
INCLUDES   operations on:
corpora cavernosa
glans penis
prepuce

64.0   **Circumcision** ♂
DEF: Removal of penis foreskin.

Operations on the Male Genital Organs

62.42–64.0

Operations on the Male Genital Organs

64.1–64.99

☑4ᵗʰ **64.1** **Diagnostic procedures on the penis**
 64.11 **Biopsy of penis** ♂
 64.19 **Other diagnostic procedures on penis** ♂
 64.2 **Local excision or destruction of lesion of penis** ♂
 EXCLUDES *biopsy of penis (64.11)*
 64.3 **Amputation of penis** ♂
☑4ᵗʰ **64.4** **Repair and plastic operation on penis**
 64.41 **Suture of laceration of penis** ♂
 64.42 **Release of chordee** ♂
 AHA: 4Q, '96, 34

 DEF: Correction of downward displacement of penis.

 64.43 **Construction of penis** ♂
 64.44 **Reconstruction of penis** ♂
 64.45 **Replantation of penis** ♂
 Reattachment of amputated penis
 64.49 **Other repair of penis** ♂
 EXCLUDES *repair of epispadias and hypospadias (58.45)*
 64.5 **Operations for sex transformation, not elsewhere classified** ♂
☑4ᵗʰ **64.9** **Other operations on male genital organs**
 64.91 **Dorsal or lateral slit of prepuce** ♂
 64.92 **Incision of penis** ♂
 64.93 **Division of penile adhesions** ♂
 64.94 **Fitting of external prosthesis of penis** ♂
 Penile prosthesis NOS
 64.95 **Insertion or replacement of non-inflatable penile prosthesis** ♂
 Insertion of semi-rigid rod prosthesis into shaft of penis
 EXCLUDES *external penile prosthesis (64.94)*
 inflatable penile prosthesis (64.97)
 plastic repair, penis (64.43-64.49)
 that associated with:
 construction (64.43)
 reconstruction (64.44)
 64.96 **Removal of internal prosthesis of penis** ♂
 Removal without replacement of non-inflatable or inflatable penile prosthesis

 64.97 **Insertion or replacement of inflatable penile prosthesis** ♂
 Insertion of cylinders into shaft of penis and placement of pump and reservoir
 EXCLUDES *external penile prosthesis (64.94)*
 non-inflatable penile prosthesis (64.95)
 plastic repair, penis (64.43-64.49)

 AHA: 2Q, '90, 26

 64.98 **Other operations on penis** ♂
 Corpora cavernosa-corpus spongiosum shunt
 Corpora-saphenous shunt
 Irrigation of corpus cavernosum
 EXCLUDES *removal of foreign body:*
 intraluminal (98.19)
 without incision (98.24)
 stretching of foreskin (99.95)

 AHA: 3Q, '92, 9

 DEF: Corpora cavernosa-corpus spongiosum shunt: Insertion of shunt between erectile tissues of penis.

 DEF: Corpora-saphenous shunt: Insertion of shunt between erectile tissue and vein of penis.

 DEF: Irrigation of corpus cavernosum: Washing of erectile tissue forming dorsum and side of penis.

 64.99 **Other** ♂
 EXCLUDES *collection of sperm for artificial insemination (99.96)*

N Newborn Age: 0   P Pediatric Age: 0-17   M Maternity Age: 12-55   A Adult Age: 15-124   **Adj** Adjunct Code   ◄► Revised Text   ● New Code   ▲ Revised Code Title

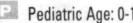

164 — Volume 3   *2006 ICD•9•CM*

12. OPERATIONS ON THE FEMALE GENITAL ORGANS (65-71)

√3rd **65 Operations on ovary**

Code also any application or administration of an adhesion barrier substance (99.77)

√4th **65.0 Oophorotomy**

Salpingo-oophorotomy

DEF: Incision into ovary.

DEF: Salpingo-oophorotomy: Incision into ovary and the fallopian tube.

65.01 Laparoscopic oophorotomy   ♀
65.09 Other oophorotomy   ♀

√4th **65.1 Diagnostic procedures on ovaries**

65.11 Aspiration biopsy of ovary   ♀
65.12 Other biopsy of ovary   ♀
65.13 Laparoscopic biopsy of ovary   ♀

AHA: 4Q, '96, 67

65.14 Other laparoscopic diagnostic procedures on ovaries   ♀
65.19 Other diagnostic procedures on ovaries   ♀

EXCLUDES   microscopic examination of specimen from ovary (91.41-91.49)

√4th **65.2 Local excision or destruction of ovarian lesion or tissue**

65.21 Marsupialization of ovarian cyst   ♀

EXCLUDES   that by laparoscope (65.23)

DEF: Exteriorized cyst to outside by incising anterior wall and suturing cut edges to create open pouch.

65.22 Wedge resection of ovary   ♀

EXCLUDES   that by laparoscope (65.24)

65.23 Laparoscopic marsupialization of ovarian cyst   ♀
65.24 Laparoscopic wedge resection of ovary   ♀
65.25 Other laparoscopic local excision or destruction of ovary   ♀
65.29 Other local excision or destruction of ovary   ♀

Bisection
Cauterization } of ovary
Partial excision

EXCLUDES   biopsy of ovary (65.11-65.13)
that by laparoscope (65.25)

√4th **65.3 Unilateral oophorectomy**

65.31 Laparoscopic unilateral oophorectomy   ♀
65.39 Other unilateral oophorectomy   ♀

EXCLUDES   that by laparoscope (65.31)

AHA: 4Q, '96, 66

√4th **65.4 Unilateral salpingo-oophorectomy**

65.41 Laparoscopic unilateral salpingo-oophorectomy   ♀

AHA: 4Q, '96, 67

65.49 Other unilateral salpingo-oophorectomy   ♀

Oophorectomy

Fallopian tube
Fimbria
Ovary
Ovarian cyst

√4th **65.5 Bilateral oophorectomy**

65.51 Other removal of both ovaries at same operative episode   ♀

Female castration

EXCLUDES   that by laparoscope (65.53)

65.52 Other removal of remaining ovary   ♀

Removal of solitary ovary

EXCLUDES   that by laparoscope (65.54)

65.53 Laparoscopic removal of both ovaries at same operative eisode   ♀
65.54 Laparoscopic removal of remaining ovary   ♀

√4th **65.6 Bilateral salpingo-oophorectomy**

65.61 Other removal of both ovaries and tubes at same operative episode   ♀

EXCLUDES   that by laparoscope (65.53)

AHA: 4Q, '96, 65

65.62 Other removal of remaining ovary and tube   ♀

Removal of solitary ovary and tube

EXCLUDES   that by laparoscope (65.54)

65.63 Laparoscopic removal of both ovaries and tubes at the same operative episode   ♀

AHA: 4Q, '96, 68

65.64 Laparoscopic removal of remaining ovary and tube   ♀

√4th **65.7 Repair of ovary**

EXCLUDES   salpingo-oophorostomy (66.72)

65.71 Other simple suture of ovary   ♀

EXCLUDES   that by laparoscope (65.74)

65.72 Other reimplantation of ovary   ♀

EXCLUDES   that by laparoscope (65.75)

DEF: Grafting and repositioning of ovary at same site.

65.73 Other salpingo-oophoroplasty   ♀

EXCLUDES   that by laparoscope (65.76)

65.74 Laparoscopic simple suture of ovary   ♀
65.75 Laparoscopic reimplantation of ovary   ♀
65.76 Laparoscopic salpingo-oophoroplasty   ♀
65.79 Other repair of ovary   ♀

Oophoropexy

√4th **65.8 Lysis of adhesions of ovary and fallopian tube**

65.81 Laparoscopic lysis of adhesions of ovary and fallopian tube   ♀

AHA: 4Q, '96, 67

65.89 Other lysis of adhesions of ovary and fallopian tube   ♀

EXCLUDES   that by laparoscope (65.81)

√4th **65.9 Other operations on ovary**

65.91 Aspiration of ovary   ♀

EXCLUDES   aspiration biopsy of ovary (65.11)

65.92 Transplantation of ovary   ♀

EXCLUDES   reimplantation of ovary (65.72, 65.75)

65.93 Manual rupture of ovarian cyst   ♀

DEF: Breaking up an ovarian cyst using manual technique or blunt instruments.

65.94 Ovarian denervation   ♀

DEF: Destruction of nerve tracts to ovary.

65.95 Release of torsion of ovary   ♀
65.99 Other   ♀

Ovarian drilling

AHA: N-D, '86, 9

√3rd
√4th Additional Digit Required   RUG III Special Care Procedure   RUG III Clinically Complex Procedure   RUG III Extensive Services Procedure   RUG III Rehab Procedure

2006 ICD•9•CM   Volume 3 — 165

Operations on the Female Genital Organs

66–66.91

Endoscopic Ligation of Fallopian Tubes

Uterus
Ovary
Ligated fallopian tube
Monitor view

Laparoscopic procedure

√3rd **66**   **Operations on fallopian tubes**
Code also any application or administration of an adhesion barrier substance (99.77)

√4th **66.0**   **Salpingotomy and salpingostomy**
    66.01   **Salpingotomy**   ♀
    66.02   **Salpingostomy**   ♀

√4th **66.1**   **Diagnostic procedures on fallopian tubes**
    66.11   **Biopsy of fallopian tube**   ♀
    66.19   **Other diagnostic procedures on fallopian tubes**   ♀

> EXCLUDES   microscopic examination of specimen from fallopian tubes (91.41-91.49)
> radiography of fallopian tubes (87.82-87.83, 87.85)
> Rubin's test (66.8)

√4th **66.2**   **Bilateral endoscopic destruction or occlusion of fallopian tubes**

> INCLUDES   bilateral endoscopic destruction or occlusion of fallopian tubes by:
>   culdoscopy   laparoscopy
>   endoscopy   peritoneoscopy
>   hysteroscopy
> endoscopic destruction of solitary fallopian tube

DEF: Endoscopic blockage or destruction of both fallopian tubes.

DEF: Bilateral endoscopic destruction or occlusion of fallopian tubes by:

Culdoscopy: Endoscopic insertion through posterior structure of vagina.
Hysteroscopy: Endoscopic insertion through uterus.
Laparoscopy: Endoscopic insertion through abdomen.
Peritoneoscopy: Endoscopic insertion through abdominal serous membrane cavity.
Endoscopic destruction of solitary fallopian tube: Endoscopic destruction of one fallopian tube.

    66.21   **Bilateral endoscopic ligation and crushing of fallopian tubes**   ♀
    66.22   **Bilateral endoscopic ligation and division of fallopian tubes**   ♀
    66.29   **Other bilateral endoscopic destruction or occlusion of fallopian tubes**   ♀

√4th **66.3**   **Other bilateral destruction or occlusion of fallopian tubes**

> INCLUDES   destruction of solitary fallopian tube
> EXCLUDES   endoscopic destruction or occlusion of fallopian tubes (66.21-66.29)

    66.31   **Other bilateral ligation and crushing of fallopian tubes**   ♀
    66.32   **Other bilateral ligation and division of fallopian tubes**   ♀
        Pomeroy operation
    66.39   **Other bilateral destruction or occlusion of fallopian tubes**   ♀
        Female sterilization operation NOS

66.4   **Total unilateral salpingectomy**   ♀

√4th **66.5**   **Total bilateral salpingectomy**   ♀

> EXCLUDES   bilateral partial salpingectomy for sterilization (66.39)
> that with oophorectomy (65.61-65.64)

    66.51   **Removal of both fallopian tubes at same operative episode**   ♀
    66.52   **Removal of remaining fallopian tube**   ♀
        Removal of solitary fallopian tube

√4th **66.6**   **Other salpingectomy**

> INCLUDES   salpingectomy by:
>   cauterization
>   coagulation
>   electrocoagulation
>   excision
> EXCLUDES   fistulectomy (66.73)

    66.61   **Excision or destruction of lesion of fallopian tube**   ♀

> EXCLUDES   biopsy of fallopian tube (66.11)

    66.62   **Salpingectomy with removal of tubal pregnancy**   ♀
        Code also any synchronous oophorectomy (65.31, 65.39)

        AHA: 3Q, '95, 15; S-O, '85, 14

    66.63   **Bilateral partial salpingectomy, not otherwise specified**   ♀
    66.69   **Other partial salpingectomy**   ♀

√4th **66.7**   **Repair of fallopian tube**
    66.71   **Simple suture of fallopian tube**   ♀
    66.72   **Salpingo-oophorostomy**   ♀
    66.73   **Salpingo-salpingostomy**   ♀
    66.74   **Salpingo-uterostomy**   ♀
    66.79   **Other repair of fallopian tube**   ♀
        Graft of fallopian tube
        Reopening of divided fallopian tube
        Salpingoplasty

        AHA: 2Q, '95, 10

DEF: Graft of fallopian: Repair of fallopian tube with implanted graft.

DEF: Reopening of divided fallopian tube: Reconnection of severed fallopian tube to restore patency.

DEF: Salpingoplasty: Plastic reconstruction of fallopian tube defect.

66.8   **Insufflation of fallopian tube**   ♀
    Insufflation of fallopian tube with:
     air
     dye
     gas
     saline
    Rubin's test

> EXCLUDES   insufflation of therapeutic agent (66.95)
> that for hysterosalpingography (87.82-87.83)

DEF: Forceful blowing of gas or liquid into fallopian tubes.

DEF: Rubin's test: Introduction of carbon dioxide gas into fallopian tubes.

√4th **66.9**   **Other operations on fallopian tubes**
    66.91   **Aspiration of fallopian tube**   ♀

N Newborn Age: 0   P Pediatric Age: 0-17   M Maternity Age: 12-55   A Adult Age: 15-124   Adj Adjunct Code   ►◄ Revised Text   ● New Code   ▲ Revised Code Title

66.92 Unilateral destruction or occlusion of fallopian tube ♀
> **EXCLUDES** *that of solitary tube (66.21-66.39)*

66.93 Implantation or replacement of prosthesis of fallopian tube ♀

66.94 Removal of prosthesis of fallopian tube ♀

66.95 Insufflation of therapeutic agent into fallopian tubes ♀

66.96 Dilation of fallopian tube ♀

66.97 Burying of fimbriae in uterine wall ♀
> **DEF:** Implantation of fallopian tube, fringed edges into uterine wall.

66.99 Other ♀
> **EXCLUDES** *lysis of adhesions of ovary and tube (65.81, 65.89)*

> **AHA:** 2Q, '94, 11

√3rd **67** **Operations on cervix**
> Code also any application or administration of an adhesion barrier substance (99.77)

67.0 Dilation of cervical canal
> **EXCLUDES** *dilation and curettage (69.01-69.09)*
> *that for induction of labor (73.1)*

√4th **67.1** Diagnostic procedures on cervix

67.11 Endocervical biopsy ♀
> **EXCLUDES** *conization of cervix (67.2)*

67.12 Other cervical biopsy ♀
> Punch biopsy of cervix NOS
> **EXCLUDES** *conization of cervix (67.2)*

67.19 Other diagnostic procedures on cervix ♀
> **EXCLUDES** *microscopic examination of specimen from cervix (91.41-91.49)*

67.2 Conization of cervix ♀
> **EXCLUDES** *that by:*
> *cryosurgery (67.33)*
> *electrosurgery (67.32)*

> **DEF:** Removal of cone-shaped section from distal cervix; cervical function preserved.

√4th **67.3** Other excision or destruction of lesion or tissue of cervix

67.31 Marsupialization of cervical cyst ♀
> **DEF:** Incision and then suturing open of a cyst in the neck of the uterus.

67.32 Destruction of lesion of cervix by cauterization ♀
> Electroconization of cervix
> LEEP (loop electrosurgical excision procedure)
> LLETZ (large loop excision of the transformation zone)

> **AHA:** 1Q, '98, 3

> **DEF:** Destruction of lesion of uterine neck by applying intense heat.

> **DEF:** Electroconization of cervix: Electrocautery excision of multilayer cone-shaped section from uterine neck.

67.33 Destruction of lesion of cervix by cryosurgery ♀
> Cryoconization of cervix
> **DEF:** Destruction of lesion of uterine neck by freezing.

> **DEF:** Cryoconization of cervix: Excision by freezing of multilayer cone-shaped section of abnormal tissue in uterine neck.

67.39 Other excision or destruction of lesion or tissue of cervix ♀
> **EXCLUDES** *biopsy of cervix (67.11-67.12)*
> *cervical fistulectomy (67.62)*
> *conization of cervix (67.2)*

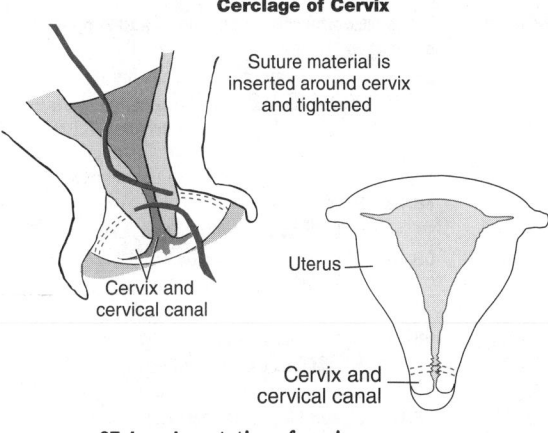

Cerclage of Cervix

Suture material is inserted around cervix and tightened

Cervix and cervical canal

Uterus

Cervix and cervical canal

67.4 Amputation of cervix ♀
> Cervicectomy with synchronous colporrhaphy
> **DEF:** Excision of lower uterine neck.

> **DEF:** Cervicectomy with synchronous colporrhaphy: Excision of lower uterine neck with suture of vaginal stump.

√4th **67.5** Repair of internal cervical os
> **AHA:** 3Q, '00, 11

> **DEF:** Repair of cervical opening defect.

67.51 Transabdominal cerclage of cervix ♀

67.59 Other repair of internal cervical os ♀
> Cerclage of isthmus uteri
> McDonald operation
> Shirodkar operation
> Transvaginal cerclage
> **EXCLUDES** *laparoscopically assisted supracervical hysterectomy [LASH] (68.31)*
> *transabdominal cerclage of cervix (67.51)*

> **DEF:** Cerclage of isthmus uteri: Placement of encircling suture in the constricted part of the between neck and body of uterus.

> **DEF:** Shirodkar operation: Placement of purse-string suture in internal cervical opening.

√4th **67.6** Other repair of cervix
> **EXCLUDES** *repair of current obstetric laceration (75.51)*

67.61 Suture of laceration of cervix ♀

67.62 Repair of fistula of cervix ♀
> Cervicosigmoidal fistulectomy
> **EXCLUDES** *fistulectomy:*
> *cervicovesical (57.84)*
> *ureterocervical (56.84)*
> *vesicocervicovaginal (57.84)*

> **DEF:** Closure of fistula in lower uterus.

> **DEF:** Cervicosigmoidal fistulectomy: Excision of abnormal passage between uterine neck and torsion of large intestine.

67.69 Other repair of cervix ♀
> Repair of old obstetric laceration of cervix

√3rd **68** **Other incision and excision of uterus**
> Code also any application or administration of an adhesion barrier substance (99.77)

68.0 Hysterotomy ♀
> Hysterotomy with removal of hydatidiform mole
> **EXCLUDES** *hysterotomy for termination of pregnancy (74.91)*

> **DEF:** Incision into the uterus.

√3rd √4th Additional Digit Required   RUG III Special Care Procedure   RUG III Clinically Complex Procedure   RUG III Extensive Services Procedure   RUG III Rehab Procedure

2006 ICD•9•CM   **Volume 3 — 167**

Operations on the Female Genital Organs

68.1–68.7

✓4ᵗʰ **68.1** **Diagnostic procedures on uterus and supporting structures**

    68.11 **Digital examination of uterus** ♀
        EXCLUDES *pelvic examination, so described (89.26)*
        postpartal manual exploration of uterine cavity (75.7)

    68.12 **Hysteroscopy** ♀
        EXCLUDES *that with biopsy (68.16)*

    68.13 **Open biopsy of uterus** ♀
        EXCLUDES *closed biopsy of uterus (68.16)*

    68.14 **Open biopsy of uterine ligaments** ♀
        EXCLUDES *closed biopsy of uterine ligaments (68.15)*

    68.15 **Closed biopsy of uterine ligaments** ♀
        Endoscopic (laparoscopy) biopsy of uterine adnexa, except ovary and fallopian tube

    68.16 **Closed biopsy of uterus** ♀
        Endoscopic (laparoscopy) (hysteroscopy) biopsy of uterus
        EXCLUDES *open biopsy of uterus (68.13)*

    68.19 **Other diagnostic procedures on uterus and supporting structures** ♀
        EXCLUDES *diagnostic:*
        aspiration curettage (69.59)
        dilation and curettage (69.09)
        microscopic examination of specimen from uterus (91.41-91.49)
        pelvic examination (89.26)
        radioisotope scan of:
        placenta (92.17)
        uterus (92.19)
        ultrasonography of uterus (88.78-88.79)
        x-ray of uterus (87.81-87.89)

✓4ᵗʰ **68.2** **Excision or destruction of lesion or tissue of uterus**

    68.21 **Division of endometrial synechiae** ♀
        Lysis of intraluminal uterine adhesions
        DEF: Separation of uterine adhesions.
        DEF: Lysis of intraluminal uterine adhesion: Surgical destruction of adhesive, fibrous structures inside uterine cavity.

    68.22 **Incision or excision of congenital septum of uterus** ♀

    68.23 **Endometrial ablation** ♀
        Dilation and curettage
        Hysteroscopic endometrial ablation
        AHA: 4Q, '96, 68
        DEF: Removal or destruction of uterine lining; usually by electrocautery or loop electrosurgical excision procedure (LEEP).

Vaginal Hysterectomy

Total hysterectomy (uterus only removed)

Total hysterectomy with bilateral salpingectomy (uterus and tubes removed)

Total hysterectomy with bilateral salpingo-oophorectomy (uterus, tubes, and ovaries removed)

68.29 **Other excision or destruction of lesion of uterus** ♀
    Uterine myomectomy
    EXCLUDES *biopsy of uterus (68.13)*
    uterine fistulectomy (69.42)
    AHA: 1Q, '96, 14

✓4ᵗʰ **68.3** **Subtotal abdominal hysterectomy**

    68.31 **Laparoscopic supracervical hysterectomy** ♀ **[LSH]**
        Classic infrafascial SEMM hysterectomy [CISH]
        Laparoscopically assisted supracervical hysterectomy [LASH]
        AHA: 4Q, '03, 98-99
        DEF: A hysterectomy that spares the cervix and maintains the integrity of the pelvic floor; SEMM version of the supracervical hysterectomy, also called the classic infrafascial Semm hysterectomy [CISH], leaves the cardinal ligaments, or lateral cervical ligaments that merge with the pelvic diaphragm intact.

    68.39 **Other subtotal abdominal hysterectomy, NOS** ♀
        Supracervical hysterectomy
        EXCLUDES *classic infrafascial SEMM hysterectomy [CISH] (68.31)*
        laparoscopic supracervical hysterectomy [LSH] (68.31)
        AHA: 4Q, '03, 98

68.4 **Total abdominal hysterectomy** ♀
    Hysterectomy:
        extended
    Code also any synchronous removal of tubes and ovaries (65.3-65.6)
    AHA: 4Q, '96, 65
    DEF: Complete excision of uterus and uterine neck through abdominal incision.

✓4ᵗʰ **68.5** **Vaginal hysterectomy**
    Code also any synchronous:
        removal of tubes and ovaries (65.31-65.64)
        repair of cystocele or rectocele (70.50-70.52)
        repair of pelvic floor (70.79)
    DEF: Complete excision of the uterus by a vaginal approach.

    68.51 **Laparoscopically assisted vaginal hysterectomy (LAVH)** ♀
        AHA: 4Q, '96, 68

    68.59 **Other vaginal hysterectomy** ♀
        EXCLUDES *laparoscopically assisted vaginal hysterectomy (68.51)*
        radical vaginal hysterectomy (68.7)

68.6 **Radical abdominal hysterectomy** ♀
    Modified radical hysterectomy
    Wertheim's operation
    Code also any synchronous:
        lymph gland dissection (40.3, 40.5)
        removal of tubes and ovaries (65.61-65.64)
        EXCLUDES *pelvic evisceration (68.8)*
    DEF: Excision of uterus, loose connective tissue and smooth muscle around uterus and vagina via abdominal approach.

68.7 **Radical vaginal hysterectomy** ♀
    Schauta operation
    Code also any synchronous:
        lymph gland dissection (40.3, 40.5)
        removal of tubes and ovaries (65.61-65.64)
    DEF: Excision of uterus, loose connective tissue and smooth muscle around uterus and vagina via vaginal approach.

N Newborn Age: 0   P Pediatric Age: 0-17   M Maternity Age: 12-55   A Adult Age: 15-124   Adj Adjunct Code   ◄ Revised Text   ● New Code   ▲ Revised Code Title

Dilation and Curettage

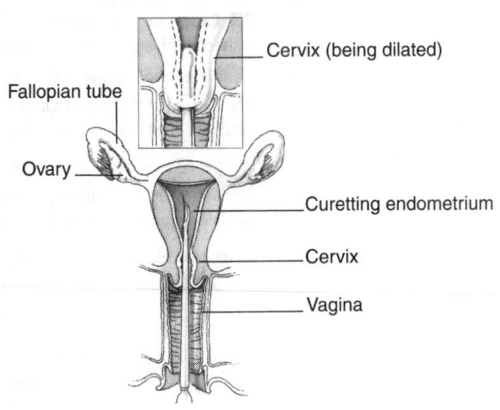

Cervix (being dilated)

Fallopian tube

Ovary

Curetting endometrium

Cervix

Vagina

68.8   **Pelvic evisceration**   ♀
Removal of ovaries, tubes, uterus, vagina, bladder, and urethra (with removal of sigmoid colon and rectum)
Code also any synchronous:
   colostomy (46.10-46.13)
   lymph gland dissection (40.3, 40.5)
   urinary diversion (56.51-56.79)

68.9   **Other and unspecified hysterectomy**   ♀
Hysterectomy NOS
> **EXCLUDES**   *abdominal hysterectomy, any approach (68.31-68.39, 68.4, 68.6)*
> *vaginal hysterectomy, any approach (68.51, 68.59, 68.7)*

✓3rd **69**   **Other operations on uterus and supporting structures**
Code also any application or administration of an adhesion barrier substance (99.77)

✓4th **69.0**   **Dilation and curettage of uterus**
> **EXCLUDES**   *aspiration curettage of uterus (69.51-69.59)*

DEF: Stretching of uterine neck to scrape tissue from walls.

69.01   **Dilation and curettage for termination of pregnancy**   ♀
AHA: 1Q, '98, 4

69.02   **Dilation and curettage following delivery or abortion**   ♀
AHA: 3Q, '93, 6

69.09   **Other dilation and curettage**   ♀
Diagnostic D and C
AHA: 1Q, '98, 4

✓4th **69.1**   **Excision or destruction of lesion or tissue of uterus and supporting structures**
69.19   **Other excision or destruction of uterus and supporting structures**   ♀
> **EXCLUDES**   *biopsy of uterine ligament (68.14)*

✓4th **69.2**   **Repair of uterine supporting structures**
69.21   **Interposition operation**   ♀
Watkins procedure
DEF: Repositioning or realignment of bladder and uterus.

69.22   **Other uterine suspension**   ♀
Hysteropexy
Manchester operation
Plication of uterine ligament
DEF: Hysteropexy: Fixation or anchoring of uterus.

DEF: Manchester operation: Fixation or anchoring of uterus with supportive banding tissue of uterine neck and vagina.

DEF: Plication of uterine ligament: Creation of tucks in supportive uterine banding tissue.

69.23   **Vaginal repair of chronic inversion of uterus**   ♀
DEF: Repositioning of inverted uterus via vaginal approach.

69.29   **Other repair of uterus and supporting structures**   ♀

69.3   **Paracervical uterine denervation**   ♀

✓4th **69.4**   **Uterine repair**
> **EXCLUDES**   *repair of current obstetric laceration (75.50-75.52)*

69.41   **Suture of laceration of uterus**   ♀
69.42   **Closure of fistula of uterus**   ♀
> **EXCLUDES**   *uterovesical fistulectomy (57.84)*

69.49   **Other repair of uterus**   ♀
Repair of old obstetric laceration of uterus

✓4th **69.5**   **Aspiration curettage of uterus**
> **EXCLUDES**   *menstrual extraction (69.6)*

69.51   **Aspiration curettage of uterus for termination of pregnancy**   ♀
Therapeutic abortion NOS

69.52   **Aspiration curettage following delivery or abortion**   ♀

69.59   **Other aspiration curettage of uterus**   ♀
AHA: 1Q, '98, 7

69.6   **Menstrual extraction or regulation**   ♀
DEF: Induction of menstruation by low pressure suction.

69.7   **Insertion of intrauterine contraceptive device**   ♀

✓4th **69.9**   **Other operations on uterus, cervix, and supporting structures**   ♀
> **EXCLUDES**   *obstetric dilation or incision of cervix (73.1, 73.93)*

69.91   **Insertion of therapeutic device into uterus**   ♀
> **EXCLUDES**   *insertion of:*
> *intrauterine contraceptive device (69.7)*
> *laminaria (69.93)*
> *obstetric insertion of bag, bougie, or pack (73.1)*

69.92   **Artificial insemination**   ♀
69.93   **Insertion of laminaria**   ♀
DEF: Placement of laminaria, a sea kelp, in cervical os to induce labor; applied for six to 12 hours.

69.94   **Manual replacement of inverted uterus**   ♀
> **EXCLUDES**   *that in immediate postpartal period (75.94)*

69.95   **Incision of cervix**   ♀
> **EXCLUDES**   *that to assist delivery (73.93)*

69.96   **Removal of cerclage material from cervix**   ♀
DEF: Removal of ring inserted to restore uterine neck competency.

69.97   **Removal of other penetrating foreign body from cervix**   ♀
> **EXCLUDES**   *removal of intraluminal foreign body from cervix (98.16)*

69.98   **Other operations on supporting structures of uterus**   ♀
> **EXCLUDES**   *biopsy of uterine ligament (68.14)*

69.99   **Other operations on cervix and uterus**   ♀
> **EXCLUDES**   *removal of:*
> *foreign body (98.16)*
> *intrauterine contraceptive device (97.71)*
> *obstetric bag, bougie, or pack (97.72)*
> *packing (97.72)*

✓3rd ✓4th Additional Digit Required   RUG III Special Care Procedure   RUG III Clinically Complex Procedure   RUG III Extensive Services Procedure   RUG III Rehab Procedure

2006 ICD•9•CM   **Volume 3 — 169**

Operations on the Female Genital Organs

70–71.09

√3rd **70**   **Operations on vagina and cul-de-sac**
Code also any application or administration of an adhesion barrier substance (99.77)

70.0   **Culdocentesis**   ♀
AHA: 2Q, '90, 26

DEF: Insertion of needle into upper vaginal vault encircling cervix to withdraw fluid.

√4th **70.1**   **Incision of vagina and cul-de-sac**

70.11   **Hymenotomy**   ♀

70.12   **Culdotomy**   ♀

DEF: Incision into pocket between terminal end of large intestine and posterior uterus.

70.13   **Lysis of intraluminal adhesions of vagina**   ♀

70.14   **Other vaginotomy**   ♀
Division of vaginal septum
Drainage of hematoma of vaginal cuff

DEF: Division of vaginal septum: Incision into partition of vaginal walls.

DEF: Drainage of hematoma of vaginal cuff: Incision into vaginal tissue to drain collected blood.

√4th **70.2**   **Diagnostic procedures on vagina and cul-de-sac**

70.21   **Vaginoscopy**   ♀

70.22   **Culdoscopy**   ♀

DEF: Endoscopic exam of pelvic viscera through incision in posterior vaginal wall.

70.23   **Biopsy of cul-de-sac**   ♀

70.24   **Vaginal biopsy**   ♀

70.29   **Other diagnostic procedures on vagina and cul-de-sac**   ♀

√4th **70.3**   **Local excision or destruction of vagina and cul-de-sac**

70.31   **Hymenectomy**   ♀

70.32   **Excision or destruction of lesion of cul-de-sac**   ♀
Endometrectomy of cul-de-sac
EXCLUDES   biopsy of cul-de-sac (70.23)

70.33   **Excision or destruction of lesion of vagina**   ♀
EXCLUDES   biopsy of vagina (70.24)
vaginal fistulectomy (70.72-70.75)

70.4   **Obliteration and total excision of vagina**   ♀
Vaginectomy
EXCLUDES   obliteration of vaginal vault (70.8)

DEF: Vaginectomy: Removal of vagina.

√4th **70.5**   **Repair of cystocele and rectocele**

70.50   **Repair of cystocele and rectocele**   ♀
DEF: Repair of anterior and posterior vaginal wall bulges.

70.51   **Repair of cystocele**   ♀
Anterior colporrhaphy (with urethrocele repair)
AHA: N-D, '84, 20

70.52   **Repair of rectocele**   ♀
Posterior colporrhaphy

√4th **70.6**   **Vaginal construction and reconstruction**

70.61   **Vaginal construction**   ♀

70.62   **Vaginal reconstruction**   ♀
AHA: N-D, '84, 20

√4th **70.7**   **Other repair of vagina**
EXCLUDES   lysis of intraluminal adhesions (70.13)
repair of current obstetric laceration (75.69)
that associated with cervical amputation (67.4)

70.71   **Suture of laceration of vagina**   ♀
AHA: N-D, '84, 20

70.72   **Repair of colovaginal fistula**   ♀
DEF: Correction of abnormal opening between midsection of large intestine and vagina.

70.73   **Repair of rectovaginal fistula**   ♀
DEF: Correction of abnormal opening between last section of large intestine and vagina.

70.74   **Repair of other vaginoenteric fistula**   ♀
DEF: Correction of abnormal opening between vagina and intestine; other than mid or last sections.

70.75   **Repair of other fistula of vagina**   ♀
EXCLUDES   repair of fistula:
rectovesicovaginal (57.83)
ureterovaginal (56.84)
urethrovaginal (58.43)
uterovaginal (69.42)
vesicocervicovaginal (57.84)
vesicosigmoidovaginal (57.83)
vesicoureterovaginal (56.84)
vesicovaginal (57.84)

70.76   **Hymenorrhaphy**   ♀
DEF: Closure of vagina with suture of hymenal ring or hymenal remnant flaps.

70.77   **Vaginal suspension and fixation**   ♀
DEF: Repair of vaginal protrusion, sinking or laxity by suturing vagina into position.

70.79   **Other repair of vagina**   ♀
Colpoperineoplasty
Repair of old obstetric laceration of vagina

70.8   **Obliteration of vaginal vault**   ♀
LeFort operation

DEF: LeFort operation: Uniting or sewing together vaginal walls.

√4th **70.9**   **Other operations on vagina and cul-de-sac**

70.91   **Other operations on vagina**   ♀
EXCLUDES   insertion of:
diaphragm (96.17)
mold (96.15)
pack (96.14)
pessary (96.18)
suppository (96.49)
removal of:
diaphragm (97.73)
foreign body (98.17)
pack (97.75)
pessary (97.74)
replacement of:
diaphragm (97.24)
pack (97.26)
pessary (97.25)
vaginal dilation (96.16)
vaginal douche (96.44)

70.92   **Other operations on cul-de-sac**   ♀
Obliteration of cul-de-sac
Repair of vaginal enterocele
AHA: 4Q, '94, 54

DEF: Repair of vaginal enterocele: Elimination of herniated cavity within pouch between last part of large intestine and posterior uterus.

√3rd **71**   **Operations on vulva and perineum**
Code also any application or administration of an adhesion barrier substance (99.77)

√4th **71.0**   **Incision of vulva and perineum**

71.01   **Lysis of vulvar adhesions**   ♀

71.09   **Other incision of vulva and perineum**   ♀
Enlargement of introitus NOS
EXCLUDES   removal of foreign body without incision (98.23)

N Newborn Age: 0   P Pediatric Age: 0-17   M Maternity Age: 12-55   A Adult Age: 15-124   Adj Adjunct Code   ►◄ Revised Text   ● New Code   ▲ Revised Code Title

Operations on the Female Genital Organs

71.1–71.9

Marsupialization

Portion of cyst and overlying skin to be excised

Cyst "unroofed"

Cyst walls sutured to skin

✓4ᵗʰ **71.1**   **Diagnostic procedures on vulva**
- **71.11**   **Biopsy of vulva**   ♀
- **71.19**   **Other diagnostic procedures on vulva**   ♀

✓4ᵗʰ **71.2**   **Operations on Bartholin's gland**
- **71.21**   **Percutaneous aspiration of Bartholin's gland (cyst)**   ♀
- **71.22**   **Incision of Bartholin's gland (cyst)**   ♀
- **71.23**   **Marsupialization of Bartholin's gland (cyst)**   ♀
  DEF: Incision and suturing open a cyst in Bartholin's gland.
- **71.24**   **Excision or other destruction of Bartholin's gland (cyst)**   ♀
- **71.29**   **Other operations on Bartholin's gland**   ♀

71.3   **Other local excision or destruction of vulva and perineum**   ♀
Division of Skene's gland
> EXCLUDES   *biopsy of vulva (71.11)*
> *vulvar fistulectomy (71.72)*

71.4   **Operations on clitoris**   ♀
Amputation of clitoris
Clitoridotomy
Female circumcision

DEF: Amputation of clitoris: Removal of clitoris.

DEF: Clitoridotomy: Incision into clitoris.

DEF: Female circumcision: Incision of skin fold over clitoris.

71.5   **Radical vulvectomy**   ♀
Code also any synchronous lymph gland dissection (40.3, 40.5)

DEF: Removal of over 80 percent of deep tissue from vulva, including tissue of abdomen, groin, labia minora, labia majora, clitoris, mons veneris, and terminal portions of urethra, vagina and other vulvar organs.

✓4ᵗʰ **71.6**   **Other vulvectomy**
- **71.61**   **Unilateral vulvectomy**   ♀
- **71.62**   **Bilateral vulvectomy**   ♀
  Vulvectomy NOS

✓4ᵗʰ **71.7**   **Repair of vulva and perineum**
> EXCLUDES   *repair of current obstetric laceration (75.69)*
- **71.71**   **Suture of laceration of vulva or perineum**   ♀
- **71.72**   **Repair of fistula of vulva or perineum**   ♀
  > EXCLUDES   *repair of fistula:*
  > *urethroperineal (58.43)*
  > *urethroperineovesical (57.84)*
  > *vaginoperineal (70.75)*
- **71.79**   **Other repair of vulva and perineum**   ♀
  Repair of old obstetric laceration of vulva or perineum
  AHA: 1Q, '97, 9

71.8   **Other operations on vulva**   ♀
> EXCLUDES   *removal of:*
> *foreign body without incision (98.23)*
> *packing (97.75)*
> *replacement of packing (97.26)*

71.9   **Other operations on female genital organs**   ♀
AHA: ▶4Q, '04, 90;◀ 1Q, '03, 13

✓3ʳᵈ / ✓4ᵗʰ Additional Digit Required   RUG III Special Care Procedure   RUG III Clinically Complex Procedure   RUG III Extensive Services Procedure   RUG III Rehab Procedure

2006 ICD•9•CM   **February 2005 • Volume 3 — 171**

Obstetrical Procedures

72–74.2

13. OBSTETRICAL PROCEDURES (72–75)

√3rd **72** **Forceps, vacuum, and breech delivery**

72.0 **Low forceps operation** ♀
     Outlet forceps operation

72.1 **Low forceps operation with episiotomy** ♀
     Outlet forceps operation with episiotomy

√4th **72.2** **Mid forceps operation**

     72.21 **Mid forceps operation with episiotomy** ♀

     72.29 **Other mid forceps operation** ♀

√4th **72.3** **High forceps operation**

     72.31 **High forceps operation with episiotomy** ♀

     72.39 **Other high forceps operation** ♀

72.4 **Forceps rotation of fetal head** ♀
     DeLee maneuver
     Key-in-lock rotation
     Kielland rotation
     Scanzoni's maneuver
     Code also any associated forceps extraction (72.0–72.39)

√4th **72.5** **Breech extraction**

     72.51 **Partial breech extraction with forceps to aftercoming head** ♀

     72.52 **Other partial breech extraction** ♀

     72.53 **Total breech extraction with forceps to aftercoming head** ♀

     72.54 **Other total breech extraction** ♀

72.6 **Forceps application to aftercoming head** ♀
     Piper forceps operation

     EXCLUDES   *partial breech extraction with forceps to aftercoming head (72.51)*
                total breech extraction with forceps to aftercoming head (72.53)

√4th **72.7** **Vacuum extraction**

     INCLUDES   Malstöm's extraction

     72.71 **Vacuum extraction with episiotomy** ♀

     72.79 **Other vacuum extraction** ♀

72.8 **Other specified instrumental delivery** ♀

72.9 **Unspecified instrumental delivery** ♀

√3rd **73** **Other procedures inducing or assisting delivery**

√4th **73.0** **Artificial rupture of membranes**

     73.01 **Induction of labor by artificial rupture of membranes** ♀
         Surgical induction NOS

         EXCLUDES   *artificial rupture of membranes after onset of labor (73.09)*

         AHA: 3Q, '00, 5

     73.09 **Other artificial rupture of membranes** ♀
         Artificial rupture of membranes at time of delivery

Breech Extraction

Breech presentation

Delivery of legs

Baby rotated for delivery of arms

Umbilicus

73.1 **Other surgical induction of labor** ♀
     Induction by cervical dilation

     EXCLUDES   *injection for abortion (75.0)*
                insertion of suppository for abortion (96.49)

√4th **73.2** **Internal and combined version and extraction**

     73.21 **Internal and combined version without extraction** ♀
         Version NOS

     73.22 **Internal and combined version with extraction** ♀

73.3 **Failed forceps** ♀
     Application of forceps without delivery
     Trial forceps

73.4 **Medical induction of labor** ♀

     EXCLUDES   *medication to augment active labor — omit code*

√4th **73.5** **Manually assisted delivery** ♀

     73.51 **Manual rotation of fetal head** ♀

     73.59 **Other manually assisted delivery** ♀
         Assisted spontaneous delivery
         Credé maneuver

     AHA: 4Q, '98, 76

73.6 **Episiotomy** ♀
     Episioproctotomy
     Episiotomy with subsequent episiorrhaphy

     EXCLUDES   *that with:*
                high forceps (72.31)
                low forceps (72.1)
                mid forceps (72.21)
                outlet forceps (72.1)
                vacuum extraction (72.71)

AHA: 1Q, '92, 10

73.8 **Operations on fetus to facilitate delivery** ♀
     Clavicotomy on fetus
     Destruction of fetus
     Needling of hydrocephalic head

√4th **73.9** **Other operations assisting delivery**

     73.91 **External version** ♀

     73.92 **Replacement of prolapsed umbilical cord** ♀

     73.93 **Incision of cervix to assist delivery** ♀
         Dührssen's incisions

     73.94 **Pubiotomy to assist delivery** ♀
         Obstetrical symphysiotomy

     73.99 **Other** ♀

         EXCLUDES   *dilation of cervix, obstetrical, to induce labor (73.1)*
                   insertion of bag or bougie to induce labor (73.1)
                   removal of cerclage material (69.96)

√3rd **74** **Cesarean section and removal of fetus**
     Code also any synchronous:
         hysterectomy (68.3-68.4, 68.6, 68.8)
         myomectomy (68.29)
         sterilization (66.31-66.39, 66.63)

74.0 **Classical cesarean section** ♀
     Transperitoneal classical cesarean section

74.1 **Low cervical cesarean section** ♀
     Lower uterine segment cesarean section

     AHA: 1Q, '01, 11

74.2 **Extraperitoneal cesarean section** ♀
     Supravesical cesarean section

N Newborn Age: 0   **P** Pediatric Age: 0-17   **M** Maternity Age: 12-55   **A** Adult Age: 15-124   **Adj** Adjunct Code   ►◄ Revised Text   ● New Code   ▲ Revised Code Title

74.3 Removal of extratubal ectopic pregnancy ♀
Removal of:
  ectopic abdominal pregnancy
  fetus from peritoneal or extraperitoneal cavity
    following uterine or tubal rupture
  EXCLUDES   *that by salpingostomy (66.02)*
  that by salpingotomy (66.01)
  that with synchronous salpingectomy
  (66.62)

AHA: 4Q, '92, 25; 2Q, '90, 25; 2Q, '90, 27; 1Q, '89, 11

74.4 Cesarean section of other specified type ♀
Peritoneal exclusion cesarean section
Transperitoneal cesarean section NOS
Vaginal cesarean section

✓4th **74.9 Cesarean section of unspecified type**
74.91 Hysterotomy to terminate pregnancy ♀
Therapeutic abortion by hysterotomy

74.99 Other cesarean section of unspecified ♀
type
Cesarean section NOS
Obstetrical abdominouterotomy
Obstetrical hysterotomy

✓3rd **75 Other obstetric operations**
75.0 Intra-amniotic injection for abortion ♀
Injection of:
  prostaglandin } for induction of
  saline }   abortion

Termination of pregnancy by intrauterine injection
  EXCLUDES   *insertion of prostaglandin suppository*
  for abortion (96.49)

75.1 Diagnostic amniocentesis ♀
75.2 Intrauterine transfusion ♀
Exchange transfusion in utero
Insertion of catheter into abdomen of fetus for
  transfusion
Code also any hysterotomy approach (68.0)

✓4th **75.3 Other intrauterine operations on fetus and amnion**
Code also any hysterotomy approach (68.0)
75.31 Amnioscopy ♀
Fetoscopy
Laparoamnioscopy

75.32 Fetal EKG (scalp) ♀
75.33 Fetal blood sampling and biopsy ♀
75.34 Other fetal monitoring ♀
Antepartum fetal nonstress test
Fetal monitoring, not otherwise specified
  EXCLUDES   *fetal pulse oximetry (75.38)*

Amniocentesis

Aspiration of amniotic fluid

75.35 Other diagnostic procedures on fetus ♀
and amnion
Intrauterine pressure determination
  EXCLUDES   *amniocentesis (75.1)*
  diagnostic procedures on
  gravid uterus and
  placenta (87.81, 88.46,
  88.78, 92.17)

75.36 Correction of fetal defect ♀
75.37 Amnioinfusion
Code also injection of antibiotic (99.21)

AHA: 4Q, '98, 76

75.38 Fetal pulse oximetry
Transcervical fetal oxygen saturation
  monitoring
Transcervical fetal SpO$_2$ monitoring

AHA: 4Q, '01, 64

DEF: Single-use sensor inserted through the birth canal
and positioned to rest against the fetal cheek, forehead,
or temple; infrared beam of light aimed at the fetal skin
is reflected back through the sensor for analysis.

75.4 Manual removal of retained placenta ♀
  EXCLUDES   *aspiration curettage (69.52)*
  dilation and curettage (69.02)

✓4th **75.5 Repair of current obstetric laceration of uterus**
75.50 Repair of current obstetric laceration ♀
of uterus, not otherwise specified
75.51 Repair of current obstetric laceration ♀
of cervix
75.52 Repair of current obstetric laceration ♀
of corpus uteri

✓4th **75.6 Repair of other current obstetric laceration**
AHA: 1Q, '92, 11

75.61 Repair of current obstetric laceration ♀
of bladder and urethra
75.62 Repair of current obstetric laceration ♀
of rectum and sphincter ani
75.69 Repair of other current obstetric ♀
laceration
Episioperineorrhaphy
Repair of:
  pelvic floor
  perineum
  vagina
  vulva
Secondary repair of episiotomy
  EXCLUDES   *repair of routine episiotomy*
  (73.6)

75.7 Manual exploration of uterine cavity, ♀
postpartum
75.8 Obstetric tamponade of uterus or vagina ♀
  EXCLUDES   *antepartum tamponade (73.1)*

✓4th **75.9 Other obstetric operations**
75.91 Evacuation of obstetrical incisional ♀
hematoma of perineum
Evacuation of hematoma of:
  episiotomy
  perineorrhaphy
75.92 Evacuation of other hematoma of vulva ♀
or vagina
75.93 Surgical correction of inverted uterus ♀
Spintelli operation
  EXCLUDES   *vaginal repair of chronic*
  inversion of uterus
  (69.23)
75.94 Manual replacement of inverted uterus ♀
75.99 Other ♀

✓3rd
✓4th   Additional Digit Required   RUG III Special Care Procedure   RUG III Clinically Complex Procedure   RUG III Extensive Services Procedure   RUG III Rehab Procedure

Operations on the Musculoskeletal System

76–76.95

14. OPERATIONS ON THE MUSCULOSKELETAL SYSTEM
(76-84)

√3ʳᵈ **76 Operations on facial bones and joints**
> EXCLUDES   *accessory sinuses (22.00-22.9)*
> *nasal bones (21.00-21.99)*
> *skull (01.01-02.99)*

√4ᵗʰ **76.0 Incision of facial bone without division**

76.01 Sequestrectomy of facial bone
Removal of necrotic bone chip from facial bone

76.09 Other incision of facial bone
Reopening of osteotomy site of facial bone
> EXCLUDES   *osteotomy associated with orthognathic surgery (76.61-76.69)*
> *removal of internal fixation device (76.97)*

√4ᵗʰ **76.1 Diagnostic procedures on facial bones and joints**

76.11 Biopsy of facial bone

76.19 Other diagnostic procedures on facial bones and joints
> EXCLUDES   *contrast arthrogram of temporomandibular joint (87.13)*
> *other x-ray (87.11-87.12, 87.14-87.16)*

AHA: N-D, '87, 12

76.2 Local excision or destruction of lesion of facial bone
> EXCLUDES   *biopsy of facial bone (76.11)*
> *excision of odontogenic lesion (24.4)*

√4ᵗʰ **76.3 Partial ostectomy of facial bone**

76.31 Partial mandibulectomy
Hemimandibulectomy
> EXCLUDES   *that associated with temporomandibular arthroplasty (76.5)*

DEF: Excision, partial of lower jawbone.

DEF: Hemimandibulectomy: Excision of one-half of lower jawbone.

76.39 Partial ostectomy of other facial bone
Hemimaxillectomy (with bonegraft or prosthesis)
AHA: J-F, '87, 14

DEF: Excision, partial of facial bone; other than lower jawbone.

DEF: Hemimaxillectomy (with bone graft or prosthesis): Excision of one side of upper jawbone and restoration with bone graft or prosthesis.

√4ᵗʰ **76.4 Excision and reconstruction of facial bones**

76.41 Total mandibulectomy with synchronous reconstruction

76.42 Other total mandibulectomy

76.43 Other reconstruction of mandible
> EXCLUDES   *genioplasty (76.67-76.68)*
> *that with synchronous total mandibulectomy (76.41)*

AHA: 2Q, '03, 13

76.44 Total ostectomy of other facial bone with synchronous reconstruction
AHA: 3Q, '93, 6

DEF: Excision, facial bone, total with reconstruction during same operative session.

76.45 Other total ostectomy of other facial bone

76.46 Other reconstruction of other facial bone
> EXCLUDES   *that with synchronous total ostectomy (76.44)*

76.5 Temporomandibular arthroplasty
AHA: 4Q, '99, 20

√4ᵗʰ **76.6 Other facial bone repair and orthognathic surgery**
Code also any synchronous:
bone graft (76.91)
synthetic implant (76.92)
> EXCLUDES   *reconstruction of facial bones (76.41-76.46)*

76.61 Closed osteoplasty [osteotomy] of mandibular ramus
Gigli saw osteotomy
DEF: Reshaping and restoration of lower jawbone projection; closed surgical field.
DEF: Gigli saw osteotomy: Plastic repair using a flexible wire with saw teeth.

76.62 Open osteoplasty [osteotomy] of mandibular ramus

76.63 Osteoplasty [osteotomy] of body of mandible

76.64 Other orthognathic surgery on mandible
Mandibular osteoplasty NOS
Segmental or subapical osteotomy
AHA: ▶2Q, '04, 9, 10◀

76.65 Segmental osteoplasty [osteotomy] of maxilla
Maxillary osteoplasty NOS

76.66 Total osteoplasty [osteotomy] of maxilla

76.67 Reduction genioplasty
Reduction mentoplasty
DEF: Reduction of protruding chin or lower jawbone.

76.68 Augmentation genioplasty
Mentoplasty: Mentoplasty:
NOS   with graft or implant
DEF: Extension of the lower jawbone to a functional position by means of plastic surgery.

76.69 Other facial bone repair
Osteoplasty of facial bone NOS

√4ᵗʰ **76.7 Reduction of facial fracture**
> INCLUDES   internal fixation

Code also any synchronous:
bone graft (76.91)
synthetic implant (76.92)
> EXCLUDES   *that of nasal bones (21.71-21.72)*

76.70 Reduction of facial fracture, not otherwise specified

76.71 Closed reduction of malar and zygomatic fracture

76.72 Open reduction of malar and zygomatic fracture

76.73 Closed reduction of maxillary fracture

76.74 Open reduction of maxillary fracture

76.75 Closed reduction of mandibular fracture

76.76 Open reduction of mandibular fracture

76.77 Open reduction of alveolar fracture
Reduction of alveolar fracture with stabilization of teeth

76.78 Other closed reduction of facial fracture
Closed reduction of orbital fracture
> EXCLUDES   *nasal bone (21.71)*

76.79 Other open reduction of facial fracture
Open reduction of orbit rim or wall
> EXCLUDES   *nasal bone (21.72)*

√4ᵗʰ **76.9 Other operations on facial bones and joints**

76.91 Bone graft to facial bone
Autogenous
Bone bank   } graft to facial
Heterogenous   bone

76.92 Insertion of synthetic implant in facial bone
Alloplastic implant to facial bone

76.93 Closed reduction of temporomandibular dislocation

76.94 Open reduction of temporomandibular dislocation

76.95 Other manipulation of temporomandibular joint

Ⓝ Newborn Age: 0   Ⓟ Pediatric Age: 0-17   Ⓜ Maternity Age: 12-55   Ⓐ Adult Age: 15-124   **Adj** Adjunct Code   ▶◀ Revised Text   ● New Code   ▲ Revised Code Title

76.96   **Injection of therapeutic substance into temporomandibular joint**

76.97   **Removal of internal fixation device from facial bone**

> **EXCLUDES**   removal of:
> dental wiring (97.33)
> external mandibular
> fixation device NEC
> (97.36)

76.99   **Other**

√3rd **77**   **Incision, excision, and division of other bones**

> **EXCLUDES**   laminectomy for decompression (03.09)
> operations on:
> accessory sinuses (22.00-22.9)
> ear ossicles (19.0-19.55)
> facial bones (76.01-76.99)
> joint structures (80.00-81.99)
> mastoid (19.9-20.99)
> nasal bones (21.00-21.99)
> skull (01.01-02.99)

The following fourth-digit subclassification is for use with appropriate categories in section 77 to identify the site. Valid fourth-digit categories are in [brackets] under each code.

0 unspecified site	**6** patella
1 scapula, clavicle, and thorax [ribs and sternum]	**7** tibia and fibula
2 humerus	**8** tarsals and metatarsals
3 radius and ulna	**9** other
4 carpals and metacarpals	Pelvic bones
5 femur	Vertebrae
	Phalanges (of foot) (of hand)

√4th **77.0**   **Sequestrectomy**
[0-9]   DEF: Excision and removal of dead bone.

√4th **77.1**   **Other incision of bone without division**
[0-9]   Reopening of osteotomy site

> **EXCLUDES**   aspiration of bone marrow, (41.31, 41.91)
> removal of internal fixation device (78.60-78.69)

AHA: For code 77.17: 1Q, '02, 13

DEF: Incision into bone without division of site.

√4th **77.2**   **Wedge osteotomy**
[0-9]

> **EXCLUDES**   that for hallux valgus (77.51)

DEF: Removal of wedge-shaped piece of bone.

√4th **77.3**   **Other division of bone**
[0-9]   Osteoarthrotomy

> **EXCLUDES**   clavicotomy of fetus (73.8)
> laminotomy or incision of vertebra (03.01-03.09)
> pubiotomy to assist delivery (73.94)
> sternotomy incidental to thoracic operation — omit code

√4th **77.4**   **Biopsy of bone**
[0-9]   AHA: 2Q, '98, 12

√4th **77.5**   **Excision and repair of bunion and other toe deformities**

77.51   **Bunionectomy with soft tissue correction and osteotomy of the first metatarsal**
DEF: Incision and removal of big toe bony prominence and reconstruction with soft tissue.

77.52   **Bunionectomy with soft tissue correction and arthrodesis**
DEF: Removal of big toe bony prominence and reconstruction with soft tissue and joint fixation.

77.53   **Other bunionectomy with soft tissue correction**

77.54   **Excision or correction of bunionette**
That with osteotomy
DEF: Resection of fifth metatarsal head via exposure of joint; includes imbrication of capsule.

Repair of Hammertoes

Corn / Callus / Hammertoe / Hemiphalengectomy / After

77.56   **Repair of hammer toe**
Fusion
Phalangectomy (partial) } of hammer toe
Filleting

DEF: Repair of clawlike toe defect by joint fusion, partial removal of toe or via traction technique.

77.57   **Repair of claw toe**
Fusion
Phalangectomy (partial)
Capsulotomy } of claw toe
Tendon lengthening

DEF: Repair of clawlike toe defect by joint fusion, partial removal of toe, joint capsule incision or lengthening of fibrous muscle attachment.

77.58   **Other excision, fusion, and repair of toes**
Cockup toe repair
Overlapping toe repair
That with use of prosthetic materials

77.59   **Other bunionectomy**
Resection of hallux valgus joint with insertion of prosthesis
DEF: Resection of hallux valgus joint with insertion of prosthesis: Cutting away part of big toe with prosthesis insertion to correct bony prominence.

√4th **77.6**   **Local excision of lesion or tissue of bone**
[0-9]

> **EXCLUDES**   biopsy of bone (77.40-77.49)
> debridement of compound fracture (79.60-79.69)

AHA: For code 77.61: 3Q, '01, 9; For code 77.65: 4Q, '04, 128; S-O, '85, 4; For code 77.67: 1Q, '02, 3; 1Q, '99, 8; For code 77.69: 2Q, '00, 18

√4th **77.7**   **Excision of bone for graft**
[0-9]   AHA: 4Q, '99, 11, 13; For code 77.71: 3Q, '03, 19; For code 77.79: 2Q, '03, 13; 4Q, '02, 107, 109-110; 2Q, '02, 16; 2Q, '00 12, 13; 4Q, '99, 11, 13

√4th **77.8**   **Other partial ostectomy**
[0-9]   Condylectomy

> **EXCLUDES**   amputation (84.00-84.19, 84.91)
> arthrectomy (80.90-80.99)
> excision of bone ends associated with:
> arthrodesis (81.00-81.29)
> arthroplasty (81.51-81.59, 81.71-81.81, 81.84)
> excision of cartilage (80.5-80.6, 80.80-80.99)
> excision of head of femur with synchronous replacement
> ▶(00.70-00.73, 81.51-81.53)◀
> hemilaminectomy (03.01-03.09)
> laminectomy (03.01-03.09)
> ostectomy for hallux valgus (77.51-77.59)
> partial amputation:
> finger (84.01)
> thumb (84.02)
> toe (84.11)
> resection of ribs incidental to thoracic operation — omit code
> that incidental to other operation — omit code

AHA: For code 77.89: 2Q, '02, 8

√3rd
√4th Additional Digit Required   ▨ RUG III Special Care Procedure   ▨ RUG III Clinically Complex Procedure   ▨ RUG III Extensive Services Procedure   ▨ RUG III Rehab Procedure

2006 ICD•9•CM   **October 2005 • Volume 3 — 175**

Operations on the Musculoskeletal System

77.9–79.1

√4th **77.9 Total ostectomy**
[0-9]
    EXCLUDES   *amputation of limb (84.00-84.19, 84.91)*
         that incidental to other operation —
         omit code

√3rd **78 Other operations on bones, except facial bones**
    EXCLUDES   *operations on:*
         accessory sinuses (22.00-22.9)
         facial bones (76.01-76.99)
         joint structures (80.00-81.99)
         nasal bones (21.00-21.99)
         skull (01.01-02.99)

The following fourth-digit subclassification is for use with categories in section 78 to identify the site. Valid fourth-digit categories are in [brackets] under each code.

0	**unspecified site**	6	**patella**
1	**scapula, clavicle, and**	7	**tibia and fibula**
	thorax [ribs and sternum]	8	**tarsals and metatarsals**
2	**humerus**	9	**other**
3	**radius and ulna**		Pelvic bones
4	**carpals and metacarpals**		Vertebrae
5	**femur**		Phalanges (of foot) (of hand)

√4th **78.0 Bone graft**
[0-9]
    Bone:
       bank graft
       graft (autogenous) (heterogenous)
    That with debridement of bone graft site (removal of
       sclerosed, fibrous, or necrotic bone or tissue)
    Transplantation of bone
    Code also any excision of bone for graft (77.70-77.79)
    EXCLUDES   *that for bone lengthening (78.30-78.39)*
    AHA: 2Q, '02, 11; 2Q, '98, 12; 3Q, '94, 10; 1Q, '91, 3

▲ √4th **78.1 Application of external fixator device**
[0-9]
    ▶Fixator with insertion of pins/wires/screws into bone
    Code also any type of fixator device, if known
       (84.71-84.73)◀
    EXCLUDES   *other immobilization, pressure, and*
         attention to wound (93.51-93.59)
    AHA: 2Q, '94, 4

√4th **78.2 Limb shortening procedures**
[0,2-5,7-9] Epiphyseal stapling   Percutaneous epiphysiodesis
    Open epiphysiodesis   Resection/osteotomy

√4th **78.3 Limb lengthening procedures**
[0,2-5,7-9] Bone graft with or without internal fixation devices
       or osteotomy
    Distraction technique with or without
       corticotomy/osteotomy
    Code also any application of an external fixation
       device (78.10-78.19)

√4th **78.4 Other repair or plastic operations on bone**
[0-9]
    Other operation on bone NEC
    Repair of malunion or nonunion fracture NEC
    EXCLUDES   *application of external fixation device*
         (78.10-78.19)
         limb lengthening procedures (78.30-78.39)
         limb shortening procedures (78.20-78.29)
         osteotomy (77.3)
         reconstruction of thumb (82.61-82.69)
         repair of pectus deformity (34.74)
         repair with bone graft (78.00-78.09)
    AHA: 3Q, '91, 20; 4Q, '88, 11; **For code 78.41:** 2Q, '02, 16;
       For code 78.47: 3Q, '91, 20; **For code 78.49:** 3Q, '04, 9;
       2Q, '03, 22; 3Q, '02, 12; 2Q, '02, 14, 15; 4Q, '99, 22; 1Q, '97, 5

√4th **78.5 Internal fixation of bone without fracture**
[0-9] **reduction**
    Internal fixation of bone (prophylactic)
    Reinsertion of internal fixation device
    Revision of displaced or broken fixation device
    EXCLUDES   *arthroplasty and arthrodesis*
         (81.00-81.85)
         bone graft (78.00-78.09)
         limb shortening procedures (78.20-78.29)
         that for fracture reduction (79.10-79.19,
         79.30-79.59)
    AHA: 2Q, '99, 11; 2Q, '94, 4; **For code 78.59:** 3Q, '04, 6; 2Q, '03, 15; 4Q, '99, 13

√4th **78.6 Removal of implanted devices from bone**
[0-9]
    External fixator device (invasive)
    Internal fixation device
    Removal of bone growth stimulator (invasive)
    Removal of internal limb lengthening devicex
    EXCLUDES   *removal of cast, splint, and traction*
         device (Kirschner wire)
         (Steinmann pin) (97.88)
         removal of skull tongs or halo traction
         device (02.95)
    AHA: 1Q, '00, 15; **For code 78.67:** 2Q, '03, 14;
       For code 78.69: 4Q, '02, 110; 2Q, '00, 18

√4th **78.7 Osteoclasis**
[0-9] **DEF:** Surgical breaking or rebreaking of bone.

√4th **78.8 Diagnostic procedures on bone, not elsewhere**
[0-9] **classified**
    EXCLUDES   *biopsy of bone (77.40-77.49)*
         magnetic resonance imaging (88.94)
         microscopic examination of specimen
         from bone (91.51-91.59)
         radioisotope scan (92.14)
         skeletal x-ray (87.21-87.29, 87.43,
         88.21-88.33)
         thermography (88.83)

√4th **78.9 Insertion of bone growth stimulator**
[0-9] Insertion of:
    bone stimulator (electrical) to aid bone healing
    osteogenic electrodes for bone growth stimulation
    totally implanted device (invasive)
    EXCLUDES   *non-invasive (transcutaneous) (surface)*
         stimulator (99.86)

√3rd **79 Reduction of fracture and dislocation**
    INCLUDES   application of cast or splint
         reduction with insertion of traction device
         (Kirschner wire) (Steinmann pin)
    Code also any:
    ▶application of external fixator device (78.10-78.19)
    type of fixator device, if known (84.71-84.73)◀
    EXCLUDES   *external fixation alone for immobilization of*
         fracture (93.51-93.56, 93.59)
         internal fixation without reduction of fracture
         (78.50-78.59)
         operations on:
         facial bones(76.70-76.79)
         nasal bones (21.71-21.72)
         orbit (76.78-76.79)
         skull (02.02)
         vertebrae (03.53)
         removal of cast or splint (97.88)
         replacement of cast or splint (97.11-97.14)
         traction alone for reduction of fracture (93.41-
         93.46)

The following fourth-digit subclassification is for use with appropriate categories in section 79 to identify the site. Valid fourth-digit categories are in [brackets] under each code.

0	**unspecified site**	5	**femur**
1	**humerus**	6	**tibia and fibula**
2	**radius and ulna**		Leg NOS
	Arm NOS	7	**tarsals and metatarsals**
3	**carpals and metacarpals**		Foot NOS
	Hand NOS	8	**phalanges of foot**
4	**phalanges of hand**	9	**other specified bone**

√4th **79.0 Closed reduction of fracture without internal**
[0-9] **fixation**
    EXCLUDES   *that for separation of epiphysis*
         (79.40-79.49)
    AHA: 2Q, '94, 3; 3Q, '89, 17; 4Q, '88, 11; **For code 79.05:** 3Q, '89, 16
    DEF: Manipulative realignment of fracture; without incision or internal fixation.

√4th **79.1 Closed reduction of fracture with internal**
[0-9] **fixation**
    EXCLUDES   *that for separation of epiphysis*
         (79.40-79.49)
    AHA: 2Q, '94, 4; 4Q, '93, 35; 1Q, '93, 27
    DEF: Manipulative realignment of fracture; with internal fixation but without incision.

N Newborn Age: 0   P Pediatric Age: 0-17   M Maternity Age: 12-55   A Adult Age: 15-124   Adj Adjunct Code   ▶◀ Revised Text   ● New Code   ▲ Revised Code Title

✓4th **79.2** **Open reduction of fracture without internal**
[0-9] **fixation**
　　　EXCLUDES　*that for separation of epiphysis*
　　　　　(79.50-79.59)

　　　AHA: 2Q, '94, 3

✓4th **79.3** **Open reduction of fracture with internal**
[0-9] **fixation**
　　　EXCLUDES　*that for separation of epiphysis*
　　　　　(79.50-79.59)

　　　AHA: 2Q, '98, 12; 3Q, '94, 10; 2Q, '94, 3; 4Q, '93, 35

　　　DEF: Realignment of fracture with incision and internal fixation.

✓4th **79.4** **Closed reduction of separated epiphysis**
[0-2,5,6,9] Reduction with or without internal fixation
　　　DEF: Manipulative reduction of expanded joint end of long bone to
　　　normal position without incision.

✓4th **79.5** **Open reduction of separated epiphysis**
[0-2,5,6,9] Reduction with or without internal fixation
　　　DEF: Reduction of expanded joint end of long bone with incision.

✓4th **79.6** **Debridement of open fracture site**
[0-9] Debridement of compound fracture
　　　AHA: 3Q, '95, 12; 3Q, '89, 16

　　　DEF: Removal of damaged tissue at fracture site.

✓4th **79.7** **Closed reduction of dislocation**
　　　INCLUDES　closed reduction (with external
　　　　　traction device)
　　　EXCLUDES　*closed reduction of dislocation of*
　　　　　temporomandibular joint (76.93)

　　DEF: Manipulative reduction of displaced joint without incision;
　　with or without external traction.

　　　79.70 **Closed reduction of dislocation of**
　　　　　unspecified site
　　　79.71 **Closed reduction of dislocation of shoulder**
　　　79.72 **Closed reduction of dislocation of elbow**
　　　79.73 **Closed reduction of dislocation of wrist**
　　　79.74 **Closed reduction of dislocation of hand and**
　　　　　finger
　　　79.75 **Closed reduction of dislocation of hip**
　　　79.76 **Closed reduction of dislocation of knee**
　　　　　AHA: N-D, '86, 7

　　　79.77 **Closed reduction of dislocation of ankle**
　　　79.78 **Closed reduction of dislocation of foot and**
　　　　　toe
　　　79.79 **Closed reduction of dislocation of other**
　　　　　specified sites

✓4th **79.8** **Open reduction of dislocation**
　　　INCLUDES　open reduction (with internal and
　　　　　external fixation devices)
　　　EXCLUDES　*open reduction of dislocation of*
　　　　　temporomandibular joint (76.94)

　　DEF: Reduction of displaced joint via incision; with or without
　　internal and external fixation.

　　　79.80 **Open reduction of dislocation of**
　　　　　unspecified site
　　　79.81 **Open reduction of dislocation of shoulder**
　　　79.82 **Open reduction of dislocation of elbow**
　　　79.83 **Open reduction of dislocation of wrist**
　　　79.84 **Open reduction of dislocation of hand and**
　　　　　finger
　　　79.85 **Open reduction of dislocation of hip**
　　　79.86 **Open reduction of dislocation of knee**
　　　79.87 **Open reduction of dislocation of ankle**
　　　79.88 **Open reduction of dislocation of foot and**
　　　　　toe
　　　79.89 **Open reduction of dislocation of other**
　　　　　specified sites

✓4th **79.9** **Unspecified operation on bone injury**
[0-9]

✓3rd **80** **Incision and excision of joint structures**
　　　INCLUDES　operations on:
　　　　　capsule of joint
　　　　　cartilage
　　　　　condyle
　　　　　ligament
　　　　　meniscus
　　　　　synovial membrane
　　　EXCLUDES　*cartilage of:*
　　　　　ear (18.01-18.9)
　　　　　nose (21.00-21.99)
　　　　　temporomandibular joint (76.01-76.99)

The following fourth-digit subclassification is for use with appropriate
categories in section 80 to identify the site:
　　　0 **unspecified site**
　　　1 **shoulder**
　　　2 **elbow**
　　　3 **wrist**
　　　4 **hand and finger**
　　　5 **hip**
　　　6 **knee**
　　　7 **ankle**
　　　8 **foot and toe**
　　　9 **other specified sites**
　　　　　Spine

✓4th **80.0** **Arthrotomy for removal of prosthesis**
　　　▶Code also any:
　　　　　insertion of (cement) (joint) spacer (84.56)
　　　　　removal of (cement) (joint) spacer (84.57)◄
　　　AHA: 2Q, '91, 18; For code 80.06: 2Q, '97, 10

　　　DEF: Incision into joint to remove prosthesis.

✓4th **80.1** **Other arthrotomy**
　　　Arthrostomy
　　　EXCLUDES　*that for:*
　　　　　arthrography (88.32)
　　　　　arthroscopy (80.20-80.29)
　　　　　injection of drug (81.92)
　　　　　operative approach — omit code

　　　DEF: Incision into joint; other than to remove prosthesis.

　　　DEF: Arthrostomy: Creation of opening into joint.

✓4th **80.2** **Arthroscopy**
　　　AHA: 3Q, '93, 5; 1Q, '93, 23

✓4th **80.3** **Biopsy of joint structure**
　　　Aspiration biopsy

✓4th **80.4** **Division of joint capsule, ligament, or cartilage**
　　　Goldner clubfoot release
　　　Heyman-Herndon(-Strong) correction of metatarsus
　　　　varus
　　　Release of:
　　　　adherent or constrictive joint capsule
　　　　joint
　　　　ligament
　　　EXCLUDES　*symphysiotomy to assist delivery*
　　　　　(73.94)
　　　　　that for:
　　　　　carpal tunnel syndrome (04.43)
　　　　　tarsal tunnel syndrome (04.44)

　　　AHA: For code 80.49: 2Q, '02, 16

　　　DEF: Incision and separation of joint tissues, including capsule,
　　　fibrous bone attachment or cartilage.

✓4th **80.5** **Excision or destruction of intervertebral disc**

　　　80.50 **Excision or destruction of intervertebral**
　　　　　disc, unspecified
　　　　　Unspecified asto excision or destruction

✓3rd ✓4th **Additional Digit Required**　RUG III Special Care Procedure　　RUG III Clinically Complex Procedure　　RUG III Extensive Services Procedure　　RUG III Rehab Procedure

2006 ICD•9•CM　　　　　October 2005 • Volume 3 — 177

80.51 Excision of intervertebral disc

Code also any concurrent spinal fusion (81.00-81.09)

Diskectomy

Level:
   cervical
   thoracic
   lumbar (lumbosacral)

Removal of herniated nucleus pulposus

That by laminotomy or hemilaminectomy

That with decompression of spinal nerve root at same level

Requires additional code for any concomitant decompression of spinal nerve root at different level from excision site

> EXCLUDES   *intervertebral chemonucleolysis (80.52)*
> *laminectomy for exploration of intraspinal canal (03.09)*
> *laminotomy for decompression of spinal nerve root only (03.09)*
> *that for insertion of (non-fusion) spinal disc replacement device (84.60-84.69)*

AHA: 4Q, '04, 133; 3Q, '03, 12; 1Q, '96, 7; 2Q, '95, 9; 2Q, '90, 27; S-O, '86, 12

DEF: Removal of intervertebral disc.

DEF: Removal of a herniated nucleus pulposus: Removal of displaced intervertebral disc, central part.

80.52 Intervertebral chemonucleolysis

With aspiration of disc fragments

With diskography

Injection of proteolytic enzyme into intervertebral space (chymopapain)

> EXCLUDES   *injection of anesthestic substance (03.91)*
> *injection of other substances (03.92)*

DEF: Destruction of intervertebral disc via injection of enzyme.

80.59 Other destruction of intervertebral disc

Destruction NEC   That by laser

AHA: 3Q, '02, 10

80.6 Excision of semilunar cartilage of knee

Excision of meniscus of knee

AHA: 2Q, '03, 18; 3Q, '00, 4; 2Q, '96, 3; 1Q, '93, 23

✓4th 80.7 Synovectomy

Complete or partial resection of synovial membrane

> EXCLUDES   *excision of Baker's cyst (83.39)*

DEF: Excision of inner membrane of joint capsule.

✓4th 80.8 Other local excision or destruction of lesion of joint

✓4th 80.9 Other excision of joint

> EXCLUDES   *cheilectomy of joint (77.80-77.89)*
> *excision of bone ends (77.80-77.89)*

Types of Grafts for Anterior Arthrodesis

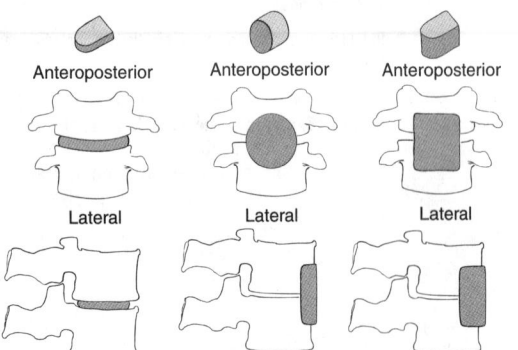

Anteroposterior   Anteroposterior   Anteroposterior

Lateral   Lateral   Lateral

✓3rd 81 Repair and plastic operations on joint structures

✓4th 81.0 Spinal fusion

> INCLUDES   arthrodesis of spine with:
>   bone graft
>   internal fixation

Code also any:
   insertion of interbody spinal fusion device (84.51)
   insertion of recombinant bone morphogenetic protein (84.52)

Code also the total number of vertebrae fused (81.62-81.64)

> EXCLUDES   *corrections of pseudarthrosis of spine (81.30-81.39)*
> *refusion of spine (81.30-81.39)*

AHA: 4Q, '03, 99

DEF: Immobilization of spinal column.

DEF: Anterior interbody fusion: Arthrodesis by excising disc and cartilage end plates with bone graft insertion between two vertebrae.

DEF: Lateral fusion: Arthrodesis by decorticating and bone grafting lateral surface of zygapophysial joint, pars interarticularis and transverse process.

DEF: Posterior fusion: Arthrodesis by decorticating and bone grafting of neural arches between right and left zygapophysial joints.

DEF: Posterolateral fusion: Arthrodesis by decorticating and bone grafting zygapophysial joint, pars interarticularis and transverse processes

81.00 Spinal fusion, not otherwise specified

81.01 Atlas-axis spinal fusion

Craniocervical fusion ⎫
C1-C2 fusion   ⎬ by anterior trans-
Occiput C2 fusion   ⎭   oral or posterior technique

81.02 Other cervical fusion, anterior technique

Arthrodesis of C2 level or below:
   anterior (interbody) technique
   anterolateral technique

AHA: 4Q, '03, 101; 1Q, '01, 6; 1Q, '96, 7

81.03 ◄Other cervical fusion, posterior technique

Arthrodesis of C2 level or below:
   posterior (interbody) technique
   posterolateral technique

81.04 Dorsal and dorsolumbar fusion, anterior technique

Arthrodesis of thoracic or thoracolumbar region:
   anterior (interbody) technique
   anterolateral technique

AHA: 3Q, '03, 19

81.05 Dorsal and dorsolumbar fusion, posterior technique

Arthrodesis of thoracic or thoracolumbar region:
   posterior (interbody) technique
   posterolateral technique

AHA: 2Q, '02, 16; 4Q, '99, 11

81.06 Lumbar and lumbosacral fusion, anterior technique

►Anterior lumbar interbody fusion (ALIF)◄

Arthrodesis of lumbar or lumbosacral region:
   anterior (interbody) technique
   anterolateral technique

AHA: 4Q, '02, 107; 4Q, '99, 11

81.07 Lumbar and lumbosacral fusion, lateral transverse process technique

AHA: 4Q, '02, 108

N Newborn Age: 0   P Pediatric Age: 0-17   M Maternity Age: 12-55   A Adult Age: 15-124   Adj Adjunct Code   ►◄ Revised Text   ● New Code   ▲ Revised Code Title

81.08   **Lumbar and lumbosacral fusion, posterior technique**
> Arthrodesis of lumbar or lumbosacral
>   region:
>   posterior (interbody) technique
>   posterolateral technique
> ▶Posterior lumbar interbody fusion (PLIF)
> Transforaminal lumbar interbody fusion
>   (TLIF)◄
>   **AHA:** 4Q, '02, 107, 109; 2Q, '00, 12, 13; 4Q, '99, 13; 2Q, '95, 9

▲   ✓4ᵗʰ **81.1**   **Arthrodesis and arthroereisis of foot and ankle**
>   INCLUDES   arthrodesis of foot and ankle with:
>   bone graft
>   external fixation device

DEF: Fixation of foot or ankle joints.

   81.11   **Ankle fusion**
> Tibiotalar fusion

   81.12   **Triple arthrodesis**
> Talus to calcaneus and calcaneus to cuboid
>   and navicular

   81.13   **Subtalar fusion**
>   EXCLUDES ▶ *arthroereisis (81.18)*◄

   81.14   **Midtarsal fusion**

   81.15   **Tarsometatarsal fusion**

   81.16   **Metatarsophalangeal fusion**

   81.17   **Other fusion of foot**

●   **81.18**   **Subtalar joint arthroereisis**

✓4ᵗʰ **81.2**   **Arthrodesis of other joint**
>   INCLUDES   arthrodesis with:
>   bone graft
>   external fixation device
>   excision of bone ends and
>   compression

   81.20   **Arthrodesis of unspecified joint**

   81.21   **Arthrodesis of hip**

   81.22   **Arthrodesis of knee**

   81.23   **Arthrodesis of shoulder**

   81.24   **Arthrodesis of elbow**

   81.25   **Carporadial fusion**

   81.26   **Metacarpocarpal fusion**

   81.27   **Metacarpophalangeal fusion**

   81.28   **Interphalangeal fusion**

   81.29   **Arthrodesis of other specified joints**

✓4ᵗʰ **81.3**   **Refusion of spine**
>   INCLUDES   arthrodesis of spine with:
>   bone graft
>   internal fixation
>   correction of pseudarthrosis of spine
> Code also any:
>   insertion of interbody spinal fusion device (84.51)
>   insertion of recombinant bone morphogenetic
>   protein (84.52)
> Code also the total number of vertebrae fused
>   (81.62-81.64)

     AHA: 4Q, '03, 99; 4Q, '01, 64

   81.30   **Refusion of spine, not otherwise specified**

   81.31   **Refusion of atlas-axis spine**
> Craniocervical fusion ⎱   by anterior transoral
> C1-C2 fusion   ⎰   or posterior
> Occiput C2 fusion   technique

   81.32   **Refusion of other cervical spine, anterior technique**
> Arthrodesis of C2 level or below:
>   anterior (interbody) technique
>   anterolateral technique

   81.33   **Refusion of other cervical spine, posterior technique**
> Arthrodesis of C2 level or below:
>   posterior (interbody) technique
>   posterolateral technique

   81.34   **Refusion of dorsal and dorsolumbar spine, anterior technique**
> Arthrodesis of thoracic or thoracolumbar
>   region:
>   anterior (interbody) technique
>   anterolateral technique

   81.35   **Refusion of dorsal and dorsolumbar spine, posterior technique**
> Arthrodesis of thoracic or thoracolumbar
>   region:
>   posterior (interbody) technique
>   posterolateral technique

   81.36   **Refusion of lumbar and lumbosacral spine, anterior technique**
> ▶Anterior lumbar interbody fusion (ALIF)◄
> Arthrodesis of lumbar or lumbosacral
>   region:
>   anterior (interbody) technique
>   anterolateral technique

   81.37   **Refusion of lumbar and lumbosacral spine, lateral transverse process technique**

   81.38   **Refusion of lumbar and lumbosacral spine, posterior technique**
> Arthrodesis of lumbar or lumbosacral
>   region:
>   posterior (interbody) technique
>   posterolateral technique
> ▶Posterior lumbar interbody fusion (PLIF)
> Transforaminal lumbar interbody fusion
>   (TLIF)◄
>   **AHA:** 4Q, '02, 110

   81.39   **Refusion of spine, not elsewhere classified**

✓4ᵗʰ **81.4**   **Other repair of joint of lower extremity**
>   INCLUDES   arthroplasty of lower extremity with:
>   external traction or fixation
>   graft of bone (chips) or cartilage
>   internal fixation device

     AHA: S-O, '85, 4

   81.40   **Repair of hip, not elsewhere classified**

   81.42   **Five-in-one repair of knee**
> Medial meniscectomy, medial collateral
>   ligament repair, vastus medialis
>   advancement, semitendinosus
>   advancement, and pes anserinus
>   transfer

   81.43   **Triad knee repair**
> Medial meniscectomy with repair of the
>   anterior cruciate ligament and the
>   medial collateral ligament
> O'Donoghue procedure

   81.44   **Patellar stabilization**
> Roux-Goldthwait operation for recurrent
>   dislocation of patella

DEF: Roux-Goldthwait operation: Stabilization of patella via lateral ligament transposed at insertion beneath undisturbed medial insertion; excision of capsule ellipse and medial patella retinaculum; capsule reefed for lateral patella hold.

Partial Hip Replacement

Acetabulum remains intact

Prosthesis

✓3ʳᵈ ✓4ᵗʰ   Additional Digit Required   RUG III Special Care Procedure   RUG III Clinically Complex Procedure   RUG III Extensive Services Procedure   RUG III Rehab Procedure

2006 ICD•9•CM   **October 2005 • Volume 3 — 179**

Operations on the Musculoskeletal System

81.45–81.66

Total Hip Replacement

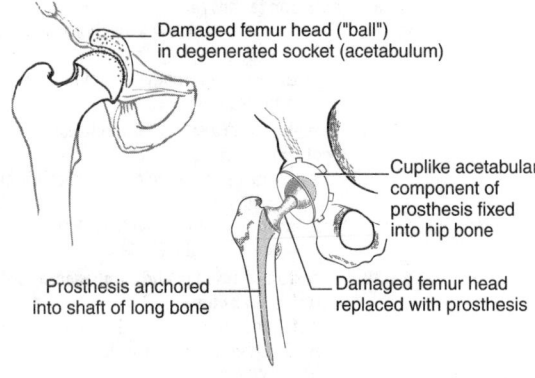

Damaged femur head ("ball") in degenerated socket (acetabulum)

Cuplike acetabular component of prosthesis fixed into hip bone

Prosthesis anchored into shaft of long bone

Damaged femur head replaced with prosthesis

Total Knee Replacement

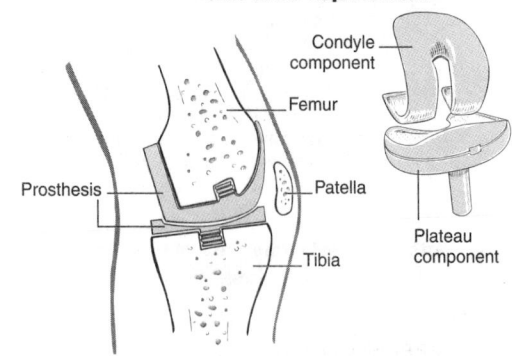

Condyle component

Femur

Prosthesis

Patella

Tibia

Plateau component

81.45   **Other repair of the cruciate ligaments**
AHA: M-A, '87, 12

81.46   **Other repair of the collateral ligaments**

81.47   **Other repair of knee**
AHA: 2Q, '03, 18; 1Q, '00, 12, 13; 1Q, '96, 3; 3Q, '93, 5

81.49   **Other repair of ankle**
AHA: 2Q, '01, 15; 3Q, '00, 4

✓4ᵗʰ **81.5**   **Joint replacement of lower extremity**

INCLUDES   arthroplasty of lower extremity with:
external traction or fixation
graft of bone (chips) or cartilage
internal fixation device or prosthesis
removal of cement spacer

AHA: S-O, '85, 4

81.51   **Total hip replacement**
Replacement of both femoral head and acetabulum by prosthesis
Total reconstruction of hip
▶Code also any type of bearing surface, if known (00.74–00.76)◀
AHA: 4Q, '04, 113; 2Q, '91, 18

DEF: Repair of both surfaces of hip joint with prosthesis.

81.52   **Partial hip replacement**
Bipolar endoprosthesis
▶Code also any type of bearing surface, if known (00.74–00.76)◀
AHA: 2Q, '91, 18

DEF: Repair of single surface of hip joint with prosthesis.

▲   **81.53**   **Revision of hip replacement, not otherwise specified**
▶Revision of hip replacement, not specified as to component(s) replaced, (acetabular, femoral or both)
Code also any:
removal of (cement) (joint) spacer (84.57)
type of bearing surface, if known (00.74–00.76)◀

EXCLUDES ▶revision of hip replacement, components specified (00.70–00.73)◀

AHA: 3Q, '97, 12

81.54   **Total knee replacement**
Bicompartmental
Tricompartmental
Unicompartmental (hemijoint)
DEF: Repair of a knee joint with prosthetic implant in one, two, or three compartments.

▲   **81.55**   **Revision of knee replacement, not otherwise specified**
▶Code also any removal of (cement) (joint) spacer (84.57)◀
EXCLUDES   arthrodesis of knee (81.22)
▶revision of knee replacement, components specified (00.80–00.84)◀

AHA: 2Q, '97, 10

81.56   **Total ankle replacement**

81.57   **Replacement of joint of foot and toe**

81.59   **Revision of joint replacement of lower extremity, not elsewhere classified**

✓4ᵗʰ **81.6**   **Other procedures on spine**
Note: Number of vertebrae
The vertebral spine consists of 25 vertebrae in the following order and number:
Cervical: C1 (atlas), C2 (axis), C3, C4, C5, C6, C7
Thoracic or Dorsal: T1, T2, T3, T4, T5, T6, T7, T8, T9, T10, T11, T12
Lumbar and Sacral: L1, L2, L3, L4, L5, S1
Coders should report only one code from the series 81.62–81.64 to show the total number of vertebrae fused on the patient.
Code also the level and approach of the fusion or refusion (81.00–81.08, 81.30–81.39)
AHA: 4Q, '03, 99

81.62   **Fusion or refusion of 2-3 vertebrae**   **Adj**
AHA: 4Q, '03, 99

81.63   **Fusion or refusion of 4-8 vertebrae**   **Adj**
AHA: 4Q, '03, 99-101

81.64   **Fusion or refusion of 9 or more vertebrae**   **Adj**
AHA: 4Q, '03, 99

81.65   **Vertebroplasty**
Injection of bone void filler (cement) (polymethacrylate) (PMMA) into the diseased or fractured vertebral body
EXCLUDES   kyphoplasty (81.66)

81.66   **Kyphoplasty**
Insertion of inflatable balloon, bone tamp, or other device to create a cavity for partial restoration of height of diseased or fractured vertebral body prior to injection of bone void filler (cement) (polymethylmethacrylate) (PMMA)
EXCLUDES   vertebroplasty (81.65)

AHA: 4Q, '04, 126

Vertebroplasty

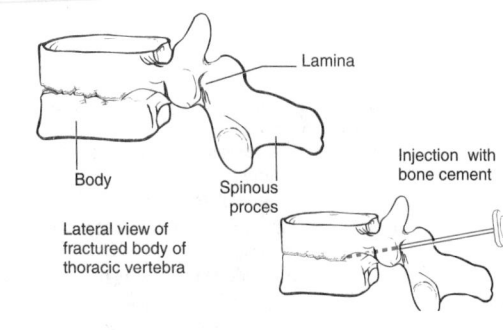

Lamina

Body

Spinous proces

Injection with bone cement

Lateral view of fractured body of thoracic vertebra

Ⓝ Newborn Age: 0   Ⓟ Pediatric Age: 0-17   Ⓜ Maternity Age: 12-55   Ⓐ Adult Age: 15-124   **Adj** Adjunct Code   ▶◀ Revised Text   ● New Code   ▲ Revised Code Title

180 — Volume 3 • October 2005   **2006 ICD•9•CM**

▶**Kyphoplasty**◀

Vertebral body
Inflatable balloon catheter
Inflated balloon
Fractured vertebra
Disc
The cavity is filled with bone cement

Arthrocentesis

Needle access into fluid filled knee joint
Femur
Patella (kneecap)
Fluid-filled joint capsule
Tibia

√4th **81.7　Arthroplasty and repair of hand, fingers, and wrist**

INCLUDES　arthroplasty of hand and finger with:
external traction or fixation
graft of bone (chips) or cartilage
internal fixation device or prosthesis

EXCLUDES　operations on muscle, tendon, and
fascia of hand (82.01-82.99)

DEF: Plastic surgery of hand, fingers and wrist joints.

81.71　Arthroplasty of metacarpophalangeal and interphalangeal joint with implant

81.72　Arthroplasty of metacarpophalangeal and interphalangeal joint without implant
AHA: 1Q, '93, 28

81.73　Total wrist replacement

81.74　Arthroplasty of carpocarpal or carpometacarpal joint with implant

81.75　Arthroplasty of carpocarpal or carpometacarpal joint without implant
AHA: 3Q, '93, 8

81.79　Other repair of hand, fingers, and wrist

√4th **81.8　Arthroplasty and repair of shoulder and elbow**

INCLUDES　arthroplasty of upper limb NEC with:
external traction or fixation
graft of bone (chips) or cartilage
internal fixation device or prosthesis

81.80　Total shoulder replacement

81.81　Partial shoulder replacement

81.82　Repair of recurrent dislocation of shoulder
AHA: 3Q, '95, 15

81.83　Other repair of shoulder
Revision of arthroplasty of shoulder
AHA: 1Q, '02, 9; 4Q, '01, 51; 2Q, '00, 14; 3Q, '93,

81.84　Total elbow replacement

81.85　Other repair of elbow

√4th **81.9　Other operations on joint structures**

81.91　Arthrocentesis
Joint aspiration
EXCLUDES　that for:
arthrography (88.32)
biopsy of joint structure
(80.30-80.39)
injection of drug (81.92)

DEF: Insertion of needle to withdraw fluid from joint.

81.92　Injection of therapeutic substance into joint or ligament
AHA: 2Q, '00, 14; 3Q, '89, 16

81.93　Suture of capsule or ligament of upper extremity
EXCLUDES　that associated with arthro-
plasty (81.71-81.75,
81.80-81.81, 81.84)

81.94　Suture of capsule or ligament of ankle and foot
EXCLUDES　that associated with arthro-
plasty (81.56-81.59)

81.95　Suture of capsule or ligament of other lower extremity
EXCLUDES　that associated with arthro-
plasty (81.51-81.55,
81.59)

81.96　Other repair of joint

81.97　Revision of joint replacement of upper extremity
Partial
Removal of cement spacer
Total
AHA: 1Q, '04, 12

81.98　Other diagnostic procedures on joint structures
EXCLUDES　arthroscopy (80.20-80.29)
biopsy of joint structure
(80.30-80.39)
microscopic examination of
specimen from joint
(91.51-91.59)
thermography (88.83)
x-ray (87.21-87.29, 88.21-
88.33)

81.99　Other

√3rd **82　Operations on muscle, tendon, and fascia of hand**
INCLUDES　operations on:
aponeurosis
synovial membrane (tendon sheath)
tendon sheath

√4th **82.0　Incision of muscle, tendon, fascia, and bursa of hand**

82.01　Exploration of tendon sheath of hand

Incision of　　　　　　} tendon sheath
Removal of rice bodies in 　of hand

EXCLUDES　division of tendon (82.11)

DEF: Incision into and exploring the hand's muscle and its accompanying supportive, connective tissue, bands, and sacs.

82.02　Myotomy of hand
EXCLUDES　myotomy for division (82.19)

DEF: Incision into hand muscle.

82.03　Bursotomy of hand

82.04　Incision and drainage of palmar or thenar space

82.09　Other incision of soft tissue of hand
EXCLUDES　incision of skin and
subcutaneous tissue
alone (86.01-86.09)

AHA: N-D, '87, 10

√4th **82.1　Division of muscle, tendon, and fascia of hand**

82.11　Tenotomy of hand
Division of tendon of hand

82.12　Fasciotomy of hand
Division of fascia of hand

82.19　Other division of soft tissue of hand
Division of muscle of hand

√3rd √4th Additional Digit Required　RUG III Special Care Procedure　RUG III Clinically Complex Procedure　RUG III Extensive Services Procedure　RUG III Rehab Procedure

2006 ICD•9•CM　　　　　　　　　　　**February 2005 • Volume 3 — 181**

√4ᵗʰ 82.2 Excision of lesion of muscle, tendon, and fascia of hand

82.21 Excision or lesion of tendon sheath of hand
Ganglionectomy of tendon sheath (wrist)

82.22 Excision of lesion of muscle of hand

82.29 Excision of other lesion of soft tissue of hand
EXCLUDES excision of lesion of skin and subcutaneous tissue (86.21-86.3)

√4ᵗʰ 82.3 Other excision of soft tissue of hand
Code also any skin graft (86.61-86.62, 86.73)
EXCLUDES excision of skin and subcutaneous tissue (86.21-86.3)

82.31 Bursectomy of hand

82.32 Excision of tendon of hand for graft
DEF: Resection and excision of fibrous tissue connecting bone to hand muscle for grafting.

82.33 Other tenonectomy of hand
Tenosynovectomy of hand
EXCLUDES excision of lesion of:
tendon (82.29)
sheath (82.21)

DEF: Removal of fibrous bands connecting muscle to bone of hand.

DEF: Tenosynovectomy of hand: Excision of fibrous band connecting muscle and bone of hand and removal of coverings.

82.34 Excision of muscle or fascia of hand for graft

82.35 Other fasciectomy of hand
Release of Dupuytren's contracture
EXCLUDES excision of lesion of fascia (82.29)

DEF: Excision of fibrous connective tissue; other than for grafting or removing lesion.

DEF: Release of Dupuytren's contracture: Excision of fibrous connective tissue to correct flexion of fingers.

82.36 Other myectomy of hand
EXCLUDES excision of lesion of muscle (82.22)

82.39 Other excision of soft tissue of hand
EXCLUDES excision of skin (86.21-86.3)
excision of soft tissue lesion (82.29)

√4ᵗʰ 82.4 Suture of muscle, tendon, and fascia of hand

82.41 Suture of tendon sheath of hand

82.42 Delayed suture of flexor tendon of hand
DEF: Suture of fibrous band between flexor muscle and bone; following initial repair.

82.43 Delayed suture of other tendon of hand

82.44 Other suture of flexor tendon of hand
EXCLUDES delayed suture of flexor tendon of hand (82.42)

82.45 Other suture of other tendon of hand
EXCLUDES delayed suture of other tendon of hand (82.43)

82.46 Suture of muscle or fascia of hand

√4ᵗʰ 82.5 Transplantation of muscle and tendon of hand
AHA: 1Q, '93, 28

82.51 Advancement of tendon of hand
DEF: Detachment of fibrous connective muscle band and bone with reattachment at advanced point of hand.

82.52 Recession of tendon of hand
DEF: Detachment of fibrous band of muscle and bone with reattachment at drawn-back point of hand.

82.53 Reattachment of tendon of hand

82.54 Reattachment of muscle of hand

82.55 Other change in hand muscle or tendon length

82.56 Other hand tendon transfer or transplantation
EXCLUDES pollicization of thumb (82.61)
transfer of finger, except thumb (82.81)
AHA: 2Q, '99, 10; 4Q, '98, 40

82.57 Other hand tendon transposition
AHA: 1Q, '93, 28; 3Q, '93, 8

82.58 Other hand muscle transfer or transplantation

82.59 Other hand muscle transposition

√4ᵗʰ 82.6 Reconstruction of thumb
INCLUDES digital transfer to act as thumb
Code also any amputation for digital transfer (84.01, 84.11)

82.61 Pollicization operation carrying over nerves and blood supply
DEF: Creation or reconstruction of a thumb with another digit, commonly the index finger.

82.69 Other reconstruction of thumb
"Cocked-hat" procedure [skin flap and bone]
Grafts:
bone
skin (pedicle) } to thumb

√4ᵗʰ 82.7 Plastic operation on hand with graft or implant

82.71 Tendon pulley reconstruction
Reconstruction for opponensplasty
DEF: Reconstruction of fibrous band between muscle and bone of hand.

82.72 Plastic operation on hand with graft of muscle or fascia

82.79 Plastic operation on hand with other graft or implant
Tendon graft to hand
AHA: J-F, '87, 6

√4ᵗʰ 82.8 Other plastic operations on hand

82.81 Transfer of finger, except thumb
EXCLUDES pollicization of thumb (82.61)

82.82 Repair of cleft hand
DEF: Correction of fissure defect of hand.

82.83 Repair of macrodactyly
DEF: Reduction in size of abnormally large fingers.

82.84 Repair of mallet finger
DEF: Repair of flexed little finger.

82.85 Other tenodesis of hand
Tendon fixation of hand NOS
DEF: Fixation of fibrous connective band between muscle and bone of hand.

82.86 Other tenoplasty of hand
Myotenoplasty of hand
DEF: Myotenoplasty of hand: Plastic repair of muscle and fibrous band connecting muscle to bone.

82.89 Other plastic operations on hand
Plication of fascia
Repair of fascial hernia
EXCLUDES that with graft or implant (82.71-82.79)

√4ᵗʰ 82.9 Other operations on muscle, tendon, and fascia of hand
EXCLUDES diagnostic procedures on soft tissue of hand (83.21-83.29)

82.91 Lysis of adhesions of hand
Freeing of adhesions of fascia, muscle, and tendon of hand
EXCLUDES decompression of carpal tunnel (04.43)
that by stretching or manipulation only (93.26)

82.92 Aspiration of bursa of hand

82.93 Aspiration of other soft tissue of hand
EXCLUDES skin and subcutaneous tissue (86.01)

N Newborn Age: 0   P Pediatric Age: 0-17   M Maternity Age: 12-55   A Adult Age: 15-124   Adj Adjunct Code   ◄ Revised Text   ● New Code   ▲ Revised Code Title

82.94   **Injection of therapeutic substance into bursa of hand**

82.95   **Injection of therapeutic substance into tendon of hand**

82.96   **Other injection of locally-acting therapeutic substance into soft tissue of hand**

> EXCLUDES   *subcutaneous or intramuscular injection (99.11-99.29)*

82.99   **Other operations on muscle, tendon, and fascia of hand**

√3rd **83**   **Operations on muscle, tendon, fascia, and bursa, except hand**

> INCLUDES   operations on:
> aponeurosis
> synovial membrane of bursa and tendon sheaths
> tendon sheaths

> EXCLUDES   *diaphragm (34.81-34.89)*
> *hand (82.01-82.99)*
> *muscles of eye (15.01-15.9)*

√4th **83.0**   **Incision of muscle, tendon, fascia, and bursa**

83.01   **Exploration of tendon sheath**
Incision of tendon sheath
Removal of rice bodies from tendon sheath
DEF: Incision of external covering of fibrous cord for exam.
DEF: Removal of rice bodies from tendon sheath: Incision and removal of small bodies resembling grains of rice.

83.02   **Myotomy**
> EXCLUDES   *cricopharyngeal myotomy (29.31)*

AHA: 2Q, '89, 18

83.03   **Bursotomy**
Removal of calcareous deposit of bursa
> EXCLUDES   *aspiration of bursa (percutaneous) (83.94)*

83.09   **Other incision of soft tissue**
Incision of fascia
> EXCLUDES   *incision of skin and subcutaneous tissue alone (86.01-86.09)*

√4th **83.1**   **Division of muscle, tendon, and fascia**

83.11   **Achillotenotomy**

83.12   **Adductor tenotomy of hip**
DEF: Incision into fibrous attachment between adductor muscle and hip bone.

83.13   **Other tenotomy**
Aponeurotomy
Division of tendon
Tendon release
Tendon transection
Tenotomy for thoracic outlet decompression
DEF: Aponeurotomy: Incision and separation of fibrous cords attaching a muscle to bone to aid movement.
DEF: Division of tendon: Separation of fibrous band connecting muscle to bone.
DEF: Tendon release: Surgical detachment of fibrous band from muscle and/or bone.
DEF: Tendon transection: Incision across width of fibrous bands between muscle and bone.
DEF: Tenotomy for thoracic outlet decompression: Incision of fibrous muscle with separation from bone to relieve compressed thoracic outlet.

83.14   **Fasciotomy**
Division of fascia
Division of iliotibial band
Fascia stripping
Release of Volkmann's contracture by fasciotomy
AHA: 3Q, '98, 8

DEF: Division of fascia: Incision to separate fibrous connective tissue.
DEF: Division of iliotibial band: Incision to separate fibrous band connecting tibial bone to muscle in flank.
DEF: Fascia stripping: Incision and lengthwise separation of fibrous connective tissue.
DEF: Release of Volkmann's contracture by fasciotomy: Divisional incision of connective tissue to correct defect in flexion of finger(s).

83.19   **Other division of soft tissue**
Division of muscle
Muscle release
Myotomy for thoracic outlet decompression
Myotomy with division
Scalenotomy
Transection of muscle

√4th **83.2**   **Diagnostic procedures on muscle, tendon, fascia, and bursa, including that of hand**

83.21   **Biopsy of soft tissue**
> EXCLUDES   *biopsy of chest wall (34.23)*
> *biopsy of skin and subcutaneous tissue (86.11)*

83.29   **Other diagnostic procedures on muscle, tendon, fascia, and bursa, including that of hand**
> EXCLUDES   *microscopic examination of specimen (91.51-91.-59)*
> *soft tissue x-ray (87.09, 87.38-87.39, 88.09, 88.35, 88.37)*
> *thermography of muscle (88.84)*

√4th **83.3**   **Excision of lesion of muscle, tendon, fascia, and bursa**
> EXCLUDES   *biopsy of soft tissue (83.21)*

83.31   **Excision of lesion of tendon sheath**
Excision of ganglion of tendon sheath, except of hand

83.32   **Excision of lesion of muscle**
Excision of:
heterotopic bone
muscle scar for release of Volkmann's contracture
myositis ossificans
DEF: Heterotopic bone: Bone lesion in muscle.
DEF: Muscle scar for release of Volkmann's contracture: Scarred muscle tissue interfering with finger flexion.
DEF: Myositis ossificans: Bony deposits in muscle.

83.39   **Excision of lesion of other soft tissue**
Excision of Baker's cyst
> EXCLUDES   *bursectomy (83.5)*
> *excision of lesion of skin and subcutaneous tissue (86.3)*
> *synovectomy (80.70-80.79)*

AHA: 2Q, '97, 6

√4th **83.4**   **Other excision of muscle, tendon, and fascia**

83.41   **Excision of tendon for graft**

83.42   **Other tenonectomy**
Excision of: Tenosynovectomy
aponeurosis
tendon sheath

83.43   **Excision of muscle or fascia for graft**

83.44   **Other fasciectomy**
DEF: Excision of fascia; other than for graft.

83.45   **Other myectomy**
Debridement of muscle NOS
Scalenectomy
AHA: 1Q, '99, 8

DEF: Scalenectomy: Removal of thoracic scaleni muscle tissue.

83.49   **Other excision of soft tissue**

83.5   **Bursectomy**
AHA: 2Q, '99, 11

√4th **83.6**   **Suture of muscle, tendon, and fascia**

83.61   **Suture of tendon sheath**

83.62   **Delayed suture of tendon**

83.63   **Rotator cuff repair**
AHA: 2Q, '93, 8

DEF: Repair of musculomembranous structure around shoulder joint capsule.

√3rd √4th Additional Digit Required   RUG III Special Care Procedure   RUG III Clinically Complex Procedure   RUG III Extensive Services Procedure   RUG III Rehab Procedure

2006 ICD•9•CM   Volume 3 — 183

Operations on the Musculoskeletal System

83.64–84.09

83.64   Other suture of tendon

Achillorrhaphy   Aponeurorrhaphy

> **EXCLUDES**   delayed suture of tendon (83.62)

DEF: Achillorrhaphy: Suture of fibrous band connecting Achilles tendon to heel bone.

DEF: Aponeurorraphy: Suture of fibrous cords connecting muscle to bone.

83.65   Other suture of muscle or fascia

Repair of diastasis recti

√4ᵗʰ   83.7   Reconstruction of muscle and tendon

> **EXCLUDES**   reconstruction of muscle and tendon associated with arthroplasty

83.71   Advancement of tendon

DEF: Detaching fibrous cord between muscle and bone with reattachment at advanced point.

83.72   Recession of tendon

DEF: Detaching fibrous cord between muscle and bone with reattachment at drawn-back point.

83.73   Reattachment of tendon

83.74   Reattachment of muscle

83.75   Tendon transfer or transplantation

83.76   Other tendon transposition

83.77   Muscle transfer or transplantation

Release of Volkmann's contracture by muscle transplantation

83.79   Other muscle transposition

√4ᵗʰ   83.8   Other plastic operations on muscle, tendon, and fascia

> **EXCLUDES**   plastic operations on muscle, tendon, and fascia associated with arthroplasty

83.81   Tendon graft

83.82   Graft of muscle or fascia

AHA: 3Q, '01, 9

83.83   Tendon pulley reconstruction

DEF: Reconstruction of fibrous cord between muscle and bone; at any site other than hand.

83.84   Release of clubfoot, not elsewhere classified

Evans operation on clubfoot

83.85   Other change in muscle or tendon length

Hamstring lengthening
Heel cord shortening
Plastic achillotenotomy
Tendon plication

DEF: Plastic achillotenotomy: Increase in heel cord length.

DEF: Tendon plication: Surgical tuck of tendon.

83.86   Quadricepsplasty

DEF: Correction of quadriceps femoris muscle.

83.87   Other plastic operations on muscle

Musculoplasty   Myoplasty

AHA: 1Q, '97, 9

83.88   Other plastic operations on tendon

Myotenoplasty   Tenodesis
Tendon fixation   Tenoplasty

83.89   Other plastic operations on fascia

Fascia lengthening   Plication of fascia
Fascioplasty

√4ᵗʰ   83.9   Other operations on muscle, tendon, fascia, and bursa

> **EXCLUDES**   nonoperative:
> manipulation (93.25-93.29)
> stretching (93.27-93.29)

83.91   Lysis of adhesions of muscle, tendon, fascia, and bursa

> **EXCLUDES**   that for tarsal tunnel syndrome (04.44)

DEF: Separation of created fibrous structures from muscle, connective tissues, bands and sacs.

83.92   Insertion or replacement of skeletal muscle stimulator

Implantation, insertion, placement, or replacement of skeletal muscle:
electrodes
stimulator

AHA: 2Q, '99, 10

83.93   Removal of skeletal muscle stimulator

83.94   Aspiration of bursa

83.95   Aspiration of other soft tissue

> **EXCLUDES**   that of skin and subcutaneous tissue (86.01)

83.96   Injection of therapeutic substance into bursa

83.97   Injection of therapeutic substance into tendon

83.98   Injection of locally-acting therapeutic substance into other soft tissue

> **EXCLUDES**   subcutaneous or intramuscular injection (99.11-99.29)

83.99   Other operations on muscle, tendon, fascia, and bursa

Suture of bursa

√3ʳᵈ   84   Other procedures on musculoskeletal system

√4ᵗʰ   84.0   Amputation of upper limb

> **EXCLUDES**   revision of amputation stump (84.3)

84.00   Upper limb amputation, not otherwise specified

Closed flap amputation
Kineplastic amputation   } of upper limb NOS
Open or guillotine amputation
Revision of current traumatic amputation

DEF: Closed flap amputation: Sewing a created skin flap over stump end of upper limb.

DEF: Kineplastic amputation: Amputation and preparation of stump of upper limb to permit movement.

DEF: Open or guillotine amputation: Straight incision across upper limb; used when primary closure is contraindicated.

DEF: Revision of current traumatic amputation: Reconstruction of traumatic amputation of upper limb to enable closure.

84.01   Amputation and disarticulation of finger

> **EXCLUDES**   ligation of supernumerary finger (86.26)

84.02   Amputation and disarticulation of thumb

84.03   Amputation through hand

Amputation through carpals

84.04   Disarticulation of wrist

84.05   Amputation through forearm

Forearm amputation

84.06   Disarticulation of elbow

DEF: Amputation of forearm through elbow joint.

84.07   Amputation through humerus

Upper arm amputation

84.08   Disarticulation of shoulder

DEF: Amputation of arm through shoulder joint.

84.09   Interthoracoscapular amputation

Forequarter amputation

DEF: Removal of upper arm, shoulder bone and collarbone.

| N | Newborn Age: 0 | P | Pediatric Age: 0-17 | M | Maternity Age: 12-55 | A | Adult Age: 15-124 | Adj | Adjunct Code | ►◄ Revised Text | ● New Code | ▲ Revised Code Title |

√4th **84.1**   **Amputation of lower limb**
> EXCLUDES   *revision of amputation stump (84.3)*

84.10   **Lower limb amputation, not otherwise specified**

Closed flap amputation
Kineplastic amputation
Open or guillotine amputation ⎫ of lower
Revision of current traumatic   ⎬ limb
    amputation   ⎭ NOS

DEF: Closed flap amputation: Sewing a created skin flap over stump of lower limb.
DEF: Kineplastic amputation: Amputation and preparation of stump of lower limb to permit movement.
DEF: Open or guillotine amputation: Straight incision across lower limb; used when primary closure is contraindicated.
DEF: Revision of current traumatic amputation: Reconstion of traumatic amputation of lower limb to enable closure.

84.11   **Amputation of toe**

Amputation through metatarsophalangeal joint
Disarticulation of toe
Metatarsal head amputation
Ray amputation of foot (disarticulation of the metatarsal head of the toe extending across the forefoot, just proximal to the metatarsophalangeal crease)
> EXCLUDES   *ligation of supernumerary toe (86.26)*

AHA: 4Q, '99, 19

84.12   **Amputation through foot**

Amputation of forefoot
Amputation through middle of foot
Chopart's amputation
Midtarsal amputation
Transmetatarsal amputation (amputation of the forefoot, including the toes)
> EXCLUDES   *Ray amputation of foot (84.11)*

AHA: 4Q, '99, 19

DEF: Amputation of forefoot: Removal of foot in front of joint between toes and body of foot.
DEF: Chopart's amputation: Removal of foot with retention of heel, ankle and other associated ankle bones.
DEF: Midtarsal amputation: Amputation of foot through tarsals.
DEF: Transmetatarsal amputation: Amputation of foot through metatarsals.

84.13   **Disarticulation of ankle**

DEF: Removal of foot through ankle bone.

84.14   **Amputation of ankle through malleoli of tibia and fibula**

84.15   **Other amputation below knee**

Amputation of leg through tibia and fibula NOS

84.16   **Disarticulation of knee**

Batch, Spitler, and McFaddin amputation
Mazet amputation
S.P. Roger's amputation
DEF: Removal of lower leg through knee joint.

84.17   **Amputation above knee**

Amputation of leg through femur
Amputation of thigh
Conversion of below-knee amputation into above-knee amputation
Supracondylar above-knee amputation
AHA: ▶1Q, '05, 16;◀ 3Q, '03, 14

84.18   **Disarticulation of hip**

DEF: Removal of leg through hip joint.

84.19   **Abdominopelvic amputation**

Hemipelvectomy
Hindquarter amputation
DEF: Removal of leg and portion of pelvic bone.
DEF: Hemipelvectomy: Removal of leg and lateral pelvis.

√4th **84.2**   **Reattachment of extremity**

AHA: 1Q, '95, 8

84.21   **Thumb reattachment**
84.22   **Finger reattachment**
84.23   **Forearm, wrist, or hand reattachment**
84.24   **Upper arm reattachment**
    Reattachment of arm NOS
84.25   **Toe reattachment**
84.26   **Foot reattachment**
84.27   **Lower leg or ankle reattachment**
    Reattachment of leg NOS
84.28   **Thigh reattachment**
84.29   **Other reattachment**

84.3   **Revision of amputation stump**

Reamputation   ⎫
Secondary closure ⎬ of stump
Trimming   ⎭
> EXCLUDES   *revision of current traumatic amputation [revision by further amputation of current injury] (84.00-84.19, 84.91)*

AHA: 4Q, '99, 15; 2Q, '98, 15; 4Q, '88, 12

√4th **84.4**   **Implantation or fitting of prosthetic limb device**

84.40   **Implantation or fitting of prosthetic limb device, not otherwise specified**
84.41   **Fitting of prosthesis of upper arm and shoulder**
84.42   **Fitting of prosthesis of lower arm and hand**
84.43   **Fitting of prosthesis of arm, not otherwise specified**
84.44   **Implantation of prosthetic device of arm**
84.45   **Fitting of prosthesis above knee**
84.46   **Fitting of prosthesis below knee**
84.47   **Fitting of prosthesis of leg, not otherwise specified**
84.48   **Implantation of prosthetic device of leg**

√4th **84.5**   **Implantation of other musculoskeletal devices and substances**
> EXCLUDES   *insertion of (non-fusion) spinal disc replacement device (84.60-84.69)*

84.51   **Insertion of interbody spinal fusion device**

Insertion of:
    cages (carbon, ceramic, metal, plastic or titanium)
    interbody fusion cage
    synthetic cages or spacers
    threaded bone dowels
Code also refusion of spine (81.30-81.39)
Code also spinal fusion (81.00-81.08)
AHA: 1Q, '04, 21; 4Q, '02, 108-110

84.52   **Insertion of recombinant bone morphogenetic protein**

rhBMP
That via collagen sponge, coral, ceramic and other carriers
Code also primary procedure performed:
    fracture repair (79.00-79.99)
    spinal fusion (81.00-81.08)
    spinal refusion (81.30-81.39)
AHA: 4Q, '02, 110

DEF: Surgical implantation of bone morphogenetic proteins (BMP) and recombinant BMP (rhBMP) to induce new bone growth formation; clinical applications include delayed unions and nonunions, fractures, and spinal fusions.

84.53   **Implantation of internal limb lengthening device with kinetic distraction**

Code also limb lengthening procedure (78.30-78.39)

√3rd / √4th   Additional Digit Required   ▓ RUG III Special Care Procedure   ▒ RUG III Clinically Complex Procedure   ▓ RUG III Extensive Services Procedure   ▒ RUG III Rehab Procedure

Operations on the Musculoskeletal System

84.54–84.99

Spinal Fusion with Metal Cage

Metal cages
support spine
until fusion
occurs

Lateral view

Anterior view

Spinal fusion
with metal cages

Detail

84.54   **Implantation of other internal limb lengthening device**
Implantation of internal limb lengthening device, not otherwise specified (NOS)
Code also limb lengthening procedure (78.30-78.39)

84.55   **Insertion of bone void filler**
Insertion of:
    acrylic cement (PMMA)
    bone void cement
    calcium based bone void filler
    polymethylmethacrylate (PMMA)
    EXCLUDES   *that with kyphoplasty (81.66)*
        that with vertebroplasty (81.65)
AHA: 4Q, '04, 128

● **84.56**   **Insertion of (cement) spacer**
Insertion of joint spacer

● **84.57**   **Removal of (cement) spacer**
Removal of joint spacer

● **84.58**   **Implantation of interspinous process decompression device**
    EXCLUDES   *fusion of spine (81.00-81.08, 81.30-81.39)*

84.59   **Insertion of other spinal devices**

✓4ᵗʰ **84.6**   **Replacement of spinal disc**
    INCLUDES   non-fusion arthroplasty of the spine with insertion of artificial disc prosthesis

84.60   **Insertion of spinal disc prosthesis, not otherwise specified**
Replacement of spinal disc, NOS
    INCLUDES   diskectomy (discectomy)

84.61   **Insertion of partial spinal disc prosthesis, cervical**
Nuclear replacement device, cervical
Partial artificial disc prosthesis (flexible), cervical
Replacement of nuclear disc (nucleus pulposus), cervical
    INCLUDES   diskectomy (discectomy)

84.62   **Insertion of total spinal disc prosthesis, cervical**
Replacement of cervical spinal disc, NOS
Replacement of total spinal disc, cervical
Total artificial disc prosthesis (flexible), cervical
    INCLUDES   diskectomy (discectomy)

84.63   **Insertion of spinal disc prosthesis, thoracic**
Artificial disc prosthesis (flexible), thoracic
Replacement of thoracic spinal disc, partial or total
    INCLUDES   diskectomy (discectomy)

84.64   **Insertion of partial spinal disc prosthesis, lumbosacral**
Nuclear replacement device, lumbar
Partial artificial disc prosthesis (flexible), lumbar
Replacement of nuclear disc (nucleus pulposus), lumbar
    INCLUDES   diskectomy (discectomy)

84.65   **Insertion of total spinal disc prosthesis, lumbosacral**
Replacement of lumbar spinal disc, NOS
Replacement of total spinal disc, lumbar
Total artificial disc prosthesis (flexible), lumbar
    INCLUDES   diskectomy (discectomy)
AHA: 4Q, '04, 133

84.66   **Revision or replacement of artificial spinal disc prosthesis, cervical**
Removal of (partial) (total) spinal disc prosthesis with synchronous insertion of new (partial) (total) spinal disc prosthesis, cervical
Repair of previously inserted spinal disc prosthesis, cervical

84.67   **Revision or replacement of artificial spinal disc prosthesis, thoracic**
Removal of (partial) (total) spinal disc prosthesis with synchronous insertion of new (partial) (total) spinal disc prosthesis, thoracic
Repair of previously inserted spinal disc prosthesis, thoracic

84.68   **Revision or replacement of artificial spinal disc prosthesis, lumbosacral**
Removal of (partial) (total) spinal disc prosthesis with synchronous insertion of new (partial) (total) spinal disc prosthesis, lumbosacral
Repair of previously inserted spinal disc prosthesis, lumbosacral

84.69   **Revision or replacement of artificial spinal disc prosthesis, not otherwise specified**
Removal of (partial) (total) spinal disc prosthesis with synchronous insertion of new (partial) (total) spinal disc prosthesis
Repair of previously inserted spinal disc prosthesis

● ✓4ᵗʰ **84.7**   **Adjunct codes for external fixator devices**
Code also any primary procedure performed:
    application of external fixator device (78.10, 78.12-78.13, 78.15, 78.17-78.19)
    reduction of fracture and dislocation (79.00-79.89)

● **84.71**   **Application of external fixator device, [Adj] monoplanar system**
    EXCLUDES   *other hybrid device or system (84.73)*
        ring device or system (84.72)

● **84.72**   **Application of external fixator device, [Adj] ring system**
Ilizarov type   Sheffield type
    EXCLUDES   *monoplanar device or system (84.71)*
        other hybrid device or system (84.73)

● **84.73**   **Application of hybrid external fixator [Adj] device**
Hybrid system using both ring and monoplanar devices
    EXCLUDES   *monoplanar device or system, when used alone (84.71)*
        ring device or system, when used alone (84.72)

✓4ᵗʰ **84.9**   **Other operations on musculoskeletal system**
    EXCLUDES   *nonoperative manipulation (93.25-93.29)*

84.91   **Amputation, not otherwise specified**

84.92   **Separation of equal conjoined twins**

84.93   **Separation of unequal conjoined twins**
Separation of conjoined twins NOS

84.99   **Other**

N Newborn Age: 0   **P** Pediatric Age: 0-17   **M** Maternity Age: 12-55   **A** Adult Age: 15-124   **Adj** Adjunct Code   ►◄ Revised Text   ● New Code   ▲ Revised Code Title

15. OPERATIONS ON THE INTEGUMENTARY SYSTEM (85-86)

√3ʳᵈ 85 Operations on the breast

INCLUDES operations on the skin and subcutaneous
tissue of:
breast ⎫ female or
previous mastectomy site ⎬ male
revision of previous mastectomy site

85.0 Mastotomy
Incision of breast (skin)
Mammotomy
EXCLUDES aspiration of breast (85.91)
removal of implant (85.94)
AHA: 1Q, '04, 3; 2Q, '90, 27

√4ᵗʰ 85.1 Diagnostic procedures on breast

**85.11 Closed [percutaneous] [needle] biopsy of
breast**
AHA: 2Q, '00, 10; 3Q, '89, 17

DEF: Mammatome biopsy: Excision of breast tissue using
a needle inserted through a small incision; followed by a
full cut circle of tissue surrounding the core biopsy to
obtain; multiple contiguous directional sampling for
definitive diagnosis and staging of cancer.

85.12 Open biopsy of breast
AHA: 3Q, '89, 17; M-A, '86, 11

DEF: Excision of breast tissue for examination.

85.19 Other diagnostic procedures on breast
EXCLUDES mammary ductogram (87.35)
mammography NEC (87.37)
manual examination (89.36)
microscopic examination of
specimen (91.61-91.69)
thermography (88.85)
ultrasonography (88.73)
xerography (87.36)

√4ᵗʰ 85.2 Excision or destruction of breast tissue
EXCLUDES mastectomy (85.41-85.48)
reduction mammoplasty (85.31-85.32)

**85.20 Excision or destruction of breast tissue, not
otherwise specified**

85.21 Local excision of lesion of breast
Lumpectomy
Removal of area of fibrosis from breast
EXCLUDES biopsy of breast (85.11-85.12)
AHA: 2Q, '90, 27; 3Q, '89, 17; M-A, '86, 11

85.22 Resection of quadrant of breast

85.23 Subtotal mastectomy
EXCLUDES quadrant resection (85.22)
AHA: 2Q, '92, 7

DEF: Excision of a large portion of breast tissue.

85.24 Excision of ectopic breast tissue
Excision of accessory nipple
DEF: Excision of breast tissue outside normal breast
region.

85.25 Excision of nipple
EXCLUDES excision of accessory nipple
(85.24)

**√4ᵗʰ 85.3 Reduction mammoplasty and subcutaneous
mammectomy**
AHA: 4Q, '95, 79, 80

85.31 Unilateral reduction mammoplasty
Unilateral:
amputative mammoplasty
size reduction mammoplasty

85.32 Bilateral reduction mammoplasty
Amputative mammoplasty
Reduction mammoplasty (for gynecomastia)

**85.33 Unilateral subcutaneous mammectomy with
synchronous implant**
EXCLUDES that without synchronous
implant (85.34)

DEF: Removal of mammary tissue, leaving skin and nipple
intact with implant of prosthesis.

**85.34 Other unilateral subcutaneous
mammectomy**
Removal of breast tissue with preservation
of skin and nipple
Subcutaneous mammectomy NOS

DEF: Excision of mammary tissue, leaving skin and nipple
intact.

**85.35 Bilateral subcutaneous mammectomy with
synchronous implant**
EXCLUDES that without synchronous
implant (85.36)

DEF: Excision of mammary tissue, both breasts, leaving
skin and nipples intact; with prosthesis.

85.36 Other bilateral subcutaneous mammectomy

√4ᵗʰ 85.4 Mastectomy

85.41 Unilateral simple mastectomy
Mastectomy: Mastectomy:
NOS   complete
DEF: Removal of one breast.

85.42 Bilateral simple mastectomy
Bilateral complete mastectomy
DEF: Removal of both breasts.

85.43 Unilateral extended simple mastectomy
Extended simple mastectomy NOS
Modified radical mastectomy
Simple mastectomy with excision of regional
lymph nodes
AHA: 2Q, '92, 7; 3Q, '91, 24; 2Q, '91, 21

DEF: Removal of one breast and lymph nodes under arm.

85.44 Bilateral extended simple mastectomy
AHA: 2Q, '92, 7; 3Q, '91, 24; 2Q, '91, 21

85.45 Unilateral radical mastectomy
Excision of breast, pectoral muscles, and
regional lymph nodes [axillary,
clavicular, supraclavicular]
Radical mastectomy NOS
AHA: 2Q, '91, 21

DEF: Removal of one breast and regional lymph nodes,
pectoral muscle and adjacent tissue.

Mastectomy

Partial mastectomy
(lumpectomy): skin
left intact

Lymph nodes

Simple mastectomy   Radical mastectomy

✓4ᵗʰ
✓5ᵗʰ Additional Digit Required   RUG III Special Care Procedure   RUG III Clinically Complex Procedure   RUG III Extensive Services Procedure   RUG III Rehab Procedure

2006 ICD•9•CM   **Volume 3 — 187**

Operations on the Integumentary System

85–85.45

Operations on the Integumentary System

85.46–86.05

85.46 Bilateral radical mastectomy
AHA: 2Q, '91, 21

85.47 Unilateral extended radical mastectomy
Excision of breast, muscles, and lymph nodes [axillary, clavicular, supraclavicular, internal mammary, and mediastinal]
Extended radical mastectomy NOS
DEF: Removal of one breast, regional and middle chest lymph nodes, chest muscle and adjacent tissue.

85.48 Bilateral extended radical mastectomy
DEF: Removal of both breasts, regional and middle chest lymph nodes, chest muscle and adjacent tissue.

√4ᵗʰ **85.5 Augmentation mammoplasty**
EXCLUDES that associated with subcutaneous mammectomy (85.33, 85.35)
AHA: 3Q, '97, 12; 4Q, '95, 76, 80
DEF: Plastic surgery to increase breast size.

85.50 Augmentation mammoplasty, not otherwise specified

85.51 Unilateral injection into breast for augmentation
AHA: 3Q, '91, 13

85.52 Bilateral injection into breast for augmentation
Injection into breast for augmentation NOS

85.53 Unilateral breast implant
AHA: 2Q, '00 18; 2Q, '98, 14

85.54 Bilateral breast implant
Breast implant NOS

85.6 Mastopexy
DEF: Anchoring of pendulous breast.

85.7 Total reconstruction of breast
AHA: 4Q, '95, 77; 1Q, '93, 27

√4ᵗʰ **85.8 Other repair and plastic operations on breast**
EXCLUDES that for:
augmentation (85.50-85.54)
reconstruction (85.7)
reduction (85.31-85.32)
AHA: 4Q, '95, 77

85.81 Suture of laceration of breast
85.82 Split-thickness graft to breast
85.83 Full-thickness graft to breast
AHA: 4Q, '95, 77

85.84 Pedicle graft to breast
AHA: 4Q, '95, 77
DEF: Implantation of transferred muscle tissue still connected to vascular source.

85.85 Muscle flap graft to breast
AHA: 4Q, '95, 77
DEF: Relocation of nipple.

85.86 Transposition of nipple
AHA: 4Q, '95, 78

85.87 Other repair or reconstruction of nipple
AHA: 4Q, '95, 78

85.89 Other mammoplasty
√4ᵗʰ **85.9 Other operations on the breast**
85.91 Aspiration of breast
EXCLUDES percutaneous biopsy of breast (85.11)

85.92 Injection of therapeutic agent into breast
EXCLUDES that for augmentation of breast (85.51-85.52)

85.93 Revision of implant of breast
AHA: 2Q, '98, 14; 4Q, '95, 76

85.94 Removal of implant of breast
AHA: 2Q, '98, 14; 3Q, '92, 4

85.95 Insertion of breast tissue expander
Insertion (soft tissue) of tissue expander (one or more) under muscle or platysma to develop skin flaps for donor use

85.96 Removal of breast tissue expander(s)
AHA: 2Q, '00, 18; 4Q, '95, 77

85.99 Other

√3ʳᵈ **86 Operations on skin and subcutaneous tissue**
INCLUDES operations on: operations on:
hair follicles subcutaneous fat pads
male perineum sudoriferous glands
nails superficial fossae
sebaceous glands
EXCLUDES those on skin of:
anus (49.01-49.99)
breast (mastectomy site) (85.0-85.99)
ear (18.01-18.9)
eyebrow (08.01-08.99)
eyelid (08.01-08.99)
female perineum (71.01-71.9)
lips (27.0-27.99)
nose (21.00-21.99)
penis (64.0-64.99)
scrotum (61.0-61.99)
vulva (71.01-71.9)

√4ᵗʰ **86.0 Incision of skin and subcutaneous tissue**
86.01 Aspiration of skin and subcutaneous tissue
Aspiration of:
abscess } of nail, skin, or
hematoma } subcutaneous
seroma } tissue
AHA: 3Q, '89, 16

86.02 Injection or tattooing of skin lesion or defect
Insertion } of filling material
Injection }
Pigmenting of skin
DEF: Pigmenting of skin: Adding color to skin.

86.03 Incision of pilonidal sinus or cyst
EXCLUDES marsupialization (86.21)

86.04 Other incision with drainage of skin and subcutaneous tissue
EXCLUDES drainage of:
fascial compartments of face and mouth (27.0)
palmar or thenar space (82.04)
pilonidal sinus or cyst (86.03)
AHA: ▶4Q, '04, 76◀

86.05 Incision with removal of foreign body or device from skin and subcutaneous tissue
Removal of loop recorder
Removal of neurostimulator pulse generator (single array, dual array)
Removal of tissue expander(s) from skin or soft tissue other than breast tissue
EXCLUDES removal of foreign body without incision (98.20-98.29)
AHA: 2Q, '96, 15; N-D, '87, 10; N-D, '86, 9

N Newborn Age: 0   P Pediatric Age: 0-17   M Maternity Age: 12-55   A Adult Age: 15-124   Adj Adjunct Code   ▶◀ Revised Text   ● New Code   ▲ Revised Code Title

86.06   Insertion of totally implantable infusion pump

Code also any associated catheterization

EXCLUDES   *insertion of totally implantable vascular access device (86.07)*

AHA: 2Q, '99, 4; 4Q, '90, 14

86.07   Insertion of totally implantable vascular access device [VAD]

Totally implanted port

EXCLUDES   *insertion of totally implantable infusion pump (86.06)*

AHA: 1Q, '01, 13; 1Q, '96, 3; 2Q, '94, 11; 3Q, '91, 13; 4Q, '90, 15

DEF: Placement of vascular access infusion catheter system under skin to allow for frequent manual infusions into blood vessel.

86.09   Other incision of skin and subcutaneous tissue

Creation of thalamic stimulator pulse generator pocket, new site

Escharotomy

Exploration:
    sinus tract, skin
    superficial fossa

Relocation of subcutaneous device pocket NEC

Reopening subcutaneous pocket for device revision without replacement

Undercutting of hair follicle

EXCLUDES   *that of:*
    cardiac pacemaker pocket, new site (37.79)
    ▶*creation of loop recorder pocket, new site and insertion/relocation of device (37.79)*
    creation of pocket for implantable, patient-activated cardiac event recorder and insertion/relocation of device (37.79)◀
    fascial compartments of face and mouth (27.0)
    ▶*removal of catheter from cranial cavity (01.27)*◀

AHA: ▶1Q, '05, 17;◀2Q, '04, 7, 8; 4Q, '00, 68; 4Q, '99, 21; 4Q, '97, 57; 3Q, '89, 17; N-D, '86, 1; N-D, '84, 6

✓4ᵗʰ 86.1   Diagnostic procedures on skin and subcutaneous tissue

86.11   Biopsy of skin and subcutaneous tissue

86.19   Other diagnostic procedures on skin and subcutaneous tissue

EXCLUDES   *microscopic examination of specimen from skin and subcutaneous tissue (91.61-91.79)*

✓4ᵗʰ 86.2   Excision or destruction of lesion or tissue of skin and subcutaneous tissue

86.21   Excision of pilonidal cyst or sinus

Marsupialization of cyst

EXCLUDES   *incision of pilonidal cyst or sinus (86.03)*

DEF: Marsupialization of cyst: Incision of cyst and suturing edges to skin to open site.

86.22   Excisional debridement of wound, infection, or burn

Removal by excision of:
    devitalized tissue
    necrosis
    slough

EXCLUDES   *debridement of:*
    abdominal wall (wound) (54.3)
    bone (77.60-77.69)
    muscle (83.45)
        of hand (82.36)
    nail (bed) (fold) (86.27)
    nonexcisional debridement of wound, infection, or burn (86.28)
    open fracture site (79.60-79.69)
    pedicle or flap graft (86.75)

AHA: ▶1Q, '05, 14;◀4Q, '04, 138; 3Q,'02, 23; 2Q, '00, 9; 1Q, '99, 8; 2Q, '92, 17; 3Q, '91, 18; 3Q, '89, 16; 4Q, '88, 5; N-D, '86, 1

86.23   Removal of nail, nailbed, or nail fold

86.24   Chemosurgery of skin

Chemical peel of skin

DEF: Chemicals applied to destroy skin tissue.

DEF: Chemical peel of skin: Chemicals used to peel skin layers.

86.25   Dermabrasion

That with laser

EXCLUDES   *dermabrasion of wound to remove embedded debris (86.28)*

DEF: Removal of wrinkled or scarred skin; with fine sandpaper, wire, brushes or laser.

86.26   Ligation of dermal appendage

EXCLUDES   *excision of preauricular appendage (18.29)*

DEF: Tying off extra skin.

86.27   Debridement of nail, nail bed, or nail fold

Removal of:
    necrosis
    slough

EXCLUDES   *removal of nail, nail bed, or nail fold (86.23)*

86.28   Nonexcisional debridement of wound infection, or burn

Debridement NOS

Maggot therapy

Removal of devitalized tissue, necrosis, and slough by such methods as:
    brushing
    irrigation (under pressure)
    scrubbing
    washing

AHA: ▶1Q, '05, 14;◀2Q, '04, 5, 6; 4Q, '03, 110; 2Q, '03, 15; 3Q, '02, 23; 2Q, '01, 18; 3Q,'91, 18; 4Q, '88, 5

DEF: Removal of damaged skin; by methods other than excision.

86.3   Other local excision or destruction of lesion or tissue of skin and subcutaneous tissue

Destruction of skin by: Destruction of skin by:
    cauterization   fulguration
    cryosurgery   laser beam
That with Z-plasty

EXCLUDES   *adipectomy (86.83)*
    biopsy of skin (86.11)
    wide or radical excision of skin (86.4)
    Z-plasty without excision (86.84)

AHA: 1Q, '96, 15; 2Q, '90, 27; 1Q, '89, 12; 3Q, '89, 18; 4Q, '88, 7

✓4ᵗʰ
✓5ᵗʰ   Additional Digit Required   RUG III Special Care Procedure   RUG III Clinically Complex Procedure   RUG III Extensive Services Procedure   RUG III Rehab Procedure

2006 ICD•9•CM   **October 2005 • Volume 3 — 189**

Operations on the Integumentary System

86.4–86.82

86.4   **Radical excision of skin lesion**

Wide excision of skin lesion involving underlying or adjacent structure

Code also any lymph node dissection (40.3-40.5)

✓4ᵗʰ **86.5**   **Suture or other closure of skin and subcutaneous tissue**

86.51   **Replantation of scalp**

86.59   **Closure of skin and subcutaneous tissue of other sites**

Adhesives (surgical) (tissue)
Staples
Sutures

> EXCLUDES   application of adhesive strips (butterfly) — omit code

AHA: 4Q, '99, 23

✓4ᵗʰ **86.6**   **Free skin graft**

> INCLUDES   excision of skin for autogenous graft
> EXCLUDES   construction or reconstruction of:
>   penis (64.43-64.44)
>   trachea (31.75)
>   vagina (70.61-70.62)

DEF: Transplantation of skin to another site.

86.60   **Free skin graft, not otherwise specified**

86.61   **Full-thickness skin graft to hand**

> EXCLUDES   heterograft (86.65)
>   homograft (86.66)

86.62   **Other skin graft to hand**

> EXCLUDES   heterograft (86.65)
>   homograft (86.66)

86.63   **Full-thickness skin graft to other sites**

> EXCLUDES   heterograft (86.65)
>   homograft (86.66)

86.64   **Hair transplant**

> EXCLUDES   hair follicle transplant to eyebrow or eyelash (08.63)

86.65   **Heterograft to skin**

Pigskin graft   Porcine graft

> EXCLUDES   application of dressing only (93.57)

AHA: 3Q,'02, 23

DEF: Implantation of nonhuman tissue.

86.66   **Homograft to skin**

Graft to skin of:
    amnionic membrane   } from donor
    skin

DEF: Implantation of tissue from human donor.

86.67   **Dermal regenerative graft**

Artificial skin, NOS
Creation of "neodermis"
Decellularized allodermis
Integumentary matrix implants
Prosthetic implant of dermal layer of skin
Regenerate dermal layer of skin

> EXCLUDES   heterograft to skin (86.65)
>   homograft to skin (86.66)

AHA: 4Q, '98, 76, 79

DEF: Replacement of dermis and epidermal layer of skin by cultured or regenerated autologous tissue; used to treat full-thickness or deep partial-thickness burns; also called cultured epidermal autograft (CEA).

86.69   **Other skin graft to other sites**

> EXCLUDES   heterograft (86.65)
>   homograft (86.66)

AHA: 4Q, '99, 15

✓4ᵗʰ **86.7**   **Pedicle grafts or flaps**

> EXCLUDES   construction or reconstruction of:
>   penis (64.43-64.44)
>   trachea (31.75)
>   vagina (70.61-70.62)

DEF: Full thickness skin and subcutaneous tissue partially attached to the body by a narrow strip of tissue so that it retains its blood supply. The unattached portion is sutured to the defect.

86.70   **Pedicle or flap graft, not otherwise specified**

86.71   **Cutting and preparation of pedicle grafts or flaps**

Elevation of pedicle from its bed
Flap design and raising
Partial cutting of pedicle or tube
Pedicle delay

> EXCLUDES   pollicization or digital transfer (82.61,82.81)
>   revision of pedicle (86.75)

AHA: 4Q, '01, 66

DEF: Elevation and preparation of tissue still attached to vascular bed; delayed implant.

DEF: Elevation of pedicle from its bed: Separation of tissue implanted from its bed.

DEF: Flap design and raising: Planing and elevation of tissue to be implanted.

86.72   **Advancement of pedicle graft**

AHA: 3Q, '99, 9, 10

86.73   **Attachment of pedicle or flap graft to hand**

> EXCLUDES   pollicization or digital transfer (82.61, 82.81)

86.74   **Attachment of pedicle or flap graft to other sites**

Attachment by: Attachment by:
   advanced flap   rotating flap
   double pedicled flap   sliding flap
   pedicle graft   tube graft

AHA: 3Q, '99, 9; 1Q, '96, 15

DEF: Fixation of tissue implant still connected to original site, other than hand.

DEF: Attachment by:

Advanced flap: Sliding tissue implant into new position.

Double pedicle flap: Implant connected to two vascular beds.

Pedicle graft: Implant connected to vascular bed.

Rotating flap: Implant rotated along curved incision.

Sliding flap: Sliding implant to site.

Tube graft: Double tissue implant to form tube with base connected to original site.

86.75   **Revision of pedicle or flap graft**

Debridement   } of pedicle or flap
Defatting   }   graft

DEF: Connection of implant still attached to its vascular tissue.

✓4ᵗʰ **86.8**   **Other repair and reconstruction of skin and subcutaneous tissue**

86.81   **Repair for facial weakness**

86.82   **Facial rhytidectomy**

Face lift

> EXCLUDES   rhytidectomy of eyelid (08.86-08.87)

DEF: Revision and tightening of excess, wrinkled facial skin.

N Newborn Age: 0   P Pediatric Age: 0-17   M Maternity Age: 12-55   A Adult Age: 15-124   Adj Adjunct Code   ◄► Revised Text   ● New Code   ▲ Revised Code Title

86.83 Size reduction plastic operation
Liposuction
Reduction of adipose tissue of:
abdominal wall (pendulous)
arms (batwing)
buttock
thighs (trochanteric lipomatosis)
> **EXCLUDES** breast (85.31-85.32)

DEF: Excision and plastic repair of excess skin and underlying tissue.

86.84 Relaxation of scar or web contracture of skin
Z-plasty of skin
> **EXCLUDES** Z-plasty with excision of lesion (86.3)

86.85 Correction of syndactyly
DEF: Plastic repair of webbed fingers or toes.

86.86 Onychoplasty
DEF: Plastic repair of nail or nail bed.

86.89 Other repair and reconstruction of skin and subcutaneous tissue
> **EXCLUDES** mentoplasty (76.67-76.68)

AHA: 4Q, '02, 107; 1Q, '00, 26; 2Q, '98, 20; 2Q, '93, 11; 2Q, '92, 17

✓4th **86.9 Other operations on skin and subcutaneous tissue**
86.91 Excision of skin for graft
Excision of skin with closure of donor site
> **EXCLUDES** that with graft at same operative episode (86.60-86.69)

86.92 Electrolysis and other epilation of skin
> **EXCLUDES** epilation of eyelid (08.91-08.93)

86.93 Insertion of tissue expander
Insertion (subcutaneous) (soft tissue) of expander (one or more) in scalp (subgaleal space), face, neck, trunk except breast, and upper and lower extremities for development of skin flaps for donor use
> **EXCLUDES** flap graft preparation (86.71)
> tissue expander, breast (85.95)

86.94 Insertion or replacement of single array neurostimulator pulse generator, not specified as rechargeable
Pulse generator (single array, single channel) for intracranial, spinal, and peripheral neurostimulator
Code also any associated lead implantation (02.93, 03.93, 04.92)
> **EXCLUDES** ▶ insertion or replacement of single array rechargeable neurostimulator pulse generator (86.97)◀

AHA: 4Q, '04, 135

86.95 Insertion or replacement of dual array neurostimulator pulse generator, not specified as rechargeable
Pulse generator (dual array, dual channel) for intracranial, spinal, and peripheral neurostimulator
Code also any associated lead implantation (02.93, 03.93, 04.92)
> **EXCLUDES** ▶ insertion or replacement of dual array rechargeable neurostimulator pulse generator (86.98)◀

86.96 Insertion or replacement of other neurostimulator pulse generator
Code also any associated lead implantation (02.93, 03.93, 04.92)
> **EXCLUDES** insertion of dual array neurostimulator pulse generator ▶(86.95, 86.98)◀
> insertion of single array neurostimulator pulse generator ▶(86.94, 86.97)◀

86.97 Insertion or replacement of single array rechargeable neurostimulator pulse generator
Rechargeable pulse generator (single array, single channel) for intracranial, spinal, and peripheral neurostimulator
Code also any associated lead implantation (02.93, 03.93, 04.92)

86.98 Insertion or replacement of dual array rechargeable neurostimulator pulse generator
Rechargeable pulse generator (dual array, dual channel) for intracranial, spinal, and peripheral neurostimulator
Code also any associated lead implantation (02.93, 03.93, 04.92)

86.99 Other
> **EXCLUDES** removal of sutures from:
> abdomen (97.83)
> head and neck (97.38)
> thorax (97.43)
> trunk NEC (97.84)
> wound catheter:
> irrigation (96.58)
> replacement (97.15)

AHA: 4Q, '97, 57; N-D, '86, 1

✓4th
✓5th Additional Digit Required   RUG III Special Care Procedure   RUG III Clinically Complex Procedure   RUG III Extensive Services Procedure   RUG III Rehab Procedure

2006 ICD•9•CM   October 2005 • Volume 3 — 191

16. MISCELLANEOUS DIAGNOSTIC AND THERAPEUTIC PROCEDURES (87-99)

√3rd **87　Diagnostic radiology**

√4th **87.0　Soft tissue x-ray of face, head, and neck**

EXCLUDES　*angiography (88.40-88.68)*

87.01　Pneumoencephalogram

DEF: Radiographic exam of cerebral ventricles and subarachnoid spaces; with injection of air or gas for contrast.

87.02　Other contrast radiogram of brain and skull

Pneumocisternogram
Pneumoventriculogram
Posterior fossa myelogram

DEF: Pneumocisternogram: Radiographic exam of subarachnoid spaces after injection of gas for contrast.

DEF: Pneumoventriculography: Radiographic exam of cerebral ventricles after injection of gas for contrast.

DEF: Posterior fossa myelogram: Radiographic exam of posterior channel of spinal cord after injection of gas or contrast.

87.03　Computerized axial tomography of head

C.A.T. scan of head

AHA: 3Q, '99, 7

87.04　Other tomography of head

87.05　Contrast dacryocystogram

DEF: Radiographic exam of tear sac after injection of contrast.

87.06　Contrast radiogram of nasopharynx

87.07　Contrast laryngogram

87.08　Cervical lymphangiogram

DEF: Radiographic exam of lymph vessels of neck; with or without contrast.

87.09　Other soft tissue x-ray of face, head, and neck

Noncontrast x-ray of:	Noncontrast x-ray of:
adenoid	salivary gland
larynx	thyroid region
nasolacrimal duct	uvula
nasopharynx	

EXCLUDES　*x-ray study of eye (95.14)*

√4th **87.1　Other x-ray of face, head, and neck**

EXCLUDES　*angiography (88.40-88.68)*

87.11　Full-mouth x-ray of teeth

87.12　Other dental x-ray

Orthodontic cephalogram or cephalometrics
Panorex examination of mandible
Root canal x-ray

87.13　Temporomandibular contrast arthrogram

87.14　Contrast radiogram of orbit

87.15　Contrast radiogram of sinus

87.16　Other x-ray of facial bones

X-ray of:	X-ray of:
frontal area	orbit
mandible	supraorbital area
maxilla	symphysis menti
nasal sinuses	zygomaticomaxillary
nose	complex

87.17　Other x-ray of skull

Lateral projection
Sagittal projection } of skull
Tangential projection

DEF: Lateral projection: Side to side view of head.

DEF: Sagittal projection: View of body in plane running midline from front to back.

DEF: Tangential projection: Views from adjacent skull surfaces.

√4th **87.2　X-ray of spine**

87.21　Contrast myelogram

DEF: Radiographic exam of space between middle and outer spinal cord coverings after injection of contrast.

87.22　Other x-ray of cervical spine

87.23　Other x-ray of thoracic spine

87.24　Other x-ray of lumbosacral spine

Sacrococcygeal x-ray

87.29　Other x-ray of spine

Spinal x-ray NOS

√4th **87.3　Soft tissue x-ray of thorax**

EXCLUDES　*angiocardiography (88.50-88.58)*
angiography (88.40-88.68)

87.31　Endotracheal bronchogram

DEF: Radiographic exam of lung, main branch, with contrast introduced through windpipe.

87.32　Other contrast bronchogram

Transcricoid bronchogram

DEF: Transcricoid bronchogram: Radiographic exam of lung, main branch, with contrast introduced through cartilage of neck.

87.33　Mediastinal pneumogram

DEF: Radiographic exam of cavity containing heart, esophagus and adjacent structures.

87.34　Intrathoracic lymphangiogram

DEF: Radiographic exam of lymphatic vessels within chest; with or without contrast.

87.35　Contrast radiogram of mammary ducts

DEF: Radiographic exam of mammary ducts; with contrast.

87.36　Xerography of breast

DEF: Radiographic exam of breast via selenium-coated plates.

87.37　Other mammography

AHA: 3Q, '89, 17; 2Q, '90, 28; N-D, '87, 1

87.38　Sinogram of chest wall

Fistulogram of chest wall

DEF: Radiographic exam of chest cavity.

DEF: Fistulogram of chest wall: Radiographic exam of abnormal opening in chest.

87.39　Other soft tissue x-ray of chest wall

√4th **87.4　Other x-ray of thorax**

EXCLUDES　*angiocardiography (88.50-88.58)*
angiography (88.40-88.68)

87.41　Computerized axial tomography of thorax

C.A.T. scan
Crystal linea scan of x-ray
　beam
Electronic subtraction } of thorax
Photoelectric response
Tomography with use of computer, x-rays, and camera

87.42　Other tomography of thorax

Cardiac tomogram

DEF: Radiographic exam of chest plane.

87.43　X-ray of ribs, sternum, and clavicle

Examination for:
　cervical rib
　fracture

87.44　Routine chest x-ray, so described

X-ray of chest NOS

87.49　Other chest x-ray

X-ray of:	X-ray of:
bronchus NOS	lung NOS
diaphragm NOS	mediastinum NOS
heart NOS	trachea NOS

N Newborn Age: 0　　P Pediatric Age: 0-17　　M Maternity Age: 12-55　　A Adult Age: 15-124　　Adj Adjunct Code　　►◄ Revised Text　　● New Code　　▲ Revised Code Title

192 — Volume 3　　　　　　　　　　　　　　　　　　　　　　　　　　　　　　　　　　　　2006 ICD•9•CM

✓4th 87.5 Biliary tract x-ray

87.51 Percutaneous hepatic cholangiogram
AHA: 2Q, '90, 28; N-D, '87, 1

DEF: Radiographic exam of bile tract of gallbladder; with needle injection of contrast into bile duct of liver.

87.52 Intravenous cholangiogram

DEF: Radiographic exam of bile ducts; with intravenous contrast injection.

87.53 Intraoperative cholangiogram
AHA: 1Q, '96, 12; 2Q, '90, 28; 3Q, '89, 18; 4Q, '88, 7

DEF: Radiographic exam of bile ducts; with contrast; following gallbladder removal.

87.54 Other cholangiogram
87.59 Other biliary tract x-ray
Cholecystogram

✓4th 87.6 Other x-ray of digestive system
87.61 Barium swallow
87.62 Upper GI series
87.63 Small bowel series
87.64 Lower GI series
87.65 Other x-ray of intestine
87.66 Contrast pancreatogram
87.69 Other digestive tract x-ray

✓4th 87.7 X-ray of urinary system
EXCLUDES angiography of renal vessels (88.45, 88.65)

87.71 Computerized axial tomography of kidney
C.A.T. scan of kidney

87.72 Other nephrotomogram

DEF: Radiographic exam of kidney plane.

87.73 Intravenous pyelogram
Diuretic infusion pyelogram

DEF: Radiographic exam of lower kidney, with intravenous contrast injection.

DEF: Diuretic infusion pyelogram: Radiographic exam of lower kidney with diuretic contrast.

87.74 Retrograde pyelogram
87.75 Percutaneous pyelogram
87.76 Retrograde cystourethrogram

DEF: Radiographic exam of bladder and urethra with contrast injected through catheter into bladder.

87.77 Other cystogram
87.78 Ileal conduitogram
AHA: M-J, '87, 11

DEF: Radiographic exam of passage created between ureter and artificial opening into abdomen.

87.79 Other x-ray of the urinary system
KUB x-ray

Ureteropyelography

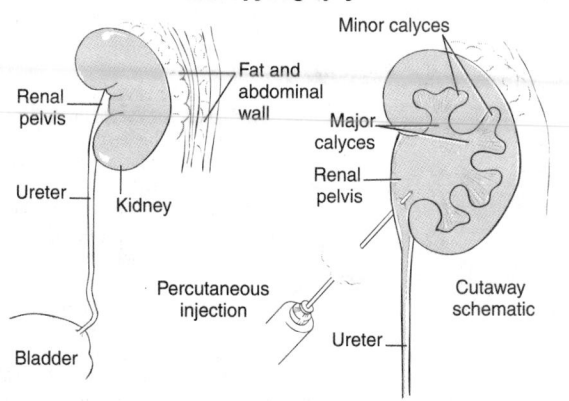

Minor calyces
Fat and abdominal wall
Renal pelvis
Major calyces
Ureter
Kidney
Renal pelvis
Percutaneous injection
Cutaway schematic
Bladder
Ureter

✓4th 87.8 X-ray of female genital organs
87.81 X-ray of gravid uterus ♀
Intrauterine cephalometry by x-ray

87.82 Gas contrast hysterosalpingogram ♀

DEF: Radiographic exam of uterus and fallopian tubes; with gas contrast.

87.83 Opaque dye contrast hysterosal-pingogram ♀
87.84 Percutaneous hysterogram ♀

DEF: Radiographic exam of uterus with contrast injected through body wall.

87.85 Other x-ray of fallopian tubes and uterus ♀
87.89 Other x-ray of female genital organs ♀

✓4th 87.9 X-ray of male genital organs
87.91 Contrast seminal vesiculogram ♂
87.92 Other x-ray of prostate and seminal vesicles ♂
87.93 Contrast epididymogram ♂
87.94 Contrast vasogram ♂
87.95 Other x-ray of epididymis and vas deferens ♂
87.99 Other x-ray of male genital organs ♂

✓3rd 88 Other diagnostic radiology and related techniques
✓4th 88.0 Soft tissue x-ray of abdomen
EXCLUDES angiography (88.40-88.68)

88.01 Computerized axial tomography of abdomen
C.A.T. scan of abdomen
EXCLUDES CA.T. scan of kidney (87.71)
AHA: 2Q, '98, 13

88.02 Other abdomen tomography
EXCLUDES nephrotomogram (87.72)

88.03 Sinogram of abdominal wall
Fistulogram of abdominal wall

DEF: Radiographic exam of abnormal abdominal passage.

88.04 Abdominal lymphangiogram

DEF: Radiographic exam of abdominal lymphatic vessels; with contrast.

88.09 Other soft tissue x-ray of abdominal wall

✓4th 88.1 Other x-ray of abdomen
88.11 Pelvic opaque dye contrast radiography
88.12 Pelvic gas contrast radiography
Pelvic pneumoperitoneum
88.13 Other peritoneal pneumogram
88.14 Retroperitoneal fistulogram
88.15 Retroperitoneal pneumogram
88.16 Other retroperitoneal x-ray
88.19 Other x-ray of abdomen
Flat plate of abdomen
AHA: 3Q, '99, 9

✓4th 88.2 Skeletal x-ray of extremities and pelvis
EXCLUDES contrast radiogram of joint (88.32)
88.21 Skeletal x-ray of shoulder and upper arm
88.22 Skeletal x-ray of elbow and forearm
88.23 Skeletal x-ray of wrist and hand
88.24 Skeletal x-ray of upper limb, not otherwise specified
88.25 Pelvimetry

DEF: Imaging of pelvic bones to measure pelvic capacity.

88.26 Other skeletal x-ray of pelvis and hip
88.27 Skeletal x-ray of thigh, knee, and lower leg
88.28 Skeletal x-ray of ankle and foot
88.29 Skeletal x-ray of lower limb, not otherwise specified

✓4th ✓5th Additional Digit Required   RUG III Special Care Procedure   RUG III Clinically Complex Procedure   RUG III Extensive Services Procedure   RUG III Rehab Procedure

2006 ICD•9•CM   Volume 3 — 193

Diagnostic and Therapeutic Procedures

88.3–88.6

√4ᵗʰ **88.3**   **Other x-ray**

     88.31   **Skeletal series**

         X-ray of whole skeleton

     88.32   **Contrast arthrogram**

         EXCLUDES   *that of temporomandibular joint (87.13)*

     88.33   **Other skeletal x-ray**

         EXCLUDES   *skeletal x-ray of:*
                extremities and pelvis (88.21-88.29)
                face, head, and neck (87.11-87.17)
                spine (87.21-87.29)
                thorax (87.43)

     88.34   **Lymphangiogram of upper limb**

     88.35   **Other soft tissue x-ray of upper limb**

     88.36   **Lymphangiogram of lower limb**

     88.37   **Other soft tissue x-ray of lower limb**

         EXCLUDES   *femoral angiography (88.48, 88.66)*

     88.38   **Other computerized axial tomography**

         C.A.T. scan NOS

         EXCLUDES   *C.A.T. scan of:*
                abdomen (88.01)
                head (87.03)
                kidney (87.71)
                thorax (87.41)

     88.39   **X-ray, other and unspecified**

√4ᵗʰ **88.4**   **Arteriography using contrast material**

         INCLUDES   angiography of arteries
                arterial puncture for injection of contrast material
                radiography of arteries (by fluoroscopy)
                retrograde arteriography

     Note: The fourth-digit subclassification identifies the site to be viewed, not the site of injection.

         EXCLUDES   *arteriography using:*
                radioisotopes or radionuclides (92.01-92.19)
                ultrasound (88.71-88.79)
                fluorescein angiography of eye (95.12)

     AHA: N-D, '85, 14

     DEF: Electromagnetic wave photography of arteries; with contrast.

     88.40   **Arteriography using contrast material, unspecified site**

     88.41   **Arteriography of cerebral arteries**

         Angiography of:
            basilar artery
            carotid (internal)
            posterior cerebral circulation
            vertebral artery

         AHA: 1Q, '00, 16; 1Q, '99, 7; 1Q, '97, 3

     88.42   **Aortography**

         Arteriography of aorta and aortic arch

         AHA: 1Q, '99, 17

     88.43   **Arteriography of pulmonary arteries**

     88.44   **Arteriography of other intrathoracic vessels**

         EXCLUDES   *angiocardiography (88.50-88.58)*
                arteriography of coronary arteries (88.55-88.57)

     88.45   **Arteriography of renal arteries**

     88.46   **Arteriography of placenta**   ♀

         Placentogram using contrast material

     88.47   **Arteriography of other intra-abdominal arteries**

         AHA: 1Q, '00, 18; N-D, '87, 4

     88.48   **Arteriography of femoral and other lower extremity arteries**

         AHA: 3Q, '03, 10; 1Q, '03, 17; 2Q, '96, 6; 2Q, '89, 17

     88.49   **Arteriography of other specified sites**

√4ᵗʰ **88.5**   **Angiocardiography using contrast material**

         INCLUDES   arterial puncture and insertion of arterial catheter for injection of contrast material
                cineangiocardiography
                selective angiocardiography

     Code also synchronous cardiac catheterization (37.21-37.23)

         EXCLUDES   *angiography of pulmonary vessels (88.43, 88.62)*

     AHA: 3Q, '92, 10; M-J, '87, 11

     DEF: Electromagnetic wave photography of heart and great vessels; with contrast.

     88.50   **Angiocardiography, not otherwise specified**

     88.51   **Angiocardiography of venae cavae**

         Inferior vena cavography
         Phlebography of vena cava (inferior) (superior)

     88.52   **Angiocardiography of right heart structures**

         Angiocardiography of:
            pulmonary valve
            right atrium
            right ventricle (outflow tract)

         EXCLUDES   *that combined with left heart angiocardiography (88.54)*

     88.53   **Angiocardiography of left heart structures**

         Angiocardiography of:
            aortic valve
            left atrium
            left ventricle (outflow tract)

         EXCLUDES   *that combined with right heart angiocardiography (88.54)*

         AHA: 1Q, '00, 20; 4Q, '88, 4

     88.54   **Combined right and left heart angiocardiography**

     88.55   **Coronary arteriography using a single catheter**

         Coronary arteriography by Sones technique
         Direct selective coronary arteriography using a single catheter

         AHA: 3Q, '02, 20

     88.56   **Coronary arteriography using two catheters**

         Coronary arteriography by:
            Judkins technique
            Ricketts and Abrams technique
         Direct selective coronary arteriography using two catheters

         AHA: 1Q, '00, 20; 4Q, '88, 4

     88.57   **Other and unspecified coronary arteriography**

         Coronary arteriography NOS

         AHA: 1Q, '00, 21

     88.58   **Negative-contrast cardiac roentgenography**

         Cardiac roentgenography with injection of carbon dioxide

√4ᵗʰ **88.6**   **Phlebography**

         INCLUDES   angiography of veins
                radiography of veins (by fluoroscopy)
                retrograde phlebography
                venipuncture for injection of contrast material
                venography using contrast material

     Note: The fourth-digit subclassification (88.60-88.67) identifies the site to be viewed, not the site of injection.

         EXCLUDES   *angiography using:*
                radioisotopes or radionuclides (92.01-92.19)
                ultrasound (88.71-88.79)
                fluorescein angiography of eye (95.12)

     DEF: Electromagnetic wave photography of veins; with contrast.

N Newborn Age: 0   P Pediatric Age: 0-17   M Maternity Age: 12-55   A Adult Age: 15-124   **Adj** Adjunct Code   ◄► Revised Text   ● New Code   ▲ Revised Code Title

88.60 **Phlebography using contrast material, unspecified site**

88.61 **Phlebography of veins of head and neck using contrast material**

88.62 **Phlebography of pulmonary veins using contrast material**

88.63 **Phlebography of other intrathoracic veins using contrast material**

88.64 **Phlebography of the portal venous system using contrast material**
　　　Splenoportogram (by splenic arteriography)

88.65 **Phlebography of other intra-abdominal veins using contrast material**

88.66 **Phlebography of femoral and other lower extremity veins using contrast material**

88.67 **Phlebography of other specified sites using contrast material**

88.68 **Impedance phlebography**

√4ᵗʰ **88.7** **Diagnostic ultrasound**
　　　INCLUDES　echography
　　　　　　non-invasive ultrasound
　　　　　　ultrasonic angiography
　　　　　　ultrasonography
　　　EXCLUDES　*intravascular imaging (adjunctive) (IVUS) (00.21-00.29)*
　　　　　　therapeutic ultrasound (00.01-00.09)
　DEF: Graphic recording of anatomical structures via high frequency, sound-wave imaging and computer graphics.

88.71 **Diagnostic ultrasound of head and neck**
　　　Determination of midline shift of brain
　　　Echoencephalography
　　　EXCLUDES　*eye (95.13)*
　　　AHA: 1Q, '92, 11

88.72 **Diagnostic ultrasound of heart**
　　　Echocardiography
　　　Transesophageal echocardiography
　　　EXCLUDES　*echocardiography of heart chambers (37.28)*
　　　　　　intracardiac echocardiography (ICE) (37.28)
　　　　　　intravascular (IVUS) imaging of coronary vessels (00.24)
　　　AHA: 4Q, '04, 121; 1Q, '04, 16; 1Q, '00, 20, 21; 1Q, '99, 6; 3Q, '98, 11

88.73 **Diagnostic ultrasound of other sites of thorax**
　　　Aortic arch ⎫
　　　Breast　　⎬ ultrasonography
　　　Lung　　 ⎭
　　　AHA: 1Q, '02, 10

88.74 **Diagnostic ultrasound of digestive system**

88.75 **Diagnostic ultrasound of urinary system**

88.76 **Diagnostic ultrasound of abdomen and retroperitoneum**
　　　AHA: 2Q, '99, 14

88.77 **Diagnostic ultrasound of peripheral vascular system**
　　　Deep vein thrombosis ultrasonic scanning
　　　EXCLUDES ▸ *adjunct vascular system procedures (00.40-00.43)*◂
　　　AHA: 4Q, '99, 17; 1Q, '99, 12; 1Q, '92, 11

88.78 **Diagnostic ultrasound of gravid uterus**　♀
　　　Intrauterine cephalometry:
　　　　echo
　　　　ultrasonic
　　　Placental localization by ultrasound

88.79 **Other diagnostic ultrasound**
　　　Ultrasonography of:　Ultrasonography of:
　　　　multiple sites　　　total body
　　　　nongravid uterus

√4ᵗʰ **88.8** **Thermography**
　　　DEF: Infrared photography to determine various body temperatures.

88.81 **Cerebral thermography**

88.82 **Ocular thermography**

88.83 **Bone thermography**
　　　Osteoarticular thermography

88.84 **Muscle thermography**

88.85 **Breast thermography**

88.86 **Blood vessel thermography**
　　　Deep vein thermography

88.89 **Thermographay of other sites**
　　　Lymph gland thermography
　　　Thermography NOS

√4ᵗʰ **88.9** **Other diagnostic imaging**

88.90 **Diagnostic imaging, not elsewhere classified**

88.91 **Magnetic resonance imaging of brain and brain stem**
　　　EXCLUDES　*intraoperative magnetic resonance imaging (88.96)*
　　　　　　real-time magnetic resonance imaging (88.96)

88.92 **Magnetic resonance imaging of chest and myocardium**

88.93 **Magnetic resonance imaging of spinal canal**
　　　Spinal cord levels:
　　　　cervical
　　　　thoracic
　　　　lumbar (lumbosacral)
　　　Spinal cord
　　　Spine

88.94 **Magnetic resonance imaging of musculoskeletal**
　　　Bone marrow blood supply
　　　Extremities (upper) (lower)

88.95 **Magnetic resonance imaging of pelvis, prostate, and bladder**

88.96 **Other intraoperative magnetic resonance imaging**
　　　iMRI
　　　Real-time magnetic resonance imaging
　　　AHA: 4Q, '02, 111

88.97 **Magnetic resonance imaging of other and unspecified sites**
　　　Abdomen　　　　Face
　　　Eye orbit　　　　Neck

88.98 **Bone mineral density studies**
　　　Dual photon absorptiometry
　　　Quantitative computed tomography (CT) studies
　　　Radiographic densitometry
　　　Single photon absorptiometry
　DEF: Dual photon absorptiometry: Measurement of bone mineral density by comparing dissipation of emission from two separate photoelectric energy peaks.
　DEF: Quantitative computed tomography (CT) studies: Computer assisted analysis of x-ray absorption through bone to determine density.
　DEF: Radiographic densiometry: Measurement of bone mineral density by degree of bone radiopacity.
　DEF: Single photon absorptiometry: Measurement of bone mineral density by degree of dissipation of emission from one photoelectric energy peaks emitted by gadolinium 153.

√3ʳᵈ **89** **Interview, evaluation, consultation, and examination**

√4ᵗʰ **89.0** **Diagnostic interview, consultation, and evaluation**
　　　EXCLUDES　*psychiatric diagnostic interview (94.11-94.19)*

89.01 **Interview and evaluation, described as brief**
　　　Abbreviated history and evaluation

89.02 **Interview and evaluation, described as limited**
　　　Interval history and evaluation

√4ᵗʰ / √5ᵗʰ　Additional Digit Required　　RUG III Special Care Procedure　　　RUG III Clinically Complex Procedure　　　RUG III Extensive Services Procedure　　　RUG III Rehab Procedure

Diagnostic and Therapeutic Procedures

89.03–89.43

89.03 **Interview and evaluation, described as comprehensive**
History and evaluation of new problem

89.04 **Other interview and evaluation**

89.05 **Diagnostic interview and evaluation, not otherwise specified**

89.06 **Consultation, described as limited**
Consultation on a single organ system

89.07 **Consultation, described as comprehensive**

89.08 **Other consultation**

89.09 **Consulation, not otherwise specified**

✓4ᵗʰ **89.1** **Anatomic and physiologic measurements and manual examinations — nervous system and sense organs**

> EXCLUDES ear examination (95.41-95.49)
> eye examination (95.01-95.26)
> the listed procedures when done as part of a general physical examination (89.7)

89.10 **Intracarotid amobarbital test**
Wada test

DEF: Amobarbital injections into internal carotid artery to induce hemiparalysis to determine the hemisphere that controls speech and language.

89.11 **Tonometry**

DEF: Pressure measurements inside eye.

89.12 **Nasal function study**
Rhinomanometry

DEF: Rhinomanometry: Measure of degree of nasal cavity obstruction.

89.13 **Neurologic examination**

89.14 **Electroencephalogram**

> EXCLUDES that with polysomnogram (89.17)

DEF: Recording of electrical currents in brain via electrodes to detect epilepsy, lesions and other encephalopathies.

89.15 **Other nonoperative neurologic function tests**
AHA: 3Q, '95, 5; 2Q, '91, 14; J-F, '87, 16; N-D, '84, 6

89.16 **Transillumination of newborn skull**

DEF: Light passed through newborn skull for diagnostic purposes.

89.17 **Polysomnogram**
Sleep recording

DEF: Graphic studies of sleep patterns.

89.18 **Other sleep disorder function tests**
Multiple sleep latency test [MSLT]

89.19 **Video and radio-telemetered electroencephalographic monitoring**
Radiographic ⎫
Video   ⎬ EEG Monitoring

AHA: 1Q, '92, 17; 2Q, '90, 27

✓4ᵗʰ **89.2** **Anatomic and physiologic measurements and manual examinations — genitourinary system**

> EXCLUDES the listed procedures when done as part of a general physical examination (89.7)

AHA: 1Q, '90, 27

89.21 **Urinary manometry**
Manometry through: Manometry through:
  indwelling ureteral   pyelostomy
  catheter   ureterostomy
  nephrostomy

DEF: Measurement of urinary pressure.

DEF: Manometry through:
  Indwelling urinary catheter: Semipermanent urinary catheter.
  Nephrostomy: Opening into pelvis of kidney.
  Pyelostomy: Opening in lower kidney.
  Ureterostomy: Opening into ureter.
  Indwelling urinary catheter: Semipermanent urinary catheter.

89.22 **Cystometrogram**

DEF: Pressure recordings at various stages of bladder filling.

89.23 **Urethral sphincter electromyogram**

89.24 **Uroflowmetry [UFR]**

DEF: Continuous recording of urine flow.

89.25 **Urethral pressure profile [UPP]**

89.26 **Gynecological examination** ♀
Pelvic examination

89.29 **Other nonoperative genitourinary system measurements**
Bioassay of urine   Urine chemistry
Renal clearance

AHA: N-D, '84, 6

✓4ᵗʰ **89.3** **Other anatomic and physiologic measurements and manual examinations**

> EXCLUDES the listed procedures when done as part of a general physical examination (89.7)

89.31 **Dental examination**
Oral mucosal survey
Periodontal survey

89.32 **Esophageal manometry**

AHA: 3Q, '96, 13

DEF: Measurement of esophageal fluid and gas pressures.

89.33 **Digital examination of enterostomy stoma**
Digital examination of colostomy stoma

89.34 **Digital examination of rectum**

89.35 **Transillumination of nasal sinuses**

89.36 **Manual examination of breast**

89.37 **Vital capacity determination**

DEF: Measurement of expelled gas volume after full inhalation.

89.38 **Other nonoperative respiratory measurements**
Plethysmography for measurement of respiratory function
Thoracic impedance plethysmography

AHA: S-O, '87, 6

DEF: Plethysmography for measurement of respiratory function: Registering changes in respiratory function as noted in blood circulation.

89.39 **Other nonoperative measurements and examinations**
¹⁴ C-Urea breath test
Basal metabolic rate [BMR]
Gastric:
  analysis
  function NEC

> EXCLUDES body measurement (93.07)
> cardiac tests (89.41-89.69)
> fundus photography (95.11)
> limb length measurement (93.06)

AHA: 2Q, '01, 9; 3Q, '00, 9; 3Q, '96, 12; 1Q, '94, 18; N-D, '84, 6

✓4ᵗʰ **89.4** **Cardiac stress tests, pacemaker and defibrillator checks**

89.41 **Cardiovascular stress test using treadmill**
AHA: 1Q, '88, 11

89.42 **Masters' two-step stress test**
AHA: 1Q, '88, 11

89.43 **Cardiovascular stress test using bicycle ergometer**
AHA: 1Q, '88, 11

DEF: Electrocardiogram during exercise on bicycle with device capable of measuring muscular, metabolic and respiratory effects of exercise.

N Newborn Age: 0   P Pediatric Age: 0-17   M Maternity Age: 12-55   A Adult Age: 15-124   Adj Adjunct Code   ►◄ Revised Text   ● New Code   ▲ Revised Code Title

89.44 Other cardiovascular stress test
Thallium stress test with or without transesophageal pacing

89.45 Artificial pacemaker rate check
Artificial pacemaker function check NOS
Bedside device check of pacemaker or cardiac resynchronization pacemaker [CRT-P]
Interrogation only without arrhythmia induction
> **EXCLUDES** electrophysiologic studies [EPS] (37.26)
> non-invasive programmed electrical stimulation [NIPS] (arrhythmia induction) (37.26)

AHA: 1Q, '02, 3

89.46 Artificial pacemaker artifact wave form check

89.47 Artificial pacemaker electrode impedance check

89.48 Artificial pacemaker voltage or amperage threshold check

89.49 Automatic implantable cardioverter/ defibrillator (AICD) check
Bedside check of an AICD or cardiac resynchronization defibrillator [CRT-D]
Checking pacing thresholds of device
Interrogation only without arrhythmia induction
> **EXCLUDES** electrophysiologic studies [EPS] (37.26)
> non-invasive programmed electrical stimulation [NIPS] (arrhythmia induction) (37.26)

AHA: ▶4Q, '04, 136◀

√4th **89.5 Other nonoperative cardiac and vascular diagnostic procedures**
> **EXCLUDES** fetal EKG (75.32)

89.50 Ambulatory cardiac monitoring
Analog devices [Holter-type]
AHA: 4Q, '99, 21; 4Q, '91, 23

89.51 Rhythm electrocardiogram
Rhythm EKG (with one to three leads)

89.52 Electrocardiogram
ECG NOS
EKG (with 12 or more leads)
AHA: 1Q, '88, 11; S-O, '87, 6

89.53 Vectorcardiogram (with ECG)

89.54 Electrographic monitoring
Telemetry
> **EXCLUDES** ambulatory cardiac monitoring (89.50)
> electrographic monitoring during surgery — omit code

AHA: 4Q, '91, 23; 1Q, '88, 11

DEF: Evaluation of heart electrical activity by continuous screen monitoring.

DEF: Telemetry: Evaluation of heart electrical activity; with radio signals at distance from patient.

89.55 Phonocardiogram with ECG lead

89.56 Carotid pulse tracing with ECG lead
> **EXCLUDES** oculoplethysmography (89.58)

89.57 Apexcardiogram (with ECG lead)
AHA: J-F, '87, 16

89.58 Plethysmogram
Penile plethysmography with nerve stimulation
> **EXCLUDES** plethysmography (for):
> measurement of respiratory function (89.38)
> thoracic impedance (89.38)

AHA: S-O, '87, 7

DEF: Determination and recording of blood pressure variations present or passing through an organ.

89.59 Other nonoperative cardiac and vascular measurements
AHA: 3Q, '03, 23; 2Q, '92, 12

√4th **89.6 Circulatory monitoring**
> **EXCLUDES** electrocardiographic monitoring during surgery — omit code

AHA: M-J, '87, 11

89.60 Continuous intra-arterial blood gas monitoring
Insertion of blood gas monitoring system and continuous monitoring of blood gases through an intra-arterial sensor
AHA: 4Q, '02, 111

89.61 Systemic arterial pressure monitoring

89.62 Central venous pressure monitoring

89.63 Pulmonary artery pressure monitoring
> **EXCLUDES** pulmonary artery wedge monitoring (89.64)

89.64 Pulmonary artery wedge monitoring
Pulmonary capillary wedge [PCW] monitoring
Swan-Ganz catheterization

DEF: Monitoring pulmonary artery pressure via catheter inserted through right lower and upper heart chambers into pulmonary artery and advancing the balloon-tip to wedge it in the distal pulmonary artery branch.

89.65 Measurement of systemic arterial blood gases
> **EXCLUDES** continuous intra-arterial blood gas monitoring (89.60)

89.66 Measurement of mixed venous blood gases

89.67 Monitoring of cardiac output by oxygen consumption technique
Fick method

DEF: Fick method: Indirect measure of cardiac output through blood volume flow over pulmonary capillaries; determines oxygen absorption by measurement of arterial oxygen content versus venous oxygen content.

89.68 Monitoring of cardiac output by other technique
Cardiac output monitor by thermodilution indicator

DEF: Cardiac output monitor by thermodilution indicator: Injection of ice cold dextrose solution into right lower heart chamber; temperature sensitive catheter monitors disappearance from beat to beat to measure expelled blood volume.

Central Venous Pressure Monitoring

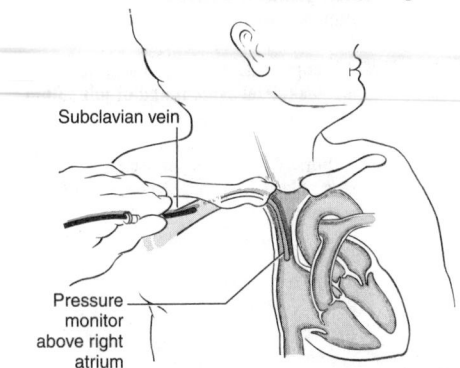

Subclavian vein

Pressure monitor above right atrium

√4th
√5th Additional Digit Required   RUG III Special Care Procedure   RUG III Clinically Complex Procedure   RUG III Extensive Services Procedure   RUG III Rehab Procedure

89.69   **Monitoring of coronary blood flow**
    Coronary blood flow monitoring by
       coincidence counting technique

89.7   **General physical examination**

89.8   **Autopsy**

√3ʳᵈ **90**   **Microscopic examination - I**

The following fourth-digit subclassification is for use with
categories in section 90 to identify type of examination:

    1   bacterial smear
    2   culture
    3   culture and sensitivity
    4   parasitology
    5   toxicology
    6   cell block and Papanicolaou smear
    9   other microscopic examination

√4ᵗʰ **90.0**   **Microscopic examination of specimen from nervous system and of spinal fluid**

√4ᵗʰ **90.1**   **Microscopic examination of specimen from endocrine gland, not elsewhere classified**

√4ᵗʰ **90.2**   **Microscopic examination of specimen from eye**

√4ᵗʰ **90.3**   **Microscopic examination of specimen from ear, nose, throat, and larynx**

√4ᵗʰ **90.4**   **Microscopic examination of specimen from trachea, bronchus, pleura, lung, and other thoracic specimen, and of sputum**

√4ᵗʰ **90.5**   **Microscopic examination of blood**

√4ᵗʰ **90.6**   **Microscopic examination of specimen from spleen and of bone marrow**

√4ᵗʰ **90.7**   **Microscopic examination of specimen from lymph node and of lymph**

√4ᵗʰ **90.8**   **Microscopic examination of specimen from upper gastrointestinal tract and of vomitus**

√4ᵗʰ **90.9**   **Microscopic examination of specimen from lower gastrointestinal tract and of stool**

√3ʳᵈ **91**   **Microscopic examination - II**

The following fourth-digit subclassification is for use with
categories in section 91 to identify type of examination:

    1   bacterial smear
    2   culture
    3   culture and sensitivity
    4   parasitology
    5   toxicology
    6   cell block and Papanicolaou smear
    9   other microscopic examination

√4ᵗʰ **91.0**   **Microscopic examination of specimen from liver, biliary tract, and pancreas**

√4ᵗʰ **91.1**   **Microscopic examination of peritoneal and retroperitoneal specimen**

√4ᵗʰ **91.2**   **Microscopic examination of specimen from kidney, ureter, perirenal and periureteral tissue**

√4ᵗʰ **91.3**   **Microscopic examination of specimen from bladder, urethra, prostate, seminal vesicle, perivesical tissue, and of urine and semen**

√4ᵗʰ **91.4**   **Microscopic examination of specimen from female genital tract**   ♀
    Amnionic sac
    Fetus

√4ᵗʰ **91.5**   **Microscopic examination of specimen from musculoskeletal system and of joint fluid**
    Microscopic examination of:

bone	ligament
bursa	muscle
cartilage	synovial membrane
fascia	tendon

√4ᵗʰ **91.6**   **Microscopic examination of specimen from skin and other integument**
    Microscopic examination of:
    hair
    nails
    skin
    EXCLUDES   *mucous membrane — code to organ site that of operative wound (91.71-91.79)*

√4ᵗʰ **91.7**   **Microscopic examination of specimen from operative wound**

√4ᵗʰ **91.8**   **Microscopic examination of specimen from other site**

√4ᵗʰ **91.9**   **Microscopic examination of specimen from unspecified site**

√3ʳᵈ **92**   **Nuclear medicine**

√4ᵗʰ **92.0**   **Radioisotope scan and function study**

    92.01   **Thyroid scan and radioisotope function studies**
       Iodine-131 uptake   Radio-iodine uptake
       Protein-bound iodine

    92.02   **Liver scan and radioisotope function study**

    92.03   **Renal scan and radioisotope function study**
       Renal clearance study

    92.04   **Gastrointestinal scan and radioisotope function study**
       Radio-cobalt B_{12} Schilling test
       Radio-iodinated triolein study

    92.05   **Cardiovascular and hematopoietic scan and radioisotope function study**
       Bone marrow
       Cardiac output
       Circulation time   ⎫ scan or function
       Radionuclide cardiac   ⎬ study
         ventriculogram
       Spleen   ⎭

       AHA: 2Q, '92, 7; 1Q, '88, 11

    92.09   **Other radioisotope function studies**

√4ᵗʰ **92.1**   **Other radioisotope scan**

    92.11   **Cerebral scan**
       Pituitary

    92.12   **Scan of other sites of head**
       EXCLUDES   *eye (95.16)*

    92.13   **Parathyroid scan**

    92.14   **Bone scan**

    92.15   **Pulmonary scan**

    92.16   **Scan of lymphatic system**

    92.17   **Placental scan**

    92.18   **Total body scan**

    92.19   **Scan of other sites**

√4ᵗʰ **92.2**   **Therapeutic radiology and nuclear medicine**
    EXCLUDES   *that for:*
       ablation of pituitary gland (07.64-07.69)
       destruction of chorioretinal lesion (14.26-14.27)

    AHA: 3Q, '92, 5

    DEF: Radiation and nuclear isotope treatment of diseased tissue.

●   **92.20**   **Infusion of liquid brachytherapy radioisotope**
       I-125 radioisotope
       Intracavitary brachytherapy
       INCLUDES   removal of radioisotope

    92.21   **Superficial radiation**
       Contact radiation [up to 150 KVP]

    92.22   **Orthovoltage radiation**
       Deep radiation [200-300 KVP]

    92.23   **Radioisotopic teleradiotherapy**
       Teleradiotherapy using:
         cobalt-60   radioactive cesium
         iodine-125

N Newborn Age: 0   **P** Pediatric Age: 0-17   **M** Maternity Age: 12-55   **A** Adult Age: 15-124   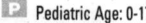 Adjunct Code   ►◄ Revised Text   ● New Code   ▲ Revised Code Title

92.24 Teleradiotherapy using photons
Megavoltage NOS
Supervoltage NOS
Use of:
   Betatron
   linear accelerator

92.25 Teleradiotherapy using electrons
Beta particles

92.26 Teleradiotherapy of other particulate radiation
Neutrons   Protons NOS

92.27 Implantation or insertion of radioactive elements
Intravascular brachytherapy
Code also incision of site
> EXCLUDES ▶ infusion of liquid brachytherapy radioisotope (92.20)◀

AHA: 1Q, '04, 3-4; 1Q, '00, 11, 12; 3Q, '94, 11; 1Q, '88, 4

92.28 Injection or instillation of radioisotopes
Injection or infusion of
   radioimmunoconjugate
Intracavitary injection or instillation
Intravenous injection or instillation
Iodine-131 [I-131] tositumomab
Radioimmunotherapy
Ytrium-90 [Y-90] ibritumomab tiuxetan
> EXCLUDES ▶ infusion of liquid brachytherapy radioisotope (92.20)◀

92.29 Other radiotherapeutic procedure

✓4ᵗʰ 92.3 Stereotactic radiosurgery
Code also stereotactic head frame application (93.59)
> EXCLUDES   stereotactic biopsy

AHA: 4Q, '98, 79; 4Q, '95, 70

DEF: Ablation of deep intracranial lesions; single procedure; placement of head frame for 3-D analysis of lesion, followed by radiation treatment from helmet attached to frame.

92.30 Stereotactic radiosurgery, not otherwise specified

92.31 Single source photon radiosurgery
High energy x-rays
Linear accelerator (LINAC)

92.32 Multi-source photon radiosurgery
Cobalt 60 radiation
Gamma irradiation

AHA: 4Q, '04, 113

92.33 Particulate radiosurgery
Particle beam radiation (cyclotron)
Proton accelerator

92.39 Stereotactic radiosurgery, not elsewhere classified

✓3ʳᵈ 93 Physical therapy, respiratory therapy, rehabilitation, and related procedures

✓4ᵗʰ 93.0 Diagnostic physical therapy
AHA: N-D, '86, 7

93.01 Functional evaluation

93.02 Orthotic evaluation

93.03 Prosthetic evaluation

93.04 Manual testing of muscle function
AHA: J-F, '87, 16

93.05 Range of motion testing
AHA: J-F, '87, 16

93.06 Measurement of limb length

93.07 Body measurement
Girth measurement
Measurement of skull circumference

93.08 Electromyography
> EXCLUDES   eye EMG (95.25)
> that with polysomnogram (89.17)
> urethral sphincter EMG (89.23)

AHA: J-F, '87, 16

DEF: Graphic recording of electrical activity of muscle.

93.09 Other diagnostic physical therapy procedure

✓4ᵗʰ 93.1 Physical therapy exercises
AHA: J-F, '87, 16; N-D, '86, 7

93.11 Assisting exercise
> EXCLUDES   assisted exercise in pool (93.31)

93.12 Other active musculoskeletal exercise

93.13 Resistive exercise

93.14 Training in joint movements

93.15 Mobilization of spine

93.16 Mobilization of other joints
> EXCLUDES   manipulation of temporomandibular joint (76.95)

93.17 Other passive musculoskeletal exercise

93.18 Breathing exercise

93.19 Exercise, not elsewhere classified

✓4ᵗʰ 93.2 Other physical therapy musculoskeletal manipulation
AHA: N-D, '86, 7

93.21 Manual and mechanical traction
> EXCLUDES   skeletal traction (93.43-93.44)
> skin traction (93.45-93.46)
> spinal traction (93.41-93.42)

93.22 Ambulation and gait training

93.23 Fitting of orthotic device

93.24 Training in use of prosthetic or orthotic device
Training in crutch walking

93.25 Forced extension of limb

93.26 Manual rupture of joint adhesions
DEF: Therapeutic application of force to rupture adhesions restricting movement.

93.27 Stretching of muscle or tendon

93.28 Stretching of fascia

93.29 Other forcible correction of deformity
AHA: N-D, 85, 11

✓4ᵗʰ 93.3 Other physical therapy therapeutic procedures

93.31 Assisted exercise in pool

93.32 Whirlpool treatment

93.33 Other hydrotherapy

93.34 Diathermy

93.35 Other heat therapy
Acupuncture with smouldering moxa
Hot packs
Hyperthermia NEC
Infrared irradiation
Moxibustion
Paraffin bath
> EXCLUDES   hyperthermia for treatment of cancer (99.85)

DEF: Moxibustion: Igniting moxa, a Chinese plant, for counterirritation of skin.

DEF: Paraffin bath: Hot wax treatment.

93.36 Cardiac retraining
DEF: Cardiac rehabilitation regimen following myocardial infarction or coronary bypass graft procedure.

93.37 Prenatal training
Training for natural childbirth

✓4ᵗʰ ✓5ᵗʰ Additional Digit Required   RUG III Special Care Procedure   RUG III Clinically Complex Procedure   RUG III Extensive Services Procedure   RUG III Rehab Procedure

93.38　Combined physical therapy without mention of the components

93.39　Other physical therapy
AHA: 4Q, '03, 105-106, 108-110; 3Q, '97, 12; 3Q, '91, 15

√4th **93.4　Skeletal traction and other traction**

93.41　Spinal traction using skull device
Traction using:　　　Traction using:
caliper tongs　　　　halo device
Crutchfield tongs　　Vinke tongs
EXCLUDES　insertion of tongs or halo traction device (02.94)

AHA: 3Q, '01, 8; 3Q, '96, 14; 2Q, '94, 3

DEF: Applying device to head to exert pulling force on spine.

93.42　Other spinal traction
Cotrel's traction
EXCLUDES　cervical collar (93.52)

DEF: Pulling force exerted on spine without skull device.

93.43　Intermittent skeletal traction

93.44　Other skeletal traction
Bryant's
Dunlop's
Lyman Smith　}　traction
Russell's

93.45　Thomas' splint traction
DEF: Thomas splint: Placement of ring around thigh, attached to rods running length of leg for therapeutic purposes.

93.46　Other skin traction of limbs
Adhesive tape traction　Buck's traction
Boot traction　　　　　Gallows traction

√4th **93.5　Other immobilization, pressure, and attention to wound**
EXCLUDES ▶external fixator device (84.71-84.73)◀
wound cleansing (96.58-96.59)

93.51　Application of plaster jacket
EXCLUDES　Minerva jacket (93.52)

93.52　Application of neck support
Application of:　　　Application of:
cervical collar　　　molded neck support
Minerva jacket

93.53　Application of other cast

93.54　Application of splint
Plaster splint　　Tray splint
EXCLUDES　periodontal splint (24.7)

93.55　Dental wiring
EXCLUDES　that for orthodontia (24.7)

93.56　Application of pressure dressing
Application of:
Gibney bandage
Robert Jones' bandage
Shanz dressing

93.57　Application of other wound dressing
Porcine wound dressing
AHA: 3Q, '02, 23

93.58　Application of pressure trousers
Application of:
anti-shock trousers
MAST trousers
vasopneumatic device
AHA: 3Q, '96, 13

93.59　Other immobilization, pressure, and attention to wound
Elastic stockings
Electronic gaiter
Intermittent pressure device
Oxygenation of wound (hyperbaric)
Stereotactic head frame application
Velpeau dressing
AHA: 3Q, '99, 7; 1Q, '99, 12, 13; 1Q, '91, 11; 1Q, '89, 12

√4th **93.6　Osteopathic manipulative treatment**

93.61　Osteopathic manipulative treatment for general mobilization
General articulatory treatment

93.62　Osteopathic manipulative treatment using high-velocity, low-amplitude forces
Thrusting forces

93.63　Osteopathic manipulative treatment using low-velocity, high-amplitude forces
Springing forces

93.64　Osteopathic manipulative treatment using isotonic, isometric forces

93.65　Osteopathic manipulative treatment using indirect forces

93.66　Osteopathic manipulative treatment to move tissue fluids
Lymphatic pump

93.67　Other specified osteopathic manipulative treatment

√4th **93.7　Speech and reading rehabilitation and rehabilitation of the blind**

93.71　Dyslexia training

93.72　Dysphasia training
DEF: Speech training to coordinate and arrange words in proper sequence.

93.73　Esophageal speech training
DEF: Speech training after voice box removal; sound is produced by vibration of air column in esophagus against the cricopharangeal sphincter.

93.74　Speech defect training

93.75　Other speech training and therapy
AHA: 4Q, '03, 105, 109; 4Q, '97, 36; 3Q, '97, 12

93.76　Training in use of lead dog for the blind

93.77　Training in braille or Moon

93.78　Other rehabilitation for the blind

√4th **93.8　Other rehabilitation therapy**

93.81　Recreational therapy
Diversional therapy
Play therapy
EXCLUDES　play psychotherapy (94.36)

93.82　Educational therapy
Education of bed-bound children
Special schooling for the handicapped

93.83　Occupational therapy
Daily living activities therapy
EXCLUDES　training in activities of daily living for the blind (93.78)

AHA: 4Q, '03, 105-106, 108-110; 3Q, '97, 12

93.84　Music therapy

93.85　Vocational rehabilitation
Sheltered employment
Vocational:
assessment
retraining
training

93.89　Rehabilitation, not elsewhere classified

√4th **93.9　Respiratory therapy**
EXCLUDES　insertion of airway (96.01-96.05)
other continuous mechanical ventilation (96.70-96.72)

93.90　Continuous positive airway pressure [CPAP]
Bi-level airway pressure
Non-invasive positive pressure (NIPPV)
AHA: 3Q, '04, 3; 1Q, '02, 12, 13; 3Q, '98, 14; 4Q, '91, 21

DEF: Noninvasive ventilation support system that augments the ability to breathe spontaneously without the insertion of an endotracheal tube or tracheostomy.

N Newborn Age: 0　　P Pediatric Age: 0-17　　M Maternity Age: 12-55　　A Adult Age: 15-124　　Adj Adjunct Code　　▶◀ Revised Text　　● New Code　　▲ Revised Code Title

93.91 Intermittent positive pressure breathing [IPPB]
    AHA: 4Q, '91, 21

93.93 Nonmechanical methods of resuscitation
    Artificial respiration
    Manual resuscitation
    Mouth-to-mouth resuscitition
    AHA: 2Q, '03, 17

93.94 Respiratory medication administered by nebulizer
    Mist therapy

93.95 Hyperbaric oxygenation
    EXCLUDES   *oxygenation of wound (93.59)*

93.96 Other oxygen enrichment
    Catalytic oxygen therapy
    Cytoreductive effect
    Oxygenators
    Oxygen therapy
    EXCLUDES   *oxygenation of wound (93.59)*

93.97 Decompression chamber

93.98 Other control of atmospheric pressure and composition
    Antigen-free air conditioning
    Helium therapy
    EXCLUDES   *inhaled nitric oxide therapy (INO) (00.12)*
    AHA: 1Q, '02, 14

93.99 Other respiratory procedures
    Continuous negative pressure ventilation [CNP]
    Postural drainage
    AHA: 4Q, '03, 108; 3Q, '99, 11; 4Q, '91, 22

√3rd **94 Procedures related to the psyche**

√4th **94.0 Psychologic evaluation and testing**

94.01 Administration of intelligence test
    Administration of:
      Stanford-Binet
      Wechsler Adult Intelligence Scale
      Wechsler Intelligence Scale for Children

94.02 Administration of psychologic test
    Administration of:
      Bender Visual-Motor Gestalt Test
      Benton Visual Retention Test
      Minnesota Multiphasic Personality Inventory
      Wechsler Memory Scale

94.03 Character analysis

94.08 Other psychologic evaluation and testing

94.09 Psychologic mental status determination, not otherwise specified

√4th **94.1 Psychiatric interviews, consultations, and evaluations**

94.11 Psychiatric mental status determination
    Clinical psychiatric mental status determination
    Evaluation for criminal responsibility
    Evaluation for testimentary capacity
    Medicolegal mental status determination
    Mental status determination NOS

94.12 Routine psychiatric visit, not otherwise specified

94.13 Psychiatric commitment evaluation
    Pre-commitment interview

94.19 Other psychiatric interview and evaluation
    Follow-up psychiatric interview NOS

√4th **94.2 Psychiatric somatotherapy**
    DEF: Biological treatment of mental disorders.

94.21 Narcoanalysis
    Narcosynthesis

94.22 Lithium therapy

94.23 Neuroleptic therapy

94.24 Chemical shock therapy

94.25 Other psychiatric drug therapy
    AHA: S-O, '86, 4

94.26 Subconvulsive electroshock therapy

94.27 Other electroshock therapy
    Electroconvulsive therapy (ECT)
    EST

94.29 Other psychiatric somatotherapy

√4th **94.3 Individual psychotherapy**

94.31 Psychoanalysis

94.32 Hypnotherapy
    Hypnodrome   Hypnosis

94.33 Behavior therapy
    Aversion therapy
    Behavior modification
    Desensitization therapy
    Extinction therapy
    Relaxation training
    Token economy

94.34 Individual therapy for psychosexual dysfunction
    EXCLUDES   *that performed in group setting (94.41)*

94.35 Crisis intervention

94.36 Play psychotherapy

94.37 Exploratory verbal psychotherapy

94.38 Supportive verbal psychotherapy

94.39 Other individual psychotherapy
    Biofeedback

√4th **94.4 Other psychotherapy and counselling**

94.41 Group therapy for psychosexual dysfunction

94.42 Family therapy

94.43 Psychodrama

94.44 Other group therapy

94.45 Drug addiction counselling

94.46 Alcoholism counselling

94.49 Other counselling

√4th **94.5 Referral for psychologic rehabilitation**

94.51 Referral for psychotherapy

94.52 Referral for psychiatric aftercare
    That in:
      halfway house
      outpatient (clinic) facility

94.53 Referral for alcoholism rehabilitation

94.54 Referral for drug addiction rehabilitation

94.55 Referral for vocational rehabilitation

94.59 Referral for other psychologic rehabilitation

√4th **94.6 Alcohol and drug rehabilitation and detoxification**
    AHA: 2Q, '91, 12

94.61 Alcohol rehabilitation
    DEF: Program designed to restore social and physical functioning, free of the dependence of alcohol.

94.62 Alcohol detoxification
    DEF: Treatment of physical symptoms during withdrawal from alcohol dependence.

94.63 Alcohol rehabilitation and detoxification

94.64 Drug rehabilitation
    DEF: Program designed to restore social and physical functioning, free of the dependence of drugs.

94.65 Drug detoxification
    DEF: Treatment of physical symptoms during withdrawal from drug dependence.

94.66 Drug rehabilitation and detoxification

94.67 Combined alcohol and drug rehabilitation

94.68 Combined alcohol and drug detoxification

94.69 Combined alcohol and drug rehabilitation and detoxification

---

√4th √5th   Additional Digit Required   ░ RUG III Special Care Procedure   ░ RUG III Clinically Complex Procedure   ░ RUG III Extensive Services Procedure   ░ RUG III Rehab Procedure

√3rd **95**   **Ophthalmologic and otologic diagnosis and treatment**

√4th **95.0**   **General and subjective eye examination**

95.01   **Limited eye examination**
Eye examination with prescription of spectacles

95.02   **Comprehensive eye examination**
Eye examination covering all aspects of the visual system

95.03   **Extended ophthalmologic work-up**
Examination (for):
glaucoma
neuro-ophthalmology
retinal disease

95.04   **Eye examination under anesthesia**
Code also type of examination

95.05   **Visual field study**

95.06   **Color vision study**

95.07   **Dark adaptation study**
DEF: Exam of eye's adaption to dark.

95.09   **Eye examination, not otherwise specified**
Vision check NOS

√4th **95.1**   **Examinations of form and structure of eye**

95.11   **Fundus photography**

95.12   **Fluorescein angiography or angioscopy of eye**

95.13   **Ultrasound study of eye**

95.14   **X-ray study of eye**

95.15   **Ocular motility study**

95.16   **P_{32} and other tracer studies of eye**

√4th **95.2**   **Objective functional tests of eye**
EXCLUDES   *that with polysomnogram (89.17)*

95.21   **Electroretinogram [ERG]**

95.22   **Electro-oculogram [EOG]**

95.23   **Visual evoked potential [VEP]**
DEF: Measuring and recording evoked visual responses of body and senses.

95.24   **Electronystagmogram [ENG]**
DEF: Monitoring of brain waves to record induced and spontaneous eye movements.

95.25   **Electromyogram of eye [EMG]**

95.26   **Tonography, provocative tests, and other glaucoma testing**

√4th **95.3**   **Special vision services**

95.31   **Fitting and dispensing of spectacles**

95.32   **Prescription, fitting, and dispensing of contact lens**

95.33   **Dispensing of other low vision aids**

95.34   **Ocular prosthetics**

95.35   **Orthoptic training**

95.36   **Ophthalmologic counselling and instruction**
Counselling in:
adaptation to visual loss
use of low vision aids

√4th **95.4**   **Nonoperative procedures related to hearing**

95.41   **Audiometry**
Békésy 5-tone audiometry
Impedance audiometry
Stapedial reflex response
Subjective audiometry
Tympanogram

95.42   **Clinical test of hearing**
Tuning fork test   Whispered speech test

95.43   **Audiological evaluation**
Audiological evaluation by:
Bárány noise machine
blindfold test
delayed feedback
masking
Weber lateralization

95.44   **Clinical vestibular function tests**
Thermal test of vestibular function

95.45   **Rotation tests**
Bárány chair
DEF: Irrigation of ear canal with warm or cold water to evaluate vestibular function.

95.46   **Other auditory and vestibular function tests**

95.47   **Hearing examination, not otherwise specified**

95.48   **Fitting of hearing aid**
EXCLUDES   *implantation of electromagnetic hearing device (20.95)*
AHA: 4Q, '89, 5

95.49   **Other nonoperative procedures related to hearing**
Adjustment (external components) of cochlear prosthetic device

√3rd **96**   **Nonoperative intubation and irrigation**

√4th **96.0**   **Nonoperative intubation of gastrointestinal and respiratory tracts**

96.01   **Insertion of nasopharyngeal airway**

96.02   **Insertion of oropharyngeal airway**

96.03   **Insertion of esophageal obturator airway**

96.04   **Insertion of endotracheal tube**

96.05   **Other intubation of respiratory tract**
AHA: 1Q, '97, 14

96.06   **Insertion of Sengstaken tube**
Esophageal tamponade
DEF: Insertion of Sengstaken tube: Nonsurgical emergency measure to stop esophageal bleeding using compression exerted by inflated balloons; additional tube ports aspirate blood and clots.

96.07   **Insertion of other (naso-) gastric tube**
Intubation for decompression
EXCLUDES   *that for enteral infusion of nutritional substance (96.6)*

96.08   **Insertion of (naso-) intestinal tube**
Miller-Abbott tube (for decompression)

96.09   **Insertion of rectal tube**
Replacement of rectal tube

√4th **96.1**   **Other nonoperative insertion**
EXCLUDES   *nasolacrimal intubation (09.44)*

96.11   **Packing of external auditory canal**

96.14   **Vaginal packing**   ♀

96.15   **Insertion of vaginal mold**   ♀

96.16   **Other vaginal dilation**   ♀

96.17   **Insertion of vaginal diaphragm**   ♀

96.18   **Insertion of other vaginal pessary**   ♀

96.19   **Rectal packing**

√4th **96.2**   **Nonoperative dilation and manipulation**

96.21   **Dilation of frontonasal duct**

Endotracheal Intubation

Laryngoscope

Larynx

Trachea

Balloon inflated above carina

N Newborn Age: 0   P Pediatric Age: 0-17   M Maternity Age: 12-55   A Adult Age: 15-124   Adj Adjunct Code   ►◄ Revised Text   ● New Code   ▲ Revised Code Title

96.22 Dilation of rectum

96.23 Dilation of anal sphincter

96.24 Dilation and manipulation of enterostomy stoma

96.25 Therapeutic distention of bladder
Intermittent distention of bladder

96.26 Manual reduction of rectal prolapse

96.27 Manual reduction of hernia

96.28 Manual reduction of enterostomy prolapse
AHA: N-D, '87, 11

96.29 Reduction of intussusception of alimentary tract
With:
   fluoroscopy
   ionizing radiation enema
   ultrasonography guidance
Hydrostatic reduction
Pneumatic reduction
> EXCLUDES   *intra-abdominal manipulation of intestine, not otherwise specified (46.80)*

AHA: 4Q, '98, 82

✓4th **96.3 Nonoperative alimentary tract irrigation, cleaning, and local instillation**

96.31 Gastric cooling
Gastric hypothermia
DEF: Reduction of internal stomach temperature.

96.32 Gastric freezing

96.33 Gastric lavage

96.34 Other irrigation of (naso-)gastric tube

96.35 Gastric gavage
DEF: Food forced into stomach.

96.36 Irrigation of gastrostomy or enterostomy

96.37 Proctoclysis
DEF: Slow introduction of large amounts of fluids into lower large intestine.

96.38 Removal of impacted feces
Removal of impaction:
   by flushing manually

96.39 Other transanal enema
Rectal irrigation
> EXCLUDES   *reduction of intussusception of alimentary tract by ionizing radiation enema (96.29)*

✓4th **96.4 Nonoperative irrigation, cleaning, and local instillation of other digestive and genitourinary organs**

96.41 Irrigation of cholecystostomy and other biliary tube

96.42 Irrigation of pancreatic tube

96.43 Digestive tract instillation, except gastric gavage

96.44 Vaginal douche   ♀

96.45 Irrigation of nephrostomy and pyelostomy

96.46 Irrigation of ureterostomy and ureteral catheter

96.47 Irrigation of cystostomy

96.48 Irrigation of other indwelling urinary catheter

96.49 Other genitourinary instillation
Insertion of prostaglandin suppository
AHA: 1Q, '01, 5

✓4th **96.5 Other nonoperative irrigation and cleaning**

96.51 Irrigation of eye
Irrigation of cornea
> EXCLUDES   *irrigation with removal of foreign body (98.21)*

96.52 Irrigation of ear
Irrigation with removal of cerumen

96.53 Irrigation of nasal passages

96.54 Dental scaling, polishing, and debridement
Dental prophylaxis   Plaque removal

96.55 Tracheostomy toilette

96.56 Other lavage of bronchus and trachea
> EXCLUDES   *diagnostic bronchoalveolar lavage (BAL) (33.24)*
>   *whole lung lavage (33.99)*

AHA: 3Q, '02, 18

96.57 Irrigation of vascular catheter
AHA: 3Q, '93, 5

96.58 Irrigation of wound catheter

96.59 Other irrigation of wound
Wound cleaning NOS
> EXCLUDES   *debridement (86.22, 86.27-86.28)*

AHA: S-O, '85, 7

96.6 Enteral infusion of concentrated-nutritional substances

✓4th **96.7 Other continuous mechanical ventilation**
> INCLUDES   Endotracheal respiratory assistance
>   Intermittent mandatory ventilation [IMV]
>   Positive end expiratory pressure [PEEP]
>   Pressure support ventilation [PSV]
>   That by tracheostomy
>   Weaning of an intubated (endotracheal tube) patient
> EXCLUDES   *bi-level airway pressure (93.90)*
>   *continuous negative pressure ventilation [CNP] (iron lung) (cuirass) (93.99)*
>   *continuous positive airway pressure [CPAP] (93.90)*
>   *intermittent positive pressure breathing [IPPB] (93.91)*
>   *non-invasive positive pressure (NIPPV) (93.90)*
>   *that by face mask (93.90-93.99)*
>   *that by nasal cannula (93.90-93.99)*
>   *that by nasal catheter (93.90-93.99)*

Code also any associated:
   endotracheal tube insertion (96.04)
   tracheostomy (31.1-31.29)

Note: Endotracheal intubation
To calculate the number of hours (duration) of continuous mechanical ventilation during a hospitalization, begin the count from the start of the (endotracheal) intubation. The duration ends with (endotracheal) extubation.

If a patient is intubated prior to admission, begin counting the duration from the time of the admission. If a patient is transferred (discharged) while intubated, the duration would end at the time of transfer (discharge).

For patients who begin on (endotracheal) intubation and subsequently have a tracheostomy performed for mechanical ventilation, the duration begins with the (endotracheal) intubation and ends when the mechanical ventilation is turned off (after the weaning period).

Tracheostomy
To calculate the number of hours of continuous mechanical ventilation during a hospitalization, begin counting the duration when mechanical ventilation is started. The duration ends when the mechanical ventilator is turned off (after the weaning period).

If a patient has received a tracheostomy prior to admission and is on mechanical ventilation at the time of admission, begin counting the duration from the time of admission. If a patient is transferred (discharged) while still on mechanical ventilation via tracheostomy, the duration would end at the time of the transfer (discharge).

AHA: ▶3Q, '04, 3;◀ 2Q, '92, 13; 4Q, '91, 16; 4Q, '91, 18; 4Q, '91, 21

✓4th Additional Digit Required   RUG III Special Care Procedure   RUG III Clinically Complex Procedure   RUG III Extensive Services Procedure   RUG III Rehab Procedure
✓5th

2006 ICD•9•CM   **February 2005 • Volume 3 — 203**

Diagnostic and Therapeutic Procedures

96.70–97.69

96.70 Continuous mechanical ventilation of unspecified duration
Mechanical ventilation NOS

96.71 Continuous mechanical ventilation for less than 96 consecutive hours
AHA: ▶3Q, '04, 11;◀ 2Q, '02, 19; 1Q, '02, 12; 1Q, '01, 6

96.72 Continuous mechanical ventilation for 96 consecutive hours or more
AHA: ▶1Q, '04, 23◀

✓3rd **97 Replacement and removal of therapeutic appliances**

✓4th **97.0 Nonoperative replacement of gastrointestinal appliance**

97.01 Replacement of (naso-)gastric or esophagostomy tube

97.02 Replacement of gastrostomy tube
AHA: 1Q, '97, 11

97.03 Replacement of tube or enterostomy device of small intestine
AHA: 1Q, '03, 10

97.04 Replacement of tube or enterostomy device of large intestine

97.05 Replacement of stent (tube) in biliary or pancreatic duct
AHA: 2Q, '99, 13

✓4th **97.1 Nonoperative replacement of musculoskeletal and integumentary system appliance**

97.11 Replacement of cast on upper limb

97.12 Replacement of cast on lower limb

97.13 Replacement of other cast

97.14 Replacement of other device for musculoskeletal immobilization

97.15 Replacement of wound catheter

97.16 Replacement of wound packing or drain
EXCLUDES   *repacking of:*
dental wound (97.22)
vulvar wound (97.26)

✓4th **97.2 Other nonoperative replacement**

97.21 Replacement of nasal packing

97.22 Replacement of dental packing

97.23 Replacement of tracheostomy tube
AHA: N-D, '87, 11

97.24 Replacement and refitting of vaginal diaphragm ♀

97.25 Replacement of other vaginal pessary ♀

97.26 Replacement of vaginal or vulvar packing or drain ♀

97.29 Other nonoperative replacements
AHA: 3Q, '99, 9; 3Q, '98, 12

✓4th **97.3 Nonoperative removal of therapeutic device from head and neck**

97.31 Removal of eye prosthesis
EXCLUDES   *removal of ocular implant (16.71)*
removal of orbital implant (16.72)

97.32 Removal of nasal packing

97.33 Removal of dental wiring

97.34 Removal of dental packing

97.35 Removal of dental prosthesis

97.36 Removal of other external mandibular fixation device

97.37 Removal of tracheostomy tube

97.38 Removal of sutures from head and neck

97.39 Removal of other therapeutic device from head and neck
EXCLUDES   *removal of skull tongs (02.94)*

✓4th **97.4 Nonoperative removal of therapeutic device from thorax**

97.41 Removal of thoracotomy tube or pleural cavity drain
AHA: 1Q, '99, 10

97.42 Removal of mediastinal drain

97.43 Removal of sutures from thorax

97.44 Nonoperative removal of heart assist system
Explantation [removal] of circulatory assist device
Explantation [removal] of percutaneous external heart assist device
Removal of extrinsic heart assist device
Removal of pVAD
Removal of percutaneous heart assist device
AHA: 4Q, '01, 65

DEF: Non-invasive removal of ventricular assist systems, or intraaortic balloon pump, which is a balloon catheter placed into the descending thoracic aorta and timed to inflate and deflate with the patient's own heart rhythm to aid blood circulation.

97.49 Removal of other device from thorax
AHA: N-D, '86, 9

✓4th **97.5 Nonoperative removal of therapeutic device from digestive system**

97.51 Removal of gastrostomy tube

97.52 Removal of tube from small intestine

97.53 Removal of tube from large intestine or appendix

97.54 Removal of cholecystostomy tube

97.55 Removal of T-tube, other bile duct tube, or liver tube
Removal of bile duct stent
AHA: 1Q, '01, 8

97.56 Removal of pancreatic tube or drain

97.59 Removal of other device from digestive system
Removal of rectal packing

✓4th **97.6 Nonoperative removal of therapeutic device from urinary system**

97.61 Removal of pyelostomy and nephrostomy tube
DEF: Nonsurgical removal of tubes from lower part of kidney.

97.62 Removal of ureterostomy tube and ureteral catheter

97.63 Removal of cystostomy tube

97.64 Removal of other urinary drainage device
Removal of indwelling urinary catheter

97.65 Removal of urethral stent

97.69 Removal of other device from urinary system

Intraaortic Balloon Pump

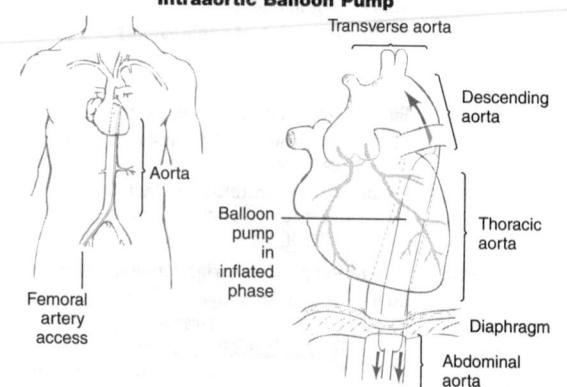

N Newborn Age: 0   P Pediatric Age: 0-17   M Maternity Age: 12-55   A Adult Age: 15-124   Adj Adjunct Code   ◄► Revised Text   ● New Code   ▲ Revised Code Title

204 — Volume 3 • February 2005   *2006 ICD•9•CM*

☑4th **97.7**   **Nonoperative removal of therapeutic device from genital system**

     97.71   **Removal of intrauterine contraceptive device**   ♀

     97.72   **Removal of intrauterine pack**   ♀

     97.73   **Removal of vaginal diaphragm**   ♀

     97.74   **Removal of other vaginal pessary**   ♀

     97.75   **Removal of vaginal or vulvar packing**   ♀

     97.79   **Removal of other device from genital tract**
         Removal of sutures

☑4th **97.8**   **Other nonoperative removal of therapeutic device**

     97.81   **Removal of retroperitoneal drainage device**

     97.82   **Removal of peritoneal drainage device**
         AHA: 2Q, '90, 28; S-O, '86, 12

     97.83   **Removal of abdominal wall sutures**

     97.84   **Removal of sutures from trunk, not elsewhere classified**

     97.85   **Removal of packing from trunk, not elsewhere classified**

     97.86   **Removal of other device from abdomen**

     97.87   **Removal of other device from trunk**

     97.88   **Removal of external immobilization device**
         Removal of: Removal of:
           brace   splint
           cast

     97.89   **Removal of other therapeutic device**

☑3rd **98**   **Nonoperative removal of foreign body or calculus**

☑4th **98.0**   **Removal of intraluminal foreign body from digestive system without incision**
         EXCLUDES   *removal of therapeutic device (97.51-97.59)*

     DEF: Retrieval of foreign body from digestive system lining without incision.

     98.01   **Removal of intraluminal foreign body from mouth without incision**

     98.02   **Removal of intraluminal foreign body from esophagus without incision**

     98.03   **Removal of intraluminal foreign body from stomach and small intestine without incision**

     98.04   **Removal of intraluminal foreign body from large intestine without incision**

     98.05   **Removal of intraluminal foreign body from rectum and anus without incision**

☑4th **98.1**   **Removal of intraluminal foreign body from other sites without incision**
         EXCLUDES   *removal of therapeutic device (97.31-97.49, 97.61-97.89)*

     98.11   **Removal of intraluminal foreign body from ear without incision**

     98.12   **Removal of intraluminal foreign body from nose without incision**

     98.13   **Removal of intraluminal foreign body from pharynx without incision**

     98.14   **Removal of intraluminal foreign body from larynx without incision**

     98.15   **Removal of intraluminal foreign body from trachea and bronchus without incision**

     98.16   **Removal of intraluminal foreign body from uterus without incision**   ♀
         EXCLUDES   *removal of intrauterine contraceptive device (97.71)*

     98.17   **Removal of intraluminal foreign body from vagina without incision**   ♀

     98.18   **Removal of intraluminal foreign body from artificial stoma without incision**

     98.19   **Removal of intraluminal foreign body from urethra without incision**

☑4th **98.2**   **Removal of other foreign body without incision**
         EXCLUDES   *removal of intraluminal foreign body (98.01-98.19)*

     98.20   **Removal of foreign body, not otherwise specified**

     98.21   **Removal of superficial foreign body from eye without incision**

     98.22   **Removal of other foreign body without incision from head and neck**
         Removal of embedded foreign body from eyelid or conjunctiva without incision

     98.23   **Removal of foreign body from vulva without incision**   ♀

     98.24   **Removal of foreign body from scrotum or penis without incision**   ♂

     98.25   **Removal of other foreign body without incision from trunk except scrotum, penis, or vulva**

     98.26   **Removal of foreign body from hand without incision**
         AHA: N-D, '87, 10

     98.27   **Removal of foreign body without incision from upper limb, except hand**

     98.28   **Removal of foreign body from foot without incision**

     98.29   **Removal of foreign body without incision from lower limb, except foot**

☑4th **98.5**   **Extracorporeal shockwave lithotripsy [ESWL]**
     Lithotriptor tank procedure
     Disintegration of stones by extracorporeal induced shockwaves
     That with insertion of stent

     DEF: Breaking of stones with high voltage condenser device synchronized with patient R waves.

     98.51   **Extracorporeal shockwave lithotripsy [ESWL] of the kidney, ureter and/or bladder**
         AHA: 4Q, '95, 73; 1Q, '89, 2

     98.52   **Extracorporeal shockwave lithotripsy [ESWL] of the gallbladder and/or bile duct**

     98.59   **Extracorporeal shockwave lithotripsy of other sites**

☑3rd **99**   **Other nonoperative procedures**

☑4th **99.0**   **Transfusion of blood and blood components**
     Use additional code for that done via catheter or cutdown (38.92-38.94)

     99.00   **Perioperative autologous transfusion of whole blood or blood components**
         Intraoperative blood collection
         Postoperative blood collection
         Salvage
         AHA: 4Q, '95, 69

         DEF: Salvaging patient blood and reinfusing it during perioperative period.

Extracorporeal Shock Wave Lithotripsy

☑4th ☑5th   Additional Digit Required   RUG III Special Care Procedure   RUG III Clinically Complex Procedure   RUG III Extensive Services Procedure   RUG III Rehab Procedure

2006 ICD•9•CM   **Volume 3 — 205**

Diagnostic and Therapeutic Procedures

99.01–99.27

99.01 **Exchange transfusion**

Transfusion: Transfusion:
    exsanguination   replacement

AHA: 2Q, '89, 15

DEF: Repetitive withdrawal of blood, replaced by donor blood.

99.02 **Transfusion of previously collected autologous blood**

Blood component

AHA: 4Q, '95, 69; 1Q, '90, 10; J-A, '85, 16

DEF: Transfusion with patient's own previously withdrawn and stored blood.

99.03 **Other transfusion of whole blood**

Transfusion: Transfusion:
    blood NOS   NOS
    hemodilution

99.04 **Transfusion of packed cells**

99.05 **Transfusion of platelets**

Transfusion of thrombocytes

99.06 **Transfusion of coagulation factors**

Transfusion of antihemophilic factor

99.07 **Transfusion of other serum**

Transfusion of plasma

    EXCLUDES   *injection [transfusion] of:*
       antivenin (99.16)
       gamma globulin (99.14)

99.08 **Transfusion of blood expander**

Transfusion of Dextran

99.09 **Transfusion of other substance**

Transfusion of:
    blood surrogate
    granulocytes

    EXCLUDES   *transplantation [transfusion] of bone marrow (41.0)*

✓4ᵗʰ **99.1** **Injection or infusion of therapeutic or prophylactic substance**

    INCLUDES   injection or infusion given:
       hypodermically ⎫
       intramuscularly ⎬ acting locally or
       intravenously ⎭ systemically

99.10 **Injection or infusion of thrombolytic agent**

Streptokinase
Tissue plasminogen activator (TPA)
Urokinase

    EXCLUDES   *aspirin — omit code*
       GP IIb/IIIa platelet inhibitors (99.20)
       heparin (99.19)
       warfarin — omit code

AHA: 2Q, '01, 7-9, 23; 4Q, '98, 83

99.11 **Injection of Rh immune globulin**

Injection of:
    Anti-D (Rhesus) globulin
    RhoGAM

99.12 **Immunization for allergy**

Desensitization

99.13 **Immunization for autoimmune disease**

99.14 **Injection of gamma globulin**

Injection of immune sera

99.15 **Parenteral infusion of concentrated nutritional substances**

Hyperalimentation
Total parenteral nutrition [TPN]
Peripheral parenteral nutrition [PPN]

AHA: 4Q, '03, 104

DEF: Administration of greater than necessary amount of nutrients via other than the alimentary canal (e.g., infusion).

99.16 **Injection of antidote**

Injection of: Injection of:
    antivenin   heavy metal antagonist

99.17 **Injection of insulin**

99.18 **Injection or infusion of electrolytes**

99.19 **Injection of anticoagulant**

    EXCLUDES   *infusion of drotrecogin alfa (activated) (00.11)*

✓4ᵗʰ **99.2** **Injection or infusion of other therapeutic or prophylactic substance**

    INCLUDES   injection or infusion given:
       hypodermically ⎫ acting locally
       intramuscularly ⎬ or system-
       intravenously ⎭ ically

Use additional code for:
    injection (into):   injection (into):
       breast (85.92)   kidney (55.96)
       bursa (82.94, 83.96)   liver (50.94)
       intraperitoneal   orbit (16.91)
         (cavity) (54.97)   other sites — see
       intrathecal (03.92)   Alphabetic Index
       joint (76.96, 81.92)
    perfusion: perfusion:
       NOS (39.97)   liver (50.93)
       intestine (46.95, 46.96)   total body (39.96)
       kidney (55.95)

99.20 **Injection or infusion of platelet inhibitor**

Glycoprotein IIB/IIIa inhibitor
GP IIB-IIIa inhibitor
GP IIB/IIIa inhibitor

    EXCLUDES   *infusion of heparin (99.19)*
       injection or infusion of thrombolytic agent (99.10)

AHA: ▶2Q, '04, 3;◀ 4Q, '02, 114; 4Q, '98, 85

99.21 **Injection of antibiotic**

    EXCLUDES   *injection or infusion of oxazolidinone class of antibiotics (00.14)*

AHA: 4Q, '98, 76; 2Q, '90, 24; M-A, '87, 9

99.22 **Injection of other anti-infective**

    EXCLUDES   *injection or infusion of oxazolidinone class of antibiotics (00.14)*

99.23 **Injection of steroid**

Injection of cortisone
Subdermal implantation of progesterone

AHA: 3Q, '00, 15; 1Q, '99, 8; 3Q, '96, 7; 3Q, '92, 9; S-O, '85, 7

99.24 **Injection of other hormone**

99.25 **Injection or infusion of cancer chemotherapeutic substance**

Chemoembolization
Injection or infusion of antineoplastic agent

    EXCLUDES   *immunotherapy, antineoplastic (00.15, 99.28)*
       implantation of chemotherapeutic agent (00.10)
       injection of radioisotope (92.28)
       injection or infusion of biological response modifier [BRM] as an antineoplastic agent (99.28)

AHA: 2Q, '03, 6, 16; 1Q, '99, 4; 1Q, '98, 6; 3Q, '96, 11; 4Q, '95, 67; 2Q, '92, 7; 1Q, '92, 12; 1Q, '88, 8; N-D, '86, 11

99.26 **Injection of tranquilizer**

99.27 **Iontophoresis**

DEF: Iontophoresis: Introduction of soluble salts into tissues via electric current.

N Newborn Age: 0   P Pediatric Age: 0-17   M Maternity Age: 12-55   A Adult Age: 15-124   Adj Adjunct Code   ▶◀ Revised Text   ● New Code   ▲ Revised Code Title

99.28 **Injection or infusion of biological response modifier [BRM] as an antineoplastic agent**

Immunotherapy, antineoplastic
Interleukin therapy
Low-dose interleukin-2 [IL-2] therapy
Tumor vaccine

EXCLUDES   *high-dose infusion inter-leukin-2 [IL-2] (00.15)*

AHA: 4Q, '03, 92; 2Q, '99, 8; 2Q, '98, 10; 4Q, '94, 51

99.29 **Injection or infusion of other therapeutic or prophylactic substance**

EXCLUDES   *administration of neuroprotective agent (99.75)*
immunization (99.31-99.59)
injection of sclerosing agent into:
    esophageal varices (42.33)
    hemorrhoids (49.42)
    veins (39.92)
injection or infusion of:
    human B-type natriuretic peptide (hBNP) (00.13)
    nesiritide (00.13)
    platelet inhibitor (99.20)
    thrombolytic agent (99.10)

AHA: 2Q, '03, 10; 3Q, '02, 19, 24; 1Q, '01, 15; 2Q, '00, 14; 1Q, '00, 8, 18, 23; 4Q, '99, 17; 3Q, '99, 21; 4Q, '98, 83; 2Q, '98, 17, 18, 23, 24; 1Q, '98, 6; 2Q, '97, 11; 1Q, '97, 3; 4Q, '95, 67; 2Q, '95, 12; 4Q, '90, 14; 2Q, '90, 23; 2Q, '89, 17; 1Q, '88, 9; N-D, '87, 4; S-O, '87, 11

✓4ᵗʰ **99.3** **Prophylactic vaccination and inoculation against certain bacterial diseases**

DEF: Administration of a killed bacteria suspension to produce immunity.

99.31 **Vaccination against cholera**
99.32 **Vaccination against typhoid and paratyphoid fever**
    Administration of TAB vaccine
99.33 **Vaccination against tuberculosis**
    Administration of BCG vaccine
99.34 **Vaccination against plague**
99.35 **Vaccination against tularemia**
99.36 **Administration of diphtheria toxoid**
EXCLUDES   *administration of:*
diphtheria antitoxin (99.58)
diphtheria-tetanus-pertussis, combined (99.39)
99.37 **Vaccination against pertussis**
EXCLUDES   *administration of diphtheria-tetanus-pertussis, combined (99.39)*
99.38 **Administration of tetanus toxoid**
EXCLUDES   *administration of:*
diphtheria-tetanus-pertussis, combined (99.39)
tetanus antitoxin (99.56)
99.39 **Administration of diphtheria-tetanus-pertussis, combined**

✓4ᵗʰ **99.4** **Prophylactic vaccination and inoculation against certain viral diseases**

DEF: Administration of a killed virus suspension to produce immunity.

99.41 **Administration of poliomyelitis vaccine**
99.42 **Vaccination against smallpox**
99.43 **Vaccination against yellow fever**
99.44 **Vaccination against rabies**

99.45 **Vaccination against measles**
EXCLUDES   *administration of measles-mumps-rubella vaccine (99.48)*
99.46 **Vaccination against mumps**
EXCLUDES   *administration of measles-mumps-rubella vaccine (99.48)*
99.47 **Vaccination against rubella**
EXCLUDES   *administration of measles-mumps-rubella vaccine (99.48)*
99.48 **Administration of measles-mumps-rubella vaccine**

✓4ᵗʰ **99.5** **Other vaccination and inoculation**

99.51 **Prophylactic vaccination against the common cold**
99.52 **Prophylactic vaccination against influenza**
99.53 **Prophylactic vaccination against arthropod-borne viral encephalitis**
99.54 **Prophylactic vaccination against other arthropod-borne viral diseases**
99.55 **Prophylactic administration of vaccine against other diseases**

Vaccination against:	Vaccination against:
anthrax	Staphylococcus
brucellosis	Streptococcus
Rocky Mountain spotted fever	typhus

AHA: 2Q, '00, 9; 1Q, '94, 10

99.56 **Administration of tetanus antitoxin**
99.57 **Administration of botulism antitoxin**
99.58 **Administration of other antitoxins**
Administration of:
    diphtheria antitoxin
    gas gangrene antitoxin
    scarlet fever antitoxin
99.59 **Other vaccination and inoculation**
Vaccination NOS
EXCLUDES   *injection of:*
gamma globulin (99.14)
Rh immune globulin (99.11)
immunization for:
allergy (99.12)
autoimmune disease (99.13)

✓4ᵗʰ **99.6** **Conversion of cardiac rhythm**
EXCLUDES   *open chest cardiac:*
electric stimulation (37.91)
massage (37.91)

AHA: 3Q, '93, 13

DEF: Correction of cardiac rhythm.

99.60 **Cardiopulmonary resuscitation, not otherwise specified**
AHA: 1Q, '94, 16

99.61 **Atrial cardioversion**
DEF: Application of electric shock to upper heart chamber to restore normal heart rhythm.

99.62 **Other electric countershock of heart**
Cardioversion:
    NOS
    external
Conversion to sinus rhythm
Defibrillation
External electrode stimulation

99.63 **Closed chest cardiac massage**
Cardiac massage NOS
Manual external cardiac massage
DEF: Application of alternating manual pressure over breastbone to restore normal heart rhythm.

✓4ᵗʰ ✓5ᵗʰ Additional Digit Required   RUG III Special Care Procedure   RUG III Clinically Complex Procedure   RUG III Extensive Services Procedure   RUG III Rehab Procedure

Diagnostic and Therapeutic Procedures

99.64–99.99

99.64 **Carotid sinus stimulation**

99.69 **Other conversion of cardiac rhythm**
AHA: 4Q, '88, 11

✓4ᵗʰ **99.7** **Therapeutic apheresis or other injection, administration, or infusion of other therapeutic or prophylactic substance**
DEF: Blood withdrawal from donor with desired portion removed (e.g., plasma, leukocytes, platelets, etc.) and retained; remainder transfused back into donor.

99.71 **Therapeutic plasmapheresis**
EXCLUDES *extracorporeal immunoadsorption [ECI] (99.76)*

99.72 **Therapeutic leukopheresis**
Therapeutic leukocytapheresis

99.73 **Therapeutic erythrocytapheresis**
Therapeutic erythropheresis
AHA: 1Q, '94, 20

99.74 **Therapeutic plateletpheresis**

99.75 **Administration of neuroprotective agent**
AHA: 4Q, '00, 68

DEF: Direct application of neuroprotective agent (e.g., nimodipine) to miinimize ischemic injury by inhibiting toxic neurotransmitters, blocking free ions, removing free radicals, and causing vasodilation.

99.76 **Extracorporeal immunoadsorption**
Removal of antibodies from plasma with protein A columns
AHA: 4Q, '02, 112

99.77 **Application or administration of adhesion barrier substance**
AHA: 4Q, '02, 113

99.78 **Aquapheresis**
Plasma water removal
Ultrafiltration [for water removal]
EXCLUDES *hemodiafiltration (39.95)*
hemodialysis (39.95)
therapeutic plasmapheresis (99.71)

99.79 **Other**
Apheresis (harvest) of stem cells
AHA: ▶1Q, '05, 16;◀ 4Q, '97, 55

✓4ᵗʰ **99.8** **Miscellaneous physical procedures**

99.81 **Hypothermia (central) (local)**
EXCLUDES *gastric cooling (96.31)*
gastric freezing (96.32)
that incidental to open heart surgery (39.62)

99.82 **Ultraviolet light therapy**
Actinotherapy

99.83 **Other phototherapy**
Phototherapy of the newborn
EXCLUDES *extracorporeal photochemotherapy (99.88)*
photocoagulation of retinal lesion (14.23-14.25, 14.33-14.35, 14.53-14.55)
AHA: 2Q, '89, 15

DEF: Treating disease with light rays of various concentrations.

99.84 **Isolation**
Isolation after contact with infectious disease
Protection of individual from his surroundings
Protection of surroundings from individual

99.85 **Hyperthermia for treatment of cancer**
Hyperthermia (adjunct therapy) induced by microwave, ultrasound, low energy radio frequency, probes (interstitial), or other means in the treatment of cancer
Code also any concurrent chemotherapy or radiation therapy
AHA: 3Q, '96, 11; 3Q, '89, 17

99.86 **Non-invasive placement of bone growth stimulator**
Transcutaneous (surface) placement of pads or patches for stimulation to aid bone healing
EXCLUDES *insertion of invasive or semi-invasive bone growth stimulators (device) (percutaneous electrodes) (78.90-78.99)*

99.88 **Therapeutic photopheresis**
Extracorporeal photochemotherapy
Extracorporeal photopheresis
EXCLUDES *other phototherapy (99.83)*
ultraviolet light therapy (99.82)
AHA: 2Q, '99, 7

DEF: Extracorporeal photochemotherapy: Treating disease with drugs that react to ultraviolet radiation or sunlight.

✓4ᵗʰ **99.9** **Other miscellaneous procedures**

99.91 **Acupuncture for anesthesia**

99.92 **Other acupuncture**
EXCLUDES *that with smouldering moxa (93.35)*

99.93 **Rectal massage (for levator spasm)**

99.94 **Prostatic massage** ♂

99.95 **Stretching of foreskin** ♂

99.96 **Collection of sperm for artificial insemination** ♂

99.97 **Fitting of denture**

99.98 **Extraction of milk from lactating breast** ♀

99.99 **Other**
Leech therapy

N Newborn Age: 0   P Pediatric Age: 0-17   M Maternity Age: 12-55   A Adult Age: 15-124   Adj Adjunct Code   ▶◀ Revised Text   ● New Code   ▲ Revised Code Title

208 — Volume 3 • October 2005

2006 ICD•9•CM

Home Health Qualifications for Medicare Coverage of Home Health Services

The criteria that must be met by the patient to qualify for Medicare coverage of home health services are specified in the following sections of the Medicare Benefit Policy Manual, Chapter 7 - Home Health Services.

20 – Conditions to be Met for Coverage of Home Health Services

Medicare covers HHA services when the following criteria are met:

1. The person to whom the services are provided is an eligible Medicare beneficiary;
2. The HHA that is providing the services to the beneficiary has in effect a valid agreement to participate in the Medicare program;
3. The beneficiary qualifies for coverage of home health services as described in §30;
4. The services for which payment is claimed are covered as described in §§40 and 50;
5. Medicare is the appropriate payer; and
6. The services for which payment is claimed are not otherwise excluded from payment.

20.1 – Reasonable and Necessary Services

20.1.1 – Background: In enacting the Medicare program, Congress recognized that the physician would play an important role in determining utilization of services. The law requires that payment can be made only if a physician certifies the need for services and establishes a plan of care. The Secretary is responsible for ensuring that Medicare covers the claimed services, including determining whether they are "reasonable and necessary."

20.1.2 – Determination of Coverage: The intermediary's decision on whether care is reasonable and necessary is based on information reflected in the home health plan of care, the OASIS as required by 42 CFR 484.55 or a medical record of the individual patient. Medicare does not deny coverage solely on the basis of the reviewer's general inferences about patients with similar diagnoses or on data related to utilization generally, but bases it upon objective clinical evidence regarding the patient's individual need for care.

20.2 – Impact of Other Available Caregivers and Other Available Coverage on Medicare Coverage of Home Health Services

Where the Medicare criteria for coverage of home health services are met, patients are entitled by law to coverage of reasonable and necessary home health services. Therefore, a patient is entitled to have the costs of reasonable and necessary services reimbursed by Medicare without regard to whether there is someone available to furnish the services. However, where a family member or other person is or will be providing services that adequately meet the patient's needs, it would not be reasonable and necessary for HHA personnel to furnish such services. Ordinarily it can be presumed that there is no able and willing person in the home to provide the services being rendered by the HHA unless the patient or family indicates otherwise and objects to the provision of the services by the HHA, or unless the HHA has first hand knowledge to the contrary.

Example 1: A patient who lives with an adult daughter and otherwise qualifies for Medicare coverage of home health services, requires the assistance of a home health aide for bathing and assistance with an exercise program to improve endurance. The daughter is unwilling to bathe her elderly father and assist him with the exercise program. Home health aide services would be reasonable and necessary.

Similarly, a patient is entitled to have the costs of reasonable and necessary home health services reimbursed by Medicare even if the patient would qualify for institutional care (e.g., hospital care or skilled nursing facility care).

Example 2: A patient who is being discharged from a hospital with a diagnosis of osteomyelitis and requires continuation of the I.V. antibiotic therapy that was begun in the hospital was found to meet the criteria for Medicare coverage of skilled nursing facility services. If the patient also meets the qualifying criteria for coverage of home health services, payment may be made for the reasonable and necessary home health services the patient needs, notwithstanding the availability of coverage in a skilled nursing facility.

Medicare payment should be made for reasonable and necessary home health services where the patient is also receiving supplemental services that do not meet Medicare's definition of skilled nursing care or home health aide services.

Example 3: A patient who needs skilled nursing care on an intermittent basis also hires a licensed practical (vocational) nurse to provide nighttime assistance while family members sleep. The care provided by the nurse, as respite to the family members, does not require the skills of a licensed nurse (as defined in §40.1) and therefore has no impact on the beneficiary's eligibility for Medicare payment of home health services even though another third party insurer may pay for that nursing care.

20.3 – Use of Utilization Screens and "Rules of Thumb"

Medicare recognizes that determinations of whether home health services are reasonable and necessary must be based on an assessment of each beneficiary's individual care needs. Therefore, denial of services based on numerical utilization screens, diagnostic screens, diagnosis or specific treatment norms is not appropriate.

30 – Conditions the Patient Must Meet to Qualify for Coverage of Home Health Services

To qualify for the Medicare home health benefit, under §§1814(a)(2)(C) and 1835(a)(2)(A) of the Act, a Medicare beneficiary must meet the following requirements:

- Be confined to the home;
- Under the care of a physician;
- Receiving services under a plan of care established and periodically reviewed by a physician;
- Be in need of skilled nursing care on an intermittent basis or physical therapy or speech-language pathology; or
- Have a continuing need for occupational therapy.

For purposes of benefit eligibility, under §§1814(a)(2)(C) and 1835(a)(2)(A) of the Act, "intermittent" means skilled nursing care that is either provided or needed on fewer than 7 days each week or less than 8 hours of each day for periods of 21 days or less (with extensions in exceptional circumstances when the need for additional care is finite and predictable).

A patient must meet each of the criteria specified in this section. Patients who meet each of these criteria are eligible to have payment made on their behalf for services discussed in §§40 and 50.

30.1 – Confined to the Home

In order for a patient to be eligible to receive covered home health services under both Part A and Part B, the law requires that a physician certify in all cases that the patient is confined to his/her home. An individual does not have to be bedridden to be considered as confined to the home. However, the condition of these patients should be such that there exists a normal inability to leave home and, consequently, leaving home would require a considerable and taxing effort. If the patient does in fact leave the home, the patient may nevertheless be considered homebound if the absences from the home are infrequent or for periods of relatively short duration, or are attributable to the need to receive medical treatment. Absences attributable to the need to receive medical treatment include but are not limited to, attendance at adult day centers to receive medical care, ongoing receipt of outpatient kidney dialysis, and the receipt of outpatient chemotherapy or radiation therapy. Any absence of an individual from the home attributable to the need to receive health care treatment, including regular absences for the purpose of participating in therapeutic, psychosocial, or medical treatment in an adult day-care program that is licensed or certified by a State, or accredited to furnish adult day-care services in a State, shall not disqualify an individual from being considered to be confined to his home. Any other absence of an individual from the home shall not so disqualify an individual if the absence is of an infrequent or of relatively short duration. For purposes of the preceding sentence, any absence for the purpose of attending a religious service shall be deemed to be an absence of infrequent or short duration. It is expected that in most instances, absences from the home that occur will be for the purpose of receiving medical treatment. However, occasional absences from the home for nonmedical purposes, e.g., an occasional trip to the barber, a walk around the block or a drive, would not necessitate a finding that the patient is not homebound if the absences are undertaken on an infrequent basis or are of relatively short duration and do not indicate that the patient has the capacity to obtain the health care provided outside rather than in the home.

Generally speaking, a patient will be considered to be homebound if he/she has a condition due to an illness or injury that restricts his/her ability to leave his/her place of residence except with the aid of supportive devices such as crutches, canes, wheelchairs, and walkers, the use of special transportation, or the assistance of another person or if leaving home is medically contraindicated. Some examples of homebound patients that illustrate the factors used to determine whether a homebound condition exists would be: (1) a patient paralyzed from a stroke who is confined to a wheelchair or requires the aid of crutches in order to walk; (2) a patient who is blind or senile and requires the assistance of another person to leave his/her residence; (3) a patient who has lost the use of his/her upper extremities and, therefore, is unable to open doors, use handrails on stairways, etc., and requires the assistance of another individual to leave his/her residence; (4) a patient in the late stages of ALS or a neurodegenerative disabilities. In determining whether the patient has the general inability to leave the home and leaves the home only infrequently or for periods of short duration, it is necessary (as is the case in determining whether skilled nursing services are intermittent) to look at the patient's condition over a period of time rather than for short periods within the home health stay. For example, a patient may leave the home (under the conditions described above, e.g., with severe and taxing effort, with the assistance of others) more frequently during a short period when, for example, the presence of visiting relatives provides a unique opportunity for such absences, than is normally the case. So long as the patient's overall condition and experience is such that he or she meets these qualifications, he or she should be considered confined to the home; (5) a patient who has just returned from a hospital stay involving surgery suffering from resultant weakness and pain and, therefore, his/her actions may be restricted by his/her physician to certain specified and limited activities such as getting out of bed only for a specified period of time, walking stairs only once a day, etc.; (6) a patient with arteriosclerotic heart disease of such severity that he/she must avoid all stress and physical activity; and (7) a patient with a psychiatric problem if the illness is manifested in part by a refusal to leave home or is of such a nature that it would not be considered safe to leave home unattended, even if he/she has no physical limitations.

The aged person who does not often travel from home because of feebleness and insecurity brought on by advanced age would not be considered confined to the home for purposes of receiving home health services unless he/she meets one of the above conditions. A patient who requires skilled care must also be determined to be confined to the home in order for home health services to be covered.

Although a patient must be confined to the home to be eligible for covered home health services, some services cannot be provided at the patient's residence because equipment is required that cannot be made available there. If the services required by a patient involve the use of such equipment, the HHA may make arrangements with a hospital, skilled nursing facility, or a rehabilitation center to provide these services on an outpatient basis. (See §50.6) However, even in these situations, for the services to be covered as home health services, the patient must be considered confined to his/her home; and to receive such outpatient services a homebound patient will generally require the use of supportive devices, special transportation, or the assistance of another person to travel to the appropriate facility.

If a question is raised as to whether a patient is confined to the home, the HHA will be asked to furnish the intermediary with the information necessary to establish that the patient is homebound as defined above.

30.1.2–Patient's Place of Residence: A patient's residence is wherever he/she makes his/her home. This may be his/her own dwelling, an apartment, a relative's home, a home for the aged, or some other type of institution. However, an institution may not be considered a patient's home if the institution meets the requirements of §§1861(e)(1) or 1819 (a)(1) of the Act. Included in this group are hospitals and skilled nursing facilities. as well as most nursing facilities under Medicaid. (See the Medicare State Operations Manual, §2166.)

Thus, if a patient is in an institution or distinct part of an institution identified above, the patient is not entitled to have payment made for home health services under either Part A or Part B since these institutions may not be considered his/her residence. When a patient remains in a participating SNF following his/her discharge from active care, the facility may not be considered his/her residence for purposes of home health coverage.

A patient may have more than one home and the Medicare rules do not prohibit a patient from having one or more places of residence. A patient, under a Medicare home health plan of care, who resides in more than one place of residence during an episode of Medicare covered home health services will not disqualify the patient's homebound status for purposes of eligibility. For example, a person may reside in a principal home and also a second vacation home, mobile home, or the home of a caretaker relative. The fact that the patient resides in more than one home and, as a result, must transit from one to the other, is not in itself, an indication that the patient is not homebound. The requirements of homebound must be met at each location (e.g., considerable taxing effort etc).

A – Assisted Living Facilities, Group Homes, and Personal Care Homes
An individual may be "confined to the home" for purposes of Medicare coverage of home health services if he or she resides in an institution that is not primarily engaged in providing to inpatients:

- Diagnostic and therapeutic services for medical diagnosis;
- Treatment;
- Care of disabled or sick persons;
- Rehabilitation services for the rehabilitation of injured, disabled, or sick
  persons;
- Skilled nursing care or related services for patients who require medical or nursing care; or
- Rehabilitation services for the rehabilitation of injured, sick, or disabled persons.

If it is determined that the assisted living facility (also called personal care homes, group homes, etc.) in which the individuals reside are not primarily engaged in providing the above services, then Medicare will cover reasonable and necessary home health care furnished to these individuals.

If it is determined that the services furnished by the home health agency are duplicative of services furnished by an assisted living facility (also called personal care homes, group homes, etc.) when provision of such care is required of the facility under State licensure requirements, claims for such services should be denied under §1862(a)(1)(A) of the Act. Section 1862(a)(1)(A) excludes services that are not necessary for the diagnosis or treatment of illness or injury or to improve the functioning of a malformed body member from Medicare coverage. Services to people who already have access to appropriate care from a willing caregiver would not be considered reasonable and necessary to the treatment of the individual's illness or injury.

Medicare coverage would not be an optional substitute for the services that a facility that is required to provide by law to its patients or where the services are included in the base contract of the facility. An individual's choice to reside in such a facility is also a choice to accept the services it holds itself out as offering to its patients.

B – Day Care Centers and Patient's Place of Residence
The current statutory definition of homebound or confined does not imply that Medicare coverage has been expanded to include adult day care services.

The law does not permit an HHA to furnish a Medicare covered billable visit to a patient under a home health plan of care outside his or her home, except in those limited circumstances where the patient needs to use medical equipment that is too cumbersome to bring to the home. Section 1861(m) of the Act stipulates that home health services provided to a patient be provided to the patient on a visiting basis in a place of residence used as the individual's home. A licensed/certified day care center does not meet the definition of a place of residence.

C – State Licensure/Certification of Day Care Facilities
Section 1861(m) of the Act, an adult day care center must be either licensed or certified by the State or accredited by a private accrediting body. State licensure or certification as an adult day care facility must be based on State interpretations of its process. For example, several States do not license adult day care facilities as a whole, but do certify some entities as Medicaid certified centers for purposes of providing adult day care under the Medicaid

home and community based waiver program. It is the responsibility of the State to determine the necessary criteria for "State certification" in such a situation. A State could determine that Medicaid certification is an acceptable standard and consider its Medicaid certified adult day care facilities to be "State certified." On the other hand, a State could determine Medicaid certification to be insufficient and require other conditions to be met before the adult day care facility is considered "State certified".

D – Determination of the Therapeutic, Medical or Psychosocial Treatment of the Patient at the Day Care Facility

It is not the obligation of the HHA to determine whether the adult day care facility is providing psychosocial treatment, but only to assure that the adult day care center is licensed/certified by the State or accrediting body. The intent of the law, in extending the homebound exception status to attendance at such adult day care facilities, recognizes that they ordinarily furnish psychosocial services.

30.2 – Services Are Provided Under a Plan of Care Established and Approved by a Physician

30.2.1 – Content of the Plan of Care: The plan of care must contain all pertinent diagnoses, including the patient's mental status, the types of services, supplies, and equipment required, the frequency of visits to be made, prognosis, rehabilitation potential, functional limitations, activities permitted, nutritional requirements, all medications and treatments, safety measures to protect against injury, instructions for timely discharge or referral, and any additional items the HHA or physician choose to include.

30.2.2 – Specificity of Orders: The orders on the plan of care must specify the type of services to be provided to the patient, both with respect to the professional who will provide them and the nature of the individual services, as well as the frequency of the services.

Example 1: SN x 7/wk x 1 wk; 3/wk x 4 wk; 2/wk x 3 wk, (skilled nursing visits 7 times per week for 1 week; 3 times per week for 4 weeks; and 2 times per week for 3 weeks) for skilled observation and evaluation of the surgical site, for teaching sterile dressing changes and to perform sterile dressing changes. The sterile change consists of (detail of procedure).

Orders for care may indicate a specific range in the frequency of visits to ensure that the most appropriate level of service is provided to home health patients. When a range of visits is ordered, the upper limit of the range is considered the specific frequency.

Example 2: SN x 2-4/wk x 4 wk; 1-2/wk x 4 wk for skilled observation and evaluation of the surgical site.

Orders for services to be furnished "as needed" or "PRN" must be accompanied by a description of the patient's medical signs and symptoms that would occasion a visit and a specific limit on the number of those visits to be made under the order before an additional physician order would have to be obtained.

30.2.3 – Who Signs the Plan of Care: The physician who signs the plan of care must be qualified to sign the physician certification as described in 42 CFR 424.22.

30.2.4 – Timeliness of Signature

A – Initial Percentage Payment

If a physician signed plan of care is not available at the beginning of the episode, the HHA may submit a RAP for the initial percentage payment based on physician verbal orders OR a referral prescribing detailed orders for the services to be rendered that is signed and dated by the physician. If the RAP submission is based on physician verbal orders, the verbal order must be recorded in the plan of care, include a description of the patient's condition and the services to be provided by the home health agency, include an attestation (relating to the physician's orders and the date received per 42 CFR 409.43), and the plan of care is copied and immediately submitted to the physician. A billable visit must be rendered prior to the submission of a RAP.

B – Final Percentage Payment

The plan of care must be signed and dated by a physician as described who meets the certification and recertification requirements of 42 CFR 424.22 and before the claim for each episode for services is submitted for the final percentage payment. Any changes in the plan of care must be signed and dated by a physician.

30.2.5 – Use of Oral (Verbal) Orders: When services are furnished based on a physician's oral order, the orders may be accepted and put in writing by personnel authorized to do so by applicable State and Federal laws and regulations, as well as by the HHA's internal policies. The orders must be signed and dated with the date of receipt by the registered nurse or qualified therapist (i.e., physical therapist, speech-language pathologist, occupational therapist, or medical social worker) responsible for furnishing or supervising

the ordered services. The orders may be signed by the supervising registered nurse or qualified therapist after the services have been rendered, as long as HHA personnel who receive the oral orders notify that nurse or therapist before the service is rendered. Thus, the rendering of a service that is based on an oral order would not be delayed pending signature of the supervising nurse or therapist. Oral orders must be countersigned and dated by the physician before the HHA bills for the care in the same way as the plan of care.

(1) Services that are provided from the beginning of the 60 day episode certification period based on a request for anticipated payment and before the physician signs the plan of care are considered to be provided under a plan of care established and approved by the physician where there is an oral order for the care prior to rendering the services which is documented in the medical record and where the services are included in a signed plan of care.

Example: The HHA acquires an oral order for I.V. medication administration for a patient to be performed on August 1. The HHA provides the I.V. medication administration August 1 and evaluates the patient's need for continued care. The physician signs the plan of care for the I.V. medication administration on August 15. The visit is covered since it is considered provided under a plan of care established and approved by the physician, and the HHA had acquired an oral order prior to the delivery of services

(2) Services that are provided in the subsequent 60 day episode certification period are considered to be provided under the subsequent plan of care where there is an oral order before the services provided in the subsequent period are furnished and the order is reflected in the medical record. However, services that are provided after the expiration of a plan of care, but before the acquisition of an oral order or a signed plan of care, cannot be considered to be provided under a plan of care.

Example 1: The patient is under a plan of care in which the physician orders I.V. medication administration every two weeks. The last day covered by the initial plan of care is July 31. The patient's next I.V. medication administration is scheduled for August 5 and the physician signs the plan of care for the new period on August 1. The I.V. medication administration on August 5 was provided under a plan of care established and approved by the physician. The episode begins on the 61 day regardless of the date of the first covered visit.

Example 2: The patient is under a plan of care in which the physician orders I.V. medication administration every two weeks. The last day covered by the plan of care is July 31. The patient's next I.V. medication administration is scheduled for August 5 and the physician does not sign the plan of care until August 6. The HHA acquires an oral order for the I.V. medication administration before the August 5 visit, and therefore the visit is considered to be provided under a plan of care established and approved by the physician. The episode begins on the 61 day regardless of the date of the first covered visit.

(3) Any increase in the frequency of services or addition of new services during a certification period must be authorized by a physician by way of a written or oral order prior to the provision of the increased or additional services.

30.2.6 – Frequency of Review of the Plan of Care: The plan of care must be reviewed and signed by the physician who established the plan of care, in consultation with HHA professional personnel, at least every 60 days. Each review of a patient's plan of care must contain the signature of the physician and the date of review.

30.2.7 – Facsimile Signatures: The plan of care or oral order may be transmitted by facsimile machine. The HHA is not required to have the original signature on file. However, the HHA is responsible for obtaining original signatures if an issue surfaces that would require verification of an original signature

30.2.8 – Alternative Signatures: HHAs that maintain patient records by computer rather than hard copy may use electronic signatures. However, all such entries must be appropriately authenticated and dated. Authentication must include signatures, written initials, or computer secure entry by a unique identifier of a primary author who has reviewed and approved the entry. The HHA must have safeguards to prevent unauthorized access to the records and a process for reconstruction of the records in the event of a system breakdown.

30.2.9 – Termination of the Plan of Care: The plan of care is considered to be terminated if the patient does not receive at least one covered skilled nursing, physical therapy, speech-language pathology service, or occupational therapy visit in a 60-day period unless the physician documents that the interval without such care is appropriate to the treatment of the patient's illness or injury.

30.2.10 – Sequence of Qualifying Services and Other Medicare Covered Home Health Services: Once patient eligibility has been confirmed and the plan of care contains physician orders for the qualifying service as well as other Medicare covered home health services, the qualifying service does not have to be rendered prior to the other Medicare covered home health services ordered in the plan of care. The sequence of visits performed by the disciplines must be dictated by the individual patient's plan of care. For example, for an eligible patient in an initial 60-day episode that has both physical therapy and occupational therapy orders in the plan of care, the sequence of the delivery of the type of therapy is irrelevant as long as the need for the qualifying service is established prior to the delivery of other Medicare covered services and the qualifying discipline provides a billable visit prior to transfer or discharge in accordance with 42 CFR 409.43(f).

Note: Dependent services provided after the final qualifying skilled service are not covered under the home health benefit, except when the dependent service was followed by a qualifying skilled service as a result of the unexpected inpatient admission or death of the patient or due to some other unanticipated event.

30.3 – Under the Care of a Physician

The patient must be under the care of a physician who is qualified to sign the physician certification and plan of care in accordance with 42 CFR 424.22.

A patient is expected to be under the care of the physician who signs the plan of care and the physician certification. It is expected, but not required for coverage, that the physician who signs the plan of care will see the patient, but there is no specified interval of time within which the patient must be seen.

30.4 – Needs Skilled Nursing Care on an Intermittent Basis or Physical Therapy or Speech-Language Pathology Services or Has Continued Need for Occupational Therapy

The patient must need one of the following types of skilled services:

1. Skilled nursing care that is

   - Reasonable and necessary as defined in §40.1;
   - Needed on an "intermittent" based as defined in §40.1; and
   - Not solely needed for venipuncture for the purposes of obtaining blood sample as defined in §40.1.2.13; or

2. Physical therapy as defined in §40.2.2; or

3. Speech-language pathology services as defined in §40.2.3; or

4. Have a continuing need for occupational therapy as defined in §§40.2.4.

   The patient has a continued need for occupational therapy when:

   1. The services which the patient requires meet the definition of "occupational therapy" services of §40.2, and

   2. The patient's eligibility for home health services has been established by virtue of a prior need for skilled nursing care (other than solely venipuncture for the purposes of obtaining a blood sample), speech-language pathology services, or physical therapy in the current or prior certification period.

   Example: A patient who is recovering from a cerebrovascular accident (CVA) has an initial plan of care that called for physical therapy, speech-language pathology services, and home health aide services. In the next certification period, the physician orders only occupational therapy and home health aide services because the patient no longer needs the skills of a physical therapist or a speech-language pathologist, but needs the services provided by the occupational therapist. The patient's need for occupational therapy qualifies him for home health services, including home health aide services (presuming that all other qualifying criteria are met).

30.5 – Physician Certification

The HHA must be acting upon a physician certification that is part of the plan of care (CMS-485) and meets the requirements of this section for HHA services to be covered.

30.5.1 – Content of the Physician Certification: The physician must certify that:

The home health services are or were needed because the patient is or was confined to the home as defined in §20.1;

The patient needs or needed skilled nursing services on an intermittent basis, (other than solely venipuncture for the purposes of obtaining a blood sample), physical therapy, or speech-language pathology services, or continues or continued to need occupational therapy after the need for skilled nursing care, physical therapy, or speech-language pathology services ceased;

A plan of care has been established and is periodically reviewed by a physician; and the services are or were furnished while the patient is or was under the care of a physician.

30.5.2 – Periodic Recertification: At the end of the 60-day episode, a decision must be made whether or not to recertify the patient for a subsequent 60-day episode. An eligible beneficiary who qualifies for a subsequent 60-day episode would start the subsequent 60-day episode on day 61. Under HHPPS, the plan of care must be reviewed and signed by the physician every 60 days unless one of the following occurs:

- A beneficiary transfers to another HHA;
- A SCIC (significant change in condition) resulting in a change in the assigned case-mix; or
- A discharge and return to the same HHA during the 60-day episode.

Medicare does not limit the number of continuous episode recertifications for beneficiaries who continue to be eligible for the home health benefit. The physician certification may cover a period less than but not greater than 60 days.

See §10.4 for counting initial and subsequent 60-day episodes and recertifications. See §10.5 for recertifications for split percentage payments.

30.5.3 – Who May Sign the Certification: The physician who signs the certification must be permitted to do so by 42 CFR 424.22.

40 – Covered Services Under a Qualifying Home Health Plan of Care

Section 1861(m)of the Act governs the Medicare home health services that may be provided to eligible beneficiaries by or under arrangements made by a participating home health agency (HHA). Section 1861(m) describes home health services as

- Part-time or intermittent skilled nursing care (other than solely venipuncture for the purposes of obtaining a blood sample);
- Part-time or intermittent home health aide services;
- Physical therapy;
- Speech-language pathology;
- Occupational therapy;
- Medical social services;
- Medical supplies (including catheters, catheter supplies, ostomy bags, supplies related to ostomy care, and a covered osteoporosis drug (as defined in §1861(kk) of the Act), but excluding other drugs and biologicals);
- Durable medical equipment while under the plan of care established by physician;
- Medical services provided by an intern or resident-in-training under an approved teaching program of the hospital in the case of an HHA which is affiliated or under common control with a hospital; and
- Services at hospitals, skilled nursing facilities, or rehabilitation centers when they involve equipment too cumbersome to bring to the home.

The term "part-time or intermittent" for purposes of coverage under §1861(m) of the Act means skilled nursing and home health aide services furnished any number of days per week as long as they are furnished (combined) less than 8 hours each day and 28 or fewer hours each week (or, subject to review on a case-by-case basis as to the need for care, less than 8 hours each day and 35 or fewer hours per week). See §50.7.

For any home health services to be covered by Medicare, the patient must meet the qualifying criteria as specified in §30, including having a need for skilled nursing care on an intermittent basis, physical therapy, speech-language pathology services, or a continuing need for occupational therapy as defined in this section.

Overview of the Home Health Agency Prospective Payment System

Section 4603 of the Balanced Budget Act of 1997, as amended by section 5101 of the Omnibus Consolidated and Emergency Supplemental Appropriations Act for Fiscal Year 1999 requires the implementation of a prospective payment system for home health agencies, consolidated billing requirements, and a number of other related changes. The prospective payment system described in this rule replaced the retrospective reasonable-cost-based system used by Medicare for the payment of home health services under Part A and Part B.

I. Home Health Agency Prospective Payment System (HHA PPS)

The unit of payment under home health PPS is a national 60-day episode rate with applicable adjustments. The episodes, rate, and adjustments to the rates are detailed in the following sections.

10.1 – National 60-Day Episode Rate

A – Services Included: The law requires the 60-day episode to include all covered home health services, including medical supplies, paid on a reasonable cost basis. That means the 60-day episode rate includes costs for the six home health disciplines and the costs for routine and nonroutine medical supplies. The six home health disciplines included in the 60-day episode rate are:

1. Skilled nursing services
2. Home health aide services;
3. Physical therapy;
4. Speech-language pathology services;
5. Occupational therapy services; and
6. Medical social services.

The 60-day episode rate also includes amounts for:

1. Nonroutine medical supplies and therapies that could have been unbundled to part B prior to PPS. See §10.12.C for those services;

2. Ongoing reporting costs associated with the outcome and assessment information set (OASIS); and

3. A one time first year of PPS cost adjustment reflecting implementation costs associated with the revised OASIS assessment schedules needed to classify patients into appropriate case-mix categories.

B – Excluded Services: The law specifically excludes durable medical equipment from the 60-day episode rate and consolidated billing requirements. DME continues to be paid on the fee schedule outside of the PPS rate.

The osteoporosis drug (injectable calcitonin), which is covered where a woman is postmenopausal and has a bone fracture. This drug is also excluded from the 60-day episode rate but must be billed by the home health agency (HHA) while a patient is under a home health plan of care since the law requires consolidated billing of osteoporosis drugs. The osteoporosis drug continues to be paid on a reasonable cost basis.

10.2 – Adjustments to the 60-Day Episode Rates

A – Case-Mix Adjustment: A case-mix methodology adjusts payment rates based on characteristics of the patient and his/her corresponding resource needs (e.g., diagnosis, clinical factors, functional factors, service needs). The 60-day episode rates are adjusted by case-mix methodology based on data elements from the OASIS. The data elements of the case-mix adjustment methodology are organized into three dimensions to capture clinical severity factors, functional severity factors, and service utilization factors influencing case mix. In the clinical, functional, and service utilization dimensions, each data element is assigned a score value. The scores are summed to determine the patient's case-mix group.

B - Labor Adjustments: The labor portion of the 60-day episode rates is adjusted to reflect the wage index based on the site of service of the beneficiary. The beneficiary's location is the determining factor for the labor adjustment. The home health PPS rates are adjusted by the pre-floor and

pre-reclassified hospital wage index. The hospital wage index is adjusted to account for the geographic reclassification of hospitals in accordance with §§1886(d)(8)(B) and 1886(d)(10) of the Social Security Act (the Act.) According to the law, geographic reclassification only applies to hospitals. Additionally, the hospital wage index has specific floors that are required by law. Because these reclassifications and floors do not apply to HHAs, the home health rates are adjusted by the pre-floor and pre-reclassified hospital wage index. NOTE: The pre-floor and pre-reclassified hospital wage index varies slightly from the numbers published in the Medicare inpatient hospital PPS regulation that reflects the floor and reclassification adjustments. The wage indices published in the home health final rule and subsequent annual updates reflect the most recent available pre-floor and pre-reclassified hospital wage index available at the time of publication.

10.3 – Continuous 60-Day Episode Recertification

Home health PPS permits continuous episode recertifications for patients who continue to be eligible for the home health benefit. Medicare does not limit the number of continuous episode recertifications for beneficiaries who continue to be eligible for the home health benefit.

10.4 – Counting 60-Day Episodes

A – Initial Episodes: The "From" date for the initial certification must match the start of care (SOC) date, which is the first billable visit date for the 60-day episode. The "To" date is up to and including the last day of the episode which is not the first day of the subsequent episode. The "To" date can be up to, but never exceed a total of 60 days that includes the SOC date plus 59 days.

B – Subsequent Episodes: If a patient continues to be eligible for the home health benefit, the home health PPS permits continuous episode recertifications. At the end of the 60-day episode, a decision must be made whether or not to recertify the patient for a subsequent 60-day episode. An eligible beneficiary who qualifies for a subsequent 60-day episode would start the subsequent 60-day episode on day 61. The "From" date for the first subsequent episode is day 61 up to including day 120. The "To" date for the subsequent episode in this example can be up to, but never exceed a total of 60 days that includes day 61 plus 59 days. Note that the certification or recertification visit can be done during a prior episode.

10.5 – Split Percentage Payment Approach to the 60-Day Episode

In order to ensure adequate cash flow to HHAs, the home health PPS has set forth a split percentage payment approach to the 60-day episode. The split percentage occurs through the request for anticipated payment (RAP) at the start of the episode and the final claim at the end of the episode. For initial episodes, there will be a 60/40 split percentage payment. An initial percentage payment of 60 percent of the episode will be paid at the beginning of the episode and a final percentage payment of 40 percent will be paid at the end of the episode, unless there is an applicable adjustment. For all subsequent episodes for beneficiaries who receive continuous home health care, the episodes will be paid at a 50/50-percentage payment split.

10.6 – Physician Signature Requirements for the Split Percentage Payments

A – Initial Percentage Payment: If a physician-signed plan of care is not available at the beginning of the episode, the HHA may submit a RAP for the initial percentage payment based on physician verbal orders OR a referral prescribing detailed orders for the services to be rendered that is signed and dated by the physician. If the RAP submission is based on a physician's verbal orders, the verbal order must be recorded in the plan of care, include a description of the patient's condition and the services to be provided by the home health agency, and include an attestation (relating to the physician's orders and the date received per Code of Federal Regulation (CFR) 42 CFR 409.43). The plan of care is copied and immediately submitted to the physician. A billable visit must be rendered prior to the submission of a RAP.

The CMS has the authority to reduce or disapprove requests for anticipated payments in situations when protecting Medicare program integrity warrants this action. Since the request for anticipated payment is based on verbal orders and is not a Medicare claim for purposes of the Act (although it is a claim for purposes of Federal, civil, criminal, and administrative law enforcement authorities, including but not limited to the Civil Monetary Penalties Law, Civil False Claims Act, and the Criminal False Claims Act), the request for anticipated payment will be canceled and recovered unless the claim is submitted within the greater of 60 days from the end of the episode or 60 days from the issuance of the request for anticipated payment.

B – Final Percentage Payment: The plan of care must be signed and dated by a physician who meets the certification and recertification requirements of 42 CFR 424.22 before the claim for each episode for services is submitted for the final percentage payment. Any changes in the plan of care must be signed and dated by a physician.

10.7 – Low Utilization Payment Adjustment (LUPA)

An episode with four or fewer visits is paid the national per visit amount by discipline adjusted by the appropriate wage index based on the site of service of the beneficiary. Such episodes of four or fewer visits are paid the wage-adjusted per visit amount for each of the visits rendered instead of the full episode amount. The national per visit amounts by discipline (skilled nursing, home health aide, physical therapy, speech-language pathology, occupational therapy, and medical social services) are updated annually by the applicable market basket for each visit type and published annually.

10.8 – Partial Episode Payment (PEP) Adjustment

A – PEP Adjustment Criteria: The PEP adjustment accounts for key intervening events in a patient's care defined as:

- A beneficiary elected transfer; or
- A discharge resulting from the beneficiary reaching the treatment goals in the original plan of care and returning to the same HHA during the 60-day episode.

The intervening event defined as the beneficiary elected transfer or discharge and return to the same HHA during the 60-day episode warrants a new 60-day episode for purposes of payment. A start of care OASIS assessment and physician certification of the new plan of care are required. When a new 60-day episode begins due to the intervening event of the beneficiary elected transfer or discharge and return to the same HHA during the 60-day episode, the original 60-day episode is proportionally adjusted to reflect the length of time the beneficiary remained under the agency's care prior to the intervening event.

B – Methodology Used to Calculate PEP Adjustment: The PEP adjustment for the original 60-day episode is calculated to reflect the length of time the beneficiary remained under the care of the original HHA based on the first billable visit date through and including the last billable visit date. The PEP adjustment is calculated by determining the actual days served by the original HHA (first billable visit date through and including last billable visit date as a proportion of 60 multiplied by the original 60-day episode payment).

C – Application of Therapy Threshold to PEP Adjusted Episode: The therapy threshold item included in the case-mix methodology used in home health PPS is not combined or prorated across episodes. Each episode whether full or proportionately adjusted is subject to the therapy threshold for purposes of case-mix adjusting the payment for that individual patient's resource needs.

D – Common Ownership Exception to PEP Adjustment: If an HHA has a significant ownership as defined in 42 CFR 424.22, then the PEP adjustment would not apply in those situations of beneficiary elected transfer. Those situations would be considered services provided under arrangement on behalf of the originating HHA by the receiving HHA with the ownership interest until the end of the episode. The common ownership exception to the transfer PEP adjustment does not apply if the beneficiary moved out of their MSA or non-MSA during the 60-day episode before the transfer to the receiving HHA.

E – Beneficiary Elected Transfer Verification: In order for a receiving HHA to accept a beneficiary elected transfer, the receiving HHA must document that the beneficiary has been informed that the initial HHA will no longer receive Medicare payment on behalf of the patient and will no longer provide Medicare covered services to the patient after the date of the patient's elected transfer in accordance with current patient rights requirements at 42 CFR 484.10(e). The receiving HHA must also document in the record that it accessed the regional home health intermediaries (RHHI) inquiry system to determine whether or not the patient was under an established home health plan of care and it must contact the initial HHA on the effective date of transfer. In the rare circumstance of a dispute between HHAs, the RHHI is responsible for working with both HHAs to resolve the dispute. If the

receiving HHA can provide documentation of its notice of patient rights on Medicare payment liability provided to the patient upon transfer and its contact of the initial HHA of the transfer date, then the initial HHA will be ineligible for payment for the period of overlap in addition to the appropriate PEP adjustment. If the receiving HHA cannot provide the appropriate documentation, the receiving HHA's RAP and/or final claim will be cancelled, and full episode payment will be provided to the initial HHA. For the receiving HHA to properly document that it contacted the initial HHA on the effective date of transfer it must maintain similar information as the initial HHA, including the same basic beneficiary information, personnel contacted, dates and times. The initial HHA must also properly document that it was contacted and it accepted the transfer. Where it disputes a transfer, the initial HHA must call its RHHI to resolve the dispute. The RHHI is responsible for working with both HHAs to resolve the dispute.

10.9 – Significant Change in Condition (SCIC) Payment Adjustment

If a patient experiences a significant change in condition during a 60-day episode that was not envisioned in the original plan of care, the 60-day episode rate may be changed with a SCIC adjustment to reflect the payment level to meet the resource needs of the patient during the 60 day episode.

A – Significant Change in Condition Adjustment Criteria: In order to receive a new case-mix assignment due to an unanticipated significant change in condition, the HHA must complete an OASIS assessment and obtain the necessary physician change orders reflecting the significant change in treatment approach in the patient's plan of care. The total significant change in condition payment adjustment is a proportional payment adjustment reflecting the time both before and after the patient experienced a significant change in condition during the 60-day episode.

B – Methodology Used to Calculate the SCIC Adjustment: The SCIC payment adjustment is calculated in two parts. The first part of the SCIC payment adjustment reflects the adjustment to the payment level prior to the patient's significant change in condition during the 60-day episode. The first part of the SCIC adjustment is determined by taking the span of days of the first billable visit date through and including the last billable visit date prior to the patient's significant change in condition as a proportion of 60 multiplied by the original episode amount. The second part of the SCIC payment adjustment reflects the adjustment to the level of payment after the significant change in the patient's condition occurs during the 60-day episode. The second part of the SCIC adjustment is calculated using the span of days of the first billable visit date through and including the last billable visit date through the balance of the 60-day episode.

The agency is not constrained to bill for a SCIC for a higher home health resource group (HHRG) if the net effect is a lower payment for the episode than if the SCIC had not occurred. Because the intent of the SCIC was not to lower the total episode payment when patients actually required more intensive services, the HHA is not forced to bill for a SCIC in this circumstance. However, where the SCIC reflects a lower HHRG due to unanticipated improvement in patient condition, the SCIC must be billed.

C – Application of Therapy Threshold to the SCIC and Relationship of Therapy Need Changes to the SCIC Adjustment: The therapy threshold item included in the case-mix methodology used in home health PPS is not combined or prorated across episodes. Since the SCIC adjustment occurs within a given 60-day episode, all therapy provided within a SCIC adjusted episode is counted toward the therapy threshold for the episode. The intermediary system will not automatically upgrade a non-therapy HHRG to a therapy HHRG when the final claim indicates 10 or more therapy visits even when 10 or more therapy visits are furnished and recorded on the claim. If the therapy threshold is the only case-mix item that requires adjustment, the HHA may cancel and resubmit a RAP with the corrected HHRG that reflects the upwardly revised therapy level. However, if the patient's actual therapy receipt as reflected on the final claim is lower than the threshold for the high therapy case-mix group projected at the initiation of the episode, the intermediary system will automatically lower the reimbursement level to the lower therapy case-mix group.

D – Relationship Between SCIC Adjustments and the Low Utilization Payment Adjustment (LUPA): The SCIC adjustment occurs within a given 60-day episode and does not restart the 60-day episode. The LUPA adjustment applies to a total 60-day episode period. As long as the total SCIC adjusted episode, comprised of both the pre-SCIC and post-SCIC parts, has more than four visits, the total episode would not be considered a LUPA situation. The LUPA applies to the total number of visits provided in a given 60-day episode.

E – Intervening Hospital of SNF Stay:- SCIC Adjustment Home health agencies have the option to discharge the patient within the scope of their own operating policies. However, an HHA discharging a patient as a result of hospital (SNF or rehab facility) admission with the patient returning to home health services at the same HHA during the 60-day episode will not be recognized by Medicare as a discharge for billing and payment purposes. An intervening hospital (SNF or rehab facility) stay will result in either an applicable SCIC adjustment or, if the resumption of care OASIS assessment upon return to home health does not indicate a change in case-mix level, a full 60-day episode will be provided spanning the start of care date prior to the hospital (SNF or rehab facility) admission, through and including the days of the hospital admission, and ending 59 days after the original start of care date.

10.10 – Outlier Payments

When cases experience an unusually high level of services in a 60-day period, Medicare systems will provide additional or "outlier" payments to the case-mix and wage-adjusted episode payment. Outlier payments can result from medically necessary high utilization in any or all-home health service disciplines. The CMS makes outlier payments when the cost of care exceeds a threshold dollar amount. The outlier threshold for each case-mix group is the episode payment amount for that group, the PEP adjustment amount for the episode, or the total SCIC adjustment amount for the episode plus a fixed dollar loss amount is the same for all case-mix groups. The outlier payment is a proportion of the amount of imputed costs beyond the threshold. The CMS calculates the imputed cost for each episode by multiplying the national per visit amount of each discipline by the number of visits in the discipline and computing the total imputed cost for all disciplines. If the imputed cost for the episode is greater than the sum of the case-mix and wage-adjusted episode payment plus the fixed dollar loss amount (the outlier threshold), a set percentage (the loss sharing ratio) of the difference between the imputed amount and outlier threshold will be paid to the HHA as a wage-adjusted outlier payment in addition to the episode payment. The amount of the outlier payment is determined as follows:

1. Calculate the case-mix and wage-adjusted episode payment;
2. Add the wage-adjusted fixed dollar loss amount. The sum of steps 1 and 2 is the outlier threshold for the episode;
3. Multiply the wage-adjusted national per visit rate for each home health discipline by the total number of visits for each home health discipline to determine the imputed cost of all visits. The result yields the total imputed costs for the episode;
4. Subtract the total imputed costs for the episode (total from Step 3) from the sum of the case-mix and wage-adjusted episode payment and the wage-adjusted fixed dollar loss amount (sum of Steps 1and 2 - outlier threshold);
5. Multiply the difference by the loss sharing ratio; and
6. The result of Step 5 is wage index adjusted. That total amount is the outlier payment for the episode.

10.11 – Discharge Issues

A – Hospice Election Mid-Episode: If a patient elects hospice before the end of the episode and there was no SCIC, PEP, or LUPA adjustment, the HHA will receive a full episode payment. Home health PPS does not change the current rules that permit a hospice patient to receive home health services for a condition unrelated to his/her reason for hospice election. Consistent with all episodes in which a patient receives four or fewer visits, the episode with four or fewer visits in which a patient elects hospice would be paid at the low utilization payment adjusted amount. In the event of a patient election of hospice during a SCIC-adjusted episode, the total SCIC-adjusted episode would constitute the full episode payment. However, the HHA is not constrained to bill for a SCIC for a higher case-mix group if the net effect is a lower payment for the episode than if the SCIC had not occurred.

B – Patient's Death: The documented event of a patient's death would result in a full episode payment, unless the death occurred in a low utilization payment adjusted episode. Consistent with all episodes in which a patient receives four or fewer visits, if the patient's death occurred during an episode with four or fewer visits, the episode would be paid at the low utilization payment adjusted amount. In the event of a patient's death during a SCIC-adjusted episode, the total SCIC-adjusted episode would constitute the full episode payment. However, the HHA is not constrained to bill for a SCIC for a higher case-mix group if the net effect is a lower payment for the episode than if the SCIC had not occurred.

C – Patient is No Longer Eligible for Home Health: (e.g., no longer homebound, no skilled need): If the patient is discharged because he or she is no longer eligible for the Medicare home health benefit and has received more than four visits, then the HHA would receive full episode payment. However, if the patient becomes subsequently eligible for the Medicare home health benefit during the same 60-day episode and later transferred to another HHA

or returned to the same HHA, then the latter situation would result in a PEP adjustment.

D – Discharge Due to Patient Refusal of Services or is a Documented Safety Threat, Abuse Threat or is Noncompliant: If the patient is discharged because he or she refuses services or becomes a documented safety, abuse, or noncompliance discharge and has received more than four visits, then the HHA would receive full episode payment unless the patient becomes subsequently eligible for the Medicare home health benefit during the same 60-day episode and later transferred to another HHA or returned to the same HHA, then the latter situation would result in a PEP adjustment.

E – Patient Becomes Managed Care Eligible Mid-Episode: If a patient's enrollment in a Medicare + Choice organization (M+CO) becomes effective mid episode, the 60-day episode payment will be made proportionally adjusted with a PEP adjustment since the patient is receiving coverage under the M+CO. Beginning with the effective date of enrollment, the M+CO will receive a capitation payment for covered services.

F – Submission of Final Claims Prior to the End of the 60-day Episode: The claim may be submitted upon discharge before the end of the 60-day episode. However, subsequent adjustments to any payments based on the claim may be made due to an intervening event resulting in a PEP adjustment or other adjustment.

G – Patient Discharge and Financial Responsibility for Part B Bundled Medical Supplies and Services: As discussed in detail under §10.12, below, the law governing the Medicare home health PPS requires the HHA to provide all bundled home health services (except DME) either directly or under arrangement while a patient is under a home health plan of care during an open episode. The HHA is responsible for providing all covered home health services (except DME) either directly or under arrangement while a patient is under a home health plan of care during an open episode. Once the patient is discharged, the HHA is no longer responsible for providing home health services including the bundled Part B medical supplies and therapy services.

H – Discharge Issues Associated with Inpatient Admission Overlapping Into Subsequent Episodes: If a patient is admitted to an inpatient facility and the inpatient stay overlaps into what would have been the subsequent episode and there is no reassessment or recertification of the patient, then the certification begins with the new start of care date after inpatient discharge.

10.12 – Consolidated Billing

For individuals under a home health plan of care payment for all services and supplies, with the exception of the osteoporosis drugs and DME, is included in the PPS episodic rate. HHAs must provide the covered home health services (except DME) either directly or under arrangement, and must bill for such covered home health services. Payment must be made to the HHA.

A - Home Health Services Subject to Consolidated Billing Requirements: The home health services included in the consolidated billing governing home health PPS are:

- Part-time or intermittent skilled nursing services;
- Part-time or intermittent home health aide services;
- Physical therapy;
- Speech-language pathology services;
- Occupational therapy;
- Medical social services;
- Routine and nonroutine medical supplies;
- Covered osteoporosis drug as defined in §1861(kk) of the Act, but excluding other drugs and biologicals;
- Medical services provided by an intern or resident-in-training of the program of the hospital in the case of an HHA that is affiliated or under common control with a hospital with an approved teaching program; and
- Home health services defined in §1861(m) provided under arrangement at hospitals, SNFs, or rehabilitation centers when they involve equipment too cumbersome to bring to the home or are furnished while the patient is at the facility to receive such services.

B - Medical Supplies: The law requires all medical supplies (routine and nonroutine) bundled to the agency while the patient is under a home health plan of care. The agency that establishes the episode is the only entity that can bill and receive payment for medical supplies during an episode for a patient under a home health plan of care. Both routine and nonroutine medical supplies are included in the base rates for every Medicare home health patient regardless of whether or not the patient requires medical supplies during the episode. Due to the consolidated billing requirements,

CMS provided additional amounts in the base rates for those nonroutine medical supplies that have a duplicate Part B code that could have been unbundled to Part B prior to PPS. See §§50.4 for detailed discussion of medical supplies.

Medical supplies used by the patient, provider, or other practitioners under arrangement on behalf of the agency (other than physicians) are subject to consolidated billing and bundled to the HHA episodic payment rate. Once a patient is discharged from home health and not under a home health plan of care, the HHA is not responsible for medical supplies.

DME, including supplies covered as DME, are paid separately from the PPS rates and are excluded from the consolidated billing requirements governing PPS. The determining factor is the medical classification of the supply, not the diagnosis of the patient. For example, infusion therapy will continue to be covered under the DME benefit separately paid from the PPS rate and excluded from the consolidated billing requirements governing PPS. The DME supplies that are currently covered and paid in accordance with the DME fee schedule as category SU are billed under the DME benefit and not included in the bundled HHA episodic payment rate. The HHAs are not required to do consolidated billing of SU supplies.

Osteoporosis drugs are included in consolidated billing under the home health benefit. However, payment is not bundled into the episodic payment rate. The HHAs must bill for osteoporosis drugs in accordance with billing instructions. Payment is in addition to the episodic payment rate.

C - Relationship between Consolidated Billing Requirements and Part B Supplies and Part B Therapies Included in the Baseline Rates That Could Have Been Unbundled Prior to PPS That No Longer Can Be Unbundled: The HHA is responsible for the services provided under arrangement on their behalf by other entities. Covered home health services at §1861(m) of the Act (except DME) are included in the baseline PPS rates and subject to the consolidated billing requirements while the patient is under a plan of care of the HHA. The time the services are bundled is while the patient is under a home health plan of care.

Physician services or nurse practitioner services that are bundled into the physician fee schedule payments are not recognized as a home health service included in the PPS rate. Supplies incident to a physician service or related to a physician service billed to the carrier are not subject to the consolidated billing requirements. The physician would not be acting as a supplier billing the DMERC in this situation.

Therapies (physical therapy, occupational therapy, and speech-language pathology services) are covered home health services that are included in the baseline rates and subject to the consolidated billing requirements. In addition to therapies that had been paid on a cost basis under home health, CMS has included in the rates additional amounts for Part B therapies that could have been unbundled prior to PPS. These therapies are subject to the consolidated billing requirements. There are revenue center codes that reflect the ranges of outpatient physical therapy, occupational therapy, and speech-language pathology services and HCPCS codes that reflect physician supplier codes that are physical therapy, occupational therapy, and speech-language pathology services by code definition and are subject to the consolidated billing requirements. Therefore, the above-mentioned therapies must be provided directly or under arrangement on behalf of the HHA while a patient is under a home health plan of care cannot be separately billed to Part B during an open 60-day episode.

D - Freedom of Choice Issues: A beneficiary exercises his or her freedom of choice for the services under the home health benefit listed in §1861(m) of the Act, including medical supplies, but excluding DME covered as a home health service by choosing the HHA. Once a home health patient chooses a particular HHA, he or she has clearly exercised freedom of choice with respect to all items and services included within the scope of the Medicare home health benefit (except DME). The HHA's consolidated billing role supersedes all other billing situations the beneficiary may wish to establish for home health services covered under the scope of the Medicare home health benefit during the certified episode.

E - Knowledge of Services Arranged for on Behalf of the HHA: The consolidated billing requirements governing home health PPS requires that the HHA provide all covered home health services (except DME) either directly or under arrangement while a patient is under a home health plan of care. Providing services either directly or under arrangement requires knowledge of the services provided during the episode. In addition, in accordance with current Medicare conditions of participation and Medicare coverage guidelines governing home health, the patient's plan of care must reflect the physician ordered services that the HHA provides either directly or under arrangement. An HHA would not be responsible for payment in the situation in which they

have no prior knowledge (unaware of physicians orders) of the services provided by an entity during an episode to a patient who is under their home health plan of care. An HHA is responsible for payment in the situation in which services are provided to a patient by another entity, under arrangement with the HHA, during an episode in which the patient is under the HHA's home health plan of care. However, it is in the best interest of future business relationships to discuss the situation with any entity that seeks payment from the HHA during an episode in an effort to resolve any misunderstanding and avoid such situations in the future.

10.13 – Change of Ownership Relationship to Episodes Under PPS

A - Change of Ownership with Assignment: When there is a change of ownership and the new owner accepts assignment of the existing provider agreement, the new owner is subject to all the terms and conditions under which the existing agreement was issued. The provider number remains the same if the new HHA owner accepts assignment of the existing provider agreement. As long as the new owner complies with the regulations governing home health PPS, billing, and payment for episodes with applicable adjustments for existing patients under an established plan of care will continue on schedule through the change in ownership with assignment. The episode would be uninterrupted spanning the date of sale. The former owner is required to file a terminating cost report. Instructions regarding when a cost report is filed are in the Provider Reimbursement Manual, §1500.

B - Change of Ownership without Assignment: When there is a change of ownership, and the new owner does not take the assignment of the existing provider agreement, the provider agreement and provider number of the former owner is terminated. The former owner will receive partial episode payment adjusted payments in accordance with the methodology set forth in the Medicare Claims Processing Manual, Chapter 10, "Home Health Agency Billing," §40.2, and 42 CFR 484.235, based on the last billable visit date for existing patients under a home health plan of care ending on or before the date of sale. The former owner is required to file a terminating cost report. The new owner cannot bill Medicare for payment until the effective date of the Medicare approval. The new HHA will not be able to participate in the Medicare program without going through the same process as any new provider, which includes an initial survey. Once the new owner is Medicare-approved, the HHA may start a new episode for purposes of payment, OASIS assessment, and certification of the home health plan of care for all new patients in accordance with the regulations governing home health PPS, effective with the date of the new provider certification.

C - Change of Ownership – Mergers: The merger of a provider corporation into another corporation constitutes a change of ownership. For information on specific procedures, refer to the State Operations Manual.

II. Clinical Model Patient Classification System

1. Background

The basic approach to the home health case-mix adjuster development was to use the patient data and other appropriate data to define alternative case-mix adjusters and then estimate their ability to explain variation in resource use over the course of a 60-day payment period.

The two basic data sources for the study are case-mix explanatory variables from the patient data on OASIS-B (supplemented by additional patient-specific items) and a resource-use variable from visit data. To arrive at an estimate of resource use from the visit logs, time is weighted by mean labor cost for the discipline providing the visit. Medicare claims were linked to the OASIS data and the visit log data to verify the visits and provide utilization measures.

Clinical judgment was used to refine the components and structure of a decision tree for assigning patients into case-mix groups. Along with clinical judgment, the relative predictive value of potential case-mix variables, their susceptibility to gaming and subjectivity, and as well as administrative implications were considered in the final resolution of the elements retained in the Clinical Model. The Clinical Model consists of 80 HHRGs. The information to assign a patient to one of the 80 HHRGs are comprised of 19 OASIS-B elements supplemented by one additional patient status item regarding projected therapy use in the 60-day episode.

B. Home Health Resource Group (HHRG) Classification System

In the HHRG case-mix classification system, patient character-istics and health status information from the OASIS-B such as "primary home care diagnosis," "ability to perform ADLs" as supplemented by projected therapy use during a 60-day episode, will be used to assign the patient to an HHRG for payment.

The HHRG system measures three dimensions of case mix.

A patient can be classified in one of 80 possible HHRG categories. The first level of the decision tree is the Clinical Dimension, which is divided into four severity groups. A patient is assigned one of four severity levels in the Clinical Dimension: minimum, low, moderate, or high clinical severity. To determine the severity group, a numeric score is applied to each answer provided to the following 12 clinical OASIS-B items: MO230 Primary Home Health Diagnosis, MO250 IV/Infusion/Parenteral/Enteral Therapies, MO390 Vision, MO420 Pain, MO460 Current Pressure Ulcer Stage, MO476 Stasis Ulcer, MO488 Surgical Wound, MO490 Dyspnea, MO530 Urinary Incontinence, MO540 Bowel Incontinence, MO550 Bowel Ostomy, MO610 Behavioral Problems. The scores are then summed. The severity level is determined by the value of the summed score.

The Functional Dimension is divided into five severity groups. A patient is assigned one of five severity levels in the Functional Dimension: minimum, low, moderate, high, or maximum functional severity. To determine the severity group, a numeric score is applied to each answer provided for the following six OASIS-B items: MO650 and MO660 Dressing Upper and Lower Body, MO670 Bathing, MO680 Toileting, MO690 Transferring, and MO700 Locomotion. The scores are then summed. The severity level for the Functional Dimension is determined by the value of the summed score.

The Services Utilization Dimension is also divided into four severity groups. A patient is assigned to one of the four following severity levels in the Services Utilization Dimension: minimum, low, moderate, or high. To determine the severity group, a numeric score is applied to each answer provided to the following OASIS-B item divided into two questions, and one supplemental item regarding projected receipt of therapy use: MO170 hospital discharge in past 14 days, MO170 inpatient rehabilitation/SNF discharge in past 14 days, and receipt of therapy. The scores are then summed. The severity level for the Services Utilization Dimension is determined by the value of the summed scores.

We are proposing a utilization proxy for the time variable corresponding to the need for 8 or more therapy hours during a 60-day episode. As a result of the Abt case-mix research, Abt determined that 10 visits of physical therapy, occupational therapy, or speech-language pathology services in any combination in a 60-day period equate to 8 hours of physical therapy, occupational therapy, or speech-language pathology services in any combination in a 60-day period. At the inception of HHA PPS, the case-mix treatment variable regarding the need for 8 or more hours of therapy in a 60-day episode were defined as 10 visits of physical therapy, occupational therapy, or speech-language pathology services in any combination furnished during the 60-day episode.

As discussed above, HHAs will project the therapy need for the patient at the start of the 60-day episode. The projection of therapy use at the start of the 60-day episode (8 hours of therapy as defined as 10 visits) will be confirmed at the end of the 60-day episode with the current line-item date visit billing requirements included on the final claim under PPS. We envision that the pricer logic at the RHHI will confirm the projection of the utilization data at the start of care with the actual utilization data submitted on the final claim. If 8 or more hours of therapy as defined as 10 therapy visits are projected at the start of the episode and confirmed at the end of the episode via the line-item date billing information on the final claim, the episode would be paid at the case-mix index level including the therapy-use variable. This assumes no adjustment for other reasons, for example, medical review etc. However, the reconciliation of projected therapy use with actual therapy use has the potential to decrease the final episode payment if the actual therapy use reported at the end of the episode on the final claim does not correspond to projected therapy use provided at the start of the episode. Depending on the results of the reporting of 15-minute increment billing, we will of course consider reverting to measure the therapy use in terms of hours by 15-minute increments rather than visits.

III. HHA PPS Framework—How the System Works

A. Start of Care

The HHA establishes the plan of care and the patient will be grouped into the appropriate case-mix category via the OASIS assessment and the additional item regarding projected number of therapy hours received in a 60-day episode at the HHA. The HHA must have all physician orders in the plan of care and a physician's signature for the plan of care before billing. The physician's orders for therapy services will be a key focus of medical review.

The HHA that initially establishes the plan of care is responsible for billing for all home health services provided under the plan of care, including nonroutine medical supplies and durable medical supplies in a 60-day episode. If a patient transfers during a 60-day episode, the responsibility for consolidating billing moves to the transfer HHA.

B. End of Episode

The final claim may contain all of the line-item date visit information for the entire 60-day episode period.

C. Recertification of 60-Day Episode Period

At the end of the 60-day episode a decision must be made to recertify the patient for another 60-day episode period. An eligible beneficiary who qualifies for a continuous 60-day episode would start the continuous 60-day episode on Day 61. A new OASIS is performed as part of the overall approach to assessment and to determine the appropriate case-mix category for the next episode. The physician's orders for services in the plan of care and the physician's certification of eligibility are required before the HHA submits a bill for the next 60-day episode period.

D. Determining Whether a Beneficiary is Under an Established Plan of Care

The national episode history by beneficiary must be created and maintained that contains beneficiary identification, provider identification, dates of service, utilization, case-mix classification codes, and discharge and transfer status indicators. CMS developed a tracking system available to both providers and RHHIs information on whether a beneficiary is under an established home health plan of care.

E. Medical Review

Section 1816 of the Act requires our contractors to conduct audits of providers' records, as needed, to ensure that payments are appropriate for the items or services furnished.

Because all Medicare-participating HHAs will be transitioned onto the new payment system on a particular calendar date, the initial medical review strategy for HHA PPS bills will be a parallel approach of random and focused medical review.

As with current Medicare medical review practice, CMS allows RHHIs to supplement their primary prepayment review activities with a limited amount of postpayment review.

F. Overpayments and Adjustments

If it is determined from proration, medical review, etc. that the preliminary case-mix-adjusted episode payment exceeds the amount ultimately due to an HHA, the overpayment may be offset against future episode payments due to the HHA for the same or other agency patients.

G. Implementation Effective Date for PPS

OCESAA requires all HHAs to be paid under PPS effective upon implementation of the system October 1, 2000. There is no transition by cost reporting period; therefore, all HHAs begin PPS on the same implementation date.

Rather than requiring the close-out of cost reports with short period cost reports, we are exploring the use of a supplemental schedule in the cost report to allocate costs and limits between pre- and post-PPS.

H. Claims Processing Transition

Under the October 1, 2000 PPS implementation date, all HHAs must bill for all eligible Medicare beneficiaries under a home health plan of care under the PPS. If an HHA has beneficiaries already under an established plan of care, all open bills for services provided September 30, 2000 or earlier will need to be closed as of September 30, 2000.

I. Quality System

Under the Medicare COPs, HHAs must develop, implement, maintain, and evaluate an effective, data-driven quality assessment and performance improvement program. The program must reflect the complexity of the HHA's organization and services, including those services provided directly or under arrangement. The HHA must take actions that result in improvements in the HHA's performance across the spectrum of care. An integral part of this approach is the additional COP requirement that HHAs use a standard core assessment data set, the Outcome and Assessment Information Set (OASIS), when evaluating patients. The OASIS is a set of valid, reliable measures, developed to assess patient outcomes to care provided in the home.

The use of a uniform patient assessment in home health is part of a broader CMS goal to develop outcome measures for all provider types. The OASIS is expected to become one of the most important aspects of the HHA's quality assessment and performance improvement efforts. By integrating a core standard assessment data set into its own more comprehensive assessment system, an HHA can use this data set as the foundation for valid and reliable information for patient assessment, care planning, and service delivery, as well as to build a strong and effective quality assessment and performance improvement program.

K. Required Schedule for Completing OASIS Supplemented by One Additional Case-Mix Item

As discussed above, the initial OASIS assessment completed at the start of care and the assessment at every subsequent follow-up recertification for beneficiaries who continue to be eligible for home health services will be the only assessments recognized for purposes of payment for the 60-day episode. The start of care OASIS must be completed at the beginning of each 60-day episode. An HHA may not bill for the initial percentage episode payment without the grouper-generated code corresponding to the complete OASIS assessment supplemented, as necessary, by the additional therapy variable for that 60-day episode. The initial OASIS assessment completed at the start of care is updated every 60 days. The initial OASIS and subsequent follow-up OASIS supplemented, as applicable, by the treatment variable regarding therapy use will also be updated on a 60-day timetable. Each 60-day follow-up OASIS supplemented by the treatment variable re-garding therapy will be the basis for case-mix adjusting each subsequent 60-day episode period for purposes of payment.

L. Relationship Between Payment and OASIS

Each Medicare home health patient is classified into an HHRG group for each 60-day episode period. The group to which the patient is classified is based on the information about the patient's clinical resource needs as reported on the OASIS-B as part of the approach to overall comprehensive assessment as required by 42 CFR 484.55 in the HHA COPs, and the ser-vices ordered in the patient's home health plan of care, includ-ing but not limited to, a physician's orders for therapy services.

Hospice Criteria for Medicare Coverage of Noncancer Hospice Care

Coverage of Hospice Services under Hospital Insurance

CMS Manual Publication 100-2, Medicare Benefits Policy Chapter 9

Summary of Changes

Physician recertification changes

Effective July 1, 2005, CMS Transmittal 458 designates the use of occurrence span code 77-Provider Liability Utilization Charged, to indicate noncovered days during a hospice billing period due to untimely physician recertification.

Nurse Practitioners as Attending Physician in Hospice

When hospice coverage is elected, the beneficiary waives all rights to Medicare Part B payments for services that are related to the treatment and management of his/her terminal illness during any period his/her hospice benefit election is in force, except for professional services of an attending physician, which may include a nurse practitioner. Nurse practitioners may not serve as or replace the medical director or physician member of an interdisciplinary group (IDG). Nurse practitioners serving as the attending physician may not certify or re-certify the terminal illness.

Hospices use revenue code 0657 to identify hospice charges for services furnished to patients by physician or nurse practitioner employees, or physicians or nurse practitioners receiving compensation from the hospice. Physician services performed by a nurse practitioner require the addition of the modifier GV in conjunction with revenue code 0657, the procedure HCPCS code is entered in FL44. Procedure codes are required in order for the FI to determine the reimbursement rate for the physician services. Appropriate procedure codes are available from the FI. Services provided by a nurse practitioner as the attending physician are not included in the CHC computation.

10 - Requirements – General

Hospice care is a benefit under the hospital insurance program. To be eligible to elect hospice care under Medicare, an individual must be entitled to Part A of Medicare and be certified as being terminally ill. An individual is considered to be terminally ill if the medical prognosis is that the individual's life expectancy is six months or less if the illness runs its normal course.

Section §1814(a)(7) of the Social Security Act (the Act) specifies that certification of terminal illness for hospice benefits shall be based on the hospice's physician's and the individual's attending physician if he/she has one or medical director's clinical judgment regarding the normal course of the individual's illness. No one other than a medical doctor or doctor of osteopathy can certify or re-certify a terminal illness. Predicting of life expectancy is not always exact. The fact that a beneficiary lives longer than expected in itself is not cause to terminate benefits. "Attending physician" is further defined in Section 20.1 and 40.2.5. Making medical prognostication of life expectancy is not always exact. If a beneficiary lives longer than expected this in itself is not cause to terminate benefits.

An individual (or his authorized representative) must elect hospice care to receive it. The first election is for a 90 day period. An individual may elect to receive Medicare coverage for an unlimited number of election periods of hospice care. The periods consist of two 90-day periods, and an unlimited number of 60-day periods. If the individual (or authorized representative) elects to receive hospice care, he or she must file an election statement with a particular hospice. Hospices obtain elections from the individual and forward them to the intermediary, which transmits them to the Common Working File (CWF) in electronic format. Once the initial election is processed, CWF maintains the beneficiary in hospice status until death or until an election termination is received.

An individual must waive all rights to Medicare payments for the duration of the election/revocation of hospice care for the following services:

Hospice care provided by a hospice other than the hospice designated by the individual (unless provided under arrangements made by the designated hospice); and

Any Medicare services that are related to the treatment of the terminal condition for which hospice care was elected or a related condition or services that are equivalent to hospice care, except for services provided by:

- The designated hospice (either directly or under arrangement);
- Another hospice under arrangements made by the designated hospice; or
- The individual's attending physician, if that physician is not an employee of the designated hospice or receiving compensation from the hospice for those services.

Medicare services for a condition completely unrelated to the terminal condition for which hospice was elected remain available to the patient if he or she is eligible for such care.

The hospice also sends a copy of the election to the carrier with jurisdiction for the hospice's geographic area. The carrier maintains the election statement in its files to use when processing physician claims.

Patients considered to be in the terminal stage of noncancer illness must meet certain criteria to be eligible for Medicare coverage of hospice care. Policies have been developed concerning noncancer hospice care. These policies were developed by the Carrier Medical Directors (CMD) Hospice Clinical Workgroup and has been reviewed by CMS Central Office, the Carrier Advisory Committee and by the hospice providers and were found not to be in conflict with any existing CMS national coverage, rules and/or regulations.

Medicare coverage of hospice care depends upon a physician's certification of an individual's prognosis of a life expectancy of six months or less if the terminal illness runs its normal course. Recognizing that determination of life expectancy during the course of a terminal illness is difficult, this intermediary has established medical criteria for determining prognosis for non-cancer diagnoses. These criteria form a reasonable approach to the determination of life expectancy based on available research, and may be revised as more research is available. Coverage of hospice care for patients not meeting the criteria in this policy may be denied. However, some patients may not meet the criteria, yet still be appropriate for hospice care, because of other comorbidities or rapid decline. Coverage for these patients may be approved on an individual consideration basis.

The criteria in each of these eight policies are considered to be the most accurate parameters to determine Medicare coverage for these specific noncancer diagnoses.

A patient will be considered to have a life expectancy of six months or less if he/she meets the non-disease specific decline in clinical status guidelines described in Part I. Alternatively, the baseline non-disease specific guidelines described in Part II plus the applicable disease specific guidelines listed in the appendix will establish the necessary expectancy.

Part I. Decline in clinical status guidelines

Patients will be considered to have a life expectancy of six months or less if there is documented evidence of decline in clinical status based on the guidelines listed below. Since determination of decline presumes assessment of the patient's status over time, it is essential that both baseline and follow-up determinations be reported where appropriate. Baseline data may be established on admission to hospice or by using existing information from records. Other clinical variables not on this list may support a six-month or less life expectancy. These should be documented in the clinical record.

These changes in clinical variables apply to patients whose decline is not considered to be reversible. They are listed in order of their likelihood to predict poor survival, the most predictive first and the least predictive last. No specific number of variables must be met, but fewer of those listed first (more predictive) and more of those listed last (least predictive) would be expected to predict longevity of six months or less.

Progression of disease as documented by worsening clinical status, symptoms, signs and laboratory results

1. Clinical Status
   a. Recurrent or intractable infections such as pneumonia, sepsis or upper urinary tract.

b. Progressive inanition as documented by:

1) Weight loss not due to reversible causes such as depression or use of diuretics

2) Decreasing anthropomorphic measurements (mid-arm circumference, abdominal girth), not due to reversible causes such as depression or use of diuretics

3) Decreasing serum albumin or cholesterol

c. Dysphagia leading to recurrent aspiration and/or inadequate oral intake documented by decreasing food portion consumption.

2. Symptoms

a. Dyspnea with increasing respiratory rate

b. Cough, intractable

c. Nausea/vomiting poorly responsive to treatment

d. Diarrhea, intractable

e. Pain requiring increasing doses of major analgesics more than briefly.

3. Signs

a. Decline in systolic blood pressure to below 90 or progressive postural hypotension

b. Ascites

c. Venous, arterial or lymphatic obstruction due to local progression or metastatic disease

d. Edema

e. Pleural/pericardial effusion

f. Weakness

g. Change in level of consciousness

4. Laboratory (When available. Lab testing is not required to establish hospice eligibility.)

a. Increasing $pCO2$ or decreasing $pO2$ or decreasing $SaO2$

b. Increasing calcium, creatinine or liver function studies

c. Increasing tumor markers (e.g. CEA, PSA)

d. Progressively decreasing or increasing serum sodium or increasing serum potassium

5. Decline in Karnofsky Performance Status (KPS) or Palliative Performance Score (PPS) from < 70% due to progression of disease.

6. Progressive decline in Functional Assessment Staging (FAST) for dementia (from =7A on the FAST)

7. Progression to dependence on assistance with additional activities of daily living. See Part II, Section 2.

8. Progressive stage 3-4 pressure ulcers in spite of optimal care.

9. Increasing emergency room visits, hospitalizations, or physician's visits related to hospice primary diagnosis

Part II. Non-disease specific baseline guidelines (both of these should be met)

A. Physiologic impairment of functional status as demonstrated by: Karnofsky Performance Status (KPS) or Palliative Performance Score (PPS) from < 70%. Note that two of the disease specific guidelines (HIV Disease, Stroke and Coma) establish a lower qualifying KPS or PPS.

B. Dependence on assistance for two or more activities of daily living (ADLs)

1. Ambulation
2. Continence
3. Transfer
4. Dressing
5. Feeding
6. Bathing

Part III. Co-morbidities – although not the primary hospice diagnosis, the presence of disease such as the following, the severity of which is likely to contribute to a life expectancy of six months or less, should be considered in determining hospice eligibility.

A. Chronic obstructive pulmonary disease

B. Congestive heart failure

C. Ischemic heart disease

D. Diabetes mellitus

E. Neurologic disease (CVA, ALS, MS, Parkinson's)

F. Renal failure

G. Liver Disease

H. Neoplasia

I. Acquired immune deficiency syndrome

J. Dementia

Hospice HIV Disease

Indications and limitations of coverage and/or medical necessity:

Patients will be considered to be in the terminal stage of their illness (life expectancy of six months or less) if they meet the following criteria (1 and 2 must be present; factors from 3 will add supporting documentation):

1. CD4+ Count < 25 cells/mcL or persistent viral load > 100,000 copies/ml, plus one of the following:

   • CNS lymphoma

   • Untreated, or not responsive to treatment, wasting (loss of 33% lean body mass)

   • Mycobacterium avium complex (MAC) bacteremia, untreated, unresponsive to treatment, or treatment refused

   • Progressive multifocal leukoencephalopathy

   • Systemic lymphoma, with advanced HIV disease and partial response to chemotherapy

   • Visceral Kaposi's sarcoma unresponsive to therapy

   • Renal failure in the absence of dialysis

   • Cryptosporidium infection

   • Toxoplasmosis, unresponsive to therapy

2. Decreased performance status, as measured by the Karnofsky Performance Status (KPS) scale, of less than 50%

3. Documentation of the following factors will support eligibility for hospice care:

   • Chronic persistent diarrhea for one year

   • Persistent serum albumin <2.5

   • Concomitant, active substance abuse

   • Age > 50 years

   • Absence of antiretroviral, chemotherapeutic and prophylactic drug therapy related specifically to HIV disease

   • Advanced AIDS dementia complex

   • Toxoplasmosis

   • Congestive heart failure, symptomatic at rest

ICD-9-CM codes that support medical necessity:
042 Human immunodeficiency virus (HIV) disease

Hospice Pulmonary Disease

Indications and limitations of coverage and/or medical necessity:

Patients will be considered to be in the terminal stage of pulmonary disease (life expectancy of six months or less) if they meet the following criteria. The criteria refer to patients with various forms of advanced pulmonary disease who eventually follow a final common pathway for end stage pulmonary disease. (1 and 2 must be present. Documentation of 3, 4, and/or 5 will lend supporting documentation.):

1. Severe chronic lung disease as documented by both a and b:

   a. Disabling dyspnea at rest, poorly or unresponsive to bronchodilators, resulting in decreased functional capacity, e.g., bed to chair existence, fatigue, and cough: (Documentation of Forced Expiratory Volume in one second (FEV1), after bronchodilator, less than 30% of predicated is objective evidence for disabling dyspnea, but is not necessary to obtain.)

   b. Progression of end stage pulmonary disease, as evidenced by prior increasing visits to the emergency department or prior hospitalizations for pulmonary infections and/or respiratory failure. (Documentation of serial decrease of FEV1 >40 ml/year is objective evidence for disease progression, but is not necessary to obtain.)

2. Hypoxemia at rest on room air, as evidenced by pO_2 ≤55 mmHg or oxygen saturation ≤88%. (These values may be obtained from recent hospital records.) Or hypercapnia, as evidenced by pCO_2 ≤250 mmHg. (This value may be obtained from recent hospital records.)

3. Cor pulmonale and right heart failure (RHF) secondary to pulmonary disease (e.g., not secondary to left heart disease or valvulopathy).

4. Unintentional progressive weight loss of greater than 10% of body weight over the preceding six months.

5. Resting tachycardia >100 beats/min.

ICD-9-CM codes that support medical necessity: There is no ICD-9-CM code for end stage pulmonary disease. Diagnoses for pulmonary disease which lead to end stage pulmonary disease will be accepted.

Hospice Stroke and Coma

Indications and limitations of coverage and/or medical necessity:

Patients will be considered to be in the terminal stage of stroke or coma (life expectancy of six months or less) if they meet the following criteria.

Acute phase of hemorrhagic or ischemic stroke (1, 2, or 3, must be present)

1. Coma or persistent vegetative state secondary to stroke, beyond three days duration
2. In post anoxic stroke, coma or severe obtundation, accompanied by severe myoclonus, persisting beyond three days past the anoxic event
3. Dysphagia, which prevents sufficient intake of foods and fluids to sustain life, in a patient who does not receive artificial nutrition and hydration

Chronic phase of hemorrhagic or ischemic stroke (1,2, or 3 must be present):

1. Post stroke dementia (all the following)
   - Stage seven or beyond according to the Functional Assessment Staging Scale
   - Unable to ambulate without assistance
   - Unable to dress without assistance
   - Unable to bathe without assistance
   - Urinary and fecal incontinence, intermittent or constant
2. Poor functional status with Karnofsky score 40% or less;
3. Poor nutritional status, whether on artificial nutrition or not, with inability to maintain sufficient fluid and calorie intake with ≥10% weight loss during the previous six months or serum albumin <2.5 gm/dl.

Coma (any etiology):

1. Comatose patients with any 3 of the following on day three of coma:
   - Abnormal brain stem response
   - Absent verbal response
   - Absent withdrawal response to pain
   - Serum creatinine >1.5 mg/dl;
   - Age over 70 years

Documentation of the following factors will support eligibility for hospice care:

1. Documentation of medical complications, in the context of progressive clinical decline, within the previous 12 months, which support a terminal prognosis:
   - Aspiration pneumonia
   - Upper urinary tract infection (pyelonephritis)
   - Sepsis
   - Refractory stage 3-4 decubitus ulcers
   - Fever recurrent after antibiotics

Documentation of diagnostic imaging factors which support poor prognosis after stroke include:

A. For non-traumatic hemorrhagic stroke:
   - Large-volume hemorrhage on CT:
     —Infratentorial: ≥20 ml.
     —Supratentorial: ≥50 ml.
   - Ventricular extension of hemorrhage.
   - Surface area of involvement of hemorrhage 30% of cerebrum.
   - Midline shift ≥1.5 cm.
   - Obstructive hydrocephalus in patient who declines, or is not a candidate for, ventriculoperitoneal shunt.

B. For thrombotic/embolic stroke:
   - Large anterior infarcts with both cortical and subcortical involvement.
   - Large bihemispheric infarcts.
   - Basilar artery occlusion.
   - Bilateral vertebral artery occlusion.

ICD-9-CM codes that support medical necessity:

430	Subarachnoid hemorrhage
431	Intracerebral hemorrhage
432.0-432.9	Other and unspecified intracranial hemorrhage
433.01	Occlusion and stenosis of precerebral arteries; Basilar artery with cerebral infarction
433.11	Carotid artery with cerebral infarction
433.21	Vertebral artery with cerebral infarction
433.31	Multiple and bilateral with cerebral infarction
433.81	Other specified precerebral artery with cerebral infarction
433.91	Unspecified precerebral artery with cerebral infarction
434.01	Cerebral thrombosis with cerebral infarction
434.11	Cerebral embolism with cerebral infarction
434.91	Cerebral artery occlusion, unspecified with cerebral infarction
436	Acute, but ill-defined, cerebrovascular disease
780.01	Coma
850.4	Concussion; with prolonged loss of consciousness, without return to pre-existing conscious level
851.05	Cortex (cerebral) contusion without mention of open intracranial wound with prolonged (more than 24 hours) loss of consciousness, without return of pre-existing conscious level
851.15	Cortex (cerebral) contusion with open intracranial wound with prolonged (more than 24 hours) loss of consciousness, without return to pre-existing conscious level
851.25	Cortex (cerebral) laceration without mention of open intracranial wound with prolonged (more than 24 hours) loss of consciousness, without return to pre-existing conscious level
851.35	Cortex (cerebral) laceration with open intracranial wound with prolonged (more than 24 hours) loss of consciousness, without return to pre-existing conscious level
851.45	Cerebellar or brain stem contusion without mention of open intracranial wound with prolonged (more than 24 hours) loss of consciousness, without return to pre-existing conscious level
851.55	Cerebellar or brain stem contusion with open intracranial wound with prolonged (more than 24 hours) loss of consciousness, without return to pre-existing conscious level
851.65	Cerebellar or brain stem laceration without mention of open intracranial wound with prolonged (more than 24 hours) loss of consciousness, without return to pre-existing conscious level
851.75	Cerebellar or brain stem laceration with open intracranial wound with prolonged (more than 24 hours) loss of consciousness, without return to pre-existing conscious level
851.85	Other and unspecified cerebral laceration and contusion, with open intracranial wound with prolonged (more than 24 hours) loss of consciousness, without return to pre-existing conscious level
851.95	Other and unspecified cerebral laceration and contusion, with open intracranial wound with prolonged (more than 24 hours) loss of consciousness, without return to pre-existing conscious level
852.05	Subarachnoid hemorrhage following injury without mention of open intracranial wound with prolonged (more than 24 hours) loss of consciousness, without return to pre-existing conscious level
852.15	Subarachnoid hemorrhage following injury without mention of open intracranial wound with prolonged (more than 24 hours) loss of consciousness, without return to pre-existing conscious level
852.25	Subdural hemorrhage following injury without mention of open intracranial wound with prolonged (more than 24 hours) loss of consciousness, without return to pre-existing conscious level
852.35	Subdural hemorrhage following injury with open intracranial wound with prolonged (more than 24 hours) loss of consciousness, without return to pre-existing conscious level
852.45	Extradural hemorrhage following injury without mention of open intracranial wound with prolonged (more than 24 hours) loss of consciousness, without return to pre-existing conscious level
852.55	Extradural hemorrhage following injury with open intracranial wound with prolonged (more than 24 hours) loss of consciousness, without return to pre-existing conscious level
853.05	Other and unspecified intracranial hemorrhage following injury; without mention of open intracranial wound with prolonged (more than 24 hours) loss of consciousness, without return to pre-existing conscious level

853.15	With open intracranial wound with prolonged (more than 24 hours) loss of consciousness, without return to pre-existing conscious level
854.05	Intracranial injury of other and unspecified nature without mention of open intracranial wound with prolonged ~more than 24 hours) loss of consciousness, without return to pre-existing conscious level
854.15	With open intracranial wound with prolonged (more than 24 hours) loss of consciousness, without return to pre-existing conscious level
997.02	Nervous system complications; iatrogenic cerebrovascular infarction or hemorrhage

Hospice Alzheimers Disease and Related Disorders

The Reisberg Functional Assessment Staging (FAST) Scale has been used for many years to describe Medicare beneficiaries with Alzheimer's disease and a prognosis of six months or less. The FAST Scale is a 16-item scale designed to parallel the progressive activity limitations associated with Alzheimer's disease. Stage 7 identifies the threshold of activity limitation that would support a six-month prognosis. The FAST Scale does not address the impact of comorbid and secondary conditions. These two variables are thus considered separately by this policy.

FAST Scale Items:

Stage #1: No difficulty, either subjectively or objectively

Stage #2: Complains of forgetting location of objects; subjective work difficulties

Stage #3: Decreased job functioning evident to coworkers; difficulty in traveling to new locations

Stage #4: Decreased ability to perform complex tasks (e.g., planning dinner for guests; handling finances)

Stage #5: Requires assistance in choosing proper clothing

Stage #6: Decreased ability to dress, bathe, and toilet independently:

- Sub-stage 6a: Difficulty putting clothing on properly
- Sub-stage 6b: Unable to bath properly; may develop fear of bathing
- Sub-stage 6c: Inability to handle mechanics of toileting (i.e., forgets to flush, does not wipe properly)
- Sub-stage 6d: Urinary incontinence
- Sub-stage 6e: Fecal incontinence

Stage #7: Loss of speech, locomotion, and consciousness:

- Sub-stage 7a: Ability to speak limited (1 to 5 words a day)
- Sub-stage 7b: All intelligible vocabulary lost
- Sub-stage 7c: Non-ambulatory
- Sub-stage 7d: Unable to sit up independently
- Sub-stage 7e: Unable to smile
- Sub-stage 7f: Unable to hold head up

Comorbid Conditions:

The significance of a given comorbid condition is best described by defining the structural/functional impairments - together with any limitation in activity - related to the comorbid condition. For example a beneficiary with Alzheimer's disease and clinically significant CHD or COPD would have specific impairments of cardiorespiratory function (e.g., dyspnea, orthopnea, wheezing, chest pain) which may or may not respond/be amenable to treatment. The identified impairments in cardiorespiratory function would be associated with both specific structural impairments of the coronary arteries or bronchial tree and may be associated with activity limitations (e.g., mobility, self-care). Ultimately, the combined effects of the Alzheimer's disease (stage 7) and any comorbid condition should be such that most beneficiaries with Alzheimer's disease and similar impairments would have a prognosis of six months or less.

Secondary Conditions:

Alzheimer's disease may be complicated by secondary conditions. The significance of a given secondary condition is best described by defining the structural/functional impairments - together with any limitation in activity - related to the secondary condition. The occurrence of secondary conditions in beneficiaries with Alzheimer's disease is facilitated by the presence of impairments in such body functions as mental functioning and movement functions. Such functional impairments contribute to the increased incidence of secondary conditions such as delirium and pressure ulcers observed in

Medicare beneficiaries with Alzheimer's Disease. Secondary conditions themselves may be associated with a new set of structural/functional impairments that may or may not respond/be amenable to treatment. Ultimately, the combined effects of the Alzheimer's disease (stage 7) and any secondary condition should be such that most beneficiaries with Alzheimer's disease and similar impairments would have a prognosis of six months or less.

The documentation of structural/functional impairments and activity limitations facilitate the selection of intervention strategies (palliative vs. curative) and provide objective criteria for determining the effects of such interventions. The documentation of these variables is thus essential in the determination of reasonable and necessary Medicare Hospice Services.

For Beneficiaries with Alzheimer's disease to be eligible for hospice the individual should have a FAST level of greater than or equal to 7 and specific comorbid or secondary conditions meeting the above criteria.

ICD-9- Codes that Support Medical Necessity

290.3	Senile dementia with delirium
331.0	Alzheimer's disease
331.11	Pick's disease
331.2	Senile degeneration of brain

Hospice Amyotrophic Lateral Sclerosis (ALS)

Indications and limitations of coverage and/or medical necessity:

General Considerations:

1. ALS tends to progress in a linear fashion over time. Thus the overall rate of decline in each patient is fairly constant and predictable, unlike many other non-cancer diseases.

2. However, no single variable deteriorates at a uniform rate in all patients. Therefore, multiple clinical parameters are required to judge the progression of ALS.

3. Although ALS usually presents in a localized anatomical area, the location of initial presentation does not correlate with survival time. By the time patients become end-stage, muscle denervation has become widespread, affecting all areas of the body, and initial predominance patterns do not persist.

4. Progression of disease differs markedly from patient to patient. Some patients decline rapidly and die quickly; others progress more slowly. For this reason, the history of the rate of progression in individual patients is important to obtain to predict prognosis.

5. In end-stage ALS, two factors are critical in determining prognosis: ability to breathe, and to a lesser extent ability to swallow. The former can be managed by artificial ventilation, and the latter by gastrostomy or other artificial feeding, unless the patient has recurrent aspiration pneumonia. While not necessarily a contraindication to hospice care, the decision to institute either artificial ventilation or artificial feeding will significantly alter six month prognosis.

6. Examination by a neurologist within three months of assessment for hospice is advised, both to confirm the diagnosis and to assist with prognosis.

Patients will be considered to be in the terminal stage of ALS (life expectancy of six months or less) if they meet the following criteria: (Must fulfill 1, 2, or 3.)

1. The patient must demonstrate critically impaired breathing capacity.
   a. Critically impaired breathing capacity as demonstrated by all the following characteristics occurring within the 12 months preceding initial hospice certification:
   - Vital capacity (VC) less than 30% of normal
   - Significant dyspnea at rest
   - Requiring supplemental oxygen at rest
   - Patient declines invasive artificial ventilation.

2. Patient must demonstrate both rapid progression of ALS and critical nutritional impairment.
   a. Rapid progression of ALS as demonstrated by all the following characteristics occurring within the 12 months preceding initial hospice certification:
   - Progression from independent ambulation to wheelchair or bed bound status;
   - Progression from normal to barely intelligible or unintelligible speech
   - Progression from normal to pureed diet;

- Progression from independence in most or all activities of daily living (ADLs) to needing major assistance by caretaker in all ADLs.

b. Critical nutritional impairment as demonstrated by all the following characteristics occurring within the 12 months preceding initial hospice certification:
- Oral intake of nutrients and fluids insufficient to sustain life;
- Continuing weight loss;
- Dehydration or hypovolemia;
- Absence of artificial feeding methods.

3. Patient must demonstrate both rapid progression of ALS and life threatening complications.
   a. Rapid progression of ALS, see 2.a. above.
   b. Life-threatening complications as demonstrated by one of the following characteristics occurring within the 12 months preceding initial hospice certification:
   - Recurrent aspiration pneumonia (with or without tube feedings);
   - Upper urinary tract infection, e.g., pyelonephritis;
   - Sepsis;
   - Recurrent fever after antibiotic therapy.

ICD-9-CM codes that support medical necessity:
335.20   Amyotrophic lateral sclerosis

Hospice Liver Disease
Indications and limitations of coverage and/or medical necessity:

Patients will be considered to be in the terminal stage of liver disease (life expectancy of six months or less) if they meet the following criteria: (1 and 2 must be present, factors from 3 will lend supporting documentation.)

1. The patient should show both a and b:
   a. Prothrombin time prolonged more than 5 seconds over control, or International Normalized Ration (INR) >1.5;
   b. Serum albumin < 2.5 gm/dl.
2. End stage liver disease is present and the patient shows at least one of the following:
   a. Ascites, refractory to treatment or patient non-complaint;
   b. Spontaneous bacterial peritonitis;
   c. Hepatorenal syndrome (elevated creatinine and BUN with oliguria (< 400 ml/day) and urine sodium concentration <10 mEq/l);
   d. Hepatic encephalopathy, refractory to treatment, or patient noncomplaint;
   e. Recurrent variceal bleeding, despite intensive therapy.
3. Documentation of the following factors will support eligibility for hospice care:
   a. Progressive malnutrition
   b. Muscle wasting with reduced strength and endurance
   c. Continued active alcoholism (>80 gm ethanol/day)
   d. Hepatocellular carcinoma
   e. HBsAg (Hepatitis B) positivity
   f. Hepatitis C refractory to interferon treatment.

Patients awaiting liver transplant who otherwise fit the above criteria may be certified for the Medicare hospice benefit, but if a donor organ is procured, the patient must be discharged from hospice.

ICD-9-CM codes that support medical necessity:
155.0   Liver, primary
571.2   Alcoholic cirrhosis of liver
571.40–571.49 Chronic hepatitis
571.5   Cirrhosis of liver without mention of alcohol
571.6   Biliary cirrhosis
572.2   Hepatic coma
572.4   Hepatorenal syndrome
573.3   Hepatitis, unspecified

Hospice Renal Disease
Indications and limitations of coverage and/or medical necessity:

Patients will be considered to be in the terminal stage of renal disease (life expectancy of six months or less) if they meet the following criteria:

Acute renal failure (1, 2, and 3 must be present; factors from 4 will lend supporting documentation):

1. The patient is not seeking dialysis or renal transplant;
2. Creatinine clearance <10 cc/min (<15 cc/min. for diabetes);
3. Serum creatinine >8.0 mg/dl (>6.0 mg/dl for diabetes)
4. Comorbid conditions:
   - Mechanical ventilation;
   - Malignancy (other organ system);
   - Chronic lung disease;
   - Advance cardiac disease;
   - Advance liver disease;
   - Sepsis;
   - Immunosuppression/AIDS
   - Albumin < 3.5 gm/dl
   - Cachexia;
   - Platelet count < 25,000;
   - Disseminated intravascular coagulation;
   - Gastrointestinal bleeding.

Chronic renal failure (1, 2, and 3 must be present; factors from 4 will lend supporting documentation):
1. The patient is not seeking dialysis or renal transplant;
2. Creatinine clearance < 10 cc/min (< 15cc/min for diabetes);
3. Serum creatinine > 8.0 mg/dl (> 6.0 mg/dl for diabetes);
4. Signs and symptoms of renal failure:
   - Uremia;
   - Oliguria (< 400 cc/day);
   - Intractable hyperkalemia (> 7.0) not responsive to treatment;
   - Uremic pericarditis;
   - Hepatorenal syndrome;
   - Intractable fluid overload, not responsive to treatment.

ICD-9-CM codes that support medical necessity:
403.11   Hypertensive kidney disease, Benign with chronic kidney disease
584.5-584.9   Acute renal failure
585.1-585.9   Chronic kidney disease (CKD)
586   Renal failure, unspecified

Hospice Heart Disease
Indications and limitations of coverage and/or medical necessity:

Patients will be considered to be in the terminal stage of heart disease (life expectancy of six months or less) if they meet the following criteria (1 and 2 must be present. Factors from 3 will add supporting documentation.):

1. At the time of initial certification or recertification for hospice, the patient is already optimally treated with diuretics and vasodilators, usually angiotensin-converting enzymes (ACE) inhibitors. (Optimally treated means that patients who are not on vasodilators have a medical reason for refusing these drugs, e.g., hypotension or renal disease.)
2. The patient has significant symptoms of recurrent congestive heart failure (CHF) at rest, and is classified as New York Heart Association (NYHA) Class IV. (Class IV Patients with heart disease have an inability to carry on any physical activity without discomfort. Symptoms of heart failure or of the anginal syndrome may be present even at rest. If any physical activity is undertaken, discomfort is increased.) Significant congestive heart failure may be documented by an ejection fraction of <20%, but is not required if not already available.
3. Documentation of the following factors will support eligibility for hospice care:
   - Treatment resistant symptomatic supraventricular or ventricular arrhythmias;
   - History of cardiac arrest or resuscitation;
   - History of unexplained syncope;
   - Brain embolism of cardiac origin;
   - Concomitant HIV disease.

ICD-9-CM codes that support medical necessity:
414.8   Other specified forms of chronic ischemic heart disease
428.0   Congestive heart failure, unspecified
428.1   Left heart failure
428.20   Systolic heart failure, Unspecified

428.21	Systolic heart failure, Acute
428.22	Systolic heart failure, Chronic
428.23	Systolic heart failure, Acute on chronic
428.30	Distolic heart failure, Unspecified
428.31	Distolic heart failure, Acute
428.32	Distolic heart failure, Chronic
428.33	Distolic heart failure, Acute on chronic
428.40	Combined systolic and diastolic heart failure, Unspecified
428.41	Combined systolic and diastolic heart failure, Acute
428.42	Combined systolic and diastolic heart failure, Chronic
428.43	Combined systolic and diastolic heart failure, Acute on chronic
428.9	Heart failure, unspecified (Specific etiology for CHF may be additionally documented.)

Skillful palliation in patients with end stage heart disease, including judicious use of diuretics and vasodilators, particularly angiotensin-covering enzyme (ACE) inhibitors, may promote survival for long periods with extremely severe symptoms. Conversely, some patients with advance coronary disease may die suddenly and unexpectedly from acute ventricular arrhythmias. Coverage of hospice care for patients not meeting the criteria in this policy may be denied. However, some patients may not meet the criteria, yet still be appropriate for hospice care, because of other comorbidities or rapid decline.

Source of Information

Social Security Act, Sections, 1102, 1812 (a)(4)and (d);1813 (a) (4); 1814 (a)(7) and (I); 1862 (a)(1),(6), and (9); 1861 (dd), 1871

42 CFR Part 418

CMS Manual Publication 100-2, Medicare Benefits Policy Chapter 9 Coverage of Hospice Services under Hospital Insurance, §10 Requirements

CMS Manual Publication 100-3, Medicare National Coverage Determinations

CMS Medicare Coverage Database:

http://www.cms.hhs.gov/mcd/search.asp?
Search: Local Coverage, policies (LMRP/LCD); Final policies only
Geographic area: all states
Coverage topics: Hospice care

Skilled Nursing Facility Background on the Resource Utilization Groups (RUG-III) Classification System

The Balanced Budget Act of 1997 requires the implementation of a Medicare Skilled Nursing Facility (SNF) prospective payment system (PPS). Background on the Resource Utilization Groups (RUG-III) classification system that is part of the new PPS for skilled nursing facilities is provided.

NOTE: This classification system employs a two stage process involving a clinical qualification stage followed by a classification stage. The clinical qualification stage includes the patient diagnoses, conditions and comorbidities, treatments and services. The classification stage involves the levels of assistance used in performing activities of daily living (ADLs) and skilled services rendered. Assignment of a resident to a specific clinical category must be based upon the patient meeting all the required qualifications for that category level.

Each of the categories of the RUG-III classification system is covered in detail in the following excerpt from the *Federal Register*. Please note that the diagnosis and procedure codes identified by St.Anthony's exclusive color coding system represent only the clinical qualification stage of the classification process. All other qualifications referred to in the explanation of the categories must be addressed. The color coding system provided is meant only as an alert to the coder that there is the potential to assign a resident to a particular category provided other qualifications are met.

Medicare Program: Prospective Payment System and Consolidated Billing for Skilled Nursing Facilities; Final Rule [Federal Register: May 12, 1998 (Volume 63, Number 91)] 42 CFR Parts 409, 410, 411, 413, 424, 483, and 489

Annual updates to the PPS rates are required by section 1888(e) of the Social Security Act, as amended by the Medicare, Medicaid, and SCHIP Balance Budget Refinement Act of 1999, and the Medicare, Medicaid, and SCHIP Benefits Improvement and Protection Act of 2000. The Prospective Payment System and Consolidated Billing for Skilled Nursing Facilities-Update; Final Rule was published in the *Federal Register*. July 31, 2001 (Volume 66, Number 147) CFR Parts 410, 411, 413, 424, and 489. In the Final Rule effective October 1, 2001, the Centers for Medicare and Medicaid Services (CMS) rebased and revised the routine market basket, modified certain variables for some of the cost categories, and implemented the transition of swing bed facilities to the SNF PPS.

Proposed Changes to RUG Classification System
CMS has proposed refining the case mix classification system under section 188(e)(4)(G0(i) of the Act by creating a new, combined Rehabilitation plus Extensive category, that better accounts for medially complex patients, as required in section 101 of the BBRA, Accordingly, the payment rates set forth in this proposed rule reflect the use of the refined 53-group RUG classification proposed. The nine groups proposed to be added to the existing RUG-III system are as follows:

RUX Rehabilitation Ultra High plus Extensive Services, High

RUL Rehabilitation Ultra High plus Extensive Services, Low

RVX Rehabilitation Very High plus Extensive Services, High

RVL Rehabilitation Very High plus Extensive Services, Low

RHX Rehabilitation High plus Extensive Services, High

RHL Rehabilitation High plus Extensive Services, Low

RMX Rehabilitation Medium plus Extensive Services, High

RML Rehabilitation Medium plus Extensive Services, Low

RLX Rehabilitation Low plus Extensive Services

Accordingly, as part of the proposed refinement, CMS proposes to increase the case mix indexes of the existing 44 RUG-III groups (as well as those of the nine proposed new Rehabilitation plus Extensive Services RUGs) by calculating a percentage increase that would increase aggregate payments.

Effective October 1, 2005 through December 31, 2005 CMS is proposing to make payment based entirely on the existing 44 group RUG-III classification system. Beginning January 1, 2006, CMS proposes to make payment based entirely on the proposed new RUG-53 classification system. Under the terms of section 101(c) of the BBRA, the temporary add-on payments for certain designated RUG-III groups will expire as of January 1, 2006. The resulting reduction in payment will be partially offset by the increase in the RUG case-mix indexes, as explained previously in section II.B.3 of the proposed rule. CMS invites comments on all aspects of implementing this proposal until January 1, 2006.

The following discussion outlines the background of the RUG III classification system and the categories of patient care.

Prospective Payment System for Skilled Nursing Facilities

1. Background on the Resource Utilization Groups (RUGs) Patient Classification System
As part of the Nursing Home Case-Mix and Quality demonstration project, Version III of the Resource Utilization Groups (RUG-III) case-mix classification system was developed to capture resource use of nursing home patients and to provide an improved method of tracking the quality of their care.

RUG-III is a 44-group model for classifying nursing home patients into homogeneous groups according to the amount and type of resources they use. The RUG-III groups are the basis for the payment indices used to establish equitable prospective payment levels for patients with different service use. Care provided directly to, or for, a patient is represented by an index score that is based on the amount of staff time, weighted by salary levels, associated with each group. That is, each RUG-III group is assigned an index score that represents the amount of nursing time and rehabilitation treatment time associated with caring for the patients who qualify for the group. The nursing weight includes both patient-specific time spent daily on behalf of each patient type by registered nurses, licensed practical nurses, and aides, as well as patient non-specific time spent by these staff members on other necessary functions such as staff education, administrative duties, and other tasks associated with maintenance of the care giving environment.

The principal goal of case-mix measurement is to identify patient characteristics associated with measured resource use. In nursing homes, no adequate models have been found for using length of stay or episode cost to explain resource use. Thus, the RUG-III nursing home case-mix system explains patient resource use on a daily basis.

The classification system was designed using resident characteristic information and measures of wage-weighted staff time. Information regarding a patient's characteristics and care needs is derived from the MDS, a set of core screening and assessment items and item definitions. The MDS is part of a standardized, comprehensive patient assessment instrument (the Resident Assessment Instrument or RAI) that all long term care facilities that are certified to participate in Medicare or Medicaid are required to use to develop individualized plans of care for each individual in the facility. The staff time measure (STM) study captured the amount of nursing staff time required to care for groups of residents over a 24-hour period and over the span of a week for therapy services.

Patient assessment and staff time data used to develop the initial version of the RUG-III classification system were collected from March to December 1990 for 7,648 patients in 202 nursing facilities in Kansas, Maine, Mississippi, South Dakota, Nebraska, Texas, and New York. Since then, two more staff time data collections have been performed on 154 Medicare certified units of hospital and freestanding facilities in 12 States (California, Colorado, Florida, Kansas, Maine, Maryland, Mississippi, New York, Ohio, South Dakota, Texas, and Washington). Only units that were judged to be providing adequate care were considered for participation in the study. Of these, the states were asked to select facilities that included 35 percent Medicare certified units, 25 percent hospital units, and two Alzheimer's units. "Unit" was defined as a nursing center such as a corridor or a floor, controlled from one nursing station. The remainder of the sample was selected by the state's demonstration project staff to represent the characteristics of the state's nursing homes.

The sample was purposefully targeted toward residents needing complex care and/or with cognitive impairments. This assured that sufficient numbers of patients with rare types of complex care needs were included in the sample. Facilities with special care units (for example, Alzheimer's or Rehabilitation units) that participated in the study were also asked to provide data from a non-specialized unit.

During the data collection, personnel on the study units electronically recorded all of the time in their work days: time providing services directly to patients; in activities related to specific patients, such as charting or consultation with family members or other members of the patient care team; as well as time that is not attributable to any particular patient, like that spent in meetings, in training, on breaks, etc. The time was allocated according to whether or not it was directly related to a particular patient, and was categorized as either patient specific time or non-patient specific time.

Those data have been used to modify the classification system to create the current RUG-III and establish updated average staff times to be salary-weighted. Analyses of the staff time data in conjunction with the patient MDS information identified three main predictors of a patient's resource utilization: (1) clinical characteristics; (2) limitations in the activities of daily living (ADLs); and (3) skilled services received. The RUG-III classification system uses these three types of variables to describe SNF patients for the purposes of determining the relative cost of caring for different types of patients (case-mix).

Analysis of the data indicated that patients with serious clinical conditions such as dehydration and respiratory infections, as well as patients who were very dependent in ADLs, require more nursing time than patients without complicating conditions. The RUG-III classification system resulting from the analyses is hierarchical. The clinical characteristics of patients, as identified by the MDS, that were associated with the greatest utilization of nursing time and rehabilitative therapy time, were used to categorize patients into the highest case-mix classification groups.

Similarly, the clinical characteristics associated with the lowest utilization of nursing time were used to categorize patients into the lowest case-mix classification group. Not all clinical characteristics are recognized separately by the classification system. Only those characteristics that were predictive of resource use and that would not introduce incentives that are considered to be negative, or not compatible with high quality patient care, are used to classify patients into RUG-III groups.

The mutually exclusive, layered categories of the RUG-III classification system describe which patient clinical characteristics, levels of assistance used in performing ADLs, and services are used to assign the patient to a RUGs group. Clinical characteristics include the patient diagnoses, conditions, and comorbidities. ADLs include bed mobility, toilet use, transfer from bed to chair, and eating. Patients receive a single RUG-III ADL score that measures the patient's ability to perform these activities (scores range from 4-18; higher scores represent greater functional dependence and a need for more assistance). Finally, treatments and services include respiratory therapy, amount of rehabilitation received, and treatments such as suctioning and intravenous medication administration.

2. The RUG-III Classification System

In the RUG-III classification system, patient characteristics and health status information from the MDS, such as "diagnoses," "ability to perform ADLs," and "treatments received," will be used to assign the patient to a resource group for payment. The RUG-III system is a hierarchy of major patient types. RUG-III consists of seven major categories that are the first level of patient classification. The major categories, in hierarchical order, are Rehabilitation, Extensive Services, Special Care, Clinically Complex, Impaired Cognition, Behavior Problems, and Reduced Physical Function. These major categories are further differentiated into 44 more specific patient groupings. Except for Rehabilitation and Extensive Services, these categories are first subdivided into groups based on the patient's ADL score. The next level of subdivision is based on nursing rehabilitation services and signs of depression.

The initial subdivision of the Rehabilitation category is based on minutes per week of rehabilitative therapy services. The second level of subdivision uses the ADL score. The Extensive Services category does not use ADL limitations except as a threshold for assignment into the category. Rather, services that require more technical clinical knowledge and skill are the variables used for

assignment of patients into this category. Examples of these services are intravenous feeding or medications and tracheostomy care.

For example, the Special Care category includes patients with quadriplegia, multiple sclerosis, surgical wound(s), open lesions, fever with vomiting, dehydration, pneumonia, tube feedings, or weight loss, those who are aphasic and need to be tube fed, those receiving treatment for 2 or more skin ulcers, and patients who are receiving radiation therapy. Any patient with one or more of these conditions, who is not receiving rehabilitation services, will be assigned to this category. The patient's assignment to one of the three groups within this category is dependent on the patient's ADL score.

The Rehabilitation category is organized differently than the clinical categories that follow in the hierarchy. Within this category, there are five sub-categories (Ultra High, Very High, High, Medium, and Low) that are then further split into the individual groups for payment. The sub-categories are defined by minutes per week of rehabilitation received by the patient, number of rehabilitation disciplines providing service, and the number of days per week on which rehabilitation services were provided. Assignment into a specific payment group is based on the patient's ability to perform certain of the activities of daily living as represented by his ADL score. As stated elsewhere, the patient is assessed on his ability to perform independently all of the activities of daily living and is assigned an ADL sum score that represents performance of the four "late loss" ADLs. The "late loss" ADLs used in the MDS ADL sum score are: eating; toileting; bed mobility; and transferring.

A brief description of the respective RUG-III categories follows.

Rehabilitation: This category includes patients who, if they were not receiving rehabilitation therapy, would qualify for one of the other RUG-III skilled care categories. This category is divided into subcategories based on the number of minutes of rehabilitative services received in a week, combinations of rehabilitation disciplines providing services, receipt of nursing rehabilitative services, and the patient ADL scores. The range of rehabilitation therapy minutes per day represented in the Rehabilitation category varies from a low of 45 minutes per week to a high of more than 720 minutes per week. Patients who qualify for assignment to the Ultra High Rehabilitation sub-category receive at least 720 minutes per week of rehabilitation therapies. At least two disciplines must be providing services: one of the disciplines must provide services 5 days each week, and the other must provide services at least 3 days each week. In contrast, patients assigned to the lowest rehabilitation sub-category, Low Rehabilitation, must receive at least 45 minutes of rehabilitative therapy services across at least 3 days each week, in addition to 6 days per week of nursing rehabilitation in two activities.

Extensive Services: To qualify for this category, patients must have, in the past 14 days, received intravenous medications, tracheostomy care, required a ventilator/respirator, required suctioning, or must have, in the past 7 days, received intravenous feeding. In addition, the patients assigned to this category will have an ADL score that is at least 7. Each patient in the extensive services category is assigned a score of 0-5 based on five criteria. The score is used to classify the patient to one of the three RUG-III groups in this category--0 or 1 will classify into the SE1 group, those with scores of 2 or 3 will go to SE 2, and those with 4 or 5 will group to SE 3. For the following five criteria, the patient receives one point for each criterion that applies to him or her. The first three criteria are presence of a clinical condition that qualifies the patient for classification to the Special Care category, Clinically Complex category, or the Cognitively Impaired category. The fourth and fifth criteria are whether the patient is receiving intravenous feeding or whether the patient is receiving intravenous medication. For example, a person who qualifies for both the Cognitively Impaired and Special Care categories will be assigned a score of 2 and will be classified into the SE 2 group. Similarly, a patient who is ventilator dependent and requires suctioning will be assigned a score of 0 and will be classified into SE1.

Special Care: Patients who are assigned to this category have at least one of the following: multiple sclerosis, cerebral palsy, quadriplegia with an ADL score of 10 or more, or receive respiratory therapy 7 days per week; have, and receive treatment for, pressure or stasis ulcers on 2 or more body sites; have a surgical wound(s) or open lesions; be tube fed with at least 26 percent of daily calorie requirements and at least 501 ml of fluid through the tube per day, and aphasic; receive radiation therapy; or have a fever in combination with dehydration, pneumonia, vomiting, weight loss, or tube feedings.

Clinically Complex: Patients qualify for this category if they are comatose, have burns, septicemia, pneumonia, internal bleeding, dehydration, dialysis, hemiplegia in combination with an ADL score of 10 or more, receive chemotherapy, tube feedings that comprise at least 26 percent of daily calorie requirements and at least 501 ml of fluid through the tube per day, treatments for foot wounds, or transfusions. Also included in this category are diabetics who receive injections 7 days per week and who have two or more physician order changes in the past 14 days as well as patients who have received oxygen therapy in the past 14 days. In order to assure inclusion of patients with unstable conditions, we also use a combination of physician visits and order changes as qualifying criteria for this category. This is a proxy measure for the amounts of skilled nursing observation, care planning, and monitoring usually required by this type of patient. The qualifying combinations of physician visit/order changes that must occur within the 14-day observation period to qualify for this category are: one or more visits with at least four order changes, or two or more visits with two or more order changes.

Impaired Cognition: Patients in this category and the following two categories frequently will not qualify for Medicare coverage although some may, due to specific circumstances. The patients in this category will have scores on the MDS 2.0 Cognition Performance Scale of 3, 4, or 5, and for two of the groups in this category will be receiving nursing rehabilitation services 6 days per week. Some patients with Alzheimer's disease or other types of dementia who have been acutely ill will classify to this category for Medicare. Under the SNF coverage guidelines, these patients could qualify based on the need for skilled nursing rehabilitation.

Behavior Only: These are patients who, in 4 of the last 7 days, exhibited behaviors that include resisting care, being combative, being physically and/or verbally abusive, wandering, socially inappropriate/disruptive behavior, and who have hallucinations or delusions.

Physical Function Reduced: The patients in this category are those who do not have any of the conditions or characteristics identified above. However, some have been documented as receiving "skilled nursing" and have been covered by Medicare in the past. With proper documentation and justification regarding the need for skilled care, Medicare may continue to cover skilled nursing services.

Coding Guidelines for Long Term Care

These guidelines for coding and reporting long term care (LTC) have been developed and approved by the cooperating parties for ICD-9-CM: American Hospital Association, American Health Information Management Association, Centers for Medicare and Medicaid Services. and the National Center for Health Statistics.

Coding and sequencing instructions in the three ICD-9-CM manuals take precedence over any guidelines. These coding guidelines have been developed to assist the user in coding and reporting in situations in which the ICD-9-CM manual does not provide direction.

In the long term care setting, ICD-9-CM diagnosis codes are assigned at admission, as conditions arise during the stay, at transfer, discharge or death of the patient. All acute and /or chronic conditions affecting the long term care of a resident should be coded

The Uniform Hospital Discharge Data Set (UHDDS) definition of the principal diagnosis applies only to inpatients in acute care, short-term, general hospitals and does not apply to LTC.

Diagnoses listed for LTC depend on the point of time of the resident's stay during which the coding is done.

The long-term care patient is assigned a first listed diagnosis describing the reason chiefly responsible for the patient's admission to the facility, or the chief reason for the patient's continued stay.

The following are examples that demonstrate the practical application of coding guidelines for Long term care facilities (LTC).

These guidelines previously appeared in the Coding Clinic for ICD-9-CM published by the American Hospital Association, 4Q, '99, 3-10.

Example 1:
The patient is discharged from the acute care hospital and admitted to the LTC with a diagnosis of acute cerebrovascular accident (CVA) with left-sided hemiparesis and dysphasia.

First listed diagnosis:
438.20, Late effects of cerebrovascular disease, Hemiplegia affecting unspecified side.

Additional diagnosis:
438.12, Late effects of cerebrovascular disease, Dysphasia.

The hemiparesis and dysphagia are late effects of the acute CVA. According to coding guidelines, list the residual condition first and the cause of the late effect in addition. The above combination codes adequately describe the residual and late effect cause. The acute CVA code, 436, is used for the initial episode of care.

The late effects residuals are conditions specified as such, or as sequelae, which may occur at any time after the onset of the causal condition.

Example 2:
A patient with progressive senile dementia, coronary artery disease, and congestive heart failure is admitted to a LTC facility after suffering a CVA and receiving treatment elsewhere. The patient has made a complete recovery from the CVA prior to admission to the LTC facility. She is admitted for long term care because of her chronic illnesses and her deteriorating mental status.

First listed diagnosis:
290.0, Senile dementia, uncomplicated

Additional diagnoses:
428.0, Congestive heart failure, unspecified
414.00, Coronary atherosclerosis.of unspecified type of vessel, native or graft
V12.59, Personal history of other diseases of the circulatory system, other

Any of the patient's chronic diseases can be listed first, since each one could be considered chiefly responsible for LTC facility admission.

Since this patient has no residuals from the CVA, it is inappropriate to use any codes from category 438.

Example 3:
A patient is admitted to the LTC facility for physical therapy from an acute care setting after treatment for acute pelvic and clavicular fractures.

First listed diagnosis:
V57.1, Care involving use of rehabilitation, Other physical therapy

Additional diagnosis:
V54.89, Other orthopedic aftercare

Do not code the fractures as acute. See AHA's Coding Clinic, 3Q,'95, 3-4, for discussion on the correct coding of healing fractures.

Example 4:
A patient is transferred to the LTC facility from the acute care hospital following treatment for a fractured [traumatic] femur in order to heal and regain strength.

First listed diagnosis:
V54.15, Aftercare for healing, traumatic fracture, upper leg

Additional diagnoses:
Code any other existing conditions that require treatment.

It is inappropriate to code the fracture as current.

Example 5:
A LTC patient develops a urinary tract infection that was subsequently treated and resolved.

First listed diagnosis:
599.0, Urinary tract infection, site not specified

Additional diagnoses:
Code any other existing conditions that require treatment.

The urinary tract infection would remain on the active problem list until resolution of the infection, after which it would no longer be correct to code or report it.

Example 6:
A patient returns to the LTC facility after hospitalization for pneumonia. The admission orders request "antibiotic continuation for three days, and then a repeat x-ray to determine pneumonia status".

First listed diagnosis:
486, Pneumonia, organism unspecified, if there is no identification of a causal organism

Additional diagnoses:
Code any other existing conditions that require treatment.

Code the pneumonia until it is resolved, after which it should no longer be coded and reported.

Example 7:
After hospitalization for pneumonia, a nursing home resident is readmitted with orders for continued antibiotic regimen for pneumonia.

Other specified residuals from a CVA several years ago are the chief reason for her original admission and continued residence in the LTC facility.

First listed diagnosis:
438.89, Other late effect of cerebrovascular disease

Additional diagnosis:
As long as the patient receives treatment for the pneumonia, it is appropriate to code it as additional.

Example 8:

After surgical treatment in the acute care setting for a wrist fracture sustained while a resident in a nursing home, the patient returns to the nursing home. The patient was admitted several years ago and has received continued care for Alzheimer's disease. Occupational therapy is ordered for the wrist, but the therapy is not the primary reason for the patient's admission.

First listed diagnosis:
331.0, Alzheimer's disease

Additional diagnosis:
V57.21, Encounter for occupational therapy.

Example 9:

Many nursing home admissions are for conditions still considered in the active care phase.

First listed diagnosis:
Code any active condition still being treated which is chiefly responsible for the admission to or which affects a resident's continued care in the LTC facility. If late effects are present, i.e., residuals present after the acute phase of an illness or injury, they should be coded. For example, assign code from category 438, Late effects of cerebrovascular disease, when a patient is admitted to a nursing home because of late effects of a CVA.

Example 10:

A patient is admitted to the LTC facility for convalescence following an acute illness or injury.

First listed diagnosis:
V66.9, Unspecified convalescence

Use only if the patient is admitted solely for convalescence and there is no definitive information in the medical record.

Selection of codes in all cases is based on documentation in the medical record of conditions treated. Codes for any late effects, signs, and symptoms present are assigned if documented.

Example 11:

A patient is transferred to a nursing home for convalescence and strengthening following major surgery. The patient's degree of debility and inability to care for himself at home are the reasons for the nursing home admission. There is a question as to the selection of symptom codes such as weakness and debility in preference to a V66 category code.

First listed diagnosis:
V58.49, Other specified aftercare following surgery

Additional diagnoses:
Code any symptoms such as gait disturbance, weakness, or pain.

Example 12:

A patient is transferred to a nursing home after hospitalization for an acute stroke. Her primary reason for admission is left hemiplegia and dysphasia, although she has a gastrostomy, created in the hospital, which will require continuing care.

First listed diagnosis:
438.20, Hemiplegia affecting unspecified side

Additional diagnoses:
438.12, Dysphasia
V55.1, Attention to artificial openings, Gastrostomy

Either 438.20 or 438.12 would qualify as first listed diagnosis, since either one could be considered chiefly responsible for admission to the LTC facility.

Example 13:

A patient is transferred to a nursing home for convalescence following a hospitalization for an acute myocardial infarction.

First listed diagnosis:
410.92, Acute myocardial infarction, unspecified site, subsequent episode of care

Additional diagnoses:
Code any other existing conditions that require treatment.

Example 14:

The reason for admission to a nursing home is stated as "deconditioning".

First listed diagnosis:
Code whatever symptoms of deconditioning, which the patient manifests, such as, weakness, gait disturbance, etc.

Additional diagnoses:
Code any other existing conditions that require treatment.

Example 15:

A LTC facility patient 's record has "mental status change" as a current condition.

First listed diagnosis:
780.99, Other general symptoms

Additional diagnoses:
Code any other existing conditions that require treatment.

Example 16:

A patient does not have a specific diagnosis, but is admitted to a LTC facility for symptoms such as weakness, debility, deterioration, or old age.

First listed diagnosis:
The correct approach is to code the symptoms related to the admission.

Additional diagnoses:
Code any other existing conditions that require treatment.

10 Steps to Correct Coding

Follow the 10 steps below to correctly code outpatient encounters for healthcare services.

Step 1: Identify the reason for the visit or encounter (i.e., a sign, symptom, diagnosis and/or condition).

The medical record documentation should accurately reflect the patient's condition, using terminology that includes specific diagnoses and symptoms, or clearly states the reasons for the encounter.

Choose the main term that best describes the reason chiefly responsible for the service provided is the most important step in coding. If symptoms are present and documented, but a definitive diagnosis has not yet been determined, code the symptoms. **Do not code conditions that are referred to as "rule out," "suspected," "probable" or "questionable."** Diagnoses often are not established at the time of the initial encounter/visit. Two or more visits may be necessary to establish the diagnosis. Code only what is documented in the available records and only to the highest degree of certainty known at the time of the patient's visit.

Step 2: After selecting the reason for the encounter, always consult the Alphabetic Index, Volume 2, before verifying code selection in the Tabular section.

The most critical rule is to begin the code selection process in the *Alphabetic Index.* Never turn to the Tabular List (Volume 1). The Index provides cross reference, essential and non-essential modifiers, and inclusion terms not found in the Tabular List. To prevent coding errors, always use both the Alphabetic Index and the Tabular List when locating and assigning a code. Always verify the code found in the Alphabetic Index in the Tabular List. First, the Index does not include the important instructional notes found in the tabular. Second, the advantage of a classification system is that like items are grouped together. A quick scan of the tabular might provide coding options for the coder that would have been missed.

Step 3: Locate the main term entry.

The Alphabetic Index is a listing of conditions. Conditions may be expressed as nouns or eponyms, with critical use of adjectives. Some conditions have multiple entries under synonyms. Reasons for encounters may be located under general terms such as admission, encounter, and examination. Other general terms such as history of or status post are used to locate factors influencing health.

Step 4: Read and interpret any notes listed with the main term or the subterm.

Notes such as common fifth-digit references and cross references are identified by italicized type. Always check any cross-references to ensure that all alternative terms are researched.

Step 5: Review entries for modifiers.

Nonessential modifiers are the terms located within parentheses following the main term entry. These parenthetical terms are supplementary words or explanatory information that may either be present or absent in the diagnostic statement and do not affect code selection. The subterms listed under the main term are essential modifiers that do affect coding assignment. Each line of indent represents a more specific code entry.

Step 6: Interpret abbreviations, cross-references, fifth digits, and brackets.

The cross-references used are "see," "see category" and "see also" indicate alternative term choices for code searches. The abbreviation NEC may follow main terms or subterms. NEC (not elsewhere classified) indicates that there is no specific code for the condition even though the medical documentation may be very specific. Is a fifth digit required? You MUST refer to the Tabular List to discover the correct code. Italicized brackets [ ] enclose a second code that must be used along with the code immediately preceding it, with the bracketed code sequenced as the secondary code. This is a

mandatory multiple code situation. Both the underlying condition and the manifestation (code in the slanted bracket) must be reported

Step 7: Choose a potential code and locate it in the Tabular List.

The coder must follow any Includes, Excludes notes, and other instructional notes, such as "Code first" and "Use additional code," listed in the tabular for the chapter, category, subcategory, and subclassification level of code selection which direct the coder to use a different or additional code.

Any codes in the Tabular range, 001.0 through 999.9, may be used to identify the diagnostic reason for the encounter. The Tabular encompasses many codes describing disease and injury classifications (e.g., infectious and parasitic diseases, neoplasms, symptoms, signs and ill-defined conditions, etc.).

Codes that describe symptoms and signs, as opposed to definitive diagnoses, should be used for reporting purposes when an established diagnosis has not been made (confirmed) by the physician. Chapter 16 of the ICD-9-CM code book, "Symptoms, Signs, and Ill-Defined Conditions" (codes 780.01-799.9) contains many, but not all, codes for symptoms.

ICD-9-CM classifies encounters with health care providers for circumstances other than a disease or injury using codes in the Supplementary Classification of Factors Influencing Health Status and Contact with Health Services (V01.0-V84). There are many occasions when circumstances other than a disease or injury are recorded as chiefly responsible for the encounter.

Step 8: Determine whether the code is at the highest level of specificity.

A code is invalid if it has not been coded to the full number of digits (greatest level of specificity) required. A three-digit code is to be used only if the category is not further subdivided. Assign four-digit codes (subcategory codes) only if there are no five-digit codes for that category. Assign five-digit codes (fifth-digit subclassification codes) for those categories mandating the use of five digits.

Step 9: Assign the code.

Having reviewed all relevant information concerning the possible code choices, assign the code that most completely describes the condition.

Repeat steps one through nine for all additional documented conditions that meet the following criteria:

- Conditions that currently exist at the time of the visit
- Conditions that require or affect patient care, treatment or management.

Step 10: Sequence codes correctly

Sequencing is defined as the order in which the codes are listed on the claim. List first the ICD-9-CM code for the diagnosis, condition, problem or other reason for the encounter/visit, which is shown in the medical record to be chiefly responsible for the services provided. List additional codes that describe any coexisting conditions. Follow the official coding guidelines (See Section IV Diagnostic Coding and reporting Guidelines for Outpatient Services) concerning proper sequencing of codes.

Coding Examples

Diagnosis: Anorexia

- Step 1: The reason for the encounters was the condition anorexia.
- Step 2. Consult the Index to Diseases.
- Step 3: Locate the main term "Anorexia," which indicates a code of 783.0.
- Step 4: There are no italicized instructional notes to interpret.
- Step 5: Note that there are two possible subterms (essential modifiers), "hysterical" and "nervosa," neither of which is documented in this instance and therefore cannot be used in code selection. The code listed next to the main term is called the default code selection.

- Step 6: There are no abbreviations, cross-references, fifth-digit notations, or brackets.
- Step 7: Turn to code 783.0 in the Tabular List and read the instructional notes. In this case the "Excludes" note indicates that anorexia determined to be of non-organic origin should be coded to Chapter 5. The diagnostic statement does not indicate non-organic origin.
- Step 8: There is no further division of the category past the fourth digit subcategory. Therefore, the subcategory code level is the highest level of specificity.
- Step 9: Therefore, the default code, 783.0 is the correct code selection.
- Step 10: Since anorexia is listed as the chief reason for the healthcare encounter, the primary or principal diagnosis is 783.0.

Diagnosis: Acute bronchitis due to staphylococcus
- Step 1: The reason for the encounters was the condition acute bronchitis due to staphylococcus.
- Step 2. Consult the Index to Diseases.
- Step 3: Locate the main term "Bronchitis."
- Step 4: There are no italicized instructional notes to interpret.
- Step 5: Review entries for modifiers. Since "acute" is not listed as a nonessential modifier, read past the "with" modifier until you find the subterm "acute or subacute" with code 466.0. Continue to search to see if the subterm "due to" appears under "acute or subacute". The subterm "due to" is present; there is no entry for staphylococcus.
- Step 6: There are no abbreviations, cross-references, fifth digit notations, or brackets.
- Step 7: Since there are no more appropriate subterms, turn to code 466.0 in the Tabular List. The Includes note under category 466.0 does refer to possible infective organism, but not to staphylococcus specifically. The note does include acute bronchitis. However, at the beginning of chapter 8, "Diseases of the Respiratory System," you will notice the "use additional code" note that tells you to assign a code to identify the infectious organism. This instructional note applies to the entire chapter.
- Step 8: There is no further division of the category past the fourth digit subcategroy. Therefore, the subcategory code level is the highest level of specificity.
- Step 9: Assign code 466.0.

Repeat steps 1-9 for any additional code assignments.

- Step 1: The reason for the encounters was the condition acute bronchitis due to staphylococcus.
- Step 2. Consult the Index to Diseases.
- Step 3: Locate the main term Staphylococcus, staphylococcal.
- Step 4: The italicized instructional notes states see condition. Locate the main term "Infection, infected, infective".
- Step 5: Review entries for modifiers. Locate the subterm "staphylococcal NEC," where you will find code 041.10 referenced.
- Step 6: The abbreviation NEC indicates that a review of the medical record may be necessary to determine if there is documentation concerning the specific type of staphylococcus.
- Step 7: Verify code 041.10 in the Tabular List. The code title is Staphylococcus, unspecified. If there is additional information identifying the organism as aureus or other, assign the appropriate code, 041.11 or 041.19. Otherwise, assign code 041.10, Staphylococcus, unspecified, as an additional code.
- Step 8: There is no further division of the category past the fifth-digit subclassification level. Therefore, the subclassification code level is the highest level of specificity. The final code assignment would be 041.10.
- Step 9: Assign code 041.10.
- Step 10: Sequence codes as directed by the instructional note for category 466. Code first 466.0 and assign code 041.10 as additional.

Diagnosis: Traveler's diarrhea
- Step 1: The reason for the encounters was the condition traveler's diarrhea.
- Step 2. Consult the Index to Diseases.
- Step 3: Locate the main term "Diarrhea" in the Alphabetic Index.
- Step 4: There are no italicized instructional notes to interpret.
- Step 5: Review entries for modifiers. Note that the nonessential modifiers (in parentheses) after the main term do not include the term "Traveler's," which means that the coder should search the subterms for the term "Traveler's." The subterm "Traveler's" has a possible code

selection, 009.2, and suggests the subterm "due to specified organism NEC 008.8."

The diagnostic statement does not include the infectious agent; therefore, code 008.8 does not apply.

- Step 6: There are no abbreviations, cross-references, fifth-digit notations, or brackets.
- Step 7: Verify code 041.10 in the Tabular List. Locate code 009.2 in the Tabular List and read all instructional notes under the main category and subcategories. The Includes notes does not list the term "Traveler's" under code 009.2. As instructed by the Alphabetic Index, you should code the condition to 009.2. The ICD-9-CM code book implies that "Traveler's diarrhea" is the same as infectious diarrhea when it is not attributed to any specified infectious agent.
- Step 8: There is no further division of the category past the fourth-digit subcategory level. Therefore, the subcategory code level is the highest level of specificity. The final code assignment would be 009.2.
- Step 9: Assign code 009.2.
- Step 10: Since infectious diarrhea is listed as the chief reason for the healthcare encounter, the primary or principal diagnosis is 009.2.

Diagnosis: Ingrown toenail, infected
- Step 1: The reason for the encounters was the condition infected ingrown toenail.
- Step 2. Consult the Index to Diseases.
- Step 3: First you must decide what the searchable main term should be. Reminder: search for condition, not anatomical site. The Alphabetic Index helps you determine the main term. Refer to "toenail" in the Alphabetic Index; the closest match is "Toe," which includes the instruction "see condition." Locate the main term "Infection" in the Alphabetic Index. The subterm toe has a subterm "nail" which refers the coder to category 681, Cellulitis and abscess of finger and toe. This does not indicate the condition ingrown toenail. The main term, therefore, is "Ingrown." A review of the Alphabetic Index takes you to "Ingrowing."
- Step 4: There are no italicized instructional notes to interpret.
- Step 5: Review the subterms. The subterm "nail" appears and lists nonessential modifiers (in parentheses) as "finger," "toe" and "infected." These nonessential modifiers complete the diagnostic statement.
- Step 6: There are no abbreviations, cross-references, fifth-digit notations, or brackets.
- Step 7: Verify code 703.0 in the Tabular List Before assigning the code, review all instructional notes under category 703 and under code 703.0. The note, "Excludes: infection, nail NOS (681.9)," can be ignored because the diagnostic statement specifies the infection is due to the ingrowing nail.
- Step 8: Therefore, the subcategory code level is the highest level of specificity. The final code assignment would be 703.0.
- Step 9: The correct code choice is 703.0, Ingrowing nail with infection.
- Step 10: Since infectious infected ingrown toenail is listed as the chief reason for the healthcare encounter, the primary or principal diagnosis is 703.0.

Home Health Qualifications for Medicare Valid Three-digit ICD-9-CM Codes

Three-digit ICD-9-CM codes are used to identify a condition or disease only when a fourth or fifth digit is not available. The following are the only ICD-9-CM codes that are valid without further specificity.

024	Glanders
025	Melioidosis
035	Erysipelas
037	Tetanus
042	Human immunodeficiency virus (HIV) infection
048	Other enterovirus diseases of central nervous system
061	Dengue
064	Viral encephalitis transmitted by other and unspecified arthropods
071	Rabies
075	Infectious mononucleosis
080	Louse-borne [epidemic] typhus
096	Late syphilis, latent
101	Vincent's angina
118	Opportunistic mycoses
124	Trichinosis
129	Intestinal parasitism, unspecified
135	Sarcoidosis
138	Late effects of acute poliomyelitis
179	Malignant neoplasm of uterus, part unspecified
181	Malignant neoplasm of placenta
185	Malignant neoplasm of prostate
193	Malignant neoplasm of thyroid gland
217	Benign neoplasm of breast
220	Benign neoplasm of ovary
226	Benign neoplasm of thyroid gland
243	Congenital hypothyroidism
260	Kwashiorkor
261	Nutritional marasmus
262	Other severe protein-calorie malnutrition
267	Ascorbic acid deficiency
311	Depressive disorder, not elsewhere classified
316	Psychic factors associated with diseases classified elsewhere
317	Mild mental retardation
319	Unspecified mental retardation
325	Phlebitis and thrombophlebitis of intracranial venous sinuses
326	Late effects of intracranial abscess or pyogenic infection
340	Multiple sclerosis
390	Rheumatic fever without mention of heart involvement
393	Chronic rheumatic pericarditis
412	Old myocardial infarction
430	Subarachnoid hemorrhage
431	Intracerebral hemorrhage
436	Acute, but ill-defined, cerebrovascular disease
452	Portal vein thrombosis
460	Acute nasopharyngitis [common cold]
462	Acute pharyngitis
463	Acute tonsillitis
470	Deviated nasal septum
475	Peritonsillar abscess
481	Pneumococcal pneumonia
485	Bronchopneumonia, organism unspecified
486	Pneumonia, organism unspecified
490	Bronchitis, not specified as acute or chronic
496	Chronic airway obstruction, not elsewhere classified
500	Coal workers' pneumoconiosis
501	Asbestosis
502	Pneumoconiosis due to other silica or silicates
503	Pneumoconiosis due to other inorganic dust
504	Pneumoconopathy due to inhalation of other dust
505	Pneumoconiosis, unspecified
514	Pulmonary congestion and hypostasis
515	Postinflammatory pulmonary fibrosis
541	Appendicitis, unqualified
542	Other appendicitis
566	Abscess of anal and rectal regions
570	Acute and subacute necrosis of liver
586	Renal failure, unspecified
587	Renal sclerosis, unspecified
591	Hydronephrosis
605	Redundant prepuce and phimosis
630	Hydatidiform mole
631	Other abnormal product of conception
632	Missed abortion
650	Delivery in a completely normal case
677	Late effect of complication of pregnancy, childbirth, and the puerperium
683	Acute lymphadenitis
684	Impetigo
700	Corns and callosities
725	Polymyalgia rheumatica
734	Flat foot
769	Respiratory distress syndrome
797	Senility without mention of psychosis
920	Contusion of face, scalp, and neck except eye(s)
931	Foreign body in ear
932	Foreign body in nose
936	Foreign body in intestine and colon
937	Foreign body in anus and rectum
938	Foreign body in digestive system, unspecified
981	Toxic effect of petroleum products
986	Toxic effect of carbon monoxide
990	Effects of radiation, unspecified
V08	Asymptomatic HIV infection status
V51	Aftercare involving the use of plastic surgery